Goldmine®

4th Edition

standard catalog of®

American RECORDS

1950-1975

Tim Neely

©2004 by Krause Publications

Published by

700 East State Street • Iola, WI 54990-0001
715-445-2214 • 888-457-2873
www.krause.com

Our toll-free number to place an order or obtain
a free catalog is (800) 258-0929.

Library of Congress Catalog Number: 2004094040

ISBN: 0-87349-831-3

Designed by Kay Sanders

Edited by Tim Neely

Printed in the United States of America

Contents

Introduction

Welcome to the fourth edition of the *Goldmine Standard Catalog of American Records 1950-1975*. We continue to be amazed and humbled by your reaction to what we've done. It's still neat to walk into a used record store and see a copy of a prior edition of this book behind the counter, dog-eared and on the verge of falling apart, because the owner has used it so thoroughly. It's still neat to hear from people who picked up the book and felt compelled to write or call or e-mail.

All the feedback has been heartwarming. We at Krause Publications believed for years that a comprehensive price guide such as this was needed, and that it would meet with a warm reception. And indeed it has; the first and third editions were complete sellouts, and the second edition came close to that mark. For this, we thank you.

If this is the first time you've encountered the *Standard Catalog*, welcome aboard!

Inside this 1,400-page book you'll find over 150,000 listings of records of four different types – 45 rpm singles, LPs, extended-play 7-inch singles, and 12-inch singles – by performers who made their first record in 1975 or earlier. Thousands of records not listed in any other price guide are in here.

The first edition, which was released in 1998, was three years in the making. In the years since, we've never stopped adding to the database that includes all this information. We've received help and suggestions from hundreds of readers located throughout the United States and around the world, all in an effort to make the information contained within as accurate and up-to-date as possible.

Unlike other price guides that claim to list as many as a million records, the *Standard Catalog* actually lists every record it includes. This book does not say, "Every 45 rpm record by Artist X on Label Y is worth between $5 and $15." Though we certainly want people to buy this book for the pricing information, there are plenty of people who buy it for the discographies, some of which can't be found anywhere else.

For regular readers, you'll see more photos in this edition of the *Standard Catalog* than in any prior edition, and more listings, too.

New features for 2004

Those who have seen prior editions of the *Standard Catalog* will notice two major changes to the listings. First is the addition of a check box before every entry. We've done this in most of our other price guides for some time; we finally have added this feature to our big-gest book. Second is a change in style of the listings, in hopes of making the book easier to read. Lines now separate the listings of each artist, so you'll know where each performer's records start and end. This also helps us add more listings in the areas where this book has had its heart from the beginning – pop, rock, R&B, soul, country & western – without increasing its price.

We have added significantly to the soul listings in the *Standard Catalog*. We have listed the entire discography of the legendary Shrine label of Washington, D.C., all of which are eagerly sought by soul collectors. We have extensively revised the prices of other soul records where necessary, and we've added many other collectible soul artists who have never appeared in a U.S. price guide before. This is an area of collecting that shows no signs of letting up, so we'll continue to add to and revise these listings in future editions.

Part of that was spurred by the 2003 publication of the *Goldmine Standard Catalog of Rhythm & Blues Records*, but our research has not stopped in that genre.

Also:

• We continue to add to our listings of pop artists of the 1950s.

• We've added every release on Lana Records, an oldies reissue label from New York that was popular in the 1960s, because we are asked about them frequently.

• We've added the entire run of the 1960s cover-record label Hit Records. A few of these have been listed before, mostly Beatles-related novelties. Now all of them are here.

• There are more extended-play singles, both the regular 45 rpm versions of the 1950s and early 1960s and the small-hole jukebox EPs of the mid 1960s to mid 1970s, listed in one place than ever before.

• We are in the process, though it is not yet complete, of making sure that virtually every performer who made the *Billboard* pop, country, R&B and easy listening charts in the 1950s and 1960s is listed. Some of them have never had a comprehensive discography compiled anywhere, not even on the Internet. Thus, a few have required extensive research.

"A change is gonna come"

With all the additions, many of which you have requested, we've had to make some tough decisions about what to include and what not to include. Both financial and technical issues make it difficult to expand the *Standard Catalog* to a larger size than it already is. So unfortunately, we've had to delete some listings that appeared in the third edition.

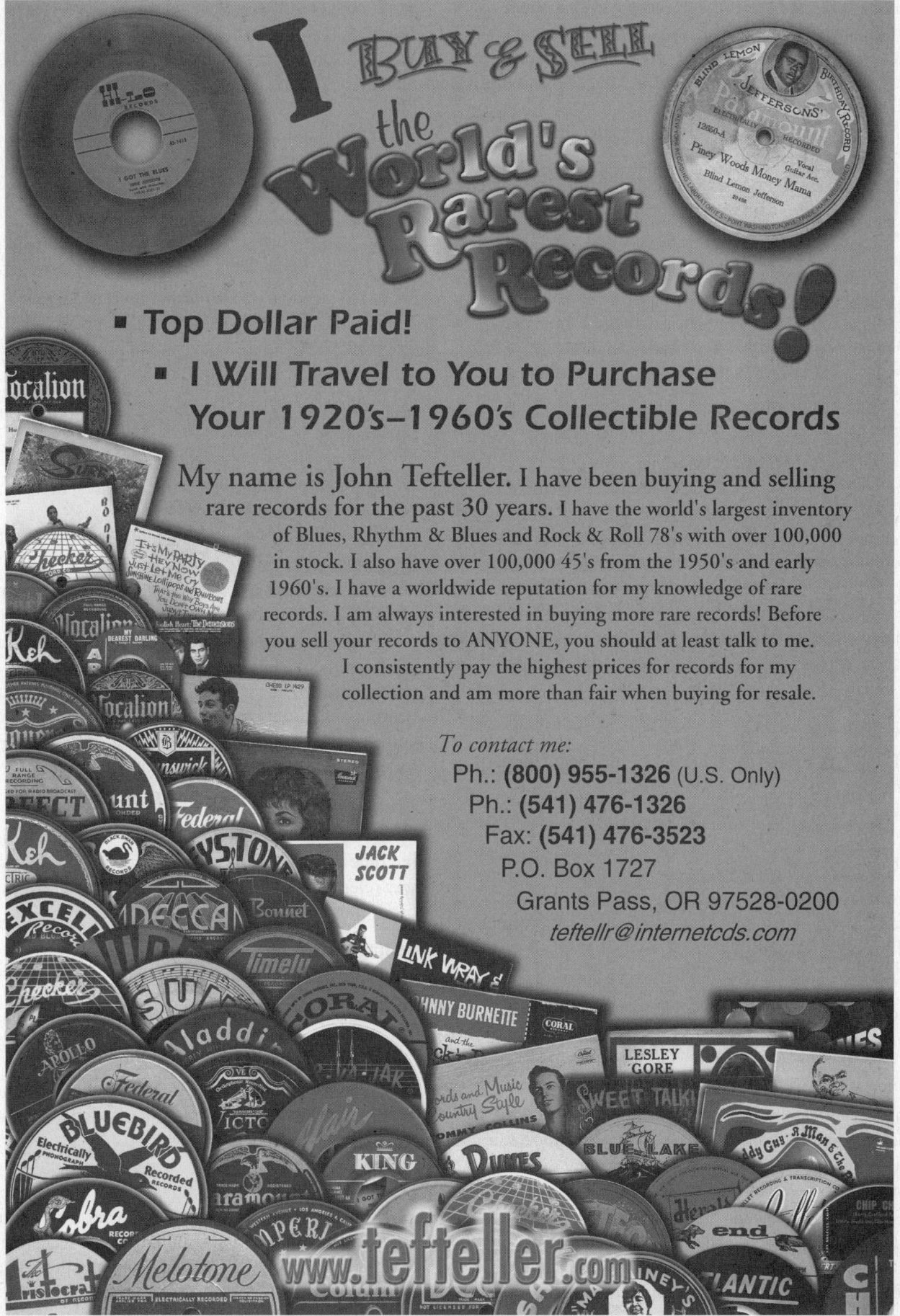

These missing listings come entirely from modern jazz, an area where our coverage was already incomplete and inconsistent. But not all jazz is gone from this book; we have retained popular jazz vocalists (Louis Armstrong and Ella Fitzgerald, for example), plus we have kept hold-overs from the swing era (Tommy Dorsey and Glenn Miller, for example, and we've added several new ones).

The artists we chose not to include this time are not gone forever; they remain in our database, and they could re-appear in a future *Standard Catalog*. All of the missing jazz artists have their LPs included in the brand-new 2nd Edition of the *Goldmine Jazz Album Price Guide,* which is scheduled for release in September 2004.

But bigger changes may be in store. We are always adding more information; alas, we are running out of room for it. We are considering altering the year range for this book to 1950-1969, then publishing a companion book of similar size covering 1970-1989 that would replace the current *Standard Catalog of American Records 1976-Present*. Most importantly, the two books would have no (or extremely few) overlapping listings. The first book would focus entirely on those artists whose first record came out in 1969 or earlier, with complete U.S. vinyl discographies to the present, and the other would focus entirely on those artists whose first record came out in 1970 or later. Let us know what you think about this proposal using the contact information found under "How you can help."

Current trends

The biggest gains in collector interest, and values, over the past two years have been in soul music, especially the so-called "Northern Soul" records – sometimes called "rare soul" or "deep soul."

To people who have no idea what "Northern Soul" means, we can't help too much; it's very difficult to define. The term was coined in the early 1970s to define the kind of soul music played in the clubs of Northern England and Scotland. (Combine the "Carolina beach music" club scene with the collecting fanaticism of many vocal group fans, and add in a dash of the competitiveness of hip-hop DJs, and you get an idea what "Northern Soul" is about.) "Northern Soul" has nothing to do with where the songs originated – they can come from Detroit, Washington, New York, New Orleans, Los Angeles, Memphis or anywhere else that soul music was recorded. Generally speaking, the more obscure the artist and/or the record, the better.

Songs that Americans ignore completely become treasured rarities overseas. The "Holy Grail" of soul music is a 45 by Frank Wilson, "Do I Love You (Indeed I Do)" on Soul S-35019. Only two copies are known to exist, both of which are promotional. One of those two sold at auction for over $20,000 in 1998.

Wilson, not to be confused with J. Frank Wilson of "Last Kiss" fame, was a staff arranger and composer at Motown. Not as well known as such giants as Holland-Dozier-Holland and Whitfield-Strong, he still had his share of involvement with hits. Among the songs he co-wrote were "Love Child" and "Up The Ladder To The Roof," both hits for the Supremes; he was the co-producer of "Keep On Truckin' " by Eddie Kendricks.

But it's his one and only single release that sets Northern Soul fans' hearts on fire.

Another area showing significant growth in interest is jazz, especially albums of the 1950s and 1960s. Values of these are increasing quickly as well. We direct those readers interested in that material to the 2004 (2nd) edition of the *Goldmine Jazz Album Price Guide* for more information.

Other rare records have maintained their value without significant increases or decreases, at least not that we can see at this time.

We are starting to see a decline in interest in albums by popular artists of the 1950s and early 1960s who have not been embraced by either oldies radio or movie producers. This is not the case with 45s of the same era, though.

We're also seeing more interest in music of the 1970s; some of the most significant gains in value were with albums by British singer Nick Drake. We've been hearing about him for years, and finally, the difficulty collectors have in finding his original American LPs is reflected in the values in this book.

Frequently asked questions

I've heard many questions over and over again in the time since the first edition of the *Standard Catalog* was released. I've tried to answer some of those that I've heard most often in the next few pages.

Selling records

How do I sell/get rid of my records?

There are many ways to do so. In general, the more time and effort you put into selling your records, the more money you're likely to get for them.

The first thing to do is to buy this book and use it. You are better off working from a position of knowing what you have rather than guessing.

Look through it and see if you have anything that is more valuable than the average. If not, or if your records are "well loved" (say, VG condition or worse), it probably isn't worth your time to work hard to sell them. Be kind to a friend: Give them to someone who collects records. Or sell them at your next garage/rummage sale for 50

cents or a buck apiece (10 cents or a quarter each for 45s). Or donate them to Goodwill, the Salvation Army, the St. Vincent De Paul Society, or some other charity with a thrift shop, and get a tax receipt. But don't throw them out! We never recommend that unless your records are in truly poor condition.

Maybe your stash has some records of above-average value, or maybe you actually took good care of your records and they are still in VG+ or better condition. You can do either of two things:

• Sell them to a dealer.
• Sell them yourself, directly to collectors.

Let's take these one at a time.

Selling to a dealer. Two important things to know when selling records to a dealer are these:

1. The prices listed in this book are RETAIL. These are NOT prices that a dealer will pay to obtain them.

2. The prices in this book are a *guide* and not holy writ.

If you go to a dealer expecting to get these prices, even more so if you've overgraded your records, you are in for a rude awakening.

For something genuinely rare, you might get 40 to 60 percent of the "book value." For many of those, all a seller has to do is pick up the phone and call the right person, and the record is sold. For less expensive records, though, don't expect to get more than 10 to 25 percent (if that) of the "book value." Sellers have overhead costs they have to recover, such as inventory, rent, utilities, postage, boxes, employees (for a store), insurance, taxes, and many more things that a dealer has to recoup by selling records to someone else. Some dealers won't even try to get records from people who say they consulted a price guide, because those sellers get delusions about what they "deserve" for their records. If this happens to you, don't say we didn't warn you.

Sometimes, the hardest part in selling to a dealer is finding one. Most large cities, and many smaller ones, have used record stores. The best way to find them in your area is to look in your local Yellow Pages. Depending on who published the phone directory, used record stores are under either the heading "Compact Discs, Tapes & Records – Retail" or "Records, Tapes & Compact Discs – Retail."

Just because you've found that store (or stores) doesn't mean they will pay you much for your records; some may not even buy them at all. From a dealer's standpoint, common records are almost literally a dime a dozen; the eyes glaze over at yet another copy of *Rumours, Frampton Comes Alive!*, *Whipped Cream and Other Delights* or *The First Family*. You might get only a token amount for a pile of records if they are all fairly common, regardless what this price guide says. But if the alternative was between getting something for them versus getting nothing for them, you'll probably be happy with the result. And you no longer have the records in your way.

Selling them direct. In the era of online auctions, this is a more appealing alternative than it used to be. Regardless what method you use, it will take longer and require more patience than selling to a dealer. Plus, if you will be dealing through the mail, you have some additional costs, most notably for good packaging and postage. But it can be worth it.

Before the Internet, you basically had two options for doing it yourself to reach the collector's market: Setting up at record shows/fairs, or advertising in record collecting magazines. And both still have their place.

For a seller, the record show is a great place to meet other collectors and dealers, get ideas and advice, and see some records you might never see anywhere else. Also, some high-value deals still take place at shows. If you like the direct interaction and the wheeling and dealing – and can resist the temptation to add to your own collection with the proceeds – then selling at a record show may be for you.

Record collector magazines have shrunk in recent years, but they still exist and remain a viable outlet for certain kinds of collectibles. They are best for selling middle-to higher-priced items that allow you to make up for the cost of the ad and still make money. And, as most serious collectors read one or the other or both magazines, an ad letting them know of your existence can pay dividends. Both serve a smaller, but more targeted, audience than an online auction.

Of the two major collecting magazines, *Goldmine* has a higher profile, a larger circulation, and more expensive ads as a result. *Discoveries* has less expensive advertising rates, but less than half of *Goldmine's* circulation. Both are published by Krause Publications; if you've never seen them, they are available at many major bookstores and independent record shops, or a sample copy of a recent issue can be obtained by calling 800-258-0929.

For most people with an accumulation of records who want to "eliminate the middleman," online has been the way to go since the late 1990s. And the most popular site for this action is eBay (www.ebay.com).

Online selling seems to draw two widely different audiences. One is much the same audience as a stand-alone record store, except on a global scale rather than a regional one. Browsers who know next to nothing about record collecting and the relative scarcity of the listed pieces are common. These are people who can sometimes be fooled into paying too much for a common

9

piece if they get caught up in "auction fever," where the thrill of bidding overwhelms their rational knowledge that the item can be had cheaper somewhere else.

The other audience drawn to online sales is the hyper-specialist, and this is often where items can justifiably go for much larger sums than in a retail store. Thanks to search engines on most of the better sites, a fan of, say, Eric Clapton can type in the words "Eric Clapton" and find nothing but the Eric Clapton-related material. People who specialize in one artist will usually pay more – sometimes a *lot* more – than someone who collects a more broad range of artists. Because they are specialists, though, they also know which items are common, so they don't get taken on the easy stuff.

As a seller, you are reaching a larger audience than you would in a record collecting magazine, but also a much less targeted one. The Internet seems to be a good place to sell lower-priced items that might take up valuable space in an expensive print ad. But many more valuable pieces sit or fetch less than they might through more traditional means. The exception seems to be with original editions of jazz albums from the 1950s and 1960s, which are rising in price significantly thanks to the online market.

To do the best at selling online:

• Use the *Goldmine* Grading Guide, which is in this introduction, or a similar guide. Don't say that your records are in "good condition" because "good" is a low grade. Unless, of course, they really are in only "good" condition.

• Grade your records conservatively, and mention any flaws with them in your description.

• Always mention the record label and number of any record you sell. I am amazed at how many auctions lack this basic information.

• Take a picture of, or scan, everything you sell, and post those images with your auctions. If possible, use multiple images. Photos can tell the potential buyer more than your words will.

• That said, don't alter the images of your items in any way, or steal someone else's better photos! Your buyers probably won't deal with you again when they find out that your "pristine" record or cover actually has serious flaws.

• Answer all of your customers' questions, no matter how arcane or trivial they may seem to you. It could be the difference between a sale and no sale.

• Make your minimum bid the lowest amount you'd be willing to take for the item. Many items sell for only the minimum.

• However, if you really want to sell, don't set that minimum too high. It is better to start an auction low and

watch the action send an item to new heights than to put a high minimum on an item. If you feel queasy, use a hidden reserve price, below which you won't sell the item.

• Charge a reasonable amount for shipping. It is expected that buyers will pay for shipping. But don't try to make a profit at it, either. If you charge more than what the Postal Service or your private shipper of choice charges to send an item, explain why.

• Once you sell the item, pack it well. Some customers will have specific requests on how they want an item sent. Listen to them!

Remember, too, that with tens of thousands of records for sale at any one time, approximately half of all records on eBay receive no bids at all. In addition to not following the advice for sellers listed above, it's possible that no one wanted to buy your record during the time your record was posted. Maybe at another time, you'll get bidders.

Will you buy my old records?

Thanks for asking, but no.

I do collect records, but only in very specific areas, which may or may not be reflected in the pages of this book. I prefer to make my contacts on my own time, not through correspondence related to my books. Neither Krause Publications nor its parent corporation, F+W Publications, Inc., engages in the buying and selling of records, so these prices are not meant as "offers to buy" or "offers to sell."

Buying records

There's a record in your catalog that I want to order in VG+ condition. Do you still have it?

No, and we never did.

This is something I've heard a few times since the *Goldmine Standard Catalog of American Records* first came out in 1999. For some reason, perhaps because of the use of the word "catalog" in the title of this book, some readers thought prior editions of this book were a list of records that the publishers or I actually had for sale.

Just so there is no confusion: This is a *price guide*, not a *sale list*. We're not selling; we're informing.

Then how do I find the records in the book?

Try the same sources you would use if you wanted to sell – used record stores, *Goldmine* and *Discoveries* magazines (both magazines offer "want list" services), record shows/fairs, the Internet, friends, yard/garage/rummage sales, flea markets, thrift shops.

Once in a while, we might list something that doesn't exist. Usually, this is a record that was scheduled by a record company but never actually released. Or in the case of 45s, the single might never have advanced

beyond the double-sided promo stage. We don't intentionally list "phantom" records.

Many collectors have informed us that they doubt certain records or sleeves exist because, in their many years of looking, they've never seen it. In cases where there is doubt, we usually note it. We do sometimes delete listings if we note the doubt of an item's existence, then no one tells us anything to allay our doubts. But we do not delete listings easily: It's easier to prove something *does* exist than something *doesn't* exist.

78 rpm records

I noticed that this book doesn't list 78s in it – you know, the real old records that break easily. Are they worth anything?

By design, the *Goldmine Standard Catalog of American Records 1950-1975* does not contain information on 78 rpm records. For many of the artists in this book, they would devour space better spent on records that actually have collector demand.

That is *not* to say that all 78s are worthless. Indeed, that is far from the case. But the vast majority of 78s that still exist have little value.

The most common 78s are, by far, by swing-era big bands and pop vocalists of the 1940s and early 1950s. Most accumulations found in attics and basements consist of this kind of material. Even in top-notch condition, these rarely get more than $5 each. (Frank Sinatra and Glenn Miller 78s can get a little more, but not much more.) Most collectors who want them already have them, and new collectors soon realize how easy they are to find and won't pay much more. Other common 78s are classical records; again, with very few exceptions, they have little collector value. That includes Enrico Caruso records, which have more sentimental than monetary value.

Most of the 78s that are sought after by collectors fit into certain narrow categories, as follows:
- Jazz of the 1920s and early 1930s by pioneers such as King Oliver;
- Post-World War II jazz by early bebop players such as Charlie Parker, especially on the Blue Note and Dial labels;
- Pre-1940 "hillbilly music" and string band records;
- Blues records of all eras and types – Robert Johnson and Charley Patton are among the hottest collectibles of this genre, but there are many others;
- Rhythm and blues records of the 1945-1959 era, though until 1957 or so, if the same record exists on both 78 and 45 with the same label and number, the 45 is almost always more valuable than the 78;
- Vogue Picture Records and other similar discs with artwork covering the entire record;
- Rock 'n' roll records;
- Almost any 78 released in 1958 and later, when the format was dying in the United States.

Also, in the 1940s and into the 1950s, record companies issued album-style collections of 78s with three or four discs by the same artist, or they issued sets of records that served as a soundtrack for a movie or Broadway play. These may have some value to the right collector, but in almost all cases, if these sets also exist as either a set of 45s or as a regular LP, the newer formats will be more collectible.

To find out more about collectible 78 rpm records, we recommend the *American Premium Record Guide, 6th Edition,* by Les Docks, also published by Krause Publications. It is strongest on 78s released before 1940, which is where most of the collecting action is.

Classical records

All my albums are classical. Are they worth anything?

Generally, they aren't worth much. Even in top condition, well over 95 percent of all classical albums are worth about what someone would have paid for them in a store when they came out, and in some cases, even less. That is the main reason that they are not included in the *Standard Catalog.*

Most of the exceptions are those that are prized by audiophiles. While this isn't all of them, the American records that fit this category are usually RCA Victor Red Seal albums with a large "LIVING STEREO" banner across the top of the front cover and a "shaded dog" on the label (so-called because the Nipper logo on the label has a darker red background than the rest of the red label). Some of these can fetch in the hundreds of dollars for near-mint copies. Also worth looking for are Mercury "Living Presence" stereo records and London stereo classical albums (sorry, Mantovani doesn't count) with a back cover that has a blue tint (these are known as "blue backs" by collectors); some of these also are sought after by audiophiles. Remember, though, that high prices only hold true for stereo copies; mono versions of the same records are almost worthless.

If you have a lot of classical albums and really want to know more about them, we recommend the privately published *Canfield Guide to Classical Recordings, 5th Edition*, available from the author, David Canfield (www.arsantiqua.com). It is only available from Canfield; do *not* contact Krause Publications about it.

Promotional records

Some of my records have white labels and/or contain words such as "Promotion Only" or "Audition

BAGS UNLIMITED
record frames

Matted LP Frames

15-3/8" x 15-3/8"
Outer Dimensions (O.D.)

silver

gold

black

Specify frame and mat color when ordering.

Kit Includes:
• 4 aluminum frame pieces, corner & hanging hardware
• Die cut colored mat
• Die cut holding mat & back mat
• Clear acrylic UF3 grade front piece (blocks 98% of harmful UV rays)

code: ALPFK*	
1	$ 31.00
3	85.50
5	130.00
10	235.00

LP Jacket Frame Kit

14" x 14" (O.D.)

Kit comes with 4 plastic side pieces, 4 connectors, and 1 sheet of crystal clear mylar. Frame pieces have a black matte finish.

code: ALPJFK	
1	$ 11.30
2	20.30
5	44.30
10	72.75
25	171.95
50	324.20

Album Art Frame

12-1/2" x 12-1/2" (O.D.)

Clear acrylic frame has three removable clips so you can change your display at any time. UV resistant.

code: AAAF	
2	$ 19.20
5	40.90
10	67.65
27	167.45
54	304.45

Jacket & Record Matted LP Frames

available in black, gold, or silver

NEW!

29-5/16" x 15-3/8" (O.D.)

Specify frame and mat color when ordering.

Kit Includes:
• 4 aluminum frame pieces, corner & hanging hardware
• Die cut colored mat
• Die cut holding mat & back mat
• Clear acrylic UF3 grade front piece (blocks 98% of harmful UV rays)
• Can be hung vertically or horizontally

code: ALPFKJR*	
1	$ 52.00
3	141.00
5	210.00
10	378.00

Encapsulation Frame Kits

12-1/2" x 12-1/2" (O.D.)

square mat

circle mat

78 Record
code: A78FK*

45 Record
code: A45FK*

NEW!

12" Picture Disc
code: A12PDFK*

Kits Include:
• Clear acrylic frame
• Die cut colored mat
• White acid-free fome-cor back
• 3 removable clips (one notched to serve as hanger)

2	$ 28.65
5	59.55
10	99.25
25	222.70
50	380.55

Specify mat color when ordering.*
For 45 kit, specify square/circle die-cut .

* MAT COLORS: Black, White, Ivory, Blue, Green, Red, Burgundy, or Pink. All mats are acid-free and buffered.

BAGS Unlimited INC

www.BagsUnlimited.com
1-800-767-2247 • Fax (585) 328-8526
7 Canal Street, Rochester, NY 14608-1910

Copy" or "Demonstration – Not for Sale" on them. What are these, and are they worth anything?

These are known generically as "promos." They were (still are) sent to radio stations, journalists, club disc jockeys and others in hopes of getting reviews or airplay, which would then spur sales. Sometimes, multiple copies are sent out to the same place to be used as contest prizes. Despite the dire warnings appearing on them about alleged ownership rights, and despite attempts by a certain auction Web site to cover its rear end, it is legal to sell them in the secondary market and always has been.

It is the policy of the *Goldmine Standard Catalog of American Records 1950-1975* to list promotional records only under certain very specific conditions. Otherwise, the listings for promos would overwhelm the listings for stock copies, and most of the records that exist are stock copies. Most promos are close duplications of the regular store copies except for a white or different-colored label or, for 45s from the late 1960s forward, having the same song on both sides, one side in mono, the other in stereo. We are not interested in documenting these "ordinary" promo records.

But not all promos are created equal.

It's probably easier to say which promotional copies are not going to fetch a premium. Those are copies that are otherwise identical to stock copies – the same label, the same number, the same everything – but are merely stamped on the front or back cover with (usually) a gold "For Promotion Only" indicator. There's nothing special about these records for the most part; any time the record company wants to create a promo, it can take a stock copy and gold-stamp it!

These are known as "designate promos" and rarely get more than 10 percent above the price of a regular stock copy, if that. For some sought-after rare items, designate promos go for much, much less than copies not so designated.

Some albums that appear to be "designate promos" do have collector value. These are copies pressed on special "audiophile vinyl," the most notable of which are the "Quiex II" pressings from the Warner-Reprise-Geffen family. Some of these fetch as much as 4-5 times the regular editions! These will *always* have a sticker on the cover advertising the "Quiex II" record within.

Also, there are records that appear to be "designate promos" from the late 1960s and early 1970s that are much more. These actually are mono copies of albums released only in stereo to the general public. These always are at least twice as valuable as the regular stock copy, as they are rare.

Other promos of little collector value are those with a hole punch in the corner. This was Capitol's preferred method of creating promos during much of the 1970s. These are never worth more than the stock copy, and usually go for less.

Also, Columbia for a time merely used a "timing strip" on the front or back cover to designate a promo; these, too, also have little extra value above the stock copy.

Promos that *do* attract interest are those with custom promotional labels. Most of the time, these are white versions of the regular label, thus the term "white label promo." Of course, the label isn't always white; sometimes it's yellow or blue or pink or some other color. But it will always have as part of the label typesetting, "Promotional Copy" or "Audition Copy" or "Demonstration" or some other such term. Sometimes, the label will be almost identical to the stock versions, but some sort of words alluding to the promotional nature of the record will have been added to the typeset copy.

What makes these promos special? They are far more likely to have been mastered from the actual master mixdown tape, rather than a several-generations-removed copy, thus making them of higher sonic quality than later editions. They are among the first to come off the presses – after all, promos get sent out before stock copies. Sometimes they are specially mastered to sound better over the air or through a store's loudspeakers. Regardless, they are sought after, and their value ranges from the same as a stock copy to as much as twice that of a stock copy. We just don't have the space to list all of them.

Another rule of thumb when it comes to promos: In most cases, the more valuable a stock copy is, the less valuable the promo is. That's because in these instances, there are fewer stock copies known to exist than the promos.

Imported records

I've got some Beatles albums that aren't listed in the book. They're on a label called Parlophone or something like that. ...I've got an Everly Brothers 45 that you list, but my copy's on London, not on Cadence. ... I've got a (fill in the blank) record, but it says "Made in West Germany." What are these, why aren't they listed, and are they worth anything?

All of these are imports, and we don't list them in this book or any other book that we publish. It's hard enough to keep track of U.S. records; if we were to add Canadian, British, German, Soviet, South African, Japanese, or Indian subcontinental (just to name a few) records, too, we'd *really* be swamped.

Alas, there's not much information available on imports, especially in the United States. Unfortunately, there are no hard and fast rules about the value of imports. Some imports are more desirable than their American counterparts, even in the United States, and some are not. Well-made, colorful Japanese (not Korean) pressings from the 1970s and forward are almost always more valuable than their U.S. equivalents.

As the Beatles' imports are the ones I am asked about most often, I do know this. Just as there are numerous label variations among American editions of Beatles records, the same is true of their British counterparts. Most Parlophone LPs and 45s that are in the States today are 1970s and 1980s pressings, when imports became more readily available with the declining quality of American-made records. Few of these have much value above 1970s Capitol pressings. However, British originals from the 1960s are every bit as valuable as Capitol originals from the 1960s, and sometimes they go for more. But they have to be true originals!

Error Pressings

I've got a record that matches one you have in the book, except for one thing. It's got the same label on both sides! When I play it, though, it plays what you say it is supposed to play. Is this rare, and is it worth anything?

Yes, it is rare. No, it is not worth anything – at least, not above and beyond a normal edition of the record.

These are known as "error pressings." The same label appearing on both sides is by far the most common of these factory mistakes. Other similar boo-boos include labels with nothing but the company name on them and records with the right labels on the wrong sides.

These records are more annoying than collectible.

Unlike stamps and coins, where there's a core of collectors who almost literally drool over stamps missing the color red and one-cent pieces pressed on dime-sized planchets, record collecting has no such collectors – or if they are out there, they collect for the novelty value and not for the monetary value. Mispressed labels are relatively common errors, though certainly not as common as correct records. We know of hundreds of different 45s and LPs that were mispressed this way.

There are only a few exceptions to the misprint rule. If an LP is otherwise correct, but the wrong record company label was used, then collectors perk up. At least two different albums over the years were released on Columbia, but some copies were issued with "Epic" labels by mistake! Some copies of an early Contours 45 that was supposed to be on Gordy were pressed on Tamla instead, with the Gordy catalog number. Also, an RCA Record Club edition of a Johnny Rivers LP, a reissue of an Imperial record, was pressed on the Warner Bros. "Burbank" palm trees label! Collectors love that kind of thing.

A collector also likes when a wrong song, or wrong mix, or alternate mix, appears. But as for flip-flopped and duplicate labels, the best thing to do is pass and look for a correct version.

Bootlegs

I've got some Beatles albums with white covers and paper inserts. They are live concerts. … I have some Beatles 45s on a label you don't list called "Deccagone" … I have some Elvis Presley EPs on Sun. …These records aren't in your book.

All of the above are bootlegs. As a matter of policy, we do not intentionally list bootlegs in any of our price guides.

A "bootleg" (as opposed to a counterfeit or reproduction; see below) is a record that never officially existed. It can be composed of material such as live concerts or studio outtakes that artists or record labels chose not to release. A bootleg can also consist of released material, but compiled in such a way that bears no resemblance to any official edition. In certain circles, both of these can have value. We see that the Elvis Sun EP bootlegs often trade in the $25 range. But if they had been legitimate Sun products, they'd sell in the hundreds or thousands. By the time Sun started issuing EPs for real, it no longer was allowed to issue Elvis Presley material in any form. Thus the Elvis Sun EPs you sometimes see on eBay are all bootlegs.

Counterfeits/Reproductions

I found a stash of mint-looking 45s that appear to be worth thousands of dollars each according to your guide. Did I stumble upon a mother lode?

Actually, you have more likely stumbled upon a collection of counterfeits or reproductions ("repro" for short). Most of the rare records in the world have been reproduced and/or counterfeited.

There is a subtle difference between a counterfeit and a repro. Basically, the repro was not originally meant to fool anyone into thinking that they had a rare original copy, whereas the counterfeit was meant to deceive. The problem is that some of the people who bought repros, which were especially popular in the pre-CD era of the 1970s (and can still be bought today, unfortunately), are dying off and not telling anyone that their records *aren't* the rare originals.

Some of the reproductions are easy to identify; others are not. The best things to do if you are offered a near-mint original that trades for thousands of dollars:

• Consider the source; is the dealer well known and reputable in the rare record field?

• Ask an expert. A reproduction being traded as a rare original hurts everyone.

• Be skeptical. If it looks too good to be true, it probably is.

Now, a primer on the most commonly encountered counterfeit record:

"Introducing the Beatles"

I have this old Beatles album. It's called *Introducing the Beatles*. It says stereophonic on it and it's on Vee Jay Records, etc., etc. I think I might have something valuable here. Do I?

The most likely answer: "No."

Perhaps no album in the history of recorded music has been counterfeited as often as Introducing *The Beatles*. Exactly where they all came from is a matter of conjecture, but the truth is that they began to emerge not too long after the album was pulled from the market in late 1964, and they continued to appear well into the 1980s. And they were available at even the most respectable kinds of record stores, including department stores that sold records.

Most of the counterfeit copies don't look that bad from the outside. They have a "Stereophonic" banner across the top of the front cover, and on the back cover, they have a list of songs including "Love Me Do" at the bottom of the first column and "P.S. I Love You" at the top of the second column. But virtually every copy with this combination on the cover is a counterfeit!

It used to be easy to know if you had a fake, but now, even most of the fakes have been in collections for 20 or more years. Here's how to tell if that *Introducing The Beatles* you have is an original.

The cover:

• If your back cover either has ads for other albums, is completely blank, or has a list of songs claiming that "Please Please Me" and "Ask Me Why" are on the record, it's probably authentic.

• If the album claims to be "Stereo" or "Stereophonic" on the cover and has a list of songs on the back that include "Love Me Do" and "P.S. I Love You," raise a warning flag. This is the most common counterfeit version. Most authentic front covers don't say "Stereophonic" on them; in the lower right corner they will say "LP 1062." Authentic copies of *Introducing The Beatles* in stereo have always been scarce; they were even scarce in 1964!

• If your cover has a brown border around the front photo, it's fake.

• If there is no shadow accompanying George Harrison, who is at the far right of the cover photo, you have a fake.

• If the cover has a yellow tint and has the word "Stereo" in the upper left, it's counterfeit.

• If you have a sealed copy, odds are it's fake. But if you feel squeamish about unsealing it, here's a way to check: Look at the word "HONEY" on the song "A Taste of Honey" listed on the back cover. If there is a small piece of the top of the letter "E" in "HONEY" missing, then it's a counterfeit. On authentic copies, the letter "E" is complete. That may be hard to see, though people who've looked for it have been able to see it. If in doubt, go ahead and unseal it, as the strongest counterfeit evidence can be found on the actual record.

The record:

• If the album cover claims to be "Stereophonic" or "Stereo" and the record label does not have any mention of stereo, odds are it's a fake.

• Where are the words "Introducing The Beatles" and "The Beatles"? Both real and phony copies have them. But on an authentic copy, the words "The Beatles" are directly underneath "Introducing The Beatles," and both lines are above the center hole. If the center hole separates "Introducing The Beatles" and "The Beatles," it's a counterfeit. *This is the easiest way to tell the real thing from a fake. All authentic copies have **both lines above the center hole!***

• If both lines are above the center hole, it has a rainbow ring around the outside of the label, and the color green is missing, it's a fake.

• Almost all real copies of the record have some sort of machine stamping in the dead wax, usually the words "Audio Matrix," the letters "MR" in a circle, or the letters "ARP." Some (not all) originals also have a numerical date scrawled in the dead wax (such as 2-12-64). No phonies have any of the above

The play test:

If you're still not sure whether your "stereo" *Introducing The Beatles* is the real thing, put Side 1 on your turntable and play it. Once you get past the bizarre omission of the "1, 2, 3" part of the count-in to "I Saw Her Standing There" (all Vee-Jay issues leave only the "Four!"), the song will be in clean, crisp, true two-track stereo, with most of the instruments coming from the left speaker and the vocals from the right speaker. If the record is mono or very poorly rechanneled stereo, and the record doesn't say "Stereo" on it, it's an authentic mono copy or a phony.

Finally, I've been asked if the counterfeits have any collector value. The short answer: No.

How to grade your records

I don't know how many times I've heard from people who think they know what they are talking about, "My records are all Mint!" Sure. And I've got some ocean front property in Arizona to sell you.

The truth is that very few records, especially from the 1950s and 1960s, are in anything close to mint, or near-mint, condition. Once you realize that, you'll have an easier time working with this book.

This book lists records in three grades of condition – Very Good, Very Good Plus, and Near Mint. For most serious collectors, Very Good is the lowest grade they will accept. And some won't even buy a Very Good copy.

So when it comes to selling records, *condition is (almost) everything!*

For most collectors, records of lower quality are only OK as placeholders – a stopgap until a better copy comes along – or as examples of truly rare records that are almost never found in more collectible condition and might be out of the collector's price range in a more lofty state.

Regular singles are usually sold with one grade, unless they have a picture sleeve. Then the picture sleeve is given a separate grade. As singles and their picture sleeves are listed separately in this book, it's easy to assign a value to each element.

Albums are usually sold with two separate grades rather than an overall grade. One grade is assigned to the cover and another to the record. In this book, we only list one grade – an overall grade. We do not list separate grades because, with few exceptions, where LPs are concerned a cover is worthless without its record, and a record is worthless without its cover. If the cover and record are in different conditions, combine the values of those conditions and divide by two to get an idea of the retail price.

Most records are graded visually. That is because most record dealers sell in quantity and don't have the time to play their entire stock. That said, some defects are easy to see, such as large scratches and warps. Others are subtle, such as groove wear from using a cheap or poorly aligned tone arm. It has been our experience that older records (1950s up to about 1971) tend to play better than they look, and newer ones (not including special pressings geared toward audiophiles) tend to play worse than they look.

When grading your records, do so under a strong light. Look at everything carefully, and then assign a grade based on your overall observations.

Some records will be worthy of a higher grade except for small defects, such as writing, tape or minor seam splits. Always mention these when selling a record! For some collectors, they will be irrelevant, but for others, they will be a deal-breaker. For all, they are important to know.

Other records will have promotional indicators such as timing strips, gold "don't sell this record or we'll take your firstborn" stamps, or other markings. Again, for some collectors, these mar the cover and make it worth less; for others, it doesn't matter, and for still others, they increase the desirability. Again, *always mention these when selling a record!*

One of the obstacles to the further growth of record collecting is poor grading and a lack of consensus as to what constitutes a "very good plus" or "near mint" record or cover. Over the years, the *Goldmine* Grading Guide has tried to standardize this. But we recognize that there are many variables to grading a record. As a seller, you are better off grading conservatively and surprising the buyer with a better record than was expected, than by grading based on wishful thinking and losing a customer.

That said, here are the standard grades for records, from best to worst:

MINT (M)

These are absolutely perfect in every way. Often rumored but rarely seen, Mint should never be used as a grade unless more than one person agrees that the record truly is in this condition. There is no set percentage of the listed Near Mint value these can bring; it is best negotiated between the buyer and seller.

NEAR MINT (NM or M–)

A good description of a NM record is "it looks like it just came from a retail store and was opened for the first time." In other words, it's nearly perfect. Many dealers won't use a grade higher than this, implying (perhaps correctly) that no record is ever truly perfect.

NM covers should have no creases, folds, seam splits or any signs of human handling. A near-mint cover also should have no cutout markings of any kind. It also will have no ring wear.

NM picture sleeves should have no creasing, ring wear or seam splits of any kind. It should look as if it has never housed a record. This is a great reason to remove your 45s from their picture sleeves and keep them separate. Just having the 45 inside the sleeve will cause damage that could reduce the grade of the sleeve.

NM records are shiny, with no visible defects. Writing, stickers or other markings cannot appear on the label, nor can any "spindle marks" from someone trying to blindly put the record on the turntable. Major factory defects also must not be present; a record and label obviously pressed off center is not Near Mint. If played, it will do so with no surface noise. (NM records are not necessarily "never played"; a record played on an excellent turntable can remain NM after many plays if the record is properly cared for.)

These are high standards, and they are *not* on a sliding scale. A record from the 1950s must meet the same standards as one from the 1990s to be near mint! It's estimated that no more than 2 to 4 percent of all records remaining from the 1950s and 1960s are truly NM. This is why they fetch such high prices. Do not assume your records are near mint. They must meet these standards to qualify!

VERY GOOD PLUS (VG+) or Excellent (E)

A good description of a VG+ record is "except for a couple minor things, this would be near mint." Most collectors and people who want to play their records will be happy with a VG+ record, especially if it is toward the high side of the grade (sometimes called VG++).

VG+ covers are close to their Near Mint counterparts. A cover might be marred by a cutout marking (cut corner, small hole punch, a cut in the spine) or promotional stamp; there might be some slight signs of handling, such as light creasing at the corners. There also can be slight signs of wear at the most vulnerable areas and even a tiny bit of ring wear. But all in all, except for a few minor imperfections, this would be a copy you could sell at retail in a store.

VG+ picture sleeves should have only minor wear. There might be some very light creasing where it is obvious that a record once resided (or still does reside). A VG+ picture sleeve might also have some very minor seam wear or a split (less than one inch long) at the bottom, the sleeve's most vulnerable location.

VG+ records may show some slight signs of wear, including light scuffs or very light scratches that do not affect the listening experience. Slight warps that do not affect the sound are OK. Minor signs of handling are OK, too, such as telltale marks around the center hole, but repeated playing has not misshaped the center hole. There may be some very light ring wear or discoloration, but it should be barely noticeable.

VERY GOOD (VG)

Many of the imperfections found on a VG+ record are more obvious on a VG record. That said, VG records – which usually go for no more than 25 percent of a Near Mint record – are among the biggest bargains in record collecting, because most of the "big money" goes for more perfect copies. For many listeners, a VG record will be worth the money.

VG covers have more signs of wear, such as minor (and we mean minor) seam splits. The most common spots for seams to split are at the bottom center, the middle of the spine, and at the upper and lower right, where the record is removed from the cover. These will not be overwhelming. Also, minor writing, tape or a sticker will detract from this cover. Other signs of handling will be more evident; ring wear, especially at the top, bottom and middle of the cover, will be visible, and it might affect the entire cover to a minor degree. Though a VG cover will still be pleasing to the eye, there is no way it could ever pass as new.

VG picture sleeves will have more signs of human handling. Ring wear in the middle of the sleeve, where the raised label of the record would reside, is obvious, though not overwhelming. Some more creases and folds might be visible. Seam splitting will be more obvious; it may appear on all three sides, though it won't be obvious upon looking. Someone might have written on it, too.

VG records have more obvious flaws. They lack most of the original gloss found on factory-fresh records. Groove wear is evident on sight, as are light scratches, deep enough to feel with a fingernail. When played, a VG record has surface noise, perhaps even an occasional audible light scratch, especially in soft passages and during a song's intro and ending. But the noise will not overpower the music otherwise. Just as with a VG cover, minor writing, tape or a sticker will detract from the label of the disc. Many collectors who have jukeboxes will use VG records in them and not think twice. They remain a fine listening experience, just not the same as if the record were in better condition.

LESSER GRADES

Good (G), Good Plus (G+) or Very Good Minus (VG–) records go for 10 to 15 percent of the Near Mint value, if you are lucky.

Good does not mean bad! The record still plays through without skipping, so it can serve as filler until something better comes along. But it has significant surface noise and groove wear, and the label is worn, with significant ring wear, heavy writing, or obvious damage caused by someone trying to remove tape or stickers and failing miserably. A Good to VG– cover will have more significant seam splits, perhaps to the point where they were taped closed, and highly obvious ring wear and heavier writing, such as the huge letters a radio station might have put on a cover to deter theft.

If the item is common, it's probably better to pass it up, but if it's something you've been seeking for a long time, get it cheap and look to upgrade.

Poor (P) and Fair (F) records go for 0 to 5 percent of the Near Mint value, if they go at all. More likely, they end up going in the trash. Records are cracked, impossibly warped, or skip and/or repeat when an attempt is made to play them. Covers are so badly seam spilt that they are fortunate to keep the record inside of it. Only the most outrageously rare records ever sell for more than a few cents in this condition – again, if they sell at all.

SEALED ALBUMS

It is best to treat sealed albums (sometimes abbreviated "SS" for "Still Sealed") with caution, especially if you are offered one as an original edition from a bygone era at an outrageous price.

For one thing, the record might have been re-sealed, regardless of intention. For example, if you see an album with a hole or indentation indicating a cutout, and there's no hole in the shrink wrap at that spot, it was re-sealed.

With a few exceptions, the only way you can tell if a record is the specific pressing you seek is to look at the record label. Often, the covers stayed the same for years. Records with back-cover dates of 1958 can have discs inside that were pressed in the 1980s! You don't really know unless you look at the record.

And you also have no way of knowing what condition the record is in. "Sealed" is *not* equivalent to "mint" or "near mint"! The record inside could have been pressed badly, or it might even be the wrong record. The author has opened sealed albums, only to find a different album inside!

Yes, legitimate sealed albums from the 1960s still exist, and sometimes they bring fancy prices. But that's only if there can be no confusion about the vintage of the record inside. Tread carefully.

Common collecting abbreviations

In addition to the letters used to designate a record's grade, it's not uncommon to see other abbreviations used in dealer advertisements. Knowing the more common ones helps to prevent confusion. Here are some:

boot: bootleg (illegal pressing)
cc: cut corner
co: cutout
coh: cut-out hole
cov, cv, cvr: cover
demo: demonstration record (synonym for promo, this is the more common term overseas)
dh: drill hole
dj: disc jockey (promotional) record
ep: extended play (can be used for both 45s and LPs)
gf: gatefold (cover)
imp: import
ins: insert
lbl: label
m, mo: monaural (mono)
m/s: mono/stereo (usually used to describe a promo single that has the same song on both sides, with the only difference in the type of sound)
nap: (does) not affect play
noc: number on cover

nol: number on label
obi: not actually an abbreviation, "obi" is the Japanese word for "sash" and is used to describe the strip of paper usually wrapped around Japanese (and occasional US) pressings of LPs
orig: original
pr, pro, promo: promotional record
ps: picture sleeve (the cover that appears with some 45s and most 7-inch extended play singles)
q: quadraphonic
re: reissue
rec: record
repro: reproduction
ri: reissue
rw: ring wear
s: stereo
sl: slight
sm: saw mark
soc: sticker on cover
sol: sticker on label
ss: still sealed
s/t: self-titled
st: stereo
sw: shrink wrap
toc: tape on cover
tol: tape on label
ts: taped seam
w/: with
wlp: white label promo
wobc: writing on back cover
woc: writing on cover
wofc: writing on front cover
wol: writing on label
wr: wear
wrp: warp
xol: "x" on label

How to read the A-Z listings

The *Goldmine Standard Catalog of American Records* arranges its listings alphabetically by artist, either by using the last name of the individual performer or the first word after "A," "An" or "The" in a group's name.

The artists' names are in **BOLD CAPITAL LETTERS.** They are alphabetized the way our computer did, so blame anything that seems way out of line on that. We have been able to "tell" the computer to sort most abbreviations and numbers as if they were spelled out completely. For example, "Dr. Hook" is found as if it were spelled "Doctor Hook."

Some artists are followed by a number or the letter (U) in parentheses. This is when we know of more than one performer using the same name and have enough knowledge to group at least some of them together. The most famous (usually, but not always, the most collectible) will be listed first, either with no number after it or the number (1) in parentheses after it. The rest will be arranged alphabetically by record label and will be followed by the appropriate parenthetical number (2), (3), and so on. This way, you'll know if there is more than one entry for the same artist name; only those names listed more than once will have the supplementary number. If a number is skipped, that particular name is outside the scope of this book, usually because they recorded after 1975. Any that we don't know where they go will be listed last with (U) for Unknown after it.

Immediately adjacent to the artist's name in many cases are cross-references or other information we feel is helpful. For some of the (1), (2), (3) artists, we tell you a little about them.

Below the artist information, we list their U.S.-released records. They are grouped in four formats, in this order: "12-Inch Singles"; "45s"; "7-Inch Extended Plays"; "Albums."

These are defined for the purposes of this book as follows:

A 12-inch single is meant to promote or make available one particular song. These rarely have a name other than that of the song being promoted. Album-sized records with three or four songs on them that are not meant to specifically "sell" one song are 12-inch extended plays, and are listed under "Albums." Sometimes we had to make a judgment call as to where to put some of these.

A **45** is a seven-inch record, usually with one song on each side. It need not have a big hole. It need not even play at 45 rpm. For simplicity's sake, we've included Columbia Microgroove 33 1/3 rpm singles of the late 1940s and early 1950s, and jukebox singles of the 1960s with one song on each side, in this category. They always have a note attached to them explaining what they are. Sometimes we list a 45 with more than one song on a side; either that's because the record was sold as a 45 or it was part of a record company's regular numbering system for 45s.

A **7-inch extended play**, a product of the 1950s and early 1960s, is a hybrid. Most of the time they contain two songs on each side and have big holes, like 45s. But they almost always came with cardboard sleeves, like albums. Until only a few years ago, price guides always treated these items as inseparable. Consumers, however, often treated EPs like 45s – they threw out the covers. Reflecting that, all EP listings here have separate lines, and values, for the cover and the record.

An **album** is defined here as a 10- or 12-inch record (never 7 inches) that has a small hole and isn't a 12-inch

single. Defining it any more than that is difficult. Some albums have only one song on a side, others have over a dozen; some play for 15 minutes, others for over an hour; some albums even play at 45 rpm rather than the standard 33 1/3 rpm. Unless noted, however, all albums are assumed to be 33 1/3s. **No 78s are listed under albums or under any other heading in this book.**

Under each format listing, the records are sorted alphabetically by label, which are printed in all capital letters, then numerically within each label, ignoring prefixes. The one exception is with RCA Victor 45s, which are arranged with the lowest numerical prefix first (for 1949-73 records), followed by APBO issues (1973-74), then PB issues (1975-76, until the label became simply "RCA" on 45s).

After many of the numbers are numbers or letters in brackets. These designate something special about the listing as follows:

DJ: some sort of promotional copy, usually for radio stations and not meant for public sale.

EP: extended play album; only used with album listings for 12-inch releases with 4 to 6 tracks and not as long as a regular album.

M: mono record.

P: partially stereo record. Rarely are records advertised as such; by carefully listening to the album, the determination has been made.

PD: picture disc (the artwork is actually part of the record; these proliferated in the late 1970s and early 1980s and tend to have inferior sound quality).

PS: picture sleeve (this is the value for the sleeve alone; combine the record and sleeve value to get an estimated worth for the two together).

Q: quadraphonic record.

R: rechanneled stereo record. These will usually be labeled with such terms as "Electronically Re-Channeled for Stereo"; "Enhanced for Stereo"; "Simulated Stereo"; or "Duophonic." But sometimes they aren't labeled as rechanneled.

S: stereo record.

10: a 10-inch LP.

(x) where x is a number: the number of records in a set. This is in parentheses inside the brackets so that in those rare instances where they exist, 10-record sets won't be confused with 10-inch LPs.

Most albums after 1968 do not have a stereo content designation. After 1968, if no designation is listed, it's probably stereo, though not necessarily. More importantly, it means that there was only one purchasing option available (except for the quadraphonic years of 1972-1977).

In the next, widest, column, we list the titles.

In the 12-inch single listings, we mention whether the version is extended, or how long it is, or something to identify it. We also mention, when known, whether a record has the same version on both sides.

For 45s, we list both the A- and B-side.

Each EP has two listings. One has its contents in order, one has the title of the EP as listed on the cover. In many cases, the title of the EP is found nowhere on the actual label – another reason to list the record and its sleeve separately. If an asterisk (*) precedes the listings of an EP, we know that these are the songs on this record, but we're not sure this is the correct order. Readers with this information are welcome to supply confirmation.

As most albums are almost worthless without a cover, they have one listing with the title as shown on the cover (assuming a title is shown on the cover). Most album listings have a prefix, usually from one to five letters. These prefixes often tell you whether your album is a first pressing and can have a considerable effect on an album's value. For proof, look up Bruce Springsteen and see what an album with a "KC" prefix goes for compared to the same title with a "PC" prefix.

The next column lists the year of release. **Please note that the year of release and the date that appears on the record (if one appears at all) are not necessarily the same!** For example, if an album had several singles taken from it, the later singles may not have come out until another year, even though all of the singles have the same year on them. Most of the "corrections" we received in year of release were caused by this confusion.

That said, some of these might be off by a year; sometimes a record is released in December of the year before or January of the year after. Other years we can only guess the decade, and the year will have a question mark in it.

The next three columns are the values in Very Good, Very Good Plus, and Near Mint condition. For all but the rarest pieces, the Very Good Plus value is twice the Very Good value, and the Near Mint value is twice the VG+ listing or four times the VG listing.

In some cases, dashes appear in the pricing column. That means that the VG or VG+ value is under $2 (bargain bin, yard sale, thrift shop material). If all three columns have dashes, there is some other reason, and we mention that in the explanatory notes below the listing. Every item with no value listed in any column is explained. If not, it's our error.

Finally, many items have a descriptive line in italics under the entry. This often purveys important information that plays a role in the above record's value, such as label design, cover design, or color of vinyl. Sometimes, relatively insignificant differences can make a huge difference in value. Just look at the Beatles or Elvis Presley listings for proof.

How to read the back listings

Because of the nature of these items, we've used a slightly different format for the four sections that appear after the letter Z. These four sections are "Original Cast Recordings," "Soundtracks," "Television Albums," and "Various Artists Collections."

Within each category, these are arranged alphabetically by the **title** of the release, again as our computer did them, and ignoring the words "A," "An," or "The." If the title starts with a number, it is sorted as if the number were spelled out, with a few exceptions. But none of the albums that start with a number are listed before the letter "A."

Underneath each title are the applicable releases, arranged alphabetically and numerically by label. Those lines start with a check box, then are followed by the label and number listed together; any applicable abbreviations in brackets (which are the same as in the rest of the book – M for mono, S for stereo, etc.); the year of release; and the prices in three grades of condition.

We still list *albums only* in the back section. There are many EPs that have various artists on them; eventually, we'll find a way to add them in.

How you can help

Since the publication of the first edition of the *Goldmine Standard Catalog of American Records 1950-1975,* we have asked for readers' help in making the book better and more complete. And you have responded: We have file cabinets full of your letters, a bulging electronic archive of your e-mailed contributions, and more jotted telephone notes than we can count. Indeed, the amount of information, and its accuracy, continues to improve with each edition.

For the first time, I am asking *not* to receive certain kinds of information. I've never asked for this material, but people send it to me anyway.

Please do *NOT* send the following, as it will be ignored:

• **Information on promos**, if the only difference between the listing in this book and your own copy is a white (or other promo-colored) label. Also, if the only difference between your promo copy and the listing in the book is that your record has the same version of the same song on both sides, one side in mono and one side in stereo, there's no need to let us know. Promos that *do* interest us are those on colored vinyl; those with a completely different number than the regular stock version; those with unique versions not released on the regular copy; and those that only exist as promos. The exception to this rule is if you have concrete evidence that a significant difference in value exists between the stock copy and the promo version. As an example, just as this book was getting finished, I got evidence that a certain stock copy was worth at least 10 times the promo copy! That is a significant difference.

• **Information on non-U.S. pressings.**

• **Years of release**, unless we have a question mark in it, or you can prove our information wrong based on chart or record company information independent of the year(s) listed on the records themselves. As mentioned earlier, the years listed on record labels and jackets often have NO relation to what year a record actually was released or was pressed.

• **Requests for pricing and values.** Don't ask me what your records are worth! That is why we compile these books. If your record isn't listed, don't assume I know what it's worth or can look it up instantly.

Here is what we are seeking more information about. We ask that, when you send information, you include the *record label and catalog number for everything*. Without this data, your updates are useless.

Stereo and other unusual 7-inch pressings of the 1958-63 era. Record companies tried numerous 7-inch alternatives to regular mono 45s in this era. We know that many labels, including Columbia, RCA Victor, MGM, Warner Bros., ABC-Paramount, Roulette, King, and even Carlton and Big Top, released stereo singles in this period. All of these are collectible, almost without regard to artist.

Extended plays. Thousands of extended-play 7-inch singles are listed in this book. Most of them are certainly collectible, and many fetch healthy sums. But some of them we still don't know about.

Anywhere you see the words "(contents unknown)," we'd like to know exactly what's on the record. What we need is Side 1 and Side 2, plus sleeve variations. As the titles of extended plays are often not listed on the records, we feel that actually listing the songs will be of greater help to the collector.

We've received good information on these records. But to make it even better, follow these guidelines:

• Use the *record* not the jacket, to determine the exact order of songs. Often, the titles on the sleeve are arranged to look better and don't necessarily correspond to the playing order.

• Not all EPs list Side 1 and Side 2 explicitly. So how do you tell? Look for the master numbers, which are usually found below the main number. On most EPs, the master number for Side 1 is one smaller than the master number for Side 2. For example, one of the Perry Como EPs listed in these pages has a Side 1 master number of "E2PW-0173" and a Side 2 number of "E2PW-0174." Another example: One of the Joni James EPs has a Side 1 master number of "57-EP-291" and a Side 2 number of "57-EP-292." You get the idea.

Also, on those EP listings with an asterisk (*) before the contents, we need confirmation of the exact order of tracks.

Jukebox singles. Our work on documenting these curious items from the 1960s and 1970s continues.

These were made exclusively for the "coin operator" trade, as jukebox distributors preferred to be called. They have small holes, usually play in stereo at 33 1/3 rpm, and contain highlights from a current LP. Usually, though not always, they contain songs *other* than the hit(s) from the album.

Some of these were the same as 45s, with one song on each side. Most of them, though, were closer in spirit to EPs, with as many as three songs per side.

If you have any that we don't list, let us know what they are, both the titles and contents. Look under "Extended Plays" above to see exactly what we seek.

Picture sleeves. Again, we didn't list a sleeve we weren't sure about. If you have something we haven't listed, let us know.

Phantom picture sleeves. Among the top picture sleeve collectors, there is a strong suspicion that at least some picture sleeves that are said to exist really do not! Thus the designation "phantom sleeve."

In here, we still list some of these, but with no values attached to them and with the following notice: "Rumored to exist, but without conclusive evidence, we will delete this from future editions." And we will do so, if no one can prove beyond a shadow of a doubt that they own legitimate U.S.-made copies of these mystery sleeves.

B-sides. Some records are listed as "(B-side unknown)." In many cases, it's because a record never got past the promo stage; in others, the record hasn't crossed too many paths. Readers have filled in hundreds of these "unknown" B-sides. If you can make some of these other B-sides known, tell us.

Very early 45s. We know that Capitol, MGM and Columbia, to name three, used different 45 rpm numbering systems in 1949-50 than the ones that became standard. Our information on these is somewhat sketchy. Again, if you have any of these (not to mention Columbia Microgroove 7-inch 33s from the era), let us know.

Early 45s on colored vinyl. Many of the early, extremely rare R&B and blues records were pressed on both black and other colors of wax (usually red). Sources conflict as to which of these are on colored vinyl only, black vinyl only, or both. Most of these are so rare that I've never seen them myself. So any authoritative help on sorting these out would be appreciated.

Late mono LPs. In 1967 and 1968, record companies quickly phased out monaural albums. Some of the mono albums are quite rare now. We're interested in what might exist that we don't have. We're also interested in deleting listings of mono albums that really don't exist.

Also, we've found that the Mercury family of labels, including Philips, Smash and Fontana, consciously packaged stereo albums inside mono sleeves in 1967. These can be identified by the stamped number starting with "2/6" in the trail-off wax, instead of starting with simply "2" (mono) or "6" (stereo). Copies of these in "true mono" may be much more rare than previously thought. If you have any of these "2/6" albums, let us know so we can indicate them.

Quadraphonic LPs. If it's not listed, we'd like to know about it. Also, if it is listed, but it never actually was released, we want to know that, too.

Photos. Sending us photos, photocopies or computer scans of items helps us, as these serve to prove the existence of the item in question.

We hope that future editions of all *Goldmine* price guides can have some cool photos of rarities. We also can accept computer scans e-mailed to us as attachments or sent on a CD-ROM.

For print use, 300 dpi or a very large photo of lower resolution that will resolve at 300 dpi at a smaller size are the only ones we now accept. Images scanned at 72 or 92 dpi that you borrowed from your, or someone else's, Web site *are not acceptable for print!* Also, make sure the scans or photos are centered (LP covers should look basically square and not like a trapezoid) and that they aren't blurry.

Some of our photos in this book and others came from computer scans. You can contact us for more information if you think you have something that might be worth putting in a future edition of any of our books.

We receive many contributions and suggestions, so not everyone's help can be acknowledged. But rest assured that even your one little correction helps in the long run.

By the way, if you sent us corrections for a prior edition of this, or any other, book I compiled, and they aren't reflected in here, there's no need to send them again; if they reached me, I still have them. As much as I enjoy receiving long lists of additions and corrections, they take much more time to dissect than shorter lists. Some items I received several years ago *still* aren't completely reflected in these pages. But I will get to them eventually; I don't dispose of anything unless I know I won't use it again. (My desk at work is proof.)

You may contact the author by mail:
Tim Neely
Standard Catalog of American Records
Krause Publications
700 E. State St.
Iola, WI 54990

or by phone:
(715) 445-2214 or 4612, ext. 782

or by e-mail:
neelyt@krause.com

If you write or e-mail, enclose a daytime phone number or return e-mail where I can reply in case I have any questions. **Because of the volume of mail and e-mail I receive, I cannot guarantee I will respond to, or even acknowledge, your inquiries, but I will try my best.**

Acknowledgments

One name appears on the cover of the *Goldmine Standard Catalog of American Records*. But a work of this magnitude would not be possible without a lot of help.

First, at Krause Publications: Paul Kennedy, Debbie Bradley, Sandi Morrison, Tammy Kuhnle and a host of people in the production and proofreading departments, plus former Krause employee Greg Loescher, whose idea this book was in the first place.

Second is to all of you who have bought this book or any other edition of the *Standard Catalog*. Your continued support enables us to do new editions. Thank you.

Third, thanks to all the people who have supplied photos for use in this and other books. We receive many photos; unfortunately, only a fraction can appear in print because most are not of a high enough quality. Many of the photos came from the author's collection and from the collections of other Krause Publications employees. Others who deserve special thanks include Kevan Budd, Betty Chrisman, Collectors Universe LLC, Alan Lowell, Gary Mack, Chuck Miller and Steve Pimper.

Next, many people have felt moved enough to write with corrections, additions and suggestions. Hundreds of people have helped make the *Goldmine Standard Catalog of American Records* the most accurate book of its kind. Here are many of those who have contributed to making the 4th Edition a success, with apologies to anyone we omitted:

Jimmy Adkins	Tim Cronin	Gary Johnson	Steve Pimper
Gene Aguilera	James Crosby	Robert Johnson	Denny Pine
Alan Aloupis	Frank DeMasi	Stephen Kauffman	David Pullen,
Anonymous	Michael Dennis	Mark Keenan	The 45 Archive
Tom Arkle	Michael Devich	Russell Kirchheuel	Lynn Pulsipher
Gary Bachman	Tom Diehl	Buster Kohlenberger	Mark Rafter
Gary Baird	John Diser	Joe Kreft	Bob Ragonese
Richard A. Banker	Jeff Drake	Francis Lecuyer	Robert Rickabaugh
Douglas Beard	Tim Dupree	Gordon Lent	Jim Rizio
Shirley Beaudoin	Keith Dutson	Dennis Listort	Dick Rosemont
Vic Bersok	Bob Eddy	Philip Liturski	Steve Schroeder
Hank Bezark	Robert H. Flowers	Ernie Mabrey	Michael Sharritt
Frank Blake	Michael Forney	Gary Mack	Stephen E. Simon
Jim Boeke	Göran Forsberg	Michael Martin,	Jeff Smedbron
Dennis Bohy	Randy French	The 45 Archive	Bruce Spizer
Dudley Boston	Rob Friedman	Karen McAlister	David Stiles
Patricia Boyles	Vanessa Gerondale	Jason McIntosh	Tom Struck
Michael Bradshaw	Dennis Gillund	John Medeiros	Ron Thornton
Gary Brenner	Gene Green	Chuck Miller	Terry Tracy
Gale Britton	Stephen Green	Greg Miller	David Tucker
Billy Brown	Albert Guzman	Bob Mohnike	Jon Urban
Bob Bruce	Dwain Hanson	Joe Moran	Scott Weiner
Danny Burgess	Larry Harrold	Cory Moris	Jeff Wells
Mark Carlson	Greg Hergert	Paul Nelson	Joel Whitburn
Floyd Cassista	Jim Hilger	Steve Perez	Paul Wilkinson
Lon Cerame	Joe Hill	Gary Phillips	Ed Worcester
Betty Chrisman	Barry Hirschberg	Glenn Phillips	Robert Ziella
Leo Costanzo	Bruce Hopkins		

Finally, I would like to dedicate this edition of the *Standard Catalog* to my mother, Judith Neely, who is very much alive to see this (and I hope she is for many more years). Her patience and understanding as her son slowly began to build a large record collection in his teenage years, and continues to build it today, are a large part of who I am today. I love you, Mom.

Tim Neely
Iola, Wisconsin
June 2004

John Kerry's rock 'n' roll past

In 1961, a seven-piece band called The Electras formed at St. Paul's, an elite prep school in New Hampshire. Like many other high-school rock bands, they were popular at school, especially with the girls. Also like many other high-school rock bands, especially in the 1960s, the Electras recorded an album's worth of songs from their repertoire in the school's band room on a reel-to-reel recorder. They pooled about $250 and had approximately 500 copies of their LP – called *The Electras* with a catalog number of ELT-201 – pressed by the RCA Custom Record Division. Most of these were sold to friends and classmates, and as so often happened, the band members moved on to bigger and better things.

Unlike other high-school rock bands, however, the bass player for The Electras was none other than future Massachusetts senator and presidential candidate John Kerry.

Little known until recently, *The Electras* suddenly has become a hot collector's item, to the point where a copy sold for over $2,500 on eBay early in 2004. It has also spurred a CD reissue of the album, and rumor has it that the band may reunite for a one-shot gig.

So if you were in New Hampshire in the early 1960s, you might want to check your LP collection for this gem.

Number	Title (A Side/B Side)	Yr	VG	VG+	NM

A

A.B. SKHY
45s
MGM

Number	Title (A Side/B Side)	Yr	VG	VG+	NM
❑ K 14086	Camel Back/Just What I Need	1969	2.00	4.00	8.00
❑ K 14086 [PS]	Camel Back/Just What I Need	1969	3.00	6.00	12.00

Albums
MGM

❑ SE-4628	A.B. Skhy	1969	3.75	7.50	15.00
❑ SE-4676	Ramblin' On	1970	3.75	7.50	15.00

A.F.O. EXECUTIVES WITH TAMI LYNN
Albums
A.F.O.

❑ 5002 [M]	A Compendium	1962	37.50	75.00	150.00

ABACO DREAM
45s
A&M

❑ 1081	Life and Death in G and A/Cat Woman	1969	2.00	4.00	8.00
❑ 1160	Another Night of Love/Chocolate Pudding	1970	2.00	4.00	8.00

ABBA Also see BJORN AND BENNY.
12-Inch Singles
ATLANTIC

❑ DSKO 81 [DJ]	Dancing Queen (same on both sides)	1976	6.25	12.50	25.00
❑ DSKO 202 [DJ]	Voulez-Vous (6:05) (same on both sides)	1979	5.00	10.00	20.00
❑ DMD 308 [DJ]	Lay All Your Love on Me/ The Day Before You Came	1980	5.00	10.00	20.00
❑ DMD 329 [DJ]	The Visitors (Long)/(Short)	1981	3.75	7.50	15.00

POLYDOR

❑ 859789-1	Dancing Queen/Take a Chance on Me	1992	2.50	5.00	10.00

45s
ATLANTIC

❑ PR 380 [DJ]	Happy New Year (mono/stereo)	1980	3.00	6.00	12.00
❑ PR 390 [DJ]	Happy New Year	1980	3.00	6.00	12.00
—One-sided promo					
❑ 3035	Waterloo/Watch Out	1974	—	2.50	5.00
❑ 3035 [PS]	Waterloo	1974	3.75	7.50	15.00
—Sleeve is promo only					
❑ 3209	Honey Honey/Dance (While the Music Still Goes On)	1974	—	2.50	5.00
❑ 3240	Hasta Manana/Ring Ring	1975	—	2.50	5.00
❑ 3265	SOS/Man in the Middle	1975	—	2.50	5.00
❑ 3310	I Do, I Do, I Do, I Do, I Do/Bang-a-Boomerang	1975	—	2.50	5.00
❑ 3315	Mamma Mia/Tropical Loveland	1976	—	2.50	5.00
❑ 3346	Fernando/Rock Me	1976	—	2.00	4.00
❑ 3346	Fernando/Tropical Loveland	1976	—	2.00	4.00
❑ 3372	Dancing Queen/That's Me	1976	—	2.00	4.00
❑ 3387	Knowing Me, Knowing You/Happy Hawaii	1977	—	2.00	4.00
❑ 3387 [PS]	Knowing Me, Knowing You/Happy Hawaii	1977	—	2.50	5.00
❑ 3434	Money, Money, Money/Crazy World	1977	—	2.00	4.00
❑ 3434 [PS]	Money, Money, Money/Crazy World	1977	—	3.00	6.00
❑ 3449	The Name of the Game/I Wonder (Departure)	1977	—	2.00	4.00
❑ 3457	Take a Chance on Me/I'm a Marionette	1978	—	2.00	4.00
❑ 3457 [PS]	Take a Chance on Me/I'm a Marionette	1978	—	3.00	6.00
❑ 3574	Does Your Mother Know/Kisses of Fire	1979	—	2.00	4.00
❑ 3574 [PS]	Does Your Mother Know/Kisses of Fire	1979	—	2.50	5.00
❑ 3609	Voulez-Vous/Angeleyes	1979	—	2.00	4.00
❑ 3609 [PS]	Voulez-Vous/Angeleyes	1979	—	2.50	5.00
❑ 3629	Chiquitita/Lovelight	1979	—	2.00	4.00
❑ 3630	Chiquitita (Spanish Version)/I Have a Dream (Spanish Version)	1979	—	2.50	5.00
❑ 3652	Gimme! Gimme! Gimme! (A Man After Midnight)/The King Has Lost His Crown	1980	—	2.00	4.00
❑ 3776	The Winner Takes It All/Elaine	1980	—	2.00	4.00
❑ 3806	Super Trouper/The Piper	1981	—	2.00	4.00
❑ 3806 [PS]	Super Trouper/The Piper	1981	—	2.00	4.00
❑ 3826	On and On and On/Lay All Your Love on Me	1981	—	2.00	4.00
❑ 3889	When All Is Said and Done/Should I Laugh or Cry	1982	—	—	3.00
❑ 3889 [PS]	When All Is Said and Done/Should I Laugh or Cry	1982	—	—	3.00
❑ 4031	The Visitors/Head Over Heels	1982	—	—	3.00
❑ 4031 [PS]	The Visitors/Head Over Heels	1982	—	—	3.00
❑ 89881	One of Us/Should I Laugh or Cry	1983	—	—	3.00
❑ 89881 [PS]	One of Us/Should I Laugh or Cry	1983	—	2.00	4.00
❑ 89948	The Day Before You Came/Cassandra	1982	—	—	3.00

CBS INTERNATIONAL

❑ DAS 40001 [DJ]	Estoy Sonando/Conociendome, Conociendote	1980	5.00	10.00	20.00
❑ DAS 40002 [DJ]	Fernando/Al Andar	1980	5.00	10.00	20.00
❑ DAS 40003 [DJ]	Dame! Dame! Dame!/Gracias Por La Musica	1980	5.00	10.00	20.00
—The above three are in Spanish, pressed in the U.S. for Hispanic markets; we don't know if stock copies exist					

Albums
ATLANTIC

❑ PR 300 [DJ]	Abba	1978	7.50	15.00	30.00
❑ PR 432 [DJ]	A Collection of Hits	1982	7.50	15.00	30.00
❑ PR 436 [(2)DJ]	The Abba Special	1983	12.50	25.00	50.00
❑ SD 16000	Voulez-Vous	1979	2.50	5.00	10.00
❑ SD 16009	Greatest Hits, Vol. 2	1979	3.00	6.00	12.00
❑ SD 16023	Super Trouper	1980	2.50	5.00	10.00
❑ SD 18101	Waterloo	1974	3.00	6.00	12.00
❑ SD 18146	Abba	1975	3.00	6.00	12.00
❑ SD 18189	Greatest Hits	1976	3.00	6.00	12.00
❑ SD 18207	Arrival	1977	3.00	6.00	12.00
❑ SD 19114	Greatest Hits	1977	2.50	5.00	10.00
❑ SD 19115	Arrival	1977	2.50	5.00	10.00
❑ SD 19164	The Album	1978	2.50	5.00	10.00
❑ SD 19332	The Visitors	1981	2.50	5.00	10.00
❑ 80036 [(2)]	The Singles — The First Ten Years	1982	3.75	7.50	15.00
❑ 80142	I Love Abba	1984	2.50	5.00	10.00
❑ 81675	Abba Live	1986	3.00	6.00	12.00

CBS INTERNATIONAL

❑ DAL 40301	Gracias Por La Musica	1980	10.00	20.00	40.00
—Spanish-language versions of some of their hits, this LP was pressed in the U.S.					

K-TEL

❑ NU 9510	The Magic of Abba	1978	3.75	7.50	15.00

NAUTILUS

❑ NR-20	Arrival	1981	7.50	15.00	30.00
—Audiophile vinyl					

ABBEY TAVERN SINGERS, THE
Albums
V.I.P.

❑ 402 [M]	We're Off to Dublin in the Green	1966	10.00	20.00	40.00
❑ S-402 [S]	We're Off to Dublin in the Green	1966	12.50	25.00	50.00

ABBOTT, BILLY, AND THE JEWELS
45s
PARKWAY

❑ 874	Groovy Baby/Come On Dance with Me	1963	5.00	10.00	20.00
❑ 905	It Isn't Fair/Hey, Good Lookin'	1964	5.00	10.00	20.00

ABRAMS, MISS, AND THE STRAWBERRY POINT SCHOOL THIRD GRADE CLASS
45s
A&M

❑ 1263	Floating Away/Wonder	1971	—	2.50	5.00

REPRISE

❑ 0928	Mill Valley/The Happiest Day of My Life	1970	—	2.00	4.00
❑ 0928 [PS]	Mill Valley/The Happiest Day of My Life	1970	—	2.50	5.00
❑ 0971	Buildin' a Heaven on Earth/This Time of Life	1970	—	2.00	4.00
❑ 1098	Green Grass/Sweet Summertime	1972	—	2.00	4.00
❑ 1136	I Never Asked/Wonder	1972	—	2.00	4.00
❑ 1322	America (Let's Get Started Again)/Running in the Green Grass	1975	—	2.00	4.00
—This one by Miss Abrams' "Fourth Grade Class"					
❑ 1322 [PS]	America (Let's Get Started Again)/Running in the Green Grass	1975	—	3.50	7.00

Albums
REPRISE

❑ MS 2098	Abrams, Miss, and the Strawberry Point School Third Grade Class	1972	3.00	6.00	12.00

ABSTRACTS, THE
45s
POMPEII

❑ 66679	Smell the Incense/See the Birdies	1968	5.00	10.00	20.00

Albums
POMPEII

❑ 6002 [M]	The Abstracts	1968	20.00	40.00	80.00
—Stereo cover with "DJ Copy Monaural" sticker; white label promo record					
❑ SD 6002 [S]	The Abstracts	1968	10.00	20.00	40.00

ACADEMICS, THE
45s
ANCHO

❑ 100	At My Front Door/Darla, My Darling	1957	20.00	40.00	80.00
❑ 101	Too Good to Be True/Heavenly Love	1957	25.00	50.00	100.00
—Reissue of Anchor 101					

ANCHOR

❑ 101	Too Good to Be True/Heavenly Love	1957	250.00	500.00	1000.
—Original edition					

ELMONT

❑ 1001/2	Drive-In Movie/Something Cool	1958	15.00	30.00	60.00

ACCENTS, THE Several different groups.
45s
ACCENT

❑ 1036	Voice of the Boyous/Where Will You Be	1956	7.50	15.00	30.00
❑ 1037	The Name Song/This Ole Body	1956	7.50	15.00	30.00

BANGAR

❑ 605	Wherever There's a Will/Howlin' for My Baby	1964	3.75	7.50	15.00
❑ 629	Searchin'/You Don't Love Me	1964	3.75	7.50	15.00
❑ 648	Road Runner/Why	1965	3.75	7.50	15.00

BRUNSWICK

❑ 55100	Wiggle Waggle/Dreamin' and Schemin'	1958	3.75	7.50	15.00
❑ 55123	I Give My Heart to You/Ching-a-Ling	1959	3.75	7.50	15.00

C-R-C

❑ 1017	I've Got Better Things to Do/ Then He Starts to Cry	1964	5.00	10.00	20.00
—Featuring Sandi					

CHALLENGE

❑ 59254	Tell Me/Better Watch Out Boy	1964	3.75	7.50	15.00
❑ 59294	Sweet Talk/Tell Me	1965	3.00	6.00	12.00

CHARTER

❑ 1017	I've Got Better Things to Do/ Then He Starts to Cry	1964	3.75	7.50	15.00
—Featuring Sandi					

COMMERCE

❑ 5012	Tell Me/Better Watch Out Boy	1964	5.00	10.00	20.00

CORAL

❑ 62151	Autumn Leaves/Anything You Want Me to Be	1959	3.75	7.50	15.00

GARRETT

❑ 4008	Wherever There's a Will/Howlin' for My Baby	1964	5.00	10.00	20.00
❑ 4014	Road Runner/Why	1965	5.00	10.00	20.00

JERDEN

❑ 728	Linda Lou/Stickey	1964	3.00	6.00	12.00
—Featuring Ron Peterson					

JUBILEE

❑ 5353	Red Light/22 Del Rio Ave.	1958	3.75	7.50	15.00

Number	Title (A Side/B Side)	Yr	VG	VG+	NM
KARATE					
❏ 529	He's the One/On the Run	1966	3.75	7.50	15.00
LIBERTY					
❏ 55813	I Really Love You/What Do You Want to Do (Little Darlin')	1965	3.00	6.00	12.00
M-PAC!					
❏ 7216	New Girl/Do You Need a Good Man	1964	5.00	10.00	20.00
MERCURY					
❏ 72154	Enchanted Garden/Tell Me Now	1963	2.50	5.00	10.00
ONE-DERFUL					
❏ 4833	You Better Think Again/Who You Gonna Love	1965	5.00	10.00	20.00
RCA VICTOR					
❏ 74-0127	Love Is a Many-Splendored Thing/ Yours Until Tomorrow	1969	—	3.00	6.00
SULTAN					
❏ 5500	Rags to Riches/Where Can I Go?	1961	15.00	30.00	60.00
VEE JAY					
❏ 484	Our Wonderful Love/A Hundred Walkin' Cats	1963	2.00	4.00	8.00

ACE
45s
ANCHOR

Number	Title (A Side/B Side)	Yr	VG	VG+	NM
❏ 21000	How Long/Sniffin' About	1975	—	2.50	5.00
❏ 21001	No Future in Your Eyes/I'm a Man	1975	—	2.50	5.00
❏ 21002	Rock & Roll Runaway/Know How It Feels	1975	—	2.50	5.00
❏ 21004	You're All That I Need/(B-side unknown)	1976	—	2.50	5.00
Albums					
ANCHOR					
❏ ANCL-2001	Five-a-Side (An Ace Album)	1975	3.00	6.00	12.00
❏ ANCL-2013	Time for Another	1975	3.00	6.00	12.00
❏ ANCL-2020	No Strings	1977	3.00	6.00	12.00

ACE, JOHNNY
45s
DUKE

Number	Title (A Side/B Side)	Yr	VG	VG+	NM
❏ 102	My Song/Follow the Rule	1952	20.00	40.00	80.00
❏ 107	Cross My Heart/Angel	1953	15.00	30.00	60.00
❏ 112	The Clock/Ace's Wild	1953	15.00	30.00	60.00
❏ 118	Saving My Love for You/Yes Baby	1953	10.00	20.00	40.00
❏ 128	Please Forgive Me/You've Been Gone So Long	1954	10.00	20.00	40.00
❏ 132	Never Let Me Go/Burley Cutie	1954	10.00	20.00	40.00
❏ 136	Pledging My Love/No Money	1954	10.00	20.00	40.00
❏ 144	Anymore/How Can You Be So Mean	1955	10.00	20.00	40.00
❏ 148	So Lonely/I'm Crazy	1956	7.50	15.00	30.00
❏ 154	Still Love You So/Don't You Know	1956	7.50	15.00	30.00
FLAIR					
❏ 1015	Midnight Hours Journey/Trouble and Me	1953	37.50	75.00	150.00
—B-side by Earl Forrest					
7-Inch Extended Plays					
DUKE					
❏ 80	Pledging My Love/Saving My Love for You// Angel/Please Forgive Me	1955	37.50	75.00	150.00
❏ 80 [PS]	Memorial Album	1955	37.50	75.00	150.00
❏ 81	The Clock/Never Let Me Go//Cross My Heart/ My Song	1955	37.50	75.00	150.00
❏ 81 [PS]	Tribute to Johnny Ace	1955	37.50	75.00	150.00
Albums					
ABC DUKE					
❏ DLPX-71	Memorial Album	1974	5.00	10.00	20.00
DUKE					
❏ DLP-70 [10]	Memorial Album for Johnny Ace	1955	400.00	800.00	1200.
❏ DLP-71 [M]	Memorial Album for Johnny Ace	1956	125.00	250.00	500.00
—With no playing card on front cover					
❏ DLP-71 [M]	Memorial Album for Johnny Ace	1961	50.00	100.00	200.00
—With playing card on front cover					
❏ DLP-71 [M]	Memorial Album for Johnny Ace	1961	2000.	3000.	4000.
—Playing card cover; red vinyl					
❏ LP-71 [R]	Memorial Album for Johnny Ace	196?	12.50	25.00	50.00
—Orange label; trail-off number is "LRS-71"					
MCA					
❏ 27014	Memorial Album	1983	2.00	4.00	8.00

ACE, SONNY
45s
ATLANTIC

Number	Title (A Side/B Side)	Yr	VG	VG+	NM
❏ 2364	Wooleh Booleh/Chili Peppers	1966	2.50	5.00	10.00

ACE SPECTRUM
12-Inch Singles
ATLANTIC

Number	Title (A Side/B Side)	Yr	VG	VG+	NM
❏ DSKO 77	Live and Learn (5:50) (same on both sides)	1976	7.50	15.00	30.00
45s					
ATLANTIC					
❏ 3012	Don't Send Nobody Else/ Don't Let Me Be Lonely Tonight	1974	12.50	25.00	50.00
❏ 3281	Trust Me/I Just Want to Spend the Night with You	1975	6.25	12.50	25.00
❏ 3296	Without You/Keep Holding On	1975	10.00	20.00	40.00
❏ 3353	Live and Learn/Just Like in the Movies	1976	5.00	10.00	20.00
Albums					
ATLANTIC					
❏ SD 7299	Inner Spectrum	1974	5.00	10.00	20.00
❏ SD 18143	Low Rent Rendezvous	1975	5.00	10.00	20.00
❏ SD 18185	Just Like in the Movies	1976	5.00	10.00	20.00

ACKLES, DAVID
45s
ELEKTRA

Number	Title (A Side/B Side)	Yr	VG	VG+	NM
❏ 45634	Down River/L.A. Route and Chicago	1968	2.00	4.00	8.00
❏ 45676	That's No Reason to Cry/Subway to the Country	1970	2.00	4.00	8.00
❏ 45712	One Night Stand/Be My Friend	1971	—	3.00	6.00
❏ 45797	Love's Enough/American Gothic	1972	—	3.00	6.00
❏ 45810	Oh California/One Night Stand	1972	—	3.00	6.00

Number	Title (A Side/B Side)	Yr	VG	VG+	NM
Albums					
COLUMBIA					
❏ KC 32466	Five & Dime	1973	3.00	6.00	12.00
ELEKTRA					
❏ EKS-74022	David Ackles	1968	3.75	7.50	15.00
❏ EKS-74060	Subway to the Country	1970	3.00	6.00	12.00
❏ EKS-75032	American Gothic	1972	3.00	6.00	12.00

ACKLIN, BARBARA
45s
BRUNSWICK

Number	Title (A Side/B Side)	Yr	VG	VG+	NM
❏ 55319	Fool, Fool, Fool (Look in the Mirror)/Your Sweet Loving	1967	2.00	4.00	8.00
❏ 55355	I've Got You Baby/Old Matchmaker	1967	2.00	4.00	8.00
❏ 55379	Love Makes a Woman/Come and See My Baby	1968	2.00	4.00	8.00
❏ 55388	Just Ain't No Love/Please Sunrise Please	1968	2.00	4.00	8.00
❏ 55388 [PS]	Just Ain't No Love/Please Sunrise Please	1968	3.75	7.50	15.00
❏ 55399	Am I the Same Girl/Be By My Side	1969	2.00	4.00	8.00
❏ 55412	Seven Days of Night/Raggedy Ride	1969	2.00	4.00	8.00
❏ 55421	After You/More Ways Than One	1969	2.00	4.00	8.00
❏ 55433	Is It Me/Someone Else's Arms	1970	2.00	4.00	8.00
❏ 55440	I Did It/I'm Living with a Memory	1970	2.00	4.00	8.00
❏ 55447	I Can't Do My Thing/Make the Man Love You	1971	2.00	4.00	8.00
❏ 55465	Lady, Lady, Lady/Stop, Look and Listen	1971	2.00	4.00	8.00
❏ 55486	I Call It Trouble/Love You Are Mine Today	1972	2.00	4.00	8.00
❏ 55501	I'm Gonna Bake a Man/I Call It Trouble	1973	—	3.00	6.00
CAPITOL					
❏ 3892	Raindrops/Here You Come Again	1974	—	2.50	5.00
❏ 4013	Special Loving/You Gave Him Everything, But I Gave Him Love	1974	—	2.50	5.00
❏ 4061	Give Me Some of Your Sweet Love/Fire Love	1975	—	2.50	5.00
SPECIAL AGENT					
❏ 203	I'm Not Mad Anymore/(B-side unknown)	196?	300.00	600.00	1200.
Albums					
BRUNSWICK					
❏ BL 754129	Great Soul Hits	1967	6.25	12.50	25.00
❏ BL 754137	Love Makes a Woman	1968	5.00	10.00	20.00
❏ BL 754148	Seven Days of Night	1969	5.00	10.00	20.00
❏ BL 754156	Someone Else's Arms	1970	5.00	10.00	20.00
❏ BL 754166	I Did It	1971	5.00	10.00	20.00
❏ BL 754187	I Call It Trouble	1972	5.00	10.00	20.00
CAPITOL					
❏ ST-11377	A Place in the Sun	1975	3.00	6.00	12.00

ACORNS, THE
45s
UNART

Number	Title (A Side/B Side)	Yr	VG	VG+	NM
❏ 2006	Angel/I'm Gonna Stick to You	1958	5.00	10.00	20.00
❏ 2015	Please Come Back/Your Name and Mine	1959	5.00	10.00	20.00

ACTION, THE
45s
CAPITOL

Number	Title (A Side/B Side)	Yr	VG	VG+	NM
❏ 5949	Never Ever/24th Hour	1967	2.00	4.00	8.00

ACUFF, ROY
45s
CAPITOL

Number	Title (A Side/B Side)	Yr	VG	VG+	NM
❏ F2385	What Will I Do/Tied Down	1953	6.25	12.50	25.00
❏ F2460	Lonesome Joe/Is It Love or Is It Lies?	1953	6.25	12.50	25.00
❏ F2548	Don't Say Goodbye/Sixteen Chickens and a Tambourine	1953	6.25	12.50	25.00
❏ F2642	Swamp Lily/Sweep Around Your Own Back Door	1953	6.25	12.50	25.00
❏ F2738	Rushing Around/Whoa Mule	1954	6.25	12.50	25.00
❏ F2820	Sunshine Special/I Closed My Heart's Door	1954	6.25	12.50	25.00
❏ F2901	I'm Planting a Rose/Streamlined Heartbreaker	1954	6.25	12.50	25.00
❏ F3064	Don't Judge Your Neighbors/ Thief Upon the Tree	1955	6.25	12.50	25.00
❏ F3115	That's What Makes the Juke Box Play/ Night Spots	1955	6.25	12.50	25.00
❏ F3209	Little Moses/Oh Those Tombs	1955	6.25	12.50	25.00
COLUMBIA					
❏ 2-357	Lonesome Old River Blues/It's Just About Time	1949	10.00	20.00	40.00
—Microgroove 33 1/3 rpm 7-inch single					
❏ 2-483	The Day They Laid Mary Away/It's All Right Now	1950	10.00	20.00	40.00
—Microgroove 33 1/3 rpm 7-inch single					
❏ 4-2792	A Plastic Heart/Your Address Unknown	1951	7.50	15.00	30.00
❏ 4-20804	Pliney Jane/Baldknob, Arkansas	1951	7.50	15.00	30.00
❏ 4-20828	Doug MacArthur/In the Shadow of the Smokies	1951	7.50	15.00	30.00
❏ 4-20858	Advice to Joe/When My Money Ran Out	1951	7.50	15.00	30.00
❏ 4-20877	Just Friends/ Thy Burdens Are Greater Than Mine	1952	6.25	12.50	25.00
❏ 4-20912	Ten Little Numbers/My Tears Don't Show	1952	6.25	12.50	25.00
❏ 4-20951	Cheating/ Don't Hang Your Dirty Linen on the Line	1952	6.25	12.50	25.00
❏ 4-21018	Wonder Is All I Do/She Isn't Guaranteed	1952	6.25	12.50	25.00
DECCA					
❏ 9-29748	Crazy Worried Mind/Along the China Coast	1955	5.00	10.00	20.00
❏ 9-29935	Goodbye Mr. Brown/Mother Hold Me Tight	1956	5.00	10.00	20.00
—With Kitty Wells					
❏ 9-30141	I Like Mountain Music/It's Hard to Love	1956	5.00	10.00	20.00
ELEKTRA					
❏ 45515	That's the Man I'm Looking For/ (B-side unknown)	1978	—	2.50	5.00
❏ 46515	Freight Train Blues/Don't Worry 'Bout the Walk	1979	—	2.50	5.00
❏ 47040	I Can't Help It (If I'm Still in Love with You)/ Cold, Cold Heart	1980	—	2.50	5.00
❏ 47480	Smokey Mountain Memories/ What Have They Done to the Trains	1982	—	2.50	5.00

Number	Title (A Side/B Side)	Yr	VG	VG+	NM
❑ 69937	Fireball Mail/The Stage	1982	—	2.50	5.00

—B-side by Boxcar Willie

HICKORY

Number	Title (A Side/B Side)	Yr	VG	VG+	NM
❑ 1073	Once More/I Don't Care (If You Don't Love Me)	1958	3.75	7.50	15.00
❑ 1081	The One I Love (Is Gone)/				
	Searchin' for Happiness	1958	3.75	7.50	15.00
❑ 1090	So Many Times/				
	They'll Never Take Her Love from Me	1958	3.75	7.50	15.00
❑ 1097	Come and Knock (On the Door of My Heart)/My				
	Love Came Back to Me	1959	3.75	7.50	15.00
❑ 1106	Nero Played His Fiddle/Write Me Sweetheart	1959	3.75	7.50	15.00
❑ 1113	Don't Know Why/Thanks for Not Telling Me	1960	3.00	6.00	12.00
❑ 1134	Mountain Guitar/Till No Longer You Care (For Me)	1960	3.00	6.00	12.00
❑ 1142	Streamlined Cannon Ball/Time Will Make You Pay	1961	3.00	6.00	12.00
❑ 1149	Little Mary/Lost John, He's Gone	1961	3.00	6.00	12.00
❑ 1160	Six More Days/Willie Boy, The Crippled Boy	1962	3.00	6.00	12.00
❑ 1178	Wabash Cannonball/Old Age Pension Check	1962	3.00	6.00	12.00
❑ 1191	Fireball Mail/The Great Speckled Bird	1962	3.00	6.00	12.00
❑ 1206	Don't Make Me Go to Bed and I'll Be Good/Pins				
	and Needles (In My Heart)	1963	3.00	6.00	12.00
❑ 1223	The Great Titanic/The Birmingham Jail	1963	3.00	6.00	12.00
❑ 1244	Low and Lonely/Wabash Cannonball	1964	2.50	5.00	10.00
❑ 1271	Do You Wonder Why/				
	Things That Might Have Been	1964	2.50	5.00	10.00
❑ 1291	Freight Train Blues/All the World Is Lonely Now	1965	2.50	5.00	10.00
❑ 1316	Life to Go/Rising Sun	1965	2.50	5.00	10.00
❑ 1331	I'm Planning a Rose/Tennessee Central	1965	2.50	5.00	10.00
❑ 1365	Pan American/Don't Tell Mama	1966	2.50	5.00	10.00
❑ 1394	Golden Treasure/Lost Highway	1966	2.50	5.00	10.00
❑ 1424	Kaw-Liga/Couldn't Believe It Was True	1966	2.50	5.00	10.00
❑ 1479	I Love You Because/I'm Movin' On	1967	2.50	5.00	10.00
❑ 1497	I'll Go On Alone/Uncle Pen	1967	2.50	5.00	10.00
❑ 1519	Don't Be Angry/				
	The Nearest Thing to Heaven Is You	1968	2.50	5.00	10.00
❑ 1581	Life to Go/Each Season Changes You	1970	2.00	4.00	8.00
❑ 1627	Somebody Touched Me/				
	Carry Me Back to the Mountains	1972	2.00	4.00	8.00
❑ 1636	A Pale Horse and His Ride/Sing a Country Song	1972	2.00	4.00	8.00
❑ 1644	Satisfied Mind/Just a Friend	1973	2.00	4.00	8.00

HICKORY/MGM

Number	Title (A Side/B Side)	Yr	VG	VG+	NM
❑ 314	Back in the Country/Jole Blon	1974	—	3.00	6.00
❑ 319	Old Time Sunshine Song/This World Can't				
	Stand Long	1974	—	3.00	6.00
❑ 336	Back Down to Atlanta/A Most Reasonable Guy	1974	—	3.00	6.00
❑ 341	Fireball Mail/Roof Top Lullaby	1975	—	3.00	6.00
❑ 348	A Whole Month of Sundays/I Can't Find a Train	1975	—	3.00	6.00
❑ 355	That's Country/Take Me Home, Country Roads	1975	—	3.00	6.00
❑ 362	Walk a Mile in Your Neighbor's Shoes/Waltz in				
	the Wind	1975	—	3.00	6.00

7-Inch Extended Plays

COLUMBIA

Number	Title (A Side/B Side)	Yr	VG	VG+	NM
❑ H 4-3 [PS]	Songs of the Smoky Mountains	195?	3.75	7.50	15.00

—Fold-open sleeve for 6-1230 and 6-1231

Number	Title (A Side/B Side)	Yr	VG	VG+	NM
❑ 6-1230	Wreck on the Highway/Fire Ball Mail//Wait for				
	the Light to Shine/Low and Lonely	195?	3.75	7.50	15.00

—Alternate numbers are "H 4-3-1" and "H 4-3-4"

Number	Title (A Side/B Side)	Yr	VG	VG+	NM
❑ 6-1231	Precious Jewel/Pins and Needles//Wabash				
	Cannon Ball/Freight Train Blues	195?	3.75	7.50	15.00

—Alternate numbers are "H 4-3-2" and "H 4-3-3"

Number	Title (A Side/B Side)	Yr	VG	VG+	NM
❑ B-2803	Wabash Cannon Ball/The Precious Jewel//				
	Freight Train Blues/Wreck on the Highway	195?	3.75	7.50	15.00
❑ B-2803 [PS]	Roy Acuff (Hall of Fame Series)	195?	3.75	7.50	15.00

Albums

CAPITOL

Number	Title (A Side/B Side)	Yr	VG	VG+	NM
❑ T 617 [M]	Songs of the Smoky Mountains	1955	15.00	30.00	60.00
❑ DT 1870 [R]	The Best of Roy Acuff	1963	5.00	10.00	20.00
❑ T 1870 [M]	The Best of Roy Acuff	1963	7.50	15.00	30.00
❑ DT 2103 [R]	The Great Roy Acuff	1964	3.75	7.50	15.00
❑ T 2103 [M]	The Great Roy Acuff	1964	6.25	12.50	25.00
❑ ST 2276 [S]	The Voice of Country Music	1965	10.00	20.00	40.00
❑ T 2276 [M]	The Voice of Country Music	1965	7.50	15.00	30.00

COLUMBIA

Number	Title (A Side/B Side)	Yr	VG	VG+	NM
❑ CL 9004 [10]	Songs of the Smoky Mountains	1949	50.00	100.00	200.00
❑ CL 9010 [10]	Old Time Barn Dance	1949	37.50	75.00	150.00
❑ CL 9013 [10]	Songs of the Saddle	1950	37.50	75.00	150.00
❑ FC 39998	Columbia Historic Edition	1985	2.50	5.00	10.00

ELEKTRA

Number	Title (A Side/B Side)	Yr	VG	VG+	NM
❑ E-C 10-1-78 [DJ]	An Interview with Roy Acuff	1978	6.25	12.50	25.00

HARMONY

Number	Title (A Side/B Side)	Yr	VG	VG+	NM
❑ HL 7082 [M]	Great Speckled Bird	1958	6.25	12.50	25.00
❑ HL 7294 [M]	That Glory Bound Train	1961	5.00	10.00	20.00
❑ HL 7342 [M]	The Great Roy Acuff	196?	3.75	7.50	15.00
❑ HL 7376 [M]	Waiting for My Call to Glory	196?	3.75	7.50	15.00

HICKORY

Number	Title (A Side/B Side)	Yr	VG	VG+	NM
❑ LPM-H-101 [M]	Once More It's Roy Acuff	1961	7.50	15.00	30.00
❑ LPM-109 [M]	King of Country Music — All-Time Greatest Hits	1962	6.25	12.50	25.00
❑ LPM-113 [M]	Roy Acuff — Star of the Grand Ole Opry	1963	6.25	12.50	25.00
❑ LPM-114 [M]	The World Is His Stage	1963	6.25	12.50	25.00
❑ LPM-115 [M]	Roy Acuff Sings American Folk Songs	1963	6.25	12.50	25.00
❑ LPM-117 [M]	Hand-Clapping Gospel Songs	1963	6.25	12.50	25.00
❑ LPM-119 [M]	Country Music Hall of Fame	1964	5.00	10.00	20.00
❑ LPM-125 [M]	Great Train Songs	1965	5.00	10.00	20.00
❑ LPM-134 [M]	Roy Acuff Sings Hank Williams	1966	10.00	20.00	40.00
❑ LPS-134 [S]	Roy Acuff Sings Hank Williams	1966	10.00	20.00	40.00
❑ LPS-139	Famous Opry Favorites	1967	5.00	10.00	20.00
❑ LPS-145	Living Legend	1968	5.00	10.00	20.00
❑ LPS-147	Treasury of Country Hits	1969	5.00	10.00	20.00
❑ LPS-156	Roy Acuff Time	1970	5.00	10.00	20.00
❑ DT-90698 [R]	Great Train Songs	1965	6.25	12.50	25.00

—Capitol Record Club edition

Number	Title (A Side/B Side)	Yr	VG	VG+	NM
❑ T-90704 [M]	King of Country Music — All-Time Greatest Hits	1966	6.25	12.50	25.00

—Capitol Record Club edition

Number	Title (A Side/B Side)	Yr	VG	VG+	NM
❑ ST-91297	Famous Opry Favorites	1967	6.25	12.50	25.00

—Capitol Record Club edition

METRO

Number	Title (A Side/B Side)	Yr	VG	VG+	NM
❑ M 508 [M]	Roy Acuff	1965	3.75	7.50	15.00
❑ MS 508 [R]	Roy Acuff	1965	2.50	5.00	10.00

MGM

Number	Title (A Side/B Side)	Yr	VG	VG+	NM
❑ E-3707 [M]	Favorite Hymns	1958	12.50	25.00	50.00
❑ E-4044 [M]	Hymn Time	1962	6.25	12.50	25.00
❑ SE-4044 [R]	Hymn Time	196?	5.00	10.00	20.00

ROUNDER

Number	Title (A Side/B Side)	Yr	VG	VG+	NM
❑ SS-23	1936-1939: Steamboat Whistle Blues	1985	2.50	5.00	10.00
❑ SS-24	1939-1941: Fly Birdie Fly	1985	2.50	5.00	10.00

ACUFF, ROY, JR.

45s

HICKORY

Number	Title (A Side/B Side)	Yr	VG	VG+	NM
❑ 1349	Baby Just Said Goodbye/Wabash Cannonball	1965	2.50	5.00	10.00
❑ 1371	Stand Tall/You Won't Ever See Me Here Again	1966	2.50	5.00	10.00
❑ 1398	I Wish It Were Me/Turn That Frown Upside Down	1966	2.50	5.00	10.00
❑ 1425	Looks Like the Sun Ain't Gonna Shine/Victim of				
	Circumstances	1966	3.00	6.00	12.00

—As "Roy Junior"

Number	Title (A Side/B Side)	Yr	VG	VG+	NM
❑ 1456	The Lament of the Cherokee Reservation				
	Indian/The Luckiest Guy in the World	1967	3.00	6.00	12.00
❑ 1476	As Long As I Live/You, You, You, You	1967	2.50	5.00	10.00
❑ 1505	My World Has Stopped/Follow Your Drum	1968	2.50	5.00	10.00
❑ 1515	Blue Train (Of the Heartbreak Line)/Thru the				
	Windows of Your House	1968	2.50	5.00	10.00
❑ 1535	The Guy Who Played Bass (So Well in Harlin				
	Mason's Band)/The Luckiest Guy in the World	1969	2.50	5.00	10.00
❑ 1551	Looks Like Baby's Gone/Through the Windows				
	of Your Mind	1969	2.50	5.00	10.00
❑ 1583	Back Down to Atlanta/Outlaw	1970	2.00	4.00	8.00
❑ 1597	Running/Street Singer	1971	2.00	4.00	8.00

HICKORY/MGM

Number	Title (A Side/B Side)	Yr	VG	VG+	NM
❑ 321	California Lady/Take Me Back	1974	—	3.00	6.00
❑ 331	Don't Worry 'Bout the Mule/Precious Memories	1974	—	3.00	6.00
❑ 344	Good Morning Country Rain/Sittin' Around the				
	Campfire	1975	—	3.00	6.00
❑ 351	Good Time and T-Bird Wine/Turpentine Blues	1975	—	3.00	6.00
❑ 358	Baby, Maybe, Some Day/When She's Thirty	1975	—	3.00	6.00

ACUFF, ROY, JR., AND SUE THOMPSON

45s

HICKORY

Number	Title (A Side/B Side)	Yr	VG	VG+	NM
❑ 1542	Thoughts/Are You Teasing Me	1969	2.50	5.00	10.00
❑ 1558	Talk Back Trembling Lips/Till I Can't Take It				
	Anymore	1970	2.00	4.00	8.00
❑ 1573	Don't Let the Stars Get In Your Eyes/Why You				
	Been Gone	1970	2.00	4.00	8.00

AD LIBS, THE   Probably all the same group.

45s

AGP

Number	Title (A Side/B Side)	Yr	VG	VG+	NM
❑ 101	New York in the Dark/Human	1968	25.00	50.00	100.00

BLUE CAT

Number	Title (A Side/B Side)	Yr	VG	VG+	NM
❑ 102	The Boy from New York City/Kicked Around	1965	3.75	7.50	15.00
❑ 114	Ask Anybody/He Ain't No Angel	1965	2.50	5.00	10.00
❑ 119	On the Corner/Oo-Wee Oh Me Oh My	1965	2.50	5.00	10.00
❑ 123	Just a Down Home Girl/Johnny My Boy	1966	2.50	5.00	10.00

CAPITOL

Number	Title (A Side/B Side)	Yr	VG	VG+	NM
❑ 2944	Love Me/Know All About You	1970	—	3.00	6.00

JOHNNIE BOY

Number	Title (A Side/B Side)	Yr	VG	VG+	NM
❑ 01	Santa's On His Way/I Stayed Home (New Year's				
	Eve)	19??	2.00	4.00	8.00

KAREN

Number	Title (A Side/B Side)	Yr	VG	VG+	NM
❑ 1527	Think of Me/Every Boy and Girl	1966	5.00	10.00	20.00

PHILIPS

Number	Title (A Side/B Side)	Yr	VG	VG+	NM
❑ 40461	Don't Ever Leave Me/You're in Love	1967	2.00	4.00	8.00

SHARE

Number	Title (A Side/B Side)	Yr	VG	VG+	NM
❑ 101	You're Just a Rolling Stone/Show a Little				
	Appreciation	1969	2.00	4.00	8.00
❑ 104	Giving Up/Appreciation	1969	2.00	4.00	8.00
❑ 106	The Boy from New York City/Nothing Worse				
	Than Being Alone	1969	2.00	4.00	8.00

ADAM, MIKE AND TIM

45s

PRESS

Number	Title (A Side/B Side)	Yr	VG	VG+	NM
❑ 9728	Little Baby/You're the Reason Why	1964	2.50	5.00	10.00

ADAM'S APPLES

45s

BRUNSWICK

Number	Title (A Side/B Side)	Yr	VG	VG+	NM
❑ 55330	Don't Take It Out on This World/Don't You Want				
	Me Home	1967	25.00	50.00	100.00
❑ 55367	You Are the One I Love/Stop Along the Way	1968	12.50	25.00	50.00

ADAMS, ART

45s

CHERRY

Number	Title (A Side/B Side)	Yr	VG	VG+	NM
❑ 1004	Rock Crazy Baby/Indian Joe	1960	25.00	50.00	100.00
❑ 1018	Dancing Doll/She Don't Live Here Anymore	1960	25.00	50.00	100.00

ADAMS, BILLY

45s

AMY

Number	Title (A Side/B Side)	Yr	VG	VG+	NM
❑ 893	You and Me/Go (Go On, Get Out of Here Now)	1963	3.00	6.00	12.00

APT

Number	Title (A Side/B Side)	Yr	VG	VG+	NM
❑ 25072	My Happiness/Big M	1962	3.00	6.00	12.00

A

Number	Title (A Side/B Side)	Yr	VG	VG+	NM
CAPITOL					
❏ 4308	Count Every Star/Peggy's Party	1959	6.25	12.50	25.00
❏ 4373	Can't Get Enough/				
	The Gods Were Angry With Me	1960	6.25	12.50	25.00
DECCA					
❏ 30724	Baby I'm Bugged/				
	Short Hair and Turtle Neck Sweater	1958	7.50	15.00	30.00
DOT					
❏ 15689	You Heard Me Knocking/				
	True Love Will Come Your Way	1958	7.50	15.00	30.00
FERN					
❏ 807	Darling Take My Hand/Tender Years	1961	6.25	12.50	25.00
❏ 808	Tattle Tale/Born to Be a Loser	1961	6.25	12.50	25.00
❏ 812	Rip Van Winkle/Sleep Baby Sleep	1961	6.25	12.50	25.00
❏ 813	Comic Strip/Call Me	1961	6.25	12.50	25.00
HOME OF THE BLUES					
❏ 239	Looking for My Baby/Had the Blues	1962	2.50	5.00	10.00
❏ 242	My Happiness/Big M	1962	5.00	10.00	20.00
NAU VOO					
❏ 802	You've Gotta Have a Duck Tail/Walking Star	1959	25.00	50.00	100.00
❏ 805	Return of the All American Boy/That's My Baby	1959	18.75	37.50	75.00
❏ 808	Blue Eyed Ella/Fun House	1959	18.75	37.50	75.00
QUINCY					
❏ 932	Rock Pretty Mama/(B-side unknown)	195?	500.00	1000.	1500.
SUN					
❏ 389	Got My Mojo Workin'/Betty and Dupree	1964	5.00	10.00	20.00
❏ 391	Trouble in My Mind/Lookin' for Mary Ann	1964	5.00	10.00	20.00
❏ 394	Reconsider Baby/Ruby Jane	1964	5.00	10.00	20.00
❏ 401	Open the Door, Richard/Rock Me Baby	1966	5.00	10.00	20.00

ADAMS, CLIFF
45s

Number	Title (A Side/B Side)	Yr	VG	VG+	NM
DOT					
❏ 16385	Funny Kind of Feeling/Keep Off My Mountain	1962	2.50	5.00	10.00

ADAMS, FAYE
45s

Number	Title (A Side/B Side)	Yr	VG	VG+	NM
ATLANTIC					
❏ 1007	Sweet Talk/Watch Out, I Told You	1953	12.50	25.00	50.00
HERALD					
❏ 416	Shake a Hand/I've Got to Leave You	1953	7.50	15.00	30.00
—Black vinyl					
❏ 416	Shake a Hand/I've Got to Leave You	1953	25.00	50.00	100.00
—Red vinyl					
❏ 419	I'll Be True/Happiness to My Soul	1953	6.25	12.50	25.00
❏ 423	Say a Prayer/Every Day	1954	6.25	12.50	25.00
❏ 429	Somebody, Somewhere, Someday/Crazy				
	Mixed-Up World	1954	6.25	12.50	25.00
❏ 434	Hurts Me to My Heart/Ain't Gonna Tell	1954	6.25	12.50	25.00
❏ 439	I Owe My Heart to You/Love Ain't Nothin' to Play				
	With	1954	6.25	12.50	25.00
❏ 444	Anything for a Friend/Your Love Has My Heart				
	Burning	1955	6.25	12.50	25.00
❏ 450	You Ain't Been True/My Greatest Desire	1955	6.25	12.50	25.00
❏ 457	Angels Tell Me/Tag Along	1955	6.25	12.50	25.00
❏ 462	No Way Out/Same Old Me	1955	6.25	12.50	25.00
❏ 470	Teen-Age Heart/Witness to the Crime	1956	6.25	12.50	25.00
❏ 480	Takin' You Back/Don't Forget to Smile	1956	6.25	12.50	25.00
❏ 489	Anytime, Anyplace, Anywhere/The Hammer				
	Keeps Knockin'	1956	6.25	12.50	25.00
❏ 512	Shake a Hand/I'll Be True	1958	5.00	10.00	20.00
IMPERIAL					
❏ 5443	Keeper of My Heart/So Much	1957	5.00	10.00	20.00
❏ 5456	Johnny Lee/You're Crazy	1957	5.00	10.00	20.00
❏ 5471	I Have a Twinkle in My Eye/Someone Like You	1957	5.00	10.00	20.00
❏ 5525	When We Kiss/Everything	1958	5.00	10.00	20.00
LIDO					
❏ 603	That's All Right/It Made Me Cry	1960	3.00	6.00	12.00
❏ 606	It Can't Be Wrong/I Waited So Long	1960	3.00	6.00	12.00
SAVOY					
❏ 1606	Cry, You Crazy Heart/Step Up and Rescue Me	1960	3.00	6.00	12.00
❏ 4357	Sinner Man/God	197?	—	2.50	5.00
WARWICK					
❏ 590	Shake a Hand/It Hurts to My Heart	1960	3.00	6.00	12.00
❏ 620	Johnny, Don't Obey My Rules	1961	3.00	6.00	12.00
❏ 638	It Can't Be Wrong/It's Nice to Know	1961	3.00	6.00	12.00
Albums					
COLLECTABLES					
❏ COL-5122	Golden Classics	1988	2.50	5.00	10.00
WARWICK					
❏ W 2031 [M]	Shake a Hand	1961	150.00	300.00	600.00

ADAMS, JERRI
45s

Number	Title (A Side/B Side)	Yr	VG	VG+	NM
COLUMBIA					
❏ 4-40279	Alone Together/Two's a Crowd When Only				
	One's in Love	1954	3.75	7.50	15.00
❏ 4-40415	Guess I Had Too Much to Dream Last Night/				
	Snow Dreams	1955	3.75	7.50	15.00
❏ 4-40615	Happiness Is a Thing Called Joe/Take My Hand,				
	Show Me the Way	1955	3.75	7.50	15.00
❏ 4-40690	If I Forget You/Walk Fast	1956	3.75	7.50	15.00
❏ 4-40888	A Little Bit of Kindness/Suddenly (The Meeting)	1957	3.00	6.00	12.00
❏ 4-40992	Looking for Someone to Love/I'm All Right Now	1957	3.00	6.00	12.00
❏ 4-41111	Every Night About This Time/My Heart Tells Me	1958	3.00	6.00	12.00
FRATERNITY					
❏ F-874	Ivory Tower/All Around This Heart	1961	2.50	5.00	10.00
7-Inch Extended Plays					
COLUMBIA					
❏ B-9162	(contents unknown)	1956	3.00	6.00	12.00
❏ B-9162 [PS]	It's Cool Inside, Vol. 2	1956	3.00	6.00	12.00

ADAMS, JOHNNY
45s

Number	Title (A Side/B Side)	Yr	VG	VG+	NM
ARIOLA AMERICA					
❏ 7701	After All the Good Is Gone/Chasing Rainbows	1978	—	2.50	5.00
❏ 7718	Selfish/One Fine Day	1978	—	2.50	5.00
ATLANTIC					
❏ 2834	More Than One Way/You Got Your Kind of Life				
	to Live	1971	2.50	5.00	10.00
❏ 2887	Salt of the Earth/I'll Carry You	1972	2.50	5.00	10.00
❏ 2905	I Wish It Would Rain/You're a Lady	1972	2.50	5.00	10.00
GAMMA					
❏ 101	Best of Luck to You/Sharing You	197?	—	3.00	6.00
GONE					
❏ 5147	Going to the City/I'm Grateful	1964	12.50	25.00	50.00
HEP ME					
❏ 132	Spanish Harlem/Feel the Beat, Feel the Heat	197?	2.00	4.00	8.00
❏ 137	After All the Good Is Gone/Chasing Rainbows	197?	2.00	4.00	8.00
❏ 147	Love Me Now/I Only Wanna Be with You	197?	—	3.00	6.00
❏ 160	I Believe in You/It Only Rains on Me	197?	—	3.00	6.00
❏ 162	I Live My Whole World at Night/(There's) No				
	Gettin' Over Me	197?	2.00	4.00	8.00
MODERN					
❏ 1036	No In Between/Don't Wait Too Long	1967	3.75	7.50	15.00
❏ 1044	One Day/Your Kind of Love	1967	3.75	7.50	15.00
PACEMAKER					
❏ 240	A Place Called Home/Spunky Onions	1965	5.00	10.00	20.00
❏ 249	When I'll Stop Loving You/A Man Will Shed a				
	Few Tears	1965	5.00	10.00	20.00
❏ 255	Let Them Talk/Operator	1965	5.00	10.00	20.00
PAID					
❏ 105	Love Me Now/I Only Want to Be with You	1980	—	3.00	6.00
❏ 117	I'm Afraid to Let You Into My Life/				
	Hell Yes I Cheated	1981	—	3.00	6.00
RIC					
❏ 961	I Won't Cry/Who Are You	1959	6.25	12.50	25.00
❏ 963	Come On/Nowhere to Go	1959	6.25	12.50	25.00
❏ 966	Bells Are Ringing/Teach Me to Forget	1960	5.00	10.00	20.00
❏ 971	Let the Wind Blow/Someone for Me	1960	5.00	10.00	20.00
❏ 976	You Can Make It If You Try/Closer to You	1960	5.00	10.00	20.00
❏ 980	Wedding Day/O, So Nice	1961	5.00	10.00	20.00
❏ 983	I Solemnly Promise/Life Is Just a Struggle	1961	5.00	10.00	20.00
❏ 986	A Losing Battle/Who's Gonna Love You	1962	5.00	10.00	20.00
❏ 992	Showdown/Tra La La	1962	5.00	10.00	20.00
RON					
❏ 995	I Want to Do Everything for You/Lonely Drifter	196?	3.75	7.50	15.00
❏ 996	Cold, Cold Heart/Coming 'Round the Mountain	196?	3.75	7.50	15.00
SSS INTERNATIONAL					
❏ 750	Release Me/You Make a New Man Out of Me	1968	3.75	7.50	15.00
❏ 770	Reconsider Me/If I Could See You One More				
	Time	1969	3.75	7.50	15.00
❏ 780	I Can't Be All Bad/In a Moment of Weakness	1969	3.75	7.50	15.00
❏ 787	Proud Woman/Real Live Livin' Hurtin' Man	1970	3.00	6.00	12.00
❏ 797	Georgia Mountain Dew/				
	Real Live Livin' Hurtin' Man	1970	3.00	6.00	12.00
❏ 809	I Won't Cry/				
	I Want to Walk Through This Life with You	197?	3.00	6.00	12.00
❏ 831	South Side of Soul Street/S				
	omething Worth Leaving For	197?	3.00	6.00	12.00
❏ 865	Too Much Pride/I Don't Worry Myself	197?	2.50	5.00	10.00
❏ 867	Kiss the Hurt Away/				
	Something Worth Leaving For	197?	2.50	5.00	10.00
❏ 870	Born to Love You/You're a Bad Habit Baby	197?	2.50	5.00	10.00
❏ 873	How Can I Prove I Love You/Just Call Me Darling	197?	2.50	5.00	10.00
WATCH					
❏ 1906	Release Me/You Make a New Man Out of Me	1968	7.50	15.00	30.00
❏ 6330	I Brought It On Myself/				
	I Believe I'll Find Happiness	196?	10.00	20.00	40.00
❏ 6333	A Part of Me/Some Day	196?	10.00	20.00	40.00
Albums					
ANALOGUE PRODUCTIONS					
❏ APP 028	Johnny Adams Sings Doc Pomus —				
	The Real Me	199?	5.00	10.00	20.00
ARIOLA AMERICA					
❏ SW 50038	After All the Good Is Gone	1978	3.75	7.50	15.00
CHELSEA					
❏ CHL 525	Stand By Me	1977	6.25	12.50	25.00
HEP ME					
❏ 159	Christmas in New Orleans	197?	3.75	7.50	15.00
ROUNDER					
❏ 2044	From the Heart	1984	3.00	6.00	12.00
❏ 2049	After Dark	1986	3.00	6.00	12.00
❏ 2059	Room with a View of the Blues	1988	3.00	6.00	12.00
❏ 2095	Walking on a Tightrope	1989	3.00	6.00	12.00
SSS INTERNATIONAL					
❏ 5	Heart and Soul	1969	5.00	10.00	20.00

ADAMS, MIKE, AND THE RED JACKETS
Albums

Number	Title (A Side/B Side)	Yr	VG	VG+	NM
CROWN					
❏ CST-255 [S]	Twist Contest	1962	7.50	15.00	30.00
❏ CST-312 [S]	Surfer's Beat	1963	7.50	15.00	30.00
—Black vinyl					
❏ CST-312 [S]	Surfer's Beat	1963	25.00	50.00	100.00
—Red vinyl					
❏ CLP-5255 [M]	Twist Contest	1962	6.25	12.50	25.00
❏ CLP-5312 [M]	Surfer's Beat	1963	6.25	12.50	25.00

Number	Title (A Side/B Side)	Yr	VG	VG+	NM

ADAMS, RICHIE
45s
BELTONE
| ❏ 1001 | No Mistakin' It/The Right Way | 1961 | 3.75 | 7.50 | 15.00 |
| ❏ 1011 | Two Initials (In a Heart)/What Took You So Long | 1961 | 3.75 | 7.50 | 15.00 |
CONGRESS
❏ 217	I Understand/Lookin' for the Blues	1964	3.75	7.50	15.00
❏ 226	Are You Changing/The King	1964	3.75	7.50	15.00
❏ 232	Slippin' Away/What Am I	1965	3.75	7.50	15.00
❏ 248	Every Window in the City/I Ain't Gonna Make It Without You	1965	3.75	7.50	15.00
❏ 256	Road to Nowhere/I Can't Escape from You	1965	15.00	30.00	60.00
IMPERIAL
❏ 5806	Something Inside of Me Died/I Got Eyes	1962	3.75	7.50	15.00
❏ 5838	My Prayer of Love/Pakistan	1962	3.75	7.50	15.00
❏ 5856	It's Worth It/Test of Love	1962	3.75	7.50	15.00
MCA
| ❏ 41182 | The Best of the Rest of Our Lives/Warm | 1980 | — | 2.00 | 4.00 |
MGM
| ❏ 13629 | You Were Mine/Better Off Without You | 1966 | 2.50 | 5.00 | 10.00 |
P.I.P.
| ❏ 6519 | Mamacita/Lisa Lisa | 1976 | — | 2.00 | 4.00 |
RIBBON
| ❏ 6910 | Lonely One/Tell Me Baby Did You Wait | 1960 | 3.00 | 6.00 | 12.00 |
| ❏ 6913 | Back to School/Don't Go, My Love, Don't Go | 1960 | 3.00 | 6.00 | 12.00 |

ADDEO, LEO
Albums
RCA CAMDEN
❏ CAL-510 [M]	Hawaii in Hi-Fi	1960	3.75	7.50	15.00
❏ CAS-510 [S]	Hawaii in Stereo	1960	5.00	10.00	20.00
❏ CAL-594 [M]	More Hawaii in Hi-Fi	1961	3.75	7.50	15.00
❏ CAS-594 [S]	More Hawaii in Hi-Fi	1961	5.00	10.00	20.00
❏ CAL-672 [M]	Great Standards with a Hawaiian Touch	1962	3.00	6.00	12.00
❏ CAS-672 [S]	Great Standards with a Hawaiian Touch	1962	3.75	7.50	15.00
❏ CAL-726 [M]	Organ and Chimes Play Christmas Carols	1962	3.00	6.00	12.00
❏ CAS-726 [S]	Organ and Chimes Play Christmas Carols	1962	3.75	7.50	15.00
❏ CAL-759 [M]	Songs of Hawaii	1963	3.00	6.00	12.00
❏ CAS-759 [S]	Songs of Hawaii	1963	3.75	7.50	15.00
❏ CAL-807 [M]	Calypso and Other Island Favorites	1963	3.00	6.00	12.00
❏ CAS-807 [S]	Calypso and Other Island Favorites	1963	3.75	7.50	15.00
❏ CAL-828 [M]	"Hello Dolly" and Other Favorites	1964	3.00	6.00	12.00
❏ CAS-828 [S]	"Hello Dolly" and Other Favorites	1964	3.75	7.50	15.00
❏ CAL-853 [M]	Hawaiian Paradise	1964	3.00	6.00	12.00
❏ CAS-853 [S]	Hawaiian Paradise	1964	3.75	7.50	15.00
❏ CAL-901 [M]	Far Away Places	1965	3.00	6.00	12.00
❏ CAS-901 [S]	Far Away Places	1965	3.75	7.50	15.00
❏ CAL-977 [M]	Musical Orchids from Hawaii	1966	3.00	6.00	12.00
❏ CAS-977 [S]	Musical Orchids from Hawaii	1966	3.75	7.50	15.00
❏ CAL-2134 [M]	"Love Is a Hurtin' Thing" and Other Favorites	1966	3.00	6.00	12.00
❏ CAS-2134 [S]	"Love Is a Hurtin' Thing" and Other Favorites	1966	3.75	7.50	15.00
❏ CAL-2211 [M]	The Magic of Hawaii	1967	3.00	6.00	12.00
❏ CAS-2211 [S]	The Magic of Hawaii	1967	3.75	7.50	15.00
RCA VICTOR
| ❏ LPM-2414 [M] | Paradise Regained | 1961 | 3.75 | 7.50 | 15.00 |
| ❏ LSA-2414 [S] | Paradise Regained | 1961 | 7.50 | 15.00 | 30.00 |

ADDEO, NICKY
45s
EARLS
| ❏ 1533 | Gloria/Bring Back Your Heart | 19?? | 2.50 | 5.00 | 10.00 |
MELODY
| ❏ 1417 | Where There Is Love/You Can Depend on Me | 1964 | 6.25 | 12.50 | 25.00 |
REVELATION
| ❏ 7-101 | Danny Boy/A Lovely Way to Spend An Evening | 1964 | 125.00 | 250.00 | 500.00 |
SAVOY
❏ 200	Gloria/Bring Back Your Heart	1963	50.00	100.00	200.00
—Black vinyl					
❏ 200	Gloria/Bring Back Your Heart	1963	75.00	150.00	300.00
—Green vinyl					
❏ 200	Gloria/Bring Back Your Heart	1963	100.00	200.00	400.00
—Red vinyl					
SELSOM
| ❏ 104 | Over the Rainbow/Fool #2 | 1965 | 50.00 | 100.00 | 200.00 |

ADDRISI, DICK
45s
VALIANT
| ❏ 742 | You're Bad/Excuse Me | 1966 | 3.00 | 6.00 | 12.00 |

ADDRISI BROTHERS, THE
45s
BELL
| ❏ 45434 | Somebody Found Her/Who Do You Think I Am | 1974 | — | 2.00 | 4.00 |
BRAD
| ❏ 003 | I'll Be True/Everybody's Happy | 1958 | 8.75 | 17.50 | 35.00 |
BUDDAH
❏ 566	Slow Dancin' Don't Turn Me On (Short)/Slow Dancin' Don't Turn Me On (Long)	1977	—	2.50	5.00
❏ 579	Does She Do It Like She Dances/Baby, Love Is a Two-Way Street	1977	—	2.00	4.00
❏ 587	Never My Love/Emergency	1977	—	2.00	4.00
COLUMBIA
❏ 45521	We've Got to Get It On Again/You Make It All Worthwhile	1972	—	2.50	5.00
❏ 45610	One Last Time/I Can Feel You	1972	—	2.50	5.00
❏ 45705	Lifetime/I Can Count on You	1972	—	2.50	5.00
DEL-FI
❏ 4116	Cherrystone/Lilies Grow High	1959	7.50	15.00	30.00
❏ 4120	Saving My Kisses/Un Jarro	1959	7.50	15.00	30.00
❏ 4125	It's Love/Back to the Old Salt Mine	1959	7.50	15.00	30.00
❏ 4130	Gonna See My Baby/Ven Ami	1959	6.25	12.50	25.00
ELEKTRA
| ❏ 47203 | Honey Come Home/Red-Eye Flight | 1981 | — | 2.00 | 4.00 |
IMPERIAL
| ❏ 5715 | What a Night for Love/Poor Little Girls | 1960 | 5.00 | 10.00 | 20.00 |
POM POM
| ❏ 4160 | The Dance Is Over/Socialite | 1962 | 6.25 | 12.50 | 25.00 |
PRIVATE STOCK
| ❏ 45,012 | Wait for Me/You Made All the Difference | 1975 | — | 2.00 | 4.00 |
SCOTTI BROTHERS
❏ 500	Ghost Dancer/Ghost Dancer	1979	—	2.00	4.00
❏ 500 [PS]	Ghost Dancer/Ghost Dancer	1979	—	3.00	6.00
—Promo-only title sleeve					
❏ 506	As Long As the Music Keeps Playing/(B-side unknown)	1979	—	2.00	4.00
VALIANT
❏ 720	Mr. Love/Side by Side	1965	3.00	6.00	12.00
❏ 6047	Love Me Baby/The Way You Look at Him	1964	3.00	6.00	12.00
❏ 6058	C'mon Home Baby/Little Miss Sad	1964	3.75	7.50	15.00
WARNER BROS.
| ❏ 5268 | The Dance Is Over (Dance with Me)/Sleeping Beauty | 1962 | 3.75 | 7.50 | 15.00 |
| ❏ 7249 | Time to Love/Good News | 1968 | 2.50 | 5.00 | 10.00 |
Albums
BUDDAH
| ❏ BDS-5694 | Addrisi Brothers | 1977 | 2.50 | 5.00 | 10.00 |
COLUMBIA
| ❏ KC 31296 | We've Got to Get It On Again | 1972 | 3.00 | 6.00 | 12.00 |

ADELPHIS, THE
45s
RIM
❏ 2020	Darlin' It's You/Kathleen	1958	25.00	50.00	100.00
—Artist's name spelled correctly as "Adelphis"					
❏ 2020	Darlin' It's You/Kathleen	1958	37.50	75.00	150.00
—Artist's name listed as "Adelphies"					

ADLIBS, THE Not to be confused with THE AD LIBS, this is a British group.
45s
INTERPHON
| ❏ 7717 | Neighbour, Neighbour/Lovely Ladies | 1965 | 2.50 | 5.00 | 10.00 |

ADMIRALS, THE
45s
KING
❏ 4772	Oh Yes/Left with a Broken Heart	1955	62.50	125.00	250.00
❏ 4782	Close Your Eyes/Give Me Love	1955	62.50	125.00	250.00
❏ 4792	It's a Sad, Sad Feeling/Ow	1955	12.50	25.00	50.00
—With Lucky Millinder					

ADMIRATIONS, THE More than one group.
45s
ATOMIC
| ❏ 12871 | Dear Lady/Memories Are Here to Stay | 195? | 50.00 | 100.00 | 200.00 |
BRUNSWICK
| ❏ 55332 | Hey Mama/Lonely Street | 1967 | 5.00 | 10.00 | 20.00 |
HULL
| ❏ 1202 | Moonlight/Ain't It Funny | 1965 | 50.00 | 100.00 | 200.00 |
KELLWAY
| ❏ 108 | Over the Rainbow/In My Younger Days | 196? | 2.50 | 5.00 | 10.00 |
MERCURY
| ❏ 71521 | The Bells of Roja Rita/Little Bo Poop | 1959 | 10.00 | 20.00 | 40.00 |
| ❏ 71883 | To the Aisle/Hey Senorita | 1962 | 50.00 | 100.00 | 200.00 |
ONE-DERFUL
| ❏ 4849 | Wait Till I Get to Know You/(Instrumental) | 1967 | 6.25 | 12.50 | 25.00 |
| ❏ 4851 | Don't Leave Me/All for You | 1967 | 6.25 | 12.50 | 25.00 |

ADORABLES, THE
45s
GOLDEN WORLD
❏ 4	Daddy Please/Deep Freeze	1964	6.25	12.50	25.00
❏ 10	School's All Over/Be	1964	6.25	12.50	25.00
❏ 25	Ooh Boy!/Devil in His Eyes	1965	10.00	20.00	40.00
PEACOCK
| ❏ 1924 | The Drive/Baby, Come and Get It | 1963 | 3.00 | 6.00 | 12.00 |

ADRIAN AND THE SUNSETS
45s
SUNSET
| ❏ 602 | Breakthrough/Cherry Pie | 1963 | 10.00 | 20.00 | 40.00 |
| ❏ 602 [PS] | Breakthrough/Cherry Pie | 1963 | 30.00 | 60.00 | 120.00 |
Albums
SUNSET
❏ 63-601 [M]	Breakthrough	1963	20.00	40.00	80.00
—Black vinyl					
❏ 63-601 [M]	Breakthrough	1963	37.50	75.00	150.00
—Multi-color vinyl					
❏ SD 63-601 [S]	Breakthrough	1963	37.50	75.00	150.00
—Black vinyl					
❏ SD 63-601 [S]	Breakthrough	1963	75.00	150.00	300.00
—Multi-color vinyl					

ADVANCEMENT, THE
Albums
PHILIPS
| ❏ PHS 600328 | The Advancement | 1969 | 10.00 | 20.00 | 40.00 |

ADVENTURERS, THE (1)
45s
COLUMBIA
| ❏ 42227 | Rock and Roll Uprising/My Mama Done Told Me | 1961 | 10.00 | 20.00 | 40.00 |

Number	Title (A Side/B Side)	Yr	VG	VG+	NM

Albums
COLUMBIA

| ❏ CL 1747 [M] | Can't Stop Twistin' | 1961 | 15.00 | 30.00 | 60.00 |
| ❏ CS 8547 [S] | Can't Stop Twistin' | 1961 | 20.00 | 40.00 | 80.00 |

ADVENTURERS, THE (U)
45s
BLUE ROCK

| ❏ 4071 | Something Bad (Is Happening)/ Nobody Can Save Me | 1968 | 2.00 | 4.00 | 8.00 |

CAPITOL

| ❏ F-4292 | Rip Van Winkle/Trail Blazer | 1959 | 3.75 | 7.50 | 15.00 |

COMPASS

| ❏ 7010 | Easy Baby/(These Days) A Good Girl Is So Hard to Find | 1967 | 2.00 | 4.00 | 8.00 |

MECCA

| ❏ A-11 | 2 O'Clock Express/Shaggin' | 1960 | 10.00 | 20.00 | 40.00 |

MIRACLE

| ❏ 1 | 2 O'Clock Express/October Days | 1960 | 5.00 | 10.00 | 20.00 |

AEROSMITH
12-Inch Singles
COLUMBIA

| ❏ CAS 2333 [DJ] | Dream On (Live) (same on both sides?) | 1986 | 3.75 | 7.50 | 15.00 |
| ❏ CAS 9965 [DJ] | Falling in Love (Is Hard on the Knees) (5 versions) | 1997 | 2.50 | 5.00 | 10.00 |

GEFFEN

❏ PRO-A-2382 [DJ]	Let the Music Do the Talking (same on both sides)	1986	2.50	5.00	10.00
❏ PRO-A-2401 [DJ]	Shela (same on both sides)	1986	2.50	5.00	10.00
❏ PRO-A-2882 [DJ]	Dude (Looks Like a Lady) (4 versions)	1987	2.00	4.00	8.00
❏ PRO-A-3138 [DJ]	Rag Doll (Extended Vacation Mix) (Rockapella) (Dub)	1988	3.75	7.50	15.00
❏ PRO-A-3810 [DJ]	Love in an Elevator (3 versions)	1989	2.50	5.00	10.00
❏ PRO-A-4117 [DJ]	The Other Side (LP Version) (Matt Dike Honky Tonk Version) (Club Mix)//Theme from "Wayne's World"/My Girl	1990	3.00	6.00	12.00
❏ 20751	Dude (Looks Like a Lady)/Simoriah//Once Is Enough/The Movie	1987	2.50	5.00	10.00

45s
COLUMBIA

❏ 38-08536	Chip Away the Stone/S.O.S.	1989	—	2.00	4.00
❏ 10034	Train Kept a-Rollin'/Spaced	1974	—	3.00	6.00
❏ 10105	S.O.S. (Too Bad)/Lord of the Thighs	1975	—	3.00	6.00
❏ 10155	Sweet Emotion/Pandora's Box	1975	—	2.50	5.00
❏ 10206	Walk This Way/Round and Round	1975	—	3.00	6.00
❏ 10253	Toys in the Attic/You See Me Crying	1975	—	3.00	6.00
❏ 10278	Dream On/Somebody	1975	—	2.50	5.00
—Contains the full-length version of A-side
❏ 10359	Last Child/Combination	1976	—	2.50	5.00
❏ 10407	Home Tonight/Pandora's Box	1976	—	2.50	5.00
❏ 10449	Walk This Way/Uncle Salty	1976	—	2.50	5.00
❏ 10516	Back in the Saddle/Nobody's Fault	1977	—	2.50	5.00
❏ 10637	Draw the Line/Bright, Light, Fright	1977	—	2.50	5.00
❏ 10699	Kings and Queens/Critical Mass	1978	—	2.50	5.00
❏ 10727	Get It Up/Milk Cow Blues	1978	—	2.50	5.00
❏ 10802	Come Together/Kings and Queens	1978	—	2.50	5.00
❏ 10880	Chip Away the Stone (Studio)//S.O.S./Chip Away the Stone (Live)	1979	—	3.00	6.00
❏ 11181	Remember (Walking in the Sand)/Bone to Bone (Coney Island White Fish Boy)	1980	—	2.50	5.00
❏ 45894	Dream On/Somebody	1973	—	3.00	6.00
—Contains a remixed, edited version of A-side
❏ 46029	Pandora's Box/Same Old Song and Dance	1974	—	3.00	6.00
❏ 78499	Falling in Love (Is Hard on the Knees)/ Fall Together	1997	—	—	2.00
—Small hole
❏ 78499 [PS]	Falling in Love (Is Hard on the Knees)/ Fall Together	1997	—	—	2.00
❏ 78569	Hole in My Soul/Falling Off	1997	—	—	2.00
❏ 78569 [PS]	Hole in My Soul/Falling Off	1997	—	—	2.00
❏ 78952	I Don't Want to Miss a Thing/Animal Crackers// Taste of India (Rock Remix)	1998	—	—	2.00
❏ 78952 [PS]	I Don't Want to Miss a Thing/Animal Crackers// Taste of India (Rock Remix)	1998	—	—	2.00
❏ 79572	Jaded/Angel's Eye	2001	—	—	3.00

GEFFEN

❏ 19143	Livin' on the Edge/Don't Stop	1993	—	—	3.00
❏ 19256	Cryin'/Walk On Down	1993	—	—	3.00
❏ 19264	Amazing/Fever	1993	—	—	3.00
❏ 19267	Crazy/Gotta Love It	1994	—	—	3.00
❏ 19377	Blind Man/Head First	1994	—	—	3.00
❏ 19927	The Other Side/My Girl	1990	—	—	3.00
❏ 19946	What It Takes/Monkey on My Back	1990	—	—	3.00
❏ 22845	Love in an Elevator/Young Lust	1989	—	—	3.00
❏ 22845 [PS]	Love in an Elevator/Young Lust	1989	—	—	3.00
❏ 27915	Rag Doll/St. John	1988	—	—	3.00
❏ 27915 [PS]	Rag Doll/St. John	1988	—	—	3.00
❏ 28240	Dude (Looks Like a Lady)/Simoriah	1987	—	—	3.00
❏ 28240 [PS]	Dude (Looks Like a Lady)/Simoriah	1987	—	—	3.00
❏ 28249	Angel/Girl Keeps Coming Apart	1987	—	—	3.00
❏ 28249 [PS]	Angel/Girl Keeps Coming Apart	1987	—	—	3.00
❏ 28814	Shela/Gypsy Boots	1986	—	2.00	4.00
❏ 28814 [PS]	Shela/Gypsy Boots	1986	—	2.50	5.00

Albums
COLUMBIA

| ❏ A3S 187 [DJ] | Pure Gold from Rock 'n' Roll's Golden Boys | 1976 | 12.50 | 25.00 | 50.00 |
| —Promo-only compilation of the first three albums |
| ❏ JC 32005 | Aerosmith | 1977 | 2.00 | 4.00 | 8.00 |
| ❏ KC 32005 | Aerosmith | 1973 | 3.00 | 6.00 | 12.00 |
| —Light blue cover, most (if not all) of which say "Featuring 'Dream On' " on front |

Number	Title (A Side/B Side)	Yr	VG	VG+	NM

| ❏ KC 32005 | Aerosmith | 1973 | 3.75 | 7.50 | 15.00 |
| —Orange cover with correct title "Walking The Dog" |
| ❏ KC 32005 | Aerosmith | 1973 | 5.00 | 10.00 | 20.00 |
| —Orange cover with back cover typo "Walking The Dig" |
| ❏ PC 32005 | Aerosmith | 1976 | 2.50 | 5.00 | 10.00 |
| —Without bar code |
| ❏ PC 32005 | Aerosmith | 1984 | 2.00 | 4.00 | 8.00 |
| —With bar code |
❏ JC 32847	Get Your Wings	1977	2.00	4.00	8.00
❏ KC 32847	Get Your Wings	1974	3.00	6.00	12.00
❏ KCQ 32847 [Q]	Get Your Wings	1974	6.25	12.50	25.00
❏ PC 32847	Get Your Wings	1976	2.50	5.00	10.00
—Without bar code
❏ PC 32847	Get Your Wings	1984	2.00	4.00	8.00
—With bar code
❏ JC 33479	Toys in the Attic	1977	2.50	5.00	10.00
❏ PC 33479	Toys in the Attic	1975	3.00	6.00	12.00
—Without bar code
❏ PC 33479	Toys in the Attic	1984	2.00	4.00	8.00
—With bar code
❏ PCQ 33479 [Q]	Toys in the Attic	1975	6.25	12.50	25.00
❏ JC 34165	Rocks	1976	2.50	5.00	10.00
—Some copies have "Rocks" in quotes on the cover, others don't; no difference in value
❏ PC 34165	Rocks	1976	3.00	6.00	12.00
—Without bar code. Some copies have "Rocks" in quotes on the cover, others don't; no difference in value
❏ PC 34165	Rocks	1984	2.00	4.00	8.00
—With bar code
❏ PCQ 34165 [Q]	Rocks	1976	6.25	12.50	25.00
❏ JC 34856	Draw the Line	1977	3.00	6.00	12.00
❏ PC 34856	Draw the Line	198?	2.00	4.00	8.00
❏ PC2 35564 [(2)]	Live! Bootleg	1978	3.75	7.50	15.00
❏ FC 36050	Night in the Ruts	1979	2.50	5.00	10.00
❏ PC 36050	Night in the Ruts	1984	2.00	4.00	8.00
❏ FC 36865	Aerosmith's Greatest Hits	1980	2.50	5.00	10.00
❏ PC 36865	Aerosmith's Greatest Hits	1984	2.00	4.00	8.00
❏ FC 38061	Rock in a Hard Place	1982	2.50	5.00	10.00
❏ PC 38061	Rock in a Hard Place	1984	2.00	4.00	8.00
❏ FC 40329	Classics Live	1986	2.50	5.00	10.00
❏ FC 40855	Classics Live, Vol. 2	1987	2.50	5.00	10.00
❏ FC 44487	Gems (1973-1982)	1989	2.50	5.00	10.00
❏ C 62088	Just Push Play	2001	2.50	5.00	10.00

GEFFEN

❏ GHS 24091	Done with Mirrors	1985	2.50	5.00	10.00
❏ GHS 24162	Permanent Vacation	1987	2.50	5.00	10.00
❏ GHS 24254	Pump	1989	2.50	5.00	10.00

AESOP'S FABLES
45s
ATCO

❏ 6508	Girl, I've Got News for You/Yes I'm Back	1967	2.00	4.00	8.00
❏ 6523	Take a Step/What's a Man to Do	1967	2.00	4.00	8.00
❏ 6565	Slow and Easy/The Truth	1968	2.00	4.00	8.00

CADET CONCEPT

❏ 7011	Temptation 'Bout to Get Me/What Is Love	1969	2.00	4.00	8.00
❏ 7016	I'm Gonna Make You Love Me/ They Go Out and Get It	1968	2.00	4.00	8.00
❏ 7016	And When It's Over/What Is Love	1969	2.00	4.00	8.00

Albums
CADET CONCEPT

| ❏ LPS-323 | In Due Time | 1969 | 5.00 | 10.00 | 20.00 |

AFDEM, JEFF, AND THE SPRINGFIELD FLUTE
Albums
BURDETTE

| ❏ 5162 | Something | 1969 | 10.00 | 20.00 | 40.00 |

AFFECTION COLLECTION, THE
45s
EVOLUTION

| ❏ 1004 | Girl/I'll Be There | 1969 | 3.00 | 6.00 | 12.00 |
| ❏ 1013 | Watch Her Walk/I Don't Mind | 1969 | 3.00 | 6.00 | 12.00 |

UNITED ARTISTS

| ❏ 50268 | In Apple Blossom Time/ Time Rests Heavy on My Hands | 1968 | 2.50 | 5.00 | 10.00 |

Albums
EVOLUTION

| ❏ 2007 | The Affection Collection | 1969 | 5.00 | 10.00 | 20.00 |

AFFINITY
Albums
PARAMOUNT

| ❏ PAS-5027 | Affinity | 1970 | 6.25 | 12.50 | 25.00 |

AFRICA
45s
ODE

| ❏ ZS7-116 | Here I Stand/Widow | 1969 | 2.00 | 4.00 | 8.00 |
| ❏ ZS7-126 | From Africa with Love/Savin' All My Love | 1969 | 2.00 | 4.00 | 8.00 |

AFRIQUE
45s
MAINSTREAM

| ❏ 5542 | Soul Makossa/Hot Mud | 1973 | — | 2.50 | 5.00 |
| ❏ 5547 | Kumbo Coming/Hot Mud | 1973 | — | 2.50 | 5.00 |

Albums
MAINSTREAM

| ❏ S-394 | Soul Makossa | 1973 | 3.00 | 6.00 | 12.00 |

AGAPE
Albums
MARK

| ❏ MRS-2170 | Gospel Hard Rock | 1971 | 30.00 | 60.00 | 120.00 |

Number	Title (A Side/B Side)	Yr	VG	VG+	NM
RENRUT					
❑ 101	Victims of Tradition	1972	30.00	60.00	120.00
AGE OF REASON, THE					
Albums					
GEORGETOWNE					
❑ (no #)	The Age of Reason	1969	37.50	75.00	150.00
AGGREGATION, THE					
45s					
LHI					
❑ 1209	Sunshine Superman/Maharish	1968	7.50	15.00	30.00
Albums					
LHI					
❑ 12008	Mind Odyssey	1967	100.00	200.00	400.00
AGRATI, DON See DON GRADY.					
AHBEZ, EDEN					
45s					
DEL-FI					
❑ 4131	Tobago/The Old Boat	1959	3.75	7.50	15.00
Albums					
DEL-FI					
❑ DFLP-1211 [M]	Eden's Island	1960	37.50	75.00	150.00
❑ DFST-1211 [S]	Eden's Island	1960	50.00	100.00	200.00
AKENS, JEWEL					
45s					
AMERICAN INT'L					
❑ 110	When Something Is Wrong with My Baby/I Just Can't Turn My Habit into Love	196?	—	3.00	6.00
CAPEHART					
❑ 5007	(Dancing) The Mashed Potatoes/ Wee Bit More of Your Lovin'	1962	3.00	6.00	12.00
COLGEMS					
❑ 66-1025	It's a Sin to Tell a Lie/You Better Move On	1968	2.00	4.00	8.00
CREST					
❑ 1098	(Dancing) The Mashed Potatoes/ Wee Bit More of Your Lovin'	1962	2.50	5.00	10.00
ERA					
❑ 104	Buenos Aires/Mississippi Syrup Sopper	1969	—	3.00	6.00
❑ 3141	The Birds and the Bees/Tic Tac Toe	1964	3.75	7.50	15.00
❑ 3142	Georgie Porgie/Around the Corner	1965	2.50	5.00	10.00
❑ 3147	You Sure Know How to Hurt a Guy/ It's the Only Way to Fly	1965	2.50	5.00	10.00
❑ 3154	You Don't Need a Crowd/I've Arrived	1965	2.50	5.00	10.00
❑ 3156	A Slice of the Pie/You Better Believe It	1965	2.50	5.00	10.00
❑ 3164	My First Lonely Night/Mama Take Your Daughter Back	1966	2.50	5.00	10.00
❑ 3207	A Slice of the Pie/ A Land Where Animals Are People	1969	2.00	4.00	8.00
MDM					
❑ 191	Christine/Please God	1988	—	2.00	4.00
—As "Jewel Akens, Mr. Birds and Bees"					
Albums					
ERA					
❑ EL-110 [M]	The Birds and the Bees	1965	7.50	15.00	30.00
❑ ES-110 [S]	The Birds and the Bees	1965	25.00	50.00	100.00
AKKERMAN, JAN Also see BRAINBOX; FOCUS.					
45s					
ATLANTIC					
❑ 3478	Crackers/(B-side unknown)	1978	—	2.00	4.00
Albums					
ATCO					
❑ SD 7032	Tabernakel	1974	3.00	6.00	12.00
ATLANTIC					
❑ SD 18210	Eli	1977	2.50	5.00	10.00
❑ SD 19159	Jan Akkerman	1978	2.50	5.00	10.00
SIRE					
❑ SAS 7407	Profile	1973	3.75	7.50	15.00
ALABAMA					
45s					
BNA					
❑ 65312	Angels Among Us/Make a Miracle	1997	—	—	3.00
—B-side credited to "Various Artists"					
GRT					
❑ 129	I Wanna Be with You Tonight/ Lovin' You Is Killin' Me	1977	3.75	7.50	15.00
❑ 129 [PS]	I Wanna Be with You Tonight/ Lovin' You Is Killin' Me	1977	5.00	10.00	20.00
MDJ					
❑ 1002-JB	My Home's in Alabama/Some Other Time, Some Other Place	1980	2.50	5.00	10.00
—Jukebox pressing with one B-side					
❑ 1002-R	My Home's in Alabama//Some Other Time, Some Other Place/Why Lady Why	1980	3.00	6.00	12.00
—Regular pressing with two B-sides					
❑ 7906	I Wanna' Come Over/Get It While It's Hot	1979	3.00	6.00	12.00
—Reissue of Sonny Limbo Int'l. 7906					
RCA					
❑ 2519-7-R	Pass It On Down/The Borderline	1990	—	—	3.00
❑ 2519-7-R [PS]	Pass It On Down/The Borderline	1990	—	2.00	4.00
❑ 2643-7-R	Jukebox in My Mind/Fire on Fire	1990	—	—	3.00
❑ 2706-7-R	Forever's As Far As I'll Go/Starting Tonight	1990	—	2.50	5.00
❑ 2778-7-R	Down Home/Goodbye (Kelly's Song)	1991	—	—	3.00
❑ 2828-7-R	Here We Are/Gulf of Mexico	1991	—	—	3.00
❑ 5003-7-R	Touch Me When We're Dancing/ Hanging Up My Travelin' Shoes	1986	—	—	3.00
❑ 5051-7-R	Christmas in Dixie/Tennessee Christmas	1986	—	2.00	4.00
❑ 5081-7-R	"You've Got" The Touch/True, True Housewife	1987	—	—	3.00
❑ 5222-7-R	Tar Top/If I Could Just See You Now	1987	—	—	3.00
❑ 5222-7-R [PS]	Tar Top/If I Could Just See You Now	1987	2.00	4.00	8.00
—Promo-only sleeve					
❑ 5328-7-R	Face to Face/Vacation	1987	—	—	3.00
❑ 6902-7-R	Fallin' Again/I Saw the Time	1988	—	—	3.00
❑ 8744-7-R	Song of the South/(I Wish It Could Always Be) '55	1988	—	—	3.00
❑ 8817-7-R	If I Had You/I Showed Her	1988	—	—	3.00
❑ 8937-7-R	Fallin' Again/Song of the South	1989	—	—	3.00
—Gold Standard Series reissue					
❑ 8948-7-R	High Cotton/"Ole" Baugh Road	1989	—	—	3.00
❑ 9083-7-R	Southern Star/Barefootin'	1989	—	—	3.00
❑ PB-12008	My Home's in Alabama/I Wanna Come Over	1980	—	2.00	4.00
❑ PB-12008 [PS]	My Home's in Alabama/I Wanna Come Over	1980	—	3.00	6.00
❑ PB-12018	Tennessee River/Can't Forget About You	1980	—	2.00	4.00
❑ PB-12091	Why Lady Why/I Wanna Come Over	1980	—	2.00	4.00
❑ PB-12091 [PS]	Why Lady Why/I Wanna Come Over	1980	—	2.50	5.00
❑ PB-12169	Old Flame/I'm Stoned	1981	—	2.00	4.00
❑ PB-12236	Feels So Right/See the Embers, Feel the Flame	1981	—	2.00	4.00
❑ PB-12288	Love in the First Degree/Ride the Train	1981	—	2.00	4.00
❑ GB-12310	Why Baby Why/My Home's in Alabama	1981	—	—	3.00
—Gold Standard Series reissue					
❑ GB-12369	Tennessee River/Old Flame	1981	—	—	3.00
—Gold Standard Series reissue					
❑ PB-13019	Mountain Music/Never Be One	1981	—	2.00	4.00
❑ PB-13019 [PS]	Mountain Music/Never Be One	1981	—	2.50	5.00
❑ PB-13210	Take Me Down/Lovin' You Is Killin' Me	1982	—	2.00	4.00
❑ PB-13294	Close Enough to Perfect/Fantasy	1982	—	2.00	4.00
❑ PB-13358	Christmas in Dixie/Christmas Is Just a Song for Us This Year	1982	—	2.50	5.00
—B-side by Louise Mandrell and R.C. Bannon					
❑ PB-13446	Dixieland Delight/A Very Special Love	1983	—	2.00	4.00
❑ GB-13489	Feels So Right/Mountain Music	1983	—	—	3.00
—Gold Standard Series reissue					
❑ GB-13492	Take Me Down/Close Enough to Perfect	1983	—	—	3.00
—Gold Standard Series reissue					
❑ PB-13524	The Closer You Get/You Turn Me On	1983	—	2.00	4.00
❑ PB-13590	Lady Down on Love/Lovin' Man	1983	—	2.00	4.00
❑ PB-13664	Christmas in Dixie/Never Be One	1983	—	2.00	4.00
❑ PB-13716	Roll On (Eighteen Wheeler)/Food on the Table	1984	—	2.00	4.00
❑ PB-13763	When We Make Love/Oklahoma Mountain Dew	1984	—	2.00	4.00
❑ GB-13786	Dixieland Delight/Lady Down on Love	1984	—	—	3.00
—Gold Standard Series reissue					
❑ PB-13840	If You're Gonna Play in Texas (You Gotta Have a Fiddle in the Band)/ I'm Not That Way Anymore	1984	—	2.00	4.00
❑ PB-13926	(There's A) Fire in the Night/Rock on the Bayou	1984	—	2.00	4.00
❑ PB-13992	There's No Way/The Boy	1985	—	2.00	4.00
❑ GB-14067	Roll On (Eighteen Wheeler)/ When We Make Love	1985	—	—	3.00
—Gold Standard Series reissue					
❑ PB-14085	Forty Hour Week (For a Livin')/As Right Now	1985	—	2.00	4.00
❑ PB-14085 [PS]	Forty Hour Week (For a Livin')/As Right Now	1985	—	2.50	5.00
❑ PB-14165	Can't Keep a Good Man Down/ If It Ain't Dixie (It Won't Do)	1985	—	2.00	4.00
❑ GB-14174	Love in the First Degree/The Closer You Get	1985	—	—	3.00
—Gold Standard Series reissue					
❑ GB-14176	(There's a) Fire in the Night/If You're Gonna Play in Texas (You Gotta Have a Fiddle in the Band)	1985	—	—	3.00
—Gold Standard Series reissue					
❑ PB-14213	Thistlehair the Christmas Bear/Santa Claus (I Still Believe in You)	1985			
—Unreleased					
❑ PB-14219	Joseph and Mary's Boy/Santa Claus (I Still Believe in You)	1985	—	2.00	4.00
❑ PB-14281	She and I/The Fans	1986	—	2.00	4.00
❑ PB-14281 [PS]	She and I/The Fans	1986	—	2.50	5.00
❑ GB-14347	There's No Way/(There's a) Fire in the Night	1986	—	—	3.00
—Gold Standard Series reissue					
❑ GB-14350	Forty Hour Week (For a Livin')/Can't Keep a Good Man Down	1986	—	—	3.00
—Gold Standard Series reissue					
❑ 60211	We Made Love/Small Stuff	2000	—	—	3.00
❑ 62059	Then Again/Hats Off	1991	—	—	3.00
❑ 62168	Born Country/Until It Happens to You	1991	—	—	3.00
❑ 62253	Take a Little Trip/Pictures and Memories	1992	—	—	3.00
❑ 62336	I'm In a Hurry (And Don't Know Why)/Sometimes Out of Touch	1992	—	—	3.00
❑ 62428	Once Upon a Lifetime/American Pride	1992	—	—	3.00
❑ 62495	Hometown Honeymoon/Homesick Fever	1993	—	—	3.00
❑ 62623	The Cheap Seats/This Love's on Me	1994	—	—	3.00
❑ 62636	Reckless/Clear Water Blues	1993	—	—	3.00
❑ 62643	Angels Among Us/Santa Claus (I Still Believe in You)	1993	—	2.00	4.00
❑ 62712	T.L.C.A.S.A.P./That Feeling	1993	—	—	3.00
❑ 62894	We Can't Love Like This Anymore/ Still Goin' Strong	1994	—	—	3.00
❑ 64273	Give Me One More Shot/Jukebox in My Mind	1995	—	—	3.00
❑ 64346	She Ain't Your Ordinary Girl/Heartbreak Express	1995	—	—	3.00
❑ 64419	In Pictures/Between the Two of Them	1995	—	—	3.00
❑ 64436	Christmas in Dixie/ Thistlehair the Christmas Bear	1995	—	—	3.00
—Reissue with edit of A-side					
❑ 64473	It Works/Katy Brought My Guitar Back Today	1996	—	—	3.00
❑ 64543	Say I/My Love Belongs to You	1996	—	—	3.00
❑ 64588	The Maker Said Take Her/Nothing Comes Close	1996	—	—	3.00
❑ 64775	Sad Lookin' Moon/Give Me One More Shot	1997	—	—	3.00
❑ 64849	Dancin', Shaggin' on the Boulevard/ Very Special Love	1997	—	—	3.00
❑ 64965	Of Course I'm Alright/ (I Wish It Could Always Be) '55	1997	—	—	3.00
❑ 65409	She's Got That Look in Her Eyes/That Feeling	1998	—	—	3.00

Number	Title (A Side/B Side)	Yr	VG	VG+	NM
❏ 65561	How Do You Fall in Love/Keepin' Up	1998	—	—	3.00
❏ 65759	God Must Have Spent a Little More Time on You/Sad Lookin' Moon	1999	—	2.00	4.00
❏ 65935	Small Stuff/God Must Have Spent a Little More Time on You	1999	—	—	3.00
❏ 69019	When It All Goes South/Feels So Right	2000	—	—	3.00

SONNY LIMBO INT'L.

❏ 7906	I Wanna' Come Over/Get It While It's Hot	1979	10.00	20.00	40.00

SUN

❏ 1173 [DJ]	I Wanna Be with You Tonight (Standard Version/Edited Version)	1982	7.50	15.00	30.00

—Promo only on yellow vinyl; stock copies were not released

Albums

ACCORD

❏ SN-7132	Pride of Dixie	1981	2.50	5.00	10.00

ALABAMA

❏ ALA-78-9-01	The Alabama Band	1978	100.00	200.00	400.00

HEARTLAND

❏ HL 1186/7 [(2)]	The Very Best of Alabama	1992	3.75	7.50	15.00

LSI

❏ 0177	Deuces Wild	1977	300.00	600.00	1200.

—As "Wild Country"

❏ 0275	Wild Country	1975	750.00	1125.	1500.

—As "Wild Country"

PLANTATION

❏ 44	Wild Country	1981	15.00	30.00	60.00

RCA

❏ 5649-1-R	The Touch	1986	2.00	4.00	8.00
❏ 6495-1-R	Just Us	1987	2.00	4.00	8.00
❏ 6825-1-R	Alabama Live	1988	2.00	4.00	8.00
❏ 8587-1-R	Southern Star	1989	2.00	4.00	8.00
❏ 9574-1-RDJ [DJ]	Open-Ended Interview	1988	7.50	15.00	30.00

RCA VICTOR

❏ AHL1-3644	My Home's in Alabama	1980	3.75	7.50	15.00
❏ AYL1-3644	My Home's in Alabama	1986	2.00	4.00	8.00

—"Best Buy Series" reissue

❏ AHL1-3930	Feels So Right	1981	2.00	4.00	8.00
❏ AHL1-4229	Mountain Music	1982	2.00	4.00	8.00
❏ AHL1-4663	The Closer You Get	1983	2.00	4.00	8.00
❏ AHL1-4939	Roll On	1984	2.00	4.00	8.00
❏ AHL1-5339	40 Hour Week	1985	2.00	4.00	8.00
❏ ASL1-7014	Christmas	1985	3.00	6.00	12.00

—Original copies have gold embossed letters on cover

❏ ASL1-7014	Christmas	1986	2.50	5.00	10.00

—Later copies have white non-embossed letters on cover

❏ AHL1-7170	Greatest Hits	1986	2.00	4.00	8.00

SOUTHWAYS

❏ 101	Pride of Dixie	1981	2.50	5.00	10.00

—Same album as on Accord

ALABAMA CHRISTIAN MOVEMENT FOR HUMAN RIGHTS CHOIR

45s

TCF

❏ 2	Do You Hear What I Hear?/The Virgin Mary	1963	3.00	6.00	12.00

ALADDINS, THE

45s

ALADDIN

❏ 3275	Remember/Cry Baby Cry	1955	50.00	100.00	200.00
❏ 3298	I Had a Dream Last Night/Get Off My Feet	1955	50.00	100.00	200.00
❏ 3314	All My Life/So Long, Farewell, Bye Bye	1956	50.00	100.00	200.00
❏ 3358	Help Me/Lord, Show Me	1957	50.00	100.00	200.00

FRANKIE

❏ 6	Dot, My Love/My Charlene	1958	100.00	200.00	400.00

WITCH

❏ 109	Please Love Me/Munch	1962	12.50	25.00	50.00
❏ 111	Our Love Will Be/Simple Simon	1962	12.50	25.00	50.00

ALAIMO, CHUCK

45s

MGM

❏ 12449	Leap Frog/That's My Desire	1957	3.75	7.50	15.00
❏ 12508	Local 60-6/How I Love You	1957	3.75	7.50	15.00
❏ 12589	Where's My Baby/Lovers Again	1957	3.75	7.50	15.00
❏ 12636	Hop in My Jalop/Rockin' in G	1958	3.75	7.50	15.00

ALAIMO, STEVE Also see THE REDCOATS; THE UNKNOWNS.

45s

ABC

❏ 10805	So Much Love/Truer Than True	1966	3.00	6.00	12.00
❏ 10833	Happy/On the Beach	1966	3.00	6.00	12.00
❏ 10873	Pardon Me (It's My First Day Alone)/Savin' All My Love	1966	3.00	6.00	12.00
❏ 10917	You Don't Love Me/You Don't Know Like I Know	1967	2.50	5.00	10.00

ABC-PARAMOUNT

❏ 10540	Love's Gonna Live Here/Let Her Go	1964	3.00	6.00	12.00
❏ 10553	Love Is a Many Splendored Thing/Fade Out	1964	3.00	6.00	12.00
❏ 10580	I Don't Know/That's What Love Will Do	1964	3.00	6.00	12.00
❏ 10605	Happy/Everybody Knows But Her	1964	3.00	6.00	12.00
❏ 10620	Real Live Girl/Need You	1965	3.00	6.00	12.00
❏ 10643	Laughing on the Outside/Tomorrow Is Another Day	1965	3.00	6.00	12.00
❏ 10680	Cast Your Fate to the Wind/Mais Oui	1965	3.00	6.00	12.00
❏ 10712	Blowin' in the Wind/Lady of the House	1965	3.00	6.00	12.00
❏ 10764	Bright Lights Big City/Once a Day	1966	3.00	6.00	12.00

ATCO

❏ 6512	New Orleans/Ooh Poo Pah Doo	1967	2.00	4.00	8.00
❏ 6560	Cuando Yo Vuelvo Ami Tierra/Todavia	1968	2.50	5.00	10.00
❏ 6561	Denver/I Do	1968	2.00	4.00	8.00
❏ 6589	1 x 1 Ain't 2/My Friend	1968	2.00	4.00	8.00

Number	Title (A Side/B Side)	Yr	VG	VG+	NM
❏ 6620	Thank You for the Sunshine Days/Watching the Trains Go	1968	2.00	4.00	8.00
❏ 6659	I'm Thankful/Afetr the Smoke Is Gone	1969	2.00	4.00	8.00

—With Betty Wright

❏ 6710	One Woman/And Then I Tripped Over Your Goodbye	1969	2.00	4.00	8.00
❏ 6732	Melissa/Smilin' in My Sleep	1970	—	3.00	6.00
❏ 6797	Can't You See/(On the) Wild Side of Life	1971	—	3.00	6.00

CHECKER

❏ 981	Big Bad Beulah/I Cried All the Way Home	1961	3.00	6.00	12.00
❏ 989	All Night Long/I'm Thankful	1961	3.00	6.00	12.00
❏ 998	The Waiting's So Hard/You Got Me Whistling	1961	3.00	6.00	12.00
❏ 1006	Mashed Potatoes/Mashed Potatoes (Part 2)	1962	3.00	6.00	12.00
❏ 1018	My Friend/Going Back to Mary	1962	3.00	6.00	12.00
❏ 1024	Cry Myself to Sleep/One Good Reason	1962	3.00	6.00	12.00
❏ 1032	Every Day I Have to Cry/Little Girl	1962	3.00	6.00	12.00
❏ 1042	A Lifetime of Loneliness/It's a Long, Long Way to Happiness	1963	3.00	6.00	12.00
❏ 1047	Don't Let the Sun Catch You Cryin'/I Told You So	1963	3.00	6.00	12.00
❏ 1054	Michael — Pt. 1/Michael — Pt. 2	1963	3.00	6.00	12.00

DADE

❏ 1800	Home by Eleven/I Wanna Kiss You	1959	12.50	25.00	50.00
❏ 1805	Love Letters/You Can Fall in Love	1959	12.50	25.00	50.00

DICKSON

❏ 6444/5	Blue Fire/My Heart Never Said Goodbye	1960	5.00	10.00	20.00

ENTRANCE

❏ 7501	When My Little Girl Is Smiling/Gemini	1971	—	2.50	5.00
❏ 7503	Thorn in Our Roses/Nobody's Fool	1971	—	2.50	5.00
❏ 7507	Amerikan Music/Nobody's Fool	1972	—	2.50	5.00
❏ 7513	Sand in My Pocket/Gemini	1972	—	2.50	5.00

IMPERIAL

❏ 5699	My Heart Never Said Goodbye/Blue Fire	1960	3.75	7.50	15.00
❏ 5717	Unchained Melody/It Happens Ev'ry Time	1961	3.75	7.50	15.00
❏ 66003	Gotta Lotta Love/Happy Pappy	1963	3.00	6.00	12.00

LIFETIME

❏ 6112/3	Jelly/The Girl Can't Help It	1957	20.00	40.00	80.00

MARLIN

❏ 6064	I Want You to Love Me/Blue Skies	1959	7.50	15.00	30.00
❏ 6065	The Weekend's Over/Girls! Girls! Girls!	1959	6.25	12.50	25.00
❏ 6067	She's My Baby/Should I Care?	1959	6.25	12.50	25.00
❏ 6103	Spooky/The Redcoats Are Coming	1961	7.50	15.00	30.00

—As "Count Stephen"

TONE LATINO

❏ 5051	Yo No Se Que Voy A Hacer Sin Ti/No Quiero Dejaria Ya	1970	2.00	4.00	8.00

7-Inch Extended Plays

CHECKER

❏ EP-5135	Don't Cry/I Wake Up Crying//Cry/Don't Let the Sun Catch You Crying	1963	20.00	40.00	80.00
❏ EP-5135 [PS]	(title unknown)	1963	20.00	40.00	80.00

Albums

ABC-PARAMOUNT

❏ 501 [M]	Starring Steve Alaimo	1965	10.00	20.00	40.00
❏ S-501 [S]	Starring Steve Alaimo	1965	12.50	25.00	50.00
❏ 531 [M]	Where the Action Is	1965	10.00	20.00	40.00
❏ S-531 [S]	Where the Action Is	1965	12.50	25.00	50.00
❏ 551 [M]	Steve Alaimo Sings and Swings	1966	10.00	20.00	40.00
❏ S-551 [S]	Steve Alaimo Sings and Swings	1966	12.50	25.00	50.00

CHECKER

❏ LP-2981 [M]	Twist with Steve Alaimo	1962	37.50	75.00	150.00
❏ LP-2983 [M]	Mashed Potatoes	1962	37.50	75.00	150.00
❏ LP-2986 [M]	Every Day I Have to Cry	1963	37.50	75.00	150.00

CROWN

❏ CST-382 [R]	Steve Alaimo	1963	3.75	7.50	15.00
❏ CLP-5382 [M]	Steve Alaimo	1963	6.25	12.50	25.00

ALAMO, TONY

45s

ALAMO

❏ 334	Something/Dreamer	1986	—	2.00	4.00

—With Kim Morris

❏ 334 [PS]	Something/Dreamer	1986	—	2.00	4.00

MGM

❏ 11390	Merry Christmas Darling/It's Christmas Time	1952	5.00	10.00	20.00

PORT

❏ 70012	Fabulous/For All We Know	1960	3.75	7.50	15.00

ALAN, LEE

45s

LEE ALAN PRESENTS

❏ (no #)	A Trip to Miami	1964	125.00	250.00	500.00

—Interviews with the Beatles; a giveaway with Lee Alan's two-page story of his trip ($200 NM)

ALBERT, MORRIS

45s

AUDIO LATINO

❏ AL-577	"Dime" Feelings/Christine	1975		2.50	5.00

—Pronounced "DEE-may," this is the Spanish version of "Feelings"

RCA

❏ GB-10937	Feelings/Memories	1977	—	—	3.00

—Gold Standard Series

❏ PB-10958	Never Let You Go/Conversation	1977	—	—	3.00
❏ PB-11089	Someone, Somehow/So Good to Me	1977	—	—	3.00

RCA VICTOR

❏ PB-10279	Feelings/This World Today Is a Mess	1975	—	2.00	4.00
❏ PB-10437	Sweet Loving Man/Christine	1975	—	2.00	4.00
❏ PB-10626	Summer in Paris/She's My Girl	1976	—	2.00	4.00
❏ PB-10706	Memories/The Same Things	1976	—	2.00	4.00

ALBERT, THE

Number	Title (A Side/B Side)	Yr	VG	VG+	NM
Albums					
RCA VICTOR					
❑ APL1-1018	Feelings	1975	2.00	4.00	8.00
❑ APL1-1496	Morris Albert	1976	2.00	4.00	8.00

ALBERT, THE
Albums
PERCEPTION

Number	Title (A Side/B Side)	Yr	VG	VG+	NM
❑ 9	The Albert	1971	5.00	10.00	20.00

ALBERTS, AL Also see FOUR ACES.
45s

Number	Title (A Side/B Side)	Yr	VG	VG+	NM
COLUMBIA					
❑ 42737	Fly Me to the Moon/Before Tomorrow Is Yesterday	1963	2.00	4.00	8.00
CORAL					
❑ 62035	Things I Didn't Say/God's Greatest Gifts	1958	2.50	5.00	10.00
❑ 62061	My Love/Willingly	1958	2.50	5.00	10.00
❑ 62083	How Soon/Love Is the Tomorrow	1959	2.50	5.00	10.00
❑ 62090	How Soon/Taking a Chance on Love	1959	2.50	5.00	10.00
❑ 62113	By You/High School	1959	2.50	5.00	10.00
DECCA					
❑ 28807	Please Tell Me/Endless	1953	3.75	7.50	15.00
MGM					
❑ 12836	Imagination/Handful of Gold	1959	2.50	5.00	10.00
❑ 12884	South of the Border/No Love But Your Love	1960	2.50	5.00	10.00
❑ 12922	Handful of Gold/Blue Bird of Happiness	1960	2.50	5.00	10.00
PRESIDENT					
❑ 711	Don't Wait for the Hearse/Heaven Needed an Angel	1961	2.00	4.00	8.00
❑ 712	Only on Sunday/Heaven Needed an Angel	1961	2.00	4.00	8.00
❑ 715	Blue O'Clock in the Morning/Till Then (I'll Never Again)	1962	2.00	4.00	8.00
❑ 719	Fly Me to the Moon/Before Tomorrow Is Yesterday	1963	3.00	6.00	12.00
SWAN					
❑ 4067	Oh My Papa/Alone	1961	2.50	5.00	10.00
❑ 4191	Mr. Sandman/Summertime in Venice	1964	2.50	5.00	10.00
VEE JAY					
❑ 568	One Has My Name, The Other Has My Heart/Mala Femina	1963	3.75	7.50	15.00
Albums					
CORAL					
❑ CRL 57259 [M]	A Man Has Got to Sing	1959	6.25	12.50	25.00
❑ CRL 757259 [S]	A Man Has Got to Sing	1959	7.50	15.00	30.00

ALDA, ALEX Actually Nick Massi of THE FOUR SEASONS.
45s

Number	Title (A Side/B Side)	Yr	VG	VG+	NM
ONE WAY					
❑ 224	The Ballad of Mr. Nixon/Little Pony	1976	—	2.50	5.00
TOPIX					
❑ 6007 [DJ]	Little Pony (one-sided)	1961	25.00	50.00	100.00

ALDEN AND THE ONE-NIGHTERS
45s

Number	Title (A Side/B Side)	Yr	VG	VG+	NM
RCA VICTOR					
❑ 47-7490	Love-O-Meter/Theme from Love-O-Meter	1959	7.50	15.00	30.00

ALDRICH, RONNIE
Albums

Number	Title (A Side/B Side)	Yr	VG	VG+	NM
LONDON					
❑ LL 3348 [M]	The Romantic Pianos of Ronnie Aldrich	1964	3.00	6.00	12.00
❑ LL 3383 [M]	Christmas with Ronnie	1964	2.50	5.00	10.00
LONDON PHASE 4					
❑ 22 [(2)]	Love Story	1971	3.75	7.50	15.00
❑ SP-44007 [S]	Melody and Percussion for Two Pianos	1961	3.75	7.50	15.00
❑ SP 44018 [S]	Ronnie Aldrich and His Two Pianos	1962	3.75	7.50	15.00
❑ SP-44029 [S]	The Magnificent Pianos of Ronnie Aldrich	1963	3.75	7.50	15.00
❑ SP 44042 [S]	The Romantic Pianos of Ronnie Aldrich	1964	3.75	7.50	15.00
❑ SP 44051 [S]	Christmas with Ronnie	1964	3.75	7.50	15.00
❑ SP-44062 [S]	Magic Moods	1965	3.00	6.00	12.00
❑ SP-44070 [S]	That Aldrich Feeling	1966	3.00	6.00	12.00
❑ SP-44081 [S]	All-Time Piano Hits	1967	3.00	6.00	12.00
❑ SP-44092 [S]	Two Pianos in Hollywood	196?	2.50	5.00	10.00
❑ SP-44108 [S]	For Young Lovers	196?	2.50	5.00	10.00

ALEXANDER, ARTHUR
45s

Number	Title (A Side/B Side)	Yr	VG	VG+	NM
BUDDAH					
❑ 492	Every Day I Have to Cry Some/Everybody Needs Somebody to Love	1975	—	2.50	5.00
❑ 522	Sharing the Night Together/She'll Throw Stones at You	1976	—	2.50	5.00
❑ 602	Sharing the Night Together/She'll Throw Stones at You	1978	—	2.00	4.00
DOT					
❑ 45-126	You Better Move On/Anna	196?	2.50	5.00	10.00
—Reissue; black label					
❑ 45-126	You Better Move On/Anna	1969	—	3.50	7.00
—Reissue; multi-color label					
❑ 16309	You Better Move On/A Shot of Rhythm and Blues	1962	5.00	10.00	20.00
❑ 16357	Where Have You Been (All My Life)/Soldier of Love	1962	5.00	10.00	20.00
❑ 16387	Anna/I Hang My Head and Cry	1962	5.00	10.00	20.00
❑ 16425	You're the Reason/Go Home Girl	1963	3.75	7.50	15.00
❑ 16454	I Wonder Where You Are Tonight/Dream Girl	1963	3.75	7.50	15.00
❑ 16509	Pretty Girls Everywhere/Baby Baby	1963	3.75	7.50	15.00
❑ 16554	Where Did Sally Go/Keep Her Guessin'	1963	3.75	7.50	15.00
❑ 16616	Black Knight/Ole John Amos	1964	3.00	6.00	12.00
❑ 16737	Detroit City/You Don't Care	1965	3.00	6.00	12.00

Number	Title (A Side/B Side)	Yr	VG	VG+	NM
JUDD					
❑ 1020	Sally Sue Brown/The Girl That Radiates That Charm	1960	12.50	25.00	50.00
—As "June Alexander"					
MONUMENT					
❑ 1060	I Need You Baby/Spanish Harlem	1968	2.00	4.00	8.00
MUSIC MILL					
❑ 1012	Hound Dog Man's Gone/So Long Baby	1977	—	3.00	6.00
SOUND STAGE 7					
❑ 2556	The Other Woman/(Baby) For You	1965	2.50	5.00	10.00
❑ 2572	Turn Around (And Try Me)/Show Me the Road	1966	2.50	5.00	10.00
❑ 2619	Set Me Free/Love's Where Life Begins	1968	2.00	4.00	8.00
❑ 2626	Bye Bye Love/Another	1969	2.00	4.00	8.00
❑ 2652	Glory Road/Cry Like a Baby	1970	2.00	4.00	8.00
WARNER BROS.					
❑ 7571	I'm Comin' Home/It Hurts to Want It So Bad	1972	—	3.00	6.00
❑ 7633	Mr. John/You Got Me Knockin'	1972	—	3.00	6.00
❑ 7658	Burning Love/It Hurts to Want It So Bad	1972	—	3.00	6.00
Albums					
DOT					
❑ DLP 3434 [M]	You Better Move On	1962	25.00	50.00	100.00
❑ DLP 25434 [S]	You Better Move On	1962	40.00	80.00	160.00
WARNER BROS.					
❑ BS 2592	Arthur Alexander	1972	6.25	12.50	25.00

ALEXANDER, JOE, AND THE CUBANS With a pre-Chess CHUCK BERRY in the band.
45s

Number	Title (A Side/B Side)	Yr	VG	VG+	NM
BALLAD					
❑ 1008	Oh Maria/I Hope These Words Will Find You Well	1954	500.00	1000.	1500.

ALEXANDER, JUNE See ARTHUR ALEXANDER.

ALEXANDER, MAX
45s

Number	Title (A Side/B Side)	Yr	VG	VG+	NM
CAPROCK					
❑ 116	Little Rome/Rock, Rock, Rock Everybody	1959	50.00	100.00	200.00

ALEXANDER AND THE GREATS
45s

Number	Title (A Side/B Side)	Yr	VG	VG+	NM
ARVEE					
❑ 5064	Swanee Stomp/Waterlogged	1963	10.00	20.00	40.00
LIMELIGHT					
❑ 3040	Do the Mustang/Hot Dang Mustang	1964	10.00	20.00	40.00

ALEXANDER'S TIMELESS BLOOZBAND
45s

Number	Title (A Side/B Side)	Yr	VG	VG+	NM
KAPP					
❑ 967	Maybe Baby/Power of Your Love	1969	3.00	6.00	12.00
MATAMAT					
❑ 101	Love So Strong/Horn Song	1967	5.00	10.00	20.00
UNI					
❑ 55044	Love So Strong/Horn Song	1967	3.75	7.50	15.00
Albums					
SMASK					
❑ 1001 [M]	Alexander's Timeless Bloozband	1967	50.00	100.00	200.00
UNI					
❑ 73021	For Sale	1968	6.25	12.50	25.00

ALFI AND HARRY
45s

Number	Title (A Side/B Side)	Yr	VG	VG+	NM
LIBERTY					
❑ 55008	The Trouble with Harry/Little Beauty	1955	6.25	12.50	25.00
❑ 55016	The Word Game Song/Persian on Excursion	1956	6.25	12.50	25.00
❑ 55066	Safari/Cloding Time	1957	6.25	12.50	25.00

ALHONA, RICHIE
45s

Number	Title (A Side/B Side)	Yr	VG	VG+	NM
FANTASY					
❑ 553	One Desire/Young Boy, Young Girl	1961	3.00	6.00	12.00
—Black vinyl					
❑ 553	One Desire/Young Boy, Young Girl	1961	7.50	15.00	30.00
—Red vinyl					
❑ 553 [PS]	One Desire/Young Boy, Young Girl	1961	7.50	15.00	30.00
❑ 556	Mama, Mama/The Pagan	1961	3.00	6.00	12.00
❑ 561	The Fool/Teenager Teenager	1962	3.00	6.00	12.00

ALICE JEAN AND THE MONDELLOS See THE MONDELLOS.

ALIOTTA-HAYNES-JEREMIAH
45s

Number	Title (A Side/B Side)	Yr	VG	VG+	NM
AMPEX					
❑ 11012	Pitter Patter/(B-side unknown)	1970	2.00	4.00	8.00
—As "Aliotta Haynes"					
❑ 11026	Tomorrow's Another Day/One Night Stand	1971	2.00	4.00	8.00
—As "Aliotta Haynes"					
SNOW QUEEN					
❑ 1000	Lake Shore Drive/(B-side unknown)	1973	5.00	10.00	20.00
Albums					
AMPEX					
❑ A-10108	Aliotta-Haynes Music	1970	5.00	10.00	20.00
—As "Aliota-Haynes"					
❑ A-10119	Aliotta-Haynes-Jeremiah	1970	5.00	10.00	20.00
BIG FOOT					
❑ 714	Lake Shore Drive	1978	6.25	12.50	25.00
LITTLE FOOT					
❑ 711	Slippin' Away	1977	5.00	10.00	20.00

ALIVE AND KICKING
45s

Number	Title (A Side/B Side)	Yr	VG	VG+	NM
ROULETTE					
❑ 7078	Tighter, Tighter/Sunday Morning	1970	—	2.50	5.00
❑ 7087	Just Let It Come/Mother Carey's Chicken	1970	—	2.50	5.00

Number	Title (A Side/B Side)	Yr	VG	VG+	NM
❏ 7094	London Bridge/You Gave Me Something	1971	—	2.50	5.00
❏ 7113	Good Ole Lovin' Back Home/Jordan	1971	—	2.50	5.00
Albums					
ROULETTE					
❏ SR 42052	Alive and Kicking	1970	5.00	10.00	20.00

ALL AMERICAN RUMBLERS, THE
Albums
GONE

❏ LP-5006 [M]	Destination Dixie	1959	12.50	25.00	50.00

ALL STARS, THE
Albums
GRAMOPHONE

❏ 20192	Boogie Woogie	196?	12.50	25.00	50.00

ALLAN, CHAD Member of the early GUESS WHO.
45s
MALA

❏ 12033	Thru the Looking Glass/Ramon's Hourglass	1968	—	3.00	6.00
REPRISE					
❏ 1003	On the Back Step/West Coast Girl	1971	—	3.00	6.00

ALLAN, DAVIE, AND THE ARROWS
45s
CUDE

❏ 101	War Path/Beyond the Blue	1963	25.00	50.00	100.00
GET HIP					
❏ GH-209	The Born Losers Theme/The Glory Stompers	1997	—	—	2.00
❏ GH-209 [PS]	The Born Losers Theme/The Glory Stompers	1997	—	—	2.00
MARC					
❏ 3223	War Path/Beyond the Blue	1963	12.50	25.00	50.00
MGM					
❏ 14299	It's the Little Things You Do/Haven't You Heard	1971	2.00	4.00	8.00
❏ 14374	Head Over Heels/Here It Comes	1972	2.00	4.00	8.00
❏ 14432	Dawn of the 7th Cavalry/Little Big Horn	1972	2.00	4.00	8.00
❏ 14560	And Evil Did Too/Pleasure Girl	1973	2.00	4.00	8.00
❏ 14650	Apache '73/Run of the Arrow	1973	2.00	4.00	8.00
MRC					
❏ 0901	Stoked on Surf/Flashback	1984	—	2.50	5.00
PRIVATE STOCK					
❏ 45,001	Touch Too Much/We Can Make It Together	1974	—	3.00	6.00
SIDEWALK					
❏ 1	Apache '65/Blue Guitar	1965	5.00	10.00	20.00
TOWER					
❏ 116	Apache '65/Blue Guitar	1965	3.75	7.50	15.00
❏ 133	Moon Dawg '65/Dance the Freddie	1965	3.00	6.00	12.00
❏ 142	Baby Ruth/I'm Looking Over a Four Leaf Clover	1965	3.00	6.00	12.00
❏ 158	Space Hop/Granny Goose	1965	3.00	6.00	12.00
❏ 267	Wild Angels Theme/UFO	1966	3.00	6.00	12.00
❏ 295	Blue's Theme/Bongo Party	1966	3.00	6.00	12.00
—As "The Arrows featuring Davie Allen"					
❏ 341	Devil's Angels/Cody's Theme	1967	3.00	6.00	12.00
❏ 381	Cycle-Delic/Blue Rides Again	1967	3.00	6.00	12.00
❏ 446	Wild in the Streets/Shape of Things to Come	1968	3.00	6.00	12.00
Albums					
TOWER					
❏ DT 5002 [R]	Apache '65	1965	7.50	15.00	30.00
❏ T 5002 [M]	Apache '65	1965	10.00	20.00	40.00
❏ DT 5043 [R]	The Wild Angels	1966	5.00	10.00	20.00
❏ T 5043 [M]	The Wild Angels	1966	7.50	15.00	30.00
❏ DT 5056 [R]	The Wild Angels, Vol. II	1967	5.00	10.00	20.00
❏ T 5056 [M]	The Wild Angels, Vol. II	1967	7.50	5.00	30.00
❏ DT 5074 [R]	Devil's Angel	1967	5.00	10.00	20.00
❏ T 5074 [M]	Devil's Angel	1967	7.50	15.00	30.00
❏ DT 5078 [R]	Blues Theme	1967	10.00	20.00	40.00
❏ T 5078 [M]	Blues Theme	1967	12.50	25.00	50.00
❏ DT 5083 [R]	Mondo Hollywood	1968	5.00	10.00	20.00
❏ T 5083 [M]	Mondo Hollywood	1968	7.50	15.00	30.00
❏ DT 5094 [R]	Cycle-Delic Sounds	1968	12.50	25.00	50.00
❏ T 5094 [M]	Cycle-Delic Sounds	1968	25.00	50.00	100.00

ALLAN & THE FLAMES
45s
CAMPBELL

❏ 225	Winter Wonderland/Till The End Of Time	1960	12.50	25.00	50.00
COLONIAL					
❏ 7006	Winter Wonderland/'Till The End of Time	1960	12.50	25.00	50.00

ALLEN, BILLY
45s
EL DORADO

❏ 505	Butterfly/Oo Wee Baby	1957	5.00	10.00	20.00
—As "Bill Allen"					
IMPERIAL					
❏ 5500	Please Give Me Something/Since I Have You	1958	25.00	50.00	100.00

ALLEN, DAVE
Albums
INTERNATIONAL ARTISTS

❏ 11	Color Blind	1969	15.00	30.00	60.00
—Original pressing					
❏ 11	Color Blind	1979	5.00	10.00	20.00
—Repressing with "RE2" and "Masterfonics" in dead wax					

ALLEN, DAYTON
Albums
GRAND AWARD

❏ GA 33-424 [M]	Why Not?	1960	6.25	12.50	25.00

ALLEN, JASON
45s
HIT

❏ 226	Everybody Loves a Clown/You've Got Your Troubles	1965	2.00	4.00	8.00
—B-side by the Spades					

ALLEN, JESSE
45s
ALADDIN

❏ 3129	Rock This Morning/Gonna Move Away from Town	1953	50.00	100.00	200.00
BAYOU					
❏ 011	Dragnet/Take It Easy	1953	25.00	50.00	100.00
CORAL					
❏ 65078	My Suffering/Let's Party	1952	50.00	100.00	200.00
IMPERIAL					
❏ 5256	Gotta Call That Number/Gonna Tell My Mama	1953	50.00	100.00	200.00
—With Audrey Walker					
❏ 5285	Sittin' and Wonderin'/I Wonder What's the Matter	1954	62.50	125.00	250.00
❏ 5303	What a Party/The Things I'm Gonna Do	1954	50.00	100.00	200.00
❏ 5315	Rockin' and Rollin'/I Love You So	1954	50.00	100.00	200.00

ALLEN, JIMMY, AND TOMMY BARTELLA
45s
AL-BRITE

❏ 1300	When Santa Comes Over The Brooklyn Bridge/What Would You Like To Have For Christmas?	1959	10.00	20.00	40.00

ALLEN, LEE
45s
ALADDIN

❏ 3334	Shimmy/Rockin' at Cosmos	1956	6.25	12.50	25.00
EMBER					
❏ 1027	Walkin' with Mr. Lee/Promenade	1957	6.25	12.50	25.00
❏ 1031	Strollin' with Mr. Lee/Boppin' at the Hop	1958	5.00	10.00	20.00
❏ 1039	Tic Toc/Chuggin'	1958	5.00	10.00	20.00
❏ 1047	Jim Jam/Short Circuit	1958	5.00	10.00	20.00
❏ 1057	Cat Walk/Creole Alley	1959	5.00	10.00	20.00
❏ 1082	Twistin' with Mr. Lee/Twist Around the Clock	1962	3.75	7.50	15.00
LOST-NITE					
❏ 416	Walkin' with Mr. Lee/Promenade	197?	—	2.50	5.00
—Reissue					
7-Inch Extended Plays					
EMBER					
❏ 103	Walkin' with Mr. Lee/Teen Dream//Promenade/Big Horn Special	1958	50.00	100.00	200.00
❏ 103 [PS]	Walkin' with Mr. Lee	1958	50.00	100.00	200.00
Albums					
EMBER					
❏ ELP-200 [M]	Walkin' with Mr. Lee	1958	125.00	250.00	500.00
—Red label					
❏ ELP-200 [M]	Walkin' with Mr. Lee	1959	50.00	100.00	200.00
—White "logs" label					
❏ ELP-200 [M]	Walkin' with Mr. Lee	1961	25.00	50.00	100.00
—Red and black label					

ALLEN, MILTON
45s
RCA VICTOR

❏ 47-6994	Love A Love A Lover/Just Look, Don't Touch, She's Mine	1957	7.50	15.00	30.00
❏ 47-7116	Don't Bug Me Baby/Jamboree	1957	12.50	25.00	50.00

ALLEN, RAY, AND THE UPBEATS
45s
BLAST

❏ 204	Peggy Sue/La Bamba	1962	7.50	15.00	30.00
SINCLAIR					
❏ 1004	Sweet Lorraine/Let Them Talk	1961	12.50	25.00	50.00
Albums					
BLAST					
❏ BLP-6804 [M]	A Tribute to Six	1962	30.00	60.00	120.00

ALLEN, REX
45s
BUENA VISTA

❏ F-341	Lazy River/Say One for Me	1959	3.75	7.50	15.00
❏ F-342	I Couldn't Care Less/Pretty Irish Girl	1959	3.75	7.50	15.00
❏ F-347	The Little Old Church in the Valley/Morgen	1959	3.75	7.50	15.00
❏ F-351	Staying Young/Forever and Ever	1959	3.75	7.50	15.00
❏ F-355	Barefoot Country Boy/Conversation with a Mule	1960	3.75	7.50	15.00
❏ F-358	The Lilacs Grow High/I'm the Man	1960	3.75	7.50	15.00
❏ F-363	Charro Bravo/I Love You So Much It Hurts	1960	3.75	7.50	15.00
❏ F-370	Dodie Ann/Pretty Irish Girl	1960	3.75	7.50	15.00
DECCA					
❏ 9-27876	Ragtime Melody/Tuck Me to Sleep in My Old 'Tucky Home	1951	6.25	12.50	25.00
❏ 9-27952	The Waltz of the Roses/As Long As the River Flows On	1952	5.00	10.00	20.00
❏ 9-28146	Till the Well Goes Dry/Rack Up the Balls Boys	1952	5.00	10.00	20.00
❏ 9-28341	Jambalaya (On the Bayou)/The Two-Faced Clock	1952	5.00	10.00	20.00
❏ 9-28446	No One Will Ever Know/Hootin' and Howlin'	1952	5.00	10.00	20.00
❏ 9-28556	Knocking on the Door/Why My Darlin' Why	1953	3.75	7.50	15.00
❏ 9-28758	Crying in the Chapel/I Thank the Lord	1953	5.00	10.00	20.00
❏ 9-28897	To Be Alone/If God Can Forgive You, So Can I	1953	5.00	10.00	20.00
❏ 9-28933	Where Did My Snowman Go?/Why Daddy?	1953	5.00	10.00	20.00
❏ 9-28998	He Played the Steel Guitar/Somewhere	1954	5.00	10.00	20.00
❏ 9-29111	Bringing Home the Bacon/I Could Cry My Heart Out	1954	3.75	7.50	15.00

Number	Title (A Side/B Side)	Yr	VG	VG+	NM
❑ 9-29168	In the Chapel in the Moonlight/				
	Chapel of Memories	1954	3.75	7.50	15.00
❑ 9-29297	You Took My Name/I'm Learning to Live	1954	5.00	10.00	20.00
❑ 9-29397	Tomorrow's Another Day to Cry/L-O-N-E-S-O-				
	M-E Letter Blues	1955	3.75	7.50	15.00
❑ 9-29586	That's What Makes the Juke Box Play/Pedro				
	Gonzales, Tennessee Lopez	1955	5.00	10.00	20.00
❑ 9-29610	Daddy, You Know What/The Albino Stallion	1955	3.75	7.50	15.00
❑ 9-29729	The Last Round-Up/I'm a Young Cowboy	1955	3.75	7.50	15.00
❑ 9-29871	The Last Frontier/Sky Boss	1956	3.00	6.00	12.00
❑ 9-30066	Trail of the Lonesome Pine/Nothin; to Do	1956	3.00	6.00	12.00
❑ 9-30204	Drango/Little White Horse	1957	3.00	6.00	12.00
❑ 9-30205	Westward Ho the Wagons/Wringle Wrangle	1957	3.00	6.00	12.00
❑ 9-30364	Money, Marbles and Chalk/				
	Flowers of San Antone	1957	3.00	6.00	12.00
❑ 9-30511	Blue Dream/Blue Light Waltz	1957	3.00	6.00	12.00
❑ 9-30651	Knock, Knock, Rattle/Invitation to the Blues	1958	6.25	12.50	25.00
❑ 9-30833	I Know the Reason Why/The Mystery of His Way	1959	3.00	6.00	12.00
❑ 9-31039	Take Me Lord/Sheltered in the Arms of the Old				
	Rugged Cross	1959	3.00	6.00	12.00
❑ 32072	A Waltz That Never Ends/				
	A Woman (Can Change a Man)	1967	2.00	4.00	8.00
❑ 32322	Tiny Bubbles/Jose Villa Lobo Alfredo Thomaso				
	Vincente Lopez	1968	—	3.00	6.00
❑ 32401	Bummin' Around/				
	When I Leave This World Behind	1968	—	3.00	6.00
❑ 32467	It Happens Over and Over Again/Sai Finis	1969	—	3.00	6.00
❑ 732612	Ain't That Beautiful Singing/A Voice	1970	—	3.00	6.00
❑ 9-46390	I've Got So Many Million Years (I Can't Count				
	'Em)/Is He Satisfied	1952	5.00	10.00	20.00
❑ 9-88161	Where Did My Snowman Go?/Why Daddy?	1953	3.75	7.50	15.00
—Yellow label "Children's Series" release					
❑ 9-88161 [PS]	Where Did My Snowman Go?/Why Daddy?	1953	7.50	15.00	30.00
HACIENDA					
❑ WWA 01	I Gotta Have My Baby Back/My Confession	196?	3.75	7.50	15.00
❑ WW 002	Lonesome Letter Blues/Love Gone Cold	196?	3.75	7.50	15.00
MCA					
❑ 41071	So Long Duke/At the Rainbow's End	1979	—	3.00	6.00
MERCURY					
❑ 5573-X45	The Roving Kind/Wresk of the John B.	1950	6.25	12.50	25.00
❑ 5597-X45	Sparrow in the Tree Top/Always You	1951	6.25	12.50	25.00
❑ 5619-X45	I'm a Sentimental Fool/Ten More Miles to Go	1951	6.25	12.50	25.00
❑ 5647-X45	Mister and Mississippi/Lonely Little Robin	1951	6.25	12.50	25.00
❑ 5713-X45	Angel to Joe/Cowpoke	1951	6.25	12.50	25.00
❑ 6297-X45	I Ain't Gonna Cry No More/You Drifted	1951	6.25	12.50	25.00
❑ 6349-X45	Naggin'/Albuquerque Polka	1951	6.25	12.50	25.00
❑ 70373	True Blue Lou-Lou-Lou/Save a Little Corner in				
	Your Heart for Me	1954	5.00	10.00	20.00
❑ 71844	Marines, Let's Go/Heartaches of a Fool	1961	2.50	5.00	10.00
❑ 71997	Don't Go Near the Indians/Touched So Deeply	1962	2.50	5.00	10.00
❑ 72071	Only the Hangman/Johnny Travers	1962	2.00	4.00	8.00
❑ 72095	Roll Up Your Sleeve/Oohin' and Aahin'	1963	2.00	4.00	8.00
❑ 72137	Silver Spoon Lonely Me/To-Ra	1963	2.00	4.00	8.00
❑ 72205	Tear After Tear/I'm Just Killing Time	1964	2.00	4.00	8.00
❑ 72205 [PS]	Tear After Tear/I'm Just Killing Time	1964	3.75	7.50	15.00
MUSICOR					
❑ 1132	Take It Back and Change It for a Boy/				
	Rodeo Twist	1965	2.00	4.00	8.00
WARNER BROS.					
❑ 5891	Jawbreaker/Change Me	1967	—	3.50	7.00
Albums					
BUENA VISTA					
❑ BV-3307 [M]	Rex Allen Sings 16 Golden Hits	1961	10.00	20.00	40.00
DECCA					
❑ DL 8402 [M]	Under Western Skies	1956	12.50	25.00	50.00
❑ DL 8776 [M]	Mister Cowboy	1959	10.00	20.00	40.00
❑ DL 75011 [S]	The Smooth Country Sound of Rex Allen	1968	5.00	10.00	20.00
❑ DL 75205	The Touch of God's Hand	1970	5.00	10.00	20.00
❑ DL 78776 [S]	Mister Cowboy	1959	15.00	30.00	60.00
HACIENDA					
❑ WWLP-101 [M]	Rex Allen Sings	1960	50.00	100.00	200.00
MERCURY					
❑ MG-20719 [M]	Faith of a Man	1962	6.25	12.50	25.00
❑ MG-20752 [M]	Rex Allen Sings and Tells Tales	1963	6.25	12.50	25.00
❑ SR-60719 [S]	Faith of a Man	1962	7.50	15.00	30.00
❑ SR-60752 [S]	Rex Allen Sings and Tells Tales	1963	7.50	15.00	30.00

ALLEN, RICHIE
45s

Number	Title (A Side/B Side)	Yr	VG	VG+	NM
ERA					
❑ 3058	Blue Holiday/Goochie Bamba	1961	5.00	10.00	20.00
IMPERIAL					
❑ 5683	Stranger from Durango/Redskin	1960	5.00	10.00	20.00
❑ 5701	Sally Ann/Why Did It End	1960	3.75	7.50	15.00
—As "Dickie Allen"					
❑ 5720	Haunted Guitar/In a Persian Market	1961	5.00	10.00	20.00
❑ 5846	Mr. Hobbs (Theme)/Comin' Back to You	1962	3.75	7.50	15.00
❑ 5865	Not So Quiet/A Touch of Blue	1962	3.75	7.50	15.00
❑ 5872	Cave Man/Room 304	1962	5.00	10.00	20.00
❑ 5885	Kick Off/Undercurrent	1962	5.00	10.00	20.00
❑ 5917	Butterscotch/Sunday Picnic	1963	3.75	7.50	15.00
❑ 5929	Foot Stomp U.S.A./Skag Along Pete	1963	5.00	10.00	20.00
❑ 5941	Surf Beater/The Rising Surf	1963	3.75	7.50	15.00
❑ 5984	The Quiet Surf/Ballad of the Surf	1963	3.75	7.50	15.00
TOWER					
❑ 273	Stranger from Durango/Nothing Good	1966	3.00	6.00	12.00
Albums					
IMPERIAL					
❑ LP-9212 [M]	Stranger from Durango	1962	10.00	20.00	40.00
❑ LP-9229 [M]	The Rising Surf	1963	20.00	40.00	80.00
❑ LP-9243 [M]	Surfer's Slide	1963	20.00	40.00	80.00
❑ LP-12212 [S]	Stranger from Durango	1962	12.50	25.00	50.00
❑ LP-12229 [S]	The Rising Surf	1963	37.50	75.00	150.00
❑ LP-12243 [S]	Surfer's Slide	1963	37.50	75.00	150.00

ALLEN, RONNIE
45s

Number	Title (A Side/B Side)	Yr	VG	VG+	NM
DAPT					
❑ 205	Flip You Over/Ronnie's Swanee	1961	10.00	20.00	40.00
SAN					
❑ 208	Juvenile Delinquent/River of Love	1959	20.00	40.00	80.00
❑ 209	High School Love/(B-side unknown)	1959	20.00	40.00	80.00
❑ 300	Gonna Get My Baby/(B-side unknown)	1959	20.00	40.00	80.00

ALLEN, STEVE
45s

Number	Title (A Side/B Side)	Yr	VG	VG+	NM
BRUNSWICK					
❑ 80228	Cinderella/Goldilocks and the Three Bears	1953	3.75	7.50	15.00
❑ 80230	But Officer/But Baby	1953	3.75	7.50	15.00
❑ 80231	Jack and the Beanstalk/				
	Snow White and the Seven Dwarfs	1953	3.75	7.50	15.00
CORAL					
❑ 61368	The Ballad of Davy Crockett/Very Square Dance	1955	3.00	6.00	12.00
❑ 61375	Tonight/Just Stay a Little While	1955	3.00	6.00	12.00
❑ 61376	I'm Glad There Is You/It Can't Be Wrong	1955	3.00	6.00	12.00
❑ 61445	The Goo Goo Doll Song/Old Betsy	1955	3.00	6.00	12.00
❑ 61485	Autumn Leaves/High and Dry	1955	3.00	6.00	12.00
❑ 61542	What Is a Wife/Memories of You	1956	3.00	6.00	12.00
❑ 61565	Don't Be That Way/Sing, Sing, Sing	1956	3.00	6.00	12.00
❑ 61566	Let's Dance/Goodbye	1956	3.00	6.00	12.00
❑ 61573	What Is a Freem?/I Never Harmed an Onion	1956	3.00	6.00	12.00
❑ 61620	Theme from "Picnic"/My Nita, Juanita	1956	3.00	6.00	12.00
❑ 61681	Lola's Theme/Conversation	1956	3.00	6.00	12.00
❑ 61707	Star Dust/The Golden Wedding Waltz	1956	3.00	6.00	12.00
❑ 61839	Do You Ever Think of Me/I Love You	1957	2.50	5.00	10.00
❑ 61877	Gotta Have Something in the Bank, Frank/				
	The Disc-Jockey's Theme Song	1957	2.50	5.00	10.00
❑ 61909	Pretend You Don't See Him/				
	But I Haven't Got Him	1957	2.50	5.00	10.00
❑ 61995	You're So Influential/When You're Smiling	1958	2.50	5.00	10.00
DOT					
❑ 15831	Hula Hoop/Love Theme from "Houseboat"	1958	2.50	5.00	10.00
❑ 15891	St. Louis Blues/Ida Sweet as Apple Cider	1959	2.50	5.00	10.00
❑ 15947	Hawaiian Punch/Follow the Leader	1959	2.50	5.00	10.00
❑ 16408	Mah Mah Limbo/Dream	1962	2.00	4.00	8.00
❑ 16457	Gravy Waltz/Preacherman	1963	2.00	4.00	8.00
❑ 16507	Quando Caliente El Sol/Leave It to Me	1963	2.00	4.00	8.00
❑ 16613	I Am the Greatest/Mouth to Mouth Resuscitation	1964	2.00	4.00	8.00
❑ 16645	Theme from "The Magic Fountain"/				
	Who's Your Sister	1964	2.00	4.00	8.00
DUNHILL					
❑ 4097	Here Comes Sgt. Pepper/Flowers and Love	1967	3.75	7.50	15.00
❑ 4127	Dance Time/Impossible	1968	—	3.00	6.00
SIGNATURE					
❑ 12003	Flattery/I Remember It Well	1959	2.50	5.00	10.00
—With Jayne Meadows					
❑ 12044	Dance Time/Impossible	1960	2.50	5.00	10.00
7-Inch Extended Plays					
CORAL					
❑ EC 82025 [PS]	Let's Dance	195?	2.50	5.00	10.00
—Cover for 2-EP set (83054, 83055)					
❑ 83054	Let's Dance/Don't Be That Way//Sing Sing Sing				
	(With a Swing)	195?	2.50	5.00	10.00
—One record of EC 82025					
❑ 83055	Stompin' at the Savoy/Memories of You//				
	Sometimes I'm Happy/Goodbye	195?	2.50	5.00	10.00
—One record of EC 82025					
Albums					
CASABLANCA					
❑ 811366-1	Funny Fone Calls	1983	2.00	4.00	8.00
—Reissue of Dot 3472					
❑ 811367-1	More Funny Fone Calls	1983	2.00	4.00	8.00
—Reissue of Dot 3517					
CORAL					
❑ CRL 57004 [M]	Music for Tonight	1955	6.25	12.50	25.00
❑ CRL 57015 [M]	Tonight at Midnight	1956	6.25	12.50	25.00
❑ CRL 57018 [M]	Jazz for Tonight	1956	6.25	12.50	25.00
❑ CRL 57019 [M]	Steve Sings	1956	6.25	12.50	25.00
❑ CRL 57028 [M]	Let's Dance	1956	6.25	12.50	25.00
❑ CRL 57048 [M]	Allen Plays Allen	1956	6.25	12.50	25.00
❑ CRL 57070 [M]	The Steve Allen Show	1957	6.25	12.50	25.00
❑ CRL 57138 [M]	Romantic Rendezvous	1957	5.00	10.00	20.00
❑ CRL 57442 [M]	Songs Everybody Knows	1964	3.75	7.50	15.00
❑ CRL 757442 [R]	Songs Everybody Knows	1964	3.00	6.00	12.00
DECCA					
❑ DL 8151 [M]	Steve Allen's All Star Jazz Concert, Vol. 1	1955	7.50	15.00	30.00
❑ DL 8152 [M]	Steve Allen's All Star Jazz Concert, Vol. 2	1955	7.50	15.00	30.00
DOT					
❑ DLP 3472 [M]	Funny Fone Calls	1963	5.00	10.00	20.00
❑ DLP 3473 [M]	12 Greatest Hits	1963	5.00	10.00	20.00
❑ DLP 3480 [M]	Bossa Nova Jazz	1963	3.75	7.50	15.00
❑ DLP 3515 [M]	Gravy Waltz and 11 Current Hits!	1963	3.75	7.50	15.00
❑ DLP 3517 [M]	More Funny Fone Calls	1963	5.00	10.00	20.00
❑ DLP 3519 [M]	Steve Allen Plays the Piano Greats	1963	3.75	7.50	15.00
❑ DLP 3530 [M]	Steve Allen Sings	1963	3.75	7.50	15.00
❑ DLP 3538 [M]	Cuano Caliente El Sol and More	1963	3.75	7.50	15.00
❑ DLP 3560 [M]	Great Ragtime Hits	1963	3.75	7.50	15.00
❑ DLP 3587 [M]	Songs from the Steve Allen TV Show	1964	3.00	6.00	12.00
❑ DLP 3597 [M]	Steve Allen, His Piano and Orchestra	1964	3.00	6.00	12.00
❑ DLP 3624 [M]	I Play for You	1965	3.00	6.00	12.00
❑ DLP 3683 [M]	Rhythm and Blues	1966	3.00	6.00	12.00

Number	Title (A Side/B Side)	Yr	VG	VG+	NM
❏ DLP 25380 [S]	Bossa Nova Jazz	1963	5.00	10.00	20.00
❏ DLP 25515 [S]	Gravy Waltz and 11 Current Hits!	1963	5.00	10.00	20.00
❏ DLP 25519 [S]	Steve Allen Plays the Piano Greats	1963	5.00	10.00	20.00
❏ DLP 25530 [S]	Steve Allen Sings	1963	5.00	10.00	20.00
❏ DLP 25538 [S]	Cuano Caliente El Sol and More	1963	5.00	10.00	20.00
❏ DLP 25560 [S]	Great Ragtime Hits	1963	5.00	10.00	20.00
❏ DLP 25587 [S]	Songs from the Steve Allen TV Show	1964	3.75	7.50	15.00
❏ DLP 25597 [S]	Steve Allen, His Piano and Orchestra	1964	3.75	7.50	15.00
❏ DLP 25624 [S]	I Play for You	1965	3.75	7.50	15.00
❏ DLP 25683 [S]	Rhythm and Blues	1966	3.75	7.50	15.00
FORUM					
❏ F-9014 [M]	Steve Allen at the Round Table	196?	5.00	10.00	20.00
❏ FS-9014 [S]	Steve Allen at the Round Table	196?	3.75	7.50	15.00
HAMILTON					
❏ HLP 132 [M]	Some of My Favorites	196?	3.00	6.00	12.00
❏ HLP 12132 [S]	Some of My Favorites	196?	3.75	7.50	15.00
ROULETTE					
❏ R-25053 [M]	Steve Allen at the Round Table	1959	6.25	12.50	25.00
❏ SR-25053 [S]	Steve Allen at the Round Table	1959	5.00	10.00	20.00
SIGNATURE					
❏ SM 1004 [M]	Man in the Street	1959	7.50	15.00	30.00
❏ SM 1021 [M]	Monday Nights	1960	7.50	15.00	30.00

ALLEN, STEVE, AND MANNY ALBAM
Albums
DOT

Number	Title (A Side/B Side)	Yr	VG	VG+	NM
❏ DLP 3194 [M]	...And All That Jazz	1959	6.25	12.50	25.00
❏ DLP 25194 [S]	...And All That Jazz	1959	5.00	10.00	20.00

ALLEN, TONY Also see THE ORIGINALS (4).
45s
ALADDIN

Number	Title (A Side/B Side)	Yr	VG	VG+	NM
❏ 3403	Time Won't Wait on You/Holy Smoke, Baby	1957	5.00	10.00	20.00
BETHLEHEM					
❏ 3002	Come-A, Come-A Baby/Just Like Before	1961	3.00	6.00	12.00
❏ 3004	It Hurts Me So/The Trakey-Doo	1962	3.00	6.00	12.00
DIG					
❏ 104	It Hurts Me So/Check Yourself	1955	5.00	10.00	20.00
❏ 109	I Found An Angel/I'm Dreaming	1956	12.50	25.00	50.00
EBB					
❏ 115	Come Back/Why in the World	1957	5.00	10.00	20.00
IMPERIAL					
❏ 5523	Strange Talk/Call My Name	1958	3.75	7.50	15.00
❏ 5547	Forgive Me/Rockin' Shoes	1958	3.75	7.50	15.00
JAMIE					
❏ 1143	Train of Love/God Gave Me You	1959	3.75	7.50	15.00
KENT					
❏ 364	Dreaming/Be My Love, Be My Love	1961	3.00	6.00	12.00
SPECIALTY					
❏ 560	Nite Owl/I	1955	12.50	25.00	50.00
❏ 570	Check Yourself Baby/Especially	1956	7.50	15.00	30.00
TAMPA					
❏ 157	Be My Love, Be My Love/Tell Me	195?	7.50	15.00	30.00
—As "The Wonders"					
ULTRA					
❏ 104	It Hurts Me So/Check Yourself	1955	7.50	15.00	30.00
UNITED ARTISTS					
❏ 50190	Now Is Forever/Triple Cross	1967	2.00	4.00	8.00
Albums					
CROWN					
❏ CST-240 [S]	Rock and Roll with Tony Allen	1961	25.00	50.00	100.00
❏ CLP-5231 [M]	Rock and Roll with Tony Allen	1960	25.00	50.00	100.00
—Black label					
❏ CLP-5231 [M]	Rock and Roll with Tony Allen	1961	15.00	30.00	60.00
—Gray label					

ALLEN, WOODY
Albums
BELL

Number	Title (A Side/B Side)	Yr	VG	VG+	NM
❏ 6008	The Wonderful Wacky World of Woody Allen	1967	5.00	10.00	20.00
CAPITOL					
❏ ST 2986	The Third Woody Allen Album	1968	6.25	12.50	25.00
CASABLANCA					
❏ NBLP2-7145 [(2)]	Woody Allen: Stand-Up Comic 1964-1968	1979	3.75	7.50	15.00
—Compilation of material from Colpix and Capitol LPs (different from either UA collection)					
COLPIX					
❏ CP 488 [M]	Woody Allen 2	1965	7.50	15.00	30.00
❏ SCP 488 [R]	Woody Allen 2	1965	6.25	12.50	25.00
❏ CP 518 [M]	Woody Allen	1964	7.50	15.00	30.00
UNITED ARTISTS					
❏ UA-LA849-J2 [(2)]	Woody Allen: Stand-Up Comic 1964-1968	1977	5.00	10.00	20.00
—Compilation of material from Colpix and Capitol LPs (different from UA 9968)					
❏ UAS 9968 [(2)]	Woody Allen: The Nightclub Years	1972	5.00	10.00	20.00
—Compilation of material from Colpix and Capitol LPs					

ALLENS, ARVEE See RITCHIE VALENS.

ALLEY CATS, THE
45s
EPIC

Number	Title (A Side/B Side)	Yr	VG	VG+	NM
❏ 9778	Lily of the West/ I Should Have Stayed at Home Tonight	1965	3.00	6.00	12.00
PHILLES					
❏ 108	Puddin N' Tain (Ask Me Again, I'll Tell You the Same)/Feel So Good	1962	6.25	12.50	25.00
PHILLES/COLLECTABLES					
❏ 3201	Puddin' and Tain/Then He Kissed Me	1985	—	3.00	6.00
—Red vinyl; part of box set "Phil Spector Wall of Sound Series Vol. 2"; B-side by the Crystals					
❏ 3201	Puddin' and Tain/Then He Kissed Me	1986	—	2.50	5.00
—Black vinyl; B-side by the Crystals					

Number	Title (A Side/B Side)	Yr	VG	VG+	NM
WHIPPET					
❏ 202	This Thing Called Love/Spang-a-Lang	1957	5.00	10.00	20.00
❏ 209	Snap, Crackle and Pop/Last Night	1958	5.00	10.00	20.00

ALLIES, THE
45s
REPRISE

Number	Title (A Side/B Side)	Yr	VG	VG+	NM
❏ 0674	I Would Love You/The Sound of Children	1968	5.00	10.00	20.00
VALIANT					
❏ 748	I'll Sell My Soul/Burning Glass	1966	10.00	20.00	40.00

ALLISON, GENE
45s
CHAMPION

Number	Title (A Side/B Side)	Yr	VG	VG+	NM
❏ 1008	Goodbye My Love/If Things Don't Change	196?	3.00	6.00	12.00
❏ 1019	Now We're Together/Understand	196?	3.00	6.00	12.00
CHEROKEE					
❏ 1022	You Gonna Be Sorry/I Know I Can Make It	196?	3.75	7.50	15.00
DECCA					
❏ 30185	You're My Baby/Somebody Somewhere	1957	3.75	7.50	15.00
MONUMENT					
❏ 876	Ev'rybody's Got a Little Problem/Now Hear This	1965	2.00	4.00	8.00
REF-O-REE					
❏ 703	Having a Party/Almost Sundown	196?	2.50	5.00	10.00
❏ 709	I Understand/Somebody Somewhere	196?	2.50	5.00	10.00
❏ 727	How Long's the Train Been Gone/You Can Make It If You Try & Have Faith	196?	2.50	5.00	10.00
❏ 729	I Understand/Almost Sundown	196?	2.50	5.00	10.00
VEE JAY					
❏ 256	You Can Make It If You Try/Hey, Hey, I Love You	1957	5.00	10.00	20.00
❏ 273	Have Faith/My Heart Remembers	1958	3.75	7.50	15.00
❏ 286	I Don't Know Why/Let's Sit and Talk	1958	3.75	7.50	15.00
❏ 299	Everything Will Be Alright/ I'm a Fool Wanting You	1958	3.75	7.50	15.00
❏ 305	Tell Me the Truth/Reap What You Sow	1959	3.75	7.50	15.00
❏ 317	Everybody But Me/I Believe in Myself	1959	3.75	7.50	15.00
❏ 329	I'll Be Waiting for You/Let There Be Women	1959	3.75	7.50	15.00
❏ 341	Why Do You Treat Me So Cold/ Oh Yeah I'm in Love	1960	3.75	7.50	15.00
❏ 365	Ask/Tell Me Sugar Baby	1960	3.75	7.50	15.00
Albums					
VEE JAY					
❏ LP-1009 [M]	Gene Allison	1959	75.00	150.00	300.00
—Maroon label					
❏ LP-1009 [M]	Gene Allison	196?	25.00	50.00	100.00
—Black label, oval or brackets logo					

ALLISON, KEITH
45s
AMY

Number	Title (A Side/B Side)	Yr	VG	VG+	NM
❏ 11024	Who Do You Love/Don't Want Nobody But You	1968	3.00	6.00	12.00
COLUMBIA					
❏ 43619	Look at Me/I Ain't Blaming You	1966	3.00	6.00	12.00
❏ 43619 [PS]	Look at Me/I Ain't Blaming You	1966	6.25	12.50	25.00
❏ 43900	Action/Glitter and Gold	1966	3.00	6.00	12.00
❏ 44028	Louise/Freeborn Man	1967	3.00	6.00	12.00
❏ 44028 [PS]	Louise/Freeborn Man	1967	6.25	12.50	25.00
❏ 44853	Birds of a Feather/To Know Her Is to Love Her	1969	2.50	5.00	10.00
❏ 45115	Everybody/Wednesday's Child	1970	2.50	5.00	10.00
WARNER BROS.					
❏ 5681	Sweet Little Rock and Roller/ The Girl Can't Help It	1965	3.00	6.00	12.00
❏ 5681 [PS]	Sweet Little Rock and Roller/ The Girl Can't Help It	1965	6.25	12.50	25.00
Albums					
COLUMBIA					
❏ CL 2641 [M]	Keith Allison In Action	1967	6.25	12.50	25.00
❏ CS 9441 [S]	Keith Allison In Action	1967	6.25	12.50	25.00

ALLISON, LUTHER
45s
GORDY

Number	Title (A Side/B Side)	Yr	VG	VG+	NM
❏ 7128	The Little Red Rooster/Raggedy and Dirty	1973	—	2.50	5.00
❏ 7137	Part Time Love/Now You Got It	1974	—	2.50	5.00
Albums					
DELMARK					
❏ DS-625	Love Me, Mama	1969	6.25	12.50	25.00
GORDY					
❏ G-964	Bad News Is Coming	1973	2.50	5.00	10.00
❏ G-967	Luther's Blues	1974	2.50	5.00	10.00
❏ G-974	Night Life	1976	2.50	5.00	10.00

ALLISONS, THE (1) British male duo.
45s
COLUMBIA

Number	Title (A Side/B Side)	Yr	VG	VG+	NM
❏ 42034	Words/Blue Tears	1961	2.50	5.00	10.00
LONDON					
❏ 1977	Are You Sure/There's One Thing More	1961	2.50	5.00	10.00
❏ 1977 [PS]	Are You Sure/There's One Thing More	1961	6.25	12.50	25.00
SMASH					
❏ 1749	Lessons in Love/Oh My Love	1962	2.50	5.00	10.00

ALLISONS, THE (2) American girl group.
45s
TIP

Number	Title (A Side/B Side)	Yr	VG	VG+	NM
❏ 1011	Surfer Street/Money	1963	10.00	20.00	40.00

ALLMAN, DUANE Of THE ALLMAN BROTHERS BAND and THE ALLMAN JOYS.
Albums
CAPRICORN

Number	Title (A Side/B Side)	Yr	VG	VG+	NM
❏ 2CP 0108 [(2)]	An Anthology	1972	5.00	10.00	20.00
❏ 2CP 0139 [(2)]	An Anthology, Vol. II	1974	5.00	10.00	20.00

Number	Title (A Side/B Side)	Yr	VG	VG+	NM
POLYDOR					
❏ PD-1-6338	The Best of Duane Allman	1981	3.00	6.00	12.00
❏ 827563-1	The Best of Duane Allman	1984	2.00	4.00	8.00

ALLMAN, DUANE AND GREGG Of THE ALLMAN BROTHERS BAND and THE ALLMAN JOYS.

45s

Number	Title (A Side/B Side)	Yr	VG	VG+	NM
BOLD					
❏ 200	Morning Dew/Morning Dew	1973	2.50	5.00	10.00
❏ 200 [DJ]	Morning Dew/Morning Dew	1973	5.00	10.00	20.00
—Promo on red vinyl					
Albums					
BOLD					
❏ 33-301	Duane and Gregg Allman	197?	3.00	6.00	12.00
—Non-gatefold cover					
❏ 33-301	Duane and Gregg Allman	1972	6.25	12.50	25.00
—Gatefold cover					

ALLMAN, GREGG Of THE ALLMAN BROTHERS BAND and THE ALLMAN JOYS. Also see ALLMAN AND WOMAN.

12-Inch Singles

Number	Title (A Side/B Side)	Yr	VG	VG+	NM
EPIC					
❏ EAS 1173 [DJ]	Can't Get Over You (same on both sides?)	1988	2.00	4.00	8.00
45s					
CAPRICORN					
❏ 0035	Midnight Rider/Multi-Colored Lady	1973	—	2.50	5.00
❏ 0042	Don't Mess Up a Good Thing/Please Call Home	1974	—	2.00	4.00
❏ 0053	Midnight Rider/Don't Mess Up a Good Thing	1975	—	2.00	4.00
—Back to Back Hits series					
❏ 0279	Cryin' Shame/One More Try	1977	—	2.00	4.00
EPIC					
❏ 06998	I'm No Angel/Lead Me On	1987	—	2.00	4.00
❏ 07215	Can't Keep Running/Anything Goes	1987	—	—	3.00
❏ 07430	Evidence of Love/Anything Goes	1987	—	—	3.00
❏ 08041	Slip Away/Every Hungry Woman	1988	—	—	3.00
7-Inch Extended Plays					
CAPRICORN					
❏ S CP 0116	Queen of Hearts/Please Call Home//Don't Mess Up a Good Thing/Midnight Rider	1973	2.50	5.00	10.00
—Jukebox issue; small hole, plays at 33 1/3 rpm					
❏ S CP 0116 [PS]	Laid Back	1973	2.50	5.00	10.00
—Part of "Little LP" series (LLP #237)					
Albums					
CAPRICORN					
❏ CP 0116	Laid Back	1973	3.00	6.00	12.00
❏ 2CP 0141 [(2)]	The Gregg Allman Tour	1974	3.75	7.50	15.00
❏ CP 0181	Playin' Up a Storm	1977	3.00	6.00	12.00
EPIC					
❏ FE 40531	I'm No Angel	1987	2.50	5.00	10.00
❏ OE 44033	Just Before the Bullets Fly	1988	2.50	5.00	10.00

ALLMAN, SHELDON

45s

Number	Title (A Side/B Side)	Yr	VG	VG+	NM
HIFI					
❏ 593	Walk on the Ground/Radioactive Mama	1960	3.00	6.00	12.00
ORIGINAL SOUND					
❏ 25	Heartbreak Boulevard/Little Black Things	1963	2.50	5.00	10.00

ALLMAN AND WOMAN GREGG ALLMAN and CHER.

45s

Number	Title (A Side/B Side)	Yr	VG	VG+	NM
WARNER BROS.					
❏ 8504	Love Me/Move Me	1977	—	2.50	5.00
Albums					
WARNER BROS.					
❏ BSK 3120	Two the Hard Way	1977	2.50	5.00	10.00

ALLMAN BROTHERS BAND, THE Also see ALLMAN AND WOMAN; THE ALLMAN JOYS; DUANE ALLMAN; DUANE AND GREGG ALLMAN; GREGG ALLMAN; DICKIE BETTS; THE HOUR GLASS.

45s

Number	Title (A Side/B Side)	Yr	VG	VG+	NM
ARISTA					
❏ 0555	Angeline/So Long	1980	—	2.00	4.00
❏ 0584	Mystery Woman/Hell and High Water	1981	—	2.00	4.00
❏ 0618	Straight from the Heart/Leavin'	1981	—	2.00	4.00
❏ 0618 [PS]	Straight from the Heart/Leavin'	1981	—	2.00	4.00
❏ 0643	Two Rights/Never Knew How Much	1981	—	2.00	4.00
CAPRICORN					
❏ 0003	Ain't Wastin' Time No More/Melissa	1972	—	2.50	5.00
❏ 0007	Melissa/Blue Sky	1972	—	2.50	5.00
❏ 0014	One Way Out/Standback	1972	—	2.50	5.00
❏ 0027	Ramblin Man/Pony Boy	1973	—	2.50	5.00
❏ 0036	Jessica/Come and Go Blues	1973	—	2.50	5.00
❏ 0050	Ain't Wastin' Time No More/Blue Sky	1974	—	2.00	4.00
—Back to Back Hits series					
❏ 0051	Ramblin' Man/Jessica	1974	—	2.00	4.00
—Back to Back Hits series					
❏ 0246	Nevertheless/Louisiana Lou and Three Card Monty John	1975	—	2.00	4.00
❏ 0320	Crazy Love/Just Ain't Easy	1979	—	2.00	4.00
❏ 0326	Can't Take It With You/Sail Away	1979	—	2.00	4.00
❏ 8003	Black Hearted Woman/Every Hungry Woman	1970	—	3.00	6.00
❏ 8011	Revival (Love Is Everywhere)/Leave My Blues at Home	1971	—	2.50	5.00
❏ 8014	Whipping Post/Midnight Rider	1971	—	2.50	5.00
EPIC					
❏ 73504	Good Clean Fun/Seven Turns	1990	—	2.00	4.00
7-Inch Extended Plays					
CAPRICORN					
❏ S CP 0111	Come and Go Blues/Wasted Words//Jessica	1973	3.00	6.00	12.00
—Jukebox issue; small hole, plays at 33 1/3 rpm					
❏ S CP 0111 [PS]	Brothers and Sisters	1973	3.00	6.00	12.00
—Part of "Little LP" series (LLP #229)					

Number	Title (A Side/B Side)	Yr	VG	VG+	NM
Albums					
ARISTA					
❏ AL 9535	Reach for the Sky	1980	2.50	5.00	10.00
❏ AL 9564	Brothers of the Road	1981	2.50	5.00	10.00
ATCO					
❏ SD 33-308	The Allman Brothers Band	1969	3.75	7.50	15.00
❏ SD 33-342	Idlewild South	1970	3.75	7.50	15.00
❏ SD 2-805 [(2)]	Beginnings	1973	5.00	10.00	20.00
CAPRICORN					
❏ 2CP 0102 [(2)]	Eat a Peach	1972	3.75	7.50	15.00
❏ CPN2 0102 [(2)]	Eat a Peach	198?	3.00	6.00	12.00
❏ CX4 0102 [(2)Q]	Eat a Peach	1974	7.50	15.00	30.00
❏ CP 0111	Brothers and Sisters	1973	3.00	6.00	12.00
❏ CPN 0111	Brothers and Sisters	198?	2.00	4.00	8.00
❏ 2CP 0131 [(2)]	The Allman Brothers Band at Fillmore East	1974	3.75	7.50	15.00
❏ CPN2 0131 [(2)]	The Allman Brothers Band at Fillmore East	198?	3.00	6.00	12.00
❏ CX4 0131 [(2)Q]	The Allman Brothers Band at Fillmore East	1974	7.50	15.00	30.00
❏ 2CX 0132 [(2)]	Beginnings	1974	3.75	7.50	15.00
❏ CPN2 0132 [(2)]	Beginnings	198?	3.00	6.00	12.00
❏ CP 0156	Win, Lose or Draw	1975	2.50	5.00	10.00
❏ CPN 0156	Win, Lose or Draw	198?	2.00	4.00	8.00
❏ 2CX 0164 [(2)]	The Road Goes On Forever	1975	3.00	6.00	12.00
❏ 2CX 0177 [(2)]	Wipe the Windows, Check the Oil, Dollar Gas	1976	3.00	6.00	12.00
❏ CPN 0196	The Allman Brothers Band	1978	2.50	5.00	10.00
❏ CPN 0197	Idlewild South	1978	2.50	5.00	10.00
❏ CPN 0218	Enlightened Rogues	1979	2.50	5.00	10.00
❏ 2-802 [(2)M]	The Allman Brothers Band at Fillmore East	1971	20.00	40.00	80.00
—Promo only; sticker on front cover says "Promotional DJ Copy Monaural Not for Sale"					
❏ SD 2-802 [(2)S]	The Allman Brothers Band at Fillmore East	1971	5.00	10.00	20.00
EPIC					
❏ E 46144	Seven Turns	1990	3.75	7.50	15.00
MOBILE FIDELITY					
❏ 1-157 [(2)]	Eat a Peach	1984	50.00	100.00	200.00
—Audiophile vinyl					
❏ 1-213	Brothers and Sisters	1994	7.50	15.00	30.00
—Audiophile vinyl					
NAUTILUS					
❏ NR-30 [(2)]	The Allman Brothers Band at Fillmore East	1982	25.00	50.00	100.00
—Audiophile vinyl					
POLYDOR					
❏ PD-1-6339	The Best of the Allman Brothers Band	1981	2.50	5.00	10.00
❏ 823273-1 [(2)]	The Allman Brothers Band at Fillmore East	1984	2.50	5.00	10.00
❏ 823653-1	The Allman Brothers Band	1984	2.00	4.00	8.00
❏ 823654-1 [(2)]	Eat a Peach	1984	2.50	5.00	10.00
❏ 823708-1	The Best of the Allman Brothers Band	1984	2.00	4.00	8.00
—Reissue of PD-1-6339					
❏ 825092-1	Brothers and Sisters	1985	2.00	4.00	8.00
❏ 839417-1 [(6)]	Dreams	1989	10.00	20.00	40.00

ALLMAN JOYS, THE Early ALLMAN BROTHERS BAND.

45s

Number	Title (A Side/B Side)	Yr	VG	VG+	NM
DIAL					
❏ 4046	Spoonful/You Deserve Each Other	1966	10.00	20.00	40.00
Albums					
DIAL					
❏ DL 6005	Early Allman	1973	3.75	7.50	15.00

ALLSUP, TOMMY

45s

Number	Title (A Side/B Side)	Yr	VG	VG+	NM
GRT					
❏ 38	I'll See Him Through/Snowbird	1971	—	3.00	6.00
Albums					
GRT					
❏ 20004	Tommy Allsup and the Tennessee Saxes Play the Hits of Tammy Wynette	1970	5.00	10.00	20.00
METROMEDIA					
❏ MM 1004	Tommy Allsup and the Nashville Survey Play the Hits of Charley Pride	1969	6.25	12.50	25.00
REPRISE					
❏ R 6182 [M]	Tommy Allsup Plays the Buddy Holly Songbook	1965	10.00	20.00	40.00
❏ RS 6182 [S]	Tommy Allsup Plays the Buddy Holly Songbook	1965	12.50	25.00	50.00

ALMA-KEYS, THE

45s

Number	Title (A Side/B Side)	Yr	VG	VG+	NM
KISKI					
❏ 2056	Please Come Back to Me/Jumpin' Twist	1962	75.00	150.00	300.00

ALMOND, JOHNNY

45s

Number	Title (A Side/B Side)	Yr	VG	VG+	NM
DERAM					
❏ 85052	Music Machine to R.K./Solar Level	1969	2.00	4.00	8.00
Albums					
DERAM					
❏ DES 18030	Music Machine	1969	3.75	7.50	15.00

ALPERT, DORE See HERB ALPERT.

ALPERT, HERB

12-Inch Singles

Number	Title (A Side/B Side)	Yr	VG	VG+	NM
A&M					
❏ 75021 2356 1	North on South St. (7 versions)	1991	2.00	4.00	8.00
❏ 75021 2359 1	Jump Street (Brighton Daze Remix Radio Edit 3:58) (LP Version 4:46) (Brighton Daze Extended Remix 6:30) (Brighton Daze Remix 6:31) (Ubiquity Mix 6:57)	1991	2.00	4.00	8.00
❏ SP-12022	Rise/Aranjuez (Mon Amour)	1979	5.00	10.00	20.00
—Clear vinyl in plastic sleeve					
❏ SP-12032	Rotation/(B-side unknown)	1979	3.75	7.50	15.00
—Clear vinyl in plastic sleeve					
❏ SP-12034	Beyond (4:14) (6:00)	1980	3.75	7.50	15.00
—Clear vinyl in plastic sleeve					
❏ SP-12042	Manhattan Melody/Besame Mucho	1981	2.00	4.00	8.00

Number	Title (A Side/B Side)	Yr	VG	VG+	NM
❏ SP-12078	Red Hot (3:45) (6:31)	1983	3.00	6.00	12.00
—Red vinyl					
❏ SP-12145	"8" Ball (Dance Mix)/(LP Version)	1985	2.00	4.00	8.00
❏ SP-12226	Keep Your Eye on Me (Extended Version)/Our Song	1987	—	3.00	6.00
❏ SP-12231	Diamonds (3 versions)	1987	—	3.00	6.00
❏ SP-12316	3 O'Clock Jump (Album Version) (12" Version) (Dub Street Mix)	1989	—	3.00	6.00
❏ SP-17127 [DJ]	Kamali (Edit) (LP)	1980	2.00	4.00	8.00
❏ SP-17163 [DJ]	Magic Man (3:45) (5:33)	1981	2.50	5.00	10.00
❏ SP-17197 [DJ]	Push and Pull/Fandango//Route 101/Love Me the Way I Am	1982	2.00	4.00	8.00
—Promo-only four-song sampler					
❏ SP-17210 [DJ]	Fandango (Specially Mixed Version) (same on both sides)	1982	2.00	4.00	8.00
❏ SP-17237 [DJ]	Garden Party (3:51)/(5:16)	1983	—	3.00	6.00
❏ SP-17499 [(3)DJ]	Making Love in the Rain (5:53) (Remix 5:50)/Diamonds (Cool Summer Mix 6:16) (Cool Summer Dance Mix 5:51) (Instrumental 5:23) (Dub Version 4:20) (7" Edit 3"50)//Keep Your Eye on Me (Extended Version 5:53)/Our Song (3:54)	1987	7.50	15.00	30.00
—Promo-only set; Record 1 is on red vinyl, Record 2 is on clear vinyl, Record 3 is on blue vinyl; comes in wide cardboard sleeve with no writing except "SP 17499" on spine					

45s
A&M

Number	Title (A Side/B Side)	Yr	VG	VG+	NM
❏ 714	Dina/You're Doin' What You Did with Me with Him	1963	2.50	5.00	10.00
—As "Dore Alpert"					
❏ 729	I'd Do It All Again/Special Kind of Love	1964	2.00	4.00	8.00
—As "Dore Alpert"					
❏ 1231	I Need You/The Lady in My Life	1988	—	—	3.00
❏ 1446	3 O'Clock Jump/Kalimba	1989	—	—	3.00
❏ 2107	Foreign Natives/Mama Way	1979	—	2.00	4.00
—With Hugh Masekela					
❏ 2151	Rise/Aranjuez (Mon Amour)	1979	—	2.00	4.00
❏ 2202	Rotation/Angelina	1979	—	2.00	4.00
❏ 2202 [PS]	Rotation/Angelina	1979	—	2.50	5.00
❏ 2221	Street Life/1980	1980	—	2.00	4.00
❏ 2221 [PS]	Street Life/1980	1980	—	2.50	5.00
❏ 2246	Beyond/Keep It Goin'	1980	—	2.00	4.00
❏ 2246 [PS]	Beyond/Keep It Goin'	1980	—	2.00	4.00
❏ 2268	Kamali/Interlude (For Erica)	1980	—	2.00	4.00
❏ 2289	Reach for the Stars/Interlude (For Erica)	1980	—	2.00	4.00
❏ 2356	Magic Man/Fantasy Island	1981	—	2.00	4.00
❏ 2356 [PS]	Magic Man/Fantasy Island	1981	—	2.50	5.00
❏ 2375	Manhattan Melody/You Smile, The Song Begins	1981	—	2.00	4.00
❏ 2422	Route 101/Angel	1982	—	2.00	4.00
❏ 2422 [PS]	Route 101/Angel	1982	—	2.50	5.00
❏ 2426	Fandango/The Lonely Bull	1982	—	—	—
—Unreleased?					
❏ 2441	Fandango/Coco Loco	1982	—	2.00	4.00
❏ 2515	Love Me the Way I Am (Quiereme Tal Como Say)/California Blues	1982	—	2.00	4.00
❏ 2562	Garden Party/Oriental Eyes	1983	—	2.00	4.00
❏ 2573	Sundown/Garden Party	1983	—	2.00	4.00
❏ 2593	Red Hot/Sundown	1983	—	2.00	4.00
❏ 2621	Oriental Eyes/Sundown	1984	—	2.00	4.00
❏ 2632	We Could Be Flying/Come What May	1984	—	2.00	4.00
—With Lani Hall					
❏ 2757	"8" Ball/Lady Love	1985	—	—	3.00
❏ 2757 [PS]	"8" Ball/Lady Love	1985	—	2.00	4.00
❏ 2779	You Are the One/Lady Love	1985	—	—	3.00
—With Brenda Russell					
❏ 2779 [PS]	You Are the One/Lady Love	1985	—	2.00	4.00
❏ 2802	African Flame/Lady Love	1985	—	—	3.00
❏ 2915	Keep Your Eye on Me/Our Song	1987	—	—	3.00
❏ 2915 [PS]	Keep Your Eye on Me/Our Song	1987	—	—	3.00
❏ 2929	Diamonds/African Flame	1987	—	—	3.00
❏ 2929 [PS]	Diamonds/African Flame	1987	—	2.50	5.00
❏ 2949	Making Love in the Rain/Rocket to the Moon	1987	—	—	3.00
❏ 2949 [PS]	Making Love in the Rain/Rocket to the Moon	1987	—	—	3.00
❏ 2973	Our Song/African Flame	1987	—	—	3.00

ANDEX

Number	Title (A Side/B Side)	Yr	VG	VG+	NM
❏ 4036	Summer School/Hully Gully	1959	2.50	5.00	10.00
—As "Herbie Alpert Sextet"					

CARNIVAL

Number	Title (A Side/B Side)	Yr	VG	VG+	NM
❏ 701	Tell It to the Birds/Fallout Shelter	1962	2.50	5.00	10.00
—As "Dore Alpert"					

CAROL

Number	Title (A Side/B Side)	Yr	VG	VG+	NM
❏ 700	Sweet Georgia Brown/Vipers Blues	1961	2.50	5.00	10.00

DOT

Number	Title (A Side/B Side)	Yr	VG	VG+	NM
❏ 16396	Fallout Shelter/Tell It to the Birds	1962	2.50	5.00	10.00
—As "Dore Alpert"					

RCA VICTOR

Number	Title (A Side/B Side)	Yr	VG	VG+	NM
❏ 47-7918	Gotta Get a Girl/Dreamland	1961	3.00	6.00	12.00
—As "Dore Alpert"					
❏ 47-7988	Little Lost Lover/Won't You Be My Valentine	1962	3.00	6.00	12.00
—As "Dore Alpert"					

Albums
A&M

Number	Title (A Side/B Side)	Yr	VG	VG+	NM
❏ SP-3714	Rise	1980	2.00	4.00	8.00
—Reissue of 4790					
❏ SP-3717	Beyond	1980	2.00	4.00	8.00
❏ SP-3728	Magic Man	1981	2.00	4.00	8.00
❏ SP-3731	Fandango	1982	2.00	4.00	8.00
❏ SP-4591	Just You and Me	1976	2.50	5.00	10.00
❏ SP-4790	Rise	1979	2.50	5.00	10.00
❏ SP-4949	Blow Your Own Horn	1983	2.00	4.00	8.00
❏ SP-5082	Wild Romance	1985	2.00	4.00	8.00
❏ SP-5125	Keep Your Eye on Me	1987	2.00	4.00	8.00

Number	Title (A Side/B Side)	Yr	VG	VG+	NM
❏ SP-5209	Under a Spanish Moon	1988	2.00	4.00	8.00
❏ SP-5273	My Abstract Heart	1989	2.00	4.00	8.00
❏ 75021 5345 1	North on South Street	1991	3.00	6.00	12.00

MOBILE FIDELITY

Number	Title (A Side/B Side)	Yr	VG	VG+	NM
❏ 1-053	Rise	1981	6.25	12.50	25.00
—Audiophile vinyl					

ALPERT, HERB, AND THE TIJUANA BRASS

12-Inch Singles
A&M

Number	Title (A Side/B Side)	Yr	VG	VG+	NM
❏ SP-12104	Bullish (3:58)/(5:49)	1984	2.00	4.00	8.00

45s
A&M

Number	Title (A Side/B Side)	Yr	VG	VG+	NM
❏ 703	The Lonely Bull (El Solo Torro)/Acapulco 1922	1962	2.50	5.00	10.00
—With pale brown label and no horn logo					
❏ 705	Marching Through Madrid/Struttin' with Maria	1963	2.00	4.00	8.00
❏ 711	Mexican Corn/Let It Be Me	1963	2.00	4.00	8.00
❏ 721	Spanish Harlem/A-Mer-I-Ca	1963	2.00	4.00	8.00
❏ 732	Mexican Drummer Man/Great Manolete	1963	2.00	4.00	8.00
❏ 742	The Mexican Shuffle/Numero Cinco	1964	2.00	4.00	8.00
❏ 751	All My Loving/El Presidente	1964	2.00	4.00	8.00
❏ 755	South of the Border/Up Cherry Street	1965	—	3.00	6.00
❏ 760	Whipped Cream/Las Mananitas	1965	—	3.00	6.00
❏ 767	El Garbanzo/Mae	1965	—	3.00	6.00
❏ 775	Taste of Honey/Third Man Theme	1965	—	3.00	6.00
❏ 787	Zorba the Greek/Tijuana Taxi	1965	—	3.00	6.00
❏ 792	What Now My Love/Spanish Flea	1966	—	3.00	6.00
❏ 792 [PS]	What Now My Love/Spanish Flea	1966	2.50	5.00	10.00
❏ 805	The Work Song/Plucky	1966	—	3.00	6.00
❏ 805 [PS]	The Work Song/Plucky	1966	2.50	5.00	10.00
❏ 813	Flamingo/So What's New	1966	—	3.00	6.00
❏ 813 [PS]	Flamingo/So What's New	1966	2.50	5.00	10.00
❏ 823	Mame/Our Day Will Come	1966	—	3.00	6.00
❏ 823 [PS]	Mame/Our Day Will Come	1966	2.50	5.00	10.00
❏ 840	Wade in the Water/Mexican Road Race	1967	—	2.50	5.00
❏ 840 [PS]	Wade in the Water/Mexican Road Race	1967	2.00	4.00	8.00
❏ 850	Casino Royale/Wall Street Rag	1967	—	2.50	5.00
❏ 850 [PS]	Casino Royale/Wall Street Rag	1967	2.00	4.00	8.00
❏ 860	The Happening/Town Without Pity	1967	—	2.50	5.00
❏ 860 [PS]	The Happening/Town Without Pity	1967	2.00	4.00	8.00
❏ 870	A Banda/Miss Frenchy Brown	1967	—	2.50	5.00
❏ 870 [PS]	A Banda/Miss Frenchy Brown	1967	2.00	4.00	8.00
❏ 890	Carmen/A Love So Fine	1967	—	2.50	5.00
❏ 890 [PS]	Carmen/A Love So Fine	1967	2.00	4.00	8.00
❏ 925	Cabaret/Slick	1968	—	2.50	5.00
❏ 925 [PS]	Cabaret/Slick	1968	2.00	4.00	8.00
❏ 929	This Guy's in Love with You/A Quiet Tear	1968	—	2.50	5.00
❏ 929 [PS]	This Guy's in Love with You/A Quiet Tear	1968	2.00	4.00	8.00
❏ 960	Yo Doy Ese Amor (This Guy's in Love with You)/A Love So Fine	1968	—	3.00	6.00
❏ 964	To Wait for Love/Bud	1968	—	2.50	5.00
❏ 964 [PS]	To Wait for Love/Bud	1968	2.00	4.00	8.00
❏ 1001	My Favorite Things/The Christmas Song	1968	—	3.00	6.00
❏ 1001 [PS]	My Favorite Things/The Christmas Song	1968	2.50	5.00	10.00
❏ 1015	She Touched Me/My Favorite Things	1969	—	2.50	5.00
❏ 1028	Monday, Monday/Treasure of San Miguel	1969	—	2.50	5.00
❏ 1043	Zazueira/Treasure of San Miguel	1969	—	2.50	5.00
❏ 1043 [PS]	Zazueira/Treasure of San Miguel	1969	—	3.00	6.00
❏ 1065	Without Her/Sandbox	1969	—	2.50	5.00
❏ 1065 [PS]	Without Her/Sandbox	1969	—	3.00	6.00
❏ 1094	Ob-La-Di, Ob-La-Da/Girl Talk	1969	—	2.50	5.00
❏ 1100	Marjorine/Warm	1969	—	2.50	5.00
❏ 1102	Marjorine/Ob-La-Di, Ob-La-Da	1969	—	2.50	5.00
❏ 1143	You Are My Life/Good Morning Mr. Sunshine	1969	—	2.50	5.00
❏ 1143 [PS]	You Are My Life/Good Morning Mr. Sunshine	1969	—	3.00	6.00
❏ 1159	The Maltese Melody/Country Lake	1969	—	2.50	5.00
❏ 1194	Brasilia/Love Potion #9	1970	—	2.00	4.00
❏ 1225	Jerusalem/Strike Up the Band	1970	—	2.00	4.00
❏ 1225 [PS]	Jerusalem/Strike Up the Band	1970	—	2.50	5.00
❏ 1237	The Bell That Couldn't Jingle/Las Mananitas	1970	—	2.50	5.00
❏ 1261	Summertime/Hurt So Bad	1971	—	2.50	5.00
❏ 1261 [PS]	Summertime/Hurt So Bad	1971	—	3.00	6.00
❏ 1284	Montezuma's Revenge/Darlin'	1971	—	2.00	4.00
❏ 1337	Without Her/Zazueira	1972	—	2.00	4.00
❏ 1337 [PS]	Without Her/Zazueira	1972	—	3.00	6.00
❏ 1420	Last Tango in Paris/Fire and Rain	1973	—	2.00	4.00
❏ 1423	The Nicest Things Happen/Last Tango in Paris	1973	—	2.00	4.00
❏ 1526	Fox Hunt/I Can't Go On Living, Baby, Without You	1974	—	2.00	4.00
❏ 1542	You Smile, the Song Begins/Save the Sunlight	1974	—	2.00	4.00
❏ 1688	Coney Island/Ratatouille	1975	—	2.00	4.00
❏ 1714	El Bimbo/Catfish	1975	—	2.00	4.00
❏ 1762	The Whistle Song (Whistlestar)/Carmine	1975	—	2.00	4.00
❏ 1852	Promenade/Musique	1976	—	2.00	4.00
❏ 1962	African Summer/You in Me	1977	—	2.00	4.00
❏ 2655	Bullish/Oriental Eyes	1984	—	2.00	4.00
—As "Herb Alpert Tijuana Brass"					
❏ 2655 [PS]	Bullish/Oriental Eyes	1984	—	2.00	4.00
❏ 2690	Struttin' on Five/Blow Your Own Horn	1984	—	2.00	4.00
—As "Herb Alpert Tijuana Brass"					

7-Inch Extended Plays
A&M

Number	Title (A Side/B Side)	Yr	VG	VG+	NM
❏ SP 410	Taste of Honey/Green Peppers/Whipped Cream//Bittersweet Samba/Lollipops and Roses/El Garbanzo	1965	2.50	5.00	10.00
—Jukebox issue; small hole, plays at 33 1/3 rpm					
❏ SP 410 [PS]	Whipped Cream and Other Delights	1965	2.50	5.00	10.00
❏ SP 412	3rd Man Theme/Cinco De Mayo/Tijuana Taxi//And the Angels Sing/Spanish Flea/A Walk in the Black Forest	1966	2.50	5.00	10.00
—Jukebox issue; small hole, plays at 33 1/3 rpm					

ALPERT, HERB/HUGH MASEKELA (left column continued)

Number	Title (A Side/B Side)	Yr	VG	VG+	NM
❑ SP 412 [PS]	Going Places!	1966	2.50	5.00	10.00
❑ SP 414	What Now My Love/Freckles/Plucky//Memories of Madrid/So What's New/Brasilia	1966	2.50	5.00	10.00
—Jukebox issue; small hole, plays at 33 1/3 rpm					
❑ SP 414 [PS]	What Now My Love	1966	2.50	5.00	10.00
Albums					
A&M					
❑ LP-101 [M]	The Lonely Bull	1962	5.00	10.00	20.00
—Originals on yellowish label with brown print					
❑ LP-101 [M]	The Lonely Bull	1963	3.75	7.50	15.00
—Second pressings with brown label and A&M logo at top					
❑ LP-101 [M]	The Lonely Bull	1964	3.00	6.00	12.00
—Third pressing with brown label and A&M logo at left					
❑ SP-101 [S]	The Lonely Bull	1962	6.25	12.50	25.00
—Original editions had this number					
❑ LP-103 [M]	Herb Alpert's Tijuana Brass, Volume 2	1963	3.75	7.50	15.00
—Brown label with A&M logo at top					
❑ LP-103 [M]	Herb Alpert's Tijuana Brass, Volume 2	1964	3.00	6.00	12.00
—Brown label with A&M logo at left					
❑ SP-103 [S]	Herb Alpert's Tijuana Brass, Volume 2	1963	5.00	10.00	20.00
—Original issues had this number					
❑ LP-108 [M]	South of the Border	1964	3.00	6.00	12.00
❑ SP-108 [S]	South of the Border	1964	5.00	10.00	20.00
—Original issues had this number					
❑ LP-110 [M]	Whipped Cream & Other Delights	1965	2.50	5.00	10.00
❑ LP-112 [M]	Going Places	1965	2.50	5.00	10.00
❑ LP-114 [M]	What Now My Love	1966	2.50	5.00	10.00
❑ LP-119 [M]	S.R.O.	1966	2.50	5.00	10.00
❑ LP-124 [M]	Sounds Like	1967	2.50	5.00	10.00
❑ SP-3101	The Lonely Bull	198?	2.00	4.00	8.00
—Reissue					
❑ SP-3113	Christmas Album	198?	2.00	4.00	8.00
—Reissue of SP-4166					
❑ SP-3157	Whipped Cream & Other Delights	198?	2.00	4.00	8.00
—Reissue					
❑ SP-3263	South of the Border	1984	2.00	4.00	8.00
❑ SP-3264	Going Places	1984	2.00	4.00	8.00
—Reissue					
❑ SP-3265	What Now My Love	1984	2.00	4.00	8.00
❑ SP-3266	The Beat of the Brass	1984	2.00	4.00	8.00
—Reissue					
❑ SP-3267	Greatest Hits	1984	2.00	4.00	8.00
—Reissue					
❑ SP-3268	Solid Brass	1984	2.00	4.00	8.00
❑ SP-3269	Greatest Hits, Vol. 2	1984	2.00	4.00	8.00
❑ SP-3521 [(2)]	Foursider	1973	3.00	6.00	12.00
❑ SP-3620	You Smile — The Song Begins	1974	2.50	5.00	10.00
❑ SP-4101 [S]	The Lonely Bull	1962	3.75	7.50	15.00
❑ SP-4103 [S]	Herb Alpert's Tijuana Brass, Volume 2	1963	3.75	7.50	15.00
❑ SP-4108 [S]	South of the Border	1964	3.75	7.50	15.00
❑ SP-4110 [S]	Whipped Cream & Other Delights	1965	3.00	6.00	12.00
❑ SP-4112 [S]	Going Places	1965	3.00	6.00	12.00
❑ SP-4114 [S]	What Now My Love	1966	3.00	6.00	12.00
❑ SP-4119 [S]	S.R.O.	1966	3.00	6.00	12.00
❑ SP-4124 [S]	Sounds Like	1967	3.00	6.00	12.00
❑ SP-4134	Herb Alpert's Ninth	1967	2.50	5.00	10.00
❑ SP-4146	The Beat of the Brass	1968	2.50	5.00	10.00
❑ SP-4166	Christmas Album	1968	3.00	6.00	12.00
❑ SP-4190	Warm	1969	2.50	5.00	10.00
❑ SP-4228	The Brass Are Comin'	1969	2.50	5.00	10.00
❑ SP-4245	Greatest Hits	1970	2.50	5.00	10.00
❑ SP-4314	Summertime	1971	2.50	5.00	10.00
❑ SP-4341	Solid Brass	1972	2.50	5.00	10.00
❑ SP-4521	Coney Island	1975	2.50	5.00	10.00
❑ SP-4627	Greatest Hits, Vol. 2	1976	2.50	5.00	10.00
❑ SP-5022	Bullish	1984	2.00	4.00	8.00
❑ SP-6011 [(2)]	Foursider	197?	2.50	5.00	10.00
—Reissue					
❑ LP-9004 [DJ]	The Best from Herb Alpert & The Tijuana Brass	196?	3.75	7.50	15.00
—Promo-only compilation					
❑ ST-90073 [S]	South of the Border	1964	5.00	10.00	20.00
—Capitol Record Club edition					
❑ T-90074 [M]	Herb Alpert's Tijuana Brass, Volume 2	1964	5.00	10.00	20.00
—Capitol Record Club edition					
❑ ST-90387 [S]	Whipped Cream & Other Delights	1965	3.75	7.50	15.00
—Capitol Record Club edition					
❑ ST-90507 [S]	Going Places	1965	5.00	10.00	20.00
—Capitol Record Club edition					
❑ T-90507 [M]	Going Places	1965	3.75	7.50	15.00
—Capitol Record Club edition					
❑ T-90655 [M]	What Now My Love	1966	3.00	6.00	12.00
—Capitol Record Club edition					
❑ SW-93870	Summertime	197?	3.00	6.00	12.00
—Capitol Record Club edition					

ALPERT, HERB/HUGH MASEKELA Also see each artist's individual listings.

45s
HORIZON

Number	Title (A Side/B Side)	Yr	VG	VG+	NM
❑ 115	Skokiaan/African Summer	1978	—	2.00	4.00
❑ 115 [PS]	Skokiaan/African Summer	1978	—	2.50	5.00
❑ 116	Lobo/African Summer	1978		2.00	4.00
Albums					
A&M					
❑ SP-3150	Herb Alpert/Hugh Masekela	198?	2.00	4.00	8.00
❑ SP-4727	Main Event	1978	2.50	5.00	10.00
HORIZON					
❑ 728	Herb Alpert/Hugh Masekela	1978	2.50	5.00	10.00

ALTAIRS, THE GEORGE BENSON was a member.

45s
AMY

Number	Title (A Side/B Side)	Yr	VG	VG+	NM
❑ 803	If You Love Me/Groove Time	1960	5.00	10.00	20.00

ALTON AND JIMMY

45s
SUN

Number	Title (A Side/B Side)	Yr	VG	VG+	NM
❑ 323	Have Faith in My Love/No More Crying the Blues	1959	6.25	12.50	25.00

ALVANS, THE

45s
MAY

Number	Title (A Side/B Side)	Yr	VG	VG+	NM
❑ 102	Love Is a Game/What Can It Be	1961	37.50	75.00	150.00

ALVIN AND BILL

45s
FERNWOOD

Number	Title (A Side/B Side)	Yr	VG	VG+	NM
❑ 124	Typing Jive/How Long	1960	15.00	30.00	60.00

AMAZING RHYTHM ACES

45s
ABC

Number	Title (A Side/B Side)	Yr	VG	VG+	NM
❑ 12078	Third Rate Romance/Mystery Train	1975	—	2.50	5.00
❑ 12142	Amazing Grace (Used to Be Her Favorite Song)/Beautiful Lie	1975	—	2.00	4.00
❑ 12202	Same Ol' Me/The End Is Not in Sight	1976	—	2.00	4.00
❑ 12242	Dancin' the Night Away/If I Just Knew What to Say	1976	—	2.00	4.00
❑ 12272	Two Can Do It Too/Living in a World Unknown	1977	—	2.00	4.00
❑ 12287	Just Between You and Me and the Wall/Never Been to the Islands	1977	—	2.00	4.00
❑ 12359	Burning the Ballroom Down/All That I Had Left (With You)	1978	—	2.00	4.00
❑ 12369	Ashes of Love/All That I Had Left (With You)	1978	—	2.00	4.00
❑ 12454	Lipstick Traces (On a Cigarette)/Whispering in the Night	1979	—	2.00	4.00
COLUMBIA					
❑ 10983	Love and Happiness/Homestead in My Heart	1979	—	2.00	4.00
WARNER BROS.					
❑ 49543	Living on Borrowed Time/What Kind of Love Is This	1980	—	2.00	4.00
❑ 49600	I Musta Died and Gone to Texas/Give Me Flowers While I'm Living	1980	—	2.00	4.00
Albums					
ABC					
❑ D-913	Stacked Deck	1975	5.00	10.00	20.00
❑ D-940	Too Stuffed to Jump	1976	3.75	7.50	15.00
❑ AB-1005	Toucan Do It Too	1977	3.75	7.50	15.00
❑ AA-1063	Burning the Ballroom Down	1978	3.75	7.50	15.00
❑ AA-1123	The Amazing Rhythm Aces	1979	5.00	10.00	20.00
COLUMBIA					
❑ JC 36083	The Amazing Rhythm Aces	1979	3.00	6.00	12.00
—Reissue of ABC 1123					
WARNER BROS.					
❑ BSK 3476	How the Hell Do You Spell Rythum?	1980	3.00	6.00	12.00

AMBASSADORS, THE (1) Male vocal group from Philadelphia.

45s
ARCTIC

Number	Title (A Side/B Side)	Yr	VG	VG+	NM
❑ 147	I Really Love You/I Can't Believe You Love Me	1969	3.00	6.00	12.00
❑ 150	Ain't Got the Love of One Girl/Music Makes You Wanna Dance	1969	2.50	5.00	10.00
❑ 153	Storm Warning/I Dig You Baby	1969	2.50	5.00	10.00
❑ 156	Can't Take My Eyes Off You/A.W.O.L.	1969	2.50	5.00	10.00
ATLANTIC					
❑ 2442	(I've Got to Find) Happiness/I'm So Proud of My Baby	1967	2.50	5.00	10.00
❑ 2491	Good Love Gone Bad/Happiness	1968	2.50	5.00	10.00
❑ 2547	We Got Love/Never Get Tired of Loving You	1968	2.50	5.00	10.00
Albums					
ARCTIC					
❑ ALPS-1005	Soul Summit	1969	6.25	12.50	25.00

AMBASSADORS, THE (2) British band known as The Saints in the U.K.

45s
DOT

Number	Title (A Side/B Side)	Yr	VG	VG+	NM
❑ 16528	Surfin' John Brown/Big Breaker	1963	7.50	15.00	30.00

AMBASSADORS, THE (U) More than one group. Some of these may go with (1) above.

45s
CUCA

Number	Title (A Side/B Side)	Yr	VG	VG+	NM
❑ 1022	Christmas Polka/Little Drummer Boy	1960	3.00	6.00	12.00
SOUND STAGE 7					
❑ 2588	If You Don't Know (You Better Ask Somebody)/There's Something on My Baby's Mind	1967	2.50	5.00	10.00
TIME					
❑ 1007	El Grippo/Can't Believe Ya	1959	3.75	7.50	15.00
TIMELY					
❑ 1001	Darling I'm Sorry/Willa-Bea	1954	100.00	200.00	400.00
UPTOWN					
❑ 734	I Need Someone/Bear With Me	1965	6.25	12.50	25.00

AMBOY DUKES, THE Also see TED NUGENT.

45s
DISCREET

Number	Title (A Side/B Side)	Yr	VG	VG+	NM
❑ 1199	Sweet Revenge/Ain't It the Truth	1974	—	3.00	6.00
—As "Ted Nugent and the Amboy Dukes"					
MAINSTREAM					
❑ 676	Baby Please Don't Go/Psalms of Aftermath	1968	3.00	6.00	12.00
❑ 684	Journey to the Center of the Mind/Mississippi Murderer	1968	3.75	7.50	15.00
❑ 693	You Talk Sunshine, I Breathe Fire/Scottish Tea	1968	3.00	6.00	12.00
❑ 700	Prodigal Man/Good Natured Emma	1969	3.00	6.00	12.00
❑ 704	For His Namesake/Loaded for Bear	1969	3.00	6.00	12.00
❑ 711	Flight of the Byrd/Ivory Castles	1969	3.00	6.00	12.00

Number	Title (A Side/B Side)	Yr	VG	VG+	NM

Albums
DISCREET
| ❑ DS 2181 | Call of the Wild | 1974 | 3.75 | 7.50 | 15.00 |
—As "Ted Nugent and the Amboy Dukes"
| ❑ DS 2203 | Tooth, Fang and Claw | 1974 | 3.75 | 7.50 | 15.00 |
—As "Ted Nugent and the Amboy Dukes"
MAINSTREAM
| ❑ S-414 | Dr. Slingshot | 1975 | 3.75 | 7.50 | 15.00 |
| ❑ S-421 | Ted Nugent and the Amboy Dukes | 1976 | 7.50 | 15.00 | 30.00 |
—Reissue of early material
| ❑ S-2-801 [(2)] | Journeys and Migrations | 1974 | 7.50 | 15.00 | 30.00 |
—Reissue of 6112 and 6118
❑ S-6104 [S]	The Amboy Dukes	1967	10.00	20.00	40.00
❑ S-6112	Journey to the Center of the Mind	1968	10.00	20.00	40.00
❑ S-6118	Migration	1968	10.00	20.00	40.00
❑ S-6125	The Best of the Original Amboy Dukes	1969	7.50	15.00	30.00
❑ 56104 [M]	The Amboy Dukes	1967	20.00	40.00	80.00
POLYDOR
❑ 24-4012	Marriage on the Rocks/Rock Bottom	1970	6.25	12.50	25.00
❑ 24-4035	Survival of the Fittest/Live	1971	6.25	12.50	25.00
—As "Ted Nugent and the Amboy Dukes"

AMBROSE SLADE See SLADE.

AMBROSIA
12-Inch Singles
WARNER BROS.
| ❑ PRO-A-1024 [DJ] | For Openers//Kid No More/How Can You Love Me | 1982 | 2.50 | 5.00 | 10.00 |
45s
FULL MOON
| ❑ 49654 | Outside/I Can't Tell You Why | 1981 | — | 2.50 | 5.00 |
—B-side by Eagles
SCEPTER
| ❑ 12373 | Shine On/Listen To Her Sing | 1973 | 2.00 | 4.00 | 8.00 |
20TH CENTURY
❑ 2207	Holdin' On to Yesterday/Make Us All Aware	1975	—	2.50	5.00
❑ 2244	Nice, Nice, Very Nice/Lover Arrive	1975	—	2.00	4.00
❑ 2310	Can't Let a Woman/The Brunt	1976	—	2.00	4.00
❑ 2327	Magical Mystery Tour/Cowboy Star	1977	—	2.50	5.00
WARNER BROS.
❑ 8640	How Much I Feel/Ready for Amarillo	1978	—	2.00	4.00
—With white label
| ❑ 8640 | How Much I Feel/Ready for Amarillo | 1978 | — | 2.50 | 5.00 |
—With "Burbank..." palm trees label
❑ 8699	Life Beyond L.A./Angola	1978	—	2.00	4.00
❑ 8817	If Heaven Could Find Me/Apothecary	1979	—	2.00	4.00
❑ 29937	Feelin' Alive Again/For Openers	1982	—	2.00	4.00
❑ 29996	How Can You Love Me/Still Not Satisfied	1982	—	2.00	4.00
❑ 49225	Biggest Part of Me/Livin' on My Own	1980	—	2.00	4.00
❑ 49508	You're the Only Woman (You & I)/Shape I'm In	1980	—	2.00	4.00
❑ 49590	Cryin' in the Rain/No Big Deal	1980	—	2.00	4.00
Albums
NAUTILUS
| ❑ NR-23 | Life Beyond L.A. | 1981 | 7.50 | 5.00 | 30.00 |
—Audiophile vinyl
20TH CENTURY
| ❑ T-434 | Ambrosia | 1975 | 2.50 | 5.00 | 10.00 |
—New cover without black border
| ❑ T-434 | Ambrosia | 1975 | 3.00 | 6.00 | 12.00 |
—Original cover with black border
| ❑ T-510 | Somewhere I've Never Traveled | 1976 | 2.50 | 5.00 | 10.00 |
—Standard cover
| ❑ T-510 | Somewhere I've Never Traveled | 1976 | 3.00 | 6.00 | 12.00 |
—Fold-open cover in the shape of a pyramid
WARNER BROS.
| ❑ BSK 3135 | Life Beyond L.A. | 1978 | 2.50 | 5.00 | 10.00 |
| ❑ BSK 3181 | Ambrosia | 1978 | 2.00 | 4.00 | 8.00 |
—Reissue of 20th Century 434
| ❑ BSK 3368 | One Eighty | 1980 | 2.50 | 5.00 | 10.00 |
| ❑ BSK 3638 | Road Island | 1982 | 2.50 | 5.00 | 10.00 |

AMECHE, DON, AND FRANCES LANGFORD
Albums
COLUMBIA
| ❑ CL 1692 | The Bickersons | 1962 | 5.00 | 10.00 | 20.00 |
—Live-in-the-studio recordings from 1961
| ❑ CL 1883 | The Bickersons Fight Back | 1962 | 5.00 | 10.00 | 20.00 |
—More live-in-the-studio recordings from 1961
| ❑ G 30523 [(2)] | The Bickersons Rematch | 1970 | 3.75 | 7.50 | 15.00 |
—Compilation of the earlier Columbia LPs
RADIOLA
| ❑ MR 1115 | The Bickersons | 198? | 3.00 | 6.00 | 12.00 |
—Compilation of radio shows
RADIOLA/MURRAY HILL
| ❑ 3MH 36721 [(3)] | Return of the Bickersons | 1987 | 5.00 | 10.00 | 20.00 |
—Compilation of radio shows

AMECHE, JIM
45s
DELTONE
| ❑ 5016 | The First Christmas Tree (Part 1)/The First Christmas Tree (Part 2) | 1964 | 2.50 | 5.00 | 10.00 |
RIC
| ❑ 137 | The First Christmas Tree (Part 1)/The First Christmas Tree (Part 2) | 1964 | 2.50 | 5.00 | 10.00 |
| ❑ 137 [PS] | The First Christmas Tree (Part 1)/The First Christmas Tree (Part 2) | 1964 | 3.00 | 6.00 | 12.00 |

Number	Title (A Side/B Side)	Yr	VG	VG+	NM

AMELIO, JOHNNY
45s
BLUE MOON
❑ 405	Jugue/Downbeat	1957	37.50	75.00	150.00
❑ 408	Jo-Ann, Jo-Ann/I'll Forever Love You	1958	25.00	50.00	100.00
❑ 410	Jugue/Jo-Ann, Jo-Ann	1958	20.00	40.00	80.00

AMEN CORNER
45s
DERAM
❑ 7521	Run, Run, Run/High in the Sky	1968	2.50	5.00	10.00
❑ 85014	Gin House Blues/I Know	1967	3.00	6.00	12.00
❑ 85021	Nema/World of Broken Hearts	1967	3.00	6.00	12.00
IMMEDIATE
❑ 5013	If Paradise Is Half As Nice/Hey Hey Girl	1968	2.50	5.00	10.00

AMERICA
45s
AMERICAN INT'L.
| ❑ 700 | California Dreamin'/See It My Way | 1979 | — | 2.50 | 5.00 |
—B-side by FDR
| ❑ 700 [PS] | California Dreamin'/See It My Way | 1979 | — | 2.50 | 5.00 |
CAPITOL
❑ 4752	Only Game in Town/High in the City	1979	—	2.00	4.00
❑ 4777	All My Life/One Morning	1979	—	2.00	4.00
❑ 4817	All Around/1960	1980	—	2.00	4.00
❑ 4915	You Could've Been the One/Catch That Train	1980	—	2.00	4.00
❑ 4950	One in a Million/Hangover	1980	—	2.00	4.00
❑ B-5142	You Can Do Magic/Even the Score	1982	—	2.00	4.00
❑ B-5177	Right Before Your Eyes/Inspector Mills	1982	—	—	3.00
❑ B-5177 [PS]	Right Before Your Eyes/Inspector Mills	1982	—	—	3.00
❑ B-5236	The Border/Sometimes Lovers	1983	—	—	3.00
❑ B-5236 [PS]	The Border/Sometimes Lovers	1983	—	—	3.00
❑ B-5275	Cast the Spirit/My Dear	1983	—	—	3.00
❑ B-5398	Special Girl/Unconditional Love	1984	—	—	3.00
❑ B-5430	(Can't Fall Asleep to a) Lullaby/Fallin' Off the World	1984	—	—	3.00
WARNER BROS.
❑ 7555	A Horse with No Name/Everyone I Meet Is From California	1972	—	3.00	6.00
❑ 7580	I Need You/Riverside	1972	—	2.50	5.00
❑ 7580 [PS]	I Need You/Riverside	1972	—	3.00	6.00
❑ 7641	Ventura Highway/Saturn Nights	1972	—	2.50	5.00
❑ 7650	A Horse with No Name/I Need You	1973	—	2.00	4.00
—"Back to Back Hits" series
❑ 7670	Don't Cross the River/To Each His Own	1972	—	2.50	5.00
❑ 7694	Only in Your Heart/Moon Song	1973	—	2.50	5.00
❑ 7725	Muskrat Love/Cornwall Blank	1973	—	2.50	5.00
❑ 7760	Rainbow Song/Willow Tree Lullaby	1973	—	2.50	5.00
❑ 7785	She's Gonna Let You Down/Green Monkey	1974	—	2.50	5.00
❑ 7839	Tin Man/In the Country	1974	—	2.50	5.00
❑ 8014	Tin Man/In the Country	1974	—	2.00	4.00
❑ 8048	Lonely People/Mad Dog	1974	—	2.50	5.00
❑ 8048 [PS]	Lonely People/Mad Dog	1974	—	3.00	6.00
❑ 8086	Sister Golden Hair/Midnight	1975	—	2.50	5.00
❑ 8118	Daisy Jane/Tomorrow	1975	—	2.50	5.00
❑ 8157	Woman Tonight/Bell Tree	1975	—	2.50	5.00
❑ 8212	Today's the Day/Hideaway (Part 2)	1976	—	2.50	5.00
❑ 8238	Amber Cascades/Who Loves You	1976	—	2.50	5.00
❑ 8285	She's Beside You/She's a Liar	1976	—	2.50	5.00
❑ 8373	God of the Sun/Down to the Water	1977	—	2.50	5.00
❑ 8397	Don't Cry Baby/Monster	1977	—	2.50	5.00
Albums
CAPITOL
❑ SO-11950	Silent Letter	1979	2.50	5.00	10.00
❑ SOO-12098	Alibi	1980	2.50	5.00	10.00
❑ ST-12209	View from the Ground	1982	2.50	5.00	10.00
❑ ST-12277	Your Move	1983	2.50	5.00	10.00
❑ ST-12370	Perspective	1984	2.50	5.00	10.00
❑ ST-12422	In Concert	1985	2.50	5.00	10.00
❑ SN-16275	Alibi	1982	2.00	4.00	8.00
❑ SN-16350	View from the Ground	1985	2.00	4.00	8.00
❑ SN-16361	Your Move	1985	2.00	4.00	8.00
WARNER BROS.
❑ BS 2576	America	1971	6.25	12.50	25.00
—First pressings omit "A Horse with No Name"
| ❑ BS 2576 | America | 1972 | 3.00 | 6.00 | 12.00 |
—With "A Horse with No Name"; green label
❑ BS 2655	Homecoming	1972	3.00	6.00	12.00
❑ BS 2728	Hat Trick	1973	3.00	6.00	12.00
❑ BS 2808	Holiday	1974	3.00	6.00	12.00
❑ BS4 2808 [Q]	Holiday	1974	5.00	10.00	20.00
❑ BS 2852	Hearts	1975	3.00	6.00	12.00
❑ BS4 2852 [Q]	Hearts	1975	5.00	10.00	20.00
❑ BS 2894	History/America's Greatest Hits	1975	3.00	6.00	12.00
❑ BS 2932	Hideaway	1976	3.00	6.00	12.00
❑ BSK 3017	Harbor	1977	3.00	6.00	12.00
❑ BSK 3110	History/America's Greatest Hits	1977	2.50	5.00	10.00
—Reissue of BS 2894 with "Burbank" palm trees label (later white labels are $8 NM)
| ❑ BSK 3136 | America/Live | 1977 | 3.00 | 6.00 | 12.00 |

AMERICAN BEATLES, THE
45s
BYP
| ❑ 1001 | She's Mine/Theme of the American Beetles | 1964 | 5.00 | 10.00 | 20.00 |
—As "The American Beetles"
ROULETTE
| ❑ 4550 | You Did It to Me/Don't Be Unkind | 1964 | 3.75 | 7.50 | 15.00 |
| ❑ 4559 | School Days/Hey Hey Girl | 1964 | 3.75 | 7.50 | 15.00 |
—As "The American Beetles"

Number	Title (A Side/B Side)	Yr	VG	VG+	NM

AMERICAN BLUES, THE — Early incarnation of ZZ TOP.

45s
AMY

Number	Title (A Side/B Side)	Yr	VG	VG+	NM
997	Your Love Is True/Say So	1967	6.25	12.50	25.00

KARMA

| 1001 | If I Were a Carpenter/(B-side unknown) | 1967 | 10.00 | 20.00 | 40.00 |

Albums
KARMA

| 1001 | The American Blues Is Here | 1967 | 100.00 | 200.00 | 400.00 |

UNI

| 73044 | The American Blues Do Their Thing | 1968 | 15.00 | 30.00 | 60.00 |

AMERICAN BLUES EXCHANGE, THE

Albums
TAYL

| TLS-1 | Blueprint | 1969 | 100.00 | 200.00 | 400.00 |

AMERICAN BREED, THE — Members of this band later formed RUFUS.

45s
ACTA

Number	Title (A Side/B Side)	Yr	VG	VG+	NM
802	I Don't Think You Know/Give Two Young Lovers a Chance	1967	2.00	4.00	8.00
804	Step Out of Your Mind/Same Old Thing	1967	2.50	5.00	10.00
808	Don't Forget About Me/Short Skirts	1967	2.00	4.00	8.00
811	Bend Me, Shape Me/Mindrocker	1967	3.00	6.00	12.00
821	Green Light/Don't It Make You Cry	1968	2.00	4.00	8.00
821 [PS]	Green Light/Don't It Make You Cry	1968	5.00	10.00	20.00
824	Ready, Willing and Able/Take Me If You Want Me	1968	2.00	4.00	8.00
827	Anyway You Want Me/Master of My Fate	1968	2.00	4.00	8.00
830	Private Zoo/Keep the Faith	1968	2.00	4.00	8.00
833	Hunky Funky/Enter Her Majesty	1969	2.00	4.00	8.00
836	Room at the Top/Walls	1969	2.00	4.00	8.00
837	Cool It/The Brain	1969	2.00	4.00	8.00

PARAMOUNT

| 0040 | Can't Make It Without You/When I'm With You | 1970 | — | 3.00 | 6.00 |
| 100 | Bend Me, Shape Me/Step Out of Your Mind | 197? | — | 3.00 | 6.00 |

Albums
ACTA

8002 [M]	The American Breed	1967	5.00	10.00	20.00
8003 [M]	Bend Me, Shape Me	1968	5.00	10.00	20.00
8006 [M]	Pumpkin, Powder, Scarlet & Green	1968	12.50	25.00	50.00
—Stock label; the cover is the same as stereo but with a "Monaural" sticker attached					
8008 [M]	Lonely Side of the City	1969	12.50	25.00	50.00
—In stereo cover with "Monaural" sticker; record is regular yellow label					
38002 [S]	The American Breed	1967	6.25	12.50	25.00
38003 [S]	Bend Me, Shape Me	1968	6.25	12.50	25.00
38006 [S]	Pumpkin, Powder, Scarlet & Green	1968	5.00	10.00	20.00
38008 [S]	Lonely Side of the City	1969	5.00	10.00	20.00

AMERICAN DREAM, THE

45s
AMPEX

| 11001 | Goodnews/I Ain't Searchin' | 1970 | 2.50 | 5.00 | 10.00 |
| 11001 [PS] | Goodnews/I Ain't Searchin' | 1970 | 3.75 | 7.50 | 15.00 |

Albums
AMPEX

| A-10101 | The American Dream | 1970 | 5.00 | 10.00 | 20.00 |
| —Produced by Todd Rundgren | | | | | |

AMERICAN EAGLE

45s
DECCA

| 32788 | Family/Gospel | 1971 | 2.00 | 4.00 | 8.00 |
| 32833 | Ballad of a Well-Known Gun/On the Rack | 1971 | 2.50 | 5.00 | 10.00 |

Albums
DECCA

| DL 75258 | American Eagle | 1971 | 5.00 | 10.00 | 20.00 |

AMERICAN FOUR, THE — With Arthur Lee, future leader of LOVE.

45s
SELMA

| 2001 | Luci Baines/Soul Food | 1964 | 12.50 | 25.00 | 50.00 |

AMERICAN REVOLUTION, THE

Albums
FLICK DISC

FL-45,002 [M]	The American Revolution	1968	12.50	25.00	50.00
—White label promo in stereo cover with "Not for Sale DJ Monaural" sticker on front					
FLS-45,002 [S]	The American Revolution	1968	6.25	12.50	25.00

AMERICAN SPRING — Formed by ex-members of THE HONEYS. Also see SPRING.

45s
COLUMBIA

| 45834 | Fallin' in Love/Shyin' Away | 1973 | 7.50 | 15.00 | 30.00 |
| 45834 [PS] | Fallin' in Love/Shyin' Away | 1973 | 15.00 | 30.00 | 60.00 |

AMES, ED — Also see THE AMES BROTHERS.

45s
HELLO LYNDON

RPKM-4426	Hello, Lyndon!/Hello, Lyndon! (Chorus)	1964	6.25	12.50	25.00
RPKM-4426 [PS]	Hello, Lyndon!/Hello, Lyndon! (Chorus)	1964	12.50	25.00	50.00
—Promotional item for Lyndon Johnson's 1964 election campaign					

RCA VICTOR

47-6791	The Bean Song/I'd Give You the World	1957	3.00	6.00	12.00
—As "Eddie Ames"					
47-8231	My Love Is Yours/Somewhere	1963	2.00	4.00	8.00
47-8245	Before I Kiss the World Goodbye/They Were You	1963	2.00	4.00	8.00
47-8320	It Only Takes a Moment/The Time Has Come	1964	2.00	4.00	8.00
47-8393	Give Me Back My Life/Monica (Love Theme from "The Carpetbaggers")	1964	2.00	4.00	8.00

Number	Title (A Side/B Side)	Yr	VG	VG+	NM
47-8483	Try to Remember/Love Is Here to Stay	1964	2.00	4.00	8.00
47-8547	Dio Mio/Weaver, Weaver	1965	2.00	4.00	8.00
47-8700	Pretty Is/Melinda	1965	2.00	4.00	8.00
47-8752	River Boy/A Man and a Woman	1965	2.00	4.00	8.00
47-8871	Gone/There's a Time for Everything	1966	2.00	4.00	8.00
47-9002	My Cup Runneth Over/It Seems a Long, Long Time	1966	2.00	4.00	8.00
47-9178	One Little Girl at a Time/Time, Time	1967	—	3.00	6.00
47-9249	Ballad of the War Wagon/Time, Time	1967	—	3.00	6.00
47-9319	Let Me So Love/When the Snow Is On the Roses	1967	—	3.00	6.00
47-9400	Who Will Answer/My Love Is Gone from Me	1967	—	3.00	6.00
47-9400 [PS]	Who Will Answer/My Love Is Gone from Me	1967	3.00	6.00	12.00
47-9517	Apologize/The Wind Will Change Tomorrow	1968	—	3.00	6.00
47-9589	I'll Stay Lonely/All My Love's Laughter	1968	—	3.00	6.00
47-9647	Kiss Her Now/Gloves, Pictures, Dreams (Doors, Mirrors and Heartaches)	1968	—	3.00	6.00
47-9682	Away in a Manger/Carry the Lord to Jerusalem	1968	—	—	—
—Unreleased					
47-9726	Changing, Changing/Six Words	1969	—	3.00	6.00
47-9864	Chippewa Town/Sing Away the World	1970	—	3.00	6.00
74-0156	2001/Son of a Travelin' Man	1969	—	3.00	6.00
74-0253	Love of the Common People/Leave Them a Flower	1969	—	3.00	6.00
74-0296	Thing Called Love/Today Is the First Day of the Rest of Our Lives	1969	—	3.00	6.00
74-0329	Honey, What's the Matter/Three Good Reasons	1970	—	2.50	5.00
74-0398	The Answer Is/Sweet, Sweet Reason	1970	—	2.50	5.00
74-0498	More Than Ever Before/The Day	1971	—	2.50	5.00
74-0551	He Gives Us All His Love/Angelica	1971	—	2.50	5.00
74-0678	And I Love You So/The Ship	1972	—	2.00	4.00
74-0726	Distant Drums/Blue Side of Lonesome	1972	—	2.00	4.00
74-0800	Lost Horizon/Question Me an Answer	1972	—	2.00	4.00
74-0883	Butterflies Are Free/The World Is a Circle	1973	—	2.00	4.00
SP-45-188 [DJ]	The Ballad Of The Christmas Donkey/Let It Snow! Let It Snow! Let It Snow!	1968	2.00	4.00	8.00

Albums
RCA CAMDEN

ACL1-0244	Do You Hear What I Hear?	1973	3.00	6.00	12.00
CAS-2536	Ed Ames	1972	3.00	6.00	12.00
CAS-2598	Somewhere, My Love	1972	3.00	6.00	12.00

RCA VICTOR

ANL1-1780	Pure Gold	1976	2.50	5.00	10.00
LPM-2781 [M]	Opening Night	1963	3.00	6.00	12.00
LSP-2781 [S]	Opening Night	1963	3.75	7.50	15.00
ANL1-2891	The Impossible Dream	1978	2.50	5.00	10.00
LPM-2944 [M]	The Ed Ames Album	1964	3.00	6.00	12.00
LSP-2944 [S]	The Ed Ames Album	1964	3.75	7.50	15.00
LPM-3390 [M]	My Kind of Songs	1965	3.00	6.00	12.00
LSP-3390 [S]	My Kind of Songs	1965	3.75	7.50	15.00
LPM-3460 [M]	It's a Man's World	1965	3.00	6.00	12.00
LSP-3460 [S]	It's a Man's World	1965	3.75	7.50	15.00
LPM-3636 [M]	More I Cannot Wish You	1966	2.50	5.00	10.00
LSP-3636 [S]	More I Cannot Wish You	1966	3.00	6.00	12.00
LPM-3774 [M]	My Cup Runneth Over	1967	2.50	5.00	10.00
LSP-3774 [S]	My Cup Runneth Over	1967	3.00	6.00	12.00
LPM-3834 [M]	Time, Time	1967	3.00	6.00	12.00
LSP-3834 [S]	Time, Time	1967	2.50	5.00	10.00
LPM-3838 [M]	Christmas with Ed Ames	1967	3.75	7.50	15.00
LSP-3838 [S]	Christmas with Ed Ames	1967	3.00	6.00	12.00
LPM-3913 [M]	When the Snow Is On the Roses	1967	3.00	6.00	12.00
LSP-3913 [S]	When the Snow Is On the Roses	1967	2.50	5.00	10.00
LPM-3961 [M]	Who Will Answer? And Other Songs of Our Time	1968	3.75	7.50	15.00
LSP-3961 [S]	Who Will Answer? And Other Songs of Our Time	1968	2.50	5.00	10.00
LPM-4028 [M]	Apologize	1968	5.00	10.00	20.00
LSP-4028 [S]	Apologize	1968	2.50	5.00	10.00
LSP-4079	The Hits of Broadway and Hollywood	1968	2.50	5.00	10.00
LSP-4128	A Time for Living, A Time for Hope	1969	2.50	5.00	10.00
LSP-4172	The Windmills of Your Mind	1969	2.50	5.00	10.00
LSP-4184	The Best of Ed Ames	1969	2.50	5.00	10.00
LSP-4249	Love of the Common People	1969	2.50	5.00	10.00
LSP-4381	Sing Away the World	1970	2.50	5.00	10.00
LSP-4385	Christmas Is the Warmest Time of the Year	1970	5.00	10.00	20.00
LSP-4453	The Songs of Bacharach and David	1971	2.50	5.00	10.00
LSP-4634	Ed Ames	1972	3.75	7.50	15.00
LSP-4683	Ed Ames Remembers Jim Reeves	1972	3.75	7.50	15.00
LSP-4808	Songs from "Lost Horizon"	1973	3.75	7.50	15.00
VPS-6023 [(2)]	This Is Ed Ames	1970	5.00	10.00	20.00

AMES, NANCY

45s
ABC

Number	Title (A Side/B Side)	Yr	VG	VG+	NM
11100	On Green Dolphin Street/Something's Gotten Hold of My Heart	1968	—	3.00	6.00

EPIC

9845	Shake a Hand/Funny Thing About It	1965	2.00	4.00	8.00
9874	I've Got a Lot of Love (Left in Me)/Friends and Lovers Forever	1965	2.00	4.00	8.00
9885	Dear Hearts and Gentle People/Friends and Lovers Forever	1966	2.00	4.00	8.00
10003	He Wore the Green Beret/War Is a Card Game	1966	2.00	4.00	8.00
10056	I Don't Want to Talk About It/Cry Softly	1966	3.00	6.00	12.00
10149	Love's Like Wine/My Story Book	1967	2.00	4.00	8.00

LIBERTY

55548	Bonsoir Cher/Cu Cu Rru Cu Cu Paloma	1963	2.50	5.00	10.00
55598	An Elizabethan Ballad (Part 1)/An Elizabethan Ballad (Part 2)	1963	2.50	5.00	10.00
55737	Malaguena Salerosa/Cu Cu Ru Cu Cu Paloma	1964	2.50	5.00	10.00
55762	It Scares Me/Let Tonight Linger On	1965	2.50	5.00	10.00

Albums
EPIC

| LN 24189 [M] | Latin Pulse | 1966 | 3.00 | 6.00 | 12.00 |
| LN 24197 [M] | As Time Goes By | 1967 | 3.00 | 6.00 | 12.00 |

Number	Title (A Side/B Side)	Yr	VG	VG+	NM
❑ LN 24238 [M]	Spiced with Brazil	1967	3.00	6.00	12.00
❑ BN 26189 [S]	Latin Pulse	1966	3.75	7.50	15.00
❑ BN 26197 [S]	As Time Goes By	1967	3.75	7.50	15.00
❑ BN 26238 [S]	Spiced with Brazil	1967	3.75	7.50	15.00
❑ BN 26378	Nancy Ames at the Americana	1968	3.00	6.00	12.00

LIBERTY

Number	Title (A Side/B Side)	Yr	VG	VG+	NM
❑ LRP-3276 [M]	The Incredible Nancy Ames	1963	3.75	7.50	15.00
❑ LRP-3299 [M]	Portrait of Nancy	1963	3.75	7.50	15.00
❑ LRP-3329 [M]	I Never Will Marry	1964	3.75	7.50	15.00
❑ LRP-3369 [M]	This Is the Girl That Is	1964	3.75	7.50	15.00
❑ LRP-3400 [M]	Let It Be Me	1965	3.75	7.50	15.00
❑ LST-7276 [S]	The Incredible Nancy Ames	1963	5.00	10.00	20.00
❑ LST-7299 [S]	Portrait of Nancy	1963	5.00	10.00	20.00
❑ LST-7329 [S]	I Never Will Marry	1964	5.00	10.00	20.00
❑ LST-7369 [S]	This Is the Girl That Is	1964	5.00	10.00	20.00
❑ LST-7400 [S]	Let It Be Me	1965	5.00	10.00	20.00

SUNSET

Number	Title (A Side/B Side)	Yr	VG	VG+	NM
❑ SUM-1109 [M]	The Versatile Nancy Ames	196?	3.00	6.00	12.00
❑ SUS-5109 [S]	The Versatile Nancy Ames	196?	3.75	7.50	15.00

AMES BROTHERS, THE Also see ED AMES.

45s

CORAL

Number	Title (A Side/B Side)	Yr	VG	VG+	NM
❑ 9-60113	White Christmas/Winter Wonderland	1950	5.00	10.00	20.00
—78 rpm version issued in 1949					
❑ 9-60140	Rag Mop/Sentimental Me	1950	6.25	12.50	25.00
—This has been proven to exist on 45 rpm					
❑ 60173	Sentimental Me/Blue Prelude	1950	3.75	7.50	15.00
❑ 60185	Dormi, Dormi/Marianna	1950	3.75	7.50	15.00
❑ 60209	Hoop-De-Doo/Stars Are the Windows of Heaven	1950	3.75	7.50	15.00
❑ 60212	Blue Prelude/Lorelei	1950	3.75	7.50	15.00
❑ 60253	Can Anyone Explain? (No, No, No!)/Sittin' 'N Starin' 'N Rockin'	1950	3.75	7.50	15.00
❑ 60267	The Twelve Days of Christmas/Wassail Song	1950	3.75	7.50	15.00
❑ 60268	Silent Night/Adeste Fideles	1950	3.75	7.50	15.00
❑ 60269	Hark! The Herald Angels Sing/It Came Upon a Midnight Clear	1950	3.75	7.50	15.00
❑ 60270	Oh, Little Town of Bethlehem/God Rest Ye Merry Gentlemen	1950	3.75	7.50	15.00
❑ 60300	Thirsty for Your Kisses/I Don't Mind Being All Alone	1950	3.75	7.50	15.00
❑ 60327	Oh Babe/To Think You've Chosen Me	1950	3.75	7.50	15.00
❑ 60333	The Thing/Music by the Angels (Lyrics by the Lord)	1950	3.75	7.50	15.00
❑ 60336	Just a Dream of You, Dear/In the Evening in the Moonlight	1950	3.75	7.50	15.00
❑ 60337	Till We Meet Again/Tell Me Your Dream	1950	3.75	7.50	15.00
❑ 60338	Meet Me Tonight in Dreamland/Moonlight Bay	1950	3.75	7.50	15.00
❑ 60339	Because/Love's Old Sweet Song	1950	3.75	7.50	15.00
❑ 60352	Loving Is Believing/Music by the Angels (Lyrics by the Lord)	1951	3.75	7.50	15.00
❑ 60363	Three Dollars and Ninety-Eight Cents/More Than I Care to Remember	1951	3.75	7.50	15.00
❑ 60385	Sentimental Me/Dormi, Dormi	1951	3.75	7.50	15.00
❑ 60386	Can Anyone Explain?/Lingering Down the Lane (Ah! La Petit Vin Blanc)	1951	3.75	7.50	15.00
❑ 60387	Lorelei/To Think You've Chosen Me	1951	3.75	7.50	15.00
❑ 60388	Stars Are the Window of Heaven/I Don't Mind Being All Alone (When I'm Alone with You)	1951	3.75	7.50	15.00
❑ 60397	Rag Mop/Hoop-De-Doo	1951	3.75	7.50	15.00
❑ 60398	Marianna/(Lift Your Glass) Sing Until the Cows Come Home	1951	3.75	7.50	15.00
❑ 60399	Clancey Lowered the Boom/More Beer	1951	3.75	7.50	15.00
❑ 60400	Noah's Ark/Bar Room Polka	1951	3.75	7.50	15.00
❑ 60404	My Love Serenade/I Love You Much Too Much	1951	3.75	7.50	15.00
❑ 60452	Too Many Women/Sometimes There Must Be Happiness	1951	3.75	7.50	15.00
❑ 60489	Wang Wang Blues/Who'll Take My Love	1951	3.75	7.50	15.00
❑ 60510	Hawaiian War Chant/Sweet Leilani	1951	3.75	7.50	15.00
❑ 60511	My Little Grass Shack/To You, Sweetheart, Aloha	1951	3.75	7.50	15.00
❑ 60512	Sing Me a Song of the Islands/Song of the Islands	1951	3.75	7.50	15.00
❑ 60513	Blue Hawaii/Moon of Manakoora	1951	3.75	7.50	15.00
❑ 60549	Only, Only You/Everything's Gonna Be Alright	1951	3.75	7.50	15.00
❑ 60566	Sentimental Journey/Undecided	1951	3.75	7.50	15.00
❑ 60572	Jolly Old St. Nicholas/Ting-a-Ling-a-Jingle	1951	3.75	7.50	15.00
❑ 60617	I Wanna Love You/I'll Still Love You	1952	3.00	6.00	12.00
❑ 60628	Mother, At Your Feet Is Kneeling/Lovely Lady Dressed in Blue	1952	3.00	6.00	12.00
❑ 60633	Deep River/Dry Bones	1952	3.00	6.00	12.00
❑ 60634	Shadrack/Swing Low, Sweet Chariot	1952	3.00	6.00	12.00
❑ 60635	Joshua Fit De Battle of Jericho/Go Down Moses	1952	3.00	6.00	12.00
❑ 60636	Blind Barnabas/Who Built the Ark	1952	3.00	6.00	12.00
❑ 60680	The Shiek of Araby/And So I Waited	1952	3.00	6.00	12.00
❑ 60751	Stardust/Crazy 'Cause I Love You	1952	3.00	6.00	12.00
❑ 60773	Auf Wiedersehn Sweetheart/Break the Bonds That Bind Me	1952	3.00	6.00	12.00
❑ 60804	Absence Makes the Heart Grow Fonder (For Someone Else)/String Along	1952	3.00	6.00	12.00
❑ 60846	My Favorite Song/Al-Lee-O! Al-Lee-Ay!	1952	3.00	6.00	12.00
❑ 60861	Sing a Song of Santa Claus/Winter's Here Again	1952	3.00	6.00	12.00
❑ 60870	Do Nothin' Till You Hear from Me/No Moon at All	1952	3.00	6.00	12.00
❑ 60885	Home on the Range/Wagon Wheels	1952	3.00	6.00	12.00
❑ 60886	Rye Whiskey/You Are My Sunshine	1952	3.00	6.00	12.00
❑ 60887	Old Faithful/Tumbling Tumbleweeds	1952	3.00	6.00	12.00
❑ 60888	The Last Round-Up/The Strawberry Roan	1952	3.00	6.00	12.00
❑ 60926	Lonely Wine/Can't I	1953	3.00	6.00	12.00
❑ 60967	At the End of a Rainbow/Candy Bar Boogie	1953	3.00	6.00	12.00
❑ 61005	Always in My Dreams/This Is Fiesta	1953	3.00	6.00	12.00
❑ 61060	Lazy River/Stardust	1953	3.00	6.00	12.00
❑ 61127	Don't Believe a Word They Say/Helen Polka	1954	3.00	6.00	12.00
❑ 61145	Don't Lie to Me/Don't Believe a Word They Say	1954	3.00	6.00	12.00
❑ 61723	Mother At Your Feet Is Kneeling/Lovely Lady Dressed in Blue	1956	3.00	6.00	12.00

EPIC

Number	Title (A Side/B Side)	Yr	VG	VG+	NM
❑ 9530	Love Me with All Your Heart/Love Is an Ocean of Emotion	1962	2.00	4.00	8.00
❑ 9591	Surrender, Surrender/Wrong Man	1963	2.00	4.00	8.00
❑ 9630	Washington Square/Knees Up, Mother Brown	1963	2.00	4.00	8.00

MCA

Number	Title (A Side/B Side)	Yr	VG	VG+	NM
❑ 60002	Rag Mop/Sentimental Me	1973	—	2.00	4.00
❑ 60005	Sentimental Journey/Undecided	1973	—	2.00	4.00
—With Les Brown					

RCA VICTOR

Number	Title (A Side/B Side)	Yr	VG	VG+	NM
❑ 47-5325	You You You/Once Upon a Tune	1953	3.00	6.00	12.00
❑ 47-5404	My Love, My Life, My Happiness/If You Want My Heart	1953	3.00	6.00	12.00
❑ 47-5530	I Can't Believe That You're in Love with Me/Boogie Woogie Maxixe	1953	3.00	6.00	12.00
❑ 47-5644	Man Is for the Woman Made/The Man with the Banjo	1954	2.50	5.00	10.00
❑ 47-5764	Leave It to Your Heart/Let's Walk and Talk	1954	2.50	5.00	10.00
❑ 47-5840	One More Time/Hopelessly	1954	2.50	5.00	10.00
❑ 47-5897	The Naughty Lady of Shady Lane/Addio	1954	2.50	5.00	10.00
❑ 47-5929	There'll Always Be a Christmas/I Got a Cold for Christmas	1954	2.50	5.00	10.00
❑ 47-6044	Sympathetic Eyes/Sweet Brown-Eyed Baby	1955	2.50	5.00	10.00
❑ 47-6117	Gotta Be This or That/Southern Cross	1955	2.50	5.00	10.00
❑ 47-6156	Wrong Again/Merci Beaucoup	1955	2.50	5.00	10.00
❑ 47-6208	My Bonnie Lassie/So Will I	1955	2.50	5.00	10.00
❑ 47-6323	My Love, Your Love/The Next Time It Happens	1955	2.50	5.00	10.00
❑ 47-6400	Forever Darling/I'm Gonna Love You	1956	2.50	5.00	10.00
❑ 47-6481	It Only Hurts for a Little While/If You Wanna See Mamie Tonight	1956	2.50	5.00	10.00
❑ 47-6608	49 Shades of Green/Summer Sweetheart	1956	2.50	5.00	10.00
❑ 47-6720	I Saw Esau/The Game of Love	1956	2.50	5.00	10.00
❑ 47-6821	I Only Know One Way to Love You/Did You Ever Get the Roses	1957	2.50	5.00	10.00
❑ 47-6851	Yeah, Yeah, Yeah/Man on Fire	1957	2.50	5.00	10.00
❑ 47-6930	Tammy/Rockin' Shoes	1957	2.50	5.00	10.00
❑ 47-7046	Melodie D'Amour/So Little Time	1957	2.50	5.00	10.00
❑ 47-7142	Little Gypsy/In Love	1958	2.50	5.00	10.00
❑ 47-7167	A Very Precious Love/Don't Leave Me Now	1958	2.50	5.00	10.00
❑ 47-7268	Stay/Little Serenade	1958	2.50	5.00	10.00
❑ 47-7315	Pussy Cat/No One But You	1958	2.50	5.00	10.00
❑ 47-7365	It's Only a Paper Moon/I Don't Know Why	1958	2.50	5.00	10.00
❑ 47-7413	Red River Rose/When the Summer Comes Again	1958	2.50	5.00	10.00
❑ 47-7474	Dancin' in the Streets/(Yes I Need) Only Your Love	1959	2.50	5.00	10.00
❑ 47-7526	Someone to Come Home To/Mason-Dixon Line	1959	2.50	5.00	10.00
❑ 47-7565	Now Hear This/Now It's Me	1959	2.50	5.00	10.00
❑ 47-7604	Take Me Along/What Do I Hear	1959	2.50	5.00	10.00
❑ 47-7655	China Doll/Christopher Sunday	1959	2.50	5.00	10.00
❑ 47-7655 [PS]	China Doll/Christopher Sunday	1959	3.75	7.50	15.00
❑ 47-7680	Quizas, Quizas, Quizas/Me Lo Digo Adela	1960	2.00	4.00	8.00
❑ 47-7742	A Hayy Pair/Carnival	1960	2.00	4.00	8.00
❑ 47-7766	Ring Them Bells/You Are My Love	1960	2.00	4.00	8.00
❑ 47-7801	Suzie Wong/There the Hot Winds Blow	1960	2.00	4.00	8.00
❑ 47-7836	Kiss from Cora/Asking for You	1961	2.00	4.00	8.00
❑ WY 491	There'll Always Be a Christmas/I Got a Cold for Christmas	1954	2.50	5.00	10.00
—From the "Little Nipper" children's series					
❑ WY 491 [PS]	There'll Always Be a Christmas/I Got a Cold for Christmas	1954	3.00	6.00	12.00
❑ H7OW-6566/7 [DJ]	I Couldn't Sleep a Wink Last Night/Por Favor	1957	6.25	12.50	25.00
—White label; "Advance Release from New RCA Victor Album Sweet Seventeen"					

7-Inch Extended Plays

CORAL

Number	Title (A Side/B Side)	Yr	VG	VG+	NM
❑ EC 81000	*Star Dust/Lazy River/Wang Wang Blues/The Sheik of Araby	1953	5.00	10.00	20.00
❑ EC 81000 [PS]	Song Time	1953	5.00	10.00	20.00
❑ EC 81021	Undecided/Sentimental Journey//Do Nothin' Til You Hear from Me/No Moon at All	195?	5.00	10.00	20.00
❑ EC 81021 [PS]	Les Brown and the Ames Brothers	195?	5.00	10.00	20.00
❑ EC 81041	*White Christmas/Winter Wonderland/Jolly Old St. Nicholas/Ting-a-Ling-a-Jingle	1954	5.00	10.00	20.00
❑ EC 81041 [PS]	Christmas Greetings from the Ames Brothers	1954	5.00	10.00	20.00
❑ EC 81042	My Favorite Song/Blue Prelude//Cruising Down the River/Oh, You Sweet One	1954	5.00	10.00	20.00
❑ EC 81042 [PS]	Favorite Songs, Vol. 1	1954	5.00	10.00	20.00
❑ EC 81043	Absence Makes the Heart Grow Fonder (For Someone Else)/String Along//Auf Wiederseh'n Sweetheart/Thirsty for Your Kisses	1954	5.00	10.00	20.00
❑ EC 81043 [PS]	Favorite Songs, Vol. 2	1954	5.00	10.00	20.00
❑ EC 81053	*In the Evening by the Moonlight/Just a Dream of You Dear/Till We Meet Again/You Tell Me Your Dream, I'll Tell You Mine	1954	5.00	10.00	20.00
❑ EC 81053 [PS]	In the Evening by the Moonlight	1954	5.00	10.00	20.00
❑ EC 81054	To You Sweetheart, Aloha/My Little Grass Shack in Kealakekua, Hawaii//Sweet Leilani/Hawaiian War Chant	1954	5.00	10.00	20.00
❑ EC 81054 [PS]	Sweet Leilani	1954	5.00	10.00	20.00
❑ EC 81060	*Home on the Range/Wagon Wheels/Rye Whiskey/You Are My Sunshine	1955	5.00	10.00	20.00
❑ EC 81060 [PS]	Home on the Range	1955	5.00	10.00	20.00
❑ EC 81100	Dry Bones/Deep River//Shadrack/Swing Low Sweet Chariot	1956	5.00	10.00	20.00
❑ EC 81100 [PS]	Favorite Spirituals	1956	5.00	10.00	20.00

Number	Title (A Side/B Side)	Yr	VG	VG+	NM
❑ 83010 [DJ]	Sing a Song of Santa Claus/Winter's Here Again//Let's Have an Old Fashioned Christmas/I've Got The Christmas Spirit	195?	3.75	7.50	15.00

—B-side by Don Cornell

RCA VICTOR

Number	Title (A Side/B Side)	Yr	VG	VG+	NM
❑ SP-45-48	Moonglow/Rag Mop/Seventeen//Two Sleepy People/When My Sugar Walks Down My Street/I Can't Give You Anything But Love	1958	5.00	10.00	20.00
❑ SP-45-48 [PS]	French's Mustard Invites You to a Platter Party with the Ames Brothers	1958	5.00	10.00	20.00
❑ LPC-112	Moonlight Serenade/And the Angels Sing//Heartaches/It's the Talk of the Town	1961	5.00	10.00	20.00

—"Compact 33 Double"; small hole, plays at 33 1/3 rpm

Number	Title (A Side/B Side)	Yr	VG	VG+	NM
❑ LPC-112 [PS]	The Ames Brothers Sing the Best of the Bands	1961	5.00	10.00	20.00
❑ 547-0329	Gotta Be This or That/Anniversary Song//Love Your Magic Spell Is Everywhere/I Can't Give You Anything But Love	1953	3.75	7.50	15.00

—Part of 2-EP set, EPB-3186

Number	Title (A Side/B Side)	Yr	VG	VG+	NM
❑ EPA-571	The Man with the Banjo/You, You, You//Man, Man Is for the Woman Made/I Can't Believe That You're in Love with Me	1955	3.75	7.50	15.00
❑ EPA-571 [PS]	The Man with the Banjo	1955	3.75	7.50	15.00
❑ EPA-680	Exactly Like You/I Only Have Eyes for You//Autumn Leaves/You're Driving Me Crazy	1955	3.75	7.50	15.00
❑ EPA-680 [PS]	Exactly Like You	1955	3.75	7.50	15.00
❑ EPA-790	It Must Be True/The Alphabet/Ol' Man River//Gotta Be This or That/Anniversary Song//That's the Way Love Goes	1956	3.75	7.50	15.00
❑ EPA-790 [PS]	The Ames Brothers	1956	3.75	7.50	15.00
❑ EPA-819	(contents unknown)	1956	3.75	7.50	15.00
❑ EPA-819 [PS]	Four Brothers, Vol. 1	1956	3.75	7.50	15.00
❑ EPA-820	(contents unknown)	1956	3.75	7.50	15.00
❑ EPA-820 [PS]	Four Brothers, Vol. 2	1956	3.75	7.50	15.00
❑ EPA 1-1541	Silver Bells/The Christmas Song//Jingle Bells/There'll Always Be a Christmas	1957	3.75	7.50	15.00
❑ EPA 1-1541 [PS]	There'll Always Be a Christmas, Vol. 1	1957	3.75	7.50	15.00
❑ EPA 2-1541	(contents unknown)	1957	3.75	7.50	15.00
❑ EPA 2-1541 [PS]	There'll Always Be a Christmas, Vol. 2	1957	3.75	7.50	15.00
❑ EPA 3-1541	*Deck the Halls/The Christmas Song/C-H-R-I-S-T-M-A-S/The Night Before Christmas/Santa Claus Is Coming to Town	1957	3.75	7.50	15.00
❑ EPA 3-1541 [PS]	There'll Always Be a Christmas, Vol. 3	1957	3.75	7.50	15.00
❑ EPB 3186 [PS]	It Must Be True	1953	3.75	7.50	15.00

—Two-pocket jacket for two-EP set

Number	Title (A Side/B Side)	Yr	VG	VG+	NM
❑ EPA-4096	Tammy/Not You Not I//That's the Way Love Goes/The Rhythm in My Heart	1957	3.75	7.50	15.00
❑ EPA-4096 [PS]	Tammy	1957	3.75	7.50	15.00
❑ EPA-4173	Melodie d'Amour/Fascination//Sayonara/Around the World	1957	3.75	7.50	15.00
❑ EPA-4173 [PS]	Melodie D'Amour	1957	3.75	7.50	15.00
❑ EPA-4213	I Don't Know Why (I Just Do)/Don't Get Around Much Anymore//For Sentimental Reasons/Oh What It Seemed to Be	1958	3.75	7.50	15.00
❑ EPA-4213 [PS]	Sentimental Mood	1958	3.75	7.50	15.00
❑ EPA-4227 [M]	Destination Moon/It's Only a Paper Moon//I'm Shooting High/Music from Out of Space	1958	3.75	7.50	15.00
❑ EPA-4227 [PS]	Destination Moon	1958	3.75	7.50	15.00
❑ ESP-4227 [PS]	Destination Moon	1958	6.25	12.50	25.00
❑ ESP-4227 [S]	Destination Moon/It's Only a Paper Moon//I'm Shooting High/Music from Out of Space	1958	6.25	12.50	25.00
❑ EPA-4320	Rag Mop/Sentimental Me//Undecided/Can Anyone Explain	1958	3.75	7.50	15.00
❑ EPA-4320 [PS]	The Best of the Ames Brothers	1958	3.75	7.50	15.00
❑ EPA-5020	You, You, You/The Naughty Lady of Shady Lane//Melodie d'Amour (Melody of Love)/Tammy	1958	3.75	7.50	15.00
❑ EPA-5020 [PS]	The Ames Brothers (Gold Standard Series)	1958	3.75	7.50	15.00

Albums

CORAL

Number	Title (A Side/B Side)	Yr	VG	VG+	NM
❑ CRL 56014 [10]	Sing a Song of Christmas	1950	12.50	25.00	50.00
❑ CRL 56017 [10]	In the Evening by the Moonlight	1951	12.50	25.00	50.00
❑ CRL 56024 [10]	Sentimental Me	1951	12.50	25.00	50.00
❑ CRL 56025 [10]	Hoop-De-Hoo	1951	12.50	25.00	50.00
❑ CRL 56042 [10]	Sweet Leilani	1951	12.50	25.00	50.00
❑ CRL 56050 [10]	Favorite Spirituals	1952	12.50	25.00	50.00
❑ CRL 56079 [10]	Home on the Range	1952	12.50	25.00	50.00
❑ CRL 56080 [10]	Merry Christmas	1952	12.50	25.00	50.00
❑ CRL 56097 [10]	Favorite Songs	1954	12.50	25.00	50.00
❑ CRL 57031 [M]	Ames Brothers Concert	1956	7.50	15.00	30.00
❑ CRL 57054 [M]	Love's Old Sweet Song	1956	7.50	15.00	30.00
❑ CRL 57166	Sounds of Christmas Harmony	1957	7.50	15.00	30.00
❑ CRL 57176 [M]	Love Serenade	1958	7.50	15.00	30.00
❑ CRL 57338 [M]	Our Golden Favorites	1960	7.50	15.00	30.00

EPIC

Number	Title (A Side/B Side)	Yr	VG	VG+	NM
❑ LN 24036 [M]	Hello Italy	1962	3.75	7.50	15.00
❑ LN 24069 [M]	Knees Up Mother Brown	1963	3.75	7.50	15.00
❑ BN 26036 [S]	Hello Italy	1962	5.00	10.00	20.00
❑ BN 26069 [S]	Knees Up Mother Brown	1963	5.00	10.00	20.00

MCA

Number	Title (A Side/B Side)	Yr	VG	VG+	NM
❑ 1510 [R]	The Ames Brothers	197?	2.50	5.00	10.00

RCA CAMDEN

Number	Title (A Side/B Side)	Yr	VG	VG+	NM
❑ CAL-571 [M]	The Ames Brothers — Sweet and Swing	1958	3.75	7.50	15.00

RCA SPECIAL PRODUCTS

Number	Title (A Side/B Side)	Yr	VG	VG+	NM
❑ DVL2-0207 [(2)]	All Their Greatest Hits	1976	3.75	7.50	15.00

RCA VICTOR

Number	Title (A Side/B Side)	Yr	VG	VG+	NM
❑ ANL1-1095e	The Best of the Ames Brothers	1975	2.50	5.00	10.00
❑ LPM-1142 [M]	Exactly Like You	1955	7.50	15.00	30.00
❑ LPM-1157 [M]	Four Brothers	1955	7.50	15.00	30.00
❑ LPM-1228 [M]	The Ames Brothers with Hugo Winterhalter	1956	7.50	15.00	30.00
❑ LPM-1487 [M]	Sweet Seventeen	1957	7.50	15.00	30.00
❑ LPM-1541 [M]	There'll Always Be a Christmas	1957	7.50	15.00	30.00

Number	Title (A Side/B Side)	Yr	VG	VG+	NM
❑ LPM-1680 [M]	Destination Moon	1958	6.25	12.50	25.00
❑ LSP-1680 [S]	Destination Moon	1958	7.50	15.00	30.00
❑ LPM-1855 [M]	Smoochin' Time	1958	6.25	12.50	25.00
❑ LSP-1855 [S]	Smoochin' Time	1958	7.50	15.00	30.00
❑ LPM-1859 [M]	The Best of the Ames Brothers	1958	6.25	12.50	25.00
❑ LSP-1859(e) [R]	The Best of the Ames Brothers	196?	5.00	10.00	20.00
❑ LPM-1954 [M]	Famous Hits of Famous Quartets	1959	5.00	10.00	20.00
❑ LSP-1954 [S]	Famous Hits of Famous Quartets	1959	6.25	12.50	25.00
❑ LPM-1998 [M]	The Ames Brothers Sing the Best in the Country	1959	5.00	10.00	20.00
❑ LSP-1998 [S]	The Ames Brothers Sing the Best in the Country	1959	6.25	12.50	25.00
❑ LPM-2009 [M]	Words and Music	1959	5.00	10.00	20.00
❑ LSP-2009 [S]	Words and Music	1959	6.25	12.50	25.00
❑ LPM-2100 [M]	Hello, Amigos	1960	5.00	10.00	20.00
❑ LSP-2100 [S]	Hello, Amigos	1960	6.25	12.50	25.00
❑ LPM-2182 [M]	The Blend and the Beat	1960	5.00	10.00	20.00
❑ LSP-2182 [S]	The Blend and the Beat	1960	6.25	12.50	25.00
❑ LPM-2273 [M]	The Best of the Bands	1960	5.00	10.00	20.00
❑ LSP-2273 [S]	The Best of the Bands	1960	6.25	12.50	25.00
❑ LPM-2876 [M]	For Sentimental Reasons	1964	3.00	6.00	12.00
❑ LSP-2876 [S]	For Sentimental Reasons	1964	3.75	7.50	15.00
❑ LPM-2981 [M]	Down Memory Lane with the Ames Brothers	1964	3.00	6.00	12.00
❑ LSP-2981 [S]	Down Memory Lane with the Ames Brothers	1964	3.75	7.50	15.00
❑ LPM-3186 [10]	It Must Be True	1954	12.50	25.00	50.00
❑ VPS-6068 [(2)]	This Is the Ames Brothers	1972	3.75	7.50	15.00

READER'S DIGEST

Number	Title (A Side/B Side)	Yr	VG	VG+	NM
❑ RDA-160 [(6)]	Sentimentally Yours	1981	6.25	12.50	25.00

VOCALION

Number	Title (A Side/B Side)	Yr	VG	VG+	NM
❑ VL 3617 [M]	The Ames Brothers	196?	3.75	7.50	15.00
❑ VL 73788 [R]	Christmas Harmony	196?	3.00	6.00	12.00

—Reissue of some Coral tracks

Number	Title (A Side/B Side)	Yr	VG	VG+	NM
❑ VL 73818	The Ames Brothers Featuring Ed Ames	196?	2.50	5.00	10.00

AMESBURY, BILL

45s

CAPITOL

Number	Title (A Side/B Side)	Yr	VG	VG+	NM
❑ 4287	I Remember/Lucky Day	1976	—	2.00	4.00

CASABLANCA

Number	Title (A Side/B Side)	Yr	VG	VG+	NM
❑ NEB 0001	Virginia (Touch Me Like You Do)/That Close to Me	1974	—	2.50	5.00
❑ NEB 0101	Rock My Roll/She's in Love	1974	—	2.50	5.00
❑ 813	Frog Man Bradley/She's in Love	1974	—	2.50	5.00
❑ 832	Every Girl in the World Tonight/(B-side unknown)	1975	—	3.00	6.00

Albums

CAPITOL

Number	Title (A Side/B Side)	Yr	VG	VG+	NM
❑ ST-11528	Can You Feel It	1976	3.00	6.00	12.00

CASABLANCA

Number	Title (A Side/B Side)	Yr	VG	VG+	NM
❑ NB 9005	Jus' a Taste of the Kid	1974	3.00	6.00	12.00

AMISH, THE

Albums

SUSSEX

Number	Title (A Side/B Side)	Yr	VG	VG+	NM
❑ SUX-7016	The Amish	1972	6.25	12.50	25.00

AMON DUUL

Albums

PROPHESY

Number	Title (A Side/B Side)	Yr	VG	VG+	NM
❑ PHS-1003	Amon Duul	1969	6.25	12.50	25.00

AMON DUUL II

45s

LIBERTY

Number	Title (A Side/B Side)	Yr	VG	VG+	NM
❑ 56196	Soda Shop Rock/Archangel's Thunderbird	1970	—	3.00	6.00

UNITED ARTISTS

Number	Title (A Side/B Side)	Yr	VG	VG+	NM
❑ XW419	Pigman/Mozambique	1974	—	2.50	5.00

Albums

ATCO

Number	Title (A Side/B Side)	Yr	VG	VG+	NM
❑ SD 36-108	Hijack	1975	2.50	5.00	10.00
❑ SD 36-119	Made in Germany	1976	2.50	5.00	10.00

UNITED ARTISTS

Number	Title (A Side/B Side)	Yr	VG	VG+	NM
❑ UA-LA017-F	Wolf City	1973	3.00	6.00	12.00
❑ UA-LA198-F	Viva La Trance	1974	3.00	6.00	12.00
❑ UAS-5586	Carnival in Babylon	1972	3.00	6.00	12.00
❑ UAS-9954 [(2)]	Dance of the Lemmings	1971	3.75	7.50	15.00

AMY AND THE JARRETTS

45s

HIT

Number	Title (A Side/B Side)	Yr	VG	VG+	NM
❑ 151	I Know Johnny Loves Me/Tobacco Road	1964	2.50	5.00	10.00

—B-side by the Roamers

ANACOSTIA

12-Inch Singles

TABU

Number	Title (A Side/B Side)	Yr	VG	VG+	NM
❑ 494	Ain't Nothing To It (5:39)/Anything for You (7:55)	1978	6.25	12.50	25.00

45s

COLUMBIA

Number	Title (A Side/B Side)	Yr	VG	VG+	NM
❑ 3-10203	All I Need/One Less Morning	1975	—	2.50	5.00
❑ 4-45685	On and Off (Part 1)/(Part 2)	1972	—	3.00	6.00
❑ 4-45820	Thick and Thin/I Just Wander	1973	—	3.00	6.00

MCA

Number	Title (A Side/B Side)	Yr	VG	VG+	NM
❑ 40838	I Can't Stop Loving Her/What Kind of Love	1977	—	3.00	6.00

ROULETTE

Number	Title (A Side/B Side)	Yr	VG	VG+	NM
❑ 7300	Love Is Never Wrong/(B-side unknown)	1980	2.00	4.00	8.00

TABU

Number	Title (A Side/B Side)	Yr	VG	VG+	NM
❑ 5506	Ain't Nothing To It/Anything for You	1978	—	2.50	5.00

Albums

MCA

Number	Title (A Side/B Side)	Yr	VG	VG+	NM
❑ 2269	Anacostia	1977	3.00	6.00	12.00

Number	Title (A Side/B Side)	Yr	VG	VG+	NM
ANASTASIA					
45s					
LAURIE					
❏ 3066	Time Bomb/That's My Kind of Love	1960	6.25	12.50	25.00
STASI					
❏ 1000	Every Road I Walk Along/Bicycle Hop	196?	50.00	100.00	200.00
❏ 1001	Seven Days a Week/Nothing Beats My Girl	196?	37.50	75.00	150.00
ANCIENT GREASE					
Albums					
MERCURY					
❏ SR-61305	Women and Children First	1970	7.50	15.00	30.00
ANDANTES, THE					
45s					
DOT					
❏ 16495	My Baby's Gone/No Yo Ru	1963	6.25	12.50	25.00
V.I.P.					
❏ 25006	If You Were Mine/(Like a) Nightmare	1964	2000.	3000.	4000.
—One of the rarest of all Motown-related 45s					
ANDERS, BERNIE					
45s					
KING					
❏ 4833	My Heart Believes/Too Late I Learned	1955	12.50	25.00	50.00
ANDERS & PONCIA					
45s					
KAMA SUTRA					
❏ 240	So It Goes/Virgin of the Night	1967	3.00	6.00	12.00
WARNER BROS.					
❏ 7271	Take His Love/I'm Beginning to Touch You	1969	2.00	4.00	8.00
❏ 7294	Make a Change (To Something Better)/Lucky	1969	2.00	4.00	8.00
Albums					
WARNER BROS.					
❏ WS 1778	The Anders & Poncia Album	1969	7.50	15.00	30.00
ANDERSEN, ERIC					
45s					
ARISTA					
❏ 0121	Ol' 55/Can't Get You Out of My Life	1975	—	2.00	4.00
❏ 0141	Be True to You/(B-side unknown)	1975	—	2.00	4.00
COLUMBIA					
❏ 45637	Is It Really Love at All/Pearl's Goodtime Blues	1972	—	2.50	5.00
❏ 45730	Blue River/More Often Than Not	1972	—	2.50	5.00
WARNER BROS.					
❏ 7231	Think About It/So Hard to Fall	1968	—	3.00	6.00
❏ 7408	Lie with Me/Secrets	1970	—	3.00	6.00
❏ 7435	Sittin' in the Sunshine/Sunshine & Flowers	1970	—	3.00	6.00
❏ 7459	Born Again/Rocky Mountain Red	1971	—	3.00	6.00
Albums					
ARISTA					
❏ AL 4033	Be True to You	1975	2.50	5.00	10.00
❏ AL 4075	Sweet Surprise	1976	2.50	5.00	10.00
❏ AL 4128	The Best Songs	1977	2.50	5.00	10.00
COLUMBIA					
❏ KC 31062	Blue River	1972	2.50	5.00	10.00
❏ PC 31062	Blue River	197?	2.00	4.00	8.00
—Reissue					
VANGUARD					
❏ VSD 7/8 [(2)]	The Best of Eric Andersen	1971	3.75	7.50	15.00
❏ VSD 6540	A Country Dream	1969	3.75	7.50	15.00
❏ VRS 9157 [M]	Today Is the Highway	1965	3.75	7.50	15.00
❏ VRS 9206 [M]	'Bout Changes and Things	1966	3.75	7.50	15.00
❏ VSD 79157 [S]	Today Is the Highway	1965	5.00	10.00	20.00
❏ VSD 79206 [S]	'Bout Changes and Things	1966	5.00	10.00	20.00
❏ VSD 79236	'Bout Changes and Things, Take 2	1968	3.75	7.50	15.00
❏ VSD 79271	More Hits from Tin Can Alley	1969	3.75	7.50	15.00
WARNER BROS.					
❏ WS 1748	Avalanche	1968	3.75	7.50	15.00
❏ WS 1806	Eric Andersen	1969	3.75	7.50	15.00
ANDERSON, BILL					
45s					
CURB					
❏ 76855	Deck of Cards/Thank You Darling	1991	—	2.50	5.00
DECCA					
❏ 9-30773	That's What It's Like to Be Lonesome/Thrill of My Life	1958	3.75	7.50	15.00
❏ 9-30914	Ninety-Nine/Back Where I Started From	1959	3.75	7.50	15.00
❏ 9-30993	Dead or Alive/It's Not the End of Everything	1959	3.75	7.50	15.00
❏ 31092	The Tip of My Fingers/No Man's Land	1960	3.00	6.00	12.00
❏ 31168	Walk Out Backwards/The Best of Strangers	1960	3.00	6.00	12.00
❏ 31262	Po' Folks/Goodbye Cruel World	1960	3.00	6.00	12.00
❏ 31358	Get a Little Dirt on Your Hands/Down Came the Rain	1962	3.00	6.00	12.00
❏ 31404	Mama Sang a Song/On and On and On	1962	2.50	5.00	10.00
❏ 31458	Still/You Made It Easy	1963	2.50	5.00	10.00
❏ 31521	8 x 10/One Mile Over — Two Miles Back	1963	2.50	5.00	10.00
❏ 31521 [PS]	8 x 10/One Mile Over — Two Miles Back	1963	5.00	10.00	20.00
❏ 31577	Five Little Fingers/Easy Come — Easy Go	1964	2.50	5.00	10.00
❏ 31630	Me/Cincinnati, Ohio	1964	2.50	5.00	10.00
❏ 31681	In Case You Ever Change Your Mind/Three A.M.	1964	2.50	5.00	10.00
❏ 31743	Certain/You Can Have Her	1965	2.50	5.00	10.00
❏ 31825	Bright Lights and Country Music/Born	1965	2.50	5.00	10.00
❏ 31890	I Love You Drops/Golden Guitar	1966	2.50	5.00	10.00
❏ 31999	I Get the Fever/The First Mrs. Jones	1966	—	4.00	8.00
❏ 32077	Get While the Gettin's Good/Something to Believe In	1967	2.00	4.00	8.00
❏ 32146	No One's Gonna Hurt You Anymore/Papa	1967	2.00	4.00	8.00
❏ 32215	Stranger on the Run/Happiness	1967	2.00	4.00	8.00
❏ 32276	Wild Week-End/Fun While It Lasted	1968	2.00	4.00	8.00
❏ 32360	Happy State of Mind/Time's Been Good to Me	1968	2.00	4.00	8.00
❏ 32417	Po' Folks' Christmas/Christmas Time's a-Coming	1968	2.00	4.00	8.00
❏ 32417 [PS]	Po' Folks' Christmas/Christmas Time's a-Coming	1968	3.75	7.50	15.00
❏ 32445	My Life (Throw It Away If I Want To)/To Be Alone	1969	—	3.50	7.00
❏ 32514	But You Know I Love You/A Picture from Life's Other Side	1969	—	3.50	7.00
❏ 32643	Love Is a Sometimes Thing/And I'm Still Missing You	1970	—	3.50	7.00
❏ 32744	Where Have All Our Heroes Gone/Loving a Memory	1970	—	3.50	7.00
❏ 32793	Always Remember/You Can Change the World	1971	—	3.50	7.00
❏ 32850	Quits/I'll Live for You	1971	—	3.50	7.00
❏ 32930	All the Lonely Women in the World/It Was Time for Me to Move Anyway	1972	—	3.50	7.00
❏ 33002	Don't She Look Good/I'm Just Gone	1972	—	3.50	7.00
MCA					
❏ 40004	If You Can Live With It (I Can Live Without It)/Let's Fall Apart	1973	—	2.00	4.00
❏ 40070	The Corner of My Life/Home and Things	1973	—	2.00	4.00
❏ 40164	World of Make Believe/Gonna Shine on It Again	1973	—	2.00	4.00
❏ 40243	Can I Come Home to You/I'm Happily Married	1974	—	2.00	4.00
❏ 40304	Every Time I Turn the Radio On/You Are My Story	1974	—	2.00	4.00
❏ 40351	I Still Feel the Same About You/Talk to Me Ohio	1975	—	2.00	4.00
❏ 40404	Country D.J./We Made Love	1975	—	2.00	4.00
❏ 40443	Thanks/Why's the Last Time Have to Be the Best	1975	—	2.00	4.00
❏ 40595	Peanuts and Diamonds/Your Love Blows Me Away	1976	—	2.00	4.00
❏ 40661	Liars One, Believers Zero/Let Me Whisper Darling One More Time	1976	—	2.00	4.00
❏ 40713	Head to Toe/Love Song for Jackie	1977	—	2.00	4.00
❏ 40794	Still the One/This Ole Suitcase	1977	—	2.00	4.00
❏ 40893	I Can't Wait Any Longer/Joanna	1978	—	2.00	4.00
❏ 40964	Double S/Married Lady	1978	—	2.00	4.00
❏ 40992	This Is a Love Song/Remembering the Good	1979	—	2.00	4.00
❏ 41060	The Dream Never Dies/One More Sexy Lady	1979	—	2.00	4.00
❏ 41150	More Than a Bedroom Thing/Love Me and I'll Be Your Best Friend	1979	—	2.00	4.00
❏ 41212	Mike Mine Night Time/Old Me and You	1980	—	2.00	4.00
❏ 41297	Rock 'N' Roll to Rock of Ages/I'm Used to the Rain	1980	—	2.00	4.00
❏ 51017	I Want That Feelin' Again/She Made Me Remember	1980	—	2.00	4.00
❏ 51052	Mister Peepers/How Married Are You, Mary Ann	1981	—	2.00	4.00
❏ 51150	Homebody/One Man Band	1981	—	2.00	4.00
❏ 51204	Whiskey Made Me Stumble (The Devil Made Me Fall)/All That Keeps Me Goin'	1981	—	2.00	4.00
SOUTHERN TRACKS					
❏ 1007	Southern Fried/You Turn the Light On	1982	—	2.50	5.00
❏ 1011	Laid Off/Lovin' Tonight	1982	—	2.50	5.00
❏ 1014	Thank You Darling/Lovin' Tonight	1983	—	2.50	5.00
❏ 1021	Son of the South/20th Century Fox	1983	—	2.50	5.00
❏ 1026	Your Eyes/I Never Get Enough of You	1984	—	2.50	5.00
❏ 1030	Speculation/We May Never Pass This Way Again	1984	—	2.50	5.00
❏ 1067	Sheet Music/Maybe Go Down	1986	—	2.50	5.00
❏ 1077	No Ordinary Memory/Sheet Music	1987	—	2.50	5.00
SWANEE					
❏ 4013	Wino the Clown/Wild Weekend	1985	—	2.50	5.00
❏ 5015	Pity Party/Don't She Look Good	1985	—	2.50	5.00
❏ 5018	When You Leave That Way, You Can Never Go Back/Quits	1985	—	2.50	5.00
TNT					
❏ 9015	City Lights/No Song to Sing	1958	20.00	40.00	80.00
Albums					
DECCA					
❏ DL 4192 [M]	Bill Anderson Sings Country Songs	1962	5.00	10.00	20.00
❏ DL 4427 [M]	Still	1963	5.00	10.00	20.00
❏ DL 4499 [M]	Bill Anderson Sings	1964	3.75	7.50	15.00
❏ DL 4600 [M]	Bill Anderson Showcase	1964	3.75	7.50	15.00
❏ DL 4646 [M]	From This Pen	1965	3.75	7.50	15.00
❏ DL 4686 [M]	Bright Lights and Country Music	1965	3.75	7.50	15.00
❏ DL 4771 [M]	I Love You Drops	1966	3.75	7.50	15.00
❏ DL 4855 [M]	Get While the Gettin's Good	1967	3.75	7.50	15.00
❏ DL 4859 [M]	Bill Anderson's Greatest Hits	1967	5.00	10.00	20.00
❏ DL 4886 [M]	I Can Do Nothing Alone	1967	6.25	12.50	25.00
❏ DXSA 7198 [(2)]	The Bill Anderson Story	1969	3.75	7.50	15.00
❏ DL 74192 [S]	Bill Anderson Sings Country Songs	1962	6.25	12.50	25.00
❏ DL 74427 [S]	Still	1963	6.25	12.50	25.00
❏ DL 74499 [S]	Bill Anderson Sings	1964	5.00	10.00	20.00
❏ DL 74600 [S]	Bill Anderson Showcase	1964	5.00	10.00	20.00
❏ DL 74646 [S]	From This Pen	1965	5.00	10.00	20.00
❏ DL 74686 [S]	Bright Lights and Country Music	1965	5.00	10.00	20.00
❏ DL 74771 [S]	I Love You Drops	1966	5.00	10.00	20.00
❏ DL 74855 [S]	Get While the Gettin's Good	1967	5.00	10.00	20.00
❏ DL 74859 [S]	Bill Anderson's Greatest Hits	1967	5.00	10.00	20.00
❏ DL 74886 [S]	I Can Do Nothing Alone	1967	5.00	10.00	20.00
❏ DL 74998	Wild Weekend	1968	3.75	7.50	15.00
❏ DL 75056	Happy State of Mind	1968	3.75	7.50	15.00
❏ DL 75142	My Life/But You Know I Love You	1969	3.75	7.50	15.00
❏ DL 75161	Bill Anderson's Christmas	1969	3.75	7.50	15.00
❏ DL 75206	Love Is a Sometimes Thing	1970	3.00	6.00	12.00
❏ DL 75254	Where Have All Our Heroes Gone?	1971	3.00	6.00	12.00
❏ DL 75275	Always Remember	1971	3.00	6.00	12.00
❏ DL 75315	Bill Anderson's Greatest Hits, Vol. 2	1971	3.00	6.00	12.00
❏ DL 75339	Singing His Praise	1972	3.00	6.00	12.00
❏ DL 75344	Bill Anderson Sings For "All the Lonely Women in the World"	1972	3.00	6.00	12.00

Number	Title (A Side/B Side)	Yr	VG	VG+	NM
❏ DL 75383	Don't She Look Good	1972	3.00	6.00	12.00
MCA					
❏ 13	Bill Anderson's Greatest Hits	1973	2.50	5.00	10.00
—Reissue of Decca 74859					
❏ 320	Bill	1973	3.00	6.00	12.00
❏ 416	"Whispering" Bill Anderson	1974	3.00	6.00	12.00
❏ 454	Every Time I Turn the Radio On/Talk to Me Ohio	1974	2.50	5.00	10.00
❏ 693	Love and Other Sad Stories	198?	2.00	4.00	8.00
—Reissue					
❏ 694	Ladies' Choice	198?	2.00	4.00	8.00
—Reissue					
❏ 766	Nashville Mirrors	198?	2.00	4.00	8.00
—Reissue					
❏ 2222	Peanuts & Diamonds & Other Jewels	1975	2.50	5.00	10.00
❏ 2264	Scorpio	1976	2.50	5.00	10.00
❏ 2371	Love and Other Sad Stories	1977	2.50	5.00	10.00
❏ 3075	Ladies' Choice	1979	2.50	5.00	10.00
❏ 3214	Nashville Mirrors	1980	2.50	5.00	10.00
❏ 4001 [(2)]	The Bill Anderson Story	1973	3.00	6.00	12.00
—Reissue of Decca 7198					
❏ 35032	Whispering	197?	2.50	5.00	10.00
MCA CORAL					
❏ 20002	I Can Do Nothing	1973	2.50	5.00	10.00
VOCALION					
❏ VL 3835 [M]	Bill Anderson's Country Style	196?	3.00	6.00	12.00
❏ VL 73835 [S]	Bill Anderson's Country Style	196?	3.75	7.50	15.00
❏ VL 73927	Just Plain Bill	197?	2.50	5.00	10.00

ANDERSON, BILL, AND JAN HOWARD
45s
DECCA

Number	Title (A Side/B Side)	Yr	VG	VG+	NM
❏ 31884	I Know You're Married (But I Love You Still)/ Time Out	1966	2.50	5.00	10.00
❏ 32197	For Loving You/The Untouchables	1967	2.00	4.00	8.00
❏ 32511	If It's All the Same to You/I Thank God for You	1969	2.00	4.00	8.00
❏ 32689	Someday We'll Be Together/ Who's the Biggest Fool	1970	2.00	4.00	8.00
❏ 32877	Dis-Satisfied/Knowing You're Mine	1971	2.00	4.00	8.00
Albums					
DECCA					
❏ DL 4959 [M]	For Loving You	1967	6.25	12.50	25.00
❏ DL 74959 [S]	For Loving You	1967	5.00	10.00	20.00
❏ DL 75184	If It's All the Same to You	1970	5.00	10.00	20.00
❏ DL 75293	Bill & Jan (Or Jan & Bill)	1972	5.00	10.00	20.00

ANDERSON, BILL, AND MARY LOU TURNER
45s
MCA

Number	Title (A Side/B Side)	Yr	VG	VG+	NM
❏ 40488	Sometimes/Circle in a Triangle	1975	—	2.00	4.00
❏ 40533	That's What Made Me Love You/Can We Still Be Friends	1976	—	2.00	4.00
❏ 40753	Where Are You Going, Billy Boy/ Sad Ole Shade of Gray	1977	—	2.00	4.00
❏ 40852	I'm Way Ahead of You/ Just Enough to Make Me Want It All	1978	—	2.00	4.00
Albums					
MCA					
❏ 2182	Sometimes	1976	3.00	6.00	12.00
❏ 2298	Billy Boy & Mary Lou	1977	3.00	6.00	12.00

ANDERSON, BROTHER JAMES
45s
SUN

Number	Title (A Side/B Side)	Yr	VG	VG+	NM
❏ 406	I'm Gonna Move in the Room with the Lord/My Soul Needs Resting	1967	12.50	25.00	50.00

ANDERSON, ELTON
45s
CAPITOL

Number	Title (A Side/B Side)	Yr	VG	VG+	NM
❏ 4762	Sick and Tired/Life Problem	1962	3.75	7.50	15.00
❏ 4830	Shed So Many Tears/That's How It's Been	1962	3.75	7.50	15.00
LANOR					
❏ 507	Humpty Dumpty Heart/Don't Touch Me Baby	1962	3.75	7.50	15.00
❏ 509	Sick and Tired/Life Problem	1962	5.00	10.00	20.00
❏ 514	I Love You So/(Sorry) I'm Gonna Have to Pass	1963	3.75	7.50	15.00
❏ 516	The Crawl (Part 1)/(Part 2)	1963	3.75	7.50	15.00
❏ 518	Bye Bye Little Angel/Don't Touch Me Baby	1963	3.75	7.50	15.00
MERCURY					
❏ 71542	Secret of Love/Cool Down Baby	1959	5.00	10.00	20.00
❏ 71643	Walking Alone/Crying Blues	1960	5.00	10.00	20.00
❏ 71777	Please Accept My Love/I Love You, Cheri	1961	5.00	10.00	20.00
TREY					
❏ 1002	Want a Come Back Home/I Love You	1959	6.25	12.50	25.00
❏ 1011	Secret of Love/Cool Down Baby	1959	6.25	12.50	25.00
VIN					
❏ 1001	Roll On Train/Shed So Many Tears	1958	7.50	15.00	30.00

ANDERSON, ERNESTINE
45s
MERCURY

Number	Title (A Side/B Side)	Yr	VG	VG+	NM
❏ 71354	My Man/Wrap Your Troubles in Dreams	1958	2.50	5.00	10.00
❏ 71423	I Don't See Me in Your Eyes Anymore/Be Mine	1959	2.50	5.00	10.00
❏ 71500	I Can Dream, Can't I/ I Heard You Cried Last Night	1959	2.50	5.00	10.00
❏ 71536	Call Me Darling/My Love Will Last	1959	2.50	5.00	10.00
❏ 71559	There Are Such Things/You, You, You	1960	2.00	4.00	8.00
❏ 71604	A Kiss to Build a Dream On/ Come On Baby, Let's Go	1960	2.00	4.00	8.00
❏ 71772	A Lover's Question/That's All I Want from You	1961	2.00	4.00	8.00
❏ 71919	See See Rider/Mound Bayou	1961	2.00	4.00	8.00
❏ 71960	Hurry Hurry/After the Lights Go Down Low	1962	2.00	4.00	8.00

SUE

Number	Title (A Side/B Side)	Yr	VG	VG+	NM
❏ 10-004	You Deserve the Best/You're Not the Guy for Me	1968	—	3.00	6.00
❏ 115	I Pity the Fool/You're Not the Guy for Me	1964	6.25	12.50	25.00
❏ 793	Keep an Eye on Love/Continental Mind	1963	6.25	12.50	25.00
❏ 803	The Best Is Yet to Come/ Will I Find My Love Today	1964	2.00	4.00	8.00
Albums					
CONCORD JAZZ					
❏ CJ-31	Hello Like Before	1977	3.00	6.00	12.00
❏ CJ-54	Live from Concord to London	1978	3.00	6.00	12.00
❏ CJ-109	Sunshine	1980	2.50	5.00	10.00
❏ CJ-147	Never Make Your Move Too Soon	1982	2.50	5.00	10.00
❏ CJ-214	Big City	1983	2.50	5.00	10.00
❏ CJ-263	When the Sun Goes Down	1985	2.50	5.00	10.00
❏ CJ-319	Be Mine Tonight	1987	2.50	5.00	10.00
MERCURY					
❏ MG-20354 [M]	Hot Cargo	1958	10.00	20.00	40.00
❏ MG-20400 [M]	Ernestine Anderson	1959	10.00	20.00	40.00
❏ MG-20492 [M]	Fascinating Ernestine	1959	10.00	20.00	40.00
❏ MG-20496 [M]	My Kinda Swing	1959	10.00	20.00	40.00
❏ MG-20582 [M]	Moanin'	1960	10.00	20.00	40.00
❏ SR-60074 [S]	Ernestine Anderson	1959	12.50	25.00	50.00
❏ SR-60171 [S]	Fascinating Ernestine	1959	12.50	25.00	50.00
❏ SR-60175 [S]	My Kinda Swing	1959	12.50	25.00	50.00
❏ SR-60242 [S]	Moanin'	1960	12.50	25.00	50.00
SUE					
❏ LP 1015 [M]	The New Sound of Ernestine Anderson	1963	5.00	10.00	20.00
WING					
❏ MGW-12281 [M]	Ernestine Anderson	1964	3.00	6.00	12.00
❏ SRW-16281 [S]	Ernestine Anderson	1964	3.75	7.50	15.00

ANDERSON, JESSE
45s
CADET

Number	Title (A Side/B Side)	Yr	VG	VG+	NM
❏ 5554	True Love Express/You're Only a Woman	1967	2.50	5.00	10.00
❏ 5588	Get Loose When You Get Loose/ Swing Too High	1968	2.50	5.00	10.00
JEWEL					
❏ 835	Help Wanted/Send Me Some Loving	1972	2.00	4.00	8.00
THOMAS					
❏ 805	I Got a Problem/Mighty Mighty	1970	3.75	7.50	15.00
❏ 807	Let Me Back In/Readings in Astrology	1970	2.50	5.00	10.00

ANDERSON, LALE
45s
KING

Number	Title (A Side/B Side)	Yr	VG	VG+	NM
❏ 5478	(A Ship Will Come) Ein Schiff Wird Kommen/ Manchmal Traum Ich Vom Kornfeld	1961	2.50	5.00	10.00

ANDERSON, LYNN
45s
CHART

Number	Title (A Side/B Side)	Yr	VG	VG+	NM
❏ 1001	Too Much of You/If This Is Love	1967	2.00	4.00	8.00
—Reissue of 1475					
❏ 1010	Promises, Promises/It Makes You Happy	1967	2.00	4.00	8.00
❏ 1026	No Another Time/The Worst Is Yet to Come	1968	2.00	4.00	8.00
❏ 1042	Big Girls Don't Cry/I Keep Forgettin'	1968	2.00	4.00	8.00
❏ 1059	Flattery Will Get You Everywhere/ A Million Shades of Blue	1968	2.00	4.00	8.00
❏ 1330	My Heart Keeps Walking the Floor/In Person	1966	2.50	5.00	10.00
❏ 1375	Ride, Ride, Ride/Tear By Tear	1966	2.00	4.00	8.00
❏ 1430	If I Kiss You (Will You Go Away)/Then Go	1967	2.00	4.00	8.00
❏ 1475	Too Much of You/If This Is Love	1967	2.50	5.00	10.00
❏ 5001	Our House Is Not a Home (If It's Never Been Loved In)/Wave Bye-Bye to the Man	1969	2.00	4.00	8.00
❏ 5013	Where's the Playground Bobby/ There Oughta Be a Law	1969	2.00	4.00	8.00
❏ 5021	That's a No No/If Silence Is Golden	1969	2.00	4.00	8.00
❏ 5040	He'd Still Love Me/All You Add Is Love	1969	2.00	4.00	8.00
❏ 5053	I've Been Everywhere/Penny for Your Thoughts	1970	2.00	4.00	8.00
❏ 5068	Rocky Top/Take Me Home	1970	—	3.50	7.00
❏ 5098	I'm Alright/Pick of the Week	1970	—	3.50	7.00
❏ 5113	It Wasn't God Who Made Honky Tonk Angels/ Be Quiet Mind	1971	—	3.50	7.00
❏ 5125	Jim Dandy/Strangers	1971	—	3.50	7.00
❏ 5136	He Even Woke Me Up to Say Goodbye/ A Pillow That Whispers	1971	—	3.50	7.00
❏ 5146	Love of the Common People/Simple Words	1971	—	3.50	7.00
❏ 5151	There Oughta Be a Law/Too Much of You	1972	—	3.50	7.00
COLUMBIA					
❏ AE7 1056 [DJ]	Frosty the Snowman/Don't Wish Me a Merry Christmas	1972	2.00	4.00	8.00
—Christmas Seals record for 1972; promo only					
❏ AE7 1056 [PS]	Frosty the Snowman/ Don't Wish Me a Merry Christmas	1972	3.00	6.00	12.00
❏ 10041	What a Man, My Man Is/ Everything's Falling in Place	1974	—	2.00	4.00
❏ 10100	He Turns It Into Love Again/ Someone to Finish What You Started	1975	—	2.00	4.00
❏ 10160	I've Never Loved Anyone More/ He Worshipped Me	1975	—	2.00	4.00
❏ 10240	Paradise/You've Got It All Together Now	1975	—	2.00	4.00
❏ 10280	All the King's Horses/ If All I Have to Do Is Just Love You	1975	—	2.00	4.00
❏ 10337	Rodeo Cowboy/Dixieland, You Will Never Die	1976	—	2.00	4.00
❏ 10401	Sweet Talkin' Man/A Good Old Country Song	1976	—	2.00	4.00
❏ 10467	Wrap Your Love All Around Your Man/I Couldn't Be Lonely (Even If I Wanted To)	1976	—	2.00	4.00
❏ 10545	I Love What Love Is Doing to Me/Will I Ever Hear Those Church Bells Ring	1977	—	2.00	4.00

A

Number	Title (A Side/B Side)	Yr	VG	VG+	NM
❑ 10597	He Ain't You/				
	It's Your Love What Keeps Me Going	1977	—	2.00	4.00
❑ 10650	We Got Love/Sunshine Man	1977	—	2.00	4.00
❑ 10721	Rising Above It All/				
	My World Begins and Ends with You	1978	—	2.00	4.00
❑ 10809	Last Love of My Life/When You Marry for Money	1978	—	2.00	4.00
❑ 10909	Isn't It Always Love/A Child with You Tonight	1979	—	2.00	4.00
❑ 11006	I Love How You Love Me/Come As You Are	1979	—	2.00	4.00
❑ 11104	Sea of Heartbreak/Say You Will	1979	—	2.00	4.00
❑ 11296	Even Cowgirls Get the Blues/See Through Me	1980	—	2.00	4.00
❑ 11374	Blue Baby Blue/The Lonely Hearts Café	1980	—	2.00	4.00
❑ 45101	Stay There 'Til I Get There/I'd Run a Mile to You	1970	—	2.50	5.00
❑ 45190	No Love at All/I Found You Just in Time	1970	—	2.50	5.00
❑ 45251	Don't Wish Me Merry Christmas/Ding-a-Ling the				
	Christmas Bell	1970	—	3.00	6.00
❑ 45251 [PS]	Don't Wish Me Merry Christmas/				
	Ding-a-Ling the Christmas Bell	1970	2.00	4.00	8.00
❑ 45252	Rose Garden/Nothing Between Us	1970	—	2.50	5.00
❑ 45356	You're My Man/I'm Gonna Write a Song	1971	—	2.00	4.00
❑ 45429	How Can I Unlove You/				
	Don't Say Things You Don't Mean	1971	—	2.00	4.00
❑ 45527	Don't Wish Me Merry Christmas/				
	Ding-a-Ling the Christmas Bell	1971	—	2.50	5.00
❑ 45529	Cry/Simple Words	1972	—	2.00	4.00
❑ 45615	Listen to a Country Song/That's What Loving				
	You Has Meant to Me	1972	—	2.00	4.00
❑ 45692	Fool Me/What's Made Milwaukee Famous	1972	—	2.00	4.00
❑ 45768	Keep Me in Mind/Rodeo	1973	—	2.00	4.00
❑ 45843	Sing About Love/				
	Home Is Where I Hang My Head	1973	—	—	—
—Canceled?					
❑ 45857	Top of the World/I Wish I Was a Little Girl Again	1973	—	2.00	4.00
❑ 45918	Sing About Love/Fickle Fortune	1973	—	2.00	4.00
❑ 46009	Smile for Me/A Man Like Your Daddy	1974	—	2.00	4.00
❑ 46056	Talkin' to the Wall/I Want to Be a Part of You	1974	—	2.00	4.00
MCA					
❑ 52408	Running from the Real Thing/				
	The Heart of the Matter	1984	—	—	3.00
MERCURY					
❑ 870528-7	Under the Boardwalk/Turn the Page	1988	—	—	3.00
❑ 872154-7	The Angel Song (Glory to God in the Highest)/				
	When a Child Is Born	1988	—	—	3.00
—With Butch Baker					
❑ 872220-7	What He Does Best/It Goes Without Saying	1988	—	—	3.00
❑ 872602-7	How Many Hearts/How Many Hearts				
	(Long Version)	1989	—	—	3.00
❑ 888209-7	Didn't We Shine/We Must Be Doing It Right	1986	—	—	3.00
❑ 888597-7	It Goes Without Saying/				
	So Little Love in the World	1987	—	—	3.00
❑ 888839-7	Read Between the Lines/If This Ain't Love	1987	—	—	3.00
PERMIAN					
❑ 82000	You Can't Lose What You Never Had/This Time				
	the Heartbreak Wins	1983	—	2.00	4.00
❑ 82001	What I Learned from Loving You/Mr. Sundown	1983	—	2.00	4.00
❑ 82003	You're Welcome To Tonight/Your Kisses Lied	1983	—	2.00	4.00
—A-side with Gary Morris					
Albums					
CHART					
❑ CHM-1001 [M]	Ride, Ride, Ride	1967	5.00	10.00	20.00
❑ CHS-1001 [S]	Ride, Ride, Ride	1967	3.75	7.50	15.00
❑ CHM-1004 [M]	Promises, Promises	1968	5.00	10.00	20.00
❑ CHS-1004 [S]	Promises, Promises	1968	3.75	7.50	15.00
❑ CHS-1008	Big Girls Don't Cry	1969	3.75	7.50	15.00
❑ CHS-1009	The Best of Lynn Anderson	1969	3.75	7.50	15.00
❑ CHS-1013	With Love, From Lynn	1969	3.75	7.50	15.00
❑ CHS-1017	At Home with Lynn	1969	3.75	7.50	15.00
❑ CHS-1022	Songs That Made Country Girls Famous	1970	3.00	6.00	12.00
❑ CHS-1028	Uptown Country Girl	1970	3.00	6.00	12.00
❑ CHS-1032	Songs My Mother Wrote	1970	3.00	6.00	12.00
❑ CHS-1037	I'm Alright	1970	3.00	6.00	12.00
❑ CHS-1040	Lynn Anderson's Greatest Hits	1971	3.00	6.00	12.00
❑ CHS-1043	Lynn Anderson with Strings	1971	3.00	6.00	12.00
❑ CHS-1050 [(2)]	Lynn Anderson	1972	3.75	7.50	15.00
COLUMBIA					
❑ CS 1025	Stay There 'Til I Get There	1970	3.00	6.00	12.00
❑ C 30099	No Love at All	1970	3.00	6.00	12.00
❑ C 30411	Rose Garden	1970	2.50	5.00	10.00
❑ PC 30411	Rose Garden	197?	2.00	4.00	8.00
—Reissue					
❑ C 30793	You're My Man	1971	2.50	5.00	10.00
❑ CG 30902 [(2)]	The World of Lynn Anderson	1971	3.00	6.00	12.00
❑ C 30925	How Can I Unlove You	1971	2.50	5.00	10.00
❑ 3C 30957	Christmas Album	198?	2.00	4.00	8.00
—Reissue of KC 30957					
❑ KC 30957	Christmas Album	1971	3.00	6.00	12.00
❑ KC 31316	Cry	1972	2.50	5.00	10.00
❑ KC 31641	Lynn Anderson's Greatest Hits	1972	2.50	5.00	10.00
❑ PC 31641	Lynn Anderson's Greatest Hits	197?	2.00	4.00	8.00
—Reissue					
❑ KC 31647	Listen to a Country Song	1972	2.50	5.00	10.00
❑ KC 32078	Keep Me in Mind	1973	2.50	5.00	10.00
❑ KC 32429	Top of the World	1973	2.50	5.00	10.00
❑ KC 32719	Queens of Country	1974	2.50	5.00	10.00
❑ KC 32941	Smile for Me	1974	2.50	5.00	10.00
❑ KC 33293	What a Man, My Man Is	1974	2.50	5.00	10.00
❑ KC 33691	I've Never Loved Anyone More	1975	2.50	5.00	10.00
❑ PC 34089	All the King's Horses	1976	2.50	5.00	10.00
❑ PC 34308	Lynn Anderson's Greatest Hits Volume II	1976	2.50	5.00	10.00
❑ PC 34439	Wrap Your Love All Around Your Man	1977	2.50	5.00	10.00
❑ JC 34871	I Love What Love Is Doing to Me/He Ain't You	1977	2.50	5.00	10.00
❑ KC 35445	From the Inside	1978	2.50	5.00	10.00
❑ JC 35776	Outlaw Is Just a State of Mind	1979	2.50	5.00	10.00
❑ JC 36568	Even Cowgirls Get the Blues	1980	2.50	5.00	10.00
❑ FC 37354	Encore	1981	2.50	5.00	10.00
❑ PC 37354	Encore	1983	2.00	4.00	8.00
—Budget-line reissue					
COLUMBIA LIMITED EDITION					
❑ LE 10053	Stay Here 'Til I Get There	197?	2.50	5.00	10.00
HARMONY					
❑ KH 32433	Singing My Song	1973	2.00	4.00	8.00
MERCURY					
❑ 834625-1	What She Does Best	1988	2.00	4.00	8.00
MOUNTAIN DEW					
❑ 7047	Lynn Anderson	197?	2.50	5.00	10.00
PERMIAN					
❑ 8205	Back	1983	2.50	5.00	10.00
PICKWICK					
❑ PTP-2049 [(2)]	Lynn Anderson	1973	3.00	6.00	12.00
❑ SPC-3267	Flower of Love	197?	2.00	4.00	8.00
❑ SPC-3296	It Makes You Happy	197?	2.00	4.00	8.00
TIME-LIFE					
❑ STW-112	Country Music	1981	2.50	5.00	10.00

ANDERSON, LYNN, AND JERRY LANE
45s

Number	Title (A Side/B Side)	Yr	VG	VG+	NM
CHART					
❑ 1003	Keeping Up Appearances/				
	You've Gotta Be the Greatest	1967	2.00	4.00	8.00
—Reissue of 1425					
❑ 1300	For Better or For Worse/We're Different	1965	2.50	5.00	10.00
❑ 1425	Keeping Up Appearances/				
	You've Gotta Be the Greatest	1967	2.50	5.00	10.00

ANDERSON, MARTY
45s

Number	Title (A Side/B Side)	Yr	VG	VG+	NM
HIT					
❑ 216	One Dyin' and a-Buryin'/I'm Henry VIII, I Am	1965	2.50	5.00	10.00
—B-side by the Chords. (2)					

ANDERSON, MILDRED
45s

Number	Title (A Side/B Side)	Yr	VG	VG+	NM
BLUESVILLE					
❑ 804	Person to Person/Connections	1960	3.75	7.50	15.00
Albums					
BLUESVILLE					
❑ BVLP-1004 [M]	Person to Person	1960	12.50	25.00	50.00
—Blue and silver label					
❑ BVLP-1004 [M]	Person to Person	1964	6.25	12.50	25.00
—Blue label with trident logo					
❑ BVLP-1017 [M]	No More in Life	1961	12.50	25.00	50.00
—Blue and silver label					
❑ BVLP-1017 [M]	No More in Life	1964	6.25	12.50	25.00
—Blue label with trident logo					

ANDERSON, SONNY
45s

Number	Title (A Side/B Side)	Yr	VG	VG+	NM
IMPERIAL					
❑ 5634	Yes, I'm Gonna Love You/Lonely, Lonely Train	1959	12.50	25.00	50.00
❑ 5689	Our Love Could Never Be/Fool	1960	12.50	25.00	50.00

ANDERSON, VICKI Also see JAMES BROWN.
45s

Number	Title (A Side/B Side)	Yr	VG	VG+	NM
BROWNSTONE					
❑ 4202	I'm Too Tough for Mr. Big Stuff/Sound Funky	1971	—	3.00	6.00
❑ 4204	I'll Work It Out/In the Land of Milk and Honey	1971	—	3.00	6.00
❑ 4307	Don't Throw Your Love in the Garbage Can/In				
	the Land of Milk and Honey	1972	—	3.00	6.00
DELUXE					
❑ 6201	Wide Awake in a Dream/Nobody Cares	1966	2.00	4.00	8.00
FONTANA					
❑ 1527	Never, Never Let You Go (Part 1)/				
	Never, Never Let You Go (Part 2)	1965	3.00	6.00	12.00
KING					
❑ 6066	You Send Me/Unchain My Heart	1967	2.00	4.00	8.00
❑ 6091	Think/Nobody Cares	1967	2.50	5.00	10.00
—A-side: With James Brown					
❑ 6109	Tears of Joy/If You Don't Give Me	1967	2.00	4.00	8.00
❑ 6138	That Feelin' Is Real/Baby Don't You Know	1967	2.00	4.00	8.00
❑ 6152	You've Got the Power/What the World Needs				
	Now Is Love	1968	2.50	5.00	10.00
—A-side: With James Brown					
❑ 6221	What the World Needs Now Is Love/				
	I'll Work It Out	1969	2.00	4.00	8.00
❑ 6251	The Answer to Mother Popcorn (I Got a Mother				
	for You)/I'll Work It Out	1969	2.00	4.00	8.00
❑ 6274	Wide Awake in a Dream/I Want to Be in the Land				
	of Milk and Honey	1969	2.00	4.00	8.00
❑ 6293	Let It Be Me/Baby, Don't You Know	1970	2.50	5.00	10.00
—A-side: With James Brown					
❑ 6314	Never Find a Love Like Mine/No More				
	Heartaches, No More Pain	1970	2.00	4.00	8.00
❑ 6377	Message from the Soul Sisters Part 1/Yesterday	1971	2.00	4.00	8.00
SMASH					
❑ 1985	I Love You/Nobody Cares	1965	2.50	5.00	10.00
TUFF					
❑ 420	I Can't Stop Loving You/I Lost a Good Man	1964	2.50	5.00	10.00

ANDREWS, CHRIS
45s

Number	Title (A Side/B Side)	Yr	VG	VG+	NM
ATCO					
❑ 6385	Yesterday Man/Too Bad You Don't Want Me	1965	2.50	5.00	10.00
❑ 6414	Something On My Mind/				
	To Whom It May Concern	1966	2.50	5.00	10.00

Number	Title (A Side/B Side)	Yr	VG	VG+	NM
RCA VICTOR					
❏ 47-9746	Pretty Belinda/Maker of Mistakes	1969	2.00	4.00	8.00
ANDREWS, JIMMY					
45s					
BLUE JAY					
❏ 5003/4	Big City Playboy/Happy Guy	196?	375.00	750.00	1500.
ANDREWS, LEE, AND THE HEARTS					
45s					
ARGO					
❏ 1000	Tear Drops/The Girl Around the Corner	1957	12.50	25.00	50.00
CASINO					
❏ 110	Baby, Come Back/I Wonder	1958	7.50	15.00	30.00
❏ 452	Try the Impossible/Nobody's Home	1958	50.00	100.00	200.00
—All-black label					
❏ 452	Try the Impossible/Nobody's Home	1958	200.00	400.00	600.00
—With playing cards on label					
CHESS					
❏ 1665	Long Lonely Nights/The Clock	1957	3.75	7.50	15.00
—All-blue label					
❏ 1665	Long Lonely Nights/The Clock	1957	10.00	20.00	40.00
—Silver-top "chess pieces" label					
❏ 1675	Tear Drops/The Girl Around the Corner	1957	5.00	10.00	20.00
—All-blue label (if a "chess pieces" label exists, we aren't aware of it)					
CRIMSON					
❏ 1002	Oh My Love/Island of Love	1967	2.00	4.00	8.00
❏ 1009	Nevertheless/Island of Love	1967	2.00	4.00	8.00
❏ 1015	I've Had It/Little Bird	1968	2.00	4.00	8.00
GOTHAM					
❏ 318	Bluebird of Happiness/Show Me the Meringue	1956	50.00	100.00	200.00
❏ 320	Lonely Room/Leona	1956	75.00	150.00	300.00
❏ 321	Just Suppose/It's Me!	1956	75.00	150.00	300.00
GRAND					
❏ 156	Teardrops/The Girl Around the Corner	1962	3.00	6.00	12.00
❏ 157	Long Lonely Nights/The Clock	1962	3.00	6.00	12.00
LANA					
❏ 110	Long Lonely Nights/The Clock	196?	—	3.00	6.00
❏ 111	Try the Impossible/Nobody's Home	196?	—	3.00	6.00
❏ 112	Teardrops/The Girl Around the Corner	196?	—	3.00	6.00
—Lana records are reissues					
LOST-NITE					
❏ 104	The Fairest/Much Too Much	196?	—	3.00	6.00
❏ 106	The Bells of St. Mary/Much Too Much	196?	—	3.00	6.00
❏ 108	The White Cliffs of Dover/Much Too Much	196?	—	3.00	6.00
❏ 110	Maybe You'll Be There/Baby Come Back	196?	—	3.00	6.00
❏ 135	The Bluebird of Happiness/ Show Me the Meringue	196?	—	3.00	6.00
❏ 136	Lonely Room/Leona	196?	—	3.00	6.00
❏ 137	Just Suppose/It's Me	196?	—	3.00	6.00
❏ 176	Teardrops/The Girl Around the Corner	196?	—	3.00	6.00
❏ 190	Long Lonely Nights/The Clock	196?	—	3.00	6.00
❏ 193	Try the Impossible/Nobody's Home	196?	—	3.00	6.00
❏ 216	All I Ask Is Love/Maybe You'll Be There	196?	—	3.00	6.00
❏ 234	Glad to Be Here/Why Do I	196?	—	3.00	6.00
—All the above Lost-Nite records (three-digit numbers) are reissues					
❏ 1001	Cold Gray Dawn/All You Can Do	1968	2.00	4.00	8.00
❏ 1004	Oh My Love/Can't Do Without You	1968	2.00	4.00	8.00
❏ 1005	Quiet As It's Kept/Island of Love	1968	2.00	4.00	8.00
—The above three are NOT reissues					
MAIN LINE					
❏ 102	Long Lonely Nights/The Clock	1957	50.00	100.00	200.00
—Black label, Philadelphia address on label					
❏ 102	Long Lonely Nights/The Clock	1957	100.00	200.00	400.00
—Green label, no address					
❏ 102	Long Lonely Nights/The Clock	1962	7.50	15.00	30.00
—Black label, no address					
❏ 105	Teardrops/The Girl Around the Corner	1962	3.00	6.00	12.00
PARKWAY					
❏ 860	I'm Sorry, Pillow/Gee, But I'm Lonesome	1962	3.75	7.50	15.00
❏ 866	Looking Back/Operator	1963	3.75	7.50	15.00
RAINBOW					
❏ 252	Maybe You'll Be There/Baby Come Back	1954	100.00	200.00	400.00
—Black vinyl					
❏ 252	Maybe You'll Be There/Baby Come Back	1954	200.00	400.00	800.00
—Red vinyl					
❏ 252	Maybe You'll Be There/Baby Come Back	1962	2.50	5.00	10.00
—Reissue with large print					
❏ 256	White Cliffs of Dover/Much Too Much	1954	375.00	750.00	1500.
—Yellow label original					
❏ 256	White Cliffs of Dover/Much Too Much	1962	2.50	5.00	10.00
—Blue label reissue					
❏ 259	The Bells of St. Mary's/The Fairest	1954	150.00	300.00	600.00
—Yellow label original					
❏ 259	The Bells of St. Mary's/The Fairest	1962	2.50	5.00	10.00
—Blue label reissue					
RCA VICTOR					
❏ 47-8929	Quiet As It's Kept/You're Taking a Long Time Coming Back	1966	2.50	5.00	10.00
SWAN					
❏ 4065	I Miss You So/I've Got to Cry	1960	25.00	50.00	100.00
❏ 4076	A Night Like This/You Gave to Me	1961	37.50	75.00	150.00
❏ 4087	P.S. I Love You/I Cried	1961	50.00	100.00	200.00
UNITED ARTISTS					
❏ 123	Try the Impossible/Nobody's Home	1958	6.25	12.50	25.00
❏ 136	Why Do I/Glad to Be Here	1958	5.00	10.00	20.00
❏ 151	Maybe You'll Be There/All I Ask Is Love	1958	5.00	10.00	20.00
❏ 162	Boom/Just Suppose	1959	5.00	10.00	20.00
❏ 592	Try the Impossible/Nobody's Home	1963	3.75	7.50	15.00

Number	Title (A Side/B Side)	Yr	VG	VG+	NM
Albums					
COLLECTABLES					
❏ COL-5003	Gotham Recording Sessions	1982	3.00	6.00	12.00
❏ COL-5028	Biggest Hits	198?	3.00	6.00	12.00
LOST-NITE					
❏ LLP-1 [10]	The Best of Lee Andrews and the Hearts, Volume 1	1981	3.00	6.00	12.00
—Red vinyl; in die-cut cover with sticker					
❏ LLP-2 [10]	The Best of Lee Andrews and the Hearts, Volume 2	1981	3.00	6.00	12.00
—Red vinyl; in die-cut cover with sticker					
❏ LP-101 [M]	Biggest Hits	1964	12.50	25.00	50.00
—Black vinyl					
❏ LP-101 [M]	Biggest Hits	1964	25.00	50.00	100.00
—Yellow vinyl					
❏ LP-113 [M]	Lee Andrews and the Hearts Live	1965	12.50	25.00	50.00
ANDREWS, PATTY Also see THE ANDREWS SISTERS.					
45s					
CAPITOL					
❏ F3159	Without Love/Where To, My Love?	1955	3.00	6.00	12.00
❏ F3228	Suddenly There's a Valley/Booga-Da-Woog	1955	3.00	6.00	12.00
❏ F3268	I'll Forgive You/The Rains Came Down	1955	3.00	6.00	12.00
❏ F3344	Daybreak Blues/I Never Will Marry	1956	3.00	6.00	12.00
❏ F3403	Friendship Ring/Music Drives Me Crazy	1956	3.00	6.00	12.00
❏ F3495	Too Old to Rock and Roll/Broken	1956	3.75	7.50	15.00
DECCA					
❏ 9-27569	Too Young/Gotta Find Somebody to Love	1951	3.75	7.50	15.00
ANDREWS, RUBY					
45s					
ABC					
❏ 12215	I Got a Bone to Pick with You/ I Don't Know How to Love You	1976	2.00	4.00	8.00
❏ 12257	Queen of the Disco/A Little Fixin' Up (Will Keep Him From Messin' Up)	1977	2.00	4.00	8.00
❏ 12286	I Wanna Be Near You/Cinderfella	1977	2.00	4.00	8.00
ICHIBAN					
❏ 90-228	I Got What I Want at Home/To the Other Woman	1990	—	2.50	5.00
ZODIAC					
❏ 1001	Let's Get a Groove Going On (Part 1)/(Part 2)	1967	25.00	50.00	100.00
❏ 1003	Johnny's Gone Away/I Just Can't Get Enough	1967	20.00	40.00	80.00
❏ 1004	Casonova (Your Playing Days Are Over)/I Just Don't Believe It	1967	2.50	5.00	10.00
❏ 1006	Hey Boy Take a Chance on Love/Come to Me	1967	5.00	10.00	20.00
❏ 1007	You Can Run (But You Can't Hide)/ Wonderful Nite	1968	3.75	7.50	15.00
❏ 1010	The Love I Need/Just Loving You	1968	20.00	40.00	80.00
❏ 1012	I Let Him Take Me (In His Arms)/I Guess That Don't Make Me a Loser	1968	3.00	6.00	12.00
❏ 1015	You Made a Believer (Out of Me)/ Where Have You Gone	1969	3.00	6.00	12.00
❏ 1016	Help Yourself (Lover)/All the Way	1969	3.00	6.00	12.00
❏ 1017	Everybody Saw You/Can You Get Away	1970	3.00	6.00	12.00
❏ 1020	You Ole Boo Boo You/Gotta Break Away	1971	2.50	5.00	10.00
❏ 1022	Hound Dog/Away from the Crowd	1971	2.50	5.00	10.00
❏ 1023	Whatever It Takes to Please You (Part 1)/(Part 2)	1971	2.50	5.00	10.00
❏ 1024	My Love Is Coming Down/Good 'n' Plenty	1971	2.50	5.00	10.00
❏ 1032	You Got to Do the Same Thing/Didn't I Fool You	197?	2.50	5.00	10.00
Albums					
ABC					
❏ AB-1002	Genuine Ruby	1977	3.75	7.50	15.00
ICHIBAN					
❏ 1104	Kiss This	1991	3.75	7.50	15.00
ZODIAC					
❏ ZS 1001	Everybody Saw You	1970	20.00	40.00	80.00
ANDREWS SISTERS, THE Also see PATTY ANDREWS; BING CROSBY.					
45s					
CAPITOL					
❏ F-3567	Crazy Arms/I Want to Linger	1956	3.00	6.00	12.00
❏ F-3583	A Child's Christmas Song/Silver Bells	1956	3.75	7.50	15.00
❏ F-3658	Rum and Coca Cola/No Baby	1957	3.00	6.00	12.00
❏ F-3707	Give Me Back My Heart/Stars, Stars	1957	3.00	6.00	12.00
❏ F-3784	By His Word/I'm Goin' Home	1957	3.00	6.00	12.00
❏ F-3869	One Mistake/Melancholy Moon	1957	3.00	6.00	12.00
❏ F-3965	Torero/Sunshine	1958	3.00	6.00	12.00
❏ F-4144	I've Got an Invitation to a Dance/ My Love Is a Kitten	1959	2.50	5.00	10.00
DECCA					
❏ 9-23605	Bei Mir Bist Du Schoen/Joseph! Joseph!	1950	3.75	7.50	15.00
❏ 9-23606	Hold Tight, Hold Tight/Well Alright	1950	3.75	7.50	15.00
❏ 9-23607	Beat Me Daddy, Eight to the Bar/Scrub Me Mama with a Boogie Beat	1950	3.75	7.50	15.00
❏ 9-23608	(I'll Be With You) In Apple Blossom Time/ Rhumba Boogie	1950	3.75	7.50	15.00
—The above four comprise a box set (9-23) originally issued on 78s					
❏ 9-23608	(I'll Be With You) In Apple Blossom Time/ Rhumba Boogie	1955	3.00	6.00	12.00
—Black label, star under the first "C" of "Decca"					
❏ 23722	Christmas Island/Winter Wonderland	1960	2.50	5.00	10.00
—With Guy Lombardo and His Royal Canadians; color bars label					
❏ 9-23722	Christmas Island/Winter Wonderland	1950	3.75	7.50	15.00
—With Guy Lombardo and His Royal Canadians; lines label					
❏ 9-23722	Christmas Island/Winter Wonderland	1955	3.00	6.00	12.00
—With Guy Lombardo and His Royal Canadians; star label					
❏ 9-24705	I Can Dream, Can't I?/ The Wedding of Lili Marlene	1950	5.00	10.00	20.00
—78 released in 1949					
❏ 9-24748	Merry Christmas Polka/Christmas Candles	1950	5.00	10.00	20.00
—With Guy Lombardo and His Royal Canadians; from "Album No. A-9-95"; 78 released in 1949					

Number	Title (A Side/B Side)	Yr	VG	VG+	NM
❑ 9-27007	I Wanna Be Loved/				
	I've Just Got to Get Out of the Habit	1950	3.75	7.50	15.00
❑ 9-27115	Can't We Talk It Over/				
	There Will Never Be Another You	1950	3.75	7.50	15.00
❑ 9-27202	The Glory of Love/A Rainy Day Refrain	1950	3.75	7.50	15.00
—With Guy Lombardo and His Royal Canadians					
❑ 9-27242	Jing-a-Ling/Parade of the Wooden Soldiers	1950	3.75	7.50	15.00
❑ 9-27251	I'd Like to Hitch a Ride with Santa Claus/(Sweet				
	Angie) The Christmas Tree Angel	1950	3.75	7.50	15.00
❑ 9-27252	A Bushel and a Peck/Guys and Dolls	1950	3.75	7.50	15.00
❑ 9-27310	Sleigh Ride/Telephone Song	1950	5.00	10.00	20.00
❑ 9-27349	Go West, Young Man/Along the Navaho Trail	1950	3.75	7.50	15.00
❑ 9-27414	A Penny a Kiss — A Penny A Hug/				
	Zing Zing, Zoom Zoom	1951	3.75	7.50	15.00
❑ 9-27421	Between Two Trees/I Wish I Knew	1951	3.75	7.50	15.00
❑ 9-27432	Three O'Clock in the Morning/				
	Lullaby of Broadway	1951	3.75	7.50	15.00
❑ 9-27537	I Remember Mama/My Mom	1951	3.75	7.50	15.00
❑ 9-27635	It Never Entered My Mind/I'm in Love Again	1951	3.75	7.50	15.00
❑ 9-27652	Night on the Waters/				
	Dimples and Cherry Cheeks	1951	3.75	7.50	15.00
❑ 9-27700	How Many Times/I Used to Love You	1951	3.75	7.50	15.00
—With Tommy Dorsey and His Orchestra					
❑ 9-27715	Can We Talk It Over/There Will Never Be				
	Another You	1951	3.75	7.50	15.00
❑ 9-27757	Carioca/Daddy	1951	3.75	7.50	15.00
❑ 9-27760	Lying in the Way/Love Is Such a Cheat	1951	3.75	7.50	15.00
❑ 9-27834	Nobody's Darling But Mine/Goodbye, Darling	1951	3.75	7.50	15.00
❑ 9-27858	The Three Bells/The Windmill Song	1951	3.75	7.50	15.00
❑ 9-27878	Blonde Sailor/All the World to Me	1951	3.75	7.50	15.00
❑ 9-27894	Down in the Valley/Red River Valley	1951	3.75	7.50	15.00
❑ 9-27910	I'm on a Seesaw of Love/Play Me a Hurtin' Tune	1951	3.75	7.50	15.00
—With Guy Lombardo and His Royal Canadians					
❑ 9-27979	Wondering/Poor Whip-Poor-Will	1952	3.75	7.50	15.00
❑ 9-28042	Why Worry/That Ever Lovin' Rag	1952	3.75	7.50	15.00
❑ 9-28116	Dreams Come Tumbling Down/Music Lessons	1952	3.75	7.50	15.00
❑ 9-28143	Linger Awhile/Wabash Blues	1952	3.75	7.50	15.00
—With Russ Morgan and His Orchestra					
❑ 9-28163	Where Is Your Wandering Mother Tonight/Hang				
	Your Head in Shame	1952	3.75	7.50	15.00
—A-side with Red Foley					
❑ 9-28276	Idle Chatter/One for the Wonder	1952	3.75	7.50	15.00
❑ 9-28294	Isle of Golden Dreams/Nalani	1952	3.00	6.00	12.00
❑ 9-28295	Kings Serenade/Cockeyed Mayor of				
	Kannakakai	1952	3.00	6.00	12.00
❑ 9-28296	Fair Hawaii/Ke Kali Nei Au	1952	3.00	6.00	12.00
❑ 9-28297	Good Night, Aloha/Malihini Mele	1952	3.00	6.00	12.00
—Above 4 with Alfred Apaka and His Orchestra					
❑ 9-28342	Adios/Carmen's Boogie	1952	3.75	7.50	15.00
❑ 9-28480	Don't Be That Way/Sing, Sing, Sing	1952	3.00	6.00	12.00
❑ 9-28481	Piccolo Pete/If I Had a Boy Like You	1952	3.00	6.00	12.00
❑ 9-28482	East of the Sun/In the Mood	1952	3.00	6.00	12.00
❑ 9-28483	Old Don Juan/The Mambo Man	1952	3.00	6.00	12.00
❑ 9-28492	No Deposit, No Return/You Blew Me a Kiss	1952	3.00	6.00	12.00
❑ 9-28680	Fugue for Tinhorns/Now That I'm in Love	1953	3.75	7.50	15.00
❑ 9-28773	You Too, You Too?/Tegucigalpa	1953	3.75	7.50	15.00
❑ 9-28929	This Little Piggie Went to Market/				
	Love Sends a Little Gift of Roses	1953	3.75	7.50	15.00
❑ 9-29149	My Love, The Blues and Me/				
	There's a Rainbow in the Valley	1954	3.75	7.50	15.00
❑ 9-29995	Rum and Coca Cola/Jack, Jack, Jack	1956	3.00	6.00	12.00
DOT					
❑ 16433	Pistol Packin' Mama/Ti-Pi-Tin	1963	2.00	4.00	8.00
❑ 16497	Mr. Bass Man/My Midnight Prison	1963	2.00	4.00	8.00
KAPP					
❑ 309	One, Two, Three, Four/I've Got to Pass Your				
	House	1959	3.00	6.00	12.00
MCA					
❑ 60012	Beer Barrel Polka/Pennsylvania Polka	1973	—	2.00	4.00
❑ 60040	Boogie Woogie Bugle Boy/Rum and Coca-Cola	1974	—	2.00	4.00
❑ 60041	Bei Mir Bist Du Schoen/(I'll Be With You) In Apple				
	Blossom Time	1974	—	2.00	4.00
❑ 60042	Don't Sit Under the Apple Tree/I Can Dream,				
	Can't I?	1974	—	2.00	4.00
❑ 65016	Take Me Out to the Ball Game/In the Good Old				
	Summertime	1973	—	2.00	4.00
❑ 65020	Christmas Island/Winter Wonderland	1973	—	2.00	4.00
—With Guy Lombardo and His Royal Canadians; black label with rainbow					
❑ 65020	Christmas Island/Winter Wonderland	1980	—	—	3.00
—With Guy Lombardo and His Royal Canadians; blue label with rainbow					
PARAMOUNT					
❑ 0257	Rum and Coca-Cola/Pennsylvania Polka	1973	—	2.50	5.00
7-Inch Extended Plays					
DECCA					
❑ ED 2006	I Can Dream, Can't I?/I Wanna Be Loved//I Don't				
	Know Why/Jealous	195?	3.75	7.50	15.00
❑ ED 2006 [PS]	The Andrews Sisters, Vol. 1	195?	3.75	7.50	15.00
Albums					
ABC					
❑ 4003	Sixteen Great Performances	1975	3.00	6.00	12.00
CAPITOL					
❑ T 790 [M]	The Andrews Sisters in Hi-Fi	1957	7.50	15.00	30.00
❑ T 860 [M]	Fresh and Fancy Free	1957	7.50	15.00	30.00
❑ T 973 [M]	The Dancing Twenties	1957	7.50	15.00	30.00
❑ DT 1924 [R]	The Hits of the Andrews Sisters	1963	3.00	6.00	12.00
❑ T 1924 [M]	The Hits of the Andrews Sisters	1963	5.00	10.00	20.00
DECCA					
❑ DL 4019 [M]	Curtain Call	1956	7.50	15.00	30.00
❑ DL 5065 [10]	Tropical Songs	1950	10.00	20.00	40.00
❑ DL 5120 [10]	The Andrews Sisters	1951	10.00	20.00	40.00
❑ DL 5155 [10]	Club 15	1951	10.00	20.00	40.00

Number	Title (A Side/B Side)	Yr	VG	VG+	NM
❑ DL 5264 [10]	Berlin Songs	1951	10.00	20.00	40.00
❑ DL 5282 [10]	Christmas Cheer	1950	10.00	20.00	40.00
—Also see "Crosby, Bing"					
❑ DL 5306 [10]	I Love to Tell the Story	1952	10.00	20.00	40.00
❑ DL 5423 [10]	My Isle of Golden Dreams	1953	10.00	20.00	40.00
❑ DL 5438 [10]	Sing, Sing, Sing	1953	10.00	20.00	40.00
❑ DL 8354 [M]	Jingle Bells	1956	7.50	15.00	30.00
❑ DL 8360 [M]	The Andrews Sisters — By Popular Demand	1957	7.50	15.00	30.00
DOT					
❑ DLP 3406 [M]	The Andrews Sisters' Greatest Hits	1962	3.75	7.50	15.00
❑ DLP 3452 [M]	Great Golden Hits	1962	3.75	7.50	15.00
❑ DLP 3529 [M]	Present	1963	3.00	6.00	12.00
❑ DLP 3567 [M]	Great Country Hits	1963	3.00	6.00	12.00
❑ DLP 3632 [M]	The Andrews Sisters Go Hawaiian	1964	3.00	6.00	12.00
❑ DLP 25406 [S]	The Andrews Sisters' Greatest Hits	1962	5.00	10.00	20.00
❑ DLP 25452 [S]	Great Golden Hits	1962	5.00	10.00	20.00
❑ DLP 25529 [S]	Present	1963	3.75	7.50	15.00
❑ DLP 25567 [S]	Great Country Hits	1963	3.75	7.50	15.00
❑ DLP 25632 [S]	The Andrews Sisters Go Hawaiian	1964	3.75	7.50	15.00
HAMILTON					
❑ HLP 124 [M]	Pennsylvania Polka	196?	3.00	6.00	12.00
❑ HLP 12124 [S]	Pennsylvania Polka	196?	3.75	7.50	15.00
MCA					
❑ 739	Near You	198?	2.00	4.00	8.00
—Reissue of Vocalion album					
❑ 908	Rarities	198?	2.00	4.00	8.00
❑ 2-4024	The Best of the Andrews Sisters	1973	3.75	7.50	15.00
❑ 2-4093 [(2)]	The Best of the Andrews Sisters, Vol. 2	197?	3.75	7.50	15.00
❑ 24015	Christmas	1987	2.00	4.00	8.00
—Reissue					
❑ 27081	Sixteen Great Performances	1980	2.00	4.00	8.00
—Reissue of ABC 4003					
❑ 27082	Boogie Woogie Bugle Girls	1980	2.00	4.00	8.00
—Reissue of Paramount 6075					
PARAMOUNT					
❑ PAS-1023	In the Mood	1974	3.75	7.50	15.00
❑ PAS-6075	Boogie Woogie Bugle Girls	1973	3.00	6.00	12.00
PICKWICK					
❑ PC-3094 [M]	Don't Sit Under the Apple Tree	196?	3.75	7.50	15.00
❑ SPC-3094 [S]	Don't Sit Under the Apple Tree	196?	3.00	6.00	12.00
❑ SPC-3382	Sing! Sing! Sing!	197?	2.50	5.00	10.00
VOCALION					
❑ VL 3611 [M]	Near You	196?	3.00	6.00	12.00

ANGEL
45s

CASABLANCA

Number	Title (A Side/B Side)	Yr	VG	VG+	NM
❑ 853	Rock and Rollers/(B-side unknown)	1976	—	2.50	5.00
❑ 878	That Magic Touch/Big Boy (Let's Do It Again)	1977	—	2.50	5.00
❑ 903	Winter Song/Can You Feel It	1977	—	2.50	5.00
❑ 903 DJ [DJ]	The Winter Song/The Christmas Song	1978	—	3.00	6.00
❑ 914	Ain't Gonna Eat Out My Heart Anymore/Flying				
	with Broken Wings (Without You)	1978	—	2.50	5.00
❑ 933	Stick Like Glue/Don't Leave Me Lonely	1978	—	2.50	5.00
❑ 963	Bad Time/Don't Take Your Love	1979	—	2.00	4.00
❑ 2240	20th Century Woman/Can You Feel It	1980	—	2.00	4.00

Albums

CASABLANCA

Number	Title (A Side/B Side)	Yr	VG	VG+	NM
❑ NBLP 7021	Angel	1975	3.00	6.00	12.00
❑ NBLP 7028	Helluva Band	1976	3.00	6.00	12.00
❑ NBLP 7043	On Earth As It Is in Heaven	1977	3.00	6.00	12.00
❑ NBLP 7085	White Hot	1977	3.00	6.00	12.00
❑ NBLP 7127	Sinful	1979	3.00	6.00	12.00
❑ NBLP 7203 [(2)]	Live Without a Net	1980	3.75	7.50	15.00

ANGEL, JOHNNY
45s

EXCELLO

Number	Title (A Side/B Side)	Yr	VG	VG+	NM
❑ 2077	I Realize/Baby I'm Confessin'	1956	6.25	12.50	25.00
FELSTED					
❑ 8633	Lady of Spain/Without Her Heart	1961	5.00	10.00	20.00
❑ 8646	Mashed Potatoe Stomp/One More Tomorrow	1962	5.00	10.00	20.00
❑ 8659	Looking for a Fool/Roller Motion	1962	5.00	10.00	20.00
GARDENA					
❑ 117	All Night Party/Baby, You've Got Soul	1961	3.75	7.50	15.00
IMPERIAL					
❑ 5673	Falling Teardrops/Doubt	1960	10.00	20.00	40.00
JAF					
❑ 2024	Lonely Nights/Seven Words	1961	3.75	7.50	15.00
LIBERTY					
❑ 55895	Summertime Blues/Biggest Part of Me	1966	2.00	4.00	8.00
POWER					
❑ 250	Starlight/The Story of Love	1959	30.00	60.00	120.00
SWAN					
❑ 4263	This Is the Night for Love/You've Been Wrong	1966	10.00	20.00	40.00
VIN					
❑ 1004	Teenage Wedding/Baby, It's Love	1958	6.25	12.50	25.00

ANGEL, JOHNNY (2) Real name: Henry Pascua
45s

CAPRICE

Number	Title (A Side/B Side)	Yr	VG	VG+	NM
❑ 2386	The Promise of Love/Fallin' in Love	1986	—	2.00	4.00
❑ 2386 [PS]	The Promise of Love/Fallin' in Love	1986	—	2.00	4.00

ANGEL, JOHNNY T.
45s

BELL

Number	Title (A Side/B Side)	Yr	VG	VG+	NM
❑ 45472	Tell Laura I Love Her/The Way I Feel Tonight	1974	—	2.00	4.00
YORKSVILLE					
❑ 45090	Tell Laura I Love Her/The Way I Feel Tonight	1974	—	3.00	6.00

A

Number	Title (A Side/B Side)	Yr	VG	VG+	NM

ANGEL, MARIAN
45s
JUBILEE

Number	Title (A Side/B Side)	Yr	VG	VG+	NM
❑ 5508	It's Gonna Be Alright/Tomorrow's Fool	1965	2.50	5.00	10.00

ANGELOU, MAYA
Albums
LIBERTY

❑ LRP-3028 [M]	Miss Calypso	1958	12.50	25.00	50.00

ANGELS, THE (1) Female vocal group.
45s
ASCOT

❑ 2139	Irresistible/Cotton Fields	1963	3.00	6.00	12.00

CAPRICE

❑ 107	'Til/A Moment Ago	1961	5.00	10.00	20.00
—With semicircular "Caprice" logo					
❑ 107	'Til/A Moment Ago	1961	7.50	15.00	30.00
—With horizontal "Caprice" logo; B-side listed as "A Moment Ago" but plays "Cotton Fields"					
❑ 112	Cry Baby Cry/That's All I Ask of You	1962	5.00	10.00	20.00
❑ 116	Everybody Loves a Lover/Blow Joe	1962	3.75	7.50	15.00
❑ 118	You Should Have Told Me/I'd Be Good for You	1962	3.75	7.50	15.00
❑ 121	Cotton Fields/A Moment Ago	1963	3.75	7.50	15.00

POLYDOR

❑ 14222	You're All I Need to Get By/ Poppa's Side of the Bed	1974	—	2.50	5.00

RCA VICTOR

❑ 47-9129	I Had a Dream I Lost You/What to Do	1967	2.50	5.00	10.00
❑ 47-9246	Go Out and Play/You'll Never Get to Heaven (If You Break My Heart)	1967	2.50	5.00	10.00
❑ 47-9404	You're the Cause of It/With Love	1967	2.50	5.00	10.00
❑ 47-9541	The Medley: Moments to Remember-Theme from A Summer Place-One Summer Night/ If I Didn't Love You	1968	2.50	5.00	10.00
❑ 47-9612	But for Love/The Man with the Green Eyes	1968	2.50	5.00	10.00
❑ 47-9681	Merry Go Round/So Nice (Samba De Verao)	1968	2.50	5.00	10.00

SMASH

❑ 1834	My Boyfriend's Back/(Love Me) Now	1963	4.00	8.00	16.00
❑ 1854	I Adore Him/Thank You and Goodnight	1963	3.75	7.50	15.00
❑ 1854 [PS]	I Adore Him/Thank You and Goodnight	1963	15.00	30.00	60.00
❑ 1870	Wow Wow Wee (He's the Boy for Me)/ Snowflakes and Teardrops	1964	3.75	7.50	15.00
❑ 1885	Little Beatle Boy/Java	1964	5.00	10.00	20.00
❑ 1915	Jamaica Joe/Dream Boy	1964	3.75	7.50	15.00
❑ 1915 [PS]	Jamaica Joe/Dream Boy	1964	15.00	30.00	60.00
❑ 1931	World Without Love/The Boy from Crosstown	1964	3.75	7.50	15.00
❑ 1931 [PS]	World Without Love/The Boy from Crosstown	1964	20.00	40.00	80.00
❑ 810325-7	My Boyfriend's Back/Thank You and Goodnight	1983	—	2.00	4.00
—Reissue in stereo					

Albums
ASCOT

❑ AM 13009 [M]	The Angels Sing—Twelve of Their Greatest Hits	1964	6.25	12.50	25.00
❑ ALS 16009 [S]	The Angels Sing—Twelve of Their Greatest Hits	1964	7.50	15.00	30.00

CAPRICE

❑ LP 1001 [M]	...And the Angels Sing	1962	30.00	60.00	120.00
❑ SLP 1001 [S]	...And the Angels Sing	1962	50.00	100.00	200.00

COLLECTABLES

❑ COL-5085	My Boyfriend's Back: Golden Classics	198?	2.50	5.00	10.00

SMASH

❑ MGS-27039 [M]	My Boyfriend's Back	1963	10.00	20.00	40.00
❑ MGS-27048 [M]	A Halo to You	1964	10.00	20.00	40.00
❑ SRS-67039 [S]	My Boyfriend's Back	1963	15.00	30.00	60.00
❑ SRS-67048 [S]	A Halo to You	1964	15.00	30.00	60.00

ANGELS, THE (2) Male vocal group.
45s
GEE

❑ 1024	Glory of Love/It's You I Love Best	1956	15.00	30.00	60.00

GRAND

❑ 115	Wedding Bells/Times Have Changed	1954	12.50	25.00	50.00
—With address on label					
❑ 115	Wedding Bells/Times Have Changed	1954	100.00	200.00	400.00
—With no address on label					
❑ 121	A Lovely Way to Spend An Evening/ You're Still My Baby	1954	12.50	25.00	50.00
—With address on label					
❑ 121	A Lovely Way to Spend An Evening/ You're Still My Baby	1954	125.00	250.00	500.00
—With no address on label					

LOST-NITE

❑ 323	Wedding Bells Are Ringing in My Ears/ Times Have Changed	197?	—	2.50	5.00
❑ 327	A Lovely Way to Spend An Evening/ You're Still My Baby	197?	—	2.50	5.00
—Reissue					

ANGELS, THE (3) Different male vocal group than (2). Also see THE SAFARIS.
45s
TAWNY

❑ 101	A Lover's Poem (To Him)/ A Lover's Poem (To Her)	1959	10.00	20.00	40.00

ANGELS, THE (U)
45s
CAMEO

❑ 250	You Turn Me On/Raining Teardrops	1963	3.75	7.50	15.00

ANGIE AND THE CHICKLETTES
45s
APT

❑ 25080	Treat Him Tender Maureen (Now That Ringo Belongs to You)/Tommy	1965	7.50	15.00	30.00

ANGLO-AMERICANS, THE
45s
CHATTAHOOCHIE

❑ 705	The Music Never Stops/Are You Ready for This?	1966	7.50	15.00	30.00

ANGLOS, THE
45s
ORBIT

❑ 201	Incense/You're Fooling Me	1965	12.50	25.00	50.00
—Steve Winwood is on this record, his first					

SCEPTER

❑ 12204	Since You've Been Gone/A Small Town Boy	1967	5.00	10.00	20.00

ANIMALS, THE Includes "Eric Burdon and the Animals." Also see ERIC BURDON; ERIC BURDON AND WAR; ALAN PRICE; HILTON VALENTINE.
12-Inch Singles
I.R.S.

❑ SP-70969 [DJ]	The Night (same on both sides)	1983	2.50	5.00	10.00

45s
ABKCO

❑ 4025	House of the Rising Sun/Bring It On Home to Me	1973	2.00	4.00	8.00
—Contains the full-length version of A-side					
❑ 4026	We Gotta Get Out of This Place/It's My Life	1973	—	2.00	4.00
❑ 4037	Don't Let Me Be Misunderstood/ Talkin' About You	1973	—	2.00	4.00
❑ 4038	I'm Cryin'/Boom Boom	1973	—	2.00	4.00

I.R.S.

❑ 9920	The Night/No John No	1983	—	2.50	5.00
❑ 9923	Love Is For All Time/It's Too Late	1983	—	2.50	5.00

JET

❑ XW-1070	Fire on the Sun/Riverside County	1977	—	3.00	6.00

MGM

❑ CS-11-5	Celebrity Scene: The Animals	1967	20.00	40.00	80.00
—Box set of five singles (13791-13795). Price includes box, all 5 singles, jukebox title strips, bio. Records are sometimes found by themselves, so they are also listed separately.					
❑ KGC 178	Gonna Take You Back to Walker/ Baby Let Me Take You Home	196?	2.00	4.00	8.00
—Reissue label					
❑ KGC 179	The House of the Rising Sun/I'm Crying	196?	2.50	5.00	10.00
—Reissue label; A-side, despite being labeled 2:58, actually plays 4:29					
❑ KGC 180	Don't Let Me Be Misunderstood/Boom Boom	196?	2.00	4.00	8.00
—Reissue label					
❑ KGC 181	We Gotta Get Out of This Place/ Don't Bring Me Down	196?	2.00	4.00	8.00
—Reissue label					
❑ KGC 182	It's My Life/Inside Looking Out	196?	2.00	4.00	8.00
—Reissue label					
❑ 13242	Gonna Send You Back to Walker (Gonna Send You Back to Georgia)/ Baby, Let Me Take You Home	1964	3.75	7.50	15.00
❑ 13264	The House of the Rising Sun/Talkin' About You	1964	3.75	7.50	15.00
❑ 13264 [PS]	The House of the Rising Sun/Talkin' About You	1964	7.50	15.00	30.00
❑ 13274	I'm Crying/Take It Easy Baby	1964	3.75	7.50	15.00
❑ 13274 [PS]	I'm Crying/Take It Easy Baby	1964	6.25	12.50	25.00
❑ 13298	Boom Boom/Blue Feeling	1964	3.75	7.50	15.00
❑ 13298 [PS]	Boom Boom/Blue Feeling	1964	6.25	12.50	25.00
❑ 13311	Don't Let Me Be Misunderstood/Club A-Go-Go	1964	3.75	7.50	15.00
❑ 13339	Bring It On Home to Me/For Miss Caulker	1965	3.00	6.00	12.00
❑ 13339 [PS]	Bring It On Home to Me/For Miss Caulker	1965	6.25	12.50	25.00
❑ 13382	We Gotta Get Out of This Place/I Can't Believe It	1965	3.00	6.00	12.00
❑ 13414	It's My Life/I'm Going to Change the World	1965	3.00	6.00	12.00
❑ 13468	Inside-Looking Out/You're On My Mind	1966	3.00	6.00	12.00
❑ 13514	Don't Bring Me Down/Cheating	1966	3.00	6.00	12.00
❑ 13582	See See Rider/She'll Return It	1966	2.50	5.00	10.00
—Starting here, records are by "Eric Burdon and the Animals"					
❑ 13636	Help Me Girl/That Ain't Where It's At	1966	2.50	5.00	10.00
❑ 13721	When I Was Young/A Girl Called Sandoz	1967	2.50	5.00	10.00
❑ 13769	San Franciscan Nights/Good Times	1967	2.50	5.00	10.00
❑ 13769 [PS]	San Franciscan Nights/Good Times	1967	6.25	12.50	25.00
❑ 13791	Don't Bring Me Down/When I Was Young	1967	3.00	6.00	12.00
❑ 13792	See See Rider/Hey Gyp	1967	3.00	6.00	12.00
❑ 13793	Inside-Looking Out/Help Me Girl	1967	3.00	6.00	12.00
❑ 13794	San Franciscan Nights/Good Times	1967	3.00	6.00	12.00
❑ 13795	It's All Meat/The Other Side of This Life	1967	3.00	6.00	12.00
❑ 13868	Monterey/Ain't That So	1967	2.50	5.00	10.00
❑ 13868 [PS]	Monterey/Ain't That So	1967	6.25	12.50	25.00
❑ 13917	Anything/It's All Meat	1968	2.50	5.00	10.00
❑ 13939	Sky Pilot (Part 1)/Sky Pilot (Part 2)	1968	2.00	4.00	8.00
—Second pressings have blue and gold labels					
❑ 13939	Sky Pilot (Part 1)/Sky Pilot (Part 2)	1968	2.50	5.00	10.00
—First pressings have black labels					
❑ 14013	River Deep, Mountain High/White Houses	1968	2.00	4.00	8.00

Albums
ABKCO

❑ AB-4226 [(2)]	The Best of the Animals	1973	3.00	6.00	12.00
❑ AB-4324 [M]	The Best of the Animals	1987	2.50	5.00	10.00
—With alternate version of "We Gotta Get Out of This Place"					

ACCORD

❑ SN-7193	Looking Back	1981	2.00	4.00	8.00
❑ SN-7235	The Animals with Eric Burdon	1982	2.00	4.00	8.00

I.R.S.

❑ SP 70037	The Ark	1983	2.50	5.00	10.00
❑ SP 70043	Rip It to Shreds: Their Greatest Hits Live	1984	2.50	5.00	10.00

JET/UA

❑ JT-LA790-H	Before We Were So Rudely Interrupted	1977	2.50	5.00	10.00
—As "The Original Animals"					

MGM

❑ E-4264 [M]	The Animals	1964	7.50	15.00	30.00
—"The House of the Rising Sun" is the edited 45 version					
❑ E-4264 [M]	The Animals	1964	25.00	50.00	100.00
—Yellow label promo					

Number	Title (A Side/B Side)	Yr	VG	VG+	NM
❑ SE-4264 [R]	The Animals	1964	6.25	12.50	25.00

—"The House of the Rising Sun" is the edited 45 version (rechanneled, like the rest of the LP)

Number	Title (A Side/B Side)	Yr	VG	VG+	NM
❑ E-4281 [M]	The Animals On Tour	1965	7.50	15.00	30.00
❑ E-4281 [M]	The Animals On Tour	1965	25.00	50.00	100.00

—Yellow label promo

❑ SE-4281 [R]	The Animals On Tour	1965	6.25	12.50	25.00
❑ E-4305 [M]	Animal Tracks	1965	10.00	20.00	40.00
❑ E-4305 [M]	Animal Tracks	1965	37.50	75.00	150.00

—Yellow label promo

❑ SE-4305 [R]	Animal Tracks	1965	7.50	15.00	30.00
❑ E-4324 [M]	The Best of the Animals	1966	5.00	10.00	20.00

—This album was the first to contain the full-length version of "House of the Rising Sun."

❑ E-4324 [M]	The Best of the Animals	1966	20.00	40.00	80.00

—Yellow label promo

❑ SE-4324 [R]	The Best of the Animals	1966	6.25	12.50	25.00
❑ E-4384 [M]	Animalization	1966	6.25	12.50	25.00
❑ E-4384 [M]	Animalization	1966	25.00	50.00	100.00

—Yellow label promo

❑ SE-4384 [P]	Animalization	1966	7.50	15.00	30.00

—All stereo except "Inside Looking Out," which is rechanneled.

❑ E-4414 [M]	Animalism	1966	6.25	12.50	25.00
❑ E-4414 [M]	Animalism	1966	25.00	50.00	100.00

—Yellow label promo

❑ SE-4414 [S]	Animalism	1966	7.50	15.00	30.00
❑ E-4433 [M]	Eric Is Here	1967	3.75	7.50	15.00
❑ SE-4433 [S]	Eric Is Here	1967	5.00	10.00	20.00
❑ E-4454 [M]	The Best of Eric Burdon and the Animals, Vol. 2	1967	5.00	10.00	20.00
❑ SE-4454 [P]	The Best of Eric Burdon and the Animals, Vol. 2	1967	5.00	10.00	20.00
❑ E-4484 [M]	Winds of Change	1967	5.00	10.00	20.00
❑ SE-4484 [S]	Winds of Change	1967	6.25	12.50	25.00
❑ E-4537 [M]	The Twain Shall Meet	1968	5.00	10.00	20.00
❑ SE-4537 [S]	The Twain Shall Meet	1968	6.25	12.50	25.00
❑ E-4553 [M]	Every One of Us	1968	12.50	25.00	50.00

—Mono is promo only (yellow label)

❑ SE-4553 [S]	Every One of Us	1968	6.25	12.50	25.00
❑ SE-4591 [(2)]	Love Is	1968	12.50	25.00	50.00
❑ SE-4602	Greatest Hits of Eric Burdon and the Animals	1969	3.75	7.50	15.00
❑ ST 90414 [R]	The Animals On Tour	1965	10.00	20.00	40.00

—Capitol Record Club edition

❑ T 90414 [M]	The Animals On Tour	1965	12.50	25.00	50.00

—Capitol Record Club edition

❑ T 90571 [M]	Animal Tracks	1965	12.50	25.00	50.00

—Capitol Record Club edition

❑ KAO 90622 [M]	The Best of the Animals	1966	10.00	20.00	40.00

—Capitol Record Club edition

❑ SKAO 90622 [R]	The Best of the Animals	1966	10.00	20.00	40.00

—Capitol Record Club edition; black label

❑ SKAO 90622 [R]	The Best of the Animals	1969	7.50	15.00	30.00

—Capitol Record Club edition; blue and gold label

❑ T 90687 [M]	The Animals	1966	12.50	25.00	50.00

—Capitol Record Club edition

❑ ST 90923 [P]	Animalization	1966	12.50	25.00	50.00

—Capitol Record Club edition

❑ T 90923 [M]	Animalization	1966	12.50	25.00	50.00

—Capitol Record Club edition

❑ ST-91550 [S]	Every One of Us	1968	10.00	20.00	40.00

—Capitol Record Club edition; black label

PICKWICK

❑ SPC-3330	The Early Animals with Eric Burdon	1971	2.00	4.00	8.00

POLYDOR

❑ 829091-1 [M]	Animalization	1986	2.00	4.00	8.00

SCEPTER CITATION

❑ 18026	The Best of the Animals	1972	2.00	4.00	8.00

SPRINGBOARD

❑ SPB-4025	The Best of the Animals	1972	2.00	4.00	8.00
❑ SPB-4065	The Night Time Is the Right Time	1973	2.00	4.00	8.00

WAND

❑ WDS-690	In the Beginning	1970	2.50	5.00	10.00

ANIMATED EGG, THE
Albums
ALSHIRE

❑ SF-32700	The Animated Egg	1967	12.50	25.00	50.00

ANITA AND TH' SO-AND-SO'S See ANITA KERR SINGERS.

ANKA, PAUL
45s
ABC-PARAMOUNT

❑ 45-PRO-104	(You Can) Share Your Love/I Talk to You (On the Telephone)	1958	7.50	15.00	30.00

—Evidently a custom pressing for Paul Anka's fan club

❑ S 296-1 [S]	(All of a Sudden) My Heart Sings/(B-side unknown)	1959	10.00	20.00	40.00
❑ S 296-2 [S]	(titles unknown)	1959	10.00	20.00	40.00
❑ S 296-3 [S]	C'est Si Bon/Comme Ci, Comme Ca	1959	10.00	20.00	40.00
❑ S 296-4 [S]	Melodie D'Amour/I Miss You So	1959	10.00	20.00	40.00
❑ S 296-5 [S]	I Love Paris/If You Love Me, Really Love Me	1959	10.00	20.00	40.00

—The above five are jukebox singles excerpting the LP "My Heart Sings"

❑ 9831	Diana/Don't Gamble with Love	1957	5.00	10.00	20.00
❑ 9855	I Love You, Baby/Tell Me That You Love Me	1957	7.50	15.00	30.00
❑ 9880	You Are My Destiny/When I Stop Loving You	1958	5.00	10.00	20.00
❑ 9907	Crazy Love/Let the Bells Keep Ringing	1958	5.00	10.00	20.00
❑ 9937	Midnight/Verboten!	1958	5.00	10.00	20.00
❑ 9956	Just Young/So It's Goodbye	1958	5.00	10.00	20.00
❑ 9956 [PS]	Just Young/So It's Goodbye	1958	—	—	—

—Rumored to exist, but without conclusive evidence, we will delete this from future editions

❑ 9987 [M]	(All of a Sudden) My Heart Sings/That's Love	1958	5.00	10.00	20.00
❑ S-9987 [S]	(All of a Sudden) My Heart Sings/That's Love	1958	12.50	25.00	50.00
❑ 10011 [M]	I Miss You So/Late Last Night	1959	3.75	7.50	15.00
❑ 10011 [PS]	I Miss You So/Late Last Night	1959	6.25	12.50	25.00
❑ S-10011 [S]	I Miss You So/Late Last Night	1959	12.50	25.00	50.00
❑ 10022 [M]	Lonely Boy/Your Love	1959	3.75	7.50	15.00
❑ S-10022 [S]	Lonely Boy/Your Love	1959	12.50	25.00	50.00
❑ 10040 [M]	Put Your Head on My Shoulder/Don't Ever Leave Me	1959	3.75	7.50	15.00
❑ 10040 [PS]	Put Your Head on My Shoulder/Don't Ever Leave Me	1959	6.25	12.50	25.00
❑ S-10040 [S]	Put Your Head on My Shoulder/Don't Ever Leave Me	1959	12.50	25.00	50.00
❑ 10064 [M]	It's Time to Cry/Something Has Changed Me	1959	3.75	7.50	15.00
❑ 10064 [PS]	It's Time to Cry/Something Has Changed Me	1959	6.25	12.50	25.00
❑ S-10064 [S]	It's Time to Cry/Something Has Changed Me	1959	12.50	25.00	50.00
❑ 10082 [M]	Puppy Love/Adam and Eve	1960	3.75	7.50	15.00
❑ 10082 [PS]	Puppy Love/Adam and Eve	1960	6.25	12.50	25.00
❑ S-10082 [S]	Puppy Love/Adam and Eve	1960	12.50	25.00	50.00
❑ 10106 [M]	My Home Town/Something Happened	1960	3.75	7.50	15.00
❑ 10106 [PS]	My Home Town/Something Happened	1960	6.25	12.50	25.00
❑ S-10106 [S]	My Home Town/Something Happened	1960	12.50	25.00	50.00
❑ 10132 [M]	Hello Young Lovers/I Love You in the Same Old Way	1960	3.75	7.50	15.00
❑ 10132 [PS]	Hello Young Lovers//I Love You in the Same Old Way	1960	6.25	12.50	25.00
❑ S-10132 [S]	Hello Young Lovers/I Love You in the Same Old Way	1960	12.50	25.00	50.00
❑ 10147 [M]	Summer's Gone/I'd Have to Share	1960	3.75	7.50	15.00
❑ 10147 [PS]	Summer's Gone/I'd Have to Share	1960	5.00	10.00	20.00
❑ S-10147 [S]	Summer's Gone/I'd Have to Share	1960	12.50	25.00	50.00
❑ 10163	Rudolph, the Red-Nosed Reindeer/I Saw Mommy Kissing Santa Claus	1960	6.25	12.50	25.00
❑ 10168 [M]	The Story of My Love/Don't Say You're Sorry	1960	3.75	7.50	15.00
❑ 10168 [PS]	The Story of My Love/Don't Say You're Sorry	1960	6.25	12.50	25.00
❑ S-10168 [S]	The Story of My Love/Don't Say You're Sorry	1960	12.50	25.00	50.00
❑ 10169	It's Christmas Everywhere/Rudolph, the Red-Nosed Reindeer	1960	4.00	8.00	16.00
❑ 10169 [PS]	It's Christmas Everywhere/Rudolph, the Red-Nosed Reindeer	1960	6.25	12.50	25.00
❑ 10194	Tonight My Love, Tonight/I'm Just a Fool Anyway	1961	3.00	6.00	12.00
❑ 10194 [PS]	Tonight My Love, Tonight/I'm Just a Fool Anyway	1961	6.25	12.50	25.00
❑ 10220	Dance On Little Girl/I Talk to You	1961	3.00	6.00	12.00
❑ 10220 [PS]	Dance On Little Girl/I Talk to You	1961	6.25	12.50	25.00
❑ 10239	Kissin' on the Phone/Cinderella	1961	3.00	6.00	12.00
❑ 10239 [PS]	Kissin' on the Phone/Cinderella	1961	6.25	12.50	25.00
❑ 10279	Loveland/The Bells at My Wedding	1961	3.00	6.00	12.00
❑ 10282	The Fools Hall of Fame/Far from the Lights of Town	1961	3.00	6.00	12.00
❑ 10311	I'd Never Find Another You/Uh Huh	1962	2.50	5.00	10.00
❑ 10338	I'm Coming Home/Cry	1962	2.50	5.00	10.00

BARNABY

❑ 2027	You're Some Kind of Friend/Why Are You Leaning on Me, Sir	1971	—	3.00	6.00

BUDDAH

❑ 252	Do I Love You/So Long City	1971	—	2.50	5.00
❑ 294	Everything's Been Changed/Jubilation	1972	—	2.50	5.00
❑ 314	Something Good Is Coming/Life Song	1972	—	2.50	5.00
❑ 337	While We're Still Young/This Is Your Song	1973	—	2.50	5.00
❑ 349	Hey Girl/You and Me Today	1973	—	2.50	5.00

COLUMBIA

❑ 03897	Hold Me 'Til the Mornin' Comes/This Is the First Time	1983	—	—	3.00
❑ 03897 [PS]	Hold Me 'Til the Mornin' Comes/This Is the First Time	1983	—	2.00	4.00
❑ 04187	Gimme the Word/No Way Out	1983	—	—	3.00

—A-side: With Karla DeVito

❑ 04407	Second Chance/Walk a Fine Line	1984	—	—	3.00
❑ 07358	No Way Out/Just for Once	1987	—	—	3.00

—A-side: Paul Anka and Julia Migenas; B-side: Migenas solo

EPIC

❑ 50298	You/Make It Up to Me in Love	1976	—	2.00	4.00

—With Odia Coates

ERIC

❑ 197	It's Time to Cry/Crazy Love	197?	—	2.00	4.00
❑ 197 [PS]	It's Time to Cry/Crazy Love	197?	—	2.50	5.00
❑ 198	(All of a Sudden) My Heart Sings/My Home Town	197?	—	2.00	4.00
❑ 198 [PS]	(All of a Sudden) My Heart Sings/My Home Town	197?	—	2.50	5.00
❑ 199	You Are My Destiny/Let the Bells Keep Ringing	197?	—	2.00	4.00
❑ 200	Diana/Don't Gamble with Love	197?	—	2.00	4.00
❑ 200 [PS]	Diana/Don't Gamble with Love	197?	—	2.50	5.00
❑ 201	Lonely Boy/I Miss You So	197?	—	2.00	4.00
❑ 201 [PS]	Lonely Boy/I Miss You So	197?	—	2.50	5.00
❑ 202	Puppy Love/Adam & Eve	197?	—	2.00	4.00
❑ 203	Put Your Head on My Shoulder/Summer's Gone	197?	—	2.00	4.00
❑ 203 [PS]	Put Your Head on My Shoulder/Summer's Gone	197?	—	2.50	5.00
❑ 204	Tonight My Love, Tonight/Dance On Little Girl	197?	—	2.00	4.00
❑ 204 [PS]	Tonight My Love, Tonight/Dance On Little Girl	197?	—	2.00	4.00

—All of the above Eric singles are reissues; all of the picture sleeves have the same photo on both sides, with the only difference between them the different song titles.

FAME

❑ XW-345	Flashback/Let Me Get to Know You	1973	—	2.00	4.00

RCA

❑ PB-11351	Lovely Lady/Brought Up in New York	1978	—	2.00	4.00
❑ PB-11351 [PS]	Lovely Lady/Brought Up in New York	1978	—	2.50	5.00
❑ PB-11395	This Is Love/I'm By Myself Again	1978	—	2.00	4.00
❑ PB-11662	As Long As We Keep Believing/Headlines	1979	—	2.00	4.00
❑ PB-11957	Rainbow/After All	1980			

—Unreleased

❑ PB-12184	We Love Each Other/Think I'm in Love Again	1981	—	—	3.00
❑ PB-12225	I've Been Waiting for You All My Life/Think I'm in Love Again	1981	—	—	3.00
❑ PB-12262	Lady Lay Down/You're Still a Part of Me	1981	—	—	3.00

Number	Title (A Side/B Side)	Yr	VG	VG+	NM
RCA VICTOR					
❑ 37-7977	Love Me Warm and Tender/I'd Like to Know	1962	6.25	12.50	25.00
—"Compact Single 33" (small hole, plays at LP speed)					
❑ 47-7977	Love Me Warm and Tender/I'd Like to Know	1962	2.50	5.00	10.00
❑ 47-7977 [PS]	Love Me Warm and Tender/I'd Like to Know	1962	5.00	10.00	20.00
❑ 47-8030	A Steel Guitar and a Glass of Wine/I Never Knew Your Name	1962	2.50	5.00	10.00
❑ 47-8030 [PS]	A Steel Guitar and a Glass of Wine/I Never Knew Your Name	1962	5.00	10.00	20.00
❑ 47-8068	Every Night (Without You)/There You Go	1962	2.50	5.00	10.00
❑ 47-8068 [PS]	Every Night (Without You)/There You Go	1962	5.00	10.00	20.00
❑ 47-8097	Eso Beso (That Kiss!)/Give Me Back My Heart	1962	2.50	5.00	10.00
❑ 47-8097 [PS]	Eso Beso (That Kiss!)/Give Me Back My Heart	1962	5.00	10.00	20.00
❑ 47-8115	Love (Makes the World Go 'Round)/Crying in the Wind	1962	2.50	5.00	10.00
❑ 47-8115 [PS]	Love (Makes the World Go 'Round)/Crying in the Wind	1962	5.00	10.00	20.00
❑ 47-8158	Think About It/At Night	1963	—	—	—
—Unreleased					
❑ 47-8170	Remember Diana/At Night	1963	2.50	5.00	10.00
❑ 47-8170 [PS]	Remember Diana/At Night	1963	5.00	10.00	20.00
❑ 47-8195	Hello Jim/You've Got the Nerve to Call This Love	1963	2.50	5.00	10.00
❑ 47-8195 [PS]	Hello Jim/You've Got the Nerve to Call This Love	1963	5.00	10.00	20.00
❑ 47-8237	Wondrous Are the Ways of Love/Hurry Up and Tell Me	1963	2.50	5.00	10.00
❑ 47-8237 [PS]	Wondrous Are the Ways of Love/Hurry Up and Tell Me	1963	5.00	10.00	20.00
❑ 47-8272	Did You Have a Happy Birthday/For No Good Reason at All	1963	2.50	5.00	10.00
❑ 47-8272 [PS]	Did You Have a Happy Birthday/For No Good Reason at All	1963	5.00	10.00	20.00
❑ 47-8311	From Rocking Horse to Rocking Chair/Cheer Up	1964	2.00	4.00	8.00
❑ 47-8311 [PS]	From Rocking Horse to Rocking Chair/Cheer Up	1964	3.75	7.50	15.00
❑ 47-8349	My Baby's Comin' Home/No, No	1964	2.00	4.00	8.00
❑ 47-8349 [PS]	My Baby's Comin' Home/No, No	1964	3.75	7.50	15.00
❑ 47-8396	In My Imagination/It's Easy to Say	1964	2.00	4.00	8.00
❑ 47-8396 [PS]	In My Imagination/It's Easy to Say	1964	3.75	7.50	15.00
❑ 47-8441	Cindy Go Home/Ogni Volta	1964	2.00	4.00	8.00
❑ 47-8441 [PS]	Cindy Go Home/Ogni Volta	1964	3.75	7.50	15.00
❑ 47-8493	Sylvia/Behind My Smile	1965	2.00	4.00	8.00
❑ 47-8595	The Loneliest Boy in the World/Dream Me Happy	1965	2.00	4.00	8.00
❑ 47-8595 [PS]	The Loneliest Boy in the World/Dream Me Happy	1965	7.50	15.00	30.00
❑ 47-8662	Every Day a Heart Is Broken/As If There Were No Tomorrow	1965	2.00	4.00	8.00
❑ 47-8764	Truly Yours/Oh, Such a Stranger	1965	2.00	4.00	8.00
❑ 47-8839	I Wish/I Went to Your Wedding	1966	2.00	4.00	8.00
❑ 47-8893	I Can't Help Loving You/Can't Get Along Very Well Without Her	1966	2.00	4.00	8.00
❑ 47-9032	Poor Old World/I'd Rather Be a Stranger	1966	2.00	4.00	8.00
❑ 47-9128	Until It's Time for You to Go/Would You Still Be My Baby	1967	2.00	4.00	8.00
❑ 47-9228	A Woman Is a Sentimental Thing/That's How Love Goes	1967	2.00	4.00	8.00
❑ 47-9457	Can't Get You Out of My Mind/When We Get There	1968	2.00	4.00	8.00
❑ 47-9648	Goodnight My Love/This Crazy World	1968	2.00	4.00	8.00
❑ 47-9767	Happy/Can't Get You Out of My Mind	1969	2.00	4.00	8.00
❑ 47-9846	Midnight Mistress/Before It's Too Late-This Land Is Your Land	1970	2.00	4.00	8.00
❑ 74-0126	In the Still of the Night/Pickin' Up the Pieces	1969	2.00	4.00	8.00
❑ 74-0164	Sincerely/Next Year	1969	2.00	4.00	8.00
❑ 47-8662 [PS]	Every Day a Heart Is Broken/As If There Were No Tomorrow	1965	7.50	15.00	30.00
❑ VP1-2502 [S]	Young, Alive and In Love/Young and Foolish	1962	10.00	20.00	40.00
❑ VP2-2502 [S]	Younger Than Springtime/You Make Me Feel So Young	1962	10.00	20.00	40.00
❑ VP3-2502 [S]	This Life of Mine/Life Is Just a Bowl of Cherries	1962	10.00	20.00	40.00
❑ VP4-2502 [S]	I Love Life/Aren't You Glad You're You?	1962	10.00	20.00	40.00
❑ VP5-2502 [S]	Falling in Love with You/You're Just in Love	1962	10.00	20.00	40.00
—The above five are 33 1/3 rpm, small hole jukebox singles excerpting the LP "Young, Alive and In Love"					
❑ GB-10180	Diana/Put Your Head on My Shoulders	1975	—	2.00	4.00
—Gold Standard Series					
❑ GB-10181	Puppy Love/Lonely Boy	1975	—	2.00	4.00
—Gold Standard Series					
❑ GB-10182	You Are My Destiny/Tonight, My Love, Tonight	1975	—	2.00	4.00
—Gold Standard Series					
RPM					
❑ 472	I Confess/Blau-Wile Deveest Fontaine	1956	20.00	40.00	80.00
❑ 499	I Confess/Blau-Wile Deveest Fontaine	1957	7.50	15.00	30.00
UNITED ARTISTS					
❑ XW-454	(You're) Having My Baby/Papa	1974	—	2.00	4.00
❑ XW-569	One Man Woman/One Woman Man//Let Me Get to Know You	1974	—	2.00	4.00
—A-side: With Odia Coates					
❑ XW-615	I Don't Like to Sleep Alone/How Can Anything Be Beautiful After You	1975	—	2.00	4.00
❑ XW-615 [PS]	I Don't Like to Sleep Alone/How Can Anything Be Beautiful After You	1975	—	2.00	4.00
❑ XW-685	(I Believe) There's Nothing Stronger Than Our Love/Today I Became a Fool	1975	—	2.00	4.00
❑ XW-737	Times of Your Life/Water Runs Deep	1975	—	2.00	4.00
❑ XW-737 [PS]	Times of Your Life/Water Runs Deep	1975	—	2.00	4.00
❑ XW-789	Anytime (I'll Be There)/Something About You	1976	—	2.00	4.00
❑ XW-911	Happier/Closing Doors	1976	—	2.00	4.00
❑ XW-945	I'll Help You/Never Gonna Fall in Love Like I Fell in Love with You	1977	—	2.00	4.00
❑ XW-972	My Best Friend's Wife/Never Gonna Fall in Love Like I Fell in Love with You	1977	—	2.00	4.00
❑ XW-1018	Tonight/Everybody Ought to Be in Love	1977	—	2.00	4.00

Number	Title (A Side/B Side)	Yr	VG	VG+	NM
❑ XW-1157	(You're) Having My Baby//One Man Woman/One Woman Man	1978	—	—	3.00
—Reissue					
❑ XW-1158	I Don't Like to Sleep Alone/Times of Your Life	1978	—	—	3.00
—Reissue					
7-Inch Extended Plays					
ABC-PARAMOUNT					
❑ C-296	So It's Goodbye/Les Filles de Paris//Melodie D'Amour/Autumn Leaves	1959	6.25	12.50	25.00
❑ C-296 [PS]	My Heart Sings	1959	6.25	12.50	25.00
❑ A-323	Diana/Puppy Love//Put Your Head on My Shoulder/Lonely Boy	1960	6.25	12.50	25.00
❑ A-323 [PS]	Four Songs from Paul Anka Sings His Big 15	1960	6.25	12.50	25.00
Albums					
ABC-PARAMOUNT					
❑ 240 [M]	Paul Anka	1958	12.50	25.00	50.00
❑ 296 [M]	My Heart Sings	1959	7.50	15.00	30.00
❑ S-296 [S]	My Heart Sings	1959	12.50	25.00	50.00
❑ 323 [M]	Paul Anka Sings His Big 15	1960	12.50	25.00	50.00
❑ S-323 [R]	Paul Anka Sings His Big 15	196?	7.50	15.00	30.00
❑ 347 [M]	Paul Anka Swings for Young Lovers	1960	7.50	15.00	30.00
❑ S-347 [S]	Paul Anka Swings for Young Lovers	1960	10.00	20.00	40.00
❑ 353 [M]	Anka at the Copa	1960	7.50	15.00	30.00
❑ S-353 [S]	Anka at the Copa	1960	10.00	20.00	40.00
❑ ABC 360 [M]	It's Christmas Everywhere	1960	7.50	15.00	30.00
❑ ABCS 360 [S]	It's Christmas Everywhere	1960	10.00	20.00	40.00
❑ 371 [M]	Strictly Instrumental	1961	7.00	15.00	30.00
❑ S-371 [S]	Strictly Instrumental	1961	10.00	20.00	40.00
❑ 390 [M]	Paul Anka Sings His Big 15, Vol. 2	1961	7.50	15.00	30.00
❑ S-390 [S]	Paul Anka Sings His Big 15, Vol. 2	1961	10.00	20.00	40.00
❑ 409 [M]	Paul Anka Sings His Big, Big 15, Volume III	1962	6.25	12.50	25.00
❑ S-409 [S]	Paul Anka Sings His Big, Big 15, Volume III	1962	7.50	15.00	30.00
❑ 420 [M]	Diana	1962	6.25	12.50	25.00
❑ S-420 [S]	Diana	1962	7.50	15.00	30.00
ACCORD					
❑ SN-7117	She's a Lady	1981	2.00	4.00	8.00
BUDDAH					
❑ BDS 5093	Paul Anka	1971	3.00	6.00	12.00
❑ BDS 5114	Jubilation	1972	3.00	6.00	12.00
❑ BDS 5622 [(2)]	This Is Anka	1974	3.75	7.50	15.00
❑ BDS 5667 [(2)]	The Essential Paul Anka	1974	3.75	7.50	15.00
COLUMBIA					
❑ FC 38442	Walk a Fine Line	1983	2.00	4.00	8.00
❑ FC 39323	Paul Anka Live	1984	2.00	4.00	8.00
LIBERTY					
❑ LN-10000	Paul Anka: His Best	1980	2.00	4.00	8.00
—Budget-line reissue					
❑ LN-10001	The Times of Your Life	1980	2.00	4.00	8.00
—Budget-line reissue					
❑ LN-10149	Feelings	1982	2.00	4.00	8.00
—Budget-line reissue					
❑ LN-10220	The Painter	1983	2.00	4.00	8.00
—Budget-line reissue					
PAIR					
❑ PDL2-1129 [(2)]	Songs I Write and Sing	1986	3.00	6.00	12.00
PICKWICK					
❑ PTP-2087 [(2)]	Paul Anka Way	197?	2.50	5.00	10.00
❑ SPC-3508	Puppy Love	1975	2.00	4.00	8.00
❑ SPC-3523	She's a Lady	1975	2.00	4.00	8.00
RANWOOD					
❑ 8203	The Very Best of Paul Anka	1981	2.00	4.00	8.00
RCA CAMDEN					
❑ ACL1-0616	My Way	1974	2.00	4.00	8.00
RCA VICTOR					
❑ ANL1-0896	Remember Diana	1975	2.50	5.00	10.00
❑ ANL1-1054	She's a Lady	1975	2.50	5.00	10.00
❑ ANL1-1584	Paul Anka Sings His Favorites	1976	2.50	5.00	10.00
❑ ANL1-2482	Songs I Wish I'd Written	1977	2.50	5.00	10.00
❑ LPM-2502 [M]	Young, Alive and In Love!	1962	3.75	7.50	15.00
—With portrait of Paul Anka on back cover					
❑ LPM-2502 [M]	Young, Alive and In Love!	1962	6.25	12.50	25.00
—With portrait of Paul Anka on front cover					
❑ LSP-2502 [S]	Young, Alive and In Love!	1962	5.00	10.00	20.00
—With portrait of Paul Anka on back cover					
❑ LSP-2502 [S]	Young, Alive and In Love!	1962	7.50	15.00	30.00
—With portrait of Paul Anka on front cover					
❑ LPM-2575 [M]	Let's Sit This One Out	1962	5.00	10.00	20.00
❑ LSP-2575 [S]	Let's Sit This One Out	1962	6.25	12.50	25.00
❑ LPM-2614 [M]	Our Man Around the World	1963	5.00	10.00	20.00
❑ LSP-2614 [S]	Our Man Around the World	1963	6.25	12.50	25.00
❑ LPM-2691 [M]	Paul Anka's 21 Golden Hits	1963	5.00	10.00	20.00
❑ LSP-2691 [S]	Paul Anka's 21 Golden Hits	1963	6.25	12.50	25.00
—LPM/LSP-2691 has re-recorded versions of ABC-Paramount hits					
❑ LPM-2744 [M]	Songs I Wish I'd Written	1963	3.75	7.50	15.00
❑ LSP-2744 [S]	Songs I Wish I'd Written	1963	5.00	10.00	20.00
❑ AFL1-2892	Listen to Your Heart	1978	2.50	5.00	10.00
❑ LPM-2996 [M]	Excitement on Park Avenue	1964	3.75	7.50	15.00
❑ LSP-2996 [S]	Excitement on Park Avenue	1964	5.00	10.00	20.00
❑ AFL1-3382	Headlines	1979	2.50	5.00	10.00
❑ LPM-3580 [M]	Strictly Nashville	1966	3.75	7.50	15.00
❑ LSP-3580 [S]	Strictly Nashville	1966	5.00	10.00	20.00
❑ AYL1-3808	Paul Anka's 21 Golden Hits	1980	2.00	4.00	8.00
—"Best Buy Series" reissue					
❑ LPM-3875 [M]	Paul Anka Live	1967	3.75	7.50	15.00
❑ LSP-3875 [S]	Paul Anka Live	1967	5.00	10.00	20.00
❑ AFL1-3926	Both Sides of Love	1981	2.50	5.00	10.00
❑ LSP-4142	Goodnight My Love	1969	3.75	7.50	15.00
❑ LSP-4203	Sincerely	1969	3.75	7.50	15.00
❑ LSP-4250	Life Goes On	1969	3.75	7.50	15.00
❑ LSP-4300	Paul Anka 70s	1970	3.75	7.50	15.00

Number	Title (A Side/B Side)	Yr	VG	VG+	NM
RHINO					
❏ RNLP-70220	The Best of Paul Anka (14 Original Hits, 1957-1961)	1986	2.50	5.00	10.00
RIVIERA					
❏ 0047 [M]	Paul Anka and Others	1959	37.50	75.00	150.00
—With Paul Anka's RPM recordings plus tracks by other artists					
SIRE					
❏ SASH-3704 [(2)]	Paul Anka Gold	1974	3.75	7.50	15.00
❏ SBK 6043 [(2)]	The Vintage Years 1957-1961	1978	3.00	6.00	12.00
UNITED ARTISTS					
❏ UA-LA314-G	Anka	1974	2.50	5.00	10.00
❏ UA-LA367-G	Feelings	1975	2.50	5.00	10.00
❏ UA-LA569-G	Times of Your Life	1975	2.50	5.00	10.00
❏ UA-LA653-G [Q]	The Painter	1976	3.00	6.00	12.00
—All copies are quadraphonic					
❏ UA-LA746-H	The Music Man	1977	2.50	5.00	10.00
❏ UA-LA922-H	Paul Anka: His Best	1978	2.50	5.00	10.00

ANKA, PAUL/GEORGE HAMILTON IV/JOHNNY NASH Also see each artist's individual listings.
45s

Number	Title (A Side/B Side)	Yr	VG	VG+	NM
ABC-PARAMOUNT					
❏ 9974	The Teen Commandments/If You Learn to Pray	1958	6.25	12.50	25.00

ANN-MARGRET Also see JOHN GARY; AL HIRT.
45s

Number	Title (A Side/B Side)	Yr	VG	VG+	NM
ARIOLA					
❏ 7511	Love Rush/For You	1979	—	3.00	6.00
AVCO EMBASSY					
❏ 4547	Today/Today	1970	3.75	7.50	15.00
—B-side by Lenny Stack					
LHI					
❏ 1	It's a Nice World to Visit/You Turned My Head Around	1969	—	3.00	6.00
❏ 2	Chico/Sleep in the Grass	1969	—	3.00	6.00
—With Lee Hazlewood					
❏ 5	The Dark End of the Street/Victims of the Night	1969	—	3.00	6.00
—With Lee Hazlewood					
❏ 11	Walk Out of My Mind/Hangin' In	1970	—	3.00	6.00
—With Lee Hazlewood					
MCA					
❏ 41186	Love Rush/For You	1980	—	2.50	5.00
❏ 41223	Midnight Message/For You	1980	—	2.50	5.00
RCA VICTOR					
❏ 37-7857	I Ain't Got Nobody/Lost Love	1961	6.25	12.50	25.00
—"Compact Single 33" (small hole, plays at LP speed)					
❏ 37-7894	I Just Don't Understand/I Don't Hurt Anymore	1961	6.25	12.50	25.00
—"Compact Single 33" (small hole, plays at LP speed)					
❏ 37-7952	It Do Me So Good/Gimme Love	1961	6.25	12.50	25.00
—"Compact Single 33" (small hole, plays at LP speed)					
❏ 47-7857	I Ain't Got Nobody/Lost Love	1961	3.00	6.00	12.00
❏ 47-7894	I Just Don't Understand/I Don't Hurt Anymore	1961	3.75	7.50	15.00
❏ 47-7894 [PS]	I Just Don't Understand/I Don't Hurt Anymore	1961	6.25	12.50	25.00
❏ 47-7952	It Do Me So Good/Gimme Love	1961	2.50	5.00	10.00
❏ 47-7952 [PS]	It Do Me So Good/Gimme Love	1961	6.25	12.50	25.00
❏ 47-7986	What Am I Supposed to Do/Let's Stop Kidding Each Other	1962	2.50	5.00	10.00
❏ 47-7986 [PS]	What Am I Supposed to Do/Let's Stop Kidding Each Other	1962	6.25	12.50	25.00
❏ 47-8061	Jim Dandy/I Was Only Kidding	1962	2.50	5.00	10.00
❏ 47-8061 [PS]	Jim Dandy/I Was Only Kidding	1962	6.25	12.50	25.00
❏ 47-8130	No More/So Did I	1963	2.50	5.00	10.00
❏ 47-8130 [PS]	No More/So Did I	1963	6.25	12.50	25.00
❏ 47-8168	Bye Bye Birdie/Take All the Kisses	1963	2.50	5.00	10.00
❏ 47-8168 [PS]	Bye Bye Birdie/Take All the Kisses	1963	6.25	12.50	25.00
❏ 47-8295	Hey Little Star/Man's Favorite Sport	1963	2.50	5.00	10.00
❏ 47-8446	He's My Man/Someday Soon	1964	2.50	5.00	10.00
❏ 47-8446 [PS]	He's My Man/Someday Soon	1964	7.50	15.00	30.00
❏ 47-8734	Mister Kiss Kiss Bang Bang/What Did I Have That I Don't Have Now	1965	2.50	5.00	10.00
❏ 47-9013	The Swinger/You've Come a Long Way from St. Louis	1966	2.50	5.00	10.00
❏ VP1-2551 [S]	Jim Dandy/Thirteen Men	1962	10.00	20.00	40.00
❏ VP2-2551 [S]	Rock and Roll Waltz/There'll Be Some Changes Made	1962	10.00	20.00	40.00
❏ VP3-2551 [S]	Make Love to Me/Tell Me, Tell Me	1962	10.00	20.00	40.00
❏ VP4-2551 [S]	C'est Si Bon/Please Don't Talk About Me When I'm Gone	1962	10.00	20.00	40.00
❏ VP5-2551 [S]	Inka Dinka Doo/Begin the Beguine	1962	10.00	20.00	40.00
—The above five are 33 1/3 rpm, small hole jukebox singles excerpting the LP "The Vivacious One"					

Albums

Number	Title (A Side/B Side)	Yr	VG	VG+	NM
MCA					
❏ 3226	Ann-Margret	1980	3.00	6.00	12.00
RCA VICTOR					
❏ LPM-2399 [M]	And Here She Is…	1961	7.50	15.00	30.00
❏ LSP-2399 [S]	And Here She Is…	1961	10.00	20.00	40.00
❏ LPM-2453 [M]	On the Way Up	1961	7.50	15.00	30.00
❏ LSP-2453 [S]	On the Way Up	1961	10.00	20.00	40.00
❏ LPM-2551 [M]	The Vivacious One	1962	7.50	15.00	30.00
❏ LSP-2551 [S]	The Vivacious One	1962	10.00	20.00	40.00
❏ LPM-2659 [M]	Bachelor's Paradise	1963	7.50	15.00	30.00
❏ LSP-2659 [S]	Bachelor's Paradise	1963	10.00	20.00	40.00
❏ LPM-3710 [M]	Songs from The Swinger and Others	1966	15.00	30.00	60.00
❏ LSP-3710 [S]	Songs from The Swinger and Others	1966	20.00	40.00	80.00

ANNETTE Also see FRANKIE AVALON AND ANNETTE FUNICELLO.
45s

Number	Title (A Side/B Side)	Yr	VG	VG+	NM
BUENA VISTA					
❏ 336	Jo Jo the Dog Faced Boy/Love Me Forever	1959	3.75	7.50	15.00
❏ 336	Jo Jo the Dog Faced Boy/Lonely Guitar	1959	5.00	10.00	20.00
❏ 339	Wild Willie/Lonely Guitar	1959	3.75	7.50	15.00
❏ 339 [PS]	Wild Willie/Lonely Guitar	1959	7.50	15.00	30.00

Number	Title (A Side/B Side)	Yr	VG	VG+	NM
❏ 344	Especially for You/My Heart Became of Age	1959	3.75	7.50	15.00
❏ 349	First Name Initial/My Heart Became of Age	1959	3.75	7.50	15.00
❏ 349 [PS]	First Name Initial/My Heart Became of Age	1959	7.50	15.00	30.00
❏ 354	O Dio Mio/It Took Dreams	1960	3.75	7.50	15.00
❏ 354 [PS]	O Dio Mio/It Took Dreams	1960	7.50	15.00	30.00
❏ 359	Train of Love/Tell Me Who's the Girl	1960	3.75	7.50	15.00
❏ 359 [PS]	Train of Love/Tell Me Who's the Girl	1960	10.00	20.00	40.00
❏ 362	Pineapple Princess/Luau Cha Cha Cha	1960	3.75	7.50	15.00
❏ 362 [PS]	Pineapple Princess/Luau Cha Cha Cha	1960	7.50	15.00	30.00
❏ 369	Talk to Me Baby/I Love You Baby	1960	3.75	7.50	15.00
❏ 369 [PS]	Talk to Me Baby/I Love You Baby	1960	7.50	15.00	30.00
❏ 374	Dream Boy/Please, Please Signore	1961	3.75	7.50	15.00
❏ 374 [PS]	Dream Boy/Please, Please Signore	1961	7.50	15.00	30.00
❏ 375	Indian Giver/Mama, Mama Rosa (Where's the Spumoni)	1961	3.75	7.50	15.00
❏ 375 [PS]	Indian Giver/Mama, Mama Rosa (Where's the Spumoni)	1961	7.50	15.00	30.00
❏ 384	Hawaiian Love Talk/Blue Muu Muu	1961	3.75	7.50	15.00
❏ 384 [PS]	Hawaiian Love Talk/Blue Muu Muu	1961	12.50	25.00	50.00
❏ 388	Dreamin' About You/Strummin' Song	1961	3.75	7.50	15.00
❏ 388 [PS]	Dreamin' About You/Strummin' Song	1961	7.50	15.00	30.00
❏ 392	That Crazy Place From Outer Space/Seven Moons (Of Batalayre)	1962	3.75	7.50	15.00
—B-side by Danny Saval and Tom Tryon					
❏ 392 [PS]	That Crazy Place From Outer Space/Seven Moons (Of Batalayre)	1962	10.00	20.00	40.00
❏ 394	The Truth About Youth/I Can't Do the Sum	1962	3.75	7.50	15.00
❏ 394 [PS]	The Truth About Youth/I Can't Do the Sum	1962	10.00	20.00	40.00
❏ 400	My Little Grass Shack/Hukilau	1962	3.75	7.50	15.00
❏ 405	He's My Ideal/Mr. Piano Man	1962	3.75	7.50	15.00
❏ 405 [PS]	He's My Ideal/Mr. Piano Man	1962	7.50	15.00	30.00
❏ 407	Bella Bella Florence/Canzone d'Amoure	1962	3.75	7.50	15.00
—With Marcochi					
❏ 407 [PS]	Bella Bella Florence/Canzone d'Amoure	1962	37.50	75.00	150.00
❏ 414	Teenage Wedding/Walkin' and Talkin'	1962	5.00	10.00	20.00
❏ 414 [PS]	Teenage Wedding/Walkin' and Talkin'	1962	150.00	300.00	600.00
❏ 427	Treat Him Nicely/Promise Me Anything	1963	3.75	7.50	15.00
❏ 427 [PS]	Treat Him Nicely/Promise Me Anything	1963	15.00	30.00	60.00
❏ 431	Merlin Jones/The Scrambled Egghead	1964	3.00	6.00	12.00
—With Tommy Kirk					
❏ 431 [PS]	Merlin Jones/The Scrambled Egghead	1964	7.50	15.00	30.00
❏ 432	Custom City/Rebel Rider	1964	5.00	10.00	20.00
❏ 432 [PS]	Custom City/Rebel Rider	1964	20.00	40.00	60.00
❏ 433	Muscle Beach Party/I Dream About Frankie	1964	3.75	7.50	15.00
❏ 433 [PS]	Muscle Beach Party/I Dream About Frankie	1964	7.50	15.00	30.00
❏ 436	Bikini Beach Party/The Clyde	1964	3.75	7.50	15.00
❏ 436 [PS]	Bikini Beach Party/The Clyde	1964	10.00	20.00	40.00
❏ 437	The Wah-Watusi/The Clyde	1964	3.00	6.00	12.00
❏ 438	Something Borrowed, Something Blue/How Will I Know My Love	1965	3.75	7.50	15.00
❏ 438 [PS]	Something Borrowed, Something Blue/How Will I Know My Love	1965	20.00	40.00	80.00
❏ 440	The Monkey's Uncle/How Will I Know My Love	1965	3.00	6.00	12.00
—With the Beach Boys backing up					
❏ 440 [PS]	The Monkey's Uncle/How Will I Know My Love	1965	5.00	10.00	20.00
❏ 442	The Boy to Love/No One Else Could Be Prouder	1965	3.00	6.00	12.00
❏ 450	No Way to Go But Up/Crystal Ball	1966	3.00	6.00	12.00
❏ 475	The Computer Wore Tennis Shoes/Merlin Jones	1970	2.00	4.00	8.00
DISNEYLAND					
❏ 102	How Will I Know My Love/Don't Jump to Conclusions	1958	6.25	15.00	30.00
❏ 102 [PS]	How Will I Know My Love/Don't Jump to Conclusions	1958	12.50	25.00	50.00
❏ 114	That Crazy Place in Outer Space/Gold Doubloons and Pieces of Eight	1958	10.00	20.00	40.00
—B-side: "Theme from the Hardy Boys"					
❏ 118	Tall Paul/Ma, He's Making Eyes at Me	1959	5.00	10.00	20.00
❏ 786	That Crazy Place From Outer Space/Happy Glow	196?	2.50	5.00	10.00
—No artist credit on label, but A-side is the same recording as Disneyland 114					
EPIC					
❏ 9829	Baby Needs Me Now/Moment of Silence	1965	6.25	12.50	25.00
—With Cecil Null					
STARVIEW					
❏ 3001	The Promised Land/In Between and Out of Love	1983	2.50	5.00	10.00
❏ 3001 [PS]	The Promised Land/In Between and Out of Love	1983	2.50	5.00	10.00
TOWER					
❏ 326	What's a Girl to Do/When You Get What You Want	1967	7.50	15.00	30.00

Albums

Number	Title (A Side/B Side)	Yr	VG	VG+	NM
BUENA VISTA					
❏ BV-3301 [M]	Annette	1959	30.00	60.00	120.00
❏ BV-3302 [M]	Annette Sings Anka	1960	25.00	50.00	100.00
❏ BV-3303 [M]	Hawaiiannette	1960	18.75	37.50	75.00
❏ BV-3304 [M]	Italiannette	1960	18.75	37.50	75.00
❏ BV-3305 [M]	Dance Annette	1961	18.75	37.50	75.00
❏ BV-3312 [M]	The Story of My Teens	1962	18.75	37.50	75.00
❏ BV-3313 [M]	Teen Street	1962	18.75	37.50	75.00
❏ BV-3314 [M]	Muscle Beach Party	1963	18.75	37.50	75.00
❏ STER-3314 [S]	Muscle Beach Party	1963	37.50	75.00	150.00
❏ BV-3316 [M]	Beach Party	1963	15.00	30.00	60.00
❏ STER-3316 [S]	Beach Party	1963	25.00	50.00	100.00
❏ BV-3320 [M]	Annette on Campus	1964	12.50	25.00	50.00
❏ STER-3320 [S]	Annette on Campus	1964	25.00	50.00	100.00
❏ BV-3324 [M]	Annette at Bikini Beach	1964	12.50	25.00	50.00
❏ STER-3324 [S]	Annette at Bikini Beach	1964	25.00	50.00	100.00
❏ BV-3325 [M]	Annette's Pajama Party	1964	10.00	20.00	40.00
❏ STER-3325 [S]	Annette's Pajama Party	1964	25.00	50.00	100.00
❏ BV-3327 [M]	Annette Sings Golden Surfin' Hits	1964	25.00	50.00	100.00
❏ STER-3327 [S]	Annette Sings Golden Surfin' Hits	1964	37.50	75.00	150.00
❏ BV-3328 [M]	Something Borrowed, Something Blue	1964	15.00	30.00	60.00

Number	Title (A Side/B Side)	Yr	VG	VG+	NM
❑ STER-3328 [P]	Something Borrowed, Something Blue	1964	25.00	50.00	100.00
❑ BV-4037	Annette Funicello	1972	12.50	25.00	50.00
RHINO					
❑ RNDF-206	The Best of Annette	1984	3.00	6.00	12.00
❑ RNLP-702 [PD]	The Best of Annette	1984	6.25	12.50	25.00

ANNETTE / HAYLEY MILLS
Albums
DISNEYLAND

Number	Title (A Side/B Side)	Yr	VG	VG+	NM
❑ DL-3508 [M]	Annette and Hayley Mills (Singing 10 of Their Greatest All-Time Hits)	1964	250.00	500.00	1000.

—*TV offer; issued with paper jacket. Though the cover says "Buena Vista Records Presents," the label is the yellow Disneyland label*

ANNIE AND THE ORPHANS
45s
CAPITOL

Number	Title (A Side/B Side)	Yr	VG	VG+	NM
❑ 5144	My Girl's Been Bitten by the Beatle Bug/ A Place Called Happiness	1964	5.00	10.00	20.00
❑ 5144 [PS]	My Girl's Been Bitten by the Beatle Bug/ A Place Called Happiness	1964	6.25	12.50	25.00

ANONYMOUS
Albums
A-MAJOR

Number	Title (A Side/B Side)	Yr	VG	VG+	NM
❑ AMLS-1002	Inside the Shadow	1976	62.50	125.00	250.00

ANT TRIP CEREMONY
Albums
C.R.C.

Number	Title (A Side/B Side)	Yr	VG	VG+	NM
❑ 2129	24 Hours	1970	150.00	300.00	600.00

ANTELL, PETE
45s
BOUNTY

Number	Title (A Side/B Side)	Yr	VG	VG+	NM
❑ 103	The Times They Are a-Changin'/Yesterrday and Tomorrow	1965	3.75	7.50	15.00
CAMEO					
❑ 234	Night Time/Something About You	1962	5.00	10.00	20.00
❑ 264	You in Disguise/Keep It Up	1963	3.75	7.50	15.00
NEW VOICE					
❑ 818	Wanting/Warm Smoke	1967	2.50	5.00	10.00

ANTHEM
Albums
BUDDAH

Number	Title (A Side/B Side)	Yr	VG	VG+	NM
❑ BDS-5071	Anthem	1971	5.00	10.00	20.00

ANTHONY, LAMONT See LAMONT DOZIER.

ANTHONY, MARK
45s
LA BELLE

Number	Title (A Side/B Side)	Yr	VG	VG+	NM
❑ 779	Mama's Twistin' with Santa/Music from Studio "D"	1962	3.00	6.00	12.00

ANTHONY, NICK
45s
ABC-PARAMOUNT

Number	Title (A Side/B Side)	Yr	VG	VG+	NM
❑ 9919	More Than Ever/You're Real Keen, Jelly Bean	1958	5.00	10.00	20.00
❑ 9985	Forbidden Love/My Baby's Gone	1958	5.00	10.00	20.00

ANTHONY, RAY
45s
CAPITOL

Number	Title (A Side/B Side)	Yr	VG	VG+	NM
❑ F794	Sitting by the Window/Dixie	1949	3.75	7.50	15.00
❑ F819	I'll See You In My Dreams/My Baby Is Blue	1950	3.00	6.00	12.00
❑ F859	Count Every Star/Bamboo	1950	3.00	6.00	12.00
❑ F923	Sentimental Me/Spaghetti Rag	1950	3.00	6.00	12.00
❑ F933	Where in the World/Candy & Cake	1950	3.00	6.00	12.00
❑ F945	Why/Little Peach from East Orange	1950	3.00	6.00	12.00
❑ F958	In the Mood/Way Down Yonder	1950	3.00	6.00	12.00
❑ F968	Autumn Nocturne/Tenderly	1950	3.00	6.00	12.00
❑ F979	Count Every Star/The Darktown Strutters Ball	1950	3.00	6.00	12.00
❑ F1001	Roses/National Emblem March	1950	3.00	6.00	12.00
❑ F1020	The Girl That I Marry/They Say It's Wonderful	1950	3.00	6.00	12.00
❑ F1040	Skip to My Lou/Scattered Toys	1950	3.00	6.00	12.00
❑ F1051	Francie/Mama Teach Me to Do the Charleston	1950	3.00	6.00	12.00
❑ F1073	Lazy Old Tune/Lackawanna Local	1950	3.00	6.00	12.00
❑ F1107	Star Dust/Young Man with a Horn	1950	3.00	6.00	12.00
❑ F1131	Can Anyone Explain/Shy Coach	1950	3.00	6.00	12.00
❑ F1169	Dixie Doodle/All of a Sudden (My Heart Sings)	1950	3.00	6.00	12.00
❑ F1190	Harbor Lights/Nevertheless (I'm in Love with You)	1950	3.00	6.00	12.00
❑ F1196	A Marshmallow World/Where Do I Go from You	1950	3.75	7.50	15.00
❑ F1249	My Heart Is Out of Town/Harlem Nocturne	1950	3.00	6.00	12.00
❑ F1280	Autumn Leaves/Mr. Anthony's Boogie	1950	3.00	6.00	12.00
❑ F1310	The Night Is Young and You're So Beautiful/All Anthony No Cleopatra	1950	3.00	6.00	12.00
❑ F1352	Be My Love/I Wonder What's Become of Sally	1951	3.00	6.00	12.00
❑ F1367	More Than I Care to Remember/Columbia, The Gem of the Ocean	1951	3.00	6.00	12.00
❑ F1490	I'll Never Know Why/Faithfully Yours	1951	3.00	6.00	12.00
❑ F1502	Mr. Anthony's Blues/Cooks Tour	1951	3.00	6.00	12.00
❑ F1522	These Things I Offer You (For a Lifetime)/ Here's To Your Illusions	1951	3.00	6.00	12.00
❑ F1556	Villa/Melancholy Rhapsody	1951	3.00	6.00	12.00
❑ F1574	Believing You/One Dance with You	1951	3.00	6.00	12.00
❑ F1583	My Truly, Truly Fair/Pretty Eyed Baby	1951	3.00	6.00	12.00
❑ F1622	Star Dust/Man with a Horn	1951	3.00	6.00	12.00
❑ F1654	Tenderly/Autumn Nocturne	1951	3.00	6.00	12.00
❑ F1664	What Is This Thing Called Love/ Harlem Nocturne	1951	3.00	6.00	12.00
❑ F1678	As Time Goes By/At Last	1954	2.50	5.00	10.00
—*Reissue*					
❑ F1679	Mr. Anthony's Boogie/I Wonder What's Become of Sally	1954	2.50	5.00	10.00
—*Reissue*					
❑ F1723	I Love the Sunshine in Your Smile/You Blew Out the Flame	1951	3.00	6.00	12.00
❑ F1739	Mary Rose/Ho Ho	1951	3.00	6.00	12.00
❑ F1758	The Fox/Rollin' Home	1951	3.00	6.00	12.00
❑ F1810	Deep Night/With All My Heart and Soul	1951	3.00	6.00	12.00
❑ F1824	Undecided/Just a Moment More	1951	3.00	6.00	12.00
❑ F1835	My Concerto/I'll Remember April	1951	3.00	6.00	12.00
❑ F1857	Brother Fats/I Remember Harlem	1951	3.00	6.00	12.00
❑ F1884	Honeydriper/Busman's Holiday	1951	3.00	6.00	12.00
❑ F1912	At Last/I'll See You in My Dreams	1952	2.50	5.00	10.00
❑ F1956	Bermuda/Broken Hearted	1952	2.50	5.00	10.00
❑ F1957	Singin' in the Rain/I Let a Song Go Out of My Heart	1952	2.50	5.00	10.00
❑ F1973	I Hear a Rhapsody/For Dancers Only	1952	2.50	5.00	10.00
❑ F2002	There Are Such Things/Moonlight Savings Time	1952	2.50	5.00	10.00
❑ F2058	Trumpet Boogie/You're Driving Me Crazy	1952	2.50	5.00	10.00
❑ 6F-2085	Slaughter on Tenth Avenue (Part I)/Slaughter on Tenth Avenue (Part II)	1952	2.50	5.00	10.00
—*Has a maroon rather than purple label*					
❑ F2104	As Time Goes By/Scatterbrain	1952	2.50	5.00	10.00
❑ F2194	Make Believe Dreams/Loaded with Love	1952	2.50	5.00	10.00
❑ F2207	Marilyn/Randles Island	1952	5.00	10.00	20.00
❑ F2251	Bunny Hop/Blow, Man, Blow	1952	3.00	6.00	12.00
❑ F2293	Idaho/People in Love	1952	2.50	5.00	10.00
❑ F2327	On the Trail/Street Scene	1953	2.50	5.00	10.00
❑ F2349	You're a Heartbreaker/Wild Horses	1953	2.50	5.00	10.00
❑ F2393	True Blue Lou/They Didn't Believe Me	1953	2.50	5.00	10.00
❑ F2427	The Hokey Pokey/Bunny Hop	1953	3.00	6.00	12.00
❑ F2451	Piccadilly Circus/Thunderbird	1953	2.50	5.00	10.00
❑ F2488	When the Saints Go Marching In/That's My Weakness Now	1953	2.50	5.00	10.00
❑ F2532	Jersey Bounce/I Guess It Was You All the Time	1953	2.50	5.00	10.00
❑ F2562	Dragnet/Dancing in the Dark	1953	3.75	7.50	15.00
❑ F2637	Sound Off/Another Dawn, Another Day	1953	2.50	5.00	10.00
❑ F2678	O Mein Papa (O! My Papa)/Secret Love	1953	2.50	5.00	10.00
❑ F2699	Tuxedo Junction/In the Mood	1954	2.50	5.00	10.00
❑ F2728	Sign Post/Air Express	1954	2.50	5.00	10.00
❑ F2777	Dance My Heart/Somewhere Beyond Tonight	1954	2.50	5.00	10.00
❑ F2860	I Don't Hurt Anymore/Cat Dancin'	1954	2.50	5.00	10.00
❑ F2896	Skokiaan/Say Hey	1954	2.50	5.00	10.00
❑ F2936	A Woman's World/Jambo	1954	2.50	5.00	10.00
❑ F3029	Heat Wave/Juke Box Special	1955	2.50	5.00	10.00
❑ F3096	Sluefoot/Something's Gotta Give	1955	2.50	5.00	10.00
❑ F3147	Learning the Blues/Mmmm Marie	1955	2.50	5.00	10.00
❑ F3176	Pete Kelly's Blues/D.C. 7	1955	2.50	5.00	10.00
❑ F3261	Flip Flop/Hurricane Anthony	1955	2.50	5.00	10.00
❑ F3319	Bullfighter Lament/Rockin' Thru Dixie	1955	2.50	5.00	10.00
❑ F3335	Madeira/Show Me the Way to Go Home	1955	2.50	5.00	10.00
❑ F3416	Chubasco (Mexican Storm Song)/Sleepwalker	1956	2.00	4.00	8.00
❑ F3500	I Am in Love/I Love You Samantha	1956	2.00	4.00	8.00
❑ F3593	Love Is Just Around the Corner/ Danciong Lovers	1956	2.00	4.00	8.00
❑ F3646	Calypso Dance/Plymouth Rock	1957	2.00	4.00	8.00
❑ F3676	The Incredible Shrinking Man/ This Could Be the Night	1957	2.00	4.00	8.00
❑ F3739	Lonely Trumpet/Cello-Phane	1957	2.00	4.00	8.00
❑ F3897	Till There Was You/Big Record	1958	2.00	4.00	8.00
❑ F4041	Peter Gunn/Tango for Two	1958	2.50	5.00	10.00
❑ F4176	Walkin' to Mother's/Bunny Hop	1959	2.50	5.00	10.00
❑ F4227	Fly Now Pay Later/707	1959	2.00	4.00	8.00
❑ F4275	Room 45/Stockholm Blues	1959	2.00	4.00	8.00
❑ 4358	Just in Time/Tres Chic	1960	2.00	4.00	8.00
❑ 4440	Atsa Nice-a/ You Know It, You Know It, You Know It	1960	2.00	4.00	8.00
❑ 4513	Gurney Slade Theme/Return to Me	1961	2.00	4.00	8.00
❑ 4603	Moliendo Café/Champs Elysses	1961	2.00	4.00	8.00
❑ 4728	Bunny Hop Twist/Tequila with a Twist	1962	2.00	4.00	8.00
❑ 4742	Worried Mind/Al Di La	1962	2.00	4.00	8.00
❑ 4834	I Almost Lost My Mind/Trouble in Mind	1962	2.00	4.00	8.00
❑ 4876	Let Me Entertain You/Wishing Star	1962	2.00	4.00	8.00
❑ 4972	Heartaches/Mexican Market Day	1963	—	3.00	6.00
❑ 5026	Toys in the Attic/Oh Steal Away	1963	—	3.00	6.00
❑ 5070	Candy Wrapper/Mr. Novak	1963	—	3.00	6.00
❑ 5149	Let's All Do the Swim/Everybody Do the Swim	1964	—	3.00	6.00
❑ 5320	Lady Bird/Tiger Tail	1964	—	3.00	6.00
❑ 5418	Skunk in a Trunk/Sabor Ami	1965	—	3.00	6.00
❑ 5468	Seventh Son/Meeting Over Yonder	1965	—	3.00	6.00
❑ 5589	It's Such a Happy Day/Bah-Yoop	1966	—	3.00	6.00
❑ 5654	Goodbye My Love/Merci Cherie	1966	—	3.00	6.00
❑ 5714	Danke Schoen/Huapango Mexicana	1966	—	3.00	6.00
❑ 5836	Gallant Men/Around the World	1967	—	2.50	5.00

7-Inch Extended Plays
CAPITOL

Number	Title (A Side/B Side)	Yr	VG	VG+	NM
❑ EAP 1-373	I Wonder What's Become of Sally/Mr. Anthony's Boogie//The Man with the Horn/ Mr. Anthony's Blues	195?	3.00	6.00	12.00
❑ EAP 1-373 [PS]	(title unknown)	195?	3.00	6.00	12.00
❑ EAP 2-373	For Dancers Only/Harlem Nocturne//Tenderly/ Stardust	195?	3.00	6.00	12.00
❑ EAP 2-373 [PS]	(title unknown)	195?	3.00	6.00	12.00
❑ EBF 373 [PS]	(title unknown)	195?	3.00	6.00	12.00
—*Gatefold cover for some versions of 1-373 and 2-373*					
❑ EAP 1-406	*Slaughter on Tenth Avenue/ On the Trail/Street Scene	195?	3.00	6.00	12.00
❑ EAP 1-406 [PS]	Ray Anthony Concert	195?	3.00	6.00	12.00

Number	Title (A Side/B Side)	Yr	VG	VG+	NM
❑ 1-476	Tuxedo Junction/Chattanooga Choo Choo//Ida/ Moonlight Serenade	195?	2.50	5.00	10.00
❑ 2-476	Serenade in Blue/Elmer's Tune// In the Mood/I Know Why	195?	2.50	5.00	10.00
❑ EBF 476 [PS]	I Remember Glenn Miller	195?	2.50	5.00	10.00

—Two-pocket cover

Number	Title (A Side/B Side)	Yr	VG	VG+	NM
❑ EAP 1-504	Cooks Tour/Idaho//Jersey Bounce/Thunderbird	1955	2.50	5.00	10.00
❑ EAP 1-504 [PS]	Ray Anthony Plays for Dancing	1955	2.50	5.00	10.00
❑ EAP 1-563	Golden Horn/Amor//The Birth of the Blues/ The Brave Bulls	195?	2.50	5.00	10.00
❑ EAP 1-563 [PS]	Golden Horn, Part 1	195?	2.50	5.00	10.00
❑ EAP 1-597	Sluefoot/Dream//Something's Gotta Give/ Thunderbird	195?	2.50	5.00	10.00
❑ EAP 1-597 [PS]	Daddy Long Legs	195?	2.50	5.00	10.00
❑ EAP 1-1181	Peter Gunn/Fallout//Walkin' to Mothers/ Dreamsville	1959	3.00	6.00	12.00
❑ EAP 1-1181 [PS]	Peter Gunn	1959	3.00	6.00	12.00

Albums

AERO SPACE

Number	Title (A Side/B Side)	Yr	VG	VG+	NM
❑ RA 1007	Around the World	197?	2.50	5.00	10.00
❑ RA 1028	Let's Go Dancing	197?	3.00	6.00	12.00

—Green vinyl; Arthur Murray promotional item; add 25 percent if certificate for a free dance lesson is included

CAPITOL

Number	Title (A Side/B Side)	Yr	VG	VG+	NM
❑ H 258 [10]	Fox Trots	195?	10.00	20.00	40.00
❑ H 292 [10]	Houseparty Hop	195?	10.00	20.00	40.00

—Reissue of L 292; purple label; "This Album Contains 8 Selections" on upper right back cover

Number	Title (A Side/B Side)	Yr	VG	VG+	NM
❑ L 292 [10]	Houseparty Hop	195?	12.50	25.00	50.00

—Original issue; maroon label; "In addition to the selections listed, this long playing record contains: PERDIDO - WAGON WHEELS" under the title on back cover

Number	Title (A Side/B Side)	Yr	VG	VG+	NM
❑ H 362 [10]	Campus Rumpus	195?	12.50	25.00	50.00
❑ H 476 [10]	I Remember Glenn Miller	1954	10.00	20.00	40.00
❑ T 563 [M]	Golden Horn	1955	3.75	7.50	15.00
❑ T 723 [M]	Dream Dancing	1956	3.75	7.50	15.00
❑ T 749 [M]	Jam Session at the Tower	1956	10.00	20.00	40.00
❑ T 831 [M]	Star Dancing	1957	3.75	7.50	15.00
❑ T 866 [M]	Young Ideas	1957	3.75	7.50	15.00
❑ T 917 [M]	Moments Together	1958	3.75	7.50	15.00
❑ T 969 [M]	The Dream Girl	1958	3.75	7.50	15.00
❑ T 1028 [M]	Dancing Over the Waves	1958	3.75	7.50	15.00
❑ T 1066 [M]	Ray Anthony Plays Steve Allen	1958	3.75	7.50	15.00
❑ T 1200 [M]	Sound Spectacular	1959	3.75	7.50	15.00
❑ ST 1252 [S]	More Dream Dancing	1959	3.75	7.50	15.00
❑ T 1252 [M]	More Dream Dancing	1959	3.00	6.00	12.00
❑ ST 1304 [S]	Like Wild!	1959	3.75	7.50	15.00
❑ T 1304 [M]	Like Wild!	1959	3.00	6.00	12.00
❑ T 1371 [M]	Arthur Murray Favorites — Fox Trots	1960	3.00	6.00	12.00
❑ ST 1420 [S]	Dancing Alone Together	1960	3.75	7.50	15.00

—Black colorband label, Capitol logo at left

Number	Title (A Side/B Side)	Yr	VG	VG+	NM
❑ ST 1420 [S]	Dancing Alone Together	1962	3.00	6.00	12.00

—Black colorband label, Capitol logo at top

Number	Title (A Side/B Side)	Yr	VG	VG+	NM
❑ T 1420 [M]	Dancing Alone Together	1960	3.00	6.00	12.00

—Black colorband label, Capitol logo at left

Number	Title (A Side/B Side)	Yr	VG	VG+	NM
❑ T 1420 [M]	Dancing Alone Together	1962	2.50	5.00	10.00

—Black colorband label, Capitol logo at top

Number	Title (A Side/B Side)	Yr	VG	VG+	NM
❑ ST 1421 [S]	The New Ray Anthony Show	1960	3.75	7.50	15.00
❑ T 1421 [M]	The New Ray Anthony Show	1960	3.00	6.00	12.00
❑ T 1477 [M]	The Hits of Ray Anthony	1960	3.00	6.00	12.00
❑ ST 1608 [S]	Dream Dancing Medley	1961	3.75	7.50	15.00
❑ T 1608 [M]	Dream Dancing Medley	1961	3.00	6.00	12.00
❑ ST 1668 [S]	Twist with Ray Anthony	1961	3.75	7.50	15.00
❑ T 1668 [M]	Twist with Ray Anthony	1961	3.00	6.00	12.00
❑ ST 1752 [S]	Worried Mind	1962	3.75	7.50	15.00
❑ T 1752 [M]	Worried Mind	1962	3.00	6.00	12.00
❑ ST 1783 [S]	I Almost Lost My Mind	1962	3.75	7.50	15.00
❑ T 1783 [M]	I Almost Lost My Mind	1962	3.00	6.00	12.00
❑ ST 1917 [S]	Smash Hits of '63	1963	3.75	7.50	15.00
❑ T 1917 [M]	Smash Hits of '63	1963	3.00	6.00	12.00
❑ ST 2043 [S]	Charade and Other Top Themes	1964	3.75	7.50	15.00
❑ T 2043 [M]	Charade and Other Top Themes	1964	3.00	6.00	12.00
❑ ST 2150 [S]	My Love, Forgive Me	1964	3.75	7.50	15.00
❑ T 2150 [M]	My Love, Forgive Me	1964	3.00	6.00	12.00
❑ ST 2188 [S]	Swim, Swim, C'mon, Let's Swim	1964	3.75	7.50	15.00
❑ T 2188 [M]	Swim, Swim, C'mon, Let's Swim	1964	3.00	6.00	12.00
❑ ST 2457 [S]	Dream Dancing Today	1966	3.75	7.50	15.00
❑ T 2457 [M]	Dream Dancing Today	1966	3.00	6.00	12.00
❑ ST 2530 [S]	Hit Songs to Remember	1966	3.75	7.50	15.00
❑ T 2530 [M]	Hit Songs to Remember	1966	3.00	6.00	12.00
❑ M-11978	Fox Trots	1979	2.50	5.00	10.00

CIRCLE

Number	Title (A Side/B Side)	Yr	VG	VG+	NM
❑ CLP-96	Sweet and Swingin' 1949-1953	1987	2.50	5.00	10.00

HINDSIGHT

Number	Title (A Side/B Side)	Yr	VG	VG+	NM
❑ HSR-240	Young Man with a Horn	1988	2.50	5.00	10.00

RANWOOD

Number	Title (A Side/B Side)	Yr	VG	VG+	NM
❑ R.8033	Now	197?	2.50	5.00	10.00

—Cover uses "R." prefix, label uses "RLP" prefix

Number	Title (A Side/B Side)	Yr	VG	VG+	NM
❑ 8059	Love Is for the Two of Us	197?	2.50	5.00	10.00
❑ 8083	I Get the Blues When It Rains	197?	2.50	5.00	10.00
❑ 8153	Golden Hits	197?	2.50	5.00	10.00

ANTHONY, RAYBURN

45s

SUN

Number	Title (A Side/B Side)	Yr	VG	VG+	NM
❑ 333	Alice Blue Gown/St. Louis Blues	1959	5.00	10.00	20.00
❑ 339	There's No Tomorrow/Who's Gonna Shoe Your Pretty Foot	1960	5.00	10.00	20.00
❑ 373	Big Dream/How Well I Know	1962	5.00	10.00	20.00

ANTHONY, TONY

45s

HERALD

Number	Title (A Side/B Side)	Yr	VG	VG+	NM
❑ 533	Peek-a-Boo/Lonely One	1959	7.50	15.00	30.00

ANTHONY AND THE SOPHOMORES Also see THE DYNAMICS (3).

45s

ABC

Number	Title (A Side/B Side)	Yr	VG	VG+	NM
❑ 10844	Heartbreak/I'll Go Through Life Loving You	1966	5.00	10.00	20.00

ABC-PARAMOUNT

Number	Title (A Side/B Side)	Yr	VG	VG+	NM
❑ 10737	Gee (But I'd Give the World)/It Depends On You	1965	5.00	10.00	20.00
❑ 10770	Get Back to You/Wild for Her	1966	5.00	10.00	20.00

GRAND

Number	Title (A Side/B Side)	Yr	VG	VG+	NM
❑ 163	Embraceable You/Beautiful Dreamer	1963	15.00	30.00	60.00

JAMIE

Number	Title (A Side/B Side)	Yr	VG	VG+	NM
❑ 1330	Serenade (From The Student Prince)/Work Out	1967	3.75	7.50	15.00
❑ 1340	One Summer Night/Work Out	1967	3.75	7.50	15.00

JASON SCOTT

Number	Title (A Side/B Side)	Yr	VG	VG+	NM
❑ 18	Embraceable You/Beautiful Dreamer	1978	—	2.00	4.00

MERCURY

Number	Title (A Side/B Side)	Yr	VG	VG+	NM
❑ 72103	Play Those Oldies Mr. D.J./Clap Your Hands	1963	15.00	30.00	60.00
❑ 72168	Swingin' at the Chariot/Better Late Than Never	1963	7.50	15.00	30.00

ANTIQUES, THE

45s

LASALLE

Number	Title (A Side/B Side)	Yr	VG	VG+	NM
❑ 0069	Go for Yourself/(B-side unknown)	196?	300.00	600.00	1200.

ANTOINETTE

45s

PARKWAY

Number	Title (A Side/B Side)	Yr	VG	VG+	NM
❑ 932	There He Goes/Little Things Mean a Lot	1964	3.00	6.00	12.00

ANTWINETTES, THE

45s

RCA VICTOR

Number	Title (A Side/B Side)	Yr	VG	VG+	NM
❑ 47-7398	Johnny/Kill It	1958	10.00	20.00	40.00

AORTA

45s

ATLANTIC

Number	Title (A Side/B Side)	Yr	VG	VG+	NM
❑ 2545	Strange/Shape of Things to Come	1968	5.00	10.00	20.00

COLUMBIA

Number	Title (A Side/B Side)	Yr	VG	VG+	NM
❑ 44870	Strange/Ode to Missy Mztsfpklk	1969	2.50	5.00	10.00

HAPPY TIGER

Number	Title (A Side/B Side)	Yr	VG	VG+	NM
❑ 567	Sandcastles/Willie Jean	1970	3.75	7.50	15.00

Albums

COLUMBIA

Number	Title (A Side/B Side)	Yr	VG	VG+	NM
❑ CS 9785	Aorta	1969	7.50	15.00	30.00

HAPPY TIGER

Number	Title (A Side/B Side)	Yr	VG	VG+	NM
❑ HT-1010	Aorta 2	1970	10.00	20.00	40.00

APHRODITE'S CHILD

45s

PHILIPS

Number	Title (A Side/B Side)	Yr	VG	VG+	NM
❑ 40536	Other People/Plastics Nevermore	1968	5.00	10.00	20.00
❑ 40587	End of the World/You Always Stand in My Way	1969	5.00	10.00	20.00

POLYDOR

Number	Title (A Side/B Side)	Yr	VG	VG+	NM
❑ 15005	Magic Mirror/I Want to Live	1969	2.00	4.00	8.00

VERTIGO

Number	Title (A Side/B Side)	Yr	VG	VG+	NM
❑ 107	Babylon/Break	1973	—	3.00	6.00

Albums

VERTIGO

Number	Title (A Side/B Side)	Yr	VG	VG+	NM
❑ VEL-2-500 [(2)]	666 (The Apocalypse of John)	1972	5.00	10.00	20.00

APOLLO 100

45s

ATCO

Number	Title (A Side/B Side)	Yr	VG	VG+	NM
❑ 7001	Dan the Banjo Man/Tidal Wave	1974	—	3.00	6.00

MEGA

Number	Title (A Side/B Side)	Yr	VG	VG+	NM
❑ 0050	Joy/Exercise in A Minor	1971	—	2.50	5.00
❑ 0069	Symphony #4, 2nd Movement/Reach for the Sky	1972	—	2.00	4.00
❑ 0080	Minuet for a Funky Lady/Telstar	1972	—	2.00	4.00

Albums

MEGA

Number	Title (A Side/B Side)	Yr	VG	VG+	NM
❑ 31-1010	Joy	1972	2.50	5.00	10.00

APPALACHIANS, THE

45s

ABC-PARAMOUNT

Number	Title (A Side/B Side)	Yr	VG	VG+	NM
❑ 10419	Bony Maronie/It Takes a Man	1963	2.50	5.00	10.00
❑ 10464	Big Betty/Hilly-Billy-Ding-Dong-Choo-Choo	1963	2.00	4.00	8.00
❑ 10498	Lawdy Miss Clawdy/Over Yonder	1963	2.00	4.00	8.00

APPALOOSA

Albums

COLUMBIA

Number	Title (A Side/B Side)	Yr	VG	VG+	NM
❑ CS 9819	Appaloosa	1969	3.75	7.50	15.00

—Produced by Al Kooper

APPELL, DAVE See THE APPLEJACKS (1).

APPLE PIE MOTHERHOOD BAND, THE

45s

ATLANTIC

Number	Title (A Side/B Side)	Yr	VG	VG+	NM
❑ 2477	Flight Path/Long Live Apple Pie	1968	2.00	4.00	8.00

Albums

ATLANTIC

Number	Title (A Side/B Side)	Yr	VG	VG+	NM
❑ SD 8189	The Apple Pie Motherhood Band	1968	6.25	12.50	25.00
❑ SD 8233	Apple Pie	1969	6.25	12.50	25.00

APPLEJACKS, THE (1) Essentially Dave Appell. The below includes his "solo" records.

45s

B.T. PUPPY

Number	Title (A Side/B Side)	Yr	VG	VG+	NM
❑ 554	The Son of a Preacher Man/Girl of the Skies	1970	2.00	4.00	8.00

—As "Dave Appell"

Number	Title (A Side/B Side)	Yr	VG	VG+	NM
CAMEO					
❏ 110	Love in the Jungle/Chitter Chatter Baby	1957	5.00	10.00	20.00
❏ 132	Dinner with Drac/No Name Theme	1958	6.25	12.50	25.00
❏ 138	Moonlight Serenade/Walk On	1958	5.00	10.00	20.00
❏ 149	Mexican Hat Rock/Stop! Red Light	1958	4.00	8.00	16.00
❏ 149	Mexican Hat Rock/Sophisticated Swing	1958	5.00	10.00	20.00
❏ 155	Rocka-Conga/Am I Blue	1958	4.00	8.00	16.00
—Later pressings have correct A-side title					
❏ 155	Rocka-Tonga/Am I Blue	1958	5.00	10.00	20.00
—First pressing contains a typographical error on A-side					
❏ 158	Bunny Hop/Night Train Stroll	1959	4.00	8.00	16.00
❏ 170	Circle Dance/Love Scene	1959	4.00	8.00	16.00
❏ 177	The Untouchables/Memories Are Made of This	1960	4.00	8.00	16.00
❏ 184	Theme from The Young Ones/September Song	1960	3.75	7.50	15.00
—As "Dave Appell and His Orchestra"					
❏ 203	Mexican Hat Twist/Let's Continental	1961	3.75	7.50	15.00
❏ 207	Happy Jose/Noivous	1961	3.75	7.50	15.00
—As "Dave Appell and His Orchestra"					
❏ 222	Struttin' in the Summertime/Any Time	1962	3.75	7.50	15.00
❏ 248	Hippies Waltz/Back in 60 Seconds	1963	3.75	7.50	15.00
❏ 283	Hot Toddy/Dance of the Hours	1963	3.75	7.50	15.00
❏ 321	She Loves You/Bongo Beach	1964	3.75	7.50	15.00
—As "Dave Appell and The Applejacks (Featuring Joe Sher on Drums)"					
DECCA					
❏ 9-29218	Smarter/My Heart Will Wait for You	1954	5.00	10.00	20.00
❏ 9-29330	Sweet Patootie Pie/Reunion	1954	5.00	10.00	20.00
Albums					
CAMEO					
❏ C-1004 [M]	Alone Together	1958	12.50	25.00	50.00
—As "Dave Appell"					

APPLEJACKS, THE (2) British band.
45s

Number	Title (A Side/B Side)	Yr	VG	VG+	NM
LONDON					
❏ 9658	Baby Jane/Tell Me When	1964	3.00	6.00	12.00
❏ 9681	Like Dreamers Do/Everybody Fall Down	1964	3.75	7.50	15.00
❏ 9709	You're the One for Me/Send Me Love	1964	3.00	6.00	12.00
❏ 9709	You're the One for Me/Three Little Words	1964	3.00	6.00	12.00

APPLEJACKS, THE (U)
45s

Number	Title (A Side/B Side)	Yr	VG	VG+	NM
PRESIDENT					
❏ 1005	Ring Around My Baby/Love Express	1956	5.00	10.00	20.00
❏ 1006	Teenage Meeting/Ooh Baby Ooh	1956	5.00	10.00	20.00
❏ 1011	Rock and Roll Story/Rainbow of Love	1956	5.00	10.00	20.00

APPLETREE THEATRE CO.
45s

Number	Title (A Side/B Side)	Yr	VG	VG+	NM
VERVE FORECAST					
❏ 5071	Hightower Square/Who Do You Think I Am	1967	3.00	6.00	12.00
❏ 5082	Lotus Flower/What a Way to Go	1968	3.00	6.00	12.00
Albums					
VERVE FORECAST					
❏ FTS-3042	Playback	1968	7.50	15.00	30.00
—RICK NELSON appears on this album					

APPRECIATIONS, THE
45s

Number	Title (A Side/B Side)	Yr	VG	VG+	NM
JUBILEE					
❏ 5525	Afraid of Love/Far from Your Love	1966	3.00	6.00	12.00
SPORT					
❏ 108	There's a Place in My Heart/She Never Really Believed Me	1967	25.00	50.00	100.00
❏ 112	It's Better to Cry/Gimme Back My Soul	1967	50.00	100.00	200.00

APRIL WINE
12-Inch Singles

Number	Title (A Side/B Side)	Yr	VG	VG+	NM
CAPITOL					
❏ SPRO-9069 [DJ]	This Could Be the Right One (same on both sides)	1984	2.50	5.00	10.00
❏ SPRO-9110 [DJ]	Sons of the Pioneers (same on both sides)	1984	2.50	5.00	10.00
❏ SPRO-9468 [DJ]	Rock Myself to Sleep (same on both sides)	1985	2.50	5.00	10.00
45s					
BIG TREE					
❏ 133	You Could Have Been a Lady/Teacher	1972	—	3.00	6.00
❏ 142	Bad Side of the Moon/Believe in Me	1972	—	2.50	5.00
❏ 15006	Come On Along/I'm on Fire for You Baby	1974	—	2.50	5.00
❏ 16010	Just Like That/Weeping Willow	1973	—	2.50	5.00
❏ 16036	Oowatanite/(B-side unknown)	1975	—	2.50	5.00
CAPITOL					
❏ 4660	Roller/Right Down to It	1978	—	2.00	4.00
❏ 4728	Get Ready for Love/ Comin' Right Down on Top of Me	1979	—	2.00	4.00
❏ 4802	Before the Dawn/Say Hello	1979	—	2.00	4.00
❏ 4828	I Like to Rock/Babes in Arms	1980	—	2.00	4.00
❏ 4859	Lady's Man/Tonite	1980	—	2.00	4.00
❏ 4975	Just Between You and Me/Big City Girls	1981	—	2.00	4.00
❏ 4975 [PS]	Just Between You and Me/Big City Girls	1981	—	2.50	5.00
—Regular sleeve					
❏ 4975 [PS]	Just Between You and Me/Big City Girls	1981	2.00	4.00	8.00
—Fold-out poster sleeve					
❏ A-5001	Sign of the Gypsy Queen/Crash and Burn	1981	—	2.00	4.00
❏ A-5001 [PS]	Sign of the Gypsy Queen/Crash and Burn	1981	—	2.50	5.00
❏ B-5133	Enough Is Enough/Ain't Got Your Love	1982	—	2.00	4.00
❏ B-5133 [PS]	Enough Is Enough/Ain't Got Your Love	1982	—	2.00	4.00
❏ B-5153	If You See Kay/Blood Money	1982	—	2.50	5.00
❏ B-5168	Tell Me Why/Runners in the Night	1982	—	2.00	4.00
❏ B-5319	This Could Be the Right One/ Really Don't Want Your Love	1984	—	—	3.00
❏ B-5319 [PS]	This Could Be the Right One/ Really Don't Want Your Love	1984	—	2.00	4.00
❏ B-5506	Rock Myself to Sleep/All It Will Ever Be	1985	—	—	3.00

Number	Title (A Side/B Side)	Yr	VG	VG+	NM
LONDON					
❏ 245	Shot Down/(B-side unknown)	1976	—	2.50	5.00
❏ 255	You Won't Dance with Me/Shot Down	1976	—	2.50	5.00
❏ 265	I'm Alive/Rock and Roll Is a Vicious Game	1977	—	2.50	5.00
Albums					
AQUARIUS					
❏ AQR 504	Electric Jewels	1973	3.75	7.50	15.00
❏ AQR 505	Live	1974	3.75	7.50	15.00
ATLANTIC					
❏ SD 19303	Stand Back	1981	2.50	5.00	10.00
—Reissue of Big Tree 89506					
BIG TREE					
❏ BTS 2012	April Wine	1972	5.00	10.00	20.00
❏ 89506	Stand Back	1975	3.75	7.50	15.00
CAPITOL					
❏ SPRO-9632/3 [DJ]	Summer Tour 1981	1981	5.00	10.00	20.00
—Promo-only sampler					
❏ ST-11852	First Glance	1979	3.00	6.00	12.00
❏ ST-12013	Harder...Faster	1979	2.50	5.00	10.00
❏ SOO-12125	The Nature of the Beast	1981	2.50	5.00	10.00
❏ ST-12218	Power Play	1982	2.50	5.00	10.00
❏ ST-12311	Animal Grace	1984	2.50	5.00	10.00
❏ SN-16245	First Glance	1982	2.00	4.00	8.00
—Budget-line reissue					
❏ SN-16322	Harder...Faster	1984	2.00	4.00	8.00
—Budget-line reissue					
❏ SN-16344	Power Play	1984	2.00	4.00	8.00
—Budget-line reissue					
❏ SN-16379	The Nature of the Beast	1986	2.00	4.00	8.00
—Budget-line reissue					
❏ C1-48418	Walking Through Fire	1988	3.00	6.00	12.00
LONDON					
❏ PS 675	The Whole World's Goin' Crazy	1976	3.75	7.50	15.00
❏ PS 699	Live at the El Mocambo	1977	3.75	7.50	15.00

AQUARIANS
45s

Number	Title (A Side/B Side)	Yr	VG	VG+	NM
UNI					
❏ 55124	Abela/Jungle Grass	1969	—	3.00	6.00
Albums					
UNI					
❏ 73053	Jungle Grass	1969	3.75	7.50	15.00

AQUATONES, THE
45s

Number	Title (A Side/B Side)	Yr	VG	VG+	NM
FARGO					
❏ 1001	You/She's the One for Me	1958	6.25	12.50	25.00
❏ 1002	Say You'll Be Mine/So Fine	1958	6.25	12.50	25.00
❏ 1003	Our First Kiss/The Drive-In	1958	6.25	12.50	25.00
❏ 1005	My Treasure/My One Desire	1959	6.25	12.50	25.00
❏ 1015	Every Time/There's a Long, Long Trail	1960	6.25	12.50	25.00
❏ 1016	Wanted/Crazy for You	1961	6.25	12.50	25.00
❏ 1022	My Treasure/Say You'll Be Mine	1962	6.25	12.50	25.00
❏ 1111	My Darling/For You, For You	1960	5.00	10.00	20.00
Albums					
FARGO					
❏ 3001 [M]	The Aquatones Sing	1964	125.00	250.00	500.00
RELIC/FARGO					
❏ 5033 [M]	The Aquatones Sing	198?	2.00	4.00	8.00

ARBORS, THE
45s

Number	Title (A Side/B Side)	Yr	VG	VG+	NM
CARNEY					
❏ 1011	A Symphony for Susan/Love Is the Light	1966	6.25	12.50	25.00
DATE					
❏ 1529	A Symphony for Susan/Love Is the Light	1966	2.50	5.00	10.00
❏ 1546	Dreamer Girl/Just Let It Happen	1967	2.50	5.00	10.00
❏ 1561	Graduation Day/I Win the Whole Wide World	1967	2.50	5.00	10.00
❏ 1570	Love for All Seasons/With You Girl	1967	2.50	5.00	10.00
❏ 1581	Valley of the Dolls/You Are the Music	1967	2.50	5.00	10.00
❏ 1581 [PS]	Valley of the Dolls/You Are the Music	1967	6.25	12.50	25.00
❏ 1601	That's the Way It Is/Graduation Day	1968	2.50	5.00	10.00
❏ 1638	The Letter/Most of All	1969	3.00	6.00	12.00
❏ 1645	I Can't Quit Her/Lovin' Tonight (Maybe Tonight)	1969	2.50	5.00	10.00
❏ 1651	Touch Me/Motet	1969	2.50	5.00	10.00
❏ 1672	Julie I Tried/Okalona River Bottom Band	1970	2.50	5.00	10.00
MERCURY					
❏ 72456	Anybody Here for Love/The Girl with the Heather Green Eyes	1965	3.00	6.00	12.00
Albums					
DATE					
❏ TEM 3003 [M]	A Symphony for Susan	1967	3.75	7.50	15.00
❏ TEM 3011 [M]	Valley of the Dolls	1967	5.00	10.00	20.00
❏ TES 4003 [S]	A Symphony for Susan	1967	3.75	7.50	15.00
❏ TES 4011 [S]	Valley of the Dolls	1967	3.75	7.50	15.00
❏ TES 4017	The Arbors Featuring I Can't Quit Her and The Letter	1969	3.75	7.50	15.00

ARCHERS, THE
45s

Number	Title (A Side/B Side)	Yr	VG	VG+	NM
LAURIE					
❏ 3207	Hey Rube/Unwind It	1963	3.75	7.50	15.00
SUMMER					
❏ 502	Motorcycle Michael/Golden Girl	196?	7.50	15.00	30.00

ARCHIBALD
45s

Number	Title (A Side/B Side)	Yr	VG	VG+	NM
IMPERIAL					
❏ 5212	Early Morning Blues/Great Big Eyes	1953	750.00	1125.	1500.
❏ 5358	Stack-O-Lee (Part 1)/Stack-O-Lee (Part 2)	1955	25.00	50.00	100.00
❏ 5563	Stack-A-Lee/Whispering Hope	1959	12.50	25.00	50.00

Number	Title (A Side/B Side)	Yr	VG	VG+	NM

ARCHIES, THE Also see RON DANTE.
12-Inch Singles
CULT

Number	Title (A Side/B Side)	Yr	VG	VG+	NM
0595	Sugar Sugar (Julian Beeston Remix '99) (Pistel Remix '99)	2000	—	3.00	6.00

45s
CALENDAR

Number	Title (A Side/B Side)	Yr	VG	VG+	NM
63-1006	Bang-Shang-a-Lang/Truck Driver	1968	2.00	4.00	8.00
63-1006 [PS]	Bang-Shang-a-Lang/Truck Driver	1968	4.00	8.00	16.00
63-1007	Feelin' So Good (S.K.O.O.B.Y.-D.O.O.)/ Love Light	1968	2.00	4.00	8.00
63-1007 [PS]	Feelin' So Good (S.K.O.O.B.Y.-D.O.O.)/ Love Light	1968	6.25	12.50	25.00
63-1008	Sugar Sugar/Melody Hill	1969	2.50	5.00	10.00

KIRSHNER

Number	Title (A Side/B Side)	Yr	VG	VG+	NM
SP-45-218 [DJ]	Sunshine (same on both sides)	1970	3.75	7.50	15.00
—Promo-only number					
63-1009	Sunshine/Over and Over	1970	2.00	4.00	8.00
63-5002	Jingle Jangle/Justine	1969	2.00	4.00	8.00
63-5003	Who's Your Baby/Senorita Rita	1970	2.00	4.00	8.00
63-5009	Everything's Alright/Together We Two	1970	2.00	4.00	8.00
63-5011	Throw a Little Love My Way/This Is Love	1971	2.00	4.00	8.00
63-5014	A Summer Prayer for Peace/Maybe I'm Wrong	1971	2.00	4.00	8.00
63-5014 [PS]	A Summer Prayer for Peace/Maybe I'm Wrong	1971	4.00	8.00	16.00
63-5018	Love Is Living in You/Hold On to Lovin'	1972	2.00	4.00	8.00
63-5021	Strangers in the Morning/Plum Crazy	1972	2.00	4.00	8.00

Albums
ACCORD

Number	Title (A Side/B Side)	Yr	VG	VG+	NM
SN-7149	Straight A's	1981	2.50	5.00	10.00

CALENDAR

Number	Title (A Side/B Side)	Yr	VG	VG+	NM
KES-101	The Archies	1968	6.25	12.50	25.00
KES-103	Everything's Archie	1969	6.25	12.50	25.00

51 WEST

Number	Title (A Side/B Side)	Yr	VG	VG+	NM
16002	The Archies	1979	2.50	5.00	10.00

KIRSHNER

Number	Title (A Side/B Side)	Yr	VG	VG+	NM
KES-103 [DJ]	Everything's Archie Box	1969	25.00	50.00	100.00
—Box with LP, photos, press kit and buttons					
KES-105	Jingle Jangle	1969	6.25	12.50	25.00
KES-107	Sunshine	1970	6.25	12.50	25.00
KES-109	The Archies Greatest Hits	1970	6.25	12.50	25.00
KES-110	This Is Love	1971	7.50	15.00	30.00

ARDELLS, THE
45s
EPIC

Number	Title (A Side/B Side)	Yr	VG	VG+	NM
9621	Eefananny/Lonely Valley	1963	3.75	7.50	15.00
9621 [PS]	Eefananny/Lonely Valley	1963	7.50	15.00	30.00
—Title sleeve with lyrics					

MARCO

Number	Title (A Side/B Side)	Yr	VG	VG+	NM
102	Every Day of the Week/Roll On	1961	7.50	15.00	30.00

SELMA

Number	Title (A Side/B Side)	Yr	VG	VG+	NM
4001	Seven Lonely Nights/You Can Fall in Love	1963	6.25	12.50	25.00

ARDEN, TONI
45s
BONFIRE

Number	Title (A Side/B Side)	Yr	VG	VG+	NM
1501	Don't You Come Home Bill Bailey/I'll Say It Again	197?	—	3.00	6.00

COLUMBIA

Number	Title (A Side/B Side)	Yr	VG	VG+	NM
1-377	I Can Dream, Can't I?/A Little Hug, a Little Kiss	1949	7.50	15.00	30.00
—Microgroove 33 1/3 rpm 7-inch single, small hole					
1-560 (?)	Mother, Mother, Mother/Rain	1950	7.50	15.00	30.00
—Microgroove 33 1/3 rpm 7-inch single, small hole					
1-630 (?)	Why/Tonight	1950	7.50	15.00	30.00
—Microgroove 33 1/3 rpm 7-inch single, small hole					
1-760 (?)	Can't We Talk It Over/Only a Moment Ago	1950	7.50	15.00	30.00
—Microgroove 33 1/3 rpm 7-inch single, small hole					
1-830 (?)	My Tears Won't Dry/And You'll Be Home	1950	7.50	15.00	30.00
—Microgroove 33 1/3 rpm 7-inch single, small hole					
1-937 (?)	Every Moment/I'm Praying to St. Christopher	1950	7.50	15.00	30.00
—Microgroove 33 1/3 rpm 7-inch single, small hole					
4-39003	My Tears Won't Dry/And You'll Be Home	1950	5.00	10.00	20.00
4-39080	Every Moment/I'm Praying to St. Christopher	1950	5.00	10.00	20.00
4-39117	My Man/Playing Our Song	1950	5.00	10.00	20.00
4-39208	Chante Moi/So Deep in Love	1951	3.75	7.50	15.00
4-39271	Too Young/Too Late Now	1951	3.75	7.50	15.00
4-39348	Little Child/Come Back to Sorrento	1951	3.75	7.50	15.00
4-39427	Wonder Why/Dark Is the Night	1951	3.75	7.50	15.00
4-39525	The Day Isn't Long Enough/ I'll Hold You In My Heart	1951	3.75	7.50	15.00
4-39577	Once/Never	1951	3.75	7.50	15.00
4-39650	Heart of Stone/There's Always My Heart	1952	3.75	7.50	15.00
4-39737	Kiss of Fire/I'm Yours	1952	3.75	7.50	15.00
4-39766	Blow Out the Candle/Where Did the Night Go	1952	3.75	7.50	15.00
4-39768	Take My Heart/Tell Your Tale, Nightingale	1952	3.75	7.50	15.00
4-39810	Remembering/One Love Too Many	1952	3.75	7.50	15.00
4-39878	Take a Chance/Sweet Forgiveness	1952	3.75	7.50	15.00
4-39911	Kiss/It's Not Their Heartache	1953	3.75	7.50	15.00
4-40019	All I Desire/Lover's Waltz	1953	3.75	7.50	15.00
—With the Four Lads					
4-40081	I Forgot More Than You'll Ever Know/Any More	1953	3.75	7.50	15.00
4-40125	Take Me Now/I Wish I Knew	1953	3.75	7.50	15.00
4-40196	In Paris and In Love/Cry, My Heart	1954	3.75	7.50	15.00
4-40225	Three Coins in the Fountain/When the Rolling Mountains Meet the Rolling Sea	1954	3.75	7.50	15.00

DECCA

Number	Title (A Side/B Side)	Yr	VG	VG+	NM
25542	Arrivederci Roma/Non Dimenticar	196?	2.00	4.00	8.00
25586	Come Back to Sorrento/Senza Mama E Namurato	196?	2.00	4.00	8.00
9-30180	Little by Little/Without Love	1957	2.50	5.00	10.00
9-30291	Like a Baby/An Empty Heart	1957	2.50	5.00	10.00
9-30396	It Takes Only One/Good Morning, Mister Love	1957	2.50	5.00	10.00
9-30507	Like You/Can You Blame Me	1957	2.50	5.00	10.00
9-30563	King Size Love/Queen of Tears	1958	2.50	5.00	10.00
9-30628	Padre/All at Once	1958	3.00	6.00	12.00
9-30732	You're Not Losing a Daughter Mama/If Your Heart Doesn't Dance	1958	2.50	5.00	10.00
9-30765	Desire Me/The Window	1958	2.50	5.00	10.00
9-30832	Just for Once/Why, Why, Why (Zon, Zon, Zon)	1959	2.50	5.00	10.00
9-30951	Only with You (You Are Me, I Am You)/ Your Touch	1959	2.50	5.00	10.00
9-30986	Besame Mucho/Anna	1959	2.50	5.00	10.00
9-31025	The Village of St. Bernadette/ Feeling Foolish in Brazil	1959	2.50	5.00	10.00
9-31139	Na Voce Na Chittara (E'o Poco E Luna) (I Only Know I Love You)/No, No, Nevermore	1960	2.00	4.00	8.00
31576	In the Summer of His Years/My Heart Is a Chapel	1963	2.00	4.00	8.00
31694	Quando, Quando, Quando/It's True, It's True	1964	2.00	4.00	8.00
7-34175 [S]	Just Say I Love Him/Anema E Core	196?	3.00	6.00	12.00
7-34176 [S]	Come Prima/Summertime in Venice	196?	3.00	6.00	12.00
7-34177 [S]	Padre/Quando, Quando, Quando	196?	3.00	6.00	12.00
7-34178 [S]	Al Di La/Retorna a Me	196?	3.00	6.00	12.00
7-34179 [S]	Guaglione/Mama	196?	3.00	6.00	12.00
—The above five are small hole, 33 1/3 rpm jukebox singles					

RCA VICTOR

Number	Title (A Side/B Side)	Yr	VG	VG+	NM
47-6142	Beware/I'll Step Aside	1955	3.00	6.00	12.00
47-6346	Are You Satisfied/ I Forgot to Remember to Forget	1956	3.75	7.50	15.00
47-6536	Believe in Love/How Sweet My Love	1956	3.00	6.00	12.00

Albums
DECCA

Number	Title (A Side/B Side)	Yr	VG	VG+	NM
DL 4375 [M]	Italian Gold	196?	3.00	6.00	12.00
DL 8651 [M]	Miss Toni Arden	1957	7.50	15.00	30.00
—Black label, silver print					
DL 8765 [M]	Sing a Song of Italy	1958	6.25	12.50	25.00
—Black label, silver print					
DL 8875 [M]	Besame	1959	5.00	10.00	20.00
—Black label, silver print					
DL 74375 [S]	Italian Gold	196?	3.75	7.50	15.00
DL 78765 [S]	Sing a Song of Italy	1959	7.50	15.00	30.00
—Maroon label, silver print					

HARMONY

Number	Title (A Side/B Side)	Yr	VG	VG+	NM
HL 7212 [M]	Exciting Toni Arden	196?	5.00	10.00	20.00

AREA CODE 615
45s
POLYDOR

Number	Title (A Side/B Side)	Yr	VG	VG+	NM
14012	Why Ask Why/Ruby	1969	—	3.00	6.00
14215	Stone Fox Chase/Sligo	1973	—	2.50	5.00

Albums
POLYDOR

Number	Title (A Side/B Side)	Yr	VG	VG+	NM
24-4002	Area Code 615	1969	5.00	10.00	20.00
24-4025	A Trip in the Country	1970	5.00	10.00	20.00

ARENA BRASS, THE
Albums
EPIC

Number	Title (A Side/B Side)	Yr	VG	VG+	NM
LN 24039 [M]	The Lonely Bull	1962	3.00	6.00	12.00
BN 26039 [S]	The Lonely Bull	1962	3.75	7.50	15.00

ARGENT Rod Argent's group after THE ZOMBIES broke up. Also see RUSS BALLARD.
45s
DATE

Number	Title (A Side/B Side)	Yr	VG	VG+	NM
1659	Liar/Schoolgirl	1970	2.50	5.00	10.00

EPIC

Number	Title (A Side/B Side)	Yr	VG	VG+	NM
10718	Rejoice/Sweet Mary	1971	—	3.00	6.00
10746	Celebration/Kingdom	1971	—	3.00	6.00
10852	Hold Your Head Up/Closer to Heaven	1972	2.00	4.00	8.00
10919	Tragedy/He's a Dynamo	1972	—	2.50	5.00
10972	God Gave Rock and Roll To You/Christmas for the Free	1973	—	2.50	5.00
11019	It's Only Money, Part 2/Losing Hold	1973	—	2.50	5.00
11137	Man for All Seasons/Music from the Spheres	1974	—	2.50	5.00
50025	The Coming of Kohoutek/Thunder and Lightning	1974	—	2.50	5.00

Albums
EPIC

Number	Title (A Side/B Side)	Yr	VG	VG+	NM
BN 26525	Argent	1970	5.00	10.00	20.00
—Yellow label					
BN 26525	Argent	1973	3.00	6.00	12.00
—Orange label					
E 30128	A Ring of Hands	1971	5.00	10.00	20.00
—Yellow label					
KE 30128	A Ring of Hands	1973	3.00	6.00	12.00
—Orange label					
KE 31556	All Together Now	1972	5.00	10.00	20.00
—Yellow label					
KE 31556	All Together Now	1973	3.00	6.00	12.00
—Orange label					
KE 32195	In Deep	1973	5.00	10.00	20.00
—Orange label					
KE 32195	In Deep	1973	6.25	12.50	25.00
—Yellow label					
PEQ 32195 [Q]	In Deep	1974	7.50	15.00	30.00
PE 32573	Nexus	1974	5.00	10.00	20.00
—Orange label					
PEG 33079 [(2)]	Encore — Live in Concert	1975	5.00	10.00	20.00
—Orange labels					
PE 33422	Circus	1975	5.00	10.00	20.00
—Orange label					
PE 33955	Anthology	1976	3.75	7.50	15.00
—Orange label					
PE 33955	Anthology	1979	2.50	5.00	10.00
—Dark blue label					

Number	Title (A Side/B Side)	Yr	VG	VG+	NM
UNITED ARTISTS					
❏ UA-LA560-G	Counterpoint	1975	3.00	6.00	12.00

ARGYLES, THE (1) See THE HOLLYWOOD ARGYLES.

ARGYLES, THE (2)
45s

Number	Title (A Side/B Side)	Yr	VG	VG+	NM
BALLY					
❏ 1030	Moonbeam/Every Time You Smile	1957	10.00	20.00	40.00

ARIELS, THE
45s

Number	Title (A Side/B Side)	Yr	VG	VG+	NM
BRENT					
❏ 7060	Feels Like I'm Cryin'/I Love You	1967	15.00	30.00	60.00

ARISTOCATS, THE
Albums

Number	Title (A Side/B Side)	Yr	VG	VG+	NM
HIFI					
❏ J-610 [M]	Boogie and Blues	1959	7.50	15.00	30.00
❏ JS-610 [S]	Boogie and Blues	1959	10.00	20.00	40.00

ARISTOCRATS, THE
45s

Number	Title (A Side/B Side)	Yr	VG	VG+	NM
ARGO					
❏ 5275	Maid of the Mist/Vagabonds	1957	6.25	12.50	25.00
ESSEX					
❏ 366	Believe Me/I'm Waiting for Ships	1954	15.00	30.00	60.00

ARKADE
45s

Number	Title (A Side/B Side)	Yr	VG	VG+	NM
ABC DUNHILL					
❏ 4247	Sing Out the Love (In My Heart)/Susan	1970	—	3.00	6.00
❏ 4268	The Morning of Our Lives/Rhythm of the People	1971	—	3.00	6.00
❏ 4268 [PS]	The Morning of Our Lives/Rhythm of the People	1971	2.50	5.00	10.00
❏ 4277	Where You Lead/Sentimental Lisa	1971	—	3.00	6.00
❏ 4286	Fool's Way of Lovin'/The Morning of Our Lives	1971	—	3.00	6.00

ARLINGTON, BRUCE
45s

Number	Title (A Side/B Side)	Yr	VG	VG+	NM
KING					
❏ 5918	You Made Me Cry/How Could You Know	1964	7.50	15.00	30.00

ARMAGEDDON (1)
Albums

Number	Title (A Side/B Side)	Yr	VG	VG+	NM
AMOS					
❏ 73075	Armageddon	1970	6.25	12.50	25.00

ARMAGEDDON (2) With KEITH RELF, ex-member of THE YARDBIRDS; his last material before his death.
Albums

Number	Title (A Side/B Side)	Yr	VG	VG+	NM
A&M					
❏ SP-4513	Armageddon	1975	5.00	10.00	20.00

ARMATRADING, JOAN
12-Inch Singles

Number	Title (A Side/B Side)	Yr	VG	VG+	NM
A&M					
❏ SP-12184 [DJ]	Kind Words (2 versions)/Figure of Speech	1986	—	3.00	6.00
❏ SP-17229 [DJ]	(I Love It When You) Call Me Names/Drop the Pilot	1983	—	3.00	6.00
❏ SP-17311 [DJ]	Temptation (7" Version)/(Album Version)	1985	—	3.00	6.00
❏ SP-17386 [DJ]	Kind Words (And a Real Good Heart) (same on both sides)	1986	—	3.00	6.00
❏ SP-17414 [DJ]	Angel Man (same on both sides)	1986	—	3.00	6.00
❏ SP-17654 [DJ]	Shouting Stage (same on both sides?)	1988	—	3.00	6.00

45s

Number	Title (A Side/B Side)	Yr	VG	VG+	NM
A&M					
❏ 1235	Living for You/I Really Must Be Going	1988	—	2.00	4.00
❏ 1452	Lonely Lady/Together in Words and Music	1973	—	2.00	4.00
❏ 1865	Love and Affection/Help Yourself	1976	—	2.50	5.00
❏ 1898	Down to Zero/Like Fire	1976	—	2.00	4.00
❏ 1914	Water with the Wine/People	1977	—	2.00	4.00
❏ 1994	Show Some Emotion/No Way Out	1977	—	2.00	4.00
❏ 2018	Warm Love/No Way Out	1978	—	2.00	4.00
❏ 2102	Bottom to the Top/Your Letter	1978	—	2.00	4.00
❏ 2113	Barefoot and Pregnant/Your Letter	1979	—	2.00	4.00
❏ 2210	Rosie/Show Some Emotion	1979	—	2.00	4.00
❏ 2224	He Wants Up/Show Some Emotion	1980	—	2.00	4.00
❏ 2240	Me Myself I/Friends	1980	—	2.00	4.00
❏ 2262	Is It Tomorrow Yet/Ma-Me-O-Beach	1980	—	2.00	4.00
❏ 2381	Weakness in Me/Crying	1981	—	2.00	4.00
❏ 2400	I Wanna Hold You/Crying	1982	—	2.00	4.00
❏ 2538	Drop the Pilot/Business Is Business	1983	—	2.00	4.00
❏ 2538 [PS]	Drop the Pilot/Business Is Business	1983	—	2.50	5.00
❏ 2564 [DJ]	(I Love It When You) Call Me Names (same on both sides)	1983	—	2.50	5.00
—Stock copies do not exist					
❏ 2622	Frustration/Heaven	1984	—	2.00	4.00
❏ 2712	Temptation/Talking to the Wall	1985	—	2.00	4.00
❏ 2751	Love Grows/Thinking Man	1985	—	2.00	4.00
❏ 2837	Kind Words (And a Real Good Heart)/Figure of Speech	1986	—	2.00	4.00
❏ 2837 [PS]	Kind Words (And a Real Good Heart)/Figure of Speech	1986	—	2.50	5.00
❏ 2868	Angel Man/Rivers on Fire	1986	—	2.00	4.00

7-Inch Extended Plays

Number	Title (A Side/B Side)	Yr	VG	VG+	NM
A&M					
❏ 2391 [DJ]	*Me Myself & I/Tall in the Saddle/Show Some Emotion/Love and Affection/Rosie/Back to the Night/People	1980	—	2.50	5.00
—White label, small hole, plays at 33 1/3 rpm					
❏ 2391 [PS]	Free Joan Armatrading	1980	—	2.50	5.00

Albums

Number	Title (A Side/B Side)	Yr	VG	VG+	NM
A&M					
❏ SP-3141	Back to the Night	1980	2.00	4.00	8.00
—Reissue					
❏ SP-3227	Whatever's For Us	1984	2.00	4.00	8.00
—Reissue					
❏ SP-3228	Joan Armatrading	1984	2.00	4.00	8.00
—Reissue					
❏ SP-3273	Show Some Emotion	1984	2.00	4.00	8.00
—Reissue					
❏ SP-3302 [EP]	How Cruel	1979	2.00	4.00	8.00
❏ SP-4382	Whatever's For Us	1974	3.00	6.00	12.00
❏ SP-4525	Back to the Night	1975	3.00	6.00	12.00
❏ SP-4588	Joan Armatrading	1976	2.50	5.00	10.00
❏ SP-4663	Show Some Emotion	1977	2.50	5.00	10.00
❏ SP-4732	To the Limit	1978	2.50	5.00	10.00
❏ SP-4809	Me Myself I	1980	2.50	5.00	10.00
❏ SP-4876	Walk Under Ladders	1981	2.50	5.00	10.00
❏ SP-4912	The Key	1983	2.50	5.00	10.00
❏ SP-4987	Track Record	1984	2.50	5.00	10.00
❏ SP-5040	Secret Secrets	1985	2.50	5.00	10.00
❏ SP-5130	Sleight of Hand	1986	2.50	5.00	10.00
❏ SP-5211	The Shouting Stage	1988	2.50	5.00	10.00
❏ 75021 5298 1	Hearts and Flowers	1990	3.75	7.50	15.00
❏ SP-8414 [DJ]	Joan Armatrading Live at the Bijou Café	1977	5.00	10.00	20.00
—Promo-only "Superstars Radio Network" issue					
❏ SP-12400 [EP]	How Cruel	1984	—	3.00	6.00
—Reissue					

ARMS, RUSSELL
45s

Number	Title (A Side/B Side)	Yr	VG	VG+	NM
EPIC					
❏ 5-9083	The "Point of View" Song/The Touch	1954	3.00	6.00	12.00
❏ 5-9109	Not As a Stranger/Don't Be Afraid to Fall in Love	1955	3.00	6.00	12.00
❏ 5-9136	Nobody Knows/Methinks	1955	3.00	6.00	12.00
ERA					
❏ 1018	Is There a Heaven/I Saw a Star	1956	2.50	5.00	10.00
❏ 1026	Cinco Robles (Five Oaks)/The World Is Made of Liza	1956	3.75	7.50	15.00
❏ 1033	Share My Love/Evangeline	1957	3.00	6.00	12.00
❏ 1040	The Bridge of San Angelo/Where Can a Wanderer Go	1957	3.00	6.00	12.00
❏ 1048	I Wonder Where's My Darlin'/I'm Tired of Pride	1957	3.00	6.00	12.00
❏ 1059	Hasta La Vista/Walkin' By Your Window	1957	3.00	6.00	12.00
❏ 1078	Blue Hawaii/Der Glockenspiel	1958	3.00	6.00	12.00
❏ 3053	Cinco Robles (Five Oaks)/The World Is Made of Lisa	1961	2.50	5.00	10.00

Albums

Number	Title (A Side/B Side)	Yr	VG	VG+	NM
ERA					
❏ EL-20013 [M]	Where Can a Wanderer Go	1957	6.25	12.50	25.00

ARMSTRONG, BRICE, AND THE AMERICAN GHOULS
45s

Number	Title (A Side/B Side)	Yr	VG	VG+	NM
DUCHESS					
❏ 1020	The Fright Before Christmas/Happy Ghoul Tide	1962	5.00	10.00	20.00

ARMSTRONG, JIMMY
45s

Number	Title (A Side/B Side)	Yr	VG	VG+	NM
BROTHERS THREE					
❏ 1001	You're Getting Next to Me Baby/Going to the Well Too Many Times	196?	100.00	200.00	400.00
ENJOY					
❏ 1016	Count the Tears/I'm Going to Lock My Heart	1964	5.00	10.00	20.00
JET SET					
❏ 768	I Won't Believe It Till I See It/I'm About to Say Goodbye	196?	10.00	20.00	40.00
SHRINE					
❏ 0102	I'm About to Say Goodbye/Mystery	1965	50.00	100.00	200.00
❏ 105	It's Gonna Take Love/I Believe I'll Love You	1965	—	—	—
—Canceled					
STOP					
❏ 105	Close to You/Hanging Out with Early Bird	1965	50.00	100.00	200.00

ARMSTRONG, LOUIS Also see BING CROSBY; ELLA FITZGERALD.
45s

Number	Title (A Side/B Side)	Yr	VG	VG+	NM
A&M					
❏ 3010	What a Wonderful World/Game of Love	1988	—	2.00	4.00
—B-side by Wayne Fontana and the Mindbenders					
❏ 3010 [PS]	What a Wonderful World/Game of Love	1988	—	2.00	4.00
—"Good Morning Vietnam" sleeve					
ABC					
❏ 10982	What a Wonderful World/Cabaret	1967	2.00	4.00	8.00
❏ 11075	Hellzapoppin/The Sunshine of Love	1968	—	3.00	6.00
❏ 11126	Hello Brother/The Sunshine of Love	1968	—	3.00	6.00
AMSTERDAM					
❏ 85013	We Shall Overcome/(Instrumental)	1970	—	3.00	6.00
❏ 85016	Give Peace a Chance/The Creator Has a Master Plan	1970	2.00	4.00	8.00
❏ 85017 [DJ]	Here Is My Heart For Christmas/His Father Wore Long Hair	1970	2.50	5.00	10.00
❏ 85019	Everybody's Talkin'/(B-side unknown)	1970	—	2.50	5.00
❏ 85021	What a Wonderful World/His Father Wore Long Hair	1971	—	2.50	5.00
AUDIO FIDELITY					
❏ 097	Ain't Gonna Give Nobody None of My Jelly Roll/Frankie & Johnny	196?	2.00	4.00	8.00
❏ 173	Bill Bailey/The Creator Has a Master Plan	1971	—	3.00	6.00
AVCO EMBASSY					
❏ 4562	Miller's Cave/You Can Have Her	1971	—	3.00	6.00
BRUNSWICK					
❏ 55318	Daydream/Northern Boulevard Blues	1967	—	3.00	6.00
❏ 55328	Louie's Dream/Step Down, Brother, Next Case	1967	—	3.00	6.00

Number	Title (A Side/B Side)	Yr	VG	VG+	NM
❑ 55350	Rosie/You'll Never Walk Alone	1967	—	3.00	6.00
❑ 55360	Happy Time/Willkomen	1968	—	3.00	6.00
❑ 55380	Talk to the Animals/I Will Wait for You	1968	—	3.00	6.00
❑ 55395	I Believe/Sunrise, Sunset	1968	—	3.00	6.00
❑ 55457	I Believe/You'll Never Walk Alone	1971	—	2.50	5.00
❑ 55474	Willkomen/Sunrise, Sunset	1972	—	2.50	5.00
❑ 55534	'Twas the Night Before Christmas/ (B-side unknown)	1976	2.00	4.00	8.00

BUENA VISTA

Number	Title (A Side/B Side)	Yr	VG	VG+	NM
❑ F-465	Ten Feet Off the Ground/'Bout Time	1968	3.75	7.50	15.00
❑ F-465 [PS]	Ten Feet Off the Ground/'Bout Time	1968	6.25	12.50	25.00
❑ F-466	The Bare Necessities/Louis	1968	3.75	7.50	15.00
❑ F-469	Bibbidi-Bobbidi-Boo/Zip-a-Dee-Doo-Dah	1968	3.75	7.50	15.00
❑ F-470	Heigh-Ho/When You Wish Upon a Star	1968	3.75	7.50	15.00
❑ F-471	The Ballad of Davy Crocket/Chim-Chim-Cheree	1968	5.00	10.00	20.00
❑ F-489	When You Wish Upon a Star/ Zip-a-Dee-Doo-Dah	1972	2.50	5.00	10.00

COLUMBIA

Number	Title (A Side/B Side)	Yr	VG	VG+	NM
❑ 40587	A Theme from the Threepenny Opera (Mack the Knife)/Back O' Town Blues	1956	3.75	7.50	15.00
❑ 40662	When the Red, Red Robin Comes Bob, Bob, Bobbin' Along/Six Foot Four	1956	3.00	6.00	12.00
❑ 40711	The Faithful Hussar/Six Foot Four	1956	3.00	6.00	12.00
❑ 41471	Mack the Knife/The Faithful Hussar	1959	2.50	5.00	10.00

CONTINENTAL

Number	Title (A Side/B Side)	Yr	VG	VG+	NM
❑ 1001	The Night Before Christmas/When the Saints Go Marching In	1971	—	2.50	5.00
❑ 1001 [PS]	The Night Before Christmas/When the Saints Go Marching In	1971	—	2.50	5.00

—With sticker: "Only 25 cents with purchase" of one of four brands of cigarette

Number	Title (A Side/B Side)	Yr	VG	VG+	NM
❑ 1001 [PS]	The Night Before Christmas/ When the Saints Go Marching In	1971	—	3.00	6.00

—With sticker: "Free with purchase" of six-pack of Fresca

DECCA

Number	Title (A Side/B Side)	Yr	VG	VG+	NM
❑ 27059	New Orleans Function (Part 1)/New Orleans Function (Part 2)	1950	5.00	10.00	20.00
❑ 27113	La Vie En Rose/C'est Si Bon	1950	5.00	10.00	20.00
❑ 27187	That's for Me (Part 1)/Russian Lullaby (Part 2)	1950	3.00	6.00	12.00
❑ 27188	That's for Me (Part 2)/Russian Lullaby (Part 1)	1950	3.00	6.00	12.00
❑ 27189	Fine and Dandy/I Surrender Dear (Part 2)	1950	3.00	6.00	12.00
❑ 27190	Baby Won't You Please Come Home/I Surrender Dear (Part 1)	1950	3.00	6.00	12.00
❑ 27191	Panama (Part 1)/Bugle Call Rag (Part 3)	1950	3.00	6.00	12.00
❑ 27192	Panama (Part 2)/Bugle Call Rag (Part 2)	1950	3.00	6.00	12.00
❑ 27193	New Orleans Function (Part 1)/ Bugle Call Rag (Part 1)	1950	3.00	6.00	12.00
❑ 27194	New Orleans Function (Part 2)/ My Bucket's Got a Hole In It	1950	3.00	6.00	12.00
❑ 27254	Sit Down You're Rockin' the Boat/ That's What the Man Said	1950	5.00	10.00	20.00
❑ 27481	If/You're Just in Love	1951	3.75	7.50	15.00
❑ 27616	Unless/That's for Me	1951	3.75	7.50	15.00
❑ 27720	(When We Are Dancing) I Get Ideas/ A Kiss to Build a Dream On	1951	3.75	7.50	15.00
❑ 27816	Because of You/Cold, Cold Heart	1951	3.75	7.50	15.00
❑ 27899	When It's Sleepy Time Down South/ It's All in the Game	1952	3.75	7.50	15.00

—With Gordon Jenkins and His Orchestra

Number	Title (A Side/B Side)	Yr	VG	VG+	NM
❑ 27931	You're the Apple of My Eye/Big Butter and Egg Man	1952	3.75	7.50	15.00
❑ 28095	Royal Garden Blues (Part 2)/ Muskrat Ramble (Part 1)	1952	3.00	6.00	12.00
❑ 28096	Royal Garden Blues (Part 1)/ Muskrat Ramble (Part 2)	1952	3.00	6.00	12.00

—Above two with Edward "Kid" Ory

Number	Title (A Side/B Side)	Yr	VG	VG+	NM
❑ 28097	Lover/Black and Blue	1952	3.00	6.00	12.00
❑ 28098	Mahogany Hall Stomp/Since I Fell for You	1952	3.00	6.00	12.00
❑ 28099	I Cried for You (Part 1)/Tea for Two (Part 2)	1952	3.00	6.00	12.00
❑ 28100	I Cried for You (Part 2)/Tea for Two (Part 1)	1952	3.00	6.00	12.00

—Above two with Velma Middleton

Number	Title (A Side/B Side)	Yr	VG	VG+	NM
❑ 28101	Stars Fell on Alabama (Part 1)/Stars Fell on Alabama (Part 2)	1952	3.00	6.00	12.00
❑ 28102	Boff Boff/C Jam Blues	1952	3.00	6.00	12.00
❑ 28103	Body and Soul (Part 1)/How High the Moon (Part 2)	1952	3.00	6.00	12.00
❑ 28104	Body and Soul (Part 2)/How High the Moon (Part 1)	1952	3.00	6.00	12.00

—Above two with Barney B

Number	Title (A Side/B Side)	Yr	VG	VG+	NM
❑ 28105	On the Sunny Side of the Street (Part 1)/That's My Desire (Part 2)	1952	3.00	6.00	12.00
❑ 28106	On the Sunny Side of the Street (Part 2)/That's My Desire (Part 1)	1952	3.00	6.00	12.00
❑ 28107	High Society/Baby Won't You Please Come Home	1952	3.00	6.00	12.00
❑ 28108	Steak Face (Part 1)/Steak Face (Part 2)	1952	3.00	6.00	12.00
❑ 28169	Back Home Again in Indiana (Part 1)/Way Down Yonder in New Orleans (Part 2)	1952	3.00	6.00	12.00
❑ 28170	Back Home Again in Indiana (Part 2)/Way Down Yonder in New Orleans (Part 1)	1952	3.00	6.00	12.00
❑ 28171	The Hucklebuck/Stardust (Part 2)	1952	3.00	6.00	12.00
❑ 28172	Baby It's Cold Outside/Stardust (Part 1)	1952	3.00	6.00	12.00
❑ 28173	Honeysuckle Rose/That's a Plenty	1952	3.00	6.00	12.00
❑ 28174	My Monday Date (Part 1)/My Monday Date (Part 4)	1952	3.00	6.00	12.00
❑ 28175	My Monday Date (Part 2)/My Monday Date (Part 3)	1952	3.00	6.00	12.00
❑ 28176	Big Daddy Blues/You Can Depend on Me	1952	3.00	6.00	12.00
❑ 28177	Kiss of Fire/Delicado	1952	3.75	7.50	15.00
❑ 28306	Once in a While/Confessin'	1952	3.75	7.50	15.00
❑ 28372	That's My Desire/Baby It's Cold Outside	1952	3.75	7.50	15.00
❑ 28394	Takes Two to Tango/I Laughed at Love	1952	3.75	7.50	15.00

Number	Title (A Side/B Side)	Yr	VG	VG+	NM
❑ 28443	White Christmas/Winter Wonderland	1952	3.75	7.50	15.00
❑ 28524	Chlo-E/Listen to the Mocking Bird	1953	3.75	7.50	15.00
❑ 28628	Your Cheatin' Heart/ Congratulations to Someone	1953	3.75	7.50	15.00
❑ 28704	April in Portugal/Ramona	1953	3.75	7.50	15.00
❑ 28803	The Dummy Song/Sittin' in the Sun	1953	3.75	7.50	15.00
❑ 28943	'Zat You, Santa Claus?/Cool Yule	1953	3.75	7.50	15.00
❑ 28995	The Gypsy/I Can't Afford to Miss This Dream	1954	3.75	7.50	15.00
❑ 29102	Basin Street Blues (Part 1)/ Basin Street Blues (Part 2)	1954	3.75	7.50	15.00
❑ 29117	On a Coconut Island/To You Sweetheart Aloha	1954	3.75	7.50	15.00
❑ 29153	The Whiffenpoof Song/Bye and Bye	1954	3.75	7.50	15.00

—With Gordon Jenkins and His Orchestra

Number	Title (A Side/B Side)	Yr	VG	VG+	NM
❑ 29256	Skokiaan (Part 1)/Skokiaan (Part 2)	1954	3.75	7.50	15.00
❑ 29280	Muskrat Ramble/Someday You'll Be Sorry	1954	3.75	7.50	15.00
❑ 29352	Trees/Spooks	1954	3.75	7.50	15.00
❑ 29421	Sincerely/Pledging My Love	1955	3.75	7.50	15.00
❑ 29546	Pretty Little Missy/Baby Your Sleep Is Showing	1955	3.75	7.50	15.00
❑ 29694	Only You (And You Alone)/Moments to Remember	1955	3.75	7.50	15.00
❑ 29710	Christmas Night in Harlem/ Christmas in New Orleans	1955	3.75	7.50	15.00
❑ 29921	Lazy Bones/Easy Street	1956	3.00	6.00	12.00

—With Gary Crosby

Number	Title (A Side/B Side)	Yr	VG	VG+	NM
❑ 30091	Blueberry Hill/That Lucky Old Sun	1956	3.00	6.00	12.00
❑ 30188	This Younger Generation/In Pursuit of Happiness	1957	2.50	5.00	10.00
❑ 30309	The Prisoner's Song/You're a Heavenly Thing	1957	2.50	5.00	10.00
❑ 30624	Nobody Knows the Trouble I've Seen/When You're Smiling	1958	2.50	5.00	10.00
❑ 30771	I Love Jazz/Mardi Gras March	1958	2.50	5.00	10.00
❑ 30860	I'll String Along with You/On My Way (Out on My Traveling Shoes)	1959	2.50	5.00	10.00
❑ 30980	Only You (And You Alone)/ Onkel Satchmo's Lullaby	1960	2.50	5.00	10.00

DOT

Number	Title (A Side/B Side)	Yr	VG	VG+	NM
❑ 15941	The Five Pennies Saints/Just the Blues	1959	2.50	5.00	10.00

—With Danny Kaye

Number	Title (A Side/B Side)	Yr	VG	VG+	NM
❑ 15991	Battle Hymn of the Republic/Lullaby in Ragtime	1959	2.50	5.00	10.00

—With Red Nichols

KAPP

Number	Title (A Side/B Side)	Yr	VG	VG+	NM
❑ 573	Hello, Dolly!/A Lot of Livin' to Do	1964	—	3.00	6.00
❑ 573 [PS]	Hello, Dolly!/A Lot of Livin' to Do	1964	2.50	5.00	10.00
❑ 597	I Still Get Jealous/Someday	1964	—	3.00	6.00
❑ 597 [PS]	I Still Get Jealous/Someday	1964	2.50	5.00	10.00
❑ 901	You Are Woman, I Am Man/Life of the Party	1968	—	3.00	6.00
❑ 977	Kinda Love Song/Someday	1969	—	3.00	6.00
❑ 2145	That's All I Want the World to Remember Me By/Hello, Dolly!	1971	—	2.50	5.00

MCA

Number	Title (A Side/B Side)	Yr	VG	VG+	NM
❑ MSS-35147	What a Wonderful World/America the Beautiful	1989	2.50	5.00	10.00

—B-side by the San Francisco Boys Chorus

Number	Title (A Side/B Side)	Yr	VG	VG+	NM
❑ MSS-35147 [PS]	What a Wonderful World/America the Beautiful	1989	2.50	5.00	10.00

—Special item for the Environmental Defense Fund

Number	Title (A Side/B Side)	Yr	VG	VG+	NM
❑ 53321	What a Wonderful World/ Dream a Little Dream of Me	1988	—	2.50	5.00

—Reissue

MERCURY

Number	Title (A Side/B Side)	Yr	VG	VG+	NM
❑ 72338	So Long Dearie/Pretty Little Missy	1964	2.00	4.00	8.00
❑ 72338 [PS]	So Long Dearie/Pretty Little Missy	1964	3.00	6.00	12.00
❑ 72371	By and By/Faith	1964	2.00	4.00	8.00
❑ 72495	Circle of Your Arms/Short But Sweet	1965	2.00	4.00	8.00
❑ 72574	Mame/Tin Roof Blues	1966	2.00	4.00	8.00
❑ 72593	Cheesecake/Bye 'N' Bye	1966	2.00	4.00	8.00

MGM

Number	Title (A Side/B Side)	Yr	VG	VG+	NM
❑ 12809	Someday You'll Be Sorry/The Beat Generation	1959	3.00	6.00	12.00

RCA VICTOR

Number	Title (A Side/B Side)	Yr	VG	VG+	NM
❑ 47-4004	Rockin' Chair/Save It, Pretty Mama	1950	3.75	7.50	15.00
❑ 47-4005	Ain't Misbehavin'/Pennies from Heaven	1950	3.75	7.50	15.00
❑ 47-4006	Saint James Infirmary/Back o' Town Blues	1950	3.75	7.50	15.00

UNITED ARTISTS

Number	Title (A Side/B Side)	Yr	VG	VG+	NM
❑ 50251	No Time Is Good Goodbye Time/We're a Home	1968	—	3.00	6.00
❑ 50617	We Have All the Time in the World/ Pretty Little Missy	1969	—	3.00	6.00

VERVE

Number	Title (A Side/B Side)	Yr	VG	VG+	NM
❑ 10182	Nobody Knows the Troubles I've Seen/ That Old Feeling	1959	3.00	6.00	12.00

7-Inch Extended Plays

COLUMBIA

Number	Title (A Side/B Side)	Yr	VG	VG+	NM
❑ 5-1192	Walkin' My Baby Back Home/You Rascal You// All of Me/Shine	195?	5.00	10.00	20.00

—Alternate numbers are "B-1523-1" and "B-1523-2"

Number	Title (A Side/B Side)	Yr	VG	VG+	NM
❑ B-1523 [PS]	Louis Armstrong Spotlight	195?	5.00	10.00	20.00

—Contains record 5-1192

Number	Title (A Side/B Side)	Yr	VG	VG+	NM
❑ B-2540	*Mack the Knife/Ain't Misbehavin'/ St. Louis Blues	1958	5.00	10.00	20.00
❑ B-2540 [PS]	Louis Armstrong (Hall of Fame Series)	1958	5.00	10.00	20.00

DECCA

Number	Title (A Side/B Side)	Yr	VG	VG+	NM
❑ ED 2012	Kiss of Fire/I'll Walk Alone//Takes Two to Tango/ Sit Down, You're Rocking the Boat	195?	3.75	7.50	15.00
❑ ED 2012 [PS]	Louis Armstrong, Vol. 1	195?	3.75	7.50	15.00
❑ ED 2126	Basin Street Blues/Otchi-Tchor-Ni-Ya	195?	3.75	7.50	15.00
❑ ED 2126 [PS]	(title unknown)	195?	3.75	7.50	15.00
❑ ED 2496	When Did You Leave Heaven/You're a Heavenly Thing//I Married an Angel/ A Sinner Kissed an Angel	195?	3.00	6.00	12.00
❑ ED 2496 [PS]	(title unknown)	195?	3.00	6.00	12.00

Albums

ABC

Number	Title (A Side/B Side)	Yr	VG	VG+	NM
❑ S-650	What a Wonderful World	1968	7.50	15.00	30.00

Number	Title (A Side/B Side)	Yr	VG	VG+	NM
ACCORD					
☐ SN-7161	Mr. Music	1982	2.50	5.00	10.00
AMSTERDAM					
☐ AMS 12009	Louis Armstrong and His Friends	1970	3.75	7.50	15.00
AUDIO FIDELITY					
☐ AFLP-1930 [M]	Louis Armstrong Plays King Oliver	1960	7.50	15.00	30.00
☐ AFLP-2128 [M]	Ain't Gonna Give Nobody None of My Jelly Roll	1964	3.75	7.50	15.00
☐ AFLP-2132 [M]	The Best of Louis Armstrong	1964	3.75	7.50	15.00
☐ AFSD-5930 [S]	Louis Armstrong Plays King Oliver	1960	10.00	20.00	40.00
☐ AFSD-6128 [S]	Ain't Gonna Give Nobody None of My Jelly Roll	1964	5.00	10.00	20.00
☐ AFSD-6132 [S]	The Best of Louis Armstrong	1964	5.00	10.00	20.00
☐ AFSD-6241	Louis Armstrong	196?	3.75	7.50	15.00
BIOGRAPH					
☐ C-5	Great Soloists	1973	3.00	6.00	12.00
☐ C-6	Louis Armstrong Plays the Blues	1973	3.00	6.00	12.00
BLUEBIRD					
☐ AXM2-5519 [(2)]	Young Louis (1932-1933)	1984	3.00	6.00	12.00
☐ 5920-1-RB [(2)]	Pops: The 1940s Small Band Sides	1987	3.75	7.50	15.00
☐ 8310-1-RB	What a Wonderful World	1988	2.50	5.00	10.00
☐ 9759-1-RB	Louis Armstrong & His Orchestra 1932-33: Laughin' Louie	1989	3.00	6.00	12.00
BRUNSWICK					
☐ BL 58004 [10]	Armstrong Classics	1950	25.00	50.00	100.00
☐ BL 754136	I Will Wait for You	1968	3.75	7.50	15.00
BUENA VISTA					
☐ BV-4044	Disney Swings the Satchmo Way	1968	10.00	20.00	40.00
CHIAROSCURO					
☐ 2002	Snake Rag	1977	3.00	6.00	12.00
☐ 2003	Great Alternatives	1977	3.00	6.00	12.00
☐ 2006	Sweetheart	1977	3.00	6.00	12.00
COLUMBIA					
☐ CL 591 [M]	Louis Armstrong Plays W.C. Handy	1954	10.00	20.00	40.00
☐ CL 708 [M]	Satch Plays Fats	1955	10.00	20.00	40.00
☐ CL 840 [M]	Ambassador Satch	1956	10.00	20.00	40.00
☐ CL 851 [M]	The Louis Armstrong Story, Volume 1	1956	7.50	15.00	30.00
☐ CL 852 [M]	The Louis Armstrong Story, Volume 2	1956	7.50	15.00	30.00
☐ CL 853 [M]	The Louis Armstrong Story, Volume 3	1956	7.50	15.00	30.00
☐ CL 854 [M]	The Louis Armstrong Story, Volume 4	1956	7.50	15.00	30.00
☐ CL 1077 [M]	Satchmo the Great	1957	7.50	15.00	30.00
☐ CL 2638 [M]	Louis Armstrong's Greatest Hits	1967	5.00	10.00	20.00
☐ ML 4383 [M]	The Louis Armstrong Story, Volume 1	1951	12.50	25.00	50.00
☐ ML 4384 [M]	The Louis Armstrong Story, Volume 2	1951	12.50	25.00	50.00
☐ ML 4385 [M]	The Louis Armstrong Story, Volume 3	1951	12.50	25.00	50.00
☐ ML 4386 [M]	The Louis Armstrong Story, Volume 4	1951	12.50	25.00	50.00
☐ CL 6335 [10]	Louis Armstrong Plays W.C. Handy, Volume 2	1955	10.00	20.00	40.00
☐ CS 9438 [R]	Louis Armstrong's Greatest Hits	1967	3.00	6.00	12.00
☐ PC 9438 [R]	Louis Armstrong's Greatest Hits	198?	2.00	4.00	8.00
—Budget-line reissue					
☐ G 30416 [(2)]	The Genius of Louis Armstrong, Vol. 1	1971	3.75	7.50	15.00
COLUMBIA MUSICAL TREASURIES					
☐ P4M 5676 [(4)]	40 Greatest Hits	197?	5.00	10.00	20.00
DECCA					
☐ DX 108 [(2)M]	Satchmo at Symphony Hall	1954	18.75	37.50	75.00
—Black labels, silver print					
☐ DX 155 [(4)M]	Satchmo, A Musical Autobiography	1956	25.00	50.00	100.00
—Black labels, silver print					
☐ DXM 155 [(4)M]	Satchmo, A Musical Autobiography	1960	10.00	20.00	40.00
—Black labels with color bars					
☐ DXB 183 [(2)M]	The Best of Louis Armstrong	196?	7.50	15.00	30.00
☐ DL 4137 [M]	Satchmo's Golden Favorites	1961	5.00	10.00	20.00
☐ DL 4227 [M]	I Love Jazz	1962	5.00	10.00	20.00
☐ DL 4230 [M]	Satchmo, A Musical Autobiography, 1926-1927	1962	6.25	12.50	25.00
☐ DL 4245 [M]	King Louis	1962	5.00	10.00	20.00
☐ DL 4330 [M]	Satchmo, A Musical Autobiography, 1928-1930	1962	6.25	12.50	25.00
☐ DL 4331 [M]	Satchmo, A Musical Autobiography, 1930-1934	1962	6.25	12.50	25.00
☐ DL 5225 [10]	New Orleans to New York	1950	18.75	37.50	75.00
☐ DL 5279 [10]	New Orleans Days	1950	18.75	37.50	75.00
☐ DL 5280 [10]	Jazz Concert	1950	18.75	37.50	75.00
☐ DL 5401 [10]	Satchmo Serenades	1952	18.75	37.50	75.00
☐ DL 5532 [10]	Latter-Day Louis	1954	18.75	37.50	75.00
☐ DL 5536 [10]	Louis Armstrong-Gordon Jenkins	1954	18.75	37.50	75.00
☐ DXSB 7183 [(2)R]	The Best of Louis Armstrong	196?	3.75	7.50	15.00
☐ DL 8037 [M]	Satchmo at Symphony Hall, Volume 1	1954	10.00	20.00	40.00
—Black label, silver print					
☐ DL 8037 [M]	Satchmo at Symphony Hall, Volume 1	1960	3.75	7.50	15.00
—Black label with color bars					
☐ DL 8038 [M]	Satchmo at Symphony Hall, Volume 2	1954	10.00	20.00	40.00
—Black label, silver print					
☐ DL 8038 [M]	Satchmo at Symphony Hall, Volume 2	1960	3.75	7.50	15.00
—Black label with color bars					
☐ DL 8041 [M]	Satchmo at Pasadena	1954	10.00	20.00	40.00
—Black label, silver print					
☐ DL 8041 [M]	Satchmo at Pasadena	1960	3.75	7.50	15.00
—Black label with color bars					
☐ DL 8126 [M]	Satchmo Sings	1955	10.00	20.00	40.00
—Black label, silver print					
☐ DL 8126 [M]	Satchmo Sings	1960	3.75	7.50	15.00
—Black label with color bars					
☐ DL 8168 [M]	Louis Armstrong at the Crescendo, Volume 1	1955	10.00	20.00	40.00
—Black label, silver print					
☐ DL 8169 [M]	Louis Armstrong at the Crescendo, Volume 2	1955	10.00	20.00	40.00
—Black label, silver print					
☐ DL 8211 [M]	Satchmo Serenades	1956	10.00	20.00	40.00
—Black label, silver print					
☐ DL 8211 [M]	Satchmo Serenades	1960	3.75	7.50	15.00
—Black label with color bars					
☐ DL 8283 [M]	New Orleans Jazz	1956	10.00	20.00	40.00
—Black label, silver print					
☐ DL 8283 [M]	New Orleans Jazz	1960	3.75	7.50	15.00
—Black label with color bars					
☐ DL 8284 [M]	Jazz Classics	1956	10.00	20.00	40.00
—Black label, silver print					
☐ DL 8284 [M]	Jazz Classics	1960	3.75	7.50	15.00
—Black label with color bars					
☐ DL 8327 [M]	Satchmo's Collector's Items	1957	10.00	20.00	40.00
—Black label, silver print					
☐ DL 8327 [M]	Satchmo's Collector's Items	1960	3.75	7.50	15.00
—Black label with color bars					
☐ DL 8329 [M]	New Orleans Nights	1957	10.00	20.00	40.00
—Black label, silver print					
☐ DL 8329 [M]	New Orleans Nights	1960	3.75	7.50	15.00
—Black label with color bars					
☐ DL 8330 [M]	Satchmo on Stage	1957	10.00	20.00	40.00
—Black label, silver print					
☐ DL 8330 [M]	Satchmo on Stage	1960	3.75	7.50	15.00
—Black label with color bars					
☐ DL 8488 [M]	Louis and the Angels	1957	10.00	20.00	40.00
—Black label, silver print					
☐ DL 8488 [M]	Louis and the Angels	1960	3.75	7.50	15.00
—Black label with color bars					
☐ DL 8741 [M]	Louis and the Good Book	1960	3.75	7.50	15.00
—Black label with color bars					
☐ DL 8781 [M]	Louis and the Good Book	1958	10.00	20.00	40.00
—Black label, silver print					
☐ DL 8840 [M]	Satchmo in Style	1958	10.00	20.00	40.00
—Black label, silver print					
☐ DL 8840 [M]	Satchmo in Style	1960	3.75	7.50	15.00
—Black label with color bars					
☐ DL 8963 [M]	Satchmo, A Musical Autobiography, 1923-1925	1960	6.25	12.50	25.00
☐ DL 9225 [M]	Rare Items (1935-1944)	196?	5.00	10.00	20.00
☐ DL 9233 [M]	Young Louis the Sideman (1924-1927)	196?	5.00	10.00	20.00
☐ DL 74137 [R]	Satchmo's Golden Favorites	1961	3.00	6.00	12.00
☐ DL 74227 [R]	I Love Jazz	1962	3.00	6.00	12.00
☐ DL 74245 [R]	King Louis	1962	3.00	6.00	12.00
☐ DL 74330 [R]	A Musical Autobiography, 1928-1930	1962	3.00	6.00	12.00
☐ DL 78963 [R]	Satchmo, A Musical Autobiography, 1923-1925	196?	3.00	6.00	12.00
☐ DL 79225 [R]	Rare Items (1935-1944)	196?	3.00	6.00	12.00
☐ DL 79233 [R]	Young Louis the Sideman (1924-1927)	196?	3.00	6.00	12.00
DISNEYLAND					
☐ STER-1341	The Wonderful World of Walt Disney	1971	5.00	10.00	20.00
—Reissue of Buena Vista 4044					
EVEREST					
☐ 3312 [R]	In Memoriam	1971	2.50	5.00	10.00
EVEREST ARCHIVE OF FOLK & JAZZ					
☐ 258	Louis "Satchmo" Armstrong	197?	3.00	6.00	12.00
☐ 312	Louis Armstrong, Vol. 2	197?	2.50	5.00	10.00
GNP CRESCENDO					
☐ 9050	Pasadena Concert, Vol. II	1987	2.50	5.00	10.00
☐ 11001 [(2)]	An Evening with Louis Armstrong	1977	3.75	7.50	15.00
HARMONY					
☐ HS 11316	Louis Armstrong	197?	3.00	6.00	12.00
☐ KH 31236	The Louis Armstrong Saga	1971	3.00	6.00	12.00
IAJRC					
☐ LP-29	Oregon State Fair, 1960	198?	2.50	5.00	10.00
JOLLY ROGER					
☐ 5009 [10]	Louis Armstrong	1954	12.50	25.00	50.00
KAPP					
☐ KL-1364 [M]	Hello, Dolly!	1964	3.00	6.00	12.00
☐ KS-3364 [S]	Hello, Dolly!	1964	3.75	7.50	15.00
MCA					
☐ 538	Hello, Dolly!	197?	2.50	5.00	10.00
—Reissue of Kapp LP					
☐ 1300	Louis and the Good Book	197?	2.50	5.00	10.00
—Reissue of Decca 8741					
☐ 1301	Young Louis the Sideman	197?	2.50	5.00	10.00
—Reissue of Decca 9233					
☐ 1304	Back in New York	197?	2.50	5.00	10.00
☐ 1306	Louis with Guest Stars	197?	2.50	5.00	10.00
☐ 1312	Swing That Music!	197?	2.50	5.00	10.00
☐ 1316	Satchmo Serenades	197?	2.50	5.00	10.00
—Reissue of Decca 8211					
☐ 1322	Satchmo's Collector's Items	197?	2.50	5.00	10.00
—Reissue of Decca 8327					
☐ 1334	Satchmo For Ever!	197?	2.50	5.00	10.00
☐ 1335	Old Favorites	197?	2.50	5.00	10.00
☐ 2-4013 [(2)]	Louis Armstrong at the Crescendo	197?	3.00	6.00	12.00
—Reissue of Decca 8168/8169 in one sleeve					
☐ 2-4035 [(2)]	The Best of Louis Armstrong	197?	3.00	6.00	12.00
—Reissue of Decca 7183					
☐ 2-4057 [(2)]	Satchmo at Symphony Hall	197?	3.00	6.00	12.00
—Reissue of Decca 108					
☐ 10006 [(4)]	Satchmo, A Musical Autobiography	197?	6.25	12.50	25.00
—Reissue of Decca 155					
☐ 25204	What a Wonderful World	1988	2.50	5.00	10.00
—Reissue of ABC 650					
☐ 42328	Louis Armstrong of New Orleans	1990	3.00	6.00	12.00
MERCURY					
☐ MG-21081 [M]	Louis Armstrong Sings Louis Armstrong	1965	3.00	6.00	12.00
☐ SR-61081 [S]	Louis Armstrong Sings Louis Armstrong	1965	3.75	7.50	15.00
METRO					
☐ M-510 [M]	Hello, Louis	1965	3.00	6.00	12.00
☐ MS-510 [S]	Hello, Louis	1965	3.75	7.50	15.00
MILESTONE					
☐ 2010	Early Portrait	197?	2.50	5.00	10.00
☐ 47017 [(2)]	Louis Armstrong and King Oliver	197?	3.00	6.00	12.00
MOSAIC					
☐ MQ8-146 [(8)]	The Complete Decca Studio Recordings of Louis Armstrong and the All-Stars	199?	37.50	75.00	150.00
PABLO					
☐ 2310941	Mack the Knife	1990	3.00	6.00	12.00

Number	Title (A Side/B Side)	Yr	VG	VG+	NM
PAIR					
❏ PDL2-1042 [(2)]	The Jazz Legend	1986	3.00	6.00	12.00
PAUSA					
❏ 9018	The Greatest of Louis Armstrong	1983	2.50	5.00	10.00
RCA VICTOR					
❏ LPT 7 [10]	Louis Armstrong Town Hall Concert	1951	20.00	40.00	80.00
❏ LJM-1005 [M]	Louis Armstrong Sings the Blues	1954	12.50	25.00	50.00
❏ LPM-1443 [M]	Town Hall Concert Plus	1957	12.50	25.00	50.00
❏ LPM-2322 [M]	A Rare Batch of Satch	1961	6.25	12.50	25.00
❏ LPM-2971 [M]	Louis Armstrong in the '30s/in the '40s	1964	5.00	10.00	20.00
❏ LSP-2971(e) [R]	Louis Armstrong in the '30s/in the '40s	1964	3.00	6.00	12.00
❏ VPM-6044 [(2)]	July 4, 1900/July 6, 1971	1971	5.00	10.00	20.00
RIVERSIDE					
❏ RLP 12-101 [M]	The Young Louis Armstrong	195?	10.00	20.00	40.00
—Blue label					
❏ RLP 12-101 [M]	The Young Louis Armstrong	1956	20.00	40.00	80.00
—White label, blue print					
❏ RLP 12-122 [M]	Louis Armstrong 1923	195?	10.00	20.00	40.00
—Blue label					
❏ RLP 12-122 [M]	Louis Armstrong 1923	1956	20.00	40.00	80.00
—White label, blue print					
❏ RLP-1001 [10]	Louis Armstrong Plays the Blues	1953	25.00	50.00	100.00
❏ RLP-1029 [10]	Louis Armstrong with King Oliver's Creole Jazz Band 1923	1953	25.00	50.00	100.00
SEAGULL					
❏ LG-8206	Greatest Hits: Live in Concert	198?	3.00	6.00	12.00
STORYVILLE					
❏ 4012	Louis Armstrong and His All-Stars	1980	2.50	5.00	10.00
SWING					
❏ SW-8450	Louis and the Big Bands	1984	2.50	5.00	10.00
TIME-LIFE					
❏ STL-J-01 [(3)]	Giants of Jazz	1978	5.00	10.00	20.00
❏ STBB-22 [(2)]	Big Bands: Louis Armstrong	1985	3.75	7.50	15.00
VANGUARD					
❏ VSD 91/92 [(2)]	Essential Louis Armstrong	1977	3.75	7.50	15.00
❏ VMS 73129	Essential Louis Armstrong, Vol. 1	1986	2.00	4.00	8.00
VERVE					
❏ MGV-4012 [M]	Louis Under the Stars	1957	12.50	25.00	50.00
❏ MGVS-4012	Louis Under the Stars	199?	6.25	12.50	25.00
—Classic Records reissue					
❏ V-4012 [M]	Louis Under the Stars	1961	5.00	10.00	20.00
❏ V6-4012 [S]	Louis Under the Stars	1961	3.75	7.50	15.00
❏ MGV-4035 [M]	I've Got the World on a String	1959	12.50	25.00	50.00
❏ MGVS-4035	I've Got the World on a String	199?	6.25	12.50	25.00
—Classic Records reissue					
❏ V-4035 [M]	I've Got the World on a String	1961	5.00	10.00	20.00
❏ V6-4035 [S]	I've Got the World on a String	1961	3.75	7.50	15.00
❏ MGVS-6044 [S]	Louis Under the Stars	1960	10.00	20.00	40.00
❏ MGVS-6101 [S]	I've Got the World on a String	1960	10.00	20.00	40.00
❏ V-8569 [M]	The Essential Louis A.	1963	3.00	6.00	12.00
❏ V6-8569 [S]	The Essential Louis A.	1963	3.75	7.50	15.00
❏ V-8595 [M]	The Best of Louis Armstrong	1964	3.00	6.00	12.00
❏ V6-8595 [S]	The Best of Louis Armstrong	1964	3.75	7.50	15.00
VOCALION					
❏ VL 3851 [M]	Here's Louis Armstrong	196?	3.75	7.50	15.00
❏ VL 73851 [R]	Here's Louis Armstrong	196?	2.50	5.00	10.00
❏ VL 73871 [R]	The One and Only Louis Armstrong	1968	2.50	5.00	10.00
WING					
❏ SR-16381	Great Louis	196?	2.50	5.00	10.00

ARMSTRONG, LOUIS, AND SIDNEY BECHET
Albums

Number	Title (A Side/B Side)	Yr	VG	VG+	NM
JOLLY ROGER					
❏ 5029 [M]	Louis Armstrong and Sidney Bechet	195?	10.00	20.00	40.00

ARMSTRONG, LOUIS, AND DUKE ELLINGTON Also see each artist's individual listings.
Albums

Number	Title (A Side/B Side)	Yr	VG	VG+	NM
MOBILE FIDELITY					
❏ 2-155 [(2)]	The Great Reunion	1984	20.00	40.00	80.00
—Audiophile vinyl					
PICKWICK					
❏ PC-3033	Louis Armstrong and Duke Ellington	196?	2.50	5.00	10.00
ROULETTE					
❏ RE-108 [(2)]	The Duke Ellington-Louis Armstrong Era	1973	3.75	7.50	15.00
❏ R 52074 [M]	Together for the First Time	1961	6.25	12.50	25.00
❏ SR 52074 [S]	Together for the First Time	1961	5.00	10.00	20.00
❏ R 52103 [M]	The Great Reunion	1963	5.00	10.00	20.00
❏ SR 52103 [S]	The Great Reunion	1963	6.25	12.50	25.00

ARMSTRONG, LOUIS/AL HIRT
Albums

Number	Title (A Side/B Side)	Yr	VG	VG+	NM
MURRAY HILL					
❏ 930633 [(4)]	Louis Armstrong and Al Hirt Play Dixieland Trumpet	197?	5.00	10.00	20.00

ARMSTRONG, LOUIS, AND THE MILLS BROTHERS Also see each artist's individual listings.
45s

Number	Title (A Side/B Side)	Yr	VG	VG+	NM
DECCA					
❏ 28984	My Walking Stick/Marie	1953	3.75	7.50	15.00

Albums

Number	Title (A Side/B Side)	Yr	VG	VG+	NM
DECCA					
❏ DL 5509 [10]	Louis Armstrong and the Mills Brothers	1954	15.00	30.00	60.00

ARMSTRONG, LOUIS, AND OSCAR PETERSON
Albums

Number	Title (A Side/B Side)	Yr	VG	VG+	NM
VERVE					
❏ MGVS-6062 [S]	Louis Armstrong Meets Oscar Peterson	1960	10.00	20.00	40.00
❏ MGV-8322 [M]	Louis Armstrong Meets Oscar Peterson	1959	12.50	25.00	50.00
❏ V-8322 [M]	Louis Armstrong Meets Oscar Peterson	1961	5.00	10.00	20.00
❏ V6-8322 [S]	Louis Armstrong Meets Oscar Peterson	1961	3.75	7.50	15.00

Number	Title (A Side/B Side)	Yr	VG	VG+	NM
ARNAZ, DESI					
45s					
COLUMBIA					
❏ 4-39937	I Love Lucy/There's a Brand New Baby	1953	10.00	20.00	40.00
RCA VICTOR					
❏ 47-2865	Tabu/Cuban Pete	1949	3.75	7.50	15.00
❏ 47-2866	Babalu/Brazil	1949	3.75	7.50	15.00
❏ 47-2867	Tico Tico/Peanut Vendor	1949	3.75	7.50	15.00
—The above three comprise a box set					
Albums					
RCA VICTOR					
❏ LPM-3096 [10]	Babalu!	1954	30.00	60.00	120.00

Number	Title (A Side/B Side)	Yr	VG	VG+	NM
ARNDT, BILL					
45s					
HIT					
❏ 21	Breaking Up Is Hard to Do/Sealed with a Kiss	1962	2.00	4.00	8.00
—B-side by Dick Swift					

Number	Title (A Side/B Side)	Yr	VG	VG+	NM
ARNELL, GINNY					
45s					
DECCA					
❏ 31104	Carnival/We	1960	3.75	7.50	15.00
❏ 31190	Look Who's Talkin'/Tell Me What You Said	1960	3.75	7.50	15.00
MGM					
❏ K13146	I'm Crying Too/Trouble's Back in Town	1963	3.00	6.00	12.00
❏ K13177	Dumb Head/How Many Times Can One Heart Break	1963	3.00	6.00	12.00
❏ K13226	He's My Little Devil/I Wish I Knew What Dress to Wear	1964	3.00	6.00	12.00
❏ K13248	Let Me Make You Smile Again/Yesterday's Memories	1964	3.00	6.00	12.00
❏ K13309	Just Like a Boy/Portrait of a Fool	1965	3.00	6.00	12.00
❏ K13362	B-I-L-L Why/A Little Bit of Love Can Hurt	1965	2.50	5.00	10.00
❏ K13403	I'm Gettin' Mad/I'm So Afraid of Loving You	1965	2.50	5.00	10.00
WARWICK					
❏ 671	No One Cares/Tribute to You	1961	6.25	12.50	25.00
❏ 680	Married to You/He Likes Me Better Than Rock and Roll	1962	5.00	10.00	20.00
Albums					
MGM					
❏ E-4228 [M]	Meet Ginny Arnell	1964	6.25	12.50	25.00
❏ SE-4228 [S]	Meet Ginny Arnell	1964	10.00	20.00	40.00

Number	Title (A Side/B Side)	Yr	VG	VG+	NM
ARNO, AUDREY					
45s					
DECCA					
❏ 31238	La Pachanga/Bei Mir Ist Nix Amore So Im Vorubergehn	1961	2.50	5.00	10.00

ARNOLD, BILLY BOY See BILLY BOY.

Number	Title (A Side/B Side)	Yr	VG	VG+	NM
ARNOLD, CALVIN					
45s					
IX CHAINS					
❏ 7009	Satisfy My Woman/You'll Do It	1975	2.50	5.00	10.00
❏ 7013	I'm Your Friendly Neighborhood Freak (Part 1)/(Part 2)	1975	2.50	5.00	10.00
SONDAY					
❏ 6005	Think I Better Rest/Portrait of a Step-Daddy	197?	2.00	4.00	8.00
SOUND STAGE 7					
❏ 45-2506	After the Love Has Gone/(B-side unknown)	1977	10.00	20.00	40.00
VENTURE					
❏ 605	Funky Way/Snatchin' Back	1967	2.50	5.00	10.00
❏ 610	Scoobie Doo/Lovely Way to Go	1968	3.75	7.50	15.00
❏ 626	Mama in Law/Miniskirt	1968	2.50	5.00	10.00
❏ 634	Just a Matter of Time/You Got to Live for Yourself	1969	2.50	5.00	10.00

Number	Title (A Side/B Side)	Yr	VG	VG+	NM
ARNOLD, EDDY					
45s					
CURB					
❏ 73088	Cattle Call (with LeAnn Rimes)/I Walk Alone	1999	—	—	3.00
MGM					
❏ 14478	So Many Ways/Once in a While	1972	—	2.50	5.00
❏ 14535	If the Whole World Stopped Lovin'/My Son, I Wish You Everything	1973	—	2.00	4.00
❏ 14600	Oh, Oh, I'm Falling in Love Again/Anyway You Want Me	1973	—	2.00	4.00
❏ 14672	She's Got Everything I Need/I'm Glad You Happened to Me	1973	—	2.00	4.00
❏ 14711	Just for Old Times Sake/I Got This Thing About You	1974	—	2.00	4.00
❏ 14734	I Wish That I Had Loved You Better/Let It Be Love	1974	—	2.00	4.00
❏ 14769	Butterfly/If You Could Only Love Me Now	1974	—	2.00	4.00
❏ 14780	Red Roses for a Blue Lady/I Will	1975	—	2.00	4.00
❏ 14827	Middle of a Memory/I Just Had You on My Mind	1975	—	2.00	4.00
RCA					
❏ 2750-7-R	You Don't Miss a Thing/Just One Time	1990	—	2.00	4.00
❏ PB-10794	Put Me Back Into Your World/Goodnight Irene	1976	—	2.00	4.00
❏ PB-10899	(I Need You) All the Time/I've Never Loved Anyone More	1977	—	2.00	4.00
❏ PB-11031	Freedom Ain't the Same as Being Free/Till You Can Make It On Your Own	1977	—	2.00	4.00
❏ PB-11133	Where Lonely People Go/Penny Arcade	1977	—	2.00	4.00
❏ PB-11257	Country Lovin'/I've So Much to Be Thankful For	1978	—	2.00	4.00
❏ PB-11319	I'm the South/You Are My Sunshine	1978	—	2.00	4.00
❏ PB-11422	If Everyone Had Someone Like You/You're a Beautiful Place to Be	1978	—	2.00	4.00
❏ PB-11537	What In Her World Did I Do/Love of My Life	1979	—	2.00	4.00
❏ PB-11668	Goodbye/You're So Good At Lovin' Me	1979	—	2.00	4.00

Number	Title (A Side/B Side)	Yr	VG	VG+	NM
❑ PB-11752	If I Ever Had to Say Goodbye to You/				
	Love of My Life	1979	—	2.00	4.00
❑ PB-11918	Let's Get It While the Gettin's Good/You Cared				
	Enough (To Give Your Very Best)	1980	—	2.00	4.00
❑ PB-12039	That's What I Get for Loving You/Undivided Love	1980	—	2.00	4.00
❑ PB-12136	Don't Look Now (But We Just Fell in Love)/				
	There's Women (Then There's My Woman)	1980	—	2.00	4.00
❑ PB-12226	Bally-Hoo Days/				
	Two Hearts Beat Better Than One	1981	—	2.00	4.00
❑ PB-13000	All I'm Missing Is You/Don't It Break Your Heart	1981	—	2.00	4.00
❑ PB-13094	Don't Give Up on Me/In Love with Loving You	1982	—	2.00	4.00
❑ PB-13339	The Valley Below/Make the World Go Away	1982	—	2.00	4.00
❑ PB-13452	The Blues Don't Care Who's Got 'Em/				
	Wooden Heart	1983	—	2.00	4.00
❑ 62598	Out of the Blue/On a Night Like This	1993	—	2.00	4.00
RCA VICTOR					
❑ 37-7861	(Jim) I Wore a Tie Today/Just Call Me Lonesome	1961	7.50	15.00	30.00

—"Compact Single 33" (small hole, plays at LP speed)

Number	Title (A Side/B Side)	Yr	VG	VG+	NM
❑ 47-2729	Anytime/What a Fool I Was	1949	—	—	—
❑ 47-2730	Bouquet of Roses/Texarkana Baby	1949	—	—	—
❑ 47-2776	I'm Thinking Tonight of My Blue Eyes/				
	Rockin' Alone	1949	—	—	—
❑ 47-2777	It Makes No Difference Now/Molly Darling	1949	—	—	—
❑ 47-2778	The Prisoner's Song/Seven Years with the				
	Wrong Woman	1949	—	—	—

—Note: The above five singles were, evidently, originally assigned by RCA Victor to the 47- series. But they were actually released on the 48- series with different numbers. The 47- versions are not known to exist.

Number	Title (A Side/B Side)	Yr	VG	VG+	NM
❑ 47-3310	That's How Much I Love You/				
	Chained to a Memory	1949	6.25	12.50	25.00
❑ 47-3311	Will the Circle Be Unbroken/				
	Who, At My Door, Is Standing	1949	6.25	12.50	25.00
❑ 47-4243	When My Blue Moon Turns to Gold Again/				
	White Azaleas	1951	5.00	10.00	20.00
❑ 47-4244	When You and I Were Young, Maggie/				
	Roll Along Kentucky Moon	1951	5.00	10.00	20.00
❑ 47-4245	That Little Boy of Mine/Sinner's Prayer	1951	5.00	10.00	20.00
❑ 47-4273	Somebody's Been Beating My Time/				
	Heart Strings	1951	5.00	10.00	20.00
❑ 47-4413	Bundle of Southern Sunshine/				
	Call Her Your Sweetheart	1951	5.00	10.00	20.00
❑ 47-4490	Take My Hand, Precious Lord/				
	Open Thy Merciful Arms	1952	5.00	10.00	20.00
❑ 47-4569	Easy on the Eyes/Anything That's Part of You	1952	5.00	10.00	20.00
❑ 47-4597	Bouquet of Roses/Texarkana Baby	1952	5.00	10.00	20.00
❑ 47-4598	It's a Sin/Anytime	1952	5.00	10.00	20.00
❑ 47-4599	That's How Much I Love You/A Heart Full of Love	1952	5.00	10.00	20.00
❑ 47-4600	I'll Hold You in My Heart (Till I Can Hold You in				
	My Arms)/Don't Rob Another Man's Castle	1952	5.00	10.00	20.00
❑ 47-4787	A Full Time Job/Shephard of My Heart	1952	5.00	10.00	20.00
❑ 47-4954	Older and Bolder/I'd Trade All My Tomorrows				
	(For Just One Yesterday)	1952	5.00	10.00	20.00
❑ 47-5020	My Desire/I Want to Thank You Lord	1952	5.00	10.00	20.00
❑ 47-5108	Eddy's Song/Condemned Without a Trial	1952	5.00	10.00	20.00
❑ 47-5189	When Your Hair Has Turned to Silver/Angry	1953	5.00	10.00	20.00
❑ 47-5192	Moonlight and Roses/Missouri Waltz	1953	5.00	10.00	20.00
❑ 47-5193	You Always Hurt the One You Love/				
	I'm Gonna Lock My Heart	1953	5.00	10.00	20.00
❑ 47-5196	The Old Rugged Cross/				
	Have Thine Own Way, Lord	1953	5.00	10.00	20.00
❑ 47-5197	Someday Somewhere/When I've Done My Best	1953	5.00	10.00	20.00
❑ 47-5305	Free Home Demonstration/				
	How's the World Treating You	1953	5.00	10.00	20.00
❑ 47-5415	Mama, Come Get Your Baby Boy/				
	If I Never Get to Heaven	1953	5.00	10.00	20.00
❑ 47-5525	I Really Don't Want to Know				
	/I'll Never Get Over You	1953	5.00	10.00	20.00
❑ 47-5601	Rose of Calvary/Prayer	1954	5.00	10.00	20.00
❑ 47-5634	My Everything/Second Fling	1954	5.00	10.00	20.00
❑ 47-5753	Chapel on the Hill/A Touch of God's Hand	1954	5.00	10.00	20.00
❑ 47-5805	This Is the Thanks I Get (For Loving You)/				
	Hep Cat Baby	1954	5.00	10.00	20.00
❑ 47-5905	Christmas Can't Be Far Away/				
	I'm Your Private Santa Claus	1954	5.00	10.00	20.00
❑ 47-6000	I've Been Thinking/Don't Forget	1955	3.75	7.50	15.00
❑ 47-6001	It Took a Miracle				
	I Always Have Someone to Turn To	1955	3.75	7.50	15.00
❑ 47-6069	Two Kinds of Love/In Time	1955	3.75	7.50	15.00
❑ 47-6139	The Cattle Call/The Kentuckian Song	1955	5.00	10.00	20.00
❑ 47-6198	Just Call Me Lonesome/That Do Make It Nice	1955	3.75	7.50	15.00
❑ 47-6290	The Richest Man/I Walked Alone Last Night	1955	3.75	7.50	15.00
❑ 47-6365	Trouble in Mind/When You Say Goodbye	1955	3.75	7.50	15.00
❑ 47-6407	Bayou Baby/Do You Know Where God Lives	1956	3.75	7.50	15.00
❑ 47-6502	You Don't Know Me/The Rockin' Mockin' Bird	1956	3.75	7.50	15.00
❑ 47-6601	Casey Jones (The Brave Engineer)/				
	You Were Mine for Awhile	1956	3.75	7.50	15.00
❑ 47-6699	The Ballad of Wes Tancred/				
	I Wouldn't Know Where to Begin	1956	3.75	7.50	15.00
❑ 47-6708	Mutual Admiration Society/If'n	1956	3.75	7.50	15.00

—With Jaye P. Morgan

Number	Title (A Side/B Side)	Yr	VG	VG+	NM
❑ 47-6773	A Dozen Hearts/A Good Lookin' Blonde	1956	3.75	7.50	15.00
❑ 47-6842	One/Do You Love Me	1957	3.00	6.00	12.00

—With Jaye P. Morgan

Number	Title (A Side/B Side)	Yr	VG	VG+	NM
❑ 47-6905	Gonna Find Me a Bluebird/Little Bit	1957	3.00	6.00	12.00
❑ 47-6975	Crazy Dream/Open Your Heart	1957	3.00	6.00	12.00
❑ 47-7040	Little Miss Sunbeam/When He Was Young	1957	3.00	6.00	12.00
❑ 47-7089	Wagon Wheels/You're Never Too Old for Everything	1957	3.00	6.00	12.00
❑ 47-7143	Too Soon to Know/I Need Somebody	1958	3.00	6.00	12.00
❑ 47-7221	Peck a Cheek/Before You Know It	1958	3.00	6.00	12.00
❑ 47-7292	The Day You Left Me/Real Love	1958	3.00	6.00	12.00
❑ 47-7340	Till You Come Back Again/I'm a Good Boy	1958	3.00	6.00	12.00

Number	Title (A Side/B Side)	Yr	VG	VG+	NM
❑ 47-7435	Chip Off the Old Block/I'll Hold You in My Heart				
	(Till I Can Hold You in My Arms)	1959	2.50	5.00	10.00
❑ 47-7542	Tennessee Stud/What's the Good				
	(Of All This Love)	1959	2.50	5.00	10.00
❑ 47-7619	Did It Rain/Sittin' By Sittin' Bull	1959	2.50	5.00	10.00
❑ 47-7661	Boot Hill/Johnny Reb, That's Me	1959	2.50	5.00	10.00
❑ 47-7727	Little Sparrow/My Arms Are a House	1960	2.50	5.00	10.00
❑ 47-7794	Before This Day Ends/Just Out of Reach	1960	2.50	5.00	10.00
❑ 47-7861	(Jim) I Wore a Tie Today/Just Call Me Lonesome	1961	2.50	5.00	10.00
❑ 47-7926	One Grain of Sand/The Worst Night of My Life	1961	2.50	5.00	10.00
❑ 47-7984	Tears Broke Out on Me/				
	I'll Do As Much for You Someday	1962	2.00	4.00	8.00
❑ 47-8048	A Little Heartache/After Loving You	1962	2.00	4.00	8.00
❑ 47-8102	Does He Mean That Much to You/Tender Touch	1962	2.00	4.00	8.00
❑ 47-8102 [PS]	Does He Mean That Much to You/Tender Touch	1962	5.00	10.00	20.00
❑ 47-8160	Yesterday's Memories/Lonely Balladeer	1963	2.00	4.00	8.00
❑ 47-8160 [PS]	Yesterday's Memories/Lonely Balladeer	1963	3.75	7.50	15.00
❑ 47-8207	A Million Years or So/Just a Ribbon	1963	2.00	4.00	8.00
❑ 47-8253	Jealous Hearted Me/I Met Her Today	1963	2.00	4.00	8.00
❑ 47-8296	Molly/The Song of the Coo Coo	1963	2.00	4.00	8.00
❑ 47-8363	Sweet Adorable You/Why	1964	—	3.00	6.00
❑ 47-8445	I Thank My Lucky Stars/I Don't Cry No More	1964	—	3.00	6.00
❑ 47-8516	What's He Doing in My World/Laura Lee	1965	—	3.00	6.00
❑ 47-8632	I'm Letting You Go/The Days Gone By	1965	—	3.00	6.00
❑ 47-8679	Make the World Go Away/The Easy Way	1965	2.00	4.00	8.00
❑ 47-8679 [PS]	Make the World Go Away/The Easy Way	1965	3.75	7.50	15.00
❑ 47-8749	I Want to Go With You/				
	Better Stop Tellin' Lies (About Me)	1965	2.00	4.00	8.00
❑ 47-8749 [PS]	I Want to Go With You/				
	Better Stop Tellin' Lies (About Me)	1965	3.75	7.50	15.00
❑ 47-8818	The Last Word in Lonesome Is Me/				
	Mary Claire Melvina Rebecca Jane	1966	—	3.00	6.00
❑ 47-8818 [PS]	The Last Word in Lonesome Is Me/Mary Claire				
	Melvina Rebecca Jane	1966	3.00	6.00	12.00
❑ 47-8869	The Tip of My Fingers/Long, Long Friendship	1966	—	3.00	6.00
❑ 47-8869 [PS]	The Tip of My Fingers/Long, Long Friendship	1966	3.00	6.00	12.00
❑ 47-8965	Somebody Like Me/Taking Chances	1966	—	3.00	6.00
❑ 47-8965 [PS]	Somebody Like Me/Taking Chances	1966	3.00	6.00	12.00
❑ 47-9027	The Angel and the Stranger/The First Word	1966	—	3.00	6.00
❑ 47-9080	Lonely Again/Love on My Mind	1967	—	3.00	6.00
❑ 47-9182	Misty Blue/Calling Mary Names	1967	—	3.00	6.00
❑ 47-9265	Turn the World Around/The Long Ride Home	1967	—	3.00	6.00
❑ 47-9368	Here Comes Heaven/Baby That's Loving	1967	—	3.00	6.00
❑ 47-9387	Jolly Old St. Nicholas/This World of Ours	1967	2.00	4.00	8.00
❑ 47-9437	Here Comes the Rain, Baby/				
	The World I Used to Know	1968	—	3.00	6.00
❑ 47-9525	It's Over/No Matter Whose Baby You Are	1968	—	3.00	6.00
❑ 47-9606	Then You Can Tell Me Goodbye/				
	Apples, Raisins and Roses	1968	—	3.00	6.00
❑ 47-9667	They Don't Make Love Like They Used To/				
	What a Wonderful World	1968	—	3.00	6.00
❑ 47-9801	Soul Deep/(Today) I Started Loving You Again	1969	—	3.00	6.00
❑ 47-9848	A Man's Kind of Woman/Living Under Pressure	1970	—	2.50	5.00
❑ 47-9889	From Heaven to Heartache/				
	Ten Times Forever More	1970	—	2.50	5.00
❑ 47-9935	Portrait of My Woman/				
	I Really Don't Want to Know	1970	—	2.50	5.00
❑ 47-9968	A Part of America Died/Call Me	1971	—	2.50	5.00
❑ 47-9993	Welcome to My World/It Ain't No Big Thing	1971	—	2.50	5.00
❑ 48-0001	Bouquet of Roses/Texarkana Baby	1949	6.25	12.50	25.00

—Second pressings: Green label, black vinyl

Number	Title (A Side/B Side)	Yr	VG	VG+	NM
❑ 48-0001	Bouquet of Roses/Texarkana Baby	1949	12.50	25.00	50.00

—Originals on green vinyl

Number	Title (A Side/B Side)	Yr	VG	VG+	NM
❑ 48-0001 [PS]	Bouquet of Roses/Texarkana Baby	1949	20.00	40.00	80.00

—Brown and dark brown title sleeve

Number	Title (A Side/B Side)	Yr	VG	VG+	NM
❑ 48-0002	Anytime/What a Fool I Was	1949	12.50	25.00	50.00

—Originals on green vinyl

Number	Title (A Side/B Side)	Yr	VG	VG+	NM
❑ 48-0002	Anytime/What a Fool I Was	195?	6.25	12.50	25.00

—Second pressings: Green label, black vinyl

Number	Title (A Side/B Side)	Yr	VG	VG+	NM
❑ 48-0016	I'm Thinking Tonight of My Blue Eyes/				
	Rockin' Alone	1949	6.25	12.50	25.00

—Second pressings: Green label, black vinyl

Number	Title (A Side/B Side)	Yr	VG	VG+	NM
❑ 48-0016	I'm Thinking Tonight of My Blue Eyes/				
	Rockin' Alone	1949	12.50	25.00	50.00

—Originals on green vinyl

Number	Title (A Side/B Side)	Yr	VG	VG+	NM
❑ 48-0017	It Makes No Difference Now/Molly Darling	1949	12.50	25.00	50.00

—Originals on green vinyl

Number	Title (A Side/B Side)	Yr	VG	VG+	NM
❑ 48-0017	It Makes No Difference Now/Molly Darling	195?	6.25	12.50	25.00

—Second pressings: Green label, black vinyl

Number	Title (A Side/B Side)	Yr	VG	VG+	NM
❑ 48-0018	The Prisoner's Song/Seven Years with the				
	Wrong Woman	1949	6.25	12.50	25.00

—Second pressings: Green label, black vinyl

Number	Title (A Side/B Side)	Yr	VG	VG+	NM
❑ 48-0018	The Prisoner's Song/				
	Seven Years with the Wrong Woman	1949	12.50	25.00	50.00

—Originals on green vinyl

Number	Title (A Side/B Side)	Yr	VG	VG+	NM
❑ 48-0019	Will the Circle Be Unbroken/Who at My Door Is				
	Standing	1949	12.50	25.00	50.00

—Originals on green vinyl

Number	Title (A Side/B Side)	Yr	VG	VG+	NM
❑ 48-0019	Will the Circle Be Unbroken/				
	Who at My Door Is Standing	195?	6.25	12.50	25.00

—Second pressings: Green label, black vinyl

Number	Title (A Side/B Side)	Yr	VG	VG+	NM
❑ 48-0025	A Heart Full of Love (For a Handful of Kisses)/				
	Then I Turned and Walked Slowly Away	1949	6.25	12.50	25.00

—Second pressings: Green label, black vinyl

Number	Title (A Side/B Side)	Yr	VG	VG+	NM
❑ 48-0025	A Heart Full of Love (For a Handful of Kisses)/				
	Then I Turned and Walked Slowly Away	1949	12.50	25.00	50.00

—Originals on green vinyl

Number	Title (A Side/B Side)	Yr	VG	VG+	NM
❑ 48-0026	Just a Little Lovin' (Will Go a Long, Long Way)/				
	My Daddy Is Only a Picture	1949	6.25	12.50	25.00

—Second pressings: Green label, black vinyl

Number	Title (A Side/B Side)	Yr	VG	VG+	NM
❑ 48-0026	Just a Little Lovin' (Will Go a Long, Long Way)/ My Daddy Is Only a Picture	1949	12.50	25.00	50.00
—Originals on green vinyl					
❑ 48-0030	I'll Hold You in My Heart (Till I Can Hold You in My Arms)/Don't Bother to Cry	1949	6.25	12.50	25.00
—Second pressings: Green label, black vinyl					
❑ 48-0030	I'll Hold You in My Heart (Till I Can Hold You in My Arms)/Don't Bother to Cry	1949	12.50	25.00	50.00
—Originals on green vinyl					
❑ 48-0042	There's Not a Thing (I Wouldn't Do for You)/Don't Rob Another Man's Castle	1949	6.25	12.50	25.00
—Second pressings: Green label, black vinyl					
❑ 48-0042	There's Not a Thing (I Wouldn't Do for You)/Don't Rob Another Man's Castle	1949	12.50	25.00	50.00
—Originals on green vinyl					
❑ 48-0080	I'm Throwing Rice (At the Girl That I Love)/Show Me the Way Back to Your Heart	1949	6.25	12.50	25.00
—Second pressings: Green label, black vinyl					
❑ 48-0080	I'm Throwing Rice (At the Girl That I Love)/Show Me the Way Back to Your Heart	1949	12.50	25.00	50.00
—Originals on green vinyl					
❑ 48-0083	One Kiss Too Many/The Echo of Your Footsteps	1949	12.50	25.00	50.00
❑ 48-0083	One Kiss Too Many/The Echo of Your Footsteps	1950	6.25	12.50	25.00
—Second pressings: Green label, black vinyl					
❑ 48-0127	C-H-R-I-S-T-M-A-S/ Will Santa Come to Shanty Town	1949	6.25	12.50	25.00
—Second pressings: Green label, black vinyl					
❑ 48-0127	C-H-R-I-S-T-M-A-S/ Will Santa Come to Shanty Town	1949	12.50	25.00	50.00
—Originals on green vinyl					
❑ 48-0136	The Nearest Thing to Heaven/The Cattle Call	1949	6.25	12.50	25.00
—Second pressings: Green label, black vinyl					
❑ 48-0136	The Nearest Thing to Heaven/The Cattle Call	1949	12.50	25.00	50.00
—Originals on green vinyl					
❑ 48-0137	There's No Wings on My Angel/You Know How Talk Gets Around	1949	6.25	12.50	25.00
—Second pressings: Green label, black vinyl					
❑ 48-0137	There's No Wings on My Angel/You Know How Talk Gets Around	1949	12.50	25.00	50.00
—Originals on green vinyl					
❑ 48-0138	Just a Little Lovin' (Will Go a Long, Long Way)/ I'm Throwing Rice (At the Girl That I Love)	1949	6.25	12.50	25.00
—Second pressings: Green label, black vinyl					
❑ 48-0138	Just a Little Lovin' (Will Go a Long, Long Way)/ I'm Throwing Rice (At the Girl That I Love)	1949	12.50	25.00	50.00
—Originals on green vinyl					
❑ 48-0150	Take Me in Your Arms and Hold Me/Mama and Daddy Broke My Heart	1949	6.25	12.50	25.00
—Second pressings: Green label, black vinyl					
❑ 48-0150	Take Me in Your Arms and Hold Me/Mama and Daddy Broke My Heart	1949	12.50	25.00	50.00
—Originals on green vinyl					
❑ 48-0165	The Lily of the Valley/Evil, Tempt Me Not	1950	6.25	12.50	25.00
—Second pressings: Green label, black vinyl					
❑ 48-0165	The Lily of the Valley/Evil, Tempt Me Not	1950	12.50	25.00	50.00
—Originals on green vinyl					
❑ 48-0166	When Jesus Beckons Me Home/Beautiful Isle	1950	6.25	12.50	25.00
—Second pressings: Green label, black vinyl					
❑ 48-0166	When Jesus Beckons Me Home/Beautiful Isle	1950	12.50	25.00	50.00
—Originals on green vinyl					
❑ 48-0167	Hills of Tomorrow/Softly and Tenderly	1950	6.25	12.50	25.00
—Second pressings: Green label, black vinyl					
❑ 48-0167	Hills of Tomorrow/Softly and Tenderly	1950	12.50	25.00	50.00
—Originals on green vinyl					
❑ 48-0174	That Wonderful Mother of Mine/Mother	1950	6.25	12.50	25.00
—Second pressings: Green label, black vinyl					
❑ 48-0174	That Wonderful Mother of Mine/Mother	1950	12.50	25.00	50.00
—Originals on green vinyl					
❑ 48-0175	Bring Roses to Her Now/I Wish I Had a Girl	1950	6.25	12.50	25.00
—Second pressings: Green label, black vinyl					
❑ 48-0175	Bring Roses to Her Now/I Wish I Had a Girl	1950	12.50	25.00	50.00
—Originals on green vinyl					
❑ 48-0176	My Mother's Sweet Voice/I Wouldn't Trade the Silver	1950	6.25	12.50	25.00
—Second pressings: Green label, black vinyl					
❑ 48-0176	My Mother's Sweet Voice/I Wouldn't Trade the Silver	1950	12.50	25.00	50.00
—Originals on green vinyl					
❑ 48-0197	To My Sorrow/Easy Rockin' Chair	1950	6.25	12.50	25.00
—Second pressings: Green label, black vinyl					
❑ 48-0197	To My Sorrow/Easy Rockin' Chair	1950	12.50	25.00	50.00
—Originals on green vinyl					
❑ 48-0198	It's a Sin/I Couldn't Believe It Was True	1950	6.25	12.50	25.00
—Second pressings: Green label, black vinyl					
❑ 48-0198	It's a Sin/I Couldn't Believe It Was True	1950	12.50	25.00	50.00
—Originals on green vinyl					
❑ 48-0199	What Is Life Without Love/ Be Sure There's No Mistake	1950	6.25	12.50	25.00
—Second pressings: Green label, black vinyl					
❑ 48-0199	What Is Life Without Love/Be Sure There's No Mistake	1950	12.50	25.00	50.00
—Originals on green vinyl					
❑ 48-0300	Little Angel with the Dirty Face/ Why Should I Cry?	1950	6.25	12.50	25.00
—Second pressings: Green label, black vinyl					
❑ 48-0300	Little Angel with the Dirty Face/ Why Should I Cry?	1950	12.50	25.00	50.00
—Originals on green vinyl					
❑ 48-0342	Cuddle Buggin' Baby/Enclosed, One Broken Heart	1950	6.25	12.50	25.00
—Second pressings: Green label, black vinyl					

Number	Title (A Side/B Side)	Yr	VG	VG+	NM
❑ 48-0342	Cuddle Buggin' Baby/ Enclosed, One Broken Heart	1950	12.50	25.00	50.00
—Originals on green vinyl					
❑ 48-0382	The Lovebug Itch/A Prison Without Walls	1950	6.25	12.50	25.00
—Second pressings: Green label, black vinyl					
❑ 48-0382	The Lovebug Itch/A Prison Without Walls	1950	12.50	25.00	50.00
—Originals on green vinyl					
❑ 48-0390	White Christmas/Santa Claus Is Comin' to Town	1950	6.25	12.50	25.00
—Second pressings: Green label, black vinyl					
❑ 48-0390	White Christmas/Santa Claus Is Comin' to Town	1950	12.50	25.00	50.00
—Originals on green vinyl					
❑ 48-0412	There's Been a Change in Me/Tie Me to Your Apron Strings Again	1950	6.25	12.50	25.00
—Second pressings: Green label, black vinyl					
❑ 48-0412	There's Been a Change in Me/Tie Me to Your Apron Strings Again	1950	12.50	25.00	50.00
—Originals on green vinyl					
❑ 48-0425	May the Good Lord Bless and Keep You/I'm Writing a Letter to the Lord	1951	5.00	10.00	20.00
—Second pressings: Green label, black vinyl					
❑ 48-0425	May the Good Lord Bless and Keep You/I'm Writing a Letter to the Lord	1951	12.50	25.00	50.00
—Originals on green vinyl					
❑ 48-0444	Kentucky Waltz/A Million Miles from Your Heart	1951	5.00	10.00	20.00
—Second pressings: Green label, black vinyl					
❑ 48-0444	Kentucky Waltz/A Million Miles from Your Heart	1951	12.50	25.00	50.00
—Originals on green vinyl					
❑ 48-0476	I Wanna Play House with You/ Something Old, Something New	1951	6.25	12.50	25.00
❑ 48-0495	Jesus and the Atheist/He Knows	1951	6.25	12.50	25.00
❑ 74-0120	Please Don't Go/Heaven Below	1969	—	2.50	5.00
❑ 74-0175	But For Love/My Lady of Love	1969	—	2.50	5.00
❑ 74-0226	You Fool/You Don't Need Me Anymore	1969	—	2.50	5.00
❑ 74-0282	Since December/Morning of Our Mind	1969	—	2.50	5.00
❑ 74-0559	I Love You Dear/Long Life, Lots of Happiness	1971	—	2.50	5.00
❑ 74-0641	Lonely People/If It's Alright with You	1972	—	2.50	5.00
❑ 74-0705	Poison Red Berries/Just Out of Reach	1972	—	2.50	5.00
❑ 74-0747	Lucy/The Last Letter	1972	—	2.50	5.00
❑ 74-0842	An Angel Sleeps Beside Me/ Sweet Bunch of Daisies	1972	—	—	—
—Unreleased					
❑ WP 239 [PS]	To Mother	1950	6.25	12.50	25.00
—Box for records 48-0174, 48-0175 and 48-0176					
❑ WP 261 [PS]	Eddy Arnold's Favorite Sacred Songs	1950	6.25	12.50	25.00
—Box for records 48-0165, 48-0166 and 48-0167					
❑ PB-10701	Cowboy/Don't Let the Good Times Roll Away	1976	—	2.00	4.00
7-Inch Extended Plays					
RCA VICTOR					
❑ 547-0099	Bouquet of Roses/It's a Sin//That's How Much I Love You/Don't Rob Another Man's Castle	1952	5.00	10.00	20.00
—Record 1 of 2-EP set EPB-3027					
❑ 547-0100	I'll Hold You in My Heart (Till I Can Hold You in My Arms)/A Heart Full of Love (For a Handful of Kisses)//Anytime/Texarkana Baby	1952	5.00	10.00	20.00
—Record 2 of 2-EP set EPB-3027					
❑ EPA 239	That Wonderful Mother of Mine/M-O-T-H-E-R//I Wouldn't Trade the Silver in My Mother's Hair/ My Mother's Sweet Voice	195?	5.00	10.00	20.00
❑ EPA 239 [PS]	To Mother	195?	5.00	10.00	20.00
❑ EPA 260	The Cattle Call/The Nearest Thing to Heaven// I'm Throwing Rice (At the Girl That I Love)/Just a Little Lovin' (Will Go a Long, Long Way)	195?	5.00	10.00	20.00
❑ EPA 260 [PS]	Eddy Arnold Sings	195?	5.00	10.00	20.00
❑ EPA 261	Beautiful Isle of Somewhere/When Jesus Beckons Me Home//(In the) Hills of Tomorrow/ Softly and Tenderly	195?	5.00	10.00	20.00
❑ EPA 261 [PS]	Eddy Arnold's Favorite Sacred Songs	195?	5.00	10.00	20.00
❑ EPA 328	White Azaleas/When My Blue Moon Turns to Gold Again//When You and I Were Young, Maggie/Roll Along Kentucky Moon	195?	5.00	10.00	20.00
❑ EPA 328 [PS]	All Time Hits from the Hills, Vol. 2	195?	5.00	10.00	20.00
❑ 547-0424	When It's Round-Up Time in Heaven/The Chapel on the Hill//'Twas the Dawn of a Beautiful Day/Prayer	1954	5.00	10.00	20.00
—Record 1 of 2-EP set EPB-3219					
❑ 547-0425	Today/Robe of Calvary//I Called on the Master/ The Touch of God's Hand	1954	5.00	10.00	20.00
—Record 2 of 2-EP set EPB-3219					
❑ EPA 427	The Old Rugged Cross/Have Thine Own Way, Lord//Someday, Somewhere/When I've Done My Best	195?	5.00	10.00	20.00
❑ EPA 427 [PS]	The Old Rugged Cross	195?	5.00	10.00	20.00
❑ EPA 428	Moonlight and Roses (Bring Mem'ries of You)/ The Missouri Waltz//I'm Gonna Lock My Heart (And Throw Away the Key)/You Always Hurt the One You Love	195?	5.00	10.00	20.00
❑ EPA 428 [PS]	All Time Favorites Vol. 1	195?	5.00	10.00	20.00
❑ EPA 429	I'm Waiting for Ships That Never Come In/I'm Gonna Sit Right Down and Write Myself a Letter//When Your Hair Has Turned to Silver (I Will Love You Just the Same)/Angry	195?	5.00	10.00	20.00
❑ EPA 429 [PS]	All Time Favorites Volume 2	195?	5.00	10.00	20.00
❑ EPA 473	C-H-R-I-S-T-M-A-S/Will Santy Come to Shanty Town//White Christmas/ Santa Claus Is Comin' to Town	1953	5.00	10.00	20.00
❑ EPA 473 [PS]	(title unknown)	1953	5.00	10.00	20.00
❑ EPA 500	Open Thy Merciful Arms/Take My Hand, Precious Lord//My Desire/I Want to Thank You, Lord	195?	5.00	10.00	20.00
❑ EPA 500 [PS]	Open Thy Merciful Arms	195?	5.00	10.00	20.00
❑ EPA 544	Beyond the Sunset/Crying in the Chapel//It Is No Secret/Whispering Hope	195?	5.00	10.00	20.00

Number	Title (A Side/B Side)	Yr	VG	VG+	NM
❑ EPA 544 [PS]	Songs of Hope and Inspiration	195?	5.00	10.00	20.00
❑ EPA 573	(contents unknown)	195?	5.00	10.00	20.00
❑ EPA 573 [PS]	I Really Don't Want to Know	195?	5.00	10.00	20.00
❑ EPA 624	(contents unknown)	195?	5.00	10.00	20.00
❑ EPA 624 [PS]	Top Hits Round-Up	195?	5.00	10.00	20.00
❑ 547-0656	Wanderin'/The Rovin' Gambler/The Lonesome Road//Careless Love/Sometimes I Feel Like a Motherless Child	1955	5.00	10.00	20.00
—Record 1 of 2-EP set EPB-1111					
❑ 547-0657	Down in the Valley/I Gave My Love a Cherry//The Wayfaring Stranger/Across the Wide Missouri	1955	5.00	10.00	20.00
—Record 2 of 2-EP set EPB-1111					
❑ EPA 712	The Cattle Call/The Richest Man (In the World)/That Do Make It Nice/Just Call Me Lonesome	195?	5.00	10.00	20.00
❑ EPA 712 [PS]	Cattle Call	195?	5.00	10.00	20.00
❑ EPA 787	Bouquet of Roses/That's How Much I Love You//I'll Hold You in My Heart (Till I Can Hold You in My Arms)/Any Time	195?	3.75	7.50	15.00
❑ EPA 787 [PS]	Anytime	195?	3.75	7.50	15.00
❑ EPA 914	You Can't Be True Dear/I Love You So Much It Hurts//So Round, So Firm, So Fully Packed/Cold, Cold Heart	195?	3.75	7.50	15.00
❑ EPA 914 [PS]	(title unknown)	195?	3.75	7.50	15.00
❑ EPA 972	A Little on the Lonely Side/Sometime//I Don't Know Why/I Cried for You	195?	3.75	7.50	15.00
❑ EPA 972 [PS]	(title unknown)	195?	3.75	7.50	15.00
❑ EPA 973	The Very Thought of You/That Old Feeling//Don't Take Your Love from Me/It Had to Be You	195?	3.75	7.50	15.00
❑ EPA 973 [PS]	(title unknown)	195?	3.75	7.50	15.00
❑ EPB-1111 [PS]	Wanderin' with Eddy Arnold	1955	5.00	10.00	20.00
—Two-pocket jacket for two-EP set (547-0656 and 547-0657)					
❑ VLP 2909	Sometimes I'm Happy/(I've Got a Woman Crazy for Me) She's Funny That Way/Then I'll Be Happy//Smile/A Little Bitty Tear/Roaming Through the Countryside	196?	3.00	6.00	12.00
—Jukebox issue; small hole, plays at 33 1/3 rpm					
❑ VLP 2909 [PS]	Sometimes I'm Happy, Sometimes I'm Blue	196?	3.00	6.00	12.00
❑ EPB 3027 [PS]	Country Classics	1952	5.00	10.00	20.00
—Two-pocket jacket for two-EP set (547-0099 and 547-0100)					
❑ EPB 3219	When It's Round-Up Time in Heaven	1954	5.00	10.00	20.00
—Two-pocket jacket for two-EP set (547-0424 and 547-0425)					
❑ VLP 3466	What's He Doin' in My World/I'm Walking Behind You//I'm Letting You Go//As Usual/The Days Gone By/Too Many Rivers	1965	3.00	6.00	12.00
—Jukebox EP, small hole, plays at 33 1/3 rpm					
❑ VLP 3466 [PS]	My World	1965	3.00	6.00	12.00
❑ VLP 3507	I Want to Go with You/Somebody Loves You/Don't Forget (I Still Love You)//One Kiss for Old Times' Sake/After Losing You/Pardon Me	1966	3.00	6.00	12.00
—Jukebox issue; small hole, plays at 33 1/3 rpm					
❑ VLP 3507 [PS]	I Want to Go with You	1966	3.00	6.00	12.00
❑ VLP 3622	Here Comes My Baby/A Thing Called Sadness/Misty Blue//Don't Touch Me/After the Laughter (Come the Tears)/The Last Word in Lonesome Is Me	1966	3.00	6.00	12.00
❑ VLP 3622 [PS]	The Last Word in Lonesome	1966	3.00	6.00	12.00
❑ VLP 3715	Somebody Like Me/Lay Some Happiness on Me/There's Always Me//Tip of My Fingers/Love on My Mind/I Love You Drops	1966	3.00	6.00	12.00
—Jukebox EP, small hole, plays at 33 1/3 rpm					
❑ VLP 3715 [PS]	Somebody Like Me	1966	3.00	6.00	12.00
❑ EPA 4109	Each Time You Leave Me/(Gonna Get Myself a) Brand New Sandman//Tennessee Hillbilly Ghost/I'll Be Satisfied	1958	3.75	7.50	15.00
❑ EPA 4109 [PS]	Eddy Arnold Time	1958	3.75	7.50	15.00
❑ EPA-5019	Anytime/Just a Little Lovin' (Will Go a Long, Long Way)//The Cattle Call/What Is Life Without Love	1958	3.75	7.50	15.00
❑ EPA-5019 [PS]	Eddy Arnold (Gold Standard Series)	1958	3.75	7.50	15.00

Albums

K-TEL

Number	Title (A Side/B Side)	Yr	VG	VG+	NM
❑ WC 307	The Living Legend of Eddy Arnold	1974	2.50	5.00	10.00

MGM

Number	Title (A Side/B Side)	Yr	VG	VG+	NM
❑ SE-4878	So Many Ways/If the Whole World Stopped Lovin'	1973	3.00	6.00	12.00
❑ SE-4912	She's Got Everything I Need	1974	3.00	6.00	12.00
❑ SE-4916	I Wish I Had Loved You Better	1974	3.00	6.00	12.00
❑ MG-1-4992	The Wonderful World of Eddy Arnold	1975	3.00	6.00	12.00
❑ MJB-5107 [(2)]	World of Hits	1976	3.00	6.00	12.00

PAIR

Number	Title (A Side/B Side)	Yr	VG	VG+	NM
❑ PDL2-1000 [(2)]	The Mellow Side of Eddy Arnold	1986	3.00	6.00	12.00

RCA

Number	Title (A Side/B Side)	Yr	VG	VG+	NM
❑ 9963-1-R	Hand-Holdin' Songs	1990	3.75	7.50	15.00

RCA CAMDEN

Number	Title (A Side/B Side)	Yr	VG	VG+	NM
❑ CAL-471 [M]	Eddy Arnold (That's How Much I Love You)	1959	5.00	10.00	20.00
❑ CAS-471(e) [R]	Eddy Arnold (That's How Much I Love You)	1966	2.50	5.00	10.00
❑ CAL-563 [M]	More Eddy Arnold	1960	5.00	10.00	20.00
❑ CAS-563(e) [R]	More Eddy Arnold	1966	2.50	5.00	10.00
❑ CAL-741 [M]	Country Songs I Love to Sing	1963	3.75	7.50	15.00
❑ CAS-741(e) [R]	Country Songs I Love to Sing	1966	2.50	5.00	10.00
❑ CAL-799 [M]	Eddy's Songs	1964	3.75	7.50	15.00
❑ CAS-799(e) [R]	Eddy's Songs	1966	2.50	5.00	10.00
❑ CAL-897 [M]	I'm Throwing Rice (At the Girl That I Love) And Other Favorites	1966	3.75	7.50	15.00
❑ CAS-897(e) [R]	I'm Throwing Rice (At the Girl That I Love) And Other Favorites	1966	2.50	5.00	10.00
❑ CAS-2501	Then You Can Tell Me Goodbye	197?	2.50	5.00	10.00

RCA VICTOR

Number	Title (A Side/B Side)	Yr	VG	VG+	NM
❑ DPL2-0051 [(2)]	The Greatest of Eddy Arnold	1973	3.75	7.50	15.00
—Special products issue; "Tele House Inc. Presents" on labels					
❑ APL1-0239	The World of Eddy Arnold	1973	3.00	6.00	12.00
❑ PRS-346	Christmas with Eddy Arnold	1971	3.75	7.50	15.00
—Special-products issue					
❑ ANL1-1078	Pure Gold	1975	2.50	5.00	10.00
❑ LPM-1111 [M]	Wanderin' with Eddy Arnold	1955	12.50	25.00	50.00
❑ LPM-1223 [M]	All-Time Favorites	1955	12.50	25.00	50.00
—New version of LPM 3117					
❑ LPM-1224 [M]	Anytime	1955	12.50	25.00	50.00
—New version of LPM 3027					
❑ LPM-1225 [M]	The Chapel on the Hill	1955	12.50	25.00	50.00
—New version of LPM 3031					
❑ LPM-1293 [M]	A Dozen Hits	1956	12.50	25.00	50.00
❑ LPM-1377 [M]	A Little on the Lonely Side	1956	12.50	25.00	50.00
❑ LPM-1484 [M]	When They Were Young	1956	12.50	25.00	50.00
❑ LPM-1575 [M]	My Darling, My Darling	1957	10.00	20.00	40.00
❑ LPM-1733 [M]	Praise Him, Praise Him	1958	10.00	20.00	40.00
❑ APL1-1817	Eddy	1976	3.00	6.00	12.00
❑ ANL1-1926	Christmas with Eddy Arnold	1976	2.50	5.00	10.00
—Reissue of LSP-2554 with similar cover to the second edition					
❑ LPM-1928 [M]	Have Guitar, Will Travel	1959	6.25	12.50	25.00
❑ LSP-1928 [S]	Have Guitar, Will Travel	1959	7.50	15.00	30.00
❑ LPM-2036 [M]	Thereby Hangs a Tale	1959	6.25	12.50	25.00
❑ LSP-2036 [S]	Thereby Hangs a Tale	1959	7.50	15.00	30.00
❑ LPM-2185 [M]	Eddy Arnold Sings Them Again	1960	6.25	12.50	25.00
❑ LSP-2185 [S]	Eddy Arnold Sings Them Again	1960	7.50	15.00	30.00
❑ LPM-2268 [M]	You Gotta Have Love	1960	6.25	12.50	25.00
❑ LSP-2268 [S]	You Gotta Have Love	1960	7.50	15.00	30.00
❑ APL1-2277	I Need You All the Time	1977	3.00	6.00	12.00
❑ LPM-2337 [M]	Let's Make Memories Tonight	1961	5.00	10.00	20.00
❑ LSP-2337 [S]	Let's Make Memories Tonight	1961	6.25	12.50	25.00
❑ LPM-2471 [M]	One More Time	1961	5.00	10.00	20.00
❑ LSP-2471 [S]	One More Time	1961	6.25	12.50	25.00
❑ LPM-2554 [M]	Christmas with Eddy Arnold	1962	5.00	10.00	20.00
❑ LSP-2554 [S]	Christmas with Eddy Arnold	1962	6.25	12.50	25.00
—Original cover; "Living Stereo" on label					
❑ LSP-2554 [S]	Christmas with Eddy Arnold	1967	3.75	7.50	15.00
—Second cover with Eddy standing in front of a Christmas tree and a "Country Music Hall of Fame" logo on front					
❑ LPM-2578 [M]	Cattle Call	1962	6.25	12.50	25.00
❑ LSP-2578 [S]	Cattle Call	1962	7.50	15.00	30.00
❑ LPM-2596 [M]	Our Man Down South	1962	6.25	12.50	25.00
❑ LSP-2596 [S]	Our Man Down South	1962	7.50	15.00	30.00
❑ LPM-2629 [M]	Faithfully Yours	1963	6.25	12.50	25.00
❑ LSP-2629 [S]	Faithfully Yours	1963	7.50	15.00	30.00
❑ LPM-2811 [M]	Folk Song Book	1964	5.00	10.00	20.00
❑ LSP-2811 [S]	Folk Song Book	1964	6.25	12.50	25.00
❑ LPM-2909 [M]	Sometimes I'm Happy, Sometimes I'm Blue	1964	5.00	10.00	20.00
❑ LSP-2909 [S]	Sometimes I'm Happy, Sometimes I'm Blue	1964	6.25	12.50	25.00
❑ LPM-2951 [M]	Pop Hits from the Country Side	1964	5.00	10.00	20.00
❑ LSP-2951 [S]	Pop Hits from the Country Side	1964	6.25	12.50	25.00
❑ LPM-3027 [10]	Anytime	1952	30.00	60.00	120.00
—Label calls this "Country Classics"					
❑ LPM-3031 [10]	All-Time Hits from the Hills	1952	25.00	50.00	100.00
❑ LPM-3117 [10]	All-Time Favorites	1953	25.00	50.00	100.00
❑ LPM-3219 [10]	When It's Roundup Time in Heaven	1954	25.00	50.00	100.00
❑ LPM-3230	An American Institution Booklet	1954	12.50	25.00	50.00
❑ LPM-3230 [10]	An American Institution	1954	25.00	50.00	100.00
❑ AHL1-3358	Somebody	1979	2.50	5.00	10.00
❑ LPM-3361 [M]	The Easy Way	1965	3.75	7.50	15.00
❑ LSP-3361 [S]	The Easy Way	1965	5.00	10.00	20.00
❑ LPM-3466 [M]	My World	1965	3.00	6.00	12.00
❑ LSP-3466 [S]	My World	1965	3.75	7.50	15.00
❑ LPM-3507 [M]	I Want to Go with You	1966	3.00	6.00	12.00
❑ LSP-3507 [S]	I Want to Go with You	1966	3.75	7.50	15.00
❑ LPM-3565 [M]	The Best of Eddy Arnold	1967	5.00	10.00	20.00
❑ LSP-3565 [S]	The Best of Eddy Arnold	1967	3.75	7.50	15.00
❑ AHL1-3606	A Legend and His Lady	1980	2.50	5.00	10.00
❑ LPM-3622 [M]	The Last Word in Lonesome	1966	3.00	6.00	12.00
❑ LSP-3622 [S]	The Last Word in Lonesome	1966	3.75	7.50	15.00
❑ AYL1-3675	The Best of Eddy Arnold	1980	2.00	4.00	8.00
—"Best Buy Series" reissue					
❑ LPM-3715 [M]	Somebody Like Me	1966	3.00	6.00	12.00
❑ LSP-3715 [S]	Somebody Like Me	1966	3.75	7.50	15.00
❑ LPM-3753 [M]	Lonely Again	1967	5.00	10.00	20.00
❑ LSP-3753 [S]	Lonely Again	1967	3.75	7.50	15.00
❑ LPM-3869 [M]	Turn the World Around	1967	5.00	10.00	20.00
❑ LSP-3869 [S]	Turn the World Around	1967	3.75	7.50	15.00
❑ AHL1-3914	A Man for All Seasons	1980	2.50	5.00	10.00
❑ LPM-3931 [M]	The Everlovin' World of Eddy Arnold	1968	10.00	20.00	40.00
❑ LSP-3931 [S]	The Everlovin' World of Eddy Arnold	1968	3.75	7.50	15.00
❑ AYL1-3937	The Best of Eddy Arnold, Volume II	1981	2.00	4.00	8.00
—"Best Buy Series" reissue					
❑ LPM-4009 [M]	The Romantic World of Eddy Arnold	1968	37.50	75.00	150.00
❑ LSP-4009 [S]	The Romantic World of Eddy Arnold	1968	3.75	7.50	15.00
❑ LSP-4089	Walkin' in Love Land	1968	3.75	7.50	15.00
❑ LSP-4110	Songs of the Young World	1969	3.75	7.50	15.00
❑ LSP-4179	The Glory of Love	1969	3.75	7.50	15.00
❑ LSP-4231	The Warmth of Eddy	1969	3.75	7.50	15.00
❑ AHL1-4263	Don't Give Up on Me	1981	2.50	5.00	10.00
❑ LSP-4304	Love & Guitars	1970	3.00	6.00	12.00
❑ LSP-4320	The Best of Eddy Arnold, Volume II	1970	3.00	6.00	12.00
❑ LSP-4471	Portrait of My Woman	1971	3.00	6.00	12.00
❑ LSP-4625	Loving Her Was Easier	1971	3.00	6.00	12.00
❑ AHL1-4661	Close Enough to Love	1983	2.50	5.00	10.00
❑ LSP-4738	Eddy Arnold Sings for Housewives and Other Ladies	1972	3.00	6.00	12.00
❑ CPL2-4885 [(2)]	The Legendary Performances (1945-1971)	1983	3.00	6.00	12.00
❑ AHL1-5467	Collector's Series	1985	2.50	5.00	10.00
❑ VPS-6032 [(2)]	This Is Eddy Arnold	1972	3.75	7.50	15.00

TIME-LIFE

Number	Title (A Side/B Side)	Yr	VG	VG+	NM
❑ STW-120	Country Music	1981	2.50	5.00	10.00

Number	Title (A Side/B Side)	Yr	VG	VG+	NM

ARNOLD, EDDY & JO ANN
45s
RCA VICTOR

| ❏ 490 | A Present For Santa Claus/Sittin' On Santa Claus' Lap | 195? | — | 2.50 | 5.00 |
| ❏ 490 [PS] | A Present For Santa Claus/Sittin' On Santa Claus' Lap | 195? | — | 2.50 | 5.00 |

ARNOLD, P.P.
45s
ATLANTIC

| ❏ 2674 | Bury Me Down by the River/Give a Hand, Take a Hand | 1969 | — | 3.00 | 6.00 |

IMMEDIATE

| ❏ 1901 | The First Cut Is the Deepest/Speak to Me | 1967 | 2.50 | 5.00 | 10.00 |
| ❏ 5006 | If You Think You're Groovy/It Hurts Me Badly | 1968 | 2.50 | 5.00 | 10.00 |

Albums
IMMEDIATE

| ❏ Z12 52016 | Kafunta | 1968 | 3.75 | 7.50 | 15.00 |

ARNOLD, VANCE, AND THE AVENGERS See JOE COCKER.

ARRIBIANS, THE
45s
J.O.B.

| ❏ 1116 | To Look at a Star/Working and Gambling | 1958 | 200.00 | 400.00 | 800.00 |

ARROGANTS, THE
45s
LUTE

| ❏ 6226 | Mirror Mirror/Canadian Sunset | 1963 | 7.50 | 15.00 | 30.00 |

ARROWS, THE See DAVIE ALLAN AND THE ARROWS.

ARS NOVA
45s
ATLANTIC

| ❏ 2625 | Sunshine and Shadows/Walk on the Sand | 1969 | — | 3.00 | 6.00 |

ELEKTRA

| ❏ 45627 | Pavan for My Lady (Fall Winter Summer and Spring)/Zoroaster | 1968 | 2.00 | 4.00 | 8.00 |
| ❏ 45631 | Fields of People/March of the Mad Duke's Circus | 1968 | 2.00 | 4.00 | 8.00 |

Albums
ATLANTIC

| ❏ SD 8221 | Sunshine and Shadows | 1969 | 3.75 | 7.50 | 15.00 |

ELEKTRA

| ❏ EKS-74020 | Ars Nova | 1968 | 3.75 | 7.50 | 15.00 |

ART OF LOVIN'
45s
MAINSTREAM

| ❏ 687 | Good Times/You've Got the Power | 1968 | 6.25 | 12.50 | 25.00 |

Albums
MAINSTREAM

| ❏ S-6113 | Art of Lovin' | 1968 | 50.00 | 100.00 | 200.00 |

ARTHUR
Albums
LHI

| ❏ 12000 | Dreams and Images | 1968 | 10.00 | 20.00 | 40.00 |

ARTISTICS, THE
45s
BRUNSWICK

❏ 55301	I'm Gonna Miss You/Hope We Have	1966	2.00	4.00	8.00
❏ 55315	Girl I Need You/Glad I Met You	1967	2.00	4.00	8.00
❏ 55326	Love Song/I'll Always Love You	1967	2.00	4.00	8.00
❏ 55342	The Chase Is On/One Last Chance	1967	2.00	4.00	8.00
❏ 55353	You Make Me Happy/Nothing But Heartaches	1967	2.00	4.00	8.00
❏ 55370	Hard to Carry On/Trouble, Heartaches and Pain	1968	2.00	4.00	8.00
❏ 55384	Lonely Old World/You Left Me	1968	2.00	4.00	8.00
❏ 55404	Walking Tall/What Happened	1969	2.00	4.00	8.00
❏ 55416	Price of Love/Yesterday's Girl	1969	2.00	4.00	8.00
❏ 55431	Just Another Heartache/Ain't It Strange	1970	2.00	4.00	8.00
❏ 55444	(I Want You To) Make My Life Over/Sugar Cane	1971	2.00	4.00	8.00
❏ 55477	Being in Love/It's Those Little Things That Count	1972	2.00	4.00	8.00
❏ 55493	She's Heaven/Look Out I'm Gonna Get You	1973	2.00	4.00	8.00

OKEH

❏ 7177	I Need Your Love/What'll I Do	1963	2.50	5.00	10.00
❏ 7193	Get My Hands on Some Lovin'/I'll Leave It Up to You	1964	2.50	5.00	10.00
❏ 7217	In Another Man's Arms/Patty Cake	1965	2.50	5.00	10.00
❏ 7232	This Heart of Mine/I'll Come Running	1965	2.50	5.00	10.00
❏ 7243	Loveland/So Much Love in My Heart	1966	2.50	5.00	10.00

Albums
BRUNSWICK

❏ BL 54123 [M]	I'm Gonna Miss You	1967	6.25	12.50	25.00
❏ BL 754123 [S]	I'm Gonna Miss You	1967	6.25	12.50	25.00
❏ BL 754139	The Articulate Artistics	1968	6.25	12.50	25.00
❏ BL 754153	What Happened	1969	6.25	12.50	25.00
❏ BL 754168	I Want You to Make My Life Over	1970	6.25	12.50	25.00
❏ BL 754195	Look Out	1973	5.00	10.00	20.00

OKEH

| ❏ OKM-12119 [M] | Get My Hands on Some Lovin' | 1967 | 20.00 | 40.00 | 80.00 |
| ❏ OKS-14119 [S] | Get My Hands on Some Lovin' | 1967 | 20.00 | 40.00 | 80.00 |

ARZACHEL
Albums
ROULETTE

| ❏ SR 42036 | Arzachel | 1969 | 37.50 | 75.00 | 150.00 |

ASCOTS, THE More than one group.
45s
ACE

| ❏ 650 | I'm Touched/Perfect Love | 1962 | 6.25 | 12.50 | 25.00 |

ARROW

| ❏ 736 | Easier Said Than Done/Is It Really You | 1958 | 7.50 | 15.00 | 30.00 |

BETHLEHEM

| ❏ 3046 | Hip Talk/She Did | 1962 | 3.75 | 7.50 | 15.00 |

DUAL-TONE

| ❏ 1120 | Acapulco Run/The Gladiator | 1963 | 15.00 | 30.00 | 60.00 |

J&S

| ❏ 1628/9 | What Love Can Do/Everything Will Be Alright | 1958 | 7.50 | 15.00 | 30.00 |

KING

| ❏ 5679 | I Don't Care One Bit/Tonight | 1962 | 7.50 | 15.00 | 30.00 |

SUPER

❏ 102	Monkey See, Monkey Do/You Can't Do That	1966	5.00	10.00	20.00
❏ 103	Midnight Hour/Midnight Hour (Part 2)	1966	5.00	10.00	20.00
❏ 104	Put Your Arms Around Me/Sookie Sookie	1966	5.00	10.00	20.00

ASGAERD
45s
THRESHOLD

| ❏ 67010 | Friends/Children of a New Born Age | 1972 | 2.50 | 5.00 | 10.00 |

Albums
THRESHOLD

| ❏ THS 6 | In the Realm of Asgaerd | 1972 | 5.00 | 10.00 | 20.00 |

ASHE, CLARENCE
45s
ABC-PARAMOUNT

| ❏ 45-10698 | Don't Open the Door on Monday Morning/Close to You | 1965 | 3.00 | 6.00 | 12.00 |

CHESS

| ❏ 1896 | Trouble I've Had/Dancing in a Dream World | 1964 | 3.75 | 7.50 | 15.00 |

J&S

❏ 1466	Trouble I've Had/Dancing in a Dream World	1964	6.25	12.50	25.00
❏ 1469	If I Could Only Lie/Why Have I Had So Much Trouble	1964	5.00	10.00	20.00
❏ 1470/1	Everything Happens to Me/New Broom Sweeps Good	1964	3.75	7.50	15.00
❏ 1472	Row Row Row Your Love/In the Middle of the Night	1965	3.75	7.50	15.00
❏ 1475/6	Don't Open the Door on Monday Morning/Close to You	1965	3.75	7.50	15.00

ASHES
45s
VAULT

❏ 924	Is There Anything I Can Do/Every Little Prayer	1966	3.00	6.00	12.00
❏ 936	Dark on You Now/Roses Gone	1967	3.00	6.00	12.00
❏ 973	Homeward Bound/Sleeping Serenade	1971	2.50	5.00	10.00

Albums
VAULT

| ❏ 125 | Ashes | 1968 | 12.50 | 25.00 | 50.00 |

ASHFORD, NICK Also see ASHFORD AND SIMPSON.
45s
ABC

| ❏ 11260 | Let's Go Get Stoned/Dead End Kids | 1970 | — | 3.00 | 6.00 |

VERVE

❏ 10463	I Don't Need No Doctor/Young Emotions	1966	2.50	5.00	10.00
❏ 10493	When I Feel the Need/Young Emotions	1967	2.50	5.00	10.00
❏ 10599	California Soul/Young Emotions	1968	2.00	4.00	8.00

ASHFORD AND SIMPSON Also see NICK ASHFORD; VALERIE SIMPSON.
12-Inch Singles
CAPITOL

❏ V-8528	Street Corner/Make It Work Again	1982	2.50	5.00	10.00
❏ V-8558	High Rise (6:05)/(Instrumental)	1983	2.00	4.00	8.00
❏ V-8570	It's Much Deeper (3:47) (6:30)	1983	2.00	4.00	8.00
❏ V-8612	Solid (Special Club Mix 6:12)/(Dub Version 5:51)	1984	2.50	5.00	10.00
❏ V-8623	Outta the World (6:05)/(6:16)	1985	2.00	4.00	8.00
❏ V-8641	Babies (unknown versions)	1985	2.00	4.00	8.00
❏ SPRO-9020/1 [DJ]	It's Much Deeper (3:47) (6:30)	1983	2.50	5.00	10.00
❏ SPRO-9951 [DJ]	Nobody Walks in L.A. (same on both sides?)	1986	2.50	5.00	10.00
❏ V-15243	Count Your Blessings/Side Effect	1986	2.00	4.00	8.00
❏ V-15259	What Becomes of Love (Edit) (LP)/It's a Rush	1986	2.00	4.00	8.00
❏ V-15272	Nobody Walks in L.A. (3 versions)/Way Ahead	1986	2.00	4.00	8.00
❏ V-15448	I'll Be There for You/Way Ahead	1989	2.00	4.00	8.00
❏ V-15487	Cookies and Cake (5 versions)	1989	—	3.50	7.00

ORPHEUS

| ❏ V-72289 | Hungry for Me Again (Edit) (LP) (Instrumental) | 1990 | 2.50 | 5.00 | 10.00 |

WARNER BROS.

| ❏ PRO-A-837 [DJ] | Nobody Knows (6:35) (same on both sides) | 1979 | 5.00 | 10.00 | 20.00 |
| ❏ DWBS 8874 | Found a Cure (7:00)/You Always Could | 1979 | 3.00 | 6.00 | 12.00 |

45s
CAPITOL

❏ B-5109	Street Corner/Make It Work Again	1982	—	—	3.00
❏ B-5109 [PS]	Street Corner/Make It Work Again	1982	—	—	3.00
❏ B-5146	Love It Away/Street Opera (Part 2)	1982	—	—	3.00
❏ B-5190	I'll Take the Whole World On/Mighty Mighty Love	1982	—	—	3.00
❏ B-5250	High-Rise/(Instrumental)	1983	—	—	3.00
❏ B-5250 [PS]	High-Rise/(Instrumental)	1983	—	—	3.00
❏ B-5284	It's Much Deeper/Working Man	1983	—	—	3.00
❏ B-5284 [PS]	It's Much Deeper/Working Man	1983	—	—	3.00
❏ B-5310	I'm Not That Tough/Side Effect	1984	—	—	3.00
❏ B-5310 [PS]	I'm Not That Tough/Side Effect	1984	—	—	3.00
❏ B-5397	Solid/Solid (Dub Version)	1984	—	—	3.00
❏ B-5397 [PS]	Solid/Solid (Dub Version)	1984	—	—	3.00
❏ B-5435	Outta the World/Outta the World (Dub)	1985	—	—	3.00
❏ B-5435 [PS]	Outta the World/Outta the World (Dub)	1985	—	—	3.00

Number	Title (A Side/B Side)	Yr	VG	VG+	NM
❑ B-5468	Babies/Street Corner	1985	—	—	3.00
❑ B-5468 [PS]	Babies/Street Corner	1985	—	—	3.00
❑ B-5598	Count Your Blessings/Side Effect	1986	—	—	3.00
❑ B-5598 [PS]	Count Your Blessings/Side Effect	1986	—	—	3.00
❑ B-5637	What Becomes of Love/It's a Rush	1986	—	—	3.00
❑ B-5666	Nobody Walks in L.A./Way Ah Way Ahead	1987	—	—	3.00
❑ B-44326	I'll Be There for You/Way Ahead	1989	—	—	3.00
❑ B-44326 [PS]	I'll Be There for You/Way Ahead	1989	—	—	3.00
❑ B-44404	Cookies and Cake/(B-side unknown)	1989	—	2.00	4.00

HOPSACK & SILK

Number	Title (A Side/B Side)	Yr	VG	VG+	NM
❑ 96-398	Been Found/I Remember All	1996	—	—	3.00

—With Maya Angelou

WARNER BROS.

Number	Title (A Side/B Side)	Yr	VG	VG+	NM
❑ 7745	(I'd Know You) Anywhere/I'm Determined	1973	—	2.00	4.00
❑ 7781	Have You Ever Tried It/Time	1974	—	2.00	4.00
❑ 7811	Main Line/Don't Fight It	1974	—	2.00	4.00
❑ 8030	Everybody's Got to Give It Up/ Over to Where You Are	1974	—	2.00	4.00
❑ 8070	Bend Me/Ain't Nothin' But a Name	1975	—	2.00	4.00
❑ 8179	It'll Come, It'll Come, It'll Come/Caretaker	1976	—	2.00	4.00
❑ 8216	Somebody Told a Lie/It Came to Me	1976	—	2.00	4.00
❑ 8286	Tried, Tested and Found True/Believe in Me	1976	—	2.00	4.00
❑ 8337	So So Satisfied/Maybe I Can Find It	1977	—	2.00	4.00
❑ 8391	Over and Over/It's You	1977	—	2.00	4.00
❑ 8453	Send It/Couldn't Get Enough	1977	—	2.00	4.00
❑ 8514	Don't Cost You Nothing/Let Love Use Me	1978	—	2.00	4.00
❑ 8571	By Way of Love's Express/Too Bad	1978	—	2.00	4.00
❑ 8651	It Seems to Hang On/Too Bad	1978	—	2.00	4.00
❑ 8710	Is It Still Good to Ya/As Long As It Holds You	1978	—	2.00	4.00
❑ 8775	Flashback/Ain't It a Shame	1979	—	2.00	4.00
❑ 8870	Found a Cure/You Always Could	1979	—	2.00	4.00
❑ 49099	Nobody Knows/Crazy	1979	—	2.00	4.00
❑ 49269	Love Don't Make It Right/Finally Got to Me	1980	—	2.00	4.00
❑ 49269 [PS]	Love Don't Make It Right/Finally Got to Me	1980	—	2.50	5.00
❑ 49594	Happy Endings/Make It to the Sky	1980	—	2.00	4.00
❑ 49646	Get Out Your Handkerchief/ You Never Left Me Alone	1980	—	2.00	4.00
❑ 49805	It Shows in the Eyes/Enough	1981	—	2.00	4.00
❑ 49867	I Need Your Light/It's the Long Run	1981	—	2.00	4.00

Albums

CAPITOL

Number	Title (A Side/B Side)	Yr	VG	VG+	NM
❑ ST-12207	Street Opera	1982	2.00	4.00	8.00
❑ ST-12282	High Rise	1983	2.00	4.00	8.00
❑ ST-12366	Solid	1984	2.00	4.00	8.00
❑ ST-12469	Real Love	1986	2.00	4.00	8.00
❑ C1-46946	Love Or Physical	1989	2.50	5.00	10.00

WARNER BROS.

Number	Title (A Side/B Side)	Yr	VG	VG+	NM
❑ BS 2739	Gimme Something Real	1973	2.50	5.00	10.00
❑ BS 2789	I Wanna Be Selfish	1974	2.50	5.00	10.00
❑ BS 2858	Come As You Are	1976	2.50	5.00	10.00
❑ BS 2992	So So Satisfied	1977	2.50	5.00	10.00
❑ BS 3088	Send It	1977	2.50	5.00	10.00
❑ BSK 3219	Is It Still Good to Ya	1978	2.50	5.00	10.00
❑ BSK 3357	Stay Free	1979	2.50	5.00	10.00
❑ HS 3458	A Musical Affair	1980	2.50	5.00	10.00
❑ 2BS 3524 [(2)]	Performance	1981	3.00	6.00	12.00

ASHKAN
Albums

SIRE

Number	Title (A Side/B Side)	Yr	VG	VG+	NM
❑ SES-97107	In from the Cold	1970	6.25	12.50	25.00

ASHLEY, DEL See DAVID GATES.

ASHLEY, JOHN
45s

CAPEHART

Number	Title (A Side/B Side)	Yr	VG	VG+	NM
❑ 5006	Little Lou/I Need Your Lovin'	1961	12.50	25.00	50.00

DOT

Number	Title (A Side/B Side)	Yr	VG	VG+	NM
❑ 15775	Born to Rock/Pickin' on the Wrong Chicken	1958	12.50	25.00	50.00
❑ 15878	My Story/Let the Good Times Roll	1958	3.75	7.50	15.00

INTRO

Number	Title (A Side/B Side)	Yr	VG	VG+	NM
❑ 6097	Bermuda/Let Yourself Go Go Go	196?	7.50	15.00	30.00

SILVER

Number	Title (A Side/B Side)	Yr	VG	VG+	NM
❑ 1002	I Want to Hear It from You/Seriously in Love	1959	6.25	12.50	25.00
❑ 1005	Cry of the Wild Goose/One Love	1960	6.25	12.50	25.00

ASHLEY, LEON
45s

ASHLEY

Number	Title (A Side/B Side)	Yr	VG	VG+	NM
❑ 22	Ain't Gonna Worry/Illusions of Life	1969	2.50	5.00	10.00
❑ 100	Our Old Love Song/She Picked Me Up	197?	2.00	4.00	8.00
❑ 350	If Love Has Died/ How Can We Divide These Little Hearts	197?	2.00	4.00	8.00
❑ 666	Lean On Me/I Ain't Got Over You Yet	197?	2.00	4.00	8.00
❑ 764	The Weakness of a Man/Most Men	197?	2.00	4.00	8.00
❑ 768	Before You Were Mine/Su-Sow	197?	2.00	4.00	8.00
❑ 2003	Laura (What's He Got That I Ain't Got)/With the Help of the Wine	1967	2.50	5.00	10.00
❑ 2003	Laura/With the Help of the Wine	1967	3.75	7.50	15.00

—Some early copies have no subtitle on A-side

Number	Title (A Side/B Side)	Yr	VG	VG+	NM
❑ 2025	Anna, I'm Taking You Home/Curtain of Sadness	1967	2.50	5.00	10.00
❑ 2075	Mental Journey/All I Can Stand	1968	2.50	5.00	10.00
❑ 4000	Flower of Love/Prayers Can't Reach Me	1968	2.50	5.00	10.00
❑ 4317	By Loving Me/Ease Up	197?	—	3.00	6.00

—Reissue

Number	Title (A Side/B Side)	Yr	VG	VG+	NM
❑ 5323	Dear Willie/Letter from Luckenbach	197?	2.00	4.00	8.00
❑ 7000	While Your Lover Sleeps/That's Alright	1968	2.50	5.00	10.00
❑ 7600	I'll Be There/If I Could See Over the Mountain	197?	2.00	4.00	8.00
❑ 9000	Walkin' Back to Birmingham/ It's All Over But the Crying	1969	2.50	5.00	10.00
❑ 35001	A Life for a Wife/The Bees Are Making Honey	197?	—	3.00	6.00

Number	Title (A Side/B Side)	Yr	VG	VG+	NM
❑ 35003	Tell Him Daddy Said Hello/Brace Up and Face It	197?	—	3.00	6.00
❑ 35004	Happy Loving You/Love Me or Leave Me	197?	—	3.00	6.00
❑ 35005	Mama's Ten/Keeping Her Memory Alive	197?	—	3.00	6.00
❑ 35008	There Ain't No Easy Way/Losing Man	197?	—	3.00	6.00
❑ 35010	Ease Up/Until Dawn	197?	—	3.00	6.00
❑ 35011	Not a Single Thing About Her (That I'd Change)/ Before the Next Teardrop Falls	197?	—	3.00	6.00
❑ 35012	The Well's Not Dry/ Guess I've Just Love You Too Long	197?	—	3.00	6.00
❑ 35013	Love Fits Me Better/Off and Running	197?	—	3.00	6.00

DOT

Number	Title (A Side/B Side)	Yr	VG	VG+	NM
❑ 16649	You Gave Me a Reason to Live/You've Got a Heartbreak	1964	3.75	7.50	15.00

GOLDBAND

Number	Title (A Side/B Side)	Yr	VG	VG+	NM
❑ 1096	Just in Her Teens/Prize Possession	1960	10.00	20.00	40.00
❑ 1104	He'll Never Go/I Was King of the Universe	1960	6.25	12.50	25.00
❑ 1124	You Win Again/Not Going Home	1962	5.00	10.00	20.00

GUSTO

Number	Title (A Side/B Side)	Yr	VG	VG+	NM
❑ GT4-2041	Laura (What's He Got That I Ain't Got)/Flower of Love	197?	—	3.00	6.00

—Reissue

IMPERIAL

Number	Title (A Side/B Side)	Yr	VG	VG+	NM
❑ 5759	The Longest Walk/Teenage Angel	1961	5.00	10.00	20.00
❑ 5795	It's Alright Baby/Court of Two Sisters	1961	5.00	10.00	20.00

TIC TOC

Number	Title (A Side/B Side)	Yr	VG	VG+	NM
❑ 111	You've Got a Heartbreak/Give Me a Reason to Live	1961	5.00	10.00	20.00

Albums

ASHLEY

Number	Title (A Side/B Side)	Yr	VG	VG+	NM
❑ 54001	The Best of Leon Ashley	197?	3.75	7.50	15.00

HILLTOP

Number	Title (A Side/B Side)	Yr	VG	VG+	NM
❑ JS-6069	Flower of Love	1968	3.75	7.50	15.00

RCA VICTOR

Number	Title (A Side/B Side)	Yr	VG	VG+	NM
❑ LPM-3900 [M]	Laura (What's He Got That I Ain't Got)	1967	7.50	15.00	30.00
❑ LSP-3900 [S]	Laura (What's He Got That I Ain't Got)	1967	5.00	10.00	20.00

ASHLEY, LEON, AND MARGIE SINGLETON Also see each artist's individual listings.
45s

ASHLEY

Number	Title (A Side/B Side)	Yr	VG	VG+	NM
❑ 600	Dear Willie (Letter from Leach)/Laura	197?	2.00	4.00	8.00
❑ 700	Love Me or Leave Me (For Love to Find)/ Here We Go Again	197?	2.00	4.00	8.00
❑ 702	Can You Live with the Way/ Watching Your Memory Grow	197?	2.00	4.00	8.00
❑ 2015	Hangin' On/Four O'Clock	1967	2.50	5.00	10.00
❑ 3000	You'll Never Be Lonely Again/ Parting of the Ways	1968	2.50	5.00	10.00
❑ 8000	Love Me or Leave Me (For Love to Find)/ Here We Go Again	1969	2.50	5.00	10.00

MONUMENT

Number	Title (A Side/B Side)	Yr	VG	VG+	NM
❑ 990	If Love Has Died/ How Can We Divide These Little Hearts	1966	3.00	6.00	12.00

Albums

ASHLEY

Number	Title (A Side/B Side)	Yr	VG	VG+	NM
❑ A-3695	New Brand of Country	197?	3.75	7.50	15.00

ASHLEY, ROBERT
45s

MERCURY

Number	Title (A Side/B Side)	Yr	VG	VG+	NM
❑ 71365	Comic Strip Rock and Roll/The Baby	1957	12.50	25.00	50.00

ASHLEY, TONY
45s

DECCA

Number	Title (A Side/B Side)	Yr	VG	VG+	NM
❑ 32240	I'll Never Be Satisfied/All Along I've Loved You	1967	5.00	10.00	20.00
❑ 32342	We Must Have Love/I Can't Put You Down	1968	5.00	10.00	20.00
❑ 32520	I'll Go Crazy/Just a Taste	1969	15.00	30.00	60.00

ASHTON, GARDNER AND DYKE
45s

CAPITOL

Number	Title (A Side/B Side)	Yr	VG	VG+	NM
❑ 2981	Hymn to Everyone/Mister Freako	1970	—	2.50	5.00
❑ 3060	Resurrection Shuffle/I'm Your Spiritual Breadman	1971	—	3.00	6.00
❑ 3206	Can You Get It/Oh Lord	1971	—	2.50	5.00
❑ 3288	Delirium/Still Got a Long Way to Go	1972	—	2.50	5.00

Albums

CAPITOL

Number	Title (A Side/B Side)	Yr	VG	VG+	NM
❑ SMAS-862	What a Bloody Long Day It's Been	1972	3.00	6.00	12.00

ASLEEP AT THE WHEEL
45s

ARISTA

Number	Title (A Side/B Side)	Yr	VG	VG+	NM
❑ 2045	Keepin' Me Up Nights/Pedernales Stroll	1990	—	—	3.00
❑ 2122	That's the Way Love Is/Beat Me, Daddy (Eight to the Bar)	1990	—	—	3.00
❑ 2178	Dance With Who Brung You/Quittin' Time	1991	—	—	3.00
❑ 12425	(Get Your Kicks on) Route 66/ Black and White Rag	1992	—	2.00	4.00

CAPITOL

Number	Title (A Side/B Side)	Yr	VG	VG+	NM
❑ 4115	The Letter That Johnny Walker Read (Part 1)/ (Part 2)	1975	—	2.50	5.00
❑ 4187	Bump Bounce Boogie/Fat Boy Rag	1975	—	2.50	5.00
❑ 4238	Nothin' Takes the Place of You/Tonight the Bartender Is on the Wrong Side of the Bar	1976	—	2.50	5.00
❑ 4319	Route 66/Shout Wa Hey	1976	—	2.50	5.00
❑ 4357	Miles and Miles of Texas/Blues for Dixie	1976	—	2.50	5.00
❑ 4393	The Trouble with Lovin' Today/Ragtime Annie	1977	—	2.50	5.00
❑ 4438	Somebody Stole His Body/Let's Face Up	1977	—	2.50	5.00
❑ 4601	Ghost Dancer/Louisiana	1978	—	2.50	5.00
❑ 4659	Texas Me & You/One O'Clock Jump	1978	—	2.50	5.00
❑ 4725	Choo Choo Ch'Boogie/Too Many Bad Habits	1979	—	2.50	5.00

Number	Title (A Side/B Side)	Yr	VG	VG+	NM
CAPITOL NASHVILLE					
❏ S7-18844	Lay Down Sally/Hightower	1995	—	2.00	4.00
EPIC					
❏ 06671	Way Down Texas Way/String of Pars	1987	—	—	3.00
❏ 06671 [PS]	Way Down Texas Way/String of Pars	1987	—	2.00	4.00
❏ 07125	House of Blue Lights/Big Foot Stomp	1987	—	—	3.00
❏ 07610	Boogie Back to Texas/Tulsa Straight Ahead	1987	—	—	3.00
❏ 07659	Blowin' Like a Bandit/String of Pars	1987	—	—	3.00
❏ 07966	Walk On By/Sugarfoot Rag	1988	—	—	3.00
❏ 08087	Hot Rod Lincoln/String of Pars	1988	—	—	3.00
❏ 08461	House of Blue Lights/Blowin' Like a Bandit	1988	—	—	3.00
—Reissue					
❏ 8-50024	You and Me Instead/Don't Ask Me Why	1974	—	2.50	5.00
❏ 8-50045	Choo Choo Ch'Boogie/Our Names Aren't Mentioned	1974	—	2.50	5.00
❏ 68620	Chattanooga Choo Choo/Sugarfoot Rag	1989	—	—	3.00
LIBERTY					
❏ S7-17715	Red Wing/Bring It On Down to My House	1993	—	2.00	4.00
❏ S7-17970	Blues for Dixie/Got a Letter from My Kid Today	1993	—	2.00	4.00
MCA					
❏ 51020	Cool as a Breeze/Don't Get Caught Out in the Rain	1980	—	2.00	4.00
UNITED ARTISTS					
❏ XW-245	Take Me Back to Tulsa/Before You Stop Loving Me	1973	—	3.00	6.00
❏ XW-344	Daddy's Advice/Drivin' Nails in My Coffin	1973	—	3.00	6.00
Albums					
ARISTA					
❏ AL-8550	Keepin' Me Up Nights	1990	3.00	6.00	12.00
CAPITOL					
❏ ST-11441	Texas Gold	1975	3.00	6.00	12.00
❏ ST-11548	Wheelin' and Dealin'	1976	3.00	6.00	12.00
❏ ST-11620	The Wheel	1977	3.00	6.00	12.00
❏ SW-11726	Collision Course	1978	3.00	6.00	12.00
❏ ST-11945	Served Live	1979	3.00	6.00	12.00
❏ SN-16306	Served Live	1984	2.00	4.00	8.00
—Budget-line reissue					
CAPITOL SPECIAL MARKETS					
❏ SL-8138	Drivin'	1980	3.00	6.00	12.00
DOT/MCA					
❏ 39036	Asleep at the Wheel	1985	2.50	5.00	10.00
EPIC					
❏ KE 33097	Asleep at the Wheel	1974	3.75	7.50	15.00
❏ PE 33097	Asleep at the Wheel	197?	2.00	4.00	8.00
—Reissue					
❏ BG 33782 [(2)]	Fathers and Sons	1974	6.25	12.50	25.00
—With Bob Wills					
❏ EG 33782 [(2)]	Fathers and Sons	197?	3.00	6.00	12.00
—Reissue					
❏ BFE 40681	10	1987	2.00	4.00	8.00
❏ FE 44213	Western Standard Time	1988	2.00	4.00	8.00
LIBERTY					
❏ LN-10296	Comin' Right At Ya!	1986	2.00	4.00	8.00
—Budget-line reissue					
MCA					
❏ 742	Framed	1982	2.00	4.00	8.00
—Reissue of 5131					
❏ 5131	Framed	1980	2.50	5.00	10.00
UNITED ARTISTS					
❏ UA-LA038-F	Comin' Right At Ya!	1973	5.00	10.00	20.00

ASSEMBLED MULTITUDE, THE
45s

Number	Title (A Side/B Side)	Yr	VG	VG+	NM
ATLANTIC					
❏ 2737	Overture from Tommy (A Rock Opera)/Mud	1970	—	2.00	4.00
❏ 2764	Woodstock/Mr. Peppercorn	1970	—	2.00	4.00
❏ 2780	Medley from "Superstar" (A Rock Opera)/Where the Wood Bine Twineth	1971	—	2.00	4.00
❏ 2870	Godfather Waltz/Mac Arthur Park	1972	—	2.00	4.00
Albums					
ATLANTIC					
❏ SD 8262	The Assembled Multitude	1970	3.00	6.00	12.00

ASSOCIATION, THE
45s

Number	Title (A Side/B Side)	Yr	VG	VG+	NM
COLUMBIA					
❏ 45602	Indian Wells Woman/Darling Be Home Soon	1972	—	2.50	5.00
❏ 45654	Come the Fall/Kicking the Gong Around	1972	—	2.50	5.00
ELEKTRA					
❏ 47094	Dreamer/You Turn the Light On	1980	—	2.00	4.00
❏ 47146	Small Town Lovers/Across the Persian Gulf	1981	—	2.00	4.00
JUBILEE					
❏ 5505	Babe I'm Gonna Leave You/Baby Can't You Hear Me Call Your Name	1965	6.25	12.50	25.00
MUMS					
❏ 6016	Names, Tags, Numbers & Labels/Rainbows Bent	1973	—	2.00	4.00
RCA VICTOR					
❏ PB-10217	One Sunday Morning/Life Is a Carnival	1975	—	2.00	4.00
VALIANT					
❏ 730	Too Many Mornings/Forty Times	1965	3.75	7.50	15.00
❏ 741	Along Comes Mary/Your Own Love	1966	3.00	6.00	12.00
❏ 747	Cherish/Don't Blame It On Me	1966	3.00	6.00	12.00
❏ 755	Pandora's Golden Heebie Jeebies/Standing Still	1966	2.50	5.00	10.00
❏ 755 [PS]	Pandora's Golden Heebie Jeebies/Standing Still	1966	5.00	10.00	20.00
❏ 758	No Fair at All/Looking Glass	1967	2.50	5.00	10.00
WARNER BROS.					
❏ 7040	Pandora's Golden Heebie Jeebies/Standing Still	1967	2.00	4.00	8.00
❏ 7041	Windy/Sometime	1967	2.50	5.00	10.00
❏ 7074	Never My Love/Requiem for the Masses	1967	2.50	5.00	10.00
—A picture sleeve is rumored to exist					
❏ 7105	Along Comes Mary/Cherish	1968	2.00	4.00	8.00
—"Back to Back Hits" series on "W7" label					
❏ 7119	Windy/Never My Love	1968	2.00	4.00	8.00
—"Back to Back Hits" series on "W7" label					
❏ 7163	Everything That Touches You/We Love Us	1968	2.00	4.00	8.00
—Orange "WB" label					
❏ 7195	Time for Livin'/Birthday Morning	1968	2.00	4.00	8.00
❏ 7229	Six Man Band/Like Always	1968	2.00	4.00	8.00
❏ 7267	Goodbye Columbus/The Time It Is Today	1969	2.00	4.00	8.00
❏ 7277	Under Branches/Hear in Here	1969	2.00	4.00	8.00
❏ 7305	Yes, I Will/I Am Up for Europe	1969	2.00	4.00	8.00
❏ 7349	Are You Ready/Dubuque Blues	1969	2.00	4.00	8.00
❏ 7372	Just About the Same/Look at Me, Look at You	1970	—	3.00	6.00
❏ 7429	Along the Way/Traveler's Guide	1970	—	3.00	6.00
❏ 7471	P.F. Sloan/Traveler's Guide	1971	—	3.00	6.00
❏ 7515	Bring Yourself Home/It's Gotta Be Real	1971	—	3.00	6.00
❏ 7524	That's Racin'/Makes Me Cry (Funny Kind of Song)	1971	—	3.00	6.00
Albums					
COLUMBIA					
❏ KC 31348	Waterbeds in Trinidad	1972	2.50	5.00	10.00
HITBOUND/REALISTIC					
❏ 51-3022	New Memories	1983	3.00	6.00	12.00
PAIR					
❏ PDL2-1061 [(2)]	Songs That Made Them Famous	1986	3.00	6.00	12.00
VALIANT					
❏ VLM-5002 [M]	And Then…Along Comes The Association	1966	5.00	10.00	20.00
❏ VLM-5004 [M]	Renaissance	1966	5.00	10.00	20.00
—With no blurb for "No Fair at All" on cover					
❏ VLM-5004 [M]	Renaissance	1967	3.75	7.50	15.00
—With blurb for "No Fair at All" on cover					
❏ VLS-25002 [S]	And Then…Along Comes The Association	1966	6.25	12.50	25.00
❏ VLS-25004 [S]	Renaissance	1966	6.25	12.50	25.00
—With no blurb for "No Fair at All" on cover					
❏ VLS-25004 [S]	Renaissance	1967	5.00	10.00	20.00
—With blurb for "No Fair at All" on cover					
WARNER BROS.					
❏ W 1696 [M]	Insight Out	1967	3.75	7.50	15.00
❏ WS 1696 [S]	Insight Out	1967	5.00	10.00	20.00
—Gold label					
❏ WS 1696 [S]	Insight Out	1968	3.00	6.00	12.00
—With "W7" logo on green label					
❏ W 1702 [M]	And Then…Along Comes The Association	1967	5.00	10.00	20.00
❏ WS 1702 [S]	And Then…Along Comes The Association	1967	3.00	6.00	12.00
—With "W7" logo on green label					
❏ WS 1702 [S]	And Then…Along Comes The Association	1967	5.00	10.00	20.00
—Gold label					
❏ WS 1704	Renaissance	1967	3.00	6.00	12.00
❏ WS 1733	Birthday	1968	3.00	6.00	12.00
—With "W7" logo on green label					
❏ WS 1767	Greatest Hits	1968	3.00	6.00	12.00
—With "W7" logo on green label					
❏ WS 1767	Greatest Hits	197?	2.00	4.00	8.00
—Any later pressing (LP in print until the late 1980s)					
❏ WS 1786	Goodbye Columbus	1969	3.00	6.00	12.00
—With "W7" logo on green label					
❏ WS 1800	The Association	1969	3.00	6.00	12.00
—With "W7" logo on green label					
❏ 2WS 1868 [(2)]	The Association "Live"	1970	3.75	7.50	15.00
❏ WS 1927	Stop Your Motor	1971	3.00	6.00	12.00
❏ ST-91317 [S]	Insight Out	1967	6.25	12.50	25.00
—Capitol Record Club edition					
❏ ST-91586	Greatest Hits	1968	5.00	10.00	20.00
—Capitol Record Club edition					
❏ STBO-93249 [(2)]	The Association "Live"	1970	5.00	10.00	20.00
—Capitol Record Club edition					

ASTORS, THE
45s

Number	Title (A Side/B Side)	Yr	VG	VG+	NM
STAX					
❏ 139	What Can It Be/Just Enough to Hurt Me	1963	20.00	40.00	80.00
❏ 170	Candy/I Found Out	1965	6.25	12.50	25.00
❏ 179	Mystery Woman/In the Twilight Zone	1965	6.25	12.50	25.00
❏ 232	Daddy Didn't Tell You/More Power to You	1967	3.00	6.00	12.00

ASTRO JETS, THE
45s

Number	Title (A Side/B Side)	Yr	VG	VG+	NM
IMPERIAL					
❏ 5760	Hide and Seek/Boom-A-Lay	1961	5.00	10.00	20.00

ASTRONAUTS, THE (1) Best known as a surf-instrumental group.
45s

Number	Title (A Side/B Side)	Yr	VG	VG+	NM
RCA VICTOR					
❏ 47-8194	Baja/Kuk	1963	5.00	10.00	20.00
❏ 47-8224	Hot Doggin'/Everyone But Me	1963	5.00	10.00	20.00
❏ 47-8224 [PS]	Hot Doggin'/Everyone But Me	1963	15.00	30.00	60.00
❏ 47-8298	Competition Coupe/Surf Party	1963	5.00	10.00	20.00
❏ 47-8364	Go Fight for Her/Swim Little Mermaid	1964	5.00	10.00	20.00
❏ 47-8419	Main Title from Ride the Wild Surf/Around and Around	1964	5.00	10.00	20.00
❏ 47-8463	I'm a Fool/Can't You See I Do	1964	5.00	10.00	20.00
❏ 47-8499	Almost Grown/My Sin Is Pride	1965	5.00	10.00	20.00
❏ 47-8545	Tomorrow's Gonna Be Another Day/Razza Matazz	1965	5.00	10.00	20.00
❏ 47-8628	It Doesn't Matter Anymore/The La La La Song	1965	5.00	10.00	20.00
❏ 47-8885	In My Car/Main Street	1966	3.75	7.50	15.00
❏ 47-9109	I Know You Rider/Better Things	1967	3.75	7.50	15.00
Albums					
RCA VICTOR					
❏ PRM-183 [M]	Rockin' with the Astronauts	1965	7.50	15.00	30.00
❏ LPM-2760 [M]	Surfin' with the Astronauts	1963	15.00	30.00	60.00

ASTRONAUTS, THE (1) / THE LIVERPOOL FIVE

Number	Title (A Side/B Side)	Yr	VG	VG+	NM
❑ LSP-2760 [S]	Surfin' with the Astronauts	1963	20.00	40.00	80.00
❑ LPM-2782 [M]	Everything Is A-OK!	1964	12.50	25.00	50.00
❑ LSP-2782 [S]	Everything Is A-OK!	1964	15.00	30.00	60.00
❑ LPM-2858 [M]	Competition Coupe	1964	15.00	30.00	60.00
❑ LSP-2858 [S]	Competition Coupe	1964	20.00	40.00	80.00
❑ LPM-2903 [M]	The Astronauts Orbit Kampus	1964	10.00	20.00	40.00
❑ LSP-2903 [S]	The Astronauts Orbit Kampus	1964	12.50	25.00	50.00
❑ LPM-3307 [M]	The Astronauts Go, Go, Go	1965	7.50	15.00	30.00
❑ LSP-3307 [S]	The Astronauts Go, Go, Go	1965	10.00	20.00	40.00
❑ LPM-3359 [M]	Favorites for You from Us	1965	7.50	15.00	30.00
❑ LSP-3359 [S]	Favorites for You from Us	1965	10.00	20.00	40.00
❑ LPM-3454 [M]	Down the Line	1966	7.50	15.00	30.00
❑ LSP-3454 [S]	Down the Line	1966	10.00	20.00	40.00
❑ LPM-3733 [M]	Travelin' Men	1967	12.50	25.00	50.00
❑ LSP-3733 [S]	Travelin' Men	1967	7.50	15.00	30.00

ASTRONAUTS, THE (1) / THE LIVERPOOL FIVE
Albums
RCA VICTOR

Number	Title (A Side/B Side)	Yr	VG	VG+	NM
❑ PRS-251 [S]	Stereo Festival	1967	25.00	50.00	100.00

—Special-prodcuts edition

ASTRONAUTS, THE (U)
45s
JAN ELL

Number	Title (A Side/B Side)	Yr	VG	VG+	NM
❑ 459	Geneva Twist/Take 17	1962	7.50	15.00	30.00

LUNEY

Number	Title (A Side/B Side)	Yr	VG	VG+	NM
❑ 100	Ridge Route/Blast Off	1962	7.50	15.00	30.00

MERCURY

Number	Title (A Side/B Side)	Yr	VG	VG+	NM
❑ 71675	Alabama Jubilee/Gadabout	1960	3.00	6.00	12.00

PALLADIUM

Number	Title (A Side/B Side)	Yr	VG	VG+	NM
❑ 610	Come Along Baby/Trying to Get to You	1962	25.00	50.00	100.00

TRIAL

Number	Title (A Side/B Side)	Yr	VG	VG+	NM
❑ 3521	Farewell/Chili Charlene	1960	50.00	100.00	200.00

VANRUS

Number	Title (A Side/B Side)	Yr	VG	VG+	NM
❑ 1000	Ski Lift/Blues Beat	1962	7.50	15.00	30.00

ASYLUM CHOIR LEON RUSSELL and MARC BENNO.
45s
SHELTER

Number	Title (A Side/B Side)	Yr	VG	VG+	NM
❑ 7313	Straight Brother/Tryin' to Stay Alive	1971	2.00	4.00	8.00

SMASH

Number	Title (A Side/B Side)	Yr	VG	VG+	NM
❑ 2186	Soul Food/Welcome to Hollywood	1968	2.00	4.00	8.00

—As "Asylum Choir"

Number	Title (A Side/B Side)	Yr	VG	VG+	NM
❑ 2204	Indian Style/Icicle Star Tree	1969	2.00	4.00	8.00

—As "Asylum Choir"
Albums
MCA

Number	Title (A Side/B Side)	Yr	VG	VG+	NM
❑ 684	Asylum Choir II	1979	2.00	4.00	8.00

—Reissue of Shelter 52010
SHELTER

Number	Title (A Side/B Side)	Yr	VG	VG+	NM
❑ SR 2120	Asylum Choir II	1974	3.00	6.00	12.00

—Reissue of 8910

Number	Title (A Side/B Side)	Yr	VG	VG+	NM
❑ SW-8910	Asylum Choir II	1971	3.75	7.50	15.00
❑ 52010	Asylum Choir II	1977	2.50	5.00	10.00

—Reissue of 2120
SMASH

Number	Title (A Side/B Side)	Yr	VG	VG+	NM
❑ SRS-67107	Look Inside the Asylum Choir	1968	7.50	15.00	30.00

—Front cover has a roll of toilet paper

Number	Title (A Side/B Side)	Yr	VG	VG+	NM
❑ SRS-67107	Look Inside the Asylum Choir	197?	3.75	7.50	15.00

—Front cover has a photo of Leon and Marc

ATKINS, CHET
45s
COLUMBIA

Number	Title (A Side/B Side)	Yr	VG	VG+	NM
❑ AE7 1776 [DJ]	East Tennessee Christmas/Winter Wonderland	1983	—	2.00	4.00
❑ CS7 2712 [DJ]	Sails/My Song	1987	—	2.00	4.00
❑ CS7 2712 [PS]	Sails/My Song	1987	—	2.00	4.00
❑ 03984	Run Don't Walk/Walk Me Home	1983	—	—	3.00
❑ 04859	The Boot and the Stone/Sunrise	1985	—	—	3.00
❑ 05662	Please Stay Tuned/Some Leather and Lace	1985	—	—	3.00
❑ 06165	The Official Beach Music/Alicia	1986	—	—	3.00
❑ 07929	I Still Can't Say Goodbye/The Mockingbird	1988	—	—	3.00

RCA

Number	Title (A Side/B Side)	Yr	VG	VG+	NM
❑ PB-10901	La Chicana/Four in the Morning	1977	—	2.00	4.00

—With Danny Davis and Floyd Cramer

Number	Title (A Side/B Side)	Yr	VG	VG+	NM
❑ PB-11071	Me and My Guitar/Cascade	1977	—	2.00	4.00
❑ PB-11892	Blind Willie/Dance with Me	1980	—	2.00	4.00
❑ PB-12064	I Can Hear Kentucky Calling Me/Strawberry Man	1980	—	2.00	4.00
❑ PB-12263	Orange Blossom Special/Ready for the Times to Get Better	1981	—	2.00	4.00

RCA VICTOR

Number	Title (A Side/B Side)	Yr	VG	VG+	NM
❑ 37-7971	Jingle Bells/Jingle Bell Rock	1961	6.25	12.50	25.00

—"Compact Single 33"; small hole, plays at 33 1/3 rpm

Number	Title (A Side/B Side)	Yr	VG	VG+	NM
❑ 47-4377	In the Mood/Sweet Bunch of Daisies	1951	6.25	12.50	25.00
❑ 47-4491	Goodbye Blues/Rainbow	1952	6.25	12.50	25.00
❑ 47-4684	Spanish Fandango/Your Mean Little Heart	1952	6.25	12.50	25.00
❑ 47-4896	Meet Mr. Callaghan/Chinatown, My Chinatown	1952	6.25	12.50	25.00
❑ 47-4922	Gallopin' on the Guitar/(B-side unknown)	1952	6.25	12.50	25.00
❑ 47-4931	Tennessee Rag/My Little Girl	1952	6.25	12.50	25.00
❑ 47-5010	Midnight/Rustic Dance	1952	6.25	12.50	25.00
❑ 47-5100	Guitar Polka/Dream Train	1952	5.00	10.00	20.00

—With Rosalie Allen

Number	Title (A Side/B Side)	Yr	VG	VG+	NM
❑ 47-5181	Fig Leaf Rag/High Rockin' Swing	1953	5.00	10.00	20.00
❑ 47-5300	Country Gentlemen/The Bells of St. Mary's	1953	5.00	10.00	20.00
❑ 47-5484	Three O'Clock in the Morning/City Slicker	1953	5.00	10.00	20.00
❑ 47-5565	Barber Shop Rag/Centipede Boogie	1953	5.00	10.00	20.00
❑ 47-5638	Wildwood Flower/Simple Simon	1954	5.00	10.00	20.00
❑ 47-5650	Georgia Camp Meeting/Jealous Hearted Me	1954	5.00	10.00	20.00

—With Minnie Pearl

Number	Title (A Side/B Side)	Yr	VG	VG+	NM
❑ 47-5704	Downhill Drag/Kentucky Derby	1954	5.00	10.00	20.00
❑ 47-5813	San Antonio Rose/Mister Misery	1954	5.00	10.00	20.00

—With Red Kirk

Number	Title (A Side/B Side)	Yr	VG	VG+	NM
❑ 47-5956	Mr. Sandman/Set a Spell	1954	5.00	10.00	20.00
❑ 47-6108	Hey Mr. Guitar/Unchained Melody	1955	3.75	7.50	15.00
❑ 47-6199	Somebody Stole My Gal/ Shine On Harvest Moon	1955	3.75	7.50	15.00
❑ 47-6314	Christmas Carols/Jingle Bells	1955	3.75	7.50	15.00
❑ 47-6366	Jean's Song/Honey	1955	3.75	7.50	15.00
❑ 47-6550	Cecilia/The Lady Loves	1956	3.75	7.50	15.00
❑ 47-6796	Trambone/Blue Echo	1957	3.75	7.50	15.00
❑ 47-6808	Tricky/Peanut Vendor	1957	3.75	7.50	15.00

—With the Rhythm Rockers

Number	Title (A Side/B Side)	Yr	VG	VG+	NM
❑ 47-6919	Martinique/Dig These Blues	1957	3.75	7.50	15.00

—With the Rhythm Rockers

Number	Title (A Side/B Side)	Yr	VG	VG+	NM
❑ 47-7048	Hidden Charms/Colonial Ballroom	1957	3.75	7.50	15.00
❑ 47-7589	Boo Boo Stick Beat/Django's Castle	1959	3.00	6.00	12.00
❑ 47-7684	One Mint Julep/Teensville	1960	3.00	6.00	12.00
❑ 47-7747	Slinkey/Rainbow's End	1960	3.00	6.00	12.00
❑ 47-7796	Hocus Pocus/ Theme from The Dark at the End of the Stairs	1960	3.00	6.00	12.00
❑ 47-7847	The Slop/Hot Mocking Bird	1961	3.00	6.00	12.00
❑ 47-7891	Man of Mystery/Windy and Warm	1961	3.00	6.00	12.00
❑ 47-7971	Jingle Bells/Jingle Bell Rock	1961	3.00	6.00	12.00
❑ 47-8029	Down Home/Melissa	1962	3.00	6.00	12.00
❑ 47-8246	Guitar Country/Waitin' for the Evening Train	1963	3.00	6.00	12.00

—With the Anita Kerr Quartet

Number	Title (A Side/B Side)	Yr	VG	VG+	NM
❑ 47-8342	Freight Train/Dobro	1964	3.00	6.00	12.00
❑ 47-8492	Travelin'/Cloudy and Cool	1965	2.50	5.00	10.00
❑ 47-8590	Yakety Axe/Letter Edged in Black	1965	2.50	5.00	10.00
❑ 47-8781	From Nashville with Love/Rhythm Guitar	1966	2.50	5.00	10.00
❑ 47-8829	Tennessee Waltz/Country Gentleman	1966	2.50	5.00	10.00
❑ 47-8927	Prissy/La Fiesta	1966	2.50	5.00	10.00
❑ 47-9116	Charlie Brown/What'd I Say	1967	2.50	5.00	10.00
❑ 47-9578	Huntin' Boots/Blue Angel	1968	2.00	4.00	8.00
❑ 47-9672	Light My Fire/Mrs. Robinson	1968	2.00	4.00	8.00
❑ 47-9725	Theme from Zorba the Greek/ Those Were the Days	1969	—	3.00	6.00
❑ 47-9824	Love Beads/Passion Flower	1969	—	3.00	6.00
❑ 47-9827	Steeplechase Lane/Love Beads	1970	—	2.50	5.00
❑ 47-9890	Tennessee Stud/Cannonball Rag	1970	—	2.50	5.00

—With Jerry Reed

Number	Title (A Side/B Side)	Yr	VG	VG+	NM
❑ 47-9956	Snowbird/Chaplain in New Shoes	1971	—	2.50	5.00
❑ 48-0062	Guitar Waltz/Barber Shop Rag	1949	6.25	12.50	25.00

—Second pressings: Green label, black vinyl

Number	Title (A Side/B Side)	Yr	VG	VG+	NM
❑ 48-0062	Guitar Waltz/Barber Shop Rag	1949	12.50	25.00	50.00

—Originals on green vinyl

Number	Title (A Side/B Side)	Yr	VG	VG+	NM
❑ 48-0089	Dance of the Goldenrod/ Telling My Troubles to My Old Guitar	1949	6.25	12.50	25.00

—Second pressings: Green label, black vinyl

Number	Title (A Side/B Side)	Yr	VG	VG+	NM
❑ 48-0089	Dance of the Goldenrod/ Telling My Troubles to My Old Guitar	1949	12.50	25.00	50.00

—Originals on green vinyl

Number	Title (A Side/B Side)	Yr	VG	VG+	NM
❑ 48-0142	Centipede Boogie/Wednesday Night Waltz	1949	6.25	12.50	25.00

—Second pressings: Green label, black vinyl

Number	Title (A Side/B Side)	Yr	VG	VG+	NM
❑ 48-0142	Centipede Boogie/Wednesday Night Waltz	1949	12.50	25.00	50.00

—Originals on green vinyl

Number	Title (A Side/B Side)	Yr	VG	VG+	NM
❑ 48-0173	One More Chance/Old Buck Dance	1950	6.25	12.50	25.00

—Originals on green vinyl

Number	Title (A Side/B Side)	Yr	VG	VG+	NM
❑ 48-0173	One More Chance/Old Buck Dance	1950	6.25	12.50	25.00

—Second pressings: Green label, black vinyl

Number	Title (A Side/B Side)	Yr	VG	VG+	NM
❑ 48-0329	Main Street Breakdown/ Under the Hickory Nut Tree	1950	6.25	12.50	25.00

—Second pressings: Green label, black vinyl

Number	Title (A Side/B Side)	Yr	VG	VG+	NM
❑ 48-0329	Main Street Breakdown /Under the Hickory Nut Tree	1950	12.50	25.00	50.00

—Originals on green vinyl

Number	Title (A Side/B Side)	Yr	VG	VG+	NM
❑ 48-0367	Boogie Man Boogie/ Was Bitten By the Same Bug Twice	1950	6.25	12.50	25.00

—Second pressings: Green label, black vinyl

Number	Title (A Side/B Side)	Yr	VG	VG+	NM
❑ 48-0367	Boogie Man Boogie/ Was Bitten By the Same Bug Twice	1950	12.50	25.00	50.00

—Originals on green vinyl

Number	Title (A Side/B Side)	Yr	VG	VG+	NM
❑ 48-0402	The Birth of the Blues/Confusin'	1950	6.25	12.50	25.00

—Second pressings: Green label, black vinyl

Number	Title (A Side/B Side)	Yr	VG	VG+	NM
❑ 48-0402	The Birth of the Blues/Confusin'	1950	12.50	25.00	50.00

—Originals on green vinyl

Number	Title (A Side/B Side)	Yr	VG	VG+	NM
❑ 48-0428	Indian Love Call/Music in My Heart	1951	6.25	12.50	25.00

—Second pressings: Green label, black vinyl

Number	Title (A Side/B Side)	Yr	VG	VG+	NM
❑ 48-0428	Indian Love Call/Music in My Heart	1951	12.50	25.00	50.00

—Originals on green vinyl

Number	Title (A Side/B Side)	Yr	VG	VG+	NM
❑ 48-0439	My Life with You/A Trinket of Shiny Gold	1951	6.25	12.50	25.00

—With the Carter Sisters

Number	Title (A Side/B Side)	Yr	VG	VG+	NM
❑ 48-0440	You're Always Brand New/Mountain Melody	1951	6.25	12.50	25.00
❑ 48-0471	Jitterbug Waltz/My Crazy Heart	1951	6.25	12.50	25.00
❑ 48-0500	Crazy Rhythm/Hybrid Corn	1951	6.25	12.50	25.00
❑ 74-0236	Delilah/Ode to Billie Joe	1969	—	2.50	5.00

—With Arthur Fiedler and the Boston Pops

Number	Title (A Side/B Side)	Yr	VG	VG+	NM
❑ 74-0536	Black Magic Woman/Wabash Blues	1971	—	2.50	5.00
❑ 74-0696	Red, White and Blue Medley/Kentucky	1972	—	2.50	5.00
❑ 74-0775	Nashtownville/Jerry's Breakdown	1972	—	2.50	5.00

—With Jerry Reed

Number	Title (A Side/B Side)	Yr	VG	VG+	NM
❑ 74-0914	Ruby, Are You Mad at Your Man/ Somewhere, My Love	1973	—	2.00	4.00
❑ 47-7847 [PS]	The Slop/Hot Mocking Bird	1961	5.00	10.00	20.00
❑ APBO-0146	Fiddlin' Around/Paramaribo	1973	—	2.00	4.00
❑ VP-1-2450 [S]	I Ain't Gonna Work Tomorrow/Never on Sunday	196?	3.75	7.50	15.00

—Jukebox issue; small hole, plays at 33 1/3 rpm

Number	Title (A Side/B Side)	Yr	VG	VG+	NM
❑ VP-2-2450 [S]	Tuxedo Junction/Give the World a Smile	196?	3.75	7.50	15.00

—Jukebox issue; small hole, plays at 33 1/3 rpm

Number	Title (A Side/B Side)	Yr	VG	VG+	NM
❑ VP-3-2450 [S]	I'm a Pilgrim/Salty Dog Drag	196?	3.75	7.50	15.00

—Jukebox issue; small hole, plays at 33 1/3 rpm

Abba, "Knowing Me, Knowing You," Atlantic 3387, picture sleeve, $2.50-$5.

Aerosmith, *Aerosmith,* Columbia KC 32005, stereo LP, original cover, $7.50-$15.

The Allman Brothers Band, *Seven Turns,* Epic E 46144, stereo LP, $7.50-$15.

The Animals, "I'm Crying," MGM K13724, picture sleeve, $12.50-$25.

Eddy Arnold, *When It's Round-Up Time in Heaven,* RCA Victor LPM-3219, 10-inch LP, $50-$100.

The Astronauts, "Hot-Doggin'," RCA Victor 47-8224, picture sleeve, $30-$60.

Number	Title (A Side/B Side)	Yr	VG	VG+	NM
❑ VP-4-2450 [S]	Steel Guitar Rag/Trambone	196?	3.75	7.50	15.00

—*Jukebox issue; small hole, plays at 33 1/3 rpm; the above 4 came in a box originally, which is worth at least as much as any of the discs*

Number	Title (A Side/B Side)	Yr	VG	VG+	NM
❑ PB-10046	The Entertainer/Dizzy Fingers	1974	—	2.00	4.00
❑ PB-10346	The Night Atlanta Burned/Old Folks of Okracoke	1975	—	2.00	4.00

—*As "The Atkins String Co."*

Number	Title	Yr	VG	VG+	NM
❑ PB-10448	Sonora/Mostly Mozart	1975	—	2.00	4.00

—*As "The Atkins String Co."*

Number	Title	Yr	VG	VG+	NM
❑ PB-10614	Frog Kissin'/Bill Cheatham	1976	—	2.00	4.00

7-Inch Extended Plays
RCA VICTOR

Number	Title (A Side/B Side)	Yr	VG	VG+	NM
❑ LPC-124	Theme from "The Dark at the Top of the Stairs"/Theme from "Picnic"//Limelight/Meet Mister Callaghan	1961	3.75	7.50	15.00

—*"Compact Double 33"; small hole, plays at 33 1/3 rpm*

Number	Title	Yr	VG	VG+	NM
❑ LPC-124 [PS]	Chet Atkins Plays Great Movie Themes	1961	5.00	10.00	20.00
❑ 547-0141	Gallopin' Guitar/Stephen Foster Medley//St. Louis Blues/Hangover Blues	1952	5.00	10.00	20.00

—*One record of 2-EP set EPB 3079*

Number	Title	Yr	VG	VG+	NM
❑ 547-0142	Black Mountain Rag/Lover, Come Back to Me//The 3rd Man Theme/Imagination	1952	5.00	10.00	20.00

—*One record of 2-EP set EPB 3079*

Number	Title	Yr	VG	VG+	NM
❑ 547-0535	South/Indiana//A Gay Ranchero/Frankie and Johnnie	1954	3.75	7.50	15.00

—*One record of 2-EP set EPB 1090*

Number	Title	Yr	VG	VG+	NM
❑ 547-0536	Alabama Jubilee/Have You Ever Been Lonely (Have You Ever Been Blue?)//Caravan/The Birth of the Blues	1954	3.75	7.50	15.00

—*One record of 2-EP set EPB 1090*

Number	Title	Yr	VG	VG+	NM
❑ EPA-588	Pagan Love Song/Sunrise Serenade//Beautiful Ohio/Avalon	1954	5.00	10.00	20.00
❑ EPA-588 [PS]	Chet Atkins and His Guitar	1954	5.00	10.00	20.00
❑ EPA-594	Tweedlee Dee/(The Wallflower) Dance with Me Henry//Cherry Pink and Apple Blossom White/Darling, Je Vous Aime Beaucoup	1955	5.00	10.00	20.00
❑ EPA-594 [PS]	Pickin' the Hits	1955	5.00	10.00	20.00
❑ EPA-685	Arkansaw Traveler/Londonderry Air//Ochi Chornya/La Golondrina	1955	5.00	10.00	20.00
❑ EPA-685 [PS]	Chet Atkins in 3 Dimensions Vol. 1: Folk	1955	5.00	10.00	20.00
❑ EPA-686	Blues in the Night/Tenderly//Little Rock Getaway/Tip-Toe Through the Tulips with Me	1955	5.00	10.00	20.00
❑ EPA-686 [PS]	Chet Atkins in 3 Dimensions Vol. 2: Popular	1955	5.00	10.00	20.00
❑ EPA-687	Minuet and Prelude/Intermezzo//Schon Rosmarin/Minute Waltz	1955	5.00	10.00	20.00
❑ EPA-687 [PS]	Chet Atkins in 3 Dimensions Vol. 3: Classical	1955	5.00	10.00	20.00
❑ EPA-796	Indian Love Call/Memphis Blues//St. Louis Blues/Black Mountain Rag	1956	5.00	10.00	20.00
❑ EPA-796 [PS]	Stringin' Along with Chet Atkins	1956	5.00	10.00	20.00
❑ 547-0919	Oh By Jingo/Indian Love Call//Alice Blue Gown/The 3rd Man Theme	1956	5.00	10.00	20.00

—*One record of 2-EP set EPB 1236*

Number	Title	Yr	VG	VG+	NM
❑ 547-0920	Memphis Blues/12th Street Rag//Gallopin' Guitar/St. Louis Blues	1956	5.00	10.00	20.00

—*One record of 2-EP set EPB 1236*

Number	Title	Yr	VG	VG+	NM
❑ EPB 1090 [PS]	A Session with Chet Atkins	1954	5.00	10.00	20.00

—*Cover for 2-EP set (547-0535, 547-0536)*

Number	Title	Yr	VG	VG+	NM
❑ EPB 1236 [PS]	Stringin' Along with Chet Atkins	1956	5.00	10.00	20.00
❑ EAP 1-1383	Swedish Rhapsody/Liza//Petite Waltz/Unchained Melody	1956	3.75	7.50	15.00
❑ EAP 1-1383 [PS]	Finger-Style Guitar, Vol. 1	1956	3.75	7.50	15.00
❑ EPA 2-1383	Heartaches/Glow Worm//Malaguena/Waltz in A Flat	1956	3.75	7.50	15.00
❑ EPA 2-1383 [PS]	Finger-Style Guitar, Vol. II	1956	3.75	7.50	15.00
❑ VLP 2450	Salty Dog Drag/Trambone/The Girl Friend of the Whirling Dervish//I'm a Pilgrim/Steel Guitar Rag/Give the World a Smile	196?	3.75	7.50	15.00

—*Jukebox issue; small hole, plays at 33 1/3 rpm*

Number	Title	Yr	VG	VG+	NM
❑ VLP 2450 [PS]	Down Home	196?	3.75	7.50	15.00
❑ EPB 3079 [PS]	Chet Atkins' Gallopin' Guitar	1952	5.00	10.00	20.00

—*Cover for 2-EP set (547-0141, 547-0142)*

Number	Title	Yr	VG	VG+	NM
❑ VLP 3316	Josephine/It Don't Mean a Thing/Rose Ann//Travelin'/Wimoweh/Say It with Soul	196?	3.75	7.50	15.00

—*Jukebox issue; small hole, plays at 33 1/3 rpm*

Number	Title	Yr	VG	VG+	NM
❑ VLP 3316 [PS]	My Favorite Guitars	196?	3.75	7.50	15.00
❑ VLP 3558	Yakety Axe/Josephine/White Silver Sands//Oh Lonesome Me/Freight Train/Cloudy and Cool	196?	3.00	6.00	12.00

—*Jukebox issue; small hole, plays at 33 1/3 rpm*

Number	Title	Yr	VG	VG+	NM
❑ VLP 3558 [PS]	The Best of Chet Atkins, Vol. 2	196?	3.00	6.00	12.00
❑ EPA-4194	Say "Si Si"/Villa//Yankee Doodle Dandy/You're Just in Love	1958	3.75	7.50	15.00
❑ EPA-4194 [PS]	Chet Atkins at Home	1958	3.75	7.50	15.00
❑ EPA-4343	In the Good Old Summertime/Bill Bailey//Sweet Bunch of Daisies/John Henry	1959	3.75	7.50	15.00
❑ EPA-4343 [PS]	Hum and Strum Along with Chet	1959	3.75	7.50	15.00
❑ EPA-5052	The Poor People of Paris (Jean's Song)/Chinatown, My Chinatown//San Antonio Rose/Country Gentleman	195?	3.75	7.50	15.00
❑ EPA-5052 [PS]	Chet Atkins (Gold Standard Series)	1958	3.75	7.50	15.00

Albums
COLUMBIA

Number	Title	Yr	VG	VG+	NM
❑ FC 38536	Work It Out with Chet Atkins C.G.P.	1983	2.50	5.00	10.00
❑ PC 38536	Work It Out with Chet Atkins C.G.P.	1985	2.00	4.00	8.00

—*Budget-line reissue*

Number	Title	Yr	VG	VG+	NM
❑ PC 39003	East Tennessee Christmas	1983	2.50	5.00	10.00
❑ FC 39591	Stay Tuned	1985	2.50	5.00	10.00
❑ FC 40256	Street Dreams	1986	2.00	4.00	8.00
❑ FC 40593	Sails	1987	2.00	4.00	8.00
❑ FC 44323	Chet Atkins, C.G.P.	1989	2.00	4.00	8.00

DOLTON

Number	Title	Yr	VG	VG+	NM
❑ BLP-16506 [M]	Play Guitar with Chet Atkins	1967	6.25	12.50	25.00
❑ BST-17506 [S]	Play Guitar with Chet Atkins	1967	7.50	15.00	30.00

PAIR

Number	Title (A Side/B Side)	Yr	VG	VG+	NM
❑ PDL2-1047 [(2)]	Tennessee Guitar Man	1985	3.00	6.00	12.00
❑ PDL2-1115 [(2)]	Guitar for All Seasons	1986	3.00	6.00	12.00

RCA CAMDEN

Number	Title	Yr	VG	VG+	NM
❑ CAL-659 [M]	Chet Atkins and His Guitar	196?	3.75	7.50	15.00
❑ CAS-659(e) [R]	Chet Atkins and His Guitar	1964	3.00	6.00	12.00
❑ CAL-753 [M]	Guitar Genius	196?	3.75	7.50	15.00
❑ CAS-753(e) [R]	Guitar Genius	196?	3.00	6.00	12.00
❑ CAL-981 [M]	Music from Nashville, My Home Town	1966	3.00	6.00	12.00
❑ CAS-981 [S]	Music from Nashville, My Home Town	1966	3.75	7.50	15.00
❑ CAL-2182 [M]	Chet	1967	3.00	6.00	12.00
❑ CAS-2182 [S]	Chet	1967	3.75	7.50	15.00
❑ CAS-2296	Relaxin' with Chet	1969	3.00	6.00	12.00
❑ CAS-2523	Chet 'n Boots	1972	3.00	6.00	12.00
❑ CAS-2555	Nashville Gold	1972	3.00	6.00	12.00
❑ CAS-2600	Finger Pickin' Good	1973	2.50	5.00	10.00
❑ ACL1-7042	Love Letters	197?	2.50	5.00	10.00

RCA RED SEAL

Number	Title	Yr	VG	VG+	NM
❑ LM-2870 [M]	The "Pops" Goes Country	1966	3.75	7.50	15.00
❑ LSC-2870 [S]	The "Pops" Goes Country	1966	5.00	10.00	20.00

—*Above two with the Boston Pops Orchestra, Arthur Fiedler, conductor*

Number	Title	Yr	VG	VG+	NM
❑ LSC-3104	Chet Picks On the Pops	1969	3.75	7.50	15.00

—*With the Boston Pops Orchestra, Arthur Fiedler, conductor*

RCA VICTOR

Number	Title	Yr	VG	VG+	NM
❑ APL1-0159	Alone	1973	3.00	6.00	12.00
❑ APD1-0329 [Q]	Superpickers	1974	5.00	10.00	20.00
❑ APL1-0329	Superpickers	1974	3.00	6.00	12.00
❑ APL1-0545	Chet Atkins Picks On Jerry Reed	1974	3.00	6.00	12.00
❑ APL1-0645	Chat Atkins Goes to the Movies	1973	3.00	6.00	12.00
❑ ANL1-0981	Chet Atkins Picks the Best	1975	2.50	5.00	10.00
❑ LPM-1090 [M]	A Session with Chet Atkins	1954	15.00	30.00	60.00

—*Red cover*

Number	Title	Yr	VG	VG+	NM
❑ LPM-1090 [M]	A Session with Chet Atkins	1961	5.00	10.00	20.00

—*Woman and guitars cover*

Number	Title	Yr	VG	VG+	NM
❑ LSP-1090(e) [R]	A Session with Chet Atkins	1967	2.50	5.00	10.00
❑ LPM-1197 [M]	Chet Atkins in Three Dimensions	1956	12.50	52.00	50.00

—*Black-and-white guitar cover*

Number	Title	Yr	VG	VG+	NM
❑ LPM-1197 [M]	Chet Atkins in Three Dimensions	1961	5.00	10.00	20.00

—*Red guitar cover*

Number	Title	Yr	VG	VG+	NM
❑ LSP-1197(e) [R]	Chet Atkins in Three Dimensions	1967	2.50	5.00	10.00
❑ APL1-1233	The Night Atlanta Burned	1975	3.00	6.00	12.00
❑ LPM-1236 [M]	Stringin' Along with Chet Atkins	1956	12.50	25.00	50.00

—*Orange cover*

Number	Title	Yr	VG	VG+	NM
❑ LPM-1236 [M]	Stringin' Along with Chet Atkins	1961	5.00	10.00	20.00

—*Full-color cover*

Number	Title	Yr	VG	VG+	NM
❑ LSP-1236(e) [R]	Stringin' Along with Chet Atkins	1967	2.50	5.00	10.00
❑ LPM-1383 [M]	Finger Style Guitar	1956	12.50	25.00	50.00

—*Chet's face not visible on cover*

Number	Title	Yr	VG	VG+	NM
❑ LPM-1383 [M]	Finger Style Guitar	1961	5.00	10.00	20.00

—*Chet's face visible on cover*

Number	Title	Yr	VG	VG+	NM
❑ LSP-1383(e) [R]	Finger Style Guitar	1962	3.00	6.00	12.00
❑ LPM-1544 [M]	Chet Atkins at Home	1957	12.50	25.00	50.00

—*Title in block letters on cover*

Number	Title	Yr	VG	VG+	NM
❑ LPM-1544 [M]	Chet Atkins at Home	1961	5.00	10.00	20.00

—*Title in script on cover*

Number	Title	Yr	VG	VG+	NM
❑ LSP-1544(e) [R]	Chet Atkins at Home	1967	2.50	5.00	10.00
❑ LPM-1577 [M]	Hi-Fi in Focus	1957	5.00	10.00	20.00

—*Guitar on cover*

Number	Title	Yr	VG	VG+	NM
❑ LPM-1577 [M]	Hi-Fi in Focus	1957	12.50	25.00	50.00

—*No guitars on cover*

Number	Title	Yr	VG	VG+	NM
❑ LSP-1577(e) [R]	Hi-Fi in Focus	196?	2.50	5.00	10.00
❑ ANL1-1935	Christmas with Chet Atkins	1976	2.00	4.00	8.00

—*Reissue of LSP-2423*

Number	Title	Yr	VG	VG+	NM
❑ APL1-1985	The Best of Chet Atkins	1975	3.00	6.00	12.00
❑ LPM-1993 [M]	Chet Atkins in Hollywood	1959	7.50	15.00	30.00

—*Night-time cover*

Number	Title	Yr	VG	VG+	NM
❑ LPM-1993 [M]	Chet Atkins in Hollywood	1961	5.00	10.00	20.00

—*Daylight "blonde" cover*

Number	Title	Yr	VG	VG+	NM
❑ LSP-1993 [S]	Chet Atkins in Hollywood	1959	12.50	25.00	50.00

—*Night-time cover*

Number	Title	Yr	VG	VG+	NM
❑ LSP-1993 [S]	Chet Atkins in Hollywood	1961	7.50	15.00	30.00

—*Daylight "blonde" cover*

Number	Title	Yr	VG	VG+	NM
❑ LPM-2025 [M]	Hum & Strum Along	1959	6.25	12.50	25.00

—*Add $10 NM if instruction book is included*

Number	Title	Yr	VG	VG+	NM
❑ LSP-2025 [S]	Hum & Strum Along	1959	10.00	20.00	40.00

—*Add $10 NM if instruction book is included*

Number	Title	Yr	VG	VG+	NM
❑ LPM-2103 [M]	Mister Guitar	1959	7.50	15.00	30.00

—*Lone guitar on cover*

Number	Title	Yr	VG	VG+	NM
❑ LPM-2103 [M]	Mister Guitar	1961	5.00	10.00	20.00

—*Guitar and woman on cover*

Number	Title	Yr	VG	VG+	NM
❑ LSP-2103 [S]	Mister Guitar	1959	12.50	25.00	50.00

—*Lone guitar on cover*

Number	Title	Yr	VG	VG+	NM
❑ LSP-2103 [S]	Mister Guitar	1961	7.50	15.00	30.00

—*Guitar and woman on cover*

Number	Title	Yr	VG	VG+	NM
❑ LPM-2161 [M]	Teensville	1960	7.50	15.00	30.00

—*Title overlaps cover photo*

Number	Title	Yr	VG	VG+	NM
❑ LPM-2161 [M]	Teensville	1961	5.00	10.00	20.00

—*Title in black strip at top of cover photo*

Number	Title	Yr	VG	VG+	NM
❑ LSP-2161 [S]	Teensville	1960	12.50	25.00	50.00

—*Title overlaps cover photo*

Number	Title	Yr	VG	VG+	NM
❑ LSP-2161 [S]	Teensville	1961	7.50	15.00	30.00

—*Title in black strip at top of cover photo*

Number	Title	Yr	VG	VG+	NM
❑ LPM-2175 [M]	The Other Chet Atkins	1960	5.00	10.00	20.00
❑ LSP-2175 [S]	The Other Chet Atkins	1960	7.50	15.00	30.00
❑ LPM-2232 [M]	Chet Atkins' Workshop	1961	5.00	10.00	20.00
❑ LSP-2232 [S]	Chet Atkins' Workshop	1961	7.50	15.00	30.00
❑ LPM-2346 [M]	The Most Popular Guitar	1961	5.00	10.00	20.00
❑ LSP-2346 [S]	The Most Popular Guitar	1961	7.50	15.00	30.00
❑ AHL1-2405	My Guitar	1977	3.00	6.00	12.00
❑ LPM-2423 [M]	Christmas with Chet Atkins	1961	7.50	15.00	30.00
❑ LSP-2423 [S]	Christmas with Chet Atkins	1961	7.50	15.00	30.00
❑ LPM-2450 [M]	Down Home	1962	5.00	10.00	20.00
❑ LSP-2450 [S]	Down Home	1962	6.25	12.50	25.00

Number	Title (A Side/B Side)	Yr	VG	VG+	NM
❑ CPL1-2503	A Legendary Performer	1977	3.00	6.00	12.00
❑ LPM-2549 [M]	Caribbean Guitar	1962	5.00	10.00	20.00
❑ LSP-2549 [S]	Caribbean Guitar	1962	6.25	12.50	25.00
❑ LPM-2601 [M]	Back Home Hymns	1962	5.00	10.00	20.00
❑ LSP-2601 [S]	Back Home Hymns	1962	6.25	12.50	25.00
❑ LPM-2616 [M]	Our Man in Nashville	1963	5.00	10.00	20.00
❑ LSP-2616 [S]	Our Man in Nashville	1963	6.25	12.50	25.00
❑ LPM-2678 [M]	Travelin'	1963	5.00	10.00	20.00
❑ LSP-2678 [S]	Travelin'	1963	6.25	12.50	25.00
❑ LPM-2719 [M]	Teen Scene	1963	5.00	10.00	20.00
❑ LSP-2719 [S]	Teen Scene	1963	6.25	12.50	25.00
❑ LPM-2783 [M]	Guitar Country	1964	3.75	7.50	15.00
❑ LSP-2783 [S]	Guitar Country	1964	5.00	10.00	20.00
❑ LPM-2887 [M]	The Best of Chet Atkins	1964	3.75	7.50	15.00
❑ LSP-2887 [S]	The Best of Chet Atkins	1964	5.00	10.00	20.00
❑ LPM-2908 [M]	Progressive Pickin'	1964	3.75	7.50	15.00
❑ LSP-2908 [S]	Progressive Pickin'	1964	5.00	10.00	20.00
❑ LPM-3079 [10]	Chet Atkins' Gallopin' Guitar	1952	37.50	75.00	150.00
❑ LPM-3169 [10]	Stringin' Along with Chet Atkins	1953	25.00	50.00	100.00
❑ AHL1-3302	The First Nashville Guitar Quartet	1979	3.00	6.00	12.00
❑ LPM-3316 [M]	My Favorite Guitars	1965	3.75	7.50	15.00
❑ LSP-3316 [S]	My Favorite Guitars	1965	5.00	10.00	20.00
❑ LPM-3429 [M]	More of That "Guitar Country"	1965	3.75	7.50	15.00
❑ LSP-3429 [S]	More of That "Guitar Country"	1965	5.00	10.00	20.00
❑ AHL1-3505	The Best of Chet On The Road…Live	1980	3.00	6.00	12.00
❑ LPM-3531 [M]	Chet Atkins Picks On the Beatles	1966	6.25	12.50	25.00
❑ LSP-3531 [S]	Chet Atkins Picks On the Beatles	1966	7.50	15.00	30.00
❑ LPM-3558 [M]	The Best of Chet Atkins, Volume 2	1966	3.00	6.00	12.00
❑ LSP-3558 [S]	The Best of Chet Atkins, Volume 2	1966	3.75	7.50	15.00
❑ LPM-3647 [M]	From Nashville with Love	1966	3.00	6.00	12.00
❑ LSP-3647 [S]	From Nashville with Love	1966	3.75	7.50	15.00
❑ LPM-3728 [M]	It's a Guitar World	1967	7.50	15.00	30.00
❑ LSP-3728 [S]	It's a Guitar World	1967	3.00	6.00	12.00
❑ AYL1-3741	The First Nashville Guitar Quartet	1981	2.00	4.00	8.00
—"Best Buy Series" reissue					
❑ LPM-3818 [M]	Chet Atkins Picks the Best	1967	7.50	15.00	30.00
❑ LSP-3818 [S]	Chet Atkins Picks the Best	1967	3.00	6.00	12.00
❑ LPM-3885 [M]	Class Guitar	1967	7.50	15.00	30.00
❑ LSP-3885 [S]	Class Guitar	1967	3.00	6.00	12.00
❑ LPM-3992 [M]	Solo Flights	1968	12.50	25.00	50.00
❑ LSP-3992 [S]	Solo Flights	1968	3.00	6.00	12.00
❑ LPM-4017 [M]	Hometown Guitar	1968	20.00	40.00	80.00
❑ LSP-4017 [S]	Hometown Guitar	1968	3.75	7.50	15.00
❑ AHL1-4044	Still Country — After All These Years	1981	2.50	5.00	10.00
❑ LSP-4061	Solid Gold '68	1968	3.75	7.50	15.00
❑ LSP-4135	Lover's Guitar	1968	3.75	7.50	15.00
❑ LSP-4244	Solid Gold '69	1969	3.00	6.00	12.00
❑ LSP-4331	Yestergroovin'	1970	3.00	6.00	12.00
❑ LSP-4396	Me & Jerry	1971	3.75	7.50	15.00
—With Jerry Reed					
❑ LSP-4464	For the Good Times	1971	3.75	7.50	15.00
❑ AHL1-4724	Great Hits of the Past	1983	2.50	5.00	10.00
❑ LSP-4754	Chet Atkins Picks the Hits	1973	3.75	7.50	15.00
❑ AHL1-5495	Collector's Series	1985	2.50	5.00	10.00
❑ VPS-6030 [(2)]	This Is Chet Atkins	1972	3.75	7.50	15.00
❑ VPXS-6079 [(2)]	Now & Then	1972	3.75	7.50	15.00
TIME-LIFE					
❑ STW-117	Country Music	1981	3.00	6.00	12.00

ATKINS, CHET, AND LES PAUL Also see each artist's individual listings.
45s
RCA

Number	Title (A Side/B Side)	Yr	VG	VG+	NM
❑ PB-11330	I'm Your Greatest Fan/Hot Toddy	1978	—	2.00	4.00
RCA VICTOR					
❑ PB-10642	Moonglow/Avalon	1976	—	2.50	5.00
Albums					
RCA VICTOR					
❑ APL1-1167	Chester and Lester	1976	3.00	6.00	12.00
❑ APL1-2786	Guitar Monsters	1978	3.00	6.00	12.00
❑ AYL1-3682	Chester and Lester	1980	2.00	4.00	8.00
—"Best Buy Series" reissue					

ATKINS, CHET, AND HANK SNOW Also see each artist's individual listings.
45s
RCA VICTOR

Number	Title (A Side/B Side)	Yr	VG	VG+	NM
❑ 47-5995	Silver Bell/Old Spinning Wheel	1954	5.00	10.00	20.00
❑ 47-6558	Reminiscing/New Spanish Two-Step	1956	3.75	7.50	15.00
❑ 47-9803	Wheels/Difficult	1969	2.00	4.00	8.00

ATKINS, CHET, AND DOC WATSON Also see each artist's individual listings.
45s
RCA

Number	Title (A Side/B Side)	Yr	VG	VG+	NM
❑ PB-12138	Medley-Tennessee Rag & Beaumont Rag/On My Way to Canaan's Land	1981	—	2.00	4.00
Albums					
RCA VICTOR					
❑ AHL1-3701	Reflections	1980	2.50	5.00	10.00

ATKINSON, SANDY
45s
HIT

Number	Title (A Side/B Side)	Yr	VG	VG+	NM
❑ 37	Mama Sang a Song/Big Girls Don't Cry	1962	2.00	4.00	8.00
—B-side by the Chellows					

ATLANTA RHYTHM SECTION Formed by ex-members of THE CANDYMEN and CLASSICS IV.
12-Inch Singles
COLUMBIA

Number	Title (A Side/B Side)	Yr	VG	VG+	NM
❑ 1271 [DJ]	Alien//Homesick/Quinella	1981	2.50	5.00	10.00
POLYDOR					
❑ PRO 121 [DJ]	Back Up Against the Wall/Doraville//Large Time/Angel (What in the World's Come Over Us)	1979	3.75	7.50	15.00
—Four-song promo-only sampler from "Are You Ready!"					

Number	Title (A Side/B Side)	Yr	VG	VG+	NM
45s					
COLUMBIA					
❑ 18-02471	Alien/Southern Exposure	1981	—	2.00	4.00
DECCA					
❑ 32928	All in Your Mind/Can't Stand It No More	1972	2.00	4.00	8.00
❑ 32948	Earnestine/Another Man's Woman	1972	2.00	4.00	8.00
❑ 33051	Back Up Against the Wall/It Must Be Done	1973	2.00	4.00	8.00
MCA					
❑ 40059	Cold Turkey, Tennessee/Conversation	1973	—	3.00	6.00
❑ 40719	All in Your Mind/Earnestine	1977	—	2.50	5.00
POLYDOR					
❑ 2001	Spooky/It's Only Music	1979	—	2.50	5.00
❑ 2039	Back Up Against the Wall/Large Time	1980	—	2.50	5.00
❑ 2079	Conversation/Indigo Passion	1980	—	2.50	5.00
❑ 2125	Putting My Faith in Love/I Ain't Much	1980	—	2.50	5.00
❑ 2142	Silver Eagle/Strictly R & R	1981	—	2.50	5.00
❑ 14248	Doraville/Who Are You Going to Run To	1974	—	2.50	5.00
❑ 14262	Angel (What in the World's Come Over Us)/Help Yourself	1975	—	2.50	5.00
❑ 14273	Get Your Head Out of Your Heart/Jesus Hearted People	1975	—	2.50	5.00
❑ 14289	Bless My Soul/Crazy	1975	—	2.50	5.00
❑ 14323	Jukin'/Beautiful Dreamer	1976	—	2.50	5.00
❑ 14339	Free Spirit/Police Police	1976	—	2.50	5.00
❑ 14373	So In to You/Everybody Gotta Go	1977	—	2.50	5.00
❑ 14397	Neon Nites/Don't Miss the Message	1977	—	2.50	5.00
❑ 14411	Dog Days/Cuban Crisis	1977	—	2.50	5.00
❑ 14459	Imaginary Lover/Silent Treatment	1978	—	2.50	5.00
❑ 14484	I'm Not Gonna Let It Bother Me Tonight/Ballad of Lois Malone	1978	—	2.50	5.00
❑ 14504	Champagne Jam/Great Escape	1978	—	2.50	5.00
❑ 14568	Do It or Die/My Song	1979	—	2.50	5.00
❑ 14582	Spooky/It's Only Music	1979	—	—	—
—Unreleased?					
Albums					
COLUMBIA					
❑ FC 37550	Quinella	1981	2.50	5.00	10.00
❑ PC 37550	Quinella	1982	2.00	4.00	8.00
—Budget-line reissue					
DECCA					
❑ DL 75265	Atlanta Rhythm Section	1972	6.25	12.50	25.00
❑ DL 75390	Back Up Against the Wall	1973	6.25	12.50	25.00
MCA					
❑ 2-4114 [(2)]	Atlanta Rhythm Section	1977	3.00	6.00	12.00
—Combines the two Decca LPs into one package					
MOBILE FIDELITY					
❑ 1-038	Champagne Jam	1981	10.00	20.00	40.00
—Audiophile vinyl					
POLYDOR					
❑ PD 6027	Third Annual Pipe Dream	1974	2.50	5.00	10.00
❑ PD 6041	Dog Days	1975	2.50	5.00	10.00
❑ PD-1-6060	Red Tape	1976	2.50	5.00	10.00
❑ PD-1-6080	A Rock and Roll Alternative	1977	[2.50]	5.00	10.00
❑ PD-1-6134	Champagne Jam	1978	2.50	5.00	10.00
❑ PD-1-6200	Underdog	1979	2.50	5.00	10.00
❑ PD-2-6236 [(2)]	Are You Ready!	1979	3.00	6.00	12.00
❑ PD-1-6285	The Boys from Doraville	1980	2.50	5.00	10.00

ATLANTICS, THE More than one group.
45s
COLUMBIA

Number	Title (A Side/B Side)	Yr	VG	VG+	NM
❑ 42877	Greensleeves/Bombera	1963	5.00	10.00	20.00
❑ 43023	War of the World/Bow Man	1964	5.00	10.00	20.00
FARO					
❑ 613	Flame of Love/Tracy	1964	3.75	7.50	15.00
—B-side by Barry White					
LINDA					
❑ 103	Boo-Hoo-Hoo/Everything Is Gonna Be All Right	1961	6.25	12.50	25.00
❑ 107	Remember the Night/Flame of Love	1962	20.00	40.00	80.00
RAMPART					
❑ 614	Let Me Call You Sweetheart/Home on the Range	1964	3.00	6.00	12.00
❑ 643	Beaver Shot/Fine, Fine, Fine	1965	2.50	5.00	10.00
❑ 647	Slopp Dance/Sonny and Cher	1965	2.50	5.00	10.00

ATOMIC ROOSTER
45s
ELEKTRA

Number	Title (A Side/B Side)	Yr	VG	VG+	NM
❑ 45727	Tomorrow Night/Play the Game	1971	—	2.50	5.00
❑ 45745	Devil's Answer/The Rock	1971	—	2.50	5.00
❑ 45766	Save Me/Never to Lose	1972	—	2.50	5.00
❑ 45800	Stand By Me/Never to Lose	1972	—	2.50	5.00
Albums					
ELEKTRA					
❑ EKS-74094	Death Walks Behind You	1971	5.00	10.00	20.00
❑ EKS-74109	In Hearing Of Atomic Rooster	1971	5.00	10.00	20.00
❑ EKS-75039	Made in England	1972	5.00	10.00	20.00
❑ EKS-75074	Atomic Rooster IV	1973	3.75	7.50	15.00

ATTILA BILLY JOEL was a member.
Albums
BACK-TRAC

Number	Title (A Side/B Side)	Yr	VG	VG+	NM
❑ P 18808	Attila	1985	2.50	5.00	10.00
EPIC					
❑ E 30030	Attila	1970	7.50	15.00	30.00

ATTITUDES
45s
DARK HORSE

Number	Title (A Side/B Side)	Yr	VG	VG+	NM
❑ 8404	Sweet Summer Music/If We Want To	1977	—	2.00	4.00
❑ 8452	Good News/In a Stranger's Arms	1977	—	2.00	4.00
❑ 10004	Ain't Love Enough/The Whole World's Crazy	1975	—	2.50	5.00

Number	Title (A Side/B Side)	Yr	VG	VG+	NM
❏ 10004 [PS]	Ain't Love Enough/The Whole World's Crazy	1975	3.00	6.00	12.00
❏ 10008	Lend a Hand/Honey Don't Leave L.A.	1976	—	2.50	5.00
❏ 10011	Sweet Summer Music/If We Want To	1976	—	2.50	5.00

Albums
DARK HORSE

❏ DH 3021	Good News	1977	2.50	5.00	10.00
❏ SP-22008	Attitudes	1976	3.00	6.00	12.00

ATTRACTIONS, THE
45s
BELL

❏ 659	Destination You/Find Me	1967	5.00	10.00	20.00
❏ 674	New Girl in the Neighborhood/That Girl Is Mine	1967	5.00	10.00	20.00
❏ 690	Why Shouldn't a Man Cry/Some of Your Time	1967	5.00	10.00	20.00

JUNE BUG

❏ 697/8	You Don't Know, Boy/Think Back	1966	6.25	12.50	25.00

ATWELL, WINIFRED
45s
COLUMBIA

❏ 43472	Snow Bells/Flea Circus	1965	—	3.00	6.00

ATWOOD THE ELECTRIC ICEMAN Actually the SIR DOUGLAS QUINTET with Atwood Allen.
45s
UNI

❏ 55216	Bossier City/Michoacan	1970	—	3.00	6.00

AUDIENCE
45s
ELEKTRA

❏ 45732	Indian Summer/It Brings a Tear	1971	—	2.50	5.00
❏ 45756	I Put a Spell on You/Nancy	1971	—	2.50	5.00
❏ 45788	Stand By the Door/Seven Sore Bruises	1972	—	2.50	5.00

Albums
ELEKTRA

❏ EKS-74100	House on the Hill	1971	3.00	6.00	12.00
❏ EKS-75026	Lunch	1972	3.00	6.00	12.00

AUDREY
45s
PLUS

❏ 104	Dear Elvis/Dear Elvis (Part 2)	1956	20.00	40.00	80.00

—Black vinyl; a red vinyl pressing has been reported but is unconfirmed

AUGER, BRIAN, TRINITY Includes "Brian Auger's Oblivion Express."
45s
ATCO

❏ 6593	This Wheel's On Fire/A Kind of Love-In	1968	2.00	4.00	8.00
—With Julie Driscoll					
❏ 6611	Black Cat/In and Out	1968	2.00	4.00	8.00
❏ 6629	Shadows of You/Road to Cairo	1968	2.00	4.00	8.00
—With Julie Driscoll					
❏ 6656	A Day in the Life/Bumpin' On Sunset	1969	2.00	4.00	8.00
❏ 6685	Save the Country/Light My Fire	1969	2.00	4.00	8.00
❏ 6685	Save the Country/The Flesh Failures (Let the Sun Shine In)	1969	2.00	4.00	8.00
❏ 6685 [DJ]	Save the Country (long/short versions)	1969	3.00	6.00	12.00

RCA VICTOR

❏ 74-0381	I Wanna Take You Higher/Listen Here	1970	—	3.00	6.00
❏ 74-0579	Maria's Wedding/Trouble	1971	—	2.50	5.00
—Group becomes "Oblivion Express"					
❏ 74-0735	Second Wind/Freedom Jazz Dance	1972	—	2.50	5.00
❏ APBO-0085	Happiness Is Just Around the Bend/Inner City Blues	1973	—	2.50	5.00
❏ APBO-0282	Straight Ahead/Beginning Again	1974	—	2.50	5.00

Albums
ATCO

❏ 33-258 [M]	Open	1968	5.00	10.00	20.00
—White label promo; no stock copies were issued in mono					
❏ SD 33-258 [S]	Open	1968	3.00	6.00	12.00
❏ SD 33-273	Definitely What!	1969	3.00	6.00	12.00
❏ SD 2-701 [(2)]	Streetnoise	1969	5.00	10.00	20.00

CAPITOL

❏ DT-136 [R]	Jools & Brian	1969	3.00	6.00	12.00
—American issue of pre-Atco material					

HEADFIRST

❏ 9702	Search Party	1981	3.75	7.50	15.00

POLYDOR

❏ PD-1-6505	Genesis	1975	3.00	6.00	12.00

RCA VICTOR

❏ AFL1-0140	Closer To It	197?	2.00	4.00	8.00
—Reissue					
❏ APL1-0140	Closer To It	1973	2.50	5.00	10.00
❏ AFL1-0454	Straight Ahead	197?	2.00	4.00	8.00
—Reissue					
❏ CPL1-0454	Straight Ahead	1974	2.50	5.00	10.00
❏ CPL1-0645	Live Oblivion	1974	2.50	5.00	10.00
❏ APL1-1210	Reinforcements	1975	2.50	5.00	10.00
❏ CPL2-1230 [(2)]	Live Oblivion, Vol. 2	1976	3.75	7.50	15.00
❏ AFL1-2249	The Best of Brian Auger	1977	2.50	5.00	10.00
❏ ANL1-2481	Live Oblivion	1977	2.00	4.00	8.00
—Reissue					
❏ LSP-4372	Befour	1970	2.50	5.00	10.00
❏ AFL1-4462	Brian Auger's Oblivion Express	197?	2.00	4.00	8.00
—Reissue					
❏ LSP-4462	Brian Auger's Oblivion Express	1971	2.50	5.00	10.00
—Starting here, group is "Oblivion Express"					
❏ LSP-4540	A Better Land	1971	2.50	5.00	10.00
❏ AFL1-4703	Second Wind	197?	2.00	4.00	8.00
—Reissue					
❏ LSP-4703	Second Wind	1972	2.50	5.00	10.00

SPRINGBOARD

❏ SPB-4044	Brian Auger	1973	2.00	4.00	8.00
—Reissue of early material					

WARNER BROS.

❏ BS 2981	Happiness Heartaches	1977	2.50	5.00	10.00
❏ BSK 3153	Encore	1978	2.50	5.00	10.00

AUGUST, JAN
45s
MERCURY

❏ 1245-X45	The Christmas Song/White Christmas	195?	3.00	6.00	12.00
❏ 5106-X45	Intermezzo/Oye Negra	1950	3.75	7.50	15.00
—78 originally issued in 1948					
❏ 5395-X45	Besame Mucho/Jan's Jam	1950	3.00	6.00	12.00
—Note: Earlier 5000-series 45s by Jan August, other than those listed, may exist					
❏ 5399-X45	Bewitched/Blue Prelude	1950	3.00	6.00	12.00
—With Jerry Murad's Harmonicats					
❏ 5400-X45	The Old Piano Roll Blues/Spain	1950	3.00	6.00	12.00
❏ 5423-X45	A Day at the Seashore/Egyptian Ella	1950	3.00	6.00	12.00
❏ 5470-X45	Clair de Lune/Scheherazade	1950	3.00	6.00	12.00
❏ 5478-X45	You've Got Me Crying Again/My Silent Love	1950	3.00	6.00	12.00
❏ 5483-X45	Deep Night/Where Do I Go from Here	1950	3.00	6.00	12.00
❏ 5497-X45	Little Gray Home/Down by the Old Mill Stream/Meet Me Tonight in Dreamland	1950	3.00	6.00	12.00
❏ 5556-X45	Babalu/Tango of Roses	1950	3.00	6.00	12.00
❏ 5589-X45	Perfidia/Jan's Cucaracha	1951	3.00	6.00	12.00
❏ 5654-X45	Dizzy Fingers/Two Lonely Hearts	1951	3.00	6.00	12.00
❏ 5723-X45	San Antonio Rose/Oriental Blues	1951	3.00	6.00	12.00
❏ 5781-X45	Ma Belle/Hot Lips	1952	3.00	6.00	12.00
❏ 5859-X45	Delicado/Just One of Those Things	1952	3.00	6.00	12.00
❏ 5900-X45	Meet Mister Callaghan/Wish You Were Here	1952	3.00	6.00	12.00
—With Jerry Murad's Harmonicats					
❏ 30000-X45	Malaguena/Miserlou	1957	2.00	4.00	8.00
—"Celebrity Series" reissue					
❏ 30001-X45	Where or When/Jalousie	1957	2.00	4.00	8.00
—"Celebrity Series" reissue					
❏ 30002-X45	Scheherazade/Clair de Lune	1957	2.00	4.00	8.00
—"Celebrity Series" reissue					
❏ 30003-X45	Intermezzo/Oye Negra	1957	2.00	4.00	8.00
❏ 70056-X45	Ti-Pi-Tin/Finesse	1953	2.50	5.00	10.00
❏ 70078-X45	Song of Lola/Habanera	1953	2.50	5.00	10.00
❏ 70144-X45	Rhumba Bells/Jamboree	1953	2.50	5.00	10.00
❏ 70206-X45	Night and Day/Dancing in the Dark	1953	2.50	5.00	10.00
❏ 70228-X45	Cow Cow Blues/Martha	1953	2.50	5.00	10.00
❏ 70250-X45	Petite Ballerina/Prince Igor	1953	2.50	5.00	10.00
❏ 70320-X45	Esplanada/Silhouettes	1954	2.50	5.00	10.00
❏ 70357-X45	Circle in the Square/Nobody Wants to Go Home	1954	2.50	5.00	10.00
❏ 70498-X45	Mambo Is In the Air/The Love Nest	1954	2.50	5.00	10.00
❏ 70541-X45	The Crazy Julius (Part 1)/(Part 2)	1955	2.50	5.00	10.00
❏ 70608-X45	Naughty Ghost/Chiqui Chiqui	1955	2.50	5.00	10.00
❏ 70711-X45	Bach Mambo/Minuet in Mambo	1955	2.50	5.00	10.00
❏ 70726-X45	I Never Knew/Skater's Waltz	1955	2.50	5.00	10.00
❏ 70875-X45	Dominique/Lovers and Lollipops	1956	2.00	4.00	8.00
❏ 71012-X45	Desert Sunrise/Nickelodeon Tango	1956	2.00	4.00	8.00
❏ 71211-X45	The Twilight Theme/Somehow You Know	1957	2.00	4.00	8.00
❏ 71964	Canadian Capers/The Volga Boat Man	1962	—	3.50	7.00

7-Inch Extended Plays
MERCURY

❏ EP-1-3005	(contents unknown)	195?	2.00	4.00	8.00
❏ EP-1-3005 [PS]	Piano Poetry	195?	2.00	4.00	8.00
❏ EP-1-3017	Misirlou/Oye Negra//Malaguena/Jalousie	195?	2.00	4.00	8.00
❏ EP-1-3017 [PS]	Piano Rhythm	195?	2.00	4.00	8.00
❏ EP-1-3022	Dancing in the Dark/September Song//Nola/Night and Day	195?	2.00	4.00	8.00
❏ EP-1-3022 [PS]	More Favorites	195?	2.00	4.00	8.00
❏ EP-1-3027	(contents unknown)	195?	2.00	4.00	8.00
❏ EP-1-3027 [PS]	Exotic Piano Rhythms	195?	2.00	4.00	8.00
❏ EP-1-3064	Dark Eyes/Intermezzo//Zigeuner/Hungarian Rhapsody	195?	2.00	4.00	8.00
❏ EP-1-3064 [PS]	Dark Eyes	195?	2.00	4.00	8.00

Albums
MERCURY

❏ MG 20072 [M]	Jan August Plays Songs to Remember	1955	6.25	12.50	25.00
❏ MG 20078 [M]	Music for the Quiet Hour	1955	6.25	12.50	25.00
❏ MG 20147 [M]	Piano Roll Blues	1955	6.25	12.50	25.00
❏ MG 20272 [M]	Cocktails and Conversation	195?	5.00	10.00	20.00
❏ MG 20273 [M]	Keyboard Waltzes	195?	5.00	10.00	20.00
❏ MG 20274 [M]	Latin Rhythms	195?	5.00	10.00	20.00
❏ MG 20408 [M]	Cha Cha Charm	1959	3.75	7.50	15.00
❏ MG 20513 [M]	Jan August Plays Great Piano Hits	195?	3.75	7.50	15.00
❏ MG 20618 [M]	Accent!	1961	3.75	7.50	15.00
❏ MG 20659 [M]	Jan August Styles the Great Pop Piano Classics	196?	3.75	7.50	15.00
❏ MG 20667 [M]	Jan August Styles the Great International Hits	196?	3.75	7.50	15.00
❏ MG 20744 [M]	Jan August Plays a Collection of 27 Popular Classical Melodies	196?	3.75	7.50	15.00
❏ MG 25087 [10]	Piano Favorites	195?	7.50	15.00	30.00
❏ MG 25136 [10]	Piano Poetry	195?	7.50	15.00	30.00
❏ SR 60082 [S]	Cha Cha Charm	1959	5.00	10.00	20.00
❏ SR 60189 [S]	Jan August Plays Great Piano Hits	195?	5.00	10.00	20.00
❏ SR 60618 [S]	Accent!	1961	5.00	10.00	20.00
❏ SR 60659 [S]	Jan August Styles the Great Pop Piano Classics	196?	5.00	10.00	20.00
❏ SR 60667 [S]	Jan August Styles the Great International Hits	196?	5.00	10.00	20.00
❏ SR 60744 [S]	Jan August Plays a Collection of 27 Popular Classical Melodies	196?	5.00	10.00	20.00

WING

❏ MGW 12129 [M]	Music for the Quiet Hour	196?	3.00	6.00	12.00
❏ MGW 12175 [M]	Christmas Favorites	196?	3.00	6.00	12.00
❏ MGW 12254 [M]	The Piano Wizardry of Jan August	196?	3.00	6.00	12.00
❏ SRW 16129 [R]	Music for the Quiet Hour	196?	2.50	5.00	10.00
❏ SRW 16254 [R]	The Piano Wizardry of Jan August	196?	2.50	5.00	10.00

Number	Title (A Side/B Side)	Yr	VG	VG+	NM
AUGUST AND DENEEN					
45s					
ABC					
❏ 11082	We Go Together/Can't Get You Out of My Head	1968	15.00	30.00	60.00
AUM					
Albums					
FILLMORE					
❏ Z 30002	Resurrection	1970	7.50	15.00	30.00
SIRE					
❏ SES-97007	Bluesvibes	1969	10.00	20.00	40.00
AUSTIN, BILL					
45s					
HIT					
❏ 05	Shout/Dr. Feelgood	1962	2.00	4.00	8.00
—B-side by Jim Porter					
❏ 06	Dear One/If a Woman Answers	1962	2.00	4.00	8.00
❏ 11	Shout! Shout! (Knock Yourself Out)/ Hide 'Nor Hair	1962	2.00	4.00	8.00
—B-side by Herbert Hunter					
❏ 82	You Can Never Stop Me Loving You/Blue Velvet	1963	2.00	4.00	8.00
—B-side by Fred York					
❏ 105	You Don't Know Me/Talking About My Baby	1964	2.00	4.00	8.00
—B-side by Harvey Frolic					
AUSTIN, DONALD					
45s					
EASTBOUND					
❏ 603	Crazy Legs/Nan Zee	1973	2.00	4.00	8.00
❏ 608	Sex Plot/Can't Understand the Strain	1973	2.00	4.00	8.00
Albums					
EASTBOUND					
❏ EB-9005	Crazy Legs	1973	7.50	15.00	30.00
AUSTIN, GENE					
45s					
FRATERNITY					
❏ 779	My Blue Heaven/Lonesome Road	1957	2.50	5.00	10.00
RCA VICTOR					
❏ 47-6880	Too Late/That's Love	1957	3.00	6.00	12.00
❏ 47-6880 [PS]	Too Late/That's Love	1957	5.00	10.00	20.00
❏ 47-6969	I Could Write a Book/A Porter's Love Song to a Chambermaid	1957	2.50	5.00	10.00
❏ 47-7117	I'm Not the Braggin' Kind/Wonder	1957	2.50	5.00	10.00
7-Inch Extended Plays					
RCA VICTOR					
❏ EPA-4057	(contents unknown)	1957	3.00	6.00	12.00
❏ EPA-4057 [PS]	The Gene Austin Story	1957	3.00	6.00	12.00
Albums					
DECCA					
❏ DL 8433 [M]	My Blue Heaven	1957	10.00	20.00	40.00
DOT					
❏ DLP 3300 [M]	Great Hits	1960	5.00	10.00	20.00
❏ DLP 25300 [S]	Great Hits	1960	6.25	12.50	25.00
FRATERNITY					
❏ F-1006 [M]	Gene Austin and His Lonesome Road	1957	5.00	10.00	20.00
RCA VICTOR					
❏ LPM-1549 [M]	Restless Heart	1957	10.00	20.00	40.00
❏ LPM-2490 [M]	My Blue Heaven	1961	6.25	12.50	25.00
❏ LPM-3200 [10]	My Blue Heaven	1953	15.00	30.00	60.00
❏ VPM-6065 [(2)]	This Is Gene Austin	1972	5.00	10.00	20.00
AUSTIN, PATTI					
12-Inch Singles					
CTI					
❏ OJL-4	Love Me by Name (same om both sides?)	1979	3.75	7.50	15.00
GRP					
❏ 4010	Through the Test of Time (4 versions)	1990	2.00	4.00	8.00
❏ 4013	Soldier Boy (3 versions)	1991	2.00	4.00	8.00
❏ 4019	Reach (7:41) (3:48) (9:48)	1992	—	3.00	6.00
QWEST					
❏ PRO-A-2076 [DJ]	It's Gonna Be Special (Dance Remix 6:30)/ (Single Edit 4:14)	1984	2.00	4.00	8.00
❏ PRO-A-2144 [DJ]	Rhythm of the Street (Edit) (LP Version)	1984	—	3.00	6.00
❏ PRO-A-2339 [DJ]	The Heat of Heat (Edit) (LP Version)	1986	—	3.00	6.00
❏ PRO-A-2516 [DJ]	Gettin' Away with Murder (Edit) (LP Version)	1986	2.50	5.00	10.00
❏ PRO-A-3271 [DJ]	Smoke Gets in Your Eyes (same on both sides?)	1988	2.50	5.00	10.00
❏ 20222	Rhythm of the Street (6:09)/ It's Gonna Be Special (6:30)	1984	2.00	4.00	8.00
❏ 20235	Shoot the Moon/Rhythm of the Street	1984	2.00	4.00	8.00
❏ 20361	Honey for the Bees (2 versions)Hot! In the Flames of Love	1985	2.00	4.00	8.00
❏ 20462	The Heat of Heat (4 versions)	1986	—	3.00	6.00
45s					
ABC					
❏ 11104	Music to My Heart/ Love 'Em and Leave 'Em Kind of Love	1968	3.75	7.50	15.00
COLUMBIA					
❏ 45337	Are We Ready for Love/Now That I Know What Loneliness Is	1971	—	2.50	5.00
❏ 45410	Black California/All Good Gifts-Day by Day	1971	—	2.50	5.00
❏ 45499	God Only Knows/Can't Forget the One I Love	1971	—	2.50	5.00
❏ 45592	Day by Day/Didn't Say a Word	1972	—	2.50	5.00
❏ 45785	Come to Him/Turn On the Music	1973	—	2.50	5.00
❏ 45906	Being with You/Take a Closer Look	1973	—	2.50	5.00
CORAL					
❏ 62455	He's Good Enough for Me/Earl	1965	5.00	10.00	20.00
❏ 62471	I Wanna Be Loved/A Most Unusual Boy	1965	5.00	10.00	20.00
❏ 62478	Someone's Gonna Cry/ You'd Better Know What You're Getting	1966	25.00	50.00	100.00
❏ 62491	Take Your Time/Take Away the Pain Stain	1966	5.00	10.00	20.00
❏ 62500	Leave a Little Love/ My Lovelight Ain't Gonna Shine	1966	5.00	10.00	20.00
❏ 62511	Got to Check You Out/ What a Difference a Day Makes	1967	5.00	10.00	20.00
❏ 62518	Only All the Time/Oh How I Need You Joe	1967	5.00	10.00	20.00
❏ 62541	I'll Keep Loving You/ You're Too Much a Part of Me	1967	5.00	10.00	20.00
❏ 62548	(I've Given) All My Love/ Why Can't We Try It Again	1968	5.00	10.00	20.00
CTI					
❏ 7	In My Life (Part 1)/In My Life (Part 2)	1973	—	2.50	5.00
—With Jerry Butler					
❏ 33	Say You Love Me/In My Life	1976	—	2.00	4.00
❏ 41	We're in Love/Golden Oldies	1977	—	2.00	4.00
❏ 51	Love Me by Name/You Fooled Me	1978	—	2.00	4.00
❏ 59	What's at the End of the Rainbow/In My Life	1978	—	2.00	4.00
❏ 9600	Body Language/People in Love	1980	—	2.00	4.00
❏ 9601	I Want You Tonight/Love Me Again	1980	—	2.00	4.00
QWEST					
❏ 27718	Smoke Gets In Your Eyes/ How Long Has This Been Goin' On?	1988	—	—	3.00
❏ 27718 [PS]	Smoke Gets In Your Eyes/ How Long Has This Been Goin' On?	1988	—	—	3.00
❏ 28573	Only a Breath Away/ Summer Is the Coldest Time of Year	1986	—	—	3.00
❏ 28659	Gettin' Away with Murder/ Anything Can Happen Here	1986	—	—	3.00
❏ 28788	The Heat of Heat/Hot in the Flames of Love	1986	—	—	3.00
❏ 28935	Honey for the Bees/Hot in the Flames of Love	1985	—	—	3.00
❏ 29136	All Behind Us Now/Fine Fine Fella (Got to Have You)	1984	—	2.00	4.00
❏ 29234	Shoot the Moon/Change Your Attitude	1984	—	2.00	4.00
❏ 29305	Rhythm of the Street/Solero	1984	—	2.00	4.00
❏ 29373	It's Gonna Be Special/Solero	1984	—	2.00	4.00
❏ 29618	How Do You Keep the Music Playing/same (Long Version)	1983	—	2.00	4.00
❏ 29727	Every Home Should Have One/Solero	1983	—	2.00	4.00
❏ 49754	Do You Love Me/Solero	1981	—	2.00	4.00
❏ 49854	Every Home Should Have One/Solero	1981	—	2.50	5.00
❏ 50036	Baby, Come to Me/Solero	1982	—	2.00	4.00
—With James Ingram					
UNITED ARTISTS					
❏ 50520	The Family Tree/Magical Boy	1969	2.00	4.00	8.00
❏ 50588	I Will Wait for You/Big Mouth	1969	2.00	4.00	8.00
❏ 50640	Your Love Made a Difference in Me/ It's Easier to Laugh Than Cry	1970	2.00	4.00	8.00
Albums					
CTI					
❏ 5001	End of a Rainbow	1976	2.50	5.00	10.00
❏ 5006	Havana Candy	1977	2.50	5.00	10.00
❏ 7086	Live at the Bottom Line	1979	2.50	5.00	10.00
❏ JZ 36503	Body Language	1980	2.50	5.00	10.00
❏ PZ 36503	Body Language	198?	2.00	4.00	8.00
—Budget-line reissue					
GRP					
❏ GR-9603	Love Is Gonna Getcha	1990	2.50	5.00	10.00
QWEST					
❏ QWS 3591	Every Home Should Have One	1981	2.00	4.00	8.00
❏ 23974	Patti Austin	1984	2.00	4.00	8.00
❏ 25276	Gettin' Away with Murder	1985	2.00	4.00	8.00
❏ 25698	The Real Me	1988	2.00	4.00	8.00
AUSTIN, SIL					
45s					
JERRI					
❏ 104	Disco Lady/Disco Music	197?	—	3.00	6.00
JUBILEE					
❏ 5153	Stagecoach/Volleyball	1954	3.75	7.50	15.00
❏ 5162	Shuffle Board/Sil's Loose	1954	3.75	7.50	15.00
❏ 5178	Crossfire (Part 1)/(Part 2)	1955	3.75	7.50	15.00
MERCURY					
❏ 30080-X45	Danny Boy/The Hungry Eye	196?	2.00	4.00	8.00
—"Celebrity Series" reissue					
❏ 70963-X45	Slow Walk/Wildwood	1956	3.75	7.50	15.00
❏ 71027-X45	Birthday Party/The Last Time	1957	3.75	7.50	15.00
❏ 71077-X45	Seven Days in Barcelona/Pretend	1957	3.75	7.50	15.00
❏ 71115-X45	He's a Real Gone Guy/Dues Day	1957	3.75	7.50	15.00
❏ 71196-X45	Fall Out/Green Blazer	1957	3.75	7.50	15.00
❏ 71305-X45	Hey Eula/Rainstorm	1958	3.00	6.00	12.00
❏ 71361-X45	Riff Raff/The Chamber	1958	3.00	6.00	12.00
❏ 71442-X45	Danny Boy/Hungry Eye	1959	3.00	6.00	12.00
❏ 71496-X45	Summertime/Ruby	1959	3.00	6.00	12.00
❏ 71543-X45	September Song/Gone Again	1959	3.00	6.00	12.00
❏ 71578	One More Time/Satisfied, Satisfied, Satisfied	1960	2.50	5.00	10.00
❏ 71627	Say Lou/Girl with a Foxy Frame	1960	2.50	5.00	10.00
❏ 71693	Why Not/When My Dreamboat Comes Home	1960	2.50	5.00	10.00
❏ 71808	The Continental Stroll (Part 1)/(Part 2)	1961	2.50	5.00	10.00
❏ 71977	Golden Twist/Tippin' In	1962	2.50	5.00	10.00
❏ 72238	Back in Your Own Back Yard/Nature Boy	1964	2.50	5.00	10.00
SEW CITY					
❏ 102	Big Boss Man/Sil's Concerto	196?	—	3.50	7.00
SSS INTERNATIONAL					
❏ 747	Honey/Lover's Holiday	1968	—	3.00	6.00
❏ 792	Massachusetts/Tara's Theme	1970	—	3.00	6.00
WING					
❏ 90075-X45	Titanic/Sil's Groove	1956	3.75	7.50	15.00
Albums					
MERCURY					
❏ MG-20237 [M]	Slow Walk Rock	1957	17.50	35.00	70.00
❏ MG-20320 [M]	Everything's Shakin'	1958	17.50	35.00	70.00

Number	Title (A Side/B Side)	Yr	VG	VG+	NM
❏ MG-20424 [M]	Sil Austin Plays Pretty for the People	1959	10.00	20.00	40.00
❏ MG-20576 [M]	Soft, Plaintive and Moody	1960	10.00	20.00	40.00
❏ MG-20663 [M]	Golden Saxophone Hits	1961	6.25	12.50	25.00
❏ MG-20755 [M]	Folk Songs	1963	3.75	7.50	15.00
❏ MG-20925 [M]	Sil Austin Plays Pretty Melodies of the World	1964	5.00	10.00	20.00
❏ MG-21126 [M]	Sil Austin Plays Pretty for the People Again	1967	5.00	10.00	20.00
❏ SR-60096 [S]	Sil Austin Plays Pretty for the People	1959	15.00	30.00	60.00
—Black label					
❏ SR-60096 [S]	Sil Austin Plays Pretty for the People	1965	5.00	10.00	20.00
—Red label, white "MERCURY" at top					
❏ SR-60096 [S]	Sil Austin Plays Pretty for the People	1974	2.50	5.00	10.00
—"Chicago styline" label					
❏ SR-60236 [S]	Soft, Plaintive and Moody	1960	15.00	30.00	60.00
❏ SR-60663 [S]	Golden Saxophone Hits	1961	7.50	15.00	30.00
❏ SR-60755 [S]	Folk Songs	1963	5.00	10.00	20.00
❏ SR-61126 [S]	Sil Austin Plays Pretty for the People Again	1967	5.00	10.00	20.00
SSS INTERNATIONAL					
❏ 4	Honey Sax	1969	3.75	7.50	15.00
❏ 8	Soft Soul with Strings	1970	3.75	7.50	15.00
❏ 14	Sil and Silver Screen	1971	3.75	7.50	15.00
❏ 23	Songs of Gold	1971	3.75	7.50	15.00
WING					
❏ SRW-16227 [S]	Everything's Shakin'	196?	3.75	7.50	15.00
❏ SRW-16369 [S]	Sil Austin Again Plays Pretty for the People	196?	3.75	7.50	15.00

AUTOSALVAGE

45s

RCA VICTOR

Number	Title (A Side/B Side)	Yr	VG	VG+	NM
❏ 47-9506	Parahighway/Rampant Generalities	1968	3.00	6.00	12.00

Albums

RCA VICTOR

Number	Title (A Side/B Side)	Yr	VG	VG+	NM
❏ LPM-3940 [M]	Autosalvage	1968	10.00	20.00	40.00
❏ LSP-3940 [S]	Autosalvage	1968	10.00	20.00	40.00

AUTRY, GENE

45s

CHALLENGE

Number	Title (A Side/B Side)	Yr	VG	VG+	NM
❏ 1009	No Back Door to Heaven/You're the Only Good Thing	1957	3.00	6.00	12.00
❏ 1010	Rudolph, the Red-Nosed Reindeer/ Here Come Santa Claus	1957	3.00	6.00	12.00
—Re-recordings of originals on Columbia					
❏ 59030	Rudolph, the Red-Nosed Reindeer/ Here Come Santa Claus	1958	3.00	6.00	12.00
❏ 59030 [PS]	Rudolph, the Red-Nosed Reindeer/ Here Come Santa Claus	1958	7.50	15.00	30.00
COLUMBIA					
❏ 4-56	Rudolph, the Red-Nosed Reindeer/ If It Doesn't Snow on Christmas	1951	5.00	10.00	20.00
—Yellow label, red print; second number on label is 90049					
❏ 4-56 [PS]	Rudolph, the Red-Nosed Reindeer/If It Doesn't Snow on Christmas	1951	6.25	12.50	25.00
—Sleeve was manufactured with a hole in the middle					
❏ 4-68	Peter Cottontail/Funny Little Bunny	1950	5.00	10.00	20.00
—Yellow label, red print; second number on label is 90063					
❏ 4-68 [PS]	Peter Cottontail/Funny Little Bunny	1950	6.25	12.50	25.00
—Sleeve was manufactured with a hole in the middle					
❏ 4-75	Frosty the Snow Man/ When Santa Claus Gets Your Letter	1951	5.00	10.00	20.00
—Yellow label, red print; second number on label is 90072					
❏ 4-75 [PS]	Frosty the Snow Man/ When Santa Claus Gets Your Letter	1951	6.25	12.50	25.00
—Sleeve was manufactured with a hole in the middle					
❏ 4-84	Here Comes Santa Claus/ He's a Chubby Little Fellow	1951	5.00	10.00	20.00
—Yellow label, red print; second number on label is 90088					
❏ 4-84 [PS]	Here Comes Santa Claus/ He's a Chubby Little Fellow	1951	6.25	12.50	25.00
—Sleeve was manufactured with a hole in the middle					
❏ 4-103	Sonny the Bunny/Bunny Round-Up	1952	5.00	10.00	20.00
—Yellow label, red print; second number on label is 90110					
❏ 4-121	Thirty-Two Feet — Eight Little Tails/(Hedrock, Coco and Joe) The Three Little Dwarfs	1952	5.00	10.00	20.00
—Yellow label, red print; second number on label is 90135					
❏ 4-121 [PS]	Thirty-Two Feet — Eight Little Tails/(Hedrock, Coco and Joe) The Three Little Dwarfs	1952	6.25	12.50	25.00
—Sleeve was manufactured with a hole in the middle					
❏ 4-122	Poppy the Puppy/He'll Be Coming Down the Chimney (Like He Always Did Before)	1952	5.00	10.00	20.00
—Yellow label, red print; second number on label is 90136					
❏ 4-122 [PS]	Poppy the Puppy/He'll Be Coming Down the Chimney (Like He Always Did Before)	1952	6.25	12.50	25.00
—Sleeve was manufactured with a hole in the middle					
❏ 2-127	Bible on the Table/I Lost My Little Darlin'	1949	12.50	25.00	50.00
—Microgroove 33 1/3 rpm 7-inch single, small hole					
❏ 4-148	Smokey the Bear/Back in the Saddle Again	1953	3.75	7.50	15.00
—Yellow label, red print; second number on label is 90168					
❏ 4-148 [PS]	Smokey the Bear/Back in the Saddle Again	1953	5.00	10.00	20.00
—All sleeves have a hole in the middle					
❏ 4-150	Merry Texas Christmas, You All!/The Night Before Christmas (In Texas, That Is)	1953	3.75	7.50	15.00
—Yellow label, red print; second number on label is 90172					
❏ 4-150 [PS]	Merry Texas Christmas, You All!/The Night Before Christmas (In Texas, That Is)	1953	5.00	10.00	20.00
—Sleeve was manufactured with a hole in the middle					
❏ 4-176	Santa Claus Is Comin' to Town/Up on the Housetop (Ho! Ho! Ho!)	1954	3.75	7.50	15.00
—Yellow label, red print					
❏ 4-176 [PS]	Santa Claus Is Comin' to Town/Up on the Housetop (Ho! Ho! Ho!)	1954	5.00	10.00	20.00
❏ 2-210 (?)	Ellie Mae/Sun Flower	1949	10.00	20.00	40.00
—Microgroove 33 1/3 rpm single					

Number	Title (A Side/B Side)	Yr	VG	VG+	NM
❏ 2-258	My Empty Heart/ I Wish I Had Stayed Over Yonder	1949	10.00	20.00	40.00
—Microgroove 33 1/3 rpm single					
❏ 4-262	Round, Round the Christmas Tree/ Merry Christmas Waltz	1955	3.75	7.50	15.00
—Yellow label, red print					
❏ 4-262 [PS]	Round, Round the Christmas Tree/ Merry Christmas Waltz	1955	5.00	10.00	20.00
❏ 4-293	Everyone's a Child at Christmas/ You Can See Old Santa Claus	1956	3.75	7.50	15.00
—Yellow label, red print					
❏ 4-293 [PS]	Everyone's a Child at Christmas/ You Can See Old Santa Claus	1956	5.00	10.00	20.00
❏ 2-336	Santa, Santa, Santa/He's a Chubby Little Fellow	1949	10.00	20.00	40.00
—Microgroove 33 1/3 rpm single					
❏ 2-350	When the Silver Colorado Turns to Gold/ Whirlwinds	1949	10.00	20.00	40.00
—Microgroove 33 1/3 rpm single					
❏ 2-370 (?)	Riders in the Sky/Cowboy Trademarks	1949	10.00	20.00	40.00
—Microgroove 33 1/3 rpm single					
❏ 1-375	Rudolph, the Red-Nosed Reindeer/If It Doesn't Snow on Christmas	1949	10.00	20.00	40.00
—Microgroove 33 1/3 rpm single					
❏ 6-375	Rudolph, the Red-Nosed Reindeer/ If It Doesn't Snow on Christmas	1950	6.25	12.50	25.00
—Reissue on 45 of a single originally on 33 1/3 Microgroove single					
❏ 2-421	Mule Train/A Cowboy's Serenade	1950	10.00	20.00	40.00
—Microgroove 33 1/3 rpm single					
❏ 2-484	Poison Ivy/A New Star Is Shining	1950	10.00	20.00	40.00
—Microgroove 33 1/3 rpm single					
❏ 2-550 (?)	Take Me Back to My Boots and Saddle/Dust	1950	10.00	20.00	40.00
—Microgroove 33 1/3 rpm single					
❏ 1-575	Peter Cottontail/Funny Little Bunny	1950	10.00	20.00	40.00
—Microgroove 33 1/3 rpm single					
❏ 1-630 (?)	Roses/The Roses I Picked for Our Wedding	1950	10.00	20.00	40.00
—Microgroove 33 1/3 rpm single					
❏ 1-741 (?)	Blue Canadian Rockies/Onteora	1950	10.00	20.00	40.00
—Microgroove 33 1/3 rpm single					
❏ 6-741 (?)	Blue Canadian Rockies/Onteora	1950	6.25	12.50	25.00
❏ 1-742	Frosty the Snow Man/ When Santa Claus Gets Your Letter	1950	10.00	20.00	40.00
—Microgroove 33 1/3 rpm single					
❏ 6-742	Frosty the Snow Man/ When Santa Claus Gets Your Letter	1950	5.00	10.00	20.00
❏ 1-767	Goodnight Irene/Texans Never Cry	1950	10.00	20.00	40.00
—Microgroove 33 1/3 rpm single					
❏ 6-767	Goodnight Irene/Texans Never Cry	1950	6.25	12.50	25.00
❏ 1-810 (?)	Little Johnny Pilgrim/Guffy the Goofy Gobbler	1950	10.00	20.00	40.00
—Microgroove 33 1/3 rpm single					
❏ 6-810 (?)	Little Johnny Pilgrim/Guffy the Goofy Gobbler	1950	6.25	12.50	25.00
❏ 2-901	Rose Colored Memories/Let Me Cry on Your Shoulder	1950	10.00	20.00	40.00
—Microgroove 33 1/3 rpm 7-inch single, small hole					
❏ 6-901	Rose Colored Memories/ Let Me Cry on Your Shoulder	1950	7.50	15.00	30.00
—Original 45 issue of 20763					
❏ 38-06189	The Statue in the Bay/God Bless America	1986	—	2.00	4.00
❏ 4-20047	You Are My Sunshine/ It Makes No Difference Now	1951	6.25	12.50	25.00
—Reissue of 78 rpm single from 1948, which itself was a reissue					
❏ 4-20084	Back in the Saddle Again/Tumbling Tumbleweeds	1951	6.25	12.50	25.00
—Reissue of 78 rpm single from 1948, which itself was a reissue					
❏ 4-20377	Here Comes Santa Claus (Down Santa Claus Lane)/An Old-Fashioned Tree	1950	5.00	10.00	20.00
—Reissue on 45 of a single originally on 78					
❏ 20709	I Love You Because/The Last Straw	1950	6.25	12.50	25.00
❏ 20727	That Silver Haired Daddy of Mine/ Mississippi Valley Blues	1950	6.25	12.50	25.00
—Reissue of 78 rpm material					
❏ 20763	Rose Colored Memories/ Let Me Cry on Your Shoulder	1950	6.25	12.50	25.00
❏ 20775	The Statue in the Bay/ The Place Where I Worship	1951	5.00	10.00	20.00
❏ 20814	At Mail Call Today/I'll Be Back	1951	5.00	10.00	20.00
—Reissue of Columbia 37041 (78)					
❏ 20865	When It's Springtime in the Rockies/I Don't Want to Set the World on Fire	1951	5.00	10.00	20.00
❏ 20899	Heartsick Soldier on Heartbreak Ridge/I'm Learning to Live	1952	3.75	7.50	15.00
❏ 20904	Am I a Pastime/I Was Just Walking Out the Door	1952	3.75	7.50	15.00
❏ 20929	Diesel Smoke, Dangerous Curves/Stop Your Gambling	1952	3.75	7.50	15.00
❏ 21035	I've Lived a Lifetime for You/Story Book of Love	1952	3.75	7.50	15.00
❏ 21144	Love Is So Misleadin'/Don't Send Your Love	1953	3.75	7.50	15.00
❏ 21207	Bimbo/Roly Poly	1954	3.75	7.50	15.00
❏ 21229	Angels in the Sky/A Voice in the Choir	1954	3.75	7.50	15.00
❏ 21252	Closing the Book/My Lazy Day	1954	3.75	7.50	15.00
❏ 21269	20-20 Vision/You're the Only Good Thing	1954	3.75	7.50	15.00
❏ 21280	I'm a Fool to Care/A Broken Promise Means a Broken Heart	1954	3.75	7.50	15.00
❏ 21304	When He Grows Tired of You/ It Just Don't Seem Like Home	1954	3.75	7.50	15.00
❏ 21329	Barney the Bashful Bullfrog/ Little Peter Pumpkin Eater	1954	3.75	7.50	15.00
❏ 21358	I'm Innocent/You're an Angel	1955	3.75	7.50	15.00
❏ 21481	You've Got to Take the Bitter with the Sweet/ Two Cheaters in Love	1956	3.75	7.50	15.00
❏ 21527	God's in the Saddle/ If Today Were the End of the World	1956	3.75	7.50	15.00
❏ 33023	Back in the Saddle Again/Tumbling Tumbleweeds	196?	2.00	4.00	8.00
—"Hall of Fame" reissue; red and black label					

Number	Title (A Side/B Side)	Yr	VG	VG+	NM
❑ 13-33165	Rudolph, the Red-Nosed Reindeer/ Here Comes Santa Claus	198?	—	—	3.00
—Reissue; gray label					
❑ 4-33165	Rudolph, the Red-Nosed Reindeer/ Here Comes Santa Claus	1969	—	2.50	5.00
—"Hall of Fame" reissue; red and black label					
❑ 4-33165 [DJ]	Rudolph, the Red-Nosed Reindeer/ Here Comes Santa Claus	1969	2.50	5.00	10.00
—"Promotion Copy Not for Sale" on red and black label above catalog number					
❑ 4-33165 [PS]	Rudolph, the Red-Nosed Reindeer/ Here Comes Santa Claus	1969	3.00	6.00	12.00
—Possibly promo-only sleeve issued for the 20th anniversary of the original release of "Rudolph"					
❑ 38610	Rudolph, the Red-Nosed Reindeer/ If It Doesn't Snow on Christmas	1951	3.75	7.50	15.00
—Second 45 issue of this song					
❑ 38907	Frosty The Snowman/ When Santa Claus Gets Your Letter	1951	3.75	7.50	15.00
—Second 45 issue of this song					
❑ 3-39086	My Heart Cries for You/Teardrops from My Eyes	1950	7.50	15.00	30.00
—Microgroove 33 1/3 rpm single					
❑ 4-39086	My Heart Cries for You/Teardrops from My Eyes	1950	5.00	10.00	20.00
❑ 39217	Sonny the Bunny/Bunny Roundup Time	1951	5.00	10.00	20.00
❑ 39347	Crime Will Never Pay/Gold Can Buy Anything	1951	3.75	7.50	15.00
❑ 39371	Mr. and Mississippi/How Long Is Forever	1951	3.75	7.50	15.00
❑ 39405	Old Soldiers Never Die/God Bless America	1951	3.75	7.50	15.00
❑ 39461	Frosty the Snow Man/An Old-Fashioned Tree	1951	3.00	6.00	12.00
❑ 39462	When Santa Claus Gets Your Letter/ He's a Chubby Little Fellow	1951	3.00	6.00	12.00
❑ 39463	Rudolph, the Red-Nosed Reindeer/Here Comes Santa Claus (Down Santa Claus Lane)	1951	3.00	6.00	12.00
❑ 39464	Santa, Santa, Santa/ If It Doesn't Snow on Christmas	1951	3.00	6.00	12.00
❑ 39542	Poppy the Puppy/He'll Be Coming Down the Chimney (Like He Always Did Before)	1951	3.75	7.50	15.00
❑ 39543	Thirty-Two Feet — Eight Little Tails/(Hedrock, Coco and Joe) The Three Little Dwarfs	1951	3.75	7.50	15.00
❑ 39808	Don't Believe a Word They Say/ God's Little Candles	1952	3.75	7.50	15.00
❑ 39876	The Night Before Christmas Song/ Look Out the Window	1952	3.75	7.50	15.00
—With Rosemary Clooney					
❑ 40092	Where Did My Snowman Go?/ Freddie the Little Fir Tree	1953	3.75	7.50	15.00
❑ 40135	I Wish My Mom Would Marry Santa Claus/ Sleigh Bells	1953	3.75	7.50	15.00
❑ 40167	Easter Morning/ The Horse with the Easter Bonnet	1954	3.75	7.50	15.00
❑ 40589	Round, Round the Christmas Tree/ Merry Christmas Tree	1955	3.75	7.50	15.00
❑ 40790	Everyone's a Child at Christmas/ You Can See Old Santa Claus	1956	3.75	7.50	15.00
❑ 40931	Johnny Reb and Billy Yank/Happy Little Island	1957	3.00	6.00	12.00
❑ 40960	Half Your Heart/Darlin' What More Can I Do	1957	3.00	6.00	12.00
❑ 44632	Back in the Saddle Again/Home on the Range	1968	2.00	4.00	8.00
CRICKET					
❑ CX-6	Rudolph, the Red-Nosed Reindeer/ Tinker Town Santa Claus	196?	3.00	6.00	12.00
—B-side by the Cricketones					
MISTLETOE					
❑ 801	Rudolph, The Red-Nosed Reindeer/ Up On The House Top	196?	2.00	4.00	8.00
REPUBLIC					
❑ 001	Back in the Saddle Again/The Last Round-Up	1977	—	2.50	5.00
❑ 326	Rudolph the Red-Nosed Reindeer/ Here Comes Santa Claus	1976	—	2.00	4.00
❑ 1405	Rudolph the Red-Nosed Reindeer/ Here Comes Santa Claus	1969	2.00	4.00	8.00
❑ 2001	Nine Little Reindeer/ Buon Natale (Means Merry Christmas)	1959	3.00	6.00	12.00
❑ 2001 [PS]	Nine Little Reindeer/ Buon Natale (Means Merry Christmas)	1959	3.00	6.00	12.00
❑ 2002	Santa's Comin' in a Whirlybird/Jingle Bells	1959	3.00	6.00	12.00
7-Inch Extended Plays					
COLUMBIA					
❑ B-270 [PS]	Merry Christmas with Gene Autry	195?	6.25	12.50	25.00
—Gatefold cover for 2-EP set (5-1067 and 5-1068)					
❑ 5-1067	Frosty the Snow Man/When Santa Claus Gets Your Letter//If It Doesn't Snow on Christmas/ Here Comes Santa Claus	195?	6.25	12.50	25.00
—Alternate numbers are B-270-1 and B-270-4					
❑ 5-1068	He's a Chubby Little Fellow/An Old Fashioned Tree//Rudolph the Red-Nosed Reindeer/ Santa, Santa, Santa	195?	6.25	12.50	25.00
—Alternate numbers are B-270-2 and B-270-3					
❑ B-2612	Rudolph the Red-Nosed Reindeer/Frosty the Snow Man//When Santa Claus Gets Your Letter/Here Come Santa Claus (Down Santa Claus Lane)	195?	5.00	10.00	20.00
❑ B-2612 [PS]	Children's Christmas (Hall of Fame Series)	195?	5.00	10.00	20.00
❑ B-2806	Mexicali Rose/Tumbling Tumbleweeds//Back in the Saddle Again/You Are My Sunshine	195?	5.00	10.00	20.00
❑ B-2806 [PS]	Gene Autry (Hall of Fame Series)	195?	5.00	10.00	20.00
Albums					
CBS SPECIAL PRODUCTS					
❑ P 18737	Golden Hits	1985	2.50	5.00	10.00
❑ P 18963	His Golden Hits	1985	2.50	5.00	10.00
❑ P 18964	Famous Favorites	1985	2.50	5.00	10.00
CHALLENGE					
❑ CHL-600 [M]	Christmas with Gene Autry	1958	12.50	25.00	50.00
COLUMBIA					
❑ CL (# unk) [10]	Easter Favorites	1949	37.50	75.00	150.00
❑ CL 677 [M]	Gene Autry and Champion — Western Adventures	1955	30.00	60.00	120.00
❑ CS 1035	Gene Autry's Country Music Hall of Fame Album	1970	3.75	7.50	15.00
❑ CL 1575 [M]	Gene Autry's Greatest Hits	1961	7.50	15.00	30.00
—Red and black label with six "eye" logos					
❑ CL 2547 [10]	Merry Christmas with Gene Autry	1954	30.00	60.00	120.00
—"House Party Series" release					
❑ CL 2568 [10]	Easter Favorites	1955	30.00	60.00	120.00
—"House Party Series" issue					
❑ CL 6020 [10]	Gene Autry's Western Classics	1949	37.50	75.00	150.00
❑ CL 6137 [10]	Merry Christmas	1950	37.50	75.00	150.00
❑ JL 8001 [10]	Gene Autry at the Rodeo	1949	37.50	75.00	150.00
❑ JL 8009 [10]	Stampede	1949	37.50	75.00	150.00
❑ JL 8012 [10]	Champion	1950	37.50	75.00	150.00
❑ HL 9001 [10]	Gene Autry's Western Classics, Volume 1	1949	37.50	75.00	150.00
❑ HL 9002 [10]	Gene Autry's Western Classics, Volume 2	1949	37.50	75.00	150.00
COLUMBIA SPECIAL PRODUCTS					
❑ P 15766	Christmas Favorites	1981	3.00	6.00	12.00
❑ P 15767	Everyone's a Child at Christmas	1981	3.00	6.00	12.00
GRAND PRIX					
❑ KS-X11 [S]	The Original Gene Autry Sings Rudolph the Red-Nosed Reindeer and Other Christmas Favorites	1961	5.00	10.00	20.00
❑ KX-11 [M]	The Original Gene Autry Sings Rudolph the Red-Nosed Reindeer and Other Christmas Favorites	1961	3.75	7.50	15.00
GUSTO					
❑ 1038	Christmas Classics	1978	2.50	5.00	10.00
HARMONY					
❑ HL 7332 [M]	Gene Autry's Great Western Hits	1965	7.50	15.00	30.00
❑ HL 7376 [M]	Back in the Saddle Again	1966	5.00	10.00	20.00
❑ HL 7399 [M]	Gene Autry Sings	1966	5.00	10.00	20.00
❑ HL 9505 [M]	Gene Autry and Champion — Western Adventures	1959	7.50	15.00	30.00
❑ HL 9550 [M]	The Original Rudolph the Red-Nosed Reindeer and Other Children's Christmas Favorites	1964	6.25	12.50	25.00
❑ HS 11199 [R]	Gene Autry Sings	1966	3.75	7.50	15.00
❑ HS 11276 [R]	Back in the Saddle Again	1966	3.75	7.50	15.00
❑ HS 14450 [R]	The Original Rudolph the Red-Nosed Reindeer and Other Children's Christmas Favorites	1964	3.00	6.00	12.00
MELODY RANCH					
❑ 101 [M]	Melody Ranch	1965	10.00	20.00	40.00
MURRAY HILL					
❑ 897296 [(4)]	Melody Ranch Radio Show	197?	15.00	30.00	60.00
—Compilation of some of Gene's radio shows in a box set					
RCA VICTOR					
❑ LPM-2623 [M]	Gene Autry's Golden Hits	1962	7.50	15.00	30.00
❑ LSP-2623 [S]	Gene Autry's Golden Hits	1962	10.00	20.00	40.00
REPUBLIC					
❑ 6011	South of the Border, All American Cowboy	1976	5.00	10.00	20.00
❑ 6012	Cowboy Hall of Fame	1976	5.00	10.00	20.00
❑ RLP 6018 [M]	Christmas with Gene Autry	1976	3.00	6.00	12.00

AVALANCHES, THE

45s

WARNER BROS.

Number	Title (A Side/B Side)	Yr	VG	VG+	NM
❑ 5407	Baby, It's Cold Outside/Avalanche	1964	3.75	7.50	15.00

Albums

WARNER BROS.

Number	Title (A Side/B Side)	Yr	VG	VG+	NM
❑ W 1525 [M]	Ski Surfin'	1963	10.00	20.00	40.00
❑ WS 1525 [S]	Ski Surfin'	1963	15.00	30.00	60.00

AVALON, FRANKIE

45s

AMOS

Number	Title (A Side/B Side)	Yr	VG	VG+	NM
❑ 127	The Star/Woman Cryin'	1969	—	2.50	5.00
BOBCAT					
❑ 04103	Such a Miracle/You're the Miracle	1983	—	2.00	4.00
CHANCELLOR					
❑ 11FX 1	Christmas Holiday/Dear Gesu Bambino	196?	5.00	10.00	20.00
❑ C-1 [DJ]	Shy Guy/Too Young to Love	1959	10.00	20.00	40.00
—Promo-only record made for "Acnecare"					
❑ 1004	Cupid/Jivin' with the Saints	1957	5.00	10.00	20.00
❑ 1006	Shy Guy/Teacher's Pet	1957	5.00	10.00	20.00
❑ 1011	Dede Dinah/Ooh La La	1958	3.75	7.50	15.00
❑ 1016	You Excite Me/Darlin'	1958	3.75	7.50	15.00
❑ 1021	Ginger Bread/Blue Betty	1958	3.75	7.50	15.00
❑ 1021 [PS]	Ginger Bread/Blue Betty	1958	10.00	20.00	40.00
❑ 1026	I'll Wait for You/What Little Girl	1958	3.75	7.50	15.00
❑ 1026 [PS]	I'll Wait for You/What Little Girl	1958	10.00	20.00	40.00
❑ 1031 [M]	Venus/I'm Broke	1959	5.00	10.00	20.00
❑ 1031 [PS]	Venus/I'm Broke	1959	10.00	20.00	40.00
❑ S-1031 [S]	Venus/I'm Broke	1959	10.00	20.00	40.00
❑ 1036 [M]	Bobby Sox to Stockings/A Boy Without a Girl	1959	3.00	6.00	12.00
—Reissues have black labels					
❑ 1036 [M]	Bobby Sox to Stockings/A Boy Without a Girl	1959	5.00	10.00	20.00
—Originals have pink labels					
❑ 1036 [PS]	Bobby Sox to Stockings/A Boy Without a Girl	1959	10.00	20.00	40.00
❑ S-1036 [S]	Bobby Sox to Stockings/A Boy Without a Girl	1959	10.00	20.00	40.00
❑ 1040 [M]	Just Ask Your Heart/Two Fools	1959	3.75	7.50	15.00
❑ 1040 [PS]	Just Ask Your Heart/Two Fools	1959	7.50	15.00	30.00
❑ S-1040 [S]	Just Ask Your Heart/Two Fools	1959	10.00	20.00	40.00
❑ 1045	Why/Swingin' on a Rainbow	1959	3.75	7.50	15.00
❑ 1045 [PS]	Why/Swingin' on a Rainbow	1959	7.50	15.00	30.00
❑ S-1045 [S]	Why/Swingin' on a Rainbow	1959	10.00	20.00	40.00
❑ 1048	Don't Throw Away All Those Teardrops/ Talk, Talk, Talk	1960	3.75	7.50	15.00
❑ 1048 [PS]	Don't Throw Away All Those Teardrops/ Talk, Talk, Talk	1960	7.50	15.00	30.00
❑ 1052	Where Are You/Tuxedo Junction	1960	3.75	7.50	15.00
❑ 1052 [PS]	Where Are You/Tuxedo Junction	1960	7.50	15.00	30.00
❑ 1056	Togetherness/Don't Let Love Pass You By	1960	3.75	7.50	15.00

Number	Title (A Side/B Side)	Yr	VG	VG+	NM
❏ 1056 [PS]	Togetherness/Don't Let Love Pass You By	1960	7.50	15.00	30.00
❏ 1065	A Perfect Love/The Puppet Song	1960	3.75	7.50	15.00
❏ 1065 [PS]	A Perfect Love/The Puppet Song	1960	7.50	15.00	30.00
❏ 1071	All of Everything/Call Me Anytime	1961	3.00	6.00	12.00
❏ 1071 [PS]	All of Everything/Call Me Anytime	1961	6.25	12.50	25.00
❏ 1077	Who Else But You/Gotta Get a Girl	1961	3.00	6.00	12.00
❏ 1081	Voyage to the Bottom of the Sea/Summer of '61	1961	3.00	6.00	12.00
❏ 1081 [PS]	Voyage to the Bottom of the Sea/Summer of '61	1961	6.25	12.50	25.00
❏ 1087	True, True Love/Married	1961	2.50	5.00	10.00
❏ 1087 [PS]	True, True Love/Married	1961	5.00	10.00	20.00
❏ 1095	Sleeping Beauty/The Lonely Bit	1961	2.50	5.00	10.00
❏ 1095 [PS]	Sleeping Beauty/The Lonely Bit	1961	5.00	10.00	20.00
❏ 1101	After You've Gone/If You Don't Think I'm Leaving	1962	2.50	5.00	10.00
❏ 1101 [PS]	After You've Gone/If You Don't Think I'm Leaving	1962	5.00	10.00	20.00
❏ 1107	You Are Mine/Ponchinello	1962	2.50	5.00	10.00
❏ 1107	You Are Mine/Italiano	1962	3.00	6.00	12.00
❏ 1107 [PS]	You Are Mine/Ponchinello	1962	5.00	10.00	20.00
❏ 1114	Venus/I'm Broke	1962	2.50	5.00	10.00
❏ 1115	A Miracle/Don't Let Me Stand in Your Way	1962	2.50	5.00	10.00
❏ 1115 [PS]	A Miracle/Don't Let Me Stand in Your Way	1962	5.00	10.00	20.00
❏ 1125	Dance the Bossa Nova/Welcome Home	1962	2.50	5.00	10.00
❏ 1125 [PS]	Dance the Bossa Nova/Welcome Home	1962	5.00	10.00	20.00
❏ 1131	My Ex-Best Friend/First Love Never Dies	1963	2.50	5.00	10.00
❏ 1134	Come Fly with Me/Girl Back Home	1963	2.50	5.00	10.00
❏ 1135	Cleopatra/Heartbeats	1963	2.50	5.00	10.00
❏ 1139	Beach Party/Don't Stop Now	1963	3.75	7.50	15.00

DE-LITE

Number	Title (A Side/B Side)	Yr	VG	VG+	NM
❏ 907	Beauty School Dropout/Midnight Lady	1978	—	2.00	4.00
❏ 907 [PS]	Beauty School Dropout/Midnight Lady	1978	—	2.50	5.00
❏ 1578	Venus/Venus (Disco Version)	1976	—	2.00	4.00
❏ 1578 [PS]	Venus/Venus (Disco Version)	1976	2.00	4.00	8.00
❏ 1582	Thank You for That Extra Sunrise/It's His Game	1976	—	2.00	4.00
❏ 1584	It's Never Too Late/Where I Leave Off (And You Begin)	1976	—	2.00	4.00
❏ 1589	Midnight Lady/Does She Wonder Where I Am	1977	—	2.00	4.00
❏ 1591	Splish Splash/When I Said I Love You	1977	—	2.00	4.00
❏ 1595	Roses Grow Beyond the Wall/Midnight Lady	1977	—	2.00	4.00

METROMEDIA

Number	Title (A Side/B Side)	Yr	VG	VG+	NM
❏ 181	Come On Back to Me Baby/Empty	1970	—	2.50	5.00
❏ 192	Heart of Everything/I Want You Near Me	1970	—	2.50	5.00

REGALIA

Number	Title (A Side/B Side)	Yr	VG	VG+	NM
❏ 5508	I'm in the Mood for Love/It's the Same Old Dream	1972	—	2.50	5.00

REPRISE

Number	Title (A Side/B Side)	Yr	VG	VG+	NM
❏ 0697	Dancing on the Stars/But I Do	1968	2.00	4.00	8.00
❏ 0796	Don't You Do It/It's Over	1968	2.00	4.00	8.00
❏ 0826	For Your Love/Why Don't They Understand	1969	2.00	4.00	8.00

UNITED ARTISTS

Number	Title (A Side/B Side)	Yr	VG	VG+	NM
❏ 728	Again/Don't Make Fun of Me	1964	2.50	5.00	10.00
❏ 748	My Love Is Here to Stay/New-Fangled, Jingle-Jangle, Swimming Suit from Paris	1964	2.50	5.00	10.00
❏ 748 [PS]	My Love Is Here to Stay/New-Fangled, Jingle-Jangle, Swimming Suit from Paris	1964	5.00	10.00	20.00
❏ 800	Moon River/Every Girl Should Get Married	1964	2.50	5.00	10.00
❏ 895	There'll Be Rainbows Again/I'll Take Sweden	1965	2.50	5.00	10.00

"X"

Number	Title (A Side/B Side)	Yr	VG	VG+	NM
❏ 0006	Trumpet Sorrento/The Rock	1954	12.50	25.00	50.00
❏ 0026	Trumpet Tarantella/Dormi, Dormi	1954	12.50	25.00	50.00

7-Inch Extended Plays

CHANCELLOR

Number	Title (A Side/B Side)	Yr	VG	VG+	NM
❏ B-5000	Shy Guy/The One I Love//Trumpet Instrumental/Undecided	1959	12.50	25.00	50.00
❏ B-5000 [PS]	The Young Frankie Avalon	1959	12.50	25.00	50.00
❏ A-5002	Too Young to Love/Into Each Life Some Rain Must Fall//Pretty Eyed Baby/I Can't Begin to Tell You	1959	12.50	25.00	50.00
❏ A-5002 [PS]	The Young Frankie Avalon	1959	12.50	25.00	50.00

"X"

Number	Title (A Side/B Side)	Yr	VG	VG+	NM
❏ EXA-20	Trumpet Taarantella/Dormi, Dormi (Sleep, My Darling)//Trumpet Sorrento/The Book	1954	12.50	25.00	50.00
❏ EXA-20 [PS]	Very Young Man with a Horn	1954	12.50	25.00	50.00

Albums

ABC

Number	Title	Yr	VG	VG+	NM
❏ ABCX-805 [R]	16 Greatest Hits	1974	3.00	6.00	12.00

CHANCELLOR

Number	Title	Yr	VG	VG+	NM
❏ CHL 5001 [M]	Frankie Avalon	1958	12.50	25.00	50.00
—Pink label					
❏ CHL 5001 [M]	Frankie Avalon	1959	10.00	20.00	40.00
—Black label					
❏ CHL 5002 [M]	The Young Frankie Avalon	1959	10.00	20.00	40.00
—Black label					
❏ CHL 5002 [M]	The Young Frankie Avalon	1959	12.50	25.00	50.00
—Pink label					
❏ CHLS 5002 [S]	The Young Frankie Avalon	1959	12.50	25.00	50.00
—Black label					
❏ CHLS 5002 [S]	The Young Frankie Avalon	1959	15.00	30.00	60.00
—Pink label					
❏ CHLX 5004 [M]	Swingin' on a Rainbow	1959	10.00	20.00	40.00
❏ CHLXS 5004 [S]	Swingin' on a Rainbow	1959	12.50	25.00	50.00
❏ CHL 5011 [M]	Summer Scene	1960	7.50	15.00	30.00
❏ CHLS 5011 [S]	Summer Scene	1960	10.00	20.00	40.00
❏ CHL 5018 [M]	A Whole Lotta Frankie	1961	7.50	15.00	30.00
❏ CHL 5022 [M]	And Now About Mr. Avalon	1961	7.50	15.00	30.00
❏ CHLS 5022 [S]	And Now About Mr. Avalon	1961	10.00	20.00	40.00
❏ CHL 5025 [M]	Italiano	1962	7.50	15.00	30.00
❏ CHLS 5025 [S]	Italiano	1962	10.00	20.00	40.00
❏ CHL 5027 [M]	You're Mine	1962	7.50	15.00	30.00
❏ CHLS 5027 [S]	You're Mine	1962	10.00	20.00	40.00
❏ CHL 5031 [M]	Frankie Avalon's Christmas Album	1962	7.50	15.00	30.00
❏ CHLS 5031 [S]	Frankie Avalon's Christmas Album	1962	10.00	20.00	40.00
❏ CHL 5032 [M]	Cleopatra Plus 13 Other Great Hits	1963	7.50	15.00	30.00
❏ CHLS 5032 [S]	Cleopatra Plus 13 Other Great Hits	1963	10.00	20.00	40.00
❏ 69801 [M]	Young and In Love	1960	10.00	20.00	40.00
—LP without the box					

Number	Title	Yr	VG	VG+	NM
❏ 69801 [M]	Young and In Love	1960	20.00	40.00	80.00
—LP in felt cover and 3-D portrait, all in box					

DE-LITE

Number	Title	Yr	VG	VG+	NM
❏ 2020	Venus	1976	3.75	7.50	15.00
❏ 9504	You're My Life	1977	3.75	7.50	15.00

EVEREST

Number	Title	Yr	VG	VG+	NM
❏ 4187	Greatest Hits	1982	2.50	5.00	10.00

LIBERTY

Number	Title	Yr	VG	VG+	NM
❏ LN-10193	Songs from Muscle Beach Party	1981	2.00	4.00	8.00
—Budget-line reissue					

MCA

Number	Title	Yr	VG	VG+	NM
❏ 27096	The Best of Frankie Avalon	1985	2.00	4.00	8.00

METROMEDIA

Number	Title	Yr	VG	VG+	NM
❏ MD-1034	I Want You Near Me	1970	3.75	7.50	15.00

SUNSET

Number	Title	Yr	VG	VG+	NM
❏ SUS-5244	Frankie Avalon	1969	3.75	7.50	15.00

TRIP

Number	Title	Yr	VG	VG+	NM
❏ 1621	16 Greatest Hits of Frankie Avalon	1977	2.50	5.00	10.00

UNITED ARTISTS

Number	Title	Yr	VG	VG+	NM
❏ UA-LA450-F	The Very Best of Frankie Avalon	1975	3.00	6.00	12.00
❏ UAL-3371 [M]	Songs from Muscle Beach Party	1964	6.25	12.50	25.00
❏ UAL-3382 [M]	Frankie Avalon's 15 Greatest Hits	1964	5.00	10.00	20.00
❏ UAS-6371 [S]	Songs from Muscle Beach Party	1964	7.50	15.00	30.00
❏ UAS-6382 [S]	Frankie Avalon's 15 Greatest Hits	1964	6.25	12.50	25.00

AVALON, FRANKIE AND FABIAN
Albums

MCA

Number	Title	Yr	VG	VG+	NM
❏ 27097	The Greatest of Frankie Avalon and Fabian	1985	2.50	5.00	10.00

AVALON, FRANKIE, AND ANNETTE FUNICELLO Also see each artist's individual listings.
45s

PACIFIC STAR

Number	Title (A Side/B Side)	Yr	VG	VG+	NM
❏ 569	(Together We Can Make a) Merry Christmas/The Night Before Christmas	1981	—	2.50	5.00
—Red vinyl					
❏ 569 [PS]	(Together We Can Make a) Merry Christmas/The Night Before Christmas	1981	—	2.50	5.00

AVALONS, THE
45s

ALADDIN

Number	Title (A Side/B Side)	Yr	VG	VG+	NM
❏ 3336	I Miss You/Love Me	1956	7.50	15.00	30.00

CASINO

Number	Title (A Side/B Side)	Yr	VG	VG+	NM
❏ 108	You Do Something to Me/You Can Count on Me	1959	50.00	100.00	200.00

DICE

Number	Title (A Side/B Side)	Yr	VG	VG+	NM
❏ 90/91	Louella/You Broke Our Hearts	1958	37.50	75.00	150.00

GROOVE

Number	Title (A Side/B Side)	Yr	VG	VG+	NM
❏ 0141	Chains Around My Heart/Och! She Flew	1956	37.50	75.00	150.00
—Black vinyl					
❏ 0141	Chains Around My Heart/Och! She Flew	1956	125.00	250.00	500.00
—Green vinyl					
❏ 0174	It's Funny But It's True/Sugar Sugar	1956	37.50	75.00	150.00

LOST-NITE

Number	Title (A Side/B Side)	Yr	VG	VG+	NM
❏ 215	Hearts Desire/Ebbtide	196?	—	2.50	5.00
—Reissue					

NPC

Number	Title (A Side/B Side)	Yr	VG	VG+	NM
❏ 302	Begin the Beguine/Malanese	1964	6.25	12.50	25.00

ROULETTE

Number	Title (A Side/B Side)	Yr	VG	VG+	NM
❏ 4568	Is It the End/Many Things from Your Window	1964	3.00	6.00	12.00

UNART

Number	Title (A Side/B Side)	Yr	VG	VG+	NM
❏ 2007	Hearts Desire/Ebbtide	1958	30.00	60.00	120.00

AVANT-GARDE, THE Game-show host CHUCK WOOLERY was in this group.
45s

COLUMBIA

Number	Title (A Side/B Side)	Yr	VG	VG+	NM
❏ 44388	Yellow Beads/Honey and Gall	1967	2.00	4.00	8.00
❏ 44590	Naturally Stoned/Honey and Gall	1968	2.00	4.00	8.00
❏ 44701	Fly with Me/Revelations Revelations	1968	2.00	4.00	8.00
—While not issued with a picture sleeve, some stock copies came with a lyric insert. Triple the value if this is included.					

AVANTIS, THE Probably more than one group.
45s

ARGO

Number	Title (A Side/B Side)	Yr	VG	VG+	NM
❏ 5436	Keep On Dancing/I Want to Dance	1963	3.75	7.50	15.00

ASTRA

Number	Title (A Side/B Side)	Yr	VG	VG+	NM
❏ 1006	Gypsy Surfer/Wax 'Em Down	1963	10.00	20.00	40.00

CHANCELLOR

Number	Title (A Side/B Side)	Yr	VG	VG+	NM
❏ 1144	Gypsy Surfer/Wax 'Em Down	1963	6.25	12.50	25.00

IKON

Number	Title (A Side/B Side)	Yr	VG	VG+	NM
❏ 115	Too Much/Mid-Night Blues	196?	6.25	12.50	25.00

PEPPER

Number	Title (A Side/B Side)	Yr	VG	VG+	NM
❏ 435	You Got a Funny Way/One Man's Poison	196?	3.00	6.00	12.00

REGENCY

Number	Title (A Side/B Side)	Yr	VG	VG+	NM
❏ 108	Do the Surfin' Granny/Surfin' Granny	1964	10.00	20.00	40.00
❏ 110	Phantom Surfer/Lucille	1964	10.00	20.00	40.00

AVENGERS VI, THE
Albums

MARK 56

Number	Title	Yr	VG	VG+	NM
❏ (# unknown)	Good Humor Presents Real Cool Hits	1966	62.50	125.00	250.00
—Custom pressing for the Good Humor ice cream company					

AVERAGE WHITE BAND
12-Inch Singles

TRACK

Number	Title	Yr	VG	VG+	NM
❏ 58831	The Spirit of Love (5 versions)	1988	2.00	4.00	8.00

Number	Title (A Side/B Side)	Yr	VG	VG+	NM
45s					
ARISTA					
❏ 0515	Let's Go Round Again/Shine	1980	—	2.00	4.00
❏ 0553	For You, For Love/Whatcha 'Gonna Do for Me	1980	—	2.00	4.00
❏ 0580	Into the Night/(B-side unknown)	1980	—	2.00	4.00
❏ 0679	Easier Said Than Done/(B-side unknown)	1982	—	2.00	4.00
❏ 1022	Cupid's in Fashion/(B-side unknown)	1982	—	2.00	4.00
ATLANTIC					
❏ 3044	Nothing You Can Do/I Just Can't Give You Up	1974	—	2.00	4.00
❏ 3229	Pick Up the Pieces/Work to Do	1974	—	2.50	5.00
❏ 3261	Cut the Cake/Person to Person	1975	—	2.00	4.00
❏ 3285	If I Ever Lose This Heaven/High Flyin' Woman	1975	—	2.00	4.00
❏ 3304	School Boy Crush/Groovin' the Night Away	1975	—	2.00	4.00
❏ 3354	Queen of My Soul/Would You Stay	1976	—	2.00	4.00
❏ 3363	Soul Searching/Love of Your Own	1976	—	2.00	4.00
❏ 3388	Cloudy/Love Your Life	1977	—	2.00	4.00
❏ 3402	Get It Up/Keepin' It To Myself	1977	—	2.00	4.00
—With Ben E. King					
❏ 3427	A Star in the Ghetto/What Is Soul?	1977	—	2.00	4.00
—With Ben E. King					
❏ 3444	Fool for You Anyway/The Message	1977	—	2.00	4.00
—With Ben E. King					
❏ 3481	Your Love Is a Miracle/One Look	1978	—	2.00	4.00
❏ 3500	Big City Lights/She's a Dream	1978	—	2.00	4.00
❏ 3563	Walk On By/Too Late to Cry	1979	—	2.00	4.00
❏ 3581	Feel No Fret/Fire Burning	1979	—	2.00	4.00
❏ 3614 [DJ]	When Will You Be Mine (same on both sides)	1979	—	2.00	4.00
—May be promo only					
MCA					
❏ 40168	This World Has Music/The Jugglers	1973	—	2.50	5.00
❏ 40196	Twilight Zone/How Can You Go Home	1974	—	2.50	5.00
Albums					
ARISTA					
❏ AB 9523	Shine	1980	2.50	5.00	10.00
❏ AB 9594	Cupid's in Fashion	1981	2.50	5.00	10.00
ATLANTIC					
❏ SD 2-1002 [(2)]	Person to Person	1977	3.00	6.00	12.00
❏ QD 7308 [Q]	Average White Band	1975	5.00	10.00	20.00
❏ SD 7308	Average White Band	1974	2.50	5.00	10.00
❏ SD 18140	Cut the Cake	1975	2.50	5.00	10.00
❏ SD 18179	Soul Searching	1976	2.50	5.00	10.00
❏ SD 19105	Benny and Us	1977	2.50	5.00	10.00
—With Ben E. King					
❏ SD 19116	Average White Band	1977	2.00	4.00	8.00
—Reissue					
❏ SD 19162	Warmer Communications	1978	2.50	5.00	10.00
❏ SD 19207	Feel No Fret	1979	2.50	5.00	10.00
❏ SD 19266	Volume VIII	1980	2.50	5.00	10.00
MCA					
❏ 345	Show Your Hands	1973	6.25	12.50	25.00
❏ 475	Put It Where You Want It	1975	2.50	5.00	10.00
—Reissue of MCA 345					
MOBILE FIDELITY					
❏ 1-245	Average White Band	1996	5.00	10.00	20.00
—Audiophile vinyl					
TRACK					
❏ 58830	Aftershock	1988	2.50	5.00	10.00

AVONS, THE (1) Male vocal group.

Number	Title (A Side/B Side)	Yr	VG	VG+	NM
45s					
ASTRA					
❏ 1023	Baby/Whisper (Softly)	1966	7.50	15.00	30.00
—Reissue of Hull material					
HULL					
❏ 717	Our Love Will Never End/I'm Sending S.O.S.	1956	12.50	25.00	50.00
—Red label					
❏ 717	Our Love Will Never End/I'm Sending S.O.S.	1956	50.00	100.00	200.00
—Black label					
❏ 722	Baby/Bonnie	1957	37.50	75.00	150.00
❏ 726	You Are So Close to Me/Gonna Catch You Nappin'	1958	30.00	60.00	120.00
❏ 728	What Will I Do/Please Come Back to Me	1958	30.00	60.00	120.00
❏ 731	What Love Can Do/On the Island	1958	30.00	60.00	120.00
❏ 744	Whisper (Softly)/If I Just (Had My Way)	196?	20.00	40.00	80.00
—Brown label					
❏ 744	Whisper (Softly)/If I Just (Had My Way)	1961	25.00	50.00	100.00
—Pink label					
❏ 744	Whisper (Softly)/If I Just (Had My Way)	1961	25.00	50.00	100.00
—White label					
❏ 754	A Girl to Call My Own/The Grass Is Greener on the Other Side	1962	20.00	40.00	80.00
—Brown label					
❏ 754	A Girl to Call My Own/The Grass Is Greener on the Other Side	1962	37.50	75.00	150.00
—White label					
Albums					
HULL					
❏ HLP-1000 [M]	The Avons	1960	175.00	350.00	700.00

AVONS, THE (U)

Number	Title (A Side/B Side)	Yr	VG	VG+	NM
45s					
A-BET					
❏ 9419	Talk to Me/Got to Get Used to You	1967	2.00	4.00	8.00
EXCELLO					
❏ 2296	Since I Met You Baby/He's My Hero	1968	2.00	4.00	8.00
GROOVE					
❏ 58-0022	Oh, Gee Baby/Push a Little Harder	1963	3.75	7.50	15.00
❏ 58-0022 [PS]	Oh, Gee Baby/Push a Little Harder	1963	7.50	15.00	30.00
❏ 58-0033	Words Written on Water/Rolling Stone	1964	3.00	6.00	12.00
❏ 58-0039	Whatever Happened to Our Love/Tonight Kiss Your Baby Goodbye	1964	3.00	6.00	12.00

Number	Title (A Side/B Side)	Yr	VG	VG+	NM
MERCURY					
❏ 71618	We Fell in Love/Pickin' Petals	1960	3.75	7.50	15.00
REF-O-REE					
❏ 700	Tell Me Baby/A Sample of My Love	196?	5.00	10.00	20.00
SOUND STAGE 7					
❏ 2561	Be Good to Your Baby/Just As Long As I Live	1966	2.50	5.00	10.00

AXTON, HOYT

Number	Title (A Side/B Side)	Yr	VG	VG+	NM
45s					
A&M					
❏ 1437	Sweet Misery/Less Than the Song	1973	—	2.50	5.00
❏ 1497	When the Morning Comes/Billie's Theme	1974	—	2.50	5.00
❏ 1541	Boney Fingers/Theme from Buster and Billie	1974	—	2.50	5.00
❏ 1607	Boney Fingers/Life Machine	1974	—	2.50	5.00
❏ 1607 [PS]	Boney Fingers/Life Machine	1974	—	3.00	6.00
❏ 1657	Nashville/Speed Trap	1974	—	2.50	5.00
❏ 1683	Lion in the Winter/No No Song	1975	—	2.50	5.00
❏ 1713	In a Young Girl's Mind/Southbound	1975	—	2.50	5.00
❏ 1811	Flash of Fire/Paid in Advance	1976	—	2.00	4.00
❏ 1864	Evangelina/Jealous Man	1976	—	2.50	5.00
BRIAR					
❏ 100	Georgia Hoss Soldier/Drinking Gourd	1961	3.75	7.50	15.00
CAPITOL					
❏ 3121	Alice in Wonderland/Have a Nice Day	1971	—	3.00	6.00
❏ 3167	California Women/Ease Your Pain	1971	—	3.00	6.00
❏ 3259	Speed Traps/Hey, Mr. Pilot Man	1972	—	3.00	6.00
COLGEMS					
❏ 66-1005	San Fernando/Ten Thousand Sunsets	1967	2.50	5.00	10.00
COLPIX					
❏ 802	Soldier's Last Letter/Speed Trap	1966	2.50	5.00	10.00
COLUMBIA					
❏ 44810	Snowblind Friend/It's All Right Now	1969	—	3.50	7.00
❏ 44850	Way Before the Time of Towns/It's All Right Now	1969	—	3.50	7.00
ELEKTRA					
❏ 47133	Flo's Yellow Rose/Lion in the Winter	1981	—	2.00	4.00
HORIZON					
❏ 2	Grizzly Bear/Gypsy Woman	1963	2.50	5.00	10.00
❏ 6	The Happy Song/We'll Sing in the Sunshine	1963	2.50	5.00	10.00
❏ 351	Greenback Dollar/Crawdad Song	1962	3.75	7.50	15.00
❏ 360	Grizzly Bear/Gypsy Woman	1963	3.00	6.00	12.00
❏ 361	This Little Light/Thunder 'N' Lightnin'	1963	3.00	6.00	12.00
❏ 362	One More Round/Greenback Dollar	1963	3.00	6.00	12.00
JEREMIAH					
❏ 1000	Della and the Dealer/In a Young Girl's Mind	1979	—	2.00	4.00
❏ 1001	A Rusty Old Halo/Gotta Keep Rollin'	1979	—	2.00	4.00
❏ 1003	Wild Bull Rider/Torpedo	1979	—	2.00	4.00
❏ 1005	Evangelina/So Hard to Give It All Up	1980	—	2.00	4.00
❏ 1006	Boozers Are Losers (When the Benders Don't End)/Politicians	1980	—	2.00	4.00
❏ 1008	Where Did the Money Go/Smile As You Go By	1980	—	2.00	4.00
❏ 1011	The Devil/Jealous Man	1981	—	2.00	4.00
❏ 1012	Win This One/Ease Your Pain	1981	—	2.00	4.00
❏ 1014	She's Too Lazy to Be Crazy/You Do Not Tango	1982	—	2.00	4.00
❏ 1015	There Stands the Glass/James Dean and the Junkman	1982	—	2.00	4.00
❏ 1016	Pistol Packin' Mama/Fearless the Wonderdog	1982	—	2.00	4.00
❏ 1017	Warm Stones and Wild Flowers/Don't Fence Me In	1983	—	2.00	4.00
❏ 1018	If You're a Cowboy/I Collect Hearts	1983	—	2.00	4.00
MCA					
❏ 40711	You're the Hangnail in My Life/Never Been to Spain	1977	—	2.00	4.00
❏ 40731	Little White Moon/Funeral of the King	1977	—	2.50	5.00
20TH FOX					
❏ 6648	Five Dollar Bill/Smoky	1966	2.50	5.00	10.00
VEE JAY					
❏ 604	L.A. Town/Double Double Dare	1964	3.00	6.00	12.00
❏ 619	Bring Your Lovin'/Tiger in the Closet	1964	3.00	6.00	12.00
❏ 659	Hush Hush Sweet Charlotte/After You've Gone	1965	2.50	5.00	10.00
Albums					
A&M					
❏ SP-3155	Life Machine	198?	2.00	4.00	8.00
—Budget-line reissue					
❏ SP-3182	Road Songs	198?	2.00	4.00	8.00
—Budget-line reissue					
❏ SP-4376	Less Than a Song	1973	2.50	5.00	10.00
❏ SP-4402	Life Machine	1974	2.50	5.00	10.00
❏ SP-4510	Southbound	1975	2.50	5.00	10.00
❏ SP-4571	Fearless	1976	2.50	5.00	10.00
❏ SP-4669	Road Songs	1977	2.50	5.00	10.00
ACCORD					
❏ SN-7197	Heartbreak Hotel	1982	2.50	5.00	10.00
ALLEGIANCE					
❏ AV-5023	Down and Out	1984	2.50	5.00	10.00
BRYLEN					
❏ BN 4400	Double Dare	1982	3.00	6.00	12.00
CAPITOL					
❏ ST-788	Joy to the World	1971	3.00	6.00	12.00
❏ SMAS-850	Country Anthem	1971	3.00	6.00	12.00
COLUMBIA					
❏ CS 9766	My Griffin Is Gone	1969	3.75	7.50	15.00
❏ KC 33103	My Griffin Is Gone	1975	2.50	5.00	10.00
❏ PC 33103	My Griffin Is Gone	1979	2.00	4.00	8.00
—Budget-line reissue					
EXODUS					
❏ EX-301 [M]	Hoyt Axton Sings Bessie Smith	1966	5.00	10.00	20.00
❏ EXS-321 [M]	Saturday's Child	1966	5.00	10.00	20.00
—Cover says stereo, record plays mono					
HORIZON					
❏ WP-1601 [M]	The Balladeer	1962	6.25	12.50	25.00
—Black label					

Number	Title (A Side/B Side)	Yr	VG	VG+	NM
❏ WP-1601 [S]	The Balladeer	1962	7.50	15.00	30.00
—Same number as mono, but with blue label					
❏ WP-1601 [M]	Greenback Dollar	1963	5.00	10.00	20.00
—Black label; two fewer songs than "The Balladeer"					
❏ WP-1601 [S]	Greenback Dollar	1963	6.25	12.50	25.00
—Blue label; two fewer songs than "The Balladeer"					
❏ SWP-1613 [S]	Thunder 'N Lightnin'	1963	7.50	15.00	30.00
❏ WP-1613 [M]	Thunder 'N Lightnin'	1963	6.25	12.50	25.00
❏ SWP-1621 [S]	Saturday's Child	1963	7.50	15.00	30.00
❏ WP-1621 [M]	Saturday's Child	1963	6.25	12.50	25.00
JEREMIAH					
❏ JH-5000	A Rusty Old Halo	1979	3.00	6.00	12.00
❏ JH-5001	Where Did the Money Go?	1980	3.00	6.00	12.00
MCA					
❏ 647	Snow Blind Friend	198?	2.00	4.00	8.00
—Budget-line reissue					
❏ 648	Free Sailin'	198?	2.00	4.00	8.00
—Budget-line reissue					
❏ 2263	Snow Blind Friend	1977	2.50	5.00	10.00
❏ 2319	Free Sailin'	1978	2.50	5.00	10.00
SURREY					
❏ S-1005 [M]	Mr. Greenback Dollar Man	1965	5.00	10.00	20.00
❏ SS-1005 [S]	Mr. Greenback Dollar Man	1965	6.25	12.50	25.00
VEE JAY					
❏ LP-1098 [M]	Hoyt Axton Explodes!	1964	6.25	12.50	25.00
❏ LPS-1098 [R]	Hoyt Axton Explodes!	1964	5.00	10.00	20.00
❏ LP-1118 [M]	The Best of Hoyt Axton	1965	5.00	10.00	20.00
❏ LPS-1118 [S]	The Best of Hoyt Axton	1965	6.25	12.50	25.00
❏ LP-1126 [M]	Greenback Dollar	1965	5.00	10.00	20.00
❏ LPS-1126 [S]	Greenback Dollar	1965	6.25	12.50	25.00
❏ LP-1127 [M]	Saturday's Child	1965	5.00	10.00	20.00
❏ LPS-1127 [S]	Saturday's Child	1965	6.25	12.50	25.00
—Reissue of Horizon 1621					
❏ LP-1128 [M]	Thunder 'N Lightnin'	1965	5.00	10.00	20.00
❏ LPS-1128 [S]	Thunder 'N Lightnin'	1965	6.25	12.50	25.00
—Reissue of Horizon 1613					
VEE JAY INTERNATIONAL					
❏ VJS-2-1005 [(2)]Gold		1974	5.00	10.00	20.00
—Compilation of older Vee Jay material					
❏ LP-6001	Long Old Road	1977	3.75	7.50	15.00
VEE JAY/DYNASTY					
❏ VJS-7306	Bessie Smith… My Way	1974	3.75	7.50	15.00

AYALA, HANK, AND THE MATADORS
45s
BACK BEAT

Number	Title (A Side/B Side)	Yr	VG	VG+	NM
❏ 530	Betty Jo/Handsome	1960	3.00	6.00	12.00
❏ 530 [PS]	Betty Jo/Handsome	1960	10.00	20.00	40.00

AYERS, ROY Includes "Roy Ayers Ubiquity."
12-Inch Singles
COLUMBIA

Number	Title (A Side/B Side)	Yr	VG	VG+	NM
❏ CAS 2804 [DJ]	I'm the One (Extended Version 7:18) (Extended Radio 5:35) (Instrumental 8:23)	1987	—	3.00	6.00
❏ 44-05115	In the Dark (5:51)/Love Is in the Feel	1984	2.00	4.00	8.00
❏ 44-05330	Hot (6:03)/(Dub)	1985	2.00	4.00	8.00
GROOVETOWN					
❏ 64361	Naste (5 versions)	1995	—	3.00	6.00
ICHIBAN					
❏ 12 PO 14 [DJ]	Fast Money (same on both sides)	1989	—	3.00	6.00
❏ 12 PO 23 [DJ]	Suave/And Then We Were One	198?	2.50	5.00	10.00

45s
COLUMBIA

Number	Title (A Side/B Side)	Yr	VG	VG+	NM
❏ 38-04653	In the Dark/Love Is in the Feel	1984	—	—	3.00
❏ 38-04821	Poo Poo La La/Sexy Sexy Sexy	1985	—	—	3.00
❏ 38-05613	Slip n' Slide/Can I See You	1985	—	—	3.00
❏ 38-05752	Hot/Virgo	1985	—	—	3.00
❏ 38-05874	Programmed for Love/For You	1986	—	—	3.00
ICHIBAN					
❏ 149	Fast Money/(Instrumental)	1987	—	2.00	4.00
❏ 157	D.C. City/(Instrumental)	1987	—	2.00	4.00
POLYDOR					
❏ 2020	Fever/I Wanna Feel It	1979	—	2.00	4.00
❏ 2037	Don't Stop the Feeling/Don't Hide Your Love	1979	—	2.00	4.00
❏ 2066	What You Won't Do for Love/Shack Up, Pack Up, It's Up (When I'm Done)	1980	—	2.00	4.00
❏ 2138	Rock Your Roll/Sigh & Feel the Vibration	1981	—	2.00	4.00
❏ 2154	Love Fantasy/Baby Bubba	1981	—	2.00	4.00
❏ 2185	There's a Master Plan/Land of Fruit and Honey	1981	—	2.00	4.00
❏ 2198	Turn Me Loose/Ooh	1982	—	2.00	4.00
❏ 2204	Fire Up the Funk/Let's Stay Together	1982	—	2.00	4.00
❏ 14078	Pretty Brown Skin/He Gives Us All His Love	1971	—	2.50	5.00
❏ 14111	He's a Superstar (Part 1)/He's a Superstar (Part 2)	1972	—	2.50	5.00
❏ 14165	Will Your Soul Be Free (Henceforth)/Rhythms of Your Mind	1973	—	2.50	5.00
❏ 14171	Red, Black and Green/Will Your Soul Be Free (Henceforth)	1973	—	2.50	5.00
❏ 14275	Magic Lady/No Question	1975	—	2.00	4.00
❏ 14294	Way of the World/2000 Black	1975	—	2.00	4.00
❏ 14316	Mystic Voyage/(B-side unknown)	1976	—	2.00	4.00
❏ 14337	The Golden Rod/Tongue Power	1976	—	2.00	4.00
❏ 14349	You and Me My Love/Hey-Uh-What You Say Come On	1976	—	2.00	4.00

Number	Title (A Side/B Side)	Yr	VG	VG+	NM
❏ 14370	Vibrations/Domelo (Give It to Me)	1977	—	2.00	4.00
❏ 14379	Searching/Come Out and Play	1977	—	2.00	4.00
❏ 14415	Running Away/Cincinnati Growl	1977	—	2.00	4.00
❏ 14451	Freaky Deaky/You Came Into My Life	1978	—	2.00	4.00
❏ 14477	Let's Do It/Melody Maker	1978	—	2.00	4.00
❏ 14509	Get On Up, Get On Down/And Don't You Say No	1978	—	2.00	4.00
❏ 14573	Love Will Bring Us Back Together/Leo	1979	—	2.00	4.00
Albums					
ATLANTIC					
❏ 1488 [M]	Virgo Vibes	1967	5.00	10.00	20.00
❏ SD 1488 [S]	Virgo Vibes	1967	3.75	7.50	15.00
❏ SD 1514	Stoned Soul Picnic	1968	5.00	10.00	20.00
❏ SD 1538	Daddy Bug	1969	5.00	10.00	20.00
❏ SD 1692	Daddy Bug & Friends	1976	3.00	6.00	12.00
COLUMBIA					
❏ FC 39422	In the Dark	1984	2.50	5.00	10.00
ICHIBAN					
❏ ICH-1028	Drive	198?	2.50	5.00	10.00
❏ ICH-1040	Wake Up	198?	2.50	5.00	10.00
POLYDOR					
❏ PD 5022	He's Coming	1972	3.00	6.00	12.00
❏ PD 5045	Red, Black and Green	1973	3.00	6.00	12.00
❏ PD 6016	Virgo Red	1973	3.00	6.00	12.00
❏ PD 6032	Change Up the Groove	1974	2.50	5.00	10.00
❏ PD 6046	A Tear to a Smile	1975	2.50	5.00	10.00
❏ PD 6057	Mystic Voyage	1976	2.50	5.00	10.00
❏ PD-1-6070	Everybody Loves the Sunshine	1976	2.50	5.00	10.00
❏ PD-1-6078	Red, Black and Green	1976	2.50	5.00	10.00
—Reissue of 5045					
❏ PD-1-6091	Vibrations	1977	2.50	5.00	10.00
❏ PD-1-6108	Lifeline	1977	2.50	5.00	10.00
❏ PD-1-6126	Let's Do It	1978	2.50	5.00	10.00
❏ PD-1-6159	You Send Me	1978	2.50	5.00	10.00
❏ PD-1-6204	Fever	1979	2.50	5.00	10.00
❏ PD-1-6246	No Stranger to Love	1979	2.50	5.00	10.00
❏ PD-1-6301	Love Fantasy	1980	2.50	5.00	10.00
❏ PD-1-6327	Africa, Center of the World	1981	2.50	5.00	10.00
❏ PD-1-6348	Feeling Good	1982	2.50	5.00	10.00
UNITED ARTISTS					
❏ UAL-3325 [M]	West Coast Vibes	1964	5.00	10.00	20.00
❏ UAS-6325 [S]	West Coast Vibes	1964	6.25	12.50	25.00

AYERS, ROY, AND WAYNE HENDERSON
12-Inch Singles
POLYDOR

Number	Title (A Side/B Side)	Yr	VG	VG+	NM
❏ PRO 071 [DJ]	Heat Of the Beat (7:06) (same on both sides)	1978	3.00	6.00	12.00

45s
POLYDOR

Number	Title (A Side/B Side)	Yr	VG	VG+	NM
❏ 2114	You Make Me Feel Like (Rockin' with You)/Million Dollar Baby (Feel So Real)	1980	—	2.00	4.00
❏ 2127	Weekend Lover/Thank You, Thank You	1980	—	—	—
—Canceled					
❏ 14523	Heat of the Beat/No Deposit No Return	1978	—	2.00	4.00
❏ 14545	Ooh Baby/Step Into Our Life	1979	—	2.00	4.00
❏ 14559	No Deposit No Return/Step Into Our Life	1979	—	2.00	4.00
Albums					
POLYDOR					
❏ PD-1-6179	Step Into Our Life	1978	2.50	5.00	10.00
❏ PD-1-6276	Prine Time	1980	2.50	5.00	10.00

AZALEAS, THE
45s
ROMULUS

Number	Title (A Side/B Side)	Yr	VG	VG+	NM
❏ 3001	Hands Off/One Drummer Can't Keep Time	1963	7.50	15.00	30.00

AZTECA
45s
COLUMBIA

Number	Title (A Side/B Side)	Yr	VG	VG+	NM
❏ 45762	Peace Everybody/Mamita Linda	1973	—	3.00	6.00
❏ 45808	Ain't Got No Special Woman/Can't Take the Funk Out of Me	1973	—	3.00	6.00
❏ 45962	Night in Nazca/Whatcha Gonna Do	1973	—	2.50	5.00
Albums					
COLUMBIA					
❏ CQ 31776 [Q]	Azteca	1974	5.00	10.00	20.00
❏ KC 31776	Azteca	1972	3.00	6.00	12.00
❏ KC 32451	Pyramid of the Sun	1973	3.00	6.00	12.00

AZTECS, THE
45s
WORLD ARTISTS

Number	Title (A Side/B Side)	Yr	VG	VG+	NM
❏ 1029	Da Doo Ron Ron/Hi-Hel Sneakers	1964	3.00	6.00	12.00
Albums					
WORLD ARTISTS					
❏ WAM-2001 [M]	Live at the Ad Lib Club of London	1964	15.00	30.00	60.00

AZTEX
45s
STAFF

Number	Title (A Side/B Side)	Yr	VG	VG+	NM
❏ (# unknown)	I Said Move/(B-side unknown)	196?	625.00	1250.	2500.

Number	Title (A Side/B Side)	Yr	VG	VG+	NM

B

B. BUMBLE AND THE STINGERS
45s
DYMO

Number	Title (A Side/B Side)	Yr	VG	VG+	NM
❑ 13	Pollywog/Slumber Party	196?	2.50	5.00	10.00

ERA BACK TO BACK HITS

❑ 038	Bumble Boogie/Angel Baby	197?	—	3.00	6.00

—B-side by Rosie and the Originals

ERIC

❑ 297	Nut Rocker/Bumble Boogie	197?	—	2.00	4.00

GOLDIES 45

❑ 2465	Bumble Boogie/School Day Blues	1973	—	2.50	5.00
❑ 2466	Nut Rocker/Nautilus	1973	—	2.50	5.00

GOLDISC

❑ 3106	Nut Rocker/Bumble Boogie	198?	—	2.00	4.00

HI OLDIES

❑ 409	Nut Rocker/Nautilus	197?	—	2.50	5.00

HIGHLAND

❑ 2001	Bumble Boogie/School Day Blues	196?	2.50	5.00	10.00

MERCURY

❑ 72614	Green Hornet Theme/Flight of the Hornet	1966	2.50	5.00	10.00
❑ 72665	Silent Movies/Twelfth Street Rag	1967	2.50	5.00	10.00

OLDIES 45

❑ 37	Nut Rocker/Nautilus	1964	2.00	4.00	8.00
❑ 065	Nut Rocker/Baby I Love You	197?	—	2.50	5.00

—B-side by Joe Weaver and the Don Juans

RENDEZVOUS

❑ 140	Bumble Boogie/School Day Blues	1961	5.00	10.00	20.00
❑ 151	Boogie Woogie/Near You	1961	3.75	7.50	15.00
❑ 160	Bee Hive/Caravan	1961	3.75	7.50	15.00
❑ 166	Nut Rocker/Nautilus	1962	3.75	7.50	15.00
❑ 174	Rockin-On-And-Off/Mashed #5	1962	3.00	6.00	12.00
❑ 179	Apple Knocker/The Moon and the Sea	1962	3.00	6.00	12.00
❑ 182	Dawn Cracker/Scales	1962	3.00	6.00	12.00
❑ 186	12th Street Rag/Canadian Sunset	1962	3.00	6.00	12.00
❑ 192	Baby Mash/Night Time Madness	1962	3.00	6.00	12.00
❑ 210	In the Mood/Chicken Chow Mein	1963	3.00	6.00	12.00

TRIAD

❑ 778	Chariots from the Stars/Funky Mud	197?	—	3.00	6.00

WAX

❑ 13	Pollywog/Slumber Party	196?	2.00	4.00	8.00

—"Wax" in large sideways print

❑ 13	Pollywog/Slumber Party	196?	2.50	5.00	10.00

—"Wax" in small vertical print

B.J. AND THE GEMINIS
45s
ATCO

❑ 6364	Scratch My Back Part 1/Scratch My Back Part 2	1965	6.25	12.50	25.00

B.R.A.T.T.S., THE
45s
TOLLIE

❑ 9024	Secret Weapon (The British Are Coming)/Jealous Kinda Woman	1964	5.00	10.00	20.00

B.T. EXPRESS
12-Inch Singles
COAST TO COAST

❑ AS 1494 [DJ]	Keep It Up (Long) (Short)	1982	3.75	7.50	15.00
❑ 4Z9-02631	Let Yourself Go/Cowboy Dancer	1981	2.00	4.00	8.00
❑ 4Z9-03247	Star Child (Spirit of the Night) (7:26)/This Must Be the Night for Love (7:26)	1982	3.75	7.50	15.00

COLUMBIA

❑ AS 403 [DJ]	Shout It Out (stereo/mono)	1977	3.75	7.50	15.00
❑ 43-60518	Let Me Be the One/Midnight Beat	1981	3.75	7.50	15.00

KING DAVIS

❑ 3661	Cover Girl (Radio Version) (Club Version)	1985	3.00	6.00	12.00

ROADSHOW

❑ 233 [DJ]	Can't Stop Groovin' Now, Wanna Do It Some More (5:54) (stereo/mono)	1976	12.50	25.00	50.00

45s
COAST TO COAST

❑ ZS5-02630	Let Yourself Go/Cowboy Dancer	1981	—	2.00	4.00
❑ ZS5-02994	Keep It Up/Dancin' Dreams	1982	—	2.00	4.00
❑ ZS4-03246	Star Child (Spirit of the Night)/This Must Be the Night for Love	1982	—	2.00	4.00

COLUMBIA

❑ 3-10346	Can't Stop Groovin' Now, Wanna Do It Some More/Herbs	1976	—	2.00	4.00
❑ 3-10399	Energy to Burn/Make Your Body Move	1976	—	2.00	4.00
❑ 3-10582	Funky Music (Don't Laugh at My Funk)/We Got It Together	1977	—	2.00	4.00
❑ 3-10649	Shout It Out/Ride On B.T.	1977	—	2.00	4.00
❑ 3-10752	You Got Something/What You Do in the Dark	1978	—	2.00	4.00
❑ 1-11200	Heart of Fire/Better Late Than Never	1980	—	2.00	4.00
❑ 1-11249	Give Up the Funk (Let's Dance)/Better Late Than Never	1980	—	2.00	4.00
❑ 1-11336	Does It Feel Good/Have Some Fun	1980	—	2.00	4.00
❑ 11400	Stretch/Just Want to Hold You	1980	—	2.00	4.00

ROADSHOW

❑ 7001	Express/Express (Disco Mix)	1975	—	2.00	4.00
❑ 7003	Give It What You Got/Peace Pipe	1975	—	2.00	4.00
❑ 7005	Close to You/(B-side unknown)	1975	—	2.00	4.00

SCEPTER

❑ 12395	Do It ('Til You're Satisfied)/(Long Version)	1974	—	2.50	5.00

Number	Title (A Side/B Side)	Yr	VG	VG+	NM

Albums
COAST TO COAST

❑ FZ 38001	Keep It Up	1982	2.50	5.00	10.00

COLLECTABLES

❑ COL-5190	Golden Classics: Express	198?	2.50	5.00	10.00

COLUMBIA

❑ PC 34178	Energy to Burn	1976	2.50	5.00	10.00
❑ PCQ 34178 [Q]	Energy to Burn	1976	3.75	7.50	15.00
❑ PC 34702	Function at the Junction	1977	2.50	5.00	10.00
❑ JC 35078	Shout!	1978	2.50	5.00	10.00
❑ JC 36333	B.T. Express 1980	1980	2.50	5.00	10.00
❑ JC 36923	Greatest Hits	1980	2.50	5.00	10.00

ROADSHOW

❑ 41001	Non-Stop	1975	3.00	6.00	12.00

ROADSHOW/SCEPTER

❑ 5117	Do It ('Til You're Satisfied)	1974	3.00	6.00	12.00

BABE RUTH
45s
CAPITOL

❑ 4219	Say No More/Elusive	1976	—	2.00	4.00

HARVEST

❑ 3553	Wells Fargo/Theme from "For A Few Dollars More"	1973	—	2.50	5.00

Albums
CAPITOL

❑ ST-11515	Kids Stuff	1976	2.50	5.00	10.00

HARVEST

❑ SW-11151	First Base	1973	3.75	7.50	15.00
❑ ST-11275	Amar Caballero	1974	3.00	6.00	12.00
❑ ST-11367	Babe Ruth	1975	2.50	5.00	10.00
❑ ST-11451	Stealin' Home	1975	2.50	5.00	10.00

BABIES, THE
45s
ABC DUNHILL

❑ 4148	I Wanna Testify/Party Time	1968	3.00	6.00	12.00

DUNHILL

❑ 4085	You Make Me Feel Like Someone/The Hand of Fate	1967	4.00	8.00	16.00
❑ 4085 [PS]	You Make Me Feel Like Someone/The Hand of Fate	1967	7.50	15.00	30.00
❑ 4101	I'm Not Asking for the World/Goodbye My Love, Goodbye	1967	3.75	7.50	15.00

BABY
45s
CHELSEA

❑ 3057	Where Did All the Money Go/(B-side unknown)	1976	—	2.50	5.00
❑ 3068	Fallen Angel/Baton Rouge	1977	—	2.50	5.00

Albums
CHELSEA

❑ CHL-517	Where Did All the Money Go	1976	2.50	5.00	10.00

LONE STARR

❑ 9782	Baby	1974	6.25	12.50	25.00

BABY BUGS, THE
45s
VEE JAY

❑ 594	Bingo/Bingo's Bongo Bingo Party	1964	6.25	12.50	25.00
❑ 594 [PS]	Bingo/Bingo's Bongo Bingo Party	1964	18.75	37.50	75.00

BABY DOLLS, THE
45s
BOOM

❑ 60002	I Will Do It ('Cause He Wants Me To)/Now That I've Lost You	1966	2.50	5.00	10.00

GAMBLE

❑ 213	Please Don't Rush Me/There You Are	1968	2.00	4.00	8.00

HOLLYWOOD

❑ 1111	Got to Get You Into My Life/Why Can't I Make Him Like You	1960	10.00	20.00	40.00

MASKE

❑ 103	Go Away Baby/I'm Lonely	1960	12.50	25.00	50.00
❑ 701	Thanks, Mr. DJ/What a Wonderful Love	1961	30.00	60.00	120.00

RCA VICTOR

❑ 47-7296	Tutti Frutti/Cause I'm in Love	1958	3.75	7.50	15.00

WARNER BROS.

❑ 5086	Hey Baby/Quiet	1959	3.00	6.00	12.00

BABY HUEY
45s
BREAKTHROUGH

❑ 1001	Just Being Careful/(B-side unknown)	196?	375.00	750.00	1500.

CURTOM

❑ 1939	Mighty Mighty Children/Mighty Mighty Children (Part 2)	1969	2.50	5.00	10.00
❑ 1962	Hard Times/Listen to Me	1971	2.50	5.00	10.00

SATELLITE

❑ 2013	Messin' with the Kid/Monkey Man	196?	5.00	10.00	20.00

U.S.A.

❑ 801	Messin' with the Kid/Just Being Careful	196?	5.00	10.00	20.00

Albums
CURTOM

❑ CRS-8007	The Living Legend	1970	10.00	20.00	40.00

BABY JANE AND THE ROCKABYES
45s
PORT

❑ 3013	Heartbreak Shop/Dance Till My Feet Get Tired	1964	7.50	15.00	30.00

Number	Title (A Side/B Side)	Yr	VG	VG+	NM
UNITED ARTISTS					
❏ 505	If You Wanna/Oh Johnny	1962	5.00	10.00	20.00
❏ 560	How Much is That Doggie in the Window/My Boy John	1963	5.00	10.00	20.00
❏ 593	Get Me to the Church on Time/Hickory Dickory Dock	1963	3.75	7.50	15.00
BABY RAY					
45s					
IMPERIAL					
❏ 66216	There's Something On Your Mind/House on Soul Hill	1966	3.75	7.50	15.00
❏ 66232	Elvira/Just Because	1967	3.75	7.50	15.00
❏ 66256	Your Sweet Love/Yours Until Tomorrow	1967	3.75	7.50	15.00
Albums					
IMPERIAL					
❏ LP-9335 [M]	Where Soul Lives	1967	6.25	12.50	25.00
❏ LP-12335 [S]	Where Soul Lives	1967	7.50	15.00	30.00
BABY RAY AND THE FERNS An early production of FRANK ZAPPA.					
45s					
DONNA					
❏ 1378	How's Your Bird/The World's Greatest Sinner	1963	50.00	100.00	200.00
BACHARACH, BURT					
45s					
A&M					
❏ 845	Alfie/Bond Street	1967	2.00	4.00	8.00
❏ 888	The Look of Love/Reach Out for Me	1967	2.00	4.00	8.00
❏ 931	Are You There (With Another Girl)/Message to Michael	1968	—	3.00	6.00
❏ 1004	The Bell That Couldn't Jingle/What the World Needs Now Is Love	1968	—	3.00	6.00
❏ 1064	I'll Never Fall in Love Again/Pacific Coast Highway	1969	—	3.00	6.00
❏ 1153	Come Touch the Sun/Raindrops Keep Fallin' on My Head	1969	—	3.00	6.00
❏ 1222	A House Is Not a Home/Any Day Now	1970	—	2.50	5.00
❏ 1241	All Kinds of People/She's Gone Away	1971	—	2.50	5.00
❏ 1241 [PS]	All Kinds of People/She's Gone Away	1971	2.00	4.00	8.00
❏ 1290	One Less Bell to Answer/Freefall	1971	—	2.50	5.00
❏ 1290 [PS]	One Less Bell to Answer/Freefall	1971	2.00	4.00	8.00
❏ 1489	Living Together, Growing Together/Something Big	1973	—	2.00	4.00
❏ 1512	Living Together, Growing Together/Reflections	1974	—	2.00	4.00
❏ 1921	I Took My Strength from You (I Had None)/Time and Tenderness	1977	—	2.00	4.00
❏ 1960	No One Remembers My Name/Futures	1977	—	2.00	4.00
❏ 2161	New York Lady/Riverboat	1979	—	2.00	4.00
KAPP					
❏ 532	Saturday Sunshine/And So Goodbye My Love	1963	2.00	4.00	8.00
❏ 657	Don't Go Breaking My Heart/Trains and Boats and Planes	1965	2.00	4.00	8.00
❏ 685	My Little Red Book/What's New Pussycat	1965	2.00	4.00	8.00
LIBERTY					
❏ 55934	Juanita's Place/Nikki	1966	2.00	4.00	8.00
UNITED ARTISTS					
❏ 50123	The Fox Trot/Ukeatalia	1967	2.00	4.00	8.00
Albums					
A&M					
❏ SP-131 [M]	Reach Out	1967	3.00	6.00	12.00
❏ SP-3501	Burt Bacharach	1971	2.50	5.00	10.00
❏ SP-3527	Living Together	1973	2.50	5.00	10.00
❏ SP-3661	Burt Bacharach's Greatest Hits	1973	2.50	5.00	10.00
❏ SP-3709	Woman	1979	2.50	5.00	10.00
❏ SP-4131 [S]	Reach Out	1967	3.00	6.00	12.00
❏ SP-4188	Make It Easy on Yourself	1969	2.50	5.00	10.00
❏ SP-4622	Futures	1977	2.50	5.00	10.00
KAPP					
❏ KS-3577	Burt Bacharach Plays His Hits	1969	3.00	6.00	12.00
MCA					
❏ 65	Burt Bacharach Plays His Hits	1973	2.00	4.00	8.00
—Reissue of Kapp LP					
BACHELORS, THE (1) British Invasion male vocal group.					
45s					
LONDON					
❏ 9584	Charmaine/Old Bill	1963	3.00	6.00	12.00
❏ 9623	Faraway Places/Is There a Chance	1964	3.00	6.00	12.00
❏ 9632	Whispering/No Light in the Window	1964	3.00	6.00	12.00
❏ 9639	Diane/Happy Land	1964	3.00	6.00	12.00
❏ 9639	Diane/I Believe	1964	3.75	7.50	15.00
❏ 9672	I Believe/Sweet Lullaby	1964	3.00	6.00	12.00
❏ 9672 [PS]	I Believe/Sweet Lullaby	1964	6.25	12.50	25.00
❏ 9693	I Wouldn't Trade You for the World/Beneath the Willow Tree	1964	3.00	6.00	12.00
❏ 9693 [PS]	I Wouldn't Trade You for the World/Beneath the Willow Tree	1964	6.25	12.50	25.00
❏ 9724	No Arms Can Ever Hold You/Oh Samuel, Don't Die	1964	3.00	6.00	12.00
❏ 9762	Marie/You Can Tell	1965	2.50	5.00	10.00
❏ 9793	Chapel in the Moonlight/The Old Wishing Well	1965	2.50	5.00	10.00
❏ 9793 [PS]	Chapel in the Moonlight/The Old Wishing Well	1965	5.00	10.00	20.00
❏ 9828	Love Me with All of Your Heart/There's No Room in My Heart	1966	2.50	5.00	10.00
❏ 20010	Can I Trust You/My Girl	1966	2.50	5.00	10.00
❏ 20018	Walk with Faith in Your Heart/Queen Molly Malone of Ireland	1966	2.50	5.00	10.00
❏ 20027	Marta/Oh How I Miss You	1967	2.00	4.00	8.00
❏ 20033	Learn to Live Without You/3 O'Clock Flamingo Street	1967	2.00	4.00	8.00
❏ 20051	Punky's Dilemma/It's a Beautiful Day	1968	2.00	4.00	8.00

Number	Title (A Side/B Side)	Yr	VG	VG+	NM
❏ 20063	Love Is All/The Colours of Love	1970	—	3.00	6.00
❏ 20071	Diamonds Are Forever/Where There's a Heartache	1971	—	3.00	6.00
Albums					
LONDON					
❏ PS 353 [S]	Presenting the Bachelors	1964	5.00	10.00	20.00
❏ PS 393 [P]	Back Again	1964	5.00	10.00	20.00
—"I Wouldn't Trade You for the World" is rechanneled.					
❏ PS 418 [S]	No Arms Can Ever Hold You	1965	5.00	10.00	20.00
❏ PS 435 [P]	Marie	1965	5.00	10.00	20.00
—"Marie" is rechanneled					
❏ PS 460 [S]	Hits of the 60's	1966	5.00	10.00	20.00
❏ PS 491 [P]	The Bachelors' Girls	1966	3.75	7.50	15.00
—"Marie" is rechanneled					
❏ PS 518 [P]	Golden All Time Hits	1967	3.75	7.50	15.00
❏ PS 528 [S]	Bachelors '68	1968	3.00	6.00	12.00
❏ PS 611	Under and Over	1972	2.50	5.00	10.00
❏ LL 3353 [M]	Presenting the Bachelors	1964	3.75	7.50	15.00
❏ LL 3393 [M]	Back Again	1964	3.75	7.50	15.00
❏ LL 3418 [M]	No Arms Can Ever Hold You	1965	3.75	7.50	15.00
❏ LL 3435 [M]	Marie	1965	3.75	7.50	15.00
❏ LL 3460 [M]	Hits of the 60's	1966	3.75	7.50	15.00
❏ LL 3491 [M]	The Bachelors' Girls	1966	3.00	6.00	12.00
❏ LL 3518 [M]	Golden All Time Hits	1967	3.75	7.50	15.00
❏ LL 3528 [M]	Bachelors '68	1968	5.00	10.00	20.00
BACHELORS, THE (2) American male vocal group.					
45s					
ALADDIN					
❏ 3210	Pretty Baby/Can't Help Loving You	1953	625.00	1250.	2500.
ROYAL ROOST					
❏ 620	I Found Love/You've Lied	1952	75.00	150.00	300.00
BACHELORS, THE (U) None of these are group (1), though some could be group (2).					
45s					
EPIC					
❏ 9369	Do the Madison/Bachelor's Club	1960	3.00	6.00	12.00
MERCURY					
❏ 8159	Yesterday's Roses/Hereafter	1949	75.00	150.00	300.00
MGM					
❏ 12668	Sometimes/Teenage Memory	1958	5.00	10.00	20.00
NATIONAL					
❏ 104	From Your Heart/A Million Teardrops	1957	6.25	12.50	25.00
❏ 115	Today, Tomorrow, Forever/I Want a Girl	1957	6.25	12.50	25.00
POPLAR					
❏ 101	After/You Know, I Know (I Love You)	1957	12.50	25.00	50.00
SMASH					
❏ 1723	The Day I Met You/Hey Little Girl	1961	3.00	6.00	12.00
BACHMAN-TURNER OVERDRIVE Also see BRAVE BELT; THE GUESS WHO.					
45s					
COMPLEAT					
❏ 127	For the Weekend/Just Look at Me Now	1984	—	2.00	4.00
❏ 133	My Sugaree/Service with a Smile	1984	—	2.00	4.00
❏ 137	My Sugaree/(B-side unknown)	1985	—	2.00	4.00
MERCURY					
❏ 73383	Gimmie Your Money Please/Little Gandy Dancer	1973	—	2.50	5.00
❏ 73417	Blue Collar/Hold Back the Water	1973	—	2.50	5.00
❏ 73457	Let It Ride/Tramp	1974	—	2.00	4.00
❏ 73487	Takin' Care of Business/Stonegates	1974	—	2.00	4.00
❏ 73622	You Ain't Seen Nothin' Yet/Free Wheelin'	1974	—	2.00	4.00
❏ 73656	Roll On Down the Highway/Sledgehammer	1975	—	2.00	4.00
❏ 73683	Hey You/Flat Broke Love	1975	—	2.00	4.00
❏ 73724	Down to the Line/She's a Devil	1975	—	2.00	4.00
❏ 73724 [PS]	Down to the Line/She's a Devil	1975	2.00	4.00	8.00
❏ 73766	Take It Like a Man/Woncha Take Me for a While	1976	—	2.00	4.00
❏ 73784	Looking Out for #1/Find Out About Love	1976	—	2.00	4.00
❏ 73843	Gimme Your Money Please/Four Wheel Drive	1976	—	2.00	4.00
❏ 73903	Freeways/My Wheels Won't Turn	1977	—	2.00	4.00
❏ 73926	Shotgun Rider/Down, Down	1977	—	2.00	4.00
❏ 73951	Life Still Goes On (I'm Lonely)/Just for You	1977	—	2.00	4.00
❏ 73987	Down the Road/A Long Time for a Little While	1978	—	2.00	4.00
❏ 74046	Heaven Tonight/Heartaches	1979	—	2.00	4.00
❏ 74062	End of the Line/Jamaica	1979	—	2.00	4.00
Albums					
COMPLEAT					
❏ CPL1-1010	Bachman-Turner Overdrive	1984	2.00	4.00	8.00
MCA/CURB					
❏ 5760	Live! Live! Live!	1986	2.00	4.00	8.00
MERCURY					
❏ SRM-1-673	Bachman-Turner Overdrive	1973	3.00	6.00	12.00
—Red label					
❏ SRM-1-673	Bachman-Turner Overdrive	1974	2.50	5.00	10.00
—Chicago skyline label					
❏ SRM-1-696	Bachman-Turner Overdrive II	1973	3.00	6.00	12.00
—Red label					
❏ SRM-1-696	Bachman-Turner Overdrive II	1974	2.50	5.00	10.00
—Chicago skyline label					
❏ SRM-1-1004	Not Fragile	1974	2.50	5.00	10.00
❏ SRM-1-1027	Four Wheel Drive	1975	2.50	5.00	10.00
❏ SRM-1-1067	Head On	1975	2.50	5.00	10.00
❏ SRM-1-1101	Best of B.T.O. (So Far)	1976	2.50	5.00	10.00
❏ SRM-1-3700	Freeways	1977	2.50	5.00	10.00
❏ SRM-1-3713	Street Action	1978	2.50	5.00	10.00
❏ SRM-1-3748	Rock N' Roll Nights	1979	2.50	5.00	10.00
❏ 822786-1	Best of B.T.O. (So Far)	1984	2.00	4.00	8.00
—Reissue of 1101					

B

Number	Title (A Side/B Side)	Yr	VG	VG+	NM
BACHS, THE					
Albums					
ROTO					
☐ PR-1044	Out of the Bachs	1967	2000.	3000.	4000.
BACK BEAT					
45s					
LAURIE					
☐ 3092	Rock and Roll Symphony, 1st and 2nd Movements	1961	5.00	10.00	20.00
BACK PORCH MAJORITY, THE					
45s					
EPIC					
☐ 9689	Friends/Hand-Me-Down Things	1964	2.50	5.00	10.00
☐ 9754	Hey Nelly Nelly/Ol' Dan Tucker	1965	2.50	5.00	10.00
☐ 9769	Smash Flops/Jack O'Diamonds	1965	2.50	5.00	10.00
☐ 9769 [PS]	Smash Flops/Jack O'Diamonds	1965	3.75	7.50	15.00
☐ 9809	Good-Time Joe/Ramblin' Man	1965	2.50	5.00	10.00
☐ 9850	The Mighty Mississippi/Song of Hope	1965	2.50	5.00	10.00
☐ 9879	Second Hand Man/That's the Way It's Gonna Be	1965	2.50	5.00	10.00
☐ 10036	Honey and Wine/Brother John	1966	2.00	4.00	8.00
☐ 10079	Once Again/Slippery Sal and Dirty Dan, the Oyster Man	1966	2.00	4.00	8.00
☐ 10129	Southtown U.S.A./This Little Light	1967	2.00	4.00	8.00
Albums					
EPIC					
☐ LN 24134 [M]	Live from Ledbetter's	1965	3.75	7.50	15.00
☐ LN 24149 [M]	Riverboat Days	1965	3.75	7.50	15.00
☐ LN 24184 [M]	That's the Way It's Gonna Be	1966	3.75	7.50	15.00
☐ LN 24319 [M]	Willy Nilly Wonder of Illusion	1967	5.00	10.00	20.00
☐ BN 26134 [S]	Live from Ledbetter's	1965	5.00	10.00	20.00
☐ BN 26149 [S]	Riverboat Days	1965	5.00	10.00	20.00
☐ BN 26184 [S]	That's the Way It's Gonna Be	1966	5.00	10.00	20.00
☐ BN 26319 [S]	Willy Nilly Wonder of Illusion	1967	3.75	7.50	15.00
BACK STREET CRAWLER					
7-Inch Extended Plays					
ATCO					
☐ PR 247 [DJ]	Hoo Doo Woman/All the Girls Are Crazy// Survivor/The Band Plays On	1975	—	3.00	6.00
—Small hole, plays at 33 1/3 rpm					
☐ PR 247 [PS]	Back Street Crawler	1975	2.00	4.00	8.00
Albums					
ATCO					
☐ SD 36-125	The Band Plays On	1975	3.00	6.00	12.00
☐ SD 36-138	2nd Street	1976	3.00	6.00	12.00
EPIC					
☐ PE 34900	Crawler	1977	2.50	5.00	10.00
—Epic titles as "Crawler"					
☐ JE 35482	Snake, Rattle and Roll	1978	2.50	5.00	10.00
BACKUS, JIM					
45s					
DICO					
☐ 101	I Was a Teenage Reindeer/The Office Party	1959	5.00	10.00	20.00
DORE					
☐ 899	Dirty Old Man/Frigid	1974	—	2.50	5.00
JUBILEE					
☐ 5330	Delicious!/I Need a Vacation	1958	3.75	7.50	15.00
—As "Jim Bakus and Friend"					
☐ 5351	Cave Man/Why Don't You Go Home for Christmas	1958	3.00	6.00	12.00
☐ 5361	Cave Man/Rock on the Roof	1959	3.00	6.00	12.00
Albums					
RCA VICTOR					
☐ LPM-1362 [M]	Mr. Magoo in Hi-Fi	1957	12.50	25.00	50.00
BACON, GAR					
45s					
BATON					
☐ 248	There's Gonna Be Rockin' Tonight/Y-I-O-U	1957	15.00	30.00	60.00
☐ 250	Justice/Pucker Up	1958	10.00	20.00	40.00
DALE					
☐ 105	Chains of Love/Mary Jane	1957	6.25	12.50	25.00
☐ 108	Dutch Treat/I'll Never Fail You	1958	7.50	15.00	30.00
OKEH					
☐ 7115	Marshall, Marshall/Too Young to Love	1959	5.00	10.00	20.00
RKO UNIQUE					
☐ 395	Lonesome Wail/You and Your Love	1957	5.00	10.00	20.00
BACON FAT					
Albums					
BLUE HORIZON					
☐ BH-4807	Grease One for Me	1970	6.25	12.50	25.00
BAD COMPANY Also see BOZ; FREE.					
12-Inch Singles					
ATLANTIC					
☐ PR 959 [DJ]	This Love (same on both sides)	1986	2.00	4.00	8.00
☐ PR 999 [DJ]	That Girl (same on both sides?)	1987	2.00	4.00	8.00
☐ 2409 [DJ]	No Smoke Without a Fire (same on both sides)	1988	2.00	4.00	8.00
45s					
ATCO					
☐ 98463	This Could Be the One/How About That	1992	—	2.00	4.00
ATLANTIC					
☐ 88939	Shake It Up/Dangerous Age	1989	—	2.00	4.00
☐ 88939 [PS]	Shake It Up/Dangerous Age	1989	—	2.00	4.00
☐ 89035	No Smoke Without a Fire/Love Attack	1988	—	2.00	4.00
☐ 89035 [PS]	No Smoke Without a Fire/Love Attack	1988	—	2.00	4.00
☐ 89299	That Girl/If I'm Sleeping	1987	—	2.00	4.00
☐ 89355	This Love/Tell It Like It Is	1986	—	2.00	4.00
☐ 89355 [PS]	This Love/Tell It Like It Is	1986	—	2.00	4.00
ATLANTIC OLDIES SERIES					
☐ 94936	If You Needed Somebody/Holy Water	1993	—	2.00	4.00
—"Reissue" of two hits that had not appeared on a U.S. vinyl 45 before					
SWAN SONG					
☐ 70015	Can't Get Enough/Little Miss Fortune	1974	—	3.00	6.00
☐ 70101	Movin' On/Easy on My Soul	1974	—	2.50	5.00
☐ 70103	Good Lovin' Gone Bad/Whiskey Bottle	1975	—	2.50	5.00
☐ 70106	Feel Like Makin' Love/Wild Fire Woman	1975	—	3.00	6.00
☐ 70108	Young Blood/Do Right by Your Woman	1976	—	2.50	5.00
☐ 70109	Honey Child/Fade Away	1976	—	2.00	4.00
☐ 70112	Burnin' Sky/Everything I Need	1976	—	2.00	4.00
☐ 70119	Rock 'N' Roll Fantasy/Crazy Circles	1979	—	2.50	5.00
☐ 70119 [PS]	Rock 'N' Roll Fantasy/Crazy Circles	1979	—	3.00	6.00
☐ 71000	Gone, Gone, Gone/Take the Time	1979	—	2.50	5.00
☐ 71000 [PS]	Gone, Gone, Gone/Take the Time	1979	—	3.00	6.00
☐ 99966	Electricland/Untie the Knot	1982	—	2.50	5.00
☐ 99966 [PS]	Electricland/Untie the Knot	1982	—	2.50	5.00
Albums					
ATCO					
☐ 91371	Holy Water	1990	3.75	7.50	15.00
ATLANTIC					
☐ 81625	10 from 6 (The Best of Bad Company)	1986	2.50	5.00	10.00
☐ 81684	Fame and Fortune	1987	2.50	5.00	10.00
☐ 81884	Dangerous Age	1988	2.50	5.00	10.00
SWAN SONG					
☐ SS 8410	Bad Company	1974	2.50	5.00	10.00
☐ SS 8413	Straight Shooter	1975	2.50	5.00	10.00
☐ SS 8415	Run with the Pack	1976	2.50	5.00	10.00
☐ SS 8500	Burnin' Sky	1977	2.50	5.00	10.00
☐ SS 8501	Bad Company	1977	2.00	4.00	8.00
☐ SS 8502	Straight Shooter	1977	2.00	4.00	8.00
☐ SS 8503	Run with the Pack	1977	2.00	4.00	8.00
☐ SS 8506	Desolation Angels	1979	2.50	5.00	10.00
☐ 90001	Rough Diamonds	1982	2.50	5.00	10.00
BADD BOYS, THE					
45s					
EPIC					
☐ 10119	Never Going Back to Georgia/River Deep Mountain High	1967	12.50	25.00	50.00
☐ 10165	Folks in a Hurry/I Told You So	1967	15.00	30.00	60.00
BADFINGER Also see GEORGE HARRISON AND FRIENDS.					
45s					
APPLE					
☐ 1803	Maybe Tomorrow/And Her Daddy's a Millionaire	1969	5.00	10.00	20.00
—By "The Iveys"; without star on label					
☐ 1803	Maybe Tomorrow/And Her Daddy's a Millionaire	1969	7.50	15.00	30.00
—By "The Iveys"; with star on label					
☐ 1815	Come and Get It/Rock of All Ages	1969	—	3.00	6.00
☐ 1815	Come and Get It/Rock of All Ages	1969	2.00	4.00	8.00
—With Capitol logo on B-side bottom					
☐ 1822	No Matter What/Carry On Till Tomorrow	1970	—	3.00	6.00
☐ 1822	No Matter What/Carry On Till Tomorrow	1970	5.00	10.00	20.00
—With star on A-side label					
☐ 1841	Day After Day/Money	1971	—	3.00	6.00
☐ 1841	Day After Day/Money	1971	5.00	10.00	20.00
—With star on A-side label					
☐ 1841 [DJ]	Day After Day/Money	1971	30.00	60.00	120.00
—White label					
☐ 1844	Baby Blue/Flying	1972	—	3.00	6.00
☐ 1844 [DJ]	Baby Blue/Flying	1972	30.00	60.00	120.00
—White label					
☐ 1844 [PS]	Baby Blue/Flying	1972	3.75	7.50	15.00
☐ 1864	Apple of My Eye/Blind Owl	1973	—	3.00	6.00
☐ P-1864 [DJ]	Apple of My Eye (mono/stereo)	1973	6.25	12.50	25.00
APPLE/AMERICOM					
☐ 1803/PM-300	Maybe Tomorrow/And Her Daddy's a Millionaire	1969	150.00	300.00	600.00
—By "The Iveys"; four-inch flexidisc sold from vending machines					
CAPITOL					
☐ S7-17487	Baby Blue/Day After Day	1993	—	—	3.00
—Blue vinyl					
☐ S7-17487	Baby Blue/Day After Day	1993	—	2.50	5.00
—Black vinyl					
ELEKTRA					
☐ 46022	Lost Inside Your Love/Come Down Hard	1979	—	2.50	5.00
☐ 46025	Love Is Gonna Come At Last/Sail Away	1979	—	2.50	5.00
RADIO					
☐ 3793	Hold On/Passin' Time	1981	—	2.50	5.00
☐ 3815	I Got You/Rock and Roll Contract	1981	—	2.50	5.00
☐ 3833	Because I Love You/Too Hung Up on You	1981	—	2.50	5.00
WARNER BROS.					
☐ 7801	I Miss You/Shine On	1974	—	3.00	6.00
Albums					
APPLE					
☐ ST-3355	Maybe Tomorrow	1969	500.00	1000.	2000.
—As "The Iveys"; album not released in US; price is for an LP slick, which does exist					
☐ ST 3364	Magic Christian Music	1970	5.00	10.00	20.00
☐ ST 3364	Magic Christian Music	1970	7.50	15.00	30.00
—With Capitol logo on Side 2 bottom					
☐ SKAO 3367	No Dice	1970	7.50	15.00	30.00
☐ SW 3387	Straight Up	1971	15.00	30.00	60.00
☐ SW 3411	Ass	1973	5.00	10.00	20.00
ELEKTRA					
☐ 6E-175	Airwaves	1979	3.00	6.00	12.00
RADIO					
☐ RR 16030	Say No More	1981	2.50	5.00	10.00

Number	Title (A Side/B Side)	Yr	VG	VG+	NM

RYKO ANALOGUE
| ❑ RALP 10189 | Day After Day | 1990 | 5.00 | 10.00 | 20.00 |

—Limited edition on clear vinyl with obi

WARNER BROS.
| ❑ BS 2762 | Badfinger | 1974 | 3.75 | 7.50 | 15.00 |
| ❑ BS 2827 | Wish You Were Here | 1974 | 3.75 | 7.50 | 15.00 |

BADGER
Albums
ATCO
| ❑ SD 7022 | One Live Badger | 1973 | 3.00 | 6.00 | 12.00 |

EPIC
| ❑ KE 32831 | White Lady | 1974 | 3.00 | 6.00 | 12.00 |

BAEZ, JOAN
45s
A&M
❑ 1334	Song of Bangladesh/Prison Trilogy (Billy Rose)	1972	—	2.50	5.00
❑ 1334 [PS]	Song of Bangladesh/Prison Trilogy (Billy Rose)	1972	2.50	5.00	10.00
❑ 1362	In the Quiet Morning/To Bobby	1972	—	2.00	4.00
❑ 1362 [PS]	In the Quiet Morning/To Bobby	1972	2.00	4.00	8.00
❑ 1393	Love Song to a Stranger/Tumbleweed	1972	—	2.00	4.00
❑ 1454	The Best of Friends/Mary Call	1973	—	2.00	4.00
❑ 1472	Less Than the Song/Windrose	1973	—	2.00	4.00
❑ 1516	Forever Young/Guantanamera	1974	—	2.00	4.00
❑ 1703	Blue Sky/Dida	1975	—	2.00	4.00
❑ 1737	Diamonds and Rust/Winds of the Old Days	1975	—	2.50	5.00
❑ 1802	Please Come to Boston/Love Song to a Stranger	1976	—	2.00	4.00
❑ 1820	Never Dreamed You'd Leave in Summer/ Children and All That Jazz	1976	—	2.00	4.00
❑ 1884	Caruso/Time Is Passing Us By	1976	—	2.00	4.00
❑ 1906	O Brother/Still Waters at Night	1977	—	2.00	4.00

DECCA
| ❑ 32890 | Silent Running/Rejoice in the Sun | 1971 | — | 3.00 | 6.00 |

GUARDIAN
| ❑ S7-19727 | No Mermaid/Diamonds and Rust | 1997 | — | — | 3.00 |

PHILCO-FORD
| ❑ HP-36 | There But For Fortune/Pack Up Your Sorrows | 1969 | 5.00 | 10.00 | 20.00 |

—4-inch plastic "Hip Pocket Record" with color sleeve

PORTRAIT
❑ 70006	I'm Blowing Away/The Altar Boy and the Sheep	1977	—	2.00	4.00
❑ 70009	Time Rag/Miracles	1977	—	2.00	4.00
❑ 70032	Light a Light/Michael	1979	—	2.00	4.00

RCA VICTOR
| ❑ 74-0568 | The Ballad of Sacco and Vanzetti/Here's to You | 1971 | — | 3.00 | 6.00 |

VANGUARD
| ❑ SPV-6 | Maria Dolores/Plane Wreck at Los Gatos (Deportee) | 1971 | — | 2.00 | 4.00 |

—Small hole, plays at 33 1/3 rpm
| ❑ SPV-6 [PS] | Maria Dolores/Plane Wreck at Los Gatos (Deportee) | 1971 | — | 2.00 | 4.00 |

—The above single and sleeve were a bonus single included with the album "Blessed Are..."; as it is sometimes found apart from the LP, we've made a separate listing, but it was never sold separately at the time
❑ 35012	Banks of the Ohio/Old Blue	1962	2.00	4.00	8.00
❑ 35013	Lonesome Road/Pal of Mine	1962	2.00	4.00	8.00
❑ 35018	What Have They Done to the Rain/ Danger Waters	1963	2.00	4.00	8.00
❑ 35023	We Shall Overcome/ What Have They Done to the Rain	1963	2.00	4.00	8.00
❑ 35026	Medley: With God on Our Side/Railroad Bill// Rambler Gambler	1964	2.00	4.00	8.00
❑ 35031	There But for Fortune/ Daddy You Been On My Mind	1965	2.00	4.00	8.00
❑ 35031 [PS]	There But for Fortune/ Daddy You Been On My Mind	1965	7.50	15.00	30.00
❑ 35040	Pack Up Your Sorrows/Swallow Song	1966	2.00	4.00	8.00
❑ 35046	Little Drummer Boy/Cantique de Noel	1966	2.50	5.00	10.00
❑ 35055	Be Not Too Hard/The North	1967	2.00	4.00	8.00
❑ 35088	Love Is Just a Four-Letter Word/Love Minus Zero-No Limit	1969	2.00	4.00	8.00
❑ 35092	If I Knew/Rock Salt and Nails	1969	2.00	4.00	8.00
❑ 35098	Four Days Gone/Hickory Wind	1969	2.00	4.00	8.00
❑ 35103	No Expectations/One Day at a Time	1970	—	3.00	6.00
❑ 35106	Sweet Sir Galahad/The Ghetto	1970	—	3.00	6.00
❑ 35114	Carry It On/Rock Salt and Nails	1970	—	3.00	6.00
❑ 35138	The Night They Drove Old Dixie Down/ When Time Is Stolen	1971	2.00	4.00	8.00
❑ 35145	Let It Be/Poor Wayfaring Stranger	1971	—	3.00	6.00
❑ 35148	Will the Circle Be Unbroken/ Just a Closer Walk with Thee	1972	—	2.50	5.00
❑ 35158	Blessed Are/The Brand New Tennessee Waltz	1972	—	2.50	5.00

Albums
A&M
| ❑ SP-3103 | Come From the Shadows | 198? | 2.00 | 4.00 | 8.00 |

—Budget-line reissue
| ❑ SP-3233 | Diamonds and Rust | 198? | 2.00 | 4.00 | 8.00 |

—Budget-line reissue
| ❑ SP-3234 | The Best of Joan C. Baez | 198? | 2.00 | 4.00 | 8.00 |

—Budget-line reissue
❑ SP-3614	Gracias A La Vida	1974	3.00	6.00	12.00
❑ SP-3704 [(2)]	From Every Stage	1976	3.00	6.00	12.00
❑ SP-4339	Come From the Shadows	1972	2.50	5.00	10.00
❑ SP-4390	Where Are You Now, My Son?	1973	2.50	5.00	10.00
❑ SP-4527	Diamonds and Rust	1975	2.50	5.00	10.00
❑ SP-4603	Gulf Winds	1976	2.50	5.00	10.00
❑ SP-4668	The Best of Joan C. Baez	1977	2.50	5.00	10.00
❑ SP-6506 [(2)]	From Every Stage	198?	2.50	5.00	10.00

—Reissue
| ❑ QU-54339 [Q] | Come From the Shadows | 1974 | 5.00 | 10.00 | 20.00 |
| ❑ QU-54527 [Q] | Diamonds and Rust | 1975 | 5.00 | 10.00 | 20.00 |

BOOK-OF-THE-MONTH
| ❑ 40-5711 [(4)] | Satisfied Mind | 1979 | 6.25 | 12.50 | 25.00 |

—With booklet

GOLD CASTLE
| ❑ D1-71309 | Recently | 1989 | 3.00 | 6.00 | 12.00 |

—Reissue of 171 009
❑ D1-71321	Diamonds and Rust in the Castle	1989	3.00	6.00	12.00
❑ D1-71324	Speaking of Dreams	1989	3.00	6.00	12.00
❑ 171009	Recently	1988	2.50	5.00	10.00

MOBILE FIDELITY
| ❑ 1-238 | Diamonds and Rust | 1996 | 15.00 | 30.00 | 60.00 |

—Audiophile vinyl

NAUTILUS
| ❑ NR-12 | Diamonds and Rust | 1980 | 10.00 | 20.00 | 40.00 |

—Audiophile vinyl

PORTRAIT
| ❑ PR 34697 | Blowin' Away | 1977 | 2.50 | 5.00 | 10.00 |
| ❑ JR 35766 | Honest Lullaby | 1979 | 2.50 | 5.00 | 10.00 |

SQUIRE
| ❑ SQ-33001 [M] | The Best of Joan Baez | 1963 | 5.00 | 10.00 | 20.00 |

VANGUARD
❑ VSD-41/42 [(2)]	The Joan Baez Ballad Book	1972	3.00	6.00	12.00
❑ VSD-49/50 [(2)]	The Contemporary Ballad Book	1974	3.00	6.00	12.00
❑ VSD-79/80 [(2)]	The Love Song Album	197?	3.00	6.00	12.00
❑ VSD-105/6 [(2)]	The Country Music Album	1979	3.00	6.00	12.00
❑ VSD-2077 [S]	Joan Baez	1960	6.25	12.50	25.00
❑ VSD-2097 [S]	Joan Baez, Vol. 2	1961	6.25	12.50	25.00
❑ VSD-2122 [S]	Joan Baez In Concert	1962	6.25	12.50	25.00
❑ VSD-2123 [S]	Joan Baez In Concert, Part 2	1963	6.25	12.50	25.00
❑ VSD-6560/1 [(2)]	The First 10 Years	1970	3.75	7.50	15.00
❑ VSD-6570/1 [(2)]	Blessed Are...	1971	3.75	7.50	15.00

—Add 50 percent if bonus 7-inch single, "Maria Dolores"/"Plane Wreck at Los Gatos (Deportee)," and its special sleeve are still in the package
❑ VRS-9078 [M]	Joan Baez	1960	5.00	10.00	20.00
❑ VRS-9094 [M]	Joan Baez, Vol. 2	1961	5.00	10.00	20.00
❑ VRS-9112 [M]	Joan Baez In Concert	1962	5.00	10.00	20.00
❑ VRS-9113 [M]	Joan Baez In Concert, Part 2	1963	5.00	10.00	20.00
❑ VRS-9160 [M]	Joan Baez/5	1964	3.75	7.50	15.00
❑ VRS-9200 [M]	Farewell, Angelina	1965	3.75	7.50	15.00
❑ VRS-9230 [M]	Noel	1966	3.75	7.50	15.00
❑ VRS-9240 [M]	Joan	1967	3.75	7.50	15.00
❑ VSQ-40001/2 [(2)Q]	Blessed Are	1973	6.25	12.50	25.00
❑ VSQ-40032 [Q]	Hits/Greatest & Others	1973	5.00	10.00	20.00
❑ VMS-73107	The Joan Baez Ballad Book, Vol. 1	1985	2.50	5.00	10.00
❑ VMS-73115	The Joan Baez Ballad Book, Vol. 2	1985	2.50	5.00	10.00
❑ VMS-73119	The Night They Drove Old Dixie Down	198?	2.50	5.00	10.00
❑ VSD-79160 [S]	Joan Baez/5	1964	5.00	10.00	20.00
❑ VSD-79200 [S]	Farewell, Angelina	1965	5.00	10.00	20.00
❑ VSD-79230 [S]	Noel	1966	5.00	10.00	20.00
❑ VSD-79240 [S]	Joan	1967	5.00	10.00	20.00
❑ VSD-79275	Baptism	1968	5.00	10.00	20.00
❑ VSD-79306/7 [(2)]	Any Day Now	1969	6.25	12.50	25.00
❑ VSD-79308	David's Album	1969	3.00	6.00	12.00
❑ VSD-79310	One Day at a Time	1970	3.00	6.00	12.00
❑ VSD-79313	Carry It On	1971	6.25	12.50	25.00

—Soundtrack album
| ❑ VSD-79332 | Hits/Greatest & Others | 1973 | 2.50 | 5.00 | 10.00 |
| ❑ VSD-79446/7 | Very Early Joan | 1981 | 3.00 | 6.00 | 12.00 |

BAG, THE
45s
DECCA
❑ 32279	Nobody's Child/Nickels 'N Dimes	1968	2.00	4.00	8.00
❑ 32409	Down and Out/Up in the Mornin'	1968	2.00	4.00	8.00
❑ 32463	Red, Purple and Blue/I Want You By My Side	1969	2.00	4.00	8.00

Albums
DECCA
| ❑ DL 75057 | Real | 1968 | 3.75 | 7.50 | 15.00 |

BAGDASARIAN, ROSS Real name of DAVID SEVILLE, who also invented THE CHIPMUNKS...
45s
CORAL
| ❑ 60544 | Come On-a My House/Oh Beauty | 1951 | 7.50 | 15.00 | 30.00 |
| ❑ 60597 | The Girl with the Tambourine/ He Says Mu-Humm | 1951 | 6.25 | 12.50 | 25.00 |

IMPERIAL
| ❑ 66379 | Jone-Cone-Phone/Spanish Pizza | 1969 | 2.50 | 5.00 | 10.00 |
| ❑ 66414 | You've Got Me on a Merry-Go-Round/You Better Open Your Eyes | 1969 | 2.50 | 5.00 | 10.00 |

LIBERTY
❑ 55013	The Bold and the Brave/See a Teardrop Fall	1956	5.00	10.00	20.00
❑ 55193	Judy/Maria from Madrid	1959	4.00	8.00	16.00
❑ 55239	Lotta Bull/(B-side unknown)	1959	4.00	8.00	16.00
❑ 55275	Lazy Lovers/One Finger Waltz	1960	4.00	8.00	16.00
❑ 55462	Armen's Theme/Russian Roulette	1962	3.75	7.50	15.00
❑ 55557	Cecelia/Gotta Get to Your House	1963	3.75	7.50	15.00
❑ 55619	Lucy, Lucy/Scalliwags and Sinners	1963	3.75	7.50	15.00
❑ 55810	La Noche/Naval Maneuver	1965	3.00	6.00	12.00
❑ 55837	Come On-a My House/Gotta Get to Your House	1965	3.00	6.00	12.00
❑ 56004	Walking Birds of Carnaby/Red Wine	1967	3.00	6.00	12.00
❑ 56043	Yallah/Naval Maneuver	1968	—	—	—

—Unreleased
| ❑ 56048 | When I Look in Your Eyes/Sands of Time | 1968 | 3.00 | 6.00 | 12.00 |
| ❑ 56165 | I Treasure Thee/Lie Lie | 1969 | 3.00 | 6.00 | 12.00 |

MERCURY
| ❑ 70254 | Let's Have a Merry, Merry Christmas/Hey Brother, Pour the Wine | 1953 | 6.25 | 12.50 | 25.00 |

Albums
LIBERTY
| ❑ LRP-3451 [M] | The Crazy, Mixed-Up World of Ross Bagdasarian | 1966 | 10.00 | 20.00 | 40.00 |
| ❑ LST-7451 [S] | The Crazy, Mixed-Up World of Ross Bagdasarian | 1966 | 12.50 | 25.00 | 50.00 |

Number	Title (A Side/B Side)	Yr	VG	VG+	NM

BAGELS, THE
45s
WARNER BROS.
| ❑ 5420 | I Wanna Hold Your Hair/ Yeah, Yeah, Yeah, Yeah | 1964 | 3.75 | 7.50 | 15.00 |

BAGGYS, THE
45s
PIPELINE
| ❑ 501 | El Surfer/El Seagull | 1963 | 10.00 | 20.00 | 40.00 |

BAILEY, DIANE
45s
SWAN
| ❑ 4079 | Golden Idol/Someone Else's Hands | 1961 | 3.00 | 6.00 | 12.00 |
| ❑ 4086 | True Blue Love/There's a Time | 1961 | 3.00 | 6.00 | 12.00 |

BAILEY, J.R.
45s
CALLA
| ❑ 158 | Love Won't Wear Off/(Instrumental) | 1968 | — | 3.00 | 6.00 |
MALA
| ❑ 12015 | Hold Back the Dawn/Too Late | 1968 | 2.00 | 4.00 | 8.00 |
MAM
| ❑ 3635 | I'll Always Be Your Lover/Not Too Long Ago | 1974 | — | 2.50 | 5.00 |
| ❑ 3639 | Everything I Want I See in You/ I Can't See Me Without You | 1974 | — | 2.50 | 5.00 |
MIDLAND INT'L
| ❑ PB-10305 | The Entertainer (If They Could Only See Me Now)/You Pass My Love (Like a Moving Train) | 1975 | — | 2.50 | 5.00 |
RCA
| ❑ PB-10799 | Super Loser/Love Still Remains | 1976 | — | 2.50 | 5.00 |
SPRING
| ❑ 3038 | I'm Still in Love with You/(B-side unknown) | 1984 | — | 2.00 | 4.00 |
TOY
| ❑ 3801 | Love, Love, Love/(B-side unknown) | 1972 | — | 3.00 | 6.00 |
| ❑ 3805 | After Hours/(B-side unknown) | 1972 | — | 3.00 | 6.00 |
UNITED ARTISTS
| ❑ XW-1215 | Alone in the Morning/Stella by Starlight | 1978 | — | 2.00 | 4.00 |
Albums
MAM
| ❑ 9 | Just Me 'N' You | 1974 | 3.00 | 6.00 | 12.00 |

BAILEY, PEARL
45s
COLUMBIA
| ❑ 4-43588 | Mame/If My Friends Could See Me Now | 1966 | — | 3.50 | 7.00 |
DECCA
| ❑ 31667 | I Was a Little Too Lonely/I'd Rather Be Rich | 1964 | — | 3.50 | 7.00 |
MERCURY
| ❑ 70926 | I Can't Rock and Roll to Save My Soul/The Gypsy Goofed | 1956 | 3.75 | 7.50 | 15.00 |
RCA VICTOR
| ❑ 74-0435 | Mama, a Rainbow/Two by Two | 1971 | — | 2.50 | 5.00 |
| ❑ 74-0510 | Close to You/A House Is Not a Home | 1971 | — | 2.50 | 5.00 |
ROULETTE
❑ 4016	Bill Bailey, Won't You Please Come Home/C'est Magnifique	1957	3.00	6.00	12.00
❑ 4167	I Got Rhythm/Summertime	1959	3.00	6.00	12.00
❑ 4206	Jingle Bells (Cha Cha Cha)/ Five Pound Box of Money	1959	5.00	10.00	20.00
❑ 4233	New Shoes/Not Now John	1960	2.50	5.00	10.00
❑ 4279	Ain't Misbehavin'/Bill Bailey, Won't You Please Come Home	1960	2.50	5.00	10.00
❑ 4415	Gee Baby (Ain't I Good to You)/You Gotta Dance	1962	2.00	4.00	8.00
❑ 4781	Look At That Face/Was It a Necessary Evil	1967	—	3.00	6.00
7-Inch Extended Plays
COLUMBIA
| ❑ B-2570 | Tired/Legalize My Name//That's Good Enough for Me/It's a Woman's Prerogative | 195? | 2.50 | 5.00 | 10.00 |
| ❑ B-2570 [PS] | Pearl Bailey (Hall of Fame Series) | 195? | 2.50 | 5.00 | 10.00 |
Albums
COLUMBIA
| ❑ CL 6099 [10] | Pearl Bailey Entertains | 1950 | 12.50 | 25.00 | 50.00 |
CORAL
❑ CRL 56068 [10]	Say Si Si	1953	12.50	25.00	50.00
❑ CRL 56078 [10]	I'm with You	1954	12.50	25.00	50.00
❑ CRL 57037 [M]	Pearl Bailey	1957	10.00	20.00	40.00
❑ CRL 57162 [M]	Cultured Pearl	1958	10.00	20.00	40.00
MERCURY
❑ MG-20187 [M]	The One and Only Pearl Bailey Sings	1956	10.00	20.00	40.00
❑ MG-20277 [M]	The Intoxicating Pearl Bailey	1957	10.00	20.00	40.00
ROULETTE
❑ SR 5004	Songs of the Bad Old Days	1975	3.00	6.00	12.00
❑ R-25012 [M]	Pearl Bailey A Broad	1957	7.50	15.00	30.00
—Black label original
| ❑ SR-25012 [R] | Pearl Bailey A Broad | 196? | 3.00 | 6.00 | 12.00 |
| ❑ R-25016 [M] | Pearl Bailey Sings for Adults Only | 1959 | 5.00 | 10.00 | 20.00 |
—Originals have a white label with colored spokes
| ❑ SR-25016 [S] | Pearl Bailey Sings for Adults Only | 1959 | 6.25 | 12.50 | 25.00 |
—Originals have a white label with colored spokes
| ❑ R-25037 [M] | St. Louis Blues | 1958 | 7.50 | 15.00 | 30.00 |
—Black label original
| ❑ SR-25037 [S] | St. Louis Blues | 1959 | 7.50 | 15.00 | 30.00 |
—Originals have a white label with colored spokes
| ❑ R-25063 [M] | Pearl Bailey Sings Porgy and Bess and Other Gershwin Melodies | 1959 | 5.00 | 10.00 | 20.00 |
—Originals have a white label with colored spokes
| ❑ SR-25063 [S] | Pearl Bailey Sings Porgy and Bess and Other Gershwin Melodies | 1959 | 6.25 | 12.50 | 25.00 |
—Originals have a white label with colored spokes

Number	Title (A Side/B Side)	Yr	VG	VG+	NM

| ❑ R-25101 [M] | More Songs for Adults Only | 1960 | 5.00 | 10.00 | 20.00 |
—Originals have a white label with colored spokes
| ❑ SR-25101 [S] | More Songs for Adults Only | 1960 | 6.25 | 12.50 | 25.00 |
—Originals have a white label with colored spokes
| ❑ R-25116 [M] | Songs of the Bad Old Days | 1960 | 5.00 | 10.00 | 20.00 |
—Originals have a white label with colored spokes
| ❑ SR-25116 [S] | Songs of the Bad Old Days | 1960 | 6.25 | 12.50 | 25.00 |
—Originals have a white label with colored spokes
| ❑ R-25125 [M] | Naughty But Nice | 1960 | 5.00 | 10.00 | 20.00 |
—Originals have a white label with colored spokes
| ❑ SR-25125 [S] | Naughty But Nice | 1960 | 6.25 | 12.50 | 25.00 |
—Originals have a white label with colored spokes
| ❑ R-25144 [M] | The Best of Pearl Bailey | 1961 | 5.00 | 10.00 | 20.00 |
—Originals have a white label with colored spokes
| ❑ SR-25144 [S] | The Best of Pearl Bailey | 1961 | 6.25 | 12.50 | 25.00 |
—Originals have a white label with colored spokes
| ❑ R-25155 [M] | Pearl Bailey Sings Songs of Harold Arlen | 1961 | 5.00 | 10.00 | 20.00 |
—Originals have a white label with colored spokes
| ❑ SR-25155 [S] | Pearl Bailey Sings Songs of Harold Arlen | 1961 | 6.25 | 12.50 | 25.00 |
—Originals have a white label with colored spokes
| ❑ R-25167 [M] | Happy Sounds | 1962 | 5.00 | 10.00 | 20.00 |
—Originals have a white label with colored spokes
| ❑ SR-25167 [S] | Happy Sounds | 1962 | 6.25 | 12.50 | 25.00 |
—Originals have a white label with colored spokes
| ❑ R-25181 [M] | Come On, Let's Play with Pearlie Mae | 1962 | 5.00 | 10.00 | 20.00 |
—Originals have a white label with colored spokes
| ❑ SR-25181 [S] | Come On, Let's Play with Pearlie Mae | 1962 | 6.25 | 12.50 | 25.00 |
—Originals have a white label with colored spokes
| ❑ R-25195 [M] | All About Good Little Girls and Bad Little Boys | 1963 | 5.00 | 10.00 | 20.00 |
—Originals have a pink and orange label
| ❑ SR-25195 [S] | All About Good Little Girls and Bad Little Boys | 1963 | 6.25 | 12.50 | 25.00 |
—Originals have a pink and orange label
| ❑ R-25222 [M] | C'est La Vie | 1963 | 5.00 | 10.00 | 20.00 |
—Originals have a pink and orange label
| ❑ SR-25222 [S] | C'est La Vie | 1963 | 6.25 | 12.50 | 25.00 |
—Originals have a pink and orange label
❑ R-25259 [M]	The Risque World of Pearl Bailey	1964	3.75	7.50	15.00
❑ SR-25259 [S]	The Risque World of Pearl Bailey	1964	5.00	10.00	20.00
❑ R-25271 [M]	Songs by James Van Heusen	1964	3.75	7.50	15.00
❑ SR-25271 [S]	Songs by James Van Heusen	1964	5.00	10.00	20.00
❑ R-25300 [M]	For Women Only	1965	3.75	7.50	15.00
❑ SR-25300 [S]	For Women Only	1965	5.00	10.00	20.00
VOCALION
❑ VL 3621 [M]	Gems by Pearl Bailey	1958	6.25	12.50	25.00

BAILEY, THOMAS
45s
FEDERAL
| ❑ 12559 | Fran/Just Won't Move | 1969 | 3.00 | 6.00 | 12.00 |
| ❑ 12567 | Wish I Was Back/Percy's Place | 1970 | 25.00 | 50.00 | 100.00 |

BAINES, VICKI
45s
LOMA
| ❑ 2078 | We Can Find True Love/Sweeter Than Sweet Things | 1967 | 3.00 | 6.00 | 12.00 |
PARKWAY
| ❑ 957 | Losing You/Got to Run | 1965 | 6.25 | 12.50 | 25.00 |
| ❑ 966 | Country Girl/Are You Kidding | 1966 | 25.00 | 50.00 | 100.00 |

BAJA MARIMBA BAND, THE Also includes records as "Julius Wechter and the Baja Marimba Band."
45s
A&M
| ❑ XMAS 1 [DJ] | The 12 Days Of Christmas/My Favorite Things | 1968 | 3.00 | 6.00 | 12.00 |
—B-side by We Five
| ❑ XMAS 1 [PS] | The 12 Days Of Christmas/My Favorite Things | 1968 | 3.75 | 7.50 | 15.00 |
—B-side by We Five
❑ 816	The Telephone Song/Portuguese Washerwoman	1966	—	2.50	5.00
❑ 824	Ghost Riders in the Sky/Sabor A Mi	1966	—	2.50	5.00
❑ 833	The Cry of the Wild Goose/Spanish Moss	1967	—	2.50	5.00
❑ 833 [PS]	The Cry of the Wild Goose/Spanish Moss	1967	2.00	4.00	8.00
❑ 843	Georgy Girl/Cabeza Arriba (Heads Up)	1967	—	2.50	5.00
❑ 862	Along Comes Mary/Wall Street Rag	1967	—	2.00	4.00
❑ 862 [PS]	Along Comes Mary/Wall Street Rag	1967	—	2.50	5.00
❑ 892	Foul Play/The Sounds of Silence	1967	—	2.00	4.00
❑ 913	Fiddler on the Roof/Sunday Mornin'	1968	—	2.00	4.00
❑ 937	Brasilia/Yes Sir, That's My Baby	1968	—	2.00	4.00
❑ 937 [PS]	Brasilia/Yes Sir, That's My Baby	1968	—	3.50	7.00
❑ 975	Little Prayer/Do You Know the Way to San Jose	1968	—	2.00	4.00
—Artist credit: "Julius Wechter & The Baja Marimba Band"
❑ 1005	Flyin' High/Les Bicyclettes de Belsize	1968	—	2.00	4.00
❑ 1047	Big Red/Ruby '68	1969	—	2.00	4.00
❑ 1078	I'll Marimba You/ I Don't Wanna Walk Without You	1969	—	2.00	4.00
—Artist credit: "Julius Wechter & The Baja Marimba Band"
❑ 1126	Fresh Air/Wave	1969	—	2.00	4.00
❑ 1136	Can You Dig It Part 1/Can You Dig It Part 2	1969	—	2.00	4.00
❑ 1186	Picasso Summer/Samba Nuevo	1970	—	2.00	4.00
❑ 1281	Spanish Flea/As Time Goes By	1971	—	2.00	4.00
—Artist credit: "Julius Wechter & The Baja Marimba Band"
ALMO
❑ 201	Comin' In the Back Door/December's Child	1963	2.00	4.00	8.00
❑ 203	Moonglow & Theme from Picnic/Acapulco 1922	1964	—	3.00	6.00
❑ 206	Pedro's Pouch/Wincle Lamoyan Coan	1964	—	3.00	6.00
❑ 207	Up Cherry Street/Woody Woodpecker Song	1964	—	3.00	6.00
❑ 211	Baja Ska/Samba De Orfeu	1964	—	3.00	6.00
❑ 216	Juarez/Guacamole	1965	—	3.00	6.00
❑ 218	Goin' Out the Side Door/Brasilia	1965	—	3.00	6.00
❑ 228	Yellow Bird/For Animals Only	1966	—	3.00	6.00
❑ 231	(How Much Is That) Doggie in the Window/ Puff (The Magic Dragon)	1966	—	3.00	6.00

Number	Title (A Side/B Side)	Yr	VG	VG+	NM
BELL					
❏ 45339	Theme from "Deep Throat"/Do You Want to Dance	1973	—	2.50	5.00
❏ 45376	Anytime of the Year/Taco Belle	1973	—	2.00	4.00
Albums					
A&M					
❏ LP-104 [M]	Baja Marimba Band	1964	2.50	5.00	10.00
—Reissue with A&M logo at left					
❏ LP-104 [M]	Baja Marimba Band	1964	3.00	6.00	12.00
—Original pressing with A&M logo at top					
❏ SP-104 [S]	Baja Marimba Band	1964	3.75	7.50	15.00
—Original number; has A&M logo at top					
❏ LP-109 [M]	Baja Marimba Band Rides Again	1965	2.50	5.00	10.00
❏ SP-109 [S]	Baja Marimba Band Rides Again	1965	3.75	7.50	15.00
—Original issues had this number					
❏ SP-113 [M]	For Animals Only	1965	2.50	5.00	10.00
❏ SP-118 [M]	Watch Out!	1966	2.50	5.00	10.00
❏ SP-123 [M]	Heads Up	1967	2.50	5.00	10.00
❏ SP-3523 [(2)]	Foursider	1972	3.00	6.00	12.00
❏ SP-4104 [S]	Baja Marimba Band	1964	3.00	6.00	12.00
—Reissue; has A&M logo at left					
❏ SP-4109 [S]	Baja Marimba Band Rides Again	1965	3.00	6.00	12.00
❏ SP-4113 [S]	For Animals Only	1965	3.00	6.00	12.00
❏ SP-4118 [S]	Watch Out!	1966	3.00	6.00	12.00
❏ SP-4123 [S]	Heads Up	1967	3.00	6.00	12.00
❏ SP-4136	Fowl Play	1968	2.50	5.00	10.00
❏ SP-4150	Do You Know the Way to San Jose?	1968	2.50	5.00	10.00
❏ SP-4167	Those Were the Days	1969	2.50	5.00	10.00
❏ SP-4200	Fresh Air	1969	2.50	5.00	10.00
❏ SP-4248	Greatest Hits	1970	2.50	5.00	10.00
❏ SP-4298	As Time Goes By	1971	2.50	5.00	10.00
BAKER, B.J.					
45s					
DECCA					
❏ 732487	The Melody Man/Anywhere	1969	2.00	4.00	8.00
BAKER, BOBBY					
45s					
SWAN					
❏ 4037	Baby Blue Eyes/Hush Our Secret	1959	3.75	7.50	15.00
BAKER, CHARLES					
HIT					
❏ 159	Where You Been/Sha La La	1964	3.75	7.50	15.00
—B-side by the Beasts					
BAKER, CHARLIE					
45s					
LIBERTY					
❏ 55226	Star of Wonder/You Crack Me Up	1959	6.25	12.50	25.00
MUNRAB					
❏ 106	Star of Wonder/You Crack Me Up	1959	37.50	75.00	150.00
BAKER, DONNIE, AND THE DEMENSIONALS					
45s					
RAINBOW					
❏ 219	Drinkin' Pop Sodee-Odee (Pop Pop)/Sleepy Time Gal	1953	15.00	30.00	60.00
—Black vinyl					
❏ 219	Drinkin' Pop Sodee-Odee (Pop Pop)/Sleepy Time Gal	1953	37.50	75.00	150.00
—Red vinyl					
BAKER, GEORGE, SELECTION					
45s					
COLOSSUS					
❏ 112	Little Gren Bag/Pretty Little Dreamer	1970	—	2.50	5.00
❏ 117	Dear Ann/Fly	1970	—	2.00	4.00
❏ 124	I Wanna Love You/Impressions	1970	—	2.00	4.00
WARNER BROS.					
❏ 8115	Paloma Blanca/Dreamboat	1975	—	2.00	4.00
❏ 8207	Baby Blue/Morning Sky	1976	—	2.00	4.00
Albums					
COLOSSUS					
❏ CS-1002	Little Green Bag	1970	5.00	10.00	20.00
WARNER BROS.					
❏ BS 2905	Paloma Blanca	1975	3.75	7.50	15.00
BAKER, GINGER, 'S AIR FORCE Includes records credited only to Ginger Baker. Also see BLIND FAITH; CREAM.					
45s					
ATCO					
❏ 6750	Man of Constant Sorrow/Doin' It	1970	—	2.50	5.00
❏ 6816	Atunde! (We Are Here) Part 1/Atunde! (We Are Here) Part 2	1971	—	2.50	5.00
Albums					
ATCO					
❏ SD 33-343	Ginger Baker's Air Force 2	1971	3.00	6.00	12.00
❏ SD 2-703 [(2)]	Ginger Baker's Air Force	1970	5.00	10.00	20.00
❏ SD 7012	Stratavarious	1972	3.00	6.00	12.00
AXIOM					
❏ 539864-1	Middle Passage	1990	3.75	7.50	15.00
CELLULOID					
❏ CEL-6126	Horses and Trees	1986	2.50	5.00	10.00
POLYDOR					
❏ 3504 [(2)]	Ginger Baker At His Best	1973	3.75	7.50	15.00
SIRE					
❏ SASD-7532	Eleven Sides of Baker	1977	2.50	5.00	10.00

Number	Title (A Side/B Side)	Yr	VG	VG+	NM
BAKER, KENNY					
45s					
ORBIT					
❏ 541	Goodbye Little Star/I'm Gonna Love You	1959	5.00	10.00	20.00
BAKER, LAVERN					
45s					
ATLANTIC					
❏ 1004	How Can You Leave a Man Like This/Soul on Fire	1953	12.50	25.00	50.00
❏ 1030	I Can't Hold Out Any Longer/I'm Living My Life for You	1954	10.00	20.00	40.00
❏ 1047	Tweedlee Dee/Tomorrow Night	1954	10.00	20.00	40.00
❏ 1057	Bop-Ting-a-Ling/That's All I Need	1955	10.00	20.00	40.00
❏ 1075	Play It Fair/That Lucky Old Sun	1955	10.00	20.00	40.00
❏ 1087	Get Up Get Up (You Sleepyhead)/My Happiness Forever	1956	6.25	12.50	25.00
❏ 1093	Fee Fee Fi Fo Fum/I'll Do the Same for You	1956	6.25	12.50	25.00
❏ 1104	I Can't Love You Enough/Still	1956	6.25	12.50	25.00
❏ 1116	Jim Dandy/Tra La La	1956	6.25	12.50	25.00
❏ 1136	Jim Dandy Got Married/The Game of Love	1957	6.25	12.50	25.00
❏ 1150	Humpty Dumpty Heart/Love Me Right	1957	6.25	12.50	25.00
❏ 1163	St.Louis Blues/Miracles	1957	6.25	12.50	25.00
❏ 1176	Substitute/Learning to Love	1958	6.25	12.50	25.00
❏ 1189	Harbor Lights/Whipper Snapper	1958	6.25	12.50	25.00
❏ 2001	It's So Fine/Why Baby Why	1958	6.25	12.50	25.00
❏ 2007	I Cried a Tear/Dix-A-Billy	1958	6.25	12.50	25.00
❏ 2021	I Waited Too Long/You're Teasing Me	1959	5.00	10.00	20.00
❏ 2033	So High So Low/If You Love Me	1959	5.00	10.00	20.00
❏ 2041	Tiny Tim/For Love of You	1959	5.00	10.00	20.00
❏ 2048	Shake a Hand/Manana	1960	5.00	10.00	20.00
❏ 2059	Wheel of Fortune/Shadows of Love	1960	3.75	7.50	15.00
❏ 2067	A Help-Each-Other Romance/How Often	1960	3.75	7.50	15.00
—With Ben E. King					
❏ 2077	Bumble Bee/My Time Will Come	1960	3.75	7.50	15.00
❏ 2090	You're the Boss/I'll Never Be Free	1961	3.75	7.50	15.00
—With Jimmy Ricks					
❏ 2099	Saved/Don Juan	1961	3.75	7.50	15.00
❏ 2109	I Didn't Know I Was Crying/Hurtin' Inside	1961	3.75	7.50	15.00
❏ 2119	Hey, Memphis/Voodoo Voodoo	1961	3.75	7.50	15.00
❏ 2137	Must I Cry Again/No Love So True	1962	3.00	6.00	12.00
❏ 2167	See See Rider/The Story of My Love	1962	3.00	6.00	12.00
❏ 2186	Trouble in Mind/Half of Your Love	1963	3.00	6.00	12.00
❏ 2203	Itty Bitty Girl/Oh, Johnny Oh, Johnny	1963	3.00	6.00	12.00
❏ 2234	You'd Better Find Yourself Another Fool/Go Away	1964	2.50	5.00	10.00
❏ 2267	Fly Me to the Moon/Ain't Gonna Cry No More	1965	2.50	5.00	10.00
ATLANTIC OLDIES SERIES					
❏ 13001	See See Rider/Jim Dandy	196?	—	2.50	5.00
—Originals have gold and black labels					
❏ 13002	I Cried a Tear/Saved	196?	—	2.50	5.00
—Originals have gold and black labels					
BRUNSWICK					
❏ 55285	Let Me Belong to You/Pledging My Love	1965	2.00	4.00	8.00
❏ 55287	Think Twice/Please Don't Hurt Me	1965	2.00	4.00	8.00
—With Jackie Wilson					
❏ 55291	One Monkey (Don't Stop the Show)/Baby	1966	2.00	4.00	8.00
❏ 55297	Batman to the Rescue/Call Me Darling	1966	2.50	5.00	10.00
❏ 55311	Nothing Like Being in Love/Wrapped, Tied and Tangled	1967	2.00	4.00	8.00
❏ 55341	Born to Lose/I Need You So	1967	2.00	4.00	8.00
❏ 55408	I'm the One to Do It/Baby	1969	—	3.00	6.00
KING					
❏ 4556	Trying/Snuff Dipper	1952	12.50	25.00	50.00
—B-side by Todd Rhodes					
❏ 4583	Must I Cry Again/Hog Maw and Cabbage Slaw	1952	12.50	25.00	50.00
—B-side by Todd Rhodes					
❏ 4601	Lost Child/Thunderball Boogie	1953	12.50	25.00	50.00
—B-side by Todd Rhodes					
7-Inch Extended Plays					
ATLANTIC					
❏ 566	(contents unknown)	1956	25.00	50.00	100.00
❏ 566 [PS]	Tweedle Dee	1956	25.00	50.00	100.00
❏ 588	*Jim Dandy/Still/Play It Fair/Tra La La	1957	20.00	40.00	80.00
❏ 588 [PS]	Jim Dandy	1957	25.00	50.00	100.00
❏ 617	(contents unknown)	1958	20.00	40.00	80.00
❏ 617 [PS]	I Cried a Tear	1958	25.00	50.00	100.00
Albums					
ATCO					
❏ SD 33-372	Her Greatest Recordings	1971	3.00	6.00	12.00
ATLANTIC					
❏ 1281 [M]	LaVern Baker Sings Bessie Smith	1958	30.00	60.00	120.00
—Black label					
❏ 1281 [M]	LaVern Baker Sings Bessie Smith	1960	7.50	15.00	30.00
—Red and purple label, "fan" logo in white					
❏ 1281 [M]	LaVern Baker Sings Bessie Smith	1963	5.00	10.00	20.00
—Red and purple label, "fan" logo in black					
❏ SD 1281 [S]	LaVern Baker Sings Bessie Smith	1959	37.50	75.00	150.00
—Green label					
❏ SD 1281 [S]	LaVern Baker Sings Bessie Smith	1960	10.00	20.00	40.00
—Green and blue label, "fan" logo in white					
❏ SD 1281 [S]	LaVern Baker Sings Bessie Smith	1963	6.25	12.50	25.00
—Green and blue label, "fan" logo in black					
❏ 8002 [M]	LaVern	1956	62.50	125.00	250.00
—Black label					
❏ 8002 [M]	LaVern	1960	7.50	15.00	30.00
—Red and purple label, "fan" logo in white					
❏ 8002 [M]	LaVern	1963	5.00	10.00	20.00
—Red and purple label, "fan" logo in black					
❏ 8007 [M]	LaVern Baker	1957	62.50	125.00	250.00
—Black label					

B

Number	Title (A Side/B Side)	Yr	VG	VG+	NM
❑ 8007 [M]	LaVern Baker	1960	7.50	15.00	30.00
—Red and purple label, "fan" logo in white					
❑ 8007 [M]	LaVern Baker	1963	5.00	10.00	20.00
—Red and purple label, "fan" logo in black					
❑ 8030 [M]	Blues Ballads	1959	50.00	100.00	200.00
—Black label					
❑ 8030 [M]	Blues Ballads	1960	7.50	15.00	30.00
—Red and purple label, "fan" logo in white					
❑ 8030 [M]	Blues Ballads	1960	37.50	75.00	150.00
—White "bullseye" label					
❑ 8030 [M]	Blues Ballads	1963	5.00	10.00	20.00
—Red and purple label, "fan" logo in black					
❑ 8036 [M]	Precious Memories	1959	50.00	100.00	200.00
—Black label					
❑ 8036 [M]	Precious Memories	1960	7.50	15.00	30.00
—Red and purple label, "fan" logo in white					
❑ 8036 [M]	Precious Memories	1960	37.50	75.00	150.00
—White "bullseye" label					
❑ 8036 [M]	Precious Memories	1963	5.00	10.00	20.00
—Red and purple label, "fan" logo in black					
❑ SD 8036 [S]	Precious Memories	1959	75.00	150.00	300.00
—Green label					
❑ SD 8036 [S]	Precious Memories	1960	10.00	20.00	40.00
—Green and blue label, "fan" logo in white					
❑ SD 8036 [S]	Precious Memories	1960	50.00	100.00	200.00
—White "bullseye" label					
❑ SD 8036 [S]	Precious Memories	1963	6.25	12.50	25.00
—Green and blue label, "fan" logo in black					
❑ 8050 [M]	Saved	1961	25.00	50.00	100.00
—Red and purple label, "fan" logo in white					
❑ 8050 [M]	Saved	1963	5.00	10.00	20.00
—Red and purple label, "fan" logo in black					
❑ SD 8050 [S]	Saved	1961	37.50	75.00	150.00
—Green and blue label, "fan" logo in white					
❑ SD 8050 [S]	Saved	1963	6.25	12.50	25.00
—Green and blue label, "fan" logo in black					
❑ 8071 [M]	See See Rider	1962	25.00	50.00	100.00
—Red and purple label, "fan" logo in white					
❑ 8071 [M]	See See Rider	1963	5.00	10.00	20.00
—Red and purple label, "fan" logo in black					
❑ SD 8071 [S]	See See Rider	1962	37.50	75.00	150.00
—Green and blue label, "fan" logo in white					
❑ SD 8071 [S]	See See Rider	1963	6.25	12.50	25.00
—Green and blue label, "fan" logo in black					
❑ 8078 [M]	The Best of LaVern Baker	1963	37.50	75.00	150.00
—Red and purple label, "fan" logo in black					
❑ 90980	LaVern Baker Sings Bessie Smith	1989	3.00	6.00	12.00
—Reissue of SD 1281					
BRUNSWICK					
❑ BL 754160	Let Me Belong to You	1970	5.00	10.00	20.00

BAKER, MICKEY "GUITAR" Also see MICKEY AND SYLVIA.
45s
ATLANTIC

Number	Title (A Side/B Side)	Yr	VG	VG+	NM
❑ 2042	Third Man Theme/Baia	1959	3.00	6.00	12.00
KING					
❑ 5951	Side Show/Steam Roller	1964	2.50	5.00	10.00
❑ 5979	Do What You Do/Night Blue	1965	2.50	5.00	10.00
MGM					
❑ 12418	Spinnin' Rock Boogie/Tricky	1957	5.00	10.00	20.00
RAINBOW					
❑ 288	Shake Walkin'/Greasy Spoon	1955	7.50	15.00	30.00
❑ 299	Bandstand Stomp/Rock with a Sock	1955	7.50	15.00	30.00
❑ 303	Old Devil Moon/Guitarambo	1955	7.50	15.00	30.00
SAVOY					
❑ 867	Guitar Mambo/Riverboat	1952	12.50	25.00	50.00
❑ 874	Love Me Baby/Oh Happy Day	1953	12.50	25.00	50.00
Albums					
ATLANTIC					
❑ 8035 [M]	The Wildest Guitar	1959	37.50	75.00	150.00
—Black label					
❑ 8035 [M]	The Wildest Guitar	1960	12.50	25.00	50.00
—Red and purple label, "fan" logo in white					
❑ SD 8035 [S]	The Wildest Guitar	1959	62.50	125.00	250.00
—Green label					
❑ SD 8035 [S]	The Wildest Guitar	1960	20.00	40.00	80.00
—Green and blue label, "fan" logo in white					
KICKING MULE					
❑ 140	The Jazz Rock Guitar of Mickey Baker	1978	3.00	6.00	12.00
❑ 142	The Blues and Jazz Guitar of Mickey Baker	1978	3.00	6.00	12.00
KING					
❑ 839 [M]	But Wild	196?	20.00	40.00	80.00
—Blue label with crown					
❑ 839 [M]	But Wild	1963	100.00	200.00	400.00
—Black label, no crown					
❑ S-839 [R]	But Wild	196?	10.00	20.00	40.00

BAKER, PENNY, AND THE PILLOWS
45s
WITCH

Number	Title (A Side/B Side)	Yr	VG	VG+	NM
❑ 123	Bring Back the Beatles/Gonna Win Him	1964	5.00	10.00	20.00
❑ 123 [PS]	Bring Back the Beatles/Gonna Win Him	1964	5.00	10.00	20.00

BAKER, RONNIE
45s
LAURIE

Number	Title (A Side/B Side)	Yr	VG	VG+	NM
❑ 3128	My Story/I Want to Be Loved	1962	15.00	30.00	60.00
❑ 3164	Land of Love/Time Told Me	1963	5.00	10.00	20.00
❑ 3250	See You in September/Young at Heart	1964	5.00	10.00	20.00

BAKER, SAM, AND NANCY COHEN
45s
HIT

Number	Title (A Side/B Side)	Yr	VG	VG+	NM
❑ 125	Once Upon a Time/No Particular Place to Go	1964	2.00	4.00	8.00
—B-side by Sammie Moore					

BAKER, SHARI
45s
HIT

Number	Title (A Side/B Side)	Yr	VG	VG+	NM
❑ 175	Don't Forget I Still Love You/My World's a Blue World	1965	2.00	4.00	8.00
—B-side by Ed Hardin					

BAKER, YVONNE Also see THE SENSATIONS.
45s
JAMIE

Number	Title (A Side/B Side)	Yr	VG	VG+	NM
❑ 1290	What a Difference Love Makes/Funny What Time Can Do	1965	3.00	6.00	12.00
MODERN					
❑ 1055	A Woman Needs a Man/My Baby Needs Me	196?	2.50	5.00	10.00
PARKWAY					
❑ 140	You Didn't Say a Word/To Prove My Love Is True	1967	25.00	50.00	100.00

BAKER GURVITZ ARMY, THE
45s
ATCO

Number	Title (A Side/B Side)	Yr	VG	VG+	NM
❑ 7043	People/(B-side unknown)	1976	—	2.50	5.00
JANUS					
❑ 248	4 Phil/Help Me	1975	—	2.50	5.00
Albums					
ATCO					
❑ SD 36-123	Elysian Encounters	1975	2.50	5.00	10.00
❑ SD 36-137	Hearts On Fire	1976	2.50	5.00	10.00
JANUS					
❑ JXS-7015	The Baker Gurvitz Army	1975	3.00	6.00	12.00

BAKER SISTERS, THE
45s
MERCURY

Number	Title (A Side/B Side)	Yr	VG	VG+	NM
❑ 70839	Too Many Teardrops/Break the String	1956	5.00	10.00	20.00
❑ 70980	Little Monster/One By One	1956	5.00	10.00	20.00
❑ 71074	Trinidaddy/Careless Love	1957	5.00	10.00	20.00
UNIQUE					
❑ 324	Last Bus Home/If You're Ever Gonna Leave Me	1956	3.75	7.50	15.00

BALDRY, LONG JOHN
45s
A&M

Number	Title (A Side/B Side)	Yr	VG	VG+	NM
❑ 974	When the Sun Comes Shining Through/Wise to the Ways of the World	1968	2.00	4.00	8.00
❑ 1041	It's Too Late Now/Long and Lonely Nights	1969	2.00	4.00	8.00
ASCOT					
❑ 2229	Bring My Baby Back to Me/Cuckoo	1967	2.50	5.00	10.00
❑ 2236	Only a Fool Breaks His Own Heart/Let Him Go	1967	2.50	5.00	10.00
EMI AMERICA					
❑ 8018	You've Lost That Lovin' Feelin'/Baldry's Out	1979	—	2.00	4.00
—A-side: With Kathi McDonald					
❑ 8018 [PS]	You've Lost That Lovin' Feelin'/Baldry's Out	1979	—	3.00	6.00
❑ 8024	A Thrill Is a Thrill/Find You	1979	—	2.00	4.00
UNITED ARTISTS					
❑ 50141	Bring My Baby Back to Me/Cuckoo	1967	2.50	5.00	10.00
WARNER BROS.					
❑ 7098	Hey Lord You Made the Night Too Long/Let the Heartaches Begin	1967	2.00	4.00	8.00
❑ 7184	Hold Back the Daybreak/Since I Lost You Baby	1968	—	3.00	6.00
❑ 7506	Don't Try to Lay No Boogie-Woogie on the King of Rock N Roll/Mr. Rubin	1971	—	3.00	6.00
❑ 7516	Don't Try to Lay No Boogie-Woogie on the King of Rock N Roll/same (Part 2)	1971	—	3.00	6.00
❑ 7597	Iko Iko/You Can't Judge a Book by Its Cover	1972	—	3.00	6.00
❑ 7617	Mother Ain't Dead/You Can't Judge a Book by Its Cover	1972	—	3.00	6.00
Albums					
ASCOT					
❑ AM-13022 [M]	Long John's Blues	1965	12.50	25.00	50.00
❑ AS-16022 [R]	Long John's Blues	1965	10.00	20.00	40.00
CASABLANCA					
❑ NBLP 7012	Good to Be Alive	1975	3.00	6.00	12.00
❑ NBLP 7035	Welcome to the Club	1976	3.00	6.00	12.00
EMI AMERICA					
❑ SW-17015	Baldry's Out	1979	2.50	5.00	10.00
❑ SW-17038	Long John Baldry	1980	2.50	5.00	10.00
UNITED ARTISTS					
❑ UAS-5543 [M]	Long John's Blues	1971	3.00	6.00	12.00
—Reissue of Ascot 13022					
WARNER BROS.					
❑ WS 1921	It Ain't Easy	1971	3.75	7.50	15.00
❑ BS 2614	Everything Stops for Tea	1973	3.00	6.00	12.00

BALDWIN, CLIVE
45s
MERCURY

Number	Title (A Side/B Side)	Yr	VG	VG+	NM
❑ 73680	Now It's Paul McCartney, Stevie Wonder, Alice Cooper, Elton John/The Disco Rag	1975	2.00	4.00	8.00

BALIN, MARTY Also see BODACIOUS D.F.; JEFFERSON AIRPLANE; JEFFERSON STARSHIP.
45s
CHALLENGE

Number	Title (A Side/B Side)	Yr	VG	VG+	NM
❑ 9146	Nobody But You/You Made Me Fall	1962	12.50	25.00	50.00
❑ 9156	I Specialize in Love/You're Alive with Love	1962	12.50	25.00	50.00

Number	Title (A Side/B Side)	Yr	VG	VG+	NM

EMI AMERICA
❏ 8084	Hearts/Freeway	1981	—	2.00	4.00
❏ 8084 [PS]	Hearts/Freeway	1981	—	2.50	5.00
❏ 8093	Atlanta Lady (Something About Your Love)/Lydia	1981	—	2.00	4.00
❏ 8153	What Love Is/Will You Forever	1983	—	2.00	4.00
❏ 8153 [PS]	What Love Is/Will You Forever	1983	—	2.50	5.00
❏ 8160	Do It for Love/Heart of Stone	1983	—	2.00	4.00
❏ 8160 [PS]	Do It for Love/Heart of Stone	1983	—	2.50	5.00

Albums
EMI AMERICA
| ❏ SPRO-9673 [DJ] | Balin | 1981 | 5.00 | 10.00 | 20.00 |
—Red vinyl
| ❏ ST-17054 | Balin | 1981 | 2.50 | 5.00 | 10.00 |
| ❏ ST-17088 | Lucky | 1983 | 2.50 | 5.00 | 10.00 |

BALL, KENNY
45s
BELL
| ❏ 45412 | Make Love to Me/Smile, Smile, Smile | 1973 | — | 2.50 | 5.00 |
DECCA
| ❏ 32083 | Greenback Theme/Red Square | 1967 | 2.00 | 4.00 | 8.00 |
| ❏ 32104 | Rosie/Harmonize | 1967 | 2.00 | 4.00 | 8.00 |
—With Max Bygraves
GUYDEN
| ❏ 2054 | Samantha/I Still Love You All | 1961 | 3.75 | 7.50 | 15.00 |
JERDEN
| ❏ 776 | 900 Miles/(I Wonder) What Becomes of Life | 1965 | 5.00 | 10.00 | 20.00 |
KAPP
❏ KJB-11	Midnight in Moscow/The Green Leaves of Summer	1964	—	3.00	6.00
❏ KJB-11 [PS]	Midnight in Moscow/The Green Leaves of Summer	1964	2.50	5.00	10.00
❏ 442	Midnight in Moscow/American Patrol	1962	3.00	6.00	12.00
❏ 451	March of the Siamese Children/Villa	1962	2.50	5.00	10.00
❏ 460	The Green Leaves of Summer/I Shall Not Be Moved	1962	2.50	5.00	10.00
❏ 483	So Do I/All Through the Night	1962	2.50	5.00	10.00
❏ 494	The Payoff/Coronet Chop Suey	1962	2.50	5.00	10.00
❏ 509	Sukiyaki/Hazelmere	1963	2.50	5.00	10.00
❏ 509	Sukiyaki/Nuages	1963	2.50	5.00	10.00
❏ 531	55 Days at Peking/Rondo	1963	2.50	5.00	10.00
❏ 554	Heartaches/High Hopes	1963	2.50	5.00	10.00
❏ 581	From Russia with Love/Acapulco 1922	1964	2.50	5.00	10.00

Albums
JAZZOLOGY
| ❏ 65 | In Concert in the USA, Volume 1 | 1979 | 2.50 | 5.00 | 10.00 |
| ❏ 66 | In Concert in the USA, Volume 2 | 1979 | 2.50 | 5.00 | 10.00 |
KAPP
❏ KL-1276 [M]	Midnight in Moscow	1962	5.00	10.00	20.00
❏ KL-1285 [M]	It's Trad	1962	5.00	10.00	20.00
❏ KL-1294 [M]	Recorded Live	1962	5.00	10.00	20.00
❏ KL-1314 [M]	More	1963	3.75	7.50	15.00
❏ KL-1340 [M]	Big Ones	1963	3.75	7.50	15.00
❏ KL-1348 [M]	Washington Square and the Best of Kenny Ball	1964	3.75	7.50	15.00
❏ KL-1392 [M]	For the Jet Set	1964	3.75	7.50	15.00
❏ KS-3276 [S]	Midnight in Moscow	1962	5.00	10.00	20.00
❏ KS-3285 [S]	It's Trad	1962	5.00	10.00	20.00
❏ KS-3294 [S]	Recorded Live	1962	5.00	10.00	20.00
❏ KS-3314 [S]	More	1963	5.00	10.00	20.00
❏ KS-3340 [S]	Big Ones	1963	5.00	10.00	20.00
❏ KS-3348 [S]	Washington Square and the Best of Kenny Ball	1964	5.00	10.00	20.00
❏ KS-3392 [S]	For the Jet Set	1964	5.00	10.00	20.00

BALLACK, ROBERT JOHN
45s
ROULETTE
| ❏ 7122 | Sweet Sounds of Music/I'm Comin' to Get You | 1972 | — | 2.50 | 5.00 |
| ❏ 7133 | Ain't No Use/Givin' Up Givin' You Up | 1972 | — | 2.50 | 5.00 |

BALLADEERS, THE
45s
DEL-FI
❏ 4123	Morning Star/Tom Gets the Last Laugh	1959	5.00	10.00	20.00
❏ 4127	Durant Jail/Turtle Dove	1959	5.00	10.00	20.00
❏ 4138	Hurtin'/Roll Call Company "J"	1960	5.00	10.00	20.00
ERA
| ❏ 3069 | A Long Way from Home/Wedding John Doe | 1962 | 3.75 | 7.50 | 15.00 |
Albums
DEL-FI
| ❏ DFLP-1204 [M] | Alive-O! | 1959 | 10.00 | 20.00 | 40.00 |
| ❏ DFST-1204 [S] | Alive-O! | 1959 | 15.00 | 30.00 | 60.00 |

BALLADS, THE
45s
VEE JAY
| ❏ 714 | I Can't See Your Love (Vocal)/(Instrumental) | 1966 | 6.25 | 12.50 | 25.00 |
VENTURE
| ❏ 615 | God Bless Our Love/My Baby Knows How to Love Her Man | 1968 | 3.75 | 7.50 | 15.00 |
| ❏ 615 | God Bless Our Love/My Baby Knows How to Love Her Man | 1968 | 5.00 | 10.00 | 20.00 |
—Original pressings call the group "The Ballards"
❏ 625	I Love You Yeah/You're the One	1968	3.75	7.50	15.00
❏ 630	Goodnight My Love/Hey Diddle Diddle	1969	3.75	7.50	15.00
❏ 637	The Gift of Love/I Wish I Knew	1969	3.75	7.50	15.00

BALLARD, FLORENCE Former member of THE SUPREMES.
45s
ABC
| ❏ 11074 | Goin' Out of My Head/It Doesn't Matter How I Say It | 1968 | 7.50 | 15.00 | 30.00 |

Number	Title (A Side/B Side)	Yr	VG	VG+	NM
❏ 11144	Love Ain't Love/Forever Faithful	1968	7.50	15.00	30.00
❏ 11144 [PS]	Love Ain't Love/Forever Faithful	1968	20.00	40.00	80.00

BALLARD, FRANK
Albums
PHILLIPS INTERNATIONAL
| ❏ 1985 [M] | Rhythm-Blues Party | 1962 | 2500. | 3750. | 5000. |

BALLARD, HANK, AND THE MIDNIGHTERS Includes records credited only to Hank Ballard. Also see THE MIDNIGHTERS; THE ROYALS (1).
45s
CHESS
| ❏ 2111 | Love, Why Is It Taking You So Long/I'm a Junkie for My Baby's Love | 1971 | — | 3.00 | 6.00 |
KING
❏ 5171	Teardrops on Your Letter/The Twist	1959	7.50	15.00	30.00
❏ 5195 [M]	Kansas City/I'll Keep You Happy	1959	6.25	12.50	25.00
❏ S-5195 [S]	Kansas City/I'll Keep You Happy	1959	12.50	25.00	50.00
❏ 5215 [M]	Sugaree/Rain Down Tears	1959	6.25	12.50	25.00
❏ S-5215 [S]	Sugaree/Rain Down Tears	1959	12.50	25.00	50.00
❏ 5245	Cute Little Ways/A House with No Windows	1959	6.25	12.50	25.00
❏ 5275	I Could Love You/Never Knew	1959	6.25	12.50	25.00
❏ 5289	Look at Little Sister/I Said I Wouldn't Beg You	1959	6.25	12.50	25.00
❏ 5312	The Coffee Grind/Waiting	1960	6.25	12.50	25.00
❏ 5341	Finger Poppin' Time/I Love You, I Love You So-o-o	1960	6.25	12.50	25.00
❏ 5400	Let's Go, Let's Go, Let's Go/If You'd Forgive Me	1960	6.25	12.50	25.00
❏ 5430	The Hoochi Coochi Coo/I'm Thinking of You	1960	5.00	10.00	20.00
❏ 5459	Let's Go Again (Where We Went Last Night)/Deep Blue Sea	1961	5.00	10.00	20.00
❏ 5491	The Continental Walk/What Is This I See	1961	5.00	10.00	20.00
❏ 5491 [PS]	The Continental Walk/What Is This I See	1961	20.00	40.00	80.00
❏ 5510	The Switch-A-Roo/The Float	1961	3.75	7.50	15.00
❏ 5513	The Big Frog/Doin' Everything	1961	3.75	7.50	15.00
—B-side by Henry Moore
❏ 5535	Nothing But Good/Keep On Dancing	1961	3.75	7.50	15.00
❏ 5550	Big Red Sunset/Can't You See — I Need a Friend	1961	3.75	7.50	15.00
❏ 5578	Do You Remember/I'm Gonna Miss You	1961	3.75	7.50	15.00
❏ 5593	Do You Know How to Twist/Broadway	1962	3.75	7.50	15.00
❏ 5601	It's Twistin' Time/Autumn Breeze	1962	3.75	7.50	15.00
❏ 5635	Good Twistin' Tonight/I'm Young	1962	3.75	7.50	15.00
❏ 5655	I Want to Thank You/Excuse Me	1962	3.75	7.50	15.00
❏ 5677	Dream World/When I Need You	1962	3.75	7.50	15.00
❏ 5693	Shaky Mae/I Love and Care for You	1962	3.75	7.50	15.00
❏ 5703	Bring Me Your Love/She's the One	1962	3.75	7.50	15.00
❏ 5713	All the Things in Life That Please You/The Rising Tide	1963	3.75	7.50	15.00
❏ 5719	The House on the Hill/That Low-Down Move	1963	3.75	7.50	15.00
❏ 5729	Christmas Time for Everyone But Me/Santa Claus Is Coming	1963	3.75	7.50	15.00
❏ 5746	How Could You Leave Your Man Alone/Walkin' and Talkin'	1963	3.75	7.50	15.00
❏ 5798	Those Lonely, Lonely Feelings/It's Love, Baby	1963	3.75	7.50	15.00
❏ 5821	Buttin' In/I'm Leavin'	1963	3.75	7.50	15.00
❏ 5835	Don't Let Temptation Turn You Around/Have Mercy, Have a Little Pity	1964	3.75	7.50	15.00
❏ 5860	Don't Fall in Love with Me/I'm So Mad with You	1964	3.75	7.50	15.00
❏ 5884	I Don't Know How to Do But One Thing/These Young Girls	1964	3.75	7.50	15.00
❏ 5901	Stay Away from My Baby/She's Got a Whole Lot of Soul	1964	3.75	7.50	15.00
❏ 5931	Daddy Rolling Stone/What's Your Name	1964	3.75	7.50	15.00
❏ 5954	Let's Get the Show on the Road/A Winner Never Quits	1964	3.75	7.50	15.00
❏ 5963	One Monkey Don't Stop No Show/What Can I Tell You	1964	3.75	7.50	15.00
❏ 5974	The Handwriting on the Wall/I Done It	1964	3.75	7.50	15.00
❏ 5996	Poppin' the Whip/You, Just You	1965	3.00	6.00	12.00
❏ 6001	I'm Just a Fool and Everybody Knows/Do It Zulu Style	1965	3.00	6.00	12.00
❏ 6018	Sloop and Slide/My Sun Is Going Down	1966	3.00	6.00	12.00
❏ 6031	I'm Ready/Togetherness	1966	3.00	6.00	12.00
❏ 6055	I Was Born to Move/He Came Alone	1966	3.00	6.00	12.00
❏ 6092	Here Comes the Hurt/Dance Till It Hurt Cha	1967	3.00	6.00	12.00
❏ 6119	You're in Real Good Hands/Unwind Yourself	1967	3.00	6.00	12.00
❏ 6131	Funky's Soul Train/Which Way Should I Turn	1967	3.00	6.00	12.00
❏ 6177	I'm Back to Stay/Come On Wit' It	1968	3.00	6.00	12.00
❏ 6196	How You Gonna Get Respect (When You Haven't Cut Your Process Yet)/Teardrops on Your Letter	1968	2.50	5.00	10.00
—As "Hank Ballard Along With The Dapps"
| ❏ 6215 | You're So Sexy/Thrill on the Hill | 1969 | 2.50 | 5.00 | 10.00 |
—As "Hank Ballard Along With The Dapps"
❏ 6228	Are You Lonely for Me Baby/With Our Sweet Lovin' Self	1969	2.50	5.00	10.00
❏ 6244	Butter Your Popcorn/Funky Soul Train	1969	3.75	7.50	15.00
❏ 6246	Come On with It/Blackenized	1969	3.75	7.50	15.00
❏ 6332	Work With Me Annie/Sexy Ways	1970	2.50	5.00	10.00
PEOPLE
| ❏ 604 | Teardrops on Your Letter/Annie Had a Baby | 1972 | — | 2.50 | 5.00 |
| ❏ 606 | With Your Sweet Lovin' Self/Finger Poppin' Time | 1972 | — | 2.50 | 5.00 |
POLYDOR
| ❏ 14128 | Finger Poppin' Time/From the Love Side | 1972 | — | 2.50 | 5.00 |
| ❏ 14166 | Going to Get a Thrill/(B-side unknown) | 1973 | — | — | — |
—Canceled?
SILVER FOX
| ❏ 23 | Sunday Morning Coming Down/Love Made a Fool of Me | 1970 | — | 3.00 | 6.00 |
STANG
❏ 5053	Let's Go Streaking/Let's Go Streaking (Part 2)	1974	—	2.50	5.00
❏ 5058	Hey There Sexy Lady/(Instrumental)	1975	—	2.50	5.00
❏ 5061	Let's Go Skinny Dipping/Love On Love	1975	—	2.50	5.00

Number	Title (A Side/B Side)	Yr	VG	VG+	NM
7-Inch Extended Plays					
KING					
❑ 435	Teardrops on Your Letter/The Twist//Cute Little Ways/House with No Windows	1959	30.00	60.00	120.00
❑ 435 [PS]	Singin' and Swingin', Vol. 1	1959	30.00	60.00	120.00
❑ 436	(contents unknown)	1959	30.00	60.00	120.00
❑ 436 [PS]	Singin' and Swingin', Vol. 2	1959	30.00	60.00	120.00
Albums					
KING					
❑ 618 [M]	Singin' and Swingin'	1959	62.50	125.00	250.00
❑ 674 [M]	The One and Only Hank Ballard	1959	62.50	125.00	250.00
—Brown cover					
❑ 674 [M]	The One and Only Hank Ballard	1960	37.50	75.00	150.00
—Green cover					
❑ 700 [M]	Mr. Rhythm and Blues	1960	37.50	75.00	150.00
❑ 740 [M]	Spotlight on Hank Ballard	1961	37.50	75.00	150.00
❑ KS-740 [S]	Spotlight on Hank Ballard	1961	75.00	150.00	300.00
❑ 748 [M]	Let's Go Again	1961	30.00	60.00	120.00
❑ 759 [M]	Dance Along	1961	30.00	60.00	120.00
❑ 781 [M]	The Twistin' Fools	1962	25.00	50.00	100.00
❑ 793 [M]	Jumpin' Hank Ballard	1962	25.00	50.00	100.00
❑ 815 [M]	The 1963 Sound of Hank Ballard	1963	25.00	50.00	100.00
❑ 867 [M]	Biggest Hits	1963	25.00	50.00	100.00
❑ 896 [M]	A Star in Your Eyes	1964	25.00	50.00	100.00
❑ 913 [M]	Those Lazy, Lazy Days	1965	17.50	35.00	70.00
❑ 927 [M]	Glad Songs, Sad Songs	1965	17.50	35.00	70.00
❑ 950 [M]	24 Hit Tunes	1966	15.00	30.00	60.00
❑ 981 [M]	24 Great Songs	1968	10.00	20.00	40.00
❑ KSD-1052	You Can't Keep a Good Man Down	1969	12.50	25.00	50.00
BALLARD, KENNY					
45s					
GENIE					
❑ 101	Lady of Stone/(B-side unknown)	196?	7.50	15.00	30.00
KAPP					
❑ 602	Mr. Magic/Oh How I Cried	1964	6.25	12.50	25.00
ROULETTE					
❑ 4716	Your Letter/I'm Losing You	1966	3.75	7.50	15.00
BALLARD, RUSS Member of ARGENT.					
12-Inch Singles					
EMI AMERICA					
❑ SPRO-9406 [DJ]	The Fire Still Burns (7" Version)/(LP Version)	1985	—	3.00	6.00
EPIC					
❑ 429 [DJ]	Cast the Spirit/Dancer	1978	3.00	6.00	12.00
45s					
EMI AMERICA					
❑ 8204	Voices/Living Without You	1984	—	2.00	4.00
❑ 8204 [PS]	Voices/Living Without You	1984	—	2.00	4.00
❑ 8217	Two Silhouettes/Playing with Fire	1984	—	2.00	4.00
❑ 8275	The Fire Still Burns/Hold On	1985	—	—	3.00
❑ 8275 [PS]	The Fire Still Burns/Hold On	1985	—	—	3.00
EPIC					
❑ 50085	You Can Do Voodoo/Danger Zone Part 2	1975	—	2.00	4.00
❑ 50211	Winning/Here I Am	1976	—	2.00	4.00
❑ 50542	Treat Her Right/What Does It Take	1978	—	2.00	4.00
❑ 50883	On the Rebound/Riding with the Angels	1980	—	2.00	4.00
❑ 51002	Breakdown/Rock and Roll Lover	1981	—	2.00	4.00
Albums					
EMI AMERICA					
❑ ST-17108	Russ Ballard	1984	2.00	4.00	8.00
❑ ST-17162	The Fire Still Burns	1985	2.00	4.00	8.00
EPIC					
❑ KE 33252	Russ Ballard	1974	2.50	5.00	10.00
❑ PE 34093	Winning	1976	2.50	5.00	10.00
❑ JE 35035	At the Third Stroke	1978	2.50	5.00	10.00
❑ JE 36186	Russ Ballard & the Barnet Dogs	1980	2.50	5.00	10.00
❑ JE 36993	Into the Fire	1981	2.50	5.00	10.00
BALLARDS, THE See THE BALLADS.					
BALLIN' JACK					
45s					
COLUMBIA					
❑ 45312	Super Highway/Only a Tear	1971	—	2.50	5.00
❑ 45464	Ballin' the Jack/Hold On	1971	—	2.50	5.00
❑ 45698	Playin' the Game/I'm the One You Need	1972	—	2.00	4.00
MERCURY					
❑ 73401	Thunder/Try to Relax	1973	—	2.50	5.00
❑ 73429	Sunday Morning/This Song	1973	—	2.50	5.00
Albums					
COLUMBIA					
❑ C 30344	Ballin' Jack	1971	2.50	5.00	10.00
❑ KC 31468	Buzzard Luck	1972	2.50	5.00	10.00
MERCURY					
❑ SRM-1-672	Special Pride	1973	2.50	5.00	10.00
BALLOON FARM, THE					
45s					
LAURIE					
❑ 3405	A Question of Temperature/Hurtin' for Your Lovin'	1967	2.50	5.00	10.00
—Second pressing corrects A-side spelling					
❑ 3405	A Question of Tempature/Hurtin' for Your Lovin'	1967	5.00	10.00	20.00
—First pressing has misspelled A-side					
❑ 3445	Hurry Up Sundown/Farmer Brown	1968	2.50	5.00	10.00
BALTIMORE AND OHIO MARCHING BAND, THE					
45s					
JUBILEE					
❑ 5592	Lapland/Condition Red	1967	—	3.00	6.00
❑ 5614	The B&O Marching Band Song/The Wanderer	1968	—	2.50	5.00

Number	Title (A Side/B Side)	Yr	VG	VG+	NM
❑ 5644	Sgt. Crunch/Typsy Gypsy	1968	—	2.50	5.00
❑ 5672	Little Arrows/(B-side unknown)	1969	—	2.50	5.00
Albums					
JUBILEE					
❑ JGS-8008	Lapland	1968	3.75	7.50	15.00
BALTINEERS, THE					
45s					
LOST-NITE					
❑ 113	Moments Like This/New Love	196?	2.00	4.00	8.00
—Reissue					
❑ 114	Tears in My Eyes/Joe's Calypso	196?	2.00	4.00	8.00
—Reissue					
TEENAGE					
❑ 1000	Moments Like This/New Love	1956	75.00	150.00	300.00
❑ 1002	Tears in My Eyes/Joe's Calypso	1956	75.00	150.00	300.00
BANANA AND THE BUNCH					
45s					
WARNER BROS.					
❑ 7621	My True Life Blues/Vanderbilt's Lament	1972	—	2.50	5.00
❑ 7626	Back in the U.S.A./My True Life Blues	1972	—	2.50	5.00
Albums					
WARNER BROS.					
❑ BS 2626	Mid Mountain Ranch	1972	3.00	6.00	12.00
BAN-LONS, THE					
45s					
FIDELITY					
❑ 4051	Highest Mountain/Hey Baby	1959	50.00	100.00	200.00
❑ 4056	I Like It/Hey Good Lookin'	1959	50.00	100.00	200.00
BANANA BOYS					
45s					
UNI					
❑ 55194	Come Into My Life/What Will Your Mama Say	1970	2.50	5.00	10.00
BANANA SPLITS, THE					
45s					
DECCA					
❑ 32391	We're the Banana Splits/Wait Til Tomorrow	1968	3.00	6.00	12.00
❑ 32429	The Tra-La-La Song (One Banana, Two Banana)/Toy Piano Melody	1968	3.00	6.00	12.00
❑ 32429 [PS]	The Tra-La-La Song (One Banana, Two Banana)/Toy Piano Melody	1968	6.25	12.50	25.00
❑ 32536	Pretty Painted Carousel/Long Live Love	1969	3.00	6.00	12.00
❑ 32536 [PS]	Pretty Painted Carousel/Long Live Love	1969	6.25	12.50	25.00
7-Inch Extended Plays					
KELLOGG'S/HANNA-BARBERA					
❑ 34578	The Tra La La Song/That's the Pretty Part of You//It's a Good Day for a Parade/The Very First Kid on My Block	1969	5.00	10.00	20.00
❑ 34578 [PS]	Kellogg's Presents The Banana Splits, Vol. 1	1969	5.00	10.00	20.00
❑ 34579	Doin' the Banana Split/I Enjoy Being a Boy (In Love with You)//The Beautiful Calliopa/Let Me Remember You Smiling	1969	5.00	10.00	20.00
❑ 34579 [PS]	Kellogg's Presents The Banana Splits, Vol. 2	1969	5.00	10.00	20.00
Albums					
DECCA					
❑ DL 75075	We're the Banana Splits	1969	50.00	100.00	200.00
BANBARRA					
45s					
UNITED ARTISTS					
❑ XW-734	Shack Up Part 1/Shack Up Part 2	1975	—	2.00	4.00
BANCHEE					
45s					
ATLANTIC					
❑ 2708	I Just Don't Know/Train of Life	1970	2.50	5.00	10.00
POLYDOR					
❑ 14104	Searcher's Life//3/4 Song	1971	2.50	5.00	10.00
Albums					
ATLANTIC					
❑ SD 8240	Banchee	1969	5.00	10.00	20.00
POLYDOR					
❑ 24-4066	Thinkin'	1971	12.50	25.00	50.00
BAND, THE Also see BOB DYLAN; RONNIE HAWKINS AND THE HAWKS; LEVON AND THE HAWKS.					
45s					
CAPITOL					
❑ 2269	The Weight/I Shall Be Released	1968	2.00	4.00	8.00
—First pressing credits "Jaime Robbie Robertson, Rick Danko, Richard Manuel, Garth Hudson, Levon Helm"					
❑ 2635	Up on Cripple Creek/The Night They Drove Old Dixie Down	1969	—	3.00	6.00
❑ 2705	Rag Mama Rag/The Unfaithful Servant	1969	—	3.00	6.00
❑ 2705 [PS]	Rag Mama Rag/The Unfaithful Servant	1969	—	3.00	6.00
❑ 2870	Time to Kill/The Shape I'm In	1970	—	3.00	6.00
❑ 3199	Life Is a Carnival/The Moon Struck One	1971	—	3.00	6.00
❑ 3249	When I Paint My Masterpiece/Where Do We Go from Here	1971	—	—	—
—Unreleased?					
❑ 3433	Don't Do It/Rag Mama Rag	1972	—	2.50	5.00
❑ 3500	Hang Up My Rock & Roll Shoes/Caledonia Mission	1972	—	2.50	5.00
❑ 3758	Ain't Got No Home/Get Up Jake	1973	—	2.50	5.00
❑ 3828	Third Man Theme/W.S. Walcott Medicine Show	1974	—	2.50	5.00
❑ 4230	Ophelia/Hobo Jungle	1976	—	2.00	4.00
❑ 4316	Twilight/Acadian Driftwood	1976	—	2.00	4.00
❑ 4361	Georgia On My Mind/The Night They Drove Old Dixie Down	1976	—	2.00	4.00
❑ 58876	The Shape I'm In/Life Is a Carnival	2000	—	2.00	4.00

Number	Title (A Side/B Side)	Yr	VG	VG+	NM

WARNER BROS.
| ❏ 8592 | Out of the Blue/The Well | 1978 | — | 2.00 | 4.00 |

Albums
CAPITOL
| ❏ STAO-132 | The Band | 1969 | 3.75 | 7.50 | 15.00 |

—Lime green label
| ❏ STAO-8-0132 | The Band | 1969 | 25.00 | 50.00 | 100.00 |

—Capitol Record Club edition with black rainbow label; we don't know if any standard versions of this album exist with this label
| ❏ SW-425 | Stage Fright | 1970 | 2.50 | 5.00 | 10.00 |

—Without tear-off wraparound cover
| ❏ SW-425 | Stage Fright | 1970 | 3.75 | 7.50 | 15.00 |

—Includes tear-off wraparound cover
| ❏ SMAS-651 | Cahoots | 1971 | 3.75 | 7.50 | 15.00 |
| ❏ SKAO 2955 | Music from Big Pink | 1968 | 6.25 | 12.50 | 25.00 |

—Black label with colorband
| ❏ SKAO 2955 | Music from Big Pink | 1969 | 3.75 | 7.50 | 15.00 |

—Lime green label
| ❏ SKAO 2955 | Music from Big Pink | 1971 | 3.75 | 7.50 | 15.00 |

—Red label, purple "C" logo at top
| ❏ SABB-11045 [(2)]Rock of Ages | | 1972 | 5.00 | 10.00 | 20.00 |
| ❏ SW-11214 | Moondog Matinee | 1973 | 2.50 | 5.00 | 10.00 |

—Without tear-off wraparound cover
| ❏ SW-11214 | Moondog Matinee | 1973 | 3.75 | 7.50 | 15.00 |

—Includes tear-off wraparound cover
❏ ST-11440	Northern Lights-Southern Cross	1975	3.00	6.00	12.00
❏ ST-11553	The Best of the Band	1976	3.00	6.00	12.00
❏ SO-11602	Islands	1977	3.00	6.00	12.00
❏ SKBO-11856 [(2)]Anthology		1978	3.75	7.50	15.00
❏ SN-16003	Cahoots	1980	2.00	4.00	8.00

—Budget-line reissue
| ❏ SN-16004 | Moondog Matinee | 1980 | 2.00 | 4.00 | 8.00 |

—Budget-line reissue
| ❏ SN-16005 | Northern Lights-Southern Cross | 1980 | 2.00 | 4.00 | 8.00 |

—Budget-line reissue
| ❏ SN-16006 | Stage Fright | 1980 | 2.00 | 4.00 | 8.00 |

—Budget-line reissue
| ❏ SN-16007 | Islands | 1980 | 2.00 | 4.00 | 8.00 |

—Budget-line reissue
| ❏ SN-16008 | Rock of Ages, Volume 1 | 1980 | 2.00 | 4.00 | 8.00 |

—Budget-line reissue
| ❏ SN-16009 | Rock of Ages, Volume 2 | 1980 | 2.00 | 4.00 | 8.00 |

—Budget-line reissue
| ❏ SN-16010 | Anthology, Volume 1 | 1980 | 2.00 | 4.00 | 8.00 |

—Budget-line reissue
| ❏ SN-16011 | Anthology, Volume 2 | 1980 | 2.00 | 4.00 | 8.00 |

—Budget-line reissue
| ❏ SN-16296 | The Band | 198? | 2.00 | 4.00 | 8.00 |

—Budget-line reissue
| ❏ SN-16331 | The Best of the Band | 198? | 2.00 | 4.00 | 8.00 |

—Budget-line reissue
MOBILE FIDELITY
| ❏ 1-039 | Music from Big Pink | 1981 | 12.50 | 25.00 | 50.00 |

—Audiophile vinyl
RHINO HANDMADE
| ❏ RHM1-7801 [(3)]The Last Waltz | | 2003 | 15.00 | 30.00 | 60.00 |

—Box set with remixed version of the album, booklet, facsimiles of tickets, posters and other ephemera, many bonus photos, and a reproduction of the cover signed by Robbie Robertson
WARNER BROS.
| ❏ PRO-A-737 [DJ]The Last Waltz Sampler | | 1978 | 5.00 | 10.00 | 20.00 |
| ❏ 3WS 3146 [(3)] The Last Waltz | | 1978 | 5.00 | 10.00 | 20.00 |

BAND OF ANGELS
45s
MUMS
| ❏ ZS8 6035 | He's Not There/So Hard Living Without You | 1975 | — | 3.00 | 6.00 |

BAND WITHOUT A NAME, THE
45s
SIDEWALK
| ❏ 913 | Theme from "Thunder Alley"/Time After Time | 1967 | 5.00 | 10.00 | 20.00 |

TOWER
| ❏ 246 | Turn On Your Love Light/Perfect Girl | 1966 | 3.75 | 7.50 | 15.00 |
| ❏ 246 [PS] | Turn On Your Love Light/Perfect Girl | 1966 | 7.50 | 15.00 | 30.00 |

BANDS OF GOLD
45s
SMASH
| ❏ 2058 | It's Over/You Won't Change Me | 1966 | 6.25 | 12.50 | 25.00 |

BANDWAGON, THE Also includes records credited to "Johnny Johnson and the Bandwagon."
45s
BELL
| ❏ 902 | Sweet Inspiration/Pride Comes Before Fall | 1970 | — | 3.00 | 6.00 |
| ❏ 953 | (Blame It) On the Pony Express/Never Let Her Go | 1971 | — | 3.00 | 6.00 |

EPIC
❏ 10255	Baby Make Your Own Sweet Music/On the Day We Fell in Love	1967	2.00	4.00	8.00
❏ 10352	Breakin' Down the Walls of Heartache/Dancin' Master	1968	2.00	4.00	8.00
❏ 10412	I Ain't Lying/You	1968	2.00	4.00	8.00

—Artist credit: "Johnny Johnson and the Bandwagon"
| ❏ 10442 | Don't Let It In/When Love Has Gone Away | 1969 | 2.00 | 4.00 | 8.00 |
| ❏ 10473 | You Blew Your Cool (And Lost Your Fool)/Let's Hang On | 1969 | 2.00 | 4.00 | 8.00 |

—Artist credit: "Johnny Johnson and the Bandwagon"
Albums
EPIC
| ❏ BN 26426 | Johnny Johnson and the Bandwagon | 1969 | 5.00 | 10.00 | 20.00 |

Number	Title (A Side/B Side)	Yr	VG	VG+	NM

BANG
45s
CAPITOL
❏ 3304	Questions/Future Shock	1972	—	2.50	5.00
❏ 3386	Keep On/Redman	1972	—	2.00	4.00
❏ 3474	No Sugar Tonight/Idealist Realist	1972	—	2.00	4.00
❏ 3622	Must Be Love/Love Sonnet	1973	—	2.00	4.00
❏ 3816	Feels Nice/Slow Down	1974	—	2.00	4.00

Albums
CAPITOL
❏ ST-11015	Bang	1972	3.75	7.50	15.00
❏ SMAS-11110	Mother/Bow to the Music	1972	3.75	7.50	15.00
❏ ST-11190	Music	1973	5.00	10.00	20.00

BANGOR FLYING CIRCUS
45s
ABC DUNHILL
| ❏ 4220 | Come On People/A Change in Our Lives | 1969 | — | 3.00 | 6.00 |
| ❏ 4223 | Mama Don't You Know/Someday I'll Find | 1970 | — | 3.00 | 6.00 |

Albums
ABC DUNHILL
| ❏ DS-50069 | Bangor Flying Circus | 1969 | 3.75 | 7.50 | 15.00 |

BANKS, BESSIE
45s
BLUE CAT
| ❏ 106 | Go Now/It Sounds Like My Baby | 1965 | 2.50 | 5.00 | 10.00 |

SPOKANE
| ❏ 4009 | Do It Now/(You Should Have Been a) Doctor | 1963 | 3.75 | 7.50 | 15.00 |

TIGER
| ❏ 102 | Go Now/It Sounds Like My Baby | 1964 | 5.00 | 10.00 | 20.00 |

VERVE
| ❏ 10519 | I Can't Make It (Without You Baby)/Need You | 1967 | 2.00 | 4.00 | 8.00 |

VOLT
| ❏ 4112 | Ain't No Easy Way/Try to Leave Me If You Can | 1974 | — | 3.00 | 6.00 |

WAND
| ❏ 163 | Do It Now/(You Should Have Been a) Doctor | 1964 | 3.00 | 6.00 | 12.00 |

BANKS, DARRELL
45s
ATCO
| ❏ 6471 | Here Come the Tears/I've Got That Feeling | 1967 | 6.25 | 12.50 | 25.00 |
| ❏ 6484 | Angel Baby Don't You Leave Me/Look Into the Eyes of a Fool | 1967 | 6.25 | 12.50 | 25.00 |

COTILLION
| ❏ 44006 | I Wanna Go Home/Love of My Woman | 1968 | 2.50 | 5.00 | 10.00 |

REVILOT
| ❏ 201 | Open the Door to Your Heart/Our Love Is In the Pocket | 1966 | 3.75 | 7.50 | 15.00 |
| ❏ 203 | Somebody (Somewhere) Needs You/Baby Whatcha Got (For Me) | 1966 | 3.75 | 7.50 | 15.00 |

VOLT
| ❏ 4014 | Just Because Your Love Has Gone/I'm the One Who Loves You | 1969 | 2.50 | 5.00 | 10.00 |
| ❏ 4026 | Beautiful Feeling/No One Blinder | 1969 | 2.50 | 5.00 | 10.00 |

Albums
ATCO
| ❏ 33-216 [M] | Darrell Banks Is Here | 1967 | 6.25 | 12.50 | 25.00 |
| ❏ SD 33-216 [S] | Darrell Banks Is Here | 1967 | 7.50 | 15.00 | 30.00 |

VOLT
| ❏ VOS-6002 | Here to Stay | 1969 | 6.25 | 12.50 | 25.00 |

BANKS, DICK
45s
LIBERTY
| ❏ 55145 | Dirty Dog/Too Late | 1958 | 10.00 | 20.00 | 40.00 |
| ❏ 55507 | Just Like You/Be Faithful to Me | 1962 | 5.00 | 10.00 | 20.00 |

BANKS, DOUG
45s
ARGO
| ❏ 5483 | I Just Keep Dancing/Baby Since You Went Away | 1964 | 15.00 | 30.00 | 60.00 |

GUYDEN
| ❏ 2082 | Ain't That Just Like a Woman/Never Say Goodbye | 1963 | 15.00 | 30.00 | 60.00 |

BANKS, EDDIE
45s
JOSIE
| ❏ 804 | Sugar Diabetes/Rock-a-Bye Blues | 1956 | 10.00 | 20.00 | 40.00 |

BANKS, HOMER
45s
GENIE
| ❏ 1000 | Hooked by Love/Lady of Stone | 1966 | 12.50 | 25.00 | 50.00 |

MINIT
❏ 32000	A Lot of Love/Fighting to Win	1966	6.25	12.50	25.00
❏ 32008	Do You Know What/60 Minutes of Your Love	1966	6.25	12.50	25.00
❏ 32020	Hooked by Love/Lady of Stone	1967	6.25	12.50	25.00

BANKS, PETER
Albums
CAPITOL/SOVEREIGN
| ❏ SMAS-11217 | Two Sides of Peter Banks | 1973 | 3.75 | 7.50 | 15.00 |

BANNED, THE
45s
FONTANA
❏ 1604	My Life Is My Own/Nothing Matters But You	1967	2.50	5.00	10.00
❏ 1616	It Couldn't Happen Here/Annie Went to Ohio	1968	2.50	5.00	10.00
❏ 1616 [PS]	It Couldn't Happen Here/Annie Went to Ohio	1968	5.00	10.00	20.00
❏ 1621	Goodbye, Groovy, Goodbye/A Blanket of Sound	1968	2.50	5.00	10.00

Number	Title (A Side/B Side)	Yr	VG	VG+	NM
45s					
DECCA					
31040	My Swing Is Broke/Windows of Blue	1959	3.75	7.50	15.00
WARNER BROS.					
5695	Follow Me/Meet Me Tonight Little Girl	1966	2.50	5.00	10.00
5868	Good Lovin' Girl/I'm So Lucky	1966	2.50	5.00	10.00
Albums					
WARNER BROS.					
W 1625 [M]	Beware the Bantams	1966	5.00	10.00	20.00
WS 1625 [S]	Beware the Bantams	1966	6.25	12.50	25.00

BAR-KAYS, THE

Number	Title (A Side/B Side)	Yr	VG	VG+	NM
12-Inch Singles					
BASIX					
1309	Old School Mega Mix/Out of My Mind	1994	2.00	4.00	8.00
MERCURY					
PRO 296-1 [DJ]	Dirty Dancer (same on both sides)	1984	—	3.00	6.00
MDS-4024	Do It (Let Me See You Shake) (Original Mix) (Instrumental)	1982	2.00	4.00	8.00
818631-1	Freakshow on the Dance Floor/Lovers Should Never Fall in Love	1984	2.00	4.00	8.00
870018-1	Don't Hang Up (4 versions)	1987	2.00	4.00	8.00
872103-1	Struck by You (Extended 12-Inch Mix) (Dub Mix) (Acapella) (7-Inch Mix)/Your Place or Mine	1989	—	3.50	7.00
872955-1	Animal (4 versions)/Time Out	1989	—	3.50	7.00
880255-1	Sexomatic (3 versions)	1984	2.00	4.00	8.00
880966-1	Your Place or Mine (Club Version) (Dub Version)	1985	2.00	4.00	8.00
884232-1	Banging the Walls (2 versions)/Gina	1985	2.00	4.00	8.00
888837-1	Certified True (3 versions)/It Be That Way Sometimes	1987	—	3.50	7.00
45s					
HIGH STACKS					
9801	Body Fine/Hey Rufus!	1999	—	—	3.00
—B-side by Rufus Thomas; artist listed as "The Barkays"					
MERCURY					
73833	Shake Your Rump to the Funk/Summer of Our Love	1976	—	2.00	4.00
73888	Too Hot to Stop (Pt. 1)/Bang Bang (Stick 'Em Up)	1977	—	2.00	4.00
73915	Spellbound/You're So Sexy	1977	—	2.00	4.00
73971	Let's Have Some Fun/Cozy	1977	—	2.00	4.00
73994	Attitudes/Can't Keep My Hands Off You	1978	—	2.00	4.00
74039	I'll Dance/Angel Eyes	1978	—	2.00	4.00
74048	Shine/Are You Being Real	1979	—	2.00	4.00
76015	Move Your Boogie Body/Love's What It's All About	1979	—	2.00	4.00
76036	Today is the Day/Loving You Is My Occupation	1980	—	2.00	4.00
76088	Boogie Body Land/Running In and Out of My Life	1980	—	2.00	4.00
76097	Body Fever/Deliver Us	1981	—	2.00	4.00
76123	Hit and Run/Say It Through Love	1981	—	2.00	4.00
76143	Freaky Behavior/Backseat Driver	1982	—	2.00	4.00
76187	Do It (Let Me See You Shake)/Feels Like I'm Falling in Love	1982	—	2.00	4.00
810435-7	She Talks to Me with Her Body/Anticipation	1983	—	2.00	4.00
818631-7	Freakshow on the Dance Floor/Lovers Should Never Fall in Love	1984	—	2.00	4.00
870018-7	Don't Hang Up/Contagious	1988	—	—	3.00
870018-7 [PS]	Don't Hang Up/Contagious	1988	—	—	3.00
870214-7	Many Mistakes/Contagious	1988	—	—	3.00
872102-7	Struck by You/Your Place or Mine	1989	—	—	3.00
872102-7 [PS]	Struck by You/Your Place or Mine	1989	—	—	3.00
872954-7	Animal/Time Out	1989	—	—	3.00
872954-7 [PS]	Animal/Time Out	1989	—	—	3.00
880045-7	Dirty Dancer/(Instrumental)	1984	—	—	3.00
880255-7	Sexomatic/Sexomatic (Bonus Beats)	1984	—	—	3.00
880966-7	Your Place or Mine/(Instrumental)	1985	—	—	3.00
884232-7	Banging the Walls/Gina	1985	—	—	3.00
888837-7	Certified True/It Be That Way Sometimes	1987	—	—	3.00
STAX					
3216	Holy Ghost/Monster	1978	—	2.50	5.00
VOLT					
148	Soul Finger/Knucklehead	1967	2.00	4.00	8.00
154	Give Everybody Some/Don't Do That	1967	—	3.00	6.00
158	A Hard Day's Night/I Want Someone	1968	—	3.00	6.00
4007	Copy Cat/In the Middle	1968	—	3.00	6.00
4011	Don't Stop Dancing/Don't Stop Dancing (Part 2)	1969	—	3.00	6.00
4019	Midnight Cowboy/A.J. The Housefly	1969	—	3.00	6.00
4033	Song and Dance/I Thank You	1970	—	3.00	6.00
4050	Montego Bay/Humpin'	1971	—	2.50	5.00
4073	Son of Shaft/Song and Dance	1972	—	2.50	5.00
4081	Dance, Dance, Dance/Memphis at Sunrise	1972	—	2.50	5.00
4092	You're the Best Thing That Ever Happened to Me/You're Still My Brother	1973	—	2.50	5.00
4097	God Is Watching/It Ain't Easy	1973	—	2.50	5.00
Albums					
ATCO					
SD 33-289	Soul Finger	1968	6.25	12.50	25.00
MERCURY					
SRM-1-1099	Too Hot to Stop	1976	2.50	5.00	10.00
SRM-1-1181	Flying High on Your Love	1977	2.50	5.00	10.00
SRM-1-3732	Light of Life	1978	2.50	5.00	10.00
SRM-1-3781	Injoy	1979	2.50	5.00	10.00
SRM-1-3844	As One	1980	2.50	5.00	10.00
SRM-1-4028	Nightcruising	1981	2.50	5.00	10.00
SRM-1-4065	Propositions	1982	2.50	5.00	10.00
818478-1	Dangerous	1984	2.50	5.00	10.00
824727-1	Banging the Wall	1985	2.50	5.00	10.00
830305-1	Contagious	1987	2.50	5.00	10.00
836774-1	Animal	1989	2.50	5.00	10.00
STAX					
4106	Money Talks	1978	2.50	5.00	10.00
4130	Gotta Groove	1979	2.50	5.00	10.00
MPS-8510	Cold Blooded	1981	2.50	5.00	10.00
MPS-8542	The Best of the Bar-Kays	1988	2.50	5.00	10.00
VOLT					
417 [M]	Soul Finger	1967	10.00	20.00	40.00
S-417 [S]	Soul Finger	1967	10.00	20.00	40.00
6004	Gotta Groove	1969	7.50	15.00	30.00
6011	Black Rock	1971	6.25	12.50	25.00
VOS-8001	Do You See What I See	1972	6.25	12.50	25.00
9504	Cold Blooded	1974	6.25	12.50	25.00

BARA, TONY

Number	Title (A Side/B Side)	Yr	VG	VG+	NM
45s					
ATCO					
6172	Rambling/Long Gone Mare	1960	3.00	6.00	12.00

BARBARA AND THE BELIEVERS

Number	Title (A Side/B Side)	Yr	VG	VG+	NM
45s					
CAPITOL					
5866	When You Wish Upon a Star/What Can Happen to Me Now	1967	4.00	8.00	16.00

BARBARA AND THE BOYS

Number	Title (A Side/B Side)	Yr	VG	VG+	NM
45s					
DOT					
15794	Hooty Sapperticker/Cobra	1958	3.75	7.50	15.00

BARBARA AND THE BROWNS

Number	Title (A Side/B Side)	Yr	VG	VG+	NM
45s					
STAX					
150	Big Party/You Belong to Her	1964	5.00	10.00	20.00
158	Please Be Honest with Me/In My Heart	1964	3.75	7.50	15.00
164	I Don't Want Trouble/My Lover	1965	3.75	7.50	15.00

BARBARIANS, THE

Number	Title (A Side/B Side)	Yr	VG	VG+	NM
45s					
JOY					
290	Hey Little Bird/You've Got to Understand	1964	12.50	25.00	50.00
LAURIE					
3308	Are You a Boy or Are You a Girl/Take It or Leave It	1965	5.00	10.00	20.00
3321	Susie Q/What the New Breed Say	1965	5.00	10.00	20.00
3326	Moulty/I'll Keep On Seeing You	1965	5.00	10.00	20.00
Albums					
LAURIE					
LLP-2033 [M]	Are You a Boy or Are You a Girl?	1966	37.50	75.00	150.00
SLP-2033 [S]	Are You a Boy or Are You a Girl?	1966	50.00	100.00	200.00
RHINO					
RNLP 008	The Barbarians	1979	3.00	6.00	12.00

BARBARY, RICHARD

Number	Title (A Side/B Side)	Yr	VG	VG+	NM
45s					
A&M					
1019	Call On Me/Like You, Babe	1969	—	3.00	6.00
SPRING					
701	Get Right/When Johnny Comes Marching Home	1967	2.00	4.00	8.00
Albums					
A&M					
SP-3010	Soul Machine	1969	5.00	10.00	20.00

BARBEES, THE Early version of THE VELVELETTES.

Number	Title (A Side/B Side)	Yr	VG	VG+	NM
45s					
STEPP					
236	The Wind/Que Pasa	1963	50.00	100.00	200.00

BARBER, CHRIS

Number	Title (A Side/B Side)	Yr	VG	VG+	NM
45s					
ATLANTIC					
2016	Hush-a-Bye/You Don't Understand	1959	3.00	6.00	12.00
LAURIE					
3022	Petite Fleur/Wild Cat Blues	1958	3.75	7.50	15.00
3022 [PS]	Petite Fleur/Wild Cat Blues	1958	6.25	12.50	25.00
3026	Rugged Cross/Thriller Rag	1959	3.00	6.00	12.00
3057	Swanee River/ Lonesome	1960	3.00	6.00	12.00
3154	It Looks Like a Big Night Tonight/King Kong	1963	3.00	6.00	12.00
LONDON					
9571V	The Loneliness of the Long Distance Runner/Valley of Roses	1963	3.00	6.00	12.00
Albums					
ATLANTIC					
1292 [M]	Here Is Chris Barber	1959	10.00	20.00	40.00
COLPIX					
CP-404 [M]	Chris Barber Plays "Trad"	1959	7.50	15.00	30.00
GHB					
GHB-40 [M]	Collaboration	1967	3.75	7.50	15.00
LAURIE					
1001 [M]	Petite Fleur	1959	10.00	20.00	40.00
LLP-1003 [M]	Trad Jazz Volume 1	1960	7.50	15.00	30.00
LLP-1009 [M]	Chris Barber's "American" Jazz Band	1962	7.50	15.00	30.00

BARBER BROTHERS, THE

Number	Title (A Side/B Side)	Yr	VG	VG+	NM
45s					
DECCA					
30753	Well All Right/How Can You Tell If It's Love	1958	3.75	7.50	15.00

BARBOUR, KEITH

Number	Title (A Side/B Side)	Yr	VG	VG+	NM
45s					
BARNABY					
2036	A Pound of Peaches/Music Sweet Music	1971	—	2.50	5.00
EPIC					
10486	Echo Park/Here I Am Losing You	1969	—	3.00	6.00
10575	Bake Me a Woman/If I Could Only Touch You	1970	—	3.00	6.00
10598	Alicia/Sweet Mary Sunday	1970	—	3.00	6.00
10652	In the Quiet of Your Love/My God and I	1970	—	3.00	6.00

B

Number	Title (A Side/B Side)	Yr	VG	VG+	NM
Albums					
EPIC					
☐ BN 26485	Echo Park	1969	5.00	10.00	20.00
BARBRA AND NEIL BARBRA STREISAND and NEIL DIAMOND.					
45s					
COLUMBIA					
☐ 3-10840	You Don't Bring Me Flowers/(Instrumental)	1978	—	2.50	5.00
BARCLAY JAMES HARVEST					
45s					
HARVEST					
☐ 3501	Thank You/Medicine Man	1972	—	2.50	5.00
MCA					
☐ 40690	Rock 'N' Roll Star/Polk Street Rag	1977	—	2.00	4.00
☐ 40795	Hymn/Our Kid's Kid	1977	—	2.00	4.00
POLYDOR					
☐ 14546	Loving Is Easy (Fantasy)/Turning in Circles	1979	—	2.00	4.00
☐ 15104	Crazy City/Child of the Universe	1975	—	2.00	4.00
☐ 15118	Titles/(B-side unknown)	197?	—	2.00	4.00
SIRE					
☐ 4105	Early Morning/Mr. Sunshine	1969	2.00	4.00	8.00
☐ 4112	Brother Thrush/Poor Wages	1969	2.00	4.00	8.00
Albums					
HARVEST					
☐ SW-11145	Baby James Harvest	1973	3.75	7.50	15.00
MCA					
☐ 2234	Octoberon	1976	2.50	5.00	10.00
☐ 2302	Gone to Earth	1977	2.50	5.00	10.00
POLYDOR					
☐ PD-1-6173	XII	1978	2.50	5.00	10.00
☐ PD-1-6267	Eyes of the Universe	1980	2.50	5.00	10.00
☐ PD-6508	Everyone Is Everybody Else	1974	3.00	6.00	12.00
☐ PD-6517	Time Honoured Ghosts	1975	3.00	6.00	12.00
SIRE					
☐ SI-4904	Back Again	1971	3.75	7.50	15.00
☐ SI-5904	Other Short Stories	1972	3.75	7.50	15.00
☐ SES-97026	Barclay James Harvest	1970	5.00	10.00	20.00
BARD, ANNETTE One of THE TEDDY BEARS.					
45s					
IMPERIAL					
☐ 5643	What Difference Does It Make/Alibi	1960	12.50	25.00	50.00
BARDS, THE (1)					
45s					
BURDETTE					
☐ 103	I Want You/Freedom Catcher	1971	2.00	4.00	8.00
CAPITOL					
☐ 2041	The Jabberwocky/Never Too Much Love	1967	2.50	5.00	10.00
☐ 2148	The Owl and the Pussycat/The Light of Love	1968	2.50	5.00	10.00
☐ 2148 [PS]	The Owl and the Pussycat/The Light of Love	1968	5.00	10.00	20.00
JERDEN					
☐ 907	Good Time Charlie's Got the Blues/Tunesmith	1969	3.00	6.00	12.00
PARROT					
☐ 337	Good Time Charlie's Got the Blues/Tunesmith	1969	2.50	5.00	10.00
☐ 344	Our Love/Jubilation	1970	2.50	5.00	10.00
☐ 351	Day by Day/Wadda Wadda	1970	2.50	5.00	10.00
PICCADILLY					
☐ 224	The Owl and the Pussycat/The Light of Love	1966	5.00	10.00	20.00
☐ 232	The Jabberwocky/My Generation	1966	3.00	6.00	12.00
☐ 242	Our Love/Jubilation	1967	3.00	6.00	12.00
BARDS, THE (2)					
45s					
DAWN					
☐ 208	I'm a Wine Drinker/Easy Going Baby	1954	62.50	125.00	250.00
☐ 209	Gravy/Avalon	1954	62.50	125.00	250.00
BARE, BOBBY By record-company accident, he also recorded as BILL PARSONS. Also see DONNIE BOWSER.					
45s					
CAPITOL					
☐ F3557	Down on the Corner of Love/Another Love Has Ended	1956	7.50	15.00	30.00
☐ F3686	Darling Don't/Life of a Fool	1957	7.50	15.00	30.00
☐ F3771	The Livin' End/Beggar	1957	7.50	15.00	30.00
COLUMBIA					
☐ 02038	Learning to Live Again/Appaloosa Rider	1981	—	2.00	4.00
☐ 0 2414	Take Me As I Am (Or Let Me Go)/White Freight Liner Blues	1981	—	2.00	4.00
☐ 02577	Dropping Out of Sight/She Is Gone	1981	—	2.00	4.00
☐ 02690	New Cut Road/Let Him Roll	1982	—	2.00	4.00
☐ 02895	If You Ain't Got Nothing (You've Got Nothing To Lose)/Golden Memories	1982	—	2.00	4.00
☐ 03135	New Cut Road/Numbers	1982	—	—	3.00
—Reissue					
☐ 03149	(I'm Not) A Candle in the Wind/Cold Day in Hell	1982	—	2.00	4.00
☐ 03334	Praise the Lord and Send Me the Money/I've Been Rained On Too	1982	—	2.00	4.00
☐ 03628	It's a Dirty Job/Caught in the Spotlight	1983	—	2.00	4.00
—A-side with Lacy J. Dalton					
☐ 03809	The Jogger/Gravy Train	1983	—	2.00	4.00
☐ 04092	Diet Song/Stacy Brown Got Two	1983	—	2.00	4.00
☐ 10690	Too Many Nights Alone/A Yard Full of Rusty Cars	1978	—	2.50	5.00
☐ 10831	Sleep Tight, Good Night Man/Hot Afternoon	1978	—	2.50	5.00
☐ 10891	Healin'/Love Is a Cold Wind	1979	—	2.00	4.00
☐ 10998	Till I Gain Control Again/I'll Feel a Whole Lot Better	1979	—	2.00	4.00
☐ 11045	No Memories Hangin' Round/This Has Happened Before	1979	—	2.00	4.00
—With Roseanne Cash					
☐ 11170	Numbers/When Hippies Get Older	1980	—	2.00	4.00
☐ 11259	Tequila Sheila/Quaaludes Again	1980	—	2.00	4.00
☐ 11365	Food Blues/Used Cars	1980	—	2.00	4.00
☐ 11408	Willie Jones/If That Ain't Love	1980	—	2.00	4.00
EMI AMERICA					
☐ 8279	When I Get Home/Party of the First Part	1985	—	—	3.00
☐ 8296	Reno and Me/Party of the First Part	1985	—	—	3.00
☐ 8317	Better Not Look Down/Wait Until Tomorrow	1986	—	—	3.00
☐ 8333	Real Good/Wait Until Tomorrow	1986	—	—	3.00
FRATERNITY					
☐ 861	I'm Hanging Up My Rifle/That's Where I Wanna Be	1959	10.00	20.00	40.00
☐ 867	Sweet Singing Sam/More Than a Poor Boy Could Give	1960	7.50	15.00	30.00
☐ 871	No Letter from My Baby/Lynchin' Party	1960	5.00	10.00	20.00
☐ 878	Book of Love/Lorena	1961	5.00	10.00	20.00
☐ 885	Sailor Man/Island of Love	1961	5.00	10.00	20.00
☐ 890	Zigzag Twist/Brooklyn Bridge	1961	5.00	10.00	20.00
☐ 892	The Day My Rainbow Fell/That Mean Old Clock	1961	5.00	10.00	20.00
MERCURY					
☐ 73097	How I Got to Memphis/It's Freezing in El Paso	1970	—	3.00	6.00
☐ 73148	Come Sundown/Woman You Have Been a Friend to Me	1970	—	3.00	6.00
☐ 73203	Please Don't Tell Me How the Story Ends/Where Have All the Seasons Gone	1971	—	3.00	6.00
☐ 73236	Short and Sweet/A Million Miles to the City	1971	—	3.00	6.00
☐ 73279	What Am I Gonna Do/Love Forever	1972	—	3.00	6.00
☐ 73317	Sylvia's Mother/Music City U.S.A.	1972	—	3.00	6.00
RCA					
☐ PB-10718	Put a Little Lovin' on Me/Those City Lights	1976	—	2.50	5.00
☐ PB-10790	Drop Kick Me, Jesus/Baby Wants to Boogie	1976	—	3.00	6.00
☐ PB-10852	Vegas/The Shelter of Your Eyes	1976	—	2.50	5.00
—A-side by Bobby and Jeannie Bare					
☐ PB-10902	Look Who I'm Cheatin' On Tonight/If You Think I'm Crazy Now (You Should Have Seen Me When I Was a Kid)	1977	—	2.50	5.00
☐ PB-11037	Red Neck Hippie Romance/Bottom Dollar	1977	—	2.50	5.00
☐ PB-11673	Hurricane Shirley/Crazy Arms	1979	—	2.50	5.00
—B-side by Willie Nelson					
RCA VICTOR					
☐ 47-8032	Shame on Me/Above and Beyond	1962	3.00	6.00	12.00
☐ 47-8083	I Don't Believe I'll Fall in Love Today/To Whom It May Concern	1962	3.00	6.00	12.00
☐ 47-8083 [PS]	I Don't Believe I'll Fall in Love Today/To Whom It May Concern	1962	6.25	12.50	25.00
☐ 47-8146	Dear Waste Basket/I'd Fight the World	1963	3.00	6.00	12.00
☐ 47-8183	Detroit City/Heart of Ice	1963	3.75	7.50	15.00
☐ 47-8183 [PS]	Detroit City/Heart of Ice	1963	6.25	12.50	25.00
☐ 47-8238	500 Miles Away from Home/It All Depends On Linda	1963	3.75	7.50	15.00
☐ 47-8294	Miller's Cave/Jeannie's Last Kiss	1963	3.00	6.00	12.00
☐ 47-8358	Have I Stayed Away Too Long/More Than a Poor Boy Can Give	1964	3.00	6.00	12.00
☐ 47-8395	He Was a Friend of Mine/When I'm Gone	1964	3.00	6.00	12.00
☐ 47-8443	Four Strong Winds/Take Me Home	1964	3.00	6.00	12.00
☐ 47-8509	Times Are Gettin' Hard/One Day at a Time	1965	2.50	5.00	10.00
☐ 47-8571	It's Alright/She Picked a Perfect Day	1965	2.50	5.00	10.00
☐ 47-8654	Just to Satisfy You/Memories	1965	2.50	5.00	10.00
☐ 47-8699	Talk Me Some Sense/Delia's Gone	1965	2.50	5.00	10.00
☐ 47-8758	In the Same Old Way/Long Black Veil	1965	2.50	5.00	10.00
☐ 47-8851	The Streets of Baltimore/She Took My Sunshine Away	1966	2.50	5.00	10.00
☐ 47-8988	Homesick/Guess I'll Move On Down the Line	1966	2.50	5.00	10.00
☐ 47-9098	Charleston Railroad Tavern/Vincennes	1967	2.00	4.00	8.00
☐ 47-9191	Come Kiss Me Love/Sandy's Crying Again	1967	2.00	4.00	8.00
☐ 47-9314	The Piney Wood Hills/They Covered Up the Old Swimmin' Hole	1967	2.00	4.00	8.00
☐ 47-9450	Find Out What's Happening/When Am I Ever Gonna Settle Down	1968	2.00	4.00	8.00
☐ 47-9568	A Little Bit Later On Down the Line/Don't Do Like I Done, Son (Do What I Say)	1968	2.00	4.00	8.00
☐ 47-9643	The Town That Broke My Heart/My Baby	1968	2.00	4.00	8.00
☐ 74-0110	(Margie's At) The Lincoln Park Inn/Rainy Day in Richmond	1969	—	3.00	6.00
☐ 74-0202	Which One Will It Be/My Frame of Mind	1969	—	3.00	6.00
☐ 74-0264	God Bless America Again/Baby, What Else Can I Do	1969	—	3.00	6.00
☐ 74-0866	I Hate Goodbyes/Fallin' Apart	1973	—	3.00	6.00
☐ 74-0918	Ride Me Down Easy/A Train That Never Runs	1973	—	3.00	6.00
☐ APBO-0063	You Know Who/Send Tomorrow to the Moon	1973	—	2.50	5.00
☐ AMAO-0119	Shame on Me/Above and Beyond	1973	—	2.50	5.00
☐ APBO-0197	Daddy What If/Restless Wind	1973	—	2.50	5.00
☐ APBO-0261	Marie Laveau/Mermaid	1974	—	2.50	5.00
☐ PB-10037	Where'd I Come From/Scarlet Ribbons	1974	—	2.50	5.00
—By "Bobby Bare, Jr., and Mommy"					
☐ PB-10096	Singin' in the Kitchen/You Are	1974	—	2.50	5.00
—As "Bobby Bare and the Family"					
☐ GB-10166	Daddy What If/Ride Me Down Easy	1975	—	—	3.00
—Gold Standard Series issue					
☐ PB-10223	Back in Huntsville Again/Warm and Free	1975	—	2.50	5.00
☐ PB-10318	Alimony/Daddy's Been Around the House Too Long	1975	—	2.50	5.00
☐ PB-10409	Cowboys and Daddys/High Plains Jamboree	1975	—	2.50	5.00
☐ GB-10495	Singin' in the Kitchen/You Are	1975	—	—	3.00
—Gold Standard Series issue					
☐ GB-10496	Marie Laveau/Mermaid	1975	—	—	3.00
—Gold Standard Series issue					
☐ GB-10497	Where'd I Come From/Scarlet Ribbons	1975	—	—	3.00
—Gold Standard Series issue					

Number	Title (A Side/B Side)	Yr	VG	VG+	NM
❏ PB-10556	The Winner/ Up Against the Wall Redneck Mother	1976	—	2.50	5.00

RICE

Number	Title (A Side/B Side)	Yr	VG	VG+	NM
❏ 5057	Christian Soldier/Dropping Out of Sight	1973	—	2.50	5.00
❏ 5060	Love Forever/A Million Miles to the City	1973	—	2.50	5.00
❏ 5066	I Took a Memory to Lunch/ It's Freezing in St. Paul	1974	—	2.50	5.00

Albums

COLUMBIA

Number	Title (A Side/B Side)	Yr	VG	VG+	NM
❏ KC 35314	Bare	1977	2.50	5.00	10.00
❏ JC 36323	Down & Dirty	1978	2.50	5.00	10.00
❏ PC 36323	Down & Dirty	198?	2.00	4.00	8.00
—Budget-line reissue					
❏ JC 36785	Drunk & Crazy	1980	2.50	5.00	10.00
❏ FC 37157	As Is	1981	2.50	5.00	10.00
❏ FC 37351	Encore	1981	2.50	5.00	10.00
❏ PC 37351	Encore	198?	2.00	4.00	8.00
—Budget-line reissue					
❏ FC 37719	Ain't Got Nothin' to Lose	1982	2.50	5.00	10.00
❏ FC 38311	Biggest Hits	1982	2.50	5.00	10.00
❏ FC 38670	Drinkin' from the Bottle, Singin' from the Heart	1983	2.50	5.00	10.00

HILLTOP

Number	Title (A Side/B Side)	Yr	VG	VG+	NM
❏ 6026	Tender Years	196?	3.00	6.00	12.00

MERCURY

Number	Title (A Side/B Side)	Yr	VG	VG+	NM
❏ SR-61290	This Is Bare Country	1970	5.00	10.00	20.00
❏ SR-61316	Where Have All the Seasons Gone	1971	5.00	10.00	20.00
❏ SR-61363	What Am I Gonna Do?	1972	5.00	10.00	20.00

PICKWICK

Number	Title (A Side/B Side)	Yr	VG	VG+	NM
❏ ACL-7003	500 Miles Away from Home	1975	2.50	5.00	10.00

RCA CAMDEN

Number	Title (A Side/B Side)	Yr	VG	VG+	NM
❏ ACL1-0150	Memphis, Tennessee	1973	3.00	6.00	12.00
❏ CAS-2290	Folsom Prison Blues	1969	3.00	6.00	12.00
❏ CAS-2465	I'm a Long Way from Home	1971	3.00	6.00	12.00

RCA VICTOR

Number	Title (A Side/B Side)	Yr	VG	VG+	NM
❏ APL1-0040	I Hate Goodbyes/Ride Me Down Easy	1973	3.75	7.50	15.00
❏ CPL2-0290 [(2)]	Bobby Bare Sings Lullabys, Legends and Lies	1973	5.00	10.00	20.00
❏ ANL1-0560	Sunday Morning	1974	2.50	5.00	10.00
❏ APL1-0700	Singin' in the Kitchen	1974	3.75	7.50	15.00
❏ APL1-0906	Hard Time Hungrys	1975	3.00	6.00	12.00
❏ APL1-1222	Cowboys and Daddys	1975	3.00	6.00	12.00
❏ APL1-1786	The Winner and Other Losers	1976	3.00	6.00	12.00
❏ APL1-2179	Me and McDill	1977	3.00	6.00	12.00
❏ LPM-2776 [M]	"Detroit City" and Other Hits	1963	5.00	10.00	20.00
❏ LSP-2776 [S]	"Detroit City" and Other Hits	1963	6.25	12.50	25.00
❏ LPM-2835 [M]	500 Miles Away from Home	1964	5.00	10.00	20.00
❏ LSP-2835 [S]	500 Miles Away from Home	1964	6.25	12.50	25.00
❏ LPM-2955 [M]	The Travelin' Bare	1964	5.00	10.00	20.00
❏ LSP-2955 [S]	The Travelin' Bare	1964	6.25	12.50	25.00
❏ LPM-3395 [M]	Constant Sorrow	1965	5.00	10.00	20.00
❏ LSP-3395 [S]	Constant Sorrow	1965	6.25	12.50	25.00
❏ LPM-3479 [M]	The Best of Bobby Bare	1965	5.00	10.00	20.00
❏ LSP-3479 [S]	The Best of Bobby Bare	1965	6.25	12.50	25.00
❏ LPM-3515 [M]	Talk Me Some Sense	1966	5.00	10.00	20.00
❏ LSP-3515 [S]	Talk Me Some Sense	1966	6.25	12.50	25.00
❏ LPM-3618 [M]	The Streets of Baltimore	1966	5.00	10.00	20.00
❏ LSP-3618 [S]	The Streets of Baltimore	1966	6.25	12.50	25.00
❏ LPM-3688 [M]	This I Believe	1966	5.00	10.00	20.00
❏ LSP-3688 [S]	This I Believe	1966	6.25	12.50	25.00
❏ LPM-3831 [M]	A Bird Named Yesterday	1967	6.25	12.50	25.00
❏ LSP-3831 [S]	A Bird Named Yesterday	1967	5.00	10.00	20.00
❏ LPM-3896 [M]	The English Country Side	1967	10.00	20.00	40.00
❏ LSP-3896 [S]	The English Country Side	1967	5.00	10.00	20.00
❏ LPM-3994 [M]	The Best of Bobby Bare — Volume 2	1968	10.00	20.00	40.00
❏ LSP-3994 [S]	The Best of Bobby Bare — Volume 2	1968	5.00	10.00	20.00
❏ AYL1-4118	Greatest Hits	1982	2.00	4.00	8.00
❏ LSP-4177	(Margie's At) The Lincoln Park Inn (And Other Controversial Country Songs)	1969	5.00	10.00	20.00
❏ LSP-4422	Real Thing	1970	3.75	7.50	15.00
❏ AHL1-5469	Collector's Series	1985	2.50	5.00	10.00
❏ VPS-6090 [(2)]	This Is Bobby Bare	1972	5.00	10.00	20.00

UNITED ARTISTS

Number	Title (A Side/B Side)	Yr	VG	VG+	NM
❏ UA-LA621-G	Bare Country	1977	3.00	6.00	12.00

BARE, BOBBY, AND SKEETER DAVIS Also see each artist's individual listings.

45s

RCA VICTOR

Number	Title (A Side/B Side)	Yr	VG	VG+	NM
❏ 47-8496	A Dear John Letter/Too Used to Being with You	1965	2.50	5.00	10.00
❏ 47-9789	Your Husband, My Wife/Before the Sunshine	1969	—	3.00	6.00

Albums

RCA VICTOR

Number	Title (A Side/B Side)	Yr	VG	VG+	NM
❏ LPM-3336 [M]	Tunes for Two	1965	5.00	10.00	20.00
❏ LSP-3336 [S]	Tunes for Two	1965	6.25	12.50	25.00
❏ LSP-4335	Your Husband, My Wife	1970	3.75	7.50	15.00

BARE, BOBBY, NORMA JEAN, & LIZ ANDERSON

45s

RCA VICTOR

Number	Title (A Side/B Side)	Yr	VG	VG+	NM
❏ 47-8963	The Game of Triangles/Bye Bye Bye	1966	2.50	5.00	10.00

Albums

RCA VICTOR

Number	Title (A Side/B Side)	Yr	VG	VG+	NM
❏ LPM-3764 [M]	The Game of Triangles	1967	6.25	12.50	25.00
❏ LSP-3764 [S]	The Game of Triangles	1967	5.00	10.00	20.00

BARE, CHARLIE

45s

HIT

Number	Title (A Side/B Side)	Yr	VG	VG+	NM
❏ 178	Do-Wacka-Do/ Ode to the Little Brown Shack Out Back	1965	2.00	4.00	8.00
—B-side by Johnny Singer					
❏ 189	King of the Road/Look of Love	1965	2.00	4.00	8.00
—B-side by Connie Dee					

BARGE, GENE

45s

CHECKER

Number	Title (A Side/B Side)	Yr	VG	VG+	NM
❏ 839	Way Down Home/Country	1954	7.50	15.00	30.00
❏ 1110	Fine Twine/The "In" Crowd	1965	2.50	5.00	10.00

LEGRAND

Number	Title (A Side/B Side)	Yr	VG	VG+	NM
❏ 1006	Thinking of You/Autumn Leaves	1961	10.00	20.00	40.00

PARAMOUNT

Number	Title (A Side/B Side)	Yr	VG	VG+	NM
❏ 0160	Love Theme from "The Godfather"/Gina	1972	—	2.50	5.00

Albums

CHECKER

Number	Title (A Side/B Side)	Yr	VG	VG+	NM
❏ LP-2994 [M]	Dance with Daddy G	1965	12.50	25.00	50.00

BARIN, PETE

45s

SABINA

Number	Title (A Side/B Side)	Yr	VG	VG+	NM
❏ 504	So Wrong/Broken Heart	1962	12.50	25.00	50.00
❏ 512	Loneliest Guy in the World/Look Out for Cindy	1962	7.50	15.00	30.00

BARITONES, THE

45s

DORE

Number	Title (A Side/B Side)	Yr	VG	VG+	NM
❏ 501	After School Rock/Sentimental Baby	1958	10.00	20.00	40.00

BARKER, DELBERT

45s

KING

Number	Title (A Side/B Side)	Yr	VG	VG+	NM
❏ 4951	That's a Sin/No Good, Robin Hood	1956	7.50	15.00	30.00
❏ 5008	Wild Heart/There Must be a Way	1957	7.50	15.00	30.00
❏ 5031	Amanda/Broken Heart	1957	7.50	15.00	30.00
❏ 6042	It Can't Last Long/Color Me Gone	1966	2.50	5.00	10.00

BARNABY BYE

45s

ATLANTIC

Number	Title (A Side/B Side)	Yr	VG	VG+	NM
❏ 2984	I Think I'm Gonna Like It/Dreamer	1973	—	2.50	5.00
❏ 3244	Take Me With You/Blonde	1975	—	2.50	5.00
❏ 3266	Can't Live This Way/Happy Was the Day We Met	1975	—	2.50	5.00

Albums

ATLANTIC

Number	Title (A Side/B Side)	Yr	VG	VG+	NM
❏ SD 7273	Room to Grow	1973	3.00	6.00	12.00
❏ SD 18104	Touch	1974	3.00	6.00	12.00

BARNES, BENNY

45s

D

Number	Title (A Side/B Side)	Yr	VG	VG+	NM
❏ 1052	Gold Records in the Snow/Happy Little Blue Bird	1959	15.00	30.00	60.00

HALL-WAY

Number	Title (A Side/B Side)	Yr	VG	VG+	NM
❏ 1203	A Bar with No Beer/Headed for Heartbreak	1964	2.50	5.00	10.00
❏ 1207	It's Good to Be Home/For a Minute There	1965	2.50	5.00	10.00

KAPP

Number	Title (A Side/B Side)	Yr	VG	VG+	NM
❏ 859	A Bar with No Beer/Headed for Heartbreak	1967	2.00	4.00	8.00
❏ 912	Sweet Suzannah/It's My Mind That's Broken	1968	2.00	4.00	8.00

MEGA

Number	Title (A Side/B Side)	Yr	VG	VG+	NM
❏ 0071	Woman, Leave My Mind Alone/I'm Just Here to Get My Baby Off My Mind	1972	—	2.50	5.00

MERCURY

Number	Title (A Side/B Side)	Yr	VG	VG+	NM
❏ 71048	Poor Man's Riches/Those Who Know	1957	5.00	10.00	20.00
❏ 71057	Poor Old Me/Penalty	1957	5.00	10.00	20.00
❏ 71119	Nickels Worth of Dreams/Mine All Mine	1957	5.00	10.00	20.00
❏ 71188	King for a Day/Your Old Stand By	1957	5.00	10.00	20.00
❏ 71284	Moon Over My Shoulder/Lonely Street	1958	6.25	12.50	25.00
❏ 71552	Beggar to a King/The Fastest Gun Alive	1959	5.00	10.00	20.00
❏ 71600	That-a Boy Willie/Token of Love	1960	5.00	10.00	20.00
❏ 71637	Pretty Little Girl/Message in the Wind	1960	5.00	10.00	20.00
❏ 71717	You're Still on My Mind/ I Think I'll Take a Walk and Disappear	1960	5.00	10.00	20.00
❏ 71806	Yearning/Go On, Go On	1961	5.00	10.00	20.00
❏ 71896	The World's Worst Loser/I Changed My Mind	1961	5.00	10.00	20.00

MUSICOR

Number	Title (A Side/B Side)	Yr	VG	VG+	NM
❏ 1100	Let Me Live As Long As I Can/ Tea Leaves Don't Lie	1965	2.00	4.00	8.00
❏ 1127	Have We Really Tried/Heartache's Comin'	1965	2.00	4.00	8.00
❏ 1169	Diesel Smoke/That's How I Need You	1966	2.00	4.00	8.00
❏ 1194	Stand By Your Window/You're Not There	1966	2.00	4.00	8.00
❏ 1223	What's the Matter with Me/Third Time Down	1966	2.00	4.00	8.00
❏ 1247	I'm Her Lover/Same Old Boat	1967	2.00	4.00	8.00
❏ 1277	Let One Call Do It All/Rosanna Martin	1967	2.00	4.00	8.00

PLAYBOY

Number	Title (A Side/B Side)	Yr	VG	VG+	NM
❏ 5808	I've Got Some Gettin' Over You to Do/ I'll Drink to That	1977	2.00	4.00	8.00
❏ 6084	Little Brown Paper Bag Blues/(B-side unknown)	1976	2.00	4.00	8.00

RCA VICTOR

Number	Title (A Side/B Side)	Yr	VG	VG+	NM
❏ 47-9830	An Old Memory Got in My Eye/ You're Everywhere	1970	—	3.00	6.00
❏ 74-0271	Pressure Cooker/To the Ones I Love	1969	—	3.00	6.00

STARDAY

Number	Title (A Side/B Side)	Yr	VG	VG+	NM
❏ 236	Once Again/No Fault of Mine	1956	7.50	15.00	30.00
❏ 262	Poor Man's Riches/Those Who Know	1956	7.50	15.00	30.00
❏ 401	You Gotta Pay/Heads You Win	1958	6.25	12.50	25.00

BARNES, BILL

45s

COLUMBIA

Number	Title (A Side/B Side)	Yr	VG	VG+	NM
❏ 4-43491	Repeat After Me/Sloop John B.	1965	2.00	4.00	8.00
❏ 4-43491 [PS]	Repeat After Me/Sloop John B.	1965	3.75	7.50	15.00

BARNES, BILLY

45s

LIBERTY

Number	Title (A Side/B Side)	Yr	VG	VG+	NM
❏ 55421	Until/To Prove My Love	1962	6.25	12.50	25.00

Number	Title (A Side/B Side)	Yr	VG	VG+	NM
UNITED ARTISTS					
❑ 148	You'd Have to Fall in Love/If You But Knew	1958	5.00	10.00	20.00
❑ 157	I'm Coming to See You/What Am I Supposed to Do	1959	5.00	10.00	20.00
❑ 218	Home Again/I Wish I Didn't Love You So	1960	5.00	10.00	20.00
❑ 311	C.C. Rider/Here Am I	1961	5.00	10.00	20.00

BARNES, DENA
45s
INFERNO

❑ 2002	Who Am I/(B-side unknown)	196?	62.50	125.00	250.00

BARNES, GEORGE
45s
DECCA

❑ 30398	Tammy/Around the World	1957	5.00	10.00	20.00
MERCURY					
❑ 71968	Transville/Spooky	1962	7.50	15.00	30.00

BARNES, J.J.
45s
BUDDAH

❑ 120	Evidence/I'll Keep Coming Back	1969	3.75	7.50	15.00
CONTEMPO					
❑ 7003	How Long/The Erroll Flynn	1977	—	2.50	5.00
GROOVESVILLE					
❑ 1006	Baby Please Come Back Home/Chains of Love	1967	3.75	7.50	15.00
❑ 1008	Now That I Got You Back/Forgive Me	1967	3.75	7.50	15.00
❑ 1009	Easy Living/(B-side unknown)	1967	4.00	8.00	16.00
INVASION					
❑ 1001	My Baby/(You Still) My Baby	1970	2.50	5.00	10.00
KABLE					
❑ 437	Won't You Let Me Know/My Love Came Tumbling Down	1960	12.50	25.00	50.00
MAGIC TOUCH					
❑ 1000	To An Early Grave/Cloudy Days	1970	2.50	5.00	10.00
MICKAY'S					
❑ 3004	Just One More Time/Hey Child, I Love You	1963	20.00	40.00	80.00
❑ 4472	Get a Hold of Yourself/Lonely No More	1964	20.00	40.00	80.00
PERCEPTION					
❑ 546	Just a Living Doll/Touching You	1974	—	3.00	6.00
REVILOT					
❑ 216	Hold On to It/Now She's Gone	1968	3.75	7.50	15.00
❑ 218	I'll Keep Coming Back/Sad Day a-Comin'	1968	3.75	7.50	15.00
❑ 222	Our Love Is in the Pocket/All Your Goodies Are Gone	1968	20.00	40.00	80.00
❑ 225	So-Called Friends/Now She's Gone	1968	3.75	7.50	15.00
RIC-TIC					
❑ 106	Please Let Me In/I Think I Found a Love	1965	3.75	7.50	15.00
❑ 110	Real Humdinger/I Ain't Gonna Do It	1966	3.75	7.50	15.00
❑ 115	Day Tripper/Don't Bring Me Bad News	1966	3.75	7.50	15.00
❑ 117	Deeper in Love/Say It	1966	3.75	7.50	15.00
RICH					
❑ 1005	Won't You Let Me Know/My Love Came Tumbling Down	1960	25.00	50.00	100.00
❑ 1737	Won't You Let Me Know/My Love Came Tumbling Down	1962	6.25	12.50	25.00
RING					
❑ 101	She Ain't Ready/Poor-Unfortunate Me	1964	6.25	12.50	25.00
SCEPTER					
❑ 1266	Just One More Time/Hey Child, I Love You	1964	7.50	15.00	30.00
VOLT					
❑ 4027	Got to Get Rid of You/Snowflakes	1969	3.75	7.50	15.00
Albums					
VOLT					
❑ VOS-6001	Rare Stamps	1969	7.50	15.00	30.00

—With Steve Mancha

BARNES, SIDNEY
45s
BLUE CAT

❑ 125	I Hurt on the Other Side/Switchy Walk	1966	37.50	75.00	150.00
CHESS					
❑ 2094	Baloney/Old Times	1970	2.50	5.00	10.00
PARACHUTE					
❑ 521	Hold On I'm Coming/Your Love Is So Good to Me	1978	—	2.00	4.00
RED BIRD					
❑ 10-039	You'll Always Be in Style/I'm So Glad	1965	10.00	20.00	40.00
❑ 10-054	I Hurt on the Other Side/Switchy Walk	1966	10.00	20.00	40.00
Albums					
PARACHUTE					
❑ 9009	Footstomp'n Music	1978	3.00	6.00	12.00

BARNES, TAWANDA
45s
A&M

❑ 1141	(You Better) Find Someone to Love/You Don't Mean It	1969	6.25	12.50	25.00

BARNETT, BILLY Not the same person as "Billy Barnette" who recorded for Parkway and Mt. Vernon in the early 1960s.
45s
TEX

❑ 105	Tired of Your Honky-Tonk Love/One Day Nearer Home	1957	62.50	125.00	250.00

BARNETTE, BILLY See BILLY JOE BURNETTE. Not the same person as BILLY BARNETT.

BARNUM, H.B.
45s
CAPITOL

❑ 2036	Baby, Love Me/The Bad Luck's on Me	1967	3.00	6.00	12.00
❑ 2139	Vaya Con Dios/What Did Sister Do	1968	2.50	5.00	10.00
❑ 2317	Happiness/It's Just a Game, Love	1968	2.50	5.00	10.00
❑ 5391	I'm a Man/The Record	1965	3.00	6.00	12.00
❑ 5440	Gimme Some/Don't Forget 127th Street	1965	3.00	6.00	12.00
❑ 5477	I Can't Help It/Dance with Me	1965	3.00	6.00	12.00
❑ 5748	Gotta Go/Nobody Wants to Hear Nobody's Trouble	1966	3.00	6.00	12.00
❑ 5932	Heartbreaker/Searchin' for My Soul	1967	5.00	10.00	20.00
DECCA					
❑ 32892	Run to Daylight/Howard Hardsell	1971	—	2.50	5.00

—B-side by Tom Patchett and Jay Tarses

ELDO					
❑ 111	Lost Love/Hallelujah	1960	3.75	7.50	15.00
IMPERIAL					
❑ 5530	Blue Moon/Tia-Juana	1958	10.00	20.00	40.00
❑ 66011	Backstage/Rented Tuxedo	1964	3.00	6.00	12.00
❑ 66046	Skakiaan (Skokiaan)/Ska Drums	1964	3.00	6.00	12.00
❑ 66063	Calpyso Blues/Three Room Flat	1964	3.00	6.00	12.00
❑ 66074	Eternal Love/So What	1964	3.00	6.00	12.00
RCA VICTOR					
❑ 47-7960	Baby Baby Baby (All the Time)/How Many More Times	1961	3.75	7.50	15.00
❑ 47-8014	Call On Me/Oh My Achin' Back	1962	3.75	7.50	15.00
❑ 47-8112	Lonely Hearts/It Hurts Too Much to Cry	1962	15.00	30.00	60.00
UNITED ARTISTS					
❑ XW338	Theme from "5 on the Back Hand Side"/Keep It Comin'	1973	—	2.50	5.00
Albums					
CAPITOL					
❑ ST 2278 [S]	Golden Boy	1965	5.00	10.00	20.00
❑ T 2278 [M]	Golden Boy	1965	3.75	7.50	15.00
❑ ST 2289 [S]	Big Hits of Detroit	1965	5.00	10.00	20.00
❑ T 2289 [M]	Big Hits of Detroit	1965	3.75	7.50	15.00
❑ ST 2583 [S]	Pop and Ice Cream Sodas	1966	5.00	10.00	20.00
❑ T 2583 [M]	Pop and Ice Cream Sodas	1966	3.75	7.50	15.00

BARONS, THE Several different groups.
45s
BELLAIRE

❑ 103	The Bandit/Wanderin'	1963	5.00	10.00	20.00
BROWNFIELD					
❑ 1035	Hope I Please You/Don't Burn It	196?	12.50	25.00	50.00
DART					
❑ 126	Lonely Loretta/Lula Mae	1959	6.25	12.50	25.00
❑ 134	Perfect Love/Until the Thirteenth Chime	1960	6.25	12.50	25.00
DECCA					
❑ 29293	Exactly Like You/Forget About Me	1954	30.00	60.00	120.00
❑ 48323	A Year and a Day/My Baby's Gone	1954	30.00	60.00	120.00
DEMON					
❑ 1520	Gravel Gert/The Fight	1959	3.75	7.50	15.00
EPIC					
❑ 9586	Don't Go Away (Pretty Little Girl)/Pledge of a Fool	1963	7.50	15.00	30.00
❑ 9747	Lucky Star/Remember Rita	1964	37.50	75.00	150.00
❑ 10093	Don't Go Away (Pretty Little Girl)/Pledge of a Fool	1966	3.75	7.50	15.00
IMPERIAL					
❑ 5343	Eternally Yours/Boom Boom	1955	30.00	60.00	120.00
❑ 5343	Eternally Yours/Boom Boom	1955	75.00	150.00	300.00

—Red vinyl, probably promo only

❑ 5359	I Know I Was Wrong/My Dream, My Love	1955	30.00	60.00	120.00
❑ 5370	Cold Kisses/Searching for You	1955	30.00	60.00	120.00
❑ 5383	So Long My Darling/Crying for You Baby	1956	30.00	60.00	120.00
❑ 5397	Don't Walk Out/Once in a Lifetime	1956	20.00	40.00	80.00
❑ 66057	Silence/I Just Go Wild Inside	1964	3.75	7.50	15.00
RCA VICTOR					
❑ 47-9034	Since You're Gone/My Smile Is Bigger (Than Your Smile)	1966	6.25	12.50	25.00
SPARTAN					
❑ 400	I've Been Hurt/Willow Weep for Me	196?	3.75	7.50	15.00
TENDER					
❑ 511	Drawbridge/(B-side unknown)	1958	3.75	7.50	15.00

BAROQUE ENSEMBLE OF THE MERSEYSIDE KAMMERMUSIKGESELLSCHAFT, THE
45s
ELEKTRA

❑ 45602	You've Got to Hide Your Love Away/Ticket to Ride	1966	3.00	6.00	12.00
Albums					
ELEKTRA					
❑ EKL-306 [M]	The Baroque Beatles Book	1966	6.25	12.50	25.00
❑ EKS-7306 [S]	The Baroque Beatles Book	1966	7.50	15.00	30.00

BAROQUES, THE
45s
CHESS

❑ 2001	Mary Jane/Iowa, A Girl's Name	1967	3.75	7.50	15.00

BARRABAS
45s
ATCO

❑ 7027	Hi Jack/Susie Wong	1975	—	2.50	5.00
❑ 7036	Mellow Blue (Long)/Checkmate	1975	—	2.50	5.00
❑ 7059	Desperately/If	1976	—	2.50	5.00
POLYDOR					
❑ 14267	Hi Jack	1974	—	—	—

—Unreleased

Albums
ATCO

❑ SD 36-110	Barrabas	1974	2.50	5.00	10.00
❑ SD 36-118	Heart of the City	1975	2.50	5.00	10.00
❑ SD 36-136	Watch Out	1976	2.50	5.00	10.00

B

Number	Title (A Side/B Side)	Yr	VG	VG+	NM
RCA VICTOR					
❏ LSP-4861	Wild Safari	1973	3.00	6.00	12.00
BARRACUDA					
45s					
RCA VICTOR					
❏ 47-9660	The Dance of St. Francis/Lady Fingers	1968	5.00	10.00	20.00
❏ 47-9660 [PS]	The Dance of St. Francis/Lady Fingers	1968	10.00	20.00	40.00
❏ 47-9743	Julie (The Song I Sing Is To You)/ Sleeping Out the Storm	1969	3.00	6.00	12.00
BARRACUDAS, THE					
Albums					
JUSTICE					
❏ JLP-143	A Plane View	1968	125.00	250.00	500.00
BARRAN, BOB					
45s					
SILVER STREAK					
❏ 311	Tom Tom Rock/Mother Goose Hop	1960	37.50	75.00	150.00
BARRETT, RICHARD					
45s					
ATLANTIC					
❏ 2142	Some Other Guy/Tricky Dicky	1962	3.75	7.50	15.00
—As "Richie Barrett"					
CRACKERJACK					
❏ 4012	Summer's Love/Let Me Down Easy	1963	3.75	7.50	15.00
GONE					
❏ 5056	Come Softly to Me/Walking Through Dreamland	1959	7.50	15.00	30.00
—With the Chantels					
❏ 5060	Summer's Love/All Is Forgiven	1959	7.50	15.00	30.00
—With the Chantels					
METRO					
❏ 20006	Lovable/Only One Way	1959	3.75	7.50	15.00
MGM					
❏ 12616	Smoke Gets In Your Eyes/Remember Me	1958	7.50	15.00	30.00
❏ 12659	Body and Soul/The Party	1958	7.50	15.00	30.00
SEVILLE					
❏ 104	Dream On/I Am Yours	1960	3.75	7.50	15.00
20TH FOX					
❏ 150	Lovely One/The Snake and the Bookworm	1959	3.75	7.50	15.00
BARRETT, SUSAN					
45s					
PHILIPS					
❏ 40147	Between Two Loves/Chico's Girl	1963	6.25	12.50	25.00
❏ 40247	The Love We Never Knew/No One But You	1964	6.25	12.50	25.00
RCA VICTOR					
❏ 47-8888	A Grain of Sand/She Gets Everything She Wants	1966	5.00	10.00	20.00
❏ 47-9017	Walking Happy/ How Can You Hold On to a Dream	1966	5.00	10.00	20.00
❏ 47-9296	What's It Gonna Be/It's No Secret	1967	12.50	25.00	50.00
❏ 47-9384	Sunny/Ev'ry Time We Say Goodbye	1967	5.00	10.00	20.00
Albums					
CAPITOL					
❏ T 1266 [M]	Mixed Emotions	1959	12.50	25.00	50.00
RCA VICTOR					
❏ LPM-3738 [M]	Susan Barrett	1967	10.00	20.00	40.00
❏ LSP-3738 [S]	Susan Barrett	1967	7.50	15.00	30.00
BARRETT, SYD Member of the earliest incarnation of PINK FLOYD.					
7-Inch Extended Plays					
CAPITOL					
❏ NR-58186	Terrapin/Octopus//Baby Lemonade/ Effervescent Elephant	1994	—	3.00	6.00
—Pink vinyl					
❏ NR-58186 [PS]	Crazy Diamond	1994	—	3.00	6.00
Albums					
CAPITOL					
❏ C1-91206	Opel	1989	5.00	10.00	20.00
HARVEST					
❏ SABB-11314 [(2)]	The Madcap Laughs/Barrett	1974	6.25	12.50	25.00
BARRI, STEVE Cohort of P.F. SLOAN. Also see THE FANTASTIC BAGGYS; THE GRASS ROOTS; THE IMAGINATIONS (2); THE INNER CIRCLE; THE LIFEGUARDS (2); PHILIP AND STEPHAN; THE RALLY PACKS; THE RINCON SURFSIDE BAND; THE STREET CLEANERS; THEMES INC.; WILLIE AND THE WHEELS.					
45s					
RONA					
❏ 1003	Down Around the Corner/Please Let It Be You	1961	10.00	20.00	40.00
❏ 1004	I Want Your Love/Story of the Ring	1961	10.00	20.00	40.00
❏ 1005	Two Different Worlds/Don't Run Away from Love	1962	10.00	20.00	40.00
❏ 1006	Never Before/Whenever You Kiss Me	1962	10.00	20.00	40.00
BARRIX, BILLY					
45s					
CHESS					
❏ 1662	Cool Off Baby/Almost	1958	5000.	7500.	10000.
—Outrageously rare rockabilly record					
BARRON KNIGHTS, THE					
45s					
DECCA					
❏ 32160	Lazy Fat People/In the Night	1967	2.50	5.00	10.00
EPIC					
❏ 9835	Pop Go the Workers Part 1/Part 2	1965	3.00	6.00	12.00
❏ 50755	The Topical Song/The Big V-asectomy	1979	—	2.50	5.00
MERCURY					
❏ 73302	Nothin' Doin'/You're All I Need	1972	—	2.50	5.00
❏ 73302 [PS]	Nothin' Doin'/You're All I Need	1972	2.50	5.00	10.00

Number	Title (A Side/B Side)	Yr	VG	VG+	NM
BARRY, GENE					
45s					
FELSTED					
❏ 8648	Moonlight Gambler/ Red Silk Stockings and Green Perfume	1961	3.00	6.00	12.00
Albums					
RCA VICTOR					
❏ LPM-2975 [M]	The Star of "Burke's Law" Sings of Love and Things	1964	6.25	12.50	25.00
❏ LSP-2975 [S]	The Star of "Burke's Law" Sings of Love and Things	1964	7.50	15.00	30.00
BARRY, JAY					
45s					
ABC-PARAMOUNT					
❏ 10154	A Picture of You/Sherry	1960	3.75	7.50	15.00
❏ 10226	Love Bank/Love Spell	1961	3.75	7.50	15.00
BARRY, JEFF Also see THE RAINDROPS.					
45s					
A&M					
❏ 1422	Walkin' in the Sun/Whatcha Wanna Do	1973	—	2.50	5.00
BELL					
❏ 45140	Sweet Saviour/Love Has Never Let Me Down	1971	—	3.00	6.00
DECCA					
❏ 31037	Never Never/It Won't Hurt	1959	5.00	10.00	20.00
❏ 31089	Lenore/Why Does the Feeling Go Away	1960	5.00	10.00	20.00
RCA VICTOR					
❏ 47-7477	It's Called Rock & Roll/Hip Couples	1959	6.25	12.50	25.00
❏ 47-7797	The Face from Outer Space/Lovely Lips	1960	6.25	12.50	25.00
❏ 47-7821	All You Need Is a Quarter/Teen Quartet	1960	6.25	12.50	25.00
RED BIRD					
❏ 10-026	I'll Still Love You/Our Love Can Still Be Saved	1965	4.00	8.00	16.00
UNITED ARTISTS					
❏ 440	We Got Love Money Can't Buy/Welcome Home	1962	4.00	8.00	16.00
❏ 50529	Much Too Young/Where It's At	1969	2.00	4.00	8.00
Albums					
A&M					
❏ SP-4393	Walkin' in the Sun	1973	3.75	7.50	15.00
BARRY, JOHN					
45s					
CAPITOL					
❏ F4212	Snap 'N Whistle/Long Long	1959	3.75	7.50	15.00
COLUMBIA					
❏ 43320	A Man Alone/Barbara's Theme	1965	2.00	4.00	8.00
❏ 43360	The Knack (And How to Get It)/The Knack (And How to Get It)	1965	2.50	5.00	10.00
—B-side by Johnny DeLittle					
❏ 43544	The Chase/Saturday Night Philosopher	1966	2.50	5.00	10.00
❏ 43801	Theme from Born Free/Goldfinger	1966	2.50	5.00	10.00
❏ 43951	Wednesday's Child/Sleep Well, My Darling	1966	2.50	5.00	10.00
❏ 44167	You Only Live Twice/ The Girl with the Sun in Her Hair	1967	2.00	4.00	8.00
❏ 44721	The Lion in Winter/To Rome	1968	2.00	4.00	8.00
❏ 44891	Midnight Cowboy/Fun City	1969	—	3.00	6.00
❏ 45062	On Her Majesty's Secret Service/ We Have All the Time in the World	1970	—	3.00	6.00
❏ 45140	Theme from "The Appointment"/ The More Things Change	1970	—	3.00	6.00
DECCA					
❏ 31815	A Man Alone (Jazz Version)/A Man Alone (Latin Version)	1965	2.50	5.00	10.00
EPIC					
❏ 10865	The Persuaders/The Girl with the Sun in Her Hair	1972	—	3.00	6.00
KING					
❏ 5495	Black Stockings/Get Lost Jack Frost	1961	3.75	7.50	15.00
MERCURY					
❏ 72261	From Russia with Love/007	1964	3.00	6.00	12.00
MGM					
❏ 13591	Born Free/Elsa at Play	1966	2.00	4.00	8.00
20TH FOX					
❏ 472	Theme from "Man in the Middle"/Barney's Blues	1964	3.00	6.00	12.00
UNITED ARTISTS					
❏ 581	James Bond Theme/March of the Mandarins	1963	3.75	7.50	15.00
❏ 581 [PS]	James Bond Theme/March of the Mandarins	1963	12.50	25.00	50.00
❏ 743	Big Shield/Zulu Stomp	1964	2.50	5.00	10.00
❏ 791	Goldfinger/Troubadour	1964	2.50	5.00	10.00
❏ 863	From Russia with Love/James Bond Theme	1965	2.50	5.00	10.00
WARNER BROS.					
❏ 7230	Highway 101/Petula	1968	—	3.00	6.00
Albums					
BULLDOG					
❏ BDL-1036	Bond by Barry	198?	2.50	5.00	10.00
COLUMBIA					
❏ C 1003	Ready When You Are, Mr. J.B.	1970	2.50	5.00	10.00
❏ CL 2493 [M]	Great Movie Sounds of John Barry	1966	3.75	7.50	15.00
❏ CL 2708 [M]	You Only Live Twice	1967	3.75	7.50	15.00
❏ CS 9293 [S]	Great Movie Sounds of John Barry	1966	5.00	10.00	20.00
❏ CS 9508 [S]	You Only Live Twice	1967	5.00	10.00	20.00
UNITED ARTISTS					
❏ UAL 3424 [M]	Goldfinger and Other Favorites	1965	3.00	6.00	12.00
❏ UAS 6424 [S]	Goldfinger and Other Favorites	1965	3.75	7.50	15.00
BARRY, LEN Former member of THE DOVELLS.					
45s					
AMY					
❏ 11026	4-5-6 (Now I'm Alone)/Funky Night	1968	—	3.00	6.00
❏ 11037	You're My Picasso, Baby/Christopher Columbus	1968	—	3.00	6.00
❏ 11047	The Child Is Born/Wouldn't It Be Beautiful	1968	—	3.00	6.00

Number	Title (A Side/B Side)	Yr	VG	VG+	NM
BUDDAH					
❑ 284	Just the Two of Us/Diggin' Life	1972	—	2.50	5.00
❑ 284 [PS]	Just the Two of Us/Diggin' Life	1972	—	3.00	6.00
CAMEO					
❑ 303	Jim Dandy/Don't Come Back	1964	3.00	6.00	12.00
❑ 318	Little White House/Hearts Are Trump	1964	3.00	6.00	12.00
DECCA					
❑ 31788	Lip Sync (To the Tongue Twisters)/At the Hop '65	1965	2.50	5.00	10.00
❑ 31827	1-2-3/Bullseye	1965	3.75	7.50	15.00
❑ 31889	Like a Baby/Happiness (Is a Girl Like You)	1966	2.50	5.00	10.00
❑ 31923	Somewhere/It's a Crying Shame	1966	2.50	5.00	10.00
❑ 31969	It's That Time of the Year/Happily Ever After	1966	2.50	5.00	10.00
❑ 32011	I Struck It Rich/Love Is	1966	2.50	5.00	10.00
❑ 32054	Would I Love You/You Baby	1966	2.50	5.00	10.00
MERCURY					
❑ 72299	Let's Do It Again/Happy Days	1964	3.00	6.00	12.00
PARAMOUNT					
❑ 0206	Heaven Plus Earth/I'm Marching to the Music	1973	—	2.50	5.00
PARKWAY					
❑ 969	Little White House/Hearts Are Trump	1966	2.00	4.00	8.00
RCA VICTOR					
❑ 47-9150	Our Song/The Moving Finger Writes	1967	2.00	4.00	8.00
❑ 47-9275	All Those Memories/Rainy Side of the Street	1967	2.00	4.00	8.00
❑ 47-9348	The ABC's of Love/Come Rain or Shine	1967	2.00	4.00	8.00
❑ 47-9464	Sweet and Funny/I Like the Way	1968	2.00	4.00	8.00
SCEPTER					
❑ 12251	Put Out the Fire/Spread It On Like Butter	1969	2.00	4.00	8.00
❑ 12263	Keem-O-Sabe/This Old World	1969	2.00	4.00	8.00
❑ 12284	Bob & Carol & Ted & Alice/In My Present State of Mind	1970	—	3.00	6.00
Albums					
BUDDAH					
❑ BDS-5105	Ups & Downs	1972	3.75	7.50	15.00
DECCA					
❑ DL 4720 [M]	1-2-3	1965	7.50	15.00	30.00
❑ DL 74720 [P]	1-2-3	1965	10.00	20.00	40.00
—"Lip Sync" is rechanneled					
RCA VICTOR					
❑ LPM-3823 [M]	My Kind of Soul	1967	6.25	12.50	25.00
❑ LSP-3823 [S]	My Kind of Soul	1967	5.00	10.00	20.00

BARRY, SANDRA

45s

Number	Title (A Side/B Side)	Yr	VG	VG+	NM
PARKWAY					
❑ 943	We Were Lovers/The End of the Line	1965	3.75	7.50	15.00
❑ 954	Question/You Can Take It from Me	1965	3.75	7.50	15.00

BARRY AND BARRY See BARRY McGUIRE AND BARRY KANE.

BARRY AND THE TAMERLANES Also see BARRY DeVORZON.

45s

Number	Title (A Side/B Side)	Yr	VG	VG+	NM
VALIANT					
❑ 703	I Wonder What She's Doing Tonight/Roberta	1965	3.00	6.00	12.00
❑ 6034	I Wonder What She's Doing Tonight/Don't Go	1963	5.00	10.00	20.00
❑ 6040	Roberta/Butterfly	1964	3.75	7.50	15.00
❑ 6046	Lucky Guy/I Don't Want to Be Your Clown	1964	3.75	7.50	15.00
❑ 6050	A Date with Judy/Pretty Things	1964	3.75	7.50	15.00
❑ 6059	Gee/Don't Cry Cindy	1964	3.75	7.50	15.00
Albums					
VALIANT					
❑ LP-406 [M]	I Wonder What She's Doing Tonight	1963	37.50	75.00	150.00
❑ LPS-406 [S]	I Wonder What She's Doing Tonight	1963	75.00	150.00	300.00

BARTEL, JON, THING

Albums

Number	Title (A Side/B Side)	Yr	VG	VG+	NM
CAPITOL					
❑ ST-274	The Jon Bartel Thing	1969	6.25	12.50	25.00

BARTEL, LOU

45s

Number	Title (A Side/B Side)	Yr	VG	VG+	NM
ABC-PARAMOUNT					
❑ 9801	Natural, Natural Baby/My Idea of Heaven	1957	6.25	12.50	25.00
❑ 9877	Blue Moon/I'm Gonna Kiss My Baby Goodnight	1957	6.25	12.50	25.00
APOLLO					
❑ 473	I Pray/(Zoom) Give Me Your Tonight	1954	37.50	75.00	150.00

BARTHOLOMEW, DAVE

45s

Number	Title (A Side/B Side)	Yr	VG	VG+	NM
DECCA					
❑ 48216	Tra La La/Teejim	1951	30.00	60.00	120.00
IMPERIAL					
❑ 5210	Who Drank the Beer While I Was in the Rear/The Rest of My Life	1952	30.00	60.00	120.00
—Dave Bartholomew records on Imperial before 5210 are unconfirmed on 45 rpm					
❑ 5249	No More Black Nights/Air Tight	1953	30.00	60.00	120.00
❑ 5273	Texas Hop/When the Saints Go Marchin' In Boogie	1954	37.50	75.00	150.00
❑ 5308	Cat Music/Jump Children	1954	30.00	60.00	120.00
❑ 5322	Another Mule/I Want to Be with Her	1955	12.50	25.00	50.00
❑ 5350	Every Night, Every Day/Four Winds	1955	12.50	25.00	50.00
❑ 5373	Shrimp and Gumbo/An Old Cowhand from a Blues Band	1956	10.00	20.00	40.00
❑ 5390	Would You/Turn Your Lamp Down Low	1956	10.00	20.00	40.00
❑ 5408	Lovin' You/Three Time Loser	1956	7.50	15.00	30.00
❑ 5438	The Monkey/The Shuffling	1957	6.25	12.50	25.00
❑ 5460	How Could You/Barrel House	1957	6.25	12.50	25.00
❑ 5481	Hard Times (The Slop)/Cinderella	1957	6.25	12.50	25.00
❑ 5560	Button Blues/Short Subjects	1959	5.00	10.00	20.00
❑ 5702	I Cried/Somebody New	1960	5.00	10.00	20.00
❑ 5714	People Are Talking/Yeah, Yeah	1961	5.00	10.00	20.00
❑ 5803	I'm Walkin'/Going to the River	1962	3.75	7.50	15.00
❑ 5835	A Sunday Kind of Love/Honky Tonk Trumpet	1962	3.75	7.50	15.00

Number	Title (A Side/B Side)	Yr	VG	VG+	NM
KING					
❑ 4482	Sweet Home Blues/Twins	1951	37.50	75.00	150.00
❑ 4508	In the Alley/I'll Never Be the Same	1952	50.00	100.00	200.00
❑ 4523	Lawdy, Lawdy, Lawd (Part 1)/Lawdy, Lawdy, Lawd (Part 2)	1952	37.50	75.00	150.00
❑ 4544	My Ding-a-Ling/Bad Habit	1952	62.50	125.00	250.00
❑ 4559	The Golden Rule/Mother Knows Best	1952	25.00	50.00	100.00
❑ 4585	High Flying Woman/Stormy Weather	1953	25.00	50.00	100.00
Albums					
BROADMOOR					
❑ BR-1201	Dave Bartholomew's New Orleans Jazz Band	1981	3.75	7.50	15.00
IMPERIAL					
❑ LP-9162 [M]	Fats Domino Presents Dave Bartholomew	1961	25.00	50.00	100.00
❑ LP-9217 [M]	New Orleans House Party	1963	25.00	50.00	100.00
❑ LP-12076 [S]	Fats Domino Presents Dave Bartholomew	1961	37.50	75.00	150.00
❑ LP-12217 [S]	New Orleans House Party	1963	37.50	75.00	150.00

BARTON, ERNIE

45s

Number	Title (A Side/B Side)	Yr	VG	VG+	NM
PHILLIPS INTERNATIONAL					
❑ 3528	Stairway of Love/Raining the Blues	1958	5.00	10.00	20.00
❑ 3541	Open the Door Richard/Shut Your Mouth	1959	37.50	75.00	150.00

BARY, HENRY

45s

Number	Title (A Side/B Side)	Yr	VG	VG+	NM
HIT					
❑ 228	One, Two, Three/Get Off of My Cloud	1965	3.00	6.00	12.00
—B-side by the Jalopy Five					

BASH, OTTO

45s

Number	Title (A Side/B Side)	Yr	VG	VG+	NM
HDS					
❑ 2008	My Babe/Straighten Up and Fly Right	1956	5.00	10.00	20.00
RCA VICTOR					
❑ 47-6426	Later Alligator/Lookout Mountain	1956	6.25	12.50	25.00
❑ 47-6585	The Elvis Blues/Later	1956	12.50	25.00	50.00

BASIC BLACK AND PEARL

45s

Number	Title (A Side/B Side)	Yr	VG	VG+	NM
POLYDOR					
❑ 15111	There'll Come a Time, There'll Come a Day/He's a Rebel	1975	—	2.50	5.00

BASIL, TONI

12-Inch Singles

Number	Title (A Side/B Side)	Yr	VG	VG+	NM
CHRYSALIS					
❑ AS 1615 [DJ]	Nobody/Rock On	1983	2.50	5.00	10.00
❑ 4V9-42708	Street Beat (Special Club Mix)/(Beat Dub)	1983	2.00	4.00	8.00
❑ 4V9-42824	Suspense/(Dub)	1984	2.00	4.00	8.00
RAZOR & TIE					
❑ 80750	Mickey (4 versions)	1999	2.50	5.00	10.00
45s					
A&M					
❑ 791	Breakaway/I'm 28	1966	50.00	100.00	200.00
CHRYSALIS					
❑ 2638	Mickey/Thief on the Loose	1982	—	—	3.00
❑ 2638 [PS]	Mickey/Thief on the Loose	1982	—	—	3.00
❑ 2665	Mickey (Spanish)/Thief on the Loose	1982	—	2.50	5.00
❑ 2665 [PS]	Mickey (Spanish)/Thief on the Loose	1982	—	2.50	5.00
❑ VS4-03537	Shoppin' from A to Z/Time After Time	1983	—	—	3.00
❑ VS4-03537 [PS]	Shoppin' from A to Z/Time After Time	1983	—	—	3.00
❑ VS4-03539	Mickey/Thief on the Loose	1983	—	2.00	4.00
—Reissue of 2638, but harder to find					
❑ VS4 42711	Street Beat/(B-side unknown)	1983	—	—	3.00
❑ VS4 42753	Over My Head/Best Performance	1983	—	—	3.00
❑ VS4 42753 [PS]	Over My Head/Best Performance	1983	—	—	3.00
RAZOR & TIE					
❑ 93018-07507	Mickey (Radio Remix)/Mickey ("Killa Klub" Edit)	1999	—	2.00	4.00
Albums					
CHRYSALIS					
❑ CHR 1410	Word of Mouth	1982	3.00	6.00	12.00
❑ FV 41410	Word of Mouth	1983	2.50	5.00	10.00
—Reissue of 1410					
❑ PV 41410	Word of Mouth	1986	2.00	4.00	8.00
—Reissue with new prefix					
❑ FV 41449	Toni Basil	1983	2.50	5.00	10.00
❑ PV 41449	Toni Basil	1986	2.00	4.00	8.00
—Reissue with new prefix					

BASKERVILLE HOUNDS, THE

45s

Number	Title (A Side/B Side)	Yr	VG	VG+	NM
AVCO EMBASSY					
❑ 4504	Hold Me/Here I Come, Miami	1968	2.50	5.00	10.00
BUDDAH					
❑ 17	Caroline/Last Night on the Back Porch	1967	2.50	5.00	10.00
DOT					
❑ 17004	Space Rock, Part 1/Space Rock, Part 2	1967	2.50	5.00	10.00
❑ 17017	Debbie/Jackie's Theme	1967	2.50	5.00	10.00
❑ 17037	Baby, Am I Losing/Never on Sunday	1967	2.50	5.00	10.00
TEMA					
❑ 125	Debbie/Jackie's Theme	1966	3.75	7.50	15.00
❑ 128	Space Rock, Part 1/Space Rock, Part 2	1966	3.75	7.50	15.00
❑ 131	Christmas Is Here (But Not For Long)/Make Me Your Man	1966	3.75	7.50	15.00
❑ 131 [PS]	Christmas Is Here (But Not For Long)/Make Me Your Man	1966	12.50	25.00	50.00
❑ 132	All You Had to Do Was Ask/Who Does She Love	1967	3.75	7.50	15.00
❑ 135	Hold Me/Here I Come, Miami	1967	3.75	7.50	15.00
Albums					
DOT					
❑ DLP-3823 [M]	The Baskerville Hounds (Featuring Space Rock, Part 2)	1967	12.50	25.00	50.00
❑ DLP-25823 [S]	The Baskerville Hounds (Featuring Space Rock, Part 2)	1967	20.00	40.00	80.00

Number	Title (A Side/B Side)	Yr	VG	VG+	NM

BASS, FONTELLA
45s
BOBBIN

Number	Title (A Side/B Side)	Yr	VG	VG+	NM
❏ 134	I Don't Hurt Anymore/Brand New Love	1962	3.75	7.50	15.00
❏ 140	Honey Bee/Bad Boy	1963	3.75	7.50	15.00

CHECKER

❏ 1097	Don't Mess Up a Good Thing/ Baby, What You Want Me to Do	1965	2.50	5.00	10.00

—With Bobby McClure

❏ 1111	You'll Miss Me (When I'm Gone)/Don't Jump	1965	2.50	5.00	10.00

—With Bobby McClure

❏ 1120	Rescue Me/Soul of the Man	1965	3.75	7.50	15.00

—Light blue label with red and black checkers

❏ 1120	Rescue Me/Soul of the Man	1965	5.00	10.00	20.00

—Red label with "Checker" vertically on left

❏ 1120	Rescue Me/Soul of the Man	1966	2.50	5.00	10.00

—Fading light blue label, no checkers

❏ 1131	Recovery/Leave It in the Hands of Love	1965	2.50	5.00	10.00
❏ 1137	I Surrender/I Can't Rest	1966	2.50	5.00	10.00
❏ 1147	Safe and Sound/You'll Never Ever Know	1966	2.50	5.00	10.00
❏ 1183	Lucky in Love/Sweet Lovin' Daddy	1967	2.50	5.00	10.00

EPIC

❏ 50341	Soon as I Touched Him/You Can Betcha in Love	1977	—	2.00	4.00

PAULA

❏ 360	Who You Gonna Blame/Hold On This Time	1972	—	2.50	5.00
❏ 367	I Need to Be Loved/I Want Everyone to Know	1972	—	2.50	5.00
❏ 376	It Sure Is Good/I'm Leaving the Choice to You	1973	—	2.50	5.00
❏ 389	Home Wrecker/ Now That I've Found a Good Thing	1973	—	2.50	5.00
❏ 393	Talking About Freedom/It's Hard to Get Back In	1974	—	2.50	5.00

Albums
CHECKER

❏ LP-2997 [M]	The "New" Look	1966	15.00	30.00	60.00

—Blue label with red and black checkers

❏ LP-2997 [M]	The "New" Look	1967	7.50	15.00	30.00

—Blue and white label

❏ LPS-2997 [S]	The "New" Look	1966	20.00	40.00	80.00

—Blue label with red and black checkers

❏ LPS-2997 [S]	The "New" Look	1967	10.00	20.00	40.00

—Blue and white label
PAULA

❏ LPS-2203	Free	1971	3.00	6.00	12.00

BASS, FONTELLA, AND TINA TURNER Also see each artist's individual listings.
45s
VESUVIUS

❏ 1002	This Would Make Me Happy/Poor Little Fool	1963	6.25	12.50	25.00

BASS, MARTHA AND FONTELLA
Albums
SOUL NOTE

❏ SN-1006	From the Root to the Source	197?	3.00	6.00	12.00

BASSEY, SHIRLEY
45s
COLUMBIA

❏ 40848	Tonight My Heart Is Crying/ If I Had a Needle and Thread	1957	3.75	7.50	15.00

EPIC

❏ 9303	As I Love You/Kiss Me Honey, Honey Kiss Me	1959	3.00	6.00	12.00

MERCURY

❏ 874412-7	No Tengo Nada (I Who Have Nothing)/ Sin Ti (Without You)	1989	—	—	3.00

MGM

❏ 12919	'S Wonderful/The Party's Over	1960	3.00	6.00	12.00

UNITED ARTISTS

❏ 0146	Diamonds Are Forever/This Is My Love	1973	—	2.00	4.00

—Silver Spotlight Series issue

❏ XW211	Never, Never, Never/Day by Day	1973	—	2.00	4.00
❏ XW318	This Is My Life/Make the World a Little Younger	1973	—	2.00	4.00
❏ 363	Reach for the Stars/You'll Never Know	1961	2.50	5.00	10.00
❏ XW387	Davy/The Trouble with Hello	1974	—	2.00	4.00
❏ 404	I'll Get By/Climb Ev'ry Mountain	1962	2.50	5.00	10.00
❏ 421	Climb Ev'ry Mountain/Where Are You	1962	2.50	5.00	10.00
❏ 503	What Kind of Fool Am I/What Now My Love	1962	2.50	5.00	10.00
❏ XW508	Goldfinger/How Can I Tell	1974	—	2.00	4.00
❏ XW509	Never, Never, Never (Grande, Grande, Grande)/ Something	1974	—	2.00	4.00
❏ 511	Above All Others/As Long As He Needs Me	1962	2.50	5.00	10.00
❏ 681	Theme from "The Victors"/How Can You Tell	1964	2.00	4.00	8.00
❏ 699	I Who Have Nothing/Imagination	1964	2.00	4.00	8.00
❏ XW717	Send In the Clowns/Living	1975	—	2.00	4.00
❏ 790	Goldfinger/Strange How Love Can Be	1964	2.50	5.00	10.00
❏ XW854	Everything That Touches You/If I Never Sing Another Song	1976	—	2.00	4.00
❏ 872	No Regrets/See-Saw Dreams	1965	2.00	4.00	8.00
❏ XW923	What I Did for Love/Feelings	1976	—	2.00	4.00
❏ 956	It's Yourself/Secrets	1965	2.00	4.00	8.00
❏ X1303	Copacabana/This Is My Life (La Vita)	1979	—	2.00	4.00
❏ X1308	Moonraker-Main Title/Moonraker-End Title	1979	—	2.00	4.00
❏ 50031	Don't Take the Lovers from the World/ Take Away	1966	—	3.00	6.00
❏ 50071	Give Me Your Love/Who Could Love Me	1966	—	3.00	6.00
❏ 50099	The Liquidator/Sunshine	1966	—	3.00	6.00
❏ 50105	I (Who Have Nothing)/Shirley	1966	—	3.00	6.00
❏ 50125	The Impossible Dream/They	1967	—	—	—

—Unreleased

❏ 50129	The Impossible Dream/Do I Look Like a Fool	1967	—	3.00	6.00
❏ 50229	Big Spender/Dangerous Games	1967	—	3.00	6.00
❏ 50312	Funny Girl/This Is My Life (La Vita)	1968	—	—	—

—Unreleased

❏ 50459	Funny Girl/This Is My Life (La Vita)	1968	—	2.50	5.00

❏ 50502	Medley: Goin' Out of My Head-You Go to My Head/I Must Know	1969	—	2.50	5.00
❏ 50544	Does Anybody Miss Me/We	1969	—	2.50	5.00
❏ 50606	Fa Fa Fa (Live for Today)/ A Bus That Never Comes	1969	—	2.50	5.00
❏ 50682	Sea and Sand/What About Today	1970	—	2.00	4.00
❏ 50698	Something/What Are You Doing the Rest of Your Life	1970	—	2.00	4.00
❏ 50770	Breakfast in Bed/Pieces of Dreams	1971	—	2.00	4.00
❏ 50833	For All We Know/What's Done Is Done Is Done	1971	—	2.00	4.00
❏ 50845	Diamonds Are Forever/For the Love of Him	1971	—	2.00	4.00
❏ 50961	And I Love You So/Jezebel	1972	—	2.00	4.00

Albums
EPIC

❏ LN 3834 [M]	The Bewitching Shirley Bassey	1962	5.00	10.00	20.00

LIBERTY

❏ LWB-111 [(2)]	Live at Carnegie Hall	198?	2.50	5.00	10.00
❏ LWB-715 [(2)]	Greatest Hits	198?	2.50	5.00	10.00
❏ LW-847	Yesterdays	198?	2.00	4.00	8.00
❏ LM-1013	Something Else	198?	2.00	4.00	8.00
❏ LN-10012	The Magic Is You	1980	2.00	4.00	8.00
❏ LN-10104	The Best of Shirley Bassey	1980	2.00	4.00	8.00
❏ LN-10180	I, Capricorn	198?	2.00	4.00	8.00
❏ LN-10252	Greatest Hits	198?	2.00	4.00	8.00
❏ LN-10262	Shirley Means Bassey	198?	2.00	4.00	8.00

MERCURY

❏ 838033-1	La Mujer	1989	3.00	6.00	12.00

MGM

❏ E-3862 [M]	The Fabulous Shirley Bassey	1960	5.00	10.00	20.00
❏ SE-3862 [S]	The Fabulous Shirley Bassey	1960	6.25	12.50	25.00
❏ E-4301 [M]	Golden Sound	1965	3.00	6.00	12.00
❏ SE-4301 [S]	Golden Sound	1965	3.75	7.50	15.00

PAIR

❏ PDL2-1057 [(2)]	Sassy Bassey	1986	3.00	6.00	12.00

PHILIPS

❏ PHM 200168 [M]	Spectacular Shirley Bassey	1965	3.00	6.00	12.00
❏ PHS 600168 [S]	Spectacular Shirley Bassey	1965	3.75	7.50	15.00

UNITED ARTISTS

❏ UA-LA055-F	Never, Never, Never	1973	2.50	5.00	10.00
❏ UA-LA111-H2 [(2)]	Live at Carnegie Hall	1973	3.75	7.50	15.00
❏ UA-LA214-G	Nobody Does It Like Me	1974	2.50	5.00	10.00
❏ UA-LA542-G	Good, Bad But Beautiful	1975	2.50	5.00	10.00
❏ UA-LA605-G	Love, Life and Feelings	1976	2.50	5.00	10.00
❏ UA-LA715-H2 [(2)]	Greatest Hits	1976	3.75	7.50	15.00
❏ UA-LA751-H	You Take My Heart Away	1977	2.50	5.00	10.00
❏ UA-LA847-H	Yesterdays	1977	2.50	5.00	10.00
❏ LM-1013	Something Else	1979	2.50	5.00	10.00
❏ UAL 3169 [M]	Shirley Bassey	1962	3.75	7.50	15.00
❏ UAL 3237 [M]	Shirley Bassey Sings the Hits from "Oliver"	1962	3.75	7.50	15.00
❏ UAL 3419 [M]	Shirley Bassey Belts the Best	1965	3.00	6.00	12.00
❏ UAL 3463 [M]	In Person	1965	3.00	6.00	12.00
❏ UAL 3545 [M]	Shirley Means Bassey	1966	3.00	6.00	12.00
❏ UAL 3565 [M]	And We Were Lovers	1967	3.00	6.00	12.00
❏ UAS 5565	I, Capricorn	1971	2.50	5.00	10.00
❏ UAS 5643	And I Love You So	1972	2.50	5.00	10.00
❏ UAS 6169 [S]	Shirley Bassey	1962	5.00	10.00	20.00
❏ UAS 6237 [S]	Shirley Bassey Sings the Hits from "Oliver"	1962	5.00	10.00	20.00
❏ UAS 6419 [S]	Shirley Bassey Belts the Best	1965	3.75	7.50	15.00
❏ UAS 6463 [S]	In Person	1965	3.75	7.50	15.00
❏ UAS 6545 [S]	Shirley Means Bassey	1966	3.75	7.50	15.00
❏ UAS 6565 [S]	And We Were Lovers	1967	3.75	7.50	15.00
❏ UAS 6675	This Is My Life	1969	3.00	6.00	12.00
❏ UAS 6713	Does Anybody Miss Me?	1969	3.00	6.00	12.00
❏ UAS 6765	Shirley Bassey Is Really "Something"	1970	2.50	5.00	10.00
❏ UAS 6797	Something Else	1971	2.50	5.00	10.00

BASTILLES, THE
45s
PHILIPS

❏ 40453	Tenderly/Vengeance	1967	5.00	10.00	20.00

BATCHELOR, RUTH
45s
PARKWAY

❏ 852	Mr. Principal/Lemon Drops Lolly Pops	1962	3.75	7.50	15.00

BATDORF & RODNEY
45s
ARISTA

❏ 0132	You Are a Song/Another Part of Me	1975	—	2.00	4.00
❏ 0159	Somewhere in the Night/Ain't It Like Home	1975	—	2.00	4.00

ASYLUM

❏ 11011	All I Need/Between the Ages	1972	—	2.50	5.00
❏ 11012	Home Again/Between the Ages	1972	—	2.50	5.00

ATLANTIC

❏ 2850	Oh My Surprise/Farm	1972	—	2.50	5.00
❏ 2863	Can You See Him/Never See His Face Again	1972	—	2.50	5.00

BATS, THE (1)
45s
HBR

❏ 445	Big Bright Eyes/Nothing at All	1965	2.50	5.00	10.00

PARROT

❏ 40013	Listen to My Heart/You Look Good Together	1967	2.50	5.00	10.00

BATS, THE (U)
45s
FLAME

❏ 5155	Batmobile/Batusi	1966	10.00	20.00	40.00

B

Number	Title (A Side/B Side)	Yr	VG	VG+	NM
BATTERED ORNAMENTS					
Albums					
HARVEST					
❑ SKAO-422	Mantle-Piece	1970	10.00	20.00	40.00
BATTIN, SKIP	Member of later versions of THE BYRDS.				
45s					
AURORA					
❑ 159	The Dating Game Theme/Night Time Girl	1966	3.75	7.50	15.00
GROOVE					
❑ 58-0055	Searchin'/She Acts Like We Never Have Met	1965	10.00	20.00	40.00
❑ 58-0065	Ten Feet Tall/What's Mine Is Mine	1965	10.00	20.00	40.00
SIGNPOST					
❑ 70010 [DJ]	Ballad of Dick Clark (mono/stereo)	1973	—	3.00	6.00
—May be promo only					
Albums					
SIGNPOST					
❑ SP 8408	Skip Battin	1972	3.00	6.00	12.00
BAUM, ALLEN					
45s					
RED ROBIN					
❑ 124	My Kinda Woman/Too Much Competition	1954	100.00	200.00	400.00
BAXTER					
45s					
PARAMOUNT					
❑ 0194	Give It All/197 Three	1973	2.00	4.00	8.00
Albums					
PARAMOUNT					
❑ PAS-6050	Baxter	1973	5.00	10.00	20.00
BAXTER, LES					
45s					
A/S					
❑ 4511	La La La/Girl on the Boulevard	1970	—	2.50	5.00
❑ 4515	Soolaimon/A Taste of Soul	1970	—	2.50	5.00
AMERICAN INT'L.					
❑ 143	Dunwich/Necronomicon	1970	—	2.50	5.00
❑ 145	Dock at Papeete/Bora Bora	1970	—	2.50	5.00
CAPITOL					
❑ F1299	Somewhere, Somehow, Someday/Tamberina	1950	3.75	7.50	15.00
❑ F1381	The Roving Kind/So Long	1951	3.75	7.50	15.00
❑ F1390	Zing Zing Zoom Zoom/When You Return	1951	3.75	7.50	15.00
❑ F1493	Because of You/Unless	1951	3.75	7.50	15.00
❑ F1546	Roller Coaster/On Top of the Ferris Wheel	1951	3.75	7.50	15.00
❑ F1584	Vanity/The World Is Mine	1951	3.75	7.50	15.00
❑ F1596	How Many Times/Bacoa	1951	3.75	7.50	15.00
❑ F1681	Because of You/Blue Tango	195?	3.00	6.00	12.00
❑ F1731	Longing for You/Sarah Kelly from Plumb Nelly	1951	3.75	7.50	15.00
❑ F1760	Somewhere, Somehow, Someday/ Because of You	1951	3.00	6.00	12.00
❑ F1773	You'll Know/Stay Awhile	1951	3.00	6.00	12.00
❑ F1785	Be Mine Tonight/California Moon	1951	3.75	7.50	15.00
❑ F1818	When/If You've Forgotten Me	1951	3.75	7.50	15.00
❑ F1839	I Remember You Love/ I Only Have One Life to Live	1951	3.75	7.50	15.00
❑ F1873	Jalousie/Shrimp Boats	1951	3.75	7.50	15.00
❑ F1887	Somebody's Been Beatin' My Time/ I Can't Help It	1951	3.75	7.50	15.00
❑ F1966	Blue Tango/Please Mr. Sun	1952	3.00	6.00	12.00
❑ F2005	Festival/Invitation	1952	3.00	6.00	12.00
❑ F2018	Wondering/God's Little Candles	1952	3.00	6.00	12.00
❑ F2053	Green Grow the Lilacs/A Day Away from You	1952	3.00	6.00	12.00
❑ F2102	I'm Yours/Kiss of Fire	1952	3.00	6.00	12.00
❑ F2106	Lonely Wine/Lost in Meditation	1952	3.00	6.00	12.00
❑ F2117	Tears/Please Say You Love Me	1952	3.00	6.00	12.00
❑ F2143	Auf Wiedersehn Sweetheart/Padam Padam	1952	3.00	6.00	12.00
❑ F2205	Till the End of the World/The Two-Faced Clock	1952	3.00	6.00	12.00
❑ F2225	Quiet Village/Indian Summer	1952	3.00	6.00	12.00
❑ F2274	Yours/Flute Salad	1952	3.00	6.00	12.00
❑ F2275	Santa Claus' Party/ Hang Your Wishes on the Tree	1952	3.00	6.00	12.00
❑ F2328	Vieni, Vieni/As Long As You Care	1953	3.00	6.00	12.00
❑ F2374	Aprin in Portugal/Suddenly	1953	3.00	6.00	12.00
❑ F2375	The Lord Is My Shepherd/My Name Is God	1953	3.00	6.00	12.00
❑ F2405	No More Goodbyes/Dance of the Flutes	1953	3.00	6.00	12.00
❑ F2457	A Little Love/Ruby	1953	3.00	6.00	12.00
❑ F2479	I Love Paris/Gigi	1953	3.00	6.00	12.00
❑ F2568	Tropicana/Julie	1953	3.00	6.00	12.00
❑ F2579	Cornflakes/Elaine	1953	3.00	6.00	12.00
❑ F2632	Love Theme from The Robe/Manhattan	1953	3.00	6.00	12.00
❑ F2705	Atlantis/The Flirtation Waltz	1954	3.00	6.00	12.00
❑ F2748	If You Were Mine/Douchka	1954	3.00	6.00	12.00
❑ F2799	Venezuela/Sea Song	1954	3.00	6.00	12.00
❑ F2845	The High and the Mighty/ More Love Than Your Love	1954	3.00	6.00	12.00
❑ F2918	Romantic Rio/When You're in Love	1954	3.00	6.00	12.00
❑ F2950	Midnight on the Cliffs/Dream Rhapsody	1954	3.00	6.00	12.00
—With Leonard Pennario					
❑ F3002	Earth Angel (Will You Be Mine)/Happy Baby	1954	3.00	6.00	12.00
❑ F3040	I Ain't Mad at You/Blue Mirage	1955	3.00	6.00	12.00
❑ F3055	Unchained Melody/Medic	1955	3.00	6.00	12.00
❑ F3120	Walke the Town and Tell the People/I'll Never Stop Loving You	1955	3.00	6.00	12.00
❑ F3195	Toy Tiger/Shrike	1955	3.00	6.00	12.00
❑ F3259	Song of the Bayou/Monika	1955	3.00	6.00	12.00
❑ F3291	The Trouble with Harry/Havana	1955	3.00	6.00	12.00
❑ F3336	The Poor People of Paris/Theme from "Helen of Troy"	1956	3.75	7.50	15.00
❑ F3404	Tango of the Drums/Sinner Man	1956	2.50	5.00	10.00
❑ F3478	Foreign Interlude/Melodia Loca	1956	2.50	5.00	10.00

Number	Title (A Side/B Side)	Yr	VG	VG+	NM
❑ F3526	Giant/There's Never Been Anyone Else But You	1956	2.50	5.00	10.00
❑ F3573	The Left Arm of Buddah/ What Happens in Buenos Aires	1956	2.50	5.00	10.00
❑ F3599	Dream Rhapsody/Midnight on the Cliffs	1956	2.50	5.00	10.00
❑ F3606	Stealin'/I'd Love to Fall Asleep	1956	2.50	5.00	10.00
—With Line Renaud					
❑ F3624	Clown on the Eiffel Tower/Woman's Devotion	1957	2.50	5.00	10.00
❑ F3653	Rain on My Window/I Dance When I Walk	1957	2.50	5.00	10.00
❑ F3704	Blue Echo/Designing Woman	1957	2.50	5.00	10.00
❑ F3728	The Lonely Whistler/Ruby Lips	1957	2.50	5.00	10.00
❑ F3768	La Panse/Manhattan	1957	2.50	5.00	10.00
❑ F3798	Search for Paradise/Ricordate Marcellino	1957	2.50	5.00	10.00
❑ F3841	Invisible Boy/ I Never Had a Dream Like This Before	1957	2.50	5.00	10.00
❑ F3887	A Farewell to Arms/ The Dance from Bonjour Tristesse	1958	2.50	5.00	10.00
❑ F4011	Love Song from Houseboat/Lily of Laguna	1958	2.50	5.00	10.00
❑ F4032	Dance, Everyone, Dance/A Chance Is All I Ask	1958	2.50	5.00	10.00
❑ F4091	Come Prima/My Heart's in Portugal	1958	2.50	5.00	10.00
❑ F4206	Tell Me, Margarita/Piccolissima Serenata	1959	2.50	5.00	10.00
❑ F4249	Sabre Dance/Milord	1959	2.50	5.00	10.00
❑ 4322	Prelude & Ben-Hur Theme/Till Tomorrow	1959	2.50	5.00	10.00
❑ 4374	Boomada/Cochi Baba	1960	2.50	5.00	10.00
❑ 4489	Pepe/Dolce Par Niente	1960	2.50	5.00	10.00
❑ 4523	Angelina/Follow Me	1961	2.50	5.00	10.00
GNP CRESCENDO					
❑ 313	Linin' Track/Baion	1964	2.00	4.00	8.00
❑ 382	And We Were Lovers/Balan Samba	1967	2.00	4.00	8.00
❑ 399	Live for Life/Free Again	1967	2.00	4.00	8.00
❑ 425	Flame Tree/Girl from Uganda	1969	—	3.00	6.00
RCA VICTOR					
❑ 47-3305	Toujours Moi/Fame	1949	5.00	10.00	20.00
❑ 47-3306	Jet/Tzezane	1949	5.00	10.00	20.00
❑ 47-3307	L'Ardente Nuit/Possession	1949	5.00	10.00	20.00
—RCA sides by "Leslie Baxter and His Orchestra"					
REPRISE					
❑ 0243	How Shall I Send Thee/ Have Yourself a Merry Little Christmas	1963	5.00	10.00	20.00
—B-side by Frank Sinatra					
❑ 20120	Theme from "The Manchurian Candidate"/ The Manchurian Beat	1962	2.50	5.00	10.00
❑ 20120 [PS]	Theme from "The Manchurian Candidate"/ The Manchurian Beat	1962	12.50	25.00	50.00
❑ 20159	Theme from "How the West Was Won"/ Theme from "Lawrence of Arabia"	1963	2.50	5.00	10.00
❑ 20165	Sail Away Ladies/Due Bonita Bandera	1963	2.50	5.00	10.00
7-Inch Extended Plays					
CAPITOL					
❑ EAP 1-447	April in Portugal/Blue Tango//Ruby/Quiet Village	195?	3.75	7.50	15.00
❑ EAP 1-447 [PS]	Blue Tango	195?	3.75	7.50	15.00
❑ EAP 1-474	Little White Lies/Miss You//Nevertheless/Mine	195?	3.00	6.00	12.00
❑ EAP 1-474 [PS]	Thinking of You, Part 1	195?	3.00	6.00	12.00
❑ EAP 2-474	Thinking of You/Speak Low//With My Eyes Wide Open I'm Dreaming/The Nearness of You	195?	3.00	6.00	12.00
❑ EAP 2-474 [PS]	Thinking of You, Part 2	195?	3.00	6.00	12.00
❑ EBF-474 [PS]	Thinking of You	195?	3.00	6.00	12.00
—Gatefold sleeve with some versions of 1-474 and 2-474					
❑ EAP 1-494	(contents unknown)	195?	3.75	7.50	15.00
❑ EAP 1-494 [PS]	Invitation	195?	3.75	7.50	15.00
❑ EAP 1-599	Blue Mirage (Don't Go)/Lonely Wine//Unchained Melody/If You've Forgotten Me	195?	3.00	6.00	12.00
❑ EAP 1-599 [PS]	Blue Mirage	195?	3.00	6.00	12.00
❑ EAP 1-672	*Wake the Town and Tell the People/The Shrike/ Toy Tiger/I'll Never Stop Loving You	1955	3.00	6.00	12.00
❑ EAP 1-672 [PS]	Wake the Town and Tell the People	1955	3.00	6.00	12.00
❑ EAP 1-730	The Poor People of Paris/Theme from "Helen of Troy"//The Trouble with Harry/If You Can Dream	1956	3.00	6.00	12.00
❑ EAP 1-730 [PS]	The Poor People of Paris	1956	3.00	6.00	12.00
Albums					
CAPITOL					
❑ H (# unknown) [10]	Music for Peace of Mind	1953	20.00	40.00	80.00
❑ DT 288 [R]	Ritual of the Savage (Le Sacre Du Sauvage)	196?	3.00	6.00	12.00
❑ H 288 [10]	Le Sacre Du Sauvage	1952	20.00	40.00	80.00
❑ T 288 [M]	Le Sacre Du Sauvage	1954	10.00	20.00	40.00
❑ T 390 [M]	Music Out of the Moon/Music for Peace of Mind	1954	10.00	20.00	40.00
❑ H 474 [10]	Thinking of You	1954	12.50	25.00	50.00
❑ T 474 [M]	Thinking of You	1954	10.00	20.00	40.00
❑ LAL 486 [M]	The Passions	1954	10.00	20.00	40.00
❑ T 594 [M]	Kaleidoscope	1955	10.00	20.00	40.00
❑ T 655 [M]	Tamboo!	1955	10.00	20.00	40.00
❑ T 733 [M]	Caribbean Moonlight	1956	10.00	20.00	40.00
❑ T 774 [M]	Skins!	1957	10.00	20.00	40.00
❑ T 780 [M]	'Round the World	1957	10.00	20.00	40.00
❑ T 843 [M]	Midnight on the Cliffs	1957	10.00	20.00	40.00
❑ T 868 [M]	Ports of Pleasure	1957	10.00	20.00	40.00
❑ T 968 [M]	Space Escapade	1958	10.00	20.00	40.00
❑ T 1012 [M]	Selections from "South Pacific"	1958	10.00	20.00	40.00
❑ T 1088 [M]	Love Is a Fabulous Thing	1958	10.00	20.00	40.00
❑ T 1117 [M]	African Jazz	1958	10.00	20.00	40.00
❑ DT 1388 [R]	Baxter's Best	1960	3.75	7.50	15.00
❑ SM-1388	Baxter's Best	197?	4.00		
❑ T 1388 [M]	Baxter's Best	1960	7.50	15.00	30.00
❑ ST 1537 [S]	Jewels of the Sea	1961	7.50	15.00	30.00
❑ T 1537 [M]	Jewels of the Sea	1961	6.25	12.50	25.00
❑ ST 1661 [S]	The Sensational Les Baxter	1962	7.50	15.00	30.00
❑ T 1661 [M]	The Sensational Les Baxter	1962	6.25	12.50	25.00
❑ ST 1846 [S]	The Original Quiet Village	1963	6.25	12.50	25.00
❑ T 1846 [M]	The Original Quiet Village	1963	5.00	10.00	20.00
❑ H 2000 [10]	Music Out of the Moon	1953	20.00	40.00	80.00
❑ T 10015 [M]	La Femme	1956	10.00	20.00	40.00
❑ M-11702	Ritual of the Savage	1977	2.50	5.00	10.00

B

Number	Title (A Side/B Side)	Yr	VG	VG+	NM
❑ SQBO-90984 [(2)]The Sounds of Adventure		1967	7.50	15.00	30.00
—Capitol Record Club exclusive					

GNP CRESCENDO
Number	Title (A Side/B Side)	Yr	VG	VG+	NM
❑ GNP-2036 [M]	Brazil Now	1967	3.75	7.50	15.00
❑ GNPS-2036 [S]	Brazil Now	1967	3.00	6.00	12.00
❑ GNPS-2042	Love Is Blue	1968	3.00	6.00	12.00
❑ GNPS-2047	Aftrican Blue	1969	3.00	6.00	12.00
❑ GNPS-2053	Moon Rock	1969	3.00	6.00	12.00

PICKWICK
Number	Title (A Side/B Side)	Yr	VG	VG+	NM
❑ PC-3011 [M]	The Fabulous Sounds of Les Baxter	196?	3.75	7.50	15.00
❑ SPC-3011 [S]	The Fabulous Sounds of Les Baxter	196?	3.75	7.50	15.00
❑ PC-3048 [M]	I Could Have Danced All Night	196?	3.75	7.50	15.00
❑ SPC-3048 [S]	I Could Have Danced All Night	196?	3.00	6.00	12.00

REPRISE
Number	Title (A Side/B Side)	Yr	VG	VG+	NM
❑ R-6036 [M]	Voices in Rhythm	1961	3.75	7.50	15.00
❑ R9-6036 [S]	Voices in Rhythm	1961	5.00	10.00	20.00
❑ R-6048 [M]	The Primitive and the Passionate	1962	3.75	7.50	15.00
❑ R9-6049 [S]	The Primitive and the Passionate	1962	5.00	10.00	20.00
❑ R-6079 [M]	Academy Award Winners '63	1963	3.75	7.50	15.00
❑ R9-6079 [S]	Academy Award Winners '63	1963	5.00	10.00	20.00
❑ R-6100 [M]	The Soul of the Drums	1963	3.75	7.50	15.00
❑ R9-6100 [S]	The Soul of the Drums	1963	5.00	10.00	20.00

BAXTER, RONNIE
45s
ATCO
Number	Title (A Side/B Side)	Yr	VG	VG+	NM
❑ 6093	Drivin' Me Out of My Mind/Afraid of Love	1957	10.00	20.00	40.00

GONE
Number	Title (A Side/B Side)	Yr	VG	VG+	NM
❑ 5036	Someone to Love Me/Gates of Heaven	1958	7.50	15.00	30.00
❑ 5041	Gates of Heaven/Prisoner of Love	1958	7.50	15.00	30.00
❑ 5050	Is It Because/I Finally Found You	1958	7.50	15.00	30.00
❑ 5058	Is It Because/I Finally Found You	1959	7.50	15.00	30.00
❑ 5084	It's Magic/If You Let Me	1960	6.25	12.50	25.00

MARK-X
Number	Title (A Side/B Side)	Yr	VG	VG+	NM
❑ 8001	It's Magic/If You Let Me	1959	3.00	6.00	12.00

BAY CITY 5 See LUIGI MARTINI AND THE BAY CITY 5.

BAY CITY ROLLERS
45s
ARISTA
Number	Title (A Side/B Side)	Yr	VG	VG+	NM
❑ 0120	Bye Bye Baby/It's for You	1975	2.50	5.00	10.00
❑ 0149	Saturday Night/Marlina	1975	—	2.00	4.00
❑ 0149 [PS]	Saturday Night/Marlina	1975	—	3.00	6.00
❑ 0170	Money Honey/Maryanne	1976	—	2.00	4.00
❑ 0170 [PS]	Money Honey/Maryanne	1976	2.00	4.00	8.00
❑ 0185	Rock and Roll Love Letter/Shanghai'd in Love	1976	—	2.00	4.00
❑ 0193	Don't Stop the Music (Long)/ Don't Stop the Music (Short)	1976	—	3.00	6.00
❑ 0205	I Only Want to Be with You/Write a Letter	1976	—	2.00	4.00
❑ 0216	Yesterday's Hero/My Lisa	1976	—	2.00	4.00
❑ 0233	Dedication/Rock N' Roller	1977	—	2.00	4.00
❑ 0233 [PS]	Dedication/Rock N' Roller	1977	—	2.50	5.00
❑ 0256	You Made Me Believe in Magic/ Dance Dance Dance	1977	—	2.00	4.00
❑ 0272	The Way I Feel Tonight/Love Power	1977	—	2.50	5.00
❑ 0272	The Way I Feel Tonight/Sweet Virginia	1977	—	2.50	5.00
❑ 0363	Where Will I Be Now/If You Were My Woman	1978	—	2.00	4.00
❑ 0476	Turn On the Radio/Hello and Welcome Home	1979	—	2.00	4.00
—As "The Rollers"					

BELL
Number	Title (A Side/B Side)	Yr	VG	VG+	NM
❑ 45169	Keep On Dancing/Alright	1972	2.50	5.00	10.00
❑ 45274	Manana/I Heard You Singing Your Song	1972	3.75	7.50	15.00
❑ 45481	Shang-a-Lang/(B-side unknown)	1974	3.75	7.50	15.00
❑ 45607	Summerlove Sensation/(B-side unknown)	1974	3.75	7.50	15.00
❑ 45618	All of Me Loves All of You/The Bump	1974	3.75	7.50	15.00

Albums
ARISTA
Number	Title (A Side/B Side)	Yr	VG	VG+	NM
❑ AL 4049	Bay City Rollers	1975	2.50	5.00	10.00
❑ AL 4071	Rock N' Roll Love Letter	1976	2.50	5.00	10.00
❑ AL 4093	Dedication	1976	2.50	5.00	10.00
❑ AB 4158	Greatest Hits	1977	2.50	5.00	10.00
❑ AB 4194	Strangers in the Wind	1978	2.50	5.00	10.00
❑ AB 4241	Elevator	1979	2.50	5.00	10.00
—As "The Rollers"					
❑ AB 7004	It's a Game	1977	2.50	5.00	10.00

BAY RIDGE, THE
45s
ATLANTIC
Number	Title (A Side/B Side)	Yr	VG	VG+	NM
❑ 2431	Back Track/I Can't Get Her Out of My Mind	1967	2.50	5.00	10.00

BAYOU BOYS, THE
45s
CHECKER
Number	Title (A Side/B Side)	Yr	VG	VG+	NM
❑ 765	Dinah/Bambalays	1952	37.50	75.00	150.00

BAYSIDERS, THE
45s
EVEREST
Number	Title (A Side/B Side)	Yr	VG	VG+	NM
❑ 19366	Over the Rainbow/My Bonnie	1960	3.75	7.50	15.00
❑ 19386	Trees/Look for the Silver Lining	1960	3.75	7.50	15.00
❑ 19393	The Bells of St. Mary's/Comin' Thru the Rye	1961	3.75	7.50	15.00

Albums
EVEREST
Number	Title (A Side/B Side)	Yr	VG	VG+	NM
❑ BRST-1124 [S]	Over the Rainbow	1961	75.00	150.00	300.00
❑ LPBR-5124 [M]	Over the Rainbow	1961	50.00	100.00	200.00

BAZUKA, TONY CAMILLO'S
45s
A&M
Number	Title (A Side/B Side)	Yr	VG	VG+	NM
❑ 1666	Dynomite Part 1/Dynomite Part 2	1975	—	2.00	4.00
❑ 1744	Bazuka Limited/Love Explosion	1975	—	2.00	4.00
❑ 1840	Theme from "Policeman"/Walkin' Tall	1976	—	2.00	4.00

VENTURE
Number	Title (A Side/B Side)	Yr	VG	VG+	NM
❑ 110	(C'est) Le Rock/Rock the Night Away	1979	—	2.00	4.00

Albums
A&M
Number	Title (A Side/B Side)	Yr	VG	VG+	NM
❑ SP-3406	Tomy Camillo's Bazuka	1975	2.50	5.00	10.00

BE-BOP DELUXE
45s
HARVEST
Number	Title (A Side/B Side)	Yr	VG	VG+	NM
❑ 4151	Sister Seagull/Maid in Heaven	1975	—	2.00	4.00
❑ 4244	Crying to the Sky/Ships in the Night	1976	—	2.00	4.00
❑ 4571	Panic in the World/Blue As a Jewel	1978	—	2.00	4.00

Albums
CAPITOL
Number	Title (A Side/B Side)	Yr	VG	VG+	NM
❑ SPRO-8486 [DJ]	Sunburst Finish	1975	6.25	12.50	25.00
—Specially banded version for radio					
❑ SN-16022	Sunburst Finish	1980	2.00	4.00	8.00
—Reissue of Harvest 11478					
❑ SN-16023	Drastic Plastic	1980	2.00	4.00	8.00
—Reissue of Harvest 11750					
❑ SN-16024	Futurama	1980	2.00	4.00	8.00
—Reissue of Harvest 11432					
❑ SN-16025	Axe Victim	1980	2.00	4.00	8.00
—Reissue of Harvest 11689					
❑ SN-16026	Modern Music	1980	2.00	4.00	8.00
—Reissue of Harvest 11575					

HARVEST
Number	Title (A Side/B Side)	Yr	VG	VG+	NM
❑ SPRO-8531 [DJ]	Be-Bop's Biggest	1978	7.50	15.00	30.00
—Promo-only compilation					
❑ ST-11432	Futurama	1975	2.50	5.00	10.00
❑ ST-11478	Sunburst Finish	1975	2.50	5.00	10.00
❑ ST-11575	Modern Music	1976	2.50	5.00	10.00
❑ SKBB-11666 [(2)]Live! In the Air Age		1977	3.00	6.00	12.00
❑ SM-11689	Axe Victim	1977	2.50	5.00	10.00
—Their first UK album; first US issue has "SM" prefix					
❑ SW-11750	Drastic Plastic	1978	2.50	5.00	10.00
❑ SKBO-11870 [(2)]The Best Of & The Rest Of Be-Bop Deluxe		1979	3.00	6.00	12.00

BEACH, BILL
45s
KING
Number	Title (A Side/B Side)	Yr	VG	VG+	NM
❑ 4940	Peg Pants/You're Gonna Like My Baby	1956	37.50	75.00	150.00

BEACH BOYS, THE Also see GLEN CAMPBELL; BRUCE JOHNSTON; BRIAN WILSON; BRIAN WILSON AND MIKE LOVE.
12-Inch Singles
CAPITOL
Number	Title (A Side/B Side)	Yr	VG	VG+	NM
❑ SPRO-9711/2 [DJ]Rock 'n' Roll to the Rescue/Good Vibrations		1986	2.50	5.00	10.00
❑ SPRO-9796 [DJ]California Dreamin' (same on both sides?)		1986	2.50	5.00	10.00

CARIBOU
Number	Title (A Side/B Side)	Yr	VG	VG+	NM
❑ AS 557 [DJ]	Here Comes the Night (Remix) (Instrumental)	1979	3.75	7.50	15.00
—Blue vinyl					
❑ 2Z8 9028	Here Comes the Night/(Instrumental)	1979	2.50	5.00	10.00
—Issued in generic "Disco Single" sleeve					
❑ 2Z8 9028 [DJ]	Here Comes the Night (Long) (Short)	1979	3.00	6.00	12.00

45s
BROTHER
Number	Title (A Side/B Side)	Yr	VG	VG+	NM
❑ 1001	Heroes and Villains/You're Welcome	1967	3.00	6.00	12.00
❑ 1001 [PS]	Heroes and Villains/You're Welcome	1967	25.00	50.00	100.00
—Not to be confused with Capitol 5826, which is a completely different sleeve					

BROTHER/REPRISE
Number	Title (A Side/B Side)	Yr	VG	VG+	NM
❑ 0101	Wouldn't It Be Nice/Sloop John B	1973	—	2.50	5.00
—"Back to Back Hits" series					
❑ 0102	God Only Knows/Caroline, No	1973	—	2.50	5.00
—"Back to Back Hits" series					
❑ 0103	Good Vibrations/Heroes and Villains	1973	—	2.50	5.00
—"Back to Back Hits" series					
❑ 0104	Darlin'/Wild Honey	1973	—	2.50	5.00
—"Back to Back Hits" series					
❑ 0105	Friends/Be Here in the Morning	1973	—	2.50	5.00
—"Back to Back Hits" series					
❑ 0106	Do It Again/Cottonfields	1973	—	2.50	5.00
—"Back to Back Hits" series					
❑ 0107	I Can Hear Music/Bluebirds Over the Mountain	1973	—	2.50	5.00
—"Back to Back Hits" series					
❑ 0118	Rock and Roll Music/It's O.K.	1977	—	2.00	4.00
—"Back to Back Hits" series					
❑ 0894	Add Some Music to Your Day/Susie Cincinnati	1970	2.00	4.00	8.00
❑ 0929	Slip On Through/This Whole World	1970	2.50	5.00	10.00
❑ 0957	It's About Time/Tears in the Morning	1970	5.00	10.00	20.00
❑ 0998	Cool, Cool Water/Forever	1971	20.00	40.00	80.00
❑ 1015	Long Promised Road/Deirdre	1971	5.00	10.00	20.00
❑ 1047	Long Promised Road/'Til I Die	1971	5.00	10.00	20.00
❑ 1058	Surf's Up/Don't Go Near the Water	1971	12.50	25.00	50.00
❑ 1091	You Need a Mess of Help to Stand Alone/ Cuddle Up	1972	7.50	15.00	30.00
❑ 1101	Marcella/Hold On Dear Brother	1972	7.50	15.00	30.00
❑ 1138	Sail On Sailor/Only With You	1972	2.50	5.00	10.00
❑ 1156	California Saga (On My Way to Sunny Californ-I-A)/Funky Pretty	1973	2.50	5.00	10.00
❑ 1310	I Can Hear Music/Let the Wind Blow	1974	2.50	5.00	10.00
❑ 1321	Child of Winter (Christmas Song)/Susie Cincinnati	1974	12.50	25.00	50.00
❑ 1321 [DJ]	Child Of Winter (Christmas Song) (mono/stereo)	1974	6.25	12.50	25.00
❑ 1325	Sail On Sailor/Only With You	1975	2.00	4.00	8.00
❑ 1336	Wouldn't It Be Nice/Caroline, No	1975	3.00	6.00	12.00
❑ 1354	Rock and Roll Music/The T M Song	1976	—	2.00	4.00
❑ 1368	It's O.K./Had to Phone Ya	1976	—	2.00	4.00
❑ 1375	Everyone's In Love with You/Susie Cincinnati	1976	—	2.00	4.00
❑ 1389	Honkin' Down the Highway/Solar System	1977	—	2.00	4.00
❑ 1394	Peggy Sue/Hey Little Tomboy	1978	—	2.00	4.00

Number	Title (A Side/B Side)	Yr	VG	VG+	NM
CANDIX					
❏ 301	Surfin'/Luau	1961	50.00	100.00	200.00
—Label says "Distributed by Era Records Sales, Inc."					
❏ 301	Surfin'/Luau	1961	75.00	150.00	300.00
—No mention of Era Records on label					
❏ 331	Surfin'/Luau	1962	50.00	100.00	200.00
CAPITOL					
❏ 2028	Wild Honey/Wind Chimes	1967	3.00	6.00	12.00
❏ 2068	Darlin'/Here Today	1967	3.00	6.00	12.00
❏ 2068 [PS]	Darlin'/Here Today	1967	5.00	10.00	20.00
❏ 2160	Friends/Little Bird	1968	3.00	6.00	12.00
❏ 2239	Do It Again/Wake the World	1968	3.00	6.00	12.00
❏ 2360	Bluebirds Over the Mountain/Never Learn Not to Love	1968	3.00	6.00	12.00
❏ 2432	I Can Hear Music/All I Want to Do	1969	3.00	6.00	12.00
❏ 2530	Break Away/Celebrate the News	1969	3.00	6.00	12.00
❏ 2765	Cottonfields/The Nearest Faraway Place	1970	5.00	10.00	20.00
❏ PRO 2936/7	Salt Lake City/Amusement Parks U.S.A.	1965	50.00	100.00	200.00
—"Courtesy of Downtown Salt Lake City Stores" promotional item					
❏ 3924	Surfin' U.S.A./The Warmth of the Sun	1974	—	2.50	5.00
❏ 4093	Little Honda/Hawaii	1975	—	2.50	5.00
❏ 4110	Barbara Ann/Little Honda	1975	—	2.50	5.00
❏ 4334	Be True to Your School/Graduation Day	1976	—	2.50	5.00
❏ 4777	Surfin' Safari/409	1962	6.25	12.50	25.00
❏ 4777 [PS]	Surfin' Safari/409	1962	20.00	40.00	80.00
❏ 4880	Ten Little Indians/County Fair	1962	7.50	15.00	30.00
❏ 4880 [PS]	Ten Little Indians/County Fair	1962	50.00	100.00	200.00
❏ 4932	Surfin' U.S.A./Shut Down	1963	6.25	12.50	25.00
—Version 2: Chuck Berry listed as composer of "Surfin' U.S.A."					
❏ 4932	Surfin' U.S.A./Shut Down	1963	6.25	12.50	25.00
—Version 1: Brian Wilson listed as composer of "Surfin' U.S.A."					
❏ 5009	Surfer Girl/Little Deuce Coupe	1963	6.25	12.50	25.00
❏ A-5030	The Beach Boys Medley/God Only Knows	1981	—	2.50	5.00
❏ 5069	Be True to Your School/In My Room	1963	6.25	12.50	25.00
❏ 5096	Little Saint Nick/The Lord's Prayer	1963	7.50	15.00	30.00
—Orange and yellow swirl label					
❏ 5096	Little Saint Nick/The Lord's Prayer	1969	4.50	9.00	18.00
—Red and orange "target" label					
❏ 5096	Little Saint Nick/The Lord's Prayer	1972	3.75	7.50	15.00
—Orange label with "Capitol" at bottom of label					
❏ 5096	Little Saint Nick/The Lord's Prayer	1978	—	2.50	5.00
—Purple label					
❏ 5096	Little Saint Nick/The Lord's Prayer	1982	—	2.50	5.00
—Black label with colorband					
❏ 5118	Fun, Fun, Fun/Why Do Fools Fall in Love	1964	5.00	10.00	20.00
—A-side songwriter listed as "Brian Wilson-Mike Love"					
❏ 5118	Fun, Fun, Fun/Why Do Fools Fall in Love	1964	6.25	12.50	25.00
—A-side songwriter listed as "Brian Wilson"					
❏ 5118 [PS]	Fun, Fun, Fun/Why Do Fools Fall in Love	1964	10.00	20.00	40.00
❏ 5174	I Get Around/Don't Worry Baby	1964	6.25	12.50	25.00
—Orange and yellow swirl label					
❏ 5174 [PS]	I Get Around/Don't Worry Baby	1964	10.00	20.00	40.00
❏ 5174	I Get Around/Don't Worry Baby	1969	3.00	6.00	12.00
—Red and orange "target" label					
❏ 5174	I Get Around/Don't Worry Baby	1972	2.00	4.00	8.00
—Orange label with "Capitol" at bottom					
❏ 5174	I Get Around/Don't Worry Baby	1978	—	2.50	5.00
—Purple label					
❏ 5174	I Get Around/Don't Worry Baby	1982	—	2.50	5.00
—Black label with colorband					
❏ 5245	When I Grow Up (To Be a Man)/She Knows Me Too Well	1964	6.25	12.50	25.00
❏ 5245 [PS]	When I Grow Up (To Be a Man)/She Knows Me Too Well	1964	10.00	20.00	40.00
—With blue border					
❏ 5245 [PS]	When I Grow Up (To Be a Man)/She Knows Me Too Well	1964	12.50	25.00	50.00
—With green border					
❏ 5306	Dance, Dance, Dance/The Warmth of the Sun	1964	6.25	12.50	25.00
❏ 5306 [PS]	Dance, Dance, Dance/The Warmth of the Sun	1964	30.00	60.00	120.00
❏ 5312	The Man with All the Toys/Blue Christmas	1964	7.50	15.00	30.00
❏ 5372	Do You Wanna Dance/Please Let Me Wonder	1965	5.00	10.00	20.00
❏ 5372 [PS]	Do You Wanna Dance/Please Let Me Wonder	1965	10.00	20.00	40.00
❏ 5395	Help Me, Rhonda/Kiss Me, Baby	1965	6.25	12.50	25.00
❏ 5395 [PS]	Help Me, Rhonda/Kiss Me, Baby	1965	10.00	20.00	40.00
❏ 5464	California Girls/Let Him Run Wild	1965	6.25	12.50	25.00
—Orange and yellow swirl label					
❏ 5464 [PS]	California Girls/Let Him Run Wild	1965	10.00	20.00	40.00
❏ 5464	California Girls/Let Him Run Wild	1969	2.50	5.00	10.00
—Red and orange "target" label					
❏ 5464	California Girls/Let Him Run Wild	1973	2.00	4.00	8.00
—Orange label with "Capitol" at bottom of label					
❏ 5464	California Girls/Let Him Run Wild	1978	—	2.50	5.00
—Purple label					
❏ 5540	The Little Girl I Once Knew/There's No Other (Like My Baby)	1965	5.00	10.00	20.00
❏ 5540 [PS]	The Little Girl I Once Knew/There's No Other (Like My Baby)	1965	10.00	20.00	40.00
❏ 5561	Barbara Ann/Girl Don't Tell Me	1965	5.00	10.00	20.00
❏ 5561 [PS]	Barbara Ann/Girl Don't Tell Me	1965	37.50	75.00	150.00
—Glossy finish					
❏ 5561 [PS]	Barbara Ann/Girl Don't Tell Me	1965	50.00	100.00	200.00
—Non-glossy finish					
❏ B-5595	Rock and Roll to the Rescue/Good Vibrations (Live in London)	1986	—	—	3.00
❏ B-5595 [PS]	Rock and Roll to the Rescue/Good Vibrations (Live in London)	1986	—	2.00	4.00
❏ 5602	Sloop John B/You're So Good to Me	1966	5.00	10.00	20.00
—Orange and yellow swirl label					
❏ 5602	Sloop John B/You're So Good to Me	1966	7.50	15.00	30.00
❏ 5602	Sloop John B/You're So Good to Me	1969	2.50	5.00	10.00
—Red and orange "target" label					
❏ 5602	Sloop John B/You're So Good to Me	1973	2.00	4.00	8.00
—Orange label with "Capitol" at bottom of label					
❏ 5602	Sloop John B/You're So Good to Me	1978	—	2.50	5.00
—Purple label					
❏ B-5630	California Dreamin'/Lady Liberty	1986	—	—	3.00
❏ 5676	Good Vibrations/Let's Go Away for Awhile	1966	5.00	10.00	20.00
❏ 5676 [PS]	Good Vibrations/Let's Go Away for Awhile	1966	7.50	15.00	30.00
❏ 5706	Wouldn't It Be Nice/God Only Knows	1966	5.00	10.00	20.00
—Even though it has a higher number, this single was released before "Good Vibrations."					
❏ 5826 [PS]	Heroes and Villains	1967	100.00	200.00	400.00
—U.S. picture sleeve for unreleased record. This sleeve, however, was exported and used in other countries.					
❏ S7-17521	409/Punchline	1993	—	2.00	4.00
❏ S7-17522	Be True to Your School/Things We Did Last Summer	1993	—	2.00	4.00
❏ S7-17523	Do You Wanna Dance/Ruby Baby	1993	—	2.00	4.00
❏ S7-18205	Merry Christmas, Baby/Santa's Beard	1994	—	2.00	4.00
—Green vinyl					
❏ S7-19765	The Man with All the Toys/We Three Kings of Orient Are	1997	—	—	3.00
❏ B-44297	Don't Worry Baby/Tequila Dreams	1989	—	2.00	4.00
—A-side: With the Everly Brothers; B-side by Dave Grusin					
❏ B-44297 [PS]	Don't Worry Baby/Tequila Dreams	1989	2.50	5.00	10.00
❏ S7-57886	Frosty the Snowman/Little Saint Nick	1992	—	2.50	5.00
—Originals on black vinyl					
❏ S7-57886	Frosty the Snowman/Little Saint Nick	1993	—	2.00	4.00
—Second pressing on green vinyl					
❏ 58745	Child of Winter (Christmas Song)/Winter Symphony	1998	—	2.00	4.00
❏ 58746	Christmas Is Here Again/Auld Lang Syne	1998	—	2.00	4.00
❏ 58747	I'll Be Home for Christmas/Little Saint Nick (Alternate Version)	1998	—	2.00	4.00
❏ 7PRO-79789 [DJ]	Still Cruisin' (same on both sides)	1989	15.00	30.00	60.00
—Vinyl is promo only					
❏ 7PRO-79841 [DJ]	Somewhere Near Japan (same on both sides)	1989	15.00	30.00	60.00
—Vinyl is promo only					
CAPITOL CUSTOM					
❏ (no #)	Spirit of America/Boogie Woodie	1963	50.00	100.00	200.00
❏ (no #) [PS]	Spirit of America/Boogie Woodie	1963	150.00	300.00	600.00
—Promo for KFWB and opening day of Wallich's Music City South Bay store					
CAPITOL STARLINE					
❏ 6059	Be True to Your School/In My Room	1965	3.75	7.50	15.00
—Originals have green swirl labels					
❏ 6060	Ten Little Indians/She Knows Me Too Well	1965	3.75	7.50	15.00
—Originals have green swirl labels					
❏ 6081	Help Me, Rhonda/Do You Wanna Dance?	1966	3.75	7.50	15.00
—Originals have green swirl labels					
❏ 6094	Surfin' U.S.A./Shut Down	1966	3.75	7.50	15.00
—Originals have green swirl labels					
❏ 6095	Surfin' Safari/409	1966	3.75	7.50	15.00
—Originals have green swirl labels					
❏ 6105	Dance, Dance, Dance/The Warmth of the Sun	1967	3.00	6.00	12.00
—Originals have red and white "target" labels					
❏ 6106	Fun, Fun, Fun/Why Do Fools Fall in Love	1967	3.00	6.00	12.00
—Originals have red and white "target" labels					
❏ 6107	Surfer Girl/Little Deuce Coupe	1967	3.00	6.00	12.00
—Originals have red and white "target" labels					
❏ 6132	Good Vibrations/Barbara Ann	1968	3.00	6.00	12.00
—Originals have red and white "target" labels					
❏ 6204	When I Grow Up (To Be a Man)/She Knows Me Too Well	197?	—	2.50	5.00
—Originals have grayish labels					
❏ 6205	Wendy/Little Honda	197?	—	2.50	5.00
—Originals have grayish labels					
❏ 6259	Barbara Ann/Little Honda	1978	—	2.00	4.00
—Originals have grayish labels					
❏ 6277	Little Saint Nick/The Lord's Prayer	1981	—	—	3.00
—Originals have blue labels					
❏ 6280	I Get Around/Don't Worry Baby	1981	—	—	3.00
—Originals have blue labels					
❏ 6289	California Girls/Let Him Run Wild	1981	—	—	3.00
—Originals have blue labels					
❏ 6295	Sloop John B/You're So Good to Me	1981	—	—	3.00
—Originals have blue labels					
CARIBOU					
❏ 02633	Come Go with Me/Don't Go Near the Water	1981	—	—	3.00
❏ 04913	Getcha Back/Male Ego	1985	—	—	3.00
❏ 04913 [PS]	Getcha Back/Male Ego	1985	—	—	3.00
❏ 05433	It's Gettin' Late/It's OK	1985	—	—	3.00
❏ 05433 [PS]	It's Gettin' Late/It's OK	1985	—	—	3.00
❏ 05624	She Believes in Love Again/It's Just a Matter of Time	1985	—	—	3.00
❏ 05624 [PS]	She Believes in Love Again/It's Just a Matter of Time	1985	—	—	3.00
❏ 9026	Here Comes the Night/Baby Blue	1979	—	2.00	4.00
❏ 9029	Good Timin'/Love Surrounds Me	1979	—	2.00	4.00
❏ 9030	Lady Lynda/Full Sail	1979	—	2.00	4.00
❏ 9031	It's a Beautiful Day/Sumahama	1979	—	2.00	4.00
❏ 9032	Goin' On/Endless Harmony	1980	—	2.00	4.00
❏ 9033	Livin' with a Heartache/Santa Ana Winds	1980	—	2.00	4.00
❏ 9034	School Day (Ring! Ring! Goes the Bell)/When Girls Get Together	1980			
—Not known to exist					
❏ 9034 [DJ]	School Day (Ring! Ring! Goes the Bell) (same on both sides)	1980	50.00	125.00	250.00
CRITIQUE					
❏ 99392	Happy Endings/California Girls	1987	—	—	3.00
—A-side with Little Richard					
❏ 99392 [PS]	Happy Endings/California Girls	1987	—	2.50	5.00
—Both the Beach Bosy and Little Richard are on the sleeve					
ELEKTRA					
❏ 69385	Kokomo/Tutti-Frutti	1988	—	—	3.00
—B-side by Little Richard					

Number	Title (A Side/B Side)	Yr	VG	VG+	NM
ERA BACK TO BACK HITS					
❑ 042	Surfer Girl/The Freeze	197?	2.00	4.00	8.00
—A-side is from the Hite Morgan sessions; B-side by Tony & Jo					
❑ 043	Surfin'/Surfin' Safari	197?	2.00	4.00	8.00
—Both sides from the Hite Morgan sessions					
FBI					
❑ 7701	East Meets West/Rhapsody	1986	5.00	10.00	20.00
—With Frankie Valli and the Four Seasons					
ODE					
❑ 66016	Wouldn't It Be Nice/The Times They Are a-Changing	1971	7.50	15.00	30.00
—B-side by Merry Clayton					
SUB POP					
❑ 363	I Just Wasn't Made for These Times/Wouldn't It Be Nice//Here Today	1996	—	2.50	5.00
—Newly released versions from the Pet Sounds box set					
❑ 363 [PS]	I Just Wasn't Made for These Times/Wouldn't It Be Nice//Here Today	1996		2.50	5.00
—Not seam sealed (folded piece of cardboard)					
X					
❑ 301	Surfin'/Luau	1961	250.00	500.00	1000.
7-Inch Extended Plays					
CAPITOL					
❑ SXA-1981	Your Summer Dream/Our Car Club/Surfer Girl/Catch a Wave/In My Room/Hawaii	1963	37.50	75.00	150.00
—Jukebox issue; small hole, plays at 33 1/3 rpm					
❑ SXA-1981 [PS] Surfer Girl		1963	37.50	75.00	150.00
❑ DU 2269	Kiss Me, Baby/Don't Hurt My Little Sister/In the Back of My Mind//I'm So Young/Good to My Baby/She Knows Me Too Well	1965	20.00	40.00	80.00
—Jukebox issue; small hole, plays at 33 1/3 rpm					
❑ DU 2269 [PS] The Beach Boys Today!		1965	20.00	40.00	80.00
❑ R-5267	Wendy/Don't Back Down//Little Honda/Hushabye	1964	15.00	30.00	60.00
❑ R-5267 [PS] 4-By the Beach Boys		1964	15.00	30.00	60.00
Albums					
ASYLUM					
❑ R 113793	Surf's Up	1972	37.50	75.00	150.00
—RCA Record Club edition, pressed with wrong labels					
BROTHER					
❑ ST 9001 [R]	Smiley Smile	1967	3.75	7.50	15.00
—"Title for this album by Barry Turnbull" on back cover					
❑ ST 9001 [R]	Smiley Smile	1967	5.00	10.00	20.00
—No mention of Barry Turnbull on cover					
❑ T 9001 [M]	Smiley Smile	1967	7.50	15.00	30.00
—"Title for this album by Barry Turnbull" on back cover					
❑ T 9001 [M]	Smiley Smile	1967	10.00	20.00	40.00
—No mention of Barry Turnbull on cover					
BROTHER/REPRISE					
❑ 2MS 2083 [(2)]	Carl and the Passions "So Tough"/Pet Sounds	1972	7.50	15.00	30.00
❑ 2MS 2083 [(2)DJ]Carl and the Passions "So Tough"/Pet Sounds		1972	12.50	25.00	50.00
—White label promo					
❑ MS 2118	Holland	1973	3.75	7.50	15.00
—Includes bonus stock-copy EP, "Mount Vernon and Fairway," in picture sleeve, taped to back cover					
❑ MS 2118 [DJ]	Holland	1973	10.00	20.00	40.00
—White label promo; includes bonus white-label promo EP, "Mount Vernon and Fairway," in picture sleeve, taped to back cover					
❑ MS 2118 [DJ]	Holland	1973	125.00	250.00	500.00
—Test pressing with "We Got Love," deleted from promos and stock copies					
❑ 2MS 2166 [(2)] Wild Honey & 20/20		1974	3.75	7.50	15.00
❑ 2MS 2167 [(2)] Friends & Smiley Smile		1974	3.75	7.50	15.00
❑ MS 2197 [M]	Pet Sounds	1974	5.00	10.00	20.00
❑ MS 2223	Good Vibrations — Best of the Beach Boys	1975	3.00	6.00	12.00
❑ MS 2251	15 Big Ones	1976	3.00	6.00	12.00
❑ MSK 2258	Love You	1977	3.00	6.00	12.00
❑ MSK 2268	M.I.U. Album	1978	3.00	6.00	12.00
❑ MSK 2280	Good Vibrations — Best of the Beach Boys	1978	2.50	5.00	10.00
❑ RS-6382	Sunflower	1970	6.25	12.50	25.00
❑ RS-6382 [DJ]	Sunflower	1970	12.50	25.00	50.00
—White label promo					
❑ RS 6453	Surf's Up	1971	5.00	10.00	20.00
❑ RS 6453 [DJ]	Surf's Up	1971	10.00	20.00	40.00
—White label promo					
❑ 2RS 6484 [(2)] The Beach Boys In Concert		1973	5.00	10.00	20.00
❑ 2RS 6484 [(2)DJ]The Beach Boys In Concert		1973	10.00	20.00	40.00
—White label promo					
❑ SKAO-93352	Sunflower	1970	50.00	100.00	200.00
—Capitol Record Club edition					
❑ R 113793	Surf's Up	1972	6.25	12.50	25.00
—RCA Record Club edition					
❑ R 130223	15 Big Ones	1976	3.75	7.50	15.00
—RCA Record Club edition					
❑ R 223569 [(2)] The Beach Boys In Concert		1973	6.25	12.50	25.00
—RCA Record Club edition					
CAPITOL					
❑ SKAO-133	20/20	1969	3.75	7.50	15.00
—"Starline" label					
❑ SKAO-133	20/20	1969	5.00	10.00	20.00
—Black label with colorband					
❑ SKAO-8-0133	20/20	1969	7.50	15.00	30.00
—Capitol Record Club edition; black label					
❑ SKAO-8-0133	20/20	1970	10.00	20.00	40.00
—Capitol Record Club edition; lime label					
❑ SWBB-253 [(2)]Close-Up		1969	7.50	15.00	30.00
—Reissue of "Surfin' U.S.A." and "All Summer Long" in one package; black labels with colorband					
❑ SWBB-253 [(2)]Close-Up		1970	10.00	20.00	40.00
—Lime labels					
❑ ST-442	Good Vibrations	1970	5.00	10.00	20.00
—Lime label (original)					
❑ ST-442	Good Vibrations	1972	6.25	12.50	25.00
—Red or orange label					

Number	Title (A Side/B Side)	Yr	VG	VG+	NM
❑ ST-8-0442	Good Vibrations	1970	7.50	15.00	30.00
—Capitol Record Club edition					
❑ STBB-500 [(2)]	All Summer Long/California Girls	1970	5.00	10.00	20.00
—Lime labels; "Special Double Play" pack; two separate LPs (abridged versions of "All Summer Long" and "Summer Days [And Summer Nights!!]") bound together					
❑ STBB-500 [(2)]	All Summer Long/California Girls	1971	6.25	12.50	25.00
—Red labels; "Special Double Play" pack; two separate LPs (abridged versions of "All Summer Long" and "Summer Days [And Summer Nights!!]") bound together					
❑ SF-501	All Summer Long	1970	2.50	5.00	10.00
—Individual record from above set					
❑ SF-8-0501	All Summer Long	1971	2.50	5.00	10.00
—Capitol Record Club edition					
❑ SF-502	California Girls	1970	2.50	5.00	10.00
—Individual record from above set					
❑ SF-8-0502	California Girls	1971	2.50	5.00	10.00
—Capitol Record Club edition					
❑ STBB-701 [(2)]	Fun, Fun, Fun/Dance, Dance, Dance	1970	5.00	10.00	20.00
—Lime labels; "Special Double Play" pack; two separate LPs (abridged versions of "Shut Down, Volume 2" and "The Beach Boys Today!") bound together					
❑ STBB-701 [(2)]	Fun, Fun, Fun/Dance, Dance, Dance	1971	6.25	12.50	25.00
—Red labels; "Special Double Play" pack; two separate LPs (abridged versions of "Shut Down, Volume 2" and "The Beach Boys Today!") bound together					
❑ SF-702	Fun, Fun, Fun	1971	2.50	5.00	10.00
—Individual record from above set					
❑ SF-8-0702	Fun, Fun, Fun	1971	2.50	5.00	10.00
—Capitol Record Club edition					
❑ SF-703	Dance, Dance, Dance	1971	2.50	5.00	10.00
—Individual record from above set					
❑ SF-8-0703	Dance, Dance, Dance	1971	2.50	5.00	10.00
—Capitol Record Club edition					
❑ DT 1808 [R]	Surfin' Safari	1962	6.25	12.50	25.00
—With only the "Duophonic" banner at top					
❑ DT 1808 [R]	Surfin' Safari	1962	20.00	40.00	80.00
—With "Capitol Full Dimensional Stereo" banner under the "Duophonic" banner					
❑ SM-1808 [M]	Surfin' Safari	197?	2.50	5.00	10.00
❑ T 1808 [M]	Surfin' Safari	1962	10.00	20.00	40.00
❑ SM-1890 [S]	Surfin' U.S.A.	197?	2.50	5.00	10.00
❑ ST 1890 [S]	Surfin' U.S.A.	1963	12.50	25.00	50.00
❑ T 1890 [M]	Surfin' U.S.A.	1963	10.00	20.00	40.00
❑ SM-1981 [S]	Surfer Girl	197?	2.50	5.00	10.00
❑ ST 1981 [S]	Surfer Girl	1963	12.50	25.00	50.00
—With reference to "their other new single record, 'Little Deuce Coupe'" in liner notes					
❑ ST 1981 [S]	Surfer Girl	1963	12.50	25.00	50.00
—With reference to The Four Freshmen in liner notes					
❑ T 1981 [M]	Surfer Girl	1963	10.00	20.00	40.00
—With reference to "their other new single record, 'Little Deuce Coupe'" in liner notes					
❑ T 1981 [M]	Surfer Girl	1963	10.00	20.00	40.00
—With reference to The Four Freshmen in liner notes					
❑ SM-1998 [S]	Little Deuce Coupe	197?	2.50	5.00	10.00
❑ ST 1998 [S]	Little Deuce Coupe	1963	10.00	20.00	40.00
❑ T 1998 [M]	Little Deuce Coupe	1963	10.00	20.00	40.00
❑ ST 2027 [P]	Shut Down, Volume 2	1964	10.00	20.00	40.00
❑ T 2027 [M]	Shut Down, Volume 2	1964	10.00	20.00	40.00
❑ ST 2110 [S]	All Summer Long	1964	7.50	15.00	30.00
—With "Don't Back Down" correctly listed on front cover					
❑ ST 2110 [S]	All Summer Long	1964	12.50	25.00	50.00
—With "Don't Break Down" erroneously listed on front cover					
❑ T 2110 [M]	All Summer Long	1964	7.50	15.00	30.00
—With "Don't Back Down" correctly listed on front cover					
❑ T 2110 [M]	All Summer Long	1964	12.50	25.00	50.00
—With "Don't Break Down" erroneously listed on front cover					
❑ SM-2164	The Beach Boys' Christmas Album	197?	2.50	5.00	10.00
❑ ST 2164 [M]	The Beach Boys' Christmas Album	1964	12.50	25.00	50.00
❑ T 2164 [M]	The Beach Boys' Christmas Album	1964	12.50	25.00	50.00
❑ SM-2198	Beach Boys Concert	197?	2.50	5.00	10.00
❑ STAO 2198 [S] Beach Boys Concert		1964	7.50	15.00	30.00
—With bound-in booklet					
❑ STAO-8-2198 [S]Beach Boys Concert		196?	20.00	40.00	80.00
—Capitol Record Club edition					
❑ TAO 2198 [M]	Beach Boys Concert	1964	7.50	15.00	30.00
—With bound-in booklet					
❑ DT 2269 [R]	The Beach Boys Today!	1965	6.25	12.50	25.00
❑ DT-8-2269 [R]	The Beach Boys Today!	1965	20.00	40.00	80.00
—Capitol Record Club edition					
❑ T 2269 [M]	The Beach Boys Today!	1965	7.50	15.00	30.00
❑ DT 2354 [R]	Summer Days (And Summer Nights!!)	1965	6.25	12.50	25.00
—With "Duophonic" banner					
❑ DT 2354 [R]	Summer Days (And Summer Nights!!)	1965	12.50	25.00	50.00
—With "New Improved Full Dimensional Stereo" banner					
❑ T 2354 [M]	Summer Days (And Summer Nights!!)	1965	7.50	15.00	30.00
❑ DMAS 2398 [R]Beach Boys Party!		1965	6.25	12.50	25.00
—Without sheet of photos					
❑ DMAS 2398 [R]Beach Boys Party!		1965	7.50	15.00	30.00
—With sheet of photos					
❑ MAS 2398 [M] Beach Boys Party!		1965	7.50	15.00	30.00
—Without sheet of photos					
❑ MAS 2398 [M] Beach Boys Party!		1965	10.00	20.00	40.00
—With sheet of photos					
❑ DT 2458 [R]	Pet Sounds	1966	7.50	15.00	30.00
❑ T 2458 [M]	Pet Sounds	1966	10.00	20.00	40.00
❑ DT 2545 [P]	Best of the Beach Boys	1966	3.00	6.00	12.00
—Black "The Star Line" label					
❑ DT 2545 [P]	Best of the Beach Boys	1966	3.75	7.50	15.00
—Black label with colorband					
❑ DT 2545 [P]	Best of the Beach Boys	1967	3.75	7.50	15.00
—Red and white "Starline" label					
❑ DT 2545 [P]	Best of the Beach Boys	1970	3.00	6.00	12.00
—Green "Starline" label					
❑ DT 2545 [P]	Best of the Beach Boys	1973	2.50	5.00	10.00
—Orange label, "Capitol" on bottom					
❑ DT 2545 [P]	Best of the Beach Boys	1978	2.50	5.00	10.00
—Purple label, large Capitol logo					

Number	Title (A Side/B Side)	Yr	VG	VG+	NM
❏ DT 2545 [P]	Best of the Beach Boys	1983	2.50	5.00	10.00
—Black label, print in colorband					
❏ T 2545 [M]	Best of the Beach Boys	1966	3.75	7.50	15.00
—Black "The Star Line" label					
❏ T 2545 [M]	Best of the Beach Boys	1966	5.00	10.00	20.00
—Black label with colorband					
❏ T 2545 [M]	Best of the Beach Boys	1967	7.50	15.00	30.00
—Red and white "Starline" label					
❏ T/DT 2580	Smile Booklet	1966	75.00	150.00	300.00
—Printed for insertion into unreleased "Smile" LP; counterfeits exist					
❏ T/DT 2580	Smile	1966	250.00	500.00	1000.
—Unreleased; price is for cover slick, which has been counterfeited					
❏ DT 2706 [P]	Best of the Beach Boys, Vol. 2	1967	3.75	7.50	15.00
—Red and while "Starline" label					
❏ DT 2706 [P]	Best of the Beach Boys, Vol. 2	1970	3.00	6.00	12.00
—Green "Starline" label					
❏ DT 2706 [P]	Best of the Beach Boys, Vol. 2	1973	2.50	5.00	10.00
—Orange label, "Capitol" on bottom					
❏ DT 2706 [P]	Best of the Beach Boys, Vol. 2	1978	2.50	5.00	10.00
—Purple label, large Capitol logo					
❏ T 2706 [M]	Best of the Beach Boys, Vol. 2	1967	6.25	12.50	25.00
❏ DTCL 2813 [(3)R]	The Beach Boys Deluxe Set	1967	12.50	25.00	50.00
—Maroon border on box; custom pressings of LPs with "DTCL" prefixes					
❏ DTCL-8-2813 [(3)R]	The Beach Boys Deluxe Set	1967	37.50	75.00	150.00
—Capitol Record Club edition; blue border on box; custom pressings of LPs with "DTCL" prefixes					
❏ TCL 2813 [(3)M]	The Beach Boys Deluxe Set	1967	62.50	125.00	250.00
—Black border on box; albums have "T" prefixes					
❏ ST 2859 [S]	Wild Honey	1967	5.00	10.00	20.00
❏ T 2859 [M]	Wild Honey	1967	10.00	20.00	40.00
❏ ST-8-2891 [R]	Smiley Smile	1968	75.00	150.00	300.00
—Capitol Record Club edition					
❏ DKAO 2893	Stack-o-Tracks	1968	12.50	25.00	50.00
—Without sheet music booklet					
❏ DKAO 2893	Stack-o-Tracks	1968	25.00	50.00	100.00
—With sheet music booklet					
❏ DKAO-8-2893	Stack-o-Tracks	1968	50.00	100.00	200.00
—Capitol Record Club edition					
❏ ST 2895	Friends	1968	6.25	12.50	25.00
❏ DKAO 2945 [P]	The Best of the Beach Boys, Vol. 3	1968	3.75	7.50	15.00
—Black label with colorband					
❏ DKAO 2945 [P]	The Best of the Beach Boys, Vol. 3	1969	5.00	10.00	20.00
—"Starline" label					
❏ PRO 3133 [DJ]	Silver Platter Service from Hollywood: The Beach Boys Christmas Special	1964	50.00	100.00	200.00
❏ SY-4572 [R]	Surfin' Safari	197?	3.00	6.00	12.00
—Orange label, Capitol logo at bottom; reissue of DT-1808 with completely different back cover and the words "... A Collector's Item ... Special Collections of Classic Hit Recordings by the Brightest Stars ..."					
❏ SVBB-11307 [(2)]	Endless Summer	1974	5.00	10.00	20.00
—Orange labels, "Capitol" on bottom; with poster					
❏ SVBB-11307 [(2)]	Endless Summer	1978	3.75	7.50	15.00
—Purple labels, large Capitol logo					
❏ SVBB-11307 [(2)]	Endless Summer	1983	3.00	6.00	12.00
—Black labels, print in colorband					
❏ SVBB-11307 [(2)]	Endless Summer	1988	3.00	6.00	12.00
—Purple labels, small Capitol logo					
❏ SVBB-11384 [(2)]	Spirit of America	1975	3.75	7.50	15.00
—Orange labels, "Capitol" on bottom					
❏ SVBB-11384 [(2)]	Spirit of America	1978	3.00	6.00	12.00
—Purple labels, large Capitol logo					
❏ SVBB-11384 [(2)]	Spirit of America	1983	2.50	5.00	10.00
—Black labels, print in colorband					
❏ SVBB-11384 [(2)]	Spirit of America	1988	2.50	5.00	10.00
—Purple labels, small Capitol logo					
❏ ST-11584	Beach Boys '69 (The Beach Boys Live in London)	1976	3.00	6.00	12.00
❏ SN-12011	Beach Boys '69 (The Beach Boys Live in London)	1979	2.50	5.00	10.00
❏ SVBB-12220 [(2)]	Sunshine Dream	1982	3.00	6.00	12.00
❏ ST-12293	Rarities	1983	3.75	7.50	15.00
❏ STBK-12396 [(2)]	Made in U.S.A.	1986	3.00	6.00	12.00
❏ N-16012 [M]	Surfin' Safari	1980	2.00	4.00	8.00
❏ SN-16013 [S]	Little Deuce Coupe	1980	2.00	4.00	8.00
❏ SN-16014 [S]	Surfer Girl	1980	2.00	4.00	8.00
❏ SN-16015 [S]	Surfin' U.S.A.	1980	2.00	4.00	8.00
❏ SN-16016 [S]	All Summer Long	1980	2.00	4.00	8.00
❏ DN-16017 [R]	California Girls	1980	2.00	4.00	8.00
❏ SN-16018 [P]	Fun, Fun, Fun	1980	2.00	4.00	8.00
—Reissue of "Shut Down, Vol. 2"					
❏ DN-16019 [R]	Dance, Dance, Dance	1981	2.00	4.00	8.00
❏ SN-16134	Beach Boys '69 (The Beach Boys Live in London)	1981	2.00	4.00	8.00
❏ SN-16156 [M]	Pet Sounds	1981	2.00	4.00	8.00
❏ SN-16157	Friends	1981	2.00	4.00	8.00
❏ SN-16158 [M]	Smiley Smile	1981	2.00	4.00	8.00
❏ SN-16159 [S]	Wild Honey	1981	2.00	4.00	8.00
❏ DN-16272 [R]	Beach Boys Party!	1982	2.00	4.00	8.00
❏ N-16273	Be True to Your School	1983	2.00	4.00	8.00
❏ DN-16318 [R]	Best of the Beach Boys, Vol. 2	1984	2.00	4.00	8.00
❏ C1-21241 [S]	Pet Sounds	1999	3.75	7.50	15.00
—True stereo version on heavyweight vinyl					
❏ C1-29628 [S]	Surfer Girl	1994	3.75	7.50	15.00
❏ C1-29629 [M]	Shut Down, Volume 2	1994	3.75	7.50	15.00
❏ C1-29630 [S]	Little Deuce Coupe	1994	3.75	7.50	15.00
❏ C1-29631 [S]	All Summer Long	1994	3.75	7.50	15.00
❏ C1-29632 [M]	The Beach Boys Today!	1994	3.75	7.50	15.00
❏ C1-29633 [M]	Summer Days (And Summer Nights!!)	1994	3.75	7.50	15.00
❏ C1-29634	Beach Boys '69 (The Beach Boys Live in London)	1994	3.75	7.50	15.00
❏ C1-29635 [M]	Smiley Smile	1994	3.75	7.50	15.00
❏ C1-29636 [S]	Wild Honey	1994	3.75	7.50	15.00
❏ C1-29637	Friends	1994	3.75	7.50	15.00
❏ C1-29638	20/20	1994	3.75	7.50	15.00
❏ C1-29640 [M]	Beach Boys Party!	1994	3.75	7.50	15.00
❏ C1-29641	Stack-o-Tracks	1994	3.75	7.50	15.00
❏ C1-29661 [M]	Surfin' Safari	1994	3.75	7.50	15.00
❏ C1-48421 [M]	Pet Sounds	1994	3.75	7.50	15.00
❏ C1-48422 [S]	Surfin' U.S.A.	1994	3.75	7.50	15.00
❏ C1-90427	Beach Boys Concert	1994	3.75	7.50	15.00
❏ C1-91318 [R]	Best of the Beach Boys	1988	3.00	6.00	12.00
—Purple label, small Capitol logo					
❏ C1-92639	Still Cruisin'	1989	3.00	6.00	12.00
❏ R 123946	Best of the Beach Boys	197?	3.75	7.50	15.00
—RCA Music Service edition					
❏ R 133854	The Beach Boys' Christmas Album	197?	3.75	7.50	15.00
—RCA Music Service edition					
❏ R 223559 [(2)]	Endless Summer	197?	6.25	12.50	25.00
—RCA Music Service edition					
❏ R 233593 [(2)]	American Summer	1975	6.25	12.50	25.00
—RCA Music Service exclusive					
❏ SF-500501	All Summer Long	1971	2.50	5.00	10.00
—Columbia Record Club edition					
❏ SF-500502	California Girls	1971	2.50	5.00	10.00
—Columbia Record Club edition					
❏ DT-502545 [P]	Best of the Beach Boys	197?	3.75	7.50	15.00
—Columbia Record Club edition					
❏ DT-502706 [P]	Best of the Beach Boys, Vol. 2	197?	3.75	7.50	15.00
—Columbia Record Club edition					
❏ SVBB-511307 [(2)]	Endless Summer	197?	6.25	12.50	25.00
—Columbia Record Club edition					
❏ SVBB-511384 [(2)]	Spirit of America	1975	5.00	10.00	20.00
—Columbia Record Club edition					

CAPITOL SPECIAL MARKETS

Number	Title (A Side/B Side)	Yr	VG	VG+	NM
❏ SLB-6994 [(2)]	Golden Years of the Beach Boys	1975	5.00	10.00	20.00
❏ SL-8114	Beach Boys Super Hits	1978	2.50	5.00	10.00
❏ SLB-8134 [(2)]	The Beach Boys	1980	5.00	10.00	20.00
❏ SL-9431	Good Vibrations from the Beach Boys	1986	3.75	7.50	15.00
—Special issue for Sunkist					

CARIBOU

Number	Title (A Side/B Side)	Yr	VG	VG+	NM
❏ JZ 35752	L.A. (Light Album)	1979	2.50	5.00	10.00
❏ JZ 35752 [DJ]	L.A. (Light Album)	1979	3.75	7.50	15.00
—White label promo					
❏ PZ 35752	L.A. (Light Album)	1980	2.00	4.00	8.00
—Budget-line reissue					
❏ FZ 36283	Keepin' the Summer Alive	1980	2.50	5.00	10.00
❏ FZ 36283 [DJ]	Keepin' the Summer Alive	1980	3.75	7.50	15.00
—White label promo					
❏ Z2X 37445 [(2)]	Ten Years of Harmony (1970-1980)	1981	3.00	6.00	12.00
❏ BFZ 39946	The Beach Boys	1985	2.50	5.00	10.00
❏ PZ 39946	The Beach Boys	1988	2.00	4.00	8.00
—Budget-line reissue					

DCC COMPACT CLASSICS

Number	Title (A Side/B Side)	Yr	VG	VG+	NM
❏ LPZ-2006 [M]	Pet Sounds	1995	30.00	60.00	120.00
—Audiophile vinyl					

ERA

Number	Title (A Side/B Side)	Yr	VG	VG+	NM
❏ HTE-805 [M]	The Beach Boys' Biggest Beach Hits	1969	3.75	7.50	15.00
—Also contains non-Beach Boys filler					

EVEREST

Number	Title (A Side/B Side)	Yr	VG	VG+	NM
❏ 4108 [M]	Rare Early Recordings	1981	2.00	4.00	8.00

GATEWAY

Number	Title (A Side/B Side)	Yr	VG	VG+	NM
❏ GSLP-10104 [M]	Surfing with the Beach Boys, the Marketts and the Frogmen	1979	2.00	4.00	8.00

MOBILE FIDELITY

Number	Title (A Side/B Side)	Yr	VG	VG+	NM
❏ 1-116	Surfer Girl	1984	7.50	15.00	30.00
—Audiophile vinyl					

ORBIT

Number	Title (A Side/B Side)	Yr	VG	VG+	NM
❏ OR 688 [M]	The Beach Boys' Greatest Hits 1961-1963	1972	3.00	6.00	12.00
—Also contains non-Beach Boys filler					

PAIR

Number	Title (A Side/B Side)	Yr	VG	VG+	NM
❏ PDL2-1068 [(2)]	For All Seasons	1986	3.75	7.50	15.00
❏ PDL2-1084 [(2)]	Golden Harmonies	1986	3.75	7.50	15.00

PICKWICK

Number	Title (A Side/B Side)	Yr	VG	VG+	NM
❏ PTP-2059 [(2)]	High Water	1973	3.00	6.00	12.00
❏ SPC-3221	Summertime Blues	1970	2.50	5.00	10.00
❏ SPC-3269	Good Vibrations	1971	2.50	5.00	10.00
❏ SPC-3309	Wow! Great Concert!	1972	2.50	5.00	10.00
❏ SPC-3351	Surfer Girl	1973	2.50	5.00	10.00
❏ SPC-3562	Little Deuce Coupe	1975	2.50	5.00	10.00

READER'S DIGEST

Number	Title (A Side/B Side)	Yr	VG	VG+	NM
❏ RBA-178 [(4)]	Their Greatest Hits and Finest Performances	1989	12.50	25.00	50.00
—Box set					

SCEPTER

Number	Title (A Side/B Side)	Yr	VG	VG+	NM
❏ CTN-18004 [M]	The Best of the Beach Boys (1961-1963)	1972	3.00	6.00	12.00
—Also contains non-Beach Boys filler					

SEARS

Number	Title (A Side/B Side)	Yr	VG	VG+	NM
❏ SPS-609	Summertime Blues	1970	12.50	25.00	50.00

SPRINGBOARD

Number	Title (A Side/B Side)	Yr	VG	VG+	NM
❏ SPB-4021 [M]	The Beach Boys 1961	1977	2.00	4.00	8.00
—Also contains non-Beach Boys filler					

SUNDAZED

Number	Title (A Side/B Side)	Yr	VG	VG+	NM
❏ LP 5005 [B]	Lost & Found!	1991	3.00	6.00	12.00
—Colored vinyl (red, yellow and light blue are known); first LP issue of the 1961 sessions from the master tapes; three tracks are stereo					

TIME-LIFE

Number	Title (A Side/B Side)	Yr	VG	VG+	NM
❏ SRNR-03 [(2)]	The Beach Boys: 1963-1967	1986	3.75	7.50	15.00
—2 LPs in box with fold-open liner notes; second cover has a portrait of the Beach Boys					
❏ SRNR-03 [(2)]	The Beach Boys: 1963-1967	1986	6.25	12.50	25.00
—2 LPs in box with fold-open liner notes; original cover portrays the Beach Boys surfing					

WAND

Number	Title (A Side/B Side)	Yr	VG	VG+	NM
❏ WDS-688 [M]	The Beach Boys' Greatest Hits 1961-1963	1972	3.00	6.00	12.00
—Also contains non-Beach Boys filler					

Number	Title (A Side/B Side)	Yr	VG	VG+	NM

BEACH BOYS, THE (2) No relation to the group that became famous.
45s
KAPP
| ❏ 289 | Bathing Beauty/On the Beach at Sunset | 1959 | 6.25 | 12.50 | 25.00 |

BEACH BUMS, THE Early BOB SEGER.
45s
ARE YOU KIDDING ME?
| ❏ 1010 | Florida Time/The Ballad of the Yellow Beret | 1966 | 15.00 | 30.00 | 60.00 |
—B-side credited to "D. Dodger"

BEACH GIRLS, THE
45s
DYNO VOX
| ❏ 202 | Goin' Places/Skiing in the Snow | 1965 | 6.25 | 12.50 | 25.00 |
VAULT
| ❏ 905 | He's My Surfin' Guy/Bobby's the Boy | 1963 | 7.50 | 15.00 | 30.00 |

BEACH NUTS, THE
45s
BANG
| ❏ 504 | Out in the Sun (Hey-O)/Someday Soon | 1965 | 12.50 | 25.00 | 50.00 |
CORONADO
| ❏ 131 | Surf Ride '65/The Last Ride | 1965 | 12.50 | 25.00 | 50.00 |
| ❏ 131 [PS] | Surf Ride '65/The Last Ride | 1965 | 15.00 | 30.00 | 60.00 |

BEACON STREET UNION, THE
45s
MGM
❏ 13865	South End Incident/Speed Kills	1967	2.50	5.00	10.00
❏ 13935	Blue Suede Shoes/Four Hundred and Five	1968	2.50	5.00	10.00
❏ 14012	May I Light Your Cigarette/Mayola	1968	2.50	5.00	10.00
Albums
MGM
❏ E-4517 [M]	The Eyes of the Beacon Street Union	1967	7.50	15.00	30.00
❏ SE-4517 [S]	The Eyes of the Beacon Street Union	1967	6.25	12.50	25.00
❏ E-4568 [M]	The Clown Died in Marvin Gardens	1968	12.50	25.00	50.00
—May be promo only (yellow label)
| ❏ SE-4568 [S] | The Clown Died in Marvin Gardens | 1968 | 6.25 | 12.50 | 25.00 |

BEAGLES, THE
45s
ERA
| ❏ 3132 | Let's All Sing Like the Birdies Sing/Deep in the Heart of Texas | 1964 | 3.75 | 7.50 | 15.00 |
| ❏ 3132 [PS] | Let's All Sing Like the Birdies Sing/Deep in the Heart of Texas | 1964 | 6.25 | 12.50 | 25.00 |
HIT
| ❏ 113 | Can't Buy Me Love/White on White | 1964 | 3.00 | 6.00 | 12.00 |
—B-side by Fred York

BEALE STREET BOYS, THE
45s
OBA
| ❏ 101 | Next Christmas/There's Nothing Greater Than A Prayer | 1960 | 15.00 | 30.00 | 60.00 |

BEAN, YOUNG BILLY See BILLY BURNETTE.

BEANS
45s
AVALANCHE
| ❏ 36011 | Bleecker Street Rain/Honky Tonk Refrigerator | 1972 | 2.00 | 4.00 | 8.00 |
Albums
AVALANCHE
| ❏ 9200 | Beans | 1971 | 5.00 | 10.00 | 20.00 |

BEAR, EDWARD See EDWARD BEAR under "E" — it's a group, not a person.

BEARD, DEAN
45s
ATLANTIC
❏ 1137	On My Mind Again/Rakin' and Scrapin'	1957	10.00	20.00	40.00
❏ 1162	Party Party/Stand By Me	1957	10.00	20.00	40.00
❏ 1182	Take Time to Love Me/Hold Me Close	1958	7.50	15.00	30.00
CANDIX
❏ 341	The Day That I Lost You/Villa Acuna	1962	3.00	6.00	12.00
CHALLENGE
❏ 59033	Egad, Charlie Brown/Keeper of the Key	1958	6.25	12.50	25.00
❏ 59048	Holding On to a Memory/Little Lover	1959	6.25	12.50	25.00
EDMORAL
❏ 1011	On My Mind Again/Rakin' and Scrapin'	1956	37.50	75.00	150.00
JOED
❏ 715	Coffee Break/Tropical Nights	1962	6.25	12.50	25.00
SIMS
❏ 299	(Are There) Honkytonks in Heaven/Pocketful of Stardust	1966	2.50	5.00	10.00
WINSTON
❏ 1063	I Don't Know How/The Red Rose	1962	3.00	6.00	12.00
❏ 1073	Don't Let the Stars Get In Your Eyes/That's How It Gets Sun Up	1963	3.00	6.00	12.00
❏ 1075	Smile Pretty for Me Temper/To Me	1963	3.00	6.00	12.00
—With Bill Graham

BEARFOOT
45s
EPIC
| ❏ 11018 | Right On/Mark Twain | 1973 | — | 2.50 | 5.00 |
Albums
EPIC
| ❏ KE 32146 | Bearfoot | 1973 | 3.00 | 6.00 | 12.00 |

BEASLEY, JIMMY
45s
MODERN
❏ 991	Ella Jane/No Love for Me	1956	6.25	12.50	25.00
❏ 996	Don't Feel Sorry for Me/Little Coquette	1956	6.25	12.50	25.00
❏ 1009	My Happiness/Jambalaya	1956	6.25	12.50	25.00
❏ 1014	Near You/I'm So Blue	1956	6.25	12.50	25.00
❏ 1018	Thinking of You/You Were Fooling	1956	6.25	12.50	25.00
❏ 1021	Johnny's House Party (Part 1)/Johnny's House Party (Part 2)	1957	6.25	12.50	25.00
❏ 1023	I Want My Baby/We Three	1957	6.25	12.50	25.00

BEAST
45s
EVOLUTION
| ❏ 1028 | Communication/Move Mountain | 1970 | — | 3.00 | 6.00 |
Albums
COTILLION
| ❏ SD 9012 | Beast | 1969 | 3.75 | 7.50 | 15.00 |
EVOLUTION
| ❏ 2017 | Beast | 1970 | 3.75 | 7.50 | 15.00 |

BEASTS, THE
45s
HIT
| ❏ 159 | Sha La La/Where You Been | 1964 | 3.75 | 7.50 | 15.00 |
—B-side by Charles Baker

BEAT BROTHERS, THE
45s
MGM
| ❏ 13201 | Nick Nack Hully Gully/Lantern Hully Gully | 1963 | 4.00 | 8.00 | 16.00 |

BEAT MERCHANTS, THE
45s
TOWER
| ❏ 127 | So Fine/You Were Made for Me | 1965 | 3.75 | 7.50 | 15.00 |
—B-side by Freddie and the Dreamers

BEAT OF THE EARTH, THE
Albums
ARDISH
| ❏ AS-001 | The Beat of the Earth | 1968 | 75.00 | 150.00 | 300.00 |
| ❏ AS-0001 | The Beat of the Earth | 1968 | 100.00 | 200.00 | 400.00 |

BEATIN' PATH, THE
45s
FONTANA
| ❏ 1583 | The Original Nothing People/I Waited So Long | 1967 | 5.00 | 10.00 | 20.00 |

BEATLE BUDDIES, THE
Albums
DIPLOMAT
| ❏ D-2313 [M] | The Beatle Buddies | 1964 | 3.75 | 7.50 | 15.00 |
| ❏ DS-2313 [S] | The Beatle Buddies | 1964 | 5.00 | 10.00 | 20.00 |

BEATLE-ETTES, THE
45s
ASSAULT
| ❏ 1893 | Yes, You Can Hold My Hand/Yes, You Can Hold My Hand (Part 2) | 1964 | 5.00 | 10.00 | 20.00 |
JAMIE
| ❏ 1270 | Dance, Beatle, Dance/We Were Meant to Be Married | 1964 | 5.00 | 10.00 | 20.00 |
JUBILEE
| ❏ 5472 | Only Seventeen/Now We're Together | 1964 | 5.00 | 10.00 | 20.00 |

BEATLES, THE Also see PETE BEST; GEORGE HARRISON; JOHN LENNON; PAUL McCARTNEY; RINGO STARR.
12-Inch Singles
(NO LABEL)
| ❏ (no #) [DJ] | Merry Christmas and Happy New Year | 1965 | 125.00 | 250.00 | 500.00 |
—Promo item from KYA Radio, San Francisco; B-side is blank
45s
(NO LABEL)
| ❏ MBRF-55551 | Decade | 1974 | — | — | — |
—A clever bootleg of radio spots for the Beatles' back catalog, compiled without authorization by two former Capitol employees.
APPLE
| ❏ Promo-1970 [DJ] | Dialogue from the Beatles' Motion Picture "Let It Be" | 1970 | 15.00 | 30.00 | 60.00 |
| ❏ 2056 | Hello Goodbye/I Am the Walrus | 1971 | 2.50 | 5.00 | 10.00 |
—Without star on A-side label
| ❏ 2056 | Hello Goodbye/I Am the Walrus | 1971 | 7.50 | 15.00 | 30.00 |
—With star on A-side label
| ❏ 2056 | Hello Goodbye/I Am the Walrus | 1975 | 5.00 | 10.00 | 20.00 |
—With "All Rights Reserved" disclaimer
| ❏ 2138 | Lady Madonna/The Inner Light | 1971 | 2.50 | 5.00 | 10.00 |
—Without star on A-side label
| ❏ 2138 | Lady Madonna/The Inner Light | 1971 | 7.50 | 15.00 | 30.00 |
—With star on A-side label
| ❏ 2138 | Lady Madonna/The Inner Light | 1975 | 5.00 | 10.00 | 20.00 |
—With "All Rights Reserved" disclaimer
| ❏ 2276 | Hey Jude/Revolution | 1968 | 2.50 | 5.00 | 10.00 |
—With "Mfd. by Apple" on label
| ❏ 2276 | Hey Jude/Revolution | 1968 | 3.75 | 7.50 | 15.00 |
—Original: With small Capitol logo on bottom of B-side label
| ❏ 2276 | Hey Jude/Revolution | 1975 | 5.00 | 10.00 | 20.00 |
—With "All Rights Reserved" disclaimer
| ❏ 2490 | Get Back/Don't Let Me Down | 1969 | 2.50 | 5.00 | 10.00 |
—With "Mfd. by Apple" on label
| ❏ 2490 | Get Back/Don't Let Me Down | 1969 | 2.50 | 5.00 | 10.00 |
—Original: With small Capitol logo on bottom of B-side label

Number	Title (A Side/B Side)	Yr	VG	VG+	NM
❑ 2490	Get Back/Don't Let Me Down	1975	5.00	10.00	20.00

—With "All Rights Reserved" disclaimer

Number	Title (A Side/B Side)	Yr	VG	VG+	NM
❑ 2531	The Ballad of John and Yoko/Old Brown Shoe	1969	2.50	5.00	10.00

—With "Mfd. by Apple" on label

| ❑ 2531 | The Ballad of John and Yoko/Old Brown Shoe | 1969 | 2.50 | 5.00 | 10.00 |

—Original: With small Capitol logo on bottom of B-side label

| ❑ 2531 [PS] | The Ballad of John and Yoko/Old Brown Shoe | 1969 | 25.00 | 50.00 | 100.00 |
| ❑ 2531 | The Ballad of John and Yoko/Old Brown Shoe | 1975 | 5.00 | 10.00 | 20.00 |

—With "All Rights Reserved" disclaimer

| ❑ 2654 | Something/Come Together | 1969 | 2.50 | 5.00 | 10.00 |

—With "Mfd. by Apple" on label

| ❑ 2654 | Something/Come Together | 1969 | 25.00 | 50.00 | 100.00 |

—Original: With small Capitol logo on bottom of B-side label

| ❑ 2654 | Something/Come Together | 1975 | 5.00 | 10.00 | 20.00 |

—With "All Rights Reserved" disclaimer

| ❑ 2764 | Let It Be/You Know My Name (Look Up My Number) | 1970 | 2.50 | 5.00 | 10.00 |

—With "Mfd. by Apple" on label

| ❑ 2764 | Let It Be/You Know My Name (Look Up My Number) | 1970 | 3.00 | 6.00 | 12.00 |

—Original: With small Capitol logo on bottom of B-side label

| ❑ 2764 [PS] | Let It Be/You Know My Name (Look Up the Number) | 1970 | 25.00 | 50.00 | 100.00 |
| ❑ 2764 | Let It Be/You Know My Name (Look Up My Number) | 1975 | 5.00 | 10.00 | 20.00 |

—With "All Rights Reserved" disclaimer

| ❑ 2832 | The Long and Winding Road/For You Blue | 1970 | 2.50 | 5.00 | 10.00 |

—With "Mfd. by Apple" on label

| ❑ 2832 | The Long and Winding Road/For You Blue | 1970 | 5.00 | 10.00 | 20.00 |

—Original: With small Capitol logo on bottom of B-side label

| ❑ 2832 [PS] | The Long and Winding Road/For You Blue | 1970 | 25.00 | 50.00 | 100.00 |
| ❑ 2832 | The Long and Winding Road/For You Blue | 1975 | 5.00 | 10.00 | 20.00 |

—With "All Rights Reserved" disclaimer

| ❑ 5112 | I Want to Hold Your Hand/I Saw Her Standing There | 1971 | 2.50 | 5.00 | 10.00 |

—Without star on label

| ❑ 5112 | I Want to Hold Your Hand/I Saw Her Standing There | 1971 | 7.50 | 15.00 | 30.00 |

—With star on label

| ❑ 5112 | I Want to Hold Your Hand/I Saw Her Standing There | 1975 | 5.00 | 10.00 | 20.00 |

—With "All Rights Reserved" disclaimer on label

| ❑ 5150 | Can't Buy Me Love/You Can't Do That | 1971 | 2.50 | 5.00 | 10.00 |

—Without star on A-side label

| ❑ 5150 | Can't Buy Me Love/You Can't Do That | 1971 | 7.50 | 15.00 | 30.00 |

—With star on A-side label

| ❑ 5150 | Can't Buy Me Love/You Can't Do That | 1975 | 3.75 | 7.50 | 15.00 |

—With "All Rights Reserved" disclaimer

| ❑ 5222 | A Hard Day's Night/I Should Have Known Better | 1971 | 2.50 | 5.00 | 10.00 |

—Without star on A-side label

| ❑ 5222 | A Hard Day's Night/I Should Have Known Better | 1971 | 7.50 | 15.00 | 30.00 |

—With star on A-side label

| ❑ 5222 | A Hard Day's Night/I Should Have Known Better | 1975 | 3.75 | 7.50 | 15.00 |

—With "All Rights Reserved" disclaimer

| ❑ 5234 | I'll Cry Instead/I'm Happy Just to Dance with You | 1971 | 2.50 | 5.00 | 10.00 |

—Without star on A-side label

| ❑ 5234 | I'll Cry Instead/I'm Happy Just to Dance with You | 1971 | 7.50 | 15.00 | 30.00 |

—With star on A-side label

| ❑ 5234 | I'll Cry Instead/I'm Happy Just to Dance with You | 1975 | 3.75 | 7.50 | 15.00 |

—With "All Rights Reserved" disclaimer

| ❑ 5235 | And I Love Her/If I Fell | 1971 | 2.50 | 5.00 | 10.00 |

—Without star on A-side label

| ❑ 5235 | And I Love Her/If I Fell | 1971 | 7.50 | 15.00 | 30.00 |

—With star on A-side label

| ❑ 5235 | And I Love Her/If I Fell | 1975 | 3.75 | 7.50 | 15.00 |

—With "All Rights Reserved" disclaimer

| ❑ 5255 | Matchbox/Slow Down | 1971 | 2.50 | 5.00 | 10.00 |

—Without star on A-side label

| ❑ 5255 | Matchbox/Slow Down | 1971 | 7.50 | 15.00 | 30.00 |

—With star on A-side label

| ❑ 5255 | Matchbox/Slow Down | 1975 | 3.75 | 7.50 | 15.00 |

—With "All Rights Reserved" disclaimer

| ❑ 5327 | I Feel Fine/She's a Woman | 1971 | 2.50 | 5.00 | 10.00 |

—Without star on A-side label

| ❑ 5327 | I Feel Fine/She's a Woman | 1971 | 7.50 | 15.00 | 30.00 |

—With star on A-side label

| ❑ 5327 | I Feel Fine/She's a Woman | 1975 | 3.75 | 7.50 | 15.00 |

—With "All Rights Reserved" disclaimer

| ❑ 5371 | Eight Days a Week/I Don't Want to Spoil the Party | 1971 | 2.50 | 5.00 | 10.00 |

—Without star on A-side label

| ❑ 5371 | Eight Days a Week/I Don't Want to Spoil the Party | 1971 | 7.50 | 15.00 | 30.00 |

—With star on A-side label

| ❑ 5371 | Eight Days a Week/I Don't Want to Spoil the Party | 1975 | 3.75 | 7.50 | 15.00 |

—With "All Rights Reserved" disclaimer

| ❑ 5407 | Ticket to Ride/Yes It Is | 1971 | 2.50 | 5.00 | 10.00 |

—Without star on A-side label

| ❑ 5407 | Ticket to Ride/Yes It Is | 1971 | 7.50 | 15.00 | 30.00 |

—With star on A-side label

| ❑ 5407 | Ticket to Ride/Yes It Is | 1975 | 3.75 | 7.50 | 15.00 |

—With "All Rights Reserved" disclaimer

| ❑ 5476 | Help!/I'm Down | 1971 | 2.50 | 5.00 | 10.00 |

—Without star on A-side label

| ❑ 5476 | Help!/I'm Down | 1971 | 7.50 | 15.00 | 30.00 |

—With star on A-side label

| ❑ 5476 | Help!/I'm Down | 1975 | 3.75 | 7.50 | 15.00 |

—With "All Rights Reserved" disclaimer

| ❑ 5498 | Yesterday/Act Naturally | 1971 | 2.50 | 5.00 | 10.00 |

—Without star on A-side label

| ❑ 5498 | Yesterday/Act Naturally | 1971 | 7.50 | 15.00 | 30.00 |

—With star on A-side label

Number	Title (A Side/B Side)	Yr	VG	VG+	NM
❑ 5498	Yesterday/Act Naturally	1975	3.75	7.50	15.00

—With "All Rights Reserved" disclaimer

| ❑ 5555 | We Can Work It Out/Day Tripper | 1971 | 2.50 | 5.00 | 10.00 |

—Without star on A-side label

| ❑ 5555 | We Can Work It Out/Day Tripper | 1971 | 7.50 | 15.00 | 30.00 |

—With star on A-side label

| ❑ 5555 | We Can Work It Out/Day Tripper | 1975 | 3.75 | 7.50 | 15.00 |

—With "All Rights Reserved" disclaimer

| ❑ 5587 | Nowhere Man/What Goes On | 1971 | 2.50 | 5.00 | 10.00 |

—Without star on A-side label

| ❑ 5587 | Nowhere Man/What Goes On | 1971 | 7.50 | 15.00 | 30.00 |

—With star on A-side label

| ❑ 5587 | Nowhere Man/What Goes On | 1975 | 3.75 | 7.50 | 15.00 |

—With "All Rights Reserved" disclaimer

| ❑ 5651 | Paperback Writer/Rain | 1971 | 2.50 | 5.00 | 10.00 |

—Without star on A-side label

| ❑ 5651 | Paperback Writer/Rain | 1971 | 7.50 | 15.00 | 30.00 |

—With star on A-side label

| ❑ 5651 | Paperback Writer/Rain | 1975 | 3.75 | 7.50 | 15.00 |

—With "All Rights Reserved" disclaimer

| ❑ 5715 | Yellow Submarine/Eleanor Rigby | 1971 | 2.50 | 5.00 | 10.00 |

—Without star on A-side label

| ❑ 5715 | Yellow Submarine/Eleanor Rigby | 1971 | 7.50 | 15.00 | 30.00 |

—With star on A-side label

| ❑ 5715 | Yellow Submarine/Eleanor Rigby | 1975 | 3.75 | 7.50 | 15.00 |

—With "All Rights Reserved" disclaimer

| ❑ 5810 | Penny Lane/Strawberry Fields Forever | 1971 | 2.50 | 5.00 | 10.00 |

—Without star on A-side label

| ❑ 5810 | Penny Lane/Strawberry Fields Forever | 1971 | 7.50 | 15.00 | 30.00 |

—With star on A-side label

| ❑ 5810 | Penny Lane/Strawberry Fields Forever | 1975 | 3.75 | 7.50 | 15.00 |

—With "All Rights Reserved" disclaimer

| ❑ 5964 | All You Need Is Love/Baby, You're a Rich Man | 1971 | 2.50 | 5.00 | 10.00 |

—Without star on A-side label

| ❑ 5964 | All You Need Is Love/Baby, You're a Rich Man | 1971 | 7.50 | 15.00 | 30.00 |

—With star on A-side label

| ❑ 5964 | All You Need Is Love/Baby, You're a Rich Man | 1975 | 3.75 | 7.50 | 15.00 |

—With "All Rights Reserved" disclaimer

| ❑ 58348 | Baby It's You/I'll Follow the Sun//Devil in Her Heart/Boys | 1995 | — | 2.00 | 4.00 |

—All 4 tracks from BBC sessions

| ❑ 58348 [PS] | Baby It's You/I'll Follow the Sun//Devil in Her Heart/Boys | 1995 | — | 2.00 | 4.00 |
| ❑ 58497 | Free as a Bird/Christmas Time (Is Here Again) | 1995 | — | 2.00 | 4.00 |

—Small center hole; all with large hole were "dinked" somewhere other than when manufactured and have little, if any, value

| ❑ 58497 [PS] | Free as a Bird/Christmas Time (Is Here Again) | 1995 | — | 2.00 | 4.00 |
| ❑ 58544 | Real Love/Baby's in Black (Live) | 1996 | — | — | 3.00 |

—Small center hole; all with large hole were "dinked" somewhere other than when manufactured and have little, if any, value

| ❑ 58544 [PS] | Real Love/Baby's in Black (Live) | 1996 | — | — | 3.00 |

APPLE/AMERICOM

| ❑ 2276/M-221 | Hey Jude/Revolution | 1969 | 75.00 | 150.00 | 300.00 |

—Four-inch flexi-disc sold in vending machines; "Hey Jude" is edited to 3:25

| ❑ 2490/M-335 | Get Back/Don't Let Me Down | 1969 | 250.00 | 500.00 | 1000. |

—Four-inch flexi-disc sold in vending machines

| ❑ 2531/M-382 | The Ballad of John and Yoko/Old Brown Shoe | 1969 | 200.00 | 400.00 | 800.00 |

—Four-inch flexi-disc sold in vending machines

| ❑ 5715 | Yellow Submarine/Eleanor Rigby | 1969 | 1000. | 1500. | 2000. |

—Four-inch flexi-disc sold in vending machines

ATCO

| ❑ 6302 | Sweet Georgia Brown/Take Out Some Insurance On Me Baby | 1964 | 50.00 | 100.00 | 200.00 |
| ❑ 6308 | Ain't She Sweet/Nobody's Child | 1964 | 12.50 | 25.00 | 50.00 |

—With "Vocal by John Lennon" on left of label

| ❑ 6308 | Ain't She Sweet/Nobody's Child | 1964 | 15.00 | 30.00 | 60.00 |

—With "Vocal by John Lennon" under "The Beatles"

| ❑ 6308 [PS] | Ain't She Sweet/Nobody's Child | 1964 | 125.00 | 250.00 | 500.00 |

—Sleeves with black and green print are reproductions

ATLANTIC

| ❑ OS-13243 | Ain't She Sweet/Sweet Georgia Brown | 1983 | 2.50 | 5.00 | 10.00 |

—"Oldies Series"

BACKSTAGE

| ❑ 1112 [DJ] | Like Dreamers Do/Love of the Loved | 1982 | 6.25 | 12.50 | 25.00 |

—Promotional 45 from "Oui" magazine

| ❑ 1122 [DJ] | Love of the Loved/Memphis | 1983 | 6.25 | 12.50 | 25.00 |

—Promotional picture disc

| ❑ 1133 [DJ] | Like Dreamers Do/Three Cool Cats | 1983 | 6.25 | 12.50 | 25.00 |

—Promotional picture disc

| ❑ 1155 [DJ] | Crying, Waiting, Hoping/Take Good Care of My Baby | 1983 | 6.25 | 12.50 | 25.00 |

BEATLES FAN CLUB

| ❑ (1964) | Season's Greetings from the Beatles | 1964 | 75.00 | 150.00 | 300.00 |

—Tri-fold soundcard

| ❑ (1965) | The Beatles Third Christmas Record | 1965 | 20.00 | 40.00 | 80.00 |

—Flexi-disc

| ❑ (1965) [PS] | The Beatles Third Christmas Record | 1965 | 25.00 | 50.00 | 100.00 |
| ❑ (1966) | Everywhere It's Christmas | 1966 | 37.50 | 75.00 | 150.00 |

—Postcard

| ❑ (1967) | Christmastime Is Here Again | 1967 | 37.50 | 75.00 | 150.00 |

—Postcard

| ❑ (1968) H-2041 | The Beatles 1968 Christmas Record | 1968 | 15.00 | 30.00 | 60.00 |

—Flexi-disc

| ❑ (1968) H-2041 [PS] | The Beatles 1968 Christmas Record | 1968 | 17.50 | 35.00 | 70.00 |
| ❑ (1969) H-2565 | Happy Christmas 1969 | 1969 | 10.00 | 20.00 | 40.00 |

—Flexi-disc

| ❑ (1969) H-2565 [PS] | Happy Christmas 1969 | 1969 | 15.00 | 30.00 | 60.00 |

CAPITOL

| ❑ 2056 | Hello Goodbye/I Am the Walrus | 1967 | 7.50 | 15.00 | 30.00 |

—Original: Orange and yellow swirl, without "A Subsidiary Of"... in perimeter label print; publishing credited to "Comet" (we're not sure which came first)

The Beatles, *Four by the Beatles,* Capitol EAP 1-2121, 7-inch EP, $200-$400 (cover and record together)

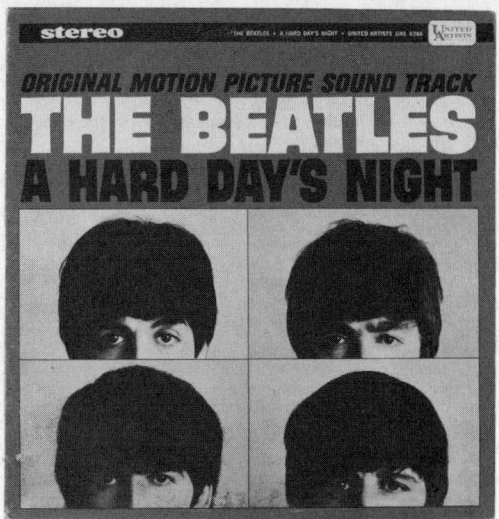

The Beatles, *A Hard Day's Night,* United Artists UAS 6366, stereo LP, original edition with black label and "I Cry Instead" listed on back cover, $100-$200.

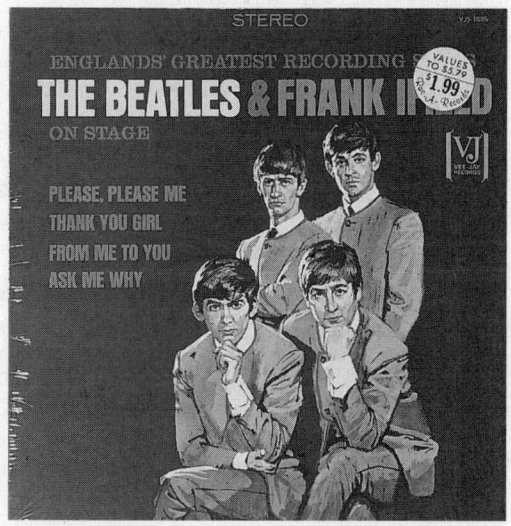

The Beatles, *The Beatles and Frank Ifield On Stage,* Vee Jay SR 1085, stereo LP, portrait of the Beatles on cover, $8,000-$12,000.

The Beatles, *Songs, Pictures and Stories of the Fabulous Beatles,* Vee Jay LP-1092, mono LP, $250-$500 (beware of counterfeits)

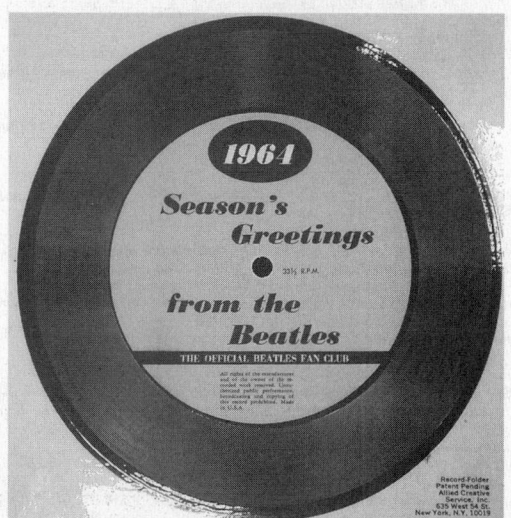

The Beatles, "Season's Greetings from the Beatles," 1964 fan club Christmas record, tri-fold soundcard, $150-$300.

The Beatles, *Yesterday and Today,* Capitol ST 2553, stereo LP with "Butcher Cover" that was never covered by a "Trunk Cover," $6,000-$8,000 and up.

Number	Title (A Side/B Side)	Yr	VG	VG+	NM
2056	Hello Goodbye/I Am the Walrus	1967	7.50	15.00	30.00

—Original: Orange and yellow swirl, without "A Subsidiary Of"... in perimeter label print; publishing credited to "Maclen" (we're not sure which came first)

Number	Title (A Side/B Side)	Yr	VG	VG+	NM
2056 [PS]	Hello Goodbye/I Am the Walrus	1967	25.00	50.00	100.00
2056	Hello Goodbye/I Am the Walrus	1968	12.50	25.00	50.00

—Orange and yellow swirl label with "A Subsidiary Of" in perimeter print

2056	Hello Goodbye/I Am the Walrus	1969	5.00	10.00	20.00

—Red and orange "target" label with Capitol round logo

2056	Hello Goodbye/I Am the Walrus	1969	15.00	30.00	60.00

—Red and orange "target" label with Capitol dome logo

2056	Hello Goodbye/I Am the Walrus	1976	—	3.00	6.00

—Orange label with "Capitol" at bottom

2056	Hello Goodbye/I Am the Walrus	1978	2.00	4.00	8.00

—Purple label; label has reeded edge

2056	Hello Goodbye/I Am the Walrus	1983	—	3.00	6.00

—Black label with colorband

2056	Hello Goodbye/I Am the Walrus	1988	—	2.50	5.00

—Purple label; label has smooth edge

P 2056 [DJ]	Hello Goodbye/I Am the Walrus	1967	62.50	125.00	250.00

—Light green label promo

2138	Lady Madonna/The Inner Light	1968	7.50	15.00	30.00

—Original: Orange and yellow swirl, without "A Subsidiary Of"... in perimeter label print

2138	Lady Madonna/The Inner Light	1968	12.50	25.00	50.00

—Orange and yellow swirl label with "A Subsidiary Of" in perimeter print

2138 [PS]	Lady Madonna/The Inner Light	1968	5.00	10.00	20.00

—"Beatles Fan Club" insert that was issued with above sleeve. Originals are glossy.

2138 [PS]	Lady Madonna/The Inner Light	1968	25.00	50.00	100.00
2138	Lady Madonna/The Inner Light	1969	5.00	10.00	20.00

—Red and orange "target" label with Capitol round logo

2138	Lady Madonna/The Inner Light	1969	15.00	30.00	60.00

—Red and orange "target" label with Capitol dome logo

2138	Lady Madonna/The Inner Light	1976	—	3.00	6.00

—Orange label with "Capitol" at bottom

2138	Lady Madonna/The Inner Light	1978	2.00	4.00	8.00

—Purple label; label has reeded edge

2138	Lady Madonna/The Inner Light	1983	—	3.00	6.00

—Black label with colorband

2138	Lady Madonna/The Inner Light	1988	—	2.50	5.00

—Purple label; label has smooth edge

P 2138 [DJ]	Lady Madonna/The Inner Light	1968	50.00	100.00	200.00

—Light green label promo

2276	Hey Jude/Revolution	1976	—	3.00	6.00

—Orange label with "Capitol" at bottom

2276	Hey Jude/Revolution	1978	2.00	4.00	8.00

—Purple label; label has reeded edge

2276	Hey Jude/Revolution	1983	—	3.00	6.00

—Black label with colorband

2276	Hey Jude/Revolution	1988	—	2.50	5.00

—Purple label; label has smooth edge

2490	Get Back/Don't Let Me Down	1976	—	3.00	6.00

—Orange label with "Capitol" at bottom

2490	Get Back/Don't Let Me Down	1978	2.00	4.00	8.00

—Purple label; label has reeded edge

2490	Get Back/Don't Let Me Down	1983	—	3.00	6.00

—Black label with colorband; "Get Back" replaced by LP version as on Let It Be

2490	Get Back/Don't Let Me Down	1988	—	2.50	5.00

—Purple label; label has smooth edge; "Get Back" replaced by LP version as on Let It Be

2531	The Ballad of John and Yoko/Old Brown Shoe	1976	—	—	—

—Orange label with "Capitol" at bottom; should exist, but not known to exist

2531	The Ballad of John and Yoko/Old Brown Shoe	1978	—	3.00	6.00

—Purple label; label has reeded edge

2531	The Ballad of John and Yoko/Old Brown Shoe	1983	—	3.50	7.00

—Black label with colorband

2531	The Ballad of John and Yoko/Old Brown Shoe	1988	—	3.00	6.00

—Purple label; label has smooth edge

2654	Something/Come Together	1976	—	3.00	6.00

—Orange label with "Capitol" at bottom

2654	Something/Come Together	1978	—	3.00	6.00

—Purple label; label has reeded edge

2654	Something/Come Together	1983	—	3.00	6.00

—Black label with colorband

2654	Something/Come Together	1988	—	2.50	5.00

—Purple label; label has smooth edge

2764	Let It Be/You Know My Name (Look Up My Number)	1976	—	3.00	6.00

—Orange label with "Capitol" at bottom

2764	Let It Be/You Know My Name (Look Up My Number)	1978	2.00	4.00	8.00

—Purple label; label has reeded edge

2764	Let It Be/You Know My Name (Look Up My Number)	1983	—	3.00	6.00

—Black label with colorband

2764	Let It Be/You Know My Name (Look Up My Number)	1988	—	2.50	5.00

—Purple label; label has smooth edge

2832	The Long and Winding Road/For You Blue	1976	—	3.00	6.00

—Orange label with "Capitol" at bottom

2832	The Long and Winding Road/For You Blue	1978	2.00	4.00	8.00

—Purple label; label has reeded edge

2832	The Long and Winding Road/For You Blue	1983	—	3.00	6.00

—Black label with colorband

2832	The Long and Winding Road/For You Blue	1988	—	2.50	5.00

—Purple label; label has smooth edge

4274	Got to Get You Into My Life/Helter Skelter	1976	—	3.00	6.00

—Original: Orange label with "Capitol" at bottom, George Martin's name not on label

4274	Got to Get You Into My Life/Helter Skelter	1976	2.50	5.00	10.00

—Orange label with "Capitol" at bottom, George Martin's name is on label

4274 [PS]	Got to Get You Into My Life/Helter Skelter	1976	—	2.50	5.00
4274	Got to Get You Into My Life/Helter Skelter	1978	—	3.00	6.00

—Purple label; label has reeded edge

4274	Got to Get You Into My Life/Helter Skelter	1983	—	3.00	6.00

—Black label with colorband

4274	Got to Get You Into My Life/Helter Skelter	1988	—	2.50	5.00

—Purple label; label has smooth edge

Number	Title (A Side/B Side)	Yr	VG	VG+	NM
P-4274 [DJ]	Got to Get You Into My Life (mono/stereo)	1976	10.00	20.00	40.00
P-4274 [DJ]	Helter Skelter (mono/stereo)	1976	10.00	20.00	40.00
4347	Ob-La-Di, Ob-La-Da/Julia	1976	2.00	4.00	8.00

—Original: Orange label with "Capitol" at bottom

4347 [PS]	Ob-La-Di, Ob-La-Da/Julia	1976	2.00	4.00	8.00

—Sleeves are individually numbered; very low numbers (under 1000) can fetch premium prices

4347	Ob-La-Di, Ob-La-Da/Julia	1978	2.00	4.00	8.00

—Purple label; label has reeded edge

4347	Ob-La-Di, Ob-La-Da/Julia	1983	—	3.00	6.00

—Black label with colorband

4347	Ob-La-Di, Ob-La-Da/Julia	1988	—	2.50	5.00

—Purple label; label has smooth edge

P-4347 [DJ]	Ob-La-Di, Ob-La-Da (mono/stereo)	1976	10.00	20.00	40.00
4506 [PS]	Girl/You're Going to Lose That Girl	1977	3.75	7.50	15.00

—Sleeve for a single that was never pressed

P-4506 [DJ]	Girl (mono/stereo)	1977	50.00	100.00	200.00

—Promo only; all colored vinyl versions are counterfeits

4612	Sgt. Pepper's Lonely Hearts Club Band-With a Little Help from My Friends/A Day in the Life	1978	2.00	4.00	8.00

—Original: Purple label; label has reeded edge

4612 [PS]	Sgt. Pepper's Lonely Hearts Club Band-With a Little Help from My Friends/A Day in the Life	1978	5.00	10.00	20.00
4612	Sgt. Pepper's Lonely Hearts Club Band-With a Little Help from My Friends/A Day in the Life	1983	—	3.00	6.00

—Black label with colorband

4612	Sgt. Pepper's Lonely Hearts Club Band-With a Little Help from My Friends/A Day in the Life	1988	—	2.50	5.00

—Purple label; label has smooth edge

P-4612 [DJ]	Sgt. Pepper's Lonely Hearts Club Band-With a Little Help from My Friends (mono/stereo)	1978	10.00	20.00	40.00
B-5100	The Beatles' Movie Medley/Fab Four on Film	1982	12.50	25.00	50.00

—Stock copy; not officially released, but some got out by mistake

B-5100 [PS]	The Beatles' Movie Medley/Fab Four on Film	1982	5.00	10.00	20.00
PB-5100 [DJ]	The Beatles' Movie Medley/Fab Four on Film	1982	6.25	12.50	25.00
B-5107	The Beatles' Movie Medley/I'm Happy Just to Dance with You	1982	—	2.50	5.00
B-5107 [PS]	The Beatles' Movie Medley/I'm Happy Just to Dance with You	1982	—	2.50	5.00
5112	I Want to Hold Your Hand/I Saw Her Standing There	1964	7.50	15.00	30.00

—Third pressings credit "Gil Music" as B-side publisher

5112	I Want to Hold Your Hand/I Saw Her Standing There	1964	8.75	17.50	35.00

—Second pressing credits "George Pincus and Sons" as B-side publisher

5112	I Want to Hold Your Hand/I Saw Her Standing There	1964	10.00	20.00	40.00

—First pressing credits "Walter Hofer" as B-side publisher

5112 [PS]	I Want to Hold Your Hand/I Saw Her Standing There	1964	25.00	50.00	100.00

—Die-cut, crops George Harrison's head in photo

5112 [PS]	I Want to Hold Your Hand/I Saw Her Standing There	1964	25.00	50.00	100.00

—Straight cut, shows all of George Harrison's head

5112 [PS]	I Want to Hold Your Hand/WMCA Good Guys	1964	500.00	1000.	2000.

—Giveaway from New York radio station with photo of WMCA DJs on rear

5112	I Want to Hold Your Hand/I Saw Her Standing There	1968	15.00	30.00	60.00

—Orange and yellow swirl label with "A Subsidiary Of" in perimeter print

5112	I Want to Hold Your Hand/I Saw Her Standing There	1969	6.25	12.50	25.00

—Red and orange "target" label, round logo

5112	I Want to Hold Your Hand/I Saw Her Standing There	1969	15.00	30.00	60.00

—Red and orange "target" label, dome logo

5112	I Want to Hold Your Hand/I Saw Her Standing There	1976	2.50	5.00	10.00

—Orange label, "Capitol" logo on bottom

5112	I Want to Hold Your Hand/I Saw Her Standing There	1978	3.75	7.50	15.00

—Purple label

5112	I Want to Hold Your Hand/I Saw Her Standing There	1984	—	2.50	5.00

—20th anniversary reissue; black print on perimeter of label (1964 pressings are white)

5112 [RS]	I Want to Hold Your Hand/I Saw Her Standing There	1984	—	3.00	6.00

—Same as 1964 sleeve except has "1984" in small print, and Paul McCartney's cigarette is airbrushed out

5112	I Want to Hold Your Hand/I Saw Her Standing There	1994	—	2.50	5.00

—30th anniversary reissue; has "7243-8-58123-7-8" engraved in record's trail-off area

5112 [PS]	I Want to Hold Your Hand/I Saw Her Standing There	1994	—	2.00	4.00

—Same as 1964 sleeve except "Reg. U.S. Pat. Off." has periods (1964s do not). Also came with a plastic sleeve with a "30th Anniversary" and UPC stickers (add 25%)

5150	Can't Buy Me Love/You Can't Do That	1964	7.50	15.00	30.00

—Original: Orange and yellow swirl, without "A Subsidiary Of"... in perimeter label print

5150	Can't Buy Me Love/You Can't Do That	1964	1000.	1500.	2000.

—Yellow and black vinyl (unauthorized); value is conjecture

5150	Can't Buy Me Love/You Can't Do That	1964	2000.	3000.	4000.

—Yellow vinyl (unauthorized); value is conjecture

5150	Can't Buy Me Love/You Can't Do That	1964	200.00	400.00	800.00

—One of the rarest Beatles picture sleeves. Numerous counterfeits exist; if in doubt, see an expert.

5150	Can't Buy Me Love/You Can't Do That	1968	12.50	25.00	50.00

—Orange and yellow swirl label with "A Subsidiary Of" in perimeter print

5150	Can't Buy Me Love/You Can't Do That	1969	6.25	12.50	25.00

—Red and orange "target" label, dome logo

5150	Can't Buy Me Love/You Can't Do That	1969	15.00	30.00	60.00

—Red and orange "target" label, round logo

5150	Can't Buy Me Love/You Can't Do That	1976	—	3.00	6.00

—Orange label with "Capitol" at bottom

5150	Can't Buy Me Love/You Can't Do That	1978	3.75	7.50	15.00

—Purple label

B-5189	Love Me Do/P.S. I Love You	1982	—	2.50	5.00

—Original: Orange and yellow swirl label, black print

B

Number	Title (A Side/B Side)	Yr	VG	VG+	NM
❏ B-5189 [PS]	Love Me Do/P.S. I Love You	1982	—	2.50	5.00
❏ B-5189	Love Me Do/P.S. I Love You	1983	—	3.00	6.00

—*Black label with colorband*

| ❏ B-5189 | Love Me Do/P.S. I Love You | 1988 | — | 2.00 | 4.00 |

—*Purple label; label has smooth edge*

| ❏ PB-5189 [DJ] | Love Me Do (same on both sides) | 1982 | 3.75 | 7.50 | 15.00 |
| ❏ 5222 | A Hard Day's Night/I Should Have Known Better | 1964 | | | |

—*Orange and yellow swirl, without "A Subsidiary Of"... in perimeter label print; second version credited only "Maclen" as publishers*

| ❏ 5222 | A Hard Day's Night/I Should Have Known Better | 1964 | 7.50 | 15.00 | 30.00 |

—*Original: Orange and yellow swirl, without "A Subsidiary Of"... in perimeter label print; first version credited both "Unart" and "Maclen" as publishers*

| ❏ 5222 [PS] | A Hard Day's Night/I Should Have Known Better | 1964 | 25.00 | 50.00 | 100.00 |
| ❏ 5222 | A Hard Day's Night/I Should Have Known Better | 1968 | 12.50 | 25.00 | 50.00 |

—*Orange and yellow swirl with "A Subsidiary Of"... on perimeter print in white*

| ❏ 5222 | A Hard Day's Night/I Should Have Known Better | 1968 | 25.00 | 50.00 | 100.00 |

—*Orange and yellow swirl with "A Subsidiary Of"... on perimeter print in black*

| ❏ 5222 | A Hard Day's Night/I Should Have Known Better | 1969 | 5.00 | 10.00 | 20.00 |

—*Red and orange "target" label with Capitol round logo*

| ❏ 5222 | A Hard Day's Night/I Should Have Known Better | 1969 | 15.00 | 30.00 | 60.00 |

—*Red and orange "target" label with Capitol dome logo*

| ❏ 5222 | A Hard Day's Night/I Should Have Known Better | 1976 | — | 3.00 | 6.00 |

—*Orange label with "Capitol" at bottom*

| ❏ 5222 | A Hard Day's Night/I Should Have Known Better | 1978 | 3.75 | 7.50 | 15.00 |

—*Purple label*

| ❏ 5234 | I'll Cry Instead/I'm Happy Just to Dance with You | 1964 | 10.00 | 20.00 | 40.00 |

—*Original: Orange and yellow swirl, without "A Subsidiary Of"... in perimeter label print*

| ❏ 5234 [PS] | I'll Cry Instead/I'm Happy Just to Dance with You | 1964 | 37.50 | 75.00 | 150.00 |
| ❏ 5234 | I'll Cry Instead/I'm Happy Just to Dance with You | 1968 | 15.00 | 30.00 | 60.00 |

—*Orange and yellow swirl label with "A Subsidiary Of" in perimeter print*

| ❏ 5234 | I'll Cry Instead/I'm Happy Just to Dance with You | 1969 | 5.00 | 10.00 | 20.00 |

—*Red and orange "target" label with Capitol round logo*

| ❏ 5234 | I'll Cry Instead/I'm Happy Just to Dance with You | 1969 | 17.50 | 35.00 | 70.00 |

—*Red and orange "target" label with Capitol dome logo*

| ❏ 5234 | I'll Cry Instead/I'm Happy Just to Dance with You | 1976 | — | 3.00 | 6.00 |

—*Orange label with "Capitol" at bottom*

| ❏ 5234 | I'll Cry Instead/I'm Happy Just to Dance with You | 1978 | 3.75 | 7.50 | 15.00 |

—*Purple label*

| ❏ 5235 | And I Love Her/If I Fell | 1964 | 7.50 | 15.00 | 30.00 |

—*Original: Orange and yellow swirl, without "A Subsidiary Of"... in perimeter label print; publishers listed as "Maclen" only*

| ❏ 5235 | And I Love Her/If I Fell | 1964 | 7.50 | 15.00 | 30.00 |

—*Original: Orange and yellow swirl, without "A Subsidiary Of"... in perimeter label print; publishers listed as "Unart" and "Maclen"*

| ❏ 5235 [PS] | And I Love Her/If I Fell | 1964 | 30.00 | 60.00 | 120.00 |
| ❏ 5235 | And I Love Her/If I Fell | 1968 | 12.50 | 25.00 | 50.00 |

—*Orange and yellow swirl with "A Subsidiary Of"... on perimeter print in white*

| ❏ 5235 | And I Love Her/If I Fell | 1968 | 18.75 | 37.50 | 75.00 |

—*Orange and yellow swirl with "A Subsidiary Of"... on perimeter print in black*

| ❏ 5235 | And I Love Her/If I Fell | 1969 | 5.00 | 10.00 | 20.00 |

—*Red and orange "target" label with Capitol dome logo*

| ❏ 5235 | And I Love Her/If I Fell | 1969 | 15.00 | 30.00 | 60.00 |

—*Red and orange "target" label with Capitol round logo*

| ❏ 5235 | And I Love Her/If I Fell | 1976 | — | 3.00 | 6.00 |

—*Orange label with "Capitol" at bottom*

| ❏ 5235 | And I Love Her/If I Fell | 1978 | 3.75 | 7.50 | 15.00 |

—*Purple label*

| ❏ 5255 | Matchbox/Slow Down | 1964 | 7.50 | 15.00 | 30.00 |

—*Original: Orange and yellow swirl, without "A Subsidiary Of"... in perimeter label print*

| ❏ 5255 [PS] | Matchbox/Slow Down | 1964 | 37.50 | 75.00 | 150.00 |
| ❏ 5255 | Matchbox/Slow Down | 1968 | 12.50 | 25.00 | 50.00 |

—*Orange and yellow swirl label with "A Subsidiary Of" in perimeter print*

| ❏ 5255 | Matchbox/Slow Down | 1969 | 5.00 | 10.00 | 20.00 |

—*Red and orange "target" label with Capitol round logo*

| ❏ 5255 | Matchbox/Slow Down | 1969 | 15.00 | 30.00 | 60.00 |

—*Red and orange "target" label with Capitol dome logo*

| ❏ 5255 | Matchbox/Slow Down | 1976 | — | 3.00 | 6.00 |

—*Orange label with "Capitol" at bottom*

| ❏ 5255 | Matchbox/Slow Down | 1978 | 3.75 | 7.50 | 15.00 |

—*Purple label*

| ❏ 5327 | I Feel Fine/She's a Woman | 1964 | 7.50 | 15.00 | 30.00 |

—*Original: Orange and yellow swirl, without "A Subsidiary Of"... in perimeter label print*

| ❏ 5327 [PS] | I Feel Fine/She's a Woman | 1964 | 20.00 | 40.00 | 80.00 |
| ❏ 5327 | I Feel Fine/She's a Woman | 1968 | 12.50 | 25.00 | 50.00 |

—*Orange and yellow swirl label with "A Subsidiary Of" in perimeter print*

| ❏ 5327 | I Feel Fine/She's a Woman | 1969 | 5.00 | 10.00 | 20.00 |

—*Red and orange "target" label with Capitol dome logo*

| ❏ 5327 | I Feel Fine/She's a Woman | 1969 | 15.00 | 30.00 | 60.00 |

—*Red and orange "target" label with Capitol round logo*

| ❏ 5327 | I Feel Fine/She's a Woman | 1976 | — | 3.00 | 6.00 |

—*Orange label with "Capitol" at bottom*

| ❏ 5327 | I Feel Fine/She's a Woman | 1978 | 3.75 | 7.50 | 15.00 |

—*Purple label*

| ❏ 5371 | Eight Days a Week/ I Don't Want to Spoil the Party | 1965 | 7.50 | 15.00 | 30.00 |

—*Original: Orange and yellow swirl, without "A Subsidiary Of"... in perimeter label print*

| ❏ 5371 [PS] | Eight Days a Week/ I Don't Want to Spoil the Party | 1965 | 6.25 | 12.50 | 25.00 |

—*Die-cut sleeve*

| ❏ 5371 [PS] | Eight Days a Week/ I Don't Want to Spoil the Party | 1965 | 18.75 | 37.50 | 75.00 |

—*Straight-cut sleeve*

| ❏ 5371 | Eight Days a Week/ I Don't Want to Spoil the Party | 1968 | 12.50 | 25.00 | 50.00 |

—*Orange and yellow swirl label with "A Subsidiary Of" in perimeter print*

| ❏ 5371 | Eight Days a Week/ I Don't Want to Spoil the Party | 1969 | 5.00 | 10.00 | 20.00 |

—*Red and orange "target" label with Capitol round logo*

| ❏ 5371 | Eight Days a Week/ I Don't Want to Spoil the Party | 1969 | 15.00 | 30.00 | 60.00 |

—*Red and orange "target" label with Capitol dome logo*

| ❏ 5371 | Eight Days a Week/ I Don't Want to Spoil the Party | 1976 | — | 3.00 | 6.00 |

—*Orange label with "Capitol" at bottom*

| ❏ 5371 | Eight Days a Week/ I Don't Want to Spoil the Party | 1978 | 3.75 | 7.50 | 15.00 |

—*Purple label*

| ❏ 5407 | Ticket to Ride/Yes It Is | 1965 | 7.50 | 15.00 | 30.00 |

—*Original: Orange and yellow swirl, without "A Subsidiary Of"... in perimeter label print*

| ❏ 5407 [PS] | Ticket to Ride/Yes It Is | 1965 | 25.00 | 50.00 | 100.00 |
| ❏ 5407 | Ticket to Ride/Yes It Is | 1968 | 12.50 | 25.00 | 50.00 |

—*Orange and yellow swirl with "A Subsidiary Of"... on perimeter print in white*

| ❏ 5407 | Ticket to Ride/Yes It Is | 1968 | 25.00 | 50.00 | 100.00 |

—*Orange and yellow swirl with "A Subsidiary Of"... on perimeter print in black*

| ❏ 5407 | Ticket to Ride/Yes It Is | 1969 | 5.00 | 10.00 | 20.00 |

—*Red and orange "target" label with Capitol round logo*

| ❏ 5407 | Ticket to Ride/Yes It Is | 1969 | 15.00 | 30.00 | 60.00 |

—*Red and orange "target" label with Capitol dome logo*

| ❏ 5407 | Ticket to Ride/Yes It Is | 1976 | — | 3.00 | 6.00 |

—*Orange label with "Capitol" at bottom*

| ❏ 5407 | Ticket to Ride/Yes It Is | 1978 | 3.75 | 7.50 | 15.00 |

—*Purple label*

| ❏ B-5439 [PS] | Leave My Kitten Alone/Ob-La-Di, Ob-La-Da | 1985 | 12.50 | 25.00 | 50.00 |

—*Sleeve for a record that was never released, not even as a promo*

| ❏ 5476 | Help!/I'm Down | 1965 | 7.50 | 15.00 | 30.00 |

—*Original: Orange and yellow swirl, without "A Subsidiary Of"... in perimeter label print*

| ❏ 5476 [PS] | Help!/I'm Down | 1965 | 18.75 | 37.50 | 75.00 |
| ❏ 5476 | Help!/I'm Down | 1968 | 12.50 | 25.00 | 50.00 |

—*Orange and yellow swirl with "A Subsidiary Of"... on perimeter print in white*

| ❏ 5476 | Help!/I'm Down | 1968 | 25.00 | 50.00 | 100.00 |

—*Orange and yellow swirl with "A Subsidiary Of"... on perimeter print in black*

| ❏ 5476 | Help!/I'm Down | 1969 | 5.00 | 10.00 | 20.00 |

—*Red and orange "target" label with Capitol round logo*

| ❏ 5476 | Help!/I'm Down | 1969 | 15.00 | 30.00 | 60.00 |

—*Red and orange "target" label with Capitol dome logo*

| ❏ 5476 | Help!/I'm Down | 1976 | — | 3.00 | 6.00 |

—*Orange label with "Capitol" at bottom*

| ❏ 5476 | Help!/I'm Down | 1978 | 3.75 | 7.50 | 15.00 |

—*Purple label*

| ❏ 5498 | Yesterday/Act Naturally | 1965 | 7.50 | 15.00 | 30.00 |

—*Original: Orange and yellow swirl, without "A Subsidiary Of"... in perimeter label print*

| ❏ 5498 [PS] | Yesterday/Act Naturally | 1965 | 25.00 | 50.00 | 100.00 |
| ❏ 5498 | Yesterday/Act Naturally | 1968 | 12.50 | 25.00 | 50.00 |

—*Orange and yellow swirl with "A Subsidiary Of"... on perimeter print in white*

| ❏ 5498 | Yesterday/Act Naturally | 1968 | 25.00 | 50.00 | 100.00 |

—*Orange and yellow swirl with "A Subsidiary Of"... on perimeter print in black*

| ❏ 5498 | Yesterday/Act Naturally | 1969 | 5.00 | 10.00 | 20.00 |

—*Red and orange "target" label with Capitol round logo*

| ❏ 5498 | Yesterday/Act Naturally | 1969 | 15.00 | 30.00 | 60.00 |

—*Red and orange "target" label with Capitol dome logo*

| ❏ 5498 | Yesterday/Act Naturally | 1976 | — | 3.00 | 6.00 |

—*Orange label with "Capitol" at bottom*

| ❏ 5498 | Yesterday/Act Naturally | 1978 | 3.75 | 7.50 | 15.00 |

—*Purple label*

| ❏ 5555 | We Can Work It Out/Day Tripper | 1965 | 7.50 | 15.00 | 30.00 |

—*Original: Orange and yellow swirl, without "A Subsidiary Of"... in perimeter label print*

| ❏ 5555 | We Can Work It Out/Day Tripper | 1968 | 12.50 | 25.00 | 50.00 |

—*Orange and yellow swirl label with "A Subsidiary Of" in perimeter print*

| ❏ 5555 | We Can Work It Out/Day Tripper | 1969 | 5.00 | 10.00 | 20.00 |

—*Red and orange "target" label with Capitol round logo*

| ❏ 5555 | We Can Work It Out/Day Tripper | 1969 | 15.00 | 30.00 | 60.00 |

—*Red and orange "target" label with Capitol dome logo*

| ❏ 5555 | We Can Work It Out/Day Tripper | 1969 | 500.00 | 1000. | 1500. |

—*Red and white "Starline" label (mispress)*

| ❏ 5555 | We Can Work It Out/Day Tripper | 1976 | — | 3.00 | 6.00 |

—*Orange label with "Capitol" at bottom*

| ❏ 5555 | We Can Work It Out/Day Tripper | 1978 | 3.75 | 7.50 | 15.00 |

—*Purple label*

| ❏ 5555 [PS] | We Can Work It Out/Day Tripper | 1978 | 15.00 | 30.00 | 60.00 |
| ❏ 5587 | Nowhere Man/What Goes On | 1966 | 6.25 | 12.50 | 25.00 |

—*Original: Orange and yellow swirl, without "A Subsidiary Of"... in perimeter label print; composers of B-side listed as "John Lennon-Paul McCartney"*

| ❏ 5587 | Nowhere Man/What Goes On | 1966 | 12.50 | 25.00 | 50.00 |

—*Orange and yellow swirl, without "A Subsidiary Of"... in perimeter label print; B-side composers listed as "Lennon-McCartney-Starkey"*

| ❏ 5587 [PS] | Nowhere Man/What Goes On | 1966 | 10.00 | 20.00 | 40.00 |
| ❏ 5587 | Nowhere Man/What Goes On | 1968 | 12.50 | 25.00 | 50.00 |

—*Orange and yellow swirl label with "A Subsidiary Of" in perimeter print*

| ❏ 5587 | Nowhere Man/What Goes On | 1969 | 5.00 | 10.00 | 20.00 |

—*Red and orange "target" label with Capitol round logo*

| ❏ 5587 | Nowhere Man/What Goes On | 1969 | 15.00 | 30.00 | 60.00 |

—*Red and orange "target" label with Capitol dome logo*

| ❏ 5587 | Nowhere Man/What Goes On | 1976 | — | 3.00 | 6.00 |

—*Orange label with "Capitol" at bottom*

| ❏ 5587 | Nowhere Man/What Goes On | 1978 | 3.75 | 7.50 | 15.00 |

—*Purple label*

| ❏ B-5624 | Twist and Shout/There's a Place | 1986 | — | 2.50 | 5.00 |

—*Black label with colorband*

| ❏ B-5624 | Twist and Shout/There's a Place | 1988 | — | 2.50 | 5.00 |

—*Purple label; label has smooth edge*

| ❏ P-B-5624 [DJ] | Twist and Shout (same on both sides) | 1986 | 3.75 | 7.50 | 15.00 |
| ❏ 5651 | Paperback Writer/Rain | 1966 | 6.25 | 12.50 | 25.00 |

—*Original: Orange and yellow swirl, without "A Subsidiary Of"... in perimeter label print*

| ❏ 5651 [PS] | Paperback Writer/Rain | 1966 | 18.75 | 37.50 | 75.00 |
| ❏ 5651 | Paperback Writer/Rain | 1968 | 12.50 | 25.00 | 50.00 |

—*Orange and yellow swirl with "A Subsidiary Of"... on perimeter print in white*

| ❏ 5651 | Paperback Writer/Rain | 1968 | 25.00 | 50.00 | 100.00 |

—*Orange and yellow swirl with "A Subsidiary Of"... on perimeter print in black*

| ❏ 5651 | Paperback Writer/Rain | 1969 | 5.00 | 10.00 | 20.00 |

—*Red and orange "target" label with Capitol round logo*

| ❏ 5651 | Paperback Writer/Rain | 1969 | 15.00 | 30.00 | 60.00 |

—*Red and orange "target" label with Capitol dome logo*

| ❏ 5651 | Paperback Writer/Rain | 1976 | — | 3.00 | 6.00 |

—*Orange label with "Capitol" at bottom*

| ❏ 5651 | Paperback Writer/Rain | 1978 | 3.75 | 7.50 | 15.00 |

—*Purple label*

Number	Title (A Side/B Side)	Yr	VG	VG+	NM
5715	Yellow Submarine/Eleanor Rigby	1966	6.25	12.50	25.00
—Original: Orange and yellow swirl, without "A Subsidiary Of"... in perimeter label print; print on perimeter is white					
5715	Yellow Submarine/Eleanor Rigby	1966	12.50	25.00	50.00
—Orange and yellow swirl, without "A Subsidiary Of"... in perimeter label print; print on perimeter is yellow (mispress)					
5715 [PS]	Yellow Submarine/Eleanor Rigby	1966	25.00	50.00	100.00
5715	Yellow Submarine/Eleanor Rigby	1968	12.50	25.00	50.00
—Orange and yellow swirl label with "A Subsidiary Of" in perimeter print					
5715	Yellow Submarine/Eleanor Rigby	1969	5.00	10.00	20.00
—Red and orange "target" label with Capitol dome logo					
5715	Yellow Submarine/Eleanor Rigby	1969	15.00	30.00	60.00
—Red and orange "target" label with Capitol round logo					
5715	Yellow Submarine/Eleanor Rigby	1976	—	3.00	6.00
—Orange label with "Capitol" at bottom					
5715	Yellow Submarine/Eleanor Rigby	1978	3.75	7.50	15.00
—Purple label					
5810	Penny Lane/Strawberry Fields Forever	1967	6.25	12.50	25.00
—Original: Orange and yellow swirl, without "A Subsidiary Of"... in perimeter label print; "Penny Lane" time listed as 3:00					
5810	Penny Lane/Strawberry Fields Forever	1967	7.50	15.00	30.00
—Orange and yellow swirl, without "A Subsidiary Of"... in perimeter label print; "Penny Lane" time listed as 2:57					
5810 [PS]	Penny Lane/Strawberry Fields Forever	1967	25.00	50.00	100.00
5810	Penny Lane/Strawberry Fields Forever	1968	12.50	25.00	50.00
—Orange and yellow swirl label with "A Subsidiary Of" in perimeter print					
5810	Penny Lane/Strawberry Fields Forever	1969	5.00	10.00	20.00
—Red and orange "target" label with Capitol round logo					
5810	Penny Lane/Strawberry Fields Forever	1969	15.00	30.00	60.00
—Red and orange "target" label with Capitol dome logo					
5810	Penny Lane/Strawberry Fields Forever	1976	—	3.00	6.00
—Orange label with "Capitol" at bottom					
5810	Penny Lane/Strawberry Fields Forever	1978	3.75	7.50	15.00
—Purple label					
P 5810 [DJ]	Penny Lane/Strawberry Fields Forever	1967	75.00	150.00	300.00
—Light green promo; most copies have an extra trumpet solo at the end of "Penny Lane"					
P 5810 [DJ]	Penny Lane/Strawberry Fields Forever	1967	150.00	300.00	600.00
—Light green promo; a few copies have no trumpet solo at the end of "Penny Lane"					
5964	All You Need Is Love/Baby, You're a Rich Man	1967	6.25	12.50	25.00
—Original: Orange and yellow swirl, without "A Subsidiary Of"... in perimeter label print					
5964 [PS]	All You Need Is Love/Baby, You're a Rich Man	1967	10.00	20.00	40.00
5964	All You Need Is Love/Baby, You're a Rich Man	1968	12.50	25.00	50.00
—Orange and yellow swirl label with "A Subsidiary Of" in perimeter print					
5964	All You Need Is Love/Baby, You're a Rich Man	1969	5.00	10.00	20.00
—Red and orange "target" label with Capitol round logo					
5964	All You Need Is Love/Baby, You're a Rich Man	1969	18.75	37.50	75.00
—Red and orange "target" label with Capitol dome logo					
5964	All You Need Is Love/Baby, You're a Rich Man	1976	—	3.00	6.00
—Orange label with "Capitol" at bottom					
5964	All You Need Is Love/Baby, You're a Rich Man	1978	3.75	7.50	15.00
—Purple label					
P 5964 [DJ]	All You Need Is Love/Baby, You're a Rich Man	1967	62.50	125.00	250.00
—Light green label promo					
S7-17488	Birthday/Taxman	1994	—	2.00	4.00
—Green vinyl					
S7-17488	Birthday/Taxman	1994	12.50	25.00	50.00
—Black vinyl "error" pressing					
S7-17688	She Loves You/I'll Get You	1994	—	2.00	4.00
—Red vinyl					
S7-17689	I Want to Hold Your Hand/This Boy	1994	—	2.00	4.00
—Clear vinyl					
S7-17690	Can't Buy Me Love/You Can't Do That	1994	—	2.00	4.00
—Gren vinyl					
S7-17691	Help!/I'm Down	1994	—	2.00	4.00
—White vinyl					
S7-17692	A Hard Day's Night/Things We Said Today	1994	—	2.00	4.00
—White vinyl					
S7-17693	All You Need Is Love/Baby You're a Rich Man	1994	—	2.00	4.00
—Pink vinyl					
S7-17694	Hey Jude/Revolution	1994	—	2.00	4.00
—Blue vinyl					
S7-17695	Let It Be/You Know My Name (Look Up My Number)	1994	—	2.00	4.00
—Yellow vinyl					
S7-17696	Yellow Submarine/Eleanor Rigby	1994	—	2.00	4.00
—Yellow vinyl					
S7-17697	Strawberry Fields Forever/Penny Lane	1994	—	2.00	4.00
—Red vinyl					
S7-17698	Something/Come Together	1994	—	2.00	4.00
—Blue vinyl					
S7-17699	Twist and Shout/There's a Place	1994	—	2.00	4.00
—Pink vinyl					
S7-17700	Here Comes the Sun/Octopus's Garden	1994	—	2.00	4.00
—Gold/orange vinyl					
S7-17701	Sgt. Pepper's Lonely Hearts Club Band-With a Little Help from My Friends/A Day in the Life	1994	—	2.00	4.00
—Clear vinyl					
S7-18888	Norwegian Wood/If I Needed Someone	1995	37.50	75.00	150.00
—Green vinyl; 1,000 pressed, given by Collectors' Choice Music to buyers of Beatles reissue LPs					
S7-18889	You've Got to Hide Your Love Away/I've Just Seen a Face	1996	—	2.00	4.00
—Gold/orange vinyl					
S7-18890	Magical Mystery Tour/The Fool on the Hill	1996	—	2.00	4.00
—Yellow vinyl					
S7-18891	Across the Universe/Two of Us	1996	—	2.00	4.00
—Clear vinyl					
S7-18892	While My Guitar Gently Weeps/Blackbird	1996	—	2.00	4.00
—Blue vinyl					
S7-18893	It's All Too Much/Only a Northern Song	1996	—	2.00	4.00
—Blue vinyl					
S7-18894	Nowhere Man/What Goes On	1996	—	2.00	4.00
—Green vinyl					
S7-18895	We Can Work It Out/Day Tripper	1996	—	2.00	4.00
—Pink vinyl					
S7-18896	Lucy in the Sky with Diamonds/When I'm 64	1996	—	2.00	4.00
—Red vinyl					
S7-18897	Here, There and Everywhere/Good Day Sunshine	1996	—	2.00	4.00
—Yellow vinyl					
S7-18898	The Long and Winding Road/For You Blue	1996	—	2.00	4.00
—Blue vinyl					
S7-18899	Got to Get You Into My Life/Helter Skelter	1996	—	2.00	4.00
—Gold/orange vinyl					
S7-18900	Ob-La-Di, Ob-La-Da/Julia	1996	—	2.00	4.00
—Clear vinyl					
S7-18901	Yesterday/Act Naturally	1996	—	2.00	4.00
—Pink vinyl					
S7-18902	Paperback Writer/Rain	1996	—	2.00	4.00
—Red vinyl					
S7-19341	Norwegian Wood (This Bird Has Flown)/If I Needed Someone	1996	—	—	3.00
S7-56785	Love Me Do/P.S. I Love You	1992	—	2.00	4.00
S7-56785	Love Me Do/P.S. I Love You	1992	7.50	15.00	30.00
—Small pressing on red vinyl "by mistake"					
72133	Roll Over Beethoven/Please Mister Postman	1964	12.50	25.00	50.00
—Orange and yellow swirl; Canadian release that was heavily imported to the U.S.					
72144	All My Loving/This Boy	1964	12.50	25.00	50.00
—Orange and yellow swirl; Canadian release that was heavily imported to the U.S.					
72144	All My Loving/This Boy	1971	25.00	50.00	100.00
—Canadian number with U.S. labels (red and orange "target" label)					
7PRO-79551/2 [DJ]	Love Me Do/P.S. I Love You	1992	6.25	12.50	25.00
7PRO-79551/2 [PS]	Love Me Do/P.S. I Love You	1992	6.25	12.50	25.00

CAPITOL STARLINE

Number	Title (A Side/B Side)	Yr	VG	VG+	NM
6061	Twist and Shout/There's a Place	1965	30.00	60.00	120.00
—Green swirl label					
6062	Love Me Do/P.S. I Love You	1965	30.00	60.00	120.00
—Green swirl label					
6063	Please Please Me/From Me to You	1965	30.00	60.00	120.00
—Green swirl label					
6064	Do You Want to Know a Secret/Thank You Girl	1965	30.00	60.00	120.00
—Green swirl label					
6065	Roll Over Beethoven/Misery	1965	30.00	60.00	120.00
—Green swirl label					
6065	Roll Over Beethoven/Misery	1971	7.50	15.00	30.00
—Red and orange "target" label					
6066	Boys/Kansas City	1965	20.00	40.00	80.00
—Green swirl label					
6066	Boys/Kansas City	1971	7.50	15.00	30.00
—Red and orange "target" label					
6278	I Want to Hold Your Hand/I Saw Her Standing There	1981	5.00	10.00	20.00
—Originals have blue labels					
6279	Can't Buy Me Love/You Can't Do That	1981	2.00	4.00	8.00
—Originals have blue labels					
6281	A Hard Day's Night/I Should Have Known Better	1981	2.00	4.00	8.00
—Originals have blue labels					
6282	I'll Cry Instead/I'm Happy Just to Dance with You	1981	2.00	4.00	8.00
—Originals have blue labels					
6283	And I Love Her/If I Fell	1981	2.00	4.00	8.00
—Originals have blue labels					
6284	Matchbox/Slow Down	1981	2.00	4.00	8.00
—Originals have blue labels					
6286	I Feel Fine/She's a Woman	1981	2.00	4.00	8.00
—Originals have blue labels					
6287	Eight Days a Week/I Don't Want to Spoil the Party	1981	2.00	4.00	8.00
—Originals have blue labels					
6288	Ticket to Ride/Yes It Is	1981	2.00	4.00	8.00
—Originals have blue labels					
6290	Help!/I'm Down	1981	2.00	4.00	8.00
—Originals have blue labels					
6291	Yesterday/Act Naturally	1981	2.00	4.00	8.00
—Originals have blue labels					
6293	We Can Work It Out/Day Tripper	1981	2.00	4.00	8.00
—Originals have blue labels					
6294	Nowhere Man/What Goes On	1981	2.00	4.00	8.00
—Originals have blue labels					
6296	Paperback Writer/Rain	1981	2.00	4.00	8.00
—Originals have blue labels					
6297	Yellow Submarine/Eleanor Rigby	1981	2.00	4.00	8.00
—Originals have blue labels					
6299	Penny Lane/Strawberry Fields Forever	1981	2.00	4.00	8.00
—Originals have blue labels					
6300	All You Need Is Love/Baby You're a Rich Man	1981	2.00	4.00	8.00
—Originals have blue labels					

CAPITOL/EVATONE

Number	Title (A Side/B Side)	Yr	VG	VG+	NM
420826cs	All My Loving/You've Got to Hide Your Love Away	1982	2.50	5.00	10.00
—Flexi-disc issued as giveaway by The Musicland Group; "Musicland" version					
420826cs	All My Loving/You've Got to Hide Your Love Away	1982	5.00	10.00	20.00
—Flexi-disc issued as giveaway by The Musicland Group; "Discount" version					
420826cs	All My Loving/You've Got to Hide Your Love Away	1982	6.25	12.50	25.00
—Flexi-disc issued as giveaway by The Musicland Group; "Sam Goody" version					
420827cs	Magical Mystery Tour/Here Comes the Sun	1982	2.50	5.00	10.00
—Flexi-disc issued as giveaway by The Musicland Group; "Musicland" version					
420827cs	Magical Mystery Tour/Here Comes the Sun	1982	5.00	10.00	20.00
—Flexi-disc issued as giveaway by The Musicland Group; "Discount" version					
420827cs	Magical Mystery Tour/Here Comes the Sun	1982	6.25	12.50	25.00
—Flexi-disc issued as giveaway by The Musicland Group; "Sam Goody" version					
420828cs	Rocky Raccoon/Why Don't We Do It in the Road?	1982	2.50	5.00	10.00
—Flexi-disc issued as giveaway by The Musicland Group; "Musicland" version					
420828cs	Rocky Raccoon/Why Don't We Do It in the Road?	1982	5.00	10.00	20.00
—Flexi-disc issued as giveaway by The Musicland Group; "Discount" version					

B

Number	Title (A Side/B Side)	Yr	VG	VG+	NM
❑ 420828cs	Rocky Raccoon/ Why Don't We Do It in the Road?	1982	6.25	12.50	25.00

—Flexi-disc issued as giveaway by The Musicland Group; "Sam Goody" version

Number	Title (A Side/B Side)	Yr	VG	VG+	NM
❑ 830771 X	Till There Was You/Three Cool Cats	1983	—	3.00	6.00

—Flexi-disc issued as giveaway with a book

| ❑ 1214825cs | German Medley | 1983 | 15.00 | 30.00 | 60.00 |

—Flexi-disc given away by House of Guitars in New York

CICADELIC/BIODISC

| ❑ 001 | A Hard Day's Night Open End Interview | 1990 | 3.75 | 7.50 | 15.00 |

—Limited edition of 700; lower numbers increase value substantially

| ❑ 001 | A Hard Day's Night Open End Interview | 1990 | 7.50 | 15.00 | 30.00 |

—"Records Etc." pressing

| ❑ 002 | Help! Open End Interview | 1990 | — | 2.50 | 5.00 |
| ❑ 002 [PS] | Help! Open End Interview | 1990 | — | 2.50 | 5.00 |

COLLECTABLES

❑ 1501	I'm Gonna Sit Right Down and Cry Over You/ Roll Over Beethoven	1982	—	—	3.00
❑ 1501 [PS]	I'm Gonna Sit Right Down and Cry Over You/ Roll Over Beethoven	1982	—	—	3.00
❑ 1502	Hippy Hippy Shake/Sweet Little Sixteen	1982	—	—	3.00
❑ 1502 [PS]	Hippy Hippy Shake/Sweet Little Sixteen	1982	—	—	3.00
❑ 1503	Lend Me Your Comb/Your Feets Too Big	1982	—	—	3.00
❑ 1503 [PS]	Lend Me Your Comb/Your Feets Too Big	1982	—	—	3.00
❑ 1504	Where Have You Been All My Life/Mr. Moonlight	1982	—	—	3.00
❑ 1504 [PS]	Where Have You Been All My Life/Mr. Moonlight	1982	—	—	3.00
❑ 1505	A Taste of Honey/Besame Mucho	1982	—	—	3.00
❑ 1505 [PS]	A Taste of Honey/Besame Mucho	1982	—	—	3.00
❑ 1506	Till There Was You/Everybody's Trying to Be My Baby	1982	—	—	3.00
❑ 1506 [PS]	Till There Was You/Everybody's Trying to Be My Baby	1982	—	—	3.00
❑ 1507	Kansas City-Hey Hey Hey Hey/Ain't Nothing Shakin Like the Leaves on a Tree	1982	—	—	3.00
❑ 1507 [PS]	Kansas City-Hey Hey Hey Hey/Ain't Nothing Shakin Like the Leaves on a Tree	1982	—	—	3.00
❑ 1508	To Know Her Is To Love Her/Little Queenie	1982	—	—	3.00
❑ 1508 [PS]	To Know Her Is To Love Her/Little Queenie	1982	—	—	3.00
❑ 1509	Falling in Love Again/Sheila	1982	—	—	3.00
❑ 1509 [PS]	Falling in Love Again/Sheila	1982	—	—	3.00
❑ 1510	Be-Bop-a-Lula/Hallelujah I Love Her So	1982	—	—	3.00
❑ 1510 [PS]	Be-Bop-a-Lula/Hallelujah I Love Her So	1982	—	—	3.00
❑ 1511	Red Sails in the Sunset/Matchbox	1982	—	—	3.00
❑ 1511 [PS]	Red Sails in the Sunset/Matchbox	1982	—	—	3.00
❑ 1512	Talkin' Bout You/Shimmy Shake	1982	—	—	3.00
❑ 1512 [PS]	Talkin' Bout You/Shimmy Shake	1982	—	—	3.00
❑ 1513	Long Tall Sally/I Remember You	1982	—	—	3.00
❑ 1513 [PS]	Long Tall Sally/I Remember You	1982	—	—	3.00
❑ 1514	Ask Me Why/Twist and Shout	1982	—	—	3.00
❑ 1514 [PS]	Ask Me Why/Twist and Shout	1982	—	—	3.00
❑ 1515	I Saw Her Standing There/Can't Help It "Blue Angel"	1982	—	—	3.00

—B-side is actually "Reminiscing"

| ❑ 1515 [PS] | I Saw Her Standing There/Can't Help It "Blue Angel" | 1982 | — | — | 3.00 |
| ❑ 1516 | I'll Try Anyway/I Don't Know Why I Do (I Just Do) | 1987 | 2.50 | 5.00 | 10.00 |

—Despite label credit to The Beatles, both are Peter Best recordings

| ❑ 1517 | She's Not the Only Girl in Town/More Than I Need Myself | 1987 | 2.50 | 5.00 | 10.00 |

—Despite label credit to The Beatles, both are Peter Best recordings

| ❑ 1518 | I'll Have Everything Too/I'm Checking Out Now Baby | 1987 | 2.50 | 5.00 | 10.00 |

—Despite label credit to The Beatles, both are Peter Best recordings

| ❑ 1519 | How'd You Get to Know Her Name/If You Can't Get Her | 1987 | 2.50 | 5.00 | 10.00 |

—Despite label credit to The Beatles, both are Peter Best recordings

| ❑ 1520 | Cry for a Shadow/Rock and Roll Music | 1987 | — | 2.50 | 5.00 |

—Despite label credit to The Beatles, B-side is a Peter Best recording

| ❑ 1521 | Let's Dance/If You Love Me Baby | 1987 | — | 3.00 | 6.00 |

—Despite label credit to The Beatles, A-side is a Tony Sheridan solo recording

| ❑ 1522 | What'd I Say/Sweet Georgia Brown | 1987 | — | 3.00 | 6.00 |

—Despite label credit to The Beatles, A-side is a Tony Sheridan solo recording

| ❑ 1523 | Ruby Baby/Ya Ya | 1987 | — | 3.00 | 6.00 |

—Despite label credit to The Beatles, both are by Tony Sheridan without the Fab Four

| ❑ 1524 | Why/I'll Try Anyway | 1987 | — | 3.00 | 6.00 |

—Despite label credit to The Beatles, B-side is a Peter Best recording

DECCA

| ❑ 31382 | My Bonnie/The Saints | 1962 | 7500. | 11250. | 15000. |

—By "Tony Sheridan and the Beat Brothers"; black label with color bars (all-black label with star under "Decca" should be a counterfeit)

| ❑ 31382 [DJ] | My Bonnie/The Saints | 1962 | 1000. | 2000. | 3000. |

—By "Tony Sheridan and the Beat Brothers"; pink label, star on label under "Decca"

EVA-TONE

| ❑ 830771X [DJ] | Til There Was You/Three Cool Cats (both on same side) | 1983 | — | 3.00 | 6.00 |

—Red plastic flexidisc; issued as giveaway with a Beatles price guide

MGM

| ❑ 13213 | My Bonnie (My Bonnie Lies Over the Ocean)/
The Saints (When the Saints Go Marching In) | 1964 | 10.00 | 20.00 | 40.00 |

—The Beatles with Tony Sheridan; no reference to LP on label

| ❑ 13213 | My Bonnie (My Bonnie Lies Over the Ocean)/
The Saints (When the Saints Go Marching In) | 1964 | 12.50 | 25.00 | 50.00 |

—The Beatles with Tony Sheridan; LP number on label

| ❑ 13213 [DJ] | My Bonnie (My Bonnie Lies Over the Ocean)/
The Saints (When the Saints Go Marching In) | 1964 | 75.00 | 150.00 | 300.00 |

—The Beatles with Tony Sheridan

| ❑ 13213 [PS] | My Bonnie (My Bonnie Lies Over the Ocean)/
The Saints (When the Saints Go Marching In) | 1964 | 30.00 | 60.00 | 120.00 |

—The Beatles with Tony Sheridan

| ❑ 13227 | Why/Cry for a Shadow | 1964 | 37.50 | 75.00 | 150.00 |

—The Beatles with Tony Sheridan

| ❑ 13227 [DJ] | Why/Cry for a Shadow | 1964 | 62.50 | 125.00 | 250.00 |

—The Beatles with Tony Sheridan

Number	Title (A Side/B Side)	Yr	VG	VG+	NM
❑ 13227 [PS]	Why/Cry for a Shadow	1964	100.00	200.00	400.00

—The Beatles with Tony Sheridan

OLDIES 45

❑ 149	Do You Want to Know a Secret/Thank You Girl	1964	3.75	7.50	15.00
❑ 150	Please Please Me/From Me to You	1964	3.75	7.50	15.00
❑ 151	Love Me Do/P.S. I Love You	1964	3.75	7.50	15.00
❑ 152	Twist and Shout/There's a Place	1964	3.75	7.50	15.00

SWAN

| ❑ 4152 | She Loves You/I'll Get You | 196? | 5.00 | 10.00 | 20.00 |

—Black label, silver print, "Don't Drop Out" not on label, smaller numbers in trailoff area

| ❑ 4152 | She Loves You/I'll Get You | 196? | 12.50 | 25.00 | 50.00 |

—White label, red or maroon print, same as above

| ❑ 4152 | She Loves You/I'll Get You | 1963 | 150.00 | 300.00 | 600.00 |

—Semi-glossy white label/blue printing

| ❑ 4152 | She Loves You/I'll Get You | 1963 | 150.00 | 300.00 | 600.00 |

—Semi-glossy white label/red print; "Don't Drop Out" not on label

| ❑ 4152 | She Loves You/I'll Get You | 1963 | 162.50 | 325.00 | 650.00 |

—Flat white label/red print, "Don't Drop Out" not on label

| ❑ 4152 | She Loves You/I'll Get You | 1963 | 162.50 | 325.00 | 650.00 |

—Semi-glossy white label/red print, "Don't Drop Out" on label

| ❑ 4152 [DJ] | She Loves You/I'll Get You | 1963 | 112.50 | 225.00 | 450.00 |

—Thin print, "Don't Drop Out" on label

| ❑ 4152 [DJ] | She Loves You/I'll Get You | 1963 | 125.00 | 250.00 | 500.00 |

—Flat white label, no "Don't Drop Out" on label

| ❑ 4152 [DJ] | She Loves You/I'll Get You | 1963 | 125.00 | 250.00 | 500.00 |

—Thick print, no "Don't Drop Out" on label

| ❑ 4152 | She Loves You/I'll Get You | 1964 | 7.50 | 15.00 | 30.00 |

—Black label, silver print, "Don't Drop Out" on label

| ❑ 4152 | She Loves You/I'll Get You | 1964 | 10.00 | 20.00 | 40.00 |

—Black label, silver print, "Don't Drop Out" not on label

| ❑ 4152 | She Loves You/I'll Get You | 1964 | 12.50 | 25.00 | 50.00 |

—Black label, silver print, "Produced by George Martin" on both labels

| ❑ 4152 | She Loves You/I'll Get You | 1964 | 12.50 | 25.00 | 50.00 |

—Black label, silver print, "Produced by George Martin" on only one label

❑ 4152 [DJ]	I'll Get You (one-sided)	1964	200.00	400.00	600.00
❑ 4152 [PS]	She Loves You/I'll Get You	1964	30.00	60.00	120.00
❑ 4182	Sie Liebt Dich (She Loves You)/I'll Get You	1964	37.50	75.00	150.00

—White label, "(She Loves You)" under "Sie Liebt Dich," wide red print

| ❑ 4182 | Sie Liebt Dich (She Loves You)/I'll Get You | 1964 | 37.50 | 75.00 | 150.00 |

—White label, "Sie Liebt Dich (She Loves You)" on one line

| ❑ 4182 | Sie Liebt Dich (She Loves You)/I'll Get You | 1964 | 37.50 | 75.00 | 150.00 |

—White label, "(She Loves You)" under "Sie Liebt Dich," narrow print

| ❑ 4182 | Sie Liebt Dich (She Loves You)/I'll Get You | 1964 | 43.75 | 87.50 | 175.00 |

—White label, "(She Loves You)" under "Sie Liebt Dich," wide orange print

| ❑ 4182 [DJ] | Sie Liebt Dich (She Loves You)/I'll Get You | 1964 | 100.00 | 200.00 | 400.00 |

—White label, "(She Loves You)" under "Sie Liebt Dich"

| ❑ 4182 [DJ] | Sie Liebt Dich (She Loves You)/I'll Get You | 1964 | 112.50 | 225.00 | 450.00 |

—White label, "Sie Liebt Dich (She Loves You)" on one line

TOLLIE

| ❑ 9001 | Twist and Shout/There's a Place | 1964 | 12.50 | 25.00 | 50.00 |

—Yellow label, black print, "TOLLIE" stands alone

| ❑ 9001 | Twist and Shout/There's a Place | 1964 | 12.50 | 25.00 | 50.00 |

—Yellow label, black print, black "tollie" in box

| ❑ 9001 | Twist and Shout/There's a Place | 1964 | 12.50 | 25.00 | 50.00 |

—Yellow label, green print, "tollie" lowercase

| ❑ 9001 | Twist and Shout/There's a Place | 1964 | 12.50 | 25.00 | 50.00 |

—Yellow label, black print, black "TOLLIE" in thin box

| ❑ 9001 | Twist and Shout/There's a Place | 1964 | 15.00 | 30.00 | 60.00 |

—Black label, silver print

| ❑ 9001 | Twist and Shout/There's a Place | 1964 | 15.00 | 30.00 | 60.00 |

—Yellow label, black print, purple "tollie" in box

| ❑ 9001 | Twist and Shout/There's a Place | 1964 | 15.00 | 30.00 | 60.00 |

—Yellow label, blue print

| ❑ 9001 | Twist and Shout/There's a Place | 1964 | 18.75 | 37.50 | 75.00 |

—Yellow label, black print, "TOLLIE" in brackets

| ❑ 9001 | Twist and Shout/There's a Place | 1964 | 20.00 | 40.00 | 80.00 |

—Yellow label, green print, "TOLLIE" uppercase

| ❑ 9001 | Twist and Shout/There's a Place | 1964 | 20.00 | 40.00 | 80.00 |

—Yellow label, purple print

| ❑ 9008 | Love Me Do/P.S. I Love You | 1964 | 12.50 | 25.00 | 50.00 |

—Yellow label, blue/green print

| ❑ 9008 | Love Me Do/P.S. I Love You | 1964 | 12.50 | 25.00 | 50.00 |

—Yellow label, black print (any logo or print variation)

| ❑ 9008 | Love Me Do/P.S. I Love You | 1964 | 15.00 | 30.00 | 60.00 |

—Black label, silver print

| ❑ 9008 [DJ] | Love Me Do/P.S. I Love You | 1964 | 100.00 | 200.00 | 400.00 |
| ❑ 9008 [PS] | Love Me Do/P.S. I Love You | 1964 | 37.50 | 75.00 | 150.00 |

UNITED ARTISTS

❑ SP-2357 [DJ]	A Hard Day's Night Theatre Lobby Spot	1964	500.00	1000.	1500.
❑ UAEP 10029 [DJ]	A Hard Day's Night Open End Interview	1964	500.00	1000.	1500.
❑ ULP-42370	Let It Be Radio Spots	1970	400.00	800.00	1200.

VEE JAY

| ❑ (no #) [PS] | We Wish You a Merry Christmas and a Happy New Year | 1964 | 20.00 | 40.00 | 80.00 |

—Used with any Vee Jay or Tollie Beatles single in 1964-65 holiday season

| ❑ Spec. DJ No. 8 | Ask Me Why/Anna | 1964 | 5000. | 7500. | 10000. |

—Though it doesn't fit into any known Vee Jay numbering system (other "Spec. DJ No." records are rumored, but none are confirmed), this is an authentic 1964 promotional release

| ❑ 498 | Please Please Me/Ask Me Why | 1963 | 300.00 | 600.00 | 900.00 |

—Correct spelling; number is "VJ 498"; thick print

| ❑ 498 | Please Please Me/Ask Me Why | 1963 | 750.00 | 1125. | 1500. |

—Misspelled "The Beattles"; number is "VJ 498"

| ❑ 498 | Please Please Me/Ask Me Why | 1963 | 800.00 | 1200. | 1600. |

—Correct spelling; number is "#498"

| ❑ 498 | Please Please Me/Ask Me Why | 1963 | 800.00 | 1200. | 1600. |

—Misspelled "The Beattles"; number is "#498"

| ❑ 498 | Please Please Me/Ask Me Why | 1963 | 1000. | 1500. | 2000. |

—Correct spelling; number is "VJ 498"; brackets label

| ❑ 498 [DJ] | Please Please Me/Ask Me Why | 1963 | 550.00 | 825.00 | 1100. |

—Misspelled "The Beattles"

| ❑ 522 | From Me to You/Thank You Girl | 1963 | 150.00 | 300.00 | 600.00 |

—Black rainbow label; "Vee Jay" in oval

Number	Title (A Side/B Side)	Yr	VG	VG+	NM
❏ 522	From Me to You/Thank You Girl	1963	200.00	400.00	800.00

—Plain black label

| ❏ 522 | From Me to You/Thank You Girl | 1963 | 300.00 | 600.00 | 900.00 |

—Black rainbow label; "VJ" in brackets

| ❏ 522 [DJ] | From Me to You/Thank You Girl | 1963 | 125.00 | 250.00 | 500.00 |
| ❏ 581 | Please Please Me/From Me to You | 1964 | 11.25 | 22.50 | 45.00 |

—Plain black label with two horizontal lines

| ❏ 581 | Please Please Me/From Me to You | 1964 | 12.50 | 25.00 | 50.00 |

—Black rainbow label, oval logo

| ❏ 581 | Please Please Me/From Me to You | 1964 | 15.00 | 30.00 | 60.00 |

—Plain black label, "VEE JAY" stands alone

| ❏ 581 | Please Please Me/From Me to You | 1964 | 15.00 | 30.00 | 60.00 |

—Plain black label, oval logo

| ❏ 581 | Please Please Me/From Me to You | 1964 | 15.00 | 30.00 | 60.00 |

—Black rainbow label, brackets logo

| ❏ 581 | Please Please Me/From Me to You | 1964 | 16.25 | 32.50 | 65.00 |

—Plain black label, "VJ" stands alone

| ❏ 581 | Please Please Me/From Me to You | 1964 | 18.75 | 37.50 | 75.00 |

—Plain black label, brackets logo

| ❏ 581 | Please Please Me/From Me to You | 1964 | 18.75 | 37.50 | 75.00 |

—Yellow label

| ❏ 581 | Please Please Me/From Me to You | 1964 | 40.00 | 80.00 | 160.00 |

—White label

| ❏ 581 | Please Please Me/From Me to You | 1964 | 62.50 | 125.00 | 250.00 |

—Purple label

| ❏ 581 [DJ] | Please Please Me/From Me to You | 1964 | 200.00 | 400.00 | 600.00 |

—White label, blue print; "Promotional Copy" on label

| ❏ 581 [DJ] | Please Please Me/From Me to You | 1964 | 300.00 | 600.00 | 900.00 |

—White label, blue print; no "Promotional Copy" on label

| ❏ 581 [PS] | Please Please Me/From Me to You | 1964 | 125.00 | 250.00 | 500.00 |
| ❏ 581 [PS] | Please Please Me/From Me to You | 1964 | 1250. | 1875. | 2500. |

—Special "The Record That Started Beatlemania" promo-only sleeve

| ❏ 587 | Do You Want to Know a Secret/Thank You Girl | 1964 | 10.00 | 20.00 | 40.00 |

—Black rainbow label, brackets logo

| ❏ 587 | Do You Want to Know a Secret/Thank You Girl | 1964 | 11.25 | 22.50 | 45.00 |

—Plain black label with two horizontal lines; "VJ" in brackets

| ❏ 587 | Do You Want to Know a Secret/Thank You Girl | 1964 | 12.50 | 25.00 | 50.00 |

—Black rainbow label, oval logo

| ❏ 587 | Do You Want to Know a Secret/Thank You Girl | 1964 | 12.50 | 25.00 | 50.00 |

—Plain black label; "VEE JAY" stands alone

| ❏ 587 | Do You Want to Know a Secret/Thank You Girl | 1964 | 16.25 | 32.50 | 65.00 |

—Plain black label; "Vee Jay" in oval

| ❏ 587 | Do You Want to Know a Secret/Thank You Girl | 1964 | 16.25 | 32.50 | 65.00 |

—Plain black label; "VJ" in brackets

| ❏ 587 | Do You Want to Know a Secret/Thank You Girl | 1964 | 16.25 | 32.50 | 65.00 |

—Plain black label; "VJ" stands alone

| ❏ 587 | Do You Want to Know a Secret/Thank You Girl | 1964 | 16.25 | 32.50 | 65.00 |

—Yellow label

| ❏ 587 [DJ] | Do You Want to Know a Secret/Thank You Girl | 1964 | 150.00 | 300.00 | 600.00 |
| ❏ 587 [PS] | Do You Want to Know a Secret/Thank You Girl | 1964 | 30.00 | 60.00 | 120.00 |

7-Inch Extended Plays

CAPITOL

| ❏ SXA-2047 | (contents unknown) | 1964 | 100.00 | 200.00 | 400.00 |

—Stereo jukebox edtion; small hole, plays at 33 1/3 rpm

| ❏ SXA-2047 [PS] | Meet the Beatles | 1964 | 150.00 | 300.00 | 600.00 |

—With all jukebox title strips intact (deduct 33 percent if missing, deduct less if material is there but not intact)

| ❏ SXA-2080 [PS] | The Beatles' Second Album | 1964 | 150.00 | 300.00 | 600.00 |

—With all jukebox title strips intact (deduct 33 percent if missing, deduct less if material is there but not intact)

| ❏ SXA-2080 [S] | Thank You Girl/Devil in Her Heart/Money (That's What I Want)//Long Tall Sally/I Call Your Name/Please Mister Postman | 1964 | 100.00 | 200.00 | 400.00 |

—33 1/3 rpm, small hole jukebox edition

| ❏ SXA-2108 [PS] | Something New | 1964 | 150.00 | 300.00 | 600.00 |

—With all jukebox title strips intact (deduct 33 percent if missing, deduct less if material is there but not intact)

| ❏ SXA-2108 [S] | (contents unknown) | 1964 | 100.00 | 200.00 | 400.00 |

—33 1/3 rpm, small hole jukebox edition

❏ EAP 1-2121	Roll Over Beethoven/This Boy//All My Loving/Please Mr. Postman	1964	25.00	50.00	100.00
❏ EAP 1-2121 [PS]	Four by the Beatles	1964	75.00	150.00	300.00
❏ PRO-2548/9 [DJ]	Open End Interview with the Beatles	1964	200.00	400.00	800.00

—33 1/3 rpm, small hole. Authentic copies have colorband along outside of label.

| ❏ PRO-2548/9 [PS] | Open End Interview with the Beatles | 1964 | 250.00 | 500.00 | 1000. |

—Contains script for interview. Authentic copies are glossy and have a die-cut thumb tab.

| ❏ PRO-2598/9 [DJ] | The Beatles Second Album Open End Interview | 1964 | 200.00 | 400.00 | 800.00 |

—33 1/3 rpm, small hole; interview plus three songs from the LP

| ❏ PRO-2598/9 [PS] | The Beatles Second Album Open End Interview | 1964 | 250.00 | 500.00 | 1000. |

—Contains script for interview

| ❏ R-5365 | Honey Don't/I'm a Loser//Mr. Moonlight/Everybody's Trying to Be My Baby | 1965 | 20.00 | 40.00 | 80.00 |
| ❏ R-5365 [PS] | 4-By the Beatles | 1965 | 50.00 | 100.00 | 200.00 |

POLYDOR

| ❏ PRO 1113-7 [DJ] | Ain't She Sweet/Cry for a Shadow//My Bonnie/The Saints | 1994 | 6.25 | 12.50 | 25.00 |
| ❏ PRO 1113-7 [PS] | Backbeat | 1994 | 6.25 | 12.50 | 25.00 |

—Picture sleeve for above sampler

VEE JAY

| ❏ 1-903 | Misery/Taste of Honey//Ask Me Why/Anna | 1964 | 10.00 | 20.00 | 40.00 |

—Black rainbow label, oval logo

| ❏ 1-903 | Misery/Taste of Honey//Ask Me Why/Anna | 1964 | 22.50 | 45.00 | 90.00 |

—Black rainbow label, brackets logo, all titles the same size

| ❏ 1-903 | Misery/Taste of Honey//Ask Me Why/Anna | 1964 | 31.25 | 62.50 | 125.00 |

—Black rainbow label, brackets logo, "Ask Me Why" in much larger print

| ❏ 1-903 | Misery/Taste of Honey//Ask Me Why/Anna | 1964 | 31.25 | 62.50 | 125.00 |

—Plain black label, oval logo

| ❏ 1-903 | Misery/Taste of Honey//Ask Me Why/Anna | 1964 | 37.50 | 75.00 | 150.00 |

—Plain black label, "VEE JAY" stands alone

| ❏ 1-903 | Misery/Taste of Honey//Ask Me Why/Anna | 1964 | 50.00 | 100.00 | 200.00 |

—Plain black label, brackets logo

| ❏ 1-903 [DJ] | Misery/Taste of Honey//Ask Me Why/Anna | 1964 | 75.00 | 150.00 | 300.00 |

—White and blue label, "Ask Me Why" in much larger print

| ❏ 1-903 [DJ] | Misery/Taste of Honey//Ask Me Why/Anna | 1964 | 100.00 | 200.00 | 400.00 |

—White and blue label, all titles the same size

| ❏ 1-903 [PS] | Souvenir of Their Visit to America | 1964 | 15.00 | 30.00 | 60.00 |

—Cardboard sleeve

| ❏ 1-903 [PS] | Souvenir of Their Visit to America | 1964 | 4000. | 6000. | 8000. |

—"Ask Me Why/The Beatles" plugged on promo-only sleeve

Albums

APPLE

| ❏ SBC-100 [M] | The Beatles' Christmas Album | 1970 | 100.00 | 200.00 | 400.00 |

—Fan club issue of the seven Christmas messages; very good counterfeits exist

| ❏ SWBO-101 [(2)] | The Beatles | 1968 | 37.50 | 75.00 | 200.00 |

—Numbered copy; includes four individual photos and large poster (included in value); because the white cover shows ring wear so readily, this is an EXTREMELY difficult album to find in near-mint condition

| ❏ SWBO-101 [(2)] | The Beatles | 197? | 15.00 | 30.00 | 60.00 |

—Un-numbered copy; includes four individual photos and large poster (included in value)

| ❏ SWBO-101 [(2)] | The Beatles | 1975 | 17.50 | 35.00 | 70.00 |

—With "All Rights Reserved" on labels; title in black on cover; photos and poster of thinner stock than originals

| ❏ SW-153 [P] | Yellow Submarine | 1969 | 12.50 | 25.00 | 50.00 |

—With Capitol logo on Side 2 bottom. "Only a Northern Song" is rechanneled.

| ❏ SW-153 [P] | Yellow Submarine | 1971 | 5.00 | 10.00 | 20.00 |

—With "Mfd. by Apple" on label

| ❏ SW-153 [P] | Yellow Submarine | 1975 | 6.25 | 12.50 | 25.00 |

—With "All Rights Reserved" on label

| ❏ SO-383 | Abbey Road | 1969 | 5.00 | 10.00 | 20.00 |

—With "Mfd. by Apple" on label; "Her Majesty" IS listed on the label

| ❏ SO-383 | Abbey Road | 1969 | 5.00 | 10.00 | 20.00 |

—With "Mfd. by Apple" on label; "Her Majesty" is NOT listed on the label

| ❏ SO-383 | Abbey Road | 1969 | 10.00 | 20.00 | 40.00 |

—With Capitol logo on Side 2 bottom; "Her Majesty" IS listed on both the jacket and the label

| ❏ SO-383 | Abbey Road | 1969 | 18.75 | 37.50 | 75.00 |

—With Capitol logo on Side 2 bottom; "Her Majesty" is NOT listed on either the jacket or the label

| ❏ SO-383 | Abbey Road | 1975 | 6.25 | 12.50 | 25.00 |

—With "All Rights Reserved" on label, either in black print or in light print along label edge (both versions exist)

| ❏ SO-385 [DJ] | The Beatles Again | 1970 | 4000. | 6000. | 8000. |

—Prototype covers with "The Beatles Again" on cover; not released to the general public. This is NOT a standard issue!

| ❏ SW-385 | Hey Jude | 1970 | 5.00 | 10.00 | 20.00 |

—With "Mfd. by Apple" on label; label calls the LP "Hey Jude"

| ❏ SW-385 | Hey Jude | 1970 | 6.25 | 12.50 | 25.00 |

—Label calls the LP "The Beatles Again"; record is "SW-385"

| ❏ SW-385 | Hey Jude | 1970 | 10.00 | 20.00 | 40.00 |

—Label calls the LP "The Beatles Again"; record is "SO-385" (this could be found in retail stores as late as 1973)

| ❏ SW-385 | Hey Jude | 1970 | 18.75 | 37.50 | 75.00 |

—With Capitol logo on Side 2 bottom; label calls the LP "Hey Jude"

| ❏ SW-385 | Hey Jude | 1975 | 6.25 | 12.50 | 25.00 |

—With "All Rights Reserved" on label; label calls the LP "Hey Jude"

| ❏ SKBO-3403 [P] | The Beatles 1962-1966 | 1973 | 7.50 | 15.00 | 30.00 |

—Custom red Apple labels. "Love Me Do" and "I Want to Hold Your Hand" are rechanneled; "She Loves You," "A Hard Day's Night," "I Feel Fine" and "Ticket to Ride" are mono; "From Me to You," "Can't Buy Me Love" and everything else is stereo.

| ❏ SKBO-3403 [P] | The Beatles 1962-1966 | 1975 | 12.50 | 25.00 | 50.00 |

—Custom red Apple labels with "All Rights Reserved" on labels

| ❏ SKBO-3404 [B] | The Beatles 1967-1970 | 1973 | 7.50 | 15.00 | 30.00 |

—Custom blue Apple labels. "Hello Goodbye" and "Penny Lane" are mono, all others stereo.

| ❏ SKBO-3404 [B] | The Beatles 1967-1970 | 1975 | 12.50 | 25.00 | 50.00 |

—Custom blue Apple labels with "All Rights Reserved" on labels

| ❏ SPRO 11206/7 [EP] | Anthology 2 Sampler | 1996 | 37.50 | 75.00 | 150.00 |

—Promo-only collection sent to college radio stations

| ❏ C1-8-31796 [(2)] | Live at the BBC | 1994 | 12.50 | 25.00 | 50.00 |
| ❏ AR-34001 | Let It Be | 1970 | 6.25 | 12.50 | 25.00 |

—Red Apple label; originals have "Bell Sound" stamped in trail-off area, counterfeits do not

| ❏ C1-8-34445 [(3)] | Anthology 1 | 1995 | 10.00 | 20.00 | 40.00 |

—All copies distributed in the U.S. were manufactured in the U.K. with no distinguishing marks (some LPs imported directly from the U.K. have "Made in England" stickers, which can be removed easily)

❏ C1-8-34448 [(3)]	Anthology 2	1996	10.00	20.00	40.00
❏ C1-8-34451 [(3)]	Anthology 3	1996	7.50	15.00	30.00
❏ C1-97036 [B]	The Beatles 1962-1966	1993	6.25	12.50	25.00

—Custom red Apple labels; red vinyl; all copies pressed in U.K; U.S. versions have a bar-code sticker over the international bar code on back cover. "Love Me Do," "Please Please Me," "From Me to You" and "She Loves You" are mono; all others are stereo.

| ❏ C1-97039 | The Beatles 1967-1970 | 1993 | 6.25 | 12.50 | 25.00 |

—Custom blue Apple labels; blue vinyl; all copies pressed in U.K.; U.S. versions have a bar-code sticker over the international bar code on back cover

APPLE FILMS

| ❏ KAL 004 [DJ] | The Yellow Submarine (A United Artists Release) | 1969 | 1000. | 1500. | 2000. |

—One-sided LP with radio spots for movie

APPLE/CAPITOL

❏ (no #) [(10)]	The Beatles Special Limited Edition	1974	300.00	600.00	1200.
❏ (no #) [(17)]	The Beatles 10th Anniversary Box Set	1974	1000.	1500.	2000.
❏ ST 2047 [P]	Meet the Beatles!	1968	10.00	20.00	40.00

—With Capitol logo on Side 2 bottom

| ❏ ST 2047 [P] | Meet the Beatles! | 1971 | 5.00 | 10.00 | 20.00 |

—With "Mfd. by Apple" on label

| ❏ ST 2047 [P] | Meet the Beatles! | 1975 | 6.25 | 12.50 | 25.00 |

—With "All Rights Reserved" on label

| ❏ ST 2080 [P] | The Beatles' Second Album | 1968 | 10.00 | 20.00 | 40.00 |

—With Capitol logo on Side 2 bottom

| ❏ ST 2080 [P] | The Beatles' Second Album | 1971 | 5.00 | 10.00 | 20.00 |

—With "Mfd. by Apple" on label

| ❏ ST 2080 [P] | The Beatles' Second Album | 1975 | 6.25 | 12.50 | 25.00 |

—With "All Rights Reserved" on label

| ❏ ST 2108 [S] | Something New | 1968 | 10.00 | 20.00 | 40.00 |

—With Capitol logo on Side 2 bottom

| ❏ ST 2108 [S] | Something New | 1971 | 5.00 | 10.00 | 20.00 |

—With "Mfd. by Apple" on label

Number	Title (A Side/B Side)	Yr	VG	VG+	NM
☐ ST 2108 [S] Something New		1975	6.25	2.50	25.00
—With "All Rights Reserved" on label					
☐ STBO 2222 [(2)P]The Beatles' Story		1968	12.50	25.00	50.00
—With Capitol logo on bottom of B-side of both records					
☐ STBO 2222 [(2)P]The Beatles' Story		1971	7.50	15.00	30.00
—With "Mfd. by Apple" on labels					
☐ STBO 2222 [(2)P]The Beatles' Story		1975	10.00	20.00	40.00
—With "All Rights Reserved" on labels					
☐ ST 2228 [P] Beatles '65		1968	10.00	20.00	40.00
—With Capitol logo on Side 2 bottom					
☐ ST 2228 [P] Beatles '65		1971	5.00	10.00	20.00
—With "Mfd. by Apple" on label					
☐ ST 2228 [P] Beatles '65		1975	6.25	12.50	25.00
—With "All Rights Reserved" on label					
☐ ST 2309 [P] The Early Beatles		1969	10.00	20.00	40.00
—With Capitol logo on Side 2 bottom					
☐ ST 2309 [P] The Early Beatles		1971	5.00	10.00	20.00
—With "Mfd. by Apple" on label					
☐ ST 2309 [P] The Early Beatles		1975	6.25	12.50	25.00
—With "All Rights Reserved" on label					
☐ ST 2358 [P] Beatles VI		1969	10.00	20.00	40.00
—With Capitol logo on Side 2 bottom					
☐ ST 2358 [P] Beatles VI		1971	5.00	10.00	20.00
—With "Mfd. by Apple" on label					
☐ ST 2358 [P] Beatles VI		1975	6.25	12.50	25.00
—With "All Rights Reserved" on label					
☐ SMAS 2386 [P]Help!		1969	10.00	20.00	40.00
—With Capitol logo on Side 2 bottom					
☐ SMAS 2386 [P]Help!		1971	5.00	10.00	20.00
—With "Mfd. by Apple" on label					
☐ SMAS 2386 [P]Help!		1975	6.25	12.50	25.00
—With "All Rights Reserved" on label					
☐ ST 2442 [S] Rubber Soul		1969	10.00	20.00	40.00
—With Capitol logo on Side 2 bottom					
☐ ST 2442 [S] Rubber Soul		1971	5.00	10.00	20.00
—With "Mfd. by Apple" on label					
☐ ST 2442 [S] Rubber Soul		1975	6.25	12.50	25.00
—With "All Rights Reserved" on label					
☐ ST 2553 [P] Yesterday and Today		1969	10.00	20.00	40.00
—With Capitol logo on Side 2 bottom					
☐ ST 2553 [P] Yesterday and Today		1971	5.00	10.00	20.00
—With "Mfd. by Apple" on label					
☐ ST 2553 [S] Yesterday and Today		1971	6.25	12.50	25.00
—With "Mfd. by Apple" on label; all 11 tracks are in true stereo. Check for a triangle in the record's trail-off area.					
☐ ST 2553 [P] Yesterday and Today		1975	6.25	12.50	25.00
—With "All Rights Reserved" on label					
☐ ST 2576 [S] Revolver		1969	10.00	20.00	40.00
—With Capitol logo on Side 2 bottom					
☐ ST 2576 [S] Revolver		1971	5.00	10.00	20.00
—With "Mfd. by Apple" on label					
☐ ST 2576 [S] Revolver		1975	6.25	12.50	25.00
—With "All Rights Reserved" on label					
☐ SMAS 2653 [S]Sgt. Pepper's Lonely Hearts Club Band		1969	10.00	20.00	40.00
—With Capitol logo on Side 2 bottom					
☐ SMAS 2653 [S]Sgt. Pepper's Lonely Hearts Club Band		1971	6.25	12.50	25.00
—With "Mfd. by Apple" on label					
☐ SMAS 2653 [S]Sgt. Pepper's Lonely Hearts Club Band		1975	6.25	12.50	25.00
—With "All Rights Reserved" on label					
☐ SMAL 2835 [P] Magical Mystery Tour		1969	10.00	20.00	40.00
—With Capitol logo on Side 2 bottom; with 24-page booklet					
☐ SMAL 2835 [P] Magical Mystery Tour		1971	5.00	10.00	20.00
—With "Mfd. by Apple" on label; with 24-page booklet					
☐ SMAL 2835 [P] Magical Mystery Tour		1975	6.25	12.50	25.00
—With "All Rights Reserved" on label; with 24-page booklet					
ATCO					
☐ 33-169 [M] Ain't She Sweet		1964	50.00	100.00	200.00
☐ 33-169 [M] Ain't She Sweet		1964	250.00	500.00	1000.
—White label promo					
☐ SD 33-169 [P] Ain't She Sweet		1964	100.00	200.00	400.00
—Tan and purple label; all four Beatles tracks are rechanneled					
☐ SD 33-169 [P] Ain't She Sweet		1969	125.00	250.00	500.00
—Yellow label					
AUDIO RARITIES					
☐ AR-2452 [M] The Complete Silver Beatles		1982	3.75	7.50	15.00
—Contains 12 Decca audition tracks					
AUDIOFIDELITY					
☐ PD-339 [M] First Movement		1982	7.50	15.00	30.00
—Contains eight Decca audition tracks; picture disc					
☐ PHX-339 [M] First Movement		1982	3.00	6.00	12.00
—Contains eight Decca audition tracks					
BACKSTAGE					
☐ 2-201 [(2)M] Like Dreamers Do		1982	10.00	20.00	40.00
—Gatefold package, individually numbered (numbers under 100 increase value significantly)					
☐ 2-201 [(2)M] Like Dreamers Do		1982	12.50	25.00	50.00
—Non-gatefold package					
☐ BSR-1111 [DJ] Like Dreamers Do		1982	12.50	25.00	50.00
—Gray vinyl promo in white sleeve					
☐ BSR-1111 [DJ] Like Dreamers Do		1982	12.50	25.00	50.00
—White vinyl promo in white sleeve					
☐ BSR-1111 [(3)M]Like Dreamers Do		1982	15.00	30.00	60.00
—Two picture discs (10 of 15 Decca audition tracks on one, interviews on the other) and one white-vinyl record (same contests as musical picture disc)					
☐ BSR-1111 [(3)M]Like Dreamers Do		1982	25.00	50.00	100.00
—Same as above, except colored-vinyl LP is gray					
☐ BSR-1165 [PD] The Beatles Talk with Jerry G.		1982	6.25	12.50	25.00
—Picture disc					
☐ BSR-1175 [PD]The Beatles Talk with Jerry G., Vol. 2		1983	6.25	12.50	25.00
—Picture disc					
CAPITOL					
☐ (no #) [(18)] The Beatles Collection Platinum Series		1984	200.00	400.00	800.00
☐ BC-13 [(14)] The Beatles Collection		1978	62.50	125.00	250.00
—American versions have "EMI" and "BC-13" on box spine; imports go for less					
☐ SWBO-101 [(2)]The Beatles		1976	7.50	15.00	30.00
—Orange label; with photos and poster					
☐ SWBO-101 [(2)]The Beatles		1978	7.50	15.00	30.00
—Purple label, large Capitol logo; with photos and poster (some copies have four photos as one perforated sheet)					
☐ SWBO-101 [(2)]The Beatles		1983	10.00	20.00	40.00
—Black label, print in colorband; with photos and poster (some copies have four photos as one perforated sheet)					
☐ SW-153 [P] Yellow Submarine		1976	3.00	6.00	12.00
—Orange label					
☐ SW-153 [P] Yellow Submarine		1978	2.50	5.00	10.00
—Purple label, large Capitol logo					
☐ SW-153 [P] Yellow Submarine		1983	3.75	7.50	15.00
—Black label, print in colorband					
☐ SJ-383 Abbey Road		1984	7.50	15.00	30.00
—New prefix; black label, print in colorband					
☐ SO-383 Abbey Road		1976	3.00	6.00	12.00
—Orange label					
☐ SO-383 Abbey Road		1978	2.50	5.00	10.00
—Purple label, large Capitol logo					
☐ SO-383 Abbey Road		1983	3.75	7.50	15.00
—Black label, print in colorband					
☐ SJ-385 Hey Jude		1984	7.50	15.00	30.00
—New prefix; black label, print in colorband					
☐ SW-385 Hey Jude		1976	3.00	6.00	12.00
—Orange label (all Capitol label versions call the LP "Hey Jude")					
☐ SW-385 Hey Jude		1978	2.50	5.00	10.00
—Purple label, large Capitol logo					
☐ SW-385 Hey Jude		1983	12.50	25.00	50.00
—Black label, print in colorband					
☐ ST 2047 [P] Meet the Beatles!		1964	30.00	60.00	120.00
—Black label with colorband; "Beatles!" on cover in tan to brown print; some labels have "ASCAP" after every title except "I Want to Hold Your Hand"; other labels have "ASCAP" after every title except "I Want to Hold Your Hand," "I Saw Her Standing There" and "I Wanna Be Your Man"; still other labels have "ASCAP" after every title except "I Want to Hold Your Hand" and "I Wanna Be Your Man"; back cover adds "Produced by George Martin" to lower left					
☐ ST 2047 [P] Meet the Beatles!		1964	37.50	75.00	150.00
—Black label with colorband; "Beatles!" on cover in tan to brown print; label has "ASCAP" after every title except "I Want to Hold Your Hand" (BMI); no producer credit on back cover (this is the second edition of this LP)					
☐ ST 2047 [P] Meet the Beatles!		1964	100.00	200.00	400.00
—Black label with colorband; "Beatles!" on cover in tan to brown print; "ASCAP" and "BMI" credits are missing on the label; no producer credit on back cover (this is the first edition of the LP)					
☐ ST 2047 [P] Meet the Beatles!		1965	18.75	37.50	75.00
—Black label with colorband; "Beatles!" on cover in green print; most of these have "Produced by George Martin" on lower left of back cover; many of these have a label giving "BMI" credit to every song except "Don't Bother Me" and "Till There Was You"					
☐ ST 2047 [P] Meet the Beatles!		1968	12.50	25.00	50.00
—Black colorband label; border print adds "A Subsidiary of Capitol Industries Inc."					
☐ ST 2047 [P] Meet the Beatles!		1969	10.00	20.00	40.00
—Lime green label					
☐ ST 2047 [P] Meet the Beatles!		1976	3.00	6.00	12.00
—Orange label					
☐ ST 2047 [P] Meet the Beatles!		1978	2.50	5.00	10.00
—Purple label, large Capitol logo					
☐ ST 2047 [P] Meet the Beatles!		1983	3.75	7.50	15.00
—Black label, print in colorband					
☐ ST-8-2047 [P] Meet the Beatles!		1969	50.00	100.00	200.00
—Capitol Record Club edition; lime green label					
☐ ST-8-2047 [P] Meet the Beatles!		1969	125.00	250.00	500.00
—Capitol Record Club edition; black label with colorband					
☐ T 2047 [M] Meet the Beatles!		1964	37.50	75.00	150.00
—Black label with colorband; "Beatles!" on cover in tan to brown print; some labels have "ASCAP" after every title except "I Want to Hold Your Hand"; other labels have "ASCAP" after every title except "I Want to Hold Your Hand," "I Saw Her Standing There" and "I Wanna Be Your Man"; still other labels have "ASCAP" after every title except "I Want to Hold Your Hand" and "I Wanna Be Your Man"; most of the back covers add "Produced by George Martin" to lower left					
☐ T 2047 [M] Meet the Beatles!		1964	50.00	100.00	200.00
—Black label with colorband; "Beatles!" on cover in tan to brown print; label has "ASCAP" after every title except "I Want to Hold Your Hand" (BMI); no producer credit on back cover (this is the second edition of this LP)					
☐ T 2047 [M] Meet the Beatles!		1964	100.00	200.00	400.00
—Black label with colorband; "Beatles!" on cover in tan to brown print; no producer credit on back cover; "ASCAP" and "BMI" credits are missing on the label (this is the first edition of the LP)					
☐ T 2047 [M] Meet the Beatles!		1965	25.00	50.00	100.00
—Black label with colorband; "Beatles!" on cover in green print; most of these have "Produced by George Martin" on lower left of back cover; many of these have a label giving "BMI" credit to every song except "Don't Bother Me" and "Till There Was You"					
☐ ST 2080 [P] The Beatles' Second Album		1964	25.00	50.00	100.00
—Black label with colorband. "She Loves You," "I'll Get You" and "You Can't Do That" are rechanneled					
☐ ST 2080 [P] The Beatles' Second Album		1968	12.50	25.00	50.00
—Black colorband label; border print adds "A Subsidiary of Capitol Industries Inc."					
☐ ST 2080 [P] The Beatles' Second Album		1969	10.00	20.00	40.00
—Lime green label					
☐ ST 2080 [P] The Beatles' Second Album		1976	3.00	6.00	12.00
—Orange label					
☐ ST 2080 [P] The Beatles' Second Album		1978	2.50	5.00	10.00
—Purple label, large Capitol logo					
☐ ST 2080 [P] The Beatles' Second Album		1983	3.75	7.50	15.00
—Black label, print in colorband					
☐ ST-8-2080 [P] The Beatles' Second Album		1964	125.00	250.00	500.00
—Capitol Record Club edition; black label with colorband					
☐ ST-8-2080 [P] The Beatles' Second Album		1969	75.00	150.00	300.00
—Capitol Record Club edition; lime green label					
☐ T 2080 [M] The Beatles' Second Album		1964	45.00	90.00	180.00
☐ ST 2108 [S] Something New		1964	20.00	40.00	80.00
—Black label with colorband					
☐ ST 2108 [S] Something New		1968	12.50	25.00	50.00
—Black colorband label; border print adds "A Subsidiary of Capitol Industries Inc."					
☐ ST 2108 [S] Something New		1969	10.00	20.00	40.00
—Lime green label					
☐ ST 2108 [S] Something New		1976	3.00	6.00	12.00
—Orange label					

BEATLES, THE
110

Number	Title (A Side/B Side)	Yr	VG	VG+	NM
❑ ST 2108 [S] Something New		1978	2.50	5.00	10.00
—Purple label, large Capitol logo					
❑ ST 2108 [S] Something New		1983	3.75	7.50	15.00
—Black label, print in colorband					
❑ ST-8-2108 [S] Something New		1964	75.00	150.00	300.00
—Capitol Record Club edition; black label with colorband					
❑ ST-8-2108 [S] Something New		1969	37.50	75.00	150.00
—Capitol Record Club edition; lime green label					
❑ ST-8-2108 [S] Something New		1969	75.00	150.00	300.00
—Longines Symphonette edition (will be stated on label); lime green label					
❑ T 2108 [M] Something New		1964	37.50	75.00	150.00
❑ STBO 2222 [(2)P]The Beatles' Story		1964	37.50	75.00	150.00
—Black label with colorband. Some of the musical snippets are rechanneled.					
❑ STBO 2222 [(2)P]The Beatles' Story		1968	20.00	40.00	80.00
—Black colorband label; border print adds "A Subsidiary of Capitol Industries Inc."					
❑ STBO 2222 [(2)P]The Beatles' Story		1969	12.50	25.00	50.00
—Lime green label					
❑ STBO 2222 [(2)P]The Beatles' Story		1976	5.00	10.00	20.00
—Orange label					
❑ STBO 2222 [(2)P]The Beatles' Story		1978	5.00	10.00	20.00
—Purple label, large Capitol logo					
❑ STBO 2222 [(2)P]The Beatles' Story		1983	10.00	20.00	40.00
—Black label, print in colorband					
❑ TBO 2222 [(2)M]The Beatles' Story		1964	50.00	100.00	200.00
❑ ST 2228 [P] Beatles '65		1964	20.00	40.00	80.00
—Black label with colorband. "She's a Woman" and "I Feel Fine" are rechanneled.					
❑ ST 2228 [P] Beatles '65		1968	12.50	25.00	50.00
—Black colorband label; border print adds "A Subsidiary of Capitol Industries Inc."					
❑ ST 2228 [P] Beatles '65		1969	10.00	20.00	40.00
—Lime green label					
❑ ST 2228 [P] Beatles '65		1976	3.00	6.00	12.00
—Orange label					
❑ ST 2228 [P] Beatles '65		1978	2.50	5.00	10.00
—Purple label, large Capitol logo					
❑ ST 2228 [P] Beatles '65		1983	3.75	7.50	15.00
—Black label, print in colorband					
❑ T 2228 [M] Beatles '65		1964	30.00	60.00	120.00
❑ ST 2309 [P] The Early Beatles		1965	25.00	50.00	100.00
—Black label with colorband. "Love Me Do" and "P.S. I Love You" are rechanneled.					
❑ ST 2309 [P] The Early Beatles		1968	12.50	25.00	50.00
—Black colorband label; border print adds "A Subsidiary of Capitol Industries Inc."					
❑ ST 2309 [P] The Early Beatles		1969	10.00	20.00	40.00
—Lime green label					
❑ ST 2309 [P] The Early Beatles		1976	3.00	6.00	12.00
—Orange label					
❑ ST 2309 [P] The Early Beatles		1978	2.50	5.00	10.00
—Purple label, large Capitol logo					
❑ ST 2309 [P] The Early Beatles		1983	6.25	12.50	25.00
—Black label, print in colorband					
❑ T 2309 [M] The Early Beatles		1965	50.00	100.00	200.00
❑ ST 2358 [P] Beatles VI		1965	18.75	37.50	75.00
—Black label with colorband; with song titles listed in correct order on back cover. "Yes It Is" is rechanneled.					
❑ ST 2358 [P] Beatles VI		1965	20.00	40.00	80.00
—Black label with colorband; with "See label for correct playing order" on back cover					
❑ ST 2358 [P] Beatles VI		1968	12.50	25.00	50.00
—Black colorband label; border print adds "A Subsidiary of Capitol Industries Inc."					
❑ ST 2358 [P] Beatles VI		1969	10.00	20.00	40.00
—Lime green label					
❑ ST 2358 [P] Beatles VI		1976	3.00	6.00	12.00
—Orange label					
❑ ST 2358 [P] Beatles VI		1978	2.50	5.00	10.00
—Purple label, large Capitol logo					
❑ ST 2358 [P] Beatles VI		1983	3.75	7.50	15.00
—Black label, print in colorband; plays in mono despite label designation					
❑ ST 2358 [M] Beatles VI		1988	20.00	40.00	80.00
—Purple label, small Capitol logo; plays in mono despite label designation					
❑ ST-8-2358 [P] Beatles VI		1965	125.00	250.00	500.00
—Capitol Record Club edition; black label with colorband					
❑ ST-8-2358 [P] Beatles VI		1969	100.00	200.00	400.00
—Capitol Record Club edition; lime green label					
❑ T 2358 [M] Beatles VI		1965	25.00	50.00	100.00
—With song titles listed in correct order on back cover					
❑ T 2358 [M] Beatles VI		1965	30.00	60.00	120.00
—With "See label for correct playing order" on back cover					
❑ MAS 2386 [M] Help!		1965	37.50	75.00	150.00
❑ SMAS 2386 [P]Help!		1965	18.75	37.50	75.00
—Black label with colorband. Has incidental music by George Martin. "Ticket to Ride" is rechanneled.					
❑ SMAS 2386 [P]Help!		1968	12.50	25.00	50.00
—Black colorband label; border print adds "A Subsidiary of Capitol Industries Inc."					
❑ SMAS 2386 [P]Help!		1969	10.00	20.00	40.00
—Lime green label					
❑ SMAS 2386 [P]Help!		1976	3.00	6.00	12.00
—Orange label					
❑ SMAS 2386 [P]Help!		1978	2.50	5.00	10.00
—Purple label, large Capitol logo					
❑ SMAS 2386 [P]Help!		1983	3.75	7.50	15.00
—Black label, print in colorband					
❑ SMAS-8-2386 [P]Help!		1965	100.00	200.00	400.00
—Capitol Record Club edition; black label with colorband; no "8" on cover					
❑ SMAS-8-2386 [P]Help!		1965	150.00	300.00	600.00
—Capitol Record Club edition; black label with colorband; with "8" on cover					
❑ SMAS-8-2386 [P]Help!		1969	50.00	100.00	200.00
—Capitol Record Club edition; lime green label; no "8" on cover					
❑ SMAS-8-2386 [P]Help!		1969	100.00	200.00	400.00
—Capitol Record Club edition; lime green label; with "8" on cover					
❑ SMAS-8-2386 [P]Help!		197?	175.00	350.00	700.00
—Longines Symphonette edition; with "Mfd. by Longines" and "8" on cover					
❑ ST 2442 [S] Rubber Soul		1965	15.00	30.00	60.00
—Black label with colorband					
❑ ST 2442 [S] Rubber Soul		1968	12.50	25.00	50.00
—Black colorband label; border print adds "A Subsidiary of Capitol Industries Inc."					
❑ ST 2442 [S] Rubber Soul		1969	10.00	20.00	40.00
—Lime green label					
❑ ST 2442 [S] Rubber Soul		1976	3.00	6.00	12.00
—Orange label					
❑ ST-8-2442 [S] Rubber Soul		1965	75.00	150.00	300.00
—Capitol Record Club edition; black label with colorband					
❑ ST-8-2442 [S] Rubber Soul		1969	50.00	100.00	200.00
—Capitol Record Club edition; lime green label					
❑ ST-8-2442 [S] Rubber Soul		1969	62.50	125.00	250.00
—Longines Symphonette edition (will be stated on label); lime green label					
❑ SW 2442 [S] Rubber Soul		1978	2.50	5.00	10.00
—Purple label, large Capitol logo					
❑ SW 2442 [S] Rubber Soul		1983	3.75	7.50	15.00
—Black label, print in colorband					
❑ T 2442 [M] Rubber Soul		1965	30.00	60.00	120.00
❑ ST 2553 [P] Yesterday and Today		1966	40.00	60.00	80.00
—Trunk cover; black label with colorband (all later variations have the trunk cover). "I'm Only Sleeping," "Dr. Robert" and "And Your Bird Can Sing" are rechanneled.					
❑ ST 2553 [P] Yesterday and Today		1966	500.00	750.00	1000.
—"Second state" butcher cover (trunk cover pasted over original cover)					
❑ ST 2553 [P] Yesterday and Today		1966	375.00	750.00	1500.
—"Third state" butcher cover (trunk cover removed, leaving butcher cover intact); cover will be about 3/16-inch narrower than other Capitol Beatles LPs; value is highly negotiable depending upon the success of removing the paste-over					
❑ ST 2553 [P] Yesterday and Today		1966	4000.	6000.	8000.
—"First state" butcher cover (never had other cover on top); cover will be the same size as other Capitol Beatles LPs					
❑ ST 2553 [P] Yesterday and Today		1968	12.50	25.00	50.00
—Black colorband label; border print adds "A Subsidiary of Capitol Industries Inc."					
❑ ST 2553 [P] Yesterday and Today		1969	10.00	20.00	40.00
—Lime green label					
❑ ST 2553 [P] Yesterday and Today		1976	3.00	6.00	12.00
—Orange label; it's possible that this and all future pressings have all 11 tracks in true stereo, but we don't know.					
❑ ST 2553 [P] Yesterday and Today		1978	2.50	5.00	10.00
—Purple label, large Capitol logo					
❑ ST 2553 [P] Yesterday and Today		1983	3.75	7.50	15.00
—Black label, print in colorband					
❑ ST-8-2553 [P] Yesterday and Today		1966	75.00	150.00	300.00
—Capitol Record Club edition; black label with colorband					
❑ ST-8-2553 [P] Yesterday and Today		1969	37.50	75.00	150.00
—Capitol Record Club edition; lime green label; all 11 tracks are in true stereo! (We don't know if the same is true of the black label version.)					
❑ T 2553 [M] Yesterday and Today		1966	37.50	75.00	150.00
—Trunk cover					
❑ T 2553 [M] Yesterday and Today		1966	250.00	500.00	1000.
—"Second state" butcher cover (trunk cover pasted over original cover)					
❑ T 2553 [M] Yesterday and Today		1966	400.00	800.00	1200.
—"Third state" butcher cover (trunk cover removed, leaving butcher cover intact); cover will be about 3/16-inch narrower than other Capitol Beatles LPs; value is highly negotiable depending upon the success of removing the paste-over					
❑ T 2553 [M] Yesterday and Today		1966	2000.	3000.	4000.
—"First state" butcher cover (never had other cover on top); cover will be the same size as other Capitol Beatles LPs					
❑ ST 2576 [S] Revolver		1966	25.00	50.00	100.00
—Black label with colorband					
❑ ST 2576 [S] Revolver		1968	12.50	25.00	50.00
—Black colorband label; border print adds "A Subsidiary of Capitol Industries Inc."					
❑ ST 2576 [S] Revolver		1969	10.00	20.00	40.00
—Lime green label					
❑ ST 2576 [S] Revolver		1970	75.00	150.00	300.00
—Red label with "target" Capitol at top (same design as lime green label)					
❑ ST 2576 [S] Revolver		1976	3.00	6.00	12.00
—Orange label					
❑ ST-8-2576 [S] Revolver		1966	100.00	200.00	400.00
—Capitol Record Club edition; black label with colorband					
❑ ST-8-2576 [S] Revolver		1969	30.00	60.00	120.00
—Capitol Record Club edition; lime green label					
❑ ST-8-2576 [S] Revolver		1973?	50.00	100.00	200.00
—Capitol Record Club edition; orange label (a very late issue, as Capitol Record Club closed in 1973)					
❑ SW 2576 [S] Revolver		1978	2.50	5.00	10.00
—Purple label, large Capitol logo					
❑ SW 2576 [S] Revolver		1983	3.75	7.50	15.00
—Black label, print in colorband					
❑ T 2576 [M] Revolver		1966	50.00	100.00	200.00
❑ 2653 Sgt. Pepper's Lonely Hearts Club Band Cut-Out Inserts		1967	—	—	3.00
❑ 2653 Sgt. Pepper's Lonely Hearts Club Band Special Inner Sleeve		1967	3.75	7.50	15.00
—Red-pink psychedelic sleeve only issued with 1967 (mono and stereo) editions					
❑ MAS 2653 [M] Sgt. Pepper's Lonely Hearts Club Band		1967	75.00	150.00	300.00
❑ SMAS 2653 [S] Sgt. Pepper's Lonely Hearts Club Band		1967	25.00	50.00	100.00
—Black label with colorband					
❑ SMAS 2653 [S]Sgt. Pepper's Lonely Hearts Club Band		1968	15.00	30.00	60.00
—Black colorband label; border print adds "A Subsidiary of Capitol Industries Inc."					
❑ SMAS 2653 [S]Sgt. Pepper's Lonely Hearts Club Band		1969	12.50	25.00	50.00
—Lime green label					
❑ SMAS 2653 [S]Sgt. Pepper's Lonely Hearts Club Band		1976	3.00	6.00	12.00
—Orange label					
❑ SMAS 2653 [S]Sgt. Pepper's Lonely Hearts Club Band		1978	2.50	5.00	10.00
—Purple label, large Capitol logo. Many copies from 1978 had a "The Original Classic" sticker on shrink wrap; it was added at the time of the release of the bomb movie version of Sgt. Pepper. Double the value if the sticker is still there.					
❑ SMAS 2653 [S]Sgt. Pepper's Lonely Hearts Club Band		1983	3.75	7.50	15.00
—Black label, print in colorband; some of these had "The Original Classic" stickers, too. Add $10 to value if it is there.					
❑ MAL 2835 [M] Magical Mystery Tour		1967	75.00	150.00	300.00
—With 24-page book bound into center of gatefold					
❑ SMAL 2835 [S] Magical Mystery Tour		1967	25.00	50.00	100.00
—Black label with colorband; with 24-page booklet. "Penny Lane," "Baby You're a Rich Man" and "All You Need Is Love" is rechanneled, as is the second half of "I Am the Walrus" (every "stereo" version of "Walrus" is this way)					

Number	Title (A Side/B Side)	Yr	VG	VG+	NM
SMAL 2835 [P]	Magical Mystery Tour	1968	15.00	30.00	60.00

—Black colorband label; border print adds "A Subsidiary of Capitol Industries Inc."; with 24-page booklet

SMAL 2835 [P]	Magical Mystery Tour	1969	12.50	25.00	50.00

—Lime green label; with 24-page booklet

SMAL 2835 [P]	Magical Mystery Tour	1976	3.00	6.00	12.00

—Orange label; with 24-page booklet

SMAL 2835 [P]	Magical Mystery Tour	1978	2.50	5.00	10.00

—Purple label, large Capitol logo; this edition did not come with booklet

SMAL 2835 [P]	Magical Mystery Tour	1983	3.75	7.50	15.00

—Black label, print in colorband; no booklet

SKBO-3403 [P]	The Beatles 1962-1966	1976	5.00	10.00	20.00

—Red labels

SKBO-3403 [P]	The Beatles 1962-1966	1976	7.50	15.00	30.00

—Blue labels (error pressing)

SKBO-3404 [B]	The Beatles 1967-1970	1976	5.00	10.00	20.00

—Blue labels

SPRO-8969	Rarities	1978	12.50	25.00	50.00

—Purple label, large Capitol logo; part of the U.S. box set The Beatles Collection (BC-13)

SKBO-11537 [(2)]	Rock 'n' Roll Music	1976	6.25	12.50	25.00
SMAS-11638	The Beatles at the Hollywood Bowl	1977	5.00	10.00	20.00

—Originals with embossed title and ticket on front cover

SMAS-11638 [DJ]	The Beatles at the Hollywood Bowl	1977	125.00	250.00	500.00

—Advance tan label promo in plain white jacket

SMAS-11638	The Beatles at the Hollywood Bowl	1980	3.75	7.50	15.00

—Second pressing without embossed title and ticket

SMAS-11638	The Beatles at the Hollywood Bowl	1989	10.00	20.00	40.00

—With UPC code on back cover

SKBL-11711 [(2)P]	Love Songs	1977	5.00	10.00	20.00

—With booklet and embossed, leather-like cover. "P.S. I Love You" and "Yes It Is" are rechanneled.

SKBL-11711 [(2)P]	Love Songs	1988	7.50	15.00	30.00

—With booklet, but without embossed cover

SEAX-11840 [PD]	Sgt. Pepper's Lonely Hearts Club Band	1978	5.00	10.00	20.00

—Picture disc; deduct 25% for cut-outs

SEBX-11841 [(2)]	The Beatles	1978	12.50	25.00	50.00

—White vinyl; with photos and poster (with number "SEBX-11841" on each)

SEBX-11842 [P]	The Beatles 1962-1966	1978	10.00	20.00	40.00

—Red vinyl

SEBX-11843 [B]	The Beatles 1967-1970	1978	10.00	20.00	40.00

—Blue vinyl

SEAX-11900 [PD]	Abbey Road	1978	10.00	20.00	40.00

—Picture disc; deduct 25% for cut-outs

SW-11921 [P]	A Hard Day's Night	1979	3.00	6.00	12.00

—Purple label, large Capitol logo

SW-11921 [P]	A Hard Day's Night	1983	3.75	7.50	15.00

—Black label, print in colorband

SW-11921 [P]	A Hard Day's Night	1988	6.25	12.50	25.00

—Purple label, small Capitol logo

SW-11922	Let It Be	1979	3.75	7.50	15.00

—Purple label, large Capitol logo; with poster and custom innersleeve

SW-11922	Let It Be	1983	3.75	7.50	15.00

—Black label, print in colorband; add 33% if poster is included

SW-11922	Let It Be	1988	6.25	12.50	25.00

—Purple label, small Capitol logo; add 20% if poster and custom innersleeve are included

SN-12009 [DJ]	Rarities	1979	75.00	150.00	300.00

—Green label; withdrawn before official release; all known copies have a plain white sleeve

SHAL-12060 [B]	Rarities	1980	3.75	7.50	15.00

—Same as above, with errors deleted and "Produced by George Martin" added to back cover

SHAL-12060 [B]	Rarities	1980	5.00	10.00	20.00

—Black label with colorband. First pressing says that "There's a Place" debuts in stereo (false) and that the screaming at the end of "Helter Skelter" was a "classic Lennon statement" (it's actually Ringo).

SV-12199	Reel Music	1982	2.50	5.00	10.00

—Standard issue with 12-page booklet

SV-12199 [DJ]	Reel Music	1982	5.00	10.00	20.00

—Yellow vinyl promo; plain white cover with 12-page booklet

SV-12199 [DJ]	Reel Music	1982	10.00	20.00	40.00

—Yellow vinyl promo; numbered back cover with 12-page booklet

SV-12245	20 Greatest Hits	1982	5.00	10.00	20.00

—Purple label, large Capitol logo. "Love Me Do" and "She Loves You" are rechanneled, the other 18 tracks are stereo

SV-12245 [P]	20 Greatest Hits	1983	5.00	10.00	20.00

—Black label, print in colorband

SV-12245 [P]	20 Greatest Hits	1988	6.25	12.50	25.00

—Purple label, small Capitol logo

SN-16020	Rock 'n' Roll Music, Volume 1	1980	2.50	5.00	10.00
SN-16021	Rock 'n' Roll Music, Volume 2	1980	2.50	5.00	10.00
C1-46435 [M]	Please Please Me	1995	3.00	6.00	12.00

—New prefix; Apple logo on back cover

CLJ-46435 [M]	Please Please Me	1987	5.00	10.00	20.00

—Black label, print in colorband; first Capitol version of original British LP

CLJ-46435 [M]	Please Please Me	1988	6.25	12.50	25.00

—Purple label, small Capitol logo

C1-46436 [M]	With the Beatles	1995	3.00	6.00	12.00

—New prefix; Apple logo on back cover

CLJ-46436 [M]	With the Beatles	1987	5.00	10.00	20.00

—Black label, print in colorband; first Capitol version of original British LP

CLJ-46436 [M]	With the Beatles	1988	6.25	12.50	25.00

—Purple label, small Capitol logo

C1-46437 [M]	A Hard Day's Night	1995	3.00	6.00	12.00

—New prefix; Apple logo on back cover

CLJ-46437 [M]	A Hard Day's Night	1987	5.00	10.00	20.00

—Black label, print in colorband; first Capitol version of original British LP

CLJ-46437 [M]	A Hard Day's Night	1988	6.25	12.50	25.00

—Purple label, small Capitol logo

C1-46438 [M]	Beatles for Sale	1995	3.00	6.00	12.00

—New prefix; Apple logo on back cover

CLJ-46438 [M]	Beatles for Sale	1987	5.00	10.00	20.00

—Black label, print in colorband; first Capitol version of original British LP

CLJ-46438 [M]	Beatles for Sale	1988	6.25	12.50	25.00

—Purple label, small Capitol logo

C1-46439 [S]	Help!	1995	3.00	6.00	12.00

—New prefix; Apple logo on back cover

CLJ-46439 [S]	Help!	1987	5.00	10.00	20.00

—Black label, print in colorband; first Capitol version of original British LP

CLJ-46439 [S]	Help!	1988	6.25	12.50	25.00

—Purple label, small Capitol logo

C1-46440 [S]	Rubber Soul	1995	3.00	6.00	12.00

—New prefix; Apple logo on back cover

CLJ-46440 [S]	Rubber Soul	1987	5.00	10.00	20.00

—Black label, print in colorband; first Capitol version of original British LP

CLJ-46440 [S]	Rubber Soul	1988	6.25	12.50	25.00

—Purple label, small Capitol logo

C1-46441 [S]	Revolver	1995	3.00	6.00	12.00

—New prefix; Apple logo on back cover

CLJ-46441 [S]	Revolver	1987	5.00	10.00	20.00

—Black label, print in colorband; first Capitol version of original British LP

CLJ-46441 [S]	Revolver	1988	6.25	12.50	25.00

—Purple label, small Capitol logo

C1-46442 [S]	Sgt. Pepper's Lonely Hearts Club Band	1988	6.25	12.50	25.00

—New number; purple label, small Capitol logo

C1-46442 [S]	Sgt. Pepper's Lonely Hearts Club Band	1995	3.00	6.00	12.00

—With Apple logo on back cover

C1-46443 [(2)]	The Beatles	1988	12.50	25.00	50.00

—New number; purple label, small Capitol logo; with photos and poster (some copies have four photos as one perforated sheet)

C1-46443 [(2)]	The Beatles	1995	5.00	10.00	20.00

—With Apple logo on back cover

C1-46445 [P]	Yellow Submarine	1988	6.25	12.50	25.00

—New number; purple label, small Capitol logo

C1-46445 [P]	Yellow Submarine	1995	3.00	6.00	12.00

—Reissue has the British liner notes, which include a review of the White Album.

C1-46446	Abbey Road	1988	6.25	12.50	25.00

—New number; purple label, small Capitol logo

C1-46446	Abbey Road	1995	3.00	6.00	12.00

—Apple logo restored to back cover on reissue

C1-46447	Let It Be	1995	3.00	6.00	12.00

—New number (the only 1995 reissue with a completely new number)

C1-48062 [P]	Magical Mystery Tour	1988	6.25	12.50	25.00

—New number; purple label, small Capitol logo; no booklet

C1-48062 [P]	Magical Mystery Tour	1992	3.00	6.00	12.00

—With Apple logo on back cover; reissue restores booklet to package

C1-90435 [P]	The Beatles 1962-1966	1988	7.50	15.00	30.00

—New number; purple labels, small Capitol logo

C1-90438 [B]	The Beatles 1967-1970	1988	7.50	15.00	30.00

—New number; purple labels, small Capitol logo

C1-90441 [P]	Meet the Beatles!	1988	6.25	12.50	25.00

—New number; purple label, small Capitol logo

C1-90442	Hey Jude	1988	6.25	12.50	25.00

—New number; purple label, small Capitol logo

C1-90443 [S]	Something New	1988	6.25	12.50	25.00

—New number; purple label, small Capitol logo

C1-90444 [P]	The Beatles' Second Album	1988	6.25	12.50	25.00

—New number; purple label, small Capitol logo

C1-90445 [M]	Beatles VI	1988	6.25	12.50	25.00

—New number; purple label, small Capitol logo; plays in mono despite label designation

C1-90446 [P]	Beatles '65	1988	6.25	12.50	25.00

—New number; purple label, small Capitol logo

C1-90447 [P]	Yesterday and Today	1988	6.25	12.50	25.00

—New number; purple label, small Capitol logo; stereo content uncertain

C1-90452 [S]	Revolver	1988	6.25	12.50	25.00

—New number; purple label, small Capitol logo

C1-90453 [S]	Rubber Soul	1988	6.25	12.50	25.00

—New number; purple label, small Capitol logo

C1-90454 [P]	Help!	1988	6.25	12.50	25.00

—New number; purple label, small Capitol logo

C1-91135 [(2)B]	Past Masters Volume 1 and 2	1988	6.25	12.50	25.00

—Some tracks are in mono, but "This Boy," "She's a Woman." "Yes It Is," and "The Inner Light" are in stereo.

BBX1-91302 [(14)]	The Beatles Deluxe Box Set	1988	75.00	150.00	300.00

CICADELIC

1960	Moviemania	1987	3.00	6.00	12.00
1961	Not a Second Time	1987	3.00	6.00	12.00
1962	Things We Said Today	1986	3.00	6.00	12.00
1963	All Our Loving	1986	3.00	6.00	12.00
1964	East Coast Invasion	1985	3.00	6.00	12.00
1965	Round the World	1986	3.00	6.00	12.00
1966	West Coast Invasion	1985	3.00	6.00	12.00
1967	From Britain with Beat!	1987	3.00	6.00	12.00
1968	Here, There and Everywhere	1988	3.00	6.00	12.00

CLARION

601 [M]	The Amazing Beatles and Other Great English Group Sounds	1966	25.00	50.00	100.00
SD 601 [P]	The Amazing Beatles and Other Great English Group Sounds	1966	50.00	100.00	200.00

—All four Beatles tracks are rechanneled

GREAT NORTHWEST

GNW 4007	Beatle Talk	1978	2.50	5.00	10.00
GNW 4007	Beatle Talk	1978	12.50	25.00	50.00

—Columbia Record Club edition; "CRC" on spine

HALL OF MUSIC

HM-1-2200 [(2)M]	Live 1962, Hamburg, Germany	1981	12.50	25.00	50.00

—Only American LP with the original Europaean contents -- "I Saw Her Standing There," "Twist and Shout," "Ask Me Why" and "Reminiscing" replace the four songs listed with the Lingasong issue

I-N-S RADIO NEWS

DOC-1 [DJ]	Beatlemania Tour Coverage	1964	750.00	1125.	1500.

—Promo-only open-end interview with script in plain white jacket

LINGASONG

LS-2-7001 [(2)DJ]	Live at the Star Club in Hamburg, Germany, 1962	1977	10.00	20.00	40.00

—Promo on black vinyl; "D.J. Copy Not for Sale" on labels

LS-2-7001 [(2)DJ]	Live at the Star Club in Hamburg, Germany, 1962	1977	50.00	100.00	200.00

—Promo only on red vinyl

Number	Title (A Side/B Side)	Yr	VG	VG+	NM

Number	Title (A Side/B Side)	Yr	VG	VG+	NM
❑ LS-2-7001 [(2)DJ]	Live at the Star Club in Hamburg, Germany, 1962	1977	75.00	150.00	300.00

—Promo only on blue vinyl

❑ LS-2-7001 [(2)R]	Live at the Star Club in Hamburg, Germany, 1962	1977	5.00	10.00	20.00

—American version contains "I'm Gonna Sit Right Down and Cry," "Where Have You Been All My Life," "Till There Was You," and "Sheila," not on imports

LLOYDS

❑ ER-MC-LTD	The Great American Tour — 1965 Live Beatlemania Concert	1965	150.00	300.00	600.00

—Another interview album from the Ed Rudy people, with a live Beatles show in the background and the songs poorly overdubbed by the Liverpool Lads

METRO

❑ M-563 [M]	This Is Where It Started	1966	25.00	50.00	100.00

—Reissue of MGM album with two of the "others" tracks deleted

❑ MS-563 [R]	This Is Where It Started	1966	37.50	75.00	150.00

—In stereo cover

❑ MS-563 [R]	This Is Where It Started	1966	50.00	100.00	200.00

—In mono cover with "Stereo" sticker

MGM

❑ E-4215 [M]	The Beatles with Tony Sheridan and Their Guests	1964	50.00	100.00	200.00

—Without "And Guests" on cover

❑ E-4215 [M]	The Beatles with Tony Sheridan and Their Guests	1964	62.50	125.00	250.00

—With "And Guests" on cover

❑ SE-4215 [R]	The Beatles with Tony Sheridan and Their Guests	1964	150.00	300.00	600.00

—With "And Guests" on cover

❑ SE-4215 [R]	The Beatles with Tony Sheridan and Their Guests	1964	200.00	400.00	800.00

—Without "And Guests" on cover

MOBILE FIDELITY

❑ BC-1 [(13)]	The Beatles Collection	1982	125.00	250.00	500.00
❑ 1-023	Abbey Road	1979	12.50	25.00	50.00

—Audiophile vinyl

❑ 1-047 [P]	Magical Mystery Tour	1980	15.00	30.00	60.00

—Audiophile vinyl; yes, this contains the rechanneled stereo versions of "Penny Lane," "Baby You're a Rich Man" and "All You Need Is Love"

❑ 2-072 [(2)]	The Beatles	1982	12.50	25.00	50.00

—Audiophile vinyl; not issued with photos or poster

❑ 1-100 [S]	Sgt. Pepper's Lonely Hearts Club Band	1985	10.00	20.00	40.00

—Audiophile vinyl

❑ UHQR 1-100 [S]	Sgt. Pepper's Lonely Hearts Club Band	1982	75.00	150.00	300.00

—Ultra High Quality release with special cover; numbered edition of 5,000; numbers under 100 fetch even more

❑ 1-101 [P]	Please Please Me	1986	10.00	20.00	40.00

—Audiophile vinyl; British version of album. "Love Me Do" and "P.S. I Love You" are rechanneled.

❑ 1-102 [S]	With the Beatles	1986	37.50	75.00	150.00

—Audiophile vinyl; British version of album. Limited run because of a damaged stamper that was not replaced.

❑ 1-103 [S]	A Hard Day's Night	1987	10.00	20.00	40.00

—Audiophile vinyl; British version of album

❑ 1-104 [S]	Beatles for Sale	1986	10.00	20.00	40.00

—Audiophile vinyl; British version of album

❑ 1-105 [S]	Help!	1985	10.00	20.00	40.00

—Audiophile vinyl; British version of album

❑ 1-106 [S]	Rubber Soul	1985	10.00	20.00	40.00

—Audiophile vinyl; British version of album

❑ 1-107 [S]	Revolver	1986	10.00	20.00	40.00

—Audiophile vinyl; British version of album

❑ 1-108 [P]	Yellow Submarine	1987	15.00	30.00	60.00

—Audiophile vinyl

❑ 1-109	Let It Be	1987	10.00	20.00	40.00

—Audiophile vinyl; gatefold cover

❑ 1-109	Let It Be	1987	50.00	100.00	200.00

—Audiophile vinyl; regular cover

ORANGE

❑ ORC-12880 [DJ]	The Silver Beatles	1985	75.00	150.00	300.00

—Test pressing; white cover with title sticker

❑ ORC-12880 [DJ]	The Silver Beatles	1985	100.00	200.00	400.00

—Test pressing; full cover cover slick folded around a white cover. Both contain all 15 Decca audition tracks

PBR INTERNATIONAL

❑ 7005/6 [(2)]	The David Wigg Interviews (The Beatles Tapes)	1978	20.00	40.00	80.00

—Blue vinyl

❑ 7005/6 [(2)]	The David Wigg Interviews (The Beatles Tapes)	1980	15.00	30.00	60.00

—Black vinyl

PHOENIX

❑ PHX-352 [M]	Silver Beatles, Volume 1	1982	3.00	6.00	12.00

—Contains seven Decca audition tracks

❑ PHX-353 [M]	Silver Beatles, Volume 2	1982	3.00	6.00	12.00

—Contains seven Decca audition tracks (different seven than Phoenix 352)

❑ P20-623	20 Hits, Beatles	1983	5.00	10.00	20.00

—With 12 Decca audition tracks, four Beatles/Tony Sheridan tracks, and four Tony Sheridan solo tracks

❑ P20-629	20 Hits, Beatles	1983	5.00	10.00	20.00

—With 20 live Hamburg tracks

PICKWICK

❑ PTP-2098 [(2)M]	The Historic First Live Recordings	1980	4.50	9.00	18.00

—Same contents as Lingasong LP, plus "Hully Gully"

❑ SPC-3661 [M]	The Beatles' First Live Recordings, Volume 1	1979	3.00	6.00	12.00
❑ SPC-3662 [M]	The Beatles' First Live Recordings, Volume 2	1979	3.00	6.00	12.00
❑ BAN-90051 [M]	Recorded Live in Hamburg, Vol. 1	1978	7.50	15.00	30.00
❑ BAN-90061 [M]	Recorded Live in Hamburg, Vol. 2	1978	7.50	15.00	30.00
❑ BAN-90071 [M]	Recorded Live in Hamburg, Vol. 3	1978	10.00	20.00	40.00

POLYDOR

❑ 24-4504 [P]	The Beatles — Circa 1960 — In the Beginning Featuring Tony Sheridan	197?	10.00	20.00	40.00

—Some copies of the record contain only the title "The Beatles -- In the Beginning"

❑ 24-4504 [P]	The Beatles — Circa 1960 — In the Beginning Featuring Tony Sheridan	1970	6.25	12.50	25.00

—Originals have gatefold cover

Number	Title (A Side/B Side)	Yr	VG	VG+	NM
❑ PD-4504 [P]	The Beatles — Circa 1960 — In the Beginning Featuring Tony Sheridan	1981	3.00	6.00	12.00

—Reissue without gatefold cover

❑ SKAO-93199 [P]	The Beatles — Circa 1960 — In the Beginning Featuring Tony Sheridan	1970	10.00	20.00	40.00

—Capitol Record Club edition

❑ 825073-1 [P]	The Beatles — Circa 1960— In the Beginning Featuring Tony Sheridan	1988	5.00	10.00	20.00

—Reissue with new number

RADIO PULSEBEAT NEWS

❑ 2	The American Tour with Ed Rudy	1964	25.00	50.00	100.00

—Yellow label; some copies came with a special edition of Teen Talk magazine (add 50%)

❑ 2	The American Tour with Ed Rudy	1980	6.25	12.50	25.00

—Blue label; authorized reissue with Beatles' photo on cover

❑ 3	1965 Talk Album — Ed Rudy with New U.S. Tour	1965	37.50	75.00	150.00

—"The Beatles" in black print under front cover photo (other versions appear to be bootlegs)

RAVEN/PVC

❑ 8911	Talk Downunder	1981	2.50	5.00	10.00
❑ 8911 [DJ]	Talk Downunder	1981	20.00	40.00	80.00

—Promo only in white cover with title sticker. Label reads "For Radio Play Only"

SAVAGE

❑ BM-69 [M]	The Savage Young Beatles	1964	37.50	75.00	150.00

—Orange label; no legitimate copy says "Stereo" on cover

❑ BM-69 [M]	The Savage Young Beatles	1964	375.00	750.00	1500.

—Yellow label, glossy orange cover

SILHOUETTE

❑ SM-10004 [PD]	Timeless	1981	5.00	10.00	20.00

—Picture disc with all interviews

❑ SM-10004 [PD]	Timeless	1981	6.25	12.50	25.00

—Picture disc with interviews plus remakes of "Imagine" and "Let It Be" (by non-Beatles)

❑ SM-10010 [PD]	Timeless II	1982	5.00	10.00	20.00

—Picture disc with mostly interviews

❑ SM-10013	The British Are Coming	1984	3.75	7.50	15.00

—Interview album with numbered sticker (very low numbers increase the value)

❑ SM-10013	The British Are Coming	1984	20.00	40.00	80.00

—Same as above, but on red vinyl

❑ SM-10013 [DJ]	The British Are Coming	1984	10.00	20.00	40.00

—White label promo; no numbered sticker

❑ SM-10015	Golden Beatles	1985	3.75	7.50	15.00
❑ SM-10015	Golden Beatles	1985	20.00	40.00	80.00

—Gold vinyl

❑ PD-83010 [PD]	The British Are Coming	1985	7.50	15.00	30.00

—Picture disc

STERLING

❑ 8895-6481	I Apologize	1966	75.00	150.00	300.00

—Same as above, but without photo

❑ 8895-6481	I Apologize	1966	100.00	200.00	400.00

—One-sided LP with John Lennon's "apology" for supposed anti-Christian remarks; includes photo

UNITED ARTISTS

❑ UA-Help-A/B [DJ]	United Artists Presents Help!	1965	500.00	1000.	1500.

—Radio spots for movie

❑ UA-Help-INT [DJ]	United Artists Presents Help!	1965	1000.	1500.	2000.

—Open-end interview with script (red label)

❑ UA-Help-Show [DJ]	United Artists Presents Help!	1965	1500.	2250.	3000.

—One-sided interview with script (blue label)

❑ SP-2359/60 [DJ]	United Artists Presents A Hard Day's Night	1964	1000.	1500.	2000.

—Open-end interview with script

❑ SP-2362/3 [DJ]	United Artists Presents A Hard Day's Night	1964	375.00	750.00	1500.

—Radio spots for movie

❑ UAL 3366 [M]	A Hard Day's Night	1964	50.00	100.00	200.00

—With "I Cry Instead" listing

❑ UAL 3366 [M]	A Hard Day's Night	1964	62.50	125.00	250.00

—With "I'll Cry Instead" listing

❑ UAL 3366 [M]	A Hard Day's Night	1964	750.00	1500.	3000.

—White label promo

❑ UAS 6366 [P]	A Hard Day's Night	1964	50.00	100.00	200.00

—With "I Cry Instead" listing

❑ UAS 6366 [P]	A Hard Day's Night	1964	62.50	125.00	250.00

—With "I'll Cry Instead" listing. Has incidental music by George Martin. All eight Beatles tracks are rechanneled; Martin's are in true stereo.

❑ UAS 6366 [P]	A Hard Day's Night	1964	6000.	9000.	12000.

—Pink vinyl; only one copy known, probably privately (and secretly) done by a pressing-plant employee

❑ UAS 6366 [P]	A Hard Day's Night	1968	12.50	25.00	50.00

—Pink and orange label

❑ UAS 6366 [P]	A Hard Day's Night	1970	12.50	25.00	50.00

—Black and orange label

❑ UAS 6366 [P]	A Hard Day's Night	1971	5.00	10.00	20.00

—Tan label

❑ UAS 6366 [P]	A Hard Day's Night	1975	5.00	10.00	20.00

—Tan label with "All Rights Reserved" in perimeter print

❑ UAS 6366 [P]	A Hard Day's Night	1977	5.00	10.00	20.00

—Sunrise label. Note: Any of the variations from 1968 on can have titles of songs incorrectly listed as "I Cry Instead" and "Tell Me Who," or only one can be wrong, or neither can be wrong. No difference in value at this time.

❑ ST-90828 [P]	A Hard Day's Night	1964	187.50	375.00	750.00

—Capitol Record Club edition

❑ T-90828 [M]	A Hard Day's Night	1964	750.00	1125.	1500.

—Capitol Record Club edition

UNITED DISTRIBUTORS

❑ UDL-2333 [M]	Dawn of the Silver Beatles	1981	12.50	25.00	50.00

—With numbered registration card (deduct 20% if missing)

❑ UDL-2333 [M]	Dawn of the Silver Beatles	1981	15.00	30.00	60.00

—Hand-stamped numbers on back cover and label; contains 10 Decca audition tracks

❑ UDL-2382 [M]	Lightning Strikes Twice	1981	15.00	30.00	60.00

—Side 1 has five Beatles' Decca audition tracks; Side 2 has live Elvis Presley performances from 1955

VEE JAY

❑ DX(S)-30	The Beatles vs. The Four Seasons Poster	1964	75.00	150.00	300.00
❑ DX-30 [(2)M]	The Beatles vs. The Four Seasons	1964	200.00	400.00	800.00

—Combines "Introducing the Beatles" with "Golden Hits of the Four Seasons" (Vee Jay 1065)

❑ DXS-30 [(2)S]	The Beatles vs. The Four Seasons	1964	1500.	2250.	3000.

—Combines "Introducing the Beatles" with "Golden Hits of the Four Seasons" (Vee Jay 1065)

Number	Title (A Side/B Side)	Yr	VG	VG+	NM
❑ 202 [M]	Hear the Beatles Tell All	1964	75.00	150.00	300.00
—Without "PRO" prefix on label					
❑ PRO 202 [DJ]	Hear the Beatles Tell All	1964	6000.	12000.	18000.
—White label promo with blue print					
❑ PRO 202 [M]	Hear the Beatles Tell All	1964	50.00	100.00	200.00
—With "PRO" prefix on label					
❑ PRO 202 [S]	Hear the Beatles Tell All	1979	2.50	5.00	10.00
—Authorized reissue in stereo					
❑ PRO 202 [PD]	Hear the Beatles Tell All	1987	5.00	10.00	20.00
—Shaped picture disc with same recordings as the black vinyl versions					
❑ LP 1062 [M]	Introducing the Beatles	1964	62.50	125.00	250.00
—Song titles cover; with "Please Please Me" and "Ask Me Why"; plain Vee Jay logo on solid black label					
❑ LP 1062 [M]	Introducing the Beatles	1964	62.50	125.00	250.00
—Song titles cover; with "Please Please Me" and "Ask Me Why"; brackets Vee Jay logo with colorband (most common authentic version)					
❑ LP 1062 [M]	Introducing the Beatles	1964	75.00	150.00	300.00
—Song titles cover; with "Please Please Me" and "Ask Me Why"; oval Vee Jay logo on solid black label					
❑ LP 1062 [M]	Introducing the Beatles	1964	75.00	150.00	300.00
—Song titles cover; with "Please Please Me" and "Ask Me Why"; oval Vee Jay logo with colorband					
❑ LP 1062 [M]	Introducing the Beatles	1964	200.00	400.00	800.00
—Song titles cover; with "Love Me Do" and "P.S. I Love You"; oval Vee Jay logo with colorband only!					
❑ LP 1062 [M]	Introducing the Beatles	1964	250.00	500.00	1000.
—Blank back cover; with "Please Please Me" and "Ask Me Why"; oval Vee Jay logo with colorband only!					
❑ LP 1062 [M]	Introducing the Beatles	1964	250.00	500.00	1000.
—Song titles cover; with "Please Please Me" and "Ask Me Why"; brackets Vee Jay logo on solid black label					
❑ LP 1062 [M]	Introducing the Beatles	1964	400.00	800.00	1200.
—Blank back cover; with "Love Me Do" and "P.S. I Love You"; oval Vee Jay logo with colorband only!					
❑ LP 1062 [M]	Introducing the Beatles	1964	1500.	2750.	4000.
—"Ad back" cover; with "Love Me Do" and "P.S. I Love You"; oval Vee Jay logo with colorband only!					
❑ SR 1062 [B]	Introducing the Beatles	1964	625.00	1250.	2500.
—Blank back cover; with "Love Me Do" and "P.S. I Love You"; oval Vee Jay logo with colorband only!					
❑ SR 1062 [B]	Introducing the Beatles	1964	3000.	5500.	8000.
—Song titles cover; with "Love Me Do" and "P.S. I Love You"; oval Vee Jay logo with colorband only! This album has been heavily counterfeited; please check the label of your copy before contacting the author. If the words "Introducing the Beatles" are above the center hole of the record, and the words "The Beatles" are below, it is automatically a counterfeit and almost worthless.					
❑ SR 1062 [B]	Introducing the Beatles	1964	4000.	8000.	12000.
—"Ad back" cover; with "Love Me Do" and "P.S. I Love You" (both mono); oval Vee Jay logo with colorband only!					
❑ SR 1062 [S]	Introducing the Beatles	1964	375.00	750.00	1500.
—Song titles cover; with "Please Please Me" and "Ask Me Why"; brackets Vee Jay logo with colorband					
❑ SR 1062 [S]	Introducing the Beatles	1964	400.00	800.00	1600.
—Song titles cover; with "Please Please Me" and "Ask Me Why"; oval Vee Jay logo with colorband					
❑ SR 1062 [S]	Introducing the Beatles	1964	400.00	800.00	1600.
—Song titles cover; with "Please Please Me" and "Ask Me Why"; plain Vee Jay logo on solid black label					
❑ LP 1085 [M]	Jolly What! The Beatles and Frank Ifield on Stage	1964	62.50	125.00	250.00
—Man in Beatle wig cover; originals have printing on spine and a dark blue/purple background (counterfeits have a black background and no spine print)					
❑ LP 1085 [M]	The Beatles and Frank Ifield on Stage	1964	2000.	3500.	5000.
—Portrait of Beatles cover; counterfeits are poorly reproduced and have no spine print					
❑ SR 1085 [B]	Jolly What! The Beatles and Frank Ifield on Stage	1964	125.00	250.00	500.00
—Man in Beatle wig cover; "Stereo" on both cover and label. "From Me to You" is mono.					
❑ SR 1085 [B]	The Beatles and Frank Ifield on Stage	1964	4000.	8000.	12000.
—Portrait of Beatles cover; "Stereo" on both cover and label					
❑ LP 1092 [M]	Songs, Pictures and Stories of the Fabulous Beatles	1964	125.00	250.00	500.00
—See above; brackets Vee Jay logo with colorband					
❑ LP 1092 [M]	Songs, Pictures and Stories of the Fabulous Beatles	1964	125.00	250.00	500.00
—See above; oval Vee Jay logo on solid black label					
❑ LP 1092 [M]	Songs, Pictures and Stories of the Fabulous Beatles	1964	125.00	250.00	500.00
—See above; plain Vee Jay logo on solid black label					
❑ LP 1092 [M]	Songs, Pictures and Stories of the Fabulous Beatles	1964	125.00	250.00	500.00
—All copies have gatefold cover with 2/3 width on front; also, all copies have "Introducing the Beatles" records. Oval Vee Jay logo with colorband.					
❑ VJS 1092 [S]	Songs, Pictures and Stories of the Fabulous Beatles	1964	800.00	1600.	2400.
—See above; brackets Vee Jay logo with colorband					
❑ VJS 1092 [S]	Songs, Pictures and Stories of the Fabulous Beatles	1964	800.00	1600.	2400.
—See above; plain Vee Jay logo on solid black label. NOTE: Any non-gatefold copy or any copy called "Songs and Pictures of the Fabulous Beatles" is a counterfeit.					
❑ VJS 1092 [S]	Songs, Pictures and Stories of the Fabulous Beatles	1964	800.00	1600.	2400.
—All copies have gatefold cover with 2/3 width on front; also, all copies have "Introducing the Beatles" records. Oval Vee Jay logo with colorband.					

BEATSTALKERS, THE
45s
PRESS

Number	Title (A Side/B Side)	Yr	VG	VG+	NM
❑ 5001	Left, Right, Left/Get a Better Hold On	1966	3.75	7.50	15.00

BEAU BRUMMELS, THE   Also see RON ELLIOTT; SAL VALENTINO.
45s
AUTUMN

Number	Title (A Side/B Side)	Yr	VG	VG+	NM
❑ 8	Laugh, Laugh/Still in Love with You Baby	1965	3.00	6.00	12.00
—Tan label					
❑ 8	Laugh, Laugh/Still in Love with You Baby	1965	3.75	7.50	15.00
—White label					
❑ 10	Just a Little/They'll Make You Cry	1965	3.75	7.50	15.00
❑ 16	You Tell Me Why/I Want You	1965	2.00	4.00	8.00
❑ 20	Don't Talk to Strangers/In Good Time	1965	2.00	4.00	8.00
❑ 24	Good Time Music/Sad Little Girl	1965	2.00	4.00	8.00

Number	Title (A Side/B Side)	Yr	VG	VG+	NM
RHINO					
❑ RNOR 4506	Laugh, Laugh/Just a Little	1984	—	2.00	4.00
❑ RNOR 4506 [PS]	Laugh, Laugh/Just a Little	1984	—	2.00	4.00
WARNER BROS.					
❑ 5813	One Too Many Mornings/She Reigns	1966	2.00	4.00	8.00
❑ 5848	Fine with Me/Here We Are Again	1966	2.00	4.00	8.00
❑ 7014	Don't Make Promises/Two Days 'Til Tomorrow	1967	2.00	4.00	8.00
❑ 7079	Magic Hollow/Lower Level	1967	2.00	4.00	8.00
❑ 7204	Are You Happy/Lift Me	1968	—	3.00	6.00
❑ 7218	I'm a Sleeper/Long Walking Down to Misery	1968	—	3.00	6.00
❑ 7260	Cherokee Girl/Deep Water	1969	—	3.00	6.00
❑ 8119	You Tell Me Why/Down to the Bottom	1975	—	2.50	5.00
Albums					
ACCORD					
❑ SN-7175	Just a Little	1982	2.50	5.00	10.00
AUTUMN					
❑ LP 103 [M]	Introducing the Beau Brummels	1965	12.50	25.00	50.00
❑ SLP 103 [S]	Introducing the Beau Brummels	1965	15.00	30.00	60.00
❑ LP 104 [M]	The Beau Brummels, Volume 2	1965	10.00	20.00	40.00
❑ SLP 104 [S]	The Beau Brummels, Volume 2	1965	12.50	25.00	50.00
JAS					
❑ 5000	Original Hits of the Beau Brummels	1976	3.75	7.50	15.00
POST					
❑ 6000	The Beau Brummels Sing	196?	3.75	7.50	15.00
RHINO					
❑ RNLP-101	The Best of the Beau Brummels	1981	2.50	5.00	10.00
❑ RNLP-102	Introducing the Beau Brummels	1981	2.50	5.00	10.00
❑ RNLP-104	From the Vaults	1981	3.00	6.00	12.00
❑ RNLP-70171	The Best of the Beau Brummels (Golden Archive Series)	1986	2.50	5.00	10.00
SUNDAZED					
❑ LP 5088	North Beach Legends	2001	3.00	6.00	12.00
❑ LP 5089	Gentle Wanderin' Ways	2001	3.00	6.00	12.00
VAULT					
❑ LP-114 [M]	Best of the Beau Brummels	1967	6.25	12.50	25.00
❑ SLP-114 [S]	Best of the Beau Brummels	1967	6.25	12.50	25.00
❑ SLP-121	Beau Brummels, Vol. 44	1968	6.25	12.50	25.00
WARNER BROS.					
❑ W 1644 [M]	Beau Brummels '66	1966	5.00	10.00	20.00
❑ WS 1644 [S]	Beau Brummels '66	1966	6.25	12.50	25.00
❑ W 1692 [M]	Triangle	1967	5.00	10.00	20.00
❑ WS 1692 [S]	Triangle	1967	6.25	12.50	25.00
❑ WS 1760	Bradley's Barn	1968	6.25	12.50	25.00
❑ BS 2842	The Beau Brummels	1975	5.00	10.00	20.00

BEAU-K'S, THE
45s
MERCURY

Number	Title (A Side/B Side)	Yr	VG	VG+	NM
❑ 72157	Packin' Up/Forget Me Not	1963	2.50	5.00	10.00
❑ 72224	A Rose and a Star/What Else Could I Do But Cry	1963	2.50	5.00	10.00

BEAU-MARKS, THE
45s
MAINSTREAM

Number	Title (A Side/B Side)	Yr	VG	VG+	NM
❑ 688	Clap Your Hands/Daddy Said	1968	2.50	5.00	10.00
PORT					
❑ 70029	Little Miss Twist/Lovely Little Lady	1962	3.75	7.50	15.00
RUST					
❑ 5035	School Is Out/Classmates	1961	5.00	10.00	20.00
❑ 5050	I'll Never Be the Same/Tender Years	1962	5.00	10.00	20.00
SHAD					
❑ 5017	Clap Your Hands/Daddy Said	1960	5.00	10.00	20.00
❑ 5021	Cause We're in Love/Billy Went a-Walkin'	1960	5.00	10.00	20.00
TIME					
❑ 1032	Oh Joan/Rockin' Blues	1961	7.50	15.00	30.00

BEAUMONT, JIMMY   Of THE SKYLINERS.
45s
BANG

Number	Title (A Side/B Side)	Yr	VG	VG+	NM
❑ 510	Tell Me/I Feel Like I'm Falling in Love	1965	5.00	10.00	20.00
❑ 525	I Never Loved Her Anyway/You Got Too Much Going for You	1966	7.50	15.00	30.00
COLPIX					
❑ 607	The End of a Story/Baion Rhythms	1961	7.50	15.00	30.00
GALLANT					
❑ 3007	Please Send Me Someone to Love/There Is No Other Love	196?	5.00	10.00	20.00
❑ 3012	Love Is a Dangerous Game/Just a Little Closer	196?	3.00	6.00	12.00
MAY					
❑ 112	Ev'rybody's Cryin'/Camera	1961	6.25	12.50	25.00
❑ 115	I Should Have Listened to Mama/Juarez	1962	6.25	12.50	25.00
❑ 120	Never Say Goodbye/I'm Gonna Try My Wings	1962	6.25	12.50	25.00
❑ 136	I'll Always Be in Love with You/Give Her My Best	1963	6.25	12.50	25.00

BEAUREGARDE
45s
INTERNATIONAL ARTISTS

Number	Title (A Side/B Side)	Yr	VG	VG+	NM
❑ 123	Popcorn Popper/Mama Never Taught Me How to Jelly Roll	1968	6.25	12.50	25.00
Albums					
EMPIRE					
❑ (no #)	Beauregarde	1969	25.00	50.00	100.00
SOUND					
❑ 7104	Beauregarde	1969	20.00	40.00	80.00

BEAVER, PAUL
Albums
RAPTURE

Number	Title (A Side/B Side)	Yr	VG	VG+	NM
❑ 11111	Perchance to Dream	196?	12.50	25.00	50.00

Number	Title (A Side/B Side)	Yr	VG	VG+	NM
BEAVER AND KRAUSE					
45s					
WARNER BROS.					
❏ 7414	People's Park/				
	Salute to the Vanishing Bald Eagle	1970	—	3.00	6.00
❏ 7485	Walkin' By the River/				
	The Saga of the Blue Beaver	1971	—	3.00	6.00
❏ 7642	Bluebird Canyon Stomp/Real Slow Drag	1972	—	3.00	6.00
Albums					
LIMELIGHT					
❏ 86069	Ragnarok — Electronic Funk	1969	7.50	15.00	30.00
WARNER BROS.					
❏ WS 1850	In a Wild Sanctuary	1969	3.75	7.50	15.00
❏ WS 1909	Gandharva	1970	3.75	7.50	15.00
❏ BS 2624	All Good Men	1972	3.75	7.50	15.00
BEAVERS, JACKEY					
45s					
CHECKER					
❏ 1102	Jack-a-Rue/Silly Boy	1965	5.00	10.00	20.00
—As "Jackey Beaver"					
❏ 1119	I Want Somebody/Slingshot	1965	5.00	10.00	20.00
—As "Jackey Beaver"					
DADE					
❏ 2041	Tryin' to Get Back to You Girl/(Part 2)	197?	2.50	5.00	10.00
MAINSTREAM					
❏ 713	When Something Is Wrong with My Baby/We're				
	Not Too Young to Fall in Love	1969	15.00	30.00	60.00
REVILOT					
❏ 208	Love That Never Grows Old/I Need My Baby	1967	250.00	500.00	1000.
SOUND STAGE 7					
❏ ZS7 1502	Someday We'll Be Together/Lover Come Back	1971	5.00	10.00	20.00
❏ ZS7 1506	Singing a Funky Song (For My Baby)/Hey Girl				
	(I Can't Stand to See You Go)	1972	2.50	5.00	10.00
❏ 2649	Hey Girl (I Can't Stand to See You Go)/Hold On	1969	3.00	6.00	12.00
❏ 2662	You Can Have Her/(B-side unknown)	1970	3.75	7.50	15.00
BEAVERS, THE					
45s					
CAPITOL					
❏ F3956	Sack Dress/Rockin' at the Drive-In	1958	6.25	12.50	25.00
❏ F4015	The Road to Happiness/Low As I Can Be	1958	5.00	10.00	20.00
BECK, BECKY LEE					
45s					
CHALLENGE					
❏ 59272	I Want a Beatle for Christmas/Puppy Dog	1964	5.00	10.00	20.00
BECK, BOBBY					
45s					
ABC-PARAMOUNT					
❏ 10099	Isle of Capri/Swinging on a Chandelier	1960	5.00	10.00	20.00
❏ 10148	The Door Is Always Open/You Got All My Love	1960	5.00	10.00	20.00
BECK, JEFF Includes the Jeff Beck Group, of whom ROD STEWART was lead singer. Also see BECK, BOGERT AND APPICE; THE YARDBIRDS.					
45s					
EPIC					
❏ 34-05595	Gets Us All in the End/You Know We Know	1985	—	2.00	4.00
❏ 10157	Beck's Bolero/Hi-Ho Silver Lining	1967	4.00	8.00	16.00
❏ 10218	Rock My Plimsoul/Tally Man	1967	4.00	8.00	16.00
❏ 10390	Blues De Luxe/Ol' Man River	1968	3.00	6.00	12.00
❏ 10484	Jailhouse Rock/Plynth (Water Down the Drain)	1969	3.00	6.00	12.00
❏ 10814	Got the Feeling/Situation	1971	2.50	5.00	10.00
❏ 10938	Definitely Maybe/Hi Ho Silver Lining	1973	2.50	5.00	10.00
❏ 50112	Constipated Duck/You Know What I Mean	1975	—	3.00	6.00
❏ 50276	Come Dancing/Head for Backstage Pass	1976	—	2.00	4.00
❏ 50914	Too Much to Lose/The FInal Peace	1980	—	2.00	4.00
Albums					
ACCORD					
❏ SN-7141	Early Anthology	1981	2.50	5.00	10.00
EPIC					
❏ AS 151 [DJ]	Everything You Always Wanted to Hear by Jeff				
	Beck But Were Afraid to Ask For	1977	5.00	10.00	20.00
—Promo-only sampler					
❏ A2S 850 [(2)DJ]	Then and Now	1981	6.25	12.50	25.00
—Promo-only sampler					
❏ BN 26413 [M]	Truth	1968	10.00	20.00	40.00
—Mono is promo only with stereo number; cover has "Mono" sticker covering the word "Stereo"					
❏ BN 26413 [S]	Truth	1973	3.75	7.50	15.00
—Yellow label					
❏ BN 26413	Truth	1973	2.50	5.00	10.00
—Orange label					
❏ PE 26413	Truth	198?	2.00	4.00	8.00
—Reissue with new prefix					
❏ BN 26478	Beck-Ola	1969	3.75	7.50	15.00
—Yellow label					
❏ BN 26478	Beck-Ola	1973	2.50	5.00	10.00
—Orange label					
❏ PE 26478	Beck-Ola	197?	2.00	4.00	8.00
—Reissue with new prefix					
❏ PE 30973	Rough and Ready	198?	2.00	4.00	8.00
—Budget-line reissue					
❏ EQ 30993 [Q]	Rough and Ready	1972	5.00	10.00	20.00
❏ KE 30993	Rough and Ready	1971	3.75	7.50	15.00
—Yellow label					
❏ KE 30993	Rough and Ready	1973	2.50	5.00	10.00
—Orange label					
❏ EQ 31331 [Q]	Jeff Beck Group	1972	5.00	10.00	20.00
❏ KE 31331	Jeff Beck Group	1972	3.75	7.50	15.00
—Yellow label					

Number	Title (A Side/B Side)	Yr	VG	VG+	NM
❏ KE 31331	Jeff Beck Group	1973	2.50	5.00	10.00
—Orange label					
❏ PE 31331	Jeff Beck Group	198?	2.00	4.00	8.00
—Budget-line reissue					
❏ PE 33409	Blow by Blow	1975	2.50	5.00	10.00
—Orange label, no bar code on cover					
❏ PE 33409	Blow by Blow	198?	2.00	4.00	8.00
—Reissue with dark blue label and bar code on cover					
❏ PEQ 33409 [Q]	Blow by Blow	1975	5.00	10.00	20.00
❏ BG 33779 [(2)]	Truth/Beck-Ola	1975	3.00	6.00	12.00
❏ PE 33849	Wired	1976	2.50	5.00	10.00
—Orange label, no bar code on cover					
❏ PE 33849	Wired	1979	2.00	4.00	8.00
—Reissue with dark blue label; with or without bar code on cover					
❏ PEQ 33849 [Q]	Wired	1976	5.00	10.00	20.00
❏ PE 34433	Jeff Beck with the Jan Hammer Group Live	1977	2.50	5.00	10.00
—Orange label, no bar code on cover					
❏ PE 34433	Jeff Beck with the Jan Hammer Group Live	198?	2.00	4.00	8.00
—Reissue with dark blue label and bar code on cover					
❏ FE 35684	There and Back	1980	2.50	5.00	10.00
❏ PE 35684	There and Back	1985	2.00	4.00	8.00
—Budget-line reissue					
❏ FE 39483	Flash	1985	2.50	5.00	10.00
❏ HE 43409	Blow by Blow	1980	7.50	15.00	30.00
—Half-speed mastered edition					
❏ HE 43849	Wired	198?	7.50	15.00	30.00
—Half-speed mastered edition					
❏ FE 44313	Jeff Beck's Guitar Shop	1989	3.75	7.50	15.00
BECK, JEFF, AND ROD STEWART Also see each artist's individual listings.					
45s					
EPIC					
❏ 34-05416	People Get Ready/Back on the Street	1985	—	—	3.00
❏ 34-05416 [PS]	People Get Ready/Back on the Street	1985	—	—	3.00
BECK, JOE					
45s					
POLYDOR					
❏ 14384	Dr. Lee/Stand Up and Be Someone	1977	—	2.00	4.00
Albums					
CTI					
❏ 8002	Beck & Sanborn	1979	2.50	5.00	10.00
—Reissue of Kudu 21 with new title					
CTI/CBS ASSOCIATED					
❏ FZ 40805	Beck & Sanborn	1987	2.50	5.00	10.00
KUDU					
❏ 21	Beck	1975	3.00	6.00	12.00
POLYDOR					
❏ PD-1-6092	Watch the Time	1976	2.50	5.00	10.00
BECK, BOGERT & APPICE Also see JEFF BECK; VANILLA FUDGE.					
45s					
EPIC					
❏ 10998	I'm So Proud/Oh to Love You	1973	2.00	4.00	8.00
❏ 11027	Lady/Oh to Love You	1973	2.00	4.00	8.00
Albums					
EPIC					
❏ CQ 32140 [Q]	Beck, Bogert & Appice	1973	5.00	10.00	20.00
❏ KE 32140	Beck, Bogert & Appice	1973	2.50	5.00	10.00
—Orange label					
❏ KE 32140	Beck, Bogert & Appice	1973	3.75	7.50	15.00
—Yellow label					
❏ PE 32140	Beck, Bogert & Appice	198?	2.00	4.00	8.00
—Budget-line reissue					
BECKER, GLORIA					
45s					
REAL					
❏ 1304	Sixteen Pounds (Housewife's Lament)/Adios to				
	Mexico City	1956	5.00	10.00	20.00
—A-side is a parody of "Sixteen Tons"					
BECKHAM, BOB					
45s					
DECCA					
❏ 30617	Tomorrow/I'm Tired of Everyone But You	1958	3.00	6.00	12.00
❏ 30861	Just As Much As Ever/Your Sweet Love	1959	3.00	6.00	12.00
❏ 31029	Crazy Arms/Beloved	1959	3.00	6.00	12.00
❏ 31029 [PS]	Crazy Arms/Beloved	1959	5.00	10.00	20.00
❏ 31089	Only the Broken Hearted/Mais Oui	1960	2.50	5.00	10.00
❏ 31132	Two Wrongs Don't Make a Right/				
	Nothing Is Forever	1960	2.50	5.00	10.00
❏ 31132 [PS]	Two Wrongs Don't Make a Right/				
	Nothing Is Forever	1960	5.00	10.00	20.00
❏ 31163	Meet Me Halfway/One More Time	1960	2.50	5.00	10.00
❏ 31239	Forget It/Like a Fool	1961	2.50	5.00	10.00
❏ 31285	How Soon (Will I Be Seeing You)/I'm Wondering	1961	2.50	5.00	10.00
❏ 31337	10,000 Teardrops				
	(And One Broken Heart)/Just Friends	1961	2.50	5.00	10.00
❏ 31391	I Cry Like a Baby/I'll Take My Chances	1962	2.00	4.00	8.00
❏ 31432	Building Memories/Memory Mountain	1962	2.00	4.00	8.00
❏ 31493	Footprints/Midnight	1963	2.00	4.00	8.00
❏ 31547	Grabbing at Rainbows/My Heart Would Know	1963	2.00	4.00	8.00
❏ 31607	Helpless/I'll Be Around	1964	2.00	4.00	8.00
MONUMENT					
❏ 1018	Cherokee Strip/				
	You Really Know How to Hurt a Guy	1967	—	3.00	6.00
❏ 1030	Lily White/Look at Them	1967	—	3.00	6.00
SMASH					
❏ 1990	Slowly Dying/It's My Heart	1965	2.00	4.00	8.00

Number	Title (A Side/B Side)	Yr	VG	VG+	NM

BECKY AND THE LOLLIPOPS
45s
EPIC
| ❑ 9736 | I Don't Care (What They Say)/My Boyfriend | 1964 | 3.00 | 6.00 | 12.00 |

BED BUGS, THE
45s
LIBERTY
| ❑ 55679 | Yeah Yeah/Lucy Lucy | 1964 | 6.25 | 12.50 | 25.00 |

BEDLAM
Albums
CHRYSALIS
| ❑ CHR-1048 | Bedlam | 1973 | 6.25 | 12.50 | 25.00 |

BEE, MOLLY
45s
CAPITOL
❑ F2258	Tennessee Tango/Kids Who Pay	1952	6.25	12.50	25.00
❑ F2285	I Saw Mommy Kissing Santa Claus/Willy Claus (Little Son of Santa Claus)	1952	5.00	10.00	20.00
❑ F2339	Honky Tonk Mountain/Nobody's Lonesome for Me	1953	5.00	10.00	20.00
❑ F2396	What'll He Do/Dancing with Someone	1953	5.00	10.00	20.00
❑ F2494	Doggie on the Highway/I'll Tell My Mommy	1953	5.00	10.00	20.00
❑ F2567	God Bless Us All/This Is My Dog	1953	5.00	10.00	20.00
❑ F2741	Remember Me/Pine Tree Pine Over Me	1954	5.00	10.00	20.00
❑ F2790	Stuffy/In the Pyrenees	1954	5.00	10.00	20.00
❑ F3865	Magic Mirror/I'm Going Steady with a Dream	1957	3.75	7.50	15.00
❑ F3968	Don't Look Back/Please Don't Talk About Me When I'm Gone	1958	3.75	7.50	15.00
❑ F4064	Five Points of a Star/After You've Gone	1958	3.75	7.50	15.00
CORAL					
❑ 9-61357	I Won't Grow Up/False Alarm	1955	5.00	10.00	20.00
DOT					
❑ 15453	Sweet Shoppe Sweetheart/From the Wrong Side of Town	1956	5.00	10.00	20.00
❑ 15517	Since I Met You Baby/I'll Be Waiting for You	1956	5.00	10.00	20.00
GRANITE					
❑ 509	She Kept On Talkin'/Baby You Got It	1974	—	3.50	7.00
❑ 515	Right or Left at Oak Street/I Got a Man	1975	—	3.50	7.00
❑ 524	California Country/(B-side unknown)	1975	—	3.50	7.00
❑ 531	I Can't Live in the Dark Anymore/(B-side unknown)	1975	—	3.50	7.00
LIBERTY					
❑ 55438	Just for the Record/Lyin' Again	1962	3.00	6.00	12.00
❑ 55543	All My Love, All My Life/She's New to You	1963	3.00	6.00	12.00
❑ 55569	I Was Only Kidding/He's My True Love	1963	3.00	6.00	12.00
❑ 55631	Some Tears Fall Dry/Johnny Liar	1963	3.00	6.00	12.00
❑ 55691	Our Secret/He Doesn't Want You	1964	3.00	6.00	12.00
MGM					
❑ 13356	Keep It a Secret/Single Girl Again	1965	2.50	5.00	10.00
❑ 13411	Together Again/I'm Gonna Change Everything	1965	2.50	5.00	10.00
❑ 13491	Losing You/Miserable Me	1966	2.50	5.00	10.00
❑ 13537	How's the World Treating You/It Keeps Right On a-Hurtin'	1966	2.50	5.00	10.00
❑ 13694	Almost Persuaded/Heartbreak U.S.A.	1967	2.50	5.00	10.00
❑ 13770	You Win Again/I Hate to See Me Go	1967	2.50	5.00	10.00
Albums					
ACCORD					
❑ 7901	Sounds Fine to Me	1982	2.50	5.00	10.00
CAPITOL					
❑ T 1097 [M]	Young Romance	1958	10.00	20.00	40.00
GRANITE					
❑ 1002	Good Golly Ms. Molly	1974	3.00	6.00	12.00
MGM					
❑ E-4303 [M]	It's Great, It's Molly Bee	1965	5.00	10.00	20.00
❑ SE-4303 [S]	It's Great, It's Molly Bee	1965	6.25	12.50	25.00
❑ E-4423 [M]	Swingin' Country	1967	5.00	10.00	20.00
❑ SE-4423 [S]	Swingin' Country	1967	6.25	12.50	25.00

BEE BEE TWINS, THE
45s
LIBERTY
| ❑ 55173 | The Night Before Christmas/Yuletide Tango | 1958 | 3.75 | 7.50 | 15.00 |

BEE GEES Also see BARRY GIBB; MAURICE GIBB; ROBIN GIBB.
12-Inch Singles
POLYDOR
❑ PRO 1068-1 [DJ]	Paying the Price of Love (Jellybean Dub Mix #1) (Edit) (Ocean Drive Dub)	1993	3.00	6.00	12.00
❑ 859165-1	Paying the Price of Love (Ocean Drive Mix 6:09) (Jellybean Mix #1 6:09) (Jellybean Mix #1 Dub Vibe 6:09)/Decadance (Classic House Mix 8:42)	1993	—	3.00	6.00
RSO					
❑ PRO 209 [DJ]	The Woman in You (5:43) (same on both sides)	1983	3.00	6.00	12.00
❑ RS 853 [DJ]	You Should Be Dancing (B-side blank)	1976	37.50	75.00	150.00
—This is for the U.S. white label promo, not for the Canadian issue					
❑ RPO 1029 [DJ]	He's a Liar (Special Dance Version)/(Instrumental)	1981	2.50	5.00	10.00
UNIVERSAL					
❑ 587696-1	This Is Where I Came In (DJ Domino Remix) (DJ Domino Remix Edit) (LP Version) (same on both sides)	2001	2.00	4.00	8.00
WARNER BROS.					
❑ PRO-A-2822 [DJ]	You Win Again (Fade) (same on both sides)	1987	2.00	4.00	8.00
❑ PRO-A-2918 [DJ]	E.S.P. (Edit) (Remix No Guitars) (Extra Sensory House Vocal) (E.S. Piano Dub)	1987	2.50	5.00	10.00
❑ PRO-A-3753 [DJ]	One (12" Club Mix) (Dub Mix) (Remix Edit) (12" Dance Version)	1989	3.00	6.00	12.00
❑ 20760	You Win Again (Extended Remix)/Backtafunk	1987	2.00	4.00	8.00

45s
ATCO
❑ 6487	New York Mining Disaster 1941 Have You Seen My Wife, Mr. Jones/I Can't See Nobody	1967	2.50	5.00	10.00
❑ 6487	New York Mining Disaster 1941/I Can't See Nobody	1967	3.00	6.00	12.00
❑ 6487 [DJ]	New York Mining Disaster 1941/I Can't See Nobody	1967	6.25	12.50	25.00
—Artist not listed on label.					
❑ 6503	To Love Somebody/Close Another Door	1967	2.50	5.00	10.00
❑ 6521	Holiday/Every Christian Lion Hearted Man Will Show You	1967	2.50	5.00	10.00
❑ 6532	(The Lights Went Out in) Massachusetts/Sir Geoffrey Saved the World	1967	2.50	5.00	10.00
❑ 6548	Words/Sinking Ships	1968	2.50	5.00	10.00
❑ 6570	Jumbo/The Singer Sang His Song	1968	2.00	4.00	8.00
❑ 6603	I've Gotta Get a Message to You/Kitty Can	1968	2.00	4.00	8.00
❑ 6639	I Started a Joke/Kilburn Towers	1969	2.00	4.00	8.00
❑ 6657	First of May/Lamplight	1969	2.00	4.00	8.00
❑ 6682	Tomorrow Tomorrow/Sun in My Morning	1969	2.00	4.00	8.00
❑ 6682 [DJ]	Tomorrow Tomorrow (Short Version 3:04)/(Long Version 4:02)	1969	3.00	6.00	12.00
—On white label with no promo markings					
❑ 6702	Don't Forget to Remember/The Lord	1969	2.50	5.00	10.00
❑ 6741	If Only I Had My Mind on Something Else/Sweetheart	1970	2.00	4.00	8.00
❑ 6752	I.O.I.O./Then You Left Me	1970	2.00	4.00	8.00
❑ 6795	Lonely Days/Man for All Seasons	1971	—	3.00	6.00
❑ 6824	How Can You Mend a Broken Heart/Country Woman	1971	—	3.00	6.00
❑ 6847	Don't Wanna Live Inside Myself/Walking Back to Waterloo	1971	—	3.00	6.00
❑ 6871	My World/On Time	1972	—	2.50	5.00
❑ 6896	Run to Me/Road to Alaska	1972	—	2.50	5.00
❑ 6909	Alive/Paper Mache, Cabbages and Kings	1972	—	2.50	5.00
EMMC					
❑ (no #)	A Personal Message from the Bee Gees/The Rescue of Bonnie Prince Wally	1979	2.50	5.00	10.00
—Official Bee Gees Fan Club record; small hole, plays at 33 1/3 rpm					
POLYDOR					
❑ 31457 1006 7	Alone/How Deep Is Your Love	1997	—	—	3.00
RSO					
❑ RP 106 [DJ]	Sgt. Pepper's Lonely Hearts Club Band/With a Little Help from My Friends (stereo/mono)	1978	3.75	7.50	15.00
—As "Lonely Hearts Club Band" (Bee Gees with Peter Frampton and Paul Nicholas); promo only					
❑ 401	Saw a New Morning/My Life Has Been a Song	1973	—	3.00	6.00
❑ 404	Wouldn't I Be Someone/Elisa	1973	—	3.00	6.00
❑ 408	Mr. Natural/It Doesn't Matter Much to Me	1974	—	3.00	6.00
❑ 410	Throw a Penny/I Can't Let Go	1974	—	3.00	6.00
❑ 501	Charade/Heavy Breathing	1974	—	3.00	6.00
❑ 510	Jive Talkin'/Wind of Change	1975	—	2.00	4.00
❑ 515	Nights on Broadway/Edge of the Universe	1975	—	2.00	4.00
❑ 515 [DJ]	Nights on Broadway (Stereo Short Version 2:52)/(Mono Short Version 2:52)	1975	2.00	4.00	8.00
❑ 519	Fanny (Be Tender With My Love)/Country Lanes	1975	—	2.00	4.00
❑ 853	You Should Be Dancing/Subway	1976	—	2.00	4.00
❑ 859	Love So Right/You Stepped Into My Life	1976	—	2.00	4.00
❑ 867	Boogie Child/Lovers	1976	—	2.00	4.00
❑ 880	Edge of the Universe/Words	1977	—	2.00	4.00
❑ 882	How Deep Is Your Love/Can't Keep a Good Man Down	1977	—	2.00	4.00
❑ 885	Stayin' Alive/If I Can't Have You	1977	—	2.00	4.00
❑ 889	Night Fever/Down the Road	1978	—	2.00	4.00
❑ 907	She's Leaving Home/Oh! Darling	1978	—	2.00	4.00
—B-side by Robin Gibb solo					
❑ 913	Too Much Heaven/Rest Your Love on Me	1978	—	2.00	4.00
❑ 913 [DJ]	Rest Your Love on Me (stereo/mono)	1979	3.00	6.00	12.00
—Promo of B-side, sent to country radio					
❑ 913 A [DJ]	Too Much Heaven (Stereo 3:15)/(Mono 3:15)	1978	2.50	5.00	10.00
—Both sides have edited versions					
❑ 918	Tragedy/Until	1979	—	2.00	4.00
❑ 918 [DJ]	Tragedy (Stereo 4:32)/(Mono 3:42)	1979	2.50	5.00	10.00
—Promo only; both sides are shorter than the 5:01 stock copy					
❑ 925	Love You Inside Out/I'm Satisfied	1979	—	2.00	4.00
❑ 1066	He's a Liar/(Instrumental)	1981	—	—	3.00
❑ 1067	Living Eyes/I Still Love You	1981	—	—	3.00
❑ 8001	Come On Over/Jive Talkin'	1980	—	2.00	4.00
—Reissue series; first time on 45 for A-side					
❑ 8003	You Should Be Dancing/Love So Right	1980	—	—	3.00
—Reissue series					
❑ 8009	Stayin' Alive/How Deep Is Your Love	1980	—	—	3.00
—Reissue series					
❑ 8010	To Love Somebody/How Can You Mend a Broken Heart	1980	—	—	3.00
—Reissue series					
❑ 8011	Lonely Days/Words	1980	—	—	3.00
—Reissue series					
❑ 8012	Nights on Broadway/Boogie Child	1980	—	—	3.00
—Reissue series					
❑ 8019	More Than a Woman/Night Fever	1980	—	2.00	4.00
—Reissue series; first time on 45 for A-side					
❑ 8022	Tragedy/Love You Inside Out	1980	—	—	3.00
—Reissue series					
❑ 8030	Too Much Heaven/Rest Your Love on Me	1980	—	—	3.00
—Reissue series					
❑ 813173-7	The Woman in You/Stayin' Alive	1983	—	—	3.00
❑ 813173-7 [PS]	The Woman in You/Stayin' Alive	1983	—	3.00	6.00
❑ 815235-7	Someone Belonging to Someone/I Love You Too Much	1983	—	—	3.00
❑ 815235-7 [PS]	Someone Belonging to Someone/I Love You Too Much	1983	—	3.00	6.00

Number	Title (A Side/B Side)	Yr	VG	VG+	NM
WARNER BROS.					
❑ PRO-S-2858 [DJ]	You Win Again (Edit) (same on both sides)	1987	2.50	5.00	10.00
❑ 22733	You Win Again/Will You Ever Let Me	1989	—	2.50	5.00
❑ 22899	One/Wing and a Prayer	1989	—	—	3.00
❑ 22899 [PS]	One/Wing and a Prayer	1989	—	—	3.00
❑ 28139	E.S.P./Overnight	1987	—	—	3.00
❑ 28139 [PS]	E.S.P./Overnight	1987	—	2.00	4.00
❑ 28351	You Win Again/Backtafunk	1987	—	—	3.00
❑ 28351 [PS]	You Win Again/Backtafunk	1987	—	—	3.00
Albums					
ATCO					
❑ 33-223 [M]	Bee Gees' 1st	1967	7.50	15.00	30.00
❑ SD 33-223 [S]	Bee Gees' 1st	1967	5.00	10.00	20.00
—Brown and purple label original					
❑ SD 33-223	Bee Gees' 1st	1969	2.50	5.00	10.00
—Yellow label reissue					
❑ 33-233 [M]	Horizontal	1968	7.50	15.00	30.00
❑ SD 33-233 [S]	Horizontal	1968	5.00	10.00	20.00
—Brown and purple label original					
❑ SD 33-233	Horizontal	1969	2.50	5.00	10.00
—Yellow label reissue					
❑ 33-253 [M]	Idea	1968	12.50	25.00	50.00
—White label promo only					
❑ SD 33-253 [S]	Idea	1968	5.00	10.00	20.00
—Brown and purple label original					
❑ SD 33-253	Idea	1969	2.50	5.00	10.00
—Yellow label reissue					
❑ 33-264 [M]	Rare, Precious & Beautiful	1968	7.50	15.00	30.00
—White label promo only					
❑ SD 33-264 [R]	Rare, Precious & Beautiful	1968	3.75	7.50	15.00
—Brown and purple label original					
❑ SD 33-264	Rare, Precious & Beautiful	1969	2.50	5.00	10.00
—Yellow label reissue					
❑ 33-292 [M]	Best of Bee Gees	1969	7.50	15.00	30.00
—White label promo only					
❑ SD 33-292 [S]	Best of Bee Gees	1969	3.00	6.00	12.00
❑ 33-321 [M]	Rare, Precious & Beautiful, Volume 2	1970	7.50	15.00	30.00
—White label promo only					
❑ SD 33-321 [R]	Rare, Precious & Beautiful, Volume 2	1970	3.00	6.00	12.00
❑ SD 33-327	Cucumber Castle	1970	3.00	6.00	12.00
❑ 33-353 [M]	2 Years On	1971	7.50	15.00	30.00
—White label promo only; "DJ Copy Monaural" sticker on cover					
❑ SD 33-353 [S]	2 Years On	1971	3.00	6.00	12.00
❑ SD 2-702 [(2)]	Odessa	1969	10.00	20.00	40.00
—Red felt cover					
❑ SD 2-702 [(2)]	Odessa	1969	20.00	40.00	80.00
—Record club editions with plain red cover					
❑ SD 7003	Trafalgar	1971	3.00	6.00	12.00
❑ SD 7012	To Whom It May Concern	1972	3.00	6.00	12.00
MOBILE FIDELITY					
❑ 1-263	Trafalgar	1996	10.00	20.00	40.00
—Audiophile vinyl					
NAUTILUS					
❑ NR-17	Spirits Having Flown	1981	7.50	15.00	30.00
❑ NR-42	Living Eyes	1982	25.00	50.00	100.00
—Record was never released; value is for test pressings					
PICKWICK					
❑ BAN-90011 [R]	Turn Around, Look at Me	1978	2.00	4.00	8.00
—Reissue of Australian recordings					
❑ BAN-90021 [R]	Monday's Rain	1978	2.00	4.00	8.00
—Reissue of Australian recordings					
❑ BAN-90031 [R]	Take Hold of That Star	1978	2.00	4.00	8.00
—Reissue of Australian recordings					
❑ BAN-90041 [R]	Peace of Mind	1978	2.00	4.00	8.00
—Reissue of Australian recordings; tracks on this LP were making their first appearance in the U.S.					
RSO					
❑ SMP-1 [DJ]	The Words and Music of Maurice, Barry and Robin Gibb	1979	12.50	25.00	50.00
—Promo-only publisher's sampler					
❑ PRO 033 [DJ]	Saturday Night Fever Special Disco Versions	1978	12.50	25.00	50.00
—Promo-only sampler; contains an otherwise unavailable extended version of "Stayin' Alive"					
❑ SO 870	Life in a Tin Can	1973	2.50	5.00	10.00
❑ SO 874	Best of Bee Gees	1973	2.50	5.00	10.00
—Reissue of Atco SD 33-292					
❑ SO 875	Best of Bee Gees, Vol. 2	1973	2.50	5.00	10.00
❑ PUB-1000 [DJ]	Unichappell Publisher's Sampler	1980	12.50	25.00	50.00
❑ RPO 1008 [DJ]	Select Disco Cuts from "Spirits Having Flown"	1979	7.50	15.00	30.00
❑ RS-1-3003	Children of the World	1976	2.50	5.00	10.00
❑ RS-1-3006	Bee Gees Gold, Volume One	1976	2.50	5.00	10.00
❑ RS-1-3007	Odessa	1976	2.50	5.00	10.00
—Condensed version of Atco original					
❑ RS-1-3024	Main Course	1977	2.00	4.00	8.00
❑ RS-1-3041	Spirits Having Flown	1979	2.50	5.00	10.00
—Some pressings have a cardboard innersleeve, others a paper innersleeve. No difference in value.					
❑ RS-1-3042 [PD]	Spirits Having Flown	1979	3.75	7.50	15.00
❑ RS-1-3098	Living Eyes	1981	2.50	5.00	10.00
❑ RS-2-3901 [(2)]	Here At Last...Bee Gees...Live	1977	3.00	6.00	12.00
❑ RS-2-4200 [(2)]	Bee Gees' Greatest	1979	3.00	6.00	12.00
❑ SO 4800	Mr. Natural	1974	2.50	5.00	10.00
❑ SO 4807	Main Course	1975	2.50	5.00	10.00
❑ 823274-1 [(2)]	Here At Last...Bee Gees...Live	1984	2.50	5.00	10.00
❑ 823658-1	Children of the World	1984	2.00	4.00	8.00
❑ 823659-1	Bee Gees Gold, Volume One	1984	2.00	4.00	8.00
❑ 825390-1 [(2)]	Bee Gees' Greatest	1984	2.50	5.00	10.00
—Gatefold replaced by single-pocket cover					
WARNER BROS.					
❑ 25541	E.S.P.	1987	2.50	5.00	10.00
❑ 25887	One	1989	3.00	6.00	12.00
BEE JAY					
45s					
CLOCK					
❑ 1743	I'll Go On/There's No One for Me	1962	6.25	12.50	25.00

Number	Title (A Side/B Side)	Yr	VG	VG+	NM
BEEFEATERS, THE Early version of THE BYRDS.					
45s					
ELEKTRA					
❑ 45013	Please Let Me Love You/Don't Be Long	1964	125.00	250.00	500.00
❑ 45013 [DJ]	Please Let Me Love You/Don't Be Long	1964	62.50	125.00	250.00
BEEHIVES, THE					
45s					
KING					
❑ 5881	I Want to Hold Your Hand/She Loves You	1964	3.75	7.50	15.00
BEES, THE At least two different groups.					
45s					
FINCH					
❑ 506	So Jealous/(B-side unknown)	196?	18.75	37.50	75.00
IMPERIAL					
❑ 5314	Toy Bell/Snatchin' Back	1954	50.00	100.00	200.00
❑ 5320	I Want to Be Loved/Get Away Baby	1954	75.00	150.00	300.00
LIVERPOOL					
❑ 62225	Voices Green and Purple/(B-side unknown)	1966	20.00	40.00	80.00
❑ 62225 [PS]	Voices Green and Purple/(B-side unknown)	1966	25.00	50.00	100.00
MIRWOOD					
❑ 5503	She's An Artist/Leave Me Be	1965	6.25	12.50	25.00
BEETHOVEN SOUL					
45s					
DOT					
❑ 17031	Good Time Gal/The Walls Are High	1967	2.00	4.00	8.00
Albums					
DOT					
❑ DLP-3821 [M]	Beethoven Soul	1967	6.25	12.50	25.00
❑ DLP-25821 [S]	Beethoven Soul	1967	6.25	12.50	25.00
BEETLES, THE					
45s					
BLUE CAT					
❑ 115	Ain't That Love/Welcome to My Heart	1965	3.75	7.50	15.00
—Also issued as "The Bouquets"					
BEGINNING OF THE END, THE					
45s					
ALSTON					
❑ 4595	Funky Nassau- Part 1/Funky Nassau - Part 2	1971	—	2.50	5.00
❑ 4599	Hey Pretty Girl/Monkey Tamarind	1971	—	2.00	4.00
❑ 4604	Come Down Baby - Part 1/ Come Down Baby - Part 2	1971	—	2.00	4.00
❑ 4605	Gee Whiz, It's Christmas/Surrey Ride	1971	—	2.00	4.00
❑ 4607	Doin' the Funky Do/Fishman	1972	—	2.00	4.00
Albums					
ALSTON					
❑ SD 33-379	Funky Nassau	1971	5.00	10.00	20.00
BEL-AIRE GIRLS, THE					
Albums					
EVEREST					
❑ STBR-1081 [S]	The Bel-Aire Girls Sing Along with the Teen-Agers	1960	20.00	40.00	80.00
❑ LPBR-5081 [M]	The Bel-Aire Girls Sing Along with the Teen-Agers	1960	15.00	30.00	60.00
BEL-AIRE POPS ORCHESTRA, THE					
Albums					
LIBERTY					
❑ LRP-3414 [M]	Jan and Dean's Pop Symphony No. 1	1965	30.00	60.00	120.00
❑ LST-7414 [S]	Jan and Dean's Pop Symphony No. 1	1965	50.00	100.00	200.00
BEL-AIRES, THE (1)					
45s					
CROWN					
❑ 126	Cherry Pie/Tick Tock	1954	12.50	25.00	50.00
FLIP					
❑ 303	This Paradise/Let's Party Awhile	1954	12.50	25.00	50.00
—Blue label					
❑ 303	This Paradise/Let's Party Awhile	1954	25.00	50.00	100.00
—Maroon label					
❑ 304	White Port and Lemon Juice/This Is Goodbye	1955	25.00	50.00	100.00
BEL-AIRES, THE (U)					
45s					
DECCA					
❑ 30631	My Yearbook/Rockin' An' Strollin'	1958	7.50	15.00	30.00
MERCURY					
❑ 71763	Knock Knock Knock (Knocking on My Door)/ Wear My Class Ring on a Ribbon	1961	3.00	6.00	12.00
NU SOUND					
❑ 1022	Palmeras/Pony Rock	1962	3.00	6.00	12.00
BELAFONTE, HARRY					
45s					
CAPITOL					
❑ F856	Whispering/ Sometimes I Feel Like a Motherless Child	1950	10.00	20.00	40.00
❑ F1018	A Farewell to Arms/I Still Get a Thrill	1950	7.50	15.00	30.00
COLUMBIA					
❑ 18-02396	Forever Young/Something to Hold On To	1981	—	2.00	4.00
GEFFEN					
❑ 27859	Day-O/Main Titles	1988	—	—	3.00
—B-side: instrumental from the "Beetlejuice" soundtrack					
❑ 27859 [PS]	Day-O/Main Titles	1988	—	—	3.00
JUBILEE					
❑ 5158	Venezuela/Annabelle Lee	1954	5.00	10.00	20.00
RCA VICTOR					
❑ 47-4676	A-Roving/Chimney Smoke	1952	3.75	7.50	15.00

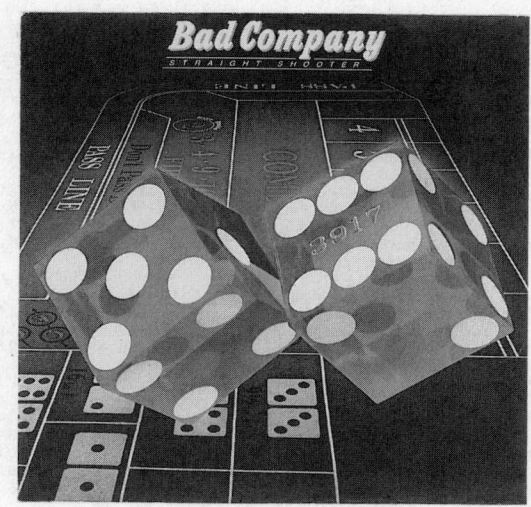

Bachman-Turner Overdrive, *Not Fragile,* Mercury SRM-1-1004, stereo LP, $5-$10.

Bad Company, *Straight Shooter,* Swan Song SS 8413, stereo LP, original edition, $5-$10.

Badfinger, *Badfinger*, Warner Bros. BS 2762, stereo LP, $7.50-$15.

The Beach Boys, "Ten Little Indians," Capitol 4880, picture sleeve, $100-$200.

The Beach Boys, *Pet Sounds,* DCC Compact Classics LPZ-2006, reissue mono LP, $60-$120.

Bee Gees, *Trafalgar,* Atco SD 7003, stereo LP, $6-$12.

The "B" tab marker appears at top right of page.

Number	Title (A Side/B Side)	Yr	VG	VG+	NM
❏ 47-4892	Man Smart (Woman Smarter)/Jerry	1952	3.75	7.50	15.00
❏ 47-5051	Scarlet Ribbons (For Her Hair)/Shenandoah	1952	3.75	7.50	15.00
❏ 47-5210	Springfield Mountain/Gomen-Nasai	1953	3.75	7.50	15.00
❏ 47-5311.	Matilda, Matilda/Suzanne	1953	3.75	7.50	15.00
❏ 47-5617	Hold 'Em Joe/I'm Just a Country Boy	1954	3.75	7.50	15.00
❏ 47-5722	Pretty As A Rainbow/Acorn in the Meadow	1954	3.75	7.50	15.00
❏ 47-5722 [PS]	Pretty As A Rainbow/Acorn in the Meadow	1954	7.50	15.00	30.00
❏ 47-5872	John Henry//(B-side unknown)	1954	3.75	7.50	15.00
❏ 47-6249	Troubles/Hello Everybody	1955	3.00	6.00	12.00
❏ 47-6458	The Blues Is Man (Part 1)/ The Blues Is Man (Part 2)	1956	3.00	6.00	12.00
❏ 47-6663	Jamaica Farewell/Once Was	1956	3.00	6.00	12.00
❏ 47-6663 [PS]	Jamaica Farewell/Once Was	1956	6.25	12.50	25.00
❏ 47-6735	Mary's Boy Child/Venezuela	1956	3.00	6.00	12.00
❏ 47-6735 [PS]	Mary's Boy Child/Venezuela	1956	6.25	12.50	25.00
❏ 47-6771	Banana Boat (Day-O)/Star-O	1956	3.00	6.00	12.00
❏ 47-6771 [PS]	Banana Boat (Day-O)/Star-O	1956	6.25	12.50	25.00
❏ 47-6780	John Henry/Tol' My Captain	1956	2.50	5.00	10.00
❏ 47-6781	Mo Mary/Lord Randall	1956	2.50	5.00	10.00
❏ 47-6782	Man Piaba/The Fox	1956	2.50	5.00	10.00
❏ 47-6782 [PS]	Man Piaba/The Fox	1956	5.00	10.00	20.00
❏ 47-6783	Man Smart (Woman Smarter)/Chimney Smoke	1956	2.50	5.00	10.00
❏ 47-6784	Unchained Melody/A-Roving	1956	2.50	5.00	10.00
❏ 47-6785	Jump Down-Spin Around/In That Great Gettin' Up Mornin'	1956	2.50	5.00	10.00
❏ 47-6786	Will His Love Be Like His Rum?/Dolly Dawn	1956	2.50	5.00	10.00
❏ 47-6787	Hosanna/I Adore Her	1956	2.50	5.00	10.00
❏ 47-6788	Come Back Liza/Brown Skin Girl	1956	2.50	5.00	10.00
❏ 47-6789	Water Boy/Noah	1956	2.50	5.00	10.00
❏ 47-6790	Danny Boy/Take My Mother Home	1956	2.50	5.00	10.00
❏ 47-6790 [PS]	Danny Boy/Take My Mother Home	1956	5.00	10.00	20.00
❏ 47-6830	Mama Look a Boo Boo (Shut Your Mouth - Go Away)/Don't Ever Love Me	1957	3.00	6.00	12.00

—Same recording as above, but new A-side title

Number	Title (A Side/B Side)	Yr	VG	VG+	NM
❏ 47-6830	Mama Look at Bubu/Don't Ever Love Me	1957	3.00	6.00	12.00
❏ 47-6830 [PS]	Mama Look at Bubu/Don't Ever Love Me	1957	6.25	12.50	25.00
❏ 47-6885	Island in the Sun/Cocoanut Woman	1957	2.50	5.00	10.00
❏ 47-7176	The Marching Saints/Did You Hear About Jerry?	1958	2.00	4.00	8.00
❏ 47-7289	Ain't That Love/The Waiting Game	1958	2.00	4.00	8.00
❏ 47-7425	I Heard the Bells on Christmas Day/Mary, Mary	1958	2.00	4.00	8.00
❏ 47-7425 [PS]	I Heard the Bells on Christmas Day/Mary, Mary	1958	3.75	7.50	15.00
❏ 47-7445	Gotta Travel On/Tarrytown	1959	2.00	4.00	8.00
❏ 47-7491	Darlin' Cora/Turn Around	1959	2.00	4.00	8.00
❏ 47-7550	Fifteen/'Round the Bay of Mexico	1959	2.00	4.00	8.00
❏ 47-7681	March Down to Jordan/Oh Freedom	1960	2.00	4.00	8.00
❏ 47-8513	Hallelujah I Love You So/In the Even' Mama	1965	—	3.00	6.00
❏ 47-8717	Little Bit of Rain/Roll On, Buddy	1965	—	3.00	6.00
❏ 47-9075	Hurry Sundown/Mama Look At Bubu	1967	—	3.00	6.00
❏ 47-9263	Sunflower/A Strange Song	1967	—	3.00	6.00
❏ 47-9406	Annie Love/I'm Just a Country Boy	1967	—	3.00	6.00
❏ 47-9542	By the Time I Get to Phoenix/Sleep Late, My Lady Friend	1968	—	3.00	6.00
❏ 74-0145	Lullabye/The Train Song	1969	—	2.50	5.00

—With Miriam Makeba

Number	Title (A Side/B Side)	Yr	VG	VG+	NM
❏ 74-0428	Circle 'Round the Sun/Something in the Way She Moves	1971	—	2.50	5.00
❏ 74-0628	Women/Pastures of Plenty	1971	—	2.50	5.00
❏ 47-6784 [PS]	Unchained Melody/A-Roving	1956	5.00	10.00	20.00
❏ 47-9263 [PS]	Sunflower/A Strange Song	1967	2.50	5.00	10.00
❏ 447-0320	Suzanne/Matilda, Matilda!	195?	2.50	5.00	10.00

—Black label, dog on top

Number	Title (A Side/B Side)	Yr	VG	VG+	NM
❏ 447-0321	Shenandoah/Scarlet Ribbons	195?	2.50	5.00	10.00

—Black label, dog on top

❏ 447-0321 [PS]	Shenandoah/Scarlet Ribbons	195?	5.00	10.00	20.00
❏ 447-0322	Hold 'Em Joe/I'm Just a Country Boy	195?	2.50	5.00	10.00

—Black label, dog on top

❏ 447-0323	Mary's Boy Child/Venezuela	195?	2.50	5.00	10.00

—Black label, dog on top

❏ 447-0324	Banana Boat (Day-O)/Jamaica Farewell	195?	2.50	5.00	10.00

—Black label, dog on top

❏ 447-0325	Mama Look A Boo Boo/Don't Ever Love Me	195?	2.50	5.00	10.00

—Black label, dog on top

❏ APBO-0093	Morningside/So Close	1973	—	2.00	4.00
❏ SP-45-181 [DJ]	By the Time I Get to Phoenix/Sleep Late, My Lady Friend	1968	3.00	6.00	12.00

—Promo-only number

7-Inch Extended Plays
CAPITOL

Number	Title (A Side/B Side)	Yr	VG	VG+	NM
❏ EAP-1-619	Close Your Eyes/Sometimes I Feel Like a Motherless Child//I Still Get a Thrill/Deep As the River	1955	3.75	7.50	15.00
❏ EAP-1-619 [PS]	Close Your Eyes	1955	3.75	7.50	15.00

JUBILEE

❏ EP 5006	Simple, Simple, Simple/Annabelle Lee//Venezuela/Only One Like Me	195?	5.00	10.00	20.00
❏ EP 5006 [PS]	Ballads by Belafonte	195?	5.00	10.00	20.00

RCA VICTOR

❏ SPD-24 [PS]	The Best of Belafonte	1956	5.00	10.00	20.00

—Box for 10-EP set plus liner-note booklet

❏ SP-45-67	Cocoanut Woman/A Woman Is a Sometime Thing//Turn Around/In the Evenin' Mama	1959	5.00	10.00	20.00
❏ SP-45-67 [PS]	RCA Victor Presents a Harry Belafonte Preview Album	1959	5.00	10.00	20.00
❏ LPC-127	Day-o/Jamaica Farewell/Man Smart (Woman Smarter)/Shenandoah	1961	2.50	5.00	10.00

—"Compact 33 Double"; small hole, plays at 33 1/3 rpm

❏ LPC-127 [PS]	Belafonte at Carnegie Hall Highlights	1961	2.50	5.00	10.00
❏ 547-0404	Mark Twain/Man Piaba//Mo Mary/Lord Randall	1954	2.50	5.00	10.00

—Record 1 of 2-EP set EPB 1022

❏ 547-0405	John Henry/Tol' My Captain//Soldier, Soldier/The Next Big River	1954	2.50	5.00	10.00

—Record 2 of 2-EP set EPB 1022

Number	Title (A Side/B Side)	Yr	VG	VG+	NM
❏ EPA 412	Shenandoah/Scarlet Ribbons (For Her Hair)//Man Smart (Woman Smarter)/Jerry (This Timber Got to Roll)	1952	3.75	7.50	15.00

—Black label, outline of dog at right

❏ EPA 412 [PS]	Harry Belafonte Sings "Man Smart" and Other Folk Songs	1952	3.00	6.00	12.00
❏ EPA 412	Shenandoah/Scarlet Ribbons (For Her Hair)//Man Smart (Woman Smarter)/Jerry (This Timber Got to Roll)	1954	2.50	5.00	10.00

—Black label, white dog at top

❏ EPA 559	Delia/The Fox//Kalenda Rock/The Drummer and the Cook	195?	3.00	6.00	12.00
❏ EPA 559 [PS]	Harry Belafonte	195?	3.00	6.00	12.00
❏ EPA 693	Take My Mother Home//Unchained Melody/Matilda	1955	3.00	6.00	12.00
❏ EPA 693 [PS]	Belafonte, Act 1	1955	3.00	6.00	12.00
❏ EPA 694	Sylvie//In That Great Gettin' Up Mornin'/Jump Down, Spin Around	1955	3.00	6.00	12.00

—With dog on label

❏ EPA 694	Sylvie//In That Great Gettin' Up Mornin'/Jump Down, Spin Around	1955	3.75	7.50	15.00

—No dog on label

❏ EPA 694 [PS]	Belafonte, Act 2	1955	3.00	6.00	12.00
❏ EPA 695	Noah//Suzanne (Every Night When the Sun Goes Down)/Waterboy	1955	2.50	5.00	10.00
❏ EPA 695 [PS]	Belafonte, Act 3	1955	2.50	5.00	10.00
❏ EPA 768	Day O/Will His Love Be Like His Rum?//Jamaica Farewell/Dolly Dawn	1956	3.00	6.00	12.00
❏ EPA 768 [PS]	Calypso	1956	3.00	6.00	12.00
❏ 547-0899	Day-O/I Do Adore Her//Brown Skin Girl/Dolly Dawn	1956	2.50	5.00	10.00

—Record 1 of 2-EP set EPB 1248

❏ 547-0900	Jamaica Farewell/Will His Love Be Like His Rum?//Star O/Hosanna	1956	2.50	5.00	10.00

—Record 2 of 2-EP set EPB 1248

❏ EPB 1022 [PS]	"Mark Twain" and Other Folk Favorites	1954	5.00	10.00	20.00

—Two-pocket jacket for two-EP set

❏ EPB 1248 [PS]	Calypso	1956	5.00	10.00	20.00

—Two-pocket jacket for two-EP set

❏ EPA 1-1402	Merci Bon Dieu//The Drummer and the Cook/Danny Boy	1956	3.00	6.00	12.00
❏ EPA 1-1402 [PS]	An Evening with Belafonte, Vol. 1	1956	3.00	6.00	12.00
❏ EPA 2-1402	Cu Cu Ru Cu Cu/Paloma//Hava Negela/When the Saints Go Marching In	1956	3.00	6.00	12.00
❏ EPA 2-1402 [PS]	An Evening with Belafonte, Vol. 2	1956	3.00	6.00	12.00
❏ EPA 3-1402	Come Oh My Love//Eden Was Like This/Shenandoah	1956	3.00	6.00	12.00
❏ EPA 3-1402 [PS]	An Evening with Belafonte, Vol. 3	1956	3.00	6.00	12.00
❏ EPA 1-1505	Haiti Cherie/Love, Love Alone//Lucy's Door/Scratch, Scratch	1957	2.50	5.00	10.00
❏ EPA 1-1505 [PS]	Belafonte Sings of the Caribbean, Vol. 1	1957	2.50	5.00	10.00
❏ EPA 2-1505	(contents unknown)	1957	2.50	5.00	10.00
❏ EPA 2-1505 [PS]	Belafonte Sings of the Caribbean, Vol. 2	1957	2.50	5.00	10.00
❏ VLP 2449	Midnight Special/Crawdad Hole//Gotta Travel On/Mule Skinner	1962	12.50	25.00	50.00

—Jukebox issue; small hole, plays at 33 1/3 rpm; Bob Dylan plays harmonica on the first track

❏ VLP 2449 [PS]	The Midnight Special	1962	12.50	25.00	50.00
❏ EPA-4084	Island in the Sun/Cocoanut Woman//Lead Man Holler	1957	3.00	6.00	12.00
❏ EPA-4084 [PS]	Island in the Sun	1957	3.00	6.00	12.00
❏ EPA 4217	Cordella Brown/Judy Drownded//Lead Man Holler/Angelique-O	1958	3.00	6.00	12.00
❏ EPA 4217 [PS]	Ballads by Belafonte	1958	3.00	6.00	12.00
❏ 599-9126	Day-O/I Do Adore Her//Jamaica Farewell/Will His Love Be Like His Rum?	1956	2.00	4.00	8.00

—Side 1 and 20 of 10-EP set SPD-24

❏ 599-9127	Dolly Dawn/Star O//The Jack-Ass Song/Hosanna	1956	2.00	4.00	8.00

—Side 2 and 19 of 10-EP set SPD-24

❏ 599-9128	Come Back Liza/Brown Skin Girl//Man Smart (Woman Smarter)/Matilda	1956	2.00	4.00	8.00

—Side 3 and 18 of 10-EP set SPD-24

❏ 599-9129	Waterboy/Suzanne (Every Night When the Sun Goes Down)//Troubles/In That Great Gettin' Up Mornin'	1956	2.00	4.00	8.00

—Side 4 and 17 of 10-EP set SPD-24

❏ 599-9130	Noah/Jump Down, Spin Around//Take My Mother Home	1956	2.00	4.00	8.00

—Side 5 and 16 of 10-EP set SPD-24

❏ 599-9131	Sylvie//Scarlet Ribbons (For Her Hair)/Unchained Melody	1956	2.00	4.00	8.00

—Side 6 and 15 of 10-EP set SPD-24

❏ 599-9132	Mark Twain/Tol' My Captain//Man Piaba/The Drummer and the Cook	1956	2.00	4.00	8.00

—Side 7 and 14 of 10-EP set SPD-24

❏ 599-9133	John Henry/Kalenda Rock//The Fox/Soldier, Soldier/The Next Big River	1956	2.00	4.00	8.00

—Side 8 and 13 of 10-EP set SPD-24

❏ 599-9134	Mo Mary/Lord Randall//Delia/Shenandoah	1956	2.00	4.00	8.00

—Side 9 and 12 of 10-EP set SPD-24

❏ 599-9135	Jerry (The Timber Got to Roll)/The Blues Is Man - Part I//Acorn in the Meadow/Hello Everybody	1956	2.00	4.00	8.00

—Side 10 and 11 of 10-EP set SPD-24

Albums
COLUMBIA

Number	Title (A Side/B Side)	Yr	VG	VG+	NM
❏ FC 37489	Loving You Is Where I Belong	1981	2.50	5.00	10.00

DCC COMPACT CLASSICS

❏ LPZ-2039	Jump Up Calypso	1997	15.00	30.00	60.00

—Audiophile vinyl

EMI

❏ E1-92247	Belafonte '89	1989	3.00	6.00	12.00

EMI MANHATAN

❏ E1-46971	Paradise in Gazankulu	1988	3.00	6.00	12.00

B

Number	Title (A Side/B Side)	Yr	VG	VG+	NM
PAIR					
❏ PDL2-1060 [(2)]The Belafonte Song Book		1986	3.00	6.00	12.00
RCA CAMDEN					
❏ ACL1-0502	Abraham, Martin and John	1974	2.50	5.00	10.00
❏ CAS-2599	Harry	1972	2.50	5.00	10.00
RCA CUSTOM EDITION					
❏ DRL1-0068	I Wish You a Merry Christmas	1973	3.75	7.50	15.00
—Reissue of LSP-2424 with two tracks deleted					
RCA VICTOR					
❏ APL1-0094	Play Me	1973	3.00	6.00	12.00
❏ ANL1-0979	Pure Gold	1975	2.50	5.00	10.00
❏ LPM-1006 [M]	Belafonte Sings the Blues	1954	12.50	25.00	50.00
—Reissued in 1958 with the same number, then re-recorded in 1959					
❏ LPM-1022 [M]	"Mark Twain" and Other Folk Favorites	1954	12.50	25.00	50.00
❏ LSP-1022(e) [R]"Mark Twain" and Other Folk Favorites		196?	3.00	6.00	12.00
❏ LPM-1150 [M]	Belafonte	1955	12.50	25.00	50.00
❏ LSP-1150(e) [R]Belafonte		196?	3.00	6.00	12.00
❏ AFL1-1248	Calypso	1977	2.50	5.00	10.00
—Reissue with new prefix					
❏ LPM-1248 [M]	Calypso	1956	7.50	15.00	30.00
❏ LSP-1248(e) [R]Calypso		196?	3.00	6.00	12.00
❏ LPM-1402 [M]	An Evening with Belafonte	1957	6.25	12.50	25.00
❏ LSP-1402(e) [R]An Evening with Belafonte		1960	3.00	6.00	12.00
—Dog on top					
❏ LSP-1402(e) [R]An Evening with Belafonte		1969	2.50	5.00	10.00
—Orange label					
❏ ANL1-1434	An Evening with Belafonte	1976	2.50	5.00	10.00
—Reissue of LSP-1402					
❏ LPM-1505 [M]	Belafonte Sings of the Caribbean	1957	7.50	15.00	30.00
❏ LSP-1505(e) [R]Belafonte Sings of the Caribbean		196?	3.00	6.00	12.00
❏ LOC-1507 [M]	Porgy and Bess	1959	5.00	10.00	20.00
❏ LSO-1507 [S]	Porgy and Bess	1959	6.25	12.50	25.00
—With Lena Horne					
❏ LPM-1887 [M]	To Wish You a Merry Christmas	1958	6.25	12.50	25.00
❏ LSP-1887 [S]	To Wish You a Merry Christmas	1958	10.00	20.00	40.00
❏ LPM-1927 [M]	Love Is a Gentle Thing	1959	5.00	10.00	20.00
❏ LSP-1927 [S]	Love Is a Gentle Thing	1959	6.25	12.50	25.00
❏ LPM-1972 [M]	Belafonte Sings the Blues	1959	5.00	10.00	20.00
❏ LSP-1972 [S]	Belafonte Sings the Blues	1959	6.25	12.50	25.00
❏ LSP-1972	Belafonte Sings the Blues	199?	6.25	12.50	25.00
—Classic Records reissue on audiophile vinyl					
❏ LPM-2022 [M]	My Lord What a Mornin'	1960	5.00	10.00	20.00
❏ LSP-2022 [S]	My Lord What a Mornin'	1960	6.25	12.50	25.00
❏ LPM-2194 [M]	Swing Dat Hammer	1961	5.00	10.00	20.00
❏ LSP-2194 [S]	Swing Dat Hammer	1961	6.25	12.50	25.00
❏ LPM-2309 [M]	At Home and Abroad	1961	5.00	10.00	20.00
❏ LSP-2309 [S]	At Home and Abroad	1961	6.25	12.50	25.00
❏ ANL1-2324	The Midnight Special	1976	2.50	5.00	10.00
—Reissue of LSP-2449					
❏ LPM-2388 [M]	Jump Up Calypso	1961	5.00	10.00	20.00
❏ LSP-2388 [S]	Jump Up Calypso	1961	6.25	12.50	25.00
❏ LPM-2449 [M]	The Midnight Special	1962	7.50	15.00	30.00
❏ LSP-2449 [S]	The Midnight Special	1962	10.00	20.00	40.00
—The above LP features Bob Dylan on harmonica on the title track, his first appearance on record					
❏ CPL1-2469	A Legendary Performer	1977	2.50	5.00	10.00
❏ LPM-2574 [M]	The Many Moods of Belafonte	1962	5.00	10.00	20.00
❏ LSP-2574 [S]	The Many Moods of Belafonte	196?	5.00	10.00	20.00
—"Stereo" on black label, "RCA Victor" in white					
❏ LSP-2574 [S]	The Many Moods of Belafonte	1962	6.25	12.50	25.00
—"Living Stereo" on label, "RCA Victor" in silver					
❏ LSP-2574 [S]	The Many Moods of Belafonte	1969	3.00	6.00	12.00
—Orange label					
❏ LPM-2626 [M]	To Wish You a Merry Christmas	1962	5.00	10.00	20.00
—Reissue of LPM-1887 with new cover and one additional track					
❏ LSP-2626 [S]	To Wish You a Merry Christmas	1962	6.25	12.50	25.00
❏ LPM-2695 [M]	Streets I Have Walked	1963	5.00	10.00	20.00
❏ LSP-2695 [S]	Streets I Have Walked	1963	6.25	12.50	25.00
❏ LPM-2953 [M]	Ballads, Blues and Boasters	1964	3.75	7.50	15.00
❏ LSP-2953 [S]	Ballads, Blues and Boasters	1964	5.00	10.00	20.00
❏ LPM-3415 [M]	An Evening with Belafonte/Mouskouri	1966	3.75	7.50	15.00
❏ LSP-3415 [S]	An Evening with Belafonte/Mouskouri	1966	5.00	10.00	20.00
—With Nana Mouskouri					
❏ LPM-3420 [M]	An Evening with Belafonte/Makeba	1965	3.75	7.50	15.00
❏ LSP-3420 [S]	An Evening with Belafonte/Makeba	1965	5.00	10.00	20.00
—With Miriam Makeba					
❏ LPM-3571 [M]	In My Quiet Room	1966	3.00	6.00	12.00
❏ LSP-3571 [S]	In My Quiet Room	1966	3.75	7.50	15.00
❏ LPM-3658 [M]	Calypso in Brass	1967	3.00	6.00	12.00
❏ LSP-3658 [S]	Calypso in Brass	1967	3.75	7.50	15.00
❏ LPM-3779 [M]	Belafonte on Campus	1967	3.00	6.00	12.00
❏ LSP-3779 [S]	Belafonte on Campus	1967	3.75	7.50	15.00
❏ AYL1-3801(e) [R]Calypso		1980	2.00	4.00	8.00
❏ AYL1-3860(e) [R]Pure Gold		1980	2.00	4.00	8.00
❏ LPM-3938 [M]	Belafonte Sings of Love	1968	3.75	7.50	15.00
❏ LSP-3938 [S]	Belafonte Sings of Love	1968	3.75	7.50	15.00
❏ LSP-4255	Homeward Bound	1969	3.75	7.50	15.00
❏ LSP-4301	By Request	1970	3.00	6.00	12.00
❏ LSP-4481	Warm Touch	1971	3.00	6.00	12.00
❏ LSP-4521	Calypso Carnival	1971	3.00	6.00	12.00
❏ LOC-6006 [(2)M]Belafonte at Carnegie Hall		1959	6.25	12.50	25.00
❏ LSO-6006 [(2)S]Belafonte at Carnegie Hall		1959	25.00	50.00	100.00
❏ LSO-6006 [(2)S]Belafonte at Carnegie Hall		1996	10.00	20.00	40.00
—Classic Records reissue on audiophile vinyl					
❏ LOC-6007 [(2)M]Belafonte Returns to Carnegie Hall		1960	5.00	10.00	20.00
❏ LSO-6007 [(2)S]Belafonte Returns to Carnegie Hall		1960	12.50	25.00	50.00
—The above LP also has tracks by Odetta, Miriam Makeba and The Chad Mitchell Trio (the latter for the first time on record)					
❏ LSO-6007 [(2)] Belafonte Returns to Carnegie Hall		1996	10.00	20.00	40.00
—Classic Records reissue on audiophile vinyl					
❏ LOC-6009 [(2)M]Belafonte at the Greek Theatre		1964	5.00	10.00	20.00
❏ LSO-6009 [(2)S]Belafonte at the Greek Theatre		1964	12.50	25.00	50.00
❏ VPS-6024 [(2)] This Is Harry Belafonte		1970	3.75	7.50	15.00

Number	Title (A Side/B Side)	Yr	VG	VG+	NM
❏ VPSX-6077 [(2)]Belafonte Live		1972	3.75	7.50	15.00
TIME-LIFE					
❏ SLGD-17 [(2)]	Legendary Singers: Harry Belafonte	1986	3.75	7.50	15.00
BELAIRS, THE					
45s					
ARVEE					
❏ A-5034	Mr. Moto/Little Brown Jug	1961	10.00	20.00	40.00
❏ A-5054	Volcanic Action/Runaway	1962	7.50	15.00	30.00
BELFAST GYPSIES, THE Also see THEM.					
45s					
LOMA					
❏ 2051	Gloria's Dream/Secret Police	1966	3.75	7.50	15.00
❏ 2060	Portland Town/People, Let's Freak Out	1966	3.75	7.50	15.00
BELL, ARCHIE, AND THE DRELLS					
12-Inch Singles					
BECKET					
❏ BKD-501	Any Time Is Right (5:25)/Why Didja Do Me (5:05)	1981	3.00	6.00	12.00
PHILADELPHIA INT'L					
❏ ASD 375 [DJ]	Glad You Could Make It (5:36)/There's No Other Like You (4:45)	1977	5.00	10.00	20.00
PHILADELPHIA INT'L.					
❏ 4Z8 3701	Strategy/We Got 'Um Dancin'	1979	3.00	6.00	12.00
45s					
ATLANTIC					
❏ 2478	Tighten Up/Tighten Up — Part 2	1968	2.00	4.00	8.00
❏ 2478	Tighten Up/Dog Eat Dog	1968	3.00	6.00	12.00
❏ 2534	I Can't Stop Dancing/You're Such a Beautiful Child	1968	—	3.50	7.00
❏ 2559	Do the Choo Choo/Love Will Rain on You	1968	—	3.50	7.00
❏ 2583	(There's Gonna Be A) Showdown/Go for What You Know	1968	—	3.50	7.00
❏ 2612	I Love My Baby/Just a Little Closer	1969	—	3.50	7.00
❏ 2644	Girl You're Too Young/Do the Hand Jive	1969	—	3.50	7.00
❏ 2663	My Balloon's Going Up/Giving Up Dancing	1969	—	3.50	7.00
❏ 2693	A World Without Music/Here I Go Again	1969	—	3.50	7.00
❏ 2721	Don't Let the Music Slip Away/Houston, Texas	1970	—	3.50	7.00
❏ 2744	I Wish/Get from the Bottom	1970	—	3.50	7.00
❏ 2769	Wrap It Up/Deal with Him	1970	—	3.50	7.00
❏ 2793	I Just Want to Fall in Love/Love at First Sight	1971	—	3.00	6.00
❏ 2829	Let the World Know/Archie's in Love	1971	—	3.00	6.00
❏ 2855	Green Power/I Can't Face You Baby	1972	—	3.00	6.00
BECKET					
❏ 45-4	Any Time Is Right/(B-side unknown)	1981	—	2.00	4.00
EAST WEST					
❏ 2048	She's My Woman/The Yankee Dance	1968	—	3.50	7.00
GLADES					
❏ 1707	Dancing to Your Music/Count the Ways	1973	—	3.00	6.00
❏ 1711	Ain't Nothing for a Man in Love/You Never Know What's On a Woman's Mind	1973	—	3.00	6.00
❏ 1718	Girls Grow Up Faster Than Boys/Love's Gonna Rain on You	1973	—	3.00	6.00
OVIDE					
❏ 228	Tighten Up/Dog Eat Dog	1967	7.50	15.00	30.00
PHILADELPHIA INT'L					
❏ 3605	Nothing Comes Easy/Right Here Is Where I Want to Be	1976	—	2.50	5.00
❏ 3615	Everybody Have a Good Time/I Bet I Can Do That Dance You're Doin'	1977	—	2.50	5.00
❏ 3632	Glad You Could Make It/There's No Other Like You	1977	—	2.50	5.00
❏ 3637	I've Been Missing You/It's Hard Not to Love You	1977	—	2.50	5.00
❏ 3651	Old People/On the Radio	1978	—	2.50	5.00
PHILADELPHIA INT'L.					
❏ 3710	Strategy/We Got 'Um Dancin'	1979	—	2.50	5.00
TSOP					
❏ 4767	I Could Dance All Night/King of the Castle	1975	—	2.50	5.00
❏ 4774	The Soul City Walk/King of the Castle	1975	—	2.50	5.00
❏ 4775	Let's Groove (Part 1)/Let's Groove (Part 2)	1976	—	2.50	5.00
WMOT					
❏ 03057	Touchin' You/(Instrumental)	1982	—	2.50	5.00
Albums					
ATLANTIC					
❏ 8181 [M]	Tighten Up	1968	12.50	25.00	50.00
❏ SD 8181 [S]	Tighten Up	1968	7.50	15.00	30.00
❏ SD 8204	I Can't Stop Dancing	1968	7.50	15.00	30.00
❏ SD 8226	There's Gonna Be a Showdown	1969	7.50	15.00	30.00
PHILADELPHIA INT'L					
❏ PZ 34323	Where Will You Go When the Party's Over	1976	2.50	5.00	10.00
❏ PZ 34855	Hard Not to Like It	1977	2.50	5.00	10.00
❏ JZ 36096	Strategy	1979	2.50	5.00	10.00
TSOP					
❏ PZ 33844	Dance Your Troubles Away	1975	2.50	5.00	10.00
BELL, CARL, AND THE NORVAIRS					
45s					
LAURIE					
❏ 3014	Birth of the Beat/Open House in Your Heart	1958	6.25	12.50	25.00
BELL, FREDDIE, AND THE BELL BOYS					
45s					
MERCURY					
❏ 70919	Stay Loose, Mother Goose/All Right, OK, You Win	1956	5.00	10.00	20.00
❏ 71075	Take the First Train Out of Town/Hey There You	1957	5.00	10.00	20.00
❏ 71105	Rockin' Is My Business/You're Gonna Be Sorry	1957	10.00	20.00	40.00
TEEN					
❏ 101	Hound Dog/Move Me Baby	1955	12.50	25.00	50.00
❏ 103	Old Town Hall/5-10-15 Hours	1955	7.50	15.00	30.00

Number	Title (A Side/B Side)	Yr	VG	VG+	NM
WING					
❑ 90066	Giddy Up a Ding Dong/I Said It and I'm Glad	1956	10.00	20.00	40.00
❑ 90082	The Hucklebuck/Rompin' and Stompin'	1956	10.00	20.00	40.00
Albums					
MERCURY					
❑ MG-20289 [M]	Rock and Roll… All Flavors	1957	50.00	100.00	200.00
20TH FOX					
❑ TF-4146 [M]	Bells Are Swinging	1964	6.25	12.50	25.00
❑ TFS-4146 [S]	Bells Are Swinging	1964	7.50	15.00	30.00

BELL, MADELINE Also see BLUE MINK.
45s

Number	Title (A Side/B Side)	Yr	VG	VG+	NM
ASCOT					
❑ 2156	You Don't Love Me No More/Don't Cross Over to My Side of the Street	1964	2.50	5.00	10.00
❑ 2180	Don't Cry My Heart/Daytime	1965	2.50	5.00	10.00
BRUT					
❑ 808	All That Love Went to Waste/A Touch of Class	1973	—	2.50	5.00
MOD					
❑ 1007	I'm Gonna Make You Love Me/Picture Me Gone	1967	3.00	6.00	12.00
PHILIPS					
❑ 40517	I'm Gonna Make You Love Me/Picture Me Gone	1968	2.00	4.00	8.00
❑ 40539	Finding You, Loving You/Doing Things Together with You	1968	—	3.00	6.00
❑ 40582	Step Inside Love/What I'm Supposed to Do	1969	—	3.00	6.00
PYE					
❑ 71061	I Always Seem to Wind Up Loving You/Your Smile	1976	—	2.00	4.00
Albums					
PHILIPS					
❑ PHS 600271	I'm Gonna Make You Love Me	1968	3.00	6.00	12.00

BELL, MAGGIE Also see STONE THE CROWS.
45s

Number	Title (A Side/B Side)	Yr	VG	VG+	NM
ATLANTIC					
❑ 3018	After Midnight/Souvenirs	1974	—	2.50	5.00
❑ 3040	Caddo Queen/Oh My My	1974	—	2.50	5.00
SWAN SONG					
❑ 70105	Wishing Well/Comin' On Strong	1975	—	2.50	5.00
❑ 99907	Here, There and Everywhere/Put Angels Around You	1983	—	2.00	4.00
—With Bobby Whitlock					
❑ 99907 [PS]	Here, There and Everywhere/Put Angels Around You	1983	—	2.00	4.00
—With Bobby Whitlock					
Albums					
ATLANTIC					
❑ SD 7293	Queen of the Night	1974	3.00	6.00	12.00
SWAN SONG					
❑ SS 8412	Suicide Sal	1975	3.00	6.00	12.00

BELL, TRUDY
45s

Number	Title (A Side/B Side)	Yr	VG	VG+	NM
PHILIPS					
❑ 40021	Willie/This Friend of Mine	1962	3.00	6.00	12.00
❑ 40055	I Remember Jimmy/A Promise and a Kiss Goodnight	1962	3.00	6.00	12.00

BELL, VINCENT
45s

Number	Title (A Side/B Side)	Yr	VG	VG+	NM
DECCA					
❑ 32224	Eleanor/Goin' Out of My Head	1967	—	3.00	6.00
❑ 32418	California Summer/A Sinner Kissed An Angel	1968	—	3.00	6.00
❑ 32483	Good Morning Starshine/Because of You	1969	—	2.50	5.00
❑ 32530	Les Bicyclettes De Belsize/The Ballad of John and Yoko	1969	—	2.50	5.00
❑ 32659	Airport Love Theme/Marilyn's Theme	1970	—	2.50	5.00
❑ 32695	Darling Lili/Nikki	1970	—	2.50	5.00
INDEPENDENT					
❑ 102	Quicksand/(B-side unknown)	1960	10.00	20.00	40.00
MUSICOR					
❑ 1068	Just a Little Kiss/Baker Street Mystery	1965	3.00	6.00	12.00
VERVE					
❑ 10308	Shindig/Whistle Stop	1963	3.00	6.00	12.00
Albums					
DECCA					
❑ DL 4938 [M]	Pop Goes the Electric Sitar	1967	5.00	10.00	20.00
❑ DL 74938 [S]	Pop Goes the Electric Sitar	1967	3.75	7.50	15.00
❑ DL 75212	Airport Love Theme	1970	3.75	7.50	15.00
MUSICOR					
❑ MM-3009 [M]	51 Motion Picture Favorites	1963	3.75	7.50	15.00
❑ MS-3009 [S]	51 Motion Picture Favorites	1963	5.00	10.00	20.00
❑ MM-3047 [M]	Big 16 Guitar Favorites	1965	3.75	7.50	15.00
❑ MS-3047 [S]	Big 16 Guitar Favorites	1965	5.00	10.00	20.00
VERVE					
❑ V-8574 [M]	Whistle Stop	1964	3.75	7.50	15.00
❑ V6-8574 [S]	Whistle Stop	1964	5.00	10.00	20.00

BELL, WILLIAM
12-Inch Singles

Number	Title (A Side/B Side)	Yr	VG	VG+	NM
WRC					
❑ 12204	Headline News/Let Him Pay the Band	1986	2.50	5.00	10.00
45s					
ATLANTIC					
❑ 13154	Everyday Will Be Like A Holiday/Winner	197?	—	2.00	4.00
—Oldies Series reissue					
KAT FAMILY					
❑ 03502	Bad Time to Break Off/The Truth in Your Eyes	1983	—	2.00	4.00
❑ 03995	Playing Hard to Get/The Truth in Your Eyes	1983	—	2.00	4.00

Number	Title (A Side/B Side)	Yr	VG	VG+	NM
MERCURY					
❑ 73839	Tryin' to Love Two/If Sex Was All We Had	1976	—	2.50	5.00
❑ 73922	Coming Back for More/You I Absolutely Positively Love	1977	—	2.00	4.00
❑ 73961	Your Love Keeps Me Goin'/Easy Comin' Out	1977	—	2.00	4.00
STAX					
❑ 0005	Private Number/Love-Eye-Tis	1968	—	2.50	5.00
—With Judy Clay					
❑ 0015	I Forgot to Be Your Lover/Bring the Curtains Down	1968	—	3.00	6.00
❑ 0017	Left-Over Love/My Baby Specializes	1968	—	2.50	5.00
—With Judy Clay					
❑ 0032	My Whole World Is Falling Down/All God's Children Got Soul	1969	—	2.50	5.00
❑ 0038	My Kind of Girl/Happy	1969	—	2.50	5.00
❑ 0043	Love's Sweet Sensation/Strung Out	1969	—	2.50	5.00
—With Mavis Staples					
❑ 0044	I Can't Stop/I Need You Woman	1969	—	2.50	5.00
—With Carla Thomas					
❑ 0054	Born Under a Bad Sign/A Smile Can't Hide a Broken Heart	1969	—	2.50	5.00
❑ 0067	All I Have to Do Is Dream/Leave the Girl Alone	1970	—	2.50	5.00
—With Carla Thomas					
❑ 0070	Lonely Soldier/Let Me Ride	1970	—	2.50	5.00
❑ 0092	A Penny for Your Thoughts/Till My Back Ain't Got No Bone	1971	—	2.50	5.00
❑ 0106	All for the Love of a Woman/I'll Be Home	1971	—	2.50	5.00
❑ 116	You Don't Miss Your Water/Formula of Love	1961	5.00	10.00	20.00
❑ 128	Any Other Way/Please Help Me I'm Falling	1962	5.00	10.00	20.00
❑ 0128	If You Really Love Him/Save Us	1972	—	2.50	5.00
❑ 132	I Told You So/What'Cha Gonna Do	1963	3.75	7.50	15.00
❑ 135	Just As I Thought/I'm Waiting on You	1963	3.75	7.50	15.00
❑ 138	Somebody Mentioned Your Name/What Can I Do to Forget	1963	3.75	7.50	15.00
❑ 141	I'll Show You/Monkeying Around	1963	3.75	7.50	15.00
❑ 146	Don't Make Something Out of Nothing/Who Will It Be Tomorrow	1964	3.00	6.00	12.00
❑ 0157	Livin' on Borrowed Time/The Man in the Street	1973	—	2.50	5.00
❑ 174	Crying All By Myself/Don't Stop Now	1965	3.00	6.00	12.00
❑ 0175	You've Got the Kind of Love I Need/I've Got to Go On Without You	1973	—	2.50	5.00
❑ 191	Share What You Got/Marching Off to War	1966	2.50	5.00	10.00
❑ 0198	All I Need Is Your Love/Gettin' What You Want	1974	—	2.50	5.00
❑ 199	Soldier's Goodbye/Never Like This Before	1966	2.50	5.00	10.00
❑ 212	Everybody Loves a Winner/You're Such a Sweet Thing	1967	2.00	4.00	8.00
❑ 0221	Get It While It's Hot/Nobody Walks Away from Love Unhurt	1974	—	2.50	5.00
❑ 227	One Plus One/Eloise (Hang On In There)	1967	2.00	4.00	8.00
❑ 237	Everyday Will Be Like a Holiday/Ain't Got No Girl	1967	2.00	4.00	8.00
❑ 248	A Tribute to a King (Otis Redding)/Every Man Oughta Have a Woman	1968	—	3.00	6.00
WRC					
❑ 202	I Don't Want to Wake Up (Feelin' Guilty)/Whatever You Want (You Got It)	1986	—	2.50	5.00
—With Janice Bulluck					
❑ 204	Headline News/Let Him Pay the Band	1986	—	2.50	5.00
Albums					
KAT FAMILY					
❑ FZ 38643	Survivor	1983	2.50	5.00	10.00
MERCURY					
❑ SRM-1-1146	Coming Back for More	1977	2.50	5.00	10.00
❑ SRM-1-1193	It's Time You Took Another Listen	1978	2.50	5.00	10.00
STAX					
❑ 719 [M]	Soul of a Bell	1967	10.00	20.00	40.00
❑ S-719 [S]	Soul of a Bell	1967	12.50	25.00	50.00
❑ ST-2014 [M]	Bound to Happen	1969	12.50	25.00	50.00
—Mono is promo only					
❑ STS-2014 [S]	Bound to Happen	1969	7.50	15.00	30.00
❑ STS-2037	Wow…	1971	7.50	15.00	30.00
❑ STS-3005	Phases of Reality	1973	5.00	10.00	20.00
❑ STS-5502	Relating	1974	5.00	10.00	20.00
❑ MPS-8541	The Best of William Bell	1988	2.50	5.00	10.00
WRC					
❑ WL-3007	On a Roll	1986	3.00	6.00	12.00

BELL HOPS, THE Probably two different groups.
45s

Number	Title (A Side/B Side)	Yr	VG	VG+	NM
BARB					
❑ 100	Angela/Ring Dang Doo Ting-a-Ling	1958	6.25	12.50	25.00
❑ 101/2	Teenage Years/Carmella	1958	6.25	12.50	25.00
DECCA					
❑ 48208	For the Rest of My Life/It Would Take a Million Years	1951	25.00	50.00	100.00
❑ 48239	I'm All Yours/Where Is Love	1951	25.00	50.00	100.00
TIN PAN ALLEY					
❑ 153	Please Don't Say No to Me/Merchant Street Blues	1956	37.50	75.00	150.00

BELL NOTES, THE
45s

Number	Title (A Side/B Side)	Yr	VG	VG+	NM
AUTOGRAPH					
❑ 204	Little Girl in Blue/Too Young or Too Old	1960	6.25	12.50	25.00
CLOCK					
❑ 71889	There She Goes/My Pledge to You	1961	5.00	10.00	20.00
MADISON					
❑ 136	Shortnin' Bread/To Each His Own	1960	5.00	10.00	20.00
❑ 141	Real Wild Child/Friendly Star	1960	5.00	10.00	20.00
TIME					
❑ 1004	I've Had It/Be Mine	1958	7.50	15.00	30.00
—First pressing on blue labels					

B

Number	Title (A Side/B Side)	Yr	VG	VG+	NM
❑ 1004	I've Had It/Be Mine	1959	6.25	12.50	25.00
—Later pressings on red labels					
❑ 1010	Old Spanish Town/She Went Thataway	1959	6.25	12.50	25.00
❑ 1013	That's Right/Betty Dear	1959	6.25	12.50	25.00
❑ 1015	You're a Big Girl Now/Don't Ask Me Why	1959	6.25	12.50	25.00
❑ 1017	White Buckskin Sneakers and Checkerboard Socks/No Dice	1959	6.25	12.50	25.00
7-Inch Extended Plays					
TIME					
❑ TEP-100	I've Had It/Be Mine//Dream Street/A Sad Guitar	1959	25.00	50.00	100.00
❑ TEP-100 [PS]	I've Had It	1959	25.00	50.00	100.00

BELL TONES, THE
45s
RAMA

Number	Title (A Side/B Side)	Yr	VG	VG+	NM
❑ 170	Heart to Heart/The Wedding	1955	50.00	100.00	200.00

BELLAMY, DAVID One-half of THE BELLAMY BROTHERS.
45s
WARNER BROS.

Number	Title (A Side/B Side)	Yr	VG	VG+	NM
❑ 8123	Baby, You're Not a Legend/Nothin' Heavy	1975	—	2.50	5.00

BELLAMY BROTHERS, THE Also see DAVID BELLAMY.
45s
ATLANTIC

Number	Title (A Side/B Side)	Yr	VG	VG+	NM
❑ 87650	All in the Name of Love/Anyway I Can	1991	—	2.00	4.00
❑ 87748	She Don't Know That She's Perfect/I Make Her Laugh	1991	—	2.00	4.00
ELEKTRA					
❑ 47431	For All the Wrong Reasons/This Time	1982	—	2.00	4.00
❑ 69850	When I'm Away from You/Long Distance Love Affair	1983	—	2.00	4.00
❑ 69999	Get Into Reggae Cowboy/We're Just a Little Ole Country Band	1982	—	2.00	4.00
MCA CURB					
❑ 52380	Forget About Me/We're Having Some Fun Now	1984	—	—	3.00
❑ 52446	The World's Greatest Lover/Rock-A-Dash	1984	—	—	3.00
❑ 52518	I Need More of You/Diesel Cafe	1984	—	—	3.00
❑ 52579	Old Hippie/Wheels	1985	—	—	3.00
❑ 52668	Lie to You for Your Love/Season of the Wind	1985	—	—	3.00
❑ 52747	Feelin' the Feelin'/The Single Man and His Wife	1985	—	—	3.00
❑ 52747 [DJ]	Feelin' the Feelin' (same on both sides)	1985	3.00	6.00	12.00
—Promo only on yellow vinyl					
❑ 52834	Country Rap/One Too Many Times	1986	—	—	3.00
❑ 52834 [DJ]	Country Rap (same on both sides)	1986	3.00	6.00	12.00
—Promo only on yellow vinyl					
❑ 52917	Too Much Is Not Enough/Restless	1986	—	—	3.00
—A-side with The Forester Sisters					
❑ 52917 [DJ]	Too Much Is Not Enough (same on both sides)	1986	3.00	6.00	12.00
—With The Forester Sisters; promo only on red vinyl					
❑ 53018	Kids of the Baby Boom/Hard on a Heart	1987	—	—	3.00
❑ 53154	Crazy from the Heart/White Trash	1987	—	—	3.00
❑ 53222	Santa Fe/White Trash	1987	—	—	3.00
❑ 53310	I'll Give You All My Love Tonight/Ying Yang	1988	—	—	3.00
❑ 53399	Rebels Without a Clue/A Little Naive	1988	—	—	3.00
❑ 53478	Big Love/The Courthouse	1988	—	—	3.00
❑ 53642	Hillbilly Hell/You're My Favorite Star	1989	—	—	3.00
❑ 53672	You'll Never Be Sorry/Hillbilly Hell	1989	—	—	3.00
❑ 53719	The Center of My Universe/Hillbilly Hell	1989	—	—	3.00
❑ 79019	I Could Be Persuaded/What's This World Coming To	1990	—	—	3.00
WARNER BROS.					
❑ 8169	Let Your Love Flow/Inside My Guitar	1975	—	2.50	5.00
❑ 8220	Hell Cat/I'm the Only Man Left Alive	1976	—	2.00	4.00
❑ 8248	Rainy, Windy, Sunshine (Roadeo Road)/Satin Sheets	1976	—	2.00	4.00
❑ 8284	Livin' in the West/Highway 2-18 (Hang On to Your Dreams)	1976	—	2.00	4.00
❑ 8350	Crossfire/Tiger Lily Lover	1977	—	2.00	4.00
❑ 8401	Can Somebody Hear Me Now/You Made Me	1977	—	2.00	4.00
❑ 8462	Hard Rockin'/Memorabilia	1977	—	2.00	4.00
❑ 8521	Bird Dog/Make Me Over	1978	—	2.00	4.00
❑ 8558	Let's Give Love a Try/Slipping Away	1978	—	2.00	4.00
❑ 8627	Tumbleweed and Rosalee/Wild Honey	1978	—	2.00	4.00
❑ 8692	Lovin' on/My Shy Anne	1978	—	2.00	4.00
❑ 8790	If I Said You Have a Beautiful Body Would You Hold It Against Me/Make Me Over	1979	—	2.00	4.00
❑ 29514	Strong Weakness/Doin' It the Hard Way	1983	—	2.00	4.00
❑ 29645	I Love Her Mind/Lazy Eyes	1983	—	2.00	4.00
❑ 29923	Redneck Girl/Let Your Love Flow	1982	—	2.00	4.00
❑ 49032	You Ain't Just Whistlin' Dixie/Blue Ribbons	1979	—	2.00	4.00
❑ 49160	Sugar Daddy/I Could Be Makin' Love to You	1980	—	2.00	4.00
❑ 49241	Dancin' Cowboys/Dead Aim	1980	—	2.00	4.00
❑ 49573	Classic Case of the Blues/Givin' Live Longer	1980	—	2.00	4.00
❑ 49639	Do You Love As Good As You Look/Givin' In to Love Again	1980	—	2.00	4.00
❑ 49729	They Could Put Me in Jail/Endangered Species	1981	—	2.00	4.00
❑ 49815	You're My Favorite Star/It's Hard to Be a Cowboy These Days	1981	—	2.00	4.00
❑ 49875	It's So Close to Christmas/Let Me Waltz Into Your Heart	1981	—	2.00	4.00
Albums					
ELEKTRA					
❑ E1-60099	When We Were Boys	1982	2.50	5.00	10.00
❑ 60210	Strong Weakness	1982	2.50	5.00	10.00
MCA CURB					
❑ 1441	Restless	1985	2.00	4.00	8.00
—Reissue of MCA 5489					
❑ 1462	Greatest Hits	1985	2.00	4.00	8.00
—Reissue of Warner Bros. 23697					
❑ 5489	Restless	1984	2.50	5.00	10.00
❑ 5586	Howard & David	1985	2.50	5.00	10.00
❑ 5721	Country Rap	1987	2.50	5.00	10.00
❑ 5812	Greatest Hits Volume Two	1986	2.50	5.00	10.00
❑ 42039	Crazy from the Heart	1987	2.50	5.00	10.00

Number	Title (A Side/B Side)	Yr	VG	VG+	NM
❑ 42224	Rebels Without a Clue	1988	2.50	5.00	10.00
❑ 42298	Greatest Hits Volume III	1989	2.50	5.00	10.00
WARNER BROS.					
❑ BS 2941	Let Your Love Flow	1976	2.50	5.00	10.00
❑ BS 3034	Plain & Fancy	1977	2.50	5.00	10.00
❑ BSK 3176	Friends	1978	2.50	5.00	10.00
❑ BSK 3347	The Two and Only	1979	2.50	5.00	10.00
❑ BSK 3408	You Can Get Crazy	1980	2.50	5.00	10.00
❑ BSK 3491	Sons of the Sun	1980	2.50	5.00	10.00
❑ 23697	Greatest Hits	1982	2.50	5.00	10.00
❑ 60210	Strong Weakness	1983	2.00	4.00	8.00
—Reissue of Elektra 60210					

BELLAND & SOMERVILLE
45s
BARNABY

Number	Title (A Side/B Side)	Yr	VG	VG+	NM
❑ 2009	Sure Seems a Lot Like Sunday/When She's Lovin'	1969	2.00	4.00	8.00

BELLES, THE
45s
HIT

Number	Title (A Side/B Side)	Yr	VG	VG+	NM
❑ 83	Sally Go 'Round the Roses/Be My Baby	1963	2.00	4.00	8.00
—B-side by the Georgettes					
❑ 96	You Don't Have to Be a Baby to Cry/There! I've Said It Again	1963	2.00	4.00	8.00
—B-side by Fred York					
❑ 101	The Boy Next Door/As Usual	1964	2.00	4.00	8.00
—B-side by Betty Williams					

BELLS, THE (1) Canadian band with male and female lead singers.
45s
MGM

Number	Title (A Side/B Side)	Yr	VG	VG+	NM
❑ 14533	Child of Mine/He Was Me, He Was You	1973	—	2.00	4.00
❑ 14624	Love Once Removed/The Singer	1973	—	2.00	4.00
POLYDOR					
❑ 15016	Fly Little White Dove, Fly/Follow the Sun	1970	—	2.00	4.00
❑ 15023	Stay Awhile/Sing a Song of Freedom	1971	—	2.50	5.00
❑ 15025	Je Vais Rester/Blanc Petit Ois Eau Blanc	1970	—	2.00	4.00
❑ 15027	I Love You Lady Dawn/Rain	1971	—	2.00	4.00
❑ 15029	She's a Lady/Sweet Sounds of Music	1971	—	2.00	4.00
❑ 15031	To Know You Is To Love You/For Better For Worse	1971	—	2.00	4.00
❑ 15036	Oh My Love/You You You	1972	—	2.00	4.00
❑ 15039	Lord, Don't You Think It's Time/Easier Said Than Done	1972	—	2.00	4.00
❑ 15063	Kris Collection/Simple Song of Freedom	1973	—	2.00	4.00
Albums					
POLYDOR					
❑ 24-4510	Fly, Little White Dove, Fly	1971	3.75	7.50	15.00
❑ 24-5503	Love, Luck & Lollypops	1972	3.75	7.50	15.00

BELLS, THE (2) Male vocal group.
45s
RAMA

Number	Title (A Side/B Side)	Yr	VG	VG+	NM
❑ 166	What Can I Tell Her Now/Let Me Love You, Love You	1955	125.00	250.00	500.00

BELLTONES, THE
45s
GRAND

Number	Title (A Side/B Side)	Yr	VG	VG+	NM
❑ 102	Estelle/Promise Love	1954	2000.	3000.	4000.
LOST-NITE					
❑ 319	Estelle/Promise Love	197?	—	2.50	5.00
—Reissue					

BELLUS, TONY
45s
ERA BACK TO BACK HITS

Number	Title (A Side/B Side)	Yr	VG	VG+	NM
❑ 048	Robbin' the Cradle/Rockin' Little Angel	197?	—	2.50	5.00
—B-side by Ray Smith					
KING					
❑ 5973	Mustang/Goodbye Baby, Goodbye	1964	3.00	6.00	12.00
NRC					
❑ 023	Robbin' the Cradle/Valentine Girl	1959	5.00	10.00	20.00
—Available with the letters "NRC" with no background, with the title of the song in either orange or blue letters; also with each letter of "NRC" in a background box. No difference in value.					
❑ 035	Hey Little Darlin'/Only Your Heart	1959	5.00	10.00	20.00
❑ 040	Little Dreams/Young Girls	1959	5.00	10.00	20.00
❑ 045	Hey Little Darlin'/Young Girls	1959	5.00	10.00	20.00
❑ 051	The End of My Love/The Echo of An Old Song	1960	5.00	10.00	20.00
—Available on both white and tan labels, no difference in value					
❑ 051 [PS]	The End of My Love/The Echo of An Old Song	1960	12.50	25.00	50.00
❑ 058	The Great Pretender/Give Me a Heart	1960	5.00	10.00	20.00
SHI-FI					
❑ 60	Seven Flags/Robbin' the Cradle	196?	12.50	25.00	50.00
❑ 60 [PS]	Seven Flags/Robbin' the Cradle	196?	12.50	25.00	50.00
—Special promotional item for "Tony Bellus' Seven Flags" International Cafe & Lounge in Kankakee, IL					
Albums					
NRC					
❑ LPA-8 [M]	Robbin' the Cradle	1960	25.00	50.00	100.00
—Black label					
❑ LPA-8 [M]	Robbin' the Cradle	1960	50.00	100.00	200.00
—Blue label					
SHI-FI					
❑ LP-11 [M]	Gems of Tony Bellus	196?	15.00	30.00	60.00

BELMONTS, THE Also see DION AND THE BELMONTS; BUDDY SHEPPARD AND THE HOLIDAYS.
45s
DOT

Number	Title (A Side/B Side)	Yr	VG	VG+	NM
❑ 17173	Reminiscing/She Only Wants to Do Her Thing	1968	3.75	7.50	15.00

Number	Title (A Side/B Side)	Yr	VG	VG+	NM
❏ 17257	Have You Heard-The Worst That Could Happen/ Answer Me My Love	1969	3.75	7.50	15.00
LAURIE					
❏ 3080	We Belong Together/Such a Long Way	1961	7.50	15.00	30.00
❏ 3631	A Brand New Song/Story Teller	1975	—	2.50	5.00
❏ 3698	Medley/You're the Only Girl for Me	198?	—	2.50	5.00
—B-side by Ernie Maresca					
SABINA					
❏ 502	I Need Some One/That American Dance	1961	6.25	12.50	25.00
❏ 503	Hombre/I Confess	1962	6.25	12.50	25.00
❏ 505	Come On Little Angel/How About Me	1962	5.00	10.00	20.00
—Greenish label					
❏ 505	Come On Little Angel/How About Me	1962	6.25	12.50	25.00
—Black label					
❏ 507	Diddle-Dee-Dum (What Happens When Your Love Has Gone)/Farewell	1962	5.00	10.00	20.00
❏ 509	Ann Marie/Ac-Cent-Tchu-Ate the Positive	1963	5.00	10.00	20.00
❏ 513	Let's Call It a Day/Walk On Boy	1963	5.00	10.00	20.00
❏ 517	More Important Things to Do/Walk On Boy	1963	5.00	10.00	20.00
❏ 519	C'mon Everybody/Why	1964	5.00	10.00	20.00
❏ 521	Summertime/Nothing in Return	1964	5.00	10.00	20.00
SABRINA					
❏ 500	Tell Me Why/Smoke from Your Cigarette	1961	6.25	12.50	25.00
❏ 501	Searching for a New Love/Don't Get Around Much Anymore	1961	6.25	12.50	25.00
STRAWBERRY					
❏ 106	Cheek to Cheek/Voyager	1976	—	2.50	5.00
SURPRISE					
❏ 1000	Tell Me Why/Smoke from Your Cigarette	1961	25.00	50.00	100.00
UNITED ARTISTS					
❏ 809	Wintertime/I Don't Know Why, I Just Do	1965	5.00	10.00	20.00
❏ 904	(Then) I Walked Away/Today My Love Has Gone Away	1965	5.00	10.00	20.00
❏ 966	I Got a Feeling/To Be with You	1965	5.00	10.00	20.00
❏ S7-19769	Wintertime/Please Come Home for Christmas	1997	—	2.00	4.00
—B-side by Dion on The Right Stuff					
❏ 50007	Come with Me/You're Like a Mystery	1966	6.25	12.50	25.00
Albums					
BUDDAH					
❏ BDS-5123	Cigars, Acapella, Candy	1972	12.50	25.00	50.00
DOT					
❏ DLP-25949	Summer Love	1969	7.50	15.00	30.00
SABINA					
❏ SALP-5001 [M]	The Belmonts' Carnival of Hits	1962	37.50	75.00	150.00
STRAWBERRY					
❏ 6001	Cheek to Cheek	1978	3.75	7.50	15.00
BELVIN, ANDY					
45s					
ATCO					
❏ 6289	Travelin' Mood/Flip Flip	1964	3.00	6.00	12.00
CANDIX					
❏ 338	Walking the Blues/Prettiest Girl	1962	5.00	10.00	20.00
VAULT					
❏ 908	Travelin' Mood/Flip Flop	1964	3.75	7.50	15.00
BELVIN, JESSE Also see THE CLIQUES; JESSE AND MARVIN.					
45s					
ALADDIN					
❏ 3431	Let Me Dream/Sugar Doll	1958	10.00	20.00	40.00
CASH					
❏ 1056	Dry Your Tears/Beware	1957	6.25	12.50	25.00
—Orange and black label					
❏ 1056	Dry Your Tears/Beware	1957	25.00	50.00	100.00
—Black and silver label					
CLASS					
❏ 267	I'm Confessin'/Deep in My Heart	1960	6.25	12.50	25.00
HOLLYWOOD					
❏ 1059	Betty My Darling/Dear Heart	1956	100.00	200.00	400.00
IMPACT					
❏ 23	Tonight My Love/Looking for Love	1962	3.75	7.50	15.00
JAMIE					
❏ 1145	Goodnight My Love (Pleasant Dreams)/My Desire	1959	5.00	10.00	20.00
KENT					
❏ 326	Sentimental Reasons/Senorita	1959	6.25	12.50	25.00
KNIGHT					
❏ 2012	Little Darling/Deacon Dan Tucker	1959	10.00	20.00	40.00
MODERN					
❏ 45x1005	Goodnight My Love (Pleasant Dreams)/Let Me Love You Tonight	1956	10.00	20.00	40.00
❏ 45x1005	Goodnight My Love (Pleasant Dreams)/I Want You With Me Xmas	1956	12.50	25.00	50.00
❏ 1013	I Need You So/Senorita	1957	7.50	15.00	30.00
❏ 1015	By My Side/Don't Close the Door	1957	7.50	15.00	30.00
❏ 1020	Sad and Lonesome/I'm Not Free	1957	7.50	15.00	30.00
❏ 1025	You Send Me/Summertime	1957	7.50	15.00	30.00
❏ 1027	My Satellite/Just to Say Hello	1957	7.50	15.00	30.00
MONEY					
❏ 208	I'm Only a Fool/Trouble and Misery	1955	15.00	30.00	60.00
RCA VICTOR					
❏ 47-7310	Volare/Ever Since We Met	1958	5.00	10.00	20.00
❏ 47-7387	Funny/Pledging My Love	1958	5.00	10.00	20.00
❏ 47-7469	Guess Who/ My Girl Is Just Enough Woman for Me	1959	5.00	10.00	20.00
❏ 47-7543	Here's a Heart/It Could've Been Worse	1959	5.00	10.00	20.00
❏ 47-7596	Give Me Love/I'll Never Be Lonely Again	1959	5.00	10.00	20.00
❏ 47-7675	Something Happens to Me/ The Door Is Always Open	1960	5.00	10.00	20.00
❏ 47-8040	Guess Who/Funny	1962	3.75	7.50	15.00

Number	Title (A Side/B Side)	Yr	VG	VG+	NM
❏ 61-7469	Guess Who/ My Girl Is Just Enough Woman for Me	1959	12.50	25.00	50.00
—"Living Stereo" (large hole, plays at 45 rpm)					
RECORDED IN HOLLYWOOD					
❏ 120	Dream Girl/Hang Your Tears Out to Dry	1951	150.00	300.00	600.00
❏ 412	Love Comes Tumbling Down/(B-side unknown)	1953	100.00	200.00	400.00
SPECIALTY					
❏ 435	Confusin' Blues/Baby Don't Go	1952	20.00	40.00	80.00
❏ 550	Gone/One Little Blessing	1955	12.50	25.00	50.00
❏ 559	Where's My Girl/Love, Love of My Life	1955	12.50	25.00	50.00
Albums					
CROWN					
❏ CLP-5145 [M]	The Casual Jesse Belvin	1959	17.50	35.00	70.00
—Black label					
❏ CLP-5145 [M]	The Casual Jesse Belvin	196?	3.75	7.50	15.00
—Gray label					
❏ CLP-5187 [M]	The Unforgettable Jesse Belvin	1959	17.50	35.00	70.00
—Black label					
❏ CLP-5187 [M]	The Unforgettable Jesse Belvin	196?	3.75	7.50	15.00
—Gray label					
RCA CAMDEN					
❏ CAL-960 [M]	Jesse Belvin's Best	1966	3.00	6.00	12.00
❏ CAS-960 [S]	Jesse Belvin's Best	1966	3.75	7.50	15.00
RCA VICTOR					
❏ LPM-2089 [M]	Just Jesse Belvin	1959	10.00	20.00	40.00
❏ LSP-2089 [S]	Just Jesse Belvin	1959	15.00	30.00	60.00
❏ LPM-2105 [M]	Mr. Easy	1960	7.50	15.00	30.00
❏ LSP-2105 [S]	Mr. Easy	1960	10.00	20.00	40.00
SPECIALTY					
❏ SP-7003	The Blues Balladeer	1990	3.75	7.50	15.00
BEN, LA BRENDA					
45s					
GORDY					
❏ 7009	Camel Walk/The Chaperone	1962	12.50	25.00	50.00
❏ 7021	I Can't Help It, I Gotta Dance/Just Be Yourself	1963	12.50	25.00	50.00
MOTOWN					
❏ 1033	Camel Walk/Chaperone	1962	100.00	200.00	400.00
BENDER, FREDDIE					
45s					
PARKWAY					
❏ 876	Miss Daisy De Lite/Let's Twist Again	1963	3.75	7.50	15.00
BENET, VICKI					
45s					
DECCA					
❏ 30044	Sam's Song (The Happy Tune)/Tea for Two	1956	3.75	7.50	15.00
LIBERTY					
❏ 55100	After My Laughter Came Tears/Always in My Heart	1957	3.75	7.50	15.00
❏ 55186	Heartstring Melody/Love Me	1959	3.00	6.00	12.00
Albums					
DECCA					
❏ DL 8233 [M]	Woman of Paris	1956	10.00	20.00	40.00
❏ DL 8381 [M]	The French Touch	1957	10.00	20.00	40.00
❏ DL 8987 [M]	Vicki Benet a Paris	1959	7.50	15.00	30.00
❏ DL 78987 [S]	Vicki Benet a Paris	1959	10.00	20.00	40.00
LIBERTY					
❏ LRP-3103 [M]	Sing to Me of Love	1960	6.25	12.50	25.00
❏ LST-7103 [S]	Sing to Me of Love	1960	7.50	15.00	30.00
BENNETT, BOYD					
45s					
KING					
❏ 1201	Precious Little Sweetheart/Wasting My Time	1953	12.50	25.00	50.00
❏ 1413	Waterloo/I've Had Enough	1954	8.75	17.50	35.00
❏ 1432	Poison Ivy/You Upset Me Baby	1955	8.75	17.50	35.00
❏ 1443	Everlovin'/Boogie at Midnight	1955	8.75	17.50	35.00
❏ 1470	Seventeen/Little Old You-All	1955	6.25	12.50	25.00
—Blue label					
❏ 1470	Seventeen/Little Old You-All	1955	8.75	17.50	35.00
—Maroon label					
❏ 1475	Tennessee Rock and Roll/Oo, Oo, Oo	1955	6.25	12.50	25.00
❏ 1494	My Boy-Flat Top/Banjo Rock and Roll	1955	6.25	12.50	25.00
❏ 4853	Desperately/The Most	1955	6.25	12.50	25.00
❏ 4874	Right Around the Corner/Partners for Life	1956	6.25	12.50	25.00
❏ 4903	Blue Suede Shoes/Mumbles Blues	1956	6.25	12.50	25.00
❏ 4925	Let Me Love You/Groovy Age	1956	6.25	12.50	25.00
❏ 4953	Hit That Jive, Jack/Rabbit-Eye Pink and Charcoal Black	1956	6.25	12.50	25.00
❏ 4985	Rockin' Up a Storm/A Lock of Your Hair	1956	6.25	12.50	25.00
❏ 5021	I'm Moving On/Big Jay Shuffle	1957	6.25	12.50	25.00
❏ 5049	Big Boy/Put the Chain on the Door	1957	6.25	12.50	25.00
❏ 5097	Sentimental Journey/Boy Meets Girl	1957	6.25	12.50	25.00
❏ 5113	Signed, Sealed and Delivered/Her Momma Doesn't Think It's Right	1958	6.25	12.50	25.00
❏ 5115	Click Clack/Move	1958	6.25	12.50	25.00
❏ 5282	High School Hop/Cool Disc Jockey	1959	6.25	12.50	25.00
❏ 5374	Seventeen/My Boy Flat Top	1960	6.25	12.50	25.00
❏ 5738	Teenage Years/Hear Me Talking	1963	3.75	7.50	15.00
MERCURY					
❏ 71409	Tight Tights/Tear It Up	1959	5.00	10.00	20.00
❏ 71479	Boogie Bear/A Boy Can Tell	1959	5.00	10.00	20.00
❏ 71537	Naughty Rock and Roll/Lover's Night	1959	5.00	10.00	20.00
❏ 71605	It's Wonderful/Amo, Amas, Amat	1960	5.00	10.00	20.00
❏ 71648	Seventeen/Sarasota	1960	5.00	10.00	20.00
❏ 71724	Hershey Bar/Big Junior	1960	5.00	10.00	20.00
❏ 71813	Coffee Break/The Brain	1961	5.00	10.00	20.00

Number	Title (A Side/B Side)	Yr	VG	VG+	NM
7-Inch Extended Plays					
KING					
❏ 377	(contents unknown)	1956	50.00	100.00	200.00
❏ 377 [PS]	Boyd Bennett	1956	75.00	150.00	300.00
❏ 383	(contents unknown)	1956	50.00	100.00	200.00
❏ 383 [PS]	Rock & Roll with Boyd Bennett & the Rockets	1956	75.00	150.00	300.00
Albums					
KING					
❏ 395-594 [M]	Boyd Bennett	1955	1500.	2750.	4000.

BENNETT, CLIFF, AND THE REBEL ROUSERS

Number	Title (A Side/B Side)	Yr	VG	VG+	NM
45s					
ABC					
❏ 10842	Got to Get You Into My Life/Baby Each Day	1966	3.75	7.50	15.00
AMY					
❏ 930	If Only You'd Reply/Three Rooms with Running Water	1965	3.75	7.50	15.00
ASCOT					
❏ 2146	Everybody Loves a Lover/My Old Stand By	1964	3.75	7.50	15.00
CAPITOL					
❏ 4621	I'm in Love with You/You've Got What I Like	1961	12.50	25.00	50.00
❏ 5309	One Way Love/I'm in Love with You	1964	3.75	7.50	15.00

BENNETT, JOE, AND THE SPARKLETONES

Number	Title (A Side/B Side)	Yr	VG	VG+	NM
45s					
ABC-PARAMOUNT					
❏ 9837	Black Slacks/Boppin' Rock Boogie	1957	7.50	15.00	30.00
❏ 9867	Penny Loafers and Bobby Socks/Rocket	1957	7.50	15.00	30.00
❏ 9885	Cotton Pickin' Rocker/I Dig You Baby	1958	7.50	15.00	30.00
❏ 9929	Little Turtle/We've Had It	1958	7.50	15.00	30.00
❏ 9959	Do the Stop/Late Again	1958	7.50	15.00	30.00
PARIS					
❏ 530	Bayou Rock/Beautiful One	1959	7.50	15.00	30.00
❏ 537	Boys Do Cry/What the Heck	1959	6.25	12.50	25.00
❏ 546	Softly/What the Heck	1960	6.25	12.50	25.00
Albums					
MCA					
❏ 1553	Black Slacks	1983	3.75	7.50	15.00

BENNETT, TONY

Number	Title (A Side/B Side)	Yr	VG	VG+	NM
45s					
BRUT					
❏ 813	All That Love Went to Waste/Some of These Days	1973	—	3.00	6.00
❏ 813 [PS]	All That Love Went to Waste/Some of These Days	1973	—	3.00	6.00
COLUMBIA					
❏ AE 28 [DJ]	My Favorite Things/I Love the Winter Weather	1970	2.00	4.00	8.00
❏ AE 28 [PS]	My Favorite Things/I Love the Winter Weather	1970	3.00	6.00	12.00
—Theme Song for 1970 Christmas Seals Campaign					
❏ 1-640 (?)	The Boulevard of Broken Dreams/I Wanna Be Loved	1950	6.25	12.50	25.00
—Microgroove 7-inch 33 1/3 rpm single					
❏ 1-670 (?)	Let's Make Love/I Can't Give You Anything But Love, Baby	1950	6.25	12.50	25.00
—Microgroove 7-inch 33 1/3 rpm single					
❏ 1-800 (?)	Sing You Sinners/Kiss You	1950	6.25	12.50	25.00
—Microgroove 7-inch 33 1/3 rpm single					
❏ 6-800 (?)	Sing You Sinners/Kiss You	1950	5.00	10.00	20.00
❏ 38-06138	Why Do People Fall in Love/Moments Like This	1986	—	—	3.00
❏ 38-07658	White Christmas/All of My Life	1987	—	—	3.00
❏ 38-07658 [PS]	White Christmas/All of My Life	1987	—	—	3.00
❏ 31272 [S]	(contents unknown)	1961	3.00	6.00	12.00
❏ 31273 [S]	(contents unknown)	1961	3.00	6.00	12.00
❏ 31274 [S]	(contents unknown)	1961	3.00	6.00	12.00
❏ 31275 [S]	(contents unknown)	1961	3.00	6.00	12.00
❏ 31276 [S]	(contents unknown)	1961	3.00	6.00	12.00
❏ 31563 [S]	(contents unknown)	1962	3.00	6.00	12.00
❏ 31564 [S]	(contents unknown)	1962	3.00	6.00	12.00
❏ 31565 [S]	(contents unknown)	1962	3.00	6.00	12.00
❏ 31566 [S]	(contents unknown)	1962	3.00	6.00	12.00
❏ 31567 [S]	(contents unknown)	1962	3.00	6.00	12.00
—Anyone who can fill in these gaps -- the above 10 all are Columbia "Stereo 7" singles -- please let us know.					
❏ 39187	Once There Lived a Fool/I Can't Give You Anything But Love, Baby	1951	3.75	7.50	15.00
❏ 39209	Beautiful Madness/Valentino Tango	1951	3.75	7.50	15.00
❏ 3-39209	Beautiful Madness/Valentino Tango	1951	6.25	12.50	25.00
—Microgroove 7-inch 33 1/3 rpm single					
❏ 39362	Because of You/I Won't Cry Anymore	1951	3.00	6.00	12.00
❏ 39449	Cold, Cold Heart/While We're Young	1951	3.00	6.00	12.00
❏ 39555	Blue Velvet/Solitaire	1951	3.00	6.00	12.00
❏ 39635	Silly Dreamer/Since My Love Has Gone	1952	3.00	6.00	12.00
❏ 4-39695	Sleepless/Somewhere Along the Way	1952	3.00	6.00	12.00
❏ 39745	Here in My Heart/I'm Lost Again	1952	3.00	6.00	12.00
❏ 39764	Have a Good Time/Please My Love	1952	3.00	6.00	12.00
❏ 39815	You Could Make Me Smile Again/Roses of Yesterday	1952	3.00	6.00	12.00
❏ 39824	Because of You/I Won't Cry Anymore	1952	2.50	5.00	10.00
❏ 39825	The Boulevard of Broken Dreams/I Wanna Be Loved	1952	2.50	5.00	10.00
❏ 39826	Once There Lived a Fool/The Valentine Tango	1952	2.50	5.00	10.00
❏ 39827	Cold, Cold Heart/While We're Young	1952	2.50	5.00	10.00
❏ 39910	Congratulations to Someone/Take Me	1953	3.00	6.00	12.00
❏ 39964	I'm the King of Broken Hearts/No One Will Ever Know	1953	3.00	6.00	12.00
❏ 40004	Someone Turned the Moon Upside Down/I'll Go	1953	3.00	6.00	12.00
❏ 40048	Rags to Riches/Here Comes That Heartache Again	1953	3.00	6.00	12.00
❏ 40121	Stranger in Paradise/Why Does It Have to Be Me	1953	3.00	6.00	12.00
❏ 40169	There'll Be No Teardrops Tonight/My Heart Won't Say Goodbye	1954	3.00	6.00	12.00

Number	Title (A Side/B Side)	Yr	VG	VG+	NM
❏ 40213	Until Yesterday/Please Driver, Once Around the Park Again	1954	3.00	6.00	12.00
❏ 40272	Cinnamon Sinner/Take Me Back Again	1954	3.00	6.00	12.00
❏ 4-40311	Not As a Stranger/Madonna, Madonna	1954	3.00	6.00	12.00
❏ 40376	Funny Thing/My Pretty Shoo-Gah	1954	3.00	6.00	12.00
❏ 40427	It's Too Soon to Know/Close Your Eyes	1955	2.50	5.00	10.00
❏ 40491	What Will I Tell My Heart/Punch and Judy Love	1955	2.50	5.00	10.00
❏ 40523	May I Never Love Again/Don't Tell Me Why	1955	2.50	5.00	10.00
❏ 40567	How Can I Replace You/Tell Me That You Love Me	1955	2.50	5.00	10.00
❏ 40598	Come Next Spring/Afraid of the Dark	1955	2.50	5.00	10.00
❏ 40632	Sing You Sinners/Capri in May	1956	2.50	5.00	10.00
❏ 40667	Can You Find It in Your Heart/Forget Her	1956	2.50	5.00	10.00
❏ 40726	From the Candy Store on the Corner to the Chapel on the Hill/Happiness Street (Corner Sunshine Square)	1956	2.50	5.00	10.00
❏ 40770	The Autumn Waltz/Just in Time	1956	2.50	5.00	10.00
❏ 40849	One Kiss Away from Heaven/Sold to the Man with the Broken Heart	1957	2.50	5.00	10.00
❏ 40907	One for My Baby (And One More for the Road)/No Hard Feelings	1957	2.50	5.00	10.00
❏ 40965	In the Middle of An Island/I Am	1957	2.50	5.00	10.00
❏ 41032	Ca, C'est L'amour/I Never Felt More Like Falling in Love	1957	2.50	5.00	10.00
❏ 41086	Love Song from Beauty and the Beast/Weary Blues From Waitin'	1957	2.50	5.00	10.00
❏ 41127	You're So Right for Me/Alone at Last	1958	2.50	5.00	10.00
❏ 41157	Crazy Rhythm/The Beat of My Heart	1958	2.50	5.00	10.00
❏ 41172	Young and Warm and Wonderful/Now I Lay Me Down to Sleep	1958	2.50	5.00	10.00
❏ 41237	Firefly/The Night That Heaven Fell	1958	2.50	5.00	10.00
❏ 41237 [PS]	Firefly/The Night That Heaven Fell	1958	5.00	10.00	20.00
❏ 41298	Love, Look Away/Blue Moon	1958	2.50	5.00	10.00
❏ 41341	It's So Peaceful in the Country/Being True to One Another	1959	2.50	5.00	10.00
❏ 41381	The Cool School/You'll Never Get Away from Me	1959	2.50	5.00	10.00
❏ 41434	Smile/You Can't Love 'Em All	1959	2.50	5.00	10.00
❏ 41520	Climb Ev'ry Mountain/Ask Anyone in Love	1959	2.50	5.00	10.00
❏ 41595	I'll Bring You a Rainbow/Ask Me (I Know)	1960	2.00	4.00	8.00
❏ 41691	Put On a Happy Face/Baby, Talk to Me	1960	2.00	4.00	8.00
❏ 41770	Till/I Am	1960	2.00	4.00	8.00
❏ 41860	Marriage-Go-Round/Somebody	1960	2.00	4.00	8.00
❏ 41874	Ramona/Follow Me	1960	2.00	4.00	8.00
❏ 41965	The Best Is Yet to Come/Marry Young	1961	2.00	4.00	8.00
❏ 42003	Toot Toot Tootsie (Goodbye)/I'm Coming Virginia	1961	2.00	4.00	8.00
❏ 42135	Close Your Eyes/Rules of the Road	1961	2.00	4.00	8.00
❏ 42219	Tender Is the Night/Comes Once in a Lifetime	1961	2.00	4.00	8.00
❏ 42332	I Left My Heart in San Francisco/Once Upon a Time	1962	2.00	4.00	8.00
❏ 42332 [PS]	I Left My Heart in San Francisco/Once Upon a Time	1962	3.75	7.50	15.00
❏ 42395	Candy Kisses/Have I Told You Lately That I Love You	1962	2.00	4.00	8.00
❏ 42634	I Wanna Be Around/I Will Live My Life for You	1962	2.00	4.00	8.00
❏ 42779	The Good Life/Spring in Manhattan	1963	2.00	4.00	8.00
❏ 42820	This Is All I Ask/True Blue Lou	1963	2.00	4.00	8.00
❏ 42886	Don't Wait Too Long/Limehouse Blues	1963	2.00	4.00	8.00
❏ 42931	The Little Boy/The Moment of Truth	1963	2.00	4.00	8.00
❏ 42996	When Joanna Loved Me/The Kid's a Dreamer	1964	2.00	4.00	8.00
❏ 42996 [DJ]	When Joanna Loved Me (same on both sides)	1964	5.00	10.00	20.00
—Promo only on red vinyl					
❏ 42996 [PS]	When Joanna Loved Me/The Kid's a Dreamer	1964	5.00	10.00	20.00
—Promo-only title sleeve with red vinyl issue; no number on sleeve					
❏ 43073	It's a Sin to Tell a Lie/A Taste of Honey	1964	2.00	4.00	8.00
❏ 43141	Who Can I Turn To (When Nobody Needs Me)/Waltz for Debby	1964	2.00	4.00	8.00
❏ 43202	The Best Thing to Be Is a Person/The Brightest Smile in Town	1964	2.00	4.00	8.00
❏ 43220	If I Ruled the World/Take the Moment	1965	—	3.00	6.00
❏ 43331	Fly Me to the Moon (In Other Words)/How Insensitive	1965	—	3.00	6.00
❏ 43431	The Shadow of Your Smile/I'll Only Miss Her When I Think of Her	1965	—	3.00	6.00
❏ 43508	Song from The Oscar/Baby Dream Your Dream	1966	—	3.00	6.00
❏ 43508 [PS]	Song from The Oscar/Baby Dream Your Dream	1966	2.50	5.00	10.00
❏ 43715	Georgia Rose/The Very Thought	1966	—	3.00	6.00
❏ 43768	A Time for Love/Touch the Earth	1966	—	3.00	6.00
❏ 43954	What Makes It Happen/Country Girl	1966	—	3.00	6.00
❏ 43954 [DJ]	What Makes It Happen/Country Girl	1966	3.75	7.50	15.00
—Orange-vinyl promo issue					
❏ 44154	Keep Smiling at Trouble/Days of Love	1967	—	2.50	5.00
❏ 44258	For Once in My Life/How Do You Say Auf Wiedersehn	1967	—	3.00	6.00
❏ 44443	The Glory of Love/A Fool of Fools	1968	—	2.50	5.00
❏ 44510	Yesterday I Heard the Rain/Sweet Georgie Fame	1968	—	2.50	5.00
❏ 44584	Hushabye Mountain/Hi-Ho	1968	—	2.50	5.00
❏ 44688	Where Is Love/My Favorite Things	1968	—	2.50	5.00
❏ 44755	People/They All Laughed	1969	—	2.50	5.00
❏ 44824	Whoever You Are, I Love You/A Place Over the Sun	1969	—	2.50	5.00
❏ 44855	What the World Needs Now Is Love/Play It Again Sam	1969	—	2.50	5.00
❏ 44947	I've Gotta Be Me/A Lonely Place	1969	—	2.50	5.00
❏ 45032	MacArthur Park/Before We Say Goodbye	1969	—	2.50	5.00
❏ 45073	Little Green Apples/Coco	1970	—	2.50	5.00
❏ 45109	Something/Eleanor Rigby	1970	—	2.50	5.00
❏ 45157	Everybody's Talkin'/Think How It's Gonna Be	1970	—	2.50	5.00
❏ 45205	Something/Think How It's Gonna Be	1970	—	2.50	5.00
❏ 45255	I'll Begin Again/I Do Not Know a Day I Did Not Love You	1970	—	2.50	5.00

Number	Title (A Side/B Side)	Yr	VG	VG+	NM
❏ 45316	(Where Do I Begin) Love Story/I'll Begin Again	1971	—	2.50	5.00
❏ 45376	I Want to Be Happy/Tea for Two	1971	—	2.50	5.00
❏ 45411	More and More/I'm Losing My Mind	1971	—	2.50	5.00
❏ 45449	Walkabout/How Beautiful Is Night	1971	—	2.50	5.00
❏ 45493	Remind Me/The Riviera	1971	—	2.50	5.00
❏ 45523	Somewhere Along the Line/The Summer Knows	1972	—	2.50	5.00
❏ 45573	Twilight World/Easy Come, Easy Go	1972	—	2.50	5.00
❏ 45613	Love/Maybe This Time	1972	—	2.50	5.00
❏ 38-79658	New York State of Mind/Don't Cry Baby	2001	—	—	3.00
—A-side with Billy Joel					
❏ JZSP 112321 [DJ]	Love Theme from "The Sandpiper" (The Shadow of Your Smile) (same on both sides)	1965	2.00	4.00	8.00
—Black vinyl promo					
IMPROV					
❏ 6976	There's Always Tomorrow (Theme Song for the United Way)/I Wish I Were in Love Again	197?	—	2.00	4.00
MGM					
❏ 14607	My Love/(B-side unknown)	1973	—	2.00	4.00
VERVE					
❏ 10690	Living Together, Growing Together/The Good Things in Life	1972	—	2.00	4.00
❏ 10702	O Solo Mio/The Good Things in Life	1973	—	2.00	4.00
❏ 10714	Tell Her It's Snowing/If I Could Go Back	1973	—	2.00	4.00
7-Inch Extended Plays					
COLUMBIA					
❏ B-314 [PS]	Because of You	195?	5.00	10.00	20.00
—Gatefold cover for 2-EP set (5-1003 and 5-1004)					
❏ 7-823	Blue Velvet/Rags to Riches/Because of You//It Amazes Me/Firefly/I Left My Heart in San Francisco	196?	2.50	5.00	10.00
—"Special Coin Operator Release"; small hole, plays at 33 1/3 rpm					
❏ 7-823 [PS]	Tony Bennett at Carnegie Hall	196?	2.50	5.00	10.00
❏ 5-1003	Because of You/The Boulevard of Broken Dreams/I Won't Cry Anymore/Cold, Cold Heart	195?	5.00	10.00	20.00
—Alternate numbers are "B-314-1" and "B-314-4"					
❏ B-1842	Stranger in Paradise/Why Does It Have to Be Me/Rags to Riches/Congratulations to Someone	195?	3.75	7.50	15.00
❏ B-1842 [PS]	Tony Bennett Spotlite	195?	3.75	7.50	15.00
❏ B-2582	*One for My Baby/I Can't Give You Anything But Love/Solitaire/Once There Lived a Fool	1959	2.50	5.00	10.00
❏ B-2582	Tony Bennett (Hall of Fame Series)	1959	2.50	5.00	10.00
❏ 7-8800	I Wanna Be Around/The Good Life/Let's Face the Music and Dance//Once Upon a Summertime/Someone to Love/Quiet Night	1964	2.50	5.00	10.00
—"Special Coin Operator Release"; small hole, plays at 33 1/3 rpm					
❏ 7-8800 [PS]	I Wanna Be Around	1964	2.50	5.00	10.00
❏ 7-9173	I Left My Heart in San Francisco/I Wanna Be Around/Quiet Nights of Quiet Stars//The Good Life/A Taste of Honey/The Best Is Yet to Come	1964	2.50	5.00	10.00
—"Special Coin Operator Release"; small hole, plays at 33 1/3 rpm					
❏ 7-9173 [PS]	Tony Bennett's Greatest Hits Volume III	1964	3.00	6.00	12.00
❏ B-9382	*These Foolish Things/I Can't Give You Anything But Love/Boulevard of Broken Dreams/I'll Be Seeing You	1957	2.50	5.00	10.00
❏ B-9382 [PS]	Tony	1957	2.50	5.00	10.00
❏ ZTEP 26851/2	Because of You/In the Middle of an Island/Cold, Cold Heart//From Rags to Riches/Come Next Spring/Can You Find It in Your Heart	1957	6.25	12.50	25.00
—Coca-Cola promotional item					
❏ ZTEP 26851/2 [PS]	Tony Bennett Autographed Edition of Hits	1957	6.25	12.50	25.00
—Coca-Cola promotional item					
Albums					
COLUMBIA					
❏ GP 14 [(2)]	Love Songs	1969	3.75	7.50	15.00
❏ C2L 23 [(2)M]	Tony Bennett at Carnegie Hall	1962	5.00	10.00	20.00
❏ CL 621 [M]	Cloud Seven	1955	10.00	20.00	40.00
❏ C2S 823 [(2)S]	Tony Bennett at Carnegie Hall	1962	6.25	12.50	25.00
❏ CL 938 [M]	Tony	1956	7.50	15.00	30.00
❏ CL 1079 [M]	The Beat of My Heart	1957	7.50	15.00	30.00
❏ CL 1186 [M]	Long Ago and Far Away	1958	7.50	15.00	30.00
❏ CL 1229 [M]	Tony's Greatest Hits	1958	7.50	15.00	30.00
❏ CL 1292 [M]	Blue Velvet	1958	7.50	15.00	30.00
❏ CL 1301 [M]	Hometown, My Hometown	1959	6.25	12.50	25.00
❏ CL 1429 [M]	To My Wonderful One	1960	6.25	12.50	25.00
❏ CL 1446 [M]	Tony Sings for Two	1960	6.25	12.50	25.00
❏ CL 1471 [M]	Alone Together	1960	6.25	12.50	25.00
❏ CL 1535 [M]	More Tony's Greatest Hits	1961	5.00	10.00	20.00
❏ CL 1559 [M]	A String of Harold Arlen	1961	5.00	10.00	20.00
❏ CL 1658 [M]	My Heart Sings	1961	5.00	10.00	20.00
❏ CL 1763 [M]	Mr. Broadway	1962	3.75	7.50	15.00
❏ CL 1869 [M]	I Left My Heart in San Francisco	1962	3.75	7.50	15.00
❏ CL 1905 [M]	Tony Bennett at Carnegie Hall Vol. 1	1963	3.75	7.50	15.00
❏ CL 2000 [M]	I Wanna Be Around	1963	3.75	7.50	15.00
❏ CL 2056 [M]	This Is All I Ask	1963	3.75	7.50	15.00
❏ CL 2141 [M]	The Many Moods of Tony	1964	3.75	7.50	15.00
❏ CL 2175 [M]	When Lights Are Low	1964	3.75	7.50	15.00
❏ CL 2285 [M]	Who Can I Turn To	1964	3.75	7.50	15.00
❏ CL 2343 [M]	If I Ruled the World — Songs for the Jet Set	1965	3.00	6.00	12.00
❏ CL 2373 [M]	Tony's Greatest Hits, Volume III	1965	3.00	6.00	12.00
❏ CL 2472 [M]	The Movie Song Album	1966	3.00	6.00	12.00
❏ CL 2507 [10]	Alone at Last with Tony Bennett	1955	15.00	30.00	60.00
❏ CL 2550 [10]	Because of You	1956	15.00	30.00	60.00
❏ CL 2560 [M]	A Time for Love	1966	3.00	6.00	12.00
❏ CL 2653 [M]	Tony Makes It Happen!	1967	3.75	7.50	15.00
❏ CL 2773 [M]	For Once in My Life	1967	7.50	15.00	30.00
❏ CL 6221 [10]	Because of You	1952	20.00	40.00	80.00
❏ CS 8107 [S]	Hometown, My Hometown	1959	10.00	20.00	40.00
❏ CS 8226 [S]	To My Wonderful One	1960	10.00	20.00	40.00
❏ CS 8242 [S]	Tony Sings for Two	1960	10.00	20.00	40.00
❏ CS 8262 [S]	Alone Together	1960	10.00	20.00	40.00

Number	Title (A Side/B Side)	Yr	VG	VG+	NM
❏ CS 8335 [S]	More Tony's Greatest Hits	1961	6.25	12.50	25.00
❏ CS 8359 [S]	A String of Harold Arlen	1961	6.25	12.50	25.00
❏ CS 8458 [S]	My Heart Sings	1961	6.25	12.50	25.00
❏ CS 8563 [S]	Mr. Broadway	1962	5.00	10.00	20.00
❏ CS 8652 [R]	Tony's Greatest Hits	1962	3.75	7.50	15.00
❏ CS 8669 [S]	I Left My Heart in San Francisco	1962	5.00	10.00	20.00
❏ PC 8669	I Left My Heart in San Francisco	198?	2.00	4.00	8.00
—Reissue with new prefix					
❏ CS 8705 [S]	Tony Bennett at Carnegie Hall Vol. 1	1963	5.00	10.00	20.00
❏ CS 8800 [S]	I Wanna Be Around	1963	6.25	12.50	25.00
❏ CS 8856 [S]	This Is All I Ask	1963	5.00	10.00	20.00
❏ CS 8941 [S]	The Many Moods of Tony	1964	5.00	10.00	20.00
❏ CS 8975 [S]	When Lights Are Low	1964	5.00	10.00	20.00
❏ CS 9085 [S]	Who Can I Turn To	1964	5.00	10.00	20.00
❏ CS 9143 [S]	If I Ruled the World — Songs for the Jet Set	1965	3.75	7.50	15.00
❏ CS 9173 [S]	Tony's Greatest Hits, Volume III	1965	3.75	7.50	15.00
❏ CS 9272 [S]	The Movie Song Album	1966	3.75	7.50	15.00
❏ CS 9360 [S]	A Time for Love	1966	3.75	7.50	15.00
❏ CS 9453 [S]	Tony Makes It Happen!	1967	3.75	7.50	15.00
❏ CS 9573 [S]	For Once in My Life	1967	3.75	7.50	15.00
❏ CS 9678	Yesterday I Heard the Rain	1968	3.75	7.50	15.00
❏ CS 9739	Snowfall: The Tony Bennett Christmas Album	1968	3.00	6.00	12.00
❏ CS 9814	Tony Bennett's Greatest Hits, Volume IV	1969	3.75	7.50	15.00
❏ CS 9882	I've Gotta Be Me	1969	3.75	7.50	15.00
❏ CS 9980	Tony Sings the Great Hits of Today!	1970	3.00	6.00	12.00
❏ C 30240	All Time Hall of Fame Hits	1971	3.00	6.00	12.00
❏ PC 30240	All Time Hall of Fame Hits	197?	2.50	5.00	10.00
—Reissue with new prefix					
❏ C 30280	Tony Bennett's "Something"	1971	3.00	6.00	12.00
❏ C 30558	Love Story	1971	3.00	6.00	12.00
❏ C 31219	Summer of '42	1972	3.00	6.00	12.00
❏ KC 31460	With Love	1972	3.00	6.00	12.00
❏ KG 31494 [(2)]	Tony Bennett's All-Time Greatest Hits	1972	3.75	7.50	15.00
❏ CG 33612 [(2)]	I Left My Heart in San Francisco/Tony Sings the Great Hits of Today!	1975	3.75	7.50	15.00
❏ FC 40344	The Art of Excellence	1986	2.50	5.00	10.00
❏ CG 40424 [(2)]	Tony Bennett Jazz	1987	3.00	6.00	12.00
❏ FC 44029	Bennett/Berlin	1987	2.50	5.00	10.00
❏ C 63668	Bennett Sings Ellington — Hot and Cool	1999	3.00	6.00	12.00
COLUMBIA LIMITED EDITION					
❏ LE 10057	For Once in My Life	197?	2.50	5.00	10.00
COLUMBIA SPECIAL PRODUCTS					
❏ CSM 552 [M]	Singer Presents Tony Bennett	1966	3.75	7.50	15.00
❏ CSS 552 [S]	Singer Presents Tony Bennett	1966	5.00	10.00	20.00
❏ C 11264	This Is All I Ask	1972	3.00	6.00	12.00
—"Distributed by Arc-Jay-Kay Distributing Co." on upper back cover					
DRG					
❏ MRS-910	Make Magnificent Music	1985	2.50	5.00	10.00
❏ DARC-2-2102 [(2)]	The Rodgers and Hart Songbook	1986	3.75	7.50	15.00
HARMONY					
❏ HS 11340	Just One of Those Things	1969	2.50	5.00	10.00
❏ KH 32171	Tony	1973	2.50	5.00	10.00
IMPROV					
❏ 7112	Life Is Beautiful	197?	3.00	6.00	12.00
❏ 7113	Tony Bennett Sings Rodgers and Hart	197?	3.00	6.00	12.00
❏ 7120	Tony Bennett Sings More Rodgers and Hart	1978	3.00	6.00	12.00
❏ 7123	Beautiful Music	1979	3.00	6.00	12.00
MGM					
❏ SE-4929	Greatest Hits, Vol. 7	1973	3.00	6.00	12.00
PAIR					
❏ PDL2-1102 [(2)]	All-Time Favorites	1986	3.00	6.00	12.00
TIME-LIFE					
❏ SLGD-10 [(2)]	Legendary Singers: Tony Bennett	1986	3.75	7.50	15.00
VERVE					
❏ MV-5088	The Good Things in Life	1972	3.00	6.00	12.00
❏ MV-5094	Listen Easy	1973	3.00	6.00	12.00

BENNETT, TONY, AND COUNT BASIE
Albums

Number	Title (A Side/B Side)	Yr	VG	VG+	NM
COLUMBIA					
❏ CL 1294 [M]	Tony Bennett In Person	1959	6.25	12.50	25.00
❏ CS 8104 [S]	Tony Bennett In Person	1959	10.00	20.00	40.00
COLUMBIA LIMITED EDITION					
❏ LE 10125	Tony Bennett In Person	197?	3.00	6.00	12.00
ROULETTE					
❏ R 25072 [M]	Count Basie Swings/Tony Bennett Sings	1961	6.25	12.50	25.00
❏ SR 25072 [S]	Count Basie Swings/Tony Bennett Sings	1961	7.50	15.00	30.00
❏ R 25231 [M]	Bennett and Basie Strike Up the Band	1963	5.00	10.00	20.00
❏ SR 25231 [S]	Bennett and Basie Strike Up the Band	1963	6.25	12.50	25.00

BENNETT, TONY, AND BILL EVANS
Albums

Number	Title (A Side/B Side)	Yr	VG	VG+	NM
DRG					
❏ MRS-901	Together Again	1985	2.00	4.00	8.00
FANTASY					
❏ F-9489	The Tony Bennett/Bill Evans Album	1975	3.00	6.00	12.00
IMPROV					
❏ 7117	Together Again	1978	3.00	6.00	12.00
MOBILE FIDELITY					
❏ 1-117	The Tony Bennett/Bill Evans Album	1981	10.00	20.00	40.00
—Audiophile vinyl					

BENNIS, BARBARA
45s

Number	Title (A Side/B Side)	Yr	VG	VG+	NM
MALA					
❏ 468	Here's My Shoulder/I Wonder What He'll Say	1963	3.00	6.00	12.00

BENNO, MARC   Also see LEON RUSSELL AND MARC BENNO.
45s

Number	Title (A Side/B Side)	Yr	VG	VG+	NM
A&M					
❏ 1327	Baby, I Love You/Speak Your Mind	1972	—	3.00	6.00

Number	Title (A Side/B Side)	Yr	VG	VG+	NM
❏ 1387	Southern Woman/Jive Fade Jive	1972	—	3.00	6.00
❏ 2184	Chasin' Rainbows/(B-side unknown)	1979	—	3.00	6.00

Albums
A&M

❏ SP-4273	Marc Benno	1970	3.00	6.00	12.00
❏ SP-4303	Minnows	1971	3.00	6.00	12.00
❏ SP-4364	Ambush	1972	3.00	6.00	12.00
❏ SP-4767	Lost in Austin	1979	2.50	5.00	10.00

BENNY AND THE BEDBUGS
45s
DCP

❏ 1008	The Beatle Beat/Roll Over Beethoven	1964	3.75	7.50	15.00
❏ 1008 [PS]	The Beatle Beat/Roll Over Beethoven	1964	6.25	12.50	25.00

BENSON, GEORGE   Also see THE ALTAIRS.
12-Inch Singles
VERVE

❏ 01028 [DJ]	El Barrio (Maw Mix 7:14) (Instrumental 5:02) (LP Version 8:29) (+1 more?)	2000	3.00	6.00	12.00
❏ 561788-1	The Ghetto (El Barrio) (4 versions)	2000	2.00	4.00	8.00

WARNER BROS.

❏ PRO-A-2026 [DJ]	Inside Love (So Personal) (5:13) (7:03) (4:08)	1983	2.50	5.00	10.00
❏ PRO-A-2251 [DJ]	20/20 (Extended Dance Mix 6:32) (same on both sides)	1984	2.00	4.00	8.00
❏ PRO-A-2617 [DJ]	Shiver (Extended) (7" Version) (Dub)/Love Is Here Tonight	1986	2.00	4.00	8.00
❏ PRO-A-3454 [DJ]	Good Habit (Remix) (Radio Version)	1988	—	3.50	7.00
❏ PRO-A-3722 [DJ]	Here, There and Everywhere (Edit) (Instrumental Edit)	1989	2.50	5.00	10.00
❏ PRO-A-6237 [DJ]	Love of My Life (same on both sides)	1993	2.50	5.00	10.00
❏ PRO-A-6242 [DJ]	Kiss and Make Up/My Heart Is Dancing/Got to Be There/I'll Be Good to You	1993	2.50	5.00	10.00
❏ PRO-A-6365 [DJ]	I'll Be Good to You (Edit) (LP Version)	1993	2.00	4.00	8.00
❏ 20110	Inside Love (So Personal) (2 versions)/In Search of a Dream	1983	—	3.00	6.00
❏ 20572	Shiver (3 versions)/Love Is Here Tonight	1986	—	3.50	7.00
❏ 20640	Teaser (3 versions)/Did You Hear Thunder	1987	—	3.50	7.00
❏ 21115	Twice the Love (Guitar Love Mix) (Guitar Love Edit) (Club Love Edit) (Club Love Dub)	1988	2.00	4.00	8.00

45s
A&M

❏ 1003	Chattanooga Choo Choo/The Shape of Things to Come	1968	—	3.00	6.00
❏ 1057	Don't Let Me Lose This Dream Part 1/Part 2	1969	—	3.00	6.00
❏ 1076	Jackie All/My Woman's Good to Me	1969	—	3.00	6.00
❏ 1124	My Cherie Amour/Tell It Like It Is	1969	—	3.00	6.00
❏ 1128	I Got a Woman Part 1/I Got a Woman Part 2	1969	—	3.00	6.00
❏ 8395	Golden Slumbers-You Never Give Me Your Money (Medley)/(B-side unknown)	1971	—	3.00	6.00

—May be promo only
ARISTA

❏ 0251	The Greatest Love of All/Ali's Theme	1977	—	2.00	4.00

—B-side by Michael Masser

❏ 0251 [PS]	The Greatest Love of All/Ali's Theme	1977	—	3.00	6.00

COLUMBIA

❏ 43684	Summertime/Ain't That Peculiar	1966	2.50	5.00	10.00
❏ 43998	The Man from Toledo/Georgia Stick	1967	2.50	5.00	10.00

CTI

❏ 25	Supership/My Latin Brother	1975	—	3.00	6.00
❏ 30	Summertime & 2001 (Part 1)/Summertime & 2001 (Part 2)	1977	—	2.50	5.00
❏ 47	Hold On, I'm Comin'/Gone	1978	—	2.50	5.00

GROOVE

❏ 0024	It Should Have Been Me #2/She Makes Me Mad	1954	10.00	20.00	40.00

PRESTIGE

❏ 317	Just Another Sunday/Shadow Dancers	1964	3.00	6.00	12.00

WARNER BROS.

❏ 8209	This Masquerade/Lady	1976	—	2.50	5.00
❏ 8268	Breezin'/Six to Four	1976	—	2.00	4.00
❏ 8360	Everything Must Change/The Wind and I	1977	—	2.00	4.00
❏ 8377	Gonna Love You More/Valdez in the Country	1977	—	2.00	4.00
❏ 8542	On Broadway/We As Love	1978	—	2.00	4.00
❏ 8542 [PS]	On Broadway/We As Love	1978	—	2.50	5.00
❏ 8604	Lady Blue/California P.M.	1978	—	2.00	4.00
❏ 8604 [PS]	Lady Blue/California P.M.	1978	—	2.50	5.00
❏ 8759	Love Ballad/You're Never Too Far from Me	1979	—	2.00	4.00
❏ 8759 [PS]	Love Ballad/You're Never Too Far from Me	1979	—	2.50	5.00
❏ 8843	Unchained Melody/Before You Go	1979	—	2.00	4.00
❏ 27537	Good Habit/Stephanie	1989	—	—	3.00
❏ 27658	Twice the Love/(Instrumental)	1989	—	—	3.00
❏ 27658 [PS]	Twice the Love/(Instrumental)	1989	—	—	3.00
❏ 27780	Let's Do It Again/Let Go	1988	—	—	3.00
❏ 27780 [PS]	Let's Do It Again/Let Go	1988	—	—	3.00
❏ 28410	Did You Hear Thunder/Teaser	1987	—	—	3.00
❏ 28523	Shiver/Love Is Here Tonight	1986	—	—	3.00
❏ 28640	Kisses in the Moonlight/Open Your Eyes (Instrumental)	1986	—	—	3.00
❏ 28640 [PS]	Kisses in the Moonlight/Open Your Eyes (Instrumental)	1986	—	—	3.00
❏ 28969	New Day/No One Emotion	1985	—	—	3.00
❏ 29042	I Just Wanna Hang Around You/Beyond the Sea (La Mer)	1985	—	—	3.00
❏ 29120	20-20/Shark Bite	1984	—	2.00	4.00
❏ 29120 [PS]	20-20/Shark Bite	1984	—	2.00	4.00
❏ 29442	In Your Eyes/Never Too Far to Fall	1983	—	2.00	4.00
❏ 29563	Lady Love Me (One More Time)/Being with You	1983	—	2.00	4.00
❏ 29649	Inside Love (So Personal)/In Search of a Dream	1983	—	2.00	4.00
❏ 29649 [PS]	Inside Love (So Personal)/In Search of a Dream	1983	—	2.00	4.00
❏ 49051	Hey Girl/Welcome Into My World	1979	—	2.00	4.00
❏ 49505	Give Me the Night/Dinorah, Dinorah	1980	—	2.00	4.00
❏ 49505 [PS]	Give Me the Night/Dinorah, Dinorah	1980	—	2.50	5.00

Number	Title (A Side/B Side)	Yr	VG	VG+	NM
❏ 49570	Love Dance/Love X Love	1980	—	2.00	4.00
❏ 49637	Midnight Love Affair/Turn Off the Lamplight	1980	—	2.00	4.00
❏ 49846	Turn Your Love Around/Nature Boy	1981	—	2.00	4.00
❏ 49846 [PS]	Turn Your Love Around/Nature Boy	1981	—	2.00	4.00
❏ 50005	Never Give Up on a Good Thing/Livin' Inside Your Love	1982	—	2.00	4.00
❏ 50005 [PS]	Never Give Up on a Good Thing/Livin' Inside Your Love	1982	—	2.00	4.00

Albums
A&M

❏ SP-3014	Shape of Things to Come	1969	5.00	10.00	20.00

—Brown label

❏ SP-3014	Shape of Things to Come	1976	3.00	6.00	12.00

—Silvery label with fading "A&M" logo

❏ SP9-3014	Shape of Things to Come	1983	3.75	7.50	15.00

—"Audio Master Plus" reissue

❏ SP-3020	Tell It Like It Is	1969	5.00	10.00	20.00

—Brown label

❏ SP-3020	Tell It Like It Is	1976	3.00	6.00	12.00

—Silvery label with fading "A&M" logo

❏ SP9-3020	Tell It Like It Is	1984	3.75	7.50	15.00

—"Audio Master Plus" reissue

❏ SP-3028	The Other Side of Abbey Road	1970	6.25	12.50	25.00

—Brown label

❏ SP-3028	The Other Side of Abbey Road	1976	3.00	6.00	12.00

—Silvery label with fading "A&M" logo

❏ SP9-3028	The Other Side of Abbey Road	1984	3.75	7.50	15.00

—"Audio Master Plus" reissue

❏ SP-3203	The Best of George Benson	1983	2.50	5.00	10.00

COLUMBIA

❏ CL 2525 [M]	The Most Exciting New Guitarist on the Jazz Scene Today — It's Uptown	1966	5.00	10.00	20.00
❏ CL 2613 [M]	The George Benson Cook Book	1967	5.00	10.00	20.00
❏ CS 9325 [S]	The Most Exciting New Guitarist on the Jazz Scene Today — It's Uptown	1966	5.00	10.00	20.00

—Red "360 Sound" label

❏ CS 9325	The Most Exciting New Guitarist on the Jazz Scene Today — It's Uptown	1976	2.50	5.00	10.00

—Orange label

❏ PC 9325	The Most Exciting New Guitarist on the Jazz Scene Today — It's Uptown	198?	2.00	4.00	8.00

—Reissue with new prefix

❏ CS 9413 [S]	The George Benson Cook Book	1967	5.00	10.00	20.00

—Red "360 Sound" label

❏ CS 9413	The George Benson Cook Book	1976	2.50	5.00	10.00

—Orange label

❏ PC 9413	The George Benson Cook Book	198?	2.00	4.00	8.00

—Reissue with new prefix

❏ CG 33569 [(2)]	Benson Burner	1976	3.00	6.00	12.00

CTI

❏ 6009	Beyond the Blue Horizon	1971	3.00	6.00	12.00
❏ 6015	White Rabbit	1972	3.00	6.00	12.00
❏ 6033	Body Talk	1973	3.00	6.00	12.00
❏ CTSQ-6033 [Q]	Body Talk	1973	5.00	10.00	20.00
❏ 6045	Bad Benson	1974	3.00	6.00	12.00
❏ 6062	Good King Bad	1976	3.00	6.00	12.00
❏ 6069	Benson & Farrell	1976	3.00	6.00	12.00
❏ 6072	George Benson In Concert — Carnegie Hall	1976	3.00	6.00	12.00
❏ 8009	White Rabbit	198?	2.50	5.00	10.00
❏ 8014	Take Five	198?	2.50	5.00	10.00
❏ 8030	Cast Your Fate to the Wind	1982	2.50	5.00	10.00
❏ 8031	Summertime: In Concert	198?	2.50	5.00	10.00

FANTASY

❏ OJC-461	New Boss Guitar	1990	3.00	6.00	12.00

—Reissue of Prestige 7310
MOBILE FIDELITY

❏ 1-011	Breezin'	1979	15.00	30.00	60.00

—Audiophile vinyl
POLYDOR

❏ PD-1-6084	Blue Benson	1976	2.50	5.00	10.00

PRESTIGE

❏ PRLP-7310 [M]	The New Boss Guitar of George Benson	1964	6.25	12.50	25.00
❏ PRST-7310 [S]	The New Boss Guitar of George Benson	1964	7.50	15.00	30.00
❏ 24072 [(2)]	George Benson & Jack McDuff	1976	3.75	7.50	15.00

VERVE

❏ V6-8749	Giblet Gravy	1968	5.00	10.00	20.00
❏ V6-8771	Goodies	1969	5.00	10.00	20.00

WARNER BROS.

❏ BS 2919	Breezin'	1976	2.50	5.00	10.00

—With "Contains This Masquerade" on front cover

❏ BS 2919	Breezin'	1976	3.75	7.50	15.00

—With no mention of "This Masquerade" on front cover

❏ BSK 2983	In Flight	1977	2.50	5.00	10.00
❏ BSK 3111	Breezin'	1977	2.00	4.00	8.00

—Reissue of 2919

❏ 2WS 3139 [(2)]	Weekend in L.A.	1978	3.00	6.00	12.00
❏ 2BSK 3277	Livin' Inside Your Love	1979	3.00	6.00	12.00
❏ HS 3453	Give Me the Night	1980	2.50	5.00	10.00
❏ 2HS 3577 [(2)]	The George Benson Collection	1981	3.00	6.00	12.00
❏ 23744	In Your Eyes	1983	2.50	5.00	10.00
❏ 25178	20/20	1985	2.50	5.00	10.00
❏ 25475	While the City Sleeps…	1986	2.50	5.00	10.00
❏ 25705	Twice the Love	1988	2.50	5.00	10.00
❏ 25907	Tenderly	1989	3.00	6.00	12.00
❏ 26295	Big Boss Band	1990	3.75	7.50	15.00

BENSON, GEORGE, AND EARL KLUGH
45s
WARNER BROS.

❏ 27975	Since You're Gone/Love Theme from "Romeo and Juliet"	1988	—	—	3.00

B

BENSON, JANE

Number	Title (A Side/B Side)	Yr	VG	VG+	NM
❏ 27975 [PS]	Since You're Gone/Love Theme from "Romeo and Juliet"	1988	—	2.00	4.00
❏ 28244	Dreamin'/Love Theme from "Romeo and Juliet"	1987	—	—	3.00

Albums
WARNER BROS.

Number	Title (A Side/B Side)	Yr	VG	VG+	NM
❏ 25580	Collaboration	1987	2.50	5.00	10.00

BENSON, JANE
45s
ATCO

Number	Title (A Side/B Side)	Yr	VG	VG+	NM
❏ 6151	Growing Up/Surrendering	1959	3.75	7.50	15.00

BENT BOLT AND THE NUTS
45s
MGM

Number	Title (A Side/B Side)	Yr	VG	VG+	NM
❏ 13635	Mechanical Man/Sweet and Sour	1966	2.00	4.00	8.00
❏ 13635 [PS]	Mechanical Man/Sweet and Sour	1966	2.50	5.00	10.00

BENTLEYS, THE
45s
SMASH

Number	Title (A Side/B Side)	Yr	VG	VG+	NM
❏ 1967	She's My Hot Rod Queen/Why Does Everybody Want to Hold My Baby	1965	6.25	12.50	25.00
❏ 1988	Did Anybody Lose a Tear/Why Didn't I Listen to Mother	1965	6.25	12.50	25.00

BENTON, BROOK Also see THE SANDMEN (2); DINAH WASHINGTON AND BROOK BENTON.
45s
ALL PLATINUM

Number	Title (A Side/B Side)	Yr	VG	VG+	NM
❏ 2364	Can't Take My Eyes Off You/Weekend with Feathers	1976	—	2.50	5.00

BRUT

Number	Title (A Side/B Side)	Yr	VG	VG+	NM
❏ 810	Lay Lady Lay/A Touch of Class	1973	—	2.50	5.00
❏ 816	South Carolina/(B-side unknown)	1973	—	2.50	5.00

COTILLION

Number	Title (A Side/B Side)	Yr	VG	VG+	NM
❏ 13107	Rainy Night in Georgia/Nothing Takes the Place of You	197?	—	2.00	4.00
—Part of "Atlantic Oldies Series"					
❏ 44007	I Just Don't Know What to Do with Myself/Do Your Own Thing	1968	2.00	4.00	8.00
❏ 44031	She Knows What to Do with 'Em/Touch 'Em with Love	1969	2.00	4.00	8.00
❏ 44034	Nothing Can Take the Place of You/Woman Without Love	1969	2.00	4.00	8.00
❏ 44057	Rainy Night in Georgia/Where Do You Go from Here	1969	2.50	5.00	10.00
❏ 44072	My Way/A Little Bit of Soap	1970	—	3.00	6.00
❏ 44078	Don't Make You Want to Go Home/I've Gotta Be Me	1970	—	3.00	6.00
❏ 44093	Shoes/Let Me Fix It	1970	—	3.00	6.00
❏ 44110	Whoever Finds This, I Love You/Heaven Help Us All	1971	—	3.00	6.00
❏ 44119	Take a Look at Your Hands/If You Think God Is Dead	1971	—	3.00	6.00
❏ 44130	Please Send Me Someone to Love/She Even Woke Me Up to Say Goodbye	1971	—	3.00	6.00
❏ 44138	A Black Child Can't Smile/If You Think God Is Dead	1971	—	3.00	6.00
❏ 44141	Soul Santa/Let Us All Get Together with the Lord	1971	2.00	4.00	8.00
❏ 44152	Movin' Day/Poor Make Believer	1972	—	3.00	6.00

EPIC

Number	Title (A Side/B Side)	Yr	VG	VG+	NM
❏ 9177	Love Made Me Your Fool/Give Me a Sign	1956	6.25	12.50	25.00
❏ 9199	The Wall/All My Love Belongs to You	1957	6.25	12.50	25.00

MERCURY

Number	Title (A Side/B Side)	Yr	VG	VG+	NM
❏ C7071 [S]	I Love Paris/All of Me	196?	5.00	10.00	20.00
—Jukebox issue, small hole, plays at 33 1/3 rpm					
❏ C7072 [S]	Blues in the Night/I Didn't Know What Time It Was	196?	5.00	10.00	20.00
—Jukebox issue, small hole, plays at 33 1/3 rpm					
❏ 30101	Merry Christmas, Happy New Year/This Time Of The Year	196?	2.00	4.00	8.00
—Reissue					
❏ 71394	It's Just a Matter of Time/Hurtin' Inside	1959	3.75	7.50	15.00
❏ 71443	Endlessly/So Close	1959	3.75	7.50	15.00
❏ 71478	Thank You Pretty Baby/With All of My Heart	1959	3.75	7.50	15.00
❏ 71512	So Many Ways/I Want You Forever	1959	3.75	7.50	15.00
❏ 71554	This Time of the Year/Nothing in the World	1959	3.75	7.50	15.00
❏ 71558	This Time of the Year/How Many Times	1959	3.75	7.50	15.00
❏ 71566	The Ties That Bind/Hither, Thither and Yon	1960	3.00	6.00	12.00
❏ 71566 [PS]	The Ties That Bind/Hither, Thither and Yon	1960	5.00	10.00	20.00
❏ 71652	Kiddio/The Same One	1960	3.00	6.00	12.00
❏ 71652 [PS]	Kiddio/The Same One	1960	5.00	10.00	20.00
❏ 71722	Fools Rush In (Where Angels Fear to Tread)/Someday You'll Want Me to Want You	1960	3.00	6.00	12.00
❏ 71722 [PS]	Fools Rush In (Where Angels Fear to Tread)/Someday You'll Want Me to Want You	1960	5.00	10.00	20.00
❏ 71730	This Time of the Year/Merry Christmas, Happy New Year	1960	3.00	6.00	12.00
❏ 71774	Think Twice/For My Baby	1961	3.00	6.00	12.00
❏ 71774 [PS]	Think Twice/For My Baby	1961	5.00	10.00	20.00
❏ 71820	The Boll Weevil Song/Your Eyes	1961	3.00	6.00	12.00
❏ 71820 [PS]	The Boll Weevil Song/Your Eyes	1961	5.00	10.00	20.00
—Back of sleeve has six albums pictured					
❏ 71820 [PS]	The Boll Weevil Song/Your Eyes	1961	6.25	12.50	25.00
—Back of sleeve has three albums pictured					
❏ 71859	Frankie and Johnny/It's Just a House Without You	1961	3.00	6.00	12.00
❏ 71859 [PS]	Frankie and Johnny/It's Just a House Without You	1961	5.00	10.00	20.00
❏ 71903	Revenge/Really Really	1961	3.00	6.00	12.00
❏ 71903 [PS]	Revenge/Really Really	1961	5.00	10.00	20.00
❏ 71912	Shadrack/The Lost Penny	1961	3.00	6.00	12.00
❏ 71912 [PS]	Shadrack/The Lost Penny	1961	5.00	10.00	20.00
❏ 71925	Walk on the Wild Side/Somewhere in the Used to Be	1962	2.50	5.00	10.00
❏ 71925 [PS]	Walk on the Wild Side/Somewhere in the Used to Be	1962	5.00	10.00	20.00
❏ 71962	Hit Record/Thanks to the Fool	1962	2.50	5.00	10.00
❏ 71962 [PS]	Hit Record/Thanks to the Fool	1962	5.00	10.00	20.00
—Blue background with orange title banner					
❏ 71962 [PS]	Hit Record/Thanks to the Fool	1962	7.50	15.00	30.00
—All-orange background with different photo					
❏ 72009	Two Tickets to Paradise/It's Alright	1962	—	—	—
—Unreleased					
❏ 72024	Lie to Me/With the Touch of Your Hand	1962	2.50	5.00	10.00
❏ 72024 [PS]	Lie to Me/With the Touch of Your Hand	1962	5.00	10.00	20.00
❏ 72055	Hotel Happiness/Still Waters Run Deep	1962	2.50	5.00	10.00
❏ 72055 [PS]	Hotel Happiness/Still Waters Run Deep	1962	5.00	10.00	20.00
❏ 72099	I Got What I Wanted/Dearer Than Life	1963	2.50	5.00	10.00
❏ 72099 [PS]	I Got What I Wanted/Dearer Than Life	1963	5.00	10.00	20.00
❏ 72135	My True Confession/Tender Years	1963	2.50	5.00	10.00
❏ 72135 [PS]	My True Confession/Tender Years	1963	5.00	10.00	20.00
❏ 72177	Two Tickets to Paradise/Don't Hate Me	1963	2.50	5.00	10.00
❏ 72177 [PS]	Two Tickets to Paradise/Don't Hate Me	1963	5.00	10.00	20.00
❏ 72214	You're All I Want for Christmas/This Time of the Year	1963	2.50	5.00	10.00
❏ 72214 [PS]	You're All I Want for Christmas/This Time of the Year	1963	6.25	12.50	25.00
❏ 72230	Going, Going, Gone/After Midnight	1963	2.50	5.00	10.00
❏ 72230 [PS]	Going, Going, Gone/After Midnight	1963	5.00	10.00	20.00
❏ 72266	Too Late to Turn Back Now/Another Cup of Coffee	1964	2.50	5.00	10.00
❏ 72266 [PS]	Too Late to Turn Back Now/Another Cup of Coffee	1964	5.00	10.00	20.00
❏ 72303	A House Is Not a Home/Come On Back	1964	2.50	5.00	10.00
❏ 72303 [PS]	A House Is Not a Home/Come On Back	1964	5.00	10.00	20.00
❏ 72333	Lumberjack/Don't Do What I Did (Do What I Say)	1964	2.50	5.00	10.00
❏ 72333 [PS]	Lumberjack/Don't Do What I Did (Do What I Say)	1964	5.00	10.00	20.00
❏ 72365	Do It Right/Please, Please Make It Easy	1964	2.50	5.00	10.00
❏ 72365 [PS]	Do It Right/Please, Please Make It Easy	1964	5.00	10.00	20.00
❏ 72398	Special Years/Where There's a Will (There's a Way)	1965	2.50	5.00	10.00
❏ 72446	Love Me Now/A-Sleepin' at the End of the Bed	1965	2.50	5.00	10.00
❏ 872796-7	It's Just a Matter of Time/Hurtin' Inside	1989	—	2.00	4.00
❏ 872798-7	Endlessly/So Many Ways	1989	—	2.00	4.00

MGM

Number	Title (A Side/B Side)	Yr	VG	VG+	NM
❏ 14440	If You've Got the Time/You Take Me Home Honey	1972	—	2.50	5.00

OKEH

Number	Title (A Side/B Side)	Yr	VG	VG+	NM
❏ 7058	The Kentuckian Song/Ooh	1955	6.25	12.50	25.00
❏ 7065	Bring Me Love/Some of My Best Friends	1956	6.25	12.50	25.00

OLDE WORLD

Number	Title (A Side/B Side)	Yr	VG	VG+	NM
❏ 1100	Makin' Love Is Good for You/Better Times	1977	—	2.50	5.00
❏ 1107	Soft/Glow Love	1978	—	2.50	5.00

POLYDOR

Number	Title (A Side/B Side)	Yr	VG	VG+	NM
❏ 2015	I Cried for You/Love Me a Little	1979	—	2.00	4.00

RCA VICTOR

Number	Title (A Side/B Side)	Yr	VG	VG+	NM
❏ 47-7489	Only Your Love/(B-side unknown)	1959	—	—	—
—Unreleased?					
❏ 47-8693	Mother Nature, Father Time/You're Mine	1965	2.50	5.00	10.00
❏ 47-8693 [PS]	Mother Nature, Father Time/You're Mine	1965	5.00	10.00	20.00
❏ 47-8768	Where There's Life/Only a Girl Like You	1965	2.50	5.00	10.00
❏ 47-8830	Too Much Good Lovin'/A Sailor Boy's Love Song	1966	2.50	5.00	10.00
❏ 47-8879	Break Her Heart/In the Evening in the Moonlight	1966	2.50	5.00	10.00
❏ 47-8944	Where Does a Man Go to Cry/The Roach Song	1966	2.50	5.00	10.00
❏ 47-8995	So True in Life, So True in Love/If You Only Knew	1966	2.50	5.00	10.00
❏ 47-9031	Our First Christmas Together/Silent Night	1966	3.00	6.00	12.00
❏ 47-9096	Wake Up/All My Love Belongs to You	1967	2.00	4.00	8.00
❏ 47-9105	Keep the Faith Baby/Going to Soulsville	1967	2.00	4.00	8.00

REPRISE

Number	Title (A Side/B Side)	Yr	VG	VG+	NM
❏ 0611	You're the Reason I'm Living/Laura (Tell Me What He's Got That I Ain't Got)	1967	2.00	4.00	8.00
❏ 0649	Glory of Love/Weakness in a Man	1967	2.00	4.00	8.00
❏ 0676	Instead (Of Loving You)/Lonely Street	1968	2.00	4.00	8.00

STAX

Number	Title (A Side/B Side)	Yr	VG	VG+	NM
❏ 0231	Winds of Change/I Keep Thinking to Myself	1974	—	2.50	5.00

VIK

Number	Title (A Side/B Side)	Yr	VG	VG+	NM
❏ 0285	I Wanna Do Everything for You/Come On Be Nice	1957	5.00	10.00	20.00
❏ 0311	A Million Miles from Nowhere/Devoted	1957	5.00	10.00	20.00
❏ 0325	Because You Love Me/Crinoline Skirt	1958	5.00	10.00	20.00
❏ 0336	Crazy in Love with You/I'm Coming Back to You	1958	5.00	10.00	20.00

7-Inch Extended Plays
MERCURY

Number	Title (A Side/B Side)	Yr	VG	VG+	NM
❏ SR-632-C	Hotel Happiness/It's Just a House Without You/The Boll Weevil Song//Think Twice/Revenge/Walk on the Wild Side	196?	3.00	6.00	12.00
❏ SR-632-C [PS]	Golden Hits, Volume 2	196?	3.00	6.00	12.00

Albums
ALL PLATINUM

Number	Title (A Side/B Side)	Yr	VG	VG+	NM
❏ 3015	This Is Brook Benton	1976	3.00	6.00	12.00

ALLEGIANCE

Number	Title (A Side/B Side)	Yr	VG	VG+	NM
❏ AV-5033	Memories Are Made of This	1986	2.50	5.00	10.00

COTILLION

Number	Title (A Side/B Side)	Yr	VG	VG+	NM
❏ SD 9002	Do Your Own Thing	1969	3.00	6.00	12.00
❏ SD 9018	Brook Benton Today	1970	3.00	6.00	12.00
❏ SD 9028	Home Style	1970	3.00	6.00	12.00
❏ SD 9050	Story Teller	1971	3.00	6.00	12.00
❏ SD 9058	The Gospel Truth	1972	3.00	6.00	12.00

EPIC

Number	Title (A Side/B Side)	Yr	VG	VG+	NM
❏ LN 3573 [M]	Brook Benton At His Best	1959	12.50	25.00	50.00

B

Number	Title (A Side/B Side)	Yr	VG	VG+	NM
HARMONY					
❑ HL 7346 [M]	The Soul of Brook Benton	196?	3.00	6.00	12.00
❑ HS 11146 [R]	The Soul of Brook Benton	196?	3.00	6.00	12.00
HMC					
❑ 830724	Beautiful Memories of Christmas	1983	3.00	6.00	12.00
MERCURY					
❑ MG-20421 [M]	It's Just a Matter of Time	1959	10.00	20.00	40.00
❑ MG-20464 [M]	Endlessly	1959	7.50	15.00	30.00
❑ MG-20565 [M]	So Many Ways I Love You	1960	7.50	15.00	30.00
❑ MG-20602 [M]	Songs I Love to Sing	1960	7.50	15.00	30.00
❑ MG-20607 [M]	Golden Hits	1961	5.00	10.00	20.00
❑ MG-20619 [M]	If You Believe	1961	5.00	10.00	20.00
❑ MG-20641 [M]	The Boll Weevil Song and 11 Other Great Hits	1961	5.00	10.00	20.00
❑ MG-20673 [M]	There Goes That Song Again	1962	5.00	10.00	20.00
❑ MG-20740 [M]	Singing the Blues — Lie to Me	1962	5.00	10.00	20.00
❑ MG-20774 [M]	Golden Hits, Volume 2	1963	5.00	10.00	20.00
❑ MG-20830 [M]	Best Ballads of Broadway	1963	5.00	10.00	20.00
❑ MG-20886 [M]	Born to Sing the Blues	1964	5.00	10.00	20.00
❑ MG-20918 [M]	On the Country Side	1964	3.75	7.50	15.00
❑ MG-20934 [M]	This Bitter Earth	1964	3.75	7.50	15.00
❑ SR-60077 [S]	It's Just a Matter of Time	1959	12.50	25.00	50.00
❑ SR-60146 [S]	Endlessly	1959	10.00	20.00	40.00
❑ SR-60225 [S]	So Many Ways I Love You	1960	10.00	2.00	40.00
❑ SR-60602 [S]	Songs I Love to Sing	1960	10.00	20.00	40.00
❑ SR-60607 [S]	Golden Hits	1961	7.50	15.00	30.00
❑ SR-60619 [S]	If You Believe	1961	7.50	15.00	30.00
❑ SR-60641 [S]	The Boll Weevil Song and 11 Other Great Hits	1961	7.50	15.00	30.00
❑ SR-60673 [S]	There Goes That Song Again	1962	7.50	15.00	30.00
❑ SR-60740 [S]	Singing the Blues — Lie to Me	1962	7.50	15.00	30.00
❑ SR-60774 [S]	Golden Hits, Volume 2	1963	7.50	15.00	30.00
❑ SR-60830 [S]	Best Ballads of Broadway	1963	6.25	12.50	25.00
❑ SR-60886 [S]	Born to Sing the Blues	1964	6.25	12.50	25.00
❑ SR-60918 [S]	On the Country Side	1964	5.00	10.00	20.00
❑ SR-60934 [S]	This Bitter Earth	1964	5.00	10.00	20.00
❑ 822321-1	It's Just a Matter of Time: His Greatest Hits	1984	2.50	5.00	10.00
MGM					
❑ SE-4874	Something for Everyone	1973	3.00	6.00	12.00
MUSICOR					
❑ 4603 [(2)]	The Best of Brook Benton	1977	3.00	6.00	12.00
PAIR					
❑ PDL2-1100 [(2)]	Brook Benton's Best	1986	3.00	6.00	12.00
RCA CAMDEN					
❑ CAL-564 [M]	Brook Benton	1960	3.75	7.50	15.00
❑ CAS-2431	I Wanna Be with You	1970	3.00	6.00	12.00
RCA VICTOR					
❑ APL1-1044	Book Benton Sings a Love Story	1975	2.50	5.00	10.00
❑ LPM-3514 [M]	That Old Feeling	1966	3.75	7.50	15.00
❑ LSP-3514 [S]	That Old Feeling	1966	5.00	10.00	20.00
❑ LPM-3526 [M]	Mother Nature, Father Time	1965	3.75	7.50	15.00
❑ LSP-3526 [S]	Mother Nature, Father Time	1965	5.00	10.00	20.00
❑ LPM-3590 [M]	My Country	1966	3.75	7.50	15.00
❑ LSP-3590 [S]	My Country	1966	5.00	10.00	20.00
REPRISE					
❑ R-6268 [M]	Laura (What's He Got That I Ain't Got)	1967	5.00	10.00	20.00
❑ RS-6268 [S]	Laura (What's He Got That I Ain't Got)	1967	3.75	7.50	15.00
RHINO					
❑ RNFP 71497 [(2)]	The Brook Benton Anthology (1959-1970)	1986	3.00	6.00	12.00
WING					
❑ MGW-12314 [M]	Brook Benton	1966	3.00	6.00	12.00
❑ SRW-16314 [S]	Brook Benton	1966	3.00	6.00	12.00

BENTON, BROOK, AND DAMITA JO Also see each artist's individual listings.
45s

Number	Title (A Side/B Side)	Yr	VG	VG+	NM
MERCURY					
❑ 72196	Yaba-Taba-Do/Almost Persuaded	1963	—	—	—
—Unreleased					
❑ 72207	Baby, You've Got It Made/Stop Foolin'	1963	2.50	5.00	10.00

BERBERIAN, JOHN, WITH THE ROCK EAST ENSEMBLE
Albums

Number	Title (A Side/B Side)	Yr	VG	VG+	NM
MAINSTREAM					
❑ S-6123	Impressions East	1969	30.00	60.00	120.00
VERVE FORECAST					
❑ FTS-3073	Middle Eastern Rock	1969	12.50	25.00	50.00

BERG, GERTRUDE
Albums

Number	Title (A Side/B Side)	Yr	VG	VG+	NM
AMY					
❑ 8007 [M]	How to Be a Jewish Mother	1965	6.25	12.50	25.00

BERGEN, POLLY
45s

Number	Title (A Side/B Side)	Yr	VG	VG+	NM
COLUMBIA					
❑ 41342	He Didn't Call/I Feel Sorry for the Boy	1959	3.00	6.00	12.00
❑ 41617	It Might As Well Be Spring/Four Seasons	1960	2.50	5.00	10.00
❑ 41675	Do It Yourself/The Party's Over	1960	2.50	5.00	10.00
❑ 41971	Bye Bye Blackbird/				
	The Happiest Girl in the World	1961	2.50	5.00	10.00
JUBILEE					
❑ 5230	No One Else Will Ever Know/Let's Make Love	1956	3.75	7.50	15.00
RCA VICTOR					
❑ 47-3886	Oh Them Dudes/I Got Tookin'	1950	3.75	7.50	15.00
❑ 47-3958	Just the Way You Are/				
	I Put My Head in the Lion's Mouth	1950	3.75	7.50	15.00
❑ 47-4022	Out of Sight/Tonda Wanda Hey	1951	3.75	7.50	15.00
Albums					
COLUMBIA					
❑ CL 994 [M]	Bergen Sings Morgan	1957	7.50	15.00	30.00
❑ CL 1031 [M]	The Party's Over	1957	7.50	15.00	30.00
❑ CL 1138 [M]	Polly and Her Pop	1958	6.25	12.50	25.00
❑ CL 1218 [M]	My Heart Sings	1959	5.00	10.00	20.00

Number	Title (A Side/B Side)	Yr	VG	VG+	NM
❑ CL 1300 [M]	All Alone by the Telephone	1959	5.00	10.00	20.00
❑ CL 1451 [M]	Four Seasons of Love	1960	5.00	10.00	20.00
❑ CL 1632 [M]	"Do Re Mi" and "Annie Get Your Gun"	1961	5.00	10.00	20.00
❑ CS 8018 [S]	My Heart Sings	1959	6.25	12.50	25.00
❑ CS 8100 [S]	All Alone by the Telephone	1959	6.25	12.50	25.00
❑ CS 8246 [S]	Four Seasons of Love	1960	6.25	12.50	25.00
❑ CS 8432 [S]	"Do Re Mi" and "Annie Get Your Gun"	1961	6.25	12.50	25.00
JUBILEE					
❑ JGL-14 [10]	Polly Bergen	1955	12.50	25.00	50.00
PHILIPS					
❑ PHM 200084 [M]	Act One — Sing, Too	1963	3.75	7.50	15.00
❑ PHS 600084 [S]	Act One — Sing, Too	1963	5.00	10.00	20.00

BERMAN, SHELLEY
Albums

Number	Title (A Side/B Side)	Yr	VG	VG+	NM
METRO					
❑ M-546 [M]	Let Me Tell You a Funny Story	1965	3.75	7.50	15.00
❑ MS-546 [R]	Let Me Tell You a Funny Story	1965	3.00	6.00	12.00
VERVE					
❑ MGV-15003 [M]	Inside Shelley Berman	1959	6.25	12.50	25.00
❑ V-15003 [M]	Inside Shelley Berman	1962	3.75	7.50	15.00
❑ V6-15003 [R]	Inside Shelley Berman	196?	3.00	6.00	12.00
❑ MGV-15007 [M]	Outside Shelley Berman	1959	6.25	12.50	25.00
❑ V-15007 [M]	Outside Shelley Berman	1962	3.75	7.50	15.00
❑ V6-15007 [R]	Outside Shelley Berman	196?	3.00	6.00	12.00
❑ MGV-15008-2 [(2)M]	Inside and Outside Shelley Berman	1959	7.50	15.00	30.00
❑ V-15008-2 [(2)M]	Inside and Outside Shelley Berman	1962	5.00	10.00	20.00
❑ MGV-15013 [M]	The Edge of Shelley Berman	1960	6.25	12.50	25.00
❑ V-15013 [M]	The Edge of Shelley Berman	1962	3.75	7.50	15.00
❑ V6-15013 [R]	The Edge of Shelley Berman	196?	3.00	6.00	12.00
❑ MGV-15027 [M]	A Personal Appearance	1961	5.00	10.00	20.00
❑ V-15027 [M]	A Personal Appearance	1962	3.75	7.50	15.00
❑ V6-15027 [R]	A Personal Appearance	196?	3.00	6.00	12.00
❑ V-15036 [M]	New Sides	1962	3.75	7.50	15.00
❑ V6-15036 [R]	New Sides	196?	3.00	6.00	12.00
❑ V-15043 [M]	The Sex Life of the Primate (And Other Bits of Gossip)	1964	5.00	10.00	20.00
❑ V6-15043 [R]	The Sex Life of the Primate (And Other Bits of Gossip)	1964	3.75	7.50	15.00
❑ V-15048 [M]	Great Moments in Comedy	1965	5.00	10.00	20.00
❑ V6-15048 [R]	Great Moments in Comedy	1965	3.75	7.50	15.00

BERMUDAS, THE
45s

Number	Title (A Side/B Side)	Yr	VG	VG+	NM
ERA					
❑ 3125	Donnie/Chu Sen Ling	1964	3.00	6.00	12.00

BERNA-DEAN
45s

Number	Title (A Side/B Side)	Yr	VG	VG+	NM
IMPERIAL					
❑ 5792	I Walk in My Sleep/Little Willie	1961	5.00	10.00	20.00
❑ 5840	He's Mine/One Gal in Town, Five Men Hagin' Around	1962	5.00	10.00	20.00
❑ 5877	Morning, Noon and Night/The World Keeps Changing	1962	5.00	10.00	20.00
❑ 5950	The President Says Walk/I Wonder	1963	5.00	10.00	20.00
❑ 5978	Hello/Sleepless Nights	1963	5.00	10.00	20.00

BERNARD, ROD
45s

Number	Title (A Side/B Side)	Yr	VG	VG+	NM
ARBEE					
❑ 101	Recorded in England/Somebody Wrote That Song for My Baby	1965	2.50	5.00	10.00
❑ 104	Gimme Back My Cadillac/ Don't You Think I've Paid Enough	1965	2.50	5.00	10.00
❑ 105	Those Were Our Songs/Just Another Lie	1966	2.50	5.00	10.00
ARGO					
❑ 5327	This Should Go On Forever/Pardon Mr. Gordon	1959	5.00	10.00	20.00
❑ 5338	You're On My Mind/My Life Is a Mystery	1959	5.00	10.00	20.00
CARL					
❑ (# unknown)	Linda Gail/Little Bitta Mama	1957	6.25	12.50	25.00
CRAZY CAJUN					
❑ 9020	Papa Thibodeaux/My Little Jollie Blonde	1978	—	2.50	5.00
HALLWAY					
❑ 1806	I Had a Girl/Wedding Bells	1963	3.75	7.50	15.00
❑ 1902	Who's Gonna Rock My Baby/Colinda	1962	3.75	7.50	15.00
❑ 1906	New Orleans Jail/Fais Do-Do	1962	3.75	7.50	15.00
❑ 1915	Forgive/I Want Somebody	1963	3.75	7.50	15.00
❑ 1917	Diggy Liggy Lo/The Clock	1963	3.75	7.50	15.00
❑ 1919	Loneliness/Boss Man's Son	1964	3.75	7.50	15.00
❑ 1922	My Own Mother-in-Law/I Might As Well	1964	3.75	7.50	15.00
JIN					
❑ 105	This Should Go On Forever/Pardon, Mr. Gordon	1958	10.00	20.00	40.00
❑ 232	Congratulations to You Darling/ You're the Reason I'm in Love	1968	2.00	4.00	8.00
❑ 237	To Have and Hold/Cajun Honey	1968	2.00	4.00	8.00
❑ 240	Big Mamou/New Orleans Jail	1969	2.00	4.00	8.00
❑ 307	Don't You Think I've Paid Enough/ Somebody Wrote That Song for Me	1974	—	2.50	5.00
❑ 325	Breaking Up Is Hard to Do/ Sometimes I Walk in My Sleep	1975	—	2.50	5.00
❑ 338	This Should Go On Forever/I Spent a Week There Last Night	1975	—	2.50	5.00
❑ 350	A Winner in Love/ I Forgot I Had These Memories of You	1975	—	2.50	5.00
❑ 373	Mardi Gras in New Orleans/Oh Mother Dear	1976	—	2.50	5.00
❑ 376	Go On, Go On/I Naver Had the One I Wanted	1976	—	2.50	5.00
MERCURY					
❑ 71507	Shedding Teardrops Over You/One More Chance	1959	5.00	10.00	20.00
❑ 71592	One of These Days/Let's Get Together Tonight	1960	5.00	10.00	20.00
❑ 71654	Two Young Fools in Love/Dance Fool Dance	1960	5.00	10.00	20.00

Number	Title (A Side/B Side)	Yr	VG	VG+	NM
❑ 71689	Sttrange Kisses/Just a Memory	1960	5.00	10.00	20.00
❑ 71767	Lonely Hearts Club/Who Knows	1961	4.00	8.00	16.00
❑ 71842	(Tell Me) Sometime/I'm Not Lonely Anymore	1961	4.00	8.00	16.00

SCEPTER

Number	Title (A Side/B Side)	Yr	VG	VG+	NM
❑ 12195	Those Were Our Songs/Recorded in England	1967	4.00	8.00	16.00

TEAR DROP

Number	Title (A Side/B Side)	Yr	VG	VG+	NM
❑ 3044	Our Teenage Love/Doing the Oo-Wa-Woo	1966	2.50	5.00	10.00
❑ 3052	You're the Reason I'm in Love/My Jole Blon	1966	2.50	5.00	10.00
❑ 3060	No Money Down/Little Green Man	1967	2.50	5.00	10.00
❑ 3117	This Should Go On Forever/Recorded in England	1969	2.00	4.00	8.00

Albums

JIN

Number	Title (A Side/B Side)	Yr	VG	VG+	NM
❑ LP-4007 [M]	Rod Bernard	196?	15.00	30.00	60.00

BERRY, BROOKS, AND SCRAPPER BLACKWELL
Albums

BLUESVILLE

Number	Title (A Side/B Side)	Yr	VG	VG+	NM
❑ BVLP-1074 [M]	My Heart Struck Sorrow	1963	20.00	40.00	80.00
—Blue label, silver print					
❑ BVLP-1074 [M]	My Heart Struck Sorrow	1964	6.25	12.50	25.00
—Blue label with trident logo					

BERRY, CHUCK Also see JOE ALEXANDER AND THE CUBANS; BO DIDDLEY/CHUCK BERRY.
45s

ATCO

Number	Title (A Side/B Side)	Yr	VG	VG+	NM
❑ 7203	Oh What a Thrill/California	1979	—	2.00	4.00

CHESS

Number	Title (A Side/B Side)	Yr	VG	VG+	NM
❑ 1604	Maybellene/Wee Wee Hours	1955	12.50	25.00	50.00
❑ 1610	Thirty Days (To Come Back Home)/Together	1955	12.50	25.00	50.00
❑ 1615	No Money Down/Down Bound Train	1956	12.50	25.00	50.00
❑ 1626	Roll Over Beethoven/Drifting Heart	1956	12.50	25.00	50.00
❑ 1635	Too Much Monkey Business/Brown Eyed Handsome Man	1956	12.50	25.00	50.00
❑ 1645	You Can't Catch Me/Havana Moon	1956	12.50	25.00	50.00
❑ 1653	School Day (Ring! Ring! Goes the Bell)/Deep Feeling	1957	12.50	25.00	50.00
❑ 1664	Oh Baby Doll/La Jaunda	1957	12.50	25.00	50.00
❑ 1671	Rock & Roll Music/Blue Feeling	1957	7.50	15.00	30.00
❑ 1683	Sweet Little Sixteen/Reelin' and Rockin'	1958	7.50	15.00	30.00
❑ 1691	Johnny B. Goode/Around and Around	1958	7.50	15.00	30.00
❑ 1697	Beautiful Delilah/Vacation Time	1958	7.50	15.00	30.00
❑ 1700	Carol/Hey Pedro	1958	7.50	15.00	30.00
❑ 1709	Sweet Little Rock and Roll/Joe Joe Gun	1958	7.50	15.00	30.00
❑ 1714	Run Rudolph Run/Merry Christmas Baby	1958	10.00	20.00	40.00
❑ 1716	Anthony Boy/That's My Desire	1959	7.50	15.00	30.00
❑ 1722	Almost Grown/Little Queenie	1959	7.50	15.00	30.00
❑ 1729	Back in the U.S.A./Memphis Tennessee	1959	7.50	15.00	30.00
❑ 1737	Broken Arrow/Childhood Sweetheart	1959	10.00	20.00	40.00
❑ 1747	Too Pooped to Pop ("Casey")/Let It Rock	1960	6.25	12.50	25.00
❑ 1754	Bye Bye Johnny/Worried Life Blues	1960	6.25	12.50	25.00
❑ 1763	I Got to Find My Baby/Mad Lad	1960	6.25	12.50	25.00
❑ 1767	Our Little Rendezvous/Jaguar and Thunderbird	1960	6.25	12.50	25.00
❑ 1779	I'm Talking About You/Little Star	1961	6.25	12.50	25.00
❑ 1799	Come On/Go-Go-Go	1961	5.00	10.00	20.00
❑ 1853	I'm Talking About You/Diploma for Two	1963	5.00	10.00	20.00
❑ 1866	Memphis/Sweet Little Sixteen	1963	5.00	10.00	20.00
❑ 1883	Nadine (Is It You?)/O Rangutang	1964	5.00	10.00	20.00
❑ 1898	No Particular Place to Go/You Two	1964	5.00	10.00	20.00
❑ 1898 [PS]	No Particular Place to Go/You Two	1964	12.50	25.00	50.00
❑ 1906	You Never Can Tell/Brenda Lee	1964	5.00	10.00	20.00
❑ 1906 [PS]	You Never Can Tell/Brenda Lee	1964	10.00	20.00	40.00
❑ 1912	Little Marie/Go Bobby Soxer	1964	3.75	7.50	15.00
❑ 1912 [PS]	Little Marie/Go Bobby Soxer	1964	10.00	20.00	40.00
❑ 1916	Promised Land/Things I Used to Do	1964	3.75	7.50	15.00
❑ 1916 [PS]	Promised Land/Things I Used to Do	1964	12.50	25.00	50.00
❑ 1926	Dear Dad/Lonely School Days	1965	3.75	7.50	15.00
❑ 1943	It Wasn't Me/Welcome Back Pretty Girl	1965	3.75	7.50	15.00
❑ 1943 [PS]	It Wasn't Me/Welcome Back Pretty Girl	1965	7.50	15.00	30.00
❑ 1963	Ramona Say Yes/Havana Moon	1966	3.75	7.50	15.00
❑ 1963	Ramona Say Yes/Lonely School Days	1966	3.75	7.50	15.00
❑ 2090	Tulane/Have Mercy Judge	1970	—	3.00	6.00
❑ 2131	My Ding-a-Ling/Johnny B. Goode	1972	—	2.00	4.00
—Orange and blue label					
❑ 2131	My Ding-a-Ling/Johnny B. Goode	1972	—	3.00	6.00
—All-blue label					
❑ 2136	Reelin' & Rockin'/Let's Boogie	1972	—	2.00	4.00
❑ 2140	Roll 'Em Pete/Bio	1973	—	2.00	4.00
❑ 2169	Baby What You Want Me to Do/Shake, Rattle and Roll	1975	—	2.00	4.00

COLLECTABLES

Number	Title (A Side/B Side)	Yr	VG	VG+	NM
❑ 3437	Run Rudolph Run/Merry Christmas Baby	199?	—	—	3.00

MERCURY

Number	Title (A Side/B Side)	Yr	VG	VG+	NM
❑ 30143	Maybellene/Sweet Little Sixteen	196?	—	3.00	6.00
❑ 30144	Memphis/School Day (Ring, Ring Goes the Bell)	196?	—	3.00	6.00
❑ 30145	Back in the U.S.A./Roll Over Beethoven	196?	—	3.00	6.00
❑ 30146	Johnny B. Goode/Rock and Roll Music	196?	—	3.00	6.00
—The Mercury 30000 series are re-recordings of the Chess hits					
❑ 72643	Club Nitty Gritty/Laugh and Cry	1966	2.50	5.00	10.00
❑ 72680	Back to Memphis/I Do Really Love You	1967	2.50	5.00	10.00
❑ 72748	It Hurts Me Too/Feelin' It	1967	2.50	5.00	10.00
❑ 72840	Louie to Frisco/Ma Dear	1968	2.50	5.00	10.00
❑ 72963	It's Too Dark in There/Good Looking Woman	1969	5.00	10.00	20.00
❑ 72963 [PS]	It's Too Dark in There/Good Looking Woman	1969	7.50	15.00	30.00

PHILCO-FORD

Number	Title (A Side/B Side)	Yr	VG	VG+	NM
❑ HP-34	Maybellene/Roll Over Beethoven	1969	5.00	10.00	20.00
—4-inch plastic "Hip Pocket Record" with color sleeve					

Number	Title (A Side/B Side)	Yr	VG	VG+	NM

7-Inch Extended Plays

CHESS

Number	Title (A Side/B Side)	Yr	VG	VG+	NM
❑ CH-5118	School Day (Ring, Ring Goes the Bell)/Wee Wee Hours//Brown Eyed Handsome Man/Too Much Monkey Business	1957	30.00	60.00	120.00
❑ CH-5118 [PS]	After School Session	1957	50.00	100.00	200.00
❑ CH-5119	Rock & Roll Music/Blue Feeling//Oh Baby Doll/La Jaunda (Espanol)	1957	25.00	50.00	100.00
❑ CH-5119 [PS]	Rock and Roll Music	1957	50.00	100.00	200.00
❑ CH-5121	Sweet Little Sixteen/Rockin' at the Philharmonic//Reelin' and Rockin'/Guitar Boogie	1958	25.00	50.00	100.00
❑ CH-5121 [PS]	Sweet Little Sixteen	1958	50.00	100.00	200.00
❑ CH-5124	(contents unknown)	1958	25.00	50.00	100.00
❑ CH-5124 [PS]	Pickin' Berries	1958	50.00	100.00	200.00
❑ EP-5126	Jo Jo Gun/Sweet Little Rock and Roller//Johnny B. Goode/Around and Around	1958	25.00	50.00	100.00
❑ EP-5126 [PS]	Sweet Little Rock and Roller	1958	50.00	100.00	200.00

Albums

ACCORD

Number	Title (A Side/B Side)	Yr	VG	VG+	NM
❑ SN-7171	Toronto Rock 'N' Roll Revival, Vol. 2	1982	2.50	5.00	10.00
❑ SN-7172	Toronto Rock 'N' Roll Revival, Vol. 3	1982	2.50	5.00	10.00

ATCO

Number	Title (A Side/B Side)	Yr	VG	VG+	NM
❑ SD 38-118	Rockit	1979	3.00	6.00	12.00

CHESS

Number	Title (A Side/B Side)	Yr	VG	VG+	NM
❑ LP-1426 [M]	After School Session	1958	50.00	100.00	200.00
❑ LPS-1426 [R]	After School Session	196?	3.00	6.00	12.00
❑ LP-1432 [M]	One Dozen Berrys	1958	50.00	100.00	200.00
❑ LPS-1432 [R]	One Dozen Berrys	196?	3.00	6.00	12.00
❑ LP-1435 [M]	Chuck Berry Is On Top	1959	45.00	90.00	180.00
❑ LPS-1435 [R]	Chuck Berry Is On Top	196?	3.00	6.00	12.00
❑ LP-1448 [M]	Rockin' at the Hops	1960	45.00	90.00	180.00
❑ LP-1456 [M]	New Juke Box Hits	1961	45.00	90.00	180.00
❑ LP-1465 [M]	Chuck Berry Twist	1962	25.00	50.00	100.00
❑ LP-1465 [M]	More Chuck Berry	1963	30.00	60.00	120.00
—Retitled version of above					
❑ LPS-1465 [R]	More Chuck Berry	196?	3.00	6.00	12.00
❑ LP-1480 [M]	Chuck Berry On Stage	1963	30.00	60.00	120.00
❑ LPS-1480 [R]	Chuck Berry On Stage	196?	3.00	6.00	12.00
❑ LP-1485 [M]	Chuck Berry's Greatest Hits	1964	30.00	60.00	120.00
❑ LPS-1485 [R]	Chuck Berry's Greatest Hits	196?	3.00	6.00	12.00
❑ LP-1488 [M]	St. Louis to Liverpool	1964	15.00	30.00	60.00
❑ LPS-1488 [S]	St. Louis to Liverpool	1964	20.00	40.00	80.00
❑ LP-1495 [M]	Chuck Berry in London	1965	7.50	15.00	30.00
❑ LPS-1495 [S]	Chuck Berry in London	1965	10.00	20.00	40.00
❑ LP-1498 [M]	Fresh Berry's	1965	7.50	15.00	30.00
❑ LPS-1498 [S]	Fresh Berry's	1965	10.00	20.00	40.00
❑ 2CH-1514 [(2)R]	Chuck Berry's Golden Decade	1972	3.75	7.50	15.00
—New cover has a pink radio					
❑ LP-1514 [(2)M]	Chuck Berry's Golden Decade	1967	10.00	20.00	40.00
❑ LPS-1514 [(2)R]	Chuck Berry's Golden Decade	1967	5.00	10.00	20.00
—Old cover does not have a pink radio					
❑ LPS-1550	Back Home	1970	5.00	10.00	20.00
❑ CH-9171	New Juke Box Hits	1986	2.50	5.00	10.00
—Reissue of 1456					
❑ CH-9186	St. Louis to Liverpool	1988	2.50	5.00	10.00
—Reissue of 1488					
❑ CH-9190	More Rock 'n' Roll Rarities	1986	2.50	5.00	10.00
❑ CH-9256	Chuck Berry Is On Top	1987	2.50	5.00	10.00
—Reissue of 1435					
❑ CH-9259	Rockin' at the Hop	1987	2.50	5.00	10.00
—Reissue of 1448					
❑ CH-9284	After School Session	1989	2.50	5.00	10.00
—Reissue of 1426					
❑ CH-9295	The London Chuck Berry Sessions	1989	2.50	5.00	10.00
—Reissue of 60020					
❑ CH-9318	Missing Berries: Rarities, Volume 3	1990	2.50	5.00	10.00
❑ CH-50008	San Fransisco Dues	1971	5.00	10.00	20.00
❑ CH-50043	Chuck Berry/Bio	1973	5.00	10.00	20.00
❑ CH-60020	The London Chuck Berry Sessions	1972	5.00	10.00	20.00
❑ 2CH-60023 [(2)]	Chuck Berry's Golden Decade, Vol. 2	1973	6.25	12.50	25.00
❑ 2CH-60028 [(2)]	Chuck Berry's Golden Decade, Vol. 3	1974	6.25	12.50	25.00
❑ CH6-80001 [(6)]	The Chess Box	1989	12.50	25.00	50.00
❑ CH2-92500 [(2)]	The Great Twenty-Eight	1983	3.00	6.00	12.00
❑ CH2-92521 [(2)]	Rock 'n' Roll Rarities	1986	3.75	7.50	15.00

EVEREST ARCHIVE OF FOLK & JAZZ

Number	Title (A Side/B Side)	Yr	VG	VG+	NM
❑ FS-321	Chuck Berry's Greatest Hits	1976	2.50	5.00	10.00

GUSTO

Number	Title (A Side/B Side)	Yr	VG	VG+	NM
❑ 0004	The Best of the Best of Chuck Berry	198?	2.50	5.00	10.00

MERCURY

Number	Title (A Side/B Side)	Yr	VG	VG+	NM
❑ SRM-2-6501 [(2)]	St. Louis to Frisco to Memphis	1972	5.00	10.00	20.00
❑ MG-21103 [M]	Chuck Berry's Golden Hits	1967	3.75	7.50	15.00
❑ MG-21123 [M]	Chuck Berry in Memphis	1967	3.75	7.50	15.00
❑ MG-21138 [M]	Love at the Fillmore Auditorium	1967	5.00	10.00	20.00
❑ SR-61103 [S]	Chuck Berry's Golden Hits	1967	3.75	7.50	15.00
❑ SR-61123 [S]	Chuck Berry in Memphis	1967	3.75	7.50	15.00
❑ SR-61138 [S]	Love at the Fillmore Auditorium	1967	5.00	10.00	20.00
❑ SR-61176	From St. Louie to Frisco	1968	5.00	10.00	20.00
❑ SR-61223	Concerto in B Goode	1969	5.00	10.00	20.00
❑ 826256-1	Chuck Berry's Golden Hits	1985	2.00	4.00	8.00
—Reissue					

PICKWICK

Number	Title (A Side/B Side)	Yr	VG	VG+	NM
❑ PTP-2061 [(2)]	Flashback	1975	3.00	6.00	12.00
❑ SPC-3327	Johnny B. Goode	1973	2.50	5.00	10.00
❑ SPC-3345	Sweet Little Rock and Roller	1974	2.50	5.00	10.00
❑ SPC-3392	Wild Berrys	1974	2.50	5.00	10.00

QUICKSILVER

Number	Title (A Side/B Side)	Yr	VG	VG+	NM
❑ QS-1017	Live Hits	198?	2.50	5.00	10.00

SSS INTERNATIONAL

Number	Title (A Side/B Side)	Yr	VG	VG+	NM
❑ 36	Chuck Berry Live	1981	2.50	5.00	10.00

B

Number	Title (A Side/B Side)	Yr	VG	VG+	NM
BERRY, DAVE					
45s					
LONDON					
❏ 9666	Memphis Tennessee/My Baby Left Me	1964	3.75	7.50	15.00
❏ 9698	The Crying Game/Don't Gimme No Lip Child	1964	4.00	8.00	16.00
❏ 9781	This Strange Effect/Now	1965	3.75	7.50	15.00
❏ 20038	Do I Still Figure in Your Life/Latisha	1968	2.00	4.00	8.00
PARROT					
❏ 40010	Picture Me Gone/Baby's Gone	1967	2.50	5.00	10.00
BERRY, JAN Includes records as "Jan Barry" and "I Jan I." Also see JAN AND DEAN.					
45s					
A&M					
❏ 1957	Little Queenie/That's the Way It Is	1977	3.75	7.50	15.00
❏ 2020	Skateboard Surfin' U.S.A. (Sidewalk Surfin' with Me)/How How I Love You	1978	3.75	7.50	15.00
LIBERTY					
❏ 55845	The Universal Coward/I Can't Wait to Love You	1965	5.00	10.00	20.00
❏ 55845 [PS]	The Universal Coward/I Can't Wait to Love You	1965	75.00	150.00	300.00
ODE					
❏ 66023	Mother Earth/Blue Moon Shuffle	1972	5.00	10.00	20.00
❏ 66034	Don't You Just Know It/Blue Moon Shuffle	1973	10.00	20.00	40.00
—With Brian Wilson on co-lead vocals on A-side					
❏ 66050	Tinsel Town/Blow Up Music	1974	5.00	10.00	20.00
—As "I Jan I"					
❏ 66120	Sing Sang a Song/Sing Sang a Song (Singalong Version)	1976	5.00	10.00	20.00
RIPPLE					
❏ 6101	Tomorrow's Teardrops/My Midsummer Night's Dream	1961	25.00	50.00	100.00
—As "Jan Barry"					
BERRY, JOHN					
45s					
DOT					
❏ 16132	Dance with Me Darlin'/Lucy Lou	1960	3.00	6.00	12.00
BERRY, KEN					
45s					
BARNABY					
❏ 2020	Lonely Street/Ain't That a Shame	1970	2.00	4.00	8.00
❏ 2034	Everyday with You/He'll Have to Go	1971	2.00	4.00	8.00
Albums					
BARNABY					
❏ Z 30014	R.F.D.	1970	6.25	12.50	25.00
❏ Z 30094	Ken Berry, R.F.D.	1970	7.50	15.00	30.00
BERRY, MIKE					
45s					
CORAL					
❏ 62341	A Tribute to Buddy Holly/Every Little Kiss	1962	15.00	30.00	60.00
❏ 62357	Don't You Think It's Time/Loneliness	1963	7.50	15.00	30.00
❏ 62483	Gonna Fall in Love/It Comes and Goes	1966	4.00	8.00	16.00
EPIC					
❏ 50748	I Am a Rocker/Boogaloo Dues	1979	—	2.00	4.00
❏ 50913	Stay Close to Me/One by One	1980	—	2.00	4.00
MCA					
❏ 40432	Don't Be Cruel/It's All Over	1975	—	2.50	5.00
Albums					
EPIC					
❏ JE 36071	I'm a Rocker	1979	2.50	5.00	10.00
SIRE					
❏ SASD 7524	Rocks in My Head	1976	3.75	7.50	15.00
BERRY, RICHARD					
45s					
FLAIR					
❏ 1016	I'm Still in Love with You/One Little Prayer	1953	20.00	40.00	80.00
❏ 1052	Bye Bye/At Last	1954	15.00	30.00	60.00
—With the Dreamers					
❏ 1055	What You Do to Me/The Big Break	1954	15.00	30.00	60.00
❏ 1058	Daddy Daddy/Baby Darling	1954	15.00	30.00	60.00
—With the Dreamers					
❏ 1064	Please Tell Me/Oh Oh Get Out of the Car	1955	12.50	25.00	50.00
❏ 1068	God Gave Me You/Doncha Go	1955	12.50	25.00	50.00
❏ 1071	Next Time/Crazy Lover	1955	12.50	25.00	50.00
❏ 1075	Together/Jelly Roll	1955	12.50	25.00	50.00
FLIP					
❏ 318	Take the Key/No Kissin' and Huggin'	1956	10.00	20.00	40.00
❏ 321	Louie, Louie/Rock, Rock, Rock	1957	10.00	20.00	40.00
❏ 321	Louie, Louie/You Are My Sunshine	1957	15.00	30.00	60.00
❏ 327	Sweet Sugar You/Rock, Rock, Rock	1957	10.00	20.00	40.00
❏ 331	You're the Girl/You Look So Good	1958	10.00	20.00	40.00
❏ 336	Heaven on Wheels/The Mess Around	1958	10.00	20.00	40.00
❏ 339	Besame Mucho/Do I, Do I	1958	7.50	15.00	30.00
❏ 349	Have Love, Will Travel/No Room	1960	7.50	15.00	30.00
❏ 352	I'll Never Ever Love Again/Somewhere There's a Rainbow	1961	7.50	15.00	30.00
❏ 360	You Look So Good/You Are My Sunshine	1962	7.50	15.00	30.00
HAPPY TIGER					
❏ 5063	Louie Louie/Rock Rock Rock	1972	2.00	4.00	8.00
K&G					
❏ 9001	I'm Your Fool/In a Really Big Way	1961	7.50	15.00	30.00
RPM					
❏ 448	Rockin' Man/Big John	1955	25.00	50.00	100.00
❏ 452	Pretty Brown Eyes/I Am Bewildered	1956	7.50	15.00	30.00
❏ 465	Angel of My Life/Yama Yama-Pretty Mama	1956	25.00	50.00	100.00
❏ 477	Wait for Me/Good Love	1956	7.50	15.00	30.00
SMASH					
❏ 1789	What Good Is a Heart/Everybody's Got a Lover But Me	1963	3.00	6.00	12.00
❏ 1811	I'm Learning/Empty Chair	1963	3.00	6.00	12.00

Number	Title (A Side/B Side)	Yr	VG	VG+	NM
WARNER BROS.					
❏ 5164	Walk Right In/It's All Right	1960	12.50	25.00	50.00
Albums					
CROWN					
❏ CST-371 [R]	Richard Berry and the Dreamers	1963	7.50	15.00	30.00
❏ CLP-5371 [M]	Richard Berry and the Dreamers	1963	15.00	30.00	60.00
PAM					
❏ 1001	Live at the Century Restaurant	1968	10.00	20.00	40.00
❏ 1002	Wild Berry	196?	10.00	20.00	40.00
BERRY KIDS, THE					
45s					
MGM					
❏ 12379	Go, Go, Go, Right Into Town/Love Me, Love	1956	20.00	40.00	80.00
❏ 12496	Rootie Tootie/Yo're My Teenage Baby	1957	20.00	40.00	80.00
BEST, BILLY, AND THE DITALIANS					
45s					
MERCURY					
❏ 72923	Baby That Takes the Cake/Time Is Getting Hard Josephine	1969	2.00	4.00	8.00
BEST, PETER (1) Former drummer with THE BEATLES.					
45s					
CAMEO					
❏ 391	Boys/Kansas City	1965	20.00	40.00	80.00
❏ 391 [PS]	Boys/Kansas City	1965	25.00	50.00	100.00
HAPPENING					
❏ 405	If You Can't Get Her/Don't Play with Me	1964	45.00	90.00	180.00
❏ 1117/8	If You Can't Get Her/The Way I Feel About You	1966	37.50	75.00	150.00
—Label credit: "Best of the Beatles (Peter Best)"					
MR. MAESTRO					
❏ 711	I Can't Do Without You Now/Keys to My Heart	1965	37.50	75.00	150.00
—Label credit: "Best of the Beatles"; blue vinyl					
❏ 711	I Can't Do Without You Now/Keys to My Heart	1965	50.00	100.00	200.00
—Label credit: "Best of the Beatles"; black vinyl					
❏ 712	Casting My Spell/I'm Blue	1965	37.50	75.00	150.00
—Black vinyl					
❏ 712	Casting My Spell/I'm Blue	1965	50.00	100.00	200.00
—Blue vinyl					
ORIGINAL BEATLES DRUMMER					
❏ 800	(I'll Try) Anyway/I Wanna Be There	1964	45.00	90.00	180.00
Albums					
PHOENIX					
❏ PHX-340	The Beatle That Time Forgot	1982	3.00	6.00	12.00
SAVAGE					
❏ BM-71	Best of the Beatles	1966	50.00	100.00	200.00
—Authentic copies have white circle around the word "Savage" and white circle around Pete Best's head on the album cover.					
BEST, PETER (2) This Peter Best is from Australia.					
45s					
CAPITOL					
❏ 2092	Carousel of Love/Want You	1968	7.50	15.00	30.00
BEST THINGS, THE					
45s					
UNITED ARTISTS					
❏ 50027	Chicks Are for Kids/You May See Me Cry	1966	2.50	5.00	10.00
BETH, KAREN					
Albums					
DECCA					
❏ DL 75148	The Joys of Life	1969	3.75	7.50	15.00
❏ DL 75247	Harvest	1970	3.75	7.50	15.00
BETTS, DICKEY Also see THE ALLMAN BROTHERS BAND.					
45s					
ARISTA					
❏ 0255	Nothing You Can Do	1977	—	2.00	4.00
❏ 0269	Bougainvilla/Sweet Virginia	1977	—	2.00	4.00
❏ 0333	Atlanta's Burning Down/Mr. Blues Man	1978	—	2.00	4.00
CAPRICORN					
❏ 0213	Kissimmee Kid/Long Time Gone	1974	—	2.50	5.00
❏ 0221	Highway Call/Rain	1975	—	2.50	5.00
Albums					
ARISTA					
❏ AL 4123	Dickey Betts & Great Southern	1977	2.50	5.00	10.00
❏ AL 4168	Atlanta's Burning Down	1978	2.50	5.00	10.00
CAPRICORN					
❏ CP 0123	Highway Call	1974	3.00	6.00	12.00
—As "Richard Betts"					
EPIC					
❏ FE 44289	Pattern Disruptive	1988	2.50	5.00	10.00
BEVEL, CHARLES					
45s					
A&M					
❏ 1481	Making a Decision/Meet "Mississippi Charles Bevel"	1973	—	2.50	5.00
❏ 1481	Black Santa Claus/Making A Decision (Bring On Sunshine)	1973	—	3.00	6.00
❏ 1501	Sally B. White/Porcupine Meat	1974	—	2.50	5.00
❏ 1608	Don't Lie to Me/It Ain't Magic	1974	—	2.50	5.00
❏ AM-8725	Black Santa Claus/Sally B. White	199?	—	—	3.00
—Reissue					
Albums					
A&M					
❏ SP-4412	Meet "Mississippi Charles"	1973	3.00	6.00	12.00

Number	Title (A Side/B Side)	Yr	VG	VG+	NM
BEVERLY SISTERS, THE					
45s					
LONDON					
❏ 1703	Greensleeves/I'll See You in My Dreams	1956	3.00	6.00	12.00
❏ 1731	Blow the Wind Southerly/Doodle Doo Doo	1957	3.00	6.00	12.00
❏ 1757	Old Enough to Know/I Remember Mama	1957	3.00	6.00	12.00
❏ 1783	Long Black Nylons/Young Cavalier	1958	3.00	6.00	12.00
❏ 1862	The Little Drummer Boy/Strawberry Fair	1958	3.00	6.00	12.00
❏ 1891	Little Donkey/Toy Dream	1960	3.00	6.00	12.00
MERCURY					
❏ 71671	Oh Ricky/Only Me	1960	3.00	6.00	12.00
ROULETTE					
❏ 4350	Flight 1203/(B-side unknown)	1961	3.00	6.00	12.00
BI-TONES, THE					
45s					
BLUE JAY					
❏ 1000	Oh How I Love You So/Beatnik Girl	1960	6.25	12.50	25.00
BIDDU ORCHESTRA					
12-Inch Singles					
EPIC					
❏ AE 348 [DJ]	Funky Tropical (4:09) (same on both sides)	1977	5.00	10.00	20.00
❏ 28-50397	Funky Tropical (6:17)/Boogiethon (5:45)	1977	5.00	10.00	20.00
45s					
COLOSSUS					
❏ 125	The Sooner I Get to You/(B-side unknown)	1970	2.00	4.00	8.00
—As "Biddu"					
EPIC					
❏ 50139	Summer of '42/Northern Dancer	1975	1.00	2.00	4.00
❏ 50173	I Could Have Danced All Night/Jump for Joy	1975	1.00	2.00	4.00
❏ 50212	Rainforest/Hot Ice	1976	—	2.00	4.00
❏ 50387	Funky Tropical/Girl You'll Be a Woman Soon	1977	—	2.00	4.00
❏ 50439	Soal Coaxing/Nirvana	1977	—	2.00	4.00
Albums					
EPIC					
❏ PE 33903	Biddu Orchestra	1975	2.50	5.00	10.00
❏ PE 34230	Rain Forest	1976	2.50	5.00	10.00
❏ PE 34723	Eastern Man	1977	2.50	5.00	10.00
BIG BEATS, THE Also see TRINI LOPEZ.					
45s					
COLUMBIA					
❏ 41072	Clark's Expedition/Big Boy	1958	6.25	12.50	25.00
❏ 41179	Rush Me/Sentimental Journey	1958	6.25	12.50	25.00
Albums					
LIBERTY					
❏ LRP-3407 [M]	The Big Beats Live	1965	7.50	15.00	30.00
❏ LST-7407 [S]	The Big Beats Live	1965	10.00	20.00	40.00
BIG BLACK No relation to the 1980s punk band of the same name.					
45s					
UNI					
❏ 55051	The Snakecharmer/Come On and Get It Baby	1968	2.00	4.00	8.00
❏ 55099	Come On Down to the Beach/Love, Sweet Like Sugarcane	1968	2.00	4.00	8.00
❏ 55293	Long Hair/Diggin' What You're Doing	1971	—	3.00	6.00
❏ 55337	Mellow/Diggin' What You're Doing	1972	—	3.00	6.00
Albums					
UNI					
❏ 73018	Elements of Now	1968	3.75	7.50	15.00
❏ 73033	Lion Walk	1969	3.75	7.50	15.00
❏ 73134	Big Black and the Blues	1972	3.75	7.50	15.00
BIG BOPPER					
45s					
D					
❏ 1008	Chantilly Lace/The Purple People Eater Meets the Witch Doctor	1958	62.50	125.00	250.00
MERCURY					
❏ 71219	Beggar to a King/Crazy Blue	1957	15.00	30.00	60.00
—As "Jape Richardson"					
❏ 71312	A Teenage Mom/Monkey Song	1958	15.00	30.00	60.00
—As "Jape Richardson"					
❏ 71343	Chantilly Lace/The Purple People Eater Meets the Witch Doctor	1958	5.00	10.00	20.00
❏ 71375	Big Bopper's Wedding/Little Red Riding Hood	1958	3.75	7.50	15.00
❏ 71416	Someone's Watching Over You/Walking Through My Dreams	1959	3.75	7.50	15.00
❏ 71451	It's the Truth, Ruth/That's What I'm Talkin' About	1959	3.75	7.50	15.00
❏ 71482	Pink Petticoats/Time Clock	1959	3.75	7.50	15.00
WING					
❏ 17000	Chantilly Lace/Someone Watching Over You	196?	2.50	5.00	10.00
—Reissue					
Albums					
MERCURY					
❏ MG-20402 [M]	Chantilly Lace	1959	125.00	250.00	500.00
—Black label					
❏ MG-20402 [M]	Chantilly Lace	196?	6.25	12.50	25.00
—Red label with twelve Mercury logos on label edge					
❏ MG-20402 [M]	Chantilly Lace	1964	50.00	100.00	200.00
—Red label with black or black & white Mercury logo at top					
❏ MG-20402 [M]	Chantilly Lace	1975	3.75	7.50	15.00
—Chicago skyline label					
❏ 832902-1 [M]	Chantilly Lace	1988	3.75	7.50	15.00
—New number, black label					
PICKWICK					
❏ SPC-3365	Chantilly Lace	1973	3.75	7.50	15.00
RHINO					
❏ R1-70164	Helloooo Baby! The Best of the Big Bopper 1954-1959	1989	3.00	6.00	12.00

Number	Title (A Side/B Side)	Yr	VG	VG+	NM
BIG BROTHER					
45s					
ALL AMERICAN					
❏ 5718	E.S.P./Brother, Where Are You	1970	10.00	20.00	40.00
Albums					
ALL-AMERICAN					
❏ 5770	Big Brother	1970	37.50	75.00	150.00
BIG BROTHER AND THE HOLDING COMPANY Also see JANIS JOPLIN.					
45s					
COLUMBIA					
❏ 44626	Piece of My Heart/Turtle Blues	1968	2.50	5.00	10.00
❏ 45284	Keep On/Home on the Strange	1970	—	3.00	6.00
❏ 45502	Black Widow Spider/Nu Boogaloo Jam	1971	—	3.00	6.00
MAINSTREAM					
❏ 657	All Is Loneliness/Blindman	1967	3.00	6.00	12.00
❏ 662	Down on Me/Call On Me	1967	3.00	6.00	12.00
❏ 666	Bye Bye Baby/Intruder	1968	3.00	6.00	12.00
❏ 675	Women Is Losers/Light Is Faster Than Sound	1968	3.00	6.00	12.00
❏ 675	Women Is Losers/Caterpillar	1968	20.00	40.00	80.00
—This is much rarer than the version with the other flip side					
❏ 678	Coo Coo/The Last Time	1968	3.00	6.00	12.00
Albums					
COLUMBIA					
❏ KCL 2900 [M]	Cheap Thrills	1968	75.00	150.00	300.00
—Red label stock copy has been confirmed					
❏ KCS 9700 [M]	Cheap Thrills	1968	25.00	50.00	100.00
—White label "Special Mono Radio Station Copy" with stereo number					
❏ KCS 9700 [S]	Cheap Thrills	1968	6.25	12.50	25.00
—Red "360 Sound" label					
❏ KCS 9700	Cheap Thrills	1970	3.00	6.00	12.00
—Orange label					
❏ PC 9700	Cheap Thrills	198?	2.00	4.00	8.00
—Reissue with new prefix					
❏ C 30222	Be a Brother	1970	5.00	10.00	20.00
❏ C 30631	Big Brother and the Holding Company	1971	5.00	10.00	20.00
—Reissue of Mainstream LP with two extra tracks					
❏ C 30738	How Hard It Is	1971	5.00	10.00	20.00
COLUMBIA SPECIAL PRODUCTS					
❏ P 13313	Big Brother and the Holding Company	197?	3.75	7.50	15.00
MAINSTREAM					
❏ S-6099 [S]	Big Brother and the Holding Company	1967	12.50	25.00	50.00
❏ 56099 [M]	Big Brother and the Holding Company	1967	25.00	50.00	100.00
BIG DADDY AND HIS BOYS					
45s					
KING					
❏ 5013	Bacon Fat/Bad Boy	1957	6.25	12.50	25.00
BIG ED AND HIS COMBO See EDDIE BURNS.					
BIG FOOT					
Albums					
WINRO					
❏ 1004	Big Foot	1969	7.50	15.00	30.00
BIG FRANK AND THE ESSENCES					
45s					
BLUE ROCK					
❏ 4012	Secret/I Won't Let Her See Me Cry	1965	50.00	100.00	200.00
PHILIPS					
❏ 40283	Secret/I Won't Let Her See Me Cry	1965	25.00	50.00	100.00
BIG GUYS, THE					
45s					
PALETTE					
❏ 5110	Walkin' the Board/Faith 7	1963	6.25	12.50	25.00
❏ 5114	Propulsion/(B-side unknown)	1964	6.25	12.50	25.00
WARNER BROS.					
❏ 7047	Hang My Head and Cry/Mr. Cupid (Don't You Call on Me)	1967	12.50	25.00	50.00
BIG MAYBELLE					
45s					
BRUNSWICK					
❏ 55234	Candy/Cry	1962	3.00	6.00	12.00
❏ 55242	Cold, Cold Heart/Why Was I Born	1963	3.00	6.00	12.00
❏ 55256	Everybody's Got a Home But Me/How Deep Is the Ocean	1963	3.00	6.00	12.00
CHESS					
❏ 1967	It's a Man's Man's Man's World/Big Maybelle Sings the Blues	1966	2.50	5.00	10.00
OKEH					
❏ 6931	Gabbin' Blues/Rain Down Rain	1953	10.00	20.00	40.00
❏ 6955	Way Back Home/Just Want Your Love	1953	10.00	20.00	40.00
❏ 6998	Send for Me/Jimmy Mule	1953	10.00	20.00	40.00
❏ 7009	My Country Man/Maybelle's Blues	1953	10.00	20.00	40.00
❏ 7026	I've Got a Feelin'/You'll Never Know	1954	7.50	15.00	30.00
❏ 7042	My Big Mistake/I'm Gettin' 'Long Alright	1954	7.50	15.00	30.00
❏ 7053	Ain't No Use/Don't Leave Poor Me	1955	7.50	15.00	30.00
❏ 7060	Whole Lotta Shakin' Goin' On/One Monkey Don't Stop No Show	1955	7.50	15.00	30.00
❏ 7066	Such a Cutie/The Other Night	1956	7.50	15.00	30.00
❏ 7069	Gabbin' Blues/New Kind of Mambo	1956	7.50	15.00	30.00
PARAMOUNT					
❏ 0237	Blame It on Your Love/See See Rider	1973	—	3.00	6.00
PORT					
❏ 3002	Let Me Go/No Better for You	1965	3.00	6.00	12.00
ROJAC					
❏ 112	96 Tears/That's Life	1966	2.50	5.00	10.00
❏ 115	I Can't Wait Any Longer/Turn the World Around the Other Way	1967	2.00	4.00	8.00

Number	Title (A Side/B Side)	Yr	VG	VG+	NM
❏ 116	Mama (He Treats Your Daughter Mean)/				
	Keep That Man	1967	2.00	4.00	8.00
❏ 118	Quittin' Time/I Can't Wait Any Longer	1967	2.00	4.00	8.00
❏ 121	Heaven Will Welcome You, Dr. King/				
	Eleanor Rigby	1968	2.50	5.00	10.00
❏ 124	How It Lies/Old Love Never Dies	1968	2.00	4.00	8.00
❏ 1003	Careless Love/My Mother's Eyes	196?	2.00	4.00	8.00
❏ 1969	Don't Pass Me By/It's Been Raining	1966	2.50	5.00	10.00
SAVOY					
❏ 1195	Candy/That's a Pretty Good Love	1956	5.00	10.00	20.00
❏ 1500	Mean to Me/Tell Me Who	1956	3.75	7.50	15.00
❏ 1512	I Don't Want to Cry/All of Me	1957	3.75	7.50	15.00
❏ 1519	Rock House/Jim	1957	3.75	7.50	15.00
❏ 1527	So Long/Ring Dang Dilly	1957	3.75	7.50	15.00
❏ 1536	Blues Early, Early (Part 1)/				
	Blues Early, Early (Part 2)	1958	3.75	7.50	15.00
❏ 1541	White Christmas/Silent Night	1958	3.75	7.50	15.00
❏ 1558	Baby Won't You Please Come Home/				
	Say It Isn't Do	1959	3.75	7.50	15.00
❏ 1572	A Good Man Is Hard to Find/Pitiful	1959	3.75	7.50	15.00
❏ 1576	Some of These Days/I Understand	1959	3.75	7.50	15.00
❏ 1583	I Got It Bad and That Ain't Good/Ramblin' Blues	1960	3.75	7.50	15.00
❏ 1583	I Got It Bad and That Ain't Good/Until the Real				
	Thing Comes Along	1960	3.75	7.50	15.00
❏ 1595	I Ain't Got Nobody/Going Home Baby	1961	3.75	7.50	15.00
SCEPTER					
❏ 1288	I Don't Want to Cry/Yesterday's Kisses	1965	3.00	6.00	12.00
Albums					
BRUNSWICK					
❏ BL 54107 [M]	What More Can a Woman Do	1962	12.50	25.00	50.00
❏ BL 754107 [S]	What More Can a Woman Do	1962	17.50	35.00	70.00
❏ BL 754142	The Gospel Soul of Big Maybelle	1968	10.00	20.00	40.00
EPIC					
❏ EE 22011 [M]	Gabbin' Blues	196?	7.50	15.00	30.00
—Reissue of Okeh recordings					
PARAMOUNT					
❏ PAS-1011 [(2)]	The Last of Big Maybelle	1973	6.25	12.50	25.00
ROJAC					
❏ RS 123	Saga of the Good Life and Hard Times	196?	10.00	20.00	40.00
❏ R 522 [M]	Got a Brand New Bag	1967	10.00	20.00	40.00
❏ RS 522 [S]	Got a Brand New Bag	1967	10.00	20.00	40.00
SAVOY					
❏ MG-14005 [M]	Big Maybelle Sings	1957	75.00	150.00	300.00
❏ MG-14011 [M]	Blues, Candy and Big Maybelle	1958	75.00	150.00	300.00
SAVOY JAZZ					
❏ SJL-1143	Roots of Rock 'n' Roll Vol. 13: Blues & Early Soul	1985	2.50	5.00	10.00
❏ SJL-1168	Blues, Candy and Big Maybelle	1986	2.50	5.00	10.00
—Reissue of 14011					
SCEPTER					
❏ S-522 [M]	The Soul of Big Maybelle	1964	10.00	20.00	40.00
❏ SS-522 [S]	The Soul of Big Maybelle	1964	12.50	25.00	50.00

BIG MOUTH
45s
SPINDIZZY

Number	Title (A Side/B Side)	Yr	VG	VG+	NM
❏ ZS7 4004	Where the Master Lives/Too Busy	1972	—	3.00	6.00

BIG STAR Alex Chilton, formerly of THE BOX TOPS, was lead singer.
45s
ARDENT

Number	Title (A Side/B Side)	Yr	VG	VG+	NM
❏ 2902	When My Baby's Beside Me/In the Street	1972	6.25	12.50	25.00
❏ 2904	Watch the Sunrise/Don't Lie to Me	1972	6.25	12.50	25.00
—With correct song on B-side. Label has the number "AS-01180" on it.					
❏ 2904	Watch the Sunrise/Don't Lie to Me	1972	12.50	25.00	50.00
—B-side plays the song "Thirteen" in error. Label has the number "AS-01127" on it.					
❏ 2909	O My Soul/Morphatoo—I'm in Love with a Girl	1974	5.00	10.00	20.00
❏ 2912	September Gurls/(B-side unknown)	1974	5.00	10.00	20.00
Albums					
ARDENT					
❏ ADS-1501	Radio City	1974	7.50	15.00	30.00
❏ ADS-2803	#1 Record	1972	6.25	12.50	25.00
PVC					
❏ 7903	Big Star's Third	1978	6.25	12.50	25.00
❏ 8933	Sister Lovers	1985	3.75	7.50	15.00
—Reissue of PVC 7903 with new title					

BIG THREE, THE Also see CASS ELLIOT.
45s
FM

Number	Title (A Side/B Side)	Yr	VG	VG+	NM
❏ 3003	The Banjo Song/Winkin' Blinkin' and Nod	1964	3.75	7.50	15.00
—Second issue, distributed by Vee Jay					
❏ 9001	Come Away/Rider	1963	3.75	7.50	15.00
❏ 9004	The Banjo Song/Winkin' Blinkin' Nod	1963	5.00	10.00	20.00
—Original issue (possibly promo only), distributed by Roulette					
ROULETTE					
❏ 4689	Nora's Dove (Dink's Song)/Grandfather's Clock	1966	2.50	5.00	10.00
TOLLIE					
❏ 9006	The Banjo Song/Winkin' Blinkin' and Nod	1964	3.00	6.00	12.00
—Third issue					
Albums					
FM					
❏ 307 [M]	The Big Three	1963	7.50	15.00	30.00
❏ S-307 [S]	The Big Three	1963	10.00	20.00	40.00
❏ 311 [M]	Live at the Recording Studio	1964	7.50	15.00	30.00
❏ S-311 [S]	Live at the Recording Studio	1964	10.00	20.00	40.00
ROULETTE					
❏ R-42000 [M]	The Big Three Featuring Cass Elliot	1967	5.00	10.00	20.00
❏ SR-42000 [S]	The Big Three Featuring Cass Elliot	1967	6.25	12.50	25.00

BIG WHEELIE AND THE HUB CAPS
45s
MCA

Number	Title (A Side/B Side)	Yr	VG	VG+	NM
❏ 40951	Sh-Boom (Life Could Be a Dream)/				
	Touch and Go	1978	—	2.50	5.00
SCEPTER					
❏ 12375	Elvis Presley Medley/Chuck Berry Medley	1973	2.50	5.00	10.00
❏ 12385	Little Richard Medley/Over the Mountain	1973	2.50	5.00	10.00
❏ 12392	Leader of the Pack/Redneck Rock and Rollers	1974	2.00	4.00	8.00
Albums					
SCEPTER					
❏ SPS-5109	Solid Grease!	1973	3.00	6.00	12.00

BIKINIS, THE
45s
DOT

Number	Title (A Side/B Side)	Yr	VG	VG+	NM
❏ 15808	Fatima the Dreamer/Kitchy Koo	1958	6.25	12.50	25.00
❏ 15872	Chop Stick Rock/A'Right, A'Ready	1958	10.00	20.00	40.00
ROULETTE					
❏ 4073	Bikini/Boogie Rock 'n' Roll	1958	6.25	12.50	25.00
TOP RANK					
❏ 2032	Crazy Vibrations/Spunky	1959	6.25	12.50	25.00

BILK, ACKER
45s
ATCO

Number	Title (A Side/B Side)	Yr	VG	VG+	NM
❏ 6160	Summer Set/Acker's Away	1960	2.50	5.00	10.00
❏ 6190	Buona Sera/Corinne, Corinna	1961	2.50	5.00	10.00
❏ 6217	Stranger on the Shore/Cieleto Lindo	1962	3.00	6.00	12.00
❏ 6230	Above the Stars/Soft Sands	1962	2.50	5.00	10.00
❏ 6238	Lonely/Lime Light	1962	2.50	5.00	10.00
❏ 6247	A Taste of Honey/Only You (& You Alone)	1963	2.00	4.00	8.00
❏ 6264	Underneath the Arches/Lady of the Lake	1963	2.00	4.00	8.00
❏ 6269	Moonlight Tango/Never Love a Stranger	1963	2.00	4.00	8.00
❏ 6282	The Harem/Train Song	1964	2.00	4.00	8.00
❏ 6311	Dream Ska/Ska Face	1964	2.00	4.00	8.00
❏ 6323	The Good Life/Theme from Warsaw Concerto	1964	2.00	4.00	8.00
❏ 6441	La Playa/When You Are There	1966	—	3.00	6.00
❏ 6514	Limehouse Blues/Wot Cher				
	(Knocked 'Em In the Old Kent Road)	1967	—	3.00	6.00
PYE					
❏ 71078	Aria/The Fool on the Hill	1976	—	2.00	4.00
REPRISE					
❏ 20090	Dardenella Part 1/Dardenella Part 2	1962	3.75	7.50	15.00
Albums					
ATCO					
❏ 33-129 [M]	Stranger on the Shore	1961	3.75	7.50	15.00
❏ SD 33-129 [S]	Stranger on the Shore	1961	5.00	10.00	20.00
❏ 33-144 [M]	Above the Stars	1962	3.75	7.50	15.00
❏ SD 33-144 [S]	Above the Stars	1962	5.00	10.00	20.00
❏ 33-150 [M]	Only You	1963	3.75	7.50	15.00
❏ SD 33-150 [S]	Only You	1963	5.00	10.00	20.00
❏ 33-158 [M]	Call Me Mister	1963	3.75	7.50	15.00
❏ SD 33-158 [S]	Call Me Mister	1963	5.00	10.00	20.00
❏ 33-168 [M]	A Touch of Latin	1964	3.00	6.00	12.00
❏ SD 33-168 [S]	A Touch of Latin	1964	3.75	7.50	15.00
❏ 33-170 [M]	Great Themes from Great Foreign Films	1965	3.00	6.00	12.00
❏ SD 33-170 [S]	Great Themes from Great Foreign Films	1965	3.75	7.50	15.00
❏ 33-181 [M]	Acker Bilk in Paris	1966	3.00	6.00	12.00
❏ SD 33-181 [S]	Acker Bilk in Paris	1966	3.75	7.50	15.00
❏ 33-197 [M]	Mood for Love	1966	3.00	6.00	12.00
❏ SD 33-197 [S]	Mood for Love	1966	3.75	7.50	15.00
GNP CRESCENDO					
❏ GNPS-2116	The Best of Acker Bilk: His Clarinet and Strings	198?	2.50	5.00	10.00
❏ GNPS-2171	The Best of Acker Bilk: His Clarinet and Strings,				
	Volume 2	198?	2.50	5.00	10.00
❏ GNPS-2191	Acker Bilk Plays Lennon and McCartney	1988	3.00	6.00	12.00
REPRISE					
❏ R-6031 [M]	A Stranger No More	1962	5.00	10.00	20.00
❏ RS-6031 [R]	A Stranger No More	1962	3.75	7.50	15.00

BILK, ACKER, AND KEN COLYER
Albums
STOMP OFF

Number	Title (A Side/B Side)	Yr	VG	VG+	NM
❏ SOS-1119	It Looks Like a Big Time Tonight	198?	2.50	5.00	10.00

BILK, ACKER, AND BENT FABRIC Also see each artist's individual listings.
45s
ATCO

Number	Title (A Side/B Side)	Yr	VG	VG+	NM
❏ 6378	Alley Cat/Stranger on the Shore	1965	—	3.00	6.00
Albums					
ATCO					
❏ 33-175 [M]	Together	1965	3.00	6.00	12.00
❏ SD 33-175 [S]	Together	1965	3.75	7.50	15.00

BILLARD, DOUG, AND THE SOUL PATROL
45s
PARKWAY

Number	Title (A Side/B Side)	Yr	VG	VG+	NM
❏ 126	Emily/Genuine Jade	1966	10.00	20.00	40.00

BILLY AND LILLIE Also see LILLIE BRYANT; BILLY FORD.
45s
ABC-PARAMOUNT

Number	Title (A Side/B Side)	Yr	VG	VG+	NM
❏ 10421	Love Me Sincerely/Whip It To Me Baby	1963	7.50	15.00	30.00
❏ 10489	Carry Me Across the Threshold/				
	Why I Love Billy (Lillie)	1963	7.50	15.00	30.00
CAMEO					
❏ 412	Nothing Moves (Without a Little Push)/				
	The Two of Us	1966	2.50	5.00	10.00
❏ 435	You Got Me by the Heart/Hear You Better Hear	1966	2.50	5.00	10.00

B

Number	Title (A Side/B Side)	Yr	VG	VG+	NM
SWAN					
❏ 4002	La Dee Dah/The Monster	1957	7.50	15.00	30.00
—"SWAN" in all capital letters; B-side by Billy Ford and the Thunderbirds					
❏ 4002	La Dee Dah/The Monster	1958	5.00	10.00	20.00
—Only the S in "Swan" is capitalized; B-side by Billy Ford and the Thunderbirds					
❏ 4005	Happiness/Creepin' Crawlin' Cryin'	1958	5.00	10.00	20.00
❏ 4011	The Greasy Spoon/Hanging On to You	1958	5.00	10.00	20.00
❏ 4020	Lucky Ladybug/I Promise You	1958	6.25	12.50	25.00
❏ 4030	Tumbled Down/A.H. Thomas the Cat	1959	3.75	7.50	15.00
❏ 4036	Bells, Bells, Bells/Honeymoonin'	1959	3.75	7.50	15.00
❏ 4042	Terrific Together/Swampy	1959	3.75	7.50	15.00
❏ 4051	Free for All/The Ins and Outs of Love	1960	3.75	7.50	15.00
❏ 4058	That's the Way the Cookie Crumbles (Ah-So)/ Over the Mountain, Across the Sea	1960	3.75	7.50	15.00
❏ 4069	Ain't Comin' Back (To You)/Bananas	1961	3.75	7.50	15.00

BILLY AND THE BEATERS See BILLY VERA.

BILLY AND THE ESSENTIALS
45s

Number	Title (A Side/B Side)	Yr	VG	VG+	NM
CAMEO					
❏ 344	Remember Me Baby/The Actor	1965	100.00	200.00	400.00
JAMIE					
❏ 1229	The Dance Is Over/Steady Girl	1962	7.50	15.00	30.00
❏ 1239	Over the Weekend/Maybe You'll Be There	1962	7.50	15.00	30.00
LANDA					
❏ 691	The Dance Is Over/Steady Girl	1962	12.50	25.00	50.00
MERCURY					
❏ 72127	Young at Heart/Lonely Weekend	1963	6.25	12.50	25.00
❏ 72210	Last Dance/Yes Sir, That's My Baby	1963	6.25	12.50	25.00
SMASH					
❏ 2045	Babalu's Wedding Day/My Way of Saying	1966	3.75	7.50	15.00
❏ 2071	Don't Cry (Sing Along with the Music)/ Baby Go Away	1966	3.00	6.00	12.00
SSS INTERNATIONAL					
❏ 706	I Wrote a Song/Oh What a Feeling	1967	3.00	6.00	12.00

BILLY BOY
45s

Number	Title (A Side/B Side)	Yr	VG	VG+	NM
COOL					
❏ 103	I Ain't Got No Money/Hello Stranger	1953	250.00	500.00	1000.
—As "Billy Boy Arnold"					
VEE JAY					
❏ 146	I Wish You Would/I Was Fooled	1955	20.00	40.00	80.00
❏ 171	I Ain't Got You/Don't Stay Out All Night	1956	20.00	40.00	80.00
—Label lists artist as "Billy Boy Arnold"					
❏ 192	Here's My Picture/You've Got Me Wrong	1956	10.00	20.00	40.00
❏ 238	Kissing at Midnight/My Heart Is Crying	1957	10.00	20.00	40.00
❏ 260	Rockinitis/Prisoner's Plea	1957	10.00	20.00	40.00
VIVID					
❏ 109	Prisoner's Plea/I Wish You Would	1964	6.25	12.50	25.00
Albums					
PRESTIGE					
❏ PRLP-7389 [M] Blues on the South Side		1965	7.50	15.00	30.00
—As "Billy Boy Arnold"					
❏ PRST-7389 [S] Blues on the South Side		1965	10.00	20.00	40.00
—As "Billy Boy Arnold"					

BILLY JOE AND THE CHECKMATES
45s

Number	Title (A Side/B Side)	Yr	VG	VG+	NM
DORE					
❏ 620	Percolator (Twist)/Round & Round & Round & Round	1961	3.75	7.50	15.00
❏ 636	Rocky's Theme/Twist That Thing	1962	3.00	6.00	12.00
❏ 643	The Chester Drag/Laughing Machine Gunner	1962	3.00	6.00	12.00
❏ 652	Chalypso Dancer/My Friend, the Rain	1962	3.00	6.00	12.00
❏ 664	Solid Gold Hubcaps/Laughing Woodpecker	1963	3.00	6.00	12.00
❏ 668	Bossville/One More Cup	1963	3.00	6.00	12.00
❏ 680	Shake, Shake, Shake/Summertime in Venice	1963	3.00	6.00	12.00
❏ 685	Last Dance/My Friend the Rain	1963	3.00	6.00	12.00
❏ 694	The Drifter/Nashville West (One More Time)	1963	3.00	6.00	12.00
❏ 697	Forbidden Planet/Slauson, Baby, Slauson	1964	3.00	6.00	12.00
❏ 703	Spotlight Dance/Zip Code	1964	3.00	6.00	12.00
❏ 720	C'mopn Everybody (Part 1)/C'mon Everybody (Part 2)	1964	3.00	6.00	12.00
❏ 728	Bells of Rome/Shadows	1965	2.50	5.00	10.00
❏ 747	Clair de Looney/Holding Hands	1966	2.50	5.00	10.00
❏ 756	Voyage to the Bottom of the Sea/Nutty Dance Instructor	1966	2.50	5.00	10.00
❏ 791	A Man and a Woman/Floatin'	1967	2.50	5.00	10.00
❏ 857	Ambrosia/Newport Beach Concerto	1971	—	3.00	6.00
❏ 871	Try It, You'll Like It/Topless Dancer	1972	—	2.50	5.00
❏ 884	Aphrodisiac (Part 1)/Aphrodisiac (Part 2)	1973	—	2.50	5.00
❏ 892	Flaky (same on both sides)	1974	—	2.50	5.00
❏ 982	Raindrops, Mem'ries, and Tears/Liuvio, Memorias, y Lagramas	1985	—	2.00	4.00

BILLY THE KID
45s

Number	Title (A Side/B Side)	Yr	VG	VG+	NM
KAPP					
❏ 261	Apron Strings/I Hardly Know You	1959	3.00	6.00	12.00

BINGHAM, J.B.
45s

Number	Title (A Side/B Side)	Yr	VG	VG+	NM
UNITED ARTISTS					
❏ XW816	All Alone by the Telephone/Live and You Learn	1976	3.75	7.50	15.00
❏ XW872	She's Gone/Keep On Walking	1976	3.75	7.50	15.00
WARNER BROS.					
❏ 7775	Sunshine/Peek-A-Boo	1974	2.50	5.00	10.00

BINKLEY, CAROLYN
45s

Number	Title (A Side/B Side)	Yr	VG	VG+	NM
COLUMBIA					
❏ 43468	I Want a Baby Brother for Christmas/All I Want for Christmas Is My Two Front Teeth	1965	2.50	5.00	10.00
❏ 43468 [PS]	I Want a Baby Brother for Christmas/All I Want for Christmas Is My Two Front Teeth	1965	3.75	7.50	15.00
❏ 4-43918	I Want a Baby Brother for Christmas/Mister Pilot	1966	2.50	5.00	10.00

BINKLEY, JIMMY
45s

Number	Title (A Side/B Side)	Yr	VG	VG+	NM
ALADDIN					
❏ 3193	Night Life/Hot Smoke	1953	30.00	60.00	120.00
CHANCE					
❏ 1134	Hey, Hey Sugar Ray/Midnite Wail	1953	50.00	100.00	200.00
CHECKER					
❏ 789	Wine, Wine, Wine/Boogie On the Hour	1954	50.00	100.00	200.00
❏ 835	Messin' Around/You Made a Boo-Boo	1956	25.00	50.00	100.00
NOTE					
❏ 10002	Why Oh Why/Blue Moon	1957	75.00	150.00	300.00

BIRD WATCHERS, THE
45s

Number	Title (A Side/B Side)	Yr	VG	VG+	NM
LAURIE					
❏ 3399	Turn Around Girl/You Got It	1967	3.00	6.00	12.00
MALA					
❏ 527	Girl I've Got News for You/Eddie's Tune	1966	7.50	15.00	30.00
❏ 536	I'm Gonna Love You Anyway/A Little Bit of Lovin'	1966	7.50	15.00	30.00
❏ 548	I'm Gonna Do It to You/I Have No Worried Mind	1966	7.50	15.00	30.00
❏ 555	Mary Mary (It's to You That I Belong)/ Cry a Little Bit	1967	7.50	15.00	30.00

BIRDSONG, EDWIN
12-Inch Singles

Number	Title (A Side/B Side)	Yr	VG	VG+	NM
PHILADELPHIA INT'L.					
❏ 2Z8 3671	Phiss-Phizz (8:38)/Goldmine (10:43)	1979	3.75	7.50	15.00
❏ 4Z8 3709 [DJ]	Lollipop (5:59) (2:52)	1979	3.75	7.50	15.00
SALSOUL					
❏ SG 363 [DJ]	Funtaztik/Win Tonight	1982	2.50	5.00	10.00
45s					
PHILADELPHIA INT'L					
❏ 3659	Kunta Dance Part 1/Kunta Dance Part 2	1978	—	2.00	4.00
❏ 3670	Phiss-Phizz/Goldmine	1979	—	2.00	4.00
POLYDOR					
❏ 14058	The Old Messiah/Use What You Got	1970	—	2.50	5.00
—With Doug McClure					
❏ 14095	It Ain't No Fun Being a Welfare Recipient/ Uncle Tom Game	1971	—	2.50	5.00
❏ 14118	My Father Preaches That God Is the Father of Us All/The Spirit of Do Do	1972	—	2.50	5.00
❏ 14186	Rising Sign/Rising Sign Climax	1973	—	2.50	5.00
❏ 14192	Rising Sign/Grow Some Flowers, You Will Learn to Love the Rain	1973	—	2.50	5.00
❏ 14224	Turn Around Hate (Communicate)/Down on the Beat	1974	—	2.50	5.00
SALSOUL					
❏ 2135	Rapper Dapper Snapper/(Instrumental)	1981	—	2.00	4.00
❏ 7019	Funtaztik/Win Tonight	1982	—	2.00	4.00
❏ 7024	She's Wrapped Too Tight (She's a Button Buster)/(Instrumental)	1982	—	2.00	4.00
Albums					
ABC DUNHILL					
❏ DSX-51036	Can't Stop the Madness	1974	3.75	7.50	15.00
PHILADELPHIA INT'L.					
❏ JZ 35758	Edwin Birdsong	1978	2.50	5.00	10.00
POLYDOR					
❏ 24-4071	What It Is	1971	3.00	6.00	12.00
❏ PD-5057	Super Natural	1973	3.00	6.00	12.00
SALSOUL					
❏ SA-8550	Funktaztic	1981	2.50	5.00	10.00

BIRKIN, JANE, AND SERGE GAINSBOURG
45s

Number	Title (A Side/B Side)	Yr	VG	VG+	NM
FONTANA					
❏ 1665	Je T'Aime...Moi Non Plus/Jane B	1969	2.00	4.00	8.00
❏ 1684	La Decadanse/Les Langues de Chat	1969	—	2.50	5.00
Albums					
FONTANA					
❏ SRF-67610	Je T'aime	1970	5.00	10.00	20.00

BIRTH CONTROL
Albums

Number	Title (A Side/B Side)	Yr	VG	VG+	NM
PROPHESY					
❏ PRS-1002	Birth Control: A New German Rock Group	1970	7.50	15.00	30.00

BISCAYNES, THE
45s

Number	Title (A Side/B Side)	Yr	VG	VG+	NM
NORTHRIDGE					
❏ 1001	Church Key/Moment of Truth	1963	15.00	30.00	60.00
—B-side by the Surfaris					
REPRISE					
❏ 20180	Church Key/Moment of Truth	1963	7.50	15.00	30.00
—B-side by the Surfaris					

BISHOP, EDDIE
45s

Number	Title (A Side/B Side)	Yr	VG	VG+	NM
ABC					
❏ 10858	Candy Man/What You're Doing to Me	1966	6.25	12.50	25.00
ABC-PARAMOUNT					
❏ 10799	What Did He Say?/Call Me	1966	15.00	30.00	60.00

B

Number	Title (A Side/B Side)	Yr	VG	VG+	NM
BISHOP, ELVIN					
45s					
CAPRICORN					
❏ 0054	Fooled Around and Fell in Love/Struttin' My Stuff	197?	—	2.00	4.00
—Hall of Fame Series					
❏ 0202	Travelin' Shoes/Fishin'	1974	—	2.50	5.00
❏ 0222	Can't Go Back/Let It Flow	1975	—	2.50	5.00
❏ 0237	Sure Feels Good/Arkansas Line	1975	—	2.50	5.00
❏ 0243	Calling All Cows/Juke Joint Jump	1975	—	2.50	5.00
❏ 0248	Silent Night (Vocal Version)/(Instrumental)	1975	2.00	4.00	8.00
❏ 0252	Fooled Around and Fell in Love/Slick Titty Boom	1976	—	2.50	5.00
❏ 0252	Fooled Around and Fell in Love/Have a Good Time	1976	—	3.00	6.00
—This is actually the second pressing, bit it's harder to find than the first					
❏ 0256	Struttin' My Stuff/Grab All the Love	1976	—	2.50	5.00
❏ 0266	Spend Some Time/Sugar Dumplin'	1976	—	2.50	5.00
❏ 0269	Keep It Cool/Yes Sir	1976	—	2.50	5.00
❏ 0285	Rock My Soul/Yes Sir	1978	—	2.00	4.00
❏ 0296	Fooled Around and Fell in Love/Travelin' Shoes	1978	—	2.00	4.00
❏ 0313	It's a Feeling/Right Now Is the Hour	1979	—	2.00	4.00
EPIC					
❏ 10926	Rock My Soul/Holler and Shout	1973	—	2.50	5.00
❏ 11022	Last Mile/Stealin' Watermelons	1973	—	2.50	5.00
FILLMORE					
❏ 7002	So Fine/(B-side unknown)	1971	—	3.00	6.00
❏ 7003	Don't Fight It, Feel It/(B-side unknown)	1971	—	3.00	6.00
❏ 7004	I Just Can't Go On/(B-side unknown)	1971	—	3.00	6.00
Albums					
ALLIGATOR					
❏ AL-4767	Big Fun	1987	2.50	5.00	10.00
CAPRICORN					
❏ CP 0134	Let It Flow	1974	3.00	6.00	12.00
❏ CP 0151	Juke Joint Jump	1975	3.00	6.00	12.00
❏ CP 0165	Struttin' My Stuff	1975	3.00	6.00	12.00
❏ CPN-0165	Struttin' My Stuff	1980	2.50	5.00	10.00
—Reissue with revised prefix and Polygram distribution					
❏ CP 0176	Hometown Boy Makes Good!	1976	3.00	6.00	12.00
❏ 2CP 0185 [(2)]	Live! Raisin' Hell	1977	3.75	7.50	15.00
❏ CPN-0215	Hog Heaven	1978	3.00	6.00	12.00
EPIC					
❏ KE 31563	Rock My Soul	1972	3.75	7.50	15.00
❏ PE 33693	The Best of Elvin Bishop	1975	3.00	6.00	12.00
FILLMORE					
❏ F 30001	Elvin Bishop Group	1969	5.00	10.00	20.00
❏ Z 30239	Feel It	1970	5.00	10.00	20.00
BISHOP, JOEY					
Albums					
ABC					
❏ ABCS-656	Joey Bishop Sings Country and Western	1968	7.50	15.00	30.00
BIT 'A SWEET					
45s					
ABC					
❏ 11125	The Second Time/2086	1968	5.00	10.00	20.00
MGM					
❏ 13695	Out of Sight, Out of Mind/It Is On, It Is Off	1967	6.25	12.50	25.00
Albums					
ABC					
❏ S-640	Hypnotic 1	1968	10.00	20.00	40.00
BJORN AND BENNY Early ABBA.					
45s					
PLAYBOY					
❏ 50014	Merry-Go-Round/People Need Love	1972	7.50	15.00	30.00
❏ 50018	Another Town, Another Train/I Am Just a Girl	1973	7.50	15.00	30.00
❏ 50025	Rock 'N Roll Band/Another Town, Another Train	1973	7.50	15.00	30.00
BLACK, BILL, 'S COMBO					
45s					
COLUMBIA					
❏ 44867	But It's Alright/Slow Action	1969	—	2.50	5.00
❏ 44983	California Dreamin'/Funky Train	1969	—	2.50	5.00
❏ 45092	Heaven Knows/One Five One Eight Chelsea	1970	—	2.50	5.00
❏ 45162	Keep the Customer Satisfied/One Five One Eight Chelsea	1970	—	2.50	5.00
HI					
❏ 2018	Smokie (Part 2)/Smokie (Part 1)	1959	5.00	10.00	20.00
❏ 2021	White Silver Sands/The Wheel	1960	5.00	10.00	20.00
❏ 2022	Josephine/Dry Bones	1960	3.75	7.50	15.00
❏ 2022 [PS]	Josephine/Dry Bones	1960	6.25	12.50	25.00
❏ 2026	Don't Be Cruel/Rollin'	1960	3.75	7.50	15.00
❏ 2026 [PS]	Don't Be Cruel/Rollin'	1960	6.25	12.50	25.00
❏ 2027	Blue Tango/Willie	1960	3.75	7.50	15.00
❏ 2027 [PS]	Blue Tango/Willie	1960	6.25	12.50	25.00
❏ 2028	Hearts of Stone/Royal Blue	1961	3.00	6.00	12.00
❏ 2029	Old Time Religion/He's Got the Whole World in His Hands	1961	10.00	20.00	40.00
—Stereo single, small hole, plays at 33 1/3 rpm					
❏ 2030	Do Lord/When the Roll Is Called Up Yonder	1961	10.00	20.00	40.00
—Stereo single, small hole, plays at 33 1/3 rpm					
❏ 2031	Down by the Riverside/It Is No Secret (What God Can Do)	1961	10.00	20.00	40.00
—Stereo single, small hole, plays at 33 1/3 rpm					
❏ 2032	When the Saints Go Marching In/(B-side unknown)	1961	10.00	20.00	40.00
—Stereo single, small hole, plays at 33 1/3 rpm					
❏ 2033	Just a Closer Walk with Thee/This Old House	1961	10.00	20.00	40.00
—Stereo single, small hole, plays at 33 1/3 rpm					
❏ 2036	Ole Buttermilk Sky/Yogi	1961	3.00	6.00	12.00
❏ 2036 [PS]	Ole Buttermilk Sky/Yogi	1961	6.25	12.50	25.00
❏ 2038	Movin'/Honky Train	1961	3.00	6.00	12.00

Number	Title (A Side/B Side)	Yr	VG	VG+	NM
❏ 2042	Twist-Her/My Girl Josephine	1961	3.00	6.00	12.00
❏ 2045	Twist-Her/Night Train	1962	10.00	20.00	40.00
—Stereo single, small hole, plays at 33 1/3 rpm					
❏ 2046	The Hucklebuck/Corrina, Corrina	1962	10.00	20.00	40.00
—Stereo single, small hole, plays at 33 1/3 rpm					
❏ 2047	Johnny B. Goode/(B-side unknown)	1962	10.00	20.00	40.00
—Stereo single, small hole, plays at 33 1/3 rpm					
❏ 2048	Josephine/My Girl Josephine	1962	10.00	20.00	40.00
—Stereo single, small hole, plays at 33 1/3 rpm					
❏ 2049	Slippin' and Slidin'/Twist with Me, Baby	1962	10.00	20.00	40.00
—Stereo single, small hole, plays at 33 1/3 rpm					
❏ 2052	Twistin' — White Silver Sands/My Babe	1962	3.00	6.00	12.00
❏ 2052 [PS]	Twistin' — White Silver Sands/My Babe	1962	6.25	12.50	25.00
❏ 2055	So What/Blues for the Red Boy	1962	3.00	6.00	12.00
❏ 2059	Joey's Song/Hot Taco	1962	3.00	6.00	12.00
❏ 2064	Do It — Rat Now/Little Jasper	1963	3.00	6.00	12.00
❏ 2069	Monkey-Shine/Love Gone	1963	3.00	6.00	12.00
❏ 2072	Comin' On/Soft Winds	1964	3.00	6.00	12.00
❏ 2077	Tequila/Raunchy	1964	3.00	6.00	12.00
❏ 2079	Little Queenie/Boo Ray	1964	3.00	6.00	12.00
❏ 2085	Come On Home/He'll Have to Go	1964	2.50	5.00	10.00
❏ 2094	Spootin'/Crazy Feeling	1965	2.50	5.00	10.00
❏ 2106	Hey, Good Lookin'/Mountain of Love	1966	2.50	5.00	10.00
❏ 2115	Rambler/You Call Everybody Darling	1966	2.50	5.00	10.00
❏ 2124	Son of Smokie/Peg Leg	1967	2.00	4.00	8.00
❏ 2145	Turn On Your Love Life/Ribbon of Darkness	1968	—	3.00	6.00
❏ 2153	Red Light/Bright Lights, Big City	1968	—	3.00	6.00
❏ 2168	Creepin' Around/The Son of Hickory Holler's Tramp	1969	—	3.00	6.00
❏ 2185	No More/Closin' Time	1971	—	2.50	5.00
❏ 2208	Daylite/Four A.M.	1972	—	2.50	5.00
❏ 2234	Smokey Bourbon Street/Mighty Fine	1973	—	2.50	5.00
❏ 2277	Soul Serenade/Pickin'	1974	—	2.00	4.00
❏ 2283	Truck Stop/Boilin' Cabbage	1975	—	2.00	4.00
❏ 2291	Almost Persuaded/Back Up and Push	1975	—	2.00	4.00
❏ 2301	Fire on the Bayou/Memphis Soul	1976	—	2.00	4.00
❏ 2311	I Can Help/Jump Back Joe	1976	—	2.00	4.00
❏ 2317	Redneck Rock/Yakety Sax	1976	—	2.00	4.00
❏ 78508	Cashin' In (A Tribute to Luther Perkins)/L.A. Blues	1978	—	2.00	4.00
MEGA					
❏ 0036	Rings/Cotton Carnival	1971	—	2.50	5.00
❏ 0052	Oh Happy Day/Sugar Cured	1971	—	2.50	5.00
❏ 0070	Harlem Nocturne/Sassy Parts	1972	—	2.50	5.00
❏ 0086	Night Train/Bluff City	1972	—	2.50	5.00
❏ 0113	Listen to the Music/Memphis Shuffle	1973	—	2.50	5.00
❏ 0117	Satin Sheets/Memphis Shuffle	1973	—	2.50	5.00
❏ 201	Smokie Part 2/Tequila	1973	—	2.50	5.00
❏ 207	Oh Happy Day/Listen to the Music	1974	—	2.00	4.00
7-Inch Extended Plays					
HI					
❏ HSP 2	My Babe/40 Miles of Bad Road/Ain't That Lovin' You Baby//What'd I Say/The Walk/Witchcraft	1962	3.75	7.50	15.00
—33 1/3 rpm jukebox single, small hole					
❏ HSP 2 [PS]	(title unknown)	1962	3.75	7.50	15.00
❏ SBG 26	T.D.'s Boogie Woogie/Tuxedo Junction/Canadian Sunset//Leap Frog/In the Mood/So Rare	196?	2.50	5.00	10.00
—33 1/3 rpm jukebox single, small hole					
❏ SBG 26 [PS]	Bill Black's Combo Goes Big Band	196?	2.50	5.00	10.00
❏ HE 22002	Honky Tonk/Cherry Pink//Singing the Blues/You Win Again	1961	10.00	20.00	40.00
❏ HE 22002 [PS]	Solid and Raunchy	1961	10.00	20.00	40.00
Albums					
COLUMBIA					
❏ CS 1055	Basic Black	1970	3.00	6.00	12.00
❏ CS 9848	Black with Sugar	1969	3.00	6.00	12.00
❏ CS 9957	Raindrops Keep Fallin' on My Head	1970	3.00	6.00	12.00
HI					
❏ 6005	Award Winners	1978	2.50	5.00	10.00
❏ 8004	Memphis Tennessee	1977	2.50	5.00	10.00
❏ HL-12001 [M]	Smokie	1960	10.00	20.00	40.00
—Orange and white label					
❏ HL-12001 [M]	Smokie	1960	15.00	30.00	60.00
—Black label with red and silver logo					
❏ HL-12002 [M]	Saxy Jazz	1960	10.00	20.00	40.00
❏ HL-12003 [M]	Solid and Raunchy	1960	10.00	20.00	40.00
❏ HL-12004 [M]	That Wonderful Feeling	1961	5.00	10.00	20.00
❏ HL-12005 [M]	Movin'	1961	5.00	10.00	20.00
❏ HL-12006 [M]	Let's Twist Her	1961	3.75	7.50	15.00
—Retitled version of above					
❏ HL-12006 [M]	Bill Black's Record Hop	1961	6.25	12.50	25.00
❏ HL-12009 [M]	The Untouchable Sound of Bill Black	1962	3.75	7.50	15.00
❏ HL-12012 [M]	Bill Black's Greatest Hits	1963	3.75	7.50	15.00
❏ HL-12013 [M]	Bill Black's Combo Goes West	1963	3.75	7.50	15.00
❏ HL-12015 [M]	Bill Black Plays the Blues	1964	3.75	7.50	15.00
❏ HL-12017 [M]	Bill Black Plays Tunes by Chuck Berry	1964	3.75	7.50	15.00
❏ HL-12020 [M]	Bill Black's Combo Goes Big Band	1964	3.75	7.50	15.00
❏ HL-12023 [M]	More Solid and Raunchy	1965	3.75	7.50	15.00
❏ HL-12027 [M]	Mr. Beat	1965	3.75	7.50	15.00
❏ HL-12032 [M]	All Timers	1966	3.00	6.00	12.00
❏ HL-12033 [M]	Black Lace	1966	3.00	6.00	12.00
❏ HL-12036 [M]	King of the Road	1966	3.00	6.00	12.00
❏ HL-12041 [M]	The Beat Goes On	1967	3.75	7.50	15.00
❏ HL-12044 [M]	Turn Your Lovelight On	1967	3.75	7.50	15.00
❏ HL-12047 [M]	Soulin' the Blues	1968	3.75	7.50	15.00
❏ SHL-32001 [R]	Smokie	1964	5.00	10.00	20.00
❏ SHL-32002 [R]	Saxy Jazz	1964	5.00	10.00	20.00
❏ SHL-32003 [R]	Solid and Raunchy	1964	5.00	10.00	20.00
❏ SHL-32004 [S]	That Wonderful Feeling	1961	6.25	12.50	25.00
❏ SHL-32005 [S]	Movin'	1961	6.25	12.50	25.00
❏ SHL-32006 [S]	Let's Twist Her	1961	5.00	10.00	20.00
—Retitled version of above					
❏ SHL-32006 [S]	Bill Black's Record Hop	1961	7.50	15.00	30.00

Number	Title (A Side/B Side)	Yr	VG	VG+	NM
❏ SHL-32009 [S] The Untouchable Sound of Bill Black		1962	5.00	10.00	20.00
❏ SHL-32012 [S] Bill Black's Greatest Hits		1963	5.00	10.00	20.00
❏ SHL-32013 [S] Bill Black's Combo Goes West		1963	5.00	10.00	20.00
❏ SHL-32015 [S] Bill Black Plays the Blues		1964	5.00	10.00	20.00
❏ SHL-32017 [S] Bill Black Plays Tunes by Chuck Berry		1964	5.00	10.00	20.00
❏ SHL-32020 [S] Bill Black's Combo Goes Big Band		1964	5.00	10.00	20.00
❏ SHL-32023 [S] More Solid and Raunchy		1965	5.00	10.00	20.00
❏ SHL-32027 [S] Mr. Beat		1965	5.00	10.00	20.00
❏ SHL-32032 [S] All Timers		1966	3.75	7.50	15.00
❏ SHL-32033 [S] Black Lace		1966	3.75	7.50	15.00
❏ SHL-32036 [S] King of the Road		1966	3.75	7.50	15.00
❏ SHL-32041 [S] The Beat Goes On		1967	3.75	7.50	15.00
❏ SHL-32044 [S] Turn Your Lovelight On		1967	3.75	7.50	15.00
❏ SHL-32047 [S] Soulin' the Blues		1968	3.75	7.50	15.00
❏ SHL-32052 Solid and Raunchy The 3rd		1969	3.75	7.50	15.00
❏ SHL-32061 More Magic		1971	3.00	6.00	12.00
❏ XSHL-32078 Bill Black's Greatest Hits, Vol. 2		1973	3.00	6.00	12.00
❏ XSHL-32088 Solid and Country		1974	3.00	6.00	12.00
❏ SHL-32093 The World's Greatest Honky Tonk Band		1975	3.00	6.00	12.00
❏ SHL-32104 It's Honky Tonk Time		1976	3.00	6.00	12.00
MEGA					
❏ MLPS-600 Bill Black Is Back		1973	3.00	6.00	12.00
❏ 31-1008 The Memphis Scene		1971	3.00	6.00	12.00
❏ 31-1014 Juke Box Favorites		1972	3.00	6.00	12.00
❏ 51-5008 Rock 'n' Roll Forever		1973	3.00	6.00	12.00

BLACK, CILLA
45s
BELL

Number	Title (A Side/B Side)	Yr	VG	VG+	NM
❏ 726	Step Inside Love/I Couldn't Take My Eyes Off You	1968	5.00	10.00	20.00
CAPITOL					
❏ 5196	You're My World/Suffer Now I Must	1964	3.75	7.50	15.00
❏ 5258	It's for You/He Won't Ask Me	1964	3.00	6.00	12.00
❏ 5373	One Little Voice/Is It Love	1965	3.00	6.00	12.00
❏ 5414	I've Been Wrong Before/My Love Came Home	1965	3.00	6.00	12.00
❏ 5595	Love's Just a Broken Heart/Yesterday	1966	3.00	6.00	12.00
❏ 5595 [PS]	Love's Just a Broken Heart/Yesterday	1966	7.50	15.00	30.00
❏ 5674	Alfie/Night Time Is Here	1966	3.00	6.00	12.00
❏ 5763	Don't Answer Me/The Right One Is Left	1966	3.00	6.00	12.00
❏ 5782	A Fool Am I/For No One	1966	3.00	6.00	12.00
DJM					
❏ 70007	What the World Needs Now Is Love/Only Forever Will Do	1969	2.00	4.00	8.00
❏ 70011	Without Him/It'll Never Happen Again	1969	2.00	4.00	8.00
❏ 70012	Surround Yourself with Sorrow/It'll Never Happen Again	1969	2.00	4.00	8.00
❏ 70014	Conversations/London Bridge	1969	2.00	4.00	8.00
❏ 70015	If I Thought You'd Ever Change Your Mind/It Feels So Good	1970	2.00	4.00	8.00
❏ 70016	If I Thought You'd Ever Change Your Mind/Conversations	1970	2.00	4.00	8.00
❏ 70018 [DJ]	Across the Universe (mono/stereo)	1970	3.00	6.00	12.00
EMI					
❏ 4003	He Was a Writer/I'll Never Run Out of You	1974	—	3.00	6.00
PRIVATE STOCK					
❏ 45,040	I'll Take a Tango/To Know Him Is To Love Him	1975	—	2.50	5.00
❏ 45,077	Fantasy/It's Now	1976	—	2.50	5.00
Albums					
CAPITOL					
❏ ST 2308 [S]	Is It Love?	1965	10.00	20.00	40.00
❏ T 2308 [M]	Is It Love?	1965	6.25	12.50	25.00

BLACK, CODY
45s
GIG

Number	Title (A Side/B Side)	Yr	VG	VG+	NM
❏ 102	It's Our Time to Fall in Love/(B-side unknown)	196?	250.00	500.00	1000.
KING					
❏ 6148	Keep On Hanging On/I'm Slowly Molding	1968	10.00	20.00	40.00

BLACK, JAY The second "Jay" of JAY AND THE AMERICANS.
12-Inch Singles
MILLENNIUM

Number	Title (A Side/B Side)	Yr	VG	VG+	NM
❏ 20614	Love Is In the Air/Please Stay	1978	3.75	7.50	15.00
ROULETTE					
❏ 2005	One Night Affair/Fill Me Up	1976	3.75	7.50	15.00
—B-side by Caress					
45s					
ATLANTIC					
❏ 3273	Dolphins/Running Scared	1975	—	2.50	5.00
MIDSONG INT'L					
❏ 72012	The Part of Me That Needs You Most/You Stole the Music	1980	—	2.00	4.00
MILLENNIUM					
❏ 618	Love Is In the Air/Please Stay	1978	—	2.50	5.00
PRIVATE STOCK					
❏ 45,058	Every Time You Walk in the Room/I'd Build a Bridge	1975	—	2.50	5.00
ROULETTE					
❏ 7198	One Night Affair/Between Two Worlds	1976	—	3.00	6.00
UNITED ARTISTS					
❏ 50116	What Will My Mary Say/Return to Me	1967	3.00	6.00	12.00
❏ 50116 [PS]	What Will My Mary Say/Return to Me	1967	6.25	12.50	25.00

BLACK, OSCAR
45s
ATLANTIC

Number	Title (A Side/B Side)	Yr	VG	VG+	NM
❏ 956	Love, Love, Love/Troubled Man Blues	1952	37.50	75.00	150.00
GROOVE					
❏ 0012	I'll Get By/Hold Me Baby	1954	15.00	30.00	60.00
—With Sue Allen					

Number	Title (A Side/B Side)	Yr	VG	VG+	NM
❏ 0102	Be My Baby/Ain't Nobody Home But Me	1955	15.00	30.00	60.00
—With Sue Allen					
❏ 0115	Baby, Please Don't Go/I'll Live My Life Alone	1955	15.00	30.00	60.00
—With Sue Allen					
❏ 0130	Think of Tomorrow/Set a Wedding Day	1955	15.00	30.00	60.00
—With Sue Allen and the Four Students					
❏ 0168	Into Each Heart (Some Tears Must Fall)/If I Cry Tomorrow	1956	12.50	25.00	50.00
—With Sue Allen					
SAVOY					
❏ 1600	I Got a Feeling/I'm a Fool to Care	1961	3.75	7.50	15.00

BLACK, TERRY
45s
DUNHILL

Number	Title (A Side/B Side)	Yr	VG	VG+	NM
❏ 4005	How Many Guys/Only Sixteen	1965	2.50	5.00	10.00
❏ 4046	Ordinary Girl/Baby's Gone	1966	2.50	5.00	10.00
TOLLIE					
❏ 9026	Unless You Care/Can't We Go Somewhere	1964	3.00	6.00	12.00
❏ 9041	Say It Again/Everyone Can Tell	1965	3.00	6.00	12.00
❏ 9041 [PS]	Say It Again/Everyone Can Tell	1965	5.00	10.00	20.00

BLACK, TERRY, AND LAUREL WARD
45s
KAMA SUTRA

Number	Title (A Side/B Side)	Yr	VG	VG+	NM
❏ 540	Goin' Down/Oh Babe	1972	—	3.00	6.00

BLACK, ZELL
45s
MOTOWN

Number	Title (A Side/B Side)	Yr	VG	VG+	NM
❏ 1281	I'd Hate Myself in the Morning/Take My Word	1973	—	2.50	5.00
❏ 1290	I Been Had by the Devil/Confession	1974	—	2.50	5.00
WARNER BROS.					
❏ 8138	Fly Me Part 1/You Make the Sun Keep Shining	1975	—	2.00	4.00
❏ 8202	Fly Me/Ride On Rider	1976	—	2.00	4.00

BLACK HEAT
45s
ATLANTIC

Number	Title (A Side/B Side)	Yr	VG	VG+	NM
❏ 2890	Street of Tears/Chip's Funk	1972	—	2.50	5.00
❏ 2934	The Jungle Part 1/The Jungle Part 2	1973	—	2.50	5.00
❏ 2987	No Time to Burn/Supercool	1973	—	2.50	5.00
❏ 3033	Check It All Out/M & M's	1974	—	2.50	5.00
❏ 3258	Drive My Car/Questions and Conclusions	1975	—	2.50	5.00
Albums					
ATLANTIC					
❏ SD 7237	Black Heat	1972	3.00	6.00	12.00
❏ SD 7294	No Time to Burn	1974	3.00	6.00	12.00
❏ SD 18128	Keep On Burnin'	1975	3.00	6.00	12.00

BLACK IVORY
45s
BUDDAH

Number	Title (A Side/B Side)	Yr	VG	VG+	NM
❏ 443	Will We Ever Come Together/Warm Inside	1975	—	2.00	4.00
❏ 489	Feel It/Daily News	1975	—	2.00	4.00
❏ 506	Love Won't You Stay/Daily News	1975	—	2.00	4.00
❏ 561	You Mean Everything to Me/White Wind	1977	—	2.00	4.00
❏ 610	Mainline/(B-side unknown)	1979	—	2.00	4.00
❏ 616	You Turned My Whole World Around/(B-side unknown)	1979	—	2.00	4.00
KWANZA/WB					
❏ 7800	No One Else Will Do/What Goes Around	1974	—	2.50	5.00
PANORAMIC					
❏ 200	You Are My Lover/(B-side unknown)	1984	—	2.00	4.00
PERCEPTION					
❏ 508	You and I/Our Future	1972	—	3.00	6.00
TODAY					
❏ 1501	Don't Turn Around/I Keep Asking You Questions	1971	—	2.50	5.00
❏ 1508	You and I/Our Future	1972	—	2.50	5.00
❏ 1511	I'll Find A Way (Loneliest Man in Town)/Surrender	1972	—	2.50	5.00
❏ 1516	Time Is Love/Got to Be There	1972	—	2.50	5.00
❏ 1520	Spinning Around/Find the One Who Loves You	1973	—	2.50	5.00
❏ 1524	We Made It/Just Leave Me Some	1973	—	2.50	5.00
Albums					
BUDDAH					
❏ BDS-5644	Feel It	1975	2.50	5.00	10.00
❏ BDS-5658	Black Ivory	1976	2.50	5.00	10.00
❏ BDS-5722	Hangin' Heavy	1979	2.50	5.00	10.00
TODAY					
❏ 1005	Don't Turn Around	1972	3.00	6.00	12.00
❏ 1008	Baby, Won't You Change Your Mind	1972	3.00	6.00	12.00

BLACK LIGHTNING
Albums
TOWER

Number	Title (A Side/B Side)	Yr	VG	VG+	NM
❏ ST 5129	Shades of Black Lightning	1968	5.00	10.00	20.00

BLACK MERDA
45s
CHESS

Number	Title (A Side/B Side)	Yr	VG	VG+	NM
❏ 2095	Reality/Cynthy-Ruth	1970	3.00	6.00	12.00
Albums					
CHESS					
❏ LP-1551	Black Merda	1970	12.50	25.00	50.00

BLACK OAK ARKANSAS
45s
ATCO

Number	Title (A Side/B Side)	Yr	VG	VG+	NM
❏ 6829	Lord Have Mercy on My Soul/Uncle Lijah	1971	—	2.50	5.00
❏ 6849	Singing the Blues/Hot and Nasty	1971	—	2.50	5.00
❏ 6878	Keep the Faith/The Big One's Still Coming	1972	—	2.00	4.00

Number	Title (A Side/B Side)	Yr	VG	VG+	NM
❏ 6893	Full Moon Ride/We Help Each Other	1972	—	2.00	4.00
❏ 6925	Hot and Nasty/Hot Rod	1973	—	2.00	4.00
❏ 6948	Jim Dandy/Red Hot Lovin'	1973	—	2.50	5.00
❏ 7003	Hey Y'all/Sting Me	1974	—	2.00	4.00
❏ 7015	Taxman/Dixie	1975	—	2.00	4.00
❏ 7019	Back Door Man/Good Stuff	1975	—	2.00	4.00
CAPRICORN					
❏ 0284	Not Fade Away/Feels So Good	1978	—	2.00	4.00
—Label lists artist as "Black Oak"					
❏ 0305	Ride with Me/Wind in Our Sails	1978	—	2.00	4.00
—Label lists artist as "Black Oak"					
ENTERPRISE					
❏ 9010	King's Row/Older Than Grandpa	1970	2.50	5.00	10.00
MCA					
❏ 40496	Strong Enough to Be Gentle/Ace in the Hole	1975	—	2.00	4.00
❏ 40536	Great Balls of Fire/Highway Pirate	1976	—	2.00	4.00
❏ 40586	A Fistful of Love/Storm of Passion	1976	—	2.00	4.00
❏ 40621	When the Band Was Singin' "Shakin' All Over"/ Bad Boy's Back in School	1976	—	2.00	4.00
Albums					
ATCO					
❏ SD 36-101	Street Party	1974	3.00	6.00	12.00
❏ SD 36-111	Ain't Life Grand	1975	3.00	6.00	12.00
❏ SD 36-128	Live! Mutha	1976	3.00	6.00	12.00
❏ SD 36-150	The Best of Black Oak Arkansas	1976	3.00	6.00	12.00
❏ SD 33-354	Black Oak Arkansas	1971	3.75	7.50	15.00
❏ 33-381 [M]	Keep the Faith	1972	7.50	15.00	30.00
—White label promo, "DJ Copy Monaural" sticker on cover; no stock copies were issued in mono					
❏ SD 33-381 [S]	Keep the Faith	1972	3.75	7.50	15.00
❏ SD 7008	If An Angel Came to See You, Would You Make Her Feel at Home?	1972	3.75	7.50	15.00
❏ QD 7019 [Q]	Raunch 'n' Roll/Live	1974	5.00	10.00	20.00
❏ SD 7019	Raunch 'n' Roll/Live	1973	3.75	7.50	15.00
❏ SD 7035	High on the Hog	1973	3.75	7.50	15.00
CAPRICORN					
❏ CP 0191	Race with the Devil	1977	3.00	6.00	12.00
❏ CP 0207	I'd Rather Be Sailing	1978	3.00	6.00	12.00
MCA					
❏ 704	X-Rated	198?	2.00	4.00	8.00
—Budget-line reissue					
❏ 2155	X-Rated	1975	3.00	6.00	12.00
❏ 2199	Balls of Fire	1976	3.00	6.00	12.00
❏ 2224	10 Year Overnight Success	1977	3.00	6.00	12.00
STAX					
❏ STS-5504	Early Times	1974	3.75	7.50	15.00

BLACK PEARL
45s
ATLANTIC

Number	Title (A Side/B Side)	Yr	VG	VG+	NM
❏ 2657	White Devil/Mr. Soul Satisfaction	1969	2.00	4.00	8.00
Albums					
ATLANTIC					
❏ SD 8220	Black Pearl	1969	6.25	12.50	25.00
PROPHESY					
❏ PRS-1001	Black Pearl — Live!	1970	6.25	12.50	25.00

BLACK SABBATH
12-Inch Singles
WARNER BROS.

Number	Title (A Side/B Side)	Yr	VG	VG+	NM
❏ PRO-A-2430 [DJ]	No Stranger to Love (4:28) (4:02)	1986	3.75	7.50	15.00
❏ PRO-A-2475 [DJ]	Danger Zone (same on both sides)	1986	3.00	6.00	12.00
45s					
WARNER BROS.					
❏ PRO 417 [DJ]	Rado Spot for Black Sabbath (same on both sides)	1970	12.50	25.00	50.00
❏ 7437	Paranoid/Wizard	1970	2.50	5.00	10.00
❏ 7530	Iron Man/Electric Funeral	1971	2.00	4.00	8.00
❏ 7625	Laguna Sunrise/Tomorrow's Dream	1972	2.00	4.00	8.00
❏ 7764	Sabbath, Bloody Sabbath/Changes	1973	2.00	4.00	8.00
❏ 7802	Iron Man/Electric Funeral	1974	2.00	4.00	8.00
❏ 8315	Rock 'N' Roll Doctor/It's Alright	1976	—	3.00	6.00
❏ 29434	Stonehenge/Trashed	1983	—	3.00	6.00
❏ 49549	Lady Evil/Children of the Sea	1980	—	3.00	6.00
Albums					
I.R.S.					
❏ 82002	Headless Cross	1989	2.50	5.00	10.00
WARNER BROS.					
❏ WS 1871	Black Sabbath	1970	3.75	7.50	15.00
—Green label					
❏ WS 1871	Black Sabbath	1973	2.50	5.00	10.00
—"Burbank" palm trees label					
❏ WS 1871	Black Sabbath	1979	2.00	4.00	8.00
—White or tan label					
❏ WS 1887	Paranoid	1971	3.75	7.50	15.00
—Green label					
❏ WS 1887	Paranoid	1973	2.50	5.00	10.00
—"Burbank" palm trees label					
❏ WS4 1887 [Q]	Paranoid	1974	7.50	15.00	30.00
—All quad copies have "Burbank" palm trees label					
❏ BS 2562	Master of Reality	1971	3.75	7.50	15.00
—Green label					
❏ BS 2562	Master of Reality Poster	1971	6.25	12.50	25.00
❏ BS 2562	Master of Reality	1973	2.50	5.00	10.00
—"Burbank" palm trees label					
❏ BS 2562	Master of Reality	1979	2.00	4.00	8.00
—White or tan label					
❏ BS 2602	Black Sabbath, Vol. 4	1972	3.75	7.50	15.00
—Green label					
❏ BS 2602	Black Sabbath, Vol. 4	1973	2.50	5.00	10.00
—"Burbank" palm trees label					
❏ BS 2602	Black Sabbath, Vol. 4	1979	2.00	4.00	8.00
—White or tan label					

Number	Title (A Side/B Side)	Yr	VG	VG+	NM
❏ BS 2695	Sabbath Bloody Sabbath	1974	3.75	7.50	15.00
—"Burbank" palm trees label					
❏ BS 2695	Sabbath Bloody Sabbath	1979	2.00	4.00	8.00
—White or tan label					
❏ BS 2822	Sabotage	1975	3.75	7.50	15.00
—"Burbank" palm trees label					
❏ BS 2822	Sabotage	1979	2.00	4.00	8.00
—White or tan label					
❏ 2BS 2923 [(2)]	We Sold Our Souls for Rock 'N' Roll	1975	5.00	10.00	20.00
—"Burbank" palm trees label					
❏ 2BS 2923 [(2)]	We Sold Our Souls for Rock 'N' Roll	1979	2.50	5.00	10.00
—White or tan label					
❏ BS 2969	Technical Ecstasy	1976	3.75	7.50	15.00
—"Burbank" palm trees label					
❏ BS 2969	Technical Ecstasy	1979	2.00	4.00	8.00
—White or tan label					
❏ BSK 3104	Paranoid	1978	2.50	5.00	10.00
—Reissue; "Burbank" palm trees label					
❏ BSK 3104	Paranoid	1979	2.00	4.00	8.00
—Reissue; white or tan label					
❏ BSK 3186	Never Say Die!	1978	3.00	6.00	12.00
❏ BSK 3372	Heaven and Hell	1980	3.00	6.00	12.00
❏ BSK 3605	Mob Rules	1981	3.00	6.00	12.00
❏ 23742 [(2)]	Live Evil	1983	3.75	7.50	15.00
❏ 23978	Born Again	1983	2.50	5.00	10.00
❏ 25337	Seventh Star	1986	2.50	5.00	10.00
❏ 25548	The Eternal Idol	1987	2.50	5.00	10.00

BLACK SATIN See THE FIVE SATINS.

BLACK SHEEP With Lou Gramm, pre-Foreigner.
45s
CAPITOL

Number	Title (A Side/B Side)	Yr	VG	VG+	NM
❏ 4012	A Little or a Lot/Broken Promises	1974	—	2.50	5.00
CHRYSALIS					
❏ 2038	Stick Around/Cruisin'	1974	—	2.50	5.00
Albums					
CAPITOL					
❏ ST-11369	Black Sheep	1974	5.00	10.00	20.00
❏ ST-11447	Encouraging Words	1975	5.00	10.00	20.00

BLACK VELVET
45s
EMBER

Number	Title (A Side/B Side)	Yr	VG	VG+	NM
❏ 702	Peace and Love Is the Message/The Clown	1970	2.50	5.00	10.00
OKEH					
❏ 7330	Come On Heart/Just Came Back	1969	3.75	7.50	15.00
Albums					
OKEH					
❏ OKS 14130	Love City	1969	6.25	12.50	25.00

BLACKBURN, LOU
45s
IMPERIAL

Number	Title (A Side/B Side)	Yr	VG	VG+	NM
❏ 5943	Grand Prix/Jazz-a-Nova	1963	7.50	15.00	30.00
❏ 5998	Two Note Samba/17 Richmond Park	1963	5.00	10.00	20.00

BLACKBYRDS, THE Also see DONALD BYRD.
45s
FANTASY

Number	Title (A Side/B Side)	Yr	VG	VG+	NM
❏ 729	Do It, Fluid/Summer Love	1974	—	2.50	5.00
❏ 736	Walking in Rhythm/The Baby	1975	—	2.00	4.00
❏ 747	Flyin' High/All I Ask	1975	—	2.00	4.00
❏ 762	Happy Music/Love So Fine	1976	—	2.00	4.00
❏ 771	Rock Creek Park/Thankful 'Bout Yourself	1976	—	2.00	4.00
❏ 787	Time Is Movin'/Lady	1977	—	2.00	4.00
❏ 794	Party Land/In Life	1977	—	2.00	4.00
❏ 809	Soft and Easy/Something Special	1977	—	2.00	4.00
❏ 819	Supernatural Feeling/Looking Ahead	1978	—	2.00	4.00
❏ 819 [PS]	Supernatural Feeling	1978	3.75	7.50	15.00
—Promo-only sleeve issued with 2:59 promos of the song					
❏ 904	What We Have Is Right/What's On Your Mind	1980	—	2.00	4.00
❏ 910	Love Don't Strike Twice/Don't Know What to Say	1981	—	2.00	4.00
❏ 914	Dancin' Dancin'/Lonelies for Your Love	1981	—	2.00	4.00
Albums					
FANTASY					
❏ FPM-4004 [Q]	Flying Start	1975	6.25	12.50	25.00
❏ F-9444	The Blackbyrds	1974	3.75	7.50	15.00
❏ F-9472	Flying Start	1974	3.75	7.50	15.00
❏ F-9490	City Life	1975	3.75	7.50	15.00
❏ F-9518	Unfinished Business	1976	3.75	7.50	15.00
❏ F-9535	Action	1977	3.00	6.00	12.00
❏ F-9570	Night Grooves	1978	3.00	6.00	12.00
❏ F-9602	Better Days	1980	3.00	6.00	12.00

BLACKFOOT, J.D.
45s
FANTASY

Number	Title (A Side/B Side)	Yr	VG	VG+	NM
❏ 741	Twilight/Done on the Ocean	1975	2.00	4.00	8.00
PHILIPS					
❏ 40625	Epitaph for a Head/Who's Nuts, Alfred	1969	3.00	6.00	12.00
❏ 40679	I've Never Seen You/One Time Woman	1970	3.00	6.00	12.00
Albums					
FANTASY					
❏ F-9468	Song of Crazy Horse	1974	5.00	10.00	20.00
❏ F-9487	Southbound and Gone	1975	5.00	10.00	20.00
MERCURY					
❏ SR-61288	The Ultimate Prophecy	1970	15.00	30.00	60.00

BLACKMAN, HONOR
Albums
LONDON

Number	Title (A Side/B Side)	Yr	VG	VG+	NM
❏ PS 408 [S]	Everything I've Got	1964	10.00	20.00	40.00
❏ LL 3408 [M]	Everything I've Got	1964	7.50	15.00	30.00

B

Number	Title (A Side/B Side)	Yr	VG	VG+	NM

BLACKWELL, OTIS
45s
ATLANTIC

Number	Title (A Side/B Side)	Yr	VG	VG+	NM
❏ 1165	Make Ready for Love/When You're Around	1957	10.00	20.00	40.00
❏ 1178	Turtle Dove/What a Coincidence	1958	10.00	20.00	40.00
CUB					
❏ 9092	Jeannie's Wedding/I'd Rather Kiss You Than Eat	1961	5.00	10.00	20.00
❏ 9107	Sister Twister/Ga Ga	1962	5.00	10.00	20.00
DATE					
❏ 1006	Don't Run Away/Handle with Care	1958	7.50	15.00	30.00
EPIC					
❏ 10654	Just Keep It Up/It's All Over Me	1970	6.25	12.50	25.00
GROOVE					
❏ 0034	Oh, What a Babe/Here I Am	1954	10.00	20.00	40.00
JAY-DEE					
❏ 784	Daddy Rolling Stone/Tears! Tears! Tears!	1953	12.50	25.00	50.00
❏ 787	You're My Love/Bartender Fill It Up Again	1954	12.50	25.00	50.00
❏ 791	On That Power Line/ Don't You Know How I Love You	1954	12.50	25.00	50.00
❏ 792	I'm Standing at the Doorway/ Nobody Met the Train	1954	12.50	25.00	50.00
❏ 794	My Josephine/Ain't Got No Time	1954	12.50	25.00	50.00
❏ 798	Go Away Mr. Blues/I'm Comin' Back Baby	1955	12.50	25.00	50.00
❏ 802	You Move Me Baby/My Poor Broken Heart	1955	12.50	25.00	50.00
❏ 808	Oh What a Wonderful Time/ Let the Daddy Hold You	1955	12.50	25.00	50.00
MGM					
❏ 13090	Kiss Away/Grandaddy of Them All	1962	5.00	10.00	20.00
RCA VICTOR					
❏ 47-5069	Wake You Fool/Please Help Me Find	1952	12.50	25.00	50.00
❏ 47-5225	The Fool That I Be/Number 000	1953	12.50	25.00	50.00
Albums					
DAVIS					
❏ 109 [M]	Singin' the Blues	1956	125.00	250.00	500.00
INNER CITY					
❏ 1032	These Are My Songs	1977	5.00	10.00	20.00

BLACKWELL, SCRAPPER
Albums
BLUESVILLE

Number	Title (A Side/B Side)	Yr	VG	VG+	NM
❏ BVLP-1047	Mr. Scrapper's Blues	1962	45.00	90.00	180.00
—Blue label, silver print					
❏ BVLP-1047	Mr. Scrapper's Blues	1964	10.00	20.00	40.00
—Blue label with trident logo					

BLACKWELLS, THE
45s
GUYDEN

Number	Title (A Side/B Side)	Yr	VG	VG+	NM
❏ 2020	Oh My Love/Holey Sombrero	1959	5.00	10.00	20.00
HICKORY					
❏ 1241	I Won't Be Perfect/Playin' Heart Strings	1964	2.50	5.00	10.00
❏ 1261	Ballad of a Young Truck Driver/She Loves the Love I Give Her	1964	2.50	5.00	10.00
❏ 1319	Little Bird/I've Been Waiting	1965	2.50	5.00	10.00
JAMIE					
❏ 1141	You Are Free, I'm Alone/The Depot	1959	3.75	7.50	15.00
❏ 1146	The Christmas Holiday/Little Match Girl	1959	5.00	10.00	20.00
❏ 1150	Always It's You/Honey, Honey	1960	3.75	7.50	15.00
❏ 1150 [PS]	Always It's You/Honey, Honey	1960	7.50	15.00	30.00
❏ 1157	Unchained Melody/Mansion on the Hill	1960	3.75	7.50	15.00
❏ 1170	You're a Habit with Me/Moulin Rouge	1960	3.75	7.50	15.00
❏ 1173	The Christmas Holiday/Little Match Girl	1960	3.75	7.50	15.00
❏ 1179	Love or Money/Big Daddy and the Cat	1961	3.00	6.00	12.00
❏ 1199	You Took Advantage of Me/"I"	1961	3.00	6.00	12.00
LIBERTY					
❏ 55750	Show Me Around/The Old Coast Road	1964	2.50	5.00	10.00

BLADES, CAROL
45s
GEE

Number	Title (A Side/B Side)	Yr	VG	VG+	NM
❏ 1029	When Will I Know/What Did I Do Wrong	1957	50.00	100.00	200.00

BLADES OF GRASS, THE
45s
JUBILEE

Number	Title (A Side/B Side)	Yr	VG	VG+	NM
❏ 5582	Happy/That's What a Boy Likes	1967	2.00	4.00	8.00
❏ 5590	Just Another Face/Baby You're a Real Good Friend of Mine	1967	2.00	4.00	8.00
❏ 5605	Help/Justah	1967	2.00	4.00	8.00
❏ 5616	You Won't Find That Girl/Charlie and Fred	1968	2.00	4.00	8.00
❏ 5622	The Way You'll Never Be/You Turned Off the Sun	1968	2.00	4.00	8.00
❏ 5635	I Love You, Alice B. Toklas/ That's What a Boy Likes	1968	2.00	4.00	8.00
❏ 5662	Love Her and Cherish Her/Pageant	1969	2.00	4.00	8.00
Albums					
JUBILEE					
❏ JGS-8007	The Blades of Grass Are Not for Smoking	1968	3.75	7.50	15.00

BLAINE, HAL
45s
ABC DUNHILL

Number	Title (A Side/B Side)	Yr	VG	VG+	NM
❏ 4181	Beverly Drive/Midnight at Fink's	1969	3.00	6.00	12.00
DUNHILL					
❏ 4006	La Bamba/Topsy '65	1965	3.75	7.50	15.00
❏ 4021	Secret Agent Man/Midnight at Pink's	1966	3.75	7.50	15.00
❏ 4049	Bang Bang Rhythm/Drums A-Go-Go	1966	3.75	7.50	15.00
❏ 4074	The Swinger/Drums A-Go-Go	1967	3.75	7.50	15.00
❏ 4091	Love-In (December)/Wiggy (November)	1967	3.75	7.50	15.00
❏ 4102	The Invaders/Secret Agent Man	1967	3.75	7.50	15.00
❏ 4142	Allegro from "Mac Arthur Park"/Drums A-Go-Go	1968	3.75	7.50	15.00

Number	Title (A Side/B Side)	Yr	VG	VG+	NM
MELODY HOUSE					
❏ 100	Slow Gate/South of Shreveport	1962	10.00	20.00	40.00
RCA VICTOR					
❏ 47-8147	Hawaii 1963/East Side Story	1963	6.25	12.50	25.00
❏ 47-8223	Dance with the Surfin' Band/ The Drummer Plays for Me	1963	6.25	12.50	25.00
❏ 47-8282	Challenger II/Gear Stripper	1963	6.25	12.50	25.00
ROCK-IT					
❏ 1000	Alamo Rock/Alamo Rock (Part 2)	1959	12.50	25.00	50.00
Albums					
ABC DUNHILL					
❏ DS-50035	Have Fun!!! Play Drums!!!	1968	10.00	20.00	40.00
—Without instruction booklet					
❏ DS-50035	Have Fun!!! Play Drums!!!	1968	12.50	25.00	50.00
—With instruction booklet					
DUNHILL					
❏ D-50002 [M]	Drums! Drums! A-Go-Go	1966	7.50	15.00	30.00
❏ DS-50002 [S]	Drums! Drums! A-Go-Go	1966	10.00	20.00	40.00
❏ D-50019 [M]	Psychedelic Percussion	1967	10.00	20.00	40.00
❏ DS-50019 [S]	Psychedelic Percussion	1967	15.00	30.00	60.00
RCA VICTOR					
❏ LPM-2834 [M]	Deuces, "T's," Roadsters & Drums	1963	25.00	50.00	100.00
❏ LSP-2834 [S]	Deuces, "T's," Roadsters & Drums	1963	37.50	75.00	150.00

BLAIR, TOM
45s
DECCA

Number	Title (A Side/B Side)	Yr	VG	VG+	NM
❏ 31223	West Coast/With My Hand on My Heart	1961	7.50	15.00	30.00
❏ 31344	Dolar Bills/Since You Are Gone	1961	7.50	15.00	30.00
DOT					
❏ 16095	Rock It/You Name It	1960	12.50	25.00	50.00
TEEN TUNES					
❏ 767	Rock It/You Name It	1960	25.00	50.00	100.00

BLAKE, HARRIETTE
45s
LTD

Number	Title (A Side/B Side)	Yr	VG	VG+	NM
❏ 403	Two of Us/Turn Around Boy	1966	3.00	6.00	12.00
❏ 409	Gee You Are/Unspoken Words	1966	3.00	6.00	12.00
MONUMENT					
❏ 1121	I Laughed Till I Cried/Tell It Like It Is	1968	2.00	4.00	8.00
MUSICOR					
❏ 1052	Love Me, Love Me/Wishin'	1965	3.00	6.00	12.00
PARKWAY					
❏ 961	Dansero/Why Did Our Love Go Wrong	1965	3.75	7.50	15.00
Albums					
HARRIETTE BLAKE					
❏ HBLP-001	This Is My Life	1976	3.75	7.50	15.00
❏ HBLP-002	My Way	1978	3.75	7.50	15.00

BLAKE, TOMMY
45s
BUDDY

Number	Title (A Side/B Side)	Yr	VG	VG+	NM
❏ 107	I'm a Fool/Kool It	1958	250.00	500.00	1000.
CHANCELLOR					
❏ 101	I Gotta Be Somewhere/ Three Cheers for the Red, White and Blue	19??	2.50	5.00	10.00
RCA VICTOR					
❏ 47-6925	Freedom/Mr. Hoody	1957	12.50	25.00	50.00
SUN					
❏ 278	Flatfoot Sam/Lordy Hoody	1957	25.00	50.00	100.00
❏ 300	Sweetie Pie/I Dig You	1958	75.00	150.00	300.00

BLAKELY, WELLINGTON
45s
VEE JAY

Number	Title (A Side/B Side)	Yr	VG	VG+	NM
❏ 104	Sailor Joe/Gypsy with a Broken Heart	1953	100.00	200.00	400.00

BLANC, MEL
45s
CAPITOL

Number	Title (A Side/B Side)	Yr	VG	VG+	NM
❏ F1330	Woody Woodpecker/Trixie and the Piano Pixie	1950	7.50	15.00	30.00
❏ F1360	I Tawt I Taw a Puddy Tat/Yosemite Sam	1951	7.50	15.00	30.00
❏ F1441	K-K-K-Katy/Flying Saucers	1951	7.50	15.00	30.00
❏ F1727	10 Little Bottles in the Sink/OKMNX	1951	7.50	15.00	30.00
❏ F1853	I Tan't Wait Till Quithmuth/Christmas Chopsticks	1951	7.50	15.00	30.00
❏ F1948	That's All Folks!/Wontcha Ever	1952	7.50	15.00	30.00
❏ F2048	Lord Bless His Soul/Morris	1952	7.50	15.00	30.00
❏ F2261	The Misses Wouldn't Approve/ I Tell My Troubles to Joe	1952	7.50	15.00	30.00
❏ F2430	Tia-Juana/Little Red Monkey	1953	6.25	12.50	25.00
❏ F2470	Somebody Stole My Gal/I Love Me	1953	6.25	12.50	25.00
❏ F2619	Ya, Das Ist Ein Christmas Tree/ I Tan't Wait Till Quithmuth	1953	7.50	15.00	30.00
❏ F2635	I'm in the Mood for Love/My Kinda Love	1953	6.25	12.50	25.00
❏ F2718	I Dess I Dotta Doe/The Lady Bird Song	1954	7.50	15.00	30.00
❏ F2764	Money/Polly Pretty Polly	1954	6.25	12.50	25.00
❏ F3902	The Hat I Got for Christmas Is Too Beeg/ Pancho's Christmas	1959	6.25	12.50	25.00
WARNER BROS.					
❏ 5129	Tweety's Twistmas Troubles/ I Keep Hearing Those Bells	1959	6.25	12.50	25.00
❏ 5156	Blimey/I Can't Fool My Heart	1960	6.25	12.50	25.00
Albums					
CAPITOL					
❏ H-436 [10]	Party Panic	1953	25.00	50.00	100.00

BLANCHARD, JACK, AND MISTY MORGAN
45s
EPIC

Number	Title (A Side/B Side)	Yr	VG	VG+	NM
❏ 11030	Cockroach Stomp/Carolina Sundown Red	1973	—	2.00	4.00
❏ 11058	Just One More Song/Why Did I Sleep So Long	1973	—	2.00	4.00

B

Number	Title (A Side/B Side)	Yr	VG	VG+	NM
❏ 11097	Something on Your Mind/				
	Here Today and Gone Tomorrow	1974	—	2.00	4.00
❏ 50023	Down to the End of the Wine/				
	You Can't Say I Didn't Try	1974	—	2.00	4.00
❏ 50082	Chorus/House	1975	—	2.00	4.00
❏ 50122	Because We Love/It's Me	1975	—	2.00	4.00
❏ 50181	I'm High on You/Let's Pretend	1975	—	2.00	4.00
❏ 50205	47 Miles (to the Georgia Line)/Motel Time	1976	—	2.00	4.00
MEGA					
❏ 0031	There Must Be More to Life/Fire Hydrant #79	1971	—	2.00	4.00
❏ 0046	Somewhere in Virginia in the Rain/				
	If Eggs Had Legs	1971	—	2.00	4.00
❏ 0063	The Legendary Chicken Fairy/The Night We				
	Heard the Voice	1972	—	2.00	4.00
❏ 0082	Miami Sidewalks/Washin' Harry Down the Sink	1972	—	2.00	4.00
❏ 0089	Second Tuesday in December/Don't It Make				
	You Want to Go Home	1972	—	2.00	4.00
❏ 0101	A Handful of Dimes/				
	It Seems Like There Ain't No Going Home	1973	—	2.00	4.00
❏ 0114	Shadows of the Leaves/Sweet Memories	1973	—	2.00	4.00
UNITED ARTISTS					
❏ XW1004	Tennessee Birdwalk/Living Together	1977	—	2.00	4.00
❏ XW1067	Heartaches/You Come So Easy to Me	1977	—	2.00	4.00
WAYSIDE					
❏ 00	Big Black Bird (Spirit of Our Love)/Autumn Song				
	(On a Yellow Day)	1969	—	2.50	5.00
—Reissue of 1028					
❏ 007	Changin' Times/Poor Jody	1969	—	2.50	5.00
❏ 010	Tennessee Bird Walk/The Clock of St. James	1970	—	2.50	5.00
❏ 013	Humphrey the Camel/A Place in My Mind	1970	—	2.50	5.00
❏ 015	You've Got Your Troubles (I've Got Mine)/				
	How I Lost 31 Pounds in 17 Days	1970	—	2.50	5.00
❏ 1024	Bethlehem Steel/No Sign of Love	1969	—	3.00	6.00
❏ 1028	Big Black Bird (Spirit of Our Love)/Autumn Song				
	(On a Yellow Day)	1969	—	3.00	6.00
Albums					
MEGA					
❏ 31-1009	Two Sides	1972	3.00	6.00	12.00
WAYSIDE					
❏ WWS 33-001	Birds of a Feather	1970	3.75	7.50	15.00

BLAND, BILLY
45s
OLD TOWN

Number	Title (A Side/B Side)	Yr	VG	VG+	NM
❏ 1016	Chicken in the Basket/The Fat Man	1956	5.00	10.00	20.00
❏ 1022	Chicken Hop/Oh You for Me	1956	5.00	10.00	20.00
❏ 1035	If I Could Be Your Man/I Had a Dream	1957	5.00	10.00	20.00
❏ 1076	Let the Little Girl Dance/Sweet Thing	1960	6.25	12.50	25.00
❏ 1082	You Were Born to Be Loved/Pardon Me	1960	3.75	7.50	15.00
❏ 1088	Make Believe Lover/Harmonys	1960	3.75	7.50	15.00
❏ 1093	Everything That Shines Ain't Gold/Keep Talkin'				
	That Sweet Talk	1960	3.75	7.50	15.00
❏ 1098	I Cross My Heart/Steady Kind	1961	3.75	7.50	15.00
❏ 1105	My Heart's On Fire/Can't Stop Her from Dancing	1961	3.75	7.50	15.00
❏ 1109	Do the Bug with Me/Uncle Bud	1962	3.75	7.50	15.00
❏ 1114	Busy Little Boy/All I Want to Do Is Cry	1961	3.75	7.50	15.00
❏ 1124	Mama Stole the Chicken/				
	I Spent My Life Loving You	1962	3.75	7.50	15.00
❏ 1128	Darling Won't You Think of Me/How Many				
	Hearts	1962	3.75	7.50	15.00
❏ 1143	Doing the Mule/Farmer in the Dell	1963	3.75	7.50	15.00
❏ 1151	A Little Touch of Your Love/Little Boy Blue	1963	3.75	7.50	15.00
ST. LAWRENCE					
❏ 1005	She's Already Married/My Divorce	1965	3.00	6.00	12.00
TIP TOP					
❏ 708	Chicken in the Basket/Chicken Hop	1958	5.00	10.00	20.00

BLAND, BOBBY Includes records by "Bobby 'Blue' Bland."
12-Inch Singles
MCA

Number	Title (A Side/B Side)	Yr	VG	VG+	NM
❏ L33-1835 [DJ]	I Feel Good, I Feel Fine/Tit for Tat/Come Fly with				
	Me/Love to See You Smile	1979	3.75	7.50	15.00

45s
ABC

Number	Title (A Side/B Side)	Yr	VG	VG+	NM
❏ 12105	Yolanda/When You Come to the End of Your				
	Road	1975	—	2.00	4.00
❏ 12134	I Take It On Home/You've Never Been This Far				
	Before	1975	—	2.00	4.00
❏ 12156	Today I Started Loving You Again/Too Far Gone	1976	—	2.00	4.00
❏ 12189	It Ain't the Real Thing/Who's Foolin' Who	1976	—	2.00	4.00
❏ 12280	The Soul of a Man/If I Weren't a Gambler	1977	—	2.00	4.00
❏ 12330	Sittin' on a Poor Man's Throne/I Intend to Take				
	Your Place	1978	—	2.00	4.00
❏ 12360	Love to See You Smile/I'm Just Your Man	1978	—	2.00	4.00
❏ 12405	Come Fly with Me/Ain't God Something	1978	—	2.00	4.00
ABC DUNHILL					
❏ 4369	This Time I'm Gone for Good/Where Baby Went	1973	—	2.50	5.00
❏ 4379	Goin' Down Slow/Up and Down World	1974	—	2.50	5.00
❏ 15003	Ain't No Love in the Heart of the City/Twenty-				
	Four Hour Blues	1974	—	2.50	5.00
❏ 15015	I Wouldn't Treat a Dog (The Way You Treated				
	Me)/I Ain't Gonna Be the First to Cry	1974	—	2.50	5.00
DUKE					
❏ 105	Lovin' Blues/I.O.U. Blues	1952	75.00	150.00	300.00
❏ 115	Army Blues/No Blow, No Show	1953	50.00	100.00	200.00
❏ 141	Time Out/It's My Life Baby	1955	15.00	30.00	60.00
❏ 146	You or None/Woke Up Screaming	1955	15.00	30.00	60.00
❏ 153	I Can't Put You Down/You've Got Bad Intentions	1956	12.50	25.00	50.00
❏ 160	I Learned My Lesson/I Don't Believe	1956	10.00	20.00	40.00
❏ 160	I Learned My Lesson/Lead Us On	1956	10.00	20.00	40.00
❏ 167	Don't Want No Woman/I Smell Trouble	1957	7.50	15.00	30.00

Number	Title (A Side/B Side)	Yr	VG	VG+	NM
❏ 170	Farther Up the Road/Sometime Tomorrow	1957	7.50	15.00	30.00
❏ 182	Teach Me/Bobby's Blues	1957	6.25	12.50	25.00
❏ 185	You Got Me Where You Want Me/Loan a				
	Helping Hand	1958	6.25	12.50	25.00
❏ 196	Little Boy Blue/Last Night	1958	6.25	12.50	25.00
❏ 300	You Did Me Wrong/I Lost Sight of the World	1959	6.25	12.50	25.00
❏ 303	Wishing Well/I'm Not Ashamed	1959	6.25	12.50	25.00
❏ 310	Is It Real/Someday	1959	6.25	12.50	25.00
❏ 314	I'll Take Care of You/That's Why	1959	6.25	12.50	25.00
❏ 318	Lead Me On/Hold Me Tenderly	1960	6.25	12.50	25.00
❏ 327	Cry Cry Cry/I've Been Wrong So Long	1960	6.25	12.50	25.00
❏ 332	I Pity the Fool/Close to You	1961	5.00	10.00	20.00
❏ 336	Don't Cry No More/How Does a Cheating				
	Woman Feel	1961	5.00	10.00	20.00
❏ 338	Ain't That Loving You/Jelly, Jelly, Jelly	1961	5.00	10.00	20.00
❏ 340	Don't Cry No More/Saint James Infirmary	1961	5.00	10.00	20.00
❏ 344	Turn On Your Love Light/You're the One (That				
	I Need)	1961	5.00	10.00	20.00
❏ 347	Who Will the Next Fool Be/Blue Moon	1962	5.00	10.00	20.00
❏ 352	Yield Not to Temptation/How Does a Cheating				
	Woman Feel	1962	5.00	10.00	20.00
❏ 355	Stormy Monday Blues/Your Friends	1962	5.00	10.00	20.00
❏ 360	That's the Way Love Is/Call On Me	1962	5.00	10.00	20.00
❏ 366	Sometimes You Gotta Cry a Little/You're Worth				
	It All	1963	3.75	7.50	15.00
❏ 369	Ain't It a Good Thing/Queen for a Day	1963	3.75	7.50	15.00
❏ 370	The Feeling Is Gone/I Can't Stop Singing	1963	3.75	7.50	15.00
❏ 375	Ain't Nothing You Can Do/Honey Child	1964	3.75	7.50	15.00
❏ 377	Share Your Love with Me/After It's Too Late	1964	2.50	5.00	10.00
❏ 383	Ain't Doing Too Bad (Part 1)/Ain't Doing Too Bad				
	(Part 2)	1964	2.50	5.00	10.00
❏ 385	These Hands (Small But Mighty)/Today	1965	2.50	5.00	10.00
❏ 386	Blind Man/Black Night	1965	2.50	5.00	10.00
❏ 390	Dust Got in Daddy's Eyes/Ain't No Telling	1965	2.50	5.00	10.00
❏ 393	I'm Too Far Gone (To Turn Around)/If You Could				
	Read My Mind	1965	2.50	5.00	10.00
❏ 402	Good Time Charlie/Good Time Charlie (Part 2)	1966	2.00	4.00	8.00
❏ 407	Poverty/Building a Fire with Hair	1966	2.00	4.00	8.00
❏ 412	Back in the Same Old Bag Again/				
	I Ain't Myself Anymore	1966	2.00	4.00	8.00
❏ 416	You're All I Need/Deep in My Soul	1967	2.00	4.00	8.00
❏ 421	That Did It/Getting Used to the Blues	1967	2.00	4.00	8.00
❏ 426	A Touch of the Blues/Shoes	1967	2.00	4.00	8.00
❏ 432	Driftin' Blues/You Could Read My Mind	1968	2.00	4.00	8.00
❏ 433	Honey Child/A Piece of Gold	1968	2.00	4.00	8.00
❏ 435	Save Your Love for Me/Share Your Love with Me	1968	2.00	4.00	8.00
❏ 440	Rockin' in the Same Old Boat/Wouldn't You				
	Rather Have Me	1968	2.00	4.00	8.00
❏ 447	Gotta Get to Know You/Baby I'm On My Way	1969	2.00	4.00	8.00
❏ 449	Chains of Love/Ask Me 'Bout Nothing				
	(But the Blues)	1969	2.00	4.00	8.00
❏ 458	If You've Got a Heart/Sad Feeling	1970	2.00	4.00	8.00
❏ 460	Lover with a Reputation/If Love Ruled the World	1970	2.00	4.00	8.00
❏ 464	Keep On Loving Me (You'll See the Change)/I				
	Just Got to Forget About You	1970	2.00	4.00	8.00
❏ 466	I'm Sorry/Yum Yum Tree	1971	2.00	4.00	8.00
❏ 471	Shape Up or Ship Out/The Love That We Share				
	(Is True)	1971	2.00	4.00	8.00
❏ 472	Do What You Set Out to Do/Ain't Nothing You				
	Can Do	1972	2.00	4.00	8.00
❏ 477	I'm So Tired/If You Could Read My Mind	1972	2.00	4.00	8.00
❏ 480	That's All There Is/I Don't Want Another				
	Mountain to Climb	1973	2.00	4.00	8.00
KENT					
❏ 378	Love You Baby/Drifting	1962	2.50	5.00	10.00
—With Ike Turner					
MALACO					
❏ 2122	Members Only/I Just Got to Know	1985	—	—	3.00
❏ 2126	Can We Make Love Tonight/In the Ghetto	1986	—	—	3.00
❏ 2133	Angel/I Hear You Thinkin'	1986	—	—	3.00
MCA					
❏ 41140	Tit for Tat/Come Fly with Me	1979	—	2.00	4.00
❏ 41197	Soon as the Weather Breaks/To Be Friends	1980	—	2.00	4.00
❏ 51068	You'd Be a Millionaire/Swat Vibrator	1981	—	—	3.00
❏ 51181	What a Difference A Day Makes/Givin' Up the				
	Streets for Love	1982	—	—	3.00
❏ 52085	Recess in Heaven/Exactly, Where It's At	1982	—	—	3.00
❏ 52136	Here We Go Again/You're About to Win	1982	—	—	3.00
❏ 52180	Is This the Blues/You're About to Win	1983	—	—	3.00
❏ 52270	If It Ain't One Thing/Tell Mr. Bland	1983	—	—	3.00
❏ 52436	Looking Back/You Got Me Loving You	1984	—	—	3.00
❏ 52482	Get Real Clean/It's Too Bad	1984	—	—	3.00
❏ 52508	You Are My Christmas/				
	New Merry Christmas Baby	1984	—	—	3.00
WAND					
❏ 1102	Honey, You've Been On My Mind/				
	You've Got Time	1965	3.75	7.50	15.00
Albums					
ABC					
❏ D-895	Get On Down with Bobby Bland	1975	3.00	6.00	12.00
❏ AB-1018	Reflections in Blue	1977	2.50	5.00	10.00
❏ AA-1075	Come Fly with Me	1978	2.50	5.00	10.00
ABC DUKE					
❏ DLPS-74	Two Steps from the Blues	197?	3.00	6.00	12.00
❏ DLP-75	Here's the Man!!!	1974	3.00	6.00	12.00
❏ DLP-77	Call On Me/That's the Way Love Is	1974	3.00	6.00	12.00
❏ DLP-78	Ain't Nothing You Can Do	1974	3.00	6.00	12.00
❏ DLP-79	The Soul of the Man	1974	3.00	6.00	12.00
❏ DLP-84	The Best of Bobby Bland	1974	3.00	6.00	12.00
❏ DLP-86	The Best of Bobby Bland, Volume 2	1974	3.00	6.00	12.00
❏ DLP-88	A Touch of the Blues	1974	3.00	6.00	12.00
❏ DLP-89	Spotlighting the Man	1974	3.00	6.00	12.00

Number	Title (A Side/B Side)	Yr	VG	VG+	NM
❑ DLP 92-2 [(2)]	Introspective of the Early Years	1974	5.00	10.00	20.00

ABC DUNHILL

Number	Title (A Side/B Side)	Yr	VG	VG+	NM
❑ DSX-50163	His California Album	1973	3.75	7.50	15.00
❑ DSX-50169	Dreamer	1974	3.75	7.50	15.00

BLUESWAY

Number	Title (A Side/B Side)	Yr	VG	VG+	NM
❑ BLS-6065	Call On Me	197?	3.75	7.50	15.00

DUKE

Number	Title (A Side/B Side)	Yr	VG	VG+	NM
❑ DLP-74 [M]	Two Steps from the Blues	1961	62.50	125.00	250.00
—Purple and yellow label					
❑ DLP-74 [M]	Two Steps from the Blues	1962	25.00	50.00	100.00
—Orange label, black vinyl					
❑ DLP-74 [M]	Two Steps from the Blues	1962	62.50	125.00	250.00
—Orange label, red vinyl					
❑ DLPS-74 [R]	Two Steps from the Blues	196?	15.00	30.00	60.00
❑ DLP-75 [M]	Here's the Man!!!	1962	25.00	50.00	100.00
—Orange label					
❑ DLP-75 [M]	Here's the Man!!!	1962	50.00	100.00	200.00
—Purple and yellow label					
❑ DLPS-75 [S]	Here's the Man!!!	196?	25.00	50.00	100.00
—Without spoken intro to "36-22-36"					
❑ DLPS-75 [S]	Here's the Man!!!	1962	50.00	100.00	200.00
—With spoken intro to "36-22-36"					
❑ DLP-77 [M]	Call On Me/That's the Way Love Is	1963	25.00	50.00	100.00
❑ DLPS-77 [S]	Call On Me/That's the Way Love Is	1963	37.50	75.00	150.00
❑ DLP-78 [M]	Ain't Nothing You Can Do	1964	20.00	40.00	80.00
❑ DLPS-78 [S]	Ain't Nothing You Can Do	1964	30.00	60.00	120.00
❑ DLP-79 [M]	The Soul of the Man	1966	20.00	40.00	80.00
❑ DLPS-79 [S]	The Soul of the Man	1966	30.00	60.00	120.00
❑ DLP-84 [M]	The Best of Bobby Bland	1967	5.00	10.00	20.00
❑ DLPS-84 [P]	The Best of Bobby Bland	1967	6.25	12.50	25.00
❑ DLP-86 [M]	The Best of Bobby Bland, Volume 2	1968	6.25	12.50	25.00
❑ DLPS-86 [P]	The Best of Bobby Bland, Volume 2	1968	5.00	10.00	20.00
❑ DLP-88 [M]	A Touch of the Blues	1968	6.25	12.50	25.00
❑ DLPS-88 [S]	A Touch of the Blues	1968	5.00	10.00	20.00
❑ DLPS-89	Spotlighting the Man	1969	5.00	10.00	20.00
❑ DLPS-90	If Loving You Is Wrong	1970	5.00	10.00	20.00

MCA

Number	Title (A Side/B Side)	Yr	VG	VG+	NM
❑ 3157	I Feel Good, I Feel Fine	1979	2.50	5.00	10.00
❑ 4172 [(2)]	Introspective of the Early Years	198?	2.50	5.00	10.00
—Reissue of Duke 92					
❑ 5145	Sweet Vibrations	1980	2.50	5.00	10.00
❑ 5233	Try Me, I'm Real	1981	2.50	5.00	10.00
❑ 5297	Here We Go Again	1982	2.50	5.00	10.00
❑ 5425	Tell Mr. Bland	1983	2.50	5.00	10.00
❑ 5503	You've Got Me Loving You	1984	2.50	5.00	10.00
❑ 27013	The Best of Bobby Bland	198?	2.00	4.00	8.00
—Reissue of Duke 84					
❑ 27036	Two Steps from the Blues	198?	2.00	4.00	8.00
—Reissue of Duke 74					
❑ 27038	Here's the Man!!!	198?	2.00	4.00	8.00
—Reissue of Duke 75					
❑ 27040	Ain't Nothing You Can Do	198?	2.00	4.00	8.00
—Reissue of Duke 78					
❑ 27041	The Soul of the Man	1984	2.00	4.00	8.00
—Reissue of Duke 79					
❑ 27042	Call On Me/That's the Way Love Is	1984	2.00	4.00	8.00
—Reissue of Duke 77					
❑ 27043	Reflections in Blue	1984	2.00	4.00	8.00
—Reissue of ABC 1018					
❑ 27044	Come Fly with Me	1984	2.00	4.00	8.00
—Reissue of ABC 1075					
❑ 27045	The Best of Bobby Bland, Volume 2	1984	2.00	4.00	8.00
—Reissue of Duke 86					
❑ 27047	A Touch of the Blues	1984	2.00	4.00	8.00
—Reissue of Duke 88					
❑ 27048	Spotlighting the Man	1984	2.00	4.00	8.00
—Reissue of Duke 89					
❑ 27073	I Feel Good, I Feel Fine	1985	2.00	4.00	8.00
—Reissue of MCA 3157					
❑ 27076	Sweet Vibrations	198?	2.00	4.00	8.00
—Reissue of 5145					

BLAND, BOBBY, AND B.B. KING Also see each artist's individual listings.
45s
ABC IMPULSE

Number	Title (A Side/B Side)	Yr	VG	VG+	NM
❑ 31006	Let the Good Times Roll/Strange Things	1976	—	2.00	4.00
❑ 31009	Everyday I Have the Blues/The Thrill Is Gone	1976	—	2.00	4.00

Albums
ABC DUNHILL

Number	Title (A Side/B Side)	Yr	VG	VG+	NM
❑ DSY-50190 [(2)]	Together for the First Time...Live	1974	3.75	7.50	15.00

ABC IMPULSE!

Number	Title (A Side/B Side)	Yr	VG	VG+	NM
❑ 9317	Together Again...Live	1976	3.00	6.00	12.00

COMMAND

Number	Title (A Side/B Side)	Yr	VG	VG+	NM
❑ CQDY-40012 [(2)Q]	Together for the First Time...Live	1974	6.25	12.50	25.00

MCA

Number	Title (A Side/B Side)	Yr	VG	VG+	NM
❑ 4160 [(2)]	Together for the First Time...Live	198?	2.50	5.00	10.00
—Reissue of ABC Dunhill 50190					
❑ 27012	Together Again...Live	198?	2.00	4.00	8.00
—Reissue of ABC Impulse! 9317					

BLANDERS, THE
45s
SMASH

Number	Title (A Side/B Side)	Yr	VG	VG+	NM
❑ 2005	Jitterbug/Desert Sands	1965	12.50	25.00	50.00

BLANE, MARCIE
45s
SEVILLE

Number	Title (A Side/B Side)	Yr	VG	VG+	NM
❑ 120	Bobby's Girl/Time to Dream	1962	5.00	10.00	20.00
—Exists with "Seville" logo straight across the top of the label, and with the "Seville" logo curving around the top of the label. No difference in value has yet been noted.					
❑ 123	What Does a Girl Do?/How Can I Tell Him	1963	4.00	8.00	16.00

Number	Title (A Side/B Side)	Yr	VG	VG+	NM
❑ 126	Little Miss Fool/Rag Time Sound	1963	4.00	8.00	16.00
❑ 128	You Gave My Number to Billy/Told You So	1963	4.00	8.00	16.00
❑ 130	Why Can't I Get a Guy/				
	Who's Going to Take My Daddy's Place	1963	4.00	8.00	16.00
❑ 133	Bobby Did/After the Laughter	1964	4.00	8.00	16.00
❑ 137	The Hurtin' Kind/She'll Break the String	1965	4.00	8.00	16.00

BLAVAT, JERRY
45s
CAMEO

Number	Title (A Side/B Side)	Yr	VG	VG+	NM
❑ 393	Discophonic Walk/				
	Back to School One More Time	1965	3.00	6.00	12.00

EPIC

Number	Title (A Side/B Side)	Yr	VG	VG+	NM
❑ 10193	Jerry's Theme/Let's Love Again	1967	3.00	6.00	12.00

FAVOR

Number	Title (A Side/B Side)	Yr	VG	VG+	NM
❑ 100	Discophonic Walk/				
	Back to School One More Time	1965	3.75	7.50	15.00

ROULETTE

Number	Title (A Side/B Side)	Yr	VG	VG+	NM
❑ 7085	Tasty (To Me)/Oh Be Joyous	1970	2.00	4.00	8.00
—With the Geatorettes					

BLAZER BOY
45s
IMPERIAL

Number	Title (A Side/B Side)	Yr	VG	VG+	NM
❑ 5199	Mornin'Train/Joe's Kid Sister	1952	25.00	50.00	100.00
❑ 5244	Surprise Blues/Waiting for My Baby	1953	25.00	50.00	100.00
❑ 5801	New Orleans Twist/That's Where It's At	1962	5.00	10.00	20.00

BLENDAIRS, THE
45s
TIN PAN ALLEY

Number	Title (A Side/B Side)	Yr	VG	VG+	NM
❑ 252	My Love Is Just for You/Repetition	1958	37.50	75.00	150.00

BLENDELLS, THE
45s
COTILLION

Number	Title (A Side/B Side)	Yr	VG	VG+	NM
❑ 44020	Night After Night/The Love That I Needed	1968	2.50	5.00	10.00

ERA BACK TO BACK HITS

Number	Title (A Side/B Side)	Yr	VG	VG+	NM
❑ 023	Dance with Me/Land of 1000 Dances	197?	—	2.50	5.00
—B-side by Cannibal and the Headhunters					

RAMPART

Number	Title (A Side/B Side)	Yr	VG	VG+	NM
❑ 641	La La La La La/Huggies Bunnies	1964	6.25	12.50	25.00

REPRISE

Number	Title (A Side/B Side)	Yr	VG	VG+	NM
❑ 0291	La La La La La/Huggies Bunnies	1964	5.00	10.00	20.00
❑ 0340	Dance with Me/Get Your Baby	1965	5.00	10.00	20.00

BLENDERS, THE Several different groups.
45s
AFO

Number	Title (A Side/B Side)	Yr	VG	VG+	NM
❑ 305	Graveyard/It Takes Time	1962	75.00	150.00	300.00

ALADDIN

Number	Title (A Side/B Side)	Yr	VG	VG+	NM
❑ 3449	Two Loves/Soda Shop	1959	250.00	500.00	1000.

CLASS

Number	Title (A Side/B Side)	Yr	VG	VG+	NM
❑ 236	My Heart's Desire/Little Rose	1958	10.00	20.00	40.00

CORTLAND

Number	Title (A Side/B Side)	Yr	VG	VG+	NM
❑ 102	Love Is a Treasure/Fisherman	1962	3.00	6.00	12.00
❑ 103	Everybody's Got a Right/What Have You Got	1962	3.00	6.00	12.00

DECCA

Number	Title (A Side/B Side)	Yr	VG	VG+	NM
❑ 27403	The Masquerade Is Over/Little Small Town Girl	1951	100.00	200.00	400.00
❑ 27587	All I Gotta Do Is Think of You/The Busiest Corner	1951	75.00	150.00	300.00
❑ 28092	Just a Little Walk with Me/I'd Be a Fool Again	1952	75.00	150.00	300.00
❑ 28241	Never in a Million Years/Memories of You	1952	75.00	150.00	300.00
❑ 48156	Gone/Honeysuckle Rose	1950	75.00	150.00	300.00
❑ 48158	Count Every Star/				
	Would I Still Be the One in Your Heart	1950	75.00	150.00	300.00
❑ 48183	I'm So Crazy for Love/What About Tonight	1950	75.00	150.00	300.00
❑ 48244	My Heart Will Never Forget/				
	You Do the Dreaming	1951	75.00	150.00	300.00

JAY DEE

Number	Title (A Side/B Side)	Yr	VG	VG+	NM
❑ 780	Don't Play Around with You/				
	You'll Never Smile Again	1953	50.00	100.00	200.00

MAR-V-LUS

Number	Title (A Side/B Side)	Yr	VG	VG+	NM
❑ 6010	Your Love Has Got Me Down/Love Is a Good Thing Going	1966	50.00	100.00	200.00

MGM

Number	Title (A Side/B Side)	Yr	VG	VG+	NM
❑ 11488	I Don't Miss You Anymore/If That's the Way You Want It Baby	1953	100.00	200.00	400.00
❑ 11531	Please Take Me Back/Isn't It a Shame	1953	100.00	200.00	400.00

RCA VICTOR

Number	Title (A Side/B Side)	Yr	VG	VG+	NM
❑ 47-6591	I've Told Every Little Star/Cecilia	1956	15.00	30.00	60.00
❑ 47-6712	Wake Up to Music/New Sensations in Sound	1956	12.50	25.00	50.00
❑ 47-7009	I'm Following You/				
	Since I Kissed My Baby Goodbye	1957	12.50	25.00	50.00

WANGER

Number	Title (A Side/B Side)	Yr	VG	VG+	NM
❑ 189	Angel/Old MacDonald	1959	6.25	12.50	25.00

WITCH

Number	Title (A Side/B Side)	Yr	VG	VG+	NM
❑ 114	Daughter/Everybody's Got a Right	1963	4.00	8.00	16.00
❑ 117	Boys Think/Squat and Squirm	1963	3.75	7.50	15.00
❑ 123	One Time/(B-side unknown)	1964	3.75	7.50	15.00

BLENDTONES, THE
45s
DON-EL

Number	Title (A Side/B Side)	Yr	VG	VG+	NM
❑ 106	She's Gone/Lights Please	1961	25.00	50.00	100.00

IMPERIAL

Number	Title (A Side/B Side)	Yr	VG	VG+	NM
❑ 5758	She's Gone/Lights Please	1961	6.25	12.50	25.00

SUCCESS

Number	Title (A Side/B Side)	Yr	VG	VG+	NM
❑ 101	Lovers/Dear Diary	1963	10.00	20.00	40.00
❑ 105	Come On Home/The Slide	1963	10.00	20.00	40.00

B

Number	Title (A Side/B Side)	Yr	VG	VG+	NM
BLESSED END					
Albums					
TNS					
❏ 248	Movin' On	1971	75.00	150.00	300.00
BLESSING, MICHAEL See MICHAEL NESMITH.					
BLEU LIGHTS, THE					
45s					
BAYSOUND					
❏ 67003	Forever/They Don't Know My Heart	1968	10.00	20.00	40.00
❏ 67007	Bony Moronie/Lonely Man's Prayer	1968	7.50	15.00	30.00
❏ 67010	Yes I Do/The End of My Dreams	1969	7.50	15.00	30.00
BLEVINS, CHUCK					
45s					
FOXIE					
❏ 7006	Sleigh Bell Rock/(B-side unknown)	1959	5.00	10.00	20.00
BLIND FAITH Also see GINGER BAKER'S AIR FORCE; ERIC CLAPTON; STEVE WINWOOD.					
45s					
POLYDOR					
❏ 871798-7	Presence of the Lord/Can't Find My Way Home	1989	—	2.00	4.00
RSO					
❏ 873	Presence of the Lord/Can't Find My Way Home	1977	2.00	4.00	8.00
—First single release from 1969 self-titled album					
Albums					
ATCO					
❏ 33-304A [M]	Blind Faith	1969	50.00	100.00	200.00
—White label promo only					
❏ SD 33-304A [S]	Blind Faith	1969	6.25	12.50	25.00
—Cover with naked girl on Side 1 and same scene without girl on Side 2					
❏ SD 33-304B [S]	Blind Faith	1969	3.75	7.50	15.00
—Cover with band photo on Side 1 and song lyrics on Side 2					
MOBILE FIDELITY					
❏ 1-186	Blind Faith	1985	10.00	20.00	40.00
—Audiophile vinyl					
RSO					
❏ RS-1-3016	Blind Faith	1977	2.50	5.00	10.00
—Reissue with naked girl on one side and band photo on the other					
❏ 825094-1	Blind Faith	1986	2.00	4.00	8.00
BLINKY					
45s					
MOTOWN					
❏ 1134	I Wouldn't Change the Man He Is/I'll Always Love You	1968	2.00	4.00	8.00
❏ 1168	How You Gonna Keep It/This Time Last Summer	1970	25.00	50.00	100.00
❏ 1233	You Get a Tangle in Your Life Line/This Man of Mine	1973	—	3.00	6.00
MOWEST					
❏ 5019	For Your Precious Love/So Tired	1972	—	3.00	6.00
❏ 5033	T'Ain't Nobody's Bizness If I Do/What More Can I Do	1973	—	2.50	5.00
SOUL					
❏ 35089	How You Gonna Keep It/This Time Last Summer	1971	—	3.00	6.00
BLISTERS, THE					
45s					
LIBERTY					
❏ 55577	Shortnin' Bread/Cookie Rockin' in Her Stockings	1963	3.00	6.00	12.00
❏ 55647	Rich in My Pocket, Poor in My Heart/Friendly Loans	1963	3.00	6.00	12.00
TITANIC					
❏ 5005	Fifty Mile Hike/Recitation	1963	5.00	10.00	20.00
BLOCH, SONNY					
45s					
BEE					
❏ 1000	Beetle Squash/Leapin' Lizards	1964	3.00	6.00	12.00
—As "Sonny Bloch's Elephants"					
REGAL					
❏ 7503	Ask Me No Questions/Hand of Faith	1958	5.00	10.00	20.00
BLODWYN PIG					
45s					
A&M					
❏ 1158	Dear Jill/Summer Day	1969	—	3.00	6.00
Albums					
A&M					
❏ SP-3180	Ahead Rings Out	1982	2.00	4.00	8.00
—Budget-line reissue					
❏ SP-4210	Ahead Rings Out	1969	3.75	7.50	15.00
❏ SP-4243	Getting to This	1970	3.75	7.50	15.00
BLOND					
45s					
FONTANA					
❏ 1673	Deep Inside My Heart/I Will Bring You Flowers in the Morning	1969	3.00	6.00	12.00
❏ 1673 [PS]	Deep Inside My Heart/I Will Bring You Flowers in the Morning	1969	4.00	8.00	16.00
Albums					
FONTANA					
❏ SRF-67067	Blond	1969	5.00	10.00	20.00
BLONDE ON BLONDE					
Albums					
JANUS					
❏ JLP-3003	Contrasts	1969	6.25	12.50	25.00

Number	Title (A Side/B Side)	Yr	VG	VG+	NM
BLOOD, SWEAT AND TEARS Also see DAVID CLAYTON-THOMAS; AL KOOPER.					
45s					
ABC					
❏ 12310	Blue Street/Somebody I Trusted	1977	—	2.00	4.00
COLUMBIA					
❏ JBQ 501 [Q]	Spinning Wheel/You've Made Me So Very Happy	1973	2.50	5.00	10.00
—"Special Coin Operator Release" in quadraphonic; contains the full-length versions of the songs (edited versions are on other 45s)					
❏ 10151	Got to Get You Into My Life/Naked Man	1975	—	2.50	5.00
❏ 10189	No Show/Yesterday's Music	1975	—	2.50	5.00
❏ 10400	You're the One/Heavy Blue	1976	—	2.50	5.00
❏ 44559	I Can't Quit Her/House in the Country	1968	2.00	4.00	8.00
❏ 44744	You've Made Me So Very Happy/Blues — Part 2	1969	—	3.00	6.00
❏ 44871	Spinning Wheel/More and More	1969	—	3.00	6.00
❏ 45008	And When I Die/Sometimes in Winter	1969	—	3.00	6.00
❏ 45204	Hi-De-Ho/The Battle	1970	—	2.50	5.00
❏ 45235	Lucretia Mac Evil/Lucretia's Reprise	1970	—	2.50	5.00
❏ 45427	Go Down Gamblin'/Valentine's Day	1971	—	2.50	5.00
❏ 45427 [PS]	Go Down Gamblin'/Valentine's Day	1971	2.00	4.00	8.00
❏ 45477	Lisa, Listen to Me/Cowboys and Indians	1971	—	2.50	5.00
❏ 45661	So Long Dixie/Alone	1972	—	2.50	5.00
❏ 45661 [PS]	So Long Dixie/Alone	1972	2.00	4.00	8.00
❏ 45755	Velvet/I Can't Move No Mountains	1973	—	2.50	5.00
❏ 45937	Roller Coaster/Inner Crisis	1973	—	2.50	5.00
❏ 45965	Save Our Ship/Song for John	1973	—	2.50	5.00
❏ 46059	Tell Me That I'm Wrong/Rock Reprise	1974	—	2.50	5.00
MCA					
❏ 41198	Nuclear Blues/Agitato	1980	—	2.00	4.00
7-Inch Extended Plays					
COLUMBIA					
❏ 7-30590	*Redemption/Lisa, Listen to Me/A Look to My Heart (duet)/A Look to My Heart (inst.)/For My Lady/Mama Gets High	1971	2.50	5.00	10.00
—Jukebox issue; small hole, plays at 33 1/3 rpm					
❏ 7-30590 [PS]	Blood, Sweat and Tears 4	1971	3.00	6.00	12.00
Albums					
ABC					
❏ 1015	Brand New Day	1977	2.50	5.00	10.00
CBS SPECIAL PRODUCTS					
❏ P 16660	Musically Speaking	1982	2.50	5.00	10.00
COLUMBIA					
❏ CS 9616 [M]	Child Is Father to the Man	1968	6.25	12.50	25.00
—White label promo only, "Special Mono Radio Station Copy" sticker on cover, with same number as stereo edition					
❏ CS 9616 [S]	Child Is Father to the Man	1968	3.75	7.50	15.00
—Red "360 Sound" label					
❏ CS 9616	Child Is Father to the Man	1970	2.50	5.00	10.00
—Orange label					
❏ PC 9619	Child Is Father to the Man	1980	2.00	4.00	8.00
❏ CS 9720	Blood, Sweat and Tears	1969	3.75	7.50	15.00
—Red "360 Sound" label					
❏ CS 9720	Blood, Sweat and Tears	1970	2.50	5.00	10.00
—Orange label					
❏ PC 9720	Blood, Sweat and Tears	1980	2.00	4.00	8.00
❏ KC 30090	Blood, Sweat and Tears 3	1970	2.50	5.00	10.00
❏ PC 30090	Blood, Sweat and Tears 3	1986	2.00	4.00	8.00
❏ KC 30590	BS&T: 4	1971	2.50	5.00	10.00
❏ CQ 30994 [Q]	Blood, Sweat and Tears	1972	5.00	10.00	20.00
❏ CQ 31170 [Q]	Blood, Sweat and Tears' Greatest Hits	1972	5.00	10.00	20.00
❏ KC 31170	Blood, Sweat and Tears' Greatest Hits	1972	2.50	5.00	10.00
—With the single versions of "You've Made Me So Very Happy," "Spinning Wheel," and "And When I Die" (all in mono)					
❏ PC 31170	Blood, Sweat and Tears' Greatest Hits	1980	2.00	4.00	8.00
❏ PCQ 31170 [Q]	Blood, Sweat and Tears' Greatest Hits	1976	4.50	9.00	18.00
—Reissue with new prefix					
❏ KC 31780	New Blood	1972	2.50	5.00	10.00
❏ KC 32180	No Sweat	1973	2.50	5.00	10.00
❏ CQ 32929 [Q]	Mirror Image	1974	5.00	10.00	20.00
❏ PC 32929	Mirror Image	1974	2.50	5.00	10.00
❏ PC 33484	New City	1975	2.50	5.00	10.00
❏ PCQ 33484 [Q]	New City	1975	3.75	7.50	15.00
❏ PC 34233	More Than Ever	1976	2.50	5.00	10.00
❏ HC 49619	Child Is Father to the Man	1981	12.50	25.00	50.00
—Half-speed mastered edition					
DIRECT DISK					
❏ SD-16605	Blood, Sweat and Tears	1981	15.00	30.00	60.00
MCA					
❏ L33-1865 [DJ]	Nuclear Blues	1980	3.75	7.50	15.00
—Promo only on gold vinyl					
❏ 3061	Nuclear Blues	1980	2.50	5.00	10.00
❏ 3227	Blood, Sweat and Tears	1981	—	—	—
—Canceled?					
MOBILE FIDELITY					
❏ 1-251	Blood, Sweat and Tears	1996	30.00	60.00	120.00
—Audiophile vinyl; fewer than 2,000 pressed					
BLOODROCK					
45s					
CAPITOL					
❏ 2736	Fatback/Gotta Find a Way	1970	—	3.00	6.00
❏ 3009	D.O.A./Children's Heritage	1971	2.00	4.00	8.00
❏ 3089	You Gotta Roll/A Certain Kind	1971	—	3.00	6.00
❏ 3161	Jessica/You Gotta Roll	1971	—	3.00	6.00
❏ 3227	Rock and Roll Candy Man/Don't Eat the Children	1971	—	3.00	6.00
❏ 3320	Erosion/Castle of Thoughts	1972	—	2.50	5.00
❏ 3399	Castle of Thoughts/D.O.A.	1972	—	2.50	5.00
❏ 3451	Help Is On the Way/Thank You Daniel Ellsburg	1972	—	2.50	5.00
❏ 3770	Voices/Thank You Daniel Ellsburg	1973	—	2.50	5.00
❏ PRO-6579/81 [DJ]	Help Is On the Way/Bloodrock Interview (By Sol Smaizys/Dennis Gray WXFM-Chicago)	1972	3.00	6.00	12.00

Number	Title (A Side/B Side)	Yr	VG	VG+	NM
Albums					
CAPITOL					
❑ ST-435	Bloodrock	1970	3.75	7.50	15.00
❑ ST-491	Bloodrock 2	1970	3.75	7.50	15.00
❑ SM-645	Bloodrock U.S.A.	197?	2.50	5.00	10.00
—Reissue with new prefix					
❑ SMAS-645	Bloodrock U.S.A.	1971	3.75	7.50	15.00
❑ SM-765	Bloodrock 3	197?	2.50	5.00	10.00
—Reissue with new prefix					
❑ ST-765	Bloodrock 3	1971	3.75	7.50	15.00
❑ SVBB-11038 [(2)]	Bloodrock Live	1972	5.00	10.00	20.00
❑ SW-11109	Bloodrock Passage	1972	3.75	7.50	15.00
❑ SMAS-11259	Whirlwind Tongues	1973	3.75	7.50	15.00
❑ SM-11417	Bloodrock 'N' Roll	1975	3.00	6.00	12.00
BLOODSTONE					
12-Inch Singles					
MOTOWN					
❑ M00017D1	Just Wanna Get the Feel of It (Vocal) (Instrumental)	1979	2.00	4.00	8.00
T-NECK					
❑ AS 1888 [DJ]	Instant Love (5:23) (same on both sides)	1984	2.00	4.00	8.00
❑ 4Z9-02863	We Go a Long Way Back/Nite Time Fun	1982	2.00	4.00	8.00
❑ 4Z9-03403	My Love Grows Stronger (Part 1 6:16) (Part 2 4:50)	1982	2.50	5.00	10.00
❑ 4Z9-05085	Bloodstone's Party (5:00) (7:03) (1:30)	1984	2.00	4.00	8.00
45s					
EPIC					
❑ 50437	Got to Find Myself Another Baby/Weeping Willow Tree	1977	—	2.00	4.00
LONDON					
❑ 1038	Girl/Judy, Judy	1972	—	2.50	5.00
❑ 1042	That's the Way We Make Our Music/This Thing Is Heavy	1972	—	2.50	5.00
❑ 1046	Natural High/Peter's Jones	1973	—	2.50	5.00
❑ 1051	Never Let You Go/You Know We've Learned	1973	—	2.50	5.00
❑ 1052	Outside Woman/Dumb Dude	1974	—	2.50	5.00
❑ 1055	That's Not How It Goes/Everybody Needs Love	1974	—	2.50	5.00
❑ 1059	I Believe You Now/I Need Time	1974	—	2.50	5.00
❑ 1061	My Little Lady/Loving You Is Just a Pastime	1975	—	2.50	5.00
❑ 1062	Give Me Your Heart/Something's Missing	1975	—	2.50	5.00
❑ 1062 [PS]	Give Me Your Heart/Something's Missing	1975	2.50	5.00	10.00
❑ 1064	Do You Wanna Do a Thing/Save Me	1976	—	2.50	5.00
❑ 1067	Just Like in the Movies/Little Linda	1976	—	2.50	5.00
MOTOWN					
❑ 1458	Just Wanna Get the Feel of It/ It's Been a Long Time	1978	—	2.00	4.00
T-NECK					
❑ ZS5-02825	We Go a Long Way Back/Nite Time Fun	1982	—	2.00	4.00
❑ ZS5-03049	Go On and Cry/(Instrumental)	1982	—	2.00	4.00
❑ ZS4-03394	My Love Grows Stronger (Part 1)/(Part 2)	1982	—	2.00	4.00
❑ ZS4-04465	Instant Love/It Feels So Good	1984	—	2.00	4.00
❑ ZS4-04592	Bloodstone's Party/Feel the Heat	1984	—	2.00	4.00
Albums					
LONDON					
❑ XPS 620	Natural High	1973	5.00	10.00	20.00
❑ XPS 634	Unreal	1973	5.00	10.00	20.00
❑ APS 647	I Need Time	1974	5.00	10.00	20.00
❑ PS 654	Riddle of the Sphinx	1975	3.75	7.50	15.00
❑ PS 671	Do a Thing?	1976	3.75	7.50	15.00
MOTOWN					
❑ M7-909	Don't Stop!	1978	3.00	6.00	12.00
T-NECK					
❑ FZ 38115	We Go a Long Way Back	1982	2.50	5.00	10.00
❑ FZ 39146	Bloodstone's Party	1984	2.50	5.00	10.00
❑ PZ 40016	Greatest Hits	1985	2.00	4.00	8.00
❑ PZ 40042	Lullaby of Broadway	1985	2.00	4.00	8.00
BLOODY MARY					
Albums					
FAMILY PRODUCTIONS					
❑ FPS-2707	Bloody Mary	1972	6.25	12.50	25.00
BLOOM, BOBBY					
45s					
EARTH					
❑ E-106	Heidi/Sign of the V	1970	2.00	4.00	8.00
KAMA SUTRA					
❑ 210	Heart of Town/Make the Radio a Little Louder	1966	3.00	6.00	12.00
—As "Bobby Mann"					
❑ 223	Love, Don't Let Me Down/Where Is the Woman	1967	2.50	5.00	10.00
❑ 229	Count on Me/Was I Dreamin'	1967	2.50	5.00	10.00
KAPP					
❑ 710	I Still Remember/Rough and Tough	1965	3.00	6.00	12.00
L&R					
❑ 157	Montego Bay/Try a Little Harder	1970	—	3.00	6.00
MAP CITY					
❑ 306	Emergency/Again 'N' Again	1970	—	3.00	6.00
MGM					
❑ 14212	Make Me Happy/This Thing I've Gotten Into	1970	—	2.50	5.00
❑ 14246	We're All Goin' Home/Careful Not to Break the Spell	1971	—	2.50	5.00
❑ 14292	We Need Each Other/You Touch Me	1971	—	2.50	5.00
❑ 14343	I Really Got It Bad for You/Until They Say Mercy	1972	—	2.50	5.00
❑ 14437	Stay on Top/Sha La Boom Boom	1972	—	2.50	5.00
❑ 14614	The Island/Oh, I Wish I Knew	1973	—	2.50	5.00
ROULETTE					
❑ 7095	Oh Yesterday/Where Are We Going	1971	—	2.50	5.00
WHITE WHALE					
❑ 285	All I Wanna Do Is Dance/Taggin' Along	1968	2.00	4.00	8.00

Number	Title (A Side/B Side)	Yr	VG	VG+	NM
Albums					
BUDDAH					
❑ BDS-5072	Where Are We Going	1971	3.00	6.00	12.00
L&R					
❑ LR-1035	The Bobby Bloom Album	1970	3.75	7.50	15.00
BLOOMFIELD, MIKE					
Albums					
COLUMBIA					
❑ CS 9883	It's Not Killing Me	1969	3.75	7.50	15.00
—Red "360 Sound" label					
❑ C2 37578 [(2)]	Bloomfield	1982	3.00	6.00	12.00
HARMONY					
❑ KH 30395	It's Not Killing Me	1971	2.50	5.00	10.00
SUNDAZED					
❑ LP 5105	I'm Cutting Out	2001	3.00	6.00	12.00
TAKOMA					
❑ C-1059	Analine	1977	2.50	5.00	10.00
❑ C-1063	Michael Bloomfield	1978	2.50	5.00	10.00
❑ C-1070	Between a Hard Place and the Ground	1979	2.50	5.00	10.00
❑ TAK-7059	Analine	198?	2.00	4.00	8.00
❑ TAK-7063	Michael Bloomfield	198?	2.00	4.00	8.00
❑ TAK-7070	Between a Hard Place and the Ground	198?	2.00	4.00	8.00
❑ TAK-7091	Cruisin' for a Bruisin'	198?	2.00	4.00	8.00
WATERHOUSE					
❑ 11	Living in the Fast Lane	1981	2.50	5.00	10.00
BLOOMFIELD, MIKE, AND NICK GRAVENITES					
Albums					
COLUMBIA					
❑ CS 9899	My Labors	1969	3.00	6.00	12.00
—Red "360 Sound" label					
❑ CS 9899	My Labors	1970	2.50	5.00	10.00
—Orange label					
BLOOMFIELD, MIKE/JOHN PAUL HAMMOND/DR. JOHN					
45s					
COLUMBIA					
❑ 45887	I Yi Yi/Pretty Thing	1973	—	3.00	6.00
Albums					
COLUMBIA					
❑ KC 32172	Triumvirate	1973	3.00	6.00	12.00
BLOOMFIELD, MIKE, AND AL KOOPER Also see each artist's individual listings.					
45s					
COLUMBIA					
❑ 44678	The Weight/Mama's Temptation	1968	—	3.00	6.00
Albums					
COLUMBIA					
❑ KGP 6 [(2)]	The Live Adventures of Mike Bloomfield & Al Kooper	1969	6.25	12.50	25.00
—Red "360 Sound" labels					
❑ PG 6 [(2)]	The Live Adventures of Mike Bloomfield & Al Kooper	197?	3.00	6.00	12.00
—Reissue with new prefix					
BLOOMFIELD, MIKE/AL KOOPER/STEVE STILLS Also see each artist's individual listings.					
45s					
COLUMBIA					
❑ 44657	Season of the Witch/Albert's Shuffle	1968	—	3.00	6.00
Albums					
COLUMBIA					
❑ CS 9701	Super Session	1968	5.00	10.00	20.00
—Red "360 Sound" label					
❑ CS 9701	Super Session	1970	2.50	5.00	10.00
—Orange label					
❑ PC 9701	Super Session	198?	2.00	4.00	8.00
—Reissue with new prefix					
❑ CQ 30991 [Q]	Super Session	1971	5.00	10.00	20.00
MOBILE FIDELITY					
❑ 1-178	Super Session	198?	10.00	20.00	40.00
—Audiophile vinyl					
BLOSSOMS, THE Probably all the same group.					
45s					
BELL					
❑ 780	You've Lost That Lovin' Feeling/Something So Wrong	1969	2.00	4.00	8.00
❑ 797	(You're My) Soul and Inspiration/Stand By	1969	2.00	4.00	8.00
❑ 857	I Ain't Got to Love Nobody Else/ Don't Take Your Love	1970	2.00	4.00	8.00
❑ 937	One Step Away/Break Your Promise	1970	2.00	4.00	8.00
CAPITOL					
❑ F3822	Move On/He Promised Me	1957	7.50	15.00	30.00
❑ F3878	Little Louie/Have Faith in Me	1958	6.25	12.50	25.00
❑ F4072	Baby Daddy-O/No Other Love	1958	6.25	12.50	25.00
CHALLENGE					
❑ 9109	Son-In-Law/I'll Wait	1961	5.00	10.00	20.00
—B-side by the Coeds					
❑ 9122	Hard to Get/Write Me a Letter	1961	5.00	10.00	20.00
❑ 9138	The Search Is Over/Big Talking Jim	1962	5.00	10.00	20.00
EEOC					
❑ 8172	Things Are Changing (same on both sides)	1965	37.50	75.00	150.00
❑ 8172 [PS]	Things Are Changing (same on both sides)	1965	37.50	75.00	150.00
—Promotional item for the Equal Employment Opportunity Commission					
EPIC					
❑ 50434	There's No Greater Love (Than Mine for You My Love)/Walking on Air	1977	—	2.50	5.00
LION					
❑ 108	Touchdown/It's All Up to You	1972	—	3.00	6.00
❑ 125	Grandma's Hands/Cherish What Is Dear to You	1972	—	3.00	6.00

B

Number	Title (A Side/B Side)	Yr	VG	VG+	NM
MGM					
❑ 13964	Tweedlee Dee/You Got Me Hummin'	1968	2.50	5.00	10.00
ODE					
❑ 101	Stoney End/Wonderful	1967	3.00	6.00	12.00
❑ 106	Cry Like a Baby/Wonderful	1968	3.00	6.00	12.00
❑ 125	Stoney End/Wonderful	1969	3.00	6.00	12.00
OKEH					
❑ 7162	I'm in Love/What Makes Love	1963	5.00	10.00	20.00
REPRISE					
❑ 0436	Good, Good Lovin'/That's When the Tears Start	1965	3.75	7.50	15.00
❑ 0475	Lover Boy/My Love, Come Home	1966	3.75	7.50	15.00
❑ 0522	Let Your Love Shine on Me/Deep Into My Heart	1966	3.75	7.50	15.00
Albums					
LION					
❑ 1007	Shockwave	1972	3.75	7.50	15.00

BLUE, DAVID

Number	Title (A Side/B Side)	Yr	VG	VG+	NM
Albums					
ASYLUM					
❑ 7E-1043	Com'n Back for More	1975	2.50	5.00	10.00
❑ 7E-1077	Cupid's Arrow	1976	2.50	5.00	10.00
❑ SD 5052	Stories	1972	3.00	6.00	12.00
❑ SD 5066	The Nice Baby and the Angel	1973	3.00	6.00	12.00
ELEKTRA					
❑ EKM-4003 [M]	David Blue	1966	5.00	10.00	20.00
❑ EKS-74003 [S]	David Blue	1966	5.00	10.00	20.00
REPRISE					
❑ RS 6296	These 23 Days in September	1968	3.75	7.50	15.00

BLUE BARONS, THE

Number	Title (A Side/B Side)	Yr	VG	VG+	NM
Albums					
PHILIPS					
❑ PHM 200017 [M]	Twist to the Great Blues Hits	1962	5.00	10.00	20.00
❑ PHS 600017 [S]	Twist to the Great Blues Hits	1962	6.25	12.50	25.00

BLUE BELLES, THE Also see PATTI LaBELLE AND THE BLUE BELLES.

Number	Title (A Side/B Side)	Yr	VG	VG+	NM
45s					
ATLANTIC					
❑ 987	The Story of a Fool/Cancel the Call	1953	37.50	75.00	150.00

BLUE CHEER

Number	Title (A Side/B Side)	Yr	VG	VG+	NM
45s					
MERCURY					
❑ 872804-7	Summertime Blues/Just a Little Bit	1989	—	2.00	4.00
—Reissue					
PHILIPS					
❑ 40516	Summertime Blues/Out of Focus	1968	3.00	6.00	12.00
❑ 40516 [PS]	Summertime Blues/Out of Focus	1968	6.25	12.50	25.00
❑ 40541	Just a Little Bit/Gypsy Ball	1968	2.50	5.00	10.00
❑ 40561	Feathers from Your Tree/Sun Cycle	1968	2.50	5.00	10.00
❑ 40561	Sun Cycle/Albert's Shuffle	1968	2.50	5.00	10.00
❑ 40561 [PS]	Feathers from Your Tree/Sun Cycle	1968	10.00	20.00	40.00
❑ 40602	West Coast Child of Sunshine/When It All Gets Old	1969	2.00	4.00	8.00
❑ 40651	All Night Long/Fortunes	1969	2.00	4.00	8.00
❑ 40664	Hello L.A., Bye-Bye Birmingham/Natural Man	1970	2.00	4.00	8.00
❑ 40682	Ain't That the Way/Fool	1970	2.00	4.00	8.00
❑ 40691	Babji (Twilight Raga)/Pilot	1971	2.00	4.00	8.00
❑ 40691	Babji (Twilight Raga)/Fool	1971	2.50	5.00	10.00
Albums					
MEGAFORCE					
❑ CAROL-1395-1	The Beast Is Back	198?	3.00	6.00	12.00
PHILIPS					
❑ PHM 200264 [M]	Vincebus Eruptum	1968	20.00	40.00	80.00
❑ PHS 600264 [S]	Vincebus Eruptum	1968	10.00	20.00	40.00
❑ PHS 600278	Outsideinside	1968	10.00	20.00	40.00
❑ PHS 600305	New! Improved! Blue Cheer	1969	10.00	20.00	40.00
❑ PHS 600333	Blue Cheer	1970	10.00	20.00	40.00
❑ PHS 600347	The Original Human Being	1970	10.00	20.00	40.00
❑ PHS 600350	Oh! Pleasant Hope	1971	10.00	20.00	40.00
RHINO					
❑ RNLP 70130	Louder Than God (The Best of Blue Cheer, 1968-1969)	1986	2.50	5.00	10.00

BLUE DIAMONDS, THE With Ernie Kador (later ERNIE K-DOE)

Number	Title (A Side/B Side)	Yr	VG	VG+	NM
45s					
SAVOY					
❑ 1134	Honey Baby/No Money	1954	15.00	30.00	60.00

BLUE HAZE

Number	Title (A Side/B Side)	Yr	VG	VG+	NM
45s					
A&M					
❑ 1357	Smoke Gets In Your Eyes/Anna Roseanna	1972	—	2.50	5.00
❑ 1426	You'll Never Walk Alone/Take Away My Heart Teresa	1973	—	2.50	5.00

BLUE JAYS, THE (1) Los Angeles-based male vocal group.

Number	Title (A Side/B Side)	Yr	VG	VG+	NM
45s					
MILESTONE					
❑ 2008	Lover's Island/You're Gonna Cry	1961	7.50	15.00	30.00
—Green label					
❑ 2008	Lover's Island/You're Gonna Cry	1961	7.50	15.00	30.00
—Light blue and white label					
❑ 2008	Lover's Island/You're Gonna Cry	1961	10.00	20.00	40.00
—Dark blue label					
❑ 2009	Tears Are Falling/Tree Tall Men	1961	7.50	15.00	30.00
❑ 2010	Let's Make Love/Rock, Rock, Rock	1962	5.00	10.00	20.00
❑ 2012	The Right to Love/Rock, Rock, Rock	1962	5.00	10.00	20.00
❑ 2014	Venus, My Love/Tall Len	1962	15.00	30.00	60.00
Albums					
MILESTONE					
❑ 1001 [M]	The Blue Jays Meet Little Caesar and the Romans	1962	25.00	50.00	100.00

BLUE JAYS, THE (2) Chicago-based (probably) male vocal group.

Number	Title (A Side/B Side)	Yr	VG	VG+	NM
45s					
CHECKER					
❑ 782	White Cliffs of Dover/Hey Poppa	1953	1000.	1500.	2000.

BLUE JAYS, THE (U)

Number	Title (A Side/B Side)	Yr	VG	VG+	NM
45s					
LAURIE					
❑ 3037	Sweet Georgia Brown/J.J.'s Blues	1959	6.25	12.50	25.00
MAP CITY					
❑ 300	Hang On/Hard Thing to Accept	1969	—	3.00	6.00
❑ 307	Freedom (Where Have You Gone)/(B-side unknown)	1971	—	3.00	6.00
❑ 311	Jackson/Wacka Wacka	1971	—	3.00	6.00
PHILIPS					
❑ 40186	Who (Will I Be Today)?/Come On Baby	1964	3.75	7.50	15.00
ROULETTE					
❑ 4169	Practical Joker/Barbara	1959	5.00	10.00	20.00
❑ 4264	Kum Ba Yah/Cave Man Love	1960	5.00	10.00	20.00
WARNER BROS.					
❑ 7299	Edgy/I'm Only Dreaming	1969	—	3.00	6.00

BLUE MAGIC

Number	Title (A Side/B Side)	Yr	VG	VG+	NM
12-Inch Singles					
COLUMBIA					
❑ 44-68789	It's Like Magic/(B-side unknown)	1989	2.00	4.00	8.00
❑ 44-68849	Secret Lover/There's a Song in My Head	1989	2.00	4.00	8.00
DEF JAM					
❑ 44-68197	Romeo and Juliet (Vocal) (Instrumental)/Couldn't Get to Sleep Last Night	1989	2.00	4.00	8.00
MIRAGE					
❑ PR 398 [DJ]	Magic # (5:00) (4:26)	1983	2.50	5.00	10.00
45s					
ATCO					
❑ 6910	Spell/Guess Who	1972	—	3.00	6.00
❑ 6930	Look Me Up/What's Come Over Me	1973	—	3.00	6.00
❑ 6949	Stop to Start/Where Have You Been	1973	—	3.00	6.00
❑ 6961	Sideshow/Just Don't Want to Be Lonely	1974	—	3.00	6.00
❑ 7004	Three Ring Circus/Welcome to the Club	1974	—	3.00	6.00
❑ 7014	Love Has Found Its Way to Me/When Ya Coming Home	1975	—	3.00	6.00
❑ 7031	Chasing Rainbows/You Won't Have to Tell Me Goodbye	1975	—	2.50	5.00
❑ 7046	Grateful Part 1/Grateful Part 2	1976	—	2.50	5.00
❑ 7052	Freak-N-Stein/Stop and Get a Hold of Yourself	1976	—	2.50	5.00
❑ 7061	Teach Me (It's Something About Love)/Spark of Love	1976	—	2.50	5.00
❑ 7090	I Waited/Can't Get You Out of My Mind	1978	—	2.00	4.00
CAPITOL					
❑ 4977	Land of Make Believe/Remember November	1981	—	3.00	6.00
COLUMBIA					
❑ 38-68900	It's Like Magic/Couldn't Get to Sleep Last Night	1989	—	2.00	4.00
❑ 38-69017	Secret Lover/There's a Song in My Head	1989	—	2.00	4.00
DEF JAM					
❑ 38-68566	Romeo and Juliet/Couldn't Get to Sleep Last Night	1989	—	2.00	4.00
LIBERTY					
❑ 56146	Can I Say I Love You/One, Two, Three	1969	2.50	5.00	10.00
MIRAGE					
❑ 99843	See Through/(B-side unknown)	1983	—	2.00	4.00
❑ 99869	Since You Been Gone/If You Move You Lose	1983	—	2.00	4.00
❑ 99914	Magic #/See Through	1983	2.00	4.00	8.00
WMOT					
❑ 4003	Summer Snow/Spark of Love	1976	—	2.50	5.00
Albums					
ATCO					
❑ SD 36-103	The Magic of the Blue	1974	3.00	6.00	12.00
❑ SD 38-104	The Message	1977	3.00	6.00	12.00
❑ SD 36-120	Thirteen Blue Magic Lane	1975	3.00	6.00	12.00
❑ SD 36-140	Mystic Dragons	1976	3.00	6.00	12.00
❑ SD 7038	Blue Magic	1974	3.00	6.00	12.00
CAPITOL					
❑ ST-12143	Welcome Back	1981	2.50	5.00	10.00
COLLECTABLES					
❑ COL-5031	The Magic of the Blue: Greatest Hits	198?	2.50	5.00	10.00
COLUMBIA					
❑ C 45092	From Out of the Blue	1989	3.00	6.00	12.00
MIRAGE					
❑ 90074	Magic #	1983	2.50	5.00	10.00
OMNI					
❑ 90527	Greatest Hits	1986	2.50	5.00	10.00

BLUE MINK Also see MADELINE BELL.

Number	Title (A Side/B Side)	Yr	VG	VG+	NM
45s					
MCA					
❑ 40031	I Can't Find the Answer/By the Devil I Was Tempted	1973	—	2.50	5.00
❑ 40091	Randy/Another Without You Day	1973	—	2.50	5.00
❑ 40230	Get Up/Loneliness	1974	—	2.50	5.00
PHILIPS					
❑ 40658	Melting Pot/But Not Forever	1969	2.00	4.00	8.00
❑ 40672	Can You Feel It Baby/(B-side unknown)	1970	2.00	4.00	8.00
❑ 40678	Good Morning Freedom/Mary Jane	1970	—	—	—
—Canceled					
❑ 40686	Our World/Respects to Mrs. Jones	1970	2.00	4.00	8.00
❑ 40697	Gasoline Alley Bred/We Have All Been Saved	1971	2.00	4.00	8.00
Albums					
MCA					
❑ 332	Blue Mink	1973	3.00	6.00	12.00
PHILIPS					
❑ PHS 600323	Melting Pot	1970	3.75	7.50	15.00
❑ PHS 600339	Real Mink	1970	3.75	7.50	15.00

Number	Title (A Side/B Side)	Yr	VG	VG+	NM

BLUE NOTES, THE (1) This group evolved into HAROLD MELVIN AND THE BLUE NOTES.
45s
COLLECTABLES

Number	Title (A Side/B Side)	Yr	VG	VG+	NM
❑ 1113	Winter Wonderland/O Holy Night	198?	—	2.00	4.00

—Reissue
JOSIE

❑ 800	If You Love Me/				
	There's Something in Your Eyes, Eloise	1956	50.00	100.00	200.00
❑ 814	Letters/With This Pen	1957	30.00	60.00	120.00

—As "Todd Randall and the Blue Notes"

❑ 823	The Retribution Blues/Wagon Wheels	1957	37.50	75.00	150.00

LOST-NITE

❑ 317	My Hero/A Good Woman	197?	—	2.50	5.00

—Reissue
PORT

❑ 70021	If You Love Me/				
	There's Something in Your Eyes, Eloise	1958	15.00	30.00	60.00

RED TOP

❑ 135	My Hero/A Good Woman	1963	7.50	15.00	30.00

3 SONS

❑ 103	WPLJ/While I'm Away	1962	7.50	15.00	30.00

UNI

❑ 55132	Got Chills and Cold Thrills/Never Gonna Leave You	1969	3.00	6.00	12.00
❑ 55201	This Time Will Be Different/Lucky Me	1970	3.00	6.00	12.00

VAL-UE

❑ 213	My Hero/A Good Woman	1960	20.00	40.00	80.00
❑ 215	Winter Wonderland/O Holy Night	1960	20.00	40.00	80.00

Albums
COLLECTABLES

❑ COL-5006	The Early Years	1982	3.00	6.00	12.00

BLUE NOTES, THE (2) Earlier male vocal group, no relation to (1).
45s
RAMA

❑ 25	If You'll Be Mine/Too Hot to Handle	1953	50.00	100.00	200.00

BLUE NOTES, THE (U) None of these appear to be by (1) or (2), but we don't know how many different groups are represented below.
45s
DOT

❑ 15692	My Steady Girl/Mighty Lou	1958	6.25	12.50	25.00

—B-side by Henry Wilson

❑ 15720	Darling of Mine/I Love Her So	1958	6.25	12.50	25.00

TNT

❑ 150	Darling of Mine/I Love Her So	1958	7.50	15.00	30.00

20TH CENTURY

❑ 1213	Blue Star/(B-side unknown)	1961	3.75	7.50	15.00

BLUE ORCHIDS, THE
45s
LONDON

❑ 9637	Love Hit Me/Don't Make Me Mad	1964	2.50	5.00	10.00
❑ 9669	Oo-Chang-a-Lang/I've Got That Feeling	1964	2.50	5.00	10.00

BLUE OYSTER CULT
12-Inch Singles
COLUMBIA

❑ AS 447 [DJ]	Godzilla (Live) (Studio Version)	1978	3.75	7.50	15.00
❑ AS 1772 [DJ]	Shooting Shark (Edit) (Album Version)/ Take Me Away/Eyes on Fire	1984	3.00	6.00	12.00
❑ CAS 2430 [DJ]	Dancin' in the Ruins (4:10) (same on both sides)	1986	2.50	5.00	10.00

45s
COLUMBIA

❑ AE7 1156 [DJ]	Godzilla (Live Version)/(Studio Version)	1978	—	3.00	6.00
❑ AE7 1156 [PS]	Godzilla (Live Version)/(Studio Version)	1978	—	3.00	6.00
❑ 18-02415	Burnin' for You/Vengeance (The Fact)	1981	—	2.00	4.00
❑ 18-02415 [DJ]	Burnin' for You (Long Version) (Short Version)	1981	—	2.50	5.00
❑ 18-02415 [PS]	Burnin' for You/Vengeance (The Fact)	1981	—	2.50	5.00
❑ 13-03137	(Don't Fear) The Reaper/Burnin' for You	1982	—	2.00	4.00

—Reissue

❑ 38-04298	Shooting Shark/Dragon Lady	1984	—	—	3.00
❑ 38-04298 [PS]	Shooting Shark/Dragon Lady	1984	—	2.00	4.00
❑ 38-04435	Take Me Away/Let Go	1984	—	—	3.00
❑ 38-05845	Dancin' in the Ruins/Shadow Warrior	1986	—	—	3.00
❑ 38-06199	Perfect Water/Spy in the House of Knight	1986	—	—	3.00
❑ 3-10046	Dominance and Submission/Career of Evil	1974	—	3.00	6.00
❑ 3-10169	Born to Be Wild/(B-side unknown)	1975	—	3.00	6.00
❑ 3-10384	(Don't Fear) The Reaper/Tattoo Vampire	1976	—	3.00	6.00
❑ 3-10560	This Ain't the Summer of Love/Debby Denise	1977	—	2.50	5.00
❑ 3-10659	Goin' Through the Motions/Searchin' for Celine	1977	—	2.50	5.00
❑ 3-10697	Godzilla/Nosferatu	1978	—	2.50	5.00
❑ 3-10725	Godzilla (Live Version)/(Studio Version)	1978	—	2.50	5.00
❑ 3-10841	We Gotta Get Out of This Place/E.T.I. (Extra Terrestrial Intelligence)	1978	—	2.50	5.00
❑ 11055	In Thee/Lonely Teardrops	1979	—	2.00	4.00
❑ 1-11145	You're Not the One (I Was Looking For)/Moon Crazy	1979	—	2.00	4.00
❑ 11-11401	Here's Johnny (The Marshall Plan)/Divine Wind	1980	—	2.00	4.00
❑ 4-45598	Cities on Flame with Rock and Roll/Before the Kiss, A Redcap	1972	2.50	5.00	10.00
❑ 4-45879	Hot Rails to Hell/Seven Screaming Diz Busters	1973	—	3.00	6.00
❑ 4-45879 [PS]	Hot Rails to Hell/Seven Screaming Diz Busters	1973	3.00	6.00	12.00
❑ 38-74716	(Don't Fear) The Reaper/Burnin' for You	1992	—	—	3.00

—Reissue
Albums
COLUMBIA

❑ KC 31063	Blue Oyster Cult	1972	3.00	6.00	12.00
❑ PC 31063	Blue Oyster Cult	197?	2.00	4.00	8.00

—Reissue with new prefix

❑ CQ 32017 [Q]	Tyranny and Mutation	1973	7.50	15.00	30.00
❑ KC 32017	Tyranny and Mutation	1973	3.00	6.00	12.00

Number	Title (A Side/B Side)	Yr	VG	VG+	NM
❑ PC 32017	Tyranny and Mutation	197?	2.00	4.00	8.00

—Reissue with new prefix

❑ CQ 32858 [Q]	Secret Treaties	1974	7.50	15.00	30.00
❑ KC 32858	Secret Treaties	1974	3.00	6.00	12.00
❑ PC 32858	Secret Treaties	197?	2.00	4.00	8.00

—Reissue with new prefix

❑ KG 33371 [(2)]	On Your Feet or On Your Knees	1975	3.75	7.50	15.00
❑ PC 34164	Agents of Fortune	1976	2.50	5.00	10.00

—Original gatefold with no bar code on cover

❑ PC 34164	Agents of Fortune	198?	2.00	4.00	8.00

—Budget-line reissue with bar code

❑ JC 35019	Spectres	1977	2.50	5.00	10.00
❑ PC 35019	Spectres	198?	2.00	4.00	8.00

—Budget-line reissue

❑ JC 35563	Some Enchanted Evening	1978	2.50	5.00	10.00
❑ PC 35563	Some Enchanted Evening	198?	2.00	4.00	8.00

—Budget-line reissue

❑ JC 36009	Mirrors	1979	2.50	5.00	10.00
❑ PC 36009	Mirrors	198?	2.00	4.00	8.00

—Budget-line reissue

❑ JC 36550	Cultosaurus Erectus	1980	2.50	5.00	10.00
❑ PC 36550	Cultosaurus Erectus	198?	2.00	4.00	8.00

—Budget-line reissue

❑ FC 37389	Fire of Unknown Origin	1981	2.50	5.00	10.00
❑ PC 37389	Fire of Unknown Origin	1984	2.00	4.00	8.00

—Budget-line reissue

❑ KG 37946 [(2)]	Extraterrestrial Live	1982	3.00	6.00	12.00
❑ FC 38947	The Revolution by Night	1983	2.50	5.00	10.00
❑ PC 38947	The Revolution by Night	1985	2.00	4.00	8.00

—Budget-line reissue

❑ FC 39979	Club Ninja	1986	2.50	5.00	10.00
❑ FC 40618	Imaginos	1988	2.50	5.00	10.00

BLUE RIDGE RANGERS, THE See JOHN FOGERTY.

BLUE RONDOS, THE
45s
PARKWAY

❑ 937	Little Baby/Baby I Go for You	1964	3.00	6.00	12.00

BLUE STARS
45s
MERCURY

❑ 70742	Lullaby of Birdland/That's My Girl	1955	2.50	5.00	10.00
❑ 70808	Mambo Italiano/Speak Low	1956	2.50	5.00	10.00
❑ 70877X45	Broadway at Basin Street/The Kissing Dance	1956	2.50	5.00	10.00
❑ 70924	Jumpin' at the Woodside/Hernando's Hideaway	1956	2.50	5.00	10.00

Albums
EMARCY

❑ MG-36067 [M]	Lullaby of Birdland	1956	10.00	20.00	40.00

BLUE SWEDE
45s
CAPITOL

❑ 3627	Hooked on a Feeling/Gotta Have Your Love	1973	2.00	4.00	8.00

EMI

❑ 3627	Hooked on a Feeling/Gotta Have Your Love	1974	—	2.50	5.00
❑ 3893	Silly Milly/Lonely Sunday Afternoon	1974	—	2.00	4.00
❑ 3938	Never My Love/Pinewood Rally	1974	—	2.00	4.00
❑ 3938 [PS]	Never My Love/Pinewood Rally	1974	—	3.00	6.00
❑ 4029	Hush-I'm Alive/Lonely Summer Afternoon	1975	—	2.00	4.00
❑ 4065	Dr. Rock and Roll/Gotta Have Your Love	1975	—	2.00	4.00

Albums
EMI

❑ ST-11266	Hooked on a Feeling	1974	2.50	5.00	10.00
❑ ST-11346	Out of the Blue	1975	2.50	5.00	10.00

BLUE THINGS, THE
45s
RCA VICTOR

❑ 47-8692	I Must Be Doing Something Wrong/La Do Da Da	1965	6.25	12.50	25.00
❑ 47-8860	Doll House/Man on the Street	1966	6.25	12.50	25.00
❑ 47-8998	Orange Rooftop of Your Mind/ One Hour Cleaners	1966	6.25	12.50	25.00
❑ 47-9203	Twist and Shout/You Can Live in Our Tree	1967	6.25	12.50	25.00
❑ 47-9308	Yes, My Friend/Somebody Help Me	1967	6.25	12.50	25.00

RUFF

❑ 1000	Mary Lou/Your Turn to Cry	1965	10.00	20.00	40.00
❑ 1002	Pretty Thing/Just Two Days Ago	1965	10.00	20.00	40.00

Albums
RCA VICTOR

❑ LPM-3603 [M]	The Blue Things	1966	30.00	60.00	120.00
❑ LSP-3603 [S]	The Blue Things	1966	45.00	90.00	180.00

BLUE TONES, THE
45s
BLUE JAY

❑ 101	I'll Love You Till the End of Time/(Instrumental)	1965	37.50	75.00	150.00

—Reissued on Swan 4200 by "The Royal Teens"

BLUE VELVET BAND, THE
45s
WARNER BROS.

❑ 7320	Hitch-Hiker/Sittin' on Top of the World	1969	2.00	4.00	8.00

Albums
WARNER BROS.

❑ WS 1802	Sweet Moments	1969	7.50	15.00	30.00

BLUENOTES, THE Probably not related to any of the groups called THE BLUE NOTES, they were a white male vocal group from North Carolina.
45s
BROOKE

❑ 111	I Don't Know What It Is/ You Can't Get Away from Love	1959	4.00	8.00	16.00
❑ 116	Forever on My Mind/I'm Gonna Find Out	1960	3.75	7.50	15.00

Number	Title (A Side/B Side)	Yr	VG	VG+	NM
❏ 116 [PS]	Forever on My Mind/I'm Gonna Find Out	1960	7.50	15.00	30.00
❏ 119	It Had to be You/Summer Love	1960	3.75	7.50	15.00

BLUES CLIMAX
Albums
HORNE

❏ JC-333	Blues Climax	1969	15.00	30.00	60.00

BLUES IMAGE
45s
ATCO

❏ 6718	Lay Your Sweet Love on Me/Outside Was Night	1969	—	2.00	4.00
❏ 6746	Ride Captain Ride/Pay My Dues	1970	—	2.50	5.00
❏ 6777	Gas Lamps and Clay/Running the Water	1970	—	2.00	4.00
❏ 6798	Rise Up/Take Me Back	1971	—	2.00	4.00
❏ 6814	Behind Every Man/It's the Truth	1971	—	2.00	4.00

Albums
ATCO

❏ SD 33-300	Blues Image	1969	6.25	12.50	25.00
❏ SD 33-317	Open	1970	5.00	10.00	20.00
❏ SD 33-346	Red, White and Blues Image	1971	5.00	10.00	20.00

BLUES MAGOOS
45s
ABC

❏ 11226	Heartbreak Hotel/I Can Feel It (Feelin' Time)	1969	2.00	4.00	8.00
❏ 11250	Never Goin' Back to Georgia/Feelin' Time	1969	2.00	4.00	8.00
❏ 11283	Gulf Coast Bound/Sea Breeze Express	1970	2.00	4.00	8.00
GANIM					
❏ 1000	Who Do You Love/Let Your Love Ride	1968	10.00	20.00	40.00
MERCURY					
❏ 72590	Tobacco Road/Sometimes I Think About You	1966	12.50	25.00	50.00
❏ 72622	(We Ain't Got) Nothin' Yet/Gotta Get Away	1966	5.00	10.00	20.00
❏ 72660	Pipe Dream/There's a Chance We Can Make It	1967	3.75	7.50	15.00
❏ 72660 [PS]	Pipe Dream/There's a Chance We Can Make It	1967	7.50	15.00	30.00
❏ 72692	One by One/Dante's Inferno	1967	3.75	7.50	15.00
❏ 72692 [PS]	One by One/Dante's Inferno	1967	7.50	15.00	30.00
❏ 72707	I Wanna Be There/Summer Is the Man	1967	2.50	5.00	10.00
❏ 72729	Life Is Just a Cher O'Bowlies/There She Goes	1967	2.50	5.00	10.00
❏ 72762	Jingle Bells/Santa Claus Is Coming to Town	1967	2.50	5.00	10.00
❏ 72838	I Can Hear the Grass Grow/Yellow Rose	1968	2.50	5.00	10.00
❏ 872806-7	(We Ain't Got) Nothin' Yet/Pipedream	1989	—	—	3.00
—Reissue					
VERVE FOLKWAYS					
❏ 5006	People Had No Faces/ So I'm Wrong and You Are Right	1966	3.75	7.50	15.00
❏ 5006	People Had No Faces/ So I'm Wrong and You Are Right	1966	5.00	10.00	20.00
—As "The Bloos Magoos"					
❏ 5044	People Had No Faces/ So I'm Wrong and You Are Right	1967	3.75	7.50	15.00

Albums
ABC

❏ S-697	Never Goin' Back to Georgia	1969	5.00	10.00	20.00
❏ S-710	Gulf Coast Bound	1970	5.00	10.00	20.00
MERCURY					
❏ MG-21096 [M]	Psychedelic Lollipop	1966	10.00	20.00	40.00
—With "21096" in trail-off; this record is mono					
❏ MG-21096 [S]	Psychedelic Lollipop	1966	10.00	20.00	40.00
—With "2/61096" in trail-off; this record plays stereo, though labeled mono					
❏ 21104/61104	Electric Comic Book Comic Book	1967	3.75	7.50	15.00
❏ MG-21104 [M]	Electric Comic Book	1967	7.50	15.00	30.00
❏ SR-61096 [S]	Psychedelic Lollipop	1966	12.50	25.00	50.00
❏ SR-61096	Psychedelic Lollipop	197?	3.00	6.00	12.00
—Reissue on Chicago skyline label					
❏ SR-61104 [S]	Electric Comic Book	1967	10.00	20.00	40.00
❏ SR-61167	Basic Blues Magoos	1968	7.50	15.00	30.00

BLUES PROJECT, THE
45s
CAPITOL

❏ 3374	Crazy Girl/Easy Lady	1972	2.00	4.00	8.00
MCA					
❏ 40154	Fly Away/Louisiana Blues	1973	—	2.50	5.00
VERVE FOLKWAYS					
❏ 5004	Back Door Man/Violets of Dawn	1966	3.75	7.50	15.00
❏ 5013	Catch the Wind/I Want to Be Your Driver	1966	3.75	7.50	15.00
❏ 5019	Where There's Smoke There's Fire/ Goin' Down Louisiana	1966	3.75	7.50	15.00
❏ 5019 [PS]	Where There's Smoke There's Fire/ Goin' Down Louisiana	1966	6.25	12.50	25.00
❏ 5032	I Can't Keep from Crying Sometimes/ The Way My Baby Walks	1966	3.75	7.50	15.00
❏ 5040	No Time Like the Right Time/Steve's Song	1967	3.00	6.00	12.00
VERVE FORECAST					
❏ 5063	Gentle Dreams/Lost in the Shuffle	1967	3.00	6.00	12.00

Albums
CAPITOL

❏ ST-782	Lazarus	1971	3.00	6.00	12.00
❏ SMAS-11017	The Blues Project	1972	3.00	6.00	12.00
MCA					
❏ 8003 [(2)]	Reunion in Central Park	1975	3.75	7.50	15.00
—Reissue of Sounds of the South LP; black rainbow labels					
❏ 25984 [(2)]	Reunion in Central Park	1987	3.00	6.00	12.00
—Reissue of MCA 8003; blue rainbow labels					
MGM					
❏ GAS-118	The Blues Project	1970	3.00	6.00	12.00
❏ M3G-4953	Archetypes	1974	3.00	6.00	12.00
RHINO					
❏ R1-70165	No Time Like the Right Time: The Best of the Blues Project	1989	3.00	6.00	12.00

Number	Title (A Side/B Side)	Yr	VG	VG+	NM
SOUNDS OF THE SOUTH					
❏ MCA2-8003 [(2)]	Reunion in Central Park	1973	5.00	10.00	20.00
—Yellow labels					
VERVE					
❏ 827918-1	Projections	1986	2.00	4.00	8.00
—Reissue					
VERVE FOLKWAYS					
❏ FT-3000 [M]	Live at the Café a Go Go	1966	5.00	10.00	20.00
❏ FTS-3000 [S]	Live at the Café a Go Go	1966	6.25	12.50	25.00
❏ FT-3008 [M]	Projections	1966	5.00	10.00	20.00
❏ FTS-3008 [S]	Projections	1966	6.25	12.50	25.00
VERVE FORECAST					
❏ FT-3000 [M]	Live at the Café a Go Go	1967	3.75	7.50	15.00
—Reissue of Verve Folkways 3000					
❏ FTS-3000 [S]	Live at the Café a Go Go	1967	5.00	10.00	20.00
—Reissue of Verve Folkways 3000					
❏ FT-3008 [M]	Projections	1967	3.75	7.50	15.00
—Reissue of Verve Folkways 3008					
❏ FTS-3008 [S]	Projections	1967	5.00	10.00	20.00
—Reissue of Verve Folkways 3008					
❏ FT-3025 [M]	The Blues Project Live at Town Hall	1967	5.00	10.00	20.00
❏ FTS-3025 [S]	The Blues Project Live at Town Hall	1967	3.75	7.50	15.00
❏ FTS-3055	Planned Obsolescence	1968	3.75	7.50	15.00
❏ FTS-3069	Flanders/Kalb/Katz, Etc.	1969	3.75	7.50	15.00
❏ FTS-3077	Best of the Blues Project	1969	3.75	7.50	15.00

BLUNSTONE, COLIN Also see THE ZOMBIES.
45s
EPIC

❏ 10826	Caroline Goodbye/Misty Roses	1972	—	2.50	5.00
❏ 10868	Say You Don't Mind/Though You Are Far Away	1972	—	2.50	5.00
❏ 10948	I Don't Believe in Miracles/I've Always Had You	1973	—	2.50	5.00
❏ 10981	Pay Me Later/I Want Some More	1973	—	2.50	5.00
❏ 11004	Andorra/Carolina Goodbye	1973	—	2.50	5.00
ROCKET					
❏ PB-11356	I'll Never Forget You/You Are the Way for Me	1978	—	2.00	4.00
❏ PB-11412	Photograph/Touch and Go	1978	—	2.00	4.00

Albums
EPIC

❏ E 30974	One Year	1972	3.00	6.00	12.00
❏ KE 31994	Ennismore	1972	3.00	6.00	12.00
❏ KE 32692	Journey	1974	3.00	6.00	12.00
ROCKET					
❏ BXL1-2093	Never Even Thought	1978	2.50	5.00	10.00

BO GRUMPUS
Albums
ATCO

❏ 33-246 [M]	Bo Grumpus	1968	7.50	15.00	30.00
❏ SD 33-246 [S]	Bo Grumpus	1968	5.00	10.00	20.00

BO PETE See NILSSON.

BOA
Albums
SNAKEFIELD

❏ SN-001	Wrong Road	1969	62.50	125.00	250.00

BOB AND BOBBIE
45s
HIT

❏ 50	Hey Paula/I Saw Linda Yesterday	1963	2.00	4.00	8.00
—B-side by Dave Gibson					
❏ 58	Young Lovers/Out of My Mind	1963	2.00	4.00	8.00
—B-side by Jackie Ott					

BOB AND EARL
45s
CHENE

❏ 103	The Sissy/(B-side unknown).	1964	2.50	5.00	10.00
CLASS					
❏ 213	That's My Desire/You Made a Boo-Boo.	1957	10.00	20.00	40.00
❏ 231	Gee Whiz/When She Walks.	1958	7.50	15.00	30.00
❏ 232	Chains of Love/Sweet Pea.	1958	7.50	15.00	30.00
❏ 247	That's My Desire/You Made a Boo-Boo.	1959	6.25	12.50	25.00
LOMA					
❏ 2004	Everybody Jerk/Just One Look in Your Eyes.	1964	2.50	5.00	10.00
MARC					
❏ 104	Harlem Shuffle/I'll Come Running.	1963	5.00	10.00	20.00
❏ 105	Puppet on a String/My Woman.	1964	5.00	10.00	20.00
MIRWOOD					
❏ 5517	Baby It's Over/Dancin' Everywhere.	1966	2.00	4.00	8.00
❏ 5526	I'll Keep Running Back/Baby, Your Time Is My Time.	1966	2.00	4.00	8.00
TEMPE					
❏ 102	Don't Ever Leave Me/Oh Baby Doll.	1962	3.75	7.50	15.00
UNI					
❏ 55196	Uh Uh No No/(Pickin' Up) Love's Vibrations.	1970	—	3.00	6.00
❏ 55248	Get Ready for the New Day/ Honey, Sugar, My Sweet Thing.	1970	—	3.00	6.00
WHITE WHALE					
❏ 310	Harlem Shuffle/I'll Come Running	1969	3.00	6.00	12.00

Albums
CRESTVIEW

❏ CRS-3055	Bob & Earl	1969	6.25	12.50	25.00
TIP					
❏ TLP-1011 [M]	Harlem Shuffle	1964	7.50	15.00	30.00
❏ TLS-9011 [S]	Harlem Shuffle	1964	12.50	25.00	50.00

BOB AND LUCILLE
45s
DITTO

❏ 121	What's the Password/Demon Lover	1962	20.00	40.00	80.00
❏ 126	Eeny-Meeny-Miney-Moe/The Big Kiss	1962	20.00	40.00	80.00

Number	Title (A Side/B Side)	Yr	VG	VG+	NM
DOT					
❑ 17327	Dream Baby/Southbound Plane	1969	2.00	4.00	8.00
—As "Bob Regan and Lucille Starr"					
KING					
❑ 5631	Eeny-Meeny-Miney-Moe/The Big Kiss	1962	7.50	15.00	30.00

BOB AND SHERI
45s

Number	Title (A Side/B Side)	Yr	VG	VG+	NM
SAFARI					
❑ 101	The Surfer Moon/Humpty Dumpty	1962	2000.	3000.	4000.
—Light blue label (other colors and colored vinyl are reproductions or counterfeits)					
❑ 101 [DJ]	The Surfer Moon/Humpty Dumpty	1962	250.00	500.00	1000.
—White label					

BOB B. SOXX AND THE BLUE JEANS
45s

Number	Title (A Side/B Side)	Yr	VG	VG+	NM
PHILLES					
❑ 107	Zip-a-Dee-Doo-Dah/Flip and Nitty	1962	5.00	10.00	20.00
❑ 110	Why Do Lovers Break Each Other's Heart?/ Dr. Kaplan's Office	1963	5.00	10.00	20.00
❑ 113	Not Too Young to Get Married/Annette	1963	5.00	10.00	20.00
PHILLES/COLLECTABLES					
❑ 3207	Not Too Young to Get Married/ There's No Other (Like My Baby)	1985	—	3.00	6.00
—Gold vinyl; part of box set "Phil Spector Wall of Sound Series Vol. 1"; B-side by the Crystals					
❑ 3207	Not Too Young to Get Married/There's No Other (Like My Baby)	1986	—	2.50	5.00
—Black vinyl; B-side by the Crystals					
❑ 3209	Why Do Lovers Break Each Other's Heart/ Zip-a-Dee Doo-Dah	1985	—	2.50	5.00
—Black vinyl					
❑ 3209	Why Do Lovers Break Each Other's Heart/ Zip-a-Dee Doo-Dah	1985	—	3.00	6.00
—Gold vinyl					
Albums					
PHILLIES					
❑ PHLP-4002 [M]	Zip-a-Dee-Doo-Dah	1963	125.00	250.00	500.00

BOB, RITA, AND PETER See BOB MARLEY AND THE WAILERS.

BOBBETTES, THE
45s

Number	Title (A Side/B Side)	Yr	VG	VG+	NM
ATLANTIC					
❑ 1144	Mr. Lee/Look at the Stars	1957	6.25	12.50	25.00
❑ 1159	Speedy/Come-a Come-a	1957	5.00	10.00	20.00
❑ 1181	Zoomy/Rock and Ree-Ah-Zole	1958	5.00	10.00	20.00
❑ 1194	The Dream/Um Bow Bow	1958	5.00	10.00	20.00
❑ 2027	Don't Say Goodnight/You Are My Sweetheart	1959	5.00	10.00	20.00
❑ 2069	I Shot Mr. Lee/Untrue Love	1960	7.50	15.00	30.00
DIAMOND					
❑ 133	Row, Row, Row/Teddy	1963	3.00	6.00	12.00
❑ 142	Close Your Eyes/Somebody Bad Stole De Wedding Bell	1963	3.00	6.00	12.00
❑ 156	My Mamma Said/Sandman	1964	3.00	6.00	12.00
❑ 166	I'm Climbing a Mountain/In Paradise	1964	3.00	6.00	12.00
❑ 181	You Ain't Seen Nothing Yet/I'm Climbing a Mountain	1965	3.00	6.00	12.00
❑ 189	Love Is Blind/Teddy	1965	3.00	6.00	12.00
END					
❑ 1093	Mr. Johnny Q/Teach Me Tonight	1961	5.00	10.00	20.00
❑ 1095	I Don't Like It Like That (Part 1)/I Don't Like It Like That (Part 2)	1961	5.00	10.00	20.00
GALLANT					
❑ 1006	Oh, My Papa/I Cried	1960	5.00	10.00	20.00
GONE					
❑ 5112	I Don't Like It Like That (Part 1)/Mr. Johnny Q	1961	3.75	7.50	15.00
JUBILEE					
❑ 5427	Over There/Loneliness	1962	3.00	6.00	12.00
❑ 5442	The Broken Heart/Mama, Papa	1962	3.00	6.00	12.00
KING					
❑ 5490	Oh My Papa/Dance With Me Georgie	1961	3.75	7.50	15.00
❑ 5551	Are You Satisfied/Looking for a Lover	1961	3.75	7.50	15.00
❑ 5623	I'm Stepping Out Tonight/My Dearest	1962	3.75	7.50	15.00
RCA VICTOR					
❑ 47-8832	I've Gotta Face the World/Having Fun	1966	3.75	7.50	15.00
❑ 47-8983	It's All Over/Happy-Go-Lucky Me	1966	3.75	7.50	15.00
TRIPLE-X					
❑ 104	I Shot Mr. Lee/Billy	1960	5.00	10.00	20.00
❑ 106	Have Mercy Baby/Dance with Me Georgie	1960	5.00	10.00	20.00

BOBBIE & BOOBIE
45s

Number	Title (A Side/B Side)	Yr	VG	VG+	NM
DICE					
❑ 480	Cool, Cool Christmas/Teenage Party	195?	50.00	100.00	200.00

BOBBIE JEAN
45s

Number	Title (A Side/B Side)	Yr	VG	VG+	NM
SUN					
❑ 342	You Burned the Bridges/Cheaters Never Win	1960	5.00	10.00	20.00

BOBBY AND BUDDY
45s

Number	Title (A Side/B Side)	Yr	VG	VG+	NM
HIT					
❑ 162	Just Give Me Time/Right or Wrong	1964	2.00	4.00	8.00
—B-side by Marty Wood					
❑ 180	Willow Weep for Me/Bless You Little Girl	1965	2.00	4.00	8.00
❑ 238	Michelle/My Love	1966	2.50	5.00	10.00
—B-side by Betty York					
❑ 246	Woman/Homeward Bound	1966	2.00	4.00	8.00
—B-side by Sammy and Theodore					

BOBBY AND CONNIE
45s

Number	Title (A Side/B Side)	Yr	VG	VG+	NM
HIT					
❑ 281	The Beat Goes On/Sock It To Me Baby	1967	2.00	4.00	8.00
—B-side by the Jalopy Five					
❑ 286	Something Stupid/Dedicated to the One I Love	1967	2.00	4.00	8.00
—B-side by the Chords (2)					

BOBBY AND HIS ORBITS
45s

Number	Title (A Side/B Side)	Yr	VG	VG+	NM
GONE					
❑ 5126	Your Cheatin' Heart/I Don't Stand a Chance	1962	6.25	12.50	25.00
SEECO					
❑ 6005	Felicia/Bandstand Dancing	1959	20.00	40.00	80.00
❑ 6030	Teen Age Love/What Do I Say (When I'm Close to You)	1960	12.50	25.00	50.00

BOBBY AND THE DUKES
45s

Number	Title (A Side/B Side)	Yr	VG	VG+	NM
PHILIPS					
❑ 40293	Ah, Ah, Ah/Come On Along with Me	1965	5.00	10.00	20.00

BOBBY THE POET See SENATOR BOBBY.

BOCEPHUS See HANK WILLIAMS, JR.

BOCKY AND THE VISIONS
45s

Number	Title (A Side/B Side)	Yr	VG	VG+	NM
PHILIPS					
❑ 40224	Mojo Hanna/Spirit of '64	1964	6.25	12.50	25.00
❑ 40242	I'm Pickin' Petals/I'm Not Worth It	1964	6.25	12.50	25.00

BODACIOUS D.F. MARTY BALIN was in this group.
Albums

Number	Title (A Side/B Side)	Yr	VG	VG+	NM
RCA VICTOR					
❑ AFL1-0206	Bodacious D.F.	1977	2.50	5.00	10.00
❑ APL1-0206	Bodacious D.F.	1973	3.75	7.50	15.00
❑ AYL1-4243	Bodacious D.F.	1982	2.00	4.00	8.00
—"Best Buy Series" reissue					

BOENZEE CRYQUE With Rusty Young, later of POCO.
45s

Number	Title (A Side/B Side)	Yr	VG	VG+	NM
CHICORY					
❑ 406	Sky Gone Gray/Still in Love with You Baby	1966	7.50	15.00	30.00
UNI					
❑ 55012	Sky Gone Gray/Still in Love with You Baby	1967	5.00	10.00	20.00
❑ 55022	Watch the Time/You Won't Believe It's True	1967	5.00	10.00	20.00

BOETCHER, CURT
45s

Number	Title (A Side/B Side)	Yr	VG	VG+	NM
ELEKTRA					
❑ 45834	I Love You More Each Day/Such a Lady	1973	—	2.50	5.00
Albums					
ELEKTRA					
❑ EKS-75037	There's an Innocent Face	1972	5.00	10.00	20.00

BOFFALONGO
45s

Number	Title (A Side/B Side)	Yr	VG	VG+	NM
UNITED ARTISTS					
❑ 50607	Tomorrow Not Today/Mr. Go Away	1969	2.00	4.00	8.00
❑ 50656	Please Stay/Mr. Go Away	1970	2.00	4.00	8.00
❑ 50699	Dancing in the Moonlight/Endless Question	1970	2.00	4.00	8.00
Albums					
UNITED ARTISTS					
❑ UAS-6726	Boffalongo	1969	5.00	10.00	20.00
❑ UAS-6770	Beyond Your Head	1970	5.00	10.00	20.00

BOHANNON
12-Inch Singles

Number	Title (A Side/B Side)	Yr	VG	VG+	NM
COMPLEAT					
❑ CK 101 [DJ]	Rock Your Body (Part 1 and 2)	1983	2.00	4.00	8.00
❑ CPD 201	Make Your Body Move/Come Back My Love	1983	—	3.50	7.00
❑ CPD 203	Don't Leave Me (same on both sides?)	1983	2.50	5.00	10.00
❑ CPD 204	Let's Start the Dance III (2 versions)	1983	2.00	4.00	8.00
❑ CPD 207	South Africa (2 versions)	1984	2.00	4.00	8.00
MCA					
❑ L33-17946 [DJ]	House Train (Extended 7:15) (Radio Edit 5:28) (Instrumental 6:48) (Bonus Beats 6:37)	1989	2.00	4.00	8.00
❑ L33-18106 [DJ]	The Gang's All Here (Vocal) (Dub)/ Over the Rainbow	1990	2.50	5.00	10.00
❑ 23522	Motions (Vocal)/(Instrumental)	1984	2.50	5.00	10.00
❑ 23967	House Train (2 versions)	1989	—	3.00	6.00
❑ 23997	The Gang's All Here/Over the Rainbow	1990	2.50	5.00	10.00
MERCURY					
❑ MK 49 [DJ]	Maybe You Can Dance (12:42)/I Found My Love	1977	3.75	7.50	15.00
❑ MK 77 [DJ]	Cut Loose (7:44)/The Beat Part 2 (6:14)	1979	2.50	5.00	10.00
❑ MK 128 [DJ]	Feel Like Dancin' (7:24)/The Funk Walk (6:02)	1980	2.50	5.00	10.00
❑ DS 2001	Bohannon Disco Symphony/Andrea	1977	3.75	7.50	15.00
❑ MDS 3002	Cut Loose (7:44)/The Beat Part 2 (6:14)	1979	3.00	6.00	12.00
❑ 888143-1	Jammin' in the Street (Part 1 6:02) (Part 2 5:12)	1986	2.00	4.00	8.00
PHASE II					
❑ AS 857 [DJ]	Throw Down the Groove (Part 1)	1980	3.00	6.00	12.00
❑ AS 961 [DJ]	Goin' for Another One/The Happy Dance	1981	3.00	6.00	12.00
❑ AS 1357 [DJ]	Take the Country to New York City (5:49)/ (Instrumental 4:31)	1982	3.00	6.00	12.00
❑ AS 1497 [DJ]	The Party Train (Parts 1 and 2)	1982	2.00	4.00	8.00
❑ 4W8-02133	Goin' for Another One/The Happy Dance	1981	3.00	6.00	12.00
❑ 4W8-02146	Foot Stompin' in the Summertime/(Instrumental)	1981	3.00	6.00	12.00
❑ 4Z9-02876	I've Got the Dance Fever (With Rap Intro)/ (Without Intro)	1982	2.50	5.00	10.00
45s					
COMPLEAT					
❑ 103	Make Your Body Move/Come Back My Love	1983	—	2.00	4.00
❑ 107	Don't Leave Me/Funkville	1983	—	2.00	4.00

Number	Title (A Side/B Side)	Yr	VG	VG+	NM
❏ 114	Wake Up/Enjoy Your Day	1983	—	2.00	4.00
❏ 118	Rock Your Body/(Instrumental)	1983	—	2.00	4.00
❏ 148	South Africa/South Africa (Special Mix)	1984	—	2.00	4.00

DAKAR

Number	Title (A Side/B Side)	Yr	VG	VG+	NM
❏ 4518	Save Their Souls/Stop and Go	1973	—	3.00	6.00
❏ 4521	The Pimpwalk/Happiness	1973	—	3.00	6.00
❏ 4525	Run It On Down Mr. DJ (Part 1)/ Run It On Down Mr. DJ (Part 2)	1973	—	3.00	6.00
❏ 4528	Fat Man/Red Bone	1974	—	3.00	6.00
❏ 4534	Happiness/Truck Stop	1974	—	3.00	6.00
❏ 4535	Keep On Dancin' (Part 1)/ Keep On Dancin' (Part 2)	1974	—	3.00	6.00
❏ 4539	South African Music (Pt. 1)/Have a Good Day	1974	—	2.50	5.00
❏ 4544	Foot Stompin' Music/Dance with Your Partner	1975	—	2.50	5.00
❏ 4549	Disco Stomp (Part 1)/Disco Stomp (Part 2)	1975	—	2.50	5.00
❏ 4551	Bohannon's Beat (Pt. 1)/East Coast Groove	1975	—	2.50	5.00
❏ 4554	Dance Your Ass Off/Happy Feeling	1976	—	2.50	5.00
❏ 4560	Gittin' Off/Come Winter	1976	—	2.50	5.00

MCA

Number	Title (A Side/B Side)	Yr	VG	VG+	NM
❏ 53685	House Train/(Instrumental)	1989	—	—	3.00
❏ 53766	The Gang's All Here/Over the Rainbow	1989	—	—	3.00

MERCURY

Number	Title (A Side/B Side)	Yr	VG	VG+	NM
❏ 73939	Bohannon Disco Symphony/Moving Fast	1977	—	2.00	4.00
❏ 73946	Just Doing My Thing/Andrea	1977	—	2.00	4.00
❏ 74015	Let's Start the Dance/I Wonder Why	1978	—	2.00	4.00
❏ 74035	Me and the Gang/Summertime Groove	1978	—	2.00	4.00
❏ 74044	Cut Loose/Listen to the Children Play	1979	—	2.00	4.00
❏ 74085	The Groove Machine/Love Floats	1979	—	2.00	4.00
❏ 76040	Feel Like Dancin'/Funk Walk	1980	—	2.00	4.00
❏ 76054	Baby I'm for Real/Hurry Mr. Sunshine	1980	—	2.00	4.00
❏ 888143-7	Jammin' in the Street/(B-side unknown)	1986	—	—	3.00

PHASE II

Number	Title (A Side/B Side)	Yr	VG	VG+	NM
❏ WS8-02062	Goin' for Another One/The Happy Dance	1981	—	2.00	4.00
❏ WS8-02145	Foot Stompin' in the Summertime/(Instrumental)	1981	—	2.00	4.00
❏ WS9-02573	Let's Start II Dance Again/Let's Start the Dance	1981	—	2.00	4.00
❏ ZS5-02682	Take the Country to New York City (Part 1 and 2)	1982	—	2.00	4.00
❏ ZS5-02897	I've Got the Dance Fever (With Rap Intro)/ (Without Intro)	1982	—	2.00	4.00
❏ ZS5-02998	The Party Train (Parts I & II)/ /Thoughts and Wishes	1982	—	2.00	4.00
❏ 5650	Throw Down the Groove (Part I)/ Throw Down the Groove (Part II)	1980	—	2.00	4.00
❏ 5651	Dance, Dance, Dance All Night/ April My Love (Part 1)	1980	—	2.00	4.00
❏ 5654	Don't Be Ashame to Call My Name/ (B-side unknown)	1981	—	2.00	4.00

Albums

COMPLEAT

Number	Title (A Side/B Side)	Yr	VG	VG+	NM
❏ CPL-1-1003	Make Your Body Move	1983	2.50	5.00	10.00
❏ CPL-1-1005	The Bohannon Drive	1984	3.00	6.00	12.00

DAKAR

Number	Title (A Side/B Side)	Yr	VG	VG+	NM
❏ 6910	Keep On Dancing	1973	3.00	6.00	12.00
❏ 76916	Insides Out	1974	3.00	6.00	12.00
❏ DK 76917	Bohannon	1975	3.75	7.50	15.00
❏ DK 76919	Dance Your Ass Off	1976	3.75	7.50	15.00
❏ DK 76921	Gittin' Off	1976	5.00	10.00	20.00

MCA

Number	Title (A Side/B Side)	Yr	VG	VG+	NM
❏ 42310	Here Comes Bohannon	1989	3.00	6.00	12.00

MERCURY

Number	Title (A Side/B Side)	Yr	VG	VG+	NM
❏ SRM-1-1159	Phase II	1977	2.50	5.00	10.00
❏ SRM-1-3710	On My Way	1978	2.50	5.00	10.00
❏ SRM-1-3728	Summertime Groove	1978	2.50	5.00	10.00
❏ SRM-1-3762	Cut Loose	1979	2.50	5.00	10.00
❏ SRM-1-3778	Too Hot to Hold	1979	2.50	5.00	10.00
❏ SRM-1-3813	Music in the Air	1980	2.50	5.00	10.00

PHASE II

Number	Title (A Side/B Side)	Yr	VG	VG+	NM
❏ JW 36867	One Step Ahead	1980	2.50	5.00	10.00
❏ FZ 37695	Alive	1981	2.50	5.00	10.00
❏ FZ 38113	Bohannon Fever	1982	2.50	5.00	10.00

BOHEMIAN VENDETTA

45s

MAINSTREAM

Number	Title (A Side/B Side)	Yr	VG	VG+	NM
❏ 681	Riddles and Fairytales/ I Wanna Touch Your Heart	1968	5.00	10.00	20.00

UNITED ARTISTS

Number	Title (A Side/B Side)	Yr	VG	VG+	NM
❏ 50174	Talk the Time/Enough	1967	6.25	12.50	25.00

Albums

MAINSTREAM

Number	Title (A Side/B Side)	Yr	VG	VG+	NM
❏ S-6106 [S]	Bohemian Vendetta	1968	50.00	100.00	200.00
❏ 56106 [M]	Bohemian Vendetta	1968	30.00	60.00	120.00

BOLDER DAMN

Albums

HIT

Number	Title (A Side/B Side)	Yr	VG	VG+	NM
❏ HRI-5061	Mourning	1971	250.00	500.00	1000.

BOLIN, TOMMY Also see THE JAMES GANG; ZEPHYR.

45s

NEMPEROR

Number	Title (A Side/B Side)	Yr	VG	VG+	NM
❏ 004	The Grind/Homeward Strut	1976	2.00	4.00	8.00
❏ 005	Savannah Woman/Marching Power	1976	2.00	4.00	8.00

Albums

COLUMBIA

Number	Title (A Side/B Side)	Yr	VG	VG+	NM
❏ PC 34329	Private Eyes	1976	3.00	6.00	12.00

—Original with no bar code on cover

Number	Title (A Side/B Side)	Yr	VG	VG+	NM
❏ PC 34329	Private Eyes	198?	2.00	4.00	8.00

—With bar code on cover

GEFFEN

Number	Title (A Side/B Side)	Yr	VG	VG+	NM
❏ 3GHS 24248 [(3)]	The Ultimate Tommy Bolin	1989	7.50	15.00	30.00

NEMPEROR

Number	Title (A Side/B Side)	Yr	VG	VG+	NM
❏ NE 436	Teaser	1975	3.00	6.00	12.00
❏ PZ 37534	Teaser	1982	2.00	4.00	8.00

BOLL WEEVILS, THE

45s

HIT

Number	Title (A Side/B Side)	Yr	VG	VG+	NM
❏ 107	Please Please Me/My Bonnie	1964	3.00	6.00	12.00

BOLTON, MICHAEL Includes records as "Michael Bolotin."

12-Inch Singles

COLUMBIA

Number	Title (A Side/B Side)	Yr	VG	VG+	NM
❏ 44-07581	(Sittin' On) The Dock of the Bay (4 versions)	1988	2.50	5.00	10.00

45s

COLUMBIA

Number	Title (A Side/B Side)	Yr	VG	VG+	NM
❏ 38-03800	Fools Game/Fighting for My Life	1983	—	2.00	4.00
❏ 38-04154	I Almost Believed You/She Did the Same Thing	1983	—	2.00	4.00
❏ 38-04823	Everybody's Crazy/She Did the Same Thing	1985	—	—	3.00
❏ 38-7322	That's What Love Is All About/Take a Look at My Face	1987	—	—	3.00

—U.S. editions are missing the usual "0" after the "38"

Number	Title (A Side/B Side)	Yr	VG	VG+	NM
❏ 38-07680	(Sittin' On) The Dock of the Bay/Call My Name	1988	—	—	3.00
❏ 38-07680 [PS]	(Sittin' On) The Dock of the Bay/Call My Name	1988	—	—	3.00
❏ 38-07680 [PS]	(Sittin' On) The Dock of the Bay/Call My Name	1988	3.00	6.00	12.00

—Promo-only sleeve with a message from Mrs. Otis Redding on the back

Number	Title (A Side/B Side)	Yr	VG	VG+	NM
❏ 38-07794	Wait on Love/I Almost Believed You	1988	—	—	3.00
❏ 38-07794 [PS]	Wait on Love/I Almost Believed You	1988	—	—	3.00
❏ 38-07983	Walk Away/The Hunger	1988	—	—	3.00
❏ 38-68909	Soul Provider/The Hunger	1989	—	—	3.00
❏ 38-73017	How Am I Supposed to Live Without You/ Forever Eyes	1989	—	—	3.00
❏ 38-73318	How Can We Be Lovers/ That's What Love Is All About	1990	—	—	3.00
❏ 38-73342	When I'm Back on My Feet Again/Walk Away	1990	—	—	3.00
❏ 38-73389	Georgia on My Mind/Take a Look at My Face	1990	—	—	3.00
❏ 38-73719	Love Is a Wonderful Thing/Soul Provider	1991	—	—	3.00
❏ 38-73889	Time, Love and Tenderness/ That's What Love Is All About	1991	—	—	3.00
❏ 38-74020	When a Man Loves a Woman/Save Me	1991	—	—	3.00
❏ 38-74184	Missing You Now/It's Only My Heart	1992	—	—	3.00
❏ 38-74733	To Love Somebody/Now That I've Found You	1992	—	—	3.00
❏ 38-74798	Reach Out I'll Be There/White Christmas	1992	—	2.00	4.00
❏ 38-77260	Said I Loved You...But I Lied/Soul Provider	1993	—	—	3.00
❏ 38-77376	Completely/That's What Love Is All About	1994	—	—	3.00
❏ 38-77991	Can I Touch You...There?/Ain't Got Nothing If You Ain't Got Love	1995	—	—	3.00

RCA

Number	Title (A Side/B Side)	Yr	VG	VG+	NM
❏ PB-10650	You Make Me Feel Like Lovin' You/ If I Had Your Lovin'	1976	2.50	5.00	10.00

—As "Michael Bolotin"

RCA VICTOR

Number	Title (A Side/B Side)	Yr	VG	VG+	NM
❏ PB-10283	Your Love/Dream While You Can	1975	2.50	5.00	10.00

—As "Michael Bolotin"

Albums

COLUMBIA

Number	Title (A Side/B Side)	Yr	VG	VG+	NM
❏ BFC 38357	Michael Bolton	1983	2.50	5.00	10.00
❏ PC 38357	Michael Bolton	1985	—	3.00	6.00

—Reissue with new prefix

Number	Title (A Side/B Side)	Yr	VG	VG+	NM
❏ BFC 39328	Everybody's Crazy	1985	2.50	5.00	10.00
❏ FC 40473	The Hunger	1987	2.00	4.00	8.00
❏ OC 45012	Soul Provider	1989	2.50	5.00	10.00
❏ C 46771	Time, Love and Tenderness	1991	3.75	7.50	15.00

RCA VICTOR

Number	Title (A Side/B Side)	Yr	VG	VG+	NM
❏ APL1-0992	Michael Bolotin	1975	5.00	10.00	20.00

—As "Michael Bolotin"

Number	Title (A Side/B Side)	Yr	VG	VG+	NM
❏ APL1-1551	Every Day of My Life	1976	5.00	10.00	20.00

—As "Michael Bolotin"

BON BONS, THE

45s

CORAL

Number	Title (A Side/B Side)	Yr	VG	VG+	NM
❏ 62402	What's Wrong with Ringo/Come On Baby	1964	15.00	30.00	60.00
❏ 62435	Everybody Wants My Boyfriend/Each Time	1964	12.50	25.00	50.00

BON-AIRES, THE

45s

RUST

Number	Title (A Side/B Side)	Yr	VG	VG+	NM
❏ TR 3	Blue Beat/(B-side unknown)	196?	7.50	15.00	30.00
❏ 5077	My Love My Love/Bye Bye	1964	5.00	10.00	20.00
❏ 5097	The Shrine of St. Ceceia/Jeanie Baby	1965	5.00	10.00	20.00

BON-AIRS, THE

45s

KING

Number	Title (A Side/B Side)	Yr	VG	VG+	NM
❏ 4975	Stop the World/Bermuda	1956	7.50	15.00	30.00

BONADUCE, DANNY One of the stars of the TV series "The Partridge Family," but he doesn't appear on any of the records.

45s

LION

Number	Title (A Side/B Side)	Yr	VG	VG+	NM
❏ 145	Blueberry You/Dreamland	1973	2.50	5.00	10.00
❏ 145 [PS]	Blueberry You/Dreamland	1973	6.25	12.50	25.00

Albums

LION

Number	Title (A Side/B Side)	Yr	VG	VG+	NM
❏ LN-1015	Danny Bonaduce	1973	15.00	30.00	60.00

BONAIRS, THE

45s

DOOTONE

Number	Title (A Side/B Side)	Yr	VG	VG+	NM
❏ 325	It's Christmas/I'm Alone Tonight	1953	37.50	75.00	150.00

—B-side by Ernie Tavares Trio

BOND, ANGELO

45s

ABC

Number	Title (A Side/B Side)	Yr	VG	VG+	NM
❏ 12077	Reach for the Moon (Poor People)/ I Never Sang for My Baby	1975	—	2.50	5.00
❏ 12135	I Love You for What You Are/Eve	1975	—	2.50	5.00

Number	Title (A Side/B Side)	Yr	VG	VG+	NM
❏ 12153	He Gained the World (But Lost His Soul)/ I Love You for What You Are	1976	—	2.50	5.00

Albums
ABC

Number	Title (A Side/B Side)	Yr	VG	VG+	NM
❏ D-889	Bondage	1975	2.50	5.00	10.00

BOND, GRAHAM
45s
ASCOT

Number	Title (A Side/B Side)	Yr	VG	VG+	NM
❏ 2211	St. James Infirmary/Wade in the Water	1966	2.50	5.00	10.00

PULSAR

Number	Title (A Side/B Side)	Yr	VG	VG+	NM
❏ 2405	Love Is the Law/The Naz	1969	2.00	4.00	8.00
❏ 2409	Crossroads of Time/Moving Towards the Light	1969	2.00	4.00	8.00
❏ 2415	Stiffened Chicken/Water, Water	1969	2.00	4.00	8.00

Albums
MERCURY

Number	Title (A Side/B Side)	Yr	VG	VG+	NM
❏ SRM-1-612	We Put Our Magick on You	1971	5.00	10.00	20.00
❏ SR-61327	Holy Magick	1970	5.00	10.00	20.00

PULSAR

Number	Title (A Side/B Side)	Yr	VG	VG+	NM
❏ 10604	Love Is the Law	1969	6.25	12.50	25.00
❏ 10606	Mighty Graham Bond	1969	6.25	12.50	25.00

WARNER BROS.

Number	Title (A Side/B Side)	Yr	VG	VG+	NM
❏ 2LS 2555 [(2)]	Solid Bond	1971	5.00	10.00	20.00

BOND, JOHNNY
45s
COLUMBIA

Number	Title (A Side/B Side)	Yr	VG	VG+	NM
❏ 2-100 (?)	Take It or Leave It Baby/Till the End of the World	1949	6.25	12.50	25.00
—Microgroove 7-inch, 33 1/3 rpm single					
❏ 2-100 (?)	Tennessee Saturday Night/A Heart Full of Love	1949	6.25	12.50	25.00
—Microgroove 7-inch, 33 1/3 rpm single					
❏ 2-200 (?)	Read It and Weep/Somebody Loves You	1950	6.25	12.50	25.00
—Microgroove 7-inch, 33 1/3 rpm single					
❏ 2-210 (?)	I'm Biting My Fingernails/I Wish I Had a Nickel	1949	6.25	12.50	25.00
—Microgroove 7-inch, 33 1/3 rpm single					
❏ 2-319	Drowning My Sorrows/Women Make a Fool Out of Me	1950	6.25	12.50	25.00
—Microgroove 7-inch, 33 1/3 rpm single					
❏ 2-400 (?)	A Petal from a Faded Rose/Put Me to Bed #2	1950	6.25	12.50	25.00
—Microgroove 7-inch, 33 1/3 rpm single					
❏ 2-532	Love Song in 32 Bars/Tennessee Kentucky & Alabam'	1950	6.25	12.50	25.00
—Microgroove 7-inch, 33 1/3 rpm single					
❏ 2-600 (?)	Cherokee Waltz/Mean Mama Boogie	1950	6.25	12.50	25.00
—Microgroove 7-inch, 33 1/3 rpm single					
❏ 20726	Under the Red, White and Blue/ Star Spangled Waltz	1950	5.00	10.00	20.00
❏ 20734	Barrel House Bessie/ It Ain't Gonna Happen to Me	1950	5.00	10.00	20.00
❏ 20738	There's a Gold Moon Shining/ Cream of Kentucky	1950	5.00	10.00	20.00
❏ 20756	I Wanna Do Something For Santa/ Jingle Bell Boogie	1950	5.00	10.00	20.00
❏ 20787	Set 'Em Up Joe/Glad Rags	1951	5.00	10.00	20.00
❏ 20808	Sick, Sober and Sorry/ Tennessee Walking Horse	1951	5.00	10.00	20.00
❏ 20844	Ten Trips to the Altar/ Keep Your Cotton Pickin' Hands	1951	5.00	10.00	20.00
❏ 20876	Broke, Disgusted and Sad/In Old New Mexico	1952	3.75	7.50	15.00
❏ 20909	I Found You Out/Alabama Boogie Boy	1952	3.75	7.50	15.00
❏ 20948	Louisiana Lucy/The Man Behind the Throttle	1952	3.75	7.50	15.00
❏ 21007	I Went to Your Wedding/Our Love Isn't Legal	1952	3.75	7.50	15.00
❏ 21041	Back Street Affair/Our Love Isn't Legal	1952	3.75	7.50	15.00
❏ 21042	Born to Be Bad/#9 Blues	1952	3.75	7.50	15.00
❏ 21066	Wildcat Boogie/Let Me Go, Devil	1953	3.75	7.50	15.00
❏ 21082	Anybody's Baby/Hills of Kentucky	1953	3.75	7.50	15.00
❏ 21113	Peace Be Still/Ninety & Nine	1953	3.75	7.50	15.00
❏ 21150	Live and Let Live/ I Wonder Where You Are Tonight	1953	3.75	7.50	15.00
❏ 21160	Wildcat Boogie/Let Me Go, Devil	1953	3.75	7.50	15.00
❏ 21186	Sweet Mama Tree Top Tall/Put a Little Sweetness in Your Love	1953	3.75	7.50	15.00
❏ 21187	Thanks/I Dreamed I Searched Heaven	1953	3.75	7.50	15.00
❏ 21222	10 Little Bottles/They Got Me	1954	3.75	7.50	15.00
❏ 21243	Firewater/Old Man Blues	1954	3.75	7.50	15.00
❏ 21294	Stealin'/My Darling Lola Lee	1954	3.75	7.50	15.00
❏ 21335	I Lose Again/Everybody Knew the Truth but Me	1954	3.75	7.50	15.00
❏ 21369	Cherokee Waltz/Glad Rags	1955	3.75	7.50	15.00
❏ 21383	Jim, Johnny & Jonas/Louisiana Swing	1955	3.75	7.50	15.00
❏ 21424	Somebody's Pushin'/Carolina Waltz	1955	3.75	7.50	15.00
❏ 21448	Remember the Alamo/Livin' It Up	1955	3.75	7.50	15.00
❏ 21494	Loaded for Bear/Six of One, Half a Dozen of the Other	1956	3.75	7.50	15.00
❏ 21521	Little Rock and Roll/I'll Be Here	1956	12.50	25.00	50.00
❏ 21565	Lonesome Train/Laughing Back the Heartaches	1956	3.75	7.50	15.00
❏ 40080	Santa Got Stuck in the Chimney/ I Said a Prayer for Santa Claus	1953	3.75	7.50	15.00
—With Jimmy Boyd					
❏ 40842	Honky Tonk Fever/Lay It on the Line	1957	3.75	7.50	15.00
❏ 40973	All I Can Do Is Cry/Sale of Broken Hearts	1957	3.75	7.50	15.00
❏ 41034	That's Just What I'll Do/Broken Doll	1957	3.75	7.50	15.00

DITTO

Number	Title (A Side/B Side)	Yr	VG	VG+	NM
❏ 120	The Tijuana Jail/Fools Paradise	1959	3.00	6.00	12.00

MGM

Number	Title (A Side/B Side)	Yr	VG	VG+	NM
❏ 10627	Rag Mop/Music! Music! Music!	1950	10.00	20.00	40.00
❏ 10751	Heart of Gold/Hey Ho Virginia Reel	1950	10.00	20.00	40.00
❏ 14596	Rose of Reynosa/Who Stole the Juke Box	1973	—	2.50	5.00

REPUBLIC

Number	Title (A Side/B Side)	Yr	VG	VG+	NM
❏ 2005	Hot Rod Lincoln/Five Minute Love Affair	1960	3.00	6.00	12.00
❏ 2008	X-15/The Way a Star Is Born	1960	3.00	6.00	12.00
❏ 2010	Side Car Cycle/Like Nothin' Man	1961	3.00	6.00	12.00
❏ 2022	Sadie Was a Lady/Buck Private's Lament	1961	3.00	6.00	12.00

SMASH

Number	Title (A Side/B Side)	Yr	VG	VG+	NM
❏ 1761	I'll Step Aside/Mister Sun	1962	2.50	5.00	10.00

STARDAY

Number	Title (A Side/B Side)	Yr	VG	VG+	NM
❏ 618	How to Succeed with Girls (Without Half-Way Trying)/Don't Mention Her Name	1963	2.00	4.00	8.00
❏ 635	True Love (Is Hard to Find)/Cimarron	1963	2.00	4.00	8.00
❏ 649	Three Sheets in the Wind/Let the Tears Begin	1963	2.00	4.00	8.00
❏ 665	Have You Seen My Baby/What Have You Done for Me Lately	1964	2.00	4.00	8.00
❏ 678	Hot Rod Surfin' Hootlebeatnanny/Don't Mama Count Anymore	1964	3.75	7.50	15.00
❏ 690	My Wicked, Wicked Ways/Bachelor Bill	1964	2.00	4.00	8.00
❏ 704	10 Little Bottles/Let It Be Me	1964	2.00	4.00	8.00
❏ 721	Sick, Sober & Sorry/ The Man Who Comes Around	1965	2.00	4.00	8.00
❏ 731	The Great Figure Eight Race/Sadie Was a Lady	1965	2.00	4.00	8.00
❏ 749	They Got Me/Silent Walls	1966	2.00	4.00	8.00
❏ 758	Fireball/Over the Hill	1966	2.00	4.00	8.00
❏ 776	Hell's Angels/A Way of Life	1966	2.00	4.00	8.00
❏ 803	Your Old Love Letters/Si Si	1967	2.00	4.00	8.00
❏ 813	I Ain't Gonna Go/Don't Bite the Hand That's Feeding You	1967	2.00	4.00	8.00
❏ 826	Bottom of the Bottle/I'm Gonna Raise Cain (While I'm Able)	1968	2.00	4.00	8.00
❏ 847	Down to Your Last Fool/Invitation to the Blues	1968	2.00	4.00	8.00
❏ 893	It Only Hurts When I Cry/ The Girl Who Carried the Torch for Me	1970	—	3.00	6.00
❏ 916	Here Come the Elephants/ Take Me Back to Tulsa	1970	—	3.00	6.00
❏ 931	The Bottle's Empty/The Late and Great Myself	1971	—	3.00	6.00
❏ 951	Put the Country Back in Country Music/Fly Me, Try Me	1972	—	3.00	6.00
❏ 7021	Hot Rod Lincoln/Barrel House Betsy	197?	—	2.50	5.00
❏ 7027	Divorce Me C.O.D./Three Sheets in the Wind	197?	—	2.50	5.00
❏ 7033	Tennessee, Kentucky and Alabam'/Glad Rags	197?	—	2.50	5.00

20TH FOX

Number	Title (A Side/B Side)	Yr	VG	VG+	NM
❏ 156	Gold Rush/The Long Tall Shadow	1959	3.00	6.00	12.00
❏ 231	Jealous Lad/A Kid Named Bell	1960	3.00	6.00	12.00

7-Inch Extended Plays
COLUMBIA

Number	Title (A Side/B Side)	Yr	VG	VG+	NM
❏ B-2820	Sick, Sober and Sorry/Love Song in 32 Bars// Ten Little Bottles/Put Me to Bed	1958	7.50	15.00	30.00
❏ B-2820 [PS]	Johnny Bond and His Red River Boys (Hall of Fame Series)	1958	7.50	15.00	30.00

REPUBLIC

Number	Title (A Side/B Side)	Yr	VG	VG+	NM
❏ 100	(contents unknown)	1960	5.00	10.00	20.00
❏ 100 [PS]	Hot Rod Lincoln	1960	5.00	10.00	20.00

Albums
CMH

Number	Title (A Side/B Side)	Yr	VG	VG+	NM
❏ 6212	The Singing Cowboy Again	1981	2.50	5.00	10.00
❏ 6213	The Return of the Singing Cowboy	1981	2.50	5.00	10.00

HARMONY

Number	Title (A Side/B Side)	Yr	VG	VG+	NM
❏ HL 7308 [M]	Johnny Bond's Best	1964	5.00	10.00	20.00
❏ HL 7353 [M]	Bottled in Bond	1965	5.00	10.00	20.00

NASHVILLE

Number	Title (A Side/B Side)	Yr	VG	VG+	NM
❏ 2054	Three Sheets to the Wind	196?	3.75	7.50	15.00

SHASTA

Number	Title (A Side/B Side)	Yr	VG	VG+	NM
❏ LP-516	Johnny Bond Rides Again	197?	3.75	7.50	15.00

STARDAY

Number	Title (A Side/B Side)	Yr	VG	VG+	NM
❏ SLP-147 [M]	That Wild, Wicked But Wonderful Wesy	1961	12.50	25.00	50.00
❏ SLP-227 [M]	Songs That Made Him Famous	1963	10.00	20.00	40.00
❏ SLP-298 [M]	Hot Rod Lincoln	1964	12.50	25.00	50.00
❏ SLP-333 [M]	Ten Little Bottles	1965	7.50	15.00	30.00
❏ SLP-354 [M]	Famous Hot Rodders I Have Known	1965	10.00	20.00	40.00
❏ SLP-368 [M]	The Man Who Comes Around	1966	6.25	12.50	25.00
❏ SLP-378 [M]	Bottles Up	1966	6.25	12.50	25.00
❏ SLP-388 [M]	The Branded Stock of Johnny Bond	1966	5.00	10.00	20.00
❏ SLP-402 [M]	Ten Nights in a Barroom	1967	5.00	10.00	20.00
❏ SLP-416	Drink Up and Go Home	1968	3.75	7.50	15.00
❏ SLP-444	The Best of Johnny Bond	1969	3.75	7.50	15.00
❏ SLP-456	Old, New, Patriotic and Blue	1970	3.75	7.50	15.00
❏ SLP-472	Here Come the Elephants	1971	3.75	7.50	15.00
❏ 954	The Best of Johnny Bond	1976	2.50	5.00	10.00

BOND, JOHNNY, AND LEFTY FRIZZELL Also see each artist's individual listings.
45s
COLUMBIA

Number	Title (A Side/B Side)	Yr	VG	VG+	NM
❏ 40934	Sick, Sober and Sorry/Lover By Appointment	1957	3.75	7.50	15.00

BOND, JOHNNY, AND RED SOVINE Also see each artist's individual listings.
45s
STARDAY

Number	Title (A Side/B Side)	Yr	VG	VG+	NM
❏ 790	The Gearjammer and the Hobo/Sweet Nellie	1966	2.50	5.00	10.00

BONDS, GARY U.S.
45s
ATCO

Number	Title (A Side/B Side)	Yr	VG	VG+	NM
❏ 6689	The Star/You Need a Personal Manager	1969	—	3.00	6.00

BLUFF CITY

Number	Title (A Side/B Side)	Yr	VG	VG+	NM
❏ 221	My Love Song/Blue Grass	1974	—	2.50	5.00

BOTANIC

Number	Title (A Side/B Side)	Yr	VG	VG+	NM
❏ 1002	I'm Glad You're Back/Funky Lies	1968	2.00	4.00	8.00

EMI AMERICA

Number	Title (A Side/B Side)	Yr	VG	VG+	NM
❏ 8079	This Little Girl/Way Back When	1981	—	2.00	4.00
❏ 8079 [PS]	This Little Girl/Way Back When	1981	—	2.50	5.00
❏ 8089	Jole Blon/Just Like a Child	1981	—	2.00	4.00
❏ 8099	Your Love/Just Like a Child	1981	—	2.00	4.00
❏ 8117	Out of Work/Bring Her Back	1982	—	2.00	4.00
❏ 8117 [PS]	Out of Work/Bring Her Back	1982	—	2.50	5.00
❏ 8133	Love's on the Line/Way Back When	1982	—	2.00	4.00
❏ 8145	Turn the Music Down/Way Back When	1982	—	2.00	4.00

B

Number	Title (A Side/B Side)	Yr	VG	VG+	NM
LEGRAND					
❏ 1003	New Orleans/Please Forgive Me	1960	3.75	7.50	15.00
—Gold and red label					
❏ 1003	New Orleans/Please Forgive Me	1960	5.00	10.00	20.00
—Original lists artist as "By-U.S. Bonds"; purple label					
❏ 1005	Not Me/Give Me One More Chance	1961	3.75	7.50	15.00
—Gold and red label					
❏ 1005	Not Me/Give Me One More Chance	1961	5.00	10.00	20.00
—Artist listed as "U.S. Bonds"; purple label					
❏ 1008	Quarter to Three/Time Ole Story	1961	3.75	7.50	15.00
—Artist listed as "U.S. Bonds"; gold and red label					
❏ 1008	Quarter to Three/Time Ole Story	1961	10.00	20.00	40.00
—Artist listed as "U.S. Bonds"; purple label					
❏ 1008 [PS]	Quarter to Three/Time Ole Story	1961	10.00	20.00	40.00
❏ 1009	School Is Out/One Million Years	1961	3.75	7.50	15.00
—Artist listed as "Gary (U.S.) Bonds" as are all later Legrand singles					
❏ 1009	School Is Out/One Million Years	1961	5.00	10.00	20.00
—Artist listed as "U.S. Bonds"					
❏ 1009 [PS]	School Is Out/One Million Years	1961	10.00	20.00	40.00
❏ 1012	School Is In/Trip to the Moon	1961	3.75	7.50	15.00
❏ 1012	School Is In/Trip to the Moon	1971	2.00	4.00	8.00
—Red label reissue					
❏ 1015	Dear Lady/Havin' So Much Fun	1961	5.00	10.00	20.00
—Original title of A-side					
❏ 1015	Dear Lady Twist/Havin' So Much Fun	1962	3.75	7.50	15.00
❏ 1018	Twist, Twist Senora/Food of Love	1962	3.75	7.50	15.00
❏ 1019	Seven Day Weekend/Gettin' a Groove	1962	3.75	7.50	15.00
❏ 1020	Copy Cat/I'll Change That Too	1962	3.75	7.50	15.00
❏ 1022	Mixed Up Faculty/I Dig This Station	1962	3.75	7.50	15.00
❏ 1025	Do the Limbo with Me/Where Did That Naughty Little Girl Go	1962	3.75	7.50	15.00
❏ 1027	I Don't Wanta Wait/What a Dream	1963	3.00	6.00	12.00
❏ 1029	No More Homework/She's Alright	1963	3.00	6.00	12.00
❏ 1030	Perdido Part 1/Perdido Part 2	1963	3.00	6.00	12.00
❏ 1031	King Kong's Monkey/My Sweet Ruby Rose	1964	3.00	6.00	12.00
❏ 1032	The Music Goes Round and Round/Ella Is Yella	1964	3.00	6.00	12.00
❏ 1034	You Little Angel You/My Little Miss America	1964	3.00	6.00	12.00
❏ 1035	Oh Yeah, Oh Yeah!/Let ❏ Oh Yeah, Oh Yeah!/Let Me Go Lover	1965	2.50	5.00	10.00
❏ 1039	Beaches U.S.A./Do the Bumpsie	1965	2.50	5.00	10.00
❏ 1040	Take Me Back to New Orleans/I'm That Kind of Guy	1966	2.50	5.00	10.00
❏ 1041	Due to Circumstances Under My Control/Slow Motion	1966	2.50	5.00	10.00
❏ 1043	Send Her Back to Me/Workin' for My Baby	1967	2.50	5.00	10.00
❏ 1045	Call Me for Christmas/Mixed Up Faculty	1967	3.00	6.00	12.00
❏ 1046	Sarah Jane/What a Crazy World	1967	2.50	5.00	10.00
MCA					
❏ 52335	One More Time Around the Block, Ophelia/Deadline U.S.A.	1984	—	2.00	4.00
—B-side by Shalamar					
❏ 52400	New Orleans/Rhythm of the Rain	1984	—	2.00	4.00
—With Neil Sedaka					
PHOENIX					
❏ 0071	Standing in the Line of Fire/Wild Nights	1984	—	2.50	5.00
❏ 0071 [PS]	Standing in the Line of Fire/Wild Nights	1984	—	2.50	5.00
PRODIGAL					
❏ 0612	Grandma's Washboard/Believing You	1975	—	2.50	5.00
SUE					
❏ 17	One Broken Heart/Can't Use You in My Business	1970	—	3.00	6.00
Albums					
EMI AMERICA					
❏ SPRO-9666 [EP]	Dedication Sampler	1981	3.75	7.50	15.00
—Promo-only sampler with limited-edition number on pink sticker					
❏ SO-17051	Dedication	1981	2.50	5.00	10.00
❏ SO-17068	On the Line	1982	2.50	5.00	10.00
LEGRAND					
❏ LLP-3001 [M]	Dance 'Til Quarter to Three	1961	25.00	50.00	100.00
❏ LLP-3002 [M]	Twist Up Calypso	1962	17.50	35.00	70.00
❏ LLP-3003 [M]	Greatest Hits of Gary U.S. Bonds	1962	17.50	35.00	70.00
MCA					
❏ 905	The Best of Gary U.S. Bonds	1984	2.50	5.00	10.00
PHOENIX					
❏ PRT 0072	Standing in the Line of Fire	1984	2.50	5.00	10.00
RHINO					
❏ RNLP-805	Certified Soul	1981	2.50	5.00	10.00

BONFIRE, MARS Real name: Dennis McCrohan. Also see SPARROW; STEPPENWOLF.

Number	Title (A Side/B Side)	Yr	VG	VG+	NM
45s					
COLUMBIA					
❏ 44772	Faster Than the Speed of Life/She	1969	2.50	5.00	10.00
❏ 44888	In Christina's Arms/Lady Moon Walker	1969	2.50	5.00	10.00
Albums					
COLUMBIA					
❏ CS 9834	Faster Than the Speed of Life	1969	3.75	7.50	15.00
UNI					
❏ 73027	Mars Bonfire	1968	5.00	10.00	20.00

BONNEVILLES, THE More than one group.

Number	Title (A Side/B Side)	Yr	VG	VG+	NM
45s					
BARRY					
❏ 104	Lorraine/Zu Zu	1962	12.50	25.00	50.00
CAPRI					
❏ 102	Give Me Your Love/Until You Say We're Through	1959	12.50	25.00	50.00
CORAL					
❏ 62273	Johnny/Freeway U.S.A.	1961	5.00	10.00	20.00
MUNICH					
❏ 103	Lorraine/Zu Zu	1960	25.00	50.00	100.00
—Black label					

Number	Title (A Side/B Side)	Yr	VG	VG+	NM
❏ 103	Lorraine/Zu Zu	1960	75.00	150.00	300.00
—Red label					
WHITEHALL					
❏ 30002	I Do/Make Believe Lovin'	1959	7.50	15.00	30.00
Albums					
DRUM BOY					
❏ DLM-1001 [M]	Meet the Bonnevilles	1963	25.00	50.00	100.00
❏ DLS-1001 [S]	Meet the Bonnevilles	1963	37.50	75.00	150.00
JUSTICE					
❏ JLP-146	Bringing It Home	196?	125.00	250.00	500.00

BONNEY, GRAHAM

Number	Title (A Side/B Side)	Yr	VG	VG+	NM
45s					
CAPITOL					
❏ 2221	I'll Be Your Baby Tonight/Back from Baltimore	1968	—	3.00	6.00
❏ 5624	Super Girl/Hill of Lovin'	1966	2.00	4.00	8.00
MIKE					
❏ 4009	Baby's Gone/Later Tonight	1966	2.00	4.00	8.00

BONNIE AND THE BUTTERFLYS

Number	Title (A Side/B Side)	Yr	VG	VG+	NM
45s					
SMASH					
❏ 1878	I Saw Him Standing There/Dust Storm	1964	5.00	10.00	20.00

BONNIE AND THE TREASURES

Number	Title (A Side/B Side)	Yr	VG	VG+	NM
45s					
PABLO					
❏ 7014	Davey, I'm So Glad It Rained/The Lonely Surfer	1964	10.00	20.00	40.00
—B-side by the Mid-Americans					
PHI-DAN					
❏ 5005	Home of the Brave/Our Song	1965	10.00	20.00	40.00

BONNIE LOU

Number	Title (A Side/B Side)	Yr	VG	VG+	NM
45s					
FRATERNITY					
❏ 808	No One Ever Lost More/Have You Ever Been Lonely	1958	3.75	7.50	15.00
❏ 812	Friction Heat/I Give My Love to You	1958	3.75	7.50	15.00
KING					
❏ 1192	Seven Lonely Days/Just Out of Reach	1953	7.50	15.00	30.00
❏ 1213	Scrap of Paper/Dancin' with Someone	1953	7.50	15.00	30.00
❏ 1237	Tennessee Wig Walk/Hand Me Down Heart	1953	7.50	15.00	30.00
❏ 1272	Papaya Mama/Since You Said Goodbye	1953	7.50	15.00	30.00
❏ 1279	Texas Polka/No Heart at All	1953	7.50	15.00	30.00
❏ 1318	Welcome Mat/Don't Stop Kissing Me Goodnight	1954	6.25	12.50	25.00
❏ 1341	Huckleberry Pie/No One	1954	6.25	12.50	25.00
❏ 1365	Wait for Me Darling/Blue Tennessee Rain	1954	3.00	6.00	25.00
❏ 1373	Two-Step Step/Please Don't Laugh When I Cry	1954	6.25	12.50	25.00
❏ 1384	Tell the World/Darlin' Why	1954	6.25	12.50	25.00
❏ 1414	Tennessee Mambo/Train Whistle Blues	1955	6.25	12.50	25.00
❏ 1436	Tweedle Dee/Finger of Suspicion	1955	6.25	12.50	25.00
❏ 1445	Danger, Heartbreak Ahead/A Rusty Old Halo	1955	6.25	12.50	25.00
❏ 1476	Drop Me a Line/Old Faithful	1955	6.25	12.50	25.00
❏ 1506	Barnyard Hop/Miss the Love	1955	6.25	12.50	25.00
❏ 4835	Daddy-O/Dancing in My Socks	1955	6.25	12.50	25.00
❏ 4864	Daddy-O/Miss the Love	1956	5.00	10.00	20.00
❏ 4895	Little Miss Bobby Sox/Beyond the Shadow of a Doubt	1956	5.00	10.00	20.00
❏ 4900	Bo Weevil/Chaperon	1956	5.00	10.00	20.00
❏ 4919	I Turn to You/Lonesome Lover	1956	5.00	10.00	20.00
❏ 4948	No Rock 'N' Roll Tonight/One Track Love	1956	6.25	12.50	25.00
❏ 5009	I Want You/Easy Love, Easy Kisses	1957	5.00	10.00	20.00
❏ 5033	Kit 'N Caboodle/Takes Two	1957	5.00	10.00	20.00
❏ 5063	Teeange Wedding/Runnin' Away	1957	5.00	10.00	20.00
❏ 5094	I'm Available/Waiting in Vain	1957	5.00	10.00	20.00
❏ 5425	Tweedle Dee/Daddy-O	1960	3.75	7.50	15.00
❏ 5865	Seven Lonely Days/Tennessee Wig Walk	1964	3.00	6.00	12.00
Albums					
KING					
❏ 595 [M]	Bonnie Lou Sings	1958	35.00	70.00	140.00

BONNIE SISTERS, THE

Number	Title (A Side/B Side)	Yr	VG	VG+	NM
45s					
RAINBOW					
❏ 45-328	I Saw Mommy Cha Cha Cha with You Know Who?/Cry Baby	1955	10.00	20.00	40.00
❏ 45-328	Cry Baby/Broken	1956	7.50	15.00	30.00
❏ 45-333	Track That Cat/Wandering Heart	1956	7.50	15.00	30.00
❏ 45-344	Confess/Shuga Duga	1956	7.50	15.00	30.00

BONNIWELL, T.S. Sean Bonniwell of THE MUSIC MACHINE.

Number	Title (A Side/B Side)	Yr	VG	VG+	NM
45s					
CAPITOL					
❏ 2551	Sleep/Where Am I to Go	1969	2.50	5.00	10.00
Albums					
CAPITOL					
❏ ST-377	Close	1969	12.50	25.00	50.00

BONNIWELL'S MUSIC MACHINE See THE MUSIC MACHINE.

BONO, SONNY See SONNY; SONNY AND CHER.

BONZO DOG BAND, THE Also see VIVIAN STANSHALL.

Number	Title (A Side/B Side)	Yr	VG	VG+	NM
45s					
IMPERIAL					
❏ 66345	I'm the Urban Spaceman/Canyons of Your Mind	1969	3.75	7.50	15.00
❏ 66373	Mr. Apollo/Ready Made	1969	3.75	7.50	15.00
—As "The Bonzo Dog Doo-Dah Band"					
UNITED ARTISTS					
❏ 50809	I'm the Urban Spaceman/Canyons of Your Mind	1971	2.50	5.00	10.00
❏ 50943	Slush/King of Scurf	1972	3.75	7.50	15.00

Number	Title (A Side/B Side)	Yr	VG	VG+	NM
Albums					
IMPERIAL					
❏ LP 9370 [M]	Gorilla	1968	5.00	10.00	20.00
—Without booklet					
❏ LP 9370 [M]	Gorilla	1968	7.50	15.00	30.00
—With booklet					
❏ LP 12370 [S]	Gorilla	1968	5.00	10.00	20.00
—Without booklet					
❏ LP 12370 [S]	Gorilla	1968	7.50	15.00	30.00
—With booklet					
❏ LP 12432	Urban Spaceman	1968	5.00	10.00	20.00
—Without booklet					
❏ LP 12432	Urban Spaceman	1968	7.50	15.00	30.00
—With booklet					
❏ LP 12445	Tadpoles	1969	5.00	10.00	20.00
❏ LP 12457	Keynsham	1969	5.00	10.00	20.00
LIBERTY					
❏ LN-10206	Some of the Best of the Bonzo Dog Band	1983	2.00	4.00	8.00
UNITED ARTISTS					
❏ UA-LA321-H2 [(2)]	The History of the Bonzos	1974	3.75	7.50	15.00
❏ UAS 5517	The Beast of the Bonzos	1971	3.75	7.50	15.00
❏ UAS 5584	Let's Make Up and Be Friendly	1972	3.75	7.50	15.00

BOOGIE KINGS, THE
45s

Number	Title (A Side/B Side)	Yr	VG	VG+	NM
MONTEL					
❏ 939	Crying Man/Two Steps from the Blues	1965	3.00	6.00	12.00
❏ 984	When She Touches Me/Philly Walk	196?	2.50	5.00	10.00
❏ 995	Elaine/Philly Walk	196?	2.50	5.00	10.00
PAULA					
❏ 260	Tell It Like It Is/Philly Walk	1967	2.50	5.00	10.00
❏ 272	Bony Maronie/I've Got Your Number	1967	2.50	5.00	10.00
PIC 1					
❏ 121	The Band Doll/She	196?	3.75	7.50	15.00
❏ 129	This Is Blue Eyed Soul/Do 'Em All	196?	3.75	7.50	15.00
❏ 133	Let It Be Me/That's Really Some Good	196?	3.75	7.50	15.00
Albums					
MONTEL					
❏ LP-104 [M]	The Boogie Kings	1966	6.25	12.50	25.00
❏ LP-109 [M]	Blue Eyed Soul	1967	6.25	12.50	25.00

BOOKENDS, THE
45s

Number	Title (A Side/B Side)	Yr	VG	VG+	NM
CAPITOL					
❏ 4667	Christmas Kisses/Let Me Walk with You	1961	3.75	7.50	15.00

BOOKER, JOHN LEE See JOHN LEE HOOKER.

BOOKER T. AND PRISCILLA Also see BOOKER T. AND THE MG'S.
45s

Number	Title (A Side/B Side)	Yr	VG	VG+	NM
A&M					
❏ 1298	The Wedding Song/She	1971	—	2.50	5.00
❏ 1487	Crippled Crow/Wild Fox	1973	—	2.50	5.00
Albums					
A&M					
❏ SP-3504 [(2)]	Booker T. and Priscilla	1971	3.75	7.50	15.00
❏ SP-4351	Home Grown	1972	2.50	5.00	10.00
❏ SP-4413	Chronicles	1973	2.50	5.00	10.00

BOOKER T. AND THE MG'S Also see BOOKER T. AND PRISCILLA; STEVE CROPPER.
12-Inch Singles

Number	Title (A Side/B Side)	Yr	VG	VG+	NM
A&M					
❏ SP-12046 [DJ]	Don't Stop Your Love/I Came to Love You	1981	3.75	7.50	15.00
—As "Booker T. Jones"					
❏ SP-17043 [DJ]	Let's Go Dancing (2 versions?)	1978	3.75	7.50	15.00
—As "Booker T. Jones"					
❏ SP-17188 [DJ]	Don't Stop Your Love (same on both sides?)	1981	3.75	7.50	15.00
—As "Booker T. Jones"					
❏ SP-20011	Don't Stop Your Love (unknown versions)	1981	3.00	6.00	12.00
—As "Booker T. Jones"					
45s					
A&M					
❏ 2100	Knockin' on Heaven's Door/Let's Go Dancin'	1978	—	2.00	4.00
—As "Booker T. Jones"					
❏ 2234	The Best of You/Let's Go Dancin'	1980	—	2.00	4.00
—As "Booker T. Jones"					
❏ 2279	Will You Be the One/Cookie	1980	—	2.00	4.00
—As "Booker T. Jones"					
❏ 2374	I Want You/You're the Best	1981	—	2.00	4.00
❏ 2394	Don't Stop Your Love/I Came to Love You	1982	—	2.00	4.00
ASYLUM					
❏ 45392	Sticky Stuff/The Stick	1977	—	2.00	4.00
❏ 45424	Grab Bag/Reincarnation	1977	—	2.00	4.00
COLUMBIA					
❏ 38-77526	Cruisin'/Just My Imagination	1994	—	2.00	4.00
EPIC					
❏ 50031	Evergreen/Song for Casey	1974	—	2.00	4.00
❏ 50078	Front Street Rag/Mama Stewart	1975	—	2.00	4.00
❏ 50149	Life Is Funny/Tennessee Voodoo	1975	—	2.00	4.00
STAX					
❏ 0001	Soul-Limbo/Heads Or Tails	1968	2.00	4.00	8.00
❏ 0013	Hang 'Em High/Over Easy	1968	2.00	4.00	8.00
❏ 0028	Time Is Tight/Johnny I Love You	1969	2.00	4.00	8.00
❏ 0037	Mrs. Robinson/Soul Clap '69	1969	2.00	4.00	8.00
❏ 0049	Slum Baby/Meditation	1969	2.00	4.00	8.00
❏ 0073	Something/Sunday Sermon	1970	—	3.00	6.00
❏ 0082	Melting Pot/Kinda Easy Like	1970	—	3.00	6.00
❏ 127	Green Onions/Behave Yourself	1962	4.00	8.00	16.00
—Blue label					
❏ 127	Green Onions/Behave Yourself	1962	5.00	10.00	20.00
—Gray label					
❏ 131	Jellybread/Aw' Mercy	1963	3.00	6.00	12.00
❏ 134	Big Train/Burnt Biscuits	1963	3.00	6.00	12.00

Number	Title (A Side/B Side)	Yr	VG	VG+	NM
❏ 134	Big Train/Home Grown	1963	3.00	6.00	12.00
❏ 137	Chinese Checkers/Plum Nellie	1963	3.00	6.00	12.00
❏ 142	Mo' Onions/Fannie Mae	1963	3.00	6.00	12.00
❏ 142	Mo' Onions/Tic Tac Toe	1963	3.00	6.00	12.00
❏ 153	Soul Dressing/MG Party	1964	2.50	5.00	10.00
❏ 161	Can't Be Still/Terrible Thing	1964	2.50	5.00	10.00
❏ 169	Boot-Leg/Outrage	1965	2.50	5.00	10.00
❏ 0169	Sugarcane/Blackride	1973	—	2.50	5.00
—As "The MG's"					
❏ 182	Red Beans and Rice/Be My Lady	1965	2.50	5.00	10.00
❏ 196	Booker-Loo/My Sweet Potato	1966	2.50	5.00	10.00
❏ 0200	Breezy/Neckbone	1974	—	2.50	5.00
—As "The MG's"					
❏ 203	Jingle Bells/Winter Wonderland	1966	3.00	6.00	12.00
❏ 211	Hip-Hug-Her/Summertime	1967	2.50	5.00	10.00
❏ 224	Groovin'/Slim Jenkin's Place	1967	2.50	5.00	10.00
❏ 236	Silver Bells/Winter Snow	1967	3.00	6.00	12.00
VOLT					
❏ 102	Green Onions/Behave Yourself	1962	7.50	15.00	30.00
Albums					
A&M					
❏ SP-4720	Try and Love Again	1978	2.50	5.00	10.00
—As "Booker T. Jones"					
❏ SP-4798	The Best of You	1979	2.50	5.00	10.00
—As "Booker T. Jones"					
❏ SP-4874	I Want You	1981	2.50	5.00	10.00
—As "Booker T. Jones"					
ASYLUM					
❏ 7E-1093	Universal Language	1977	2.50	5.00	10.00
ATLANTIC					
❏ 8202 [M]	The Best of Booker T. and the MG's	1968	12.50	25.00	50.00
—Mono is white label promo only					
❏ SD 8202 [S]	The Best of Booker T. and the MG's	1968	5.00	10.00	20.00
❏ 81285	The Best of Booker T. and the MG's	1985	2.00	4.00	8.00
EPIC					
❏ KE 33143	Evergreen	1974	3.00	6.00	12.00
MCA					
❏ 6282	The Runaway	1989	3.00	6.00	12.00
—As "Booker T. Jones"					
STAX					
❏ ST-701 [M]	Green Onions	1962	17.50	35.00	70.00
❏ STS-701 [R]	Green Onions	1966	12.50	25.00	50.00
❏ ST-705 [M]	Soul Dressing	1965	17.50	35.00	70.00
❏ STS-705 [R]	Soul Dressing	1966	12.50	25.00	50.00
❏ ST-711 [M]	And Now…Booker T. and the MG's	1966	12.50	25.00	50.00
❏ STS-711 [S]	And Now…Booker T. and the MG's	1966	20.00	40.00	80.00
❏ ST-713 [M]	In the Christmas Spirit	1966	100.00	200.00	400.00
—Fingers and piano keys cover					
❏ ST-713 [M]	In the Christmas Spirit	1967	50.00	100.00	200.00
—Same as above; Santa Claus cover					
❏ STS-713 [S]	In the Christmas Spirit	1966	100.00	200.00	400.00
—Fingers and piano keys cover					
❏ STS-713 [S]	In the Christmas Spirit	1967	50.00	100.00	200.00
—Santa Claus cover					
❏ ST-717 [M]	Hip Hug-Her	1967	10.00	20.00	40.00
❏ STS-717 [S]	Hip Hug-Her	1967	12.50	25.00	50.00
❏ STS-724	Doin' Our Thing	1968	12.50	25.00	50.00
❏ STS-2001	Soul Limbo	1968	6.25	12.50	25.00
❏ STS-2006	Uptight	1969	6.25	12.50	25.00
❏ STS-2009	The Booker T. Set	1969	6.25	12.50	25.00
❏ STS-2027	McLemore Avenue	1970	6.25	12.50	25.00
❏ STS-2033	Booker T. and the MG's Greatest Hits	1970	3.75	7.50	15.00
❏ STS-2035	Melting Pot	1971	3.75	7.50	15.00
❏ STX-4104	Free Ride	1978	2.50	5.00	10.00
❏ STX-4113	Soul Limbo	198?	2.50	5.00	10.00
—Reissue of 2001					
❏ MPS-8505	Booker T. and the MG's Greatest Hits	1981	2.50	5.00	10.00
❏ MPS-8521	Melting Pot	198?	2.50	5.00	10.00
—Reissue of 2035					
❏ MPS-8531	The Booker T. Set	1987	2.50	5.00	10.00
—Reissue of 2009					
❏ MPS-8552	McLemore Avenue	1990	3.00	6.00	12.00
—Reissue of 2027					
SUNDAZED					
❏ LP 5042	Soul Dressing	2000	3.75	7.50	15.00
—Reissue on 180-gram vinyl					
❏ LP 5043	And Now! Booker T. and the MG's	2000	3.75	7.50	15.00
—Reissue on 180-gram vinyl					
❏ LP 5053	In the Christmas Spirit	2000	3.75	7.50	15.00
—Reissue on 180-gram vinyl					
❏ LP 5079	Green Onions	2002	3.00	6.00	12.00
—Reissue on 180-gram vinyl					
❏ LP 5080	Hip Hug-Her	2002	3.00	6.00	12.00
—Reissue on 180-gram vinyl					

BOOMERANG
45s

Number	Title (A Side/B Side)	Yr	VG	VG+	NM
RCA VICTOR					
❏ 74-0508	Mockingbird/Montreal Jail	1971	2.00	4.00	8.00
❏ 74-0580	Juke It/Hard Times	1971	2.00	4.00	8.00
Albums					
RCA VICTOR					
❏ LSP-4577	Boomerang	1971	5.00	10.00	20.00

BOONE, DANIEL
45s

Number	Title (A Side/B Side)	Yr	VG	VG+	NM
EPIC					
❏ 10787	Daddy Don't You Walk So Fast/Tiger Woman	1971	—	2.50	5.00
MERCURY					
❏ 73281	Beautiful Sunday/Truly Julie	1972	—	2.50	5.00
❏ 73339	Annabelle/Sleepyhead	1972	—	2.00	4.00
❏ 73357	Crying/Sunshine Lover	1973	—	2.00	4.00

B

Number	Title (A Side/B Side)	Yr	VG	VG+	NM
73428	Skydiver/Do You Thank the Lord	1973	—	2.00	4.00
73461	Love Spell/Lilly, I Love You	1974	—	2.00	4.00

PYE

Number	Title (A Side/B Side)	Yr	VG	VG+	NM
71007	A Rock 'N Roll Band/Singing Backing Vocal with a Rock 'N Roll Band	1975	—	2.00	4.00
71011	Run, Tell the People/Rock 'N' Roll Bum	1975	—	2.00	4.00
71041	Run, Tell the People/(B-side unknown)	1976	—	2.00	4.00
71052	I Think of You/(B-side unknown)	1976	—	2.00	4.00

Albums

MERCURY

Number	Title (A Side/B Side)	Yr	VG	VG+	NM
SRM-1-649	Beautiful Sunday	1972	2.50	5.00	10.00

BOONE, PAT Also see THE BOONES.

45s

BUENA VISTA

Number	Title (A Side/B Side)	Yr	VG	VG+	NM
487	Little Green Tree/The Sounds of Christmas	1973	—	3.50	7.00

CAPITOL

Number	Title (A Side/B Side)	Yr	VG	VG+	NM
2763	What Are You Doing the Rest of Your Life/Now I'm Saved	1970	—	2.50	5.00
2860	Picking Up Pebbles/Oh My God	1970	—	2.50	5.00

DOT

Number	Title (A Side/B Side)	Yr	VG	VG+	NM
S-200 [S]	With the Wind and the Rain in Your Hair/Good Rockin' Tonight	1959	10.00	20.00	40.00
S-203 [S]	For a Penny/The Wang Dang Taffy Apple Tango	1959	10.00	20.00	40.00
S-207 [S]	Twixt Twlve and Twenty/Rock Boll Weevil	1959	10.00	20.00	40.00
S-211 [S]	Fools Hall of Fame/The Brightest Wishing Star	1959	10.00	20.00	40.00
S-218 [S]	Beyond the Sunset/My Faithful Heart	1959	10.00	20.00	40.00
S-220 [S]	(Welcome) New Lovers/Words	1960	10.00	20.00	40.00
S-221 [S]	Walking the Floor Over You/Spring Rain	1960	10.00	20.00	40.00
S-228 [S]	Delia Gone/Candy Street	1960	10.00	20.00	40.00
15338	Two Hearts/Tra La La	1955	5.00	10.00	20.00
15377	Ain't That a Shame/Tennessee Saturday Night	1955	5.00	10.00	20.00
15422	At My Front Door/No Other Arms	1955	5.00	10.00	20.00
15435	Gee Whittakers!/Take the Time	1955	5.00	10.00	20.00
15443	Tutti Frutti/I'll Be Home	1956	5.00	10.00	20.00
15457	Long Tall Sally/Just As Long As I'm with You	1956	5.00	10.00	20.00
15472	I Almost Lost My Mind/I'm in Love with You	1956	5.00	10.00	20.00
15490	Friendly Persuasion (Thee I Love)/Chains of Love	1956	3.75	7.50	15.00
—Second pressing on black label					
15490	Friendly Persuasion (Thee I Love)/Chains of Love	1956		10.00	20.00
—Original on maroon label					
15521	Don't Forbid Me/Anastasia	1956	3.75	7.50	15.00
15545	Why Baby Why/I'm Waiting Just for You	1957	3.75	7.50	15.00
15570	Love Letters in the Sand/Bernardine	1957	3.75	7.50	15.00
15570 [PS]	Love Letters in the Sand/Bernardine	1957	7.50	15.00	30.00
15602	Remember You're Mine/There's a Gold Mine in the Sky	1957	3.75	7.50	15.00
15660	April Love/When the Swallows Come Back to Capistrano	1957	3.75	7.50	15.00
15690	It's Too Soon to Know/A Wonderful Time Up There	1958	3.75	7.50	15.00
15750	Sugar Moon/Cherie, I Love You	1958	3.75	7.50	15.00
15750 [PS]	Sugar Moon/Cherie, I Love You	1958	7.50	15.00	30.00
15785	If Dreams Came True/That's How Much I Love You	1958	3.75	7.50	15.00
15825	Gee, But It's Lonely/For My Good Fortune	1958	3.75	7.50	15.00
15840	I'll Remember Tonight/The Mardi Gras March	1958	3.75	7.50	15.00
15840 [PS]	I'll Remember Tonight/The Mardi Gras March	1958	7.50	15.00	30.00
15888 [M]	With the Wind and the Rain in Your Hair/Good Rockin' Tonight	1959	3.75	7.50	15.00
15914 [M]	For a Penny/The Wang Dang Taffy Apple Tango	1959	3.75	7.50	15.00
15955 [M]	Twixt Twlve and Twenty/Rock Boll Weevil	1959	3.75	7.50	15.00
15955 [PS]	Twixt Twlve and Twenty/Rock Boll Weevil	1959	7.50	15.00	30.00
15982 [M]	Fools Hall of Fame/The Brightest Wishing Star	1959	3.75	7.50	15.00
15982 [PS]	Fools Hall of Fame/The Brightest Wishing Star	1959	7.50	15.00	30.00
16006 [M]	Beyond the Sunset/My Faithful Heart	1959	3.75	7.50	15.00
16015	To the Center of the Earth Part 1/Part 2	1959	5.00	10.00	20.00
16028	Ain't That a Shame/I'll Be Home	1960	2.50	5.00	10.00
16033	I Almost Lost My Mind/Friendly Persuasion	1960	2.50	5.00	10.00
16034	Don't Forbid Me/April Love	1960	2.50	5.00	10.00
16035	Love Letters in the Sand/A Wonderful Time Up There	1960	2.50	5.00	10.00
16048	(Welcome) New Lovers/Words	1960	3.00	6.00	12.00
16048 [PS]	(Welcome) New Lovers/Words	1960	5.00	10.00	20.00
16073	Walking the Floor Over You/Spring Rain	1960	3.00	6.00	12.00
16073 [PS]	Walking the Floor Over You/Spring Rain	1960	5.00	10.00	20.00
16122	Delia Gone/Candy Street	1960	3.00	6.00	12.00
16152	Dear John/Alabam	1960	3.00	6.00	12.00
16176	The Exodus Song (This Land Is Mine)/There's a Moon Out Tonight	1961	3.00	6.00	12.00
16190	Cherry Pink and Apple Blossom White/On Both Sides	1961	3.00	6.00	12.00
16209	Moody River/A Thousand Years	1961	3.75	7.50	15.00
16244	Big Cold Wind/That's My Desire	1961	3.00	6.00	12.00
16278	Louella/(B-side unknown)	1961	—	—	—
—Unreleased?					
16284	Johnny Will/Just Let Me Dream	1961	3.00	6.00	12.00
16312	I'll See You in My Dreams/Pictures in the Fire	1961	3.00	6.00	12.00
16349	Quando, Quando, Quando (Tell Me When)/Willing and Eager	1962	2.50	5.00	10.00
16368	Speedy Gonzales/The Locket	1962	3.00	6.00	12.00
16391	Ten Lonely Guys/Lover's Lane	1962	2.50	5.00	10.00
16416	In the Room/Mexican Joe	1963	2.50	5.00	10.00
16439	Days of Wine and Roses/Meditation	1963	2.50	5.00	10.00
16474	Always You and Me/Main Attraction	1963	2.50	5.00	10.00
16494	Tie Me Kangaroo Down Sport/I Feel Like Crying	1963	2.50	5.00	10.00
16498	Amore Baciami/Gondoli Gondola	1963	2.50	5.00	10.00
16498	Main Attraction/Si Si Si	1963	2.50	5.00	10.00
16525	Love Me/Mr. Moon	1963	2.50	5.00	10.00
16547	Santa's Coming in a Whirleybird/Oh Holy Night	1963	2.50	5.00	10.00
16559	Some Enchanted Evening/That's Me	1963	2.50	5.00	10.00
16576	I Like What You Do/Never Put It in Writing	1964	2.00	4.00	8.00
16598	I Understand (Just How You Feel)/Rosemarie	1964	2.00	4.00	8.00
16626	Side by Side/I'll Never Be Free	1964	2.00	4.00	8.00
—By "Pat and Shirley Boone"					
16641	Sincerely/Don't You Just Know It	1964	2.00	4.00	8.00
16658	Beach Girl/Little Honda	1964	7.50	15.00	30.00
16668	Goodbye, Charlie/Love, Who Needs It	1964	2.00	4.00	8.00
16684	I'd Rather Die Young/I Want It That Way	1964	2.00	4.00	8.00
16699	Blueberry Hill/Heartaches	1965	2.00	4.00	8.00
16707	Baby Elephant Walk/Say Goodbye	1965	2.00	4.00	8.00
16728	Pearly Shells/Crazy Arms	1965	2.00	4.00	8.00
16738	Mickey Mouse/(Welcome) New Lovers	1965	2.00	4.00	8.00
16738	Mickey Mouse/Time Marches On	1965	2.00	4.00	8.00
16754	Rainy Days/With My Eyes Wide Open I'm Dreaming	1965	2.00	4.00	8.00
16785	I Love You So Much It Hurts/Meet Me Tonight in Dreamland	1965	2.00	4.00	8.00
16808	A Man Alone/Run to Me, Baby	1966	2.00	4.00	8.00
16825	As Tears Go By/Judith	1966	2.00	4.00	8.00
16836	It Seems Like Yesterday/Well Remembered, Highly Thought Of Love Affair	1966	2.00	4.00	8.00
16871	Five Miles from Home/Don't Put Your Feet in the Lemonade	1966	2.00	4.00	8.00
16903	Wrath of Grapes/You Don't Need Me Anymore	1966	2.00	4.00	8.00
16933	Wish You Were Here, Buddy/Love for You	1966	2.00	4.00	8.00
16998	Hurry Sundown/What If They Gave a War and Nobody Came	1967	—	3.00	6.00
17018	Have You Heard (It's All Over)/Me	1967	—	3.00	6.00
17027	In the Mirror of Your Mind/Swanee Is a River	1967	—	3.00	6.00
17045	By the Time I Get to Phoenix/Ride Ride Ride	1967	—	3.00	6.00
17056	The Green Kentucky Hills of Home/You Mean All the World to Me	1967	—	3.00	6.00
17076	It's a Happening World/Emily	1968	—	3.00	6.00
17098	500 Miles/I Had a Dream	1968	—	3.00	6.00
17122	Gonna Find Me a Bluebird/Deafening Roar of Silence	1968	—	3.00	6.00
17156	Beyond One Memory/September Blues	1968	—	3.00	6.00

HITSVILLE

Number	Title (A Side/B Side)	Yr	VG	VG+	NM
6037	Texas Woman/It's Gone	1976	—	2.50	5.00
6042	Oklahoma Sunshine/Won't Be Home Tonight	1976	—	2.50	5.00
6047	Country Days and Country Nights/Lovelight Comes a-Shining	1976	—	2.50	5.00
6054	Colorado Country Morning/Don't Want to Fall Away from You	1977	—	2.50	5.00

LAMB & LION

Number	Title (A Side/B Side)	Yr	VG	VG+	NM
818	It's OK to Be a Kid at Christmas/Don't Let the Season Pass You By	1979	—	2.50	5.00

LION

Number	Title (A Side/B Side)	Yr	VG	VG+	NM
106	Mr. Blue/Song of the Children of Israel (Exodus)	1972	—	2.50	5.00
—With the Boone Girls					
119	I Believe in Music/Children Learn What They Live	1972	—	2.50	5.00
—With the Boone Family					
126	Empty Chairs/If You're Gonna Make a Fool of Somebody	1972	—	2.50	5.00

MC

Number	Title (A Side/B Side)	Yr	VG	VG+	NM
5001	Whatever Happened to the Good Old Honky Tonk/Ain't Going Down in the Ground Before My Time	1977	—	2.50	5.00

MELODYLAND

Number	Title (A Side/B Side)	Yr	VG	VG+	NM
6001	Candy Lips/Young Girl	1974	—	2.50	5.00
6005	Indiana Girl/Young Girl	1975	—	2.50	5.00
6018	I'd Do It with You/Yester-Me, Yester-You, Yesterday	1975	—	2.50	5.00
—A-side with Shirley Boone					
6029	Glory Train/U.F.O.	1976	—	2.50	5.00

MGM

Number	Title (A Side/B Side)	Yr	VG	VG+	NM
14242	All for the Love of Sunshine/M.I.A-P.O.W.	1971	—	2.50	5.00
14282	C'mon, Give a Hand/Where There's a Heartache	1971	—	2.50	5.00
14470	I Saw the Light/Great Speckled Bird	1972	—	2.50	5.00
14521	Tying the Pieces Together/Hayden Carter	1973	—	2.00	4.00
14521 [PS]	Tying the Pieces Together/Hayden Carter	1973	—	2.50	5.00
14601	Everything Begins and Ends with You/Golden Rocket	1973	—	2.00	4.00

REPUBLIC

Number	Title (A Side/B Side)	Yr	VG	VG+	NM
7049	My Heart Belongs to You/Until You Tell Me So	1953	6.25	12.50	25.00
7062	Remember to Be Mine/Half Way Chance with You	1953	6.25	12.50	25.00
7084	I Need Someone/Love You Madly	1954	6.25	12.50	25.00
7119	My Heart Belongs to You/I Need Someone	1955	5.00	10.00	20.00

TETRAGRAMMATON

Number	Title (A Side/B Side)	Yr	VG	VG+	NM
1516	July, You're a Woman/Break My Mind	1969	—	2.50	5.00
1529	Never Goin' Back/What's Gnawing at Me	1969	—	2.50	5.00
1540	You Win Again/Good Morning, Dear	1969	—	2.50	5.00

WARNER BROS.

Number	Title (A Side/B Side)	Yr	VG	VG+	NM
49097	Midnight/Can You Feel the Love	1979	—	2.00	4.00
—By "Pat and Shirley Boone"					
49255	Hostage Prayer/Love's Got a Way of Hanging On	1980	—	2.00	4.00
49596	Colorado Country Morning/Whatever Happened to the Good Old Honky Tonk	1980	—	2.00	4.00
49691	Won't Be Home Tonight/Throw It Away	1981	—	2.00	4.00

7-Inch Extended Plays

DOT

Number	Title (A Side/B Side)	Yr	VG	VG+	NM
DEP-1049	At My Front Door/Tennessee Saturday Night//Ain't That a Shame/Two Hearts	1956	5.00	10.00	20.00
DEP-1049 [PS]	Pat Boone	1956	5.00	10.00	20.00
DEP-1053	Treasure of Love/B-I-N-G-O//Hoboken Baby/Am I Seeing Angels	1956	5.00	10.00	20.00
DEP-1053 [PS]	Pat On Mike	1956	5.00	10.00	20.00

Number	Title (A Side/B Side)	Yr	VG	VG+	NM
❑ DEP-1054	Coax Me A Little/The Mocking Bird In The Willow Tree//Indiana Holiday/Marry Me, Marry Me	1956	5.00	10.00	20.00
❑ DEP-1054 [PS]	Pat Boone Sings Songs from Friendly Persuasion	1956	5.00	10.00	20.00
❑ DEP-1055	Don't Forbid Me/Why Did I Choose You?//Rock Me Baby/The Fat Man	1957	5.00	10.00	20.00
❑ DEP-1055 [PS]	A Date with Pat Boone	1957	5.00	10.00	20.00
❑ DEP-1056	Just a Closer Walk with Thee/Peace in the Valley//He'll Understand/Steal Away	1957	5.00	10.00	20.00
❑ DEP-1056 [PS]	A Closer Walk with Thee	1957	5.00	10.00	20.00
❑ DEP-1057	Technique/Cathedral in the Pines//Louella/Without My Love	1957	5.00	10.00	20.00
❑ DEP-1057 [PS]	Four by Pat	1957	5.00	10.00	20.00
❑ DEP-1062	White Christmas/Silent Night//Jingle Bells/Santa Claus Is Comin' to Town	1957	7.50	15.00	30.00
❑ DEP-1062 [PS]	... And a Very Merry Christmas	1957	7.50	15.00	30.00
❑ DEP-1064	Chattanooga Shoe Shine Boy/Harbor Lights//Tutti Frutti/I'll Be Home	195?	3.75	7.50	15.00
❑ DEP-1064 [PS]	Tutti Frutti	195?	3.75	7.50	15.00
❑ DEP-1068	The Lord's Prayer/I Believe//Ave Maria/He	195?	3.75	7.50	15.00
❑ DEP-1068 [PS]	The Lord's Prayer	195?	3.75	7.50	15.00
❑ DEP-1069	Autumn Leaves/Blueberry Hill//Cold, Cold Heart/St. Louis Blues	1958	5.00	10.00	20.00
❑ DEP-1069 [PS]	Star Dust	1958	5.00	10.00	20.00
❑ DEP-1075	Loyalty/Bourbon Street Blues//Bigger Than Texas/A Fiddle, A Rifle, An Axe and a Bible	1958	3.75	7.50	15.00
❑ DEP-1075 [PS]	Mardi Gras	1958	3.75	7.50	15.00
❑ DEP-1076	*You Can't Be True, Dear/My Happiness//Now Is the Hour/Side by Side	1959	3.75	7.50	15.00
❑ DEP-1076 [PS]	Side by Side	1959	3.75	7.50	15.00
—By "Pat & Shirley Boone"					
❑ DEP-1081	Beyond The Sunset/It Is No Secret//My God Is Real (Yes, God Is Real)/Yield Not To Temptation	195?	3.75	7.50	15.00
❑ DEP-1081 [PS]	Hymns We Love	195?	3.75	7.50	15.00
❑ DEP-1082	Tenderly/Fascination//True Love/Maybe You'll Be There	196?	3.75	7.50	15.00
❑ DEP-1082 [PS]	Tenderly	196?	3.75	7.50	15.00
❑ DEP-1083	(contents unknown)	196?	3.75	7.50	15.00
❑ DEP-1083 [PS]	Pat's Great Hits	196?	3.75	7.50	15.00
❑ DEP-1086	(contents unknown)	196?	3.75	7.50	15.00
❑ DEP-1086 [PS]	I'm in the Mood for Love	196?	3.75	7.50	15.00
❑ DEP-1090	(contents unknown)	196?	3.75	7.50	15.00
❑ DEP-1090 [PS]	Beyond the Sunset	196?	3.75	7.50	15.00
❑ DEP-1091	The Faithful Heart/To the Center of the Earth//Twice as Tall/My Love Is Like a Red, Red Rose	196?	3.75	7.50	15.00
❑ DEP-1091 [PS]	Journey to the Center of the Earth	196?	3.75	7.50	15.00
❑ DEP-1098	All Hands on Deck/There's No One Like You//I've Got It Made/Somewhere There's Home	196?	3.75	7.50	15.00
❑ DEP-1098 [PS]	All Hands On Deck	196?	3.75	7.50	15.00

Albums

ABC

Number	Title	Yr	VG	VG+	NM
❑ 4006	16 Great Performances	1975	2.50	5.00	10.00

BIBLE VOICE

❑ 7076	The Solution to Crisis-America	1970	3.00	6.00	12.00

DOT

❑ DLP-3012 [M]	Pat Boone	1956	12.50	25.00	50.00
—Maroon label					
❑ DLP-3012 [M]	Pat Boone	1957	6.25	12.50	25.00
—Black label					
❑ DLP-3030 [M]	Howdy!	1956	12.50	25.00	50.00
—Maroon label					
❑ DLP-3030 [M]	Howdy!	1957	6.25	12.50	25.00
—Black label					
❑ DLP-3050 [M]	Pat	1957	6.25	12.50	25.00
❑ DLP-3068 [M]	Hymns We Love	1957	6.25	12.50	25.00
❑ DLP-3071 [M]	Pat's Great Hits	1957	6.25	12.50	25.00
❑ DLP-3077 [M]	Pat Boone Sings Irving Berlin	1958	5.00	10.00	20.00
❑ DLP-3118 [M]	Star Dust	1958	5.00	10.00	20.00
❑ DLP-3121 [M]	Yes Indeed!	1958	5.00	10.00	20.00
❑ DLP-3158 [M]	Pat Boone Sings	1959	5.00	10.00	20.00
❑ DLP-3180 [M]	Tenderly	1959	5.00	10.00	20.00
❑ DLP-3199 [M]	Side by Side	1959	5.00	10.00	20.00
❑ DLP-3222 [M]	White Christmas	1959	6.25	12.50	25.00
❑ DLP-3234 [M]	He Leadeth Me	1960	3.75	7.50	15.00
❑ DLP-3261 [M]	Pat's Great Hits Volume 2	1960	3.75	7.50	15.00
❑ DLP-3270 [M]	Moonglow	1960	3.75	7.50	15.00
❑ DLP-3285 [M]	This and That	1960	3.75	7.50	15.00
❑ DLP-3346 [M]	Great! Great! Great!	1961	3.75	7.50	15.00
❑ DLP-3384 [M]	Moody River	1961	3.00	6.00	12.00
❑ DLP-3386 [M]	My God and I	1961	3.00	6.00	12.00
❑ DLP-3399 [M]	I'll See You in My Dreams	1961	3.00	6.00	12.00
❑ DLP-3402 [M]	Pat Boone Reads from the Holy Bible	1962	3.75	7.50	15.00
❑ DLP-3455 [M]	Pat Boone's Golden Hits	1962	3.00	6.00	12.00
❑ DLP-3475 [M]	I Love You Truly	1962	3.00	6.00	12.00
❑ DLP-3501 [M]	Pat Boone Sings Guess Who?	1963	12.50	25.00	50.00
❑ DLP-3504 [M]	Pat Boone Sings "Days of Wine and Roses" and Other Great Movie Themes	1963	3.00	6.00	12.00
❑ DLP-3513 [M]	Sing Along Without Pat Boone	1963	3.00	6.00	12.00
❑ DLP-3520 [M]	The Star Spangled Banner	1963	3.00	6.00	12.00
❑ DLP-3534 [M]	Tie Me Kangaroo Down, Sport	1963	3.00	6.00	12.00
❑ DLP-3546 [M]	The Touch of Your Lips	1963	3.00	6.00	12.00
❑ DLP-3582 [M]	The Lord's Prayer And Other Great Hymns	1964	3.00	6.00	12.00
❑ DLP-3594 [M]	Boss Beat	1964	3.00	6.00	12.00
❑ DLP-3601 [M]	Blest Be the Tie That Binds	1965	3.00	6.00	12.00
❑ DLP-3606 [M]	Near You	1965	3.00	6.00	12.00
❑ DLP-3626 [M]	The Golden Era of Country Hits	1965	3.00	6.00	12.00
❑ DLP-3650 [M]	My 10th Anniversary with Dot Records	1965	3.00	6.00	12.00
❑ DLP-3667 [M]	Winner of the Reader's Digest Poll	1965	3.00	6.00	12.00
❑ DLP-3685 [M]	Great Hits of 1965	1965	3.00	6.00	12.00
❑ DLP-3748 [M]	Memories	1966	3.00	6.00	12.00
❑ DLP-3764 [M]	Wish You Were Here, Buddy	1966	3.00	6.00	12.00

Number	Title	Yr	VG	VG+	NM
❑ DLP-3770 [M]	Christmas Is a-Comin'	1966	3.00	6.00	12.00
❑ DLP-3798 [M]	How Great Thou Art	1967	3.75	7.50	15.00
❑ DLP-3805 [M]	I Was Kaiser Bill's Batman	1967	3.75	7.50	15.00
❑ DLP-3814 [M]	15 Hits of Pat Boone	1967	3.75	7.50	15.00
❑ DLP-3876 [M]	Look Ahead	1968	3.75	7.50	15.00
❑ DLP-25068 [S]	Hymns We Love	1959	7.50	15.00	30.00
❑ DLP-25071 [P]	Pat's Great Hits	1959	7.50	15.00	30.00
❑ DLP-25077 [S]	Pat Boone Sings Irving Berlin	1959	6.25	12.50	25.00
❑ DLP-25118 [S]	Star Dust	1959	6.25	12.50	25.00
❑ DLP-25121 [S]	Yes Indeed!	1959	6.25	12.50	25.00
❑ DLP-25158 [S]	Pat Boone Sings	1959	6.25	12.50	25.00
❑ DLP-25180 [S]	Tenderly	1959	6.25	12.50	25.00
❑ DLP-25199 [S]	Side by Side	1959	6.25	12.50	25.00
❑ DLP-25222 [S]	White Christmas	1959	7.50	15.00	30.00
❑ DLP-25234 [S]	He Leadeth Me	1960	5.00	10.00	20.00
❑ DLP-25261 [S]	Pat's Great Hits Volume 2	1960	5.00	10.00	20.00
❑ DLP-25270 [S]	Moonglow	1960	5.00	10.00	20.00
—Black vinyl					
❑ DLP-25270 [S]	Moonglow	1960	12.50	25.00	50.00
—Blue vinyl					
❑ DLP-25285 [S]	This and That	1960	5.00	10.00	20.00
❑ DLP-25346 [S]	Great! Great! Great!	1961	5.00	10.00	20.00
❑ DLP-25384 [S]	Moody River	1961	3.75	7.50	15.00
❑ DLP-25386 [S]	My God and I	1961	3.75	7.50	15.00
❑ DLP-25399 [S]	I'll See You in My Dreams	1961	3.75	7.50	15.00
❑ DLP-25455 [S]	Pat Boone's Golden Hits	1962	3.75	7.50	15.00
❑ DLP-25475 [S]	I Love You Truly	1962	3.75	7.50	15.00
❑ DLP-25501 [S]	Pat Boone Sings Guess Who?	1963	20.00	40.00	80.00
❑ DLP-25504 [S]	Pat Boone Sings "Days of Wine and Roses" and Other Great Movie Themes	1963	3.75	7.50	15.00
❑ DLP-25513 [S]	Sing Along Without Pat Boone	1963	3.75	7.50	15.00
❑ DLP-25520 [S]	The Star Spangled Banner	1963	3.75	7.50	15.00
❑ DLP-25534 [S]	Tie Me Kangaroo Down, Sport	1963	3.75	7.50	15.00
❑ DLP-25546 [S]	The Touch of Your Lips	1963	3.75	7.50	15.00
❑ DLP-25573 [R]	Pat Boone	1964	3.00	6.00	12.00
❑ DLP-25582 [S]	The Lord's Prayer And Other Great Hymns	1964	3.75	7.50	15.00
❑ DLP-25594 [S]	Boss Beat	1964	3.75	7.50	15.00
❑ DLP-25601 [S]	Blest Be the Tie That Binds	1965	3.75	7.50	15.00
❑ DLP-25606 [S]	Near You	1965	3.75	7.50	15.00
❑ DLP-25626 [S]	The Golden Era of Country Hits	1965	3.75	7.50	15.00
❑ DLP-25650 [S]	My 10th Anniversary with Dot Records	1965	3.75	7.50	15.00
❑ DLP-25667 [S]	Winner of the Reader's Digest Poll	1965	3.75	7.50	15.00
❑ DLP-25685 [S]	Great Hits of 1965	1965	3.75	7.50	15.00
❑ DLP-25748 [S]	Memories	1966	3.75	7.50	15.00
❑ DLP-25764 [S]	Wish You Were Here, Buddy	1966	3.75	7.50	15.00
❑ DLP-25770 [S]	Christmas Is a-Comin'	1966	3.75	7.50	15.00
❑ DLP-25798 [S]	How Great Thou Art	1967	3.00	6.00	12.00
❑ DLP-25805 [S]	I Was Kaiser Bill's Batman	1967	3.00	6.00	12.00
❑ DLP-25814 [S]	15 Hits of Pat Boone	1967	3.00	6.00	12.00
❑ DLP-25876 [S]	Look Ahead	1968	3.00	6.00	12.00

HAMILTON

❑ HLP-118 [M]	12 Great Hits	196?	3.00	6.00	12.00
❑ HLP-12118 [S]	12 Great Hits	196?	3.00	6.00	12.00

HITSVILLE

❑ H6-405	Texas Woman	1976	3.00	6.00	12.00

LAMB & LION

❑ 1002	New Songs of the Jesus People	197?	3.00	6.00	12.00
❑ 1004	Pat Boone and the First Nashville Jesus Band	197?	3.00	6.00	12.00
❑ 1005	Christian People, Vol. 1	197?	2.50	5.00	10.00
❑ 1006	The Family Who Prays	197?	2.50	5.00	10.00
❑ 1007	Born Again	197?	2.50	5.00	10.00
❑ 1008	All in the Boone Family	1972	2.50	5.00	10.00
❑ 1013	S-A-V-E-D	197?	2.50	5.00	10.00
❑ 1016	Songs from the Inner Court	197?	2.50	5.00	10.00
❑ 5000	The Pat Boone Family in the Holy Land	197?	2.50	5.00	10.00

MCA

❑ 658	16 Great Performances	1980	2.00	4.00	8.00
❑ 6020 [(2)]	The Best of Pat Boone	1980	3.00	6.00	12.00
❑ 15028 [S]	White Christmas	198?	2.50	5.00	10.00
—Reissue of Dot LP					

MELODYLAND

❑ 6-501	The Country Side of Pat Boone	1975	3.00	6.00	12.00

MGM

❑ SE-4899	I Love You More and More Every Day	1973	2.50	5.00	10.00

PARAMOUNT

❑ 1024 [(2)]	Pat Boone's Greatest Hymns	1974	3.75	7.50	15.00
❑ 1043 [(2)]	Pat Boone's Greatest Hits	1974	3.75	7.50	15.00

PICKWICK

❑ SPC-1024	White Christmas	1979	2.50	5.00	10.00
❑ SPC-3079	True Love	196?	2.50	5.00	10.00
❑ SPC-3107	Love Me Tender	196?	2.50	5.00	10.00
❑ SPC-3123	Canadian Sunset	196?	2.50	5.00	10.00
❑ SPC-3145	Favorite Hymns	197?	2.50	5.00	10.00
❑ SPC-3219	You've Lost That Lovin' Feeling	197?	2.50	5.00	10.00
❑ SPC-3568	The Old Rugged Cross	1978	2.00	4.00	8.00
❑ SPC-3597	Great Hits	1978	2.00	4.00	8.00

SUPREME

❑ SS-2060	Rapture	1970	3.00	6.00	12.00

TETRAGRAMMATON

❑ T-118	Departure	1969	3.00	6.00	12.00

WORD

❑ WST-8536	The Pat Boone Family	1970	2.50	5.00	10.00
❑ WST-8664	Hymns We Love	197?	2.50	5.00	10.00
❑ WST-8711	He Leadeth Me	197?	2.50	5.00	10.00
❑ WST-8725	The Star-Spangled Banner	197?	2.50	5.00	10.00
❑ WST-8738	I Believe	198?	2.00	4.00	8.00

B

Number	Title (A Side/B Side)	Yr	VG	VG+	NM

BOONES, THE
45s
MOTOWN

Number	Title (A Side/B Side)	Yr	VG	VG+	NM
❑ 1314	Please Mr. Postman/Friend	1974	—	2.50	5.00

—As "The Pat Boone Family"

| ❑ 1334 | When The Lovelight Starts Shining Through His Eyes/Viva Espana | 1975 | — | 2.50 | 5.00 |
| ❑ 1389 | My Guy/When the Lovelight Starts Shining Through His Eyes | 1976 | — | 2.50 | 5.00 |

WARNER BROS.

| ❑ 8385 [DJ] | Hasta Manana (mono/stereo) | 1977 | — | 2.50 | 5.00 |

—Stock copy not known to exist

| ❑ 8446 | He's a Rebel/You Light Up My Life | 1977 | — | 3.00 | 6.00 |

—B-side by Debby Boone

BOOT
45s
AGAPE

| ❑ 9008 | Hey Little Girl/Liza Brown | 1972 | 2.00 | 4.00 | 8.00 |

Albums
AGAPE

| ❑ 2601 | Boot | 1972 | 6.25 | 12.50 | 25.00 |

BOOTLES, THE
45s
GNP CRESCENDO

| ❑ 311 | I'll Let You Hold My Hand/Never Till Now | 1964 | 3.75 | 7.50 | 15.00 |

BOP-A-LOOS, THE
45s
MERCURY

❑ 70552	Teach Me Tonight/South Parkway Mambo	1955	5.00	10.00	20.00
❑ 70553	Tweedle Dee/Bongo Mambo	1955	5.00	10.00	20.00
❑ 70568	Hearts of Stone/Miracle Mambo	1955	5.00	10.00	20.00
❑ 70569	Sincerely/Cuban Carnival	1955	5.00	10.00	20.00

BOP-CHORDS, THE
45s
HOLIDAY

| ❑ 2601 | Castle in the Sky/My Darling to You | 1957 | 50.00 | 100.00 | 200.00 |

—Black label

| ❑ 2601 | Castle in the Sky/My Darling to You | 196? | 6.25 | 12.50 | 25.00 |

—Red label, single line

| ❑ 2601 | Castle in the Sky/My Darling to You | 196? | 12.50 | 25.00 | 50.00 |

—Red label, double lines

| ❑ 2603 | When I Woke Up This Morning/I Really Love You | 1957 | 50.00 | 100.00 | 200.00 |

—Black label

| ❑ 2603 | When I Woke Up This Morning/I Really Love You | 196? | 12.50 | 25.00 | 50.00 |

—Red label
LOST-NITE

| ❑ 175 | Castle in the Sky/My Darling to You | 196? | — | 3.00 | 6.00 |

—Reissue

| ❑ 188 | When I Woke Up This Morning/I Really Love You | 196? | — | 3.00 | 6.00 |

—Reissue

BORDERSONG With Ann and Nancy Wilson, later of HEART.
45s
GREAT NORTHWEST

| ❑ 704 | She's a Good Woman/Morning | 1976 | 6.25 | 12.50 | 25.00 |

Albums
REAL GOOD

| ❑ 1001 | Morning | 1975 | 17.50 | 35.00 | 70.00 |

BOSSTONES, THE
45s
BOSS

| ❑ 401 | Mope-Itty Mope/Wings of an Angel | 1959 | 25.00 | 50.00 | 100.00 |

—As "Boss Tones"

| ❑ 501 | Mope-Itty Mope/Wings of an Angel | 1959 | 50.00 | 100.00 | 200.00 |

—As "Bosstones"
LOST-NITE

| ❑ 107 | Mope-Itty Mope/Wings of an Angel | 196? | — | 3.00 | 6.00 |

—Yellow label with "street lamp" logo
V-TONE

| ❑ 208 | Mope-Itty Mope/Wings of an Angel | 1960 | 15.00 | 30.00 | 60.00 |

BOSTIC, EARL
45s
KING

❑ 4444	Sleep/September Song	1951	7.50	15.00	30.00
❑ 4454	Always/How Could It Have Been You and I	1951	7.50	15.00	30.00
❑ 4475	Flamingo/I'm Getting Sentimental Over You	1951	7.50	15.00	30.00
❑ 4491	I Got Loaded/Chains of Love	1951	10.00	20.00	40.00
❑ 4511	The Moon Is Low/Lover Come Back to Me	1952	6.25	12.50	25.00
❑ 4536	Linger Awhile/Velvet Sunset	1952	6.25	12.50	25.00
❑ 4550	Moonglow/Ain't Misbehavin'	1952	6.25	12.50	25.00
❑ 4570	For You/Smoke Gets In Your Eyes	1952	6.25	12.50	25.00
❑ 4586	You Go to My Head/Hour of Parting	1953	6.25	12.50	25.00
❑ 4603	The Sheik of Araby/Steamwhistle Jump	1953	6.25	12.50	25.00
❑ 4623	Cherokee/The Song Is Ended	1953	6.25	12.50	25.00
❑ 4644	Melancholy Serenade/What, No Pearls	1953	6.25	12.50	25.00
❑ 4653	The Very Thought of You/Memories	1953	6.25	12.50	25.00
❑ 4674	Deep Purple/Smoke Rings	1953	6.25	12.50	25.00
❑ 4683	Off Shore/Don't You Do It	1953	6.25	12.50	25.00
❑ 4699	My Heart at Thy Sweet Voice/Cracked Ice	1954	5.00	10.00	20.00
❑ 4708	Jungle Drums/Danube Waves	1954	5.00	10.00	20.00
❑ 4723	Blue Skies/Mambolino	1954	5.00	10.00	20.00
❑ 4730	These Foolish Things/Mambostic	1954	5.00	10.00	20.00
❑ 4741	Ubangi Stomp/Time on My Hands	1954	5.00	10.00	20.00
❑ 4754	Song of the Islands/Liebestraum	1954	5.00	10.00	20.00
❑ 4765	Embraceable You/Night and Day	1955	5.00	10.00	20.00
❑ 4776	Melody of Love/Sweet Lorraine	1955	5.00	10.00	20.00
❑ 4790	Cocktails for Two/When Your Lover Has Gone	1955	5.00	10.00	20.00
❑ 4799	Remember/Cherry Bean	1955	5.00	10.00	20.00
❑ 4815	East of the Sun/Dream	1955	5.00	10.00	20.00
❑ 4829	For All We Know/Beyond the Blue Horizon	1955	5.00	10.00	20.00
❑ 4845	O Solo Mio/Poeme	1955	5.00	10.00	20.00
❑ 4883	I Love You Truly/'Cause You're My Lover	1956	3.75	7.50	15.00
❑ 4905	Bugle Call Rag/I'll String Along with You	1956	3.75	7.50	15.00
❑ 4943	Roses of Picardy/Where or When	1956	3.75	7.50	15.00
❑ 4978	Harlem Nocturne/I Hear a Rhapsody	1956	3.75	7.50	15.00
❑ 5025	Too Fine for Crying/Avalon	1957	3.75	7.50	15.00
❑ 5041	Temptation/September Song	1957	3.75	7.50	15.00
❑ 5056	She's Funny That Way/Exercise	1957	3.75	7.50	15.00
❑ 5071	Vienna, City of My Dreams/Just Too Shy	1957	3.75	7.50	15.00
❑ 5081	A Gay Day/Answer Me	1957	3.75	7.50	15.00
❑ 5092	Josephine/Jeannie I Dream of Lilac Time	1957	3.75	7.50	15.00
❑ 5106	Southern Fried/No Name Jive	1958	3.75	7.50	15.00
❑ 5120	Lester Leaps In/Pompton Turnpike	1958	3.75	7.50	15.00
❑ 5127	Honeysuckle Rose/Back Beat	1958	3.75	7.50	15.00
❑ 5133	Woodchopper's Ball/John's Idea	1958	3.75	7.50	15.00
❑ 5136	Twilight Time/Over Waves Rock	1958	3.75	7.50	15.00
❑ 5144	Pinkie/Home Sweet Home Rock	1958	3.75	7.50	15.00
❑ 5152	Goodnight Sweetheart/Indian Boogie Woogie	1958	3.75	7.50	15.00
❑ 5161	Red Skin Cha Cha/Rockin' with Richard	1958	3.75	7.50	15.00
❑ 5175	My Reverie Cha Cha/Barcarole	1959	3.00	6.00	12.00
❑ 5190	Up There in Orbit/Sweet Pea	1959	3.00	6.00	12.00
❑ 5203	Up There in Orbit (Part 1)/ Up There in Orbit (Part 2)	1959	3.00	6.00	12.00
❑ 5209	La Cucaracha Cha Cha/Dancing in the Dark	1959	3.00	6.00	12.00
❑ 5229	Who Cares/Feeling Cool	1959	3.00	6.00	12.00
❑ 5252	White Horse/Dark Eyes	1959	3.00	6.00	12.00
❑ 5263	Gondola/Once in a While	1959	3.00	6.00	12.00
❑ 5290	Tut-Strut/All the Things You Are	1959	3.00	6.00	12.00
❑ 5301	Ebb Tide/Hildegarde	1959	3.00	6.00	12.00
❑ 5309	Let's Move Out/I Burned Your Letter	1960	3.00	6.00	12.00
❑ 5314	Off Shore/Hello '60	1960	3.00	6.00	12.00
❑ 5317	Elegie/Out of Nowhere	1960	3.00	6.00	12.00
❑ 5345	Make Believe/A Gay Day	1960	3.00	6.00	12.00
❑ 5362	Tuxedo Junction/Polonaise	1960	3.00	6.00	12.00
❑ 5402	720 in the Books/Just in Time	1960	3.00	6.00	12.00
❑ 5454	That Old Black Magic/ Full Moon and Empty Arms	1961	2.50	5.00	10.00
❑ 5477	Jersey Bounce/Because of You	1961	2.50	5.00	10.00
❑ 5564	The Thrill Is Gone/April in Portugal	1961	2.50	5.00	10.00
❑ 5600	How Deep Is the Ocean/Wrap It	1962	2.50	5.00	10.00
❑ 5636	Dark Eyes/People Will Say We're in Love	1962	2.50	5.00	10.00
❑ 5661	More Than You Know/Don't Blame Me	1962	2.50	5.00	10.00
❑ 5683	Ducky/Deep in My Heart	1962	2.50	5.00	10.00
❑ 5699	Autumn Leaves/Anita's Theme	1962	2.50	5.00	10.00
❑ 5711	El Choclo Bossa Nova/My Reverie	1963	2.50	5.00	10.00
❑ 5742	Cherry Pink (And Apple Blossom White)/ Your Cheatin' Heart	1963	2.50	5.00	10.00
❑ 5776	Love Letters in the Sand/Tammy	1963	2.50	5.00	10.00
❑ 5819	Apple Cake/Don't Do It Please	1963	2.50	5.00	10.00
❑ 5839	Telstar Drive/Fast Track	1964	2.00	4.00	8.00
❑ 5861	Let's Dance Little Girl/Summertime	1964	2.00	4.00	8.00
❑ 5900	Make Believe/Star Gazer	1964	2.00	4.00	8.00
❑ 5925	The Pink Panther/Lawrence of Arabia	1964	2.00	4.00	8.00
❑ 5944	From Russia with Love/My Special Dream	1964	2.00	4.00	8.00
❑ 5955	Theme from The Unforgiven/Dominique	1964	2.00	4.00	8.00
❑ 5961	Hello Dolly/Walk on the Wild Side	1964	2.00	4.00	8.00
❑ 5977	More/Charade	1965	2.00	4.00	8.00
❑ 6254	September Song/Harlem Nocturne	1969	—	2.50	5.00

7-Inch Extended Plays
KING

❑ EP-200	Flamingo/Swing Low Sweet Boogie//I Can't Give You Anything But Love/The Moon Is Low	195?	6.25	12.50	25.00
❑ EP-200 [PS]	Earl Bostic and His Alto Sax, Vol. 1	195?	6.25	12.50	25.00
❑ EP 201	*Sleep/Earl's Imagination/Lover Come Back to Me/I'm Gettin' Sentimental Over You	1953	6.25	12.50	25.00
❑ EP 201 [PS]	Earl Bostic and His Alto Sax, Vol. 2	1953	6.25	12.50	25.00
❑ EP 202	*Always/Linger Awhile/Merry Widow/ Earl Blows a Fuse	1953	6.25	12.50	25.00
❑ EP 202 [PS]	Earl Bostic and His Alto Sax, Vol. 3	1953	6.25	12.50	25.00
❑ EP 203	*Deep Purple/Velvet Sunset/Choppin' It Down/ You Go to My Head	1953	6.25	12.50	25.00
❑ EP 203 [PS]	Earl Bostic and His Alto Sax, Vol. 4	1953	6.25	12.50	25.00
❑ EP 204	*Cherokee/Seven Steps/No Name Blues/ Don't You Do It	1953	6.25	12.50	25.00
❑ EP 204 [PS]	Earl Bostic and His Alto Sax, Vol. 5	1953	6.25	12.50	25.00
❑ EP 205	*Moonglow/For You/Blip Boogie/Wrap It Up	1953	6.25	12.50	25.00
❑ EP 205 [PS]	Earl Bostic and His Alto Sax, Vol. 6	1953	6.25	12.50	25.00
❑ EP 206	*Filibuster/The Sheik of Araby/Smoke Gets in Your Eyes/The Hour of Parting	1953	6.25	12.50	25.00
❑ EP 206 [PS]	Earl Bostic and His Alto Sax, Vol. 7	1953	6.25	12.50	25.00
❑ EP 207	*Serenade/Ain't Misbehavin'/Smoke Rings/ Steamwhistle Jump	1953	6.25	12.50	25.00
❑ EP 207 [PS]	Earl Bostic and His Alto Sax, Vol. 8	1953	6.25	12.50	25.00
❑ EP 245	Melancholy Serenade/What! No Pearls// The Very Thought of You/Memories	1954	5.00	10.00	20.00
❑ EP 245 [PS]	Earl Bostic and His Alto Sax, Vol. 9	1954	5.00	10.00	20.00
❑ EP 284	*Jungle Drums/The Song Is Ended/ Off Shore/Cracked Ice	1954	5.00	10.00	20.00
❑ EP 284 [PS]	Earl Bostic and His Alto Sax, Vol. 10	1954	5.00	10.00	20.00
❑ EP 285	*Danube Waves/My Heart at Thy Sweet Voice/ Poeme/O Sole Mio	1954	5.00	10.00	20.00
❑ EP 285 [PS]	Earl Bostic and His Alto Sax, Vol. 11	1954	5.00	10.00	20.00
❑ EP 347	*Mambostic/Time on My Hands/Mambolino/ Ven-A-Mi	1955	5.00	10.00	20.00
❑ EP 347 [PS]	Earl Bostic and His Alto Sax, Vol. 12	1955	5.00	10.00	20.00
❑ KEP 350	Blue Skies/Ubangi Stomp//Song of the Islands/ These Foolish Things	1955	5.00	10.00	20.00
❑ KEP 350 [PS]	The Artistry of Earl Bostic, Vol. 13	1955	5.00	10.00	20.00

Number	Title (A Side/B Side)	Yr	VG	VG+	NM
❏ EP 355	*Cherry Bean/Liebestraum/Night and Day/ Embraceable You	1955	5.00	10.00	20.00
❏ EP 355 [PS]	Earl Bostic and His Alto Sax, Vol. 14	1955	5.00	10.00	20.00
❏ EP 363	*Melody of Love/Cocktails for Two/Blue Moon/ Remember	1955	5.00	10.00	20.00
❏ EP 363 [PS]	Earl Bostic and His Alto Sax, Vol. 15	1955	5.00	10.00	20.00
❏ EP 375	*Dream/Beyond the Blue Horizon/East of the Sun/For All We Know	1956	5.00	10.00	20.00
❏ EP 375 [PS]	Earl Bostic with Strings, Vol. 16	1956	5.00	10.00	20.00
❏ EP 381	*Bugle Call Rag/I'll String Along with You/I Love You Truly/'Cause You're My Lover	1956	5.00	10.00	20.00
❏ EP 381 [PS]	Bostic Blows, Vol. 17	1956	5.00	10.00	20.00
❏ KEP 398	Harlem Nocturne/I Hear a Rhapsody//Roses of Picardy/Where or When	1957	5.00	10.00	20.00
❏ KEP 398 [PS]	Earl Bostic, Vol. 18	1957	5.00	10.00	20.00
❏ EP-405	*She's Funny That Way/How Deep Is the Ocean/ Avalon/September Song	1958	5.00	10.00	20.00
❏ EP-405 [PS]	Earl Bostic Dance Time	1958	5.00	10.00	20.00
❏ EP-406	*Temptation/Sweet Lorraine/Away/Exercise	1958	5.00	10.00	20.00
❏ EP-406 [PS]	Alto-Tude	1958	5.00	10.00	20.00
❏ EP-409	*Just Too Shy/Laura/Josephine/A Gay Day	1958	5.00	10.00	20.00
❏ EP-409 [PS]	Earl Bostic for Listening and Dancing	1958	5.00	10.00	20.00
❏ EP-410	*Jeannine I Dream of Lilac Time/Answer Me/ Vienna, My City of Dreams/Make Believe	1958	5.00	10.00	20.00
❏ EP-410 [PS]	Bostic Plays	1958	5.00	10.00	20.00
❏ EP-414	*Southern Fried/Jersey Bounce/Jumpin' at the Woodside/Tuxedo Junction	1958	5.00	10.00	20.00
❏ EP-414 [PS]	Hits of the Swing Age, Vol. 1	1958	5.00	10.00	20.00
❏ EP-415	*720 in the Books/Air Mail Special/Pompton Turnpike/Woodchopper's Ball	1958	5.00	10.00	20.00
❏ EP-415 [PS]	Hits of the Swing Age, Vol. 2	1958	5.00	10.00	20.00
❏ EP-416	*Night Train/Stompin' at the Savoy/Honeysuckle Rose/No Name Jive	1958	5.00	10.00	20.00
❏ EP-416 [PS]	Hits of the Swing Age, Vol. 3	1958	5.00	10.00	20.00
❏ EP-417	(contents unknown)	1958	5.00	10.00	20.00
❏ EP-417 [PS]	Showcase of Swinging Dance Hits, Vol. 1	1958	5.00	10.00	20.00
❏ EP-418	Two O'Clock Jump/Back Beat//John's Idea/ Royal Garden Blues	1958	5.00	10.00	20.00
❏ EP-418 [PS]	Showcase of Swinging Dance Hits, Vol. 2	1958	5.00	10.00	20.00
❏ EP-419	(contents unknown)	1958	5.00	10.00	20.00
❏ EP-419 [PS]	Showcase of Swinging Dance Hits, Vol. 3	1958	5.00	10.00	20.00
❏ EP-420	Twilight Time/Stairway to the Stars//Rockin' with Richard/Be My Love	1958		10.00	20.00
❏ EP-420 [PS]	Alto Magic in Hi Fi, Vol. 1	1958	5.00	10.00	20.00
❏ EP-421	(contents unknown)	1958	5.00	10.00	20.00
❏ EP-421 [PS]	Alto Magic in Hi Fi, Vol. 2	1958	5.00	10.00	20.00
❏ EP-422	C Jam Blues/Wee-Gee Board//The Wrecking Rock/Home Sweet Home Rock	1958		10.00	20.00
❏ EP-422 [PS]	Alto Magic in Hi Fi, Vol. 3	1958	5.00	10.00	20.00
ROYALE					
❏ EP 367	The Man I Love/All On//Hurricane Blues/The Major and the Minor	195?	3.75	7.50	15.00
❏ EP 367 [PS]	His Saxophone and Orchestra	195?	3.75	7.50	15.00
Albums					
GRAND PRIX					
❏ K-404 [M]	The Earl of Bostic	196?	3.75	7.50	15.00
❏ KS-404 [R]	The Earl of Bostic	196?	3.00	6.00	12.00
❏ K-416 [M]	Wild Man	196?	3.75	7.50	15.00
❏ KS-416 [R]	Wild Man	196?	3.00	6.00	12.00
KING					
❏ 295-64 [10]	Earl Bostic and His Alto Sax	1951	50.00	100.00	200.00
—Black vinyl					
❏ 295-64 [10]	Earl Bostic and His Alto Sax	1951	100.00	200.00	400.00
—Red vinyl					
❏ 295-65 [10]	Earl Bostic and His Alto Sax	1951	50.00	100.00	200.00
—Black vinyl					
❏ 295-65 [10]	Earl Bostic and His Alto Sax	1951	100.00	200.00	400.00
—Red vinyl					
❏ 295-66 [10]	Earl Bostic and His Alto Sax	1951	50.00	100.00	200.00
—Black vinyl					
❏ 295-66 [10]	Earl Bostic and His Alto Sax	1951	100.00	200.00	400.00
—Red vinyl					
❏ 295-72 [10]	Earl Bostic and His Alto Sax	1952	50.00	100.00	200.00
❏ 295-76 [10]	Earl Bostic and His Alto Sax	1952	50.00	100.00	200.00
❏ 295-77 [10]	Earl Bostic and His Alto Sax	1952	50.00	100.00	200.00
❏ 295-78 [10]	Earl Bostic and His Alto Sax	1952	50.00	100.00	200.00
❏ 295-79 [10]	Earl Bostic and His Alto Sax	1952	50.00	100.00	200.00
❏ 295-95 [10]	Earl Bostic Plays the Old Standards	1954	50.00	100.00	200.00
❏ 295-103 [10]	Earl Bostic and His Alto Sax	1954	50.00	100.00	200.00
❏ 395-500 [M]	Dance to the Best of Bostic	195?	20.00	40.00	80.00
—Second cover with girl in a swimsuit pictured					
❏ 395-500 [M]	Dance to the Best of Bostic	1956	25.00	50.00	100.00
—Original cover with Earl Bostic pictured					
❏ 395-503 [M]	Bostic for You	1956	25.00	50.00	100.00
❏ 395-515 [M]	Alto-Tude	1956	25.00	50.00	100.00
❏ 395-525 [M]	Dance Time	1956	20.00	40.00	80.00
❏ 395-529 [M]	Let's Dance with Earl Bostic	1956	20.00	40.00	80.00
❏ 395-547 [M]	Invitation to Dance	1956	20.00	40.00	80.00
❏ 558 [M]	C'mon and Dance with Earl Bostic	1956	20.00	40.00	80.00
❏ KS-558 [S]	C'mon and Dance with Earl Bostic	1959	37.50	75.00	150.00
❏ 571 [M]	Hits of the Swing Age	1957	20.00	40.00	80.00
❏ 583 [M]	Showcase of Swinging Dance Hits	1958	20.00	40.00	80.00
❏ 597 [M]	Alto Magic in Hi-Fi	1958	20.00	40.00	80.00
❏ KS-597 [S]	Alto Magic in Hi-Fi	1959	37.50	75.00	150.00
❏ 602 [M]	Sweet Tunes of the Fantastic Fifties	1959	12.50	25.00	50.00
❏ KSD-602 [S]	Sweet Tunes of the Fantastic Fifties	1959	25.00	50.00	100.00
❏ 613 [M]	Bostic Workshop	1959	12.50	25.00	50.00
❏ KS-613 [S]	Bostic Workshop	1959	25.00	50.00	100.00
❏ 620 [M]	Sweet Tunes from the Roaring Twenties	1959	12.50	25.00	50.00
❏ KS-620 [S]	Sweet Tunes from the Roaring Twenties	1959	25.00	50.00	100.00
❏ 632 [M]	Sweet Tunes of the Swinging Thirties	1959	12.50	25.00	50.00
❏ KS-632 [S]	Sweet Tunes of the Swinging Thirties	1959	25.00	50.00	100.00

Number	Title (A Side/B Side)	Yr	VG	VG+	NM
❏ 640 [M]	Sweet Tunes of the Sentimental Forties	1960	12.50	25.00	50.00
❏ KS-640 [S]	Sweet Tunes of the Sentimental Forties	1960	20.00	40.00	80.00
❏ 662 [M]	Musical Pearls	1960	12.50	25.00	50.00
❏ KS-662 [S]	Musical Pearls	1960	20.00	40.00	80.00
❏ 705 [M]	Hit Tunes of Big Broadway Shows	1960	12.50	25.00	50.00
❏ KS-705 [S]	Hit Tunes of Big Broadway Shows	1960	20.00	40.00	80.00
❏ 786 [M]	By Popular Demand	1961	12.50	25.00	50.00
❏ 827 [M]	Earl Bostic Plays Bossa Nova	1963	12.50	25.00	50.00
❏ 838 [M]	Songs of the Fantastic Fifties, Volume 2	1963	12.50	25.00	50.00
❏ 846 [M]	Jazz As I Feel It	1963	12.50	25.00	50.00
❏ 881 [M]	The Best of Earl Bostic, Volume 2	1964	12.50	25.00	50.00
❏ 900 [M]	The New Sound	1964	12.50	25.00	50.00
❏ 921 [M]	The Great Hits of 1964	1964	12.50	25.00	50.00
❏ 947 [M]	24 Songs That Earl Loved the Most	1966	10.00	20.00	40.00
❏ KS-1048 [S]	Harlem Nocturne	1969	6.25	12.50	25.00
❏ K-5010X	14 Original Greatest Hits	1977	3.00	6.00	12.00
PHILIPS					
❏ PHM 200262 [M]	The Song Is Not Ended	1967	6.25	12.50	25.00
❏ PHS 600262 [S]	The Song Is Not Ended	1967	6.25	12.50	25.00

BOSTIC, EARL, AND BILL DOGGETT Also see each artist's individual listings.

45s

KING

Number	Title (A Side/B Side)	Yr	VG	VG+	NM
❏ 4930	Mean to Me/Bo-Do Rock	1956	3.75	7.50	15.00
❏ 4954	Indiana/Bubbins Rock	1956	3.75	7.50	15.00
❏ 5427	Special Delivery Stomp/Earl's Dog	1960	2.50	5.00	10.00

7-Inch Extended Plays

KING

Number	Title (A Side/B Side)	Yr	VG	VG+	NM
❏ EP-397	*Bubbins Rock/Indiana/The Bo-Do Rock/Mean to Me	1957	5.00	10.00	20.00
❏ EP-397 [PS]	Bill Doggett — Earl Bostic	1957	5.00	10.00	20.00

BOSTIC, EARL/JIMMY LUNCEFORD

Albums

ALLEGRO ELITE

Number	Title (A Side/B Side)	Yr	VG	VG+	NM
❏ 4053 [10]	Earl Bostic/Jimmy Lunceford Orchestras	195?	10.00	20.00	40.00

BOSTICK, CALVIN

45s

CHESS

Number	Title (A Side/B Side)	Yr	VG	VG+	NM
❏ 1530	Christmas Won't Be Christmas Without You/ Four-Eleven Boogie	1952	37.50	75.00	150.00

BOSTON CRABS, THE

45s

CAPITOL

Number	Title (A Side/B Side)	Yr	VG	VG+	NM
❏ 5493	Down in Mexico/Who?	1965	2.50	5.00	10.00
TOWER					
❏ 368	Gin House/Leave My Woman Alone	1967	2.50	5.00	10.00

BOTKIN, PERRY, JR.

45s

A&M

Number	Title (A Side/B Side)	Yr	VG	VG+	NM
❏ 1856	Nadia's Theme (The Young and the Restless)/ Down the Line	1976	2.50	5.00	10.00
—Original issue; Barry DeVorzon's name was added after he threatened legal action					
❏ 1856 [PS]	Nadia's Theme (The Young and the Restless)/ Down the Line	1976	2.50	5.00	10.00
—Sleeve with only Perry Botkin Jr.'s name on it (see above listing)					
❏ 1967	Looking for Home/Lovers	1977	—	2.00	4.00
❏ 1990	Bridges/Love Theme from Aspen	1977	—	2.00	4.00
DECCA					
❏ 30912	The Execution Theme/Waltz of the Hunter	1959	3.00	6.00	12.00
MGM					
❏ 14357	Soley Soley/(B-side unknown)	1972		2.50	5.00
—As "Perry Botkin, Inc."					
❏ 14379	Bless the Beasts and Children/Lost	1972		2.50	5.00
PRIDE					
❏ 1005	Journey to Moscow/Ellie's Theme	1972		2.50	5.00
VALIANT					
❏ 719	Where Does Love Go (Instrumental)/Where Does Love Go (Vocal)	1965	2.00	4.00	8.00
—B-side by Charles Boyer					
❏ 6025	Careless Love/Wabash Cannonball	1962	2.50	5.00	10.00

BOUCHER, PEGI

45s

HIBACK

Number	Title (A Side/B Side)	Yr	VG	VG+	NM
❏ 101	The Christmas Clock/Christmas Tree Heaven	1966	2.00	4.00	8.00
❏ 101 [PS]	The Christmas Clock/Christmas Tree Heaven	1966	3.75	7.50	15.00

BOUGALIEU

45s

ROULETTE

Number	Title (A Side/B Side)	Yr	VG	VG+	NM
❏ 4767	Let's Do Wrong/When I Was a Child	1967	6.25	12.50	25.00
❏ 4776	Let's Do Wrong/When I Was a Child	1967	3.75	7.50	15.00

BOUQUETS

45s

BLUE CAT

Number	Title (A Side/B Side)	Yr	VG	VG+	NM
❏ 115	Welcome to My Heart/Ain't That Love	1965	7.50	15.00	30.00
MALA					
❏ 472	I Love Him So/No Love at All	1964	3.75	7.50	15.00
VEST					
❏ 8000	Yeah Babe/Girls, Girls	1963	3.75	7.50	15.00

BOW STREET RUNNERS, THE

Albums

B.T. PUPPY

Number	Title (A Side/B Side)	Yr	VG	VG+	NM
❏ BTPS-1026	The Bow Street Runners	1969	500.00	750.00	1000.
SUNDAZED					
❏ LP 5029	The Bow Street Runners	199?	2.50	5.00	10.00
—Reissue of B.T. Puppy LP					

Number	Title (A Side/B Side)	Yr	VG	VG+	NM

BOWEN, JIMMY
45s
CAPEHART

Number	Title (A Side/B Side)	Yr	VG	VG+	NM
❑ 5005	Teenage Dreamworld/It's Against the Law	1962	5.00	10.00	20.00
❑ 5005 [PS]	Teenage Dreamworld/It's Against the Law	1962	12.50	25.00	50.00

CREST
| ❑ 1085 | Don't Drop It/Somebody to Love | 1961 | 5.00 | 10.00 | 20.00 |

REPRISE
❑ 0264	The Biggest Lover in Town/The Big Bus	1964	2.50	5.00	10.00
❑ 0358	The Golden Eagle/Spanish Cricket	1965	2.50	5.00	10.00
❑ 0450	Wonder Mother/Captain Gorgeous	1966	2.50	5.00	10.00
❑ 0592	Raunchy/It's Such a Pretty World Today	1967	2.50	5.00	10.00

ROULETTE
❑ 4001	I'm Stickin' With You/Ever Lovin' Fingers	1957	5.00	10.00	20.00
—With the Rhythm Orchids					
❑ 4010	Warm Up to Me Baby/I Trusted You	1957	5.00	10.00	20.00
❑ 4017	Ever Since That Night/Don't Tell Me Your Troubles	1957	5.00	10.00	20.00
❑ 4023	Cross Over/It's Shameful	1957	5.00	10.00	20.00
❑ 4057	Can She Kiss/Keeping You	1958	5.00	10.00	20.00
❑ 4083	By the Light of the Silvery Moon/The Two Step	1958	5.00	10.00	20.00
❑ 4102	My Kind of Woman/Blue Moon	1958	5.00	10.00	20.00
❑ 4122	Always Faithful/Wish I Were Tied to You	1958	5.00	10.00	20.00
❑ 4175	You're Just Wasting Your Time/Walkin' on Air	1959	5.00	10.00	20.00
❑ 4224	Oh Yeah! Oh Yeah! Mm Mm/Your Loving Arms	1960	5.00	10.00	20.00

TRIPLE D
| ❑ 798 | I'm Stickin' With You/Party Doll | 1956 | 250.00 | 500.00 | 1000. |
| —B-side by Buddy Knox | | | | | |

7-Inch Extended Plays
ROULETTE
| ❑ EPR-1-302 | I'm Stickin' with You/Warm Up to Me Baby// Raggedy Anne/Ever Since That Night | 1957 | 50.00 | 100.00 | 200.00 |
| ❑ EPR-1-302 [PS] | Jimmy Bowen | 1957 | 50.00 | 100.00 | 200.00 |

Albums
REPRISE
| ❑ R-6210 [M] | Sunday Morning with the Comics | 1966 | 7.50 | 15.00 | 30.00 |
| ❑ RS-6210 [S] | Sunday Morning with the Comics | 1966 | 10.00 | 20.00 | 40.00 |

ROULETTE
❑ R 25004 [M]	Jimmy Bowen	1957	75.00	150.00	300.00
—Black and silver label					
❑ R 25004 [M]	Jimmy Bowen	1958	37.50	75.00	150.00
—Red label					
❑ R 25004 [M]	Jimmy Bowen	198?	3.00	6.00	12.00
—Reissue for Publishers Central Bureau (it says so on the jacket)					

BOWENS, PRIVATE CHARLES
45s
ROJAC
| ❑ 111 | Christmas In Viet Nam/(B-side unknown) | 196? | 15.00 | 30.00 | 60.00 |

BOWIE, DAVID
12-Inch Singles
BACKSTREET
| ❑ L33-1759 [DJ] | Cat People (Putting Out Fire) (6:41) (4:08) | 1982 | 3.00 | 6.00 | 12.00 |

EMI
| ❑ SPRO-04547 [DJ] | Fame 90 (House Mix) (Hip Hop Mix)/(Queen Latifah's Rap Version) (Bonus Beats Instrumental) (Acapulco Rap) | 1990 | 3.75 | 7.50 | 15.00 |
| ❑ V-56163 | Fame 90 (With Queen Latifah Mix) (House Mix) (Gass Mix)/(Hip Hop Mix) (Absolutely Nothing Premeditated/Epic Mix) | 1990 | 2.00 | 4.00 | 8.00 |

EMI AMERICA
❑ V-7805	Let's Dance (Long Version)/Cat People (Putting Out Fire)	1983	2.00	4.00	8.00
❑ V-7809	China Girl/Shake It	1983	2.50	5.00	10.00
❑ V-7811	Modern Love/Modern Love (Live)	1983	2.50	5.00	10.00
❑ V-7838	Blue Jean (Extended Dance Mix)/Dancing with the Big Boys (Extended Dance Mix) (Extended Dub Mix)	1984	2.00	4.00	8.00
❑ V-7846	Tonight (Vocal Dance Mix 4:29) (Dub 4:18)/ Tumble and Twirl (Extended 5:03)	1984	2.00	4.00	8.00
❑ VG-7858	Loving the Alien (2 versions)/Don't Look Down	1985	3.00	6.00	12.00
—With gatefold sleeve and poster					
❑ SEAV-7860	Loving the Alien (Extended Dance Mix) (Extended Dub Mix)/Don't Look Down (Extended Dance Mix)	1985	3.75	7.50	15.00
—Picture disc					
❑ SPRO-9221/2 [DJ]	Blue Jean/Dancing with the Big Boys	1984	3.75	7.50	15.00
❑ SPRO-9295 [DJ]	Tonight (same on both sides)	1984	3.00	6.00	12.00
❑ SPRO 9670/99 [DJ]	Underground (Album Version) (Edited Version)	1986	3.00	6.00	12.00
❑ SPRO-9904/5 [DJ]	Let's Dance (2 versions)/Cat People (Putting Out Fire)	1983	3.00	6.00	12.00
❑ SPRO-9951/2 [DJ]	China Girl (Long)/Shake It (Long)	1983	3.75	7.50	15.00
❑ SPRO-9985 [DJ]	Day In Day Out (Single Version) (same on both sides)	1987	2.50	5.00	10.00
❑ SPRO-9996/7 [DJ]	Day In Day Out (7" Dance Edit) (Extended Dance Mix)/(Edited Dance Mix)	1987	3.75	7.50	15.00
❑ V-19205	Absolute Beginners (Full Length)/(Dub)	1986	2.00	4.00	8.00
❑ V-19210	Underground (Extended Dance Mix)/(Dub Mix) (Instrumental Version)	1986	2.00	4.00	8.00
❑ V-19217	Magic Dance (A Dance Mix)//Magic Dance (Dub)/Within You	1986	2.00	4.00	8.00
❑ V-19234	Day In Day Out (Extended Dance Mix) (Extended Dub Mix)/Julie	1987	2.50	5.00	10.00
❑ V-19239	Day In Day Out (Groucho Mix) (Extended Dance Mix) (Single Version)	1984	3.75	7.50	15.00
❑ V-19247	Time Will Crawl (2 versions)/Girls (2 versions)	1987	2.50	5.00	10.00
❑ V-19255	Never Let Me Down (Extended Dance Remix) (7" Remix Edit) (Dub) (Acapella) (Instrumental)/'87 and Cry (Edit)	1987	2.50	5.00	10.00
❑ SPRO-79090 [DJ]	Never Let Me Down (same on both sides)	1987	2.50	5.00	10.00
❑ SPRO-79209 [DJ]	Too Dizzy (same on both sides)	1987	5.00	10.00	20.00

RCA
❑ DJL1-3255 [DJ]	Star (Live)//What in the World (Live)/Breaking Glass (Live)	1978	6.25	12.50	25.00
—Promo sampler from the Stage LP; white vinyl (black vinyl versions are counterfeits)					
❑ DJL1-3795 [DJ]	Space Oddity/Ashes to Ashes (Edited) (medley)/ /Ashes to Ashes (LP Version)	1980	5.00	10.00	20.00
—Without stamps					
❑ DJL1-3795 [DJ]	Space Oddity/Ashes to Ashes (Edited) (medley)/ /Ashes to Ashes (LP Version)	1980	7.50	15.00	30.00
—Also known as "The Continuing Story of Major Tom"; with set of stamps					
❑ JD-11151 [DJ]	Heroes (Long Version 6:07) (Edited Version 3:31)	1977	6.25	12.50	25.00
❑ PC-11204 [DJ]	Beauty and the Beast/Fame	1978	7.50	15.00	30.00
❑ JD-11306 [DJ]	Peter and the Wolf (Part 1 5:52) (Part 2 8:47)/ (B-side blank)	1978	7.50	15.00	30.00
❑ PD-11886	John I'm Only Dancing (Again)/Golden Years	1980	3.00	6.00	12.00
❑ JD-12079	Ashes to Ashes/Fashion	1980	—	—	—
—Canceled					
❑ JD-12140 [DJ]	Fashion (4:45) (3:23)	1981	3.00	6.00	12.00
❑ PD-12145	Fashion/Scream Like a Baby	1980	3.00	6.00	12.00
❑ PD-12249	Up the Hills Backwards/Crystal Japan	1981	5.00	10.00	20.00
—Includes sheet of stamps					
❑ PD-13770	1984/TVC 15	1984	2.00	4.00	8.00

SAVAGE
❑ 50039 [DJ]	Jump They Say (5 versions)/Pallas Athena	1993	3.00	6.00	12.00
❑ 50042	Jump They Say (5 versions)/Pallas Athena	1993	2.50	5.00	10.00
❑ 50045 [DJ]	Black Tie White Noise (Extended Remix) (Club Mix) (Trance Mix)/(Digi Funky's Lush Mix) (Supa Pump Mix) (Funky Crossover Mix) (Extended Urban Mix)	1993	3.75	7.50	15.00

VIRGIN
❑ SPRO-11038 [DJ]	The Hearts Filthy Lesson (Good Karma Mix) (Alt. Mix) (Original Mix)/(Rubber Mix) (Filthy Mix)	1995	3.00	6.00	12.00
❑ SPRO-11513 [DJ]	Hallo Spaceboy (12" Remix) (7" Remix)/(Lost in Space Mix) (Double Click Mix)	1995	3.75	7.50	15.00
❑ SPRO-12217 [DJ]	Little Wonder (Junior Vasquez Club Mix) (Album Version)/(Danny Saber Dance Mix) (Junior Vasquez Club Dub)	1997	3.00	6.00	12.00
❑ SPRO-12249 [DJ]	Dead Man Walking (Moby Mix 1) (House Mix)/ (Album Version) (Moby Mix 2)	1997	3.00	6.00	12.00
❑ Y-38618	I'm Afraid of Americans (6 versions)	1997	2.50	5.00	10.00

WARNER BROS.
| ❑ 40575 | Real Cool World (4 versions) | 1992 | 2.50 | 5.00 | 10.00 |

45s
BACKSTREET
❑ 52024	Cat People (Putting Out Fire)/Paul's Theme (Jogging Chase)	1982	—	—	3.00
—B-side by Georgio Moroder					
❑ 52024 [PS]	Cat People (Putting Out Fire)/Paul's Theme (Jogging Chase)	1982	—	—	3.00

DERAM
| ❑ 85009 | Rubber Band/There Is a Happy Land | 1967 | 25.00 | 50.00 | 100.00 |
| ❑ 85016 | Love You Till Tuesday/Did You Ever Have a Dream | 1967 | 25.00 | 50.00 | 100.00 |

EMI AMERICA
❑ B-8158	Let's Dance/Cat People (Putting Out Fire)	1983	—	—	3.00
❑ B-8158 [PS]	Let's Dance/Cat People (Putting Out Fire)	1983	—	—	3.00
❑ B-8165	China Girl/Shake It	1983	—	—	3.00
❑ B-8165 [PS]	China Girl/Shake It	1983	—	3.00	6.00
❑ B-8177	Modern Love/Modern Love (Live)	1983	—	—	3.00
❑ B-8177 [PS]	Modern Love/Modern Love (Live)	1983	—	—	3.00
❑ B-8190	Without You/Criminal World	1984	—	—	3.00
❑ B-8190 [PS]	Without You/Criminal World	1984	—	—	3.00
❑ B-8231	Blue Jean/Dancin' with the Big Boys	1984	—	—	3.00
—Second pressing on black vinyl					
❑ B-8231	Blue Jean/Dancin' with the Big Boys	1984	—	3.00	6.00
—First pressing on blue vinyl					
❑ B-8231 [PS]	Blue Jean/Dancin' with the Big Boys	1984	—	—	3.00
—Both colors of vinyl have the same picture sleeve					
❑ B-8246	Tonight/Tumble and Twirl	1984	—	—	3.00
❑ B-8246 [PS]	Tonight/Tumble and Twirl	1984	—	2.50	5.00
—Fold-out poster sleeve					
❑ B-8251	This Is Not America/(Instrumental)	1984	—	—	3.00
—With the Pat Metheny Group					
❑ B-8251 [PS]	This Is Not America/(Instrumental)	1984	—	—	3.00
❑ BG-8271	Loving the Alien/Don't Look Down	1985	—	—	3.00
❑ BG-8271 [PS]	Loving the Alien/Don't Look Down	1985	—	2.50	5.00
—Gatefold sleeve					
❑ B-8308	Absolute Beginners/(Dub Mix)	1986	—	—	3.00
❑ B-8308 [PS]	Absolute Beginners/(Dub Mix)	1986	—	—	3.00
❑ B-8323	Underground/(instrumental)	1986	—	—	3.00
❑ B-8323 [PS]	Underground/(instrumental)	1986	—	—	3.00
❑ B-8380	Day In Day Out/Julie	1987	—	—	3.00
❑ B-8380 [PS]	Day In Day Out/Julie	1987	—	—	3.00
❑ B-43020	Time Will Crawl/Girls	1987	—	—	3.00
❑ B-43020 [PS]	Time Will Crawl/Girls	1987	3.75	7.50	15.00
❑ B-43031	Never Let Me Down/'87 and Cry	1987	—	—	3.00
❑ B-43031 [PS]	Never Let Me Down/'87 and Cry	1987	—	—	3.00

LONDON
| ❑ 20079 | The Laughing Gnome/ The Gospel According to Tony Day | 1973 | 12.50 | 25.00 | 50.00 |

MERCURY
❑ 72949	Space Oddity/Wild-Eyed Boy from Freecloud	1969	12.50	25.00	50.00
❑ 73075	Memory of a Free Festival Part 1/Part 2	1970	50.00	100.00	200.00
❑ 73173 [DJ]	All the Madmen (mono/stereo)	1971	37.50	75.00	150.00
—May be promo only					

RCA
❑ PB-10664	TVC 15/We Are the Dead	1976	—	3.00	6.00
❑ PB-10736	Stay/Word on a Wing	1976	—	3.00	6.00
❑ PB-10905	Sound and Vision/A New Career in a New Town	1977	—	3.00	6.00

Number	Title (A Side/B Side)	Yr	VG	VG+	NM
❑ GB-10938	Fame/Golden Years	1977	—	—	3.00
—Gold Standard Series issue					
❑ PB-11017	Be My Wife/The Speed of Life	1977	2.00	4.00	8.00
❑ PB-11121	Heroes/V-2 Schneider	1977	2.00	4.00	8.00
❑ PB-11190	Beauty and the Beast/Sense of Doubt	1978	2.00	4.00	8.00
❑ PB-11585	Boys Keep Swinging/Fantastic Voyage	1979	—	3.00	6.00
❑ PB-11661	D.J./Fantastic Voyage	1979	2.00	4.00	8.00
❑ PB-11724	Look Back in Anger/Repetition	1979	—	3.00	6.00
❑ PB-11887	John I'm Only Dancing 1972/Joe the Lion	1980	—	3.00	6.00
❑ PB-12078	Ashes to Ashes/It's No Game	1980	—	2.50	5.00
❑ PB-12078 [PS]	Ashes to Ashes/It's No Game	1980	—	2.50	5.00
—The standard US picture sleeve has David Bowie holding a shoe and looking into it; other variations may exist, but we don't know about them yet					
❑ JE-12087 [DJ]	Fashion/It's No Game/Teenage Wildlife	1980	100.00	200.00	400.00
❑ PB-12134	Fashion/Scream Like a Baby	1980	—	2.50	5.00
❑ PB-12134 [PS]	Fashion/Scream Like a Baby	1980	—	2.50	5.00
❑ PH-13400	Peace on Earth-Little Drummer Boy/Fantastic Voyage	1982	—	2.50	5.00
—A-side with Bing Crosby					
❑ PH-13400 [PS]	Peace on Earth-Little Drummer Boy/Fantastic Voyage	1982	2.50	5.00	10.00
—A-side with Bing Crosby					
❑ PB-13660	White Light-White Heat/Cracked Actor	1983	—	2.50	5.00
❑ PB-13660 [PS]	White Light-White Heat/Cracked Actor	1983	—	2.50	5.00
❑ PB-13769	1984/TVC 15	1984	—	2.50	5.00
❑ PB-13769 [PS]	1984/TVC 15	1984	—	2.50	5.00
RCA VICTOR					
❑ 74-0605	Changes/Andy Warhol	1971	2.50	5.00	10.00
—Orange label (original)					
❑ 74-0605	Changes/Andy Warhol	1974	—	3.00	6.00
—Tan or gray label					
❑ 74-0719	Starman/Suffragette City	1972	—	3.00	6.00
❑ 74-0719 [PS]	Starman/Suffragette City	1972	7.50	15.00	30.00
❑ 74-0838	The Jean Genie/Hang On to Yourself	1972	—	3.00	6.00
❑ 74-0876	Space Oddity/The Man Who Sold the World	1973	—	3.00	6.00
❑ 74-0876 [PS]	Space Oddity/The Man Who Sold the World	1973	5.00	10.00	20.00
❑ APBO-0001	Time/The Prettiest Star	1973	—	3.00	6.00
❑ APBO-0001 [PS]	Time/The Prettiest Star	1973	200.00	400.00	800.00
❑ APBO-0028	Let's Spend the Night Together/Lady Grinning Soul	1973	—	3.00	6.00
❑ APBO-0160	Sorrow/Amsterdam	1973	—	3.00	6.00
❑ APBO-0287	Rebel Rebel/Lady Grinning Soul	1974	2.50	5.00	10.00
—All copies contain an alternate mix of "Rebel, Rebel"					
❑ APBO-0293	Diamond Dogs/Holy Holy	1974	2.50	5.00	10.00
—Part of U.S. numbering system, but released only outside the U.S.					
❑ PB-10026	1984/Queen Bitch	1974	—	3.00	6.00
❑ PB-10105	Rock and Roll with Me/Panic in Detroit	1974	—	3.00	6.00
❑ JB-10152 [DJ]	Young Americans (3:11) (5:10)	1975	2.50	5.00	10.00
❑ PB-10152	Young Americans/Knock on Wood	1975	—	3.00	6.00
—Orange label (West Coast pressing)					
❑ PB-10152	Young Americans/Knock on Wood	1975	—	3.00	6.00
—Tan label (Indianapolis pressing)					
❑ JB-10320 [DJ]	Fame (Long Version 4:12)/(Short Version 3:30)	1975	3.00	6.00	12.00
—Promo-only edition; stock copies contain the 3:30 version					
❑ PB-10320	Fame/Right	1975	—	3.00	6.00
—Orange label (West Coast pressing)					
❑ PB-10320	Fame/Right	1975	—	3.00	6.00
—Tan label (Indianapolis pressing)					
❑ PB-10441	Golden Years/Can You Hear Me	1975	—	3.00	6.00
❑ GB-10468	Changes/Andy Warhol	1975	—	2.00	4.00
—Gold Standard Series issue					
❑ GB-10469	Young Americans/Knock on Wood	1975	—	2.00	4.00
—Gold Standard Series issue					
❑ GB-10470	Space Oddity/The Man Who Sold the World	1975	—	2.00	4.00
—Gold Standard Series issue					
VIRGIN					
❑ S7-19517	Dead Man Walking/Little Wonder	1997	—	2.00	4.00
❑ 58833	Changes/Rebel Rebel	2000	—	2.00	4.00
❑ 58834	Fame/Golden Years	2000	—	2.00	4.00
—Both are full-length versions, not the single edits					
❑ 58835	Let's Dance (single edit)/Modern Love	2000	—	2.00	4.00
WARNER BROS.					
❑ 5815	Can't Stop Thinking About Me/And I Say to Myself	1966	100.00	200.00	400.00
—As "David Bowie and the Lower Third"					

7-Inch Extended Plays
RCA VICTOR

Number	Title (A Side/B Side)	Yr	VG	VG+	NM
❑ 45-103 [DJ]	Space Oddity/Moonage Daydream//Life on Mars?/It Ain't Easy	1972	7.50	15.00	30.00
❑ 45-103 [PS]	David Bowie	1972	7.50	15.00	30.00

Albums
COLUMBIA

Number	Title (A Side/B Side)	Yr	VG	VG+	NM
❑ C 86630	Heathen	2002	3.00	6.00	12.00
DERAM					
❑ DE 16003 [M]	David Bowie	1967	30.00	60.00	120.00
❑ DES 18003 [S]	David Bowie	1967	37.50	75.00	150.00
EMI AMERICA					
❑ SPRO 9960/1 [(2)DJ]	Let's Talk	1983	6.25	12.50	25.00
—Promo-only interview album					
❑ SO-17093	Let's Dance	1983	2.50	5.00	10.00
❑ SJ-17138	Tonight	1984	2.50	5.00	10.00
❑ PJ-17267	Never Let Me Down	1987	2.50	5.00	10.00
❑ SPRO-79112/3 [DJ]	Never Let Me Down: The Interview	1987	6.25	12.50	25.00
❑ R 153730	Let's Dance	1983	3.00	6.00	12.00
—RCA Music Service edition					
❑ R 174212	Never Let Me Down	1987	3.00	6.00	12.00
—BMG Direct Marketing edition					
LONDON					
❑ PS 628/9 [(2)]	Images 1966-1967	1973	12.50	25.00	50.00
—Original pressings have dark blue and silver labels. Later pressings, if any, are worth at least 50% less.					
❑ LC 50007	Starting Point	1977	3.00	6.00	12.00

Number	Title (A Side/B Side)	Yr	VG	VG+	NM
MERCURY					
❑ SR 61246	Man of Words, Man of Music	1969	37.50	75.00	150.00
❑ SR 61325	The Man Who Sold the World	1970	10.00	20.00	40.00
—An often-counterfeited album; originals have matrix numbers stamped in the trail-off area					
MOBILE FIDELITY					
❑ 1-064	The Rise and Fall of Ziggy Stardust and the Spiders from Mars	1983	12.50	25.00	50.00
—Audiophile vinyl					
❑ 1-083	Let's Dance	1984	7.50	15.00	30.00
—Audiophile vinyl					
RCA RED SEAL					
❑ ARL1-2743	Peter and the Wolf	1978	5.00	10.00	20.00
—With the Philadelphia Orchestra conducted by Eugene Ormandy; black vinyl					
❑ ARL1-2743	Peter and the Wolf	1978	5.00	10.00	20.00
—With the Philadelphia Orchestra conducted by Eugene Ormandy; green vinyl					
RCA VICTOR					
❑ AFL1-0291	Pin Ups	1978	2.50	5.00	10.00
—Reissue					
❑ APL1-0291	Pin Ups	1973	5.00	10.00	20.00
❑ CPL1-0576	Diamond Dogs	1974	5.00	10.00	20.00
—Standard issue, with dog's genitals airbrushed					
❑ CPL1-0576	Diamond Dogs	1974	1000.	2000.	4000.
—Original copies have cover with dog's genitals clearly visible. Almost all were destroyed prior to release.					
❑ CPL2-0771 [(2)]	David Live	1974	5.00	10.00	20.00
—At time of release, available with either orange or tan labels					
❑ CPL2-0771 [(2)]	David Live	1976	3.00	6.00	12.00
—Reissue with black label, dog near top					
❑ APL1-0998	Young Americans	1975	3.00	6.00	12.00
—At time of release, available with either orange or tan label					
❑ APL1-0998	Young Americans	1976	2.50	5.00	10.00
—Black label					
❑ AQK1-0998	Young Americans	1984	2.50	5.00	10.00
—Reissue					
❑ APL1-1327	Station to Station	1976	2.50	5.00	10.00
—Black label					
❑ APL1-1327	Station to Station	1976	3.00	6.00	12.00
—Originals have a brown label					
❑ AQK1-1327	Station to Station	1984	2.50	5.00	10.00
—Reissue					
❑ AFL1-1732	Changesonebowie	1978	2.50	5.00	10.00
—Reissue					
❑ APL1-1732	Changesonebowie	1976	5.00	5.00	10.00
❑ AQL1-1732	Changesonebowie	1984	2.50	5.00	10.00
—Reissue					
❑ APL1-2030	Low	1977	2.50	5.00	10.00
❑ AFL1-2522	"Heroes"	1977	2.50	5.00	10.00
❑ DJL1-2697 [DJ]	Bowie Now	1978	15.00	30.00	60.00
❑ CPL2-2913 [(2)]	Stage	1978	5.00	10.00	20.00
❑ DJL3-3016 [DJ]	An Evening with David Bowie	1978	12.50	25.00	50.00
—Music and interview for "Superstars Radio Network"					
❑ AQL1-3254	Lodger	1979	2.50	5.00	10.00
❑ DJL1-3545 [DJ]	1980 All Clear	1980	6.25	12.50	25.00
—Promo-only compilation					
❑ AQL1-3647	Scary Monsters	1980	2.50	5.00	10.00
❑ DJL1-3829 [DJ]	College Radio Series	1980	6.25	12.50	25.00
❑ DJL1-3829-A [DJ]	Special Radio Series	1980	6.25	12.50	25.00
—Same material as DJL1-3829					
❑ DJL1-3840 [DJ]	Scary Monsters Interview	1980	5.00	10.00	20.00
❑ AYL1-3843	The Rise and Fall of Ziggy Stardust and the Spiders from Mars	1980	2.00	4.00	8.00
—Reissue					
❑ AYL1-3844	Hunky Dory	1980	2.00	4.00	8.00
—Reissue					
❑ AYL1-3856	Low	1980	2.00	4.00	8.00
—Reissue					
❑ AYL1-3857	"Heroes"	1980	2.00	4.00	8.00
—Reissue					
❑ AYL1-3889	Diamond Dogs	1980	2.00	4.00	8.00
—Reissue					
❑ AYL1-3890	Aladdin Sane	1980	2.00	4.00	8.00
—Reissue					
❑ AFL1-4202	Changestwobowie	1981	2.50	5.00	10.00
❑ AYL1-4234	Lodger	1981	2.00	4.00	8.00
—Reissue					
❑ CPL1-4346 [EP]	David Bowie in Berthold Brecht's Baal	1982	2.50	5.00	10.00
❑ LSP-4623	Hunky Dory	1972	5.00	10.00	20.00
❑ AYL1-4653	Pin Ups	1982	2.00	4.00	8.00
—Reissue					
❑ AFL1-4702	The Rise and Fall of Ziggy Stardust and the Spiders from Mars	1977	2.50	5.00	10.00
—Reissue					
❑ LSP-4702	The Rise and Fall of Ziggy Stardust and the Spiders from Mars	1972	5.00	10.00	20.00
—Orange label					
❑ LSP-4702	The Rise and Fall of Ziggy Stardust and the Spiders from Mars	1975	3.00	6.00	12.00
—Tan label					
❑ AFL1-4792	Golden Years	1983	2.50	5.00	10.00
❑ LSP-4813	Space Oddity	1973	5.00	10.00	20.00
—Reissue of Mercury SR-61246; add 1/3 if bonus poster is enclosed					
❑ LSP-4816	The Man Who Sold the World	1973	5.00	10.00	20.00
—Reissue of Mercury SR-61325; add 1/3 if bonus poster is enclosed					
❑ AFL1-4852	Aladdin Sane	1977	2.50	5.00	10.00
—Reissue					
❑ LSP-4852	Aladdin Sane	1973	5.00	10.00	20.00
—Orange label is original (deduct 50% for tan labels)					
❑ CPL2-4862 [(2)]	Ziggy Stardust, The Motion Picture	1983	5.00	10.00	20.00
❑ CPL2-4862 [(2)DJ]	Ziggy Stardust, The Motion Picture	1983	12.50	25.00	50.00
—Promo version on clear vinyl					
❑ AFL1-4919	Fame and Fashion	1984	2.50	5.00	10.00

B

Harry Belafonte, *Jump Up Calypso*, RCA Victor LSP-2388, stereo LP, $12.50-$25.

Brook Benton, *Brook Benton*, RCA Camden CAL-564, mono LP, $7.50-$15.

Chuck Berry, "You Never Can Tell," Chess 1906, picture sleeve, $20-$40.

Cilla Black, "Yesterday," Capitol 5595, picture sleeve, $15-$30.

Blue Cheer, *Vincebus Eruptum*, Philips PHS 600-264, stereo LP, $20-$40.

David Bowie, *David Bowie*, RCA Victor 45-103, promo-only 7-inch EP, $30-$60 (cover and record together).

Number	Title (A Side/B Side)	Yr	VG	VG+	NM
RYKO ANALOGUE					
❏ RALP 0120/1/2 [(6)]Sound + Vision		1989	20.00	40.00	80.00
—Six-LP box set on clear vinyl with three gatefold cardboard inner sleeves					
❏ RALP 0131 [(2)]Space Oddity		1990	5.00	10.00	20.00
—Clear vinyl with "Limited Edition" obi					
❏ RALP 0132 [(2)]The Man Who Sold the World		1990	5.00	10.00	20.00
—Clear vinyl with "Limited Edition" obi					
❏ RALP 0133 [(2)]Hunky Dory		1990	5.00	10.00	20.00
—Clear vinyl with "Limited Edition" obi					
❏ RALP 0134 [(2)]The Rise and Fall of Ziggy Stardust and the Spiders from Mars		1990	5.00	10.00	20.00
—Clear vinyl with "Limited Edition" obi					
❏ RALP 0135 Aladdin Sane		1990	5.00	10.00	20.00
—Clear vinyl with "Limited Edition" obi					
❏ RALP 0136 Pin Ups		1990	5.00	10.00	20.00
—Clear vinyl with "Limited Edition" obi					
❏ RALP 0137 Diamond Dogs		1990	5.00	10.00	20.00
—Clear vinyl with "Limited Edition" obi; genitals on dog are restored					
❏ RALP 0138/9 [(2)]David Live		1990	5.00	10.00	20.00
—Clear vinyl with "Limited Edition" obi					
❏ RALP 0171 [(2)]Changesbowie		1990	5.00	10.00	20.00
—Clear vinyl with "Limited Edition" obi					
❏ LSD-4702 [DJ] The Rise and Fall of Ziggy Stardust and the Spiders from Mars		1990	25.00	50.00	100.00
—Special promo-only package with both the LP and CD versions					

BOX TOPS, THE Lead singer Alex Chilton was later in BIG STAR.
45s

Number	Title (A Side/B Side)	Yr	VG	VG+	NM
ARISTA					
❏ 9488	Sweet Cream Ladies/Neon Rainbow	1986	—	—	3.00
—"Flashback" oldies series					
BELL					
❏ 865	Come On Honey/You Keep Tightening Up on Me	1970	2.00	4.00	8.00
❏ 923	Let Me Go/Got to Hold On to You	1970	2.00	4.00	8.00
❏ 981	King's Highway/Since I've Been Gone	1971	2.00	4.00	8.00
GUSTO					
❏ 2112	The Letter/Cry Like a Baby	1981	—	2.00	4.00
—Re-recordings					
HI					
❏ 2228	It's All Over/Sugar Creek Woman	1972	—	3.00	6.00
❏ 2242	Hold On Girl/Angel	1973	—	3.00	6.00
MALA					
❏ 565	The Letter/Happy Times	1967	3.00	6.00	12.00
❏ 580	Neon Rainbow/Everything I Am	1967	2.50	5.00	10.00
❏ 593	Cry Like a Baby/The Door You Closed to Me	1968	3.00	6.00	12.00
❏ 12005	Choo Choo Train/Fields of Clover	1968	2.50	5.00	10.00
❏ 12017	I Met Her in Church/People Gonna Talk	1968	2.50	5.00	10.00
❏ 12035	Sweet Cream Ladies, Forward March/I See Only Sunshine	1968	2.50	5.00	10.00
❏ 12038	I Shall Be Released/I Must Be the Devil	1969	2.50	5.00	10.00
❏ 12040	Soul Deep/The Happy Song	1969	2.50	5.00	10.00
❏ 12042	Turn On a Dream/Together	1969	2.50	5.00	10.00
PHILCO-FORD					
❏ HP-27	The Letter/Happy Times	1968	5.00	10.00	20.00
—4-inch plastic "Hip Pocket Record" with color sleeve					
SPHERE SOUND					
❏ 77001	The Letter/Happy Times	1969	2.50	5.00	10.00
—Blue label; reissue					
❏ 77001	The Letter/Happy Times	1970	2.00	4.00	8.00
—Silver label; reissue					
❏ 77002	Cry Like a Baby/The Door You Closed to Me	1970	2.00	4.00	8.00
—Silver label; reissue					
STAX					
❏ 0199	It's Gonna Be O.K./Willobee and Dale	1974	—	3.00	6.00
Albums					
BELL					
❏ 6011 [M]	The Letter/Neon Rainbow	1967	6.25	12.50	25.00
❏ S-6011 [S]	The Letter/Neon Rainbow	1967	5.00	10.00	20.00
❏ 6017	Cry Like a Baby	1968	5.00	10.00	20.00
❏ 6023	Non-Stop	1968	5.00	10.00	20.00
❏ 6025	The Box Tops Super Hits	1968	5.00	10.00	20.00
❏ 6032	Dimensions	1969	5.00	10.00	20.00
RHINO					
❏ RNLP-161	The Greatest Hits	1982	3.00	6.00	12.00

BOXER, KARL
45s

Number	Title (A Side/B Side)	Yr	VG	VG+	NM
DOT					
❏ 16853	Hava Nagila/A Piece of the Action	1966	5.00	10.00	20.00

BOYCE, TOMMY Also see TOMMY BOYCE AND BOBBY HART.
45s

Number	Title (A Side/B Side)	Yr	VG	VG+	NM
A&M					
❏ 809	Sunday, The Day Before Monday/The Green Grass (Is Turning Brown)	1966	3.75	7.50	15.00
❏ 826	In Case the Wind Should Blow/Simon Smith and the Amazing Dancing Bear	1966	6.25	12.50	25.00
CAPITOL					
❏ 3136	Alice My Sweet/Eve Laurain	1971	—	2.50	5.00
CHELSEA					
❏ BCBO-0101	Thank God for Rock and Roll/Krush on Kris	1973	—	2.50	5.00
—As "Christopher Cloud"					
❏ 78-0118	Zip-a-Dee-Doo-Dah/Interpretation of War	1973	—	2.50	5.00
—As "Christopher Cloud"					
COLPIX					
❏ 794	Let's Go Where the Action Is/(Instrumental)	1966	5.00	10.00	20.00
DOT					
❏ 16117	The Gypsy Song/Give Me the Clue	1960	5.00	10.00	20.00
MGM					
❏ 13400	Pretty Thing (You Look Out of Sight Tonight)/I Don't Have to Worry 'Bout You	1965	3.75	7.50	15.00
❏ 13429	Little Suzy Somethin'/Pee's N' Que's	1965	3.75	7.50	15.00

Number	Title (A Side/B Side)	Yr	VG	VG+	NM
R-DELL					
❏ 111	Betty Jean/I'm Not Sure	1960	6.25	12.50	25.00
RCA VICTOR					
❏ 47-7975	Along Came Linda/You Look So Lonely	1961	5.00	10.00	20.00
❏ 47-8025	Come Here Joanne/The Way I Used to Do	1962	5.00	10.00	20.00
❏ 47-8074	I'll Remember Carol/Too Late for Tears	1962	5.00	10.00	20.00
❏ 47-8126	Have You Had a Change of Heart/Sweet Little Baby, I Care	1963	5.00	10.00	20.00
❏ 47-8208	Don't Be Afraid/A Million Things to Say	1963	5.00	10.00	20.00
WOW					
❏ 345	Is It True/Little One	1961	5.00	10.00	20.00
Albums					
RCA CAMDEN					
❏ CAL-2202 [M]	Tommy Boyce	1967	5.00	10.00	20.00
❏ CAS-2202 [S]	Tommy Boyce	1967	6.25	12.50	25.00

BOYCE, TOMMY, AND BOBBY HART Also see each artist's individual listings.
45s

Number	Title (A Side/B Side)	Yr	VG	VG+	NM
A&M					
❏ 858	Out and About/My Little Chickadee	1967	2.50	5.00	10.00
❏ 858 [PS]	Out and About/My Little Chickadee	1967	5.00	10.00	20.00
❏ 874	Sometimes She's a Little Girl/Love Every Day	1967	2.50	5.00	10.00
❏ 874 [PS]	Sometimes She's a Little Girl/Love Every Day	1967	5.00	10.00	20.00
❏ 893	I Wonder What She's Doing Tonight/The Ambushers	1967	3.00	6.00	12.00
❏ 893 [PS]	I Wonder What She's Doing Tonight/The Ambushers	1967	5.00	10.00	20.00
❏ 919	Goodbye Baby (I Don't Want to See You Cry)/Where Angels Go, Trouble Follows	1968	2.50	5.00	10.00
❏ 919 [PS]	Goodbye Baby (I Don't Want to See You Cry)/Where Angels Go, Trouble Follows	1968	5.00	10.00	20.00
❏ 948	Alice Long (You're Still My Favorite Girlfriend)/P.O. Box 9847	1968	2.50	5.00	10.00
❏ 948 [PS]	Alice Long (You're Still My Favorite Girlfriend)/P.O. Box 9847	1968	5.00	10.00	20.00
❏ 993	We're All Going to the Same Place/6 + 6	1968	2.50	5.00	10.00
❏ 993 [PS]	We're All Going to the Same Place/6 + 6	1968	2.50	5.00	10.00
❏ 1017	Maybe Somebody Heard/It's All Happening on the Inside	1969	2.00	4.00	8.00
❏ 1031	L.U.V. (Let Us Vote)/I Wanna Be Free	1969	2.00	4.00	8.00
❏ 1031 [PS]	L.U.V. (Let Us Vote)/I Wanna Be Free	1969	3.75	7.50	15.00
AQUARIAN					
❏ 380	I'll Blow You a Kiss in the Wind/Smilin'	1970	—	2.00	4.00
❏ 380 [PS]	I'll Blow You a Kiss in the Wind/Smilin'	1970	—	3.00	6.00
Albums					
A&M					
❏ LP-126 [M]	Test Patterns	1967	5.00	10.00	20.00
❏ LP-143 [M]	I Wonder What She's Doing Tonite?	1968	7.50	15.00	30.00
❏ SP-4126 [S]	Test Patterns	1967	5.00	10.00	20.00
❏ SP-4143 [S]	I Wonder What She's Doing Tonite?	1968	5.00	10.00	20.00
❏ SP-4162	It's All Happening on the Inside	1968	5.00	10.00	20.00

BOYD, EDDIE
45s

Number	Title (A Side/B Side)	Yr	VG	VG+	NM
ART TONE					
❏ 832	I'm Comin' Home/Operator	1962	3.75	7.50	15.00
BEA & BABY					
❏ 101	I'm Comin' Home/Thank You Baby	1959	3.75	7.50	15.00
❏ 107	Blue Monday Blues/The Blues Is Here to Stay	1959	3.75	7.50	15.00
❏ 108	Come Home/You've Got to Reap What You Sow	1959	3.75	7.50	15.00
CHESS					
❏ 1523	Cool Kind Treatment/Rosa Lee Swing	1952	25.00	50.00	100.00
❏ 1533	24 Hours/The Tickler	1953	25.00	50.00	100.00
—Black vinyl					
❏ 1533	24 Hours/The Tickler	1953	100.00	200.00	400.00
—Red vinyl					
❏ 1541	Third Degree/Back Beat	1953	50.00	100.00	200.00
—Black vinyl					
❏ 1541	Third Degree/Back Beat	1953	125.00	250.00	500.00
—Red vinyl					
❏ 1552	That's When I Miss You So/Tortured Soul	1953	20.00	40.00	80.00
❏ 1561	Nothing But Trouble/Picture in the Frame	1954	15.00	30.00	60.00
❏ 1573	Hush Baby, Don't You Cry/Came Home This Morning	1954	15.00	30.00	60.00
❏ 1576	Driftin'/Rattin' and Runnin' Around	1954	15.00	30.00	60.00
❏ 1582	The Story of Bill/Please Help Me	1954	15.00	30.00	60.00
❏ 1595	The Nightmare Is Over/Real Good Feeling	1955	12.50	25.00	50.00
❏ 1606	I'm a Prisoner/I've Been Deceived	1955	12.50	25.00	50.00
❏ 1621	Don't/Life Gets to Be a Burden	1956	10.00	20.00	40.00
❏ 1634	Just a Fool/Four Leaf Clover	1956	10.00	20.00	40.00
❏ 1660	I Got a Woman/Hotel Blues	1957	10.00	20.00	40.00
❏ 1674	I Got the Blues/She's the One	1957	10.00	20.00	40.00
HERALD					
❏ 406	Lonesome for My Baby/I'm Goin' Downtown	1953	100.00	200.00	400.00
J.O.B.					
❏ 1007	Five Long Years/Blue Coat Man	1952	37.50	75.00	150.00
—Black vinyl					
❏ 1007	Five Long Years/Blue Coat Man	1952	75.00	150.00	300.00
—Red vinyl					
❏ 1009	It's Miserable to Be Alone/I'm Pleading	1953	75.00	150.00	300.00
❏ 1114	I Love You/Save Her Doctor	1957	15.00	30.00	60.00
RCA VICTOR					
❏ 50-0006	What Makes These Things Happen/Chicago Is Just That Way	1950	30.00	60.00	120.00
—Gray label, orange vinyl					

BOYD, JIMMY Also see ROSEMARY CLOONEY; FRANKIE LAINE.
45s

Number	Title (A Side/B Side)	Yr	VG	VG+	NM
CAPITOL					
❏ 4967	Day Dreamer/I've Got It Made	1963	2.50	5.00	10.00

B

Number	Title (A Side/B Side)	Yr	VG	VG+	NM
COLUMBIA					
❏ 4-152	I Saw Mommy Kissing Santa Claus/Thumbelina	1952	5.00	10.00	20.00
—Yellow-label Children's Series issue; alternate number is 90174					
❏ 4-152 [PS]	I Saw Mommy Kissing Santa Claus/Thumbelina	1952	6.25	12.50	25.00
❏ 4-183	Santa Got Stuck in the Chimney/I Said a Prayer for Santa Claus	1953	3.75	7.50	15.00
—Yellow-label Children's Series issue					
❏ 4-183 [PS]	Santa Got Stuck in the Chimney/I Said a Prayer for Santa Claus	1953	5.00	10.00	20.00
❏ 21571	Rockin' Down the Mississippi/Crazy Mixed Up Blues	1956	12.50	25.00	50.00
❏ 39696	God's Little Candles/Owl Lullaby	1952	3.75	7.50	15.00
❏ 39733	Little Train A-Chuggin'/Needle In, Needle Out	1952	3.75	7.50	15.00
❏ 39871	I Saw Mommy Kissing Santa Claus/Thumbelina	1952	3.75	7.50	15.00
❏ 39927	Early Bird/I'll Stay in the House	1953	3.75	7.50	15.00
❏ 39955	My Bunny and My Sister Sue/Two Easter Sunday Sweethearts	1953	3.75	7.50	15.00
❏ 40007	Playmates/Shoo Fly Pie and Apple Pan Dowdy	1953	3.75	7.50	15.00
❏ 40049	Marco, the Polo Pony/God Bless Us All	1953	3.75	7.50	15.00
❏ 40070	I Saw Mommy Kissing Santa Claus/Santa Claus Is Coming to Town	1953	3.00	6.00	12.00
❏ 40071	Winter Wonderland/Here Comes Santa Claus	1953	3.00	6.00	12.00
❏ 40072	Silent Night, Holy Night/Frosty the Snowman	1953	3.00	6.00	12.00
❏ 40073	The Little Match Girl/Rudolph, the Red-Nosed Reindeer	1953	3.00	6.00	12.00
❏ 40080	Santa Got Stuck in the Chimney/I Said a Prayer for Santa Claus	1953	3.75	7.50	15.00
—With Johnny Bond					
❏ 40138	I've Got Those "Wake Up Seven-Thirty, Wash Your Ears They're Dirty, Eat Your Eggs and Oatmeal, Rush to School" Blues/Jelly on My Head	1954	5.00	10.00	20.00
❏ 40181	Little Bonny Bunny/Jimmy, Roll Me Gently	1954	3.75	7.50	15.00
❏ 40218	I'm So Glad (I'm a Little Boy and You're a Little Girl)/Kitty in the Basket	1954	3.75	7.50	15.00
—With Gayla Peevey					
❏ 40253	Ma I Miss Your Apple Pie/Shepherd Boy	1954	3.75	7.50	15.00
❏ 40304	Little Sir Echo/The Little White Duck	1954	3.75	7.50	15.00
❏ 40365	I Saw Mommy Do the Mambo (With You Know Who)/Santa Claus Blues	1954	3.75	7.50	15.00
❏ 40504	I Want a Haircut with a Moon on Top/How Come	1955	3.00	6.00	12.00
❏ 40601	Reindeer Rock/A Kiss for Christmas	1955	5.00	10.00	20.00
❏ 40756	Don't Forget to Say Your Prayers/Little Dog	1956	3.00	6.00	12.00
❏ 40881	I Wanna Go Steady/Gonna Take My Heart on a Hayride	1957	3.00	6.00	12.00
❏ 41547	Dennis the Menace/Little Josey	1960	5.00	10.00	20.00
—With Rosemary Clooney					
DOT					
❏ 16126	Dusty/Jambalaya	1960	3.00	6.00	12.00
IMPERIAL					
❏ 66166	I Would Never Do That/Lazy Me	1966	2.00	4.00	8.00
❏ 66206	She Chased Me/Will I Cry	1966	2.00	4.00	8.00
❏ 66233	So Young and So Fine/I Would Never Do That	1967	2.00	4.00	8.00
JUBILEE					
❏ 5316	Don't Tempt Me/High School Social	1958	3.00	6.00	12.00
MGM					
❏ 12788	Cream Puff/I Love You So Much	1959	15.00	30.00	60.00
VEE JAY					
❏ 620	All Alone/In Love In Vain	1964	2.50	5.00	10.00
❏ 686	That's What I'll Give to You/My Home Town	1965	2.50	5.00	10.00
7-Inch Extended Plays					
COLUMBIA					
❏ B-1913	I Saw Mommy Kissing Santa Claus/Jingle Bells/I Said a Prayer For Santa Claus/Santa Got Stuck In The Chimney	195?	3.00	6.00	12.00
❏ B-1913 [PS]	Jimmy Boyd	195?	3.75	7.50	15.00
Albums					
COLUMBIA					
❏ CL 2543 [10]	I Saw Mommy Kissing Santa Claus	1955	10.00	20.00	40.00
—"House Party Series" reissue					
❏ CL 6270 [10]	Christmas with Jimmy Boyd	1953	25.00	50.00	100.00

BOYD, MICKEY, AND THE PLAIN VIEWERS See THE STRING-A-LONGS.

BOYFRIENDS, THE Also known as THE FIVE DISCS.
45s
KAPP

❏ 569	Let's Fall in Love/Oh Lana	1964	25.00	50.00	100.00

BOZ Boz Burrell, later of KING CRIMSON and BAD COMPANY.
45s
EPIC

❏ 10097	Baby Song/Pinocchio	1966	2.50	5.00	10.00
❏ 10097 [PS]	Baby Song/Pinocchio	1966	3.75	7.50	15.00

BOZE, CALVIN
45s
ALADDIN

❏ 3045	Waiting and Drinking/If You Ever Had the Blues	1950	37.50	75.00	150.00
❏ 3055	Safronia Blues/Angel City Blues	1950	37.50	75.00	150.00
❏ 3065	Lizzie Lou/Lizzie Lou (Part 2)	1950	37.50	75.00	150.00
❏ 3072	Stinkin' from Drinkin'/Look Out for Tomorrow Today	1950	25.00	50.00	100.00
❏ 3079	Beat Street on Saturday Night/Choo Choo Ch'Boogieing My Baby Back Home	1951	25.00	50.00	100.00
❏ 3086	Slippin' and Slidin'/Baby, You're Tops with Me	1951	25.00	50.00	100.00
❏ 3100	I've Got News for You/I Can't Stop Crying	1951	20.00	40.00	80.00
❏ 3110	I'm Gonna Steam Off the Stamp/Fish Tail	1952	20.00	40.00	80.00
❏ 3122	Hey, Lawdy Miss Clawdy/My Friend Told Me	1952	20.00	40.00	80.00
❏ 3132	Good Time Sue/Keep Your Nose Out of My Business	1952	15.00	30.00	60.00
❏ 3142	The Blue Tango/The Glory of Love	1952	15.00	30.00	60.00
❏ 3143	Blue Shuffle/Popside	1952	15.00	30.00	60.00

Number	Title (A Side/B Side)	Yr	VG	VG+	NM
❏ 3147	Looped/Blow Man Blow	1952	15.00	30.00	60.00
❏ 3160	Havin' a Time/Shamrock	1953	12.50	25.00	50.00
❏ 3181	That Other Woman/Shoot De Pistol	1953	12.50	25.00	50.00
IMPERIAL					
❏ 5844	Shamrock/Safronia B	1962	3.00	6.00	12.00

BRACELETS, THE
45s
CONGRESS

❏ 104	I'll Play Along/Waddle, Waddle	1962	4.00	8.00	16.00
20TH CENTURY-FOX					
❏ 539	You Better Move On/You're Just Fooling Yourself	1964	3.00	6.00	12.00

BRADEN, JOHN
45s
A&M

❏ 1066	What a Friend We Have in Jesus/Hand Me Down Man	1969	2.50	5.00	10.00
Albums					
A&M					
❏ SP-4172	John Braden	1969	3.75	7.50	15.00

BRADLEY, BERRY
45s
HIT

❏ 88	That Sunday, That Summer/Don't Think Twice, It's All Right	1963	2.00	4.00	8.00
—B-side by Jimmy, Wayne and Betty					

BRADLEY, HAROLD
45s
COLUMBIA

❏ 4-42694	Devil Woman/Walk On By	1963	2.50	5.00	10.00
❏ 4-42830	Maria Elena/A La Orilla Del Lago	1963	2.50	5.00	10.00
❏ 4-43043	Sugarfoot Rag/Wildwood Flower	1964	2.00	4.00	8.00
Albums					
COLUMBIA					
❏ CL 2014 [M]	Bossa Nova Goes to Nashville	1963	3.00	6.00	12.00
❏ CL 2073 [M]	Misty Guitar	1963	3.00	6.00	12.00
❏ CL 2456 [M]	Guitar for Lovers Only	1966	3.00	6.00	12.00
❏ CS 8814 [S]	Bossa Nova Goes to Nashville	1963	3.75	7.50	15.00
❏ CS 8873 [S]	Misty Guitar	1963	3.75	7.50	15.00
❏ CS 9256 [S]	Guitar for Lovers Only	1966	3.75	7.50	15.00
HARMONY					
❏ H 31324	Guitar for Sentimental Lovers	1971	3.00	6.00	12.00

BRADLEY, JAN
45s
CHESS

❏ 1845	Mama Didn't Lie/Lovers Like Me	1962	2.50	5.00	10.00
❏ 1851	These Tears/Baby What Can I Do	1963	2.00	4.00	8.00
❏ 1884	Curfew Blues/Pack My Things	1964	2.00	4.00	8.00
❏ 1897	Please Mr. D.J./Two of a Kind	1964	2.00	4.00	8.00
❏ 1919	I'm Over You/The Brush-Off	1964	2.00	4.00	8.00
❏ 1975	Just a Summer Memory/He'll Wait for Me	1966	—	3.00	6.00
❏ 1996	Trust Me/Things a Woman Needs	1967	—	3.00	6.00
❏ 2023	Your Kind of Love/It's Just Your Way	1967	—	3.00	6.00
❏ 2043	You Have Me What's Missing/Nights in New York City	1968	—	3.00	6.00
FORMAL					
❏ 1044	Mama Didn't Lie/Lovers Like Me	1962	50.00	100.00	200.00
❏ 1048	Dear Sears and Roebuck/(B-side unknown)	1963	3.00	6.00	12.00
HOOTENANNY					
❏ 1	Christmas Time (Part 1)/Christmas Time (Part 2)	1962	3.00	6.00	12.00

BRADSHAW, JACK
45s
DECCA

❏ 29654	My Heart, My Heart/Flirting with You	1955	6.25	12.50	25.00
GLENN					
❏ 754	No, No/Welcome Heart	1955	15.00	30.00	60.00
❏ 755	I Got What You Need/You Hurt Me	195?	15.00	30.00	60.00
MAR-VEL					
❏ 750	Don't Tease Me/Don't Cause Me to Hate You	1954	25.00	50.00	100.00
❏ 751	Searchin'/My Heart, My Heart	1955	15.00	30.00	60.00
❏ 752	It Just Ain't Right/Naughty Girls	1955	15.00	30.00	60.00
❏ 753	Jo Jo/Men Are Weak	1955	25.00	50.00	100.00
❏ 756	Saturday Night Special/Out of the Picture	195?	15.00	30.00	60.00

BRADSHAW, TINY
45s
KING

❏ 4376	After You've Gone/Boogie Green	1950	15.00	30.00	60.00
❏ 4397	Butterfly/I'm Going to Have Myself a Ball	1950	15.00	30.00	60.00
❏ 4417	Breaking Up the House/If You Don't Love Me, Tell Me So	1950	15.00	30.00	60.00
❏ 4427	Walk That Mess/One, Two, Three, Kick Blues	1951	15.00	30.00	60.00
❏ 4447	Brad's Blues/Two Dry Bones on the Pantry Shelf	1951	15.00	30.00	60.00
❏ 4457	Bradshaw Boogie/Walkin' the Chalk Line	1951	15.00	30.00	60.00
❏ 4467	I'm a High Ballin' Daddy/You Came By	1951	15.00	30.00	60.00
❏ 4487	T-99/Long Time Baby	1951	50.00	100.00	200.00
❏ 4497	The Train Kept a-Rollin'/Knockin' Blues	1951	50.00	100.00	200.00
❏ 4537	Mailman's Sack/Newspaper Boy Blues	1952	50.00	100.00	200.00
❏ 4547	Rippin' and Runnin'/Lay It on the Line	1952	50.00	100.00	200.00
❏ 4577	Strange/Soft	1952	12.50	25.00	50.00
❏ 4621	The Blues Came Pouring In/Heavy Juice	1953	12.50	25.00	50.00
❏ 4664	South of the Orient/Later	1953	12.50	25.00	50.00
❏ 4687	Powder Puff/Ping Pong	1953	12.50	25.00	50.00
❏ 4713	Don't Worry 'Bout Me/Overflow	1954	10.00	20.00	40.00
❏ 4727	Spider Web/The Gypsey	1954	10.00	20.00	40.00
❏ 4747	A Stack of Dollars/Cat Fruit	1954	10.00	20.00	40.00

Number	Title (A Side/B Side)	Yr	VG	VG+	NM
❑ 4757	Light/Choice	1954	10.00	20.00	40.00
❑ 4777	Cat Nap/Stomping Room Only	1955	10.00	20.00	40.00
❑ 4787	Phantom Turnpike/Come On	1955	10.00	20.00	40.00
❑ 5114	Short Shorts/Bushes	1958	6.25	12.50	25.00

7-Inch Extended Plays
KING

Number	Title (A Side/B Side)	Yr	VG	VG+	NM
❑ EP 208	*Soft/Well Oh Well/Heavy Juice/The Train Kept a-Rollin'	195?	10.00	20.00	40.00
❑ EP 208 [PS]	Tiny Bradshaw	195?	10.00	20.00	40.00
❑ EP 248	Off and On/Free for All//South of the Orient/Later	195?	10.00	20.00	40.00
❑ EP 248 [PS]	Tiny Bradshaw, Vol. 2	195?	10.00	20.00	40.00
❑ EP 307	*Ping Pong/Powder Puff/Spider Web/Overflow	195?	10.00	20.00	40.00
❑ EP 307 [PS]	Tiny Bradshaw Plays, Vol. 4	195?	10.00	20.00	40.00

Albums
KING

Number	Title (A Side/B Side)	Yr	VG	VG+	NM
❑ 295-74 [10]	Off and On	1955	250.00	500.00	1000.
❑ 395-501 [M]	Selections	1956	175.00	350.00	700.00
❑ 653 [M]	Great Composer	1960	75.00	150.00	300.00
❑ 953 [M]	24 Great Songs	1966	10.00	20.00	40.00

BRADY, JUNE AND GEORGE
45s
ABC-PARAMOUNT

Number	Title (A Side/B Side)	Yr	VG	VG+	NM
❑ 9893	Sweetheart, Sweetheart/You're My Love	1958	5.00	10.00	20.00

BRADY BUNCH, THE Also see CHRIS KNIGHT; MIKE LOOKINLAND; MAUREEN McCORMICK; EVE PLUMB; BARRY WILLIAMS.
45s
PARAMOUNT

Number	Title (A Side/B Side)	Yr	VG	VG+	NM
❑ 0062	Frosty the Snowman/Silver Bells	1970	3.00	6.00	12.00
❑ 0062 [PS]	Frosty the Snowman/Silver Bells	1970	7.50	15.00	30.00
❑ 0141	We Can Make the World a Whole Lot Brighter/Time to Change	1972	3.00	6.00	12.00
❑ 0167	Time to Change/We'll Always Be Friends	1972	3.00	6.00	12.00
❑ 0205	Zuckerman's Famous Pig/Charlotte's Web	1973	3.00	6.00	12.00
❑ 0205 [PS]	Zuckerman's Famous Pig/Charlotte's Web	1973	5.00	10.00	20.00
❑ 0229	I'd Love You to Want Me/Everything I Do	1973	3.00	6.00	12.00

—As "The Brady Bunch Kids"
Albums
PARAMOUNT

Number	Title (A Side/B Side)	Yr	VG	VG+	NM
❑ PAS-5026	Merry Christmas from the Brady Bunch	1971	20.00	40.00	80.00
❑ PAS-6032	Meet the Brady Bunch	1972	12.50	25.00	50.00
❑ PAS-6037	The Kids from the Brady Bunch	1972	10.00	20.00	40.00
❑ PAS-6058	The Brady Bunch Phonograph Record	1973	20.00	40.00	80.00

BRAINBOX With JAN AKKERMAN, later of FOCUS.
45s
CAPITOL

Number	Title (A Side/B Side)	Yr	VG	VG+	NM
❑ 2943	Alpha & Omega/Cruel Train	1970	2.00	4.00	8.00

ELEKTRA

Number	Title (A Side/B Side)	Yr	VG	VG+	NM
❑ 45673	Woman's Gone/Down Man	1969	2.00	4.00	8.00

Albums
CAPITOL

Number	Title (A Side/B Side)	Yr	VG	VG+	NM
❑ ST-596	Brainbox	1970	3.75	7.50	15.00

BRAMLETT, BONNIE Half of DELANEY AND BONNIE.
45s
CAPRICORN

Number	Title (A Side/B Side)	Yr	VG	VG+	NM
❑ 0229	Higher and Higher/It's Time	1975	—	2.00	4.00
❑ 0262	Let's Go, Let's Go, Let's Go/Never Gonna Give You Up	1976	—	2.00	4.00
❑ 0306	Except for Real/I've Just Seen a Face	1978	—	2.00	4.00

COLUMBIA

Number	Title (A Side/B Side)	Yr	VG	VG+	NM
❑ 45897	Good Vibrations/How Glad I Am	1973	—	2.50	5.00

Albums
CAPRICORN

Number	Title (A Side/B Side)	Yr	VG	VG+	NM
❑ CP 0148	It's Time	1975	3.00	6.00	12.00
❑ CP 0169	Lady's Choice	1976	3.00	6.00	12.00
❑ CP 0190	Memories	1978	3.00	6.00	12.00

COLUMBIA

Number	Title (A Side/B Side)	Yr	VG	VG+	NM
❑ KC 31786	Sweet Bonnie Bramlett	1973	3.75	7.50	15.00

BRAMLETT, DELANEY Half of DELANEY AND BONNIE.
45s
COLUMBIA

Number	Title (A Side/B Side)	Yr	VG	VG+	NM
❑ 45696	I'm Not Your Lover, I'm Your Lover/Over and Over	1972	—	2.50	5.00
❑ 45781	We Can't Be Seen Together/Thank God	1973	—	2.50	5.00
❑ 45950	Are You a Beatle or a Rolling Stone/California Rain	1973	2.50	5.00	10.00

CREAM

Number	Title (A Side/B Side)	Yr	VG	VG+	NM
❑ 8147	What's a Little Love/I Love to Love You	1981	—	2.00	4.00

—By "Delaney and Bekka Bramlett"
GNP CRESCENDO

Number	Title (A Side/B Side)	Yr	VG	VG+	NM
❑ 328	Heartbreak Hotel/You Never Looked Sweeter	1964	3.75	7.50	15.00
❑ 339	Liverpool Lou/You Have No Choice	1965	3.75	7.50	15.00
❑ 363	Without Your Love/A Better Man Than He	1965	3.75	7.50	15.00

INDEPENDENCE

Number	Title (A Side/B Side)	Yr	VG	VG+	NM
❑ 76	Guess I Must Be Dreaming/Don't Let It	1967	3.75	7.50	15.00

Albums
COLUMBIA

Number	Title (A Side/B Side)	Yr	VG	VG+	NM
❑ KC 31631	Some Things Coming	1972	3.00	6.00	12.00
❑ KC 32420	Moblus Strip	1973	3.00	6.00	12.00

MGM

Number	Title (A Side/B Side)	Yr	VG	VG+	NM
❑ M3G-5011	Giving Birth to a Song	1975	2.50	5.00	10.00

PRODIGAL

Number	Title (A Side/B Side)	Yr	VG	VG+	NM
❑ P6-10017S1	Class Reunion	1977	2.50	5.00	10.00

BRANT, BOBBY
45s
EASTWEST

Number	Title (A Side/B Side)	Yr	VG	VG+	NM
❑ 124	Piano Nellie/I Found a New Love	1959	25.00	50.00	100.00

WHITE ROCK

Number	Title (A Side/B Side)	Yr	VG	VG+	NM
❑ 1114	Piano Nellie/I Found a New Love	1959	37.50	75.00	150.00

BRASS RING, THE
45s
ABC DUNHILL

Number	Title (A Side/B Side)	Yr	VG	VG+	NM
❑ 4164	For the Love of Ivy/Theme from The Odd Couple	1968	—	3.00	6.00

DUNHILL

Number	Title (A Side/B Side)	Yr	VG	VG+	NM
❑ 4023	The Phoenix Love Theme (Sensa Fine)/Lightning Bug	1966	—	3.00	6.00
❑ 4036	Lara's Theme/Secret Love	1966	—	3.00	6.00
❑ 4047	California Dreamin'/Samba de Orfeu	1966	—	3.00	6.00
❑ 4059	Lapland/Patricia	1966	—	3.00	6.00
❑ 4065	The Dis-Advantages of You/The Dating Game	1967	—	3.00	6.00
❑ 4090	Love in the Open Air/Wait for Me	1967	5.00	10.00	20.00
❑ 4090 [PS]	Love in the Open Air/Wait for Me	1967	7.50	15.00	30.00

—Sleeve says this is "Paul McCartney's first non-Beatles song"

Number	Title (A Side/B Side)	Yr	VG	VG+	NM
❑ 4108	Monday, Monday/Flower Ring	1967	—	3.00	6.00
❑ 4132	Cherry Pink & Apple Blossom White/Adoro (Don't Tempt Me)	1968	—	3.00	6.00

7-Inch Extended Plays
ABC DUNHILL

Number	Title (A Side/B Side)	Yr	VG	VG+	NM
❑ LP-DS-50044 [DJ]	Mrs. Robinson/This Guy's in Love with You/For Love of Ivy//Do You Know the Way to San Jose/Love Is Blue/Honey	1969	3.00	6.00	12.00

—Small hole, 33 1/3 rpm jukebox EP

Number	Title (A Side/B Side)	Yr	VG	VG+	NM
❑ LP-DS-50044 [PS]	Only Love	1969	3.00	6.00	12.00

Albums
ABC DUNHILL

Number	Title (A Side/B Side)	Yr	VG	VG+	NM
❑ DS-50034	Gazpacho	1968	3.00	6.00	12.00
❑ DS-50044	Only Love	1969	3.00	6.00	12.00
❑ DS-50051	The Best of the Brass Ring	1970	2.50	5.00	10.00

DUNHILL

Number	Title (A Side/B Side)	Yr	VG	VG+	NM
❑ D 50008 [M]	Love Theme from The Flight of the Phoenix	1966	3.00	6.00	12.00
❑ DS 50008 [S]	Love Theme from The Flight of the Phoenix	1966	3.75	7.50	15.00
❑ D 50012 [M]	Lara's Theme	1966	3.00	6.00	12.00
❑ DS 50012 [S]	Lara's Theme	1966	3.75	7.50	15.00
❑ D 50015 [M]	Sunday Night at the Movies	1967	3.00	6.00	12.00
❑ DS 50015 [S]	Sunday Night at the Movies	1967	3.75	7.50	15.00
❑ D 50017 [M]	The Dis-Advantages of You	1967	3.00	6.00	12.00
❑ DS 50017 [S]	The Dis-Advantages of You	1967	3.75	7.50	15.00
❑ D 50023 [M]	The Now Sound	1967	3.00	6.00	12.00
❑ DS 50023 [S]	The Now Sound	1967	3.75	7.50	15.00
❑ ST-91039 [S]	Lara's Theme	1966	5.00	10.00	20.00

—Capitol Record Club edition
PROJECT 3

Number	Title (A Side/B Side)	Yr	VG	VG+	NM
❑ 5067	The Brass Ring	1972	2.50	5.00	10.00

BRAUTIGAN, RICHARD
Albums
HARVEST

Number	Title (A Side/B Side)	Yr	VG	VG+	NM
❑ ST-424	Listening to Richard Brautigan	1970	7.50	15.00	30.00

BRAVE BELT Also see BACHMAN-TURNER OVERDRIVE.
45s
REPRISE

Number	Title (A Side/B Side)	Yr	VG	VG+	NM
❑ 1039	Holy Train/Crazy Arms-Crazy Eyes	1971	—	2.50	5.00
❑ 1061	Never Comin' Home/Can You Feel It	1971	—	2.50	5.00
❑ 1083	Another Way Out/Dunrobin's Gone	1972	—	2.50	5.00

Albums
REPRISE

Number	Title (A Side/B Side)	Yr	VG	VG+	NM
❑ MS 2057	Brave Belt II	1972	3.00	6.00	12.00
❑ MS 2210	Bachman-Turner-Bachman As Brave Belt	1974	2.50	5.00	10.00
❑ RS 6447	Brave Belt	1971	3.00	6.00	12.00

BRAVE NEW WORLD
45s
EPIC

Number	Title (A Side/B Side)	Yr	VG	VG+	NM
❑ 10123	It's Tomorrow/Cried	1967	5.00	10.00	20.00

BREAD Also see DAVID GATES; JIMMY GRIFFIN.
45s
ELEKTRA

Number	Title (A Side/B Side)	Yr	VG	VG+	NM
❑ 45365	Lost Without Your Love/Change of Heart	1976	—	2.00	4.00
❑ 45389	Hooked on You/Our Lady of Sorrow	1977	—	2.00	4.00
❑ 45666	Dismal Day/Anyway You Want Me	1969	2.00	4.00	8.00
❑ 45668	Could I/You Can't Measure the Cost	1969	—	3.00	6.00
❑ 45686	Make It With You/Why Do You Keep Me Waiting	1970	—	2.00	4.00

—Yellow and black label

Number	Title (A Side/B Side)	Yr	VG	VG+	NM
❑ 45686	Make It With You/Why Do You Keep Me Waiting	1970	—	2.00	4.00

—Red, black and white label

Number	Title (A Side/B Side)	Yr	VG	VG+	NM
❑ 45701	It Don't Matter to Me/Call on Me	1970	—	2.00	4.00
❑ 45701 [PS]	It Don't Matter to Me/Call on Me	1970	2.00	4.00	8.00
❑ 45711	Let Your Love Go/Too Much Love	1971	—	2.00	4.00
❑ 45720	If/Take Comfort	1971	—	2.00	4.00
❑ 45720 [PS]	If/Take Comfort	1971	2.00	4.00	8.00
❑ 45740	Mother Freedom/Life in Your Love	1971	—	2.00	4.00
❑ 45751	Baby I'm-a Want You/Truckin'	1971	—	2.00	4.00
❑ 45765	Everything I Own/I Don't Love You	1972	—	2.00	4.00
❑ 45784	Diary/Down on My Knees	1972	—	2.00	4.00
❑ 45803	The Guitar Man/Just Like Yesterday	1972	—	2.00	4.00
❑ 45818	Sweet Surrender/Make It By Yourself	1972	—	2.00	4.00
❑ 45832	Aubrey/Didn't Even Know Her Name	1973	—	2.00	4.00

Albums
ELEKTRA

Number	Title (A Side/B Side)	Yr	VG	VG+	NM
❑ BRD-1 [DJ]	Bread	1971	5.00	10.00	20.00

—In-store sampler; very similar to the future LP "The Best of Bread"

Number	Title (A Side/B Side)	Yr	VG	VG+	NM
❑ 6E-108	The Best of Bread	1977	2.00	4.00	8.00

—Reissue of 75056

Number	Title (A Side/B Side)	Yr	VG	VG+	NM
❑ 6E-110	The Best of Bread, Volume 2	1977	2.00	4.00	8.00

—Reissue of 7E-1005

Number	Title (A Side/B Side)	Yr	VG	VG+	NM
❏ 7E-1005	The Best of Bread, Volume 2	1974	3.00	6.00	12.00
❏ 7E-1094	Lost Without Your Love	1976	2.50	5.00	10.00
❏ EQ-5015 [Q]	Baby I'm-a Want You	1974	5.00	10.00	20.00
❏ EQ-5056 [Q]	The Best of Bread	1973	5.00	10.00	20.00
❏ 60414	Anthology of Bread	1985	2.50	5.00	10.00
❏ EKS-74044	Bread	1969	3.75	7.50	15.00
—Red label with large stylized "E"					
❏ EKS-74044	Bread	1971	2.50	5.00	10.00
—Butterfly label					
❏ EKS-74076	On the Waters	1970	3.75	7.50	15.00
—Red label with large stylized "E"					
❏ EKS-74076	On the Waters	1971	2.50	5.00	10.00
—Butterfly label					
❏ EKS-74086	Manna	1971	3.00	6.00	12.00
❏ EKS-75015	Baby I'm-a Want You	197?	2.50	5.00	10.00
—Front photo is not raised					
❏ EKS-75015	Baby I'm-a Want You	1971	3.75	7.50	15.00
—Gatefold with raised photo on front					
❏ EKS-75047	Guitar Man	1972	3.00	6.00	12.00
❏ EKS-75056	The Best of Bread	1973	3.00	6.00	12.00

BREAD, LOVE AND DREAMS
Albums
LONDON

Number	Title (A Side/B Side)	Yr	VG	VG+	NM
❏ PS 566	Bread, Love and Dreams	1969	7.50	15.00	30.00

BREAKAWAYS, THE
45s
CAMEO

Number	Title (A Side/B Side)	Yr	VG	VG+	NM
❏ 323	That's How It Goes/He Doesn't Love Me	1964	3.75	7.50	15.00
LONDON INT'L.					
❏ 10526	That Boy of Mine/Here She Comes	1963	3.00	6.00	12.00
MELBOURNE					
❏ 1805	Granada/The Flipper	1964	3.00	6.00	12.00

BREAKERS, THE
45s
AMY

Number	Title (A Side/B Side)	Yr	VG	VG+	NM
❏ 938	Don't Send Me No Flowers (I Ain't Dead Yet)/ Love of My Life	1965	3.75	7.50	15.00
BRANA					
❏ 1001/2	Kama-Kaze/Surf Breaker	1963	15.00	30.00	60.00
DJB					
❏ 116	Jet Stream/Beach Head	1964	12.50	25.00	50.00
❏ 116	Super Jet Rumble/Beach Head	1964	12.50	25.00	50.00
—Revised A-side title					
IMPACT					
❏ 14	Surfin' Tragedy/Surf Bird	1963	6.25	12.50	25.00
—Black vinyl					
❏ 14	Surfin' Tragedy/Surf Bird	1963	20.00	40.00	80.00
—Gold vinyl					
JERDEN					
❏ 789	All My Nights, All My Days/Better for the Both of Us	1966	5.00	10.00	20.00
MARSH					
❏ 206	Balboa Memories/Long Way Home	1963	12.50	25.00	50.00
RIVERTON					
❏ 102	All My Nights, All My Days/Better for the Both of Us	1966	10.00	20.00	40.00

BREEDLOVE, JIMMY
45s
ATCO

Number	Title (A Side/B Side)	Yr	VG	VG+	NM
❏ 6094	That's My Baby/Over Somebody Else's Shoulder	1957	6.25	12.50	25.00
❏ 6105	I Can Still Hear You Say You Love Me/ I Wish I Were Twins	1957	6.25	12.50	25.00
DIAMOND					
❏ 144	Jealous Fool/Lil' Ol' Me	1963	7.50	15.00	30.00
EPIC					
❏ 9270	Could This Be Love/This Too Shall Pass Away	1958	5.00	10.00	20.00
❏ 9283	Love Is All We Need/Lovable	1958	5.00	10.00	20.00
❏ 9289	Love Is All We Need/ Oo-Wee Good Gosh A-Mighty	1958	5.00	10.00	20.00
❏ 9319	All Is Forgiven/I Say Hello	1959	5.00	10.00	20.00
❏ 9360	To Belong/Waiting for You	1960	5.00	10.00	20.00
JUBILEE					
❏ 5551	Jealous Fool/The Greatest Love (Nothing Less, Nothing More)	1966	2.50	5.00	10.00
OKEH					
❏ 7145	Anytime You Want Me/My Guardian Angel	1962	3.00	6.00	12.00
❏ 7152	Don't Let It Happen/Queen Bee	1962	3.00	6.00	12.00
ROULETTE					
❏ 7010	I Can't Help Lovin' You/I Saw You	1968	2.00	4.00	8.00

7-Inch Extended Plays
RCA CAMDEN

Number	Title (A Side/B Side)	Yr	VG	VG+	NM
❏ CEP-447	(contents unknown)	1958	6.25	12.50	25.00
❏ CEP-447 [PS]	Rock 'n' Roll Music	1958	6.25	12.50	25.00

Albums
RCA CAMDEN

Number	Title (A Side/B Side)	Yr	VG	VG+	NM
❏ CAL-430 [M]	Rock 'N' Roll Hits	1958	10.00	20.00	40.00

BREEN, BOBBY
45s
CHIC

Number	Title (A Side/B Side)	Yr	VG	VG+	NM
❏ 1003	If the Night Could Tell You/Wait	1956	3.75	7.50	15.00
❏ 1013	We Will Make Love/Rainbow	1957	3.75	7.50	15.00
LYRIC					
❏ 105	It's a Sin/Valley of Romance	196?	5.00	10.00	20.00
MOTOWN					
❏ 1053	How Can We Tell Him/Better Late Than Never	1964	6.25	12.50	25.00

Number	Title (A Side/B Side)	Yr	VG	VG+	NM
❏ 1059	You're Just Like You/Here Comes That Heartache	1964	6.25	12.50	25.00
❏ 1059 [PS]	You're Just Like You/Here Comes That Heartache	1964	10.00	20.00	40.00
NRC					
❏ 055	Hawaii Calls/Theme from A Summer Place	1960	2.50	5.00	10.00

Albums
LONDON

Number	Title (A Side/B Side)	Yr	VG	VG+	NM
❏ LB 270 [10]	Songs at Yuletide	1953	12.50	25.00	50.00

BREMERS, BEVERLY
45s
BRUT

Number	Title (A Side/B Side)	Yr	VG	VG+	NM
❏ 513	I Just Need Some Music/Let It Play On	197?	—	3.00	6.00
❏ 513 [PS]	I Just Need Some Music/Let It Play On	197?	2.50	5.00	10.00
COLUMBIA					
❏ 10180	What I Did for Love/You're Precious to Me	1975	—	2.50	5.00
❏ 10451	The Prisoner/Flight 309 to Tennessee	1976	—	2.50	5.00
SCEPTER					
❏ 12315	Don't Say You Don't Remember/Get Smart Girl	1971	—	3.00	6.00
❏ 12332	When Michael Calls/Toy Girl	1971	—	2.50	5.00
❏ 12348	We're Free/Colors of Love	1972	—	2.50	5.00
❏ 12348 [PS]	We're Free/Colors of Love	1972	2.50	5.00	10.00
❏ 12363	I'll Make You Music/ I Made a Man Out of You, Jimmy	1972	—	2.50	5.00
❏ 12370	Heaven Help Us/All That's Left Is the Music	1973	—	2.50	5.00
❏ 12378	Run to Her/Baby I Don't Know You	1973	—	2.50	5.00
❏ 12380	Daddy's Coming Home/A Little Bit of Love	1973	—	2.50	5.00
❏ 12391	Sing a Happy Song/Get Smart Girl	1974	—	2.50	5.00
❏ 12399	One Day at a Time/Get Up in the Morning	1975	—	2.50	5.00

Albums
SCEPTER

Number	Title (A Side/B Side)	Yr	VG	VG+	NM
❏ SPS-5102	I'll Make You Music	1972	2.50	5.00	10.00

BRENDA AND THE TABULATIONS
12-Inch Singles
CHOCOLATE CITY

Number	Title (A Side/B Side)	Yr	VG	VG+	NM
❏ CCD 20006	(I'm a) Superstar (unknown versions)	1977	3.75	7.50	15.00

45s
CHOCOLATE CITY

Number	Title (A Side/B Side)	Yr	VG	VG+	NM
❏ 004	Home to Myself/Leave Me Alone	1976	—	2.00	4.00
❏ 009	(I'm a) Superstar/Take It or Leave It	1977	—	2.00	4.00
❏ 012	Let's Go All the Way (Down)/I Keep Coming Back for More	1977	—	2.00	4.00
DIONN					
❏ 500	Dry Your Eyes/The Wash	1967	2.50	5.00	10.00
❏ 501	Who's Lovin' You/Stay Together Young Lovers	1967	2.50	5.00	10.00
❏ 503	Just Once in a Lifetime/Hey Boy	1967	2.50	5.00	10.00
❏ 504	When You're Gone/Hey Boy	1967	2.50	5.00	10.00
❏ 507	To the One I Love/Baby You're So Right	1968	2.50	5.00	10.00
❏ 509	I Can't Get Over You/That's in the Past	1968	2.50	5.00	10.00
❏ 511	Reason to Live/Hey Boy	1968	2.50	5.00	10.00
❏ 512	That's the Price You Have to Pay/I Wish I Hadn't Done What I Did	1969	2.50	5.00	10.00
EPIC					
❏ 10898	Little Bit of Love/Let Me Be Happy	1972	—	3.00	6.00
❏ 10954	One Girl Too Late/The Magic of Your Love	1973	—	3.00	6.00
❏ 11000	Key to My Heart/Love Is Just a Carnival	1973	—	3.00	6.00
❏ 11059	I'm in Love/Walk On In	1973	—	3.00	6.00
❏ 50081	Let Me Be Happy/Little Bit of Love	1975	—	2.00	4.00
PHILCO-FORD					
❏ HP-40	Dry Your Eyes/When You're Gone	1969	5.00	10.00	20.00
—4-inch plastic "Hip Pocket Record" with color sleeve					
TOP & BOTTOM					
❏ 401	The Touch of You/Stop Sneaking Around	1969	2.00	4.00	8.00
❏ 403	And My Heart Sang (Tra La La)/Lies, Lies, Lies	1970	2.00	4.00	8.00
❏ 404	Don't Make Me Over/You've Changed	1970	2.00	4.00	8.00
❏ 406	A Child No One Wanted/'Scuse Us All	1970	2.00	4.00	8.00
❏ 407	Right on the Tip of My Tongue/Always and Forever	1971	2.00	4.00	8.00
❏ 408	A Part of You/Where There's a Will	1971	2.00	4.00	8.00
❏ 411	Why Didn't I Think of That/A Love You Can Depend On	1971	2.00	4.00	8.00

Albums
CHOCOLATE CITY

Number	Title (A Side/B Side)	Yr	VG	VG+	NM
❏ 2002	I Keep Coming Back for More	1977	2.50	5.00	10.00
DIONN					
❏ LPM-2000 [M]	Dry Your Eyes	1967	10.00	20.00	40.00
❏ LPS-2000 [S]	Dry Your Eyes	1967	12.50	25.00	50.00
TOP & BOTTOM					
❏ 100	Brenda and the Tabulations	1970	5.00	10.00	20.00

BRENNAN, WALTER
45s
DOT

Number	Title (A Side/B Side)	Yr	VG	VG+	NM
❏ 16066	Dutchman's Gold/Back to the Farm	1960	3.00	6.00	12.00
❏ 16066 [PS]	Dutchman's Gold/Back to the Farm	1960	5.00	10.00	20.00
❏ 16136	Space Mice/The Thievin' Stranger	1960	3.00	6.00	12.00
❏ 16136 [PS]	Space Mice/The Thievin' Stranger	1960	6.25	12.50	25.00
❏ 16348	Tribute to a Dog/Life Gets Tee-Jus Don't It	1962	3.00	6.00	12.00
EVEREST					
❏ 19365	Noah's Ark (Part 1)/Noah's Ark (Part 2)	1960	3.00	6.00	12.00
KAPP					
❏ 2126	Grandad/Man Needs to Know	1971	—	3.00	6.00
LIBERTY					
❏ 55436	Old Rivers/The Epic Ride of John B. Glenn	1962	3.00	6.00	12.00
❏ 55477	Houdini/The Old Kelly Place	1962	3.00	6.00	12.00
❏ 55477 [PS]	Houdini/The Old Kelly Place	1962	5.00	10.00	20.00
❏ 55508	Mama Sang a Song/Who Will Take Gramma	1962	3.00	6.00	12.00
❏ 55518	Henry Had A Merry Christmas/White Christmas	1962	3.00	6.00	12.00

Number	Title (A Side/B Side)	Yr	VG	VG+	NM
❏ 55518 [PS]	Henry Had A Merry Christmas/White Christmas	1962	5.00	10.00	20.00
❏ 55617	Keep a-Movin' Old Man/Waiting for a Train	1963	3.00	6.00	12.00
LONDON					
❏ 141	Yesterday, When I Was Young/Time	1970	—	3.00	6.00
RPC					
❏ 502	Knight in Bright Armor/The Soul of Big Jack Dunn	1961	3.00	6.00	12.00
UNITED ARTISTS					
❏ 0055	Old Rivers/Mama Sang a Song	1973	—	2.00	4.00
—Silver Spotlight Series issue					
Albums					
DOT					
❏ DLP-3309 [M]	Dutchman's Gold	1960	6.25	12.50	25.00
❏ DLP-25309 [S]	Dutchman's Gold	1960	7.50	15.00	30.00
EVEREST					
❏ SDBR-1103 [S]	World of Miracles	1960	7.50	15.00	30.00
❏ SDBR-1123 [S]	The President: A Musical Biography of Our Chief Executive	1960	7.50	15.00	30.00
❏ LPBR-5103 [M]	World of Miracles	1960	6.25	12.50	25.00
❏ LPBR-5123 [M]	The President: A Musical Biography of Our Chief Executive	1960	6.25	12.50	25.00
HAMILTON					
❏ HLP-159 [M]	Dutchman's Gold	1965	3.00	6.00	12.00
❏ HLP-12159 [S]	Dutchman's Gold	1965	3.00	6.00	12.00
LIBERTY					
❏ LRP-3233 [M]	Old Rivers	1962	5.00	10.00	20.00
❏ LRP-3241 [M]	The President: A Musical Biography of Our Chief Executive	1962	3.75	7.50	15.00
—Reissue of Everest 5123					
❏ LRP-3244 [M]	World of Miracles	1962	3.75	7.50	15.00
—Reissue of Everest 5103					
❏ LRP-3257 [M]	'Twas the Night Before Christmas Back Home	1962	5.00	10.00	20.00
❏ LRP-3266 [M]	Mama Sang a Song	1963	5.00	10.00	20.00
❏ LRP-3317 [M]	Talkin' from the Heart	1964	5.00	10.00	20.00
❏ LRP-3372 [M]	Gunfight at the O.K. Corral	1964	5.00	10.00	20.00
❏ LST-7233 [S]	Old Rivers	1962	6.25	12.50	25.00
❏ LST-7241 [S]	The President: A Musical Biography of Our Chief Executive	1962	5.00	10.00	20.00
—Reissue of Everest 1123					
❏ LST-7244 [S]	World of Miracles	1962	5.00	10.00	20.00
—Reissue of Everest 1103					
❏ LST-7257 [S]	'Twas the Night Before Christmas Back Home	1962	6.25	12.50	25.00
❏ LST-7266 [S]	Mama Sang a Song	1963	6.25	12.50	25.00
❏ LST-7317 [S]	Talkin' from the Heart	1964	6.25	12.50	25.00
❏ LST-7372 [S]	Gunfight at the O.K. Corral	1964	6.25	12.50	25.00
LONDON					
❏ PS 577	Yesterday, When I Was Young	1970	3.75	7.50	15.00
R.P.C.					
❏ 108 [M]	By the Fireside	1961	7.50	15.00	30.00
❏ 108S [S]	By the Fireside	1961	10.00	20.00	40.00
SUNSET					
❏ SUM-1100 [M]	Country Heart	1966	3.00	6.00	12.00
❏ SUS-5100 [S]	Country Heart	1966	3.00	6.00	12.00
❏ SUS-5269	God and Country	1970	2.50	5.00	10.00
UNITED ARTISTS					
❏ UA-LA438-E	The Very Best of Walter Brennan	1975	3.00	6.00	12.00

BRENSTON, JACKIE
45s
CHESS

Number	Title (A Side/B Side)	Yr	VG	VG+	NM
❏ 1458	Rocket "88"/Come Back Where You Belong	1951	5000.	7500.	10000.
—Early rockabilly classic; obscenely rare, even though the 45s were pressed later					
❏ 1469	In My Real Gone Rocket/Tuckered Out	1951	500.00	750.00	1000.
❏ 1472	Juiced/Independent Woman	1951	500.00	750.00	1000.
❏ 1496	Leo the Louse/Hi-Ho Baby	1952	125.00	250.00	500.00
❏ 1532	Blues Got Me Again/Starvation	1953	62.50	125.00	250.00
FEDERAL					
❏ 12283	What Can It Be?/Gonna Wait for My Chance	1956	12.50	25.00	50.00
❏ 12291	Much Later/The Mistreater	1957	12.50	25.00	50.00
SUE					
❏ 736	Trouble Up the Road/You Ain't the One	1961	5.00	10.00	20.00

BRENT, CAROLYN
45s
CONGRESS

Number	Title (A Side/B Side)	Yr	VG	VG+	NM
❏ 213	My Man (Mon Homme)/Rose of Washington Square	1964	2.00	4.00	8.00

BRENT, RONNIE
45s
COLT 45

Number	Title (A Side/B Side)	Yr	VG	VG+	NM
❏ 101	Crazy Feeling/Shirley Ann	1959	6.25	12.50	25.00
❏ 109	Cowboys and Indians/Flow Gently	1959	6.25	12.50	25.00
UNITED ARTISTS					
❏ 108	My Sweet Verlene/Love	1958	10.00	20.00	40.00

BRENT, TONY
45s
ROULETTE

Number	Title (A Side/B Side)	Yr	VG	VG+	NM
❏ 4113	Girl of My Dreams/Don't Play That Melody	1958	3.00	6.00	12.00

BREWER, TERESA
45s
ABC

Number	Title (A Side/B Side)	Yr	VG	VG+	NM
❏ 10909	Jimmy/Thoroughly Modern Millie	1967	—	2.50	5.00
AMSTERDAM					
❏ 85024	Day by Day/Somewhere There's Someone Who Loves You	1972	—	2.00	4.00
❏ 85025	A Simple Song/Singing a Doo-Dah Song	1973	—	2.00	4.00
❏ 85027	Music, Music, Music/School Days	1973	—	2.00	4.00
❏ 85028	Music to the Man/Another Useless Day	1973	—	2.00	4.00

Number	Title (A Side/B Side)	Yr	VG	VG+	NM
❏ 85029	Bo Weevil/Bei Mir Bist Du Schoen (Means That You're Grand)	1974	—	2.00	4.00
CORAL					
❏ 60591	Sing, Sing, Sing/I Don't Care	1952	3.00	6.00	12.00
❏ 60645	Lovin' Machine/Noodlin' Bay	1952	3.00	6.00	12.00
❏ 60676	Gonna Get Along Without You Now/Roll Them Roly-Poly Eyes	1952	3.00	6.00	12.00
❏ 60755	I Hear the Bluebells/Kisses on Paper	1952	3.00	6.00	12.00
❏ 60775	Rhode Island Red/En-Thuz-E-Uz-E-As-M	1952	3.00	6.00	12.00
—With Eileen Barton					
❏ 60873	Till I Waltz Again with You/Hello Bluebird	1952	3.00	6.00	12.00
❏ 60953	Breakin' the Blues/Dancing with Someone	1953	3.00	6.00	12.00
❏ 60994	Too Much Mustard/Into Each Life Some Rain Must Fall	1953	3.00	6.00	12.00
❏ 61043	Ricochet (Rick O'Shay)/Too Young to Tango	1953	3.00	6.00	12.00
❏ 61066	Bell Bottom Blues/Our Heartbreaking Waltz	1953	3.00	6.00	12.00
❏ 61067	I Guess It Was You All the Time/ Baby, Baby, Baby	1953	3.00	6.00	12.00
❏ 61078	I Saw Mommy Kissing Santa Claus/ Ebenezer Scrooge	1953	3.00	6.00	12.00
❏ 61079	I Just Can't Wait Till Christmas/ Too Fat for the Chimney	1953	3.00	6.00	12.00
❏ 61152	Jilted/Le Grand Tour de L'Amour	1954	3.00	6.00	12.00
❏ 61197	Skinnie Minnie (Fish Tart)/ I Had Someone Else Before I Had You	1954	3.00	6.00	12.00
❏ 61225	Au Revoir/Danger Signs	1954	3.00	6.00	12.00
❏ 61286	Time/My Sweetie Went Away	1954	3.00	6.00	12.00
❏ 61315	Let Me Go, Lover/The Moon Is On Fire	1954	3.00	6.00	12.00
❏ 61339	I Gotta Go Get My Baby/ What More Is There to Say	1955		6.00	12.00
❏ 61362	How Important Can It Be?/Pledging My Love	1955	3.00	6.00	12.00
❏ 61366	Tweedle Dee/Rock Love	1955	3.00	6.00	12.00
❏ 61394	Silver Dollar/I Don't Want to Be Lonely Tonight	1955	3.00	6.00	12.00
❏ 61448	The Banjo's Back in Town/ How to Be Very, Very Popular	1955	3.00	6.00	12.00
❏ 61500	Baby Be My Toy/So Doggone Lonely	1955	3.00	6.00	12.00
❏ 61528	Shoot It Again/You're Telling Our Secrets	1955	3.00	6.00	12.00
❏ 61548	A Good Man Is Hard to Find/It's Siesta Time	1956	2.50	5.00	10.00
❏ 61590	A Tear Fell/Bo Weevil	1956	2.50	5.00	10.00
❏ 61636	A Sweet Old Fashioned Girl/Goodbye John	1956	2.50	5.00	10.00
❏ 61700	I Love Mickey/Keep Your Cotton Pickin' Hands Off My Baby	1956	6.25	12.50	25.00
❏ 61700 [PS]	I Love Mickey/Keep Your Cotton Pickin' Hands Off My Baby	1956	12.50	25.00	50.00
❏ 61737	Mutual Admiration Society/Crazy with Love	1956	2.50	5.00	10.00
❏ 61776	How Lonely Can One Be/I'm Drowning My Sorrows	1957	2.50	5.00	10.00
❏ 61805	Empty Arms/The Ricky Tick Song	1957	2.50	5.00	10.00
❏ 61850	Lula Rock-a Hula/Teardrops in My Heart	1957	2.50	5.00	10.00
❏ 61878	It's the Same Old Jazz/Born to Love	1957	2.50	5.00	10.00
❏ 61898	You Send Me/Would I Were	1957	2.50	5.00	10.00
❏ 61912	Listen My Children/Hush-a-Bye, Wink-a-Bye	1957	2.50	5.00	10.00
❏ 61944	Lost a Little Puppy/Because Him Is a Baby	1958	2.50	5.00	10.00
❏ 61944 [PS]	Lost a Little Puppy/Because Him Is a Baby	1958	3.75	7.50	15.00
❏ 61948	There's Nothing As Lonesome As Saturday Night/Whirlpool	1958	2.50	5.00	10.00
❏ 61983	Saturday Dance/I Think the World of You	1958	2.50	5.00	10.00
❏ 62013	Pickle Up a Doodle/The Rain Falls on Everybody	1958	2.50	5.00	10.00
❏ 62033	The Hula Hoop Song/So Shy	1958	2.50	5.00	10.00
❏ 62057	The One Rose (That's Left in My Heart)/Satellite	1958	2.50	5.00	10.00
❏ 62058	Jingle Bell Rock/I Like Christmas	1958	2.50	5.00	10.00
❏ 62084	Heavenly Lover/Fair Weather Sweetheart	1959	2.50	5.00	10.00
❏ 62126	Bye Bye Baby Goodbye/Chain of Friendship	1959	2.50	5.00	10.00
❏ 62150	Mexicali Rose/If You Like-A Me	1959	2.50	5.00	10.00
❏ 62167	Peace of Mind/Venetian Sunset	1960	2.00	4.00	8.00
❏ 62167 [PS]	Peace of Mind/Venetian Sunset	1960	2.50	5.00	10.00
❏ 62197	If There Are Stars in My Eyes/ How Do You Know It's Love	1960	2.00	4.00	8.00
❏ 62197 [PS]	If There Are Stars in My Eyes/ How Do You Know It's Love	1960	3.00	6.00	12.00
❏ 62219	Anymore/That Piano Man	1960	2.00	4.00	8.00
❏ 62219 [PS]	Anymore/That Piano Man	1960	2.50	5.00	10.00
❏ 62236	Have You Ever Been Lonely (Have You Ever Been Blue)/When Do You Love Me	1960	2.00	4.00	8.00
❏ 62253	Whippoorwill/Older and Wiser	1961	2.00	4.00	8.00
❏ 62265	Milord/I've Got My Fingers Crossed	1961	2.00	4.00	8.00
❏ 62278	Sea Shell/Little Miss Belong to No One	1961	2.00	4.00	8.00
❏ 62299	Step Right Up/Pretty Lookin' Boy	1961	2.00	4.00	8.00
❏ 62306	Another/I Want You to Worry	1962	2.00	4.00	8.00
❏ 62316	You Came a Long Way from St. Louis/ One Heart Less to Break	1962	2.00	4.00	8.00
❏ 62428	Cry Baby/I Hear the Angels Singing	1964	—	3.00	6.00
❏ 69039	Too Fat For The Chimney/ I Just Can't Wait Till Christmas	1953	3.75	7.50	15.00
—Maroon label with silver print					
DOCTOR JAZZ					
❏ WS4-03835	Classic Medley #1/Jimmy Dorsey Medley	1983	—	2.00	4.00
❏ WS4-04114	No Way Conway/Sittin' Here Cryin'	1983	—	2.00	4.00
LONDON					
❏ 1083	Oceana Roll/Wang Wang Blues	1951	3.75	7.50	15.00
❏ 1085	If You Don't Marry Me/I Wish I Wuz	1951	3.75	7.50	15.00
❏ 1086	Longing for You/Jazz Me Blues	1951	3.75	7.50	15.00
❏ 30023	Music! Music! Music! (Put Another Nickel In)/Copenhagen	1950	3.75	7.50	15.00
❏ 30100	Choo'n Gum/(B-side unknown)	1950	3.75	7.50	15.00
PHILIPS					
❏ 40077	The Ballad of Lover's Hill/Not Like a Sister	1962	2.00	4.00	8.00
❏ 40095	She'll Never Love You/The Thrill Is Gone	1963	2.00	4.00	8.00
❏ 40120	Second Hand Love/Stand-In	1963	2.00	4.00	8.00
❏ 40135	He Understands Me/ Just Before We Say Goodbye	1963	2.00	4.00	8.00
❏ 40177	Come On In/Simple Things	1964	—	3.00	6.00
❏ 40227	Dang Me (Dern You)/Mama Never Told Me	1964	—	3.00	6.00
❏ 40253	Goldfinger/Make Room for One More Fool	1965	—	3.00	6.00

B

Number	Title (A Side/B Side)	Yr	VG	VG+	NM
❏ 40282	Supercalifragilisticexpialidocious/ I've Grown Accustomed to His Face	1965	—	3.00	6.00
❏ 40310	Say Something Sweet to Your Sweetheart/ What About Time	1965	—	3.00	6.00
❏ 40345	Little Bitty Grain of Sand/Little Buddy	1965	—	3.00	6.00
❏ 40367	Handle with Care/I Can't Remember Ever Loving You	1966	—	3.00	6.00
❏ 40389	Evil on Your Mind/Ain't Had No Lovin'	1966	—	3.00	6.00
PROJECT 3					
❏ #100	Come Follow the Band/(B-side unknown)	1982	—	2.00	4.00
SIGNATURE					
❏ 101	A Natural Feelin' for You/Some Songs	197?	—	2.50	5.00
❏ 101 [PS]	A Natural Feelin' for You/Some Songs	197?	—	2.50	5.00
❏ WS4-04654	The Pilgrim (Chapter #33)/School Days	1984	—	2.00	4.00
❏ PB-10100	Am I Asking Too Much of You/Willie Burgundy	1974	—	2.00	4.00
❏ PB-10173	Unliberated Woman/(B-side unknown)	1975	—	2.00	4.00
❏ PB-10609	Music, Music, Music/Where Did the Good Times Go	1976	—	2.00	4.00
SSS INTERNATIONAL					
❏ 735	Live a Little/Step to the Rear	1968	—	2.50	5.00
❏ 744	Ride-A-Roo/A Woman's World	1968	—	2.50	5.00
TERESA BREWER					
❏ TB-1 [DJ]	Take a Message to Jesus (same on both sides)	198?	—	2.00	4.00

7-Inch Extended Plays

CORAL

Number	Title (A Side/B Side)	Yr	VG	VG+	NM
❏ EC 81008	Sing, Sing, Sing/I Don't Care//Gonna Get Along Without Ya Now/Roll Them Roly Boly Eyes	195?	3.00	6.00	12.00
❏ EC 81008 [PS]	Sing, Sing, Sing	195?	3.00	6.00	12.00
❏ EC 81034	(contents unknown)	195?	3.00	6.00	12.00
❏ EC 81034 [PS]	'Til I Waltz Again with You	195?	3.00	6.00	12.00
❏ EC 81072	(contents unknown)	195?	3.00	6.00	12.00
❏ EC 81072 [PS]	Teresa Brewer	195?	3.00	6.00	12.00
❏ EC 81085	(contents unknown)	195?	3.00	6.00	12.00
❏ EC 81085 [PS]	A Bouquet of Hits from Teresa Brewer, Part 1	195?	3.00	6.00	12.00
❏ EC 81086	Chicago Style/My Sweetie Went Away//Baby, Baby, Baby/Jilted	195?	3.00	6.00	12.00
❏ EC 81086 [PS]	A Bouquet of Hits from Teresa Brewer, Part 2	195?	3.00	6.00	12.00
❏ EC 81108	Ricochet (Rick-O-Shay)/Too Young to Tango// Bell Bottom Blues/Our Heartbreaking Waltz	195?	3.00	6.00	12.00
❏ EC 81108 [PS]	Teresa Brewer Favorites	195?	3.00	6.00	12.00
❏ EC 81115	How Important Can It Be?/Rock Love//Pledging My Love/Tweedlee Dee	1955	3.00	6.00	12.00
❏ EC 81115 [PS]	Especially for You...	1955	3.00	6.00	12.00
❏ EC 81162	(contents unknown)	195?	3.00	6.00	12.00
❏ EC 81162 [PS]	Miss Music	195?	3.00	6.00	12.00
❏ EC 81175	(contents unknown)	1959	3.00	6.00	12.00
❏ EC 81175 [PS]	When Your Lover Has Gone	1959	3.00	6.00	12.00
❏ EC 81176 [M]	The Dixieland Band/When the Saints Go Marching In//Bill Bailey, Won't You Please Come Home/Basin Street Blues	1959	3.00	6.00	12.00
❏ EC 81176 [PS]	Teresa Brewer and the Dixieland Band	1959	3.00	6.00	12.00
❏ EC 7-81176 [S]	The Dixieland Band/When the Saints Go Marching In//Bill Bailey, Won't You Please Come Home/Basin Street Blues	1959	5.00	10.00	20.00
❏ EC7-81176 [PS]	Teresa Brewer and the Dixieland Band	1959	5.00	10.00	20.00
❏ EC 81178	(contents unknown)	195?	3.00	6.00	12.00
❏ EC 81178 [PS]	Kiss Me	195?	3.00	6.00	12.00
❏ EC 81510	Empty Arms/A Tear Fell//Ricochet/Till I Waltz Again with You	195?	3.00	6.00	12.00
❏ EC 81510 [PS]	Teresa Brewer (Silver Star Series)	195?	3.00	6.00	12.00
❏ EC 82023 [PS]	Music, Music, Music	195?	3.00	6.00	12.00

—Cover for 2-EP set (83052 and 83053)

Number	Title (A Side/B Side)	Yr	VG	VG+	NM
❏ 83052	(Put Another Nickel In) Music! Music! Music!/At Sundown//My Buddy/Sundown	195?	3.00	6.00	12.00

—"Side 1" and "Side 2" of 2-EP set EC 82023

Number	Title (A Side/B Side)	Yr	VG	VG+	NM
❏ 83053	Where the Black-Eyed Susans Grow/When I Leave the World Behind//Darkness on the Delta/A Good Man Is Hard to Find	195?	3.00	6.00	12.00

—"Side 3" and "Side 4" of 2-EP set EC 82023

LONDON

Number	Title (A Side/B Side)	Yr	VG	VG+	NM
❏ BEP 6039	Music, Music, Music/Copenhagen//Honky Tonkin'/Ol' Man Mose	1952	5.00	10.00	20.00
❏ BEP 6039 [PS]	Teresa Brewer	1952	5.00	10.00	20.00
❏ BEP 6041	*The Jazz Me Blues/Longing for You/I Wish I Wuz/If You Don't Marry Me	1952	5.00	10.00	20.00
❏ BEP 6041 [PS]	Teresa Brewer, Vol. 2	1952	5.00	10.00	20.00
PHILIPS					
❏ PHS 811-C	Ain't Had No Living/Once a Day/Another//Make the World Go Away/Anymore/Baby	196?	5.00	10.00	15.00
❏ PHS 811-C	Ain't Had No Living/Once a Day/Another//Make the World Go Away/Anymore/Baby	196?	5.00	10.00	15.00

—Jukebox issue; small hole, plays at 33 1/3 rpm

Number	Title (A Side/B Side)	Yr	VG	VG+	NM
❏ PHS 811-C [PS]	Gold Country	196?	5.00	10.00	15.00
RCA					
❏ ZE-11882	Jingle Bells/Santa Claus Is Comin' to Town-The Christmas Song//Deck The Halls/Away in a Manger	1979	2.50	5.00	10.00

—Name of EP is "Merry Christmas From Teresa Brewer"; picture label, no PS

Albums

AMSTERDAM

Number	Title (A Side/B Side)	Yr	VG	VG+	NM
❏ 12012	The Doo Dah Song	1973	2.50	5.00	10.00
❏ 12013	Music, Music, Music	1973	2.50	5.00	10.00
❏ 12015	Teresa Brewer In London	1974	2.50	5.00	10.00
COLUMBIA					
❏ FC 37363	A Sophisticated Lady	1981	2.50	5.00	10.00
❏ PC 37363	A Sophisticated Lady	198?	2.00	4.00	8.00

—Budget-line reissue

CORAL

Number	Title (A Side/B Side)	Yr	VG	VG+	NM
❏ CXB 7 [(2)M]	The Best of Teresa Brewer	1965	5.00	10.00	20.00
❏ CXSB 7 [(2)P]	The Best of Teresa Brewer	1965	5.00	10.00	20.00
❏ CRL 56072 [10]	A Bouquet of Hits	1952	10.00	20.00	40.00

Number	Title (A Side/B Side)	Yr	VG	VG+	NM
❏ CRL 56093 [10]	Till I Waltz Again with You	1953	10.00	20.00	40.00
❏ CRL 57027 [M]	Music, Music, Music	1955	7.50	15.00	30.00
❏ CRL 57053 [M]	Teresa	1956	7.50	15.00	30.00
❏ CRL 57135 [M]	For Teenagers in Love	1957	7.50	15.00	30.00
❏ CRL 57144 [M]	Teresa Brewer At Christmas Time	1957	7.50	15.00	30.00
❏ CRL 57179 [M]	Miss Music	1958	7.50	15.00	30.00
❏ CRL 57232 [M]	Time for Teresa	1958	7.50	15.00	30.00
❏ CRL 57245 [M]	Teresa Brewer and the Dixieland Band	1958	5.00	10.00	20.00
❏ 57297 [M]	Heavenly Lover	1959	5.00	10.00	20.00
❏ CRL 57297 [M]	When Your Lover Has Gone	1958	5.00	10.00	20.00
❏ CRL 57315 [M]	Ridin' High	1960	5.00	10.00	20.00
❏ CRL 57329 [M]	Naughty, Naughty, Naughty	1960	5.00	10.00	20.00
❏ CRL 57351 [M]	My Golden Favorites	1960	5.00	10.00	20.00
❏ CRL 57361 [M]	Songs Everybody Knows	1961	5.00	10.00	20.00
❏ CRL 57374 [M]	Aloha from Teresa	1961	5.00	10.00	20.00
❏ CRL 57414 [M]	Don't Mess with Tess	1962	5.00	10.00	20.00
❏ CRL 757245 [S]	Teresa Brewer and the Dixieland Band	1958	7.50	15.00	30.00
❏ CRL 757297 [S]	When Your Lover Has Gone	1959	7.50	15.00	30.00
❏ CRL 757315 [S]	Ridin' High	1960	6.25	12.50	25.00
❏ CRL 757329 [S]	Naughty, Naughty, Naughty	1960	6.25	12.50	25.00
❏ CRL 757351 [R]	My Golden Favorites	1960	5.00	10.00	20.00
❏ CRL 757361 [S]	Songs Everybody Knows	1961	6.25	12.50	25.00
❏ CRL 757374 [S]	Aloha from Teresa	1961	6.25	12.50	25.00
❏ CRL 757414 [S]	Don't Mess with Tess	1962	6.25	12.50	25.00
DOCTOR JAZZ					
❏ ASLP 804	Good News	198?	2.50	5.00	10.00
❏ FW 38534	I Dig Big Band Singers	1983	2.50	5.00	10.00
❏ W2X 39521 [(2)]	Live at Carnegie Hall and Montreux, Switzerland	1984	3.00	6.00	12.00
❏ FW 40232	Midnight Café	1986	2.50	5.00	10.00
❏ FW 40951	Good News	198?	2.00	4.00	8.00
FLYING DUTCHMAN					
❏ BSL1-0577	Good News	1974	3.00	6.00	12.00
LONDON					
❏ APB-1006 [10]	Teresa Brewer	1951	12.50	25.00	50.00
PHILIPS					
❏ PHM 200062 [M]	Teresa Brewer's Greatest Hits	1962	3.75	7.50	15.00
❏ PHM 200099 [M]	Terrific Teresa	1963	3.75	7.50	15.00
❏ PHM 200119 [M]	Moments to Remember	1964	3.00	6.00	12.00
❏ PHM 200147 [M]	Golden Hits of 1964	1964	3.00	6.00	12.00
❏ PHM 200163 [M]	Dear Heart/Goldfinger	1965	3.00	6.00	12.00
❏ PHM 200200 [M]	Songs for Our Fighting Men	1966	3.00	6.00	12.00
❏ PHM 200216 [M]	Gold Country	1966	3.00	6.00	12.00
❏ PHM 200230 [M]	Texas Leather and Mexican Lace	1967	3.75	7.50	15.00
❏ PHS 600062 [S]	Teresa Brewer's Greatest Hits	1962	5.00	10.00	20.00
❏ PHS 600099 [S]	Terrific Teresa	1963	5.00	10.00	20.00
❏ PHS 600119 [S]	Moments to Remember	1964	3.75	7.50	15.00
❏ PHS 600147 [S]	Golden Hits of 1964	1964	3.75	7.50	15.00
❏ PHS 600163 [S]	Dear Heart/Goldfinger	1965	3.75	7.50	15.00
❏ PHS 600200 [S]	Songs for Our Fighting Men	1966	3.75	7.50	15.00
❏ PHS 600216 [S]	Gold Country	1966	3.75	7.50	15.00
❏ PHS 600230 [S]	Texas Leather and Mexican Lace	1967	3.00	6.00	12.00
PROJECT 3					
❏ 5108	Come Follow the Band	1982	2.50	5.00	10.00
RCA VICTOR					
❏ ANL1-1131	The Best of Teresa Brewer	1975	2.50	5.00	10.00
SIGNATURE					
❏ FW 39421	Teresa Brewer In London	1984	2.00	4.00	8.00

—Reissue of Amsterdam 12015

Number	Title (A Side/B Side)	Yr	VG	VG+	NM
❏ PW 40113	Teresa Brewer At Christmas Time	1985	2.50	5.00	10.00

—Reissue of Coral 57144

VOCALION

Number	Title (A Side/B Side)	Yr	VG	VG+	NM
❏ VL 3693 [M]	Teresa Brewer	1966	3.00	6.00	12.00
❏ VL 73847 [R]	Here's Teresa Brewer	1969	2.50	5.00	10.00

BREWER, TERESA, AND SVEND ASMUSSEN

Albums

DOCTOR JAZZ

Number	Title (A Side/B Side)	Yr	VG	VG+	NM
❏ FW 40233	On the Good Ship Lollipop	1987	2.50	5.00	10.00

BREWER, TERESA, AND COUNT BASIE

Albums

DOCTOR JAZZ

Number	Title (A Side/B Side)	Yr	VG	VG+	NM
❏ FW 38836	Songs of Bessie Smith	1984	2.00	4.00	8.00
FLYING DUTCHMAN					
❏ FD 10161	Songs of Bessie Smith	1973	3.00	6.00	12.00

BREWER, TERESA, AND DON CORNELL Also see each artist's individual listings.

45s

CORAL

Number	Title (A Side/B Side)	Yr	VG	VG+	NM
❏ 60829	You'll Never Get Away/The Hookey Song	1952	3.00	6.00	12.00
❏ 61027	The Glad Song/What Happened to the Music	1953	3.00	6.00	12.00

7-Inch Extended Plays

CORAL

Number	Title (A Side/B Side)	Yr	VG	VG+	NM
❏ EC 81073	(contents unknown)	195?	3.00	6.00	12.00
❏ EC 81073 [PS]	Don Cornell and Teresa Brewer	195?	3.00	6.00	12.00

BREWER, TERESA, AND MERCER ELLINGTON

Albums

DOCTOR JAZZ

Number	Title (A Side/B Side)	Yr	VG	VG+	NM
❏ FW 40031	The Cotton Connection	1985	2.50	5.00	10.00

BREWER, TERESA, AND STEPHANE GRAPPELLI

Albums

DOCTOR JAZZ

Number	Title (A Side/B Side)	Yr	VG	VG+	NM
❏ FW 38448	On the Road Again	198?	2.50	5.00	10.00

BREWER AND SHIPLEY

45s

A&M

Number	Title (A Side/B Side)	Yr	VG	VG+	NM
❏ 905	The Keeper of the Keys/I Can't See Her	1968	2.00	4.00	8.00

—Artist reads "Michael Brewer and Tom Shipley"

Number	Title (A Side/B Side)	Yr	VG	VG+	NM
❏ 938	Green Bamboo/Truly Right	1968	2.00	4.00	8.00

—Artist reads "Michael Brewer and Tom Shipley"

Number	Title (A Side/B Side)	Yr	VG	VG+	NM
❏ 996	Dreamin' in the Shade/Tame and Changes	1968	2.00	4.00	8.00

Number	Title (A Side/B Side)	Yr	VG	VG+	NM
BUDDAH					
❏ 154	Rise Up Easy Rider/Boomerang	1970	—	2.00	4.00
CAPITOL					
❏ 3933	Fair Play/How Are You	1974	—	2.00	4.00
❏ 4105	Brain Damage/Rock and Roll Hostage	1975	—	2.00	4.00
KAMA SUTRA					
❏ 512	People Love Each Other/Witchi-Tai-To	1970	—	2.00	4.00
❏ 516	One Toke Over the Line/Oh Mommy	1970	—	2.50	5.00
❏ 524	Tarkio Road/Seems Like a Long Time	1971	—	2.00	4.00
❏ 539	Shake Off the Demon/Indian Summer	1972	—	2.00	4.00
❏ 547	Natural Child/Yankee Lady	1972	—	2.00	4.00
❏ 567	Black Sky/Fly, Fly Fly	1972	—	2.00	4.00
Albums					
A&M					
❏ SP-4154	Down in L.A.	1968	3.75	7.50	15.00
CAPITOL					
❏ ST-11261	ST-11261	1974	2.50	5.00	10.00
❏ ST-11402	Welcome to Riddle Bridge	1975	2.50	5.00	10.00
KAMA SUTRA					
❏ KSBS-2016	Weeds	1969	3.00	6.00	12.00
❏ KSBS-2024	Tarkio	1970	3.00	6.00	12.00
—LP label calls this "Tarkio Road"					
❏ KSBS-2039	Shake Off the Demon	1971	3.00	6.00	12.00
❏ KSBS-2058	Rural Space	1972	3.00	6.00	12.00
❏ KSBS 2613-2 [(2)]	The Best... Brewer & Shipley	1976	3.75	7.50	15.00
BRIAN, NEIL					
45s					
JAMIE					
❏ 1216	Lucky Coin/A Fool Was I	1962	5.00	10.00	20.00
PARKWAY					
❏ 886	My Haunted Heart/Three Rows Over	1963	5.00	10.00	20.00
❏ 895	I Made Her Forget/Lilac and Spanish Moss	1964	5.00	10.00	20.00
20TH CENTURY FOX					
❏ 6686	Running Scared/Barefoot Girl	1967	3.00	6.00	12.00
BRIDGE, THE See THE BROOKLYN BRIDGE.					
BRIGADE, THE					
Albums					
BAND'N VOCAL					
❏ 1066	Last Laugh	1970	1000.	1500.	2000.
BRIGADIERS, THE					
45s					
MALA					
❏ 441	The Cry of the Wild Goose/Dixie Brigade	1961	5.00	10.00	20.00
BRIGANDS, THE					
45s					
EPIC					
❏ 10011	(Would I Still Be) Her Big Man/I'm a Patient Man	1966	5.00	10.00	20.00
BRIGG					
Albums					
SUSQUEHANNA					
❏ LP-301	Brigg	1973	45.00	90.00	180.00
BRIGGS, LILLIAN					
45s					
ABC-PARAMOUNT					
❏ 10253	I Want You to Be My Baby/I'm Burning for You	1961	2.50	5.00	10.00
CORAL					
❏ 62108	Rag Mop/Smile for the People	1959	2.50	5.00	10.00
❏ 62136	Blues in the Night/Is There a Man in the House	1959	2.50	5.00	10.00
❏ 62156	Hooray for the Rock/Diddy Boppers	1959	2.50	5.00	10.00
❏ 62193	Be Mine/Not a Soul	1960	2.50	5.00	10.00
❏ 62223	I Care for You/That's What It's Like to Be Lonesome	1960	2.50	5.00	10.00
EPIC					
❏ 9115	I Want You to Be My Baby/Don't Stay Away Too Long	1955	7.50	15.00	30.00
❏ 9120	Give Me a Band and My Baby/It Could've Been Me	1955	7.50	15.00	30.00
❏ 9138	Rock and Roll-y Poly Santa Claus/Can't Stop	1955	7.50	15.00	30.00
❏ 9141	Follow the Leader/That's the Only Way to Live	1956	5.00	10.00	20.00
❏ 9151	Eddie, My Love/Teens in Jeans from New Orleans	1956	5.00	10.00	20.00
❏ 9166	The Gypsy Goofed/Too Close for Comfort	1956	5.00	10.00	20.00
❏ 9190	I'll Be Gone/Mean Words	1956	5.00	10.00	20.00
❏ 9214	Sugar Blues/Boogie Blues	1957	3.75	7.50	15.00
❏ 9249	She Sells Sea Shells/I	1957	3.75	7.50	15.00
SUNBEAM					
❏ 104	Come Home/Till We Meet Again	1958	3.00	6.00	12.00
❏ 114	Hey Ba Ba Re Bop/I've Got Your Heart	1958	3.00	6.00	12.00
7-Inch Extended Plays					
EPIC					
❏ B-7163	(contents unknown)	1956	10.00	20.00	40.00
❏ B-7163 [PS]	High Priestess of Rock 'n' Roll	1956	10.00	20.00	40.00
BRIGHTER SIDE OF DARKNESS					
45s					
MAGIC TOUCH					
❏ 9011	He Made You Mine/Disco Ball	197?	—	3.00	6.00
STAR-VUE					
❏ 1028	Oh Baby/Because I Love You	197?	7.50	15.00	30.00
20TH CENTURY					
❏ 2002	Love Jones/I'm the Guy	1972	2.00	4.00	8.00
❏ 2021	Just a Little Bit/Something to Remember You By	1973	3.75	7.50	15.00
❏ 2034	I Owe You Love/Summer Ride	1973	2.50	5.00	10.00
Albums					
20TH CENTURY					
❏ T-405	Love Jones	1973	7.50	15.00	30.00

Number	Title (A Side/B Side)	Yr	VG	VG+	NM
BRIGHTONES, THE					
45s					
WARNER BROS.					
❏ 5472	Swim, Swim, Swim/Rumors	1964	5.00	10.00	20.00
BRIGMAN, GEORGE					
Albums					
SOLID					
❏ SR-001	Jungle Rot	1975	30.00	60.00	120.00
BRIKS, THE					
45s					
BISMARK					
❏ 1013	Foolish Baby/Can You See Me	1966	50.00	100.00	200.00
DOT					
❏ 16876	Foolish Baby/Can You See Me	1966	6.25	12.50	25.00
BRIMSTONE					
Albums					
BRIMSTONE					
❏ (no #)	Paper Winged Dreams	1968	50.00	100.00	200.00
BRIMSTONES, THE					
45s					
MGM					
❏ 13653	It's All Over But the Crying/What Is This Life	1966	5.00	10.00	20.00
WORLD PACIFIC					
❏ 77834	Cold Hearted Woman/I'm in Misery	1966	7.50	15.00	30.00
BRINSLEY SCHWARZ Featuring Nick Lowe and Ian Gomm.					
45s					
CAPITOL					
❏ 3004	Rock and Roll Women/Hymn to Be	1970	2.00	4.00	8.00
UNITED ARTISTS					
❏ 50915	Nightingale/Silver Pistol	1972	—	3.00	6.00
❏ 50976	Nervous on the Road/Happy Doing What We're Doing	1972	—	3.00	6.00
Albums					
CAPITOL					
❏ ST-589	Brinsley Schwarz	1970	5.00	10.00	20.00
❏ ST-744	Despite It All	1971	5.00	10.00	20.00
❏ SWBC-11869 [(2)]	Brinsley Schwarz	1978	3.75	7.50	15.00
LIBERTY					
❏ LN 10145	Silver Pistol	1980	2.50	5.00	10.00
—10-track reissue					
❏ LN 10146	Nervous on the Road	1981	2.50	5.00	10.00
—10-track reissue					
UNITED ARTISTS					
❏ UAS-5566	Silver Pistol	1972	3.75	7.50	15.00
❏ UAS-5647	Nervous on the Road	1972	3.75	7.50	15.00
BRISTOL, JOHNNY Also see JOHNNY AND JACKEY.					
45s					
ATLANTIC					
❏ 3360	Do It to My Mind/Love to Take a Chance to Taste the Wine	1976	—	2.00	4.00
❏ 3391	You Turned Me On to Love/I Sho Like Groovin' with You	1977	—	2.00	4.00
❏ 3421	Waiting on Love/She's So Amazing	1977	—	2.00	4.00
❏ 3501	When He Comes (You Will Know)/Strangers in the Dark Corners	1978	—	2.00	4.00
❏ 3526	Why Stop Now/When He Comes (You Will Know)	1978	—	2.00	4.00
HANDSHAKE					
❏ 02594	Take Me Down/Loving and Free	1981	—	2.00	4.00
❏ 5300	My Guy/My Girl//Now	1980	—	2.00	4.00
—A-side with Amii Stewart					
❏ 5304	Love No Longer Has a Hold on Me/Until I See You Again	1981	—	2.00	4.00
MGM					
❏ 14715	Hang On In There Baby/Take Care of You for Me	1974	—	2.50	5.00
❏ 14762	You and I/It Don't Hurt No More	1974	—	2.50	5.00
❏ 14792	Leave My World/All Goodbyes Aren't Good	1975	—	2.50	5.00
❏ 14814	Love Takes Tears/Go On and Dream	1975	—	2.50	5.00
POLYDOR					
❏ 813982-7	Hang On In There Baby/Stand By Me	1983	—	—	3.00
—Reissue					
Albums					
ATLANTIC					
❏ SD 18197	Bristol's Creme	1976	2.50	5.00	10.00
❏ SD 19184	Strangers	1978	2.50	5.00	10.00
HANDSHAKE					
❏ FW 37666	Free to Be Me	1981	2.50	5.00	10.00
MGM					
❏ M3G-4959	Hang On In There Baby	1974	3.00	6.00	12.00
❏ M3G-4983	Feeling the Magic	1975	3.00	6.00	12.00
BRITISH CASUALS, THE See THE CASUALS (3).					
BROADWAY SINGERS, THE					
45s					
HIT					
❏ 214	I'll Never Find Another You/Come Back to Me	1965	2.00	4.00	8.00
—B-side by William Randolph					
BROGUES, THE Two members became part of QUICKSILVER MESSENGER SERVICE.					
45s					
CHALLENGE					
❏ 59311	But Now I'm Fine/Someday	1965	7.50	15.00	30.00
❏ 59316	I Ain't No Miracle Worker/Don't Shoot Me Down	1965	7.50	15.00	30.00
TWILIGHT					
❏ 408	But Now I'm Fine/Early Bird	1965	10.00	20.00	40.00
❏ 408	But Now I'm Fine/Someday	1965	10.00	20.00	40.00

Number	Title (A Side/B Side)	Yr	VG	VG+	NM

BROMBERG, DAVID
45s
COLUMBIA

Number	Title (A Side/B Side)	Yr	VG	VG+	NM
❏ 45612	The Holdup/Suffer to Sing the Blues	1972	—	3.00	6.00
❏ 45767	Sharon/Hardworkin' John	1973	2.00	4.00	8.00

FANTASY

❏ 785	Such a Night/Bluebirds	1977	—	2.00	4.00
❏ 812	Battle of Bull Run Medley/I Want to Go Home	1978	—	2.00	4.00
❏ 854	Don't Let Your Deal Go Down/My Own House	1979	—	2.00	4.00

Albums
COLUMBIA

❏ C 31104	David Bromberg	1972	3.00	6.00	12.00
❏ PC 31104	David Bromberg	198?	2.00	4.00	8.00
—Budget-line reissue					
❏ KC 31753	Demon in Disguise	1973	3.00	6.00	12.00
❏ PC 31753	Demon in Disguise	198?	2.00	4.00	8.00
—Budget-line reissue					
❏ KC 32717	Wanted Dead or Alive	1974	3.00	6.00	12.00
❏ PC 33397	Midnight on the Water	1975	3.00	6.00	12.00
—Original with no bar code					
❏ PC 33397	Midnight on the Water	198?	2.00	4.00	8.00
—Budget-line reissue with bar code					
❏ PC 34467	The Best of David Bromberg: Out of the Blues	1976	3.00	6.00	12.00
—Original with no bar code					
❏ PC 34467	The Best of David Bromberg: Out of the Blues	198?	2.00	4.00	8.00
—Budget-line reissue with bar code					

FANTASY

❏ 9540	Reckless Abandon	1977	3.00	6.00	12.00
❏ 9555	Bandit in a Bathing Suit	1978	2.50	5.00	10.00
❏ 9572	My Own House	1979	2.50	5.00	10.00
❏ 9590	You Should See the Rest of the Band	1980	2.50	5.00	10.00
❏ 79007 [(2)]	How Late'll Ya Play 'Til?	1976	3.75	7.50	15.00

ROUNDER

❏ 3110	Sideman Serenade	1989	3.00	6.00	12.00

BRONZETTES, THE
45s
PARKWAY

❏ 929	Hot Spot/Run, Run, You Little Fool	1964	3.00	6.00	12.00

BROOKLYN BRIDGE, THE Also see JOHNNY MAESTRO.
45s
BUDDAH

❏ 60	Little Red Boat by the River/From My Window	1968	—	3.00	6.00
❏ 75	Worst That Could Happen/Your Kite, My Kite	1968	2.00	4.00	8.00
❏ 95	Welcome Me Love/Blessed Is the Rain	1969	—	3.00	6.00
❏ 126	Your Husband, My Wife/Upside Down	1969	—	3.00	6.00
❏ 139	You'll Never Walk Alone/Minstrel Sunday	1969	—	3.00	6.00
❏ 162	Free as the Wind/He's Not a Happy Man	1970	—	3.00	6.00
❏ 179	Down by the River/Look Again	1970	—	3.00	6.00
❏ 193	Day Is Done/Easy Way	1970	—	3.00	6.00
❏ 193	Day Is Done/Opposites	1970	—	3.00	6.00
❏ 199	Nights in White Satin/Cynthia	1971	2.00	4.00	8.00
❏ 230	Wednesday in Your Garden (mono/stereo)	1971	2.00	4.00	8.00
—Stock copy unknown					
❏ 293	Man in a Band/Bruno's Place	1972	2.00	4.00	8.00
❏ 317	I Feel Free (mono/stereo)	1972	2.50	5.00	10.00
—As "The Bridge"; stock copy unknown					

COLLECTABLES

❏ 3997	Have Yourself A Merry Little Christmas/ A Christmas Long Ago (Jingle Jingle)	199?	—	—	3.00
—As "Johnny Maestro and the Brooklyn Bridge"; B-side by the Echelons					

Albums
BUDDAH

❏ BDS-5034	Brooklyn Bridge	1969	5.00	10.00	20.00
❏ BDS-5042	The Second Brooklyn Bridge	1969	5.00	10.00	20.00
❏ BDS-5065	The Brooklyn Bridge	1970	5.00	10.00	20.00
❏ BDS-5107	Bridge in Blue	1972	5.00	10.00	20.00

COLLECTABLES

❏ COL-5015	The Greatest Hits	198?	3.00	6.00	12.00
—As "Johnny Maestro and the Brooklyn Bridge"					

BROOKS, BOBBY
45s
HIT

❏ 109	See the Funny Little Clown/ My Heart Belongs to Only You	1964	2.00	4.00	8.00
❏ 120	A World Without Love/Chapel of Love	1964	2.00	4.00	8.00
—B-side by the Flower Sisters					
❏ 123	Tell Me Why/Be Anything (But Be Mine)	1964	2.00	4.00	8.00
—B-side by Connie Dee					
❏ 127	Don't Let the Sun Catch You Crying/ I'll Touch a Star	1964	2.00	4.00	8.00
❏ 143	It Hurts to Be in Love/Do Wah Diddy Diddy	1964	3.75	7.50	15.00
—B-side by Bobby Cash					
❏ 146	Last Kiss/A Summer Song	1964	2.00	4.00	8.00
❏ 156	Mountain of Love/Be Yourself	1964	2.50	5.00	10.00
❏ 176	Wise Like Solomon/Hold What You've Got	1965	2.00	4.00	8.00
—B-side by the Jalopy Five					
❏ 192	She's Come of Age/Eight Days a Week	1965	3.00	6.00	12.00
—B-side by the Jalopy Five					
❏ 199	Hearts Are Funny Things/Goodnight	1965	2.00	4.00	8.00
—B-side by Ed Hardin					
❏ 202	I Must Be Seeing Things/Once a Cheater, Always a Cheater	1965	2.00	4.00	8.00
—B-side by Connie Dee					
❏ 219	What's New Pussycat?/Down in the Boondocks	1965	2.00	4.00	8.00
—B-side by Ed Hardin					
❏ 231	England Swings/A Taste of Honey	1965	2.00	4.00	8.00
—B-side by the Nashville Five					

❏ 255	Rainy Day Women #12 and 35/When a Man Loves a Woman	1966	2.00	4.00	8.00
—B-side by Leroy Jones					
❏ 269	If I Were a Carpenter/Poor Side of Town	1966	2.00	4.00	8.00
—B-side by Bobby Sims					

BROOKS, CHUCK, AND THE SHARPIES
45s
DUB

❏ 2844	Spinning My Wheels/You Make Me Feel Mean	1958	75.00	150.00	300.00

BROOKS, DONNIE
45s
CHALLENGE

❏ 59331	I Call Your Name/Be Fair	1966	2.00	4.00	8.00
❏ 59344	Pink Carousel/Mission Man	1966	2.00	4.00	8.00

ERA

❏ 3004	Lil' Sweetheart/If You're Lookin'	1959	5.00	10.00	20.00
❏ 3007	White Orchid/Sway and Move with the Beat	1959	5.00	10.00	20.00
❏ 3014	The Devil Ain't a Man/How Long	1960	5.00	10.00	20.00
❏ 3018	Mission Bell/Do It for Me	1960	5.00	10.00	20.00
❏ 3028	Doll House/Round Robin	1960	3.75	7.50	15.00
❏ 3028 [PS]	Doll House/Round Robin	1960	6.25	12.50	25.00
❏ 3042	Memphis/That's Why	1961	3.75	7.50	15.00
❏ 3042 [PS]	Memphis/That's Why	1961	6.25	12.50	25.00
❏ 3049	All I Can Give/Wishbone	1961	3.75	7.50	15.00
❏ 3052	Boomerang/How Long	1961	3.75	7.50	15.00
❏ 3059	Sweet Lorraine/Up to My Ears in Tears	1961	3.75	7.50	15.00
❏ 3063	Goodnight Judy/Your Little Boy's Gone Home	1961	3.75	7.50	15.00
❏ 3071	My Favorite Kind of Face/He Stole Flo	1962	3.75	7.50	15.00
❏ 3077	Oh You Beautiful Doll/Just a Bystander	1962	3.75	7.50	15.00
❏ 3095	Cries My Heart/It's Not That Easy	1962	3.75	7.50	15.00
❏ 3194	Blue Soldier/Love Is Funny That Way	1968	2.00	4.00	8.00

HAPPY TIGER

❏ 526	Abracadabra/I Know You as a Woman	1970	—	2.50	5.00
❏ 544	Hush/I Know You as a Woman	1970	—	2.50	5.00
❏ 551	My God and I/Pink Carousel	1970	—	2.50	5.00
❏ 566	(I Wanna) Have You for Myself/Rub-a-Dub-Dub	1971	—	2.50	5.00
❏ 579	I'm Gonna Make You Love Me/Pink Carousel	1971	—	2.50	5.00

MIDSONG INT'L.

❏ 1007	Big John/Get Fame, Son	1978	—	2.00	4.00

OAK

❏ 1019	The Song That I Sing Is For You/Country Dude	1971	—	2.50	5.00

REPRISE

❏ 0261	Gone/Girl Machine	1964	2.50	5.00	10.00
❏ 0311	Can't Help Lovin' You/Pickin' Up the Pieces	1964	2.50	5.00	10.00
❏ 0363	Hey, Little Girl/I Never Get to Love You	1965	2.50	5.00	10.00

YARDBIRD

❏ 8006	Sunglasses on the Sand/Sunshine, Summertime and Love	1968	—	3.00	6.00
❏ 8008	Hush/Sunshine, Summertime and Love	1968	—	3.00	6.00
❏ 8010	Tree Trimming Time/(Instrumental)	1968	—	3.00	6.00

Albums
ERA

❏ EL-105 [M]	The Happiest	1961	37.50	75.00	150.00

BROOKS, DUSTY, AND HIS TONES WITH JUANITA BROWN
45s
SUN

❏ 182	Heaven or Fire/Tears and Wine	1953	1500.	2250.	3000.

BROOKS, ELKIE
45s
A&M

❏ 1781	Where Do We Go from Here (Rich Man's Woman)/Roll Me Over	1976	—	2.50	5.00
❏ 1935	You Did Something for Me/Pearl's a Singer	1977	—	2.50	5.00
❏ 1953	Sunshine After the Rain/ You Did Something for Me	1977	—	2.50	5.00
❏ 1968	Love Potion No. 9/ Honey, Can I Put You on Your Clothes	1977	—	2.50	5.00
❏ 2068	Since You Went Away/Too Precious	1978	—	2.00	4.00
❏ 2271	Paint Your Pretty Pictures/Pull On the Rope	1980	—	2.00	4.00

PARROT

❏ 9699	Nothin' Left to Do But Cry/Strange Tho It Seems	1964	2.50	5.00	10.00

Albums
A&M

❏ SP-4554	Rich Man's Woman	1975	2.50	5.00	10.00
❏ SP-4631	Two Days Away	1977	2.50	5.00	10.00
❏ SP-4695	Shooting Star	1977	2.50	5.00	10.00

BROOKS, JOHN
45s
HIT

❏ 251	Soul and Inspiration/Good Lovin'	1966	3.00	6.00	12.00
—B-side by the Spartas					

BROOKS BROTHERS, THE
45s
LONDON

❏ 1987	Warpaint/Sometimes	1961	3.75	7.50	15.00
❏ 9668	Once in Awhile/Poor Plan	1964	2.50	5.00	10.00
—As "The Brooks"					

LONDON INT'L.

❏ 10501	Ain't Gonna Wash for a Week/One Last Kiss	1962	3.00	6.00	12.00
❏ 10515	Too Scared/Tell Tale	1962	3.00	6.00	12.00

BROONZY, BIG BILL
45s
CHESS

❏ 1546	Little City Woman/Lonesome	1953	100.00	200.00	400.00

Number	Title (A Side/B Side)	Yr	VG	VG+	NM
MERCURY					
❏ 8160	You've Been Mistreating Me/I Stay Blue All the Time	1951	7.50	15.00	30.00
—*Released on 78 in 1949*					
❏ 8261	Willie Mae Blues/Hollerin' the Blues	1951	7.50	15.00	30.00
❏ 8271	Hey Hey/Walkin' the Lonesome Road	1952	7.50	15.00	30.00
❏ 8284	Mopper's Blues/I Know She Will	1952	7.50	15.00	30.00
❏ 70039	South Bound Train/Leavin' Day	1953	6.25	12.50	25.00
❏ 71352	Tomorrow/Hey Hey	1958	5.00	10.00	20.00
Albums					
BIOGRAPH					
❏ C-15	Big Bill Broonzy 1932-1942	197?	2.50	5.00	10.00
CHESS					
❏ LP-1468 [M]	Big Bill Broonzy and Washboard Sam	1962	40.00	80.00	160.00
COLUMBIA					
❏ WL 111 [M]	Big Bill's Blues	1958	25.00	50.00	100.00
DIAL					
❏ LP-306 [10]	Blues Concert	1952	37.50	75.00	150.00
EMARCY					
❏ MG-26034 [10]	Folk Blues	1954	30.00	60.00	120.00
❏ MG-36137 [M]	Blues by Broonzy	1958	25.00	50.00	100.00
EPIC					
❏ EE 22017 [M]	Big Bill's Blues	196?	5.00	10.00	20.00
EVEREST ARCHIVE OF FOLK & JAZZ					
❏ 213	Big Bill Broonzy	1967	3.00	6.00	12.00
FOLKWAYS					
❏ FA-2315 [M]	Big Bill Broonzy	1957	12.50	25.00	50.00
❏ FA-2326 [M]	Country Blues	1957	12.50	25.00	50.00
❏ FG-3586 [M]	His Songs and Story	195?	12.50	25.00	50.00
❏ 31005 [R]	Big Bill Sings Country Blues	196?	3.75	7.50	15.00
GNP CRESCENDO					
❏ 10004	Feeling Low Down	1974	2.50	5.00	10.00
❏ 10009	Lonesome Road Blues	1975	2.50	5.00	10.00
MERCURY					
❏ MG-20822 [M]	Big Bill Broonzy — Memorial	1963	7.50	15.00	30.00
❏ MG-20905 [M]	Remembering Big Bill Broonzy	1964	7.50	15.00	30.00
❏ SR-60822 [R]	Big Bill Broonzy — Memorial	1963	5.00	10.00	20.00
❏ SR-60905 [R]	Remembering Big Bill Broonzy	1964	5.00	10.00	20.00
PERIOD					
❏ SLP-1114 [M]	Big Bill Broonzy Sings (Blues)	1956	37.50	75.00	150.00
❏ SLP-1209 [M]	Big Bill Broonzy Sings and Josh White Comes a-Visiting	1958	17.50	35.00	70.00
PORTRAIT MASTERS					
❏ RJ 44089	Big Bill's Blues	1988	3.75	7.50	15.00
—*Reissue of Columbia 111*					
SMITHSONIAN FOLKWAYS					
❏ SF-40023	Big Bill Broonzy Sings Folk Songs	1989	3.00	6.00	12.00
VERVE					
❏ MGV-3000-5 [(5)M]	The Big Bill Broonzy Story	1959	50.00	100.00	200.00
❏ MGV-3001 [M]	Last Session, Vol. 1	1959	12.50	25.00	50.00
❏ MGV-3002 [M]	Last Session, Vol. 2	1959	12.50	25.00	50.00
❏ MGV-3003 [M]	Last Session, Vol. 3	1959	12.50	25.00	50.00
YAZOO					
❏ L-1011	The Young Big Bill Broonzy	1969	3.75	7.50	15.00
❏ L-1035	Do That Guitar Rag	197?	3.75	7.50	15.00

BROTH
Albums
Number	Title (A Side/B Side)	Yr	VG	VG+	NM
MERCURY					
❏ SR-61298	Broth	1970	5.00	10.00	20.00

BROTHER FOX AND TAR BABY
45s
Number	Title (A Side/B Side)	Yr	VG	VG+	NM
CAPITOL					
❏ 2940	Electric Chair/Steel Dog Man	1970	2.50	5.00	10.00
Albums					
CAPITOL					
❏ ST-544	Brother Fox and Tar Baby	1970	7.50	15.00	30.00
ORACLE					
❏ 1001	Brother Fox and Tar Baby	1969	7.50	15.00	30.00

BROTHER SISTERS, THE
45s
Number	Title (A Side/B Side)	Yr	VG	VG+	NM
MERCURY					
❏ 71195	Alone (Why Must I Be Alone)/Pass Me the Mustard	1957	5.00	10.00	20.00
❏ 71678	Strawberry Shortcake/Crystal Ball	1960	5.00	10.00	20.00

BROTHERHOOD OF MAN, THE
45s
Number	Title (A Side/B Side)	Yr	VG	VG+	NM
BELL					
❏ 45456	When Love Catches Up on You/(B-side unknown)	1974	—	2.00	4.00
DERAM					
❏ 85056	Love One Another/A Little Bit of Heaven	1970	—	3.00	6.00
❏ 85059	United We Stand/Say a Prayer	1970	—	3.00	6.00
❏ 85065	Where Are You Going To My Love/Living in the Land of Love	1970	—	2.50	5.00
❏ 85070	This Boy/You Can Depend on Me	1971	—	2.50	5.00
❏ 85073	Reach Out Your Hand/A Better Tomorrow	1971	—	2.50	5.00
❏ 85077	Sing in the Sunshine/You and I	1971	—	2.50	5.00
❏ 85078	California Sunday Morning/Do Your Thing	1972	—	2.50	5.00
❏ 85081	Say a Prayer/Follow Me	1972	—	2.50	5.00
MERCURY					
❏ 882118-7	United We Stand/My Baby Loves Lovin'	1986	—	2.00	4.00
—*Reissue; B-side by White Plains*					
PRIVATE STOCK					
❏ 45,148	Oh Boy (The Mood I'm In)/(B-side unknown)	1977	—	2.50	5.00
❏ 45,165	Angelo/All Night	1977	—	2.50	5.00

Number	Title (A Side/B Side)	Yr	VG	VG+	NM
PYE					
❏ 71043	Spring of 1912/(B-side unknown)	1976	—	3.00	6.00
❏ 71066	Save Your Kisses for Me/Let's Love Together	1976	—	2.50	5.00
❏ 71076	Sweet Lady from Georgia/Sugar Honey Love	1976	—	2.50	5.00
Albums					
DERAM					
❏ DES 18046	United We Stand	1970	3.75	7.50	15.00

BROTHERS, THE
45s
Number	Title (A Side/B Side)	Yr	VG	VG+	NM
ARGO					
❏ 5318	Lazy Susan/Deep Sleep	1958	5.00	10.00	20.00
❏ 5329	Sioux City Sue/Deep Sleep	1959	5.00	10.00	20.00
CHECKER					
❏ 995	My True Love/One Lonely Heart	1961	3.75	7.50	15.00

BROTHERS AND SISTERS
45s
Number	Title (A Side/B Side)	Yr	VG	VG+	NM
ODE					
❏ 121	The Mighty Quinn/Chimes of Freedom	1969	2.00	4.00	8.00
❏ 123	Mr. Tambourine Man/The Times They Are a-Changing	1969	2.00	4.00	8.00

BROTHERS CAIN, THE
45s
Number	Title (A Side/B Side)	Yr	VG	VG+	NM
ACTA					
❏ 810	Better Times/Pupil Alexander	1967	6.25	12.50	25.00
❏ 820	It Sure Is Groovy/Anyway You Like It	1968	6.25	12.50	25.00
MERCURY					
❏ 72437	In Love with One/Two Wrongs	1965	6.25	12.50	25.00

BROTHERS FOUR, THE
45s
Number	Title (A Side/B Side)	Yr	VG	VG+	NM
COLUMBIA					
❏ S7 31089 [S]	Hey Hey My Honey/Low Bridge	1961	3.00	6.00	12.00
❏ S7 31090 [S]	The Lilies Grow High/Ballad of Sam Hill	1961	3.00	6.00	12.00
❏ S7 31091 [S]	Abilene/Frogg	1961	3.00	6.00	12.00
❏ S7 31092 [S]	Betty and Dupree/Pastures of Plenty	1961	3.00	6.00	12.00
❏ S7 31093 [S]	Island Woman/This Land Is Your Land	1961	3.00	6.00	12.00
—*The above five are "Stereo Seven" 33 1/3 rpm jukebox singles from set "JS 7-25" entitled "Roamin' with the Brothers Four"*					
❏ 41461	Chicka Mucha Hi Di/Darlin' Won't You Wait	1959	2.50	5.00	10.00
❏ 41571	Greenfields/Angelique-O	1960	2.00	4.00	8.00
❏ 41571 [PS]	Greenfields/Angelique-O	1960	3.00	6.00	12.00
❏ 41692	My Tani/Ellie Lou	1960	2.00	4.00	8.00
❏ 41692 [PS]	My Tani/Ellie Lou	1960	3.00	6.00	12.00
❏ 41808	The Green Leaves of Summer/Beautiful Brown Eyes	1960	2.00	4.00	8.00
❏ 41808 [PS]	The Green Leaves of Summer/Beautiful Brown Eyes	1960	3.00	6.00	12.00
❏ 41958	Frogg/Sweet Rosyanne	1961	2.00	4.00	8.00
❏ 41958 [PS]	Frogg/Sweet Rosyanne	1961	3.00	6.00	12.00
❏ 42142	My Woman Left Me/Nobody Knows	1961	2.00	4.00	8.00
❏ 42235	What Child Is This/Christmas Bells	1961	2.50	5.00	10.00
❏ 42256	Blue Water Line/Summer Days Alone	1962	2.00	4.00	8.00
❏ 42256 [PS]	Blue Water Line/Summer Days Alone	1962	3.00	6.00	12.00
❏ 42391	Darlin' Sporty Jenny/Slowly, Slowly	1962	2.00	4.00	8.00
❏ 42450	This Train/Summertime	1962	2.00	4.00	8.00
❏ 42450 [PS]	This Train/Summertime	1962	3.00	6.00	12.00
❏ 42507	Five Weeks in a Balloon/Land of the Midnight Sun	1962	2.00	4.00	8.00
❏ 42507 [PS]	Five Weeks in a Balloon/Land of the Midnight Sun	1962	3.00	6.00	12.00
❏ 42586	The Tavern Song/25 Minutes to Go	1962	2.00	4.00	8.00
❏ 42586 [PS]	The Tavern Song/25 Minutes to Go	1962	5.00	10.00	20.00
❏ 42756	Ringing Bells/Welcome Home Sally	1963	2.00	4.00	8.00
❏ 42787	55 Days at Peking/All for the Love of a Girl	1963	2.00	4.00	8.00
❏ 42888	Four Strong Winds/John B. Sails	1963	2.00	4.00	8.00
❏ 42927	Hootenanny Saturday Night/Across the Sea	1963	2.00	4.00	8.00
❏ 43025	Seven Daffodils/San Francisco Bay Blues	1964	2.00	4.00	8.00
❏ 43147	Take This Hammer/Little Play Soldier	1964	2.00	4.00	8.00
❏ 43211	Somewhere/Turn Around	1965	—	3.00	6.00
❏ 43317	Come Kiss Me Love/Lazy Harry's	1965	—	3.00	6.00
❏ 43404	Try to Remember/Sakura	1965	—	3.00	6.00
❏ 43493	It Was a Very Good Year/Wild Colonial Boy	1965	—	3.00	6.00
❏ 43547	Ratman and Bobbin in the Clipper Caper/Muleskinner	1966	3.75	7.50	15.00
❏ 43621	Nowhere Man/If I Fell	1966	2.50	5.00	10.00
❏ 43825	Changes/For Emily, Whenever I May Find Her	1966	—	3.00	6.00
❏ 43919	I'll Be Home for Christmas/'Twas the Night Before Christmas	1966	2.00	4.00	8.00
❏ 43984	All I Need Is You/And Then the Sun Came Down	1967	—	3.00	6.00
❏ 44058	Ain't No More Cane on the Brazos/Shenandoah	1967	—	3.00	6.00
❏ 44175	The First Time Ever/Walkin' Backwards Down the Road	1967	—	3.00	6.00
❏ 44278	Here Today and Gone Tomorrow/No Sad Songs from Me	1967	—	3.00	6.00
❏ 44578	I'm Falling Down/Sweet Dreams, Sweet Runaway Child	1968	—	2.50	5.00
❏ 44832	Skip a Rope/Strangest Dream	1969	—	2.50	5.00
FANTASY					
❏ 640	Going Back to Big Sur/Here I Go Again	1970	—	2.50	5.00
Albums					
COLUMBIA					
❏ CL 1402 [M]	The Brothers Four	1960	3.00	6.00	12.00
❏ CL 1479 [M]	Rally 'Round the Brothers Four	1960	3.00	6.00	12.00
❏ CL 1578 [M]	B.M.O.C. (Best Music On/Off Campus)	1961	3.00	6.00	12.00
❏ CL 1625 [M]	Roamin'	1961	3.00	6.00	12.00
❏ CL 1697 [M]	The Brothers Four Song Book	1961	3.00	6.00	12.00
❏ CL 1803 [M]	The Brothers Four's Greatest Hits	1962	3.00	6.00	12.00
❏ CL 1828 [M]	The Brothers Four: In Person	1962	3.00	6.00	12.00
❏ CL 1946 [M]	Cross Country Concert	1963	3.00	6.00	12.00
❏ CL 2033 [M]	The Big Folk Hits	1963	3.00	6.00	12.00
❏ CL 2128 [M]	The Brothers Four Sing of Our Times	1964	3.00	6.00	12.00

B

Number	Title (A Side/B Side)	Yr	VG	VG+	NM
❑ CL 2213 [M]	More Big Folk Hits	1964	3.00	6.00	12.00
❑ CL 2305 [M]	The Honey Wind Blows	1965	3.00	6.00	12.00
❑ CL 2379 [M]	Try to Remember	1965	3.00	6.00	12.00
❑ CL 2502 [M]	A Beatles' Songbook (The Brothers Four Sing Lennon/McCartney)	1966	3.75	7.50	15.00
❑ CL 2702 [M]	A New World's Record	1967	3.75	7.50	15.00

—Corrected cover, with the guitarist using his right hand, as he does in real life

| ❑ CL 2702 [M] | A New World's Record | 1967 | 6.25 | 12.50 | 25.00 |

—Original cover has a flopped image on the front cover, which makes it appear as if the guitarist is left-handed

❑ CS 8197 [S]	The Brothers Four	1960	3.75	7.50	15.00
❑ CS 8270 [S]	Rally 'Round the Brothers Four	1960	3.75	7.50	15.00
❑ CS 8378 [S]	B.M.O.C. (Best Music On/Off Campus)	1961	3.75	7.50	15.00
❑ CS 8425 [S]	Roamin'	1961	3.75	7.50	15.00
❑ CS 8497 [S]	The Brothers Four Song Book	1961	3.75	7.50	15.00
❑ CS 8603 [S]	The Brothers Four's Greatest Hits	1962	3.75	7.50	15.00

—Red "360 Sound" label

| ❑ CS 8603 | The Brothers Four's Greatest Hits | 1970 | 2.50 | 5.00 | 10.00 |

—Orange label

| ❑ PC 8603 | The Brothers Four's Greatest Hits | 198? | 2.00 | 4.00 | 8.00 |

—Reissue with new prefix

❑ CS 8628 [S]	The Brothers Four: In Person	1962	3.75	7.50	15.00
❑ CS 8746 [S]	Cross Country Concert	1963	3.75	7.50	15.00
❑ CS 8833 [S]	The Big Folk Hits	1963	3.75	7.50	15.00
❑ CS 8928 [S]	The Brothers Four Sing of Our Times	1964	3.75	7.50	15.00
❑ CS 9013 [S]	More Big Folk Hits	1964	3.75	7.50	15.00
❑ CS 9105 [S]	The Honey Wind Blows	1965	3.75	7.50	15.00
❑ CS 9179 [S]	Try to Remember	1965	3.75	7.50	15.00
❑ CS 9302 [S]	A Beatles' Songbook (The Brothers Four Sing Lennon/McCartney)	1966	5.00	10.00	20.00
❑ CS 9502 [S]	A New World's Record	1967	3.00	6.00	12.00

—Corrected cover, with the guitarist using his right hand, as he does in real life

| ❑ CS 9502 [S] | A New World's Record | 1967 | 5.00 | 10.00 | 20.00 |

—Original cover has a flopped image on the front cover, which makes it appear as if the guitarist is left-handed

| ❑ CS 9818 | Let's Get Together | 1969 | 3.00 | 6.00 | 12.00 |

FANTASY

| ❑ 8400 | The Brothers Four 1970 | 1970 | 2.50 | 5.00 | 10.00 |

FIRST AMERICAN

❑ 7705	The Brothers Four Now	1978	2.50	5.00	10.00
❑ 7722 [(2)]	Greenfields and Other Gold	1980	3.00	6.00	12.00
❑ 7728	New Gold	1981	2.50	5.00	10.00

HARMONY

| ❑ HS 11341 | Four Strong Winds | 1969 | 2.50 | 5.00 | 10.00 |
| ❑ H 31505 | Great Songs of Our Times | 1972 | 2.50 | 5.00 | 10.00 |

BROTHERS GRIMM, THE
45s
MERCURY

| ❑ 72512 | A Man Needs Love/Looky, Looky | 1966 | 2.50 | 5.00 | 10.00 |

BROWN, AL
45s
AMY

❑ 804	The Madison/Mo' Madison	1960	6.25	12.50	25.00
❑ 806	It's True 'Bout Love/Sweet Little Love	1960	5.00	10.00	20.00
❑ 811	Take Me Back/Mention Me	1960	5.00	10.00	20.00
❑ 829	Route 66/Shimmy Swing	1961	5.00	10.00	20.00

Albums
AMY

| ❑ A-1 [M] | Madison Dance Party | 1960 | 10.00 | 20.00 | 40.00 |
| ❑ AS-1 [S] | Madison Dance Party | 1960 | 12.50 | 25.00 | 50.00 |

BROWN, ARTHUR, THE CRAZY WORLD OF
45s
ATLANTIC

| ❑ 2556 | Fire/Rest Cure | 1968 | 2.50 | 5.00 | 10.00 |

MERCURY

| ❑ 873504-7 | Fire/Rest Cure | 1990 | — | — | 3.00 |

—Reissue

TRACK

| ❑ 2582 | I Put a Spell on You/Nightmare | 1968 | 2.00 | 4.00 | 8.00 |

Albums
GULL

| ❑ GU6-405 | Dance | 1975 | 3.00 | 6.00 | 12.00 |

PASSPORT

| ❑ 98003 | Journey | 1974 | 3.00 | 6.00 | 12.00 |

TRACK

| ❑ SD 8198 | The Crazy World of Arthur Brown | 1968 | 6.25 | 12.50 | 25.00 |

BROWN, BILLY (1)
45s
CHALLENGE

| ❑ 59396 | One of the Ten Most Wanted Women/Open Arms | 1969 | 2.00 | 4.00 | 8.00 |

COLUMBIA

❑ 4-20766	Jealous Stars/I Never Knew I'd Miss You	1950	12.50	25.00	50.00
❑ 4-20789	Trusting Heart/I Hope I Don't Live Long Enough to Lose You	1951	12.50	25.00	50.00
❑ 4-20936	Tight Wad/I'm Sending Back Everything But Memories	1952	12.50	25.00	50.00
❑ 4-20982	Don't Hold Back/Rich in Love	1952	12.50	25.00	50.00
❑ 4-41029	Did We Have a Party/It's Love	1957	10.00	20.00	40.00
❑ 4-41100	Meet Me in the Alley, Sally/I Wanted You	1958	12.50	25.00	50.00
❑ 4-41297	Flip Out/Echo Mountain	1958	10.00	20.00	40.00
❑ 4-41380	Run 'Em Off/He'll Have to Go	1959	10.00	20.00	40.00

DECCA

| ❑ 9-29559 | Drunk-Drunk Again/High Heels But No Soul | 1955 | 5.00 | 10.00 | 20.00 |

REPUBLIC

| ❑ 2004 | The Last Letter/Be Honest with Me | 1960 | 3.75 | 7.50 | 15.00 |
| ❑ 2007 | Just Out of Reach/Lost Weekend | 1960 | 3.75 | 7.50 | 15.00 |

Number	Title (A Side/B Side)	Yr	VG	VG+	NM
❑ 2012	Look Out Heart (Here Comes Love)/It Don't Take Long to Learn	1961	3.75	7.50	15.00

STARS

| ❑ 552 | Did We Have a Party/It's Love | 1957 | 25.00 | 50.00 | 100.00 |

BROWN, BUSTER
45s
FIRE

❑ 507	Sugar Babe/I'm Going — But I'll Be Back	1962	5.00	10.00	20.00
❑ 516	Raise a Rucks Tonight/Gonna Love My Baby	1962	5.00	10.00	20.00
❑ 1008	Fannie Mae/Lost in a Dream	1959	6.25	12.50	25.00
❑ 1020	The Madison Shuffle/John Henry	1960	5.00	10.00	20.00
❑ 1023	Is You Is or Is You Ain't My Baby/Don't Dog Your Woman	1960	5.00	10.00	20.00
❑ 1032	Sincerely/Doctor Brown	1960	5.00	10.00	20.00
❑ 1040	Blues When It Rains/Good News	1961	5.00	10.00	20.00
❑ 2021	Sugar Babe/Don't Dog Your Woman	1962	3.75	7.50	15.00

LOST-NITE

| ❑ 448 | Fannie Mae/Is You Is or Is You Ain't My Baby | 197? | — | 3.00 | 6.00 |

—Reissue

RCA VICTOR

| ❑ PB-10023 | Eloise/Fallin' Out of Love | 1974 | — | 2.50 | 5.00 |

WHITE WHALE

| ❑ 316 | The Proud One/I've Got It Made | 1969 | 2.50 | 5.00 | 10.00 |

Albums
COLLECTABLES

| ❑ COL-5110 | Golden Classics: The New King of the Blues | 198? | 2.50 | 5.00 | 10.00 |

FIRE

| ❑ FLP-102 [M] | The New King of the Blues | 1961 | 75.00 | 150.00 | 300.00 |

—Red and black label, white cover

| ❑ FLP-102 [M] | The New King of the Blues | 1961 | 100.00 | 200.00 | 400.00 |

—Red and black label, purple cover

| ❑ FLP-102 [M] | The New King of the Blues | 1961 | 175.00 | 350.00 | 700.00 |

—White and red label

SOUFFLE

| ❑ 2014 | Get Down | 1973 | 3.00 | 6.00 | 12.00 |

BROWN, CHARLES
45s
ACE

| ❑ 561 | Educated Fool/I Want to Go Back Home | 1959 | 3.00 | 6.00 | 12.00 |

—With Amos Milburn

| ❑ 599 | Love's Like a River/Boys Will Be Boys | 1960 | 3.00 | 6.00 | 12.00 |
| ❑ 599 | Love's Like a River/Sing My Blues Tonight | 1960 | 3.00 | 6.00 | 12.00 |

ALADDIN

| ❑ 3076 | Black Night/Once There Was a Fool | 1951 | 37.50 | 75.00 | 150.00 |

—Charles Brown records on Aladdin prior to 3076 are unconfirmed on 45 rpm

❑ 3091	I'll Always Be in Love with You/The Message	1951	20.00	40.00	80.00
❑ 3092	Seven Long Days/Don't Fool with My Heart	1951	20.00	40.00	80.00
❑ 3116	Hard Times/Tender Heart	1952	20.00	40.00	80.00
❑ 3120	Still Water/My Last Affair	1952	20.00	40.00	80.00
❑ 3138	See/Without Your Love	1952	20.00	40.00	80.00
❑ 3157	Rollin' Like a Pebble in the Sand/Alley Batting	1952	20.00	40.00	80.00
❑ 3163	Evening Shadows/Moonrise	1953	15.00	30.00	60.00
❑ 3176	Take Me/Rising Sun	1953	15.00	30.00	60.00
❑ 3191	Lonesome Feeling/I Lost Everything	1953	15.00	30.00	60.00
❑ 3200	All My Life/Don't Leave Me Poor	1953	15.00	30.00	60.00
❑ 3209	P.S. I Love You/Cryin' and Driftin' Blues	1953	15.00	30.00	60.00
❑ 3220	Everybody's Got Trouble/I Fool Around with You	1954	10.00	20.00	40.00
❑ 3235	Let's Walk/Crying Mercy	1954	10.00	20.00	40.00
❑ 3254	My Silent Love/Foolish	1954	10.00	20.00	40.00
❑ 3272	By the Bend of the River/Honey Slipper	1955	7.50	15.00	30.00
❑ 3284	Night After Night/Walk with Me	1955	7.50	15.00	30.00
❑ 3290	Hot Lips and Seven Kisses/Fools' Paradise	1955	7.50	15.00	30.00
❑ 3296	My Heart Is Mended/Trees, Trees	1955	7.50	15.00	30.00
❑ 3316	Please Don't Drive Me Away/One Minute to One	1956	6.25	12.50	25.00
❑ 3342	Soothe Me/I'll Always Be in Love with You	1956	6.25	12.50	25.00
❑ 3348	Merry Christmas, Baby/Black Night	1956	6.25	12.50	25.00
❑ 3366	Please Believe Me/It's a Sin to Tell a Lie	1957	5.00	10.00	20.00
❑ 3423	Hard Times/Ooh, Ooh Sugar	1958	5.00	10.00	20.00

BLUES SPECTRUM

| ❑ 17 | Merry Christmas, Baby/Rockin' Blues | 197? | — | 3.00 | 6.00 |

BLUESWAY

| ❑ 61031 | Merry Christmas, Baby/Rainy, Rainy Day | 1969 | — | 3.00 | 6.00 |

CASH

| ❑ 1052 | Lost in the Night/I Sold My Heart to the Junkman | 1957 | 7.50 | 15.00 | 30.00 |

—B-side by the Basin Street Boys

CHARLENA

| ❑ 001 | Please Come Home For Christmas/Santa Claus Santa Claus | 197? | — | 2.00 | 4.00 |
| ❑ 001 [PS] | Please Come Home For Christmas/Santa Claus Santa Claus | 197? | — | 2.50 | 5.00 |

EASTWEST

| ❑ 106 | When Did You Leave Heaven/We've Got a Lot in Common | 1958 | 5.00 | 10.00 | 20.00 |

EMI

| ❑ S7-18213 | Please Come Home for Christmas/Merry Christmas Baby | 1994 | — | 2.00 | 4.00 |

—Green vinyl

GALAXY

| ❑ 762 | I'm Gonna Push On/Cry No More | 1968 | 2.50 | 5.00 | 10.00 |
| ❑ 766 | Abraham, Martin, and John/(B-side unknown) | 1968 | 2.50 | 5.00 | 10.00 |

HOLLYWOOD

| ❑ 1006 | Pleading for Your Love/The Best I Can Do | 1954 | 10.00 | 20.00 | 40.00 |
| ❑ 1021 | Merry Christmas Baby/Sleigh Ride | 1954 | 5.00 | 10.00 | 20.00 |

—Charles Brown's first recording of the A-side, released on 78 on Exclusive 254 (1946); B-side by Lloyd Glenn; maroon label

| ❑ 1021 | Merry Christmas Baby/Sleigh Ride | 196? | 2.00 | 4.00 | 8.00 |

—B-side by Lloyd Glenn; color label

| ❑ 1021 | Merry Christmas Baby/Sleigh Ride | 197? | — | 2.50 | 5.00 |

—B-side by Lloyd Glenn; black label

Number	Title (A Side/B Side)	Yr	VG	VG+	NM
IMPERIAL					
❑ 5830	Fool's Paradise/Lonesome Feeling	1962	2.50	5.00	10.00
❑ 5902	Merry Christmas Baby/I Lost Everything	1962	2.50	5.00	10.00
❑ 5905	Black Night/Drifting Blues	1963	2.50	5.00	10.00
❑ 5961	I'm Savin' My Love for You/ Please Don't Drive Me Away	1963	2.50	5.00	10.00
JEWEL					
❑ 814	Christmas in Heaven/Just a Blessing	1970	—	3.00	6.00
❑ 815	Merry Christmas Baby/ Please Come Home for Christmas	1970	—	3.00	6.00
❑ 830	I Don't Know/For You	1972	—	2.50	5.00
❑ 838	I've Got Your Love/I Just Can't Get Over You	1973	—	2.50	5.00
❑ 847	Please Come Home for Christmas/ Christmas in Heaven	1974	—	2.50	5.00
KENT					
❑ 501	Merry Christmas Baby/3 O'Clock Blues	1968	2.50	5.00	10.00
KING					
❑ 5405	Please Come Home for Christmas/ Christmas (Comes But Once a Year)	1960	3.00	6.00	12.00
—B-side by Amos Milburn; original blue label					
❑ 5405	Please Come Home for Christmas/ Christmas (Comes But Once a Year)	1970	—	3.00	6.00
—B-side by Amos Milburn; black label					
❑ 5439	Angel Baby/Baby Oh Baby	1961	3.00	6.00	12.00
❑ 5464	I Wanna Go Back Home/My Little Baby	1961	3.00	6.00	12.00
—With Amos Milburn					
❑ 5523	Butterfly/This Fool Has Learned	1961	3.00	6.00	12.00
❑ 5530	Christmas in Heaven/ It's Christmas All Year 'Round	1961	3.00	6.00	12.00
❑ 5570	Without a Friend/If You Play with Cats	1961	3.00	6.00	12.00
❑ 5722	I'm Just a Drifter/ I Don't Want Your Rambling Letters	1963	2.50	5.00	10.00
❑ 5726	It's Christmas Time/Christmas Finds Me Lonely	1963	2.50	5.00	10.00
❑ 5731	Christmas Questions/Wrap Yourself in a Christmas Package	1963	2.50	5.00	10.00
❑ 5802	If You Don't Believe I'm Crying/I Wanna Be Close	1963	2.50	5.00	10.00
❑ 5825	Lucky Dreamer/Too Fine for Crying	1963	2.50	5.00	10.00
❑ 5852	Blow Out All the Candles/Come Home	1964	2.50	5.00	10.00
❑ 5946	Christmas Blues/My Most Miserable Christmas	1964	2.50	5.00	10.00
❑ 5947	Christmas Comes (But Once a Year)/Bringin' In a Brand New Year	1964	2.50	5.00	10.00
❑ 6094	Regardless/The Plan	1967	2.00	4.00	8.00
❑ 6192	Hang On a Little Longer/Black Night	1968	2.00	4.00	8.00
❑ 6194	Merry Christmas, Baby/ Let's Make Every Day Christmas	1968	2.00	4.00	8.00
❑ 6420	For the Good Times/Lonesome and Driftin'	1973	—	2.50	5.00
LIBERTY					
❑ 1393	Merry Christmas, Baby/Silent Night	1980	—	2.50	5.00
—B-side by Baby Washington					
❑ 5902	Merry Christmas, Baby/I Lost Everything	196?	2.00	4.00	8.00
—Reissue of Imperial 5902					
LILLY					
❑ 506	Bon Voyage/Bye and Bye	1962	2.50	5.00	10.00
MAINSTREAM					
❑ 607	Pledging My Love/Tomorrow Night	1965	2.00	4.00	8.00
NOLA					
❑ 702	Standing on the Outside/I'll Love You (If You Let Me)	1965	2.00	4.00	8.00
SWING TIME					
❑ 238	Merry Christmas, Baby/Lost In The Night	195?	25.00	50.00	100.00
—Originally released on 78, but a 45 does exist					
❑ 253	I'll Miss You/New Orleans Blues	1952	30.00	60.00	120.00
❑ 259	Be Fair with Me/Sunny Road	1952	30.00	60.00	120.00
TEEM					
❑ 1008	Merry Christmas Baby/ Christmas Finds Me Oh So Sad	19??	—	3.00	6.00
UNITED ARTISTS					
❑ 0085	Drifting Blues/Black Night	1973	—	2.00	4.00
—Silver Spotlight Series issue					
❑ 0086	I Lost Everything/Lonesome Feeling	1973	—	2.00	4.00
—Silver Spotlight Series issue					
❑ XW582	Merry Christmas Baby//(B-side unknown)	1974	—	2.50	5.00
UPSIDE					
❑ PRO 002	Santa Claus Boogie (one-sided)	1986	—	2.00	4.00
—Flexidisc					
❑ PRO 002 [PS]	Santa Claus Boogie	1986	—	2.00	4.00
Albums					
ALADDIN					
❑ LP-702 [10]	Mood Music	1952	1500.	2750.	4000.
—Black vinyl					
❑ LP-702 [10]	Mood Music	1952	3000.	5250.	7500.
—Red vinyl					
❑ LP-809 [M]	Mood Music	1956	—	—	—
—Unreleased?					
ALLIGATOR					
❑ AL-4771	One More for the Road	1989	3.00	6.00	12.00
BIG TOWN					
❑ 1003	Merry Christmas Baby	1977	3.00	6.00	12.00
❑ 1005	Music Maestro Please	1978	2.50	5.00	10.00
BLUESWAY					
❑ BLS-6039	Charles Brown — Legend	1970	6.25	12.50	25.00
BULLSEYE BLUES					
❑ BB-9501	All My Life	1990	5.00	10.00	20.00
IMPERIAL					
❑ LP-9178 [M]	Charles Brown Sings Million Sellers	1961	100.00	200.00	400.00
JEWEL					
❑ 5006	Blues 'N' Brown	1972	3.00	6.00	12.00
KING					
❑ 775 [M]	Charles Brown Sings Christmas Songs	1961	37.50	75.00	150.00

Number	Title (A Side/B Side)	Yr	VG	VG+	NM
❑ KS-775 [S]	Charles Brown Sings Christmas Songs	1963	75.00	150.00	300.00
—Stereo copies (whether true stereo or rechanneled, we don't know) exist on blue labels with "King" in block letters (no crown)					
❑ 878 [M]	The Great Charles Brown	1963	50.00	100.00	200.00
MAINSTREAM					
❑ S-6007 [S]	Boss of the Blues	1965	7.50	15.00	30.00
❑ S-6035 [S]	Ballads My Way	1965	7.50	15.00	30.00
❑ 56007 [M]	Boss of the Blues	1965	5.00	10.00	20.00
❑ 56035 [M]	Ballads My Way	1965	5.00	10.00	20.00
MOSAIC					
❑ MQ7-153 [(7)]	The Complete Aladdin Recordings of Charles Brown	1994	37.50	75.00	150.00
SCORE					
❑ SLP-4011 [M]	Driftin' Blues	1958	100.00	200.00	400.00
❑ SLP-4036 [M]	More Blues with Charles Brown	1959	—	—	—
—Unreleased					

BROWN, CHARLIE
45s
HIT

Number	Title (A Side/B Side)	Yr	VG	VG+	NM
❑ 164	Legend of Daniel Boone/Ballad of Daniel Boone	1964	2.00	4.00	8.00
—B-side by Ricky Dickens					

BROWN, CLARENCE "GATEMOUTH"
45s
PEACOCK

Number	Title (A Side/B Side)	Yr	VG	VG+	NM
❑ 1600	Baby Take It Easy/Just Got Lucky	1952	100.00	200.00	400.00
❑ 1607	Dirty Work at the Crossroads/You Got Money	1952	62.50	125.00	250.00
❑ 1617	Boogie Uproar/Hurry Back Good News	1953	50.00	100.00	200.00
❑ 1619	Please Tell Me Baby/Gate Walks to Board	1953	50.00	100.00	200.00
❑ 1633	Midnight Hour/For Now So Long	1954	37.50	75.00	150.00
❑ 1637	Okie Dokie Stomp/Depression Blues	1954	37.50	75.00	150.00
❑ 1653	Gate's Salty Blues/Rock My Blues Away	1955	25.00	50.00	100.00
❑ 1662	Ain't That Dandy/September Song	1956	20.00	40.00	80.00
❑ 1692	Just Before Dawn/Swinging the Gate	1958	10.00	20.00	40.00

BROWN, ESTELLE One of the SWEET INSPIRATIONS.
45s
UNITED ARTISTS

Number	Title (A Side/B Side)	Yr	VG	VG+	NM
❑ 727	You Got Just What You Asked For/Stick Close	1964	2.50	5.00	10.00

BROWN, FRED
45s
HIT

Number	Title (A Side/B Side)	Yr	VG	VG+	NM
❑ 60	Can't Get Used to Losing You/Baby Workout	1963	2.00	4.00	8.00
—B-side by Leroy Jones					

BROWN, FRED X.
45s
HIT

Number	Title (A Side/B Side)	Yr	VG	VG+	NM
❑ 16	The Man Who Shot Liberty Valance/It Keeps Right On a-Hurtin'	1962	2.00	4.00	8.00

BROWN, GENE
45s
DOT

Number	Title (A Side/B Side)	Yr	VG	VG+	NM
❑ 15709	Playing with My Heart Again/Big Door	1958	15.00	30.00	60.00

BROWN, GEORGE WASHINGTON See VAN DYKE PARKS.

BROWN, JAMES Also see VICKI ANDERSON; BOBBY BYRD; LYN COLLINS; FRED WESLEY AND THE JB'S.
12-Inch Singles
POLYDOR

Number	Title (A Side/B Side)	Yr	VG	VG+	NM
❑ PRO 040 [DJ]	Eyesight/The Spank	1978	3.75	7.50	15.00
❑ PRO 059 [DJ]	For Goodness Sake, Look at Those Cakes (11:04) (same on both sides)	1978	6.25	12.50	25.00
❑ PRO 086 [DJ]	It's Too Funky in Here (6:33) (same on both sides)	1979	5.00	10.00	20.00
❑ PRO 100 [DJ]	Star Generation (8:07) (4:21)	1979	5.00	10.00	20.00
❑ PD-510	It's Too Funky in Here (6:33)/Are We Really Dancing	1979	3.75	7.50	15.00
SCOTTI BROTHERS					
❑ ZAS 2241 [DJ]	Living in America (4:50) (same on both sides)	1985	3.75	7.50	15.00
❑ 4Z9-05310	Living in America (LP Version) (Dance Mix) (Instrumental)	1985	2.00	4.00	8.00
❑ 4Z9-05943	Gravity (Extended Dance Mix) (7" Edit) (12" Dub Mix)/The Big G (Dig This Mess)	1986	2.00	4.00	8.00
❑ 4Z9-05990	How Do You Stop (Special Extended Remix)/ Goliath (Special Extended Remix)	1986	2.50	5.00	10.00
❑ 4Z9-07805	I'm Real/Tribute	1988	2.00	4.00	8.00
❑ 4Z9-07863	Static (3 versions)/Godfather Runnin' the Joint	1988	2.50	5.00	10.00
❑ 4Z9-08130	Time to Get Busy (Full Force Remix) (Single Version)/Busy J.B. (Full Force Remix) (Single Version)	1988	2.00	4.00	8.00
❑ 75286	(So Tired of Standing Still We Got to) Move On (5 versions)	1991	2.50	5.00	10.00
❑ 75352 [(2)]	Can't Get Any Harder (4 versions)	1993	3.00	6.00	12.00
❑ 78034	Respect Me (6 versions)	1995	2.50	5.00	10.00
❑ 78094	Hooked on Brown (Long) (Radio Edit 1) (Radio Edit 2)	1996	3.75	7.50	15.00
T.K. DISCO					
❑ TKD 452	Rapp Payback (Where Iz Moses) (Part 1 7:00)/ (Part 2 3:28)	1980	3.00	6.00	12.00
45s					
A&M					
❑ 3022	I Got You (I Feel Good)/Nowhere to Run	1988	—	2.00	4.00
—B-side by Martha and the Vandellas					
❑ 3022 [PS]	I Got You (I Feel Good)/Nowhere to Run	1988	—	2.00	4.00
—"Good Morning Vietnam" sleeve					
AUGUSTA SOUND					
❑ 94023	Bring It On ... Bring It On/The Night Time Is the Right Time (To Be With the One That You Love)	1983	—	2.00	4.00

B

Number	Title (A Side/B Side)	Yr	VG	VG+	NM
❏ 94023 [PS]	Bring It On ... Bring It On/The Night Time Is the Right Time (To Be With the One That You Love)	1983	—	2.00	4.00

BACKSTREET

Number	Title (A Side/B Side)	Yr	VG	VG+	NM
❏ 52215	King of Soul/Theme from Doctor Detroit	1983	—	—	3.00

—B-side by Devo

BETHLEHEM

Number	Title (A Side/B Side)	Yr	VG	VG+	NM
❏ 3089	I Loves You Porgy/Yours and Mine	1969	3.75	7.50	15.00
❏ 3098	A Man Has to Go Back to the Crossroads/The Drunk	1969	3.75	7.50	15.00

FEDERAL

Number	Title (A Side/B Side)	Yr	VG	VG+	NM
❏ 12258	Please, Please, Please/Why Do You Do Me?	1956	10.00	20.00	40.00
❏ 12264	I Don't Know/I Feel That Old Feeling Coming On	1956	6.25	12.50	25.00
❏ 12277	No, No, No, No/Hold My Baby's Hand	1956	6.25	12.50	25.00
❏ 12289	Just Won't Do Right/Let's Make It	1957	6.25	12.50	25.00
❏ 12290	I Won't Plead No More/Chonnie On Chon	1957	6.25	12.50	25.00
❏ 12292	Gonna Try/Can't Be the Same	1957	6.25	12.50	25.00
❏ 12295	Love or a Game/Messing with the Blues	1957	6.25	12.50	25.00
❏ 12300	I Walked Alone/You're Mine, You're Mine	1957	6.25	12.50	25.00
❏ 12311	Baby Cries Over the Ocean/That Dood It	1957	6.25	12.50	25.00
❏ 12316	Begging, Begging/That's When I Lost My Heart	1958	6.25	12.50	25.00
❏ 12337	Try Me/Tell Me What I Did Wrong	1958	7.50	15.00	30.00
❏ 12348	I Want You So Bad/There Must Be a Reason	1959	5.00	10.00	20.00
❏ 12352 [M]	I've Got to Change/It Hurts to Tell You	1959	5.00	10.00	20.00
❏ S-12352 [S]	I've Got to Change/It Hurts to Tell You	1959	12.50	25.00	50.00
❏ 12361 [M]	Don't Let It Happen to Me/Good Good Lovin'	1959	5.00	10.00	20.00
❏ S-12361 [S]	Don't Let It Happen to Me/Good Good Lovin'	1959	12.50	25.00	50.00
❏ 12364	It Was You/Got to Cry	1959	5.00	10.00	20.00
❏ 12369	I'll Go Crazy/I Know It's True	1960	5.00	10.00	20.00
❏ 12370	Think/You've Got the Power	1960	5.00	10.00	20.00
❏ 12378	This Old Heart/I Wonder When You're Coming Home	1960	5.00	10.00	20.00

KING

Number	Title (A Side/B Side)	Yr	VG	VG+	NM
❏ 5423	The Bells/And I Do Just What I Want	1960	3.75	7.50	15.00
❏ 5438	The Scratch/Hold It	1961	3.75	7.50	15.00
❏ 5442	Bewildered/If You Want Me	1961	3.75	7.50	15.00
❏ 5466	I Don't Mind/Love Don't Love Nobody	1961	3.75	7.50	15.00
❏ 5485	Sticky/Suds	1961	3.75	7.50	15.00
❏ 5519	Night Flying/Cross Firing	1961	3.75	7.50	15.00
❏ 5524	Baby You're Right/I'll Never, Never Let You Go	1961	3.75	7.50	15.00
❏ 5547	Just You and Me, Darling/I Love You, Yes I Do	1961	3.75	7.50	15.00
❏ 5573	Lost Someone/Cross Firing	1961	3.75	7.50	15.00
❏ 5614	Night Train/Why Does Everything Happen to Me	1962	3.75	7.50	15.00
❏ 5654	Tell Me Why/Say So Long	1962	3.75	7.50	15.00

—With Yvonne Fair

Number	Title (A Side/B Side)	Yr	VG	VG+	NM
❏ 5657	Shout and Shimmy/Come Over Here	1962	3.75	7.50	15.00
❏ 5672	Mashed Potatoes U.S.A./You Don't Have to Go	1962	3.75	7.50	15.00
❏ 5687	It Hurts to Be in Love/You Can Make It If You Try	1962	3.75	7.50	15.00

—With Yvonne Fair

Number	Title (A Side/B Side)	Yr	VG	VG+	NM
❏ 5698	(Can You) Feel It Part 1/(Can You) Feel It Part 2	1962	3.75	7.50	15.00
❏ 5701	Three Hearts in a Tangle/I've Got Money	1962	3.75	7.50	15.00
❏ 5710	Like a Baby/Every Beat of My Heart	1963	3.75	7.50	15.00
❏ 5739	Prisoner of Love/Choo Choo	1963	3.75	7.50	15.00
❏ 5767	These Foolish Things/Can You Feel It — Part 1	1963	3.75	7.50	15.00
❏ 5803	Signed, Sealed and Delivered/Waiting in Vain	1963	3.75	7.50	15.00
❏ 5829	The Bells/I've Got to Change	1963	3.75	7.50	15.00
❏ 5842	Oh Baby Don't You Weep (Part 1)/Oh Baby Don't You Weep (Part 2)	1964	3.75	7.50	15.00
❏ 5842 [PS]	Oh Baby Don't You Weep (Part 1)/Oh Baby Don't You Weep (Part 2)	1964	6.25	12.50	25.00
❏ 5853	Please, Please, Please/In the Wee Wee Hours	1964	3.75	7.50	15.00
❏ 5876	How Long Darling/Again	1964	3.75	7.50	15.00
❏ 5899	So Long/Dancin' Little Thing	1964	3.75	7.50	15.00
❏ 5922	Tell Me What You're Gonna Do/I Don't Care	1964	3.75	7.50	15.00
❏ 5952	Think/Try Me	1964	3.75	7.50	15.00
❏ 5956	Fine Old Foxy Self/Medley	1964	3.75	7.50	15.00
❏ 5968	Have Mercy Baby/Just Won't Do Right	1964	3.75	7.50	15.00
❏ 5995	This Old Heart/It Was You	1965	3.00	6.00	12.00
❏ 5999	Papa's Got a Brand New Bag Part I/Papa's Got a Brand New Bag Part II	1965	3.75	7.50	15.00
❏ 6015	I Got You (I Feel Good)/I Can't Help It (I Just Do, Do, Do)	1965	3.75	7.50	15.00
❏ 6020	I'll Go Crazy/Lost Someone	1966	3.00	6.00	12.00
❏ 6025	Ain't That a Groove Part I/Ain't That a Groove Part II	1966	3.00	6.00	12.00
❏ 6029	Prisoner of Love/I've Got to Change	1966	3.00	6.00	12.00
❏ 6033	Come Over Here/Tell Me What You're Gonna Do	1966	3.00	6.00	12.00
❏ 6035	It's a Man's Man's Man's World/Is It Yes Or Is It No?	1966	3.00	6.00	12.00
❏ 6037	I've Got Money/Just Won't Do Right	1966	3.00	6.00	12.00
❏ 6040	I Don't Care/It Was You	1966	3.00	6.00	12.00
❏ 6044	This Old Heart/How Long Darling	1966	3.00	6.00	12.00
❏ 6048	Money Won't Change You Part 1/Money Won't Change You Part 2	1966	3.00	6.00	12.00
❏ 6056	Don't Be a Drop-Out/Tell Me That You Love Me	1966	3.00	6.00	12.00
❏ 6064	The Christmas Song (Version 1)/The Christmas Song (Version 2)	1966	3.75	7.50	15.00
❏ 6065	Sweet Little Baby Boy (Part 1)/Sweet Little Baby Boy (Part 2)	1966	3.00	6.00	12.00
❏ 6071	Bring It Up/Nobody Knows	1967	3.00	6.00	12.00
❏ 6072	Let's Make Christmas Mean Something This Year (Part 1)/Let's Make Christmas Mean Something This Year (Part 2)	1967	3.00	6.00	12.00
❏ 6086	Kansas City/Stone Fox	1967	3.00	6.00	12.00
❏ 6091	Think/Nobody Cares	1967	3.00	6.00	12.00

—A-side: With Vicki Anderson; B-side: Vicki Anderson solo

Number	Title (A Side/B Side)	Yr	VG	VG+	NM
❏ 6100	Let Yourself Go/Good Rockin' Tonight	1967	3.00	6.00	12.00
❏ 6110	Cold Sweat — Part 1/Cold Sweat — Part 2	1967	3.00	6.00	12.00
❏ 6111	Mona Lisa/It Won't Be Me	1967	15.00	30.00	60.00

—Evidently not released or pulled shortly after release

Number	Title (A Side/B Side)	Yr	VG	VG+	NM
❏ 6112	America Is My Home — Part 1/America Is My Home — Part 2	1967	3.00	6.00	12.00

Number	Title (A Side/B Side)	Yr	VG	VG+	NM
❏ 6122	Get It Together (Part 1)/Get It Together (Part 2)	1967	3.00	6.00	12.00
❏ 6133	The Soul of J.B./Funky Soul #1	1967	3.00	6.00	12.00
❏ 6141	I Guess I'll Have to Cry, Cry, Cry/Just Plain Funk	1967	3.00	6.00	12.00
❏ 6144	I Can't Stand Myself (When You Touch Me)/There Was a Time	1967	3.00	6.00	12.00
❏ 6151	You've Got to Change Your Mind/I'll Lose My Mind	1968	3.00	6.00	12.00

—A-side: With Bobby Byrd; B-side: Bobby Byrd solo

Number	Title (A Side/B Side)	Yr	VG	VG+	NM
❏ 6152	You've Got the Power/What the World Needs Now Is Love	1968	3.00	6.00	12.00

—A-side: With Vicki Anderson; B-side: Vicki Anderson solo

Number	Title (A Side/B Side)	Yr	VG	VG+	NM
❏ 6155	I Got the Feelin'/If I Ruled the World	1968	3.00	6.00	12.00
❏ 6159	Maybe Good, Maybe Bad (Part 1)/(Part 2)	1968	3.75	7.50	15.00
❏ 6164	Here I Go/Shhhh	1968	3.00	6.00	12.00
❏ 6166	Licking Stick — Licking Stick (Part 1)/Licking — Licking Stick (Part 2)	1968	3.00	6.00	12.00
❏ 6187	Say It Loud — I'm Black and I'm Proud (Part 1)/Say It Loud — I'm Black and I'm Proud (Part 2)	1968	2.50	5.00	10.00
❏ 6187	Say It Loud — I'm Black and I'm Proud (Part 1)/Say It Loud — I'm Black But I'm Proud (Part 2)	1968	6.25	12.50	25.00

—Some copies have the above erroneous title on both sides

Number	Title (A Side/B Side)	Yr	VG	VG+	NM
❏ 6198	Goodbye My Love/Shades of Brown	1968	2.50	5.00	10.00
❏ 6203	Santa Claus Go Straight to the Ghetto/You Know It	1968	2.50	5.00	10.00
❏ 6204	Believers Shall Enjoy/Tit for Tat (Ain't No Turning Back)	1968	2.50	5.00	10.00
❏ 6205	Let's Unite the World at Christmas/In the Middle (Part 1)	1968	2.50	5.00	10.00
❏ 6206	In the Middle (Part 2)/Tit for Tat (Ain't No Turning Back)	1969	2.50	5.00	10.00

—A-side: With Marva Whitney

Number	Title (A Side/B Side)	Yr	VG	VG+	NM
❏ 6213	Give It Up or Turnit A Loose/I'll Lose My Mind	1969	2.50	5.00	10.00
❏ 6216	Shades of Brown (Part 2)/A Talk with the News	1969	2.50	5.00	10.00

—B-side by Steve Soul

Number	Title (A Side/B Side)	Yr	VG	VG+	NM
❏ 6218	You Got to Have a Job/I'm Tired, I'm Tired, I'm Tired	1969	2.50	5.00	10.00

—A-side with Marva Whitney; B-side: Marva Whitney solo

Number	Title (A Side/B Side)	Yr	VG	VG+	NM
❏ 6222	Soul Pride (Part 1)/Soul Pride (Part 2)	1969	2.50	5.00	10.00
❏ 6223	You've Got to Have a Mother for Me (Part 1)/You've Got to Have a Mother for Me (Part 2)	1969	2.50	5.00	10.00
❏ 6224	I Don't Want Nobody to Give Me Nothing (Open Up the Door, I'll Get It Myself) Part 1/Part 2	1969	2.50	5.00	10.00
❏ 6235	Little Groove Maker (Part 1)/Any Day Now	1969	2.50	5.00	10.00
❏ 6235	Little Groove Maker (Part 1)/I'm Shook	1969	2.50	5.00	10.00
❏ 6240	The Popcorn/The Chicken	1969	2.50	5.00	10.00
❏ 6245	Mother Popcorn (You Got to Have a Mother for Me) Part 1/Mother Popcorn (You Got to Have a Mother for Me) Part 2	1969	2.50	5.00	10.00
❏ 6250	Lowdown Popcorn/Top of the Stack	1969	2.50	5.00	10.00
❏ 6255	Let a Man Come In and Do the Popcorn Part One/Sometime	1969	2.50	5.00	10.00
❏ 6258	World (Part 1)/World (Part 2)	1969	2.50	5.00	10.00
❏ 6273	I'm Not Demanding (Part 1)/I'm Not Demanding (Part 2)	1969	2.50	5.00	10.00
❏ 6275	Part Two (Let a Man Come In and Do the Popcorn)/Get a Little Hipper	1969	2.50	5.00	10.00
❏ 6277	It's Christmas Time (Part 1)/It's Christmas Time (Part 2)	1969	2.50	5.00	10.00
❏ 6280	Ain't It Funky Now (Part 1)/Ain't It Funky Now (Part 2)	1970	2.00	4.00	8.00
❏ 6290	Funky Drummer (Part 1)/Funky Drummer (Part 2)	1970	2.00	4.00	8.00
❏ 6292	It's a New Day (Part 1)/It's a New Day (Part 2)	1970	2.00	4.00	8.00
❏ 6293	Let It Be Me/Baby Don't You Know	1970	2.00	4.00	8.00

—A-side: With Vicki Anderson; B-side: Vicki Anderson solo

Number	Title (A Side/B Side)	Yr	VG	VG+	NM
❏ 6300	Talkin' Loud and Sayin' Nothing (Part 1)/Talkin' Loud and Sayin' Nothing (Part 2)	1970	2.00	4.00	8.00
❏ 6310	Brother Rapp (Part 1) & (Part 2)/Bewildered	1970	2.00	4.00	8.00
❏ 6318	Get Up (I Feel Like Being A) Sex Machine (Part 1)/Get Up (I Feel Like Being A) Sex Machine (Part 2)	1970	2.00	4.00	8.00
❏ 6322	I'm Not Demanding (Part 1)/I'm Not Demanding (Part 2)	1970	2.00	4.00	8.00
❏ 6329	Super Bad (Part 1 & Part 2)/Super Bad (Part 3)	1970	2.00	4.00	8.00
❏ 6329	Call Me Super Bad (Part 1 & Part 2)/Call Me Super Bad (Part 3)	1970	5.00	10.00	20.00

—First pressing: Note longer title

Number	Title (A Side/B Side)	Yr	VG	VG+	NM
❏ 6339	Hey America/(Instrumental)	1970	2.00	4.00	8.00
❏ 6339 [PS]	Hey America/(Instrumental)	1970	3.75	7.50	15.00
❏ 6340	Santa Claus Is Definitely Here to Stay/(Instrumental)	1970	2.00	4.00	8.00
❏ 6340 [PS]	Santa Claus Is Definitely Here to Stay/(Instrumental)	1970	7.50	15.00	30.00
❏ 6347	Get Up, Get Into It, Get Involved Pt. 1/Get Up, Get Into It, Get Involved Pt. 2	1971	2.00	4.00	8.00
❏ 6359	Talking Loud and Saying Nothing — Part 1/Talking Loud and Saying Nothing — Part 2	1971	2.00	4.00	8.00
❏ 6363	I Cried/World (Part 2)	1971	2.00	4.00	8.00
❏ 6366	Spinning Wheel (Part 1)/Spinning Wheel (Part 2)	1971	2.00	4.00	8.00
❏ 6368	Soul Power Pt. 1/Soul Power Pt 2 & Pt. 3	1971	2.00	4.00	8.00

MERCURY

Number	Title (A Side/B Side)	Yr	VG	VG+	NM
❏ 885190-7	Prisoner of Love/Please, Please, Please	1986	—	2.00	4.00

—Reissue

Number	Title (A Side/B Side)	Yr	VG	VG+	NM
❏ 885194-7	Get on the Good Foot/Give It Up or Turnit A Loose	1986	—	2.00	4.00

—Reissue

PEOPLE

Number	Title (A Side/B Side)	Yr	VG	VG+	NM
❏ 664	Everybody Wanna Be Funky One More Time Pt. 1/Everybody Wanna Be Funky One More Time Pt. 2	1976	—	2.50	5.00
❏ 2500	Escape-ism (Part 1)/Escape-ism (Parts 2 & 3)	1971	—	3.00	6.00
❏ 2501	Hot Pants Pt. 1 (She Got to Use What She Got to Get What She Wants)/Hot Pants Pt. 2	1971	—	3.00	6.00

Number	Title (A Side/B Side)	Yr	VG	VG+	NM
POLYDOR					
❏ 2005	Star Generation/Women Are Something Else	1979	—	2.50	5.00
❏ 2034	The Original Disco Man/Let the Boogie Do the Rest	1979	—	2.50	5.00
❏ 2054	Regrets/Stone Cold Drag	1979	—	2.50	5.00
❏ 2078	Let the Funk Flow/Sometimes That's All There Is	1980	—	2.50	5.00
❏ 2129	Get Up Offa That Thing/It's Too Funky in Here	1980	—	2.50	5.00
❏ 2167	Give the Bass Player Some Part 1/Part 2	1981	—	2.50	5.00
❏ 14088	Make It Funky Part 1/Make It Funky Part 2	1971	—	3.00	6.00
❏ 14098	My Part/Make It Funky, Part 3// Make It Funky, Part 4	1971	—	3.00	6.00
❏ 14100	I'm a Greedy Man Part 1/I'm a Greedy Man Part 2	1971	—	3.00	6.00
❏ 14109	Talking Loud and Saying Nothing Part 1/Part 2	1972	—	3.00	6.00
❏ 14110	Nothing Beats a Try But a Fail/Hot Pants Road	1972	—	—	—
—Unreleased					
❏ 14116	King Heroin/Theme from King Heroin	1972	—	3.00	6.00
❏ 14116 [PS]	King Heroin/Theme from King Heroin	1972	2.50	5.00	10.00
❏ 14125	There It Is Part 1/There It Is Part 2	1972	—	3.00	6.00
❏ 14129	Honky Tonk Part 1/Honky Tonk Part 2	1972	—	3.00	6.00
—Artist credit: "James Brown Soul Train"					
❏ 14139	Get On the Good Foot Part 1/Get On the Good Foot Part 2	1972	—	3.00	6.00
❏ 14153	I Got a Bag of My Own/Public Enemy #1	1972	—	3.00	6.00
❏ 14155	I Got a Bag of My Own/I Know It's True	1972	7.50	15.00	30.00
—Manufactured in U.S. for export					
❏ 14157	What My Baby Needs Now Is a Little More Lovin'/ This Guy-This Girl's in Love	1972	—	3.00	6.00
—With Lyn Collins					
❏ 14161	Santa Claus Goes Straight to the Ghetto/Sweet Little Baby Boy	1972	—	3.00	6.00
❏ 14162	I Got Ants in My Pants (and I want to dance) Part 1/Part 15 and 16	1973	—	2.50	5.00
❏ 14168	Down and Out in New York City/Mama's Dead	1973	—	2.50	5.00
❏ 14169	The Boss/Like It Is, Like It Was	1973	—	2.50	5.00
❏ 14177	Think/Something	1973	—	2.50	5.00
❏ 14185	Think/Something	1973	—	2.50	5.00
❏ 14193	Woman Part 1/Woman Part 2	1973	—	2.50	5.00
❏ 14194	Sexy, Sexy, Sexy/Slaughter Theme	1973	—	2.50	5.00
❏ 14199	Let It Be Me/It's All Right	1973	—	—	—
—With Lyn Collins; canceled?					
❏ 14206	I Got a Good Thing Part 1/ I Got a Good Thing Part 2	1973	—	—	—
—Canceled?					
❏ 14210	Stoned to the Bone Part 1/ Stoned to the Bone Part 2	1973	—	2.50	5.00
—Notice corrected title					
❏ 14210	Stone to the Bone Part 1/ Stone to the Bone Part 2	1973	2.50	5.00	10.00
❏ 14223	The Payback Part 1/The Payback Part 2	1974	—	2.50	5.00
❏ 14223 [PS]	The Payback Part 1/The Payback Part 2	1974	2.50	5.00	10.00
❏ 14244	My Thang/Public Enemy No. 1	1974	—	2.50	5.00
❏ 14255	Papa Don't Take No Mess Part 1/Part 2	1974	—	2.50	5.00
❏ 14258	Funky President (People It's Bad)/Coldblooded	1974	—	2.50	5.00
❏ 14268	Reality/I Need Your Love So Bad	1975	—	2.50	5.00
❏ 14270	Sex Machine Part 1/Sex Machine Part 2	1975	—	2.50	5.00
❏ 14274	Thank You For Letting Me Be Myself And... Part 1/Part 2	1975	—	2.50	5.00
❏ 14279	Dead On It Part 1/Dead On It Part 2	1975	—	—	—
—Unreleased					
❏ 14281	Hustle (Dead On It) Part 1/Hustle (Dead On It) Part 2	1975	—	2.50	5.00
❏ 14295	Superbad, Superslick Part 1/Superbad, Superslick Part 2	1975	—	2.50	5.00
❏ 14301	Hot (I Need to Be Loved, Loved, Loved, Loved)/ Superbad, Superslick	1975	—	2.50	5.00
❏ 14302	Dooley's Junkyard Dogs Part 1/Part 2	1975	—	2.50	5.00
❏ 14304	(I Love You) For Sentimental Reasons/ Goodnight My Love	1976	—	2.50	5.00
❏ 14326	Get Up Offa That Thing/Release the Pressure	1976	—	2.50	5.00
❏ 14354	I Refuse to Lose/Home Again	1976	—	2.50	5.00
❏ 14360	Bodyheat Part 1/Bodyheat Part 2	1976	—	2.50	5.00
❏ 14388	Kiss in 77/Woman	1977	—	2.50	5.00
❏ 14409	Give Me Some Skin/People Wake Up and Live	1977	—	2.50	5.00
—With the J.B.'s					
❏ 14433	Take Me Higher and Groove Me/Summertime	1977	—	2.50	5.00
—B-side by Martha and James					
❏ 14438	If You Don't Give a Doggone About It/People Who Criticize	1977	—	2.50	5.00
—With the New J.B.'s					
❏ 14460	Love Me Tender/Have a Happy Day	1978	—	2.50	5.00
—With the New J.B.'s					
❏ 14465	Eyesight/I Never Never Never Will Forget	1978	—	2.50	5.00
❏ 14487	The Spank/Love Me Tender	1978	—	2.50	5.00
❏ 14512	Nature Part 1/Nature Part 2	1978	—	2.50	5.00
❏ 14522	For Goodness Sakes, Look at Those Cakes Part 1/Part 2	1979	—	2.50	5.00
❏ 14540	Someone to Talk To Part 1/Someone to Talk To Part 2	1979	—	2.50	5.00
❏ 14557	It's Too Funky in Here/Are We Really Dancing	1979	—	2.50	5.00
❏ 871804-7	Think/Lost Someone	1989	—	—	3.00
—Reissue					
❏ 871808-7	Out of Sight/Maybe the Last Time	1989	—	—	3.00
—Reissue					
❏ 871810-7	I Got You (I Feel Good)/Papa's Got a Brand New Bag	1989	—	—	3.00
—Reissue					
❏ 887500-7	(Get Up I Feel Like Being a) Sex Machine/ Vincent's Theme	1988	—	—	3.00
—B-side by Ethan James					
❏ 887500-7 [PS]	(Get Up I Feel Like Being a) Sex Machine/ Vincent's Theme	1988	—	2.00	4.00
—B-side by Ethan James					

Number	Title (A Side/B Side)	Yr	VG	VG+	NM
SCOTTI BROTHERS					
❏ ZS4-05682	Living in America/Farewell	1985	—	—	3.00
—B-side by Vince Di Cola					
❏ ZS4-05682 [PS]	Living in America/Farewell	1985	—	—	3.00
❏ ZS4-06275	Gravity/Gravity (Dub Mix)	1986	—	—	3.00
❏ ZS4-06275 [PS]	Gravity/Gravity (Dub Mix)	1986	—	—	3.00
❏ ZS4-06568	How Do You Stop/House of Rock	1987	—	—	3.00
❏ ZS4-06568 [PS]	How Do You Stop/House of Rock	1987	—	—	3.00
❏ ZS4-07090	Let's Get Personal/Repeat the Beat	1987	—	—	3.00
❏ ZS4-07783	I'm Real/Tribute	1988	—	—	3.00
❏ ZS4-07783 [PS]	I'm Real/Tribute	1988	—	—	3.00
❏ ZS4-07975	Static/Godfather Runnin' the Joint	1988	—	—	3.00
❏ ZS4-08088	Time to Get Busy/Busy J.B.	1988	—	—	3.00
❏ ZS4-68559	It's Your Money $/You and Me	1989	—	—	3.00
❏ 75286	(So Tired of Standing Still We Got to) Move On/ You Are My Everything	1991	—	2.00	4.00
SMASH					
❏ 1898	Caldonia/Evil	1964	3.00	6.00	12.00
❏ 1898	Caledonia/Evil	1964	3.00	6.00	12.00
❏ 1898 [PS]	Caledonia/Evil	1964	6.25	12.50	25.00
❏ 1908	The Things That I Used to Do/Out of the Blue	1964	3.00	6.00	12.00
❏ 1908 [PS]	The Things That I Used to Do/Out of the Blue	1964	10.00	20.00	40.00
❏ 1919	Out of Sight/Maybe the Last Time	1964	3.00	6.00	12.00
❏ 1919 [PS]	Out of Sight/Maybe the Last Time	1964	10.00	20.00	40.00
❏ 1949	Who's Afraid of Virginia Woolf? Part 1/Part 2	1964			
—Unreleased					
❏ 1975	Devil's Hideaway/ Who's Afraid of Virginia Woolf?	1965	2.50	5.00	10.00
❏ 1989	I Got You/Only You	1965	12.50	25.00	50.00
—Withdrawn					
❏ 2008	Try Me/Papa's Got a Brand New Bag	1965	2.50	5.00	10.00
❏ 2028	New Breed Part 1/New Breed Part 2	1966	2.50	5.00	10.00
❏ 2042	James Brown's Boo-Ga-Loo/ Lost in the Mood of Changes	1966	2.50	5.00	10.00
❏ 2064	Let's Go Get Stoned/Our Day Will Come	1966	2.50	5.00	10.00
❏ 2093	Jimmy Mack/What Do You Like	1967	2.50	5.00	10.00
T.K.					
❏ 1039	Rapp Payback (Where Iz Moses) Part 1/Part 2	1980	—	2.00	4.00
❏ 1042	Stay with Me/Smokin' and Drinkin'	1981	—	2.00	4.00
7-Inch Extended Plays					
KING					
❏ EP-430	*Please, Please, Please/That's When I Lost My Heart/Try Me/Tell Me What I Did Wrong	1959	50.00	100.00	200.00
❏ EP-430 [PS]	Please, Please, Please	1959	100.00	200.00	400.00
❏ 826	(contents unknown)	1963	20.00	40.00	80.00
❏ 826 [PS]	Live at the Apollo	1963	30.00	60.00	120.00
SMASH					
❏ SRS 707-C	New Breed/Lost in the Mood of Changes/Hooks/ /Jabo/Fat Bag (Part 1)/Fat Bag❏ (Part 2)	196?	12.50	25.00	50.00
—Jukebox issue; small hole, plays at 33 1/3 rpm					
❏ SRS 707-C [PS]	James Brown Plays New Breed (The Boo-Ga-Loo)	196?	12.50	25.00	50.00
—Jukebox issue; small hole, plays at 33 1/3 rpm					
Albums					
HRB					
❏ 1004 [(2)]	The Fabulous James Brown	1974	6.25	12.50	25.00
KING					
❏ 610 [M]	Please Please Please	1958	300.00	600.00	1200.
—"Woman's and man's legs" cover; "King" on label is two inches wide					
❏ 610 [M]	Please Please Please	1961	250.00	500.00	1000.
—"Woman's and man's legs" cover; "King" on label is three inches wide					
❏ 635 [M]	Try Me!	1959	225.00	450.00	900.00
—"Woman with cigarette and gun" cover; "King" on label is two inches wide					
❏ 635 [M]	Try Me!	1961	150.00	300.00	600.00
—"Woman with cigarette and gun" cover; "King" on label is three inches wide					
❏ 683 [M]	Think!	1960	225.00	450.00	900.00
—"Baby" cover; "King" on label is two inches wide					
❏ 683 [M]	Think!	1961	150.00	300.00	600.00
—"Baby" cover; "King" on label is three inches wide					
❏ 683 [M]	Think!	1963	25.00	50.00	100.00
—James Brown photo cover; "crownless" King label					
❏ 683 [M]	Think!	1966	12.50	25.00	50.00
—James Brown photo cover; "crown" King label					
❏ 743 [M]	The Amazing James Brown	1961	125.00	250.00	500.00
—"James Brown in suit" cover					
❏ 743 [M]	The Amazing James Brown	1963	37.50	75.00	150.00
—White title cover; "crownless" King label					
❏ 743 [M]	The Amazing James Brown	1966	125.00	250.00	500.00
—White title cover with "James Brown" in huge letters; "crown" King label					
❏ 771 [M]	Night Train	1961	75.00	150.00	300.00
—Original title					
❏ 771 [M]	Twist Around	1962	62.50	125.00	250.00
—Second title					
❏ 771 [M]	Jump Around	1963	50.00	100.00	200.00
—Third title					
❏ KS-771 [S]	Jump Around	1963	75.00	150.00	300.00
—Stereo copies of King 771 only exist with this title					
❏ 780 [M]	Good Good Twistin'	1962	50.00	100.00	200.00
—"Good Good Twistin' " on either label or cover, or both					
❏ 780 [M]	Shout and Shimmy	1962	62.50	125.00	250.00
—"Shout and Shimmy" on both cover and label					
❏ 780 [M]	Excitement	1963	37.50	75.00	150.00
—Third title; "crownless" King label					
❏ 780 [M]	Excitement	1966	12.50	25.00	50.00
—Third title; "crown" King label					
❏ 804 [M]	James Brown & His Famous Flames Tour the U.S.A.	1962	37.50	125.00	250.00
—"Crownless" King label					
❏ 804 [M]	James Brown & His Famous Flames Tour the U.S.A.	1966	12.50	25.00	50.00
—"Crown" King label					

B

Number	Title (A Side/B Side)	Yr	VG	VG+	NM
❏ 826 [M]	Live at the Apollo	1963	37.50	75.00	150.00
—Other King albums on back cover; "crownless" King label					
❏ 826 [M]	Live at the Apollo	1963	50.00	100.00	200.00
—Custom back cover; "crownless" King label					
❏ 826 [M]	Live at the Apollo	1963	200.00	400.00	800.00
—White label promo, banded for airplay					
❏ 826 [M]	Live at the Apollo	1966	12.50	25.00	50.00
—"Crown" King label					
❏ KS-826 [S]	Live at the Apollo	1963	50.00	100.00	200.00
—Other King albums on back cover; "crownless" King label					
❏ KS-826 [S]	Live at the Apollo	1963	75.00	150.00	300.00
—Custom back cover; "crownless" King label					
❏ KS-826 [S]	Live at the Apollo	1966	17.50	35.00	70.00
—"Crown" King label					
❏ 851 [M]	Prisoner of Love	1963	25.00	50.00	100.00
—Other King albums on back cover; "crownless" King label					
❏ 851 [M]	Prisoner of Love	1963	50.00	100.00	200.00
—Custom back cover; "crownless" King label					
❏ 851 [M]	Prisoner of Love	1966	12.50	25.00	50.00
—"Crown" King label					
❏ 883 [M]	Pure Dynamite! Live at the Royal	1964	50.00	100.00	200.00
—"Crownless" King label					
❏ 883 [M]	Pure Dynamite! Live at the Royal	1964	200.00	400.00	800.00
—White label promo; banded for airplay					
❏ 883 [M]	Pure Dynamite! Live at the Royal	1966	12.50	25.00	50.00
—"Crown" King label					
❏ 909 [M]	Please Please Please	1964	25.00	50.00	100.00
—Reissue of 610; "crownless" King label					
❏ 909 [M]	Please Please Please	1966	12.50	25.00	50.00
—"Crown" King label					
❏ 919 [M]	The Unbeatable James Brown — 16 Hits	1964	25.00	50.00	100.00
—Reissue of 635; "crownless" King label					
❏ 919 [M]	The Unbeatable James Brown — 16 Hits	1966	12.50	25.00	50.00
—"Crown" King label					
❏ 938 [M]	Papa's Got a Brand New Bag	1965	20.00	40.00	80.00
—Red cover; "crownless" King label					
❏ 938 [M]	Papa's Got a Brand New Bag	1966	10.00	20.00	40.00
—"Crown" King label					
❏ 938 [M]	Papa's Got a Brand New Bag	1966	12.50	25.00	50.00
—Green cover; "crownless" King label					
❏ LPS-938 [P]	Papa's Got a Brand New Bag	1965	25.00	50.00	100.00
—Red cover; "crownless" King label					
❏ LPS-938 [P]	Papa's Got a Brand New Bag	1966	12.50	25.00	50.00
—"Crown" King label					
❏ LPS-938 [P]	Papa's Got a Brand New Bag	1966	15.00	30.00	60.00
—Green cover; "crownless" King label					
❏ 946 [M]	I Got You (I Feel Good)	1966	10.00	20.00	40.00
—"Crown" King label					
❏ 946 [M]	I Got You (I Feel Good)	1966	25.00	50.00	100.00
—"Crownless" King label					
❏ LPS-946 [S]	I Got You (I Feel Good)	1966	12.50	25.00	50.00
—"Crown" King label					
❏ LPS-946 [S]	I Got You (I Feel Good)	1966	37.50	75.00	150.00
—"Crownless" King label					
❏ 961 [M]	Mighty Instrumentals	1966	25.00	50.00	100.00
❏ LPS-961 [S]	Mighty Instrumentals	1966	37.50	75.00	150.00
❏ 985 [M]	It's a Man's Man's Man's World	1966	12.50	25.00	50.00
❏ KS-985 [S]	It's a Man's Man's Man's World	1966	17.50	35.00	70.00
❏ 1010 [M]	Christmas Songs	1966	25.00	50.00	100.00
—Wreath on gray wall, no song titles on back					
❏ 1010 [M]	Christmas Songs	1967	20.00	40.00	80.00
—Wreath on white wall, song titles are on back					
❏ KS-1010 [S]	Christmas Songs	1966	37.50	75.00	150.00
—Wreath on gray wall, no song titles on back					
❏ KS-1010 [S]	Christmas Songs	1967	25.00	50.00	100.00
—Wreath on white wall, song titles are on back					
❏ 1016 [M]	Raw Soul	1967	12.50	25.00	50.00
❏ KS-1016 [P]	Raw Soul	1967	17.50	35.00	70.00
❏ 1018 [M]	Live at the Garden	1967	20.00	40.00	80.00
❏ 1018 [M]	Live at the Garden	1967	100.00	200.00	400.00
—Black label promo; banded for airplay					
❏ KS-1018 [S]	Live at the Garden	1967	25.00	50.00	100.00
❏ 1020 [M]	Cold Sweat	1967	12.50	25.00	50.00
❏ KS-1020 [S]	Cold Sweat	1967	17.50	35.00	70.00
❏ LPS-1022 [(2)]	Live at the Apollo, Volume II	1968	17.50	35.00	70.00
❏ LPS-1024	James Brown Presents His Show of Tomorrow	1968	12.50	25.00	50.00
—Various-artists album					
❏ LPS-1030	I Can't Stand Myself (When You Touch Me)	1968	12.50	25.00	50.00
❏ LPS-1031	I Got the Feelin'	1968	12.50	25.00	50.00
❏ LPS-1034	James Brown Plays Nothing But Soul	1968	12.50	25.00	50.00
❏ LPS-1038	Thinking About Little Willie John and a Few Nice Things	1968	12.50	25.00	50.00
❏ KS-1040	A Soulful Christmas	1968	20.00	40.00	80.00
❏ KS-1047	Say It Loud — I'm Black and I'm Proud	1969	12.50	25.00	50.00
❏ KS-1051	Gettin' Down To It	1969	12.50	25.00	50.00
❏ KSD-1055	James Brown Plays & Directs The Popcorn	1969	10.00	20.00	40.00
❏ KSD-1063	It's a Mother	1969	10.00	20.00	40.00
❏ KSD-1092	Ain't It Funky	1970	10.00	20.00	40.00
❏ KSD-1095	It's a New Day So Let a Man Come In	1970	10.00	20.00	40.00
❏ KSD-1100	Soul on Top	1970	10.00	20.00	40.00
❏ KSD-1110	Sho Is Funky Down Here	1971	10.00	20.00	40.00
❏ KSD-1115 [(2)]	Sex Machine	1970	12.50	25.00	50.00
❏ KSD-1124	Hey America!	1970	10.00	20.00	40.00
❏ KSD-1127	Super Bad	1971	10.00	20.00	40.00
POLYDOR					
❏ 25-3003 [(2)]	Revolution of the Mind — Live at the Apollo, Volume III	1971	15.00	30.00	60.00
❏ PD2-3004 [(2)]	Get On the Good Foot	1972	15.00	30.00	60.00
❏ PD2-3007 [(2)]	The Payback	1973	12.50	25.00	50.00
❏ 24-4054	Hot Pants	1971	10.00	20.00	40.00
❏ PD-5028	There It Is	1972	10.00	20.00	40.00
❏ SC-5401	James Brown Soul Classics	1972	6.25	12.50	25.00
❏ SC-5402	Soul Classics, Volume 2	1973	6.25	12.50	25.00
❏ PD-6014	Black Caesar	1973	12.50	25.00	50.00
❏ PD-6015	Slaughter's Big Rip-Off	1973	12.50	25.00	50.00
❏ PD-1-6039	Reality	1975	10.00	20.00	40.00
❏ PD-1-6042	Sex Machine Today	1975	10.00	20.00	40.00
❏ PD-1-6054	Everybody's Doin' the Hustle & Dead On the Double Bump	1975	10.00	20.00	40.00
❏ PD-1-6059	Hot	1976	10.00	20.00	40.00
❏ PD-1-6071	Get Up Offa That Thing	1976	10.00	20.00	40.00
❏ PD-1-6093	Bodyheat	1976	10.00	20.00	40.00
❏ PD-1-6111	Mutha's Nature	1977	10.00	20.00	40.00
❏ PD-1-6140	Jam/1980s	1978	10.00	20.00	40.00
❏ PD-1-6181	Take a Look at Those Cakes	1978	7.50	15.00	30.00
❏ PD-1-6212	The Original Disco Man	1979	7.50	15.00	30.00
❏ PD-1-6258	People	1980	7.50	15.00	30.00
❏ PD-2-6290 [(2)]	James Brown…Live/Hot on the One	1980	12.50	25.00	50.00
❏ PD-1-6318	Nonstop!	1981	7.50	15.00	30.00
❏ PD-1-6340	The Best of James Brown	1981	5.00	10.00	20.00
❏ PD-2-9001 [(2)]	Hell	1974	20.00	40.00	80.00
❏ PD-2-9004 [(2)]	Sex Machine Live	1976	12.50	25.00	50.00
❏ 821231-1	Ain't That a Groove: The James Brown Story 1966-1969	1984	3.75	7.50	15.00
❏ 821232-1	Doing It to Death: The James Brown Story 1970-1973	1984	3.75	7.50	15.00
❏ 823275-1	The Best of James Brown	1984	3.00	6.00	12.00
—Reissue of 6340					
❏ 827439-1	Dead on the Heavy Funk: The James Brown Story 1974-1978	1985	3.75	7.50	15.00
❏ 829254-1 [(2)]	Solid Gold: 30 Golden Hits	1985	5.00	10.00	20.00
❏ 829417-1	James Brown's Funky People	1986	3.75	7.50	15.00
—Various-artists LP					
❏ 829624-1	In the Jungle Groove	1986	3.75	7.50	15.00
❏ 835857-1	James Brown's Funky People 2	1988	3.75	7.50	15.00
—Various-artists compilation					
❏ 837126-1	Motherlode	1988	3.75	7.50	15.00
RHINO					
❏ RNLP-217	Live at the Apollo, Volume 2, Part 1	1985	3.75	7.50	15.00
❏ RNLP-218	Live at the Apollo, Volume 2, Part 2	1985	3.75	7.50	15.00
❏ RNLP-219	Greatest Hits (1964-1968)	1986	3.75	7.50	15.00
❏ R1 70194	Santa's Got a Brand New Bag	1986	2.50	5.00	10.00
—Reissue of King material					
❏ R1-70217	Live at the Apollo, Volume 2, Part 1	1988	3.00	6.00	12.00
—Reissue of 217					
❏ R1-70218	Live at the Apollo, Volume 2, Part 2	1988	3.00	6.00	12.00
—Reissue of 218					
❏ R1-70219	Greatest Hits (1964-1968)	1988	3.00	6.00	12.00
—Reissue of 219					
SCOTTI BROTHERS					
❏ FZ 40380	Gravity	1986	3.00	6.00	12.00
❏ FZ 44241	I'm Real	1988	3.00	6.00	12.00
❏ FZ 45164	Soul Session Live	1989	3.75	7.50	15.00
❏ 75225-1	Love Overdue	1991	5.00	10.00	20.00
SMASH					
❏ MGS-27054 [M]	Showtime	1964	7.50	15.00	30.00
❏ MGS-27057 [M]	Grits & Soul	1965	7.50	15.00	30.00
❏ MGS-27058 [M]	Out of Sight	1965	25.00	50.00	100.00
❏ MGS-27072 [M]	James Brown Plays James Brown — Today & Yesterday	1965	7.50	15.00	30.00
❏ MGS-27080 [M]	James Brown Plays New Breed	1966	7.50	15.00	30.00
❏ MGS-27084 [M]	Handful of Soul	1966	7.50	15.00	30.00
❏ MGS-27087 [M]	The James Brown Show	1967	7.50	15.00	30.00
—Various-artists LP					
❏ MGS-27093 [M]	James Brown Plays the Real Thing	1967	7.50	15.00	30.00
❏ SRS-67054 [S]	Showtime	1964	10.00	2.00	40.00
❏ SRS-67057 [S]	Grits & Soul	1965	10.00	20.00	40.00
❏ SRS-67058 [S]	Out of Sight	1965	37.50	75.00	150.00
❏ SRS-67072 [S]	James Brown Plays James Brown — Today & Yesterday	1965	10.00	20.00	40.00
❏ SRS-67080 [S]	James Brown Plays New Breed	1966	10.00	2.00	40.00
❏ SRS-67084 [S]	Handful of Soul	1966	10.00	20.00	40.00
❏ SRS-67087 [S]	The James Brown Show	1967	10.00	2.00	40.00
—Various-artists LP					
❏ SRS-67093 [S]	James Brown Plays the Real Thing	1967	10.00	20.00	40.00
❏ SRS-67109 [S]	James Brown Sings Out of Sight	1968	7.50	15.00	30.00
—Abridged reissue of 67058					
SOLID SMOKE					
❏ SS-8006	Live and Lowdown at the Apollo, Vol. 1	1980	3.00	6.00	12.00
❏ SS-8013	Can Your Heart Stand It	1981	3.00	6.00	12.00
❏ SS-8023	The Federal Years, Part 1	198?	3.00	6.00	12.00
❏ SS-8024	The Federal Years, Part 2	198?	3.00	6.00	12.00
T.K.					
❏ 615	Soul Syndrome	1980	7.50	15.00	30.00

BROWN, JAMES (2) The MGM James Brown is not the same person as the others.
45s
MGM

Number	Title (A Side/B Side)	Yr	VG	VG+	NM
❏ 11987	The Berry Tree/I Lost When I Found You	1955	3.00	6.00	12.00
❏ 12011	The Kentuckian Song/The Man from Laramie	1955	3.00	6.00	12.00
❏ 12080	The White Buffalo/It's Lonesome Out Tonight	1955	3.00	6.00	12.00

BROWN, JERICHO
45s
DEL-FI

Number	Title (A Side/B Side)	Yr	VG	VG+	NM
❏ 4103	I Need You/Lonesome Drifter	1958	6.25	12.50	25.00
RKO UNIQUE					
❏ 412	Little Neva/Darling I Love Thee	1957	7.50	15.00	30.00
WARNER BROS.					
❏ 5161	Look for a Star/Don't You Know	1960	3.00	6.00	12.00
❏ 5213	Rovin' Eye/Someday She'll Come Along	1961	2.50	5.00	10.00
❏ 5381	Lonely Birthday/Paper Rose and Candy Ring	1963	2.50	5.00	10.00
❏ 5408	I'll Be Gone/He's Taken My Baby	1964	2.50	5.00	10.00
❏ 5458	I'm Watching You/Wisdom of a Fool	1964	2.50	5.00	10.00

Number	Title (A Side/B Side)	Yr	VG	VG+	NM

BROWN, JIM ED Also see THE BROWNS.
45s
RCA

Number	Title (A Side/B Side)	Yr	VG	VG+	NM
❏ PB-10619	Let Me Love You Where It Hurts/I Love You All Over Again	1976	—	2.00	4.00
❏ PB-10786	I've Rode with the Best/Close the Door	1976	—	2.00	4.00
❏ PB-11134	When I Touch Her There/Mexican Joe	1977	—	2.00	4.00
❏ PB-11742	You're the Part of Me/Changes	1979	—	2.00	4.00

RCA VICTOR

Number	Title (A Side/B Side)	Yr	VG	VG+	NM
❏ 47-8566	I Heard from a Memory Last Night/Just to Satisfy You	1965	2.00	4.00	8.00
❏ 47-8644	I'm Just a Country Boy/To Be or Not to Be	1965	2.00	4.00	8.00
❏ 47-8766	Regular on My Mind/The Mounties	1966	2.00	4.00	8.00
❏ 47-8867	A Taste of Heaven/Paint Me the Color of Your Wall	1966	2.00	4.00	8.00
❏ 47-8997	The Last Laugh/Party Girl	1966	2.00	4.00	8.00
❏ 47-9077	You Can Have Her/If You Were Mine, Mary	1967	2.00	4.00	8.00
❏ 47-9192	Pop a Top/Too Good to Be True	1967	2.00	4.00	8.00
❏ 47-9329	Bottle, Bottle/It Doesn't Know Any Better	1967	2.00	4.00	8.00
❏ 47-9434	The Cajun Stripper/You'll Never Know	1968	2.00	4.00	8.00
❏ 47-9518	The Enemy/I Just Came from There	1968	2.00	4.00	8.00
❏ 47-9616	Jack and Jill/Honky Tonkin'	1968	2.00	4.00	8.00
❏ 47-9677	Longest Beer of the Night/What's a Girl Like You	1968	—	3.00	6.00
❏ 47-9810	Lift Ring, Pull Open/Going Up the Country	1970	—	3.00	6.00
❏ 47-9858	Baby, I Tried/The City Cries at Night	1970	—	3.00	6.00
❏ 47-9909	Morning/How to Lose a Good Woman	1970	—	3.00	6.00
❏ 47-9965	Angel's Sunday/Every Mile of the Way	1971	—	3.00	6.00
❏ 74-0114	Man and Wife Time/Healing Hands of Time	1969	—	3.00	6.00
❏ 74-0190	The Three Bells/Beyond the Shadow	1969	—	3.00	6.00
❏ 74-0274	Ginger Is Gentle and Waiting for Me/ Drink Boys Drink	1969	—	3.00	6.00
❏ 74-0509	She's Leavin' (Bonnie, Please Don't Go)/ Love Is Worth the Tryin'	1971	—	3.00	6.00
❏ 74-0642	Evening/You Keep Right On Loving Me	1972	—	3.00	6.00
❏ 74-0712	How I Love Them Old Songs/Close	1972	—	3.00	6.00
❏ 74-0785	All I Had to Do/Triangle	1972	—	3.00	6.00
❏ 74-0846	Unbelievable Love/ If Her Blue Eyes Don't Get You	1972	—	3.00	6.00
❏ 74-0928	Southern Loving/How Long Does It Take a Memory to Drown	1973	—	3.00	6.00
❏ APBO-0059	Broad-Minded Man/Helpin' You Get Over Him	1973	—	2.50	5.00
❏ APBO-0180	Sometime Sunshine/Louisiana Woman	1973	—	2.50	5.00
❏ APBO-0267	It's That Time of Night/If Wishes Were Horses	1974	—	2.50	5.00
❏ PB-10047	Get Up I Think I Love You/A Nickel for the Fiddler	1974	—	2.50	5.00
❏ PB-10131	Don Junior/Who's Gonna Love Me	1974	—	2.50	5.00
❏ PB-10233	Barroom Pal, Goodtime Gals/ Nearer My Love to You	1975	—	2.50	5.00
❏ PB-10370	Fine Time to Get the Blues/Sweet Song	1975	—	2.50	5.00
❏ PB-10531	Another Morning/An Old Flame Never Dies	1975	—	2.50	5.00

Albums
RCA CAMDEN

Number	Title (A Side/B Side)	Yr	VG	VG+	NM
❏ ACL1-0197	Hey Good Lookin'	1973	2.50	5.00	10.00
❏ ACL1-0618	The Three Bells	1974	2.50	5.00	10.00
❏ CAS-2496	Gentle on My Mind	1971	2.50	5.00	10.00
❏ CAS-2549	Country Cream	1972	2.50	5.00	10.00

RCA VICTOR

Number	Title (A Side/B Side)	Yr	VG	VG+	NM
❏ APL1-0172	Bar-Rooms & Pop-A-Tops	1973	3.75	7.50	15.00
❏ APL1-0324	Best of Jim Ed Brown	1973	3.75	7.50	15.00
❏ APL1-0572	It's That Time of Night	1974	3.75	7.50	15.00
❏ ANL1-1215	It's That Time of Night	1975	2.50	5.00	10.00
—Reissue of 0572					
❏ LPM-3569 [M]	Alone with You	1966	5.00	10.00	20.00
❏ LSP-3569 [S]	Alone with You	1966	6.25	12.50	25.00
❏ LPM-3744 [M]	Just Jim	1967	6.25	12.50	25.00
❏ LSP-3744 [S]	Just Jim	1967	5.00	10.00	20.00
❏ LPM-3853 [M]	Gems by Jim	1967	6.25	12.50	25.00
❏ LSP-3853 [S]	Gems by Jim	1967	5.00	10.00	20.00
❏ LPM-3942 [M]	Bottle, Bottle	1968	10.00	20.00	40.00
❏ LSP-3942 [S]	Bottle, Bottle	1968	5.00	10.00	20.00
❏ LSP-4011	Country's Best on Record	1968	5.00	10.00	20.00
❏ LSP-4130	This Is My Best!	1968	5.00	10.00	20.00
❏ LSP-4175	Jim Ed Sings the Browns	1969	5.00	10.00	20.00
❏ LSP-4262	Going Up the Country	1970	3.75	7.50	15.00
❏ LSP-4366	Just for You	1970	3.75	7.50	15.00
❏ LSP-4461	Morning	1971	3.75	7.50	15.00
❏ LSP-4525	Angel's Sunday	1971	3.75	7.50	15.00
❏ LSP-4614	She's Leavin'	1971	3.75	7.50	15.00
❏ LSP-4713	Evening	1972	3.75	7.50	15.00
❏ LSP-4755	Brown Is Blue	1972	3.75	7.50	15.00

BROWN, JOE, AND THE BRUVVERS
45s
BELL

Number	Title (A Side/B Side)	Yr	VG	VG+	NM
❏ 45364 [DJ]	Hey Mama (mono/stereo)	1973	—	3.00	6.00
—May be promo only					

CAMEO

Number	Title (A Side/B Side)	Yr	VG	VG+	NM
❏ 241	It Only Took a Minute/ All Things Bright and Beautiful	1963	3.00	6.00	12.00

DOT

Number	Title (A Side/B Side)	Yr	VG	VG+	NM
❏ 16508	Hava Nagila/That's What Love Will Do	1963	3.00	6.00	12.00

HICKORY

Number	Title (A Side/B Side)	Yr	VG	VG+	NM
❏ 1329	Sally Ann/Little Ukulele	1965	2.50	5.00	10.00

JAMIE

Number	Title (A Side/B Side)	Yr	VG	VG+	NM
❏ 1298	Lonely Circus/Teardrops in the Rain	1965	2.50	5.00	10.00
❏ 1327	Sea of Heartbreak/Mrs. O's Theme	1966	2.50	5.00	10.00

KAPP

Number	Title (A Side/B Side)	Yr	VG	VG+	NM
❏ 2068	Adieu, Monsieur Le Professeur/ Diamonds of Dew	1969	—	3.00	6.00

LONDON INT'L.

Number	Title (A Side/B Side)	Yr	VG	VG+	NM
❏ 10507	What a Crazy World We're Living In/Popcorn	1962	3.75	7.50	15.00
❏ 10517	A Picture of You/A Lay-About's Lament	1962	3.75	7.50	15.00
❏ 10522	Your Tender Look/The Other Side of Town	1962	3.75	7.50	15.00

STELLAR

Number	Title (A Side/B Side)	Yr	VG	VG+	NM
❏ 1504	Hava Nagila/That's What Love Will Do	1963	3.75	7.50	15.00

VERTIGO

Number	Title (A Side/B Side)	Yr	VG	VG+	NM
❏ 201	I Was Lost/Cincinnati Floor	1974	—	2.50	5.00
—As "Brown's Home Brew"					

WARNER BROS.

Number	Title (A Side/B Side)	Yr	VG	VG+	NM
❏ 7055	With a Little Help from My Friends/Won't You Show Me Around	1967	2.00	4.00	8.00

BROWN, MAXINE (1)
45s
ABC-PARAMOUNT

Number	Title (A Side/B Side)	Yr	VG	VG+	NM
❏ 10235	I Don't Need You No More/Think of Me	1961	3.00	6.00	12.00
❏ 10255	After All We've Been Through Together/My Life	1961	3.00	6.00	12.00
❏ 10290	I Got a Funny Kind of Feeling/What I Don't Know	1962	3.00	6.00	12.00
❏ 10315	Forget Him/A Man	1962	3.00	6.00	12.00
❏ 10327	No Time for Cryin'/Wanting You	1962	3.00	6.00	12.00
❏ 10343	I Kneel at Your Throne/If I Knew Then	1962	3.00	6.00	12.00
❏ 10370	Promise Me Anything/Am I Falling in Love	1962	3.00	6.00	12.00
❏ 10388	Life Goes On Just the Same/ If You Have No Real Objections	1962	3.00	6.00	12.00

AVCO

Number	Title (A Side/B Side)	Yr	VG	VG+	NM
❏ 4585	Always and Forever/Make Love to Me	1971	—	2.50	5.00
❏ 4604	Treat Me Like a Lady/I.O.U.	1972	—	2.50	5.00
❏ 4612	Picked Up, Packed and Went Away/(B-side unknown)	1972	—	2.50	5.00

COMMONWEALTH UNITED

Number	Title (A Side/B Side)	Yr	VG	VG+	NM
❏ 3001	We'll Cry Together/Darling Be Home Soon	1969	—	3.00	6.00
❏ 3008	I Can't Get Along Without You/Reason to Believe	1970	—	3.00	6.00

EPIC

Number	Title (A Side/B Side)	Yr	VG	VG+	NM
❏ 10334	Seems You've Forsaken My Love/ Plum Outa Sight	1968	2.50	5.00	10.00
❏ 10424	Love in Them There Hills/From Loving You	1968	2.50	5.00	10.00

NOMAR

Number	Title (A Side/B Side)	Yr	VG	VG+	NM
❏ 103	All in My Mind/Harry, Let's Marry	1960	3.75	7.50	15.00
❏ 106	Funny/Now That You've Gone	1961	3.75	7.50	15.00
❏ 107	Heaven in Your Arms/Maxine's Place	1961	3.75	7.50	15.00
—B-side by Frankie and the Flips					

WAND

Number	Title (A Side/B Side)	Yr	VG	VG+	NM
❏ 135	Ask Me/Yesterday's Kisses	1963	2.50	5.00	10.00
❏ 135 [PS]	Ask Me/Yesterday's Kisses	1963	12.50	25.00	50.00
❏ 142	Coming Back to You/Since I Found You	1963	2.50	5.00	10.00
❏ 152	Little Girl Lost/You Upset My Soul	1964	2.00	4.00	8.00
❏ 158	I Cry Alone/Put Yourself in My Place	1964	2.00	4.00	8.00
❏ 162	Oh No Not My Baby/You Upset My Soul	1964	3.00	6.00	12.00
❏ 173	It's Gonna Be Alright/You Do Something to Me	1965	2.00	4.00	8.00
❏ 185	Anything for a Laugh/One Step at a Time	1965	2.00	4.00	8.00
❏ 1104	If You Gotta Make a Fool of Somebody/ You're in Love	1965	2.00	4.00	8.00
❏ 1117	One in a Million/Anything You Do Is Alright	1966	2.00	4.00	8.00
❏ 1128	We Can Work It Out/Let Me Give You My Lovin'	1966	2.00	4.00	8.00
❏ 1145	I Don't Need Anything/The Secret of Livin'	1967	2.00	4.00	8.00
❏ 1179	Soul Serenade/He's the Only Guy I'll Ever Love	1968	2.00	4.00	8.00

Albums
COLLECTABLES

Number	Title (A Side/B Side)	Yr	VG	VG+	NM
❏ COL-5116	Golden Classics	198?	3.00	6.00	12.00

COMMONWEALTH UNITED

Number	Title (A Side/B Side)	Yr	VG	VG+	NM
❏ CU-6001	We'll Cry Together	1969	5.00	10.00	20.00

GUEST STAR

Number	Title (A Side/B Side)	Yr	VG	VG+	NM
❏ GS-1911 [M]	Maxine Brown	1964	3.00	6.00	12.00

WAND

Number	Title (A Side/B Side)	Yr	VG	VG+	NM
❏ LP-656 [M]	The Fabulous Sound of Maxine Brown	1963	12.50	25.00	50.00
❏ WDS-656 [S]	The Fabulous Sound of Maxine Brown	1963	15.00	30.00	60.00
❏ WD-663 [M]	Spotlight on Maxine Brown	1965	7.50	15.00	30.00
❏ WDS-663 [S]	Spotlight on Maxine Brown	1965	10.00	20.00	40.00
❏ WD-684 [M]	Maxine Brown's Greatest Hits	1967	5.00	10.00	20.00
❏ WDS-684 [S]	Maxine Brown's Greatest Hits	1967	6.25	12.50	25.00
❏ DT-91012 [R]	The Fabulous Sound of Maxine Brown	196?	12.50	25.00	50.00
—Capitol Record Club edition					

BROWN, NAPPY
45s
ICHIBAN

Number	Title (A Side/B Side)	Yr	VG	VG+	NM
❏ 206	Lemon Squeezin' Daddy/Small Red Apples	1989	—	2.50	5.00

SAVOY

Number	Title (A Side/B Side)	Yr	VG	VG+	NM
❏ 1129	That Man/I Wonder	1954	7.50	15.00	30.00
❏ 1135	Is It True, Is It True/Two-Faced Woman	1954	7.50	15.00	30.00
❏ 1155	Don't Be Angry/It's Really You	1955	6.25	12.50	25.00
❏ 1162	Piddly Patter Patter/There'll Come a Day	1955	6.25	12.50	25.00
❏ 1176	Doodle I Love You/Sittin' in the Dark	1955	6.25	12.50	25.00
❏ 1187	Open Up That Door/Pleasing You	1956	6.25	12.50	25.00
❏ 1196	Am I/Love Baby	1956	6.25	12.50	25.00
❏ 1506	Little by Little/I'm Getting Lonesome	1956	5.00	10.00	20.00
❏ 1511	Pretty Girl (Yea Yea Yea)/I'm Gonna Get You	1957	5.00	10.00	20.00
❏ 1514	Goody Goody Gum Drops/Bye Bye Baby	1957	5.00	10.00	20.00
❏ 1525	The Right Time/Oh You Don't Know	1957	5.00	10.00	20.00
❏ 1530	If You Need Some Lovin'/I'm in the Mood	1958	5.00	10.00	20.00
❏ 1547	Skidy Wo/I Cried Like a Baby	1958	5.00	10.00	20.00
❏ 1551	It Don't Hurt No More/My Baby	1958	5.00	10.00	20.00
❏ 1555	You're Going to Need Someone/Skiddy Woe	1958	5.00	10.00	20.00
❏ 1562	A Long Time/All Right Now	1959	5.00	10.00	20.00
❏ 1569	This Is My Confession/For Those Who Love	1959	5.00	10.00	20.00
❏ 1575	I Cried Like a Baby/So Deep	1959	5.00	10.00	20.00
❏ 1579	Give Me Your Love/Too Shy	1959	5.00	10.00	20.00
❏ 1582	Down in the Alley/My Baby Knows	1960	3.75	7.50	15.00
❏ 1587	Baby, Cry, Cry, Cry, Baby/ What's Come Over You	1960	3.75	7.50	15.00
❏ 1588	Apple of My Eye/My Baby I Got News for You	1960	3.75	7.50	15.00
❏ 1592	The Hole I'm In/Nobody Can Say	1960	3.75	7.50	15.00
❏ 1594	Coal Miner/Honnie-Bonnie	1961	3.75	7.50	15.00
❏ 1598	Don't Be Angry/Any Time Is the Right Time	1961	3.75	7.50	15.00

Number	Title (A Side/B Side)	Yr	VG	VG+	NM
❏ 1616	Didn't You Know/I've Had My Fun	1962	3.75	7.50	15.00
❏ 1621	Lock on the Door/	1963			
	So Glad I Don't Have to Cry No More	1963	3.75	7.50	15.00

Albums
BLACK TOP

❏ BT-1039	Something Gonna Jump Out the Bushes	1987	3.75	7.50	15.00

ICHIBAN

❏ ICH-1056	Apples and Lemons	1990	3.00	6.00	12.00

KING SNAKE/ICHIBAN

❏ ICH-9006	Aw! Shucks	1991	3.75	7.50	15.00

LANDSLIDE

❏ LD 1008	Tore Up	1984	3.75	7.50	15.00

MELTONE

❏ 1502	Deep Sea Diver	1989	3.75	7.50	15.00

SAVOY

❏ MG-14002 [M]	Nappy Brown Sings	1958	100.00	200.00	400.00
❏ MG-14025 [M]	The Right Time	1960	62.50	125.00	250.00
❏ 14427	Nappy Brown	1977	3.00	6.00	12.00

SAVOY JAZZ

❏ SJL-1149	Don't Be Angry	1984	2.50	5.00	10.00

BROWN, ODELL
45s
CADET

❏ 5570	Mellow Yellow/Quiet Village	1967	2.00	4.00	8.00
❏ 5591	The Look of Love/No More Water in the Well	1968	2.00	4.00	8.00
❏ 5624	The Weight/Think About It	1968	2.00	4.00	8.00

Albums
CADET

❏ LP-775 [M]	Raising the Roof	1966	3.75	7.50	15.00
❏ LPS-775 [S]	Raising the Roof	1966	5.00	10.00	20.00
❏ LP-788 [M]	Mellow Yellow	1967	5.00	10.00	20.00
❏ LPS-788 [S]	Mellow Yellow	1967	3.75	7.50	15.00
❏ LP-800 [M]	Ducky	1967	5.00	10.00	20.00
❏ LPS-800 [S]	Ducky	1967	3.75	7.50	15.00
❏ LPS-823	Odell Brown Plays Otis Redding	1969	3.75	7.50	15.00
❏ LPS-838	Free Delivery	1970	3.75	7.50	15.00

PAULA

❏ 4005	Odell Brown	1974	3.00	6.00	12.00

BROWN, RAY, AND THE WHISPERS
45s
GNP CRESCENDO

❏ 357	Fool, Fool, Fool/Pride	1965	5.00	10.00	20.00

PARKWAY

❏ 951	20 Miles/Devoted to You	1965	7.50	15.00	30.00

BROWN, RITCHIE
45s
HIT

❏ 240	Uptight (Everything's Alright)/California Dreamin'	1966	2.50	5.00	10.00

—B-side by the Jalopy Five

BROWN, ROY
45s
BLUESWAY

❏ 61002	New Orleans Women/Standing on Broadway (Watching the Girls)	1967	2.00	4.00	8.00

DELUXE

❏ 3318	Big Town/Train Time Blues	1951	50.00	100.00	200.00

—Roy Brown singles on DeLuxe before 3318 are unconfirmed on 45 rpm

❏ 3318	Big Town/Train Time Blues	1951	100.00	200.00	400.00

—Blue vinyl

❏ 3319	Bar Room Blues/Good Rockin' Man	1951	50.00	100.00	200.00

—Black vinyl

❏ 3319	Bar Room Blues/Good Rockin' Man	1951	100.00	200.00	400.00

—Blue vinyl

❏ 3323	I've Got the Last Laugh Now/Brown Angel	1951	50.00	100.00	200.00

—Black vinyl

❏ 3323	I've Got the Last Laugh Now/Brown Angel	1951	100.00	200.00	400.00

—Blue vinyl

HOME OF THE BLUES

❏ 107	Don't Break My Heart/A Man with the Blues	1960	6.25	12.50	25.00
❏ 110	Tired of Being Alone/Rocking All the Time	1960	6.25	12.50	25.00
❏ 115	Oh So Wonderful/Sugar Baby	1961	6.25	12.50	25.00
❏ 122	Rock and Roll Jamboree/I Need a Friend	1961	6.25	12.50	25.00

IMPERIAL

❏ 5422	Everybody/Saturday Night	1957	7.50	15.00	30.00
❏ 5427	Party Doll/I'm Sticking with You	1957	7.50	15.00	30.00
❏ 5439	Let the Four Winds Blow/Diddy-Y-Diddy-O	1957	7.50	15.00	30.00
❏ 5455	I'm Convicted of Love/I'm Ready to Play	1957	7.50	15.00	30.00
❏ 5469	Tick of the Clock/Slow Down Little Eva	1957	7.50	15.00	30.00
❏ 5489	Ain't Gonna Do It/Sail On Little Girl	1958	7.50	15.00	30.00
❏ 5510	Hip Shakin' Baby/Be My Love Tonight	1958	7.50	15.00	30.00
❏ 5969	Let the Four Winds Blow/Diddy-Yi-Diddy-Yo	1963	5.00	10.00	20.00

KING

❏ 4602	Travelin' Man/Hurry, Hurry Baby	1953	15.00	30.00	60.00
❏ 4609	Grandpa Stole My Baby/Money Can't Buy Love	1953	15.00	30.00	60.00
❏ 4704	Trouble at Midnight/Bootlegging Baby	1954	15.00	30.00	60.00
❏ 4715	Up Jumped the Devil/This Is My Last Goodbye	1954	15.00	30.00	60.00
❏ 4722	No Love at All/Don't Let It Rain	1954	15.00	30.00	60.00
❏ 4731	Ain't It a Shame/Gal from Kokomo	1954	15.00	30.00	60.00
❏ 4743	Worried Life Blues/Black Diamond	1954	15.00	30.00	60.00
❏ 4761	Fannie Brown Got Married/Queen of Diamonds	1955	12.50	25.00	50.00
❏ 4816	Shake 'Em Up Baby/Letter to Baby	1955	12.50	25.00	50.00
❏ 4834	My Little Angel Child/She's Gone Too Long	1955	12.50	25.00	50.00
❏ 5178	La-Dee-Dah-Dee/Melinda	1959	5.00	10.00	20.00
❏ 5207	I Never Had It So Good/Rinky Dinky Doo	1959	5.00	10.00	20.00
❏ 5218	Hard Luck Blues/Good Looking and Forty	1959	5.00	10.00	20.00
❏ 5247	School Bell Rock/Ain't No Rocking No More	1959	5.00	10.00	20.00

Number	Title (A Side/B Side)	Yr	VG	VG+	NM
❏ 5333	Ain't Got No Blues Today/Adorable One	1960	5.00	10.00	20.00
❏ 5521	Mighty Mighty Man/Good Man Blues	1961	5.00	10.00	20.00

MERCURY

❏ 73166	It's My Fault Darling/Love for Sale	1970	—	3.00	6.00
❏ 73219	Mail Man Blues/Hunky Funky Woman	1971	—	3.00	6.00

Albums
BLUESWAY

❏ BLS-6019	The Blues Are Brown	1968	6.25	12.50	25.00
❏ BLS-6056	Hard Times	1973	6.25	12.50	25.00

EPIC

❏ E 30473	Live at Monterey	1971	6.25	12.50	25.00

INTERMEDIA

❏ QS-5027	Good Rockin' Tonight	198?	2.50	5.00	10.00

KING

❏ 956 [M]	Roy Brown Sings 24 Hits	1966	12.50	25.00	50.00
❏ KS-956 [R]	Roy Brown Sings 24 Hits	1966	12.50	25.00	50.00
❏ KS-1130	Hard Luck Blues	1971	6.25	12.50	25.00

BROWN, ROY / WYNONIE HARRIS
Albums
KING

❏ 607 [M]	Battle of the Blues	1958	150.00	300.00	600.00
❏ 627 [M]	Battle of the Blues, Volume 2	1959	200.00	400.00	800.00

BROWN, ROY / WYNONIE HARRIS / EDDIE VINSON
Albums
KING

❏ 668 [M]	Battle of the Blues, Volume 4	1960	625.00	1250.	2500.

BROWN, RUTH
45s
ATLANTIC

❏ 893	Happiness Is a Thing Called Joe/Love Me Baby	197?	2.50	5.00	10.00

—Reissue 45 on glossy yellow label with black "fan" logo (there was no 45 of this in the 1950s)

❏ 919	Teardrops from My Eyes/				
	Am I Making the Same Mistake	1950	100.00	200.00	400.00

—This and Atlantic 914 were the label's first two 45s.

❏ 948	Shine On—Big Bright Moon Shine On/				
	Without My Love	1951	15.00	30.00	60.00

—Ruth Brown records on Atlantic before 948 (except as listed) are unconfirmed on 45 rpm

❏ 962	5-10-15 Hours/Be Anything But Be Mine	1952	12.50	25.00	50.00
❏ 973	Daddy Daddy/Have a Good Time	1952	12.50	25.00	50.00
❏ 978	Three Letters/Good for Nothing Joe	1952	12.50	25.00	50.00
❏ 986	(Mama) He Treats Your Daughter Mean/				
	R.B. Blues	1953	15.00	30.00	60.00
❏ 993	Wild Wild Young Men/Mend Your Ways	1953	10.00	20.00	40.00
❏ 1005	The Tears Keep Tumblin' Down/				
	I Would If I Could	1953	7.50	15.00	30.00
❏ 1018	Love Contest/If You Don't Want Me	1954	7.50	15.00	30.00
❏ 1023	Sentimental Journey/It's All in Your Mind	1954	7.50	15.00	30.00
❏ 1027	If I Had Any Sense/Hello Little Boy	1954	7.50	15.00	30.00
❏ 1036	Oh What a Dream/Please Don't Freeze	1954	7.50	15.00	30.00
❏ 1044	Somebody Touch Me/Mambo Baby	1954	7.50	15.00	30.00
❏ 1051	Ever Since My Baby's Been Gone/				
	Bye Bye Young Men	1955	7.50	15.00	30.00
❏ 1059	I Can See Everybody's Baby/				
	As Long As I'm Moving	1955	7.50	15.00	30.00
❏ 1072	What'd I Say/It's Love Baby (24 Hours of the Day)	1955	7.50	15.00	30.00
❏ 1077	Love Has Joined Us Together/I Gotta Have You	1955	7.50	15.00	30.00

—With Clyde McPhatter

❏ 1082	Old Man River/I Want to Do More	1956	6.25	12.50	25.00
❏ 1091	Sweet Baby of Mine/I'm Getting Right	1956	6.25	12.50	25.00
❏ 1102	I Want to Be Loved/Mom, Oh Mom	1956	6.25	12.50	25.00
❏ 1113	Smooth Operator/I Still Love You	1956	6.25	12.50	25.00
❏ 1125	Lucky Lips/My Heart Is Breaking Over You	1957	6.25	12.50	25.00
❏ 1140	When I Get You Baby/One More Time	1957	6.25	12.50	25.00
❏ 1153	Show Me/I Hope We Meet	1957	6.25	12.50	25.00
❏ 1166	A New Love/Look Me Up	1957	6.25	12.50	25.00
❏ 1177	Book of Lies/Just Too Much	1958	6.25	12.50	25.00
❏ 1197	This Little Girl's Gone Rockin'/Why Me	1958	6.25	12.50	25.00
❏ 2008	Mama, He Treats Your Daughter Mean/				
	I'll Step Aside	1958	5.00	10.00	20.00
❏ 2015	5-10-15 Hours/Itty Bitty Girl	1959	5.00	10.00	20.00
❏ 2026	Jack O'Diamonds/I Can't Hear a Word You Say	1959	5.00	10.00	20.00
❏ 2035	I Don't Know/Papa Daddy	1959	5.00	10.00	20.00
❏ 2052	Don't Deceive Me/I Burned Your Letter	1960	5.00	10.00	20.00
❏ 2064	The Door Is Still Open/What I Wouldn't Give	1960	5.00	10.00	20.00
❏ 2075	Taking Care of Business/Honey Boy	1960	5.00	10.00	20.00
❏ 2088	Sure 'Nuff/Here He Comes	1961	3.75	7.50	15.00
❏ 2104	It Tears Me All to Pieces/Anyone But You	1961	3.75	7.50	15.00

DECCA

❏ 31598	What Happened to You/Yes Sir That's My Baby	1964	2.50	5.00	10.00
❏ 31640	Come a Little Closer/I Love Him and I Know It	1964	2.50	5.00	10.00

MAINSTREAM

❏ 611	On the Good Ship Lollipop/Hurry On Down	1965	2.50	5.00	10.00

PHILIPS

❏ 40028	Shake a Hand/Say It Again	1962	3.00	6.00	12.00
❏ 40056	Mama (He Treats Your Daughter Mean)/				
	Hold My Hand	1962	3.00	6.00	12.00
❏ 40086	He Tells Me with His Eyes/If You Don't Tell Nobody	1963	3.00	6.00	12.00
❏ 40119	Satisfied/If You Don't Tell Nobody	1963	3.00	6.00	12.00

7-Inch Extended Plays
ATLANTIC

❏ 505	Teardrops from My Eyes/5-10-15//Mama He Treats Your Daughter Mean/So Long	1953	25.00	50.00	100.00
❏ 505 [PS]	Ruth Brown Sings	1953	37.50	75.00	150.00
❏ 585	*Lucky Lips/Mambo Baby/Smooth Operator/ Oh What a Dream	1957	15.00	30.00	60.00
❏ 585 [PS]	Ruth Brown	1957	30.00	60.00	120.00

Number	Title (A Side/B Side)	Yr	VG	VG+	NM

Albums

ATLANTIC

❏ 1308 [M]	Last Date with Ruth Brown	1959	50.00	100.00	200.00
—Black label					
❏ 1308 [M]	Last Date with Ruth Brown	1961	12.50	25.00	50.00
—Red and purple label, "fan" logo in white					
❏ SD 1308 [S]	Last Date with Ruth Brown	1959	75.00	150.00	300.00
—Green label					
❏ SD 1308 [S]	Last Date with Ruth Brown	1961	15.00	30.00	60.00
—Blue and green label, "fan" logo in white					
❏ 8004 [M]	Ruth Brown	1957	50.00	100.00	200.00
—Black label					
❏ 8004 [M]	Ruth Brown	1960	37.50	75.00	150.00
—White "bullseye" label					
❏ 8004 [M]	Ruth Brown	1961	12.50	25.00	50.00
—Red and purple label, "fan" logo in white					
❏ 8026 [M]	Miss Rhythm	1959	50.00	100.00	200.00
—Black label					
❏ 8026 [M]	Miss Rhythm	1960	37.50	75.00	150.00
—White "bullseye" label					
❏ 8026 [M]	Miss Rhythm	1961	12.50	25.00	50.00
—Red and purple label, "fan" logo in white					
❏ 8080 [M]	The Best of Ruth Brown	1963	10.00	20.00	40.00

DOBRE

| ❏ 1041 | You Don't Know Me | 1978 | 3.00 | 6.00 | 12.00 |

FANTASY

| ❏ F-9661 | Have a Good Time | 1988 | 3.00 | 6.00 | 12.00 |
| ❏ F-9662 | Blues on Broadway | 1989 | 3.00 | 6.00 | 12.00 |

ICHIBAN

| ❏ SPEG-4023 | Brown, Black and Beautiful | 198? | 3.00 | 6.00 | 12.00 |

MAINSTREAM

❏ 369	Softly	1972	3.00	6.00	12.00
❏ S-6034 [S]	Ruth Brown '65	1965	7.50	15.00	30.00
❏ 56034 [M]	Ruth Brown '65	1965	6.25	12.50	25.00

PHILIPS

❏ PHM 200028 [M]	Along Comes Ruth	1962	10.00	20.00	40.00
❏ PHM 200055 [M]	Gospel Time	1962	7.50	15.00	30.00
❏ PHS 600028 [S]	Along Comes Ruth	1962	12.50	25.00	50.00
❏ PHS 600055 [S]	Gospel Time	1962	10.00	20.00	40.00

SKYE

| ❏ SK-13 | Black Is Brown and Brown Is Beautiful | 1970 | 3.75 | 7.50 | 15.00 |

BROWN, SKIPPY
45s

CHANCE

| ❏ 1129 | So Many Days/Tale of Woe | 1953 | 62.50 | 125.00 | 250.00 |

BROWN, TOMMY
45s

ABC-PARAMOUNT

| ❏ 10632 | Ain't So/Well, There Goes My Heart | 1965 | 3.00 | 6.00 | 12.00 |

DOT

| ❏ 16130 | Tra-La-La/Weepin' and Cryin' | 1960 | 3.75 | 7.50 | 15.00 |

GROOVE

| ❏ 0132 | Don't Leave Me/Won't You Forgive Me | 1955 | 7.50 | 15.00 | 30.00 |
| ❏ 0143 | The Thrill Is Gone/Gambler's Prayer | 1956 | 7.50 | 15.00 | 30.00 |

IMPERIAL

| ❏ 5476 | Rock Away My Blues/Someday, Somewhere | 1957 | 12.50 | 25.00 | 50.00 |
| ❏ 5533 | Just for You/A Heart with No Feeling | 1958 | 7.50 | 15.00 | 30.00 |

KING

| ❏ 4658 | How Much Do You Think I Can Stand/Fore Day Train | 1953 | 37.50 | 75.00 | 150.00 |
| ❏ 4679 | Goodbye, I'm Gone/Since You Left Me Dear | 1953 | 15.00 | 30.00 | 60.00 |

UNITED

| ❏ 183 | Remember Me/Southern Woman | 1956 | 37.50 | 75.00 | 150.00 |

BROWN, WINI
45s

COLUMBIA

❏ 1-872	A Good Man Is Hard to Find/This Is the Last Time	1950	10.00	20.00	40.00
—Microgroove 7-inch, 33 1/3 rpm single					
❏ 6-872	A Good Man Is Hard to Find/This Is the Last Time	1950	7.50	15.00	30.00

JARO

| ❏ 77018 | Gone Again/Johnny with the Gentle Hand | 1960 | 5.00 | 10.00 | 20.00 |

MERCURY

❏ 5870	Here in My Heart/Your Happiness Is Mine	1952	50.00	100.00	200.00
❏ 8270	Be Anything — Be Mine/Heaven Knows Why	1952	50.00	100.00	200.00
❏ 70062	Tear Down the Sky/Can't Stand No More	1953	25.00	50.00	100.00

RCA VICTOR

| ❏ 47-6970 | Available Lover/It's All in Your Mind | 1957 | 5.00 | 10.00 | 20.00 |

Albums

SAVOY JAZZ

| ❏ SJL-1163 [M] | Miss Brown for You | 1986 | 2.50 | 5.00 | 10.00 |

BROWN SUGAR
45s

CAPITOL

| ❏ 4198 | The Game Is Over (What's the Matter with You)/I'm Going Through Changes Now | 1976 | — | 2.50 | 5.00 |
| ❏ 4367 | Lay Some Lovin' on Me/Don't Tie Me Down | 1976 | — | 2.50 | 5.00 |

CHELSEA

❏ 78-0125	Loneliness (Will Bring Us Together Again)/Don't Hold Back	1973	2.50	5.00	10.00
❏ BCBO-0149	Didn't I/Moonlight and Taming You	1973	2.50	5.00	10.00
❏ BCBO-0239	Dance to the Music/Love Can Bring You Down	1974	2.50	5.00	10.00

Albums

CHELSEA

| ❏ BCL-0368 | Brown Sugar Featuring Clydie King | 1973 | 5.00 | 10.00 | 20.00 |

Number	Title (A Side/B Side)	Yr	VG	VG+	NM

BROWN'S HOME BREW See JOE BROWN AND THE BRUVVERS.

BROWNE, JACKSON
45s

ASYLUM

❏ 11004	Doctor My Eyes/Looking Into You	1972	—	2.50	5.00
❏ 11006	Rock Me on the Water/Something Fine	1972	—	2.00	4.00
❏ 11023	Redneck Friend/Those Times You've Come	1973	—	2.00	4.00
❏ 11030	Ready or Not/Take It Easy	1974	—	2.00	4.00
❏ 45227	Walking Slow/Before the Deluge	1975	—	2.00	4.00
❏ 45242	Fountains of Sorrow/The Late Show	1975	—	2.00	4.00
❏ 45379	Here Come Those Tears Again/Linda Paloma	1976	—	2.00	4.00
❏ 45399	The Pretender/Daddy's Tune	1977	—	2.00	4.00
❏ 45460	Running on Empty/Nothing But Time	1978	—	2.00	4.00
❏ 45460 [PS]	Running on Empty/Nothing But Time	1978	—	2.50	5.00
❏ 45485-A/B	Stay/Rosie	1978	—	2.50	5.00
❏ 45485-A/B [PS]	Stay/Rosie	1978	—	2.50	5.00
❏ 45485-A/C	Stay/The Load-Out	1978	—	2.00	4.00
❏ 45543	You Love the Thunder/The Road	1978	—	2.00	4.00
❏ 45543 [PS]	You Love the Thunder/The Road	1978	—	2.50	5.00
❏ 47003	Boulevard/Call It a Loan	1980	—	2.00	4.00
❏ 47003 [PS]	Boulevard/Call It a Loan	1980	—	2.50	5.00
❏ 47036	That Girl Could Sing/Of Missing Persons	1980	—	2.00	4.00
❏ 69543	In the Shape of a Heart/Voice of America	1986	—	—	3.00
❏ 69543 [PS]	In the Shape of a Heart/Voice of America	1986	—	3.00	6.00
❏ 69566	For America/Till I Go Down	1986	—	—	3.00
❏ 69566 [PS]	For America/Till I Go Down	1986	—	—	3.00
❏ 69764	For a Rocker/Downtown	1984	—	—	3.00
❏ 69764 [PS]	For a Rocker/Downtown	1984	—	—	3.00
❏ 69791	Tender Is the Night/On the Day	1983	—	—	3.00
❏ 69791 [PS]	Tender Is the Night/On the Day	1983	—	—	3.00
❏ 69826	Lawyers in Love/Say It Isn't True	1983	—	—	3.00
❏ 69826 [PS]	Lawyers in Love/Say It Isn't True	1983	—	—	3.00
❏ 69982	Somebody's Baby/The Crow on the Cradle [w/ Graham Nash & David Lindley]	1982	—	2.00	4.00
❏ 69982 [PS]	Somebody's Baby/The Crow on the Cradle [w/ Graham Nash & David Lindley]	1982	—	2.00	4.00

ELEKTRA

❏ 69262	Chasing You Into the Light/How Long	1989	—	2.50	5.00
❏ 69284	Anything Can Happen/Lights and Virtues	1989	—	2.50	5.00
❏ 69292	World in Motion/My Personal Revenge	1989	—	2.00	4.00

Albums

ASYLUM

❏ 6E-107	The Pretender	1977	2.50	5.00	10.00
—Reissue of 7E-1079					
❏ 6E-113	Running on Empty	1977	2.50	5.00	10.00
❏ 5E-511	Hold Out	1979	2.50	5.00	10.00
❏ 7E-1017	Late for the Sky	1974	3.00	6.00	12.00
❏ EQ-1017 [Q]	Late for the Sky	1974	7.50	15.00	30.00
❏ 7E-1079	The Pretender	1976	3.00	6.00	12.00
❏ SD 5051	Jackson Browne (Saturate Before Using)	1972	2.00	4.00	8.00
—Standard cover					
❏ SD 5051	Jackson Browne (Saturate Before Using)	1972	3.00	6.00	12.00
—Burlap cover; "clouds" label					
❏ SD 5051	Jackson Browne (Saturate Before Using)	1972	4.00	8.00	16.00
—Burlap cover, opens at right side; white label with "Asylum Records" logo in a circle at top					
❏ SD 5051	Jackson Browne (Saturate Before Using)	1972	5.00	10.00	20.00
—Burlap cover, opens at top; white label with "Asylum Records" logo in a circle at top					
❏ SD 5067	For Everyman	1973	3.00	6.00	12.00
❏ 60268	Lawyers in Love	1983	2.50	5.00	10.00
❏ 60457	Lives in the Balance	1986	2.50	5.00	10.00

ELEKTRA

| ❏ 60830 | World in Motion | 1989 | 2.50 | 5.00 | 10.00 |

MOBILE FIDELITY

| ❏ 1-055 | The Pretender | 1981 | 6.25 | 12.50 | 25.00 |
| —Audiophile vinyl | | | | | |

NINA MUSIC PUBLISHING

| ❏ (no #) [(2)] | Songs by Jackson Browne | 1967 | 1000. | 1500. | 2000. |
| —Publisher's demo in plain cardboard jacket; three sides performed by Jackson Browne, one side by Steve Noonan | | | | | |

BROWNETTES, THE
45s

KING

| ❏ 6153 | Baby, Don't You Know/Never Find a Love Like Mine | 1968 | 5.00 | 10.00 | 20.00 |

BROWNS, THE Also see JIM ED BROWN.
45s

FABOR

❏ 107	Rio De Janeiro/Lookin' Back to See	1954	6.25	12.50	25.00
—All on Fabor as "Jim Edward and Maxine Brown"					
❏ 112	Why Am I Falling/Itsy Witsy Bitsy Me	1954	6.25	12.50	25.00
❏ 118	Here Today and Gone Tomorrow/Draggin' Main Street	1955	6.25	12.50	25.00
❏ 122	Do Memories Haunt You/Jungle Magic	1955	6.25	12.50	25.00
❏ 126	You Thought I Thought/Here Today and Gone Tomorrow	1955	6.25	12.50	25.00

RCA VICTOR

❏ 37-7866	Ground Hog/Angel's Dolly	1961	6.25	12.50	25.00
—"Compact Single 33" (small hole, plays at LP speed)					
❏ 37-7917	Whispering Wine/My Baby's Gone	1961	6.25	12.50	25.00
—"Compact Single 33" (small hole, plays at LP speed)					
❏ 37-7969	Foolish Pride/Alpha and Omega	1961	6.25	12.50	25.00
—"Compact Single 33" (small hole, plays at LP speed)					
❏ 47-6480	I Take the Chance/Goo Goo Da Da	1956	5.00	10.00	20.00
—As "Jim Edward and Maxine Brown"					
❏ 47-6628	Here Today and Gone Tomorrow/Looking Back to See	1956	5.00	10.00	20.00
❏ 47-6629	Do Memories Haunt You/Draggin' Main Street	1956	5.00	10.00	20.00

B

Number	Title (A Side/B Side)	Yr	VG	VG+	NM
❑ 47-6631	Just As Long As You Love Me/Don't Tell Me Your Troubles	1956	5.00	10.00	20.00
—As "Jim Edward, Maxine and Bonnie Brown"					
❑ 47-6730	A Man with a Plan/Just a Lot of Sweet Talk	1956	5.00	10.00	20.00
—As "Jim, Maxine and Bonnie Brown"					
❑ 47-6823	Money/It Takes a Long Train with a Red Caboose	1957	3.75	7.50	15.00
❑ 47-6918	I'm in Heaven/Getting Used to Being Lonely	1957	3.75	7.50	15.00
—As "Jim, Maxine and Bonnie Brown"					
❑ 47-6995	I Heard the Bluebirds Sing/The Last Thing I Want	1957	3.75	7.50	15.00
—As "Jim, Maxine and Bonnie Brown"					
❑ 47-7110	The Man in the Moon/ True Love Goes Far Beyond	1957	3.75	7.50	15.00
❑ 47-7208	Crazy Dreams/Ain't No Way in the World	1958	3.75	7.50	15.00
❑ 47-7311	Would You Care?/The Trot	1958	3.75	7.50	15.00
❑ 47-7427	Beyond the Shadow/This Time I Would Know	1958	3.75	7.50	15.00
❑ 47-7555	The Three Bells/Heaven Fell Last Night	1959	3.00	6.00	12.00
❑ 47-7614	Scarlet Ribbons (For Her Hair)/Blue Bells Ring	1959	3.00	6.00	12.00
❑ 47-7700	The Old Lamplighter/Teen-Ex	1960	3.00	6.00	12.00
❑ 47-7700 [PS]	The Old Lamplighter/Teen-Ex	1960	6.25	12.50	25.00
❑ 47-7755	Lonely Little Robin/Margo (The Ninth of May)	1960	3.00	6.00	12.00
❑ 47-7755 [PS]	Lonely Little Robin/Margo (The Ninth of May)	1960	6.25	12.50	25.00
❑ 47-7780	The Whiffenpoof Song/Brighten the Corner Where You Are	1960	3.00	6.00	12.00
❑ 47-7780 [PS]	The Whiffenpoof Song/Brighten the Corner Where You Are	1960	6.25	12.50	25.00
❑ 47-7804	Send Me the Pillow You Dream On/You're So Much a Part of Me	1960	3.00	6.00	12.00
❑ 47-7820	Blue Christmas/Greenwillow Christmas	1960	3.00	6.00	12.00
❑ 47-7866	Ground Hog/Angel's Dolly	1961	2.50	5.00	10.00
❑ 47-7917	Whispering Wine/My Baby's Gone	1961	2.50	5.00	10.00
❑ 47-7969	Foolish Pride/Alpha and Omega	1961	2.50	5.00	10.00
❑ 47-7997	Buttons and Bows/Remember Me	1962	2.50	5.00	10.00
❑ 47-8066	It's Just a Little Heartache/The Old Master Painter	1962	2.50	5.00	10.00
❑ 47-8198	The Twelfth Rose/Watching My World Fall Apart	1963	2.50	5.00	10.00
❑ 47-8242	Oh, No!/Dear Teresa	1963	2.50	5.00	10.00
❑ 47-8348	Then I'll Stop Loving You/I Know My Place	1964	2.00	4.00	8.00
❑ 47-8423	Everybody's Darlin', Plus Mine/The Outskirts of Town	1964	2.00	4.00	8.00
❑ 47-8495	I Feel Like Crying/No Sad Songs for Me	1965	2.00	4.00	8.00
❑ 47-8603	You Can't Grow Peaches on a Cherry Tree/A Little Too Much to Dream	1965	2.00	4.00	8.00
❑ 47-8714	Meadowgreen/One Take Away One	1965	2.00	4.00	8.00
❑ 47-8838	I'd Just Be Fool Enough/Springtime	1966	2.00	4.00	8.00
❑ 47-8942	Coming Back to You/Gigawachem	1966	2.00	4.00	8.00
❑ 47-9153	I Hear It Now/He Will Set Your Fields on Fire	1967	2.00	4.00	8.00
❑ 47-9364	Big Daddy/I Will Bring You Water	1967	2.00	4.00	8.00
❑ 61-7555 [S]	The Three Bells/Heaven Fell Last Night	1959	6.25	12.50	25.00
—"Living Stereo" (large hole, plays at 45 rpm)					
❑ 61-7614 [S]	Scarlet Ribbons (For Her Hair)/Blue Bells Ring	1959	6.25	12.50	25.00
—"Living Stereo" (large hole, plays at 45 rpm)					
❑ 61-7700 [S]	The Old Lamplighter/Teen-Ex	1960	6.25	12.50	25.00
—"Living Stereo" (large hole, plays at 45 rpm)					
❑ 61-7755 [S]	Lonely Little Robin/Margo (The Ninth of May)	1960	6.25	12.50	25.00
—"Living Stereo" (large hole, plays at 45 rpm)					
❑ 61-7780 [S]	The Whiffenpoof Song/Brighten the Corner Where You Are	1960	6.25	12.50	25.00
—"Living Stereo" (large hole, plays at 45 rpm)					
❑ 61-7804 [S]	Send Me the Pillow You Dream On/ You're So Much a Part of Me	1960	6.25	12.50	25.00
—"Living Stereo" (large hole, plays at 45 rpm)					

7-Inch Extended Plays

RCA VICTOR

Number	Title (A Side/B Side)	Yr	VG	VG+	NM
❑ EPA-4347	The Three Bells/Be My Love//The Man in the Moon/This Time I Would Know	1959	3.75	7.50	15.00
❑ EPA-4347 [PS]	The Browns Sing The 3 Bells	1959	3.75	7.50	15.00
❑ EPA-4352	Scarlet Ribbons/I Still Do//Love Me Tender/ We Should Be Together	1959	3.75	7.50	15.00
❑ EPA-4352 [PS]	Scarlet Ribbons	1959	3.75	7.50	15.00
❑ EPA-4364	The Old Lamplighter/Oh! My Pa-Pa//True Love/ The Enchanted Sea	1960	3.75	7.50	15.00
❑ EPA-4364 [PS]	The Old Lamplighter	1960	3.75	7.50	15.00

Albums

RCA CAMDEN

Number	Title (A Side/B Side)	Yr	VG	VG+	NM
❑ CAL-885 [M]	I Heard the Bluebirds Sing	1965	3.00	6.00	12.00
❑ CAS-885 [S]	I Heard the Bluebirds Sing	1965	3.00	6.00	12.00
❑ CAL-2142 [M]	Big Ones from the Country	1967	3.00	6.00	12.00
❑ CAS-2142 [S]	Big Ones from the Country	1967	2.50	5.00	10.00
❑ CAS-2262	The Browns Sing a Harvest of Country Songs	1968	2.50	5.00	10.00

RCA VICTOR

Number	Title (A Side/B Side)	Yr	VG	VG+	NM
❑ ANL1-1083	The Best of the Browns	1975	2.50	5.00	10.00
❑ LPM-1438 [M]	Jim Edward, Maxine and Bonnie Brown	1957	12.50	25.00	50.00
❑ LPM-2144 [M]	Sweet Sounds by the Browns	1959	7.50	15.00	30.00
❑ LSP-2144 [S]	Sweet Sounds by the Browns	1959	10.00	20.00	40.00
❑ LPM-2174 [M]	Town and Country	1960	5.00	10.00	20.00
❑ LSP-2174 [S]	Town and Country	1960	6.25	12.50	25.00
❑ LPM-2260 [M]	The Browns Sing Their Hits	1960	5.00	10.00	20.00
❑ LSP-2260 [S]	The Browns Sing Their Hits	1960	6.25	12.50	25.00
❑ LPM-2333 [M]	Our Favorite Folk Songs	1961	5.00	10.00	20.00
❑ LSP-2333 [S]	Our Favorite Folk Songs	1961	6.25	12.50	25.00
❑ LPM-2345 [M]	The Little Brown Church Hymnal	1961	5.00	10.00	20.00
❑ LSP-2345 [S]	The Little Brown Church Hymnal	1961	6.25	12.50	25.00
❑ LPM-2784 [M]	Grand Ole Opry Favorites	1963	3.75	7.50	15.00
❑ LSP-2784 [S]	Grand Ole Opry Favorites	1963	5.00	10.00	20.00
❑ LPM-2860 [M]	This Young Land	1964	3.75	7.50	15.00
❑ LSP-2860 [S]	This Young Land	1964	5.00	10.00	20.00
❑ LPM-2987 [M]	Three Shades of Brown	1964	3.75	7.50	15.00
❑ LSP-2987 [S]	Three Shades of Brown	1964	5.00	10.00	20.00
❑ LPM-3423 [M]	When Love Is Gone	1965	3.75	7.50	15.00
❑ LSP-3423 [S]	When Love Is Gone	1965	5.00	10.00	20.00
❑ LPM-3561 [M]	The Best of the Browns	1966	3.75	7.50	15.00
❑ LSP-3561 [S]	The Best of the Browns	1966	5.00	10.00	20.00

Number	Title (A Side/B Side)	Yr	VG	VG+	NM
❑ LPM-3668 [M]	Our Kind of Country	1966	3.75	7.50	15.00
❑ LSP-3668 [S]	Our Kind of Country	1966	5.00	10.00	20.00
❑ LPM-3798 [M]	The Old Country Church	1967	5.00	10.00	20.00
❑ LSP-3798 [S]	The Old Country Church	1967	3.75	7.50	15.00

BROWNSVILLE STATION

45s

BIG TREE

Number	Title (A Side/B Side)	Yr	VG	VG+	NM
❑ 144	Rock with the Music/(B-side unknown)	1972	—	2.50	5.00
❑ 156	The Red Back Spider/Rock with the Music	1972	—	2.50	5.00
❑ 161	Let Your Yeah Be Yeah/Mister Robert	1973	—	2.50	5.00
❑ 15005	I'm the Leader of the Gang/Fast Phyllis	1974	—	2.00	4.00
❑ 15005	I'm the Leader of the Gang/ Meet Me on the Fourth Floor	1974	—	2.00	4.00
❑ 16001	Kings of the Party/Ostrich	1974	—	2.00	4.00
❑ 16011	Smokin' in the Boy's Room/Barefootin'	1973	—	2.50	5.00
❑ 16029	I Got It Bad for You/Mama Don't Allow No Parkin'	1974	—	2.00	4.00

EPIC

Number	Title (A Side/B Side)	Yr	VG	VG+	NM
❑ 50695	Love Stealer/Fever	1979	—	2.00	4.00
—As "Brownsville"					

HIDEOUT

Number	Title (A Side/B Side)	Yr	VG	VG+	NM
❑ 1957	Rock and Roll Holiday/Jailhouse Rock	1969	3.00	6.00	12.00

POLYDOR

Number	Title (A Side/B Side)	Yr	VG	VG+	NM
❑ 14017	Rock and Roll Holiday/Jailhouse Rock	1969	—	2.50	5.00

PRIVATE STOCK

Number	Title (A Side/B Side)	Yr	VG	VG+	NM
❑ 45,149	Lady (Put the Light on Me)/Rockers and Rollers	1977	—	2.00	4.00
❑ 45,167	The Martian Boogie/Mr. Johnson Sez	1977	—	2.00	4.00

WARNER BROS.

Number	Title (A Side/B Side)	Yr	VG	VG+	NM
❑ 7441	Be-Bop Confidential/City Life	1970	2.00	4.00	8.00
❑ 7456	Roadrunner/Do the Bosco	1971	2.00	4.00	8.00
❑ 7501	That's Fine/Tell Me All About It	1971	2.00	4.00	8.00

Albums

BIG TREE

Number	Title (A Side/B Side)	Yr	VG	VG+	NM
❑ BTS-2010	A Night on the Town	1972	3.00	6.00	12.00
❑ BTS-2102	Yeah!	1973	3.00	6.00	12.00
❑ BT 89500	School Punks	1974	3.00	6.00	12.00
❑ BT 89510	Motor City Connection	1975	3.00	6.00	12.00

EPIC

Number	Title (A Side/B Side)	Yr	VG	VG+	NM
❑ JE 35606	Air Special	1978	2.50	5.00	10.00
❑ JE 35606 [DJ]	Air Special	1978	5.00	10.00	20.00
—Orange vinyl promo					

PALLADIUM

Number	Title (A Side/B Side)	Yr	VG	VG+	NM
❑ P-1004	Brownsville Station	1970	7.50	15.00	30.00

PRIVATE STOCK

Number	Title (A Side/B Side)	Yr	VG	VG+	NM
❑ PS-2026	Brownsville Station	1977	2.50	5.00	10.00

WARNER BROS.

Number	Title (A Side/B Side)	Yr	VG	VG+	NM
❑ WS 1888	No B.S.	1970	3.75	7.50	15.00

BRUBECK, DAVE

45s

ATLANTIC

Number	Title (A Side/B Side)	Yr	VG	VG+	NM
❑ 3015	Three to Get Ready/Blue Rondo (A La Turk)	1974	—	2.00	4.00

COLUMBIA

Number	Title (A Side/B Side)	Yr	VG	VG+	NM
❑ 30719 [S]	(contents unknown)	1960	3.00	6.00	12.00
❑ 30720 [S]	(contents unknown)	1960	3.00	6.00	12.00
❑ 30721 [S]	(contents unknown)	1960	3.00	6.00	12.00
❑ 30722 [S]	(contents unknown)	1960	3.00	6.00	12.00
❑ 30723 [S]	(contents unknown)	1960	3.00	6.00	12.00
❑ 30899 [S]	(contents unknown)	1961	3.00	6.00	12.00
❑ 30900 [S]	(contents unknown)	1961	3.00	6.00	12.00
❑ 30901 [S]	(contents unknown)	1961	3.00	6.00	12.00
❑ 30902 [S]	(contents unknown)	1961	3.00	6.00	12.00
❑ 30903 [S]	(contents unknown)	1961	3.00	6.00	12.00
❑ 31312 [S]	(contents unknown)	1962	3.00	6.00	12.00
❑ 31313 [S]	(contents unknown)	1962	3.00	6.00	12.00
❑ 31314 [S]	(contents unknown)	1962	3.00	6.00	12.00
❑ 31315 [S]	(contents unknown)	1962	3.00	6.00	12.00
❑ 31316 [S]	(contents unknown)	1962	3.00	6.00	12.00
—Anyone who can fill in these gaps -- the above 15 all are Columbia "Stereo 7" singles -- please let us know.					
❑ 31443 [S]	Charles Matthew Hallelujah/Maria	1962	3.00	6.00	12.00
❑ 31444 [S]	Someday My Prince Will Come/ I'm in a Dancing Mood	1962	3.00	6.00	12.00
❑ 31445 [S]	Tangerine/The Duke	1962	3.00	6.00	12.00
❑ 31446 [S]	Far More Blue/Gone with the Wind	1962	3.00	6.00	12.00
❑ 31447 [S]	Take the "A" Train/Camptown Races	1962	3.00	6.00	12.00
❑ 40776	Lover/I'm in a Dancin' Mood	1956	3.00	6.00	12.00
❑ 41479	Take Five/Blue Rondo A La Turk	1960	3.00	6.00	12.00
❑ 41485	Camptown Races/Shortnin' Bread	1959	3.00	6.00	12.00
❑ 42068	Paradiddle Joe/Briar Bush	1961	2.50	5.00	10.00
❑ 42228	Unsquare Dance/It's a Raggy Waltz	1961	2.50	5.00	10.00
❑ 42228 [PS]	Unsquare Dance/It's a Raggy Waltz	1961	3.75	7.50	15.00
❑ 42404	Countdown/Eleven Four	1962	2.50	5.00	10.00
❑ 42404 [PS]	Countdown/Eleven Four	1962	3.75	7.50	15.00
❑ 42651	Bossa Nova U.S.A./This Can't Be Love	1962	2.50	5.00	10.00
❑ 42675	Bossa Nova U.S.A./Camptown Races	1963	2.00	4.00	8.00
❑ 42804	Summer Song/Three to Get Ready	1963	2.00	4.00	8.00
❑ 42920	Cable Car/Theme from Elementals	1963	2.00	4.00	8.00
❑ 43091	Unisphere/Toki's Theme	1964	2.00	4.00	8.00
❑ 43133	Mr. Broadway/Toki's Theme	1964	2.00	4.00	8.00
❑ 43409	Happy Bandito/Bag O' Heat	1965	2.00	4.00	8.00
❑ 43663	Three to Get Ready/Done Her Wrong	1966	2.00	4.00	8.00
❑ 44345	Raga Theme for Ragu/Do Not Fold, Staple, Spindle or Mutilate	1968	2.00	4.00	8.00
❑ 44844	Broke Blues/Blues Roots	1969	—	3.00	6.00

FANTASY

Number	Title (A Side/B Side)	Yr	VG	VG+	NM
❑ 501	Lullaby in Rhythm/You Stepped Out of a Dream	1952	3.75	7.50	15.00
❑ 502	Singing in the Rain/I'll Remember April	1952	3.75	7.50	15.00
❑ 503	Body & Soul/Let's Fall in Love	1952	3.75	7.50	15.00
❑ 504	Indiana/Laura	1952	3.75	7.50	15.00
—The above four records comprised a box set					

Number	Title (A Side/B Side)	Yr	VG	VG+	NM
❏ 505	Blue Moon/Tea for Two	1952	3.75	7.50	15.00
❏ 506	Undecided/That Old Black Magic	1952	3.75	7.50	15.00
❏ 507	September Song/Sweet Georgia Brown	1952	3.75	7.50	15.00
❏ 508	'S Wonderful/Spring Is Here	1952	3.75	7.50	15.00

—The above four records comprised a box set

Number	Title (A Side/B Side)	Yr	VG	VG+	NM
❏ 509	The Way You Look Tonight/Love Walked In	1953	3.75	7.50	15.00
❏ 510	September in the Rain/ What Is This Thing Called Love	1953	3.75	7.50	15.00
❏ 511	Prelude/Fugue on Bob's Theme	1953	3.75	7.50	15.00
❏ 512	Ipca/Let's Fall in Love	1953	3.75	7.50	15.00

—The above four records comprised a box set

Number	Title (A Side/B Side)	Yr	VG	VG+	NM
❏ 513	Avalon/Perfidia	1953	3.75	7.50	15.00
❏ 514	Always/I Didn't Know What Time It Was	1953	3.75	7.50	15.00
❏ 515	Squeeze Me/How High the Moon	1953	3.75	7.50	15.00
❏ 516	Too Marvelous for Words/Heart and Soul	1953	3.75	7.50	15.00

—The above four records comprised a box set

Number	Title (A Side/B Side)	Yr	VG	VG+	NM
❏ 517	Somebody Loves Me/Crazy Chris	1953	3.75	7.50	15.00
❏ 518	A Foggy Day/Lyons Bust (Theme)	1953	3.75	7.50	15.00
❏ 519	Mam'selle/Me and My Shadow	1953	3.75	7.50	15.00
❏ 520	At a Perfume Counter/Frenesi	1953	3.75	7.50	15.00

—The above four records comprised a box set

Number	Title (A Side/B Side)	Yr	VG	VG+	NM
❏ 521	This Can't Be Love/Look for the Silver Lining	1953	3.75	7.50	15.00
❏ 523	Just One of Those Things/My Romance	1953	3.75	7.50	15.00
❏ 524	Stardust/Lulu's Back in Town	1953	3.75	7.50	15.00
❏ 526	Alice in Wonderland/All the Things You Are	1953	3.75	7.50	15.00
❏ 527	On a Little Street in Singapore/I May Be Wrong	195?	3.75	7.50	15.00
❏ 530	The Trolley Song/My Heart Stood Still	195?	3.75	7.50	15.00
❏ 535	The Trolley Song/The Trolley Song Rehearsal	195?	5.00	10.00	20.00
❏ 549	The Piper/Soliloquy	195?	3.75	7.50	15.00
❏ 558	The Trolley Song/Crazy Chris	1961	3.00	6.00	12.00

7-Inch Extended Plays
COLUMBIA

Number	Title (A Side/B Side)	Yr	VG	VG+	NM
❏ B-435 [PS]	Jazz Goes to College Vol. I	1955	2.50	5.00	10.00
—Dual-pocket sleeve for 1940 and 1941					
❏ B-436 [PS]	Jazz Goes to College Vol. II	1955	2.50	5.00	10.00
—Dual-pocket sleeve for 1942 and 1943					
❏ B-465 [PS]	Dave Brubeck at Storyville: 1954 (Vol. 1)	1955	2.50	5.00	10.00
—Dual-pocket sleeve for 2016 and 2017					
❏ B-473 [PS]	Brubeck Time	1955	2.50	5.00	10.00
—Dual-pocket sleeve for 2067 and 2068					
❏ B-699 [PS]	Jazz Red Hot and Cool	1956	3.00	6.00	12.00
—Triple-pocket sleeve for 2280, 2281 and 2282					
❏ 5-1940	Balcony Rock (Beg.)/Le Souk	1955	2.50	5.00	10.00
—Alternate numbers are "B-435-1" and "B-435-4"					
❏ 5-1941	Balcony Rock (Concl.)/Out of Nowhere	1955	2.50	5.00	10.00
—Alternate numbers are "B-435-2" and "B-435-3"					
❏ 5-1942	Take the "A" Train/The Song Is You	1955	2.50	5.00	10.00
—Alternate numbers are "B-436-1" and "B-436-4"					
❏ 5-1943	I Want to Be Happy/Don't Worry 'Bout Me	1955	2.50	5.00	10.00
—Alternate numbers are "B-436-2" and "B-436-3"					
❏ 5-2016	On the Alamo (Beginning)/Here Lies Love	1955	2.50	5.00	10.00
—Alternate numbers are "B-465-1" and "B-465-4"					
❏ 5-2017	On the Alamo (Conclusion)/ Don't Worry 'Bout Me	1955	2.50	5.00	10.00
—Alternate numbers are "B-465-2" and "B-465-3"					
❏ 5-2067	A Fine Romance/Brother, Can You Spare a Dime	1955	2.50	5.00	10.00
—Alternate numbers are "B-473-1" and "B-473-4"					
❏ 5-2068	Pennies from Heaven/Why Do I Love You	1955	2.50	5.00	10.00
—Alternate numbers are "B-473-2" and "B-473-3"					
❏ 5-2280	Lover/Love Walked In	1956	3.00	6.00	12.00
❏ 5-2281	Little Girl Blue/Indiana	1956	3.00	6.00	12.00
❏ 5-2282	*The Duke/Fare Thee Well, Annabelle/ Sometimes I'm Happy	1956	3.00	6.00	12.00
❏ B-2552	Laura/Sometimes I'm Happy	195?	2.50	5.00	10.00
❏ B-2552 [PS]	The Dave Brubeck Quartet (Hall of Fame Series)	195?	2.50	5.00	10.00

FANTASY

Number	Title (A Side/B Side)	Yr	VG	VG+	NM
❏ EP 4014	Blue Moon/Let's Fall in Love	195?	3.75	7.50	15.00
—Red vinyl					
❏ EP 4014 [PS]	The Brubeck Quartet at Storyville	195?	3.75	7.50	15.00
—Title not on front cover; it's on the notes on the back					
❏ EP 4019	How High the Moon//Serenades Suite/ Playland-at-the-Beach	195?	3.75	7.50	15.00
—Green vinyl					
❏ EP 4019 [PS]	Old Sounds from San Francisco, Volume 1	195?	3.75	7.50	15.00
❏ EP 4020	The Prisoner's Song/Schizophrenic Scherzo/ Rondo//You Go to My Head/ Laura/Closing Theme	195?	3.75	7.50	15.00
—Red vinyl					
❏ EP 4020 [PS]	Old Sounds from San Francisco, Volume 2	195?	3.75	7.50	15.00

Albums
ATLANTIC

Number	Title (A Side/B Side)	Yr	VG	VG+	NM
❏ SD 2-317 [(2)]	The Art of Dave Brubeck: The Fantasy Years	1975	3.75	7.50	15.00
❏ SD 1606	Truth Is Fallen	1972	3.00	6.00	12.00
❏ SD 1607	The Last Set at Newport	1972	3.00	6.00	12.00
❏ SD 1641	We're All Together Again for the First Time	1973	3.00	6.00	12.00
❏ SD 1645	Two Generations of Brubeck	1974	3.00	6.00	12.00
❏ SD 1660	Brother, The Great Spirit Made Us All	1974	3.00	6.00	12.00
❏ SD 1684	All the Things We Are	1976	3.00	6.00	12.00

BOOK-OF-THE-MONTH

Number	Title (A Side/B Side)	Yr	VG	VG+	NM
❏ 80-5547 [(3)]	Early Fantasies	1980	5.00	10.00	20.00

COLUMBIA

Number	Title (A Side/B Side)	Yr	VG	VG+	NM
❏ C2L 26 [(2)M]	The Dave Brubeck Quartet at Carnegie Hall	1963	6.25	12.50	25.00
—Red "Guaranteed High Fidelity" label					
❏ C2L 26 [(2)M]	The Dave Brubeck Quartet at Carnegie Hall	1966	3.75	7.50	15.00
—Red "360 Sound" label					
❏ CL 566 [M]	Jazz Goes to College	1954	20.00	40.00	80.00
—Dark red label, gold print; released at the same time as 6321 and 6322					
❏ CL 566 [M]	Jazz Goes to College	1955	12.50	25.00	50.00
—Red/black label with six "eye" logos					
❏ CL 566 [M]	Jazz Goes to College	1962	5.00	10.00	20.00
—Red "Guaranteed High Fidelity" label					

Number	Title (A Side/B Side)	Yr	VG	VG+	NM
❏ CL 566 [M]	Jazz Goes to College	1966	3.00	6.00	12.00
—Red "360 Sound" label					
❏ CL 590 [M]	Dave Brubeck at Storyville: 1954	1954	20.00	40.00	80.00
—Dark red label, gold print; released at the same time as 6330 and 6331					
❏ CL 590 [M]	Dave Brubeck at Storyville: 1954	1955	12.50	25.00	50.00
—Red/black label with six "eye" logos					
❏ CL 590 [M]	Dave Brubeck at Storyville: 1954	1962	5.00	10.00	20.00
—Red "Guaranteed High Fidelity" label					
❏ CL 590 [M]	Dave Brubeck at Storyville: 1954	1966	3.00	6.00	12.00
—Red "360 Sound" label					
❏ CL 622 [M]	Brubeck Time	1955	15.00	30.00	60.00
—Red/black label with six "eye" logos					
❏ CL 622 [M]	Brubeck Time	1962	5.00	10.00	20.00
—Red "Guaranteed High Fidelity" label					
❏ CL 622 [M]	Brubeck Time	1966	3.00	6.00	12.00
—Red "360 Sound" label					
❏ CL 699 [M]	Jazz: Red Hot and Cool	1955	15.00	30.00	60.00
—Red/black label with six "eye" logos					
❏ CL 699 [M]	Jazz: Red Hot and Cool	1962	5.00	10.00	20.00
—Red "Guaranteed High Fidelity" label					
❏ CL 699 [M]	Jazz: Red Hot and Cool	1966	3.00	6.00	12.00
—Red "360 Sound" label					
❏ C2S 826 [(2)S]	The Dave Brubeck Quartet at Carnegie Hall	1963	7.50	15.00	30.00
—Red label, "360 Sound" in black					
❏ C2S 826 [(2)S]	The Dave Brubeck Quartet at Carnegie Hall	1966	5.00	10.00	20.00
—Red label, "360 Sound" in white					
❏ C2S 826 [(2)]	The Dave Brubeck Quartet at Carnegie Hall	1971	3.75	7.50	15.00
—Orange label					
❏ CL 878 [M]	Brubeck Plays Brubeck	1956	15.00	30.00	60.00
—Red/black label with six "eye" logos					
❏ CL 878 [M]	Brubeck Plays Brubeck	1962	5.00	10.00	20.00
—Red "Guaranteed High Fidelity" label					
❏ CL 878 [M]	Brubeck Plays Brubeck	1966	3.00	6.00	12.00
—Red "360 Sound" label					
❏ CL 932 [M]	American Jazz Festival at Newport '56	1956	12.50	25.00	50.00
—Red/black label with six "eye" logos					
❏ CL 932 [M]	American Jazz Festival at Newport '56	1962	5.00	10.00	20.00
—Red "Guaranteed High Fidelity" label					
❏ CL 984 [M]	Jazz Impressions of the U.S.A.	1957	12.50	25.00	50.00
—Red/black label with six "eye" logos					
❏ CL 984 [M]	Jazz Impressions of the U.S.A.	1962	5.00	10.00	20.00
—Red "Guaranteed High Fidelity" label					
❏ CL 984 [M]	Jazz Impressions of the U.S.A.	1966	3.00	6.00	12.00
—Red "360 Sound" label					
❏ CL 1034 [M]	Jazz Goes to Junior College	1957	10.00	20.00	40.00
—Red/black label with six "eye" logos					
❏ CL 1034 [M]	Jazz Goes to Junior College	1962	5.00	10.00	20.00
—Red "Guaranteed High Fidelity" label					
❏ CL 1034 [M]	Jazz Goes to Junior College	1966	3.00	6.00	12.00
—Red "360 Sound" label					
❏ CL 1059 [M]	Dave Digs Disney	1957	10.00	20.00	40.00
—Red/black label with six "eye" logos					
❏ CL 1059 [M]	Dave Digs Disney	1962	5.00	10.00	20.00
—Red "Guaranteed High Fidelity" label					
❏ CL 1059 [M]	Dave Digs Disney	1966	3.00	6.00	12.00
—Red "360 Sound" label					
❏ CL 1168 [M]	The Dave Brubeck Quartet in Europe	1958	10.00	20.00	40.00
—Red/black label with six "eye" logos					
❏ CL 1168 [M]	The Dave Brubeck Quartet in Europe	1962	5.00	10.00	20.00
—Red "Guaranteed High Fidelity" label					
❏ CL 1168 [M]	The Dave Brubeck Quartet in Europe	1966	3.00	6.00	12.00
—Red "360 Sound" label					
❏ CL 1249 [M]	Newport 1958	1958	10.00	20.00	40.00
—Red/black label with six "eye" logos					
❏ CL 1249 [M]	Newport 1958	1962	5.00	10.00	20.00
—Red "Guaranteed High Fidelity" label					
❏ CL 1249 [M]	Newport 1958	1966	3.00	6.00	12.00
—Red "360 Sound" label					
❏ CL 1251 [M]	Jazz Impressions of Eurasia	1958	10.00	20.00	40.00
—Red/black label with six "eye" logos					
❏ CL 1251 [M]	Jazz Impressions of Eurasia	1962	5.00	10.00	20.00
—Red "Guaranteed High Fidelity" label					
❏ CL 1251 [M]	Jazz Impressions of Eurasia	1966	3.00	6.00	12.00
—Red "360 Sound" label					
❏ CL 1347 [M]	Gone with the Wind	1959	10.00	20.00	40.00
—Red/black label with six "eye" logos					
❏ CL 1347 [M]	Gone with the Wind	1962	5.00	10.00	20.00
—Red "Guaranteed High Fidelity" label					
❏ CL 1347 [M]	Gone with the Wind	1966	3.00	6.00	12.00
—Red "360 Sound" label					
❏ CL 1397 [M]	Time Out	1960	6.25	12.50	25.00
—Red/black label with six "eye" logos					
❏ CL 1397 [M]	Time Out Featuring "Take Five"	1962	3.75	7.50	15.00
—Red "Guaranteed High Fidelity" label; beginning with this issue, the cover was altered to emphasize the hit					
❏ CL 1397 [M]	Time Out Featuring "Take Five"	1966	3.00	6.00	12.00
—Red "360 Sound" label					
❏ CL 1439 [M]	Southern Scene	1960	6.25	12.50	25.00
—Red/black label with six "eye" logos					
❏ CL 1439 [M]	Southern Scene	1962	3.75	7.50	15.00
—Red "Guaranteed High Fidelity" label					
❏ CL 1439 [M]	Southern Scene	1966	3.00	6.00	12.00
—Red "360 Sound" label					
❏ CL 1454 [M]	The Riddle	1960	6.25	12.50	25.00
—Red/black label with six "eye" logos					
❏ CL 1454 [M]	The Riddle	1962	3.75	7.50	15.00
—Red "Guaranteed High Fidelity" label					
❏ CL 1454 [M]	The Riddle	1966	3.00	6.00	12.00
—Red "360 Sound" label					
❏ CL 1466 [M]	Bernstein Plays Brubeck Plays Bernstein	1960	6.25	12.50	25.00
—Red/black label with six "eye" logos					
❏ CL 1466 [M]	Bernstein Plays Brubeck Plays Bernstein	1962	3.75	7.50	15.00
—Red "Guaranteed High Fidelity" label					

B

Number	Title (A Side/B Side)	Yr	VG	VG+	NM
CL 1466 [M]	Bernstein Plays Brubeck Plays Bernstein	1966	3.00	6.00	12.00
—Red "360 Sound" label					
CL 1553 [M]	Brubeck and Rushing	1961	6.25	12.50	25.00
—Red/black label with six "eye" logos					
CL 1553 [M]	Brubeck and Rushing	1962	3.75	7.50	15.00
—Red "Guaranteed High Fidelity" label					
CL 1553 [M]	Brubeck and Rushing	1966	3.00	6.00	12.00
—Red "360 Sound" label					
CL 1609 [M]	Tonight Only!	1961	6.25	12.50	25.00
—Red/black label with six "eye" logos					
CL 1609 [M]	Tonight Only!	1962	3.75	7.50	15.00
—Red "Guaranteed High Fidelity" label					
CL 1609 [M]	Tonight Only!	1966	3.00	6.00	12.00
—Red "360 Sound" label					
CL 1690 [M]	Time Further Out	1961	6.25	12.50	25.00
—Red/black label with six "eye" logos					
CL 1690 [M]	Time Further Out	1962	3.75	7.50	15.00
—Red "Guaranteed High Fidelity" label					
CL 1690 [M]	Time Further Out	1966	3.00	6.00	12.00
—Red "360 Sound" label					
CL 1775 [M]	Countdown — Time in Outer Space	1962	3.75	7.50	15.00
—Red "Guaranteed High Fidelity" label					
CL 1775 [M]	Countdown — Time in Outer Space	1962	7.50	15.00	30.00
—Red/black label with six "eye" logos					
CL 1775 [M]	Countdown — Time in Outer Space	1966	3.00	6.00	12.00
—Red "360 Sound" label					
CL 1963 [M]	Brandenburg Gate Revisited	1963	5.00	10.00	20.00
—Red "Guaranteed High Fidelity" label					
CL 1963 [M]	Brandenburg Gate Revisited	1966	3.00	6.00	12.00
—Red "360 Sound" label					
CL 1998 [M]	Bossa Nova U.S.A.	1963	5.00	10.00	20.00
—Red "Guaranteed High Fidelity" label					
CL 1998 [M]	Bossa Nova U.S.A.	1966	3.00	6.00	12.00
—Red "360 Sound" label					
CL 2127 [M]	Time Changes	1964	5.00	10.00	20.00
—Red "Guaranteed High Fidelity" label					
CL 2127 [M]	Time Changes	1966	3.00	6.00	12.00
—Red "360 Sound" label					
CL 2212 [M]	Jazz Impressions of Japan	1964	5.00	10.00	20.00
—Red "Guaranteed High Fidelity" label					
CL 2212 [M]	Jazz Impressions of Japan	1966	3.00	6.00	12.00
—Red "360 Sound" label					
CL 2275 [M]	Jazz Impressions of New York	1965	5.00	10.00	20.00
—Red "Guaranteed High Fidelity" label					
CL 2275 [M]	Jazz Impressions of New York	1966	3.00	6.00	12.00
—Red "360 Sound" label					
CL 2316 [M]	Take Five	1965	5.00	10.00	20.00
—Red "Guaranteed High Fidelity" label					
CL 2316 [M]	Take Five	1966	3.00	6.00	12.00
—Red "360 Sound" label					
CL 2348 [M]	Angel Eyes	1965	5.00	10.00	20.00
—Red "Guaranteed High Fidelity" label					
CL 2348 [M]	Angel Eyes	1966	3.00	6.00	12.00
—Red "360 Sound" label					
CL 2437 [M]	My Favorite Things	1966	3.75	7.50	15.00
CL 2484 [M]	Dave Brubeck's Greatest Hits	1966	3.75	7.50	15.00
CL 2512 [M]	Time In	1966	3.75	7.50	15.00
CL 2602 [M]	Anything Goes! Dave Brubeck Quartet Plays Cole Porter	1966	3.75	7.50	15.00
CL 2695 [M]	Bravo Brubeck!	1967	5.00	10.00	20.00
CL 2712 [M]	Jackpot	1967	5.00	10.00	20.00
CL 6321 [10]	Jazz Goes to College, Volume 1	1954	25.00	50.00	100.00
CL 6322 [10]	Jazz Goes to College, Volume 2	1954	25.00	50.00	100.00
CL 6330 [10]	Dave Brubeck at Storyville: 1954, Volume 1	1954	20.00	40.00	80.00
CL 6331 [10]	Dave Brubeck at Storyville: 1954, Volume 2	1954	20.00	40.00	80.00
CS 8058 [S]	Jazz Impressions of Eurasia	1959	12.50	25.00	50.00
—Red/black label with six "eye" logos					
CS 8058 [S]	Jazz Impressions of Eurasia	1962	6.25	12.50	25.00
—Red label, "360 Sound" in black					
CS 8058 [S]	Jazz Impressions of Eurasia	1966	3.75	7.50	15.00
—Red label, "360 Sound" in white					
CS 8082 [S]	Newport 1958	1959	12.50	25.00	50.00
—Red/black label with six "eye" logos					
CS 8082 [S]	Newport 1958	1962	6.25	12.50	25.00
—Red label, "360 Sound" in black					
CS 8082 [S]	Newport 1958	1966	3.75	7.50	15.00
—Red label, "360 Sound" in white					
CS 8090 [S]	Dave Digs Disney	1959	12.50	25.00	50.00
—Red/black label with six "eye" logos					
CS 8090 [S]	Dave Digs Disney	1962	6.25	12.50	25.00
—Red label, "360 Sound" in black					
CS 8090 [S]	Dave Digs Disney	1966	3.75	7.50	15.00
—Red label, "360 Sound" in white					
CS 8156 [S]	Gone with the Wind	1959	12.50	25.00	50.00
—Red/black label with six "eye" logos					
CS 8156 [S]	Gone with the Wind	1962	6.25	12.50	25.00
—Red label, "360 Sound" in black					
CS 8156 [S]	Gone with the Wind	1966	3.75	7.50	15.00
—Red label, "360 Sound" in white					
CS 8156	Gone with the Wind	1971	3.00	6.00	12.00
—Orange label					
CS 8192 [S]	Time Out	1960	7.50	15.00	30.00
—Red/black label with six "eye" logos					
CS 8192 [S]	Time Out Featuring "Take Five"	1962	5.00	10.00	20.00
—Red label, "360 Sound" in black; beginning with this issue, the cover was altered to emphasize the hit					
CS 8192 [S]	Time Out Featuring "Take Five"	1966	3.75	7.50	15.00
—Red label, "360 Sound" in white					
CS 8192	Time Out Featuring "Take Five"	1971	3.00	6.00	12.00
—Orange label					
CS 8192	Time Out	1995	7.50	15.00	30.00
—Audiophile vinyl, distributed by Classic Records					
PC 8192	Time Out	1981	2.00	4.00	8.00
—Reissue with new prefix					
CS 8235 [S]	Southern Scene	1960	7.50	15.00	30.00
—Red/black label with six "eye" logos					
CS 8235 [S]	Southern Scene	1962	5.00	10.00	20.00
—Red label, "360 Sound" in black					
CS 8235 [S]	Southern Scene	1966	3.75	7.50	15.00
—Red label, "360 Sound" in white					
CS 8248 [S]	The Riddle	1960	7.50	15.00	30.00
—Red/black label with six "eye" logos					
CS 8248 [S]	The Riddle	1962	5.00	10.00	20.00
—Red label, "360 Sound" in black					
CS 8248 [S]	The Riddle	1966	3.75	7.50	15.00
—Red label, "360 Sound" in white					
CS 8257 [S]	Brubeck Plays Bernstein Plays Brubeck	1960	7.50	15.00	30.00
—Red/black label with six "eye" logos					
CS 8257 [S]	Brubeck Plays Bernstein Plays Brubeck	1962	5.00	10.00	20.00
—Red label, "360 Sound" in black					
CS 8257 [S]	Brubeck Plays Bernstein Plays Brubeck	1966	3.75	7.50	15.00
—Red label, "360 Sound" in white					
CS 8257	Brubeck Plays Bernstein Plays Brubeck	1971	3.00	6.00	12.00
—Orange label					
CS 8353 [S]	Brubeck and Rushing	1961	7.50	15.00	30.00
—Red/black label with six "eye" logos					
CS 8353 [S]	Brubeck and Rushing	1962	5.00	10.00	20.00
—Red label, "360 Sound" in black					
CS 8353 [S]	Brubeck and Rushing	1966	3.75	7.50	15.00
—Red label, "360 Sound" in white					
CS 8409 [S]	Tonight Only!	1961	7.50	15.00	30.00
—Red/black label with six "eye" logos					
CS 8409 [S]	Tonight Only!	1962	5.00	10.00	20.00
—Red label, "360 Sound" in black					
CS 8409 [S]	Tonight Only!	1966	3.75	7.50	15.00
—Red label, "360 Sound" in white					
CS 8490 [S]	Time Further Out	1961	7.50	15.00	30.00
—Red/black label with six "eye" logos					
CS 8490 [S]	Time Further Out	1962	5.00	10.00	20.00
—Red label, "360 Sound" in black					
CS 8490 [S]	Time Further Out	1966	3.75	7.50	15.00
—Red label, "360 Sound" in white					
CS 8490	Time Further Out	1971	3.00	6.00	12.00
—Orange label					
PC 8490	Time Further Out	1981	2.00	4.00	8.00
—Reissue with new prefix					
CS 8575 [S]	Countdown — Time in Outer Space	1962	5.00	10.00	20.00
—Red label, "360 Sound" in black					
CS 8575 [S]	Countdown — Time in Outer Space	1962	10.00	20.00	40.00
—Red/black label with six "eye" logos					
CS 8575 [S]	Countdown — Time in Outer Space	1966	3.75	7.50	15.00
—Red label, "360 Sound" in white					
CS 8645 [R]	Jazz: Red Hot and Cool	1963	3.75	7.50	15.00
—Red label, "360 Sound" in black					
CS 8645 [R]	Jazz: Red Hot and Cool	1966	3.00	6.00	12.00
—Red label, "360 Sound" in white					
CS 8763 [S]	Brandenburg Gate Revisited	1963	6.25	12.50	25.00
—Red label, "360 Sound" in black					
CS 8763 [S]	Brandenburg Gate Revisited	1966	3.75	7.50	15.00
—Red label, "360 Sound" in white					
CS 8798 [S]	Bossa Nova U.S.A.	1963	6.25	12.50	25.00
—Red label, "360 Sound" in black					
CS 8798 [S]	Bossa Nova U.S.A.	1966	3.75	7.50	15.00
—Red label, "360 Sound" in white					
CS 8927 [S]	Time Changes	1964	6.25	12.50	25.00
—Red label, "360 Sound" in black					
CS 8927 [S]	Time Changes	1966	3.75	7.50	15.00
—Red label, "360 Sound" in white					
CS 9012 [S]	Jazz Impressions of Japan	1964	6.25	12.50	25.00
—Red label, "360 Sound" in black					
CS 9012 [S]	Jazz Impressions of Japan	1966	3.75	7.50	15.00
—Red label, "360 Sound" in white					
CS 9012	Jazz Impressions of Japan	1971	3.00	6.00	12.00
—Orange label					
PC 9012	Jazz Impressions of Japan	1981	2.00	4.00	8.00
—Reissue with new prefix					
CS 9075 [S]	Jazz Impressions of New York	1965	6.25	12.50	25.00
—Red label, "360 Sound" in black					
CS 9075 [S]	Jazz Impressions of New York	1966	3.75	7.50	15.00
—Red label, "360 Sound" in white					
CS 9075	Jazz Impressions of New York	1971	3.00	6.00	12.00
—Orange label					
PC 9075	Jazz Impressions of New York	1981	2.00	4.00	8.00
—Reissue with new prefix					
CS 9116 [S]	Take Five	1965	6.25	12.50	25.00
—Red label, "360 Sound" in black					
CS 9116 [S]	Take Five	1966	3.75	7.50	15.00
—Red label, "360 Sound" in white					
CS 9148 [S]	Angel Eyes	1965	6.25	12.50	25.00
—Red label, "360 Sound" in black					
CS 9148 [S]	Angel Eyes	1966	3.75	7.50	15.00
—Red label, "360 Sound" in black					
CS 9237 [S]	My Favorite Things	1966	5.00	10.00	20.00
—Red "360 Sound" label					
CS 9284 [S]	Dave Brubeck's Greatest Hits	1966	5.00	10.00	20.00
—Red "360 Sound" label					
CS 9284	Dave Brubeck's Greatest Hits	1971	3.00	6.00	12.00
—Orange label					
PC 9284	Dave Brubeck's Greatest Hits	1981	2.00	4.00	8.00
—Reissue with new prefix					
CS 9312 [S]	Time In	1966	5.00	10.00	20.00
—Red "360 Sound" label					
CS 9312	Time In	1971	3.00	6.00	12.00
—Orange label					
PC 9312	Time In	1981	2.00	4.00	8.00
—Reissue with new prefix					

Number	Title (A Side/B Side)	Yr	VG	VG+	NM
❑ CS 9402 [S]	Anything Goes! Dave Brubeck Quartet Plays Cole Porter	1966	5.00	10.00	20.00
—Red "360 Sound" label					
❑ CS 9402	Anything Goes! Dave Brubeck Quartet Plays Cole Porter	1971	3.00	6.00	12.00
—Orange label					
❑ PC 9402	Anything Goes! Dave Brubeck Quartet Plays Cole Porter	1981	2.00	4.00	8.00
—Reissue with new prefix					
❑ CS 9495 [S]	Bravo Brubeck!	1967	3.75	7.50	15.00
—Red "360 Sound" label					
❑ CS 9495	Bravo Brubeck!	1971	3.00	6.00	12.00
—Orange label					
❑ CS 9512 [S]	Jackpot	1967	3.75	7.50	15.00
—Red "360 Sound" label					
❑ CS 9572	The Last Time We Saw Paris	1971	3.00	6.00	12.00
—Orange label					
❑ CS 9672	The Last Time We Saw Paris	1968	3.75	7.50	15.00
—Red "360 Sound" label					
❑ CS 9704	Compadres	1968	3.75	7.50	15.00
—Red "360 Sound" label					
❑ CS 9704	Compadres	1971	3.00	6.00	12.00
—Orange label					
❑ CS 9749	Blues Roots	1969	3.75	7.50	15.00
—Red "360 Sound" label					
❑ CS 9749	Blues Roots	1971	3.00	6.00	12.00
—Orange label					
❑ CS 9897	Brubeck in Amsterdam	1969	3.75	7.50	15.00
—Red "360 Sound" label					
❑ CS 9897	Brubeck in Amsterdam	1971	3.00	6.00	12.00
—Orange label					
❑ C 30522	The Summit Sessions	1971	3.00	6.00	12.00
❑ G 30625 [(2)]	Adventures in Time	1971	3.75	7.50	15.00
❑ KG 31298 [(2)]	Brubeck On Campus	1972	3.75	7.50	15.00
❑ KC 32143	Brubeck at the Berlin Philharmonic	1973	3.00	6.00	12.00
❑ KG 32761 [(2)]	All-Time Greatest Hits	1974	3.75	7.50	15.00
❑ CG 33666 [(2)]	Gone with the Wind/Time Out	1975	3.75	7.50	15.00
❑ PC 37022	A Place in Time	1981	2.50	5.00	10.00
—Reissue of Odyssey LP					
COLUMBIA JAZZ MASTERPIECES					
❑ CJ 40455	The Dave Brubeck Quartet Plays Music from West Side Story and Other Shows and Films	1987	2.50	5.00	10.00
❑ CJ 40585	Time Out	1987	2.50	5.00	10.00
❑ CJ 40627	Gone with the Wind	1987	2.50	5.00	10.00
❑ CJ 45149	Jazz Goes to College	1989	2.50	5.00	10.00
COLUMBIA LIMITED EDITION					
❑ LE 10013	Gone with the Wind	197?	2.50	5.00	10.00
CONCORD JAZZ					
❑ CJ-103	Back Home	1979	2.50	5.00	10.00
❑ CJ-129	Tritonis	1980	2.50	5.00	10.00
❑ CJ-178	Paper Moon	1982	2.50	5.00	10.00
❑ CJ-198	Concord on a Summer Night	1982	2.50	5.00	10.00
❑ CJ-259	For Iola	1985	2.50	5.00	10.00
❑ CJ-299	Reflections	1986	2.50	5.00	10.00
❑ CJ-317	Blue Rondo	1987	2.50	5.00	10.00
❑ CJ-353	Moscow Night	1988	2.50	5.00	10.00
CROWN					
❑ CLP-5406 [M]	The Greats	196?	3.75	7.50	15.00
❑ CLP 5470 [M]	Dave Brubeck and the George Nielson Quartet	196?	3.75	7.50	15.00
DECCA					
❑ DXSA 7202 [(2)]	The Light in the Wilderness	1968	3.75	7.50	15.00
—Records are individually numbered "DL 710,155" and "DL 710,156"					
❑ DL 710175	The Gates of Justice	1969	3.00	6.00	12.00
❑ DL 710181	Brubeck/Mulligan/Cincinnati	1971	3.00	6.00	12.00
DIRECT DISK					
❑ 106 [(2)]	A Cut Above	1979	6.25	12.50	25.00
FANTASY					
❑ 3-1 [10]	Dave Brubeck Trio	1951	37.50	75.00	150.00
❑ 3-2 [10]	Dave Brubeck Trio	1951	37.50	75.00	150.00
❑ 3-3 [10]	Dave Brubeck Octet	1951	37.50	75.00	150.00
❑ 3-4 [10]	Dave Brubeck Trio	1952	37.50	75.00	150.00
❑ 3-5 [10]	Dave Brubeck Quartet with Paul Desmond	1952	37.50	75.00	150.00
❑ 3-7 [10]	Dave Brubeck Quartet with Paul Desmond	1952	37.50	75.00	150.00
❑ 3-8 [10]	Jazz at Storyville	1953	37.50	75.00	150.00
❑ 3-10 [10]	Jazz at the Blackhawk	1953	37.50	75.00	150.00
❑ 3-11 [10]	Jazz at Oberlin	1953	37.50	75.00	150.00
❑ 3-13 [10]	Jazz at the College of the Pacific	1954	37.50	75.00	150.00
❑ 3-16 [10]	Old Sounds from San Francisco	1954	37.50	75.00	150.00
❑ 3-20 [10]	Paul and Dave's Jazz Interwoven	1955	37.50	75.00	150.00
❑ OJC-046	Jazz at Oberlin	198?	2.50	5.00	10.00
—Reissue of 3245					
❑ OJC-047	Jazz at the College of the Pacific	198?	2.50	5.00	10.00
—Reissue of 3223					
❑ OJC-101	The Dave Brubeck Octet	198?	2.50	5.00	10.00
—Reissue of Fantasy 3239					
❑ OJC-150	Re-Union	198?	2.50	5.00	10.00
❑ OJC-200	Brubeck A La Mode	1985	2.50	5.00	10.00
❑ OJC-236	Near Myth	1986	2.50	5.00	10.00
—Reissue of Fantasy 3319					
❑ 3204 [M]	Dave Brubeck Trio	195?	15.00	30.00	60.00
—Black vinyl, red label, non-flexible vinyl					
❑ 3204 [M]	Dave Brubeck Trio	1956	25.00	50.00	100.00
—Dark red vinyl; reissue of 3-1					
❑ 3204 [M]	Dave Brubeck Trio	196?	10.00	20.00	40.00
—Black vinyl, red label, flexible vinyl					
❑ 3205 [M]	Dave Brubeck Trio: Distinctive Rhythm Instrumentals	195?	15.00	30.00	60.00
—Black vinyl, red label, non-flexible vinyl					
❑ 3205 [M]	Dave Brubeck Trio: Distinctive Rhythm Instrumentals	1956	25.00	50.00	100.00
—Dark red vinyl; reissue of 3-2					
❑ 3205 [M]	Dave Brubeck Trio: Distinctive Rhythm Instrumentals	196?	10.00	20.00	40.00
❑ 3210 [M]	Jazz at the Blackhawk	195?	15.00	30.00	60.00
—Black vinyl, red label, non-flexible vinyl					
❑ 3210 [M]	Jazz at the Blackhawk	1956	25.00	50.00	100.00
—Dark red vinyl; reissue of 3-10					
❑ 3210 [M]	Jazz at the Blackhawk	196?	10.00	20.00	40.00
—Black vinyl, red label, flexible vinyl					
❑ 3223 [M]	Jazz at the College of the Pacific	195?	15.00	30.00	60.00
—Black vinyl, red label, non-flexible vinyl					
❑ 3223 [M]	Jazz at the College of the Pacific	1956	25.00	50.00	100.00
—Dark red vinyl; reissue of 3-13					
❑ 3223 [M]	Jazz at the College of the Pacific	196?	10.00	20.00	40.00
—Black vinyl, red label, flexible vinyl					
❑ 3229 [M]	Brubeck-Desmond	195?	15.00	30.00	60.00
—Black vinyl, red label, non-flexible vinyl					
❑ 3229 [M]	Brubeck-Desmond	1956	25.00	50.00	100.00
—Dark red vinyl; reissue of 3-5					
❑ 3229 [M]	Brubeck-Desmond	196?	10.00	20.00	40.00
—Black vinyl, red label, flexible vinyl					
❑ 3230 [M]	Dave Brubeck Quartet	195?	15.00	30.00	60.00
—Black vinyl, red label, non-flexible vinyl					
❑ 3230 [M]	Dave Brubeck Quartet	1956	25.00	50.00	100.00
—Dark red vinyl; reissue of 3-7					
❑ 3230 [M]	Dave Brubeck Quartet	196?	10.00	20.00	40.00
—Black vinyl, red label, flexible vinyl					
❑ 3239 [M]	Dave Brubeck Octet	195?	15.00	30.00	60.00
—Black vinyl, red label, non-flexible vinyl					
❑ 3239 [M]	Dave Brubeck Octet	1956	25.00	50.00	100.00
—Dark red vinyl; reissue of 3-3					
❑ 3239 [M]	Dave Brubeck Octet	196?	10.00	20.00	40.00
—Black vinyl, red label, flexible vinyl					
❑ 3240 [M]	Brubeck Desmond: Jazz at Storyville	195?	15.00	30.00	60.00
—Black vinyl, red label, non-flexible vinyl					
❑ 3240 [M]	Brubeck Desmond: Jazz at Storyville	1957	25.00	50.00	100.00
—Dark red vinyl; reissue of 3-8					
❑ 3240 [M]	Brubeck Desmond: Jazz at Storyville	196?	10.00	20.00	40.00
—Black vinyl, red label, flexible vinyl					
❑ 3245 [M]	Jazz at Oberlin	195?	15.00	30.00	60.00
—Black vinyl, red label, non-flexible vinyl					
❑ 3245 [M]	Jazz at Oberlin	1957	25.00	50.00	100.00
—Dark red vinyl; reissue of 3-11					
❑ 3245 [M]	Jazz at Oberlin	196?	10.00	20.00	40.00
—Black vinyl, red label, flexible vinyl					
❑ 3249 [M]	Brubeck & Desmond at Wilshire-Ebell	195?	15.00	30.00	60.00
—Black vinyl, red label, non-flexible vinyl					
❑ 3249 [M]	Brubeck & Desmond at Wilshire-Ebell	1957	25.00	50.00	100.00
—Dark red vinyl					
❑ 3249 [M]	Brubeck & Desmond at Wilshire-Ebell	196?	10.00	20.00	40.00
—Black vinyl, red label, flexible vinyl					
❑ 3259 [M]	Dave Brubeck Plays and Plays and Plays and Plays and…	195?	10.00	20.00	40.00
—Black vinyl, red label, non-flexible vinyl					
❑ 3259 [M]	Dave Brubeck Plays and Plays and Plays and Plays and…	1958	15.00	30.00	60.00
—Red vinyl					
❑ 3259 [M]	Dave Brubeck Plays and Plays and Plays and Plays and…	196?	7.50	15.00	30.00
—Black vinyl, red label, flexible vinyl					
❑ 3268 [M]	Re-Union	195?	10.00	20.00	40.00
—Black vinyl, red label, non-flexible vinyl					
❑ 3268 [M]	Re-Union	1958	15.00	30.00	60.00
—Red vinyl					
❑ 3268 [M]	Re-Union	196?	7.50	15.00	30.00
—Black vinyl, red label, flexible vinyl					
❑ 3298 [M]	Two Knights at the Black Hawk	1959	10.00	20.00	40.00
—Black vinyl, red label, non-flexible vinyl					
❑ 3298 [M]	Two Knights at the Black Hawk	1959	15.00	30.00	60.00
—Red vinyl					
❑ 3298 [M]	Two Knights at the Black Hawk	196?	7.50	15.00	30.00
—Black vinyl, red label, flexible vinyl					
❑ 3301 [M]	Brubeck A La Mode	196?	7.50	15.00	30.00
—Black vinyl, red label, flexible vinyl					
❑ 3301 [M]	Brubeck A La Mode	1960	10.00	20.00	40.00
—Black vinyl, red label, non-flexible vinyl					
❑ 3301 [M]	Brubeck A La Mode	1960	15.00	30.00	60.00
—Red vinyl					
❑ 3319 [M]	Near-Myth	196?	7.50	15.00	30.00
—Black vinyl, red label, flexible vinyl					
❑ 3319 [M]	Near-Myth	1961	10.00	20.00	40.00
—Black vinyl, red label, non-flexible vinyl					
❑ 3319 [M]	Near-Myth	1961	15.00	30.00	60.00
—Red vinyl					
❑ 3331 [M]	Dave Brubeck Trio Featuring Cal Tjader	196?	7.50	15.00	30.00
—Black vinyl, red label, flexible vinyl					
❑ 3331 [M]	Dave Brubeck Trio Featuring Cal Tjader	1962	10.00	20.00	40.00
—Black vinyl, red label, non-flexible vinyl					
❑ 3331 [M]	Dave Brubeck Trio Featuring Cal Tjader	1962	15.00	30.00	60.00
—Red vinyl					
❑ 3332 [M]	Brubeck Tjader	196?	7.50	15.00	30.00
—Black vinyl, red label, flexible vinyl					
❑ 3332 [M]	Brubeck Tjader	1962	10.00	20.00	40.00
—Black vinyl, red label, non-flexible vinyl					
❑ 3332 [M]	Brubeck Tjader	1962	15.00	30.00	60.00
—Red vinyl					
❑ MPF-4528	Greatest Hits from the Fantasy Years	198?	2.50	5.00	10.00
❑ 8007 [S]	Re-Union	196?	5.00	10.00	20.00
—Black vinyl, blue label, flexible vinyl					
❑ 8007 [S]	Re-Union	196?	7.50	15.00	30.00
—Black vinyl, blue label, non-flexible vinyl					
❑ 8007 [S]	Re-Union	1962	12.50	25.00	50.00
—Blue vinyl					

Number	Title (A Side/B Side)	Yr	VG	VG+	NM
❏ 8047 [S]	Brubeck A La Mode	196?	5.00	10.00	20.00
—Black vinyl, blue label, flexible vinyl					
❏ 8047 [S]	Brubeck A La Mode	196?	7.50	15.00	30.00
—Black vinyl, blue label, non-flexible vinyl					
❏ 8047 [S]	Brubeck A La Mode	1962	12.50	25.00	50.00
—Blue vinyl					
❏ 8063 [S]	Near-Myth	196?	5.00	10.00	20.00
—Black vinyl, blue label, flexible vinyl					
❏ 8063 [S]	Near-Myth	196?	7.50	15.00	30.00
—Black vinyl, blue label, non-flexible vinyl					
❏ 8063 [S]	Near-Myth	1962	12.50	25.00	50.00
—Blue vinyl					
❏ 8069 [R]	Jazz at Oberlin	196?	3.75	7.50	15.00
—Black vinyl, blue label, flexible vinyl					
❏ 8069 [R]	Jazz at Oberlin	196?	5.00	10.00	20.00
—Black vinyl, blue label, non-flexible vinyl					
❏ 8069 [R]	Jazz at Oberlin	1962	10.00	20.00	40.00
—Blue vinyl					
❏ 8073 [R]	Dave Brubeck Trio Featuring Cal Tjader	196?	3.75	7.50	15.00
—Black vinyl, blue label, flexible vinyl					
❏ 8073 [R]	Dave Brubeck Trio Featuring Cal Tjader	1962	5.00	10.00	20.00
—Black vinyl, blue label, non-flexible vinyl					
❏ 8073 [R]	Dave Brubeck Trio Featuring Cal Tjader	1962	10.00	20.00	40.00
—Blue vinyl					
❏ 8074 [R]	Brubeck Tjader	196?	3.75	7.50	15.00
—Black vinyl, blue label, flexible vinyl					
❏ 8074 [R]	Brubeck Tjader	1962	5.00	10.00	20.00
—Black vinyl, blue label, non-flexible vinyl					
❏ 8074 [R]	Brubeck Tjader	1962	10.00	20.00	40.00
—Blue vinyl					
❏ 8078 [R]	Jazz at the College of the Pacific	196?	3.75	7.50	15.00
—Black vinyl, blue label, flexible vinyl					
❏ 8078 [R]	Jazz at the College of the Pacific	196?	5.00	10.00	20.00
—Black vinyl, blue label, non-flexible vinyl					
❏ 8078 [R]	Jazz at the College of the Pacific	1962	10.00	20.00	40.00
—Blue vinyl					
❏ 8080 [R]	Jazz at Storyville	196?	3.75	7.50	15.00
—Black vinyl, blue label, flexible vinyl					
❏ 8080 [R]	Jazz at Storyville	1962	5.00	10.00	20.00
—Black vinyl, blue label, non-flexible vinyl					
❏ 8080 [R]	Jazz at Storyville	1962	10.00	20.00	40.00
—Blue vinyl					
❏ 8081 [R]	Two Knights at the Blackhawk	196?	3.75	7.50	15.00
—Black vinyl, blue label, flexible vinyl					
❏ 8081 [R]	Two Knights at the Blackhawk	1962	5.00	10.00	20.00
—Black vinyl, blue label, non-flexible vinyl					
❏ 8081 [R]	Two Knights at the Blackhawk	1962	10.00	20.00	40.00
—Blue vinyl					
❏ 8092 [R]	Brubeck-Desmond	196?	3.75	7.50	15.00
—Black vinyl, blue label, flexible vinyl					
❏ 8092 [R]	Brubeck-Desmond	1962	5.00	10.00	20.00
—Black vinyl, blue label, non-flexible vinyl					
❏ 8092 [R]	Brubeck-Desmond	1962	10.00	20.00	40.00
—Blue vinyl					
❏ 8093 [R]	Dave Brubeck Quartet	196?	3.75	7.50	15.00
—Black vinyl, blue label, flexible vinyl					
❏ 8093 [R]	Dave Brubeck Quartet	1962	5.00	10.00	20.00
—Black vinyl, blue label, non-flexible vinyl					
❏ 8093 [R]	Dave Brubeck Quartet	1962	10.00	2.00	40.00
—Blue vinyl					
❏ 8094 [R]	Dave Brubeck Octet	196?	3.75	7.50	15.00
—Black vinyl, blue label, flexible vinyl					
❏ 8094 [R]	Dave Brubeck Octet	1962	5.00	10.00	20.00
—Black vinyl, blue label, non-flexible vinyl					
❏ 8094 [R]	Dave Brubeck Octet	1962	10.00	20.00	40.00
—Blue vinyl					
❏ 8095 [S]	Brubeck and Desmond at Wilshire-Ebell	196?	5.00	10.00	20.00
—Black vinyl, blue label, flexible vinyl					
❏ 8095 [S]	Brubeck and Desmond at Wilshire-Ebell	1962	7.50	15.00	30.00
—Black vinyl, blue label, non-flexible vinyl					
❏ 8095 [S]	Brubeck and Desmond at Wilshire-Ebell	1962	12.50	25.00	50.00
—Blue vinyl					
❏ 24726 [(2)]	The Dave Brubeck Trio	198?	3.75	7.50	15.00
❏ 24727 [(2)]	Brubeck-Desmond	1982	3.75	7.50	15.00
❏ 24728 [(2)]	Stardust	198?	3.75	7.50	15.00
HARMONY					
❏ HS 11253	Instant Brubeck	1968	3.00	6.00	12.00
❏ HS 11336	Gone with the Wind	1969	3.00	6.00	12.00
HORIZON					
❏ SP-703	1975: The Duets	1975	3.00	6.00	12.00
❏ SP-714	The Dave Brubeck Quartet 25th Anniversary	1976	3.00	6.00	12.00
JAZZTONE					
❏ J-1272 [M]	Best of Brubeck	195?	10.00	20.00	40.00
MOBILE FIDELITY					
❏ 1-216	We're All Together Again for the First Time	1994	15.00	30.00	60.00
—Audiophile vinyl					
MOON					
❏ 028	St. Louis Blues	1992	5.00	10.00	20.00
ODYSSEY					
❏ 32160248	A Place in Time	197?	3.00	6.00	12.00
TOMATO					
❏ 7018	The New Brubeck Quartet at Montreux	1978	3.00	6.00	12.00

BRUCE, ED

45s

Number	Title (A Side/B Side)	Yr	VG	VG+	NM
EPIC					
❏ 50424	When I Die, Just Let Me Go to Texas/ I've Not Forgotten Marie	1977	—	2.00	4.00
❏ 50475	Star Studded Nights/Wedding Dress	1977	—	2.00	4.00
❏ 50503	Love Somebody to Death/I Can't Seem to Get the Hang of Telling Her Goodbye	1977	—	2.00	4.00
❏ 50544	Man Made of Glass/ Never Take Candy from a Stranger	1978	—	2.00	4.00

Number	Title (A Side/B Side)	Yr	VG	VG+	NM
❏ 50613	The Man That Turned My Mama On/Give My Old Memory a Call	1978	—	2.00	4.00
❏ 50645	Angeline/Give My Old Memory a Call	1978	—	2.00	4.00
MCA					
❏ 41201	Diane/Blue Umbrella	1980	—	—	3.00
❏ 41273	The Last Cowboy Song/The Outlaw and the Stranger	1980	—	—	3.00
❏ 51018	Girls, Women & Ladies/The Last Thing She Said	1980	—	—	3.00
❏ 51076	Evil Angel/Easy Temptations	1981	—	—	3.00
❏ 51139	(When You Fall in Love) Everything's a Waltz/ Thirty-Nine and Holding	1982	—	—	3.00
❏ 51210	You're the Best Break This Old Heart Ever Had/ It Just Makes Me Want You More	1982	—	—	3.00
❏ 52036	Love's Found You and Me/I Take the Chance	1982	—	—	3.00
❏ 52109	Ever, Never Lovin' You/Theme from "Bret Maverick"	1982	—	—	3.00
❏ 52156	My First Taste of Texas/One More Shot of "Old Back Home Again"	1983	—	—	3.00
❏ 52210	You're Not Leaving Here Tonight/I Think I'm in Love	1983	—	—	3.00
❏ 52251	If It Was Easy/You've Got Her Eyes	1983	—	—	3.00
❏ 52295	After All/It Would Take a Fool	1983	—	—	3.00
❏ 52433	Tell 'Em I've Gone Crazy/Birds of Paradise	1984	—	—	3.00
MONUMENT					
❏ 1118	Song for Jenny/Puzzles	1968	—	3.00	6.00
❏ 1138	Everybody Wants to Get to Heaven/When a Man Becomes a Man	1969	—	3.00	6.00
❏ 1155	Hey Porter/The Love of My Heart	1969	—	3.00	6.00
RCA					
❏ 5005-7-R	Fools for Each Other/Memphis Roots	1986	—	—	3.00
—A-side with Lynn Anderson					
❏ 5077-7-R	Quietly Crazy/Memphis Routes	1986	—	—	3.00
❏ JB-13937 [DJ]		1984	2.00	4.00	8.00
—Promo only on green vinyl					
❏ JB-13937 [PS]		1984	2.00	4.00	8.00
—Possibly promo-only sleeve with "RCA Records and Coors Present Ed Bruce" on it					
❏ PB-13937	You Turn Me On Like a Radio/If It Ain't Love	1984	—	—	3.00
❏ PB-14037	When Givin' Up Was Easy/Texas Girl, I'm Closing In on You	1985	—	—	3.00
❏ PB-14150	If It Ain't Love/The Migrant	1985	—	—	3.00
❏ PB-14305	Nights/Fifteen to Forty-Three (Man in the Middle)	1986	—	—	3.00
RCA VICTOR					
❏ 47-7842	Flight 303/Spun Gold	1961	3.75	7.50	15.00
❏ 47-9044	Walker's Woods/Lonesome Is Me	1966	2.00	4.00	8.00
❏ 47-9155	Last Train to Clarksville/I'm Getting Better	1967	2.00	4.00	8.00
❏ 47-9315	The Price I Pay to Stay/If I Could Just Go Home	1967	2.00	4.00	8.00
❏ 47-9394	Shadows of Her Mind/Her Sweet Love and the Baby	1967	2.00	4.00	8.00
❏ 47-9475	I'll Take You Away/Give More Than You Take	1968	2.00	4.00	8.00
❏ 47-9553	Painted Girls and Wine/Ninety-Seven More to Go	1968	2.00	4.00	8.00
❏ 61-7842 [S]	Flight 303/Spun Gold	1961	7.50	15.00	30.00
—"Living Stereo" (large hole, plays at 45 rpm)					
SUN					
❏ 276	Rock Boppin' Baby/More Than Yesterday	1957	7.50	15.00	30.00
—As "Edwin Bruce"					
❏ 292	Sweet Woman/Part of My Life	1958	10.00	20.00	40.00
—As "Edwin Bruce"					
UNITED ARTISTS					
❏ XW204	A House in New Orleans/Good Jelly Jones	1973	—	2.00	4.00
❏ XW353	July, You're a Woman/The Rain in Baby's Life	1973	—	2.00	4.00
❏ XW403	It's Not What She Done/The Devil Ain't a Lonely Woman's Friend	1974	—	2.00	4.00
❏ XW732	Mammas Don't Let Your Babies Grow Up to Be Cowboys/It's Not What She's Done (It's What You Didn't Do)	1975	—	2.50	5.00
❏ XW774	The Littlest Cowboy Rides Again/The Feel of Being Gone	1976	—	2.00	4.00
❏ XW811	Sleep All Mornin'/Working Man's Prayer	1976	—	2.00	4.00
❏ XW862	For Love's Own Sake/When Wide Open Spaces and Cowboys Are Gone	1976	—	2.00	4.00
WAND					
❏ 136	It's Coming to Me/The Greatest Man	1963	3.00	6.00	12.00
❏ 156	I'm Gonna Have a Party/Half a Love	1964	3.00	6.00	12.00

Albums

Number	Title	Yr	VG	VG+	NM
EPIC					
❏ KE 35043	Tennesseean	1977	2.50	5.00	10.00
❏ KE 35541	Cowboys and Dreamers	1978	2.50	5.00	10.00
MCA					
❏ 3242	Ed Bruce	1980	2.50	5.00	10.00
❏ 5188	One to One	1981	2.50	5.00	10.00
❏ 5323	I Write It Down	1982	2.50	5.00	10.00
❏ 5416	You're Not Leaving Here Tonight	1983	2.50	5.00	10.00
❏ 5511	Tell 'Em I've Gone Crazy	1984	2.50	5.00	10.00
❏ 5577	Greatest Hits	1985	2.50	5.00	10.00
❏ 27068	Ed Bruce	198?	2.00	4.00	8.00
—Reissue of 3242					
MONUMENT					
❏ SLP-18118	Shades	1969	5.00	10.00	20.00
RCA VICTOR					
❏ LPM-3948 [M]	If I Could Just Go Home	1968	12.50	25.00	50.00
❏ LSP-3948 [S]	If I Could Just Go Home	1968	6.25	12.50	25.00
❏ AHL1-5324	Homecoming	1985	2.50	5.00	10.00
❏ AHL1-5808	Night Things	1986	2.50	5.00	10.00
UNITED ARTISTS					
❏ UA-LA613-G	Ed Bruce	1976	3.00	6.00	12.00

Number	Title (A Side/B Side)	Yr	VG	VG+	NM

BRUCE, JACK Ex-member of CREAM.
45s
RSO

Number	Title (A Side/B Side)	Yr	VG	VG+	NM
❏ 507	Keep It Down/Keep On Wondering	1975	—	2.50	5.00

Albums
ATCO

❏ SD 33-306	Songs for a Tailor	1969	3.75	7.50	15.00
❏ SD 33-349	Things We Like	1971	3.75	7.50	15.00
❏ SD 33-365	Harmony Row	1971	3.75	7.50	15.00

EPIC

❏ JE 36827	I've Always Wanted to Do This	1980	2.50	5.00	10.00
❏ FE 45279	A Question of Time	1989	3.75	7.50	15.00

POLYDOR

❏ PD2-3505 [(2)]	Jack Bruce At His Best	1972	3.75	7.50	15.00

RSO

❏ RS-1-3021	How's Tricks	1977	2.50	5.00	10.00
❏ SO 4805	Out of the Storm	1974	2.50	5.00	10.00

BRUCE, JACK/ROBIN TROWER Also see each artist's individual listings.
Albums
CHRYSALIS

❏ CHR 1352	Truce	1982	2.50	5.00	10.00
❏ PV 41352	Truce	1983	2.00	4.00	8.00

—Reissue

BRUCE, LENNY
Albums
BIZARRE

❏ 2XS 6329 [(2)]	The Berkeley Concert	1969	6.25	12.50	25.00

DOUGLAS

❏ 2	To Is a Preposition, Come Is a Verb	196?	5.00	10.00	20.00
❏ 788	The Essential Lenny Bruce Politics	1968	5.00	10.00	20.00
❏ Z 30872	What I Was Arrested For	1971	3.75	7.50	15.00

—Reissue of 2
FANTASY

❏ FP-1 [DJ]	The Promo Album	196?	50.00	100.00	200.00

—Promo-only compilation of material from albums 7001, 7003, 7007 and 7011

❏ 7001 [M]	Interviews of Our Times	1959	10.00	20.00	40.00

—Non-flexible black vinyl; cover changed to blue tint

❏ 7001 [M]	Interviews of Our Times	1959	25.00	50.00	100.00

—Opaque, non-flexible red vinyl; tan cover with Lenny Bruce's name blacked out throughout the back

❏ 7001 [M]	Interviews of Our Times	1962	5.00	10.00	20.00

—Flexible black vinyl

❏ 7001 [M]	Interviews of Our Times	1962	10.00	20.00	40.00

—Translucent, flexible red vinyl

❏ 7003 [M]	The Sick Humor of Lenny Bruce	1959	10.00	20.00	40.00

—Non-flexible black vinyl

❏ 7003 [M]	The Sick Humor of Lenny Bruce	1959	25.00	50.00	100.00

—Opaque, non-flexible red vinyl

❏ 7003 [M]	The Sick Humor of Lenny Bruce	1962	5.00	10.00	20.00

—Flexible black vinyl

❏ 7003 [M]	The Sick Humor of Lenny Bruce	1962	10.00	20.00	40.00

—Translucent, flexible red vinyl

❏ 7007 [M]	I Am Not a Nut, Elect Me	1960	10.00	20.00	40.00

—Non-flexible black vinyl

❏ 7007 [M]	I Am Not a Nut, Elect Me	1960	25.00	50.00	100.00

—Opaque, non-flexible red vinyl

❏ 7007 [M]	I Am Not a Nut, Elect Me	1962	5.00	10.00	20.00

—Flexible black vinyl

❏ 7007 [M]	I Am Not a Nut, Elect Me	1962	10.00	20.00	40.00

—Translucent, flexible red vinyl

❏ 7011 [M]	Lenny Bruce, American	1961	10.00	20.00	40.00

—Non-flexible black vinyl

❏ 7011 [M]	Lenny Bruce, American	1961	25.00	50.00	100.00

—Opaque, non-flexible red vinyl

❏ 7011 [M]	Lenny Bruce, American	1962	5.00	10.00	20.00

—Flexible black vinyl

❏ 7011 [M]	Lenny Bruce, American	1962	10.00	20.00	40.00

—Translucent, flexible red vinyl

❏ 7012 [M]	The Best of Lenny Bruce	1962	5.00	10.00	20.00

—Black vinyl

❏ 7012 [M]	The Best of Lenny Bruce	1962	12.50	25.00	50.00

—Red vinyl

❏ 7017	Thank You Masked Man	1971	3.75	7.50	15.00
❏ 34201 [(3)]	Lenny Bruce at the Curran Theater	1971	10.00	20.00	40.00
❏ 79003 [(2)]	The Real Lenny Bruce	1975	5.00	10.00	20.00

LENNY BRUCE

❏ LB-3001/2 [M]	Lenny Bruce Is Out Again	196?	75.00	150.00	300.00

—Privately pressed version with white labels and Lenny's address on cover

❏ LB-9001/2 [10]	Warning: Sale of This Album...	1962	125.00	250.00	500.00

—Privately pressed LP with routines used as evidence in Lenny's obscenity trial
PHILLIES

❏ PHLP-4010 [M]	Lenny Bruce Is Out Again	1966	25.00	50.00	100.00

—Reissue of Lenny Bruce 3001/2
UNITED ARTISTS

❏ UAL 3580 [M]	The Midnight Concert	1967	6.25	12.50	25.00
❏ UAS 6580	The Midnight Concert	1967	5.00	10.00	20.00
❏ UAS 6794	The Midnight Concert	1972	3.75	7.50	15.00

—Reissue of 6580

❏ UAS 9800 [(3)]	Lenny Bruce/Carnegie Hall	1972	6.25	12.50	25.00

WARNER/SPECTOR

❏ SP 9101	The Law, the Language and Lenny Bruce	1975	3.75	7.50	15.00

BRUCE, TOMMY
45s
CAPITOL

❏ 4403	Ain't Misbehavin'/Got the Water Boilin'	1960	3.00	6.00	12.00
❏ 5354	It's Driving Me Wild/Over Suzanne	1965	2.50	5.00	10.00

BRUCE AND TERRY BRUCE JOHNSTON and TERRY MELCHER.
45s
COLUMBIA

❏ 42956	Custom Machine/Makaha at Midnight	1964	5.00	10.00	20.00
❏ 43055	Summer Means Fun/Yeah!	1964	5.00	10.00	20.00
❏ 43238	I Love You Model T/Carmen	1965	5.00	10.00	20.00
❏ 43378	Raining in My Heart/Four Strong Winds	1965	4.00	8.00	16.00
❏ 43479	Thank You Baby/Come Love	1965	4.00	8.00	16.00
❏ 43582	Don't Run Away/Girl It's All Right Now	1966	4.00	8.00	16.00

EQUINOX

❏ PB-10238	Rebecca/Take It to Mexico	1975	2.50	5.00	10.00

—As "Bruce Johnston and Terry Melcher"

BRUINS, THE
45s
COMET

❏ 2167	Nobody But You/One More Try	1964	6.25	12.50	25.00

GENERAL AMERICAN

❏ 721	Go On and Cry/Can't Believe That You've Grown Up	1965	10.00	20.00	40.00

ROULETTE

❏ 4566	Believe Me/The Slide	1964	5.00	10.00	20.00

BRUNO, BRUCE
45s
ROULETTE

❏ 4386	Hey Little One/Some Time, Some Place	1961	5.00	10.00	20.00
❏ 4427	Venus in Blue Jeans/Dear Joanne	1962	5.00	10.00	20.00

BRUTE FORCE
45s
B.T. PUPPY

❏ 561	War/Overture to Hello	1970	2.00	4.00	8.00

COLUMBIA

❏ 44091	Cudd'ly/In Jim's Garage	1967	2.00	4.00	8.00
❏ 44371	Brute's Party/Toys for Tots	1967	2.00	4.00	8.00

WARNER BROS.

❏ 7224	Adam & Evening/The Purpose of a Circus	1968	2.00	4.00	8.00

Albums
B.T. PUPPY

❏ BTPS-1015	Extemporaneous	1971	1000.	1500.	2000.

COLUMBIA

❏ CL 2615 [M]	I, Brute Force — Confections of Love	1967	5.00	10.00	20.00
❏ CS 9415 [S]	I, Brute Force — Confections of Love	1967	5.00	10.00	20.00

EMBRYO

❏ 522	Brute Force	1970	5.00	10.00	20.00

BRYAN, BILLY See GENE PITNEY.

BRYAN, WES
45s
CLOCK

❏ 1013	Honey Baby/So Blue Over You	1959	5.00	10.00	20.00

ROULETTE

❏ 4289	I Guess I'll Never Know/Melodie D'Amour	1960	3.75	7.50	15.00

UNITED ARTISTS

❏ 102	Tiny Spacemen/Lonesome Love	1957	7.50	15.00	30.00
❏ 102 [PS]	Tiny Spacemen/Lonesome Love	1957	15.00	30.00	60.00
❏ 122	Wait for Me Baby/Freeze!	1958	6.25	12.50	25.00

BRYANT, ANITA
45s
ANITA BRYANT MINISTRIES

❏ 1-413	Gospel Medley/Nostalgia Medley	1980	3.75	7.50	15.00

—Small hole, plays at 33 1/3 rpm

❏ 1-413 [PS]	Gospel Medley/Nostalgia Medley	1980	3.75	7.50	15.00

CARLTON

❏ ST 118-1 [S]	Just in Time/Till There Was You	1959	3.75	7.50	15.00
❏ ST 118-2 [S]	Hello Young Lovers/Mr. Wonderful	1959	3.75	7.50	15.00
❏ ST 118-3 [S]	Anyone Would Love You/The Party's Over	1959	3.75	7.50	15.00
❏ ST 118-4 [S]	Promise Me a Rose/Wouldn't It Be Lovely	1959	3.75	7.50	15.00
❏ ST 118-5 [S]	Small World/Love Look Away	1959	3.75	7.50	15.00

—The above five are jukebox singles excerpting the LP "Anita Bryant"

❏ 473	Be Good, Be Careful, Be Mine/Dance On	1958	3.75	7.50	15.00
❏ 512	Till There Was You/Little George	1959	2.50	5.00	10.00
❏ 518	Six Boys and Seven Girls/The Blessings of Love	1959	2.50	5.00	10.00
❏ 523	Promise Me a Rose (A Slight Detail)/Do-Re-Mi	1959	2.50	5.00	10.00
❏ 528	Paper Roses/Mixed Emotions	1960	2.00	4.00	8.00
❏ 530	In My Little Corner of the World/Anyone Would Love You	1960	2.00	4.00	8.00
❏ 535	One of the Lucky Ones/Love Look Away	1960	2.00	4.00	8.00
❏ 537	Wonderland by Night/Pictures	1960	2.00	4.00	8.00
❏ 538	A Texan and a Girl from Mexico/He's Not Good Enough for You	1961	2.00	4.00	8.00
❏ 547	I Can't Do It By Myself/An Angel Cried	1961	2.00	4.00	8.00
❏ 553	Lonesome for You Mama/A Place Called Happiness	1961	2.00	4.00	8.00

COLUMBIA

❏ 31570 [S]	(contents unknown)	1962	2.50	5.00	10.00
❏ 31571 [S]	(contents unknown)	1962	2.50	5.00	10.00
❏ 31572 [S]	(contents unknown)	1962	2.50	5.00	10.00
❏ 31573 [S]	(contents unknown)	1962	2.50	5.00	10.00
❏ 31574 [S]	(contents unknown)	1962	2.50	5.00	10.00

—Anyone who can fill in these gaps -- the above 5 all are Columbia "Stereo 7" singles -- please let us know.

❏ 42148	The Wedding/Seven Kinds of Lonesome	1961	2.00	4.00	8.00
❏ 42148 [PS]	The Wedding/Seven Kinds of Lonesome	1961	2.50	5.00	10.00
❏ 42257	Step by Step, Little By Little/Cold, Cold Winter	1962	—	3.00	6.00
❏ 42257 [PS]	Step by Step, Little By Little/Cold, Cold Winter	1962	2.50	5.00	10.00
❏ 42438	One More Time with Billy/Free	1962	—	3.00	6.00
❏ 42515	Moonlight Melody/I'm Not a Child Anymore	1962	—	3.00	6.00

Number	Title (A Side/B Side)	Yr	VG	VG+	NM
❏ 42515 [PS]	Moonlight Melody/I'm Not a Child Anymore	1962	2.50	5.00	10.00
❏ 42629	A-Sleepin' at the Foot of the Bed/Wishing It Was You	1962	—	3.00	6.00
❏ 42739	Our Winter Love/Honest John	1963	—	3.00	6.00
❏ 42803	A Wound Time Can't Erase/Will I Cry in September	1963	—	3.00	6.00
❏ 42847	Hey Good Lookin'/You're the Only Star (In My Blue Heaven)	1963	—	3.00	6.00
❏ 42847	Hey Good Lookin'/Bonaparte's Retreat	1963	2.00	4.00	8.00
❏ 43037	The World of Lonely People/It's Better to Cry Today Than Cry Tomorrow	1964	—	3.00	6.00
❏ 43106	Laughing on the Outside/Welcome, Welcome Home	1964	—	3.00	6.00
❏ 43205	Tell Me/I Don't Understand	1965	—	3.00	6.00
❏ 43436	My Mind's Playing Tricks on Me Again/Just Say Auf Wiedersehn	1965	—	3.00	6.00
❏ 43494	Another Year, Another Love, Another Heartache/Everything in the Garden	1965	—	3.00	6.00
❏ 43928	Battle Hymn of the Republic/The Star-Spangled Banner	1966	—	3.00	6.00
❏ 44067	Sticks and Stones/Tomorrow Belongs to Me	1967	—	2.50	5.00
❏ 44193	The Man in the Raincoat/Love Is (Everything You Are)	1967	—	2.50	5.00
❏ 44193 [PS]	The Man in the Raincoat/Love Is (Everything You Are)	1967	2.00	4.00	8.00
❏ 44247	Some Sunday in the Middle of the Week/Little Love Words	1967	—	2.50	5.00
❏ 44324	I Don't See Me in Your Eyes Anymore/Happy Time	1967	—	2.50	5.00
❏ 44341	Do You Hear What I Hear/Away in the Manger	1967	2.00	4.00	8.00
❏ 44341 [PS]	Do You Hear What I Hear/Away in the Manger	1967	2.50	5.00	10.00
❏ 44427	Something in Your Smile/Yellow Days	1968	—	2.50	5.00
❏ 44471	Try to Remember/My Cup Runneth Over	1968	—	2.50	5.00
❏ 44569	Blue Summer/Silver and Blue	1968	—	2.50	5.00
❏ 44654	Let the Heartaches Begin/Sister Sarah	1968	—	2.50	5.00
DISNEYLAND					
❏ DL-560	The Orange Bird Song/Orange Tree	1971	2.00	4.00	8.00
❏ DL-560 [PS]	The Orange Bird Song/Orange Tree	1971	3.75	7.50	15.00
Albums					
CARLTON					
❏ LP-118 [M]	Anita Bryant	1959	5.00	10.00	20.00
❏ STLP-118 [S]	Anita Bryant	1959	7.50	15.00	30.00
❏ LP-127 [M]	Hear Anita Bryant in Your Home Tonight	1960	5.00	10.00	20.00
❏ STLP-127 [S]	Hear Anita Bryant in Your Home Tonight	1960	6.25	12.50	25.00
❏ LP-132 [M]	In My Little Corner of the World	1961	5.00	10.00	20.00
❏ STLP-132 [S]	In My Little Corner of the World	1961	6.25	12.50	25.00
COLUMBIA					
❏ CL 1719 [M]	Kisses Sweeter Than Wine	1961	3.75	7.50	15.00
❏ CL 1767 [M]	Abiding Love	1962	3.75	7.50	15.00
❏ CL 1885 [M]	In a Velvet Mood	1962	3.00	6.00	12.00
❏ CL 1956 [M]	Anita Bryant's Greatest Hits	1963	3.00	6.00	12.00
❏ CL 2035 [M]	As Long As He Needs Me	1963	3.00	6.00	12.00
❏ CL 2069 [M]	Country's Best	1964	3.00	6.00	12.00
❏ CL 2222 [M]	World of Lonely People	1964	3.00	6.00	12.00
❏ CL 2573 [M]	Mine Eyes Have Seen the Glory	1966	3.00	6.00	12.00
❏ CL 2706 [M]	I Believe	1967	3.75	7.50	15.00
❏ CL 2720 [M]	Do You Hear What I Hear?	1967	3.75	7.50	15.00
❏ CS 8519 [S]	Kisses Sweeter Than Wine	1961	5.00	10.00	20.00
❏ CS 8567 [S]	Abiding Love	1962	5.00	10.00	20.00
❏ CS 8685 [S]	In a Velvet Mood	1962	3.75	7.50	15.00
❏ CS 8756 [S]	Anita Bryant's Greatest Hits	1963	3.75	7.50	15.00
❏ CS 8835 [S]	As Long As He Needs Me	1963	3.75	7.50	15.00
❏ CS 8869 [S]	Country's Best	1964	3.75	7.50	15.00
❏ CS 9022 [S]	World of Lonely People	1964	3.75	7.50	15.00
❏ CS 9373 [S]	Mine Eyes Have Seen the Glory	1966	3.75	7.50	15.00
❏ CS 9506 [S]	I Believe	1967	3.00	6.00	12.00
❏ CS 9520 [S]	Do You Hear What I Hear?	1967	2.50	5.00	10.00
❏ CS 9607	In Remembrance of You (The Story of a Love Affair)	1968	3.00	6.00	12.00
❏ CS 9642	How Great Thou Art	1968	3.00	6.00	12.00
COLUMBIA SPECIAL PRODUCTS					
❏ CSS 900	The Sunshine Tree	1970	3.00	6.00	12.00
HARMONY					
❏ HL 9557 [M]	ABC Stories of Jesus	196?	3.00	6.00	12.00
❏ HS 11280	Anita Bryant	1968	2.50	5.00	10.00
❏ HS 11330	Little Things Mean a Lot	1969	2.50	5.00	10.00
❏ HS 11395	A World Without Love	1970	2.50	5.00	10.00
❏ H 31181	You'll Never Walk Alone	1972	2.50	5.00	10.00
MYRRH					
❏ MSB-6513	Naturally	197?	3.00	6.00	12.00
WORD					
❏ WST-8532	Abide with Me	1970	3.00	6.00	12.00
❏ WST-8540	Love Lifted Me	1971	3.00	6.00	12.00
❏ WST-8558	The Miracle of Christmas	197?	2.50	5.00	10.00
❏ WST-8571	Battle Hymn of the Republic	1972	3.00	6.00	12.00
❏ WST-8631	This Is My Story	1975	3.00	6.00	12.00
❏ WST-8652	Hymns	1976	3.00	6.00	12.00
❏ WST-8670	Old Fashioned Prayin'	1977	3.00	6.00	12.00
❏ 8785	Singing a New Song	198?	2.50	5.00	10.00

BRYANT, J.D.
45s
SHRINE

Number	Title (A Side/B Side)	Yr	VG	VG+	NM
❏ 108	I Won't Be Coming Back/Walk On	1966	1500.	2750.	4000.

BRYANT, JAY DEE
45s
ENJOY

Number	Title (A Side/B Side)	Yr	VG	VG+	NM
❏ 2017	You're Hurting Me/Get It	1964	6.25	12.50	25.00
HERALD					
❏ 570	Come Summer/I Could Have Cried	1962	7.50	15.00	30.00

ISLAND

Number	Title (A Side/B Side)	Yr	VG	VG+	NM
❏ 008	I Want to Thank You Baby/Standing Ovation for Love	1975	7.50	15.00	30.00
JOSIE					
❏ 998	You Don't Know/Let Me Fix It for You	1968	12.50	25.00	50.00

BRYANT, LILLIE Of BILLY AND LILLIE.
45s
SWAN

Number	Title (A Side/B Side)	Yr	VG	VG+	NM
❏ 4029	Smokey Grey Eyes/I'll Never Be Free	1959	3.00	6.00	12.00

BRYANT, RAY
45s
ATLANTIC JAZZ

Number	Title (A Side/B Side)	Yr	VG	VG+	NM
❏ 5102	Let It Be/Shake-A-Lady	1971	—	2.00	4.00
CADET					
❏ 5535	Gotta Travel On/It Was a Very Good Year	1966	—	3.00	6.00
❏ 5558	If You Go Away/Slow Freight	1967	—	3.00	6.00
❏ 5575	Ode to Billie Joe/Ramblin'	1967	—	3.00	6.00
❏ 5580	City Tribal Dance/Little Suzie	1967	—	3.00	6.00
❏ 5587	Pata Pata/Doing My Thing	1968	—	3.00	6.00
❏ 5598	To Sir with Love/Dinner on the Grounds	1968	—	2.50	5.00
❏ 5615	Mrs. Robinson/Poochie	1968	—	2.50	5.00
❏ 5625	Little Green Apples/Up Above the Rock	1968	—	2.50	5.00
❏ 5639	After Hours/Quizas, Quizas, Quizas	1969	—	2.50	5.00
COLUMBIA					
❏ 31339 [S]	(contents unknown)	1961	3.00	6.00	12.00
❏ 31340 [S]	(contents unknown)	1961	3.00	6.00	12.00
❏ 31341 [S]	(contents unknown)	1961	3.00	6.00	12.00
❏ 31342 [S]	(contents unknown)	1961	3.00	6.00	12.00
❏ 31343 [S]	(contents unknown)	1961	3.00	6.00	12.00

—Anyone who can fill in these gaps -- the above 5 all are Columbia "Stereo 7" singles -- please let us know.

Number	Title (A Side/B Side)	Yr	VG	VG+	NM
❏ 41553	Little Suzie (Part 1)/Little Suzie (Part 2)	1960	2.50	5.00	10.00
❏ 41628	The Madison Time (Part 1)/The Madison Time (Part 2)	1960	2.50	5.00	10.00
❏ 41628 [PS]	The Madison Time (Part 1)/The Madison Time (Part 2)	1960	3.75	7.50	15.00
❏ 41761	C Jam Blues (Part 1)/C Jam Blues (Part 2)	1960	2.50	5.00	10.00
❏ 41940	Sack O' Woe/Walk No More	1961	2.50	5.00	10.00
❏ 42015	Moonrise/First Lady	1961	2.50	5.00	10.00
❏ 42390	After Hours/Tonk	1962	2.50	5.00	10.00
MCA					
❏ 53322	The Madison Time/Mama Didn't Lie	1988	—	—	3.00

—B-side by Jan Bradley

Number	Title (A Side/B Side)	Yr	VG	VG+	NM
❏ 53322 [PS]	The Madison Time/Mama Didn't Lie	1988	—	—	3.00
NEW JAZZ					
❏ 505	Joy/Stocking Feet	1959	3.00	6.00	12.00
SIGNATURE					
❏ 12026	Little Suzie (Part 2)/Little Suzie (Part 4)	1960	3.00	6.00	12.00
SUE					
❏ 108	Shake a Lady/Blues March	1964	2.00	4.00	8.00
❏ 125	Goldfinger/Adalia	1965	2.00	4.00	8.00
❏ 801	Glissamba/Joey	1963	2.00	4.00	8.00
Albums					
ATLANTIC					
❏ SD 1564	MCMLXX	1970	3.75	7.50	15.00
❏ SD 1626	Alone at Montreux	1972	3.00	6.00	12.00
CADET					
❏ LP-767 [M]	Gotta Travel On	1966	3.75	7.50	15.00
❏ LPS-767 [S]	Gotta Travel On	1966	5.00	10.00	20.00
❏ LP-778 [M]	Lonesome Traveler	1966	3.75	7.50	15.00
❏ LPS-778 [S]	Lonesome Traveler	1966	5.00	10.00	20.00
❏ LP-781 [M]	Slow Freight	1967	3.75	7.50	15.00
❏ LPS-781 [S]	Slow Freight	1967	5.00	10.00	20.00
❏ LP-793 [M]	The Ray Bryant Touch	1967	5.00	10.00	20.00
❏ LPS-793 [S]	The Ray Bryant Touch	1967	3.75	7.50	15.00
❏ LP-801 [M]	Take a Bryant Step	1967	5.00	10.00	20.00
❏ LPS-801 [S]	Take a Bryant Step	1967	3.75	7.50	15.00
❏ LPS-818	Up Above the Rock	1968	3.75	7.50	15.00
❏ LPS-830	Sound Ray	1969	3.75	7.50	15.00
❏ 50038 [(2)]	It Was a Very Good Year	1973	3.75	7.50	15.00
❏ 50052	In the Cut	1974	3.00	6.00	12.00
CLASSIC JAZZ					
❏ 130	Hot Turkey	198?	2.50	5.00	10.00
COLUMBIA					
❏ CL 1449 [M]	Little Susie	1960	5.00	10.00	20.00
❏ CL 1476 [M]	The Madison Time	1960	6.25	12.50	25.00
❏ CL 1633 [M]	Con Alma	1961	5.00	10.00	20.00
❏ CL 1746 [M]	Dancing the Big Twist	1962	5.00	10.00	20.00
❏ CL 1867 [M]	Hollywood Jazz Beat	1962	5.00	10.00	20.00
❏ CS 8244 [S]	Little Susie	1960	6.25	12.50	25.00
❏ CS 8276 [S]	The Madison Time	1960	7.50	15.00	30.00
❏ CS 8433 [S]	Con Alma	1961	6.25	12.50	25.00
❏ CS 8546 [S]	Dancing the Big Twist	1962	6.25	12.50	25.00
❏ CS 8667 [S]	Hollywood Jazz Beat	1962	6.25	12.50	25.00
COLUMBIA JAZZ MASTERPIECES					
❏ CJ 44058	Con Alma	1988	2.50	5.00	10.00
EMARCY					
❏ 832235-1	Ray Bryant Plays Basie and Ellington	1987	3.00	6.00	12.00
❏ 832589-1	The Ray Bryant Trio Today	1988	3.00	6.00	12.00
❏ 836368-1	Golden Earrings	1989	3.00	6.00	12.00
EPIC					
❏ LN 3279 [M]	Ray Bryant Trio	1956	17.50	35.00	70.00
FANTASY					
❏ OJC-213	Alone with the Blues	1987	2.50	5.00	10.00

—Reissue

Number	Title (A Side/B Side)	Yr	VG	VG+	NM
❏ OJC-371	Montreux '77	1989	2.50	5.00	10.00

—Reissue of Pablo Live 2308 201

Number	Title (A Side/B Side)	Yr	VG	VG+	NM
NEW JAZZ					
❏ NJLP-8213 [M] Alone with the Blues		1959	12.50	25.00	50.00
—*Purple label*					
❏ NJLP-8213 [M] Alone with the Blues		1965	6.25	12.50	25.00
—*Blue label with trident logo*					
❏ NJLP-8227 [M] Ray Bryant Trio		1959	12.50	25.00	50.00
—*Purple label; reissue of Prestige 7098*					
❏ NJLP-8227 [M] Ray Bryant Trio		1965	6.25	12.50	25.00
—*Blue label with trident logo*					
PABLO					
❏ 2310764	Here's Ray Bryant	1976	2.50	5.00	10.00
❏ 2310798	Solo Flight	1977	2.50	5.00	10.00
❏ 2310820	All Blues	1978	2.50	5.00	10.00
❏ 2310860	Potpourri	1981	2.50	5.00	10.00
❏ 2405402	The Best of Ray Bryant	198?	2.50	5.00	10.00
PABLO LIVE					
❏ 2308201	Montreux '77	1977	2.50	5.00	10.00
PRESTIGE					
❏ PRLP-7098 [M] Ray Bryant Trio		1957	17.50	35.00	70.00
❏ PRLP-7837	Alone with the Blues	1971	3.75	7.50	15.00
—*Reissue of New Jazz 8213*					
❏ PRT-7837	Alone with the Blues	1973	3.00	6.00	12.00
—*Reissue; "Distributed by Fantasy Records, Berkeley, California" on label*					
❏ 24038 [(2)]	Me and the Blues	1973	3.75	7.50	15.00
SIGNATURE					
❏ SM-6008 [M]	Ray Bryant Plays	1960	50.00	100.00	200.00
❏ SS-6008 [S]	Ray Bryant Plays	1960	62.50	125.00	250.00
SUE					
❏ LP-1016 [M]	Groove House	1963	10.00	20.00	40.00
❏ LPS-1016 [S]	Groove House	1963	12.50	25.00	50.00
❏ LP-1019 [M]	Live at Basin Street	1964	10.00	20.00	40.00
❏ LPS-1019 [S]	Live at Basin Street	1964	12.50	25.00	50.00
❏ LP-1032 [M]	Cold Turkey	1964	10.00	20.00	40.00
❏ LPS-1032 [S]	Cold Turkey	1964	12.50	25.00	50.00
❏ LP-1036 [M]	Ray Bryant Soul	1965	10.00	20.00	40.00
❏ LPS-1036 [S]	Ray Bryant Soul	1965	12.50	25.00	50.00
BRYDS, THE					
45s					
REYNARD					
❏ 10038	Your Lies/Why Did You Have to Break My Heart	1965	100.00	200.00	400.00
BRYNDLE Andrew Gold, Karla Bonoff, Wendy Waldman, Kenny Edwards.					
45s					
A&M					
❏ 1252	Let's Go Home and Start Again/Woke Up This Morning	1971	2.50	5.00	10.00
BUBBLE PUPPY, THE Also see DEMIAN.					
45s					
INTERNATIONAL ARTISTS					
❏ 128	Hot Smoke and Sasafrass/Lonely	1969	5.00	10.00	20.00
❏ 133	Beginning/If I Had a Reason	1969	6.25	12.50	25.00
❏ 136	Days of Our Time/Thinkin' About Thinkin'	1969	6.25	12.50	25.00
❏ 138	What Do You See/Hurry Sundown	1970	6.25	12.50	25.00
❏ 138 [DJ]	What Do You See/Hurry Sundown	1970	12.50	25.00	50.00
—*Green vinyl promo*					
Albums					
INTERNATIONAL ARTISTS					
❏ 10	A Gathering of Promises	1969	25.00	50.00	100.00
—*Original does not have "Masterfonics" in the dead wax*					
❏ 10	A Gathering of Promises	1979	6.25	12.50	25.00
—*Reissue has "Masterfonics" in the dead wax*					
BUBI AND BOB					
45s					
SPHINX					
❏ 1201	The Mummy/Biscayne Beat	1959	7.50	15.00	30.00
BUCCANEERS, THE					
45s					
RAINBOW					
❏ 211	Dear Ruth/Fine Brown Flame	1953	200.00	400.00	800.00
RAMA					
❏ 21	The Stars Will Remember/Come Back My Love	1954	500.00	1000.	2000.
❏ 24	In the Mission of St. Augustine/You Did Me Wrong	1954	500.00	1000.	2000.
SOUTHERN					
❏ 101	Dear Ruth/Fine Brown Flame	1953	2000.	3000.	4000.
—*All copies are on red vinyl*					
BUCHANAN, BILL Also see BUCHANAN AND ANCELL; BUCHANAN AND CELLA; BUCHANAN AND GOODMAN; BUCHANAN AND GREENFIELD.					
45s					
GONE					
❏ 5032	The Thing/Happy Day	1958	7.50	15.00	30.00
UNITED ARTISTS					
❏ 531	The Night Before Halloween/Beware	1962	3.75	7.50	15.00
BUCHANAN, ROY					
45s					
ATLANTIC					
❏ 3342	Keep What You Got/Caruso	1976	—	2.00	4.00
❏ 3414	The Circle/Green Onions	1977	—	2.00	4.00
❏ 3433	The Circle/(B-side unknown)	1977	—	2.00	4.00
POLYDOR					
❏ 14149	Haunted House/Cajun	1972	—	2.50	5.00
❏ 14174	Filthy Teddy/Thank You Lord	1973	—	2.50	5.00
❏ 14178	Sweet Dreams/John's Blues	1973	—	2.50	5.00
❏ 14265	Rescue Me/I'm a Ram	1974	—	2.50	5.00
SWAN					
❏ 4088	Mule Train Stomp/Pretty Please	1961	3.00	6.00	12.00

Number	Title (A Side/B Side)	Yr	VG	VG+	NM
Albums					
ALLIGATOR					
❏ AL-4741	When a Guitar Plays the Blues	1985	2.50	5.00	10.00
❏ AL-4747	Dancing on the Edge	1986	2.50	5.00	10.00
❏ AL-4756	Hot Wires	1988	2.50	5.00	10.00
ATLANTIC					
❏ SD 18170	A Street Called Straight	1976	3.00	6.00	12.00
❏ SD 18219	Loading Zone	1977	3.00	6.00	12.00
❏ SD 19138	Loading Zone	1978	2.00	4.00	8.00
—*Reissue of 18219*					
❏ SD 19170	You're Not Alone	1978	3.00	6.00	12.00
BIOYA					
❏ MM-519	Buch and the Snake Stretchers	1971	50.00	100.00	200.00
POLYDOR					
❏ PD-5033	Roy Buchanan	1972	3.75	7.50	15.00
❏ PD-5046	Second Album	1973	3.75	7.50	15.00
❏ PD-6020	That's What I Am Here For	1974	3.75	7.50	15.00
❏ PD-6035	In the Beginning	1974	3.75	7.50	15.00
❏ PD-6048	Live Stock	1975	3.75	7.50	15.00
WATERHOUSE					
❏ 12	My Babe	1981	2.50	5.00	10.00
BUCHANAN AND ANCELL Also see BILL BUCHANAN.					
45s					
FLYING SAUCER					
❏ 501	The Creature/Meet the Creature	1957	10.00	20.00	40.00
BUCHANAN AND CELLA Also see BILL BUCHANAN.					
45s					
ABC-PARAMOUNT					
❏ 10033	String Along with Pal-O-Mine/More and More String Along with Pal-O-Mine	1959	6.25	12.50	25.00
BUCHANAN AND GOODMAN Also see BILL BUCHANAN; DICKIE GOODMAN.					
45s					
COMIC					
❏ 500	Flying Saucer the Third/The Cha Cha Lesson	1959	10.00	20.00	40.00
LUNIVERSE					
❏ 101	The Flying Saucer Part 1/The Flying Saucer Part 2	1956	12.50	25.00	50.00
—*Most labels have the entire word "Luniverse" typeset*					
❏ 101	The Flying Saucer Part 1/The Flying Saucer Part 2	1956	25.00	50.00	100.00
—*Original labels have a handwritten "L" at the beginning of the printed word "Universe"*					
❏ 101X	Back to Earth Part 1/Back to Earth Part 2	1956	50.00	100.00	200.00
❏ 102	Buchanan and Goodman On Trial/Crazy	1956	10.00	20.00	40.00
❏ 102X	Public Opinion Part 1/Public Opinion Part 2	1956	—	—	—
—*Not known to exist*					
❏ 103	The Banana Boat Story/The Mystery (In Slow Motion)	1957	10.00	20.00	40.00
❏ 105	Flying Saucer The 2nd/Martian Melody	1957	10.00	20.00	40.00
❏ 107	Santa and the Satellite Part 1/Santa and the Satellite Part 2	1957	10.00	20.00	40.00
❏ 108	The Flying Saucer Goes West/Saucer Serenade	1958	10.00	20.00	40.00
NOVELTY					
❏ 301	Frankenstein of '59/Frankenstein Returns	1959	10.00	20.00	40.00
BUCHANAN AND GREENFIELD Also see BILL BUCHANAN.					
45s					
NOVEL					
❏ 711	The Invasion/What a Lovely Party	1964	7.50	15.00	30.00
—*Originals have all-red labels*					
❏ 711	The Invasion/What a Lovely Party	1972	2.00	4.00	8.00
—*Red and white label reissue*					
BUCHANAN BROTHERS Early version of CASHMAN, PISTILLI AND WEST.					
45s					
EVENT					
❏ 201	Get Down with the People/You Don't Know	1970	—	3.00	6.00
❏ 205	Don't Stop Now/You Don't Know	1971	—	3.00	6.00
❏ 3302	Medicine Man (Part 1)/Medicine Man (Part 2)	1969	—	3.00	6.00
❏ 3305	Son of a Lovin' Man/I'll Never Get Enough	1969	—	3.00	6.00
❏ 3307	A Feeling That I Get/The Last Time	1969	—	3.00	6.00
❏ 3308	Sad Song with a Happy Soul/Rusianna	1970	—	3.00	6.00
Albums					
EVENT					
❏ ES-101	Medicine Man	1969	6.25	12.50	25.00
BUCHANANS, THE					
45s					
HIT					
❏ 277	Kind of a Drag/98.6	1967	2.00	4.00	8.00
—*B-side by the Jalopy Five*					
BUCK, CHARLIE					
45s					
TAD					
❏ 104	I Wish I Were A Christmas Tree/We Can't Miss This Christmas	1962	3.00	6.00	12.00
BUCKEYES, THE					
45s					
DELUXE					
❏ 6110	Since I Fell for You/My Only You	1957	75.00	150.00	300.00
❏ 6126	Dottie Baby/Begging You Please	1957	100.00	200.00	400.00
BUCKINGHAM NICKS Lindsey Buckingham and Stephanie (later known as Stevie) Nicks. Also see FLEETWOOD MAC.					
45s					
POLYDOR					
❏ 14209	Don't Let Me Down Again/The Races Are Run	1973	12.50	25.00	50.00
❏ 14229	Crying in the Night/Without a Leg to Stand On	1974	12.50	25.00	50.00
❏ 14335	Don't Let Me Down Again/Crystal	1976	7.50	15.00	30.00
❏ 14428	Crying in the Night/Stephanie	1977	7.50	15.00	30.00
❏ 14428 [PS]	Crying in the Night/Stephanie	1977	15.00	30.00	60.00

B

Number	Title (A Side/B Side)	Yr	VG	VG+	NM
Albums					
POLYDOR					
❑ PD-5058	Buckingham Nicks	1973	10.00	20.00	40.00
—Gatefold cover					
❑ PD-5058	Buckingham Nicks	1975	3.00	6.00	12.00
—Regular cover					

BUCKINGHAMS, THE (1) Chicago band. Also see THE FALLING PEBBLES.

Number	Title (A Side/B Side)	Yr	VG	VG+	NM
45s					
COLUMBIA					
❑ 44053	Don't You Care/Why Don't You Love Me	1967	2.00	4.00	8.00
❑ 44053 [PS]	Don't You Care/Why Don't You Love Me	1967	3.00	6.00	12.00
❑ 44182	Mercy, Mercy, Mercy/You Are Gone	1967	2.00	4.00	8.00
❑ 44182 [PS]	Mercy, Mercy, Mercy/You Are Gone	1967	3.00	6.00	12.00
❑ 44254	Hey Baby (They're Playing Our Song)/And Our Love	1967	2.00	4.00	8.00
❑ 44254 [PS]	Hey Baby (They're Playing Our Song)/And Our Love	1967	3.00	6.00	12.00
❑ 44378	Susan/Foreign Policy	1967	2.00	4.00	8.00
❑ 44378 [PS]	Susan/Foreign Policy	1967	3.00	6.00	12.00
❑ 44533	Back in Love Again/You Misunderstand Me	1968	2.00	4.00	8.00
❑ 44533 [PS]	Back in Love Again/You Misunderstand Me	1968	3.00	6.00	12.00
❑ 44672	Where Did You Come From/Song of the Breeze	1968	2.00	4.00	8.00
❑ 44672 [PS]	Where Did You Come From/Song of the Breeze	1968	3.00	6.00	12.00
❑ 44790	This Is How Much I Love You/Can't You Find the Words	1969	2.00	4.00	8.00
❑ 44790 [PS]	This Is How Much I Love You/Can't You Find the Words	1969	3.00	6.00	12.00
❑ 44923	It's a Beautiful Day/Difference of Opinion	1969	2.00	4.00	8.00
❑ 45066	It Took Forever/I Got a Feelin'	1970	2.00	4.00	8.00
PHILCO-FORD					
❑ HP-14	Kind of a Drag/Lawdy Miss Clawdy	1968	5.00	10.00	20.00
—4-inch plastic "Hip Pocket Record" with color sleeve					
RED LABEL					
❑ 71001	Veronica/Can We Talk About It	1985	—	2.00	4.00
❑ 71001 [PS]	Veronica/Can We Talk About It	1985	—	2.50	5.00
SPECTRASOUND					
❑ 4618	Sweets for My Sweet/Beginner's Love	1967	5.00	10.00	20.00
U.S.A.					
❑ 844	I'll Go Crazy/I Don't Wanna Cry	1966	3.00	6.00	12.00
❑ 848	I Call Your Name/Makin' Up and Breakin' Up	1966	3.00	6.00	12.00
❑ 853	I've Been Wrong/Love Ain't Enough	1966	3.00	6.00	12.00
❑ 860	Kind of a Drag/You Make Me Feel So Good	1966	3.75	7.50	15.00
—Light blue label with all dark blue printing					
❑ 860	Kind of a Drag/You Make Me Feel So Good	1966	3.75	7.50	15.00
—Light blue label with red, white, blue and black printing					
❑ 869	Lawdy Miss Clawdy/I Call Your Name	1967	3.00	6.00	12.00
❑ 869	Lawdy Miss Clawdy/Making Up and Breaking Up	1967	3.00	6.00	12.00
❑ 873	Summertime/Don't Want to Cry	1967	3.00	6.00	12.00
Albums					
COLUMBIA					
❑ CL 2669 [M]	Time & Charges	1967	6.25	12.50	25.00
❑ CL 2798 [M]	Portraits	1968	6.25	12.50	25.00
❑ CS 9469 [S]	Time & Charges	1967	5.00	10.00	20.00
❑ CS 9598 [S]	Portraits	1968	5.00	10.00	20.00
❑ CS 9703	In One Ear and Gone Tomorrow	1968	5.00	10.00	20.00
❑ CS 9812	The Buckinghams Greatest Hits	1969	5.00	10.00	20.00
—Red "360 Sound" label					
❑ CS 9812	The Buckinghams Greatest Hits	1970	3.00	6.00	12.00
—Orange label					
❑ PC 9812	The Buckinghams Greatest Hits	198?	2.00	4.00	8.00
—Reissue with new prefix					
❑ KG 33333 [(2)]	Made in Chicago	1975	5.00	10.00	20.00
U.S.A.					
❑ 107 [M]	Kind of a Drag	1967	7.50	15.00	30.00
—Without "I'm a Man"					
❑ 107 [M]	Kind of a Drag	1967	150.00	300.00	600.00
—With "I'm a Man"					
❑ 107 [S]	Kind of a Drag	1967	10.00	20.00	40.00
—No known stereo copy has "I'm a Man"					

BUCKINGHAMS, THE (2) These two records are not by group (1).

Number	Title (A Side/B Side)	Yr	VG	VG+	NM
45s					
LAURIE					
❑ 3258	Gonna Say Goodbye/Many Times	1964	2.50	5.00	10.00
SEG-WAY					
❑ 1004	Lobo Lobo/Rockin' Piper	1962	2.50	5.00	10.00

BUCKLEY, LORD

Number	Title (A Side/B Side)	Yr	VG	VG+	NM
Albums					
CRESTVIEW					
❑ CRV-801 [M]	The Best of Lord Buckley	1963	12.50	25.00	50.00
❑ CRV7-801 [S]	The Best of Lord Buckley	1963	15.00	30.00	60.00
ELEKTRA					
❑ EKS-74047	The Best of Lord Buckley	1969	6.25	12.50	25.00
—Reissue of Crestview 7-801					
RCA VICTOR					
❑ LPM-3246 [10]	Hipsters, Flipsters and Finger Poppin' Daddies, Knock Me Your Lobes	1955	75.00	150.00	300.00
REPRISE					
❑ RS 6389	A Most Immaculately Hip Aristocrat	1970	6.25	12.50	25.00
—Reissue of Straight 1054					
STRAIGHT					
❑ STS-1054	A Most Immaculately Hip Aristocrat	1970	10.00	20.00	40.00
VAYA					
❑ 101/2 [M]	Euphoria, Volume 1	1955	37.50	75.00	150.00
❑ 107/8 [M]	Euphoria, Volume 2	1955	50.00	100.00	200.00
❑ 1715 [10]	Euphoria	195?	75.00	150.00	300.00
—Red vinyl					
WORLD PACIFIC					
❑ WP-1279 [M]	The Way Out Humor of Lord Buckley	1959	25.00	50.00	100.00
—With correct "Way Out Humor" on the back cover					

Number	Title (A Side/B Side)	Yr	VG	VG+	NM
❑ WP-1279 [M]	The Way Out Humor of Lord Buckley	1959	30.00	60.00	120.00
—With "Far Out Humor" on the back cover					
❑ WP-1815 [M]	Lord Buckley in Concert	1964	12.50	25.00	50.00
—Reissue of 1279					
❑ WP-1849 [M]	Blowing His Mind (and Yours, Too)	1966	12.50	25.00	50.00
❑ WPS-21879	Buckley's Best	1968	10.00	20.00	40.00
❑ WPS-21889	Bad Rapping of the Marquis de Sade	1969	7.50	15.00	30.00

BUCKLEY, TIM

Number	Title (A Side/B Side)	Yr	VG	VG+	NM
45s					
DISCREET					
❑ 1187	Quicksand/Stone in Love	1973	—	3.00	6.00
❑ 1189	Dolphins/Honey Man	1974	—	3.00	6.00
❑ 1311	Wanda Lu/Who Could Deny You	1974	—	3.00	6.00
ELEKTRA					
❑ 45606	Grief in My Soul/Wings	1966	2.00	4.00	8.00
❑ 45612	Aren't You the Girl/Strange Street Affair Down Under	1967	2.00	4.00	8.00
❑ 45618	Once Upon a Time/Lady Give Me Your Heart	1967	2.00	4.00	8.00
❑ 45623	Morning Glory/Once I Was	1967	2.00	4.00	8.00
WARNER BROS.					
❑ 7623	Move with Me/Nighthawkin'	1972	—	3.00	6.00
Albums					
DISCREET					
❑ MS 2157	Sefronia	1973	3.75	7.50	15.00
❑ DS 2201	Look at the Fool	1974	3.75	7.50	15.00
ELEKTRA					
❑ EKL-318 [M]	Goodbye and Hello	1967	6.25	12.50	25.00
—Original issue					
❑ EKL-4004 [M]	Tim Buckley	1966	3.75	7.50	15.00
❑ EKL-4028 [M]	Goodbye and Hello	1968	—	—	—
—Reissue of 318; may not exist with this number					
❑ EKS-7318 [S]	Goodbye and Hello	1967	6.25	12.50	25.00
—Original issue; tan/brown/silvery label					
❑ EKS-74004 [S]	Tim Buckley	1966	5.00	10.00	20.00
❑ EKS-74028 [S]	Goodbye and Hello	1968	5.00	10.00	20.00
—Brown labels; reissue of 7318					
❑ EKS-74028 [S]	Goodbye and Hello	1975	2.50	5.00	10.00
—Butterfly label with Warner Communications logo					
❑ EKS-74045	Happy Sad	1969	5.00	10.00	20.00
❑ EKS-74074	Lorca	1970	5.00	10.00	20.00
RHINO					
❑ RNLP-112	The Best of Tim Buckley	1985	2.50	5.00	10.00
STRAIGHT					
❑ STS-1060	Blue Afternoon	1969	7.50	15.00	30.00
WARNER BROS.					
❑ WS 1842	Blue Afternoon	1970	3.75	7.50	15.00
❑ WS 1881	Starsailor	1970	3.75	7.50	15.00
❑ BS 2631	Greetings from L.A.	1972	3.75	7.50	15.00

BUCKNER, JOE

Number	Title (A Side/B Side)	Yr	VG	VG+	NM
45s					
VEE JAY					
❑ 141	Why Don't Cha/How Can I Let Her Go	1955	6.25	12.50	25.00
❑ 172	One More Mile/Straight and Ready	1956	6.25	12.50	25.00
—B-side by Tommy Dean					

BUCKWHEAT

Number	Title (A Side/B Side)	Yr	VG	VG+	NM
Albums					
LONDON					
❑ PS 595	Buckwheat	1971	3.75	7.50	15.00
❑ PS 609	Movin' On	1972	3.00	6.00	12.00
❑ XPS 621	Charade	1972	3.00	6.00	12.00
❑ XPS 635	Hot Tracks	1973	3.00	6.00	12.00

BUD AND TRAVIS

Number	Title (A Side/B Side)	Yr	VG	VG+	NM
45s					
LIBERTY					
❑ 55202	Truly Do/Bonsoir Dame	1959	2.50	5.00	10.00
❑ 55221	Poor Boy/Jenny on a Horse	1959	2.50	5.00	10.00
❑ 55235	Cloudy Summer Afternoon/E Labas	1959	2.50	5.00	10.00
❑ 55259	Come to the Dance/Carmen Carmelia	1960	2.00	4.00	8.00
❑ 55284	Ballad of the Alamo/The Green Leaves of Summer	1960	2.00	4.00	8.00
❑ 55612	Tomorrow Is a Long Time/Haiti	1963	—	3.00	6.00
❑ 55681	Maria Cristina/Sabras Que Te Quiero	1964	—	3.00	6.00
❑ 55713	How Long, How Long Blues/Gimmie Some	1964	—	3.00	6.00
❑ 55764	I Talk to the Trees/Moment in the Sun	1965	—	3.00	6.00
❑ 55803	Cold Summer/Girl Sittin' Up in a Tree	1965	—	3.00	6.00
WORLD PACIFIC					
❑ 801	Raspberries Strawberries/Mexican Wedding Song	1959	3.00	6.00	12.00
Albums					
LIBERTY					
❑ LRP-3125 [M]	Bud and Travis	1959	7.50	15.00	30.00
❑ LRP-3138 [M]	Spotlight On Bud and Travis	1960	5.00	10.00	20.00
❑ LRP-3222 [M]	Bud and Travis In Concert at the Santa Monica Civic Auditorium, Vol. 2	1961	5.00	10.00	20.00
❑ LRP-3295 [M]	Naturally	1963	5.00	10.00	20.00
❑ LRP-3341 [M]	Perspective on Bud and Travis	1964	5.00	10.00	20.00
❑ LRP-3386 [M]	Bud and Travis In Person (At the Cellar Door)	1964	5.00	10.00	20.00
❑ LRP-3398 [M]	The Latin Album	1965	5.00	10.00	20.00
❑ LST-7125 [S]	Bud and Travis	1959	10.00	20.00	40.00
❑ LST-7138 [S]	Spotlight On Bud and Travis	1960	6.25	12.50	25.00
❑ LST-7222 [S]	Bud and Travis In Concert at the Santa Monica Civic Auditorium, Vol. 2	1961	6.25	12.50	25.00
❑ LST-7295 [S]	Naturally	1963	6.25	12.50	25.00
❑ LST-7341 [S]	Perspective on Bud and Travis	1964	6.25	12.50	25.00
❑ LST-7386 [S]	Bud and Travis In Person (At the Cellar Door)	1964	6.25	12.50	25.00
❑ LST-7398 [S]	The Latin Album	1965	6.25	12.50	25.00
❑ LDM-11001 [(2)M]	Bud and Travis...In Concert	1960	6.25	12.50	25.00
❑ LDS-12001 [(2)S]	Bud and Travis...In Concert	1960	7.50	15.00	30.00

Number	Title (A Side/B Side)	Yr	VG	VG+	NM
SUNSET					
❏ SUM-1154 [M]	Bud and Travis	1967	3.00	6.00	12.00
❏ SUS-5154 [S]	Bud and Travis	1967	3.00	6.00	12.00

BUDD, BILLY
45s
JUBILEE

Number	Title (A Side/B Side)	Yr	VG	VG+	NM
❏ 5583	Like I Want You Too/Love Revolution	1967	2.00	4.00	8.00
20TH CENTURY-FOX					
❏ 502	Why Are You Running/The Girl of the Year	1964	2.00	4.00	8.00

BUDDIES, THE Several different groups.
45s
COMET

Number	Title (A Side/B Side)	Yr	VG	VG+	NM
❏ 2143	Hully Gully Baby/Must Be True Love	1961	6.25	12.50	25.00
DECCA					
❏ 29840	The Most Happy Fella/Two Skeletons on a Tin Roof	1956	3.75	7.50	15.00
❏ 29953	Bag of Bones/Every Time the Phone Rings	1956	3.75	7.50	15.00
❏ 30355	A Prom and a Promise/The Lottery	1957	3.75	7.50	15.00
❏ 31920	Duckman Part 1/Duckman Part 2	1966	2.00	4.00	8.00
GLORY					
❏ 230	I Stole Your Heart/I Waited	1955	37.50	75.00	150.00
OKEH					
❏ 7123	Castle of Love/Give Me Your Love	1959	3.75	7.50	15.00
SWAN					
❏ 4073	Spooky Spider/Lebone Delada	1961	3.75	7.50	15.00
❏ 4170	The Beatle/Pulsebeat	1964	6.25	12.50	25.00
TIARA					
❏ 6121	She's a Loser/Heartless	1959	6.25	12.50	25.00
Albums					
WING					
❏ MGW-12293 [M]	The Buddies and the Compacts	1965	12.50	25.00	50.00
❏ MGW-12306 [M]	Go Go with the Buddies	1965	12.50	25.00	50.00
❏ SRW-16293 [S]	The Buddies and the Compacts	1965	20.00	40.00	80.00
❏ SRW-16306 [S]	Go Go with the Buddies	1965	20.00	40.00	80.00

BUDGIE
45s
KAPP

Number	Title (A Side/B Side)	Yr	VG	VG+	NM
❏ 2152	Nude Disintegrating Parachutist Woman/Crash Course	1971	—	2.50	5.00
❏ 2185	Stranded/Whiskey River	1972	—	2.50	5.00
MCA					
❏ 40367	Honey/I Ain't No Mountain	1975	—	2.50	5.00
Albums					
A&M					
❏ SP-4593	If I Were Brittania I'd Waive the Rules	1976	3.75	7.50	15.00
❏ SP-4618	Bandolier	1977	3.75	7.50	15.00
❏ SP-4675	Impeckable	1978	3.75	7.50	15.00
KAPP					
❏ KS-3656	Budgie	1971	7.50	15.00	30.00
❏ KS-3669	Squawk	1972	7.50	15.00	30.00
MCA					
❏ 429	In for the Kill	1973	5.00	10.00	20.00

BUFFALO NICKEL JUGBAND, THE
Albums
HAPPY TIGER

Number	Title (A Side/B Side)	Yr	VG	VG+	NM
❏ 1018	The Buffalo Nickel Jugband	1971	6.25	12.50	25.00

BUFFALO SPRINGFIELD Also see DEWEY MARTIN AND MEDICINE BALL; JIM MESSINA; STEPHEN STILLS; NEIL YOUNG.
45s
ATCO

Number	Title (A Side/B Side)	Yr	VG	VG+	NM
❏ 6428	Nowadays Clancy Can't Even Sing/Go And Say Goodbye	1966	5.00	10.00	20.00
❏ 6452	Everybody's Wrong/Burned	1966	5.00	10.00	20.00
❏ 6459	For What It's Worth (Stop, Hey, What's That Sound)/Do I Have to Come Right Out and Say It	1967	3.00	6.00	12.00
❏ 6459	For What It's Worth/Do I Have to Come Right Out and Say It	1967	3.75	7.50	15.00
❏ 6499	Bluebird/Mr. Soul	1967	5.00	10.00	20.00
❏ 6519	Rock 'N' Roll Woman/A Child's Claim to Fame	1967	2.50	5.00	10.00
❏ 6545	Expecting to Fly/Everydays	1968	2.50	5.00	10.00
❏ 6572	Uno Mundo/Merry-Go-Round	1968	2.50	5.00	10.00
❏ 6602	Special Care/Kind Woman	1968	2.50	5.00	10.00
❏ 6615	Four Days Gone/On the Way Home	1968	2.50	5.00	10.00
Albums					
ATCO					
❏ SD 38-105 [S]	Retrospective/The Best of Buffalo Springfield	197?	2.00	4.00	8.00
—Reissue of 33-283					
❏ 33-200 [M]	Buffalo Springfield	1967	50.00	100.00	200.00
—With "Baby Don't Scold Me"					
❏ 33-200A [M]	Buffalo Springfield	1967	6.25	12.50	25.00
—With "For What It's Worth" replacing "Baby Don't Scold Me"					
❏ SD 33-200 [S]	Buffalo Springfield	1967	50.00	100.00	200.00
—With "Baby Don't Scold Me"					
❏ SD 33-200A [S]	Buffalo Springfield	1967	6.25	12.50	25.00
—With "For What It's Worth" replacing "Baby Don't Scold Me"; purple and brown label					
❏ SD 33-200A [S]	Buffalo Springfield	1969	3.75	7.50	15.00
—Reissue on yellow label					
❏ SD 33-200A [S]	Buffalo Springfield	197?	2.00	4.00	8.00
—Later white or gray label					
❏ 33-226 [M]	Buffalo Springfield Again	1967	20.00	40.00	80.00
❏ SD 33-226 [S]	Buffalo Springfield Again	1967	6.25	12.50	25.00
—Purple and brown label					
❏ SD 33-226 [S]	Buffalo Springfield Again	1969	3.75	7.50	15.00
—Reissue on yellow label					
❏ SD 33-226 [S]	Buffalo Springfield Again	197?	2.00	4.00	8.00
—Later white or gray label					

Number	Title (A Side/B Side)	Yr	VG	VG+	NM
❏ 33-256 [M]	Last Time Around	1968	30.00	60.00	120.00
—White label promo only					
❏ SD 33-256 [S]	Last Time Around	1968	7.50	15.00	30.00
—Purple and brown label					
❏ SD 33-256 [S]	Last Time Around	1969	3.75	7.50	15.00
—Reissue on yellow label					
❏ SD 33-256 [S]	Last Time Around	197?	2.00	4.00	8.00
—Later white or gray label					
❏ 33-283 [M]	Retrospective/The Best of Buffalo Springfield	1969	25.00	50.00	100.00
—White label promo only					
❏ SD 33-283 [S]	Retrospective/The Best of Buffalo Springfield	1969	5.00	10.00	20.00
—Yellow label					
❏ SD 2-806 [(2)]	Buffalo Springfield	197?	3.00	6.00	12.00
—Later white or gray label					
❏ SD 2-806 [(2)]	Buffalo Springfield	1973	5.00	10.00	20.00
—Yellow label					

BUFFETT, JIMMY
45s
ABC

Number	Title (A Side/B Side)	Yr	VG	VG+	NM
❏ 11399 [DJ]	He Went to Paris (stereo/mono)	1973	3.00	6.00	12.00
—Number may have been assigned by mistake; double-sided promotional copies are known to exist; regular copies are on ABC Dunhill 4372					
❏ 12113	Door Number Three/Dallas	1975	—	2.50	5.00
❏ 12143	Big Red/Havana Daydreamin'	1975	—	2.50	5.00
❏ 12175	The Captain and the Kid/Cliches	1976	—	2.50	5.00
❏ 12200	Something So Feminine About a Mandolin/ Woman Goin' Crazy on Caroline Street	1976	—	2.50	5.00
❏ 12254	Margaritaville/Miss You So Badly	1977	—	2.00	4.00
❏ 12305	Changes in Latitudes, Changes in Attitudes/ Landfall	1977	—	2.00	4.00
❏ 12305 [PS]	Changes in Latitudes, Changes in Attitudes/ Landfall	1977	—	3.00	6.00
❏ 12358	Cheeseburger in Paradise/African Friend	1978	—	2.00	4.00
❏ 12391	Livingston Saturday Night/Cowboy in the Jungle	1978	—	2.00	4.00
❏ 12428	Manana/The Coast of Marsailles	1978	—	2.00	4.00
ABC DUNHILL					
❏ 4348	The Great Filling Station Hold Up/Why Don't We Get Drunk	1973	2.00	4.00	8.00
❏ 4353	The Great Filling Station Hold Up/They Can't Dance Like Carmen No More	1973	—	2.00	4.00
❏ 4359	Grapefruit-Juicy Fruit/I Found Me a Home	1973	—	2.00	4.00
❏ 4372	He Went to Paris/Peanut Butter Conspiracy	1973	—	2.00	4.00
❏ 4378	Ringling, Ringling/Saxophones	1974	—	2.00	4.00
❏ 4385	Come Monday/The Wino and I Know	1974	—	2.50	5.00
❏ 15008	Come Monday/The Wino and I Know	1974	—	2.00	4.00
❏ 15011	Brand New Country Star/Pencil Thin Moustache	1974	—	2.00	4.00
❏ 15029	Presents to Send You/A Pirate Looks at Forty	1975	—	2.00	4.00
ASYLUM					
❏ 69890	I Don't Know (Spicoli's Theme)/She's My Baby (And She's Out of Control)	1982	—	2.00	4.00
—B-side by Palmer & Jost					
BARNABY					
❏ 2013	The Christian/Richard Frost	1970	2.50	5.00	10.00
❏ 2019	He Ain't Free/There Ain't Nothing Soft About Hard Times	1970	2.50	5.00	10.00
❏ 2023	Captain America/Truckstop Salvation	1970	2.50	5.00	10.00
FULL MOON					
❏ 49659	Survive/Send Me Somebody to Love	1981	—	2.00	4.00
—B-side by Kathy Walker					
FULL MOON/ASYLUM					
❏ 47073	Hello Texas/Lyin' Eyes [by the Eagles]	1980	—	2.50	5.00
ISLAND					
❏ 562144-7	Pacing the Cage/I Will Play for Gumbo	1999	—	—	3.00
MCA					
❏ S45-17084 [DJ]	Christmas In The Caribbean (same on both sides)	1985	—	2.50	5.00
❏ 41109	Fins/Dreamsicle	1979	—	2.00	4.00
❏ 41161	Volcano/Stranded on a Sandbar	1979	—	2.00	4.00
❏ 41199	Boat Drinks/Survive	1980	—	2.00	4.00
❏ 51061	It's My Job/Little Miss Magic	1981	—	2.00	4.00
❏ 51105	Stars Fell on Alabama/Growing Older But Not Up	1981	—	2.00	4.00
❏ 52013	It's Midnight And I'm Not Famous Yet/When Salome Plays the Drum	1982	—	2.00	4.00
❏ 52050	If I Could Just Get It on Paper/Where's the Party	1982	—	2.00	4.00
❏ 52298	One Particular Harbour/Distantly in Love	1983	—	2.00	4.00
❏ 52333	Brown Eyed Girl/Twelve Volt Man	1984	—	2.00	4.00
❏ 52438	When the Wild Life Betrays Me/Ragtop Day	1984	—	2.00	4.00
❏ 52438 [PS]	When the Wild Life Betrays Me/Ragtop Day	1984	—	2.00	4.00
❏ 52499	Come to the Moon/Bigger Than the Both of Us	1984	—	2.00	4.00
❏ 52550	Who's the Blond Stranger/She's Going Out of My Mind	1985	—	—	3.00
❏ 52607	Gypies in the Palace/Jolly Mon Sing	1985	—	—	3.00
❏ 52664	If the Phone Doesn't Ring, It's Me/Frank and Lola	1985	—	—	3.00
❏ 52752	Please Bypass This Heart/Beyond the End	1986	—	—	3.00
❏ 52849	I Love the Now/No Plane on Sunday	1986	—	—	3.00
❏ 52932	Creola/You'll Never Work in Dis Bidness Again	1986	—	—	3.00
❏ 52932 [PS]	Creola/You'll Never Work in Dis Bidness Again	1986	—	2.00	4.00
❏ 53035	Take It Back/Floridays	1987	—	—	3.00
❏ 53360	Homemade Music/L'air de la Louisiane	1988	—	—	3.00
❏ 53360 [PS]	Homemade Music/L'air de la Louisiane	1988	—	2.00	4.00
❏ 53396	Bring Back the Magic/That's What Living Is to Me	1988	—	—	3.00
❏ 53396 [PS]	Bring Back the Magic/That's What Living Is to Me	1988	—	2.00	4.00
❏ 53675	Take Another Road/Off to See the Lizard	1989	—	—	3.00
❏ 54680	Another Saturday Night/Souvenirs	1993	—	—	3.00
Albums					
ABC					
❏ SPDJ-43 [DJ]	Special Jimmy Buffett Sampler	1978	5.00	10.00	20.00
❏ D-914	Havana Daydreamin'	1976	3.00	6.00	12.00
❏ AB-990	Changes in Latitudes, Changes in Attitudes	1977	3.00	6.00	12.00
❏ AK-1008 [(2)]	You Had to Be There	1978	3.75	7.50	15.00
❏ AA-1046	Son of a Son of a Sailor	1978	3.00	6.00	12.00

Number	Title (A Side/B Side)	Yr	VG	VG+	NM
ABC DUNHILL					
❏ DSD-50132	Living and Dying in 3/4 Time	1973	3.75	7.50	15.00
❏ DSX-50150	A White Sport Coat and a Pink Crustaceon	1974	3.75	7.50	15.00
❏ DSD-50183	A1A	1975	3.75	7.50	15.00
BARNABY					
❏ BR-6014	High Cumberland Jubilee	1975	10.00	20.00	40.00
❏ Z 30093	Down to Earth	1970	25.00	50.00	100.00
MCA					
❏ 5102	Volcano	1979	2.50	5.00	10.00
❏ 5169	Coconut Telegraph	1981	2.50	5.00	10.00
❏ 5285	Somewhere Over China	1982	2.50	5.00	10.00
❏ 5447	One Particular Harbour	1983	2.50	5.00	10.00
❏ 5512	Riddles in the Sand	1984	2.50	5.00	10.00
❏ 5600	Last Mango in Paris	1985	2.50	5.00	10.00
❏ 5633	Songs You Know By Heart — Jimmy Buffett's Greatest Hit(s)	1985	2.50	5.00	10.00
❏ 5730	Floridays	1986	2.50	5.00	10.00
❏ 2-6005 [(2)]	You Had to Be There	1981	2.50	5.00	10.00
❏ 6314	Off to See the Lizard	1989	2.50	5.00	10.00
❏ 37023	Havana Daydreamin'	1981	2.00	4.00	8.00
❏ 37024	Son of a Son of a Sailor	1981	2.00	4.00	8.00
❏ 37025	Living and Dying in 3/4 Time	1981	2.00	4.00	8.00
❏ 37026	A White Sport Coat and a Pink Crustaceon	1981	2.00	4.00	8.00
❏ 37027	A1A	1981	2.00	4.00	8.00
❏ 37150	Changes in Latitudes, Changes in Attitudes	1982	2.00	4.00	8.00
❏ 37156	Volcano	1982	2.00	4.00	8.00
❏ 37246	Somewhere Over China	1984	2.00	4.00	8.00
❏ 42093	Hot Water	1988	2.50	5.00	10.00

BUG COLLECTORS, THE
45s
CATCH

Number	Title (A Side/B Side)	Yr	VG	VG+	NM
❏ 103	The Beatle Bug/Thief in the Night	1964	5.00	10.00	20.00

BUG MEN, THE See THE STRING-A-LONGS.

BUGALOOS, THE
45s
CAPITOL

Number	Title (A Side/B Side)	Yr	VG	VG+	NM
❏ 2946	Senses of Our World/For a Friend	1970	3.00	6.00	12.00

Albums
CAPITOL

| ❏ SW-621 | The Bugaloos | 1970 | 7.50 | 15.00 | 30.00 |

BUGGS, THE
45s
SOMA

| ❏ 1413 | The Buggs vs. The Beatles/She Loves You | 1964 | 6.25 | 12.50 | 25.00 |

Albums
CORONET

| ❏ CX-212 [M] | The Beatle Beat | 1964 | 5.00 | 10.00 | 20.00 |
| ❏ CXS-212 [R] | The Beatle Beat | 1964 | 3.00 | 6.00 | 12.00 |

BUGS, THE
45s
HIT

| ❏ 106 | She Loves You/Dawn (Go Away) | 1964 | 3.00 | 6.00 | 12.00 |

—B-side by the Chellows

| ❏ 111 | Twist and Shout/Stay | 1964 | 3.00 | 6.00 | 12.00 |

—B-side by the Chellows

| ❏ 161 | Any Way You Want It/Sidewalk Surfin' | 1964 | 3.00 | 6.00 | 12.00 |

—B-side by the Jalopy Five

BULLDOG With Gene Cornish and Dino Danelli, ex-members of THE RASCALS.
45s
BUDDAH

| ❏ 414 | Bad Bad Girl/I Tried to Sleep | 1974 | — | 2.00 | 4.00 |

DECCA

| ❏ 32996 | Good Times Are Comin'/No | 1972 | — | 2.00 | 4.00 |

GUYDEN

| ❏ 5001 | Man of Constant Sorrow/Inner Spring | 1971 | — | 2.50 | 5.00 |

MCA

| ❏ 40014 | I'm a Madman/Are You Really Happy Together | 1973 | — | 2.00 | 4.00 |
| ❏ 40050 | I Tip My Hat/I'm a Madman | 1973 | — | 2.00 | 4.00 |

Albums
BUDDAH

| ❏ BDS-5600 | Smasher | 1974 | 3.75 | 7.50 | 15.00 |

DECCA

| ❏ DL 75370 | Bulldog | 1972 | 5.00 | 10.00 | 20.00 |

BULLDOGS, THE
45s
MERCURY

| ❏ 72262 | John, Paul, George and Ringo/What Do I See | 1964 | 5.00 | 10.00 | 20.00 |

BUNCH, THE
Albums
A&M

| ❏ SP-4354 | The Bunch | 1973 | 6.25 | 12.50 | 25.00 |

BUNKERS, THE
45s
RCA VICTOR

| ❏ 74-0962 | They Can't Take That Away from Me/Oh Babe, What Would You Say | 1973 | — | 3.00 | 6.00 |
| ❏ 74-0962 [PS] | They Can't Take That Away from Me/Oh Babe, What Would You Say | 1973 | 2.50 | 5.00 | 10.00 |

Albums
RCA VICTOR

| ❏ APL1-0102 | Archie and Edith Side by Side | 1973 | 5.00 | 10.00 | 20.00 |

BUONO, VICTOR
45s
DORE

Number	Title (A Side/B Side)	Yr	VG	VG+	NM
❏ 864	Fat Man's Prayer/Bless Me Doctor	1971	—	3.00	6.00

Albums
DORE

| ❏ 325 | Heavy! | 1971 | 3.75 | 7.50 | 15.00 |

BUOYS, THE
45s
POLYDOR

| ❏ 14201 | Liza's Last Ride/Downtown Singer | 1973 | — | 3.00 | 6.00 |

SCEPTER

❏ 12254	These Days/Don't You Know It's Over	1969	2.00	4.00	8.00
❏ 12275	Timothy/It Feels Good	1970	2.50	5.00	10.00
❏ 12275 [PS]	Timothy/It Feels Good	1970	5.00	10.00	20.00
❏ 12318	Give Up Your Guns/Prince of Thieves	1971	2.00	4.00	8.00
❏ 12331	Tell Me Heaven Is Here/Bloodknot	1971	2.00	4.00	8.00

Albums
SCEPTER

| ❏ SPS-593 | Timothy | 1971 | 6.25 | 12.50 | 25.00 |

BURDEN, RAY
45s
CULLMAN

| ❏ 6407 | Christmas Is Here At Last/Santa, Bring Me A Gal | 1958 | 12.50 | 25.00 | 50.00 |

BURDETTE, LEW
45s
DOT

| ❏ 15672 | Three Strikes and You're Out/Mary Lou | 1957 | 6.25 | 12.50 | 25.00 |

BURDON, ERIC Also see THE ANIMALS; ERIC BURDON AND WAR.
45s
CAPITOL

❏ 3997	The Real Me/Letter from the County Farm	1974	—	2.50	5.00
❏ 3997 [PS]	The Real Me/Letter from the County Farm	1974	3.00	6.00	12.00
❏ 4007	Ring of Fire/The Real Me	1974	—	2.50	5.00

MGM

| ❏ 14296 | Headin' for Home/Soledad | 1971 | — | 2.50 | 5.00 |

—With Jimmy Witherspoon
UNITED ARTISTS

| ❏ 50842 | Headin' for Home/Soledad | 1971 | — | — | — |

—With Jimmy Witherspoon; assigned to MGM
Albums
CAPITOL

| ❏ ST-11359 | Sun Secrets | 1974 | 3.00 | 6.00 | 12.00 |
| ❏ S?A?11426 | Stop | 1975 | 5.00 | 10.00 | 20.00 |

—Cover shaped like a hexagon

| ❏ ST-11426 | Stop | 1975 | 3.00 | 6.00 | 12.00 |

—Regular square cover
GNP CRESCENDO

| ❏ GNPS-2194 | Wicked Man | 1988 | 2.50 | 5.00 | 10.00 |

LAX

| ❏ PW 37110 | Sun Secrets | 1981 | 2.50 | 5.00 | 10.00 |

—Reissue of Capitol 11359
STRIPED HORSE

| ❏ SHL 2006 | I Used to Be an Animal | 1988 | 2.50 | 5.00 | 10.00 |

BURDON, ERIC, AND THE ANIMALS See THE ANIMALS.

BURDON, ERIC, AND WAR Also see ERIC BURDON; WAR.
45s
ABC

| ❏ 12244 | Magic Mountain/Home Dream | 1977 | — | 2.50 | 5.00 |

MGM

❏ 14118	Spill the Wine/Magic Mountain	1970	—	3.00	6.00
❏ 14118 [PS]	Spill the Wine/Magic Mountain	1970	3.00	6.00	12.00
❏ 14196	They Can't Take Away Our Music/Home Cookin'	1970	—	2.50	5.00

Albums
ABC

| ❏ D-988 | Love Is All Around | 1976 | 3.00 | 6.00 | 12.00 |

—As "War Featuring Eric Burdon"
LAX

| ❏ PW 37109 | Spill the Wine | 1981 | 2.50 | 5.00 | 10.00 |

—Reissue of MGM 4663 with new title
MGM

| ❏ SE-4663 | Eric Burdon Declares "War" | 1970 | 3.75 | 7.50 | 15.00 |
| ❏ SE-4710-2 [(2)] | The Black Man's Burdon | 1970 | 5.00 | 10.00 | 20.00 |

—Add 50% if the package includes an "Official War Bond," entitling the bearer to $1 off any Eric Burdon and War concert before December 31, 1973

BURGESS, DAVE Also see THE CHAMPS.
45s
CHALLENGE

| ❏ 1001 | Don't Cry. For You I Love/Fire in the Eyes | 1957 | 6.25 | 12.50 | 25.00 |

—As "Dave Dupree"

| ❏ 1002 | Flame of Love/Well, It Isn't Fair | 1957 | 6.25 | 12.50 | 25.00 |

—As "Dave Dupree"

| ❏ 1005 | A Job Well Done/Our Tomorrow | 1957 | 6.25 | 12.50 | 25.00 |

—As "Dave Dupree"

| ❏ 1008 | I'm Available/Who's Gonna Cry | 1957 | 6.25 | 12.50 | 25.00 |
| ❏ 1018 | Take This Love/Maybelle | 1958 | 5.00 | 10.00 | 20.00 |

—As "Dave Burgess and the Champs"

❏ 59032	Lovey Dovey Baby/I Hang My Head and Cry	1958	5.00	10.00	20.00
❏ 59037	I Don't Want to Know/Lulu	1959	5.00	10.00	20.00
❏ 59045	Everlovin'/Just for Me	1959	5.00	10.00	20.00
❏ 59101	Without You/Are You Teasing Me	1961	5.00	10.00	20.00

OKEH

| ❏ 7002 | Don't Put a Dent in My Heart/Judalina | 1953 | 6.25 | 12.50 | 25.00 |
| ❏ 7044 | Gratefully Yours/Too Late for Tears | 1954 | 6.25 | 12.50 | 25.00 |

Number	Title (A Side/B Side)	Yr	VG	VG+	NM
TAMPA					
❑ 104	Down, Down/Don't Turn Your Back on Love	1955	6.25	12.50	25.00
❑ 105	I Love Paris/Five Foot Two, Eyes of Blue	1955	6.25	12.50	25.00

BURGESS, SONNY
45s
Number	Title (A Side/B Side)	Yr	VG	VG+	NM
PHILLIPS INT'L.					
❑ 3551	Sadie's Back in Town/Kiss Goodnight	1960	7.50	15.00	30.00
SUN					
❑ 247	Red Headed Woman/We Wanna Boogie	1956	37.50	75.00	150.00
❑ 263	Ain't Got a Thing/Restless	1957	20.00	40.00	80.00
❑ 285	My Bucket's Got a Hole in It/Sweet Misery	1958	12.50	25.00	50.00
❑ 304	Thunderbird/Itchy	1958	7.50	15.00	30.00

BURKE, BUDDY
45s
Number	Title (A Side/B Side)	Yr	VG	VG+	NM
BULLSEYE					
❑ 1002	That Big Old Moon/Street of Sorrows	195?	37.50	75.00	150.00

BURKE, SOLOMON
12-Inch Singles
Number	Title (A Side/B Side)	Yr	VG	VG+	NM
INFINITY					
❑ L33-1023 [DJ]	Sidewalks, Fences and Walls (3:39) (5:15)	1979	3.00	6.00	12.00

45s
Number	Title (A Side/B Side)	Yr	VG	VG+	NM
ABC DUNHILL					
❑ 4388	Midnight and You/I Have a Dream	1974	—	2.50	5.00
❑ 15009	Midnight and You/I Have a Dream	1974	—	2.00	4.00
AMHERST					
❑ 736	Please Don't You Say Goodbye to Me/See That Girl	1978	—	2.00	4.00
APOLLO					
❑ 485	Christmas Presents/When I'm All Alone	1955	7.50	15.00	30.00
❑ 487	I'm in Love/Why Do Me That Way	1956	6.25	12.50	25.00
❑ 491	I'm All Alone/To Thee	1956	6.25	12.50	25.00
❑ 500	No Man Walks Alone/Walking in a Dream	1956	6.25	12.50	25.00
❑ 505	A Picture of You/You Can Run But You Can't Hide	1957	6.25	12.50	25.00
❑ 511	I Need You Tonight/This Is It	1957	6.25	12.50	25.00
❑ 512	For You and You Alone/You Are My One Love	1957	6.25	12.50	25.00
❑ 522	They Always Say/Don't Cry	1958	6.25	12.50	25.00
❑ 527	My Heart Is a Chapel/This Is It	1958	6.25	12.50	25.00
ATLANTIC					
❑ 2089	Keep the Magic Working/How Many Times	1961	5.00	10.00	20.00
❑ 2114	Just Out of Reach (Of My Two Open Arms)/Be-Bop Grandma	1961	5.00	10.00	20.00
❑ 2131	Cry to Me/I Almost Lost My Mind	1962	5.00	10.00	20.00
❑ 2147	Down in the Valley/I'm Hanging Up My Heart for You	1962	3.75	7.50	15.00
❑ 2157	I Really Don't Want to Know/Tonight My Heart She Is Crying (Love Is a Bird)	1962	3.75	7.50	15.00
❑ 2170	Go On Back to Him/I Said I Was Sorry	1962	3.75	7.50	15.00
❑ 2180	Words/Home in Your Heart	1963	3.75	7.50	15.00
❑ 2185	If You Need Me/You Can Make It If You Try	1963	3.75	7.50	15.00
❑ 2196	Can't Nobody Love You/Stupidity	1963	3.75	7.50	15.00
❑ 2205	You're Good for Me/Beautiful Brown Eyes	1963	3.75	7.50	15.00
❑ 2218	He'll Have to Go/Rockin' Soul	1964	3.75	7.50	15.00
❑ 2226	Goodbye Baby (Baby Goodbye)/Someone to Love Me	1964	3.75	7.50	15.00
❑ 2241	Everybody Needs Somebody to Love/Looking for My Baby	1964	3.75	7.50	15.00
❑ 2254	Yes I Do/Won't You Give Him (One More Chance)	1964	3.75	7.50	15.00
❑ 2259	The Price/More Rockin' Soul	1964	3.75	7.50	15.00
❑ 2276	Got to Get You Off My Mind/Peepin'	1965	3.75	7.50	15.00
❑ 2288	Tonight's the Night/Maggie's Farm	1965	3.75	7.50	15.00
❑ 2299	Someone Is Watching/Dance, Dance, Dance	1965	3.00	6.00	12.00
❑ 2308	Only Love (Can Save Me Now)/A Little Girl That Loves Me	1965	3.00	6.00	12.00
❑ 2314	Baby Come On Home/(No, No, No) Can't Stop Lovin' You Now	1965	3.00	6.00	12.00
❑ 2327	I Feel a Sin Coming On/Mountain of Pride	1966	2.50	5.00	10.00
❑ 2345	Suddenly/Lawdy Miss Clawdy	1966	2.50	5.00	10.00
❑ 2349	Keep Looking/Don't Want You No More	1966	2.50	5.00	10.00
❑ 2359	When She Touches Me/Woman How Do You Make Me Love You Like I Do	1966	2.50	5.00	10.00
❑ 2369	Presents for Christmas/A Tear Fell	1966	3.00	6.00	12.00
❑ 2378	Keep a Light in the Window Till I Come Home/Time Is a Thief	1967	2.50	5.00	10.00
❑ 2416	Take Me (Just As I Am)/Stayed Away Too Long	1967	2.50	5.00	10.00
❑ 2459	It's Been a Change/Detroit City	1967	2.50	5.00	10.00
❑ 2483	Party People/Need Your Love So Bad	1968	2.50	5.00	10.00
❑ 2507	I Wish I Knew (How It Would Feel to Be Free)/It's Just a Matter of Time Baby	1968	2.50	5.00	10.00
❑ 2527	Save it/Meet Me in Church	1968	2.50	5.00	10.00
❑ 2566	Get Out of My Life Woman/What'd I Say	1968	2.50	5.00	10.00
BELL					
❑ 759	Up Tight Good Woman/I Can't Stop	1969	2.00	4.00	8.00
❑ 783	Proud Mary/What Am I Living For	1969	2.00	4.00	8.00
❑ 806	That Lucky Old Sun/How Big a Fool	1969	2.00	4.00	8.00
❑ 829	I'm Gonna Stay Right Here/Generation of Revelations	1969	2.00	4.00	8.00
❑ 891	God Knows I Love You/In the Ghetto	1970	—	3.00	6.00
CHESS					
❑ 401	I'll Never Stop Loving You (Never Ever Song)/The Do Right Song	1976	—	3.00	6.00
❑ 2159	You and Your Baby Blues/I'm Leaving on That Late, Late Train	1975	—	2.00	4.00
❑ 2172	Let Me Wrap My Arms Around You/Everlasting Love	1975	—	2.00	4.00
INFINITY					
❑ 50046	Sidewalks, Fences and Walls/Boo-Hoo-Hoo (Cra-Cra-Craya)	1979	—	2.50	5.00

Number	Title (A Side/B Side)	Yr	VG	VG+	NM
MALA					
❑ 420	This Little Ring/I'm Not Afraid	1960	5.00	10.00	20.00
MCI					
❑ 712842	You're All I Want for Christmas/No Place Like Home	198?	2.00	4.00	8.00
—B-side by Rayne					
MGM					
❑ 14185	Lookin' Out My Back Door/All for the Love of Sunshine	1970	—	3.00	6.00
❑ 14221	The Electronic Magnetism (That's Heavy, Baby)/Bridge of Life	1971	—	3.00	6.00
❑ 14279	J.C. I Know Who You Are/The Things Love Will Make You Do	1971	—	3.00	6.00
❑ 14302	The Night They Drove Old Dixie Down/PSR 1983	1971	—	3.00	6.00
❑ 14353	Love's Street and Fool's Road/I Got to Tell It	1972	—	3.00	6.00
❑ 14402	We're Almost Home/Fight Back	1972	—	3.00	6.00
❑ 14402 [PS]	We're Almost Home/Fight Back	1972	3.00	6.00	12.00
❑ 14425	Get Up and Do Something for Yourself/We're Almost Home	1972	—	3.00	6.00
❑ 14571	Shambala/Love Thy Neighbor	1973	—	3.00	6.00
❑ 14651	Georgia Up North/Here Comes the Train	1973	—	3.00	6.00
POINTBLANK					
❑ S7-19520	Oooooooyou/Today Is Your Birthday	1997	—	2.00	4.00
PRIDE					
❑ 1017	I Can't Stop Loving You (Part 1)/I Can't Stop Loving You (Part 2)	1972	—	3.00	6.00
❑ 1022	All I Want for Christmas/I Can't Stop Loving You (Part 1)	1972	—	3.00	6.00
❑ 1028	My Prayer/Ookie Bookie Man	1973	—	3.00	6.00
❑ 1038	Sentimental Journey/Vaya Con Dios	1973	—	3.00	6.00
—With Lady Lee					

Albums
Number	Title	Yr	VG	VG+	NM
ABC DUNHILL					
❑ DSX-50161	I Have a Dream	1974	3.00	6.00	12.00
AMHERST					
❑ AMH-1018	Please Don't You Say Goodbye to Me	1978	3.00	6.00	12.00
APOLLO					
❑ ALP-498 [M]	Solomon Burke	1962	125.00	250.00	500.00
ATLANTIC					
❑ 8067 [M]	Solomon Burke's Greatest Hits	1962	12.50	25.00	50.00
❑ SD 8067 [S]	Solomon Burke's Greatest Hits	1962	20.00	40.00	80.00
❑ 8085 [M]	If You Need Me	1963	12.50	25.00	50.00
❑ SD 8085 [S]	If You Need Me	1963	20.00	40.00	80.00
❑ 8096 [M]	Rock N' Soul	1964	12.50	25.00	50.00
❑ SD 8096 [S]	Rock N' Soul	1964	20.00	40.00	80.00
❑ 8109 [M]	The Best of Solomon Burke	1965	7.50	15.00	30.00
❑ SD 8109 [S]	The Best of Solomon Burke	1965	10.00	20.00	40.00
❑ SD 8158	King Solomon	1968	6.25	12.50	25.00
❑ SD 8185	I Wish I Knew	1968	6.25	12.50	25.00
BELL					
❑ 6033	Proud Mary	1969	5.00	10.00	20.00
CHESS					
❑ CH-19002	Back to My Roots	1976	3.00	6.00	12.00
❑ CH-60042	Music to Make Love By	1975	3.00	6.00	12.00
CLARION					
❑ 607 [M]	I Almost Lost My Mind	1966	5.00	10.00	20.00
❑ SD 607 [S]	I Almost Lost My Mind	1966	6.25	12.50	25.00
INFINITY					
❑ INF-9024	Sidewalks, Fences and Walls	1979	3.00	6.00	12.00
KENWOOD					
❑ LP-498 [M]	Solomon Burke	1964	50.00	100.00	200.00
—Reissue of Apollo 498					
MGM					
❑ SE-4767	Electronic Magnetism	1971	3.75	7.50	15.00
❑ SE-4830	King Heavy	1972	3.75	7.50	15.00
PRIDE					
❑ 0011	The History of Solomon Burke	1972	3.75	7.50	15.00
ROUNDER					
❑ 2042/3 [(2)]	Soul Alive!	1984	3.00	6.00	12.00
❑ 2053	A Change Is Gonna Come	1986	2.50	5.00	10.00
SAVOY					
❑ 14660	Solomon Burke	1981	2.50	5.00	10.00
❑ 14679	Into My Life	1982	2.50	5.00	10.00
❑ 14717	Take Me, Shake Me	1983	2.50	5.00	10.00

BURLAND, SASCHA & THE SKIPJACK CHOIR
45s
Number	Title (A Side/B Side)	Yr	VG	VG+	NM
COLUMBIA					
❑ 42009	Gorilla Walk/Hole in My Soul	1960	5.00	10.00	20.00
RCA VICTOR					
❑ 47-8277	Have Yourself a Merry Little Christmas/The Chickens Are in the Chimes	1963	7.50	15.00	30.00
❑ 47-8277 [PS]	Have Yourself a Merry Little Christmas/The Chickens Are in the Chimes	1963	10.00	20.00	40.00

BURNETT, FRANCES
45s
Number	Title (A Side/B Side)	Yr	VG	VG+	NM
CORAL					
❑ 62092	Come to Me/So Many Tears	1959	25.00	50.00	100.00
❑ 62127	Please Remember Me/How I Miss You So	1959	25.00	50.00	100.00
❑ 62164	I Love Him So/Too Proud	1960	25.00	50.00	100.00
❑ 62214	She Was Taking My Baby/Sweetie	1960	25.00	50.00	100.00
DECCA					
❑ 30571	Spin the Wheel/A Promise Made a Fool of Me	1958	30.00	60.00	120.00

BURNETTE, BILLY Also see FLEETWOOD MAC. Not to be confused with Billy Joe Burnette.
12-Inch Singles
Number	Title (A Side/B Side)	Yr	VG	VG+	NM
MCA CURB					
❑ L33-17065 [DJ]	Roll Over/Guitar Bug	1985	2.50	5.00	10.00

B

Number	Title (A Side/B Side)	Yr	VG	VG+	NM
45s					
A&M					
❏ 743	Just Because We're Kids/Little Girl, Big Love	1964	6.25	12.50	25.00
—As "Young Billy Bean"; A-side written by Dr. Seuss!					
❏ 1794	Baby/Just Another Love Song	1976	—	2.50	5.00
CAPRICORN					
❏ 18525	I Still Remember (How to Miss You)/I Recovered, I Survived	1993	—	—	3.00
❏ 18751	Tangled Up in Texas/Into the Storm	1992	—	—	3.00
COLUMBIA					
❏ 02527	Let the New Love Begin/I Don't Know Why	1981	—	2.00	4.00
❏ 02699	The Bigger the Love/I Don't Know Why	1982	—	2.00	4.00
❏ 11380	Don't Say No/Rockin' L.A.	1980	—	2.00	4.00
❏ 11432	Oh Susan/Sittin' On Ready	1981	—	2.00	4.00
ENTRANCE					
❏ 7515	Broken Hearted/I'm Always Wondering	1972	—	2.50	5.00
MCA CURB					
❏ 52626	Ain't It Just Like Love/Guitar Bug	1985	—	—	3.00
❏ 52710	Who's Using Your Heart Tonight/It Ain't Over	1985	—	—	3.00
❏ 52749	It's Not Easy/Try Me	1985	—	—	3.00
❏ 52852	Soldier of Love/Guitar Bug	1986	—	—	3.00
POLYDOR					
❏ 2024	What's a Little Love Between Friends/Precious Times	1979	—	2.00	4.00
❏ 14530	Dreamin' My Way Back to You/Shoo-Be-Doo	1979	—	2.00	4.00
❏ 14549	Believe What You Say/Mississippi Line	1979	—	2.00	4.00
WARNER BROS.					
❏ 7327	Frog Prince/One Extreme to the Other	1969	2.00	4.00	8.00
❏ 19042	Nothin' to Do (And All Night to Do It)/Can't Get Over You	1992	—	—	3.00
Albums					
COLUMBIA					
❏ JC 36792	Billy Burnette	1980	2.50	5.00	10.00
❏ FC 37460	Gimme You	1981	2.50	5.00	10.00
ENTRANCE					
❏ Z 31228	Billy Burnette	1972	5.00	10.00	20.00
MCA CURB					
❏ 5604	Try Me	1985	2.50	5.00	10.00
POLYDOR					
❏ PD-1-6187	Billy Burnette	1979	2.50	5.00	10.00

BURNETTE, BILLY JOE

Number	Title (A Side/B Side)	Yr	VG	VG+	NM
45s					
BADGER					
❏ 1004	Three Flags/(B-side unknown)	1989	—	3.00	6.00
❏ 2003	Help Me Make It Through the Night/(B-side unknown)	198?	—	3.00	6.00
❏ 2005	Anything to Keep from Going Home/(B-side unknown)	198?	—	3.00	6.00
❏ 2008	Our Last Goodbye/(B-side unknown)	198?	—	3.00	6.00
GUSTO					
❏ 167	Welcome Home Elvis/Haven't Seen Mama in Years	1977	2.00	4.00	8.00
❏ 9009	The Colonel and the King/Walk Again in the Hills	1978	3.00	6.00	12.00
—May be promo only					
K-ARK					
❏ 961	Blow Smoke on a Kangaroo/Have I Told You Lately	1970	2.00	4.00	8.00
MT. VERNON					
❏ 500	Stomp, Shake & Twist/Don't Let Our Love Go Wrong	1962	200.00	400.00	800.00
—As "Billy Barnette"					
❏ 501	Billy the Kid/I've Got a Heart	1962	100.00	200.00	400.00
PARKWAY					
❏ 826	Two Brothers/Marlene	1961	6.25	12.50	25.00
—As "Billy Barnette"					
Albums					
GUSTO					
❏ 994	Welcome Home, Elvis	1977	3.75	7.50	15.00

BURNETTE, DORSEY Also see DORSEY AND JOHNNY BURNETTE.

Number	Title (A Side/B Side)	Yr	VG	VG+	NM
45s					
ABBOTT					
❏ 188	Let's Fall in Love/The Devil's Queen	1956	12.50	25.00	50.00
❏ 190	At a Distance/Jungle Magic	1957	12.50	25.00	50.00
CALLIOPE					
❏ 8004	Things I Treasure/One Mornin'	1977	—	3.00	6.00
❏ 8012	Soon As I Touched Her/Dear Hearted Children	1977	—	3.00	6.00
CAPITOL					
❏ 3073	New Orleans Woman/After the Long Drive Home	1971	—	2.50	5.00
❏ 3190	Shelby County Penal Farm/Children of the Universe	1971	—	2.50	5.00
❏ 3307	In the Spring (The Roses Always Turn Red)/The Same Old You, The Same Old Me	1972	—	2.50	5.00
❏ 3404	I Just Couldn't Let Her Walk Away/Church Bells	1972	—	2.50	5.00
❏ 3463	Cry Mama/Lonely to Be Alone	1972	—	2.50	5.00
❏ 3529	I Let Another Good One Get Away/Take Your Weapons, Lay 'Em Down	1973	—	2.50	5.00
❏ 3588	Keep Out of My Dreams/Mama, Mama	1973	—	2.50	5.00
❏ 3678	Darlin' (Don't Come Back)/Sweet Lovin' Woman	1973	—	2.50	5.00
❏ 3796	It Happens Every Time/Mr. Jukebox, Sing a Lullaby	1973	—	2.50	5.00
❏ 3829	Bob, All the Playboys, and Me/The Bootleggers	1974	—	2.50	5.00
❏ 3887	Daddy Loves You Honey/True Romance Forgiving	1974	—	2.50	5.00
❏ 3963	What Ladies Can Do (When They Want To)/Tangerine	1974	—	2.50	5.00
CEE-JAM					
❏ 16	Bertha Lou/'Til the Law Says Stop	1957	20.00	40.00	80.00

Number	Title (A Side/B Side)	Yr	VG	VG+	NM
DOT					
❏ 16230	Rainin' in My Heart/A Full House	1961	4.00	8.00	16.00
❏ 16230	Rainin'/A Full House	1961	6.25	12.50	25.00
❏ 16265	The Feminine Touch/Sad Boy	1961	4.00	8.00	16.00
❏ 16305	A Country Boy in the Army/A Dying Ember	1961	4.00	8.00	16.00
ELEKTRA					
❏ 46513	Here I Go Again/What Would It Profit Me	1979	—	2.00	4.00
❏ 46586	B.J. Kick-a-Beaux/What Would It Profit Me	1980	—	2.00	4.00
ERA					
❏ 3012	(There Was a)Tall Oak Tree/Juarez Town	1960	5.00	10.00	20.00
❏ 3019	Hey Little One/Big Rock Candy Mountain	1960	4.00	8.00	16.00
❏ 3025	The Ghost of Billy Malloo/Red Roses	1960	4.00	8.00	16.00
❏ 3033	The River and the Mountain/This Hotel	1960	4.00	8.00	16.00
❏ 3033 [PS]	The River and the Mountain/This Hotel	1960	10.00	20.00	40.00
❏ 3041	Hard Rock Mine/(It's No) Sin	1961	4.00	8.00	16.00
❏ 3045	Great Shakin' Fever/That's Me Without You	1961	4.00	8.00	16.00
HAPPY TIGER					
❏ 546	To Be a Man/Fly Away and Hurry Home	1970	—	3.00	6.00
❏ 563	One Lump Sum/Call Me Lowdown	1970	—	3.00	6.00
HICKORY					
❏ 1458	The House That Jack Built/Ain't That Fine	1967	2.00	4.00	8.00
IMPERIAL					
❏ 5561	Try/You Came as a Miracle	1959	6.25	12.50	25.00
❏ 5597	Lonely Train/Misery	1959	6.25	12.50	25.00
❏ 5668	Way in the Middle of the Night/Your Love	1960	6.25	12.50	25.00
❏ 5756	House with a Tin Roof Top/Circle Rock	1961	6.25	12.50	25.00
❏ 5987	House with a Tin Roof Top/Circle Rock	1963	3.75	7.50	15.00
LIBERTY					
❏ 56087	The Greatest Love/Thin Little Simple Little Plain Little Girl	1969	—	3.00	6.00
MEL-O-DY					
❏ 113	Little Acorn/Cold As Usual	1964	3.75	7.50	15.00
❏ 116	Jimmy Brown/Everybody's Angel	1964	3.75	7.50	15.00
❏ 118	Long Long Time Ago/Ever Since the World Began	1964	3.75	7.50	15.00
MELODYLAND					
❏ 6007	Molly (I Ain't Gettin' Any Younger)/She's Feeling Low	1975	—	2.50	5.00
❏ 6019	Lyin' in Her Arms Again/Doggone the Dogs	1975	—	2.50	5.00
❏ 6031	Ain't No Heartbreak/I Dreamed I Saw	1976	—	2.50	5.00
MERCURY					
❏ 72546	To Remember/In the Morning	1966			
—Unreleased?					
MUSIC FACTORY					
❏ 417	I'll Walk Away/Son, You've Got to Make It Alone	1968	2.00	4.00	8.00
REPRISE					
❏ 0246	Four for Texas/Foolish Pride	1963	3.75	7.50	15.00
❏ 0246 [PS]	Four for Texas/Foolish Pride	1963	10.00	20.00	40.00
❏ 20093	Castle in the Sky/Boys Keep Hanging Around	1962	3.75	7.50	15.00
❏ 20121	Darling Jane/I'm a Waitin' For Ya Baby	1962	3.75	7.50	15.00
❏ 20177	Invisible Chains/Pebbles	1963	3.75	7.50	15.00
❏ 20208	One of the Lonely/Where's the Girl	1963	3.75	7.50	15.00
SMASH					
❏ 2029	To Remember/In the Morning	1966	2.50	5.00	10.00
❏ 2039	If You Want to Love Somebody/Teach Me Little Children	1966	2.50	5.00	10.00
❏ 2062	Tall Oak Tree/I Just Can't Be Tamed	1966	2.50	5.00	10.00
U.S. NAVY					
❏ (# unknown)	Be a Navy Man	196?	10.00	20.00	40.00
❏ (# unknown) [PS]	Be a Navy Man	196?	5.00	10.00	20.00
Albums					
CALLIOPE					
❏ CAL 7006	Things I Treasure	1977	3.00	6.00	12.00
CAPITOL					
❏ ST-11094	Here and Now	1972	3.75	7.50	15.00
❏ ST-11219	Dorsey Burnette	1973	3.75	7.50	15.00
DOT					
❏ DLP-3456 [M]	Dorsey Burnette Sings	1963	10.00	20.00	40.00
❏ DLP-25456 [S]	Dorsey Burnette Sings	1963	12.50	25.00	50.00
ERA					
❏ EL-102 [M]	Tall Oak Tree	1960	37.50	75.00	150.00
❏ ES-102 [S]	Tall Oak Tree	1960	75.00	150.00	300.00
❏ ES-800 [M]	Dorsey Burnette's Greatest Hits	1969	6.25	12.50	25.00
GUSTO					
❏ 0050	The Golden Hits of Dorsey Burnette	197?	3.00	6.00	12.00

BURNETTE, DORSEY AND JOHNNY Also see each artist's individual listings.

Number	Title (A Side/B Side)	Yr	VG	VG+	NM
45s					
CORAL					
❏ 62190	Blues Stay Away from Me/Midnight Train	1960	50.00	100.00	200.00
—As "Johnny and Dorsey Burnette"					
IMPERIAL					
❏ 5509	Warm Love/My Honey	1958	25.00	50.00	100.00
—As "Burnette Brothers"					
REPRISE					
❏ 20153	It Don't Take Much/Hey Sue	1963	5.00	10.00	20.00
Albums					
SOLID SMOKE					
❏ SS-8005	Together Again	1978	3.75	7.50	15.00

BURNETTE, JOHNNY Includes the Rock 'N' Roll Trio. Also see DORSEY AND JOHNNY BURNETTE.

Number	Title (A Side/B Side)	Yr	VG	VG+	NM
45s					
CAPITOL					
❏ 5023	All Week Long/It Isn't There	1963	3.75	7.50	15.00
❏ 5114	You Taught Me the Way to Love You/The Opposite	1964	3.75	7.50	15.00
❏ 5176	Walkin' Talkin' Doll/Sweet Suzie	1964	3.75	7.50	15.00
CHANCELLOR					
❏ 1116	I Wanna Thank Your Folks/The Giant	1962	3.75	7.50	15.00

Number	Title (A Side/B Side)	Yr	VG	VG+	NM
❏ 1123	Party Girl/Tag Along	1962	3.75	7.50	15.00
❏ 1129	Remember Me/Time Is Not Enough	1962	3.75	7.50	15.00
CORAL					
❏ 61651	Tear It Up/You're Undecided	1956	75.00	150.00	300.00
❏ 61675	Midnight Train/Oh Baby Babe	1956	75.00	150.00	300.00
❏ 61719	The Train Kept a-Rollin'/Honey Hush	1956	62.50	125.00	250.00
❏ 61758	Lonesome Train/I Just Found Out	1956	75.00	150.00	300.00
❏ 61829	Eager Beaver Baby/Touch Me	1957	75.00	150.00	300.00
❏ 61869	Drinkin' Wine Spo-Dee-O-Dee/Butterfingers	1957	75.00	150.00	300.00
❏ 61918	Rock Billy Boogie/If You Want It Enough	1957	75.00	150.00	300.00
FREEDOM					
❏ 44001	I'm Restless/Kiss Me	1958	20.00	40.00	80.00
❏ 44011	Gumbo/Me and the Bear	1959	20.00	40.00	80.00
❏ 44017	Sweet Baby Doll/I'll Never Love Again	1959	20.00	40.00	80.00
LIBERTY					
❏ 55222	Settin' the Woods on Fire/Kentucky Waltz	1959	5.00	10.00	20.00
❏ 55243	Don't Do It/Patrick Henry	1959	5.00	10.00	20.00
❏ 55258	Dreamin'/Cincinnati Fireball	1960	5.00	10.00	20.00
❏ 55285	You're Sixteen/I Beg Your Pardon	1960	5.00	10.00	20.00
❏ 55285 [PS]	You're Sixteen/I Beg Your Pardon	1960	12.50	25.00	50.00
❏ 55298	Little Boy Sad/(I Go) Down to the River	1961	3.75	7.50	15.00
❏ 55298 [PS]	Little Boy Sad/(I Go) Down to the River	1961	10.00	20.00	40.00
❏ 55318	Big Big World/Ballad of the One Eyed Jacks	1961	3.75	7.50	15.00
❏ 55318 [PS]	Big Big World/Ballad of the One Eyed Jacks	1961	10.00	20.00	40.00
❏ 55345	Girls/I've Got a Lot of Things to Do	1961	3.75	7.50	15.00
❏ 55377	Honestly I Do/Fools Like Me	1961	3.75	7.50	15.00
❏ 55379	God, Country and My Baby/Honestly I Do	1961	3.75	7.50	15.00
❏ 55416	Clown Shoes/The Way I Am	1962	3.75	7.50	15.00
❏ 55448	The Fool of the Year/The Poorest Boy in Town	1962	3.75	7.50	15.00
❏ 55489	Damn the Defiant/Lonesome Waters	1962	3.75	7.50	15.00
MAGIC LAMP					
❏ 515	Bigger Man/Less Than a Heartache	1964	12.50	25.00	50.00
❏ 515 [PS]	Bigger Man/Less Than a Heartache	1964	75.00	150.00	300.00
SAHARA					
❏ 512	Fountain of Love/What a Summer Day	1964	3.75	7.50	15.00
UNITED ARTISTS					
❏ 0018	Dreamin'/Little Boy Sad	1973	—	2.00	4.00
—Silver Spotlight Series issue					
❏ 0019	You're Sixteen/God, Country and My Baby	1973	—	2.00	4.00
—Silver Spotlight Series issue					
VON					
❏ 1006	You're Undecided/Go, Mule, Go	1954	1500.	2250.	3000.
7-Inch Extended Plays					
LIBERTY					
❏ LSX-1004	Dreamin'/Love Me//Settin' the Woods on Fire/ Please Help Me, I'm Falling	1960	25.00	50.00	100.00
❏ LSX-1004 [PS]	Dreamin'	1960	37.50	75.00	150.00
❏ LSX-1011	Little Boy Sad/Don't Do It/You're Sixteen/I Go Down to the River	1961	25.00	50.00	100.00
❏ LSX-1011 [PS]	Johnny Burnette's Hits	1961	37.50	75.00	150.00
Albums					
CORAL					
❏ CRL 57080 [M]	Johnny Burnette & the Rock 'N' Roll Trio	1956	2000.	4000.	6000.
—Originals have maroon labels, machine-stamped (not engraved) numbers in the dead wax, printing on jacket's spine and "Printed in U.S.A." in lower right of back cover					
LIBERTY					
❏ LRP-3179 [M]	Dreamin'	1960	10.00	20.00	40.00
❏ LRP-3183 [M]	Johnny Burnette	1961	10.00	20.00	40.00
❏ LRP-3190 [M]	Johnny Burnette Sings	1961	10.00	20.00	40.00
❏ LRP-3206 [M]	Johnny Burnette's Hits and Other Favorites	1962	10.00	20.00	40.00
❏ LRP-3255 [M]	Roses Are Red	1962	10.00	20.00	40.00
❏ LRP-3389 [M]	The Johnny Burnette Story	1964	10.00	20.00	40.00
❏ LST-7179 [S]	Dreamin'	1960	15.00	30.00	60.00
❏ LST-7183 [S]	Johnny Burnette	1961	15.00	30.00	60.00
❏ LST-7190 [S]	Johnny Burnette Sings	1961	15.00	30.00	60.00
❏ LST-7206 [S]	Johnny Burnette's Hits and Other Favorites	1962	12.50	25.00	50.00
❏ LST-7255 [S]	Roses Are Red	1962	12.50	25.00	50.00
❏ LST-7389 [S]	The Johnny Burnette Story	1964	12.50	25.00	50.00
MCA					
❏ 1513	Listen to Johnny Burnette and the Rock 'N' Roll Trio	1982	2.50	5.00	10.00
SOLID SMOKE					
❏ SS-8001	Tear It Up	1978	3.75	7.50	15.00
—Black viinyl					
❏ SS-8001	Tear It Up	1978	7.50	15.00	30.00
—Blue vinyl					
SUNSET					
❏ SUM-1179 [M]	Dreamin'	1967	3.75	7.50	15.00
❏ SUS-5179 [S]	Dreamin'	1967	5.00	10.00	20.00
UNITED ARTISTS					
❏ UA-LA432-G	The Very Best of Johnny Burnette	1975	2.50	5.00	10.00

BURNETTE BROTHERS See DORSEY AND JOHNNY BURNETTE.

BURNING BUSH, THE
45s
MERCURY

Number	Title (A Side/B Side)	Yr	VG	VG+	NM
❏ 72657	Keep On Burning/Evil Eye	1967	5.00	10.00	20.00

BURNS, EDDIE
45s
CHECKER

Number	Title (A Side/B Side)	Yr	VG	VG+	NM
❏ 790	Biscuit Baking Mama/Superstition	1954	75.00	150.00	300.00
—As "Big Ed and His Combo"					
CHESS					
❏ 1672	Treat Me Like I Treat You/ Don't Cha Leave Me Baby	1957	10.00	20.00	40.00
DELUXE					
❏ 6024	Hello Miss Jessie Lee/Dealing with the Devil	1953	50.00	100.00	200.00
HARVEY					
❏ 111	Orange Driver/Hard Hearted Woman	1962	25.00	50.00	100.00

Number	Title (A Side/B Side)	Yr	VG	VG+	NM
❏ 115	The Thing to Do/Mean and Evil (Baby)	1962	7.50	15.00	30.00
❏ 118	Orange Driver/Messin' with My Bread	1962	7.50	15.00	30.00
JVB					
❏ 82	Treat Me Like I Treat You/ Don't Cha Leave Me Baby	1957	25.00	50.00	100.00

BURNS, RANDY
45s
MERCURY

Number	Title (A Side/B Side)	Yr	VG	VG+	NM
❏ 73198	Living in the Country/17 Years on the River	1971	—	3.00	6.00
POLYDOR					
❏ 14143	Hold On/Country Rain	1972	—	3.00	6.00
Albums					
ESP-DISK'					
❏ 1039	Songs of Love and War	1966	6.25	12.50	25.00
❏ 1089	Evening of the Magician	1968	6.25	12.50	25.00
❏ 2007	Song for an Uncertain Lady	1971	3.75	7.50	15.00
MERCURY					
❏ SR-61329	Randy Burns and the Skydog Band	1971	3.00	6.00	12.00
POLYDOR					
❏ PD-5030	I'm a Lover, Not a Fool	1972	3.00	6.00	12.00
❏ PD-5049	Still On Our Feet	1973	3.00	6.00	12.00

BURNT SUITE
Albums
B.J.W.

Number	Title (A Side/B Side)	Yr	VG	VG+	NM
❏ 9	Burnt Suite	1967	50.00	100.00	200.00

BURRAGE, HAROLD
45s
ALADDIN

Number	Title (A Side/B Side)	Yr	VG	VG+	NM
❏ 3194	Sweet Brown Gal/Way Down Boogie	1953	15.00	30.00	60.00
COBRA					
❏ 5004	One More Dance/You Eat Too Much	1956	12.50	25.00	50.00
❏ 5012	Messed Up/I Don't Care Who Knows	1957	12.50	25.00	50.00
❏ 5018	Satisfied/Stop for the Red Light	1957	12.50	25.00	50.00
❏ 5022	She Knocks Me Out/A Heart	1958	12.50	25.00	50.00
❏ 5026	Betty Jean/I Cry for You	1958	12.50	25.00	50.00
DECCA					
❏ 48175	Hi Ya/I Need You Baby	1950	25.00	50.00	100.00
M-PAC!					
❏ 7201	The Master Key/Faith and Understanding	1963	2.50	5.00	10.00
❏ 7204	Long Ways Together/I'll Take One	1963	2.50	5.00	10.00
❏ 7210	That's a Friend/Everybody's Dancing	1964	2.50	5.00	10.00
❏ 7211	Baby I'm Alright/Fifty-Fifty	1964	2.50	5.00	10.00
❏ 7222	Your Friend/Take Me Now	1965	2.50	5.00	10.00
❏ 7225	Got to Find a Way/How You Fix Your Mouth	1965	3.00	6.00	12.00
❏ 7229	More Power to You/A Long Way Together	1966	2.50	5.00	10.00
❏ 7234	Take Me Now/You Make Me So Happy	1966	2.50	5.00	10.00
STATES					
❏ 144	Feel So Fine/You're Gonna Cry	1955	30.00	60.00	120.00
—Black vinyl					
❏ 144	Feel So Fine/You're Gonna Cry	1955	62.50	125.00	250.00
—Red vinyl					
VEE JAY					
❏ 318	What You Don't Know/Crying for My Baby	1959	6.25	12.50	25.00
VIVID					
❏ 102	Betty Jean/I Cry for You	1959	10.00	20.00	40.00

BURRITO BROTHERS, THE See THE FLYING BURRITO BROTHERS.

BURROUGHS, WILLIAM
Albums
ESP-DISK'

Number	Title (A Side/B Side)	Yr	VG	VG+	NM
❏ 1050 [M]	Call Me Burroughs	1967	25.00	50.00	100.00

BURTON, JAMES
45s
PHILIPS

Number	Title (A Side/B Side)	Yr	VG	VG+	NM
❏ 40137	Swamp Surfer/Everybody Listen to the Dobro	1963	10.00	20.00	40.00
—As "Jimmy Dobro"					

BUSH, DICK
45s
ERA

Number	Title (A Side/B Side)	Yr	VG	VG+	NM
❏ 1067	Hollywood Party/Exactly	1957	12.50	25.00	50.00

BUSTERS, THE
45s
ARLEN

Number	Title (A Side/B Side)	Yr	VG	VG+	NM
❏ 735	Bust Out/Astronaut's	1963	5.00	10.00	20.00
❏ 740	All American Surfer/Pine Tree Hop	1963	5.00	10.00	20.00
❏ 745	Heartaches/Torrid Zone	1964	5.00	10.00	20.00
UNITED ARTISTS					
❏ 0145	Bust Out/The Green Mosquito	1973	—	2.50	5.00
—Silver Spotlight Series issue; B-side by the Tune Rockers					

BUTANES, THE
45s
ENRICA

Number	Title (A Side/B Side)	Yr	VG	VG+	NM
❏ 1007	Don't Forget I Love You/That My Desire	1961	6.25	12.50	25.00

BUTLER, CARL Also see CARL BUTLER AND PEARL.
45s
CAPITOL

Number	Title (A Side/B Side)	Yr	VG	VG+	NM
❏ F1335	Heartbreak Express/White Rose	1950	7.50	15.00	30.00
❏ F1399	Plastic Man/Country Mile	1950	6.25	12.50	25.00
❏ F1454	Shake, Rattle & Roll/No Guarantee on My Heart	1951	6.25	12.50	25.00
❏ F1541	Our Last Rendezvous/I Live My Life Alone	1951	5.00	10.00	20.00
❏ F1701	Linda Lou/No Trespassing	1951	5.00	10.00	20.00
❏ F1813	A String of Empties/You Plus Me	1951	5.00	10.00	20.00
❏ F1891	Blue Million Tears/River of Love	1951	5.00	10.00	20.00
❏ F1996	Alone Without You/Vicious Lies	1952	5.00	10.00	20.00

Number	Title (A Side/B Side)	Yr	VG	VG+	NM
☐ F2084	Penny for Your Thoughts/				
	Everything Will Be the Same	1952	5.00	10.00	20.00
☐ F2158	Stepping on My Heart/I Need You So	1952	5.00	10.00	20.00
COLUMBIA					
☐ 4-21353	Angel Band/Hallelujah We Shall Rise	1955	5.00	10.00	20.00
☐ 4-21407	Wedding Day/If I Could Spend My Heartaches	1955	5.00	10.00	20.00
☐ 4-21455	It's My Sin/Borrowed Love	1955	5.00	10.00	20.00
☐ 4-40874	Your Cold Heart Told Me So/I Know What It				
	Means to Be Lonesome	1957	3.75	7.50	15.00
☐ 40994	River of Tears/Cry, You Fool, Cry	1957	3.00	6.00	12.00
☐ 41119	If You've Got the Money (I've Got the Time)/				
	Nothing I'd Rather Do	1958	2.50	5.00	10.00
☐ 41205	Jealous Heart/So Close	1958	2.50	5.00	10.00
☐ 41263	Baby I'm a-Waitin'/My Cajun Baby	1958	2.50	5.00	10.00
☐ 41368	I Like to Pretend/Oh, How I Miss You	1959	2.50	5.00	10.00
☐ 41475	Remember the Alamo/Grief in My Heart	1959	2.50	5.00	10.00
☐ 41560	You Jes' Don't Steal from a Poor Man/				
	Cry, You Fool, Cry	1960	2.50	5.00	10.00
☐ 41674	The Door/I Know Why I Cry	1960	2.50	5.00	10.00
☐ 41869	I'm a Prisoner of Love/For the First Time	1960	2.50	5.00	10.00
☐ 41997	Honky Tonkitis/You Were the Orchid	1961	2.50	5.00	10.00
☐ 42306	Have You Run Out of Lies/				
	If I Had Only Met You First	1962	2.50	5.00	10.00
☐ 42593	Don't Let Me Cross Over/Wonder Drug	1962	2.50	5.00	10.00
OKEH					
☐ 18003	Just for Fooling Around/				
	You Can't Insure a House of Dreams	1954	3.75	7.50	15.00
☐ 18012	Crowded Out/My Heart Tells Me	1954	3.75	7.50	15.00
☐ 18018	So Close/It's Wrong to Be Jealous	1954	3.75	7.50	15.00
☐ 18032	A Victim of Lies/				
	I Just Said Goodbye to My Dreams	1955	3.75	7.50	15.00
☐ 18039	That's All Right/I'll Go Steppin' Too	1955	5.00	10.00	20.00
☐ 18052	Kisses Don't Lie/				
	I Wouldn't Change You If I Could	1955	3.75	7.50	15.00
Albums					
COLUMBIA					
☐ CL 2002 [M]	Don't Let Me Cross Over	1963	5.00	10.00	20.00
☐ CS 8802 [S]	Don't Let Me Cross Over	1963	6.25	12.50	25.00
HARMONY					
☐ HL 7385 [M]	The Great Carl Butler Sings	1966	3.00	6.00	12.00
☐ HS 11185 [S]	The Great Carl Butler Sings	1966	3.75	7.50	15.00
☐ H 30674	For the First Time	1971	3.00	6.00	12.00

BUTLER, CARL, AND PEARL Also see CARL BUTLER.
45s

Number	Title (A Side/B Side)	Yr	VG	VG+	NM
CHART					
☐ 5145	Temptation Keeps Twisting Her Arm/I'm So				
	Close to Loving You	1972	—	2.00	4.00
☐ 5160	She Didn't Come Home/Two of a Kind	1972	—	2.00	4.00
☐ 5191	Heartaches for Lunch/Fifteen Years Ago	1973	—	2.00	4.00
COLUMBIA					
☐ 42778	Loving Arms/Who'll Be Next	1963	2.00	4.00	8.00
☐ 42892	Too Late to Try Again/My Tears Don't Show	1963	2.00	4.00	8.00
☐ 43030	I'm Hanging Up the Phone/Just a Message	1964	2.00	4.00	8.00
☐ 43102	Forbidden Street/When the Door Swings Shut	1964	2.00	4.00	8.00
☐ 43210	Just Thought I'd Let You Know/				
	We'd Destroy Each Other	1965	2.00	4.00	8.00
☐ 43335	Beers and Tears/Can I Draw the Line	1965	2.00	4.00	8.00
☐ 43433	Our Ship of Love/It's Called Cheating	1965	2.00	4.00	8.00
☐ 43536	Little Mac/Wrong Generation	1966	2.00	4.00	8.00
☐ 43685	Little Pedro/Cell 29	1966	2.00	4.00	8.00
☐ 43869	Same Old Me Lovin' Same Old You/				
	Dreaming of a Little Cabin	1966	2.00	4.00	8.00
☐ 44043	Wild Goose Chase/Lost	1967	—	3.00	6.00
☐ 44252	Guilty of Love/For a Minute	1967	—	3.00	6.00
☐ 44447	If You Should Ever Stop Loving Me/				
	If I'd Only Met You First	1968	—	3.00	6.00
☐ 44587	Punish Me Tomorrow/Goodbye Tennessee	1968	—	3.00	6.00
☐ 44694	I Never Got Over You/I Started Loving You Again	1968	—	3.00	6.00
☐ 44862	We'll Sweep Out the Ashes in the Morning/Your				
	Way of Life	1969	—	3.00	6.00
☐ 45112	Used to Own This Train/Caution	1970	—	2.50	5.00
☐ 45228	Bottoms Up/Let the Sun Shine on the People	1970	—	2.50	5.00
Albums					
CHART					
☐ 1051	Temptation Keeps Twistin' Her Arm	1972	3.75	7.50	15.00
COLUMBIA					
☐ CS 1039	Carl and Pearl Butler's Greatest Hits	1970	3.75	7.50	15.00
☐ CL 2125 [M]	Loving Arms	1964	5.00	10.00	20.00
☐ CL 2308 [M]	The Old and the New	1965	3.75	7.50	15.00
☐ CL 2640 [M]	Avenue of Prayer	1967	5.00	10.00	20.00
☐ CS 8925 [S]	Loving Arms	1964	6.25	12.50	25.00
☐ CS 9108 [S]	The Old and the New	1965	5.00	10.00	20.00
☐ CS 9440 [S]	Avenue of Prayer	1967	3.75	7.50	15.00
☐ CS 9651	Our Country World	1968	3.75	7.50	15.00
☐ CS 9769	Honky Tonkin'	1969	3.75	7.50	15.00
HARMONY					
☐ H 31182	Watch and Pray	1972	3.00	6.00	12.00

BUTLER, FREDDIE
45s

Number	Title (A Side/B Side)	Yr	VG	VG+	NM
KAPP					
☐ 819	This Thing/There Was a Time	1967	3.75	7.50	15.00
WHEELSVILLE					
☐ 10001	Save Your Love for Me/(B-side unknown)	196?	250.00	500.00	1000.
Albums					
KAPP					
☐ KS-3519	With a Dab of Soul	1968	7.50	15.00	30.00

BUTLER, JERRY Also see GENE CHANDLER; BETTY EVERETT; THE IMPRESSIONS.
12-Inch Singles

Number	Title (A Side/B Side)	Yr	VG	VG+	NM
MOTOWN					
☐ M00004D1	Chalk It Up/Vitamin U	1977	5.00	10.00	20.00
—B-side by Smokey Robinson					
PHILADELPHIA INT'L					
☐ 3664	(I'm Just Thinking About) Cooling Out/Are You				
	Lonely Tonight	1978	2.50	5.00	10.00
45s					
ABNER					
☐ 1024	Lost/One by One	1959	7.50	15.00	30.00
☐ 1028	Hold Me Darling/Rainbow Valley	1959	7.50	15.00	30.00
☐ 1030	I Was Wrong/Couldn't Go to Sleep	1959	7.50	15.00	30.00
☐ 1035	A Lonely Soldier/I Found a Love	1960	7.50	15.00	30.00
FOUNTAIN					
☐ 400	No Love Without Changes/All the Way	1982	—	3.00	6.00
ICHIBAN					
☐ 269	Angel Flying Too Close to the Ground/You're the				
	Only One	1992	—	—	3.00
☐ 290	Need to Belong/Sure Feels Good	1993	—	—	3.00
LOST-NITE					
☐ 273	A Lonely Soldier/I Found a Love	197?	—	2.50	5.00
—Reissue					
☐ 279	He Will Break Your Heart/Thanks to You	197?	—	2.50	5.00
—Reissue					
☐ 284	Moon River/Aware of Love	197?	—	2.50	5.00
—Reissue					
☐ 291	Make It Easy on Yourself/It's Too Late	197?	—	2.50	5.00
—Reissue					
☐ 306	Need to Belong/Giving Up on Love	197?	—	2.50	5.00
☐ 312	I Stand Accused/You Can Run	197?	—	2.50	5.00
MCA					
☐ 52177	Let's Talk It Over/Especially You	1983	—	2.00	4.00
—With Stix Hooper; B-side by Stix Hooper solo					
MERCURY					
☐ 72592	Love (Oh How Sweet It Is)/Loneliness	1966	2.50	5.00	10.00
☐ 72625	You Make Me Feel Like Someone/				
	For What You Made of Me	1966	2.50	5.00	10.00
☐ 72648	I Dig You Baby/Some Kinda Magic	1966	2.50	5.00	10.00
☐ 72676	Why Do I Lose You/You Walked Into My Life	1967	2.50	5.00	10.00
☐ 72698	You Don't Know What You've Got Until You Lose				
	It/The Way I Love You	1967	2.50	5.00	10.00
☐ 72721	Mr. Dream Merchant/'Cause I Love You So	1967	2.50	5.00	10.00
☐ 72764	Lost/You Don't Know What You've Got				
	Until You Lose It	1968	2.00	4.00	8.00
☐ 72798	Never Give You Up/Beside You	1968	2.00	4.00	8.00
☐ 72850	Hey, Western Union Man/Just Can't Forget				
	About You	1968	2.00	4.00	8.00
☐ 72876	Are You Happy/I Still Love You	1968	2.00	4.00	8.00
☐ 72898	Only the Strong Survive/				
	Just Because I Really Love You	1969	2.00	4.00	8.00
☐ 72929	Moody Woman/Go Away — Find Yourself	1969	2.00	4.00	8.00
☐ 72960	What's the Use of Breaking Up/Brand New Me	1969	2.00	4.00	8.00
☐ 72991	Don't Let Love Hang You Up/				
	Walking Around in Teardrops	1969	2.00	4.00	8.00
☐ 73015	Got to See If I Can't Get Mommy (To Come Back				
	Home)/I Forgot to Remember	1970	2.00	4.00	8.00
☐ 73045	I Could Write a Book/Since I Lost You, Baby	1970	2.00	4.00	8.00
☐ 73101	Where Are You Going/You Can Fly	1970	2.00	4.00	8.00
☐ 73131	How Does It Feel/Special Memory	1970	2.00	4.00	8.00
☐ 73169	If It's Real What I Feel/Why Are You Leaving Me	1971	—	3.00	6.00
☐ 73210	How Did We Lose It baby/Do You Finally Need				
	a Friend	1971	—	3.00	6.00
☐ 73241	Walk Easy My Son/Let Me Be	1971	—	3.00	6.00
☐ 73290	I Only Have Eyes for You/A Prayer	1972	—	3.00	6.00
☐ 73335	One Night Affair/Life's Unfortunate Song	1972	—	3.00	6.00
☐ 73443	Power of Love/What Do You Do on a Sunday				
	Afternoon	1973	—	3.00	6.00
☐ 73459	That's How Heartaches Are Made/Too Many				
	Danger Signs	1974	—	3.00	6.00
☐ 73495	Take the Time to Tell Her/High Stepper	1974	—	3.00	6.00
☐ 73629	You and Me Against the World/Playing on You	1974	—	3.00	6.00
☐ 872914-7	Only the Strong Survive/Lost	1989	—	—	3.00
—Reissue					
☐ 872916-7	Never Give You Up/Hey, Western Union Man	1989	—	—	3.00
—Reissue					
MISTLETOE					
☐ 803	Silent Night/O Holy Night	1974	—	2.50	5.00
MOTOWN					
☐ 1403	The Devil in Mrs. Jones/Don't Wanna Be				
	Reminded	1976	—	2.50	5.00
☐ 1403 [PS]	The Devil in Mrs. Jones/Don't Wanna Be				
	Reminded	1976	2.50	5.00	10.00
☐ 1414	I Wanna Do It to You/I Don't Wanna Be				
	Reminded	1977	—	2.50	5.00
☐ 1421	Chalk It Up/I Don't Want Nobody to Know	1977	—	2.50	5.00
☐ 1422	It's a Lifetime Thing/Kiss Me Now	1977	—	2.50	5.00
—With Thelma Houston					
PHILADELPHIA INT'L					
☐ 3113	Don't Be Ashamed/Best Love I Ever Had	1980	—	2.00	4.00
☐ 3117	Tell Me Girl (Why It Has to End)/We've Got This				
	Feeling Again	1980	—	2.00	4.00
☐ 3656	(I'm Just Thinking About) Cooling Out/Are You				
	Lonely Tonight	1978	—	2.00	4.00
☐ 3673	I'm Glad to Be Back/Nothing Says I Love You				
	Like I Love You	1979	—	2.00	4.00
☐ 3683	Let's Make Love/Dream World	1979	—	2.00	4.00
VEE JAY					
☐ 354	He Will Break Your Heart/Thanks to You	1960	5.00	10.00	20.00
☐ 371	Silent Night/O Holy Night	1960	5.00	10.00	20.00
☐ 375	Find Another Girl/When Trouble Calls	1961	3.75	7.50	15.00

Number	Title (A Side/B Side)	Yr	VG	VG+	NM
❏ 390	I See a Fool/I'm a Telling You	1961	3.75	7.50	15.00
❏ 396	For Your Precious Love/Sweet Was the Wine	1961	3.75	7.50	15.00
❏ 405	Moon River/Aware of Love	1961	3.75	7.50	15.00
❏ 426	Isle of Sirens/Chi Town	1962	3.75	7.50	15.00
❏ 451	Make It Easy on Yourself/It's Too Late	1962	3.75	7.50	15.00
❏ 463	You Can Run/I'm the One	1962	3.75	7.50	15.00
❏ 475	Theme from Taras Bulba (Wishing Star)/You Go Right Through Me	1963	3.00	6.00	12.00
❏ 475 [PS]	Theme from Taras Bulba (Wishing Star)/You Go Right Through Me	1963	10.00	20.00	40.00
❏ 486	You Won't Be Sorry/Whatever You Want	1963	3.00	6.00	12.00
❏ 526	Strawberries/I Almost Lost My Head	1963	3.00	6.00	12.00
❏ 534	Where's the Girl?/How Beautifully You Lie	1963	3.00	6.00	12.00
❏ 556	Just a Little Bit/A Woman with Soul	1963	3.00	6.00	12.00
❏ 567	Need to Belong/Give Me Your Love	1963	3.00	6.00	12.00
❏ 588	Giving Up on Love/I've Been Trying	1964	3.00	6.00	12.00
❏ 598	I Stand Accused/I Don't Want to Hear Anymore	1964	3.00	6.00	12.00
❏ 598 [PS]	I Stand Accused/I Don't Want to Hear Anymore	1964	7.50	15.00	30.00
❏ 651	Good Times/I've Grown Accustomed to Her Face	1965	3.00	6.00	12.00
❏ 696	I Can't Stand to See You Cry/Nobody Needs Your Love	1965	3.00	6.00	12.00
❏ 707	Believe in Me/Just for You	1965	3.00	6.00	12.00
❏ 711	Moon River/Make It Easy on Yourself	1966	3.00	6.00	12.00
❏ 715	For Your Precious Love/Give It Up	1966	3.00	6.00	12.00

Albums

ABNER
Number	Title (A Side/B Side)	Yr	VG	VG+	NM
❏ R-2001 [M]	Jerry Butler, Esq.	1959	100.00	200.00	400.00

BUDDAH
| ❏ BDS-4001 | The Very Best of Jerry Butler | 1969 | 3.75 | 7.50 | 15.00 |

FOUNTAIN
| ❏ FR 2-82-1 | Ice 'n Hot | 1982 | 2.50 | 5.00 | 10.00 |

MERCURY
❏ SRM-1-689	The Power of Love	1973	3.75	7.50	15.00
❏ SRM-1-1006	Sweet Sixteen	1974	3.75	7.50	15.00
❏ SRM-2-7502 [(2)]	The Spice of Life	1972	5.00	10.00	20.00
❏ MG-21005 [M]	The Soul Artistry of Jerry Butler	1967	5.00	10.00	20.00
❏ MG-21146 [M]	Mr. Dream Merchant	1967	5.00	10.00	20.00
❏ SR-61005 [S]	The Soul Artistry of Jerry Butler	1967	3.75	7.50	15.00
❏ SR-61146 [S]	Mr. Dream Merchant	1967	3.75	7.50	15.00
❏ SR-61151	Jerry Butler's Golden Hits Live	1968	3.75	7.50	15.00
❏ SR-61171	The Soul Goes On	1968	3.75	7.50	15.00
❏ SR-61198	The Ice Man Cometh	1968	3.75	7.50	15.00
❏ SR-61234	Ice On Ice	1969	3.75	7.50	15.00
❏ SR-61269	You & Me	1970	3.75	7.50	15.00
❏ SR-61281	The Best of Jerry Butler	1970	3.75	7.50	15.00
❏ SR-61320	Jerry Butler Sings Assorted Sounds	1971	3.75	7.50	15.00
❏ SR-61347	The Sagittarius Movement	1971	3.75	7.50	15.00
❏ 810369-1	The Best of Jerry Butler	1983	2.50	5.00	10.00
❏ 822212-1	Only the Strong Survive: The Great Philadelphia Hits	1984	2.50	5.00	10.00

MOTOWN
❏ M6-850	Love's on the Menu	1976	3.00	6.00	12.00
❏ M6-878	Suite for the Single Girl	1977	2.50	5.00	10.00
❏ M6-892	It All Comes Out in My Songs	1977	2.50	5.00	10.00

PHILADELPHIA INT'L.
| ❏ JZ 35510 | Nothing Says I Love You Like I Love You | 1978 | 2.50 | 5.00 | 10.00 |
| ❏ JZ 36413 | The Best Love I Ever Had | 1979 | 2.50 | 5.00 | 10.00 |

RHINO
| ❏ RNLP-216 | The Best of Jerry Butler (1958-1969) | 1984 | 2.50 | 5.00 | 10.00 |

TRADITION
| ❏ TLP-2068 | Starring Jerry Butler | 1969 | 3.75 | 7.50 | 15.00 |

TRIP
| ❏ 8011 [(2)] | All Time Hits | 1972 | 3.75 | 7.50 | 15.00 |

UNITED ARTISTS
| ❏ UA-LA498-E | The Very Best of Jerry Butler | 1975 | 2.50 | 5.00 | 10.00 |

VEE JAY
❏ VJLP2-1003 [(2)]	Jerry Butler Gold	198?	3.75	7.50	15.00
❏ LP-1027 [M]	Jerry Butler, Esquire	1960	37.50	75.00	150.00
—Reissue of Abner 2001					
❏ LP-1029 [M]	He Will Break Your Heart	1960	20.00	40.00	80.00
❏ LP-1034 [M]	Love Me	1961	12.50	25.00	50.00
—Reissue of 1027					
❏ LP-1038 [M]	Aware of Love	1961	10.00	20.00	40.00
❏ SR-1038 [S]	Aware of Love	1961	12.50	25.00	50.00
❏ LP-1046 [M]	Moon River	1962	10.00	20.00	40.00
❏ SR-1046 [S]	Moon River	1962	12.50	25.00	50.00
❏ VJLP-1046	Moon River	1985	2.50	5.00	10.00
—Reissue of original 1046; has softer vinyl					
❏ LP-1048 [M]	The Best of Jerry Butler	1962	6.25	12.50	25.00
❏ SR-1048 [P]	The Best of Jerry Butler	1962	7.50	15.00	30.00
❏ VJLP-1048	The Best of Jerry Butler	1985	2.50	5.00	10.00
—Reissue of original 1048; has softer vinyl					
❏ LP-1057 [M]	Folk Songs	1963	6.25	12.50	25.00
❏ SR-1057 [S]	Folk Songs	1963	7.50	15.00	30.00
❏ LP-1075 [M]	For Your Precious Love	1963	6.25	12.50	25.00
❏ SR-1075 [S]	For Your Precious Love	1963	7.50	15.00	30.00
❏ LP-1076 [M]	Giving Up On Love/Need to Belong	1963	6.25	12.50	25.00
❏ VJS-1076 [S]	Giving Up On Love/Need to Belong	1963	7.50	15.00	30.00
❏ LP-1119 [M]	More of the Best of Jerry Butler	1965	6.25	12.50	25.00
❏ VJS-1119 [S]	More of the Best of Jerry Butler	1965	7.50	15.00	30.00
❏ D1-74807	He Will Break Your Heart	1989	3.00	6.00	12.00

BUTLER, JERRY, AND BRENDA LEE EAGER Also see each artist's individual listings.
45s
MERCURY
Number	Title (A Side/B Side)	Yr	VG	VG+	NM
❏ 73255	Ain't Understanding Mellow/Windy City Soul	1971	—	3.00	6.00
❏ 73301	(They Long to Be) Close to You/You Can't Always Tell	1972	—	3.00	6.00
❏ 73395	Can't Understand It/How Long Will It Last	1973	—	3.00	6.00
❏ 73422	We Were Lovers, We Were Friends/The Love We Had Stays On My Mind	1973	—	3.00	6.00

Albums

MERCURY
Number	Title (A Side/B Side)	Yr	VG	VG+	NM
❏ SRM-1-660	The Love We Have	1973	3.75	7.50	15.00

BUTLER, JERRY, AND THE IMPRESSIONS See THE IMPRESSIONS.

BUTLER, JIMMY
45s
GEM
| ❏ 222 | Trim Your Tree/Cruelty For Kindness | 1954 | 12.50 | 25.00 | 50.00 |

BUTLER, JOE Also see THE LOVIN' SPOONFUL.
45s
KAMA SUTRA
| ❏ 264 | Revelation, Revolution '69/War Games | 1969 | 2.00 | 4.00 | 8.00 |
| ❏ 264 [PS] | Revelation, Revolution '69/War Games | 1969 | 5.00 | 10.00 | 20.00 |

BUTLERS, THE
45s
ROUSER
| ❏ 1017 | Because of My Heart/(B-side unknown) | 196? | 1000. | 2000. | 3000. |

BUTTERFIELD, PAUL
45s
BEARSVILLE
| ❏ 49706 | Living in Memphis/Footprints on the Windshield (Upside Down) | 1981 | — | 2.00 | 4.00 |

ELEKTRA
❏ 45016	Got My Mojo Working/Mellow Down Easy	1964	2.50	5.00	10.00
❏ 45609	Come On In/I Got a Mind to Give Up Living	1967	2.50	5.00	10.00
❏ 45620	Run Out of Time/One More Heartache	1967	2.50	5.00	10.00
❏ 45620 [PS]	Run Out of Time/One More Heartache	1967	5.00	10.00	20.00
❏ 45643	In My Own Dream/(B-side unknown)	1968	3.00	6.00	12.00
❏ 45658	Where Did My Baby Go/In My Own Dream	1969	2.50	5.00	10.00
❏ 45692	Love March/(B-side unknown)	1970	3.00	6.00	12.00

Albums

AMHERST
| ❏ AMH-3305 | The Legendary Paul Butterfield Rides Again | 1986 | 3.00 | 6.00 | 12.00 |

BEARSVILLE
❏ BR 2119	Paul Butterfield's Better Days	1973	3.00	6.00	12.00
❏ BR 2170	It All Comes Back	1973	3.00	6.00	12.00
❏ BR 6960	Put It In Your Ear	1976	3.00	6.00	12.00
❏ BRK 6995	North-South	1978	3.00	6.00	12.00

ELEKTRA
❏ EKL-294 [M]	The Paul Butterfield Blues Band	1965	5.00	10.00	20.00
—Gold label with guitar player					
❏ EKL-294 [M]	The Paul Butterfield Blues Band	1966	3.75	7.50	15.00
—Brown label					
❏ EKL-315 [M]	East-West	1966	5.00	10.00	20.00
—Gold label with guitar player					
❏ EKL-315 [M]	East-West	1967	3.75	7.50	15.00
—Brown label					
❏ 7E-2001 [(2)]	The Butterfield Blues Band/Live	1970	6.25	12.50	25.00
❏ 7E-2005 [(2)]	Golden Butter/The Best of the Paul Butterfield Blues Band	1972	6.25	12.50	25.00
❏ EKL-4015 [M]	The Resurrection of Pigboy Crabshaw	1967	7.50	15.00	30.00
❏ EKS-7294 [S]	The Paul Butterfield Blues Band	1965	6.25	12.50	25.00
—Gold label with guitar player					
❏ EKS-7294 [S]	The Paul Butterfield Blues Band	1966	5.00	10.00	20.00
—Brown label					
❏ EKS-7294 [S]	The Paul Butterfield Blues Band	1969	3.75	7.50	15.00
—Red label with large stylized "E"					
❏ EKS-7294 [S]	The Paul Butterfield Blues Band	1971	3.00	6.00	12.00
—Butterfly label					
❏ EKS-7315 [S]	East-West	1966	6.25	12.50	25.00
—Gold label with guitar player					
❏ EKS-7315 [S]	East-West	1966	5.00	10.00	20.00
—Brown label					
❏ EKS-7315 [S]	East-West	1969	3.75	7.50	15.00
—Red label with large stylized "E"					
❏ EKS-7315 [S]	East-West	1971	3.00	6.00	12.00
—Butterfly label					
❏ EKS-74015 [S]	The Resurrection of Pigboy Crabshaw	1967	5.00	10.00	20.00
—Brown label					
❏ EKS-74015 [S]	The Resurrection of Pigboy Crabshaw	1969	3.75	7.50	15.00
—Red label with large stylized "E"					
❏ EKS-74015 [S]	The Resurrection of Pigboy Crabshaw	1971	3.00	6.00	12.00
—Butterfly label					
❏ EKS-74025	In My Own Dream	1968	5.00	10.00	20.00
—Brown label					
❏ EKS-74025	In My Own Dream	1969	3.75	7.50	15.00
—Red label with large stylized "E"					
❏ EKS-74025	In My Own Dream	1971	3.00	6.00	12.00
—Butterfly label					
❏ EKS-74053	Keep On Moving	1969	5.00	10.00	20.00
—Red label with large stylized "E"					
❏ EKS-74053	Keep On Moving	1971	3.00	6.00	12.00
—Butterfly label					
❏ EKS-75013	Sometimes I Just Feel Like Smilin'	1971	5.00	10.00	20.00

RHINO
❏ RNLP-70877	Paul Butterfield's Better Days	1987	2.00	4.00	8.00
—Reissue of Bearsville 2119					
❏ RNLP-70878	It All Comes Back	1987	2.00	4.00	8.00
—Reissue of Bearsville 2170					
❏ RNLP-70879	Put It In Your Ear	1987	2.00	4.00	8.00
—Reissue of Bearsville 6960					
❏ RNLP-70880	North-South	1987	2.00	4.00	8.00
—Reissue of Bearsville 6995					

SUNDAZED
❏ LP 5095 [S]	The Paul Butterfield Blues Band	2001	3.00	6.00	12.00
—Reissue on 180-gram vinyl					
❏ LP 5096	East-West	2001	3.00	6.00	12.00
—Reissue on 180-gram vinyl					

Walter Brennan, "Space Mice," Dot 45-16136, picture sleeve, $12.50-$25.

Teresa Brewer, *Music, Music, Music,* Coral EC 82023, 2-EP set, $17.50-$35 (cover and both records together).

The Buckinghams, "Don't You Care," Columbia 4-44053, picture sleeve, $6-$12.

Buffalo Springfield, *Buffalo Springfield,* Atco SD 33-200-A, stereo LP with "For What It's Worth" and purple/brown label, $12.50-$25.

Solomon Burke, *Proud Mary,* Bell 6033, stereo LP, $10-$20.

The Byrds, *Preflyte,* Together ST-T-1001, stereo LP, $12.50-$25.

Number	Title (A Side/B Side)	Yr	VG	VG+	NM

BUTTERFLYS, THE
45s
RED BIRD

Number	Title (A Side/B Side)	Yr	VG	VG+	NM
❑ 10-009	Goodnight Baby/The Swim	1964	6.25	12.50	25.00
❑ 10-016	I Wonder/Gee, Baby, Gee	1964	6.25	12.50	25.00

BUTTS BAND With Robbie Krieger and John Densmore of THE DOORS.
12-Inch Singles
RHINO

❑ RNTI 403	Kinky Reggae/Get Up, Stand Up	1983	6.25	12.50	25.00

—*As "The Krieger-Densmore Reggae Bonanza"*
45s
BLUE THUMB

❑ 242	Pop a Top/Baja Bus	1973	2.00	4.00	8.00
❑ 252	I Won't Be Alone Anymore/Kansas City	1974	2.00	4.00	8.00
❑ 263	Get Up, Stand Up/Mike's Blues	1975	2.00	4.00	8.00

Albums
BLUE THUMB

❑ BTS-53	Butts Band	1973	3.00	6.00	12.00
❑ BTS-6018	Hear and Now	1975	3.00	6.00	12.00

BYE BYES, THE
45s
MERCURY

❑ 71530	Blonde Hair, Blue Eyes, Ruby Red Lips/Do You	1959	3.75	7.50	15.00

BYRD, BOBBY Two different artists have this name. For records on the Cash, Jamie and Sage & Sand labels, see BOBBY DAY.
45s
ABC

❑ 11134	Here Is My Everything/Loving You	1968	2.50	5.00	10.00

—*With Vicki Anderson*
BANG

❑ 562	Whatcha Gonna Do About It/If She's There	1968	—	3.00	6.00

BROWNSTONE

❑ 4203	Hot Pants - I'm Coming, Coming, I'm Coming	1971	—	3.00	6.00
❑ 4205	Keep On Doin' What You're Doin'/Let Me Know	1971	—	3.00	6.00
❑ 4206	If You Got a Love You Better (Hold On to It)/You Have Got to Change Your Mind	1972	—	3.00	6.00
❑ 4208	Never Get Enough/My Concerto	1972	—	3.00	6.00
❑ 4209	Sayin' It and Doin' It Are Two Different Things/Never Get Enough	1972	—	3.00	6.00
❑ 4210	Signed, Sealed and Delivered/I Need Help (I Can't Do It Alone)	1973	—	3.00	6.00

FEDERAL

❑ 12486	They Are Sayin'/I Found Out	1963	3.75	7.50	15.00

INTERNATIONAL BROTHERS

❑ 901	Back from the Dead/The Way to Get Down	1975	—	3.00	6.00

KING

❑ 6069	I Found Out/I'll Keep Pressing On	1967	—	3.00	6.00
❑ 6126	Funky Soul #1 (Part 1)/Funky Soul #1 (Part 2)	1967	—	3.00	6.00
❑ 6151	You've Got to Change Your Mind/I'll Lose My Mind	1968	2.50	5.00	10.00

—*A-side with James Brown*

❑ 6165	You Gave My Heart a Brand New Song/Concerto	1968	—	3.00	6.00
❑ 6289	You Gave My Heart a New Song/Hang-Ups We Don't Need	1970	—	3.00	6.00
❑ 6308	I'm Not to Blame/It's I Who Loves You (It's Not Him Anymore)	1970	—	3.00	6.00
❑ 6323	I Need Help (Part 1)/I Need Help (Part 2)	1970	—	3.00	6.00
❑ 6342	You've Got to Change Your Mind/You Got to Have a Job (If You Don't Work You Can't Eat)	1970	—	3.00	6.00
❑ 6378	I Know You Got Soul/It's I Who Love You (It's Not Him Anymore)	1971	—	3.00	6.00

KWANZA/WB

❑ 7703	On the Move/Try It Again	1973	—	3.00	6.00

SMASH

❑ 1903	Write Me a Letter/I Love You So	1964	2.00	4.00	8.00
❑ 1928	I'm Lonely/I've Got a Girl	1964	2.00	4.00	8.00
❑ 1964	No One Like My Baby/We Are In Love	1965	2.00	4.00	8.00
❑ 1984	Time Will Make a Change/The Way I Feel	1965	2.00	4.00	8.00
❑ 2003	You're Gonna Need My Lovin'/Let Me Know	1965	2.00	4.00	8.00
❑ 2018	Lost in the Mood of Changes/Oh, What a Nite	1966	2.00	4.00	8.00
❑ 2052	Ain't No Use/Let Me Know	1966	2.00	4.00	8.00

Albums
KING

❑ KS-1118	I Need Help	1970	50.00	100.00	200.00

BYRD, BOBBY, AND THE IMPALAS See BOBBY DAY.

BYRD, CURTIS
45s
CANDIX

❑ 340	Pretty Woman/Turn Some More Lights On	1962	6.25	12.50	25.00

BYRD, ROBERT, AND THE BIRDIES See BOBBY DAY.

BYRDS, THE Also see SKIP BATTIN; THE BEEFEATERS; GENE CLARK; DAVID CROSBY; ROGER McGUINN; GRAM PARSONS.
45s
ASYLUM

❑ 11016	Full Circle/Long Live the King	1973	—	2.50	5.00
❑ 11019	Cowgirl in the Sand/Long Live the King	1973	—	2.50	5.00

COLUMBIA

❑ 43271	Mr. Tambourine Man/I Knew I'd Want You	1965	3.75	7.50	15.00
❑ 43271 [DJ]	Mr. Tambourine Man (same on both sides)	1965	37.50	75.00	150.00

—*Red vinyl promo*

❑ 43271 [PS]	Mr. Tambourine Man	1965	150.00	150.00	300.00

—*Promo-only sleeve promoting the Byrds' appeance on the TV show Hullabaloo*

❑ 43332	All I Really Want to Do/I'll Feel a Whole Lot Better	1965	3.75	7.50	15.00
❑ 43332 [DJ]	All I Really Want to Do (same on both sides)	1965	25.00	50.00	100.00

—*Red vinyl promo*

Number	Title (A Side/B Side)	Yr	VG	VG+	NM
❑ 43332 [DJ]	I'll Feel a Whole Lot Better (same on both sides)	1965	30.00	60.00	120.00

—*Red vinyl promo*

❑ 4-43391	The Times They Are a-Changin'/She Don't Care About Time	1965	—	—	—

—*Scheduled but never released*

❑ 4-43391 [PS]	The Times They Are a-Changin'/She Don't Care About Time	1965	125.00	250.00	500.00

—*Picture sleeve for unreleased single*

❑ 43424	Turn! Turn! Turn! (To Everything There Is a Season)/She Don't Care About Time	1965	3.75	7.50	15.00
❑ 43424 [DJ]	Turn! Turn! Turn! (To Everything There Is a Season) (same on both sides)	1965	25.00	50.00	100.00

—*Red vinyl promo*

❑ 43501	It Won't Be Wrong/Set You Free This Time	1965	3.00	6.00	12.00
❑ 43578	Eight Miles High/Why	1966	3.00	6.00	12.00
❑ 43578 [PS]	Eight Miles High/Why	1966	15.00	30.00	60.00
❑ 43702	5 D (Fifth Dimension)/Captain Soul	1966	3.00	6.00	12.00
❑ 43766	Mr. Spaceman/What's Happening	1966	3.00	6.00	12.00
❑ 43987	So You Want to Be a Rock 'N' Roll Star/Everybody's Been Burned	1967	3.00	6.00	12.00
❑ 44054	My Back Pages/Renaissance Fair	1967	3.00	6.00	12.00
❑ 44157	Have You Seen Her Face/Don't Make Waves	1967	2.50	5.00	10.00
❑ 44157 [PS]	Have You Seen Her Face/Don't Make Waves	1967	10.00	20.00	40.00
❑ 44230	Lady Friend/Old John Robertson	1967	2.50	5.00	10.00
❑ 44362	Goin' Back/Change Is Now	1967	2.00	4.00	8.00
❑ 44499	Artificial Energy/You Ain't Going Nowhere	1968	2.00	4.00	8.00
❑ 44643	Pretty Boy Floyd/I Am a Pilgrim	1968	2.00	4.00	8.00
❑ 44746	Drug Store Truck Drivin' Man/Bad Night at the Whiskey	1969	2.00	4.00	8.00
❑ 44868	Lay Lady Lay/Old Blue	1969	2.00	4.00	8.00
❑ 44990	Wasn't Born to Follow/Ballad of Easy Rider	1969	2.00	4.00	8.00
❑ 44990	Ballad of Easy Rider/Oil in My Lamp	1969	2.50	5.00	10.00
❑ 45071	Jesus Is Just Alright/It's All Over Now, Baby Blue	1970	2.00	4.00	8.00
❑ 45259	Chestnut Mare/Just a Season	1970	—	3.00	6.00
❑ 45440	Glory Glory/Citizen Kane	1971	—	3.00	6.00
❑ 45514	America's Great National Pastime/Farther Along	1971	—	3.00	6.00
❑ 45761	Jesus Is Just Alright/Mr. Spaceman	1973	2.50	5.00	10.00
❑ JZSP 116476 [DJ]	He Was a Friend of Mine (same on both sides)	1966	10.00	20.00	40.00

7-Inch Extended Plays
COLUMBIA

❑ ZLP 116003/4 [DJ]	A Special Open-End Interview with the Byrds Talking About Their New LP "Fifth Dimension"	1966	30.00	60.00	120.00

—*Promo-only interview; plays at 33 1/3 rpm*

❑ ZLP 116003/4 [PS]	A Special Open-End Interview with the Byrds Talking About Their New LP "Fifth Dimension"	1966	45.00	90.00	180.00

COLUMBIA/SCHOLASTIC

❑ CV 10287	Lover of the Bayou/So You Want to Be a Rock and Roll Star//Chimes of Freedom/Goin' Back	1971	7.50	15.00	30.00
❑ CV 10287 [PS]	The Byrds	1971	7.50	15.00	30.00

Albums
ASYLUM

❑ 5058 [M]	Byrds	1973	10.00	20.00	40.00

—*Mono is white label promo only; "dj copy monaural" sticker on stereo cover*

❑ SD 5058 [S]	Byrds	1973	3.00	6.00	12.00

COLUMBIA

❑ CL 2372 [M]	Mr. Tambourine Man	1965	10.00	20.00	40.00

—*"Guaranteed High Fidelity" on label*

❑ CL 2372 [M]	Mr. Tambourine Man	1966	7.50	15.00	30.00

—*"360 Sound Mono" on label*

❑ CL 2454 [M]	Turn! Turn! Turn!	1965	7.50	15.00	30.00
❑ CL 2549 [M]	Fifth Dimension (5D)	1966	7.50	15.00	30.00
❑ CL 2642 [M]	Younger Than Yesterday	1967	7.50	15.00	30.00
❑ CL 2716 [M]	The Byrds' Greatest Hits	1967	7.50	15.00	30.00
❑ CL 2775 [M]	The Notorious Byrd Brothers	1968	12.50	25.00	50.00
❑ CS 9172 [S]	Mr. Tambourine Man	1965	10.00	20.00	40.00

—*Red label, "360 Sound" in black*

❑ CS 9172 [S]	Mr. Tambourine Man	1966	6.25	12.50	25.00

—*Red label, "360 Sound" in white*

❑ CS 9172 [S]	Mr. Tambourine Man	1971	2.50	5.00	10.00

—*Orange label*

❑ PC 9172 [S]	Mr. Tambourine Man	198?	2.00	4.00	8.00

—*Reissue with new prefix*

❑ CS 9254 [S]	Turn! Turn! Turn!	1965	6.25	12.50	25.00

—*Red "360 Sound" label*

❑ CS 9254 [S]	Turn! Turn! Turn!	1971	2.50	5.00	10.00

—*Orange label*

❑ PC 9254 [S]	Turn! Turn! Turn!	198?	2.00	4.00	8.00

—*Reissue with new prefix*

❑ CS 9349 [S]	Fifth Dimension (5D)	1966	6.25	12.50	25.00

—*Red "360 Sound" label*

❑ CS 9349 [S]	Fifth Dimension (5D)	1971	2.50	5.00	10.00

—*Orange label*

❑ PC 9349 [S]	Fifth Dimension (5D)	198?	2.00	4.00	8.00

—*Reissue with new prefix*

❑ CS 9442 [S]	Younger Than Yesterday	1967	6.25	12.50	25.00

—*Red "360 Sound" label*

❑ CS 9442 [S]	Younger Than Yesterday	1971	2.50	5.00	10.00

—*Orange label*

❑ PC 9442 [S]	Younger Than Yesterday	198?	2.00	4.00	8.00

—*Reissue with new prefix*

❑ CS 9516 [S]	The Byrds' Greatest Hits	1967	5.00	10.00	20.00

—*Red "360 Sound" label*

❑ KCS 9516 [S]	The Byrds' Greatest Hits	1971	2.50	5.00	10.00

—*Orange label*

❑ PC 9516 [S]	The Byrds' Greatest Hits	197?	2.00	4.00	8.00

—*Reissue with another new prefix*

❑ CS 9575 [S]	The Notorious Byrd Brothers	1968	5.00	10.00	20.00

—*Red "360 Sound" label*

❑ CS 9575 [S]	The Notorious Byrd Brothers	1971	2.50	5.00	10.00

—*Orange label*

❑ PC 9575 [S]	The Notorious Byrd Brothers	198?	2.00	4.00	8.00

—*Reissue with new prefix*

❑ CS 9670 [M]	Sweetheart of the Rodeo	1968	25.00	50.00	100.00

—*"Special Mono Radio Station Copy" with white label*

❑ CS 9670 [S]	Sweetheart of the Rodeo	1968	5.00	10.00	20.00

—*Red "360 Sound" label*

Number	Title (A Side/B Side)	Yr	VG	VG+	NM
❏ CS 9670 [S]	Sweetheart of the Rodeo	1971	2.50	5.00	10.00
—Orange label					
❏ PC 9670 [S]	Sweetheart of the Rodeo	198?	2.00	4.00	8.00
—Reissue with new prefix					
❏ CS 9755 [S]	Dr. Byrds and Mr. Hyde	1969	5.00	10.00	20.00
—Red "360 Sound" label					
❏ CS 9755 [S]	Dr. Byrds and Mr. Hyde	1971	2.50	5.00	10.00
—Orange label					
❏ PC 9755 [S]	Dr. Byrds and Mr. Hyde	198?	2.00	4.00	8.00
—Reissue with new prefix					
❏ CS 9942 [S]	Ballad of Easy Rider	1969	5.00	10.00	20.00
—Red "360 Sound" label					
❏ CS 9942 [S]	Ballad of Easy Rider	1971	2.50	5.00	10.00
—Orange label					
❏ PC 9942	Ballad of Easy Rider	1984	2.00	4.00	8.00
—Reissue with new prefix					
❏ G 30127 [(2)]	The Byrds (Untitled)	1970	3.75	7.50	15.00
—Without "Kathleen" listed on back cover					
❏ G 30127 [(2)]	The Byrds (Untitled)	1970	5.00	10.00	20.00
—With "Kathleen" listed on back cover (it is not on the set)					
❏ KC 30640	Byrdmaniax	1971	3.00	6.00	12.00
❏ C 31050	Farther Along	1971	3.00	6.00	12.00
❏ C 31795	The Best of the Byrds (Greatest Hits, Volume II)	197?	2.50	5.00	10.00
—Reissue with new prefix					
❏ KC 31795	The Best of the Byrds (Greatest Hits, Volume II)	1972	3.00	6.00	12.00
❏ PC 31795	The Best of the Byrds (Greatest Hits, Volume II)	198?	2.00	4.00	8.00
—Reissue with another new prefix					
❏ C 32183	Preflyte	197?	2.50	5.00	10.00
—Reissue with new prefix					
❏ KC 32183	Preflyte	1973	3.00	6.00	12.00
—Reissue of Together LP					
❏ CG 33645 [(2)]	Mr. Tambourine Man/Turn! Turn! Turn!	1976	3.75	7.50	15.00
❏ PC 36293	The Byrds Play Dylan	1980	2.50	5.00	10.00
❏ FC 37335	The Original Singles Volume 1 (1965-1967)	1981	2.50	5.00	10.00
❏ PC 37335	The Original Singles Volume 1 (1965-1967)	1985	2.00	4.00	8.00
—Budget-line reissue					
COLUMBIA LIMITED EDITION					
❏ LE 10215	Farther Along	197?	3.75	7.50	15.00
—Reissue of 31050					
PAIR					
❏ PDL2-1040 [(2)]	The Very Best of the Byrds	1986	3.00	6.00	12.00
RE-FLYTE					
❏ MH-70318	Never Before	1987	3.00	6.00	12.00
—Released by Muuray Hill Records via mail order					
RHINO					
❏ R1-70244	In the Beginning	1988	2.50	5.00	10.00
SUNDAZED					
❏ LP 5057	Mr. Tambourine Man	1999	3.75	7.50	15.00
—Reissue on 180-gram vinyl					
❏ LP 5058	Turn! Turn! Turn!	1999	3.75	7.50	15.00
—Reissue on 180-gram vinyl					
❏ LP 5059	Fifth Dimension	1999	3.75	7.50	15.00
—Reissue on 180-gram vinyl					
❏ LP 5060	Younger Than Yesterday	1999	3.75	7.50	15.00
—Reissue on 180-gram vinyl					
❏ LP 5061	Sanctuary	2000	3.00	6.00	12.00
❏ LP 5065	Sanctuary II	2000	3.00	6.00	12.00
❏ LP 5066	Sanctuary III	2001	3.00	6.00	12.00
❏ LP 5090	Sanctuary IV	2002	3.00	6.00	12.00
❏ LP 5114 [(2)]	The Preflyte Sessions	2001	3.75	7.50	15.00
❏ LP 5130 [(2)]	The Columbia Singles '65-'67	2001	3.75	7:50	15.00
TOGETHER					
❏ ST-T-1001	Preflyte	1969	6.25	12.50	25.00

BYRNES, EDD
45s
WARNER BROS.

Number	Title (A Side/B Side)	Yr	VG	VG+	NM
❏ 5047 [M]	Kookie, Kookie (Lend Me Your Comb)/You're the Top	1959	5.00	10.00	20.00
—A-side by Edward Byrnes and Connie Stevens; B-side by Edward Byrnes					
❏ 5047 [PS]	Kookie, Kookie (Lend Me Your Comb)/ You're the Top	1959	10.00	20.00	40.00
—A-side by Edward Byrnes and Connie Stevens; B-side by Edward Byrnes					
❏ S-5047 [S]	Kookie, Kookie (Lend Me Your Comb)/ You're the Top	1959	12.50	25.00	50.00
❏ 5087	Like I Love You/Kookie's Mad Pad	1959	4.00	8.00	16.00
—Artist credit: "Edd Byrnes and Friend"					
❏ 5087 [PS]	Like I Love You/Kookie's Mad Pad	1959	10.00	20.00	40.00
—Artist credit: "Edd Byrnes and Friend"					
❏ 5114	Kookie's Love Song Part 1/Kookie's Love Song Part 2	1959	4.00	8.00	16.00
—With the Mary Kay Trio					
❏ 5114 [PS]	Kookie's Love Song Part 1/Kookie's Love Song Part 2	1959	10.00	20.00	40.00
—With the Mary Kay Trio					
❏ 5121	Yulesville/Lonely Christmas	1959	4.00	8.00	16.00
❏ 5121 [PS]	Yulesville/Lonely Christmas	1959	10.00	20.00	40.00

7-Inch Extended Plays
WARNER BROS.

Number	Title (A Side/B Side)	Yr	VG	VG+	NM
❏ EA 1309	Hot Broad Rock/I Don't Dig You, Kookie// Saturday Night on Sunset Strip/The Kookie Cha-Cha-Cha	1959	12.50	25.00	50.00
❏ EA 1309 [PS]	Kookie	1959	12.50	25.00	50.00

Albums
WARNER BROS.

Number	Title (A Side/B Side)	Yr	VG	VG+	NM
❏ W 1309 [M]	Kookie	1959	25.00	50.00	100.00
❏ W/WS 1309	Kookie Bonus Photo	1959	12.50	25.00	50.00
❏ WS 1309 [S]	Kookie	1959	30.00	60.00	120.00

BYRON, LORD DOUGLAS
45s
DOT

Number	Title (A Side/B Side)	Yr	VG	VG+	NM
❏ 16685	Surfin' Santa/The Drink That Makes You Shrink	1964	7.50	15.00	30.00
UNION					
❏ 505	Big Bad Ho-Dad/Coffee House	1962	10.00	20.00	40.00
—B-side by the Continentals					

C

C.A. QUINTET, THE
45s
CANDY FLOSS

Number	Title (A Side/B Side)	Yr	VG	VG+	NM
❏ 102	Smooth as Silk/Dr. of Philosophy	1968	20.00	40.00	80.00
FALCON					
❏ 70	Mickey's Monkey/I Want You to Love Me Girl	1967	25.00	50.00	100.00
❏ 71	Blow to My Soul/She's Got to Be True	1967	25.00	50.00	100.00

Albums
CANDY FLOSS

Number	Title (A Side/B Side)	Yr	VG	VG+	NM
❏ 7764	A Trip Through Hell	1969	500.00	1000.	1500.
SUNDAZED					
❏ LP-5037 [(2)]	Trip Thru Hell	1997	3.75	7.50	15.00

C.C.S.
45s
BELL

Number	Title (A Side/B Side)	Yr	VG	VG+	NM
❏ 45396	The Band Played the Boogie/Hang It On Me	1973	—	2.00	4.00
RAK					
❏ ZS7 4501	Whole Lotta Love/Boom Boom	1971	—	3.00	6.00
❏ ZS7 4502	Walking/Lookin' for Fun	1971	—	2.50	5.00
❏ ZS7 4507	Save the World/The Tap Turns On the Water	1972	—	2.50	5.00

Albums
RAK

Number	Title (A Side/B Side)	Yr	VG	VG+	NM
❏ Z 30559	Whole Lotta Love	1971	5.00	10.00	20.00
❏ KZ 31569	C.C.S.	1972	5.00	10.00	20.00

C.K. STRONG
45s
EPIC

Number	Title (A Side/B Side)	Yr	VG	VG+	NM
❏ 5-10534	Stormbird/Daddy	1969	2.50	5.00	10.00

Albums
EPIC

Number	Title (A Side/B Side)	Yr	VG	VG+	NM
❏ BN 26473	C.K. Strong	1969	5.00	10.00	20.00

C.L. AND THE PICTURES Also see CURTIS LEE.
45s
DUNES

Number	Title (A Side/B Side)	Yr	VG	VG+	NM
❏ 2010	I'm Asking Forgiveness/Let's Take a Ride	1962	6.25	12.50	25.00
❏ 2017	Afraid/Mary Go 'Round	1962	6.25	12.50	25.00
❏ 2023	I'm Sorry/That's What's Happening	1963	6.25	12.50	25.00
JAMIE					
❏ 1398	You Really Slipped One By Me/The Same People (That You Meet Going Up, You Meet Coming Down)	1971	3.75	7.50	15.00
—As "C.L. Weldon and the Pictures"					
MONUMENT					
❏ 854	He'll Only Hurt You/Talking About My Baby	1964	5.00	10.00	20.00
❏ 888	Could This Be Magic/Yolanda	1965	5.00	10.00	20.00
❏ 958	Baby, Not Now/Jigsaw Puzzle	1966	5.00	10.00	20.00

C-NOTES, THE
45s
EVERLAST

Number	Title (A Side/B Side)	Yr	VG	VG+	NM
❏ 5005	On Your Mark/From Now On	1957	12.50	25.00	50.00

C.O.D.'S, THE
45s
KELLMAC

Number	Title (A Side/B Side)	Yr	VG	VG+	NM
❏ 1003	Michael/Cry No More	1965	3.00	6.00	12.00
❏ 1005	Pretty Baby/I'm a Good Guy	1965	5.00	10.00	20.00
❏ 1008	I'm Looking Out for Me/I'll Come Running Back to You	1966	5.00	10.00	20.00
❏ 1010	She's Fire/It Must Be You	1966	375.00	750.00	1500.
❏ 1012	Coming Back Girl/It Must Be Love	1966	25.00	50.00	100.00

C-QUENTS, THE
45s
CAPETOWN

Number	Title (A Side/B Side)	Yr	VG	VG+	NM
❏ 4027	All I Want for Christmas Is You/ Merry Christmas, Baby	1962	75.00	150.00	300.00
ESSICA					
❏ 004	Dearest One/It's You and Me	196?	7.50	15.00	30.00

CABINEERS, THE
45s
PRESTIGE

Number	Title (A Side/B Side)	Yr	VG	VG+	NM
❏ 904	Each Time/(B-side unknown)	1952	75.00	150.00	300.00
❏ 917	Baby Mine/(B-side unknown)	1953	100.00	200.00	400.00

CABOT, SEBASTIAN
45s
MGM

Number	Title (A Side/B Side)	Yr	VG	VG+	NM
❏ 13650	It Ain't Me Babe/And Mostly They Sing	1966	3.75	7.50	15.00

Albums
MGM

Number	Title (A Side/B Side)	Yr	VG	VG+	NM
❏ E-4431 [M]	Sebastian Cabot, Actor; Bob Dylan, Poet: A Dramatic Reading with Music	1967	7.50	15.00	30.00
❏ SE-4431 [S]	Sebastian Cabot, Actor; Bob Dylan, Poet: A Dramatic Reading with Music	1967	10.00	20.00	40.00

CACTUS With Tim Bogert and Carmen Appice, ex-VANILLA FUDGE.
45s
ATCO

Number	Title (A Side/B Side)	Yr	VG	VG+	NM
❏ 6782	Brother Bill/You Can't Judge a Book By Its Cover	1971	2.00	4.00	8.00
❏ 6811	Long Tall Sally/Rock 'n' Roll Christian	1971	2.00	4.00	8.00
❏ 6842	Token Chokin'/Alaska	1971	2.00	4.00	8.00
❏ 6872	The Booger Man/Cold Bear	1972	—	3.00	6.00
❏ 6901	Bringing Me Down/Bad Mother Boogie	1972	—	3.00	6.00

Albums
ATCO

Number	Title (A Side/B Side)	Yr	VG	VG+	NM
❏ SD 33-340	Cactus	1970	5.00	10.00	20.00
❏ SD 33-356	One Way...Or Another	1971	5.00	10.00	20.00
❏ SD 33-377	Restrictions	1971	5.00	10.00	20.00
❏ SD 7011	'Ot 'N' Sweaty	1972	5.00	10.00	20.00

CADETS, THE Also see THE JACKS.

45s

Number	Title (A Side/B Side)	Yr	VG	VG+	NM
JAN-LAR					
❏ 102	Don't/Car Crash	1960	15.00	30.00	60.00
MODERN					
❏ 956	Don't Be Angry/I Cried	1955	12.50	25.00	50.00
❏ 960	Rollin' Stone/Fine Lookin' Baby	1955	12.50	25.00	50.00
❏ 963	I Cried/Fine Lookin' Baby	1955	10.00	20.00	40.00
❏ 969	Annie Met Henry/So Will I	1955	10.00	20.00	40.00
❏ 971	Do You Wanna Rock/If It Is Wrong	1956	25.00	50.00	100.00
❏ 985	Church Bells May Ring/Heartbreak Hotel	1956	10.00	20.00	40.00
❏ 994	Stranded in the Jungle/I Want You	1956	10.00	20.00	40.00
❏ 1000	I Got Loaded/Dancin' Dan	1956	10.00	20.00	40.00
❏ 1006	Fools Rush In/I'll Be Spinning	1956	10.00	20.00	40.00
❏ 1012	Heaven Help Me/Love Bandit	1957	10.00	20.00	40.00
❏ 1017	Wiggle Waggle Woo/You Belong to Me	1957	10.00	20.00	40.00
❏ 1019	Pretty Evey/Rum, Jamaica Rum	1957	12.50	25.00	50.00
—As "Aaron Collins and the Cadets"					
❏ 1024	Hands Across the Table/Love Can Do Most Anything	1957	10.00	20.00	40.00
—As "Will Jones and the Cadets"					
❏ 1026	Ring Chimes/Baby Ya Know	1957	10.00	20.00	40.00
SHERWOOD					
❏ 211	One More Chance/I'm Looking for a Job	1960	12.50	25.00	50.00

Albums

Number	Title	Yr	VG	VG+	NM
CROWN					
❏ CST-370 [R]	The Cadets	1963	25.00	50.00	100.00
❏ CLP-5015 [M]	Rockin' 'n' Reelin'	1957	62.50	125.00	250.00
—Black label					
❏ CLP-5370 [M]	The Cadets	1963	37.50	75.00	150.00
MODERN					
❏ LPM-1215 [M]	Rockin' 'n' Reelin'	1956	—	—	—
—Canceled					
RELIC					
❏ 5025	The Cadets' Greatest Hits	197?	3.00	6.00	12.00

CADETS, THE (2) Nashville studio group. Also see ED HARDIN.

45s

Number	Title (A Side/B Side)	Yr	VG	VG+	NM
HIT					
❏ 284	Happy Together/There's a Kind of Hush	1967	2.00	4.00	8.00
—B-side by the Chellows					

CADILLACS, THE

45s

Number	Title (A Side/B Side)	Yr	VG	VG+	NM
ARTIC					
❏ 101	Fool/The Right Kind of Lovin'	1964	25.00	50.00	100.00
CAPITOL					
❏ 4825	Groovy, Groovy Love/White Gardenia	1962	5.00	10.00	20.00
❏ 4935	La Bomba/I Saw You	1963	5.00	10.00	20.00
—As "Bobby Ray and the Cadillacs"					
JOSIE					
❏ 765	Gloria/I Wonder Why	1954	175.00	350.00	700.00
—Original with "joz" logo at top					
❏ 765	Gloria/I Wonder Why	196?	6.25	12.50	25.00
—Reissue with 1960s label					
❏ 769	Wishing Well/I Want to Know About Love	1954	125.00	250.00	500.00
❏ 773	Sympathy/No Chance	1955	25.00	50.00	100.00
❏ 778	Widow Lady/Down the Road	1955	50.00	100.00	200.00
❏ 785	Speedoo/Let Me Explain	1955	15.00	30.00	60.00
❏ 792	Zoom/You Are	1956	12.50	25.00	50.00
❏ 798	Woe Is Me/Betty My Love	1956	12.50	25.00	50.00
❏ 805	The Girl I Love/That's All I Need	1956	25.00	50.00	100.00
❏ 807	Rudolph the Red-Nosed Reindeer/Shack-a Doo	1956	10.00	20.00	40.00
❏ 812	Sugar Sugar/About That Girl Named Lou	1957	10.00	20.00	40.00
❏ 820	My Girl Friend/Broken Heart	1957	12.50	25.00	50.00
❏ 821	Lucy/Hurry Home	1957	10.00	20.00	40.00
—As "The Original Cadillacs"					
❏ 829	Buzz-Buzz-Buzz/Yes, Yes Baby	1957	10.00	20.00	40.00
—As "The Original Cadillacs"					
❏ 836	Speedo Is Back/A' Looka Here	1958	7.50	15.00	30.00
❏ 842	Holy Smoke Baby/I Want to Know	1958	7.50	15.00	30.00
❏ 846	Peek-a-Book/Oh, Oh Lolita	1958	7.50	15.00	30.00
❏ 857	Copy Cat/Jay Walker	1959	7.50	15.00	30.00
❏ 861	Cool It Fool/Please Mr. Johnson	1959	7.50	15.00	30.00
❏ 866 [M]	Romeo/Always My Darling	1959	7.50	15.00	30.00
❏ 870	Dumbell/Bad Dan McGoon	1959	7.50	15.00	30.00
❏ 876	Tell Me Today/It's Love	1960	7.50	15.00	30.00
❏ 883	That's Why/The Boogie Man	1960	7.50	15.00	30.00
❏ 915	Wayward Wanderer/I'll Never Let You Go	1963	5.00	10.00	20.00
—As "The Original Cadillacs"					
JUBILEE					
❏ 8010 [S]	Romeo/Always My Darling	1959	15.00	30.00	60.00
LANA					
❏ 118	Speedo/Baby It's All Right	196?	—	3.00	6.00
—Reissue					
❏ 119	Gloria/Hey Bob E Re Bob	196?	—	3.00	6.00
—Reissue					
MERCURY					
❏ 71738	I'm Willing/Thrill Me So	1961	25.00	50.00	100.00
POLYDOR					
❏ 14031	Deep in the Heart of the Ghetto (Part 1)/Deep in the Heart of the Ghetto (Part 2)	1969	3.75	7.50	15.00
—As "The Original Cadillacs"					
ROULETTE					
❏ 4654	Let's Get Together/She's My Connection	1965	5.00	10.00	20.00
SMASH					
❏ 1712	You Are to Blame/What to Bet	1961	6.25	12.50	25.00

Albums

Number	Title	Yr	VG	VG+	NM
HARLEM HIT PARADE					
❏ 5009	Cruisin' with the Cadillacs	197?	2.50	5.00	10.00
JUBILEE					
❏ JGM-1045 [M]	The Fabulous Cadillacs	1957	100.00	200.00	400.00
—Blue label					
❏ JGM-1045 [M]	The Fabulous Cadillacs	1959	62.50	125.00	250.00
—Flat black label					
❏ JGM-1045 [M]	The Fabulous Cadillacs	1960	25.00	50.00	100.00
—Glossy black label					
❏ JGM-1089 [M]	The Crazy Cadillacs	1959	75.00	150.00	300.00
—Flat black label					
❏ JGM-1089 [M]	The Crazy Cadillacs	1960	25.00	50.00	100.00
—Glossy black label					
❏ JGM-5009 [M]	Twisting with the Cadillacs	1962	50.00	100.00	200.00
MURRAY HILL					
❏ 1195	The Very Best of the Cadillacs	198?	3.75	7.50	15.00
❏ 1285 [(5)]	The Cadillacs	198?	10.00	20.00	40.00
—Box set					

CADILLACS, THE/ THE ORIOLES Also see each artist's individual listings.

Albums

Number	Title	Yr	VG	VG+	NM
JUBILEE					
❏ JGM-1117 [M]	The Cadillacs Meet the Orioles	1961	50.00	100.00	200.00

CAESAR AND CLEO See SONNY AND CHER.

CAGLE, WADE

45s

Number	Title (A Side/B Side)	Yr	VG	VG+	NM
SUN					
❏ 360	Groovy Train/Highland Rock	1961	6.25	12.50	25.00

CAHPERONES, THE See THE CHAPERONES.

CAIN

Albums

Number	Title	Yr	VG	VG+	NM
A.S.I.					
❏ 204	A Pound of Flesh	1974	15.00	30.00	60.00
❏ 214	Stinger	1975	10.00	20.00	40.00

CAIOLA, AL

45s

Number	Title (A Side/B Side)	Yr	VG	VG+	NM
AVALANCHE					
❏ XW290	And I Love You So/Live and Let Die	1973	—	2.50	5.00
RCA VICTOR					
❏ 47-5252	Anna/Cachita	1953	3.75	7.50	15.00
❏ 47-5315	Pianola/The Donkey Serenade	1953	3.75	7.50	15.00
❏ 47-5400	Cumana/El Cumbanchero	1953	3.75	7.50	15.00
❏ 47-5949	Steel Guitar Rag/Stardust	1954	3.75	7.50	15.00
❏ 47-6101	A Song of India (Mambo)/Rapid Fire (Samba)	1955	3.75	7.50	15.00
❏ 47-6404	Antilles/Corsage (Her First Corsage)	1955	3.75	7.50	15.00
REGENT					
❏ 7500	Flamenco Love/(B-side unknown)	1956	3.75	7.50	15.00
UNITED ARTISTS					
❏ 261	The Magnificent Seven/The Lonely Rebel	1960	3.00	6.00	12.00
❏ 302	Bonanza/Bounty Hunter	1961	2.50	5.00	10.00
❏ 347	Autumn in Cheyenne/Speak Low	1961	2.00	4.00	8.00
❏ 400	Rollerama/Stampede	1962	2.00	4.00	8.00
❏ 438	Experiment in Terror/Sergeants Three March	1962	2.50	5.00	10.00
❏ 499	Katusha/Love Is Like Champagne	1962	2.00	4.00	8.00
❏ 545	Guitar Boogie/Kalinka	1963	2.00	4.00	8.00
❏ 577	Mexicali Rose/Mexicali Rose	1963	2.00	4.00	8.00
❏ 586	Gunsmoke/Ciao	1963	2.50	5.00	10.00
❏ 608	James Bond Theme/(B-side unknown)	1963	3.00	6.00	12.00
❏ 646	La Donna Nel Mondo/Redigo	1963	2.00	4.00	8.00
❏ 677	Burke's Law Theme/Smoke Signals	1963	2.50	5.00	10.00
❏ 711	From Russia with Love/Mexican Summer	1964	2.50	5.00	10.00
❏ 736	The Guns of Navarone/Theme from A Summer Place	1964	—	—	—
—Canceled					
❏ 740	Theme from The World of the Brothers Grimm/Baby Elephant Walk	1964	—	—	—
—Canceled					
❏ 747	On the Trail/Wheels West	1964	2.00	4.00	8.00
❏ 787	Tuff Guitar/Hound Dog	1964	2.00	4.00	8.00
❏ 814	Brash Brannigan/Hunky Funky	1965	2.00	4.00	8.00
❏ 855	Gabrielle/Ring of Fire	1965	2.00	4.00	8.00
❏ 882	Forget Domani/Glory Boys	1965	2.00	4.00	8.00
❏ 932	Theme from "The Trials of O'Brien"/Walkin' Down the Line	1965	2.00	4.00	8.00
❏ 983	Batman Theme/Karelia	1966	3.00	6.00	12.00
❏ 50037	Duel at Diablo/Sugar Me Sweet	1966	—	3.00	6.00
❏ 50070	Hill Country Theme/Quedate Un Rato Mas	1966	—	3.00	6.00
❏ 50098	Return of the Seven/The Rat Patrol	1966	2.00	4.00	8.00
❏ 50159	Eight on the Lam/Sailor from Gibraltar	1967	—	3.00	6.00
❏ 50214	Tiny Bubbles/Stag or Drag	1967	—	3.00	6.00
❏ 50231	Never Pick Up a Stranger/Sleep Walk	1967	—	3.00	6.00
❏ 50237	Bossa Nova Noel/Holiday on Skis	1967	2.50	5.00	10.00
—With Riz Ortolani					
❏ 50252	Here Is Where I Belong/The Sound of Music	1968	—	2.50	5.00
❏ 50288	Scalphunter's Theme/Theme for November	1968	—	2.50	5.00
❏ 50471	The High Chaparral/Master Jack	1969	—	3.00	6.00
❏ 50519	Infinity Blue/Soul American	1969	—	2.50	5.00
❏ 50571	Stiletto/Guitar Woman	1969	—	2.50	5.00

Albums

Number	Title	Yr	VG	VG+	NM
ATCO					
❏ 33-117 [M]	Music for Space Squirrels	1960	6.25	12.50	25.00
❏ SD 33-117 [S]	Music for Space Squirrels	1960	7.50	15.00	30.00
AVALANCHE					
❏ AV-LA058-F	The Magnificent Seven Ride '73	1973	2.50	5.00	10.00
❏ 9201	The Magnificent Seven	1972	3.00	6.00	12.00
AVCO EMBASSY					
❏ 33019	Bonanza Guitars/50 Years of the Greatest Country Music	1971	2.50	5.00	10.00
BAINBRIDGE					
❏ 1010	Soft Guitars	198?	2.00	4.00	8.00
❏ 1023	Italian Guitars	198?	2.00	4.00	8.00
❏ 1030	Guitar of Plenty	1980	2.00	4.00	8.00
CHANCELLOR					
❏ CHL-5008 [M]	Great Pickin'	1960	6.25	12.50	25.00
❏ CHS-5008 [S]	Great Pickin'	1960	7.50	15.00	30.00
PICKWICK					
❏ SPC-3034	Italian Style	196?	3.00	6.00	12.00
RCA CAMDEN					
❏ CAL-710 [M]	The Guitar Style of Al Caiola	1962	3.00	6.00	12.00
❏ CAS-710 [S]	The Guitar Style of Al Caiola	1962	3.75	7.50	15.00
❏ CAS-2569	Music from "The Godfather"	1972	2.50	5.00	10.00

C

Number	Title (A Side/B Side)	Yr	VG	VG+	NM
RCA VICTOR					
❏ LPM-2031 [M]	High Strung	1959	6.25	12.50	25.00
❏ LSP-2031 [S]	High Strung	1959	7.50	15.00	30.00
ROULETTE					
❏ R 25108 [M]	Salute Italia	1960	5.00	10.00	20.00
❏ SR 25108 [S]	Salute Italia	1960	6.25	12.50	25.00
❏ SR-42008	Roman Guitar	1968	2.50	5.00	10.00
SAVOY					
❏ MG-12033 [M]	Deep in a Dream	1955	10.00	20.00	40.00
❏ MG-12057 [M]	Serenade in Blue	1956	10.00	20.00	40.00
SUNSET					
❏ SUS-5292	Guitar in Love	1970	2.50	5.00	10.00
TIME					
❏ S-2000 [S]	Percussion and Guitars	1960	6.25	12.50	25.00
❏ S-2006 [S]	Percussion Espanol	1960	6.25	12.50	25.00
❏ S-2026 [S]	Percussion Espanol, Vol. 2	1960	6.25	12.50	25.00
❏ S-2039 [S]	Spanish Guitars	1960	6.25	12.50	25.00
❏ S-2101 [S]	Gershwin and Guitars	1961	6.25	12.50	25.00
❏ 52000 [M]	Percussion and Guitars	1960	5.00	10.00	20.00
❏ 52006 [M]	Percussion Espanol	1960	5.00	10.00	20.00
❏ 52026 [M]	Percussion Espanol, Vol. 2	1960	5.00	10.00	20.00
❏ 52039 [M]	Spanish Guitars	1960	5.00	10.00	20.00
❏ 52101 [M]	Gershwin and Guitars	1961	5.00	10.00	20.00
UNITED ARTISTS					
❏ UAL-3133 [M]	The Magnificent Seven	1960	5.00	10.00	20.00
❏ UAL-3142 [M]	Golden Instrumental Hits	1961	3.00	6.00	12.00
❏ UAL-3161 [M]	Hit Instrumentals from TV Westerns	1961	3.75	7.50	15.00
❏ UAL-3180 [M]	Solid Gold Guitar	1962	3.00	6.00	12.00
❏ UAL-3228 [M]	Midnight Dance Party	1962	3.00	6.00	12.00
❏ UAL-3240 [M]	Golden Guitar	1962	3.00	6.00	12.00
❏ UAL-3255 [M]	City Guy Goes Country	1963	3.00	6.00	12.00
❏ UAL-3256 [M]	Acapulco 1922 and The Lonely Bull	1963	3.00	6.00	12.00
❏ UAL-3263 [M]	Paradise Village	1963	3.00	6.00	12.00
❏ UAL-3276 [M]	Ciao	1963	3.00	6.00	12.00
❏ UAL-3280 [M]	Give Me the Simple Life	1963	3.00	6.00	12.00
❏ UAL-3299 [M]	Cleopatra and All That Jazz	1963	6.25	12.50	25.00
❏ UAL-3310 [M]	The Best of Al Caiola	1964	3.00	6.00	12.00
❏ UAL-3330 [M]	50 Fabulous Guitar Favorites	1964	3.00	6.00	12.00
❏ UAL-3354 [M]	50 Fabulous Italian Favorites	1964	3.00	6.00	12.00
❏ UAL-3362 [M]	On the Trail	1964	3.00	6.00	12.00
❏ UAL-3389 [M]	Tuff Guitar	1965	3.00	6.00	12.00
❏ UAL-3403 [M]	Guitar for Lovers	1965	3.00	6.00	12.00
❏ UAL-3405 [M]	Have Guitar Will Travel	1965	3.00	6.00	12.00
❏ UAL-3418 [M]	Solid Gold Guitar Goes Hawaiian	1965	3.00	6.00	12.00
❏ UAL-3435 [M]	Sounds for Spies and Private Eyes	1965	3.75	7.50	15.00
❏ UAL-3454 [M]	Tuff Guitar English Style	1966	3.00	6.00	12.00
❏ UAS-6133 [S]	The Magnificent Seven	1960	6.25	12.50	25.00
❏ UAS-6142 [S]	Golden Instrumental Hits	1961	3.75	7.50	15.00
❏ UAS-6161 [S]	Hit Instrumentals from TV Westerns	1961	5.00	10.00	20.00
❏ UAS-6180 [S]	Solid Gold Guitar	1962	3.75	7.50	15.00
❏ UAS-6228 [S]	Midnight Dance Party	1962	3.75	7.50	15.00
❏ UAS-6240 [S]	Golden Guitar	1962	3.75	7.50	15.00
❏ UAS-6255 [S]	City Guy Goes Country	1963	3.75	7.50	15.00
❏ UAS-6256 [S]	Acapulco 1922 and The Lonely Bull	1963	3.75	7.50	15.00
❏ UAS-6263 [S]	Paradise Village	1963	3.75	7.50	15.00
❏ UAS-6276 [S]	Ciao	1963	3.75	7.50	15.00
❏ UAS-6280 [S]	Give Me the Simple Life	1963	3.75	7.50	15.00
❏ UAS-6299 [S]	Cleopatra and All That Jazz	1963	7.50	15.00	30.00
❏ UAS-6310 [S]	The Best of Al Caiola	1964	3.75	7.50	15.00
❏ UAS-6330 [S]	50 Fabulous Guitar Favorites	1964	3.75	7.50	15.00
❏ UAS-6354 [S]	50 Fabulous Italian Favorites	1964	3.75	7.50	15.00
❏ UAS-6362 [S]	On the Trail	1964	3.75	7.50	15.00
❏ UAS-6389 [S]	Tuff Guitar	1965	3.75	7.50	15.00
❏ UAS-6403 [S]	Guitar for Lovers	1965	3.75	7.50	15.00
❏ UAS-6405 [S]	Have Guitar Will Travel	1965	3.75	7.50	15.00
❏ UAS-6418 [S]	Solid Gold Guitar Goes Hawaiian	1965	3.75	7.50	15.00
❏ UAS-6435 [S]	Sounds for Spies and Private Eyes	1965	5.00	10.00	20.00
❏ UAS-6454 [S]	Tuff Guitar English Style	1966	3.75	7.50	15.00
❏ UAS-6712 [S]	Let the Sunshine In	1969	2.50	5.00	10.00

CAIROS, THE
45s

Number	Title (A Side/B Side)	Yr	VG	VG+	NM
SHRINE					
❏ 111	Stop Overlooking Me/Don't Fight It	1966	300.00	600.00	1200.

CAKE, THE
45s

Number	Title (A Side/B Side)	Yr	VG	VG+	NM
DECCA					
❏ 32179	Mockingbird/Baby That's Me	1967	2.50	5.00	10.00
❏ 32212	You Can Have Him/I Know	1967	2.50	5.00	10.00
❏ 32212 [PS]	You Can Have Him/I Know	1967	7.50	15.00	30.00
❏ 32235	Fire Fly/Rainbow Wood	1967	2.50	5.00	10.00
❏ 32347	PT 280/Have You Heard the News 'Bout Miss Molly	1968	2.50	5.00	10.00

Albums

Number	Title (A Side/B Side)	Yr	VG	VG+	NM
DECCA					
❏ DL 4927 [M]	The Cake	1967	5.00	10.00	20.00
❏ DL 74927 [S]	The Cake	1967	6.25	12.50	25.00
❏ DL 75039	A Slice of the Cake	1968	6.25	12.50	25.00

CALDWELL, LOUISE HARRISON
Albums

Number	Title (A Side/B Side)	Yr	VG	VG+	NM
RECAR					
❏ 2012 [M]	All About the Beatles	1965	37.50	75.00	150.00
—Without insert					
❏ 2012 [M]	All About the Beatles	1965	50.00	100.00	200.00
—With insert					

CALE, J.J.
45s

Number	Title (A Side/B Side)	Yr	VG	VG+	NM
LIBERTY					
❏ 55840	Dick Tracy/It's a Go-Go Place	1965	3.75	7.50	15.00
❏ 55881	Outside Lookin' In/In Our Time	1966	3.75	7.50	15.00
❏ 55931	After Midnight/Slow Motion	1966	3.75	7.50	15.00
MCA					
❏ 51095	Carry On/Deep Dark Dungeon	1981	—	2.00	4.00
MERCURY					
❏ 76145	Devil in Disguise/Drifter's Wife	1982	—	—	3.00
❏ 814497-7	Losers/Reality	1983	—	—	3.00

Number	Title (A Side/B Side)	Yr	VG	VG+	NM
SHELTER					
❏ 7306	Magnolia/Crazy Mama	1971	2.00	4.00	8.00
❏ 7314	Crazy Mama/Don't Go to Strangers	1971	—	3.00	6.00
❏ 7321	After Midnight/Crying Eyes	1972	—	3.00	6.00
❏ 7326	Lies/Riding Home	1972	—	3.00	6.00
❏ 7332	Going Down/Louisiana Women	1973	—	3.00	6.00
❏ 40238	Cajun Moon/Starbound	1974	—	2.50	5.00
❏ 40290	I'll Be There/Precious Memories	1974	—	2.50	5.00
❏ 40366	I Got the Same Old Blues/Rock and Roll Records	1975	—	2.50	5.00
❏ 62002	Hey Baby/Cocaine	1976	—	3.00	6.00

Albums

Number	Title (A Side/B Side)	Yr	VG	VG+	NM
MCA					
❏ 5158	Shades	1981	2.50	5.00	10.00
❏ 37102	5	1981	2.00	4.00	8.00
—Reissue of Shelter 3163					
❏ 37103	Troubadour	1981	2.00	4.00	8.00
—Reissue of Shelter 52002					
❏ 37104	Naturally	1981	2.00	4.00	8.00
—Reissue of Shelter 52009					
❏ 37105	Really	1981	2.00	4.00	8.00
—Reissue of Shelter 52012					
❏ 37106	Okie	1981	2.00	4.00	8.00
—Reissue of Shelter 52019					
MERCURY					
❏ SRM-1-4038	Grasshopper	1982	2.50	5.00	10.00
❏ 810313-1	5	1983	—	3.00	6.00
—Reissue of MCA 37102					
❏ 810314-1	Really	1983	—	3.00	6.00
—Reissue of MCA 37105					
❏ 811152-1	#8	1983	2.50	5.00	10.00
❏ 818633-1	Special Edition	1984	2.50	5.00	10.00
❏ 822888-1	Grasshopper	1985	—	3.00	6.00
—Reissue of 4038					
SHELTER					
❏ 2107	Okie	1974	3.75	7.50	15.00
❏ 2122	Naturally	1974	3.00	6.00	12.00
—Reissue of SW-8908					
❏ 2123	Really	1974	3.00	6.00	12.00
—Reissue of 8912					
❏ 3163	5	1979	3.00	6.00	12.00
❏ SW-8908	Naturally	1971	3.75	7.50	15.00
❏ SW-8912	Really	1972	3.75	7.50	15.00
❏ 52002	Troubadour	1976	3.75	7.50	15.00
❏ 52009	Naturally	1977	2.50	5.00	10.00
—Reissue of 2122					
❏ 52012	Really	1977	2.50	5.00	10.00
—Reissue of 2123					
❏ 52015	Okie	1977	2.50	5.00	10.00
—Reissue of 2107					
SILVERTONE					
❏ 1306-1-J	Travel-Log	1990	3.00	6.00	12.00

CALE, JOHN Also see THE VELVET UNDERGROUND.
12-Inch Singles

Number	Title (A Side/B Side)	Yr	VG	VG+	NM
A&M					
❏ SP-17154 [DJ]	Dead or Alive/Honi Soit	1981	2.50	5.00	10.00

45s

Number	Title (A Side/B Side)	Yr	VG	VG+	NM
A&M					
❏ 2329	Dead or Alive/Honi Soit	1981	—	2.50	5.00
COLUMBIA					
❏ 4-45154	Cleo/Fairweather Friend	1970	2.50	5.00	10.00
❏ 4-45266	Big White Cloud/Gideon's Bible	1970	2.50	5.00	10.00
REPRISE					
❏ 1108	Legs Larry at Television Center/Days of Steam	1972	2.50	5.00	10.00
SPY/I.R.S.					
❏ 9008	Ready for War/Rosegarden Funeral of Sores	1979	—	3.00	6.00
❏ 9008 [PS]	Ready for War/Rosegarden Funeral of Sores	1979	—	3.00	6.00

Albums

Number	Title (A Side/B Side)	Yr	VG	VG+	NM
A&M					
❏ SP-4849	Honi Soit	1981	2.50	5.00	10.00
ANTILLES					
❏ AN-7063	Guts	198?	3.00	6.00	12.00
—Reissue of Island 9459					
COLUMBIA					
❏ CS 1037	Vintage Violence	1970	6.25	12.50	25.00
—Red "360 Sound" label					
❏ CS 1037	Vintage Violence	1971	3.75	7.50	15.00
—Orange label					
❏ C 30131	Church of Anthrax	1971	3.75	7.50	15.00
ISLAND					
❏ IXP-2 [DJ]	Hear Fear	1975	15.00	30.00	60.00
—Promo-only interview album					
❏ IT-8401	Caribbean Sunset	1984	2.50	5.00	10.00
❏ IT-8402	John Cale Comes Alive	1984	2.50	5.00	10.00
❏ ILPS 9301	Fear	1975	5.00	10.00	20.00
❏ ILPS 9317	Slow Dazzle	1975	3.75	7.50	15.00
❏ ILPS 9350	Helen of Troy	1975	5.00	10.00	20.00
❏ ILPS 9459	Guts	1977	5.00	10.00	20.00
OPAL/WARNER BROS.					
❏ 26024	Words for the Dying	1989	3.00	6.00	12.00
PASSPORT					
❏ PB 6019	Music for a New Society	1982	3.00	6.00	12.00
PVC					
❏ 8947	Artificial Intelligence	1985	3.75	7.50	15.00
REPRISE					
❏ MS 2079	The Academy in Peril	1972	6.25	12.50	25.00
❏ MS 2131	Paris, 1919	1973	6.25	12.50	25.00
SPY/I.R.S.					
❏ SP-004	Sabotage/Live	1980	3.75	7.50	15.00

CALIFORNIA
45s

Number	Title (A Side/B Side)	Yr	VG	VG+	NM
LAURIE					
❏ 3612	See You in September/Ivy Ivy	1974	—	2.00	4.00
❏ 3639	Song of a Thousand Voices/ Abraham, Martin and John	1976	—	2.00	4.00

Number	Title (A Side/B Side)	Yr	VG	VG+	NM
❏ 3647	Jeans On/Doo-Wop Music	1976	—	2.00	4.00
❏ 3651	I'm Just Thinking of You/Doo-Wop Music	1977	—	2.00	4.00
❏ 3695	Summer Fun Medley/Paris	1981	—	2.00	4.00

RCA

Number	Title (A Side/B Side)	Yr	VG	VG+	NM
❏ PB-11769	Everybody Needs a Little Help/I'm a Poet	1979	2.50	5.00	10.00

RSO

| ❏ 901 | I Can Hear Music/Love's Supposed to Be That Way | 1978 | 2.50 | 5.00 | 10.00 |

WARNER BROS.

| ❏ 8253 | Happy in Hollywood/Music, Music, Music | 1976 | 2.50 | 5.00 | 10.00 |
| ❏ 8307 | (Just to Let You Know) I Love You So/Happy in Hollywood | 1977 | 2.50 | 5.00 | 10.00 |

CALIFORNIA, RANDY   Also see SPIRIT.
45s
EPIC

| ❏ 10927 | Walkin' the Dog/Live for the Day | 1972 | 2.00 | 4.00 | 8.00 |

Albums
EPIC

❏ KE 31755	Kapt. Kopter & the Fabulous Twirly Birds	1972	6.25	12.50	25.00
—Yellow label					
❏ KE 31755	Kapt. Kopter & the Fabulous Twirly Birds	1973	3.00	6.00	12.00
—Orange label					

CALIFORNIA MUSIC
45s
EQUINOX

❏ PB-10120	Don't Worry Baby/Ten Years' Harmony	1974	3.75	7.50	15.00
❏ PB-10363	Why Do Fools Fall in Love/Don't Worry Baby	1975	3.75	7.50	15.00
❏ PB-10572	Jamaica Farewell/California Music	1976	3.75	7.50	15.00

CALIFORNIA POPPY PICKERS, THE
Albums
ALSHIRE

| ❏ S-5153 | Hair-Aquarius | 1969 | 7.50 | 15.00 | 30.00 |
| ❏ S-5167 | Honky Tonk Women | 1970 | 10.00 | 20.00 | 40.00 |

CALIFORNIANS, THE (1)
45s
CRAZY HORSE

| ❏ 1318 | Nausea Beast/Glass Disguise | 1969 | 2.50 | 5.00 | 10.00 |

CALIFORNIANS, THE (2)   JESSE BELVIN appears on this record.
45s
FEDERAL

| ❏ 12231 | My Angel/Heavenly Ruby | 1955 | 75.00 | 150.00 | 300.00 |

CALLENDER, BOBBY
45s
CORAL

| ❏ 62517 | You've Really Got a Hold on Me/I Can't Get Over You | 1967 | 2.50 | 5.00 | 10.00 |
| ❏ 62528 | Sweet Song of Life/Vicissitude (Or a Day at Jaffry's) | 1967 | 2.50 | 5.00 | 10.00 |

MGM

| ❏ 13965 | Rainbow/Symphonic Pictures | 1968 | 3.00 | 6.00 | 12.00 |

ROULETTE

| ❏ 4471 | Little Star/Love and Kisses | 1963 | 4.00 | 8.00 | 16.00 |

CALVANES, THE
45s
DECK

| ❏ 579 | Dreamworld/5, 7 or 9 | 1958 | 25.00 | 50.00 | 100.00 |
| ❏ 580 | My Love Song/Horror Pictures | 1958 | 25.00 | 50.00 | 100.00 |

DOOTONE

| ❏ 371 | Crazy Over You/Don't Take Your Love from Me | 1956 | 50.00 | 100.00 | 200.00 |
| ❏ 380 | One More Kiss/Florabelle | 1956 | 50.00 | 100.00 | 200.00 |

7-Inch Extended Plays
DOOTONE

| ❏ 205 | *They Call Me Fool/One More Kiss/Don't Take Your Love from Me/Crazy Over You | 1956 | 100.00 | 200.00 | 400.00 |
| ❏ 205 [PS] | Voices for Lovers | 1956 | 150.00 | 300.00 | 600.00 |

CAMBRIDGE, GODFREY
Albums
EPIC

❏ FLM 13101 [M]	Ready or Not...Here's Godfrey Cambridge	1964	5.00	10.00	20.00
❏ FLM 13102 [M]	Them Cotton Pickin' Days Is Over	1965	5.00	10.00	20.00
❏ FLM 13108 [M]	Godfrey Cambridge Toys with the World	1966	5.00	10.00	20.00
❏ FLM 13115 [M]	The Godfrey Cambridge Show Live at the Aladdin	1968	5.00	10.00	20.00
❏ FLS 15101 [S]	Ready or Not...Here's Godfrey Cambridge	1964	5.00	10.00	20.00
❏ FLS 15102 [S]	Them Cotton Pickin' Days Is Over	1965	5.00	10.00	20.00
❏ FLS 15108 [S]	Godfrey Cambridge Toys with the World	1966	5.00	10.00	20.00
❏ FLS 15115 [S]	The Godfrey Cambridge Show Live at the Aladdin	1968	5.00	10.00	20.00

CAMEL
45s
JANUS

| ❏ 262 | Another Night/Lunar Sea | 1976 | — | 3.00 | 6.00 |

Albums
ARISTA

| ❏ AB 4206 | Breathless | 1979 | 2.50 | 5.00 | 10.00 |
| ❏ AB 4254 | I Can See Your House from Here | 1980 | 2.50 | 5.00 | 10.00 |

JANUS

❏ 7009	Mirage	1974	3.00	6.00	12.00
❏ 7016	The Snow Goose	1975	3.00	6.00	12.00
❏ 7024	Moonmadness	1976	3.00	6.00	12.00
❏ 7035	Rain Dances	1977	3.00	6.00	12.00

LONDON

| ❏ 820166-1 | Pressure Points | 1987 | 2.50 | 5.00 | 10.00 |

PASSPORT

❏ PB-6008	Nude	198?	2.50	5.00	10.00
❏ PB-6013	The Single Factor	198?	2.50	5.00	10.00
❏ PB-9855	Mirage	198?	2.00	4.00	8.00
—Reissue of Janus 7009					
❏ PB-9856	The Snow Goose	198?	2.00	4.00	8.00
—Reissue of Janus 7016					
❏ PB-9857	Moonmadness	198?	2.00	4.00	8.00
—Reissue of Janus 7024					
❏ PB-9858	Rain Dances	198?	2.00	4.00	8.00
—Reissue of Janus 7035					

CAMELOTS, THE
45s
AANKO

| ❏ 1001 | Your Way/Don't Leave Me Baby | 1963 | 20.00 | 40.00 | 80.00 |
| ❏ 1004 | Sunday Kind of Love/My Imagination | 1963 | 20.00 | 40.00 | 80.00 |

CAMEO

| ❏ 334 | Don't Leave Me Baby/Love Call | 1964 | 7.50 | 15.00 | 30.00 |
| —B-side by the Ebonaires | | | | | |

COMET

| ❏ 930 | Scratch/Charge | 1962 | 3.75 | 7.50 | 15.00 |

CRIMSON

| ❏ 1001 | Don't Leave Me Baby/The Letter | 1963 | 7.50 | 15.00 | 30.00 |

DREAM

| ❏ 1001 | Your Way/I Wonder | 1967 | 2.00 | 4.00 | 8.00 |

EMBER

| ❏ 1108 | Pocahontas/Searching for My Baby | 1964 | 5.00 | 10.00 | 20.00 |

LAURIE

| ❏ 3239 | Marie/Daddy's Going Away Again | 1964 | 5.00 | 10.00 | 20.00 |
| —As "The Harps" | | | | | |

LOST-NITE

| ❏ 247 | Don't Leave Me Baby/The Letter | | — | 2.50 | 5.00 |
| —Reissue | | | | | |

NIX

| ❏ 101 | Lulu/Never Been in Love Before | 1961 | 5.00 | 10.00 | 20.00 |

RELIC

❏ 530	Chain of Broken Hearts/Rat Race	196?	2.00	4.00	8.00
—B-side by the Bootleggers					
❏ 541	Dance Girl/That's My Baby	1965	2.00	4.00	8.00
—B-side by the Suns					

TIMES SQUARE

| ❏ 32 | Dance Girl/That's My Baby | 1964 | 2.50 | 5.00 | 10.00 |
| —B-side by the Suns | | | | | |

7-Inch Extended Plays
CLIFTON/UGHA

| ❏ EP 507/1 | Music to My Ears/Daddy's Going Away//Pocahontas/Don't Leave Me Baby | 1981 | — | 2.50 | 5.00 |
| ❏ EP 507/1 [PS] | (title unknown) | 1981 | — | 2.50 | 5.00 |

CAMEO
12-Inch Singles
ATLANTA ARTISTA

| ❏ PRO 282-1 [DJ] | Talkin' Out the Side of Your Neck (same on both sides) | 1984 | 5.00 | 10.00 | 20.00 |

ATLANTA ARTISTS

❏ PRO 217-1 [DJ]	Slow Movin' (2 versions?)	1983	5.00	10.00	20.00
❏ PRO 291-1 [DJ]	Hangin' Downtown (same on both sides)	1984	2.50	5.00	10.00
❏ PRO 543-1 [DJ]	She's Mine (2 versions)	1986	2.50	5.00	10.00
❏ PRO 839-1 [DJ]	I Want It Now (same on both sides)	1990	3.75	7.50	15.00
❏ PRO 868-1 [DJ]	Close Quarters (2 versions) (same on both sides)	1990	3.00	6.00	12.00
❏ 812053-1	Style (5:08) (5:19)	1983	3.00	6.00	12.00
❏ 818384-1	She's Strange (Club Mix 6:42) (LP Version 7:21)	1984	2.50	5.00	10.00
❏ 870587-1	You Make Me Work (3 versions)/DKWIG	1988	2.00	4.00	8.00
❏ 872315-1	Skin I'm In (3 versions)/Honey	1988	2.50	5.00	10.00
❏ 874051-1	Pretty Girls (12" Remix) (12" Dub) (7" Remix) (7" Dub)	1989	2.50	5.00	10.00
❏ 875589-1	I Want It Now (12" Edit) (Rough Mix) (Then Dub) (Now Dub)	1990	2.50	5.00	10.00
❏ 878199-1	Close Quarters (4 versions)/Honey	1990	2.00	4.00	8.00
❏ 880038-1	Talkin' Out the Side of Your Neck/She's Strange (Rap Version)	1984	3.75	7.50	15.00
❏ 880744-1	Attack Me with Your Love (Extended Version 6:31) (7" Dance Remix 4:15)	1985	3.00	6.00	12.00
❏ 884010-1	Single Life (6:30)/I've Got Your Image	1985	2.50	5.00	10.00
❏ 884270-1	A Good-Bye (5:41)/Little Boys-Dangerous Toys	1985	3.00	6.00	12.00
❏ 884933-1	Word Up (3 versions)/Urban Warrior	1986	2.50	5.00	10.00
❏ 888193-1	Candy/She's Strange	1986	2.50	5.00	10.00
❏ 888385-1	Back and Forth (12" Club Remix 6:30) (Dub Mix 6:01) (7" Version 3:47)/You Can Have the World	1987	2.50	5.00	10.00

CHOCOLATE CITY

❏ CCD 20005 [DJ]	Rigor Mortis (Disco Mix 6:14)/(Mono Mix 3:12)	1977	10.00	20.00	40.00
❏ CCD 20007 [DJ]	Post Mortem/(B-side blank)	1977	6.25	12.50	25.00
❏ CCD 20013 [DJ]	It's Serious/(B-side blank)	1978	7.50	15.00	30.00
❏ CCD 20014 [DJ]	Find My Way/Rigor Mortis//(B-side blank)	1978	7.50	15.00	30.00
❏ CCD 20016 [DJ]	I Just Want to Be/(B-side blank)	1979	7.50	15.00	30.00
❏ CCD 20020 [DJ]	We're Goin' Out Tonight (4:41)/(B-side blank)	1980	6.25	12.50	25.00
❏ CCD 20022	Shake Your Pants (5:59) (4:01)	1980	5.00	10.00	20.00
❏ CCD 20028	Keep It Hot/Your Love Takes Me Out	1980	5.00	10.00	20.00
❏ CCD 20034	Don't Be So Cool (4:23)/I Never Knew (4:34)	1981	5.00	10.00	20.00
❏ CCD 20035 [DJ]	Just Be Yourself (4:20) (same on both sides)	1982	5.00	10.00	20.00
❏ CCD 20037	Alligator Woman//(B-side blank?)	1982	3.75	7.50	15.00
❏ CCD 20038	Flirt (2 versions)	1982	5.00	10.00	20.00
❏ CCD 20039	Flirt (3 versions)	1982	5.00	10.00	20.00

REPRISE

❏ PRO-A-5224 [DJ]	Emotional Violence (Edit) (LP Version)	1992	5.00	10.00	20.00
❏ PRO-A-5625 [DJ]	Raw But Tasty (Rap Remix) (Funk Mix) (Raw Remix) (Dub) (Ronnie's Mix)	1992	3.75	7.50	15.00
❏ 40392	Money (Reese Revamp Mix) (Reese Hardcore Instrumental) (Hardsell Mix)/Front Street	1992	7.50	15.00	30.00

45s
ATLANTA ARTISTS

❏ PRO 272-7 [DJ]	She's Strange (Rap)/(Edit)	1984	2.50	5.00	10.00
❏ 812054-7	Style/Enjoy Your Life	1983	—	—	3.00
❏ 812472-7	Can't Help Falling in Love/For You	1983	—	—	3.00
❏ 814077-7	Slow Movin'/For You	1983	—	—	3.00
❏ 818384-7	She's Strange/Tribute to Bob Marley	1984	—	—	3.00
❏ 818870-7	Talkin' Out the Side of Your Neck/Leve-Toi	1984	—	—	3.00
❏ 870587-7	You Make Me Work/DKWIG	1988	—	—	3.00
❏ 870587-7 [PS]	You Make Me Work/DKWIG	1988	—	—	3.00

Number	Title (A Side/B Side)	Yr	VG	VG+	NM
☐ 872314-7	Skin I'm In/Honey	1988	—	—	3.00
☐ 872314-7 [PS]	Skin I'm In/Honey	1988	—	—	3.00
☐ 872918-7	Single Life/She's Strange	1989	—	—	3.00
—Reissue					
☐ 874050-7	Pretty Girls/Pretty Girls (Dub)	1989	—	—	3.00
☐ 874050-7 [PS]	Pretty Girls/Pretty Girls (Dub)	1989	—	—	3.00
☐ 875588-7	I Want It Now/DKWIG	1990	—	—	3.00
☐ 878198-7	Close Quarters/Honey	1990	—	—	3.00
☐ 880169-7	Hangin' Downtown/Cameo's Dance	1984	—	—	3.00
☐ 880744-7	Attack Me With Your Love/Love You Anyway	1985	—	—	3.00
☐ 884010-7	Single Life/I've Got Your Image	1985	—	—	3.00
☐ 884270-7	A Good-Bye/Little Boys-Dangerous Toys	1985	—	—	3.00
☐ 884933-7	Word Up/Urban Warrior	1986	—	—	3.00
☐ 884933-7 [PS]	Word Up/Urban Warrior	1986	—	—	3.00
☐ 888193-7	Candy/She's Strange	1986	—	—	3.00
☐ 888193-7 [PS]	Candy/She's Strange	1986	—	—	3.00
☐ 888385-7	Back and Forth/You Can Have the World	1987	—	—	3.00
☐ 888385-7 [PS]	Back and Forth/You Can Have the World	1987	—	—	3.00
☐ 888711-7	Don't Be Lonely/I've Got Your Image	1987	—	—	3.00
☐ 888876-7	She's Mine/I've Got Your Image	1987	—	—	3.00
CHOCOLATE CITY					
☐ 001	Find My Way/Good Company	1975	—	2.50	5.00
☐ 005	Rigor Mortis/Stand By My Side	1976	—	2.50	5.00
☐ 008	Find My Way/Rigor Mortis	1977	—	2.00	4.00
☐ 010	Post Mortem/Smile	1977	—	2.00	4.00
☐ 011	Funk Funk/Good Time	1977	—	2.00	4.00
☐ 013	It's Serious/Inflation	1978	—	2.00	4.00
☐ 014	It's Over/Inflation	1978	—	2.00	4.00
☐ 016	Insane/I Want You	1978	—	2.00	4.00
☐ 018	Give Love a Chance/Two of Us	1979	—	2.00	4.00
☐ 019	I Just Want to Be/The Rock	1979	—	2.00	4.00
☐ 3202	Sparkle/Macho	1979	—	2.00	4.00
☐ 3206	We're Goin' Out Tonight/One the One	1980	—	2.00	4.00
☐ 3210	Shake Your Pants/I Came for You	1980	—	2.00	4.00
☐ 3219	Keep It Hot/I Came for You	1980	—	2.00	4.00
☐ 3222	Feel Me/Is This the Way	1981	—	2.00	4.00
☐ 3225	Freaky Dancin'/Better Days	1981	—	2.00	4.00
☐ 3227	I Like It/The Sound Table	1981	—	2.00	4.00
☐ 3231	Just Be Yourself/Use It or Lose It	1982	—	2.00	4.00
☐ 3233	Flirt/Owe It All to You	1982	—	2.00	4.00
☐ 3235	Alligator Woman/Soul Away	1982	—	2.00	4.00
Albums					
ATLANTA ARTISTS					
☐ 811072-1	Style	1983	2.50	5.00	10.00
☐ 814984-1	She's Strange	1984	2.50	5.00	10.00
☐ 824546-1	Single Life	1985	2.50	5.00	10.00
☐ 830265-1	Word Up!	1986	2.50	5.00	10.00
☐ 836002-1	Machismo	1988	2.50	5.00	10.00
☐ 846297-1	Real Men..Wear Black	1990	3.00	6.00	12.00
CHOCOLATE CITY					
☐ CCLP 2003	Cardiac Arrest	1977	3.00	6.00	12.00
☐ CCLP 2004	We All Know Who We Are	1978	3.00	6.00	12.00
☐ CCLP 2006	Ugly Ego	1978	3.00	6.00	12.00
☐ CCLP 2008	Secret Omen	1979	3.00	6.00	12.00
☐ CCLP 2011	Cameosis	1980	3.00	6.00	12.00
☐ CCLP 2016	Feel Me	1980	3.00	6.00	12.00
☐ CCLP 2019	Knights of the Sound Table	1981	3.00	6.00	12.00
☐ CCLP 2021	Alligator Woman	1982	3.00	6.00	12.00

CAMEOS, THE
45s

Number	Title (A Side/B Side)	Yr	VG	VG+	NM
CAMEO					
☐ 123	Merry Christmas/New Year's Eve	1957	37.50	75.00	150.00
☐ 123	Merry Christmas/New Year's Eve	197?	2.50	5.00	10.00
—Reproduction of the original 1957 release					
DEAN					
☐ 504	Lost Lover/Wait Up	1961	37.50	75.00	150.00
JOHNSON					
☐ 108	Lost Lover/Wait Up	1961	20.00	40.00	80.00
MATADOR					
☐ 1813	Never Before/Canadian Sunset	1963	6.25	12.50	25.00

CAMERON, JIMMY AND VELLA
45s

Number	Title (A Side/B Side)	Yr	VG	VG+	NM
REPRISE					
☐ 0483	Lovin' You Is Such a Groove/I Know a Place	1966	7.50	15.00	30.00
UNLIMITED GOLD					
☐ 1422	Mornin' Time/There Is No Other Love	1980	—	2.00	4.00

CAMP, THE
45s

Number	Title (A Side/B Side)	Yr	VG	VG+	NM
SCEPTER					
☐ 12159	Marching/Long Long Trail	1966	20.00	40.00	80.00

CAMPANELLA, DAVID, AND THE DELLCHORDS
45s

Number	Title (A Side/B Side)	Yr	VG	VG+	NM
KANE					
☐ 25593	Over the Rainbow/Everything's That Way	1959	15.00	30.00	60.00

CAMPBELL, CHOKER
45s

Number	Title (A Side/B Side)	Yr	VG	VG+	NM
APT					
☐ 25011	Walk Awhile/Walking on Thin-Soled Shoes	1958	15.00	30.00	60.00
ATLANTIC					
☐ 1014	Last Call for Whiskey/How Could You Do This	1953	10.00	20.00	40.00
☐ 1038	Have You Seen My Baby/Jackie Mambo	1954	10.00	20.00	40.00
FORTUNE					
☐ 808	Frankie and Johnny/Rocking and Jumping	1953	15.00	30.00	60.00
MOTOWN					
☐ 1072	Come See About Me/Pride and Joy	1964	6.25	12.50	25.00
Albums					
MOTOWN					
☐ M-620 [M]	Hits of the Sixties	1964	25.00	50.00	100.00
☐ MS-620 [S]	Hits of the Sixties	1964	37.50	75.00	150.00

Number	Title (A Side/B Side)	Yr	VG	VG+	NM

CAMPBELL, EDDIE Also see EDDIE AND ERNIE.
45s

Number	Title (A Side/B Side)	Yr	VG	VG+	NM
ARTCO					
☐ 45-103	Contagious Love/Why Do You Treat Me Like You Do	1967	300.00	600.00	1200.

CAMPBELL, GLEN Also see THE BEACH BOYS; THE CHAMPS; GEE CEES.

Number	Title (A Side/B Side)	Yr	VG	VG+	NM
ATLANTIC AMERICA					
☐ 99525	Call Home/Sweet 16	1986	—	—	3.00
☐ 99559	Cowpoke/Rag Doll	1986	—	—	3.00
☐ 99600	It's Just a Matter of Time/Gene Autry, My Hero	1985	—	—	3.00
☐ 99600 [PS]	It's Just a Matter of Time/Gene Autry, My Hero	1985	—	2.00	4.00
☐ 99647	(Love Always) Letter to Home/An American Trilogy	1985	—	—	3.00
☐ 99691	A Lady Like You/Tennessee	1984	—	—	3.00
☐ 99768	Faithless Love/Scene of the Crime	1984	—	—	3.00
☐ 99893	On the Wings of My Victory/A Few Good Men	1983	—	—	3.00
☐ 99930	I Love How You Love Me/Hang On Baby (Ease My Mind)	1983	—	—	3.00
☐ 99967	Old Home Town/Heartache #3	1982	—	2.00	4.00
☐ 99967 [PS]	Old Home Town/Heartache #3	1982	—	2.00	4.00
CAPEHART					
☐ 5008	Death Valley/Nothin' Better Than a Pretty Woman	1961	6.25	12.50	25.00
CAPITOL					
☐ 2015	By the Time I Get to Phoenix/ You've Still Got a Place in My Heart	1967	—	3.50	7.00
☐ 2076	Hey Little One/My Baby's Gone	1968	—	3.50	7.00
☐ 2076 [PS]	Hey Little One/My Baby's Gone	1968	3.00	6.00	12.00
☐ 2146	I Wanna Live/That's All That Matters	1968	—	3.50	7.00
☐ 2224	Dreams of the Everyday Housewife/Kelli Ho-Down	1968	—	3.50	7.00
☐ 2302	Wichita Lineman/Fate of Man	1968	—	3.00	6.00
☐ 2336	Christmas Is for Children/There's No Place Like Home	1968	2.00	4.00	8.00
☐ 2428	Galveston/How Come Every Time I Itch I Wind Up Scratchin' You	1969	—	3.00	6.00
☐ 2494	Where's the Playground Susie/Arkansas	1969	—	3.00	6.00
☐ 2573	True Grit/Hava Nagila	1969	—	3.00	6.00
☐ 2659	Try a Little Kindness/Lonely My Lonely Friend	1969	—	3.00	6.00
☐ 2718	Honey Come Back/Where Do You Go	1970	—	3.00	6.00
☐ 2787	Oh Happy Day/Someone Above	1970	—	3.00	6.00
☐ 2843	Everything a Man Could Ever Need/Norwood (Me and My Guitar)	1970	—	3.00	6.00
☐ 2905	It's Only Make Believe/ Pave Your Way Into Tomorrow	1970	—	3.00	6.00
☐ 3062	Dream Baby (How Long Must I Dream)/ Here and Now	1971	—	3.00	6.00
☐ 3123	The Last Time I Saw Her/Bach Talk	1971	—	3.00	6.00
☐ 3254	Oklahoma Sunday Morning/ Everybody's Got to Go There Sometime	1972	—	3.00	6.00
☐ 3305	Manhattan, Kansas/Wayfaring Stranger	1972	—	3.00	6.00
☐ 3382	We All Pull the Load/Wherefore and Why	1972	—	3.50	7.00
☐ 3411	I Will Never Pass This Way Again/ We All Pull the Load	1972	—	3.00	6.00
☐ 3483	One Last Time/All My Tomorrows	1972	—	3.00	6.00
☐ 3509	I Believe in Christmas/New Snow on the Roof	1972	—	3.00	6.00
☐ 3548	I Knew Jesus (Before He Was a Star)/ On This Road	1973	—	2.50	5.00
☐ 3669	Bring Back My Yesterday/Beautiful Love Song	1973	—	2.50	5.00
☐ 3735	Wherefore and Why/Give Me Back That Old Familiar Feeling	1973	—	2.50	5.00
☐ 3808	Houston (I'm Coming to See You)/Honestly Love	1973	—	2.50	5.00
☐ 3926	Bonaparte's Retreat/Too Many Mornings	1974	—	2.50	5.00
☐ 3988	It's a Sin When You Love Somebody/If I Were Loving You	1974	—	2.50	5.00
☐ 4095	Rhinestone Cowboy/Lovelight	1975	—	2.00	4.00
☐ 4155	Country Boy (You Got Your Feet in L.A.)/ Record Collector's Dream	1975	—	2.00	4.00
☐ 4245	Then You Can Tell Me Goodbye-Don't Pull Your Love/I Miss You Tonight	1976	—	2.00	4.00
☐ 4288	See You on Sunday/Bloodline	1976	—	2.00	4.00
☐ 4376	Southern Nights/William Tell Overture	1976	—	2.00	4.00
☐ 4445	Sunflower/How High Did We Go	1977	—	2.00	4.00
☐ 4515	God Must Have Blessed America/Amazing Grace	1977	—	2.00	4.00
☐ 4584	Another Fine Mess/Can You Fool	1978	—	2.00	4.00
☐ 4638	Can You Fool/Let's All Sing a Song About It	1978	—	2.00	4.00
☐ 4682	I'm Gonna Love You/Love Takes You Higher	1979	—	2.00	4.00
☐ 4715	California/Never Tell You No Lies	1979	—	2.00	4.00
☐ 4769	Hound Dog Man/Tennessee Home	1979	—	2.00	4.00
☐ 4783	Too Late to Worry — Too Blue to Cry/How Do I Tell My Heart Not to Break	1962	3.75	7.50	15.00
☐ 4799	My Prayer/Don't Lose Me in the Confusion	1979	—	2.00	4.00
☐ 4856	Long Black Limousine/Here I Am	1962	2.50	5.00	10.00
☐ 4856 [PS]	Long Black Limousine/Here I Am	1962	5.00	10.00	20.00
☐ 4865	Somethin' 'Bout You Baby I Like/ Late Night Confession	1980	—	2.00	4.00
—With Rita Coolidge					
☐ 4867	Kentucky Means Paradise/Truck Driving Man	1962	3.75	7.50	15.00
—As "The Green River Boys Featuring Glen Campbell"					
☐ 4909	Hollywood Smiles/Hooked on Love	1980	—	2.00	4.00
☐ 4925	Oh My Darling/Prima Donna	1963	3.00	6.00	12.00
☐ 4959	I Don't Want to Know Your Name/Daisy a Day	1981	—	2.00	4.00
☐ 4986	Why Don't We Just Sleep on It Tonight/ It's Your World	1981	—	2.00	4.00
—With Tanya Tucker					
☐ 4990	Divorce Me C.O.D./Dark as a Dungeon	1963	3.00	6.00	12.00
☐ 5037	As Far As I'm Concerned/Same Old Places	1963	3.00	6.00	12.00
☐ 5172	Let Me Tell You About Mary/ Through the Eyes of a Child	1964	3.00	6.00	12.00
☐ 5279	Summer, Winter, Spring and Fall/ Heartaches Can Be Fun	1964	3.00	6.00	12.00
☐ 5279 [PS]	Summer, Winter, Spring and Fall/ Heartaches Can Be Fun	1964	6.25	12.50	25.00
☐ 5360	It's a Woman's World/Tomorrow Never Comes	1965	3.00	6.00	12.00

Number	Title (A Side/B Side)	Yr	VG	VG+	NM
❏ 5441	Guess I'm Dumb/That's All Right	1965	30.00	60.00	120.00
—A Brian Wilson "Pet Sounds"-like production					
❏ 5504	The Universal Soldier/Spanish Shades	1965	2.50	5.00	10.00
❏ 5545	Less of Me/Private John Q	1965	2.50	5.00	10.00
❏ 5638	Can't You See I'm Tryin'/Satisfied Mind	1966	2.50	5.00	10.00
❏ 5773	Burning Bridges/Only the Lonely	1966	2.50	5.00	10.00
❏ 5854	I Gotta Have My Baby Back/Just to Satisfy You	1967	2.50	5.00	10.00
❏ 5939	Gentle on My Mind/Just Another Man	1967	2.00	4.00	8.00
—Orange and yellow swirl, without "A Subsidiary Of"... in perimeter label print					
❏ 5939	Gentle on My Mind/Just Another Man	1968	—	3.00	6.00
—Orange and yellow swirl label with "A Subsidiary Of" in perimeter print					
❏ 7PRO-79107	On a Good Night (same on both sides)	1990	—	3.00	6.00
—Vinyl is promo only					
❏ 7PRO-79966	Walkin' in the Sun (same on both sides)	1990	—	3.00	6.00
—Vinyl is promo only					
CAPITOL CREATIVE PRODUCTS					
❏ 54	Homeward Bound/(Sittin' On) The Dock of the Bay//Mary in the Morning	1969	2.00	4.00	8.00
CAPITOL NASHVILLE					
❏ 7PRO-79279	Somebody's Leavin' (same on both sides)	1990	—	3.00	6.00
—Vinyl is promo only					
❏ 7PRO-79494	Unconditional Love (same on both sides)	1991	—	3.00	6.00
—Vinyl is promo only					
CENECO					
❏ 1324	Dreams for Sale/I've Got to Win	1961	6.25	12.50	25.00
❏ 1356	I Wonder/You, You, You	1961	5.00	10.00	20.00
COMPLEAT					
❏ 113	Letting Go/(Instrumental)	1983	—	2.00	4.00
CREST					
❏ 1087	Turn Around, Look at Me/Brenda	1961	5.00	10.00	20.00
❏ 1096	The Miracle of Love/Once More	1962	3.75	7.50	15.00
EVEREST					
❏ 2500	Delight, Arkansas/Walk Right In	1969	—	3.00	6.00
LIBERTY					
❏ S7-18214	Blue Christmas/Feliz Navidad	1994	—	2.50	5.00
—B-side on EMI Latin by Jose Feliciano; red vinyl					
MCA					
❏ 41323	Dream Lover/Bronco	1980	—	2.00	4.00
—A-side with Tanya Tucker					
❏ 53108	The Hand That Rocks the Cradle/Arkansas	1987	—	—	3.00
—A-side with Steve Wariner					
❏ 53172	Still Within the Sound of My Voice/In My Life	1987	—	—	3.00
❏ 53218	I Have You/I'm a One Woman Man	1987	—	—	3.00
❏ 53245	I Remember You/For Sure, For Certain, Forever, For Always	1988	—	—	3.00
❏ 53426	Heart of the Matter/Light Years	1988	—	—	3.00
❏ 53493	More Than Enough/Our Movie	1989	—	—	3.00
MIRAGE					
❏ 3845	I Love My Truck/Melody's Melody	1981	—	2.00	4.00
STARDAY					
❏ 853	For the Love of a Woman/Smokey Blue Eyes	1968	2.00	4.00	8.00
UNIVERSAL					
❏ UVL-66024	She's Gone, Gone, Gone/William Tell Overture	1989	—	2.00	4.00
WARNER BROS.					
❏ 49609	Any Which Way You Can/Medley from Any Which Way You Can	1980	—	2.00	4.00
—B-side by Texas Opera Company					

Albums

ATLANTIC AMERICA

Number	Title (A Side/B Side)	Yr	VG	VG+	NM
❏ 90016	Old Home Town	1983	2.00	4.00	8.00
❏ 90164	Letter to Home	1984	2.00	4.00	8.00
❏ 90483	It's Just a Matter of Time	1985	2.00	4.00	8.00
CAPITOL					
❏ SM-103	Wichita Lineman	1977	2.00	4.00	8.00
—Reissue with new prefix					
❏ ST-103	Wichita Lineman	1968	3.75	7.50	15.00
❏ ST-8-0103	Wichita Lineman	1968	5.00	10.00	20.00
—Capitol Record Club edition					
❏ ST-210	Galveston	1969	3.75	7.50	15.00
❏ STBO-268	Glen Campbell — "Live"	1969	5.00	10.00	20.00
❏ SM-389	Try a Little Kindness	1977	2.00	4.00	8.00
—Reissue with new prefix					
❏ SW-389	Try a Little Kindness	1970	3.00	6.00	12.00
❏ SW-443	Oh Happy Day	1970	3.00	6.00	12.00
❏ SW-493	The Glen Campbell Goodtime Album	1970	3.00	6.00	12.00
❏ SM-733	The Last Time I Saw Her	1977	2.00	4.00	8.00
—Reissue with new prefix					
❏ SW-733	The Last Time I Saw Her	1971	3.00	6.00	12.00
❏ SW-752	Glen Campbell's Greatest Hits	1971	3.00	6.00	12.00
❏ ST 1810 [S]	Big Bluegrass Special	1962	25.00	50.00	100.00
—As "The Green River Boys Featuring Glen Campbell"					
❏ T 1810 [M]	Big Bluegrass Special	1962	20.00	40.00	80.00
—As "The Green River Boys Featuring Glen Campbell"					
❏ ST 1881 [S]	Too Late to Worry, Too Blue to Cry	1963	6.25	12.50	25.00
❏ T 1881 [M]	Too Late to Worry, Too Blue to Cry	1963	5.00	10.00	20.00
❏ ST 2023 [S]	The Astounding 12-String Guitar of Glen Campbell	1964	5.00	10.00	20.00
❏ T 2023 [M]	The Astounding 12-String Guitar of Glen Campbell	1964	3.75	7.50	15.00
❏ ST 2392 [S]	The Big Bad Rock Guitar of Glen Campbell	1965	5.00	10.00	20.00
❏ T 2392 [M]	The Big Bad Rock Guitar of Glen Campbell	1965	3.75	7.50	15.00
❏ ST 2679 [S]	Burning Bridges	1967	3.75	7.50	15.00
❏ T 2679 [M]	Burning Bridges	1967	3.75	7.50	15.00
❏ ST 2809 [S]	Gentle on My Mind	1967	3.75	7.50	15.00
❏ T 2809 [M]	Gentle on My Mind	1967	3.75	7.50	15.00
❏ ST 2851 [S]	By the Time I Get to Phoenix	1967	3.75	7.50	15.00
❏ T 2851 [M]	By the Time I Get to Phoenix	1967	3.75	7.50	15.00
❏ ST 2878 [S]	Hey, Little One	1968	3.75	7.50	15.00
❏ T 2878 [M]	Hey, Little One	1968	6.25	12.50	25.00
❏ ST 2907	A New Place in the Sun	1968	3.75	7.50	15.00
❏ ST 2978	That Christmas Feeling	1968	3.75	7.50	15.00
❏ SW-11117	Glen Travis Campbell	1972	2.50	5.00	10.00
❏ SW-11185	I Knew Jesus (Before He Was a Star)	1973	2.50	5.00	10.00
❏ SW-11253	I Remember Hank Williams	1973	2.50	5.00	10.00
❏ SW-11293	Houston (I'm Comin' to See You)	1974	2.50	5.00	10.00
❏ SW-11336	Reunion (The Songs of Jimmy Webb)	1974	2.50	5.00	10.00

Number	Title (A Side/B Side)	Yr	VG	VG+	NM
❏ SM-11407	Arkansas	1977	2.00	4.00	8.00
—Reissue with new prefix					
❏ SW-11407	Arkansas	1975	2.50	5.00	10.00
❏ SW-11430	Rhinestone Cowboy	1975	2.50	5.00	10.00
❏ SW-11516	Bloodline	1976	2.50	5.00	10.00
❏ ST-11577	The Best of Glen Campbell	1976	2.50	5.00	10.00
❏ SO-11601	Southern Nights	1977	2.50	5.00	10.00
❏ SWBC-11707 [(2)]	Live at the Royal Festival Hall	1977	3.00	6.00	12.00
❏ SW-11722	Basic	1978	2.50	5.00	10.00
❏ SM-11960	Gentle on My Mind	1979	2.00	4.00	8.00
—Reissue of 2809					
❏ SOO-12008	Highwayman	1979	2.50	5.00	10.00
❏ SM-12040	By the Time I Get to Phoenix	1979	2.00	4.00	8.00
—Reissue of 2851					
❏ SOO-12075	Somethin' 'Bout You Baby I Like	1980	2.50	5.00	10.00
❏ SOO-12124	It's the World Gone Crazy	1981	2.50	5.00	10.00
❏ SN-16029	Rhinestone Cowboy	1980	—	3.00	6.00
—Budget-line reissue					
❏ SN-16030	Southern Nights	1980	—	3.00	6.00
—Budget-line reissue					
❏ SN-16031	Glen Travis Campbell	1980	—	3.00	6.00
—Budget-line reissue					
❏ SN-16160	Wichita Lineman	1981	—	3.00	6.00
—Budget-line reissue					
❏ SN-16258	Hey Little Girl	1982	—	3.00	6.00
—Budget-line reissue					
❏ SN-16259	Galveston	1982	—	3.00	6.00
—Budget-line reissue					
❏ SN-16297	Glen Campbell's Greatest Hits	1984	—	3.00	6.00
—Budget-line reissue					
❏ SN-16335	The Best of Glen Campbell	1984	—	3.00	6.00
—Budget-line reissue					
❏ SWAK-93157	Limited Collector's Edition	1970	5.00	10.00	20.00
—Capitol Record Club exclusive; includes tour program					
LONGINES SYMPHONETTE					
❏ LS-218 [(5)]	Glen Campbell's Golden Favorites	1972	6.25	12.50	25.00
MCA					
❏ 42009	Still Within the Sound of My Voice	1987	2.00	4.00	8.00
❏ 42210	Light Years	1988	2.00	4.00	8.00
PAIR					
❏ PDL2-1089 [(2)]	All-Time Favorites	1986	3.00	6.00	12.00
PICKWICK					
❏ PTP-2048 [(2)]	Only the Lonely	197?	2.50	5.00	10.00
❏ PC-3052 [M]	The 12 String Guitar of Glen Campbell	196?	3.00	6.00	12.00
❏ SPC-3052 [S]	The 12 String Guitar of Glen Campbell	196?	2.50	5.00	10.00
❏ SPC-3134	A Satisfied Mind	197?	2.00	4.00	8.00
❏ SPC-3274	The Glen Campbell Album	197?	2.00	4.00	8.00
❏ SPC-3346	I'll Paint You a Song	197?	2.00	4.00	8.00
STARDAY					
❏ SLP-424	Country Soul	1968	3.75	7.50	15.00
❏ SLP-437	Country Music Star #1	1969	3.75	7.50	15.00
SURREY					
❏ S 1007 [M]	Country Shindig	196?	3.00	6.00	12.00

CAMPBELL, GLEN, AND BOBBIE GENTRY Also see each artist's individual listings.

45s

CAPITOL

Number	Title (A Side/B Side)	Yr	VG	VG+	NM
❏ 2314	Less of Me/Morning Glory	1968	—	3.00	6.00
❏ 2387	Let It Be Me/Little Green Apples	1969	—	3.00	6.00
❏ 2745	All I Have to Do Is Dream/Less of Me	1970	—	3.00	6.00

Albums

CAPITOL

Number	Title (A Side/B Side)	Yr	VG	VG+	NM
❏ ST 2928	Bobbie Gentry & Glen Campbell	1968	3.75	7.50	15.00
❏ ST 8-2928	Bobbie Gentry & Glen Campbell	1968	5.00	10.00	20.00
—Capitol Record Club edition					

CAMPBELL, JO ANN

45s

ABC-PARAMOUNT

Number	Title (A Side/B Side)	Yr	VG	VG+	NM
❏ 10134 [M]	A Kookie Little Paradise/Bobby, Bobby, Bobby	1960	6.25	12.50	25.00
❏ S-10134 [S]	A Kookie Little Paradise/Bobby, Bobby, Bobby	1960	12.50	25.00	50.00
❏ 10172	But Maybe This Year/Crazy Daisy	1960	5.00	10.00	20.00
❏ 10200	Motorcycle Michael/Puka Puka Pants	1961	5.00	10.00	20.00
❏ 10224	Eddie My Love/It Wasn't Right	1961	5.00	10.00	20.00
❏ 10258	Mama Don't Wait/Duane	1961	5.00	10.00	20.00
❏ 10300	I Changed My Mind Jack/You Made Me Love You	1962	5.00	10.00	20.00
❏ 10335	Amateur Night/I Wish It Would Rain All Summer	1962	5.00	10.00	20.00
CAMEO					
❏ 223	I'm the Girl from Wolverton Mountain/Sloppy Joe	1962	5.00	10.00	20.00
❏ 237	Let Me Do It My Way/Mr. Fix-It Man	1962	5.00	10.00	20.00
❏ 249	Mother Please/Waitin' for Love	1963	5.00	10.00	20.00
EL DORADO					
❏ 504	Forever Young/Come On Baby	1957	10.00	20.00	40.00
❏ 509	Funny Thing/I Can't Give You Anything But Love	1957	10.00	20.00	40.00
GONE					
❏ 5014	Wait a Minute/I'm in Love with You	1957	7.50	15.00	30.00
❏ 5014	Wait a Minute/It's True	1957	10.00	20.00	40.00
❏ 5021	You're Driving Me Mad/Rock and Roll Love	1958	7.50	15.00	30.00
❏ 5027	Whassa Matter with You/You-Oo	1958	7.50	15.00	30.00
❏ 5037	I Really, Really Love You/I'm Nobody's Baby Now	1958	7.50	15.00	30.00
❏ 5049	Happy New Year Baby/Tall Boy	1958	7.50	15.00	30.00
❏ 5055	Mama/Nervous	1959	7.50	15.00	30.00
❏ 5068	Beach Comber/I Ain't Got No Steady Date	1959	7.50	15.00	30.00
POINT					
❏ 4	I'm Coming Home Late Tonight/Wherever You Go	1956	10.00	20.00	40.00
RORI					
❏ 711	Jim Dandy/Five Minutes More	1962	5.00	10.00	20.00

Albums

ABC-PARAMOUNT

Number	Title (A Side/B Side)	Yr	VG	VG+	NM
❏ 393 [M]	Twistin' and Listenin'	1962	20.00	40.00	80.00
❏ S-393 [S]	Twistin' and Listenin'	1962	25.00	50.00	100.00
CAMEO					
❏ C-1026 [M]	All the Hits of Jo Ann Campbell	1962	12.50	25.00	50.00
❏ SC-1026 [S]	All the Hits of Jo Ann Campbell	1962	25.00	50.00	100.00

Number	Title (A Side/B Side)	Yr	VG	VG+	NM
CORONET					
❑ CX-199 [M]	Starring Jo Ann Campbell	196?	5.00	10.00	20.00
❑ CXS-199 [R]	Starring Jo Ann Campbell	196?	3.00	6.00	12.00
END					
❑ LP-306 [M]	I'm Nobody's Baby	1959	37.50	75.00	150.00

CAMPBELL, JOHN
45s
HIT
| ❑ 64 | If You Wanna Be Happy/Ain't That a Shame | 1963 | 2.00 | 4.00 | 8.00 |
—B-side by the Chellows

CAMPERS, THE Includes SONNY CURTIS and THE CRICKETS (1).
45s
PARKWAY
| ❑ 974 | The Ballad of Batman/The Batmobile | 1966 | 7.50 | 15.00 | 30.00 |
| ❑ 974 | The Ballad of Batman/The Batmobile | 1966 | 8.75 | 17.50 | 35.00 |
—Original label credit: "The Camps"

CAMPI, RAY
45s
COLPIX
❑ 166	French Fries/Hear What I Wanna Hear	1960	3.75	7.50	15.00
D					
❑ 1047	The Ballad of Donna and Peggy Sue/A Man I Met (Tribute to The Big Bopper)	1959	10.00	20.00	40.00
DOMINO					
❑ 700	My Screamin' Screamin' Meemie/With You	1958	7.50	15.00	30.00
DOT					
❑ 15617	It Ain't Me/Give That Love to Me	1957	15.00	30.00	60.00
ROLLIN' ROCK					
❑ 006	Eager Boy/Dobroggie	1978	—	2.50	5.00
❑ 008	Tore Up/If It's All the Same to You	1978	—	2.50	5.00
❑ 014	Sixteen Chicks/Pan American Boogie	1979	—	2.50	5.00
❑ 019	My Baby Left Me/A Li'l Bit of Heartache	1979	—	2.50	5.00
❑ 027	Wrong, Wrong, Wrong/Booze It	1980	—	2.00	4.00
❑ 029	Scrumptious Baby/I Didn't Mean to Be Mean	1980	—	2.00	4.00
❑ 031	Merle's Boogie-Woogie-Missouri/Sweet Temptation Guitar Rag	1980	—	2.00	4.00
—With Merle Travis					
❑ 038	Rockin' at the Ritz/Quit Your Triplin'	1981	—	2.00	4.00
❑ 044	Rattlin' Daddy/Wild One	1981	—	2.00	4.00
❑ 046	Texas Sands/How Long Can You Feel	1982	—	2.00	4.00
❑ 047	Sweet Woman Blues/The Newest Wave	1982	—	2.00	4.00
❑ 052	Rockabilly Man/Hollywood Cats	1983	—	2.00	4.00
TNT					
❑ 145	Caterpillar/Play It Cool	1958	75.00	150.00	300.00
WINSOR					
❑ 6401	Billie Jean/Shenandoah	1964	7.50	15.00	30.00
Albums					
ROLLIN' ROCK					
❑ 023	Rockabilly Music	1979	3.00	6.00	12.00
ROUNDER					
❑ 3046	Rockin' at the Ritz	198?	2.50	5.00	10.00
❑ 3047	Gone, Gone, Gone	198?	2.50	5.00	10.00

CAMPS, THE See THE CAMPERS.

CANADIAN BEADLES, THE
45s
TIDE
❑ 2203	I Think I'm Gonna Cry/I'll Show You the Way	1964	3.75	7.50	15.00
❑ 2206	I'm Coming Home/Love Walk Away	1964	3.75	7.50	15.00
—As "Vic, Paul and Bruce"					
Albums					
TIDE					
❑ 2005 [M]	Three Faces North	1964	12.50	25.00	50.00

CANARIES, THE
45s
B.T. PUPPY
❑ 557	I'll Cry Again/Baby Don't Surprise Me	1970	2.00	4.00	8.00
DIMENSION					
❑ 1047	I'm Sorry Baby/Runaround Ronnie	1965	3.75	7.50	15.00
Albums					
B.T. PUPPY					
❑ BTS-1007	Flying High with the Canaries	1970	25.00	50.00	100.00

CANDLELIGHTERS, THE
45s
DELTA
| ❑ 203 | Would You Do the Same for Me/(B-side unknown) | 1958 | 200.00 | 400.00 | 800.00 |

CANDY AND THE KISSES
45s
CAMEO
❑ 336	The 81/Two Happy People	1964	5.00	10.00	20.00
❑ 355	Soldier Boy (Of Mine)/Shakin' Time	1964	5.00	10.00	20.00
DECCA					
❑ 32415	Chains of Love/Someone Out There	1968	—	3.00	6.00
LOST-NITE					
❑ 229	The 81/Two Happy People	196?	—	2.50	5.00
—Reissue					
SCEPTER					
❑ 12106	Keep On Searchin'/Together	1965	3.75	7.50	15.00
❑ 12125	Sweet and Lovely/Out in the Streets Again	1965	3.75	7.50	15.00
❑ 12136	Tonight's the Night/The Last Time	1966	3.00	6.00	12.00

CANDY STORE, THE
Albums
DECCA
| ❑ DL 75147 | Turned-On Christmas | 1969 | 6.25 | 12.50 | 25.00 |

Number	Title (A Side/B Side)	Yr	VG	VG+	NM
CANDYMEN, THE					
45s					
ABC					
❑ 10995	Georgia Pines/Movies in My Mind	1967	2.00	4.00	8.00
❑ 11023	Deep in the Night/Stone Blues Man	1967	2.00	4.00	8.00
❑ 11048	Sentimental Lady/Ways	1968	2.00	4.00	8.00
❑ 11077	Candy Man/Crowded Room	1968	2.00	4.00	8.00
❑ 11141	Go and Tell the People/It's Gonna Get Good in a Minute	1968	2.00	4.00	8.00
❑ 11175	I'll Never Forget/Lonely Eyes	1969	2.00	4.00	8.00
LIBERTY					
❑ 56172	Happy Tonight/Papers	1970	2.00	4.00	8.00
Albums					
ABC					
❑ 616 [M]	The Candymen	1967	6.25	12.50	25.00
❑ S-616 [S]	The Candymen	1967	5.00	10.00	20.00
❑ S-633	The Candymen Bring You Candypower	1968	5.00	10.00	20.00

CANNED HEAT
45s
ALA
❑ 1996	C.C. Shooter/Harley Davidson Blues	1984	—	2.50	5.00
—As "Heat Brothers '84"					
ATLANTIC					
❑ 3010	One More River to Cross/Highway 401	1974	—	2.00	4.00
❑ 3236	The Harder They Come/Rock 'N' Roll Show	1975	—	2.00	4.00
CAPITOL					
❑ S7-57890	Christmas Blues/Christmas Is the Time to Say "I Love You"	1992	—	2.00	4.00
—B-side by Billy Squier					
LIBERTY					
❑ 55979	Rolin' and Tumblin'/Bullfrog Blues	1967	2.00	4.00	8.00
❑ 55979 [PS]	Rolin' and Tumblin'/Bullfrog Blues	1967	3.00	6.00	12.00
❑ 56005	Evil Woman/The World Is a Jug	1967	2.00	4.00	8.00
❑ 56038	On the Road Again/Boogie Music	1968	—	3.00	6.00
❑ 56077	Going Up the Country/One Kind Favor	1968	—	3.00	6.00
❑ 56077 [PS]	Going Up the Country/One Kind Favor	1968	3.75	7.50	15.00
❑ 56079	Christmas Blues/The Chipmunk Song	1968	6.25	12.50	25.00
—B-side with the Chipmunks					
❑ 56097	Time Was/Low Down	1969	—	3.00	6.00
❑ 56127	Sic 'Em Pigs/Poor Man	1969	—	3.00	6.00
❑ 56140	Change My Ways/Get Off My Back	1969	—	3.00	6.00
❑ 56151	Let's Work Together/I'm Her Man	1970	—	3.00	6.00
❑ 56180	Future Blues/Going Up the Country	1970	—	3.00	6.00
❑ 56217	My TIme Ain't Long/Wooly Bully	1970	—	3.00	6.00
UNITED ARTISTS					
❑ 0058	On the Road Again/This Was	1973	—	2.00	4.00
—"Silver Spotlight Series" reissue					
❑ 0059	Going Up the Country/Let's Work Together	1973	—	2.00	4.00
—"Silver Spotlight Series" reissue					
❑ XW167	Rock and Roll Music/Lookin' for My Rainbow	1973	—	2.50	5.00
❑ XW243 [DJ]	Harley Davidson Blues (mono/stereo)	1973	—	3.00	6.00
—Stock copy apparently does not exist					
❑ 50831	Long Way from L.A./Hill's Stomp	1971	—	2.50	5.00
❑ 50892	Rockin' with the King/I Don't Care What You Tell Me	1972	—	2.50	5.00
❑ 50927	Sneakin' Around/Cherokee Dance	1972	—	2.50	5.00
Albums					
ACCORD					
❑ SN-7144	Captured Live	1981	2.50	5.00	10.00
ATLANTIC					
❑ SD 7289	One More River to Cross	1973	3.75	7.50	15.00
DALI					
❑ DCLP-89022	Reheated	1990	3.75	7.50	15.00
JANUS					
❑ JLS-3009	Vintage — Canned Heat	1969	3.75	7.50	15.00
LIBERTY					
❑ LRP-3526 [M]	Canned Heat	1967	6.25	12.50	25.00
❑ LRP-3541 [M]	Boogie with Canned Heat	1968	10.00	20.00	40.00
—Stock copy in stereo cover with "Audition Mono LP Not for Sale" sticker					
❑ LST-7526 [S]	Canned Heat	1967	5.00	10.00	20.00
❑ LST-7541 [S]	Boogie with Canned Heat	1968	5.00	10.00	20.00
❑ LST-7618	Hallelujah	1969	5.00	10.00	20.00
❑ LN-10105	Boogie with Canned Heat	1981	2.00	4.00	8.00
—Budget-line reissue					
❑ LN-10106	Canned Heat Cook Book (The Best of Canned Heat)	1981	2.00	4.00	8.00
—Budget-line reissue					
❑ LST-11000	Canned Heat Cook Book (The Best of Canned Heat)	1969	5.00	10.00	20.00
❑ LST-11002	Future Blues	1970	3.75	7.50	15.00
❑ LST-27200 [(2)]	Living the Blues	1968	6.25	12.50	25.00
PICKWICK					
❑ SPC-3364	Live at Topanga Canyon	197?	2.50	5.00	10.00
❑ SPC-3614	Boogie	1978	2.50	5.00	10.00
SCEPTER					
❑ CTN-18017	The Best of Canned Heat	1972	2.50	5.00	10.00
SUNSET					
❑ SUS-5298	Collage	1971	2.50	5.00	10.00
TAKOMA					
❑ 7066	The Human Condition	1980	3.00	6.00	12.00
UNITED ARTISTS					
❑ UA-LA049-F	The New Age	1973	3.75	7.50	15.00
❑ LM-1015	Boogie with Canned Heat	1980	3.00	6.00	12.00
—Reissue of Liberty 7541					
❑ UAS-5509	Canned Heat Concert (Recorded Live in Europe)	1971	3.75	7.50	15.00
❑ UAS-5557	Historical Figures and Ancient Heads	1972	3.75	7.50	15.00
❑ UAS-9955 [(2)]	Living the Blues	1971	5.00	10.00	20.00
—Reissue of Liberty 27200					
WAND					
❑ WDS-693	Live at Topanga Canyon	1970	6.25	12.50	25.00

Number	Title (A Side/B Side)	Yr	VG	VG+	NM

CANNED HEAT AND JOHN LEE HOOKER See JOHN LEE HOOKER AND CANNED HEAT

CANNIBAL AND THE HEADHUNTERS

45s

AIRES

Number	Title (A Side/B Side)	Yr	VG	VG+	NM
❑ 1001	Mean So Much/Dance By the Light	1968	3.75	7.50	15.00

CAPITOL

| ❑ 2393 | Get It On Up (Get Up the Courage)/Mean So Much | 1969 | 3.75 | 7.50 | 15.00 |

DATE

| ❑ 1516 | La Bamba/Zulu King | 1966 | 3.75 | 7.50 | 15.00 |
| ❑ 1525 | Land of 1,000 Dances/Love Bird | 1966 | 3.75 | 7.50 | 15.00 |

ERA BACK TO BACK HITS

| ❑ 023 | Land of 1,000 Dances/Dance with Me | 197? | — | 2.50 | 5.00 |

—B-side by the Blendells

RAMPART

❑ 642	Land of 1,000 Dances/ I'll Show You How to Love Me	1964	5.00	10.00	20.00
❑ 644	Here Comes Love/Nau Ninny Nau	1965	3.75	7.50	15.00
❑ 646	I Need Your Loving/Follow the Music	1965	3.75	7.50	15.00
❑ 654	Out of Sight/Please Baby Please	1965	3.75	7.50	15.00

Albums

DATE

| ❑ TEM 3001 [M] | Land of 1000 Dances | 1966 | 7.50 | 15.00 | 30.00 |
| ❑ TES 4001 [S] | Land of 1000 Dances | 1966 | 10.00 | 20.00 | 40.00 |

RAMPART

| ❑ RM-3302 [M] | Land of 1000 Dances | 1965 | 12.50 | 25.00 | 50.00 |
| ❑ RS-3302 [S] | Land of 1000 Dances | 1965 | 17.50 | 35.00 | 70.00 |

CANNON, ACE

45s

FERNWOOD

| ❑ 117 | Big Shot/Rest | 1960 | 7.50 | 15.00 | 30.00 |

—As "Johnny Cannon"

| ❑ 135 | Summertime/Hoe Down Rock | 1963 | 5.00 | 10.00 | 20.00 |
| ❑ 137 | Big Shot/Tie Me to Your Apron Strings Again | 1964 | 5.00 | 10.00 | 20.00 |

HI

❑ 2040	Tuff/Sittin' Tight	1961	4.00	8.00	16.00
❑ 2051	Blues (Stay Away from Me)/Blues in My Heart	1962	3.75	7.50	15.00
❑ 2057	Volare/Looking Back	1962	3.00	6.00	12.00
❑ 2063	Love Letters/Since I Met You Baby	1963	3.00	6.00	12.00
❑ 2065	Cottonfields/Mildew	1963	3.00	6.00	12.00
❑ 2065 [PS]	Cottonfields/Mildew	1963	5.00	10.00	20.00
❑ 2070	Swanee River/Moanin' the Blues	1963	3.00	6.00	12.00
❑ 2070 [PS]	Swanee River/Moanin' the Blues	1963	5.00	10.00	20.00
❑ 2074	Searchin'/Love Letters in the Sand	1964	2.50	5.00	10.00
❑ 2078	The Great Pretender/Gone	1964	2.50	5.00	10.00
❑ 2081	Empty Arms/Sunday Blues	1964	2.50	5.00	10.00
❑ 2084	Blue Christmas/Here Comes Santa Claus	1964	2.50	5.00	10.00
❑ 2089	Sea Cruise/Gold Coins	1965	2.00	4.00	8.00
❑ 2096	Up Shore/Ishapan	1965	2.00	4.00	8.00
❑ 2101	Funny (How Time Slips Away)/Saxy Lullaby	1966	2.00	4.00	8.00
❑ 2107	Mocking Bird Rock/Dedicated to the One I Love	1966	2.00	4.00	8.00
❑ 2111	More/Spanish Eyes	1966	2.00	4.00	8.00
❑ 2117	Wonderland by Night/As Time Goes By	1966	2.00	4.00	8.00
❑ 2127	I Walk the Line/Memory	1967	2.00	4.00	8.00
❑ 2136	White Silver Sands/San Antonio Rose	1967	2.00	4.00	8.00
❑ 2144	Sleep Walk/By the Time I Get to Phoenix	1968	—	3.00	6.00
❑ 2148	Alley Cat/Cannonball	1968	—	3.00	6.00
❑ 2155	If I Had a Hammer/Soul for Sale	1969	—	3.00	6.00
❑ 2166	Amen/Down By the Riverside	1969	—	3.00	6.00
❑ 2174	Ruby, Don't Take Your Love to Town/ I Can't Stop Loving You	1970	—	3.00	6.00
❑ 2180	Rainy Night in Georgia/Lodi	1970	—	3.00	6.00
❑ 2187	Chicken Fried Soul/Chunck	1971	—	2.50	5.00
❑ 2192	Me and Bobby McGee/Sweet Caroline	1971	—	2.50	5.00
❑ 2199	Easy Loving/Misty Blue	1971	—	2.50	5.00
❑ 2210	Lovesick Blues/Cold, Cold Heart	1972	—	2.50	5.00
❑ 2220	Wabash Cannonball/To Get to You	1972	—	2.50	5.00
❑ 2231	Tuffer Than Tuff/The Green Door	1973	—	2.00	4.00
❑ 2238	Ruff/Baby Don't Get Hooked on Me	1973	—	2.00	4.00
❑ 2256	Country Comfort/Closin' Time's a Downer	1973	—	2.00	4.00
❑ 2261	Last Date/Methilda	1974	—	2.00	4.00
❑ 2273	There Goes My Everything/Tennessee Saturday Night	1974	—	2.00	4.00
❑ 2286	Peace in the Valley/Raunchy	1975	—	2.00	4.00
❑ 2299	Walk On By/Malt Liquor	1975	—	2.00	4.00
❑ 2313	Blue Eyes Crying in the Rain/I'll Fly Away	1976	—	2.00	4.00
❑ 78516	It Was Almost Like a Song/(B-side unknown)	1978	—	2.00	4.00
❑ 78526	Don't It Make My Brown Eyes Blue/ Blanket on the Ground	1978	—	2.00	4.00

LOUIS (LOUISE?)

| ❑ 2001 | Tuff/Sittin' Tight | 1961 | 7.50 | 15.00 | 30.00 |

SANTO

| ❑ 503 | Sugar Blues/38 Special | 1962 | 3.75 | 7.50 | 15.00 |
| ❑ 506 | Big Shot/Rest | 1962 | 3.75 | 7.50 | 15.00 |

7-Inch Extended Plays

HI

| ❑ SBG-60 | By the Time I Get to Pheonix/Green, Green Grass of Home/Turn On Your Love Light// Sleep Walking/Woman, Woman/Laura (What's He Got That I Ain't Got) | 1968 | 2.50 | 5.00 | 10.00 |

—Jukebox issue; small hole, plays at 33 1/3 rpm

| ❑ SBG-60 [PS] | The Incomparable Sax of Ace Cannon | 1968 | 2.50 | 5.00 | 10.00 |

Albums

ALLEGIANCE

| ❑ AV-5024 | Ace in the Whole | 1986 | 2.00 | 4.00 | 8.00 |

HI

❑ 6006	After Hours	1978	2.50	5.00	10.00
❑ 8003	Sax Man	1977	2.50	5.00	10.00
❑ 8008	Cannon Country	1979	2.50	5.00	10.00
❑ HL-12007 [M]	Tuff Sax	1962	6.25	12.50	25.00
❑ HL-12008 [M]	Looking Back	1962	6.25	12.50	25.00
❑ HL-12014 [M]	The Moanin' Sax of Ace Cannon	1963	6.25	12.50	25.00
❑ HL-12016 [M]	Aces Hi	1964	5.00	10.00	20.00
❑ HL-12019 [M]	The Great Show Tunes	1964	5.00	10.00	20.00
❑ HL-12022 [M]	Christmas Cheer	1964	5.00	10.00	20.00
❑ HL-12025 [M]	Ace Cannon Live	1965	3.75	7.50	15.00
❑ HL-12028 [M]	Nashville Hits	1965	3.75	7.50	15.00
❑ HL-12030 [M]	Sweet and Tuff	1966	3.75	7.50	15.00
❑ HL-12035 [M]	The Misty Sax of Ace Cannon	1967	5.00	10.00	20.00
❑ HL-12040 [M]	Memphis Golden Hits	1967	5.00	10.00	20.00
❑ SHL-32007 [S]	Tuff Sax	1962	7.50	15.00	30.00
❑ SHL-32008 [S]	Looking Back	1962	7.50	15.00	30.00
❑ SHL-32014 [S]	The Moanin' Sax of Ace Cannon	1963	7.50	15.00	30.00
❑ SHL-32016 [S]	Aces Hi	1964	6.25	12.50	25.00
❑ SHL-32019 [S]	The Great Show Tunes	1964	6.25	12.50	25.00
❑ SHL-32022 [S]	Christmas Cheer	1964	6.25	12.50	25.00
❑ SHL-32025 [S]	Ace Cannon Live	1965	5.00	10.00	20.00
❑ SHL-32028 [S]	Nashville Hits	1965	5.00	10.00	20.00
❑ SHL-32030 [S]	Sweet and Tuff	1966	5.00	10.00	20.00
❑ SHL-32035 [S]	The Misty Sax of Ace Cannon	1967	3.75	7.50	15.00
❑ SHL-32040 [S]	Memphis Golden Hits	1967	3.75	7.50	15.00
❑ SHL-32043	The Incomparable Sax of Ace Cannon	1968	3.75	7.50	15.00
❑ SHL-32046	In the Spotlight	1968	3.75	7.50	15.00
❑ SHL-32051	The Ace of Sax	1969	3.75	7.50	15.00
❑ SHL-32057	The Happy and Mellow Sax of Ace Cannon	1970	3.00	6.00	12.00
❑ SHL-32060	Cool 'n Saxy	1971	3.00	6.00	12.00
❑ SHL-32067	Blowing Wild	1971	3.00	6.00	12.00
❑ SHL-32071	Cannon Country	1972	3.00	6.00	12.00
❑ SHL-32072/3 [(2)]	Aces Back to Back	1972	3.75	7.50	15.00
❑ SHL-32076	Baby Don't Get Hooked on Me	1973	2.50	5.00	10.00
❑ SHL-32080	Country Comfort	1974	2.50	5.00	10.00
❑ SHL-32086	That Music City Feeling	1974	2.50	5.00	10.00
❑ SHL-32090	Super Sax Country Style	1975	2.50	5.00	10.00
❑ SHL-32101	Peace in the Valley	1976	2.50	5.00	10.00

CANNON, FREDDY

45s

AMHERST

| ❑ 201 | Dance to the Bop/(She's a) Mean Rebel Rouser | 1983 | — | 2.00 | 4.00 |
| ❑ 327 | Rockin' in My Socks/Rockin' in My Socks | 1988 | — | 3.00 | 6.00 |

BUDDAH

| ❑ 242 | Rockin' Robin/Red Valley | 1971 | 2.50 | 5.00 | 10.00 |

CLARIDGE

| ❑ 401 | Palisades Park/Way Down Yonder in New Orleans | 1975 | — | 3.00 | 6.00 |
| ❑ 416 | Sugar/Sugar (Part 2) | 1976 | — | 3.00 | 6.00 |

HQ

| ❑ (no #) [DJ] | Kennywood Park/With a Little Love | 1987 | — | 3.00 | 6.00 |
| ❑ (no #) [PS] | Kennywood Park/With a Little Love | 1987 | 2.00 | 4.00 | 8.00 |

—Promotional item for KDKA Radio, Pittsburgh, Pa.

MCA

| ❑ 40269 | Rock and Roll ABC's/Superman | 1974 | 3.75 | 7.50 | 15.00 |

METROMEDIA

| ❑ 262 | If You've Got the Time/Take Me Back | 1972 | 2.50 | 5.00 | 10.00 |

MIASOUND

| ❑ 1002 | Let's Put the Fun Back in Rock and Roll/ Your Mama Ain't Always Right | 1981 | — | 3.00 | 6.00 |

—With the Belmonts

RADIO ACTIVE GOLD

| ❑ 64 | Rockin' Robin/Red Valley | 197? | — | 2.50 | 5.00 |

ROYAL AMERICAN

❑ 2	Charged-Up, Turned-On Rock-N-Roll Singer/I Ain't Much, But I'm Yours	1970	2.50	5.00	10.00
❑ 11	Nite Time Lady/I Ain't Much, But I'm Yours	1970	2.50	5.00	10.00
❑ 288	Strawberry Wine/Blossom Dear	1969	2.50	5.00	10.00

SIRE

| ❑ 4103 | Beautiful Downtown Burbank/ If You Give Me a Title | 1969 | 2.50 | 5.00 | 10.00 |

SWAN

❑ 4031	Tallahassee Lassie/You Know	1959	5.00	10.00	20.00
❑ 4038	Okefenokee/Kookie Hat	1959	5.00	10.00	20.00
❑ 4043	Way Down Yonder in New Orleans/Fractured	1959	5.00	10.00	20.00
❑ 4043 [PS]	Way Down Yonder in New Orleans/Fractured	1959	7.50	15.00	30.00
❑ 4050	Chattanooga Shoe Shine Boy/Boston "My Home Town"	1960	3.75	7.50	15.00
❑ 4050 [PS]	Chattanooga Shoe Shine Boy/Boston "My Home Town"	1960	7.50	15.00	30.00
❑ 4053	Jump Over/The Urge	1960	3.75	7.50	15.00
❑ 4053 [PS]	Jump Over/The Urge	1960	7.50	15.00	30.00
❑ 4057	Happy Shades of Blue/(Kwa-Na-Va-Ka) Cuernavaca Choo Choo	1960	3.75	7.50	15.00
❑ 4057 [PS]	Happy Shades of Blue/(Kwa-Na-Va-Ka) Cuernavaca Choo Choo	1960	7.50	15.00	30.00
❑ 4061	Humdinger/My Blue Heaven	1960	3.75	7.50	15.00
❑ 4061 [PS]	Humdinger/My Blue Heaven	1960	7.50	15.00	30.00
❑ 4066	Muskrat Ramble/Two Thousand-88	1961	3.75	7.50	15.00
❑ 4066 [PS]	Muskrat Ramble/Two Thousand-88	1961	7.50	15.00	30.00
❑ 4071	Buzz Buzz A-Diddle It/Opportunity	1961	3.75	7.50	15.00
❑ 4078	Transistor Sister/Walk to the Moon	1961	3.75	7.50	15.00
❑ 4078 [PS]	Transistor Sister/Walk to the Moon	1961	7.50	15.00	30.00
❑ 4083	For Me and My Gal/Blue Plate Special	1961	3.75	7.50	15.00
❑ 4096	Teen Queen of the Week/Wild Guy	1962	3.75	7.50	15.00
❑ 4106	Palisades Park/June, July and August	1962	4.00	8.00	16.00
❑ 4117	What's Gonna Happen When Summer's Done/ Broadway	1962	3.75	7.50	15.00
❑ 4122	If You Were a Rock and Roll Record/ The Truth, Ruth	1962	3.75	7.50	15.00
❑ 4132	Come On and Love Me/Four Letter Man	1963	3.00	6.00	12.00
❑ 4139	Patty Baby/Betty Jean	1963	3.00	6.00	12.00
❑ 4149	Everybody Monkey/Oh Gloria	1963	6.25	12.50	25.00
❑ 4155	Do What the Hippies Do/That's the Way Girls Are	1963	3.00	6.00	12.00
❑ 4168	What a Party/Sweet Georgia Brown	1964	3.00	6.00	12.00
❑ 4178	The Ups and Downs of Love/It's Been Nice	1964	6.25	12.50	25.00

WARNER BROS.

❑ 5409	Abigail Beecher/All American Girl	1964	3.00	6.00	12.00
❑ 5434	OK Wheeler, The Used Car Dealer/ Odie Cologne	1964	3.00	6.00	12.00
❑ 5448	Summertime U.S.A./Gotta Good Thing Goin'	1964	3.00	6.00	12.00
❑ 5487	Little Autograph Seeker/Too Much Monkey Business	1964	3.00	6.00	12.00
❑ 5615	Little Miss A-Go-Go/In the Night	1965	3.00	6.00	12.00
❑ 5615 [PS]	Little Miss A-Go-Go/In the Night	1965	6.25	12.50	25.00
❑ 5645	Action/Beachwood City	1965	3.75	7.50	15.00

Number	Title (A Side/B Side)	Yr	VG	VG+	NM
❑ 5666	Let Me Show You Where It's At/				
	The Old Rag Man	1965	3.00	6.00	12.00
❑ 5673	She's Something Else/Little Bitty Corrine	1965	3.00	6.00	12.00
❑ 5693	The Dedication Song/Come On, Come On	1966	3.00	6.00	12.00
❑ 5810	The Greatest Show on Earth/Hokie Pokie Girl	1966	3.00	6.00	12.00
❑ 5832	The Laughing Song/Natalie	1966	3.00	6.00	12.00
❑ 5859	Run for the Sun/Use Your Imagination	1966	3.00	6.00	12.00
❑ 5876	A Happy Clown/In My Wildest Dreams	1966	6.25	12.50	25.00
❑ 7019	Maverick's Flat/Run to the Poet Man	1967	6.25	12.50	25.00
❑ 7075	20th Century Fox/Cincinnati Woman	1967	6.25	12.50	25.00
WE MAKE ROCK & ROLL					
❑ 1601	Rock Around the Clock/Sock It to the Judge	1968	—	3.00	6.00
❑ 1604	Sea Cruise/She's a Friday Night Fox	1968	—	3.00	6.00
Albums					
RHINO					
❑ RNLP-210	14 Booming Hits	1982	2.50	5.00	10.00
SWAN					
❑ LP-502 [M]	The Explosive! Freddy Cannon	1960	30.00	60.00	120.00
❑ LPS-502 [S]	The Explosive! Freddy Cannon	1960	75.00	150.00	300.00
❑ LP-504 [M]	Happy Shades of Blue	1960	37.50	75.00	150.00
❑ LP-505 [M]	Solid Gold Hits	1961	37.50	75.00	150.00
❑ LP-507 [M]	Freddy Cannon at Palisades Park	1962	37.50	75.00	150.00
❑ LP-511 [M]	Freddy Cannon Steps Out	1963	37.50	75.00	150.00
WARNER BROS.					
❑ W 1544 [M]	Freddie Cannon	1964	7.50	15.00	30.00
❑ WS 1544 [S]	Freddie Cannon	1964	10.00	20.00	40.00
❑ W 1612 [M]	Action!	1965	7.50	15.00	30.00
❑ WS 1612 [S]	Action!	1965	10.00	20.00	40.00
❑ W 1628 [M]	Freddy Cannon's Greatest Hits	1966	7.50	15.00	30.00
❑ WS 1628 [S]	Freddy Cannon's Greatest Hits	1966	10.00	20.00	40.00

CANNON, GUS
Albums
STAX

Number	Title (A Side/B Side)	Yr	VG	VG+	NM
❑ ST-702 [M]	Walk Right In	1962	150.00	300.00	600.00

CANNON, JACKIE
45s
CHAN

Number	Title (A Side/B Side)	Yr	VG	VG+	NM
❑ 103	Proof of Your Love/Chill Bumps	1961	10.00	20.00	40.00
CHESS					
❑ 1807	Proof of Your Love/Chill Bumps	1961	3.75	7.50	15.00

CANNON, JOHNNY See ACE CANNON.

CANO, EDDIE
45s
DUNHILL

Number	Title (A Side/B Side)	Yr	VG	VG+	NM
❑ 4072	Monday, Monday/Slip Slip	1967	—	3.00	6.00
❑ 4075	Amy's Theme/La Bamba	1967	—	3.00	6.00
GNP CRESCENDO					
❑ 172	La Casita/Hava Nagilah	1962	2.00	4.00	8.00
❑ 187	Line for Lyons/Tin Tin Deo	1962	2.00	4.00	8.00
REPRISE					
❑ 0237	Danke Schoen/Our Day Will Come	1963	2.00	4.00	8.00
❑ 0254	What Now My Love/Theme from Snow Angel	1963	2.00	4.00	8.00
❑ 0382	Tortilla Flats (Part 1)/Tortilla Flats (Part 2)	1965	2.00	4.00	8.00
❑ 20075	A Taste of Honey/Panchita	1962	2.00	4.00	8.00
❑ 20113	Barsonova Brown/Greenfields	1962	2.00	4.00	8.00
❑ 20147	Days of Wine and Roses/Our Day Will Come	1963	2.00	4.00	8.00
Albums					
ATCO					
❑ 33-184 [M]	On Broadway	1966	2.50	5.00	10.00
❑ SD 33-184 [S]	On Broadway	1966	3.00	6.00	12.00
DUNHILL					
❑ D-50018 [M]	Brought Back Live from P.J.'s	1967	3.00	6.00	12.00
❑ DS-50018 [S]	Brought Back Live from P.J.'s	1967	2.50	5.00	10.00
GNP CRESCENDO					
❑ GNP-77 [M]	A Taste of Cano	1963	3.00	6.00	12.00
❑ GNPS-77 [S]	A Taste of Cano	1963	3.75	7.50	15.00
PICKWICK					
❑ SPC-3017	25 Latin Dance Favorites	196?	2.50	5.00	10.00
RCA VICTOR					
❑ LPM-1672 [M]	Time for Cha Cha Cha	1958	3.75	7.50	15.00
REPRISE					
❑ R-6030 [M]	Eddie Cano at P.J.'s	1962	3.00	6.00	12.00
❑ R9-6030 [S]	Eddie Cano at P.J.'s	1962	3.75	7.50	15.00
❑ R-6055 [M]	Here Is the Fabulous Eddie Cano	1963	3.00	6.00	12.00
❑ R9-6055 [S]	Here Is the Fabulous Eddie Cano	1963	3.75	7.50	15.00
❑ R-6068 [M]	Cano Plays Mancini	1963	3.00	6.00	12.00
❑ R9-6068 [S]	Cano Plays Mancini	1963	3.75	7.50	15.00
❑ R-6105 [M]	Danke Schoen	1963	3.00	6.00	12.00
❑ R9-6105 [S]	Danke Schoen	1963	3.75	7.50	15.00
❑ R-6124 [M]	Broadway — Right Now!	1964	3.00	6.00	12.00
❑ R9-6124 [S]	Broadway — Right Now!	1964	3.75	7.50	15.00
❑ R-6145 [M]	The Sound of Music	1965	3.00	6.00	12.00
❑ RS-6145 [S]	The Sound of Music	1965	3.75	7.50	15.00

CANTRELL, LANA
45s
POLYDOR

Number	Title (A Side/B Side)	Yr	VG	VG+	NM
❑ 14261	Like a Sunday Morning/Good Times	1974	—	2.00	4.00
RCA VICTOR					
❑ 47-8978	Breakfast at Tiffany's/Since I Fell for You	1966	—	3.00	6.00
❑ 47-9089	Confession/Theme from The Sand Pebbles	1967	—	3.00	6.00
❑ 47-9205	Sunshine/How Can I Hurt You	1967	—	3.00	6.00
❑ 47-9391	On the Good Ship Lollipop/				
	When You Wish Upon a Star	1967	—	3.00	6.00
❑ 47-9526	The Music Played/Just a Little Lovin'	1968	—	3.00	6.00
❑ 47-9619	The Good Times We Had/Catch the Wind	1968	—	3.00	6.00
❑ 74-0103	Your Mother Should Know/Mr. Bojangles	1969	—	3.00	6.00
❑ 74-0173	All the Things You Are/If I Say No	1969	—	3.00	6.00
❑ 74-0268	I Let the Moment Slip By/Tomorrow Is the First				
	Day of the Rest of My Life	1969	—	3.00	6.00
Albums					
RCA VICTOR					
❑ LPM-3755 [M]	And Then There Was Lana	1967	3.75	7.50	15.00
❑ LSP-3755 [S]	And Then There Was Lana	1967	3.00	6.00	12.00

C

Number	Title (A Side/B Side)	Yr	VG	VG+	NM
❑ LPM-3862 [M]	Another Shade of Lana	1967	3.75	7.50	15.00
❑ LSP-3862 [S]	Another Shade of Lana	1967	3.00	6.00	12.00
❑ LPM-3947 [M]	Act III	1968	3.75	7.50	15.00
❑ LSP-3947 [S]	Act III	1968	3.00	6.00	12.00
❑ LSP-4121	Lana!	1968	3.00	6.00	12.00
❑ LSP-4121	Now or Then	1969	3.00	6.00	12.00
❑ LSP-4263	The 6th Lana	1970	3.00	6.00	12.00

CAP-TANS, THE
45s
ANNA

Number	Title (A Side/B Side)	Yr	VG	VG+	NM
❑ 1122	I'm Afraid/Tight Skirts and Crazy Sweaters	1960	75.00	15.00	30.00
CORAL					
❑ 65071	Asking/Who Can I Turn To	1951	75.00	150.00	300.00
DOT					
❑ 15114	I'm So Crazy for Love/With All My Love	1953	25.00	50.00	100.00
GOTHAM					
❑ 233	My, My, My, Ain't She Pretty/Never Be Lonely	1950	100.00	200.00	400.00
❑ 268	I Thought I Could Forget You/				
	Waiting at the Station	1951	75.00	150.00	300.00

CAPALDI, JIM Also see TRAFFIC.
12-Inch Singles
ATLANTIC

Number	Title (A Side/B Side)	Yr	VG	VG+	NM
❑ PR 545 [DJ]	Tonight You're Mine (same on both sides)	1983	2.50	5.00	10.00
❑ DMD 786 [DJ]	I'll Keep Holding On/(Instrumental)	1984	2.00	4.00	8.00
ISLAND					
❑ PR 2491 [DJ]	Something So Strong (same on both sides)	1988	2.00	4.00	8.00
RSO					
❑ RPO 1014 [DJ]	Shoe Shine (7:39) (same on both sides)	1979	3.00	6.00	12.00
45s					
ATLANTIC					
❑ 89625	I'll Keep Holding On/Tales of Power	1984	—	2.00	4.00
❑ 89783 [DJ]	Tonight You're Mine (same on both sides)	1983	—	2.00	4.00
—May be promo only					
❑ 89799	Living on the Edge/Gifts of Unknown Things	1983	—	—	3.00
❑ 89849	That's Love/Runaway	1983	—	—	3.00
❑ 89849 [PS]	That's Love/Runaway	1983	—	2.00	4.00
ISLAND					
❑ 003	It's All Right/Whale Meat Again	1974	—	2.50	5.00
❑ 025	It's All Up to You/I've Got So Much Lovin'	1975	—	2.50	5.00
❑ 045	Love Hurts/Sugar Honey	1976	—	2.00	4.00
❑ 055	Goodbye Love/(B-side unknown)	1976	—	2.00	4.00
❑ 067	Goodnight and Good Morning/				
	Short Cut Draw Blood	1976	—	2.00	4.00
❑ 1204	Eve/Going Down Slow All the Way	1972	—	3.00	6.00
❑ 1205	Oh How We Danced/Open Your Heart	1972	—	3.00	6.00
❑ 1216	Tricky Dicky Rides Again/Love Is All You Can Try	1973	—	2.50	5.00
❑ 99220	Some Came Running/Favela Music	1989	—	—	3.00
❑ 99220 [PS]	Some Came Running/Favela Music	1989	—	—	3.00
❑ 99266	Something So Strong/Child in the Storm	1988	—	—	3.00
❑ 99266 [PS]	Something So Strong/Child in the Storm	1988	—	—	3.00
RSO					
❑ 912	Daughter of the Night/I'm Gonna Do It	1978	—	2.00	4.00
Albums					
ANTILLIES					
❑ 7050	Short Cut Draw Blood	198?	2.00	4.00	8.00
—Reissue of Island 9336					
ATLANTIC					
❑ 80059	Fierce Heart	1983	2.50	5.00	10.00
❑ 80182	One Man Mission	1984	2.50	5.00	10.00
ISLAND					
❑ ILPS 9254	Whale Meat Again	1974	2.50	5.00	10.00
❑ SW-9314	Oh How We Danced	1972	3.00	6.00	12.00
❑ ILPS 9336	Short Cut Draw Blood	1976	2.50	5.00	10.00
❑ 91024	Some Came Running	1988	2.50	5.00	10.00
RSO					
❑ RS-1-3037	Daughter of the Night	1978	2.50	5.00	10.00
❑ RS-1-3050	Electric Nights	1979	2.50	5.00	10.00

CAPEHART, JERRY
45s
CASH

Number	Title (A Side/B Side)	Yr	VG	VG+	NM
❑ 1021	Walkin' Stick Boogie/Rollin'	1956	50.00	100.00	200.00
—With Eddie and Hank Cochran					
CREST					
❑ 1101	Song of New Orleans/The Young and Blue				
	(Theme)	1962	12.50	25.00	50.00

CAPERS, THE
45s
DORE

Number	Title (A Side/B Side)	Yr	VG	VG+	NM
❑ 587	Rockin' Round the Mountain/				
	What Is This Thing Called Love	1961	3.00	6.00	12.00
VEE JAY					
❑ 297	Miss You My Dear/Early One Morning	1958	6.25	12.50	25.00
❑ 315	Candy Store Blues/High School Diploma	1959	6.25	12.50	25.00

CAPERS & CARSON See HEDGE & DONNA.

CAPITAL CITY ROCKETS
45s
ELEKTRA

Number	Title (A Side/B Side)	Yr	VG	VG+	NM
❑ 45855	Breakfast in Bed/Grab Your Honey	1973	2.00	4.00	8.00
❑ 45872	Little Bit O' Fun/Ten Hole Dollars	1973	2.00	4.00	8.00
Albums					
ELEKTRA					
❑ EKS-75079	Capital City Rockets	1973	5.00	10.00	20.00

CAPITOLS, THE (1) Detroit-based R&B vocal group.
45s
KAREN

Number	Title (A Side/B Side)	Yr	VG	VG+	NM
❑ 1524	Cool Jerk/Hello Stranger	1966	3.75	7.50	15.00
❑ 1525	I Got to Handle It/Zig Zagging	1966	2.50	5.00	10.00
❑ 1526	We Got a Thing That's In the Groove/Tired				
	Running from You	1966	2.50	5.00	10.00
❑ 1534	Patty Cake/Take a Chance on Me Baby	1967	2.50	5.00	10.00
❑ 1536	Cool Pearl/Don't Say Maybe Baby	1967	2.50	5.00	10.00

Number	Title (A Side/B Side)	Yr	VG	VG+	NM
❑ 1537	Cool Jerk '68/Afro Twist	1968	2.50	5.00	10.00
❑ 1543	Soul Brother, Soul Sister/Ain't That Terrible	1968	2.50	5.00	10.00
❑ 1546	Soul Soul/When You're in Trouble	1969	2.50	5.00	10.00
❑ 1549	I Thought She Loved Me/When You're in Trouble	1969	2.50	5.00	10.00
Albums					
ATCO					
❑ 33-190 [M]	Dance the Cool Jerk	1966	10.00	20.00	40.00
❑ SD 33-190 [S]	Dance the Cool Jerk	1966	12.50	25.00	50.00
❑ 33-201 [M]	We Got a Thing That's In the Groove	1966	10.00	20.00	40.00
❑ SD 33-201 [S]	We Got a Thing That's In the Groove	1966	12.50	25.00	50.00
COLLECTABLES					
❑ COL-5105	Golden Classics	1988	2.50	5.00	10.00
SOLID SMOKE					
❑ 8019	The Capitols: Their Greatest Hits	1983	3.00	6.00	12.00

CAPITOLS, THE (2) Not group (1).
45s
CARLTON

Number	Title (A Side/B Side)	Yr	VG	VG+	NM
❑ 461	I Let Her Go/I've Got a Girl	1958	150.00	300.00	600.00

CAPITOLS, THE (U) None of these is by group (1), though it's possible that one or more is by group (2).
45s
CINDY

Number	Title (A Side/B Side)	Yr	VG	VG+	NM
❑ 3002	Rosemary/Millie	1957	50.00	100.00	200.00
GATEWAY					
❑ 721	Day By Day/Little Things	1964	75.00	150.00	300.00
PET					
❑ 807	Angel of Love/'Cause I Love You	1958	50.00	100.00	200.00
TRIUMPH					
❑ 601	Three O'Clock Rock/Write Me a Love Letter	1959	7.50	15.00	30.00

CAPONE, SUSAN
45s
PILGRIM

Number	Title (A Side/B Side)	Yr	VG	VG+	NM
❑ 704	I'll Be Dancing/Four or Five Hundred Kisses	1956	6.25	12.50	25.00
❑ 718	Click-I-Dee, Click-I-Dee/Maybe Someday	1956	6.25	12.50	25.00

CAPRIS, THE (1) Italian male vocal group from New York.
45s
AMBIENT SOUND

Number	Title (A Side/B Side)	Yr	VG	VG+	NM
❑ ZS5-02697	There's a Moon Out Again/Morse Code of Love	1982	—	3.00	6.00
CANDLELITE					
❑ 422	Oh, My Darling/Rock Pretty Baby	196?	3.00	6.00	12.00
LIFETIME					
❑ 1001/2	Oh My Darling/Rock Pretty Baby	1961	25.00	50.00	100.00
LOST-NITE					
❑ 101	There's a Moon Out Tonight/Indian Girl	196?	2.00	4.00	8.00
—Yellow label reissue					
❑ 101	There's a Moon Out Tonight/Indian Girl	1961	17.50	35.00	70.00
—Pink label original; black vinyl					
❑ 101	There's a Moon Out Tonight/Indian Girl	1961	37.50	75.00	150.00
—Pink label original; red vinyl					
❑ 148	Little Girl/When	196?	2.00	4.00	8.00
MR. PEEKE					
❑ 118	Limbo/From the Vine Came the Grape	1963	5.00	10.00	20.00
OLD TOWN					
❑ 1094	There's a Moon Out Tonight/Indian Girl	1961	7.50	15.00	30.00
—Light blue label					
❑ 1094	There's a Moon Out Tonight/Indian Girl	1962	5.00	10.00	20.00
—Mostly black label					
❑ 1099	Where I Fell in Love/Some People Think	1961	7.50	15.00	30.00
❑ 1103	Tears in My Eyes/Why Do I Cry	1961	7.50	15.00	30.00
❑ 1107	Girl in My Dreams/My Island in the Sun	1961	7.50	15.00	30.00
PLANET					
❑ 1010	There's a Moon Out Tonight/Indian Girl	1958	400.00	800.00	1200.
SABRE					
❑ 201/2	My Promise to You/Bop! Bop! Bop!	1959	37.50	75.00	150.00
TROMMERS					
❑ 101	There's a Moon Out Tonight/Indian Girl	1961	6.25	12.50	25.00
—Red label					
❑ 101	There's a Moon Out Tonight/Indian Girl	1961	6.25	12.50	25.00
—White label (not a promo)					
20TH CENTURY					
❑ 1201	My Weakness/Yes, My Baby, Please!	1957	15.00	30.00	60.00
Albums					
AMBIENT SOUND					
❑ FW 37714	There's a Moon Out Again	1982	3.75	7.50	15.00
COLLECTABLES					
❑ COL-5016	There's a Moon Out Tonight	198?	3.00	6.00	12.00

CAPRIS, THE (2) Different male vocal group than (1).
45s
GOTHAM

Number	Title (A Side/B Side)	Yr	VG	VG+	NM
❑ 304	God Only Knows/ That's What You're Doing to Me	1954	30.00	60.00	120.00
—Red label					
❑ 304	God Only Knows/ That's What You're Doing to Me	1954	150.00	300.00	600.00
—Blue label					
❑ 304	God Only Knows/ That's What You're Doing to Me	1956	20.00	40.00	80.00
—Yellow label					
❑ 306	It Was Moonglow/Too Poor to Love	1955	50.00	100.00	200.00
❑ 308	It's a Miracle/Let's Linger Awhile	1956	30.00	60.00	120.00
LOST-NITE					
❑ 112	God Only Knows/ That's What You're Doing to Me	196?	2.00	4.00	8.00
Albums					
COLLECTABLES					
❑ COL-5000	Gotham Recording Stars	198?	3.00	6.00	12.00

CAPTAIN AND TENNILLE
45s
A&M

Number	Title (A Side/B Side)	Yr	VG	VG+	NM
❑ 1624	The Way I Want to Touch You/Disney Girls	1974	—	3.00	6.00
❑ 1672	Love Will Keep Us Together/Gentle Stranger	1975	—	2.00	4.00

Number	Title (A Side/B Side)	Yr	VG	VG+	NM
❑ 1672 [PS]	Love Will Keep Us Together/Gentle Stranger	1975	—	3.00	6.00
❑ 1715	Por Amor Vivremos (Love Will Keep Us Together)/Broddy Bounce	1975	—	2.50	5.00
❑ 1725	The Way I Want to Touch You/Broddy Bounce	1975	—	2.00	4.00
❑ 1725 [PS]	The Way I Want to Touch You/Broddy Bounce	1975	—	3.00	6.00
❑ 1774	Como Yo Quiero Sentorte (The Way I Want to Touch You)/El Rebote de Broddy	1975	2.00	4.00	8.00
❑ 1782	Lonely Night (Angel Face)/ Smile for Me One More Time	1976	—	2.00	4.00
❑ 1782 [PS]	Lonely Night (Angel Face)/ Smile for Me One More Time	1976	—	3.00	6.00
❑ 1817	Shop Around/Butterscotch Castle	1976	—	2.00	4.00
❑ 1817 [PS]	Shop Around/Butterscotch Castle	1976	—	3.00	6.00
❑ 1870	Muskrat Love/Honey Come Love Me	1976	—	2.00	4.00
❑ 1870 [PS]	Muskrat Love/Honey Come Love Me	1976	—	3.00	6.00
❑ 1894	Song of Joy/Wedding Song (There Is Love)	1976	—	—	—
—Canceled; issued on 8601					
❑ 1912	Can't Stop Dancin'/ Mis Canciones (The Good Songs)	1977	—	2.00	4.00
❑ 1912 [PS]	Can't Stop Dancin'/ Mis Canciones (The Good Songs)	1977	—	3.00	6.00
❑ 1944	Come In from the Rain/ We Never Really Said Goodbye	1977	—	2.00	4.00
❑ 1944 [PS]	Come In from the Rain/ We Never Really Said Goodbye	1977	—	3.00	6.00
❑ 1970	Circles/1954 Boogie Blues	1977	—	2.00	4.00
❑ 2027	I'm On My Way/We Never Really Said Goodbye	1978	—	2.00	4.00
❑ 2027 [PS]	I'm On My Way/We Never Really Said Goodbye	1978	—	3.00	6.00
❑ 2063	You Never Done It Like That/"D" Keyboard Blues	1978	—	2.00	4.00
❑ 2063 [PS]	You Never Done It Like That/"D" Keyboard Blues	1978	—	3.00	6.00
❑ 2106	You Need a Woman Tonight/ Love Me Like a Baby	1978	—	2.00	4.00
❑ 2106 [PS]	You Need a Woman Tonight/ Love Me Like a Baby	1978	—	3.00	6.00
❑ 8600	Lonely Night (Angel Face)/Shop Around	1977	—	2.00	4.00
—"A&M Forget Me Nots" series; green and yellow labels					
❑ 8600	Lonely Night (Angel Face)/Shop Around	1977	—	3.00	6.00
❑ 8600	Lonely Night (Angel Face)/Shop Around	198?	—	—	3.00
—"A&M Memories" series; white label, pink and black print					
❑ 8601	Song of Joy/Wedding Song (There Is Love)	1977	—	2.00	4.00
—"A&M Forget Me Nots" series; green and yellow labels					
❑ 8601	Song of Joy/Wedding Song (There Is Love)	1977	—	3.00	6.00
❑ 8601	Song of Joy/Wedding Song (There Is Love)	198?	—	—	3.00
—"A&M Memories" series; white label, pink and black print					
BUTTERSCOTCH CASTLE					
❑ 001	The Way I Want to Touch You/Disney Girls	1974	20.00	40.00	80.00
CASABLANCA					
❑ 2215	Do That To Me One More Time/Deep in the Dark	1979	—	2.00	4.00
❑ 2243	Love on a Shoestring/How Can You Be So Cold	1980	—	2.00	4.00
❑ 2247	Amame Una Vez Mas (Do That To Me One More Time)/Deep in the Dark	1980	2.00	4.00	8.00
❑ 2264	Happy Together (A Fantasy)/ Baby You Still Got It	1980	—	2.00	4.00
❑ 2320	This Is Not the First Time/Gentle Stranger	1980	—	2.00	4.00
❑ 2328	Don't Forget Me/Keep Our Love Warm	1981	—	2.00	4.00
JOYCE					
❑ 101	The Way I Want to Tocuh You/Disney Girls	1974	10.00	20.00	40.00
PUREBRED					
❑ 0001	Tahoe Snow/Here Comes Santa Claus	198?	—	2.50	5.00
❑ 0001 [PS]	Tahoe Snow/Here Comes Santa Claus	198?	—	3.00	5.00
Albums					
A&M					
❑ SP-3105	Captain & Tennille's Greatest Hits	198?	2.00	4.00	8.00
—Reissue of 4667					
❑ SP-3405	Love Will Keep Us Together	1975	3.00	6.00	12.00
❑ SP-4552	Love Will Keep Us Together	1975	2.50	5.00	10.00
—Reissue of 3405					
❑ SP-4561	Por Amor Vivremos	1975	3.00	6.00	12.00
❑ SP-4570	Song of Joy	1976	2.50	5.00	10.00
❑ SP-4667	Captain & Tennille's Greatest Hits	1977	2.50	5.00	10.00
❑ SP-4700	Come In From the Rain	1977	2.50	5.00	10.00
❑ SP-4707	Dream	1978	2.50	5.00	10.00
❑ QU-54552 [Q]	Love Will Keep Us Together	1975	3.75	7.50	15.00
CASABLANCA					
❑ NBLP 7188	Make Your Move	1979	2.50	5.00	10.00
❑ NBLP 7250	Keeping Our Love Warm	1980	2.50	5.00	10.00

CAPTAIN BEEFHEART Also see FRANK ZAPPA.
45s
A&M

Number	Title (A Side/B Side)	Yr	VG	VG+	NM
❑ 794	Diddy Wah Diddy/ Who Do You Think You're Fooling	1966	10.00	20.00	40.00
❑ 818	Moonchild/Here I Am, Here I Always Am	1966	12.50	25.00	50.00
BUDDAH					
❑ 9	Yellow Brick Road/Abba Zaba	1967	3.75	7.50	15.00
❑ 108	Plastic Factory/Where There's Woman	1969	3.75	7.50	15.00
MERCURY					
❑ 73494	I Got Love on My Mind/Upon the My-O-My	1974	2.00	4.00	8.00
REPRISE					
❑ PRO 547 [DJ]	Too Much Time/Low Yo Yo Stuff	1973	5.00	10.00	20.00
❑ PRO 547 [PS]	Too Much Time/Low Yo Yo Stuff	1973	10.00	20.00	40.00
—Gatefold cardboard sleeve					
❑ 1068	Click Clack/I'm Gonna Boogalize You Baby	1972	3.75	7.50	15.00
❑ 1133	Too Much Time/My Head Is My Only House Unless It Rains	1972	3.75	7.50	15.00
VIRGIN/EPIC					
❑ 14-03190	Ice Cream for Crow/Light Reflected Off the Oceans of the Moon	1982	—	2.50	5.00
❑ 14-03190 [PS]	Ice Cream for Crow/Light Reflected Off the Oceans of the Moon	1982	—	3.00	6.00
Albums					
A&M					
❑ SP-12510 [EP]	The Legendary A&M Sessions	1984	2.50	5.00	10.00
BLUE THUMB					
❑ BTS-1	Strictly Personal	1968	12.50	25.00	50.00
—Black label, unbanded sides					
❑ BTS-1	Strictly Personal	1969	7.50	15.00	30.00
—White label, unbanded sides					

Number	Title (A Side/B Side)	Yr	VG	VG+	NM
❏ BTS-1	Strictly Personal	197?	5.00	10.00	20.00
—White label, banded sides					
BUDDAH					
❏ 1001/5001	Safe As Milk "Baby Jesus" Bumper Sticker	1967	6.25	12.50	25.00
❏ BDM-1001 [M]	Safe As Milk	1967	25.00	50.00	100.00
❏ BDS-5001 [S]	Safe As Milk	1967	15.00	30.00	60.00
❏ BDS-5063	Safe As Milk	1969	6.25	12.50	25.00
❏ BDS-5077	Mirror Man	197?	6.25	12.50	25.00
—Regular cover					
❏ BDS-5077	Mirror Man	1971	12.50	25.00	50.00
—Die-cut gatefold cover					
MERCURY					
❏ SRM-1-709	Unconditionally Guaranteed	1974	3.75	7.50	15.00
❏ SRM-1-1018	Bluejeans and Moonbeams	1975	5.00	10.00	20.00
REPRISE					
❏ 2MS 2027 [(2)]	Trout Mask Replica	1970	7.50	15.00	30.00
—Stock copy with 2027 labels and 2027 jacket					
❏ MS 2050	The Spotlight Kid	1971	5.00	10.00	20.00
❏ MS 2115	Clear Spot	1972	5.00	10.00	20.00
❏ RS 6420	Lick My Decals Off, Baby	1970	5.00	10.00	20.00
STRAIGHT					
❏ 2 STS-1053 [(2)]	Trout Mask Replica	1969	62.50	125.00	250.00
—Stock copy with 1053 labels (this has been confirmed to exist)					
❏ 2 STS-1053 [(2)DJ]	Trout Mask Replica	1969	50.00	100.00	200.00
—White label promo with 1053 labels					
❏ 2MS 2027 [(2)]	Trout Mask Replica	1969	15.00	30.00	60.00
—Stock copy with 2027 labels inside 1053 jacket					
❏ 2MS 2027 [(2)DJ]	Trout Mask Replica	1969	37.50	75.00	150.00
—White label promo with 2027 labels inside 1053 jacket					
❏ RS 6420	Lick My Decals Off, Baby	1970	12.50	25.00	50.00
VERVE FORECAST					
❏ FTS-3054	Captain Beefheart and the Magic Band	1968	—	—	—
—Canceled					
VIRGIN					
❏ VA 13148	Doc at the Radar Station	1980	3.00	6.00	12.00
VIRGIN/EPIC					
❏ ARE 38274	Ice Cream for Crow	1982	3.00	6.00	12.00
WARNER BROS.					
❏ (no #)	Bat Chain Puller	1978	100.00	200.00	400.00
—Test pressing with different selections than stock version					
❏ BSK 3256	Shiny Beast (Bat Chain Puller)	1978	3.00	6.00	12.00

CAPTAIN BEYOND
45s
CAPRICORN

Number	Title (A Side/B Side)	Yr	VG	VG+	NM
❏ 0013	As the Moon Speaks (Return)/A Thousand Days of Yesterdays (Time Since Come & Gone)	1972	—	3.00	6.00
❏ 0029	Drifting in Space/Sufficiently Breathless	1973	—	3.00	6.00
Albums					
CAPRICORN					
❏ CP 0105	Captain Beyond	1972	3.75	7.50	15.00
—Later covers are normal					
❏ CP 0105	Captain Beyond	1972	7.50	15.00	30.00
—Original covers are 3-D					
❏ CP 0115	Sufficiently Breathless	1973	3.75	7.50	15.00
WARNER BROS.					
❏ BS 3047	Dawn Explosion	1977	2.50	5.00	10.00

CAPTAIN ZAP AND THE MOTORTOWN CUT-UPS
45s
MOTOWN

Number	Title (A Side/B Side)	Yr	VG	VG+	NM
❏ 1151	The Luney Landing/The Luney Take-Off	1969	5.00	10.00	20.00

CAPTIVATIONS, THE
45s
GARPAX

Number	Title (A Side/B Side)	Yr	VG	VG+	NM
❏ 44179	Red Hot Scrambler-Go/Speed Shift	1964	7.50	15.00	30.00
PENTACLE					
❏ 1635	Red Hot Scramblers-Go/Speed Shift	1964	15.00	30.00	60.00

CARAVAN
45s
LONDON

Number	Title (A Side/B Side)	Yr	VG	VG+	NM
❏ 20065	Love to Love You/Golf Girl	1971	—	3.00	6.00
❏ 20080	Headloss/(B-side unknown)	1973	—	3.00	6.00
VERVE FORECAST					
❏ 5102	A Place of My Own/Ride	1969	2.50	5.00	10.00
Albums					
ARISTA					
❏ AL 4088	Blind Dog	1976	2.50	5.00	10.00
BTM					
❏ 5000	Cunning Stunts	1975	2.50	5.00	10.00
LONDON					
❏ PS 582	If I Could Do It All Over Again…	1971	3.75	7.50	15.00
❏ PS 593	In the Land of the Grey & Pink	1971	3.75	7.50	15.00
❏ XPS 615	Waterloo Lily	1972	3.75	7.50	15.00
❏ XPS 637	For Girls Who Grow Plump in the Night	1973	3.75	7.50	15.00
❏ XPS 650	Caravan and the New Symphonia	1974	3.75	7.50	15.00
❏ LC 50011	The Best of Caravan	1978	2.50	5.00	10.00
VERVE FORECAST					
❏ FTS-3066	Caravan	1969	10.00	20.00	40.00

CARAVAN, JIMMY
Albums
TOWER

Number	Title (A Side/B Side)	Yr	VG	VG+	NM
❏ ST 5103 [S]	Look Into the Flower	1968	5.00	10.00	20.00
❏ T 5103 [M]	Look Into the Flower	1968	12.50	25.00	50.00
VAULT					
❏ 9007	Hey Jude	1969	5.00	10.00	20.00

CARAVELLES, THE (1) British female vocal group.
45s
SMASH

Number	Title (A Side/B Side)	Yr	VG	VG+	NM
❏ 1852	You Don't Have to Be a Baby to Cry/ The Last One to Know	1963	3.75	7.50	15.00
❏ 1869	Have You Ever Been Lonely/ Don't Blow Your Cool	1964	3.00	6.00	12.00

Number	Title (A Side/B Side)	Yr	VG	VG+	NM
❏ 1901	You Are Here/How Can I Be Sure	1964	3.00	6.00	12.00
❏ 1958	I Don't Care If the Sun Don't Shine/I Like a Man	1964	3.00	6.00	12.00
Albums					
SMASH					
❏ MGS-27044 [M]	You Don't Have to Be a Baby to Cry	1963	15.00	30.00	60.00
❏ SRS-67044 [R]	You Don't Have to Be a Baby to Cry	1963	15.00	30.00	60.00

CARAVELLES, THE (U) These may or may not be the same group, but they are definitely not group (1).
45s
JOEY

Number	Title (A Side/B Side)	Yr	VG	VG+	NM
❏ 301	Falling for You/Shake Baby	1963	37.50	75.00	150.00
❏ 6208	One Little Kiss/Twistin' Marie	1962	25.00	50.00	100.00
STARMAKER					
❏ 1925	Pink Lips/Angry Angel	1961	6.25	12.50	25.00

CARBO, CHUCK Also see THE SPIDERS (1).
45s
ACE

Number	Title (A Side/B Side)	Yr	VG	VG+	NM
❏ 631	Tears, Tears and More Tears/I Shouldn't, But I Do	1961	3.00	6.00	12.00
❏ 666	Out on a Limb/Getting Out	1962	3.00	6.00	12.00
IMPERIAL					
❏ 5405	That's the Way to Win My Heart/Goodbye	1956	6.25	12.50	25.00
❏ 5423	Honey Bee/That's My Desire	1957	7.50	15.00	30.00
❏ 5452	The Bells Are Ringing/Poor Boy	1957	5.00	10.00	20.00
❏ 5479	I Miss You/The Times	1957	5.00	10.00	20.00
INSTANT					
❏ 3240	In the Night/Run. Henry	1962	3.00	6.00	12.00
❏ 3254	Two Tables Away/What Does It Take	1962	3.00	6.00	12.00
REX					
❏ 1003	Promises/Be My Girl	1959	3.75	7.50	15.00
❏ 1011	Lucy Brown/A Picture of You	1960	3.75	7.50	15.00
❏ 1012	Blue Velvet/It's You	1960	3.75	7.50	15.00

CARDBOARD ZEPPELIN Supposedly a pseudonym for THE REGENTS.
45s
LAURIE

Number	Title (A Side/B Side)	Yr	VG	VG+	NM
❏ 3433	City Lights/Ten Story Building	1968	6.25	12.50	25.00

CARDINALS, THE (1) Baltimore-based male vocal group.
45s
ATLANTIC

Number	Title (A Side/B Side)	Yr	VG	VG+	NM
❏ 952	I'll Always Love You/Pretty Baby Blues	1952	100.00	200.00	400.00
—Cardinals records on Atlantic before 952 are unconfirmed on 45 rpm					
❏ 958	Wheel of Fortune/Kiss Me Baby	1952	150.00	300.00	600.00
❏ 972	The Bump/She Rocks	1952	75.00	150.00	300.00
❏ 995	You Are My Only Love/Lovie Darling	1953	100.00	200.00	400.00
❏ 1025	Please Baby/Under a Blanket of Blue	1954	50.00	100.00	200.00
❏ 1054	The Door Is Still Open/Misirlou	1955	20.00	40.00	80.00
❏ 1067	Come Back My Love/Two Things I Love	1955	25.00	50.00	100.00
❏ 1079	Lovely Girl/There Goes My Heart to You	1955	25.00	50.00	100.00
❏ 1090	Choo Choo/Off Shore	1956	12.50	25.00	50.00
❏ 1103	The End of the Story/ I Won't Make You Cry Anymore	1956	12.50	25.00	50.00
❏ 1126	Near You/One Love	1957	10.00	20.00	40.00

CARDINALS, THE (2)
45s
CHA CHA

Number	Title (A Side/B Side)	Yr	VG	VG+	NM
❏ 740	I Want You/Tomato Juice	1966	7.50	15.00	30.00
❏ 740 [PS]	I Want You/Tomato Juice	1966	12.50	25.00	50.00
❏ 741	Go Go Baby/Hatchet Face	1966	6.25	12.50	25.00
❏ 742	Saturday Night/I'm Gonna Tell on You	1966	6.25	12.50	25.00
❏ 748	When You're Away/I'm Gonna Tell on You	1966	6.25	12.50	25.00

CARE PACKAGE
45s
JUBILEE

Number	Title (A Side/B Side)	Yr	VG	VG+	NM
❏ 5599	To Discover/World of Thursday	1967	2.50	5.00	10.00
Albums					
LIBERTY					
❏ LST-7647	Keep On Keepin' On	1970	6.25	12.50	25.00

CAREFREES, THE
45s
LONDON INT'L.

Number	Title (A Side/B Side)	Yr	VG	VG+	NM
❏ 10614	We Love You Beatles/Hot Blooded Lover	1964	5.00	10.00	20.00
—Gold label					
❏ 10614	We Love You Beatles/Hot Blooded Lover	1964	5.00	10.00	20.00
—Red label					
❏ 10614 [PS]	We Love You Beatles/Hot Blooded Lover	1964	10.00	20.00	40.00
❏ 10615	Paddy Whack/Aren't You Glad You're You	1964	3.75	7.50	15.00
Albums					
LONDON					
❏ PS 379 [S]	From England! The Carefrees	1964	25.00	50.00	100.00
❏ LL 3379 [M]	From England! The Carefrees	1964	20.00	40.00	80.00

CARETAKERS, THE
45s
ABC

Number	Title (A Side/B Side)	Yr	VG	VG+	NM
❏ 11110	Get Off My Tulips/Bee Side Blues	1968	3.00	6.00	12.00

CARGILL, HENSON
45s
ARCO

Number	Title (A Side/B Side)	Yr	VG	VG+	NM
❏ 6605	Big Town/How Long Is Never	1967	2.00	4.00	8.00
ATLANTIC					
❏ 4007	Some Old California Memory/ A Writer of Verses and a Singer of Songs	1973	—	2.00	4.00
❏ 4016	She Still Comes to Me (To Pour the Wine)/ But You Know I Love You	1974	—	2.00	4.00
❏ 4021	Stop and Smell the Roses/Strawberry Wine	1974	—	2.00	4.00
COPPER MOUNTAIN					
❏ 201	Silence on the Line/Forever in Blue Jeans	1979	—	2.00	4.00
❏ 589	Have a Good Day/(B-side unknown)	1980	—	2.00	4.00
ELEKTRA					
❏ 45234	Deep in the Heart of Dixie/It Hurts the Man	1975	—	2.00	4.00
❏ 45273	Something to Hold On To/Now and Then	1975	—	2.00	4.00

Number	Title (A Side/B Side)	Yr	VG	VG+	NM
MEGA					
❏ 0030	Pencil Marks on the Wall/Momma's Waiting	1971	—	2.50	5.00
❏ 0043	Naked and Crying/Afraid to Rock the Boat	1971	—	2.50	5.00
❏ 0060	I Can't Face the Bed Alone/Daddy Don't You Walk So Fast	1972	—	2.50	5.00
❏ 0074	Oklahoma Hell/She Likes Warm Summer Days	1972	—	2.50	5.00
❏ 0090	Red Skies Over Georgia/1932	1972	—	2.50	5.00
❏ 0100	Running from the Rain/My '47 Chevy, My Honky Tonk Guitar, and Me	1973	—	2.50	5.00
MONUMENT					
❏ 1041	Skip a Rope/Very Well Traveled Man	1967	—	3.00	6.00
❏ 1065	Row Row Row/Six White Horses	1968	—	3.00	6.00
❏ 1084	She Thinks I'm On That Train/It Just Don't Take Me Long to Say Goodbye	1968	—	3.00	6.00
❏ 1106	A Candle for Amy/Wild Flower	1968	—	3.00	6.00
❏ 1122	None of My Business/So Many Ways of Saying She's Gone	1969	—	3.00	6.00
❏ 1142	This Generation Shall Not Pass/Little Girls and Little Boys	1969	—	3.00	6.00
❏ 1158	Then the Baby Came/Hemphill, Kentucky, Consolidated Coal Mine	1969	—	3.00	6.00
❏ 1178	Silver Bells/The Little Drummer Boy	1969	2.00	4.00	8.00
❏ 1184	Me & Bobby McGee/What's My Name	1970	—	3.00	6.00
❏ 1198	The Most Uncomplicated Goodbye I've Ever Heard/Four Shades of Love	1970	—	3.00	6.00
❏ 1209	Bless 'Em All/How Much Do Mommies Cost?	1970	—	3.00	6.00
TOWER					
❏ 400	Picking White Cotton/Joe, Jesse and I	1968	2.00	4.00	8.00
Albums					
ATLANTIC					
❏ SD 7279	This Is Henson Cargill Country	1973	3.00	6.00	12.00
HARMONY					
❏ KH 31397	Welcome to My World	1972	2.50	5.00	10.00
MEGA					
❏ 31-1016	On the Road	1972	3.75	7.50	15.00
MONUMENT					
❏ SLP-18094	Skip a Rope	1968	5.00	10.00	20.00
❏ SLP-18103	Coming On Strong	1968	5.00	10.00	20.00
❏ SLP-18117	None of My Business	1969	5.00	10.00	20.00
❏ SLP-18137	Uncomplicated	1970	5.00	10.00	20.00

CARIANS, THE   Also see THE CORDIALS.
45s

Number	Title (A Side/B Side)	Yr	VG	VG+	NM
INDIGO					
❏ 136	She's Gone/Snooty Friends	1961	25.00	50.00	100.00
MAGENTA					
❏ 04	Only a Dream/Girls	1961	12.50	25.00	50.00

CARLA AND RUFUS   See RUFUS AND CARLA.

CARLE, BOBBY, AND THE BLENDAIRES
45s

Number	Title (A Side/B Side)	Yr	VG	VG+	NM
DECCA					
❏ 30938	I Got It Bad and That Ain't Good/Guaranteed	1959	7.50	15.00	30.00

CARLIN, GEORGE
45s

Number	Title (A Side/B Side)	Yr	VG	VG+	NM
LITTLE DAVID					
❏ 720	Eleven O'Clock News (Part 1)/Eleven O'Clock News (Part 2)	1971	—	3.00	6.00
❏ 731	New News (Part 1)/New News (Part 2)	1974	—	3.00	6.00
❏ 736	Head Lines (Part 1)/Head Lines (Part 2)	1977	—	3.00	6.00
RCA VICTOR					
❏ 47-9110	Winderful WINO/Al Sleet, Your Hippy Dippy Weatherman	1967	2.50	5.00	10.00
7-Inch Extended Plays					
ATLANTIC					
❏ EP-PR-409 [DJ]*Have a Nice Day/Rice Krispies/Second, Third, Fifth, Sixth Announcements/Join the Book Club/Ice Box Man		1981	2.50	5.00	10.00
❏ EP-PR-409 [PS]A Place for My Stuff		1981	2.50	5.00	10.00
Albums					
ATLANTIC					
❏ SD 19326	A Place for My Stuff	1981	2.50	5.00	10.00
EARDRUM					
❏ 1001	Carlin On Campus	1984	2.50	5.00	10.00
❏ 90523	Playin' with Your Head	1986	2.50	5.00	10.00
❏ 90972	What Am I Doing in New Jersey?	1988	2.50	5.00	10.00
ERA					
❏ EL 103 [M]	George Carlin and Jack Burns At the Playboy Club Tonight	1960	6.25	12.50	25.00
❏ E 600	The Original George Carlin	1972	3.00	6.00	12.00
LAFF					
❏ A 219	Killer Carlin	1981	2.50	5.00	10.00
—Reissue of Era material					
LITTLE DAVID					
❏ LD 1004	Class Clown	1972	2.50	5.00	10.00
❏ LD 1005	Occupation: Foole	1973	2.50	5.00	10.00
❏ LD 1008	An Evening with Wally Londo	1975	2.50	5.00	10.00
❏ LD 1075	On the Road	1977	2.50	5.00	10.00
❏ LD 1076	Indecent Exposure (Some of the Best of George Carlin)	1978	2.50	5.00	10.00
❏ LD 3003	Toledo Window Box	1974	2.50	5.00	10.00
❏ LD 7214	FM & AM	1972	2.50	5.00	10.00
❏ 90129	Toledo Window Box	1983	2.00	4.00	8.00
—Reissue of 3003					
❏ 90241	The George Carlin Collection	1984	2.00	4.00	8.00
RCA CAMDEN					
❏ CAS-2566	Take-Offs and Put-Ons	1972	2.50	5.00	10.00
RCA VICTOR					
❏ LPM-3772 [M]	Take-Offs and Put-Ons	1967	5.00	10.00	20.00
❏ LSP-3772 [S]	Take-Offs and Put-Ons	1967	3.75	7.50	15.00

Number	Title (A Side/B Side)	Yr	VG	VG+	NM
CARLO					
45s					
LAURIE					
❏ 3063	Happy Time/Rockin' Rocket	1960	5.00	10.00	20.00
—As "Carlo and Jimmy"					
❏ 3151	Baby Doll/Write Me a Letter	1962	7.50	15.00	30.00
❏ 3157	Little Orphan Girl/Mairzy Doats	1963	7.50	15.00	30.00
❏ 3175	Five Minutes More/The Story of Love	1963	7.50	15.00	30.00
❏ 3227	Ring-a-Ling/Stranger in My Arms	1964	12.50	25.00	50.00
RAFTIS					
❏ 110	Claudine/Fever	1970	3.00	6.00	12.00

CARLOS, WALTER   In the early 1980s, he became a she (Wendy Carlos). It's possible that many of the early LPs were reissued with the new name on them, but we have not confirmed this.
45s

Number	Title (A Side/B Side)	Yr	VG	VG+	NM
COLUMBIA					
❏ 8-3322 [PS]	A Second Chance for Bach!	1969	5.00	10.00	20.00
—Promo-only sleeve that came with JZSP 139195/6					
❏ 44803	Brandenberg Concerto No. 3 in G Major/Two-Part Invention in F Major	1969	2.50	5.00	10.00
❏ 45033	Third Movement, Brandenburg Concerto No. 4 in D Major/Scarliotta Sonata	1969	2.50	5.00	10.00
❏ JZSP 139195/6 [DJ]Third Movement, Brandenburg Concerto No. 3 (mono/stereo)		1969	3.00	6.00	12.00
Albums					
CBS MASTERWORKS					
❏ M 39340	Digital Moonscapes	1984	2.50	5.00	10.00
—As "Wendy Carlos"					
COLUMBIA					
❏ KG 31236 [(2)]	Sonic Seasonings	1972	3.75	7.50	15.00
❏ KC 31480	Walter Carlos' Clockwork Orange	1972	3.00	6.00	12.00
COLUMBIA MASTERWORKS					
❏ MS 7194	Switched-On Bach	1968	3.75	7.50	15.00
—"Standing Bach" cover; gray label with "360 Sound Stereo"					
❏ MS 7194	Switched-On Bach	1968	12.50	25.00	50.00
—"Sitting Bach" (sometimes called "Constipated Bach") cover that was quickly replaced; gray label with "360 Sound Stereo"					
❏ MS 7194	Switched-On Bach	1970	3.00	6.00	12.00
—Gray label with orange Columbia logos and no "360 Sound Stereo"					
❏ MS 7194	Switched-On Bach	198?	3.75	7.50	15.00
—Later reissue under the name "Wendy Carlos"; bar code on back cover					
❏ MS 7286	The Well-Tempered Synthesizer	1969	3.75	7.50	15.00
—Gray label with "360 Sound Stereo"					
❏ MS 7286	The Well-Tempered Synthesizer	1970	3.00	6.00	12.00
—Gray label with orange Columbia logos and no "360 Sound Stereo"					
❏ M 32088	Walter Carlos By Request	1973	3.00	6.00	12.00
❏ KM 32659	More Switched-On Bach	1974	3.00	6.00	12.00
❏ M2X 35895 [(2)]Switched-On Brandenburgs		1979	3.75	7.50	15.00
❏ HM 45950	Switched-On Brandenburgs Vol. 1	1980	25.00	50.00	100.00
—Half-speed mastered edition					
❏ HM 47194	Switched-On Bach	198?	7.50	15.00	30.00
—Half-speed mastered edition					

CARLTON, CARL
12-Inch Singles

Number	Title (A Side/B Side)	Yr	VG	VG+	NM
CASABLANCA					
❏ 880949-1	Private Property (Club Mix 6:43) (Dub Version 6:23)	1985	2.50	5.00	10.00
❏ 884274-1	Slipped, Tripped (Fooled Around and Fell in Love) (Special Club Remix) (Dub Version)/Hot	1986	3.00	6.00	12.00
RCA					
❏ PD-13314	Baby I Need Your Loving (5:56)/Everyone Can Be a Star	1982	2.50	5.00	10.00
❏ PD-13407	Swing That Sexy Thang/Just One Kiss	1982	2.50	5.00	10.00
20TH CENTURY					
❏ TCD-129	She's a Bad Mama Jama (She's Built, She's Stacked)/This Feeling's Rated X-Tra	1981	5.00	10.00	20.00
45s					
ABC					
❏ 11378	You Can't Stop a Man in Love/You Times Me Plus Love	1973	—	2.50	5.00
❏ 12059	Smokin' Room/Signed, Sealed, Delivered, I'm Yours	1974	—	2.50	5.00
❏ 12089	Morning, Noon and Nightime/Our Day Will Come	1975	—	2.50	5.00
❏ 12166	Ain't Gonna Tell Nobody (About You)/Live for Today, Not for Tomorrow	1976	—	2.50	5.00
❏ 12226	Let's Groove/Live for Today, Not for Tomorrow	1976	—	2.50	5.00
BACK BEAT					
❏ 588	Competition Ain't Nothin'/Three Way Love	1968	—	3.00	6.00
—As "Little Carl Carlton"					
❏ 598	46 Drums — 1 Guitar/Why Don't They Leave Us Alone	1968	—	3.00	6.00
—As "Little Carl Carlton"					
❏ 603	Look at Mary Wonder (How I Got Over)/Bad for Each Other	1969	—	3.00	6.00
❏ 610	Don't Walk Away/Hold On a Little Longer	1969	—	3.00	6.00
❏ 613	Drop By My Place/Two Timer	1970	—	3.00	6.00
—As "Little Carl Carlton"					
❏ 617	I Can Feel It/You've Got So Much (To Learn About Love)	1970	—	3.00	6.00
❏ 619	Sure Miss Loving You/Wild Child	1970	—	3.00	6.00
❏ 621	Wild Child/Look at Mary Wonder (How I Got Over)	1971	—	3.00	6.00
❏ 624	The Generation Gap/Where Have You Been	1972	—	3.00	6.00
❏ 627	I Won't Let That Chump Break Your Heart/Why Don't They Leave Us Alone	1972	—	3.00	6.00
❏ 629	It Ain't Been Easy/I Wanna Be Your Main Squeeze	1973	—	3.00	6.00
❏ 630	Everlasting Love/I Wanna Be Your Main Squeeze	1974	2.00	4.00	8.00
❏ 27001	Everlasting Love/I Wanna Be Your Main Squeeze	1974	—	2.50	5.00
CASABLANCA					
❏ 880949-7	Private Property/Mama's Boy	1985	—	—	3.00
❏ 884274-7	Slipped, Tripped (Fooled Around and Fell in Love)/Hot	1986	—	—	3.00

C

Number	Title (A Side/B Side)	Yr	VG	VG+	NM
GOLDEN WORLD					
❑ 23	Nothin' No Sweeter Than Love/I Love True Love	1965	6.25	12.50	25.00
LANDO					
❑ 8527	So What/(B-side unknown)	1965	12.50	25.00	50.00
MERCURY					
❑ 73969	Something's Wrong/You, You	1977	—	2.00	4.00
RCA					
❑ PB-13313	Baby I Need Your Loving/Everyone Can Be a Star	1982	—	2.00	4.00
❑ PB-13406	Swing That Sexy Thang/Just One Kiss	1982	—	2.00	4.00
20TH CENTURY					
❑ 2459	This Feeling's Rated X-Tra/Fighting in the Name of Love	1980	—	2.00	4.00
❑ 2488	She's a Bad Mama Jama (She's Built, She's Stacked)/This Feeling's Rated X-Tra	1981	—	2.00	4.00
❑ 2513	Let Me Love You Till the Morning Comes/Sexy Lady	1982	—	2.00	4.00
❑ 2601	I Think It's Gonna Be Alright/Let Me Love You Till the Morning Comes	1982	—	2.00	4.00
Albums					
ABC					
❑ D-857	Everlasting Love	1974	3.00	6.00	12.00
❑ D-910	I Wanna Be with You	1975	3.00	6.00	12.00
BACK BEAT					
❑ BBLX-71	Can't Stop a Man in Love	1973	3.75	7.50	15.00
CASABLANCA					
❑ 822705-1	Private Property	1985	2.50	5.00	10.00
RCA VICTOR					
❑ AFL1-4425	The Bad C.C.	1982	2.50	5.00	10.00
20TH CENTURY					
❑ T-628	Carl Carlton	1981	2.50	5.00	10.00
CARLTON, LARRY					
12-Inch Singles					
WARNER BROS.					
❑ PRO-A-2043 [DJ]	Tequila (2 versions)	1983	2.00	4.00	8.00
45s					
BLUE THUMB					
❑ 227	An American Family/(B-side unknown)	1973	2.00	4.00	8.00
MCA					
❑ S45-17400 [DJ]	Hello Tomorrow (same on both sides)	1987	—	3.00	6.00
❑ 52844	Smiles and Smiles to Go/Carrying You	1986	—	—	3.00
❑ 52844 [PS]	Smiles and Smiles to Go/Carrying You	1986	—	—	3.00
❑ 53319	Minute by Minute/Hello Tomorrow	1987	—	—	3.00
UNI					
❑ 55080	The Odd Couple/Monday, Monday	1968	2.50	5.00	10.00
❑ 55120	Moon People/Son of a Preacher Man	1969	2.00	4.00	8.00
WARNER BROS.					
❑ 8694	Room 335/Where Did You Come From	1978	—	2.00	4.00
❑ 29590	Tequila/L.A., N.Y.	1983	—	2.00	4.00
❑ 29977	Song for Katie/10:00 P.M.	1982	—	2.00	4.00
❑ 50019	Sleepwalk/Frenchman's Flat	1982	—	2.00	4.00
Albums					
BLUE THUMB					
❑ BTS-46	Singing/Playing	1972	3.75	7.50	15.00
GRP					
❑ 9611	Collection	1990	3.00	6.00	12.00
MCA					
❑ 5689	Alone/But Never Alone	1986	2.00	4.00	8.00
❑ 6237	On Solid Ground	1989	2.00	4.00	8.00
❑ 6322	Christmas at Our House	1989	2.50	5.00	10.00
❑ 42003	Discovery	1987	2.00	4.00	8.00
UNI					
❑ 73036	With a Little Help from My Friends	1968	5.00	10.00	20.00
WARNER BROS.					
❑ BSK 3221	Larry Carlton	1978	2.50	5.00	10.00
❑ BSK 3380	Strikes Twice	1980	2.50	5.00	10.00
❑ BSK 3635	Sleepwalk	1981	2.50	5.00	10.00
❑ 23834	Friends	1983	2.00	4.00	8.00
CARMEL SISTERS, THE Also see CAROL CONNORS.					
45s					
COLPIX					
❑ 767	Go, Go, G.T.O./Sunny Winter	1965	75.00	150.00	300.00
—As "Carol and Cheryl"					
JUBILEE					
❑ 5464	Joey's Comin' Home/The Rumor	1963	5.00	10.00	20.00
CARMEN, ERIC Also see CYRUS ERIE; THE QUICK; RASPBERRIES.					
12-Inch Singles					
GEFFEN					
❑ 20294	I Wanna Hear It from Your Lips (2 versions)	1984	2.00	4.00	8.00
45s					
ARISTA					
❑ 0165	All By Myself/Everything	1975	—	2.00	4.00
❑ 0184	Never Gonna Fall in Love Again/No Hard Feelings	1976	—	2.00	4.00
❑ 0200	Sunrise/My Girl	1976	—	2.00	4.00
❑ 0266	She Did It/Someday	1977	—	2.00	4.00
❑ 0266 [PS]	She Did It/Someday	1977	—	3.00	6.00
❑ 0295	Boats Against the Current/Take It or Leave It	1977	—	2.00	4.00
❑ 0319	Marathon Man/I Think I Found Myself	1978	—	2.00	4.00
❑ 0354	Change of Heart/Hey Deanie	1978	—	2.00	4.00
❑ 0384	Baby I Need Your Lovin'/Heaven Can Wait	1979	—	2.00	4.00
❑ 0435	Haven't We Come a Long Way/End of the World	1979	—	2.00	4.00
❑ 0506	It Hurts Too Much/You Need Some Lovin'	1980	—	2.00	4.00
❑ 0550	All for Love/Tonight You're Mine	1980	—	2.00	4.00
❑ 9686	Make Me Lose Control/That's Rock 'N' Roll	1988	—	—	3.00
❑ 9686 [PS]	Make Me Lose Control/That's Rock 'N' Roll	1988	—	—	3.00
❑ 9736	Boats Against the Current/No Hard Feelings	1988	—	—	3.00
❑ 9746	Reason to Try/Sunrise	1988	—	—	3.00
❑ 9746 [PS]	Reason to Try/Sunrise	1988	—	—	3.00
COOL					
❑ 101	The Rock Stops Here (same on both sides)	1988	—	—	3.00
❑ 101 [PS]	The Rock Stops Here (same on both sides)	1988	—	—	3.00
—Semi-promotional record used to promote Cleveland's candidacy for the site of the Rock and Roll Hall of Fame					

Number	Title (A Side/B Side)	Yr	VG	VG+	NM
EPIC					
❑ 10669	I'll Hold Out My Hand/It Won't Be the Same Without You	1970	—	—	—
—Not known to exist					
GEFFEN					
❑ 29032	I'm Through with Love/Maybe My Baby	1985	—	—	3.00
❑ 29032 [PS]	I'm Through with Love/Maybe My Baby	1985	—	—	3.00
❑ 29118	I Wanna Hear It from Your Lips/Spotlight	1985	—	—	3.00
❑ 29118 [PS]	I Wanna Hear It from Your Lips/Spotlight	1985	—	—	3.00
RCA					
❑ 5315-7-R	Hungry Eyes/Where Are You Tonight	1987	—	—	3.00
Albums					
ARISTA					
❑ AL 4057	Eric Carmen	1975	2.00	4.00	8.00
—Regular non-shiny gold cover					
❑ AL 4057	Eric Carmen	1975	3.00	6.00	12.00
—Shiny, simulated gold foil cover					
❑ AQ 4057 [Q]	Eric Carmen	1975	4.50	9.00	18.00
❑ AB 4124	Boats Against the Current	1977	2.00	4.00	8.00
❑ AB 4184	Change of Heart	1978	2.00	4.00	8.00
❑ AL 8547	The Best of Eric Carmen	1988	2.00	4.00	8.00
—Reissues add "Make Me Lose Control"					
❑ AL 8547	The Best of Eric Carmen	1988	3.75	7.50	15.00
—Original copies do not contain "Make Me Lose Control"					
❑ AL 9513	Tonight You're Mine	1980	2.00	4.00	8.00
GEFFEN					
❑ GHS 24042	Eric Carmen	1985	2.00	4.00	8.00
CARMICHAEL, BILL					
45s					
HIT					
❑ 38	Limbo Rock/Don't Hang Up	1962	2.00	4.00	8.00
—B-side by the Dacrons					
❑ 45	It's Up to You/Tell Him	1962	2.00	4.00	8.00
—B-side by Peggy Gaines					
CARMICHAEL, SANDY					
45s					
HIT					
❑ 35	Don't Go Near the Indians/Return to Sender	1962	2.00	4.00	8.00
—B-side by Ed Hardin					
CARNATIONS, THE Several different groups.					
45s					
DERBY					
❑ 789	Tree in the Meadow/Clown of the Masquerade	1952	100.00	200.00	400.00
ENRICA					
❑ 1001	Gimme, Gimme, Gimme/Love, Open My Heart	1959	6.25	12.50	25.00
FRATERNITY					
❑ 863	Red Wing/Casual	1960	6.25	12.50	25.00
LAURIE					
❑ 3163	Punctuation/Funny Time	1963	6.25	12.50	25.00
LESCAY					
❑ 3002	Long Tall Girl/Is There Such a World	1961	25.00	50.00	100.00
LOST-NITE					
❑ 145	Long Tall Girl/Is There Such a World	196?	—	3.00	6.00
—Reissue					
SAVOY					
❑ 1172	Angels Sent You to Me/Night Time Is the Right Time	1955	15.00	30.00	60.00
TERRY-TONE					
❑ 199	Barbary Coast/Sleepy Hollow	1960	10.00	20.00	40.00
UNIVERSITY					
❑ 606	Leap Year/A Wing and a Prayer	1960	6.25	12.50	25.00
CARNE, JUDY					
45s					
REPRISE					
❑ 0680	Sock It To Me/Right, Said Fred	1968	2.50	5.00	10.00
CARNES, KIM Also see GENE COTTON; KENNY ROGERS; BARBRA STREISAND.					
12-Inch Singles					
EMI AMERICA					
❑ V-7815	Invisible Hands (Dance Mix) (FM Mix)	1983	2.50	5.00	10.00
❑ V-7819	You Make My Heart Beat Faster (And That's All That Matters) (Dance Mix) (Instrumental)	1983	3.00	6.00	12.00
❑ V-7829	Hurricane (Extended Vocal Version 5:18) (Instrumental 4:47)	1984	3.00	6.00	12.00
❑ V-7851	Invitation to Dance (Vocal Dance Mix) (Instrumental Dance Mix)	1985	2.50	5.00	10.00
❑ V-7857	Crazy in the Night (Barking at Airplanes) (Dance Mix 5:10) (Part II Dub Mix 4:59)	1985	2.50	5.00	10.00
❑ V-7863	Abadabadango (2 versions)/He Makes the Sun Rise	1985	2.50	5.00	10.00
❑ SPRO-9022/3 [DJ]	Invisible Hands (Dance Mix) (FM Mix)	1983	2.50	5.00	10.00
❑ SPRO 9036/7 [DJ]	It Hurts So Bad/What Am I Gonna Do	1979	3.00	6.00	12.00
❑ SPRO-9042/3 [DJ]	Invisible Hands (FM Mix)/You Make My Heart Beat Faster (And That's All That Matters)	1983	3.00	6.00	12.00
❑ SPRO-9118/9 [DJ]	Hurricane (Extended Vocal Version 5:18) (Instrumental 4:47)	1984	3.75	7.50	15.00
❑ SPRO-9670/1 [DJ]	Draw of the Cards (Short Version 3:58) (Long Mix 4:54)	1981	5.00	10.00	20.00
❑ SPRO-9702/3 [DJ]	Divided Hearts (Club Mix 7:29) (Red Mix 4:47) (Dub 6:08) (Instrumental 4:21)	1986	3.00	6.00	12.00
❑ SPRO 9821 [DJ]	Voyeur (same on both sides)	1982	2.50	5.00	10.00
❑ SPRO 9845 [DJ]	Voyeur (Extended Version) (same on both sides?)	1982	3.00	6.00	12.00
45s					
A&M					
❑ 1748	Somewhere in the Night/Hang On to Your Airplane (Honeymoon)	1975	—	2.50	5.00
❑ 1767	You're a Part of Me/Hang On to Your Airplane (Honeymoon)	1975	—	2.50	5.00
❑ 1807 [DJ]	Bad Seed (mono/stereo)	1976	2.00	4.00	8.00
—No stock copies issued					
❑ 1902	The Last Thing You Ever Wanted to Do/Let Your Love Come Easy	1977	—	2.50	5.00

Number	Title (A Side/B Side)	Yr	VG	VG+	NM
❏ 1943	Sailin'/He'll Come Home	1977	—	2.50	5.00
AMOS					
❏ 165	I Won't Call You Back/To Love	1971	2.00	4.00	8.00
❏ 166	To Love Somebody/Fell in Love with a Poet	1971	2.00	4.00	8.00
❏ 167	It's Love That Keeps It All Together/Long and Lonely Memeories	1971	2.00	4.00	8.00
—With Dave Ellingson					
EMI AMERICA					
❏ 8010	Losing Love/Looking for a Big Night	1979	—	2.50	5.00
❏ 8011	It Hurts So Bad/Lookin' for a Big Night	1979	—	2.50	5.00
❏ 8014	What Am I Gonna Do/Goodnight Moon	1979	—	2.50	5.00
❏ 8045	More Love/Changin'	1980	—	2.00	4.00
❏ 8045 [PS]	More Love/Changin'	1980	—	3.00	6.00
❏ 8058	Cry Like a Baby/In the Chill of the Night	1980	—	2.00	4.00
❏ 8069	Mas Amor/Changin'	1980	2.00	4.00	8.00
❏ 8077	Bette Davis Eyes/Miss You Tonight	1981	—	2.00	4.00
❏ 8077 [PS]	Bette Davis Eyes/Miss You Tonight	1981	—	2.00	4.00
❏ A-8087	Draw of the Cards/Break the Rules Tonite (Out of School)	1981	—	2.00	4.00
❏ A-8087 [PS]	Draw of the Cards/Break the Rules Tonite (Out of School)	1981	—	2.00	4.00
❏ A-8098	Mistaken Identity/Jamaica Sunday Morning	1981	—	2.00	4.00
❏ A-8098 [PS]	Mistaken Identity/Jamaica Sunday Morning	1981	—	2.00	4.00
❏ B-8127	Voyeur/Thrill of the Grill	1982	—	—	3.00
❏ B-8127 [PS]	Voyeur/Thrill of the Grill	1982	—	—	3.00
❏ B-8147	Does It Make You Remember/ Take It on the Chin	1982	—	—	3.00
❏ B-8147 [PS]	Does It Make You Remember/ Take It on the Chin	1982	—	—	3.00
❏ B-8154	Say You Don't Know Me/ Breakin' Away from Society	1983	—	2.50	5.00
❏ B-8181	Invisible Hands/I'll Be Here Where the Heart Is	1983	—	—	3.00
❏ B-8181 [PS]	Invisible Hands/I'll Be Here Where the Heart Is	1983	—	—	3.00
❏ B-8191	You Make My Heart Beat Faster (And That's All That Matters)/Hangin' On by a Thread	1984	—	—	3.00
❏ B-8191 [PS]	You Make My Heart Beat Faster (And That's All That Matters)/Hangin' On by a Thread	1984	—	—	3.00
❏ B-8202	I Pretend/Hurricane	1984	—	—	3.00
❏ B-8202 [PS]	I Pretend/Hurricane	1984	—	—	3.00
❏ B-8250	Invitation to Dance/Breakthrough	1984	—	—	3.00
—B-side by Haven					
❏ B-8250 [PS]	Invitation to Dance/Breakthrough	1984	—	—	3.00
❏ B-8267	Crazy in the Night (Barking at Airplanes)/Oliver (Voice on the Radio)	1985	—	—	3.00
❏ B-8267 [PS]	Crazy in the Night (Barking at Airplanes)/Oliver (Voice on the Radio)	1985	—	—	3.00
❏ B-8281	Abadabadango/He Makes the Sun Rise (Orpheus)	1985	—	—	3.00
❏ B-8281 [PS]	Abadabadango/He Makes the Sun Rise (Orpheus)	1985	—	—	3.00
❏ B-8290	Rough Edges/Begging for Favors (Learning How Things Work)	1985	—	2.00	4.00
❏ B-8322	Divided Hearts/You Say You Love Me (But I Know You Don't)	1986	—	—	3.00
❏ B-8322 [PS]	Divided Hearts/You Say You Love Me (But I Know You Don't)	1986	—	—	3.00
❏ B-8335	I'd Lie to You for Your Love/Black and White	1986	—	2.00	4.00
MCA					
❏ S45-17682 [DJ]	Crazy in Love/(New Version)	1988	—	2.50	5.00
❏ 53387	Speed of the Sound of Loneliness/Blood from the Bandit	1988	—	—	3.00
❏ 53433	Crazy in Love/Blood from the Bandit	1988	—	—	3.00
❏ 53433 [PS]	Crazy in Love/Blood from the Bandit	1988	—	2.00	4.00
❏ 53494	Fantastic Fire of Love/Brass and Batons	1989	—	—	3.00
Albums					
A&M					
❏ SP-3114	Sailin'	198?	2.00	4.00	8.00
—Budget-line reissue					
❏ SP-3204	The Best of Kim Carnes	1982	2.50	5.00	10.00
❏ SP-4548	Kim Carnes	1975	3.00	6.00	12.00
❏ SP-4606	Sailin'	1976	3.00	6.00	12.00
AMOS					
❏ AAS 7016	Rest on Me	1971	5.00	10.00	20.00
EMI AMERICA					
❏ SW-17004	St. Vincent's Court	1978	2.50	5.00	10.00
❏ SW-17030	Romance Dance	1980	2.50	5.00	10.00
❏ SO-17052	Mistaken Identity	1981	2.50	5.00	10.00
❏ SO-17078	Voyeur	1982	2.50	5.00	10.00
❏ SO-17107	Café Racers	1983	2.50	5.00	10.00
❏ SO-17159	Barking at Airplanes	1985	2.50	5.00	10.00
❏ ST-17198	Light House	1986	2.00	4.00	8.00
MCA					
❏ 914	The Early Years	1984	2.00	4.00	8.00
❏ 42200	View from the House	1988	2.00	4.00	8.00
MOBILE FIDELITY					
❏ 1-073	Mistaken Identity	1982	6.25	12.50	25.00
—Audiophile vinyl					

CARNIVAL
45s
UNITED ARTISTS

Number	Title (A Side/B Side)	Yr	VG	VG+	NM
❏ 50749	Where There's a Heartache (There Must Be a Heart)/The Truth About It	1971	—	2.50	5.00
❏ 50749 [PS]	Where There's a Heartache (There Must Be a Heart)/The Truth About It	1971	3.00	6.00	12.00
WORLD PACIFIC					
❏ 77932	Laia Ladaia/Calito de Carnival	1969	—	3.00	6.00
Albums					
WORLD PACIFIC					
❏ ST-21894	The Carnival	1969	3.00	6.00	12.00

CARO, NYDIA
45s
ROULETTE

Number	Title (A Side/B Side)	Yr	VG	VG+	NM
❏ 4588	Ask Me What I Want for Christmas/ Hey Johnny What	1964	3.00	6.00	12.00
❏ 4588 [PS]	Ask Me What I Want for Christmas/ Hey Johnny What	1964	5.00	10.00	20.00

CAROL AND CHERYL See THE CARMEL SISTERS.

CAROL AND GERRI
45s
MGM

Number	Title (A Side/B Side)	Yr	VG	VG+	NM
❏ 13568	How Can I Ever Find the Way/On You, Heartache Looks Good	1966	10.00	20.00	40.00

CAROL, LINDA AND CATHY
45s
UNITED

Number	Title (A Side/B Side)	Yr	VG	VG+	NM
❏ 216	Merry Christmas/ I Don't Wanna Be Last On Santa's List	1957	5.00	10.00	20.00

CAROLINA SLIM
Albums
SHARP

Number	Title (A Side/B Side)	Yr	VG	VG+	NM
❏ 2002 [M]	Blues from the Cotton Fields	195?	62.50	125.00	250.00

CAROLS, THE (1) Female group.
45s
LAMP

Number	Title (A Side/B Side)	Yr	VG	VG+	NM
❏ 2001	My Search Is Over/Keko	1957	12.50	25.00	50.00

CAROLS, THE (2) Male group.
45s
SAVOY

Number	Title (A Side/B Side)	Yr	VG	VG+	NM
❏ 896	Fifty Million Women/I Got a Feelin'	1953	37.50	75.00	150.00

CAROUSEL, THE
45s
ABC

Number	Title (A Side/B Side)	Yr	VG	VG+	NM
❏ 10953	One Mistake/Only One for Me	1967	3.00	6.00	12.00
TEEN TOWN					
❏ 108	I've Been with You/What Will You Do for Me	1969	3.75	7.50	15.00
❏ 116	To Say Goodbye/I Get Along Indefinitely	1969	3.75	7.50	15.00

CAROUSELS, THE Possibly more than one group.
45s
ABC-PARAMOUNT

Number	Title (A Side/B Side)	Yr	VG	VG+	NM
❏ 10233	Symptoms of Love/The Hush of Love	1961	6.25	12.50	25.00
AUTUMN					
❏ 13	Beneath the Willow/Sail Away	1965	2.50	5.00	10.00
GONE					
❏ 5118	If You Want To/Pretty Little Thing	1961	7.50	15.00	30.00
❏ 5118	You Can Come If You Want To/Pretty Little Thing	1961	12.50	25.00	50.00
❏ 5131	Never Let Him Go/Dirty Tricks	1962	6.25	12.50	25.00
GUYDEN					
❏ 2102	I Wanna Fly/Something Else	1964	3.00	6.00	12.00
JAGUAR					
❏ 3029	Drive-In Movie/Rendezvous	1959	15.00	30.00	60.00
SPRY					
❏ 116	I've Cried Enough/Did I Cry Enough	1962	37.50	75.00	150.00

CARP Actor Gary Busey was in this group.
45s
EPIC

Number	Title (A Side/B Side)	Yr	VG	VG+	NM
❏ 10632	Save the Delta Queen/ Mammoth Mountain Blues	1970	2.00	4.00	8.00
❏ 10647	Pine Creek Bridge/Page 258	1970	2.00	4.00	8.00
Albums					
EPIC					
❏ E 30212	Carp	1970	6.25	12.50	25.00

CARPENTERS
45s
A&M

Number	Title (A Side/B Side)	Yr	VG	VG+	NM
❏ 1142	Ticket to Ride/Your Wonderful Parade	1969	2.50	5.00	10.00
❏ 1183	(They Long to Be) Close to You/I Kept On Loving You	1970	—	2.50	5.00
❏ 1217	We've Only Just Begun/All of My Life	1970	—	2.50	5.00
❏ 1217 [PS]	We've Only Just Begun/All of My Life	1970	—	3.00	6.00
❏ 1236	Merry Christmas Darling/Mr. Guder	1970	—	3.00	6.00
—A-side vocal is different than later releases of this song					
❏ 1236 [PS]	Merry Christmas Darling/Mr. Guder	1970	2.00	4.00	8.00
❏ 1243	For All We Know/Don't Be Afraid	1971	—	2.00	4.00
❏ 1243 [PS]	For All We Know/Don't Be Afraid	1971	—	3.00	6.00
❏ 1260	Rainy Days and Mondays/Saturday	1971	—	2.00	4.00
❏ 1260 [PS]	Rainy Days and Mondays/Saturday	1971	—	3.00	6.00
❏ 1289	Superstar/Bless the Beasts and Children	1971	—	2.00	4.00
❏ 1289 [PS]	Superstar/Bless the Beasts and Children	1971	—	3.00	6.00
❏ 1322	Hurting Each Other/Maybe It's You	1972	—	2.00	4.00
❏ 1322 [PS]	Hurting Each Other/Maybe It's You	1972	—	3.00	6.00
❏ 1351	It's Going to Take Some Time/Flat Baroque	1972	—	2.00	4.00
❏ 1351 [PS]	It's Going to Take Some Time/Flat Baroque	1972	—	3.00	6.00
❏ 1367	Goodbye to Love/Crystal Lullaby	1972	—	2.00	4.00
❏ 1367 [PS]	Goodbye to Love/Crystal Lullaby	1972	—	3.00	6.00
❏ 1391	Top of the World/Druscilla Penny	1972	—	—	—
—Unreleased					
❏ 1413	Sing/Druscilla Penny	1973	—	2.00	4.00
❏ 1413 [PS]	Sing/Druscilla Penny	1973	—	3.00	6.00
❏ 1446	Yesterday Once More/Road Ode	1973	—	2.00	4.00
❏ 1446 [PS]	Yesterday Once More/Road Ode	1973	—	3.00	6.00
❏ 1468	Top of the World/Heather	1973	—	—	3.00
—Second pressings have silvery labels					
❏ 1468	Top of the World/Heather	1973	—	2.00	4.00
—Originals have brown labels					
❏ 1468 [PS]	Top of the World/Heather	1973	—	3.00	6.00
❏ 1521	I Won't Last a Day Without You/One Love	1974	—	2.00	4.00
❏ 1521 [PS]	I Won't Last a Day Without You/One Love	1974	—	3.00	6.00
❏ 1646	Please Mister Postman/This Masquerade	1974	—	2.00	4.00
❏ 1646 [PS]	Please Mister Postman/This Masquerade	1974	—	3.00	6.00
❏ 1648	Santa Claus Is Coming to Town/Merry Christmas Darling	1974	—	2.50	5.00
❏ 1648 [PS]	Santa Claus Is Coming to Town/Merry Christmas Darling	1974	2.50	5.00	10.00
❏ 1677	Only Yesterday/Happy	1975	—	2.00	4.00
❏ 1677 [PS]	Only Yesterday/Happy	1975	—	3.00	6.00
❏ 1721	Solitaire/Love Me for What I Am	1975	—	2.00	4.00

Number	Title (A Side/B Side)	Yr	VG	VG+	NM
❑ 1721 [PS]	Solitaire/Love Me for What I Am	1975	—	3.00	6.00
❑ 1800	There's a Kind of Hush (All Over the World)/(I'm Caught Between) Goodbye and I Love You	1976	—	2.00	4.00
❑ 1800 [PS]	There's a Kind of Hush (All Over the World)/(I'm Caught Between) Goodbye and I Love You	1976	—	3.00	6.00
❑ 1828	I Need to Be in Love/Sandy	1976	—	2.00	4.00
❑ 1859	Goofus/Boat to Sail	1976	—	2.00	4.00
❑ 1940	All You Get from Love Is a Love Song/I Have You	1977	—	2.00	4.00
❑ 1978	Calling Occupants of Interplanetary Craft/Can't Smile Without You	1977	—	2.00	4.00
❑ 1978 [PS]	Calling Occupants of Interplanetary Craft/Can't Smile Without You	1977	—	3.00	6.00
❑ 1991	The Christmas Song/Merry Christmas Darling	1977	—	2.50	5.00
❑ 1991 [PS]	The Christmas Song/Merry Christmas Darling	1977	2.00	4.00	8.00
❑ 2008	Sweet, Sweet Smile/I Have You	1978	—	2.00	4.00
❑ 2097	I Believe You/B'wana She No Home	1978	—	2.00	4.00
❑ 2344	Touch Me When We're Dancing/Because We Are in Love (The Wedding Song)	1981	—	2.00	4.00
❑ 2344 [PS]	Touch Me When We're Dancing/Because We Are in Love (The Wedding Song)	1981	—	2.00	4.00
❑ 2370	(Want You) Back in My Life Again/Somebody's Been Lyin'	1981	—	2.00	4.00
❑ 2386	Those Good Old Dreams/When It's Gone	1981	—	2.00	4.00
❑ 2405	Beechwood 4-5789/Two Sides	1982	—	2.00	4.00
❑ 2585	Make Believe It's Your First Time/Look to Your Dreams	1983	—	2.00	4.00
❑ 2585 [PS]	Make Believe It's Your First Time/Look to Your Dreams	1983	—	2.50	4.00
❑ 2620	Sailing on the Tide/Your Baby Doesn't Love You Anymore	1984	—	2.00	4.00
❑ 2700	Do You Hear What I Hear/Little Altar Boy	1984	2.50	5.00	10.00
❑ 2735	Yesterday Once More/(They Long to Be) Close to You-We've Only Just Begun	1985	5.00	10.00	20.00
❑ 2735 [PS]	Yesterday Once More/(They Long to Be) Close to You-We've Only Just Begun	1985	5.00	10.00	20.00
❑ 8620	Christmas Song/Merry Christmas Darling	1977	—	2.50	5.00

—"Forget Me Nots" green and gold label

❑ 8620 [PS]	Christmas Song/Merry Christmas Darling	1977	2.50	5.00	10.00
❑ 8629	Calling Occupants of Interplanetary Craft/Don't Cry for Me Argentina	1980	—	2.50	5.00
❑ 8629 [PS]	Calling Occupants of Interplanetary Craft/Don't Cry for Me Argentina	1980	3.75	7.50	15.00
❑ 8667	Honolulu City Lights/I Just Fall in Love Again	1986	—	2.50	5.00
❑ 8667 [PS]	Honolulu City Lights/I Just Fall in Love Again	1986	2.50	5.00	10.00
❑ SP-17001	Yesterday Once More/Rainy Days and Mondays	1978	12.50	25.00	50.00

—This 45 was contained in one of six different "Superstar Teaching Machine" packages. The price includes the record, a poster of the Carpenters, and a book of reading exercises.

MAGIC LAMP

| ❑ 704 | I'll Be Yours/Looking for Love | 1967 | 500.00 | 1000. | 2000. |

—As "Karen Carpenter", but Richard also was on this record

7-Inch Extended Plays

A&M

| ❑ LLP 3502 | Bacharach-David Hit Medley//Superstar/Let Me Be the One/For All We Know | 1971 | 3.75 | 7.50 | 15.00 |

—Jukebox issue; small hole, plays at 33 1/3 rpm

| ❑ LLP 3502 [PS] | Carpenters | 1971 | 3.75 | 7.50 | 15.00 |

—Part of "Little LP" series (LLP #151)

| ❑ LLP 3519 | Fun, Fun, Fun/The End of the World/Da Doo Ron Ron (When He Walked Me Home)/Deadman's Curve//Johnny Angel/The Night Has a Thousand Eyes/Our Day Will Come/One Fine Day | 1973 | 5.00 | 10.00 | 20.00 |

—Jukebox issue; small hole, plays at 33 1/3 rpm

| ❑ LLP 3519 [PS] | Now & Then | 1973 | 5.00 | 10.00 | 20.00 |

—Part of "Little LP" series (LLP #222)

| ❑ LLP 3601 | Ticket to Ride/(They Long to Be) Close to You/We've Only Just Begun/Top of the World/Rainy Days and Mondays | 1973 | 5.00 | 10.00 | 20.00 |

—Jukebox issue; small hole, plays at 33 1/3 rpm

| ❑ LLP 3601 [PS] | The Singles 1969-1973 | 1973 | 5.00 | 10.00 | 20.00 |

—Part of "Little LP" series (LLP #238)

| ❑ LLP 4271 | Help/Baby It's You/I'll Never Fall in Love Again/Love Is Surrender/Maybe It's You/(They Long to be) Close to You | 1970 | 3.75 | 7.50 | 15.00 |

—Jukebox issue; small hole, plays at 33 1/3 rpm

| ❑ LLP 4271 [PS] | Close to You | 1970 | 3.75 | 7.50 | 15.00 |

—Part of "Little LP" series (LLP #125)

Albums

A&M

| ❑ SP-3184 | Close to You | 1982 | 2.00 | 4.00 | 8.00 |

—Reissue of 4271

| ❑ SP-3197 | A Kind of Hush | 1982 | 2.00 | 4.00 | 8.00 |

—Reissue of 4581

| ❑ SP-3199 | Passage | 1982 | 2.00 | 4.00 | 8.00 |

—Reissue of 4703

| ❑ SP-3210 | Christmas Portrait | 198? | 2.00 | 4.00 | 8.00 |

—Reissue of SP-4726

❑ SP-3270	An Old-Fashioned Christmas	1984	2.50	5.00	10.00
❑ SP-3502	Carpenters	1971	3.00	6.00	12.00
❑ SP-3511	A Song for You	1972	3.00	6.00	12.00
❑ SP-3519	Now & Then	1973	3.00	6.00	12.00
❑ SP-3601	The Singles 1969-1973	1973	3.00	6.00	12.00
❑ SP-3723	Made in America	1981	3.00	6.00	12.00
❑ SP-4205	Offering	1969	20.00	40.00	80.00
❑ SP-4205	Ticket to Ride	1970	3.00	6.00	12.00

—Reissue of "Offering" with new title and cover

❑ SP-4271	Close to You	1970	3.00	6.00	12.00
❑ SP-4530	Horizon	1975	3.00	6.00	12.00
❑ SP-4581	A Kind of Hush	1976	3.00	6.00	12.00
❑ SP-4703	Passage	1977	3.00	6.00	12.00
❑ SP-4726	Christmas Portrait	1978	3.75	7.50	15.00
❑ SP-4954	Voice of the Heart	1983	3.00	6.00	12.00
❑ SP-5172	An Old Fashioned Christmas	1987	2.00	4.00	8.00

—Reissue of 3270 (record still says 3270 but cover is 5172)

| ❑ SP-6601 [(2)] | Yesterday Once More | 1985 | 3.75 | 7.50 | 15.00 |
| ❑ QU-53502 [Q] | Carpenters | 1974 | — | — | — |

—Not released

Number	Title (A Side/B Side)	Yr	VG	VG+	NM
❑ QU-53511 [Q]	A Song for You	1974	—	—	—

—Not released

❑ QU-53519 [Q]	Now & Then	1974	5.00	10.00	20.00
❑ QU-53601 [Q]	The Singles 1969-1973	1974	5.00	10.00	20.00
❑ QU-54271 [Q]	Close to You	1974	—	—	—

—Not released

| ❑ QU-54530 [Q] | Horizon | 1975 | 5.00 | 10.00 | 20.00 |
| ❑ SMAS-94398 | A Song for You | 1972 | 5.00 | 10.00 | 20.00 |

—Capitol Record Club edition; unlike the standard edition, the cover is smooth and not textured

CARPETS, THE
45s
FEDERAL

| ❑ 12257 | Why Do I/Let Her Go | 1956 | 50.00 | 100.00 | 200.00 |
| ❑ 12269 | Lonely Me/Chicken Backs | 1956 | 50.00 | 100.00 | 200.00 |

CARR, CATHY
45s
CORAL

❑ 60907	Heartbroken/Half Pink Boogie	1953	3.00	6.00	12.00
❑ 60988	I Just Can't Get That Melody Out of My Mind/Somebody Told You a Lie	1953	3.00	6.00	12.00
❑ 61092	I'll Cry at Your Wedding/Cryin' for the Caroline's	1953	3.00	6.00	12.00
❑ 61646	I'll Cry at Your Wedding/Heartbroken	1956	2.50	5.00	10.00

FRATERNITY

❑ 718	Morning, Noon and Night/Toward Evening	1955	5.00	10.00	20.00
❑ 734	Ivory Tower/Please Please Believe Me	1956	3.75	7.50	15.00
❑ 743	Heart Hideaway/The Boy on Page 35	1956	3.75	7.50	15.00
❑ 750	Oh Baby/Waltzing to the Blues	1956	3.75	7.50	15.00
❑ 757	It Looks Like Love/Una Momenta	1957	3.00	6.00	12.00
❑ 765	Wild Honey/Speak for Yourself John	1957	3.00	6.00	12.00
❑ 782	House of Heartache/Presents from the Past	1957	3.00	6.00	12.00
❑ 793	Doll Baby/Don't Come to My Party	1958	3.00	6.00	12.00

LAURIE

❑ 3133	Ivory Tower/Should I Believe Him	1962	2.50	5.00	10.00
❑ 3147	Sailorboy/Next Time a Band Plays a Waltz	1962	2.50	5.00	10.00
❑ 3161	I Waded in the Water/In Place of You	1963	2.50	5.00	10.00
❑ 3206	My Favorite Song/The Ghost of a Broken Heart	1963	2.50	5.00	10.00
❑ 3378	When You Come Home Again/The Ghost of a Broken Heart	1967	—	3.00	6.00

ROULETTE

❑ 4107	To Know Him Is to Love Him/Put Away the Invitation	1958	3.00	6.00	12.00
❑ 4125	First Anniversary/With Love	1959	3.00	6.00	12.00
❑ 4152 [M]	I'm Gonna Change Him/The Little Things You Do	1959	3.00	6.00	12.00
❑ SSR-4152 [S]	I'm Gonna Change Him/The Little Things You Do	1959	7.50	15.00	30.00
❑ 4187	Shy/Personal Secret	1959	3.00	6.00	12.00
❑ 4219	Little Sister/Dark River	1960	3.00	6.00	12.00
❑ 4248	A Little Time/What Do I Do Now	1960	3.00	6.00	12.00
❑ 4296	I Want to Be Your Pet/Golden Locket	1960	3.00	6.00	12.00
❑ 4323	Johnny's Song/Someone Told You a Lie	1961	3.00	6.00	12.00
❑ 4367	Yearning/Baseball He Loves	1961	3.00	6.00	12.00
❑ 4383	I Can't Begin to Tell You/You're Breaking My Heart	1961	3.00	6.00	12.00

SMASH

| ❑ 1726 | Footprints in the Snow/Nein, Nein, Fraulein | 1961 | 3.00 | 6.00 | 12.00 |

Albums
DOT

| ❑ DLP-3674 [M] | Ivory Tower | 1966 | 6.25 | 12.50 | 25.00 |
| ❑ DLP-25674 [S] | Ivory Tower | 1966 | 6.25 | 12.50 | 25.00 |

FRATERNITY

| ❑ 1005 [M] | Ivory Tower | 1957 | 30.00 | 60.00 | 120.00 |

ROULETTE

| ❑ R 25077 [M] | Shy | 1959 | 10.00 | 20.00 | 40.00 |
| ❑ SR 25077 [S] | Shy | 1959 | 12.50 | 25.00 | 50.00 |

CARR, JAMES
45s
ATLANTIC

| ❑ 2803 | Hold On/I'll Put It to You | 1971 | 3.00 | 6.00 | 12.00 |

GOLDWAX

❑ 108	You Don't Want Me/Only Fools Run Away	1965	7.50	15.00	30.00
❑ 112	I Can't Make It/Lovers' Competition	1965	7.50	15.00	30.00
❑ 119	He's Better Than You/Talk Talk	1965	7.50	15.00	30.00
❑ 302	You've Got My Mind Messed Up/That's What I Want to Know	1966	5.00	10.00	20.00
❑ 309	Love Attack/Come Back to Me Baby	1966	3.75	7.50	15.00
❑ 311	Pouring Water on a Drowning Man/Forgetting You	1966	3.75	7.50	15.00
❑ 317	The Dark End of the Street/Lovable Girl	1967	4.00	8.00	16.00
❑ 323	Let It Happen/A Losing Game	1967	3.75	7.50	15.00
❑ 328	I'm a Fool for You/Gonna Send You Back to Georgia	1967	3.75	7.50	15.00
❑ 332	A Man Needs a Woman/Stronger Than Love	1968	3.75	7.50	15.00
❑ 335	Life Turned Her That Way/A Message to Young Lovers	1968	3.75	7.50	15.00
❑ 338	Freedom Train/That's the Way Love Turned Out for Me	1968	3.75	7.50	15.00
❑ 340	To Love Somebody/These Ain't Teardrops	1969	3.75	7.50	15.00
❑ 343	Everybody Needs Somebody/Row, Row Your Boat	1969	3.75	7.50	15.00

Albums
GOLDWAX

| ❑ 3001S | You Got My Mind Messed Up | 1968 | 37.50 | 75.00 | 150.00 |
| ❑ 3002S | A Man Needs a Woman | 1968 | 37.50 | 75.00 | 150.00 |

CARR, VIKKI
45s
COLUMBIA

❑ AS 85 [DJ]	It Came Upon A Midnight Clear/Wind Me Up	1971	—	2.00	4.00
❑ AS 85 [PS]	It Came Upon A Midnight Clear/Wind Me Up	1971	2.00	4.00	8.00
❑ 10058	One Hell of a Woman/Wind Me Up	1974	—	2.00	4.00
❑ 10122	Hoy (Today)/El Pajaro Herido	1975	—	2.00	4.00
❑ 10214	Puttin' Myself in Your Hands (Gettin' Ready to Move)/I Don't Want a Sometimes Man	1975	—	2.00	4.00
❑ 45208	Ain't No Mountain High Enough/Call My Heart Your Home	1970	—	2.50	5.00
❑ 45296	I'll Be Home/Call My Heart Your Home	1971	—	2.00	4.00

C

Number	Title (A Side/B Side)	Yr	VG	VG+	NM
❏ 45403	Six Weeks Every Summer (Christmas Every Day)/If You Could Read My Mind	1971	—	2.00	4.00
❏ 45454	I Can't Give Back the Love I Feel for You/I've Never Been a Woman Before	1971	—	2.00	4.00
❏ 45510	I'd Do It All Again/I'm Gonna Love You	1971	—	2.00	4.00
❏ 45622	Cabaret/The Big Hurt	1972	—	2.00	4.00
❏ 45658	Y Volvere/Grande, Grande, Grande	1972	—	2.50	5.00
❏ 45750	Reflections/Let the Band Play On	1973	—	2.00	4.00
❏ 45809	Ms. America/We Didn't Know the Time of Day	1973	—	2.00	4.00
❏ 45955	Have You Heard the News/Leave a Little Room	1973	—	2.50	5.00
❏ 46033	Borrowed Time/Sleeping Between Two People	1974	—	2.00	4.00
LIBERTY					
❏ 55465	I'll Walk the Rest of the Way/Beside a Bridge	1962	2.50	5.00	10.00
❏ 55493	He's a Rebel/Be My Love	1962	5.00	10.00	20.00
—Recorded about the same time, and with many of the same musicians, as The Crystals' classic version.					
❏ 55564	The Rose and the Butterfly/From 9 to 5	1963	2.50	5.00	10.00
❏ 55620	San Francisco/Irma La Douce	1963	2.50	5.00	10.00
❏ 55620	San Francisco/Look Again	1963	2.50	5.00	10.00
❏ 55640	Right Kind of Woman/Poor Butterfly, Stay	1963	2.50	5.00	10.00
❏ 55736	Forget You/Her Little Heart Went to Loveland	1964	2.00	4.00	8.00
❏ 55783	Should I Follow/Don't Talk to Me (Spanish)	1965	2.00	4.00	8.00
❏ 55804	Theme from "Peyton Place"/Unforgettable	1965	2.00	4.00	8.00
❏ 55839	I Only Have Eyes for You/None But the Lonely Heart	1965	2.00	4.00	8.00
❏ 55857	The Silencers/Santiago	1966	—	3.00	6.00
❏ 55857 [PS]	The Silencers/Santiago	1966	2.50	5.00	10.00
❏ 55869	Heartaches/True Love's a Blessing	1966	—	3.00	6.00
❏ 55897	My Heart Reminds Me (Part 1)/My Heart Reminds Me (Part 2)	1966	—	3.00	6.00
❏ 55917	It Must Be Him/So Nice	1966	2.00	4.00	8.00
❏ 55937	Until Today/Now I Know the Feeling	1966	—	3.00	6.00
❏ 55976	Fly Away/Sunshine	1967	—	3.00	6.00
❏ 55986	It Must Be Him/That's All	1967	—	3.00	6.00
❏ 56012	The Lesson/One More Mountain	1968	—	2.50	5.00
❏ 56012 [PS]	The Lesson/One More Mountain	1968	2.50	5.00	10.00
❏ 56026	She'll Be There/Your Heart Is Free Just Like the Wind	1968	—	2.50	5.00
❏ 56039	Nothing to Lose/Don't Break My Pretty Balloon	1968	—	2.50	5.00
❏ 56062	Happy Together/Dissatisfied Man	1968	—	2.50	5.00
❏ 56092	With Pen in Hand/Can't Take My Eyes Off You	1969	—	2.50	5.00
❏ 56132	Eternity/I Will Wait for Love	1969	—	2.50	5.00
❏ 56185	Make It Rain/Singing My Song	1970	—	2.50	5.00
UNITED ARTISTS					
❏ 0097	It Must Be Him/The Lesson	1973	—	2.00	4.00
—"Silver Spotlight Series" reissue					
❏ 0098	With Pen in Hand/Eternity	1973	—	2.00	4.00
—"Silver Spotlight Series" reissue					
Albums					
COLUMBIA					
❏ C 30662	Vikki Carr's Love Story	1971	2.50	5.00	10.00
❏ C 31040	Superstar	1971	2.50	5.00	10.00
❏ KC 31453	The First Time Ever (I Saw Your Face)	1972	2.50	5.00	10.00
❏ KC 31470	Canta En Espanol	1972	2.50	5.00	10.00
❏ KC 32251	Ms. America	1973	2.50	5.00	10.00
❏ KG 32656 [(2)]	Live at the Greek Theatre	1973	3.00	6.00	12.00
❏ KC 32860	One Hell of a Woman	1974	2.50	5.00	10.00
❏ PC 33340	Hoy (Today)	1975	2.50	5.00	10.00
❏ CG 33609 [(2)]	Love Story/The First Time Ever	1976	3.00	6.00	12.00
LIBERTY					
❏ LRP-3314 [M]	Color Her Great	1963	3.75	7.50	15.00
❏ LRP-3354 [M]	Discovery!	1964	3.75	7.50	15.00
❏ LRP-3383 [M]	Discovery! Volume Two	1964	3.75	7.50	15.00
❏ LRP-3420 [M]	The Anatomy of Love	1965	3.75	7.50	15.00
❏ LRP-3456 [M]	The Way of Today	1966	3.75	7.50	15.00
❏ LRP-3506 [M]	Intimate Excitement	1967	5.00	10.00	20.00
❏ LRP-3533 [M]	It Must Be Him	1967	5.00	10.00	20.00
❏ LRP-3548 [M]	Vikki	1968	7.50	15.00	30.00
—Mono stock copy inside stereo cover with "Audition Mono LP Not for Sale" sticker					
❏ LST-7314 [S]	Color Her Great	1963	5.00	10.00	20.00
❏ LST-7354 [S]	Discovery!	1964	5.00	10.00	20.00
❏ LST-7383 [S]	Discovery! Volume Two	1964	5.00	10.00	20.00
❏ LST-7420 [S]	The Anatomy of Love	1965	5.00	10.00	20.00
❏ LST-7456 [S]	The Way of Today	1966	5.00	10.00	20.00
❏ LST-7506 [S]	Intimate Excitement	1967	3.75	7.50	15.00
❏ LST-7533 [S]	It Must Be Him	1967	3.75	7.50	15.00
❏ LST-7548 [S]	Vikki	1968	3.75	7.50	15.00
❏ LST-7565	Don't Break My Pretty Balloon	1969	3.75	7.50	15.00
❏ LST-7604	For Once in My Life	1969	3.75	7.50	15.00
❏ LN-10108	The Best of Vikki Carr	1981	2.00	4.00	8.00
❏ LST-11001	Nashville by Carr	1970	3.75	7.50	15.00
PAIR					
❏ PDL2-1082 [(2)]	From the Heart	1986	3.00	6.00	12.00
PICKWICK					
❏ SPC-3587	Intimate	1978	2.00	4.00	8.00
❏ SPC-3613	Unforgettable	1978	2.00	4.00	8.00
SUNSET					
❏ SUS-5228	That's All	1969	2.50	5.00	10.00
❏ SUS-5293	Unforgettable	1971	2.50	5.00	10.00
UNITED ARTISTS					
❏ UA-LA089-G [(2)]	Vikki Carr's Golden Songbook/Superpak	1973	3.00	6.00	12.00
❏ UA-LA244-G	The Very Best of Vikki Carr	1974	2.50	5.00	10.00
❏ LM-1006	It Must Be Him	1980	2.50	5.00	10.00
—Abridged reissue of Liberty 7533					
❏ UAS-5581 [(2)]	The Best of Vikki Carr	1972	3.00	6.00	12.00
❏ UAS-6813	The Ways to Love a Man	1972	2.50	5.00	10.00

CARROLL, ANDREA

45s

Number	Title (A Side/B Side)	Yr	VG	VG+	NM
BIG TOP					
❏ 515	The Doolang/This Time Tomorrow	1964	10.00	20.00	40.00
❏ 3156	It Hurts to Be Sixteen/Why Am I So Shy	1963	5.00	10.00	20.00
EPIC					
❏ 9438	I've Got a Date with Frankie/Young and Lonely	1961	25.00	50.00	100.00
❏ 9450	Please Don't Talk to the Lifeguard/Room of Memories	1961	5.00	10.00	20.00
❏ 9471	Gee Dad/The Charm on My Arm	1961	5.00	10.00	20.00
❏ 9471 [PS]	Gee Dad/The Charm on My Arm	1961	10.00	20.00	40.00
❏ 9523	Miss Happiness/Fifteen Shades of Pink	1962	5.00	10.00	20.00

Number	Title (A Side/B Side)	Yr	VG	VG+	NM
RCA VICTOR					
❏ 47-8618	Mr. Music Man/Sally Fool	1965	5.00	10.00	20.00
UNITED ARTISTS					
❏ 982	The World Isn't Big Enough/She Gets Everything She Wants	1966	5.00	10.00	20.00
❏ 50039	Hey, Beach Boy/Why Should We Take the Easy Way Out	1966	7.50	15.00	30.00

CARROLL, ANDREA /BEVERLY WARREN Also see each artist's individual listings.

Albums

Number	Title (A Side/B Side)	Yr	VG	VG+	NM
B.T. PUPPY					
❏ BTS-1017	Andrea Carroll and Beverly Warren Side By Side	1971	37.50	75.00	150.00

CARROLL, BERNADETTE

45s

Number	Title (A Side/B Side)	Yr	VG	VG+	NM
JULIA					
❏ 1106	My Heart Stood Still/Sweet Sugar Sweet	1962	3.75	7.50	15.00
LAURIE					
❏ 3217	Nicky/All the Way Home I Cried	1964	3.75	7.50	15.00
—The Four Seasons sing backup on this record					
❏ 3238	Party Girl/I Don't Wanna Know	1964	3.75	7.50	15.00
❏ 3268	Happy Birthday/Homecoming Party	1964	3.75	7.50	15.00
❏ 3278	The Hero/One Little Lie	1964	3.75	7.50	15.00
❏ 3311	Circus Girl/Don't Hurt Me	1965	3.75	7.50	15.00
❏ 3320	He's Just a Playboy/Try Your Luck	1965	3.75	7.50	15.00

CARROLL, DELORES, AND THE FOUR TOPS Also see THE FOUR TOPS.

45s

Number	Title (A Side/B Side)	Yr	VG	VG+	NM
CHATEAU					
❏ 2002	Everybody Knows/I Just Can't Keep the Tears from Tumblin' Down	1956	75.00	150.00	300.00

CARROLL, JIM Not the same Jim Carroll as the Jim Carroll Band ("People Who Died" in 1981).

45s

Number	Title (A Side/B Side)	Yr	VG	VG+	NM
A&M					
❏ 1329	On and On/I Don't Know	1972	—	2.50	5.00
❏ 1360	Save Me/I Got Plenty	1972	—	2.50	5.00
Albums					
A&M					
❏ SP-4323	Jim Carroll	1971	3.00	6.00	12.00

CARROLL, JOHNNY

45s

Number	Title (A Side/B Side)	Yr	VG	VG+	NM
DECCA					
❏ 29940	Rock and Roll Ruby/Tryin' to Get to You	1956	37.50	75.00	150.00
❏ 29941	Wild, Wild Women/Corrine, Corrina	1956	37.50	75.00	150.00
❏ 30013	Hot Rock/Crazy, Crazy	1956	37.50	75.00	150.00
PHILLIPS INT'L.					
❏ 3520	That's the Way I Love/I'll Wait	1957	50.00	100.00	200.00
SARG					
❏ 144	I'll Think of You/Stars Come Down	1956	20.00	40.00	80.00
WARNER BROS.					
❏ 5042	Bandstand Doll/The Swing	1958	7.50	15.00	30.00
❏ 5080	Lost Without You/Sugar	1959	7.50	15.00	30.00
Albums					
HMG/HIGHTONE					
❏ HT 6602	Texabilly	1997	2.50	5.00	10.00

CARROLL, RONNIE

45s

Number	Title (A Side/B Side)	Yr	VG	VG+	NM
PHILIPS					
❏ 40110	Say Wonderful Things/Please Tell Me Your Name	1963	3.00	6.00	12.00
❏ 40388	Tomorrow/Wait for Me	1966	2.50	5.00	10.00

CARROLL, WAYNE

45s

Number	Title (A Side/B Side)	Yr	VG	VG+	NM
KING					
❏ 5123	Chicken Out/Cindy Lee	1958	12.50	25.00	50.00
❏ 5134	Rockin' Chair Momma/There's Been a Change in Me	1958	12.50	25.00	50.00
❏ 5146	He Cheated/Wall Around Your Heart	1958	12.50	25.00	50.00

CARROLL BROTHERS, THE

45s

Number	Title (A Side/B Side)	Yr	VG	VG+	NM
CAMEO					
❏ 140	(My Gal Is) Red Hot/Dearly Beloved	1959	20.00	40.00	80.00
❏ 213	Don't Knock the Twist/Bo Diddley	1962	5.00	10.00	20.00
❏ 221	Sweet Georgia Brown/Boot It	1962	5.00	10.00	20.00
FELSTED					
❏ 8550	Movin' Day/I Found You	1959	5.00	10.00	20.00
Albums					
CAMEO					
❏ C-1015 [M]	College Twist Party	1962	6.25	12.50	25.00
❏ SC-1015 [S]	College Twist Party	1962	10.00	20.00	40.00

CARSON, MARTHA

45s

Number	Title (A Side/B Side)	Yr	VG	VG+	NM
CAPITOL					
❏ F1900	Satisfied/Hide Me Rock of Ages	1951	3.75	7.50	15.00
❏ F1982	Weighed the Balance/You Sure Do Need Him Now	1952	3.75	7.50	15.00
❏ F2077	I Wanna Rest/Old Blind Barnabas	1952	3.75	7.50	15.00
❏ F2145	Beyond the Shadow/I'm Gonna Walk and Talk with the Lord	1952	3.75	7.50	15.00
❏ F2180	He Will Set Your Fields on Fire/When God Dips His Love	1952	3.75	7.50	15.00
❏ F2252	Fear Not/Cryin' Holy Unto the Lord	1952	3.75	7.50	15.00
❏ F2342	There's a Higher Power/Inspiration from Above	1953	3.75	7.50	15.00
❏ F2477	Ask and You Shall Receive/I Feel It in My Soul	1953	3.75	7.50	15.00
❏ F2634	Singing on the Other Side/I've Got a Better Place to Go	1953	3.75	7.50	15.00
❏ F2740	Lazarus/Bye & Bye	1954	3.75	7.50	15.00
❏ F2825	I Bowed Down/He'll Part the Water	1954	3.75	7.50	15.00
❏ F2969	Christmas Time Is Here/Peace On Earth (At Christmas Time)	1954	3.75	7.50	15.00
❏ F3045	It's Alright/Counting My Blessings	1955	3.75	7.50	15.00
❏ 4437	Everything's All Right/High on the Hill	1960	3.00	6.00	12.00

Number	Title (A Side/B Side)	Yr	VG	VG+	NM
RCA VICTOR					
❏ 47-6293	Laugh a Little More/Let the Light Shine on Me	1955	5.00	10.00	20.00
❏ 47-6413	David and Goliath/I Want to Rest a Little While	1956	5.00	10.00	20.00
❏ 47-6510	Dixieland Roll/Music Drives Me Crazy	1956	5.00	10.00	20.00
❏ 47-6603	All These Things/Faith Is the Key	1956	5.00	10.00	20.00
❏ 47-6724	Get That Golden Key/He Was There	1956	5.00	10.00	20.00
❏ 47-6861	Satisfied/Let the Light Shine on Me	1957	3.75	7.50	15.00
❏ 47-6948	Now Stop/Just Whistle or Call	1957	3.75	7.50	15.00
SIMS					
❏ 144	Everybody Needs Somebody/It Takes a Lot of Lovin'	1963	2.50	5.00	10.00
7-Inch Extended Plays					
CAPITOL					
❏ EAP 1-449	*Satisfied/Cryin' Holy Unto the Lord/I Wanna Rest/I'm Gonna Walk and Talk with My Lord	1954	3.75	7.50	15.00
❏ EAP 1-449 [PS]	Gospel Songs	1954	3.75	7.50	15.00
Albums					
CAPITOL					
❏ ST 1507 [S]	Satisfied	1960	7.50	15.00	30.00
❏ T 1507 [M]	Satisfied	1960	6.25	12.50	25.00
❏ ST 1607 [S]	A Talk with the Lord	1961	7.50	15.00	30.00
❏ T 1607 [M]	A Talk with the Lord	1961	6.25	12.50	25.00
RCA VICTOR					
❏ LPM-1145 [M]	Journey to the Sky	1955	10.00	20.00	40.00
❏ LPM-1490 [M]	Rock-a My Soul	1957	12.50	25.00	50.00
SIMS					
❏ LP-100 [M]	Martha Carson	196?	6.25	12.50	25.00
CARTER, BRENDA					
45s					
MUSICOR					
❏ 1353	Everything's Found a Home with Me But You/Mama and the Teacher	1969	—	3.50	7.00
❏ 1386	Miss Nosy Brown/Shadow from Her Eyes	1969	—	3.50	7.00
❏ 1399	Life of Riley's/While You're Forgetting Me	1970	—	3.50	7.00
CARTER, CALVIN					
45s					
VEE JAY					
❏ 419	The Roach/What'd I Say	1962	3.75	7.50	15.00
❏ 436	Twisting Bones/Crazy Little Mama Twist	1962	3.75	7.50	15.00
—As "The Cal Carter Singers"					
❏ 439	Mashed Potatoes/Wimoweh	1962	3.75	7.50	15.00
Albums					
VEE JAY					
❏ LP-1041 [M]	Twist with Calvin Carter	1962	25.00	50.00	100.00
❏ SR-1041 [S]	Twist with Calvin Carter	1962	37.50	75.00	150.00
CARTER, CLARENCE					
45s					
ABC					
❏ 12058	Warning/On Your Way Down	1974	—	2.00	4.00
❏ 12094	Everything Comes Up Roses/A Very Special Love Song	1975	—	2.00	4.00
❏ 12130	I Got Caught/Take It All Off	1975	—	2.00	4.00
❏ 12162	Dear Abby/Love Ain't Here No More	1976	—	2.00	4.00
❏ 12224	Heart Full of Song/All Messed Up	1976	—	2.00	4.00
ATLANTIC					
❏ 2461	I Can't See Myself/Looking for a Fox	1967	—	3.00	6.00
❏ 2508	Slip Away/Funky Fever	1968	2.00	4.00	8.00
❏ 2569	Too Weak to Fight/Let Me Comfort You	1968	—	3.00	6.00
❏ 2576	Back Door Santa/That Old Time Feeling	1968	2.00	4.00	8.00
❏ 2605	Snatching It Back/Making Love	1969	—	3.00	6.00
❏ 2642	The Feeling Is Right/You Can't Miss What You Can't Measure	1969	—	3.00	6.00
❏ 2660	Doin' Our Thing/I Smell a Rat	1969	—	3.00	6.00
❏ 2702	Take It Off Him and Put It On Me/A Few Troubles I've Had	1970	—	3.00	6.00
❏ 2726	I Can't Leave Your Love Alone/Devil Woman	1970	—	3.00	6.00
❏ 2748	Patches/Say It One More Time	1970	—	3.00	6.00
❏ 2774	It's All in Your Mind/Till I Can't Take It Anymore	1970	—	3.00	6.00
❏ 2801	The Court Room/Getting the Bills	1971	—	3.00	6.00
❏ 2818	Slipped, Tripped, and Fell in Love/I Hate to Love and Run	1971	—	3.00	6.00
❏ 2842	I'm the One/Scratch My Back	1971	—	3.00	6.00
❏ 2875	If You Can't Beat 'Em/Lonesomest Lonesome	1972	—	3.00	6.00
—With Candi Carter					
FAME					
❏ XW179	Put On Your Shoes and Walk/I Found Somebody New	1973	—	2.50	5.00
❏ XW250	Sixty Minute Man/Mother-in-Law	1973	—	2.50	5.00
❏ XW330	I'm the Midnight Special/I Got Another Woman	1973	—	2.50	5.00
❏ XW415	Love's Trying to Come to You/Heartbreak Woman	1974	—	2.50	5.00
❏ 1010	Tell Daddy/I Stayed Away Too Long	1966	3.00	6.00	12.00
❏ 1013	Thread the Needle/Don't Make My Baby Cry	1967	3.00	6.00	12.00
❏ 1016	Road of Love/She Ain't Gonna Do Right	1967	3.00	6.00	12.00
❏ 91006	Back in Your Arms/Holdin' Out	1972	—	2.50	5.00
ICHIBAN					
❏ 101	Messin' with My Mind/I Was in the Neighborhood	1986	—	—	3.00
❏ 106	If You Let Me Take You Home/So You're Leaving Me	1986	—	—	3.00
❏ 108	Strokin'/Love Me with Feelin'	1987	2.00	4.00	8.00
❏ 116	Doctor C.C./I Stayed Away Too Long	1987	—	—	3.00
❏ 131	Grandpa Can't Find His Kate/What'd I Say	1988	—	—	3.00
❏ 135	Trying to Sleep Tonight/(B-side unknown)	1988	—	—	3.00
❏ 158	I'm Just Not Good/I'm the Best	1989	—	—	3.00
❏ 164	Why Do I Stay Here and Take This Shit fro You/It's a Man Down There	1989	—	—	3.00
❏ 213	In Between a Rock and a Hard Place/Dance to the Blues	1990	—	—	3.00
❏ 222	Things Ain't Like They Used to Be/Pickin' 'Em Up, Layin' 'Em Down	1990	—	—	3.00
❏ 238	I Ain't Leaving, Girl/If You See My Lady	1991	—	—	3.00
❏ 262	"G" Spot/Hot Dog	1992	—	—	3.00
❏ 275	Hand Me Down Love/Let's Get a Quickie	1992	—	—	3.00

Number	Title (A Side/B Side)	Yr	VG	VG+	NM
RONN					
❏ 90	I Couldn't Refuse Your Love/What Was I Supposed to Do?	1977	—	2.50	5.00
VENTURE					
❏ 130	Jimmy's Disco/Searching	1980	—	2.00	4.00
❏ 141	Let's Burn/If I Stay	1980	—	2.00	4.00
❏ 145	It's a Monster Thang/If I Were Yours	1981	—	2.00	4.00
❏ 147	Can We Slip Away Again/If I Were Yours	1981	—	2.00	4.00
7-Inch Extended Plays					
ATLANTIC					
❏ EP 1021 [DJ]	Bad News/Soul Deep//I Can't Do Without You/I Smell a Rat	1969	3.75	7.50	15.00
—Promo only; white label, large hole					
❏ EP 1021 [PS]	Testifyin'	1969	5.00	10.00	20.00
—Promo only; white label, large hole					
Albums					
ABC					
❏ X-833	Real	1974	3.75	7.50	15.00
❏ X-896	Loneliness & Temptation	1975	3.75	7.50	15.00
❏ X-943	A Heart Full of Song	1976	3.75	7.50	15.00
ATLANTIC					
❏ SD 8192	This Is Clarence Carter	1968	7.50	15.00	30.00
❏ SD 8199	The Dynamic Clarence Carter	1969	7.50	15.00	30.00
❏ SD 8238	Testifyin'	1969	7.50	15.00	30.00
❏ 8267 [M]	Patches	1970	15.00	30.00	60.00
—Mono is white label promo only; "d/j copy monaural" sticker on stereo cover					
❏ SD 8267 [S]	Patches	1970	7.50	15.00	30.00
❏ SD 8282	The Best of Clarence Carter	1971	5.00	10.00	20.00
FAME					
❏ FM-LA186-F	Sixty Minutes	1973	3.75	7.50	15.00
ICHIBAN					
❏ ICH-1001	Messin' with My Mind	1986	3.00	6.00	12.00
❏ ICH-1003	Dr. C.C.	1986	3.00	6.00	12.00
❏ ICH-1016	Hooked on Love	1987	3.00	6.00	12.00
❏ ICH-1032	Touch of Blues	1988	3.00	6.00	12.00
❏ ICH-1068	Between a Rock and a Hard Place	1989	3.00	6.00	12.00
❏ ICH-1116	The Best of Clarence Carter: The Dr.'s Greatest Presciptions	1991	3.00	6.00	12.00
VENTURE					
❏ VL 1005	Let's Burn	1980	2.50	5.00	10.00
❏ VL 1009	Mr. Clarence Carter In Person	1981	2.50	5.00	10.00
CARTER, MEL					
45s					
AMOS					
❏ 132	Everything Stops for a Little While/This Is My Life	1970	—	3.00	6.00
❏ 139	Kiss Tomorrow Goodbye/This Is My Life	1970	—	3.00	6.00
ARWIN					
❏ 123	Sugar/I'm Coming Home	1960	3.75	7.50	15.00
BELL					
❏ 743	Didn't We/I Pretend	1968	—	3.00	6.00
❏ 775	Another Saturday Night/Coming From You	1969	—	3.00	6.00
CREAM					
❏ 8041	You Changed My Life Again/(B-side unknown)	1980	—	2.00	4.00
❏ 8143	Who's Right, Who's Wrong/I Don't Wanna Get Over You	1981	—	2.00	4.00
DERBY					
❏ 1003	When a Boy Falls in Love/So Wonderful	1963	3.00	6.00	12.00
❏ 1005	Time of Young Love/Wonderful Love	1963	3.00	6.00	12.00
❏ 1008	Why I Call Her Mine/After the Party, the Meeting Is Sweeter	1964	3.00	6.00	12.00
IMPERIAL					
❏ 66052	'Deed I Do/What's On Your Mind	1964	2.00	4.00	8.00
❏ 66078	I'll Never Be Free/The Richest Man Alive	1964	2.00	4.00	8.00
❏ 66101	High Noon/I Just Can't Imagine	1965	2.00	4.00	8.00
❏ 66113	Hold Me, Thrill Me, Kiss Me/Sweet Little Girl	1965	2.50	5.00	10.00
❏ 66138	(All of a Sudden) My Heart Sings/When I Hold the Hand of the One I Love	1965	2.00	4.00	8.00
❏ 66148	Love Is All We Need/I Wish I Didn't Love You So	1965	2.00	4.00	8.00
❏ 66165	Band of Gold/Detour	1966	2.00	4.00	8.00
❏ 66183	You You You/If You Lose Her	1966	2.00	4.00	8.00
❏ 66208	Take Good Care of Her/Tar and Cement	1966	2.00	4.00	8.00
❏ 66228	As Time Goes By/Look to the Rainbow	1966	2.00	4.00	8.00
LIBERTY					
❏ MLC-1 [DJ]	The Star Spangled Banner (same on both sides)	196?	3.00	6.00	12.00
—Promo only; "This record is issued by Liberty Records as a Public Service" on label					
❏ 55970	Edelweiss/For Once in My Life	1968	—	3.00	6.00
❏ 55987	Star Dust/Enter Laughing	1967	—	3.00	6.00
❏ 56000	Be My Love/Look Into My Love	1967	—	3.00	6.00
❏ 56015	Excuse Me/The Other Woman	1968	—	3.00	6.00
PRIVATE STOCK					
❏ 45,057	Put a Little Love Away/Dancing for Dimes	1975	—	2.00	4.00
❏ 45,087	My Coloring Book	1976	—	2.00	4.00
ROMAR					
❏ 711	She Is Me/Do Me Wrong, But Do Me	1973	—	2.00	4.00
❏ 714	Treasure of Love/Do Me Wrong, But Do Me	1973	—	2.00	4.00
❏ 716	I Only Have Eyes for You/Treasure of Love	1974	—	2.00	4.00
Albums					
AMOS					
❏ 7010	This Is My Life	1971	3.00	6.00	12.00
DERBY					
❏ LPM-702 [M]	When a Boy Falls in Love	1963	75.00	150.00	300.00
IMPERIAL					
❏ LP-9289 [M]	Hold Me, Thrill Me, Kiss Me	1965	3.75	7.50	15.00
❏ LP-9300 [M]	All of a Sudden My Heart Sings	1966	3.75	7.50	15.00
❏ LP-9319 [M]	Easy Listening	1966	3.75	7.50	15.00
❏ LP-12289 [S]	Hold Me, Thrill Me, Kiss Me	1965	5.00	10.00	20.00
❏ LP-12300 [S]	All of a Sudden My Heart Sings	1966	5.00	10.00	20.00
❏ LP-12319 [S]	Easy Listening	1966	5.00	10.00	20.00
SUNSET					
❏ SUS-5227	Mel Carter	1968	2.50	5.00	10.00
❏ SUS-5295	Easy Goin'	1970	2.50	5.00	10.00

Number	Title (A Side/B Side)	Yr	VG	VG+	NM

CARTER, SONNY
45s
CARLTON
| ❏ 481 | Crying Over You/My Lonely Life | 1959 | — | — | — |

—Unreleased?

DOT
| ❏ 15921 | Crying Over You/My Lonely Life | 1959 | 7.50 | 15.00 | 30.00 |

KING
| ❏ 4739 | There Is No Greater Love/Oh Baby | 1954 | 12.50 | 25.00 | 50.00 |
| ❏ 4756 | It's Strange but True/I Solemnly Swear | 1954 | 12.50 | 25.00 | 50.00 |

CARTER, WILF See MONTANA SLIM.

CARTER FAMILY, THE
45s
COLUMBIA
❏ 3-10387	Papa's Sugar/In the Pines				
	(The Longest Train I Ever Saw)	1976	—	2.50	5.00
❏ 3-10502	My Father's Fiddle/My Ship Will Sail	1977	—	2.50	5.00
❏ 4-20920	Fair and Tender Ladies/Foggy Mountain Top	1952	6.25	12.50	25.00
❏ 4-20974	I Never Will Marry/				
	The Sun's Gonna Shine in My Back Door	1952	6.25	12.50	25.00
❏ 4-20986	Amazing Grace/Softly and Tenderly	1952	6.25	12.50	25.00
❏ 4-21184	You Are My Flower/				
	I Ain't Gonna Work Tomorrow	1953	6.25	12.50	25.00
❏ 4-21233	Love, Oh Crazy Love/Time's a Wastin'	1954	6.25	12.50	25.00
❏ 4-21316	Are You Afraid to Remember Me/				
	He Went Slippin' Around	1954	6.25	12.50	25.00
❏ 4-43004	Keep on the Sunny Side/Fair and Tender Ladies	1964	2.50	5.00	10.00
❏ 4-43235	Farewell/You Win Again	1965	2.50	5.00	10.00
❏ 4-43579	I Walk the Line/For Lovin' Me	1966	2.00	4.00	8.00
❏ 4-44136	Once Around the Briar Patch/Bye Bye	1967	2.00	4.00	8.00
❏ 4-44982	If I Live Long Enough/Break My Mind	1969	2.00	4.00	8.00
❏ 4-45428	A Song to Mama/One More Summer in Virginia	1971	2.00	4.00	8.00
❏ 4-45581	Travelin' Minstrel Band/2001				
	(Ballad to the Future)	1972	—	3.50	7.00
❏ 4-45679	The World Needs a Melody/A Bird with Broken				
	Wings Can't Fly	1972	—	3.50	7.00

—As "The Carter Family with Johnny Cash"

LIBERTY
| ❏ 55501 | Fourteen Carat Nothing/Get Up Early in the | | | | |
| | Morning | 1962 | 3.00 | 6.00 | 12.00 |

MERCURY
| ❏ 870397-7 | Dixie Darlin'/Ain't Gonna Work Tomorrow | 1988 | — | 2.00 | 4.00 |

Albums
ACME
| ❏ LP-1 [M] | All Time Favorites | 1960 | 50.00 | 100.00 | 200.00 |
| ❏ LP-2 [M] | In Memory of A.P. Carter | 1960 | 50.00 | 100.00 | 200.00 |

COLUMBIA
❏ CL 2319 [M]	The Best of the Carter Family	1965	3.75	7.50	15.00
❏ CL 2617 [M]	Country Album	1967	6.25	12.50	25.00
❏ CS 9119 [S]	The Best of the Carter Family	1965	5.00	10.00	20.00
❏ CS 9417 [S]	Country Album	1967	5.00	10.00	20.00
❏ KC 31454	Travelin' Minstrel Band	1972	5.00	10.00	20.00
❏ KC 33084	Three Generations	1974	5.00	10.00	20.00
❏ KC 34266	Country's First Family	1976	5.00	10.00	20.00

DECCA
| ❏ DL 4404 [M] | A Collection of Favorites by the Carter Family | 1963 | 7.50 | 15.00 | 30.00 |
| ❏ DL 4557 [M] | More Favorites by the Carter Family | 1964 | 7.50 | 15.00 | 30.00 |

LIBERTY
| ❏ LRP-3230 [M] | The Carter Family Album | 1962 | 7.50 | 15.00 | 30.00 |
| ❏ LST-7230 [S] | The Carter Family Album | 1962 | 10.00 | 20.00 | 40.00 |

RCA CAMDEN
| ❏ ACL1-0047 [R] | My Old Cottage Home | 1973 | 2.50 | 5.00 | 10.00 |
| ❏ CAL-586 [M] | The Original and Great Carter Family | 1960 | 3.75 | 7.50 | 15.00 |

—Two-tone blue label with "RCA Camden" at top

| ❏ CAL-586 [M] | The Original and Great Carter Family | 1969 | 2.50 | 5.00 | 10.00 |

—All-blue label with "RCA" on its side at left and "Camden" straight at right (reissue)

❏ CAL-2473 [M]	Lonesome Pine Special	1971	3.00	6.00	12.00
❏ CAS-2554(e) [R]	More Golden Gems from the Original				
	Carter Family	1972	2.50	5.00	10.00

RCA VICTOR
| ❏ LPM-2772 [M] | 'Mid the Green Fields of Virginia | 1963 | 10.00 | 20.00 | 40.00 |
| ❏ LSP-2772 [R] | 'Mid the Green Fields of Virginia | 1963 | 5.00 | 10.00 | 20.00 |

STARDAY
| ❏ SLP-248 [M] | Echoes of the Carter Family | 1963 | 10.00 | 20.00 | 40.00 |

CARTEY, RIC
45s
ABC-PARAMOUNT
| ❏ 10415 | Poor Me/Something in My Eye | 1963 | 3.00 | 6.00 | 12.00 |

NRC
| ❏ 503 | My Heart Belongs to You/ | | | | |
| | Scratching on the Screen | 1959 | 12.50 | 25.00 | 50.00 |

RCA VICTOR
❏ 47-6751	Young Love/Oooh-Eee	1956	20.00	40.00	80.00
❏ 47-6828	Heart Throb/I Wancha to Know	1957	20.00	40.00	80.00
❏ 47-6920	Let Me Tell You About Love/				
	Born to Love One Woman	1957	30.00	60.00	120.00
❏ 47-7011	My Babe/Hello Down Easy	1957	30.00	60.00	120.00

STARS
| ❏ 539 | Young Love/Oooh-Eee | 1956 | 37.50 | 75.00 | 150.00 |

CARTOONE
45s
ATLANTIC
❏ 2598	Mr. Poor Man/Knik Knak Man	1969	2.00	4.00	8.00
❏ 2630	Reflections on a Common Theme/				
	Penny for the Sun	1969	—	3.00	6.00

Albums
ATLANTIC
| ❏ SD 8219 | Cartoone | 1969 | 5.00 | 10.00 | 20.00 |

CARVETTES, THE
45s
COPA
| ❏ 200-1/2 | A Lover's Prayer/Never Gonna Leave Me | 1959 | 200.00 | 400.00 | 800.00 |

CASANOVAS, THE
45s
APOLLO
❏ 471	That's All/Are You for Real	1955	25.00	50.00	100.00
❏ 474	It's Been a Long Time/Hush-a-Mecca	1955	37.50	75.00	150.00
❏ 477	I Don't Want You to Go/Please Be My Love	1955	37.50	75.00	150.00
❏ 483	My Baby's Love/Sleepy Head Mama	1956	37.50	75.00	150.00
❏ 519	Please Be Mine/For You and You Alone	1957	25.00	50.00	100.00
❏ 523	(I Got a) Good Lookin' Baby/You Are My Queen	1957	25.00	50.00	100.00

CASCADES, THE Probably all the same group.
45s
ARWIN
| ❏ 132 | Cheryl's Going Home/Truly Julie's Blues | 1966 | 2.00 | 4.00 | 8.00 |
| ❏ 134 | Midnight Lace/All's Fair in Love and War | 1966 | 2.00 | 4.00 | 8.00 |

CANBASE
| ❏ 714 | I Started a Joke/Sweet America | 1972 | — | 2.50 | 5.00 |

CHARTER
❏ 1018	She Was Never Mine (To Really Lose)/				
	My Best Girl	1964	3.75	7.50	15.00
❏ 1018	She Was Never Really Mine (To Lose)/				
	My Best Girl	1964	5.00	10.00	20.00

ERA BACK TO BACK HITS
| ❏ 027 | Rhythm of the Rain/Harlem Shuffle | 197? | — | 2.50 | 5.00 |

—A-side is a re-recording; B-side by Bob and Earl

LIBERTY
| ❏ 55822 | She'll Love Again/I Bet You Won't Stay | 1965 | 2.50 | 5.00 | 10.00 |

LONDON
| ❏ 177 | Two-Sided Man/The Woman's A Girl | 1972 | — | 2.50 | 5.00 |

PROBE
| ❏ 453 | Two-Sided Man/Everyone Is Blossoming | 1968 | 2.00 | 4.00 | 8.00 |
| ❏ 453 [PS] | Two-Sided Man/Everyone Is Blossoming | 1968 | 3.75 | 7.50 | 15.00 |

RCA VICTOR
❏ 47-8206	Cinderella/A Little Like Lovin'	1963	3.75	7.50	15.00
❏ 47-8268	For Your Sweet Love/Jeannie	1963	3.00	6.00	12.00
❏ 47-8321	Little Betty Falling Star/Those Were the Good				
	Old Days	1964	3.75	7.50	15.00
❏ 47-8402	I Dare You to Cry/Awake	1964	3.00	6.00	12.00
❏ 47-8206 [PS]	Cinderella/A Little Like Lovin'	1963	5.00	10.00	20.00

RENEE
| ❏ 105 | Pains in My Heart/One That I Can Spare | 19?? | 5.00 | 10.00 | 20.00 |

SMASH
| ❏ 2083 | Hey Little Girl of Mine/Blue Hours | 1967 | 2.00 | 4.00 | 8.00 |
| ❏ 2101 | Flying on the Ground/Main Street | 1967 | 2.00 | 4.00 | 8.00 |

UNI
❏ 55152	Maybe the Rain Will Fall/Naggin' Cries	1969	2.00	4.00	8.00
❏ 55169	Indian River/Big City Country Boy	1969	2.00	4.00	8.00
❏ 55200	But For Love/Hazel Autumn Cocoa Brown	1970	2.00	4.00	8.00
❏ 55231	April, May, June and July/Big Ugly Sky	1970	2.00	4.00	8.00

VALIANT
❏ 6021	There's a Reason/Second Chance	1962	6.25	12.50	25.00
❏ 6026	Rhythm of the Rain/Let Me Be	1962	5.00	10.00	20.00
❏ 6028	Shy Girl/The Last Leaf	1963	3.75	7.50	15.00
❏ 6032	I Wanna Be Your Lover/My First Day Alone	1963	3.75	7.50	15.00

WARNER BROS.
| ❏ 7114 | Rhythm of the Rain/The Last Leaf | 1968 | — | 2.50 | 5.00 |

—"Back to Back Hits" series; originals on green "W7" label

Albums
UNI
| ❏ 73069 | Maybe the Rain Will Fall | 1969 | 6.25 | 12.50 | 25.00 |

VALIANT
| ❏ W 405 [M] | Rhythm of the Rain | 1963 | 37.50 | 75.00 | 150.00 |
| ❏ WS 405 [S] | Rhythm of the Rain | 1963 | 75.00 | 150.00 | 300.00 |

CASEY, AL Also see DUANE EDDY.
45s
BLUE HORIZON
| ❏ 925 | Cookin'/Hot Foot | 1962 | 6.25 | 12.50 | 25.00 |

DOT
| ❏ 15524 | A Fool's Blues/Juice | 1956 | 7.50 | 15.00 | 30.00 |
| ❏ 15563 | Guitar Man/Come What May | 1957 | 10.00 | 20.00 | 40.00 |

HIGHLAND
| ❏ 1002 | Got the Teenage Blues/(B-side unknown) | 1959 | 10.00 | 20.00 | 40.00 |
| ❏ 1004 | Night Beat/The Stinger | 1960 | 6.25 | 12.50 | 25.00 |

LIBERTY
| ❏ 55117 | Willa Mae/She Gotta Shake | 1957 | 5.00 | 10.00 | 20.00 |

MCI
| ❏ 1005 | Pink Panther/If I Told You | 1965 | 3.75 | 7.50 | 15.00 |

STACY
❏ 925	Cookin'/Hot Foot	1962	3.75	7.50	15.00
❏ 936	Jivin' Around/Doin' the Shotish	1962	3.75	7.50	15.00
❏ 950	Laughin'/Chicken Feathers	1962	3.75	7.50	15.00
❏ 956	Doin' It/Monte Carlo	1963	3.75	7.50	15.00
❏ 961	Full House/Indian Love Call	1963	3.75	7.50	15.00
❏ 962	Surfin' Hootenanny/Easy Pickin'	1963	5.00	10.00	20.00

—Black vinyl

| ❏ 962 | Surfin' Hootenanny/Easy Pickin' | 1963 | 10.00 | 20.00 | 40.00 |

—Red vinyl

| ❏ 964 | Surfin' Blues/Guitars, Guitars, Guitars | 1963 | 3.75 | 7.50 | 15.00 |
| ❏ 971 | Cookin'/What Are We Gonna Do in '64 | 1964 | 3.75 | 7.50 | 15.00 |

UNITED ARTISTS
| ❏ 158 | The Stinger/Keep Talking | 1959 | 6.25 | 12.50 | 25.00 |
| ❏ 494 | Jivin' Around/Doin' the Shotish | 1962 | 6.25 | 12.50 | 25.00 |

Albums
STACY
| ❏ STM-100 [M] | Surfin' Hootenanny | 1963 | 75.00 | 150.00 | 300.00 |
| ❏ STS-100 [S] | Surfin' Hootenanny | 1963 | 100.00 | 200.00 | 400.00 |

SUNDAZED
| ❏ LP-5026 | Surfin' Hootenanny | 1996 | 2.50 | 5.00 | 10.00 |

CASEY, AL (2)
Albums
MOODSVILLE
| ❏ MVLP-12 [M] | The Al Casey Quartet | 1960 | 12.50 | 25.00 | 50.00 |

—Green label

Number	Title (A Side/B Side)	Yr	VG	VG+	NM
❑ MVLP-12 [M]	The Al Casey Quartet	1965	6.25	12.50	25.00

—Blue label, trident logo at right

SWINGVILLE

Number	Title (A Side/B Side)	Yr	VG	VG+	NM
❑ SVLP-2007 [M]	Buck Jumpin'	1960	12.50	25.00	50.00

—Purple label

| ❑ SVLP-2007 [M] | Buck Jumpin' | 1965 | 6.25 | 12.50 | 25.00 |

—Blue label, trident logo at right

CASH, ALVIN
45s
CHESS

Number	Title (A Side/B Side)	Yr	VG	VG+	NM
❑ 2098	Getaway/Saddle Up	1970	2.00	4.00	8.00

DAKAR

| ❑ 4559 | Doin' the Ali Shuffle/The Feeling | 1976 | — | 2.50 | 5.00 |

MAR-V-LUS

❑ 6002	Twine Time/The Bump	1964	3.75	7.50	15.00
❑ 6005	The Barracuda/Do It One More Time	1965	2.50	5.00	10.00
❑ 6006	Un-Wind the Twine/The Penguin	1965	2.50	5.00	10.00
❑ 6009	Boston Monkey/Unwind the Twine	1965	2.50	5.00	10.00
❑ 6012	The Philly Freeze/No Deposit No Return	1966	2.50	5.00	10.00
❑ 6014	Alvin's Boo-Ga-Loo/Let's Do Some Good Timing	1966	2.50	5.00	10.00
❑ 6015	Doin' the Ali Shuffle/Feel So Good	1967	2.50	5.00	10.00
❑ 6019	Different Strokes for Different Folks/The Change	1967	2.50	5.00	10.00

SEVENTY-7

| ❑ 112 | Alvin's Doing His Thing/It's a Party | 1972 | — | 3.00 | 6.00 |
| ❑ 118 | Doin' the Creep/Party Time | 1972 | — | 3.00 | 6.00 |

SOUND STAGE 7

| ❑ 1509 | Funky Washing Machine/I Don't Want It | 1973 | — | 3.00 | 6.00 |

TODDLIN' TOWN

❑ 104	Alvin's Bag/Whip It On Me	1968	2.00	4.00	8.00
❑ 111	Keep On Dancing/(Instrumental)	1968	2.00	4.00	8.00
❑ 119	Funky '69/Moaning and Groaning	1969	2.00	4.00	8.00
❑ 124	Poppin' Popcorn/(Instrumental)	1969	2.00	4.00	8.00

WESTBOUND

| ❑ 159 | Stone Thing (Part 1)/Stone Thing (Part 2) | 1970 | 2.00 | 4.00 | 8.00 |

Albums
MAR-V-LUS

| ❑ 1827 [M] | Twine Time | 1965 | 7.50 | 15.00 | 30.00 |

CASH, BOBBY
45s
HIT

| ❑ 143 | Do Wah Diddy Diddy/It Hurts to Be in Love | 1964 | 3.75 | 7.50 | 15.00 |

—B-side by Bobby Brooks

KING

❑ 5844	Mona Lisa/Teen Love	1964	7.50	15.00	30.00
❑ 5864	Only Make Believe/Run, Fool, Run	1964	7.50	15.00	30.00
❑ 5894	The Answer to My Dreams/I Don't Need Your Love and Kisses	1964	7.50	15.00	30.00

CASH, EDDIE
45s
PEAK

| ❑ 1001 | Doing All Right/Land of Promises | 1958 | 30.00 | 60.00 | 120.00 |
| ❑ 1010 | Come On Home/(B-side unknown) | 1960 | 3.75 | 7.50 | 15.00 |

ROULETTE

| ❑ 4380 | Stormy Weather/Lonely Island | 1961 | 3.00 | 6.00 | 12.00 |

TODD

| ❑ 1057 | Thinkin' Man/Livin' Lovin' Temptation | 1960 | 3.00 | 6.00 | 12.00 |

CASH, JOE
45s
HIT

| ❑ 17 | A Steel Guitar and a Glass of Wine/Playboy | 1962 | 2.00 | 4.00 | 8.00 |

—B-side by Peggy Gaines

| ❑ 47 | The Night Has a Thousand Eyes/Loop-De-Loop | 1963 | 2.00 | 4.00 | 8.00 |

—B-side by Herbert Hunter

CASH, JOHNNY
12-Inch Singles
COLUMBIA

| ❑ AS 921 [DJ] | Without Love (one-sided) | 1980 | 3.75 | 7.50 | 15.00 |

—Black B-side has etched autographs of Johnny Cash and Nick Lowe

45s
A&M

| ❑ 2291 | The Death of Me/One More Shot | 1980 | — | 2.00 | 4.00 |

—With Levon Helm

AMERICAN

| ❑ 18091 | Drive On/Delia's Gone | 1994 | — | 2.00 | 4.00 |

CACHET

| ❑ 4504 | Wings in the Morning/What on Earth | 1980 | — | 2.50 | 5.00 |
| ❑ 4504 [PS] | Wings in the Morning/What on Earth | 1980 | — | 2.50 | 5.00 |

COLUMBIA

❑ 02189	Mobile Bay/The Hard Way	1981	—	2.00	4.00
❑ 02669	The Reverend Mr. Black/Chattanooga City Limit Sign	1982	—	2.00	4.00
❑ 03058	Georgia on a Fast Train/Sing a Song	1982	—	2.00	4.00
❑ 03317	Fair Weather Friends/Ain't Gonna Hobo No More	1982	—	2.00	4.00
❑ 03524	I'll Cross Over Jordan Some Day/We Must Believe in Magic	1983	—	2.00	4.00
❑ 04060	I'm Ragged, But I'm Right/Brand New Dance	1983	—	2.00	4.00
❑ 04227	Johnny 99/New Cut Road	1983	—	—	3.00
❑ 04428	That's the Truth/Joshua Gone Barbados	1984	—	—	3.00
❑ 04513	The Chicken in Black/The Battle of Nashville	1984	—	—	3.00
❑ 04740	They Killed Him/The Three Bells	1985	—	—	3.00

—With the Carter Family

| ❑ 04860 | Crazy Old Soldier/It Ain't Gonna Worry My Mind | 1985 | — | — | 3.00 |

—A-side: Ray Charles and Johnny Cash; B-side: Ray Charles and Mickey Gilley

| ❑ 04881 | Highwayman/The Human Condition | 1985 | — | — | 3.00 |

—A-side: Willie Nelson/Waylon Jennings/Johnny Cash/Kris Kristofferson; B-side: Nelson, Cash

| ❑ 04881 [PS] | Highwayman/The Human Condition | 1985 | — | 2.50 | 5.00 |

—A-side: Willie Nelson/Waylon Jennings/Johnny Cash/Kris Kristofferson; B-side: Nelson, Cash

| ❑ 05594 | Desperadoes Waiting for a Train/The Twentieth Century Is Almost Over | 1985 | — | — | 3.00 |

—A-side: Willie Nelson/Waylon Jennings/Johnny Cash/Kris Kristofferson; B-side: Nelson, Cash

| ❑ 05672 | I'm Leaving Now/Easy Street | 1985 | — | — | 3.00 |

Number	Title (A Side/B Side)	Yr	VG	VG+	NM
❑ 08406	Highwayman/Desperadoes Waiting for a Train	1988	—	—	3.00

—Waylon Jennings/Willie Nelson/Johnny Cash/Kris Kristofferson; reissue

| ❑ 10011 | The Junkie and the Juicehead/Crystal Chandeliers and Burgundy | 1974 | — | 2.50 | 5.00 |
| ❑ 10048 | Father and Daughter, Father and Son/Don't Take Your Love to Town | 1974 | — | 2.50 | 5.00 |

—With Rosey Nix

❑ 10066	The Lady Came from Baltimore/Lonesome to the Bone	1974	—	2.50	5.00
❑ 10116	My Old Kentucky Home (Turpentine and Dandelion Wine)/Hard Times Comin'	1975	—	2.50	5.00
❑ 10177	Look at Them Beans/All Around Cowboy	1975	—	2.50	5.00
❑ 10237	Texas — 1947/I Hardly Ever Sing Beer Drinking Songs	1975	—	2.50	5.00
❑ 10279	Strawberry Cake/I Got Stripes	1975	—	2.50	5.00
❑ 10321	One Piece at a Time/Go On Blues	1976	—	2.50	5.00
❑ 10381	Sold Out of Flagpoles/Mountain Lady	1976	—	2.50	5.00
❑ 10424	It's All Over/Ridin' on the Cotton Belt	1976	—	2.50	5.00
❑ 10483	The Last Gunfighter Ballad/City Jail	1977	—	2.50	5.00
❑ 10587	Lady/Hit the Road and Go	1977	—	2.50	5.00
❑ 10623	After the Ball/Calilou	1977	—	2.50	5.00
❑ 10681	I Would Like to See You Again/Lately	1978	—	2.50	5.00
❑ 10817	Gone Girl/I'm Alright Now	1978	—	2.50	5.00
❑ 10855	It'll Be Her/It Comes and Goes	1978	—	2.50	5.00
❑ 10888	I Will Rock and Roll with You/A Song for the Life	1979	—	2.50	5.00
❑ 10961	(Ghost) Riders in the Sky/I'm Gonna Sit on the Porch and Pick on My Guitar	1979	—	2.50	5.00
❑ 10961 [PS]	(Ghost) Riders in the Sky/I'm Gonna Sit on the Porch and Pick on My Guitar	1979	—	3.00	6.00
❑ 11103	I'll Say It's True/Cocaine Blues	1979	—	2.50	5.00
❑ 11237	Bull Rider/Lonesome to the Bone	1980	—	2.00	4.00
❑ 11283	Song of a Patriot/She's a Go-er	1980	—	2.00	4.00
❑ 11340	Cold Lonesome Morning/The Cowboy Who Started the Fight	1980	—	2.00	4.00
❑ 11399	The Last Time/Rockabilly Blues (Texas 1965)	1980	—	2.00	4.00
❑ 11424	Without Love/It Ain't Nothing New Babe	1981	—	2.00	4.00
❑ S7 30843 [S]	Loading Coal/Slow Rider	1960	7.50	15.00	30.00
❑ S7 30844 [S]	Lumberjack/Dorrance of Ponchartrain	1960	7.50	15.00	30.00
❑ S7 30845 [S]	When Papa Played the Dobro/Going to Memphis	1960	7.50	15.00	30.00
❑ S7 30846 [S]	Old Doc Brown/Boss Jack	1960	7.50	15.00	30.00

—The above four are "Stereo Seven" 33 1/3 rpm jukebox singles from set "JS 7-12" and the album "Ride This Train"

| ❑ S7 30847 [S] | One More Ride/Run Softly, Blue River | 1960 | 7.50 | 15.00 | 30.00 |

—"Stereo Seven" 33 1/3 rpm jukebox single from "JS 7-12," but from the album "The Fabulous Johnny Cash"

❑ 31109 [S]	Seasons of My Heart/I Couldn't Keep from Crying	1961	7.50	15.00	30.00
❑ 31110 [S]	My Shoes Keep Walking Back to You/Time Changes Everything	1961	7.50	15.00	30.00
❑ 31111 [S]	Transfusion Blues/I'd Just Be Fool Enough (To Fall)	1961	7.50	15.00	30.00
❑ 31112 [S]	I'm So Lonesome I Could Cry/I Will Miss You When You Go	1961	7.50	15.00	30.00
❑ S7 31113 [S]	Just One More/Honky Tonk Girl	1961	7.50	15.00	30.00

—The above five are "Stereo Seven" 33 1/3 rpm jukebox singles from set "JS 7-29" entitled "Now There Was a Song"

| ❑ 3-38990 | Hey Porter/Big River | 1964 | 7.50 | 15.00 | 30.00 |

—Jukebox single, small hole, plays at 33 1/3 rpm; rather than the usual rainbow "target" label of Columbia "Stereo Seven" singles, this one has green labels

❑ 41251	All Over Again/What Do I Care	1958	3.75	7.50	15.00
❑ 41251 [PS]	All Over Again/What Do I Care	1958	10.00	20.00	40.00
❑ 41313	Don't Take Your Guns to Town/I Still Miss Someone	1959	3.75	7.50	15.00
❑ 41313 [PS]	Don't Take Your Guns to Town/I Still Miss Someone	1959	10.00	20.00	40.00
❑ 41371	Frankie's Man, Johnny/You, Dreamer, You	1959	3.75	7.50	15.00
❑ 41427	I Got Stripes/Five Feet High and Rising	1959	3.75	7.50	15.00
❑ 41481	The Little Drummer Boy/I'll Remember You	1959	3.75	7.50	15.00
❑ 41481 [PS]	The Little Drummer Boy/I'll Remember You	1959	10.00	20.00	40.00
❑ 41618	Seasons of My Heart/Smiling Bill McCall	1960	3.75	7.50	15.00
❑ 41707	Second Honemoon/Honky Tonk Girl	1960	3.75	7.50	15.00
❑ 41804	Going to Memphis/Loading Coal	1960	3.75	7.50	15.00
❑ 41920	Girl in Saskatoon/Locomotive Man	1960	3.75	7.50	15.00
❑ 41995	The Rebel-Johnny Yuma/Forty Shades of Green	1961	3.00	6.00	12.00
❑ 41995 [PS]	The Rebel-Johnny Yuma/Forty Shades of Green	1961	6.25	12.50	25.00
❑ 42147	Tennessee Flat Top Box/Tall Men	1961	3.00	6.00	12.00
❑ 42147 [PS]	Tennessee Flat Top Box/Tall Men	1961	6.25	12.50	25.00
❑ 42301	The Big Battle/What I've Learned	1962	3.00	6.00	12.00
❑ 42301 [PS]	The Big Battle/What I've Learned	1962	6.25	12.50	25.00
❑ 42425	In the Jailhouse Now/A Little at a Time	1962	3.00	6.00	12.00
❑ 42425 [PS]	In the Jailhouse Now/A Little at a Time	1962	6.25	12.50	25.00
❑ 42512	Bonanza!/Pick a Bale o' Cotton	1962	3.00	6.00	12.00
❑ 42615	Peace in the Valley/Were You There	1962	3.00	6.00	12.00

—With the Carter Family

❑ 42665	Busted/Send a Picture of Mother	1963	2.50	5.00	10.00
❑ 42665 [PS]	Busted/Send a Picture of Mother	1963	6.25	12.50	25.00
❑ 42788	Ring of Fire/I'd Still Be There	1963	2.50	5.00	10.00
❑ 42788 [DJ]	Ring of Fire (same on both sides)	1963	10.00	20.00	40.00

—Red vinyl promo

❑ 42788 [PS]	Ring of Fire/I'd Still Be There	1963	7.50	15.00	30.00
❑ 42880	The Matador/Still in Town	1963	2.50	5.00	10.00
❑ 42880 [PS]	The Matador/Still in Town	1963	5.00	10.00	20.00
❑ 4-42964	Understand Your Man/Dark as a Dungeon	1964	2.50	5.00	10.00
❑ 4-42964 [DJ]	Understand Your Man (same on both sides)	1964	10.00	20.00	40.00

—Red vinyl, white label promo

❑ 43058	The Ballad of Ira Hayes/Bad News	1964	2.50	5.00	10.00
❑ 4-43145	It Ain't Me, Babe/Time and Time Again	1964	2.50	5.00	10.00
❑ 4-43145 [DJ]	It Ain't Me, Babe (same on both sides)	1964	10.00	20.00	40.00

—Red vinyl, white label promo

❑ 43206	Orange Blossom Special/All of God's Children Ain't Free	1965	2.00	4.00	8.00
❑ 43313	Mister Garfield/Streets or Laredo	1965	2.00	4.00	8.00
❑ 43342	The Sons of Katie Elder/A Certain Kinda Hurtin'	1965	2.00	4.00	8.00
❑ 43420	Happy to Be with You/Pickin' Time	1965	2.00	4.00	8.00
❑ 43496	The One on the Right Is On the Left/Cotton Pickin' Hands	1965	2.00	4.00	8.00
❑ 43673	Everybody Loves a Nut/Austin Prison	1966	—	3.00	6.00
❑ 43763	Boa Constrictor/Bottom of a Mountain	1966	—	3.00	6.00

C

Number	Title (A Side/B Side)	Yr	VG	VG+	NM
❑ 43921	You Beat All I Ever Saw/Put the Sugar to Bed	1966	—	3.00	6.00
❑ 44288	The Wind Changes/Red Velvet	1967	—	3.00	6.00
❑ 44373	Rosanna's Going Wild/Roll Call	1967	—	3.00	6.00
❑ 44373 [PS]	Rosanna's Going Wild/Roll Call	1967	2.50	5.00	10.00
❑ 44513	Folsom Prison Blues/The Folk Singer	1968	—	3.00	6.00
❑ 44513 [PS]	Folsom Prison Blues/The Folk Singer	1968	2.50	5.00	10.00
❑ 44689	Daddy Sang Bass/He Turned the Water Into Wine	1968	—	3.00	6.00
❑ 44944	A Boy Named Sue/San Quentin	1969	—	3.00	6.00
❑ 45020	Blistered/See Ruby Fall	1969	—	3.00	6.00
❑ 45134	What Is Truth/Sing a Traveling Song	1970	—	2.50	5.00
❑ 45211	Sunday Morning Coming Down/I'm Gonna Try to Be That Way	1970	—	2.50	5.00
❑ 45269	Flesh and Blood/This Side of the Law	1970	—	2.50	5.00
❑ 45339	Man in Black/Little Bit of Yesterday	1971	—	2.50	5.00
❑ 45393	Singing in Viet Nam Talking Blues/You've Got a New Light Shining	1971	—	2.50	5.00
❑ 45460	Papa Was a Good Man/I Promise You	1971	—	2.50	5.00
❑ 45534	A Thing Called Love/Daddy	1972	—	2.50	5.00
❑ 45590	Kate/Miracle Man	1972	—	2.50	5.00
❑ 45660	Oney/Country Trash	1972	—	2.50	5.00
❑ 45740	Any Old Wind That Blows/Kentucky Straight	1972	—	2.50	5.00
❑ 45786	Children/Last Summer	1973	—	2.50	5.00
❑ 45938	Pick the Wildwood Flower/Diamonds in the Rough	1973	—	2.50	5.00
—With Mother Maybelle and the Carter Family					
❑ 45979	Christmas As I Knew It/That Christmasy Feeling	1973	—	2.50	5.00
—With Tommy Cash					
❑ 45997	Orleans Parish Prison/Jacob Green	1974	—	2.50	5.00
❑ 46028	Ragged Old Flag/Don't Go Near the Water	1974	—	2.50	5.00
❑ CS7 56799 [DJ]	Folsom Prison Blues (Live)/I'll Remember You	2002	—	3.00	6.00
—Promo-only 70th birthday tribute; both tracks previously unreleased; label is a replica of the 1957-58 yellow and black 45 label					
❑ CS7 56799 [PS]	Folsom Prison Blues (Live)/I'll Remember You	2002	—	3.00	6.00
—Cardboard sleeve					
❑ 60516	The Baron/I Will Dance with You	1981	—	2.00	4.00
❑ 69067	Ragged Old Flag/I'm Leaving Now	1989	—	—	3.00
❑ 73233	America Remains/Silver Stallion	1990	—	—	3.00
—Waylon Jennings/Willie Nelson/Johnny Cash/Kris Kristofferson					
❑ 73381	Born and Raised in Black and White/Texas	1990	—	—	3.00
—The Highwaymen (Waylon Jennings/Willie Nelson/Johnny Cash/Kris Kristofferson)					
❑ 73572	American Remains/Texas	1990	—	—	3.00
—The Highwaymen (Waylon Jennings/Willie Nelson/Johnny Cash/Kris Kristofferson)					
EPIC					
❑ 50778	There Ain't No Good Chain Gang/I Wish I Was Crazy Again	1979	—	2.50	5.00
—Johnny Cash/Waylon Jennings					
LIBERTY					
❑ S7-18486	It Is What It Is/The Devil's Right Hand	1995	—	—	3.00
—By The Highwaymen					
MERCURY					
❑ 870010-7	W. Lee O'Daniel (And the Light Crust Dough Boys)/Letters from Homes	1987	—	—	3.00
❑ 870237-7	Cry, Cry, Cry/Get Rhythm	1988	—	—	3.00
❑ 870688-7	Tennessee Flat Top Box/That Old Wheel	1988	—	—	3.00
—A-side with Hank Williams, Jr.					
❑ 872420-7	Ballad of a Teenage Queen/Get Rhythm	1988	—	—	3.00
—With Roseanne Cash and the Everly Brothers					
❑ 874562-7	The Last of the Drifters/Water from the Wells of Home	1989	—	—	3.00
—A-side with Tom T. Hall					
❑ 875626-7	Cat's in the Cradle/I Love You, Love You	1990	—	—	3.00
❑ 878292-7	Goin' By the Book/Beans for Breakfast	1990	—	—	3.00
❑ 878710-7	The Greatest Cowboy of Them All/Hey Porter	1990	—	—	3.00
❑ 878968-7	The Mystery of Life/I'm an Easy Rider	1990	—	—	3.00
❑ 888459-7	The Night Hank Williams Came to Town/I'd Rather Have You	1987	—	—	3.00
❑ 888719-7	Sixteen Tons/The Ballad of Barbara	1987	—	—	3.00
❑ 888838-7	Let Him Roll/My Ship Will Sail	1987	—	—	3.00
SCOTTI BROS.					
❑ 02803	The General Lee/Duelin' Dukes	1982	—	2.00	4.00
—Narration on B-side: Sorrell Booke					
SMASH					
❑ 884934-7	Sixteen Candles/Rock & Roll (Fais-Do-Do)	1986	—	2.00	4.00
—With Jerry Lee Lewis, Roy Orbison and Carl Perkins					
❑ 888142-7	We Remember the King/Class of '55	1987	—	2.00	4.00
—With Jerry Lee Lewis, Roy Orbison and Carl Perkins; B-side by Carl Perkins solo					
SUN					
❑ 7-36/39	Folsom Prison Blues/I Walk the Line	1969	5.00	10.00	20.00
—"Premium" on label; possibly a giveaway with specially marked packages of Dr Pepper soda					
❑ 221	Hey Porter/Cry, Cry, Cry	1955	10.00	20.00	40.00
❑ 232	Folsom Prison Blues/So Doggone Lonesome	1956	7.50	15.00	30.00
❑ 241	I Walk the Line/Get Rhythm	1956	10.00	20.00	40.00
❑ 258	Train of Love/There You Go	1956	7.50	15.00	30.00
❑ 266	Next in Line/Don't Make Me Go	1957	7.50	15.00	30.00
❑ 279	Home of the Blues/Give My Love to Rose	1957	7.50	15.00	30.00
❑ 283	Ballad of a Teenage Queen/Big River	1958	6.25	12.50	25.00
❑ 295	Guess Things Happen That Way/Come In Stranger	1958	6.25	12.50	25.00
❑ 295 [PS]	Guess Things Happen That Way/Come In Stranger	1958	10.00	20.00	40.00
❑ 302	The Ways of a Woman in Love/You're the Nearest Thing to Heaven	1958	6.25	12.50	25.00
❑ 309	It's Just About Time/Just Thought You'd Like to Know	1958	6.25	12.50	25.00
❑ 316	Luther Played the Boogie/Thanks a Lot	1959	5.00	10.00	20.00
❑ 321	Katy Too/I Forgot to Remember to Forget	1959	5.00	10.00	20.00
❑ 331	Goodbye Little Darlin'/You Tell Me	1959	5.00	10.00	20.00
❑ 334	Straight A's in Love/I Love You Because	1960	5.00	10.00	20.00
❑ 343	The Story of a Broken Heart/Down the Street to 301	1960	5.00	10.00	20.00
❑ 347	Mean Eyed Cat/Port of Lonely Hearts	1960	5.00	10.00	20.00
❑ 355	Oh Lonesome Me/Life Goes On	1961	5.00	10.00	20.00
❑ 363	Sugartime/My Treasurer	1961	5.00	10.00	20.00
❑ 376	Born to Lose/Blue Train	1962	5.00	10.00	20.00
❑ 392	Wide Open Road/Belshazar	1964	5.00	10.00	20.00
❑ 1103	Get Rhythm/Hey Porter	1969	—	3.00	6.00
❑ 1111	Rock Island Line/Next in Line	1970	—	3.00	6.00
❑ 1121	Big River/Come In Stranger	1971	—	2.50	5.00

Number	Title (A Side/B Side)	Yr	VG	VG+	NM
7-Inch Extended Plays					
COLUMBIA					
❑ B-2155	The Rebel — Johnny Yuma/Remember the Alamo//The Ballad of Boot Hill/Lorena	1961	3.75	7.50	15.00
❑ B-2155 [PS]	The Rebel — Johnny Yuma	1961	3.75	7.50	15.00
❑ 7-9639	Folsom Prison Blues/The Long Black Veil/I Got Stripes//Cocaine Blues/Jackson/Dirty Old Egg-Sucking Dog	1968	3.00	6.00	12.00
—Jukebox issue; small hole, plays at 33 1/3 rpm					
❑ 7-9639 [PS]	Johnny Cash at Folsom Prison	1968	3.00	6.00	12.00
❑ 7-9943	I've Got a Thing About Trains/Wrinkled, Crinkled Wadded Dollar Bill/Southwind//To Beat the Devil/Sing a Traveling Song	1970	3.00	6.00	12.00
—Jukebox issue; small hole, plays at 33 1/3 rpm					
❑ 7-9943 [PS]	Hello, I'm Johnny Cash	1970	3.00	6.00	12.00
❑ B-12531	Run Softly, Blue River/That's All Over//I Still Miss Someone/Supper-Time	1958	3.00	6.00	12.00
❑ B-12531 [PS]	The Fabulous Johnny Cash, Vol. I	1958	3.00	6.00	12.00
❑ B-12532	Frankie's Man, Johnny/The Troubadour//Don't Take Your Guns to Town/That's Enough	1958	3.00	6.00	12.00
❑ B-12532 [PS]	The Fabulous Johnny Cash, Vol. II	1958	3.00	6.00	12.00
❑ B-12533	I'd Rather Die Young/One More Ride//Pickin' Time/Shepherd of My Heart	1958	3.00	6.00	12.00
❑ B-12533 [PS]	The Fabulous Johnny Cash, Vol. III	1958	3.00	6.00	12.00
❑ B-12841	It Was Jesus/I Saw a Man//Are All the Children In?/The Old Account	1959	3.00	6.00	12.00
❑ B-12841 [PS]	Hymns by Johnny Cash, Vol. I	1959	3.00	6.00	12.00
❑ B-12842	Lead Me Gently Home/Swing Low, Sweet Chariot//Snow in His Hair/Lead Me Father	1959	3.00	6.00	12.00
❑ B-12842 [PS]	Hymns by Johnny Cash, Vol. II	1959	3.00	6.00	12.00
❑ B-12843	I Call Him/These Things Shall Pass//He'll Be a Friend/God Will	1959	3.00	6.00	12.00
❑ B-12843 [PS]	Hymns by Johnny Cash, Vol. III	1959	3.00	6.00	12.00
❑ B-13391	*Drink to Me/Five Feet High and Rising/The Man on the Hill/Hank and Joe and Me	1959	3.00	6.00	12.00
❑ B-13391 [PS]	Songs of Our Soil, Vol. I	1959	3.00	6.00	12.00
❑ B-13392	*Grandfather's Clock/It Could Be You (Instead of Him)/Old Apache Squaw/Don't Step on Mother's Roses	1959	3.00	6.00	12.00
❑ B-13392 [PS]	Songs of Our Soil, Vol. II	1959	3.00	6.00	12.00
❑ B-13393	Old Apache Squaw/Don't Step on Mother's Roses//My Grandfather's Clock/It Could Be You	1959	3.00	6.00	12.00
❑ B-13393 [PS]	Songs of Our Soil, Vol. III	1959	3.00	6.00	12.00
❑ B-14631	Seasons of My Heart/I Feel Better All Over//I Couldn't Keep from Crying/Time Changes Everything	1960	3.00	6.00	12.00
❑ B-14631 [PS]	Now, There Was a Song, Vol. I	1960	3.00	6.00	12.00
❑ B-14632	My Shoes Just Keep Walking Back to You/I'd Just Be Fool Enough (To Fall)//Transfusion Blues/Why Do You Punish Me	1960	3.00	6.00	12.00
❑ B-14632 [PS]	Now, There Was a Song, Vol. II	1960	3.00	6.00	12.00
❑ B-14633	I Will Miss You When You Go/I'm So Lonesome I Could Cry//Just One More/Honky Tonk Girl	1960	3.00	6.00	12.00
❑ B-14633 [PS]	Now, There Was a Song, Vol. III	1960	3.00	6.00	12.00
SUN					
❑ EPA-111	I Can't Help It/You Win Again//Hey Good Lookin'/I Could Never Be Ashamed	1956	10.00	20.00	40.00
❑ EPA-111 [PS]	Johnny Cash Sings Hank Williams	1956	15.00	30.00	60.00
❑ EPA-112	Rock Island Line/I Heard That Lonesome Whistle//Country Boy/If the Good Lord's Willin'	1956	7.50	15.00	30.00
❑ EPA-112 [PS]	Country Boy	1956	12.50	25.00	50.00
❑ EPA-113	I Walk the Line/The Wreck of the Old '97//Folsom Prison Blues/Doin' My Time	1958	7.50	15.00	30.00
❑ EPA-113 [PS]	I Walk the Line	1958	12.50	25.00	50.00
❑ EPA-114	The Ways of a Woman in Love/Next in Line//Guess Things Happen That Way/Train of Love	1958	7.50	15.00	30.00
❑ EPA-114 [PS]	His Top Hits	1958	12.50	25.00	50.00
❑ SEP-116	You're the Nearest Thing to Heaven/I Can't Help It//Home of the Blues/Big River	1959	7.50	15.00	30.00
❑ SEP-116 [PS]	Home of the Blues	1959	12.50	25.00	50.00
❑ SEP-117	So Doggone Lonesome/I Was There When It Happened//Cry, Cry, Cry/Remember Me	1958	7.50	15.00	30.00
❑ SEP-117 [PS]	Johnny Cash	1958	12.50	25.00	50.00
Albums					
ACCORD					
❑ SN-7134	I Walk the Line	1983	2.50	5.00	10.00
❑ SN-7208	Years Gone By	1983	2.50	5.00	10.00
ALLEGIANCE					
❑ AV-5017	The First Years	1986	2.50	5.00	10.00
AMERICAN					
❑ 43097	Unchained	1996	3.00	6.00	12.00
❑ 45520	American Recordings	1994	5.00	10.00	20.00
❑ 440-063336-1 [(2)]	American IV: The Man Comes Around	2002	5.00	10.00	20.00
ARCHIVE OF FOLK MUSIC					
❑ 278	Johnny Cash	198?	3.00	6.00	12.00
CACHET					
❑ 9001	A Believer Sings the Truth	1979	3.75	7.50	15.00
COLUMBIA					
❑ GP 29 [(2)]	The World of Johnny Cash	1970	3.75	7.50	15.00
❑ C2L 38 [(2)M]	Ballads of the True West	1965	6.25	12.50	25.00
❑ C2S 838 [(2)S]	Ballads of the True West	1965	6.25	12.50	25.00
❑ CL 1253 [M]	The Fabulous Johnny Cash	1958	5.00	10.00	20.00
❑ CL 1284 [M]	Hymns by Johnny Cash	1959	6.25	12.50	25.00
❑ CL 1339 [M]	Songs of Our Soil	1959	6.25	12.50	25.00
❑ CL 1463 [M]	Now, There Was a Song!	1960	6.25	12.50	25.00
❑ CL 1464 [M]	Ride This Train	1960	6.25	12.50	25.00
❑ CL 1622 [M]	The Lure of the Grand Canyon	1961	10.00	20.00	40.00
—Cash narrates; with Andre Kostelanetz and His Orchestra					
❑ CL 1722 [M]	Hymns from the Heart	1962	5.00	10.00	20.00
❑ CL 1802 [M]	The Sound of Johnny Cash	1962	5.00	10.00	20.00
❑ CL 1930 [M]	Blood, Sweat & Tears	1963	5.00	10.00	20.00
❑ STS 2004 [(2)]		196?	5.00	10.00	20.00
—"Columbia Star Series" release; has "360 Sound" labels					
❑ CL 2052 [M]	Ring of Fire (The Best of Johnny Cash)	1963	5.00	10.00	20.00
❑ CL 2117 [M]	The Christmas Spirit	1963	6.25	12.50	25.00
❑ CL 2190 [M]	I Walk the Line	1964	3.75	7.50	15.00
❑ CL 2248 [M]	Bitter Tears (Ballads of the American Indian)	1964	3.75	7.50	15.00

C

Number	Title (A Side/B Side)	Yr	VG	VG+	NM
❏ CL 2309 [M]	Orange Blossom Special	1965	3.75	7.50	15.00
❏ CL 2446 [M]	Mean as Hell	1965	3.75	7.50	15.00
❏ CL 2492 [M]	Everybody Loves a Nut	1966	3.75	7.50	15.00
❏ CL 2537 [M]	That's What You Get for Lovin' Me	1966	3.75	7.50	15.00
❏ CL 2647 [M]	From Sea to Shining Sea	1967	5.00	10.00	20.00
❏ CL 2678 [M]	Johnny Cash's Greatest Hits, Volume 1	1967	5.00	10.00	20.00
❏ CS 8122 [S]	The Fabulous Johnny Cash	1959	10.00	20.00	40.00
❏ CS 8125 [S]	Hymns by Johnny Cash	1959	10.00	20.00	40.00
❏ CS 8148 [S]	Songs of Our Soil	1959	10.00	20.00	40.00
❏ CS 8254 [S]	Now, There Was a Song!	1960	10.00	20.00	40.00
❏ CS 8255 [S]	Ride This Train	1960	10.00	20.00	40.00
❏ CS 8255 [S]	Ride This Train	197?	2.50	5.00	10.00
—Reissue on orange label					
❏ CS 8422 [S]	The Lure of the Grand Canyon	1961	12.50	25.00	50.00
—Cash narrates; with Andre Kostelanetz and His Orchestra					
❏ CS 8522 [S]	Hymns from the Heart	1962	7.50	15.00	30.00
❏ CS 8602 [S]	The Sound of Johnny Cash	1962	7.50	15.00	30.00
❏ CS 8730 [S]	Blood, Sweat & Tears	1963	6.25	12.50	25.00
❏ CS 8852 [S]	Ring of Fire (The Best of Johnny Cash)	1963	6.25	12.50	25.00
❏ CS 8917 [S]	The Christmas Spirit	1963	7.50	15.00	30.00
❏ CS 8990 [S]	I Walk the Line	1964	5.00	10.00	20.00
❏ CS 9048 [S]	Bitter Tears (Ballads of the American Indian)	1964	5.00	10.00	20.00
❏ CS 9109 [S]	Orange Blossom Special	1965	5.00	10.00	20.00
❏ CS 9246 [S]	Mean as Hell	1965	5.00	10.00	20.00
❏ CS 9292 [S]	Everybody Loves a Nut	1966	5.00	10.00	20.00
❏ CS 9337 [S]	That's What You Get for Lovin' Me	1966	5.00	10.00	20.00
❏ CS 9447 [S]	From Sea to Shining Sea	1967	5.00	10.00	20.00
❏ CS 9478 [S]	Johnny Cash's Greatest Hits, Volume 1	1967	5.00	10.00	20.00
❏ CS 9639 [M]	Johnny Cash at Folsom Prison	1968	12.50	25.00	50.00
—Mono is white label promo only with stereo number; "Special Mono Radio Station Copy" sticker on cover					
❏ CS 9639 [S]	Johnny Cash at Folsom Prison	1968	5.00	10.00	20.00
❏ KCS 9726	The Holy Land	1969	3.75	7.50	15.00
❏ CS 9827	Johnny Cash at San Quentin	1969	3.00	6.00	12.00
❏ KCS 9943	Hello, I'm Johnny Cash	1970	3.00	6.00	12.00
❏ C 30100	The Johnny Cash Show	1970	3.00	6.00	12.00
❏ S 30397	I Walk the Line	1970	3.00	6.00	12.00
—Soundtrack from movie					
❏ KC 30550	Man in Black	1971	3.00	6.00	12.00
❏ KC 30887	The Johnny Cash Collection (His Greatest Hits, Volume II)	1971	3.00	6.00	12.00
❏ CQ 30961 [Q]	Johnny Cash at San Quentin	1971	5.00	10.00	20.00
❏ KC 31256	Give My Love to Rose	1972	3.00	6.00	12.00
❏ KC 31332	A Thing Called Love	1972	3.00	6.00	12.00
❏ KC 31645	Johnny Cash: America (A 200-Year Salute in Story and Song)	1972	3.00	6.00	12.00
❏ KC 32091	Any Old Wind That Blows	1973	3.00	6.00	12.00
❏ C 32240	Sunday Morning Coming Down	1973	3.00	6.00	12.00
❏ C 32253	The Gospel Road	1973	3.00	6.00	12.00
❏ CG 32253 [(2)]	The Gospel Road	1973	6.25	12.50	25.00
❏ KC 32898	Children's Album	1974	3.00	6.00	12.00
❏ C 32917	The Ragged Old Flag	1974	3.00	6.00	12.00
❏ C 32951	Five Feet High and Rising	1974	3.00	6.00	12.00
❏ KC 33086	The Junkie and the Juicehead	1974	3.00	6.00	12.00
❏ C 33087	Johnny Cash Sings Precious Memories	1974	3.00	6.00	12.00
❏ KC 33370	John R. Cash	1975	3.00	6.00	12.00
❏ CG 33639 [(2)]	Johnny Cash at Folsom Prison/Johnny Cash at San Quentin	1974	3.75	7.50	15.00
❏ KC 33814	Look at Them Beans	1975	3.00	6.00	12.00
❏ KC 34088	Strawberry Cake	1976	3.00	6.00	12.00
❏ KC 34193	One Piece at a Time	1976	3.00	6.00	12.00
❏ JC 34314	The Last Gunfighter Ballad	1977	3.00	6.00	12.00
❏ JC 34833	The Rambler	1977	3.00	6.00	12.00
❏ KC 35313	I Would Like to See You Again	1978	2.50	5.00	10.00
❏ JC 35637	Johnny Cash's Greatest Hits, Volume 3	1978	3.00	6.00	12.00
❏ KC 35646	Gone Girl	1978	3.00	6.00	12.00
❏ JC 36086	Silver	1979	3.00	6.00	12.00
❏ JC 36779	Rockabilly Blues	1980	2.50	5.00	10.00
❏ JC 36866	Classic Christmas	1980	3.00	6.00	12.00
❏ FC 37179	The Baron	1981	2.50	5.00	10.00
❏ FC 37355	Encore	1981	2.50	5.00	10.00
❏ PC 38074	A Believer Sings the Truth	1985	2.00	4.00	8.00
—Reissue of Priority 38074					
❏ FC 38094	The Adventures of Johnny Cash	1982	2.50	5.00	10.00
❏ FC 38317	Johnny Cash's Biggest Hits	1982	2.50	5.00	10.00
❏ FC 38696	Johnny 99	1983	2.50	5.00	10.00
❏ PC 38696	Johnny 99	1986	2.00	4.00	8.00
—Budget-line reissue					
❏ FC 39951	Rainbow	1985	2.50	5.00	10.00
❏ FC 40056	Highwayman	1985	2.50	5.00	10.00
—Waylon Jennings/Willie Nelson/Johnny Cash/Kris Kristofferson					
❏ C 45240	Highwayman 2	1990	3.75	7.50	15.00
—Waylon Jennings/Willie Nelson/Johnny Cash/Kris Kristofferson					
COLUMBIA LIMITED EDITION					
❏ LE 10063 [S]	The Fabulous Johnny Cash	197?	3.75	7.50	15.00
—Reissue of 8122					
COLUMBIA SPECIAL PRODUCTS					
❏ 363	Legends and Love Songs	196?	5.00	10.00	20.00
❏ P 13043	Destination Victoria Station	1977	10.00	20.00	40.00
—Alternate number is "VS 150"					
❏ P 13832	Hello, I'm Johnny Cash	1977	3.00	6.00	12.00
DORAL/CSP					
❏ (# unknown)	Doral Presents Johnny Cash	1972	10.00	20.00	40.00
—Mail-order offer from Doral cigarettes					
EVEREST					
❏ 276	Johnny Cash	19??	3.00	6.00	12.00
HARMONY					
❏ HS 11249	Golden Sounds of Country Music	1968	3.00	6.00	12.00
❏ HS 11342	Johnny Cash	1969	3.00	6.00	12.00
❏ KH 30138	The Walls of a Prison	1970	3.00	6.00	12.00
❏ KH 30916	Understand Your Man	1971	3.00	6.00	12.00
❏ KH 31602	The Johnny Cash Songbook	1972	3.00	6.00	12.00
❏ KH 32388	Ballads of the American Indian	1973	3.00	6.00	12.00
MERCURY					
❏ 832031-1	Johnny Cash Is Coming to Town	1987	2.50	5.00	10.00
❏ 834778-1	Water from the Wells of Home	1988	2.50	5.00	10.00
PAIR					
❏ PDL2-1107 [(2)]	Classic Cash	1986	3.75	7.50	15.00

Number	Title (A Side/B Side)	Yr	VG	VG+	NM
POWER PAK					
❏ 246	Country Gold	198?	2.50	5.00	10.00
PRIORITY					
❏ UG 32253 [(2)]	The Gospel Road	1981	3.75	7.50	15.00
—Reissue of Columbia album of the same name					
❏ PU 33087	Johnny Cash Sings Precious Memories	1982	3.00	6.00	12.00
—Reissue of Columbia album of the same name					
❏ PU 38074	A Believer Sings the Truth	1982	3.00	6.00	12.00
—Reissue of Cachet album					
RHINO					
❏ RNLP 70229	The Vintage Years	1987	3.00	6.00	12.00
SHARE					
❏ 5000	I Walk the Line	197?	3.00	6.00	12.00
❏ 5001	Folsom Prison Blues	197?	3.00	6.00	12.00
❏ 5002	The Blue Train	197?	3.00	6.00	12.00
❏ 5003	Johnny Cash Sings the Greatest Hits	197?	3.00	6.00	12.00
SUN					
❏ LP-100	Original Golden Hits, Volume I	1969	3.00	6.00	12.00
❏ LP-101	Original Golden Hits, Volume II	1969	3.00	6.00	12.00
❏ LP-104	Story Songs of the Trains and Rivers	1969	3.00	6.00	12.00
❏ LP-105	Get Rhythm	1969	3.00	6.00	12.00
❏ LP-106	Showtime	1969	3.00	6.00	12.00
❏ LP-115	The Singing Story Teller	1970	3.00	6.00	12.00
❏ LP-118 [(2)]	Johnny Cash — The Legend	1970	5.00	10.00	20.00
❏ LP-122	The Rough Cut King of Country Music	1971	3.00	6.00	12.00
❏ LP-126 [(2)]	Johnny Cash: The Man, The World, His Music	1971	5.00	10.00	20.00
❏ LP-127	Original Golden Hits, Volume III	1972	3.00	6.00	12.00
❏ LP-139	I Walk the Line	1979	2.50	5.00	10.00
❏ LP-140	Folsom Prison Blues	1979	2.50	5.00	10.00
❏ LP-141	The Blue Train	1979	2.50	5.00	10.00
❏ LP-142	Johnny Cash Sings the Greatest Hits	1979	2.50	5.00	10.00
❏ 1002	Superbilly (1955-58)	198?	2.50	5.00	10.00
❏ 1006	The Original Johnny Cash	1980	2.50	5.00	10.00
❏ SLP-1220 [M]	Johnny Cash with His Hot and Blue Guitar	1956	25.00	50.00	100.00
❏ SLP-1220 [R]	Johnny Cash with His Hot and Blue Guitar	196?	5.00	10.00	20.00
—Reissue in rechanneled stereo; front cover says "STEREO"					
❏ SLP-1235 [M]	The Songs That Made Him Famous	1958	25.00	50.00	100.00
❏ SLP-1235 [R]	The Songs That Made Him Famous	196?	5.00	10.00	20.00
—Reissue in rechanneled stereo; front cover says "STEREO"					
❏ SLP-1240 [M]	Johnny Cash's Greatest!	1959	12.50	25.00	50.00
❏ SLP-1245 [R]	Johnny Cash Sings Hank Williams	196?	5.00	10.00	20.00
—Reissue in rechanneled stereo; front cover says "STEREO"					
❏ SLP-1245 [M]	Johnny Cash Sings Hank Williams	1960	12.50	25.00	50.00
❏ SLP-1255 [R]	Now Here's Johnny Cash	196?	5.00	10.00	20.00
—Reissue in rechanneled stereo; front cover says "STEREO"					
❏ SLP-1255 [M]	Now Here's Johnny Cash	1961	12.50	25.00	50.00
❏ SLP-1270 [M]	All Aboard the Blue Train	1963	12.50	25.00	50.00
❏ SLP-1275 [M]	The Original Sun Sound of Johnny Cash	1965	12.50	25.00	50.00
❏ DT-90668 [R]	The Songs That Made Him Famous	1966	6.25	12.50	25.00
—Capitol Record Club edition					
❏ T-90668 [M]	The Songs That Made Him Famous	1966	10.00	20.00	40.00
—Capitol Record Club edition					
❏ DT-90678 [R]	Now Here's Johnny Cash	1966	5.00	10.00	20.00
—Capitol Record Club edition					
❏ DT-91284 [R]	Johnny Cash Sings Hank Williams	196?	6.25	12.50	25.00
—Capitol Record Club edition					
❏ T-91284 [M]	Johnny Cash Sings Hank Williams	196?	10.00	20.00	40.00
—Capitol Record Club edition					
❏ DT-91458 [R]	All Aboard the Blue Train	196?	6.25	12.50	25.00
—Capitol Record Club edition					
❏ ST-92085	Original Golden Hits, Volume I	1969	5.00	10.00	20.00
—Capitol Record Club edition; uses older Sun label					
❏ ST-92086	Original Golden Hits, Volume II	1969	5.00	10.00	20.00
—Capitol Record Club edition; uses older Sun label					
❏ SQBO-93213 [(2)]	The Greatness of Johnny Cash	197?	5.00	10.00	20.00
—Capitol Record Club exclusive					
SUNDAZED					
❏ LP-5170	Town Hall Party Live! 1958	2003	3.75	7.50	15.00
—Reissue on 180-gram vinyl					
❏ LP-5171	Town Hall Party Live! 1959	2003	3.75	7.50	15.00
—Reissue on 180-gram vinyl					
❏ LP-5176	Blood, Sweat & Tears	2003	3.75	7.50	15.00
—Reissue on 180-gram vinyl					
TIME-LIFE					
❏ TLCS-3 [(3)]	Country & Western Classics	1982	5.00	10.00	20.00
❏ STW-108	Country Music	1981	3.00	6.00	12.00
WORD					
❏ WR-8333	Believe in Him	1986	3.00	6.00	12.00

CASH, JOHNNY, AND JUNE CARTER

45s

COLUMBIA

Number	Title (A Side/B Side)	Yr	VG	VG+	NM
❏ 10436	Old Time Feeling/Far Side Banks of Jordan	1976	—	2.50	5.00
❏ 44011	Jackson/Pack Up Your Sorrows	1967	—	3.00	6.00
❏ 44158	Long-Legged Guitar Pickin' Man/You'll Be All Right	1967	—	3.00	6.00
❏ 45064	If I Were a Carpenter/'Cause I Love You	1970	—	2.50	5.00
❏ 45431	No Need to Worry/I'll Be Loving You	1971	—	2.50	5.00
❏ 45631	If I Had a Hammer/I Gotta Go	1972	—	2.50	5.00
❏ 45758	The Loving Gift/Help Me Make It Through the Night	1973	—	2.50	5.00
❏ 45890	Praise the Lord and Pass the Soup/The Ballad of Barbara	1973	—	2.50	5.00
❏ 45929	Allegheny/We're for Love	1973	—	2.50	5.00

Albums

COLUMBIA

Number	Title (A Side/B Side)	Yr	VG	VG+	NM
❏ CL 2728 [M]	Carryin' On with Johnny Cash and June Carter	1967	5.00	10.00	20.00
❏ CS 9528 [S]	Carryin' On with Johnny Cash and June Carter	1967	5.00	10.00	20.00
❏ KC 32443	Johnny Cash and His Woman	1973	3.75	7.50	15.00

CASH, JOHNNY, AND WAYLON JENNINGS   Also see each artist's individual listings.

45s

COLUMBIA

Number	Title (A Side/B Side)	Yr	VG	VG+	NM
❏ 05896	Even Cowgirls Get the Blues/American by Birth	1986	—	—	3.00
❏ 06287	The Ballad of $40/Field of Diamonds	1986	—	—	3.00
❏ 10742	There Ain't No Good Chain Gang/I Wish I Was Crazy Again	1978	—	2.50	5.00

Number	Title (A Side/B Side)	Yr	VG	VG+	NM
CASH, JOHNNY/TAMMY WYNETTE					
Albums					
COLUMBIA MUSICAL TREASURIES					
❑ DS 608 [(2)]	The King/The Queen	1969	3.75	7.50	15.00
—One record by Johnny Cash, the other by Tammy Wynette					
❑ P4S 5376 [(4)]	The King/The Queen	1969	6.25	12.50	25.00
—Box set; two records by Johnny Cash, two records by Tammy Wynette; records are individually numbered from DS 562 through DS 565					
CASHMAN, TERRY Also see BUCHANAN BROTHERS; CASHMAN AND WEST; CASHMAN, PISTILLI AND WEST.					
45s					
BOOM					
❑ 60005	Try Me/Pretty Face	1966	3.75	7.50	15.00
LIFESONG					
❑ 45015	Baby, Baby I Love You/We'll Be Together	1976	—	2.00	4.00
❑ 45021	The Dreamer/Football U.S.A.	1977	—	2.00	4.00
❑ 45086	Willie, Mickey and "The Duke" (Talkin' Baseball)/It's So Easy to Sing a Love Song	1980	—	2.50	5.00
❑ 45086 [PS]	Willie, Mickey and "The Duke" (Talkin' Baseball)/It's So Easy to Sing a Love Song	1980	2.50	5.00	10.00
❑ 45087	Baseball (America's National Pastime)/Willie, Mickey and "The Duke" (Talkin' Baseball)	1981	—	2.50	5.00
❑ 45087 [PS]	Baseball (America's National Pastime)/Willie, Mickey and "The Duke" (Talkin' Baseball)	1981	2.50	5.00	10.00
❑ 45096	Talkin' Baseball (Philadelphia Phillies Version)/Baby, Baby I Love You	1982	—	2.00	4.00
❑ 45096 [PS]	Talkin' Baseball (Philadelphia Phillies Version)/Baby, Baby I Love You	1982	—	2.00	4.00
—Green "Talkin' Baseball" sleeve with custom sticker					
❑ 45097	Talkin' Baseball (New York Yankees Version)/Baby, Baby I Love You	1982	—	2.00	4.00
❑ 45097 [PS]	Talkin' Baseball (New York Yankees Version)/Baby, Baby I Love You	1982	—	2.00	4.00
—Green "Talkin' Baseball" sleeve with custom sticker					
❑ 45098	Talkin' Baseball (Los Angeles Dodgers Version)/Baby, Baby I Love You	1982	—	2.00	4.00
❑ 45098 [PS]	Talkin' Baseball (Los Angeles Dodgers Version)/Baby, Baby I Love You	1982	—	2.00	4.00
—Green "Talkin' Baseball" sleeve with custom sticker					
❑ 45099	Talkin' Baseball (Cleveland Indians Version)/Baby, Baby I Love You	1982	—	2.00	4.00
❑ 45099 [PS]	Talkin' Baseball (Cleveland Indians Version)/Baby, Baby I Love You	1982	—	2.00	4.00
—Green "Talkin' Baseball" sleeve with custom sticker					
❑ 45100	Talkin' Baseball (Texas Rangers Version)/Baby, Baby I Love You	1982	—	2.00	4.00
❑ 45100 [PS]	Talkin' Baseball (Texas Rangers Version)/Baby, Baby I Love You	1982	—	2.00	4.00
—Green "Talkin' Baseball" sleeve with custom sticker					
❑ 45101	Talkin' Baseball (Cincinnati Reds Version)/Baby, Baby I Love You	1982	—	2.00	4.00
❑ 45101 [PS]	Talkin' Baseball (Cincinnati Reds Version)/Baby, Baby I Love You	1982	—	2.00	4.00
—Green "Talkin' Baseball" sleeve with custom sticker					
❑ 45102	Talkin' Baseball (San Francisco Giants Version)/Baby, Baby I Love You	1982	—	2.00	4.00
❑ 45102 [PS]	Talkin' Baseball (San Francisco Giants Version)/Baby, Baby I Love You	1982	—	2.00	4.00
—Green "Talkin' Baseball" sleeve with custom sticker					
❑ 45103	Talkin' Baseball (Detroit Tigers Version)/Baby, Baby I Love You	1982	—	2.00	4.00
❑ 45103 [PS]	Talkin' Baseball (Detroit Tigers Version)/Baby, Baby I Love You	1982	—	2.00	4.00
—Green "Talkin' Baseball" sleeve with custom sticker					
❑ 45104CC	Talkin' Baseball (Baseball and the Cubs)/Baby, Baby I Love You	1982	—	2.00	4.00
❑ 45104CC [PS]	Talkin' Baseball (Special Cubs Version)/Baby, Baby I Love You	1982	—	3.00	6.00
—Green "Talkin' Baseball" sleeve with square Chicago Cubs sticker					
❑ 45105	Talkin' Baseball (Baltimore Orioles Version)/Baby, Baby I Love You	1982	—	2.00	4.00
❑ 45105 [PS]	Talkin' Baseball/Baby, Baby I Love You	1982	—	2.00	4.00
—Green "Talkin' Baseball" sleeve with "For Orioles Fans" custom sticker					
❑ 45105 [PS]	Talkin' Baseball (Baltimore Orioles Version)/Baby, Baby I Love You	1982	—	2.50	5.00
—Orange sleeve with photo of Cal Ripken Jr.					
❑ 45106	Talkin' Baseball (Boston Red Sox Version)/Baby, Baby I Love You	1982	—	2.00	4.00
❑ 45106 [PS]	Talkin' Baseball (Boston Red Sox Version)/Baby, Baby I Love You	1982	—	2.00	4.00
—Green "Talkin' Baseball" sleeve with custom sticker					
❑ 45107	Talkin' Baseball (St. Louis Cardinals Version)/Baby, Baby I Love You	1982	—	2.00	4.00
❑ 45107 [PS]	Talkin' Baseball (St. Louis Cardinals Version)/Baby, Baby I Love You	1982	—	2.00	4.00
—Green "Talkin' Baseball" sleeve with custom sticker					
❑ 45108	Talkin' Baseball (New York Mets Version)/Baby, Baby I Love You	1982	—	2.00	4.00
❑ 45108 [PS]	Talkin' Baseball (New York Mets Version)/Baby, Baby I Love You	1982	—	2.00	4.00
—Green "Talkin' Baseball" sleeve with custom sticker					
❑ 45109	Talkin' Baseball (Pittsburgh Pirates Version)/Baby, Baby I Love You	1982	—	2.00	4.00
❑ 45109 [PS]	Talkin' Baseball (Pittsburgh Pirates Version)/Baby, Baby I Love You	1982	—	2.00	4.00
—Green "Talkin' Baseball" sleeve with custom sticker					
❑ 45110	Talkin' Baseball (Atlanta Braves Version)/Baby, Baby I Love You	1982	—	2.00	4.00
❑ 45110 [PS]	Talkin' Baseball (Atlanta Braves Version)/Baby, Baby I Love You	1982	—	2.00	4.00
—Green "Talkin' Baseball" sleeve with custom sticker					
❑ 45111	Talkin' Baseball (Kansas City Royals Version)/Baby, Baby I Love You	1982	—	2.00	4.00
❑ 45111 [PS]	Talkin' Baseball (Kansas City Royals Version)/Baby, Baby I Love You	1982	—	2.00	4.00
—Green "Talkin' Baseball" sleeve with custom sticker					

Number	Title (A Side/B Side)	Yr	VG	VG+	NM
❑ 45112	Talkin' Baseball (Houston Astros Version)/Baby, Baby I Love You	1982	—	2.00	4.00
❑ 45112 [PS]	Talkin' Baseball (Houston Astros Version)/Baby, Baby I Love You	1982	—	2.00	4.00
—Green "Talkin' Baseball" sleeve with custom sticker					
❑ 45113	Talkin' Baseball (Milwaukee Brewers Version)/Baby, Baby I Love You	1982	—	2.00	4.00
❑ 45113 [PS]	Talkin' Baseball (Milwaukee Brewers Version)/Baby, Baby I Love You	1982	—	2.00	4.00
—Green "Talkin' Baseball" sleeve with custom sticker					
❑ 45114	Talkin' Baseball (Minnesota Twins Version)/Baby, Baby I Love You	1982	—	2.00	4.00
❑ 45114 [PS]	Talkin' Baseball (Minnesota Twins Version)/Baby, Baby I Love You	1982	—	2.00	4.00
—Green "Talkin' Baseball" sleeve with custom sticker					
❑ 45115	Talkin' Baseball (Montreal Expos Version)/Baby, Baby I Love You	1982	—	2.00	4.00
❑ 45115 [PS]	Talkin' Baseball (Montreal Expos Version)/Baby, Baby I Love You	1982	—	2.00	4.00
—Green "Talkin' Baseball" sleeve with custom sticker					
❑ 45117	Cooperstown (The Town Where Baseball Lives)/Baseball Ballet	1983	—	2.50	5.00
❑ 45119	The Earl of Baltimore/Baseball Ballet	1983	—	2.00	4.00
❑ 45121 [DJ]	Football U.S.A. (same on both sides)	1983	—	2.00	4.00
—May be promo only					
METROSTAR					
❑ M-4585-2	There Must Be Something Inside (A Tribute to Pete Rose)/Baseball's Red Machine (Talkin' Baseball, Cincinnati Reds)	1985	2.50	5.00	10.00
Albums					
LIFESONG					
❑ LS 6006	Terry Cashman	1976	3.00	6.00	12.00
❑ LS 8137	Talkin' Baseball	1981	3.75	7.50	15.00
❑ PZ 34999	Terry Cashman	1977	2.50	5.00	10.00
—Reissue of 6006					
CASHMAN AND WEST Also see TERY CASHMAN.					
45s					
ABC DUNHILL					
❑ 4324	American City Suite/I Belong to You	1972	—	3.00	6.00
❑ 4324 [PS]	American City Suite/I Belong to You	1972	2.00	4.00	8.00
❑ 4333	Songman/If You Were a Rainbow	1972	—	2.50	5.00
❑ 4349	The King of Rock 'N Roll/Somebody Stole the Sun	1973	—	2.50	5.00
❑ 4380	Is It Raining in New York City/Will You Be My Baby	1973	—	2.50	5.00
❑ 15021	Lifesong/I Could Feel the Morning	1974	—	2.50	5.00
LIFESONG					
❑ 45000	American City Suite/A Friend Is Dying	1975	—	2.50	5.00
Albums					
ABC DUNHILL					
❑ DSX-50126	A Song or Two	1972	3.00	6.00	12.00
❑ DSX-50141	Moondog Serenade	1973	3.00	6.00	12.00
❑ DSX-50179	Lifesong	1974	3.00	6.00	12.00
CASHMAN, PISTILLI AND WEST Also see BUCHANAN BROTHERS; TERRY CASHMAN; CASHMAN AND WEST; GENE PISTILLI.					
45s					
ABC					
❑ 11047	But for Love/Song That Never Comes	1968	2.00	4.00	8.00
❑ 11079	Spring Has a Tear in Her Eye/Little Girl	1968	2.00	4.00	8.00
❑ 11111	My Side of the Sky/You Can Write a Song	1968	2.00	4.00	8.00
CAPITOL					
❑ 2462	Some of My Best Friends Are People/Sausalito	1969	—	3.00	6.00
❑ 2582	Proud Mary-Dock of the Bay/Sister John	1969	—	3.00	6.00
❑ 2671	Signs/Dolphins	1969	—	3.00	6.00
❑ 2747	She Never Looked Better/Goodbye Jo	1970	—	3.00	6.00
❑ 2863	Midnight Man/Automatic Pilot	1970	—	3.00	6.00
Albums					
ABC					
❑ ABCS-629	Bound to Happen	1968	5.00	10.00	20.00
CAPITOL					
❑ ST-211	Cashman, Pistilli, and West	1969	3.75	7.50	15.00
CASHMERES, THE Possibly more than one group.					
45s					
HEM					
❑ 1000	Show Stopper/(B-side unknown)	1965	2500.	3750.	5000.
HERALD					
❑ 474	Little Dream Girl/Do I Upset You	1956	20.00	40.00	80.00
JOSIE					
❑ 894	Life Line/Where Have You Been	1961	3.00	6.00	12.00
LAKE					
❑ 703	Everything's Gonna Be Alright/Four Lonely Nights	1960	7.50	15.00	30.00
❑ 705	Satisfied/Satisfied (Part 2)	1961	6.25	12.50	25.00
LAURIE					
❑ 3078	I Believe in St. Nick/A Very Special Birthday	1960	10.00	20.00	40.00
❑ 3088	I Gotta Go/Singing Waters	1961	6.25	12.50	25.00
❑ 3105	Poppa Said/Bobby Come On Home	1961	6.25	12.50	25.00
MERCURY					
❑ 70501	My Sentimental Heart/Yes, Yes, Yes	1954	20.00	40.00	80.00
❑ 70617	Don't Let It Happen Again/Boom Mag-Azeno-Vip Vay	1955	20.00	40.00	80.00
❑ 70679	There's a Rumor/Second Hand Heart	1955	20.00	40.00	80.00
RELIC					
❑ 1005	Satisfied/Satisfied (Part 2)	1970	—	3.00	6.00
CASINOS, THE (1) Male vocal group from Cincinnati.					
45s					
BUCCANEER					
❑ 3000	Then You Can Tell Me Goodbye/I Still Love You	196?	2.00	4.00	8.00
—Reissue of Fraternity release					
FRATERNITY					
❑ 944	She's Out of Sight/The Gallop	1965	2.50	5.00	10.00
❑ 949	Right There Beside You/The Gallop	1965	2.50	5.00	10.00
❑ 977	Then You Can Tell Me Goodbye/I Still Love You	1967	3.00	6.00	12.00

Number	Title (A Side/B Side)	Yr	VG	VG+	NM
❏ 985	It's All Over Now/Tailor Made	1967	2.50	5.00	10.00
❏ 987	Forever and a Night/How Long Has It Been	1967	2.50	5.00	10.00
❏ 995	When I Stop Dreaming/Please Love	1967	2.50	5.00	10.00
❏ 997	Bye Bye Love/Walk Through This World with Me	1967	2.50	5.00	10.00
❏ 1020	These Are the Things We'll Share/				
	Casinos Having Fun	1969	2.50	5.00	10.00
❏ 1028	I Wish I Were Anyone But Me/				
	I Just Want to Stay Here	1969	2.50	5.00	10.00
❏ 1200	Father John/The Old Saloon	1970	2.50	5.00	10.00
❏ 1201	Wisdom of Love/My House	1970	2.50	5.00	10.00
❏ 1250	Loving Her Was Easier/A Restless Wind	1971	2.50	5.00	10.00
MILLION					
❏ 13	I'm Walking Behind You/Angels Were All Asleep	1972	2.50	5.00	10.00
—As "Gene Hughes and the Casinos"					
UNITED ARTISTS					
❏ 50255	Here I Am/Peggy	1968	2.50	5.00	10.00
—As "Gene Hughes and the Casinos"					
❏ 50313	Nobody's Child/Leaving Makes the Rain				
	Come Down	1968	2.50	5.00	10.00
—As "Gene Hughes and the Casinos"					

Albums
FRATERNITY

❏ LP-1019 [M]	Then You Can Tell Me Goodbye	1967	10.00	20.00	40.00
❏ LPS-1019 [S]	Then You Can Tell Me Goodbye	1967	15.00	30.00	60.00

CASINOS, THE (U) Some of these no doubt are group (1), but not all of them are, and we're not sure which is which.
45s
AIRTOWN

❏ 002	That's the Way/Too Good to Be True	1967	3.75	7.50	15.00
ALTO					
❏ 2002	I Like It Like That/Baby Don't Do It	1961	7.50	15.00	30.00
CASINO					
❏ 111	My Love for You/Why Am I a Fool	1960	10.00	20.00	40.00
CERTRON					
❏ 10015	Coal River/(B-side unknown)	1970	—	3.00	6.00
ITZY					
❏ 2	Do You Recall?/The Swim	1964	12.50	25.00	50.00
NAME					
❏ 7739	Do You Recall?/The Swim	1962	62.50	125.00	250.00
OLIMPIC					
❏ 251	Do You Recall?/The Swim	1963	37.50	75.00	150.00
SIMS					
❏ 306	Moon River/Soul Serenade	1966	3.00	6.00	12.00
TERRY					
❏ 115	Gee Whiz/Lovely One	1964	15.00	30.00	60.00
❏ 116	That's the Way/Too Good to Be True	1964	12.50	25.00	50.00

CASSIDY, DAVID Also see THE PARTRIDGE FAMILY.
45s
BELL

❏ 45150	Cherish/All I Want to Do Is Touch You	1971	—	2.50	5.00
❏ 45150 [PS]	Cherish/All I Want to Do Is Touch You	1971	—	3.00	6.00
❏ 45187	Could It Be Forever/Blind Hope	1972	—	2.00	4.00
❏ 45187 [PS]	Could It Be Forever/Blind Hope	1972	—	3.00	6.00
❏ 45220	How Can I Be Sure/Ricky's Tune	1972	—	2.00	4.00
❏ 45260	Rock Me Baby/Two Time Loser	1972	—	2.00	4.00
❏ 45386	Daydream/Can't Go Home Again	1973	—	2.00	4.00
❏ 45413	Daydreamer/The Puppy Song	1973	—	2.00	4.00
❏ 45605	Breaking Up Is Hard to Do/Please Please Me	1974	—	2.00	4.00
MCA					
❏ 41101	Hurt So Bad/Once a Fool	1979	—	2.00	4.00
❏ 41101 [PS]	Hurt So Bad/Once a Fool	1979	—	2.50	5.00
RCA					
❏ PB-10788	I'll Have to Go Away (Saying Goodbye)/Gettin'				
	It in the Streets	1976	2.00	4.00	8.00
❏ PB-10921	Saying Goodbye Ain't Easy (We'll Have to Go				
	Away)/Rosa's Cantina	1977	2.00	4.00	8.00
RCA VICTOR					
❏ PB-10321	Get It Up for Love/Love In Bloom	1975	2.50	5.00	10.00
❏ PB-10405	This Could Be the Night/Darlin'	1975	2.50	5.00	10.00
❏ PB-10585	Tomorrow/Bedtime	1976	2.50	5.00	10.00
❏ PB-10647	Breakin' Down Again/On Fire	1976	2.50	5.00	10.00

Albums
BELL

❏ 1109	Rock Me Baby	1972	5.00	10.00	20.00
❏ 1132	Dreams Are Nothing More Than Wishes	1973	5.00	10.00	20.00
❏ 1312	Cassidy Live	1974	6.25	12.50	25.00
❏ 1321	David Cassidy's Greatest Hits	1974	3.75	7.50	15.00
❏ 6070	Cherish	1972	5.00	10.00	20.00
RCA VICTOR					
❏ APL1-1066	The Higher They Climb…	1975	3.75	7.50	15.00
—Black vinyl					
❏ APL1-1066	The Higher They Climb…	1975	25.00	50.00	100.00
—Blue vinyl					
❏ APL1-1309	Home Is Where the Heart Is	1976	3.75	7.50	15.00
❏ APL1-1852	Gettin' It in the Street	1976	10.00	20.00	40.00

CASSIDY, TED
45s
CAPITOL

❏ 5503	The Lurch/Wesley	1965	5.00	10.00	20.00
❏ 5503 [PS]	The Lurch/Wesley	1965	30.00	60.00	120.00

CASTALEERS, THE
45s
DONNA

❏ 1349	That's Why I Cry/My Baby's All Right	1961	6.25	12.50	25.00
FELSTED					
❏ 8504	Come Back/Hi-Fi Baby	1958	12.50	25.00	50.00
❏ 8512	Lonely Boy/My Bull Fightin' Baby	1958	10.00	20.00	40.00
❏ 8585	You're My Dream/I'll Be Around	1959	15.00	30.00	60.00
PLANET					
❏ 44	That's Why I Cry/My Baby's All Right	1961	10.00	20.00	40.00

CASTANETS, THE
45s
TCF

Number	Title (A Side/B Side)	Yr	VG	VG+	NM
❏ 1	I Love Him/Funky Wunky Piano	1963	2.50	5.00	10.00

CASTAWAYS, THE (1) Garage rock band from Minnesota.
45s
BEAR

❏ 2000	I Feel So Fine/Hit the Road Jack	1967	10.00	20.00	40.00
ERA BACK TO BACK HITS					
❏ 016	Liar, Liar/Surfin' Bird	197?	—	2.50	5.00
—B-side by the Trashmen					
ERIC					
❏ 247	Liar, Liar/Surfin' Bird	197?	—	2.50	5.00
—B-side by the Trashmen; reissue					
FONTANA					
❏ 1615	Walking in Different Circles/Just On High	1968	3.75	7.50	15.00
❏ 1626	Lavender Popcorn/What Kind of Face	1968	3.75	7.50	15.00
LANA					
❏ 151	Liar, Liar/Sam	196?	2.00	4.00	8.00
—Oldies reissue					
SOMA					
❏ 1433	Liar, Liar/Sam	1965	3.75	7.50	15.00
❏ 1442	Goodbye Babe/A Man's Gotta Be a Man	1965	3.00	6.00	12.00
❏ 1461	Girl in Love/Should Happen to Me	1966	3.00	6.00	12.00
❏ 1469	Liar, Liar/Surfin' Bird	1966	3.00	6.00	12.00
—B-side by the Trashmen					
TAUNAH					
❏ 7745	(I) Feel So Fine/Hit the Road Jack	1967	3.00	6.00	12.00

CASTAWAYS, THE (2) Not sure who they are, but they are not (1), (3) or (4).
45s
CAPITOL

❏ 4340	The Twitch/Vibrations	1960	3.00	6.00	12.00

CASTAWAYS, THE (3) Not sure who they are, but they are not (1), (2) or (4).
45s
EXCELLO

❏ 2038	I Wish/Teasin'	1954	10.00	20.00	40.00

CASTAWAYS, THE (4) Different group, probably from California.
45s
GNP CRESCENDO

❏ 302	Tarzan/Wild Boy	1963	2.50	5.00	10.00
❏ 310	Moritat/Pass It Around	1964	2.50	5.00	10.00

CASTAWAYS, THE (U) May go with (4) above, or possibly not.
45s
WITCH

❏ 124	Don't You Just Know It/I Go Ape	1964	7.50	15.00	30.00

CASTELLES, THE
45s
ATCO

❏ 6069	Happy and Gay/Hey Baby Baby	1956	25.00	50.00	100.00
CLASSIC ARTISTS					
❏ 114	At Christmas Time/One Little Teardrop	1989	—	2.00	4.00
GRAND					
❏ 101	My Girl Awaits Me/Sweetness	1954	500.00	1000.	2000.
—Blue label original					
❏ 103	This Silver Ring/Wonder Why	1954	500.00	1000.	2000.
—Glossy yellow label original					
❏ 105	Do You Remember/If You Were the Only Girl	1954	375.00	750.00	1500.
—Glossy yellow label original					
❏ 109	Baby Can't You See/Over a Cup of Coffee	1954	500.00	1000.	2000.
—Blue label original					
❏ 114	Marcella/I'm a Fool to Care	1955	400.00	800.00	1200.
—Cream label original					
❏ 122	My Wedding Day/Heavenly Father	1955	1750.	3500.	7000.
—Cream label original					
LOST-NITE					
❏ 318	My Girl Awaits Me/Sweetness	197?	—	2.50	5.00
—Reissue					
❏ 320	This Silver Ring/Wonder Why	197?	—	2.50	5.00
—Reissue					
❏ 322	Do You Remember/If You Were the Only Girl	197?	—	2.50	5.00
—Reissue					
❏ 324	Baby Can't You See/Over a Cup of Coffee	197?	—	2.50	5.00
—Reissue					
❏ 326	Marcella/I'm a Fool to Care	197?	—	2.50	5.00
—Reissue					
❏ 328	My Wedding Day/Heavenly Father	197?	—	2.50	5.00
—Reissue					

Albums
COLLECTABLES

❏ COL-5002	The Sweet Sounds of the Castelles	198?	3.00	6.00	12.00

CASTELLS, THE
45s
BLACK GOLD

❏ 306	Save a Chance/Children Who Dream	196?	2.00	4.00	8.00
DECCA					
❏ 31834	Just Walk Away/An Angel Cried	1965	3.75	7.50	15.00
❏ 31967	Life Goes On/I Thought You'd Like That	1966	3.75	7.50	15.00
ERA					
❏ 3038	Little Sad Eyes/Romeo	1961	6.25	12.50	25.00
❏ 3048	Sacred/I Get Dreamy	1961	6.25	12.50	25.00
❏ 3057	My Miracle/Make Believe Wedding	1961	5.00	10.00	20.00
❏ 3064	The Vision of You/Stiki De Boom Boom	1961	5.00	10.00	20.00
❏ 3073	So This Is Love/On the Street of Tears	1962	5.00	10.00	20.00
❏ 3083	Oh, What It Seemed to Be/				
	Stand There, Mountain	1962	5.00	10.00	20.00
❏ 3089	Echoes in the Night/The Only One	1962	5.00	10.00	20.00
❏ 3098	Clown Prince/Eternal Spring, Eternal Love	1962	5.00	10.00	20.00
❏ 3102	Little Sad Eyes/Initials	1963	5.00	10.00	20.00
❏ 3107	Some Enchanted Evening/				
	What Do Little Girls Dream Of	1963	5.00	10.00	20.00

Number	Title (A Side/B Side)	Yr	VG	VG+	NM
LAURIE					
❏ 3444	I'd Like to Know/Rocky Ridges	1968	2.50	5.00	10.00
UNITED ARTISTS					
❏ 50324	Two Lovers/Jerusalem	1968	2.50	5.00	10.00
WARNER BROS.					
❏ 5421	I Do/Teardrops	1964	20.00	40.00	80.00
—A-side written and produced by Brian Wilson					
❏ 5445	Could This Be Magic/Shinny Up Your Own Side	1964	7.50	15.00	30.00
❏ 5486	Love Finds a Way/Tell Her If I Could	1964	5.00	10.00	20.00
Albums					
ERA					
❏ EL-109 [M]	So This Is Love	1962	30.00	60.00	120.00
❏ ES-109 [S]	So This Is Love	1962	100.00	200.00	400.00

CASTLE, JOEY
45s

Number	Title (A Side/B Side)	Yr	VG	VG+	NM
HEADLINE					
❏ 1008	Rock and Roll Daddy-O/Wild Love	1959	100.00	200.00	400.00
RCA VICTOR					
❏ 47-7283	That Ain't Nothin' But Right/ Come A Little Closer Baby	1958	15.00	30.00	60.00

CASTLE, TONY
45s

Number	Title (A Side/B Side)	Yr	VG	VG+	NM
EASTWEST					
❏ 107	Terry/Young and In Love	1958	7.50	15.00	30.00
GONE					
❏ 5099	Salty/Salty, Part 2	1961	5.00	10.00	20.00
❏ 5099	Salty/Hi Lili, Hi Lo	1961	6.25	12.50	25.00
❏ 5105	Sincerely/Tara's Themes	1961	5.00	10.00	20.00
❏ 5107	Seems Like Old Times/ The Loneliest Girl in the World	1961	5.00	10.00	20.00
TREY					
❏ 3002	Kiss Me Goodnight/The Fool	1960	6.25	12.50	25.00

CASTLE KINGS, THE
45s

Number	Title (A Side/B Side)	Yr	VG	VG+	NM
ATLANTIC					
❏ 2107	You Can Get Him Frankenstein/Loch Lomond	1961	7.50	15.00	30.00
—Produced by Phil Spector					
❏ 2158	Jeanette/The Caissons Go Rolling Along	1962	3.75	7.50	15.00

CASTLEMAN, BOOMER
45s

Number	Title (A Side/B Side)	Yr	VG	VG+	NM
BNA					
❏ 006	Summertime Blues/(B-side unknown)	198?	—	3.00	6.00
❏ 007	Hot Day in the South/Losin' My Touch	198?	—	3.00	6.00
GRT					
❏ 069	That House Up On the Hill/Chihuahua	1976	—	3.00	6.00
❏ 082	Mississippi Mud/(B-side unknown)	1976	—	3.00	6.00
MUMS					
❏ ZS8 6038	Judy Mae/Three Feet High and Growing	1975	—	3.00	6.00

CASTON, BOBBY
45s

Number	Title (A Side/B Side)	Yr	VG	VG+	NM
ATLAS					
❏ 1103	Call Me Darling/Why Wasn't I Told	1958	25.00	50.00	100.00

CASTOR, JIMMY, BUNCH Also see THE CLINTONIAN CUBS.
12-Inch Singles

Number	Title (A Side/B Side)	Yr	VG	VG+	NM
CATAWBA					
❏ 4Z9-05299	Godzilla (Vocal 4:28) (Instrumental)	1985	2.00	4.00	8.00
COTILLION					
❏ DSKO 183 [DJ]	Don't Do That! (7:08) (same on both sides)	1979	3.75	7.50	15.00
❏ DSKO 206 [DJ]	Party People (6:30) (same on both sides)	1979	5.00	10.00	20.00
❏ DK 4731	Don't Do That! (7:08)/Psych-Out (6:55)	1979	5.00	10.00	20.00
DREAM					
❏ DG 707	Amazon (Long Version 5:45) (Short Version 3:45) (Dub 7:30) (Bonus Acapella 1:45)	1984	5.00	10.00	20.00
❏ DG 708	It Gets to Me (Vocal 6:33) (Short Version 3:45) (Dub 6:30) (Bonus Beats Acapella 2:15)	1984	3.75	7.50	15.00
SALSOUL					
❏ SG 361	E-Man Boogie/Any Way, Any Where, Any Time	1982	3.75	7.50	15.00
45s					
ATLANTIC					
❏ 3011	Maggie (Part 1)/Maggie (Part 2)	1974	—	2.50	5.00
❏ 3045	Everything Man (E-Man)/Heaven Kissed	1974	—	2.50	5.00
❏ 3232	The Bertha Butt Boogie (Part 1)/ The Bertha Butt Boogie (Part 2)	1975	—	2.50	5.00
❏ 3270	Potential/Daniel	1975	—	2.50	5.00
❏ 3295	King Kong (Part 1)/King Kong (Part 2)	1975	—	2.50	5.00
❏ 3302	The Christmas Song (Chestnuts Roasting on an Open Fire)/Merry Christmas	1975	—	3.50	7.00
❏ 3316	Supersound/Drifting	1976	—	2.00	4.00
❏ 3331	Bom Bom/What's Best	1976	—	2.00	4.00
❏ 3362	Everything Is Beautiful to Me/ The Magic Is in the Music	1976	—	2.00	4.00
❏ 3369 [DJ]	I Don't Wanna Lose You (mono/stereo)	1976	—	2.50	5.00
—May be promo-only					
❏ 3375	Space Age/Dracula	1976	—	2.00	4.00
❏ 3396	I Love a Mellow Groove/I Don't Want to Lose You	1977	—	2.00	4.00
❏ 3424	The Return of Leroy (Part 1)/The Return of Leroy (Part 2)	1977	—	2.00	4.00
❏ 3451	Magnolia/TR-7	1978	—	2.00	4.00
❏ 3455	Maximum Stimulation/It Was You	1978	—	2.00	4.00
ATOMIC					
❏ 100	Somebody Mentioned Your Name/ This Girl of Mine	1957	125.00	250.00	500.00
CAPITOL					
❏ 2358	Hey Shorty (Part 1)/Hey Shorty (Part 2)	1968	2.00	4.00	8.00
❏ 2487	Psycho Man/The Real McCoy	1969	2.00	4.00	8.00
❏ 2634	Helpless/Make Me	1969	2.00	4.00	8.00
CATAWBA					
❏ ZS4-05676	Godzilla/(Instrumental)	1985	—	2.00	4.00
COMPASS					
❏ 7019	Soul Sister/Rattlesnake	1968	2.00	4.00	8.00

Number	Title (A Side/B Side)	Yr	VG	VG+	NM
COTILLION					
❏ 44253	Don't Do That!/Don't Do That! (Part 2)	1979	—	2.00	4.00
❏ 45004	Party People/I Just Wanna Stop	1979	—	2.00	4.00
DECCA					
❏ 31963	In a Boogaloo Bag (Part 1)/In a Boogaloo Bag (Part 2)	1966	2.50	5.00	10.00
DREAM					
❏ D7-0359	Don't Cry Out Loud/(Instrumental)	1983	—	2.50	5.00
❏ D7-0360	Amazon/She's an Amazon	1984	—	2.50	5.00
❏ D 70361	It Gets to Me/(Instrumental)	1984	—	2.50	5.00
DRIVE					
❏ 6271	Bertha Butt Encounters Vadar/Mystery of Me	1978	—	2.00	4.00
❏ 6276	You Light Up My Life/Let It Out	1978	—	2.00	4.00
HULL					
❏ 758	Poor Loser/Oh Suzzana	1963	5.00	10.00	20.00
LONG DISTANCE					
❏ 702	Can't Help Falling in Love with You/Stay with Me (Spend the Night)	1980	—	2.50	5.00
RCA VICTOR					
❏ 48-1024	Say Leroy (The Creature from the Black Lagoon Is Your Father) (Parts 1 & 2)	1972	—	2.50	5.00
❏ 48-1029	Troglodyte (Cave Man)/I Promise to Remember	1972	—	3.00	6.00
❏ 74-0583	My Brightest Day/You Better Be Good	1971	—	2.50	5.00
❏ 74-0763	Luther the Anthropod/Party Life	1972	—	2.50	5.00
❏ 74-0836	Paradise/The First Time Ever I Saw Your Face	1972	—	2.50	5.00
❏ 74-0953	Soul Serenade/Purple Haze-Foxey Lady (Tribute to Jimi Hendrix)	1973	—	2.50	5.00
❏ APBO-0047	How Beautiful You Are/I'm Not a Child Anymore	1973	—	2.50	5.00
❏ AMBO-0120	Troglodyte (Cave Man)/Luther the Anthropod	1973	—	2.00	4.00
—Gold Standard Series					
SALSOUL					
❏ 7018	E-Man Boogie/Any Way, Any Where, Any Time	1982	—	2.00	4.00
❏ 7058	E-Man Boogie '83/It's Just Begun	1983	—	2.00	4.00
SMASH					
❏ 2069	Hey, Leroy, Your Mama's Calling You/Ham Hocks Espanol	1966	2.00	4.00	8.00
❏ 2085	Just You Girl/Magic Saxophone	1967	2.00	4.00	8.00
❏ 2099	Leroy Is In the Army/Dry	1967	2.00	4.00	8.00
❏ 2120	Jamaica Farewell/Mini-Sonata	1967	2.00	4.00	8.00
WING					
❏ 90078	I Promise/I Know the Meaning of Love	1956	30.00	60.00	120.00
Albums					
ATLANTIC					
❏ SD 7305	The Everything Man	1974	2.50	5.00	10.00
❏ SD 18124	Butt Of Course	1975	2.50	5.00	10.00
❏ SD 18150	Supersound	1975	2.50	5.00	10.00
❏ SD 18186	E-Man Groovin'	1976	2.50	5.00	10.00
❏ SD 19111	Maximum Stimulation	1977	2.50	5.00	10.00
COTILLION					
❏ SD 5215	The Jimmy Castor Bunch	1979	3.00	6.00	12.00
DRIVE					
❏ 407	Let It Out	1978	3.00	6.00	12.00
LONG DISTANCE					
❏ 1201	C	1980	3.00	6.00	12.00
RCA VICTOR					
❏ APD1-0103 [Q]	Dimension III	1973	5.00	10.00	20.00
—All copies are quadraphonic					
❏ APL1-0313	The Everything Man	1974	3.75	7.50	15.00
❏ LSP-4640	It's Just Begun	1972	3.75	7.50	15.00
❏ LSP-4783	Phase Two	1972	3.75	7.50	15.00
SMASH					
❏ MGS-27091 [M]	Hey Leroy!	1967	10.00	20.00	40.00
❏ SRS-67091 [S]	Hey Leroy!	1967	10.00	20.00	40.00

CASTROES, THE
45s

Number	Title (A Side/B Side)	Yr	VG	VG+	NM
GRAND					
❏ 2002	Dearest Darling/Dance with Me	1959	37.50	75.00	150.00

CASUAL ASSOCIATION, THE
45s

Number	Title (A Side/B Side)	Yr	VG	VG+	NM
PARKWAY					
❏ 158	Georgy Girl/Nickels and Dimes	1967	3.00	6.00	12.00

CASUALAIRS, THE
45s

Number	Title (A Side/B Side)	Yr	VG	VG+	NM
AUTUMN					
❏ 21	Just For You/This Is a Mean World	1965	6.25	12.50	25.00
CRAIG					
❏ 5001	Bossa Nova Twist/Cruising	1962	10.00	20.00	40.00
MONA-LEE					
❏ 136	At the Dance/Satsfied	1959	10.00	20.00	40.00

CASUALS, THE (1) See THE ORIGINAL CASUALS.

CASUALS, THE (2)
45s

Number	Title (A Side/B Side)	Yr	VG	VG+	NM
DOT					
❏ 15557	Somebody Help Me/My Love Song for You	1957	6.25	12.50	25.00
❏ 15671	Hello Love/Till You Come Back to Me	1957	6.25	12.50	25.00

CASUALS, THE (3) British group.
45s

Number	Title (A Side/B Side)	Yr	VG	VG+	NM
MAINSTREAM					
❏ 692	I've Got Something Too/Jesamine (A Butterfly Child)	1968	2.50	5.00	10.00
❏ 697	Touched/Toy	1968	2.50	5.00	10.00
—As "The British Casuals"					

CASUALS, THE (4)
45s

Number	Title (A Side/B Side)	Yr	VG	VG+	NM
MINARET					
❏ 109	Money/Big Hammer	1963	3.75	7.50	15.00
MONUMENT					
❏ 905	Promise Her Anything (But Give Her Love)/Walk	1965	3.00	6.00	12.00
❏ 937	Walk Away/If You Don't	1966	3.00	6.00	12.00

Number	Title (A Side/B Side)	Yr	VG	VG+	NM
SOUND STAGE 7					
2534	Mustang 2 + 2/Play Me a Sad Song	1964	3.75	7.50	15.00

CAT MOTHER AND THE ALL NIGHT NEWS BOYS
45s

Number	Title (A Side/B Side)	Yr	VG	VG+	NM
POLYDOR					
14002	Good Old Rock 'N Roll/Bad News	1969	2.00	4.00	8.00
14007	Can You Dance to It/Marie	1969	—	3.00	6.00

—Both of the above were produced by Jimi Hendrix

Number	Title (A Side/B Side)	Yr	VG	VG+	NM
14029	Last Go-Round/I Must Be Dreaming	1970	—	3.00	6.00
14126	Letter to the President/Ode to Oregon	1972	—	3.00	6.00
14138	She Came from a Different World/Three and Me	1972	—	3.00	6.00

Albums

Number	Title (A Side/B Side)	Yr	VG	VG+	NM
POLYDOR					
24-4001	The Street Giveth…And the Street Taketh Away	1969	6.25	12.50	25.00

—Produced by Jimi Hendrix

Number	Title (A Side/B Side)	Yr	VG	VG+	NM
24-4023	Albion Doo-Wah	1970	3.75	7.50	15.00
PD-5017	Cat Mother	1972	3.75	7.50	15.00
PD-5042	Last Chance Dance	1972	3.75	7.50	15.00

CATALINAS, THE (1) Studio band of Los Angeles session pros.
45s

Number	Title (A Side/B Side)	Yr	VG	VG+	NM
RIC					
113	Banzai Wipeout/Beach Walkin'	1964	6.25	12.50	25.00
164	Boss Barracuda/Surfer Boy	1965	6.25	12.50	25.00
SIMS					
134	Bail Out/Bulletin	1963	3.75	7.50	15.00
Albums					
RIC					
M-1006 [M]	Fun, Fun, Fun	1964	25.00	50.00	100.00
S-1006 [S]	Fun, Fun, Fun	1964	37.50	75.00	150.00

CATALINAS, THE (2) Five-man vocal group.
45s

Number	Title (A Side/B Side)	Yr	VG	VG+	NM
LITTLE					
811/2	Give Me Your Love/Castle of Love	1957	50.00	100.00	200.00

CATALINAS, THE (U)
45s

Number	Title (A Side/B Side)	Yr	VG	VG+	NM
BACK BEAT					
513	Speechless/Flying Formation with You	1958	7.50	15.00	30.00
DEE JAY					
1010	Bail Out/Bulletin	1963	10.00	20.00	40.00
DIAL					
3008	Cha Cha Joe/Echo One	1963	3.00	6.00	12.00
GLORY					
285	Marlene/With Your Girl — Yeah!	1958	5.00	10.00	20.00
ORIGINAL SOUND					
48	Your Tender Lips/Gonna Tell	1964	3.00	6.00	12.00
RITA					
1006	Ring of Stars/Wooly Wooly Willie	1960	5.00	10.00	20.00
SCEPTER					
12188	Tick Tock/You Haven't the Right	1967	3.75	7.50	15.00
20TH FOX					
286	Sweetheart/Unchained Melody	1962	7.50	15.00	30.00
299	Safari/Pretty Little Nashville Girl	1962	7.50	15.00	30.00

CATANOOGA CATS, THE
Albums

Number	Title (A Side/B Side)	Yr	VG	VG+	NM
FORWARD					
ST-F-1018	The Catanooga Cats	1969	10.00	20.00	40.00

CATHY JEAN AND THE ROOMATES Also see THE ROOMATES.
45s

Number	Title (A Side/B Side)	Yr	VG	VG+	NM
PHILIPS					
40106	My Heart Belongs to Only You/I Only Want You	1963	5.00	10.00	20.00

—As "Cathy Jean"

Number	Title (A Side/B Side)	Yr	VG	VG+	NM
40143	Double Trouble/Believe Me	1963	5.00	10.00	20.00

—As "Cathy Jean"

Number	Title (A Side/B Side)	Yr	VG	VG+	NM
VALMOR					
007	Please Love Me Forever/Canadian Sunset	1961	3.75	7.50	15.00

—Black label

Number	Title (A Side/B Side)	Yr	VG	VG+	NM
007	Please Love Me Forever/Canadian Sunset	1961	6.25	12.50	25.00

—Red label

Number	Title (A Side/B Side)	Yr	VG	VG+	NM
007 [PS]	Please Love Me Forever/Canadian Sunset	1961	17.50	35.00	70.00

—Sleeve is promo only

Number	Title (A Side/B Side)	Yr	VG	VG+	NM
009	Make Me Smile Again/Sugar Cake	1961	6.25	12.50	25.00
011	I Only Want You/One Love	1961	5.00	10.00	20.00
016	Please Tell Me/Sugar Cake	1962	5.00	10.00	20.00
Albums					
VALMOR					
78 [M]	Great Oldies	1962	200.00	400.00	800.00

—Reissue of 789 with titles on cover and no group shot

Number	Title (A Side/B Side)	Yr	VG	VG+	NM
789 [M]	At the Hop!	1961	225.00	450.00	900.00

CAUTIONS, THE
45s

Number	Title (A Side/B Side)	Yr	VG	VG+	NM
SHRINE					
104	Watch Your Step/Is It Right	1965	175.00	350.00	700.00
115	No Other Way/Poor Loser	1966	200.00	400.00	800.00

CAVALIERE, FELIX Also see FELIX AND THE ESCORTS; THE RASCALS.
45s

Number	Title (A Side/B Side)	Yr	VG	VG+	NM
BEARSVILLE					
0300	High Price to Pay/Mountain Men	1974	—	2.50	5.00
0302	Everlasting Love/Future Train	1975	—	3.00	6.00
0305	Never Felt Love Before/Love Came	1975	—	3.00	6.00
EPIC					
9-50785	Castles in the Air/Outside Your Window	1979	—	2.00	4.00
9-50829	Only a Lonely Heart Sees/You Turned Me Around	1980	—	2.00	4.00
9-50880	Good to Have Love Back/Dancin' the Night Away	1980	—	2.00	4.00
Albums					
BEARSVILLE					
BR 6955	Felix Cavaliere	1974	3.00	6.00	12.00
BR 6958	Destiny	1975	3.00	6.00	12.00

Number	Title (A Side/B Side)	Yr	VG	VG+	NM
EPIC					
JE 35990	Castles in the Air	1979	2.50	5.00	10.00

CAVALIERS, THE (1) Washington, D.C. group renowned in "Northern Soul" circles.
45s

Number	Title (A Side/B Side)	Yr	VG	VG+	NM
RCA VICTOR					
47-9054	Dance Little Girl/Hold On to My Baby	1966	25.00	50.00	100.00
47-9321	I Really Love You/I've Gotta Find Her	1967	20.00	40.00	80.00
SHRINE					
119	Do What I Need/Tighten Up	1966	300.00	600.00	1200.

CAVALIERS, THE (U) None of these are by group (1).
45s

Number	Title (A Side/B Side)	Yr	VG	VG+	NM
APT					
25004	Dance, Dance, Dance/Play By the Rules of Love	1958	10.00	20.00	40.00
CORAL					
62245	Teen Fever/Funky	1961	3.00	6.00	12.00
DECCA					
29556	Somewhere, Sometime, Someday/Honor Bright	1955	3.75	7.50	15.00
GALENA					
1277	Blowin' Smoke/Ten More Miles	1962	5.00	10.00	20.00
MUSIC WORLD					
101	The Magic Age of Sixteen/So Young, So Warm, So Beautiful	1963	7.50	15.00	30.00
NRC					
028	Dreamy Bikini/Charm Bracelet	1959	3.75	7.50	15.00

CAVE DWELLERS, THE
45s

Number	Title (A Side/B Side)	Yr	VG	VG+	NM
ABC-PARAMOUNT					
10735	Sinking Feeling/Sling My Rock	1965	5.00	10.00	20.00

CELEBRITYS, THE
45s

Number	Title (A Side/B Side)	Yr	VG	VG+	NM
CAROLINE					
2301	Juanita/(B-side unknown)	1956	150.00	300.00	600.00
2302	Absent Minded/We Made Romance	1956	150.00	300.00	600.00

CELLOS, THE
45s

Number	Title (A Side/B Side)	Yr	VG	VG+	NM
APOLLO					
510	Rang Tang Ding Dong (I Am the Japanese Sandman)/You Took My Love	1957	6.25	12.50	25.00
510	Rang Tang Ding Dong/You Took My Love	1957	20.00	40.00	80.00
515	Under Your Spell/The Juicy Crocodile	1957	12.50	25.00	50.00
516	The Be-Bop Mouse/Girlie That I Love	1957	12.50	25.00	50.00
524	I Beg for Your Love/What's the Matter with You	1958	15.00	30.00	60.00

CELTICS, THE
45s

Number	Title (A Side/B Side)	Yr	VG	VG+	NM
AL-JACK'S					
0002	Can You Remember/Send Me Someone to Love	1958	2500.	3750.	5000.
WAR CONN					
2216	Darline, Darling/Only the Lonely	1962	100.00	200.00	400.00

CENTIPEDE
Albums

Number	Title (A Side/B Side)	Yr	VG	VG+	NM
RCA VICTOR					
CPL2-5042 [(2)]September Energy		1974	12.50	25.00	50.00

CENTRAL NERVOUS SYSTEM
45s

Number	Title (A Side/B Side)	Yr	VG	VG+	NM
LAURIE					
3421	It Takes All Kinds/I'm Still Hung Up on You	1968	2.50	5.00	10.00
3446	Alice in Wonderland/Something Happened to Me	1968	2.50	5.00	10.00
Albums					
MUSIC FACTORY					
MF-12003 [M]	I Could Have Danced All Night	1968	7.50	15.00	30.00

—White label promo only (no stock copies were issued in mono)

Number	Title (A Side/B Side)	Yr	VG	VG+	NM
MFS-12003 [S]	I Could Have Danced All Night	1968	5.00	10.00	20.00

CENTURIES, THE
45s

Number	Title (A Side/B Side)	Yr	VG	VG+	NM
CLEOPATRA					
2	The Outer Limits/Polynesian Paradise	1963	7.50	15.00	30.00
3	Jack 23/4th Dimension	1964	7.50	15.00	30.00

CENTURIONS, THE
Albums

Number	Title (A Side/B Side)	Yr	VG	VG+	NM
DEL-FI					
DFLP-1228 [M] Surfer's Pajama Party		1963	25.00	50.00	100.00
DFST-1228 [S] Surfer's Pajama Party		1963	50.00	100.00	200.00

—Above has the same title and number, and almost the same cover, as the album of the same name by Bruce Johnston, but the contents are different

CESANA
Albums

Number	Title (A Side/B Side)	Yr	VG	VG+	NM
MODERN					
M-100 [M]	Tender Emotions	1964	5.00	10.00	20.00

CEYLEIB PEOPLE, THE
45s

Number	Title (A Side/B Side)	Yr	VG	VG+	NM
VAULT					
940	Changes/Ceyladd Seyta	1968	5.00	10.00	20.00
Albums					
VAULT					
LP-117	Tanyet	1968	15.00	30.00	60.00

CHAD AND JEREMY Also see CHAD AND JILL STUART.
45s

Number	Title (A Side/B Side)	Yr	VG	VG+	NM
CAPITOL STARLINE					
6087	A Summer Song/Willow Weep for Me	1966	2.00	4.00	8.00

—Green and white swirl label

Number	Title (A Side/B Side)	Yr	VG	VG+	NM
COLUMBIA					
43277	Before and After/Fare Thee Well	1965	2.50	5.00	10.00
43277 [DJ]	Before and After (same on both sides)	1965	10.00	20.00	40.00

—Promo only on red vinyl

Number	Title (A Side/B Side)	Yr	VG	VG+	NM
❏ 43277 [PS]	Before and After/Fare Thee Well	1965	12.50	25.00	50.00

—Basically identical to the more common "I Don't Want to Lose You Baby," except that on this sleeve, the blurbs on the front and back begin "Columbia Records Proudly Introduces..."

Number	Title (A Side/B Side)	Yr	VG	VG+	NM
❏ 43339	I Don't Wanna Lose You Baby/Pennies	1965	2.00	4.00	8.00
❏ 43339 [PS]	I Don't Wanna Lose You Baby/Pennies	1965	5.00	10.00	20.00

—Basically identical to the "Before and After" sleeve, except that this one has the words "Columbia Records Proudly Presents..." on front and back

Number	Title (A Side/B Side)	Yr	VG	VG+	NM
❏ 43414	I Have Dreamed/Should I?	1966	2.00	4.00	8.00
❏ 43490	Teenage Failure/Early Morning Rain	1965	2.00	4.00	8.00
❏ 43490 [PS]	Teenage Failure/Early Morning Rain	1965	5.00	10.00	20.00
❏ 43682	Distant Shores/Last Night	1966	2.00	4.00	8.00
❏ 43682 [PS]	Distant Shores/Last Night	1966	5.00	10.00	20.00
❏ 43807	You Are She/I Won't Cry	1966	2.00	4.00	8.00
❏ 43807 [PS]	You Are She/I Won't Cry	1966	5.00	10.00	20.00
❏ 44131	Rest in Peace/Family Way	1967	2.00	4.00	8.00
❏ 44379	Painted Dayglow Smile/Editorial	1967	2.00	4.00	8.00
❏ 44525	Sister Marie/Rest in Peace	1968	2.00	4.00	8.00
❏ 44660	Paxton Quigley's Had the Course/You Need Feet	1968	2.00	4.00	8.00
❏ 44660 [PS]	Paxton Quigley's Had the Course/You Need Feet	1968	4.00	8.00	16.00

—Promo-only sleeve of a Nazi military rally

LANA

Number	Title (A Side/B Side)	Yr	VG	VG+	NM
❏ 145	Yesterday's Gone/Lemon Tree	196?	—	3.00	6.00

—Oldies reissue

Number	Title (A Side/B Side)	Yr	VG	VG+	NM
❏ 146	A Summer Song/No Tears for Johnny	196?	—	3.00	6.00

ROCSHIRE

Number	Title (A Side/B Side)	Yr	VG	VG+	NM
❏ 95046	Bite the Bullet/How Many Trains	1983	—	2.00	4.00
❏ 95050 [DJ]	Bite the Bullet/Interview	1983	3.00	6.00	12.00
❏ 95061	Dreams/Zanzibar Sunset	1983	—	2.00	4.00

WORLD ARTISTS

Number	Title (A Side/B Side)	Yr	VG	VG+	NM
❏ 1021	Yesterday's Gone/Lemon Tree	1964	2.50	5.00	10.00

—As "Chad Stuart and Jeremy Clyde"

Number	Title (A Side/B Side)	Yr	VG	VG+	NM
❏ 1027	A Summer Song/No Tears for Johnny	1964	2.50	5.00	10.00

—As "Chad Stuart and Jeremy Clyde"

Number	Title (A Side/B Side)	Yr	VG	VG+	NM
❏ 1034	Willow Weep for Me/If She Was Mine	1964	2.50	5.00	10.00
❏ 1034 [PS]	Willow Weep for Me/If She Was Mine	1964	5.00	10.00	20.00
❏ 1041	If I Loved You/Donna, Donna	1965	2.50	5.00	10.00
❏ 1041 [PS]	If I Loved You/Donna, Donna	1965	5.00	10.00	20.00
❏ 1052	What Do You Want with Me/A Very Good Year	1965	2.50	5.00	10.00

—As "Chad Stuart and Jeremy Clyde"

Number	Title (A Side/B Side)	Yr	VG	VG+	NM
❏ 1052 [PS]	What Do You Want with Me/A Very Good Year	1965	12.50	25.00	50.00

—As "Chad Stuart and Jeremy Clyde"

Number	Title (A Side/B Side)	Yr	VG	VG+	NM
❏ 1056	From a Window/My Coloring Book	1965	2.50	5.00	10.00
❏ 1060	September in the Rain/Only for the Young	1965	2.50	5.00	10.00

Albums
CAPITOL

Number	Title (A Side/B Side)	Yr	VG	VG+	NM
❏ ST 2470 [P]	The Best of Chad and Jeremy	1966	3.00	6.00	12.00

—Black label with colorband

Number	Title (A Side/B Side)	Yr	VG	VG+	NM
❏ ST 2470 [P]	The Best of Chad and Jeremy	1967	2.50	5.00	10.00

—"Starline" label

Number	Title (A Side/B Side)	Yr	VG	VG+	NM
❏ T 2470 [M]	The Best of Chad and Jeremy	1966	2.50	5.00	10.00

—Black label with colorband

Number	Title (A Side/B Side)	Yr	VG	VG+	NM
❏ T 2470 [M]	The Best of Chad and Jeremy	1967	2.00	4.00	8.00

—"Starline" label

Number	Title (A Side/B Side)	Yr	VG	VG+	NM
❏ STT 2546 [P]	More Chad and Jeremy	1966	3.00	6.00	12.00
❏ TT 2546 [M]	More Chad and Jeremy	1966	2.50	5.00	10.00
❏ SN-16135 [P]	The Best of Chad and Jeremy	1980	2.00	4.00	8.00

—Budget-line reissue

COLUMBIA

Number	Title (A Side/B Side)	Yr	VG	VG+	NM
❏ CL 2374 [M]	Before and After	1965	5.00	10.00	20.00
❏ CL 2398 [M]	I Don't Want to Lose You Baby	1966	6.25	12.50	25.00
❏ CL 2564 [M]	Distant Shores	1966	5.00	10.00	20.00
❏ CL 2671 [M]	Of Cabbages and Kings	1967	5.00	10.00	20.00
❏ CL 2899 [M]	The Ark	1968	6.25	12.50	25.00
❏ CS 9174 [S]	Before and After	1965	7.50	15.00	30.00
❏ CS 9198 [S]	I Don't Want to Lose You Baby	1966	10.00	20.00	40.00
❏ CS 9364 [P]	Distant Shores	1966	6.25	12.50	25.00

—"Distant Shores" is rechanneled

Number	Title (A Side/B Side)	Yr	VG	VG+	NM
❏ CS 9471 [S]	Of Cabbages and Kings	1967	6.25	12.50	25.00
❏ CS 9699 [S]	The Arc	1968	6.25	12.50	25.00

—Some copies spell the LP title this way on the cover

Number	Title (A Side/B Side)	Yr	VG	VG+	NM
❏ CS 9699 [S]	The Ark	1968	6.25	12.50	25.00

—Correct spelling of LP title on cover

FIDU

Number	Title (A Side/B Side)	Yr	VG	VG+	NM
❏ FM-101 [M]	5 + 10 = 15 Fabulous Hits	1966	2.50	5.00	10.00
❏ FS-101 [P]	5 + 10 = 15 Fabulous Hits	1966	3.00	6.00	12.00

HARMONY

Number	Title (A Side/B Side)	Yr	VG	VG+	NM
❏ HS 11357 [S]	Chad and Jeremy	1973	2.00	4.00	8.00

ROCSHIRE

Number	Title (A Side/B Side)	Yr	VG	VG+	NM
❏ XR-22018	Chad Stuart and Jeremy Clyde	1983	2.50	5.00	10.00

WORLD ARTISTS

Number	Title (A Side/B Side)	Yr	VG	VG+	NM
❏ WAM-2002 [M]	Yesterday's Gone	1964	3.00	6.00	12.00
❏ WAM-2005 [M]	Chad and Jeremy Sing for You	1965	3.00	6.00	12.00
❏ WAS-3002 [P]	Yesterday's Gone	1964	3.75	7.50	15.00

—"Yesterday's Gone" is rechanneled.

Number	Title (A Side/B Side)	Yr	VG	VG+	NM
❏ WAS-3005 [S]	Chad and Jeremy Sing for You	1965	3.75	7.50	15.00

CHAFFIN, ERNIE
45s
SUN

Number	Title (A Side/B Side)	Yr	VG	VG+	NM
❏ 262	Feelin' Low/Lonesome for My Baby	1957	7.50	15.00	30.00
❏ 275	Laughin' and Jokin'/I'm Lonesome	1957	7.50	15.00	30.00
❏ 307	Nothing Can Change My Love for You/Born to Lose	1958	6.25	12.50	25.00
❏ 320	Don't Ever Leave Me/Miracle of You	1959	6.25	12.50	25.00

CHAIN REACTION This Chain Reaction includes Steve Tallarico, later known as Steve Tyler of AEROSMITH.
45s
DATE

Number	Title (A Side/B Side)	Yr	VG	VG+	NM
❏ 1538	When I Needed You/The Sun	1966	7.50	15.00	30.00

CHAIRMEN OF THE BOARD
45s
INVICTUS

Number	Title (A Side/B Side)	Yr	VG	VG+	NM
❏ 1251	Finder's Keepers/Finder's Keepers (Part 2)	1973	—	2.50	5.00
❏ 1263	Life & Death/Love with Me, Love with Me	1974	—	2.50	5.00
❏ 1268	Everybody Party All Night/Morning Glory	1974	—	2.50	5.00
❏ 1271	Let's Have Some Fun/Love at First Sight	1974	—	2.50	5.00
❏ 1276	The Skin I'm In/Love at First Sight	1975	—	2.50	5.00
❏ 1278	You've Got Extra Added Power in Your Love/Someone Just Like You	1975	—	2.50	5.00
❏ 9074	Give Me Just a Little More Time/Since the Days of Pigtails	1970	—	3.00	6.00
❏ 9078	(You've Got Me) Dangling on a String/I'll Come Crawling	1970	—	2.50	5.00
❏ 9079	Everything's Tuesday/Patches	1970	—	2.50	5.00
❏ 9081	Pay to the Piper/Bless You	1970	—	2.50	5.00
❏ 9081 [PS]	Pay to the Piper/Bless You	1970	2.50	5.00	10.00
❏ 9086	Chairman of the Board/When Will She Tell Me She Needs Me	1971	—	2.50	5.00
❏ 9089	Hanging On (To) A Memory/Tracked and Trapped	1971	—	2.50	5.00
❏ 9099	Try On My Love for Size/Working on a Building of Love	1971	—	2.50	5.00
❏ 9103	Men Are Getting Scarce/Bravo! Hurray!	1971	—	2.50	5.00
❏ 9106	Bittersweet/Elmo James	1972	—	2.50	5.00
❏ 9122	Everybody's Got a Song to Sing/Working on a Building of Love	1972	—	2.50	5.00
❏ 9126	Let Me Down Easy/I Can't Find Myself	1972	—	2.50	5.00

Albums
INVICTUS

Number	Title (A Side/B Side)	Yr	VG	VG+	NM
❏ ST-7300	Chairmen of the Board (Featuring "Give Me Just a Little More Time")	1970	10.00	20.00	40.00
❏ SKAO-7304	In Session	1970	10.00	20.00	40.00
❏ ST-9801	Bittersweet	1972	10.00	20.00	40.00
❏ KZ 32526	The Skin I'm In	1974	10.00	20.00	40.00

CHAKACHAS, THE
45s
AVCO

Number	Title (A Side/B Side)	Yr	VG	VG+	NM
❏ 4596	Judas Kiss/Stories	1972	—	2.50	5.00

JANUS

Number	Title (A Side/B Side)	Yr	VG	VG+	NM
❏ 237	Africa Yama (Part 1)/Africa Yama (Part 2)	1974	—	2.50	5.00

POLYDOR

Number	Title (A Side/B Side)	Yr	VG	VG+	NM
❏ 15030	Jungle Fever/Cha Ka Cha	1972	—	3.00	6.00
❏ 15102	Jungle Fever '75/Liza (And Brook)	1975	—	2.00	4.00

Albums
POLYDOR

Number	Title (A Side/B Side)	Yr	VG	VG+	NM
❏ PD-5504	Jungle Fever	1972	3.75	7.50	15.00

CHAKIRIS, GEORGE
45s
CAPITOL

Number	Title (A Side/B Side)	Yr	VG	VG+	NM
❏ 4844	Maria/Once Upon a Time	1962	2.00	4.00	8.00
❏ 4892	My Coloring Book/I've Got Your Number	1962	2.00	4.00	8.00
❏ 5113	My Place/Love Being Here with You	1964	2.00	4.00	8.00
❏ 5209	Invisible Tears/Not for Me	1964	2.00	4.00	8.00
❏ 5426	Days of the Waltz/Finding Words for Spring	1965	2.00	4.00	8.00
❏ 5458	Blue Summer/Ship of Fools	1965	2.00	4.00	8.00

HORIZON

Number	Title (A Side/B Side)	Yr	VG	VG+	NM
❏ 356	But Not for Me/Embraceable You	1962	3.00	6.00	12.00
❏ 363	Cool/Embraceable You	1962	3.00	6.00	12.00

Albums
CAPITOL

Number	Title (A Side/B Side)	Yr	VG	VG+	NM
❏ ST 1750 [S]	George Chakiris	1962	5.00	10.00	20.00
❏ T 1750 [M]	George Chakiris	1962	3.75	7.50	15.00
❏ ST 1813 [S]	Memories Are Made of These	1963	5.00	10.00	20.00
❏ T 1813 [M]	Memories Are Made of These	1963	3.75	7.50	15.00
❏ ST 2391 [S]	It's Been a Swingin' Summer	1965	3.75	7.50	15.00
❏ T 2391 [M]	It's Been a Swingin' Summer	1965	3.00	6.00	12.00

HORIZON

Number	Title (A Side/B Side)	Yr	VG	VG+	NM
❏ ST-1610 [S]	The Gershwin Songbook	1962	5.00	10.00	20.00
❏ WP-1610 [M]	The Gershwin Songbook	1962	3.75	7.50	15.00

CHAKRAS, THE
45s
REPRISE

Number	Title (A Side/B Side)	Yr	VG	VG+	NM
❏ 0838	Things We Said Today/Just with You	1969	3.75	7.50	15.00
❏ 0859	Agnes Vandalism/City Boy	1969	3.75	7.50	15.00

CHALETS, THE
45s
DART

Number	Title (A Side/B Side)	Yr	VG	VG+	NM
❏ 1026	Who's Laughing-Who's Crying/Fat Fat Fat! Mom-Mi-O	1961	6.25	12.50	25.00

LAURIE

Number	Title (A Side/B Side)	Yr	VG	VG+	NM
❏ 3348	She's Not the Marrying Type/(Theme from) She's Not the Marrying Type	1966	3.00	6.00	12.00

MUSICNOTE

Number	Title (A Side/B Side)	Yr	VG	VG+	NM
❏ 1001	Who's Laughing-Who's Crying/Fat Fat Fat! Mom-Mi-O	1962	5.00	10.00	20.00

TRU-LITE

Number	Title (A Side/B Side)	Yr	VG	VG+	NM
❏ 1001	Who's Laughing-Who's Crying/Mom-Mia	1961	12.50	25.00	50.00

CHALLENGERS, THE (1) California surf and instrumental group.
45s
GNP CRESCENDO

Number	Title (A Side/B Side)	Yr	VG	VG+	NM
❏ 362	The Man from U.N.C.L.E./Summer Nights	1965	2.50	5.00	10.00
❏ 362	The Man from U.N.C.L.E./The Streets of London	1965	2.50	5.00	10.00
❏ 368	Walk with Me/How Could It	1966	2.50	5.00	10.00
❏ 376	Wipe Out/North Beach	1966	2.50	5.00	10.00
❏ 380	Milord/What If It Should Rain	1966	2.50	5.00	10.00
❏ 396	The Water Country/Everything to Me	1967	2.50	5.00	10.00
❏ 400	Color Me In/Before You	1968	2.50	5.00	10.00
❏ 412	Chitty Chitty Bang Bang/Lonely Little Girl	1968	2.50	5.00	10.00

TRIUMPH

Number	Title (A Side/B Side)	Yr	VG	VG+	NM
❏ 112	Pipeline/Asphalt Spinner	1966	7.50	15.00	30.00

VAULT

Number	Title (A Side/B Side)	Yr	VG	VG+	NM
❏ 900	Bull Dog/Torquay	1963	5.00	10.00	20.00
❏ 902	Moondawg/Tidal Wave	1963	5.00	10.00	20.00
❏ 904	Foot Tapper/On the Move	1963	5.00	10.00	20.00
❏ 910	Hot Rod Hootenanny/Maybellene	1964	7.50	15.00	30.00
❏ 913	Hot Rod Show/K-39	1964	7.50	15.00	30.00
❏ 918	Channel Nine/Can't Seem to Make You Mine	1965	5.00	10.00	20.00

Number	Title (A Side/B Side)	Yr	VG	VG+	NM
Albums					
FANTASY					
❑ F-9443	Where Were You in the Summer of '62	1973	3.00	6.00	12.00
GNP CRESCENDO					
❑ GNP-609 [(2)M]	25 Great Instrumental Hits	1967	6.25	12.50	25.00
❑ GNPS-609 [(2)S]	25 Great Instrumental Hits	1967	5.00	10.00	20.00
❑ GNP-2010 [M]	The Challengers at the Teenage Fair	1965	5.00	10.00	20.00
❑ GNPS-2010 [S]	The Challengers at the Teenage Fair	1965	6.25	12.50	25.00
❑ GNP-2018 [M]	The Man from U.N.C.L.E.	1965	5.00	10.00	20.00
❑ GNPS-2018 [S]	The Man from U.N.C.L.E.	1965	6.25	12.50	25.00
❑ GNP-2025 [M]	California Kicks	1966	5.00	10.00	20.00
❑ GNPS-2025 [S]	California Kicks	1966	6.25	12.50	25.00
❑ GNP-2030 [M]	Billy Strange and the Challengers	1966	5.00	10.00	20.00
❑ GNPS-2030 [S]	Billy Strange and the Challengers	1966	6.25	12.50	25.00
❑ GNP-2031 [M]	Wipe Out	1966	5.00	10.00	20.00
❑ GNPS-2031 [S]	Wipe Out	1966	6.25	12.50	25.00
❑ GNPS-2045	Light My Fire with Classical Gas	1968	5.00	10.00	20.00
❑ GNPS-2056	Vanilla Funk	1970	5.00	10.00	20.00
❑ GNPS-2093	Sidewalk Surfing	1975	3.00	6.00	12.00
RHINO					
❑ RNLP-053	Best of the Challengers	1982	2.50	5.00	10.00
TRIUMPH					
❑ TR-100 [M]	The Challengers Go Sidewalk Surfing	1965	5.00	10.00	20.00
❑ TRS-100 [S]	The Challengers Go Sidewalk Surfing	1965	6.25	12.50	25.00
VAULT					
❑ LP-100 [M]	Surfbeat	1963	12.50	25.00	50.00
❑ VS-100 [S]	Surfbeat	1963	20.00	40.00	80.00
—Black vinyl					
❑ VS-100 [S]	Surfbeat	1963	62.50	12.50	250.00
—Orange vinyl					
❑ VS-100 [S]	Surfbeat	1963	62.50	125.00	250.00
—Red vinyl					
❑ VS-100 [S]	Surfbeat	1963	62.50	125.00	250.00
—Yellow vinyl					
❑ LP-101 [M]	Surfin' with the Challengers	1963	12.50	25.00	50.00
—Altered title					
❑ LP-101 [M]	Lloyd Thaxton Goes Surfin' with the Challengers	1963	15.00	30.00	60.00
—Original title					
❑ VS-101 [S]	Surfin' with the Challengers	1963	20.00	40.00	80.00
—Altered title; black vinyl					
❑ VS-101 [S]	Lloyd Thaxton Goes Surfin' with the Challengers	1963	25.00	50.00	100.00
—Original title; black vinyl					
❑ VS-101 [S]	(Lloyd Thaxton Goes) Surfin' with the Challengers	1963	62.50	125.00	250.00
—Either title; blue vinyl					
❑ VS-101 [S]	(Lloyd Thaxton Goes) Surfin' with the Challengers	1963	62.50	125.00	250.00
—Either title; orange vinyl					
❑ VS-101 [S]	(Lloyd Thaxton Goes) Surfin' with the Challengers	1963	62.50	125.00	250.00
—Either title; red vinyl					
❑ VS-101 [S]	(Lloyd Thaxton Goes) Surfin' with the Challengers	1963	62.50	125.00	250.00
—Either title; yellow vinyl					
❑ LP-102 [M]	The Challengers On The Move	1963	10.00	20.00	40.00
❑ VS-102 [S]	The Challengers On The Move	1963	15.00	30.00	60.00
❑ LP-107 [M]	K-39	1964	20.00	40.00	80.00
❑ LP-109 [M]	The Surf's Up	1965	10.00	20.00	40.00
❑ VS-109 [S]	The Surf's Up	1965	15.00	30.00	60.00
❑ LP-110 [M]	The Challengers A-Go-Go	1966	7.50	15.00	30.00
❑ VS-110 [S]	The Challengers A-Go-Go	1966	10.00	20.00	40.00
❑ LP-111 [M]	The Challengers' Greatest Hits	1967	6.25	12.50	25.00
❑ VS-111 [S]	The Challengers' Greatest Hits	1967	6.25	12.50	25.00

CHALLENGERS, THE (2) Mid-1960s R&B group.
45s
CHESS

Number	Title (A Side/B Side)	Yr	VG	VG+	NM
❑ 1957	Tossin' and Turnin'/Don;t You Know It	1966	2.50	5.00	10.00

CHALLENGERS, THE (3) Members of this group later recorded as THE OLYMPICS.
45s
MELATONE

Number	Title (A Side/B Side)	Yr	VG	VG+	NM
❑ 1002	I Can Tell/The Mambo Beat	1956	75.00	150.00	300.00

CHALLENGERS, THE (4) Members of this group later recorded as UNDERGROUND SUNSHINE.
45s
NIGHT OWL

Number	Title (A Side/B Side)	Yr	VG	VG+	NM
❑ 6794	I Wanna Hold You/The Challengers Take a Ride on the Jefferson Airplane	1967	7.50	15.00	30.00

CHALLENGERS, THE (5) British group.
45s
TRIODEX

Number	Title (A Side/B Side)	Yr	VG	VG+	NM
❑ 102	Goofus/Lazy Twist	1960	5.00	10.00	20.00
❑ 107	Deadline/Cry of the Wild Goose	1961	5.00	10.00	20.00

CHALLENGERS, THE (U) May be another record by group (2), but we're not sure.
45s
CUCA

Number	Title (A Side/B Side)	Yr	VG	VG+	NM
❑ 1500	Hear My Message/I Wanna Hold You	1968	2.00	4.00	8.00

CHALLENGERS III, THE
45s
TRI-PHI

Number	Title (A Side/B Side)	Yr	VG	VG+	NM
❑ 1012	Stay/Honey, Honey, Honey	1962	7.50	15.00	30.00
—As "The Challengers"					
❑ 1012	Stay/Honey, Honey, Honey	1962	12.50	25.00	50.00
—As "The Challengers III"					
❑ 1020	Every Day/I Hear an Echo	1963	12.50	25.00	50.00

CHAMAELEON CHURCH Chevy Chase was in this group.
45s
MGM

Number	Title (A Side/B Side)	Yr	VG	VG+	NM
❑ 13929	Your Golden Love/Camillia I Changing	1968	3.00	6.00	12.00
Albums					
MGM					
❑ SE-4574	Chamaeleon Church	1968	5.00	10.00	20.00

Number	Title (A Side/B Side)	Yr	VG	VG+	NM
CHAMBERLAIN, RICHARD					
45s					
MCA					
❑ 40691	Secret Kingdom/The Slipper and the Rose Waltz	1977	—	2.00	4.00
MGM					
❑ K13075	Theme from Dr. Kildare (Three Stars Will Shine Tonight)/A Kiss to Build a Dream On	1962	2.50	5.00	10.00
❑ K13075 [PS]	Theme from Dr. Kildare (Three Stars Will Shine Tonight)/A Kiss to Build a Dream On	1962	5.00	10.00	20.00
❑ K13097	Love Me Tender/All I Do Is Dream of You	1962	2.50	5.00	10.00
❑ K13097 [PS]	Love Me Tender/All I Do Is Dream of You	1962	5.00	10.00	20.00
❑ K13121	All I Have to Do Is Dream/Hi-Lili, Hi-Lo	1963	2.50	5.00	10.00
❑ K13121 [PS]	All I Have to Do Is Dream/Hi-Lili, Hi-Lo	1963	5.00	10.00	20.00
❑ K13148	I Will Love You/True Love	1963	2.50	5.00	10.00
❑ K13148 [PS]	I Will Love You/True Love	1963	5.00	10.00	20.00
❑ K13170	Blue Guitar/They Long to Be Close to You	1963	2.50	5.00	10.00
❑ K13170 [PS]	Blue Guitar/They Long to Be Close to You	1963	5.00	10.00	20.00
❑ K13205	Stella By Starlight/Georgia on My Mind	1964	2.00	4.00	8.00
❑ K13205 [PS]	Stella By Starlight/Georgia on My Mind	1964	5.00	10.00	20.00
❑ K13285	Rome Will Never Leave You/You Always Hurt the One You Love	1964	2.00	4.00	8.00
❑ K13285 [PS]	Rome Will Never Leave You/You Always Hurt the One You Love	1964	3.75	7.50	15.00
❑ K13340	Joy in the Morning/April Love	1965	2.50	5.00	10.00
❑ K13340 [PS]	Joy in the Morning/April Love	1965	5.00	10.00	20.00
Albums					
METRO					
❑ M-564 [M]	Richard Chamberlain Sings	1966	3.00	6.00	12.00
❑ MS-564 [S]	Richard Chamberlain Sings	1966	3.00	6.00	12.00
MGM					
❑ E-4088 [M]	Richard Chamberlain Sings	1962	3.75	7.50	15.00
❑ SE-4088 [S]	Richard Chamberlain Sings	1962	5.00	10.00	20.00
❑ E-4185 [M]	Twilight of Honor	1963	3.75	7.50	15.00
❑ SE-4185 [S]	Twilight of Honor	1963	5.00	10.00	20.00
❑ E-4287 [M]	Joy in the Morning	1965	3.75	7.50	15.00
❑ SE-4287 [S]	Joy in the Morning	1965	5.00	10.00	20.00
❑ ST 90512 [S]	Richard Chamberlain Sings	1965	7.50	15.00	30.00
—Capitol Record Club edition					
❑ T 90512 [M]	Richard Chamberlain Sings	1965	6.25	12.50	25.00
—Capitol Record Club edition					

CHAMBERLAIN, WILT "THE STILT"
45s
END

Number	Title (A Side/B Side)	Yr	VG	VG+	NM
❑ 1066	By the River/That's Easy to Say	1960	6.25	12.50	25.00

CHAMBERS BROTHERS, THE
45s
AVCO

Number	Title (A Side/B Side)	Yr	VG	VG+	NM
❑ 4632	Let's Go, Let's Go, Let's Go/Do You Believe in Magic	1974	—	2.00	4.00
❑ 4638	1-2-3/Looking Back	1974	—	2.00	4.00
❑ 4657	Miss Lady Brown/Stealin' Watermelons	1975	—	2.00	4.00
COLUMBIA					
❑ 4-43816	Time Has Come Today (2:37)/Dinah	1966	3.00	6.00	12.00
—A-side is a different recording than the later hit, both vocally and instrumentally					
❑ 43957	All Strung Out Over You/Falling in Love	1967	—	3.00	6.00
❑ 44080	Please Don't Leave Me/I Can't Stand It	1967	—	3.00	6.00
❑ 44296	Uptown/Love Me Like the Rain	1967	—	3.00	6.00
❑ 4-44414	Time Has Come Today (4:45)/People Get Ready	1968	2.00	4.00	8.00
—Hit version; label refers to the album "The Time Has Come"					
❑ 4-44414	Time Has Come Today (3:05)/People Get Ready	1968	2.50	5.00	10.00
—No reference to the album "The Time Has Come"; despite the listed time, this plays the 4:45 hit version (master number in trail-off ends in "3B"); we're not sure if stock copies list 3:05 and play 3:05, too					
❑ 4-44414 [DJ]	Time Has Come Today (3:05) (same on both sides)	1968	3.75	7.50	15.00
—"Special Rush Reservice" on label; this plays a 3:05 edit of the long LP version (master numbers in trail-off end in "1B" on one side and "1F" on the other)					
❑ 4-44679	I Can't Turn You Loose/Do Your Thing	1968	—	3.00	6.00
❑ 4-44679 [PS]	I Can't Turn You Loose/Do Your Thing	1968	2.50	5.00	10.00
❑ 44779	Are You Ready/You Got the Power to Turn Me On	1969	—	3.00	6.00
❑ 44890	Wake Up/Everybody Needs Someone	1969	—	3.00	6.00
❑ 44986	Have a Little Faith/Baby Takes Care of Business	1969	—	2.50	5.00
❑ 4-45055	Merry Christmas, Happy New Year/Did You Stop to Pray This Morning	1969	—	3.00	6.00
❑ 45088	Love, Peace and Happiness/If You Want Me To	1970	—	2.50	5.00
❑ 45146	To Love Somebody/Let's Do It	1970	—	2.50	5.00
❑ 45277	Love, Peace and Happiness/Funky	1970	—	2.50	5.00
❑ 45394	When the Evening Comes/New Generation	1971	—	2.50	5.00
❑ 45488	Heaven/(By the Hair on) My Chinny Chin Chin	1971	—	3.00	6.00
❑ 45518	Merry Christmas, Happy New Year!/Did You Stop to Pray This Morning	1971	—	3.00	6.00
❑ 45837	Boogie Children/You Make the Magic	1973	—	3.00	6.00
ROXBURY					
❑ 2034	Bring It On Down Front Pretty Mama/Midnight Blue	1976	—	2.50	5.00
VAULT					
❑ 920	Call Me/Seventeen	1965	3.75	7.50	15.00
❑ 923	Pretty Girls Everywhere/Love Me Like the Rain	1966	3.00	6.00	12.00
❑ 945	Shout Part 1/Shout Part 2	1968	2.00	4.00	8.00
❑ 955	Just a Closer Walk with Thee/Girls We Love You	1969	—	3.00	6.00
❑ 967	House of the Rising Sun/Blues Get Off My Shoulder	1970	—	3.00	6.00
Albums					
AVCO					
❑ 11013	Unbonded	1974	3.00	6.00	12.00
❑ 69003	Night Move	1975	5.00	10.00	20.00
COLUMBIA					
❑ KGP 20 [(2)]	Love, Peace and Happiness	1969	6.25	12.50	25.00
❑ CL 2722 [M]	The Time Has Come	1967	7.50	15.00	30.00
❑ CS 9522 [S]	The Time Has Come	1967	5.00	10.00	20.00
—Red "360 Sound" label					
❑ CS 9522	The Time Has Come	1971	3.00	6.00	12.00
—Orange label					

Number	Title (A Side/B Side)	Yr	VG	VG+	NM
❏ PC 9522	The Time Has Come	198?	2.00	4.00	8.00
—Reissue with new prefix					
❏ CS 9671	A New Time — A New Day	1968	5.00	10.00	20.00
❏ C 30032	New Generation	1970	3.75	7.50	15.00
❏ C 30871	The Chambers Brothers' Greatest Hits	1971	3.75	7.50	15.00
❏ PC 30871	The Chambers Brothers' Greatest Hits	198?	2.00	4.00	8.00
—Reissue with new prefix					
❏ KC 31158	Oh My God	1972	—	—	—
—Canceled					
❏ CG 33642 [(2)]	The Time Has Come/A New Time — A New Day	1975	3.75	7.50	15.00
FANTASY					
❏ 24718 [(2)]	The Best of the Chambers Brothers	1973	3.75	7.50	15.00
FOLKWAYS					
❏ 31008	Groovin' Time	1968	3.75	7.50	15.00
ROXBURY					
❏ RLX-106	Live In Concert on Mars	1976	7.50	15.00	30.00
VAULT					
❏ LP-115 [M]	The Chambers Brothers Now	1967	3.75	7.50	15.00
❏ VS-115 [S]	The Chambers Brothers Now	1967	3.75	7.50	15.00
❏ VS-120	The Chambers Brothers Shout	1968	3.75	7.50	15.00
❏ VS-128	Feelin' the Blues	1969	3.75	7.50	15.00
❏ VS-135 [(2)]	The Chambers Brothers Greatest Hits	1970	5.00	10.00	20.00
❏ LP-9003 [M]	People Get Ready	1966	5.00	10.00	20.00
❏ LPS-9003 [S]	People Get Ready	1966	6.25	12.50	25.00

CHAMP, BILLY
45s
ABC-PARAMOUNT

Number	Title (A Side/B Side)	Yr	VG	VG+	NM
❏ 10518	Believe Me/Hush-A-Bye	1964	7.50	15.00	30.00

CHAMPLAINS, THE FRED PARRIS of THE FIVE SATINS is the lead voice.
45s
UNITED ARTISTS

Number	Title (A Side/B Side)	Yr	VG	VG+	NM
❏ 346	Ding Dong/Have You Changed Your Mind	1961	10.00	20.00	40.00

CHAMPS, THE Also see DAVE BURGESS; GLEN CAMPBELL; CHUCK RIO; SEALS AND CROFTS.
45s
CHALLENGE

Number	Title (A Side/B Side)	Yr	VG	VG+	NM
❏ 1016	Tequila/Train to Nowhere	1958	6.25	12.50	25.00
❏ 1016	Tequila/Train to Nowhere	1958	150.00	300.00	600.00
—Blue vinyl (one known to exist)					
❏ 9113	The Shoddy Shoddy/Sombrero	1961	5.00	10.00	20.00
❏ 9116	Cantina/Panic Button	1961	5.00	10.00	20.00
❏ 9131	Tequila Twist/Limbo Rock	1961	5.00	10.00	20.00
❏ 9140	Experiment in Terror/La Cucaracha	1962	3.75	7.50	15.00
❏ 9143	What a Country/I've Just Seen Her	1962	3.75	7.50	15.00
❏ 9162	Limbo Dance/Latin Limbo	1962	3.75	7.50	15.00
❏ 9174	Varsity Rock/That Did It	1962	3.75	7.50	15.00
❏ 9180	Mr. Cool//3/4 Mash	1963	3.75	7.50	15.00
❏ 9189	Nik Nak/Shades	1963	3.75	7.50	15.00
❏ 9199	Cactus Juice/Roots	1963	3.75	7.50	15.00
❏ 59007	El Rancho Rock/Midnighter	1958	5.00	10.00	20.00
❏ 59018	Chariot Rock/Subway	1958	5.00	10.00	20.00
❏ 59026	Turnpike/Rockin' Mary	1958	5.00	10.00	20.00
❏ 59035	Gone Train/Beatnik	1958	5.00	10.00	20.00
❏ 59043	Moonlight Bay/Caramba	1959	5.00	10.00	20.00
❏ 59049	Night Train/The Rattler	1959	5.00	10.00	20.00
❏ 59053	Sky High/Double Eagle Rock	1959	5.00	10.00	20.00
❏ 59063	Too Much Tequila/Twenty Thousand Leagues	1960	5.00	10.00	20.00
❏ 59076	Red Eye/The Little Matador	1960	5.00	10.00	20.00
❏ 59086	Alley Cat/Coconut Grove	1960	5.00	10.00	20.00
❏ 59097	The Face/Tough Train	1960	5.00	10.00	20.00
❏ 59103	Hokey Pokey/Jumping Bean	1961	5.00	10.00	20.00
❏ 59219	San Juan/Jalisco	1963	3.75	7.50	15.00
❏ 59236	Switzerland/Only the Young	1964	3.75	7.50	15.00
❏ 59263	Fraternity Waltz/Kahlua	1964	3.75	7.50	15.00
❏ 59276	French 75/Bright Lights, Big City	1965	3.75	7.50	15.00
❏ 59314	The Man from Durango/Red Pepper	1965	3.75	7.50	15.00
❏ 59322	Anna/Buckaroo	1965	3.75	7.50	15.00
LANA					
❏ 155	Tequila/Sky High	196?	2.00	4.00	8.00
—Possibly re-recorded version of A-side					
REPUBLIC					
❏ 246	Tequila '76 (Long)/Tequila '76 (Short)	1976	2.00	4.00	8.00
❏ 246 [PS]	Tequila '76 (Long)/Tequila '76 (Short)	1976	2.00	4.00	8.00
WE'RE BACK					
❏ 1	Tequila '77/From Me to You	1977	2.00	4.00	8.00

7-Inch Extended Plays
CHALLENGE

Number	Title (A Side/B Side)	Yr	VG	VG+	NM
❏ EP-7100	Tequila/I'll Be There//Train to Nowhere/Lollipop	1958	37.50	75.00	150.00
❏ EP-7100 [PS]	Tequila	1958	37.50	75.00	150.00

Albums
CHALLENGE

Number	Title (A Side/B Side)	Yr	VG	VG+	NM
❏ CHL-601 [M]	Go Champs Go	1958	62.50	125.00	250.00
❏ CHL-601 [M]	Go Champs Go	1958	800.00	1600.	2400.
—Blue vinyl					
❏ CHL-605 [M]	Everybody's Rockin' with the Champs	1959	50.00	100.00	200.00
❏ CHL-613 [M]	Great Dance Hits	1962	30.00	60.00	120.00
❏ CHL-614 [M]	All American Music from the Champs	1962	30.00	60.00	120.00
❏ CHS-2500 [S]	Everybody's Rockin' with the Champs	1959	75.00	150.00	300.00
❏ CHS-2513 [S]	Great Dance Hits	1962	50.00	100.00	200.00
❏ CHS-2514 [S]	All American Music from the Champs	1962	50.00	100.00	200.00

CHANCE, NOLAN
45s
BUNKY

Number	Title (A Side/B Side)	Yr	VG	VG+	NM
❏ 161	Just Like the Weather/(B-side unknown)	1965	300.00	600.00	1200.
CONSTELLATION					
❏ 144	She's Gone/If He Makes You	1965	6.25	12.50	25.00
❏ 161	Don't Use Me/Just Like the Weather	1965	30.00	60.00	120.00

CHANCERS, THE
45s
DOT

Number	Title (A Side/B Side)	Yr	VG	VG+	NM
❏ 15870	Shirley Ann/My One	1958	7.50	15.00	30.00

CHANDELLES, THE
45s
DOT

Number	Title (A Side/B Side)	Yr	VG	VG+	NM
❏ 16553	El Gato/Jetster	1963	6.25	12.50	25.00

CHANDLER, DENIECE See DENIECE WILLIAMS.

CHANDLER, GENE Includes records as "The Duke of Earl." Also see THE DUKAYS.
12-Inch Singles
CHI-SOUND

Number	Title (A Side/B Side)	Yr	VG	VG+	NM
❏ TCD 68	Get Down (8:14) (same on both sides)	1978	3.75	7.50	15.00
❏ TCD 73	Get Down/Contact	1979	3.75	7.50	15.00
—B-side by Edwin Starr					
❏ TCD 110	Does She Have a Friend?/Let Me Make Love to You	1980	2.50	5.00	10.00
❏ CH-2001	I'll Make the Living If You Make the Loving Worthwhile (Disco Version 6:10)/Time Is a Thief	1982	3.75	7.50	15.00
20TH CENTURY					
❏ TCD 80	When You're #1 (8:59)/I'll Remember You	1979	5.00	10.00	20.00
❏ TCD 98	Do What Comes So Natural (5:00)/That Funky Disco Rhythm (5:39)	1979	3.75	7.50	15.00

45s
BRUNSWICK

Number	Title (A Side/B Side)	Yr	VG	VG+	NM
❏ 55312	Girl Don't Care/My Love	1967	2.00	4.00	8.00
❏ 55339	There Goes the Lover/Tell Me What I Can Do	1967	2.00	4.00	8.00
❏ 55383	There Was a Time/Those Were the Good Old Days	1968	2.00	4.00	8.00
❏ 55394	Teacher, Teacher/Pit of Loneliness	1968	2.00	4.00	8.00
❏ 55413	Eleanor Rigby/Familiar Footsteps	1969	2.00	4.00	8.00
❏ 55425	This Bitter Earth/Suicide	1969	2.00	4.00	8.00
CHECKER					
❏ 1155	I Fooled You This Time/Such a Pretty Thing	1966	2.00	4.00	8.00
❏ 1165	To Be a Lover/After the Laughter	1967	2.00	4.00	8.00
❏ 1190	I Won't Need You/No Peace, No Satisfaction	1967	2.00	4.00	8.00
❏ 1199	River of Tears/It's Time to Settle Down	1968	2.00	4.00	8.00
❏ 1220	Go Back Home/In My Baby's House	1969	2.00	4.00	8.00
CHI-SOUND					
❏ 1001	I'll Make the Living If You Make the Loving Worthwhile/(B-side unknown)	1982	—	2.50	5.00
❏ 1168	Give Me the Cue/Tomorrow We May Not Feel the Same	1978	—	2.00	4.00
❏ 2386	Get Down/I'm the Traveling Kind	1978	—	2.00	4.00
❏ 2404	Please Sunrise/Greatest Love Ever Known	1979	—	2.00	4.00
❏ 2411	When You're #1/I'll Remember You	1979	—	2.50	5.00
❏ 2451	Does She Have a Friend?/Let Me Make Love to You	1980	—	2.00	4.00
❏ 2468	Lay Me Gently/You've Been So Good to Me	1980	—	2.00	4.00
❏ 2480	Rainbow '80/I'll Be There	1980	—	2.00	4.00
❏ 2494	I'm Attracted to You/I've Got to Meet You	1981	—	2.00	4.00
❏ 2507	Love Is the Answer/Godsend	1981	—	2.00	4.00
CONSTELLATION					
❏ 104	From Day to Day/It's No Good for Me	1963	2.50	5.00	10.00
❏ 110	Pretty Little Girl/A Little Like Lovin'	1963	2.50	5.00	10.00
❏ 112	Think Nothing About It/Wish You Were Here	1964	2.50	5.00	10.00
❏ 114	Soul Hootenanny (Part 1)/Soul Hootenanny (Part 2)	1964	2.50	5.00	10.00
❏ 124	A Song Called Soul/You Left Me	1964	2.50	5.00	10.00
❏ 130	Just Be True/A Song Called Soul	1964	2.50	5.00	10.00
❏ 136	Bless Our Love/London Town	1964	2.50	5.00	10.00
❏ 141	What Now/If You Can't Be True	1964	2.50	5.00	10.00
❏ 146	You Can't Hurt Me No More/Everybody Let's Dance	1965	2.00	4.00	8.00
❏ 149	Nothing Can Stop Me/The Big Lie	1965	2.00	4.00	8.00
❏ 158	Rainbow '65 (Part 1)/Rainbow '65 (Part 2)	1965	2.00	4.00	8.00
❏ 160	Good Times/No One Can Love You	1965	2.00	4.00	8.00
❏ 164	Here Come the Tears/Soul Hootenanny (Part 2)	1965	2.00	4.00	8.00
❏ 166	Baby That's Love/Bet You Never Thought	1966	2.00	4.00	8.00
❏ 167	(I'm Just a) Fool for You/Buddy Ain't It a Shame	1966	2.00	4.00	8.00
❏ 169	I Can Take Care of Myself/If I Can't Save It	1966	2.00	4.00	8.00
❏ 172	Mr. Big Shot/I Hate to Be the One to Say	1966	2.00	4.00	8.00
CURTOM					
❏ 1979	Don't Have to Be Lyin' Babe (Part 1)/Don't Have to Be Lyin' Babe (Part 2)	1973	—	2.50	5.00
❏ 1986	Baby I Still Love You/I Understand	1973	—	2.50	5.00
❏ 1992	Without You Here/Just Be There	1973	—	2.50	5.00
FASTFIRE					
❏ 7003	Haven't I Heard That Line Before/You'll Never Be Free of Me	1985	—	2.50	5.00
❏ 7005	Lucy/Please You Tonight	1986	—	2.50	5.00
LOST-NITE					
❏ 310	Duke of Earl/Rainbow	197?	—	2.50	5.00
MERCURY					
❏ 73083	Groovy Situation/Not the Marrying Kind	1970	—	3.00	6.00
❏ 73121	Simply Call It Love/Give Me a Chance	1970	—	3.00	6.00
❏ 73206	You're a Lady/Stone Cold Feeling	1971	—	3.00	6.00
❏ 73258	Yes I'm Ready (If I Don't Get to Go)/Pillars of Glass	1971	—	3.00	6.00
SALSOUL					
❏ 7051	You're the One/I Keep Comin' Back for More	1983	—	2.00	4.00
—With Jaime Lynn					
20TH CENTURY					
❏ 2411	When You're #1/I'll Remember You	1979	—	2.00	4.00
❏ 2428	Do What Comes So Natural/That Funky Disco Rhythm	1979	—	2.00	4.00
VEE JAY					
❏ 416	Duke of Earl/Kissin' in the Kitchen	1961	6.25	12.50	25.00
❏ 416	Duke of Earl/Kissin' in the Kitchen	1962	5.00	10.00	20.00
—Some later pressings as "The Duke of Earl"					
❏ 440	Walk On with the Duke/London Town	1962	3.75	7.50	15.00
—As "The Duke of Earl"					
❏ 450	Daddy's Home/The Big Lie	1962	3.75	7.50	15.00
—As "The Duke of Earl"					
❏ 455	I'll Follow You/You Left Me	1962	3.75	7.50	15.00
—As "The Duke of Earl"					
❏ 461	Tear for Tear/Miracle After Miracle	1962	3.75	7.50	15.00
❏ 468	You Threw a Lucky Punch/Rainbow	1962	3.75	7.50	15.00
❏ 511	Check Yourself/Forgive Me	1963	3.75	7.50	15.00
❏ 536	Baby, That's Love/Man's Temptation	1963	3.75	7.50	15.00

Number	Title (A Side/B Side)	Yr	VG	VG+	NM
Albums					
BRUNSWICK					
☐ BL 54124 [M]	The Girl Don't Care	1967	6.25	12.50	25.00
☐ BL 754124 [S]	The Girl Don't Care	1967	5.00	10.00	20.00
☐ BL 754131	There Was a Time	1968	5.00	10.00	20.00
☐ BL 754149	The Two Sides of Gene Chandler	1969	5.00	10.00	20.00
CHECKER					
☐ LP-3003 [M]	The Duke of Soul	1967	12.50	25.00	50.00
☐ LPS-3003 [R]	The Duke of Soul	1967	7.50	15.00	30.00
CHI-SOUND					
☐ T-578	Get Down	1978	2.50	5.00	10.00
CONSTELLATION					
☐ LP 1421 [M]	Greatest Hits by Gene Chandler	1964	12.50	25.00	50.00
☐ LP 1423 [M]	Just Be True	1964	12.50	25.00	50.00
☐ LP 1425 [M]	Gene Chandler — Live On Stage in '65	1965	12.50	25.00	50.00
MERCURY					
☐ SR-61304	The Gene Chandler Situation	1970	3.75	7.50	15.00
SOLID SMOKE					
☐ SS-8027	Stroll On with the Duke	198?	2.50	5.00	10.00
20TH CENTURY					
☐ T-605	Gene Chandler '80	1980	2.50	5.00	10.00
☐ T-625	Ear Candy	1980	2.50	5.00	10.00
☐ T-629	Here's to Love	1981	2.50	5.00	10.00
VEE JAY					
☐ LP-1040 [M]	The Duke of Earl	1962	30.00	60.00	120.00
☐ SR-1040 [M]	The Duke of Earl	196?	12.50	25.00	50.00

—*"Stereophonic" on front; no "Important Notice..." on back; record plays mono. Most labels are all-black with "VJ" in brackets. This was a semi-authorized reissue after ex-Vee Jay executives bought the company's remnants in bankruptcy court in 1966.*

Number	Title (A Side/B Side)	Yr	VG	VG+	NM
☐ SR-1040 [S]	The Duke of Earl	1962	62.50	125.00	250.00

—*"Stereo" sticker on mono cover; "Stereo" on record labels*

Number	Title (A Side/B Side)	Yr	VG	VG+	NM
☐ SR-1040 [S]	The Duke of Earl	1962	200.00	400.00	800.00

—*"Stereophonic" on front cover; top back cover contains note that begins: "Important Notice...This Is a Stereophonic Record"; "Stereo" on record labels*

Number	Title (A Side/B Side)	Yr	VG	VG+	NM
☐ VJLP-1040	The Duke of Earl	198?	2.50	5.00	10.00

—*Mid-1980s authorized reissue*

CHANDLER, GENE, AND BARBARA ACKLIN Also see each artist's individual listings.

Number	Title (A Side/B Side)	Yr	VG	VG+	NM
45s					
BRUNSWICK					
☐ 55366	Love Won't Start/Show Me the Way to Go	1968	2.00	4.00	8.00
☐ 55387	From the Teacher to the Preacher/Anywhere But Nowhere	1968	2.00	4.00	8.00
☐ 55405	Little Green Apples/Will I Find You	1969	2.00	4.00	8.00

CHANDLER, GENE, AND JERRY BUTLER Also see each artist's individual listings.

Number	Title (A Side/B Side)	Yr	VG	VG+	NM
45s					
MERCURY					
☐ 73163	You Just Can't Win (By Making the Same Mistake)/The Show Is Grooving	1971	—	3.00	6.00
☐ 73195	Two and Two (Take This Woman Off the Corner)/Everybody Is Waiting	1971	—	3.00	6.00
Albums					
MERCURY					
☐ SR-61330	Gene & Jerry — One & One	1971	3.75	7.50	15.00

CHANDLER, JEFF

Number	Title (A Side/B Side)	Yr	VG	VG+	NM
45s					
DECCA					
☐ 9-29004	I Should Care/More Than Anyone	1954	3.75	7.50	15.00
☐ 9-29175	Lamplight/That's All She's Waiting to Hear	1954	3.00	6.00	12.00
☐ 9-29345	Always/Everything Happens to Me	1955	3.00	6.00	12.00
☐ 9-29405	My Prayer/When Spring Comes	1955	3.00	6.00	12.00
☐ 9-29532	Shaner Maidel/Foxfire	1955	3.00	6.00	12.00
☐ 9-29600	Only the Very Young/A Little Love Can Go a Long, Long Way	1955	3.00	6.00	12.00
LIBERTY					
☐ 55092	Half of My Heart/Hold Me	1957	2.50	5.00	10.00
Albums					
LIBERTY					
☐ LRP-3067 [M]	Jeff Chandler Sings to You	1957	10.00	20.00	40.00
☐ LRP-3074 [M]	Warm and Easy	1958	10.00	20.00	40.00
SUNSET					
☐ SUS-5127	Sincerely Yours	1969	3.00	6.00	12.00

CHANDLER, KENNY

Number	Title (A Side/B Side)	Yr	VG	VG+	NM
45s					
AMY					
☐ 890	I Don't Know Why/Happy to Be Unhappy	1963	2.50	5.00	10.00
CORAL					
☐ 62309	It Might Have Been/Yours and Yours Alone	1962	2.50	5.00	10.00
EPIC					
☐ 9758	Come Softly to Me/S.O.S. (Sweet On Susie)	1965	2.00	4.00	8.00
☐ 10009	I'll Be Coming Back/Sunshine Sweetheart	1966	2.00	4.00	8.00
LAURIE					
☐ 3140	Man on the Run/Leave Me If You Want To	1962	2.50	5.00	10.00
☐ 3158	Heart/Wait for Me	1963	2.50	5.00	10.00
☐ 3181	I Tell Myself/I Can't Stand Tears at a Party	1963	2.50	5.00	10.00
TOWER					
☐ 354	Sleep/Nickles and Dimes	1967	2.00	4.00	8.00
☐ 405	Beyond Love/Charity	1968	2.00	4.00	8.00
UNITED ARTISTS					
☐ 342	The Magic Ring/Drums	1961	3.00	6.00	12.00
☐ 384	Please Mr. Mountain/What Kind of Love Is Yours	1961	3.00	6.00	12.00

CHANDLER, LORRAINE

Number	Title (A Side/B Side)	Yr	VG	VG+	NM
45s					
GIANT					
☐ 703	What Can I Do/Tell Me You're Mine	1966	15.00	30.00	60.00
RCA VICTOR					
☐ 47-8810	What Can I Do/Tell Me You're Mine	1966	7.50	15.00	30.00
☐ 47-8980	I Can't Hold On/She Don't Want You	1966	7.50	15.00	30.00
☐ 47-9349	I Can't Change/Oh How I Need Your Love	1967	12.50	25.00	50.00

CHANELS, THE See THE FIVE CHANELS.

CHANGIN' TIMES, THE

Number	Title (A Side/B Side)	Yr	VG	VG+	NM
45s					
BELL					
☐ 675	Free Spirit/You Just Seem to Know	1967	5.00	10.00	20.00
☐ 711	Show Me the Way to Go Home/When the Good Sun Shines	1968	5.00	10.00	20.00
PHILIPS					
☐ 40320	Pied Piper/Thank You Babe	1965	5.00	10.00	20.00
☐ 40341	How Is the Air Up There/Young and Innocent Girl	1965	5.00	10.00	20.00
☐ 40368	Goin' Lovin' with You/I Should Have Brought Her Home	1966	3.75	7.50	15.00
☐ 40401	Aladdin/All in the Mind of a Young Girl	1966	3.75	7.50	15.00

CHANGING SCENE, THE

Number	Title (A Side/B Side)	Yr	VG	VG+	NM
45s					
FONTANA					
☐ 1669	Is It Really Worth It/Sing Me Something Pretty	1969	3.00	6.00	12.00

CHANNEL, BRUCE

Number	Title (A Side/B Side)	Yr	VG	VG+	NM
45s					
ELEKTRA					
☐ 46587	One More Last Chance/That's the Truth, Ruth	1980	—	2.00	4.00
KING					
☐ 5294	Will I Ever Love Again/Blow Down Baby	1959	7.50	15.00	30.00
☐ 5331	Now or Never/Boy, This Stuff Kills Me	1960	7.50	15.00	30.00
☐ 5620	Now or Never/Will I Ever Love Again	1962	5.00	10.00	20.00
LE CAM					
☐ 122	Going Back to Louisiana/Forget Me Not	1964	2.50	5.00	10.00
☐ 125	My Baby/Blue Monday	1964	2.50	5.00	10.00
☐ 953	Hey! Baby/Dream Girl	1961	10.00	20.00	40.00
☐ 1117	A Presley Medley/A Man Without a Woman	1977	—	2.50	5.00
☐ 7277	The King Is Free (Love Me)/Funky Dude	1977	—	2.50	5.00
—B-side by Andy and the Dude					
MALA					
☐ 579	Mr. Bus Driver/It's Me	1967	2.50	5.00	10.00
☐ 592	Keep On/Barbara Allen	1968	2.50	5.00	10.00
☐ 12011	California/Water the Family Tree	1968	2.50	5.00	10.00
☐ 12027	Try Me/Nobody	1968	2.50	5.00	10.00
☐ 12041	The Web/Mrs. P	1969	2.50	5.00	10.00
MANCO					
☐ 1035	Run Romance, Run/Don't Leave Me	1962	5.00	10.00	20.00
MEL-O-DY					
☐ 112	That's What's Happenin'/Satisfied Mind	1964	3.75	7.50	15.00
☐ 114	You Make Me Happy/You Never Looked Better	1964	3.75	7.50	15.00
SMASH					
☐ 1731	Hey! Baby/Dream Girl	1962	5.00	10.00	20.00
☐ 1752	Number One Man/If Only I Had Known	1962	3.75	7.50	15.00
☐ 1769	Come On Baby/Mine Exclusively	1962	3.75	7.50	15.00
☐ 1780	Stand Tough/Somewhere in This Town	1962	3.75	7.50	15.00
☐ 1780 [PS]	Stand Tough/Somewhere in This Town	1962	7.50	15.00	30.00
☐ 1792	Oh Baby/Let's Hurt Together	1962	3.75	7.50	15.00
☐ 1826	No Other Baby/Night People	1963	3.75	7.50	15.00
☐ 1826 [PS]	No Other Baby/Night People	1963	7.50	15.00	30.00
☐ 1838	The Dipsy Doodle/Send Her Home	1963	3.75	7.50	15.00
☐ 1838 [PS]	The Dipsy Doodle/Send Her Home	1963	7.50	15.00	30.00
TEENAGER					
☐ 601	Run Romance, Run/Don't Leave Me	1960	7.50	15.00	30.00
Albums					
SMASH					
☐ MGS-27008 [M]	Hey! Baby (And 11 Other Songs About Your Baby)	1962	25.00	50.00	100.00
☐ SRS-67008 [R]	Hey! Baby (And 11 Other Songs About Your Baby)	1962	15.00	30.00	60.00

CHANNELLS, THE See THE CHANNELS (2).

CHANNELS, THE (1) Group led by Earl Lewis.

Number	Title (A Side/B Side)	Yr	VG	VG+	NM
45s					
CHANNEL					
☐ 1000	Gloria/You Said You Loved Me	1971	2.50	5.00	10.00
—Black vinyl					
☐ 1000	Gloria/You Said You Loved Me	1971	5.00	10.00	20.00
—Red vinyl					
☐ 1001	We Belong Together/Hey Girl, I'm in Love with You	1972	2.50	5.00	10.00
☐ 1002	You Got What It Takes/Crazy Mixed-Up World	1972	2.50	5.00	10.00
☐ 1003	Close Your Eyes/Work with Me Annie	1973	2.50	5.00	10.00
☐ 1004	Over Again/In My Arms to Stay	1973	2.50	5.00	10.00
☐ 1006	A Thousand Miles Away/Don't Let the Green Grass Fool You	1974	2.50	5.00	10.00
FIRE					
☐ 1001	My Heart Is Sad/The Girl Next Door	1959	12.50	25.00	50.00
—As "Earl Lewis and the Channels"					
FURY					
☐ 1021	Bye Bye Baby/My Love Will Never Die	1959	12.50	25.00	50.00
☐ 1071	Bye Bye Baby/My Love Will Never Die	1963	10.00	20.00	40.00
GONE					
☐ 5012	That's My Desire/Stay As You Are	1957	15.00	30.00	60.00
☐ 5019	Altar of Love/All Alone	1957	15.00	30.00	60.00
LANA					
☐ 122	The Closer You Are/Sad Song	196?	2.50	5.00	10.00
☐ 123	That's My Desire/My Love Will Never Die	196?	2.50	5.00	10.00
LOST-NITE					
☐ 348	The Closer You Are/Now You Know	197?	—	2.50	5.00
—Reissue					
☐ 350	The Gleam in Your Eyes/Stars in the Sky	197?	—	2.50	5.00
—Reissue					
☐ 352	I Really Love You/What Do You Do	197?	—	2.50	5.00
—Reissue					
☐ 354	Flames in My Heart/My Lovin' Baby	197?	—	2.50	5.00
—Reissue					
☐ 356	Bye Bye Baby/My Love Will Never Die	197?	—	2.50	5.00
—Reissue					
☐ 359	My Heart Is Sad/The Girl Next Door	197?	—	2.50	5.00
—Reissue					

Number	Title (A Side/B Side)	Yr	VG	VG+	NM
PORT					
❏ 70014	The Closer You Are/Now You Know	1960	6.25	12.50	25.00
—Reissue of Whirlin' Disc 100					
❏ 70017	The Gleam in Your Eyes/Stars in the Sky	1960	6.25	12.50	25.00
—Reissue of Whirlin' Disc 102					
❏ 70022	Flames in My Heart/My Lovin' Baby	1961	6.25	12.50	25.00
—Reissue of Whirlin' Disc 109					
❏ 70023	I Really Love You/What Do You Do	1961	6.25	12.50	25.00
—Reissue of Whirlin' Disc 107					
RARE BIRD					
❏ 5017	She Blew My Mind/Breaking Up Is Hard to Do	1971	2.50	5.00	10.00
WHIRLIN' DISC					
❏ 100	The Closer You Are/Now You Know	1956	25.00	50.00	100.00
—Label name is all caps, but not in block letters					
❏ 100	The Closer You Are/Now You Know	1956	50.00	100.00	200.00
—Block-letter label name; publisher listed as "Spinning Wheel Music"					
❏ 100	The Closer You Are/Now You Know	1956	62.50	125.00	250.00
—Block-letter label name; publisher listed as "Bob-Dan Music"					
❏ 102	The Gleam in Your Eyes/Stars in the Sky	1956	50.00	100.00	200.00
❏ 107	I Really Love You/What Do You Do	1957	50.00	100.00	200.00
❏ 109	Flames in My Heart/My Lovin' Baby	1957	50.00	100.00	200.00
Albums					
COLLECTABLES					
❏ COL-5012	New York's Finest: The Best of Earl Lewis and the Channels	198?	3.00	6.00	12.00
LOST-NITE					
❏ LLP-15 [10]	The Channels	1981	3.00	6.00	12.00
—Red vinyl					
❏ LLP-16 [10]	The Channels	1981	3.00	6.00	12.00
—Red vinyl					

CHANNELS, THE (2) Group led by Tony and Gene Williams.

45s

Number	Title (A Side/B Side)	Yr	VG	VG+	NM
ENJOY					
❏ 2001	Sad Song/My Love	1963	6.25	12.50	25.00
GROOVE					
❏ 58-0046	Anything You Do/I've Got My Eyes on You	1964	6.25	12.50	25.00
❏ 58-0061	Old Chinatown/You Can Count on Me	1965	6.25	12.50	25.00
HIT RECORD					
❏ 700	In My Arms to Stay/You Hurt Me	1963	10.00	20.00	40.00
—As "The Channells"					

CHANNELS, THE (3) Neither of the above.

45s

Number	Title (A Side/B Side)	Yr	VG	VG+	NM
MERCURY					
❏ 71501	Earthquake/Jungle Lights	1959	3.00	6.00	12.00

CHANTAY'S

45s

Number	Title (A Side/B Side)	Yr	VG	VG+	NM
DOT					
❏ 145	Pipeline/Move It	1966	2.00	4.00	8.00
—Reissue; black label					
❏ 145	Pipeline/Move It	1969	—	3.00	6.00
—Reissue; orange-red label					
❏ 16440	Pipeline/Move It	1963	6.25	12.50	25.00
❏ 16492	Monsoon/Scotch Highs	1963	5.00	10.00	20.00
DOWNEY					
❏ 104	Pipeline/Move It	1963	15.00	30.00	60.00
❏ 108	Monsoon/Scotch Highs	1963	7.50	15.00	30.00
❏ 116	Space Probe/Continental Missile	1964	5.00	10.00	20.00
❏ 120	Only If You Care/Love Can Be Cruel	1964	5.00	10.00	20.00
❏ 126	Beyond/I'll Be Back Someday	1964	5.00	10.00	20.00
❏ 130	Three Coins in the Fountain/Greens	1965	5.00	10.00	20.00
Albums					
DOT					
❏ DLP 3516 [M]	Pipeline	1963	12.50	25.00	50.00
❏ DLP 3771 [M]	Two Sides of the Chantays	1966	12.50	25.00	50.00
❏ DLP 25516 [S]	Pipeline	1963	20.00	40.00	80.00
❏ DLP 25771 [S]	Two Sides of the Chantays	1966	20.00	40.00	80.00
DOWNEY					
❏ DLP-1002 [M]	Pipeline	1963	55.00	110.00	220.00
❏ DLPS-1002 [S]	Pipeline	1963	87.50	175.00	350.00

CHANTECLAIRS, THE

45s

Number	Title (A Side/B Side)	Yr	VG	VG+	NM
DOT					
❏ 1227	Baby Please/Someday Love Will Come My Way	1954	18.75	37.50	75.00
❏ 15404	Believe Me, Beloved/I've Never Been There	1955	15.00	30.00	60.00

CHANTELS, THE Also see ARLENE SMITH; THE VENEERS.

45s

Number	Title (A Side/B Side)	Yr	VG	VG+	NM
CARLTON					
❏ 555	Look in My Eyes/Glad to Be Back	1961	5.00	10.00	20.00
❏ 564	Still/Well, I Told You	1961	5.00	10.00	20.00
❏ 569	Summertime/Here It Comes Again	1962	5.00	10.00	20.00
END					
❏ 1001	He's Gone/The Plea	1957	20.00	40.00	80.00
—Black label					
❏ 1005	Maybe/Come My Little Baby	1957	20.00	40.00	80.00
—Black label					
❏ 1005	Maybe/Come My Little Baby	1958	10.00	20.00	40.00
—Gray (white) label					
❏ 1005	Maybe/Come My Little Baby	1959	5.00	10.00	20.00
—Multi-color label					
❏ 1015	Every Night/Whoever You Are	1958	7.50	15.00	30.00
—Gray (white) label					
❏ 1015	Every Night/Whoever You Are	1959	5.00	10.00	20.00
—Multi-color label					
❏ 1020	I Love You So/How Could You Call It Off	1958	10.00	20.00	40.00
❏ 1026	Prayer/Sure of Love	1958	6.25	12.50	25.00
❏ 1030	If You Try/Congratulations	1958	6.25	12.50	25.00
❏ 1037	Never Let Go/I Can't Take It	1959	6.25	12.50	25.00
❏ 1048	I'm Confessin'/Goodbye to Love	1959	6.25	12.50	25.00
❏ 1069	Whoever You Are/How Could You Call It Off	1960	6.25	12.50	25.00
❏ 1103	Believe Me (My Angel)/I	1961	15.00	30.00	60.00
—Originally released on Princeton 102 as "The Veneers"					
❏ 1105	There's Our Song Again/I'm the Girl	1961	6.25	12.50	25.00

Number	Title (A Side/B Side)	Yr	VG	VG+	NM
LANA					
❏ 100	Look in My Eyes/Glad to Be Back	196?	2.00	4.00	8.00
—Oldies reissue					
LUDIX					
❏ 101	Eternally/Swamp Water	1963	5.00	10.00	20.00
❏ 106	That's Why I'm Happy/Some Tears Fall Dry	1963	5.00	10.00	20.00
RCA VICTOR					
❏ 74-0347	I'm Gonna Win Him Back/Love Makes All the Difference in the World	1970	2.50	5.00	10.00
ROULETTE					
❏ 7064	Maybe/He's Gone	1969	2.50	5.00	10.00
TCF HALL					
❏ 123	Take Me As I Am/There's No Forgetting Me	1965	3.75	7.50	15.00
VERVE					
❏ 10387	You're Welcome to My Heart/Soul of a Soldier	1966	3.75	7.50	15.00
❏ 10435	Indian Giver/It's Just Me	1966	3.75	7.50	15.00
7-Inch Extended Plays					
END					
❏ 201	Sure of Love/Prayee//I Love You So/ How Could You Call It Off	1958	37.50	75.00	150.00
❏ 201 [PS]	I Love You So	1958	62.50	125.00	250.00
❏ 202	(contents unknown)	1958	25.00	50.00	100.00
❏ 202 [PS]	C'est Si Bon	1958	50.00	100.00	200.00
Albums					
CARLTON					
❏ LP-144 [M]	The Chantels On Tour/Look in My Eyes	1962	50.00	100.00	200.00
❏ STLP-144 [P]	The Chantels On Tour/Look in My Eyes	1962	100.00	200.00	400.00
—Eight tracks are true stereo, two are mono, two are rechanneled					
END					
❏ END-301 [R]	We Are the Chantels	197?	6.25	12.50	25.00
—Reissue in rechanneled stereo; orange bar through center hole and "END" on both sides of center hole					
❏ LP-301 [M]	We Are the Chantels	1958	500.00	1000.	1500.
—Group photo on front cover; gray label with "11-17-58" in trail-off wax					
❏ LP-301 [M]	We Are the Chantels	1959	100.00	200.00	400.00
—Jukebox on front cover; gray label, "11-17-58" in trail-off wax					
❏ LP-301 [M]	We Are the Chantels	1962	50.00	100.00	200.00
—Jukebox on front cover; gray label, "1962" in trail-off wax					
❏ LP-301 [M]	We Are the Chantels	1965	20.00	40.00	80.00
—Jukebox on front cover; multicolor label, "8-65" in trail-off wax					
❏ LP-301 [M]	We Are the Chantels	1965	25.00	50.00	100.00
—Jukebox on front cover; gray label, "8-65" in trail-off wax					
❏ LP-312 [M]	There's Our Song Again	1962	30.00	60.00	120.00
FORUM					
❏ F-9104 [M]	The Chantels Sing Their Favorites	1964	12.50	25.00	50.00
❏ FS-9104 [R]	The Chantels Sing Their Favorites	1964	6.25	12.50	25.00

CHANTERS, THE (1)

45s

Number	Title (A Side/B Side)	Yr	VG	VG+	NM
COMBO					
❏ 78	Why/Watts	1954	125.00	250.00	500.00
❏ 92	I Love You/Hot Mamma	1955	100.00	200.00	400.00
DELUXE					
❏ 6162	My My Darling/I Need Your Tenderness (I Love You Darling)	1958	12.50	25.00	50.00
❏ 6166	Row Your Boat/Stars in the Skies	1958	5.00	10.00	20.00
—Yellow label					
❏ 6166	Row Your Boat/Stars in the Skies	1958	10.00	20.00	40.00
—Black label					
❏ 6172	Angel Darling/Five Little Kisses	1958	12.50	25.00	50.00
❏ 6177	No, No, No/Over the Rainbow	1958	10.00	20.00	40.00
❏ 6191	No, No, No/I Make This Pledge (To You)	1961	7.50	15.00	30.00
❏ 6194	My My Darling/At My Door	1961	10.00	20.00	40.00
❏ 6200	Row Your Boat/No, No, No	1963	7.50	15.00	30.00
KEM					
❏ 2740	Lonesome Me/Golden Apple	1955	75.00	150.00	300.00
RPM					
❏ 415	Tell Me, Thrill Me/She Wants to Mambo	1954	75.00	150.00	300.00

CHANTERS, THE (2)

45s

Number	Title (A Side/B Side)	Yr	VG	VG+	NM
MGM					
❏ 13750	Free As A Bird/Bongo, Bongo	1967	—	3.00	6.00

CHANTEURS, THE With Eugene Record, later of THE CHI-LITES.

45s

Number	Title (A Side/B Side)	Yr	VG	VG+	NM
VEE JAY					
❏ 519	You've Got a Great Love/The Grizzly Bear	1963	5.00	10.00	20.00

CHANTONES, THE

45s

Number	Title (A Side/B Side)	Yr	VG	VG+	NM
CAPITOL					
❏ 4661	Stormy Weather/Sweet Georgia Brown	1961	6.25	12.50	25.00
CARLTON					
❏ 485	Five Little Numbers/It's Just a Summer Love	1958	7.50	15.00	30.00
TOP RANK					
❏ 2066	Don't Open That Door/Tangerock	1960	6.25	12.50	25.00

CHANTS, THE (1) British soul group.

45s

Number	Title (A Side/B Side)	Yr	VG	VG+	NM
CAMEO					
❏ 277	I Don't Care/Come Go with Me	1963	5.00	10.00	20.00
❏ 297	I Could Write a Book/A Thousand Stars	1964	5.00	10.00	20.00
INTERPHON					
❏ 7703	She's Mine/Then I'll Be Home	1964	3.75	7.50	15.00

CHANTS, THE (U) None of these are by group (1), but we doubt all of them are by the same group.

45s

Number	Title (A Side/B Side)	Yr	VG	VG+	NM
CAPITOL					
❏ F3949	Lost and Found/Close Friends	1958	5.00	10.00	20.00
CHECKER					
❏ 1209	Surfside/Chicken 'N' Gravy	1968	2.00	4.00	8.00
EKO					
❏ 3567/77	Respectable/Kiss Me Goodbye	1961	7.50	15.00	30.00
MGM					
❏ 13008	Respectable/Kiss Me Goodbye	1961	5.00	10.00	20.00

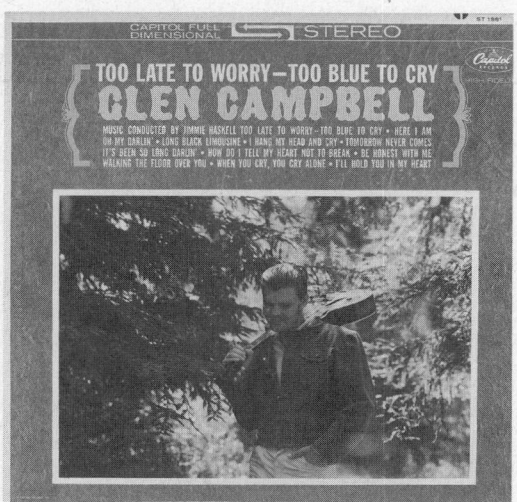

Glen Campbell, *Too Late to Worry, Too Blue to Cry,* Capitol ST 1881, stereo LP, black label, $12.50-$25

Canned Heat, *Boogie with Canned Heat,* Liberty LST-7541, stereo LP, $10-$20.

Johnny Cash, *Ring of Fire,* Columbia CL 2052, mono LP, $10-$20.

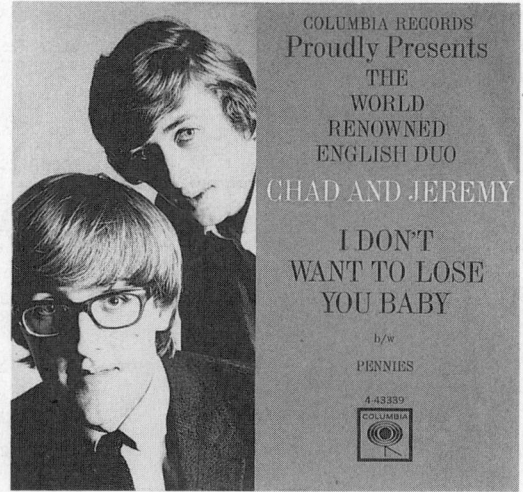

Chad and Jeremy, "I Don't Want to Lose You Baby," Columbia 4-43339, picture sleeve, $10-$20.

The Champs, *Tequila,* Challenge EP-7100, 7-inch EP, $150-$300 (cover and record together).

The Chantels, *We Are the Chantels,* End LP-301, mono LP, group photo on cover, gray label, $1,000-$1,500.

Number	Title (A Side/B Side)	Yr	VG	VG+	NM
NITE OWL					
❏ 40	Heaven and Paradise/When I'm With You	196?	5.00	10.00	20.00
—Blue vinyl					
❏ 40	Heaven and Paradise/When I'm With You	196?	5.00	10.00	20.00
—Red vinyl					
❏ 40	Heaven and Paradise/When I'm With You	196?	5.00	10.00	20.00
—Yellow vinyl					
❏ 40	Heaven and Paradise/When I'm With You	1960	10.00	20.00	40.00
—Black label, black vinyl					
❏ 40	Heaven and Paradise/When I'm With You	1960	75.00	150.00	300.00
—Maroon label original					
U.W.R.					
❏ 4243	Rockin' Santa/Respectable	1962	6.25	12.50	25.00
VERVE					
❏ 10244	Dick Tracy/Choo Choo	1961	5.00	10.00	20.00
CHAPEL, JEAN					
45s					
CHALLENGE					
❏ 59350	Tell It Like It Is/I'm Your Woman	1966	2.00	4.00	8.00
❏ 59362	You Can Take Me/Stamp Out Loneliness	1967	2.00	4.00	8.00
❏ 59370	In the Reach of Your Arms/This Waltz Is Mine	1967	2.00	4.00	8.00
❏ 59376	Hungry Eyes/Green Paper	1967	2.00	4.00	8.00
❏ 59381	Dino's TV Door/If I Never Get You	1967	2.00	4.00	8.00
❏ 59386	See and Ye Shall Find/I Really Go for You	1968	2.00	4.00	8.00
KAPP					
❏ 2034	Bluebird Ridge/I Started Loving You Again	1969	—	3.00	6.00
❏ 2082	I'm Your Woman/The Roll Call	1970	—	3.00	6.00
RCA VICTOR					
❏ 47-6681	I Won't Be Rockin' Tonight/Welcome to the Club	1956	10.00	20.00	40.00
❏ 47-6892	Oo-Ba La Baby/I Had a Dream	1957	6.25	12.50	25.00
SMASH					
❏ 1829	Don't Let Go/Your Tender Love	1963	3.00	6.00	12.00
SUN					
❏ 244	I Won't Be Rockin' Tonight/Welcome to the Club	1956	12.50	25.00	50.00
CHAPERONES, THE					
45s					
JOSIE					
❏ 880	Dance with Me/Cruise to the Moon	1960	6.25	12.50	25.00
—With correct group name on label					
❏ 880	Dance with Me/Cruise to the Moon	1960	37.50	75.00	150.00
—With typographical error listing group as "The Cahperones"					
❏ 885	Shining Star/My Shadow and Me	1960	6.25	12.50	25.00
❏ 891	Man from the Moon/Blueberry Sweet	1961	12.50	25.00	50.00
CHAPIN, HARRY Also see THE CHAPINS.					
45s					
BOARDWALK					
❏ NB7-11-119	Story of a Love/Salt and Pepper	1981	—	2.00	4.00
❏ 5700	Sequel/I Finally Found It Sandy	1980	—	2.00	4.00
❏ 5705	Remember When the Music/Northwest 222	1981	—	2.00	4.00
ELEKTRA					
❏ 45203	Cat's in the Cradle/Vacancy	1974	—	2.00	4.00
❏ 45236	I Wanna Learn a Love Song/She Sings Songs Without Words	1975	—	2.00	4.00
❏ 45264	Dreams Go By/Sandy	1975	—	2.00	4.00
❏ 45285	Tangled-Up Puppet/Dirt Get Under the Fingernails	1975	—	2.00	4.00
❏ 45304	Star Tripper/The Rock	1976	—	2.00	4.00
❏ 45327	Better Place to Be (Part 1)/Better Place to Be (Part 2)	1976	—	2.00	4.00
❏ 45368	Corey's Coming/If My Mary Were Here	1976	—	2.00	4.00
❏ 45426	Dance Band on the Titanic/I Wonder What Happened to Him	1977	—	2.00	4.00
❏ 45445	My Old Lady/I'd Do It for You, Jane	1977	—	2.00	4.00
❏ 45497	I Wonder What Would Happen to This World/If You Want to Feel	1978	—	2.00	4.00
❏ 45524	Flowers Are Red/Jenny	1978	—	2.00	4.00
❏ 45770	Taxi/Empty	1972	—	2.50	5.00
❏ 45792	Could You Put Your Light On, Please?/Any Old Kind of Day	1972	—	2.00	4.00
❏ 45811	Sunday Morning Sunshine/Burning Herself	1972	—	2.00	4.00
❏ 45828	Better Place to Be/Winter Song	1973	—	2.00	4.00
❏ 45874	WOLD/Short Stories	1973	—	2.00	4.00
❏ 45893	What Made America Famous/Old College Avenue	1974	—	2.00	4.00
Albums					
BOARDWALK					
❏ FW 36872	Sequel	1980	2.50	5.00	10.00
ELEKTRA					
❏ 6E-142	Living Room Suite	1978	2.50	5.00	10.00
❏ 9E-301 [(2)]	Dance Band on the Titanic	1977	3.00	6.00	12.00
❏ BB-703 [(2)]	Legends of the Lost and Found — New Greatest Stories Live	1979	3.00	6.00	12.00
❏ 7E-1012	Verities & Balderdash	1974	2.50	5.00	10.00
❏ 7E-1041	Portrait Gallery	1975	2.50	5.00	10.00
❏ 7E-1082	On the Road to Kingdom Come	1976	2.50	5.00	10.00
❏ 7E-2009 [(2)]	Greatest Stories Live	1976	3.00	6.00	12.00
❏ 8E-6003 [(2)]	Greatest Stories Live	1978	2.50	5.00	10.00
—Reissue of 7E-2009					
❏ 60413	Anthology of Harry Chapin	1985	2.50	5.00	10.00
❏ EKS-75023	Heads and Tales	1972	2.50	5.00	10.00
❏ EKS-75042	Sniper and Other Love Songs	1972	2.50	5.00	10.00
❏ EKS-75065	Short Stories	1973	2.50	5.00	10.00
CHAPINS, THE HARRY CHAPIN; Steve Chapin; Tom Chapin.					
45s					
EPIC					
❏ 10761	Workin' On My Life/The Only Thing (You Ever Really Have to Do Is Die)	1971	3.00	6.00	12.00
ROCK-LAND					
❏ 664	Old Time Movies/Not Your Kind	1966	3.75	7.50	15.00
❏ 664 [PS]	Old Time Movies/Not Your Kind	1966	6.25	12.50	25.00

Number	Title (A Side/B Side)	Yr	VG	VG+	NM
Albums					
ROCK-LAND					
❏ RR-66 [M]	Chapin Music	1966	7.50	15.00	30.00
—As "The Chapin Brothers"					
CHAPMAN, GRADY					
45s					
IMPERIAL					
❏ 5591	Garden of Memories/Tell Me That You Care	1959	3.00	6.00	12.00
❏ 5611	Come Away/Let's Talk About Us	1959	3.00	6.00	12.00
KNIGHT					
❏ 2003	Say You Will Be Mine/Starlight, Starbright	1958	7.50	15.00	30.00
MERCURY					
❏ 71632	Sweet Thing/I Know What I Want	1960	3.00	6.00	12.00
❏ 71698	Ambush/My Life Would Be Worth Living	1960	12.50	25.00	50.00
❏ 71771	I'll Never Question Your Love/This, That, 'N the Other	1961	3.00	6.00	12.00
MONEY					
❏ 204	I Need You So/Don't Blooper	1955	75.00	150.00	300.00
ZEPHYR					
❏ 016	My Love Will Never Change/Smiling	1957	7.50	15.00	30.00
CHARGERS, THE Also see JESSE BELVIN.					
45s					
RCA VICTOR					
❏ 47-7301	Old MacDonald/Dandelion	1958	7.50	15.00	30.00
CHARIOT					
Albums					
NATIONAL GENERAL					
❏ NG-2003	Chariot	1971	12.50	25.00	50.00
CHARIOTEERS, THE Also see BILLY WILLIAMS.					
45s					
COLUMBIA					
❏ 1-168	A Kiss and a Rose/A Cottage in Old Donegal	1949	150.00	300.00	600.00
—Microgroove 7-inch, 33 1/3 rpm single					
❏ 1-363	This Side of Heaven/Hawaiian Sunset	1949	150.00	300.00	600.00
—Microgroove 7-inch, 33 1/3 rpm single					
JOSIE					
❏ 787	I've Got My Heart on My Sleeve/Don't Play No Mambo	1955	20.00	40.00	80.00
MGM					
❏ 12569	The Candles/I Didn't Mean to Be Mean to You	1957	20.00	40.00	80.00
RCA VICTOR					
❏ 47-6098	Easy Does It/Tremble, Tremble, Tremble	1955	20.00	40.00	80.00
Albums					
COLUMBIA					
❏ CL 6014 [10]	Sweet and Low	1949	75.00	150.00	300.00
HARMONY					
❏ HL 7089 [M]	The Charioteers with Billy Williams	1957	25.00	50.00	100.00
CHARISMA					
45s					
ROULETTE					
❏ 7075	What's It Like/(B-side unknown)	1970	2.00	4.00	8.00
❏ 7096	Bizwambi/(B-side unknown)	1971	2.00	4.00	8.00
Albums					
ROULETTE					
❏ SR-42037	Charisma	1970	5.00	10.00	20.00
CHARITY					
45s					
PHILIPS					
❏ 40614	Never Change Your Mind/Windy City Woman	1969	2.50	5.00	10.00
UNI					
❏ 55159	Never Change Your Mind/I Still Love You	1969	2.00	4.00	8.00
Albums					
UNI					
❏ 73061	Charity Now	1969	6.25	12.50	25.00
CHARLATANS, THE					
45s					
KAPP					
❏ 779	The Shadow Knows/32-20	1967	12.50	25.00	50.00
❏ 779 [PS]	The Shadow Knows/32-20	1967	20.00	40.00	80.00
PHILIPS					
❏ 40610	High Coin/When I Go Sailin' By	1969	10.00	20.00	40.00
❏ 40610 [PS]	High Coin/When I Go Sailin' By	1969	20.00	40.00	80.00
—Sleeve is promo only					
❏ 44824 [DJ]	Date: May 19, 1969	1969	15.00	30.00	60.00
—One-sided, promo only					
Albums					
PHILIPS					
❏ PHS 600309	The Charlatans	1969	25.00	50.00	100.00
CHARLENE					
45s					
ARIOLA AMERICA					
❏ 7696	Are You Free/We Know	1977	—	2.50	5.00
MOTOWN					
❏ 1262	Give It One More Try/Relove	1973	2.00	4.00	8.00
❏ 1285	All That Love Went to Waste/Give It One More Try	1973	2.00	4.00	8.00
❏ 1492	Hungry/I Won't Remember Ever Loving You	1980	—	2.00	4.00
❏ 1611	I've Never Been to Me/Somewhere in My Life	1982	—	—	3.00
❏ 1621	Nunca He Ido A Mi/If I Could See Myself	1982	—	2.00	4.00
❏ 1650	Used to Be/I Want to Come Back As a Song	1982	—	—	3.00
—A-side with Stevie Wonder					
❏ 1650 [PS]	Used to Be/I Want to Come Back As A Song	1982	—	—	3.00
❏ 1663	I Want to Go Back There Again/Richie's Song	1983	—	—	3.00
❏ 1734	We're Both in Love with You/I Want the World to Know He's Mine	1984	—	—	3.00
❏ 1761	Hit and Run Lover/Last Song	1984	—	—	3.00
PRODIGAL					
❏ 0632	It Ain't Easy Coming Down/On My Way to You	1977	—	2.50	5.00
❏ 0633	Freddie/(B-side unknown)	1977	—	2.50	5.00

Number	Title (A Side/B Side)	Yr	VG	VG+	NM
❏ 0633 [PS]	Freddie/(B-side unknown)	1977	2.00	5.00	10.00
❏ 0636	I've Never Been to Me/				
	It's Really Nice to Be in Love Again	1977	5.00	10.00	20.00
Albums					
MOTOWN					
❏ 6007 ML	Charlene	1981	2.50	5.00	10.00
❏ 6027 ML	Used to Be	1982	2.50	5.00	10.00
❏ 6090 ML	Hit and Run Lover	1985	2.50	5.00	10.00
PRODIGAL					
❏ P6-10015	Charlene	1976	5.00	10.00	20.00
❏ P6-10018	Songs of Love	1977	5.00	10.00	20.00

CHARLES, BOBBY
45s
Number	Title (A Side/B Side)	Yr	VG	VG+	NM
BEARSVILLE					
❏ 0010	Small Town Talk/Save Me Jesus	1973	—	2.00	4.00
CHESS					
❏ 1609	Later Alligator/On Bended Knee	1955	12.50	25.00	50.00
❏ 1617	Why Did You Leave/Don't You Know I Love You	1956	12.50	25.00	50.00
❏ 1628	Only Time Will Tell/Take It Easy. Greasy	1956	12.50	25.00	50.00
❏ 1638	Laura Lee/No Use Knocking	1956	12.50	25.00	50.00
❏ 1647	Put Your Arms Around Me/				
	Why Can't You, Honey	1957	10.00	20.00	40.00
❏ 1658	No More/You Can Suit Yourself	1957	10.00	20.00	40.00
❏ 1670	One Eyed Jack/Yea Yea Baby	1957	10.00	20.00	40.00
IMPERIAL					
❏ 5542	Since She's Gone/At the Jamboree	1958	5.00	10.00	20.00
❏ 5557	Oh Yeah/Since I Lost You	1958	5.00	10.00	20.00
❏ 5579	The Town Is Talking/What Can I Do	1959	5.00	10.00	20.00
❏ 5642	Bye Bye Baby/Those Eyes	1960	5.00	10.00	20.00
❏ 5681	What a Party/I Just Want You	1960	5.00	10.00	20.00
❏ 5691	Four Winds/Nothing Sweet As You	1960	5.00	10.00	20.00
JEWEL					
❏ 728	Everybody's Laughing/Everybody Knows	1964	2.50	5.00	10.00
❏ 729	Goodnight Irene/I Hope	1964	2.50	5.00	10.00
❏ 735	Ain't Misbehavin'/Preacher's Daughter	1964	2.50	5.00	10.00
❏ 740	Oh Lonesome Me/One More Glass of Wine	1964	2.50	5.00	10.00
PAULA					
❏ 226	The Walk/Worrying Over You	1965	2.50	5.00	10.00
Albums					
CHESS					
❏ CH 9175	Chess Masters	1984	3.75	7.50	15.00

CHARLES, DON
45s
Number	Title (A Side/B Side)	Yr	VG	VG+	NM
WORLD ARTISTS					
❏ 1031	She's Mine/Big Talk from a Little Man	1964	2.50	5.00	10.00

CHARLES, JIMMY
45s
Number	Title (A Side/B Side)	Yr	VG	VG+	NM
PROMO					
❏ 1002	A Million to One/Hop Scotch Hop	1960	3.75	7.50	15.00
❏ 1002	A Million to One/Hop Scotch Polka	1960	5.00	10.00	20.00
❏ 1003	The Age for Love/Follow the Swallow	1960	3.75	7.50	15.00
❏ 1003 [PS]	The Age for Love/Follow the Swallow	1960	5.00	10.00	20.00
❏ 1004	Santa Won't Be Blue This Christmas/I Saw Mommy Kissing Santa Claus	1960	3.75	7.50	15.00
❏ 1004 [PS]	Santa Won't Be Blue This Christmas/I Saw Mommy Kissing Santa Claus	1960	5.00	10.00	20.00
❏ 1005	Christmasville U.S.A./A Little White Mouse Called Steve	1960	3.75	7.50	15.00
❏ 1005 [PS]	Christmasville U.S.A./A Little White Mouse Called Steve	1960	5.00	10.00	20.00
❏ 1006	I Wonder How It Feels to Fall in Love/Just Whistle for Me	1961	3.75	7.50	15.00

CHARLES, RAY   Also see BILLY JOEL.
12-Inch Singles
Number	Title (A Side/B Side)	Yr	VG	VG+	NM
COLUMBIA					
❏ CAS 1421 [DJ]	I Wish I'd Never Loved You at All (same on both sides?)	1988	3.00	6.00	12.00
WARNER BROS.					
❏ PRO-A-4425 [DJ]	I'll Take Care of You (same on both sides)	1990	3.75	7.50	15.00
❏ PRO-A-4696 [DJ]	Living Without You (same on both sides)	1990	3.00	6.00	12.00
❏ PRO-A-5977 [DJ]	A Song for You (same on both sides)	1993	2.50	5.00	10.00

45s
Number	Title (A Side/B Side)	Yr	VG	VG+	NM
ABC					
❏ 10808	Let's Go Get Stoned/At the Train	1966	2.00	4.00	8.00
❏ 10840	I Chose to Sing the Blues/Hopelessly	1966	2.00	4.00	8.00
❏ 10865	Please Say You're Fooling/I Don't Need No Doctor	1966	2.00	4.00	8.00
❏ 10901	I Want to Talk About You/Something Inside Me	1967	2.00	4.00	8.00
❏ 10938	Here We Go Again/Somebody Ought to Write a Book About It	1967	2.00	4.00	8.00
❏ 10970	In the Heat of the Night/Somebody's Got to Change	1967	2.00	4.00	8.00
❏ 11009	Yesterday/Never Had Enough of Nothing Yet	1967	2.00	4.00	8.00
❏ 11045	That's a Lie/Go On Home	1968	2.00	4.00	8.00
❏ 11045 [PS]	That's a Lie/Go On Home	1968	3.75	7.50	15.00
❏ 11090	Eleanor Rigby/Understanding	1968	2.00	4.00	8.00
❏ 11133	Sweet Young Thing Like You/ Listen, They're Playing Our Song	1968	2.00	4.00	8.00
❏ 11170	If It Wasn't for Bad Luck/When I Stop Dreaming	1969	2.00	4.00	8.00
—With Jimmy Lewis					
❏ 11193	I'll Be Your Servant/ I Don't Know What Time It Was	1969	2.00	4.00	8.00
❏ 11213	Let Me Love You/I'm Satisfied	1969	2.00	4.00	8.00
❏ 11239	We Can Make It/I Can't Stop Loving You Baby	1969	2.00	4.00	8.00
❏ 11251	Someone to Watch Over Me/Claudie Mae	1969	2.00	4.00	8.00
❏ 11259	Laughin' and Clownin'/That Thing Called Love	1970	2.00	4.00	8.00
❏ 11271	If You Were Mine/Till I Can't Take It Anymore	1970	2.00	4.00	8.00
❏ 11291	Don't Change on Me/Sweet Memories	1971	2.00	4.00	8.00
❏ 11308	Feel So Bad/Your Love Is So Doggone Good	1971	—	3.00	6.00
❏ 11317	What Am I Living For/Tired of My Tears	1971	—	3.00	6.00
❏ 11329	Look What They've Done to My Song, Ma/ America the Beautiful	1972	2.50	5.00	10.00
❏ 11337	Hey Mister/There'll Be No Peace Without All Men as One	1972	—	3.00	6.00

Number	Title (A Side/B Side)	Yr	VG	VG+	NM
❏ 11344	Every Saturday Night/Take Me Home, Country Roads	1973	—	3.00	6.00
❏ 11351	I Can Make It Through the Days (But Oh Those Lonely Nights)/Ring of Fire	1973	—	3.00	6.00
ABC-PARAMOUNT					
❏ 410-5 [S]	You Win Again/Careless Love	1962	5.00	10.00	20.00
—33 1/3 rpm jukebox single, small hole					
❏ 465-1 [S]	Busted/(B-side unknown)	1963	5.00	10.00	20.00
❏ 465-2 [S]	That Lucky Old Sun/(B-side unknown)	1963	5.00	10.00	20.00
❏ 465-3 [S]	Ol' Man River/(B-side unknown)	1963	5.00	10.00	20.00
❏ 465-4 [S]	Ol' Man Time/(B-side unknown)	1963	5.00	10.00	20.00
—The above four are 33 1/3 rpm, 7-inch jukebox singles with small holes, excerpted from the LP "Ingredients in a Recipe for Soul"					
❏ 480-1 [S]	Don't Cry Baby/Teardrops from My Eyes	1964	5.00	10.00	20.00
❏ 480-2 [S]	Baby, Don't You Cry/Cry Me a River	1964	5.00	10.00	20.00
❏ 480-3 [S]	I Cried for You/Cry	1964	5.00	10.00	20.00
❏ 480-4 [S]	A Tear Fell/No One to Cry To	1964	5.00	10.00	20.00
❏ 480-5 [S]	You've Got Me Crying Again/ After My Laughter Came Tears	1964	5.00	10.00	20.00
—The above five are 33 1/3 rpm, small hole jukebox singles excerpted from the LP "Sweet and Sour Tears"					
❏ 10081	My Baby/Who You Gonna Love	1960	3.75	7.50	15.00
❏ 10118	Sticks and Stones/Worried Life Blues	1960	3.00	6.00	12.00
❏ 10135	Georgia on My Mind/ Carry Me Back to Old Virginny	1960	3.75	7.50	15.00
❏ 10141	Them That Got/I Wonder	1960	3.00	6.00	12.00
❏ 10164	Ruby/Heard Hearted Woman	1960	3.00	6.00	12.00
❏ 10244	Hit the Road Jack/The Danger Zone	1961	3.75	7.50	15.00
❏ 10266	Unchain My Heart/But on the Other Hand, Baby	1961	3.75	7.50	15.00
❏ 10314	Hide 'Nor Hair/At the Club	1962	3.00	6.00	12.00
❏ 10330	I Can't Stop Loving You/Born to Lose	1962	3.75	7.50	15.00
❏ 10345	You Don't Know Me/Careless Love	1962	3.75	7.50	15.00
❏ 10375	You Are My Sunshine/Your Cheating Heart	1962	3.00	6.00	12.00
❏ 10405	Don't Set Me Free/The Brightest Smile in Town	1963	3.00	6.00	12.00
❏ 10435	Take These Chains from My Heart/ No Letter Today	1963	3.75	7.50	15.00
❏ 10453	No One/Without Love (There Is Nothing)	1963	3.75	7.50	15.00
❏ 10481	Busted/Making Believe	1963	3.75	7.50	15.00
❏ 10509	That Lucky Old Sun/Ol' Man Time	1963	3.00	6.00	12.00
❏ 10530	Baby Don't You Cry/My Heart Cries for You	1964	3.00	6.00	12.00
❏ 10557	My Baby Don't Dig Me/Something's Wrong	1964	3.00	6.00	12.00
❏ 10571	No One to Cry To/A Tear Fell	1964	3.00	6.00	12.00
❏ 10588	Smack Dab in the Middle/I Wake Up Crying	1964	3.00	6.00	12.00
❏ 10609	Makin' Whoopee/(Instrumental)	1964	3.00	6.00	12.00
❏ 10615	Cry/Teardrops from My Eyes	1965	3.00	6.00	12.00
❏ 10649	I Gotta Woman (Part 1)/I Gotta Woman (Part 2)	1965	3.00	6.00	12.00
❏ 10663	Without a Song (Part 1)/Without a Song (Part 2)	1965	3.00	6.00	12.00
❏ 10700	I'm a Fool to Care/Love's Gonna Live Here	1965	3.00	6.00	12.00
❏ 10720	The Cincinnati Kid/That's All I Am to You	1965	3.00	6.00	12.00
❏ 10739	Crying Time/ When My Dreamboat Comes Home	1965	3.75	7.50	15.00
❏ 10785	Together Again/ You're Just About to Lose Your Clown	1966	3.00	6.00	12.00
ATLANTIC					
❏ 976	Roll with Me Baby/The Midnight Hour	1952	125.00	250.00	500.00
❏ 984	The Sun's Gonna Shine Again/ Jumpin' in the Morning	1953	100.00	200.00	400.00
❏ 999	Mess Around/Funny (But I Still Love You)	1953	50.00	100.00	200.00
❏ 1008	Feelin' Sad/Heartbreaker	1953	25.00	50.00	100.00
❏ 1021	It Should've Been Me/Sinner's Prayer	1954	12.50	25.00	50.00
❏ 1037	Don't You Know/Losing Hand	1954	7.50	15.00	30.00
❏ 1050	I've Got a Woman/Come Back	1954	12.50	25.00	50.00
❏ 1063	This Little Girl of Mine/A Fool for You	1955	7.50	15.00	30.00
❏ 1076	Blackjack/Greenbacks	1955	7.50	15.00	30.00
❏ 1085	Drown in My Own Tears/Mary Ann	1956	6.25	12.50	25.00
❏ 1096	Hallelujah, I Love Her So/What Would I Do Without You	1956	5.00	10.00	20.00
❏ 1108	Lonely Avenue/Leave My Woman Alone	1956	5.00	10.00	20.00
❏ 1124	I Want to Know/Ain't That Love	1957	5.00	10.00	20.00
❏ 1143	It's All Right/Get On the Right Track Baby	1957	5.00	10.00	20.00
❏ 1154	Swanee River Rock (Talkin' 'Bout That River)/I Want a Little Girl	1957	5.00	10.00	20.00
❏ 1172	Talkin' 'Bout You/What Kind of a Man Are You	1958	3.75	7.50	15.00
❏ 1180	Yes Indeed/I Had a Dream	1958	3.75	7.50	15.00
—With the Cookies					
❏ 1196	My Bonnie/You Be My Baby	1958	3.75	7.50	15.00
❏ 2006	Rockhouse (Part 1)/Rockhouse (Part 2)	1958	3.75	7.50	15.00
❏ 2010	(Night Time Is) The Right Time/Tell All the World About You	1959	3.75	7.50	15.00
❏ 2022	Tell Me How Do You Feel/That's Enough	1959	3.75	7.50	15.00
❏ 2031	What'd I Say (Part I)/What'd I Say (Part II)	1959	5.00	10.00	20.00
❏ 2043	I'm Movin' On/I Believe to My Soul	1959	3.00	6.00	12.00
❏ 2047	Let the Good Times Roll/Don't Let the Sun Catch You Cryin'	1960	3.00	6.00	12.00
❏ 2055	Heartbreaker/Just for a Thrill	1960	3.00	6.00	12.00
❏ 2068	Tell the Truth/Sweet Sixteen Bars	1960	3.00	6.00	12.00
❏ 2084	Come Rain or Come Shine/ Tell Me You'll Wait for Me	1960	3.00	6.00	12.00
❏ 2094	Early in the Morning/A Bit of Soul	1961	3.00	6.00	12.00
❏ 2106	Am I Blue/It Should've Been Me	1961	3.00	6.00	12.00
❏ 2118	I Wonder Who/Hard Times (No One Knows Better Than I)	1961	3.00	6.00	12.00
❏ 2174	Carryin' That Load/Feelin' Sad	1963	2.50	5.00	10.00
❏ 2239	Talkin' 'Bout You/In a Little Spanish Town	1964	2.50	5.00	10.00
❏ 2470	Come Rain or Come Shine/ Tell Me You'll Wait for Me	1968	2.50	5.00	10.00
❏ 3443	I Can See Clearly Now/Anonymous Love	1977	—	2.50	5.00
❏ 3473	A Peace That We Never Could Enjoy/ Game Number Nine	1978	—	2.50	5.00
❏ 3527	Riding Thumb/You Forgot Your Memories	1978	—	2.50	5.00
❏ 3549 [DJ]	Christmas Time (same on both sides)	1978	—	3.00	6.00
—May be promo-only					
❏ 3611	Some Enchanted Evening/20th Century Fox	1979	—	2.50	5.00
❏ 3634	Just Because/Love Me or Set Me Free	1979	—	2.50	5.00
❏ 3762	Compared To What/ Now That We've Found Each Other	1980	—	2.50	5.00
❏ 5005	Doodlin' (Part 1)/Doodlin' (Part 2)	1960	3.75	7.50	15.00
BARONET					
❏ 7111	See See Rider/I Used to be So Happy	1960	3.00	6.00	12.00
❏ 7111 [PS]	See See Rider/I Used to be So Happy	1960	6.25	12.50	25.00

Number	Title (A Side/B Side)	Yr	VG	VG+	NM
COLUMBIA					
38-03429	String Bean/Born to Love Me	1982	—	2.00	4.00
38-03810	You Feel Good All Over/ 3/4 Time	1983	—	—	3.00
38-04083	Ain't Your Memory Got No Pride at All/I Don't Want No Strangers Sleeping in My Bed	1983	—	—	3.00
38-04297	We Didn't See a Thing/I Wish You Were Here Tonight	1983	—	—	3.00
—A-side with George Jones and Chet Atkins					
38-04420	Do I Ever Cross Your Mind/They Call It Love	1984	—	—	3.00
38-04500	Woman (Sensuous Woman)/ I Was On Georgia Time	1984	—	—	3.00
38-04531	Rock and Roll Shoes/Then I'll Be Over You	1984	—	—	3.00
—Ray Charles and B.J. Thomas					
38-04715	Seven Spanish Angels/Who Cares	1984	—	—	3.00
—A-side with Willie Nelson; B-side with Janie Frickie					
38-04860	It Ain't Gonna Worry My Mind/Crazy Old Soldier	1985	—	—	3.00
—A-side with Mickey Gilley; B-side with Johnny Cash					
38-05575	Two Old Cats Like Us/Little Hotel Room	1985	—	—	3.00
—A-side with Hank Williams, Jr.; B-side with Merle Haggard					
38-06172	Pages of My Mind/Slip Away	1986	—	—	3.00
38-06370	Dixie Moon/A Little Bit of Heaven	1986	—	—	3.00
38-08393	Seven Spanish Angels/It Ain't Gonna Worry My Mind	1988	—	—	3.00
—Reissue; A-side with Willie Nelson, B-side with Mickey Gilley					
CROSSOVER					
973	Come Live with Me/Everybody Sing	1973	—	2.50	5.00
974	Louise/Somebody	1974	—	2.50	5.00
981	Living for the City/Then We'll Be Home	1975	—	2.50	5.00
985	America the Beautiful/Sunshine	1976	—	3.00	6.00
—A-side is a different recording than that on the B-side of ABC 11329					
IMPULSE!					
200	One Mint Julep/Let's Go	1961	2.50	5.00	10.00
202	I've Got News for You/ I'm Gonna Move to the Outskirts of Town	1961	2.50	5.00	10.00
RCA					
PB-10800	Oh Lawd, I'm On My Way/ Oh Bess, Where's My Bess	1976	—	2.50	5.00
ROCKIN'					
504	Walkin' and Talkin' (To Myself)/I'm Wonderin' and Wonderin'	1952	75.00	150.00	300.00
SITTIN' IN WITH					
641	Baby Let Me Hear You Call My Name/ Guitar Blues	1952	75.00	150.00	300.00
SWING TIME					
250	Baby, Let Me Hold Your Hand/Lonely Boy	1951	125.00	250.00	500.00
—Ray Charles records on Swing Time before 250 are unconfirmed on 45 rpm					
274	Kissa Me Baby/I'm Glad for Your Sake	1952	125.00	250.00	500.00
300	Baby Let Me Hear You Call My Name/ Guitar Blues	1952	125.00	250.00	500.00
326	The Snow Is Falling/Misery in My Heart	1953	125.00	250.00	500.00
TANGERINE					
1015	Booty Butt/Sidewinder	1971	—	3.00	6.00
TIME					
1026	I Found My Baby/Guitar Blues	1960	3.75	7.50	15.00
1054	Why Did You Go/Back Home	1962	3.00	6.00	12.00
WARNER BROS.					
18611	A Song for You/I Can't Get Enough	1993	—	—	3.00
49608	Beers to You/Cotton-Eyed Clint	1980	—	2.50	5.00
—A-side with Clint Eastwood; B-side by Texas Opera Company					
7-Inch Extended Plays					
ABC-PARAMOUNT					
EP 410	Half As Much/I Love You So Much It Hurts//You Win Again/It Makes No Difference Now	196?	7.50	15.00	30.00
—Jukebox issue; small hole, plays at 33 1/3 rpm					
EP 410 [PS]	Modern Sounds in Country and Western Music	196?	7.50	15.00	30.00
EP A-410	I Can't Stop Loving You/Born to Lose//You Don't Know Me/Careless Love	1962	6.25	12.50	25.00
EP A-410 [PS]	Modern Sounds in Country and Western Music	1962	6.25	12.50	25.00
EP 415	Them That Got/Unchain My Heart/Hit the Road Jack//Sticks and Stones/I Wonder/The Danger Zone	1962	7.50	15.00	30.00
—Jukebox issue; small hole, plays at 33 1/3 rpm					
EP 415 [PS]	Ray Charles' Greatest Hits	1962	7.50	15.00	30.00
ATLANTIC					
EP 587	*Ain't That Love/Greenbacks/Drown in My Own Tears/Hallelujah I Love Her So	1956	25.00	50.00	100.00
EP 587 [PS]	Ray Charles	1956	25.00	50.00	100.00
EP 597	(contents unknown)	1957	25.00	50.00	100.00
EP 597 [PS]	The Great Ray Charles	1957	25.00	50.00	100.00
EP 607	*A Fool for You/Mary Ann/Blackjack/Lonely Avenue	1958	25.00	50.00	100.00
EP 607 [PS]	Rock with Ray Charles	1958	25.00	50.00	100.00
EP 619	*Let the Good Times Roll/Come Rain or Come Shine/Don't Let the Sun Catch You Cryin'/Alexander's Ragtime Band	1959	25.00	50.00	100.00
EP 619 [PS]	The Genius of Ray Charles	1959	25.00	50.00	100.00
Albums					
ABC					
S-335 [S]	The Genius Hits the Road	1967	3.00	6.00	12.00
S-355 [S]	Dedicated to You	1967	3.00	6.00	12.00
S-410 [S]	Modern Sounds in Country and Western Music	1967	3.00	6.00	12.00
S-415 [S]	Ray Charles' Greatest Hits	1967	3.00	6.00	12.00
S-435 [S]	Modern Sounds in Country and Western Music (Volume Two)	1967	3.00	6.00	12.00
S-465 [S]	Ingredients in a Recipe for Soul	1967	3.00	6.00	12.00
S-480 [S]	Sweet & Sour Tears	1967	3.00	6.00	12.00
S-495 [S]	Have a Smile with Me	1967	3.00	6.00	12.00
S-500 [S]	Ray Charles Live in Concert	1967	3.00	6.00	12.00
S-520 [S]	Together Again	1967	3.00	6.00	12.00
S-544 [S]	Crying Time	1967	3.00	6.00	12.00
S-550 [S]	Ray's Moods	1967	3.00	6.00	12.00
590X [(2)M]	A Man and His Soul	1967	3.75	7.50	15.00
S-590X [(2)S]	A Man and His Soul	1967	5.00	10.00	20.00
595 [M]	Ray Charles Invites You to Listen	1967	5.00	10.00	20.00
S-595 [S]	Ray Charles Invites You to Listen	1967	3.75	7.50	15.00
S-625	A Portrait of Ray	1968	3.00	6.00	12.00
S-675	I'm All Yours — Baby!	1969	3.00	6.00	12.00

Number	Title (A Side/B Side)	Yr	VG	VG+	NM
S-695	Doing His Thing	1969	3.00	6.00	12.00
S-707	Love Country Style	1971	3.00	6.00	12.00
S-726	Volcanic Action of My Soul	1971	3.00	6.00	12.00
H-731 [(2)]	A 25th Anniversary in Show Business Salute to Ray Charles	1971	3.75	7.50	15.00
X-755	A Message from the People	1972	3.00	6.00	12.00
X-765	Through the Eyes of Love	1972	3.00	6.00	12.00
X-781/2 [(2)]	All-Time Great Country & Western Hits	1973	3.75	7.50	15.00
QBO-91036 [(2)M]	The Ray Charles Story	1967	7.50	15.00	30.00
—Capitol Record Club exclusive					
SQBO-91036 [(2)S]	The Ray Charles Story	1967	6.25	12.50	25.00
—Capitol Record Club exclusive					
ST-91233 [S]	Ray Charles Invites You to Listen	1967	3.75	7.50	15.00
—Capitol Record Club edition					
ABC IMPULSE!					
AS-2 [S]	Genius + Soul = Jazz	1968	3.00	6.00	12.00
ABC-PARAMOUNT					
335 [M]	The Genius Hits the Road	1960	5.00	10.00	20.00
S-335 [S]	The Genius Hits the Road	1960	7.50	15.00	30.00
355 [M]	Dedicated to You	1961	5.00	10.00	20.00
S-355 [S]	Dedicated to You	1961	7.50	15.00	30.00
410 [M]	Modern Sounds in Country and Western Music	1962	6.25	12.50	25.00
S-410 [S]	Modern Sounds in Country and Western Music	1962	7.50	15.00	30.00
415 [M]	Ray Charles' Greatest Hits	1962	5.00	10.00	20.00
S-415 [S]	Ray Charles' Greatest Hits	1962	6.25	12.50	25.00
435 [M]	Modern Sounds in Country and Western Music (Volume Two)	1962	5.00	10.00	20.00
S-435 [S]	Modern Sounds in Country and Western Music (Volume Two)	1962	6.25	12.50	25.00
465 [M]	Ingredients in a Recipe for Soul	1963	5.00	10.00	20.00
S-465 [S]	Ingredients in a Recipe for Soul	1963	6.25	12.50	25.00
480 [M]	Sweet & Sour Tears	1964	5.00	10.00	20.00
S-480 [S]	Sweet & Sour Tears	1964	6.25	12.50	25.00
495 [M]	Have a Smile with Me	1964	5.00	10.00	20.00
S-495 [S]	Have a Smile with Me	1964	6.25	12.50	25.00
500 [M]	Ray Charles Live in Concert	1965	3.75	7.50	15.00
S-500 [S]	Ray Charles Live in Concert	1965	5.00	10.00	20.00
520 [M]	Together Again	196?	3.75	7.50	15.00
—Retitled version of "Country and Western Meets Rhythm and Blues"					
520 [M]	Country & Western Meets Rhythm & Blues	1965	3.75	7.50	15.00
S-520 [S]	Together Again	196?	5.00	10.00	20.00
—Retitled version of "Country and Western Meets Rhythm and Blues"					
S-520 [S]	Country & Western Meets Rhythm & Blues	1965	5.00	10.00	20.00
544 [M]	Crying Time	1966	3.75	7.50	15.00
S-544 [S]	Crying Time	1966	5.00	10.00	20.00
550 [M]	Ray's Moods	1966	3.75	7.50	15.00
S-550 [S]	Ray's Moods	1966	5.00	10.00	20.00
ST-90144 [S]	Ray Charles Live in Concert	1965	5.00	10.00	20.00
—Capitol Record Club edition					
T-90144 [M]	Ray Charles Live in Concert	1965	5.00	10.00	20.00
—Capitol Record Club edition					
ST-90625 [S]	Crying Time	1966	5.00	10.00	20.00
—Capitol Record Club edition					
T-90625 [M]	Crying Time	1966	5.00	10.00	20.00
—Capitol Record Club edition					
ST-90847 [S]	Together Again	1966	6.25	12.50	25.00
—Capitol Record Club edition					
ST-90929 [S]	Ray's Moods	1966	6.25	12.50	25.00
—Capitol Record Club edition					
ATLANTIC					
SD 2-503 [(2)]	Ray Charles Live	1973	3.75	7.50	15.00
2-900 [(2)M]	The Ray Charles Story	1962	10.00	20.00	40.00
1259 [M]	The Great Ray Charles	1957	12.50	25.00	50.00
—Black label					
1259 [M]	The Great Ray Charles	1960	6.25	12.50	25.00
—Red and white label, white fan logo on right					
1259 [M]	The Great Ray Charles	1962	5.00	10.00	20.00
—Red and white label, black fan logo on right					
SD 1259 [S]	The Great Ray Charles	1959	12.50	25.00	50.00
—Green label					
SD 1259 [S]	The Great Ray Charles	1960	6.25	12.50	25.00
—Blue and green label, white fan logo on right					
SD 1259 [S]	The Great Ray Charles	1962	5.00	10.00	20.00
—Blue and green label, black fan logo on right					
1289 [M]	Ray Charles at Newport	1958	12.50	25.00	50.00
—Black label					
1289 [M]	Ray Charles at Newport	1960	6.25	12.50	25.00
—Red and white label, white fan logo on right					
1289 [M]	Ray Charles at Newport	1962	5.00	10.00	20.00
—Red and white label, black fan logo on right					
SD 1289 [S]	Ray Charles at Newport	1959	12.50	25.00	50.00
—Green label					
SD 1289 [S]	Ray Charles at Newport	1960	6.25	12.50	25.00
—Blue and green label, white fan logo on right					
SD 1289 [S]	Ray Charles at Newport	1962	5.00	10.00	20.00
—Blue and green label, black fan logo on right					
1312 [M]	The Genius of Ray Charles	1960	6.25	12.50	25.00
—Red and white label, white fan logo on right					
1312 [M]	The Genius of Ray Charles	1960	10.00	20.00	40.00
—Black label					
1312 [M]	The Genius of Ray Charles	1960	10.00	20.00	40.00
—White "bullseye" label					
1312 [M]	The Genius of Ray Charles	1962	5.00	10.00	20.00
—Red and white label, black fan logo on right					
SD 1312 [S]	The Genius of Ray Charles	1960	6.25	12.50	25.00
—Blue and green label, white fan logo on right					
SD 1312 [S]	The Genius of Ray Charles	1960	12.50	25.00	50.00
—Green label					
SD 1312 [S]	The Genius of Ray Charles	1960	12.50	25.00	50.00
—White "bullseye" label					
SD 1312 [S]	The Genius of Ray Charles	1962	5.00	10.00	20.00
—Blue and green label, black fan logo on right					
SD 1312 [S]	The Genius of Ray Charles	1968	5.00	10.00	20.00
—Brown and purple label					
1369 [M]	The Genius After Hours	1961	6.25	12.50	25.00
—Red and white label, white fan logo on right					
1369 [M]	The Genius After Hours	1962	5.00	10.00	20.00
—Red and white label, black fan logo on right					

Number	Title (A Side/B Side)	Yr	VG	VG+	NM
❑ SD 1369 [S]	The Genius After Hours	1961	7.50	15.00	30.00
—Blue and green label, white fan logo on right					
❑ SD 1369 [S]	The Genius After Hours	1962	6.25	12.50	25.00
—Blue and green label, black fan logo on right					
❑ SD 1543	The Best of Ray Charles	1970	3.00	6.00	12.00
❑ 3700 [(6)]	Ray Charles: A Life in Music	198?	12.50	25.00	50.00
❑ SD 7101 [S]	The Great Hits of Ray Charles Recorded on 8-Track Stereo	1966	6.25	12.50	25.00
❑ 8006 [M]	Ray Charles (Rock and Roll)	1957	22.50	45.00	90.00
—Black label					
❑ 8006 [M]	Ray Charles (Rock and Roll)	1960	6.25	12.50	25.00
—Red and white label, white fan logo on right					
❑ 8006 [M]	Hallelujah! I Love Her So	1962	5.00	10.00	20.00
—Red and white label, black fan logo on right; retitled version					
❑ 8025 [M]	Yes, Indeed!	1958	12.50	25.00	50.00
—Black label; cover has screaming girls					
❑ 8025 [M]	Yes, Indeed!	1960	6.25	12.50	25.00
—Red and white label, white fan logo on right; cover has screaming girls					
❑ 8025 [M]	Yes, Indeed!	1962	5.00	10.00	20.00
—Red and white label, black fan logo on right; cover has Ray on it					
❑ 8029 [M]	What'd I Say	1959	12.50	25.00	50.00
—Black label					
❑ 8029 [M]	What'd I Say	1960	6.25	12.50	25.00
—Red and white label, white fan logo on right					
❑ 8029 [M]	What'd I Say	1960	10.00	20.00	40.00
—White "bullseye" label					
❑ 8029 [M]	What'd I Say	1962	5.00	10.00	20.00
—Red and white label, black fan logo on right					
❑ 8039 [M]	Ray Charles In Person	1960	6.25	12.50	25.00
—Red and white label, white fan logo on right					
❑ 8039 [M]	Ray Charles In Person	1960	10.00	20.00	40.00
—Black label					
❑ 8039 [M]	Ray Charles In Person	1962	5.00	10.00	20.00
—Red and white label, black fan logo on right					
❑ 8052 [M]	The Genius Sings the Blues	1961	6.25	12.50	25.00
—Red and white label, white fan logo on right					
❑ 8052 [M]	The Genius Sings the Blues	1962	5.00	10.00	20.00
—Red and white label, black fan logo on right					
❑ 8054 [M]	Do the Twist!	1961	6.25	12.50	25.00
—Red and white label, white fan logo on right					
❑ 8054 [M]	Do the Twist!	1962	5.00	10.00	20.00
—Red and white label, black fan logo on right					
❑ 8063 [M]	The Ray Charles Story, Volume 1	1962	5.00	10.00	20.00
❑ 8064 [M]	The Ray Charles Story, Volume 2	1962	5.00	10.00	20.00
❑ 8083 [M]	The Ray Charles Story, Volume 3	1963	5.00	10.00	20.00
❑ 8094 [M]	The Ray Charles Story, Volume 4	1964	5.00	10.00	20.00
❑ SD 8094 [S]	The Ray Charles Story, Volume 4	1964	6.25	12.50	25.00
❑ SD 19142	True to Life	1977	3.00	6.00	12.00
❑ SD 19199	Love and Peace	1978	3.00	6.00	12.00
❑ SD 19251	Ain't It So	1979	3.00	6.00	12.00
❑ SD 19281	Brother Ray Is At It Again	1980	3.00	6.00	12.00
❑ 90464	The Genius After Hours	1986	2.50	5.00	10.00
—Reissue					
BARONET					
❑ B-111 [M]	The Artistry of Ray Charles	196?	3.00	6.00	12.00
❑ BS-111 [R]	The Artistry of Ray Charles	196?	2.50	5.00	10.00
❑ B-117 [M]	The Great Ray Charles	196?	3.00	6.00	12.00
❑ BS-117 [R]	The Great Ray Charles	196?	2.50	5.00	10.00
BLUESWAY					
❑ 6053	The Genius Live	1973	3.00	6.00	12.00
COLUMBIA					
❑ AS 1920 [DJ]	Friendship Radio Show	1984	5.00	10.00	20.00
❑ FC 38293	Wish You Were Here Tonight	1983	2.50	5.00	10.00
❑ PC 38293	Wish You Were Here Tonight	1985	2.00	4.00	8.00
—Budget-line reissue					
❑ FC 38990	Do I Ever Cross Your Mind	1984	2.50	5.00	10.00
❑ FC 39415	Friendship	1985	2.50	5.00	10.00
❑ FC 40125	The Spirit of Christmas	1985	2.50	5.00	10.00
❑ FC 40338	From the Pages of My Mind	1986	2.50	5.00	10.00
❑ FC 45062	Seven Spanish Angels and Other Hits (1982-1986)	1989	3.00	6.00	12.00
CORONET					
❑ CX-173 [M]	Ray Charles	196?	3.00	6.00	12.00
❑ CXS-173 [R]	Ray Charles	196?	2.50	5.00	10.00
CROSSOVER					
❑ 9000	Come Live with Me	1974	3.00	6.00	12.00
❑ 9005	Renaissance	1975	3.00	6.00	12.00
❑ 9007	My Kind of Jazz, Part 3	1976	3.00	6.00	12.00
DCC COMPACT CLASSICS					
❑ LPZ-2012	Greatest Country and Western Hits	1995	25.00	50.00	100.00
—Audiophile vinyl					
DUNHILL COMPACT CLASSICS					
❑ DZL-038	Genius + Soul = Jazz	1988	3.75	7.50	15.00
—Clear vinyl reissue					
EVEREST ARCHIVE OF FOLK & JAZZ					
❑ 244	Ray Charles	1970	3.00	6.00	12.00
❑ 292	Ray Charles, Vol. 2	197?	2.50	5.00	10.00
❑ 358	Rockin' with Ray	1979	2.50	5.00	10.00
HOLLYWOOD					
❑ 504 [M]	The Original Ray Charles	1959	37.50	75.00	150.00
❑ 505 [M]	The Fabuolus Ray Charles	1959	37.50	75.00	150.00
IMPULSE!					
❑ A-2 [M]	Genius + Soul = Jazz	1961	6.25	12.50	25.00
❑ AS-2 [S]	Genius + Soul = Jazz	1961	7.50	15.00	30.00
INTERMEDIA					
❑ QS-5013	Goin' Down Slow	198?	2.50	5.00	10.00
LONGINES SYMPHONETTE					
❑ 95647 [(5)]	The Greatest Hits of Ray Charles	1974	10.00	20.00	40.00
PAIR					
❑ PDL2-1139 [(2)]	The Real Ray Charles	1986	3.00	6.00	12.00
PREMIER					
❑ PM 2004 [M]	The Great Ray Charles	196?	3.00	6.00	12.00
❑ PS 2004 [R]	The Great Ray Charles	196?	2.50	5.00	10.00
❑ PS-6001 [R]	Fantastic Ray Charles	196?	2.50	5.00	10.00
RHINO					
❑ R1-70097	Greatest Hits, Volume 1	1988	2.50	5.00	10.00
❑ R1-70098	Greatest Hits, Volume 2	1988	2.50	5.00	10.00
❑ R1-70099	Modern Sounds in Country and Western Music	1988	2.50	5.00	10.00

Number	Title (A Side/B Side)	Yr	VG	VG+	NM
TANGERINE					
❑ 1512	My Kind of Jazz	1970	3.00	6.00	12.00
❑ 1516	My Kind of Jazz No. II	1973	3.00	6.00	12.00
WARNER BROS.					
❑ 26343	Would You Believe?	1990	3.75	7.50	15.00

CHARLES, RAY / HARRY BELAFONTE Also see each artist's individual listings.
Albums

Number	Title (A Side/B Side)	Yr	VG	VG+	NM
CORONET					
❑ CX-203 [M]	The Greatest Ever	196?	3.00	6.00	12.00
❑ CXS-203 [R]	The Greatest Ever	196?	2.50	5.00	10.00

CHARLES, RAY, AND BETTY CARTER
45s

Number	Title (A Side/B Side)	Yr	VG	VG+	NM
ABC-PARAMOUNT					
❑ 10298	Baby It's Cold Outside/We'll Be Together Again	1962	2.50	5.00	10.00
Albums					
ABC					
❑ S-385 [S]	Ray Charles and Betty Carter	1967	5.00	10.00	20.00
—Reissue of ABC-Paramount ABCS-385					
ABC-PARAMOUNT					
❑ ABC-385 [M]	Ray Charles and Betty Carter	1961	10.00	20.00	40.00
❑ ABCS-385 [S]	Ray Charles and Betty Carter	1961	15.00	30.00	60.00
DCC COMPACT CLASSICS					
❑ LPZ-2005	Ray Charles and Betty Carter	1995	37.50	75.00	150.00
—Audiophile vinyl					
DUNHILL COMPACT CLASSICS					
❑ DZL-039	Ray Charles and Betty Carter	1988	3.75	7.50	15.00
—Clear vinyl reissue					

CHARLES, RAY/IVORY JOE HUNTER/JIMMY RUSHING Also see RAY CHARLES; IVORY JOE HUNTER.
Albums

Number	Title (A Side/B Side)	Yr	VG	VG+	NM
DESIGN					
❑ DLP-909 [M]	Three of a Kind	196?	3.00	6.00	12.00
❑ DLS-909 [R]	Three of a Kind	196?	2.50	5.00	10.00

CHARLES, RAY, AND MILT JACKSON
7-Inch Extended Plays

Number	Title (A Side/B Side)	Yr	VG	VG+	NM
ATLANTIC					
❑ 614	Blue Funk/Cosmic Ray	1958	17.50	35.00	70.00
❑ 614 [PS]	Soul Brothers	1958	17.50	35.00	70.00
Albums					
ATLANTIC					
❑ 1279 [M]	Soul Brothers	1958	12.50	25.00	50.00
—Black label					
❑ 1279 [M]	Soul Brothers	1960	6.25	12.50	25.00
—Red and white label, white fan logo on right					
❑ 1279 [M]	Soul Brothers	1962	5.00	10.00	20.00
—Red and white label, black fan logo on right					
❑ SD 1279 [S]	Soul Brothers	1959	12.50	25.00	50.00
—Green label					
❑ SD 1279 [S]	Soul Brothers	1960	6.25	12.50	25.00
—Blue and green label, white fan logo on right					
❑ SD 1279 [S]	Soul Brothers	1962	5.00	10.00	20.00
—Blue and green label, black fan logo on right					
❑ 1360 [M]	Soul Meeting	1961	6.25	12.50	25.00
—Red and white label, white fan logo on right					
❑ 1360 [M]	Soul Meeting	1962	5.00	10.00	20.00
—Red and white label, black fan logo on right					
❑ SD 1360 [S]	Soul Meeting	1961	7.50	15.00	30.00
—Blue and green label, white fan logo on right					
❑ SD 1360 [S]	Soul Meeting	1962	6.25	12.50	25.00
—Blue and green label, black fan logo on right					

CHARLES, RAY, AND CLEO LAINE
Albums

Number	Title (A Side/B Side)	Yr	VG	VG+	NM
RCA VICTOR					
❑ CPL2-1831 [(2)]	Porgy & Bess	1976	3.75	7.50	15.00
❑ DJL1-2163	Porgy & Bess	1976	5.00	10.00	20.00
—Promo-only excerpts from 2-record set					

CHARLES, RAY, SINGERS No relation to the above Ray Charles.
45s

Number	Title (A Side/B Side)	Yr	VG	VG+	NM
COMMAND					
❑ SE# 41SD [S]	Misty/East of the Sun	196?	2.00	4.00	8.00
—Jukebox issue; small hole, plays at 33 1/3 rpm					
❑ 4046	Love Me with All Your Heart/Sweet Little Mountain Bird	1964	—	3.00	6.00
—With the Ray Charles Singers receiving a more "apt" credit					
❑ 4046	Love Me with All Your Heart/Sweet Little Mountain Bird	1964	2.50	5.00	10.00
—The LP title "Something Special for Young Lovers" is in bold, with "The Ray Charles Singers" in tiny print at bottom					
❑ 4049	Al Di La/Till the End of Time	1964	—	3.00	6.00
❑ 4057	One More Time/Bluesette	1964	—	3.00	6.00
❑ 4059	This Is My Prayer/A Toy for a Boy	1965	—	3.00	6.00
❑ 4070	Hey, Pretty Pussycat/The Nut Song	1965	—	3.00	6.00
❑ 4073	My Love, Forgive Me/My Guitar and My Song	1965	—	3.00	6.00
❑ 4074	Christmas Is a Birthday/A Toy for a Boy	1965	2.50	5.00	10.00
❑ 4079	One of Those Songs/To You	1966	—	2.50	5.00
❑ 4082	Blue Roses/My World (Il Mondo)	1966	—	2.50	5.00
❑ 4085	It's Time to Sing/Promises	1966	—	2.50	5.00
❑ 4086	Minneapolis/The Bells	1966	—	2.50	5.00
❑ 4090	Don't Cry/There's No Place Like Home	1967	—	2.50	5.00
❑ 4092	Birds of a Feather/Step By Step	1967	—	2.50	5.00
❑ 4096	Bless Your Heart/Little By Little and Step By Step	1967	—	2.50	5.00
❑ 4103	Then You Can Tell Me Goodbye/Blame It on Me	1968	—	2.50	5.00
❑ 4105	Take Me Along/Walkin' Lonely	1968	—	2.50	5.00
❑ 4115	I Can See It Now/Quiz Me	1968	—	2.50	5.00
❑ 4123	I Wish I Knew How It Would Feel to Be Free/Let Go	1969	—	2.00	4.00
❑ 4130	Holly/Summer Warning	1969	—	2.00	4.00
❑ 4135	Move Me, O Wondrous Music/I'll Fly Away	1969	—	2.00	4.00
DECCA					
❑ 30834	Hip Hop/A Touch of Pink	1959	2.50	5.00	10.00
MGM					
❑ 12068	Autumn Leaves/Early Autumn	1955	2.50	5.00	10.00
❑ 12108	Autumn in New York/Autumn in Rome	1955	2.50	5.00	10.00

C

Number	Title (A Side/B Side)	Yr	VG	VG+	NM
❑ 12217	Spring Is Here/Spring! Spring! Spring!	1956	2.50	5.00	10.00
❑ 12274	June Night/When the Red, Red Robin Comes Bob, Bob, Bobbin' Along	1956	2.50	5.00	10.00
❑ 12333	September in the Rain/'Tis Autumn	1956	2.50	5.00	10.00
❑ 12363	Moonlight in Vermont/Button Up Your Overcoat	1956	2.50	5.00	10.00
❑ 12413	I've Got My Love to Keep Me Warm/When Winter Comes	1957	2.50	5.00	10.00
❑ 12445	Mam'selle/Madamoiselle de Paris	1957	2.50	5.00	10.00
❑ 12470	When It's Springtime in the Rockies/Lovelier Than Ever	1957	2.50	5.00	10.00
❑ 12507	Around the World/Take a Trip to Memory Lane	1957	2.50	5.00	10.00
❑ 12524	Lazy Afternoon/Mountain Greenery	1957	2.50	5.00	10.00
❑ 12563	The Things We Did Last Summer/Shine On Harvest Moon	1957	2.50	5.00	10.00
❑ 12606	Let It Snow, Let It Snow, Let It Snow/You're My Girl	1957	3.00	6.00	12.00

7-Inch Extended Plays

MGM

Number	Title (A Side/B Side)	Yr	VG	VG+	NM
❑ X-1503	Here's to My Lady/You Must Have Been a Beautiful Baby//The Very Thought of You/You're Getting to Be a Habit with Me	1957	2.50	5.00	10.00
❑ X-1503 [PS]	Here's to My Lady, Vol. 1	1957	2.50	5.00	10.00

Albums

ABC

Number	Title (A Side/B Side)	Yr	VG	VG+	NM
❑ X-772	Moods of Love	1973	2.50	5.00	10.00

ATCO

| ❑ SD 33-263 | Memories of a Middle-Aged Movie Fan | 1970 | 2.50 | 5.00 | 10.00 |

COMMAND

❑ 33-827 [M]	Something Wonderful	1961	2.50	5.00	10.00
❑ SD 827 [S]	Something Wonderful	1961	3.00	6.00	12.00
❑ 33-839 [M]	Rome Revisited	1962	2.50	5.00	10.00
❑ SD 839 [S]	Rome Revisited	1962	3.00	6.00	12.00
❑ 33-845 [M]	Paradise Islands	1962	2.50	5.00	10.00
❑ SD 845 [S]	Paradise Islands	1962	3.00	6.00	12.00
❑ 33-866 [M]	Something Special for Young Lovers	1964	2.50	5.00	10.00
❑ SD 866 [S]	Something Special for Young Lovers	1964	3.00	6.00	12.00
❑ 33-870 [M]	Al-Di-La and Other Extra Special Songs for Young Lovers	1964	2.50	5.00	10.00
❑ SD 870 [S]	Al-Di-La and Other Extra Special Songs for Young Lovers	1964	3.00	6.00	12.00
❑ 33-874 [M]	Songs for Lonesome Lovers	1964	2.50	5.00	10.00
❑ SD 874 [S]	Songs for Lonesome Lovers	1964	3.00	6.00	12.00
❑ 33-876 [M]	Command Performances	1965	2.50	5.00	10.00
❑ SD 876 [S]	Command Performances	1965	3.00	6.00	12.00
❑ 33-886 [M]	Songs for Latin Lovers	1965	2.50	5.00	10.00
❑ SD 886 [S]	Songs for Latin Lovers	1965	3.00	6.00	12.00
❑ 33-890 [M]	Young Lovers on Broadway	1965	2.50	5.00	10.00
❑ SD 890 [S]	Young Lovers on Broadway	1965	3.00	6.00	12.00
❑ 33-896 [M]	Command Performances Vol. 2	1966	2.50	5.00	10.00
❑ SD 896 [S]	Command Performances Vol. 2	1966	3.00	6.00	12.00
❑ 33-898 [M]	One of Those Songs	1966	2.50	5.00	10.00
❑ SD 898 [S]	One of Those Songs	1966	3.00	6.00	12.00
❑ 33-903 [M]	What the World Needs Now Is Love	1966	2.50	5.00	10.00
❑ SD 903 [S]	What the World Needs Now Is Love	1966	3.00	6.00	12.00
❑ 33-914 [M]	Special Something	1967	3.00	6.00	12.00
❑ SD 914 [S]	Special Something	1967	2.50	5.00	10.00
❑ SD 923	At the Movies	1968	2.50	5.00	10.00
❑ SD 926	Take Me Along	1968	2.50	5.00	10.00
❑ SD 936	MacArthur Park	1969	2.50	5.00	10.00
❑ SD 949	Move Me, O Wondrous Music	1969	2.50	5.00	10.00
❑ CQ-40005 [Q]	Love Me with All of Your Heart	1972	3.75	7.50	15.00

DECCA

❑ DL 8787 [M]	Highest Fidelity — Love and Marriage	1958	3.00	6.00	12.00
❑ DL 8838 [M]	Sunrise Serenade	1958	3.00	6.00	12.00
❑ DL 8874 [M]	In the Evening by the Moonlight	1959	3.00	6.00	12.00
❑ DL 8940 [M]	We Gather Together — Beloved Hymns	1959	3.00	6.00	12.00
❑ DL 8988 [M]	Deep Night	1960	3.00	6.00	12.00
❑ DL 78787 [S]	Highest Fidelity — Love and Marriage	1958	3.75	7.50	15.00
❑ DL 78838 [S]	Sunrise Serenade	1958	3.75	7.50	15.00
❑ DL 78874 [S]	In the Evening by the Moonlight	1959	3.75	7.50	15.00
❑ DL 78940 [S]	We Gather Together — Beloved Hymns	1959	3.75	7.50	15.00
❑ DL 78988 [S]	Deep Night	1960	3.75	7.50	15.00

MCA

| ❑ 4162 [(2)] | The Best of the Ray Charles Singers | 1980 | 2.50 | 5.00 | 10.00 |

METRO

| ❑ M-507 [M] | Spring, Spring, Spring | 1965 | 2.50 | 5.00 | 10.00 |
| ❑ MS-507 [S] | Spring, Spring, Spring | 1965 | 2.50 | 5.00 | 10.00 |

MGM

❑ E-3387 [M]	Winter Wonderland	1956	3.75	7.50	15.00
—Yellow label					
❑ E-3387 [M]	Winter Wonderland	1960	3.00	6.00	12.00
—Black label					
❑ E-3568 [M]	Here's to My Lady	1957	3.75	7.50	15.00
—Yellow label					
❑ E-3568 [M]	Here's to My Lady	1960	3.00	6.00	12.00
—Black label					
❑ E-4163 [M]	Autumn Moods	1963	3.00	6.00	12.00
❑ SE-4163 [S]	Autumn Moods	1963	3.00	6.00	12.00
❑ E-4164 [M]	Songs for a Lazy Summer Afternoon	1963	3.00	6.00	12.00
❑ SE-4164 [S]	Songs for a Lazy Summer Afternoon	1963	3.00	6.00	12.00
❑ E-4165 [M]	We Love Paris	1963	3.00	6.00	12.00
❑ SE-4165 [S]	We Love Paris	1963	3.00	6.00	12.00
❑ E-4166 [M]	Christmas at Home	1963	3.00	6.00	12.00
❑ SE-4166 [S]	Christmas at Home	1963	3.00	6.00	12.00
❑ E-4257 [M]	The Very Best of the Ray Charles Singers	1964	3.00	6.00	12.00
❑ SE-4257 [S]	The Very Best of the Ray Charles Singers	1964	3.00	6.00	12.00

SOMERSET

❑ P-21400 [M]	Quiet Moments for Young Lovers	196?	2.50	5.00	10.00
❑ SF-21400 [S]	Quiet Moments for Young Lovers	196?	2.50	5.00	10.00
❑ P-21500 [M]	Young Lovers in Far Away Places	196?	2.50	5.00	10.00
❑ SF-21500 [S]	Young Lovers in Far Away Places	196?	2.50	5.00	10.00

VOCALION

| ❑ VL 3784 [M] | Love Is a Many-Splendored Thing | 196? | 2.50 | 5.00 | 10.00 |
| ❑ VL 73784 [S] | Love Is a Many-Splendored Thing | 196? | 2.50 | 5.00 | 10.00 |

CHARLES, SONNY   Also see THE CHECKMATES LTD.

45s

FRATERNITY

Number	Title (A Side/B Side)	Yr	VG	VG+	NM
❑ 935	Speechless/These Two Feet	1964	4.00	8.00	12.00

HIGHRISE

| ❑ 2001 | Put It in a Magazine/The Week-End Father Song | 1982 | — | 2.50 | 5.00 |
| ❑ 2006 | Always on My Mind/One-Eyed Jacks | 1983 | — | 2.50 | 5.00 |

RCA VICTOR

| ❑ 74-0645 | It's Alright in the City/Nicasio | 1972 | — | 3.00 | 6.00 |

Albums

HIGHRISE

| ❑ HR-102 | The Sun Still Shines | 1982 | 3.00 | 6.00 | 12.00 |

CHARLES AND CARL

45s

RED ROBIN

| ❑ 137 | Lucky Star/One More Chance | 1955 | 25.00 | 50.00 | 100.00 |

CHARLES RIVER VALLEY BOYS, THE

Albums

ELEKTRA

| ❑ EKL-4006 [M] | Beatle Country | 1967 | 5.00 | 10.00 | 20.00 |
| ❑ EKS-74006 [S] | Beatle Country | 1967 | 6.25 | 12.50 | 25.00 |

CHARLETTES, THE

45s

ANGIE

| ❑ 1002 | The Fight's Not Over/Whatever Happened to Our Love | 1963 | 6.25 | 12.50 | 25.00 |

CHARMAINES, THE

45s

DOT

| ❑ 16351 | Where Is the Boy Tonight/On the Wagon | 1961 | 5.00 | 10.00 | 20.00 |

CHARMERS, THE (1)   Female group.

45s

ALADDIN

| ❑ 3337 | All Alone/Johnny My Dear | 1956 | 15.00 | 30.00 | 60.00 |
| ❑ 3341 | He's Gone/Oh! Yes | 1956 | 15.00 | 30.00 | 60.00 |

IMPERIAL

| ❑ 5957 | All Alone/Johnny My Dear | 1963 | 3.00 | 6.00 | 12.00 |
| —Reissue of Aladdin 3337 | | | | | |

CHARMERS, THE (2)   Another female group, not the same as group (1).

45s

CENTRAL

| ❑ 1002 | The Beating of My Heart/Why Does It Have to Be Me | 1954 | 200.00 | 400.00 | 800.00 |
| ❑ 1006 | Tony, My Darling/In the Rain | 1954 | 250.00 | 500.00 | 1000. |

LOST-NITE

❑ 141	Tony, My Darling/In the Rain	196?	2.00	4.00	8.00
—Reissue					
❑ 142	The Beating of My Heart/Why Does It Have to Be Me	1954	2.00	4.00	8.00
—Reissue					

TIMELY

| ❑ 1009 | I Was Wrong/The Mambo | 1955 | 250.00 | 500.00 | 1000. |
| ❑ 1011 | The Church on the Hill/Battle Axe | 1955 | 250.00 | 500.00 | 1000. |

CHARMERS, THE (U)   Probably none of these are group (1) or (2), but which ones go together, we don't yet know.

45s

CO-REC

| ❑ 101 | The Letter/Watch What You Do | 1963 | 5.00 | 10.00 | 20.00 |

JAF

| ❑ 2021 | Little Fool/Hard to Get | 1961 | 6.25 | 12.50 | 25.00 |

LAURIE

❑ 3142	My Kind of Love/Johnny	1962	5.00	10.00	20.00
❑ 3173	Shy Guy/I Cried	1963	5.00	10.00	20.00
❑ 3203	Work It Out/Sweet Talk	1963	5.00	10.00	20.00

LOUIS

| ❑ 6806 | It's a Funny Way We Met/Where's the Boy | 1965 | 3.00 | 6.00 | 12.00 |

PIP

| ❑ 8000 | Looking for Trouble/After You Walk Me Home | 1964 | 3.00 | 6.00 | 12.00 |

SILHOUETTE

| ❑ 522 | Rock, Rhythm and Blues/Letters Don't Have Arms | 1957 | 15.00 | 30.00 | 60.00 |

SURE SHOT

| ❑ 104 | Lessons from the Stars/My Love | 1963 | 75.00 | 150.00 | 300.00 |

TERRACE

| ❑ 7512 | Visiting Day/Whatever Happened to Baby Jane | 1962 | 6.25 | 12.50 | 25.00 |

CHARMETTES, THE

45s

FEDERAL

| ❑ 12345 | Johnny, Johnny/School Letter | 1959 | 10.00 | 20.00 | 40.00 |

HI

| ❑ 2003 | My Love with All My Heart/Skating in Blue Light | 1958 | 5.00 | 10.00 | 20.00 |

KAPP

| ❑ 547 | Please Don't Kiss Me Again/What Is a Tear | 1963 | 7.50 | 15.00 | 30.00 |
| ❑ 570 | Oozi-Oozi-Ooh/He's a Wise Guy | 1964 | 6.25 | 12.50 | 25.00 |

MALA

| ❑ 491 | My Lover Is a Boy Scout/Mailbox | 1964 | 3.00 | 6.00 | 12.00 |

TRI-DISC

| ❑ 103 | Why Oh Why/On a Night Like Tonight | 1962 | 6.25 | 12.50 | 25.00 |

WORLD ARTISTS

| ❑ 1053 | Stop the Wedding (Preacher Man)/Sugar Boy | 1965 | 6.25 | 12.50 | 25.00 |

CHARMS, THE   Also see OTIS WILLIAMS AND THE CHARMS.

45s

CHART

❑ 608	Love's Our Inspiration/Love, Love Stick Stov	1956	10.00	20.00	40.00
❑ 613	Heart of a Rose/I Offer You	1956	10.00	20.00	40.00
❑ 623	I'll Be True/Boom Diddy Boom Boom	1956	10.00	20.00	40.00

DELUXE

| ❑ 6000 | Heaven Only Knows/Loving Baby | 1953 | 125.00 | 250.00 | 500.00 |
| ❑ 6014 | Happy Are We/What Do You Know About That | 1953 | 100.00 | 200.00 | 400.00 |

Number	Title (A Side/B Side)	Yr	VG	VG+	NM
❑ 6034	Bye Bye Baby/Please Believe in Me	1954	100.00	200.00	400.00
❑ 6050	Quiet Please/55 Seconds	1954	100.00	200.00	400.00
❑ 6056	Come to Me Baby/My Baby, Dearest Darling	1954	50.00	100.00	200.00
❑ 6062	Hearts of Stone/Who Knows	1954	12.50	25.00	50.00
❑ 6065	Two Hearts/The First Time We Met	1954	12.50	25.00	50.00
❑ 6072	Crazy, Crazy Love/Mambo Sh-Mambo	1955	12.50	25.00	50.00
❑ 6076	Ling, Ting, Tong/Bazoom (I Need Your Lovin')	1955	12.50	25.00	50.00
❑ 6080	Ko Ko Mo (I Love You So)/Whadya Want?	1955	12.50	25.00	50.00
❑ 6082	Whadya Want?/Crazy, Crazy Love	1955	10.00	20.00	40.00
❑ 6087	When We Get Married/Let the Happenings Happen	1955	10.00	20.00	40.00
❑ 6089	One Fine Day/It's You, You, You	1955	10.00	20.00	40.00

ROCKIN'

| ❑ 516 | Heaven Only Knows/Loving Baby | 1953 | 200.00 | 400.00 | 800.00 |

7-Inch Extended Plays

DELUXE

| ❑ EP-357 | *Hearts of Stone/Bazoom (I Need Your Lovin')/Ling Ting Tong/Crazy, Crazy Love | 1955 | 100.00 | 200.00 | 400.00 |
| ❑ EP-357 [PS] | Hits by the Charms | 1955 | 100.00 | 200.00 | 400.00 |

CHARTERS, THE May all be the same group.
45s

ALVA

| ❑ 1001 | I Lost You/My Little Girl | 1963 | 75.00 | 150.00 | 300.00 |

MEL-O-DY

| ❑ 104 | Trouble Lover/Show Me Some Sign | 1962 | 500.00 | 1000. | 2000. |

MERRY-GO-ROUND

| ❑ 103 | Lost in a Dream/This Makes Me Mad | 1963 | 15.00 | 30.00 | 60.00 |

TARX

| ❑ 1003 | My Rose/El Merengue | 1962 | 25.00 | 50.00 | 100.00 |

CHARTS, THE
45s

EVERLAST

❑ 5001	Deserie/Zoop	1957	20.00	40.00	80.00
❑ 5002	Dance Girl/Why Do You Cry	1957	20.00	40.00	80.00
❑ 5006	You're the Reason (I'm in Love)/I've Been Wondering	1958	15.00	30.00	60.00
❑ 5008	I Told You So/All Because of Love	1958	15.00	30.00	60.00
❑ 5010	My Diane/All Because of You	1958	17.50	35.00	70.00
❑ 5026	Deserie/Zoop	1963	6.25	12.50	25.00

GUYDEN

| ❑ 2021 | For the Birds/Ooba-Gooba | 1959 | 5.00 | 10.00 | 20.00 |

LANA

| ❑ 117 | Deserie/I Wanna Take You Home | 196? | 2.00 | 4.00 | 8.00 |

LOST-NITE

❑ 173	Deserie/Zoop	196?	—	3.00	6.00
—Reissue					
❑ 180	Dance Girl/Why Do You Cry	196?	—	3.00	6.00
—Reissue					
❑ 186	You're the Reason (I'm in Love)/I've Been Wondering	196?	—	3.00	6.00
—Reissue					
❑ 377	My Diane/Baby Be Mine	197?	—	2.50	5.00
—Reissue					
❑ 381	I Told You So/All Because of Love	197?	—	2.50	5.00
—Reissue					

WAND

| ❑ 1112 | Deserie/Fell in Love with Your Baby | 1966 | 6.25 | 12.50 | 25.00 |
| ❑ 1124 | Livin' the Night Life/Nobody Made You Love Me | 1966 | 15.00 | 30.00 | 60.00 |

Albums

COLLECTABLES

| ❑ COL-5029 | Greatest Hits | 1986 | 3.00 | 6.00 | 12.00 |

LOST-NITE

| ❑ LLP-10 [10] | The Charts | 1981 | 3.00 | 6.00 | 12.00 |
| —Red vinyl | | | | | |

CHASE
45s

EPIC

❑ 5-10738	Get It On/River	1971	—	2.50	5.00
❑ 5-10775	Handbags and Gladrags/Open Up Wide	1971	—	2.00	4.00
❑ 5-10806	So Many People/Paint It Sad	1971	—	2.00	4.00
❑ 5-10853	I Can Feel It/Cronus (Saturn)	1972	—	2.00	4.00
❑ 5-11113	Run Back to Mama/Weird Song Number 1	1974	—	2.00	4.00
❑ 8-50027	Love Is on the Way/Bochawa	1974	—	2.00	4.00

Albums

EPIC

❑ E 30472	Chase	1971	3.00	6.00	12.00
❑ EQ 30472 [Q]	Chase	1973	5.00	10.00	20.00
❑ KE 31097	Ennea	1972	3.00	6.00	12.00
❑ EQ 32572 [Q]	Pure Music	1974	5.00	10.00	20.00
❑ KE 32572	Pure Music	1974	3.00	6.00	12.00
❑ EG 33737 [(2)]	Chase/Ennea	1976	3.75	7.50	15.00

CHAVELLES, THE
45s

VITA

| ❑ 127 | Valley of Love/Red Tape | 1956 | 37.50 | 75.00 | 150.00 |

CHAVIS BROTHERS, THE
45s

ASCOT

| ❑ 2177 | Torture Me/Humpty Dumpty Time | 1965 | 3.00 | 6.00 | 12.00 |

CLOCK

| ❑ 1025 | I Love You/So Tired | 1960 | 6.25 | 12.50 | 25.00 |

CORAL

| ❑ 62270 | Old Time Rock and Roll/Baby, Don't Leave Me | 1961 | 7.50 | 15.00 | 30.00 |
| —As "The Five Chavis Brothers" | | | | | |

PARKWAY

| ❑ 851 | Slippin' and Slidin'/Good Old Mountain Dew | 1962 | 3.75 | 7.50 | 15.00 |

CHECKER, CHUBBY Also see BOBBY RYDELL; DEE DEE SHARP.
12-Inch Singles

AMHERST

| ❑ AMH-D-4 | The Rub (5:02)/Move It (4:45) | 1976 | 5.00 | 10.00 | 20.00 |

Number	Title (A Side/B Side)	Yr	VG	VG+	NM
SEA BRIGHT					
❑ 7128	Read You Like a Book (Extended Version) (Radio Version)	1986	2.00	4.00	8.00

45s

ABKCO

❑ 4001	The Twist/Loddy Lo	1972	—	2.50	5.00
❑ 4002	The Hucklebuck/Pony Time	1972	—	2.50	5.00
❑ 4003	Limbo Rock/Let's Twist Again	1972	—	2.50	5.00
❑ 4004	Hey Bobba Needle/Hooka Tooka	1972	—	2.50	5.00
❑ 4027	Slow Twistin'/Birdland	1973	—	2.50	5.00

AMHERST

| ❑ 716 | The Rub/Move It | 1976 | — | 2.00 | 4.00 |

BUDDAH

| ❑ 100 | Back in the U.S.S.R./Windy Cream | 1969 | 3.00 | 6.00 | 12.00 |

MCA

❑ 51233	Running/Is Tonight the Night	1982	—	2.50	5.00
❑ 52015	Running/Is Tonight the Night	1982	—	2.00	4.00
❑ 52043	Harder Than Diamond/Your Love	1982	—	2.00	4.00

PARKWAY

❑ 003 [DJ]	Never on Sunday/Alouette	1962	10.00	20.00	40.00
—Yellow label, black print, promo only					
❑ 004 [DJ]	Love Is Like a Twist/Peppermint Twist	1962	10.00	20.00	40.00
—Yellow label, black print, promo only					
❑ 005 [DJ]	Your Lips and Mine/Dear Lady Twist	1962	10.00	20.00	40.00
—Yellow label, black print, promo only					
❑ 006 [DJ]	The Jet/The Ray Charles-ton	1962	7.50	15.00	30.00
❑ 105	You Got the Power/Looking at Tomorrow	1966	3.75	7.50	15.00
❑ 112	Karate Monkey/Her Heart	1966	3.75	7.50	15.00
❑ 804	The Class/Schooldays, Oh Schooldays	1959	7.50	15.00	30.00
❑ 808	Samson and Delilah/Whole Lotta Laughin'	1959	6.25	12.50	25.00
❑ 810	Dancing Dinosaur/Those Private Eyes (Keep Watchin' Me)	1960	6.25	12.50	25.00
—The existence of both 808 and 810 has been confirmed					
❑ 811	The Twist/Toot	1960	5.00	10.00	20.00
—Second pressings have orange label with black print					
❑ 811	The Twist/Toot	1960	7.50	15.00	30.00
—First pressings have white label with blue print					
❑ 811	The Twist/Twistin' U.S.A.	1961	3.75	7.50	15.00
❑ 811 [DJ]	The Twist/Twistin' U.S.A.	1961	37.50	75.00	150.00
—Promo copy on yellow vinyl					
❑ 811 [DJ]	The Twist/Twistin' U.S.A.	1961	50.00	100.00	200.00
—Promo copy on red vinyl					
❑ 811 [PS]	The Twist/Twistin' U.S.A.	1961	6.25	12.50	25.00
❑ 813	The Hucklebuck/Whole Lotta Shakin' Goin' On	1960	3.75	7.50	15.00
❑ 818	Pony Time/Oh, Susannah	1960	3.75	7.50	15.00
❑ 822	Dance the Mess Around/Good, Good Lovin'	1961	3.75	7.50	15.00
❑ 824	Let's Twist Again/Everything's Gonna Be Alright	1961	3.75	7.50	15.00
❑ 824	Let's Twist Again/Everything's Gonna Be Alright	1961	50.00	100.00	200.00
—Orange vinyl					
❑ 824 [PS]	Let's Twist Again/Everything's Gonna Be Alright	1961	6.25	12.50	25.00
❑ 830	The Fly/That's the Way It Goes	1961	3.75	7.50	15.00
❑ 830 [PS]	The Fly/That's the Way It Goes	1961	6.25	12.50	25.00
❑ 835	Slow Twistin'/La Paloma Twist	1962	3.75	7.50	15.00
—Features female vocal by Dee Dee Sharp					
❑ 835 [PS]	Slow Twistin'/La Paloma Twist	1962	6.25	12.50	25.00
❑ 842	Dancin' Party/Gotta Get Myself Together	1962	3.75	7.50	15.00
❑ 842 [PS]	Dancin' Party/Gotta Get Myself Together	1962	6.25	12.50	25.00
❑ 849	Limbo Rock/Popeye The Hitch-Hiker	1962	3.75	7.50	15.00
❑ 849 [PS]	Limbo Rock/Popeye The Hitch-Hiker	1962	6.25	12.50	25.00
❑ 862	Twenty Miles/Let's Limbo Some More	1963	3.75	7.50	15.00
❑ 862 [PS]	Twenty Miles/Let's Limbo Some More	1963	6.25	12.50	25.00
❑ 873	Birdland/Black Cloud	1963	3.75	7.50	15.00
❑ 873 [PS]	Birdland/Black Cloud	1963	6.25	12.50	25.00
❑ 879	Surf Party/Twist It Up	1963	3.75	7.50	15.00
❑ 879 [PS]	Surf Party/Twist It Up	1963	6.25	12.50	25.00
❑ 890	Loddy Lo/Hooka Tooka	1963	3.75	7.50	15.00
❑ 890	Loddy Lo/Everything's Gonna Be Alright	1963	4.00	8.00	16.00
❑ 890 [PS]	Loddy Lo/Hooka Tooka	1963	6.25	12.50	25.00
❑ 890 [PS]	Loddy Lo/Everything's Gonna Be Alright	1963	7.00	14.00	28.00
❑ 907	Hey Bobba Needle/Spread Joy	1964	3.75	7.50	15.00
❑ 907 [PS]	Hey Bobba Needle/Spread Joy	1964	6.25	12.50	25.00
❑ 920	Lazy Elsie Molly/Rosie	1964	3.75	7.50	15.00
❑ 920 [PS]	Lazy Elsie Molly/Rosie	1964	6.25	12.50	25.00
❑ 922	She Wants T'Swim/You Better Believe It, Baby	1964	3.00	6.00	12.00
❑ 922 [PS]	She Wants T'Swim/You Better Believe It, Baby	1964	6.25	12.50	25.00
❑ 936	Lovely, Lovely (Loverly, Loverly)/The Weekend's Here	1964	3.00	6.00	12.00
❑ 936 [PS]	Lovely, Lovely (Loverly, Loverly)/The Weekend's Here	1964	6.25	12.50	25.00
❑ 949	Let's Do the Freddie/(At the) Discotheque	1965	3.00	6.00	12.00
—Original A-side title (number is P-949-A) and probably correct B-side title					
❑ 949	Do the Freddie/(Do the) Discotheque	1965	5.00	10.00	20.00
—Reissue with new A-side title (number is P-949-C) and probably incorrect B-side title					
❑ 959	Everything's Wrong/Cu Me La Be-Stay	1965	3.00	6.00	12.00
❑ 965	You Just Don't Know/Two Hearts Make One Love	1965	100.00	200.00	400.00
❑ 989	Hey You! Little Boo-Ga-Loo/Pussy Cat	1966	3.00	6.00	12.00

SEA BRIGHT

| ❑ 5128 | Read You Like a Book/(B-side unknown) | 1986 | — | 2.00 | 4.00 |

TIN PAN APPLE

❑ 887571-7 [PS]	The Twist (Yo, Twist!)/(Buffapella)	1988	—	—	3.00
❑ 887571-7 [PS]	The Twist (Yo, Twist!)/(Buffapella)	1988	—	—	3.00
—"Stupid def vocals" on a Fat Boys record					

20TH CENTURY

| ❑ 2040 | Reggae My Way/Gypsy | 1973 | — | 2.50 | 5.00 |
| ❑ 2075 | She's a Bad Woman/Happiness Is a Girl Like You | 1974 | — | 2.50 | 5.00 |

7-Inch Extended Plays

PARKWAY

❑ 5001	The Ray Charles-ton/The Mess Around//The Jet/The Continental Walk	1961	15.00	30.00	60.00
—Small hole, plays at 33 1/3 rpm					
❑ 5001 [PS]	Chubby Checker	1961	15.00	30.00	60.00
—Paper die-cut sleeve					

Albums

ABKCO

| ❑ 4219 [(2)] | Chubby Checker's Greatest Hits | 1972 | 5.00 | 10.00 | 20.00 |

C

Number	Title (A Side/B Side)	Yr	VG	VG+	NM
EVEREST					
❏ 4111	Chubby Checker's Greatest Hits	1981	3.00	6.00	12.00
MCA					
❏ 5291	The Change Has Come	1982	2.50	5.00	10.00
PARKWAY					
❏ P 7001 [M]	Twist with Chubby Checker	1960	10.00	20.00	40.00
—All-orange label					
❏ P 7001 [M]	Twist with Chubby Checker	1962	7.50	15.00	30.00
—Orange and yellow label					
❏ P 7002 [M]	For Twisters Only	1960	10.00	20.00	40.00
—All-orange label					
❏ P 7002 [M]	For Twisters Only	1962	7.50	15.00	30.00
—Orange and yellow label					
❏ P 7003 [M]	It's Pony Time	1961	10.00	20.00	40.00
—All-orange label					
❏ P 7003 [M]	It's Pony Time	1962	7.50	15.00	30.00
—Orange and yellow label					
❏ P 7004 [M]	Let's Twist Again	1961	10.00	20.00	40.00
—All-orange label					
❏ P 7004 [M]	Let's Twist Again	1962	7.50	15.00	30.00
—Orange and yellow label					
❏ P 7007 [M]	Your Twist Party	1961	10.00	20.00	40.00
—All-orange label					
❏ P 7007 [M]	Your Twist Party	1962	7.50	15.00	30.00
—Orange and yellow label					
❏ P 7008 [M]	Twistin' Round the World	1962	7.50	15.00	30.00
❏ SP 7008 [B]	Twistin' Round the World	1962	10.00	20.00	40.00
❏ P 7009 [M]	For Teen Twisters Only	1962	7.50	15.00	30.00
❏ SP 7009 [S]	For Teen Twisters Only	1962	10.00	20.00	40.00
❏ P 7014 [M]	All the Hits (For Your Dancin' Party)	1962	7.50	15.00	30.00
❏ P 7020 [M]	Limbo Party	1962	7.50	15.00	30.00
❏ SP 7020 [S]	Limbo Party	1962	10.00	20.00	40.00
❏ P 7022 [M]	Chubby Checker's Biggest Hits	1962	7.50	15.00	30.00
❏ SP 7022 [R]	Chubby Checker's Biggest Hits	1962	7.50	15.00	30.00
❏ P 7026 [M]	Chubby Checker In Person	1963	7.50	15.00	30.00
❏ SP 7026 [S]	Chubby Checker In Person	1963	10.00	20.00	40.00
—The above record is labeled "Twist It Up"					
❏ P 7027 [M]	Let's Limbo Some More	1963	7.50	15.00	30.00
❏ SP 7027 [S]	Let's Limbo Some More	1963	10.00	20.00	40.00
❏ P 7030 [M]	Beach Party	1963	7.50	15.00	30.00
❏ SP 7030 [S]	Beach Party	1963	10.00	20.00	40.00
❏ P 7036 [M]	Chubby Checker With Sy Oliver and His Orchestra	1964	7.50	15.00	30.00
❏ SP 7036 [S]	Chubby Checker With Sy Oliver and His Orchestra	1964	10.00	20.00	40.00
❏ P 7040 [M]	Folk Album	1964	7.50	15.00	30.00
❏ SP 7040 [S]	Folk Album	1964	10.00	20.00	40.00
❏ P 7045 [M]	Discotheque	1965	7.50	15.00	30.00
❏ SP 7045 [S]	Discotheque	1965	10.00	20.00	40.00
❏ P 7048 [M]	Chubby Checker's Eighteen Golden Hits	1966	7.50	15.00	30.00
❏ SP 7048 [P]	Chubby Checker's Eighteen Golden Hits	1966	10.00	20.00	40.00

CHECKERLADS, THE
45s
RCA VICTOR

Number	Title (A Side/B Side)	Yr	VG	VG+	NM
❏ 47-8986	Shake Yourself Down/Baby Send for Me	1966	6.25	12.50	25.00

CHECKERS, THE (1)
45s
FEDERAL

Number	Title (A Side/B Side)	Yr	VG	VG+	NM
❏ 12355	So Fine/Sentimental Heart	1959	12.50	25.00	50.00
❏ 12375	White Cliffs of Dover/Let Me Come Back	1960	12.50	25.00	50.00
KING					
❏ 4558	Flame in My Heart/Oh, Oh, Oh Baby	1952	250.00	500.00	1000.
❏ 4581	Night's Curtains/Let Me Come Back	1952	250.00	500.00	1000.
❏ 4596	My Prayer Tonight/Love Wasn't There	1953	250.00	500.00	1000.
❏ 4626	Ghost of My Baby/I Wanna Know	1953	200.00	400.00	800.00
❏ 4673	I Promise You/You Never Had It So Good	1953	125.00	250.00	500.00
❏ 4675	White Cliffs of Dover/Without a Song	1953	125.00	250.00	500.00
❏ 4710	House with No Windows/Don't Stop Dan	1954	125.00	250.00	500.00
❏ 4719	Over the Rainbow/You've Been Fooling Around	1954	100.00	200.00	400.00
❏ 4751	I Wasn't Thinking, I Was Drinking/Mama's Daughter	1954	125.00	250.00	500.00
❏ 4764	Trying to Hold My Girl/Can't Find My Sadie	1955	125.00	250.00	500.00
❏ 5156	Heaven Only Knows/Nine More Miles	1958	100.00	200.00	400.00
❏ 5592	Over the Rainbow/Love Wasn't There	1962	5.00	10.00	20.00
—As "The Original Checkers"					

CHECKERS, THE (2) Different group than (1).
45s
ARVEE

Number	Title (A Side/B Side)	Yr	VG	VG+	NM
❏ 5035	Skooby Doo (Part 1)/Skooby Doo (Part 2)	1961	5.00	10.00	20.00
❏ 5037	Swingin' Summer/Skooby Doo	1961	5.00	10.00	20.00

CHECKERS, THE (3) Not the same group as (1) though on the same label. Also see THE FIVE WINGS.
45s
KING

Number	Title (A Side/B Side)	Yr	VG	VG+	NM
❏ 5199	Teardrops Are Falling/Rock-A-Locka	1959	15.00	30.00	60.00
—Originally released as King 4781 by The Five Wings					

CHECKERS, THE (U) Some of these may be the same group as (2), but not all of them.
45s
DOTTIE

Number	Title (A Side/B Side)	Yr	VG	VG+	NM
❏ 1001	Big Car/Buzz	196?	5.00	10.00	20.00
JERDEN					
❏ 710	Black Cat/Soft Blue	1963	5.00	10.00	20.00
MERCURY					
❏ 72354	Red Ball Express/Come Back Home	1964	3.00	6.00	12.00
SKYLA					
❏ 1120	Blue Saturday/Cascade	1961	5.00	10.00	20.00

CHECKMATES, THE
Albums
JUSTICE

Number	Title (A Side/B Side)	Yr	VG	VG+	NM
❏ JLP-149	The Checkmates	1966	100.00	200.00	400.00

CHECKMATES LTD., THE Also see SONNY CHARLES.
45s
A&M

Number	Title (A Side/B Side)	Yr	VG	VG+	NM
❏ 1006	Spanish Harlem/Baby Don't You Get Crazy	1968	2.00	4.00	8.00
❏ 1040	Love Is All I Have to Give/Never Should Have Lied	1969	2.00	4.00	8.00
❏ 1053	Black Pearl/Lazy Susan	1969	2.50	5.00	10.00
—As "Sonny Charles and the Checkmates Ltd."					
❏ 1127	Spanish Harlem/Proud Mary	1969	2.00	4.00	8.00
—As "Sonny Charles and the Checkmates Ltd."					
❏ 1130	Proud Mary/Do You Love Your Baby	1969	2.00	4.00	8.00
—As "Sonny Charles and the Checkmates Ltd."					
CAPITOL					
❏ 5603	Do the Walk/Glad for You	1966	5.00	10.00	20.00
❏ 5753	I Can Hear the Rain/Kissin' Her and Cryin' for You	1966	7.50	15.00	30.00
❏ 5814	Please Don't Take My World Away/Mastered the Art of Love	1966	5.00	10.00	20.00
❏ 5922	Walk in the Sunlight/A & I	1967	5.00	10.00	20.00
FANTASY					
❏ 800	Let's Do It/Take All the Time You Need	1977	—	2.50	5.00
❏ 823	Greedy for Your Love/That's How It Feels (When Two People Fall in Love)	1978	—	2.50	5.00
GREEDY					
❏ 111	I'm Laying My Heart on the Line/Make Love to Your Mind	1977	—	2.50	5.00
POLYDOR					
❏ 14313	All Alone by the Telephone/Body Language	1976	—	2.50	5.00
Albums					
A&M					
❏ SP-4183	Love Is All I Have to Give	1969	6.25	12.50	25.00
CAPITOL					
❏ ST 2840 [S]	Live at Caesar's Palace	1968	5.00	10.00	20.00
❏ T 2840 [M]	Live at Caesar's Palace	1968	7.50	15.00	30.00
FANTASY					
❏ 9541	We Got the Moves	1978	3.75	7.50	15.00

CHEECH AND CHONG
45s
MCA

Number	Title (A Side/B Side)	Yr	VG	VG+	NM
❏ 52655	Born in East L.A./I'm a (Modern) Man	1985	—	—	3.00
❏ 52655 [PS]	Born in East L.A./I'm a (Modern) Man	1985	—	2.00	4.00
❏ 52732	I'm Not Home Right Now/Hot Saki	1985	—	—	3.00
❏ 52732 [PS]	I'm Not Home Right Now/Hot Saki	1985	—	2.00	4.00
ODE					
❏ 50471	Bloat On (Featuring the Bloaters)/Just Say "Right On"	1977	—	2.00	4.00
❏ 50471 [PS]	Bloat On (Featuring the Bloaters)/Just Say "Right On"	1977	—	3.00	6.00
❏ 50499	Santa Claus and His Old Lady/Rudolph the Red-Nosed Reindeer	1977	2.50	5.00	10.00
❏ 66021	Santa Claus and His Old Lady/Dave	1971	2.00	4.00	8.00
❏ 66021 [PS]	Santa Claus and His Old Lady/Dave	1971	3.00	6.00	12.00
❏ 66038	Basketball Jones/Don't Bug Me	1973	—	2.50	5.00
❏ 66038 [PS]	Basketball Jones/Don't Bug Me	1973	—	3.00	6.00
❏ 66041	Sister Mary Elephant/Wink Dinkerson	1974	—	2.50	5.00
❏ 66041 [PS]	Sister Mary Elephant/Wink Dinkerson	1974	—	3.00	6.00
❏ 66049	Earache My Eye (Featuring Alice Bowie)/Turn That Thing Down	1974	—	—	—
—Unreleased?					
❏ 66102	Earache My Eye (Featuring Alice Bowie)/Turn That Thing Down	1974	—	2.00	4.00
❏ 66102 [PS]	Earache My Eye (Featuring Alice Bowie)/Turn That Thing Down	1974	—	3.00	6.00
❏ 66104	Black Lassie (Featuring Johnny Stash)/Coming Attractions	1974	—	2.00	4.00
❏ 66104 [PS]	Black Lassie (Featuring Johnny Stash)/Coming Attractions	1974	—	3.00	6.00
❏ 66115	How I Spent My Summer Vacation, Or A Day at the Beach with Pedro and Man (Part 1/Part 2)	1975	—	2.00	4.00
❏ 66124	Framed/Pedro's Request	1976	—	2.00	4.00
WARNER BROS.					
❏ 8666	Up in Smoke/Rock Fight	1978	—	2.50	5.00
❏ 8666 [PS]	Up in Smoke/Rock Fight	1978	2.50	5.00	10.00
Albums					
MCA					
❏ 5640	Get Out of My Room	1985	2.00	4.00	8.00
ODE					
❏ PE 34947	Cheech and Chong	1977	2.50	5.00	10.00
—Reissue of 77010					
❏ PE 34951	Los Cochinos	1977	2.50	5.00	10.00
—Reissue of 77019					
❏ PE 34954	Cheech and Chong's Wedding Album	1977	2.50	5.00	10.00
—Reissue of 77025					
❏ PE 34960	Sleeping Beauty	1977	2.50	5.00	10.00
—Reissue of 77040					
❏ SP-77010	Cheech and Chong	1971	3.00	6.00	12.00
❏ SP-77014	Big Bambu	1972	3.00	6.00	12.00
—Add 50% if rolling paper is still enclosed					
❏ SP-77019	Los Cochinos	1973	3.00	6.00	12.00
❏ SP-77025	Cheech and Chong's Wedding Album	1974	3.00	6.00	12.00
❏ SP-77040	Sleeping Beauty	1976	3.00	6.00	12.00
WARNER BROS.					
❏ BSK 3249	Up in Smoke	1978	2.50	5.00	10.00
❏ BSK 3250	Cheech and Chong	1978	2.00	4.00	8.00
❏ BSK 3251	Big Bambu	1978	2.00	4.00	8.00
❏ BSK 3252	Los Cochinos	1978	2.00	4.00	8.00
❏ BSK 3253	Cheech and Chong's Wedding Album	1978	2.00	4.00	8.00
❏ BSK 3254	Sleeping Beauty	1978	2.00	4.00	8.00
❏ HS 3391	Let's Make a New Dope Deal	1980	2.50	5.00	10.00
❏ BSK 3614	Cheech and Chong's Greatest Hit	1982	2.00	4.00	8.00

CHEERIOS, THE
45s
GOLDEN OLDIES

Number	Title (A Side/B Side)	Yr	VG	VG+	NM
❏ 1	Ding Dong Honeymoon/Where Are You Tonight	196?	5.00	10.00	20.00
INFINITY					
❏ 011	Ding Dong Honeymoon/Where Are You Tonight	1961	100.00	200.00	400.00

Number	Title (A Side/B Side)	Yr	VG	VG+	NM

CHEERS, THE 1970s game-show host Bert Convy was a member.
45s
CAPITOL

Number	Title (A Side/B Side)	Yr	VG	VG+	NM
❏ F2921	Bazoom (I Need Your Lovin')/Arrividerci	1954	6.25	12.50	25.00
❏ F2921	I Need Your Lovin' (Bazoom)/Arrividerci	1954	10.00	20.00	40.00
❏ F3019	Whadaya Want/Bernie's Tune	1955	6.25	12.50	25.00
❏ F3075	Can't We Be More Than Friends/Blueberries	1955	6.25	12.50	25.00
❏ F3146	I Must Be Dreaming/Fancy Meeting You Here	1955	6.25	12.50	25.00
❏ F3219	Black Denim Trousers and Motorcycle Boots/Some Night in Alaska	1955	6.25	12.50	25.00
❏ F3219	Black Denim Trousers/Some Night in Alaska	1955	6.25	12.50	25.00

—Shorter A-side title; we're not sure which came first

❏ F3353	The Chicken/Don't Do Anything	1956	5.00	10.00	20.00
❏ F3409	Heaven on Earth/Que Pasa Muchacha	1956	5.00	10.00	20.00

MERCURY

❏ 71083	Chug Chug Toot Toot/Big Feet	1957	3.75	7.50	15.00
❏ 71100	Two Hearts/You Never Have the Time	1957	3.75	7.50	15.00

—As "Bert Convy and the Cheers"
NRC

❏ 5003	Hold That Line/Blue Serenade	1958	3.75	7.50	15.00

CHEETAHS, THE
45s
PHILIPS

❏ 40239	Mecca/That Goodnight Kiss	1964	2.50	5.00	10.00

CHELLOWS, THE
45s
HIT

❏ 30	Sherry/Teenage Idol	1962	2.00	4.00	8.00

—As "The Four Chellows"; B-side by Barney Fox

❏ 37	Big Girls Don't Cry/Mama Sang a Song	1962	2.00	4.00	8.00

—B-side by Sandy Atkinson

❏ 51	Walk Like a Man/Send Me Some Lovin'	1963	2.00	4.00	8.00

—B-side by Leroy Jones

❏ 64	Ain't That a Shame/If You Wanna Be Happy	1963	2.00	4.00	8.00

—B-side by John Campbell

❏ 77	Candy Girl/Hello Muddah, Hello Faddah	1963	2.00	4.00	8.00

—B-side by Dick Martin

❏ 106	Dawn (Go Away)/She Loves You	1964	3.00	6.00	12.00

—B-side by the Bugs

❏ 111	Stay/Twist and Shout	1964	3.00	6.00	12.00

—B-side by the Bugs

❏ 115	Ronnie/Dead Man's Curve	1964	2.00	4.00	8.00

—B-side by the Roamers

❏ 134	Rag Doll/A Hard Day's Night	1964	2.00	4.00	8.00

—B-side by the Jalopy Five

❏ 160	Big Man in Town/We Build a 409	1964	3.00	6.00	12.00

—B-side by the Roamers

❏ 187	Bye Bye Baby/This Diamond Ring	1965	2.00	4.00	8.00
❏ 203	The Sun Will Still Shine/Don't Let Me Be Misunderstood	1965	2.50	5.00	10.00

—B-side by the Chords (2)

❏ 220	California Girls/Help!	1965	3.00	6.00	12.00

—B-side by the Jalopy Five

❏ 237	Barbara Ann/No Matter What Shape (Your Stomach's In)	1966	2.00	4.00	8.00

—B-side by the Upsetters

❏ 241	Working My Way Back to You/These Boots Are Made for Walking	1966	2.00	4.00	8.00

—B-side by Betty Richards

❏ 247	The Cheater/Sure Gonna Miss Her	1966	2.00	4.00	8.00

—B-side by Ed Hardin

❏ 248	Time Won't Let Me/Secret Agent Man	1966	2.00	4.00	8.00

—B-side by Marty Woods

❏ 252	Gloria/Monday, Monday	1966	3.00	6.00	12.00

—B-side by the Jalopy Five

❏ 262	Little Red Riding Hood/Wild Thing	1966	2.00	4.00	8.00

—B-side by the Jalopy Five

❏ 264	Bus Stop/Cherish	1966	2.00	4.00	8.00
❏ 270	Reach Out I'll Be There/Satisfied Mind	1966	2.00	4.00	8.00

—B-side by Leroy Jones

❏ 278	Nashville Cats/Georgy Girl	1967	2.00	4.00	8.00

—B-side by the Chords (2)

❏ 283	Ruby Tuesday/Then You Can Tell Me Goodbye	1967	2.00	4.00	8.00

—B-side by the Jalopy Five

❏ 284	There's a Kind of Hush/Happy Together	1967	2.00	4.00	8.00

—B-side by the Cadets (2)

❏ 288	Western Union/Get Me to the World on Time	1967	2.00	4.00	8.00
❏ 292	Him or Me — What's It Gonna Be?/Creeque Alley	1967	2.00	4.00	8.00

—B-side by the Chords (2)

❏ 295	Somebody to Love/Groovin'	1967	2.00	4.00	8.00

—B-side by the Jalopy Five

❏ 298	Little Bit o' Soul/I Take It Back	1967	2.00	4.00	8.00

—B-side by Kathy Shannon

❏ 305	Never My Love/Gimme Little Sign	1967	2.00	4.00	8.00

—B-side by Bergen Justice

❏ 308	Holiday/Incense and Peppermints	1967	2.00	4.00	8.00

—B-side by the Chords (2)

CHELSEA Future Kiss member Peter Criss (as "Peter Cris") played drums on this LP.
Albums
DECCA

❏ DL 75262	The Chelsea Album	1972	37.50	75.00	150.00

CHER Also see ALLMAN AND WOMAN; SONNY AND CHER.
12-Inch Singles
CASABLANCA

❏ NBD 20150 [DJ]	Take Me Home (7:30)/(B-side blank)	1979	6.25	12.50	25.00
❏ NBD 20168	Take Me Home (7:30)/Wasn't It Good (7:03)	1979	3.75	7.50	15.00
❏ NBD 20189 [DJ]	Hell on Wheels (Disco Remix 7:13)/Git Down (Guitar Groupie) (Disco Remix 7:14)	1979	6.25	12.50	25.00

GEFFEN

❏ PRO-A-3154 [DJ]	Skin Deep (Extended Dance Mix) (Dub) (Bonus Beats) (Percapella)	1987	2.50	5.00	10.00
❏ PRO-A-4295 [DJ]	Love and Understanding (unknown versions)	1991	2.00	4.00	8.00

❏ 20937	Skin Deep (Extended Dance Mix 7:48) (Dub 5:40) (Bonus Beats 3:40)/Perfection	1988	3.00	6.00	12.00
❏ 21657	Love and Understanding (5 versions)/Trail of Broken Hearts	1991	2.00	4.00	8.00
❏ 22230	The Shoop Shoop Song (It's In His Kiss) (4 versions)	1990	3.75	7.50	15.00

REPRISE

❏ PRO-A-8015 [DJ]	One by One (5 versions)	1995	3.00	6.00	12.00
❏ PRO-A-8375 [DJ]	Paradise Is Here (Sunrise Mix 6:50) (Padapella 8:20)/(Glow Stick Dub 8:30) (Tribal Beats 5:54)	1995	3.00	6.00	12.00
❏ PRO-A-8428 [DJ]	One by One (Junior's Pride Mix) (Bonus Beats) (Piano Dub)/Walking in Memphis (Shut Up and Dance Mix) (Rated PG Mix)	1996	2.50	5.00	10.00
❏ 43643	One by One (4 versions)/I Wouldn't Treat a Dog (The Way You Treated Me)	1996	2.50	5.00	10.00
❏ 43759 [(2)]	Paradise Is Here (Junior's Arena Anthem) (Glow Stick Mix) (Runway Mix) (Give Me the Night Dub)//(Padapella) (Glow Stick Dub) (Tribal Beats) (Sunrise Mix)	1996	3.75	7.50	15.00
❏ 43759-A [DJ]	Paradise Is Here (Junior's Arena Anthem 10:45) (Glow Stick Mix 8:33) (Runway Mix 8:32) (Give Me the Night Dub 8:35)	1996	3.00	6.00	12.00

—Promo version is only one record
WARNER BROS.

❏ PRO-A-4208 [(2)DJ]	All or Nothing (Danny Tenaglia Cherbot Vocadub)/(Danny Tenaglia International Mix)//(Danny Tenaglia Inchermental)/(Metro Radio Mix) (Cherbots)	1999	3.75	7.50	15.00
❏ PRO-A-9719 [(2)DJ]	Strong Enough (8 versions)	1999	3.75	7.50	15.00
❏ PRO-A-9926-A [(2)DJ]	All or Nothing (5 versions)	1999	3.75	7.50	15.00
❏ 44576 [(2)]	Believe (8 versions)	1998	3.00	6.00	12.00
❏ 44644 [(2)]	Strong Enough (8 versions)	1999	2.50	5.00	10.00
❏ 44774 [(2)]	All or Nothing (8 versions)	1999	2.50	5.00	10.00

45s
ANNETTE

❏ 1000	Ringo I Love You/Beatles Blues	1964	175.00	350.00	700.00

—As "Bonnie Jo Mason"; a Phil Spector production
ATCO

❏ 6658	Yours Until Tomorrow/Thought of Loving You	1969	—	3.00	6.00
❏ 6684	I Walk on Gilded Splinters/Chastity's Song	1969	—	3.00	6.00
❏ 6704	For What It's Worth/Hangin' On	1969	—	3.00	6.00
❏ 6713	You've Made Me So Very Happy/First Time	1969	—	3.00	6.00
❏ 6793	Superstar/First Time	1971	—	3.00	6.00
❏ 6868	Lay Baby Lay/(Just Enough to Keep Me) Hangin' On	1972	—	2.50	5.00

CASABLANCA

❏ 965	Take Me Home/My Song (Too Far Gone)	1979	—	2.00	4.00
❏ 987	Wasn't It Good/It's Too Late to Love Me Now	1979	—	2.00	4.00
❏ 2208	Hell on Wheels/Git Down (Guitar Groupie)	1979	—	2.00	4.00
❏ 2228	Holdin' Out for Love/Boys and Girls	1979	—	2.00	4.00

COLUMBIA

❏ 18-02850	Rudy/Do I Ever Cross Your Mind	1982	—	2.00	4.00
❏ 18-02850 [PS]	Rudy/Do I Ever Cross Your Mind	1982	—	2.50	5.00
❏ 18-03150	I Paralyze/Walk With Me	1982	—	2.00	4.00

GEFFEN

❏ 19023	Love and Understanding/Trail of Broken Hearts	1991	—	2.00	4.00
❏ 19105	Save Up All Your Tears/A World Without Heroes	1991	—	—	3.00
❏ 19659	The Shoop Shoop Song (It's In His Kiss)/Love on a Rooftop	1990	—	—	3.00
❏ 19953	Heart of Stone/All Because of You	1990	—	—	3.00
❏ 22844	Just Like Jesse James/Starting Over	1989	—	—	3.00
❏ 22886	If I Could Turn Back Time/Some Guys	1989	—	—	3.00
❏ 22886 [PS]	If I Could Turn Back Time/Some Guys	1989	—	2.50	5.00
❏ 27529	After All (Love Theme from "Chances Are")/Dangerous Times	1989	—	—	3.00

—A-side with Peter Cetera

❏ 27529 [PS]	After All (Love Theme from "Chances Are")/Dangerous Times	1989	—	2.50	5.00
❏ 27742	Main Man/(It's Been Hard Enough) Gettin' Over You	1988	—	—	3.00
❏ 27742 [PS]	Main Man/(It's Been Hard Enough) Gettin' Over You	1988	—	—	3.00
❏ 27894	Skin Deep/Perfection	1988	—	—	3.00
❏ 27894 [PS]	Skin Deep/Perfection	1988	—	—	3.00
❏ 27986	We All Sleep Alone/Working Girl	1988	—	—	3.00
❏ 27986 [PS]	We All Sleep Alone/Working Girl	1988	—	—	3.00
❏ 28191	I Found Someone/Dangerous Times	1987	—	—	3.00
❏ 28191 [PS]	I Found Someone/Dangerous Times	1987	—	—	3.00

IMPERIAL

❏ 66081	Dream Baby/Stan Quetzal	1964	10.00	20.00	40.00

—By "Cherilyn"

❏ 66114	All I Really Want to Do/I'm Gonna Love You	1965	3.00	6.00	12.00
❏ 66136	Where Do You Go/See See Blues	1965	3.00	6.00	12.00
❏ 66160	Bang Bang (My Baby Shot Me Down)/Needles and Pins	1966	3.00	6.00	12.00
❏ 66160	Bang Bang (My Baby Shot Me Down)/Our Day Will Come	1966	3.00	6.00	12.00
❏ 66192	Alfie/She's No Better Than Me	1966	2.50	5.00	10.00
❏ 66217	Behind the Door/Magic in the Air	1966	2.50	5.00	10.00
❏ 66223	Dream Baby/Mama (When My Dollies Have Babies)	1966	2.50	5.00	10.00
❏ 66252	Hey Joe/Our Day Will Come	1967	2.50	5.00	10.00
❏ 66261	You Better Sit Down Kids/Mama (When My Dollies Have Babies)	1967	2.50	5.00	10.00
❏ 66261	You Better Sit Down Kids/Elusive Butterfly	1967	3.00	6.00	12.00
❏ 66282	Click Song Number One/But I Can't Love You More	1968	2.00	4.00	8.00
❏ 66307	Take Me for a Little While/A Song Called Children	1968	2.00	4.00	8.00

KAPP

❏ 2134	Classified 1-A/Don't Put It on Me	1971	—	3.00	6.00
❏ 2146	Gypsys, Tramps and Thieves/He'll Never Know	1971	—	2.00	4.00

—Multi-color label; black Kapp logo stands alone

❏ 2146	Gypsys, Tramps and Thieves/He'll Never Know	1971	—	2.50	5.00

—Multi-color label; white Kapp logo in black box

❏ 2146	Gypsys, Tramps and Thieves/He'll Never Know	1971	—	3.00	6.00

—Black label

❏ 2158	The Way of Love/Don't Put It on Me	1972	—	2.00	4.00

C

Number	Title (A Side/B Side)	Yr	VG	VG+	NM
❑ 2171	Living in a House Divided/One Honest Man	1972	—	2.00	4.00
❑ 2184	Don't Hide Your Love/First Time	1972	—	2.00	4.00
MCA					
❑ 40039	Am I Blue/How Long Has This Been Going On	1973	—	2.00	4.00
❑ 40102	Half-Breed/Melody	1973	—	2.00	4.00
❑ 40161	Dark Lady/Two People Clinging to a Thread	1973	—	2.00	4.00
❑ 40245	Train of Thought/Dixie Girl	1974	—	2.00	4.00
❑ 40273	I Saw a Man and He Danced With His Wife/I Hate to Sleep Alone	1974	—	2.00	4.00
❑ 40324	Carousel Man/When You Find Out Where You're Going Let Me Know	1974	—	2.00	4.00
❑ 40375	Rescue Me/Dixie Girl	1975	—	2.00	4.00
REPRISE					
❑ 17695	One by One/I Wouldn't Treat a Dog (The Way You Treated Me)	1996	—	—	3.00
UNITED ARTISTS					
❑ 0106	All I Really Want to Do/Where Do You Go	1973	—	2.00	4.00
—"Silver Spotlight Series" reissue					
❑ 0107	Bang Bang (My Baby Shot Me Down)/You Better Sit Down Kids	1973	—	2.00	4.00
—"Silver Spotlight Series" reissue					
❑ XW511	Sunny/Alfie	1974	—	2.00	4.00
❑ 50864	Reason to Believe/Will You Still Love Me Tomorrow	1971	—	2.00	4.00
❑ 50974	Old Man River/Our Day Will Come	1972	—	2.00	4.00
WARNER BROS.					
❑ 8096	Geronimo's Cadillac/These Days	1975	—	2.00	4.00
❑ 8263	Borrowed Time/Long Distance Love Affair	1976	—	2.00	4.00
❑ 8311	Pirate/Send the Man Over	1976	—	2.00	4.00
❑ 8366	War Paint and Soft Feathers/Sand the Man Over	1977	—	2.00	4.00
❑ 17119	Believe (Album Version)/(Xenomania Mix)	1998	—	—	3.00
WARNER/SPECTOR					
❑ 0400	Baby, I Love You/A Woman's Story	1974	2.50	5.00	10.00
❑ 0402	A Love Like Yours/Just Enough to Keep Me Hangin' On	1975	2.50	5.00	10.00
—With Nilsson					
Albums					
ATCO					
❑ 33-298 [M]	3614 Jackson Highway	1969	7.50	15.00	30.00
—White label promo only (no stock copies issued in mono)					
❑ SD 33-298 [S]	3614 Jackson Highway	1969	5.00	10.00	20.00
CASABLANCA					
❑ NBLP-7133	Take Me Home	1979	2.50	5.00	10.00
❑ NBPIX-7133 [PD]	Take Me Home	1979	12.50	25.00	50.00
❑ NBLP-7184	Prisoner	1980	2.50	5.00	10.00
COLUMBIA					
❑ FC 38096	I Paralyze	1982	2.50	5.00	10.00
GEFFEN					
❑ GHS 24164	Cher	1987	2.50	5.00	10.00
❑ GHS 24239	Heart of Stone	1989	2.50	5.00	10.00
—Later cover with larger picture of Cher and no rock					
❑ GHS 24239	Heart of Stone	1989	3.75	7.50	15.00
—Original cover with Cher in heart-shaped pose next to "skeleton rock"					
IMPERIAL					
❑ LP-9292 [M]	All I Really Want to Do	1965	5.00	10.00	20.00
❑ LP-9301 [M]	The Sonny Side of Cher	1966	5.00	10.00	20.00
❑ LP-9320 [M]	Cher	1966	3.75	7.50	15.00
❑ LP-9358 [M]	With Love — Cher	1967	3.75	7.50	15.00
❑ LP-12292 [S]	All I Really Want to Do	1965	6.25	12.50	25.00
❑ LP-12301 [S]	The Sonny Side of Cher	1966	6.25	12.50	25.00
❑ LP-12320 [S]	Cher	1966	5.00	10.00	20.00
❑ LP-12358 [S]	With Love — Cher	1967	5.00	10.00	20.00
❑ LP-12373 [M]	Backstage	1968	10.00	20.00	40.00
—Stereo cover with designate mono sticker attached; label is stock					
❑ LP-12373 [S]	Backstage	1968	5.00	10.00	20.00
❑ LP-12406	Cher's Golden Greats	1968	5.00	10.00	20.00
KAPP					
❑ KS-3649	Gypsys, Tramps & Thieves	1971	3.75	7.50	15.00
—Retitled version of above LP; red and orange swirl label					
❑ KS-3649	Cher	1971	5.00	10.00	20.00
—Original title of LP (without "Gypsys, Tramps & Thieves" title on front cover)					
❑ KRS-5514	Foxy Lady	1972	3.75	7.50	15.00
❑ KRS-5549	Gypsys, Tramps & Thieves	1972	3.75	7.50	15.00
—Reissue of 3649; black label					
❑ SW-94485	Foxy Lady	1972	5.00	10.00	20.00
—Capitol Record Club edition					
LIBERTY					
❑ LN-10110	The Very Best of Cher, Vol. 1	1981	2.00	4.00	8.00
❑ LN-10111	The Very Best of Cher, Vol. 2	1981	2.00	4.00	8.00
MCA					
❑ 624	Cher	197?	2.50	5.00	10.00
❑ 2101	Bittersweet White Light	1973	3.00	6.00	12.00
❑ 2104	Half-Breed	1973	3.00	6.00	12.00
❑ 2113	Dark Lady	1974	3.00	6.00	12.00
❑ 2127	Greatest Hits	1974	3.00	6.00	12.00
❑ 37028	Greatest Hits	1981	2.00	4.00	8.00
—Reissue of MCA 2127					
PICKWICK					
❑ SPC-3619	This Is Cher	1978	2.50	5.00	10.00
SPRINGBOARD					
❑ SPB-4028	Cher's Greatest Hits	197?	2.50	5.00	10.00
❑ SPB-4029	Cher Sings the Hits	197?	2.50	5.00	10.00
SUNSET					
❑ SUS-5276	This Is Cher	1970	3.75	7.50	15.00
UNITED ARTISTS					
❑ UXS-88 [(2)]	Cher Superpak	1971	5.00	10.00	20.00
❑ UXS-89 [(2)]	Cher Superpak, Vol. II	1972	5.00	10.00	20.00
—The above are reissues of Imperial recordings					
❑ UA-LA237-G	The Very Best of Cher	1974	3.00	6.00	12.00
❑ UA-LA377-E	The Very Best of Cher	1975	2.50	5.00	10.00
❑ UA-LA435-E	The Very Best of Cher, Vol. 2	1975	3.00	6.00	12.00
WARNER BROS.					
❑ BS 2850	Stars	1975	3.00	6.00	12.00
❑ BS 2898	I'd Rather Believe in You	1976	3.00	6.00	12.00
❑ BS 3046	Cherished	1977	3.00	6.00	12.00

Number	Title (A Side/B Side)	Yr	VG	VG+	NM
CHEROKEE					
45s					
ABC					
❑ 11295	Rosiana/All the Way Home	1971	2.00	4.00	8.00
❑ 11295 [PS]	Rosiana/All the Way Home	1971	3.00	6.00	12.00
❑ 11304	Girl, I've Got News for You/All the Way Home	1971	2.00	4.00	8.00
Albums					
ABC					
❑ ABCS-719	Cherokee	1970	5.00	10.00	20.00
CHEROKEES, THE (1)					
45s					
CHALLENGE					
❑ 9135	Cherokee Stomp/Uprisin'	1961	5.00	10.00	20.00
CHEROKEES, THE (2) Male vocal group.					
45s					
GRAND					
❑ 106	Rainbow of Love/I Had a Thrill	1954	250.00	500.00	1000.
❑ 110	Please Tell Me So/Remember When	1954	250.00	500.00	1000.
LOST-NITE					
❑ 321	Rainbow of Love/I Had a Thrill	197?	—	2.50	5.00
—Reissue					
❑ 325	Please Tell Me So/Remember When	197?	—	2.50	5.00
—Reissue					
PEACOCK					
❑ 1656	Drip Drip/Is She Real	1955	50.00	100.00	200.00
CHEROKEES, THE (3)					
45s					
GUYDEN					
❑ 2044	Cherokee/Harlem Nocturne	1960	3.75	7.50	15.00
❑ 2044 [PS]	Cherokee/Harlem Nocturne	1960	7.50	15.00	30.00
CHEROKEES, THE (4) British band.					
45s					
MGM					
❑ 13334	Seven Daffodils/Wondrous Place	1964	3.75	7.50	15.00
❑ 13433	Dig a Little Deeper/I Will Never Turn My Back on You	1965	5.00	10.00	20.00
CHEROKEES, THE (5) FRED PARRIS of THE FIVE SATINS was a member.					
45s					
UNITED ARTISTS					
❑ 367	My Heavenly Angel/Bed Bug	1961	25.00	50.00	100.00
CHERRY, DON					
45s					
COLUMBIA					
❑ 40421	Tell It To Me Again/Clean Break	1955	3.00	6.00	12.00
❑ 40492	Be My Darling Once Again/You Still Mean the Same to Me	1955	3.00	6.00	12.00
❑ 40544	What Am I Trying to Forget/Fifty Million Salty Kisses	1955	3.00	6.00	12.00
❑ 40597	Band of Gold/Rumble Boogie	1955	3.75	7.50	15.00
❑ 40665	Wild Cherry/I'm Still a King to You	1956	2.50	5.00	10.00
❑ 40705	Ghost Town/I'll Be Around	1956	2.50	5.00	10.00
❑ 40746	Namely You/If I Had My Druthers	1956	2.50	5.00	10.00
❑ 40804	Give Me More/The Story of Sherry	1956	2.50	5.00	10.00
❑ 40828	The Last Dance/Don't You Worry Your Pretty Little Head	1957	2.50	5.00	10.00
❑ 40885	Mr. Teardrop/April Age	1957	2.50	5.00	10.00
❑ 40958	There's a Place Called Heaven/Fourteen Carat Gold	1957	2.50	5.00	10.00
❑ 41014	I Keep Running Away from You/A Ferryboat Named Minerva	1957	2.50	5.00	10.00
❑ 41077	It'll Be Me/Love Me, If You Will	1957	2.50	5.00	10.00
❑ 41134	The Glide/Another Time, Another Place	1958	2.50	5.00	10.00
❑ 41259	Big Bad Wolf/I Look for a Love	1958	2.50	5.00	10.00
❑ 41351	Hasty Heart/The Golden Age	1959	2.50	5.00	10.00
DECCA					
❑ 27244	I'll Always Love You/Maybe on Sunday	1950	3.75	7.50	15.00
—With Eileen Wilson					
❑ 27245	I Need You So/Can't Seem to Laugh Anymore	1950	3.75	7.50	15.00
❑ 27435	Seven Wonders of the World/When You Return	1951	3.00	6.00	12.00
❑ 27475	Chapel of the Roses/Beautiful Madness	1951	3.00	6.00	12.00
❑ 27484	I Apologize/Bring Back the Thrill	1951	3.00	6.00	12.00
❑ 27535	Don't Cry/Don't Leave Me Now	1951	3.00	6.00	12.00
❑ 27618	Powder Blue/Vanity	1951	3.00	6.00	12.00
❑ 27626	My Life's Desire/I Can See You	1951	3.00	6.00	12.00
❑ 27633	Far, Far Away/Star of Hope	1951	3.00	6.00	12.00
—With Eileen Wilson					
❑ 27717	Belle, Belle, My Liberty Belle/Cara Cara Bella Bella	1951	3.00	6.00	12.00
❑ 27755	The Sweetest Waltz/I Will Never Change	1951	3.00	6.00	12.00
❑ 27807	The Lamp of Faith/Sin Ain't Nothing	1951	3.00	6.00	12.00
❑ 27836	I Can't Help It/Grievin' My Heart Out for You	1951	3.00	6.00	12.00
❑ 27904	Neither Am I/Take Me Back	1951	3.00	6.00	12.00
❑ 27944	I'll Sing to You/Your Sentimental Heart	1952	3.00	6.00	12.00
❑ 28050	It Doesn't Matter Where I Go/Sentimental Tears	1952	3.00	6.00	12.00
❑ 28153	Wonder/My Mother's Pearl	1952	3.00	6.00	12.00
❑ 28292	My Name Is Morgan, But It Ain't J.P./Pretty Girl	1952	3.00	6.00	12.00
❑ 28368	It's Been So Long, Darling/Silver Dew on the Blue Grass Tonight	1952	3.00	6.00	12.00
❑ 28452	I Don't Want to Set the World on Fire/From Your Lips Only	1952	3.00	6.00	12.00
❑ 28477	How Long/Second Star to the Right	1952	3.00	6.00	12.00
❑ 28548	Lover's Quarrel/Changeable	1953	3.00	6.00	12.00
❑ 28635	All By Myself/If They Should Ask Me	1953	3.00	6.00	12.00
❑ 28768	If You See Sally/I Got to Pass Your House to Get to My House	1953	3.00	6.00	12.00
❑ 28789	No Stone Unturned/Till the Moon Turns Green	1953	3.00	6.00	12.00
❑ 28844	Too Long/For Now and Always	1953	3.00	6.00	12.00
❑ 29005	I'm Through with Love/You Didn't Have to Tell Me	1954	2.50	5.00	10.00
❑ 29142	Lulu's Back in Town/Anyplace, Anytime, Anywhere	1954	2.50	5.00	10.00
❑ 29322	Where Can You Be/I'm Just a Country Boy	1954	2.50	5.00	10.00

C

Number	Title (A Side/B Side)	Yr	VG	VG+	NM
❑ 29444	Home Again/Sip of Moonlight	1955	2.50	5.00	10.00
❑ 29807	The Thrill Is Gone/Wanted, Someone to Love Me	1956	2.50	5.00	10.00

MONUMENT

Number	Title (A Side/B Side)	Yr	VG	VG+	NM
❑ 45-232	Come Sundown/Love Is Gone for Good	1977	—	2.50	5.00
❑ 45-269	Six Weeks Every Summer, Christmas Every Day/Play Her Back to Yesterday	1978	—	2.50	5.00
❑ 880	More I Cannot Do/Sweet Sugar	1965	2.00	4.00	8.00
❑ 898	The Story of My Life/Things Called Sadness	1965	2.00	4.00	8.00
❑ 930	Don't Change/I Love You Drops	1966	2.00	4.00	8.00
❑ 947	Tip of My Fingers/After I'm Number One	1966	2.00	4.00	8.00
❑ 971	I Know Love/Married	1966	2.00	4.00	8.00
❑ 989	There Goes My Everything/I Don't Wanna Go Home	1966	2.00	4.00	8.00
❑ 1008	I Live to Love You/I Run to the Door	1967	—	3.00	6.00
❑ 1027	That Lucky Old Sun/No Hearts and Flowers	1967	—	3.00	6.00
❑ 1045	Theme from "Will Penny" (Lonely Rider)/Here Comes the Rain	1967	—	3.00	6.00
❑ 1062	Good Morning/Let Me Lead the Way	1968	—	3.00	6.00
❑ 1088	Take a Message to Mary/In My Youth	1968	—	3.00	6.00
❑ 1130	Whippoorwill/To Think You've Chosen Me	1969	—	3.00	6.00
❑ 1147	Days of Sand and Shovels/That Woman's Coming Home	1969	—	3.00	6.00
❑ 1156	I'll Catch the Sun/Ain't You Glad You're Living, Joe	1969	—	3.00	6.00
❑ 1185	Lilacs in Winter/Look for Me Tomorrow	1970	—	3.00	6.00
❑ 1201	Between Winston-Salem and Nashville, Tennessee/Just a Drop of Rain	1970	—	3.00	6.00
❑ 1222	Statue of a Fool/Ev'ry Body Else	1970	—	3.00	6.00
❑ 8530	Freedom Come, Freedom Go/Have You Ever Been to Georgia	1971	—	2.50	5.00
❑ 8542	For a Moment You Slipped My Mind/Is It Any Wonder	1972	—	2.50	5.00
❑ 8557	The Riddle Song/Wonder Where They're Going	1972	—	2.50	5.00
❑ 8578	When You Leave Amarillo, Turn Out the Lights/Cajun Fiddler	1973	—	2.50	5.00
❑ 8603	Going Away Party/The Old Rugged Cross	1974	—	2.50	5.00
❑ 8704	The Good Old Days Are Right Now/Pleasing You (As Long As I Live)	1976	—	2.50	5.00

STRAND

Number	Title (A Side/B Side)	Yr	VG	VG+	NM
❑ 25005	Vanity/Summer School Blues	1959	2.50	5.00	10.00

VERVE

Number	Title (A Side/B Side)	Yr	VG	VG+	NM
❑ 10270	Then You Can Tell Me Goodbye/When I Found I'd Lost	1962	2.50	5.00	10.00

WARWICK

Number	Title (A Side/B Side)	Yr	VG	VG+	NM
❑ 597	Hair of Gold/Somebody Cares for Me	1960	2.50	5.00	10.00

7-Inch Extended Plays

COLUMBIA

Number	Title (A Side/B Side)	Yr	VG	VG+	NM
❑ B-8931	When the Sun Comes Out/Love Is Just Around the Corner//For You/I'll String Along with You	195?	3.00	6.00	12.00
❑ B-8931 [PS]	Swingin' for Two, Part 1	195?	3.00	6.00	12.00
❑ B-8932	I Didn't Know About You/So Rare//I'm Yours/I'm Gonna Sit Right Down and Write Myself a Letter	195?	3.00	6.00	12.00
❑ B-8932 [PS]	Swingin' for Two, Part 2	195?	3.00	6.00	12.00

Albums

COLUMBIA

Number	Title (A Side/B Side)	Yr	VG	VG+	NM
❑ CL 893 [M]	Swingin' for Two	1956	6.25	12.50	25.00

MONUMENT

Number	Title (A Side/B Side)	Yr	VG	VG+	NM
❑ MLP-8049 [M]	Don Cherry Smashes	1966	3.00	6.00	12.00
❑ MLP-8075 [M]	There Goes My Everything	1967	3.75	7.50	15.00
❑ 8601 [(2)]	The World of Don Cherry	197?	3.00	6.00	12.00
—Reissue of 32334					
❑ SLP-18049 [S]	Don Cherry Smashes	1966	3.75	7.50	15.00
❑ SLP-18075 [S]	There Goes My Everything	1967	3.00	6.00	12.00
❑ SLP-18088	Let It Be Me	1968	3.00	6.00	12.00
❑ SLP-18109	Take a Message to Mary	1969	3.00	6.00	12.00
❑ SLP-18124	Don Cherry	1970	3.00	6.00	12.00
❑ KZG 32334 [(2)]	The World of Don Cherry	1972	3.75	7.50	15.00

CHERRY PEOPLE, THE

45s

HERITAGE

Number	Title (A Side/B Side)	Yr	VG	VG+	NM
❑ 801	And Suddenly/Imagination	1968	2.00	4.00	8.00
❑ 801 [PS]	And Suddenly/Imagination	1968	3.75	7.50	15.00
❑ 807	Gotta Get Back to the Good Life/I'm the One Who Loves You	1968	2.00	4.00	8.00
❑ 807 [PS]	Gotta Get Back to the Good Life/I'm the One Who Loves You	1968	3.75	7.50	15.00
❑ 810	Feelings/Mr. Hyde	1969	2.00	4.00	8.00
❑ 810 [PS]	Feelings/Mr. Hyde	1969	3.75	7.50	15.00
❑ 815	Light of Love/On to Something New	1969	2.00	4.00	8.00

Albums

HERITAGE

Number	Title (A Side/B Side)	Yr	VG	VG+	NM
❑ HT 35000 [M]	The Cherry People	1968	10.00	20.00	40.00
—Stereo cover with "Mono" and "DJ" stickers attached; all records appear to be white label promos					
❑ HTS 35000 [S]	The Cherry People	1968	5.00	10.00	20.00

CHERRY SLUSH

45s

U.S.A.

Number	Title (A Side/B Side)	Yr	VG	VG+	NM
❑ 895	I Cannot Stop You/Don't Walk Away	1968	5.00	10.00	20.00
❑ 904	Gotta Take It Easy/Day Don't Come	1968	5.00	10.00	20.00

CHESS, TUBBY, AND HIS CANDY STRIPE TWISTERS

Albums

GRAND PRIX

Number	Title (A Side/B Side)	Yr	VG	VG+	NM
❑ K-187 [M]	Do the Twist	1962	3.75	7.50	15.00
❑ KS-187 [S]	Do the Twist	1962	5.00	10.00	20.00

CHESTER, GARY

Albums

DCP

Number	Title (A Side/B Side)	Yr	VG	VG+	NM
❑ DCL 3803 [M]	Yeah, Yeah, Yeah	1964	5.00	10.00	20.00
❑ DCS 6803 [S]	Yeah, Yeah, Yeah	1964	6.25	12.50	25.00

CHESTERFIELDS, THE (1)

45s

A&M

Number	Title (A Side/B Side)	Yr	VG	VG+	NM
❑ 2041	That Is Rock and Roll/Why Do Fools Fall in Love	1978	—	2.50	5.00

CHESTERFIELDS, THE (2)

45s

CHESS

Number	Title (A Side/B Side)	Yr	VG	VG+	NM
❑ 1559	I'm in Heaven/All Messed Up	1954	100.00	200.00	400.00

CHESTERFIELDS, THE (3)

45s

CUB

Number	Title (A Side/B Side)	Yr	VG	VG+	NM
❑ 9008	I Got Fired/Meet Me at the Candy Store	1958	6.25	12.50	25.00

CHESTERFIELDS, THE (4)

45s

PHILIPS

Number	Title (A Side/B Side)	Yr	VG	VG+	NM
❑ 40060	A Dream Is But a Dream/You Walked Away	1962	50.00	100.00	200.00

CHESTERS, THE See LITTLE ANTHONY AND THE IMPERIALS.

CHESTNUT, MORRIS

45s

AMY

Number	Title (A Side/B Side)	Yr	VG	VG+	NM
❑ 981	Too Darned Soulful/You Don't Love Me Anymore	1967	62.50	125.00	250.00

CHEVRONS, THE

45s

BRENT

Number	Title (A Side/B Side)	Yr	VG	VG+	NM
❑ 7000	That Comes With Love/Don't Be Heartless	1959	12.50	25.00	50.00
❑ 7007	Lullabye/The Day After Forever	1959	12.50	25.00	50.00
❑ 7015	Little Darlin'/Little Star	1960	12.50	25.00	50.00

TIME

Number	Title (A Side/B Side)	Yr	VG	VG+	NM
❑ 1	Come Go with Me/I'm in Love Again	1960	10.00	20.00	40.00

Albums

TIME

Number	Title (A Side/B Side)	Yr	VG	VG+	NM
❑ T-10008 [M]	Sing-a-Long Rock & Roll	1961	20.00	40.00	80.00

CHI-LITES, THE

12-Inch Singles

CHI-SOUND

Number	Title (A Side/B Side)	Yr	VG	VG+	NM
❑ TCD 121 [DJ]	Have You Seen Her (Long Version 5:28) (Short Version 3:39)	1981	3.75	7.50	15.00
❑ TCD 122	Have You Seen Her/Super Mad (About You Baby)	1981	3.00	6.00	12.00
❑ TCD 132 [DJ]	Me and You (stereo/mono)	1981	2.50	5.00	10.00
❑ TCD 136	Hot on a Thing (Called Love) (6:16)/Whole Lot of Good, Good Lovin'	1981	3.00	6.00	12.00
❑ TCD 138	Try My Side (Of Love)/Get Down with Me	1982	3.00	6.00	12.00

ICHIBAN

Number	Title (A Side/B Side)	Yr	VG	VG+	NM
❑ 12 PO 46	There's a Change (same on both sides)	1990	—	3.50	7.00
❑ 12 PO 55	Eternity (3 versions)	199?	—	3.50	7.00
❑ 12 PO 61	Solid Love Affair/Happy Music	199?	—	3.50	7.00

NUANCE

Number	Title (A Side/B Side)	Yr	VG	VG+	NM
❑ NU 1252	Hard Act to Follow (Vocal 5:24) (House Mix 6:57) (Vocal Edit 4:04)	1985	—	3.50	7.00

PRIVATE I

Number	Title (A Side/B Side)	Yr	VG	VG+	NM
❑ 4Z9-04962	Stop What You're Doin' (Club Version 6:17) (Instrumental 3:32)	1984	2.50	5.00	10.00
❑ 4Z9-05016	Gimme Whatcha Got (Club Version 6:20) (Dub Mix)	1984	2.50	5.00	10.00

T.K. DISCO

Number	Title (A Side/B Side)	Yr	VG	VG+	NM
❑ TKD-414	Higher (8:14)/Stay a Little Longer	1979	3.00	6.00	12.00

45s

BLUE ROCK

Number	Title (A Side/B Side)	Yr	VG	VG+	NM
❑ 4007	I'm So Jealous/The Mix-Mix Song	1965	6.25	12.50	25.00
❑ 4020	Doing the Snatch/Bassology	1965	6.25	12.50	25.00
❑ 4037	Never No More/She's Mine	1965	12.50	25.00	50.00

BRUNSWICK

Number	Title (A Side/B Side)	Yr	VG	VG+	NM
❑ 55398	Give It Away/What Do I Wish For	1969	2.00	4.00	8.00
❑ 55414	Let Me Be the Man My Daddy Was/The Twelfth of Never	1969	2.00	4.00	8.00
❑ 55422	I'm Gonna Make You Love Me/To Change My Love	1969	2.00	4.00	8.00
❑ 55426	24 Hours of Sadness/You're No Longer Part of My Heart	1970	2.00	4.00	8.00
❑ 55438	I Like Your Lovin' (Do You Like Mine)/You're No Longer Part of My Heart	1970	2.00	4.00	8.00
❑ 55442	Are You My Woman (Tell Me So)/Troubles A-Comin'	1970	2.00	4.00	8.00
❑ 55450	(For God's Sake) Give More Power to the People/Troubles A-Comin'	1971	2.00	4.00	8.00
❑ 55455	We Are Neighbors/What Do I Wish For	1971	2.00	4.00	8.00
❑ 55458	I Want to Pay You back (For Loving Me)/Love Uprising	1971	2.00	4.00	8.00
❑ 55462	Have You Seen Her/Yes I'm Ready	1971	—	3.00	6.00
❑ 55471	Oh Girl/Being in Love	1972	—	3.00	6.00
❑ 55478	The Coldest Days of My Life (Part 1)/The Coldest Days of My Life (Part 2)	1972	—	3.00	6.00
❑ 55483	A Lonely Man/The Man and the Woman (The Boy and the Girl)	1972	—	3.00	6.00
❑ 55489	We Need Order/Living in the Footsteps of Another Man	1972	—	3.00	6.00
❑ 55491	A Letter to Myself/Sally	1973	—	3.00	6.00
❑ 55496	My Heart Just Keeps On Breakin'/Just Two Teenage Kids	1973	—	3.00	6.00
❑ 55500	Stoned Out of My Mind/Someone Else's Arms	1973	—	3.00	6.00
❑ 55502	I Found Someone/Marriage License	1973	—	3.00	6.00
❑ 55505	Homely Girl/Never Had It So Good and Felt So Bad	1974	—	3.00	6.00
❑ 55512	There Will Never Be Any Peace (Until God Is Seated at the Conference Table)/Too Good to Be Forgotten	1974	—	3.00	6.00
❑ 55514	You Got to Be the One/Happiness Is Your Middle Name	1974	—	3.00	6.00
❑ 55515	Toby/That's How Long	1974	—	3.00	6.00

Number	Title (A Side/B Side)	Yr	VG	VG+	NM
55520	It's Time for Love/Here I Am	1975	—	3.00	6.00
55522	Don't Burn No Bridges/(Instrumental)	1975	—	3.00	6.00

—With Jackie Wilson

Number	Title (A Side/B Side)	Yr	VG	VG+	NM
55525	The Devil Is Doing His Work/I'm Not a Gambler	1976	—	3.00	6.00
55528	You Don't Have to Go/(Instrumental)	1976	—	3.00	6.00
55546	First Time/Marriage License	1978	—	2.50	5.00

CHI-SOUND

Number	Title (A Side/B Side)	Yr	VG	VG+	NM
2472	Heavenly Body/Strung Out	1980	—	2.00	4.00
2481	Have You Seen Her/Super Mad (About You Baby)	1981	—	2.00	4.00
2495	All I Wanna Do Is Make Love to You/Round and Round	1981	—	2.00	4.00
2503	Me and You/Tell Me Where It Hurts	1981	—	2.00	4.00
2600	Hot on a Thing (Called Love)/Whole Lot of Good Lovin'	1982	—	2.00	4.00
2604	Try My Side (Of Love)/Get Down with Me	1982	—	2.00	4.00

DAKAR

Number	Title (A Side/B Side)	Yr	VG	VG+	NM
600	Baby It's Time/Price of Love	1968	3.00	6.00	12.00

—As "Marshall and the Chi-Lites"

DARAN

Number	Title (A Side/B Side)	Yr	VG	VG+	NM
011	One by One/You Did That to Me	1964	25.00	50.00	100.00

—As "The Hi-Lites"

Number	Title (A Side/B Side)	Yr	VG	VG+	NM
0111	Pretty Girl/Love Bandit	1966	12.50	25.00	50.00

—As "Marshall and the Chi-Lites"

Number	Title (A Side/B Side)	Yr	VG	VG+	NM
222	I'm So Jealous/The Mix-Mix Song	1964	25.00	50.00	100.00

—As "The Hi-Lites"

ICHIBAN

Number	Title (A Side/B Side)	Yr	VG	VG+	NM
90-205	There's a Change/Happy Music	1990	—	2.00	4.00

INPHASION

Number	Title (A Side/B Side)	Yr	VG	VG+	NM
7205	Higher/Stay a Little Longer	1979	—	2.50	5.00
7208	The Only One for Me (One in a Million)/You Won't Be Lonely Too Long	1979	—	2.50	5.00

JA-WES

Number	Title (A Side/B Side)	Yr	VG	VG+	NM
0888	You Did That to Me/I Won't Care About You	1966	3.75	7.50	15.00

LARC

Number	Title (A Side/B Side)	Yr	VG	VG+	NM
81015	Bottom's Up/Bottom's Up Groove	1983	—	2.00	4.00
81023	Bad Motor Scooter/I Just Wanna Hold You	1983	—	2.00	4.00

MERCURY

Number	Title (A Side/B Side)	Yr	VG	VG+	NM
73844	Happy Being Lonely/Love Can Be Dangerous	1976	—	2.50	5.00
73886	Vanishing Love/I Turn Away	1977	—	2.50	5.00
73934	My First Mistake/Stop Still	1977	—	2.50	5.00
73954	If I Had a Girl/I've Got Love on My Mind	1977	—	2.50	5.00

NUANCE

Number	Title (A Side/B Side)	Yr	VG	VG+	NM
752	Hard Act to Follow/(Instrumental)	1985	—	2.00	4.00

PRIVATE I

Number	Title (A Side/B Side)	Yr	VG	VG+	NM
ZS4-04365	Stop What You're Doin'/Little Girl	1984	—	—	3.00
ZS4-04484	Gimme Whatcha Got/Let Today Come Back Tomorrow	1984	—	—	3.00

REVUE

Number	Title (A Side/B Side)	Yr	VG	VG+	NM
11005	Love Is Gone/Love Me	1967	3.00	6.00	12.00
11018	(Um, Um) My Baby Loves Me/That's My Baby for You	1968	3.00	6.00	12.00

Albums

BRUNSWICK

Number	Title (A Side/B Side)	Yr	VG	VG+	NM
BL 754152	Give It Away	1969	6.25	12.50	25.00
BL 754165	I Like Your Lovin', Do You Like Mine?	1970	6.25	12.50	25.00
BL 754170	(For God's Sake) Give More Power to the People	1971	6.25	12.50	25.00
BL 754179	A Lonely Man	1972	6.25	12.50	25.00
BL 754184	The Chi-Lites Greatest Hits	1972	6.25	12.50	25.00
BL 754188	A Letter to Myself	1973	6.25	12.50	25.00
BL 754197	Chi-Lites	1973	6.25	12.50	25.00
BL 754200	Toby	1974	6.25	12.50	25.00
BL 754204	Half a Love	1975	6.25	12.50	25.00
BL 754208	The Chi-Lites Greatest Hits, Volume 2	1976	6.25	12.50	25.00

CHI-SOUND

Number	Title (A Side/B Side)	Yr	VG	VG+	NM
T-619	Heavenly Body	1980	3.75	7.50	15.00
T-635	Me and You	1982	3.75	7.50	15.00

EPIC

Number	Title (A Side/B Side)	Yr	VG	VG+	NM
PE 38627	Greatest Hits	1983	2.50	5.00	10.00

ICHIBAN

Number	Title (A Side/B Side)	Yr	VG	VG+	NM
ICH-1057	Just Say You Love Me	198?	2.50	5.00	10.00

LARC

Number	Title (A Side/B Side)	Yr	VG	VG+	NM
8103	Bottom's Up	1983	3.00	6.00	12.00

MERCURY

Number	Title (A Side/B Side)	Yr	VG	VG+	NM
SRM-1-1118	Happy Being Lonely	1976	3.75	7.50	15.00
SRM-1-1147	Fantastic	1977	3.75	7.50	15.00

PRIVATE I

Number	Title (A Side/B Side)	Yr	VG	VG+	NM
FZ 39316	Steppin' Out	1984	2.50	5.00	10.00
PZ 39316	Steppin' Out	1985	2.00	4.00	8.00

—Budget-line reissue

CHIC-LETS, THE
45s

JOSIE

Number	Title (A Side/B Side)	Yr	VG	VG+	NM
919	I Want You to Be My Boyfriend/Don't Goof on Me	1964	3.75	7.50	15.00

CHICAGO
12-Inch Singles

COLUMBIA

Number	Title (A Side/B Side)	Yr	VG	VG+	NM
AS 539 [DJ]	No Tell Lover (3:49) (4:15)	1979	5.00	10.00	20.00

WARNER BROS.

Number	Title (A Side/B Side)	Yr	VG	VG+	NM
PRO-A-2134 [DJ]	Stay the Night (same on both sides)	1984	3.75	7.50	15.00
PRO-A-2183 [DJ]	Hard Habit to Break (Edit) (LP Version)	1984	3.00	6.00	12.00
PRO-A-2256 [DJ]	Along Comes a Woman (Remix) (same on both sides)	1985	3.00	6.00	12.00
PRO-A-2293 [DJ]	Along Comes a Woman (Dance Mix 6:12) (same on both sides)	1985	2.50	5.00	10.00
PRO-A-2560 [DJ]	25 or 6 to 4 (same on both sides)	1986	3.00	6.00	12.00

45s

COLUMBIA

Number	Title (A Side/B Side)	Yr	VG	VG+	NM
10049	Wishing You Were Here/Life Saver	1974	—	2.50	5.00
10092	Harry Truman/Till We Meet Again	1975	—	2.50	5.00
10092 [PS]	Harry Truman/Till We Meet Again	1975	—	3.00	6.00
10131	Old Days/Hideaway	1975	—	2.50	5.00
10200	Brand New Love Affair/Hideaway	1975	—	2.50	5.00
3-10360	Another Rainy Day in New York City/Hope for Love	1976	—	2.50	5.00
3-10390	If You Leave Me Now/Together Again	1976	—	2.50	5.00
3-10523	You Are On My Mind/Gently I'll Wake You	1977	—	2.50	5.00
3-10620	Baby, What a Big Surprise/Takin' It On Uptown	1977	—	2.50	5.00
3-10620 [PS]	Baby, What a Big Surprise/Takin' It On Uptown	1977	3.75	7.50	15.00

—Sleeve appears to be promo only

Number	Title (A Side/B Side)	Yr	VG	VG+	NM
3-10683	Little One/Till the End of Time	1978	—	2.50	5.00
3-10737	Take Me Back to Chicago/Policeman	1978	—	2.50	5.00
3-10845	Alive Again/Love Was New	1978	—	2.50	5.00
3-10879	No Tell Lover/Take a Chance	1979	—	2.50	5.00
3-10935	Gone Long Gone/The Greatest Love on Earth	1979	—	2.00	4.00
1-11061	Must Have Been Crazy/Closer to You	1979	—	2.00	4.00
1-11124	Street Player/Window Dreamin'	1979	—	2.00	4.00
1-11341	Song for You/I'd Rather Be Rich	1980	—	—	—

—Canceled?

Number	Title (A Side/B Side)	Yr	VG	VG+	NM
1-11345	Thunder and Lightning/I'd Rather Be Rich	1980	—	2.00	4.00
11-11376	Song for You/The American Dream	1980	—	2.00	4.00
4-44909	Questions 67 and 68/Listen	1969	2.00	4.00	8.00
4-44909 [DJ]	Questions 67 and 68 (3:07)/(4:45)	1969	3.00	6.00	12.00

—Both versions mono; A-side "Edited Version" has a master number of "JZSP 151568"; B-side's master number is "JZSP 151534"

Number	Title (A Side/B Side)	Yr	VG	VG+	NM
4-44909 [PS]	Questions 67 and 68/Listen	1969	3.00	6.00	12.00
45011	Beginnings/Poem 58	1969	—	3.00	6.00
45127	Make Me Smile/Colour My World	1970	—	2.50	5.00
45127 [PS]	Make Me Smile/Colour My World	1970	2.00	4.00	8.00
45194	25 or 6 to 4/Where Do We Go from Here	1970	—	2.50	5.00
4-45264	Does Anybody Really Know What Time It Is?/Listen	1970	—	2.50	5.00
4-45264 [DJ]	Does Anybody Really Know What Time It Is? (3:17)/(2:53)	1970	2.50	5.00	10.00

—A-side master number is "JZSP 154094"; B-side master number is "JZSP 154096"

Number	Title (A Side/B Side)	Yr	VG	VG+	NM
4-45264 [PS]	Does Anybody Really Know What Time It Is?/Listen	1970	2.50	5.00	10.00
45331	Free/Free Country	1971	—	2.50	5.00
45331 [PS]	Free/Free Country	1971	2.00	4.00	8.00
45370	Lowdown/Loneliness Is Just a Word	1971	—	2.50	5.00
45370 [PS]	Lowdown/Loneliness Is Just a Word	1971	2.00	4.00	8.00
45417	Beginnings/Colour My World	1971	—	2.50	5.00
45417 [PS]	Beginnings/Colour My World	1971	2.00	4.00	8.00
45467	Questions 67 and 68/I'm a Man	1971	—	2.50	5.00
45657	Saturday in the Park/Alma Mater	1972	—	2.50	5.00
45717	Dialogue (Parts 1 and 2)/Now That You've Gone	1972	—	2.50	5.00
45717 [PS]	Dialogue (Parts 1 and 2)/Now That You've Gone	1972	—	3.00	6.00
45880	Feelin' Stronger Every Day/Jenny	1973	—	2.50	5.00
45933	Just You 'N' Me/Critic's Choice	1973	—	2.50	5.00
46020	(I've Been) Searchin' So Long/Byblos	1974	—	2.50	5.00
46062	Call On Me/Prelude to Aire	1974	—	2.50	5.00

FULL MOON

Number	Title (A Side/B Side)	Yr	VG	VG+	NM
29798	What You're Missing/Rescue You	1983	—	2.00	4.00
29911	Love Me Tomorrow/Bad Advice	1982	—	2.00	4.00
29979	Hard to Say I'm Sorry/Sonny Think Twice	1982	—	2.00	4.00

REPRISE

Number	Title (A Side/B Side)	Yr	VG	VG+	NM
19466	Chasin' the Wind/Only Time Can Heal the Wounded	1991	—	—	3.00
22741	What Kind of Man Would I Be?/25 or 6 to 4	1990	—	—	3.00
22741 [PS]	What Kind of Man Would I Be?/25 or 6 to 4	1990	—	2.50	3.00
22985	We Can Last Forever/One More Day	1989	—	—	3.00
27757	You're Not Alone/It's Alright	1988	—	—	3.00
27757 [PS]	You're Not Alone/It's Alright	1988	—	—	3.00
27766	Look Away/Come In from the Night	1988	—	—	3.00
27766 [PS]	Look Away/Come In from the Night	1988	—	—	3.00
27855	I Don't Wanna Live Without Your Love/I Stand Up	1988	—	—	3.00
27855 [PS]	I Don't Wanna Live Without Your Love/I Stand Up	1988	—	—	3.00

WARNER BROS.

Number	Title (A Side/B Side)	Yr	VG	VG+	NM
28283	Niagara Falls/I Believe	1987	—	—	3.00
28283 [PS]	Niagara Falls/I Believe	1987	—	2.50	3.00
28424	If She Would Have Been Faithful.../Forever	1987	—	—	3.00
28424 [PS]	If She Would Have Been Faithful.../Forever	1987	—	—	3.00
28512	Will You Still Love Me/25 or 6 to 4	1986	—	—	3.00
28628	25 or 6 to 4/One More Day	1986	—	—	3.00
28628 [PS]	25 or 6 to 4/One More Day	1986	—	—	3.00
29082	Along Comes a Woman/We Can't Stop the Hurtin'	1985	—	—	3.00
29126	You're the Inspiration/Once in a Lifetime	1984	—	—	3.00
29214	Hard Habit to Break/Remember the Feeling	1984	—	—	3.00
29214 [PS]	Hard Habit to Break/Remember the Feeling	1984	—	—	3.00
29306	Stay the Night/Only You	1984	—	—	3.00
29306 [PS]	Stay the Night/Only You	1984	—	—	3.00

7-Inch Extended Plays

COLUMBIA

Number	Title (A Side/B Side)	Yr	VG	VG+	NM
7-KGP 24	Movin' In/Wake Up Sunshine/To Be Free/West Virginia Fantasies/Colour My World/It Better End Soon, 2nd Movement	1970	2.50	5.00	10.00

—Jukebox issue; small hole, plays at 33 1/3 rpm

Number	Title (A Side/B Side)	Yr	VG	VG+	NM
7-KGP 24 [PS]	Chicago	1970	2.50	5.00	10.00
7-30110	Canon/Once Upon a Time/Mother//Loneliness Is Just a Word/What Else Can I Say/At the Sunrise	1971	2.50	5.00	10.00

—Jukebox issue; small hole, plays at 33 1/3 rpm

Number	Title (A Side/B Side)	Yr	VG	VG+	NM
7-30110 [PS]	Chicago III	1971	2.50	5.00	10.00
7-32400	Chicago VI	1973	2.50	5.00	10.00
7-32400	What's This World Comin' To/Darlin' Bear//Discovery/In Terms of Two	1973	2.50	5.00	10.00

—Jukebox issue; small hole, plays at 33 1/3 rpm

Albums

ACCORD

Number	Title (A Side/B Side)	Yr	VG	VG+	NM
SN-7140	Toronto Rock 'n Roll Revival, Part I	1982	3.00	6.00	12.00

—Reissue of Magnum LP

COLUMBIA

Number	Title (A Side/B Side)	Yr	VG	VG+	NM
(no #) [(17)]	Chicago	1976	62.50	125.00	250.00

—Promo-only set: The first 10 Chicago LPs with gold stamps on covers, box, side panel and wraparound

Number	Title (A Side/B Side)	Yr	VG	VG+	NM
GP 8 [(2)]	Chicago Transit Authority	1969	6.25	12.50	25.00

—Red labels with "360 Sound" at bottom

Number	Title (A Side/B Side)	Yr	VG	VG+	NM
GP 8 [(2)]	Chicago Transit Authority	1970	3.75	7.50	15.00

—Orange labels; most copies add a Roman numeral "I" to the title on spine

Number	Title (A Side/B Side)	Yr	VG	VG+	NM
❑ KGP 24 [(2)]	Chicago II	1970	3.75	7.50	15.00
—Orange labels					
❑ KGP 24 [(2)]	Chicago II	1970	6.25	12.50	25.00
—Red labels with "360 Sound" at bottom; label and spine call the album "Chicago II"					
❑ KGP 24 [(2)]	Chicago	1970	10.00	20.00	40.00
—Red labels with "360 Sound" at bottom; label and spine call the album "Chicago"					
❑ C2 30110 [(2)]	Chicago III	1971	3.75	7.50	15.00
❑ C2Q 30110 [(2)Q]	Chicago III	1974	7.50	15.00	30.00
❑ KG 30863 [(2)]	Chicago at Carnegie Hall, Vol. 1 & 2	1971	3.75	7.50	15.00
—First half of the 4-LP box, possibly for Columbia Record Club only					
❑ KG 30864 [(2)]	Chicago at Carnegie Hall, Vol. 3 & 4	1971	3.75	7.50	15.00
—Second half of the 4-LP box, possibly for Columbia Record Club only					
❑ C4Q 30865 [(4)Q]	Chicago at Carnegie Hall	1971	—	—	—
—Scheduled but never released					
❑ C4X 30865	Chicago at Carnegie Hall	1971	7.50	15.00	30.00
—With box, 4 posters and program; deduct for missing items					
❑ CQ 31102 [Q]	Chicago V	1974	6.25	12.50	25.00
❑ KC 31102	Chicago V	1972	3.75	7.50	15.00
❑ CQ 32400 [Q]	Chicago VI	1974	6.25	12.50	25.00
❑ KC 32400	Chicago VI	1973	3.00	6.00	12.00
❑ C2 32810 [(2)]	Chicago VII	1974	3.75	7.50	15.00
❑ C2Q 32810 [(2)Q]	Chicago VII	1974	7.50	15.00	30.00
❑ PC 33100	Chicago VIII	1975	3.00	6.00	12.00
❑ PCQ 33100 [Q]	Chicago VIII	1975	6.25	12.50	25.00
❑ GQ 33255 [(2)Q]	Chicago Transit Authority	1975	6.25	12.50	25.00
❑ GQ 33258 [(2)Q]	Chicago II	1975	6.25	12.50	25.00
❑ PC 33900	Chicago IX — Chicago's Greatest Hits	1975	2.50	5.00	10.00
❑ PCQ 33900 [Q]	Chicago IX — Chicago's Greatest Hits	1975	6.25	12.50	25.00
❑ PC 34200	Chicago X	1976	2.50	5.00	10.00
❑ PCQ 34200 [Q]	Chicago X	1976	6.25	12.50	25.00
❑ JC 34860	Chicago XI	1977	2.50	5.00	10.00
❑ FC 35512	Hot Streets	1978	2.50	5.00	10.00
❑ FC 36105	Chicago 13	1979	3.00	6.00	12.00
❑ FC 36517	Chicago XIV	1980	3.00	6.00	12.00
❑ FC 37682	Chicago — Greatest Hits, Volume II	1981	3.00	6.00	12.00
❑ PC 38590	If You Leave Me Now	1982	3.00	6.00	12.00
❑ PC 39579	Take Me Back to Chicago	1983	3.00	6.00	12.00
❑ HC 43900	Chicago IX — Chicago's Greatest Hits	1982	7.50	15.00	30.00
—Half-speed mastered edition					
❑ HC 44200	Chicago X	1982	10.00	20.00	40.00
—Half-speed mastered edition					
FULL MOON					
❑ 23689	Chicago 16	1982	2.00	4.00	8.00
MAGNUM					
❑ MR 604	Chicago Transit Authority Live in Concert	1978	5.00	10.00	20.00
—Taken from their 1969 Toronto Rock 'n Roll Revival performance					
MOBILE FIDELITY					
❑ 2-128 [(2)]	Chicago Transit Authority	1983	20.00	40.00	80.00
—Audiophile vinyl					
REPRISE					
❑ 25714	Chicago 19	1988	2.00	4.00	8.00
❑ 26080	Greatest Hits 1982-1989	1989	2.50	5.00	10.00
❑ R 110533	Twenty 1	1991	5.00	10.00	20.00
—BMG Direct Marketing version					
WARNER BROS.					
❑ 25060 [DJ]	Chicago 17	1984	5.00	10.00	20.00
—Promo pressing on Quiex II vinyl					
❑ 25060	Chicago 17	1984	2.00	4.00	8.00
❑ 25509	Chicago 18	1986	2.00	4.00	8.00

CHICAGO CUBS, THE
45s
CHESS
| ❑ 2075 | Pennant Fever/Slide | 1969 | 3.00 | 6.00 | 12.00 |
| ❑ 2075 [PS] | Pennant Fever/Slide | 1969 | 7.50 | 15.00 | 30.00 |

CHICKEN SHACK Also see CHRISTINE McVIE.
45s
BLUE HORIZON
❑ 100	Tears in the Wind/The Things You Put Me Through	1970	—	3.00	6.00
❑ 302	Maudie/Diary of Your Life	1972	—	3.00	6.00
DERAM					
❑ 7537	As Time Goes Passing By/(B-side unknown)	1972	—	2.50	5.00
EPIC					
❑ 10414	Six Nights in Seven/Worried About My Woman	1968	2.50	5.00	10.00

Albums
BLUE HORIZON
❑ BH 4809	Accept Chicken Shack	1970	6.25	12.50	25.00
❑ BH 7705	O.K. Ken?	1969	6.25	12.50	25.00
❑ BH 7706	100-Ton Chicken	1969	6.25	12.50	25.00
DERAM					
❑ DES 18063	Imagination Lady	1972	5.00	10.00	20.00
EPIC					
❑ LN 24414 [M]	Forty Blue Fingers, Freshly Packed and Ready to Serve	1968	25.00	50.00	100.00
❑ BN 26414 [S]	Forty Blue Fingers, Freshly Packed and Ready to Serve	1968	7.50	15.00	30.00
LONDON					
❑ XPS 632	Unlucky Boy	1973	5.00	10.00	20.00

CHIEFTAINS, THE
45s
ISLAND
❑ 048	Love Theme from "Barry Lyndon"/Timpan Reel	1976	—	3.00	6.00
SHANACHIE					
❑ 702	Cotton Eyed Joe/The Gold Ring	1981	2.50	5.00	10.00

Albums
COLUMBIA
❑ JC 35612	The Chieftains 7	1979	3.00	6.00	12.00
❑ PC 35612	The Chieftains 7	198?	2.00	4.00	8.00
—Budget-line reissue					
❑ JC 35726	The Chieftains 8	1980	3.00	6.00	12.00
❑ JC 36401	Boil the Breakfast Early	1981	3.00	6.00	12.00
❑ PC 36401	Boil the Breakfast Early	198?	2.00	4.00	8.00
—Budget-line reissue					

Number	Title (A Side/B Side)	Yr	VG	VG+	NM
ISLAND					
❑ ILPS 9334	The Chieftains 5	1975	3.00	6.00	12.00
—Black label original					
❑ ILPS 9364	The Chieftains 1	1976	3.00	6.00	12.00
—Black label original; first US issue					
❑ ILPS 9365	The Chieftains 2	1976	3.00	6.00	12.00
—Black label original; first US issue					
❑ ILPS 9379	The Chieftains 3	1976	3.00	6.00	12.00
—Black label original; first US issue					
❑ ILPS 9380	The Chieftains 4	1976	3.00	6.00	12.00
—Black label original; first US issue					
❑ ILPS 9432	Bonaparte's Retreat	1977	3.00	6.00	12.00
❑ ILPS 9501	The Chieftains Live	1978	3.00	6.00	12.00
RCA					
❑ 6358-1-R	Celtic Wedding	1987	2.50	5.00	10.00
❑ 7858-1-R	A Chieftains Celebration	1989	3.00	6.00	12.00
SHANACHIE					
❑ 79019	Cotton-Eyed Joe	198?	2.50	5.00	10.00
❑ 79021	The Chieftains 1	1982	2.50	5.00	10.00
—Reissue of Island 9364					
❑ 79022	The Chieftains 2	198?	2.50	5.00	10.00
—Reissue of Island 9365					
❑ 79023	The Chieftains 3	198?	2.50	5.00	10.00
—Reissue of Island 9379					
❑ 79024	The Chieftains 4	198?	2.50	5.00	10.00
—Reissue of Island 9380					
❑ 79025	The Chieftains 5	198?	2.50	5.00	10.00
—Reissue of Island 9334					
❑ 79026	Bonaparte's Retreat	198?	2.50	5.00	10.00
—Reissue of Island 9432					
❑ 79036	Year of the French	1983	2.50	5.00	10.00
❑ 79050	The Chieftains in China	198?	2.50	5.00	10.00
❑ 79051	The Ballad of Iron Horse	198?	2.50	5.00	10.00

CHIFFONS, THE
45s
B.T. PUPPY
❑ 558	Secret Love/Strange, Strange Feeling	1970	2.50	5.00	10.00
BIG DEAL					
❑ 6003	Tonight's the Night/Do You Know	1960	20.00	40.00	80.00
BUDDAH					
❑ 171	So Much in Love/Strange, Strange Feeling	1970	2.50	5.00	10.00
LAURIE					
❑ 3152	He's So Fine/Oh My Love	1963	5.00	10.00	20.00
❑ 3152	He's So Fine/Oh My Lover	1963	5.00	10.00	20.00
—Both B-side titles have been advertised; we're not sure which came first					
❑ 3166	Lucky Me/Why Am I So Shy?	1963	3.75	7.50	15.00
❑ 3179	One Fine Day/Why Am I So Shy	1963	5.00	10.00	20.00
❑ 3195	A Love So Fine/Only My Friend	1963	3.00	6.00	12.00
❑ 3212	I Have a Boyfriend/I'm Gonna Dry My Eyes	1963	3.00	6.00	12.00
❑ 3224	Tonight I Met an Angel/Easy to Love	1964	3.00	6.00	12.00
❑ 3262	Sailor Boy/When Summer's Through	1964	3.00	6.00	12.00
❑ 3275	What Am I Gonna Do with You/Strange, Strange Feeling	1964	3.00	6.00	12.00
❑ 3301	Nobody Knows What's Going On (In My Mind But Me)/Did You Ever Go Steady	1965	3.00	6.00	12.00
❑ 3301	Nobody Knows What's Going On (In My Mind But Me)/The Real Thing	1965	3.00	6.00	12.00
❑ 3318	Tonight I'm Gonna Dream/Heavenly Place	1965	3.00	6.00	12.00
❑ 3340	Sweet Talkin' Guy/Did You Ever Go Steady	1966	3.75	7.50	15.00
❑ 3350	Out of This World/Just a Boy	1966	2.50	5.00	10.00
❑ 3357	Stop, Look, Listen/March	1966	2.50	5.00	10.00
❑ 3364	My Boyfriend's Back/I Got Plenty of Nuttin'	1966	2.50	5.00	10.00
❑ 3377	If I Knew Then/Keep the Boy Happy	1967	2.50	5.00	10.00
❑ 3423	Just for Tonight/Keep the Boy Happy	1968	2.50	5.00	10.00
❑ 3423	Just for Tonight/Teach Me How	1968	2.50	5.00	10.00
❑ 3460	Up on the Bridge/March	1968	2.50	5.00	10.00
❑ 3497	Love Me Like You're Gonna Lose Me/Three Dips of Ice Cream	1969	2.50	5.00	10.00
❑ 3630	My Sweet Lord/Main Nerve	1975	2.50	5.00	10.00
❑ 3648	Dream, Dream, Dream/Oh My Lover	1976	2.50	5.00	10.00
REPRISE					
❑ 20103	After Last Night/Doctor of Hearts	1962	5.00	10.00	20.00
RUST					
❑ 5070	When the Boy's Happy (The Girl's Happy Too)/Hockaday, Part 1	1963	6.25	12.50	25.00
—As "The Four Pennies"					
❑ 5071	Dry Your Eyes/My Block	1963	6.25	12.50	25.00
—As "The Four Pennies"					
WILDCAT					
❑ 601	Never Never/No More Tomorrows	1961	6.25	12.50	25.00

Albums
B.T. PUPPY
❑ S-1011	My Secret Love	1970	100.00	200.00	400.00
COLLECTABLES					
❑ COL-5042	Golden Classics	198?	3.00	6.00	12.00
LAURIE					
❑ LLP-2018 [M]	He's So Fine	1963	30.00	60.00	120.00
❑ LLP-2020 [M]	One Fine Day	1963	50.00	100.00	200.00
❑ LLP-2036 [M]	Sweet Talkin' Guy	1966	25.00	50.00	100.00
❑ SLP-2036 [S]	Sweet Talkin' Guy	1966	37.50	75.00	150.00
❑ 4001	Everything You Always Wanted to Hear by the Chiffons	1975	5.00	10.00	20.00
❑ DT-90075 [R]	He's So Fine	1965	50.00	100.00	200.00
—Capitol Record Club edition					
❑ ST-90779 [S]	Sweet Talkin' Guy	1966	50.00	100.00	200.00
—Capitol Record Club edition					

CHILDREN, THE
45s
ATCO
❑ 6633	Maypole/I'll Be Your Sunshine	1968	5.00	10.00	20.00
CINEMA					
❑ 025	Pills/(B-side unknown)	1968	7.50	15.00	30.00
LARAMIE					
❑ 666	Picture Me/(B-side unknown)	1967	10.00	20.00	40.00

Number	Title (A Side/B Side)	Yr	VG	VG+	NM

MAP CITY
❑ 304	What If I/Evil Woman	1970	3.00	6.00	12.00

ODE
❑ 66005	From the Very Start/Such a Fine Night	1970	5.00	10.00	20.00
❑ 66013	Fire King/Hand of a Lady	1971	5.00	10.00	20.00

Albums
ATCO
❑ SD 33-271	Rebirth	1968	6.25	12.50	25.00

CINEMA
❑ CLP-1	Rebirth	1968	37.50	75.00	150.00

CHILLIWACK Also see THE COLLECTORS.
12-Inch Singles
MILLENNIUM
❑ JD-11821 [DJ]	Tell It to the Telephone/(B-side blank)	1981	2.00	4.00	8.00
❑ JD-13116 [DJ]	Whatcha Gonna Do (Extended Dance Mix 6:06) (LP Version 3:50)	1982	2.50	5.00	10.00
❑ YD-13118	Secret Information/Really Don't Mind	1982	2.00	4.00	8.00

45s
A&M
❑ 1310	Lonesome Mary/Ridin'	1971	2.00	4.00	8.00
❑ 1395	Ground Hog/Nothin' to Do	1972	2.00	4.00	8.00

MILLENNIUM
❑ YB-11813	My Girl (Gone, Gone, Gone)/Sign Here	1981	—	2.00	4.00
❑ YB-13102	I Believe/Living in Stereo	1981	—	2.00	4.00
❑ YB-13110	Whatcha Gonna Do/Really Don't Mind	1982	—	2.00	4.00
❑ YB-13117	Secret Information/Really Don't Mind	1982	—	2.00	4.00
❑ YB-13123	Lean On Me/Night Time	1983	—	—	—
—Canceled					

MUSHROOM
❑ 7022	California Girl/Reach	1976	—	2.50	5.00
❑ 7024	Fly By Night/Mary Lou and Me	1977	—	2.50	5.00
❑ 7025	Something Better/Rain-O	1977	—	2.50	5.00
❑ 7028	Baby Blue/Something Better	1977	—	2.50	5.00
❑ 7033	Arms of Mary/I Wanna Be the One	1978	—	2.50	5.00
❑ 7038	Never Be the Same/I Wanna Be the One	1978	—	2.50	5.00
❑ 7046	Communication Breakdown/Are You With Me	1980	—	2.50	5.00

PARROT
❑ 350	I Must Have Been Blind/Chain Train	1970	2.00	4.00	8.00
❑ 357	Everyday/Sundown	1970	2.00	4.00	8.00

SIRE
❑ 716	Crazy Talk/In and Out	1974	—	2.50	5.00
❑ 718	Come On Over/Time Don't Mean a Thing to You	1975	—	2.50	5.00
❑ 720	If You Want My Love/Train's a-Comin' Back	1975	—	2.50	5.00
❑ 723	Last Day in December/Magnolia	1976	—	2.50	5.00

Albums
A&M
❑ SP-3509 [(2)]	Chilliwack	1971	6.25	12.50	25.00
❑ SP-4375	All Over You	1972	3.75	7.50	15.00

MILLENNIUM
❑ BXL1-7759	Wanna Be a Star	1981	2.50	5.00	10.00
❑ BXL1-7766	Opus X	1982	2.50	5.00	10.00

MUSHROOM
❑ MRS-5006	Dreams, Dreams, Dreams	1977	3.00	6.00	12.00
❑ MRS-5011	Lights from the Valley	1978	3.00	6.00	12.00
❑ MRS-5015	Breakdown in Paradise	1980	3.00	6.00	12.00

PARROT
❑ PAS 71040	Chilliwack	1970	5.00	10.00	20.00

SIRE
❑ SASD-7506	Chilliwack	1975	3.75	7.50	15.00
❑ SASD-7511	Rockerbox	1976	3.75	7.50	15.00

CHIMES, THE (1)
45s
LAURIE
❑ 3211	Whose Heart Are You Breaking Now/Baby's Coming Home	1963	3.75	7.50	15.00

LOST-NITE
❑ 208	Once in Awhile/Summer Night	196?	—	2.50	5.00
—Reissue					

METRO
❑ 1	Whose Heart Are You Breaking Now/Baby's Coming Home	1963	10.00	20.00	40.00

TAG
❑ 444	Once in Awhile/Summer Night	1960	10.00	20.00	40.00
—Light blue label					
❑ 444	Once in Awhile/Summer Night	1960	10.00	20.00	40.00
—Maroon label					
❑ 444	Once in Awhile/Oh, How I Love You So	1960	12.50	25.00	50.00
—B-side is actually by a group called the Bi-Tones, though credited to the Chimes					
❑ 445	I'm in the Mood for Love/Only Love	1961	7.50	15.00	30.00
❑ 447	Let's Fall in Love/Dream Girl	1961	6.25	12.50	25.00
❑ 450	Paradise/My Love	1961	7.50	15.00	30.00

CHIMES, THE (2) On the Arrow label, see FREDDIE SCOTT.

CHIMES, THE (3) On the Flair label, see THE FLAIRS.

CHIMES, THE (U) Some of these may be group (1).
45s
HOUSE OF BEAUTY
❑ 3	Tears from An Angel's Eyes/(B-side unknown)	1959	20.00	40.00	80.00

LIMELIGHT
❑ 3000	Cry, Baby, Cry/Angel Child	1963	6.25	12.50	25.00
❑ 3002	Du Wap/Stop, Look and Listen	1963	6.25	12.50	25.00

RESERVE
❑ 120	When School Starts Again/Nervous Heart	1957	10.00	20.00	40.00

ROYAL ROOST
❑ 577	Dearest Darling/A Fool Was I	1955	175.00	350.00	700.00

SPECIALTY
❑ 555	Tears on My Pillow/Cindy Lou	1955	15.00	30.00	60.00
❑ 574	Chop Chop/Pretty Little Girl	1956	15.00	30.00	60.00

CHIPMUNKS, THE, DAVID SEVILLE AND Listings only include the "original" group, which made recordings from 1958-68. Also see ROSS BAGDASARIAN; DAVID SEVILLE.
45s
DOT
❑ 16997	Apple Picker/Sorry About That, Herb	1967	3.00	6.00	12.00

Number	Title (A Side/B Side)	Yr	VG	VG+	NM

EMI
❑ S7-17645	The Chipmunk Song/Frosty the Snowman	1993	—	2.00	4.00
—Green vinyl					

LIBERTY
❑ 55168	The Chipmunk Song/Almost Good	1958	6.25	12.50	25.00
—Blue-green label					
❑ 55168	The Chipmunk Song/Almost Good	1958	7.50	15.00	30.00
—Black label					
❑ 55168	The Chipmunk Song/Almost Good	1958	7.50	15.00	30.00
—Dark blue label					
❑ 55179	Alvin's Harmonica/Mediocre	1959	5.00	10.00	20.00
❑ 55200 [M]	Ragtime Cowboy Joe/Flip Side	1959	5.00	10.00	20.00
❑ 55200 [PS]	Ragtime Cowboy Joe/Flip Side	1959	10.00	20.00	40.00
❑ 55233	Alvin's Orchestra/Copyright 1960	1960	3.75	7.50	15.00
❑ 55233 [PS]	Alvin's Orchestra/Copyright 1960	1960	10.00	20.00	40.00
❑ 55246	Coming 'Round the Mountain/Sing a Goofy Song	1960	3.75	7.50	15.00
❑ 55246 [PS]	Coming 'Round the Mountain/Sing a Goofy Song	1960	10.00	20.00	40.00
❑ 55250	The Chipmunk Song/Alvin's Harmonica	1959	3.75	7.50	15.00
—Blue-green label, no horizontal lines					
❑ 55250 [PS]	The Chipmunk Song/Alvin's Harmonica	1959	10.00	20.00	40.00
—Sleeve has Chipmunks depicted somewhat like real chipmunks					
❑ 55250	The Chipmunk Song/Alvin's Harmonica	1961	3.00	6.00	12.00
—Blue-green label with horizontal lines					
❑ 55250 [PS]	The Chipmunk Song/Alvin's Harmonica	1961	7.50	15.00	30.00
—Sleeve has Chipmunks depicted as the familiar cartoon characters					
❑ 55277	Alvin for President/Sack Time	1960	3.75	7.50	15.00
❑ 55277 [PS]	Alvin for President/Sack Time	1960	10.00	20.00	40.00
❑ 55289	Rudolph, the Red-Nosed Reindeer/Spain	1960	3.75	7.50	15.00
❑ 55289 [PS]	Rudolph, the Red-Nosed Reindeer/Spain	1960	10.00	20.00	40.00
❑ 55424	The Alvin Twist/I Wish I Could Speak French	1962	3.75	7.50	15.00
❑ 55452	America the Beautiful/My Wild Irish Rose	1962	3.75	7.50	15.00
❑ 55544	Alvin's All Star Chipmunk Band/Old MacDonald Cha Cha Cha	1963	3.75	7.50	15.00
❑ 55544 [PS]	Alvin's All Star Chipmunk Band/Old MacDonald Cha Cha Cha	1963	10.00	20.00	40.00
❑ 55632	Eefin' Alvin/Flip Side	1963	3.75	7.50	15.00
❑ 55635	The Night Before Christmas/Wonderful Day	1963	3.75	7.50	15.00
❑ 55635 [PS]	The Night Before Christmas/Wonderful Day	1963	7.50	15.00	30.00
❑ 55734	All My Lovin'/Do You Want to Know a Secret	1964	3.75	7.50	15.00
❑ 55773	Do-Re-Mi/Supercalifragilisticexpialidocious	1965	3.00	6.00	12.00
❑ 55832	I'm Henry VIII, I Am/What's New Pussycat	1965	3.00	6.00	12.00
❑ 56079	The Chipmunk Song/Christmas Blues	1968	4.00	8.00	16.00
—With Canned Heat					
❑ 77200 [S]	Ragtime Cowboy Joe/Flip Side	1959	10.00	20.00	40.00

SUNSET
❑ 61002	Talk to the Animals/My Friend the Doctor	1968	2.50	5.00	10.00
❑ 61002 [PS]	Talk to the Animals/My Friend the Doctor	1968	3.75	7.50	15.00
❑ 61003	Chitty Chitty Bang Bang/Hushabye Mountain	1968	2.50	5.00	10.00
❑ 61003 [PS]	Chitty Chitty Bang Bang/Hushabye Mountain	1968	3.75	7.50	15.00

UNITED ARTISTS
❑ 0056	The Chipmunk Song/Ragtime Cowboy Joe	1973	2.00	4.00	8.00
—"Silver Spotlight Series" reissue					
❑ 0057	Alvin's Harmonica/Rudolph, the Red-Nosed Reindeer	1973	2.00	4.00	8.00
—"Silver Spotlight Series" reissue					
❑ XW576	The Chipmunk Song/Rudolph, the Red-Nosed Reindeer	1974	—	3.00	6.00

7-Inch Extended Plays
LIBERTY
❑ LSX-1007	The Chipmunk Song/Ragtime Cowboy Joe// Alvin's Harmonica/If You Love Me	1960	7.50	15.00	30.00
❑ LSX-1007 [PS]	Let's All Sing with the Chipmunks	1960	12.50	25.00	50.00
❑ LSX-1016	Rudolph the Red-Nosed Reindeer/Jingle Bells/ /Frosty the Snowman/Santa Claus Is Comin' to Town	1962	5.00	10.00	20.00
❑ LSX-1016 [PS]	Christmas with the Chipmunks	1962	12.50	25.00	50.00
❑ LSX-1017	Wonderful Day/Christmas Time//Deck The Halls/The Night Before Christmas	1963	5.00	10.00	20.00
❑ LSX-1017 [PS]	Christmas with the Chipmunks, Volume 2	1963	12.50	25.00	50.00

Albums
LIBERTY
❑ LM-1070	Christmas with the Chipmunks	1980	2.00	4.00	8.00
—Reissue with two tracks omitted					
❑ LRP-3132 [M]	Let's All Sing with the Chipmunks	1959	7.50	15.00	30.00
—Black vinyl; original cover features "realistic" chipmunks and no reference to "The Alvin Show"					
❑ LRP-3132 [M]	Let's All Sing with the Chipmunks	1959	15.00	30.00	60.00
—Red vinyl					
❑ LRP-3132 [M]	Let's All Sing with the Chipmunks	1961	5.00	10.00	20.00
—Second cover features the "cartoon" Chipmunks and a reference to "The Alvin Show"					
❑ LRP-3159 [M]	Sing Again with the Chipmunks	1960	10.00	20.00	40.00
—Original cover features "realistic" chipmunks					
❑ LRP-3159 [M]	Sing Again with the Chipmunks	1961	5.00	10.00	20.00
—Second cover features the "cartoon" Chipmunks					
❑ LRP-3170 [M]	Around the World with the Chipmunks	1960	10.00	20.00	40.00
—Original cover features "realistic" chipmunks on and near a plane					
❑ LRP-3170 [M]	Around the World with the Chipmunks	1961	5.00	10.00	20.00
—Second cover features the "cartoon" Chipmunks on and near a camel					
❑ LRP-3209 [M]	The Alvin Show	1961	6.25	12.50	25.00
❑ LRP-3229 [M]	The Chipmunks Songbook	1962	6.25	12.50	25.00
❑ LRP-3256 [M]	Christmas with the Chipmunks	1962	6.25	12.50	25.00
❑ LRP-3334 [M]	Christmas with the Chipmunks, Vol. 2	1963	6.25	12.50	25.00
❑ LRP-3388 [M]	The Chipmunks Sing the Beatles Hits	1964	7.50	15.00	30.00
❑ LRP-3405 [M]	The Chipmunks Sing with Children	1965	5.00	10.00	20.00
❑ LRP-3424 [M]	The Chipmunks A-Go-Go	1965	5.00	10.00	20.00
❑ LST-7132 [S]	Let's All Sing with the Chipmunks	1959	10.00	20.00	40.00
—Black vinyl; original cover features "realistic" chipmunks and no reference to "The Alvin Show"					
❑ LST-7132 [S]	Let's All Sing with the Chipmunks	1959	20.00	40.00	80.00
—Red vinyl					
❑ LST-7132 [S]	Let's All Sing with the Chipmunks	1961	6.25	12.50	25.00
—Second cover features the "cartoon" Chipmunks and a reference to "The Alvin Show"					
❑ LST-7159 [S]	Sing Again with the Chipmunks	1960	12.50	25.00	50.00
—Original cover features "realistic" chipmunks					
❑ LST-7159 [S]	Sing Again with the Chipmunks	1961	6.25	12.50	25.00
—Second cover features the "cartoon" Chipmunks					
❑ LST-7170 [S]	Around the World with the Chipmunks	1960	6.25	12.50	25.00
—Second cover features the "cartoon" Chipmunks on and near a camel					

C

Number	Title (A Side/B Side)	Yr	VG	VG+	NM
❑ LST-7170 [S]	Around the World with the Chipmunks	1960	12.50	25.00	50.00
—Original covers have "realistic" chipmunks on and near a plane.					
❑ LST-7209 [S]	The Alvin Show	1961	7.50	15.00	30.00
❑ LST-7229 [S]	The Chipmunks Songbook	1962	7.50	15.00	30.00
❑ LST-7256 [S]	Christmas with the Chipmunks	1962	7.50	15.00	30.00
❑ LST-7334 [S]	Christmas with the Chipmunks, Vol. 2	1963	7.50	15.00	30.00
❑ LST-7388 [S]	The Chipmunks Sing the Beatles Hits	1964	10.00	20.00	40.00
❑ LST-7405 [S]	The Chipmunks Sing with Children	1965	6.25	12.50	25.00
❑ LST-7424 [S]	The Chipmunks A-Go-Go	1965	6.25	12.50	25.00
MISTLETOE					
❑ MLP-1216	Christmas with the Chipmunks	197?	2.00	4.00	8.00
—Reissue of Liberty LST-7256					
❑ MLP-1217	Christmas with the Chipmunks, Vol. 2	197?	2.00	4.00	8.00
—Reissue of Liberty LST-7334					
PICKWICK					
❑ SPC-1034	Christmas with the Chipmunks	1980	2.50	5.00	10.00
❑ SPC-1035	The Twelve Days of Christmas with The Chipmunks	1980	2.50	5.00	10.00
—Reissue of "Christmas with the Chipmunks, Vol. 2"					
SUNSET					
❑ LST-7334 [S]	Christmas with the Chipmunks, Vol. 2	1968	5.00	10.00	20.00
—Budget-line reissue of Liberty LST-7334					
❑ LST-7424 [S]	The Chipmunks A-Go-Go	196?	3.75	7.50	15.00
—Same cover as Liberty 7424, but with "SUNSET" sticker at upper right					
UNITED ARTISTS					
❑ UA-LA352-E2 [(2)]	Christmas with the Chipmunks	1974	5.00	10.00	20.00
—Entire contents of both original Liberty LPs					

CHIPS, THE (1) Male vocal group.
45s
JOSIE

Number	Title (A Side/B Side)	Yr	VG	VG+	NM
❑ 803	Rubber Biscuit/Oh My Darlin'	1956	25.00	50.00	100.00

CHIPS, THE (2)
45s
PHILIPS

Number	Title (A Side/B Side)	Yr	VG	VG+	NM
❑ 40520	Mixed Up Shook Up Girl/Break It Gently	1968	2.50	5.00	10.00
❑ 40520 [PS]	Mixed Up Shook Up Girl/Break It Gently	1968	10.00	20.00	40.00

CHIPS, THE (3) Memphis group.
45s
SATELLITE

Number	Title (A Side/B Side)	Yr	VG	VG+	NM
❑ 105	As You can See/You Make Me Feel So Good	1961	30.00	60.00	120.00

CHIPS, THE (4)
45s
STRAND

Number	Title (A Side/B Side)	Yr	VG	VG+	NM
❑ 25027	Darling (I Need Your Love)/You're On My Side	1961	10.00	20.00	40.00
VENICE					
❑ 101	Darling (I Need Your Love)/You're On My Side	1961	30.00	60.00	120.00

CHIPS, THE (5) Lead singer: JOE SOUTH.
45s
TOLLIE

Number	Title (A Side/B Side)	Yr	VG	VG+	NM
❑ 9042	Party People/Long Lonely Winter	1965	2.50	5.00	10.00

CHIPS, THE (U)
45s
EMBER

Number	Title (A Side/B Side)	Yr	VG	VG+	NM
❑ 1077	What a Lie/Bye, Bye, My Love	1961	5.00	10.00	20.00

CHOCO AND HIS MALIMBA DRUM RHYTHMS
Albums
AUDIO FIDELITY

Number	Title (A Side/B Side)	Yr	VG	VG+	NM
❑ AFLP-2102 [M]	African Latin Voodoo Drums	1962	5.00	10.00	20.00
❑ AFSD-6102 [S]	African Latin Voodoo Drums	1962	7.50	15.00	30.00

CHOCOLATE WATCH BAND, THE
45s
TOWER

Number	Title (A Side/B Side)	Yr	VG	VG+	NM
❑ 373	Are You Gonna Be There (At the Love-In)/No Way Out	1967	12.50	25.00	50.00
UPTOWN					
❑ 740	Baby Blue/Sweet Young Thing	1967	75.00	150.00	300.00
❑ 749	Misty Lane/She Weaves a Tender Trap	1967	12.50	25.00	50.00
Albums					
RHINO					
❑ RNLP-108	The Best of the Chocolate Watch Band	1983	3.00	6.00	12.00
TOWER					
❑ ST 5096 [S]	No Way Out	1967	100.00	200.00	400.00
❑ T 5096 [M]	No Way Out	1967	75.00	150.00	300.00
❑ ST 5106 [S]	The Inner Mystique	1968	75.00	150.00	300.00
❑ T 5106 [M]	The Inner Mystique	1968	100.00	200.00	400.00
❑ ST 5153	One Step Beyond	1969	75.00	150.00	300.00

CHOIR, THE Two members went on to form the RASPBERRIES.
45s
CANADIAN AMERICAN

Number	Title (A Side/B Side)	Yr	VG	VG+	NM
❑ 203	It's Cold Outside/I'm Goin' Home	1967	10.00	20.00	40.00
INTREPID					
❑ 75020	Gonna Have a Good Time Tonight/ So Much Love	1970	5.00	10.00	20.00
ROULETTE					
❑ 4738	It's Cold Outside/I'm Goin' Home	1967	3.75	7.50	15.00
❑ 4760	No One Here to Play With/ Don't You Feel a Little Sorry for Me	1967	3.75	7.50	15.00
❑ 7005	Changin' My Mind/When You Were With Me	1968	3.75	7.50	15.00
Albums					
SUNDAZED					
❑ LP 5009	Choir Practice	1992	2.50	5.00	10.00

CHORDCATS, THE See THE CHORDS.

CHORDETTES, THE
45s
ATLANTIC

Number	Title (A Side/B Side)	Yr	VG	VG+	NM
❑ 89310	Lollipop/Never on Sunday	1986	—	—	3.00
❑ 89310 [PS]	Lollipop/Never on Sunday	1986	—	—	3.00
CADENCE					
❑ 1239	It's You, It's You I Love/ True Love Goes on and On	1954	3.75	7.50	15.00
❑ 1247	Mr. Sandman/I Don't Wanna See You Cryin'	1954	3.75	7.50	15.00
❑ 1259	Lonely Lips/The Dudelsack Song	1955	3.00	6.00	12.00
❑ 1267	Hummingbird/I Told a Lie	1955	3.00	6.00	12.00
❑ 1273	The Wedding/I Don't Know, I Don't Care	1955	3.00	6.00	12.00
❑ 1284	Eddie My Love/Whispering Willie	1956	3.00	6.00	12.00
❑ 1291	Born to Be with You/Love Never Changes	1956	3.00	6.00	12.00
❑ 1299	Lay Down Your Arms/Teen Age Goodnight	1956	3.00	6.00	12.00
❑ 1307	Come Home to My Arms/(Fifi's) Walking the Poodle	1957	3.00	6.00	12.00
❑ 1319	Echo of Love/Like a Baby	1957	3.00	6.00	12.00
❑ 1330	Just Between You and Me/Soft Sands	1957	3.00	6.00	12.00
❑ 1341	Photographs/Baby of Mine	1957	3.00	6.00	12.00
❑ 1345	Lollipop/Baby Come-a Back-a	1958	3.75	7.50	15.00
❑ 1349	Zorro/Love Is a Two-Way Street	1958	3.00	6.00	12.00
❑ 1349 [PS]	Zorro/Love Is a Two-Way Street	1958	6.25	12.50	25.00
❑ 1361	No Other Arms, No Other Lips/ We Should Be Together	1959	2.50	5.00	10.00
❑ 1366	A Girl's Work Is Never Done/No Wheels	1959	2.50	5.00	10.00
❑ 1366 [PS]	A Girl's Work Is Never Done/No Wheels	1959	6.25	12.50	25.00
❑ 1367	Forever/Ho Hum	1959	2.50	5.00	10.00
❑ 1382	All My Sorrows/A Broken Vow	1960	2.50	5.00	10.00
❑ 1402	Never on Sunday/A Faraway Star	1961	2.50	5.00	10.00
❑ 1412	The Exodus Song/Theme from Goodbye Again (Say No More-It's Goodbye)	1961	2.50	5.00	10.00
❑ 1417	Adios/White Rose of Athens	1962	2.50	5.00	10.00
❑ 1425	In the Deep Blue Sea/All My Sorrows	1962	2.50	5.00	10.00
❑ 1442	True Love Goes on and On/All My Sorrows	1963	2.50	5.00	10.00
COLUMBIA					
❑ 38756	When You Were Sweet Sixteen/Moonlight Bay	1950	3.75	7.50	15.00
❑ 38757	Carry Me Back to Old Virginny/Ballin' the Jack	1950	3.75	7.50	15.00
❑ 38758	Tell Me Why/Shine On Harvest Moon	1950	3.75	7.50	15.00
❑ 38759	I'd Love to Live in Loveland (With a Love Like You)/When Day Is Done	1950	3.75	7.50	15.00
—The above four comprise box set B-201					
❑ 39251	Runnin' Wild/Alice Blue Gown	1951	3.75	7.50	15.00
❑ 39252	Love Me and the World Is Mine/ Lonesome That's All	1951	3.75	7.50	15.00
❑ 39253	Moonlight on the Ganges/ Let the Rest of the World Go By	1951	3.75	7.50	15.00
❑ 39254	The World Is Waiting for the Sunrise/ Love's Old Sweet Song	1951	3.75	7.50	15.00
❑ 39793	Carolina Moon//The Anniversary Waltz/ Sentimental Journey	1952	3.75	7.50	15.00
❑ 39794	A Little Street Where Old Friends Meet//Basin Street Blues + 1	1952	3.75	7.50	15.00
❑ 39795	Drifting and Dreaming + 1//I'm Drifting Back to Dreamland/Angry	1952	3.75	7.50	15.00
❑ 39796	S'posin'/The Sweetheart of Sigma Chi// Kentucky Babe/In the Sweet Long Ago	1952	3.75	7.50	15.00

7-Inch Extended Plays
CADENCE

Number	Title (A Side/B Side)	Yr	VG	VG+	NM
❑ CEP 101	Mr. Sandman/Hummingbird//Born to Be with You/Soft Sands	1956	3.75	7.50	15.00
❑ CEP 101 [PS]	The Chordettes	1956	3.75	7.50	15.00
❑ CEP 102	Just Between You and Me/Eddie My Love//Lay Down Your Arms/Teen Age Goodnight	1957	3.75	7.50	15.00
❑ CEP 102 [PS]	The Chordettes	1957	3.75	7.50	15.00
COLUMBIA					
❑ B-401 [PS]	The Chordettes Sing Your Requests	195?	3.00	6.00	12.00
—Double-pocket sleeve for 1878 and 1879					
❑ 5-1878	Wait Till the Sun Shines Nellie/They Say It's Wonderful//Wonderful One/Darkness on the Delta	195?	3.00	6.00	12.00
❑ 5-1879	I Wonder Who's Kissing Her Now?/ For Me and My Gal//I Believe/Down Among the Sheltering Pines	195?	3.00	6.00	12.00

Albums
BARNABY

Number	Title (A Side/B Side)	Yr	VG	VG+	NM
❑ BR-4003	All the Very Best of the Chordettes	1976	3.00	6.00	12.00
CADENCE					
❑ CLP-1002 [10]	Close Harmony	1955	12.50	25.00	50.00
❑ CLP-3001 [M]	The Chordettes	1957	10.00	20.00	40.00
❑ CLP-3020 [M]	Barbershop Harmony	1958	10.00	20.00	40.00
❑ CLP-3056 [M]	Never on Sunday	1962	5.00	10.00	20.00
❑ CLP-25056 [S]	Never on Sunday	1962	7.50	15.00	30.00
COLUMBIA					
❑ CL 956 [M]	Listen	1955	12.50	25.00	50.00
❑ CL 2519 [10]	The Chordettes	1955	10.00	20.00	40.00
❑ CL 6111 [10]	Harmony Time	1950	12.50	25.00	50.00
❑ CL 6170 [10]	Harmony Time, Vol. 2	1951	12.50	25.00	50.00
❑ CL 6218 [10]	Harmony Encores	1952	12.50	25.00	50.00
❑ CL 6285 [10]	Your Requests	1953	12.50	25.00	50.00
HARMONY					
❑ HL 7164 [M]	The Chordettes	196?	3.75	7.50	15.00
RHINO					
❑ R1-70849	The Best of the Chordettes	1989	3.00	6.00	12.00

CHORDS, THE
45s
ATCO

Number	Title (A Side/B Side)	Yr	VG	VG+	NM
❑ 6213	Sh-Boom/Little Maiden	1961	3.75	7.50	15.00
—As "The Sh-Booms"					
ATLANTIC					
❑ 2074	Blue Moon/Short Skirts	1960	5.00	10.00	20.00
—As "The Sh-Booms"					
CASINO					
❑ 451	Tears in Your Eyes/Don't Be a Jumpin' Jack	1958	7.50	15.00	30.00
CAT					
❑ 104	Sh-Boom/Little Maiden	1954	15.00	30.00	60.00
❑ 104	Sh-Boom/Cross Over the Bridge	1954	30.00	60.00	120.00
❑ 109	Zippety Zum (I'm in Love)/Bless You (For Being an Angel)	1954	10.00	20.00	40.00
❑ 112	A Girl to Love/Hold Me Baby	1955	10.00	20.00	40.00
—As "The Chordcats"					

Number	Title (A Side/B Side)	Yr	VG	VG+	NM
❑ 117	Could It Be/Pretty Wild	1955	10.00	20.00	40.00
—As "The Sh-Booms"					
METRO					
❑ 20015	Elephant Walk/Pretty Face	1959	5.00	10.00	20.00
VIK					
❑ 0295	I Don't Want to Set the World on Fire/Lu Lu	1957	7.50	15.00	30.00
—As "The Sh-Booms"					

CHORDS, THE (2) Nashville studio group.
45s

Number	Title (A Side/B Side)	Yr	VG	VG+	NM
HIT					
❑ 163	Two Plus Two/Mr. Lonely	1964	2.00	4.00	8.00
—B-side by Fred York					
❑ 174	Have You Been There/Downtown	1965	2.00	4.00	8.00
—B-side by Betty York					
❑ 186	The Jolly Green Giant/Ring Telephone	1965	2.00	4.00	8.00
—B-side by Connie Dee					
❑ 203	Don't Let Me Be Misunderstood/The Sun Will Still Shine	1965	2.50	5.00	10.00
—B-side by the Chellows					
❑ 212	Mrs. Brown You've Got a Lovely Daughter/Where Were You	1965	2.50	5.00	10.00
❑ 216	I'm Henry VIII, I Am/One Dyin' and a-Buryin'	1965	2.50	5.00	10.00
—B-side by Marty Anderson					
❑ 232	Over and Over/We Can Work It Out	1965	3.00	6.00	12.00
—B-side by the Jalopy Five					
❑ 233	Fever/Make the World Go Away	1965	2.00	4.00	8.00
—B-side by Johnny Singer					
❑ 236	As Tears Go By/Five O'Clock World	1966	3.00	6.00	12.00
—B-side by the McCalls					
❑ 242	Listen People/Ballad of the Green Berets	1966	2.00	4.00	8.00
—B-side by Herb Eaton					
❑ 254	Leaning on the Lamp Post/How Does That Grab You Darlin'	1966	2.00	4.00	8.00
—B-side by Betty Richards					
❑ 256	A Groovy Kind of Love/Green Grass	1966	2.00	4.00	8.00
—B-side by Ed Hardin					
❑ 263	This Door Swings Both Ways/Mother's Little Helper	1966	2.50	5.00	10.00
—B-side by the Jalopy Five					
❑ 265	Dandy/Sunshine Superman	1966	2.00	4.00	8.00
—B-side by Joe King					
❑ 271	Have You Seen Your Mother, Baby/The Hair on My Chinny Chin Chin	1966	2.50	5.00	10.00
—B-side by the Jalopy Five					
❑ 272	Snoopy vs. the Red Baron/That's Life	1966	2.00	4.00	8.00
—B-side by Bobby Sims					
❑ 278	Georgy Girl/Nashville Cats	1967	2.00	4.00	8.00
—B-side by the Chellows					
❑ 282	Pretty Ballerina/Baby I Need Your Lovin'	1967	2.00	4.00	8.00
—B-side by Ed Hardin					
❑ 286	Dedicated to the One I Love/Something Stupid	1967	2.00	4.00	8.00
—B-side by Bobby and Connie					
❑ 291	Don't You Care/You Got What It Takes	1967	2.00	4.00	8.00
❑ 292	Creeque Alley/Him or Me — What's It Gonna Be?	1967	2.00	4.00	8.00
—B-side by the Chellows					
❑ 294	Mirage/Release Me	1967	2.00	4.00	8.00
—B-side by Ed Hardin					
❑ 299	Up, Up and Away/Windy	1967	2.00	4.00	8.00
—B-side by the Jalopy Five					
❑ 300	Carrie-Anne/Pleasant Valley Sunday	1967	2.00	4.00	8.00
—B-side by the Jalopy Five					
❑ 302	Mercy, Mercy, Mercy/Light My Fire	1967	2.00	4.00	8.00
—B-side by the Fantastics					
❑ 303	White Rabbit/Ode to Billie Joe	1967	2.00	4.00	8.00
—B-side by Kathy Shannon					
❑ 307	The Letter/Dandelion	1967	2.50	5.00	10.00
—B-side by the Jalopy Five					
❑ 308	Incense and Peppermints/Holiday	1967	2.00	4.00	8.00
—B-side by the Chellows					
❑ 314	Massachusetts/Pata Pata	1967	2.00	4.00	8.00
—B-side by the Fantastics					
❑ 319	I Can Take or Leave Your Loving/Love Is Blue	1968	2.00	4.00	8.00
—B-side by the New Society Group					
❑ 325	The Unicorn/Young Girl	1968	2.00	4.00	8.00
—B-side by the Jalopy Five					
❑ 326	Lady Madonna/A Beautiful Morning	1968	2.00	4.00	8.00
—B-side by the Classmates					
❑ 332	Reach Out of the Darkness/D.W. Washburn	1968	2.00	4.00	8.00
—B-side by the Jalopy Five					
❑ 335	Turn Around, Look at Me/The Look of Love	1968	2.00	4.00	8.00
—B-side by the Classmates					
❑ 337	Sunshine of Your Love/You Keep Me Hangin' On	1968	2.00	4.00	8.00
—B-side by Leroy Jones					
❑ 339	Hello, I Love You/Dreams of the Everyday Housewife	1968	2.00	4.00	8.00
—B-side by Bobby Sims					
❑ 342	Born to Be Wild/Revolution	1968	2.50	5.00	10.00
—B-side by the Jalopy Five					
❑ 344	My Special Angel/Over You	1968	2.00	4.00	8.00
—B-side by the Fantastics					
❑ 346	Girl Watcher/Those Were the Days	1968	2.00	4.00	8.00
—B-side by Kathy Shannon					
❑ 353	Worst That Could Happen/Son-of-a-Preacher-Man	1969	2.00	4.00	8.00
—B-side by Kathy Shannon					

CHOSEN FEW, THE Many different groups.
45s

Number	Title (A Side/B Side)	Yr	VG	VG+	NM
AUTUMN					
❑ 17	Nobody But Me/I Think It's Time	1965	2.50	5.00	10.00
CANADIAN AMERICAN					
❑ 202	Cute Thing/One of Those Songs	1967	3.00	6.00	12.00
CANUSA					
❑ 504	Summer's Love/Hey Joe	1967	3.75	7.50	15.00
CANYON					
❑ 1000	Talking All the Love I Can/Birth of a Playboy	196?	2.50	5.00	10.00

Number	Title (A Side/B Side)	Yr	VG	VG+	NM
CO-OP					
❑ 510	Why Can't I Love You/La La La La La	1966	3.00	6.00	12.00
❑ 511	Summer's Love/(Instrumental)	1967	3.00	6.00	12.00
CRYSTAL					
❑ 1107	You're a Big Girl Now/(B-side unknown)	196?	2.50	5.00	10.00
DART					
❑ 1080	Foolin' Around with Me/We Walk Together	1967	2.00	4.00	8.00
DENIM					
❑ 1092	Pink Clouds and Lemonade/Stop in the Name of Love	196?	2.00	4.00	8.00
LIBERTY					
❑ 55919	Synthetic Man/The Last Man Alive	1966	2.50	5.00	10.00
❑ 55962	Asian Chrome/Earth Above, Sky Below	1967	2.50	5.00	10.00
NORTH BEACH					
❑ 1003	Nobody But Me/I Think It's Time	1965	3.75	7.50	15.00
PLAYBOY					
❑ 106	I've Had It/Ask Me Baby	196?	2.50	5.00	10.00
POWER INTERNATIONAL					
❑ 872	Another Goodbye/Forget About the Past	1966	10.00	20.00	40.00
RCA VICTOR					
❑ 74-0217	Maybe the Rain Will Fall/Deeper In	1969	2.00	4.00	8.00
❑ 74-0254	I'll Never Change You/Talk with Me	1969	2.00	4.00	8.00
ROULETTE					
❑ 7015	Footsee/You Can Never Be Wrong	1968	2.00	4.00	8.00
Albums					
MAPLE					
❑ 6000	Takin' All the Love I Can	196?	5.00	10.00	20.00
RCA VICTOR					
❑ LSP-4242	The Chosen Few	1969	5.00	10.00	20.00

CHRISTIAN, DIANE
45s

Number	Title (A Side/B Side)	Yr	VG	VG+	NM
BELL					
❑ 610	It Happened One Night/Wonderful Guy	1965	2.50	5.00	10.00
❑ 617	Little Boy/Why Don't the Boy Leave Me Alone	1965	2.50	5.00	10.00
SMASH					
❑ 1862	Has Anybody Seen My Boyfriend/There's So Much About My Baby	1963	2.50	5.00	10.00

CHRISTIAN, NEIL
45s

Number	Title (A Side/B Side)	Yr	VG	VG+	NM
MORNING STAR					
❑ 517	That's Nice/She's Got the Action	19??	2.00	4.00	8.00
RCA VICTOR					
❑ 47-8828	That's Nice/She's Got the Action	1966	2.00	4.00	8.00

CHRISTIAN, ROGER
45s

Number	Title (A Side/B Side)	Yr	VG	VG+	NM
RENDEZVOUS					
❑ 195	The Meaning of Merry Christmas/Little Mary Christmas	1962	6.25	12.50	25.00

CHRISTIE
45s

Number	Title (A Side/B Side)	Yr	VG	VG+	NM
EPIC					
❑ 10626	Yellow River/Down the Mississippi Line	1970	—	2.50	5.00
❑ 10695	San Bernadino/Here I Am	1971	—	2.00	4.00
❑ 10732	Man of Many Faces/Country Sam	1971	—	2.00	4.00
Albums					
EPIC					
❑ E 30403	Yellow River	1970	3.75	7.50	15.00

CHRISTIE, LOU Also see THE CLASSICS (2); THE CLAMS; THE CRITTERS.
45s

Number	Title (A Side/B Side)	Yr	VG	VG+	NM
ALCAR					
❑ 207	Close Your Eyes/Funny Thing	1963	6.25	12.50	25.00
❑ 208	You're With It/Tomorrow Will Come	1963	6.25	12.50	25.00
AMERICAN MUSIC MAKERS					
❑ 006	The Jury/Little Did I Know	1963	7.50	15.00	30.00
BUDDAH					
❑ 65	Genesis and the Third Verse/Rake Up the Leaves	1968	2.00	4.00	8.00
❑ 76	Canterbury Road/Saints of Aquarius	1969	2.00	4.00	8.00
❑ 116	I'm Gonna Make You Mine/I'm Gonna Get Married	1969	—	3.00	6.00
❑ 149	Are You Getting Any Sunshine/It'll Take Time	1970	—	2.50	5.00
❑ 163	Love Is Over/She Sold Me Magic	1970	—	2.50	5.00
❑ 192	Indian Lady/Glory River	1970	—	2.50	5.00
❑ 231 [DJ]	Waco (same on both sides)	1971	—	3.00	6.00
—Stock copy does not exist					
❑ 235	Waco/Lighthouse	1971	—	2.50	5.00
❑ 257	Mickey's Monkey/She Sold Me Magic	1971	6.25	12.50	25.00
❑ 285	Sing Me, Sing Me/Paper Song	1972	—	2.50	5.00
❑ 285 [PS]	Sing Me, Sing Me/Paper Song	1972	2.50	5.00	10.00
—Sleeve appears to be promo only					
❑ 312	Shuffle On Down to Pittsburgh/I'm Gonna Get Married	1972	5.00	10.00	20.00
C&C					
❑ 102	The Gypsy Cried/Red Sails in the Sunset	1962	50.00	100.00	200.00
CO & CE					
❑ 235	Outside the Gates of Heaven/All That Glitters Isn't Gold	1966	2.50	5.00	10.00
COLPIX					
❑ 735	Merry-Go-Round/Guitars and Bongos	1964	3.00	6.00	12.00
❑ 753	Pot of Gold/Have I Sinned	1964	3.00	6.00	12.00
❑ 770	Make Summer Last Forever/Why Did You Do It Baby	1965	3.00	6.00	12.00
❑ 778	A Teenager in Love/Back Track	1965	3.00	6.00	12.00
❑ 799	Cryin' on My Knees/Big Time	1966	3.00	6.00	12.00
❑ 799 [PS]	Cryin' on My Knees/Big Time	1966	6.25	12.50	25.00
COLUMBIA					
❑ 44062	Shake Hands and Walk Away Cryin'/Escape	1967	3.75	7.50	15.00
❑ 44177	Self Expression/Back to the Days of the Romans	1967	3.75	7.50	15.00
❑ 44240	(I Remember) Gina/Escape	1967	3.75	7.50	15.00
❑ 44338	Back to the Days of the Romans/Don't Stop Me	1967	3.75	7.50	15.00
EPIC					
❑ 8-50244	Summer in Malibu/Ridin' in My Van	1976	3.75	7.50	15.00

Number	Title (A Side/B Side)	Yr	VG	VG+	NM
LIFESONG					
❑ 1775	Theme from "People" (Part 1)/Theme from "People" (Part 2)	1978	12.50	25.00	50.00
—As "Sacco"					
MGM					
❑ 13412	Lightnin' Strikes/Cryin' in the Streets	1965	3.75	7.50	15.00
❑ 13473	Rhapsody in the Rain/Trapeze	1966	3.75	7.50	15.00
—Revised A-side has altered lyrics: "We fell in love in the rain/And in this car, love came like a falling star." Matrix number in dead wax is "66-XY-308 D.J."					
❑ 13473	Rhapsody in the Rain/Trapeze	1966	5.00	10.00	20.00
—Original version of A-side had racy (by 1966 standards) lyrics: "We were makin' out in the rain/And in this car, our love went much too far." Matrix number in dead wax is "66-XY-308"					
❑ 13473 [PS]	Rhapsody in the Rain/Trapeze	1966	5.00	10.00	20.00
❑ 13533	Painter/Du Ronda	1966	2.50	5.00	10.00
❑ 13533 [PS]	Painter/Du Ronda	1966	5.00	10.00	20.00
❑ 13576	If My Car Could Only Talk/Song of Lita	1966	2.50	5.00	10.00
❑ 13623	Since I Don't Have You/Wild Life's in Season	1966	2.50	5.00	10.00
MIDLAND INT'L.					
❑ MB-10848	You're Gonna Make Love to Me/Fantasies	1976	3.75	7.50	15.00
❑ MB-10959	Spanish Wine/Dancing in the Sand	1977	3.75	7.50	15.00
MIDSONG INT'L.					
❑ 72013	Don't Knock My Love (Short)/Don't Knock My Love (Long)	1980	2.50	5.00	10.00
—With Pia Zadora					
PLATEAU					
❑ 4551	Guardian Angels/(B-side unknown)	1981	10.00	20.00	40.00
RHINO					
❑ 90105	O Holy Night (same on both sides)	1991	—	3.00	6.00
—With the University of Pittsburgh Men's Glee Club					
ROULETTE					
❑ 4457	The Gypsy Cried/Red Sails in the Sunset	1963	3.75	7.50	15.00
—Pink label					
❑ 4457	The Gypsy Cried/Red Sails in the Sunset	1963	5.00	10.00	20.00
—White label with spokes					
❑ 4457	The Gypsy Cried/Red Sails in the Sunset	1964	2.50	5.00	10.00
—Orange and yellow label					
❑ 4481	Two Faces Have I/All That Glitters Isn't Gold	1963	3.75	7.50	15.00
❑ 4504	How Many Teardrops/You and I (Have a Right to Cry)	1963	3.00	6.00	12.00
❑ 4527	Shy Boy/It Can Happen	1963	3.00	6.00	12.00
❑ 4545	Stay/There They Go	1964	3.75	7.50	15.00
❑ 4554	Maybe You'll Be There/When You Dance	1964	6.25	12.50	25.00
SLIPPED DISC					
❑ 45270	Summer Days/The One and Only Original Sunshine Kid	1976	3.75	7.50	15.00
THREE BROTHERS					
❑ 400	Blue Canadian Rocky Dream/Wilma Lee and Stoney	1973	2.00	4.00	8.00
❑ 402	Beyond the Blue Horizon/Saddle the Wind	1974	—	2.50	5.00
❑ 403	You Were the One/Good Morning	1974	2.00	4.00	8.00
❑ 405	Hey You Cajun/Sunbeam	1974	2.50	5.00	10.00
WORLD					
❑ 1002	The Jury/Little Did I Know	1963	7.50	15.00	30.00
Albums					
BUDDAH					
❑ BDS-5052	I'm Gonna Make You Mine	1969	3.75	7.50	15.00
❑ BDS-5073	Paint America Love	1971	3.75	7.50	15.00
CO & CE					
❑ LP-1231 [M]	Lou Christie Strikes Back	1966	10.00	20.00	40.00
—The front cover and spine use this title, but the back cover and label use "Lou Christie Strikes Again"					
COLPIX					
❑ CP-4001 [M]	Lou Christie Strikes Again	1966	7.50	5.00	30.00
❑ SCP-4001 [S]	Lou Christie Strikes Again	1966	12.50	25.00	50.00
51 WEST					
❑ P 18260	Lou Christie Does Detroit	1983	3.75	7.50	15.00
MGM					
❑ E-4360 [M]	Lightnin' Strikes	1966	3.75	7.50	15.00
❑ SE-4360 [S]	Lightnin' Strikes	1966	5.00	10.00	20.00
❑ E-4394 [M]	Painter of Hits	1966	3.75	7.50	15.00
❑ SE-4394 [S]	Painter of Hits	1966	5.00	10.00	20.00
RHINO					
❑ R1-70246	EnLightnin'Ment: The Best of Lou Christie	1988	3.00	6.00	12.00
ROULETTE					
❑ R 25208 [M]	Lou Christie	1963	10.00	20.00	40.00
—White wall in background on front cover					
❑ R 25208 [M]	Lou Christie	1963	12.50	25.00	50.00
—Blue background on front cover					
❑ SR 25208 [S]	Lou Christie	1963	15.00	30.00	60.00
—White wall in background on front cover					
❑ SR 25208 [S]	Lou Christie	1963	20.00	40.00	80.00
—Blue background on front cover					
❑ R 25332 [M]	Lou Christie Strikes Again	1966	6.25	12.50	25.00
❑ SR 25332 [S]	Lou Christie Strikes Again	1966	7.50	15.00	30.00
SPIN-O-RAMA					
❑ M-173 [M]	Starring Lou Christie and the Classics	1966	5.00	10.00	20.00
❑ S-173 [S]	Starring Lou Christie and the Classics	1966	3.00	6.00	12.00
—The above LP also includes other artists					
THREE BROTHERS					
❑ THB-2000	Lou Christie	1973	5.00	10.00	20.00
CHRISTIE, SUSAN					
45s					
COLUMBIA					
❑ 43595	I Love Onions/Take Me As You Find Me	1966	2.50	5.00	10.00
❑ 43595 [PS]	I Love Onions/Take Me As You Find Me	1966	12.50	25.00	50.00
❑ 44117	Tonight You Belong to Me/Toy Balloon	1967	—	3.00	6.00
❑ 44327	All I Have to Do Is Dream/Anywhere You Are	1967	—	3.00	6.00
CHRISTMAS SPIRIT, THE (1) William B. Williams, narrator.					
45s					
DUEL					
❑ 503	It's Christmas/A World to Grow Up In	1961	3.00	6.00	12.00

Number	Title (A Side/B Side)	Yr	VG	VG+	NM
CHRISTMAS SPIRIT, THE (2) Members of THE TURTLES with LINDA RONSTADT.					
45s					
WHITE WHALE					
❑ 290	Christmas Is My Time of Year/Will You Still Believe	1968	20.00	40.00	80.00
CHRISTOPHER, JORDAN					
45s					
JUBILEE					
❑ 5440	Goodbye My Love/Broken Hearted Boy	1962	2.50	5.00	10.00
❑ 5440 [PS]	Goodbye My Love/Broken Hearted Boy	1962	6.25	12.50	25.00
UNITED ARTISTS					
❑ 954	The Knack/Big Time	1965	2.00	4.00	8.00
❑ 954 [PS]	The Knack/Big Time	1965	6.25	12.50	25.00
❑ 993	Hello Lover/Taste of Honey	1966	2.00	4.00	8.00
❑ 50049	Put Your Tears Away/World Down on Your Knees	1966	2.00	4.00	8.00
❑ 50072	When That I Was (A Little Tiny Boy)/(B-side unknown)	1966	2.00	4.00	8.00
❑ 50131	To Live a Lie/Angelica	1967	2.00	4.00	8.00
Albums					
UNITED ARTISTS					
❑ UAL 3479 [M]	Jordan Christopher Has the Knack	1966	5.00	10.00	20.00
❑ UAS 6479 [S]	Jordan Christopher Has the Knack	1966	6.25	12.50	25.00
CHRISTOPHER, TONY					
45s					
HIT					
❑ 56	What Will My Mary Say/South Street	1963	2.00	4.00	8.00
—B-side by the Dacrons					
CHRISTOPHER (1)					
45s					
BELL					
❑ 679	Hey Girl/Every Boy in the World	1967	3.75	7.50	15.00
DATE					
❑ 1664	Spring/Santa Ana Winds	1970	3.00	6.00	12.00
Albums					
BELL					
❑ 1203	R.P.M.	1970	5.00	10.00	20.00
CHRISTOPHER (2) Band from North Carolina.					
Albums					
CHRIS-TEE					
❑ 12411	What'cha Gonna Do	1970	1500.	2250.	3000.
—100 copies were pressed					
CHRISTOPHER (3) Band from Texas.					
Albums					
METROMEDIA					
❑ 1024	Christopher	1970	75.00	150.00	300.00
CHRISTOPHER (U)					
45s					
DOT					
❑ 17133	Valerie/Sunday Life	1968	3.75	7.50	15.00
WOODEN NICKEL					
❑ BWBO-0207	Get Me Goin' the Right Direction/Henry's Highway Fillin' Station	1974	—	3.00	6.00
CHRISTY, DON See SONNY.					
CHRISTY, JUNE					
45s					
CAPITOL					
❑ F1207	He Can Come Back Any Time He Wants To/A Mile Down the Highway	1950	5.00	10.00	20.00
❑ F1647	Get Happy/I'll Remember April	1951	3.00	6.00	12.00
—Reissue					
❑ F2163	Live Oak Tree/The Man I Love	1952	3.75	7.50	15.00
❑ F2199	Bei Mir Bist Du Schoen/Some Folks Do	1952	3.75	7.50	15.00
❑ F2308	My Heart Belongs to Only You/I Was a Fool	1952	3.75	7.50	15.00
❑ F2384	I've Got a Letter/Let Me Share Your Name	1953	3.75	7.50	15.00
❑ F2432	Great Scot/I Lived When I Met You	1953	3.75	7.50	15.00
❑ F2590	Not I/Whee Baby	1953	3.75	7.50	15.00
❑ F2765	First Thing You Know/Magazines Are Magic	1954	3.75	7.50	15.00
❑ F3213	Pete Kelly's Blues/Kicks	1955	3.00	6.00	12.00
❑ F3375	I Never Wanna Look Into Those Eyes Again/Look Out Up There	1956	3.00	6.00	12.00
❑ F3471	Intrigue/You Took Advantage of Me	1956	3.00	6.00	12.00
❑ 4864	One Note Samba/Bossa Nova	1963	2.00	4.00	8.00
7-Inch Extended Plays					
CAPITOL					
❑ EAP 1-448	My Heart Belongs to Only You/Get Happy/The Man I Love/I Lived When I Met You	195?	5.00	10.00	20.00
❑ EAP 1-448 [PS]	Get Happy with June Christy	195?	5.00	10.00	20.00
Albums					
CAPITOL					
❑ H 516 [10]	Something Cool	1954	20.00	40.00	80.00
❑ SM-516 [R]	Something Cool	197?	2.50	5.00	10.00
❑ ST 516 [S]	Something Cool	196?	3.75	7.50	15.00
—Re-recording of the original mono LP					
❑ T 516 [M]	Something Cool	1955	12.50	25.00	50.00
—Turquoise label					
❑ T 516 [M]	Something Cool	1959	6.25	12.50	25.00
—Black label with colorband, logo at left					
❑ T 516 [M]	Something Cool	196?	3.75	7.50	15.00
—Black label with colorband, logo at top					
❑ T 656 [M]	Duets	1955	10.00	20.00	40.00
—Turquoise label					
❑ T 725 [M]	The Misty Miss Christy	1956	10.00	20.00	40.00
—Turquoise label					
❑ T 833 [M]	June — Fair and Warmer!	1957	10.00	20.00	40.00
—Turquoise label					
❑ T 902 [M]	Gone for the Day	1957	10.00	20.00	40.00
—Turquoise label					
❑ T 1006 [M]	This Is June Christy!	1958	10.00	20.00	40.00
—Turquoise label					

C

Number	Title (A Side/B Side)	Yr	VG	VG+	NM
❑ ST 1076 [S]	June's Got Rhythm	1958	10.00	20.00	40.00
—Black label with colorband, Capitol logo at left					
❑ T 1076 [M]	June's Got Rhythm	1958	7.50	15.00	30.00
—Black label with colorband, Capitol logo at left					
❑ ST 1114 [S]	The Song Is June!	1959	10.00	20.00	40.00
—Black label with colorband, Capitol logo at left					
❑ T 1114 [M]	The Song Is June!	1959	7.50	15.00	30.00
—Black label with colorband, Capitol logo at left					
❑ ST 1202 [S]	June Christy Recalls Those Kenton Days	1959	10.00	20.00	40.00
—Black label with colorband, Capitol logo at left					
❑ T 1202 [M]	June Christy Recalls Those Kenton Days	1959	7.50	15.00	30.00
—Black label with colorband, Capitol logo at left					
❑ ST 1308 [S]	Ballads for Night People	1959	10.00	20.00	40.00
—Black label with colorband, Capitol logo at left					
❑ T 1308 [M]	Ballads for Night People	1959	7.50	15.00	30.00
—Black label with colorband, Capitol logo at left					
❑ STBO 1327 [(2)S]Road Show		1960	10.00	20.00	40.00
—Black label with colorband, Capitol logo at left					
❑ TBO 1327 [(2)M]Road Show		1960	7.50	15.00	30.00
—Black label with colorband, Capitol logo at left					
❑ ST 1398 [S]	The Cool School	1960	10.00	20.00	40.00
—Black label with colorband, Capitol logo at left					
❑ T 1398 [M]	The Cool School	1960	7.50	15.00	30.00
—Black label with colorband, Capitol logo at left					
❑ ST 1498 [S]	Off Beat	1961	12.50	25.00	50.00
—Black label with colorband, Capitol logo at left					
❑ T 1498 [M]	Off Beat	1961	10.00	20.00	40.00
—Black label with colorband, Capitol logo at left					
❑ ST 1586 [S]	Do-Re-Mi	1961	12.50	25.00	50.00
—Black label with colorband, Capitol logo at left					
❑ T 1586 [M]	Do-Re-Mi	1961	10.00	20.00	40.00
—Black label with colorband, Capitol logo at left					
❑ ST 1605 [S]	That Time of Year	1961	12.50	25.00	50.00
—Black label with colorband, Capitol logo at left					
❑ T 1605 [M]	That Time of Year	1961	10.00	20.00	40.00
—Black label with colorband, Capitol logo at left					
❑ ST 1693 [S]	The Best of June Christy	1962	7.50	15.00	30.00
—Black logo with colorband					
❑ T 1693 [M]	The Best of June Christy	1962	6.25	12.50	25.00
—Black label with colorband					
❑ ST 1845 [S]	Big Band Specials	1962	6.25	12.50	25.00
❑ T 1845 [M]	Big Band Specials	1962	5.00	10.00	20.00
❑ ST 1953 [S]	The Intimate June Christy	1963	6.25	12.50	25.00
❑ T 1953 [M]	The Intimate June Christy	1963	5.00	10.00	20.00
❑ ST 2410 [S]	Something Broadway, Something Latin	1965	7.50	15.00	30.00
❑ T 2410 [M]	Something Broadway, Something Latin	1965	6.25	12.50	25.00
❑ SM-11961	The Best of June Christy	1979	2.50	5.00	10.00
DISCOVERY					
❑ DS-836	Impromptu	1982	3.00	6.00	12.00
❑ DS-911	Interlude	1986	2.50	5.00	10.00
❑ DS-919	The Misty Miss Christy	1986	2.50	5.00	10.00
HINDSIGHT					
❑ HSR-219	June Christy, Vol. 1	1986	2.50	5.00	10.00
❑ HSR-235	June Christy, Vol. 2	1988	2.50	5.00	10.00
PAUSA					
❑ 9039	Big Band Specials	198?	2.50	5.00	10.00

CHRYSALIS
Albums
MGM

Number	Title (A Side/B Side)	Yr	VG	VG+	NM
❑ SE-4547	Definition	1968	7.50	15.00	30.00

CHUBBY AND THE TURNPIKES Some members later were in TAVARES.
45s
CAPITOL

Number	Title (A Side/B Side)	Yr	VG	VG+	NM
❑ 5840	I Didn't Try/I Know the Inside Story	1967	7.50	15.00	30.00

CHUCK-A-LUCKS, THE
45s
BOW

Number	Title (A Side/B Side)	Yr	VG	VG+	NM
❑ 305	Heaven Knows/Chuck-a-Luck	1957	12.50	25.00	50.00
CANDLELITE					
❑ 424	Heaven Knows/Chuck-a-Luck	196?	3.00	6.00	12.00
JUBILEE					
❑ 5415	Tarzan's Date/Unconditional Surrender	1961	5.00	10.00	20.00
LIN					
❑ 5010	Who Am I?/The Devil's Train	1958	6.25	12.50	25.00
❑ 5014	The Magic of First Love/Disc Jockey Fever	1958	12.50	25.00	50.00
MEL-O-DY					
❑ 106	Sugar Cane Curtain/Dingbat Diller	1963	6.25	12.50	25.00
WARNER BROS.					
❑ 5198	Long John/Pick Up and Deliver	1961	5.00	10.00	20.00
❑ 5234	Cotton Pickin' Love/I'm Hospitalized Over You	1961	5.00	10.00	20.00

CHUCKLES, THE Also see THE THREE CHUCKLES.
45s
ABC-PARAMOUNT

Number	Title (A Side/B Side)	Yr	VG	VG+	NM
❑ 10276	Runaround/Lonely Traveler	1961	3.75	7.50	15.00

CHURCH, EUGENE Also see THE CLIQUES.
45s
CLASS

Number	Title (A Side/B Side)	Yr	VG	VG+	NM
❑ 235	Pretty Girls Everywhere/For the Rest of My Life	1958	6.25	12.50	25.00
❑ 254	Miami/I Ain't Goin' for That	1959	3.00	6.00	12.00
❑ 261	Jack of All Trades/Without Soul	1959	3.00	6.00	12.00
❑ 266	The Struttin' Kind/That's What's Happenin'	1960	3.00	6.00	12.00
KING					
❑ 5545	Mind Your Own Business/You Got the Right Idea	1961	3.00	6.00	12.00
❑ 5589	That's All I Need/Geneva	1962	2.50	5.00	10.00
❑ 5610	Light of the Moon/I'm Your Taboo Man	1962	2.50	5.00	10.00
❑ 5659	The Right Girl, the Right Time/ Pretty Baby Won't You Come On Home	1962	2.50	5.00	10.00
❑ 5715	Sixteen Tons/ Time Has Brought About a Change	1963	2.50	5.00	10.00
RENDEZVOUS					
❑ 132	Good News/Polly	1960	3.00	6.00	12.00
SPECIALTY					
❑ 604	How Long/Open Up Your Heart	1957	5.00	10.00	20.00

Number	Title (A Side/B Side)	Yr	VG	VG+	NM
WORLD PACIFIC					
❑ 77866	Dollar Bill/U Maka Hanna	1967	3.75	7.50	15.00

CHURCH STREET FIVE, THE
45s
LEGRAND

Number	Title (A Side/B Side)	Yr	VG	VG+	NM
❑ 1004	A Night with Daddy "G" Part 1/Part 2	1961	3.75	7.50	15.00
—Red, gold and white "shield" label					
❑ 1004	A Night with Daddy "G" Part 1/Part 2	1961	6.25	12.50	25.00
—Purple label original					
❑ 1010	Fallen Arches/Everybody's Happy	1961	5.00	10.00	20.00
❑ 1014	Church Street Walk/I'm Gonna Sue	1961	5.00	10.00	20.00
❑ 1021	Daddy G Rides Again/Hey Now	1962	5.00	10.00	20.00
❑ 1026	Moonlight in Vermont/Sing a Song Children	1963	5.00	10.00	20.00

CINDERELLAS, THE (1) Female vocal group.
45s
COLUMBIA

Number	Title (A Side/B Side)	Yr	VG	VG+	NM
❑ 41540	The Trouble with Boys/Puppy Dog	1959	3.75	7.50	15.00
DECCA					
❑ 30830	Mr. Dee Jay/Yum Yum Yum	1959	6.25	12.50	25.00
❑ 30925	I Was Only 15/You Never Shoulda Gone Away	1959	6.25	12.50	25.00

CINDERELLAS, THE (2) Another female vocal group.
45s
DIMENSION

Number	Title (A Side/B Side)	Yr	VG	VG+	NM
❑ 1026	Baby, Baby, I Still Love You/ Please Don't Wake Me	1964	10.00	20.00	40.00
MERCURY					
❑ 72394	Fairy Tale/Mr. Happy Love	1965	2.50	5.00	10.00

CINDERS, THE
45s
ORIGINAL SOUND

Number	Title (A Side/B Side)	Yr	VG	VG+	NM
❑ 43	I'll Follow You/The Story	1964	2.50	5.00	10.00
WARNER BROS.					
❑ 5326	The Cinnamon Cinder/C'mon Wobble	1962	3.00	6.00	12.00

CINDY AND LINDY
45s
ABC-PARAMOUNT

Number	Title (A Side/B Side)	Yr	VG	VG+	NM
❑ 9847	The Language of Love/Brigette's Song	1957	6.25	12.50	25.00
❑ 9886	Shakin'/Sittin' It Out	1958	6.25	12.50	25.00
CORAL					
❑ 62008	The Wonder That Is You/ I'll String Along with You	1958	5.00	10.00	20.00
❑ 62072	Saturday Night in Tia-Juana/ You Can't Mail an Elephant	1959	5.00	10.00	20.00
❑ 62119	Before and After/Big Bells and Bongo Drummers	1959	5.00	10.00	20.00
❑ 62165	Let's Go Steady/There Are Such Things	1960	5.00	10.00	20.00
PILGRIM					
❑ 702	Let's Go Steady/The Wedding Is Over	1956	3.75	7.50	15.00
❑ 705	Hungry Heart/Livin' and Bein' Loved	1956	3.75	7.50	15.00

CINNAMON ANGELS May be the same group as THE CINNAMONS.
45s
B.T. PUPPY

Number	Title (A Side/B Side)	Yr	VG	VG+	NM
❑ 559	Calypso Girl/Let's Be Sweethearts	1970	2.00	4.00	8.00

CINNAMONS, THE
B.T. PUPPY

Number	Title (A Side/B Side)	Yr	VG	VG+	NM
❑ 503	I'm Not Gonna Worry/Strange, Strange Feeling	1964	2.00	4.00	8.00
❑ 508	Mr. Cupid '65/Dance to the Music	1965	2.00	4.00	8.00

CIRCUS
45s
METROMEDIA

Number	Title (A Side/B Side)	Yr	VG	VG+	NM
❑ 68-0112	Feel So Right/Jonah's Fable	1973	—	2.50	5.00
❑ 265	Stop, Wait and Listen/I Need Your Love	1972	—	3.00	6.00
Albums					
METROMEDIA					
❑ 7401	Circus	1973	7.50	15.00	30.00

CIRCUS MAXIMUS Group features JERRY JEFF WALKER.
45s
VANGUARD

Number	Title (A Side/B Side)	Yr	VG	VG+	NM
❑ 35063	Lonely Man/Negative Dreamer Girl	1968	5.00	10.00	20.00
Albums					
VANGUARD					
❑ VRS-9260 [M]	Circus Maximus	1967	5.00	10.00	20.00
❑ VSD-79260 [S]	Circus Maximus	1967	6.25	12.50	25.00
❑ VSD-79274	Neverland Revisited	1968	6.25	12.50	25.00

CITATIONS, THE More than one group.
45s
BALLAD

Number	Title (A Side/B Side)	Yr	VG	VG+	NM
❑ 101	I Will Stand By You/To Win the Race	1967	25.00	50.00	100.00
CANADIAN AMERICAN					
❑ 136	Mystery of Love/Magic Eyes	1962	7.50	15.00	30.00
—As "Nicki North and the Citations"					
DON-EL					
❑ 113	It Hurts Me/Kiss in the Night	1961	10.00	20.00	40.00
EPIC					
❑ 9603	Moon Race/Slippin' and Slidin'	1963	6.25	12.50	25.00
FRATERNITY					
❑ 910	The Girl Next Door/Ten Miles from Nowhere	1963	5.00	10.00	20.00
❑ 992	The Girl Next Door/Ten Miles from Nowhere	1967	3.00	6.00	12.00
MERCURY					
❑ 72286	Chicago/The Stomp	1964	3.75	7.50	15.00
MGM					
❑ 13373	That Girl of Mine/Down Went the Curtain	1965	5.00	10.00	20.00
PRINCESS					
❑ 54	Carmen P./Everybody Philly	1965	7.50	15.00	30.00
ROULETTE					
❑ 4623	Carmen P./Everybody Philly	1965	3.75	7.50	15.00

Ray Charles, *Ray Charles (Rock & Roll),* Atlantic 8006, mono LP, black label, $45-$90.

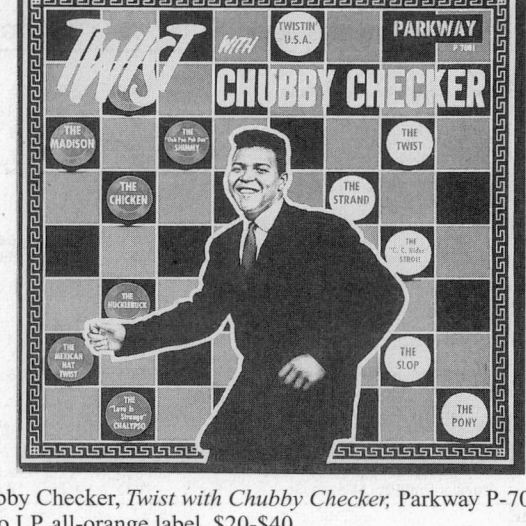

Chubby Checker, *Twist with Chubby Checker,* Parkway P-7001, mono LP, all-orange label, $20-$40.

Chicago, "Harry Truman," Columbia 3-10092, picture sleeve, $3-$6.

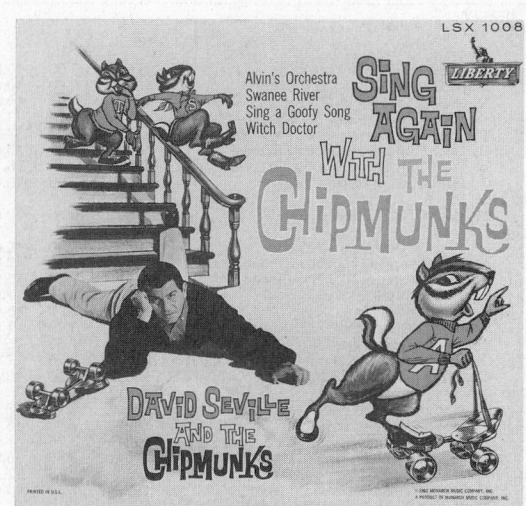

The Chipmunks, *Sing Again with the Chipmunks,* Liberty LSX-1008, 7-inch EP, $40-$80 (cover and record together).

Lou Christie, "Rhapsody in the Rain," MGM K13473, picture sleeve, $10-$20.

Jimmy Clanton, "Come Back," Ace 600, picture sleeve, $15-$30.

Number	Title (A Side/B Side)	Yr	VG	VG+	NM
SARA					
❏ 3301	Moon Race/Slippin' and Slidin'	1963	12.50	25.00	50.00
SWAN					
❏ 4062	Fiddlin' Around/Fire Ritual	1960	10.00	20.00	40.00
VANGEE					
❏ 301	The Girl Next Door/Ten Miles from Nowhere	1963	10.00	20.00	40.00

CITY, THE CAROLE KING was a member.
45s
ODE

Number	Title (A Side/B Side)	Yr	VG	VG+	NM
❏ 113	Snow Queen/Paradise Alley	1968	3.00	6.00	12.00
❏ 117	That Old Sweet Rule/Why Are You Leaving	1968	3.00	6.00	12.00
❏ 119	(Hi-De-Ho) That Old Sweet Roll/ Why Are You Leaving	1969	3.00	6.00	12.00
Albums					
ODE					
❏ Z12 44012	Now That Everything's Been Said	1968	20.00	40.00	80.00
—Color front cover					
❏ Z12 44012	Now That Everything's Been Said	1971	3.00	6.00	12.00
—Black & white front cover					

CITY SURFERS, THE
45s
CAPITOL

Number	Title (A Side/B Side)	Yr	VG	VG+	NM
❏ 5002	Beach Ball/Sun Tan Baby	1963	6.25	12.50	25.00
❏ 5052	Powder Puff/Fifty Miles to Go	1963	6.25	12.50	25.00

CLAMS, THE
45s
THREE BROTHERS

Number	Title (A Side/B Side)	Yr	VG	VG+	NM
❏ 404	Close to You/First Time Ever I Saw Your Face	1974	2.50	5.00	10.00
—LOU CHRISTIE appears on this record					

CLANTON, JIMMY
45s
ACE

Number	Title (A Side/B Side)	Yr	VG	VG+	NM
❏ 537	I Trusted You/That's You Baby	1958	5.00	10.00	20.00
❏ 546	Just a Dream/You Aim to Please	1958	5.00	10.00	20.00
❏ 551	A Letter to An Angel/A Part of Me	1958	5.00	10.00	20.00
❏ 560	My Love Is Strong/Ship on a Stormy Sea	1959	3.75	7.50	15.00
❏ 567 [M]	My Own True Love/Little Boy in Love	1959	3.75	7.50	15.00
❏ 567 [PS]	My Own True Love/Little Boy in Love	1959	7.50	15.00	30.00
❏ 567 [S]	My Own True Love/Little Boy in Love	1959	7.50	15.00	30.00
❏ 575	Go, Jimmy, Go/I Trusted You	1959	5.00	10.00	20.00
—Normal white label					
❏ 575	Go, Jimmy, Go/I Trusted You	1959	6.25	12.50	25.00
—Purple label					
❏ 575 [PS]	Go, Jimmy, Go/I Trusted You	1959	7.50	15.00	30.00
❏ 585	Another Sleepless Night/I'm Gonna Try	1960	3.75	7.50	15.00
❏ 585 [PS]	Another Sleepless Night/I'm Gonna Try	1960	7.50	15.00	30.00
❏ 600	Come Back/Wait	1960	3.75	7.50	15.00
❏ 600 [PS]	Come Back/Wait	1960	7.50	15.00	30.00
❏ 607	What Am I Gonna Do/If I	1961	3.75	7.50	15.00
❏ 607 [PS]	What Am I Gonna Do/If I	1961	7.50	15.00	30.00
❏ 616	Down the Aisle/No Longer Blue	1961	3.75	7.50	15.00
❏ 616 [PS]	Down the Aisle/No Longer Blue	1961	7.50	15.00	30.00
—With Mary Ann Mobley					
❏ 622	I Just Wanna Make Love/Don't Look at Me	1961	3.75	7.50	15.00
❏ 622 [PS]	I Just Wanna Make Love/Don't Look at Me	1961	7.50	15.00	30.00
❏ 634	Lucky in Love with You/Not Like a Brother	1961	3.75	7.50	15.00
❏ 634 [PS]	Lucky in Love with You/Not Like a Brother	1961	7.50	15.00	30.00
❏ 641	Twist On Little Girl/Wayward Love	1962	3.75	7.50	15.00
❏ 641 [PS]	Twist On Little Girl/Wayward Love	1962	7.50	15.00	30.00
❏ 642	Twist On Little Girl/Wayward Love//Green Light/ Happy Times	1962	12.50	25.00	50.00
❏ 642 [PS]	Teenage Millionaire	1962	12.50	25.00	50.00
❏ 655	Just a Moment/Because I Do	1962	3.75	7.50	15.00
❏ 655 [PS]	Just a Moment/Because I Do	1962	7.50	15.00	30.00
❏ 664 [DJ]	Venus in Blue Jeans/Highway Bound	1962	6.25	12.50	25.00
—No stock copies exist with this catalog number					
❏ 668	Heart Hotel/Many Dreams	1963	3.00	6.00	12.00
❏ 8001	Venus in Blue Jeans/Highway Bound	1962	3.75	7.50	15.00
❏ 8005	Darkest Street in Town/Dreams of a Fool	1962	2.50	5.00	10.00
❏ 8006	Endless Nights/Another Day, Another Heartache	1963	2.50	5.00	10.00
❏ 8006 [PS]	Endless Nights/ Another Day, Another Heartache	1963	5.00	10.00	20.00
❏ 8007	Cindy/I Care Enough (To Give the Very Best)	1963	2.50	5.00	10.00
IMPERIAL					
❏ 66242	Absence of Lisa/C'mon Jim	1967	2.00	4.00	8.00
❏ 66274	Calico Junction/I'll Be Loving You	1968	2.00	4.00	8.00
LAURIE					
❏ 3508	Curly/The Girl Who Cried Love (Once Too Often)	1969	2.00	4.00	8.00
❏ 3508	Curly/I'll Never Forget Your Love	1969	2.50	5.00	10.00
❏ 3534	Tell Me/I'll Never Forget Your Love	1969	2.00	4.00	8.00
MALA					
❏ 500	Hurting Each Other/ Don't Keep Your Friends Away	1965	2.50	5.00	10.00
❏ 516	Everything I Touch Turns to Tears/ That Special Way	1965	2.50	5.00	10.00
PHILIPS					
❏ 40161	Red Don't Go with Blue/ All the Words in the World	1963	2.50	5.00	10.00
❏ 40181	I'll Step Aside/I Won't Cry Anymore	1964	2.50	5.00	10.00
❏ 40208	If I'm a Fool for Loving You/A Million Drums	1964	2.50	5.00	10.00
❏ 40219	Follow the Sun/Lock the Windows	1964	2.50	5.00	10.00
SPIRAL					
❏ 3406	The Coolest Hot Pants/(Instrumental)	1971	—	2.50	5.00
STARCREST					
❏ 078 [DJ]	Old Rock 'N Roller (mono/stereo)	1978	—	2.50	5.00
—May be promo only					
STARFIRE					
❏ 104	I Wanna Go Home/You Kissed a Fool Goodbye	1976	—	2.50	5.00
UNITED ARTISTS					
❏ (no #)	Teenage Millionaire	1961	7.50	15.00	30.00
—Cardboard record; B-side promotes the movie of the same name					
VIN					
❏ 1028	What Am I Living For/Wedding Blues	1962	2.50	5.00	10.00

7-Inch Extended Plays
ACE

Number	Title (A Side/B Side)	Yr	VG	VG+	NM
❏ 101	(contents unknown)	1959	25.00	50.00	100.00
❏ 101 [PS]	Jimmy Clanton	1959	25.00	50.00	100.00
❏ 102	(contents unknown)	1959	37.50	75.00	150.00
❏ 102 [PS]	Thinking of You	1959	37.50	75.00	150.00
Albums					
ACE					
❏ DLP-100	Jimmy's Happy/Jimmy's Blue Poster	1960	20.00	40.00	80.00
❏ DLP-100 [M]	Jimmy's Happy/Jimmy's Blue	1960	37.50	75.00	150.00
—Black vinyl; also released as two separate albums, 1007 and 1008					
❏ DLP-100 [M]	Jimmy's Happy/Jimmy's Blue	1960	100.00	200.00	400.00
—The "Happy" album is red vinyl, the "Blue" album is blue					
❏ 1001 [M]	Just a Dream	1959	30.00	60.00	120.00
❏ 1007 [M]	Jimmy's Happy	1960	10.00	20.00	40.00
❏ 1008 [M]	Jimmy's Blue	1960	10.00	20.00	40.00
❏ 1011 [M]	My Best to You	1960	25.00	50.00	100.00
❏ 1014 [M]	Teenage Millionaire	1961	25.00	50.00	100.00
❏ 1026 [M]	Venus in Blue Jeans	1962	25.00	50.00	100.00
PHILIPS					
❏ PHM 200154 [M]	The Best of Jimmy Clanton	1964	6.25	12.50	25.00
❏ PHS 600154 [S]	The Best of Jimmy Clanton	1964	7.50	15.00	30.00

CLANTON, JIMMY/BRISTOW HOOPER
Albums
DESIGN

Number	Title (A Side/B Side)	Yr	VG	VG+	NM
❏ DLP-176 [M]	Jimmy Clanton and Bristow Hooper	196?	3.75	7.50	15.00
❏ DLS-176 [R]	Jimmy Clanton and Bristow Hooper	196?	2.50	5.00	10.00

CLAP
Albums
NOVA SOL

Number	Title (A Side/B Side)	Yr	VG	VG+	NM
❏ 1001	Have You Reached Yet?	1970	250.00	500.00	1000.

CLAPTON, ERIC Also see BLIND FAITH; CREAM; DEREK AND THE DOMINOS; GEORGE HARRISON AND FRIENDS; B.B. KING; JOHN MAYALL; THE YARDBIRDS.
12-Inch Singles
DUCK

Number	Title (A Side/B Side)	Yr	VG	VG+	NM
❏ PRO-A-2000 [DJ]	I've Got a Rock n' Roll Heart (same on both sides)	1983	5.00	10.00	20.00
❏ PRO-A-2248 [DJ]	Forever Man (same on both sides)	1985	2.50	5.00	10.00
❏ PRO-A-2306 [DJ]	See What Love Can Do (same on both sides)	1985	3.75	7.50	15.00
❏ PRO-A-2578 [DJ]	Tearing Us Apart (same on both sides)	1986	5.00	10.00	20.00
—With Tina Turner					
❏ PRO-A-2616 [DJ]	It's In the Way That You Use It (same on both sides)	1986	3.75	7.50	15.00
❏ PRO-A-2683 [DJ]	Miss You (same on both sides)	1986	5.00	10.00	20.00
❏ PRO-A-2700 [DJ]	Run (same on both sides)	1986	3.75	7.50	15.00
REPRISE					
❏ PRO-A-4200 [(2)DJ]	(I) Get Lost (David Morales Club Mix 8:11) (David Morales Club Mix with Guitar Intro 8:27) (Stereo Dub 7:31) (Stereo Beats 7:40) (Yost Nothing Without U Mix 7:36) (Yost Nothing Without U Radio Edit 4:01) (Yost Lost & Found Dub 8:03) (Yost Acoustic Tears Mix 7:54)	1999	6.25	12.50	25.00
❏ PRO-A-4203 [DJ]	(I) Get Lost (Lost & Found Dub 8:03) (Stereo Dub 7:31)	1999	3.75	7.50	15.00
❏ PRO-A-9350 [DJ]	Pilgrim (Organized Noize Mix) (Organized Noize Instrumental) (Acappella) (Keith Crouch Mix) (Keith Crouch Instrumental) (Background Acappella) (Remix Edit)	1998	5.00	10.00	20.00
❏ 43855	Rip Stop (4 versions)/ Seven (Blackmarket Roll Out Mix)	1997	2.50	5.00	10.00
RSO					
❏ RPO 1005 [DJ]	Promises/Watch Out for Lucy	1978	7.50	15.00	30.00
45s					
ATCO					
❏ 6784	After Midnight/Easy Now	1970	—	3.00	6.00
DUCK					
❏ 28279	Tearing Us Apart/Hold On	1987	—	—	3.00
—A-side with Tina Turner					
❏ 28279 [PS]	Tearing Us Apart/Hold On	1987	—	—	3.00
❏ 28391	Behind the Sun/Grand Illusion	1987	—	—	3.00
❏ 28514	It's in the Way That You Use It/Grand Illusion	1986	—	—	3.00
❏ 28514 [PS]	It's in the Way That You Use It/Grand Illusion	1986	—	—	3.00
❏ 28986	See What Love Can Do/She's Waiting	1985	—	—	3.00
❏ 29081	Forever Man/Too Bad	1985	—	—	3.00
❏ 29081 [PS]	Forever Man/Too Bad	1985	—	—	3.00
❏ 29647	Pretty Girl/The Shape You're In	1983	—	2.00	4.00
❏ 29780	I've Got a Rock n' Roll Heart/Man in Love	1983	—	2.00	4.00
—Silver label with Duck logo					
POLYDOR					
❏ 15049	Let It Rain/Easy Now	1972	—	3.00	6.00
❏ 15056	Bell Bottom Blues/Little Wing	1972	—	2.50	5.00
—Reissue of Derek and the Dominos recordings, but under Clapton's name					
❏ 887403-7	After Midnight/I Can't Stand It	1988	—	—	3.00
❏ 887403-7 [PS]	After Midnight/I Can't Stand It	1988	—	—	3.00
REPRISE					
❏ 17621	Change the World/Danny Boy	1996	—	2.00	4.00
❏ 18044	Motherless Child/Driftin'	1994	—	2.00	4.00
❏ 18787	Layla/Signe	1992	—	2.00	4.00
❏ 19038	Tears in Heaven/Tracks and Lines	1992	—	2.50	5.00
❏ 22732	Pretending/Before You Accuse Me	1989	—	2.00	4.00
❏ 22732 [PS]	Pretending/Before You Accuse Me	1989	—	—	3.00
RSO					
❏ 409	I Shot the Sheriff/Give Me Strength	1974	—	2.50	5.00
❏ 500	I Shot the Sheriff/Give Me Strength	1974	—	2.00	4.00
❏ 503	Willie and the Hand Jive/Main Line Florida	1975	—	2.00	4.00
❏ 509	Swing Low Sweet Chariot/Pretty Blue Eyes	1975	—	2.00	4.00
❏ 513	Knockin' on Heaven's Door/Someone Like You	1975	—	2.00	4.00
❏ 861	Hello Old Friend/All Our Pastimes	1976	—	2.00	4.00
❏ 868	Carnival/Hungry	1976	—	2.00	4.00
❏ 886	Lay Down Sally/Next Time You See Her	1978	—	2.00	4.00
❏ 895	Wonderful Tonight/Peaches and Diesel	1978	—	2.00	4.00
❏ 910	Promises/Watch Out for Lucy	1978	—	2.00	4.00
❏ 928	Tulsa Time/Cocaine	1979	—	2.50	5.00
—Studio versions of the two songs					

Number	Title (A Side/B Side)	Yr	VG	VG+	NM
❑ 1039	Tulsa Time/Cocaine	1980	—	2.00	4.00
—Live versions of the two songs					
❑ 1051	Blues Power/Early in the Morning	1980	—	2.00	4.00
❑ 1060	I Can't Stand It/Black Rose	1981	—	2.00	4.00
❑ 1064	Another Ticket/Rita Mae	1981	—	2.00	4.00
❑ 1064 [PS]	Another Ticket/Rita Mae	1981	—	2.50	5.00
WARNER BROS.					
❑ 29780	I've Got a Rock n' Roll Heart/Man in Love	1983	—	2.50	5.00
—Original pressing on white WB label					
Albums					
ATCO					
❑ 33-329 [DJ]	Eric Clapton	1970	25.00	50.00	100.00
—Mono pressing is promo only					
❑ SD 33-329	Eric Clapton	1970	5.00	10.00	20.00
❑ SD 33-329	Eric Clapton	1970	50.00	100.00	200.00
—Odd pressing with alternate takes of "After Midnight" and "Blues Power" plus remixes of other tracks. Look for "CTH" in trail-off area.					
❑ SD 2-803 [(2)]	History of Eric Clapton	1972	5.00	10.00	20.00
—Contains tracks from the Yardbirds, John Mayall's Bluesbreakers, Cream, Blind Faith, and solo records					
DUCK					
❑ 23773	Money and Cigarettes	1983	2.50	5.00	10.00
❑ 25186	Behind the Sun	1985	2.50	5.00	10.00
❑ 25476	August	1986	2.50	5.00	10.00
MOBILE FIDELITY					
❑ 1-030	Slowhand	1980	17.50	35.00	70.00
—Audiophile vinyl					
❑ 1-220	Eric Clapton	1995	6.25	12.50	25.00
—Audiophile vinyl					
NAUTILUS					
❑ NR-32 [(2)]	Just One Night	1981	37.50	75.00	150.00
—Audiophile vinyl					
POLYDOR					
❑ PD 3503 [(2)]	Eric Clapton at His Best	1972	5.00	10.00	20.00
—Compiles tracks from his first solo album plus Derek and the Dominos					
❑ 24-5526	Clapton	1973	3.75	7.50	15.00
—Compiles tracks from his first solo album plus Derek and the Dominos					
❑ SKBO-94837 [(2)]	Eric Clapton at His Best	1972	7.50	15.00	30.00
—Capitol Record Club edition					
❑ 835261-1 [(6)]	Crossroads	1988	12.50	25.00	50.00
—Box set; contains material from all phases of his career					
REPRISE					
❑ 26074	Journeyman	1989	3.00	6.00	12.00
❑ W1-26420 [(2)]	24 Nights	1991	6.25	12.50	25.00
—Vinyl copies released only through Columbia House					
RSO					
❑ PRO 035 [DJ]	Slowhand	1977	10.00	20.00	40.00
—White vinyl promo sampler					
❑ SO 877	Eric Clapton's Rainbow Concert	1973	3.75	7.50	15.00
❑ RPO-1009 [DJ]	Limited Backless	1978	12.50	25.00	50.00
—White vinyl promo					
❑ RS-1-3004	No Reason to Cry	1976	3.00	6.00	12.00
❑ RS-1-3008	Eric Clapton	1977	3.00	6.00	12.00
—Reissue of Atco LP of the same name					
❑ RS-1-3023	461 Ocean Boulevard	1977	3.00	6.00	12.00
—Reissue of RSO 4801					
❑ RS-1-3030	Slowhand	1977	3.00	6.00	12.00
❑ RS-1-3039	Backless	1978	3.00	6.00	12.00
❑ RX-1-3095	Another Ticket	1981	2.50	5.00	10.00
❑ RS-1-3099	Time Pieces/The Best of Eric Clapton	1982	2.50	5.00	10.00
❑ RS-2-4202 [(2)]	Just One Night	1980	3.75	7.50	15.00
❑ QD 4801 [Q]	461 Ocean Boulevard	1974	6.25	12.50	25.00
❑ SO 4801	461 Ocean Boulevard	1974	3.00	6.00	12.00
—With "Better Make It Through the Day"					
❑ SO 4801	461 Ocean Boulevard	1974	3.75	7.50	15.00
—With "Give Me Strength"					
❑ QD 4806 [Q]	There's One in Every Crowd	1975	6.25	12.50	25.00
❑ SO 4806	There's One in Every Crowd	1975	3.00	6.00	12.00
❑ SO 4809	E.C. Was Here	1975	3.00	6.00	12.00
❑ 811697-1	461 Ocean Boulevard	198?	2.00	4.00	8.00
—Reissue of RSO 3023					
❑ 823276-1	Slowhand	1983	2.00	4.00	8.00
—Reissue of RSO 3030					
❑ 825093-1	Eric Clapton	1984	2.00	4.00	8.00
—Reissue of RSO 3008					
❑ 825382-1	Time Pieces/The Best of Eric Clapton	1984	2.00	4.00	8.00
—Reissue of RSO 3099					
❑ 825391-1 [(2)]	Just One Night	1984	2.50	5.00	10.00
—Reissue of RSO 4202					
❑ 827579-1	Another Ticket	1985	2.00	4.00	8.00
—Reissue of RSO 3095					

CLARA AND THE CLEFTONES See CLARA WILSON AND THE CLEFTONES.

CLAREMONTS, THE
45s
APOLLO

Number	Title (A Side/B Side)	Yr	VG	VG+	NM
❑ 517	Why Keep Me Dreaming/Angel of Romance	1957	15.00	30.00	60.00
❑ 751	Why Keep Me Dreaming/Angel of Romance	1963	6.25	12.50	25.00

CLARK, CHRIS
45s
MOTOWN

Number	Title (A Side/B Side)	Yr	VG	VG+	NM
❑ 1114	From Head to Toe/The Beginning of the End	1967	3.75	7.50	15.00
❑ 1121	Whisper You Love Me Boy/The Beginning of the End	1968	3.75	7.50	15.00
V.I.P.					
❑ 25031	Do Right, Baby, Do Right/Don't Be Too Long	1965	3.75	7.50	15.00
❑ 25038	Love's Gone Bad/Put Yourself in My Place	1965	5.00	10.00	20.00
—Same song as above A-side, but with corrected title					
❑ 25038	Love's Gone Mad/Put Yourself in My Place	1965	15.00	30.00	60.00
❑ 25041	I Love You/I Want to Go Back There Again	1966	3.75	7.50	15.00
Albums					
MOTOWN					
❑ M-664 [M]	Soul Sounds	1967	12.50	25.00	50.00
❑ MS-664 [S]	Soul Sounds	1967	15.00	30.00	60.00

WEED

Number	Title (A Side/B Side)	Yr	VG	VG+	NM
❑ 801	C.C. Rides Again	1969	20.00	40.00	80.00

CLARK, CLAUDINE
45s
CHANCELLOR

Number	Title (A Side/B Side)	Yr	VG	VG+	NM
❑ 1113	Party Lights/Disappointed	1962	5.00	10.00	20.00
—exists on two different labels					
❑ 1124	Telephone Game/Walkin' Through a Cemetery	1962	3.00	6.00	12.00
❑ 1130	Walk Me Home/Who Will You Hurt	1963	3.00	6.00	12.00
HERALD					
❑ 523	Teenage Blues/Angel of Happiness	1958	10.00	20.00	40.00
JAMIE					
❑ 1279	Moon Madness/(The Strength) To Be Strong	1964	2.50	5.00	10.00
❑ 1291	Buttered Popcorn/A Sometimes Thing	1964	2.50	5.00	10.00
TCF HALL					
❑ 18	Foxy/Standin' on Tip Toes	196?	2.50	5.00	10.00
Albums					
CHANCELLOR					
❑ CHL-5029 [M]	Party Lights	1962	62.50	125.00	250.00

CLARK, DAVE, FIVE
45s
CONGRESS

Number	Title (A Side/B Side)	Yr	VG	VG+	NM
❑ 212	I Knew It All the Time/That's What I Said	1964	5.00	10.00	20.00
❑ 212 [PS]	I Knew It All the Time/That's What I Said	1964	10.00	20.00	40.00
EPIC					
❑ 9656	Glad All Over/I Know You	1964	3.75	7.50	15.00
❑ 9656 [PS]	Glad All Over/I Know You	1964	5.00	10.00	20.00
❑ 9671	Bits and Pieces/All of the Time	1964	3.00	6.00	12.00
❑ 9678	Do You Love Me/Chaquita	1964	3.00	6.00	12.00
❑ 9692	Can't You See That She's Mine/No TIme to Lose	1964	3.00	6.00	12.00
❑ 9692 [PS]	Can't You See That She's Mine/No TIme to Lose	1964	5.00	10.00	20.00
❑ 9704	Because/Theme Without a Name	1964	3.00	6.00	12.00
❑ 9704 [PS]	Because/Theme Without a Name	1964	5.00	10.00	20.00
❑ 9722	Everybody Knows (I Still Love You)/Ol' Sol	1964	3.00	6.00	12.00
❑ 9722 [PS]	Everybody Knows (I Still Love You)/Ol' Sol	1964	5.00	10.00	20.00
❑ 9739	Any Way You Want It/Crying Over You	1964	3.00	6.00	12.00
❑ 9763	Come Home/Your Turn to Cry	1965	3.00	6.00	12.00
❑ 9763 [PS]	Come Home/Your Turn to Cry	1965	5.00	10.00	20.00
❑ 9786	Reelin' and Rockin'/I'm Thinking	1965	3.00	6.00	12.00
❑ 9811	I Like It Like That/Hurting Inside	1965	3.00	6.00	12.00
❑ 9811 [PS]	I Like It Like That/Hurting Inside	1965	5.00	10.00	20.00
❑ 9833	Catch Us If You Can/On the Move	1965	3.00	6.00	12.00
❑ 9833 [PS]	Catch Us If You Can/On the Move	1965	5.00	10.00	20.00
❑ 9863	Over and Over/I'll Be Yours (My Love)	1965	3.00	6.00	12.00
❑ 9863 [DJ]	Over and Over (same on both sides)	1965	10.00	20.00	40.00
—Promo only on red vinyl					
❑ 9863 [PS]	Over and Over/I'll Be Yours (My Love)	1965	5.00	10.00	20.00
❑ 9863 [PS]	Over and Over	1965	100.00	200.00	400.00
—Promo-only black and white sleeve					
❑ 9882	At the Scene/I Miss You	1966	3.00	6.00	12.00
❑ 9882 [PS]	At the Scene/I Miss You	1966	5.00	10.00	20.00
❑ 10004	Try Too Hard/All Night Long	1966	3.00	6.00	12.00
❑ 10004 [PS]	Try Too Hard/All Night Long	1966	5.00	10.00	20.00
❑ 10031	Please Tell Me Why/Look Before You Leap	1966	3.00	6.00	12.00
❑ 10031 [PS]	Please Tell Me Why/Look Before You Leap	1966	5.00	10.00	20.00
❑ 10053	Satisfied with You/Don't Let Me Down	1966	3.00	6.00	12.00
❑ 10053 [PS]	Satisfied with You/Don't Let Me Down	1966	5.00	10.00	20.00
❑ 10076	Nineteen Days/Sitting Here Baby	1966	3.00	6.00	12.00
❑ 10076 [DJ]	Nineteen Days (same on both sides)	1966	10.00	20.00	40.00
—Promo only on red vinyl					
❑ 10076 [PS]	Nineteen Days/Sitting Here Baby	1966	5.00	10.00	20.00
❑ 10114	I've Got to Have a Reason/Good Time Woman	1966	3.00	6.00	12.00
❑ 10114 [PS]	I've Got to Have a Reason/Good Time Woman	1966	5.00	10.00	20.00
❑ 10144	You Got What It Takes/Doctor Rhythm	1967	3.00	6.00	12.00
❑ 10144 [PS]	You Got What It Takes/Doctor Rhythm	1967	5.00	10.00	20.00
❑ 10179	You Must Have Been a Beautiful Baby/Man in the Pin Stripe Suit	1967	3.00	6.00	12.00
❑ 10179 [PS]	You Must Have Been a Beautiful Baby/Man in the Pin Stripe Suit	1967	6.25	12.50	25.00
❑ 10209	A Little Bit Now/You Don't Play Me Around	1967	3.75	7.50	15.00
❑ 10209 [PS]	A Little Bit Now/You Don't Play Me Around	1967	5.00	10.00	20.00
❑ 10244	Red and Blue/Concentration Baby	1967	3.75	7.50	15.00
❑ 10265	Everybody Knows/Inside and Out	1967	3.75	7.50	15.00
❑ 10265 [PS]	Everybody Knows/Inside and Out	1967	7.50	15.00	30.00
❑ 10265/60 [DJ]	Everybody Knows/Best of Both Worlds	1968	6.25	12.50	25.00
—B-side by Lulu; odd promo					
❑ 10325	Please Stay/Forget	1968	3.75	7.50	15.00
❑ 10375	Red Balloon/Maze of Love	1968	3.75	7.50	15.00
❑ 10375 [PS]	Red Balloon/Maze of Love	1968	6.25	12.50	25.00
❑ 10476	Paradise (Is Half As Nice)/34-06	1969	3.75	7.50	15.00
❑ 10476 [PS]	Paradise (Is Half As Nice)/34-06	1969	7.50	15.00	30.00
❑ 10509	If Somebody Loves You/Best Day's Work	1969	3.75	7.50	15.00
❑ 10547	Bring It On Home to Me/Darling, I Love You	1969	3.75	7.50	15.00
❑ 10547 [PS]	Bring It On Home to Me/Darling, I Love You	1969	5.00	10.00	20.00
❑ 10635	Here Comes Summer/Five by Five	1970	3.75	7.50	15.00
❑ 10684	Good Old Rock and Roll (Medley)/One Night	1970	5.00	10.00	20.00
❑ 10684 [PS]	Good Old Rock and Roll (Medley)/One Night	1970	7.50	15.00	30.00
❑ 10704	Southern Man/If You Wanna See Me Cry	1971	10.00	20.00	40.00
❑ 10768	Won't You Be My Lady/Into Your Life	1971	5.00	10.00	20.00
❑ 10894	Rub It In/I'm Sorry Baby	1972	5.00	10.00	20.00
EPIC MEMORY LANE					
❑ 2225	Glad All Over/Bits and Pieces	1972	—	2.00	4.00
❑ 2230	Because/Do You Love Me	1972	—	2.00	4.00
❑ 2234	Any Way You Want It/Can't You See That She's Mine	1972	—	2.00	4.00
❑ 2239	I Like It Like That/Everybody Knows (I Still Love You)	1972	—	2.00	4.00
❑ 2248	Over and Over/Catch Us If You Can	1972	—	2.00	4.00
❑ 2294	Bring It On Home to Me/If Somebody Loves You	1972	—	2.00	4.00
❑ 2313	I Like It That/Can't You See That She's Mine	1972	—	2.00	4.00
❑ 2316	Come Home/You Got What It Takes	1972	—	2.00	4.00
HOLLYWOOD					
❑ 65909	Over and Over/You Got What It Takes	1993	—	2.00	4.00
❑ 65909 [PS]	Over and Over/You Got What It Takes	1993	—	3.00	6.00
❑ 65910	I Like It Like That/Reelin' and Rockin'	1993	—	2.00	4.00
❑ 65910 [PS]	I Like It Like That/Reelin' and Rockin'	1993	—	3.00	6.00

C

Number	Title (A Side/B Side)	Yr	VG	VG+	NM
❏ 65911	Glad All Over/Bits and Pieces	1993	—	2.00	4.00
❏ 65911 [PS]	Glad All Over/Bits and Pieces	1993	—	3.00	6.00
❏ 65912	Do You Love Me/Can't You See That She's Mine	1993	—	2.00	4.00
❏ 65912 [PS]	Do You Love Me/Can't You See That She's Mine	1993	—	3.00	6.00
❏ 65913	Catch Us If You Can/Try Too Hard	1993	—	2.00	4.00
❏ 65913 [PS]	Catch Us If You Can/Try Too Hard	1993	—	3.00	6.00
❏ 65914	Because/Everybody Knows (I Still Love You)	1993	—	2.00	4.00
❏ 65914 [PS]	Because/Everybody Knows (I Still Love You)	1993	—	3.00	6.00
❏ 65915	Any Way You Want It/Come Home	1993	—	2.00	4.00
❏ 65915 [PS]	Any Way You Want It/Come Home	1993	—	3.00	6.00

JUBILEE

| ❏ 5476 | Chaquita/In Your Heart | 1964 | 7.50 | 15.00 | 30.00 |

LAURIE

| ❏ 3188 | I Walk the Line/First Love | 1963 | — | — | — |

—Not known to exist

RUST

| ❏ 5078 | I Walk the Line/First Love | 1964 | 10.00 | 20.00 | 40.00 |

7-Inch Extended Plays
EPIC

| ❏ E 26185 | Over and Over/Can't You See That She's Mine/
I Like It Like That//Catch Us If You Can/
Because/Glad All Over | 1966 | 17.50 | 35.00 | 70.00 |

—33 1/3 rpm, small hole, jukebox edition

| ❏ E 26185 [PS] | The Dave Clark Five's Greatest Hits | 1966 | 17.50 | 35.00 | 70.00 |
| ❏ E 26221 | Try Too Hard/Please Tell Me Why/Reelin' and
Rockin'//Satisfied with You/At the Scene/All
Night Long | 1966 | 17.50 | 35.00 | 70.00 |

—33 1/3 rpm, small hole, jukebox edition

| ❏ E 26221 [PS] | More Greatest Hits | 1966 | 17.50 | 35.00 | 70.00 |

Albums
CORTLEIGH

| ❏ C-1073 [M] | The Dave Clark Five with Ricky Astor | 1964 | 7.50 | 15.00 | 30.00 |

—With two early DC5 tracks and assorted other stuff by other artists

| ❏ CS-1073 [R] | The Dave Clark Five with Ricky Astor | 1964 | 3.75 | 7.50 | 15.00 |

—With two early DC5 tracks and assorted other stuff by other artists

CROWN

| ❏ CST-400 [R] | The Dave Clark Five with the Playbacks | 1964 | 3.75 | 7.50 | 15.00 |

—With two early DC5 tracks and assorted other stuff by other artists

| ❏ CST-473 [R] | Chaquita/In Your Heart | 1964 | 3.75 | 7.50 | 15.00 |

—With two early DC5 tracks and assorted other stuff by other artists

| ❏ CST-644 [R] | The Dave Clark Five with the Playbacks | 196? | 3.00 | 6.00 | 12.00 |

—Reissue

| ❏ CLP-5400 [M] | The Dave Clark Five with the Playbacks | 1964 | 7.50 | 15.00 | 30.00 |

—With two early DC5 tracks and assorted other stuff by other artists

| ❏ CLP-5473 [M] | Chaquita/In Your Heart | 1964 | 7.50 | 15.00 | 30.00 |

—With two early DC5 tracks and assorted other stuff by other artists

CUSTOM

| ❏ CS 1098 [R] | The Dave Clark Five with the Playbacks | 196? | 3.00 | 6.00 | 12.00 |

—Reissue

EPIC

| ❏ LN 24093 [M] | Glad All Over | 1964 | 10.00 | 20.00 | 40.00 |

—Group photo with instruments

| ❏ LN 24093 [M] | Glad All Over | 1964 | 20.00 | 40.00 | 80.00 |

—Group photo, no instruments

❏ LN 24104 [M]	The Dave Clark Five Return	1964	10.00	20.00	40.00
❏ LN 24117 [M]	American Tour	1964	10.00	20.00	40.00
❏ LN 24128 [M]	Coast to Coast	1965	10.00	20.00	40.00
❏ LN 24139 [M]	Weekend in London	1965	10.00	20.00	40.00
❏ LN 24162 [M]	Having a Wild Weekend	1965	10.00	20.00	40.00
❏ LN 24178 [M]	I Like It Like That	1965	10.00	20.00	40.00
❏ LN 24185 [M]	The Dave Clark Five's Greatest Hits	1966	6.25	12.50	25.00
❏ LN 24198 [M]	Try Too Hard	1966	7.50	15.00	30.00
❏ LN 24212 [M]	Satisfied with You	1966	7.50	15.00	30.00
❏ LN 24221 [M]	More Greatest Hits	1966	6.25	12.50	25.00
❏ LN 24236 [M]	5 by 5	1967	7.50	15.00	30.00
❏ LN 24312 [M]	You Got What It Takes	1967	7.50	15.00	30.00
❏ LN 24354 [M]	Everybody Knows	1968	7.50	15.00	30.00
❏ BN 26093 [R]	Glad All Over	1964	7.50	15.00	30.00

—Group photo with instruments

| ❏ BN 26093 [R] | Glad All Over | 1964 | 12.50 | 25.00 | 50.00 |

—Group photo, no instruments

❏ BN 26104 [R]	The Dave Clark Five Return	1964	7.50	15.00	30.00
❏ BN 26117 [R]	American Tour	1964	7.50	15.00	30.00
❏ BN 26128 [R]	Coast to Coast	1965	7.50	15.00	30.00
❏ BN 26139 [R]	Weekend in London	1965	7.50	15.00	30.00
❏ BN 26162 [R]	Having a Wild Weekend	1965	7.50	15.00	30.00
❏ BN 26178 [R]	I Like It Like That	1965	7.50	15.00	30.00
❏ BN 26185 [R]	The Dave Clark Five's Greatest Hits	1966	5.00	10.00	20.00

—Yellow label

| ❏ BN 26185 [R] | The Dave Clark Five's Greatest Hits | 1973 | 10.00 | 20.00 | 40.00 |

—Orange label

❏ BN 26198 [R]	Try Too Hard	1966	6.25	12.50	25.00
❏ BN 26212 [R]	Satisfied with You	1966	6.25	12.50	25.00
❏ BN 26221 [R]	More Greatest Hits	1966	5.00	10.00	20.00
❏ BN 26236 [S]	5 by 5	1967	10.00	20.00	40.00
❏ BN 26312 [S]	You Got What It Takes	1967	10.00	20.00	40.00
❏ BN 26354 [S]	Everybody Knows	1968	10.00	20.00	40.00
❏ EG 30434 [(2)S]	The Dave Clark Five	1971	25.00	50.00	100.00

—Twenty hits and near-hits, all in true stereo! Yellow label.

| ❏ EG 30434 [(2)S] | The Dave Clark Five | 1973 | 20.00 | 40.00 | 80.00 |

—Twenty hits and near-hits, all in true stereo! Orange label.

| ❏ KEG 33459 [(2)M] | Glad All Over Again | 1975 | 12.50 | 25.00 | 50.00 |
| ❏ XEM 77238/9 [DJ] | The Dave Clark Five Interview | 1964 | 150.00 | 300.00 | 600.00 |

CLARK, DEE Also see THE DELEGATES (3); KOOL GENTS.
45s
ABNER

| ❏ (no #) [DJ] | Blues Get Off My Shoulder (B-side blank) | 1959 | 25.00 | 50.00 | 100.00 |

—White label; noted as "Special D.J. Release from Latest E.P."

❏ 1019	Nobody But You/When I Call on You	1958	6.25	12.50	25.00
❏ 1026	Just Keep It Up/Whispering Grass	1959	6.25	12.50	25.00
❏ 1029	Hey Little Girl/If It Wasn't for Love	1959	6.25	12.50	25.00
❏ 1029 [PS]	Hey Little Girl/If It Wasn't for Love	1959	10.00	20.00	40.00
❏ 1032	How About That/Blues Get Off My Shoulder	1959	6.25	12.50	25.00
❏ 1037	At My Front Door/Cling-a-Ling	1960	6.25	12.50	25.00

CHELSEA

| ❏ 3025 | Ride a Wild Horse/(Instrumental) | 1975 | — | 2.50 | 5.00 |

Number	Title (A Side/B Side)	Yr	VG	VG+	NM
COLUMBIA					
❏ 44200	In These Very Tender Moments/Lost Girl	1967	2.00	4.00	8.00
CONSTELLATION					
❏ 108	Crossfire Time/I'm Going Home	1963	3.00	6.00	12.00
❏ 113	It's Raining/That's My Girl	1964	3.00	6.00	12.00
❏ 120	Come Closer/That's My Girl	1964	3.00	6.00	12.00
❏ 132	Warm Summer Breeze/Heartbreak	1964	3.00	6.00	12.00
❏ 142	Ain't Gonna Be Your Fool/In My Apartment	1964	3.00	6.00	12.00
❏ 147	T.C.B./It's Impossible	1965	3.00	6.00	12.00
❏ 155	I Can't Run Away/She's My Baby	1965	3.00	6.00	12.00
❏ 165	I Don't Need (Nobody Like You)/Hot Potatoe	1966	3.00	6.00	12.00
❏ 173	Old Fashion Love/I'm Goin' Home	1966	3.00	6.00	12.00
FALCON					
❏ 1002	Gloria/Kangaroo Hop	1957	7.50	15.00	30.00
❏ 1005	Seven Nights/24 Boy Friends	1957	10.00	20.00	40.00
❏ 1009	Oh Little Girl/Wondering	1958	10.00	20.00	40.00
LIBERTY					
❏ 56152	24 Hours of Loneliness/ Where Did All the Good Times Go	1970	—	2.50	5.00
LOST-NITE					
❏ 303	Raindrops/I Want to Love You	197?	—	2.50	5.00

—Reissue

UNITED ARTISTS					
❏ 50759	You Can Make Me Feel So Good/Old Time Religion	1971	—	2.50	5.00
VEE JAY					
❏ 355	You're Looking Good/Gloria	1960	3.75	7.50	15.00
❏ 372	Your Friends/Because I Love You	1961	3.75	7.50	15.00
❏ 383	Raindrops/I Want to Love You	1961	5.00	10.00	20.00
❏ 394	Gotos Delluvia (Raindrops)/Livin' with Vivian	1961	3.75	7.50	15.00

—B-side by Al Smith

❏ 409	Don't Walk Away from Me/ You're Telling Our Secrets	1961	3.75	7.50	15.00
❏ 428	You Are Like the Wind/Drums in My Heart	1962	3.75	7.50	15.00
❏ 443	Dance On Little Girl/Fever	1962	3.75	7.50	15.00
❏ 462	I'm Going Back to School/Nobody But You	1962	3.75	7.50	15.00
❏ 487	I'm a Soldier Boy/Shook Up Over You	1963	3.75	7.50	15.00
❏ 532	How Is He Treating You/The Jones Boy	1963	3.75	7.50	15.00
❏ 548	Walking My Dog/Nobody But Me	1963	3.75	7.50	15.00
WAND					
❏ 1177	Nobody But You (Part 1)/Nobody But You (Part 2)	1968	2.00	4.00	8.00
WARNER BROS.					
❏ 7720	Raindrops '73/I'm a Happy Man	1973	—	2.50	5.00

7-Inch Extended Plays
ABNER

| ❏ 900 | (contents unknown) | 1959 | 30.00 | 60.00 | 120.00 |
| ❏ 900 [PS] | Dee Clark | 1959 | 30.00 | 60.00 | 120.00 |

Albums
ABNER

❏ LP-2000 [M]	Dee Clark	1959	30.00	60.00	120.00
❏ SR-2000 [S]	Dee Clark	1959	87.50	175.00	350.00
❏ LP-2002 [M]	How About That	1960	20.00	40.00	80.00
❏ SR-2002 [S]	How About That	1960	30.00	60.00	120.00

SOLID SMOKE

| ❏ 8026 | His Best Recordings | 1983 | 2.50 | 5.00 | 10.00 |

SUNSET

| ❏ SUS-5217 | Wondering | 1968 | 3.00 | 6.00 | 12.00 |

VEE JAY

❏ LP-1019 [M]	You're Looking Good	1960	12.50	25.00	50.00
❏ LP-1037 [M]	Hold On, It's Dee Clark	1961	12.50	25.00	50.00
❏ SR-1037 [S]	Hold On, It's Dee Clark	1961	25.00	50.00	100.00
❏ LP-1047 [M]	The Best of Dee Clark	1964	12.50	25.00	50.00
❏ SR-1047 [S]	The Best of Dee Clark	1964	25.00	50.00	100.00
❏ VJLP-1047	The Best of Dee Clark	1986	3.00	6.00	12.00

—Authorized reissue

CLARK, DICK See VARIOUS ARTISTS COLLECTIONS.

CLARK, DOUG, AND THE HOT NUTS
45s
JUBILEE

| ❏ 5536 | Baby Let Me Bang Your Box Part 1/
Baby Let Me Bang Your Box Part 2 | 1966 | 5.00 | 10.00 | 20.00 |
| ❏ 5546 | Milk the Cow/Go, Doug, Go | 1966 | 3.75 | 7.50 | 15.00 |

Albums
GROSS

❏ 101	Nuts to You	196?	7.50	15.00	30.00
❏ 102	On Campus	196?	7.50	15.00	30.00
❏ 103	Homecoming	196?	7.50	15.00	30.00
❏ 104	Rush Week	1967	7.50	15.00	30.00
❏ 105	Panty Raid	196?	7.50	15.00	30.00
❏ 106	Summer Session	196?	7.50	15.00	30.00
❏ 107	Hell Night	196?	7.50	15.00	30.00
❏ 108	Freak Out	196?	7.50	15.00	30.00
❏ 109	With a Hat On	196?	7.50	15.00	30.00

CLARK, FRANK
45s
HIT

| ❏ 29 | Ramblin' Rose/
Send Me the Pillow You Dream On | 1962 | 2.00 | 4.00 | 8.00 |

—B-side by Fred York

| ❏ 69 | Those Lazy-Hazy-Crazy Days of Summer/
Blue on Blue | 1963 | 2.00 | 4.00 | 8.00 |

—B-side by John Preston

CLARK, GENE Also see THE BYRDS.
45s
ASYLUM

| ❏ 45222 | Life's Greatest Fool/From a Silver Petal | 1974 | — | 2.50 | 5.00 |

COLUMBIA

❏ 43903	Echoes/I Found You	1966	3.75	7.50	15.00
❏ 43903 [PS]	Echoes/I Found You	1966	75.00	150.00	300.00
❏ 44088	Is Yours Mine/So You Say You Lost Your Baby	1967	3.75	7.50	15.00

RSO

| ❏ 876 | Home Run King/Lonely Saturday | 1977 | — | 2.50 | 5.00 |

Number	Title (A Side/B Side)	Yr	VG	VG+	NM
Albums					
A&M					
❑ SP-4292	White Light	1971	3.75	7.50	15.00
ASYLUM					
❑ 7E-1016	No Other	1974	3.75	7.50	15.00
COLUMBIA					
❑ CL 2618 [M]	Gene Clark with the Gosdin Brothers	1967	7.50	15.00	30.00
❑ CS 9418 [S]	Gene Clark with the Gosdin Brothers	1967	12.50	25.00	50.00
❑ KC 31123	Early L.A. Sessions	1972	3.75	7.50	15.00
RSO					
❑ RS-1-3011	Two Sides to Every Story	1976	5.00	10.00	20.00
SUNDAZED					
❑ LP 5062	Gene Clark with the Gosdin Brothers	2000	3.75	7.50	15.00
—Reissue of Columbia LP					
TAKOMA					
❑ TAK-7112	Firebyrd	1984	2.50	5.00	10.00

CLARK, PETULA

Number	Title (A Side/B Side)	Yr	VG	VG+	NM
45s					
ABC DUNHILL					
❑ 15007	Never Been a Horse That Couldn't Be Rode/				
	I'm the Woman You Need	1974	—	2.50	5.00
❑ 15019	Loving Arms/I'm the Woman You Need	1974	—	2.50	5.00
CORAL					
❑ 60971	Song of the Mermaid/Tell Me Truly	1953	6.25	12.50	25.00
❑ 61077	Where Did My Snowman Go/Three Little Kittens	1953	6.25	12.50	25.00
ESSEX					
❑ (# unknown)	Majorca/Fascinating Rhythm	1955	—	—	—
—We have not been able to confirm this record's existence. Readers?					
IMPERIAL					
❑ 5582	The Little Blue Man/Baby Lover	1959	5.00	10.00	20.00
❑ 5600	Where Do I Go from Here/Mama's Talkin' Soft	1959	5.00	10.00	20.00
❑ 5655	Now That I Need You/I Love a Violin	1960	5.00	10.00	20.00
KING					
❑ 1371	The Little Shoemaker/Helpless	1954	6.25	12.50	25.00
LAURIE					
❑ 3143	Jumble Sale/The Road	1962	3.75	7.50	15.00
❑ 3156	I Will Follow Him/Darling Cheri	1963	3.75	7.50	15.00
❑ 3236	Elle Est Finie/J'ai Tout Oublie	1964	3.75	7.50	15.00
❑ 3259	In Love/The Road	1964	3.75	7.50	15.00
❑ 3316	In Love/Darling Cheri	1965	3.00	6.00	12.00
❑ 3573	Jumble Sale/The Road	1971	—	3.00	6.00
LONDON INT'L.					
❑ 10504	My Friend the Sea/With All My Love	1962	3.75	7.50	15.00
❑ 10510	I'm Counting on You/Some Other World	1962	3.75	7.50	15.00
❑ 10516	Tender Love/Whistlin' for the Moon	1962	3.75	7.50	15.00
MGM					
❑ 12049	The Pendulum Song/Romance in Rome	1955	6.25	12.50	25.00
❑ 14392	My Guy/Little Bit of Lovin'	1972	—	2.50	5.00
❑ 14431	Wedding Song (There Is Love)/				
	Song Without End	1972	—	2.50	5.00
❑ 14511	Serenade of Love/I Can't Remember	1973	—	2.50	5.00
❑ 14577	Gratification/I Can't Remember	1973	—	2.50	5.00
❑ 14673	Silver Spoon/Fixing to Live	1973	—	2.50	5.00
❑ 14708	Come On Home/The Old Fashioned Way	1974	—	2.50	5.00
SCOTTI BROS.					
❑ 02676	Natural Love/Because I Love Him	1982	—	2.00	4.00
❑ 02979	Blue Eyes Crying in the Rain/Love Won't Always				
	Pass You By	1982	—	2.00	4.00
❑ 03171	Dreamin' with My Eyes Wide Open/Afterglow	1982	—	2.00	4.00
WARNER BROS.					
❑ 5494	Downtown/You'd Better Love Me	1964	2.50	5.00	10.00
—Later pressings have orange labels					
❑ 5494	Downtown/You'd Better Love Me	1964	3.75	7.50	15.00
—Originals have red labels with arrows					
❑ 5612	I Know a Place/Jack and John	1965	2.50	5.00	10.00
❑ 5643	You'd Better Come Home/Heart	1965	2.50	5.00	10.00
❑ 5661	Round Every Corner/Two Rivers	1965	2.50	5.00	10.00
❑ 5684	My Love/Where Am I Going	1965	2.50	5.00	10.00
❑ 5802	A Sign of the Times/Time for Love	1966	2.50	5.00	10.00
❑ 5835	I Couldn't Live Without Your Love/				
	Your Way of Life	1966	2.50	5.00	10.00
❑ 5863	Who Am I/Love Is a Long Journey	1966	2.50	5.00	10.00
❑ 5882	Color My World/Take Me Home Again	1966	2.50	5.00	10.00
❑ 7002	This Is My Song/High	1967	2.50	5.00	10.00
❑ 7049	Don't Sleep in the Subway/Here Comes the				
	Morning	1967	2.50	5.00	10.00
❑ 7073	The Cat in the Window (The Bird in the Sky)/				
	Fancy Dancin' Man	1967	2.50	5.00	10.00
❑ 7097	The Other Man's Grass Is Always Greener/At				
	the Crossroads	1967	2.50	5.00	10.00
❑ 7170	Kiss Me Goodbye/I've Got Love Going for Me	1968	2.00	4.00	8.00
—Later pressings have green labels with "W7" logo					
❑ 7170	Kiss Me Goodbye/I've Got Love Going for Me	1968	2.50	5.00	10.00
—Originals have orange labels					
❑ 7216	Don't Give Up/Every Time I See a Rainbow	1968	2.00	4.00	8.00
❑ 7244	American Boys/Look to the Sky	1968	2.00	4.00	8.00
❑ 7275	Happy Heart/Love Is the Only Thing	1969	2.00	4.00	8.00
❑ 7310	Look at Mine/If Somebody Loves You	1969	2.00	4.00	8.00
❑ 7343	No One Better Than You/Things Bright and				
	Beautiful	1969	2.00	4.00	8.00
❑ 7422	Beautiful Sounds/The Song Is Love	1970	2.00	4.00	8.00
❑ 7467	The Song of My Life/Couldn't Sleep	1971	2.00	4.00	8.00
❑ 7484	I Don't Know How to Love Him				
	(Superstar)/Maybe	1971	2.00	4.00	8.00
WARWICK					
❑ 652	Romeo/Isn't It a Lovely Day	1961	5.00	10.00	20.00
7-Inch Extended Plays					
WARNER BROS.					
❑ S 1743	Have Another Dream on Me/Your Love Is				
	Everywhere/One in a Million//The Sun Shines				
	Out of Your Shoes/Days/Why Can't I Cry?	1968	3.00	6.00	12.00
—Jukebox issue; small hole, plays at 33 1/3 rpm					
❑ S 1743 [PS]	Petula	1968	—	—	12.00
Albums					
COCA-COLA					
❑ 103 [DJ]	Petula Clark Swings the Jingle	1966	37.50	75.00	150.00
GNP CRESCENDO					
❑ 2069	Live at the Royal Albert Hall	1972	2.50	5.00	10.00
❑ 2170	The Greatest Hits of Petula Clark	1984	2.00	4.00	8.00
IMPERIAL					
❑ LP-9079 [M]	Pet Clark	1959	12.50	25.00	50.00
❑ LP-9281 [M]	Uptown with Petula Clark	1965	5.00	10.00	20.00
—Reissue of Imperial 9079					
❑ LP-12027 [S]	Pet Clark	1959	20.00	40.00	80.00
❑ LP-12281 [S]	Uptown with Petula Clark	1965	6.25	12.50	25.00
—Reissue of Imperial 12079					
JANGO					
❑ 779	Give It a Try	1986	2.50	5.00	10.00
LAURIE					
❑ LLP-2032 [M]	In Love!	1965	3.75	7.50	15.00
❑ SLP-2032 [S]	In Love!	1965	3.75	7.50	15.00
❑ ST-90497 [S]	In Love!	1965	5.00	10.00	20.00
—Capitol Record Club edition					
MGM					
❑ SE-4859	Pet Clark Now	1972	2.50	5.00	10.00
PREMIER					
❑ PM-9016 [M]	The English Sound Starring Petula Clark	1965	3.00	6.00	12.00
❑ PS-9016 [S]	The English Sound Starring Petula Clark	1965	3.75	7.50	15.00
ROULETTE					
❑ 1 [(3)]	Petula	1975	5.00	10.00	20.00
SUNSET					
❑ SUM-1101 [M]	This Is Petula Clark	1965	3.00	6.00	12.00
❑ SUS-5101 [S]	This Is Petula Clark	1965	3.75	7.50	15.00
WARNER BROS.					
❑ W 1590 [M]	Downtown	1965	3.75	7.50	15.00
—Originals have gray labels					
❑ W 1590 [M]	Downtown	1966	3.00	6.00	12.00
—Reissues have gold labels					
❑ WS 1590 [S]	Downtown	1965	5.00	10.00	20.00
—Originals have gold labels					
❑ W 1598 [M]	I Know a Place	1965	3.75	7.50	15.00
—Originals have gray labels					
❑ W 1598 [M]	I Know a Place	1966	3.00	6.00	12.00
—Reissues have gold labels					
❑ WS 1598 [S]	I Know a Place	1965	5.00	10.00	20.00
—Originals have gold labels					
❑ WS 1598 [S]	I Know a Place	1968	3.00	6.00	12.00
—Green label with "W7" logo in box at top					
❑ W 1608 [M]	The World's Greatest International Hits	1965	3.00	6.00	12.00
—Reissues have gold labels					
❑ W 1608 [M]	The World's Greatest International Hits	1965	3.75	7.50	15.00
—Originals have gray labels					
❑ WS 1608 [S]	The World's Greatest International Hits	1965	5.00	10.00	20.00
—Originals have gold labels					
❑ W 1630 [M]	My Love	1966	2.50	5.00	10.00
❑ WS 1630 [S]	My Love	1966	3.00	6.00	12.00
❑ W 1645 [M]	I Couldn't Live Without Your Love	1966	2.50	5.00	10.00
❑ WS 1645 [S]	I Couldn't Live Without Your Love	1966	3.00	6.00	12.00
❑ W 1673 [M]	Color My World/Who Am I	1967	2.50	5.00	10.00
❑ WS 1673 [S]	Color My World/Who Am I	1967	3.00	6.00	12.00
❑ W 1698 [M]	These Are My Songs	1967	2.50	5.00	10.00
❑ WS 1698 [S]	These Are My Songs	1967	3.00	6.00	12.00
❑ W 1719 [M]	The Other Man's Grass Is Always Greener	1968	3.00	6.00	12.00
❑ WS 1719 [P]	The Other Man's Grass Is Always Greener	1968	3.00	6.00	12.00
—"The Other Man's Grass Is Always Greener" is rechanneled.					
❑ W 1743 [M]	Petula	1968	3.00	6.00	12.00
❑ WS 1743 [S]	Petula	1968	3.00	6.00	12.00
❑ WS 1765	Greatest Hits, Volume I	1968	2.50	5.00	10.00
❑ WS 1789	Portrait of Petula	1969	2.50	5.00	10.00
❑ WS 1823	Just Pet	1969	2.50	5.00	10.00
❑ WS 1862	Memphis	1970	2.50	5.00	10.00
❑ WS 1865	Warm and Tender (The Song of My Life)	1971	2.50	5.00	10.00
❑ ST-91348 [S]	These Are My Songs	1967	3.75	7.50	15.00
—Capitol Record Club edition					
❑ ST-91598	Greatest Hits, Volume I	1968	3.75	7.50	15.00
—Capitol Record Club edition					
❑ SQBO-93215 [(2)P]	Hits...My Way	1969	6.25	12.50	25.00
—Capitol Record Club exclusive; "The Other Man's Grass Is Always Greener" is rechanneled.					

CLARK, ROY

Number	Title (A Side/B Side)	Yr	VG	VG+	NM
45s					
ABC					
❑ 12328	Must You Throw Dirt in My Face/Lazy River	1978	—	2.00	4.00
❑ 12365	Where Have You Been All of My Life/Near You	1978	—	2.00	4.00
❑ 12402	The Happy Days/Shoulder to Shoulder				
	(Arm and Arm)	1978	—	2.00	4.00
❑ 12437	Is It Hot in Here				
	(Or Is It Me)/Jolly Ho (Happy Hour)	1978	—	2.00	4.00
—With Buck Trent					
ABC DOT					
❑ 17530	Dear God/Take Good Care of Her	1974	—	2.00	4.00
❑ 17545	You're Gonna Love Yourself in the Morning/				
	Banjoy	1975	—	2.00	4.00
❑ 17565	Heart to Heart/Someone Cares for You	1975	—	2.00	4.00
❑ 17605	If I Had to Do It All Over Again/It Sure Looks				
	Good on You	1976	—	2.00	4.00
❑ 17626	Think Summer/Whatever Happened to Gauze	1976	—	2.00	4.00
❑ 17667	I Have a Dream, I Have a Love/Half a Love	1976	—	2.00	4.00
❑ 17712	We Can't Build a Fire in the Rain/I'm So				
	Lonesome I Could Cry	1977	—	2.00	4.00
CAPITOL					
❑ 4595	Under the Double Eagle/Black Sapphire	1961	3.00	6.00	12.00
❑ 4670	Texas Twist/Wildwood Twist	1961	3.00	6.00	12.00
❑ 4794	Talk About a Party/As Long As I'm Movin'	1962	3.00	6.00	12.00
❑ 4956	The Tip of My Fingers/Spooky Movies	1963	2.50	5.00	10.00
❑ 5047	Good Time Charlie/Application for Love	1963	2.50	5.00	10.00
❑ 5099	Through the Eyes of a Fool/Sweet Violets	1964	2.50	5.00	10.00
❑ 5163	Take Me As I Am/If You'll Pardon Me	1964	2.50	5.00	10.00
❑ 5233	It's My Way/I'm Forgetting Now	1964	2.50	5.00	10.00
❑ 5300	Alabama Jubilee/Down Yonder	1964	2.50	5.00	10.00
❑ 5350	When the Wind Blows In Chicago/				
	Live Fast, Love Hard, Die Young	1965	2.50	5.00	10.00
❑ 5445	The Color of Her Love Is Blue/				
	Too Pooped to Pop	1965	2.50	5.00	10.00

Number	Title (A Side/B Side)	Yr	VG	VG+	NM
❏ 5512	So Much to Remember/				
	Turn Around and Look Again	1965	2.50	5.00	10.00
❏ 5565	Malaguena/Overdue Blues	1965	2.50	5.00	10.00
❏ 5619	Rose Colored Glasses/Everybody Watches Me	1966	2.50	5.00	10.00
❏ 5664	Hey Sweet Thing/If You Want It, Come and Get It	1966	2.50	5.00	10.00
—With Mary Taylor					
❏ 5770	St. Louis Blues/Just a Closer Walk with Thee	1966	2.50	5.00	10.00
CHURCHILL					
❏ 52469	Another Lonely Night With You/(Instrumental)	1984	—	2.00	4.00
❏ 94002	Paradise Knife and Gun Club/I Don't Care	1982	—	2.50	5.00
❏ 94007	Tennessee Saturday Night/Tumbling				
	Tumbleweeds	1982	—	2.50	5.00
❏ 94007 [PS]	Tennessee Saturday Night/Tumbling				
	Tumbleweeds	1982	—	3.00	6.00
❏ 94011	Here We Go Again/Early in the Morning	1982	—	2.50	5.00
❏ 94016	Christmas Wouldn't Be Christmas Without You/				
	A Way Without Words	1982	—	3.00	6.00
❏ 94016 [PS]	Christmas Wouldn't Be Christmas Without You/				
	A Way Without Words	1982	—	3.00	6.00
❏ 94017	I'm a Booger/A Way Without Words	1983	—	2.50	5.00
❏ 94025	Wildwood Flower/Southern Nights	1983	—	2.50	5.00
DOT					
❏ 17117	Do You Believe This Town/				
	It Just Happened That Way	1968	—	3.00	6.00
❏ 17187	Love Is Just a State of Mind/Look to the Sky	1968	—	3.00	6.00
❏ 17246	Yesterday, When I Was Young/Just Another				
	Man	1969	—	2.50	5.00
❏ 17299	September Song/For the Life of Me	1969	—	2.50	5.00
❏ 17324	Right or Left at Oak Street/I Need to Be Needed	1969	—	2.50	5.00
❏ 17335	Then She's a Lover/Say Amen	1969	—	2.50	5.00
❏ 17349	I Never Picked Cotton/Lonesome Too Long	1970	—	2.50	5.00
❏ 17355	Thank God and Greyhound/Strangers	1970	—	2.50	5.00
❏ 17368	A Simple Thing As Love/I'd Fight the World	1971	—	2.50	5.00
❏ 17370	(Where Do I Begin) Love Story/Theme from				
	"Love Story"	1971	—	2.50	5.00
❏ 17386	She Cried/Back in the Race	1971	—	2.50	5.00
❏ 17395	Magnificent Sanctuary Bird/Be Ready	1971	—	2.50	5.00
❏ 17413	I'll Take the Time/Ode to a Critter	1972	—	2.50	5.00
❏ 17426	The Lawrence Welk—Hee Haw Counter-				
	Revolution Polka/When the Wind Blows	1972	—	2.50	5.00
❏ 17449	Come Live with Me/Darby's Castle	1973	—	2.50	5.00
❏ 17458	Riders in the Sky/Roy's Guitar Boogie	1973	—	2.50	5.00
❏ 17480	Somewhere Between Love and Tomorrow/I'll				
	Paint You a Song	1973	—	2.50	5.00
❏ 17498	Honeymoon Feelin'/I Really Don't Want to Know	1974	—	2.50	5.00
❏ 17518	The Great Divide/Chomp'n	1974	—	2.50	5.00
HALLMARK					
❏ 0001	What a Wonderful World/(Instrumental)	1989	—	2.50	5.00
❏ 0004	But, She Loves Me/(B-side unknown)	1989	—	2.50	5.00
MCA					
❏ 41122	Caldonia/Four O'Clock in the Morning	1979	—	2.00	4.00
❏ 41153	Chain Gang of Love/Why Don't We Go				
	Somewhere and Love	1979	—	2.00	4.00
❏ 41208	If There Were Only Time for Love/				
	Then I'll Be Over You	1980	—	2.00	4.00
❏ 41288	For Love's Own Sake/				
	They'll Never Take Her Love from Me	1980	—	2.00	4.00
❏ 51031	I Ain't Got Nobody/				
	Play Me a Little Traveling Music	1980	—	2.00	4.00
❏ 51079	She Can't Give It Away/				
	Dig a Little Deeper in the Well	1981	—	2.00	4.00
❏ 51111	Love Takes Two/Come Sundown	1981	—	2.00	4.00
SILVER DOLLAR					
❏ 0001	Tobacco Road/Black Sapphire	1986	—	2.50	5.00
❏ 0001 [PS]	Tobacco Road/Black Sapphire	1986	2.00	4.00	8.00
❏ 0004	Juke Box Saturday Night/Night Life	1986	—	2.50	5.00
SONGBIRD					
❏ 51167	The Last Word in Jesus Is Us/Shinin' Face	1981	—	2.00	4.00
TOWER					
❏ 331	Orange Blossom Special/The Great Pretender	1967	2.00	4.00	8.00
Albums					
ABC					
❏ AB-1053	Labor of Love	1978	2.50	5.00	10.00
ABC DOT					
❏ DOSD-2001	Roy Clark/The Entertainer	1974	2.50	5.00	10.00
❏ DOSD-2005	Roy Clark, Family & Friends	1974	2.50	5.00	10.00
❏ DOSD-2010	Classic Clark	1974	2.50	5.00	10.00
❏ DOSD-2030	Roy Clark's Greatest Hits — Volume 1	1975	2.50	5.00	10.00
❏ DOSD-2041	Heart to Heart	1975	2.50	5.00	10.00
❏ DOSD-2054	Roy Clark In Concert	1976	2.50	5.00	10.00
❏ DO-2072 [(2)]	My Music and Me/Vocal & Instrumental	1977	3.00	6.00	12.00
❏ DO-2099	Hookin' It	1977	2.50	5.00	10.00
—Reissue of Record 2 of 2072					
CAPITOL					
❏ SKAO-369	The Greatest!	1969	3.00	6.00	12.00
❏ SM-369	The Greatest!	197?	2.50	5.00	10.00
—Reissue with new prefix					
❏ ST 1780 [S]	The Lightning Fingers of Roy Clark	1962	6.25	12.50	25.00
❏ T 1780 [M]	The Lightning Fingers of Roy Clark	1962	5.00	10.00	20.00
❏ ST 1972 [S]	The Tip of My Fingers	1963	6.25	12.50	25.00
❏ T 1972 [M]	The Tip of My Fingers	1963	5.00	10.00	20.00
❏ ST 2031 [S]	Happy to Be Unhappy	1964	6.25	12.50	25.00
❏ T 2031 [M]	Happy to Be Unhappy	1964	5.00	10.00	20.00
❏ SM-2425	The Roy Clark Guitar Spectacular	197?	2.50	5.00	10.00
—Reissue with new prefix					
❏ ST 2425 [S]	The Roy Clark Guitar Spectacular	1965	6.25	12.50	25.00
❏ T 2425 [M]	The Roy Clark Guitar Spectacular	1965	5.00	10.00	20.00
❏ ST 2452 [S]	Roy Clark Sings Lonesome Love Ballads	1966	6.25	12.50	25.00
❏ T 2452 [M]	Roy Clark Sings Lonesome Love Ballads	1966	5.00	10.00	20.00
❏ ST 2535 [S]	Stringing Along with the Blues	1966	6.25	12.50	25.00
❏ T 2535 [M]	Stringing Along with the Blues	1966	5.00	10.00	20.00
❏ SABB-11264 [(2)]	The Entertainer of the Year	1974	3.75	7.50	15.00
❏ SM-11412	So Much to Remember	1975	2.50	5.00	10.00
❏ SM-12032	The Tip of My Fingers	1980	2.00	4.00	8.00
❏ SN-16161	The Greatest!	198?	2.00	4.00	8.00
❏ SN-16227	The Lightning Fingers of Roy Clark	198?	2.00	4.00	8.00
CHURCHILL					
❏ 9421	The Roy Clark Show Live from Austin City Limits	1982	2.50	5.00	10.00
❏ 9425	Turned Loose	1982	2.50	5.00	10.00

Number	Title (A Side/B Side)	Yr	VG	VG+	NM
DOT					
❏ DOS-000112	The Special Talents of Roy Clark	1973	3.00	6.00	12.00
❏ DLP-25863	Urban, Suburban	1968	3.00	6.00	12.00
❏ DLP-25895	Do You Believe This Roy Clark	1968	3.00	6.00	12.00
❏ DLP-25953	Yesterday, When I Was Young	1969	3.00	6.00	12.00
❏ DLP-25972	The Everlovin' Soul of Roy Clark	1969	3.00	6.00	12.00
❏ DLP-25977	The Other Side of Roy Clark	1970	3.00	6.00	12.00
❏ DLP-25980	I Never Picked Cotton	1970	3.00	6.00	12.00
❏ DOS-25986	The Best of Roy Clark	1971	3.00	6.00	12.00
❏ DOS-25990	The Incredible Roy Clark	1971	3.00	6.00	12.00
❏ DOS-25993	The Magnificent Sanctuary Band	1971	3.00	6.00	12.00
❏ DOS-25997	Roy Clark Country!	1972	3.00	6.00	12.00
❏ DOS-26005	Roy Clark Live!	1972	3.00	6.00	12.00
❏ DOS-26008	Roy Clark/Superpicker	1973	3.00	6.00	12.00
❏ DOS-26010	Come Live with Me	1973	3.00	6.00	12.00
❏ DOS-26018	Roy Clark's Family Album	1973	3.00	6.00	12.00
❏ ST-93117	The Everlovin' Soul of Roy Clark	1969	3.75	7.50	15.00
—Capitol Record Club edition with old-style black Dot label with multi-color logo					
❏ ST-94463	Roy Clark Country!	1972	3.75	7.50	15.00
—Capitol Record Club edition					
HILLTOP					
❏ 6046	Roy Clartk	196?	3.75	7.50	15.00
❏ 6080	Silver Threads and Golden Needles	1970	2.50	5.00	10.00
❏ 6094	He'll Have to Go	1970	2.50	5.00	10.00
❏ 6135	Take Me As I Am	197?	2.50	5.00	10.00
❏ 6154	Honky Tonk	197?	2.50	5.00	10.00
MCA					
❏ 675	Labor of Love	1980	2.00	4.00	8.00
❏ 676	Heart to Heart	1980	2.00	4.00	8.00
❏ 677	Hookin' It	1980	2.00	4.00	8.00
❏ 678	Yesterday, When I Was Young	198?	2.00	4.00	8.00
❏ 679	Roy Clark/Superpicker	198?	2.00	4.00	8.00
❏ 811	Back to the Country	198?	2.00	4.00	8.00
❏ 3161	Makin' Music	1980	2.50	5.00	10.00
—With Gatemouth Brown					
❏ 3189	My Music	1980	2.50	5.00	10.00
❏ 27015	The Best of Roy Clark	198?	2.00	4.00	8.00
❏ 27050	Roy Clark's Greatest Hits — Volume 1	198?	2.00	4.00	8.00
❏ 37130	Banjo Bandits	198?	2.00	4.00	8.00
—With Buck Trent					
❏ 37131	A Pair of Fives (Banjos, That Is)	198?	2.00	4.00	8.00
❏ 37132	Roy Clark In Concert	198?	2.00	4.00	8.00
❏ 37134	Roy Clark Live!	198?	2.00	4.00	8.00
❏ 37142	My Music	198?	2.00	4.00	8.00
PAIR					
❏ PDL2-1088 [(2)]	Country Standard Time	1986	3.00	6.00	12.00
PICKWICK					
❏ PTP-2043 [(2)]	Roy Clark	1973	3.00	6.00	12.00
❏ PTP-2093 [(2)]	The Entertainer of the Year	1978	3.00	6.00	12.00
SONGBIRD					
❏ 5260	The Last Word in Jesus Is Us	1981	2.50	5.00	10.00
TOWER					
❏ ST 5055 [S]	Roy Clark Live	1967	5.00	10.00	20.00
❏ T 5055 [M]	Roy Clark Live	1967	3.75	7.50	15.00
❏ DT 5118 [R]	In the Mood	1968	3.75	7.50	15.00
WORD					
❏ 8654	Roy Clark Sings Gospel	1975	3.00	6.00	12.00

CLARK, ROY, AND BUCK TRENT
Albums

ABC

Number	Title (A Side/B Side)	Yr	VG	VG+	NM
❏ AY-1084	Banjo Bandits	1978	2.50	5.00	10.00
ABC DOT					
❏ 2015	A Pair of Fives (Banjos, That Is)	1975	2.50	5.00	10.00

CLARK, SANFORD
45s

DOT

Number	Title (A Side/B Side)	Yr	VG	VG+	NM
❏ 15481	The Fool/Lonesome for a Letter	1956	6.25	12.50	25.00
—Second pressings have black labels					
❏ 15481	The Fool/Lonesome for a Letter	1956	12.50	25.00	50.00
—Originals have maroon labels					
❏ 15516	A Cheat/Usta Be My Baby	1956	6.25	12.50	25.00
❏ 15534	Oooo Baby/9 Lb. Hammer	1957	6.25	12.50	25.00
❏ 15556	The Glory of Love/Darling Dear	1957	6.25	12.50	25.00
❏ 15585	Love Charms/Loo-Be-Doo	1957	6.25	12.50	25.00
❏ 15646	Swanee River Rock/				
	The Man Who Made an Angel Cry	1957	6.25	12.50	25.00
❏ 15738	Modern Romance/Travelin' Man	1958	37.50	75.00	150.00
JAMIE					
❏ 1107	Sing 'Em Some Blues/Still as the Night	1958	5.00	10.00	20.00
❏ 1120	Bad Luck/My Jealousy	1959	5.00	10.00	20.00
❏ 1129	Run Boy Run/New Kind of Fool	1959	5.00	10.00	20.00
❏ 1153	Go On Home/Pledging My Love	1960	5.00	10.00	20.00
LHI					
❏ 1203	The Son of Hickory Holler's Tramp/				
	Black Widow Spider	1968	2.00	4.00	8.00
❏ 1213	Love Me Till Then/Farm Labor Camp No. 2	1968	2.00	4.00	8.00
MCI					
❏ 1003	The Fool/Lonesome for a Letter	1956	50.00	100.00	200.00
RAMCO					
❏ 1972	The Fool '66/Step Aside	1966	3.75	7.50	15.00
❏ 1976	Shades/Once Upon a Time	1966	3.00	6.00	12.00
❏ 1979	They Call Me Country/Climbin' the Walls	1967	3.00	6.00	12.00
❏ 1987	It's Nothing to Me/Calling All Hearts	1967	3.00	6.00	12.00
❏ 1992	The Big Lie/Where's the Floor	1967	3.00	6.00	12.00
TREY					
❏ 3016	It Hurts Me Too/Guess It's Love	1961	5.00	10.00	20.00
WARNER BROS.					
❏ 5473	She Taught Me/Just Blessin'	1964	3.75	7.50	15.00
❏ 5624	Houston/Hard Feelings	1965	3.75	7.50	15.00
Albums					
LHI					
❏ 12003	Return of the Fool	1968	15.00	30.00	60.00

Number	Title (A Side/B Side)	Yr	VG	VG+	NM

CLARKE, ALLAN Also see THE HOLLIES.
45s
ASYLUM

Number	Title (A Side/B Side)	Yr	VG	VG+	NM
❑ 45313	Light a Light/				
	If You Think You Know How to Love Me	1976	—	2.00	4.00

ATLANTIC

❑ 3459	(I Will Be Your) Shadow in the Street/				
	The Passenger	1978	—	2.00	4.00
❑ 3497	I Wasn't Born Yesterday/The Man Who				
	Manufactured Daydreams	1978	—	2.00	4.00
❑ 3522	I'm Betting My Life on You/				
	Who's Goin' Out the Back Door	1978	—	2.00	4.00

ELEKTRA

❑ 46617	Slipstream/Imagination's Child	1979	—	2.00	4.00
❑ 47019	The Only Ones/Driving the Doomsday Cars	1980	—	2.00	4.00

EPIC

❑ 5-10914	Baby It's Alright with Me/Ruby	1972	—	2.00	4.00

Albums
ASYLUM

❑ 7E-1056	I've Got Time	1976	2.50	5.00	10.00

ATLANTIC

❑ SD 19175	I Wasn't Born Yesterday	1978	2.50	5.00	10.00

ELEKTRA

❑ 6E-267	Legendary Heroes	1980	2.50	5.00	10.00

EPIC

❑ KE 31757	My Real Name Is 'Arold	1972	3.75	7.50	15.00

CLASS-AIRES, THE
45s
HONEY BEE

❑ (# unknown)	Too Old to Cry/My Tears Start to Fall	195?	500.00	1000.	2000.

Albums
HONEY BEE

❑ (# unknown)	Tears Start to Fall	195?	75.00	150.00	300.00

CLASS-NOTES, THE
45s
DOT

❑ 15786	You Inspire Me/Goodness Gracious	1958	7.50	15.00	30.00

HAMILTON

❑ 50011	Take It Back/Bessie's House	1959	15.00	30.00	60.00

CLASSIC IV, THE
45s
ALGONQUIN

❑ 1650	Limbo Under The Christmas Tree/				
	Early Christmas	1962	7.50	15.00	30.00

TWIST

❑ 1001	Island of Paradise/Heavenly Bliss	1962	25.00	50.00	100.00

CLASSICS, THE (1) Brooklyn vocal group led by Emil Stucchio.
45s
BED-STUY

❑ 222	Again/The Way You Look Tonight	196?	2.50	5.00	10.00

DART

❑ 1015	So in Love/Cinderella	1960	7.50	15.00	30.00
❑ 1024	Life Is But a Dream, Sweetheart/That's the Way	1961	50.00	100.00	200.00
❑ 1032	Angel Angela/Eenie Minie Mo	1961	12.50	25.00	50.00

LOST-NITE

❑ 200	Till Then/Eenie Minie Mo	196?	—	2.50	5.00
—Reissue					

MERCURY

❑ 71829	Life Is But a Dream, Sweetheart/That's the Way	1961	6.25	12.50	25.00

MUSICNOTE

❑ 118	P.S. I Love You/Wrap Your Troubles in Dreams	1963	6.25	12.50	25.00
❑ 1116	Till Then/Eenie Minie Mo	1963	6.25	12.50	25.00
—Black vinyl, blue label					
❑ 1116	Till Then/Eenie Minie Mo	1963	7.50	15.00	30.00
—Black vinyl, yellow label					
❑ 1116	Till Then/Eenie Minie Mo	1963	25.00	50.00	100.00
—Gold vinyl					
❑ 1116	Till Then/Eenie Minie Mo	1963	37.50	75.00	150.00
—Multi-color vinyl					

MUSICTONE

❑ 1114	So in Love/Cinderella	1963	5.00	10.00	20.00
❑ 6131	Too Young/Who's Laughing, Who's Crying	1964	5.00	10.00	20.00

PICCOLO

❑ 500	I Apologize/Love for Today	1965	6.25	12.50	25.00

STORK

❑ STK-2	You'll Never Know/Dancing with You	1964	6.25	12.50	25.00

STREAM LINE

❑ 1028	Life Is But a Dream, Sweetheart/Nuttin' in the				
	Noggin	1961	6.25	12.50	25.00

CLASSICS, THE (2) With LOU CHRISTIE.
45s
STARR

❑ 508	Close Your Eyes/Funny Things	1960	50.00	100.00	200.00
—Reissued on Alcar with Lou Christie's name prominently mentioned					

CLASSICS, THE (3) Canadian group.
45s
JERDEN

❑ 742	Till I Met You/It Didn't Take Much	1964	7.50	15.00	30.00

CLASSICS, THE (U) Some of these could be group (1); none of them are group (2); probably none of these are group (3).
45s
CLASS

❑ 219	If Only the Sky Was a Mirror/				
	Gosh, But This Is Love	1958	17.50	35.00	70.00

CREST

❑ 1063	Let Me Dream/You're the Prettiest One	1959	20.00	40.00	80.00

MV

❑ 1000	Christmas Is Here/(B-side unknown)	19??	2.50	5.00	10.00

Number	Title (A Side/B Side)	Yr	VG	VG+	NM

PROMO

❑ 1010	Blue Moon/Little Boy Lost	1961	7.50	15.00	30.00
—As "Herb Lance and the Classics"					

RO-ANN

❑ 1002	Je Vous Aime/Burning Desire	1959	250.00	500.00	1000.

SHELTER

❑ 7318	Mr. Fire Coal-Man/Flashing My Whip	1972	—	2.50	5.00
—B-side by Hugh Roy					

TOP RANK

❑ 2061	You're Everything/Burning Love	1960	6.25	12.50	25.00

YAN-G

❑ 4665	So Glad That I Found You/(B-side unknown)	196?	500.00	1000.	2000.

CLASSICS IV
45s
ARLEN

❑ 746	Don't Make Me Wait/It's Too Late	1964	5.00	10.00	20.00

CAPITOL

❑ 5710	Cry Baby/Pollyanna	1966	3.75	7.50	15.00
—As "The Classics"					
❑ 5816	Little Darlin'/Nothing to Lose	1966	3.75	7.50	15.00

IMPERIAL

❑ 66259	Spooky/Poor People	1967	2.00	4.00	8.00
❑ 66293	Soul Train/Strange Changes	1968	2.00	4.00	8.00
❑ 66304	Mama's and Papa's/Waves	1968	2.00	4.00	8.00
❑ 66328	Stormy/24 Hours of Loneliness	1968	2.00	4.00	8.00
❑ 66328	Stormy/Ladies' Man	1968	5.00	10.00	20.00
❑ 66352	Traces/Mary, Mary Row Your Boat	1969	2.00	4.00	8.00
❑ 66378	Everyday With You Girl/Sentimental Lady	1969	2.00	4.00	8.00
❑ 66393	Change of Heart/Rainy Day	1969	—	3.00	6.00
—Starting here, "Dennis Yost and the Classics IV"					
❑ 66424	Midnight/The Comic	1969	—	3.00	6.00
❑ 66439	The Funniest Thing/Nobody Loves You But Me	1970	—	3.00	6.00

LIBERTY

❑ 56182	God Knows I Loved Her/We Miss You	1970	—	3.00	6.00
❑ 56200	Where Did All the Good Times Go/				
	Ain't It the Truth	1970	—	3.00	6.00

MGM

❑ 14785	My First Day Without You/Lovin' Each Other	1975	—	2.00	4.00

MGM SOUTH

❑ 7002	What Am I Crying For/All in Your Mind	1972	—	2.50	5.00
❑ 7012	Rosanna/One Man Show	1973	—	2.50	5.00
❑ 7016	Save the Sunlight/Make Me Believe It	1973	—	2.50	5.00
❑ 7020	I Knew It Would Happen/				
	Love Me or Leave Me Alone	1973	—	2.50	5.00
❑ 7027	It's Now Winter's Day/Losing My Mind	1974	—	2.50	5.00

UNITED ARTISTS

❑ 0125	Stormy/Spooky	1973	—	2.00	4.00
—"Silver Spotlight Series" reissue					
❑ 0126	Traces/Everyday with You Girl	1973	—	2.00	4.00
—"Silver Spotlight Series" reissue					
❑ 50777	Most of All/It's Time for Love	1971	—	2.50	5.00
❑ 50805	Cherry Hill Park/Pick Up the Pieces	1971	—	2.50	5.00

Albums
ACCORD

❑ SN-7107	Stormy	1981	2.50	5.00	10.00

IMPERIAL

❑ LP-12371	Spooky	1968	5.00	10.00	20.00
❑ LP-12407	Mamas and Papas/Soul Train	1969	5.00	10.00	20.00
❑ LP-12429	Traces	1969	5.00	10.00	20.00
❑ LP-16000	Dennis Yost & the Classics IV/				
	Golden Greats - Volume I	1969	5.00	10.00	20.00

LIBERTY

❑ LN-10109	The Very Best of the Classics IV	198?	2.00	4.00	8.00
❑ LST-11003	Song	1970	3.75	7.50	15.00

MGM SOUTH

❑ 702	Dennis Yost and the Classics IV	1973	3.75	7.50	15.00

UNITED ARTISTS

❑ UA-LA446-E	The Very Best of the Classics IV	1975	3.00	6.00	12.00

CLASSMATES, THE
45s
HIT

❑ 324	Tighten Up/Cowboys to Girls	1968	2.00	4.00	8.00
—B-side by the Fantastics					
❑ 326	A Beautiful Morning/Lady Madonna	1968	2.00	4.00	8.00
—B-side by the Chords (2)					
❑ 335	The Look of Love/Turn Around, Look at Me	1968	2.00	4.00	8.00
—B-side by the Chords (2)					
❑ 338	Classical Gas/People Got to Be Free	1968	2.00	4.00	8.00
❑ 345	Suzie-Q/Midnight Confessions	1968	2.00	4.00	8.00
—B-side by the Jalopy Five					

CLAY, CASSIUS
45s
COLUMBIA

❑ 43007	Stand By Me/I Am the Greatest	1964	6.25	12.50	25.00
❑ 43007 [PS]	Stand By Me/I Am the Greatest	1964	12.50	25.00	50.00
❑ ZSP 75717/77185 [DJ]	The Prediction/Will the Real Sonny				
	Liston Please Fall Down	1964	10.00	20.00	40.00
❑ ZSP 75717/77185 [PS]	The Prediction/Will the Real Sonny				
	Liston Please Fall Down	1964	20.00	40.00	80.00

Albums
COLUMBIA

❑ CL 2093 [M]	I Am the Greatest!	1963	10.00	20.00	40.00
❑ CS 8893 [S]	I Am the Greatest!	1963	12.50	25.00	50.00

CLAY, CHRIS
45s
VELTONE

❑ 111	Santa Under Analysis Part 1/Santa Under				
	Analysis Part 2	1960	6.25	12.50	25.00

CLAY, JOE
45s
VIK

❑ 0211	Duck Tail/Sixteen Chicks	1956	25.00	50.00	100.00
❑ 0218	Get On the Right Track/Cracker Jack	1956	25.00	50.00	100.00

C

Number	Title (A Side/B Side)	Yr	VG	VG+	NM

CLAY, JUDY Also see WILLIAM BELL, BILLY VERA.
45s
ATLANTIC

Number	Title (A Side/B Side)	Yr	VG	VG+	NM
❑ 2669	Get Together/Sister Pitiful	1969	—	3.00	6.00
❑ 2697	Greatest Love/Saving All for You	1969	—	3.00	6.00

EMBER

❑ 1080	More Than You Know/ I Thought I'd Gotten Over You	1961	3.00	6.00	12.00
❑ 1085	Stormy Weather/Do You Think That's Right	1962	3.00	6.00	12.00

SCEPTER

❑ 1273	My Arms Aren't Strong Enough/That's All	1964	2.00	4.00	8.00
❑ 1281	Lonely People Do Foolish Things/I'm Comin' Home	1964	2.00	4.00	8.00
❑ 12135	The Way You Look Tonight/ Haven't You Got What It Takes	1966	2.00	4.00	8.00
❑ 12157	He's the Kind of Guy/You Busted My Mind	1966	2.00	4.00	8.00
❑ 12218	I Want You/He's the Kind of Guy	1968	2.00	4.00	8.00

STAX

❑ 0006	Bed of Roses/Remove the Clouds	1968	—	3.00	6.00
❑ 0026	It Ain't Long Enough/Give Love to Save Love	1969	—	3.00	6.00
❑ 230	You Can't Run Away from Your Heart/ It Takes a Lot of Good Love	1967	2.00	4.00	8.00

CLAY, OTIS
45s
COTILLION

❑ 44001	She's About a Mover/You Don't Miss Your Water	1968	2.00	4.00	8.00
❑ 44009	Do Right Woman, Do Right Man/ That Kind of Lovin'	1968	—	3.50	7.00
❑ 44068	Pouring Water on a Drowning Man/Hard Working Women	1970	—	3.50	7.00
❑ 44101	Is It Over/I'm Qualified	1970	—	3.50	7.00

DAKAR

❑ 610	Baby Jane/You Hurt Me for the Last Time	1969	—	3.50	7.00

ECHO

❑ 2002	Check It Out/Messing with My Mind	1975	2.50	5.00	10.00

ELKA

❑ 301	Turn Back the Hands of Time/Good Lovin'	197?	2.00	4.00	8.00

GLADES

❑ 1736	All I Need Is You/Special Kind of Soul	1976	2.50	5.00	10.00

HI

❑ 2206	Home Is Where the Heart Is/Brand New Thing	1972	—	3.00	6.00
❑ 2214	Precious Precious/Too Many Hands	1972	—	3.00	6.00
❑ 2226	Trying to Live My Life Without You/ Let Me Be the One	1972	—	3.50	7.00
❑ 2239	I Can't Make It Alone/ I Didn't Know the Meaning of Pain	1973	—	3.00	6.00
❑ 2252	If I Could Reach Out/I Die a Little Bit Each Day	1973	—	3.00	6.00
❑ 2266	Woman Don't Live Here No More/You Can't Escape the Hands of Love	1974	—	3.00	6.00
❑ 2270	You Did Something to Me/I Was Jealous	1974	—	3.00	6.00

KAYVETTE

❑ 5130	All Because of Your Love/Today My World Fell	1977	—	2.50	5.00
❑ 5133	Let Me In/Sweet Woman's Love	1977	—	2.50	5.00

ONE-DERFUL!

❑ 4834	Three Is a Crowd/Flame in Your Heart	1965	2.50	5.00	10.00
❑ 4837	I Paid the Price/Tired of Falling In (And Out of) Love	1966	2.50	5.00	10.00
❑ 4841	I Testify/I'm Satisfied	1966	2.50	5.00	10.00
❑ 4846	Flame in Your Heart/It's Easier Said, Than Done	1967	2.00	4.00	8.00
❑ 4848	That's How It Is (When You're in Love)/ Show Place	1967	2.00	4.00	8.00
❑ 4850	A Lasting Love/Got to Find a Way	1967	2.00	4.00	8.00
❑ 4852	Don't Pass Me By/ That'll Get You What You Want	1968	2.00	4.00	8.00

Albums
HI

❑ HLP 6003	I Can't Take It	1977	3.75	7.50	15.00
❑ SHL 32075	Trying to Live My Life Without You	1972	5.00	10.00	20.00

ROOSTER BLUES

❑ R-7609 [(2)]	Soul Man: Live in Japan	1985	3.75	7.50	15.00

CLAY, TOM
45s
BIG TOP

❑ 3055	The Little Boy/That's All	1960	5.00	10.00	20.00

CHANT

❑ 103	Marry Me/(B-side unknown)	1959	25.00	50.00	100.00

IBBB

❑ ZTSC 97436/7	Remember, We Don't Like Them, We Love Them: Official IBBB Interview	1964	37.50	75.00	150.00

—Interviews with the Beatles
MOWEST

❑ 5002	What the World Needs Now Is Love/Abraham, Martin and John//The Victors	1971	—	2.50	5.00

—Blue and yellow label

❑ 5002	What the World Needs Now Is Love/Abraham, Martin and John//The Victors	1971	—	3.00	6.00

—Mostly orange label

❑ 5007	Whatever Happened to Love/Baby I Need Your Loving	1971	—	2.00	4.00

Albums
MOWEST

❑ 103	What the World Needs Now Is Love	1971	3.75	7.50	15.00

CLAYTON, MERRY
45s
CAPITOL

❑ 4984	It's In His Kiss/The Magic of Romance	1963	2.50	5.00	10.00
❑ 5100	Usher Boy/Nothing Left to Do But Cry	1963	2.50	5.00	10.00
❑ 5164	Beg Me/La La Jace Song	1964	2.50	5.00	10.00
❑ 5243	This Is My Dream/The Knocks on the Door	1964	2.50	5.00	10.00

MCA

❑ 41195	Emotion/Let Me Make You Cry a Little Longer	1980	—	2.00	4.00
❑ 41266	You're Always There When I Need You/When the World Turns Blue	1980	—	2.00	4.00

ODE

❑ 66003	Gimme Shelter/Good Girls	1970	—	2.50	5.00
❑ 66007	Country Road/Forget It, I Got It	1970	—	2.50	5.00
❑ 66011	Lift Every Voice and Sing/ I Ain't Gonna Worry My Life Away	1970	—	2.50	5.00
❑ 66016	The Times They Are a-Changing/ Wouldn't It Be Nice	1971	7.50	15.00	30.00

—B-side by the Beach Boys

❑ 66018	After All This Time/Whatever	1971	—	2.00	4.00
❑ 66020	Steamroller/After All This Time	1971	—	2.00	4.00
❑ 66024	Southern Man/Oh No, Not My Baby	1972	—	2.00	4.00
❑ 66030	Oh No, Not My Baby/Suspicious Minds	1972	—	2.00	4.00
❑ 66108	The Acid Queen/Eyesight to the Blind	1975	—	2.00	4.00

—B-side by Richie Havens

❑ 66110	Keep Your Eye on the Sparrow/ Love Grows Up Slow	1975	—	2.00	4.00
❑ 66116	One More Ride/If I Lose	1976	—	2.00	4.00

RCA

❑ 6989-7-R	Yes/In the Still of the Night	1988	—	—	3.00

—B-side by the Five Satins

❑ 8917-7-R	Almost Paradise/Hungry Eyes	1989	—	—	3.00

—B-side with Eric Carmen
Albums
MCA

❑ 3200	Emotion	1980	2.50	5.00	10.00

ODE

❑ PE 34948	Merry Clayton	1977	2.00	4.00	8.00
❑ PE 34957	Keep Your Eye on the Sparrow	1977	2.00	4.00	8.00
❑ SP-77001	Gimme Shelter	1970	3.75	7.50	15.00
❑ SP-77012	Merry Clayton	1971	3.00	6.00	12.00
❑ SP-77030	Keep Your Eye on the Sparrow	1975	3.00	6.00	12.00

CLAYTON-THOMAS, DAVID Also see BLOOD, SWEAT AND TEARS.
45s
ATCO

❑ 6347	Hey Hey Hey Hey/Walk That Walk	1965	3.75	7.50	15.00

COLUMBIA

❑ 45569	Sing a Song/We're All Meat from the Same Bone	1972	—	2.50	5.00
❑ 45603	North Beach Racetrack/ Magnificent Sanctuary Band	1972	—	2.50	5.00
❑ 45675	Yesterday's Music/Falling by Degrees	1972	—	2.50	5.00

DECCA

❑ 32556	Say Boss Man/Done Somebody Wrong	1969	2.50	5.00	10.00

EPIC

❑ 34-03792	I Can't Blame a Broken Heart/ Some Hearts Get All the Breaks	1983	—	2.00	4.00

RCA VICTOR

❑ 74-0966	Hernando's Hideaway/Harmony Junction	1973	—	2.00	4.00
❑ APBO-0078	Workin' on the Railroad/Prof. Longhair	1973	—	2.00	4.00
❑ APBO-0216	Yolanda/Workin' on the Railroad	1974	—	2.00	4.00
❑ APBO-0296	Take the Money and Run/Anytime... Babe	1974	—	2.00	4.00

ROULETTE

❑ 7048	No, No, No/Monopoly	1969	2.50	5.00	10.00

TOWER

❑ 206	Take Me Back/Out of the Sunshine	1966	3.00	6.00	12.00
❑ 263	Born with the Blues/Brainwashed	1966	3.00	6.00	12.00

Albums
ABC

❑ AA-1104	Clayton	1978	2.50	5.00	10.00

COLUMBIA

❑ KC 31000	David Clayton-Thomas	1972	3.75	7.50	15.00
❑ KC 31700	Tequila Sunrise	1972	3.75	7.50	15.00

DECCA

❑ DL 75146	David Clayton-Thomas!	1969	5.00	10.00	20.00

RCA VICTOR

❑ APD1-0173 [Q]	David Clayton-Thomas	1973	5.00	10.00	20.00
❑ APL1-0173	David Clayton-Thomas	1973	3.00	6.00	12.00

CLEAN LIVING
45s
VANGUARD

❑ 35162	In Heaven There Is No Beer/Backwoods Girl	1972	—	2.50	5.00
❑ 35170	Old Time Music/Jenny Regardless	1973	—	2.00	4.00
❑ 35171	Far North Again/Me and You	1973	—	2.00	4.00

Albums
VANGUARD

❑ VSD-79318	Clean Living	1972	2.50	5.00	10.00
❑ VSD-79334	Meadow Muffin	1973	2.50	5.00	10.00

CLEANLINESS AND GODLINESS SKIFFLE BAND, THE Also see THE MASKED MARAUDERS.
Albums
VANGUARD

❑ VSD-79285	Greatest Hits	1968	6.25	12.50	25.00

CLEAR LIGHT Also see CLIFF DeYOUNG.
45s
ELEKTRA

❑ 45622	She's Ready to Be Free/Black Roses	1967	3.00	6.00	12.00
❑ 45626	They Who Have Nothing/ Ballad of Freddie and Larry	1968	3.00	6.00	12.00

Albums
ELEKTRA

❑ EKL-4011 [M]	Clear Light	1967	6.25	12.50	25.00
❑ EKS-74011 [S]	Clear Light	1967	6.25	12.50	25.00

SUNDAZED

❑ LP 5125	Clear Light	2002	3.00	6.00	12.00

—Reissue on 180-gram vinyl

CLEARY, DON
Albums
PALOMINO

❑ 302 [M]	Don Cleary Sings Traditional Cowboy Songs	1966	12.50	25.00	50.00

Number	Title (A Side/B Side)	Yr	VG	VG+	NM

CLEAVER, ELDRIDGE

Albums

MORE
- ❑ 4000 [M] — Soul On Wax — 1968 — 6.25 — 12.50 — 25.00

CLEE-SHAYS, THE

45s

TRIUMPH
- ❑ 65 — The Man from U.N.C.L.E./Dynamite — 1966 — 5.00 — 10.00 — 20.00

CLEFS OF LAVENDER HILL, THE

45s

DATE
- ❑ 1510 — Stop! — Get a Ticket/First Tell Me Why — 1966 — 5.00 — 10.00 — 20.00
- ❑ 1530 — One More Time/So I'll Try — 1966 — 5.00 — 10.00 — 20.00
- ❑ 1533 — Play with Fire/It Won't Be Long — 1966 — 5.00 — 10.00 — 20.00
- ❑ 1567 — Gimme One Good Reason/Oh, Say My Love — 1967 — 5.00 — 10.00 — 20.00

THAMES
- ❑ 100 — Stop! — Get a Ticket/First Tell Me Why — 1966 — 10.00 — 20.00 — 40.00

CLEFTONES, THE

45s

CLASSIC ARTISTS
- ❑ 121 — She's So Fine/Trudy — 1990 — — — 2.00 — 4.00

GEE
- ❑ 1000 — You Baby You/I Was Dreaming — 1955 — 15.00 — 30.00 — 60.00
- ❑ 1011 — Little Girl of Mine/You're Driving Me Mad — 1956 — 10.00 — 20.00 — 40.00
- ❑ 1016 — Can't We Be Sweethearts/Niki-Hoeky — 1956 — 10.00 — 20.00 — 40.00
- ❑ 1025 — String Around My Heart/Happy Memories — 1956 — 10.00 — 20.00 — 40.00
- ❑ 1031 — Why You Do Me Like You Do/ I Like Your Style of Making Love — 1957 — 10.00 — 20.00 — 40.00
- ❑ 1038 — See You Next Year/Ten Pairs of Shoes — 1957 — 10.00 — 20.00 — 40.00
- ❑ 1041 — Hey Babe/What Did I Do That Was Wrong — 1957 — 10.00 — 20.00 — 40.00
- ❑ 1048 — Lover Boy/Beginners in Love — 1958 — 7.50 — 15.00 — 30.00
- ❑ 1064 — Heart and Soul/How Do You Feel — 1961 — 6.25 — 12.50 — 25.00
- ❑ 1067 — (I Love You) For Sentimental Reasons/ 'Deed I Do — 1961 — 5.00 — 10.00 — 20.00
- ❑ 1074 — Earth Angel/Blues in the Night — 1961 — 5.00 — 10.00 — 20.00
- ❑ 1077 — Again/Do You — 1961 — 5.00 — 10.00 — 20.00
- ❑ 1079 — Lover Come Back to Me/There She Goes — 1962 — 5.00 — 10.00 — 20.00
- ❑ 1080 — How Deep Is the Ocean/Some Kinda Blue — 1962 — 5.00 — 10.00 — 20.00

OLD TOWN
- ❑ 1011 — The Masquerade Is Over/My Dearest Darling — 1955 — 125.00 — 250.00 — 500.00

ROULETTE
- ❑ 4094 — Trudy/She's So Fine — 1958 — 6.25 — 12.50 — 25.00
- ❑ 4161 — Mish Mash Baby/Cuzin Casanova — 1959 — 6.25 — 12.50 — 25.00
- ❑ 4302 — She's Gone/Shadows on the Very Last Row — 1960 — 6.25 — 12.50 — 25.00

WARE
- ❑ 6001 — She's Forgotten You/Right from the Git Go — 1964 — 3.75 — 7.50 — 15.00

Albums

GEE
- ❑ GLP-705 [M] — Heart and Soul — 1961 — 50.00 — 100.00 — 200.00
- ❑ SGLP-705 [S] — Heart and Soul — 1961 — 125.00 — 250.00 — 500.00
- ❑ GLP-707 [M] — For Sentimental Reasons — 1961 — 62.50 — 125.00 — 250.00
- ❑ SGLP-707 [S] — For Sentimental Reasons — 1961 — 300.00 — 600.00 — 1200.

CLEMENT, JACK

45s

ELEKTRA
- ❑ 45397 — Just Because You Ask Me To/When I Dream — 1977 — — — 2.00 — 4.00
- ❑ 45474 — We Must Believe in Magic/When I Dream — 1978 — — — 2.00 — 4.00
- ❑ 45518 — All I Want to Do in Life/It'll Be Her — 1978 — — — 2.00 — 4.00
- ❑ 45547 — Gone Girl/There She Goes — 1978 — — — 2.00 — 4.00

HALLWAY
- ❑ 1796 — Time After Time After Time/ My Voice Is Changing — 1963 — 3.75 — 7.50 — 15.00

JMI
- ❑ 10 — The One on the Right Is the One on the Left/The Child That's in the Manger — 1972 — — — 3.00 — 6.00
- ❑ 14 — She Thinks I Still Care/Never Give a Heartache a Place to Go — 1973 — — — 3.00 — 6.00
- ❑ 20 — Steal Away/(B-side unknown) — 1973 — — — 3.00 — 6.00
- ❑ 43 — The One on the Right Is on the Left/Feet — 1974 — — — 3.00 — 6.00

RCA VICTOR
- ❑ 47-7602 — Whole Lotta Lookin'/Edge of Town — 1959 — 3.75 — 7.50 — 15.00

SUN
- ❑ 291 — Ten Years/Your Lover Boy — 1958 — 6.25 — 12.50 — 25.00
- ❑ 311 — The Black Haired Man/Wrong — 1958 — 6.25 — 12.50 — 25.00

Albums

ELEKTRA
- ❑ 6E-122 — All I Want to Do in Life — 1978 — 3.00 — 6.00 — 12.00

CLEMENTINO, CLAIRETTE

45s

CAPITOL
- ❑ 5003 — Everywhere/See Me — 1963 — 2.50 — 5.00 — 10.00
- ❑ 5003 [PS] — Everywhere/See Me — 1963 — 3.75 — 7.50 — 15.00
- ❑ 5081 — Adonis/Bless My Soul — 1963 — 2.50 — 5.00 — 10.00
- ❑ 5177 — Since I Fell in Love with You/It's Happening to Me — 1964 — 2.50 — 5.00 — 10.00
- ❑ 5276 — He Don't Want Your Love Anymore/Never Love a Wandering Boy — 1964 — 2.50 — 5.00 — 10.00

CLIBURN, VAN

45s

RCA VICTOR
- ❑ SP-45-102 [DJ] — Romantic Theme (from MacDowell Piano Concerto No. 2 in D Minor, Op. 23) (same on both sides) — 1960 — 2.50 — 5.00 — 10.00
- —Promo-only single release
- ❑ SP-45-102 [PS] — Romantic Theme (from MacDowell Piano Concerto No. 2 in D Minor, Op. 23) — 1960 — 5.00 — 10.00 — 20.00

Albums

RCA VICTOR RED SEAL
- ❑ LM-2252 [M] — Tchaikovsky: Piano Concerto No. 1 — 1958 — 5.00 — 10.00 — 20.00
- ❑ LSC-2252 [S] — Tchaikovsky: Piano Concerto No. 1 — 1958 — 6.25 — 12.50 — 25.00
- —"Shaded dog" pressing ("Living Stereo" on label)

Number	Title (A Side/B Side)	Yr	VG	VG+	NM

- ❑ LSC-2252 [S] — Tchaikovsky: Piano Concerto No. 1 — 1965 — 3.75 — 7.50 — 15.00
- —"White dog" pressing ("Stereo" on label)
- ❑ LSC-2252 [S] — Tchaikovsky: Piano Concerto No. 1 — 1969 — 3.00 — 6.00 — 12.00
- —"No dog" pressing ("RCA" sideways at left)
- ❑ LSC-2252 [S] — Tchaikovsky: Piano Concerto No. 1 — 1976 — 2.00 — 4.00 — 8.00
- —"Late dog" pressing (dog near top)
- ❑ LM-2355 [M] — Rachmaninoff: Piano Concerto No. 3 — 1959 — 5.00 — 10.00 — 20.00
- ❑ LSC-2355 [S] — Rachmaninoff: Piano Concerto No. 3 — 1959 — 6.25 — 12.50 — 25.00
- —"Shaded dog" pressing ("Living Stereo" on label)
- ❑ LSC-2355 [S] — Rachmaninoff: Piano Concerto No. 3 — 1965 — 3.75 — 7.50 — 15.00
- —"White dog" pressing ("Stereo" on label)
- ❑ LSC-2355 [S] — Rachmaninoff: Piano Concerto No. 3 — 1969 — 3.00 — 6.00 — 12.00
- —"No dog" pressing ("RCA" sideways at left)
- ❑ LM-2455 [M] — Schumann: Piano Concerto in A Minor — 1960 — 3.75 — 7.50 — 15.00
- ❑ LSC-2455 [S] — Schumann: Piano Concerto in A Minor — 1960 — 5.00 — 10.00 — 20.00
- —"Shaded dog" pressing ("Living Stereo" on label)
- ❑ LSC-2455 [S] — Schumann: Piano Concerto in A Minor — 1965 — 3.75 — 7.50 — 15.00
- —"White dog" pressing ("Stereo" on label)
- ❑ LSC-2455 [S] — Schumann: Piano Concerto in A Minor — 1969 — 3.00 — 6.00 — 12.00
- —"No dog" pressing ("RCA" sideways at left)
- ❑ LM-2507 [M] — Prokofiev: Piano Concerto No. 3; MacDowell: Piano Concerto No. 2 — 1961 — 3.75 — 7.50 — 15.00
- ❑ LSC-2507 [S] — Prokofiev: Piano Concerto No. 3; MacDowell: Piano Concerto No. 2 — 1961 — 7.50 — 15.00 — 30.00
- —"Shaded dog" pressing ("Living Stereo" on label)
- ❑ LSC-2507 [S] — Prokofiev: Piano Concerto No. 3; MacDowell: Piano Concerto No. 2 — 1965 — 7.50 — 15.00 — 30.00
- —"White dog" pressing ("Stereo" on label)
- ❑ LSC-2507 [S] — Prokofiev: Piano Concerto No. 3; MacDowell: Piano Concerto No. 2 — 1969 — 3.00 — 6.00 — 12.00
- —"No dog" pressing ("RCA" sideways at left)
- ❑ LM-2562 [M] — Beethoven: Piano Concerto No. 5 (Emperor Concerto) — 1961 — 3.75 — 7.50 — 15.00
- ❑ LSC-2562 [S] — Beethoven: Piano Concerto No. 5 (Emperor Concerto) — 1961 — 5.00 — 10.00 — 20.00
- —"Shaded dog" pressing ("Living Stereo" on label)
- ❑ LSC-2562 [S] — Beethoven: Piano Concerto No. 5 (Emperor Concerto) — 1964 — 5.00 — 10.00 — 20.00
- —"White dog" pressing ("Stereo" on label)
- ❑ LSC-2562 [S] — Beethoven: Piano Concerto No. 5 (Emperor Concerto) — 1969 — 3.00 — 6.00 — 12.00
- —"No dog" pressing ("RCA" sideways at left)
- ❑ LM-2576 [M] — My Favorite Chopin — 1962 — 3.75 — 7.50 — 15.00
- ❑ LSC-2576 [S] — My Favorite Chopin — 1962 — 5.00 — 10.00 — 20.00
- —"Shaded dog" pressing ("Living Stereo" on label)
- ❑ LSC-2576 [S] — My Favorite Chopin — 1965 — 3.75 — 7.50 — 15.00
- —"White dog" pressing ("Stereo" on label)
- ❑ LSC-2576 [S] — My Favorite Chopin — 1969 — 3.00 — 6.00 — 12.00
- —"No dog" pressing ("RCA" sideways at left)
- ❑ LSC-2576 [S] — My Favorite Chopin — 1976 — 2.00 — 4.00 — 8.00
- —"Late dog" pressing (dog near top)
- ❑ LM-2581 [M] — Brahms: Piano Concerto No. 2 — 1962 — 3.75 — 7.50 — 15.00
- ❑ LSC-2581 [S] — Brahms: Piano Concerto No. 2 — 1962 — 5.00 — 10.00 — 20.00
- —"Shaded dog" pressing ("Living Stereo" on label)
- ❑ LSC-2581 [S] — Brahms: Piano Concerto No. 2 — 1965 — 3.75 — 7.50 — 15.00
- —"White dog" pressing ("Stereo" on label)
- ❑ LSC-2581 [S] — Brahms: Piano Concerto No. 2 — 1969 — 3.00 — 6.00 — 12.00
- —"No dog" pressing ("RCA" sideways at left)
- ❑ LSC-2581 [S] — Brahms: Piano Concerto No. 2 — 1976 — 2.00 — 4.00 — 8.00
- —"Late dog" pressing (dog near top)
- ❑ LM-2601 [M] — Rachmaninoff: Piano Concerto No. 2 — 1962 — 3.75 — 7.50 — 15.00
- ❑ LSC-2601 [S] — Rachmaninoff: Piano Concerto No. 2 — 1962 — 3.75 — 7.50 — 15.00
- —"White dog" pressing ("Stereo" on label)
- ❑ LSC-2601 [S] — Rachmaninoff: Piano Concerto No. 2 — 1962 — 5.00 — 10.00 — 20.00
- —"Shaded dog" pressing ("Living Stereo" on label)
- ❑ LSC-2601 [S] — Rachmaninoff: Piano Concerto No. 2 — 1969 — 3.00 — 6.00 — 12.00
- —"No dog" pressing ("RCA" sideways at left)
- ❑ LM-2680 [M] — Beethoven: Piano Concerto No. 4 — 1963 — 3.00 — 6.00 — 12.00
- ❑ LSC-2680 [S] — Beethoven: Piano Concerto No. 4 — 1963 — 3.75 — 7.50 — 15.00
- —"Shaded dog" pressing ("Living Stereo" on label)
- ❑ LSC-2680 [S] — Beethoven: Piano Concerto No. 4 — 1965 — 3.00 — 6.00 — 12.00
- —"White dog" pressing ("Stereo" on label)
- ❑ LSC-2680 [S] — Beethoven: Piano Concerto No. 4 — 1969 — 2.50 — 5.00 — 10.00
- —"No dog" pressing ("RCA" sideways at left)
- ❑ LSC-3323 — The World's Favorite Piano Music — 196? — 3.00 — 6.00 — 12.00
- ❑ ARP1-4441 — Tchaikovsky: Piano Concerto No. 1 — 198? — 2.50 — 5.00 — 10.00
- —Half-speed mastered reissue
- ❑ ARP1-4688 — Rachmaninoff: Piano Concerto No. 3 — 198? — 2.50 — 5.00 — 10.00
- —Half-speed mastered reissue

CLICKETTES, THE

45s

CHECKER
- ❑ 1060 — I Just Can't Help It/(Instrumental) — 1963 — 5.00 — 10.00 — 20.00

DICE
- ❑ 83/84 — Jive Time Turkey/A Teenager's First Love — 1959 — 37.50 — 75.00 — 150.00
- ❑ 92/93 — To Be a Part of You/Because of My Best Friend — 1959 — 30.00 — 60.00 — 120.00
- ❑ 94/95 — Warm, Soft and Lovely/Why Oh Why — 1959 — 30.00 — 60.00 — 120.00
- ❑ 96/97 — Lover's Prayer/Grateful — 1959 — 17.50 — 35.00 — 70.00
- ❑ 96/97 — Lover's Prayer/Grateful — 1959 — 37.50 — 75.00 — 150.00
- —With distribution by Memo Record Corp.
- ❑ 100 — But Not for Me/I Love You I Swear — 1960 — 30.00 — 60.00 — 120.00

GUYDEN
- ❑ 2043 — Where Is He/The Lone Lover — 1960 — 7.50 — 15.00 — 30.00

LOST-NITE
- ❑ 138 — Lover's Prayer/Grateful — 196? — 2.00 — 4.00 — 8.00
- —Reissue
- ❑ 139 — Because of My Best Friend/Grateful — 196? — 2.00 — 4.00 — 8.00
- ❑ 140 — To Be a Part of You/Grateful — 196? — 2.00 — 4.00 — 8.00

TUFF
- ❑ 373 — I Just Can't Help It/(Instrumental) — 1964 — 5.00 — 10.00 — 20.00

CLICKS, THE

45s

JOSIE
- ❑ 780 — Come Back to Me/Peace and Commitment — 1955 — 75.00 — 150.00 — 300.00

Number	Title (A Side/B Side)	Yr	VG	VG+	NM

CLIFF, BENNY
45s
DRIFT

❏ 1441	Shake Um Um Rock/The Breaking Point	1959	1000.	2000.	3000.

CLIFF, JIMMY
12-Inch Singles
COLUMBIA

❏ CAS 1185 [DJ]	Hanging Fire (Edit) (12" Mix) (Dub)	1987	2.00	4.00	8.00
❏ CAS 1351 [DJ]	Soar Like an Eagle (same on both sides)	198?	2.50	5.00	10.00
❏ AS 1809 [DJ]	We All Are One (same on both sides)	1983	2.50	5.00	10.00
❏ CAS 2380 [DJ]	Seven Day Weekend (same on both sides)	1986	2.50	5.00	10.00
—With Elvis Costello					
❏ 44-03045	Special/Peace Officer (Dub Version)	1982	3.00	6.00	12.00
❏ 44-03507	Treat the Youths Right (6:49)/ Roots Radical (6:51)	1983	2.50	5.00	10.00
❏ 44-04126	Reggae Night (Remix 6:17) (Dub Mix 6:12)	1983	2.50	5.00	10.00
❏ 44-04966	We All Are One (2 versions)	1983	2.50	5.00	10.00
❏ 44-05029	Reggae Night (Remix) (Dub)	1984	2.50	5.00	10.00
❏ 44-05235	Hot Shot (Extended) (Instrumental) (7" Version)	1985	—	3.50	7.00
❏ 44-07565	Love Me, Love Me (Popstand Remix) (Jimmy Love Dub) (Perc-apella) (Chant-apella)	1988	2.00	4.00	8.00

45s
A&M

❏ 1146	Wonderful World, Beautiful People/Waterfall	1969	2.00	4.00	8.00
❏ 1146 [PS]	Wonderful World, Beautiful People/Waterfall	1969	3.00	6.00	12.00
❏ 1167	Come Into My Life/Viet Nam	1970	2.00	4.00	8.00
❏ 1167 [PS]	Come Into My Life/Viet Nam	1970	3.00	6.00	12.00
❏ 1201	You Can Get It If You Really Want/Be Aware	1970	2.00	4.00	8.00
❏ 1270	Goodbye Yesterday/Let's Seize the Time	1971	2.00	4.00	8.00
COLUMBIA					
❏ 38-03216	Special/Peace Officer	1982	—	2.00	4.00
❏ 38-04141	Reggae Night/Love Heights	1983	—	2.00	4.00
❏ 38-04335	We All Are One/Roots Woman	1984	—	2.00	4.00
❏ 38-05396	Hot Shot/Modern World	1985	—	2.00	4.00
❏ 38-05716	American Sweet/Reggae Movement	1985	—	2.00	4.00
❏ 38-06135	Seven Day Weekend/Brightest Star	1986	—	2.00	4.00
—A-side with Elvis Costello					
❏ 38-06235	Club Paradise/Third World People	1986	—	—	3.00
❏ 38-06235 [PS]	Club Paradise/Third World People	1986	—	2.00	4.00
❏ 38-07692	Love Me, Love Me/Sunshine in the Music	1988	—	2.00	4.00
MCA					
❏ 51043	I Am the Living/Love Again	1981	—	2.50	5.00
❏ 51094	Another Summer/It's the Beginning of the End	1981	—	2.50	5.00
❏ 51211	My Philosophy/Shelter of Your Love	1981	—	2.00	4.00
REPRISE					
❏ 1177	Black Queen/Born to Win	1973	—	3.00	6.00
❏ 1315	You Can't Be Wrong and Get Right/Music Maker	1974	—	3.00	6.00
❏ 1383	The Harder They Come/Viet Nam	1977	2.50	5.00	10.00
VEEP					
❏ 1265	Aim and Ambition/Give and Take	1967	3.75	7.50	15.00
❏ 1276	That's the Way Life Goes/Thank You	1968	3.75	7.50	15.00

Albums
A&M

❏ SP-3189	Wonderful World, Beautiful People	198?	2.00	4.00	8.00
—Reissue of 4251					
❏ SP-4251	Wonderful World, Beautiful People	1970	6.25	12.50	25.00
COLUMBIA					
❏ FC 38099	Special	1982	2.50	5.00	10.00
❏ PC 38099	Special	198?	2.00	4.00	8.00
—Budget-line reissue					
❏ FC 38986	The Power and the Glory	1983	2.50	5.00	10.00
❏ PC 38996	The Power and the Glory	1985	2.00	4.00	8.00
—Budget-line reissue					
❏ FC 40002	Cliff Hanger	1985	2.50	5.00	10.00
❏ FC 40845	Hanging Fire	1988	2.50	5.00	10.00
ISLAND					
❏ SW-9343	Struggling Man	1973	5.00	10.00	20.00
MANGO					
❏ ILPS 9235	Struggling Man	197?	3.00	6.00	12.00
—Reissue of Island SW-9343					
MCA					
❏ 813	I Am the Living	198?	2.00	4.00	8.00
—Reissue of 5153					
❏ 820	Give the People What They Want	198?	2.00	4.00	8.00
—Reissue of 5217					
❏ 5153	I Am the Living	1980	3.00	6.00	12.00
❏ 5217	Give the People What They Want	1981	3.00	6.00	12.00
REPRISE					
❏ MS 2147	Unlimited	1973	3.75	7.50	15.00
❏ MS 2188	Music Maker	1974	3.75	7.50	15.00
❏ MS 2218	Follow My Mind	1975	3.75	7.50	15.00
❏ MS 2256	In Concert: The Best of Jimmy Cliff	1976	3.75	7.50	15.00
VEEP					
❏ VPS-16536	Can't Get Enough of It	1969	10.00	20.00	40.00
WARNER BROS.					
❏ BSK 3240	Give Thankx	1978	3.00	6.00	12.00

CLIFF, BUZZ
45s
A&M

❏ 878	Just Can't Wait/On My Way	1967	2.50	5.00	10.00
CAPITOL					
❏ 5880	Bored to Tears/Swing in My Back Yard	1967	2.50	5.00	10.00
COLUMBIA					
❏ 41774	Blue Lagoon/Hello, Mr. Moonlight	1960	5.00	10.00	20.00
❏ 41774 [PS]	Blue Lagoon/Mr. Moonlight	1960	25.00	50.00	100.00
—Sleeve calls B-side "Mr. Moonlight"; may be promo only					
❏ 41876	Baby Sittin' Boogie/Driftwood	1960	5.00	10.00	20.00
❏ 41876	Baby Sitter Boogie/Driftwood	1960	6.25	12.50	25.00
❏ 41876 [PS]	Baby Sittin' Boogie/Driftwood	1960	12.50	25.00	50.00
❏ 41876	Baby Sittin' Boogie/Driftwood	1972	2.50	5.00	10.00
—Gray label					
❏ 41979	Three Little Fishes/Just Because	1961	5.00	10.00	20.00
❏ 41979 [PS]	Three Little Fishes/Just Because	1961	12.50	25.00	50.00
❏ 42019	I'll Never Forget/The Awakening	1961	12.50	25.00	50.00
❏ 42019 [PS]	I'll Never Forget/The Awakening	1961	20.00	40.00	80.00

Number	Title (A Side/B Side)	Yr	VG	VG+	NM
❏ 42177	Moving Day/Loneliness	1961	5.00	10.00	20.00
❏ 42177 [PS]	Moving Day/Loneliness	1961	12.50	25.00	50.00
❏ 42290	Forever/Magic Circle	1962	6.25	12.50	25.00
❏ 42290 [PS]	Forever/Magic Circle	1962	12.50	25.00	50.00
DOT					
❏ 17329	(Baby I Could Be) So Good At Loving You/ Children Are Crying Aloud	1970	—	3.00	6.00
❏ 17344	Procter and Gunther/I Am the River	1971	—	3.00	6.00
RCA VICTOR					
❏ 47-8935	Until Then/Let Her Go (It's All Right)	1966	3.00	6.00	12.00
ROULETTE					
❏ 4451	No One Loves Me Like You Do/More Dead Than Alive	1962	3.75	7.50	15.00

Albums
COLUMBIA

❏ CL 1616 [M]	Baby Sittin' with Buzz	1961	25.00	50.00	100.00
❏ CS 8416 [S]	Baby Sittin' with Buzz	1961	37.50	75.00	150.00
DOT					
❏ DLP-25965	See Your Way Clear	1969	7.50	15.00	30.00

CLIFFORD, DOUG Of CREEDENCE CLEARWATER REVIVAL.
45s
FANTASY

❏ 686	Latin Music/Take a Train	1972	—	2.50	5.00
❏ 686 [PS]	Latin Music/Take a Train	1972	—	3.00	6.00
Albums					
FANTASY					
❏ 9411	Cosmo	1972	3.75	7.50	15.00

CLIFFORD, MIKE
45s
AMERICAN INT'L.

❏ 138	Broken Hearted Man/When Cindy When	1970	—	2.50	5.00
❏ 158	Do Your Own Thing/ You Better Start Singing Soon	1971	—	2.50	5.00
❏ 171	You Say Love/It's a Dream Way	1970	—	2.00	4.00
CAMEO					
❏ 381	Before I Loved Her/Shirl Girl	1965	2.50	5.00	10.00
❏ 395	Out in the Country/Courtin'	1966	2.50	5.00	10.00
COLUMBIA					
❏ 41862	Stranger/Poor Little Girl	1960	3.00	6.00	12.00
❏ 41862 [PS]	Stranger/Poor Little Girl	1960	7.50	15.00	30.00
❏ 41964	Look in Any Window/Uh Huh	1961	3.00	6.00	12.00
❏ 42029	Pretty Little Girl in the Yellow Dress/At Last	1961	3.00	6.00	12.00
❏ 42226	When We Marry/Bombay	1961	3.00	6.00	12.00
❏ 42226 [PS]	When We Marry/Bombay	1961	6.25	12.50	25.00
❏ 42335	Joanna/Mary, Mary	1962	3.00	6.00	12.00
LIBERTY					
❏ 55207	Should I/Whisper Whisper	1959	3.75	7.50	15.00
—With Patience and Prudence					
❏ 55219	I Don't Know Why/I'm Afraid to Say I Love You	1959	3.00	6.00	12.00
SIDEWALK					
❏ 917	Send Her Flowers/ This Time, Time May Be Wrong	1967	2.00	4.00	8.00
❏ 939	Gas Hassle/Mary Jane	1968	2.00	4.00	8.00
UNITED ARTISTS					
❏ 489	Close to Cathy/She's Just Another Girl	1962	3.00	6.00	12.00
❏ 557	What to Do with Laurie/That's What They Said	1963	2.50	5.00	10.00
❏ 588	Danny's Dream/One Boy Too Late	1963	2.50	5.00	10.00
❏ 614	Gee, I Don't Remember/Cotton Dresses	1963	2.50	5.00	10.00
❏ 713	It Had Better Be Tonight/ All the Colors of the Rainbow	1964	2.50	5.00	10.00
❏ 763	See You in September/ One By One, The Roses Died	1964	2.50	5.00	10.00
❏ 794	Don't Make Her Cry/Barbara's Theme	1964	2.50	5.00	10.00
❏ 823	How to Murder Your Wife/Here's To My Lover	1965	2.50	5.00	10.00

Albums
UNITED ARTISTS

❏ UAL-3409 [M]	For the Love of Mike	1965	5.00	10.00	20.00
❏ UAS-6409 [S]	For the Love of Mike	1965	6.25	12.50	25.00

CLIMATES, THE
45s
HOLIDAY INN

❏ 2206	Don't Be Cruel/Tell Him Tonite	1967	3.00	6.00	12.00
SUN					
❏ 404	No You for Me/Breaking Up Again	1967	6.25	12.50	25.00

CLIMAX With Sonny Geraci, formerly of THE OUTSIDERS.
45s
CAROUSEL

❏ 30050	Hard Rock Group/(B-side unknown)	1971	—	2.50	5.00
❏ 30055	Precious and Few/Park Preserve	1971	—	2.50	5.00
PARAMOUNT					
❏ 0023	You've Gotta Try/Friendship	1970	—	3.00	6.00
ROCKY ROAD					
❏ 30055	Precious and Few/Park Preserve	1972	—	2.00	4.00
—Reissue of Carousel 30055					
❏ 30061	Life and Breath/If It Feels Good, Do It	1972	—	2.00	4.00
❏ 30064	Caroline This Time/Rainbow Rides Are Free	1972	—	2.00	4.00
❏ 30072	Rock and Roll Heaven/Face the Music	1973	—	2.50	5.00
❏ 30074	Walking in the Georgia Rain/(B-side unknown)	1973	—	2.00	4.00
❏ 30077	It's Gonna Get Better/(B-side unknown)	1974	—	2.00	4.00

Albums
ROCKY ROAD

❏ 3506	Climax	1972	3.75	7.50	15.00

CLIMAX BLUES BAND Includes records as "Climax Chicago Blues Band."
12-Inch Singles
WARNER BROS.

❏ PRO-A-807 [DJ]	Fat City/Summer Rain/Children of the Nightime	1979	2.50	5.00	10.00

45s
SIRE

❏ 351	Reap What I've Sowed/(B-side unknown)	1971	2.00	4.00	8.00
❏ 358	Hey Mama/That's All	1972	2.00	4.00	8.00
❏ 705	Shake Your Love/Mule on the Dole	1973	2.00	4.00	8.00
❏ 712	Goin' to New York/I Am Constant	1974	—	3.00	6.00

Number	Title (A Side/B Side)	Yr	VG	VG+	NM
❑ 713	Sense of Direction/Losin' the Humbles	1974	—	3.00	6.00
❑ 715	Reaching Out/Milwaukee Truckin' Blues	1974	—	3.00	6.00
❑ 721	Using the Power/Running Out of Time	1975	—	3.00	6.00
❑ 736	Couldn't Get It Right/Sav'ry Gravy	1977	—	2.50	5.00
❑ 747	Together and Free/Berlin Blues	1977	—	2.00	4.00
❑ 1026	Makin' Love/Gospel Singer	1978	—	2.00	4.00
❑ 1031	Mistress Moonshine/Teardrops	1978	—	2.00	4.00
❑ 49012	Children of the Nightime/Long Distance Love	1979	—	2.00	4.00
❑ 49098	Summer Rain/Money in Your Pocket	1979	—	2.00	4.00

WARNER BROS.

Number	Title (A Side/B Side)	Yr	VG	VG+	NM
❑ 49605	Gotta Have More Love/One for Me and You	1980	—	2.00	4.00
❑ 49669	I Love You/Horizontalized	1981	—	2.50	5.00
❑ 49850	Darlin'/This Time You're the Singer	1981	—	2.00	4.00
❑ 50018	Breakdown/Shake It Lucy	1982	—	2.00	4.00

Albums

SIRE

Number	Title (A Side/B Side)	Yr	VG	VG+	NM
❑ SRK 3334	Real to Reel	1979	2.50	5.00	10.00
❑ SES-4901	#3	1971	3.75	7.50	15.00
❑ SES-5903	Tightly Knit	1972	3.75	7.50	15.00
❑ SR 6003	The Climax Chicago Blues Band	1978	2.50	5.00	10.00
❑ SR 6004	Lot of Bottle	1977	2.50	5.00	10.00
❑ SR 6008	Tightly Knit	1977	2.50	5.00	10.00
❑ 2XS 6013 [(2)]	FM/Live	1977	3.00	6.00	12.00
❑ SR 6016	Stamp Album	1977	2.50	5.00	10.00
❑ SR 6033	The Climax Chicago Blues Band Plays On	1978	2.50	5.00	10.00
❑ SRK 6056	Shine On	1978	2.50	5.00	10.00
❑ SES-7402	Rich Man	1972	3.75	7.50	15.00
❑ SAS-2-7411 [(2)]	FM/Live	1973	3.75	7.50	15.00
❑ SAS-7501	Sense of Direction	1974	3.00	6.00	12.00
❑ SASD-7507	Stamp Album	1975	3.00	6.00	12.00
❑ SASD-7523	Gold Plated	1976	3.00	6.00	12.00
❑ SES-97013	The Climax Chicago Blues Band	1969	3.75	7.50	15.00
❑ SES-97023	The Climax Chicago Blues Band Plays On	1970	3.75	7.50	15.00

VIRGIN/EPIC

Number	Title (A Side/B Side)	Yr	VG	VG+	NM
❑ FE 38631	Sample and Hold	1983	2.50	5.00	10.00

WARNER BROS.

Number	Title (A Side/B Side)	Yr	VG	VG+	NM
❑ BSK 3493	Flying the Flag	1981	3.00	6.00	12.00
❑ BSK 3623	Lucky for Some	1982	2.50	5.00	10.00

CLIMBERS, THE
45s

J&S

Number	Title (A Side/B Side)	Yr	VG	VG+	NM
❑ 1652/3	My Darlin' Dear/Angels in Heaven Know I Love You	1957	25.00	50.00	100.00
❑ 1658	I Love You/Train, Car, Boat or Plane	1957	200.00	400.00	800.00

CLINE, PATSY
45s

CORAL

Number	Title (A Side/B Side)	Yr	VG	VG+	NM
❑ 61464	A Church, a Courtroom, Then Goodbye/Honky Tonk Merry-Go-Round	1955	7.50	15.00	30.00
❑ 61523	Turn the Cards Slowly/Hidin' Out	1955	7.50	15.00	30.00
❑ 61583	I Love You Honey/Come Right In	1956	6.25	12.50	25.00

DECCA

Number	Title (A Side/B Side)	Yr	VG	VG+	NM
❑ 25673	South of the Border/San Antonio Rose	1965	3.00	6.00	12.00
❑ 25686	I Love You So Much It Hurts/Seven Lonely Days	1966	3.00	6.00	12.00
❑ 25694	Shoes/Half As Much	1966	3.00	6.00	12.00
❑ 25699	Lonely Street/You Were Only Fooling (While I Was Falling in Love)	1966	3.00	6.00	12.00
❑ 25707	That's My Desire/Foolin' 'Round	1967	3.00	6.00	12.00
❑ 25712	You Took Him Off My Hands/Does Your Heart Beat for Me	196?	3.00	6.00	12.00
❑ 25718	Have You Ever Been Lonely/Hidin' Out	196?	3.00	6.00	12.00
❑ 25724	True Love/Love, Love, Love Me Honey Do	196?	3.00	6.00	12.00
❑ 25732	Always/Pick Me Up on Your Way Down	196?	3.00	6.00	12.00
❑ 25738	Too Many Secrets/You Made Me Love You	196?	3.00	6.00	12.00
❑ 25744	Anytime/In Care of the Blues	196?	3.00	6.00	12.00
❑ 25747	Crazy Arms/The Wayward Wind	196?	3.00	6.00	12.00
❑ 29963	Stop, Look and Listen/I've Loved and Lost Again	1956	5.00	10.00	20.00
❑ 30221	Walkin' After Midnight/A Poor Man's Roses (Or a Rich Man's Gold)	1957	5.00	10.00	20.00
❑ 30221 [PS]	Walkin' After Midnight/A Poor Man's Roses (Or a Rich Man's Gold)	1957	20.00	40.00	80.00
❑ 30339	Try Again/Today, Tomorrow and Forever	1957	3.75	7.50	15.00
❑ 30406	Three Cigarettes in an Ashtray/A Stranger in My Arms	1957	3.75	7.50	15.00
❑ 30504	I Don't Wanta/Then You'll Know	1957	3.75	7.50	15.00
❑ 30542	Stop the World/Walking Dream	1958	3.75	7.50	15.00
❑ 30659	Come On In/Let the Teardrops Fall	1958	3.75	7.50	15.00
❑ 30706	Never No More/I Can See an Angel	1958	3.75	7.50	15.00
❑ 30746	Just Out of Reach (Of My Two Open Arms)/If I Could See The World	1958	3.75	7.50	15.00
❑ 30794	Dear God/He Will Do for You	1958	3.75	7.50	15.00
❑ 30846	Yes, I Understand/Cry Not for Me	1959	3.75	7.50	15.00
❑ 30929	Got a Lot of Rhythm in My Soul/I'm Blue Again	1959	5.00	10.00	20.00
❑ 31061	Lovesick Blues/How Can I Face Tomorrow	1960	3.00	6.00	12.00
❑ 31128	There He Goes/Crazy Dream	1960	3.00	6.00	12.00
❑ 31205	I Fall to Pieces/Lovin' in Vain	1961	3.00	6.00	12.00
❑ 31317	Crazy/Who Can I Count On	1961	3.00	6.00	12.00
❑ 31354	She's Got You/Strange	1962	3.00	6.00	12.00
❑ 31377	When I Get Thru with You (You'll Love Me Too)/Imagine That	1962	3.00	6.00	12.00
❑ 31377 [PS]	When I Get Thru with You (You'll Love Me Too)/Imagine That	1962	6.25	12.50	25.00
❑ 31406	So Wrong/You're Stronger Than Me	1962	3.00	6.00	12.00
❑ 31429	Heartaches/Why Can't He Be You	1962	3.00	6.00	12.00
❑ 31455	Leavin' On Your Mind/Tra La Le La Triangle	1963	2.50	5.00	10.00
❑ 31455 [PS]	Leavin' On Your Mind/Tra La Le La Triangle	1963	6.25	12.50	25.00
❑ 31483	Sweet Dreams (Of You)/Back in Baby's Arms	1963	2.50	5.00	10.00
❑ 31522	Faded Love/Blue Moon of Kentucky	1963	2.50	5.00	10.00
❑ 31552	When You Need a Laugh/I'll Sail My Ship Alone	1963	2.50	5.00	10.00
❑ 31588	Your Kinda Love/Someday You'll Want Me to Love You	1964	2.50	5.00	10.00
❑ 31616	Love Letters in the Sand/That's How a Heartache Begins	1964	2.50	5.00	10.00
❑ 31671	He Called Me Baby/Bill Bailey Won't You Please Come Home	1964	2.50	5.00	10.00
❑ 31754	Your Cheatin' Heart/I Can't Help It (If I'm Still in Love with You)	1965	2.50	5.00	10.00

Number	Title (A Side/B Side)	Yr	VG	VG+	NM
❑ 7-34130 [S]	Foolin' 'Round/The Wayward Wind	1962	5.00	10.00	20.00
❑ 7-34131 [S]	South of the Border (Down Mexico Way)/I Love You So Much It Hurts	1962	5.00	10.00	20.00
❑ 7-34132 [S]	Crazy/Seven Lonely Days	1962	6.25	12.50	25.00
❑ 7-34133 [S]	San Antonio Rose/True Love	1962	5.00	10.00	20.00

—The above four are 33 1/3, small hole jukebox singles

EVEREST

Number	Title (A Side/B Side)	Yr	VG	VG+	NM
❑ 2011	Then You'll Know/Hungry for Love	1963	3.00	6.00	12.00
❑ 2020	Walking After Midnight/That Wonderful Someone	1963	3.00	6.00	12.00
❑ 2031	I Can See an Angel/Just Out of Reach	1963	3.00	6.00	12.00
❑ 2039	I've Loved and Lost Again/I Love You Honey	1964	2.50	5.00	10.00
❑ 2045	In Care of the Blues/If I Could See the World (Through the Eyes of a Child)	1964	2.50	5.00	10.00
❑ 2052	Got a Lot of Rhythm (In My Soul)/Love Me, Love Me, Honey Do	1964	2.50	5.00	10.00
❑ 2060	Crazy Dream/There He Goes	1965	2.50	5.00	10.00
❑ 20005	I Don't Wanta/I Can't Forget	1962	3.75	7.50	15.00

4 STAR

Number	Title (A Side/B Side)	Yr	VG	VG+	NM
❑ AP-39 [DJ]	Dear God/He Will Do for You	195?	7.50	15.00	30.00

—4 Star promo-only item

Number	Title (A Side/B Side)	Yr	VG	VG+	NM
❑ 1033	Life's Railway to Heaven/If I Could See the World	1978	—	2.50	5.00

KAPP

Number	Title (A Side/B Side)	Yr	VG	VG+	NM
❑ 659	Just a Closer Walk with Thee	1965	3.75	7.50	15.00

—One-sided release, possibly promo only

MCA

Number	Title (A Side/B Side)	Yr	VG	VG+	NM
❑ 41303	Always/I Sail My Ship Alone	1980	—	2.00	4.00
❑ 51038	I Fall to Pieces/True Love	1980	—	2.00	4.00
❑ 52052	So Wrong/I Fall to Pieces	1982	—	—	3.00

—A-side: With Jim Reeves (electronically created duet)

Number	Title (A Side/B Side)	Yr	VG	VG+	NM
❑ 52684	Sweet Dreams/Blue Moon of Kentucky	1985	—	—	3.00
❑ 60061	Walkin' After Midnight/South of the Border (Down Mexico Way)	1973	—	2.50	5.00

—Reissue; black label with rainbow

Number	Title (A Side/B Side)	Yr	VG	VG+	NM
❑ 60062	I Fall to Pieces/He Called Me Baby	1973	—	2.50	5.00

—Reissue; black label with rainbow

Number	Title (A Side/B Side)	Yr	VG	VG+	NM
❑ 60063	Crazy/Your Cheatin' Heart	1973	—	2.50	5.00

—Reissue; black label with rainbow

Number	Title (A Side/B Side)	Yr	VG	VG+	NM
❑ 60063	Crazy/Your Cheatin' Heart	1980	—	—	3.00

—Reissue; blue label with rainbow

Number	Title (A Side/B Side)	Yr	VG	VG+	NM
❑ 60102	Pick Me Up on Your Way Down/Crazy Arms	1973	—	2.50	5.00

—Reissue; black label with rainbow

RCA

Number	Title (A Side/B Side)	Yr	VG	VG+	NM
❑ PB-12346	Have You Ever Been Lonely (Have You Ever Been Blue)/Welcome to My World	1981	—	—	3.00

—With Jim Reeves (electronically created duet)

STARDAY

Number	Title (A Side/B Side)	Yr	VG	VG+	NM
❑ 7030	Walking After Midnight/Lovesick Blues	1965	2.50	5.00	10.00
❑ 8024	Walking After Midnight/Lovesick Blues	1971	—	3.00	6.00

7-Inch Extended Plays

CORAL

Number	Title (A Side/B Side)	Yr	VG	VG+	NM
❑ EC 81159	*Honky Tonk Merry-Go-Round/A Church, a Courtroom, and Then Goodbye/Turn the Cards Slowly/Hidin' Out	1958	6.25	12.50	25.00
❑ EC 81159 [PS]	Songs by Patsy Cline	1958	7.50	15.00	30.00

DECCA

Number	Title (A Side/B Side)	Yr	VG	VG+	NM
❑ ED 2542	That Wonderful Someone/Three Cigarettes (In an Ashtray)//Hungry for Love/Fingerprints	1958	5.00	10.00	20.00
❑ ED 2542 [PS]	Patsy Cline	1958	5.00	10.00	20.00
❑ ED 2703	*I Fall to Pieces/Lovin' in Vain//Lovesick Blues/There He Goes	1961	3.75	7.50	15.00
❑ ED 2703 [PS]	Patsy Cline	1961	3.75	7.50	15.00
❑ ED 2707	Crazy/Foolin' Around//Who Can I Count On/South of the Border	1961	3.75	7.50	15.00
❑ ED 2707 [PS]	Patsy Cline	1961	3.75	7.50	15.00
❑ ED 2719	*She's Got You/Strange/The Wayward Wind/I Love You So Much It Hurts	1962	3.75	7.50	15.00
❑ ED 2719 [PS]	She's Got You	1962	3.75	7.50	15.00
❑ ED 2729	So Wrong/You're Stronger Than Me//Heartaches/Your Cheatin' Heart	1962	3.75	7.50	15.00
❑ ED 2729 [PS]	Patsy Cline	1962	3.75	7.50	15.00
❑ ED 2757	*Leavin' on Your Mind/Tra La La La La La Triangle/Half As Much/Lonely Street	1963	3.75	7.50	15.00
❑ ED 2757 [PS]	Leavin' on Your Mind	1963	3.75	7.50	15.00
❑ ED 2759	Just a Closer Walk with Thee/Life's Railroad to Heaven//Dear God/He Will Do for You	1963	3.75	7.50	15.00
❑ ED 2759 [PS]	Dear God	1963	3.75	7.50	15.00
❑ ED 2768	I'm Blue Again/How Can I Face Tomorrow//I'm Moving Along/How Love Love Me Honey Do	1964	3.75	7.50	15.00
❑ ED 2768 [PS]	How Can I Face Tomorrow	1964	3.75	7.50	15.00
❑ ED 2770	Someday You'll Want Me to Want You/Faded Love//When You Need a Laugh/I'll Sail My Ship Alone	1964	3.75	7.50	15.00
❑ ED 2770 [PS]	Someday You'll Want Me to Want You	1964	3.75	7.50	15.00
❑ ED 2794	(contents unknown)	1965	3.75	7.50	15.00
❑ ED 2794 [PS]	Portrait of Patsy Cline	1965	3.75	7.50	15.00
❑ ED 2802	(contents unknown)	1965	3.75	7.50	15.00
❑ ED 2802 [PS]	Love Letters in the Sand	1965	3.75	7.50	15.00
❑ 7-34180	Strange/South of the Border/Sweet Dreams (Of You)/I Fall to Pieces/I Love You So Much It Hurts/A Poor Man's Roses (Or a Rich Man's Gold)	196?	5.00	10.00	20.00

—Jukebox issue; small hole, plays at 33 1/3 rpm

Number	Title (A Side/B Side)	Yr	VG	VG+	NM
❑ 7-34180	The Patsy Cline Story	196?	5.00	10.00	20.00

—Number on cover is "DXSB 7176"

Number	Title (A Side/B Side)	Yr	VG	VG+	NM
❑ 7-34285	That's How a Heartache Begins/Lovesick Blues//Bill Bailey, Won't You Please Come Home//There He Goes/I'm Blue Again/Shoes	196?	5.00	10.00	20.00

—Jukebox issue; small hole, plays at 33 1/3 rpm

Number	Title (A Side/B Side)	Yr	VG	VG+	NM
❑ 7-34285 [PS]	That's How a Heartache Begins	196?	5.00	10.00	20.00
❑ DL 34822	She's Got You/Crazy/South of the Border//I Fall to Pieces/Sweet Dreams/Walking After Midnight	197?	3.75	7.50	15.00

—Jukebox issue; small hole, plays at 33 1/3 rpm

Number	Title (A Side/B Side)	Yr	VG	VG+	NM
❑ DL 34822 [PS]	The Patsy Cline Story	197?	3.75	7.50	15.00

—Part of "Little LP" series (LLP # 131)

Number	Title (A Side/B Side)	Yr	VG	VG+	NM
4 STAR					
❑ EPF-16 [DJ]	Try Again/Turn the Cards Slowly//Come On In/ Stop Look and Listen	195?	12.50	25.00	50.00

—*Sometimes said to be on the "Patsy Cline" label, but it is a 4 Star promo-only item; not issued with cover?*

Number	Title	Yr	VG	VG+	NM
❑ EP-21 [DJ]	Three Cigarettes (In an Ashtray)/Hungry for Love//Fingerprints/That Wonderful Someone	195?	12.50	25.00	50.00

—*Sometimes said to be on the "Patsy Cline" label, but it is a 4 Star promo-only item; not issued with cover?*

Number	Title	Yr	VG	VG+	NM
❑ EP-31 [DJ]	Just Out of Reach/Come On In//Let the Tear Drops Fall/Don't Ever Leave Me Again	195?	12.50	25.00	50.00

—*Sometimes said to be on the "Patsy Cline" label, but it is a 4 Star promo-only item; not issued with cover?*

Number	Title	Yr	VG	VG+	NM
❑ EP-38 [DJ]	Just Out of Reach/I Can See an Angel//If I Could See the World (Through the Eyes of a Child)/ Never No More	195?	12.50	25.00	50.00

—*4 Star promo-only item; not issued with cover?*

Number	Title	Yr	VG	VG+	NM
❑ EP-41 [DJ]	Cry Not for Me/Yes, I Understand//Am I That Easy to Forget/Such Is Life	1959	10.00	20.00	40.00

—*B-side by Carl Belew; sometimes said to be on the "Patsy Cline" label, but it is a 4 Star promo-only item; not issued with cover?*

Number	Title	Yr	VG	VG+	NM
❑ EP-43 [DJ]	How Can I Face Tomorrow/A Church, a Courtroom, Then Goodbye//That's What I Get for Loving You/My Baby's Not Here (In Town Tonight)	1959	10.00	20.00	40.00

—*B-side by Carl Belew; sometimes said to be on the "Patsy Cline" label, but it is a 4 Star promo-only item; not issued with cover?*

Albums

Number	Title	Yr	VG	VG+	NM
ACCORD					
❑ SN-7153	Let the Teardrops Fall	1981	2.50	5.00	10.00
ALLEGIANCE					
❑ AV-5021	Stop, Look and Listen	198?	2.50	5.00	10.00
DECCA					
❑ DXB 176 [(2)M]	The Patsy Cline Story	1963	10.00	20.00	40.00
❑ DL 4202 [M]	Patsy Cline Showcase	1961	10.00	20.00	40.00
❑ DL 4282 [M]	Sentimentally Yours	1962	7.50	15.00	30.00
❑ DL 4508 [M]	A Portrait of Patsy Cline	1964	7.50	15.00	30.00
❑ DL 4586 [M]	That's How a Heartache Begins	1964	7.50	15.00	30.00
❑ DL 4854 [M]	Patsy Cline's Greatest Hits	1967	5.00	10.00	20.00
❑ DXSB 7176 [(2)S]	The Patsy Cline Story	1963	12.50	25.00	50.00
❑ DL 8611 [M]	Patsy Cline	1957	25.00	50.00	100.00
—*Black label with silver print*					
❑ DL 8611 [M]	Patsy Cline	1960	12.50	25.00	50.00
—*Black label with color bars*					
❑ DL 74202 [S]	Patsy Cline Showcase	1961	12.50	25.00	50.00
❑ DL 74282 [S]	Sentimentally Yours	1962	10.00	20.00	40.00
❑ DL 74508 [S]	A Portrait of Patsy Cline	1964	10.00	20.00	40.00
❑ DL 74586 [S]	That's How a Heartache Begins	1964	10.00	20.00	40.00
❑ DL 74854 [S]	Patsy Cline's Greatest Hits	1967	6.25	12.50	25.00
EVEREST					
❑ 1200 [R]	Golden Hits	1962	3.00	6.00	12.00
❑ 1204 [R]	Encores	1962	3.00	6.00	12.00
❑ 1217 [R]	In Memoriam	1963	3.00	6.00	12.00
❑ 1229 [R]	Reflections	1964	3.00	6.00	12.00
❑ 5200 [M]	Golden Hits	1962	5.00	10.00	20.00
❑ 5204 [M]	Encores	1962	5.00	10.00	20.00
❑ 5217 [M]	In Memoriam	1963	5.00	10.00	20.00
❑ 5223 [M]	Legend	1963	5.00	10.00	20.00
❑ 5229 [M]	Reflections	1964	5.00	10.00	20.00
❑ ST-90070 [R]	Golden Hits	1962	3.75	7.50	15.00
—*Capitol Record Club edition*					
HILLTOP					
❑ 6001 [M]	Today, Tomorrow, Forever	1965	3.00	6.00	12.00
❑ S-6001 [R]	Today, Tomorrow, Forever	1965	2.50	5.00	10.00
❑ 6016 [M]	I Can't Forget You	1966	3.00	6.00	12.00
❑ S-6016 [R]	I Can't Forget You	1966	2.50	5.00	10.00
❑ S-6039	Stop the World	1968	2.50	5.00	10.00
❑ JS-6072	In Care of the Blues	1969	2.50	5.00	10.00
❑ 6148	Country Music Hall of Fame	197?	2.50	5.00	10.00
MCA					
❑ 12	Patsy Cline's Greatest Hits	1973	3.00	6.00	12.00
—*Reissue of Decca 74854; black label with rainbow*					
❑ 12	Patsy Cline's Greatest Hits	1977	2.50	5.00	10.00
—*Tan label*					
❑ 12	Patsy Cline's Greatest Hits	1980	2.00	4.00	8.00
—*Blue label with rainbow*					
❑ 87	Patsy Cline Showcase	1973	3.00	6.00	12.00
—*Reissue of Decca 74202; black label with rainbow*					
❑ 90	Sentimentally Yours	1973	3.00	6.00	12.00
—*Reissue of Decca 74282; black label with rainbow*					
❑ 224	A Portrait of Patsy Cline	1973	3.00	6.00	12.00
—*Reissue of Decca 74508; black label with rainbow*					
❑ 736	The Great Patsy Cline	198?	2.50	5.00	10.00
—*Reissue of Vocalion 73872*					
❑ 738	Here's Patsy Cline	198?	2.50	5.00	10.00
—*Reissue of Vocalion 73753*					
❑ 1440	Stop, Look and Listen	198?	2.00	4.00	8.00
❑ 1463	Today, Tomorrow and Forever	198?	2.00	4.00	8.00
❑ 3263	Always	1980	3.75	7.50	15.00
❑ 4038 [(2)]	The Patsy Cline Story	1974	3.75	7.50	15.00
—*Reissue of Decca 7176;; black labels with rainbow*					
❑ 6149	Sweet Dreams — The Life and Times of Patsy Cline	1985	2.50	5.00	10.00
❑ 27069	Always	198?	2.00	4.00	8.00
❑ 42142	Live at the Opry	1988	2.50	5.00	10.00
❑ 42284	Live Volume 2	1989	3.00	6.00	12.00
METRO					
❑ M-540 [M]	Gotta Lot of Rhythm in My Soul	1965	3.00	6.00	12.00
❑ MS-540 [R]	Gotta Lot of Rhythm in My Soul	1965	2.50	5.00	10.00
RHINO					
❑ R1-70048	Her First Recordings, Vol. 1: Walkin' Dreams	1989	3.00	6.00	12.00
❑ R1-70049	Her First Recordings, Vol. 2: Hungry for Love	1989	3.00	6.00	12.00
❑ R1-70050	Her First Recordings, Vol. 3: The Rockin' Side	1989	3.00	6.00	12.00
SEARS					
❑ SP-102 [M]	Walkin' After Midnight	196?	7.50	15.00	30.00
❑ SPS-102 [R]	Walkin' After Midnight	196?	5.00	10.00	20.00
❑ SPS-127	In Care of the Blues	1968	6.25	12.50	25.00

Number	Title (A Side/B Side)	Yr	VG	VG+	NM
VOCALION					
❑ VL 3753 [M]	Here's Patsy Cline	1965	3.00	6.00	12.00
❑ VL 73753 [R]	Here's Patsy Cline	1965	2.50	5.00	10.00
❑ VL 73872	Country Great!	1969	2.50	5.00	10.00

CLINTON, GEORGE   Also see FUNKADELIC; PARLIAMENT; THE PARLIAMENTS.

12-Inch Singles

Number	Title	Yr	VG	VG+	NM
CAPITOL					
❑ V-8538	Loopzilla (5:58) (8:48)	1982	3.75	7.50	15.00
❑ V-8544	Atomic Dog (Album Version) (Single Version)	1982	6.25	12.50	25.00
❑ V-8572	Nubian Nut (LP Version 5:59)/Free Alterations	1983	2.50	5.00	10.00
❑ V-8580	Quickie/Last Dance	1984	3.00	6.00	12.00
❑ V-8581	Last Dance/Get Dressed	1984	2.50	5.00	10.00
❑ V-8603	Atomic Dog (Atomic Mix Long Version) (Instrumental)	1984	3.75	7.50	15.00
❑ V-8642	Double Oh-Oh (For Your Ears Only Mashed Mix) (LP Version) (Mixing Parts)	1985	2.50	5.00	10.00
❑ V-8653	Bullet Proof (Extended)/Silly Millameter	1985	3.00	6.00	12.00
❑ SPRO-9038/9 [DJ]	Nubian Nut (LP Version) (Single Version)	1983	2.50	5.00	10.00
❑ SPRO-9065/70 [DJ]	Last Dance (LP Version) (Single Version)	1984	3.00	6.00	12.00
❑ SPRO-9136 [DJ]	Quickie (same on both sides?)	1984	3.75	7.50	15.00
❑ SPRO-9628 [DJ]	Do Fries Go with That Shake (Thick Mix) (same on both sides)	1986	3.75	7.50	15.00
❑ SPRO-9728/9 [DJ]	Hey Good Lookin' (Rush This Mix 7:52) (Mirror Mix 4:33) (Marvelous Mix 5:35)	1986	2.50	5.00	10.00
❑ SPRO-9825/6 [DJ]	Loopzilla (Single Mix 4:13) (Broadcast Version 6:36)	1982	7.50	15.00	30.00
❑ V-15219	Do Fries Go with That Shake (10:15)/Scratch Medley: Do Fries Go with That Shake-Pleasures of Exhaustion (12:36)	1986	3.00	6.00	12.00
❑ V-15241	Hey Good Lookin' (Rush This Mix) (Mirror Mix) (Marvelous Mix)	1986	3.00	6.00	12.00
❑ V-15263	R&B Skeletons (In the Closet)/Nubian Nut	1986	2.50	5.00	10.00
❑ V-15562	Atomic Dog (Special Atomic Mix) (LP Version) (Instrumental)	1990	2.50	5.00	10.00
❑ 53576	Atomic Dog (2 versions)/Knee Deep/Hey Good Lookin'/Do Fries Go with That Shake	2000	2.00	4.00	8.00
—*Red vinyl*					
❑ SPRO-79901 [DJ]	Atomic Dog (Special Atomic Mix) (same on both sides)	1990	3.00	6.00	12.00
550 MUSIC					
❑ BAS 7697 [DJ]	If Anybody Gets Funked Up (It's Gonna Be You) (4 versions)	1996	3.75	7.50	15.00
❑ BAS 7906 [DJ]	If Anybody Gets Funked Up (It's Gonna Be You) (6 versions)	1996	2.50	5.00	10.00
❑ BAS 8309 [DJ]	Summer Swim (LP Version) (Edit Version) (Instrumental) (Acappella)	1996	3.75	7.50	15.00
❑ 46-78391	Summer Swim (6 versions)	1996	2.50	5.00	10.00
FOX					
❑ 10013	Erotic City (Extended Sweat Mix) (Groovestramental)/Stomp (LP Version) (Sir Nose Goes On)	1994	3.00	6.00	12.00
INTERSOUND					
❑ 9284	Ain't Nuthin' But a Jam Y'All (4:02) (Instrumental)	1997	3.00	6.00	12.00
—*With the Dazz Band*					
PAISLEY PARK					
❑ PRO-A-3717 [DJ]	Tweakin' (Edit) (LP Version)	1989	2.00	4.00	8.00
❑ PRO-A-5995 [DJ]	Martial Law (Hey Man... Smell My Finger) (Single Version 4:14) (LP Version 7:13)	1993	2.50	5.00	10.00
❑ PRO-A-5998 [(2)DJ]	Martial Law (Hey Man... Smell My Finger) (Scratch & Sniff Mix 7:37) (Where's Your Finger Been Mix 7:28) (Smell My Finger Mix 9:05) (Stank Finger Mix) (2 Phunky Finger Mix) (Middle Finger Instrumental Mix) (Somethin' Stinks and I Want Some Bonus Beats Mix) (Single Version Edit)	1993	3.75	7.50	15.00
—*One record is red vinyl, the other is green*					
❑ 21157	Why Should I Dog U Out? (4 versions)	1989	2.50	5.00	10.00
❑ 21337	Tweakin' (A-Mix) (Dub Mix) (C-Mixapella) (Radio Remix) (Hysterical Remix)	1989	2.50	5.00	10.00
❑ 41057	Paint the White House Black (3 versions)/Picture This/Booty	1993	2.50	5.00	10.00

45s

Number	Title	Yr	VG	VG+	NM
ABC					
❑ 12040	Hold On to Your Lady/ Nothing in This Whole World	1974	—	3.50	7.00
CAPITOL					
❑ B-5160	Loopzilla/Pot Sharing Tots	1982	—	2.00	4.00
❑ B-5201	Atomic Dog/(Instrumental)	1983	—	2.00	4.00
❑ B-5201 [PS]	Atomic Dog/(Instrumental)	1983	—	3.00	6.00
❑ B-5222	Get Dressed/Free Alterations	1983	—	2.00	4.00
❑ B-5222 [PS]	Get Dressed/Free Alterations	1983	—	2.00	4.00
❑ B-5296	Nubian Nut/Free Alterations	1983	—	2.00	4.00
❑ B-5296 [PS]	Nubian Nut/Free Alterations	1983	—	2.00	4.00
❑ B-5324	Quickie/Last Dance	1984	—	2.00	4.00
❑ B-5324 [PS]	Quickie/Last Dance	1984	—	2.00	4.00
❑ B-5332	Last Dance/Get Dressed	1984	—	2.00	4.00
❑ B-5332 [PS]	Last Dance/Get Dressed	1984	—	2.00	4.00
❑ B-5473	Double Oh-Oh/Bangladesh	1985	—	2.00	4.00
❑ B-5473 [PS]	Double Oh-Oh/Bangladesh	1985	—	2.00	4.00
❑ B-5504	Bullet Proof/Silly Millimeter	1985	—	2.00	4.00
❑ B-5558	Do Fries Go With That Shake/Pleasure of Exhaustion (Do It Till I Drop)	1986	—	2.00	4.00
❑ B-5602	Hey Good Lookin' (Remix)/Hey Good Lookin' (Mirror Mix)	1986	—	2.00	4.00
❑ B-5642	R&B Skeletons (In the Closet)/Nubian Nut	1986	—	2.00	4.00
FOX					
❑ 10012	Stomp/Pump It Up	1994	—	2.50	5.00
—*B-side by Mudhoney*					
❑ 10012 [PS]	Stomp/Pump It Up	1994	—	2.50	5.00
PAISLEY PARK					
❑ PRO-S-3438 [DJ]	Why Should I Dog U Out? (same on both sides?)	1989	—	3.00	6.00
❑ 22790	Tweakin'/French Kiss	1989	—	2.00	4.00
❑ 27557	Why Should I Dog U Out?/(Instrumental)	1989	—	—	3.00
❑ 27557 [PS]	Why Should I Dog U Out?/(Instrumental)	1989	—	—	3.00

Number	Title (A Side/B Side)	Yr	VG	VG+	NM

Albums

ABC

| ❏ D-831 | The George Clinton Band Arrives | 1974 | 3.75 | 7.50 | 15.00 |

CAPITOL

❏ ST-12246	Computer Games	1982	2.50	5.00	10.00
❏ ST-12308	You Shouldn't-Nuf Bit Fish	1984	2.50	5.00	10.00
❏ ST-12417	Some of My Best Jokes Are Friends	1985	2.50	5.00	10.00
❏ ST-12481	R&B Skeletons in the Closet	1986	2.50	5.00	10.00
❏ MLP-15021 [EP]	The Mothership Connection Live from Houston, Texas	1986	3.75	7.50	15.00
❏ C1-33911 [(2)]	Greatest Funkin' Hits	1996	3.00	6.00	12.00
—Red vinyl					
❏ CJ-48424	The Best of George Clinton	1987	2.50	5.00	10.00

550 MUSIC

| ❏ B2 67144 [(2)] | T.A.P.O.A.F.O.M. — The Awesome Power of a Fully Operational Mothership | 1996 | 3.75 | 7.50 | 15.00 |
| —Red vinyl | | | | | |

INVICTUS

| ❏ ST-9815 | Black Vampire | 1973 | 5.00 | 10.00 | 20.00 |

PAISLEY PARK

❏ PRO-A-6537 [(2)DJ]	Hey Man... Smell My Finger	1993	6.25	12.50	25.00
—Promo-only vinyl issue					
❏ 25994	The Cinderella Theory	1989	3.00	6.00	12.00

WARNER BROS.

| ❏ 25887 | George Clinton Presents Our Gang Funky | 1988 | 2.50 | 5.00 | 10.00 |
| ❏ 25991 | Under a Nouveau Groove | 1989 | 2.50 | 5.00 | 10.00 |

CLINTONIAN CUBS, THE JIMMY CASTOR was a member.
45s

MY BROTHERS

| ❏ 508 | She's Just My Size/Confusion | 1960 | 75.00 | 150.00 | 300.00 |

CLIQUE, THE (1) Texas band.
45s

CINEMA

| ❏ 001 | Stay By Me/Splash One | 1967 | 7.50 | 15.00 | 30.00 |

SCEPTER

| ❏ 12202 | Stay By Me/Splash One | 1967 | 5.00 | 10.00 | 20.00 |
| ❏ 12212 | Gotta Get Away/Love Ain't Easy | 1967 | 5.00 | 10.00 | 20.00 |

WHITE WHALE

❏ 312	Superman/Shadow of Your Love	1969	3.00	6.00	12.00
❏ 323	Sugar on Sunday/Superman	1969	3.75	7.50	15.00
❏ 333	Soul Mate/I'll Hold Out My Hand	1969	2.50	5.00	10.00
❏ 338	I'm Alive/Sparkle and Shine	1970	2.50	5.00	10.00
❏ 361	Memphis/Southbound Wind	1970	2.50	5.00	10.00
❏ 367 [DJ]	Judy, Judy, Judy (same on both sides)	1970	3.00	6.00	12.00
—May be promo only					

Albums

WHITE WHALE

| ❏ WWS-7126 | The Clique | 1969 | 5.00 | 10.00 | 20.00 |

CLIQUE, THE (2) British band.
45s

ABC-PARAMOUNT

| ❏ 10655 | She Ain't No Good/Time, Time, Time | 1965 | 2.50 | 5.00 | 10.00 |

CLIQUE, THE (U) This could be an early record by group (1) or a later record by group (2).
45s

LAURIE

| ❏ 3365 | Sun Come Up/Drifter's Melody | 1966 | 2.50 | 5.00 | 10.00 |

CLIQUES, THE Also see JESSE BELVIN; EUGENE CHURCH.
45s

MODERN

❏ 987	Girl in My Dreams/I Wanna Know Why	1956	7.50	15.00	30.00
—Black label					
❏ 987	Girl in My Dreams/I Wanna Know Why	1956	12.50	25.00	50.00
—Blue label					
❏ 995	My Desire/I'm in Love with a Gal	1956	7.50	15.00	30.00

CLOONEY, ROSEMARY
45s

COLUMBIA

❏ 4-123	Suzy Snowflake/Little Red Riding Hood's Christmas	1951	3.75	7.50	15.00
—Yellow-label Children's Series record; alternate number is 90137					
❏ 4-123 [PS]	Suzy Snowflake/Little Red Riding Hood's Christmas	1951	5.00	10.00	20.00
❏ 4-149	The Night Before Christmas Song/Look Out the Window (The Winter Song)	1952	3.75	7.50	15.00
—With Gene Autry; yellow-label Children's Series record; alternate number is 90170					
❏ 4-149 [PS]	The Night Before Christmas Song/Look Out the Window (The Winter Song)	1952	5.00	10.00	20.00
❏ 4-175	Winter Wonderland/Christmas Song	1954	3.75	7.50	15.00
—Yellow-label Children's Series record					
❏ 4-175 [PS]	Winter Wonderland/Christmas Song	1954	5.00	10.00	20.00
❏ B-319 [PS]	Hollywood's Best	1952	3.00	6.00	12.00
—Box for records 39852-39855					
❏ 4-21423	Go On By/I Whsiper Your Name	1955	6.25	12.50	25.00
❏ 38988	C-H-R-I-S-T-M-A-S/Bless This House	1950	5.00	10.00	20.00
❏ 39054	The Place Where I Worship/House of Singing Bamboo	1950	3.75	7.50	15.00
❏ 39141	Cherry Pies/Love Means Love	1951	3.75	7.50	15.00
❏ 39158	Sentimental Music/The Face	1951	3.75	7.50	15.00
❏ 39185	I Still Feel the Same/When Apples Grow on Cherry Trees	1951	3.75	7.50	15.00
❏ 39212	Beautiful Brown Eyes/Shot Gun Boogie	1951	3.75	7.50	15.00
❏ 39333	Mixed Emotions/Kentucky Waltz	1951	3.75	7.50	15.00
❏ 39467	Come On-a My House/Rose of the Mountain	1951	3.75	7.50	15.00
❏ 39535	I'm Waiting Just for You/If Teardrops Were Pennies	1951	3.75	7.50	15.00
❏ 39536	I Wish I Wuz/Mixed Emotions	1951	3.75	7.50	15.00
❏ 39591	Find Me/I Only Saw Him Once	1951	3.75	7.50	15.00
❏ 39612	Suzy Snowflake/Little Red Riding Hood's Christmas	1951	3.75	7.50	15.00
❏ 39631	Be My Life's Companion/Why Don't You	1952	3.75	7.50	15.00
❏ 39648	Tenderly/Did Anyone Call	1952	3.75	7.50	15.00
❏ 39710	Half As Much/Poor Whippoorwill	1952	3.75	7.50	15.00

Number	Title (A Side/B Side)	Yr	VG	VG+	NM

❏ 39730	Tenderly/Be Anything (But Be Mine)	1952	3.00	6.00	12.00
—B-side by Champ Butler; part of a various artists 4-record box set					
❏ 39767	Botch-a-Me (Ba-Ba-Baciami Piccina)/On the First Warm Day	1952	3.75	7.50	15.00
❏ 39812	Too Old to Cut the Mustard/Good for Nothing	1952	3.75	7.50	15.00
—A-side with Marlene Dietrich					
❏ 39813	Blues in the Night/Who Kissed Me Last Night	1952	3.75	7.50	15.00
❏ 39852	You'll Never Know/In the Cool, Cool, Cool of the Evening	1952	3.00	6.00	12.00
—Sides 1 and 8 of B-319					
❏ 39853	On the Atchison, Topeka and the Santa Fe/When You Wish Upon a Star	1952	3.00	6.00	12.00
—Sides 2 and 7 of B-319					
❏ 39854	It Might As Well Be Spring/The Continental	1952	3.00	6.00	12.00
—Sides 3 and 6 of B-319					
❏ 39855	Over the Rainbow/Sweet Leilani	1952	3.00	6.00	12.00
—Sides 4 and 5 of B-319					
❏ 39876	The Night Before Christmas Song/Look Out the Window (The Winter Song)	1952	3.75	7.50	15.00
—With Gene Autry					
❏ 39892	If I Had a Penny/You're After My Own Heart	1952	3.75	7.50	15.00
❏ 39905	You'll Never Know/The Continental	1952	3.75	7.50	15.00
❏ 39931	What Would You Do/I Laughed Until I Cried	1953	3.75	7.50	15.00
❏ 39943	Lovely Weather for Ducks/Haven't Got a Worry	1953	3.75	7.50	15.00
❏ 39980	Dot's Nice — Donna Fight/It's the Same	1953	3.75	7.50	15.00
—With Marlene Dietrich					
❏ 40003	When I See You/It Just Happened to Happen to Me	1953	3.75	7.50	15.00
❏ 40024	Stick with Me/Cheegah, Choonem	1953	3.75	7.50	15.00
❏ 40031	Blues in the Night/Tenderly	1953	3.00	6.00	12.00
❏ 40102	C-H-R-I-S-T-M-A-S/Happy Christmas, Little Friend	1953	3.75	7.50	15.00
❏ 40142	My Baby Rocks Me/When You Love Someone	1953	3.75	7.50	15.00
❏ 40144	Man (Uh-Huh)/Woman (Uh-Huh)	1953	3.75	7.50	15.00
—B-side by Jose Ferrer					
❏ 40158	Red Garters/A Man and a Woman	1954	3.00	6.00	12.00
❏ 40159	Bad News/A Dime and a Dollar	1954	3.00	6.00	12.00
—With Guy Mitchell					
❏ 40160	Brave Man/Meet a Happy Guy	1954	3.00	6.00	12.00
—With Guy Mitchell					
❏ 40161	This Is Greater Than I Thought/Good Intentions	1954	3.00	6.00	12.00
—With Joanne Gilbert					
❏ 40187	Brave Man/Tomorrow I'll Dream and Remember	1954	3.75	7.50	15.00
❏ 40266	Hey There/This Ole House	1954	3.75	7.50	15.00
❏ 40305	Sisters/Love, You Didn't Do Right by Me	1954	3.75	7.50	15.00
—A-side by Betty Clooney					
❏ 40317	(Let's Give) A Christmas Present to Santa Claus/March of the Christmas Toys	1954	3.75	7.50	15.00
—With Jose Ferrer					
❏ 40355	White Christmas/Count Your Blessings	1954	3.00	6.00	12.00
❏ 40356	Mandy/The Best Things Happen While Dancing	1954	3.00	6.00	12.00
❏ 40357	Sisters/Snow	1954	3.00	6.00	12.00
—A-side with Betty Clooney					
❏ 40358	Love, You Didn't Do Right By Me/Gee, I Wish I Was Back in the Army	1954	3.00	6.00	12.00
❏ 40361	Mambo Italiano/We'll Be Together Again	1954	3.75	7.50	15.00
❏ 40370	Count Your Blessings Instead of Sheep/White Christmas	1954	3.75	7.50	15.00
❏ 40407	Mr. and Mrs./Marry the Man	1955	3.00	6.00	12.00
—With Jose Ferrer					
❏ 40434	Brahms' Lullaby/Where Will the Dimple Be	1955	3.00	6.00	12.00
❏ 40496	It Might As Well Be Spring/When You Wish Upon a Star	1955	3.00	6.00	12.00
❏ 40498	A Touch of the Blues/Love Among the Young	1955	3.00	6.00	12.00
❏ 40534	Sailor Boy Have Talk to Me in English/Go On By	1954	3.00	6.00	12.00
❏ 40579	Pet Me, Poppa/Wake Me	1955	3.00	6.00	12.00
❏ 40616	Memories of You/It's Bad for Me	1955	3.00	6.00	12.00
—With Benny Goodman					
❏ 40619	The Key to My Heart/Little Girl at Heart	1955	3.00	6.00	12.00
❏ 40625	A Fine Romance/Goodbye	1955	3.00	6.00	12.00
—With Benny Goodman					
❏ 40676	I Could Have Danced All Night/I've Grown Accustomed to Your Face	1956	3.00	6.00	12.00
❏ 40701	Sophisticated Lady/Grievin'	1956	3.00	6.00	12.00
❏ 40723	Hello, Young Lovers/Peachy, Peachy	1956	3.00	6.00	12.00
❏ 40774	Come Rain or Come Shine/It's a Nuisance Having You Around	1956	3.00	6.00	12.00
❏ 40808	He'll Be Comin' Down the Chimney/Mommy Can I Keep the Kitten	1956	3.00	6.00	12.00
—With "Her Sister Gail"					
❏ 40812	(Don't That Take the) Rag Offen the Bush/Love Is a Feeling	1956	3.00	6.00	12.00
❏ 40835	Mangos/Independent (On My Own)	1957	3.00	6.00	12.00
❏ 40917	Sing Little Birdie Sing/Who Dot Mon, Mon	1957	3.00	6.00	12.00
❏ 40981	Colors/That's How It Is	1957	3.00	6.00	12.00
❏ 41053	Tonight/Love and Affection	1957	3.00	6.00	12.00
❏ 41107	You Don't Know Him/Surprise	1958	3.00	6.00	12.00
❏ 50007	Come On-a My House/(B-side unknown)	1954	2.50	5.00	10.00
—Early "Hall of Fame Series" issue					

CORAL

| ❏ 62137 | A Touch of the Blues/I Wish I Were in Love Again | 1959 | 2.50 | 5.00 | 10.00 |

DOT

| ❏ 17100 | One Less Bell to Answer/Let Me Down Easy | 1968 | — | 3.00 | 6.00 |

GIBSON MUSICARDS

❏ 100G 27104 [PS]	Happy Birthday, Dear Mother	1955	5.00	10.00	20.00
—7x7 card that comes with GIB-6... Others are likely to exist, but we haven't documented them yet.					
❏ GIB-6	Happy Birthday, Dear Mother/(B-side blank)	1955	5.00	10.00	20.00

MGM

❏ 12654	Morning Music of Montmartre/Give It All You Got	1958	2.50	5.00	10.00
—With Jose Ferrer					
❏ 12655	Hey, Madame/You're So Right for Me	1958	2.50	5.00	10.00
—With Jose Ferrer					
❏ 12760	It's a Boy/The Loudenboomer Bird	1958	2.50	5.00	10.00
❏ 12823	Love Eyes/Flattery	1959	2.50	5.00	10.00
❏ 13349	I Wonder/For You	1959	2.50	5.00	10.00
	I'm Glad It's You/Love and Learn	1965	—	3.00	6.00

Number	Title (A Side/B Side)	Yr	VG	VG+	NM
RCA VICTOR					
❏ 47-7707	Watermelon Heart/Summertime Love	1960	2.50	5.00	10.00
—With Perez Prado					
❏ 47-7754	Many a Wonderful Moment/Vaya Vaya	1960	2.50	5.00	10.00
❏ 47-7754 [PS]	Many a Wonderful Moment/Vaya Vaya	1960	3.75	7.50	15.00
❏ 47-7806	Danke Schoen/Swing Me	1960	2.50	5.00	10.00
❏ 47-7819	Hey Look Me Over/What Takes My Fancy	1960	2.50	5.00	10.00
❏ 47-7887	Theme from Return to Peyton Place/ Without Love	1961	2.50	5.00	10.00
❏ 47-7948	Give Myself a Party/ If I Can Stay Away Long Enough	1961	2.50	5.00	10.00
REPRISE					
❏ 0327	A Spoonful of Sugar/Stay Awake	1964	2.00	4.00	8.00
❏ 20145	I Will Follow Him (Chariot)/ The Rose and the Butterfly	1963	2.00	4.00	8.00
❏ 20173	Mixed Emotions/The Prisoner's Song	1963	2.00	4.00	8.00
❏ 20173	The Prisoner's Song/Mixed Emotions	1963	2.00	4.00	8.00
❏ 20222	Helo Faithless/A Hundred Years from Today	1963	2.00	4.00	8.00
7-Inch Extended Plays					
COLUMBIA					
❏ B-1901	White Christmas/Mandy//Snow / Gee, I Wish I Was Back In The Army	195?	3.00	6.00	12.00
❏ B-1901 [PS]	White Christmas Volume 2	195?	3.00	6.00	12.00
❏ B-1932	Hey There/This Ole House//The Little Shoemaker (La Petit Cordonnier)/ Love Is a Beautiful Stranger	195?	3.00	6.00	12.00
❏ B-1932 [PS]	(title unknown)	195?	3.00	6.00	12.00
❏ B-2524	*Come On-a My House/Mixed Emotions/ Mambo Italiano/Tenderly	1957	3.00	6.00	12.00
❏ B-2524 [PS]	Rosemary Clooney (Hall of Fame Series)	1957	3.00	6.00	12.00
❏ B-2525	*Hey There/Botch-A-Me/Half as Much// This Ole House	1957	3.00	6.00	12.00
❏ B-2525 [PS]	Rosemary Clooney (Hall of Fame Series)	1957	3.00	6.00	12.00
❏ B-2550	*Be My Life's Companion/Blame It on My Youth/ Blues in the Night/Why Fight the Feeling?	1958	3.00	6.00	12.00
❏ B-2550 [PS]	Rosemary Clooney (Hall of Fame Series)	1958	3.00	6.00	12.00
❏ B-10061	(contents unknown)	1957	3.00	6.00	12.00
❏ B-10061 [PS]	Ring Around the Rosie, Vol. 1	1957	3.00	6.00	12.00
❏ B-10062	(contents unknown)	1957	3.00	6.00	12.00
❏ B-10062 [PS]	Ring Around the Rosie, Vol. 2	1957	3.00	6.00	12.00
❏ B-10063	(contents unknown)	1957	3.00	6.00	12.00
❏ B-10063 [PS]	Ring Around the Rosie, Vol. 3	1957	3.00	6.00	12.00
❏ ZTV-60077/8	Tenderly/Hey There//Half as Much/I Could Have Danced All Night	195?	3.75	7.50	15.00
Albums					
COLUMBIA					
❏ CL 585 [M]	Hollywood's Best	1955	12.50	25.00	50.00
❏ CL 872 [M]	Blue Rose	1956	10.00	20.00	40.00
❏ CL 969 [M]	Clooney Tunes	1957	20.00	40.00	80.00
❏ CL 1006 [M]	Ring Around the Rosie	1957	10.00	20.00	40.00
—With the Hi-Lo's					
❏ CL 1230 [M]	Rosie's Greatest Hits	1958	10.00	20.00	40.00
—Six "eye" logos on label					
❏ CL 1230 [M]	Rosie's Greatest Hits	1962	6.25	12.50	25.00
—"Guaranteed High Fidelity" on label					
❏ CL 1230 [M]	Rosie's Greatest Hits	1965	3.75	7.50	15.00
—"360 Sound Mono" on label					
❏ CL 2525 [10]	Tenderly	1955	12.50	25.00	50.00
❏ CL 2569 [10]	Children's Favorites	1955	12.50	25.00	50.00
❏ CL 2572 [10]	A Date with the King	1956	12.50	25.00	50.00
❏ CL 2581 [10]	On Stage	1956	12.50	25.00	50.00
❏ CL 2597 [10]	My Fair Lady	1956	12.50	25.00	50.00
❏ CL 6224 [10]	Hollywood's Best	1952	15.00	30.00	60.00
❏ CL 6297 [10]	Rosemary Clooney (While We're Young)	1954	15.00	30.00	60.00
❏ CL 6338 [10]	White Christmas	1954	15.00	30.00	60.00
COLUMBIA SPECIAL PRODUCTS					
❏ P 13083	Hollywood's Best	197?	3.00	6.00	12.00
❏ P 13085	Blue Rose	197?	3.00	6.00	12.00
❏ P 14382	Come On-a My House	197?	3.00	6.00	12.00
CONCORD JAZZ					
❏ CJ-47	Everything's Coming Up Rosie	1978	3.00	6.00	12.00
❏ CJ-60	Rosie Sings Bing	1979	3.00	6.00	12.00
❏ CJ-81	Here's to My Lady	1979	3.00	6.00	12.00
❏ CJ-112	Rosemary Clooney Sings Ira Gershwin	1980	3.00	6.00	12.00
❏ CJ-144	With Love	1981	3.00	6.00	12.00
❏ CJ-185	Rosemary Clooney Sings Cole Porter	1982	3.00	6.00	12.00
❏ CJ-210	Rosemary Clooney Sings Harold Arlen	1983	3.00	6.00	12.00
❏ CJ-226	My Buddy	1984	3.00	6.00	12.00
—With Woody Herman					
❏ CJ-255	Rosemary Clooney Sings the Music of Irving Berlin	1985		6.00	12.00
❏ CJ-282	Rosemary Clooney Sings Ballads	1985	3.00	6.00	12.00
❏ CJ-308	Rosemary Clooney Sings the Music of Jimmy Van Heusen	1987	3.00	6.00	12.00
❏ CJ-333	Rosemary Clooney Sings the Lyrics of Johnny Mercer	1988	3.00	6.00	12.00
❏ CJ-364	Show Tunes	1989	3.00	6.00	12.00
CORAL					
❏ CRL 57266 [M]	Swing Around Rosie	1959	7.50	15.00	30.00
❏ CRL 757266 [S]	Swing Around Rosie	1959	10.00	20.00	40.00
HARMONY					
❏ HL 7123 [M]	Rosemary Clooney in High Fidelity	195?	6.25	12.50	25.00
❏ HL 7213 [M]	Hollywood Hits	195?	6.25	12.50	25.00
❏ HL 7454 [M]	Mixed Emotions	1968	5.00	10.00	20.00
❏ HL 9501 [M]	Rosemary Clooney Sings for Children	196?	5.00	10.00	20.00
❏ HS 11254 [R]	Mixed Emotions	1968	3.00	6.00	12.00
HINDSIGHT					
❏ HSR-234	Rosemary Clooney 1951-1952	1988	2.50	5.00	10.00
HOLIDAY					
❏ 1946	Christmas with Rosemary Clooney	1981	2.50	5.00	10.00
MGM					
❏ E-3687 [M]	Oh, Captain!	1958	10.00	20.00	40.00
❏ E-3782 [M]	Hymns from the Heart	1959	7.50	15.00	30.00
❏ SE-3782 [S]	Hymns from the Heart	1959	10.00	20.00	40.00
❏ E-3834 [M]	Rosie Clooney Swings Softly	1960	7.50	15.00	30.00
❏ SE-3834 [S]	Rosie Clooney Swings Softly	1960	10.00	20.00	40.00

Number	Title (A Side/B Side)	Yr	VG	VG+	NM
MISTLETOE					
❏ MLP-1234	Christmas with Rosemary Clooney	1978	3.00	6.00	12.00
RCA VICTOR					
❏ LPM-2133 [M]	A Touch of Tabasco	1960	5.00	10.00	20.00
❏ LSP-2133 [S]	A Touch of Tabasco	1960	7.50	15.00	30.00
❏ LPM-2212 [M]	Clap Hands, Here Comes Rosie	1960	5.00	10.00	20.00
❏ LSP-2212 [S]	Clap Hands, Here Comes Rosie	1960	7.50	15.00	30.00
❏ LPM-2265 [M]	Rosie Solves the Swingin' Riddle	1961	5.00	10.00	20.00
❏ LSP-2265 [S]	Rosie Solves the Swingin' Riddle	1961	7.50	15.00	30.00
❏ LPM-2565 [M]	Country Hits from the Heart	1963	5.00	10.00	20.00
❏ LSP-2565 [S]	Country Hits from the Heart	1963	7.50	15.00	30.00
REPRISE					
❏ R-6088 [M]	Love	1963	7.50	15.00	30.00
❏ R9-6088 [S]	Love	1963	10.00	20.00	40.00
❏ R-6108 [M]	Thanks for Nothing	1964	7.50	15.00	30.00
❏ RS-6108 [S]	Thanks for Nothing	1964	10.00	20.00	40.00
TIME-LIFE					
❏ SLGD-16 [(2)]	Legendary Singers: Rosemary Clooney	1986	3.75	7.50	15.00

CLOONEY, ROSEMARY, AND JIMMY BOYD Also see each artist's individual listings.
45s
COLUMBIA

Number	Title (A Side/B Side)	Yr	VG	VG+	NM
❏ 4-39988	Dennis the Menace/Little Josey	1953	5.00	10.00	20.00

CLOONEY, ROSEMARY, AND BING CROSBY
Albums
CAPITOL

Number	Title (A Side/B Side)	Yr	VG	VG+	NM
❏ ST 2300 [S]	That Travelin' Two-Beat	1965	7.50	15.00	30.00
❏ T 2300 [M]	That Travelin' Two-Beat	1965	5.00	10.00	20.00
RCA CAMDEN					
❏ CAS-2330	Rendezvous	1968	3.75	7.50	15.00
RCA VICTOR					
❏ LPM-1854 [M]	Fancy Meeting You Here	1958	5.00	10.00	20.00
❏ LSP-1854 [S]	Fancy Meeting You Here	1958	7.50	15.00	30.00

CLOONEY SISTERS, THE Also see ROSEMARY CLOONEY.
Albums
EPIC

Number	Title (A Side/B Side)	Yr	VG	VG+	NM
❏ LN 3160 [M]	The Clooney Sisters with Tony Pastor	1956	15.00	30.00	60.00

CLOUD, CHRISTOPHER See TOMMY BOYCE.

CLOVER, TIMOTHY
Albums
TOWER

Number	Title (A Side/B Side)	Yr	VG	VG+	NM
❏ ST 5114	A Harvard Square Affair	1968	5.00	10.00	20.00

CLOVERS, THE
45s
ATLANTIC

Number	Title (A Side/B Side)	Yr	VG	VG+	NM
❏ 934	Don't You Know I Love You/Skylark	1951	250.00	500.00	1000.
❏ 944	Fool, Fool, Fool/Needless	1951	62.50	125.00	250.00
❏ 963	One Mint Julep/Middle of the Night	1952	25.00	50.00	100.00
—Yellow label, no "fan" logo					
❏ 963	One Mint Julep/Middle of the Night	1961	6.25	12.50	25.00
—Red label, no "fan" logo					
❏ 969	Ting-A-Ling/Wonder Where My Baby's Gone	1952	25.00	50.00	100.00
❏ 977	I Played the Fool/Hey, Miss Fannie	1952	62.50	125.00	250.00
❏ 989	Yes, It's You/Crawlin'	1953	15.00	30.00	60.00
❏ 1000	Good Lovin'/Here Goes a Fool	1953	20.00	40.00	80.00
❏ 1010	Comin' On/The Feeling Is So Good	1953	37.50	75.00	150.00
❏ 1022	Lovey Dovey/Little Mama	1954	12.50	25.00	50.00
❏ 1035	Your Cash Ain't Nothin' But Trash/I've Got My Eyes on You	1954	12.50	25.00	50.00
❏ 1046	I Confess/Alrighty, Oh Sweetie	1954	12.50	25.00	50.00
❏ 1052	Blue Velvet/If You Love Me (Why Don't You Tell Me So)	1955	15.00	30.00	60.00
❏ 1060	Love Bug/In the Morning Time	1955	12.50	25.00	50.00
❏ 1073	Nip Sip/If I Could Be Loved By You	1955	12.50	25.00	50.00
❏ 1083	Devil or Angel/Hey, Doll Baby	1956	10.00	20.00	40.00
—Red label, no "fan" logo					
❏ 1083	Devil or Angel/Hey, Doll Baby	1956	50.00	100.00	200.00
—Yellow label, no "fan" logo					
❏ 1083	Devil or Angel/Hey, Doll Baby	1956	2000.	3000.	4000.
—Red label, no "fan" logo; red vinyl; value is conjecture					
❏ 1094	Love, Love, Love/Your Tender Lips	1956	10.00	20.00	40.00
❏ 1107	From the Bottom of My Heart/Bring Me Love	1956	7.50	15.00	30.00
❏ 1118	A Lonely Fool/Baby, Baby, Oh My Darling	1956	7.50	15.00	30.00
❏ 1129	Here Comes Romance/You Good-Looking Woman	1957	7.50	15.00	30.00
❏ 1139	I-I-I Love You/So Young	1957	7.50	15.00	30.00
❏ 1152	There's No Tomorrow/Down in the Alley	1957	7.50	15.00	30.00
❏ 1175	Wishing for Your Love/All About You	1958	7.50	15.00	30.00
❏ 2129	Drive It Home/The Bootie Green	1961	5.00	10.00	20.00
BRUNSWICK					
❏ 55249	Love! Love! Love!/The Kickapoo	1963	3.00	6.00	12.00
JOSIE					
❏ 992	For Days/Too Long Without Some Loving	1968	2.50	5.00	10.00
❏ 997	Try My Lovin' On You/Sweet Side of a Soulful Woman	1968	2.50	5.00	10.00
LANA					
❏ 113	Love Potion No. 9/Hey Little Girl	196?	2.00	4.00	8.00
—B-side by the Deltones					
❏ 114	Devil or Angel/Since I Met You	196?	2.00	4.00	8.00
—B-side by the Deltones					
POPLAR					
❏ 110	The Gossip Wheel/Please Come On to Me	1958	6.25	12.50	25.00
❏ 111	The Good Old Summertime/Idaho	1958	6.25	12.50	25.00
PORT					
❏ 3004	Poor Baby/He Sure Could Hypnotize	1965	2.50	5.00	10.00
PORWIN					
❏ 1001/2	Stop Pretending/One More Time	1963	3.75	7.50	15.00
—As "Buddy Bailey and the Clovers"					
❏ 1004	It's All in the Game/That's What I Will Be	1963	3.75	7.50	15.00
—As "Buddy Bailey and the Clovers"					
STENTON					
❏ 7001	Please Mr. Sun/Gimme, Gimme, Gimme	1961	20.00	40.00	80.00
—As "Tippie and the Clovermen"					

Number	Title (A Side/B Side)	Yr	VG	VG+	NM
TIGER					
❏ 201	Bossa Nova Baby/The Bossa Nova (My Heart Said)	1962	3.75	7.50	15.00
—As "Tippie and the Clovers"					
UNITED ARTISTS					
❏ 0133	Love Potion #9/Stay Awhile	1973	—	2.00	4.00
—"Silver Spotlight Series" reissue					
❏ 174	Rock and Roll Tango/That Old Black Magic	1959	6.25	12.50	25.00
❏ 180	Love Potion #9/Stay Awhile	1959	6.25	12.50	25.00
❏ 209	One Mint Julep/Lovey	1960	6.25	12.50	25.00
❏ 227	Easy Lovin'/I'm Confessin' That I Love You	1960	6.25	12.50	25.00
❏ 263	Yes It's You/Burning Fire	1960	6.25	12.50	25.00
❏ 307	The Honeydripper/Have Gun	1961	6.25	12.50	25.00
WINLEY					
❏ 255	Let Me Hold You/Wrapped Up in a Dream	1961	3.75	7.50	15.00
❏ 265	I Need You Now/Gotta Quit You	1962	3.75	7.50	15.00
❏ 265	They're Rockin' Down the Street/Be My Baby	1962	3.75	7.50	15.00
—As "The Fabulous Clovers"					
7-Inch Extended Plays					
ATLANTIC					
❏ 504	One Mint Julep/Fool, Fool, Fool//Hey, Miss Fannie/I Played the Fool	1953	50.00	100.00	200.00
❏ 504 [PS]	The Clovers Sing	1953	50.00	100.00	200.00
❏ 537	(contents unknown)	1954	37.50	75.00	150.00
❏ 537 [PS]	The Clovers Sing	1954	50.00	100.00	200.00
❏ 590	*Love, Love, Love/Devil or Angel/Blue Velvet/ From the Bottom of My Heart	1955	37.50	75.00	150.00
❏ 590 [PS]	The Clovers	1955	50.00	100.00	200.00
Albums					
ATCO					
❏ SD 33-374	Their Greatest Recordings/The Early Years	1971	3.00	6.00	12.00
ATLANTIC					
❏ 1248 [M]	The Clovers	1956	150.00	300.00	600.00
❏ 8009 [M]	The Clovers	1957	100.00	200.00	400.00
—Reissue of 1248 on the "pop" series; black label					
❏ 8009 [M]	The Clovers	1960	75.00	150.00	300.00
—White "bullseye" label					
❏ 8009 [M]	The Clovers	1961	50.00	100.00	200.00
—Red and white label					
❏ 8034 [M]	Dance Party	1959	100.00	200.00	400.00
—Black label					
❏ 8034 [M]	Dance Party	1960	75.00	150.00	300.00
—White "bullseye" label					
❏ 8034 [M]	Dance Party	1961	50.00	100.00	200.00
—Red and white label					
GRAND PRIX					
❏ K-428 [M]	The Original Love Potion Number Nine	1964	7.50	15.00	30.00
❏ KS-428 [R]	The Original Love Potion Number Nine	1964	3.00	6.00	12.00
POPLAR					
❏ 1001 [M]	The Clovers In Clover	1958	100.00	200.00	400.00
UNITED ARTISTS					
❏ UAL-3033 [M]	The Clovers In Clover	1959	75.00	150.00	300.00
❏ UAL-3099 [M]	Love Potion Number Nine	1959	62.50	125.00	250.00
❏ UAS-6033 [R]	The Clovers In Clover	196?	50.00	100.00	200.00
❏ UAS-6099 [S]	Love Potion Number Nine	1959	125.00	250.00	500.00

CLOWNEY, DAVID See DAVE "BABY" CORTEZ.

CLUSTERS, THE
45s

Number	Title (A Side/B Side)	Yr	VG	VG+	NM
END					
❏ 1115	Pardon My Heart/Darling Can't You Tell	1962	10.00	20.00	40.00
EPIC					
❏ 9330	Forecast of Our Love/Long Legged Maggie	1959	20.00	40.00	80.00
TEE GEE					
❏ 102	Pardon My Heart/Darling Can't You Tell	1958	30.00	60.00	120.00
—With Gone distribution mentioned; publishing by Real Gone Music					
❏ 102	Pardon My Heart/Darling Can't You Tell	1958	75.00	150.00	300.00
—No mention of Gone distribution					
❏ 102	Pardon My Heart/Darling Can't You Tell	1958	75.00	150.00	300.00
—With Gone distribution mentioned; publishing by Emkay Music					

COASTERS, THE Also see THE ROBINS.
45s

Number	Title (A Side/B Side)	Yr	VG	VG+	NM
AMERICAN INT'L.					
❏ 1122	If I Had a Hammer/If I Had a Hammer (Disco Version)	1976	—	2.50	5.00
—As "The World Famous Coasters"					
ATCO					
❏ 6064	Down in Mexico/Turtle Dovin'	1956	20.00	40.00	80.00
❏ 6073	One Kiss Led to Another/Brazil	1956	15.00	30.00	60.00
❏ 6087	Searchin'/Young Blood	1957	6.25	12.50	25.00
—White and yellow label					
❏ 6087	Searchin'/Young Blood	1957	17.50	35.00	70.00
—Maroon label (first pressing)					
❏ 6098	Idol with the Golden Head/(When She Wants Good Lovin') My Baby Comes to Me	1957	10.00	20.00	40.00
❏ 6104	Sweet Georgia Brown/What Is the Secret of Your Success	1957	10.00	20.00	40.00
❏ 6111	Dance!/Gee, Golly	1958	10.00	20.00	40.00
❏ 6116	Yakety Yak/Zing Went the Strings of My Heart	1958	6.25	12.50	25.00
❏ 6126	The Shadow Knows/Sorry But I'm Gonna Have to Pass	1958	6.25	12.50	25.00
❏ 6132 [M]	Charlie Brown/Three Cool Cats	1959	6.25	12.50	25.00
❏ SD-45-6132 [S]	Charlie Brown/Three Cool Cats	1959	15.00	30.00	60.00
—Blue label, silver print, "Stereo" under the "O" of "Atco"					
❏ 6141	Along Came Jones/That Is Rock and Roll	1959	5.00	10.00	20.00
❏ 6146	Poison Ivy/I'm a Hog for You	1959	5.00	10.00	20.00
❏ 6153	Run Red Run/What About Us	1959	5.00	10.00	20.00
❏ 6163	Besame Mucho (Part 1)/Besame Mucho (Part 2)	1960	6.25	12.50	25.00
❏ 6168	Wake Me, Shake Me/Stewball	1960	6.25	12.50	25.00
❏ 6178	Shoppin' for Clothes/The Snake and the Book Worm	1960	6.25	12.50	25.00
❏ 6186	Thumbin' a Ride/Wait a Minute	1961	5.00	10.00	20.00
❏ 6192	Little Egypt (Ying-Yang)/Keep On Rolling	1961	5.00	10.00	20.00
❏ 6204	Girls, Girls, Girls (Part 1)/Girls, Girls, Girls (Part 2)	1961	5.00	10.00	20.00
❏ 6210	Bad Blood/(Ain't That) Just Like Me	1961	5.00	10.00	20.00

Number	Title (A Side/B Side)	Yr	VG	VG+	NM
❏ 6219	Teach Me How to Shimmy/Ridin' Hood	1962	5.00	10.00	20.00
❏ 6234	The Climb/(Instrumental)	1962	5.00	10.00	20.00
❏ 6251	The P.T.A./Bull Tick Waltz	1962	5.00	10.00	20.00
❏ 6287	Speedo's Back in Town/T'Ain't Nothin' to Me	1964	3.75	7.50	15.00
❏ 6300	Lovey Dovey/Bad Detective	1964	3.75	7.50	15.00
❏ 6321	Wild One/I Must Be Dreaming	1964	3.75	7.50	15.00
❏ 6341	Hungry/Lady Like	1965	3.75	7.50	15.00
❏ 6356	Money Honey/Let's Go Get Stoned	1965	3.75	7.50	15.00
❏ 6379	Bell Bottom Slacks and a Chinese Kimono (She's My Little Spodee-O)/Crazy Baby	1965	6.25	12.50	25.00
❏ 6407	Saturday Night Fish Fry/She's a Yum Yum	1966	3.75	7.50	15.00
ATLANTIC					
❏ 89361	Yakety Yak/Stand By Me	1986	—	—	3.00
❏ 89361 [PS]	Yakety Yak/Stand By Me	1986	—	—	3.00
—B-side by Ben E. King. See listing of this record under "King, Ben E." for more information.					
CHELAN					
❏ 2000	Searchin' '75/Young BLood	1975		2.50	5.00
—As "The Coasters 2+2"					
DATE					
❏ 1552	Soul Pad/Down Home Girl	1967	5.00	10.00	20.00
❏ 1607	Everybody's Woman/She Can	1968	5.00	10.00	20.00
❏ 1617	D.W. Washburn/Everybody's Woman	1968	5.00	10.00	20.00
KING					
❏ 6385	Love Potion #9/D.W. Washburn	1972	—	3.00	6.00
❏ 6389	Cool Jerk/Talkin' 'Bout a Woman	1972	—	3.00	6.00
❏ 6404	Soul Pad/D.W. Washburn	1972	—	3.00	6.00
SAL WA					
❏ 1001	Take It Easy, Greasy/You Move Me	1975	—	2.50	5.00
TURNTABLE					
❏ 504	Act Right/The World Is Changing	1969	2.50	5.00	10.00
7-Inch Extended Plays					
ATCO					
❏ 4501	Searchin'/Young Blood//(When She Wants Good Lovin') My Baby Comes to Me/Idol with the Golden Head	1958	37.50	75.00	150.00
❏ 4501 [PS]	Rock and Roll with the Coasters	1958	50.00	100.00	200.00
❏ 4503	Yakety Yak/Framed//Loop De Loop Mambo/Riot in Cell Block Number Nine	1959	50.00	100.00	200.00
❏ 4503 [PS]	Keep Rockin' with the Coasters	1959	50.00	100.00	200.00
❏ 4506	*Charlie Brown/Three Cool Cats/The Shadow Knows/Sorry But I'm Gonna Have to Pass	1959	37.50	75.00	150.00
❏ 4506 [PS]	The Coasters	1959	37.50	75.00	150.00
❏ 4507	Along Came Jones/That Is Rock & Roll//Dance!/ Gee, Golly	1959	37.50	75.00	150.00
❏ 4507 [PS]	The Coasters' Top Hits	1959	37.50	75.00	150.00
Albums					
ATCO					
❏ 33-101 [M]	The Coasters	1958	75.00	150.00	300.00
—Yellow "harp" label					
❏ 33-101 [M]	The Coasters	196?	15.00	30.00	60.00
—Gold and dark blue label					
❏ 33-111 [M]	The Coasters' Greatest Hits	1959	37.50	75.00	150.00
—Yellow "harp" label					
❏ 33-111 [M]	The Coasters' Greatest Hits	196?	15.00	30.00	60.00
—Gold and gray label					
❏ 33-123 [M]	One By One	196?	15.00	30.00	60.00
—Gold and gray label					
❏ 33-123 [M]	One By One	1960	37.50	75.00	150.00
—Yellow "harp" label					
❏ SD 33-123 [S]	One By One	196?	37.50	75.00	150.00
—Purple and brown label					
❏ SD 33-123 [S]	One By One	1960	100.00	200.00	400.00
—Yellow "harp" label					
❏ 33-135 [M]	Coast Along with the Coasters	1962	25.00	50.00	100.00
—Gold and gray label					
❏ SD 33-135 [P]	Coast Along with the Coasters	1962	37.50	75.00	150.00
—Purple and brown label; "Wait a Minute" is rechanneled					
❏ SD 33-371	Their Greatest Recordings/The Early Years	1971	5.00	10.00	20.00
CLARION					
❏ 605 [M]	That Is Rock and Roll	1965	10.00	20.00	40.00
❏ SD 605 [S]	That Is Rock and Roll	1965	12.50	25.00	50.00
KING					
❏ KS-1146	The Coasters On Broadway	1971	6.25	12.50	25.00
POWER PAK					
❏ 310	Greatest Hits	198?	2.50	5.00	10.00
TRIP					
❏ 8028	It Ain't Sanitary	197?	3.00	6.00	12.00

COBRAS, THE (1) Stevie Ray Vaughan was a member of this Cobras.
45s

Number	Title (A Side/B Side)	Yr	VG	VG+	NM
ARMADILLO					
❏ 79-1	Blow Joe Blow (Crazy 'Bout a Saxophone)/ Sugaree	1980	25.00	50.00	100.00

COBRAS, THE (2)
45s

Number	Title (A Side/B Side)	Yr	VG	VG+	NM
CASINO					
❏ 1309	La La/Goodbye Molly	1963	20.00	40.00	80.00
LOST-NITE					
❏ 230	La La/Goodbye Molly	196?	—	2.50	5.00
—Reissue					
SWAN					
❏ 4176	La La/Goodbye Molly	1964	6.25	12.50	25.00

COBRAS, THE (3)
45s

Number	Title (A Side/B Side)	Yr	VG	VG+	NM
MODERN					
❏ 964	Cindy/I Will Return	1955	37.50	75.00	150.00
—Revised spelling of A-side					
❏ 964	Sindy/I Will Return	1955	75.00	150.00	300.00
—Original spelling of A-side					

COBRAS, THE (U) These may be by group (2), but we're not sure.
45s

Number	Title (A Side/B Side)	Yr	VG	VG+	NM
MONOGRAM					
❏ 519	Thumpin'/Don't Even Know Your Name	1964	3.00	6.00	12.00
STAX					
❏ 148	Shake Up/Restless	1964	3.75	7.50	15.00

Number	Title (A Side/B Side)	Yr	VG	VG+	NM

COCHRAN, EDDIE Also see COCHRAN BROTHERS; JEWEL AND EDDIE.
45s
CAPEHART

Number	Title (A Side/B Side)	Yr	VG	VG+	NM
❑ 5003	Rough Stuff/Our Love	1960	6.25	12.50	25.00
❑ 5003 [PS]	Rough Stuff/Our Love	1960	50.00	100.00	200.00

CREST

❑ 1026	Skinny Jim/Half Loved	1956	75.00	150.00	300.00

LIBERTY

❑ 55056	Sittin' in the Balcony/Dark Lonely Street	1957	7.50	15.00	30.00
❑ 55070	Mean When I'm Mad/One Kiss	1957	7.50	15.00	30.00
❑ 55070 [PS]	Mean When I'm Mad/One Kiss	1957	500.00	1000.	1500.
❑ 55087	Drive In Show/Am I Blue	1957	7.50	15.00	30.00
❑ 55112	Twenty Flight Rock/Cradle Baby	1957	37.50	75.00	150.00
❑ 55123	Jeannie, Jeannie, Jeannie/Pocketful of Hearts	1958	7.50	15.00	30.00
❑ 55138	Pretty Girl/Theresa	1958	8.75	17.50	35.00
❑ 55144	Summertime Blues/Live Again	1958	7.50	15.00	30.00
❑ 55166	C'mon Everybody/Don't Ever Let Me Go	1958	7.50	15.00	30.00
❑ 55177	Teen Age Heaven/I Remember	1959	7.50	15.00	30.00
❑ 55177	Teenage Heaven/I Remember	1959	10.00	20.00	40.00
—Note difference in title					
❑ 55203	The Boll Weevil Song/Somethin' Else	1959	7.50	15.00	30.00
❑ 55217	Hallelujah I Love Her So/Little Angel	1959	7.50	15.00	30.00
❑ 55242	Three Steps to Heaven/Cut Across Shorty	1960	10.00	20.00	40.00
❑ 55278	Lonely/Sweetie Pie	1960	6.25	12.50	25.00
❑ 55389	Weekend/Lonely	1961	7.50	15.00	30.00

UNITED ARTISTS

❑ 0014	Summertime Blues/Cut Across Shorty	1973	—	2.00	4.00
❑ 0015	C'mon Everybody/Twenty Flight Rock	1973	—	2.00	4.00
❑ 0016	Sittin' in the Balcony/Somethin' Else	1973	—	2.00	4.00
—0014, 0015, 0016 are "Silver Spotlight Series" reissues					

7-Inch Extended Plays
LIBERTY

❑ LEP 1-3061	Sittin' in the Balcony/Proud of You//Stockings and Shoes/Have I Told You Lately That I Love You	1958	50.00	100.00	200.00
❑ LEP 1-3061 [PS]	Singin' to My Baby (Part One)	1958	50.00	100.00	200.00
❑ LEP 2-3061	(contents unknown)	1958	50.00	100.00	200.00
❑ LEP 2-3061 [PS]	Singin' to My Baby (Part Two)	1958	50.00	100.00	200.00
❑ LEP 3-3061	(contents unknown)	1958	50.00	100.00	200.00
❑ LEP 3-3061 [PS]	Singin' to My Baby (Part Three)	1958	50.00	100.00	200.00

Albums
LIBERTY

❑ LRP-3061 [M]	Singin' to My Baby	1957	200.00	400.00	800.00
—Green label					
❑ LRP-3061 [M]	Singin' to My Baby	1960	75.00	150.00	300.00
—Black label					
❑ LRP-3172 [M]	Eddie Cochran (12 of His Biggest Hits)	1960	30.00	60.00	120.00
❑ LRP-3220 [M]	Never to Be Forgotten	1962	25.00	50.00	100.00
❑ LN-10137	Singin' to My Baby	198?	3.00	6.00	12.00
—Budget-line reissue					
❑ LN-10204	Great Hits	198?	2.00	4.00	8.00

SUNSET

❑ SUM-1123 [M]	Summertime Blues	1966	10.00	20.00	40.00
❑ SUS-5123 [R]	Summertime Blues	1966	6.25	12.50	25.00

UNITED ARTISTS

❑ UA-LA428-E	The Very Best of Eddie Cochran	1975	3.00	6.00	12.00
❑ UAS-9959 [(2)]	Legendary Masters Series #4	1972	6.25	12.50	25.00

COCHRAN, HANK Also see COCHRAN BROTHERS.
45s
CAPITOL

❑ 4585	Willie/Uphill All the Way	1978	—	2.00	4.00
—A-side with Merle Haggard					
❑ 4635	Ain't Life Hell/I'm Going With You This Time	1978	—	2.50	5.00
—With Willie Nelson					

DOT

❑ 17361	One Night for Willie/Back to His	1970	—	3.00	6.00

ELEKTRA

❑ 46596	Make the World Go Away/I Don't Do Windows	1980	—	2.00	4.00
❑ 47062	A Little Bitty Tear/He's Got You	1980	—	2.00	4.00

GAYLORD

❑ 6426	Yesterday's Memories/When You Gotta Go (You Gotta Go)	1963	3.00	6.00	12.00
❑ 6431	A Good Country Song/Same Old Hurt	1963	3.00	6.00	12.00
❑ 6432	Just for the Record/If She Could See Me Now	1963	3.00	6.00	12.00

LIBERTY

❑ 55402	Lonely Little Mansion/Has Anybody Seen Me Lately	1962	3.00	6.00	12.00
❑ 55461	Sally Was a Good Old Girl/The Picture Behind the Picture	1962	3.00	6.00	12.00
❑ 55498	I'd Fight the World/Lucy, Let Your Lovelight Shine	1962	3.00	6.00	12.00
❑ 55520	I Remember/Private John Q	1963	2.50	5.00	10.00
❑ 55644	Tootsie's Orchid Lounge/Go On Home	1963	2.50	5.00	10.00

MONUMENT

❑ 994	All of Me Belongs to You/I Just Burned a Dream	1967	—	3.00	6.00
❑ 1012	It Couldn't Happen to a Nicer Guy/Tootsie's Orchid Lounge	1967	—	3.00	6.00
❑ 1033	A Happy Goodbye/Speak Well of Me to the Kids	1967	—	3.00	6.00
❑ 1051	Has Anybody Seen Me Lately/I Woke Up	1968	—	3.00	6.00

RCA VICTOR

❑ 47-8329	My Baby's His Baby Now/What Kind of Bird Is That	1964	2.50	5.00	10.00
❑ 47-8457	I Want to Go with You/Sad Songs and Waltzes	1964	2.50	5.00	10.00
❑ 47-8528	Somewhere in My Dreams/Going in Training	1965	2.50	5.00	10.00
❑ 47-8616	Who's Gonna/Let's Be Different	1965	2.50	5.00	10.00
❑ 47-8694	Hank Today and Him Tomorrow/I'm Alone	1965	2.50	5.00	10.00
❑ 47-8827	The Crying Section/Only You Can Make Me Well	1966	2.00	4.00	8.00
❑ 47-8955	That's What I'll Say/I Lie a Lot	1966	2.00	4.00	8.00

Albums
CAPITOL

❑ ST-11807	With a Little Help from His Friends	1978	3.00	6.00	12.00

ELEKTRA

❑ 6E-277	Make the World Go Away	1980	2.50	5.00	10.00

MONUMENT

❑ SLP-18089	The Heart of Hank	1968	5.00	10.00	20.00

RCA VICTOR

❑ LPM-3303 [M]	Hits from the Heart	1965	5.00	10.00	20.00
❑ LSP-3303 [S]	Hits from the Heart	1965	6.25	12.50	25.00
❑ LPM-3431 [M]	Going in Training	1965	5.00	10.00	20.00
❑ LSP-3431 [S]	Going in Training	1965	6.25	12.50	25.00

COCHRAN, JACKIE LEE
45s
ABC-PARAMOUNT

❑ 9930	Buy a Car/I Want You	1958	20.00	40.00	80.00

DECCA

❑ 30206	Ruby Pearl/Mama Don't You Think I Know	1957	30.00	60.00	120.00

JAGUAR

❑ 3031	Georgia Lee Brown/I Wanna See You	1959	30.00	60.00	120.00

SIMS

❑ 107	Hip Shakin' Mama/Riverside Jump	1956	50.00	100.00	200.00

SPRY

❑ 120	Pity Me/Endless Love	1959	62.50	125.00	250.00

VIV

❑ 988	I Want You/Buy a Car	1958	37.50	75.00	150.00

COCHRAN, WAYNE
45s
BETHLEHEM

❑ 3097	Hey Jude/Eleanor Rigby	1970	—	3.00	6.00

CHESS

❑ 2020	When My Baby Cries/Some-a Your Sweet Lovin'	1967	2.00	4.00	8.00
❑ 2029	Get Ready/Hootchie Cootchie Man	1967	2.00	4.00	8.00
❑ 2054	You Can't Judge a Book By Its Cover/Up in My Mind	1968	2.00	4.00	8.00

EPIC

❑ 10859	Do You Like the Sound of Music/Everybody's Been Cuttin' In on My Groove	1972	—	2.50	5.00
❑ 10893	Long, Long Day/Sleepless Nights	1972	—	2.50	5.00

KING

❑ 5832	Little Orphan Annie/Monkey, Monkey	1963	3.00	6.00	12.00
❑ 5856	Last Kiss/I Dreamed, I Gambled, I Lost	1964	3.00	6.00	12.00
❑ 5874	Cindy Marie/The Coo	1964	3.00	6.00	12.00
❑ 5950	Mr. Lonely/Wrong Number, Wrong Gal	1964	3.00	6.00	12.00
❑ 5994	You Left the Water Running/Think	1965	3.00	6.00	12.00
❑ 6358	Let Me Come with You (Part 1)/Let Me Come with You (Part 2)	1971	—	3.00	6.00

MERCURY

❑ 72507	Harlem Shuffle/Somebody Please	1965	2.50	5.00	10.00
❑ 72552	Got Down with It/No Rest for the Wicked	1966	2.50	5.00	10.00
❑ 72623	Goin' Back to Miami/I'm in Trouble	1966	2.50	5.00	10.00

SCOTTIE

❑ 1303	My Little Girl/The Coo	1959	5.00	10.00	20.00

Albums
BETHLEHEM

❑ 10002	High and Ridin'	1970	3.75	7.50	15.00

CHESS

❑ LPS-1519	Wayne Cochran!	1968	10.00	20.00	40.00

EPIC

❑ KE 30889	Cochran	1972	3.75	7.50	15.00

KING

❑ KS-1116	Alive and Well	1970	5.00	10.00	20.00

COCHRAN BROTHERS EDDIE COCHRAN and HANK COCHRAN, who are not brothers.
45s
EKKO

❑ 1003	Mr. Fiddle/Two Blue Singing Stars	1955	62.50	125.00	250.00
❑ 1005	Guilty Conscience/Your Tomorrow Never Comes	1955	62.50	125.00	250.00
❑ 3001	Tired and Sleepy/Fool's Paradise	1956	75.00	150.00	300.00

COCKBURN, BRUCE
12-Inch Singles
GOLD MOUNTAIN

❑ GG-81209 [DJ]	Lovers in a Dangerous Time/Nicaragua	1984	3.00	6.00	12.00
❑ GG-81210 [DJ]	Lovers in a Dangerous Time (LP Version) (Live)	1984	3.00	6.00	12.00

MCA

❑ L33-17139 [DJ]	Call It Democracy (Edit) (same on both sides)	1986	3.00	6.00	12.00
❑ L33-17182 [DJ]	See How I Miss You (same on both sides)	1986	2.50	5.00	10.00
❑ L33-17203 [DJ]	People See Through You (same on both sides)	1986	2.50	5.00	10.00

MILLENNIUM

❑ JD-11822 [DJ]	Radio Shoes/(B-side blank)	1981	5.00	10.00	20.00
—With custom picture cover					

45s
GOLD MOUNTAIN

❑ 82009	Lovers in a Dangerous Time/Sahara Gold	1984	—	3.00	6.00
❑ 82013	If I Had a Rocket Launcher/Nicaragua	1984	—	3.00	6.00

MILLENNIUM

❑ YB-11786	Wondering Where the Lions Are/After the Rain	1979	—	2.00	4.00
❑ YB-11795	Rumours of Glory/You Get Bigger As You Go	1980	—	2.50	5.00
❑ YB-11798	Tokyo/Guerrilla Betrayed	1980	—	3.00	6.00
❑ YB-11806	The Coldest Night of the Year/Lord of the Starfields	1981	—	3.00	6.00
❑ YB-11820	Radio Shoes/(B-side unknown)	1981	—	3.00	6.00

Albums
EPIC

❑ E 30812	True North	1971	5.00	10.00	20.00
❑ KE 31768	Sunwheel Dance	1972	5.00	10.00	20.00

GOLD CASTLE

❑ D1-71320	Big Circumstance	1988	2.00	4.00	8.00
❑ 171005-1 [(2)]	Waiting for a Miracle	1987	3.00	6.00	12.00
❑ 171008-1	The Trouble with Normal	1987	2.00	4.00	8.00
—Reissue of Gold Mountain GM-3283					
❑ 171009-1	Dancing in the Dragon's Jaws	1987	2.00	4.00	8.00
—Reissue of Gold Mountain GM-3276					
❑ 171010-1	Stealing Fire	1987	2.00	4.00	8.00
—Reissue of Gold Mountain GM-80012					

GOLD MOUNTAIN

❑ GM-3276	Dancing in the Dragon's Jaws	1985	2.00	4.00	8.00
—Reissue of Millennium BXL1-7747					
❑ GM-3283	The Trouble with Normal	1985	2.00	4.00	8.00

C

Number	Title (A Side/B Side)	Yr	VG	VG+	NM
❏ GM-80012	Stealing Fire	1984	2.00	4.00	8.00
ISLAND					
❏ ILTN 9463	In the Falling Dark	1976	3.00	6.00	12.00
❏ ILTA 9475 [(2)]	Circles in the Stream	1977	3.75	7.50	15.00
❏ ILSP 9528	Furhter Adventures of	1978	3.00	6.00	12.00
MCA					
❏ 5772	World of Wonders	1986	2.00	4.00	8.00
MILLENNIUM					
❏ DJL1-(# unknown)	[DJ]Selected Cuts from 1980 U.S. Tour	1980	12.50	25.00	50.00
—Promo-only four-song live EP					
❏ DJL1-3583	[DJ]RCA Special Radio Series	1980	5.00	10.00	20.00
—Promo-only music and interview					
❏ DJL1-3830	[DJ]RCA College Radio Series, Vol. II	1980	5.00	10.00	20.00
—Promo-only music and interview					
❏ BXL1-7747	Dancing in the Dragon's Jaws	1979	2.50	5.00	10.00
❏ BXL1-7752	Humans	1980	2.50	5.00	10.00
❏ BXL1-7757	Resume	1981	2.50	5.00	10.00
❏ BXL1-7761	Inner City Front	1981	2.50	5.00	10.00

COCKER, JOE
12-Inch Singles
CAPITOL

Number	Title (A Side/B Side)	Yr	VG	VG+	NM
❏ SPRO-9144/5	[DJ]Civilized Man/Tempted	1984	2.00	4.00	8.00
❏ SPRO 9660	[DJ]You Can Leave Your Hat On (LP Version 4:14) (same on both sides)	1986	2.00	4.00	8.00
❏ V-15237	You Can Leave Your Hat On (Extended Dressed Mix 6:22) (Acacussion Mix 4:01) (LP Version 4:14)	1986	3.75	7.50	15.00
❏ SPRO 79246	[DJ]Two Wrongs (same on both sides)	1988	2.50	5.00	10.00

45s
A&M

Number	Title (A Side/B Side)	Yr	VG	VG+	NM
❏ 928	Marjorine/New Age of the Lily	1968	2.50	5.00	10.00
❏ 991	With a Little Help from My Friends/Something's Coming On	1968	2.50	5.00	10.00
❏ 1063	Feeling Alright/Sandpaper Cadillac	1969	—	3.00	6.00
—Reissued in 1971 with the same number					
❏ 1112	Delta Lady/She's So Good to Me	1969	—	2.50	5.00
❏ 1147	She Came In Through the Bathroom Window/Change in Louise	1969	—	2.50	5.00
❏ 1147 [PS]	She Came In Through the Bathroom Window/Change in Louise	1969	—	3.00	6.00
❏ 1174	The Letter/Space Captain	1970	—	2.50	5.00
❏ 1174 [PS]	The Letter/Space Captain	1970	—	3.00	6.00
❏ 1200	Cry Me a River/Give Peace a Chance	1970	—	2.50	5.00
❏ 1200	Cry Me a River/Please Give Peace a Chance	1970	—	2.50	5.00
❏ 1200 [PS]	Cry Me a River/Give Peace a Chance	1970	—	3.00	6.00
❏ 1258	High Time We Went/Black-Eyed Blues	1971	—	2.00	4.00
❏ 1258 [PS]	High Time We Went/Black-Eyed Blues	1971	—	3.00	6.00
❏ 1370	Midnight Rider/Woman to Woman	1972	—	2.00	4.00
❏ 1370 [PS]	Midnight Rider/Woman to Woman	1972	—	3.00	6.00
❏ 1407	Pardon Me Sir/St. James Infirmary Blues	1973	—	2.00	4.00
❏ 1407 [PS]	Pardon Me Sir/St. James Infirmary Blues	1973	—	3.00	6.00
❏ 1539	Put Out the Light/If I Love You	1974	—	2.00	4.00
❏ 1539 [PS]	Put Out the Light/If I Love You	1974	—	3.00	6.00
❏ 1626	I Can Stand a Little Rain/I Get Mad	1974	—	2.00	4.00
❏ 1641	You Are So Beautiful/It's a Sin When You Love Somebody	1974	—	2.00	4.00
❏ 1749	I Think It's Going to Rain Today/Oh Mama	1975	—	2.00	4.00
❏ 1758	Jamaica Say You Will/It's All Over But the Shoutin'	1975	—	2.00	4.00
❏ 1805	The Man in Me (Part 1)/The Man in Me (Part 2)	1976	—	2.00	4.00
❏ 1830	Jealous Kind/You Came Along	1976	—	2.00	4.00
❏ 1855	I Broke Down/You Came Along	1976	—	2.00	4.00
❏ 2019	Feeling Alright/Cry Me a River	1978	—	2.00	4.00
ASYLUM					
❏ 45540	Fun Time/Watching the River Flow	1978	—	2.00	4.00
❏ 46001	Lady Put the Light Out/Wasted Years	1978	—	2.00	4.00
CAPITOL					
❏ B-5338	Civilized Man/A Girl Like You	1984	—	—	3.00
❏ B-5338 [PS]	Civilized Man/A Girl Like You	1984	—	2.00	4.00
❏ B-5390	Crazy in Love/Come On In	1984	—	—	3.00
❏ B-5412	Edge of a Dream/Tempted	1984	—	—	3.00
❏ B-5412 [PS]	Edge of a Dream/Tempted	1984	—	2.00	4.00
❏ B-5557	Shelter Me/Tell Me There's a Way	1986	—	—	3.00
❏ B-5589	You Can Leave Your Hat On/Long Drag of the Cigarette	1986	—	2.50	5.00
❏ B-5589 [PS]	You Can Leave Your Hat On/Long Drag of the Cigarette	1986	—	3.00	6.00
❏ B-5626	Don't Drink the Water/Don't You Love Me Anymore	1986	—	—	3.00
❏ S7-18124	The Simple Things/Unchain My Heart (90's Version)	1994	—	—	3.00
—White vinyl					
❏ B-44072	Unchain My Heart/Satisfied	1987	—	—	3.00
❏ B-44072 [PS]	Unchain My Heart/Satisfied	1987	—	—	3.00
❏ B-44101	Two Wrongs (Don't Make a Right)/Isolation	1987	—	—	3.00
❏ B-44182	A Woman Loves a Man/La Vie En Rose	1988	—	—	3.00
—B-side by Edith Piaf					
❏ B-44182 [PS]	A Woman Loves a Man/La Vie En Rose	1988	—	—	3.00
❏ NR-44590	Living in the Promiseland/She Came In Through the Bathroom Window (Live)	1990	—	2.00	4.00
❏ S7-57988	Feels Like Forever/When the Night Comes	1992	—	—	3.00
❏ 7PRO-79025	[DJ]What Are You Doing with a Fool Like Me (same on both sides)	1990	—	2.50	5.00
—Vinyl is promo only					
❏ 7PRO-79711	[DJ]When the Night Comes (same on both sides)	1989	—	2.50	5.00
—Vinyl is promo only					
ISLAND					
❏ 99875	Throw It Away/Easy Rider	1983	—	2.00	4.00
MCA					
❏ 51177	I'm So Glad I'm Standing Here Today/Standing Tall	1981	—	2.00	4.00
—With the Crusaders					
❏ 51222	This Old World's Too Funky for Me/Standing Tall	1981	—	2.00	4.00
—With the Crusaders					
❏ 53077	Love Lives On/On My Way to You	1987	—	2.00	4.00
❏ 53077 [PS]	Love Lives On/On My Way to You	1987	—	2.00	4.00

Number	Title (A Side/B Side)	Yr	VG	VG+	NM
PHILIPS					
❏ 40255	I'll Cry Instead/Precious Words	1965	10.00	20.00	40.00
—Artist listed as "Joe Cocker"					
❏ 40255	I'll Cry Instead/Precious Words	1965	10.00	20.00	40.00
—Originally by "Vance Arnold and the Avengers"					
THE RIGHT STUFF					
❏ S7-19857	Human Touch/One Step Up	1998	—	—	3.00
—B-side by Paul Cebar					

Albums
A&M

Number	Title (A Side/B Side)	Yr	VG	VG+	NM
❏ SP-3106	With a Little Help from My Friends	1980	2.00	4.00	8.00
❏ SP-3175	I Can Stand a Little Rain	1980	2.00	4.00	8.00
❏ SP-3257	Joe Cocker's Greatest Hits	1982	2.00	4.00	8.00
❏ SP-3633	I Can Stand a Little Rain	1974	2.50	5.00	10.00
❏ SP-4182	With a Little Help from My Friends	1969	3.00	6.00	12.00
—Brown label					
❏ SP-4182	With a Little Help from My Friends	1974	2.50	5.00	10.00
—Silver label					
❏ SP-4224	Joe Cocker!	1969	3.00	6.00	12.00
—Brown label					
❏ SP-4224	Joe Cocker!	1974	2.50	5.00	10.00
—Silver label					
❏ SP-4368	Joe Cocker	1972	3.00	6.00	12.00
—Brown label					
❏ SP-4368	Joe Cocker	1974	2.50	5.00	10.00
—Silver label					
❏ SP-4529	Jamaica Say You Will	1975	2.50	5.00	10.00
❏ SP-4574	Stingray	1976	2.50	5.00	10.00
❏ SP-4670	Joe Cocker's Greatest Hits	1977	2.50	5.00	10.00
❏ SP-6002 [(2)]	Mad Dogs and Englishmen	1970	3.75	7.50	15.00
—Brown labels					
❏ SP-6002 [(2)]	Mad Dogs and Englishmen	1974	3.00	6.00	12.00
—Silver labels					
❏ QU-54182 [Q]	With a Little Help from My Friends	1974	—	—	—
—Not released					
❏ QU-54224 [Q]	Joe Cocker!	1974	—	—	—
—Not released					
ASYLUM					
❏ 6E-145	Luxury You Can Afford	1978	2.50	5.00	10.00
❏ DP-400 [PD]	Luxury You Can Afford	1978	3.75	7.50	15.00
CAPITOL					
❏ ST-12335	Civilized Man	1984	2.50	5.00	10.00
❏ ST-12394	Cocker	1986	2.50	5.00	10.00
❏ CLT-48285	Unchain My Heart	1988	2.50	5.00	10.00
❏ C1-92861	One Night of Sin	1989	3.00	6.00	12.00
ISLAND					
❏ IL 9750	Sheffield Steel	1982	2.50	5.00	10.00
❏ 90096	One More Time	1983	2.50	5.00	10.00
MOBILE FIDELITY					
❏ 1-223	Sheffield Steel	1995	10.00	20.00	40.00
—Audiophile vinyl					

COCKER, JOE, AND JENNIFER WARNES Also see each artist's individual listings.
45s
ISLAND

Number	Title (A Side/B Side)	Yr	VG	VG+	NM
❏ 99996	Up Where We Belong/Sweet Li'l Woman	1982	—	2.00	4.00
❏ 99996 [PS]	Up Where We Belong/Sweet Li'l Woman	1982	—	2.00	4.00

COE, DAVID ALLAN
45s
COLUMBIA

Number	Title (A Side/B Side)	Yr	VG	VG+	NM
❏ 11-02118	Tennessee Whiskey/The Bottle (In My Hand)	1981	—	2.00	4.00
❏ 18-02492	(Sittin' On) The Dock of the Bay/I Love Robbin's Trains	1981	—	2.00	4.00
❏ 18-02612	Juanita/I'll Always Be a Fool for You	1981	—	2.00	4.00
❏ 18-02678	Now I Lay Me Down to Cheat/If I Knew	1981	—	2.00	4.00
❏ 18-02815	Take Time to Know Her/London Homesick Blues	1982	—	2.00	4.00
❏ 18-03022	What Made You Change Your Mind/Pouring Water on a Drowning Man	1982	—	2.00	4.00
❏ 13-03129	Jack Daniel's, If You Please/Tennessee Whiskey	1982	—	—	3.00
—Hall of Fame Series reissue					
❏ 38-03343	Whiskey, Whiskey (Take My Mind)/Those Low Down Blues	1982	—	2.00	4.00
❏ 38-03778	The Ride/Son of a Rebel Son	1983	—	2.00	4.00
❏ 38-03997	Cheap Thrills/You Never Even Call Me by My Name	1983	—	2.00	4.00
❏ 38-03997 [PS]	Cheap Thrills/You Never Even Call Me by My Name	1983	—	3.00	6.00
❏ 38-04136	Crazy Old Soldier/Drinkin' to Forget	1983	—	2.00	4.00
❏ 38-04396	Mona Lisa Lost Her Smile/Someone Special	1984	—	2.00	4.00
❏ 38-04553	It's Great to Be Single Again/Sweet Angeline	1984	—	2.00	4.00
❏ 38-04688	She Used to Love Me a Lot/For Lovers Only (Part IV)	1984	—	2.00	4.00
❏ 38-04846	Don't Cry Darlin'/You're the Only Song I Sing Today	1985	—	2.00	4.00
❏ 38-05451	My Elusive Dreams/Call Me the Breeze	1985	—	2.00	4.00
❏ 38-05631	I'm Gonna Hurt Her on the Radio/He Has to Pay (For What I Get for Free)	1985	—	2.00	4.00
❏ 38-05876	A Country Boy (Who Rolled the Rock Away)/Take My Advice	1986	—	2.00	4.00
❏ 38-06227	I've Already Cheated on You/Take My Advice	1986	—	2.00	4.00
—A-side with Willie Nelson					
❏ 38-06346	Son of the South/Gemini Girl	1986	—	2.00	4.00
❏ 38-06661	Need a Little Time Off for Bad Behavior/It's a Matter of Life and Death	1987	—	2.00	4.00
❏ 38-07129	Tanya Montana/The Ten Commandments of Love	1987	—	2.00	4.00
❏ 38-08527	Love Is a Never Ending War/Action Speaks Louder Than Words	1989	—	2.00	4.00
❏ 3-10024	(If I Could Climb) The Walls of the Bottle/Another Pretty Country Song	1974	—	2.50	5.00
❏ 3-10093	Would You Be My Lady/Rock and Roll Holiday	1975	—	2.50	5.00
❏ 3-10159	You Never Even Called Me By My Name/Would You Lay with Me (In a Field of Stone)	1975	—	3.00	6.00
❏ 3-10254	Longhaired Redneck/Family Reunion	1975	—	2.50	5.00
❏ 3-10323	When She's Got Me (Where She Wants Me)/Living on the Run	1976	—	2.50	5.00

Number	Title (A Side/B Side)	Yr	VG	VG+	NM
☐ 3-10395	Willie, Waylon and Me/Please Come to Boston	1976	—	2.50	5.00
☐ 3-10475	Lately I've Been Thinking Too Much Lately/ Under Rachel's Wings	1977	—	2.50	5.00
☐ 3-10583	Just to Prove My Love for You/Play Me a Sad Song	1977	—	2.50	5.00
☐ 3-10621	Face to Face/Play Me a Sad Song	1977	—	2.50	5.00
☐ 3-10701	Divers Do It Deeper/Million Dollar Memories	1978	—	2.50	5.00
☐ 3-10753	You Can Count on Me/Bad Impressions	1978	—	2.50	5.00
☐ 3-10816	If This Is Just a Game/Tomorrow's Another Day	1978	—	2.50	5.00
☐ 3-10860	Bright Morning Light/Suicide	1978	—	2.50	5.00
☐ 3-10911	Jack Daniel's, If You Please/Human Emotions	1979	—	2.50	5.00
☐ 1-11098	X's and O's (Kisses and Hugs)/Gone (Like)	1979	—	2.50	5.00
☐ 1-11167	Loving You Comes So Natural/Lost	1979	—	2.50	5.00
—With Johnny Rodriguez					
☐ 1-11230	The Great Nashville Railroad Disaster (True Story)/Take It Easy Rider	1980	—	2.50	5.00
☐ 1-11277	Get a Little Dirt on Your Hands/What Can I Do	1980	—	2.50	5.00
—A-side with Bill Anderson					
☐ 1-11352	Hank Williams Jr., Jr./I've Got Something to Say	1980	—	2.50	5.00
☐ 4-46012	Sad Country Song/Atlantic Song	1974	—	3.00	6.00
☐ 11-60501	Stand By Your Man/Take This Job and Shove It	1981	—	2.00	4.00
KAT FAMILY					
☐ ZS4-04258	Ride 'Em Cowboy/Yesterday's Wine	1983	—	2.00	4.00
PLANTATION					
☐ 99	How High's the Watergate, Martha/Tricky Dicky, The Only Son of King Fu	1973	2.00	4.00	8.00
☐ 104	Keep Those Big Wheels Rolling/Memphis in My Blood	1973	2.00	4.00	8.00
SSS INTERNATIONAL					
☐ 804	Penitentiary Blues/Monkey David Wine	1971	—	—	—
—Canceled					
☐ 825	Tobacco Road/Death Row	1971	2.50	5.00	10.00
☐ 864	Two-Tone Brown/Funeral Parlor Blues	1972	2.50	5.00	10.00
Albums					
COLUMBIA					
☐ KC 32942	Mysterious Rhinestone Cowboy	1974	3.00	6.00	12.00
☐ PC 32942	Mysterious Rhinestone Cowboy	197?	2.50	5.00	10.00
—Early reissue with new prefix and no bar code					
☐ KC 33085	Once Upon a Rhyme	1975	3.00	6.00	12.00
☐ PC 33085	Once Upon a Rhyme	197?	2.50	5.00	10.00
—Early reissue with new prefix and no bar code					
☐ PC 33916	Longhaired Redneck	1976	2.50	5.00	10.00
☐ PC 34310	David Allan Coe Rides Again	1977	2.50	5.00	10.00
☐ PC 34780	Tattoo	1977	2.50	5.00	10.00
☐ KC 35306	Family Album	1978	2.50	5.00	10.00
☐ KC 35535	Human Emotions — Happy Side/Su-I-Side	1978	2.50	5.00	10.00
☐ KC 35627	Greatest Hits	1978	2.50	5.00	10.00
☐ PC 35627	Greatest Hits	198?	2.00	4.00	8.00
—Budget-line reissue					
☐ KC 35789	Spectrum, VII	1979	2.50	5.00	10.00
☐ JC 36277	Compass Point	1980	2.50	5.00	10.00
☐ PC 36277	Compass Point	198?	2.00	4.00	8.00
—Budget-line reissue with new prefix					
☐ JC 36489	I've Got Something to Say	1980	2.50	5.00	10.00
☐ PC 36489	I've Got Something to Say	198?	2.00	4.00	8.00
—Budget-line reissue with new prefix					
☐ JC 36970	Invictus (Means) Unconquered	1981	2.50	5.00	10.00
☐ PC 36970	Invictus (Means) Unconquered	198?	2.00	4.00	8.00
—Budget-line reissue with new prefix					
☐ FC 37352	Encore	1981	2.50	5.00	10.00
☐ PC 37352	Encore	198?	2.00	4.00	8.00
—Budget-line reissue with new prefix					
☐ FC 37454	Tennessee Whiskey	1981	2.50	5.00	10.00
☐ PC 37454	Tennessee Whiskey	198?	2.00	4.00	8.00
—Budget-line reissue with new prefix					
☐ FC 37736	Rough Rider	1982	2.50	5.00	10.00
☐ PC 37736	Rough Rider	198?	2.00	4.00	8.00
—Budget-line reissue with new prefix					
☐ FC 38093	D.A.C.	1982	2.50	5.00	10.00
☐ FC 38318	Biggest Hits	1982	2.50	5.00	10.00
☐ FC 38535	Castles in the Sand	1983	2.50	5.00	10.00
☐ PC 38535	Castles in the Sand	1985	2.00	4.00	8.00
—Budget-line reissue with new prefix					
☐ FC 38926	Hello In There	1983	2.50	5.00	10.00
☐ FC 39269	Just Divorced	1984	2.50	5.00	10.00
☐ PC 39269	Just Divorced	1986	2.00	4.00	8.00
—Budget-line reissue with new prefix					
☐ KC2 39585 [(2)]	For the Record — The First 10 Years	1984	3.00	6.00	12.00
☐ FC 39617	Darlin', Darlin'	1985	2.50	5.00	10.00
☐ FC 40195	Unchained	1985	2.50	5.00	10.00
☐ FC 40346	Son of the South	1986	2.50	5.00	10.00
☐ FC 40571	A Matter of Life... And Death	1987	2.50	5.00	10.00
☐ FC 45057	Crazy Daddy	1989	2.50	5.00	10.00
PAIR					
☐ PDL2-1075 [(2)]	Best of David Allan Coe	1986	3.00	6.00	12.00
PLANTATION					
☐ 507	Texas Moon	197?	3.75	7.50	15.00
SSS INTERNATIONAL					
☐ 9	Penitentiary Blues	1977	20.00	40.00	80.00
COE, JAMIE					
45s					
ABC-PARAMOUNT					
☐ 10120	Goodbye, My Love, Goodbye/There's Never Been a Night	1960	5.00	10.00	20.00
☐ 10149	The Story of Jesse James/Say You	1960	5.00	10.00	20.00
☐ 10203	I'm Gettin' Married/Two Dozen and a Half	1961	5.00	10.00	20.00
☐ 10267	How Low Is Low/Little Darling, Little Darling	1961	5.00	10.00	20.00
ADDISON					
☐ 15001	Summertime Symphony/There's Gonna Be a Day	1959	5.00	10.00	20.00
☐ 15003	I'll Go On Loving You/School Day Blues	1959	5.00	10.00	20.00
BIG TOP					
☐ 3107	Cleopatra/But Yesterday	1962	5.00	10.00	20.00
☐ 3139	The Fool/I've Got That Feeling Again	1963	5.00	10.00	20.00
CAMEO					
☐ 424	Greenback Dollar/But Yesterday	1966	3.75	7.50	15.00

Number	Title (A Side/B Side)	Yr	VG	VG+	NM
ENTERPRISE					
☐ 5005	The Dealer/Close Your Eyes	1964	3.00	6.00	12.00
☐ 5050	My Girl/I Cried on My Pillow	1964	3.00	6.00	12.00
☐ 5055	Good Enough for a King/I Was the One	1965	3.00	6.00	12.00
☐ 5070	The One Who Really Loves You/A Long Time Ago	1965	—	6.00	12.00
☐ 5080	Greenback Dollar/But Yesterday	1965	5.00	10.00	20.00
☐ 5095	First Girl/Very Few	1966	3.75	7.50	15.00
REPRISE					
☐ 0295	Close Your Eyes/The Dealer	1964	3.00	6.00	12.00
COFFEE, RED					
45s					
WARNER BROS.					
☐ 5128	Ducky Christmas/Jolly Jingle Bells	1959	3.75	7.50	15.00
COFFEY, DENNIS					
12-Inch Singles					
WESTBOUND					
☐ DSKO 117 [DJ]	Calling Planet Earth (5:06) (same on both sides)	1978	3.00	6.00	12.00
45s					
SUSSEX					
☐ 208	Getting It On/Summertime Girl	1970	—	2.50	5.00
☐ 226	Scorpio/Sad Angel	1971	—	2.50	5.00
☐ 233	Taurus/Can You Feel It	1972	—	2.50	5.00
☐ 237	Ride, Sally, Ride/Getting It On	1972	—	2.50	5.00
☐ 251	Capricorn's Thing/Lonely Moon Child	1973	—	2.50	5.00
☐ 511	Theme from "Enter the Dragon"/Junction Flats	1973	—	2.50	5.00
☐ 631	Getting It On '75/Chicano	1974	—	2.50	5.00
WARNER BROS.					
☐ 7769	Theme from "Black Belt Jones"/Love Theme from "Black Belt Jones"	1974	—	2.50	5.00
WESTBOUND					
☐ 5020	Finger Lickin' Good/Wild Child	1975	—	2.00	4.00
☐ 5028	Honky Tonk/El Tigre	1976	—	2.00	4.00
☐ 55402	Our Love Goes On Forever/Back Home	1977	—	2.00	4.00
☐ 55414	Calling Planet Earth/A Sweet Taste of Sin	1978	—	2.00	4.00
Albums					
ORPHEUS					
☐ D1-75617	Under the Moonlight	1989	3.00	6.00	12.00
SUSSEX					
☐ SUX-7004	Evolution	1971	3.00	6.00	12.00
☐ SUX-7010	Goin' for Myself	1972	3.00	6.00	12.00
☐ SUX-7021	Electric Coffey	1972	3.00	6.00	12.00
☐ SUX-8031	Instant Coffey	1974	3.00	6.00	12.00
WESTBOUND					
☐ W-212	Finger Lickin' Good	1975	2.50	5.00	10.00
☐ WD 300	Home	1977	2.50	5.00	10.00
☐ 6105	The Sweet Taste of Sin	1978	2.50	5.00	10.00
COGAN, ALMA					
45s					
AMERICAN ARTS					
☐ 4	I Love You Much Too Much/Tennessee Waltz	1964	2.50	5.00	10.00
CAPITOL					
☐ F4170	Mama Says/Last Night on the Back Porch	1959	3.00	6.00	12.00
☐ 4547	Cowboy Jimmy Joe/Just Couldn't Resist Her with Her Pocket Transistor	1961	3.00	6.00	12.00
LAURIE					
☐ TL 18	Snakes Snails and Puppy Dog Tails/How Many Days How Many Nights	1965	2.50	5.00	10.00
RCA VICTOR					
☐ 47-6063	Blue Again/Paper Kisses	1955	3.75	7.50	15.00
☐ 47-6236	Got N' Idea/Give a Fool a Chance	1955	3.75	7.50	15.00
☐ 47-6405	Twenty Tiny Fingers/Never Do a Tango with an Eskimo	1956	3.00	6.00	12.00
☐ 47-6573	Willie Can/Pickin' a Chicken	1956	3.00	6.00	12.00
COHEN, LEONARD					
45s					
COLUMBIA					
☐ 44439	Suzanne/Hey, That's No Way to Say Goodbye	1968	—	3.00	6.00
☐ 44827	Bird on the Wire/Seems So Long Ago (Nancy)	1969	—	3.00	6.00
☐ 45852	Nancy/Passing Thru	1973	—	2.50	5.00
Albums					
COLUMBIA					
☐ CL 2733 [M]	Leonard Cohen	1967	6.25	12.50	25.00
☐ CS 9533 [S]	Leonard Cohen	1967	3.00	6.00	12.00
—Red "360 Sound" label					
☐ CS 9533 [S]	Leonard Cohen	1970	2.50	5.00	10.00
—Orange label					
☐ PC 9533	Leonard Cohen	198?	2.00	4.00	8.00
—Reissue with new prefix					
☐ CS 9767	Songs From a Room	1969	3.00	6.00	12.00
—Red "360 Sound" label					
☐ CS 9767	Songs From a Room	1970	2.50	5.00	10.00
—Orange label					
☐ PC 9767	Songs From a Room	198?	2.00	4.00	8.00
—Reissue with new prefix					
☐ C 30103	Songs of Love and Hate	1971	3.00	6.00	12.00
☐ PC 30103	Songs of Love and Hate	198?	2.00	4.00	8.00
—Budget-line reissue					
☐ KC 31724	Leonard Cohen: Live Songs	1973	3.00	6.00	12.00
☐ KC 33167	New Skin for the Old Ceremony	1974	3.00	6.00	12.00
☐ PC 34077	The Best of Leonard Cohen	1975	2.50	5.00	10.00
—No bar code					
☐ PC 34077	The Best of Leonard Cohen	198?	2.00	4.00	8.00
—Reissue with bar code					
☐ JC 36264	Recent Songs	1979	2.50	5.00	10.00
☐ PC 36264	Recent Songs	198?	2.00	4.00	8.00
—Budget-line reissue					
☐ FC 44191	I'm Your Man	1988	2.50	5.00	10.00
PASSPORT					
☐ PB-6045	Various Positions	1985	2.50	5.00	10.00
WARNER BROS.					
☐ BSK 3125	Death of a Ladies' Man	1977	2.50	5.00	10.00

Number	Title (A Side/B Side)	Yr	VG	VG+	NM
COHEN, MYRON					
45s					
CORAL					
❏ 61280	Mr. and Mrs./Soup and Fish	1954	3.00	6.00	12.00
Albums					
AUDIO FIDELITY					
❏ 701 [M]	Myron Cohen	196?	5.00	10.00	20.00
RCA VICTOR					
❏ LPM-3534 [M]	Everybody Gotta Be Someplace	1966	3.00	6.00	12.00
❏ LSP-3534 [S]	Everybody Gotta Be Someplace	1966	3.75	7.50	15.00
❏ LPM-3791 [M]	It's Not a Question	1967	3.00	6.00	12.00
❏ LSP-3791 [S]	It's Not a Question	1967	3.75	7.50	15.00
❏ VPS-6052 [(2)]	This Is Myron Cohen	1972	3.75	7.50	15.00
COINS, THE					
45s					
GEE					
❏ 10	Cheatin' Baby/Blue, Can't Get No Place with You	1954	500.00	1000.	2000.
❏ 11	Look at Me Girl/S.R. Blues	1954	500.00	1000.	2000.
❏ 1007	Look at Me Girl/Two Loves Have I	1956	150.00	300.00	600.00
—B-side by the Colonials					
MODEL					
❏ 2001	Loretta/Please	1955	500.00	1000.	2000.
COLD BLOOD					
45s					
ABC					
❏ 12173	I Get Off on You/We Came Down Here	1976	—	2.00	4.00
—As "Lydia Pense and Cold Blood"					
REPRISE					
❏ 1092	Down to the Bone/Valdes in the Country	1972	—	2.50	5.00
❏ 1157	Baby I Love You/Livin' Your Dream	1973	—	2.50	5.00
SAN FRANCISCO					
❏ 60	You Got Me Hummin'/If You Will	1970	—	3.00	6.00
❏ 61	I Wish I Knew How It Would Feel to Be Free/I'ma Good Woman	1970	—	3.00	6.00
❏ 62	Too Many People/I Can't Stay	1970	—	3.00	6.00
❏ 66	Understanding/Shop Talk	1971	—	3.00	6.00
Albums					
ABC					
❏ D-917	Lydia Pense and Cold Blood	1976	2.50	5.00	10.00
REPRISE					
❏ MS 2074	First Taste of Sin	1972	3.00	6.00	12.00
❏ MS 2130	Thriller!	1973	3.00	6.00	12.00
SAN FRANCISCO					
❏ SD 200	Cold Blood	1969	5.00	10.00	20.00
❏ SD 205	Sisyphus	1970	5.00	10.00	20.00
WARNER BROS.					
❏ BS 2806	Lydia	1974	2.50	5.00	10.00
COLDER, BEN See SHEB WOOLEY.					
COLE, ANN					
45s					
BATON					
❏ 218	Are You Satisfied?/Darling Don't Hurt Me	1955	5.00	10.00	20.00
❏ 224	Easy Easy Baby/New Love	1956	5.00	10.00	20.00
❏ 229	I'm Waiting for You/My Tearful Heart	1956	5.00	10.00	20.00
❏ 232	In the Chapel/Each Day	1956	6.25	12.50	25.00
❏ 237	Got My Mo-Jo Working/I've Got a Little Boy	1957	10.00	20.00	40.00
❏ 243	You're Mine/No Star Is Lost	1957	5.00	10.00	20.00
❏ 247	Give Me Love or Nothing/I've Got Nothing Working Now	1957	5.00	10.00	20.00
❏ 258	Love in My Heart/Summer Nights	1958	5.00	10.00	20.00
MGM					
❏ 12954	In the Chapel/Plain As the Nose on Your Face	1960	3.75	7.50	15.00
ROULETTE					
❏ 4452	Don't Stop the Wedding/Have Fun	1962	3.75	7.50	15.00
SIR					
❏ 272	Nobody But Me/That's Enough	1959	3.75	7.50	15.00
❏ 275	A Love of My Own/Brand New House	1960	3.75	7.50	15.00
TIMELY					
❏ 1006	Danny Boy/Smilin' Through	1954	6.25	12.50	25.00
❏ 1007	I'll Find a Way/Oh Love of Mine	1954	6.25	12.50	25.00
❏ 1010	So Proud of You/Down in the Valley	1955	6.25	12.50	25.00
COLE, COZY					
45s					
BETHLEHEM					
❏ 3067	Big Boss/Cozy and Bossa	1963	2.00	4.00	8.00
COLUMBIA					
❏ 43657	Whole Lotta Shakin' Goin' On/Watch It	1966	2.00	4.00	8.00
CORAL					
❏ 62339	Big Noise from Winnetka (Part 1)/Big Noise from Winnetka (Part 2)	1962	2.00	4.00	8.00
❏ 62379	Rockin' Drummer/Sing, Sing, Sing (With a Swing)	1963	2.00	4.00	8.00
—With Gary Chester					
❏ 62395	Ol' Man Moses/Christopher Columbus	1964	2.00	4.00	8.00
❏ 62417	Cozy Beat/Night Beach	1964	2.00	4.00	8.00
FELSTED					
❏ 8546	Caravan Part 1/Caravan Part 2	1959	2.50	5.00	10.00
GRAND AWARD					
❏ 1023	Caravan Part 1/Caravan Part 2	1959	3.00	6.00	12.00
KING					
❏ 5222	Blow-Up/Flop-Down	1959	2.50	5.00	10.00
❏ 5242	Strange/D Natural Rock	1959	2.50	5.00	10.00
❏ 5254	Melody of a Dreamer/Soft	1959	2.50	5.00	10.00
❏ 5265	Boy Meets Girl/Playtime Blues	1959	2.50	5.00	10.00
—With Lee Parker					
❏ 5287	Stain Glass/D'Mitri	1959	2.50	5.00	10.00
❏ 5303	Play, Cozy, Play/Cozy's Mambo	1960	2.50	5.00	10.00
❏ 5316	Blockhead/Teen-Age Ideas	1960	2.50	5.00	10.00
❏ 5337	Drum Fever/Bag of Tricks	1960	2.50	5.00	10.00
❏ 5363	Cozy's Corner/Red Ball	1960	2.50	5.00	10.00
❏ 5390	Ha Ha Cha-Cha/The Pogo Hop	1960	2.50	5.00	10.00

Number	Title (A Side/B Side)	Yr	VG	VG+	NM
LOVE					
❏ 5003/4	Topsy I/Topsy II	1958	3.75	7.50	15.00
❏ 5014	Turvy I/Turvy II	1958	3.00	6.00	12.00
MERCURY					
❏ 71385	St. Louis Blues/Father Cooperates	1958	3.00	6.00	12.00
MGM					
❏ 11794	Hound Dog Special/Terrible Sight	1954	3.00	6.00	12.00
Albums					
AUDITION					
❏ 33-5943 [M]	Cozy Cole	1955	12.50	25.00	50.00
BETHLEHEM					
❏ BCP-21 [M]	Jazz at the Metropole Café	1955	12.50	25.00	50.00
CHARLIE PARKER					
❏ PLP-403 [M]	A Cozy Conaption of Carmen	1962	5.00	10.00	20.00
❏ PLP-403S [S]	A Cozy Conaption of Carmen	1962	6.25	12.50	25.00
COLUMBIA					
❏ CL 2553 [M]	It's a Rockin' Thing	1965	3.75	7.50	15.00
❏ CS 9353 [S]	It's a Rockin' Thing	1965	5.00	10.00	20.00
CORAL					
❏ CRL 57423 [M]	Drum Beat Dancing Feet	1962	3.75	7.50	15.00
❏ CRL 57457 [M]	It's a Cozy World	1964	3.75	7.50	15.00
❏ CRL 757423 [S]	Drum Beat Dancing Feet	1962	5.00	10.00	20.00
❏ CRL 757457 [S]	It's a Cozy World	1964	5.00	10.00	20.00
FELSTED					
❏ 2002 [S]	Cozy's Caravan/Earl's Backroom	1958	10.00	20.00	40.00
❏ 7002 [M]	Cozy's Caravan/Earl's Backroom	1958	12.50	25.00	50.00
GRAND AWARD					
❏ GA 33-334 [M]	After Hours	1956	10.00	20.00	40.00
KING					
❏ 673 [M]	Cozy Cole	1959	15.00	30.00	60.00
❏ KS-673 [S]	Cozy Cole	1959	37.50	75.00	150.00
LOVE					
❏ 500M [M]	Topsy	1959	25.00	50.00	100.00
❏ 500S [S]	Topsy	1959	50.00	100.00	200.00
PARIS					
❏ 122 [M]	Cozy Cole and His All-Stars	1958	12.50	25.00	50.00
PLYMOUTH					
❏ P 12-155 [M]	Cozy Cole and His All Stars	195?	7.50	15.00	30.00
SAVOY					
❏ MG-12197 [M]	Concerto for Cozy	196?	5.00	10.00	20.00
WHO'S WHO IN JAZZ					
❏ 21003	Lionel Hampton Presents Cozy Cole & Marty Napoleon	1977	2.50	5.00	10.00
COLE, COZY/JIMMY MCPARTLAND					
Albums					
WALDORF MUSIC HALL					
❏ MH 33-162 [10]	After Hours	195?	12.50	25.00	50.00
COLE, DON					
45s					
COED					
❏ 548	Free Flight/Squad Car	1961	5.00	10.00	20.00
GUYDEN					
❏ 2059	Lie Detector Machine/Born to Be with You	1961	25.00	50.00	100.00
KENT					
❏ 305	Saturday Night Party Time/Sweet Lovin' Honey	1958	20.00	40.00	80.00
RPM					
❏ 502	Snake Eyed Mama/Kiss of Love	1957	50.00	100.00	200.00
—With Al Casey					
COLE, JERRY					
45s					
CAPITOL					
❏ 5056	Midnight Mary/Land of Dreams	1963	3.00	6.00	12.00
❏ 5106	Pokey/One Color Blues	1964	2.50	5.00	10.00
❏ 5141	Night Rumble/Boss Dance	1964	2.50	5.00	10.00
❏ 5265	Meet Me on the Corner/Life Will Go On	1964	2.50	5.00	10.00
❏ 5394	Every Window in the City/Come On Over to My Place	1965	2.50	5.00	10.00
Albums					
BEAT ROCKET					
❏ BR 117	Guitars A-Go-Go!	2000	3.00	6.00	12.00
❏ BR 118	Wild Strings!	2001	3.00	6.00	12.00
CAPITOL					
❏ ST 2044 [S]	Outer Limits	1963	20.00	40.00	80.00
❏ T 2044 [M]	Outer Limits	1963	12.50	25.00	50.00
❏ (S)T 2061	Hot Rod Dance Party Bonus Photo	1964	6.25	12.50	25.00
❏ ST 2061 [S]	Hot Rod Dance Party	1964	25.00	50.00	100.00
❏ T 2061 [M]	Hot Rod Dance Party	1964	20.00	40.00	80.00
❏ ST 2112 [S]	Surf Age	1964	25.00	50.00	100.00
—With bonus single missing					
❏ ST 2112 [S]	Surf Age	1964	30.00	60.00	120.00
—With bonus single by Dick Dale, "Thunder Wave"/"Spanish Kiss"					
❏ T 2112 [M]	Surf Age	1964	20.00	40.00	80.00
—With bonus single missing					
❏ T 2112 [M]	Surf Age	1964	25.00	50.00	100.00
—With bonus single by Dick Dale, "Thunder Wave"/"Spanish Kiss"					
LIBERTY					
❏ LRP-3362 [M]	Sounds of the Big Irons	1964	12.50	25.00	50.00
❏ LST-7362 [S]	Sounds of the Big Irons	1964	15.00	30.00	60.00
COLE, NAT KING Includes reissues of material by the King Cole Trio.					
45s					
AMERICAN PIE					
❏ 9067	The Christmas Song/Ramblin' Rose	198?	—	2.50	5.00
—Reissue					
CAPITOL					
❏ 54-529	These Foolish Things/Cole Capers	1949	5.00	10.00	20.00
—Part of "CCF-156"					
❏ F529	These Foolish Things/Cole Capers	1950	3.75	7.50	15.00
—Part of "CCF-156"; reissue of 54-529					
❏ 54-530	Three Little Words/I'll Never Be the Same	1949	5.00	10.00	20.00
—Part of "CCF-156"					
❏ F530	Three Little Words/I'll Never Be the Same	1950	3.75	7.50	15.00
—Part of "CCF-156"; reissue of 54-530					

Number	Title (A Side/B Side)	Yr	VG	VG+	NM
❑ 54-531	Blues in My Shower/How High the Moon	1949	5.00	10.00	20.00
—Part of "CCF-156"					
❑ F531	Blues in My Shower/How High the Moon	1950	3.75	7.50	15.00
—Part of "CCF-156"; reissue of 54-531					
❑ F606	Lillian/Lush Life	1949	3.75	7.50	15.00
—Add 1/3 if "O.C." (optional center) is still in the center of the record					
❑ 54-680	(It's Easy to See) The Trouble with Me Is You/ Who Do You Know in Heaven	1949	5.00	10.00	20.00
❑ F883	It's Only a Paper Moon/Embraceable You	1950	5.00	10.00	20.00
—As "The King Cole Trio"					
❑ F889	I Almost Lost My Mind/Baby Won't You Say You Love Me	1950	3.75	7.50	15.00
—Nat King Cole records on Capitol before F889 are unconfirmed on 45 rpm, except as listed					
❑ F1010	Mona Lisa/The Greatest Inventor (Of Them All)	1950	3.75	7.50	15.00
❑ F1030	I Don't Know Why/ You're the Cream in My Coffee	1950	3.75	7.50	15.00
❑ F1032	I'm in the Mood for Love/Don't Blame Me	1950	3.75	7.50	15.00
❑ F1033	(I Love You) For Sentimental Reasons/I Can't See for Lookin'	1950	3.75	7.50	15.00
❑ F1034	Little Girl/What Can I Say	1950	3.75	7.50	15.00
❑ F1035	Portrait of Jenny/Lost April	1950	3.75	7.50	15.00
❑ F1036	Exactly Like You/That's What	1950	3.75	7.50	15.00
❑ F1037	Sweet Georgia Brown/I Know That You Know	1950	3.75	7.50	15.00
❑ F1038	This Way Out/Rex Rhumba	1950	3.75	7.50	15.00
❑ F1068	I'll Never Say "Never Again" Again/A Little Bit Independent	1950	5.00	10.00	20.00
❑ F1133	Home (When Shadows Fall)/Tunnel of Love	1950	3.75	7.50	15.00
❑ F1176	Get Out and Get Under/Hey, Not Now	1950	3.75	7.50	15.00
❑ F1184	Orange Colored Sky/Jambo	1950	3.75	7.50	15.00
❑ F1203	Frosty the Snow Man/A Little Christmas Tree	1950	7.50	15.00	30.00
❑ F1270	Time Out for Tears/Get to Gettin'	1951	3.00	6.00	12.00
❑ F1365	Jet/Magic Tree	1951	3.00	6.00	12.00
❑ F1401	Always You/Destination Moon	1951	3.00	6.00	12.00
❑ F1449	Too Young/That's My Girl	1951	3.00	6.00	12.00
❑ F1468	Red Sails in the Sunset/Little Child	1951	3.00	6.00	12.00
❑ F1501	Because of Rain/Song of Delilah	1951	3.00	6.00	12.00
❑ F1565	Early American/My Brother	1951	3.00	6.00	12.00
❑ F1613	Sweet Lorraine/Kee-Mo Ky-Mo	1951	3.00	6.00	12.00
❑ F1627	Lost April/Calypso Blues	1951	3.00	6.00	12.00
❑ F1650	Embraceable You/It's Only a Paper Moon	1951	2.50	5.00	10.00
—As "The King Cole Trio"					
❑ F1663	Nature Boy/For All We Know	1951	2.50	5.00	10.00
❑ F1669	Makin' Whoopee/This Is My Night to Dream	1951	2.50	5.00	10.00
❑ F1672	Lush Life/I Miss You So	1951	2.50	5.00	10.00
❑ F1673	Mona Lisa/No Moon at All	1951	2.50	5.00	10.00
❑ F1674	Too Young/(I Love You) For Sentimental Reasons	1952	2.50	5.00	10.00
❑ F1689	Pretend/Unforgettable	1954	2.50	5.00	10.00
—Most of the Capitol 1600 series were reissues, some of material from 78s					
❑ F1747	Make Believe Land/I'll Always Remember You	1951	3.00	6.00	12.00
❑ F1808	Unforgettable/My First, My Last Love	1951	3.00	6.00	12.00
❑ F1815	I Still See Elisa/You're OK for TV	1951	3.00	6.00	12.00
❑ F1863	Walkin'/I'm Hurtin'	1951	3.00	6.00	12.00
❑ F1893	Here's to My Lady/Miss Me	1951	3.00	6.00	12.00
❑ F1925	Wine, Women and Song/A Weaver of My Dreams	1952	3.00	6.00	12.00
❑ F1968	You Weren't There/You Will Never Grow Old	1952	2.50	5.00	10.00
❑ F1994	Easter Sunday Morning/Summer Is a Comin' On	1952	2.50	5.00	10.00
❑ SXE-2-2008 [S]	When My Sugar Walks Down the Street/Warm and Willing	196?	2.50	5.00	10.00
—"Capitol Compact 33," small hole, plays at 33 1/3 rpm					
❑ F2069	Somewhere Along the Way/What Does It Take to Make You Take Me	1952	2.50	5.00	10.00
❑ 2088	Thank You, Pretty Baby/Brazilian Love Song	1968	—	3.00	6.00
❑ F2130	Walking My Baby Back Home/Funny (Not Much)	1952	2.50	5.00	10.00
❑ F2212	Because You're Mine/I'm Never Satisfied	1952	2.50	5.00	10.00
❑ F2230	Faith Can Move Mountains/The Ruby and the Pearl	1952	2.50	5.00	10.00
❑ F2309	Strange/How (Do I Go About It)	1952	2.50	5.00	10.00
❑ F2346	Pretend/Don't Let Your Eyes Go Shopping	1953	2.50	5.00	10.00
❑ F2389	Can't I/Blue Gardenia	1953	2.50	5.00	10.00
❑ 2451	I'm Gonna Laugh You Right Out of My Life/ People	1969	—	3.00	6.00
❑ F2459	I Am in Love/My Flaming Heart	1953	2.50	5.00	10.00
❑ F2498	Return to Paradise/Angel Eyes	1953	2.50	5.00	10.00
❑ F2540	A Fool Was I/If Love Is Good to Me	1953	2.50	5.00	10.00
❑ F2610	Lover Come Back to Me/That's All	1953	2.50	5.00	10.00
❑ F2616	Mrs. Santa Claus/The Little Boy That Santa Claus Forgot	1953	5.00	10.00	20.00
❑ F2687	Answer Me, My Love/Why	1953	2.50	5.00	10.00
❑ F2754	It Happens to Be Me/Alone Too Long	1954	2.50	5.00	10.00
❑ F2803	Make Her Mine/I Envy	1954	2.50	5.00	10.00
❑ F2897	Smile/It's Crazy	1954	2.50	5.00	10.00
❑ F2949	Hajji Baba (Persian Lament)/Unbelievable	1954	2.50	5.00	10.00
❑ F2955	The Christmas Song (Merry Christmas to You)/ My Two Front Teeth (All I Want for Christmas)	1954	5.00	10.00	20.00
❑ F2985	Open Up the Doghouse/Long, Long Ago	1954	3.75	7.50	15.00
—With Dean Martin					
❑ F3027	Darling Je Vous Aime Beaucoup/The Sand and the Sea	1955	2.50	5.00	10.00
❑ F3095	A Blossom Fell/If I May	1955	3.75	7.50	15.00
—B-side with the Four Knights					
❑ F3136	My One Sin/Blues from Kiss Me Deadly	1955	2.50	5.00	10.00
❑ F3234	Forgive My Heart/Someone You Love	1955	2.50	5.00	10.00
❑ F3305	Take Me Back to Toyland/I'm Gonna Laugh You Right Out of My Life	1955	5.00	10.00	20.00
❑ F3328	Ask Me/Nothing Ever Changes My Love for You	1956	2.50	5.00	10.00
❑ F3390	Too Young to Go Steady/Never Let Me Go	1956	2.50	5.00	10.00
❑ F3456	That's All There Is to That/My Dream Sonata	1956	2.50	5.00	10.00
❑ F3551	Night Lights/To the Ends of the Earth	1956	2.50	5.00	10.00
❑ F3560	Mrs. Santa Claus/Take Me Back to Toyland	1956	3.75	7.50	15.00
❑ 3561	The Christmas Song (Merry Christmas to You)/ The Little Boy That Santa Claus Forgot	1960	2.00	4.00	8.00
—Purple label, Capitol logo on side					
❑ 3561	The Christmas Song (Merry Christmas to You)/ The Little Boy That Santa Claus Forgot	1962	—	3.00	6.00
—Orange and yellow swirl label					
❑ 3561	The Christmas Song (Merry Christmas to You)/ The Little Boy That Santa Claus Forgot	1973	—	2.00	4.00
—Orange label with "Capitol" at bottom					
❑ F3561	The Christmas Song (Merry Christmas to You)/ The Little Boy That Santa Claus Forgot	1956	3.75	7.50	15.00
—Original with "F" prefix, Capitol logo on top					
❑ F3619	Ballerina/You Are My First Love	1957	2.50	5.00	10.00
❑ F3702	When Rock and Roll Come to Trinidad/ China Gate	1957	3.75	7.50	15.00
❑ F3737	Send for Me/My Personal Possession	1957	3.75	7.50	15.00
—B-side with the Four Knights					
❑ F3782	With You on My Mind/ The Song of Raintree County	1957	2.50	5.00	10.00
❑ F3860	Angel Smile/Back in My Arms	1957	2.50	5.00	10.00
❑ F3939	Looking Back/Do I Like It	1958	2.50	5.00	10.00
❑ F4004	Come Closer to Me/Nothing in the World	1958	2.50	5.00	10.00
❑ F4056	Non Dimentica (Don't Forget)/ Bend a Little My Way	1958	2.50	5.00	10.00
❑ F4125	Madrid/Give Me Your Love	1959	2.50	5.00	10.00
❑ F4184	You Made Me Love You/I Must Be Dreaming	1959	2.50	5.00	10.00
❑ F4248	Sweet Bird of Youth/Midnight Flyer	1959	2.50	5.00	10.00
❑ F4248 [PS]	Sweet Bird of Youth/Midnight Flyer	1959	7.50	15.00	30.00
❑ 4301	The Happiest Christmas Tree/Buon Natale	1959	3.00	6.00	12.00
❑ 4301 [PS]	The Happiest Christmas Tree/Buon Natale	1959	6.25	12.50	25.00
❑ 4325	What'cha Gonna Do/Time and the River	1960	2.00	4.00	8.00
❑ 4369	Is It Better to Have Loved and Lost/That's You	1960	2.00	4.00	8.00
❑ 4393	My Love/Steady	1960	2.00	4.00	8.00
❑ 4481	If I Knew/World in My Arms	1960	2.00	4.00	8.00
❑ 4519	Illusion/When It's Summer	1961	2.00	4.00	8.00
❑ 4555	Goodnight, Little Leaguer/ The First Baseball Game	1961	2.00	4.00	8.00
❑ 4555 [PS]	Goodnight, Little Leaguer/ The First Baseball Game	1961	5.00	10.00	20.00
❑ 4582	Take a Fool's Advice/Make It Last	1961	2.00	4.00	8.00
❑ 4623	Let True Love Begin/Cappuccina	1961	2.00	4.00	8.00
❑ 4672	Magic Moment/Step Right Up	1961	2.00	4.00	8.00
❑ 4714	Look No Further/The Right Thing to Say	1962	2.00	4.00	8.00
❑ 4804	Ramblin' Rose/Good Times	1962	3.00	6.00	12.00
❑ 4804 [PS]	Ramblin' Rose/Good Times	1962	5.00	10.00	20.00
❑ 4870	Dear Lonely Hearts/Who's Next in Line	1962	3.00	6.00	12.00
❑ 4870 [PS]	Dear Lonely Hearts/Who's Next in Line	1962	5.00	10.00	20.00
❑ 4919	All Over the World/Nothing Goes Up (Without Coming Down)	1963	2.00	4.00	8.00
❑ 4965	Those Lazy-Hazy-Crazy Days of Summer/ In the Cool of Day	1963	3.00	6.00	12.00
❑ 4965 [PS]	Those Lazy-Hazy-Crazy Days of Summer/ In the Cool of Day	1963	5.00	10.00	20.00
❑ 5027	That Sunday, That Summer/Mr. Wishing Well	1963	3.00	6.00	12.00
❑ 5125	My True Carrie, Love/A Rag a Bone, A Hank of Hair	1964	2.00	4.00	8.00
❑ 5155	I Don't Want to Be Hurt Anymore/People	1964	2.00	4.00	8.00
❑ 5219	Marnie and More of the Amore	1964	2.00	4.00	8.00
❑ 5261	L-O-V-E/I Don't Want to See Tomorrow	1964	2.00	4.00	8.00
❑ 5412	The Ballad of Cat Ballou/ They Can't Make Her Cry	1965	2.00	4.00	8.00
—With Stubby Kay					
❑ 5412 [PS]	The Ballad of Cat Ballou/ They Can't Make Her Cry	1965	3.75	7.50	15.00
❑ 5486	Wanderlust/You'll See	1965	2.00	4.00	8.00
❑ 5549	One Sun/Looking Back	1965	2.00	4.00	8.00
❑ 5683	Let Me Tell You, Babe/For the Want of a Kiss	1966	2.00	4.00	8.00
❑ F15509	Straighten Up and Fly Right/Nature Boy	1950	3.75	7.50	15.00
—All the Capitol 15000 series on 45s are from multi-disc box sets					
❑ F15510	You Call It Madness/The Frim Fram Sauce	1950	3.75	7.50	15.00
❑ F15511	(Get Your Kicks on) Route 66/Gee Baby Ain't I Been Good to You	1950	3.75	7.50	15.00
❑ F15552	Yes Sir That's My Baby/I Used to Love You	1950	3.75	7.50	15.00
❑ F15553	For All We Know/'Tis Autumn	1950	3.75	7.50	15.00
❑ F15554	Bop Kick/Laugh Cool Clown	1950	3.75	7.50	15.00
❑ F15564	Sweet Lorraine/It's Only a Paper Moon	1950	3.75	7.50	15.00
❑ F15565	The Man I Love/Body and Soul	1950	3.75	7.50	15.00
❑ F15566	Embraceable You/ What Is This Thing Called Love	1950	3.75	7.50	15.00
❑ F15643	Jumpin' at Capitol/Love for Sale	1950	3.75	7.50	15.00
—B-side by Benny Carter Orchestra					
❑ F15728	Makin' Whoopee/Honeysuckle Rose	1951	3.00	6.00	12.00
❑ F15729	I'll String Along with You/ Too Marvelous for Words	1951	3.00	6.00	12.00
❑ F15730	This Is My Night to Dream/Rhumba Azul	1951	3.00	6.00	12.00
❑ F15843	Return Trip/St. Louis Blues	1952	3.00	6.00	12.00
—B-side by Freddie Slack					
❑ F15868	Penthouse Serenade/If I Should Lose You	1952	3.00	6.00	12.00
❑ F15869	Somebody Loves Me/ Down by the Old Mill Stream	1952	3.00	6.00	12.00
❑ F15870	Laura/Polka Dots and Moonbeams	1952	3.00	6.00	12.00
❑ F15922	Walkin' My Baby Back Home/Kay's Lament	1952	3.00	6.00	12.00
—B-side by Kay Starr					
❑ S7-19764	Mrs. Santa Claus/Take Me Back to Toyland	1997	—	—	3.00
❑ S7-57887	The Christmas Song/O Holy Night	1992	—	2.00	4.00
—Originals on black vinyl					
❑ S7-57887	The Christmas Song/O Holy Night	1993	—	2.00	4.00
—Second pressing on red vinyl					
❑ F90036	(All I Want for Christmas Is) My Two Front Teeth/ The Christmas Song (Merry Christmas To You)	1949	5.00	10.00	20.00
—B-side is the original King Cole Trio hit version, possibly its only U.S. release on 45					
TAMPA					
❑ 134	Vom-Vim-Veedle/All for You	1957	3.00	6.00	12.00
❑ 134 [PS]	Vom-Vim-Veedle/All for You	1957	6.25	12.50	25.00

7-Inch Extended Plays

CAPITOL

Number	Title (A Side/B Side)	Yr	VG	VG+	NM
❑ EAP 1-332	(contents unknown)	195?	3.00	6.00	12.00
❑ EAP 1-332 [PS]	Penthouse Serenade, Part 1	195?	3.00	6.00	12.00
❑ EAP 2-332	(contents unknown)	195?	3.00	6.00	12.00
❑ EAP 2-332 [PS]	Penthouse Serenade, Part 2	195?	3.00	6.00	12.00
❑ EBF-332 [PS]	Penthouse Serenade	195?	3.75	7.50	15.00
—Gatefold sleeve for some copies of 1-332 and 2-332					

C

Number	Title (A Side/B Side)	Yr	VG	VG+	NM
❏ EAP 1-357	Unforgettable/Portrait of Jennie//(I Love You) For Sentimental Reasons/ Red Sails in the Sunset	195?	3.00	6.00	12.00
❏ EAP 1-357 [PS]	Unforgettable Songs by Nat King Cole, Part 1	195?	3.00	6.00	12.00
❏ EAP 2-357	What'll I Do/Lost April//Too Young/Mona Lisa	195?	3.00	6.00	12.00
❏ EAP 2-357 [PS]	Unforgettable Songs by Nat King Cole, Part 2	195?	3.00	6.00	12.00
❏ EAP 3-357	Answer Me, My Love/Hajji Baba// Pretend/Make Her Mine	195?	3.00	6.00	12.00
❏ EAP 3-357 [PS]	Unforgettable Songs by Nat King Cole, Part 3	195?	3.00	6.00	12.00
❏ EBF-357 [PS]	Unforgettable	195?	3.75	7.50	15.00
—Gatefold sleeve for some copies of 1-357 and 2-357					
❏ EAP 1-420	*Love Is Here to Stay/A Handful of Stars/Almost Like Being in Love/Tenderly	1954	3.00	6.00	12.00
❏ EAP 1-420 [PS]	Two in Love, Part 1	1954	3.00	6.00	12.00
❏ EAP 2-420	*A Little Street Where Old Friends Meet/This Can't Be Love/Dinner for One Please, James/ There Goes My Heart	1954	3.00	6.00	12.00
❏ EAP 2-420 [PS]	Two in Love, Part 2	1954	3.00	6.00	12.00
❏ EPA 1-500	*Lover Come Back/Pretend/ A Fool Was I/I'm Hurtin'	1954	3.00	6.00	12.00
❏ EPA 1-500 [PS]	Songs by Nat King Cole	1954	3.00	6.00	12.00
❏ EAP 1-514	(contents unknown)	1954	3.00	6.00	12.00
❏ EAP 1-514 [PS]	Tenth Anniversary Album, Part 1	1954	3.00	6.00	12.00
❏ EAP 2-514	(contents unknown)	1954	3.00	6.00	12.00
❏ EAP 2-514 [PS]	Tenth Anniversary Album, Part 2	1954	3.00	6.00	12.00
❏ EAP 3-514	The Love Nest/But All I've Got Is Me//Lovelight/ Where Were You	1954	3.00	6.00	12.00
❏ EAP 3-514 [PS]	Tenth Anniversary Album, Part 3	1954	3.00	6.00	12.00
❏ EAP 4-514	Peaches/I Can't Be Bothered//Mother Nature and Father Time/Wish I Were Somebody Else	1954	3.00	6.00	12.00
❏ EAP 4-514 [PS]	Tenth Anniversary Album, Part 4	1954	3.00	6.00	12.00
❏ EBF 1-514 [PS]	Tenth Anniversary Album, Parts 1 and 2	1954	5.00	10.00	20.00
—Gatefold sleeve for some editions of EAP 1-514 and 2-514					
❏ EBF 2-514 [PS]	Tenth Anniversary Album, Parts 3 and 4	1954	10.00	20.00	
—Gatefold sleeve for some editions of EAP 3-514 and 4-514					
❏ EAP 1-633	Darling, Je Vous Aime Beaucoup/If I May//A Blossom Fell/The Sand and the Sea	1955	3.00	6.00	12.00
❏ EAP 1-633 [PS]	Moods in Song	1955	3.00	6.00	12.00
❏ EAP 1-782	Sometimes I'm Happy//Just You, Just Me/When I Grow Too Old to Dream	1956	2.50	5.00	10.00
❏ EAP 1-782 [PS]	After Midnight, Part 1	1956	2.50	5.00	10.00
❏ EAP 2-782	Lonely One/I Know That You Know// Sweet Lorraine	1956	2.50	5.00	10.00
❏ EAP 2-782 [PS]	After Midnight, Part 2	1956	2.50	5.00	10.00
❏ EAP 3-782	You're Looking at Me//Caravan/ (Get Your Kicks on) Route 66	1956	2.50	5.00	10.00
❏ EAP 3-782 [PS]	After Midnight, Part 3	1956	2.50	5.00	10.00
❏ EAP 4-782	It's Only a Paper Moon/Don't Let It Go to Your Head//Blame It On My Youth	1956	2.50	5.00	10.00
❏ EAP 4-782 [PS]	After Midnight, Part 4	1956	2.50	5.00	10.00
❏ EBF 1-782 [PS]	After Midnight, Parts 1 & 2	1956	5.00	10.00	20.00
—Gatefold sleeve for some editions of EAP 1-782 and 2-782					
❏ EAP 1-801	Night Lights/Nothing Ever Changes My Love for You//To the Ends of the Earth/My Dream Sonata	1957	3.00	6.00	12.00
❏ EAP 1-801 [PS]	Night Lights	1957	3.00	6.00	12.00
❏ EAP 1-813	Around the World/Fascination//An Affair to Remember (Our Love Affair)/There's a Gold Mine in the Sky	1957	3.00	6.00	12.00
❏ EAP 1-813 [PS]	Around the World	1957	3.00	6.00	12.00
❏ EAP 1-824	Love Is the Thing/Stay as Sweet as You Are// When I Fall in Love/Where Can I Go Without You?	1957	3.00	6.00	12.00
❏ EAP 1-824 [PS]	Love Is the Thing, Part 1	1957	3.00	6.00	12.00
❏ EAP 2-824	Maybe It's Because I Love You Too Much/It's All in the Game//Stardust/When Sunny Gets Blue	1957	3.00	6.00	12.00
❏ EAP 2-824 [PS]	Love Is the Thing, Part 2	1957	3.00	6.00	12.00
❏ EAP 3-824	(contents unknown)	1957	3.00	6.00	12.00
❏ EAP 3-824 [PS]	Love Is the Thing, Part 3	1957	3.00	6.00	12.00
❏ EAP 1-903	(contents unknown)	195?	3.00	6.00	12.00
❏ EAP 1-903 [PS]	Just One of Those Things, Part 1	195?	3.00	6.00	12.00
❏ EAP 2-903	Don't Get Around Much Anymore/The Party's Over//Once in a While/Just for the Fun of It	195?	3.00	6.00	12.00
❏ EAP 2-903 [PS]	Just One of Those Things, Part 2	195?	3.00	6.00	12.00
❏ EAP 3-903	(contents unknown)	195?	3.00	6.00	12.00
❏ EAP 3-903 [PS]	Just One of Those Things, Part 3	195?	3.00	6.00	12.00
❏ EAP 1-960	Looking Back/Send for Me//Do I Like It/ Angel Smile	1958	2.50	5.00	10.00
❏ EAP 1-960 [PS]	Looking Back	1958	2.50	5.00	10.00
❏ EAP 1-993	*Overture (Introducing "Love Theme" and "Hesitating Blues")/Harlem Blues/ Yellow Dog Blues/St. Louis Blues	1958	3.00	6.00	12.00
❏ EAP 1-993 [PS]	St. Louis Blues, Part 1	1958	3.00	6.00	12.00
❏ EAP 2-993	(contents unknown)	1958	3.00	6.00	12.00
❏ EAP 2-993 [PS]	St. Louis Blues, Part 2	1958	3.00	6.00	12.00
❏ EAP 3-993	Stay/Joe Turner's Blues//Beale Street Blues/ Careless Love	1958	3.00	6.00	12.00
❏ EAP 3-993 [PS]	St. Louis Blues, Part 3	1958	3.00	6.00	12.00
❏ EAP 1-1031	*Cachito/Maria Elena/Las Mananitas/Quizas, Quizas, Quizas	1958	3.00	6.00	12.00
❏ EAP 1-1031 [PS]	Cole Espanol, Part 1	1958	3.00	6.00	12.00
❏ EAP 2-1031	(contents unknown)	1958	3.00	6.00	12.00
❏ EAP 2-1031 [PS]	Cole Espanol, Part 2	1958	3.00	6.00	12.00
❏ EAP 3-1031	(contents unknown)	1958	3.00	6.00	12.00
❏ EAP 3-1031 [PS]	Cole Espanol, Part 3	1958	3.00	6.00	12.00
❏ EAP 1-1084	Paradise/Cherchez La Femme//Impossible/ Found A Million Dollar Baby (In A Five And Ten Cent Store)	195?	2.50	5.00	10.00
❏ EAP 1-1084 [PS]	The Very Thought of You, Part 1	195?	2.50	5.00	10.00
❏ EAP 2-1084	(contents unknown)	195?	2.50	5.00	10.00
❏ EAP 2-1084 [PS]	The Very Thought of You, Part 2	195?	2.50	5.00	10.00
❏ EAP-1138	(contents unknown)	195?	2.50	5.00	10.00
❏ EAP-1138 [PS]	Non Dimenticar	195?	2.50	5.00	10.00
❏ EAP 1346	(contents unknown)	195?	2.50	5.00	10.00
❏ EAP 1346 [PS]	The Happiest Christmas Tree	195?	2.50	5.00	10.00
❏ EAP-1500	(contents unknown)	196?	2.50	5.00	10.00
❏ EAP-1500 [PS]	Songs by Nat King Cole	196?	2.50	5.00	10.00
❏ EAP-1535	(contents unknown)	195?	2.50	5.00	10.00
❏ EAP-1535 [PS]	By the Beautiful Sea	195?	2.50	5.00	10.00

Number	Title (A Side/B Side)	Yr	VG	VG+	NM
❏ EAP-1696	(contents unknown)	196?	2.50	5.00	10.00
❏ EAP-1696 [PS]	Love Songs by Nat King Cole	196?	2.50	5.00	10.00
❏ EAP-1709	(contents unknown)	196?	2.50	5.00	10.00
❏ EAP-1709 [PS]	Strip for Action	196?	2.50	5.00	10.00
❏ SXA-2195	Your Love/My Kind of Girl/Three Little Words// L-O-V-E/Coquette/More	1965	2.50	5.00	10.00
—33 1/3 rpm, small hole					
❏ SXA-2195 [PS]	L-O-V-E	1965	2.50	5.00	10.00
❏ EAP 1-9026	The Christmas Song/Mrs. Santa Claus//Frosty The Snowman/The Little Christmas Tree	195?	3.00	6.00	12.00
❏ EAP 1-9026 [PS]	The Christmas Song	195?	3.00	6.00	12.00
❏ EAP 1-9110	*Somewhere Along the Way/Funny (Not Much)/ Walkin' My Baby Back Home/Faith Can Move Mountains	195?	3.75	7.50	15.00
❏ EAP 1-9110 [PS]	Nat King Cole's Top Pops, Part I	195?	3.75	7.50	15.00
❏ EAP 2-9110	*Because You're Mine/I'm Never Satisfied/The Ruby and the Pearl/A Weaver of Dreams	195?	3.75	7.50	15.00
❏ EAP 2-9110 [PS]	Nat King Cole's Top Pops, Part II	195?	3.75	7.50	15.00
❏ EAP 1-9120	If I Give My Heart To You/Hold My Hand//Pappa Loves Mambo/Teach Me Tonight	1954	3.00	6.00	12.00
❏ EAP 1-9120 [PS]	Nat King Cole Sings	1954	3.00	6.00	12.00
❏ EAP 1-9128	Love Is a Many-Splendored Thing/Breezin' Along with the Breeze//Autumn Leaves/You Are My Sunshine	1955	3.00	6.00	12.00
❏ EAP 1-9128 [PS]	Nat King Cole	1955	3.00	6.00	12.00

Albums

CAMAY

Number	Title (A Side/B Side)	Yr	VG	VG+	NM
❏ CA-3004	Nat King Cole	196?	3.00	6.00	12.00

CAPITOL

Number	Title (A Side/B Side)	Yr	VG	VG+	NM
❏ H 8 [10]	The King Cole Trio	1950	25.00	50.00	100.00
❏ H 29 [10]	The King Cole Trio, Volume 2	1950	25.00	50.00	100.00
❏ H 59 [10]	The King Cole Trio, Volume 3	1950	25.00	50.00	100.00
❏ H 156 [10]	Nat King Cole at the Piano	1950	25.00	50.00	100.00
❏ H 177 [10]	The King Cole Trio, Volume 4	1950	17.50	35.00	70.00
❏ H 213 [10]	Harvest of Hits	1950	17.50	35.00	70.00
❏ H 220 [10]	The Nat King Cole Trio	1950	15.00	30.00	60.00
❏ DWBB-252 [(2)]	Close-Up	1969	3.75	7.50	15.00
—Reissue of 680 and 1891					
❏ ST-310	There! I've Said It Again	1969	3.00	6.00	12.00
❏ H 332 [10]	Penthouse Serenade	1951	15.00	30.00	60.00
❏ T 332 [M]	Penthouse Serenade	1955	10.00	20.00	40.00
❏ DT 357 [R]	Unforgettable	1965	3.00	6.00	12.00
❏ H 357 [10]	Unforgettable	1952	15.00	30.00	60.00
❏ SM-357	Unforgettable	197?	2.00	4.00	8.00
—Reissue with new prefix					
❏ T 357 [M]	Unforgettable	1955	10.00	20.00	40.00
—Turquoise label					
❏ T 357 [M]	Unforgettable	1958	7.50	15.00	30.00
—Black label with colorband, "Capitol" at left					
❏ T 357 [M]	Unforgettable	1962	5.00	10.00	20.00
—Black label with colorband, "Capitol" at top					
❏ SKAO-373	Nat King Cole's Greatest	1969	3.00	6.00	12.00
❏ DT 420 [R]	Nat King Cole Sings for Two in Love	1963	3.75	7.50	15.00
❏ H 420 [10]	Nat King Cole Sings for Two in Love	1953	12.50	25.00	50.00
❏ T 420 [M]	Nat King Cole Sings for Two in Love	1955	10.00	20.00	40.00
—Turquoise label					
❏ T 420 [M]	Nat King Cole Sings for Two in Love	1958	7.50	15.00	30.00
—Black label with colorband, "Capitol" at left					
❏ T 420 [M]	Nat King Cole Sings for Two in Love	1962	5.00	10.00	20.00
—Black label with colorband, "Capitol" at top					
❏ STBB-503 [(2)]	Walkin' My Baby Back Home/A Blossom Fell	1970	3.75	7.50	15.00
❏ H 514 [10]	Tenth Anniversary Album	1954	12.50	25.00	50.00
❏ W 514 [M]	Tenth Anniversary Album	1955	10.00	20.00	40.00
❏ T 591 [M]	Vocal Classics	1955	10.00	20.00	40.00
❏ T 592 [M]	Instrumental Classics	1955	10.00	20.00	40.00
❏ DT 680 [R]	Ballads of the Day	1963	3.75	7.50	15.00
—Black label with colorband					
❏ T 680 [M]	Ballads of the Day	1956	10.00	20.00	40.00
—Turquoise label					
❏ T 680 [M]	Ballads of the Day	1958	7.50	15.00	30.00
—Black label with colorband, "Capitol" at left					
❏ T 680 [M]	Ballads of the Day	1962	5.00	10.00	20.00
—Black label with colorband, "Capitol" at top					
❏ W 689 [M]	The Piano Style of Nat King Cole	1956	10.00	20.00	40.00
—Turquoise label					
❏ W 689 [M]	The Piano Style of Nat King Cole	1958	7.50	15.00	30.00
—Black label with colorband, "Capitol" at left					
❏ W 689 [M]	The Piano Style of Nat King Cole	1962	5.00	10.00	20.00
—Black label with colorband, "Capitol" at top					
❏ W 782 [M]	After Midnight	1956	10.00	20.00	40.00
—Turquoise label					
❏ W 782 [M]	After Midnight	1958	7.50	15.00	30.00
—Black label with colorband, "Capitol" at left					
❏ W 782 [M]	After Midnight	1962	5.00	10.00	20.00
—Black label with colorband, "Capitol" at top					
❏ SM-824	Love Is the Thing	197?	2.00	4.00	8.00
—Reissue with new prefix					
❏ SW 824 [S]	Love Is the Thing	1959	7.50	15.00	30.00
—Black label with colorband, "Capitol" at left					
❏ SW 824 [S]	Love Is the Thing	1962	5.00	10.00	20.00
—Black label with colorband, "Capitol" at top					
❏ SW 824 [S]	Love Is the Thing	1969	3.00	6.00	12.00
—Lime green label					
❏ W 824 [M]	Love Is the Thing	1957	10.00	20.00	40.00
—Turquoise or gray label					
❏ W 824 [M]	Love Is the Thing	1958	7.50	15.00	30.00
—Black label with colorband, "Capitol" at left					
❏ W 824 [M]	Love Is the Thing	1962	5.00	10.00	20.00
—Black label with colorband, "Capitol" at top					
❏ DT 870 [R]	This Is Nat "King" Cole	1963	3.75	7.50	15.00
—Black label with colorband					
❏ T 870 [M]	This Is Nat "King" Cole	1957	10.00	20.00	40.00
—Turquoise or gray label					
❏ T 870 [M]	This Is Nat "King" Cole	1958	7.50	15.00	30.00
—Black label with colorband, "Capitol" at left					
❏ T 870 [M]	This Is Nat "King" Cole	1962	5.00	10.00	20.00
—Black label with colorband, "Capitol" at top					

Number	Title (A Side/B Side)	Yr	VG	VG+	NM
❑ SW 903 [S] Just One of Those Things		1959	7.50	15.00	30.00
—Black label with colorband, "Capitol" at left					
❑ SW 903 [S] Just One of Those Things		1962	5.00	10.00	20.00
—Black label with colorband, "Capitol" at left					
❑ W 903 [M] Just One of Those Things		1957	10.00	20.00	40.00
—Turquoise or gray label					
❑ W 903 [M] Just One of Those Things		1958	7.50	15.00	30.00
—Black label with colorband, "Capitol" at left					
❑ W 903 [M] Just One of Those Things		1962	5.00	10.00	20.00
—Black label with colorband, "Capitol" at top					
❑ SW 993 [S] St. Louis Blues		1959	12.50	25.00	50.00
—Black label with colorband, "Capitol" at left					
❑ W 993 [M] St. Louis Blues		1958	12.50	25.00	50.00
—Turquoise or gray label					
❑ W 993 [M] St. Louis Blues		1962	10.00	20.00	40.00
—Black label with colorband, "Capitol" at left					
❑ DW 1031 [R] Cole Espanol		196?	3.75	7.50	15.00
—Black label with colorband					
❑ SM-1031 Cole Espanol		197?	2.00	4.00	8.00
—Reissue with new prefix					
❑ W 1031 [M] Cole Espanol		1958	7.50	15.00	30.00
—Black label with colorband, "Capitol" at left					
❑ W 1031 [M] Cole Espanol		1962	5.00	10.00	20.00
—Black label with colorband, "Capitol" at top					
❑ SW 1084 [S] The Very Thought of You		1959	7.50	15.00	30.00
—Black label with colorband, "Capitol" at left					
❑ SW 1084 [S] The Very Thought of You		1962	5.00	10.00	20.00
—Black label with colorband, "Capitol" at top					
❑ W 1084 [M] The Very Thought of You		1958	7.50	15.00	30.00
—Black label with colorband, "Capitol" at left					
❑ W 1084 [M] The Very Thought of You		1962	5.00	10.00	20.00
—Black label with colorband, "Capitol" at top					
❑ SW 1120 [S] Welcome to the Club		1959	10.00	20.00	40.00
—Black label with colorband, "Capitol" at left					
❑ W 1120 [M] Welcome to the Club		1959	7.50	15.00	30.00
—Black label with colorband, "Capitol" at left					
❑ SW 1190 [S] To Whom It May Concern		1959	10.00	20.00	40.00
—Black label with colorband, "Capitol" at left					
❑ W 1190 [M] To Whom It May Concern		1959	7.50	15.00	30.00
—Black label with colorband, "Capitol" at left					
❑ SW 1220 [S] A Mis Amigos		1959	10.00	20.00	40.00
—Black label with colorband, "Capitol" at left					
❑ SW 1220 [S] A Mis Amigos		1962	6.25	12.50	25.00
—Black label with colorband, "Capitol" at top					
❑ W 1220 [M] A Mis Amigos		1959	7.50	15.00	30.00
—Black label with colorband, "Capitol" at left					
❑ W 1220 [M] A Mis Amigos		1962	5.00	10.00	20.00
—Black label with colorband, "Capitol" at top					
❑ SW 1249 [S] Every Time I Feel the Spirit		1960	7.50	15.00	30.00
—Black label with colorband, "Capitol" at left					
❑ W 1249 [M] Every Time I Feel the Spirit		1960	6.25	12.50	25.00
—Black label with colorband, "Capitol" at left					
❑ SW 1331 [S] Tell Me About Yourself		1960	7.50	15.00	30.00
—Black label with colorband, "Capitol" at left					
❑ W 1331 [M] Tell Me About Yourself		1960	6.25	12.50	25.00
—Black label with colorband, "Capitol" at left					
❑ SWAK 1392 [S] Wild Is Love		1960	7.50	15.00	30.00
—Black label with colorband, "Capitol" at left					
❑ WAK 1392 [M] Wild Is Love		1960	6.25	12.50	25.00
—Black label with colorband, "Capitol" at left					
❑ SW 1444 [S] The Magic of Christmas		1960	5.00	10.00	20.00
❑ W 1444 [M] The Magic of Christmas		1960	5.00	10.00	20.00
❑ SW 1574 [S] The Touch of Your Lips		1961	6.25	12.50	25.00
—Black label with colorband, "Capitol" at left					
❑ SW 1574 [S] The Touch of Your Lips		1962	5.00	10.00	20.00
—Black label with colorband, "Capitol" at top					
❑ W 1574 [M] The Touch of Your Lips		1961	5.00	10.00	20.00
—Black label with colorband, "Capitol" at left					
❑ W 1574 [M] The Touch of Your Lips		1962	3.75	7.50	15.00
—Black label with colorband, "Capitol" at top					
❑ SWCL 1613 [(3)S] The Nat King Cole Story		1961	7.50	15.00	30.00
❑ WCL 1613 [(3)M] The Nat King Cole Story		1961	6.25	12.50	25.00
❑ SM-1675 Nat King Cole Sings/George Shearing Plays		197?	2.00	4.00	8.00
—Reissue with new prefix					
❑ SW 1675 [S] Nat King Cole Sings/George Shearing Plays		1962	7.50	15.00	30.00
—Black label with colorband, "Capitol" at left					
❑ SW 1675 [S] Nat King Cole Sings/George Shearing Plays		1963	5.00	10.00	20.00
—Black label with colorband, "Capitol" at top					
❑ W 1675 [M] Nat King Cole Sings/George Shearing Plays		1962	6.25	12.50	25.00
—Black label with colorband, "Capitol" at left					
❑ W 1675 [M] Nat King Cole Sings/George Shearing Plays		1963	3.75	7.50	15.00
—Black label with colorband, "Capitol" at top					
❑ SW 1713 [S] Nat King Cole Sings the Blues		1962	6.25	12.50	25.00
—Black label with colorband, "Capitol" at left					
❑ W 1713 [M] Nat King Cole Sings the Blues		1962	5.00	10.00	20.00
—Black label with colorband, "Capitol" at left					
❑ SM-1749 More Cole Espanol		197?	2.00	4.00	8.00
—Reissue with new prefix					
❑ SW 1749 [S] More Cole Espanol		1962	7.50	15.00	30.00
—Black label with colorband, "Capitol" at left					
❑ SW 1749 [S] More Cole Espanol		1963	5.00	10.00	20.00
—Black label with colorband, "Capitol" at top					
❑ W 1749 [M] More Cole Espanol		1962	6.25	12.50	25.00
—Black label with colorband, "Capitol" at left					
❑ W 1749 [M] More Cole Espanol		1963	3.75	7.50	15.00
—Black label with colorband, "Capitol" at top					
❑ ST 1793 [S] Ramblin' Rose		1962	5.00	10.00	20.00
❑ T 1793 [M] Ramblin' Rose		1962	3.75	7.50	15.00
❑ ST 1838 [S] Dear Lonely Hearts		1962	5.00	10.00	20.00
❑ T 1838 [M] Dear Lonely Hearts		1962	3.75	7.50	15.00
❑ SW 1859 [S] Where Did Everyone Go?		1963	5.00	10.00	20.00
❑ W 1859 [M] Where Did Everyone Go?		1963	3.75	7.50	15.00
❑ DT 1891 [R] Nat King Cole's Top Pops		1963	3.00	6.00	12.00
❑ T 1891 [M] Nat King Cole's Top Pops		1963	3.75	7.50	15.00
❑ SW 1926 [S] The Nat King Cole Story, Volume 1		1962	3.75	7.50	15.00
❑ W 1926 [M] The Nat King Cole Story, Volume 1		1962	3.00	6.00	12.00
❑ SW 1927 [S] The Nat King Cole Story, Volume 2		1963	3.75	7.50	15.00
❑ W 1927 [M] The Nat King Cole Story, Volume 2		1963	3.00	6.00	12.00
❑ SW 1928 [S] The Nat King Cole Story, Volume 3		1963	3.75	7.50	15.00
❑ W 1928 [M] The Nat King Cole Story, Volume 3		1963	3.00	6.00	12.00
❑ SW 1929 [S] Nat King Cole Sings the Blues, Volume 2		1963	5.00	10.00	20.00
❑ W 1929 [M] Nat King Cole Sings the Blues, Volume 2		1963	3.75	7.50	15.00
❑ ST 1932 [S] Those Lazy-Hazy-Crazy Days of Summer		1963	5.00	10.00	20.00
❑ T 1932 [M] Those Lazy-Hazy-Crazy Days of Summer		1963	3.75	7.50	15.00
❑ SM-1967 The Christmas Song		197?	2.00	4.00	8.00
—Budget-line reissue					
❑ SW 1967 [S] The Christmas Song		1962	3.75	7.50	15.00
—Black label with colorband					
❑ SW 1967 [S] The Christmas Song		1969	3.00	6.00	12.00
—Lime-green label					
❑ SW 1967 [S] The Christmas Song		1971	3.00	6.00	12.00
—Red label					
❑ SW 1967 [S] The Christmas Song		1973	2.50	5.00	10.00
—Orange label, "Capitol" at bottom					
❑ W 1967 [M] The Christmas Song		1962	3.75	7.50	15.00
—Reissue of W 1444 with title song added and another deleted					
❑ SW 2008 [S] Let's Face the Music		1963	5.00	10.00	20.00
❑ W 2008 [M] Let's Face the Music		1963	3.75	7.50	15.00
❑ SM-2117 My Fair Lady		197?	2.00	4.00	8.00
—Reissue with new prefix					
❑ SW 2117 [S] My Fair Lady		1964	5.00	10.00	20.00
—Black label with colorband					
❑ SW 2117 [S] My Fair Lady		1969	3.00	6.00	12.00
—Lime green label					
❑ W 2117 [M] My Fair Lady		1964	3.75	7.50	15.00
❑ ST 2118 [S] I Don't Want to Be Hurt Anymore		1964	5.00	10.00	20.00
❑ T 2118 [M] I Don't Want to Be Hurt Anymore		1964	3.75	7.50	15.00
❑ ST 2195 [S] L-O-V-E		1965	5.00	10.00	20.00
❑ T 2195 [M] L-O-V-E		1965	3.75	7.50	15.00
❑ T 2311 [M] The Nat King Cole Trio		1965	3.00	6.00	12.00
❑ ST 2340 [S] Songs from "Cat Ballou" and Other Motion Pictures		1965	3.75	7.50	15.00
❑ T 2340 [M] Songs from "Cat Ballou" and Other Motion Pictures		1965	3.00	6.00	12.00
❑ DT 2348 [R] Nature Boy		1965	3.00	6.00	12.00
❑ T 2348 [M] Nature Boy		1965	3.75	7.50	15.00
❑ ST 2361 [S] Looking Back		1965	3.75	7.50	15.00
❑ T 2361 [M] Looking Back		1965	3.00	6.00	12.00
❑ MAS 2434 [M] Nat King Cole at the Sands		1966	3.00	6.00	12.00
❑ SM-2434 Nat King Cole at the Sands		197?	2.00	4.00	8.00
—Reissue with new prefix					
❑ SMAS 2434 [S] Nat King Cole at the Sands		1966	3.75	7.50	15.00
❑ ST 2454 [S] Hymns and Spirituals		1966	3.75	7.50	15.00
❑ T 2454 [M] Hymns and Spirituals		1966	3.00	6.00	12.00
❑ T 2529 [M] The Vintage Years		1966	3.00	6.00	12.00
❑ ST 2558 [S] The Great Songs!		1966	3.75	7.50	15.00
❑ T 2558 [M] The Great Songs!		1966	3.00	6.00	12.00
❑ ST 2680 [S] Sincerely, Nat King Cole		1967	3.00	6.00	12.00
❑ T 2680 [M] Sincerely, Nat King Cole		1967	3.75	7.50	15.00
❑ ST 2759 [S] Thank You Pretty Baby		1967	3.00	6.00	12.00
❑ T 2759 [M] Thank You Pretty Baby		1967	3.75	7.50	15.00
❑ ST 2820 [S] Beautiful Ballads		1967	3.00	6.00	12.00
❑ T 2820 [M] Beautiful Ballads		1967	3.75	7.50	15.00
❑ STCL 2873 [(3)P] The Nat King Cole Deluxe Set		1968	6.25	12.50	25.00
❑ TCL 2873 [(3)M] The Nat King Cole Deluxe Set		1968	7.50	15.00	30.00
❑ SKAO 2944 The Best of Nat King Cole		1968	3.00	6.00	12.00
❑ H 9110 [10] Eight Top Pops		1954	12.50	25.00	50.00
❑ M-11033 [M] Trio Days		1972	3.75	7.50	15.00
❑ SWAK-11355 Love Is Here to Stay		1974	3.00	6.00	12.00
❑ SM-11796 After Midnight		1978	2.50	5.00	10.00
❑ SM-11804 Songs from "Cat Ballou" and Other Motion Pictures		1978	2.50	5.00	10.00
❑ SM-11882 Looking Back		1979	2.50	5.00	10.00
❑ ST-12219 16 Grandes Exitos		1982	2.50	5.00	10.00
❑ SN-16032 Ramblin' Rose		1980	2.00	4.00	8.00
❑ SN-16033 The Nat King Cole Story, Volume 1		1980	2.00	4.00	8.00
❑ SN-16034 The Nat King Cole Story, Volume 2		1980	2.00	4.00	8.00
❑ SN-16035 The Nat King Cole Story, Volume 3		1980	2.00	4.00	8.00
❑ SN-16036 The Best of Nat King Cole		1980	2.00	4.00	8.00
❑ SN-16037 Wild Is Love		1980	2.00	4.00	8.00
❑ SN-16136 A Mis Amigos		1980	2.00	4.00	8.00
❑ SN-16137 St. Louis Blues		1980	2.00	4.00	8.00
❑ SN-16162 Unforgettable		1981	2.00	4.00	8.00
❑ SN-16163 Love Is the Thing		1981	2.00	4.00	8.00
❑ DN-16164 Walkin' My Baby Back Home		1981	2.00	4.00	8.00
❑ DN-16165 A Blossom Fell		1981	2.00	4.00	8.00
❑ N-16166 Cole Espanol		1981	2.00	4.00	8.00
❑ SN-16167 More Cole Espanol		1981	2.00	4.00	8.00
❑ N-16260 The Best of the King Cole Trio — Volume 1		1982	2.00	4.00	8.00
❑ N-16281 The Best of the King Cole Trio — Volume 2		1982	2.00	4.00	8.00
❑ SQBO 90938 [(2)] The Velvet Moods of Nat King Cole		1967	6.25	12.50	25.00
—Capitol Record Club exclusive					
❑ SQBO 91278 [(2)] The Swingin' Moods of Nat King Cole		1967	6.25	12.50	25.00
—Capitol Record Club exclusive					
❑ SQBO-93741 [(2)] The Man and His Music		197?	5.00	10.00	20.00
—Capitol Record Club exclusive; with booklet					
DCC COMPACT CLASSICS					
❑ LPZ-2029 Love Is the Thing		1997	30.00	60.00	120.00
—Audiophile vinyl					
❑ LPZ-2047 The Very Thought of You		1998	25.00	50.00	100.00
—Audiophile vinyl					
❑ LPZ-2061 [(2)] The Greatest Hits		1998	30.00	60.00	120.00
—Audiophile vinyl					
DECCA					
❑ DL 8260 [M] In the Beginning		1956	10.00	20.00	40.00
—Black label, silver print					
❑ DL 8260 [M] In the Beginning		1960	6.25	12.50	25.00
—Black label with color bars					
EVEREST ARCHIVE OF FOLK & JAZZ					
❑ 290 Nature Boy		197?	2.50	5.00	10.00
MARK 56					
❑ 739 [(2)] Early 1940s		197?	3.75	7.50	15.00
MCA					
❑ 4020 [(2)] From the Very Beginning		1973	3.00	6.00	12.00

Number	Title (A Side/B Side)	Yr	VG	VG+	NM
MOBILE FIDELITY					
❏ 1-081	Nat King Cole Sings/George Shearing Plays	1981	10.00	20.00	40.00
—Audiophile vinyl					
MOSAIC					
❏ MR27-138 [(27)]	The Complete Capitol Recordings of the Nat King Cole Trio	1991	200.00	400.00	800.00
PAIR					
❏ PDL2-1025 [(2)]	Weaver of Dreams	1986	3.00	6.00	12.00
❏ PDL2-1026 [(2)]	Love Moods	1986	3.00	6.00	12.00
❏ PDL2-1128 [(2)]	Tenderly	1986	3.00	6.00	12.00
PICKWICK					
❏ PTP-2058 [(2)]	Nature Boy	1973	3.00	6.00	12.00
❏ SPC-3046	Love Is a Many Splendored Thing	196?	2.50	5.00	10.00
❏ SPC-3071	When You're Smiling	196?	2.50	5.00	10.00
❏ SPC-3105	Stay As Sweet As You Are	196?	2.50	5.00	10.00
❏ SPC-3154	You're My Everything	197?	2.50	5.00	10.00
❏ SPC-3249	Nature Boy	197?	2.50	5.00	10.00
SAVOY JAZZ					
❏ SJL-1205	Nat King Cole & The King Cole Trio	1989	3.00	6.00	12.00
SCORE					
❏ SLP-4019 [M]	The King Cole Trio and Lester Young	1957	20.00	40.00	80.00
TIME-LIFE					
❏ SLGD-01 [(2)]	Legendary Singers: Nat King Cole	1985	3.75	7.50	15.00
❏ SLGD-15 [(2)]	Legendary Singers: Nat King Cole: Take Two	1986	3.75	7.50	15.00
TRIP					
❏ 7	The Nat "King" Cole Trio	197?	3.00	6.00	12.00
VERVE					
❏ VSP-14 [M]	Nat Cole at JATP	1966	3.75	7.50	15.00
❏ VSPS-14 [R]	Nat Cole at JATP	1966	3.00	6.00	12.00
❏ VSP-25 [M]	Nat Cole at JATP 2	1966	3.75	7.50	15.00
❏ VSPS-25 [R]	Nat Cole at JATP 2	1966	3.00	6.00	12.00

COLE, NATALIE

12-Inch Singles

Number	Title (A Side/B Side)	Yr	VG	VG+	NM
CAPITOL					
❏ SPRO-8990/1 [DJ]	I'm Catching Hell (Living Here Alone) (7:28) (stereo/mono)	1978	3.75	7.50	15.00
ELEKTRA					
❏ ED 6256 [(2)DJ]	Livin' for Love (unknown versions)	2000	3.00	6.00	12.00
❏ 67153 [(2)]	Livin' for Love (Hex HQ2 Club Mix) (Acappella) (Frankie Knuckles Classic Club Mix) (Album Version) (Hex HQ2 Instrumental) (Hex HQ2 Radio Mix) (Frankie Knuckles Classic Instrumental) (Frankie Knuckles Dubbin' 4 Love)	2000	2.50	5.00	10.00
EMI					
❏ SPRO 04265 [DJ]	Miss You Like Crazy (same on both sides?)	1989	2.50	5.00	10.00
❏ SPRO 04441/2 [DJ]	As a Matter of Fact (4 versions)	1989	2.50	5.00	10.00
❏ SPRO 04449 [DJ]	Starting Over Again (same on both sides?)	1989	3.75	7.50	15.00
❏ V-56161	Wild Women Do (7 versions)	1990	2.00	4.00	8.00
EMI MANHATTAN					
❏ V-56084	Pink Cadillac (Radio Version) (Club Vocal) (Bass It Dub)/I Wanna Be That Woman	1988	2.50	5.00	10.00
EPIC					
❏ AS 1748 [DJ]	Keep It on the Outside/I Won't Deny You	1983	2.00	4.00	8.00
❏ 49-04001	Too Much Mister/Where's Your Angel	1983	2.00	4.00	8.00
MANHATTAN					
❏ V-56053	Jump Start (Extended Remix) (Dub Version) (Radio Edit)/More Than Stars	1987	2.00	4.00	8.00
❏ SPRO-79136/7 [DJ]	Jump Start (Extended Version) (Car Mix) (Deluxe Dub Mix)	1987	3.00	6.00	12.00
❏ SPRO-79154 [DJ]	I Live for Your Love (same on both sides?)	1987	2.50	5.00	10.00
MODERN					
❏ DMD 903 [DJ]	Secrets (Extended) (LP Version)	1985	2.50	5.00	10.00
❏ 96841	Secrets (Extended) (Instrumental)	1985	2.00	4.00	8.00
❏ 96885	Dangerous (Extended Dance Mix) (Dub Mix) (Acappella)	1985	2.50	5.00	10.00

45s

Number	Title (A Side/B Side)	Yr	VG	VG+	NM
CAPITOL					
❏ 4109	This Will Be/Joey	1975	—	2.50	5.00
❏ 4193	Inseparable/How Come You Won't Stay Here	1975	—	2.00	4.00
❏ 4259	Sophisticated Lady (She's a Different Lady)/Good Morning Heartache	1976	—	2.00	4.00
❏ 4328	Mr. Melody/Not Like Mine	1976	—	2.00	4.00
❏ 4360	I've Got Love on My Mind/Unpredictable You	1976	—	2.00	4.00
❏ 4439	Party Lights/Peaceful Living	1977	—	2.00	4.00
❏ 4509	Our Love/La Costa	1977	—	2.00	4.00
❏ 4572	Annie Mae/Just Can't Stay Away	1978	—	2.00	4.00
❏ 4623	Lucy in the Sky with Diamonds/Lovers	1978	—	2.00	4.00
❏ 4690	Stand By/Who Will Carry On	1979	—	2.00	4.00
❏ 4722	Sorry/You're So Good	1979	—	2.00	4.00
❏ 4767	Your Lonely Heart/The Winner	1979	—	2.00	4.00
❏ 4869	Someone That I Used to Love/Don't Look Back	1980	—	2.00	4.00
❏ 4924	Hold On/Paradise	1980	—	2.00	4.00
❏ A-5021	You Were Right Girl/Across the Nation	1981	—	2.00	4.00
❏ A-5045	Nothin' But a Fool/The Joke Is On You	1981	—	2.00	4.00
ELEKTRA					
❏ 64816	The Christmas Song (Chestnuts Roasting on an Open Fire)/Nature Boy	1991	—	2.00	4.00
❏ 64875	Unforgettable/Cottage for Sale	1991	—	2.00	4.00
EMI					
❏ B-50185	Miss You Like Crazy/Good to Be Back	1989	—	—	3.00
❏ B-50185 [PS]	Miss You Like Crazy/Good to Be Back	1989	—	2.50	5.00
❏ B-50213	I Do/Miss You Like Crazy	1989	—	—	3.00
❏ B-50231	As a Matter of Fact/(B-side unknown)	1989	—	2.50	5.00
EMI MANHATTAN					
❏ B-50117	Pink Cadillac/I Wanna Be That Woman	1988	—	—	3.00
❏ B-50138	When I Fall in Love/Pink Cadillac	1988	—	—	3.00
❏ B-50138 [PS]	When I Fall in Love/Pink Cadillac	1988	—	2.00	4.00
EPIC					
❏ 34-04000	Too Much Mister/Where's Your Angel	1983	—	2.00	4.00
❏ 34-04147	Keep 'Em on the Outside/I Won't Deny You	1983	—	2.00	4.00
GEFFEN					
❏ 28152	Over You/After Midnite	1987	—	—	3.00
—With Ray Parker Jr.					
MANHATTAN					
❏ B-50073	Jump Start/More Than Stars	1987	—	—	3.00
❏ B-50073 [PS]	Jump Start/More Than Stars	1987	—	2.00	4.00

Number	Title (A Side/B Side)	Yr	VG	VG+	NM
❏ B-50094	I Live for Your Love/More Than the Stars	1987	—	—	3.00
❏ B-50094 [PS]	I Live for Your Love/More Than the Stars	1987	—	2.00	4.00
MODERN					
❏ 99589	Secrets/Nobody's Soldier	1985	—	—	3.00
❏ 99630	A Little Bit of Heaven/When I Need It Bad, You Got It Good	1985	—	—	3.00
❏ 99648	Dangerous/Love Is On the Way	1985	—	—	3.00
❏ 99648 [PS]	Dangerous/Love Is On the Way	1985	—	—	3.00
Albums					
CAPITOL					
❏ ST-11429	Inseparable	1975	2.50	5.00	10.00
❏ ST-11517	Natalie	1976	2.50	5.00	10.00
❏ SO-11600	Unpredictable	1977	2.50	5.00	10.00
❏ SW-11708	Thankful	1978	2.50	5.00	10.00
❏ SKBL-11709 [(2)]	Natalie..Live!	1978	3.00	6.00	12.00
❏ SO-11928	I Love You So	1979	2.50	5.00	10.00
❏ ST-12079	Don't Look Back	1980	2.50	5.00	10.00
❏ ST-12165	Happy Love	1981	2.50	5.00	10.00
❏ ST-12242	A Collection	1982	2.50	5.00	10.00
❏ SN-16038	Inseparable	198?	2.00	4.00	8.00
—Budget-line reissue					
❏ SN-16310	A Collection	1985	2.00	4.00	8.00
—Budget-line reissue					
ELEKTRA					
❏ 61049 [(2)]	Unforgettable	1991	5.00	10.00	20.00
EMI					
❏ E1-48902	Good to Be Back	1989	2.50	5.00	10.00
EPIC					
❏ FE 38280	I'm Ready	1983	2.50	5.00	10.00
MANHATTAN					
❏ 53051	Everlasting	1987	2.50	5.00	10.00
MOBILE FIDELITY					
❏ 1-032	Thankful	1980	5.00	10.00	20.00
—Audiophile vinyl					
MODERN					
❏ 90270	Dangerous	1985	2.50	5.00	10.00

COLE, NATALIE, AND PEABO BRYSON

45s

Number	Title (A Side/B Side)	Yr	VG	VG+	NM
CAPITOL					
❏ 4804	Gimme Some Time/Love Will Find You	1979	—	2.00	4.00
❏ 4826	What You Won't Do for Love/Your Lonely Heart	1980	—	2.00	4.00
Albums					
CAPITOL					
❏ SOO-12025	We're the Best of Friends	1979	2.50	5.00	10.00

COLE, TONY

45s

Number	Title (A Side/B Side)	Yr	VG	VG+	NM
20TH CENTURY					
❏ 2001	Suite: Man and Woman/All I Meant to Do	1972	2.50	5.00	10.00
❏ 2011	The King Is Dead/Ruby	1973	2.50	5.00	10.00
❏ 2055	Scorpio/Mermaid	1973	2.50	5.00	10.00
Albums					
20TH CENTURY					
❏ T-403	If the Music Stops	1972	3.00	6.00	12.00
❏ T-416	Magnificently Mad	1973	3.00	6.00	12.00

COLEMAN, RAY

45s

Number	Title (A Side/B Side)	Yr	VG	VG+	NM
ARCADE					
❏ 147	Jukebox Rock and Roll/Rock, Chicken Rock	1957	50.00	100.00	200.00

COLESON, BETTY

45s

Number	Title (A Side/B Side)	Yr	VG	VG+	NM
HIT					
❏ 93	Dominique/Since I Fell for You	1963	2.00	4.00	8.00
—B-side by Tom Tripp					
❏ 131	The Girl from Ipanema/Dang Me	1964	2.00	4.00	8.00
—B-side by Harvey Frolic					
❏ 144	We'll Sing in the Sunshine/Tottle-Dee Doodle, Dee Doo	1964	2.00	4.00	8.00
—B-side by Jackie Preston					
❏ 173	The Wedding/Song of Love	1965	2.00	4.00	8.00
—B-side by William Randolph					
❏ 201	I Know a Place/I'm in a Very Romantic Mood	1965	2.00	4.00	8.00
—B-side by William Randolph					

COLLAGE, THE

45s

Number	Title (A Side/B Side)	Yr	VG	VG+	NM
SMASH					
❏ 2135	Any Day's a Sunday Afternoon/Lookin' at a Baby	1967	2.00	4.00	8.00
❏ 2135 [PS]	Any Day's a Sunday Afternoon/Lookin' at a Baby	1967	3.75	7.50	15.00
❏ 2150	Driftin'/Any Day's a Sunday Afternoon	1968	2.00	4.00	8.00
❏ 2170	The Story of Rock & Roll/Virginia Day's Ragtime Stories	1968	2.00	4.00	8.00

COLLECTORS, THE   Early incarnation of CHILLIWACK.

45s

Number	Title (A Side/B Side)	Yr	VG	VG+	NM
VALIANT					
❏ 760	Old Man/Looking at a Baby	1967	7.50	15.00	30.00
WARNER BROS.					
❏ 7059	Listen to the Words/Fisherwoman	1967	5.00	10.00	20.00
❏ 7159	Make It Easy/Fat Bird	1968	5.00	10.00	20.00
❏ 7194	Lydia Purple/I Ain't No Rich Man	1968	3.00	6.00	12.00
❏ 7194	Lydia Purple/She (Will O' the Wind)	1968	3.75	7.50	15.00
❏ 7300	Early Morning/My Love Delights Me	1969	3.00	6.00	12.00
Albums					
WARNER BROS.					
❏ W 1746 [M]	The Collectors	1968	12.50	25.00	50.00
—May be white label promo only					
❏ WS 1746 [S]	The Collectors	1968	6.25	12.50	25.00
❏ WS 1774	Grass and Wild Strawberries	1969	6.25	12.50	25.00

COLLEGIANS, THE (1)

45s

Number	Title (A Side/B Side)	Yr	VG	VG+	NM
LOST-NITE					
❏ 123	Zoom, Zoom, Zoom/On Your Merry Way	196?	2.00	4.00	8.00
—Reissue					

Number	Title (A Side/B Side)	Yr	VG	VG+	NM
❏ 158	Let's Go for a Ride/Heavenly Night	196?	—	3.00	6.00
—Reissue					
WINLEY					
❏ 224	Zoom, Zoom, Zoom/On Your Merry Way	1958	12.50	25.00	50.00
❏ 261	Oh I Need Your Love/Tonite, Oh Tonite	1962	7.50	15.00	30.00
❏ 263	Right Around the Corner/	1962	7.50	15.00	30.00
	Teenie Weenie Little Bit				
X-TRA					
❏ 108	Let's Go for a Ride/Heavenly Night	1958	75.00	150.00	300.00
—Small print label (title and artist about 1/8-inch high)					
❏ 108	Let's Go for a Ride/Heavenly Night	1961	15.00	30.00	60.00
—Large print label (title and artist about 1/4-inch high)					
Albums					
LOST-NITE					
❏ LLP-5 [10]	The Best of the Collegians	1981	2.50	5.00	10.00
—Red vinyl					
WINLEY					
❏ LP-6004 [M]	Sing Along with the Collegians	195?	100.00	200.00	400.00

COLLEGIANS, THE (U) Some of these may be by group (1), but others are not.

45s

Number	Title (A Side/B Side)	Yr	VG	VG+	NM
CAT					
❏ 110	Rickety Tickety Melody/The Sackbut, the	1954	6.25	12.50	25.00
	Psaltery and the Dulcimer				
GROOVE					
❏ 0163	Blue Solitude/Please Let Me Be the One	1956	10.00	20.00	40.00
HILLTOP					
❏ 1866	Nomad/Fred's Boogie	1960	5.00	10.00	20.00
❏ 1867	The Saints (Part 1)/The Saints (Part 2)	1960	5.00	10.00	20.00
❏ 1868	Cookin'/Happy Parakeet	1961	5.00	10.00	20.00
HUDCO					
❏ STAR-1/2	Ooh Poo Pah Doo/Silver Dollar	196?	3.00	6.00	12.00
POST					
❏ 10002	I'm Ready/Grandma Told Me So	1962	5.00	10.00	20.00

COLLINS, ALBERT

45s

Number	Title (A Side/B Side)	Yr	VG	VG+	NM
GREAT SCOTT					
❏ 007	Albert's Alley/Defrost	1963	7.50	15.00	30.00
HALLWAY					
❏ 1913	Albert's Alley/Defrost	1963	5.00	10.00	20.00
❏ 1920	Frosty/Tremble	1964	7.50	15.00	30.00
❏ 1925	Backstroke/Thaw Out	1964	5.00	10.00	20.00
IMPERIAL					
❏ 66351	Ain't Got Time/Got a Good Thing Goin'	1969	2.00	4.00	8.00
❏ 66391	Do the Sissy/Turnin' On	1969	2.00	4.00	8.00
❏ 66412	Conversation for Collins/And Then It Started	1969	2.00	4.00	8.00
	Raining				
KANGAROO					
❏ 103	Freeze/(B-side unknown)	1958	15.00	30.00	60.00
❏ 104	Collins Shuffle/(B-side unknown)	1958	15.00	30.00	60.00
LIBERTY					
❏ 56184	Coon 'n Collards/Do What You Want to Do	1970	2.00	4.00	8.00
TCF HALL					
❏ 104	Sno Cone (Part 1)/Sno Cone (Part 2)	1965	2.50	5.00	10.00
❏ 116	Dyin' Flu/Hot 'N' Cold	1966	2.50	5.00	10.00
❏ 127	Frost Bite/Don't Lose Your Cool	1966	2.50	5.00	10.00
TUMBLEWEED					
❏ 1007	Eight Days on the Road/(B-side unknown)	1972	2.00	4.00	8.00
20TH FOX					
❏ 6708	Cookin' Catfish/Taking My Time	1968	2.00	4.00	8.00
Albums					
ALLIGATOR					
❏ AL-4713	Ice Pickin'	1978	2.50	5.00	10.00
❏ AL-4719	Frostbite	1980	2.50	5.00	10.00
❏ AL-4725	Frozen Alive!	1981	2.50	5.00	10.00
❏ AL-4730	Don't Lose Your Cool	1983	2.50	5.00	10.00
❏ AL-4733	Live in Japan	1984	2.50	5.00	10.00
❏ AL-4743	Showdown!	1985	2.50	5.00	10.00
—With Robert Cray and Johnny Copeland					
❏ AL-4752	Cold Snap	1986	2.50	5.00	10.00
BLUE THUMB					
❏ BTS 8	Truckin' with Albert Collins	1969	6.25	12.50	25.00
—Reissue of TCF Hall LP					
IMPERIAL					
❏ LP-12428	Love Can Be Found Anywhere	1968	7.50	15.00	30.00
❏ LP-12438	Trash Talkin'	1969	7.50	15.00	30.00
❏ LP-12449	The Compleat Albert Collins	1970	7.50	15.00	30.00
MOBILE FIDELITY					
❏ 1-217	Showdown!	1995	7.50	15.00	30.00
—With Robert Cray and Johnny Copeland; audiophile vinyl					
❏ 1-226	Cold Snap	1995	5.00	10.00	20.00
—Audiophile vinyl					
TCF HALL					
❏ 8002 [M]	The Cool Sound of Albert Collins	1965	75.00	150.00	300.00
TUMBLEWEED					
❏ TWS-103	There's Gotta Be a Change	1971	3.75	7.50	15.00

COLLINS, BIG TOM

45s

Number	Title (A Side/B Side)	Yr	VG	VG+	NM
KING					
❏ 4483	Heartache Blues/Real Good Feeling	1951	25.00	50.00	100.00
❏ 4568	Heart Breaking Woman/Watchin' My Stuff	1952	25.00	50.00	100.00

COLLINS, EDDIE

45s

Number	Title (A Side/B Side)	Yr	VG	VG+	NM
FERNWOOD					
❏ 104	Patience Baby/Can't Face Life Alone	1958	25.00	50.00	100.00

COLLINS, GLENDA

45s

Number	Title (A Side/B Side)	Yr	VG	VG+	NM
LAWN					
❏ 250	Lollipop/Everybody's Gotta Fall in Love	1965	2.50	5.00	10.00

COLLINS, JUDY

45s

Number	Title (A Side/B Side)	Yr	VG	VG+	NM
ELEKTRA					
❏ 45008	Turn, Turn, Turn/Farewell	1963	2.50	5.00	10.00
❏ 45253	Send In the Clowns/Houses	1975	—	2.50	5.00
—Large print label (original)					
❏ 45253	Send In the Clowns/Houses	1977	—	2.00	4.00
—Small print label (reissue)					
❏ 45289	Angel, Spread Your Wings/The Moon Is a Harsh	1975	—	2.00	4.00
	Mistress				
❏ 45355	Bread and Roses/Out of Control	1976	—	2.00	4.00
❏ 45355 [PS]	Bread and Roses/Out of Control	1976	—	3.00	6.00
❏ 45372	Everything Must Change/Special Delivery	1976	—	2.00	4.00
❏ 45415	Born to the Breed/Special Delivery	1977	—	2.00	4.00
❏ 45601	I'll Keep It With Mine/Thirsty Boots	1965	2.00	4.00	8.00
❏ 45610	I Think It's Going to Rain Today/Hard Lovin'	1966	2.00	4.00	8.00
	Losers				
❏ 45639	Both Sides Now/	1968	—	3.00	6.00
	Who Knows Where the Time Goes				
—Yellow and black label					
❏ 45639	Both Sides Now/	1968	2.00	4.00	8.00
	Who Knows Where the Time Goes				
—Red, white and black label					
❏ 45649	Someday Soon/My Father	1969	—	3.00	6.00
❏ 45657	Chelsea Morning/Pretty Polly	1969	—	3.00	6.00
❏ 45657 [PS]	Chelsea Morning/Pretty Polly	1969	3.75	7.50	15.00
❏ 45680	Pack Up Your Sorrows/Turn, Turn, Turn	1970	—	2.50	5.00
❏ 45709	Amazing Grace/Nightingale II	1971	—	2.50	5.00
❏ 45755	Open the Door/Innisfree	1971	—	2.50	5.00
❏ 45813	In My Life/Sunny Goodge Street	1972	—	2.00	4.00
❏ 45831	Cook with Honey/So Begins the Task	1973	—	2.00	4.00
❏ 45849	The Hostage/Secret Gardens	1973	—	2.00	4.00
❏ 46020	Hard Times for Lovers/Happy End	1979	—	2.00	4.00
❏ 46020 [PS]	Hard Times for Lovers/Happy End	1979	—	3.00	6.00
❏ 46050	Where or When/Dorothy	1979	—	2.00	4.00
❏ 46623	Bright Morning Star/Almost Free	1980	—	2.00	4.00
❏ 46651	The Rainbow Connection/Running for My Life	1980	—	2.00	4.00
❏ 47243	Memory/The Life You Dream	1981	—	2.00	4.00
❏ 47434	It's Gonna Be One of Those Nights/Mama Mama	1982	—	2.00	4.00
❏ 47437 [DJ]	Drink a Round to Ireland (stereo)/(mono)	1982	2.50	5.00	10.00
—Promo only on green vinyl					
❏ 69662	Only You/Dream On	1985	—	—	3.00
❏ 69697	Home Again/Dream On	1984	—	2.00	4.00
—A-side with T.G. Sheppard					
Albums					
DCC COMPACT CLASSICS					
❏ LPZ-2067	Colors of the Day/The Best of Judy Collins	1998	6.25	12.50	25.00
—Audiophile vinyl					
DIRECT DISK					
❏ SD-16607	Judith	1980	10.00	20.00	40.00
—Audiophile vinyl					
ELEKTRA					
❏ JC-1 [DJ]	Judy Collins	1967	3.75	7.50	15.00
—Promo-only compilation of six songs, each in mono on one side, stereo on the other					
❏ 6E-111	Judith	1977	2.00	4.00	8.00
—Reissue of 7E-1032					
❏ 6E-171	Hard Times for Lovers	1979	2.50	5.00	10.00
❏ EKL-209 [M]	Maid of Constant Sorrow	1961	10.00	20.00	40.00
—"Guitar player" label					
❏ EKL-209 [M]	Maid of Constant Sorrow	1966	5.00	10.00	20.00
—Gold/tan label					
❏ EKL-222 [M]	Golden Apples of the Sun	1962	7.50	15.00	30.00
—"Guitar player" label					
❏ EKL-222 [M]	Golden Apples of the Sun	1966	5.00	10.00	20.00
—Gold/tan label					
❏ EKL-243 [M]	Judy Collins #3	1963	7.50	15.00	30.00
—"Guitar player" label					
❏ EKL-243 [M]	Judy Collins #3	1966	5.00	10.00	20.00
—Gold/tan label					
❏ 6E-253	Running for My Life	1980	2.50	5.00	10.00
❏ EKL-280 [M]	Judy Collins' Concert	1964	7.50	15.00	30.00
—"Guitar player" label					
❏ EKL-280 [M]	Judy Collins' Concert	1966	5.00	10.00	20.00
—Gold/tan label					
❏ EKL-300 [M]	Judy Collins' Fifth Album	1965	7.50	15.00	30.00
—"Guitar player" label					
❏ EKL-300 [M]	Judy Collins' Fifth Album	1966	5.00	10.00	20.00
—Gold/tan label					
❏ EKL-320 [M]	In My Life	1966	5.00	10.00	20.00
❏ DS 500	Judy	1969	3.75	7.50	15.00
—Columbia Record Club exclusive; red label with large stylized "E"					
❏ 7E-1032	Judith	1975	3.00	6.00	12.00
❏ EQ-1032 [Q]	Judith	1975	5.00	10.00	20.00
❏ 7E-1076	Bread and Roses	1976	2.50	5.00	10.00
❏ EKL-4012 [M]	Wildflowers	1967	6.25	12.50	25.00
❏ EQ-5030 [Q]	Colors of the Day/The Best of Judy Collins	1973	5.00	10.00	20.00
❏ 8E-6002 [(2)]	So Early in the Spring: The First 15 Years	1977	3.00	6.00	12.00
❏ EKS-7209 [R]	Maid of Constant Sorrow	1964	5.00	10.00	20.00
—"Guitar player" label (first edition)					
❏ EKS-7209 [R]	Maid of Constant Sorrow	1966	3.00	6.00	12.00
—Gold/tan label or red label with large stylized "E"					
❏ EKS-7209 [R]	Maid of Constant Sorrow	1971	2.50	5.00	10.00
—Butterfly label, no Warner Communications logo					
❏ EKS-7209 [R]	Maid of Constant Sorrow	1975	2.00	4.00	8.00
—Any label with Warner Communications logo					
❏ EKS-7222 [R]	Golden Apples of the Sun	196?	3.00	6.00	12.00
—Gold/tan label or red label with large stylized "E"					
❏ EKS-7222 [R]	Golden Apples of the Sun	1971	2.50	5.00	10.00
—Butterfly label, no Warner Communications logo					
❏ EKS-7222 [R]	Golden Apples of the Sun	1975	2.00	4.00	8.00
—Any label with Warner Communications logo					
❏ EKS-7243 [S]	Judy Collins #3	1963	10.00	20.00	40.00
—"Guitar player" label					
❏ EKS-7243 [S]	Judy Collins #3	1966	6.25	12.50	25.00
—Gold/tan label					
❏ EKS-7243 [S]	Judy Collins #3	1969	3.75	7.50	15.00
—Red label with large stylized "E"					

Number	Title (A Side/B Side)	Yr	VG	VG+	NM
❏ EKS-7243 [S] Judy Collins #3		1971	2.50	5.00	10.00
—Butterfly label, no Warner Communications logo					
❏ EKS-7243 [S] Judy Collins #3		1975	2.00	4.00	8.00
—Any label with Warner Communications logo					
❏ EKS-7280 [S] Judy Collins' Concert		1964	10.00	20.00	40.00
—"Guitar player" label					
❏ EKS-7280 [S] Judy Collins' Concert		1966	6.25	12.50	25.00
—Gold/tan label					
❏ EKS-7280 [S] Judy Collins' Concert		1969	3.75	7.50	15.00
—Red label with large stylized "E"					
❏ EKS-7280 [S] Judy Collins' Concert		1971	3.00	6.00	12.00
—Butterfly label, no Warner Communications logo					
❏ EKS-7280 [S] Judy Collins' Concert		1975	2.00	4.00	8.00
—Any label with Warner Communications logo					
❏ EKS-7300 [S] Judy Collins' Fifth Album		1965	10.00	20.00	40.00
—"Guitar player" label					
❏ EKS-7300 [S] Judy Collins' Fifth Album		1966	6.25	12.50	25.00
—Gold/tan label					
❏ EKS-7300 [S] Judy Collins' Fifth Album		1969	3.75	7.50	15.00
—Red label with large stylized "E"					
❏ EKS-7300 [S] Judy Collins' Fifth Album		1971	3.00	6.00	12.00
—Butterfly label, no Warner Communications logo					
❏ EKS-7300 [S] Judy Collins' Fifth Album		1975	2.00	4.00	8.00
—Any label with Warner Communications logo					
❏ EKS-7320 [S] In My Life		1966	6.25	12.50	25.00
❏ 60001 Times of Our Lives		1982	2.50	5.00	10.00
❏ 60304 Home Again		1985	2.50	5.00	10.00
❏ EKS-74012 [S] Wildflowers		1967	5.00	10.00	20.00
—Gold/tan label					
❏ EKS-74012 [S] Wildflowers		1969	3.75	7.50	15.00
—Red label with large stylized "E"					
❏ EKS-74012 [S] Wildflowers		1971	3.00	6.00	12.00
—Butterfly label, no Warner Communications logo					
❏ EKS-74012 [S] Wildflowers		1975	2.00	4.00	8.00
—Any label with Warner Communications logo					
❏ EKS-74027 In My Life		1968	5.00	10.00	20.00
—Reissue of 7320; gold/tan label					
❏ EKS-74027 In My Life		1969	3.75	7.50	15.00
—Red label with large stylized "E"					
❏ EKS-74027 In My Life		1971	3.00	6.00	12.00
—Butterfly label, no Warner Communications logo					
❏ EKS-74027 In My Life		1975	2.00	4.00	8.00
—Any label with Warner Communications logo					
❏ EKS-74033 Who Knows Where the Time Goes		1968	5.00	10.00	20.00
—Gold/tan label					
❏ EKS-74033 Who Knows Where the Time Goes		1969	3.75	7.50	15.00
—Red label with large stylized "E"					
❏ EKS-74033 Who Knows Where the Time Goes		1971	3.00	6.00	12.00
—Butterfly label, no Warner Communications logo					
❏ EKS-74033 Who Knows Where the Time Goes		1975	2.00	4.00	8.00
—Any label with Warner Communications logo					
❏ EKS-74055 Recollections		1969	3.75	7.50	15.00
—Red label with large stylized "E"					
❏ EKS-74055 Recollections		1971	3.00	6.00	12.00
—Butterfly label, no Warner Communications logo					
❏ EKS-74055 Recollections		1975	2.00	4.00	8.00
—Any label with Warner Communications logo					
❏ EKS-75010 Whales & Nightingales		1970	3.00	6.00	12.00
—Butterfly label, no Warner Communications logo					
❏ EKS-75010 Whales & Nightingales		1975	2.00	4.00	8.00
—Any label with Warner Communications logo					
❏ EKS-75014 Living		1971	3.00	6.00	12.00
—Butterfly label, no Warner Communications logo					
❏ EKS-75014 Living		1975	2.00	4.00	8.00
—Any label with Warner Communications logo					
❏ EKS-75030 Colors of the Day/The Best of Judy Collins		1972	3.00	6.00	12.00
—Butterfly label, no Warner Communications logo					
❏ EKS-75030 Colors of the Day/The Best of Judy Collins		1975	2.00	4.00	8.00
—Any label with Warner Communications logo					
❏ EKS-75053 True Stories and Other Dreams		1973	3.00	6.00	12.00
—Butterfly label					
❏ EKS-75053 True Stories and Other Dreams		1980	2.00	4.00	8.00
—Red or red/black label					
GOLD CASTLE					
❏ D1-71302 Trust Your Heart		1989	3.00	6.00	12.00
—Reissue of 171002					
❏ D1-71318 Sanity and Grace		1989	3.00	6.00	12.00
❏ 171002 Trust Your Heart		1988	3.00	6.00	12.00
PAIR					
❏ PDL2-1141 [(2)] Her Finest Hour		1986	3.00	6.00	12.00
WARNER SPECIAL PRODUCTS					
❏ 61-6462 [(4)] Judy Collins		1981	20.00	40.00	80.00
—Book-of-the-Month Club exclusive					

COLLINS, LYN Also see JAMES BROWN.
45s

Number	Title (A Side/B Side)	Yr	VG	VG+	NM
KING					
❏ 6373 Wheels of Life/Just Won't Do Right		1971	12.50	25.00	50.00
PEOPLE					
❏ 608 Think (About It)/Ain't No Sunshine		1972	6.25	12.50	25.00
❏ 615 Me and My Baby Got a Good Thing Goin'/I'll Never Let You Break My Heart Again		1972	3.75	7.50	15.00
❏ 618 Mama Feel Good/Fly Me to the Moon		1973	5.00	10.00	20.00
❏ 623 How Long Can I Keep It Up (Part 1)/How Long Can I Keep It Up (Part 2)		1973	5.00	10.00	20.00
❏ 626 Take Me As I Am/Make the World a Better Place		1973	5.00	10.00	20.00
❏ 630 We Want to Parrty, Parrty, Parrty/You Can't Beat Two People in Love		1973	5.00	10.00	20.00
❏ 633 Take Me Just As I Am/Don't Make Me Over		1973	3.00	6.00	12.00
❏ 636 Give It Up or Turnit A Loose/What the World Needs Now Is Love		1974	7.50	15.00	30.00
❏ 641 Wide Awake in a Dream/Rock Me Again & Again & Again & Again & Again		1974	7.50	15.00	30.00
❏ 650 Rock Me Again & Again & Again & Again & Again/You Can't Love Me If You Don't Respect Me		1974	7.50	15.00	30.00
❏ 657 Baby Don't Do It/How Long Can I Keep It Up		1975	5.00	10.00	20.00
❏ 659 If You Don't Know Me By Now/Baby Don't Do It		1975	5.00	10.00	20.00
❏ 662 Mr. Big Stuff/Rock Me Again & Again & Again & Again & Again		1975	6.25	12.50	25.00
POLYDOR					
❏ 14107 Wheels of Life/Just Won't Do Right		1971	5.00	10.00	20.00
—Reissue of King 6373					
Albums					
PEOPLE					
❏ PE-5602 Think (About It)		1972	37.50	75.00	150.00
—This album has been "reissued"; be careful of sealed copies					
❏ PE-6605 Check Me Out		1975	25.00	50.00	100.00
—This album has been "reissued"; be careful of sealed copies					

COLOGNES, THE
45s

Number	Title (A Side/B Side)	Yr	VG	VG+	NM
LUMMTONE					
❏ 102 A River Flows/A Bird and a Bee		1960	37.50	75.00	150.00

COLORADO With members of THE FIREBALLS.
45s

Number	Title (A Side/B Side)	Yr	VG	VG+	NM
UNI					
❏ 55280 My Babe/Country Comfort		1971	—	3.00	6.00
❏ 55302 Dogwood/Moonshine		1971	—	3.00	6.00

COLOSSEUM
45s

Number	Title (A Side/B Side)	Yr	VG	VG+	NM
ABC DUNHILL					
❏ 4200 Those Who Are About to Die Salute You/Walking in the Park		1969	2.00	4.00	8.00
❏ 4211 Kettle/Plenty Hard Luck		1969	2.00	4.00	8.00
Albums					
ABC DUNHILL					
❏ DS-50062 Those Who Are About to Die Salute You		1969	5.00	10.00	20.00
❏ DS-50079 The Grass Is Green		1970	5.00	10.00	20.00
❏ DSX-50101 Daughter of Time		1971	3.75	7.50	15.00
WARNER BROS.					
❏ PRO 500 [DJ] Colosseum Live		1972	3.75	7.50	15.00
—Highlights for radio					
❏ 2WS 1942 [(2)] Colosseum Live		1972	3.75	7.50	15.00

COLOURS
45s

Number	Title (A Side/B Side)	Yr	VG	VG+	NM
DOT					
❏ 17181 Hyannis Port Soul/Run Away from Here		1968	2.00	4.00	8.00
Albums					
DOT					
❏ DLP-3854 [M] Colours		1968	12.50	25.00	50.00
—Record has a black label, resembling a stock copy, but it is in a stereo cover with "Monaural" and "Promotional Copy Not for Sale" stickers on front					
❏ DLP-25854 [S] Colours		1968	6.25	12.50	25.00
❏ DLP-25935 Atmosphere		1969	6.25	12.50	25.00

COLTER, JESSI Also see DUANE AND MIRRIAM EDDY; WAYLON JENNINGS; WAYLON AND JESSI.
45s

Number	Title (A Side/B Side)	Yr	VG	VG+	NM
CAPITOL					
❏ 4009 I'm Not Lisa/For the First Time		1974	—	2.00	4.00
❏ 4087 What's Happened to Blue Eyes/You Ain't Never Been Loved (Like I'm Gonna Love You)		1975	—	2.00	4.00
❏ 4200 It's Morning (And I Still Love You)/Would You Walk with Me (To the Lilies)		1975	—	2.00	4.00
❏ 4252 Without You/All My Life I've Been Your Love		1976	—	2.00	4.00
❏ 4325 I Thought I Heard You Calling My Name/You Hung the Moon (Didn't You Waylon)		1976	—	2.00	4.00
❏ 4472 I Belong to Him/There Ain't No Rain		1977	—	2.00	4.00
❏ 4641 Maybe You Should've Been Listening/My Cowboy's Last Ride		1978	—	2.00	4.00
❏ 4696 Love Me Back to Sleep/Don't You Think I Felt It Too		1979	—	2.00	4.00
❏ 5073 Holdin' On/(B-side unknown)		1981	—	2.00	4.00
❏ 5113 Nobody Else But You/Ain't Makin' No Headlines		1982	—	2.00	4.00
JAMIE					
❏ 1193 I Cried Long Enough/Making Believe		1961	7.50	15.00	30.00
—As "Mirriam Johnson"					
RCA VICTOR					
❏ 47-9826 Cry Softly/If She's Where You Like Livin'		1970	—	2.50	5.00
❏ 47-9962 The Golden Rocket/You Mean to Say		1971	—	2.50	5.00
❏ 74-0280 Take a Message to Laura/I Ain't the One		1969	—	2.50	5.00
❏ 74-0780 You Don't Need Me, Do You/I Don't Wanna Be a One-Night Stand		1972	—	2.50	5.00
❏ PB-10309 He Called Me Baby/Take a Message to Laura		1975	—	2.50	5.00
Albums					
CAPITOL					
❏ ST-11363 I'm Jessi Colter		1975	2.50	5.00	10.00
❏ ST-11477 Jessi		1976	2.50	5.00	10.00
❏ ST-11543 Diamond in the Rough		1976	2.50	5.00	10.00
❏ ST-11583 Mirriam		1977	2.50	5.00	10.00
❏ ST-11863 That's the Way a Cowboy Rocks and Rolls		1978	2.50	5.00	10.00
❏ ST-12185 Ridin' Shotgun		1981	2.50	5.00	10.00
❏ ST-511863 That's the Way a Cowboy Rocks and Rolls		1978	3.00	6.00	12.00
—Columbia House edition					
RCA VICTOR					
❏ LSP-4333 Country Star		1970	5.00	10.00	20.00

COLTON, TONY
45s

Number	Title (A Side/B Side)	Yr	VG	VG+	NM
ABC-PARAMOUNT					
❏ 10705 I Stand Accused/Further On Down the Track		1965	3.75	7.50	15.00
❏ 10792 You're Wrong Baby/Have You Lost Your Mind		1966	3.75	7.50	15.00
ROULETTE					
❏ 4475 Tell the World/Goodbye Cindy, Goodbye		1963	3.75	7.50	15.00

COLTRANE, CHI
45s

Number	Title (A Side/B Side)	Yr	VG	VG+	NM
CLOUDS					
❏ 10 What's Happening to Me (It's a Spell)/Changes		1978	—	2.00	4.00
COLUMBIA					
❏ 45640 Thunder and Lightning/Time to Come In		1972	—	2.50	5.00

Number	Title (A Side/B Side)	Yr	VG	VG+	NM
❏ 45749	It's Really Come to This/Go Like Elijah	1972	—	2.50	5.00
❏ 45802	Turn Me Around/You Are My Friend	1973	—	2.50	5.00
❏ 45960	Myself to You/Who Every Told You	1973	—	2.00	4.00

Albums
COLUMBIA

Number	Title (A Side/B Side)	Yr	VG	VG+	NM
❏ KC 31275	Chi Coltrane	1972	3.00	6.00	12.00
❏ KC 32463	Let It Ride	1973	3.00	6.00	12.00

COLTRANE, JOHN Also see MILES DAVIS; THELONIOUS MONK.
45s
ATLANTIC

Number	Title (A Side/B Side)	Yr	VG	VG+	NM
❏ 5003	Cousin Mary/Naimi	1960	2.50	5.00	10.00
❏ 5012	My Favorite Things (Part 1)/My Favorite Things (Part 2)	1961	3.00	6.00	12.00

BLUE NOTE

❏ 1691	Blue Train (Part 1)/Blue Train (Part 2)	1957	3.75	7.50	15.00

IMPULSE!

❏ 203	Easy to Remember/Greensleeves	1961	2.50	5.00	10.00
❏ 212	Nancy (With the Laughing Face)/Up 'Gainst the Wall	1962	2.50	5.00	10.00
❏ 218	Lush Life/My One and Only Love	1963	2.50	5.00	10.00

—With Johnny Hartman

PRESTIGE

❏ 107	Time Was (Part 1)/Time Was (Part 2)	195?	3.00	6.00	12.00
❏ 122	Things Ain't What They Used to Be (Part 1)/Things Ain't What They Used to Be (Part 2)	195?	3.00	6.00	12.00
❏ 139	Good Bait (Part 1)/Good Bait (Part 2)	195?	3.00	6.00	12.00
❏ 249	Lush Life/I Love You	1960	3.00	6.00	12.00
❏ 267	Stardust/Love Thy Neighbor	1961	3.00	6.00	12.00
❏ 315	Dakar/The Believer	1963	2.50	5.00	10.00
❏ 394	By the Numbers (Part 1)/By the Numbers (Part 2)	196?	2.00	4.00	8.00

—With Red Garland

❏ 415	Breathless/I Love You	196?	2.00	4.00	8.00

7-Inch Extended Plays
IMPULSE!

❏ EP AS-40	My One and Only/Lush Life	1963	5.00	10.00	20.00

—Jukebox issue; small hole, plays at 33 1/3 rpm

❏ EP AS-40 [PS]	John Coltrane + Johnny Hartman	1963	5.00	10.00	20.00

Albums
ABC IMPULSE!

Number	Title	Yr	VG	VG+	NM
❏ AS-6 [S]	Africa/Brass	1968	3.75	7.50	15.00
❏ AS-10 [S]	Live at the Village Vanguard	1968	3.75	7.50	15.00
❏ AS-21 [S]	Coltrane	1968	3.75	7.50	15.00
❏ AS-30 [S]	Duke Ellington and John Coltrane	1968	3.75	7.50	15.00
❏ AS-32 [S]	Ballads	1968	3.75	7.50	15.00
❏ AS-40 [S]	John Coltrane + Johnny Hartman	1968	3.75	7.50	15.00
❏ AS-42 [S]	Impressions	1968	3.75	7.50	15.00
❏ AS-50 [S]	Coltrane Live at Birdland	1968	3.75	7.50	15.00
❏ AS-66 [S]	Crescent	1968	3.75	7.50	15.00
❏ AS-77 [S]	A Love Supreme	1968	3.75	7.50	15.00
❏ AS-85 [S]	The John Coltrane Quartet Plays	1968	3.75	7.50	15.00
❏ AS-94 [S]	New Thing at Newport	1968	3.75	7.50	15.00
❏ AS-95 [S]	Ascension	1968	3.75	7.50	15.00

—With "Edition II" in dead wax

❏ AS-9106 [S]	Kulu Se Mama	1968	3.75	7.50	15.00
❏ AS-9110 [S]	Meditations	1968	3.75	7.50	15.00
❏ AS-9120 [S]	Expression	1968	3.75	7.50	15.00
❏ AS-9124 [S]	Live at the Village Vanguard Again!	1968	3.75	7.50	15.00
❏ AS-9140 [S]	Om	1968	3.75	7.50	15.00
❏ AS-9148	Cosmic Music	1969	5.00	10.00	20.00

—Credited to "Alice and John Coltrane"; reissue of Coltrane LP

❏ AS-9161	Selflessness	1969	5.00	10.00	20.00
❏ AS-9195	Transition	1969	5.00	10.00	20.00
❏ AS-9200 [(2)]	Greatest Years	1971	5.00	10.00	20.00
❏ AS-9202 [(2)]	Live in Seattle	1971	5.00	10.00	20.00
❏ AS-9211	Sun Ship	1971	5.00	10.00	20.00
❏ AS-9223 [(2)]	Greatest Years, Volume 2	1973	3.75	7.50	15.00
❏ AS-9225	Infinity	1973	3.00	6.00	12.00
❏ IA-9246 [(2)]	Concert Japan	1973	3.75	7.50	15.00
❏ IA-9273	Africa/Brass, Volume 2	1974	3.00	6.00	12.00
❏ IA-9277	Interstellar Space	1974	3.00	6.00	12.00
❏ IA-9278 [(2)]	Greatest Years, Volume 3	1974	3.75	7.50	15.00
❏ IA-9306 [(2)]	The Gentle Side of John Coltrane	1976	3.75	7.50	15.00
❏ IA-9325 [(2)]	The Other Village Vanguard Tapes	1977	3.75	7.50	15.00
❏ IA-9332	First Meditations	1978	3.00	6.00	12.00
❏ IZ-9345 [(2)]	The Mastery of John Coltrane Vol. 1: Feelin' Good	1978	3.00	6.00	12.00
❏ IZ-9346 [(2)]	The Mastery of John Coltrane Vol. 2: Different Drum	1978	3.00	6.00	12.00
❏ IA-9360	The Mastery of John Coltrane Vol. 3: Jupiter Variation	1978	3.00	6.00	12.00
❏ IZ-9361 [(2)]	The Mastery of John Coltrane Vol. 4: Trane's Moods	1978	3.00	6.00	12.00

ATLANTIC

❏ SD 2-313 [(2)]	The Art of John Coltrane	1973	3.75	7.50	15.00
❏ 1311 [M]	Giant Steps	1959	12.50	25.00	50.00

—Black label

❏ 1311 [M]	Giant Steps	1960	6.25	12.50	25.00

—Orange and purple label, white fan logo

❏ 1311 [M]	Giant Steps	1962	3.75	7.50	15.00

—Orange and purple label, black fan logo

❏ SD 1311 [S]	Giant Steps	1959	15.00	30.00	60.00

—Green label

❏ SD 1311 [S]	Giant Steps	1959	17.50	35.00	70.00

—"Bullseye" label

❏ SD 1311 [S]	Giant Steps	1960	6.25	12.50	25.00

—Green and blue label, white fan logo

❏ SD 1311 [S]	Giant Steps	1962	2.75	7.50	15.00

—Green and blue label, black fan logo

❏ SD 1311 [S]	Giant Steps	1969	3.00	6.00	12.00

—Red and green label

❏ 1354 [M]	Coltrane Jazz	1960	7.50	15.00	30.00

—Orange and purple label, white fan logo

❏ 1354 [M]	Coltrane Jazz	1962	3.75	7.50	15.00

—Orange and purple label, black fan logo

❏ SD 1354 [S]	Coltrane Jazz	1960	7.50	15.00	30.00

—Green and blue label, white fan logo

Number	Title	Yr	VG	VG+	NM
❏ SD 1354 [S]	Coltrane Jazz	1962	3.75	7.50	15.00

—Green and blue label, black fan logo

❏ SD 1354 [S]	Coltrane Jazz	1969	3.00	6.00	12.00

—Red and green label

❏ 1361 [M]	My Favorite Things	1961	7.50	15.00	30.00

—Orange and purple label, white fan logo

❏ 1361 [M]	My Favorite Things	1962	3.75	7.50	15.00

—Orange and purple label, black fan logo

❏ SD 1361 [S]	My Favorite Things	1961	7.50	15.00	30.00

—Green and blue label, white fan logo

❏ SD 1361 [S]	My Favorite Things	1962	3.75	7.50	15.00

—Green and blue label, black fan logo

❏ SD 1361 [S]	My Favorite Things	1969	3.00	6.00	12.00

—Red and green label

❏ 1373 [M]	Ole' Coltrane	1961	7.50	15.00	30.00

—Orange and purple label, white fan logo

❏ 1373 [M]	Ole' Coltrane	1962	3.75	7.50	15.00

—Orange and purple label, black fan logo

❏ SD 1373 [S]	Ole' Coltrane	1961	7.50	15.00	30.00

—Green and blue label, white fan logo

❏ SD 1373 [S]	Ole' Coltrane	1962	3.75	7.50	15.00

—Green and blue label, black fan logo

❏ SD 1373 [S]	Ole' Coltrane	1969	3.00	6.00	12.00

—Red and green label

❏ 1382 [M]	Coltrane Plays the Blues	1962	7.50	15.00	30.00
❏ SD 1382 [S]	Coltrane Plays the Blues	1962	7.50	51.00	30.00

—Green and blue label, black fan logo

❏ SD 1382 [S]	Coltrane Plays the Blues	1969	3.00	6.00	12.00

—Red and green label

❏ 1419 [M]	Coltrane's Sound	1964	6.25	12.50	25.00
❏ SD 1419 [S]	Coltrane's Sound	1964	6.25	12.50	25.00

—Green and blue label, black fan logo

❏ SD 1419 [S]	Coltrane's Sound	1969	3.00	6.00	12.00

—Red and green label

❏ 1451 [M]	The Avant Garde	1966	6.25	12.50	25.00
❏ SD 1451 [S]	The Avant Garde	1966	6.25	12.50	25.00

—Green and blue label, black fan logo

❏ SD 1451 [S]	The Avant Garde	1969	3.00	6.00	12.00

—Red and green label

❏ SD 1541	The Best of John Coltrane	1970	3.00	6.00	12.00
❏ SD 1553	The Coltrane Legacy	1971	3.00	6.00	12.00
❏ 90041	The Avant-Garde	1983	2.50	5.00	10.00
❏ 90462	Countdown	1986	2.50	5.00	10.00

ATLANTIC/RHINO

❏ R1-71984 [(12)]	The Heavyweight Champion: The Complete Atlantic Recordings	1995	62.50	125.00	250.00

—Box set with liner notes; albums pressed on 150-gram vinyl

ATLANTIC/RHINO HANDMADE

❏ RHM1-7784 [(12)]	The Heavyweight Champion: The Complete Atlantic Recordings (Year 2000 Second Edition)	2000	50.00	100.00	200.00

—"Year 2000 Second Edition" at lower right back cover; limited, numbered edition of 1,500 copies on 180-gram vinyl

❏ RHM1-7784 [(12)]	The Heavyweight Champion: The Complete Atlantic Recordings (Year 2000 Second Edition)	2000	50.00	100.00	200.00

—"Year 2000 Second Edition" on lower left back cover; limited edition of 1,500, un-numbered, on 180-gram vinyl; pressed in the U.S. for export

BLUE NOTE

❏ BLP-1577 [M]	Blue Train	1957	25.00	50.00	100.00

—Regular version, W. 63rd St., NYC address on label

❏ BLP-1577 [M]	Blue Train	1957	37.50	75.00	150.00

—"Deep groove" version (deep indentation under label on both sides)

❏ BLP-1577 [M]	Blue Train	196?	7.50	15.00	30.00

—New York, USA address on label

❏ BST-1577 [S]	Blue Train	1959	20.00	40.00	80.00

—Regular version, W. 63rd St., NYC address on label

❏ BST-1577 [S]	Blue Train	1959	30.00	60.00	120.00

—"Deep groove" version (deep indentation under label on both sides)

❏ BST-1577 [S]	Blue Train	196?	6.25	12.50	25.00

—New York, USA address on label

❏ B1-46095	Blue Train	1997	3.75	7.50	15.00
❏ B1-81577	Blue Train	1988	2.50	5.00	10.00

—Reissue with new prefix

❏ BST-81577	Blue Train	1967	3.75	7.50	15.00

—"A Division of Liberty Records" on label

❏ BST-81577	Blue Train	198?	2.50	5.00	10.00

—"The Finest in Jazz Since 1939" reissue

COLTRANE

❏ AU-4950	Cosmic Music	1966	75.00	150.00	300.00
❏ AU-5000	Cosmic Music	1966	50.00	100.00	200.00

DCC COMPACT CLASSICS

❏ LPZ-2032	Lush Life	1997	15.00	30.00	60.00

—Audiophile vinyl

FANTASY

❏ OJC-020	Coltrane	198?	2.50	5.00	10.00
❏ OJC-021	Soultrane	198?	2.50	5.00	10.00
❏ OJC-078	Settin' the Pace	198?	2.50	5.00	10.00
❏ OJC-127	Tenor Conclave	1991	3.00	6.00	12.00
❏ OJC-131	Lush Life	198?	2.50	5.00	10.00
❏ OJC-189	Traneing In	1986	2.50	5.00	10.00
❏ OJC-246	Standard Coltrane	1987	2.50	5.00	10.00
❏ OJC-292	Interplay for Two Trumpets and Two Tenors	1988	2.50	5.00	10.00
❏ OJC-352	Black Pearls	1989	2.50	5.00	10.00
❏ OJC-393	Dakar	1989	2.50	5.00	10.00
❏ OJC-394	Last Trane	1989	2.50	5.00	10.00
❏ OJC-415	Bahia	1990	3.00	6.00	12.00
❏ OJC-460	Cattin' with Coltrane and Quinichette	1990	3.00	6.00	12.00

GRP/IMPULSE!

❏ GR-155	A Love Supreme	1995	3.75	7.50	15.00
❏ GR-156	Ballads	1995	3.75	7.50	15.00
❏ GR-157	John Coltrane + Johnny Hartman	1995	3.75	7.50	15.00
❏ IMP-166	Duke Ellington and John Coltrane	1997	3.75	7.50	15.00
❏ IMP-167	Sun Ship	1997	3.75	7.50	15.00
❏ IMP-169	Stellar Regions	1995	3.75	7.50	15.00
❏ IMP-198	Coltrane Live at Birdland	1997	3.75	7.50	15.00
❏ IMP-200	Crescent	1997	3.75	7.50	15.00
❏ IMP-213	Live at the Village Vanguard Again!	1997	3.75	7.50	15.00

Number	Title (A Side/B Side)	Yr	VG	VG+	NM
❏ IMP-214	The John Coltrane Quartet Plays	1997	3.75	7.50	15.00
❏ IMP-215	Coltrane	1997	3.75	7.50	15.00
IMPULSE!					
❏ A-6 [M]	Africa/Brass	1961	7.50	15.00	30.00
❏ AS-6 [S]	Africa/Brass	1961	10.00	20.00	40.00
❏ A-10 [M]	Live at the Village Vanguard	1962	7.50	15.00	30.00
❏ AS-10 [S]	Live at the Village Vanguard	1962	10.00	20.00	40.00
❏ A-21 [M]	Coltrane	1962	7.50	15.00	30.00
❏ AS-21 [S]	Coltrane	1962	10.00	20.00	40.00
❏ A-30 [M]	Duke Ellington and John Coltrane	1963	7.50	15.00	30.00
❏ AS-30 [S]	Duke Ellington and John Coltrane	1963	10.00	20.00	40.00
❏ A-32 [M]	Ballads	1963	7.50	15.00	30.00
❏ AS-32 [S]	Ballads	1963	10.00	20.00	40.00
❏ A-40 [M]	John Coltrane + Johnny Hartman	1963	10.00	20.00	40.00
❏ AS-40 [S]	John Coltrane + Johnny Hartman	1963	12.50	25.00	50.00
❏ A-42 [M]	Impressions	1963	6.25	12.50	25.00
❏ AS-42 [S]	Impressions	1963	7.50	15.00	30.00
❏ A-50 [M]	Coltrane Live at Birdland	1963	6.25	12.50	25.00
❏ AS-50 [S]	Coltrane Live at Birdland	1963	7.50	15.00	30.00
❏ A-66 [M]	Crescent	1964	6.25	12.50	25.00
❏ AS-66 [S]	Crescent	1964	7.50	15.00	30.00
❏ A-77 [M]	A Love Supreme	1965	7.50	15.00	30.00
❏ AS-77 [S]	A Love Supreme	1965	10.00	20.00	40.00
❏ A-85 [M]	The John Coltrane Quartet Plays	1965	6.25	12.50	25.00
❏ AS-85 [S]	The John Coltrane Quartet Plays	1965	7.50	15.00	30.00
❏ A-94 [M]	New Thing at Newport	1965	6.25	12.50	25.00
❏ AS-94 [S]	New Thing at Newport	1965	7.50	15.00	30.00
❏ A-95 [M]	Ascension	1965	20.00	40.00	80.00
—Without "Edition II" in dead wax					
❏ A-95 [M]	Ascension	1966	6.25	12.50	25.00
—With "Edition II" in dead wax					
❏ AS-95 [S]	Ascension	1965	25.00	50.00	100.00
—Without "Edition II" in dead wax					
❏ AS-95 [S]	Ascension	1966	7.50	15.00	30.00
—With "Edition II" in dead wax					
❏ A-9106 [M]	Kulu Se Mama	1966	6.25	12.50	25.00
❏ AS-9106 [S]	Kulu Se Mama	1966	7.50	15.00	30.00
❏ A-9110 [M]	Meditations	1966	6.25	12.50	25.00
❏ AS-9110 [S]	Meditations	1966	7.50	15.00	30.00
❏ A-9120 [M]	Expression	1967	7.50	15.00	30.00
❏ AS-9120 [S]	Expression	1967	6.25	12.50	25.00
❏ A-9124 [M]	Live at the Village Vanguard Again!	1967	7.50	15.00	30.00
❏ AS-9124 [S]	Live at the Village Vanguard Again!	1967	6.25	12.50	25.00
❏ A-9140 [M]	Om	1967	7.50	15.00	30.00
❏ AS-9140 [S]	Om	1967	6.25	12.50	25.00
MCA					
❏ 4131 [(2)]	Greatest Years	1981	2.50	5.00	10.00
❏ 4132 [(2)]	Greatest Years, Volume 2	1981	2.50	5.00	10.00
❏ 4133 [(2)]	Greatest Years, Volume 3	1981	2.50	5.00	10.00
❏ 4134 [(2)]	Live in Seattle	1981	2.50	5.00	10.00
❏ 4135 [(2)]	Concert Japan	1981	2.50	5.00	10.00
❏ 4136 [(2)]	The Gentle Side of John Coltrane	1981	2.50	5.00	10.00
❏ 4137 [(2)]	The Other Village Vanguard Tapes	1981	2.50	5.00	10.00
❏ 4138 [(2)]	The Mastery of John Coltrane Vol. 1: Feelin' Good	1981	2.50	5.00	10.00
❏ 4139 [(2)]	The Mastery of John Coltrane Vol. 2: Different Drum	1981	2.50	5.00	10.00
❏ 4140 [(2)]	The Mastery of John Coltrane Vol. 4: Trane's Moods	1981	2.50	5.00	10.00
❏ 29007	Africa/Brass	1981	2.00	4.00	8.00
❏ 29008	Africa/Brass, Volume 2	1981	2.00	4.00	8.00
❏ 29009	Live at the Village Vanguard	1981	2.00	4.00	8.00
❏ 29010	Live at the Village Vanguard Again!	1981	2.00	4.00	8.00
❏ 29011	Coltrane	1981	2.00	4.00	8.00
❏ 29012	Ballads	1981	2.00	4.00	8.00
❏ 29013	John Coltrane + Johnny Hartman	1981	2.00	4.00	8.00
❏ 29014	Impressions	1981	2.00	4.00	8.00
❏ 29015	Coltrane Live at Birdland	1981	2.00	4.00	8.00
❏ 29016	Crescent	1981	2.00	4.00	8.00
❏ 29017	A Love Supreme	1981	2.00	4.00	8.00
❏ 29018	The John Coltrane Quartet Plays	1981	2.00	4.00	8.00
❏ 29019	New Thing at Newport	1981	2.00	4.00	8.00
❏ 29020	Ascension	1981	2.00	4.00	8.00
❏ 29021	Kulu Se Mama	1981	2.00	4.00	8.00
❏ 29022	Meditations	1981	2.00	4.00	8.00
❏ 29023	Expression	1981	2.00	4.00	8.00
❏ 29024	Om	1981	2.00	4.00	8.00
❏ 29025	Cosmic Music	1981	2.00	4.00	8.00
❏ 29026	Selflessness	1981	2.00	4.00	8.00
❏ 29027	Transition	1981	2.00	4.00	8.00
❏ 29028	Sun Ship	1981	2.00	4.00	8.00
❏ 29029	Interstellar Space	1981	2.00	4.00	8.00
❏ 29030	First Meditations	1981	2.00	4.00	8.00
❏ 29031	The Mastery of John Coltrane Vol. 3: Jupiter Variation	1981	2.00	4.00	8.00
❏ 29032	Duke Ellington and John Coltrane	1981	2.00	4.00	8.00
MCA/IMPULSE!					
❏ 5660	A Love Supreme	1986	2.50	5.00	10.00
❏ 5661	John Coltrane + Johnny Hartman	1986	2.50	5.00	10.00
❏ 5883	Coltrane	1987	2.50	5.00	10.00
❏ 5885	Ballads	1987	2.50	5.00	10.00
❏ 5887	Impressions	1987	2.50	5.00	10.00
❏ 5889	Crescent	1987	2.50	5.00	10.00
❏ 33109	Coltrane Live at Birdland	198?	2.50	5.00	10.00
❏ 33110	The John Coltrane Quartet Plays	198?	2.50	5.00	10.00
❏ 39103	Duke Ellington and John Coltrane	1988	2.50	5.00	10.00
❏ 39118	Om	1988	2.50	5.00	10.00
❏ 39136	Live at the Village Vanguard	1988	2.50	5.00	10.00
❏ 42231	Africa/Brass	1988	2.50	5.00	10.00
❏ 42232	Africa/Brass, Volume 2	1988	2.50	5.00	10.00
PABLO					
❏ 2405417	The Best of John Coltrane	198?	2.50	5.00	10.00
PABLO LIVE					
❏ 2308217	The Paris Concert	1980	3.00	6.00	12.00
❏ 2308222	European Tour	1981	3.00	6.00	12.00
❏ 2308227	Bye Bye Blackbird	1981	3.00	6.00	12.00
❏ 2620101 [(2)]	Afro Blue Impressions	198?	3.00	6.00	12.00

Number	Title (A Side/B Side)	Yr	VG	VG+	NM
PRESTIGE					
❏ PRLP-7105 [M]	Coltrane	1957	25.00	50.00	100.00
—Yellow label					
❏ PRLP-7105 [M]	Coltrane	1964	7.50	15.00	30.00
—Blue label with trident logo					
❏ PRLP-7123 [M]	John Coltrane and the Red Garland Trio	1957	25.00	50.00	100.00
—Yellow label					
❏ PRLP-7123 [M]	Traneing In	1964	7.50	15.00	30.00
—Blue label with trident logo; reissue with new title					
❏ PRLP-7142 [M]	Soultrane	1958	20.00	40.00	80.00
—Yellow label					
❏ PRLP-7142 [M]	Soultrane	1964	6.25	12.50	25.00
—Blue label with trident logo					
❏ PRLP-7158 [M]	Cattin' with Coltrane and Quinichette	1959	20.00	40.00	80.00
—Yellow label					
❏ PRLP-7158 [M]	Cattin' with Coltrane and Quinichette	1964	6.25	12.50	25.00
—Blue label with trident logo					
❏ PRLP-7188 [M]	Lush Life	1960	20.00	40.00	80.00
—Yellow label					
❏ PRLP-7188 [M]	Lush Life	1964	6.25	12.50	25.00
—Blue label with trident logo					
❏ PRLP-7213 [M]	Settin' the Pace	1961	20.00	40.00	80.00
—Yellow label					
❏ PRLP-7213 [M]	Settin' the Pace	1964	6.25	12.50	25.00
—Blue label with trident logo					
❏ PRLP-7243 [M]	Standard Coltrane	1962	10.00	20.00	40.00
—Yellow label					
❏ PRLP-7243 [M]	Standard Coltrane	1964	6.25	12.50	25.00
—Blue label with trident logo					
❏ PRST-7243 [S]	Standard Coltrane	1962	12.50	25.00	50.00
—Silver label					
❏ PRST-7243 [S]	Standard Coltrane	1964	6.25	12.50	25.00
—Blue label with trident logo					
❏ PRLP-7247 [M]	Mating Call	1962	10.00	20.00	40.00
—Yellow label					
❏ PRLP-7247 [M]	Mating Call	1964	6.25	12.50	25.00
—Blue label with trident logo					
❏ PRST-7247 [R]	Mating Call	196?	6.25	12.50	25.00
—Silver label					
❏ PRST-7247 [R]	Mating Call	1964	5.00	10.00	20.00
—Blue label with trident logo					
❏ PRLP-7249 [M]	Tenor Conclave	1962	10.00	20.00	40.00
—Yellow label					
❏ PRLP-7249 [M]	Tenor Conclave	1964	6.25	12.50	25.00
—Blue label with trident logo					
❏ PRST-7249 [R]	Tenor Conclave	196?	6.25	12.50	25.00
—Silver label					
❏ PRST-7249 [R]	Tenor Conclave	1964	5.00	10.00	20.00
—Blue label with trident logo					
❏ PRLP-7268 [M]	Stardust	1963	10.00	20.00	40.00
—Yellow label					
❏ PRLP-7268 [M]	Stardust	1964	6.25	12.50	25.00
—Blue label with trident logo					
❏ PRST-7268 [S]	Stardust	1963	10.00	20.00	40.00
—Silver label					
❏ PRST-7268 [S]	Stardust	1964	6.25	12.50	25.00
—Blue label with trident logo					
❏ PRLP-7280 [M]	Dakar	1963	10.00	20.00	40.00
—Yellow label					
❏ PRLP-7280 [M]	Dakar	1964	6.25	12.50	25.00
—Blue label with trident logo					
❏ PRST-7280 [S]	Dakar	1963	10.00	20.00	40.00
—Silver label					
❏ PRST-7280 [S]	Dakar	1964	6.25	12.50	25.00
—Blue label with trident logo					
❏ PRLP-7292 [M]	The Believer	1964	6.25	12.50	25.00
—Blue label with trident logo					
❏ PRLP-7292 [M]	The Believer	1964	10.00	20.00	40.00
—Yellow label					
❏ PRST-7292 [S]	The Believer	1964	6.25	12.50	25.00
—Blue label with trident logo					
❏ PRST-7292 [S]	The Believer	1964	10.00	20.00	40.00
—Silver label					
❏ PRLP-7316 [M]	Black Pearls	1964	6.25	12.50	25.00
—Blue label with trident logo					
❏ PRLP-7316 [M]	Black Pearls	1964	10.00	20.00	40.00
—Yellow label					
❏ PRST-7316 [S]	Black Pearls	1964	6.25	12.50	25.00
—Blue label with trident logo					
❏ PRST-7316 [S]	Black Pearls	1964	10.00	20.00	40.00
—Silver label					
❏ PRLP-7353 [M]	Bahia	1965	6.25	12.50	25.00
❏ PRST-7353 [S]	Bahia	1965	6.25	12.50	25.00
❏ PRLP-7378 [M]	The Last Trane	1965	6.25	12.50	25.00
❏ PRST-7378 [S]	The Last Trane	1965	6.25	12.50	25.00
❏ PRLP-7426 [M]	John Coltrane Plays for Lovers	1966	6.25	12.50	25.00
❏ PRST-7426 [S]	John Coltrane Plays for Lovers	1966	6.25	12.50	25.00
❏ PRLP-7531 [M]	Soultrane	1967	6.25	12.50	25.00
❏ PRST-7531 [R]	Soultrane	1967	3.00	6.00	12.00
❏ PRST-7581 [R]	Lush Life	1968	3.00	6.00	12.00
❏ PRST-7609 [R]	The First Trane	1969	3.00	6.00	12.00
❏ PRST-7651 [R]	Traneing In	1969	3.00	6.00	12.00
❏ PRST-7670 [R]	Two Tenors	1969	3.00	6.00	12.00
❏ PRST-7725	Mating Call	1970	3.00	6.00	12.00
❏ PRST-7746	Trane's Reign	1970	3.00	6.00	12.00
❏ PRST-7825	The Master	1971	3.00	6.00	12.00
❏ 24003 [(2)]	John Coltrane	1972	3.75	7.50	15.00
❏ 24014 [(2)]	More Lasting Than Bronze	1973	3.75	7.50	15.00
❏ 24037 [(2)]	Black Pearls	1974	3.75	7.50	15.00
❏ 24056 [(2)]	The Stardust Session	197?	3.75	7.50	15.00
❏ 24069 [(2)]	Wheelin'	197?	3.00	6.00	12.00
❏ 24084 [(2)]	On a Misty Night	198?	3.00	6.00	12.00
❏ 24094 [(2)]	Rain or Shine	198?	3.00	6.00	12.00
❏ 24104 [(2)]	Dakar	198?	3.00	6.00	12.00
❏ 24110 [(2)]	Bahia	198?	3.00	6.00	12.00
RHINO					
❏ R1-75203	Giant Steps	2003	3.75	7.50	15.00
—Reissue on 180-gram vinyl					

Number	Title (A Side/B Side)	Yr	VG	VG+	NM
SOLID STATE					
❑ SM-17025 [M]	Coltrane Time	1968	6.25	12.50	25.00
❑ SS-18025 [S]	Coltrane Time	1968	3.75	7.50	15.00
TRIP					
❑ 5001 [(2)]	Trane Tracks	1974	3.75	7.50	15.00
UNITED ARTISTS					
❑ UAS-5638	Coltrane Time	1972	3.00	6.00	12.00
—Reissue of 15001					
❑ UAJ-14001 [M]	Coltrane Time	1962	10.00	20.00	40.00
❑ UAJS-15001 [S]	Coltrane Time	1962	12.50	25.00	50.00

COLTS, THE
45s

Number	Title (A Side/B Side)	Yr	VG	VG+	NM
ANTLER					
❑ 4003	Never No More/The Shiek of Araby	1959	10.00	20.00	40.00
❑ 4007	Guiding Angel/The Shiek of Araby	1959	10.00	20.00	40.00
MAMBO					
❑ 112	Adorable/Lips Red as Wine	1955	100.00	200.00	400.00
PLAZA					
❑ 505	Hey, Pretty Baby/Sweet Sixteen	1962	5.00	10.00	20.00
VITA					
❑ 112	Adorable/Lips Red as Wine	1955	37.50	75.00	150.00
❑ 121	Honey Bun/Sweet Sixteen	1955	30.00	60.00	120.00
❑ 130	Never No More/Hey You Shoo-Bee-Ooh-Bee	1956	30.00	60.00	120.00

COLUMBUS PHARAOHS, THE
45s

Number	Title (A Side/B Side)	Yr	VG	VG+	NM
ESTA					
❑ 290	Give Me Your Love/China Girl	1958	250.00	500.00	1000.

COLWELL-WINFIELD BLUES BAND, THE
45s

Number	Title (A Side/B Side)	Yr	VG	VG+	NM
VERVE FORECAST					
❑ 5098	Cold Wind Blues/Free Will Fantasy	1968	2.50	5.00	10.00
Albums					
VERVE FORECAST					
❑ FTS-3056	Cold Wind Blues	1968	5.00	10.00	20.00
ZA-ZOO					
❑ 1	Live Bust	1971	7.50	15.00	30.00

COLYER, KEN
45s

Number	Title (A Side/B Side)	Yr	VG	VG+	NM
LONDON					
❑ 1655	Down by the Riverside/Take This Hammer	1956	3.00	6.00	12.00
❑ 1674	Casey Jones/Streamline Train	1956	3.00	6.00	12.00
Albums					
GHB					
❑ 161	Live at the 100 Club	198?	2.50	5.00	10.00
LONDON					
❑ PB 904 [10]	New Orleans to London	1954	12.50	25.00	50.00
❑ LL 1340 [M]	Back to the Delta	1956	10.00	20.00	40.00
❑ LL 1618 [M]	Club Session with Colyer	1957	10.00	20.00	40.00
STORYVILLE					
❑ SLP-144	Ken's Early Days	197?	3.00	6.00	12.00

COMBINATIONS, THE
45s

Number	Title (A Side/B Side)	Yr	VG	VG+	NM
KELLMAC					
❑ 1007	Why/Come Back	1966	7.50	15.00	30.00
❑ 1011	What'cha Gonna Do/Like I Never Did Before	1966	375.00	750.00	1500.

COMFORTABLE CHAIR, THE
45s

Number	Title (A Side/B Side)	Yr	VG	VG+	NM
ODE					
❑ 109	Be Me/Some Soon, Some Day	1968	2.50	5.00	10.00
❑ 112	I'll See You/Now	1968	2.50	5.00	10.00
Albums					
ODE					
❑ Z12 44005	The Comfortable Chair	1968	5.00	10.00	20.00

COMMANDER CODY AND HIS LOST PLANET AIRMEN
Includes records as "Commander Cody Band" and "Commander Cody."
45s

Number	Title (A Side/B Side)	Yr	VG	VG+	NM
ARISTA					
❑ 0271	Seven-Eleven/You Snooze You Lose	1977	—	2.00	4.00
❑ 0344	Thank You Lone Ranger/My Day	1978	—	2.00	4.00
DOT					
❑ 17487	Daddy's Drinking Up Our Christmas/ Honeysuckle Honey	1973	—	3.00	6.00
❑ 17500	Diggy Liggy Lo/Outgoing Person	1974	—	2.50	5.00
PARAMOUNT					
❑ 0130	Lost in the Ozone/Midnight Shift	1971	—	3.00	6.00
❑ 0130 [PS]	Lost in the Ozone/Midnight Shift	1971	2.50	5.00	10.00
❑ 0146	Hot Rod Lincoln/My Home in My Hand	1972	—	3.00	6.00
❑ 0169	Beat Me Daddy, Eight to the Bar/Daddy's Gonna Treat You Right	1972	—	3.00	6.00
❑ 0169 [PS]	Beat Me Daddy, Eight to the Bar/Daddy's Gonna Treat You Right	1972	2.50	5.00	10.00
❑ 0178	Truck Stop Rock/Mama Hated Diesels	1972	—	3.00	6.00
❑ 0178 [PS]	Truck Stop Rock/Mama Hated Diesels	1972	2.50	5.00	10.00
❑ 0193	Semi-Truck/Watch My .38	1973	—	3.00	6.00
❑ 0216	Smoke! Smoke! Smoke! (That Cigarette)/Rock That Boogie	1973	—	3.00	6.00
❑ 0216 [PS]	Smoke! Smoke! Smoke! (That Cigarette)/Rock That Boogie	1973	2.50	5.00	10.00
❑ 0278	Riot in Cell Block No. 9/Oh, Momma Momma	1974	—	3.00	6.00
WARNER BROS.					
❑ 8073	Don't Let Go/Keep On Lovin' Her	1975	—	2.00	4.00
❑ 8164	It's Gonna Be One of Those Nights/ Roll Your Own	1975	—	2.00	4.00
Albums					
ARISTA					
❑ AL 4125	Rock 'N' Roll Again	1977	2.50	5.00	10.00
❑ AB 4183	Flying Dreams	1978	3.75	7.50	15.00
BLIND PIG					
❑ BP-2086	Let's Rock	1986	2.50	5.00	10.00

Number	Title (A Side/B Side)	Yr	VG	VG+	NM
MCA					
❑ 659	Live from Deep in the Heart of Texas	1980	2.00	4.00	8.00
—Reissue of Paramount 1017					
❑ 660	Country Casanova	1980	2.00	4.00	8.00
—Reissue of Paramount 6054					
❑ 661	Hot Licks, Cold Steel & Truckers Favorites	1980	2.00	4.00	8.00
—Reissue of Paramount 6031					
❑ 37101	Lost in the Ozone	1980	2.00	4.00	8.00
—Reissue of Paramount 6017					
PARAMOUNT					
❑ PAS-1017	Live from Deep in the Heart of Texas	1974	3.00	6.00	12.00
❑ PAS-6017	Lost in the Ozone	1971	3.75	7.50	15.00
❑ PAS-6031	Hot Licks, Cold Steel & Truckers Favorites	1972	3.00	6.00	12.00
❑ PAS-6054	Country Casanova	1973	3.00	6.00	12.00
WARNER BROS.					
❑ BS 2847	Commander Cody and His Lost Planet Airmen	1975	2.50	5.00	10.00
❑ BS 2883	Tales from the Ozone	1975	2.50	5.00	10.00
❑ 2LS 2939 [(2)]	We've Got a Live One Here!	1976	3.00	6.00	12.00

COMMERCIALS, THE
45s

Number	Title (A Side/B Side)	Yr	VG	VG+	NM
DAYHILL					
❑ 2012	Power in Your Love/I Guess, I Guess, I Guess	196?	7.50	15.00	30.00

COMMODORES
Popular 1970s and 1980s soul group. Few, if any, of their records use the word "The" before "Commodores."
12-Inch Singles

Number	Title (A Side/B Side)	Yr	VG	VG+	NM
MOTOWN					
❑ M 00007D1	Brick House (6:11) (same on both sides)	1977	3.75	7.50	15.00
❑ PR-56 [DJ]	Still (5:51)/Sail On (5:35)	1979	5.00	10.00	20.00
❑ PR-70 [DJ]	Jesus Is Love (Short Version 4:26) (Long Version 6:04)	1980	5.00	10.00	20.00
❑ PR-87 [DJ]	Keep On Taking Me Higher (5:18)/ Why You Wanna Try Me (4:36)	1981	3.00	6.00	12.00
❑ PR-166 [DJ]	Nightshift (Radio Edit of Club Mix 4:48) (Club Mix 7:02) (Dub Mix 7:12)	1985	3.00	6.00	12.00
❑ 4533MG	Nightshift (Edit of Club Mix 4:48) (Club Mix 7:02) (Instrumentakl Mix 7:12)	1985	2.00	4.00	8.00
❑ 4535MG	Animal Instinct (Club Mix 9:46)/ Lightin' Up the Night	1985	2.00	4.00	8.00
POLYDOR					
❑ PRO 467-1 [DJ]	Goin' to the Bank (Club Mix) (Dub)	1986	3.00	6.00	12.00
❑ PRO 501-1 [DJ]	United in Love (Edit) (LP Version)	1986	2.00	4.00	8.00
❑ PRO 641-1 [DJ]	Solitaire (same on both sides)	1988	2.50	5.00	10.00
❑ PRO 684-1 [DJ]	Homeless (same on both sides)	1988	2.00	4.00	8.00
❑ 871371-1	Grrip (6 versions)	1989	2.00	4.00	8.00
❑ 885358-1	Goin' to the Bank (7:17) (4:19)	1986	2.00	4.00	8.00
❑ 885538-1	Take It from Me (4 versions)/I Wanna Rock You	1987	2.00	4.00	8.00

45s

Number	Title (A Side/B Side)	Yr	VG	VG+	NM
MOTOWN					
❑ 1268	Are You Happy/There's a Song in My Heart	1973	—	3.00	6.00
❑ 1307	Machine Gun/There's a Song in My Heart	1974	—	2.50	5.00
❑ 1307 [DJ]	Machine Gun (stereo/mono)	1974	3.75	7.50	15.00
—Promo only on red vinyl					
❑ 1319	I Feel Sanctified/It Is As Good As You Make It	1974	—	2.50	5.00
❑ 1338	Slippery When Wet/The Bump	1975	—	2.50	5.00
❑ 1361	This Is Your Life/Look What You've Done to Me	1975	—	2.50	5.00
❑ 1366	Wide Open/(B-side unassigned)	1975	—	—	—
—Unreleased					
❑ 1381	Sweet Love/Better Never Than Forever	1976	—	2.00	4.00
❑ 1381 [DJ]	Sweet Love (stereo/mono)	1976	3.75	7.50	15.00
—Promo only on yellow vinyl					
❑ 1394	Come Inside/Time	1976	—	—	—
—Unreleased					
❑ 1399	High on Sunshine/Thumpin' Music	1976	—	—	—
—Unreleased					
❑ 1402	Just to Be Close to You/Thumpin' Music	1976	—	2.00	4.00
❑ 1408	Fancy Dancer/Cebu	1977	—	2.00	4.00
❑ 1418	Easy/Can't Let You Tease Me	1977	—	2.00	4.00
❑ 1425	Brick House/Captain Quickdraw	1977	—	2.00	4.00
❑ 1432	Too Hot Ta Trot/Funky Situation	1977	—	2.00	4.00
❑ 1443	Three Times a Lady/ Look What You've Done to Me	1978	—	2.00	4.00
❑ 1452	Flying High/X-Rated Movie	1978	—	2.00	4.00
❑ 1457	Say Yeah/(B-side unassigned)	1978	—	—	—
—Unreleased					
❑ 1466	Sail On/Thumpin' Music	1979	—	2.00	4.00
❑ 1474	Still/Such a Woman	1979	—	2.00	4.00
❑ 1479	Wonderland/Lovin' You	1979	—	2.00	4.00
❑ 1489	Old Fashion Love/Sexy Lady	1980	—	2.00	4.00
❑ 1495	Heroes/Funky Situation	1980	—	2.00	4.00
❑ 1502	Jesus Is Love/Mighty Spirit	1980	—	3.00	6.00
❑ 1514	Lady (You Bring Me Up)/Gettin' It	1981	—	2.00	4.00
❑ 1527	Oh No/Lovin' You	1981	—	2.00	4.00
❑ 1604	Why You Wanna Try Me/X-Rated Movie	1982	—	2.00	4.00
❑ 1651	Painted Pictures/Reach High	1982	—	—	3.00
❑ 1661	Sexy Lady/Reach High	1983	—	—	3.00
❑ 1694	Only You/Cebu	1983	—	—	3.00
❑ 1719	Been Lovin' You/Turn Off the Lights	1984	—	—	3.00
❑ 1773	Nightshift/I Keep Running	1985	—	—	3.00
❑ 1773 [PS]	Nightshift/I Keep Running	1985	—	3.00	6.00
❑ 1788	Animal Instinct/Lightin' Up the Sky	1985	—	—	3.00
❑ 1802	Janet/I'm in Love	1985	—	—	3.00
MOWEST					
❑ 5009	I'm Looking for Love/At the Zoo	1972	2.00	4.00	8.00
❑ 5038	Determination/Don't You Be Worried	1973	2.00	4.00	8.00
POLYDOR					
❑ 871370-7	Grrip/Ain't Giving Up	1989	—	—	3.00
❑ 885358-7	Goin' to the Bank/Serious Love	1986	—	—	3.00
❑ 885358-7 [PS]	Goin' to the Bank/Serious Love	1986	—	—	3.00
❑ 885538-7	Take It from Me/I Wanna Rock You	1987	—	—	3.00
❑ 885538-7 [PS]	Take It from Me/I Wanna Rock You	1987	—	—	3.00
❑ 885760-7	United in Love/Talk to Me	1987	—	—	3.00
❑ 885760-7 [PS]	United in Love/Talk to Me	1987	—	—	3.00
❑ 887939-7	Solitaire/Stretchhh	1988	—	—	3.00
❑ 887939-7 [PS]	Solitaire/Stretchhh	1988	—	—	3.00

Albums

MOTOWN

Number	Title (A Side/B Side)	Yr	VG	VG+	NM
❏ PR 39 [DJ]	1978 Platinum Tour	1978	5.00	10.00	20.00

—Promo-only compilation

Number	Title (A Side/B Side)	Yr	VG	VG+	NM
❏ M5-121V1	Machine Gun	1981	2.50	5.00	10.00

—Reissue

Number	Title (A Side/B Side)	Yr	VG	VG+	NM
❏ M5-179V1	Movin' On	1981	2.00	4.00	8.00
❏ M5-222V1	Commodores	1982	2.00	4.00	8.00
❏ M5-240V1	Caught in the Act	1982	2.00	4.00	8.00
❏ M6-798	Machine Gun	1974	3.75	7.50	15.00
❏ M6-820	Caught in the Act	1975	2.50	5.00	10.00
❏ M6-848	Movin' On	1975	2.50	5.00	10.00
❏ M6-867	Hot on the Tracks	1976	2.50	5.00	10.00
❏ M7-884	Commodores	1977	2.50	5.00	10.00
❏ M9-894 [(2)]	Commodores Live!	1977	3.00	6.00	12.00
❏ M7-902	Natural High	1978	2.50	5.00	10.00
❏ M7-912	Commodores' Greatest Hits	1978	2.50	5.00	10.00
❏ M8-926	Midnight Magic	1979	2.50	5.00	10.00
❏ M8-939	Heroes	1980	2.50	5.00	10.00
❏ M8-955	In the Pocket	1981	2.50	5.00	10.00
❏ 5257 ML	Hot on the Tracks	1983	2.00	4.00	8.00
❏ 5293 ML	Natural High	1983	2.00	4.00	8.00
❏ 6028 ML	All the Great Hits	1982	2.50	5.00	10.00
❏ 6044 ML2 [(2)]	Anthology	1983	3.00	6.00	12.00
❏ 6054 ML	Commodores 13	1983	2.50	5.00	10.00
❏ 6124 ML	Nightshift	1985	2.50	5.00	10.00

POLYDOR

Number	Title (A Side/B Side)	Yr	VG	VG+	NM
❏ 831194-1	United	1986	2.50	5.00	10.00
❏ 835369-1	Rock Solid	1988	2.50	5.00	10.00

COMMODORES, THE None of the below are the popular 1970s-1980s group, but they aren't all the same group, either.

45s

ATLANTIC

Number	Title (A Side/B Side)	Yr	VG	VG+	NM
❏ 2633	Keep On Dancing/Rise Up	1969	2.00	4.00	8.00

BRUNSWICK

Number	Title (A Side/B Side)	Yr	VG	VG+	NM
❏ 55126	Laughing with Tears/Who Dat	1959	5.00	10.00	20.00

CHALLENGE

Number	Title (A Side/B Side)	Yr	VG	VG+	NM
❏ 1004	Sweet Angel/Not a Day Goes By	1957	5.00	10.00	20.00
❏ 1007	Faith/I'll Be There	1957	5.00	10.00	20.00

DOT

Number	Title (A Side/B Side)	Yr	VG	VG+	NM
❏ 15372	Uranium/Riding on a Train	1955	6.25	12.50	25.00
❏ 15425	Cream Puff/Close to My Heart	1955	6.25	12.50	25.00
❏ 15439	Speedoo/Whole Lotta Shakin' Goin' On	1956	6.25	12.50	25.00
❏ 15461	Two Loves Have I/Who Said I Said That	1956	6.25	12.50	25.00

COMMON PEOPLE, THE

Albums

CAPITOL

Number	Title (A Side/B Side)	Yr	VG	VG+	NM
❏ ST-266	Of the People/By the People/For the People/From the Common People	1969	25.00	50.00	100.00

COMO, PERRY

45s

RCA

Number	Title (A Side/B Side)	Yr	VG	VG+	NM
❏ 9096-7-R [DJ]	I May Never Pass This Way Again (same on both sides)	1989	—	2.50	5.00

—Promotional record for Christmas Seals

Number	Title (A Side/B Side)	Yr	VG	VG+	NM
❏ PB-10122	Christmas Dream/Christ Is Born	1976	—	—	3.00

—Reissue; black label, dog near top

Number	Title (A Side/B Side)	Yr	VG	VG+	NM
❏ PB-11185	Girl You Made It Happen/Where You're Concerned	1977	—	—	3.00
❏ PB-11434	When I Wanted You/Forever	1978	—	—	3.00
❏ PB-12028	Colors of My Life/Someone Is Waiting	1980	—	—	3.00
❏ PB-12088	Not While I'm Around/When	1980	—	—	3.00
❏ PB-12146	You Are My World/Regrets	1981	—	—	3.00
❏ PB-13069	Goodbye for Now (Theme from "Reds")/Jason	1982	—	—	3.00
❏ PB-13307	I Wish It Could Be Christmas Forever/Toyland	1982	—	2.00	4.00
❏ PB-13453	So It Goes/Fancy Dancer	1983	—	—	3.00
❏ PB-13613	As My Love for You/The Second Time	1983	—	—	3.00
❏ PB-13690	The Best of Times/Song of the Sand (La Da Da Da)	1983	—	—	3.00
❏ PB-13690 [PS]	The Best of Times/Song of the Sand (La Da Da Da)	1983	—	3.00	6.00

RCA VICTOR

Number	Title (A Side/B Side)	Yr	VG	VG+	NM
❏ 47-2728	Because/If You Had All the World and All the Gold	1949	3.75	7.50	15.00
❏ 47-2747	What'll I Do?/Love Me or Leave Me	1949	3.75	7.50	15.00
❏ 47-2843	When Your Hair Has Turned to Silver/When Day Is Done	1949	3.75	7.50	15.00
❏ 47-2844	Carolina Moon/Body and Soul	1949	3.75	7.50	15.00
❏ 47-2845	I'm Always Chasing Rainbows/If We Can't Be the Same Old Sweethearts, We'll Just Be the Same Old Friends	1949	3.75	7.50	15.00

—The above three comprise box set WP 187, "A Sentimental Date with Perry"

Number	Title (A Side/B Side)	Yr	VG	VG+	NM
❏ 47-2886	Prisoner of Love/Temptation	1949	3.75	7.50	15.00
❏ 47-2887	Till the End of Time/Because	1949	3.75	7.50	15.00
❏ 47-2888	When You Were Sweet Sixteen/Song of Songs	1949	3.75	7.50	15.00
❏ 47-2892	Forever and Ever/I Don't See Me in Your Eyes Anymore	1949	3.75	7.50	15.00
❏ 47-2896	Bali Ha'i/Some Enchanted Evening	1949	3.75	7.50	15.00
❏ 47-2899	"A" You're Adorable/When Is Sometime?	1949	3.75	7.50	15.00
❏ 47-2919	Every Time I Meet You/Two Little, New Little, Blue Little Eyes	1949	3.75	7.50	15.00
❏ 47-2931	Let's Take an Old-Fashioned Walk/Just One Way to Say I Love You	1949	3.75	7.50	15.00
❏ 47-2969	That Christmas Feeling/Winter Wonderland	1949	5.00	10.00	20.00
❏ 47-2970	I'll Be Home for Christmas/Santa Claus Is Coming to Town	1949	5.00	10.00	20.00
❏ 47-2971	Silent Night/White Christmas	1949	5.00	10.00	20.00
❏ 47-2972	Jingle Bells/O Come All Ye Faithful	1949	5.00	10.00	20.00
❏ 47-2997	Give Me Your Hand/I Wish I Had a Record	1949	3.75	7.50	15.00
❏ 47-3036	A Dreamer's Holiday/The Meadows of Heaven	1949	3.75	7.50	15.00
❏ 47-3211	Please Believe Me/Did Anyone Ever Tell You, Mrs. Murphy	1949	3.75	7.50	15.00
❏ 47-3229	Easter Parade/Song of Songs	1949	3.75	7.50	15.00
❏ 47-3229	With a Song in My Heart/Blue Room	1949	3.75	7.50	15.00
❏ 47-3267	Far Away Places/Missouri Waltz	1949	3.75	7.50	15.00

Number	Title (A Side/B Side)	Yr	VG	VG+	NM
❏ 47-3763	If You Were Only Mine/Let's Go to the Church	1950	3.00	6.00	12.00
❏ 47-3850	Bless This House/The Rosary	1950	3.00	6.00	12.00
❏ 47-3851	Mother Dear O Pray For Me/Hoy God, We Praise Thy Name	1950	3.00	6.00	12.00
❏ 47-3852	Rock of Ages/Prayer of Thanksgiving	1950	3.00	6.00	12.00
❏ 47-3905	Patricia/Watchin' the Trains Go By	1950	3.00	6.00	12.00
❏ 47-3922	The Best Thing for You/Marrying for Love	1950	3.00	6.00	12.00
❏ 47-3930	A Bushel and a Peck/She's a Lady	1950	3.00	6.00	12.00

—With Betty Hutton

Number	Title (A Side/B Side)	Yr	VG	VG+	NM
❏ 47-3931	Marchita/So Long Sally	1950	3.00	6.00	12.00
❏ 47-3933	The Christmas Symphony/There Is No Christmas Like a Home Christmas	1950	3.75	7.50	15.00
❏ 47-3997	If/Zing, Zing, Zoom, Zoom	1950	3.00	6.00	12.00
❏ 47-4033	Without a Song/More Than You Know	1951	3.00	6.00	12.00
❏ 47-4034	It's Only a Paper Moon/Me and My Shadow	1951	3.00	6.00	12.00
❏ 47-4035	That Old Gang of Mine/I Found a Million Dollar Baby	1951	3.00	6.00	12.00
❏ 47-4081	Tumbling Tumbleweeds/You Don't Know What Lonesome Is	1951	3.00	6.00	12.00

—With the Sons of the Pioneers

Number	Title (A Side/B Side)	Yr	VG	VG+	NM
❏ 47-4112	Hello Young Lovers/We Kissed in a Shadow	1951	3.00	6.00	12.00
❏ 47-4158	There's No Boat Like a Rowboat/There's a Big Blue Cloud (Next to Heaven)	1951	3.00	6.00	12.00
❏ 47-4203	Surprising/Cara Cara Bella Bella	1951	3.00	6.00	12.00
❏ 47-4314	It's Beginning to Look Like Christmas/There Is No Christmas Like a Home Christmas	1951	3.75	7.50	15.00
❏ 47-4445	Garden in the Rain/Oh, How I Miss You Tonight	1952	3.00	6.00	12.00
❏ 47-4453	Please Mr. Sun/Tulips and Heather	1952	3.00	6.00	12.00
❏ 47-4527	You'll Never Walk Alone/Over the Rainbow	1952	3.00	6.00	12.00
❏ 47-4528	Black Moonlight/I Concentrate on You	1952	3.00	6.00	12.00
❏ 47-4529	My Heart Stood Still/If There's Someone	1952	3.00	6.00	12.00
❏ 47-4530	Summertime/While We're Young	1952	3.00	6.00	12.00
❏ 47-4631	One Little Candle/It's Easter Time	1952	3.00	6.00	12.00
❏ 47-4687	Why Did You Leave Me/Lonesome, That's All	1952	3.00	6.00	12.00
❏ 47-4707	Childhood Is a Meadow/One Little Candle	1952	3.00	6.00	12.00
❏ 47-4744	Maybe/Watermelon Weather	1952	3.00	6.00	12.00

—With Eddie Fisher

Number	Title (A Side/B Side)	Yr	VG	VG+	NM
❏ 47-4877	My Love and Devotion/Sweethearts' Holiday	1952	3.00	6.00	12.00
❏ 47-5064	Don't Let the Stars Get In Your Eyes/Lies	1952	3.00	6.00	12.00
❏ 47-5152	Wild Horses/I Confess	1953	3.00	6.00	12.00
❏ 47-5277	Say You're Mine Again/My One and Only Heart	1953	3.00	6.00	12.00
❏ 47-5317	No Other Love/Keep It Gay	1953	3.00	6.00	12.00
❏ 47-5317 [PS]	No Other Love/Keep It Gay	1953	5.00	10.00	20.00
❏ 47-5447	You Alone (Solo Tu)/Pa-Paya Mama	1953	3.00	6.00	12.00
❏ 47-5571	I Believe/Onward Christian Soldiers	1953	3.00	6.00	12.00
❏ 47-5572	Act of Contrition/Good Night Sweet Jesus	1953	3.00	6.00	12.00
❏ 47-5573	Abide with Me/Nearer, My God, To Thee	1953	3.00	6.00	12.00
❏ 47-5574	Eli, Eli/Kol Niore	1953	3.00	6.00	12.00
❏ 47-5647	Wanted/Look Out the Window	1954	3.00	6.00	12.00
❏ 47-5749	Hit and Run Affair/There Never Was a Night So Beautiful	1954	3.00	6.00	12.00
❏ 47-5857	Papa Loves Mambo/The Things I Didn't Do	1954	3.00	6.00	12.00
❏ 47-5950	(There's No Place Like) Home for the Holidays/Silk Stockings	1954	3.00	6.00	12.00
❏ 47-5994	Ko Ko Mo (I Love You So)/You'll Always Be My Lifetime Sweetheart	1955	2.50	5.00	10.00
❏ 47-6059	Door of Dreams/Nobody	1955	2.50	5.00	10.00
❏ 47-6137	Chee Chee O-Chee (Sang the Little Bird)/Two Lost Souls	1955	2.50	5.00	10.00

—With Jaye P. Morgan

Number	Title (A Side/B Side)	Yr	VG	VG+	NM
❏ 47-6192	Tina Marie/Fooled	1955	2.50	5.00	10.00
❏ 47-6294	All at Once You Love Her/The Rose Tattoo	1955	2.50	5.00	10.00
❏ 47-6321	Home for the Holidays/God Rest Ye Merry Gentlemen	1955	3.00	6.00	12.00
❏ 47-6427	Hot Diggity (Dog Ziggity Boom)/Juke Box Baby	1956	2.50	5.00	10.00
❏ 47-6554	More/Glendora	1956	2.50	5.00	10.00
❏ 47-6590	Somebody Up There Likes Me/Dream Along with Me	1956	2.50	5.00	10.00
❏ 47-6590 [PS]	Somebody Up There Likes Me/Dream Along with Me	1956	7.50	15.00	30.00
❏ 47-6670	Moonlight Love/Chincherinchee	1956	2.50	5.00	10.00
❏ 47-6815	Round and Round/Mi Casa, Su Casa (My House Is Your House)	1957	2.50	5.00	10.00
❏ 47-6904	The Girl with the Golden Braids/My Little Baby	1957	2.50	5.00	10.00
❏ 47-6991	Dancin'/Marchin' Along to the Blues	1957	2.50	5.00	10.00
❏ 47-7050	Just Born (To Be Your Baby)/Ivy Rose	1957	2.50	5.00	10.00
❏ 47-7128	Catch a Falling Star/Magic Moments	1957	3.00	6.00	12.00
❏ 47-7202	Kewpie Doll/Dance Only with Me	1958	2.50	5.00	10.00
❏ 47-7274	Moon Talk/Beats There a Heart So True	1958	2.50	5.00	10.00
❏ 47-7353	Love Makes the World Go 'Round/Mandolins in the Moonlight	1958	2.50	5.00	10.00
❏ 47-7464	Tomboy/Kiss Me and Kiss Me and Kiss Me	1959	2.50	5.00	10.00
❏ 47-7541	I Know/You Are in Love	1959	2.50	5.00	10.00
❏ 47-7541 [PS]	I Know/You Are in Love	1959	6.25	12.50	25.00
❏ 47-7628	I May Never Pass This Way Again/A Still Small Voice	1959	2.50	5.00	10.00
❏ 47-7650	Ave Maria/The Lord's Prayer	1959	2.50	5.00	10.00
❏ 47-7650 [PS]	Ave Maria/The Lord's Prayer	1959	7.50	15.00	30.00
❏ 47-7670	Delaware/I Know What God Is	1960	2.00	4.00	8.00
❏ 47-7812	Make Someone Happy/Gone Is My Love	1960	2.00	4.00	8.00
❏ 47-7962	You're Following Me/Especially for the Young	1961	2.00	4.00	8.00
❏ 47-8004	Caterina/The Island of Forgotten Lovers	1962	2.00	4.00	8.00
❏ 47-8004 [PS]	Caterina/The Island of Forgotten Lovers	1962	5.00	10.00	20.00
❏ 47-8186	(I Love You) Don't You Forget It/One More Mountain	1963	2.00	4.00	8.00
❏ 47-8186 [PS]	(I Love You) Don't You Forget It/One More Mountain	1963	5.00	10.00	20.00
❏ 47-8533	Dream On Little Dreamer/My Own Peculiar Way	1965	2.00	4.00	8.00
❏ 47-8533 [PS]	Dream On Little Dreamer/My Own Peculiar Way	1965	5.00	10.00	20.00
❏ 47-8636	Oowee, Oowee/Summer Wind	1965	2.00	4.00	8.00
❏ 47-8722	Meet Me at the Altar/Bye, Bye, Little Girl	1965	2.00	4.00	8.00
❏ 47-8823	Stay with Me/Coo Coo Roo Coo Coo Paloma	1966	2.00	4.00	8.00
❏ 47-8945	Forget Domani/One Day Is Like Another	1966	2.00	4.00	8.00
❏ 47-9165	Stop! And Think It Over/How Beautiful the World Can Be	1967	—	3.00	6.00
❏ 47-9262	I Looked Back/A World of Love (That I Found)	1967	—	3.00	6.00
❏ 47-9356	What Love Is Made Of/You Made It That Way	1967	—	3.00	6.00
❏ 47-9367	Christmas Bells/Love Is a Christmas Rose	1967	2.00	4.00	8.00
❏ 47-9367 [PS]	Christmas Bells/Love Is a Christmas Rose	1967	2.50	5.00	10.00

Number	Title (A Side/B Side)	Yr	VG	VG+	NM
47-9448	The Father of Girls/Somebody Makes It So	1968	—	2.50	5.00
47-9533	Happy Man/Another Go-Round	1968	—	2.50	5.00
47-9683	There Is No Christmas Like a Home Christmas/ Christmas Eve	1968	—	3.00	6.00
47-9722	Seattle/Sunshine Wine	1969	—	2.50	5.00
52-0071	Ave Maria/The Lord's Prayer	1949	3.00	6.00	12.00
—Black vinyl reissue					
52-0071	Ave Maria/The Lord's Prayer	1949	6.25	12.50	25.00
—Blue vinyl original					
74-0193	Happiness Comes, Happiness Goes/That's All This Old World Needs	1969	—	2.00	4.00
74-0356	Don't Leave Me/ Love Is Spreading All Over the World	1970	—	2.00	4.00
74-0387	It's Impossible/Long Life. Lots of Happiness	1970	—	2.50	5.00
74-0436	Don't Leave Me/ Love Is Spreading All Over the World	1971	—	2.00	4.00
74-0444	El Condor Pasa/I Think of You	1971	—	2.00	4.00
74-0518	My Days of Loving You/ Yesterday I Heard the Rain	1971	—	2.00	4.00
74-0906	And I Love Her So/Love Looks So Good on You	1973	—	2.00	4.00
447-0110	Ave Maria/The Lord's Prayer	1955	3.00	6.00	12.00
447-0810	Silent Night/O Come, All Ye Faithful	196?	—	2.50	5.00
447-0811	That Christmas Feeling/ I'll Be Home For Christmas	196?	—	2.50	5.00
447-0812	Home for the Holidays/ God Rest Ye Merry Gentlemen	196?	—	2.50	5.00
WBY 43	'Twas the Night Before Christmas/ The Twelve Days of Christmas	1953	3.75	7.50	15.00
APBO-0096	Love Don't Care/Walk Right Back	1973	—	2.00	4.00
SP-45-119 [DJ]	(There's No Place Like) Home For The Holidays/ I'll Be Home For Christmas	1962	3.00	6.00	12.00
APBO-0225	Beyond Tomorrow/It All Seems to Fall Into Line	1974	—	2.00	4.00
APBO-0274	Weave Me the Sunshine/ I Don't Know What He Told You	1974	—	2.00	4.00
E3VW 1339/F7OW 9047 [DJ]	Rudolph The Red-Nosed Reindeer/Rudolph The Red-Nosed Reindeer	1955		3.75	7.50
—B-side by the Three Suns					
K2NW 6096/7 [DJ]	(Intro) I May Never Pass This Way Again/ (Alternate Intro) I May Never Pass This Way Again	1959	3.00	6.00	12.00
—Promotional record for Christmas Seals					
PB-10045	In These Crazy Times/Temptation	1974	—	—	3.00
PB-10122	Christmas Dream/Christ Is Born	1974	—	2.00	4.00
—Gray label					
GB-10174	Catch a Falling Star/Dream Along with Me	1975	—	—	3.00
—Gold Standard Series					
GB-10175	Hot Diggity (Dog Ziggity Boom)/Don't Let the Stars Get In Your Eyes	1975	—	—	3.00
—Gold Standard Series					
GB-10176	Prisoner of Love/Magic Moments	1975	—	—	3.00
—Gold Standard Series					
GB-10177	Round and Round/Wanted	1975	—	—	3.00
—Gold Standard Series					
PB-10257	Wonderful Baby/World of Dreams	1975	—	—	3.00
PB-10402	Just Out of Reach/Love Put a Song in My Heart	1975	—	2.00	4.00
GB-10471	And I Love You So/Love Looks So Good on You	1975	—	—	3.00
—Gold Standard Series					
PB-10604	Then You Can Tell Me Goodbye/The Grass Keeps Right On Growing	1976	—	—	3.00

USAF

Number	Title (A Side/B Side)	Yr	VG	VG+	NM
85/86 [DJ]	"Special Christmas Show" Home For The Holidays/Merry Merry Christmas To You	195?	3.75	7.50	15.00
—B-side by Art Mooney					

7-Inch Extended Plays

RCA CAMDEN

Number	Title (A Side/B Side)	Yr	VG	VG+	NM
CAE-410	Without a Song/More Than You Know//Me and My Shadow/Dream Along with Me	195?	2.00	4.00	8.00
CAE-410 [PS]	Dream Along with Me	195?	2.00	4.00	8.00

RCA VICTOR

Number	Title (A Side/B Side)	Yr	VG	VG+	NM
EYA-19	The Story of the First Christmas//Santa Claus Is Coming to Town/Jingle Bells	195?	3.75	7.50	15.00
—"Little Nipper" Children's Series issue					
SPD-27 [PS]	Perry Como	195?	3.75	7.50	15.00
—Box for 10-EP set plus booklet					
SPD-28	South of the Border/Because/Bless This House/ /Breezin' Along with the Breeze/Lies/You'll Never Walk Alone	1957	5.00	10.00	20.00
SPD-28 [PS]	Kleenex Tissues Presents Perry Como Highlighter	1957	5.00	10.00	20.00
547-0033	When Day Is Done/Carolina Moon//What'll I Do/ If We Can't Be the Same Old Sweethearts We'll Just Be the Same Old Friends	1952	2.50	5.00	10.00
—Part of 2-EP set EPB 3035					
547-0034	I'm Always Chasing Rainbows/Love Me or Leave Me//Body and Soul/When Your Hair Has Turned to Silver (I Will Love You Just the Same)	1952	2.50	5.00	10.00
—Part of 2-EP set EPB 3035					
SP-45-55	Hot Diggity/Patricia/Lazy Bones//Dream Along with Me/Land of Dreams/Bewitched	1958	5.00	10.00	20.00
—Songs are by, in order: Perry Como/Perez Prado/Kay Starr//Perry Como/Eddie Heywood/Gogi Grant					
SP-45-55 [PS]	Kleenex Tissues Presents RCA Victor's '59 Highlighter: Perry Como and His Friends	1958	5.00	10.00	20.00
547-0059	Prisoner of Love/Because//When You Were Sweet Sixteen/Far Away Places	1952	2.50	5.00	10.00
—Part of 2-EP set EPB 3044					
LPC-109	(contents unknown)	1961	3.00	6.00	12.00
—"Compact 33 Double"; small hole, plays at 33 1/3 rpm					
LPC-109 [PS]	Till the End of Time	1961	3.00	6.00	12.00
547-0116	That Christmas Feeling/I'll Be Home for Christmas//Silent Night/O Come, All Ye Faithful	1952	3.00	6.00	12.00
—Record 1 of 2-EP set EPB 3023					
547-0117	Jingle Bells/White Christmas//Santa Claus Is Coming to Town/Winter Wonderland	1952	3.00	6.00	12.00
—Record 2 of 2-EP set EPB 3023					
EPA-293	(contents unknown)	195?	3.00	6.00	12.00
EPA-293 [PS]	Perry Como Sings His Favorite Songs of Worship	195?	3.00	6.00	12.00
EPA-405	Blues in the Night/Wabash Blues//I Got It Bad and That Ain't Good/The Birth of the Blues	1952	3.75	7.50	15.00
EPA-405 [PS]	(title unknown)	1952	3.75	7.50	15.00
EPA-409	Some Enchanted Evening/Bali Ha'i//Hello, Young Lovers/We Kiss in a Shadow	1952	3.00	6.00	12.00
EPA-409 [PS]	Perry Como Sings the Hits from Broadway Shows	1952	3.00	6.00	12.00
EPA-410	Ave Maria/The Lord's Prayer//Mother Dear, O Pray for Me/Holy God We Praise Thy Name	1952	3.00	6.00	12.00
EPA-410 [PS]	Songs of Faith	1952	3.00	6.00	12.00
EPA-451	(contents unknown)	195?	3.00	6.00	12.00
EPA-451 [PS]	Perry Como Sings the Hits from Broadway Shows	195?	3.00	6.00	12.00
547-0454	A Hubba-Hubba-Hubba (Dig You Later)/Till the End of Time//Don't Let the Stars Get In Your Eyes/Wanted	1954	2.50	5.00	10.00
—Record 1 of 2-EP set EPB 3224					
547-0455	Temptation/Prisoner of Love//When You Were Sweet Sixteen/Because	1954	2.50	5.00	10.00
—Record 2 of 2-EP set EPB 3224					
EPA-496	The Night Before Christmas/God Rest Ye Merry, Gentlemen//The 12 Days of Christmas/C-H-R-I-S-T-M-A-S	195?	3.00	6.00	12.00
EPA-496 [PS]	Around the Christmas Tree	195?	3.00	6.00	12.00
EPA-497	(contents unknown)	195?	3.00	6.00	12.00
EPA-497 [PS]	Around the Christmas Tree	195?	3.00	6.00	12.00
EPA-514	Remember/When Day Is Done//One Alone/The Birth of the Blues	1954	3.00	6.00	12.00
EPA-514 [PS]	(title unknown)	1954	3.00	6.00	12.00
EPA-563	Wanted/You Alone//Pa-Paya Mama/ No Other Love	1954	3.00	6.00	12.00
EPA-563 [PS]	Wanted	1954	3.00	6.00	12.00
EPA-642	For Me and My Gal/My Funny Valentine//It Happened in Monterey/It's the Talk of the Town	1955	3.00	6.00	12.00
EPA-642 [PS]	P.C.	1955	3.00	6.00	12.00
EPA-728	(contents unknown)	1955	3.00	6.00	12.00
EPA-728 [PS]	Perry Como Sings Hits from Broadway Shows	1955	3.00	6.00	12.00
EPA-738	(contents unknown)	1955	3.00	6.00	12.00
EPA-738 [PS]	Relaxing with Perry Como	1955	3.00	6.00	12.00
EPA-739	With a Song in My Heart/Love Me or Leave Me/ Lies//Body and Soul/No Other Love	1955	3.00	6.00	12.00
EPA-739 [PS]	A Sentimental Date with Perry Como	1955	3.00	6.00	12.00
547-0834	With a Song in My Heart/Love Me or Leave Me/ Lies//Carolina Moon/Blue Room	1955	2.50	5.00	10.00
—Part of 2-EP set EPB 1177					
547-0835	Body and Soul/No Other Love//When Day Is Done/What'll I Do?	1955	2.50	5.00	10.00
—Part of 2-EP set EPB 1177					
EPA-903	(contents unknown)	1956	3.00	6.00	12.00
EPA-903 [PS]	Perry Como Sings	1956	3.00	6.00	12.00
EPA-920	Santa Claus Is Comin' to Town/Frosty the Snow Man/Winter Wonderland//Rudolph, the Red-Nosed Reindeer/Jingle Bells	1956	3.00	6.00	12.00
EPA-920 [PS]	Perry Como Sings Merry Christmas Music	1956	3.00	6.00	12.00
547-1048	(contents unknown)	1955	2.50	5.00	10.00
—Part of 2-EP set EPB 1243					
547-1049	Joy to the World/White Christmas//God Rest Ye Merry, Gentlemen/The Christmas Song	1955	2.50	5.00	10.00
—Part of 2-EP set EPB 1243					
EPB 1177 [PS]	A Sentimental Date with Perry Como	1955	3.00	6.00	12.00
—Gatefold cover for 2-EP set (547-0834, 547-0835)					
EPB 1243 [PS]	Perry Como Sings Merry Christmas Music	1955	5.00	10.00	20.00
—Cover for 2-EP set					
EPA 1-1463	Swinging Down the Lane/South of the Border// Honey, Honey (Bless Your Heart)/Angry	1957	2.50	5.00	10.00
EPA 1-1463 [PS]	We Get Letters, Vol. 1	1957	2.50	5.00	10.00
EPB 3023 [PS]	Perry Como Sings Merry Christmas Music	1952	3.00	6.00	12.00
—Double-pocket cover for 547-0116 and 547-0117					
EPB 3035 [PS]	A Sentimental Date with Perry	1952	2.50	5.00	10.00
—Double-pocket cover for 547-0033 and 547-0034					
EPB 3044 [PS]	Supper Club Favorites	1952	2.50	5.00	10.00
—Two-pocket jacket for two-EP set					
EPB 3224 [PS]	Como's Golden Records	1954	2.50	5.00	10.00
—Double-pocket cover for 547-0454 and 547-0455					
EPA-4285 [M]	Accentuate the Positive/Red Sails in the Sunset/ /Birth of the Blues/It Had to Be You	1958	2.50	5.00	10.00
EPA-4285 [PS]	(title unknown)	1958	2.50	5.00	10.00
ESP-4285 [PS]	(title unknown)	1958	5.00	10.00	20.00
ESP-4285 [S]	Accentuate the Positive/Red Sails in the Sunset/ /Birth of the Blues/It Had to Be You	1958	5.00	10.00	20.00
EPA-4326	A Still Small Voice/I May Never Pass This Way Again//He's Got the Whole World in His Hands/ When You Come to the End of the Day	1958	2.50	5.00	10.00
EPA-4326 [PS]	(title unknown)	1958	2.50	5.00	10.00
EPA-5012	*Don't Let the Stars Get In Your Eyes/Wanted/ Papa Loves Mambo/Hot Diggity (Dog Ziggity Boom)	1958	2.50	5.00	10.00
EPA-5012 [PS]	Como's Golden Records	1958	2.50	5.00	10.00
EPA-5029	Round and Round/When You Were Sweet Sixteen//Till the End of Time/A Hubba Hubba Hubba	1958	2.50	5.00	10.00
EPA-5029 [PS]	Como's Golden Records, Volume 2	1958	2.50	5.00	10.00
EPA-5030	Temptation/Mi Casa, Su Casa//Prisoner of Love/ Because	1958	2.50	5.00	10.00
EPA-5030 [PS]	Como's Golden Records, Volume 3	1958	2.50	5.00	10.00
EPA-5044	You'll Never Walk Alone/No Other Love//Song of Songs/Some Enchanted Evening	1958	2.50	5.00	10.00
EPA-5044 [PS]	You'll Never Walk Alone (Gold Standard Series)	1958	2.50	5.00	10.00
EPA-5109	Juke Box Baby/Catch a Falling Star//Tina Marie/ Magic Moments	1959	2.50	5.00	10.00
EPA-5109 [PS]	(title unknown)	1959	2.50	5.00	10.00
EPA-5128	Ko Ko Mo/Glendora//Hoop-De-Doo/Far Away Places	1959	2.50	5.00	10.00
EPA-5128 [PS]	Perry Como (Gold Standard Series)	1959	2.50	5.00	10.00
599-9156	For Me and My Gal/As Time Goes By//I Believe/ When Day Is Done	1957	2.00	4.00	8.00
—Side 1 and 20 of 10-EP set SPD-27					

C

Number	Title (A Side/B Side)	Yr	VG	VG+	NM
❑ 599-9157	Far Away Places/Till the End of Time//Don't Let the Stars Get In Your Eyes/Bali Ha'l	1957	2.00	4.00	8.00
—Side 2 and 19 of 10-EP set SPD 27					
❑ 599-9158	It's a Good Day/My Funny Valentine//You'll Never Walk Alone/Hello Young Lovers	1957	2.00	4.00	8.00
—Side 3 and 18 of 10-EP set SPD 27					
❑ 599-9159	If There Is Someone Lovelier Than You/Over the Rainbow//Body and Soul/Lies	1957	2.00	4.00	8.00
—Side 4 and 17 of 10-EP set SPD 27					
❑ 599-9160	Temptation/Black Moonlight//All at Once You Love Her/Look Out the Window	1957	2.00	4.00	8.00
—Side 5 and 16 of 10-EP set SPD 27					
❑ 599-9161	If/When You Were Sweet Sixteen//I've Got the World on a String/You Do Something To Me	1957	2.00	4.00	8.00
—Side 6 and 15 of 10-EP set SPD 27					
❑ 599-9162	Prisoner of Love/Carolina Moon//One for My Baby/In the Still of the Night	1957	2.00	4.00	8.00
—Side 7 and 14 of 10-EP set SPD 27					
❑ 599-9163	What'll I Do/Blue Moon//Hot Diggity (Dog Ziggity Boom)/It Happened in Monterey	1957	2.00	4.00	8.00
—Side 8 and 13 of 10-EP set SPD 27					
❑ 599-9164	With a Song in My Heart/No Other Love//Breezin' Along with the Breeze/It's the Talk of the Town	1957	2.00	4.00	8.00
—Side 9 and 12 of 10-EP set SPD 27					
❑ 599-9165	Wanted/Love Me or Leave Me//Pa-Paya Mama/I Gotta Right to Sing the Blues	1957	2.00	4.00	8.00
—Side 10 and 11 of 10-EP set SPD 27					
Albums					
PAIR					
❑ PDL2-1001 [(2)]	Easy Listening	1986	3.00	6.00	12.00
❑ PDL2-1038 [(2)]	Love Moods	1986	3.00	6.00	12.00
❑ PDL2-1112 [(2)]	Blue Skies	1986	3.00	6.00	12.00
PICKWICK					
❑ CAS-660 [R]	Perry Como Sings Merry Christmas Music	1977	2.00	4.00	8.00
—Reissue of RCA Camden CAS-660 with another new cover					
RCA					
❑ 6368-1-R	Perry Como Today	1988	2.50	5.00	10.00
RCA CAMDEN					
❑ CAL-403 [M]	Dream Along with Me	1957	5.00	10.00	20.00
❑ CAS-403(e) [R]	Dream Along with Me	1962	2.50	5.00	10.00
❑ CAL-440 [M]	Perry Como Sings Just for You	1958	3.75	7.50	15.00
❑ CAS-440(e) [R]	Perry Como Sings Just for You	1962	2.50	5.00	10.00
❑ CAL-511 [M]	Como's Wednesday Night Music Hall	1959	5.00	10.00	20.00
❑ CAL-582 [M]	Dreamer's Holiday	1960	3.75	7.50	15.00
❑ CAL-660 [M]	Perry Como Sings Merry Christmas Music	1961	3.00	6.00	12.00
—Reissue of RCA Victor LPM-1243 with new cover					
❑ CAS-660(e) [R]	Perry Como Sings Merry Christmas Music	1961	2.50	5.00	10.00
❑ CAL-694 [M]	Make Someone Happy	1962	3.00	6.00	12.00
❑ CAL-742 [M]	An Evening with Perry Como	196?	3.75	7.50	15.00
❑ CAL-805 [M]	Love Makes the World Go 'Round	1964	3.00	6.00	12.00
❑ CAS-805 [S]	Love Makes the World Go 'Round	1964	2.50	5.00	10.00
❑ CAL-858 [M]	Somebody Loves Me	1965	3.00	6.00	12.00
❑ CAS-858 [S]	Somebody Loves Me	1965	2.50	5.00	10.00
❑ CAL-941 [M]	No Other Love	1966	3.00	6.00	12.00
❑ CAS-941 [S]	No Other Love	1966	2.50	5.00	10.00
❑ CAL-2122 [M]	Hello Young Lovers	1967	3.75	7.50	15.00
❑ CAS-2122 [R]	Hello Young Lovers	1967	2.50	5.00	10.00
❑ CAL-2201 [M]	You Are Never Far Away	1968	3.75	7.50	15.00
❑ CAS-2201 [S]	You Are Never Far Away	1968	2.50	5.00	10.00
❑ CAS-2299	The Lord's Prayer	1968	2.50	5.00	10.00
❑ CAS-2482	Door of Dreams	1971	2.50	5.00	10.00
❑ CAS-2547	The Shadow of Your Smile	1972	2.50	5.00	10.00
❑ CAS-2609	Dream On Little Dreamer	1972	2.50	5.00	10.00
❑ CXS-9002 [(2)]	Easy Listening	1972	3.00	6.00	12.00
RCA CUSTOM EDITION					
❑ DRL1-0010	Seattle	1973	3.00	6.00	12.00
RCA SPECIAL PRODUCTS					
❑ DPL1-0193	By Special Request	1974	3.00	6.00	12.00
—Sold only at Sylvania dealers					
RCA VICTOR					
❑ LPM-51 [10]	Merry Christmas	1951	10.00	20.00	40.00
❑ APD1-0100 [Q]	And I Love You So	1974	3.75	7.50	15.00
❑ APL1-0100	And I Love You So	1973	2.50	5.00	10.00
❑ ACL1-0444	The Sweetest Sounds	1974	2.50	5.00	10.00
❑ APD1-0585 [Q]	Perry	1974	3.75	7.50	15.00
❑ CPL1-0585	Perry	1974	2.50	5.00	10.00
❑ APD1-0863 [Q]	Just Out of Reach	1975	3.75	7.50	15.00
❑ APL1-0863	Just Out of Reach	1975	2.50	5.00	10.00
❑ ANL1-0972	Pure Gold	1975	2.50	5.00	10.00
❑ LSPX-1001	Perry Como at the International Hotel, Las Vegas	1970	3.75	7.50	15.00
❑ LOP-1004 [M]	Saturday Night with Mr. C.	1958	6.25	12.50	25.00
❑ LOP-1007 [M]	Como's Golden Records	1958	6.25	12.50	25.00
❑ LPM-1085 [M]	So Smooth	1955	7.50	15.00	30.00
❑ LPM-1172 [M]	I Believe	1956	7.50	15.00	30.00
❑ LSP-1172(e) [R]	I Believe	1962	3.00	6.00	12.00
❑ LPM-1176 [M]	Relaxing with Perry Como	1956	7.50	15.00	30.00
❑ LPM-1177 [M]	A Sentimental Date with Perry Como	1956	7.50	15.00	30.00
❑ LPM-1191 [M]	Hits from Broadway Shows	1956	7.50	15.00	30.00
❑ LPM-1243 [M]	Perry Como Sings Merry Christmas Music	1956	7.50	15.00	30.00
❑ LPM-1463 [M]	We Get Letters	1957	6.25	12.50	25.00
❑ CPL1-1752	A Legendary Performer	1976	2.50	5.00	10.00
❑ LPM-1885 [M]	When You Come to the End of the Day	1958	5.00	10.00	20.00
❑ LSP-1885 [S]	When You Come to the End of the Day	1958	7.50	15.00	30.00
❑ ANL1-1929	The Perry Como Christmas Album	1976	2.00	4.00	8.00
—Budget-line reissue of LSP-4016					
❑ LPM-1971 [M]	Saturday Night with Mr. C.	1959	5.00	10.00	20.00
—Reissue of LOP-1004					
❑ LSP-1971(e) [R]	Saturday Night with Mr. C.	1962	3.00	6.00	12.00
❑ AFL1-1981	Como's Golden Records	1977	2.50	5.00	10.00
—Reissue with new prefix					
❑ LPM-1981 [M]	Como's Golden Records	1959	5.00	10.00	20.00
—Reissue of LOP-1007					
❑ LSP-1981(e) [R]	Como's Golden Records	1962	3.00	6.00	12.00
❑ LPM-2010 [M]	Como Swings	1959	5.00	10.00	20.00
❑ LSP-2010 [S]	Como Swings	1959	6.25	12.50	25.00

Number	Title (A Side/B Side)	Yr	VG	VG+	NM
❑ LPM-2066 [M]	Season's Greetings from Perry Como	1959	5.00	10.00	20.00
—Later front covers have "LPM-2066" in upper right, inside RCA Victor box					
❑ LPM-2066 [M]	Season's Greetings from Perry Como	1959	6.25	12.50	25.00
—Original front covers have "LPM-2066" in lower left corner					
❑ LSP-2066 [S]	Season's Greetings from Perry Como	1959	6.25	12.50	25.00
❑ LPM-2343 [M]	For the Young at Heart	1960	3.75	7.50	15.00
❑ LSP-2343 [S]	For the Young at Heart	1960	5.00	10.00	20.00
❑ LPM-2390 [M]	Sing to Me, Mr. C.	1961	3.75	7.50	15.00
❑ LSP-2390 [S]	Sing to Me, Mr. C.	1961	5.00	10.00	20.00
❑ ANL1-2485	Especially for You	1977	2.50	5.00	10.00
❑ LPM-2567 [M]	By Request	1962	3.75	7.50	15.00
❑ LSP-2567 [S]	By Request	1962	5.00	10.00	20.00
❑ LPM-2630 [M]	The Best of Irving Berlin's Songs from "Mr. President"	1962	3.75	7.50	15.00
❑ LSP-2630 [S]	The Best of Irving Berlin's Songs from "Mr. President"	1962	5.00	10.00	20.00
❑ AFL1-2641	Where You're Concerned	1978	2.50	5.00	10.00
❑ LPM-2708 [M]	The Songs I Love	1963	3.75	7.50	15.00
❑ LSP-2708 [S]	The Songs I Love	1963	5.00	10.00	20.00
❑ ANL1-2969(e)	Over the Rainbow	1976	2.50	5.00	10.00
❑ LPM-3013 [10]	TV Favorites	1952	10.00	20.00	40.00
❑ LPM-3035 [10]	A Sentimental Date with Perry Como	1952	10.00	20.00	40.00
❑ LPM-3044 [10]	Supper Club Favorites	1952	10.00	20.00	40.00
❑ LPM-3124 [10]	Hits from Broadway Shows	1953	10.00	20.00	40.00
❑ LPM-3133 [10]	Around the Christmas Tree	1953	10.00	20.00	40.00
❑ LPM-3188 [10]	I Believe	1954	10.00	20.00	40.00
❑ LPM-3224 [10]	Como's Golden Records	1954	10.00	20.00	40.00
❑ LPM-3396 [M]	The Scene Changes	1965	3.00	6.00	12.00
❑ LSP-3396 [S]	The Scene Changes	1965	3.75	7.50	15.00
❑ LPM-3552 [M]	Lightly Latin	1966	3.00	6.00	12.00
❑ LSP-3552 [S]	Lightly Latin	1966	3.75	7.50	15.00
❑ LPM-3608 [M]	Perry Como in Italy	1966	3.00	6.00	12.00
❑ LSP-3608 [S]	Perry Como in Italy	1966	3.75	7.50	15.00
❑ AFL1-3629	Perry Como	1980	2.50	5.00	10.00
❑ AYL1-3672	And I Love You So	1980	2.00	4.00	8.00
—Reissue					
❑ AYL1-3802	Como's Golden Records	1981	2.00	4.00	8.00
—Reissue					
❑ AYL1-3803	Where You're Concerned	1981	2.00	4.00	8.00
—Reissue					
❑ AYL1-3804	It's Impossible	1981	2.00	4.00	8.00
—Reissue					
❑ LSP-4016	The Perry Como Christmas Album	1968	3.00	6.00	12.00
❑ LSP-4052	Look to Your Heart	1968	3.75	7.50	15.00
❑ LSP-4183	Seattle	1969	3.75	7.50	15.00
❑ AFL1-4272	So It Goes	1983	2.50	5.00	10.00
❑ AFL1-4473	It's Impossible	1977	2.50	5.00	10.00
—Reissue with new prefix					
❑ LSP-4473	It's Impossible	1970	3.75	7.50	15.00
❑ AYL1-4526	I Wish It Could Be Christmas Forever	1982	2.50	5.00	10.00
❑ AFL1-4539	I Think of You	1977	2.50	5.00	10.00
—Reissue with new prefix					
❑ LSP-4539	I Think of You	1971	3.75	7.50	15.00
❑ VPS-6026 [(2)]	This Is Perry Como	1970	3.75	7.50	15.00
❑ VPS-6067 [(2)]	This Is Perry Como, Volume 2	1972	3.75	7.50	15.00
READER'S DIGEST					
❑ RDA-144/D	Christmas with Perry Como	1983	2.50	5.00	10.00
TIME-LIFE					
❑ SLGD-04 [(2)]	Legendary Singers: Perry Como	1985	3.75	7.50	15.00

COMO, PERRY, AND THE FONTANE SISTERS Also see each artist's individual listings.

45s

RCA VICTOR

Number	Title (A Side/B Side)	Yr	VG	VG+	NM
❑ 47-3082	I Wanna Go Home (With You)/Hush Little Darlin'	1949	3.75	7.50	15.00
❑ 47-3113	Bibbidi-Bobbidi-Boo/A Dream Is a Wish Your Heart Makes	1949	3.75	7.50	15.00
❑ 47-3747	Hoop-Dee-Doo/On the Outgoing Tide	1950	3.00	6.00	12.00
❑ 47-3846	I Cross My Fingers/If You Were My Girl	1950	3.00	6.00	12.00
❑ 47-3945	You're Just in Love/It's a Lovely Day Today	1950	3.00	6.00	12.00
❑ 47-4269	Rollin' Stone/With All My Heart and Soul	1951	3.00	6.00	12.00
❑ 47-4344	Here's to My Lady/If Wishes Were Kisses	1951	3.00	6.00	12.00
❑ 47-4542	Noodlin' Rag/Play Me a Hurtin' Tune	1952	3.00	6.00	12.00
❑ 47-4959	To Know You (Is to Love You)/My Lady Loves to Dance	1952		6.00	12.00
❑ 47-5524	Silver Bells/Kissing Bridge	1953		6.00	12.00

COMPANIONS, THE More than one group.

45s

AMY

Number	Title (A Side/B Side)	Yr	VG	VG+	NM
❑ 852	No Fool Am I/How Could You	1962	25.00	50.00	100.00

ARLEN

Number	Title (A Side/B Side)	Yr	VG	VG+	NM
❑ 722	These Foolish Things/It's Too Late	1963	20.00	40.00	80.00

BROOK'S

Number	Title (A Side/B Side)	Yr	VG	VG+	NM
❑ 100	Why, Oh Why Baby/I Didn't Know (You Got Married)	1959	15.00	30.00	60.00

COLUMBIA

Number	Title (A Side/B Side)	Yr	VG	VG+	NM
❑ 42279	I'll Always Love You/A Little Bit of Blue	1962	7.50	15.00	30.00

DOVE

Number	Title (A Side/B Side)	Yr	VG	VG+	NM
❑ 240	Falling/Oh, What a Feeling!	1958	30.00	60.00	120.00

FEDERAL

Number	Title (A Side/B Side)	Yr	VG	VG+	NM
❑ 12397	Why, Oh Why Baby/I Didn't Know (You Got Married)	1960	7.50	15.00	30.00

GENERAL AMERICAN

Number	Title (A Side/B Side)	Yr	VG	VG+	NM
❑ 711	Be Yourself/Help a Lonely Guy	1962	5.00	10.00	20.00

GINA

Number	Title (A Side/B Side)	Yr	VG	VG+	NM
❑ 722	These Foolish Things/It's Too Late	1963	12.50	25.00	50.00

COMPETITORS, THE

45s

DOT

Number	Title (A Side/B Side)	Yr	VG	VG+	NM
❑ 16560	Power Shift/Little Stick Nomad	1963	10.00	20.00	40.00

Albums

DOT

Number	Title (A Side/B Side)	Yr	VG	VG+	NM
❑ DLP-3542 [M]	Hits of the Street and Strip	1963	37.50	75.00	150.00
❑ DLP-25542 [S]	Hits of the Street and Strip	1963	50.00	100.00	200.00

Number	Title (A Side/B Side)	Yr	VG	VG+	NM

COMPLIMENTS, THE
45s
CONGRESS
| ❏ 243 | Shake It Up, Shake It Down/ You Are My Sunshine | 1965 | 12.50 | 25.00 | 50.00 |
| ❏ 252 | The Time of Her Life/Everybody Loves a Lover | 1965 | 12.50 | 25.00 | 50.00 |

MIDAS
| ❏ 304 | Borrow 'Til Morning/Beware, Beware | 1968 | 7.50 | 15.00 | 30.00 |

COMPOSERS, THE
45s
AMPEN
| ❏ 221 | Woe Is Me/Elephant Drag | 196? | 75.00 | 150.00 | 300.00 |

ERA
| ❏ 3118 | I Had a Dream/You and Yours | 1963 | 5.00 | 10.00 | 20.00 |

COMSTOCK, BOBBY
45s
ASCOT
❏ 2164	Right Hand Man/Always	1964	3.75	7.50	15.00
❏ 2175	I'm a Man/I'll Make You Glad	1965	3.00	6.00	12.00
❏ 2193	This Magic Moment/Shotgun Sally	1965	3.00	6.00	12.00
❏ 2216	Can't Judge a Book/Out of Sight	1966	3.00	6.00	12.00

ATLANTIC
| ❏ 2051 | Jambalaya/Let's Talk It Over | 1960 | 5.00 | 10.00 | 20.00 |

BLAZE
| ❏ 349 | Tennessee Waltz/Sweet Talk | 1959 | 6.25 | 12.50 | 25.00 |

FESTIVAL
| ❏ 25000 | Garden of Eden/Piece of Paper | 1961 | 5.00 | 10.00 | 20.00 |

JUBILEE
| ❏ 5392 | Bony Maronie/Do That Little Thing | 1960 | 5.00 | 10.00 | 20.00 |
| ❏ 5396 | Jezebel/Your Big Brown Eyes | 1961 | 5.00 | 10.00 | 20.00 |

LAWN
❏ 202	Let's Stomp/I Want to Do It	1963	3.75	7.50	15.00
❏ 210	Susie Baby/Take a Walk	1963	3.75	7.50	15.00
❏ 217	The Chicken Back/Sunny	1963	3.75	7.50	15.00
❏ 219	Your Boyfriend's Back/This Little Love of Mine	1963	5.00	10.00	20.00
❏ 224	I Can't Help Myself/Run My Heart	1963	3.75	7.50	15.00
❏ 229	The Beatle Bounce/Since You Been Gone	1964	5.00	10.00	20.00
❏ 232	Can It Be True/Ain't That Just Like Me	1964	3.75	7.50	15.00
❏ 255	I Wanna Do It/This Little Love of Mine	1965	3.00	6.00	12.00

LOST-NITE
| ❏ 227 | Let's Stomp/I Want to Do It | 196? | — | 2.50 | 5.00 |
—Reissue

MOHAWK
| ❏ 124 | The Wayward Wind/Everyday Blues | 1960 | 5.00 | 10.00 | 20.00 |

TRIUMPH
| ❏ 602 | Jealous Fool/Zig Zag | 1959 | 6.25 | 12.50 | 25.00 |

Albums
ASCOT
| ❏ AM-13026 [M] | Out of Sight | 1966 | 6.25 | 12.50 | 25.00 |
| ❏ AS-16026 [S] | Out of Sight | 1966 | 7.50 | 15.00 | 30.00 |

CONCORDS, THE (1)
45s
BOOM
| ❏ 60021 | Down the Aisle of Love/I Feel Love Comin' | 1966 | 10.00 | 20.00 | 40.00 |

EPIC
| ❏ 9697 | Should I Cry/It's Our Wedding Day | 1964 | 15.00 | 30.00 | 60.00 |

GRAMERCY
| ❏ 304 | Cross My Heart/Our Last Goodbye | 1961 | 12.50 | 25.00 | 50.00 |
—No candy canes on label
| ❏ 304 | Cross My Heart/Our Last Goodbye | 1961 | 50.00 | 100.00 | 200.00 |
—With candy canes on label
| ❏ 305 | My Dreams/Scarlet Ribbons | 1961 | 10.00 | 20.00 | 40.00 |

HERALD
| ❏ 576 | Marlene/Our Love Wasn't Meant to Be | 1962 | 6.25 | 12.50 | 25.00 |
| ❏ 578 | Cold and Frosty Morning/Don't Go Now | 1963 | 7.50 | 15.00 | 30.00 |

POLYDOR
| ❏ 14036 | Down the Aisle of Love/I Feel a Love Comin' On | 1970 | 3.00 | 6.00 | 12.00 |

RCA VICTOR
| ❏ 47-7911 | Again/The Boy Most Likely | 1961 | 7.50 | 15.00 | 30.00 |

RUST
| ❏ 5048 | One Step from Heaven/Away | 1962 | 7.50 | 15.00 | 30.00 |

CONCORDS, THE (2)
45s
EMBER
| ❏ 1007 | I'm Satisfied with Rock 'N' Roll/ I'll Always Say Please | 1956 | 15.00 | 30.00 | 60.00 |

HARLEM
| ❏ 2328 | Candlelight/Monticello | 1954 | 150.00 | 300.00 | 600.00 |

CONCORDS, THE (U) Probably a Nashville studio group and no relation to the others, but we're not sure.
45s
HIT
| ❏ 121 | Diane/Walk On By | 1964 | 2.00 | 4.00 | 8.00 |
—B-side by Mary Jones

CONDELLO
45s
SCEPTER
| ❏ 12233 | Crystal Clear/See What Tomorrow Brings | 1968 | 3.00 | 6.00 | 12.00 |

Albums
SCEPTER
| ❏ SPS-542 | Phase 1 | 1968 | 10.00 | 20.00 | 40.00 |

CONDORS, THE
45s
HUNTER
| ❏ 2503/4 | Swetest Angel/Little Curly Top | 1960 | 250.00 | 500.00 | 1000. |

CONEY ISLAND KIDS, THE
45s
JOSIE
| ❏ 791 | I Love It/Red Light, Green Light | 1956 | 7.50 | 15.00 | 30.00 |

Number	Title (A Side/B Side)	Yr	VG	VG+	NM

| ❏ 802 | We Want a Rock & Roll President/Thwistle Rock and Thwistle Roll | 1956 | 7.50 | 15.00 | 30.00 |
| ❏ 809 | Popcorn and Candy/Not You, Pie Face | 1957 | 7.50 | 15.00 | 30.00 |

JUBILEE
| ❏ 5215 | Moonlight Beach/Baby Baby You | 1955 | 10.00 | 20.00 | 40.00 |

CONFESSIONS, THE
45s
EPIC
| ❏ 9474 | Be-Bop Baby/Before You Change Your Mind | 1961 | 6.25 | 12.50 | 25.00 |

CONLEY, ARTHUR
45s
ATCO
❏ 6463	Sweet Soul Music/Let's Go Steady	1967	2.50	5.00	10.00
❏ 6494	Shake, Rattle and Roll/ You Don't Have to See Me	1967	2.00	4.00	8.00
❏ 6529	Whole Lot of Woman/Love Comes and Goes	1967	2.00	4.00	8.00
❏ 6563	Funky Street/Put Our Love Together	1968	2.00	4.00	8.00
❏ 6588	People Sure Act Funny/Burning Fire	1968	2.00	4.00	8.00
❏ 6622	Is That You Love/Aunt Dora's Love Soul Shack	1968	2.00	4.00	8.00
❏ 6640	Ob-La-Di, Ob-La-Da/Otis Sleep On	1968	2.00	4.00	8.00
❏ 6661	Speak Her Name/Run On	1969	—	3.00	6.00
❏ 6706	Star Review/Love Sure Is a Powerful Thing	1969	—	3.00	6.00
❏ 6733	Hurt/They Call the Wind Maria	1970	—	3.00	6.00
❏ 6747	God Bless/(Your Love Has Brought Me A) Mighty Long Way	1970	—	3.00	6.00
❏ 6790	Nobody's Fault But Mine/Day-O	1970	—	3.00	6.00

CAPRICORN
❏ 0001	More Sweet Soul Music/Walking on Eggs	1972	2.50	5.00	10.00
❏ 0006	Rita/More Sweet Soul Music	1972	2.00	4.00	8.00
❏ 0047	Bless You/It's So Nice	1973	2.00	4.00	8.00
❏ 8017	I'm Living Good/I'm So Glad You're Here	1971	2.50	5.00	10.00

FAME
| ❏ 1007 | I Can't Stop/In the Same Old Way | 1966 | 3.75 | 7.50 | 15.00 |
| ❏ 1009 | Take Me (Just As I Am)/ I'm Gonna Forget About You | 1966 | 3.75 | 7.50 | 15.00 |

JOTIS
| ❏ 470 | I'm a Lonely Stranger/Where Lead Me | 1965 | 5.00 | 10.00 | 20.00 |
| ❏ 472 | Who's Fooling Who/There's a Place for Us | 1966 | 5.00 | 10.00 | 20.00 |

PHILCO-FORD
| ❏ HP-15 | Sweet Soul Music/You Don't Have to See Me | 1968 | 3.75 | 7.50 | 15.00 |
—4-inch plastic "Hip Pocket Record" with color sleeve

Albums
ATCO
❏ 33-215 [M]	Sweet Soul Music	1967	10.00	20.00	40.00
❏ SD 33-215 [S]	Sweet Soul Music	1967	7.50	15.00	30.00
❏ 33-220 [M]	Shake, Rattle & Roll	1967	10.00	20.00	40.00
❏ SD 33-220 [S]	Shake, Rattle & Roll	1967	7.50	15.00	30.00
❏ SD 33-243	Soul Directions	1968	7.50	15.00	30.00
❏ SD 33-276	More Sweet Soul	1969	7.50	15.00	30.00

CONNIE AND CLARA
45s
HIT
| ❏ 61 | I Will Follow Him/Take These Chains from My Heart | 1963 | 2.00 | 4.00 | 8.00 |
—B-side by Herbert Hunter

CONNIFF, RAY Includes the Ray Conniff Singers.
45s
BRUNSWICK
| ❏ 55020 | Beamy Boy Boogie/Super Chief | 1957 | 2.50 | 5.00 | 10.00 |

COLUMBIA
❏ 10002	The Entertainer/I Understand Just How You Feel	1974	—	2.00	4.00
❏ 10097	Sing Along Song/Ecstasy	1975	—	2.00	4.00
❏ 10164	I Need You Baby/On the Run	1975	—	2.00	4.00
❏ 3-10294	Paloma Blanca/Lara's Theme from "Doctor Zhivago"	1976	—	2.00	4.00
❏ 3-10375	Moments to Remember/Vera's Theme	1976	—	2.00	4.00
❏ 3-10416	Song from M*A*S*H/Theme from "Love Story"	1976	—	2.00	4.00
❏ S7 30447 [S]	Love Is a Many-Splendored Thing/Please	1959	2.50	5.00	10.00
—"Stereo Seven" single (small hole, plays at 33 1/3 rpm)
❏ 30909 [S]	(titles unknown)	1960	2.50	5.00	10.00
❏ 30910 [S]	(titles unknown)	1960	2.50	5.00	10.00
❏ S7 30911 [S]	Moments to Remember/My Foolish Heart	1960	2.50	5.00	10.00
❏ 30912 [S]	(titles unknown)	1960	2.50	5.00	10.00
❏ 30913 [S]	(titles unknown)	1960	2.50	5.00	10.00
—The above five are "Stereo Seven" 33 1/3 rpm jukebox singles from set "JS 7-20" entitled "Memories Are Made of This"
❏ 31119 [S]	(titles unknown)	1961	2.50	5.00	10.00
❏ 31120 [S]	(titles unknown)	1961	2.50	5.00	10.00
❏ 31121 [S]	(titles unknown)	1961	2.50	5.00	10.00
❏ 31122 [S]	(titles unknown)	1961	2.50	5.00	10.00
❏ 31123 [S]	(titles unknown)	1961	2.50	5.00	10.00
❏ 31463 [S]	(titles unknown)	1962	2.50	5.00	10.00
❏ 31464 [S]	(titles unknown)	1962	2.50	5.00	10.00
❏ 31465 [S]	(titles unknown)	1962	2.50	5.00	10.00
❏ 31466 [S]	(titles unknown)	1962	2.50	5.00	10.00
❏ S7 31467 [S]	Green Eyes/Lisbon Antigua	1962	2.50	5.00	10.00
❏ 31555 [S]	(titles unknown)	1962	2.50	5.00	10.00
❏ 31556 [S]	(titles unknown)	1962	2.50	5.00	10.00
❏ 31557 [S]	(titles unknown)	1962	2.50	5.00	10.00
❏ 31558 [S]	(titles unknown)	1962	2.50	5.00	10.00
❏ 31559 [S]	(titles unknown)	1962	2.50	5.00	10.00
—The above 20 all are Columbia "Stereo 7" singles
❏ 4-40660	Begin the Beguine/Stardust	1956	2.50	5.00	10.00
❏ 40775	'S Wonderful/Wagon Wheels	1957	2.50	5.00	10.00
❏ 40862	Three Way Love/Cuddle Up a Little Closer	1957	2.50	5.00	10.00
❏ 40991	Walkin' and Whistlin'/Melody for Two Guitars	1957	2.00	4.00	8.00
❏ 41040	Theme from Perry Mason/Symphony of Love	1957	3.00	6.00	12.00
❏ 41242	Tchaikovsky's First Piano Concerto/Schubert's Serenade	1958	2.00	4.00	8.00
❏ 41349	Oklahoma/On the Street Where You Live	1959	2.00	4.00	8.00
❏ 41404	They Tried to Tell Me/Early Evening	1959	2.00	4.00	8.00
❏ 41444	Christmas Bride/Silver Bells	1959	3.00	6.00	12.00
❏ 41582	None But the Lonely Heart (Improvisation)/ Warsaw Concerto	1960	2.00	4.00	8.00

Number	Title (A Side/B Side)	Yr	VG	VG+	NM
❏ 41696	Theme from Perry Mason/Walkin; and Whistlin'	1960	2.00	4.00	8.00
❏ 41776	Besame Mucho/Brazil	1960	—	—	—
—Canceled					
❏ 41800	Midnight Lace — Part I/Midnight Lace — Part II	1960	2.00	4.00	8.00
❏ 42007	Golden Earrings/The Thrill Is Gone	1961	—	3.00	6.00
❏ 42695	Popsy/Scarlet	1963	2.00	4.00	8.00
❏ 4-42893	Sweet Sue, Just You/How Am I to Know	1963	2.00	4.00	8.00
❏ 42967	Blue Moon/Honeycomb	1964	—	3.00	6.00
❏ 42967 [DJ]	Blue Moon/Honeycomb	1964	3.00	6.00	12.00
—Blue vinyl promo; white label, blue print					
❏ 43061	Invisible Tears/Singing the Blues	1964	—	3.00	6.00
❏ 43168	Melodie D'Amour/If I Knew Then	1964	—	3.00	6.00
❏ 43352	Happiness Is/Miss You	1965	—	3.00	6.00
❏ 43448	The Real Meaning of Christmas/ Go Tell It on the Mountain	1965	2.00	4.00	8.00
❏ 43503	Jamaica Farewell/The Sheik of Araby	1966	—	3.00	6.00
❏ 43626	Somewhere, My Love/Midsummer in Sweden	1966	—	3.00	6.00
❏ 43626 [DJ]	Somewhere, My Love (same on both sides)	1966	3.00	6.00	12.00
—Promo only on red vinyl					
❏ 43814	Lookin' for Love/It Takes Two	1966	—	3.00	6.00
❏ 43939	Mame/Wednesday's Child	1966	—	3.00	6.00
❏ 44055	The World Will Smile Again/"17"	1967	—	3.00	6.00
❏ 44192	Moonlight Brings Memories/Wonderful Season of Summer	1967	—	3.00	6.00
❏ 44298	The Hulilau Song/One Paddle Two Paddle	1967	—	3.00	6.00
❏ 44422	Winds of Change/We're a Home	1968	—	2.50	5.00
❏ 44536	A Certain Girl/Sounds of Silence	1968	—	2.50	5.00
❏ 44645	People/Look Homeward Angel	1968	—	2.50	5.00
❏ 44724	I've Got My Eyes on You/Dear World	1968	—	2.50	5.00
❏ 44872	I Love How You Love Me/Hold Me Tight	1969	—	2.50	5.00
❏ 44933	A Banda/La Felicidad	1969	—	2.50	5.00
❏ 45002	Love at First Sight/Love Made a Fool of Me	1969	—	2.50	5.00
❏ 45070	Jean/The Power of Love	1970	—	2.50	5.00
❏ 45137	Half and Half (A Song for Sarah)/Walk in the Spring Rain	1970	—	2.50	5.00
❏ 45187	Songs Are For Lovers/These Are My Flowers	1970	—	2.50	5.00
❏ 45267	Everybody Knows/Loss of Love	1970	—	2.50	5.00
❏ 45333	Love Story/Out of the Darkness	1971	—	2.00	4.00
❏ 45363	El Condor Pasa/Rosa	1971	—	2.00	4.00
❏ 45443	Tijuana Taxi/Happy Together	1971	—	2.00	4.00
❏ 45528	We Must Forget We Ever Met/Where Were You	1972	—	2.00	4.00
❏ 45543	Theme from "Summer of '42"/Imagine	1972	—	2.00	4.00
❏ 45595	With Every Beat of My Heart/Sleepy Shores	1972	—	2.00	4.00
❏ 45687	Where Is the Love/Because	1972	—	2.00	4.00
❏ 45687 [PS]	Where Is the Love/Because	1972	—	3.00	6.00
❏ 45782	Face on the Wind/A Man Without a Vision	1973	—	2.00	4.00
❏ 45823	Charlotte's Web/Someone	1973	—	2.00	4.00
❏ 45893	Harmony/Bah, Bah, Conniff Sprach	1973	—	2.00	4.00
❏ 45996	The Most Beautiful Girl/Beyond Tomorrow	1974	—	2.00	4.00
❏ JZSP 111913/4 [DJ]	The Real Meaning of Christmas/ Go Tell It on the Mountain	1965	2.50	5.00	10.00
—Black vinyl					
❏ JZSP 111913/4 [DJ]	The Real Meaning of Christmas/ Go Tell It on the Mountain	1965	3.00	6.00	12.00
—Green vinyl					
CORAL					
❏ 61371	Beamy Boy Boogie/Super Chief	1955	3.00	6.00	12.00
7-Inch Extended Plays					
COLUMBIA					
❏ B-2578	*'S Wonderful/I Get a Kick Out of You/Begin the Beguine/That Old Black Magic	1958	2.50	5.00	10.00
❏ B-2578 [PS]	Ray Conniff (Hall of Fame Series)	1958	2.50	5.00	10.00
❏ B-9251	*'S Wonderful/Dancing in the Dark/ Speak Low/Begin the Beguine	1956	2.50	5.00	10.00
❏ B-9251 [PS]	'S Wonderful	1956	2.50	5.00	10.00
❏ B-10043	(title unknown)	1956	3.00	6.00	12.00
❏ B-10043	Hand Around/Play a Gittar Solo//The Spinner/ Honky Tonk Rock-a-Round	1956	3.00	6.00	12.00
❏ B-10743	In the Still of the Night/Someone to Watch Over Me//Be My Love/Where or When	1957	2.50	5.00	10.00
❏ B-10743 [PS]	'S Marvelous	1957	2.50	5.00	10.00
❏ B-11631	*Theme from Tchaikovsky's First Piano Concerto/Theme from Swan Lake Ballet/ Theme from Rachmaninoff's Second Piano Concerto/Theme from Tchaikovsky's Fifth Symphony	195?	2.50	5.00	10.00
❏ B-11631 [PS]	Concert in Rhythm	195?	2.50	5.00	10.00
Albums					
COLUMBIA					
❏ GP 3 [(2)]	Here We Come a-Caroling/Ray Conniff's World of Hits	1968	3.75	7.50	15.00
❏ CL 925 [M]	'S Wonderful!	1956	5.00	10.00	20.00
—Red and black label with six "eye" logos					
❏ CL 1004 [M]	Dance the Bop	1957	7.50	15.00	30.00
—Red and black label with six "eye" logos; includes instruction booklet					
❏ CS 1022	Bridge Over Troubled Water	1970	2.50	5.00	10.00
❏ CL 1074 [M]	'S Marvelous	1957	3.75	7.50	15.00
❏ CL 1137 [M]	'S Awful Nice	1958	3.75	7.50	15.00
❏ CL 1163 [M]	Concert in Rhythm	1958	3.75	7.50	15.00
❏ CL 1252 [M]	Broadway in Rhythm	1959	3.75	7.50	15.00
❏ CL 1310 [M]	Hollywood in Rhythm	1959	3.75	7.50	15.00
❏ CL 1334 [M]	It's the Talk of the Town	1959	3.00	6.00	12.00
❏ CL 1390 [M]	Christmas with Conniff	1959	3.75	7.50	15.00
❏ CL 1415 [M]	Concert in Rhythm — Volume II	1960	3.00	6.00	12.00
❏ CL 1489 [M]	Young at Heart	1960	3.00	6.00	12.00
❏ CL 1490 [M]	Say It With Music (A Touch of Latin)	1960	3.00	6.00	12.00
❏ CL 1574 [M]	Memories Are Made of This	1961	3.00	6.00	12.00
❏ CL 1642 [M]	Somebody Loves Me	1961	3.00	6.00	12.00
❏ CL 1720 [M]	So Much in Love	1962	3.00	6.00	12.00
❏ CL 1776 [M]	'S Continental	1962	3.00	6.00	12.00
❏ CL 1878 [M]	Rhapsody in Rhythm	1962	3.00	6.00	12.00
❏ CL 1892 [M]	We Wish You a Merry Christmas	1962	3.75	7.50	15.00
❏ CL 1949 [M]	The Happy Beat	1963	3.00	6.00	12.00
❏ CL 2022 [M]	Just Kiddin' Around	1963	3.00	6.00	12.00
❏ CL 2118 [M]	You Make Me Feel So Young	1964	3.00	6.00	12.00
❏ CL 2150 [M]	Speak to Me of Love	1964	2.50	5.00	10.00
❏ CL 2210 [M]	Friendly Persuasion	1964	2.50	5.00	10.00
❏ CL 2264 [M]	Invisible Tears	1964	2.50	5.00	10.00

Number	Title (A Side/B Side)	Yr	VG	VG+	NM
❏ CL 2352 [M]	Love Affair	1965	2.50	5.00	10.00
❏ CL 2366 [M]	Music from Mary Poppins, The Sound of Music, My Fair Lady & Other Great Movie Themes	1965	2.50	5.00	10.00
❏ CL 2406 [M]	Here We Come a-Caroling	1965	3.00	6.00	12.00
❏ CL 2461 [M]	Happiness Is	1966	2.50	5.00	10.00
❏ CL 2500 [M]	Ray Conniff's World of Hits	1966	3.00	6.00	12.00
❏ CL 2519 [M]	Somewhere My Love	1966	3.00	6.00	12.00
❏ CL 2608 [M]	En Espanol	1967	3.00	6.00	12.00
❏ CL 2676 [M]	This Is My Song	1967	3.00	6.00	12.00
❏ CL 2747 [M]	Hawaiian Album	1967	3.00	6.00	12.00
❏ CL 2795 [M]	It Must Be Him	1968	3.75	7.50	15.00
❏ CS 8001 [S]	'S Awful Nice	1958	5.00	10.00	20.00
—Red and black label with six "eye" logos					
❏ CS 8022 [S]	Concert in Rhythm	1958	5.00	10.00	20.00
—Red and black label with six "eye" logos					
❏ PC 8022	Concert in Rhythm	1988	—	3.00	6.00
—Reissue with new prefix					
❏ CS 8037 [S]	'S Marvelous	1958	5.00	10.00	20.00
—Red and black label with six "eye" logos					
❏ CS 8064 [S]	Broadway in Rhythm	1959	5.00	10.00	20.00
—Red and black label with six "eye" logos					
❏ CS 8117 [S]	Hollywood in Rhythm	1959	5.00	10.00	20.00
—Red and black label with six "eye" logos					
❏ CS 8143 [S]	It's the Talk of the Town	1959	3.75	7.50	15.00
❏ CS 8155 [S]	Conniff Meets Butterfield	1959	6.25	12.50	25.00
—Red and black label with six "eye" logos					
❏ CS 8185 [S]	Christmas with Conniff	1959	3.00	6.00	12.00
❏ CS 8212 [S]	Concert in Rhythm — Volume II	1960	3.75	7.50	15.00
❏ CS 8281 [S]	Young at Heart	1960	3.75	7.50	15.00
❏ CS 8282 [S]	Say It With Music (A Touch of Latin)	1960	3.75	7.50	15.00
❏ CS 8374 [S]	Memories Are Made of This	1961	3.75	7.50	15.00
❏ CS 8442 [S]	Somebody Loves Me	1961	3.75	7.50	15.00
❏ CS 8520 [S]	So Much in Love	1962	3.75	7.50	15.00
❏ CS 8576 [S]	'S Continental	1962	3.75	7.50	15.00
❏ CS 8678 [S]	Rhapsody in Rhythm	1962	3.75	7.50	15.00
❏ CS 8692 [S]	We Wish You a Merry Christmas	1962	3.00	6.00	12.00
❏ CS 8749 [S]	The Happy Beat	1963	3.75	7.50	15.00
❏ CS 8822 [S]	Just Kiddin' Around	1963	3.75	7.50	15.00
❏ CS 8918 [S]	You Make Me Feel So Young	1964	3.75	7.50	15.00
❏ CS 8950 [S]	Speak to Me of Love	1964	3.00	6.00	12.00
❏ CS 9064 [S]	Invisible Tears	1964	3.00	6.00	12.00
❏ CS 9110 [S]	Friendly Persuasion	1964	3.00	6.00	12.00
❏ CS 9152 [S]	Love Affair	1965	3.00	6.00	12.00
❏ CS 9166 [S]	Music from Mary Poppins, The Sound of Music, My Fair Lady & Other Great Movie Themes	1965	3.00	6.00	12.00
❏ CS 9206 [S]	Here We Come a-Caroling	1965	2.50	5.00	10.00
❏ CS 9261 [S]	Happiness Is	1966	3.00	6.00	12.00
❏ CS 9300 [S]	Ray Conniff's World of Hits	1966	2.50	5.00	10.00
❏ CS 9319 [S]	Somewhere My Love	1966	2.50	5.00	10.00
❏ PC 9319	Somewhere My Love	198?	—	3.00	6.00
—Reissue with new prefix					
❏ CS 9408 [S]	En Espanol	1967	2.50	5.00	10.00
❏ CS 9476 [S]	This Is My Song	1967	2.50	5.00	10.00
❏ CS 9547 [S]	Hawaiian Album	1967	2.50	5.00	10.00
❏ PC 9547	Hawaiian Album	198?	—	3.00	6.00
—Reissue with new prefix					
❏ CS 9595 [S]	It Must Be Him	1968	2.50	5.00	10.00
❏ CS 9661	Honey	1968	2.50	5.00	10.00
❏ CS 9712	Turn Around Look at Me	1968	2.50	5.00	10.00
❏ CS 9777	I Love How You Love Me	1969	2.50	5.00	10.00
❏ CS 9839	Ray Conniff's Greatest Hits	1969	2.50	5.00	10.00
❏ PC 9839	Ray Conniff's Greatest Hits	198?	—	3.00	6.00
—Reissue with new prefix					
❏ CS 9920	Jean	1969	2.50	5.00	10.00
❏ G 30122 [(2)]	Concert in Stereo/Live at the Sahara/Tahoe	1970	3.75	7.50	15.00
❏ C 30410	We've Only Just Begun	1970	2.50	5.00	10.00
❏ C 30498	Love Story	1971	2.50	5.00	10.00
❏ CQ 30498 [Q]	Love Story	1972	3.75	7.50	15.00
❏ C 30755	Great Contemporary Instrumental Hits	1971	2.50	5.00	10.00
❏ KC 31220	I'd Like to Teach the World to Sing	1972	2.50	5.00	10.00
❏ CQ 31473 [Q]	Love Theme from "The Godfather"	1972	3.75	7.50	15.00
❏ KC 31473	Love Theme from "The Godfather"	1972	2.50	5.00	10.00
❏ CQ 31629 [Q]	Alone Again (Naturally)	1972	3.75	7.50	15.00
❏ KC 31629	Alone Again (Naturally)	1972	2.50	5.00	10.00
❏ KC 32090	I Can See Clearly Now	1973	2.50	5.00	10.00
❏ KC 32376	You Are the Sunshine of My Life	1973	2.50	5.00	10.00
❏ C 32413	Charlotte's Web	1973	2.50	5.00	10.00
❏ CQ 32553 [Q]	Harmony	1973	3.75	7.50	15.00
❏ KC 32553	Harmony	1973	2.50	5.00	10.00
❏ CQ 32802 [Q]	The Way We Were	1974	3.75	7.50	15.00
❏ KC 32802	The Way We Were	1974	2.50	5.00	10.00
❏ CQ 33139 [Q]	The Happy Sound	1974	3.75	7.50	15.00
❏ KC 33139	The Happy Sound	1974	2.50	5.00	10.00
❏ CQ 33332 [Q]	Laughter in the Rain	1975	3.75	7.50	15.00
❏ CQ 33564 [Q]	Another Somebody Done Somebody Wrong Song	1975	3.75	7.50	15.00
❏ KC 33564	Another Somebody Done Somebody Wrong Song	1975	2.50	5.00	10.00
❏ CG 33603 [(2)]	Somewhere My Love/Bridge Over Troubled Water	1975	3.00	6.00	12.00
❏ CQ 33884 [Q]	Love Will Keep Us Together	1975	3.75	7.50	15.00
❏ KC 33884	Love Will Keep Us Together	1975	2.50	5.00	10.00
❏ CQ 34040 [Q]	I Write the Songs	1976	3.75	7.50	15.00
❏ KC 34040	I Write the Songs	1976	2.50	5.00	10.00
❏ CQ 34170 [Q]	Send In the Clowns	1976	3.75	7.50	15.00
❏ KC 34170	Send In the Clowns	1976	2.50	5.00	10.00
❏ CQ 34312 [Q]	S.W.A.T.	1976	3.75	7.50	15.00
❏ KC 34312	S.W.A.T.	1976	2.50	5.00	10.00
❏ PC 34477	After the Lovin'	1977	2.50	5.00	10.00
❏ JC 35659	Ray Conniff Plays the Bee Gees and Other Hits	1978	2.50	5.00	10.00
❏ PC 36255	I Will Survive	1979	2.50	5.00	10.00
❏ JC 36749	Perfect "10" Classics	1980	2.50	5.00	10.00
❏ FC 38072	The Nashville Connection	1981	2.50	5.00	10.00
❏ PC 38300	Christmas Album	1982	2.50	5.00	10.00
❏ PC 39470	Christmas Caroling	1984	2.50	5.00	10.00
❏ FC 40384	Say You, Say Me	1986	2.50	5.00	10.00
❏ FC 40152	Always in My Heart	1988	2.50	5.00	10.00
HARMONY					
❏ HS 11346	Love Is a Many-Splendored Thing	1969	2.50	5.00	10.00
❏ KH 30134	The Impossible Dream	1970	2.50	5.00	10.00

Number	Title (A Side/B Side)	Yr	VG	VG+	NM

CONNORS, CAROL Also see THE CARMEL SISTERS; THE TEDDY BEARS.
45s
CAPITOL
| ❑ 5152 | Never/Angel, My Angel | 1964 | 6.25 | 12.50 | 25.00 |

COLUMBIA
❑ 41976	You Are My Answer/My Diary	1961	6.25	12.50	25.00
❑ 42155	Listen to the Beat/My Special Boy	1961	6.25	12.50	25.00
❑ 42337	That's All It Takes/What Do You See in Him	1962	6.25	12.50	25.00

ERA
| ❑ 3084 | Two Rivers/Big, Big Love | 1962 | 7.50 | 15.00 | 30.00 |
| ❑ 3096 | Tommy Go Away/I Wanna Know | 1962 | 7.50 | 15.00 | 30.00 |

MIRA
| ❑ 219 | Lonely Little Beach Girl/ My Baby Looks, But He Don't Touch | 1965 | 6.25 | 12.50 | 25.00 |
| ❑ 219 [PS] | Lonely Little Beach Girl/ My Baby Looks, But He Don't Touch | 1965 | 12.50 | 25.00 | 50.00 |

N.T.C.
| ❑ 3131 | Yum Yum Yamaha | 1964 | 12.50 | 25.00 | 50.00 |
—One-sided single
| ❑ 3131 [PS] | Yum Yum Yamaha | 1964 | 25.00 | 50.00 | 100.00 |

CONNORS, NORMAN
12-Inch Singles
ARISTA
| ❑ SP-99 [DJ] | Take It to the Limit (same on both sides?) | 1980 | 3.75 | 7.50 | 15.00 |

CAPITOL
| ❑ V-15376 | You're My One and Only Love (5 versions) | 1988 | 2.50 | 5.00 | 10.00 |

45s
ARISTA
❑ 0343	This Is Your Life/Captain Connors	1978	—	2.00	4.00
❑ 0377	Wouldn't You Like to See/Listen	1978	—	2.00	4.00
❑ 0443	Your Love/Disco Land	1979	—	2.00	4.00
❑ 0460	Hand Me Gently/Be There In the Morning	1979	—	2.00	4.00
❑ 0548	Take It to the Limit/You Bring Me Joy	1980	—	2.00	4.00
❑ 0581	Melancholy Fire/You've Been On My Mind	1980	—	2.00	4.00
❑ 0632	She's Gone/Mr. C.	1981	—	2.00	4.00

BUDDAH
❑ 499	Valentine Love/Aria	1975	—	2.50	5.00
❑ 534	We Both Need Each Other/You Are My Starship	1976	—	3.00	6.00
❑ 542	You Are My Starship/Bubbles	1976	—	2.50	5.00
❑ 554	Betcha By Golly Wow/Kwasi	1976	—	2.50	5.00
❑ 570	Once I've Been There/Romantic Journey	1977	—	2.50	5.00
❑ 580	For You Everything/Give the Drummer Some	1977	—	2.50	5.00

CAPITOL
| ❑ B-44110 | I Am Your Melody/Samba for Maria | 1988 | — | — | 3.00 |
| ❑ B-44159 | You're My One and Only Love/I Am Your Melody | 1988 | — | — | 3.00 |

THE RIGHT STUFF
| ❑ 58849 | Didn't I (Blow Your Mind This Time)/River of Love | 2000 | — | — | 3.00 |

Albums
ACCORD
| ❑ SN-7210 | Just Imagine | 1982 | 2.00 | 4.00 | 8.00 |

ARISTA
❑ AB 4177	This Is Your Life	1978	2.50	5.00	10.00
❑ AB 4216	Invitation	1979	2.50	5.00	10.00
❑ AL 9534	Take It to the Limit	1980	2.50	5.00	10.00
❑ AL 9575	Mr. C.	1981	2.50	5.00	10.00

BUDDAH
❑ BDS-5142	Love from the Sun	1973	3.00	6.00	12.00
❑ BDS-5611	Slewfoot	1974	3.00	6.00	12.00
❑ BDS-5643	Saturday Night Special	1975	2.50	5.00	10.00
❑ BDS-5655	You Are My Starship	1976	2.50	5.00	10.00
❑ BDS-5674	Dance of Magic	1977	5.00	10.00	20.00
—Reissue of Cobblestone 9024
| ❑ BDS-5675 | Dark of Light | 1977 | 5.00 | 10.00 | 20.00 |
—Reissue of Cobblestone 9035
| ❑ BDS-5682 | Romantic Journey | 1977 | 2.50 | 5.00 | 10.00 |
| ❑ BDS-5716 | The Best of Norman Connors & Friends | 1978 | 2.50 | 5.00 | 10.00 |

CAPITOL
| ❑ C1-48515 | Passion | 1988 | 2.50 | 5.00 | 10.00 |

COBBLESTONE
| ❑ 9024 | Dance of Magic | 1972 | 6.25 | 12.50 | 25.00 |
| ❑ 9035 | Dark of Light | 1973 | 6.25 | 12.50 | 25.00 |

CONNY
45s
CAPITOL
| ❑ 4526 | Midi Midnette/Little Girl | 1961 | 3.00 | 6.00 | 12.00 |

CONRAD, BOB
45s
WARNER BROS.
❑ 5211	I Want You (Pretty Baby)/Ballin' the Jack	1961	2.50	5.00	10.00
❑ 5211 [PS]	I Want You (Pretty Baby)/Ballin' the Jack	1961	6.25	12.50	25.00
❑ 5242	Bye, Bye Baby/Love You	1961	2.50	5.00	10.00
❑ 5242 [PS]	Bye, Bye Baby/Love You	1961	6.25	12.50	25.00
❑ 5267	Keep It Up/Noah's Ark	1962	2.50	5.00	10.00
❑ 5306	Crazy Magician/I Just Gotta Have You	1962	2.50	5.00	10.00
❑ 5317	Cindy Is Gone/Again	1962	2.50	5.00	10.00

CONRAD, JESS
45s
LONDON
| ❑ 1967 | Mystery Girl/Just the Two of Us | 1961 | 3.00 | 6.00 | 12.00 |
| ❑ 2005 | Little Ship/Walk Away | 1961 | 3.00 | 6.00 | 12.00 |

CONSORTS, THE
45s
APT
| ❑ 25066 | Please Be Mine/Time After Time | 1962 | 30.00 | 60.00 | 120.00 |

COUSINS
| ❑ 1004 | Please Be Mine/Time After Time | 1961 | 100.00 | 200.00 | 400.00 |

CONTENDERS, THE More than one group.
45s
BETH
| ❑ 1001 | I'll Show You How to Love/(B-side unknown) | 195? | 5.00 | 10.00 | 20.00 |

BLUE SKY
| ❑ 105 | Mr. Dee Jay/Yes I Do | 1959 | 150.00 | 300.00 | 600.00 |

CHATTAHOOCHIE
| ❑ 644 | The Dune Bugy/Go Ahead | 1964 | 6.25 | 12.50 | 25.00 |
| ❑ 656 | Johnny B. Goode/Rise 'N' Shine | 1964 | 6.25 | 12.50 | 25.00 |

JACKPOT
| ❑ 48002 | Tequila Song/Wild Man | 1959 | 10.00 | 20.00 | 40.00 |

JAVA
| ❑ 101 | The Clock/Look at Me | 196? | 6.25 | 12.50 | 25.00 |
—Red label
| ❑ 101 | The Clock/Look at Me | 196? | 25.00 | 50.00 | 100.00 |
—Gold label

CONTINENTAL GEMS, THE
45s
GUYDEN
| ❑ 2091 | My Love Will Follow You/Everywhere | 1963 | 100.00 | 200.00 | 400.00 |

CONTINENTALS, THE (1)
45s
ERA
| ❑ 3003 | Cool Penguin/Soap Sudz | 1959 | 5.00 | 10.00 | 20.00 |

PENGUIN
| ❑ 1002 | Cool Penguin/Soap Sudz | 1959 | 10.00 | 20.00 | 40.00 |

CONTINENTALS, THE (2)
45s
LOST-NITE
| ❑ 349 | Dear Lord/Fine Fine Frame | 197? | — | 2.50 | 5.00 |
—Reissue
| ❑ 351 | Picture of Love/Soft and Sweet | 197? | — | 2.50 | 5.00 |
—Reissue
PORT
| ❑ 70018 | Dear Lord/Fine Fine Frame | 1960 | 7.50 | 15.00 | 30.00 |
| ❑ 70024 | Picture of Love/Soft and Sweet | 1961 | 7.50 | 15.00 | 30.00 |

WHIRLIN' DISC
| ❑ 101 | Dear Lord/Fine Fine Frame | 1956 | 50.00 | 100.00 | 200.00 |
| ❑ 105 | Picture of Love/Soft and Sweet | 1957 | 50.00 | 100.00 | 200.00 |

CONTINENTALS, THE (3)
45s
RAMA
| ❑ 190 | You Are An Angel/Giddy Up a Ding Dong | 1956 | 37.50 | 75.00 | 150.00 |
—Red label
| ❑ 190 | You Are An Angel/Giddy Up a Ding Dong | 1956 | 375.00 | 750.00 | 1500. |
—Blue label

CONTINENTALS, THE (U) Some of these may be groups (1), (2) or (3); many are not.
45s
AOK
| ❑ 1025 | Take Me/She Wants You | 1966 | 6.25 | 12.50 | 25.00 |

BOLO
| ❑ 720 | I'm Coming Home/The Turnaround | 1960 | 7.50 | 15.00 | 30.00 |

CUCA
| ❑ 1063 | Tic-Toc/Sue | 1961 | 7.50 | 15.00 | 30.00 |

DAVIS
| ❑ 466 | Don't Do It, Baby/Tongue Twister | 1959 | 10.00 | 20.00 | 40.00 |

HUNTER
| ❑ 3503 | It Doesn't Matter/Whisper It | 1960 | 300.00 | 600.00 | 1200. |

KEY
| ❑ 517 | Take a Gamble on Me/Meanwhile Back at the Ranch | 1956 | 25.00 | 50.00 | 100.00 |

LIFETIME
| ❑ 1019 | Cathy's Clown/Maybe Baby | 1966 | 2.50 | 5.00 | 10.00 |

VANDAN
| ❑ 8067 | No Money No Luck Blues/Pink Champagne | 196? | 5.00 | 10.00 | 20.00 |

CONTOURS, THE
12-Inch Singles
MOTOWN
| ❑ 4611MG | Do You Love Me (6:26) (Edited Version 2:37) (Original Version 2:53) | 1988 | 3.75 | 7.50 | 15.00 |

45s
GORDY
❑ 7005	Do You Love Me/Move Mr. Man	1962	5.00	10.00	20.00
❑ 7012	Shake Sherry/You Better Get in Line	1963	3.75	7.50	15.00
❑ 7016	Don't Let Her Be Your Baby/It Must Be Love	1963	3.00	6.00	12.00
❑ 7019	Pa I Need a Car/You Get Ugly	1963	3.00	6.00	12.00
❑ 7029	Can You Do It/I'll Stand By You	1964	3.00	6.00	12.00
❑ 7037	Can You Jerk Like Me/That Day When She Needed Me	1964	3.00	6.00	12.00
❑ 7044	First I Look at the Purse/Searching for a Girl	1965	3.00	6.00	12.00
❑ 7052	Just a Little Misunderstanding/Determination	1966	3.00	6.00	12.00
❑ 7059	It's So Hard Being a Loser/Your Love Grows More Precious Every Day	1967	3.00	6.00	12.00

HOB
| ❑ 116 | I'm So Glad/Yours Is My Heart Alone | 1961 | 30.00 | 60.00 | 120.00 |

MOTOWN
| ❑ 1008 | Whole Lotta Woman/Come On and Be Mine | 1961 | 125.00 | 250.00 | 500.00 |
| ❑ 1012 | The Stretch/Funny | 1962 | 200.00 | 400.00 | 800.00 |

MOTOWN YESTERYEAR
| ❑ 448 | Do You Love Me/Shake Sherry | 1972 | — | 2.00 | 4.00 |
| ❑ 448 [PS] | Do You Love Me/Shake Sherry | 1988 | — | 2.50 | 5.00 |
—"Dirty Dancing" sleeve; without cut-out hole
ROCKET
| ❑ 41192 | I'm a Winner/Makes Me Wanna Come Back | 1980 | — | 2.00 | 4.00 |

TAMLA
| ❑ 7012 | Shake Sherry/You Better Get in Line | 1963 | 37.50 | 75.00 | 150.00 |
—Tamla label used in error for a Gordy release

Albums
GORDY
| ❑ G 901 [M] | Do You Love Me? | 1962 | 125.00 | 250.00 | 500.00 |

MOTOWN
| ❑ M5-188V1 | Do You Love Me? | 1981 | 2.50 | 5.00 | 10.00 |

The Dave Clark Five, "You Must Have Been a Beautiful Baby,"
Epic 5-10179, picture sleeve, $12.50-$25.

Petula Clark, *Downtown,* Warner Bros. W 1590, mono LP, gray
label, $7.50-$15.

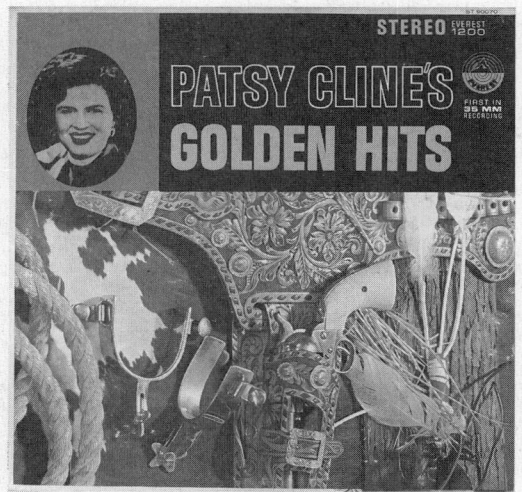

Patsy Cline, *Golden Hits,* Everest ST 90070, rechanneled
stereo LP, Capitol Record Club edition, $7.50-$15.

Joe Cocker, "The Letter," A&M 1174, picture sleeve,
$3-$6.

Perry Como, *Saturday Night with Mr. C,* RCA Victor
LSP-1971, stereo LP, $15-$30.

Sam Cooke, *Sam Cooke Sings,* RCA Victor LPC-126,
"Compact 33 Double" EP, $20-$40 (cover and record
together).

Number	Title (A Side/B Side)	Yr	VG	VG+	NM

CONVINCERS, THE
45s
MOVIN'

Number	Title (A Side/B Side)	Yr	VG	VG+	NM
❏ 100	Rejected Love/Go Back Baby	1962	100.00	200.00	400.00

CONWAY, JULIE
Albums
HARMONY

Number	Title (A Side/B Side)	Yr	VG	VG+	NM
❏ HL 7143 [M]	Good Housekeeping's Plan for Reducing Off-the-Record	1960	5.00	10.00	20.00

COODER, RY   Also see THE ROLLING STONES.
12-Inch Singles
WARNER BROS.

Number	Title (A Side/B Side)	Yr	VG	VG+	NM
❏ PRO-A-943 [DJ]	Crazy 'Bout an Automobile/If Walls Could Talk/ The Very Thing That Makes You Rich/ Look at Granny Run	1981	5.00	10.00	20.00

45s
MUSICOR

Number	Title (A Side/B Side)	Yr	VG	VG+	NM
❏ 1148	Life Game/1983	1966	2.50	5.00	10.00

REPRISE

Number	Title (A Side/B Side)	Yr	VG	VG+	NM
❏ 0910	Goin' to Brownsville/Available Space	1970	—	3.00	6.00
❏ 0940	Alimony/Pigmeat	1970	—	3.00	6.00
❏ 1009	Dark Is the Night/On a Monday	1971	—	3.00	6.00
❏ 1071	Billy the Kid/Money Honey	1972	—	3.00	6.00
❏ 1167	Billy the Kid/Boomer's Story	1973	—	3.00	6.00

WARNER BROS.

Number	Title (A Side/B Side)	Yr	VG	VG+	NM
❏ 8384	School Is Out/Jesus on the Mainline	1977	—	2.50	5.00
❏ 27945	Get Rhythm/Get Back to Okinawa	1988	—	2.00	4.00
❏ 28158	All Shook Up/Get Your Lies Straight	1987	—	2.00	4.00
❏ 28158 [PS]	All Shook Up/Get Your Lies Straight	1987	—	2.00	4.00
❏ 28723	Crossroads/Feel It (Bad Blues)	1986	—	2.00	4.00
❏ 28725	Tell Me Something Slick/Billy and Annie	1986	—	2.00	4.00
❏ 49055	Down in Hollywood/Little Sister	1979	—	2.50	5.00
❏ 49081	The Very Thing That Makes You Rich/ Little Sister	1979	—	2.50	5.00
❏ 49677	Girls from Texas/Borderline	1981	—	2.00	4.00
❏ 49704	Crazy 'Bout an Automobile/Borderline	1981	—	2.00	4.00

Albums
MOBILE FIDELITY

Number	Title (A Side/B Side)	Yr	VG	VG+	NM
❏ 1-085	Jazz	198?	100.00	200.00	400.00

—Audiophile vinyl
REPRISE

Number	Title (A Side/B Side)	Yr	VG	VG+	NM
❏ PRO 588 [DJ]	The Ry Cooder Radio Show	1976	25.00	50.00	100.00
❏ MS 2052	Into the Purple Valley	1972	3.00	6.00	12.00
❏ MS 2117	Boomer's Story	1973	3.00	6.00	12.00
❏ MS 2179	Paradise and Lunch	1974	3.00	6.00	12.00
❏ MS 2254	Chicken Skin Music	1976	3.00	6.00	12.00
❏ RS-6402	Ry Cooder	1969	3.75	7.50	15.00

—Two-tone orange label with "r:" and "W7" logos

Number	Title (A Side/B Side)	Yr	VG	VG+	NM
❏ RS-6402	Ry Cooder	1970	3.00	6.00	12.00

—No "W7" on label; one-tone orange (almost tan) label
WARNER BROS.

Number	Title (A Side/B Side)	Yr	VG	VG+	NM
❏ BS 3059	Show Time	1977	2.50	5.00	10.00
❏ BSK 3197	Jazz	1978	2.50	5.00	10.00
❏ BSK 3358	Bop Till You Drop	1979	2.50	5.00	10.00
❏ HS 3448	The Long Riders	1980	2.50	5.00	10.00
❏ BSK 3489	Borderline	1980	2.50	5.00	10.00
❏ BSK 3651	The Slide Area	1982	2.50	5.00	10.00
❏ 25270	Paris, Texas	1984	2.50	5.00	10.00
❏ 25399	Crossroads	1986	2.50	5.00	10.00
❏ 25639	Get Rhythm	1987	2.50	5.00	10.00
❏ 25996	Johnny Handsome	1989	2.50	5.00	10.00

COOK, KEN
45s
PHILLIPS INT'L.

Number	Title (A Side/B Side)	Yr	VG	VG+	NM
❏ 3534	I Was a Fool/Crazy Baby	1959	12.50	25.00	50.00

—Roy Orbison appears on this record (uncredited)

COOK, PETER, AND DUDLEY MOORE
45s
PARROT

Number	Title (A Side/B Side)	Yr	VG	VG+	NM
❏ 3016	Bedazzled/Love Me	1967	2.00	4.00	8.00

COOKE, SAM
45s
CHERIE

Number	Title (A Side/B Side)	Yr	VG	VG+	NM
❏ 4501	Darling I Need You Now/Win Your Love for Me	1971	2.00	4.00	8.00

KEEN

Number	Title (A Side/B Side)	Yr	VG	VG+	NM
❏ 8-1001	You Send Me/Love You Most of All	1960	3.75	7.50	15.00

—Gold label; early reissue series

Number	Title (A Side/B Side)	Yr	VG	VG+	NM
❏ 3-2005	Stealing Kisses/All of My Life	1958	6.25	12.50	25.00
❏ 3-2006 [M]	Win Your Love for Me/Love Song from "Houseboat" (Almost in Your Arms)	1958	6.25	12.50	25.00
❏ 5-2006 [S]	Win Your Love for Me/Love Song from "Houseboat" (Almost in Your Arms)	1959	25.00	50.00	100.00

—Blue vinyl

Number	Title (A Side/B Side)	Yr	VG	VG+	NM
❏ 3-2008	Love You Most of All/Blue Moon	1958	6.25	12.50	25.00
❏ 3-2018 [M]	Everybody Likes to Cha Cha Cha/ Little Things You Do	1959	6.25	12.50	25.00
❏ 5-2018 [S]	Everybody Likes to Cha Cha Cha/ Little Things You Do	1959	10.00	20.00	40.00
❏ 2022 [M]	Only Sixteen/Let's Go Steady Again	1959	6.25	12.50	25.00
❏ 5-2022 [S]	Only Sixteen/Let's Go Steady Again	1959	12.50	25.00	50.00
❏ 2101	Summertime/Summertime (Part 2)	1959	6.25	12.50	25.00
❏ 8-2105	There! I've Said It Again/ One Hour Ahead of the Posse	1959	6.25	12.50	25.00
❏ 2118	Steal Away/So Glamorous	1960	5.00	10.00	20.00
❏ 2122	Mary, Mary Lou/Eee-Yi-Ee-Yi-Oh	1960	5.00	10.00	20.00
❏ 4009	You Were Made for Me/Lonely Island	1958	6.25	12.50	25.00
❏ 3-4013	You Send Me/Summertime	195?	5.00	10.00	20.00

—Multicolor label; note slightly different number than original (34013)

Number	Title (A Side/B Side)	Yr	VG	VG+	NM
❏ 34002	(I Love You) For Sentimental Reasons/ Desire Me	1958	6.25	12.50	25.00

—Black label

Number	Title (A Side/B Side)	Yr	VG	VG+	NM
❏ 34013	You Send Me/Summertime	1957	6.25	12.50	25.00

—Black label (original)

Number	Title (A Side/B Side)	Yr	VG	VG+	NM
❏ 82111	'T'ain't Nobody's Bizness (If I Do)/No One	1960	6.25	12.50	25.00
❏ 82112	Wonderful World/Along the Navajo Trail	1960	5.00	10.00	20.00
❏ 82117	With You/I Thank God	1960	5.00	10.00	20.00

RCA

Number	Title (A Side/B Side)	Yr	VG	VG+	NM
❏ PB-14146	Bring It On Home to Me/ Nothing Can Change This Love	1985	2.00	4.00	8.00

RCA VICTOR

Number	Title (A Side/B Side)	Yr	VG	VG+	NM
❏ 37-7853	That's It-I Quit-I'm Movin' On/What Do You Say	1961	15.00	30.00	60.00

—"Compact Single 33" (small hole, plays at LP speed)

Number	Title (A Side/B Side)	Yr	VG	VG+	NM
❏ 47-7701	Teenage Sonata/If You Were the Only Girl	1960	5.00	10.00	20.00
❏ 47-7730	You Understand Me/I Belong to Your Heart	1960	3.75	7.50	15.00
❏ 47-7730 [PS]	You Understand Me/I Belong to Your Heart	1960	6.25	12.50	25.00
❏ 47-7783	Chain Gang/I Fall in Love Every Day	1960	3.75	7.50	15.00
❏ 47-7783 [PS]	Chain Gang/I Fall in Love Every Day	1960	6.25	12.50	25.00
❏ 47-7816	Sad Mood/Love Me	1960	3.75	7.50	15.00
❏ 47-7853	That's It-I Quit-I'm Movin' On/What Do You Say	1961	3.75	7.50	15.00
❏ 47-7883	Cupid/Farewell, My Darling	1961	3.75	7.50	15.00
❏ 47-7883 [PS]	Cupid/Farewell, My Darling	1961	6.25	12.50	25.00
❏ 47-7927	Feel It/It's All Right	1961	3.75	7.50	15.00
❏ 47-7927 [PS]	Feel It/It's All Right	1961	6.25	12.50	25.00
❏ 47-7983	Twistin' the Night Away/One More Time	1962	3.75	7.50	15.00
❏ 47-8036	Bring It On Home to Me/Having a Party	1962	3.75	7.50	15.00
❏ 47-8088	Nothing Can Change This Love/Somebody Have Mercy	1962	3.75	7.50	15.00
❏ 47-8088 [PS]	Nothing Can Change This Love/Somebody Have Mercy	1962	6.25	12.50	25.00
❏ 47-8129	Send Me Some Lovin'/Baby, Baby, Baby	1963	3.75	7.50	15.00
❏ 47-8129 [PS]	Send Me Some Lovin'/Baby, Baby, Baby	1963	6.25	12.50	25.00
❏ 47-8164	Another Saturday Night/Love Will Find a Way	1963	3.75	7.50	15.00
❏ 47-8164 [PS]	Another Saturday Night/Love Will Find a Way	1963	6.25	12.50	25.00
❏ 47-8215	Frankie and Johnny/Cool Train	1963	3.00	6.00	12.00
❏ 47-8215 [PS]	Frankie and Johnny/Cool Train	1963	6.25	12.50	25.00
❏ 47-8247	Little Red Rooster/You Gotta Move	1963	3.00	6.00	12.00
❏ 47-8247 [PS]	Little Red Rooster/You Gotta Move	1963	6.25	12.50	25.00
❏ 47-8299	Good News/Basin Street Blues	1963	3.00	6.00	12.00
❏ 47-8299	Ain't That Good News/Basin Street Blues	1963	5.00	10.00	20.00

—Original A-side title (or a scarce reissue)

Number	Title (A Side/B Side)	Yr	VG	VG+	NM
❏ 47-8368	Good Times/Tennessee Waltz	1964	3.00	6.00	12.00
❏ 47-8426	Cousin of Mine/That's Where It's At	1964	3.00	6.00	12.00
❏ 47-8486	Shake/A Change Is Gonna Come	1964	3.00	6.00	12.00
❏ 47-8539	It's Got the Whole World Shakin'/Ease My Troublin' Mind	1965	2.50	5.00	10.00
❏ 47-8586	When a Boy Falls in Love/The Piper	1965	2.50	5.00	10.00
❏ 47-8631	Sugar Dumpling/Bridge of Tears	1965	2.50	5.00	10.00
❏ 47-8631 [PS]	Sugar Dumpling/Bridge of Tears	1965	6.25	12.50	25.00
❏ 47-8751	Feel It/That's All	1965	2.50	5.00	10.00
❏ 47-8803	Let's Go Steady Again/Trouble Blues	1966	2.50	5.00	10.00
❏ 47-8934	Meet Me at Mary's Place/If I Had a Hammer	1966	2.50	5.00	10.00
❏ SP-45-173 [DJ]	A Change Is Gonna Come (same on both sides)	1968	12.50	25.00	50.00

—Promo-only number; this appears to be a radio reissue in the wake of events going on in 1968

Number	Title (A Side/B Side)	Yr	VG	VG+	NM
❏ VP-3-2555 [S]	The Twist/Movin' & Groovin'	196?	6.25	12.50	25.00

—Small hole, plays at 33 1/3 rpm

Number	Title (A Side/B Side)	Yr	VG	VG+	NM
❏ VP-4-2555 [S]	Somebody Have Mercy/Camptown Girl	196?	6.25	12.50	25.00

—Small hole, plays at 33 1/3 rpm
SAR

Number	Title (A Side/B Side)	Yr	VG	VG+	NM
❏ 122 [DJ]	Just for You/Made for Me	1961	25.00	50.00	100.00

—Promo only (some copies have "Audition" on label, sone do not); possibly made as leverage during contract renegotiation at RCA Victor
SPECIALTY

Number	Title (A Side/B Side)	Yr	VG	VG+	NM
❏ 596	Forever/Lovable	1957	7.50	15.00	30.00

—As "Dale Cook"

Number	Title (A Side/B Side)	Yr	VG	VG+	NM
❏ 619	I'll Come Running Back to You/Forever	1957	7.50	15.00	30.00
❏ 627	That's All I Need to Know/I Don't Want to Cry	1958	7.50	15.00	30.00
❏ 667	Happy in Love/I Need You Now	1959	7.50	15.00	30.00
❏ 921	Must Jesus Bear the Cross Alone/ The Last Mile of the Way	1970	2.50	5.00	10.00

—With the Soul Stirrers

Number	Title (A Side/B Side)	Yr	VG	VG+	NM
❏ 928	Just Another Day/Christ Is All	1973	2.50	5.00	10.00

—With the Soul Stirrers

Number	Title (A Side/B Side)	Yr	VG	VG+	NM
❏ 930	That's Heaven to Me/Lord, Remember Me	1974	2.50	5.00	10.00

—With the Soul Stirrers
7-Inch Extended Plays
KEEN

Number	Title (A Side/B Side)	Yr	VG	VG+	NM
❏ B-2001	The Bells of Saint Mary's/Tammy// Moonlight in Vermont/So Long	1958	20.00	40.00	80.00
❏ B-2001 [PS]	Songs by Sam Cooke, Volume 1	1958	20.00	40.00	80.00
❏ B-2002	*You Send Me/The Lonesome Road/That Lucky Old Sun/Canadian Sunset	1958	20.00	40.00	80.00
❏ B-2002 [PS]	Songs by Sam Cooke, Volume 2	1958	20.00	40.00	80.00
❏ B-2003	Summertime/Danny Boy//Around the World/Ol' Man River	1958	20.00	40.00	80.00
❏ B-2003 [PS]	Songs by Sam Cooke, Volume 3	1958	20.00	40.00	80.00
❏ B-2006	*Mary, Mary Lou/The Gypsy/Oh, Look at Me Now/Someday	1958	20.00	40.00	80.00
❏ B-2006 [PS]	Encore, Volume 1	1958	20.00	40.00	80.00
❏ B-2007	*When I Fall in Love/I Cover the Waterfront/ Running Wild/Today I Sing the Blues	1958	20.00	40.00	80.00
❏ B-2007 [PS]	Encore, Volume 2	1958	20.00	40.00	80.00
❏ B-2008	It's the Talk of the Town/Along the Navajo Trail/ /My Foolish Heart/Accentuate the Positive	1958	20.00	40.00	80.00
❏ B-2008 [PS]	Encore, Volume 3	1958	20.00	40.00	80.00
❏ B-2010	Love Song from Houseboat/Lonely Island//Win Your Love for Me/All of My Life	1959	20.00	40.00	80.00
❏ B-2010 [PS]	Sam Cooke Sings His Hits	1959	20.00	40.00	80.00
❏ B-2012	Let's Call the Whole Thing Off/God Bless the Child//Comes Love/Lover Girl	1959	20.00	40.00	80.00
❏ B-2012 [PS]	Tribute to the Lady, Volume 1	1959	20.00	40.00	80.00
❏ B-2013	(contents unknown)	1959	20.00	40.00	80.00
❏ B-2013 [PS]	Tribute to the Lady, Volume 2	1959	20.00	40.00	80.00
❏ B-2014	(contents unknown)	1959	20.00	40.00	80.00
❏ B-2014 [PS]	Tribute to the Lady, Volume 3	1959	20.00	40.00	80.00

RCA VICTOR

Number	Title (A Side/B Side)	Yr	VG	VG+	NM
❏ LPC-126	Chain Gang/If You Were the Only Girl//Teenage Sonata/You Understand Me	1961	5.00	10.00	20.00
❏ LPC-126 [PS]	Sam Cooke Sings	1961	5.00	10.00	20.00
❏ EPA-4375	Another Saturday Night/You Send Me//Only Sixteen/Bring It On Home to Me	1963	5.00	10.00	20.00
❏ EPA-4375 [PS]	Another Saturday Night	1963	5.00	10.00	20.00

C

Number	Title (A Side/B Side)	Yr	VG	VG+	NM
Albums					
ABKCO					
❑ 1124-1	Sam Cooke's Night Beat	1995	3.00	6.00	12.00
—Reissue					
❑ 2970-1	Sam Cooke at the Copa	1988	3.00	6.00	12.00
—Reissue					
FAMOUS					
❑ 502	Sam's Songs	1969	10.00	20.00	40.00
❑ 505	Only Sixteen	1969	10.00	20.00	40.00
❑ 508	So Wonderful	1969	10.00	20.00	40.00
❑ 509	You Send Me	1969	10.00	20.00	40.00
❑ 512	Cha-Cha-Cha	1969	10.00	20.00	40.00
51 WEST					
❑ Q 16032	My Foolish Heart	198?	3.00	6.00	12.00
KEEN					
❑ A-2001 [M]	Sam Cooke	1958	50.00	100.00	200.00
❑ A-2003 [M]	Encore	1958	50.00	100.00	200.00
❑ A-2004 [M]	Tribute to the Lady	1959	37.50	75.00	150.00
❑ AS-2004 [S]	Tribute to the Lady	1959	50.00	100.00	200.00
❑ 86101 [M]	Hit Kit	1959	62.50	125.00	250.00
❑ 86103 [M]	I Thank God	1960	100.00	200.00	400.00
❑ 86106 [M]	The Wonderful World of Sam Cooke	1960	87.50	1175.	350.00
PAIR					
❑ PDL2-1006 [(2)]	You Send Me	1986	3.75	7.50	15.00
RCA CAMDEN					
❑ ACS1-0445	You Send Me	1974	3.00	6.00	12.00
❑ CAL-2264 [M]	The One and Only Sam Cooke	1967	5.00	10.00	20.00
❑ CAS-2264 [R]	The One and Only Sam Cooke	1967	3.00	6.00	12.00
❑ CAS-2433	Sam Cooke	1970	3.00	6.00	12.00
❑ CAS-2610	The Unforgettable Sam Cooke	1972	3.00	6.00	12.00
RCA VICTOR					
❑ LPM-2221 [M]	Cooke's Tour	1960	10.00	20.00	40.00
❑ LSP-2221 [S]	Cooke's Tour	1960	12.50	25.00	50.00
❑ LPM-2236 [M]	Hits of the 50's	1960	10.00	20.00	40.00
❑ LSP-2236 [S]	Hits of the 50's	1960	12.50	25.00	50.00
❑ LPM-2293 [M]	Swing Low	1960	10.00	20.00	40.00
❑ LSP-2293 [S]	Swing Low	1960	12.50	25.00	50.00
❑ LPM-2392 [M]	My Kind of Blues	1961	10.00	20.00	40.00
❑ LSP-2392 [S]	My Kind of Blues	1961	12.50	25.00	50.00
❑ LPM-2555 [M]	Twistin' the Night Away	1962	10.00	20.00	40.00
❑ LSP-2555 [S]	Twistin' the Night Away	1962	12.50	25.00	50.00
❑ AFL1-2625	The Best of Sam Cooke	1977	3.00	6.00	12.00
—Reissue with new prefix					
❑ LPM-2625 [M]	The Best of Sam Cooke	1962	7.50	15.00	30.00
❑ LSP-2625 [R]	The Best of Sam Cooke	1962	5.00	10.00	20.00
❑ ANL1-2658	Sam Cooke at the Copa	1977	3.00	6.00	12.00
—Reissue of LSP-2970					
❑ LPM-2673 [M]	Mr. Soul	1963	7.50	15.00	30.00
❑ LSP-2673 [S]	Mr. Soul	1963	10.00	20.00	40.00
❑ LPM-2709 [M]	Night Beat	1963	7.50	15.00	30.00
❑ LSP-2709 [S]	Night Beat	1963	10.00	20.00	40.00
❑ LPM-2899 [M]	Ain't That Good News	1964	7.50	15.00	30.00
❑ LSP-2899 [S]	Ain't That Good News	1964	10.00	20.00	40.00
❑ LPM-2970 [M]	Sam Cooke at the Copa	1964	7.50	15.00	30.00
❑ LSP-2970 [S]	Sam Cooke at the Copa	1964	10.00	20.00	40.00
❑ LPM-3367 [M]	Shake	1965	6.25	12.50	25.00
❑ LSP-3367 [S]	Shake	1965	7.50	15.00	30.00
❑ LPM-3373 [M]	The Best of Sam Cooke, Volume 2	1965	6.25	12.50	25.00
❑ LSP-3373 [S]	The Best of Sam Cooke, Volume 2	1965	7.50	15.00	30.00
❑ LPM-3435 [M]	Try a Little Love	1965	6.25	12.50	25.00
❑ LSP-3435 [S]	Try a Little Love	1965	7.50	15.00	30.00
❑ LPM-3517 [M]	The Unforgettable Sam Cooke	1966	5.00	10.00	20.00
❑ LSP-3517 [S]	The Unforgettable Sam Cooke	1966	6.25	12.50	25.00
❑ AYL1-3863	The Best of Sam Cooke	1981	2.00	4.00	8.00
—Budget-line reissue					
❑ LPM-3991 [M]	The Man Who Invented Soul	1968	12.50	25.00	50.00
❑ LSP-3991 [S]	The Man Who Invented Soul	1968	6.25	12.50	25.00
❑ AFL1-5181	Live at the Harlem Square Club, 1963	1985	3.00	6.00	12.00
❑ VPS-6027 [(2)]	This Is Sam Cooke	1970	5.00	10.00	20.00
❑ CPL2-7127 [(2)]	The Man and His Music	1986	3.75	7.50	15.00
SPECIALTY					
❑ SPS-2106	Sam Cooke and the Soul Stirrers	1970	3.75	7.50	15.00
❑ SPS-2116	The Gospel Soul of Sam Cooke, Vol. 1	1970	3.75	7.50	15.00
❑ SPS-2119	Two Sides of Sam Cooke	1970	3.75	7.50	15.00
❑ SPS-2128	The Gospel Soul of Sam Cooke, Vol. 2	197?	3.75	7.50	15.00
❑ SPS-2146	That's Heaven to Me	197?	3.75	7.50	15.00
TRIP					
❑ 8030 [(2)]	The Golden Sound of Sam Cooke	1972	3.75	7.50	15.00
UPFRONT					
❑ 160	The Billie Holiday Story	1973	3.75	7.50	15.00

COOKER, JOHN LEE See JOHN LEE HOOKER.

COOKIE AND HIS CUPCAKES

Number	Title (A Side/B Side)	Yr	VG	VG+	NM
45s					
CHESS					
❑ 1848	Got You On My Mind/I've Been So Lonely	1963	3.75	7.50	15.00
JUDD					
❑ 1002	Matilda/Married Life	1958	7.50	15.00	30.00
—Without "h" in A-side title					
❑ 1002	Mathilda/Married Life	1958	12.50	25.00	50.00
—With "h" in A-side title					
❑ 1015	Until Then/Close Up the Back Door	1959	10.00	20.00	40.00
KHOURY'S					
❑ 703	Mathilda/Married Life	1958	15.00	30.00	60.00
LYRIC					
❑ 1003	Mathilda/I'm Twisted	1963	5.00	10.00	20.00
❑ 1004	Got You On My Mind/I've Been So Lonely	1963	5.00	10.00	20.00
❑ 1008	All My Lovin' Baby/I Heard That Story Before	196?	5.00	10.00	20.00
❑ 1009	Breaking Up Is Hard to Do/I Cried	196?	5.00	10.00	20.00
❑ 1012	Until Then/Close Up the Back Door	196?	3.75	7.50	15.00
❑ 1015	Hey Little School Girl/Charged with Cheating	196?	3.75	7.50	15.00
❑ 1016	Walking Down the Aisle/Even Though	196?	3.75	7.50	15.00
❑ 1017	Long Time Ago/Kissing Someone Else	196?	3.75	7.50	15.00
❑ 1020	Belinda/Trouble in My Life	196?	3.75	7.50	15.00
MERCURY					
❑ 71748	Matilda Has Finally Come Back/As Part of Everything	1961	5.00	10.00	20.00

Number	Title (A Side/B Side)	Yr	VG	VG+	NM
PAULA					
❑ 221	Mathilda/I'm Twisted	1965	3.00	6.00	12.00
❑ 230	Belinda/Trouble in My Life	1965	2.50	5.00	10.00

COOKIES, THE

Number	Title (A Side/B Side)	Yr	VG	VG+	NM
45s					
ATLANTIC					
❑ 1061	Precious Love/Later, Later	1955	7.50	15.00	30.00
❑ 1084	In Paradise/Passing Time	1956	7.50	15.00	30.00
❑ 1110	Down By the River/My Lover	1956	6.25	12.50	25.00
❑ 2079	Passing Time/In Paradise	1960	5.00	10.00	20.00
DIMENSION					
❑ 1002	Chains/Stranger in My Arms	1962	5.00	10.00	20.00
❑ 1008	Don't Say Nothin' Bad (About My Baby)/Softly in the Night	1963	3.75	7.50	15.00
❑ 1008	Don't Say Nothin' Bad/Softly in the Night	1963	5.00	10.00	20.00
❑ 1012	I Want a Boy for My Birthday/Will Power	1963	3.75	7.50	15.00
❑ 1020	Girls Grow Up Faster Than Boys/Only to Other People	1963	3.75	7.50	15.00
❑ 1032	I Never Dreamed/The Old Crowd	1964	3.75	7.50	15.00
JOSIE					
❑ 822	King of Hearts/Hippy-Dippy-Daddy	1957	7.50	15.00	30.00
LAMP					
❑ 8008	Don't Let Go/All Night Mambo	1954	10.00	20.00	40.00
WARNER BROS.					
❑ 7025	All My Trials/Wounded	1967	2.50	5.00	10.00
❑ 7047	Mr. Cupid (Don't You Call on Me)/Hang My Head and Cry	1967	2.50	5.00	10.00
—B-side by the Big Guys					

COOKIES, THE/LITTLE EVA/CAROLE KING

Number	Title (A Side/B Side)	Yr	VG	VG+	NM
Albums					
DIMENSION					
❑ DLP-6001 [M]	The Dimension Dolls, Vol. 1	1964	62.50	125.00	250.00

COOL, CALVIN, AND THE SURF KNOBS

Number	Title (A Side/B Side)	Yr	VG	VG+	NM
45s					
CHARTER					
❑ 7	Beach Bash/El Tocolote	1963	10.00	20.00	40.00
Albums					
CHARTER					
❑ CLP-103 [M]	The Surfer's Beat	1963	10.00	20.00	40.00
❑ CLS-103 [S]	The Surfer's Beat	1963	12.50	25.00	50.00

COOL HEAT See WIND.

COOL SOUNDS, THE

Number	Title (A Side/B Side)	Yr	VG	VG+	NM
45s					
PULSAR					
❑ 2421	Comin' Home (Free)/Rag Doll	1969	12.50	25.00	50.00
WARNER BROS.					
❑ 7538	I'll Take You Back/Where Do We Go from Here	1971	7.50	15.00	30.00
❑ 7575	A Love Like Ours Could Last a Million Years or More/Who Can I Turn To	1972	7.50	15.00	30.00
❑ 7615	Boy Wonder/Free	1972	7.50	15.00	30.00

COOLBREEZERS, THE

Number	Title (A Side/B Side)	Yr	VG	VG+	NM
45s					
ABC-PARAMOUNT					
❑ 9865	You Know I Go for You/My Brother	1957	25.00	50.00	100.00
BALE					
❑ 100/101	The Greatest Love of All/Eda Weda Bug	1958	15.00	30.00	60.00
❑ 102/103	Let Christmas Ring/Hello, Mister New Year	1958	50.00	100.00	200.00
EBONY					
❑ 1015	Won't You Come In/Pack Your Bags and Go	1956	125.00	250.00	500.00
—As "The Little Coolbreezers"					

COOLIDGE, RITA Also see KRIS KRISTOFFERSON AND RITA COOLIDGE.

Number	Title (A Side/B Side)	Yr	VG	VG+	NM
45s					
A&M					
❑ 1256	Crazy Love/Mountains	1971	—	2.50	5.00
❑ 1271	Mud Island/I Believe in You	1971	—	2.50	5.00
❑ 1324	Lay My Burden Down/Nice Feelin'	1972	—	2.00	4.00
❑ 1353	Most Likely You Go Your Way/Family Full of Soul	1972	—	2.00	4.00
❑ 1398	Fever/My Crew	1972	—	2.00	4.00
❑ 1398 [PS]	Fever/My Crew	1972	—	3.00	6.00
❑ 1414	Donut Man/Whiskey, Whiskey	1973	—	2.00	4.00
❑ 1545	Hold an Old Friend's Hand/Mama Lou	1974	—	2.00	4.00
❑ 1642	Love Has No Pride/Heaven's Dream	1974	—	2.00	4.00
❑ 1792	Am I Blue/Star	1976	—	2.00	4.00
❑ 1816	Late Again/Keep the Candle Burning	1976	—	2.00	4.00
❑ 1922	(Your Love Has Lifted Me) Higher and Higher/Who's to Bless and Who's to Blame	1977	—	2.00	4.00
❑ 1922 [PS]	(Your Love Has Lifted Me) Higher and Higher/Who's to Bless and Who's to Blame	1977	—	3.00	6.00
❑ 1965	We're All Alone/Southern Lady	1977	—	2.00	4.00
❑ 1965 [PS]	We're All Alone/Southern Lady	1977	—	2.00	4.00
❑ 2004	The Way You Do the Things You Do/I Feel the Burden (Being Lifted Off My Shoulders)	1977	—	2.00	4.00
❑ 2004 [PS]	The Way You Do the Things You Do/I Feel the Burden (Being Lifted Off My Shoulders)	1977	—	2.00	4.00
❑ 2058	You/Only You Know and I Know	1978	—	2.00	4.00
❑ 2058 [PS]	You/Only You Know and I Know	1978	—	2.00	4.00
❑ 2090	Love Me Again/The Jealous Kind	1978	—	2.00	4.00
❑ 2169	One Fine Day/Sweet Emotions	1979	—	2.00	4.00
❑ 2199	I'd Rather Leave While I'm in Love/Sweet Emotions	1979	—	2.00	4.00
❑ 2281	Fool That I Am/Can She Keep You Satisfied	1980	—	2.00	4.00
❑ 2318	Words/Born Under a Bad Sign	1981	—	2.00	4.00
❑ 2361	The Closer You Get/Take It Home	1981	—	2.00	4.00
❑ 2385	Wishin' and Hopin'/I Did My Part	1981	—	2.00	4.00
❑ 2541	I'll Never Let You Go/Shadow in the Night	1983	—	—	3.00
❑ 2546 [DJ]	I Will Never Let You Go (same on both sides)	1983	—	2.00	4.00
—Stock copies do not exist					
❑ 2551	All Time High/(Instrumental)	1983	—	—	3.00
❑ 2551 [PS]	All Time High/(Instrumental)	1983	—	2.50	5.00
❑ 2586	Only You/Shadow in the Night	1983	—	—	3.00
❑ 2634	Something Said Love/Survivor	1984	—	—	3.00

Number	Title (A Side/B Side)	Yr	VG	VG+	NM
PEPPER					
❏ 442	Rainbow Child/Secret Places, Hiding Faces	1969	2.00	4.00	8.00
❏ 443	Turn Around and Love You/				
	Walking in the Morning	1969	2.00	4.00	8.00
Albums					
A&M					
❏ SP-3107	Rita Coolidge	198?	2.00	4.00	8.00
—Budget-line reissue					
❏ SP-3130	Nice Feelin'	198?	2.00	4.00	8.00
—Budget-line reissue					
❏ SP-3163	Anytime…Anywhere	198?	2.00	4.00	8.00
—Budget-line reissue					
❏ SP-3238	Greatest Hits	198?	2.00	4.00	8.00
—Budget-line reissue					
❏ SP-3627	Fall Into Spring	1974	2.50	5.00	10.00
❏ SP-3727	Heartbreak Radio	1981	2.50	5.00	10.00
❏ SP-4291	Rita Coolidge	1971	2.50	5.00	10.00
❏ SP-4325	Nice Feelin'	1971	2.50	5.00	10.00
❏ SP-4370	The Lady's Not for Sale	1972	2.50	5.00	10.00
❏ SP-4531	It's Only Love	1975	2.50	5.00	10.00
❏ SP-4616	Anytime…Anywhere	1977	2.50	5.00	10.00
❏ SP-4669	Love Me Again	1978	2.50	5.00	10.00
❏ SP-4781	Satisfied	1979	2.50	5.00	10.00
❏ SP-4836	Greatest Hits	1981	2.50	5.00	10.00
❏ SP-4914	Never Let You Go	1983	2.50	5.00	10.00
❏ SP-5003	Inside the Fire	1984	2.50	5.00	10.00
NAUTILUS					
❏ NR-16	Anytime…Anywhere	1981	6.25	12.50	25.00
—Audiophile vinyl					
COOPER, ALICE Also see NAZZ (2); THE SPIDERS (2).					
12-Inch Singles					
EPIC					
❏ EAS 1347 [DJ]	I Got a Line on You (same on both sides)	1988	2.50	5.00	10.00
❏ EAS 1663 [DJ]	Poison (same on both sides)	1989	2.50	5.00	10.00
❏ EAS 1686 [DJ]	Trash (same on both sides)	1989	2.50	5.00	10.00
MCA					
❏ L33-17177 [DJ]	He's Back (The Man Behind the Mask) (same on both sides)	1986	2.50	5.00	10.00
❏ L33-17205 [DJ]	Give It Up (same on both sides)	1986	2.50	5.00	10.00
❏ L33-17416 [DJ]	Freedom (same on both sides)	1987	2.50	5.00	10.00
WARNER BROS.					
❏ PRO-A-864 [DJ]	Clones (We're All)/Model Citizen	1980	5.00	10.00	20.00
❏ PRO-A-1059 [DJ]	I Like Girls (same on both sides)	1981	5.00	10.00	20.00
45s					
ATLANTIC					
❏ 3254	Only Women/Cold Ethyl	1975	—	2.50	5.00
❏ 3280	Department of Youth/Some Folks	1975	—	2.50	5.00
❏ 3298	Welcome to My Nightmare/Cold Ethyl	1975	—	2.50	5.00
EPIC					
❏ 34-08114	I Got a Line on You/Livin' on the Edge	1988	—	—	3.00
—B-side by Britney Fox					
❏ 34-68958	Poison/Trash	1989	—	—	3.00
❏ 34-73085	House of Fire/Ballad of Dwight Fry	1989	—	—	3.00
❏ 34-73785	Hey Stoopid/It Rained All Night	1991	—	—	3.00
❏ 34-73983	Love's a Loaded Gun/Fire	1991	—	—	3.00
MCA					
❏ 52904	He's Back (The Man Behind the Mask)/Billion Dollar Baby	1986	—	—	3.00
❏ 52904 [PS]	He's Back (The Man Behind the Mask)/Billion Dollar Baby	1986	—	—	3.00
❏ 53212	Freedom/Time to Kill	1987	—	—	3.00
❏ 53212 [PS]	Freedom/Time to Kill	1987	—	—	3.00
STRAIGHT					
❏ 101	Reflected/Living	1969	75.00	150.00	300.00
—Promos worth about 10% of this value					
WARNER BROS.					
❏ GWB 7141	Eighteen/Caught in a Dream	1972	—	2.00	4.00
—"Back to Back Hits" series; green label					
❏ GWB 7141	Eighteen/Caught in a Dream	1973	—	—	3.00
—"Back to Back Hits" series; "Burbank" palm trees label					
❏ 7398	Shoe Salesman/Return of the Spiders	1970	5.00	10.00	20.00
❏ 7449	Eighteen/Body	1971	—	2.50	5.00
❏ 7490	Caught in a Dream/Hallowed Be My Name	1971	—	2.50	5.00
❏ 7529	Under My Wheels/Desperado	1971	—	2.50	5.00
❏ 7568	Be My Lover/Yeah, Yeah, Yeah	1972	—	2.50	5.00
❏ 7596	School's Out/Gutter Cat	1972	—	2.50	5.00
❏ 7596 [PS]	School's Out/Gutter Cat	1972	2.50	5.00	10.00
❏ 7631	Elected/Luney Tune	1972	—	2.50	5.00
❏ 7631 [PS]	Elected/Luney Tune	1972	2.50	5.00	10.00
❏ 7673	Hello Hurray/Generation Landslide	1972	—	2.50	5.00
❏ 7691	No More Mr. Nice Guy/Raped and Freezin'	1973	—	2.50	5.00
❏ 7724	Billion Dollar Babies/Mary Ann	1973	—	2.50	5.00
❏ 7762	Teenage Lament '74/Hard Hearted Alice	1973	—	2.50	5.00
❏ 7783	Muscle of Love/Crazy Little Child	1974	—	2.50	5.00
❏ 8023	I'm Eighteen/Muscle of Love	1974	—	2.50	5.00
❏ 8228	I Never Cry/Go to Hell	1976	—	2.00	4.00
❏ 8349	You and Me/It's Hot Tonight	1977	—	2.00	4.00
❏ 8349 [PS]	You and Me/It's Hot Tonight	1977	2.00	4.00	8.00
❏ 8448	(No More) Love at Your Convenience/I Never Wrote Those Songs	1977	—	2.50	5.00
❏ 8607	School's Out/Eighteen	1978	2.00	4.00	8.00
❏ 8695	How You Gonna See Me Now/No Tricks	1978	—	2.50	5.00
❏ 8760	From the Inside/Nurse Rosetta	1979	—	2.00	4.00
❏ 29828	I Am the Future/Tag, You're It	1982	—	2.00	4.00
❏ 29928	I Like Girls/Zorro's Ascent	1982	—	2.00	4.00
❏ 49204	Clones (We're All)/Model Citizen	1980	—	2.00	4.00
❏ 49204 [PS]	Clones (We're All)/Model Citizen	1980	—	2.50	5.00
❏ 49526	Dance Yourself to Death/Talk Talk	1980	—	2.00	4.00
❏ 49780	You Want It, You Got It/ Who Do You Think We Are	1981	—	2.00	4.00
❏ 49848	Generation Landslide '81/Seven and Seven Is	1981	—	2.00	4.00
7-Inch Extended Plays					
WARNER BROS.					
❏ S 2748	Working Up a Sweat/Never Been Sold Before// Muscle of Love/Teenage Lament	1973	5.00	10.00	20.00
—Jukebox issue; small hole, plays at 33 1/3 rpm					

Number	Title (A Side/B Side)	Yr	VG	VG+	NM
❏ S 2748 [PS]	Muscle of Love	1973	5.00	10.00	20.00
—Part of "Little LP" series (LLP #235)					
Albums					
ACCORD					
❏ SN-7162	Toronto Rock 'n' Roll Revival 1969	1981	3.00	6.00	12.00
ATLANTIC					
❏ SD 18130	Welcome to My Nightmare	1975	2.50	5.00	10.00
❏ SD 19157	Welcome to My Nightmare	1978	2.00	4.00	8.00
—Reissue of 18130					
EPIC					
❏ OE 45137	Trash	1989	3.00	6.00	12.00
❏ E 46786	Hey Stoopid	1991	3.75	7.50	15.00
MCA					
❏ 5761	Constrictor	1986	2.00	4.00	8.00
❏ 42091	Raise Your Fist and Yell	1987	2.00	4.00	8.00
MOBILE FIDELITY					
❏ 1-063	Welcome to My Nightmare	1980	12.50	25.00	50.00
—Audiophile vinyl					
PAIR					
❏ PDL2-1163 [(2)]	A Man Called Alice	1987	3.75	7.50	15.00
STRAIGHT					
❏ STS-1051	Pretties for You	1969	37.50	75.00	150.00
—Yellow label stock copy					
❏ STS-1051 [DJ]	Pretties for You	1969	50.00	100.00	200.00
—White label promo					
❏ WS 1840	Pretties for You	1970	15.00	30.00	60.00
—Pink label stock copy					
❏ WS 1845	Easy Action	1970	7.50	15.00	30.00
—Pink label stock copy; "Alice Cooper" in white on cover					
❏ WS 1845	Easy Action	1970	12.50	25.00	50.00
—Pink label stock copy; "Alice Cooper" in black on cover					
❏ WS 1845 [DJ]	Easy Action	1970	25.00	50.00	100.00
—White label promo					
❏ WS 1883	Love It to Death	1971	12.50	25.00	50.00
—Pink label stock copy					
❏ WS 1883 [DJ]	Love It to Death	1971	25.00	50.00	100.00
—White label promo					
WARNER BROS.					
❏ PRO 789 [DJ]	The Alice Cooper Radio Show	1978	6.25	12.50	25.00
❏ WS 1840	Pretties for You	1973	5.00	10.00	20.00
—"Burbank" palm trees label; comes in Straight cover					
❏ WS 1883	Love It to Death	1971	3.00	6.00	12.00
—Version 4: Green "WB" label; with "I'm Eighteen" box and Alice's protruding thumb airbrushed off the cover					
❏ WS 1883	Love It to Death	1971	5.00	10.00	20.00
—Version 2: Green "WB" label; same as above, but has a white box reading "Contains the Hit 'I'm Eighteen' "					
❏ WS 1883	Love It to Death	1971	5.00	10.00	20.00
—Version 3: Green "WB" label; cover has large white areas at top and bottom with lower half of the photo cropped out					
❏ WS 1883	Love It to Death	1971	7.50	15.00	30.00
—Version 1: Green "WB" label; cover has Alice's thumb sticking out in such a way that it appears to be another part of the body					
❏ BS 2567	Killer	1971	7.50	15.00	30.00
—Early copies have an attached 1972 calendar/poster					
❏ BS 2567	Killer	1972	3.00	6.00	12.00
—Later copies no longer have the calendar/poster					
❏ BS 2623	School's Out	1972	3.00	6.00	12.00
—No panties, with song titles listed					
❏ BS 2623	School's Out	1972	5.00	10.00	20.00
—Back cover does not list song titles, but panties are missing					
❏ BS 2623	School's Out	1972	7.50	15.00	30.00
—With paper panties intact; back cover lists song titles					
❏ BS 2623	School's Out	1972	10.00	20.00	40.00
—With paper panties intact; back cover does not list song titles					
❏ BS 2685	Billion Dollar Babies	1973	3.00	6.00	12.00
—Green "WB" label					
❏ BS4 2685 [Q]	Billion Dollar Babies	1974	6.25	12.50	25.00
❏ BS 2748	Muscle of Love	1973	2.50	5.00	10.00
❏ BS4 2748 [Q]	Muscle of Love	1974	6.25	12.50	25.00
❏ BS4 2803 [Q]	Alice Cooper's Greatest Hits	1974	—	—	—
—Not released					
❏ W 2803	Alice Cooper's Greatest Hits	1974	2.50	5.00	10.00
❏ BS 2896	Alice Cooper Goes to Hell	1976	2.50	5.00	10.00
❏ BSK 3027	Lace and Whiskey	1977	2.50	5.00	10.00
❏ BSK 3107	Alice Cooper's Greatest Hits	1977	2.00	4.00	8.00
—Reissue of BS 2803					
❏ BSK 3138	The Alice Cooper Show	1977	2.50	5.00	10.00
❏ BSK 3263	From the Inside	1978	2.50	5.00	10.00
❏ BSK 3436	Flush the Fashion	1980	2.50	5.00	10.00
❏ BSK 3581	Special Forces	1981	2.50	5.00	10.00
❏ 23719	Zipper Catches Skin	1982	2.50	5.00	10.00
❏ 23969	Da Da	1983	2.50	5.00	10.00

COOPER, BO See RON DANTE.

COOPER, CHRISTINE

45s

PARKWAY

Number	Title (A Side/B Side)	Yr	VG	VG+	NM
❏ 122	I Must Have You (Or No One)/Good Looks (They Don't Count)	1966	3.75	7.50	15.00
❏ 971	S.O.S./Say What You Feel	1966	6.25	12.50	25.00
❏ 983	(They Call Him) A Bad Boy/ Heartaches Away My Boy	1966	10.00	20.00	40.00

COOPER, DOLLY

45s

DOT

Number	Title (A Side/B Side)	Yr	VG	VG+	NM
❏ 15495	Big Rock Inn/I'm Looking Through Your Window	1956	3.00	6.00	12.00
❏ 15535	The Confession of a Fool/Tell Me, Tell Me	1957	3.00	6.00	12.00
EBB					
❏ 109	Wild Love/Time Brings About a Change	1957	3.00	6.00	12.00
MODERN					
❏ 965	My Man/Ay La Bas	1955	10.00	20.00	40.00
❏ 977	Teenage Prayer/Down So Long	1956	12.50	25.00	50.00
❏ 986	Teenage Wedding Bells/ Every Day and Every Night	1956	12.50	25.00	50.00

Number	Title (A Side/B Side)	Yr	VG	VG+	NM
SAVOY					
❑ 1121	You Gotta Be Good to Yourself/				
	Love Can't Be Blind	1954	5.00	10.00	20.00

COOPER, LES, AND THE SOUL ROCKERS Also see THE EMPIRES (1).

Number	Title (A Side/B Side)	Yr	VG	VG+	NM
45s					
ARRAWAK					
❑ 1008	I Can Do the Soul Jerk/At the World's Fair	1965	3.00	6.00	12.00
ATCO					
❑ 6644	Gonna Have a Lotta Fun/Thank God for You	1969	2.00	4.00	8.00
DIMENSION					
❑ 1023	Motor City/Swobblin'	1963	5.00	10.00	20.00
ENJOY					
❑ 2024	Owee Baby/Let's Do the Boston Monkey	1965	2.50	5.00	10.00
EVERLAST					
❑ 5016	Twistin'/Dig Yourself	1963	3.00	6.00	12.00
❑ 5019	Wiggle Wobble/Dig Yourself	1963	3.75	7.50	15.00
❑ 5023	Garbage Can/Bossa Nova Dance	1963	3.00	6.00	12.00
LOST-NITE					
❑ 388	Wiggle Wobble/Dig Yourself	197?	—	2.50	5.00
—Reissue					
Albums					
EVERLAST					
❑ ELP-202 [M]	Wiggle Wobble	1963	12.50	25.00	50.00

COOPER, PAT

Number	Title (A Side/B Side)	Yr	VG	VG+	NM
45s					
UNITED ARTISTS					
❑ 922	Everyone Is Equal/Mama's Moo-Len-Yenna				
	(The Eggplant Song)	1965	—	3.50	7.00
❑ 938	Mama's Moo-Len-Yenna (The Eggplant Song)/				
	The More You Make, The More You Spend	1965	—	3.50	7.00
❑ 50113	The Pepperoni Kid/Little Red Scooter	1967	—	3.50	7.00
❑ 50294	You Don't Have to Be Italian/Conchetta	1968	—	3.00	6.00
❑ 50641	It's the Italian in Me/I Don't Wanna Go Home	1970	—	3.00	6.00
Albums					
UNITED ARTISTS					
❑ UAL 3446 [M]	Our Hero...Pat Cooper	1966	3.00	6.00	12.00
❑ UAL 3548 [M]	Spaghetti Sauce & Other Delights	1966	3.00	6.00	12.00
❑ UAS 6446 [S]	Our Hero...Pat Cooper	1966	3.75	7.50	15.00
❑ UAS 6548 [S]	Spaghetti Sauce & Other Delights	1966	3.75	7.50	15.00
❑ UAS 6600	You Don't Have to Be Italian To Like Pat Cooper	1968	3.00	6.00	12.00
❑ UAS 6690	More Saucy Stories from... Pat Cooper	1969	3.00	6.00	12.00

COOPERETTES, THE

Number	Title (A Side/B Side)	Yr	VG	VG+	NM
45s					
ABC					
❑ 11156	Peace Maker/Trouble	1968	3.00	6.00	12.00
❑ 11197	Spiral Road/Trouble	1969	3.00	6.00	12.00
BRUNSWICK					
❑ 55296	Goodbye School/Goodbye School (Part 2)	1966	3.75	7.50	15.00
❑ 55307	Don't Trust Him/Everything's Wrong	1966	3.75	7.50	15.00
❑ 55329	(Life Has) No Meaning Now/Shing-a-Ling	1967	6.25	12.50	25.00

COPAS, COWBOY

Number	Title (A Side/B Side)	Yr	VG	VG+	NM
45s					
DOT					
❑ 15668	Blue Kimono/Breeze	1957	5.00	10.00	20.00
❑ 15735	Circle Rock/My Little Red Wagon	1958	15.00	30.00	60.00
❑ 15847	A World That's Real/Looking for an Angel	1958	5.00	10.00	20.00
KING					
❑ 951	The Strange Little Girl/You'll Never See Me Cry	1951	10.00	20.00	40.00
❑ 964	Tennessee Flat Guitar/I Love You	1951	7.50	15.00	30.00
❑ 980	I'm Glad I'm On the Inside/				
	Four Books in the Bible	1951	7.50	15.00	30.00
❑ 1000	'Tis Sweet to Be Remembered/Because of You	1951	7.50	15.00	30.00
❑ 1003	O Little Town of Bethlehem/It Came Upon the				
	Midnight Clear	1951	7.50	15.00	30.00
❑ 1004	White Christmas/Jingle Bells	1951	7.50	15.00	30.00
❑ 1034	Copy Cat/Those Gone and Left Me Blues	1952	7.50	15.00	30.00
❑ 1040	I'll Pay the Price/'Tis Sweet to Be Remembered	1951	7.50	15.00	30.00
❑ 1046	Four Bare Walls and a Ceiling/				
	I Can't Stop Loving You	1952	7.50	15.00	30.00
❑ 1064	Boomerang/It's Enough to Make Anyone Cry	1952	7.50	15.00	30.00
❑ 1080	Golden Moon/I Can't Remember to Forget	1952	7.50	15.00	30.00
❑ 1136	I've Grown So Used to You/				
	It's No Sin to Love You	1952	7.50	15.00	30.00
❑ 1139	Purple Rose/Some Fine Morning	1952	7.50	15.00	30.00
❑ 1151	Feelin' Low/Love Me Now	1952	7.50	15.00	30.00
❑ 1166	Doll of Clay/If Wishes Were Horses	1953	6.25	12.50	25.00
❑ 1200	I Can't Go On/A Wreath at the Door of My Heart	1953	6.25	12.50	25.00
❑ 1234	Tennessee Senorita/				
	If You Will Let Me Be Your Love	1953	6.25	12.50	25.00
❑ 1253	Look What I Got/Will You Forgive	1953	6.25	12.50	25.00
❑ 1274	Blue Waltz/A Heartache Ago	1953	6.25	12.50	25.00
❑ 1306	He Stands By His Window/The Man Upstairs	1954	6.25	12.50	25.00
❑ 1313	Unwanted Alone/Sorry	1954	6.25	12.50	25.00
❑ 1329	I'll Be There/I'm a Stranger in My Home	1954	6.25	12.50	25.00
❑ 1359	Return to Sender/I'll Waltz with You	1954	6.25	12.50	25.00
❑ 1386	Carbon Copy/I'm Glad for Your Sake	1954	6.25	12.50	25.00
❑ 1407	When I Lost You/Why Should I Want Her	1954	6.25	12.50	25.00
❑ 1424	Hello Darling/The Talking Mule	1955	6.25	12.50	25.00
❑ 1444	The Stone Was Rolled Away/The Silver That				
	Nailed Him to the Cross	1955	6.25	12.50	25.00
❑ 1456	Pledging My Love/Shamed of Myself	1955	6.25	12.50	25.00
❑ 1464	The Party's Over/Summer Kisses	1955	6.25	12.50	25.00
❑ 1486	Tragic Romance/Listen to My Heart	1955	6.25	12.50	25.00
❑ 1507	Blue Yesterday/Tell Me More	1955	6.25	12.50	25.00
❑ 4865	Any Old Time/Don't Shake Hands with the Devil	1956	5.00	10.00	20.00
❑ 5270	Tennessee Waltz/Signed, Sealed and Delivered	1959	3.75	7.50	15.00
—As "Lloyd Copas"					
❑ 5392	Carolina Sunshine Girl/Rose of Tennessee	1960	3.75	7.50	15.00
❑ 5437	A Stranger in My Home/				
	Old Faithful and True Love	1960	3.75	7.50	15.00
❑ 5479	It's a Shame/				
	You Walked Right Out of My Dreams	1961	3.75	7.50	15.00
❑ 5544	It's a Lonely World/				
	Don't Let Them Change Your Mind	1961	3.75	7.50	15.00

C

Number	Title (A Side/B Side)	Yr	VG	VG+	NM
❑ 5571	Sweet Thing/Signed, Sealed, Then Forgotten	1961	3.75	7.50	15.00
❑ 5638	I Built a Fence Around My Heart/				
	My Blues Are Gone	1962	3.75	7.50	15.00
❑ 5676	When Jesus Beckons Me Home/I Saw the Light	1962	3.75	7.50	15.00
❑ 5733	Signed, Sealed and Delivered/				
	The Hopes of a Broken Heart	1963	3.00	6.00	12.00
❑ 5734	Breeze/The Road of Broken Hearts	1963	3.00	6.00	12.00
STARDAY					
❑ 476	Mom and Dad's Affair/Black Cloud Risin'	1959	3.75	7.50	15.00
❑ 493	South Pacific Shore/That's All I Can Remember	1960	3.75	7.50	15.00
❑ 501	Alabam/I Can	1960	5.00	10.00	20.00
❑ 524	I Have a Friend/The Hem of His Garment	1960	3.75	7.50	15.00
❑ 528	Sittin' Flat on Ready/Midnight in Heaven	1960	3.75	7.50	15.00
❑ 542	Flat Top/True Love (Is the Greatest Thing)	1961	3.75	7.50	15.00
❑ 552	Sunny Tennessee/Dreaming	1961	3.75	7.50	15.00
❑ 559	Signed, Sealed and Delivered/New Filipino				
	Baby	1961	3.75	7.50	15.00
❑ 573	Sal/A Thousand Miles of Ocean	1961	3.75	7.50	15.00
❑ 585	There'll Come a Time Someday/				
	Seven Seas from You	1962	3.75	7.50	15.00
❑ 595	Sold the Farm/Table in the Corner	1962	3.75	7.50	15.00
❑ 606	Bury Me Face Down/Heart on the Run	1962	3.75	7.50	15.00
❑ 612	Family Reunion/Smoke on the Water	1962	3.75	7.50	15.00
❑ 621	Goodbye Kisses/The Gypsy Girl	1963	3.00	6.00	12.00
❑ 641	Louisian/Break Away, Break Away	1963	3.00	6.00	12.00
❑ 658	Autobiography/The Rainbow and the Rose	1963	3.00	6.00	12.00
❑ 685	Old Man's Story/Pretty Diamonds	1964	3.00	6.00	12.00
❑ 708	Ride in My Little Red Wagon/Black Eyed Susie	1965	2.50	5.00	10.00
❑ 729	Waltzing with Sin/Blue Kimono	1965	2.50	5.00	10.00
❑ 750	Cowboy's Deck of Cards/Beyond the Sunset	1966	2.50	5.00	10.00
❑ 7000	Alabam/Goodbye Kisses	197?	—	2.50	5.00
❑ 7001	Signed, Sealed and Delivered/				
	New Filipino Baby	197?	—	2.50	5.00
❑ 7015	I Dreamed of a Hillbilly Heaven/Tragic Romance	197?	—	2.50	5.00
❑ 8006	Signed, Sealed and Delivered/Hillbilly Heaven	197?	—	2.50	5.00
❑ 8029	Alabam/Filipino Baby	197?	—	2.50	5.00
Albums					
KING					
❑ 553 [M]	Cowboy Copas Sings His All-Time Hits	1957	25.00	50.00	100.00
❑ 556 [M]	Favorite Sacred Songs	1957	20.00	40.00	80.00
❑ 619 [M]	Sacred Songs by Cowboy Copas	1959	20.00	40.00	80.00
❑ 714 [M]	Tragic Tales of Love and Life	1960	20.00	40.00	80.00
❑ 720 [M]	Broken Hearted Melodies	1960	20.00	40.00	80.00
❑ 817 [M]	Country Gentleman of Song	1963	10.00	20.00	40.00
❑ 824 [M]	As You Remember Cowboy Copas	1963	10.00	20.00	40.00
❑ 894 [M]	Cowboy Copas Hymns	1964	10.00	20.00	40.00
STARDAY					
❑ SLP-118 [M]	All Time Country Music Great	1960	10.00	20.00	40.00
❑ SLP-133 [M]	Inspirational Songs	1961	10.00	20.00	40.00
❑ SLP-144 [M]	Cowboy Copas	1961	10.00	20.00	40.00
❑ SLP-157 [M]	Opry Star Spotlight on Cowboy Copas	1962	10.00	20.00	40.00
❑ SLP-175 [M]	Mister Country Music	1962	10.00	20.00	40.00
❑ SLP-184 [M]	Songs That Made Him Famous	1962	10.00	20.00	40.00
❑ SLP-208 [M]	Country Music Entertainer #1	1963	10.00	20.00	40.00
❑ SLP-212 [M]	Beyond the Sunset	1963	10.00	20.00	40.00
❑ SLP-234 [M]	The Unforgettable Cowboy Copas	1963	10.00	20.00	40.00
❑ SLP-247 [M]	Star of the Grand Ole Opry	1963	10.00	20.00	40.00
❑ SLP-268 [M]	Cowboy Copas and His Friends	1964	10.00	20.00	40.00
❑ SLP-317 [M]	The Legend Lives On	1965	7.50	15.00	30.00
❑ SLP (9)-347 [(2)R]	The Cowboy Copas Story	1965	6.25	12.50	25.00
❑ SLP-347 [(2)M]	The Cowboy Copas Story	1965	7.50	15.00	30.00
❑ SLP-458	The Best of Cowboy Copas	1970	3.75	7.50	15.00

COPAS, COWBOY, AND HAWKSHAW HAWKINS Also see each artist's individual listings.

Number	Title (A Side/B Side)	Yr	VG	VG+	NM
Albums					
KING					
❑ 835 [M]	In Memory	1963	10.00	20.00	40.00
❑ 850 [M]	The Legend of Cowboy Copas and Hawkshaw				
	Hawkins	1964	10.00	20.00	40.00
❑ 984 [M]	24 Great Hits	1968	6.25	12.50	25.00

COPAS, COWBOY/HAWKSHAW HAWKINS/PATSY CLINE Also see each artist's individual listings.

Number	Title (A Side/B Side)	Yr	VG	VG+	NM
Albums					
STARDAY					
❑ SLP-346 [M]	Gone But Not Forgotten	1965	7.50	15.00	30.00

COPASETICS, THE

Number	Title (A Side/B Side)	Yr	VG	VG+	NM
45s					
PREMIUM					
❑ 409	Believe in Me/Collegian	1956	50.00	100.00	200.00

COPELAND, KEN

Number	Title (A Side/B Side)	Yr	VG	VG+	NM
45s					
DOT					
❑ 15686	Where the Rio Rosa Flows/				
	Locked in the Arms of Love	1958	3.75	7.50	15.00
IMPERIAL					
❑ 5432	Pledge of Love/Night Air	1957	5.00	10.00	20.00
—B-side by The Mints					
❑ 5453	Teenage/Bed of Lies	1957	5.00	10.00	20.00
❑ 5466	I Want to Go Steady/I Would Give My Heart	1957	5.00	10.00	20.00
LIN					
❑ 5007	Pledge of Love/Night Air	1957	10.00	20.00	40.00
—B-side by The Mints					
❑ 5017	Fanny Brown/Chaser of Hearts	1957	10.00	20.00	40.00

COPPER PLATED INTEGRATED CIRCUIT, THE

Number	Title (A Side/B Side)	Yr	VG	VG+	NM
Albums					
COMMAND					
❑ RS-945 SD	Plugged In Pop	1969	6.25	12.50	25.00

COPS 'N ROBBERS

Number	Title (A Side/B Side)	Yr	VG	VG+	NM
45s					
CORAL					
❑ 62466	I Could Have Danced All Night/				
	Just Keep Right On	1965	2.50	5.00	10.00
❑ 62473	It's All Over Now, Baby Blue/I Found Out	1965	2.50	5.00	10.00

Number	Title (A Side/B Side)	Yr	VG	VG+	NM
PARROT					
❏ 9716	St. James Infirmary/There's Got to Be a Reason	1964	2.50	5.00	10.00
CORDEL, PAT Also see THE ELEGANTS.					
45s					
CLUB					
❏ 1011	Darling, Come Back/My My Tears	1956	500.00	1000.	1500.
—And the Crescents					
MICHELLE					
❏ 503	Darling, Come Back/My My Tears	1959	37.50	75.00	150.00
—And the Elegants					
VICTORY					
❏ 1001	Darling, Come Back/My My Tears	1963	20.00	40.00	80.00
—And the Elegants					
CORDELLS, THE					
45s					
BARGAIN					
❏ 5004	The Beat of My Heart/Laid Off	1962	12.50	25.00	50.00
BULLSEYE					
❏ 1017	Believe in Me/Please Don't Go	1958	25.00	50.00	100.00
CORDET, LOUISE					
45s					
LONDON					
❏ 9560	I'm Just a Baby/In a Matter of Moments	1963	3.00	6.00	12.00
CORDIALS, THE Several different groups.					
45s					
BETHLEHEM					
❏ 3019	What's the Matter with Me/I'm Not Crying Anymore	1961	6.25	12.50	25.00
CORDIAL					
❏ 1001	I'm Ashamed/Sentimental Jorney	1960	25.00	50.00	100.00
FELSTED					
❏ 8653	Once in a Lifetime/What Kind of Fool Am I	1962	7.50	15.00	30.00
LIBERTY					
❏ 55784	Oh, How I Love Her/You Can't Believe in Love	1965	6.25	12.50	25.00
REVEILLE					
❏ 106	Eternal Love/The International Twist	1962	75.00	150.00	300.00
7 ARTS					
❏ 707	Dawn Is Almost Here/Keep An Eye	1961	25.00	50.00	100.00
WHIP					
❏ 276	Listen My Heart/My Heart's Desire	1961	62.50	125.00	250.00
Albums					
CATAMOUNT					
❏ 902	Blue Eyed Soul	1967	6.25	12.50	25.00
CORDOVANS, THE					
45s					
JOHNSON					
❏ 731	Come On Baby/My Heart	1960	6.25	12.50	25.00
COREY, JILL					
45s					
COLUMBIA					
❏ 4-40123	Rose of Calvary/Minneapolis	1953	3.75	7.50	15.00
❏ 4-40177	Cleo and Meo/Do You Know What Lips Are For	1954	3.00	6.00	12.00
—With the Four Lads					
❏ 4-40188	Should I Tell/A Good Night's Work	1954	3.00	6.00	12.00
❏ 4-40268	One God/He Is a Man (I Am a Woman)	1954	3.00	6.00	12.00
❏ 4-40327	Where Are You/Number One Boy	1954	3.00	6.00	12.00
❏ 4-40410	Edward/I'm Not at All in Love	1955	3.00	6.00	12.00
❏ 4-40502	That's All I Need/Come to Me for Everything	1955	3.00	6.00	12.00
❏ 4-40566	Look! Look!/Ching-a-Ling	1955	3.00	6.00	12.00
❏ 4-40627	First Love/Wait for Tomorrow	1955	3.00	6.00	12.00
❏ 4-40687	Your Prayers Are Always Answered/Summer Nights	1956	3.00	6.00	12.00
❏ 4-40743	What Am I to Do/Let Him Know	1956	3.00	6.00	12.00
❏ 4-40794	I Love My Baby (My Baby Loves Me)/Egghead	1956	3.00	6.00	12.00
❏ 4-40878	Let It Be Me/Make Like a Bunny, Honey	1957	3.75	7.50	15.00
—With Jimmy Carroll; A-side is the first English-language recording of the song, which later was a hit for several other artists					
❏ 4-40955	Love Me to Pieces/Love	1957	3.00	6.00	12.00
❏ 4-41023	I Feel Pretty/How Can I Tell	1957	3.00	6.00	12.00
❏ 4-41068	I Told a Lie to My Darlin'/Exactly Like You	1957	3.00	6.00	12.00
❏ 4-41108	Give It All You've Got/Uh Huh, Oh Yeah	1958	3.00	6.00	12.00
❏ 4-41164	Loveable/Sweet Sugar Lips	1958	3.00	6.00	12.00
❏ 4-41202	Big Daddy/Wherefore Art Thou, Romeo	1958	3.00	6.00	12.00
❏ 4-41300	I Found a New Baby/My Reverie	1958	3.00	6.00	12.00
❏ 4-41360	Dream Boy/Love Will Find Out the Way	1959	2.50	5.00	10.00
❏ 4-41435	The President Song/Have I Told You Lately That I Love You	1959	2.50	5.00	10.00
❏ 4-41498	I Can't Hide a Mountain/Seems Like Old Times	1959	2.50	5.00	10.00
❏ 4-41621	Have You Ever Been Lonely/I Gotta Have My Baby Back	1960	2.50	5.00	10.00
❏ 4-41772	Stick 'Em Up Stuck Up/Ten Gallon Hat	1960	2.50	5.00	10.00
MERCURY					
❏ 71913	I Miss You Already/It's Only Me	1962	2.50	5.00	10.00
Albums					
COLUMBIA					
❏ CL 1095 [M]	Sometimes I'm Happy, Sometimes I'm Blue	1957	7.50	15.00	30.00
COREY, JOHN					
45s					
VEE JAY					
❏ 466	Pollyanna/I'll Forget	1962	7.50	15.00	30.00
—Backing group: The Four Seasons					
❏ 514	Hey Little Runaround/The Prettiest Girl I've Kissed Today	1963	2.50	5.00	10.00
CORNELIUS BROTHERS AND SISTER ROSE					
45s					
PLATINUM					
❏ 105/6	Treat Her Like a Lady/Over at My Place	1970	3.00	6.00	12.00
UNITED ARTISTS					
❏ 0131	Treat Her Like a Lady/Over at My Place	1973	—	2.00	4.00
—"Silver Spotlight Series" reissue					

Number	Title (A Side/B Side)	Yr	VG	VG+	NM
❏ XW208	Let Me Down Easy/Gonna Be Sweet for You	1973	—	2.50	5.00
❏ XW313	I Just Can't Stop Loving You/These Lonely Nights	1973	—	2.50	5.00
❏ XW377	Big Time Lover/Wonderful Tune	1974	—	2.50	5.00
❏ XW512	Too Late to Turn Back Now/Don't Ever Be Lonely (A Poor Little Fool Like Me)	1974	—	2.00	4.00
—Reissue					
❏ XW533	Trouble Child/Got to Testify	1974	—	2.50	5.00
❏ XW534	Since I Found My Baby/I Love Music	1974	—	2.50	5.00
❏ 50721	Treat Her Like a Lady/Over at My Place	1970	—	2.50	5.00
❏ 50910	Too Late to Turn Back Now/Lift Your Love Higher	1972	—	2.50	5.00
❏ 50954	Don't Ever Be Lonely (A Poor Little Fool Like Me)/I'm So Glad to Be Loved by You	1972	—	2.50	5.00
❏ 50996	I'm Never Gonna Be Alone Anymore/Let's Stay Together	1972	—	2.50	5.00
Albums					
UNITED ARTISTS					
❏ UA-LA593-G	Greatest Hits	1976	3.00	6.00	12.00
❏ UAS-5568	Cornelius Brothers and Sister Rose	1972	3.75	7.50	15.00
CORNELL, DON Also see TERESA BREWER.					
45s					
ABC-PARAMOUNT					
❏ 10687	Italian Wedding Song/Please Lie to Me	1965	—	3.00	6.00
❏ 10740	Dingle Ling, Dingle Ling/Careless Hands	1965	—	3.00	6.00
CORAL					
❏ 60659	I'll Walk Alone/That's the Chance You Take	1952	3.00	6.00	12.00
❏ 60690	I'm Yours/My Mother's Pearls	1952	3.00	6.00	12.00
❏ 60748	This Is the Beginning of the End/I Can't Cry Anymore	1952	3.00	6.00	12.00
❏ 60859	Let's Have an Old Fashioned Christmas/I've Got the Christmas Spirit	1952	3.75	7.50	15.00
❏ 60860	I/Be Fair	1952	3.00	6.00	12.00
❏ 60900	For You/I Was Lucky	1953	2.50	5.00	10.00
❏ 60901	Stay As Sweet As You Are/We Three (My Echo, My Shadow and Me)	1953	2.50	5.00	10.00
❏ 60902	It Isn't Fair/Something to Remember You By	1953	2.50	5.00	10.00
❏ 60903	S'posin/If You Were Only Mine	1953	2.50	5.00	10.00
❏ 60968	There's No Escape/Many Are the Times	1953	3.00	6.00	12.00
❏ 61011	Who Loves Me/When the Hands of the Clock Pray at Midnight	1953	3.00	6.00	12.00
❏ 61030	Please Play Our Song (Mister Record Man)/If I Should Love Again	1953	3.00	6.00	12.00
❏ 61068	I'm Yearning/You're On Trial	1953	3.00	6.00	12.00
❏ 61125	Hold Me/Size 12	1954	3.00	6.00	12.00
❏ 61171	Believe in Me/Little Lucy	1954	3.00	6.00	12.00
❏ 61206	Hold My Hand/I'm Blessed	1954	3.00	6.00	12.00
❏ 61253	No Man Is an Island/All at Once	1954	3.00	6.00	12.00
❏ 61333	Athena/No Man Is an Island	1955	2.50	5.00	10.00
❏ 61367	When You Are in Love/Give Me Your Love	1955	2.50	5.00	10.00
❏ 61393	Most of All/The Door Is Still Open to My Heart	1955	2.50	5.00	10.00
❏ 61407	Unchained Melody/All of You	1955	2.50	5.00	10.00
❏ 61467	The Bible Tells Me So/Love Is a Many-Splendored Thing	1955	2.50	5.00	10.00
❏ 61521	Young Abe Lincoln/Dream World	1955	2.50	5.00	10.00
❏ 61549	Make a Wish/There Once Was a Beautiful...	1955	2.50	5.00	10.00
❏ 61584	Teenage Meeting (Gonna Rock It Up Right)/I Still Have a Prayer	1956	3.75	7.50	15.00
❏ 61613	Rock Island Line/Na-Ne-Na-Na	1956	2.50	5.00	10.00
❏ 61631	But Love Me/Fort Knox	1956	2.50	5.00	10.00
❏ 61659	Grazie/Could You	1956	2.50	5.00	10.00
❏ 61687	Heaven Only Knows/Life Is a Song	1956	2.50	5.00	10.00
❏ 61721	See-Saw/From the Bottom of My Heart	1956	2.50	5.00	10.00
❏ 61757	Let's Be Friends/Ma-Ma Pa-Pa Cha-Cha	1956	2.50	5.00	10.00
❏ 61790	Afternoon in Madrid/Let's Get Lost	1957	2.50	5.00	10.00
❏ 61811	Sittin' in the Balcony/My Faith, My Hope, My Love	1957	2.50	5.00	10.00
❏ 61817	Mama Guitar/A Face in the Crowd	1957	2.50	5.00	10.00
❏ 61854	Mailman, Bring Me No More Blues/No Matter What	1957	2.50	5.00	10.00
❏ 61905	Non Dimentica/Before It's Time to Say Goodnight	1957	2.50	5.00	10.00
❏ 61993	You Go to My Head/Village in Capri	1958	2.50	5.00	10.00
❏ 62019	But Not Your Heart/Once More	1958	2.50	5.00	10.00
DOT					
❏ 15938	Heart of My Heart/This Earth Is Mine	1959	2.00	4.00	8.00
❏ 16044	I/Size 12	1960	2.00	4.00	8.00
JUBILEE					
❏ 5423	Night Train to Memphis/Bring Down the Curtain	1962	2.00	4.00	8.00
RCA VICTOR					
❏ 47-2914	Baby It's Cold Outside/Whispering Waters	1949	3.75	7.50	15.00
—With Laura Leslie					
❏ 47-3239	Come Back to Me/My Baby Is Blue	1949	3.75	7.50	15.00
❏ 47-3776	You Dreamer You/I Surrender Dear	1950	3.75	7.50	15.00
❏ 47-3839	You Wonderful You/Hawaii	1950	3.75	7.50	15.00
❏ 47-3884	I Need You So/It Couldn't Happen to a Sweeter Girl	1950	3.75	7.50	15.00
❏ 47-3909	Au Revoir Again/A Whistle and a Prayer	1950	3.75	7.50	15.00
❏ 47-3950	Take Me in Your Arms/The Breeze	1950	3.75	7.50	15.00
❏ 47-3991	Sue Me/Velvet Lips	1950	3.75	7.50	15.00
❏ 47-4042	Wedding Bells/Let a Smile Be Your Umbrella	1951	3.00	6.00	12.00
❏ 47-4043	Was That the Human Thing to Do/That Old Feeling	1951	3.00	6.00	12.00
❏ 47-4044	I'll Be Seeing You/When I Take My Sugar to Tea	1951	3.00	6.00	12.00
❏ 47-4083	My Inspiration/You Can't Tell a Lie to Your Heart	1951	3.75	7.50	15.00
❏ 47-4149	Why Don't You Tell Me So/If I Had Another Chance	1951	3.75	7.50	15.00
ROULETTE					
❏ 4355	The Flying Trapeze/Wish I Was	1961	2.00	4.00	8.00
SIGNATURE					
❏ 12002	Forever Couldn't Be Long Enough/Sempre Amore	1959	2.00	4.00	8.00
❏ 12020	Forever/There's Still Time Brother	1959	2.00	4.00	8.00
❏ 12027	Grateful/Only Time Will Tell	1960	2.00	4.00	8.00
❏ 12032	Your Kiss/I Have But One Heart	1960	2.00	4.00	8.00
20TH FOX					
❏ 515	If You Love Her Tell Her So/You Know You Don't Want Me	1964	2.00	4.00	8.00

C

Number	Title (A Side/B Side)	Yr	VG	VG+	NM

7-Inch Extended Plays

CORAL

Number	Title (A Side/B Side)	Yr	VG	VG+	NM
❏ EC 81002	I'm Yours/This Is the Beginning of the End//I'll Walk Alone/(I've Cried Until) I Can't Cry Anymore	1953	3.00	6.00	12.00
❏ EC 81002 [PS]	I'm Yours	1953	3.00	6.00	12.00
❏ EC 81118	Most of All/All of You//Unchained Melody/ Danger Heartbreak Ahead	1955	2.50	5.00	10.00
❏ EC 81118 [PS]	Your Date with Don ...	1955	2.50	5.00	10.00
❏ EC 81501	Hold My Hand/I'm Yours//It Isn't Fair/I'll Walk Alone	195?	3.00	6.00	12.00
❏ EC 81501 [PS]	Don Cornell	195?	3.00	6.00	12.00
❏ 83010 [DJ]	Let's Have an Old Fashioned Christmas/I've Got the Christmas Spirit//Sing a Song Of Santa Claus/Winter's Here Again	195?	3.75	7.50	15.00

—B-side by the Ames Brothers

RCA CAMDEN

Number	Title (A Side/B Side)	Yr	VG	VG+	NM
❏ CAE-239	The Breeze (Bringin' My Honey Back to Me)/Are You Lonesome Tonight//Wedding Bells Are Breaking Up That Old Gang of Mine//Have You Ever Been Lonely	195?	2.50	5.00	10.00
❏ CAE-239 [PS]	Don Cornell	195?	2.50	5.00	10.00

RCA VICTOR

Number	Title (A Side/B Side)	Yr	VG	VG+	NM
❏ 547-0242	It Isn't Fair/Take Me in Your Arms//I Surrender Dear/I Need You So	1952	3.00	6.00	12.00

—One record of 2-EP set EPB-3116; Side 1, track 1 credited to "Swing and Sway with Sammy Kaye, vocal refrain by Don Cornell"

Number	Title (A Side/B Side)	Yr	VG	VG+	NM
❏ 547-0243	Come Back to Me/Why Don't You Tell Me So//Au Revoir Again/(The Breeze) Bringin' My Honey Back to Me	1952	3.00	6.00	12.00

—One record of 2-EP set EPB-3116

Number	Title (A Side/B Side)	Yr	VG	VG+	NM
❏ EPB 3116 [PS]	Don Cornell Sings	1952	3.75	7.50	15.00

—Fold-open cover for 2-EP set (547-0242, 547-0243)

Albums

ABC-PARAMOUNT

Number	Title (A Side/B Side)	Yr	VG	VG+	NM
❏ ABC-537 [M]	Incomparable	1966	3.00	6.00	12.00
❏ ABCS-537 [S]	Incomparable	1966	3.75	7.50	15.00

CORAL

Number	Title (A Side/B Side)	Yr	VG	VG+	NM
❏ CRL 57055 [M]	Don	1955	7.50	15.00	30.00
❏ CRL 57133 [M]	For Teenagers Only	1957	7.50	15.00	30.00

DOT

Number	Title (A Side/B Side)	Yr	VG	VG+	NM
❏ DLP-3160 [M]	Don Cornell's Great Hits	1959	6.25	12.50	25.00
❏ DLP-25160 [S]	Don Cornell's Great Hits	1959	7.50	15.00	30.00

MOVIETONE

Number	Title (A Side/B Side)	Yr	VG	VG+	NM
❏ 71013 [M]	I Wish You Love	1966	3.00	6.00	12.00
❏ S-72013 [S]	I Wish You Love	1966	3.75	7.50	15.00

SIGNATURE

Number	Title (A Side/B Side)	Yr	VG	VG+	NM
❏ SM-1001 [M]	Don Cornell Sings Love Songs	1960	5.00	10.00	20.00
❏ SS-1001 [S]	Don Cornell Sings Love Songs	1960	6.25	12.50	25.00

VOCALION

Number	Title (A Side/B Side)	Yr	VG	VG+	NM
❏ VL 3657 [M]	Don Cornell	196?	3.00	6.00	12.00

CORNELL, DON; JOHNNY DESMOND; ALAN DALE

45s

CORAL

Number	Title (A Side/B Side)	Yr	VG	VG+	NM
❏ 61076	The Gang That Sang "Heart of My Heart"/I Think I'll Fall in Love Today	1953	3.00	6.00	12.00

CORNELLS, THE

45s

GAREX

Number	Title (A Side/B Side)	Yr	VG	VG+	NM
❏ 100	Mama's Little Baby/Wak-A-Cha	1962	7.50	15.00	30.00
❏ 102	Malibu Surf/Agua Caliente	1963	7.50	15.00	30.00
❏ 201	Beach Bound/Lone Star Stomp	1963	7.50	15.00	30.00
❏ 206	Surf Fever/Do the Slauson	1963	7.50	15.00	30.00

Albums

GAREX

Number	Title (A Side/B Side)	Yr	VG	VG+	NM
❏ LPGA-100 [M]	Beach Bound	1963	125.00	250.00	500.00

SUNDAZED

Number	Title (A Side/B Side)	Yr	VG	VG+	NM
❏ LP-5013	Surf Fever!	199?	2.50	5.00	10.00

CORNISH, GENE Also see THE RASCALS.

45s

DAWN

Number	Title (A Side/B Side)	Yr	VG	VG+	NM
❏ 550	Let's Do the Capri/Lonely I Will Say	1964	7.50	15.00	30.00
❏ 551	I Wanna Be a Beatle/Oh Misery	1964	10.00	20.00	40.00

VASSAR

Number	Title (A Side/B Side)	Yr	VG	VG+	NM
❏ 319	Since I Lost You/Winner Take All	1962	5.00	10.00	20.00
❏ 321	My Baby Ran Away from Me/Now the Story Can Be Told	1962	6.25	12.50	25.00

CORONETS, THE

45s

CHESS

Number	Title (A Side/B Side)	Yr	VG	VG+	NM
❏ 1549	Nadine/I'm All Alone	1953	50.00	100.00	200.00

—Silver top label

Number	Title (A Side/B Side)	Yr	VG	VG+	NM
❏ 1549	Nadine/I'm All Alone	1958	3.00	6.00	12.00

—All-blue label

Number	Title (A Side/B Side)	Yr	VG	VG+	NM
❏ 1553	It Would Be Heavenly/Baby's Coming Home	1953	100.00	200.00	400.00

—Black vinyl

Number	Title (A Side/B Side)	Yr	VG	VG+	NM
❏ 1553	It Would Be Heavenly/Baby's Coming Home	1953	200.00	400.00	800.00

—Red vinyl

GROOVE

Number	Title (A Side/B Side)	Yr	VG	VG+	NM
❏ 0114	I Love You More/Crime Doesn't Pay	1955	25.00	50.00	100.00
❏ 0116	The Bible Tells Me So/Hush	1955	37.50	75.00	150.00

STERLING

Number	Title (A Side/B Side)	Yr	VG	VG+	NM
❏ 903	Don't Deprive Me/Little Boy	1955	62.50	125.00	250.00

CORPORATION, THE

45s

CAPITOL

Number	Title (A Side/B Side)	Yr	VG	VG+	NM
❏ 2467	Highway/I Want to Get Out of My Grave	1969	3.75	7.50	15.00

CUCA

Number	Title (A Side/B Side)	Yr	VG	VG+	NM
❏ 1496	You Make Me Feel Good/Sitting by the Sea	1968	3.75	7.50	15.00

Albums

AGE OF AQUARIUS

Number	Title (A Side/B Side)	Yr	VG	VG+	NM
❏ 4150	Get On Our Swing	1968	7.50	15.00	30.00
❏ 4250	Hassles in My Mind	1969	7.50	15.00	30.00

CAPITOL

Number	Title (A Side/B Side)	Yr	VG	VG+	NM
❏ ST-175	The Corporation	1969	12.50	25.00	50.00

CORPUS

Albums

ACORN

Number	Title (A Side/B Side)	Yr	VG	VG+	NM
❏ 1001	Creation: A Child	1971	75.00	150.00	300.00

CORSAIRS, THE

45s

HY-TONE

Number	Title (A Side/B Side)	Yr	VG	VG+	NM
❏ 110	Goodbye Darling/Rock Lilly Rock	1957	375.00	750.00	1500.

SMASH

Number	Title (A Side/B Side)	Yr	VG	VG+	NM
❏ 1715	Time Waits/It Won't Be a Sin	1961	3.75	7.50	15.00

TUFF

Number	Title (A Side/B Side)	Yr	VG	VG+	NM
❏ 375	Save a Little Monkey/(Instrumental)	1963	2.50	5.00	10.00
❏ 402	On the Spanish Side/The Change in You	1964	2.50	5.00	10.00

TUFF/CHESS

Number	Title (A Side/B Side)	Yr	VG	VG+	NM
❏ 1808	Smoky Places/Thinkin'	1961	6.25	12.50	25.00
❏ 1818	I'll Take You HJome/Sittin' on Your Doorstep	1962	3.00	6.00	12.00
❏ 1830	Dancing Shadows/While	1962	3.00	6.00	12.00
❏ 1840	At the Stroke of Midnight/Listen to My Little Heart	1962	3.00	6.00	12.00
❏ 1847	Stormy/It's Almost Sunday Morning	1963	3.00	6.00	12.00

CORT, BOB

45s

LONDON

Number	Title (A Side/B Side)	Yr	VG	VG+	NM
❏ 1713	Don't You Rock Me Daddy-O/It Takes a Worried Man to Sing a Worried Blues	1957	3.75	7.50	15.00
❏ 1742	Freight Train/Roll Jen Jenkins	1957	3.00	6.00	12.00
❏ 1748	Maggie Mae/Jessamine	1957	3.00	6.00	12.00

—With Liz Winters

CORTEZ, DAVE "BABY"

45s

ALL PLATINUM

Number	Title (A Side/B Side)	Yr	VG	VG+	NM
❏ 2339	Funky Robot (Part 1)/Funky Robot (Part 2)	1972	—	2.50	5.00
❏ 2342	Unaddressed Letter/Funky Robot (Part 1)	1972	—	2.50	5.00
❏ 2343	Someone Has Taken Your Place/Born Funky	1973	—	2.50	5.00
❏ 2345	Hell Street Junction/(Instrumental)	1973	—	2.50	5.00
❏ 2347	Soul Walkin'/(B-side unknown)	1974	—	2.50	5.00

ARGO

Number	Title (A Side/B Side)	Yr	VG	VG+	NM
❏ 5462	Let It Be You/I'm Gonna Stay	1964	2.50	5.00	10.00

CHESS

Number	Title (A Side/B Side)	Yr	VG	VG+	NM
❏ 1829	Rinky Dink/Getting Right	1962	2.50	5.00	10.00
❏ 1834	Happy Weekend/Fiddle Sticks	1962	2.50	5.00	10.00
❏ 1842	Tweedle Dee/Gift of Love	1962	2.50	5.00	10.00
❏ 1850	Hot Cakes! 1st Serving/Hot Cakes! 2nd Serving	1963	2.00	4.00	8.00
❏ 1861	Organ Shout/Precious You	1963	2.00	4.00	8.00
❏ 1874	Happy Feet/Gettin' to the Point	1963	2.00	4.00	8.00

CLOCK

Number	Title (A Side/B Side)	Yr	VG	VG+	NM
❏ 1006	You're the Girl/Eeny Meeny Minie Mo	1958	5.00	10.00	20.00
❏ 1009	The Happy Organ/Love Me As I Love You	1959	5.00	10.00	20.00
❏ 1012	The Whistling Organ/I'm Happy	1959	3.00	6.00	12.00
❏ 1014	Piano Shuffle/It's a Sin to Tell a Lie	1959	3.00	6.00	12.00
❏ 1016	Dave's Special/Whispers	1959	3.00	6.00	12.00
❏ 1020	You're Just Right/Deep in the Heart of Texas	1960	3.00	6.00	12.00
❏ 1021	You're the Girl/I'm Happy	1960	3.00	6.00	12.00
❏ 1024	Cat Nip/Talk Is Cheap	1960	3.00	6.00	12.00
❏ 1031	Hurricane/The Shift	1960	3.00	6.00	12.00
❏ 1034	Summertime/Walking with You	1961	3.00	6.00	12.00
❏ 1036	Tootsie/Second Chance	1961	3.00	6.00	12.00
❏ 71824	Tootsie/Second Chance	1961	2.50	5.00	10.00
❏ 71851	The Happy Organ/Piano Shuffle	1961	2.50	5.00	10.00
❏ 71875	C'mon and Stomp/Calypso Love Song	1961	2.50	5.00	10.00

EMBER

Number	Title (A Side/B Side)	Yr	VG	VG+	NM
❏ 1011	Soft Lights/Movin' and Groovin'	1956	10.00	20.00	40.00

—As "David Clowney"

EMIT

Number	Title (A Side/B Side)	Yr	VG	VG+	NM
❏ 301	Fiesta/Hey-Hey-Hey	1962	2.50	5.00	10.00

EPIC

Number	Title (A Side/B Side)	Yr	VG	VG+	NM
❏ 9732	Poppin' Popcorn/The Question	1964	2.50	5.00	10.00

JULIA

Number	Title (A Side/B Side)	Yr	VG	VG+	NM
❏ 1829	Rinky Dink/Getting Right	1962	6.25	12.50	25.00

OKEH

Number	Title (A Side/B Side)	Yr	VG	VG+	NM
❏ 7102	You Give Me Heebie Jeebies/Honey Baby	1958	5.00	10.00	20.00
❏ 7208	Popping Popcorn/The Question (Do You Love Me)	1964	2.00	4.00	8.00

PARIS

Number	Title (A Side/B Side)	Yr	VG	VG+	NM
❏ 513	Shakin'/Hoot Owl	1958	7.50	15.00	30.00

—As "Dave Clowney"

ROULETTE

Number	Title (A Side/B Side)	Yr	VG	VG+	NM
❏ 4628	Tweetie Pie/Things Ain't What They Used to Be	1965	2.00	4.00	8.00
❏ 4679	Count Down/Summertime	1966	2.00	4.00	8.00
❏ 4693	Sticks and Stones/Do Any Dance	1966	2.00	4.00	8.00
❏ 4717	Belly Rub (Part 1)/Belly Rub (Part 2)	1967	2.00	4.00	8.00
❏ 4759	Hula Hoop/Come Back	1967	2.00	4.00	8.00
❏ 4783	Hot Chocolate/Soul Groovin'	1967	2.00	4.00	8.00

T-NECK

Number	Title (A Side/B Side)	Yr	VG	VG+	NM
❏ 907	I Turned You On/I Know Who You Been Socking It To	1969	—	3.00	6.00
❏ 913	Save Me/My Little Girl	1969	—	3.00	6.00

WINLEY

Number	Title (A Side/B Side)	Yr	VG	VG+	NM
❏ 259	Jamin' (Part 1)/Jamin' (Part 2)	1961	2.50	5.00	10.00
❏ 262	Skins and Sounds/Little Paris Melody	1962	2.50	5.00	10.00
❏ 267	Scotty (Part 1)/Scotty (Part 2)	1962	2.50	5.00	10.00

7-Inch Extended Plays

CLOCK

Number	Title (A Side/B Side)	Yr	VG	VG+	NM
❏ EP 1-4039-C	The Happy Organ/The Whistling Organ//Catnip/ Deep in the Heart of Texas	1959	6.25	12.50	25.00
❏ EP 1-4039-C [PS]	Dave "Baby" Cortez and His Happy Organ	1959	6.25	12.50	25.00

RCA VICTOR

Number	Title (A Side/B Side)	Yr	VG	VG+	NM
❏ EPA-4342 [M]	*The Happy Organ/Love Me As I Love You/ Dave's Special/You're the Girl	1959	3.00	6.00	12.00
❏ EPA-4342 [PS]	The Happy Organ	1959	3.00	6.00	12.00
❏ ESP-4342 [PS]	The Happy Organ	1959	5.00	10.00	20.00

Number	Title (A Side/B Side)	Yr	VG	VG+	NM
❏ ESP-4342 [S]	*The Happy Organ/Love Me As I Love You/ Dave's Special/You're the Girl	1959	5.00	10.00	20.00

Albums

CHESS

Number	Title (A Side/B Side)	Yr	VG	VG+	NM
❏ LP-1473 [M]	Rinky Dink	1962	12.50	25.00	50.00

CLOCK

❏ C-331 [M]	Dave "Baby" Cortez	1960	10.00	20.00	40.00
❏ CS-331 [S]	Dave "Baby" Cortez	1960	12.50	25.00	50.00
❏ MGC-20647 [M]	Dave "Baby" Cortez	1961	7.50	15.00	30.00
❏ SRC-60647 [S]	Dave "Baby" Cortez	1961	10.00	20.00	40.00

CORONET

❏ CX-201 [M]	The Whistling Organ	196?	3.75	7.50	15.00

DESIGN

❏ DLP-163 [R]	The Happy Organ	1962	3.00	6.00	12.00

METRO

❏ M-550 [M]	The Fabulous Organ of Dave "Baby" Cortez	1965	3.75	7.50	15.00
❏ MS-550 [R]	The Fabulous Organ of Dave "Baby" Cortez	1965	3.00	6.00	12.00

RCA VICTOR

❏ LPM-2099 [M]	The Happy Organ	1959	20.00	40.00	80.00
❏ LSP-2099 [S]	The Happy Organ	1959	25.00	50.00	100.00

ROULETTE

❏ R-25298 [M]	Organ Shindig	1965	5.00	10.00	20.00
❏ SR-25298 [S]	Organ Shindig	1965	6.25	12.50	25.00
❏ R-25315 [M]	Tweety Pie	1966	5.00	10.00	20.00
❏ SR-25315 [S]	Tweety Pie	1966	6.25	12.50	25.00
❏ R-25328 [M]	In Orbit with Dave "Baby" Cortez	1966	5.00	10.00	20.00
❏ SR-25328 [S]	In Orbit with Dave "Baby" Cortez	1966	6.25	12.50	25.00

T-NECK

❏ TNS-3005	The Isley Brothers Way	1970	5.00	10.00	20.00

CORVELLS, THE
45s

ABC-PARAMOUNT

❏ 10324	Take My Love/Daisy	1962	50.00	100.00	200.00

BLAST

❏ 203	The Bells/Don't Forget	1961	37.50	75.00	150.00

CUB

❏ 9122	One (Is Such a Lonely Number)/ The Joke's On Me	1963	5.00	10.00	20.00

LIDO

❏ 509	We Made a Vow/Miss Jones	1957	50.00	100.00	200.00

LUPINE

❏ 104	He's So Fine/Baby Sitting	1962	6.25	12.50	25.00

TIP TOP

❏ 509	We Made a Vow/Miss Jones	1957	75.00	150.00	300.00

COSBY, BILL
45s

CAPITOL

❏ 4258	Yes, Yes, Yes/Ben	1976	—	2.00	4.00
❏ 4299	I Luv Myself Better Than I Luv Myself/Do It To Me	1976	—	2.00	4.00
❏ 4501	Boogie on Your Face/What's in a Slang	1977	—	2.00	4.00
❏ 4523	Merry Christmas Mama (Vocal)/(Instrumental)	1977	5.00	10.00	20.00

TETRAGRAMMATON

❏ 1539	Football/Golf	1969	—	3.00	6.00

UNI

❏ 55184	Hikky Burr/Hikky Burr	1969	—	3.00	6.00

—A-side with the Bunions; B-side by the Bradford Band

❏ 55223	Grover Henson Feels Forgotten/(Instrumental)	1970	—	3.00	6.00
❏ 55247	Hybish Skybish/Martin's Funeral	1970	—	2.50	5.00

—With Bad Foot Brown

WARNER BROS.

❏ 5499	Stand Still for My Lovin'/When I Marry	1965	2.50	5.00	10.00
❏ 7072	Little Ole Man (Uptight-Everything's Alright)/ Hush Hush	1967	2.00	4.00	8.00
❏ 7096	Hooray for the Salvation Army Band/Ursalena	1968	2.00	4.00	8.00
❏ 7126	Little Ole Man (Uptight-Everything's Alright)/ Funky North Philly	1969	—	3.00	6.00

—Hall of Fame Hits (originals have green labels with "W7" logo)

❏ 7171	Funky North Philly/Stop, Look and Listen	1968	2.00	4.00	8.00

Albums

CAPITOL

❏ ST-11530	Bill Cosby Is Not Himself These Days, Rat Own, Rat Own, Rat Own	1976	2.50	5.00	10.00
❏ ST-11590	My Father Confused Me…What Must I Do? What Must I Do?	1977	2.50	5.00	10.00
❏ ST-11683	Let's Boogie (Disco Bill)	1977	2.50	5.00	10.00
❏ ST-11731	Bill's Best Friend	1978	2.50	5.00	10.00

GEFFEN

❏ GHS 24104	Those of You With or Without Children, You'll Understand	1986	2.50	5.00	10.00

MCA

❏ 169	When I Was a Kid	197?	2.00	4.00	8.00

—Reissue of Uni 73100

❏ 333	Fat Albert	1973	2.50	5.00	10.00
❏ 553	For Adults Only	197?	2.00	4.00	8.00

—Reissue of Uni 73112

❏ 554	Inside the Mind of Bill Cosby	197?	2.00	4.00	8.00

—Reissue of Uni 73139

❏ 8005 [(2)]	Bill	197?	3.00	6.00	12.00

MOTOWN

❏ 5364 ML	Bill Cosby "Himself"	198?	2.50	5.00	10.00

—Reissue of 6026 with new cover

❏ 6026 ML	Bill Cosby "Himself"	1982	2.50	5.00	10.00

TETRAGRAMMATON

❏ TD-5100 [(2)]	8:15 12:15	1969	5.00	10.00	20.00

UNI

❏ 73066	Bill Cosby	1969	2.50	5.00	10.00
❏ 73082	"Live" Madison Square Garden Center	1970	2.50	5.00	10.00
❏ 73100	When I Was a Kid	1971	2.50	5.00	10.00
❏ 73101	Bill Cosby Talks to Kids About Drugs	1971	3.75	7.50	15.00
❏ 73112	For Adults Only	1971	2.50	5.00	10.00
❏ 73139	Inside the Mind of Bill Cosby	1972	2.50	5.00	10.00

WARNER BROS.

❏ PRO 249 [DJ]	Radio Sampler Album — The Best of Bill Cosby	1969	5.00	10.00	20.00

—Promo LP with edits of 12 tracks for radio use

❏ W 1518 [M]	Bill Cosby Is a Very Funny Fellow Right!	1964	3.75	7.50	15.00
❏ W 1567 [M]	I Started Out as a Child	1964	3.75	7.50	15.00
❏ WS 1567 [S]	I Started Out as a Child	1964	5.00	10.00	20.00
❏ W 1606 [M]	Why Is There Air?	1965	3.75	7.50	15.00
❏ WS 1606 [S]	Why Is There Air?	1965	5.00	10.00	20.00

—Gold label

❏ W 1634 [M]	Wonderfulness	1966	3.75	7.50	15.00
❏ WS 1634 [S]	Wonderfulness	1966	3.75	7.50	15.00

—Gold label

❏ W 1691 [M]	Revenge	1967	3.75	7.50	15.00
❏ W 1709 [M]	Bill Cosby Sings/Silver Throat	1967	3.75	7.50	15.00
❏ WS 1709 [S]	Bill Cosby Sings/Silver Throat	1967	3.00	6.00	12.00
❏ W 1728 [M]	Bill Cosby Sings/Hooray for the Salvation Army Band	1968	3.75	7.50	15.00
❏ WS 1728 [S]	Bill Cosby Sings/Hooray for the Salvation Army Band	1968	3.00	6.00	12.00
❏ W 1734 [M]	To Russell, My Brother, Whom I Slept With	1968	3.75	7.50	15.00
❏ WS 1734 [S]	To Russell, My Brother, Whom I Slept With	1968	3.00	6.00	12.00
❏ WS 1757	200 M.P.H.	1968	3.00	6.00	12.00
❏ WS 1770	It's True! It's True!	1969	3.00	6.00	12.00
❏ WS 1798	The Best of Bill Cosby	1969	3.00	6.00	12.00
❏ WS 1836	More of the Best of Bill Cosby	1970	3.00	6.00	12.00

COSMIC RAYS, THE
45s

SATURN

❏ 222	Bye Bye/Someone's in Love	1960	750.00	1500.	3000.
❏ 401	Daddy's Gonna Tell You No Lies/Dreaming	1960	500.00	1000.	2000.

COSMO, TONY
45s

FLING

❏ 716	Wise to You/Ponytail Annie and Crewcut Joe	1960	3.00	6.00	12.00
❏ 716 [PS]	Wise to You/Ponytail Annie and Crewcut Joe	1960	6.25	12.50	25.00

ROULETTE

❏ 4265	A Teenager for President/Give Me Some	1960	2.50	5.00	10.00

VANN

❏ 100	Big Party/Tiny Hands and Funny Dimples	1961	3.75	7.50	15.00

COSTA, DON
45s

ABC-PARAMOUNT

❏ 9693	Flamenco Love/Heart of Paris	1956	3.75	7.50	15.00
❏ 9717	Magic Melody/Lullaby to an Angel	1956	3.75	7.50	15.00
❏ 9729	For Me and My Gal/Beer Barrel Polka	1956	3.75	7.50	15.00
❏ 9770	Around the World/Everybody Loves Pierre	1956	3.75	7.50	15.00
❏ 9783	By the Fireside/C'est Ca!	1957	3.75	7.50	15.00
❏ 9835	Bella Nunziata/Tennessee Tulip	1957	3.75	7.50	15.00
❏ 9943	Bing Bang Bong/Almost in Your Arms	1958	3.75	7.50	15.00

COLUMBIA

❏ 4-42307	Flamenco Guitar/Sugar Blues	1962	2.50	5.00	10.00
❏ 4-42442	Theme from The Miracle Worker/Hully Gully	1962	2.50	5.00	10.00
❏ 4-42494	Theme from The Wonderful World of the Brothers Grimm/Above the Stars	1962	2.50	5.00	10.00
❏ 4-42705	Diamonds/The Harem	1963	2.00	4.00	8.00
❏ 4-42785	Losing You/Tamoure	1963	2.00	4.00	8.00

DCP

❏ 1100	Theme from "Golden Boy"/Main Street	1964	2.00	4.00	8.00
❏ 1121	If I Had a Hammer/Put Your Head on My Shoulder	1964	2.00	4.00	8.00
❏ 1124	I Will Wait for You/Pretty Blue Eyes	1965	2.00	4.00	8.00
❏ 1132	How to Murder Your Wife/Elise	1965	2.00	4.00	8.00

DCP INTERNATIONAL

❏ 1002	Love Theme from "Tom Jones"/Off Broadway	1964	2.00	4.00	8.00

ESSEX

❏ 405	Under the Linden Tree/Safe in the Harbor	1955	3.75	7.50	15.00

JAMIE

❏ 1123	I'm in Heaven/The Main One	1959	3.00	6.00	12.00

MERCURY

❏ 72841	Mrs. Robinson/Sound of Silence	1968	—	3.50	7.00
❏ 72932	Love So Fine/On the South Side of Chicago	1969	2.00	4.00	8.00

MGM

❏ K13520	Theme from "A Study in Terror"/Titoli	1966	—	3.50	7.00
❏ K14201	Gemini Trip/Rosy's Theme (From Ryan's Daughter)	1970	—	3.00	6.00
❏ K14467	Gone/Song for Anna	1972	—	3.00	6.00

UNITED ARTISTS

❏ 035	Never on Sunday/Theme from The Unforgiven	1973	—	2.50	5.00

—"Silver Spotlight Series"

❏ 190	I'll Walk the Line/Cat Walk	1959	3.00	6.00	12.00
❏ 221	Theme from "The Unforgiven"/Streets of Paris	1960	2.50	5.00	10.00
❏ 221 [PS]	Theme from "The Unforgiven"/Streets of Paris	1960	12.50	25.00	50.00

—Promo-only sleeve with photos of Audrey Hepburn and Burt Lancaster

❏ 234	Never on Sunday/The Sound of Love	1960	2.50	5.00	10.00
❏ 234 [PS]	Never on Sunday/The Sound of Love	1960	6.25	12.50	25.00
❏ 286	The Misfits/Chi-Chi	1961	3.00	6.00	12.00
❏ 286 [PS]	The Misfits/Chi-Chi	1961	10.00	20.00	40.00

—With photos of Clark Gable, Marilyn Monroe and Montgomery Clift

❏ 318	How in the World/That's the Way with Love	1961	2.50	5.00	10.00
❏ 349	La La La/These Things Remain	1961	2.50	5.00	10.00
❏ 1500	Never on Sunday/Exodus	196?	—	3.00	6.00

—B-side by Ferrante and Teicher; "Silver Series" reissue

❏ 1523	The Song from Moulin Rouge/Laura	196?	—	3.00	6.00

—"Silver Series" issue

❏ 1524	An Affair to Remember/Invitation	196?	—	3.00	6.00

—"Silver Series" issue

❏ 1525	The Third Man Theme/From Here to Eternity	196?	—	3.00	6.00

—"Silver Series" issue

❏ 1526	Stella by Starlight/Picnic	196?	—	3.00	6.00

—"Silver Series" issue

❏ 1602	Never on Sunday/Theme from The Unforgiven	196?	—	3.00	6.00

—"Silver Series" issue

VERVE

❏ 10511	Illya Darling/Trini's Tune	1967	2.00	4.00	8.00
❏ 10511 [PS]	Illya Darling/Trini's Tune	1967	3.75	7.50	15.00
❏ 10558	Theme from Valley of the Dolls/Up, Up and Away	1967	—	3.50	7.00
❏ 10559	Can't Take My Eyes Off You/Society's Child	1967	—	3.50	7.00

C

Number	Title (A Side/B Side)	Yr	VG	VG+	NM
Albums					
ABC-PARAMOUNT					
❑ ABC-107 [M]	Music to Break a Lease	1956	6.25	12.50	25.00
❑ ABC-212 [M]	Music to Break a Sub-Lease	1958	6.25	12.50	25.00
❑ ABC-362 [M]	Don Costa Conducts His 15 Hits	1961	6.25	12.50	25.00
COLUMBIA					
❑ CL 1880 [M]	Hollywood Premiere	1962	3.75	7.50	15.00
❑ CL 2041 [M]	Hits! Hits!	1963	3.75	7.50	15.00
❑ CS 8680 [S]	Hollywood Premiere	1962	6.25	12.50	25.00
❑ CS 8841 [S]	Hits! Hits! Hits!	1963	6.25	12.50	25.00
DCP INTERNATIONAL					
❑ DCL 3802 [M]	The Golden Touch	1964	3.00	6.00	12.00
❑ DCL 3806 [M]	Don Costa Plays Music from Umbrellas of Cherbourg and Other Film Music	1965	3.00	6.00	12.00
❑ DCS 6802 [S]	The Golden Touch	1964	3.75	7.50	15.00
❑ DCS 6806 [S]	Don Costa Plays Music from Umbrellas of Cherbourg and Other Film Music	1965	3.75	7.50	15.00
HARMONY					
❑ HL 7347 [M]	Days of Wine and Roses and Other Great Hits	1965	3.00	6.00	12.00
❑ HS 11147 [S]	Days of Wine and Roses and Other Great Hits	1965	3.75	7.50	15.00
MERCURY					
❑ SR 61177	Instrumental Versions of Simon and Garfunkel	1968	5.00	10.00	20.00
❑ SR 61216	The Don Costa Concept	1969	5.00	10.00	20.00
UNITED ARTISTS					
❑ UAL 3119 [M]	The Unforgiven	1960	5.00	10.00	20.00
❑ UAL 3134 [M]	Magnificent Motion Picture Music	1960	3.75	7.50	15.00
❑ WW 3513 [M]	The Sound of the Million Sellers	1960	3.75	7.50	15.00
❑ UAS 6134 [S]	Magnificent Motion Picture Music	1960	5.00	10.00	20.00
❑ WW 7501 [M]	Echoing Voices and Trombones	1960	5.00	10.00	20.00
❑ WWS 8501 [S]	Echoing Voices and Trombones	1960	7.50	15.00	30.00
❑ WWS 8513 [S]	The Sound of the Million Sellers	1960	6.25	12.50	25.00
VERVE					
❑ V-8702 [M]	Modern Delights	1967	5.00	10.00	20.00
❑ V6-8702 [S]	Modern Delights	1967	3.75	7.50	15.00
COTTON, GENE					
45s					
(NO LABEL)					
❑ NR-16361 [DJ]	Child Of Peace (same on both sides)	1981	2.00	4.00	8.00
ABC					
❑ 12087	Country Spirit/Damn It All	1975	—	2.50	5.00
❑ 12137	Let Your Love Flow/Keepin' It on the Road	1975	—	2.50	5.00
❑ 12227	You've Got Me Runnin'/It's Over, Goodbye	1976	—	2.50	5.00
❑ 12250	Rain On/A Song for You	1977	—	2.50	5.00
❑ 12282	My Love Comes Alive/Sweet Destiny	1977	—	2.50	5.00
ARIOLA AMERICA					
❑ 7675	Before My Heart Finds Out/Like a Sunday in Salem	1977	—	2.50	5.00
❑ 7723	Like a Sunday in Salem (The Amos and Andy Song)/Shine On (You Got to Shine On)	1978	—	2.00	4.00
❑ 7778	Michael/Ocean of Love	1979	—	2.00	4.00
KNOLL					
❑ 5002	If I Could Get You (Into My Life)/Rained On Before	1982	—	2.50	5.00
MYRRH					
❑ 116	American Indian Blues/Lessons of History	1973	—	3.00	6.00
❑ 117	Lean On One Another/(B-side unknown)	1973	—	3.00	6.00
❑ 123	Great American Noel/Mrs. Oliver	1973	—	3.00	6.00
❑ 137	Sunshine Roses/Mrs. Oliver	1974	—	3.00	6.00
Albums					
ABC					
❑ D-933	For All the Young Writers	1975	2.50	5.00	10.00
❑ D-983	Rain On	1977	2.50	5.00	10.00
ARIOLA AMERICA					
❑ SW-50031	Save the Dancer	1978	2.50	5.00	10.00
❑ SW-50070	No Strings Attached	1979	2.50	5.00	10.00
KNOLL					
❑ 1001	Eclipse of the Blue Moon	1981	2.50	5.00	10.00
MYRRH					
❑ MSB-6517	In the Gray of the Morning	1973	3.00	6.00	12.00
❑ MSB-6524	Liberty	1974	3.00	6.00	12.00
COTTON, GENE, AND KIM CARNES Also see each artist's individual listings.					
45s					
ARIOLA AMERICA					
❑ 7704	You're a Part of Me/Shine On (You Got to Shine On)	1978	—	2.50	5.00
COTTON, JAMES					
45s					
BUDDAH					
❑ 461	Boogie Thing/Fever	1975	—	2.50	5.00
❑ 468	Rocket 88/One More Mile	1975	—	2.50	5.00
LOMA					
❑ 2042	Laying in the Weeds/Complete This Order	1966	3.00	6.00	12.00
SUN					
❑ 199	My Baby/Straighten Up, Baby	1954	375.00	750.00	1500.
❑ 206	Cotton Crop Blues/Hold Me in Your Arms	1954	450.00	900.00	1800.
VERVE FORECAST					
❑ 5053	Good Time Charlie/Off the Wall	1967	2.50	5.00	10.00
❑ 5066	Feelin' Good/Don't Start Me Talkin'	1967	2.50	5.00	10.00
❑ 5107	The Coach's Better Days/(B-side unknown)	1969	2.00	4.00	8.00
Albums					
ALLIGATOR					
❑ AL-4737	High Compression	1984	2.50	5.00	10.00
❑ AL-4746	Live from Chicago	1986	2.50	5.00	10.00
ANTONE'S					
❑ ANT-0007	James Cotton Live	1988	3.00	6.00	12.00
BLIND PIG					
❑ BP-2587	Take Me Back	1987	2.50	5.00	10.00
BUDDAH					
❑ BDS-5620	100% Cotton	1974	3.00	6.00	12.00
❑ BDS-5650	High Energy	1975	3.00	6.00	12.00
❑ BDS-5661 [(2)]	Live & On the Move!	1976	3.75	7.50	15.00

Number	Title (A Side/B Side)	Yr	VG	VG+	NM
CAPITOL					
❑ SM-814	Taking Care of Business	197?	2.50	5.00	10.00
—Reissue with new prefix					
❑ ST-814	Taking Care of Business	1971	3.75	7.50	15.00
INTERMEDIA					
❑ QS-5006	Dealing with the Devil	198?	2.50	5.00	10.00
❑ QS-5011	Two Sides of the Blues	198?	2.50	5.00	10.00
VANGUARD					
❑ VSD-79283	Cut You Loose!	1969	3.75	7.50	15.00
VERVE FORECAST					
❑ FT-3023 [M]	The James Cotton Blues Band	1967	6.25	12.50	25.00
❑ FTS-3023 [S]	The James Cotton Blues Band	1967	5.00	10.00	20.00
❑ FTS-3038	Pure Cotton	1968	5.00	10.00	20.00
COTTON PICKERS, THE					
Albums					
PHILIPS					
❑ PHM 200025 [M]	Country Guitar	1962	5.00	10.00	20.00
❑ PHS 600025 [S]	Country Guitar	1962	6.25	12.50	25.00
COUNT FIVE, THE					
45s					
DOUBLE SHOT					
❑ 104	Psychotic Reaction/They're Gonna Get You	1966	3.00	6.00	12.00
—Later pressings, with label logo at side					
❑ 104	Psychotic Reaction/They're Gonna Get You	1966	3.75	7.50	15.00
—First pressing, with label logo at top					
❑ 106	Peace of Mind/The Morning After	1966	3.00	6.00	12.00
❑ 110	You Must Believe Me/Teeny Bopper, Teeny Bopper	1967	3.00	6.00	12.00
❑ 115	Merry-Go-Round/Contrast	1967	3.00	6.00	12.00
❑ 125	Declaration of Independence/Revelation in Slow Motion	1968	3.00	6.00	12.00
❑ 141	Mailman/Pretty Big Mouth	1969	3.00	6.00	12.00
Albums					
DOUBLE SHOT					
❑ DSM-1001 [M]	Psychotic Reaction	1966	10.00	20.00	40.00
❑ DSS-5001 [R]	Psychotic Reaction	1966	6.25	12.50	25.00
COUNT ROCKIN' SIDNEY See ROCKIN' SIDNEY.					
COUNT STEPHEN See STEVE ALAIMO.					
COUNTRY BOYS, THE Also see DAVID GATES.					
45s					
DEL-FI					
❑ 4245	The Okie Surfer/Blue Surf	1964	10.00	20.00	40.00
COUNTRY HAMS, THE See PAUL McCARTNEY.					
COUNTRY JOE AND THE FISH Includes releases by "Country Joe McDonald."					
45s					
FANTASY					
❑ 758	Breakfast for Two/Lost My Connection	1976	—	2.00	4.00
❑ 765	Save the Whales/Oh Jamaica	1976	—	2.00	4.00
❑ 780	Love Is a Fire/I Need You	1976	—	2.00	4.00
❑ 814	Southern Cross/Coyote	1978	—	2.00	4.00
❑ 822	Bring Back the Sixties, Man/Sunshine Through My Window	1978	—	2.00	4.00
❑ 876	Private Parts/Take Time Out	1979	—	2.00	4.00
PHILCO-FORD					
❑ HP-35	Not So Sweet Martha Lorraine/Masked Marauder	1969	6.25	12.50	25.00
—4-inch plastic "Hip Pocket Record" with color sleeve					
VANGUARD					
❑ 35052	Not So Sweet Martha Lorraine/The Masked Marauder	1967	2.50	5.00	10.00
❑ 35059	Janis (Part 1)/Janis (Part 2)	1967	2.50	5.00	10.00
❑ 35061	Who Am I/Thursday	1968	2.50	5.00	10.00
❑ 35061 [PS]	Who Am I/Thursday	1968	5.00	10.00	20.00
❑ 35068	Rock and Soul (Part 1)/Rock and Soul (Part 2)	1968	2.50	5.00	10.00
❑ 35090	Here I Go Again/Baby, You're Driving Me Crazy	1969	2.00	4.00	8.00
❑ 35112	I-Feel-Like-I'm-Fixin'-to-Die Rag/Janis	1970	2.00	4.00	8.00
❑ 35133	Hold On, It's Coming/Playing with Fire	1971	—	2.50	5.00
—Starting here, as "Country Joe McDonald"					
❑ 35150	Hang On/Hand of Man	1972	—	2.50	5.00
❑ 35161	Fantasy/I Seen a Rocket	1972	—	2.50	5.00
❑ 35181	Doctor Hip/Satisfactorily	1973	—	2.00	4.00
❑ 35184	Chloe/Jesse James	1974	—	2.00	4.00
7-Inch Extended Plays					
RAG BABY					
❑ 1001	(contents unknown)	1966	25.00	50.00	100.00
❑ 1001 [PS]	Rag Baby	1966	50.00	100.00	200.00
—Actually an envelope in which the record came					
Albums					
CUSTOM FIDELITY					
❑ CFS-2348	Joe McDonald	1968	500.00	750.00	1000.
—Recorded in 1964, 200 copies were pressed for Joe McDonald.					
FANTASY					
❑ 9495	Paradise with an Ocean View	1975	2.50	5.00	10.00
❑ 9511	Love Is a Fire	1976	2.50	5.00	10.00
❑ 9525	Goodbye Blues	1977	2.50	5.00	10.00
❑ 9530	Reunion	1977	3.00	6.00	12.00
❑ 9544	Rock and Roll Music From the Planet Earth	1978	2.50	5.00	10.00
❑ 9586	Leisure Suite	1980	2.50	5.00	10.00
FIRST AMERICAN					
❑ PIC-3309	The Early Years	1979	2.50	5.00	10.00
MOBLIE FIDELITY					
❑ 1-056	Paradise with an Ocean View	1981	7.50	15.00	30.00
—Audiophile vinyl					
VANGUARD					
❑ VSD-27/28 [(2)]	The Life and Times of Country Joe & the Fish From Haight-Ashbury to Woodstock	1971	5.00	10.00	20.00
❑ VSD-85/86 [(2)]	The Essential Country Joe	1977	3.00	6.00	12.00
❑ VSD-6545	Country Joe & The Fish/Greatest Hits	1969	5.00	10.00	20.00
❑ VSD-6546	Thinking of Woody	1969	3.75	7.50	15.00
❑ VSD-6555	C.J. Fish	1970	5.00	10.00	20.00
❑ VSD-6557	Tonight I'm Singing Just for You	1970	3.75	7.50	15.00

Number	Title (A Side/B Side)	Yr	VG	VG+	NM
❏ VRS-9244 [M]	Electric Music for the Mind and Body	1967	5.00	10.00	20.00
—Gold label					
❏ VRS-9244 [M]	Electric Music for the Mind and Body	1967	25.00	50.00	100.00
—Black label					
❏ 9266/79266	I-Feel-Like-I'm-Fixin'-to-Die "Fish Game" Poster	1967	2.50	5.00	10.00
❏ VRS-9266 [M]	I-Feel-Like-I'm-Fixin'-to-Die	1967	5.00	10.00	20.00
❏ VSQ-40004/5 [(2)Q]	The Life and Times of Country Joe & the Fish From Haight-Ashbury to Woodstock	197?	10.00	20.00	40.00
❏ VSD-79244 [S]	Electric Music for the Mind and Body	1967	5.00	10.00	20.00
—Gold label					
❏ VSD-79244 [S]	Electric Music for the Mind and Body	1967	12.50	25.00	50.00
—Black label					
❏ VSD-79266 [S]	I-Feel-Like-I'm-Fixin'-to-Die	1967	5.00	10.00	20.00
❏ VSD-79277	Together	1968	5.00	10.00	20.00
❏ VSD-79299	Here We Are Again	1969	5.00	10.00	20.00
❏ VSD-79304	Hold On It's Coming	1971	3.75	7.50	15.00
❏ VSD-79315	War, War, War	1971	3.75	7.50	15.00
❏ VSD-79316	Incredible! Live!	1972	3.00	6.00	12.00
❏ VSD-79328	Paris Sessions	1973	3.00	6.00	12.00
❏ VSD-79348	Country Joe	1974	3.00	6.00	12.00

COUNTS, THE (1) Male vocal group from Indianapolis.
45s
DOT

Number	Title (A Side/B Side)	Yr	VG	VG+	NM
❏ 1188	Darling Dear/I Need You Always	1954	15.00	30.00	60.00
❏ 1199	Hot Tamales/Baby Don't You Know	1954	12.50	25.00	50.00
❏ 1210	My Dear, My Darling/She Won't Say Yes	1954	10.00	20.00	40.00
❏ 1226	Baby I Want You/Waitin' Around for You	1954	10.00	20.00	40.00
❏ 1235	Wailin' Little Mama/Let Me Go	1955	7.50	15.00	30.00
❏ 1243	From This Day On/Love and Understanding	1955	7.50	15.00	30.00
❏ 1265	I Need You Tonight/Sally Walker	1955	7.50	15.00	30.00
❏ 1275	To Our Love/Heartbreaker	1956	6.25	12.50	25.00
❏ 16105	Darling Dear/I Need You Always	1960	5.00	10.00	20.00

NOTE

Number	Title (A Side/B Side)	Yr	VG	VG+	NM
❏ 20000	Sweet Names/I Guess I Brought It All on Myself	1956	50.00	100.00	200.00

COUNTS, THE (2) Detroit-based funk group.
45s
AWARE

Number	Title (A Side/B Side)	Yr	VG	VG+	NM
❏ 038	Funk/Too Bad	1974	—	2.50	5.00
❏ 046	Sacrifice/Funk Pump	1974	—	2.50	5.00
❏ 049	At the Fair/I'm the Music	1975	—	2.50	5.00
❏ 054	Magic Ride/Short Cut	1975	—	2.50	5.00

WESTBOUND

Number	Title (A Side/B Side)	Yr	VG	VG+	NM
❏ 191	Thinking Single/Why Not Start All Over Again	1972	—	2.50	5.00

Albums
AWARE

Number	Title (A Side/B Side)	Yr	VG	VG+	NM
❏ 2002	Love Sign	1973	6.25	12.50	25.00
❏ 2006	Funk Pump	1975	5.00	10.00	20.00

WESTBOUND

Number	Title (A Side/B Side)	Yr	VG	VG+	NM
❏ 2011	What's Up Front That Counts	1972	7.50	15.00	30.00

COUNTS, THE (U) It appears as if none of these are by group (1) or (2), and they aren't all by the same group.
45s
COUNT

Number	Title (A Side/B Side)	Yr	VG	VG+	NM
❏ 5	The Beat/After Beat	196?	5.00	10.00	20.00

MANCO

Number	Title (A Side/B Side)	Yr	VG	VG+	NM
❏ 1060	Surfer's Paradise/Chug-a-Lug	1964	10.00	20.00	40.00

MERCURY

Number	Title (A Side/B Side)	Yr	VG	VG+	NM
❏ 71318	Shake the Town/Teenage Guy and Girl	1958	3.75	7.50	15.00

PANORAMA

Number	Title (A Side/B Side)	Yr	VG	VG+	NM
❏ 9	Chitlins, Etc./Clyde, Clyde, The Cow's Outside	1965	2.50	5.00	10.00
❏ 33	Come Now/Since I Fell for You	1966	2.50	5.00	10.00

SEA CREST

Number	Title (A Side/B Side)	Yr	VG	VG+	NM
❏ 6003	Turn On Song/Enchanted Sea	1964	10.00	20.00	40.00
❏ 6004	Doggin'/And Then I Cried	1964	3.75	7.50	15.00

SHRINE

Number	Title (A Side/B Side)	Yr	VG	VG+	NM
❏ 117	Peaches Baby/My Only Love	1966	1000.	2000.	3000.

SMASH

Number	Title (A Side/B Side)	Yr	VG	VG+	NM
❏ 1821	Stormy Weather/True Love's Gone	1963	2.50	5.00	10.00

YES

Number	Title (A Side/B Side)	Yr	VG	VG+	NM
❏ 102	Stronger Than Ever/Gospel Truth	196?	100.00	200.00	400.00
❏ 103	Ask the Lonely/If You Don't Love Me	196?	100.00	200.00	400.00

COURCY, JOANNE
45s
TWIRL

Number	Title (A Side/B Side)	Yr	VG	VG+	NM
❏ 2020	Silly Girl/My Poor Broken Heart	1966	7.50	15.00	30.00
❏ 2026	I Got the Power/I'm Gonna Keep You	1966	175.00	350.00	700.00

COURTLAND, JEROME
Albums
JUBILEE

Number	Title (A Side/B Side)	Yr	VG	VG+	NM
❏ LP 22 [10]	Through a Long and Sleepless Night	1955	10.00	20.00	40.00

COURTNEY, LOU
45s
BUDDAH

Number	Title (A Side/B Side)	Yr	VG	VG+	NM
❏ 121	Let Me Turn You On/Tryin' to Find My Woman	1969	2.00	4.00	8.00

EPIC

Number	Title (A Side/B Side)	Yr	VG	VG+	NM
❏ 11062	What Do You Want Me to Do/Beware	1973	—	2.50	5.00
❏ 11088	I Don't Need Nobody Else/Why	1974	—	2.50	5.00
❏ 50046	The Best Thing a Man Can Do for His Woman/I'm Serious About Lovin' You	1974	—	2.50	5.00
❏ 50070	Just to Let Him Break Your Heart/Somebody New Is Lovin' You	1975	—	2.50	5.00

IMPERIAL

Number	Title (A Side/B Side)	Yr	VG	VG+	NM
❏ 66006	Come On Home/The Man with the Cigar	1963	3.00	6.00	12.00
❏ 66043	Little Old Love Maker/Professional Lover	1964	3.00	6.00	12.00

PHILIPS

Number	Title (A Side/B Side)	Yr	VG	VG+	NM
❏ 40287	I Watched You Slowly Slip Away/I'll Cry If I Want To	1965	25.00	50.00	100.00

POP-SIDE

Number	Title (A Side/B Side)	Yr	VG	VG+	NM
❏ 4594	Hey Joyce/I'm Mad About You	1967	2.50	5.00	10.00
❏ 4596	If the Shoe Fits/It's Love Now	1968	2.50	5.00	10.00

RIVERSIDE

Number	Title (A Side/B Side)	Yr	VG	VG+	NM
❏ 4588	Skate Now/I Can Always Tell	1966	2.50	5.00	10.00
❏ 4589	Do the Thing/Man Is Lonely	1967	2.50	5.00	10.00
❏ 4591	You Ain't Ready/I've Got Just the Thing	1967	2.50	5.00	10.00

VERVE

Number	Title (A Side/B Side)	Yr	VG	VG+	NM
❏ 10602	Do the Horse/Rubber Neckin'	1968	2.00	4.00	8.00
❏ 10631	Please Stay/You Can Give Your Love to Me	1968	2.00	4.00	8.00

Albums
EPIC

Number	Title (A Side/B Side)	Yr	VG	VG+	NM
❏ KE 33011	I'm in Need of Love	1974	3.00	6.00	12.00

RCA VICTOR

Number	Title (A Side/B Side)	Yr	VG	VG+	NM
❏ APL1-1969	Buffalo Smoke	1976	3.00	6.00	12.00

RIVERSIDE

Number	Title (A Side/B Side)	Yr	VG	VG+	NM
❏ 92000	Skate Now (Shing-a-Ling)	1967	6.25	12.50	25.00

COURTSHIP, THE
45s
TAMLA

Number	Title (A Side/B Side)	Yr	VG	VG+	NM
❏ 54217	It's the Same Old Love/Last Row, First Balcony	1972	—	2.50	5.00
❏ 54227	Oops, It Just Slipped Out/Love Ain't Love	1973	—	2.50	5.00

COURVALE, KEITH
45s
DOT

Number	Title (A Side/B Side)	Yr	VG	VG+	NM
❏ 15844	Trapped Love/Steelworker Blues	1958	25.00	50.00	100.00

COUSINS, THE (1)
45s
DECCA

Number	Title (A Side/B Side)	Yr	VG	VG+	NM
❏ 30609	I'm in Love with You/Be Nice to Me	1958	5.00	10.00	20.00

FIDELITY

Number	Title (A Side/B Side)	Yr	VG	VG+	NM
❏ 3010	Love Is Blind/How We'll Love	1959	7.50	15.00	30.00

COUSINS, THE (2)
45s
PARKWAY

Number	Title (A Side/B Side)	Yr	VG	VG+	NM
❏ 823	St. Louis Blues/No One Knows	1961	3.75	7.50	15.00
❏ 848	When My Baby Smiles at Me/Some of These Days	1962	3.00	6.00	12.00
❏ 870	Sweet Georgia Brown/Outside the Wall	1963	3.00	6.00	12.00

Albums
PARKWAY

Number	Title (A Side/B Side)	Yr	VG	VG+	NM
❏ P-7005 [M]	Music of the Strip	1961	5.00	10.00	20.00
❏ SP-7005 [S]	Music of the Strip	1961	6.25	12.50	25.00

COUSINS, THE (U) Neither group (1) nor group (2).
45s
VERSATILE

Number	Title (A Side/B Side)	Yr	VG	VG+	NM
❏ 105	Down That Lonely Road/(B-side unknown)	1960	20.00	40.00	80.00

WYNNE

Number	Title (A Side/B Side)	Yr	VG	VG+	NM
❏ 132	Guilty/(B-side unknown)	1959	125.00	250.00	500.00

COVAY, DON Also see THE SOLDIER BOYS.
45s
ARNOLD

Number	Title (A Side/B Side)	Yr	VG	VG+	NM
❏ 1002	Pony Time/Love Boat	1961	3.00	6.00	12.00
—As "Don Covay and the Goodtimers"					
❏ 1002	Pony Time/Love Boat	1961	6.25	12.50	25.00
—As "The Goodtimers"					

ATLANTIC

Number	Title (A Side/B Side)	Yr	VG	VG+	NM
❏ 1147	Bip Bop Bip/Silver Dollar	1957	20.00	40.00	80.00
—As "Pretty Boy"					
❏ 2280	The Boomerang/Daddy Loves Baby	1965	2.50	5.00	10.00
❏ 2286	Please Do Something/A Woman's Love	1965	2.50	5.00	10.00
❏ 2301	See Saw/I Never Get Enough of Your Love	1965	2.50	5.00	10.00
❏ 2323	Sookie Sookie/Watching the Late Late Shoe	1966	2.50	5.00	10.00
❏ 2340	You Put Something On Me/Iron Out the Rough Spots	1966	2.50	5.00	10.00
❏ 2357	Somebody's Got to Love You/Temptation Was Too Strong	1966	2.50	5.00	10.00
❏ 2375	Shing-Aling '67/I Was There	1967	2.50	5.00	10.00
❏ 2407	40 Days — 40 Nights/The Usual Place	1967	2.50	5.00	10.00
❏ 2440	You've Got Me on the Critical List/Never Had No Love	1967	2.50	5.00	10.00
❏ 2481	Chain of Fools/Prove It	1968	2.50	5.00	10.00
❏ 2494	Don't Let Go/It's In the Wind	1968	2.50	5.00	10.00
❏ 2521	Gonna Send You Back to Your Mama/House on the Corner	1968	2.50	5.00	10.00
❏ 2565	I Stole Some Love/Snake in the Grass	1968	2.50	5.00	10.00
❏ 2609	Sweet Pea/C.C. Rider Blues	1969	2.50	5.00	10.00
❏ 2666	Ice Cream Man (The Gimmie Game)/Black Woman	1969	2.50	5.00	10.00
❏ 2725	Everything I Do Goin' Be Funky/Key to the Kighway	1970	2.00	4.00	8.00
❏ 2742	Soul Stirrer/Sookie Sookie	1970	2.00	4.00	8.00

BIG

Number	Title (A Side/B Side)	Yr	VG	VG+	NM
❏ 617	Switchin' in the Kitchen/Rockin' the Mule	1958	20.00	40.00	80.00
—As "Pretty Boy"					

BIG TOP

Number	Title (A Side/B Side)	Yr	VG	VG+	NM
❏ 3060	Hey There/I'm Coming Down with the Blues	1960	3.75	7.50	15.00

BLAZE

Number	Title (A Side/B Side)	Yr	VG	VG+	NM
❏ 350	Standing in the Doorway/(B-side unknown)	1958	7.50	15.00	30.00

CAMEO

Number	Title (A Side/B Side)	Yr	VG	VG+	NM
❏ 239	The Popeye Waddle/One Little Bot Had Money	1962	3.00	6.00	12.00
❏ 251	Wiggle Wobble/Do the Bug	1963	3.00	6.00	12.00

COLUMBIA

Number	Title (A Side/B Side)	Yr	VG	VG+	NM
❏ 41981	Shake Wid the Snake/Every Which-a Way	1961	5.00	10.00	20.00
❏ 42058	Hand Jive Workout/See About Me	1961	5.00	10.00	20.00
❏ 42197	Now That I Need You/Teen Life Swag	1961	25.00	50.00	100.00

EPIC

Number	Title (A Side/B Side)	Yr	VG	VG+	NM
❏ 9484	It's Twistin' Time/Twistin' Train	1961	3.75	7.50	15.00
—As "The Goodtimers"					

JANUS

Number	Title (A Side/B Side)	Yr	VG	VG+	NM
❏ 164	Sweet Thang/Standing in the Grits Line	1971	—	3.00	6.00
❏ 181	Daddy Please Don't Go Out/Shoes Under My Bed	1972	—	3.00	6.00

Number	Title (A Side/B Side)	Yr	VG	VG+	NM
LANDA					
❑ 704	You're Good for Me/Truth of the Lite	1965	2.50	5.00	10.00
MERCURY					
❑ 71385	I Was Checkin' Out She Was Checkin' In/Money	1973	—	3.00	6.00
❑ 71430	Somebody's Been Enjoying My Home/Bad Mouthing	1973	—	3.00	6.00
❑ 71469	It's Better to Have (And Don't Need)/Leave Him (Part 1)	1974	—	3.00	6.00
❑ 73311	Overtime Man/Dungeon #3	1972	—	3.00	6.00
❑ 73648	Rumble in the Jungle/We Can't Make It No More	1975	—	3.00	6.00
NEWMAN					
❑ 500	Badd Boy//(Instrumental)	1980	—	2.50	5.00
PARKWAY					
❑ 894	Ain't That Silly/Turn It On	1964	3.00	6.00	12.00
❑ 910	The Froog/One Little Boy Had Money	1964	3.00	6.00	12.00
PHILADELPHIA INT'L.					
❑ 3594	Right Time for Love/No Tell Motel	1976	—	2.50	5.00
❑ 3602	Travelin' in Heavy Traffic/Once You Have It	1976	—	2.50	5.00
ROSEMART					
❑ 801	Mercy Mercy/Can't Stay Away	1964	3.75	7.50	15.00
❑ 802	Take This Hurt Off Me/Please Don't Let Me Know	1964	3.00	6.00	12.00
SUE					
❑ 709	Betty Jean/Believe It or Not	1958	7.50	15.00	30.00
U-VON					
❑ 102	Back to the Roots (Part 1)/Back to the Roots (Part 2)	1977	—	2.50	5.00
Albums					
ATLANTIC					
❑ 8104 [M]	Mercy	1965	10.00	20.00	40.00
❑ SD 8104 [S]	Mercy	1965	12.50	25.00	50.00
❑ 8120 [M]	See Saw	1966	10.00	20.00	40.00
❑ SD 8120 [S]	See Saw	1966	12.50	25.00	50.00
❑ SD 8237	The House of Blue Lights	1969	6.25	12.50	25.00
JANUS					
❑ 3038	Different Strokes for Different Folks	1972	3.75	7.50	15.00
MERCURY					
❑ SRM-1-653	Super Dude I	1973	3.00	6.00	12.00
❑ SRM-1-1020	Hot Blood	1974	3.00	6.00	12.00
❑ 835030-1	Checkin' In with Don Covay	1988	2.50	5.00	10.00
PHILADELPHIA INT'L.					
❑ PZ 33958	Travelin' In Heavy Traffic	1977	2.50	5.00	10.00

COVEN
45s
Number	Title (A Side/B Side)	Yr	VG	VG+	NM
ABC					
❑ 11377	One Tin Soldier (The Legend of Billy Jack)/I Think You Always Knew	1973	—	3.00	6.00
BUDDAH					
❑ 440	I Need a Hundred of You/(B-side unknown)	1974	—	2.00	4.00
LION					
❑ 192	Nightingale/Jailhouse Rock	1972	—	2.00	4.00
MERCURY					
❑ 72973	Wicked Woman/White Witch of Rose Hall	1969	—	3.00	6.00
❑ 72973 [PS]	Wicked Woman/White Witch of Rose Hall	1969	2.50	5.00	10.00
MGM					
❑ 14308	One Tin Soldier/I Guess It's a Beautiful Day Today	1971	—	2.50	5.00
❑ 14348	Nightingale/Jailhouse Rock	1972	—	2.00	4.00
SGC					
❑ 003	I Shall Be Released/I've Come Too Far	1968	—	3.00	6.00
WARNER BROS.					
❑ BJS 0101	One Tin Soldier, The Legend of Billy Jack/Johnnie	1973	—	2.00	4.00
—*B-side by Teresa Kelly*					
❑ 7509	One Tin Soldier, The Legend of Billy Jack/Say Goodbye, 'Cause You're Leavin'	1971	—	2.50	5.00
Albums					
BUDDAH					
❑ BDS-5614	Blood on the Snow	1974	3.00	6.00	12.00
MERCURY					
❑ SR 61239	Witchcraft Destroys Minds and Reaps Souls	1969	3.75	7.50	15.00
MGM					
❑ SE-4801	Coven	1971	3.00	6.00	12.00

COWSILL, BILL Also see THE COWSILLS.
45s
Number	Title (A Side/B Side)	Yr	VG	VG+	NM
MGM					
❑ 14166	When Everybody's Here/I Wish I Could Say the Same About You	1970	—	3.00	6.00
Albums					
MGM					
❑ SE-4706	Nervous Breakthrough	1970	3.75	7.50	15.00

COWSILL, JOHN Also see THE COWSILLS.
45s
Number	Title (A Side/B Side)	Yr	VG	VG+	NM
MGM					
❑ 14003	Path of Love/Captain Sad and His Ship of Fools	1968	2.00	4.00	8.00

COWSILL, SUSAN Also see THE COWSILLS.
45s
Number	Title (A Side/B Side)	Yr	VG	VG+	NM
WARNER BROS.					
❑ 8232	It Might As Well Rain Until September/Mohammad's Radio	1976	—	2.50	5.00
❑ 8333	The Next Time That I See You/I Think of You	1977	—	2.50	5.00

COWSILLS, THE Also see BILL COWSILL; JOHN COWSILL; SUSAN COWSILL.
45s
Number	Title (A Side/B Side)	Yr	VG	VG+	NM
GASATANKA/ROCKVILLE					
❑ 6139	Christmastime (Song for Marissa)/Some Good Years	1993	—	—	3.00
—*Green vinyl*					
❑ 6139	Christmastime (Song For Marisa)/Some Good Years	1993	—	2.00	4.00
—*Clear vinyl*					
❑ 6139 [PS]	Christmastime (Song for Marissa)/Some Good Years	1993	—	—	3.00

Number	Title (A Side/B Side)	Yr	VG	VG+	NM
JODA					
❑ 103	All I Really Wanta Be Is Me/And the Next Day, Too	1965	7.50	15.00	30.00
LONDON					
❑ 149	On My Side/There Is No Child	1971	2.00	4.00	8.00
❑ 153	You/Crystal Claps	1971	2.00	4.00	8.00
❑ 170	Blue Road/Covered Wagon	1972	2.00	4.00	8.00
MGM					
❑ 13810	The Rain, the Park and Other Things/River Blue	1967	2.50	5.00	10.00
❑ 13810 [PS]	The Rain, the Park and Other Things/River Blue	1967	3.00	6.00	12.00
❑ 13886	We Can Fly/A Time for Remembrance	1967	2.00	4.00	8.00
❑ 13886 [PS]	We Can Fly/A Time for Remembrance	1967	3.00	6.00	12.00
❑ 13909	In Need of a Friend/Mister Flynn	1968	2.00	4.00	8.00
❑ 13909 [PS]	In Need of a Friend/Mister Flynn	1968	3.00	6.00	12.00
❑ 13944	Indian Lake/Newspaper Blanket	1968	2.00	4.00	8.00
—*Second pressings have blue and gold labels*					
❑ 13944	Indian Lake/Newspaper Blanket	1968	2.50	5.00	10.00
—*First pressings have black labels*					
❑ 13944 [PS]	Indian Lake/Newspaper Blanket	1968	3.00	6.00	12.00
❑ 13981	Poor Baby/Meet Me at the Wishing Well	1968	2.00	4.00	8.00
❑ 14011	The Impossible Years/Candy Kid	1968	2.00	4.00	8.00
❑ 14026	Hair/What Is Happy	1969	3.00	6.00	12.00
❑ 14063	The Prophecy of Daniel and John the Divine (Six-Six-Six)/Gotta Get Away from It All	1969	2.00	4.00	8.00
❑ 14063 [PS]	The Prophecy of Daniel and John the Divine (Six-Six-Six)/Gotta Get Away from It All	1969	3.75	7.50	15.00
❑ 14084	Silver Threads and Golden Needles/Love, American Style	1969	2.50	5.00	10.00
❑ 14084 [PS]	Silver Threads and Golden Needles/Love, American Style	1969	3.00	6.00	12.00
❑ 14106	Start to Love/Two by Two	1970	2.00	4.00	8.00
PHILIPS					
❑ 40382	Most of All/Siamese Cat	1966	2.50	5.00	10.00
❑ 40382 [PS]	Most of All/Siamese Cat	1966	3.75	7.50	15.00
❑ 40406	Party Girl/What's It Gonna Be Like	1966	2.50	5.00	10.00
❑ 40437	A Most Peculiar Man/Could It Be, Let Me Know	1967	2.50	5.00	10.00
7-Inch Extended Plays					
MGM					
❑ PEP-1	The Milk Song/All My Days//Nothing to Do/The Fun Song	1969	2.50	5.00	10.00
—*American Dairy Association promotional item*					
❑ PEP-1 [PS]	The Cowsills Collector's Record	1969	6.25	12.50	25.00
—*American Dairy Association promotional item*					
Albums					
LONDON					
❑ PS 587	On My Side	1971	7.50	15.00	30.00
MGM					
❑ GAS-103	The Cowsills (Golden Archive Series)	1970	3.75	7.50	15.00
❑ E-4498 [M]	The Cowsills	1967	5.00	10.00	20.00
❑ SE-4498 [S]	The Cowsills	1967	3.75	7.50	15.00
❑ E-4534 [M]	We Can Fly	1968	7.50	15.00	30.00
—*Appears to exist only as a yellow label promo*					
❑ SE-4534 [S]	We Can Fly	1968	3.75	7.50	15.00
❑ E-4554 [M]	Captain Sad and His Ship of Fools	1968	10.00	20.00	40.00
—*Mono appears to be yellow label promo only*					
❑ SE-4554 [S]	Captain Sad and His Ship of Fools	1968	3.75	7.50	15.00
❑ SE-4597	The Best of the Cowsills	1968	3.75	7.50	15.00
❑ SE-4619	The Cowsills in Concert	1969	3.75	7.50	15.00
❑ SE-4639	II X II	1969	5.00	10.00	20.00
WING					
❑ SRW-16354	The Cowsills Plus the Lincoln Park Zoo	1968	3.00	6.00	12.00

COXON'S ARMY Pat Benatar was in this group.
Albums
Number	Title (A Side/B Side)	Yr	VG	VG+	NM
TRACE					
❑ (# unknown)	Coxon's Army	1975	100.00	200.00	400.00

CRABBY APPLETON
45s
Number	Title (A Side/B Side)	Yr	VG	VG+	NM
ELEKTRA					
❑ 45687	Go Back/Try	1970	—	3.00	6.00
❑ 45702	Lucy/Some Madness	1970	—	2.50	5.00
❑ 45716	Grab On/Can't Live My Life	1971	—	2.50	5.00
❑ 45754	It's So Hard/Tomorrow Is a New Day	1971	—	2.50	5.00
❑ 45781	Love Can Change Everything/Smokin' in the Mornin'	1972	—	2.50	5.00
Albums					
ELEKTRA					
❑ EKS-74067	Crabby Appleton	1970	3.75	7.50	15.00
❑ EKS-74106	Rotten to the Core!	1971	3.75	7.50	15.00

CRACK THE SKY
45s
Number	Title (A Side/B Side)	Yr	VG	VG+	NM
LIFESONG					
❑ 1763	Give Myself to You/A Night on the Town (With Snow White)	1978	—	2.00	4.00
❑ 1764	Long Nights/Give Myself to You	1978	—	2.00	4.00
❑ 1782	I Am the Walrus/Lighten Up McGraw	1979	—	2.00	4.00
❑ 45003	She's a Dancer/Robots for Ronnie	1976	—	2.00	4.00
❑ 45016	We Want Mine (We Don't Want Your Money)/Invaders from Mars	1976	—	2.00	4.00
❑ 45081	Techni-Generation/Suspicion	1980	—	2.00	4.00
Albums					
GRUDGE					
❑ 4500-1-F	From the Greenhouse	1989	2.50	5.00	10.00
LIFESONG					
❑ LS 6000	Crack the Sky	1975	3.75	7.50	15.00
❑ LS 6005	Animal Notes	1976	3.75	7.50	15.00
❑ LS 6015	Safety in Numbers	1976	3.75	7.50	15.00
❑ LS 8133	Photoflamingo	1981	2.50	5.00	10.00
❑ PZ 34994	Crack the Sky	1977	2.50	5.00	10.00
—*Reissue of 6000*					
❑ PZ 34998	Animal Notes	1977	2.50	5.00	10.00
—*Reissue of 6004*					
❑ PZ 35041	Safety in Numbers	1978	2.50	5.00	10.00
—*Reissue of 6015*					
❑ PZ 35620	Live Sky	1978	3.00	6.00	12.00

C

Number	Title (A Side/B Side)	Yr	VG	VG+	NM

CRADDOCK, BILLY "CRASH" Also recorded as "Bill Craddock" and "Crash Craddock," both included below.

45s

ABC

Number	Title (A Side/B Side)	Yr	VG	VG+	NM
❏ 11342	Afraid I'll Want to Love Her One More Time/Treat Her Right	1972	—	3.00	6.00
❏ 11349	Don't Be Angry/I'm a White Boy	1973	—	3.00	6.00
❏ 11364	Slippin' and Slidin'/Living Example	1973	—	3.00	6.00
❏ 11379	'Till the Water Stops Runnin'/What Does a Loser Say	1973	—	3.00	6.00
❏ 11412	Sweet Magnolia Blossom/Home Is Such a Lonely Place to Go	1973	—	3.00	6.00
❏ 11437	Rub It In/It's Hard to Love a Hungry, Worried Man	1974	—	3.00	6.00
❏ 12013	Rub It In/It's Hard to Love a Hungry, Worried Man	1974	—	2.00	4.00
❏ 12036	Ruby, Baby/Walk When Love Walks	1974	—	2.50	5.00
❏ 12068	Still Thinkin' 'Bout You/Stay a Little Longer in Your Bed	1975	—	2.50	5.00
❏ 12104	I Love the Blues and the Boogie Woogie/No Deposit, No Return	1975	—	2.50	5.00
❏ 12335	Another Woman/The Words Still Rhyme	1978	—	2.00	4.00
❏ 12357	Think I'll Go Somewhere (And Cry Myself to Sleep)/It All Came Back	1978	—	2.00	4.00
❏ 12384	Don Juan/Things Are Mostly Fine	1978	—	2.00	4.00

ABC DOT

Number	Title (A Side/B Side)	Yr	VG	VG+	NM
❏ 17584	Easy As Pie/She's Mine	1975	—	2.50	5.00
❏ 17619	Walk Softly/She's About a Mover	1976	—	2.50	5.00
❏ 17635	You Rubbed It In All Wrong/I Need Somebody to Love Me	1976	—	2.50	5.00
❏ 17659	Broken Down in Tiny Pieces/Shake It Easy	1976	—	2.50	5.00
❏ 17682	Just a Little Thing/The First Time	1977	—	2.50	5.00
❏ 17701	A Tear Fell/A Piece of the Rock	1977	—	2.50	5.00
❏ 17723	The First Time/Walk When Love Walks	1977	—	2.50	5.00

ATLANTIC

Number	Title (A Side/B Side)	Yr	VG	VG+	NM
❏ 88851	Just Another Miserable Day (Here in Paradise)/Softly Diana	1989	—	—	3.00
❏ 88851 [PS]	Just Another Miserable Day (Here in Paradise)/Softly Diana	1989	—	2.00	4.00

CAPITOL

Number	Title (A Side/B Side)	Yr	VG	VG+	NM
❏ 4545	I Cheated on a Good Woman's Love/Not a Day Goes By	1978	—	2.00	4.00
❏ 4575	I've Been Too Long Lonely Baby/Jailhouse Rock	1978	—	2.00	4.00
❏ 4624	Hubba Hubba/Let's Go Back to the Beginning	1978	—	2.00	4.00
❏ 4672	If I Could Write a Song As Beautiful As You/Never Ending	1978	—	2.00	4.00
❏ 4707	My Mama Never Heard Me Sing/As Long As I Live	1979	—	2.00	4.00
❏ 4753	Robinhood/We Never Made It to Chicago	1979	—	2.00	4.00
❏ 4792	Till I Stop Shaking/Sneak Out of Love with You	1979	—	2.00	4.00
❏ 4838	I Just Had You on My Mind/You Just Wanta Be Mine	1980	—	2.00	4.00
❏ 4875	Sea Cruise/She's Got Legs	1980	—	2.00	4.00
❏ 4935	A Real Cowboy (You Say You're)/One Dream Coming, One Dream Going	1980	—	2.00	4.00
❏ 4972	It Was You/Betty Ruth	1981	—	2.00	4.00
❏ 5011	I Just Need You For Tonight/Leave Your Love A-Smokin'	1981	—	2.00	4.00
❏ 5051	Now That the Feeling's Gone/She's Good to Me	1981	—	2.00	4.00
❏ 5139	Love Busted/Darlin' Take Care of Yourself	1982	—	2.00	4.00
❏ 5170	The New Will Never Wear Off on You/Hold Me Tight	1982	—	2.00	4.00

CARTWHEEL

Number	Title (A Side/B Side)	Yr	VG	VG+	NM
❏ 193	Knock Three Times/The Best I Ever Had	1971	—	3.50	7.00
❏ 196	Dream Lover/I Ran Out of Time	1971	—	3.50	7.00
❏ 201	You Better Move On/Confidence and Common Sense	1971	—	3.50	7.00
❏ 210	Ain't Nothin' Shakin' (But the Leaves on the Trees)/She's My Angel	1972	—	3.50	7.00
❏ 216	I'm Gonna Knock on Your Door/What He Don't Know	1972	—	3.50	7.00
❏ 222	Afraid I'll Want to Love Her One More Time/Treat Her Right	1972	3.00	6.00	12.00

CEE CEE

Number	Title (A Side/B Side)	Yr	VG	VG+	NM
❏ 5400	Tell Me When I'm Hot/When the Feeling Is Right	1983	—	2.50	5.00

CHART

Number	Title (A Side/B Side)	Yr	VG	VG+	NM
❏ 1004	Go On Home Girl/Learning to Live Without You	1967	2.00	4.00	8.00
❏ 1025	Your Love Is What Is/Anything That's Part of You	1968	2.00	4.00	8.00
❏ 1415	There Ought to Be a Law/Two Arms Full of Lonely	1966	2.50	5.00	10.00
❏ 1450	Whipping Boy/The Love We Live Without	1967	2.50	5.00	10.00
❏ 5126	Go On Home Girl/Whipping Boy	1971	2.00	4.00	8.00
❏ 5154	Your Love Is What Is/Whipping Boy	1972	2.00	4.00	8.00

COLONIAL

Number	Title (A Side/B Side)	Yr	VG	VG+	NM
❏ 721	Bird Doggin'/Millionaire	1958	10.00	20.00	40.00

COLUMBIA

Number	Title (A Side/B Side)	Yr	VG	VG+	NM
❏ 41316	Am I to Be the One/I Miss You So Much	1959	6.25	12.50	25.00
❏ 41367	Sweetie Pie/Blabbermouth	1959	7.50	15.00	30.00
❏ 41470	Don't Destroy Me/Boom Boom Baby	1959	6.25	12.50	25.00
❏ 41470 [PS]	Don't Destroy Me/Boom Boom Baby	1959	12.50	25.00	50.00
❏ 41536	I Want That/Since She Turned Seventeen	1960	7.50	15.00	30.00
❏ 41619	All I Want Is You/Letter of Love	1960	6.25	12.50	25.00
❏ 41619 [PS]	All I Want Is You/Letter of Love	1960	12.50	25.00	50.00
❏ 41677	One Last Kiss/Is It True or False	1960	5.00	10.00	20.00
❏ 41822	Heavenly Love/Good Time Billy	1961	5.00	10.00	20.00

DATE

Number	Title (A Side/B Side)	Yr	VG	VG+	NM
❏ 1007	Lulu Lee/Ah, Poor Little Baby	1958	10.00	20.00	40.00

KING

Number	Title (A Side/B Side)	Yr	VG	VG+	NM
❏ 5912	Betty, Betty/Right Around the Corner	1964	6.25	12.50	25.00
❏ 5924	My Baby's Got Flat Feet/One Heartache Too Many	1964	6.25	12.50	25.00
❏ 5964	Teardrops on Your Letter/Love You More Everyday	1964	5.00	10.00	20.00

MERCURY

Number	Title (A Side/B Side)	Yr	VG	VG+	NM
❏ 71811	Truly True/How Lonely He Must Be	1961	5.00	10.00	20.00
❏ 71862	A Diamond Is Forever/Old King Cole	1962	6.25	12.50	25.00

Albums

ABC

Number	Title (A Side/B Side)	Yr	VG	VG+	NM
❏ X-777	Two Sides of "Crash"	1973	3.75	7.50	15.00
—Retitled version of above					
❏ X-777	Afraid I'll Want to Love Her One More Time	1973	6.25	12.50	25.00
❏ X-788	Mr. Country Rock	1973	3.75	7.50	15.00
❏ X-817	Rub It In	1974	3.00	6.00	12.00
—Multicolor label					
❏ X-817	Rub It In	1974	3.75	7.50	15.00
—Black label					
❏ X-850	Greatest Hits — Volume One	1975	3.00	6.00	12.00
❏ ABCD-875	Still Thinkin' Bout You	1975	3.00	6.00	12.00
❏ AB-1078	Billy "Crash" Craddock Sings His Greatest Hits	1978	2.50	5.00	10.00

ABC DOT

Number	Title (A Side/B Side)	Yr	VG	VG+	NM
❏ DOSD-2040	Easy As Pie	1976	3.00	6.00	12.00
❏ 2063	Crash	1976	3.00	6.00	12.00
❏ 2082	Live!	1977	3.00	6.00	12.00

ATLANTIC

Number	Title (A Side/B Side)	Yr	VG	VG+	NM
❏ 82012	Back on Track	1989	3.00	6.00	12.00

CAPITOL

Number	Title (A Side/B Side)	Yr	VG	VG+	NM
❏ ST-11758	Billy "Crash" Craddock	1978	2.50	5.00	10.00
❏ SW-11853	Turning Up and Turning On	1978	2.50	5.00	10.00
❏ ST-11946	Laughing and Crying, Living and Dying	1979	2.50	5.00	10.00
❏ ST-12054	Changes	1980	2.50	5.00	10.00
❏ ST-12249	The New Will Never Wear Off	1981	2.50	5.00	10.00
❏ ST-12304	Greatest Hits	1983	2.50	5.00	10.00

CARTWHEEL

Number	Title (A Side/B Side)	Yr	VG	VG+	NM
❏ 193	Knock Three Times	1971	5.00	10.00	20.00
❏ 05001	You Better Move On	1972	5.00	10.00	20.00

CHART

Number	Title (A Side/B Side)	Yr	VG	VG+	NM
❏ 1053	The Best of Billy Crash Craddock	1973	3.75	7.50	15.00

HARMONY

Number	Title (A Side/B Side)	Yr	VG	VG+	NM
❏ KH 32186	Billy "Crash" Craddock	1973	3.00	6.00	12.00

KING

Number	Title (A Side/B Side)	Yr	VG	VG+	NM
❏ 912 [M]	I'm Tore Up	1964	25.00	50.00	100.00

MCA

Number	Title (A Side/B Side)	Yr	VG	VG+	NM
❏ 662	Greatest Hits — Volume One	1981	2.00	4.00	8.00
—Reissue of ABC 850					
❏ 663	Billy "Crash" Craddock Sings His Greatest Hits	1981	2.00	4.00	8.00
—Reissue of ABC 1078					
❏ 664	Easy As Pie	1981	2.00	4.00	8.00
—Reissue of ABC Dot 2040					
❏ 665	Live!	1981	2.00	4.00	8.00
—Reissue of ABC Dot 2082					
❏ 666	The First Time	1981	2.00	4.00	8.00
❏ 4165 [(2)]	The Best of Billy "Crash" Craddock	198?	3.00	6.00	12.00

MCA DOT

Number	Title (A Side/B Side)	Yr	VG	VG+	NM
❏ 39054	Crash Craddock	1986	2.50	5.00	10.00

STARDAY

Number	Title (A Side/B Side)	Yr	VG	VG+	NM
❏ 3005	16 Favorite Hits	1978	2.50	5.00	10.00

CRAIG, JIMMY

45s

BRILL

Number	Title (A Side/B Side)	Yr	VG	VG+	NM
❏ 1	All for You/Gonna Love My Baby	1959	20.00	40.00	80.00

IMPERIAL

Number	Title (A Side/B Side)	Yr	VG	VG+	NM
❏ 5592	Walking in Darkness/Oh Little Girl	1959	3.75	7.50	15.00

WARWICK

Number	Title (A Side/B Side)	Yr	VG	VG+	NM
❏ 542	Drifter/Let Me Stay	1960	3.75	7.50	15.00

CRAIG, THE

45s

FONTANA

Number	Title (A Side/B Side)	Yr	VG	VG+	NM
❏ 1579	I Must Be Mad/Suspense	1967	6.25	12.50	25.00

CRAMER, FLOYD

45s

ABBOTT

Number	Title (A Side/B Side)	Yr	VG	VG+	NM
❏ 142	Little Brown Jug/Dancin' Diane	1953	3.75	7.50	15.00
❏ 146	Fancy Pants/Five Foot Two, Eyes of Blue	1953	3.75	7.50	15.00
—Black vinyl					
❏ 146	Fancy Pants/Five Foot Two, Eyes of Blue	1953	5.00	10.00	20.00
—Red vinyl					
❏ 159	Jolly Cholly/Oh! Suzanna	1954	3.75	7.50	15.00
❏ 181	Rag-a-tag/Aunt Dinah's Quilting Party	1955	3.75	7.50	15.00

MGM

Number	Title (A Side/B Side)	Yr	VG	VG+	NM
❏ 11990	Sweet Adeline/Howdy Ma'm	1955	3.00	6.00	12.00
❏ 12059	Piano Rag/Jealous, Cold, Cheatin' Heart	1955	3.00	6.00	12.00
❏ 12161	Battle Hymn of the Republic/Dixie	1955	3.00	6.00	12.00
❏ 12242	Succotash/Tennessee Central (#9)	1956	3.00	6.00	12.00
❏ 12306	Pretty Blue Jeans/Good Time Cakewalk	1956	3.00	6.00	12.00
❏ 12442	Rio Grande Valley/Slap Happy	1957	3.00	6.00	12.00
❏ 12520	Waltz with Cramer/Funny Face	1957	3.00	6.00	12.00
❏ 12619	Herman's Theme/Country Gentleman	1958	3.00	6.00	12.00

RCA

Number	Title (A Side/B Side)	Yr	VG	VG+	NM
❏ PB-10761	I'm Thinking Tonight of My Blue Eyes/Hang On Sloopy	1976	—	2.00	4.00
❏ PB-10901	La Chicana/Four in the Morning	1977	—	2.00	4.00
—With Chet Atkins and Danny Davis					
❏ PB-10908	Rhythm of the Rain/Prelude to Love	1977	—	2.00	4.00
❏ PB-10908 [PS]	Rhythm of the Rain/Prelude to Love	1977	2.00	4.00	8.00
—Sleeve may be promo only (with "JH" prefix)					
❏ PB-11065	Coming Home/The Hurt	1977	—	2.00	4.00
❏ PB-11163	Looking for Mr. Goodbar/Father Time	1977	—	2.00	4.00
❏ PB-11284	Root Beer Rag/Morning Dew	1978	—	2.00	4.00
❏ PB-11394	The Main Street Electrical Parade/Singing in the Country Rain	1978	—	2.00	4.00
❏ PB-11432	Our Winter Love/For Lovers' Sake	1978	—	2.00	4.00
❏ PB-11576	Georgia on My Mind/Boogie Woogie	1979	—	2.00	4.00
❏ PB-11715	A Never Ending Love/Last Date	1979	—	2.00	4.00
❏ PB-11916	Dallas/Lover's Minuet	1980	—	—	3.00
❏ PB-11916 [PS]	Dallas/Lover's Minuet	1980	—	3.00	6.00
❏ PB-12195	Sleepy Shores/Help Me Make It Through the Night	1981	—	—	3.00
❏ PB-12272	High Noon/Lone Ranger	1981	—	—	3.00

RCA VICTOR

Number	Title (A Side/B Side)	Yr	VG	VG+	NM
❏ 47-7156	Flip, Flop and Fly/Sophisticated Swing	1958	2.50	5.00	10.00
❏ 47-7250	Mumble Jumble/Cryin'	1958	2.50	5.00	10.00

Number	Title (A Side/B Side)	Yr	VG	VG+	NM
❏ 47-7388	Rumpus/The Big Chihuahua	1958	2.50	5.00	10.00
❏ 47-7775	Last Date/Sweetie Baby	1960	3.00	6.00	12.00
❏ 47-7840	On the Rebound/Mood Indigo	1961	3.00	6.00	12.00
❏ 47-7840 [PS]	On the Rebound/Mood Indigo	1961	5.00	10.00	20.00
❏ 47-7893	San Antonio Rose/I Can Just Imagine	1961	2.50	5.00	10.00
❏ 47-7907	Your Last Goodbye/Hang On	1961	2.50	5.00	10.00
❏ 47-7907 [PS]	Your Last Goodbye/Hang On	1961	5.00	10.00	20.00
❏ 47-7978	Chattanooga Choo Choo/Let's Go	1962	2.00	4.00	8.00
❏ 47-8013	Lovesick Blues/The First Hurt	1962	2.00	4.00	8.00
❏ 47-8041	Hot Pepper/For Those That Cry	1962	2.00	4.00	8.00
❏ 47-8084	Swing Low/Losers Weepers	1962	2.00	4.00	8.00
❏ 47-8116	Java/Melissa	1962	2.00	4.00	8.00
❏ 47-8171	(These Are) The Young Years/Kaapsedri	1963	2.00	4.00	8.00
❏ 47-8171 [PS]	(These Are) The Young Years/Kaapsedri	1963	3.75	7.50	15.00
❏ 47-8217	How High the Moon/Satan's Doll	1963	2.00	4.00	8.00
❏ 47-8217 [PS]	How High the Moon/Satan's Doll	1963	3.75	7.50	15.00
❏ 47-8265	The Hucklebuck/Heartless Heart	1963	2.00	4.00	8.00
❏ 47-8325	Want Me/Naomi	1964	2.00	4.00	8.00
❏ 47-8414	Tomorrow's Gone/Shrum	1964	2.00	4.00	8.00
❏ 47-8541	Town Square/Long Walk Home	1965	2.00	4.00	8.00
❏ 47-8899	Strangers in the Night/				
	You've Lost That Lovin' Feelin'	1966	—	3.00	6.00
❏ 47-9065	Stood Up/Good Vibrations	1967	—	3.00	6.00
❏ 47-9157	I Wanna Be Free/Papa Gene's Blues	1967	—	3.00	6.00
❏ 47-9237	Theme for Sam/For No One	1967	—	3.00	6.00
❏ 47-9396	Gentle on My Mind/By the Time I Get to Phoenix	1967	—	3.00	6.00
❏ 47-9841	Theme from Room 222/Leaving on a Jet Plane	1970	—	2.00	4.00
❏ 47-9874	Fancy Free/Is This Tomorrow	1970	—	2.00	4.00
❏ 47-9940	For the Good Times/Everything Is Beautiful	1971	—	2.00	4.00
❏ 47-9978	Makin' Up/Theme from "Flight of the Doves"	1971	—	2.00	4.00
❏ 74-0152	Games People Play/Ob-La-Di, Ob-La-Da	1969	—	2.50	5.00
❏ 74-0209	Seattle/Lovin' Season	1969	—	2.50	5.00
❏ 74-0621	Corn Crib Symphony/Your Last Goodbye	1971	—	2.00	4.00
❏ 74-0674	Hony Tonk (Part 2)/Detour	1972	—	2.00	4.00
❏ 74-0821	Quiet Girl/Smile	1972	—	2.00	4.00
❏ 74-0869	Tonight's the Night/Crystal Chandelier	1973	—	2.00	4.00
❏ 47-8084 [PS]	Swing Low/Losers Weepers	1962	2.50	5.00	10.00
❏ APBO-0012	Lonely Street/The Battle of New Orleans	1973	—	2.00	4.00
❏ APBO-0214	Theme from "The Young and the Restless"/				
	Boogie, Boogie, Boogie	1974	—	2.00	4.00
❏ VP-3-2544	I Can't Help It/Kaw-Liga	1962	2.00	4.00	8.00
—Stereo jukebox issue; small hole, plays at 33 1/3 rpm					
❏ PB-10076	Forever/Flip, Flop and Fly	1974	—	2.00	4.00
❏ PB-10336	The Last Farewell/My Melody of Love	1975	—	2.00	4.00
❏ PB-10533	Eres Tu (Touch the Wind)/Faded Love	1975	—	2.00	4.00
❏ PB-10597	Tonight's the Night/Candy Pants	1976	—	2.00	4.00
SIMS					
❏ 121	Fancy Pants/Five Foot Two, Eyes of Blue	1961	2.00	4.00	8.00
STEP ONE					
❏ 454	Christmas Medley//We Wish You A Merry				
	Christmas/I'll Be Home For Christmas	1992		2.50	5.00
—Red vinyl					

7-Inch Extended Plays
RCA VICTOR

Number	Title (A Side/B Side)	Yr	VG	VG+	NM
❏ DJEO-0272 [DJ]	Behind Closed Doors/The Most Beautiful Girl//				
	Star Spangled Banner/Top of the World	1974	2.50	5.00	10.00
❏ EPA-4377	Last Date/San Antonio Rose//Flip, Flop and Bop/				
	Chattanooga Choo Choo	1961	2.50	5.00	10.00
❏ EPA-4377 [PS]	Last Date	1961	2.50	5.00	10.00

Albums
MGM

Number	Title (A Side/B Side)	Yr	VG	VG+	NM
❏ E-3502 [M]	That Honky-Tonk Piano	1957	10.00	20.00	40.00
❏ E-4223 [M]	Floyd Cramer Goes Honky Tonkin'	1964	3.75	7.50	15.00
❏ SE-4223 [R]	Floyd Cramer Goes Honky Tonkin'	1964	3.00	6.00	12.00
❏ SE-4666	Floyd Cramer Goes Honky Tonkin'	1970	3.00	6.00	12.00
—Reissue of 4223					
PAIR					
❏ PDL2-1049 [(2)]	Country Classics	1986	3.00	6.00	12.00
RCA					
❏ 5621-1-R	Our Class Reunion	1987	2.50	5.00	10.00
RCA CAMDEN					
❏ ACL2-0128 [(2)]	Floyd Cramer Plays the Big Hits	1973	3.00	6.00	12.00
❏ ACL1-0563	Spotlight On Floyd Cramer	1974	2.50	5.00	10.00
❏ CAL-874 [M]	The Magic Touch	1965	3.00	6.00	12.00
❏ CAS-874(e) [P]	The Magic Touch	1965	3.00	6.00	12.00
—Even though this album is labeled "Stereo Electronically Reprocessed," nine of the 10 tracks are in true stereo					
❏ CAL-2104 [M]	Distinctive Piano Styling	196?	3.00	6.00	12.00
❏ CAS-2104 [S]	Distinctive Piano Styling	196?	3.00	6.00	12.00
❏ CAL-2152 [M]	Night Train	1967	3.00	6.00	12.00
❏ CAS-2152 [S]	Night Train	1967	3.00	6.00	12.00
❏ CAS-2508	Almost Persuaded	1971	3.00	6.00	12.00
❏ CXS-9016 [(2)]	A Date with Floyd Cramer	1972	3.75	7.50	15.00
RCA VICTOR					
❏ APD1-0155 [Q]	Super Country Hits	1973	3.75	7.50	15.00
—All copies are in quadraphonic					
❏ APD1-0299 [Q]	Class of '73	1973	3.75	7.50	15.00
❏ APL1-0299	Class of '73	1973	3.00	6.00	12.00
❏ APD1-0469 [Q]	The Young and the Restless	1974	3.75	7.50	15.00
❏ APL1-0469	The Young and the Restless	1974	3.00	6.00	12.00
❏ APL1-0661	Floyd Cramer In Concert	1974	3.00	6.00	12.00
❏ APD1-0893 [Q]	Piano Masterpieces (1900-75)	1975	3.75	7.50	15.00
❏ APL1-0893	Piano Masterpieces (1900-75)	1975	2.50	5.00	10.00
❏ APD1-1191 [Q]	Class of '74 and '75	1975	3.75	7.50	15.00
❏ APL1-1191	Class of '74 and '75	1975	2.50	5.00	10.00
❏ APD1-1541 [Q]	Floyd Cramer Country	1976	3.75	7.50	15.00
❏ APL1-1541	Floyd Cramer Country	1976	2.50	5.00	10.00
❏ LPM-2151 [M]	Hello Blues	1960	3.75	7.50	15.00
❏ LSP-2151 [S]	Hello Blues	1960	5.00	10.00	20.00
❏ APL1-2278	Floyd Cramer & the Keyboard Kick Band	1977	2.50	5.00	10.00
❏ ANL1-2344	Hits from Country Hall	1977	2.50	5.00	10.00
❏ LPM-2350 [M]	Last Date	1961	5.00	10.00	20.00
❏ LSP-2350 [S]	Last Date	1961	6.25	12.50	25.00
❏ LPM-2359 [M]	On the Rebound	1961	3.75	7.50	15.00
❏ LSP-2359 [S]	On the Rebound	1961	5.00	10.00	20.00
❏ LPM-2428 [M]	Floyd Cramer Gets Organ-ized	1962	3.75	7.50	15.00
❏ LSP-2428 [S]	Floyd Cramer Gets Organ-ized	1962	5.00	10.00	20.00
❏ LPM-2466 [M]	America's Biggest Selling Pianist	1962	3.75	7.50	15.00

Number	Title (A Side/B Side)	Yr	VG	VG+	NM
❏ LSP-2466 [S]	America's Biggest Selling Pianist	1962	5.00	10.00	20.00
❏ LPM-2544 [M]	I Remember Hank Williams	1962	3.75	7.50	15.00
❏ LSP-2544 [S]	I Remember Hank Williams	1962	5.00	10.00	20.00
❏ LPM-2642 [M]	Swing Along	1963	3.75	7.50	15.00
❏ LSP-2642 [S]	Swing Along	1963	5.00	10.00	20.00
❏ AHL1-2644	Looking for Mr. Goodbar	1978	2.50	5.00	10.00
❏ LPM-2701 [M]	Comin' On	1963	3.75	7.50	15.00
❏ LSP-2701 [S]	Comin' On	1963	5.00	10.00	20.00
❏ LPM-2800 [M]	Country Piano — City Strings	1964	3.75	7.50	15.00
❏ LSP-2800 [S]	Country Piano — City Strings	1964	5.00	10.00	20.00
❏ LPM-2883 [M]	Cramer at the Console	1964	3.75	7.50	15.00
❏ LSP-2883 [S]	Cramer at the Console	1964	5.00	10.00	20.00
❏ LPM-2888 [M]	The Best of Floyd Cramer	1964	3.00	6.00	12.00
❏ LSP-2888 [S]	The Best of Floyd Cramer	1964	3.75	7.50	15.00
❏ AHL1-3209	Super Hits	1979	2.50	5.00	10.00
❏ LPM-3318 [M]	Hits from the Country Hall of Fame	1965	3.75	7.50	15.00
❏ LSP-3318 [S]	Hits from the Country Hall of Fame	1965	5.00	10.00	20.00
❏ LPM-3405 [M]	Class of '65	1965	3.00	6.00	12.00
❏ LSP-3405 [S]	Class of '65	1965	3.75	7.50	15.00
❏ ANL1-3469	Floyd Cramer In Concert	1979	2.00	4.00	8.00
❏ AHL1-3487	Last Date	1979	2.50	5.00	10.00
❏ LPM-3533 [M]	The Big Ones	1966	3.00	6.00	12.00
❏ LSP-3533 [S]	The Big Ones	1966	3.75	7.50	15.00
❏ AHL1-3613	Dallas	1980	2.50	5.00	10.00
❏ LPM-3650 [M]	Class of '66	1966	3.00	6.00	12.00
❏ LSP-3650 [S]	Class of '66	1966	3.75	7.50	15.00
❏ AYL1-3745	Piano Masterpieces (1900-75)	1980	2.00	4.00	8.00
❏ LPM-3746 [M]	Here's What's Happening!	1967	3.75	7.50	15.00
❏ LSP-3746 [S]	Here's What's Happening!	1967	3.75	7.50	15.00
❏ LPM-3811 [M]	Floyd Cramer Plays the Monkees	1967	3.75	7.50	15.00
❏ LSP-3811 [S]	Floyd Cramer Plays the Monkees	1967	3.75	7.50	15.00
❏ LPM-3827 [M]	Class of '67	1967	3.75	7.50	15.00
❏ LSP-3827 [S]	Class of '67	1967	3.75	7.50	15.00
❏ LPM-3828 [M]	We Wish You a Merry Christmas	1967	7.50	15.00	30.00
❏ LSP-3828 [S]	We Wish You a Merry Christmas	1967	3.00	6.00	12.00
❏ AYL1-3900	The Best of Floyd Cramer	1981	2.00	4.00	8.00
❏ LPM-3925 [M]	Floyd Cramer Plays Country Classics	1968	5.00	10.00	20.00
❏ LSP-3925 [S]	Floyd Cramer Plays Country Classics	1968	3.75	7.50	15.00
❏ AYL1-4008	Great Country Hits	1981	2.00	4.00	8.00
❏ LPM-4025 [M]	Class of '68	1968	—	—	—
—Canceled?					
❏ LSP-4025 [S]	Class of '68	1968	3.75	7.50	15.00
❏ LSP-4070	MacArthur Park	1968	3.75	7.50	15.00
❏ LSP-4091	The Best of Floyd Cramer, Volume 2	1969	3.75	7.50	15.00
❏ AHL1-4119	Best of the West	1982	2.50	5.00	10.00
❏ LSP-4162	Class of '69	1969	3.75	7.50	15.00
❏ LSP-4220	Floyd Cramer Plays More Country Classics	1969	3.75	7.50	15.00
❏ LSP-4312	The Big Ones, Volume II	1970	3.75	7.50	15.00
❏ LSP-4367	Floyd Cramer with the Music City Pops	1970	3.75	7.50	15.00
❏ LSP-4437	Class of '70	1970	3.75	7.50	15.00
❏ LSP-4500	Sounds of Sunday	1971	3.75	7.50	15.00
❏ LSP-4590	Class of '71	1971	3.75	7.50	15.00
❏ LSP-4676	Detours	1972	3.75	7.50	15.00
❏ LSP-4772	Class of '72	1972	3.75	7.50	15.00
❏ LSP-4821	Best of the Class of…	1973	3.75	7.50	15.00
❏ AHL1-5452	Collector's Series	1985	2.50	5.00	10.00
❏ VPS-6031 [(2)]	This Is Floyd Cramer	1970	5.00	10.00	20.00

CRANE, BOB
45s
EPIC

Number	Title (A Side/B Side)	Yr	VG	VG+	NM
❏ 10038	Theme from Get Smart/Happy Feet	1966	3.00	6.00	12.00
❏ 10038 [PS]	Theme from Get Smart/Happy Feet	1966	7.50	15.00	30.00
❏ 10108	Theme from Hogan's Heroes/Theme from "F"				
	Troop	1966	3.00	6.00	12.00

Albums
EPIC

Number	Title (A Side/B Side)	Yr	VG	VG+	NM
❏ LN 24224 [M]	The Funny Side of TV	1966	6.25	12.50	25.00
❏ BN 26224 [S]	The Funny Side of TV	1966	7.50	15.00	30.00

CRANE, LES
45s
WARNER BROS.

Number	Title (A Side/B Side)	Yr	VG	VG+	NM
❏ 7520	Desiderata/A Different Drummer	1971	—	2.50	5.00
❏ 7520 [PS]	Desiderata/A Different Drummer	1971	—	3.00	6.00
❏ 7548	Desiderata (Spanish)/Desiderata (English)	1972	—	3.00	6.00
❏ 7582	Children Learn What They Live/The Wilderness	1972	—	2.00	4.00

Albums
WARNER BROS.

Number	Title (A Side/B Side)	Yr	VG	VG+	NM
❏ BS 2570	Desiderata	1971	2.50	5.00	10.00
❏ SW-94266	Desiderata	1972	3.00	6.00	12.00
—Capitol Record Club edition					

CRANE, SHERRY
45s
SUN

Number	Title (A Side/B Side)	Yr	VG	VG+	NM
❏ 328	Willie Willie/Winnie the Parakeet	1959	6.25	12.50	25.00

CRAWFORD, BOBBY Also see THE CRAWFORD BROTHERS.
45s
DEL-FI

Number	Title (A Side/B Side)	Yr	VG	VG+	NM
❏ 4211	Mrs. Smith, Please Wake Up/				
	That Little Old Lovemaker Me	1963	3.75	7.50	15.00
❏ 4236	I Want to Be a Good Guy/(B-side unknown)	1964	3.75	7.50	15.00

CRAWFORD, CAROLYN
45s
MERCURY

Number	Title (A Side/B Side)	Yr	VG	VG+	NM
❏ 74036	Coming On Strong/Love Song for You	1978	—	2.50	5.00
—Mercury titles as "Caroline Crawford"					
❏ 74054	You'll Wait/Breakdown	1979	—	2.50	5.00
❏ 76013	The Strut/I'll Be Here for You	1979	—	2.50	5.00
MOTOWN					
❏ 1050	Forget About Me/Devil in His Heart	1963	10.00	20.00	40.00
❏ 1064	My Smile Is Just a Frown (Turned Upside Down)/				
	I'll Come Running	1964	5.00	10.00	20.00
—Revised version of A-side title					

C

Number	Title (A Side/B Side)	Yr	VG	VG+	NM
❏ 1064	My Smile Is Just a Frown Turned Upside Down/				
	I'll Come Running	1964	12.50	25.00	50.00
—Original version of A-side title					
❏ 1070	My Heart/When Someone's Good to You	1964	10.00	20.00	40.00
PHILADELPHIA INT'L.					
❏ 3553	Just Got to Be More Careful/				
	Saving All the Love I Got for You	1974	—	2.50	5.00
❏ 3570	It Takes Two to Make One/No Matter How Bad				
	Things Are, I Still Love You	1975	—	2.50	5.00
❏ 3580	Good & Plenty/If You Move, You Lose	1975	—	2.50	5.00

CRAWFORD, HANK
45s
ATLANTIC

Number	Title (A Side/B Side)	Yr	VG	VG+	NM
❏ 5013	Misty (Part 1)/Misty (Part 2)	1961	2.50	5.00	10.00
❏ 5016	Easy Living/Playmates	1961	2.50	5.00	10.00
❏ 5022	Don't Cry Baby/The Peeper	1962	2.50	5.00	10.00
❏ 5030	Blueberry Hill/Any Time	1963	2.50	5.00	10.00
❏ 5033	Skunky Green/Whispering Grass	1963	2.50	5.00	10.00
❏ 5039	Shake a-Plenty/Mellow Down	1964	2.50	5.00	10.00
❏ 5042	Merry Christmas Baby/Read 'Em and Weep	1964	2.50	5.00	10.00
❏ 5049	Don't Get Around Much Anymore/				
	Bluff City Blues	1966	2.00	4.00	8.00
❏ 5066	Soul Shoutin'/				
	Who Can I Turn To When Nobody Needs Me	1968	2.00	4.00	8.00
❏ 5079	Smoky City/Hush Puppies	1969	2.00	4.00	8.00
KUDU					
❏ 905	Brian's Song/				
	In the Wee Small Hours of the Morning	1972	—	2.50	5.00
❏ 908	Help Me Make It Through the Night/Uncle Funky	1972	—	2.50	5.00
❏ 911	The Christmas Song/Winter Wonderland	1974	—	2.50	5.00
❏ 923	Sho Is Funky/(B-side unknown)	1975	—	2.50	5.00
❏ 944	Daytime Friends/I Don't Want No Happy Songs	1978	—	2.50	5.00

Albums
ATLANTIC

Number	Title (A Side/B Side)	Yr	VG	VG+	NM
❏ SD 2-315 [(2)]	The Art of Hank Crawford	1973	3.75	7.50	15.00
❏ 1356 [M]	More Soul	1960	5.00	10.00	20.00
—Purple and red label, white fan logo					
❏ 1356 [M]	More Soul	1962	3.00	6.00	12.00
—Purple and red label, black fan logo					
❏ SD 1356 [S]	More Soul	1960	6.25	12.50	25.00
—Green and blue label, white fan logo					
❏ SD 1356 [S]	More Soul	1962	3.75	7.50	15.00
—Green and blue label, black fan logo					
❏ 1372 [M]	The Soul Clinic	1961	5.00	10.00	20.00
—Purple and red label, white fan logo					
❏ 1372 [M]	The Soul Clinic	1962	3.00	6.00	12.00
—Purple and red label, black fan logo					
❏ SD 1372 [S]	The Soul Clinic	1961	6.25	12.50	25.00
—Green and blue label, white fan logo					
❏ SD 1372 [S]	The Soul Clinic	1962	3.75	7.50	15.00
—Green and blue label, black fan logo					
❏ 1387 [M]	From the Heart	1962	3.75	7.50	15.00
❏ SD 1387 [S]	From the Heart	1962	5.00	10.00	20.00
❏ 1405 [M]	Soul of the Ballad	1963	3.75	7.50	15.00
❏ SD 1405 [S]	Soul of the Ballad	1963	5.00	10.00	20.00
❏ 1423 [M]	True Blue	1964	3.75	7.50	15.00
❏ SD 1423 [S]	True Blue	1964	5.00	10.00	20.00
❏ 1436 [M]	Dig These Blues	1965	3.75	7.50	15.00
❏ SD 1436 [S]	Dig These Blues	1965	5.00	10.00	20.00
❏ 1455 [M]	After Hours	1966	3.75	7.50	15.00
❏ SD 1455 [S]	After Hours	1966	5.00	10.00	20.00
❏ 1470 [M]	Mr. Blues	1967	5.00	10.00	20.00
❏ SD 1470 [S]	Mr. Blues	1967	3.75	7.50	15.00
❏ SD 1503	Double Cross	1968	3.75	7.50	15.00
❏ SD 1523	Mr. Blues Plays Lady Soul	1969	3.75	7.50	15.00
❏ SD 1557	The Best of Hank Crawford	1970	3.75	7.50	15.00
COTILLION					
❏ SD 18003	It's a Funny Thing to Do	1971	3.00	6.00	12.00
KUDU					
❏ 06	Help Me Make It	1972	3.00	6.00	12.00
❏ 08	We've Got a Good Thing	1973	3.00	6.00	12.00
❏ 15	Wildflower	1974	3.00	6.00	12.00
❏ 19	Don't You Worry 'Bout a Thing	1975	3.00	6.00	12.00
❏ 26	I Hear a Symphony	1976	3.00	6.00	12.00
❏ 33	Hank Crawford's Back	1977	3.00	6.00	12.00
❏ 35	Tico Rico	1977	3.00	6.00	12.00
❏ 39	Cajun Sunrise	1979	3.00	6.00	12.00
MILESTONE					
❏ 9112	Midnight Ramble	1983	2.50	5.00	10.00
❏ 9119	Indigo Blue	1984	2.50	5.00	10.00
❏ 9129	Down on the Deuce	1985	2.50	5.00	10.00
❏ 9140	Roadhouse Symphony	1986	2.50	5.00	10.00
❏ 9149	Mr. Chips	1987	2.50	5.00	10.00
❏ 9168	Night Beat	1988	2.50	5.00	10.00
❏ 9182	Groove Master	1990	3.00	6.00	12.00
MOBILE FIDELITY					
❏ 1-224	Soul of the Ballad	1995	6.25	12.50	25.00
—Audiophile vinyl					

CRAWFORD, HANK, AND JIMMY McGRIFF Also see each artist's individual listings.
Albums
MILESTONE

Number	Title (A Side/B Side)	Yr	VG	VG+	NM
❏ 9142	Soul Survivors	1986	2.50	5.00	10.00
❏ 9153	Steppin' Up	1988	2.50	5.00	10.00
❏ 9177	On the Blue Side	1990	3.00	6.00	12.00

CRAWFORD, JOHNNY Also see THE CRAWFORD BROTHERS.
45s
DEL-FI

Number	Title (A Side/B Side)	Yr	VG	VG+	NM
❏ 4162	Daydreams/So Goes the Story	1961	3.75	7.50	15.00
❏ 4162 [PS]	Daydreams/So Goes the Story	1961	6.25	12.50	25.00
❏ 4165	Your Love Is Growing Cold/Treasure	1961	3.75	7.50	15.00
❏ 4165 [PS]	Your Love Is Growing Cold/Treasure	1961	6.25	12.50	25.00
❏ 4172	Patti Ann/Donna	1962	3.75	7.50	15.00
❏ 4178	Cindy's Birthday/Something Special	1962	3.75	7.50	15.00
❏ 4178 [PS]	Cindy's Birthday/Something Special	1962	6.25	12.50	25.00
❏ 4181	Your Nose Is Gonna Grow/Mr. Blue	1962	3.75	7.50	15.00

Number	Title (A Side/B Side)	Yr	VG	VG+	NM
❏ 4181 [PS]	Your Nose Is Gonna Grow/Mr. Blue	1962	6.25	12.50	25.00
❏ 4188	Rumors/No One Really Loves a Clown	1962	3.75	7.50	15.00
❏ 4188 [PS]	Rumors/No One Really Loves a Clown	1962	6.25	12.50	25.00
❏ 4193	Proud/Lonesome Town	1963	3.75	7.50	15.00
❏ 4203	Cry on My Shoulder/When I Fall in Love	1963	3.75	7.50	15.00
❏ 4215	What Happened to Janie/Petite Chanson	1963	3.75	7.50	15.00
❏ 4221	Cindy's Gonna Cry/Debbie	1963	3.75	7.50	15.00
❏ 4229	Sandy/Ol' Shorty	1963	3.75	7.50	15.00
❏ 4231	Judy Loves Me/Living in the Past	1963	3.75	7.50	15.00
❏ 4242	The Girl Next Door (Once Upon a Time)/				
	Sittin' and Watchin'	1964	3.75	7.50	15.00
❏ 4305	Am I Too Young/Janie Please Believe It	1965	3.75	7.50	15.00
SIDEWALK					
❏ 932	Angelica/Everybody Has Their Day	1968	3.00	6.00	12.00
❏ 941	Good Guys Finish Last/				
	Everyone Should Own a Dream	1968	3.00	6.00	12.00
WYNNE					
❏ 124	Dance with the Dolly				
	(With the Hole in Her Stocking)/Ask	1958	5.00	10.00	20.00

Albums
DEL-FI

Number	Title (A Side/B Side)	Yr	VG	VG+	NM
❏ DFLP-1220 [M]	The Captivating Johnny Crawford	1962	10.00	20.00	40.00
❏ DFLP-1223 [M]	A Young Man's Fancy	1962	7.50	15.00	30.00
❏ DFST-1223 [S]	A Young Man's Fancy	1962	10.00	20.00	40.00
❏ DFLP-1224 [M]	Rumors	1963	7.50	15.00	30.00
❏ DFST-1224 [S]	Rumors	1963	10.00	20.00	40.00
❏ DFLP-1229 [M]	His Greatest Hits	1963	7.50	15.00	30.00
❏ DFST-1229 [S]	His Greatest Hits	1963	10.00	20.00	40.00
❏ DFLP-1248 [M]	Greatest Hits, Volume 2	1964	5.00	10.00	20.00
❏ DFST-1248 [S]	Greatest Hits, Volume 2	1964	6.25	12.50	25.00
GUEST STAR					
❏ GS-1470 [M]	Johnny Crawford	196?	5.00	10.00	20.00
❏ GSS-1470 [S]	Johnny Crawford	196?	6.25	12.50	25.00
RHINO					
❏ RNDF-202	The Best of Johnny Crawford	1982	3.00	6.00	12.00
SUPREME					
❏ M-110 [M]	Songs from "The Restless Ones"	1965	5.00	10.00	20.00
❏ MS-210 [S]	Songs from "The Restless Ones"	1965	6.25	12.50	25.00

CRAWFORD, ODESSA
45s
HIT

Number	Title (A Side/B Side)	Yr	VG	VG+	NM
❏ 289	I Never Loved a Man the Way I Love You/				
	Bernadette	1967	2.00	4.00	8.00
—B-side by the Fantastics					

CRAWFORD BROTHERS, THE Also see BOBBY CRAWFORD; JOHNNY CRAWFORD.
45s
DEL-FI

Number	Title (A Side/B Side)	Yr	VG	VG+	NM
❏ 4191	Good Buddies/You Gotta Wear Shoes	1963	3.75	7.50	15.00
❏ 4191 [PS]	Good Buddies/You Gotta Wear Shoes	1963	6.25	12.50	25.00

CRAWLER See BACK STREET CRAWLER.

CRAYNE, LESLIE 'UGGAMS' See LESLIE UGGAMS.

CRAYONS, THE
45s
COUNSEL

Number	Title (A Side/B Side)	Yr	VG	VG+	NM
❏ 122	Love at First Sight/I Saw You	1963	7.50	15.00	30.00

CRAYTON, PEE WEE
45s
ALADDIN

Number	Title (A Side/B Side)	Yr	VG	VG+	NM
❏ 3112	When It Rains It Pours/Daybreak	1952	25.00	50.00	100.00
❏ 3112	When It Rains It Pours/Daybreak	1952	500.00	1000.	1500.
—Green vinyl					
EDCO					
❏ 1009	Ev'ry Night About This Time/(B-side unknown)	196?	6.25	12.50	25.00
❏ 1010	Money Tree/When Darkness Falls	196?	6.25	12.50	25.00
FOX					
❏ 10069	Give Me One More Chance/(B-side unknown)	196?	7.50	15.00	30.00
GUYDEN					
❏ 2048	I'm Still in Love with You/Time on My Hands	1961	3.75	7.50	15.00
IMPERIAL					
❏ 5288	Do Unto Others/Every Dog Has a Day	1954	50.00	100.00	200.00
❏ 5297	Wine-O/Hurry Hurry	1954	125.00	250.00	500.00
❏ 5321	I Need Your Love/You Know — Yeah	1955	12.50	25.00	50.00
❏ 5338	My Idea About You/I Got News for You	1955	12.50	25.00	50.00
❏ 5345	Eyes Full of Tears/Runnin' Wild	1955	12.50	25.00	50.00
❏ 5353	Yours Truly/Be Faithful	1955	12.50	25.00	50.00
JAMIE					
❏ 1190	'Tain't Nobody's Business If I Do/				
	Little Bitty Things	1961	3.75	7.50	15.00
MODERN					
❏ 892	Cool Evening/Have You Lost Your Love for Me	1951	25.00	50.00	100.00
POST					
❏ 2007	Don't Go!/I Must Go On	1955	10.00	20.00	40.00
RECORDED IN HOLLYWOOD					
❏ 408	Pappy's Blues/Crying and Walking	1954	25.00	50.00	100.00
❏ 426	Baby Pat the Floor/I'm Your Prisoner	1954	25.00	50.00	100.00
SMASH					
❏ 1774	Sabre Twist/Hillbilly Blues	1962	3.00	6.00	12.00
VEE JAY					
❏ 214	A Frosty Night/The Telephone Is Ringing	1956	10.00	20.00	40.00
❏ 252	I Don't Care/I Found My Peace of Mind	1957	10.00	20.00	40.00
❏ 266	Fiddle Dee Dee/Is This the Price I Pay	1957	10.00	20.00	40.00

Albums
CROWN

Number	Title (A Side/B Side)	Yr	VG	VG+	NM
❏ CLP-5175 [M]	Pee Wee Crayton	1959	25.00	50.00	100.00
—Black label					
❏ CLP-5175 [M]	Pee Wee Crayton	196?	5.00	10.00	20.00
—Gray label					
VANGUARD					
❏ VSD-6566	The Things I Used to Do	1971	3.75	7.50	15.00

C

Number	Title (A Side/B Side)	Yr	VG	VG+	NM
CRAZY ELEPHANT					
45s					
BELL					
❑ 763	Gimme Gimme Good Lovin'/				
	Dark Part of My Mind	1969	2.00	4.00	8.00
❑ 804	Pam/Sunshine, Red Wine	1969	—	3.00	6.00
❑ 817	Gimme Some More/My Babe (Honey Pie)	1969	—	3.00	6.00
❑ 846	There's a Better Day a-Comin' (Na, Na, Na, Na)/				
	Space Buggy	1969	—	3.00	6.00
❑ 875	Land Rover/There Ain't No Umbopo	1970	—	3.00	6.00
Albums					
BELL					
❑ 6034	Crazy Elephant	1969	5.00	10.00	20.00
CRAZY HORSE Also see NEIL YOUNG.					
45s					
EPIC					
❑ 10925	Rock and Roll Band/Outside Lookin' In	1972	—	2.50	5.00
M.O.C.					
❑ 671	Love/High on Lovin'	1967	3.00	6.00	12.00
REPRISE					
❑ 1007	Downtown/Crow Jane Lady	1971	—	2.50	5.00
❑ 1025	Dance, Dance, Dance/Carolay	1971	—	2.50	5.00
❑ 1046	Beggars Day/Dirty, Dirty	1971	—	2.50	5.00
❑ 1075	All Alone Now/One Thing I Love	1972	—	2.50	5.00
Albums					
EPIC					
❑ KE 31710	Crazy Horse at Crooked Lane	1972	3.75	7.50	15.00
RCA VICTOR					
❑ AFL1-3054	Crazy Moon	1978	3.00	6.00	12.00
REPRISE					
❑ MS 2059	Loose	1972	3.75	7.50	15.00
❑ RS 6438	Crazy Horse	1971	3.75	7.50	15.00
CRAZY OTTO					
45s					
DECCA					
❑ 29403	Glad Rag Doll/Smiles	1955	3.00	6.00	12.00
—Later pressings credited to "Crazy Otto"					
❑ 29403	Glad Rag Doll/Smiles	1955	5.00	10.00	20.00
—Original pressings credited to "Happy Otto"					
❑ 29449	My Melancholy Baby/In the Mood	1955	2.50	5.00	10.00
❑ 29503	Crazy Otto Rag/Twelfth Street Rag	1955	2.50	5.00	10.00
❑ 29571	Oh Johnny, Oh Johnny, Oh!/Palestine	1955	2.50	5.00	10.00
❑ 29658	The Marching Otto Medley (Part 1)/The				
	Marching Otto Medley (Part 2)	1955	3.00	6.00	12.00
—As "Marching Otto"					
❑ 29673	If You Knew Susie/				
	Somebody Else Is Taking My Place	1955	2.50	5.00	10.00
❑ 29753	Tin Pan Alley Medley/Gaslight Medley	1955	2.50	5.00	10.00
❑ 29980	Alabamy Bound/Das Ist Musik	1956	2.00	4.00	8.00
❑ 30093	Derby Hat Medley/Swingin' Door Medley	1956	2.00	4.00	8.00
❑ 30377	Happy Piano Medley/Good Evening Friends				
	Medley	1957	2.00	4.00	8.00
❑ 30608	Zippy Medley/Bouncy Medley	1958	2.00	4.00	8.00
❑ 30818	Chopin's Polonaise/Sunrise Serenade	1959	2.00	4.00	8.00
❑ 31185	Medley: Sleigh Ride-Winter Wonderland-White				
	Christmas/Medley: Rudolph The Red-Nosed				
	Reindeer-I Saw Mommy.Kissing Santa Claus-				
	Jingle Bells	1960	3.00	6.00	12.00
❑ 31235	Piccadilly/Spanish Holiday	1961	2.00	4.00	8.00
MGM					
❑ 13101	Alley Cat/Cheerio Choo Choo	1962	2.00	4.00	8.00
7-Inch Extended Plays					
DECCA					
❑ ED 2201	Smiles/Glad Rag Doll//In the Mood/My				
	Melancholy Baby	1955	2.50	5.00	10.00
❑ ED 2201 [PS]	Crazy Otto, Part 1	1955	2.50	5.00	10.00
❑ ED 2202	Beautiful Ohio/Paddlin' Madelin' Home//S-H-I-				
	N-E/Lights Out	1955	2.50	5.00	10.00
❑ ED 2202 [PS]	Crazy Otto, Part 2	1955	2.50	5.00	10.00
❑ ED 2260	Alabamy Bound/Indiana (Back Home Again in				
	Indiana)//If You Knew Susie (Like I Know				
	Susie)/I'll Always Be in Love with You	1956	2.50	5.00	10.00
❑ ED 2260 [PS]	Crazy Otto Rides Again, Volume 1	1956	2.50	5.00	10.00
❑ ED 2261	Somebody Else Is Taking My Place/Mammy o'				
	Mine//The Darktown Strutters' Ball/Rag Mop	1956	2.50	5.00	10.00
❑ ED 2261 [PS]	Crazy Otto Rides Again, Volume 2	1956	2.50	5.00	10.00
❑ ED 2263	The Crazy Otto Rag/Twelfth Street Rag//Oh				
	Johnny, Oh Johnny, Oh!/Palesteena	1956	2.50	5.00	10.00
❑ ED 2263 [PS]	Crazy Otto Rides Again, Volume 3	1956	2.50	5.00	10.00
❑ ED 2431	The Man with the Banjo/Let There Be Love//We				
	Could Make Such Beautiful Music/				
	Exactly Like You	195?	2.00	4.00	8.00
❑ ED 2431 [PS]	Not-So-Crazy Otto, Part 3	195?	2.00	4.00	8.00
❑ ED 2569	(contents unknown)	1957	2.00	4.00	8.00
❑ ED 2569 [PS]	Crazy Otto's Back in Town	1957	2.00	4.00	8.00
❑ ED 2600	(contents unknown)	1958	2.00	4.00	8.00
❑ ED 2600 [PS]	Honky Tonk Piano	1958	2.00	4.00	8.00
Albums					
DECCA					
❑ DL 4157 [M]	Have Piano, Will Travel	1961	3.75	7.50	15.00
❑ DL 8113 [M]	Crazy Otto	1955	5.00	10.00	20.00
—Black label, silver print					
❑ DL 8113 [M]	Crazy Otto	1960	3.00	6.00	12.00
—Black label with color bars					
❑ DL 8163 [M]	Crazy Otto Rides Again	1956	5.00	10.00	20.00
❑ DL 8367 [M]	Not So Crazy	1956	5.00	10.00	20.00
❑ DL 8627 [M]	Crazy Otto's Back in Town	1957	3.75	7.50	15.00
❑ DL 8737 [M]	Honky Tonk Piano	1958	3.75	7.50	15.00
❑ DL 8919 [M]	Golden Award Songs	1960	3.75	7.50	15.00
❑ DL 74157 [S]	Have Piano, Will Travel	1961	5.00	10.00	20.00
❑ DL 78919 [S]	Golden Award Songs	1960	5.00	10.00	20.00
MGM					
❑ E-4150 [M]	Crazy Otto Plays Crazy Tunes	1963	3.00	6.00	12.00
❑ SE-4150 [S]	Crazy Otto Plays Crazy Tunes	1963	3.75	7.50	15.00
VOCALION					
❑ VL 3663 [M]	Crazy Otto Goes Sentimental	196?	3.00	6.00	12.00

Number	Title (A Side/B Side)	Yr	VG	VG+	NM
CREACH, PAPA JOHN Also see HOT TUNA; JEFFERSON AIRPLANE; JEFFERSON STARSHIP.					
45s					
BUDDAH					
❑ 509	I'm the Fiddle Man/Joyce	1975	—	2.00	4.00
DJM					
❑ 1102	All the World Loves a Winner/Southern Strut	1979	—	2.00	4.00
GRUNT					
❑ 65-0501	Over the Rainbow/The Janitor Drives a Cadillac	1971	—	2.50	5.00
❑ 65-0505	Papa John's Down Home Blues/String Jet Rock	1971	—	2.50	5.00
❑ 65-0508	Filthy Funky (Part 1)/Filthy Funky (Part 2)	1972	—	2.50	5.00
Albums					
BUDDAH					
❑ BDS-5649	I'm the Fiddle Man	1975	3.00	6.00	12.00
❑ BDS-5660	Rock Father	1977	3.00	6.00	12.00
DJM					
❑ 11	Cat & Fiddle	1977	3.00	6.00	12.00
❑ 18	Inphasion	1978	3.00	6.00	12.00
GRUNT					
❑ BFL1-0418	Playing My Fiddle for You	1974	3.75	7.50	15.00
❑ BXL1-1003	Papa John Creach	197?	3.00	6.00	12.00
—Reissue with new prefix					
❑ FTR-1003	Papa John Creach	1971	3.75	7.50	15.00
❑ BXL1-1009	Filthy!	197?	3.00	6.00	12.00
—Reissue with new prefix					
❑ FTR-1009	Filthy!	1972	3.75	7.50	15.00
CREAM Also see GINGER BAKER'S AIR FORCE; JACK BRUCE; ERIC CLAPTON.					
45s					
ATCO					
❑ 6462	I Feel Free/N.S.U.	1967	3.75	7.50	15.00
❑ 6488	Strange Brew/Tales of Brave Ulysses	1967	3.75	7.50	15.00
❑ 6522	Spoonful/Spoonful (Part 2)	1967	3.75	7.50	15.00
❑ 6544	Sunshine of Your Love/SWLABR	1968	2.00	4.00	8.00
❑ 6575	Anyone for Tennis/Pressed Rat and Warthog	1968	2.00	4.00	8.00
❑ 6617	White Room/Those Were the Days	1968	2.00	4.00	8.00
❑ 6646	Crossroads/Passing the Time	1969	2.00	4.00	8.00
❑ 6668	Badge/What a Bringdown	1969	2.00	4.00	8.00
❑ 6708	Sweet Wine/Lawdy Mama	1969	2.50	5.00	10.00
Albums					
ATCO					
❑ 33-206 [M]	Fresh Cream	1967	12.50	25.00	50.00
❑ SD 33-206 [S]	Fresh Cream	1967	7.50	15.00	30.00
—Purple and brown labels					
❑ SD 33-206 [S]	Fresh Cream	1969	3.75	7.50	15.00
—Yellow labels					
❑ 33-232 [M]	Disraeli Gears	1967	12.50	25.00	50.00
❑ SD 33-232 [S]	Disraeli Gears	1967	7.50	15.00	30.00
—Purple and brown labels					
❑ SD 33-232 [S]	Disraeli Gears	1969	3.75	7.50	15.00
—Yellow labels					
❑ SD 33-291	Best of Cream	1969	6.25	12.50	25.00
❑ SD 33-328	Live Cream	1970	6.25	12.50	25.00
❑ 2-700 [(2)M]	Wheels of Fire	1968	50.00	100.00	200.00
—White label promo; no stock copies are mono					
❑ SD 2-700 [(2)S]	Wheels of Fire	1968	12.50	25.00	50.00
—Purple and brown labels; foil-like cover					
❑ SD 2-700 [(2)S]	Wheels of Fire	1969	5.00	10.00	20.00
—Yellow labels; dull gray cover					
❑ SD 7001	Goodbye	1969	3.75	7.50	15.00
—Yellow labels					
❑ SD 7001	Goodbye	1969	7.50	15.00	30.00
—Purple and brown labels; deduct 33% if poster is missing					
❑ SD 7005	Live Cream — Volume II	1972	6.25	12.50	25.00
DCC COMPACT CLASSICS					
❑ LPZ-2015	Fresh Cream	1996	25.00	50.00	100.00
—Audiophile vinyl					
MOBILE FIDELITY					
❑ 2-066 [(2)]	Wheels of Fire	1980	22.50	45.00	90.00
—Audiophile vinyl					
❑ 1-264	Goodbye	1996	—	—	—
—Audiophile vinyl; canceled					
POLYDOR					
❑ 24-3502 [(2)]	Heavy Cream	1972	3.75	7.50	15.00
❑ 24-5529	Off the Top	1973	3.75	7.50	15.00
RSO					
❑ 015 [(2)DJ]	Classic Cuts	1978	10.00	20.00	40.00
—Promo-only compilation					
❑ RS-1-3009	Fresh Cream	1977	3.00	6.00	12.00
❑ RS-1-3010	Disraeli Gears	1977	3.00	6.00	12.00
❑ RS-1-3012	Best of Cream	1977	3.00	6.00	12.00
❑ RS-1-3013	Goodbye	1977	3.00	6.00	12.00
❑ RS-1-3014	Live Cream	1977	3.00	6.00	12.00
❑ RS-1-3015	Live Cream — Volume 2	1977	3.00	6.00	12.00
❑ RS-2-3802 [(2)S]	Wheels of Fire	1977	3.75	7.50	15.00
SPRINGBOARD					
❑ SPB 4037	Early Cream	1972	3.75	7.50	15.00
CREATION, THE					
45s					
DECCA					
❑ 32155	If I Stay Too Long/Nightmares	1967	3.00	6.00	12.00
❑ 32227	How Does It Feel to Feel/Life Is Just Beginning	1967	3.00	6.00	12.00
PLANET					
❑ 116	Making Time/Try and Stop Me	1966	3.75	7.50	15.00
❑ 119	Painter Man/Biff Bang Pow	1966	3.75	7.50	15.00
CREATION OF SUNLIGHT					
Albums					
WINDI					
❑ 1001	Creation of Sunlight	1968	150.00	300.00	600.00
CREATIONS, THE Many different groups.					
45s					
GLOBE					
❑ 102	Just Remember Me/Times Are Changing	1967	5.00	10.00	20.00
❑ 103	I've Got to Find Her/Times Are Changing	1967	5.00	10.00	20.00
❑ 1000	Oh Baby/Plenty of Love	1967	5.00	10.00	20.00

Number	Title (A Side/B Side)	Yr	VG	VG+	NM
JAMIE					
❏ 1197	The Bells/Shang Shang	1961	6.25	12.50	25.00
LIDO					
❏ 501	You Are My Darling/There Goes the Girl I Love	1956	75.00	150.00	300.00
MEL-O-DY					
❏ 101	This Is Our Night/You're My Inspiration	1962	—	—	—
MERIDIAN					
❏ 7550	The Wedding/I've Got a Feeling	1962	25.00	50.00	100.00
PATTI-JO					
❏ 1703	Seventeen/You'll Always Be Mine	1962	50.00	100.00	200.00
PENNY					
❏ 9022	Lady Luck/We're in Love	1962	15.00	30.00	60.00
PINE CREST					
❏ 101	Woke Up in the Morning/ Strolling Through the Park	1961	100.00	200.00	400.00
RADIANT					
❏ 103	Don't Listen to What Others Say/Don't Listen to What Others Say, Part 2	1964	6.25	12.50	25.00
TAKE TEN					
❏ 1501	Lady Luck/We're in Love	1963	7.50	15.00	30.00
TIP TOP					
❏ 400	Every Night I Pray/Mommy and Daddy	1956	50.00	100.00	200.00
❏ 501	You Are My Darling/There Goes the Girl I Love	1956	50.00	100.00	200.00
—At least one source claims this is a bootleg.					
TOP HAT					
❏ 1003	Crash/Chickie Darling	1964	10.00	20.00	40.00
❏ 1003 [PS]	Crash/Chickie Darling	1964	20.00	40.00	80.00
❏ 1004	Don't Be Mean/41 Willies	1965	12.50	235.00	50.00
❏ 1004 [PS]	Don't Be Mean/41 Willies	1965	25.00	50.00	100.00
VIRTUE					
❏ 2517	I'm So in Love with You/Save the People	1971	—	3.00	6.00
❏ 2518	Don't Let Me Down/The Price I Have to Pay	1971	—	3.00	6.00
❏ 2520	Nothing Too Good for You/You Mean So Much	1972	—	3.00	6.00
❏ 2521	You Make Me Feel So Good/ That's How Strong My Love Is	1972	—	3.00	6.00
❏ 2522	How Sweetly Simple/Lovin' Simple	1973	—	3.00	6.00
ZODIAC					
❏ 1005	A Dream/Foot Steps	1967	2.00	4.00	8.00

CREATIVE SOURCE
45s
Number	Title (A Side/B Side)	Yr	VG	VG+	NM
POLYDOR					
❏ 14291	Pass the Feelin' On/Turn On to Music	1975	—	2.50	5.00
❏ 14334	I'll Find You Anywhere/Singin' Funky Music	1976	—	—	—
—Canceled					
SUSSEX					
❏ 501	You Can't Hide Love/Lovesville	1973	—	2.50	5.00
❏ 508	You're Too Good to Be True/Oh Love	1973	—	2.50	5.00
❏ 509	Who Is He and What Is He to You (Part 1)/Who Is He and What Is He to You (Part 2)	1974	—	2.50	5.00
❏ 622	Keep On Movin'/I Just Can't See Myself Without You	1974	—	2.50	5.00
❏ 632	Migration/I Just Can't See Myself Without You	1974	—	2.50	5.00
Albums					
POLYDOR					
❏ PD-1-6052	Pass the Feelin' On	1975	3.00	6.00	12.00
❏ PD-1-6065	Consider the Source	1976	3.00	6.00	12.00
SUSSEX					
❏ SUS-8027	Creative Source	1973	3.75	7.50	15.00
❏ SUS-8035	Migration	1974	3.75	7.50	15.00

CREATORS, THE (1)
45s
Number	Title (A Side/B Side)	Yr	VG	VG+	NM
DOOTO					
❏ 463	I've Had You/Drafted, Volunteered, Enlisted	1961	6.25	12.50	25.00
DORE					
❏ 635	Too Far to Turn Around/ Hello There, Mister Grave Digger	1962	15.00	30.00	60.00

CREATORS, THE (2)
45s
Number	Title (A Side/B Side)	Yr	VG	VG+	NM
EPIC					
❏ 9605	Crazy Love/Cross Fire	1963	3.75	7.50	15.00
HI-Q					
❏ 5021	Wear My Ring/Booga Bear	1961	6.25	12.50	25.00
—Bold print label					
❏ 5021	Wear My Ring/Booga Bear	1961	20.00	40.00	80.00
—Normal print label					
TIME					
❏ 1038	Do You Remember/ There's Going to Be an Angel	1961	6.25	12.50	25.00

CREATORS, THE (3)
45s
Number	Title (A Side/B Side)	Yr	VG	VG+	NM
PHILIPS					
❏ 40058	Boy, He's Got It/Yeah, He's Got It	1962	6.25	12.50	25.00
❏ 40083	I'll Stay Home (New Year's Eve)/ Shoom Ba Boom	1962	75.00	150.00	300.00
T-KAY					
❏ 110	I'll Never, Never Do It Again/Boy, He's Got It!	1962	20.00	40.00	80.00

CREATURES, THE
45s
Number	Title (A Side/B Side)	Yr	VG	VG+	NM
COLUMBIA					
❏ 43689	Night Is Warm/String Along	1966	2.50	5.00	10.00
❏ 43894	Looking at Tomorrow/Someone Needs You	1967	2.00	4.00	8.00

CREEDENCE CLEARWATER REVIVAL Also see DOUG CLIFFORD; JOHN FOGERTY; TOM FOGERTY; TOMMY FOGERTY AND THE BLUE VELVETS; THE GOLLIWOGS.
12-Inch Singles
Number	Title (A Side/B Side)	Yr	VG	VG+	NM
FANTASY					
❏ 759-D-LP [DJ]	I Heard It Through the Grapevine (11:05) (same on both sides)	1976	5.00	10.00	20.00
45s
FANTASY					
❏ 616	Suzie Q (Part One)/Suzie Q (Part Two)	1968	—	3.00	6.00
❏ 617	I Put a Spell on You/Walk on the Water	1968	2.00	4.00	8.00

Number	Title (A Side/B Side)	Yr	VG	VG+	NM
❏ 619	Proud Mary/Born on the Bayou	1969	—	3.00	6.00
❏ 622	Bad Moon Rising/Lodi	1969	—	3.00	6.00
❏ 625	Green River/Commotion	1969	—	3.00	6.00
❏ 634	Down on the Corner/Fortunate Son	1969	—	3.00	6.00
❏ 634 [PS]	Down on the Corner/Fortunate Son	1969	3.00	6.00	12.00
❏ 637	Travelin' Band/Who'll Stop the Rain	1970	—	3.00	6.00
❏ 637 [PS]	Travelin' Band/Who'll Stop the Rain	1970	3.00	6.00	12.00
❏ 641	Up Around the Bend/Run Through the Jungle	1970	—	3.00	6.00
❏ 641 [PS]	Up Around the Bend/Run Through the Jungle	1970	3.00	6.00	12.00
❏ 645	Lookin' Out My Back Door/ Long As I Can See the Light	1970	—	3.00	6.00
❏ 645 [PS]	Lookin' Out My Back Door/ Long As I Can See the Light	1970	3.00	6.00	12.00
❏ 655	Have You Ever Seen the Rain/Hey Tonight	1971	—	3.00	6.00
❏ 665	Sweet Hitch-Hiker/Door to Door	1971	—	3.00	6.00
❏ 665 [PS]	Sweet Hitch-Hiker/Door to Door	1971	3.00	6.00	12.00
❏ 676	Someday Never Comes/Tearin' Up the Country	1972	—	3.00	6.00
❏ 759	I Heard It Through the Grapevine/ Good Golly Miss Molly	1976	—	2.00	4.00
❏ 759 [PS]	I Heard It Through the Grapevine/ Good Golly Miss Molly	1976	—	2.50	5.00
❏ 908	Tombstone Shadow/Commotion	1981	—	2.00	4.00
❏ 917	Medley U.S.A./Bad Moon Rising	1981	—	2.00	4.00
❏ 920	Cotton Fields/Lodi	1981	—	2.00	4.00
❏ 957	Medley (from "I Heard It Through the Grapevine" to "Up Around the Bend")/Medley (from "Proud Mary" to "Lodi")	1985	2.50	5.00	10.00
❏ 2832/3 [DJ]	45 Revolutions Per Minute (Part 1)/45 Revolutions Per Minute (Part 2)	1970	10.00	20.00	40.00
❏ 2832/3 [PS]	45 Revolutions Per Minute (Part 1)/45 Revolutions Per Minute (Part 2)	1970	15.00	30.00	60.00
SCORPIO					
❏ 412	Porterville/Call It Pretending	1968	20.00	40.00	80.00
Albums					
ANALOGUE PRODUCTIONS					
❏ AAPP-8382	Creedence Clearwater Revival	2002	6.25	12.50	25.00
—Audiophile edition on heavy vinyl					
❏ AAPP-8387	Bayou Country	2002	6.25	12.50	25.00
—Audiophile edition on heavy vinyl					
❏ AAPP-8393	Green River	2002	6.25	12.50	25.00
—Audiophile edition on heavy vinyl					
❏ AAPP-8397	Willie and the Poor Boys	2002	6.25	12.50	25.00
—Audiophile edition on heavy vinyl					
❏ AAPP-8402	Cosmo's Factory	2002	6.25	12.50	25.00
—Audiophile edition on heavy vinyl					
❏ AAPP-9404	Mardi Gras	2002	6.25	12.50	25.00
—Audiophile edition on heavy vinyl					
DCC COMPACT CLASSICS					
❏ LPZ-2019	Willie and the Poor Boys	1996	12.50	25.00	50.00
—Audiophile vinyl					
FANTASY					
❏ CCR-1 [(2)]	Live in Europe	1973	3.00	6.00	12.00
❏ CCR-2 [(2)]	Chronicle (The 20 Greatest Hits)	1976	3.75	7.50	15.00
—Brown labels					
❏ CCR-2 [(2)]	Chronicle (The 20 Greatest Hits)	1979	3.00	6.00	12.00
—Whitish or light blue labels					
❏ CCR-3 [(2)]	Chronicle, Volume 2	1987	3.75	7.50	15.00
❏ CCR-68 [(2)]	Creedence Clearwater Revival 1968/69	1981	3.00	6.00	12.00
—Compilation of 8382 and 8387					
❏ CCR-69 [(2)]	Creedence Clearwater Revival 1969	1981	3.00	6.00	12.00
—Compilation of 8393 and 8397					
❏ CCR-70 [(2)]	Creedence Clearwater Revival 1970	1981	3.00	6.00	12.00
—Compilation of 8402 and 8410					
❏ FPM-4001 [Q]	Creedence Gold	1975	12.50	25.00	50.00
❏ MPF-4501	The Royal Albert Hall Concert	1980	3.75	7.50	15.00
—Album withdrawn and changed when it was discovered this didn't come from the Royal Albert Hall					
❏ MPF-4501	The Concert	1981	2.50	5.00	10.00
—Retitled version					
❏ MPF-4509	Creedence Country	1981	2.50	5.00	10.00
❏ ORC-4512	Creedence Clearwater Revival	1981	2.00	4.00	8.00
—Reissue of 8382					
❏ ORC-4513	Bayou Country	1981	2.00	4.00	8.00
—Reissue of 8387					
❏ ORC-4514	Green River	1981	2.00	4.00	8.00
—Reissue of 8393					
❏ ORC-4515	Willy and the Poor Boys	1981	2.00	4.00	8.00
—Reissue of 8397					
❏ ORC-4516	Cosmo's Factory	1981	2.00	4.00	8.00
—Reissue of 8402					
❏ ORC-4517	Pendulum	1981	2.00	4.00	8.00
—Reissue of 8410					
❏ ORC-4518	Mardi Gras	1981	2.00	4.00	8.00
—Reissue of 9404					
❏ MPF-4522	The Movie Album	1985	2.00	4.00	8.00
❏ ORC-4526 [(2)]	Live in Europe	1986	2.50	5.00	10.00
❏ F-8382	Creedence Clearwater Revival	1968	3.75	7.50	15.00
—With "Susie Q" mentioned on the front cover; dark blue label					
❏ F-8382	Creedence Clearwater Revival	1968	6.25	12.50	25.00
—With no reference to "Susie Q" on the front cover					
❏ F-8382 [DJ]	Creedence Clearwater Revival	1968	20.00	40.00	80.00
—White label promo					
❏ F-8382	Creedence Clearwater Revival	1973	2.50	5.00	10.00
—Brown label					
❏ F-8387	Bayou Country	1969	3.75	7.50	15.00
—Dark blue label					
❏ F-8387 [DJ]	Bayou Country	1969	20.00	40.00	80.00
—White label promo					
❏ F-8387	Bayou Country	1973	2.50	5.00	10.00
—Brown label					
❏ F-8393	Green River	1969	3.75	7.50	15.00
—Dark blue label					
❏ F-8393 [DJ]	Green River	1969	20.00	40.00	80.00
—White label promo					
❏ F-8393	Green River	1973	2.50	5.00	10.00
—Brown label					
❏ F-8397	Willy and the Poor Boys	1969	3.75	7.50	15.00
—Dark blue label					

Number	Title (A Side/B Side)	Yr	VG	VG+	NM
❏ F-8397 [DJ]	Willy and the Poor Boys	1969	20.00	40.00	80.00
—White label promo					
❏ F-8397	Willy and the Poor Boys	1973	2.50	5.00	10.00
—Brown label					
❏ F-8402	Cosmo's Factory	1970	3.75	7.50	15.00
—Dark blue label					
❏ F-8402 [DJ]	Cosmo's Factory	1970	20.00	40.00	80.00
—White label promo					
❏ F-8402	Cosmo's Factory	1973	2.50	5.00	10.00
—Brown label					
❏ F-8410	Pendulum	1970	3.75	7.50	15.00
—Dark blue label					
❏ F-8410	Pendulum	1973	2.50	5.00	10.00
—Brown label					
❏ F-9404	Mardi Gras	1972	3.75	7.50	15.00
—Dark blue label					
❏ F-9404	Mardi Gras	1973	2.50	5.00	10.00
—Brown label					
❏ F-9418	Creedence Gold	1972	2.50	5.00	10.00
❏ F-9430	More Creedence Gold	1973	2.50	5.00	10.00
❏ F-9621	Chooglin'	1982	2.00	4.00	8.00
HEARTLAND					
❏ HR 2039 [(3)]	Creedence Clearwater Revival	1990	3.75	7.50	15.00
K-TEL					
❏ NU 9360	The Best of Creedence Clearwater Revival — 20 Super Hits	1978	3.75	7.50	15.00
MOBILE FIDELITY					
❏ 1-037	Cosmo's Factory	1979	17.50	35.00	70.00
—Audiophile vinyl					
TIME-LIFE					
❏ SCLR-18 [(2)]	Classic Rock: Creedence Clearwater Revival	1989	3.75	7.50	15.00

CRESCENDOS, THE (1) Nashville-based vocal group.
45s

Number	Title (A Side/B Side)	Yr	VG	VG+	NM
NASCO					
❏ 6005	Oh Julie/My Little Girl	1957	6.25	12.50	25.00
❏ 6009	School Girl/Crazy Hop	1958	6.25	12.50	25.00
❏ 6009 [PS]	School Girl/Crazy Hop	1958	12.50	25.00	50.00
❏ 6021	Rainy Sunday/Young and In Love	1958	6.25	12.50	25.00
❏ 6021 [PS]	Rainy Sunday/Young and In Love	1958	12.50	25.00	50.00
NASHBORO					
❏ (no #) [PS]	The Crescendos	1957	12.50	25.00	50.00
—Large-hole omnibus sleeve, often found with "Oh Julie," but may have been used on other Nasco singles					
TAP					
❏ 7027	Oh Julie/Angel Face	1962	3.75	7.50	15.00
❏ 7027 [PS]	Oh Julie/Angel Face	1962	6.25	12.50	25.00

Albums

Number	Title (A Side/B Side)	Yr	VG	VG+	NM
GUEST STAR					
❏ G-1453 [M]	Oh Julie	1962	12.50	25.00	50.00
❏ GS-1453 [R]	Oh Julie	1962	5.00	10.00	20.00

CRESCENDOS, THE (2)
45s

Number	Title (A Side/B Side)	Yr	VG	VG+	NM
ATLANTIC					
❏ 1109	Sweet Dreams/Finders Keepers	1956	7.50	15.00	30.00
❏ 2014	I'll Be Seeing You/Sweet Dreams	1959	3.75	7.50	15.00

CRESCENDOS, THE (U) Some of these may be group (1); it's unlikely that any are group (2).
45s

Number	Title (A Side/B Side)	Yr	VG	VG+	NM
DOMAIN					
❏ 1025	A Fellow Needs a Girl/Black Cat	1964	3.75	7.50	15.00
IMPRO					
❏ 5006	Tidal Wave/Crescendo Special	1962	10.00	20.00	40.00
NU SOUND					
❏ 1007	Count Down/Hawk Walk	1961	7.50	15.00	30.00
❏ 1014	Sweet Talk/Movin' Wild	1961	7.50	15.00	30.00
SCARLET					
❏ 4007	Strange Love/Let's Take a Walk	1960	7.50	15.00	30.00
❏ 4009	Angel Face/I'm So Ashamed	1961	12.50	25.00	50.00

CRESCHENDOS, THE
45s

Number	Title (A Side/B Side)	Yr	VG	VG+	NM
GONE					
❏ 5100	My Heart's Desire/Take My Heart	1961	7.50	15.00	30.00
MUSIC CITY					
❏ 831	My Heart's Desire/Take My Heart	1960	50.00	100.00	200.00
—Maroon label					
❏ 831	My Heart's Desire/Take My Heart	1960	100.00	200.00	400.00
—Green label					
❏ 831	My Heart's Desire/Take My Heart	1961	12.50	25.00	50.00
—Black label					
❏ 839	Teenage Prayer/I Don't Mind	1961	62.50	125.00	250.00
SATURN					
❏ 404	Surfing Strip/Hanging Ten	1963	12.50	25.00	50.00

CRESENTS, THE
45s

Number	Title (A Side/B Side)	Yr	VG	VG+	NM
JOYCE					
❏ 102	Everybody Knew But Me/Rosemarie	1957	62.50	125.00	250.00

CRESTONES, THE
45s

Number	Title (A Side/B Side)	Yr	VG	VG+	NM
MARKIE					
❏ 117	She's a Bad Motorcycle/Grasshopper Dance	1963	12.50	25.00	50.00
U.S.A.					
❏ 835	My Girl/The Chopper	1965	3.00	6.00	12.00

CRESTS, THE Also see JOHNNY MAESTRO.
45s

Number	Title (A Side/B Side)	Yr	VG	VG+	NM
COED					
❏ 501	Pretty Little Angel/I Thank the Moon	1958	10.00	20.00	40.00
—"Coed" in red and black print					
❏ 501	Pretty Little Angel/I Thank the Moon	1958	37.50	75.00	150.00
—"Coed" in red print					
❏ 506	16 Candles/Beside You	1958	7.50	15.00	30.00
❏ 509	Six Nights a Week/I Do	1959	6.25	12.50	25.00

Number	Title (A Side/B Side)	Yr	VG	VG+	NM
❏ 511	Flower of Love/Molly Mae	1959	6.25	12.50	25.00
❏ 515	The Angels Listened In/I Thank the Moon	1959	7.50	15.00	30.00
❏ 521	A Year Ago Tonight/Paper Clown	1959	6.25	12.50	25.00
❏ 525	Step by Step/Gee (But I'd Give the World)	1960	6.25	12.50	25.00
❏ 531	Trouble in Paradise/Always You	1960	6.25	12.50	25.00
❏ 535	Journey of Love/If My Heart Could Write a Letter	1960	5.00	10.00	20.00
❏ 537	Isn't It Amazing/Molly Mae	1960	5.00	10.00	20.00
❏ 543	I Remember (In the Still of the Night)/ Good Golly Miss Molly	1961	6.25	12.50	25.00
❏ 561	Little Miracles/Baby I Gotta Know	1962	7.50	15.00	30.00
CORAL					
❏ 62403	You Blew Out the Candles/ A Love to Last a Lifetime	1964	7.50	15.00	30.00
HARVEY					
❏ 5002	Sixteen Candles/My Juanita	1981	2.50	5.00	10.00
—Red vinyl					
JOYCE					
❏ 103	My Juanita/Sweetest One	1957	75.00	150.00	300.00
—Label name: "JoYce"					
❏ 103	My Juanita/Sweetest One	1959	12.50	25.00	50.00
—Label name: "Joyce"					
❏ 105	No One to Love/Wish She Was Mine	1957	75.00	150.00	300.00
KING TUT					
❏ 172	Earth Angel/Tweedlee Dee	197?	2.00	4.00	8.00
LANA					
❏ 101	16 Candles/Besides You	196?	2.00	4.00	8.00
—Oldies reissue					
❏ 102	Trouble in Paradise/I Thank the Moon	196?	2.00	4.00	8.00
—Oldies reissue					
❏ 103	Step by Step/Gee (But I'd Give the World)	196?	2.00	4.00	8.00
—Oldies reissue					
LOST-NITE					
❏ 156	No One to Love/Wish She Was Mine	196?	—	3.00	6.00
—Reissue					
❏ 163	Six Nights a Week/I Do	196?	—	3.00	6.00
—Reissue					
❏ 166	Step by Step/Gee (But I'd Give the World)	196?	—	3.00	6.00
—Reissue					
❏ 168	16 Candles/Beside You	196?	—	3.00	6.00
—Reissue					
❏ 171	The Angels Listened In/I Thank the Moon	196?	—	3.00	6.00
—Reissue					
❏ 209	My Juanita/Sweetest One	196?	—	3.00	6.00
—Reissue					
❏ 211	Flower of Love/Molly Mae	196?	—	3.00	6.00
—Reissue					
❏ 229	Pretty Little Angel/I Thank the Moon	196?	—	2.50	5.00
—Reissue					
MUSICTONE					
❏ 1106	My Juanita/Sweetest One	1961	5.00	10.00	20.00
SCEPTER					
❏ 12112	I'm Stepping Out of the Picture/Afraid of Love	1965	3.75	7.50	15.00
SELMA					
❏ 311	Guilty/Number One with Me	1962	6.25	12.50	25.00
—A-side does not have spoken intro					
❏ 311	Guilty/Number One with Me	1962	18.75	37.50	75.00
—A-side has spoken intro					
❏ 4000	Did I Remember/Tears Will Fall	1963	7.50	15.00	30.00
TIMES SQUARE					
❏ 2	No One to Love/Wish She Was Mine	1962	5.00	10.00	20.00
—Red vinyl					
❏ 6	Baby/I Love You So	1964	3.75	7.50	15.00
❏ 97	Baby/I Love You So	1964	3.00	6.00	12.00
TRANS ATLAS					
❏ 696	The Actor/Three Tears in a Bucket	1962	7.50	15.00	30.00

7-Inch Extended Plays

Number	Title (A Side/B Side)	Yr	VG	VG+	NM
COED					
❏ EPC-101	The Angels Listened In/Flower of Love//16 Candles/Six Nights a Week	1959	100.00	200.00	400.00
❏ EPC-101 [PS]	The Angels Listened In	1959	100.00	200.00	400.00

Albums

Number	Title (A Side/B Side)	Yr	VG	VG+	NM
COED					
❏ LPC-901 [M]	The Crests Sing All Biggies	1960	50.00	100.00	200.00
—Red label					
❏ LPC-901 [M]	The Crests Sing All Biggies	1960	100.00	200.00	400.00
—Yellow label, black print					
❏ LPC-904 [M]	The Best of the Crests/16 Fabulous Hits	1961	100.00	200.00	400.00
—Label simply calls this "16 Fabulous Hits"					
COLLECTABLES					
❏ COL-5009	Greatest Hits	1982	3.00	6.00	12.00
POST					
❏ 3000	The Crests Sing	196?	10.00	20.00	40.00
RHINO					
❏ R1-70948	The Best of the Crests	1989	3.00	6.00	12.00

CRESTS, THE (2) Nashville studio group.
45s

Number	Title (A Side/B Side)	Yr	VG	VG+	NM
HIT					
❏ 227	You're the One/Treat Her Right	1965	2.00	4.00	8.00
—B-side by Cal York and the Roamers					

CREW CUTS, THE
45s

Number	Title (A Side/B Side)	Yr	VG	VG+	NM
ABC-PARAMOUNT					
❏ 10450	Hip-Huggers/You're a Star, Donna, Donna	1963	3.00	6.00	12.00
CHESS					
❏ 1892	Ain't That Nice/Yeah, Yeah, She Wants Me	1964	2.50	5.00	10.00
FIREBIRD					
❏ 1805	My Heart Belongs to Only You/You've Been In	1970	—	2.50	5.00
4 CORNERS OF THE WORLD					
❏ 120	Don't Be Angry/Earth Angel	1962	2.50	5.00	10.00
MERCURY					
❏ 70341	Crazy 'Bout You Baby/Angela Mia	1954	5.00	10.00	20.00
❏ 70404	Sh-Boom/I Spoke Too Soon	1954	6.25	12.50	25.00
❏ 70404	Sh-Boom/I Spoke Too Soon	1954	12.50	25.00	50.00
—7-inch 78 rpm on vinyl					

Number	Title (A Side/B Side)	Yr	VG	VG+	NM
❑ 70404 [PS]	Sh-Boom/I Spoke Too Soon	1954	25.00	50.00	100.00

—Sleeve accompanying the 78: "PopSi Hit Record of the Month"

Number	Title (A Side/B Side)	Yr	VG	VG+	NM
❑ 70443	Oop-Shoop/Do Me Good Baby	1954	3.75	7.50	15.00
❑ 70490	All I Wanna Do/The Barking Dog	1954	3.75	7.50	15.00
❑ 70491	Dance, Mr. Snowman, Dance/Twinkle Toes	1954	3.75	7.50	15.00
❑ 70494	The Whippenpoof Song/Varsity Drag	1954	3.75	7.50	15.00
❑ 70529	Ko Ko Mo (I Love You So)/Earth Angel	1955	3.75	7.50	15.00
❑ 70597	Don't Be Angry/Chop Chop Boom	1955	3.75	7.50	15.00
❑ 70598	Unchained Melody/Two Hearts, Two Kisses	1955	3.75	7.50	15.00
❑ 70634	A Story Untold/Carmen's Boogie	1955	3.75	7.50	15.00
❑ 70668	Gum Drop/Song of the Fool	1955	3.75	7.50	15.00
❑ 70710	Slam! Bam!/Are You Having Any Fun	1955	3.75	7.50	15.00
❑ 70741	Angels in the Sky/Mostly Martha	1955	3.75	7.50	15.00
❑ 70782	Seven Days/That's Your Mistake	1956	3.75	7.50	15.00
❑ 70840	Out of the Picture/Honey Hair, Sugar Lips, Eyes of Blue	1956	3.75	7.50	15.00
❑ 70890	Tell Me Why/Rebel in Town	1956	3.75	7.50	15.00
❑ 70922	Bei Mir Bist Du Schoen/Thirteen Going on Fourteen	1956	3.75	7.50	15.00
❑ 70977	Love in a Home/Keeper of the Flame	1956	3.75	7.50	15.00
❑ 70988	The Varsity Drag/Halls of Ivy	1956	3.75	7.50	15.00
❑ 71022	Young Love/Little by Little	1956	3.75	7.50	15.00
❑ 71076	The Angelus/Whatever, Whenever. Whoever	1957	3.75	7.50	15.00
❑ 71125	Suzie Q/Such a Shame	1957	3.75	7.50	15.00
❑ 71168	I Sit in My Window/Hey, You Face	1957	3.75	7.50	15.00
❑ 71223	I Like It Like That/Be My Only Love	1957	3.75	7.50	15.00

RCA VICTOR

Number	Title (A Side/B Side)	Yr	VG	VG+	NM
❑ 47-7320	Forever My Darling/Hey Stella	1958	3.00	6.00	12.00
❑ 47-7359	That's My Desire/Baby Be Mine	1958	3.00	6.00	12.00
❑ 47-7446	Fraternity Pin/Can You Hear Me	1959	3.00	6.00	12.00
❑ 47-7509	Gone, Gone, Gone/Someone in Heaven	1959	3.00	6.00	12.00
❑ 47-7577	Bermuda/Kin-Ni-Ki-Nic	1959	3.00	6.00	12.00
❑ 47-7667	It Is No Secret/No, No, Nevermore	1960	3.00	6.00	12.00
❑ 47-7734	American Beauty Rose/The Shrine on Top of the Hill	1960	3.00	6.00	12.00
❑ 47-7759	Aura Lee/Going to Church on Sunday	1960	3.00	6.00	12.00

VEE JAY

Number	Title (A Side/B Side)	Yr	VG	VG+	NM
❑ 569	The Three Bells/Spanish Is the Loving Tongue	1963	3.00	6.00	12.00

WARWICK

Number	Title (A Side/B Side)	Yr	VG	VG+	NM
❑ 558	Over the Mountain/Searchin'	1960	3.00	6.00	12.00
❑ 585	You and the Angels/I Care for You	1960	3.00	6.00	12.00
❑ 595	Malaguena/Why Not	1960	3.00	6.00	12.00
❑ 623	The Legend of Gunga Din/Number One with Me	1961	3.00	6.00	12.00

WHALE

Number	Title (A Side/B Side)	Yr	VG	VG+	NM
❑ 507	Twistin' All the World/Electric Chair	1962	3.00	6.00	12.00
❑ 508	Laura Love/Little Donkey	1962	3.00	6.00	12.00
❑ 509	Hush Little Baby/Ti-Pi-Tum	1962	3.00	6.00	12.00

7-Inch Extended Plays

MERCURY

Number	Title (A Side/B Side)	Yr	VG	VG+	NM
❑ EP-1-3274	Down the Old Ox Road/The Whiffenpoof Song//We're Working Our Way Through College/Varsity Drag	1956	3.00	6.00	12.00
❑ EP-1-3274 [PS]	The Crew Cuts On Campus	1956	3.00	6.00	12.00
❑ EP-1-3275	Buckle Down, Winsocki/Betty Co-Ed//You Gotta Be a Football Hero/Collegiate	195?	3.00	6.00	12.00
❑ EP-1-3275 [PS]	3 Cheers for the Crew Cuts	195?	3.00	6.00	12.00
❑ EP-1-3325	Carmen's Boogie/Here//Red Hot Serenade/When, When, When	195?	3.00	6.00	12.00
❑ EP-1-3325 [PS]	Crew Cuts Go Long Hair	195?	3.00	6.00	12.00

Albums

CAMAY

Number	Title (A Side/B Side)	Yr	VG	VG+	NM
❑ CA-1002 [M]	The Great New Sound of the Crew Cuts	196?	5.00	10.00	20.00
❑ CA-3002 [S]	The Great New Sound of the Crew Cuts	196?	6.25	12.50	25.00

MERCURY

Number	Title (A Side/B Side)	Yr	VG	VG+	NM
❑ MG-20067 [M]	The Crew Cuts Go Longhair	1955	12.50	25.00	50.00
❑ MG-20140 [M]	The Crew Cuts On Campus	1956	12.50	25.00	50.00
❑ MG-20143 [M]	Crew Cut Capers	1956	12.50	25.00	50.00
❑ MG-20144 [M]	Rock and Roll Bash	1956	20.00	40.00	80.00
❑ MG-20199 [M]	Music A La Carte	1957	12.50	25.00	50.00
❑ MG-25200 [10]	The Crew Cuts On Campus	1956	20.00	40.00	80.00

PICADILLY

Number	Title (A Side/B Side)	Yr	VG	VG+	NM
❑ PIC-3560	The Wonderful Happy Crazy Innocent World	1980	2.50	5.00	10.00

RCA VICTOR

Number	Title (A Side/B Side)	Yr	VG	VG+	NM
❑ PR-102 [M]	The Crew Cuts Sing Out!	1960	6.25	12.50	25.00
❑ PR-129 [M]	The Crew Cuts Have a Ball	1960	6.25	12.50	25.00

—Produced for Ebonite bowling balls; Side 2 has "Bowling Tips by Top Stars"

Number	Title (A Side/B Side)	Yr	VG	VG+	NM
❑ LPM-1933 [M]	Surprise Package	1958	7.50	15.00	30.00
❑ LSP-1933 [S]	Surprise Package	1959	10.00	20.00	40.00
❑ LPM-2037 [M]	The Crew Cuts Sing	1959	7.50	15.00	30.00
❑ LSP-2037 [S]	The Crew Cuts Sing	1959	10.00	20.00	40.00
❑ LPM-2067 [M]	You Must Have Been a Beautiful Baby	1960	7.50	15.00	30.00
❑ LSP-2067 [S]	You Must Have Been a Beautiful Baby	1960	10.00	20.00	40.00

WING

Number	Title (A Side/B Side)	Yr	VG	VG+	NM
❑ MGW-12125 [M]	Rock and Roll Bash	196?	6.25	12.50	25.00
❑ MGW-12145 [M]	The Crew Cuts On Campus	196?	5.00	10.00	20.00
❑ MGW-12177 [M]	The Crew Cuts	196?	5.00	10.00	20.00
❑ MGW-12180 [M]	High School Favorites	196?	5.00	10.00	20.00
❑ MGW-12195 [M]	The Crew Cuts Sing the Masters	196?	5.00	10.00	20.00

CREWE, BOB Includes records as "The Bob Crewe Generation" and similar names.

45s

ABC-PARAMOUNT

Number	Title (A Side/B Side)	Yr	VG	VG+	NM
❑ 10204	Swingin' Family Tree/La La Loretta	1961	3.00	6.00	12.00
❑ 10246	One More Lie/I'm Goin' Home (On My Way)	1961	3.00	6.00	12.00
❑ 10273	Another Day/Come to Me	1961	3.00	6.00	12.00

BRUNSWICK

Number	Title (A Side/B Side)	Yr	VG	VG+	NM
❑ 55021	I Can't Shake the Blues/Torn and Tattered Heart	1957	3.75	7.50	15.00

CORAL

Number	Title (A Side/B Side)	Yr	VG	VG+	NM
❑ 61688	Melody for Lovers/Can't Get Away from It	1956	3.75	7.50	15.00

CREWE

Number	Title (A Side/B Side)	Yr	VG	VG+	NM
❑ 605	Dandylion/Day By Day & Prepare Ye	1971	—	2.50	5.00

DYNO VOICE

Number	Title (A Side/B Side)	Yr	VG	VG+	NM
❑ 229	Music to Watch Girls By/Girls on the Rocks	1966	2.00	4.00	8.00
❑ 231	After the Ball/One More Year	1967	—		3.00
❑ 233	Mini Skirts in Moscow, or ... /Theme for a Lazy Girl	1967	—		3.00	6.00

Number	Title (A Side/B Side)	Yr	VG	VG+	NM
❑ 233 [PS]	Mini Skirts in Moscow, or ... /Theme for a Lazy Girl	1967	2.50	5.00	10.00
❑ 237	A Lover's Concerto/You Only Live Twice	1967	—	3.00	6.00
❑ 902	Birds of Britain/I Will Wait for You	1968	—	3.00	6.00
❑ 906	Winter Warm/Song from Moulin Rouge	1968	—	3.00	6.00
❑ 915	To Give (The Reason I Live)/Battle Hymn of the Republic	1968	—	3.00	6.00
❑ 928	Angel Is Love/Black Queen's Beads	1968	—	3.00	6.00

ELEKTRA

Number	Title (A Side/B Side)	Yr	VG	VG+	NM
❑ 45346	Time for You and Me/Free (Medley)	1976	—	2.00	4.00
❑ 45380	Menage a Trois/I Am Free-Keep Walkin'	1976	—	2.00	4.00
❑ 45404	It Took a Long Time (For the First Time in My Life)/In Another Life	1977	—	2.00	4.00
❑ 45425	Marriage Made in Heaven/In Another Life	1977	—	2.00	4.00

JUBILEE

Number	Title (A Side/B Side)	Yr	VG	VG+	NM
❑ 5148	Cash Register Heart/Change of Heart	1954	5.00	10.00	20.00
❑ 5164	Punch/It's All Over	1954	5.00	10.00	20.00

MELBA

Number	Title (A Side/B Side)	Yr	VG	VG+	NM
❑ 119	Guessin' Games/Don't Call Me Chicken	1957	3.75	7.50	15.00

METROMEDIA

Number	Title (A Side/B Side)	Yr	VG	VG+	NM
❑ 229	Mammy Blue/Better Be Gone	1972	—	2.50	5.00
❑ 243	Takin' Care of Each Other/(B-side unknown)	1972	—	2.50	5.00

PHILIPS

Number	Title (A Side/B Side)	Yr	VG	VG+	NM
❑ 40241	Rag Doll/Ronnie	1964	2.00	4.00	8.00
❑ 40241 [PS]	Rag Doll/Ronnie	1964	3.75	7.50	15.00

—Has photo of the Four Seasons on it; the sleeve even looks as if it belongs to a Four Seasons record until you read a bit more closely!

SPOTLIGHT

Number	Title (A Side/B Side)	Yr	VG	VG+	NM
❑ 387	The Rhythm and the Blues/The Bumblebee	1955	6.25	12.50	25.00
❑ 393	Penny Nickel Dime Quarter (On a Teenage Date)/How Long	1956	5.00	10.00	20.00

20TH CENTURY

Number	Title (A Side/B Side)	Yr	VG	VG+	NM
❑ 2271	Street Talk/Street Talk (Part 2)	1976	—	2.00	4.00

VIK

Number	Title (A Side/B Side)	Yr	VG	VG+	NM
❑ 0307	Charm Bracelet/Do Be Do Be Do	1957	6.25	12.50	25.00
❑ 0333	Of Sun, the Sea and the Sand/Sweet Talk	1958	5.00	10.00	20.00

WARWICK

Number	Title (A Side/B Side)	Yr	VG	VG+	NM
❑ 519	The Whippenpoof Song/Let's Pretend	1959	3.00	6.00	12.00
❑ 534	Cool Time/Quite a Picture	1960	3.00	6.00	12.00
❑ 553	Silhouettes/Let's Get Serious	1960	3.00	6.00	12.00
❑ 579	Little Girl of Mine/To Ev'ry Girl, To Ev'ry Boy	1960	3.00	6.00	12.00
❑ 601	Oh, How I Miss You Tonight/Ev'rytime	1960	3.00	6.00	12.00
❑ 616	She's Only Wonderful/On the Street Where You Live	1961	3.00	6.00	12.00

Albums

CGC

Number	Title (A Side/B Side)	Yr	VG	VG+	NM
❑ 1000	Let Me Touch You	1970	3.00	6.00	12.00

DYNO VOICE

Number	Title (A Side/B Side)	Yr	VG	VG+	NM
❑ DV-1902 [M]	Music to Watch Birds By	1967	3.75	7.50	15.00
❑ DV-1906 [M]	The Bob Crewe Generation In Classic Form	1968	3.75	7.50	15.00
❑ DV-9003 [M]	Music to Watch Girls By	1967	3.75	7.50	15.00
❑ DVS-9003 [S]	Music to Watch Girls By	1967	3.00	6.00	12.00
❑ DV-31902 [S]	Music to Watch Birds By	1967	3.00	6.00	12.00
❑ DV-31906 [S]	The Bob Crewe Generation In Classic Form	1968	3.00	6.00	12.00

ELEKTRA

Number	Title (A Side/B Side)	Yr	VG	VG+	NM
❑ 7E-1083	Street Talk	1976	3.00	6.00	12.00
❑ 7E-1103	Motivation	1977	3.00	6.00	12.00

PHILIPS

Number	Title (A Side/B Side)	Yr	VG	VG+	NM
❑ PHM 200150 [M]	All the Song Hits of the Four Seasons	1964	6.25	12.50	25.00
❑ PHM 200238 [M]	Bob Crewe Plays the Four Seasons' Hits	1967	5.00	10.00	20.00
❑ PHS 600150 [S]	All the Song Hits of the Four Seasons	1964	7.50	15.00	30.00
❑ PHS 600238 [S]	Bob Crewe Plays the Four Seasons' Hits	1967	3.75	7.50	15.00

WARWICK

Number	Title (A Side/B Side)	Yr	VG	VG+	NM
❑ W-2009 [M]	Kicks	1960	6.25	12.50	25.00
❑ WST-2009 [S]	Kicks	1960	12.50	25.00	50.00
❑ W-2034 [M]	Crazy in the Heart	1961	6.25	12.50	25.00
❑ WST-2034 [S]	Crazy in the Heart	1961	12.50	25.00	50.00

CRIBBINS, BERNARD

45s

CAPITOL

Number	Title (A Side/B Side)	Yr	VG	VG+	NM
❑ 5933	When I'm Sixty-Four/Oh My Word	1967	2.50	5.00	10.00

UNITED ARTISTS

Number	Title (A Side/B Side)	Yr	VG	VG+	NM
❑ 907	Right Said Fred/Quietly Bonkers	1965	2.50	5.00	10.00

CRICKETS, THE (1) BUDDY HOLLY's group. Includes records credited to "The Crickets" both during and after Holly's life. Also see SONNY CURTIS; IVAN; NIKI SULLIVAN.

45s

BARNABY

Number	Title (A Side/B Side)	Yr	VG	VG+	NM
❑ 2061	Rockin' 50's Rock 'N' Roll/True Love Ways	1972	5.00	10.00	20.00

BRUNSWICK

Number	Title (A Side/B Side)	Yr	VG	VG+	NM
❑ 55009	That'll Be the Day/I'm Lookin' for Someone to Love	1957	12.50	25.00	50.00
❑ 55035	Oh, Boy!/Not Fade Away	1957	12.50	25.00	50.00
❑ 55053	Maybe Baby/Tell Me How	1958	12.50	25.00	50.00
❑ 55072	Think It Over/Fool's Paradise	1958	12.50	25.00	50.00
❑ 55094	It's So Easy/Lonesome Tears	1958	12.50	25.00	50.00
❑ 55124	Love's Made a Fool of You/Someone, Someone	1959	10.00	20.00	40.00
❑ 55153	When You Ask About Love/Deborah	1959	10.00	20.00	40.00

CORAL

Number	Title (A Side/B Side)	Yr	VG	VG+	NM
❑ 62198	More Than I Can Say/Baby, My Heart	1960	10.00	20.00	40.00
❑ 62238	Peggy Sue Got Married/Don't Cha Know	1960	10.00	20.00	40.00
❑ 62407	Maybe Baby/Not Fade Away	1964	7.50	15.00	30.00

EPIC

Number	Title (A Side/B Side)	Yr	VG	VG+	NM
❑ 34-08028	T-Shirt/Hollywould	1988	—	2.50	5.00
❑ 34-08028 [PS]	T-Shirt/Hollywould	1988	—	2.50	5.00

LIBERTY

Number	Title (A Side/B Side)	Yr	VG	VG+	NM
❑ 55392	He's Old Enough to Know Better/I'm Feeling Better	1961	6.25	12.50	25.00
❑ 55441	Don't Ever Change/I'm Not a Bad Boy	1962	6.25	12.50	25.00
❑ 55492	I Believe in You/Parisian Girl	1962	6.25	12.50	25.00
❑ 55495	Little Hollywood Girl/Parisian Girl	1962	6.25	12.50	25.00
❑ 55540	My Little Girl/Teardrops Fall Like Rain	1963	6.25	12.50	25.00
❑ 55603	Don't Say You Love Me/April Avenue	1963	6.25	12.50	25.00
❑ 55660	Lonely Avenue/You Can't Be In-Between	1964	6.25	12.50	25.00
❑ 55668	Please, Please Me/From Me to You	1964	12.50	25.00	50.00
❑ 55696	(They Call Her) La Bomba/All Over You	1964	6.25	12.50	25.00

Number	Title (A Side/B Side)	Yr	VG	VG+	NM
❑ 55742	We Gotta Get Together/ I Think I've Caught the Blues	1964	6.25	12.50	25.00
❑ 55767	Everybody's Got a Little Problem/Now Hear This	1965	6.25	12.50	25.00
MGM					
❑ 14541	Hayride/Wasn't It Nice	1973	3.75	7.50	15.00
MUSIC FACTORY					
❑ 415	Million Dollar Movie/A Million Miles Apart	1968	5.00	10.00	20.00
7-Inch Extended Plays					
BRUNSWICK					
❑ EB 71036	*I'm Looking for Someone to Love/That'll Be the Day/Not Fade Away/Oh! Boy	1957	75.00	150.00	300.00
❑ EB 71036 [PS]	The Chirping Crickets	1957	75.00	150.00	300.00
❑ EB 71038	*Maybe Baby/Rock Me My Baby/Send Me Some Lovin'/Tell Me How	1958	62.50	125.00	250.00
❑ EB 71038 [PS]	The Sound of the Crickets	1958	62.50	125.00	250.00
Albums					
BARNABY					
❑ Z 30268	Rockin' 50's Rock 'N' Roll	1970	6.25	12.50	25.00
BRUNSWICK					
❑ BL 54038 [M]	The "Chirping" Crickets	1957	200.00	400.00	800.00
—Textured cover					
❑ BL 54038 [M]	The "Chirping" Crickets	1958	150.00	300.00	600.00
—Regular cover					
CORAL					
❑ CRL 57320 [M]	In Style with the Crickets	1960	50.00	100.00	200.00
❑ CRL 757320 [S]	In Style with the Crickets	1960	100.00	200.00	400.00
EPIC					
❑ FE 44446	T-Shirt	1988	3.75	7.50	15.00
LIBERTY					
❑ LRP-3272 [M]	Something Old, Something New, Something Blue, Somethin' Else	1962	37.50	75.00	150.00
❑ LRP-3351 [M]	California Sun/She Loves You	1964	25.00	50.00	100.00
❑ LST-7272 [S]	Something Old, Something New, Something Blue, Somethin' Else	1962	50.00	100.00	200.00
❑ LST-7351 [S]	California Sun/She Loves You	1964	37.50	75.00	150.00
VERTIGO					
❑ VEL-1020	Remnants	1973	5.00	10.00	20.00

CRICKETS, THE (2) Black vocal group featuring Dean Barlow.
45s

Number	Title (A Side/B Side)	Yr	VG	VG+	NM
DAVIS					
❑ 459	I'm Going to Live My Life Alone/ Man from the Moon	1958	15.00	30.00	60.00
JAY DEE					
❑ 777	Dreams and Wishes/When I Met You	1953	50.00	100.00	200.00
❑ 781	Fine As Wine/I'm Not the Same One You Love	1953	50.00	100.00	200.00
❑ 785	Changing Partners/Your Love	1954	37.50	75.00	150.00
❑ 786	Just You/My Little Baby's Shoes	1954	37.50	75.00	150.00
❑ 789	Are You Looking for a Sweetheart/ Never Give Up Hope	1954	37.50	75.00	150.00
❑ 795	I'm Going to Live My Life Alone/ Man from the Moon	1954	37.50	75.00	150.00
MGM					
❑ 11428	You're Mine/Milk and Gin	1953	62.50	125.00	250.00
❑ 11507	I'll Cry No More/For You I Have Eyes	1953	50.00	100.00	200.00
Albums					
RELIC					
❑ LP-5040	The Crickets Featuring Dean Barlow	1987	2.50	5.00	10.00

CRISS, GARY
12-Inch Singles

Number	Title (A Side/B Side)	Yr	VG	VG+	NM
SALSOUL					
❑ 2059	Rio De Janeiro/My Rio Lady	1978	2.50	5.00	10.00
❑ 2074	Brazilian Nights (6:14)/Amazon Queen (7:08)	1978	5.00	10.00	20.00
45s					
DIAMOND					
❑ 114	Welcome Home to My Heart/ Our Favorite Melodies	1962	3.00	6.00	12.00
❑ 122	My Heavenly Angel/The Girl I Told You About	1962	3.00	6.00	12.00
❑ 127	Long Lonely Nights/I Still Miss You So	1963	2.50	5.00	10.00
❑ 145	Little Joe/Sweet, Warm and Soft	1963	2.50	5.00	10.00
❑ 182	Hands of My Baby/If This Is Goodbye	1965	2.00	4.00	8.00
❑ 190	My Baby Left Me/This Love of Mine	1965	2.00	4.00	8.00
❑ 228	Welcome Home to My Heart/Hands Off Buddy	1967	5.00	10.00	20.00
SALSOUL					
❑ 2082	Brazilian Nights/Amazon Queen	1979	—	3.00	6.00
STRAND					
❑ 25044	Good Golly Miss Molly/I'll Love Only You	1961	7.50	15.00	30.00

CRITTERS, THE
45s

Number	Title (A Side/B Side)	Yr	VG	VG+	NM
KAPP					
❑ 727	He'll Make You Cry/Children & Flowers	1965	2.50	5.00	10.00
❑ 752	Younger Girl/Gone for a While	1966	3.00	6.00	12.00
❑ 769	Mr. Dieingly Sad/It Won't Be That Way	1966	3.00	6.00	12.00
❑ 769 [PS]	Mr. Dieingly Sad/It Won't Be That Way	1966	5.00	10.00	20.00
❑ 793	Bad Misunderstanding/Forever or No More	1966	2.50	5.00	10.00
❑ 805	Marryin' Kind of Love/New York Bound	1967	2.50	5.00	10.00
❑ 838	Don't Let the Rain Fall Down on Me/Walk Like a Man Again	1967	2.50	5.00	10.00
❑ 858	Little Girl/Dancing in the Streets	1967	2.50	5.00	10.00
MUSICOR					
❑ 1044	I'm Gonna Give/Georgianna	1964	5.00	10.00	20.00
PRANCER					
❑ 6001	No One But You/I'm Telling Everyone	1969	2.00	4.00	8.00
PROJECT 3					
❑ 1326	Good Morning Sunshine/A Moment of Being with You	1968	2.00	4.00	8.00
❑ 1332	Touch 'N' Go/Younger Generation	1968	2.00	4.00	8.00
❑ 1349	Cool Sunday Morning/Lisa, But Not the Same	1969	2.00	4.00	8.00
❑ 1363	She Said She Loved Him/I Just Want to Sit Right Here and Look at You	1969	2.00	4.00	8.00
Albums					
KAPP					
❑ KL-1485 [M]	Younger Girl	1966	7.50	15.00	30.00
❑ KS-3485 [S]	Younger Girl	1966	10.00	20.00	40.00

Number	Title (A Side/B Side)	Yr	VG	VG+	NM
PROJECT 3					
❑ PR 4001SD	Touch 'n Go with the Critters	1968	7.50	15.00	30.00
❑ PR 4002SD	The Critters	1969	7.50	15.00	30.00

CRITTERS, THE /THE YOUNG RASCALS/LOU CHRISTIE
Albums

Number	Title (A Side/B Side)	Yr	VG	VG+	NM
BOUTIQUE					
❑ CA-1079 [M]	A Taste of the Critters & The Young Rascals & Lou Christie	1966	10.00	20.00	40.00

CROCE, JIM
45s

Number	Title (A Side/B Side)	Yr	VG	VG+	NM
ABC					
❑ 11328	You Don't Mess Around with Jim/Photographs and Memories	1972	—	2.00	4.00
❑ 11335	Operator (That's Not the Way It Feels)/ Rapid Roy (The Stock Car Boy)	1972	—	2.00	4.00
❑ 11346	One Less Set of Footsteps/ It Doesn't Have to Be That Way	1973	—	2.00	4.00
❑ 11359	Bad, Bad Leroy Brown/A Good Time Man Like Me Ain't Got No Business (Singin' the Blues)	1973	—	2.00	4.00
—Regular ABC logo					
❑ 11359	Bad, Bad Leroy Brown/A Good Time Man Like Me Ain't Got No Business (Singin' the Blues)	1973	—	2.50	5.00
—ABC logo in children's building blocks					
❑ 11389	I Got a Name/Alabama Rain	1973	—	2.00	4.00
❑ 11405	Time in a Bottle/Hard Time Losin' Man	1973	—	2.00	4.00
❑ 11413	It Doesn't Have to Be That Way/ Roller Derby Queen	1973	—	2.00	4.00
❑ 11413 [PS]	It Doesn't Have to Be That Way/ Roller Derby Queen	1973	—	2.50	5.00
❑ 11424	I'll Have to Say I Love You in a Song/ Salon and Saloon	1974	—	2.00	4.00
❑ 11447	Workin' at the Car Wash Blues/Thursday	1974	—	2.00	4.00
❑ 12015	Workin' at the Car Wash Blues/Thursday	1974	—	2.50	5.00
LIFESONG					
❑ 45001	Chain Gang Medley/Stone Walls	1975	—	2.00	4.00
❑ 45005	Maybe Tomorrow/Mississippi Lady	1976	—	2.00	4.00
❑ 45018 [DJ]	It Doesn't Have to Be That Way (mono/stereo)	1976	—	2.50	5.00
—Promo-only release; Lifesong sleeve has custom sticker (add $4)					
21 RECORDS					
❑ 94969	Workin' at the Car Wash Blues/Rapid Roy (The Stock Car Boy)	1987	—	—	3.00
❑ 94970	It Doesn't Have to Be That Way/Time in a Bottle	1987	—	—	3.00
❑ 94971	I'll Have to Say I Love You in a Song/I Got a Name	1987	—	—	3.00
❑ 94972	You Don't Mess Around with Jim/Photographs and Memories	1987	—	—	3.00
❑ 94973	Bad, Bad Leroy Brown/Operator (That's Not the Way It Feels)	1987	—	—	3.00
7-Inch Extended Plays					
ABC					
❑ PRO-769	Dreamin' Again/One Less Set of Footsteps/Next Time, This Time//Roller Derby Queen/A Good Time Man Like Me Ain't Got No Business (Singin' the Blues)/Bad, Bad Leroy Brown	1973	2.50	5.00	10.00
—Jukebox issue; small hole, plays at 33 1/3 rpm					
❑ PRO-769 [PS]	Life and Times	1973	2.50	5.00	10.00
—Part of "Little LP" series (LLP #232)					
Albums					
ABC					
❑ ABCX-756	You Don't Mess Around with Jim	1972	5.00	10.00	20.00
—Original covers have no green box advertising "Time in a Bottle"					
❑ ABCX-756	You Don't Mess Around with Jim	1973	3.75	7.50	15.00
—Posthumous covers have a green box advertising "Time in a Bottle"					
❑ ABCX-769	Life and Times	1973	3.75	7.50	15.00
❑ ABCX-797	I Got a Name	1973	3.75	7.50	15.00
❑ ABCD-835	Photographs & Memories/His Greatest Hits	1974	3.75	7.50	15.00
CAPITOL					
❑ SMAS-315	Jim and Ingrid Croce	1970	7.50	15.00	30.00
COMMAND					
❑ QD-40006 [Q]	You Don't Mess Around with Jim	1974	7.50	15.00	30.00
—With wide border around the outside of front cover					
❑ QD-40006 [Q]	You Don't Mess Around with Jim	1974	6.25	12.50	25.00
—Without border around outside of front cover					
❑ QD-40007 [Q]	Life and Times	1974	6.25	12.50	25.00
❑ QD-40008 [Q]	I Got a Name	1974	6.25	12.50	25.00
❑ QD-40020 [Q]	Photographs & Memories/His Greatest Hits	1974	6.25	12.50	25.00
CROCE					
❑ 101	Facets	1966	75.00	150.00	300.00
DCC COMPACT CLASSICS					
❑ LPZ-2054	His Greatest Recordings	1998	10.00	20.00	40.00
—Audiophile vinyl					
LIFESONG					
❑ LS 900 [(2)]	The Faces I've Been	1975	3.75	7.50	15.00
❑ LS 6007	Time in a Bottle — Jim Croce's Greatest Love Songs	1976	3.00	6.00	12.00
❑ JZ 34993	You Don't Mess Around with Jim	1978	2.50	5.00	10.00
❑ JZ 35000	Time in a Bottle — Jim Croce's Greatest Love Songs	1978	2.50	5.00	10.00
❑ JZ 35008	Life and Times	1978	2.50	5.00	10.00
❑ JZ 35009	I Got a Name	1978	2.50	5.00	10.00
❑ JZ 35010	Photographs & Memories/His Greatest Hits	1978	2.50	5.00	10.00
❑ JZ 35571	Bad, Bad Leroy Brown: Jim Croce's Greatest Character Songs	1978	2.50	5.00	10.00
MOBILE FIDELITY					
❑ 1-079	You Don't Mess Around with Jim	1981	10.00	20.00	40.00
—Audiophile vinyl					
PICKWICK					
❑ SPC-3332	Another Day, Another Town	1973	2.50	5.00	10.00
—Reissue of Capitol LP					
21 RECORDS					
❑ 90467	Photographs & Memories/His Greatest Hits	1985	2.00	4.00	8.00
❑ 90468	Time in a Bottle — Jim Croce's Greatest Love Songs	1985	2.00	4.00	8.00
❑ 90469	Down the Highway	1985	2.50	5.00	10.00

C

Number	Title (A Side/B Side)	Yr	VG	VG+	NM

CROCKETT, HOWARD
45s
DOT

Number	Title (A Side/B Side)	Yr	VG	VG+	NM
❏ 15593	If You'll Let Me/You've Got Me Lyin'	1957	12.50	25.00	50.00
❏ 15701	The Night Rider/Branded	1958	10.00	20.00	40.00
❏ 17457	The House Where Momma Lived/Last Will and Testament (Of a Drinking Man)	1973	—	3.00	6.00
❏ 17482	I Feel More Like Myself Than I Did a While Ago/ I'd Like to Be Everybody for Just One Day	1973	—	3.00	6.00
❏ 17509	The Calling/Pictures and Memories	1974	—	3.00	6.00

MANCO

Number	Title (A Side/B Side)	Yr	VG	VG+	NM
❏ 1002	Sluefoot the Bear/Polly Ann	1960	12.50	25.00	50.00
❏ 1012	That Old Juke Box/Steamboat Bill	1961	7.50	15.00	30.00
❏ 1023	Just a Poor Man/I've Got You Worried Too	1961	7.50	15.00	30.00

MEL-O-DY

Number	Title (A Side/B Side)	Yr	VG	VG+	NM
❏ 109	The Big Wheel/That Silver-Haired Daddy of Mine	1963	6.25	12.50	25.00
❏ 111	Bringing In the Gold/I've Been a Long Time Leaving	1963	6.25	12.50	25.00
❏ 115	My Lil's Run Off/Spanish Lace and Memories	1964	6.25	12.50	25.00
❏ 119	Put Me in Your Pocket/The Miles	1964	6.25	12.50	25.00
❏ 121	All the Good Times Are Gone/The Great Titanic	1965	6.25	12.50	25.00

SMASH

Number	Title (A Side/B Side)	Yr	VG	VG+	NM
❏ 1721	Deep Elm Dave/Going Down to Soldiers	1961	10.00	20.00	40.00
❏ 1750	Break Away Billy Boy/Out of Bounds Again	1962	10.00	20.00	40.00
❏ 1782	Jessie and the Glendale Train/Trail of Tears	1962	20.00	40.00	80.00

STOP

Number	Title (A Side/B Side)	Yr	VG	VG+	NM
❏ 136	The Big Cat/You're Messin' Up My Mind	1968	2.00	4.00	8.00
❏ 172	The Big Day/You Can't Get to All of 'Em Jack	1968	2.00	4.00	8.00
❏ 210	Soap and Water/A Man with No Face	1969	2.00	4.00	8.00
❏ 238	Where Were You/The Story of Bango	1969	2.00	4.00	8.00
❏ 250	The Law Says/Ask Little Brother	1969	2.00	4.00	8.00

CROME SYRCUS, THE
45s
COMMAND

Number	Title (A Side/B Side)	Yr	VG	VG+	NM
❏ 4111	Cover Up/Take It Like a Man	1968	2.50	5.00	10.00

JERDEN

Number	Title (A Side/B Side)	Yr	VG	VG+	NM
❏ 921	Elevator Operator/Lord in Black	196?	3.00	6.00	12.00

PICCADILLY

Number	Title (A Side/B Side)	Yr	VG	VG+	NM
❏ 256	Lord in Black/Long Hard Road	196?	3.00	6.00	12.00

Albums
COMMAND

Number	Title (A Side/B Side)	Yr	VG	VG+	NM
❏ RS 925 SD	The Love Cycle	1968	10.00	20.00	40.00

CROPPER, STEVE Also see BOOKER T. AND THE MG's; MAR-KEYS.
45s
MCA

Number	Title (A Side/B Side)	Yr	VG	VG+	NM
❏ 51078	Playin' My Thang/Why Do You Say You Love Me	1981	—	2.00	4.00
❏ 51115	Sandy Beaches/Fly	1981	—	2.00	4.00
❏ 52103	Night After Night/634-5789	1982	—	2.00	4.00

Albums
MCA

Number	Title (A Side/B Side)	Yr	VG	VG+	NM
❏ 5171	Playin' My Thang	1980	2.50	5.00	10.00
❏ 5340	Night After Night	1982	2.50	5.00	10.00

VOLT

Number	Title (A Side/B Side)	Yr	VG	VG+	NM
❏ VOS-6006	With a Little Help from My Friends	1970	3.75	7.50	15.00

CROSBY, BING Includes most of his duets with other performers. Crosby was past his peak of popularity when 45s and LPs were introduced; while much of his material showed up on these formats, many of his 1930s and 1940s releases did not. The list below is exhaustive as to the availability of Bing's music on vinyl, but probably not complete; it's likely that other singles in the 23000, 24000 and 25000 series exist on 45s, as well as other EPs. Also see DAVID BOWIE; FRANK SINATRA.
45s
AMOS

Number	Title (A Side/B Side)	Yr	VG	VG+	NM
❏ 111	Hey Jude/Lonely Street	1969	—	3.00	6.00
❏ 116	It's All in the Game/More and More	1969	—	2.50	5.00

BING CROSBY

Number	Title (A Side/B Side)	Yr	VG	VG+	NM
❏ (no #) [DJ]	How Lovely Is Christmas/Never Be Afraid	195?	5.00	10.00	20.00

—Crowley's Milk promotional item

CAPITOL

Number	Title (A Side/B Side)	Yr	VG	VG+	NM
❏ F-3695	Man on Fire/Seven Nights a Week	1957	3.00	6.00	12.00
❏ 4548	Simple Love Affair/That's How I Met Your Mother	1978	—	2.00	4.00
❏ 5088	Do You Hear What I Hear/Christmas Dinner Country Style	1963	2.00	4.00	8.00
❏ S7-19766	Do You Hear What I Hear?/I Wish You a Merry Christmas	1997	—	—	3.00

COLUMBIA

Number	Title (A Side/B Side)	Yr	VG	VG+	NM
❏ 41104	Straight Down the Middle/Tomorrow's My Lucky Day	1958	3.00	6.00	12.00
❏ 41387	Say One for Me/I Couldn't Care Less	1959	3.00	6.00	12.00
❏ 41496	The Secret of Christmas/Just What I Wanted for Christmas	1959	3.75	7.50	15.00

DAYBREAK

Number	Title (A Side/B Side)	Yr	VG	VG+	NM
❏ 1001	A Time to Be Jolly/And the Bells Rang	1971	—	2.50	5.00

—Yellow label

Number	Title (A Side/B Side)	Yr	VG	VG+	NM
❏ 1001	A Time to Be Jolly/And the Bells Rang	1971	—	3.00	6.00

—Black label

Number	Title (A Side/B Side)	Yr	VG	VG+	NM
❏ 1001 [PS]	A Time to Be Jolly/And the Bells Rang	1971	—	2.50	5.00

DECCA

Number	Title (A Side/B Side)	Yr	VG	VG+	NM
❏ 9-65 [(4)]	Merry Christmas	1950	12.50	25.00	50.00

—Includes records 23281, 23777, 23778 and 23779 (also priced separately) and box

Number	Title (A Side/B Side)	Yr	VG	VG+	NM
❏ 9-66 [(4)]	Christmas Greetings	1950	12.50	25.00	50.00

—Includes records and box

Number	Title (A Side/B Side)	Yr	VG	VG+	NM
❏ 1-256 [PS]	Jingle Bells/Santa's Coming	19??	3.75	7.50	15.00

—With the Andrews Sisters; alternate number is 23281

Number	Title (A Side/B Side)	Yr	VG	VG+	NM
❏ 23281	Jingle Bells/Santa Claus Is Comin' to Town	1950	3.00	6.00	12.00

—With the Andrews Sisters; lines label; Sides 1 and 2 of "Album No. 9-65"

Number	Title (A Side/B Side)	Yr	VG	VG+	NM
❏ 9-23484	Pistol Packin' Mama/Don't Fence Me In	1950	3.00	6.00	12.00

—With the Andrews Sisters; "lines" label

Number	Title (A Side/B Side)	Yr	VG	VG+	NM
❏ 9-23484	Pistol Packin' Mama/Don't Fence Me In	1955	2.50	5.00	10.00

—With the Andrews Sisters; star under "Decca"

Number	Title (A Side/B Side)	Yr	VG	VG+	NM
❏ 23495	McNamara's Band/Dear Old Donegal	1950	3.00	6.00	12.00

—Reissue of 78; part of "Album No. 9-31"

Number	Title (A Side/B Side)	Yr	VG	VG+	NM
❏ 23777	Silent Night/Adeste Fideles (O Come All Ye Faithful)	1950	3.00	6.00	12.00

—Lines label; Sides 3 and 4 of "Album No. 9-65"

Number	Title (A Side/B Side)	Yr	VG	VG+	NM
❏ 23777	Silent Night/Adeste Fideles (O Come All Ye Faithful)	1955	2.50	5.00	10.00

—Star on label

Number	Title (A Side/B Side)	Yr	VG	VG+	NM
❏ 23777	Silent Night/Adeste Fideles (O Come All Ye Faithful)	1960	2.00	4.00	8.00

—Color bars on label

Number	Title (A Side/B Side)	Yr	VG	VG+	NM
❏ 23777 [PS]	Silent Night/Adeste Fideles (O Come All Ye Faithful)	1960	3.75	7.50	15.00

—Sleeve came with early 1960s pressings

Number	Title (A Side/B Side)	Yr	VG	VG+	NM
❏ 23778	White Christmas/God Rest Ye Merry Gentlemen	1960	2.00	4.00	8.00

—Color bars on label

Number	Title (A Side/B Side)	Yr	VG	VG+	NM
❏ 23778 [PS]	White Christmas/God Rest Ye Merry Gentlemen	1960	3.75	7.50	15.00

—Sleeve came with early 1960s pressings

Number	Title (A Side/B Side)	Yr	VG	VG+	NM
❏ 9-23778	White Christmas/God Rest Ye Merry Gentlemen	1950	3.00	6.00	12.00

—Lines label; Sides 5 and 6 of "Album No. 9-65"

Number	Title (A Side/B Side)	Yr	VG	VG+	NM
❏ 9-23778	White Christmas/God Rest Ye Merry Gentlemen	1955	2.50	5.00	10.00

—Star on label

Number	Title (A Side/B Side)	Yr	VG	VG+	NM
❏ 23779	I'll Be Home for Christmas (If Only in My Dreams)/Faith of Our Fathers	1950	3.00	6.00	12.00

—Lines label; Sides 7 and 8 of "Album No. 9-65"

Number	Title (A Side/B Side)	Yr	VG	VG+	NM
❏ 23786	Who Threw the Overalls in Mrs. Murphy's Chowder?/It's the Same Old Overalls	1950	3.00	6.00	12.00

—Reissue of 78; part of "Album No. 9-31"

Number	Title (A Side/B Side)	Yr	VG	VG+	NM
❏ 23787	Did Your Mother Come from Ireland?/Where the River Shannon Flows	1950	3.00	6.00	12.00

—Reissue of 78; part of "Album No. 9-31"

Number	Title (A Side/B Side)	Yr	VG	VG+	NM
❏ 23789	Too-Ra-Loo-Ra-Loo-Ral/I'll Take You Home Again Kathleen	1950	3.00	6.00	12.00

—Reissue of 78; part of "Album No. 9-31"

Number	Title (A Side/B Side)	Yr	VG	VG+	NM
❏ 24659	You're All I Want for Christmas/The First Noel	1950	3.75	7.50	15.00

—78 rpm issued in 1949; lines label

Number	Title (A Side/B Side)	Yr	VG	VG+	NM
❏ 25003	Take Me Back to My Boots and Saddle/My Little Buckaroo	1950	3.00	6.00	12.00

—Reissue of 78; part of "Album No. 9-145"

Number	Title (A Side/B Side)	Yr	VG	VG+	NM
❏ 25020	Clementine/The Old Oaken Bucket	1950	3.00	6.00	12.00

—Reissue of 78; part of "Album No. 9-145"

Number	Title (A Side/B Side)	Yr	VG	VG+	NM
❏ 25497	Sierra Sue/Along the Santa Fe Trail	1950	3.00	6.00	12.00

—Reissue of 78; part of "Album No. 9-145"

Number	Title (A Side/B Side)	Yr	VG	VG+	NM
❏ 25520	Memories Are Made of This/My Blue Heaven	1961	—	3.00	6.00
❏ 25540	Moments to Remember/Vaya Con Dios	1961	—	3.00	6.00
❏ 25643	Avalon/On the Alamo	1964	—	3.00	6.00
❏ 25661	Chinatown, My Chinatown/I'm Confessin' (That I Love You)	1965	—	3.00	6.00
❏ 25665	Between the Devil and the Deep Blue Sea/ Georgia on My Mind	1965	—	3.00	6.00
❏ 27013	Jamboree Jones/Dixieland Band	1950	3.00	6.00	12.00
❏ 27018	I Didn't Slip, I Wasn't Pushed, I Fell/So Tall a Tree	1950	3.00	6.00	12.00
❏ 27019	Home Cookin'/When the Sun Goes Down	1950	3.00	6.00	12.00
❏ 27111	La Vie En Rose/I Cross My Fingers	1950	3.00	6.00	12.00
❏ 27112	Play a Simple Melody/Sam's Song	1950	3.00	6.00	12.00

—By "Gary Crosby and Friend" (guess who the friend is)

Number	Title (A Side/B Side)	Yr	VG	VG+	NM
❏ 27117	All My Love/The Friendly Islands	1950	3.00	6.00	12.00
❏ 27143	This Could Be Forever/Helpless	1950	3.00	6.00	12.00

—With Louanne Hogan

Number	Title (A Side/B Side)	Yr	VG	VG+	NM
❏ 27158	Ave Maria/Home Sweet Home	1950	3.00	6.00	12.00
❏ 27159	Rudolph, the Red-Nosed Reindeer/The Teddy Bear's Picnic	1950	3.00	6.00	12.00
❏ 27159/30126 [DJ]	Rudolph The Red-Nosed Reindeer/I Heard The Bells On Christmas Day	1956	5.00	10.00	20.00

—Green label promo with two different numbers on the record!

Number	Title (A Side/B Side)	Yr	VG	VG+	NM
❏ 27173	Life Is So Peculiar/High on the List	1950	3.00	6.00	12.00

—With the Andrews Sisters

Number	Title (A Side/B Side)	Yr	VG	VG+	NM
❏ 27219	Harbor Lights/Beyond the Reef	1950	3.00	6.00	12.00
❏ 27228	Mele Kalikimaka/Poppa Santa Claus	1950	3.00	6.00	12.00

—With the Andrews Sisters

Number	Title (A Side/B Side)	Yr	VG	VG+	NM
❏ 27229	Silver Bells/That Christmas Feeling	1950	3.00	6.00	12.00

—A-side with Carol Richards

Number	Title (A Side/B Side)	Yr	VG	VG+	NM
❏ 27230	A Marshmallow World/Looks Like a Cold, Cold Winter	1950	3.00	6.00	12.00
❏ 27231	Autumn Leaves/This Is the Time	1950	3.00	6.00	12.00
❏ 27232	If I Were a Bell/I've Never Been in Love Before	1950	3.00	6.00	12.00

—A-side with Patti Andrews

Number	Title (A Side/B Side)	Yr	VG	VG+	NM
❏ 27241	And You'll Be Mine/Accidents Will Happen	1950	3.00	6.00	12.00
❏ 27249	A Crosby Christmas (Part 1)/A Crosby Christmas (Part 2)	1950	—	—	—

—As "Gary, Phillip, Dennis, Lindsay and Bing Crosby"; unreleased on this number?

Number	Title (A Side/B Side)	Yr	VG	VG+	NM
❏ 27250	The Best Thing for You/Marrying for Love	1950	3.00	6.00	12.00
❏ 27263	Wouldn't It Be Funny/One More for the Blue and White	1950	3.00	6.00	12.00
❏ 27264	Accidents Will Happen/Milady	1950	3.00	6.00	12.00

—With Dorothy Kirsten

Number	Title (A Side/B Side)	Yr	VG	VG+	NM
❏ 27275	Oh! What a Beautiful Morning/People Will Say We're in Love	1950	2.50	5.00	10.00
❏ 27276	If I Loved You/Close As Pages in a Book	1950	2.50	5.00	10.00
❏ 27277	They Say It's Wonderful/I Love You	1950	2.50	5.00	10.00
❏ 27278	Evalina/The Eagle and Me	1950	2.50	5.00	10.00
❏ 27404	May the Good Lord Bless and Keep You/A Perfect Day	1951	2.50	5.00	10.00
❏ 27441	An Early American/My Own Bit of Land	1951	2.50	5.00	10.00
❏ 27443	The Meadows of Heaven/The Last Mile Home	1951	2.50	5.00	10.00
❏ 27461	Then You've Never Been Blue/You Gotta Show Me	1951	2.50	5.00	10.00
❏ 27477	Sparrow in the Tree Top/Forsaking All Others	1951	2.50	5.00	10.00

—With the Andrews Sisters

Number	Title (A Side/B Side)	Yr	VG	VG+	NM
❏ 27478	St. Patrick's Day Parade/With My Shillelagh Under My Arm	1951	2.50	5.00	10.00
❏ 27483	Sentimental Music/Any Town Is Paris When You're Young	1951	2.50	5.00	10.00
❏ 27500	Feudin' and Fightin'/Goodbye, My Lovers, Goodbye	1951	2.50	5.00	10.00
❏ 27505	When My Dreamboat Comes Home/Walking the Floor Over You	1951	2.50	5.00	10.00
❏ 27536	Silver Moon/More I Cannot Wish You	1951	2.50	5.00	10.00
❏ 27536	Maria Bonita/Quizas, Quizas, Quizas	1951	2.50	5.00	10.00
❏ 27549	Yours Is My Heart Alone/Beautiful Love	1951	2.50	5.00	10.00

Number	Title (A Side/B Side)	Yr	VG	VG+	NM
❑ 27550	I Kiss Your Hand, Madame/				
	The Kiss in Your Eyes	1951	2.50	5.00	10.00
❑ 27551	Girl of My Dreams/I'll Remember April	1951	2.50	5.00	10.00
❑ 27553	Country Style/Home Cookin'	1951	2.50	5.00	10.00
❑ 27554	I Only Want a Buddy — Not a Sweetheart/When				
	the White Azaleas Start Blooming	1951	2.50	5.00	10.00
❑ 27555	Weddin' Day/(B-side unknown)	1951	2.50	5.00	10.00
—With the Andrews Sisters					
❑ 27577	Moonlight Bay/				
	When You and I Were Young Maggie Blues	1951	2.50	5.00	10.00
—As "Gary and Bing Crosby"					
❑ 27588	Hello Young Lovers/Something Wonderful	1951	2.50	5.00	10.00
❑ 27589	Getting to Know You/I Whistle a Happy Tune	1951	2.50	5.00	10.00
❑ 27595	With This Ring I Thee Wed/Here Ends the				
	Rainbow	1951	2.50	5.00	10.00
❑ 27605	Going My Way/Swinging on a Star	1951	2.50	5.00	10.00
❑ 27606	Old Soldiers Never Die/My Own Bit of Land	1951	2.50	5.00	10.00
❑ 27631	Black Ball Ferry Line/The Yodeling Ghost	1951	2.50	5.00	10.00
—With the Andrews Sisters					
❑ 27643	I Might Be Your Once in a While/Indian Summer	1951	2.50	5.00	10.00
❑ 27653	(Why Did I Twll You I Was Going to) Shanghai/				
	I've Got to Fall in Love Again	1951	2.50	5.00	10.00
❑ 27667	Row, Row, Row/Love Me or Leave Me	1951	2.50	5.00	10.00
❑ 27678	In the Cool, Cool, Cool of the Evening/Misto				
	Christophe Columbo	1951	2.50	5.00	10.00
—With Jane Wyman					
❑ 27679	Your Own Little House/Bonne Nuit	1951	2.50	5.00	10.00
❑ 27768	I Will Remember You/The Loneliness of Evening	1951	2.50	5.00	10.00
❑ 27830	Domino/When the World Was Young	1951	2.50	5.00	10.00
❑ 9-27831	Christmas in Killarney/It's Beginning to Look like				
	Christmas	1951	3.75	7.50	15.00
❑ 27852	A Weaver of Dreams/I Still See Alisa	1951	2.50	5.00	10.00
❑ 27934	At Last, At Last!/The Isle of Innisfree	1952	2.50	5.00	10.00
❑ 27951	Copacabana/Granada	1952	2.50	5.00	10.00
❑ 28048	2 Shillelagh O'Sullivan/That Tumbledown Shack				
	in Athlone	1952	2.50	5.00	10.00
❑ 28061	Don't Ever Be Afraid to Go Home/Rosaleen	1952	2.50	5.00	10.00
❑ 28195	Galway Bay/The Isle of Innisfree	1952	2.50	5.00	10.00
❑ 28210	Mine/You've Got Me Where You Want Me	1952	3.00	6.00	12.00
—With Judy Garland					
❑ 28217	Just for You/A Flight of Fancy	1952	2.50	5.00	10.00
❑ 28254	On the 10:10 from Ten-Ten-Tennessee/				
	Just for You	1952	2.50	5.00	10.00
❑ 28255	Zing a Little Zong/The Maiden of Guadaloupe	1952	2.50	5.00	10.00
—With Jane Wyman					
❑ 28256	The Live Oak Tree/I'll Si-Si You in Bahia	1952	2.50	5.00	10.00
—With the Andrews Sisters					
❑ 28261	The Bells of St. Mary's/Kathleen	1952	2.50	5.00	10.00
❑ 28265	Till the End of the World/Just a Little Lovin'	1952	2.50	5.00	10.00
—With Grady Martin					
❑ 28303	Poinciana/Symphony	1952	2.50	5.00	10.00
❑ 28319	Deep in the Heart of Texas/Do You Care	1952	2.50	5.00	10.00
❑ 28419	Cool Water/South Rampart Street Parade	1952	2.50	5.00	10.00
—With the Andrews Sisters					
❑ 28463	Sleigh Ride/Little Jack Frost Get Lost	1952	3.75	7.50	15.00
❑ 28470	Open Up Your Heart/You Don't Know What				
	Lonesome Is	1952	2.50	5.00	10.00
❑ 28511	Sleigh Bell Serenade/Keep It a Secret	1952	3.75	7.50	15.00
❑ 28513	The Road to Bali/Chicago Style	1952	2.50	5.00	10.00
—With Bob Hope					
❑ 28514	Merry Go Run Around/Hoot Mon	1952	2.50	5.00	10.00
—With Peggy Lee and Bob Hope					
❑ 28515	To See You/Moonflowers	1952	2.50	5.00	10.00
—B-side by Peggy Lee					
❑ 28581	Hush-a-Bye/Mother Darlin'	1953	2.50	5.00	10.00
❑ 28610	A Quiet Girl/Ohio	1953	2.50	5.00	10.00
❑ 28683	I Love My Baby (My Baby Loves Me)/There's				
	Music in You	1953	2.50	5.00	10.00
❑ 28733	Tenderfoot/Walk Me By the River	1953	2.50	5.00	10.00
❑ 28743	It Had to Be You/Granada	1953	2.50	5.00	10.00
❑ 28805	Magic Window/Cela Mi Est Egal	1953	2.50	5.00	10.00
❑ 28814	Mademoiselle de Paris/Embrasse — Moi Bien	1953	2.50	5.00	10.00
❑ 28955	Down By the Riverside/				
	What a Little Moonlight Can Do	1953	2.50	5.00	10.00
—As "Bing and Gary Crosby"					
❑ 28963	Ida! Sweet as Apple Cider/I Can't Believe				
	ThatYou're in Love	1953	2.50	5.00	10.00
❑ 28969	Y'All Come/Changing Partners	1954	2.50	5.00	10.00
❑ 29024	Secret Love/My Love, My Love	1954	2.50	5.00	10.00
❑ 29054	Young at Heart/I Get So Lonely	1954	2.50	5.00	10.00
❑ 29144	If You Love Me (Really Love Me)/Liebchen	1954	2.50	5.00	10.00
❑ 29147	Call of the South/Cornbelt Symphony	1954	2.50	5.00	10.00
—As "Bing and Gary Crosby"					
❑ 29212	In the Good Old Summertime/Oh Tell Me Why				
	(The Stars Do Shine)	1954	2.50	5.00	10.00
❑ 29251	Count Your Blessings Instead of Sheep/What				
	Can You Do with a General	1954	2.50	5.00	10.00
❑ 29341	Old Man-Mandy/Gee, I Wish I Was Back in the				
	Army	1954	2.50	5.00	10.00
❑ 29342	White Christmas/Snow	1954	3.75	7.50	15.00
—A-side with Danny Kaye; B-side by Peggy Lee and Trudi Stevens					
❑ 29357	The Song from Desiree/Who Gave You the				
	Roses	1954	2.50	5.00	10.00
❑ 29376	River/Tobermory Bay	1954	2.50	5.00	10.00
❑ 29409	Dissertation on State of Bliss/It's Mine, It's Yours	1955	2.50	5.00	10.00
❑ 29410	The Land Around Us/The Search Is Through	1955	2.50	5.00	10.00
❑ 29483	Farewell/Jim, Johnny & Jonah	1955	2.50	5.00	10.00
❑ 29493	Silver Moon/Nobody	1955	2.50	5.00	10.00
❑ 29568	She Is the Sunshine of Virginia/(All She'd Say				
	Was) Uh-Huh	1955	2.50	5.00	10.00
❑ 29634	You Are My Sunshine/				
	Nobody's Darling But Mine	1955	2.50	5.00	10.00
❑ 29636	Angel Bells/Let's Harmonize	1955	2.50	5.00	10.00
❑ 29777	The First Snowfall/The Next Time It Happens	1956	2.00	4.00	8.00
❑ 29790	Christmas Is A-Comin'/Is Christmas Only a Tree	1955	3.00	6.00	12.00
❑ 29817	John Barleycorn/When You're in Love	1956	2.00	4.00	8.00
❑ 29850	In a Little Spanish Town ('Twas On a Night Like				
	This)/Ol' Man River	1956	2.00	4.00	8.00
❑ 29981	Honeysucle Rose/Swanee	1956	2.00	4.00	8.00
❑ 30023	When My Baby Smiles at Me/April Showers	1956	2.00	4.00	8.00
❑ 30082	Now Is the Hour/Tumbling Tumbleweeds	1956	2.00	4.00	8.00
❑ 30120	Around the World/Love in a Home	1956	2.50	5.00	10.00
❑ 30126	I Heard the Bells on Christmas Day/				
	Christmas Is a-Comin'	1956	3.00	6.00	12.00
❑ 30126 [DJ]	I Heard the Bells on Christmas Day/				
	Christmas Is a-Comin'	1956	3.00	6.00	12.00
—Pink label, black type					
❑ 30262	Around the World/Around the World	1957	2.00	4.00	8.00
—B-side by Victor Young					
❑ 30262 [PS]	Around the World/Around the World	1957	3.75	7.50	15.00
❑ 30488	Chinatown My Chinatown/Alabamy Bound	1957	2.00	4.00	8.00
❑ 30555	Gigi/Trust Your Destiny to Your Star	1958	2.00	4.00	8.00
❑ 30828	Rain/Church Bells	1959	2.00	4.00	8.00
❑ 38031 [DJ]	Around the World/Mississippi Mud	1957	2.50	5.00	10.00
—Green label					
❑ 38031 [PS]	Around the World/Mississippi Mud	1957	5.00	10.00	20.00
❑ 40181	A Crosby Christmas (Part 1)/A Crosby				
	Christmas (Part 2)	1950	7.50	15.00	30.00
—As "Gary, Phillip, Dennis, Lindsay and Bing Crosby"					
KAPP					
❑ 196	How Lovely Is Christmas/My Own Individual Star	1957	3.00	6.00	12.00
❑ 196 [PS]	How Lovely Is Christmas/My Own Individual Star	1957	5.00	10.00	20.00
LITTLE GOLDEN					
❑ EP407	Boy At A Window/How Lovely Is Christmas	195?	2.50	5.00	10.00
❑ EP407 [PS]	Boy At A Window/How Lovely Is Christmas	195?	3.00	6.00	12.00
LONDON					
❑ 20095	There's Nothing I Haven't Sung About/				
	The Way We Were	1977	—	2.00	4.00
MCA					
❑ 38056	Rudolph The Red-Nosed Reindeer/				
	I Heard The Bells On Christmas Day	198?	—	2.00	4.00
❑ 40830	White Christmas/When the Blue of the Night				
	Meets the Gold of the Day	1977	—	2.50	5.00
❑ 40830 [PS]	White Christmas/When the Blue of the Night				
	Meets the Gold of the Day	1977	—	2.50	5.00
❑ 65019	Jingle Bells/Santa Claus Is Comin' to Town	1973	—	2.00	4.00
—With the Andrews Sisters; black label with rainbow					
❑ 65019	Jingle Bells/Santa Claus Is Comin' to Town	1980	—	—	3.00
—With the Andrews Sisters; blue label with rainbow					
❑ 65021	Silent Night/Adeste Fideles				
	(O Come All Ye Faithful)	1973	—	2.00	4.00
—Black label with rainbow					
❑ 65021	Silent Night/Adeste Fideles				
	(O Come All Ye Faithful)	1980	—	—	3.00
—Blue label with rainbow					
❑ 65022	White Christmas/God Rest Ye Merry Gentlemen	1973	—	2.00	4.00
—Black label with rainbow					
❑ 65022	White Christmas/God Rest Ye Merry Gentlemen	1980	—	—	3.00
—Blue label with rainbow					
MGM					
❑ 12946	The Second Time Around/Incurably Romantic	1960	2.00	4.00	8.00
P.I.P.					
❑ 8903	Where the Rainbow Ends/				
	What's More American	197?	—	2.50	5.00
POLYDOR					
❑ 14452	Yesterday, When I Was Young/June in January	1978	—	2.00	4.00
RCA VICTOR					
❑ 47-7695	It's a Good Day/The Music of Home	1960	2.00	4.00	8.00
REPRISE					
❑ 0283	Don't Be a Do-Badder/The Hukilau Song	1964	—	3.00	6.00
❑ 0315	It's Christmas Time Again/Christmas Candles	1964	3.00	6.00	12.00
—With Fred Waring and the Pennsylvanians					
❑ 0315 [PS]	It's Christmas Time Again/Christmas Candles	1964	3.75	7.50	15.00
❑ 0424	The White World of Winter/The Secret of				
	Christmas	1965	2.00	4.00	8.00
❑ 0478	How Green Was My Valley/Far from Home	1966	—	2.50	5.00
❑ 0645	Step to the Rear/What Do We Do with the World	1967	—	2.50	5.00
UNITED ARTISTS					
❑ XW700	Send In the Clowns/That's What Life Is All About	1975	—	2.00	4.00
VERVE					
❑ 2025	I've Got Five Dollars/Mountain Greenery	1956	2.50	5.00	10.00
WARNER BROS.					
❑ PRO 146 [DJ]	I Wish You a Merry Christmas/Winter				
	Wonderland//The Littlest Angel	1962	5.00	10.00	20.00
7-Inch Extended Plays					
DECCA					
❑ ED 547 [PS]	Merry Christmas	195?	6.25	12.50	25.00
—Cover for 2-EP set					
❑ ED 561 [PS]	Christmas Greetings	195?	6.25	12.50	25.00
—Cover for 2-EP set (91129 and 91130)					
❑ ED 581 [PS]	Stardust	195?	5.00	10.00	20.00
—Cover for 2-EP set					
❑ ED 662 [PS]	Down Memory Lane	195?	5.00	10.00	20.00
—Cover for 2-EP set					
❑ ED 850 [PS]	A Christmas Sing with Bing Around the World	195?	5.00	10.00	20.00
—Gatefold cover for 91835, 91836 and 91837					
❑ ED 1800 [PS]	Old Masters	195?	5.00	10.00	20.00
—Box for records 91611 through 91619					
❑ ED 2000	Red Sails in the Sunset/Far Away Places//				
	Harbor Lights/On Treasure Island	195?	3.00	6.00	12.00
❑ ED 2000 [PS]	Bing Crosby, Vol. 1	195?	3.00	6.00	12.00
❑ ED 2036	*Going My Way/Swinging on a Star/Too-Ra-				
	Loo-Ra-Loo-Ral/The Day After Forever	195?	3.00	6.00	12.00
❑ ED 2036 [PS]	Going My Way	195?	3.00	6.00	12.00
❑ ED 2107	Do You Ever Think of Me/I Never Knew//				
	Somebody Loves Me/After You've Gone	195?	3.00	6.00	12.00
❑ ED 2107 [PS]	Some Fine Old Chestnuts, Vol. 1	195?	3.00	6.00	12.00
❑ ED 2108	Sleepy Time Gal/Dinah/I Never Knew/I Can't				
	Give You Anything But Love	1954	3.00	6.00	12.00
❑ ED 2108 [PS]	Some Fine Old Chestnuts, Vol. 2	1954	3.00	6.00	12.00
❑ ED 2426	April Showers/When My Baby Smiles at Me//My				
	Blue Heaven/A Little Kiss Each Morning (A				
	Little Kiss Each Night)	195?	3.75	7.50	15.00
❑ ED 2426 [PS]	Song I Wish I Had Sung the First Time Around...				
	Part 1	195?	3.75	7.50	15.00

Number	Title (A Side/B Side)	Yr	VG	VG+	NM
❏ ED 2427	Prisoner of Love/Ain't Misbehavin'//Paper Doll/This Love of Mine	1956	3.75	7.50	15.00
❏ ED 2427 [PS]	Song I Wish I Had Sung the First Time Around... Part 2	1956	3.75	7.50	15.00
❏ ED 2535	When I Take My Sugar to Tea/On the Alamo//I'm Confessin' (That I Love You)/Between the Devil and the Deep Blue Sea	195?	3.00	6.00	12.00
❏ ED 2535 [PS]	New Tricks...	195?	3.00	6.00	12.00
❏ ED 2547	Silent Night, Holy Night/Adeste Fideles//White Christmas/Jingle Bells	195?	3.00	6.00	12.00
❏ ED 2547 [PS]	Christmas Time	195?	3.00	6.00	12.00
❏ ED 2659	Silver Bells/The Christmas Song//Christmas Carols/God Rest Ye Merry Gentlemen	195?	3.00	6.00	12.00
❏ ED 2659 [PS]	Christmas Songs	195?	3.00	6.00	12.00
❏ 7-38274	The First Nowell/Medley: Deck The Hall-Away In A Manger-I Saw Three Ships//God Rest Ye Merry, Gentlemen/Jingle Bells	196?	3.00	6.00	12.00
❏ 7-38274 [PS]	General Electric Wishes You a Merry Christmas	196?	3.00	6.00	12.00
❏ 91123	Silent Night/Adeste Fideles//White Christmas/God Rest Ye Merry Gentlemen	195?	3.00	6.00	12.00
—Part of 2-EP set ED 547					
❏ 91124	I'll Be Home for Christmas/Faith of Our Fathers//Jingle Bells/Santa Claus Is Comin' to Town	195?	3.00	6.00	12.00
—Part of 2-EP set ED 547					
❏ 91129	Here Comes Santa Claus/Twelve Days of Christmas//You're All I Want for Christmas/The First Nowell	195?	3.00	6.00	12.00
—Part of 2-EP set ED 561					
❏ 91130	Christmas Carols, Part 1/Christmas Carols, Part 2//The Christmas Song/O, Fir Tree Dark	195?	3.00	6.00	12.00
—Part of 2-EP set ED 561					
❏ 91168	I Cried for You/My Melancholy Baby//Star Dust/Deep Purple	195?	3.00	6.00	12.00
—Part of 2-EP set ED 581					
❏ 91169	The One Rose/Moonlight and Shadows//A Blue Serenade/S'posin'	195?	3.00	6.00	12.00
—Part of 2-EP set ED 581					
❏ 91289	Please/I Found a Million Dollar Baby//I Wonder What's Become of Sally/Mary's a Grand Old Name	195?	3.00	6.00	12.00
—Part of 2-EP set ED 662					
❏ 91290	I'm Waiting for Ships That Never Come In/When Day Is Done//I Don't Want to Walk Without You/Moonlight Cocktail	195?	3.00	6.00	12.00
—Part of 2-EP set ED 662					
❏ 91611	Someday, Sweetheart/Would You//How Soon/I'll See You in My Dreams	195?	2.00	4.00	8.00
—Side 1 and Side 18 of ED 1800					
❏ 91612	(contents unknown)	195?	2.00	4.00	8.00
—Side 2 and Side 17 of ED 1800					
❏ 91613	Dear Old Girl/You Must Have Been a Beautiful Baby//Sweet Lorraine/The One I Love (Belongs to Somebody Else)	195?	2.00	4.00	8.00
—Side 3 and Side 16 of ED 1800					
❏ 91614	It's the Dreamer in Me/My Reverie//I Want My Mama/So in Love	195?	2.00	4.00	8.00
—Side 4 and Side 15 of ED 1800					
❏ 91615	Old Folks/Don't Be That Way//On Behalf of the Visiting Firemen/One Sweet Letter from You	195?	2.00	4.00	8.00
—Side 5 and Side 14 of ED 1800					
❏ 91616	Mr. Crosby and Mr. Mercer/The Moon of Manakoora//Pretending/These Foolish Things (Remind Me of You)	195?	2.00	4.00	8.00
—Side 6 and Side 13 of ED 1800					
❏ 91617	Lazy/It's the Talk of the Town//And the Angels Sing/On the Atchison, Topeka and the Santa Fe	195?	2.00	4.00	8.00
—Side 7 and Side 12 of ED 1800					
❏ 91618	What's New/If I Knew Then (What I Know Now)//A Gal in Calico/Bue Beautiful	195?	2.00	4.00	8.00
—Side 8 and Side 11 of ED 1800					
❏ 91619	My Buddy/I Ain't Got Nobody (And Nobody Cares for Me)//Mister Meadowlark/Imagination	195?	2.00	4.00	8.00
—Side 9 and Side 10 of ED 1800					
❏ 91836	Happy Holiday/Joy to the World/Hark! The Herald Angels Sing//God Rest Ye Merry Gentlemen/O Little Town of Bethlehem/Silent Night	195?	2.00	4.00	8.00
—Side 1 and Side 6 of ED 850; titles not listed on labels					
❏ 91837	White Christmas/Adeste Fideles/We Three Kings of Orient Are//Away in a Manger/Thou Descendeth from the Stars (Descendi de la Stelli)/Deck the Hall	195?	2.00	4.00	8.00
—Side 2 and Side 5 of ED 850; titles not listed on labels					
❏ 91838	The First Noel/Carol of the Bells//What Christmas Means to Me//Good King Wenceslas/Jesus, Sweet Savior (Jesus, Sauveur Adorable)/Angels We Have Heard on High	195?	2.00	4.00	8.00
—Side 3 and Side 4 of ED 850; song titles not listed on labels					
RCA VICTOR					
❏ EPA 3-1473	Mack the Knife/Tell Me//Down Among the Sheltering Palms/Mama Loved Papa	1957	2.00	4.00	8.00
❏ EPA 3-1473 [PS]	Bing with a Beat	1957	2.50	5.00	10.00
Albums					
AMOS					
❏ AAS-7001	Hey Jude/Hey Bing!	1969	3.00	6.00	12.00
BIOGRAPH					
❏ M-1	When the Blue of the Night Meets the Gold of the Day	197?	2.50	5.00	10.00
❏ C-13	Bing Crosby 1929-33	1973	3.00	6.00	12.00
BRUNSWICK					
❏ BL 54005 [M]	The Voice of Bing in the 1930s	1957	6.25	12.50	25.00
❏ BL 58000 [10]	Bing Crosby, Volume 1	1950	12.50	25.00	50.00
❏ BL 58001 [10]	Bing Crosby, Volume 2	1950	12.50	25.00	50.00
CAPITOL					
❏ ST 2300 [S]	That Travelin' Two-Beat	1965	5.00	10.00	20.00
❏ T 2300 [M]	That Travelin' Two-Beat	1965	3.75	7.50	15.00

Number	Title (A Side/B Side)	Yr	VG	VG+	NM
❏ ST 2346 [S]	Great Country Hits	1965	5.00	10.00	20.00
❏ T 2346 [M]	Great Country Hits	1965	3.75	7.50	15.00
❏ SM-11732	Bing Crosby's Christmas Classics	1977	2.50	5.00	10.00
—"A Capitol Re-Issue"; same recordings as on Warner Bros. 1484					
❏ SM-11736	That Travelin' Two-Beat	1977	2.50	5.00	10.00
❏ SM-11737	Great Country Hits	1977	2.50	5.00	10.00
❏ SM-11738	Bing Crosby Classics, Vol. 1	1977	2.50	5.00	10.00
❏ SM-11739	Bing Crosby Classics, Vol. 2	1977	2.50	5.00	10.00
❏ SM-11740	Bing Crosby Classics, Vol. 3	1977	2.50	5.00	10.00
COLUMBIA					
❏ C2L 43 [(2)]	Bing in Hollywood 1930-1934	196?	3.75	7.50	15.00
—Red "360 Sound" labels					
❏ C2L 43 [(2)]	Bing in Hollywood 1930-1934	1971	3.00	6.00	12.00
—Orange labels					
❏ CL 2502 [10]	Der Bingle	1955	10.00	20.00	40.00
❏ CL 6027 [10]	Crosby Classics	1949	12.50	25.00	50.00
❏ CL 6105 [10]	Crosby Classics, Volume 2	1950	12.50	25.00	50.00
❏ C 35093	Bing Crosby Collection, Vol. 1	1977	2.50	5.00	10.00
❏ C 35094	Bing Crosby Collection, Vol. 2	1977	2.50	5.00	10.00
❏ C4X 44229 [(4)]	The Crooner: The Columbia Years	1988	10.00	20.00	40.00
COLUMBIA SPECIAL PRODUCTS					
❏ P 14369	Bing	197?	2.50	5.00	10.00
DAYBREAK					
❏ 2006	A Time to Be Jolly	1971	3.00	6.00	12.00
❏ 2014	Bing and Basie	1972	3.00	6.00	12.00
DECCA					
❏ DX 151 [(5)M]	Bing: A Musical Autobiography	195?	37.50	75.00	150.00
❏ DX 152 [(3)M]	Old Masters	195?	37.50	75.00	150.00
❏ DXB 184 [(2)M]	The Best of Bing	1965	6.25	12.50	25.00
❏ DL 4086 [M]	My Golden Favorites	1961	6.25	12.50	25.00
❏ DL 4250 [M]	Bing's Hollywood: Easy to Remember	1962	6.25	12.50	25.00
❏ DL 4251 [M]	Bing's Hollywood: Pennies from Heaven	1962	6.25	12.50	25.00
❏ DL 4252 [M]	Bing's Hollywood: Pocket Full of Dreams	1962	6.25	12.50	25.00
❏ DL 4253 [M]	Bing's Hollywood: East Side of Heaven	1962	6.25	12.50	25.00
❏ DL 4254 [M]	Bing's Hollywood: The Road Begins	1962	6.25	12.50	25.00
❏ DL 4255 [M]	Bing's Hollywood: Only Forever	1962	6.25	12.50	25.00
❏ DL 4256 [M]	Bing's Hollywood: Holiday Inn	1962	6.25	12.50	25.00
❏ DL 4257 [M]	Bing's Hollywood: Swinging on a Star	1962	6.25	12.50	25.00
❏ DL 4258 [M]	Bing's Hollywood: Accentuate the Positive	1962	6.25	12.50	25.00
❏ DL 4259 [M]	Bing's Hollywood: Blue Skies	1962	6.25	12.50	25.00
❏ DL 4260 [M]	Bing's Hollywood: But Beautiful	1962	6.25	12.50	25.00
❏ DL 4261 [M]	Bing's Hollywood: Sunshine Cake	1962	6.25	12.50	25.00
❏ DL 4262 [M]	Bing's Hollywood: Cool of the Evening	1962	6.25	12.50	25.00
❏ DL 4263 [M]	Bing's Hollywood: Zing a Little Zong	1962	6.25	12.50	25.00
❏ DL 4264 [M]	Bing's Hollywood: Anything Goes	1962	6.25	12.50	25.00
❏ DL 4281 [M]	Holiday in Europe	1962	6.25	12.50	25.00
❏ DL 4283	Two Favorite Stories by Bing Crosby	1962	6.25	12.50	25.00
❏ DL 4415 [M]	Songs Everybody Knows	1964	6.25	12.50	25.00
❏ DLP 5000 [10]	Hits from Musical Comedies	1949	12.50	25.00	50.00
❏ DLP 5001 [10]	Jerome Kern Songs	1949	12.50	25.00	50.00
❏ DLP 5010 [10]	Stephen Foster Songs	1949	12.50	25.00	50.00
❏ DLP 5011 [10]	El Bingo	1949	12.50	25.00	50.00
❏ DLP 5019 [10]	Merry Christmas	1949	15.00	30.00	60.00
❏ DLP 5020 [10]	Christmas Greetings	1949	15.00	30.00	60.00
❏ DL 5028 [10]	Auld Lang Syne	1950	12.50	25.00	50.00
❏ DL 5037 [10]	St. Patrick's Day	1950	12.50	25.00	50.00
❏ DL 5039 [10]	St. Valentine's Day	1950	12.50	25.00	50.00
❏ DL 5042 [10]	Blue Skies	1950	12.50	25.00	50.00
❏ DL 5052 [10]	Going My Way/The Bells of St. Mary's	1950	15.00	30.00	60.00
❏ DL 5063 [10]	Don't Fence Me In	1950	12.50	25.00	50.00
❏ DL 5064 [10]	Cole Porter Songs	1950	12.50	25.00	50.00
❏ DL 5081 [10]	Songs by Gershwin	1950	12.50	25.00	50.00
❏ DL 5102 [10]	Blue of the Night	1950	12.50	25.00	50.00
❏ DL 5107 [10]	Cowboy Songs	1950	12.50	25.00	50.00
❏ DL 5119 [10]	Drifting and Dreaming	1950	12.50	25.00	50.00
❏ DL 5122 [10]	Hawaiian Songs	1950	12.50	25.00	50.00
❏ DL 5126 [10]	Stardust	1950	12.50	25.00	50.00
❏ DL 5129 [10]	Cowboy Songs, Volume 2	1950	12.50	25.00	50.00
❏ DL 5220 [10]	Bing Sings Hits	1950	12.50	25.00	50.00
❏ DL 5272 [10]	Top o' the Morning/The Emperor Waltz	1950	12.50	25.00	50.00
❏ DL 5284 [10]	Mr. Music	1950	12.50	25.00	50.00
❏ DL 5298 [10]	Hits from Broadway Shows	1951	12.50	25.00	50.00
❏ DL 5299 [10]	Favorite Hawaiian Songs	1951	12.50	25.00	50.00
❏ DL 5302 [10]	Go West, Young Man	1951	12.50	25.00	50.00
❏ DL 5310 [10]	Way Back Home	1951	12.50	25.00	50.00
❏ DL 5323 [10]	Bing and the Dixieland Bands	1951	12.50	25.00	50.00
❏ DL 5326 [10]	Yours Is My Heart Alone	1951	12.50	25.00	50.00
❏ DL 5331 [10]	Country Style	1951	12.50	25.00	50.00
❏ DL 5340 [10]	Down Memory Lane	1951	12.50	25.00	50.00
❏ DL 5343 [10]	Down Memory Lane, Volume 2	1951	12.50	25.00	50.00
❏ DL 5351 [10]	Beloved Hymns	1951	12.50	25.00	50.00
❏ DL 5355 [10]	Bing Sings Victor Herbert	1951	12.50	25.00	50.00
❏ DL 5390 [10]	Bing and Connee	1953	12.50	25.00	50.00
—With Connee Boswell					
❏ DL 5403 [10]	When Irish Eyes Are Smiling	1952	12.50	25.00	50.00
❏ DL 5417 [10]	Just for You	1952	12.50	25.00	50.00
❏ DL 5444 [10]	The Road to Bali	1952	15.00	30.00	60.00
❏ DL 5499 [10]	Song Hits of Paris/Le Bing	1953	12.50	25.00	50.00
❏ DL 5508 [10]	Some Fine Old Chestnuts	1953	12.50	25.00	50.00
❏ DL 5520 [10]	Bing Sings the Hits	1954	12.50	25.00	50.00
❏ DL 5556 [10]	Country Girl/Little Boy Lost/Anything Goes	1954	12.50	25.00	50.00
❏ DL 6000 [10]	Two Favorite Stories by Bing Crosby	1950	15.00	30.00	60.00
❏ DL 6001 [10]	Ichabod/Rip Van Winkle	1950	12.50	25.00	50.00
❏ DL 6008 [10]	Collector's Classics: Mississippi/Here Is My Heart	1951	15.00	30.00	60.00
❏ DL 6009 [10]	Collector's Classics: Anything Goes/Two for Tonight	1951	15.00	30.00	60.00
❏ DL 6010 [10]	Collector's Classics: Rhythm on the Range/Pennies from Heaven	1951	15.00	30.00	60.00
❏ DL 6011 [10]	Collector's Classics: Waikiki Wedding	1951	15.00	30.00	60.00
❏ DL 6012 [10]	Collector's Classics: Paris Honeymoon	1951	15.00	30.00	60.00
❏ DL 6013 [10]	Collector's Classics: The Star Maker/Doctor Rhythm	1951	15.00	30.00	60.00
❏ DL 6014 [10]	Collector's Classics: Big Broadcast of 1936	1951	15.00	30.00	60.00
❏ DL 6015 [10]	Collector's Classics: The Road to Singapore/If I Had My Way	1951	15.00	30.00	60.00
❏ DXSB 7184 [(2)R]	The Best of Bing	1965	3.75	7.50	15.00
❏ DL 8020 [M]	The Man Without a Country/What So Proudly We Hail	1950	10.00	20.00	40.00

Number	Title (A Side/B Side)	Yr	VG	VG+	NM
❏ DL 8110 [M]	Lullaby Time	1955	10.00	20.00	40.00
❏ DL 8128 [M]	Merry Christmas	1955	10.00	20.00	40.00
—Expanded version of 10-inch LP; all-black label					
❏ DL 8128 [M]	Merry Christmas	1960	6.25	12.50	25.00
—Reissue on black label with color bars					
❏ DL 8178 [M]	Merry Christmas	196?	15.00	30.00	60.00
—Black label with color bars; at least one copy is known to exist on red vinyl					
❏ DL 8207 [M]	Shillelaghs and Shamrocks	1956	10.00	20.00	40.00
❏ DL 8210 [M]	Home on the Range	1956	10.00	20.00	40.00
❏ DL 8262 [M]	When Irish Eyes Are Smiling	1956	10.00	20.00	40.00
❏ DL 8269 [M]	Drifting and Dreaming	1956	10.00	20.00	40.00
❏ DL 8269 [M]	Blue Hawaii	1956	10.00	20.00	40.00
❏ DL 8272 [M]	High Tor	1956	100.00	200.00	400.00
❏ DL 8318 [M]	Anything Goes	1956	12.50	25.00	50.00
❏ DL 8352 [M]	Song I Wish I Had Sung…The First Time Around	1956	10.00	20.00	40.00
❏ DL 8365 [M]	Twilight on the Trail	1957	10.00	20.00	40.00
❏ DL 8374 [M]	Some Fine Old Chestnuts	1957	10.00	20.00	40.00
❏ DL 8419 [M]	A Christmas Sing with Bing Around the World	1957	10.00	20.00	40.00
❏ DL 8493 [M]	Bing and the Dixieland Bands	1957	10.00	20.00	40.00
❏ DL 8575 [M]	New Tricks	1957	10.00	20.00	40.00
❏ DL 8687 [M]	Around the World	1958	10.00	20.00	40.00
❏ DL 8780 [M]	Bing in Paris	1958	10.00	20.00	40.00
❏ DL 8781 [M]	That Christmas Feeling	1958	7.50	15.00	30.00
—Expanded version of DL 5020; all-black label, textured cover					
❏ DL 8781 [M]	That Christmas Feeling	1960	5.00	10.00	20.00
—Reissue on black label with color bars, smooth cover					
❏ DL 8846 [M]	In a Little Spanish Town	1959	7.50	15.00	30.00
❏ DL 9054 [M]	Bing: A Musical Autobiography 1927-1934	1961	10.00	20.00	40.00
❏ DL 9064 [M]	Bing: A Musical Autobiography 1934-1941	1961	10.00	20.00	40.00
❏ DL 9067 [M]	Bing: A Musical Autobiography 1941-44	1961	10.00	20.00	40.00
❏ DL 9077 [M]	Bing: A Musical Autobiography 1944-47	1961	10.00	20.00	40.00
❏ DL 9078 [M]	Bing: A Musical Autobiography 1947-1953	1961	10.00	20.00	40.00
❏ DL 9106 [M]	Ichabod/Rip Van Winkle	1962	6.25	12.50	25.00
❏ DL 34522	Favorite Songs of Christmas	1968	3.75	7.50	15.00
—Decca Records Custom Division pressing					
❏ DL 74281 [R]	Holiday in Europe	1962	3.75	7.50	15.00
❏ DL 74283 [R]	The Small One	1962	2.50	5.00	10.00
❏ DL 74415 [R]	Songs Everybody Knows	1964	3.75	7.50	15.00
❏ DL 78128 [R]	Merry Christmas	196?	2.50	5.00	10.00
❏ DL 78207 [R]	Shillelaghs and Shamrocks	196?	2.50	5.00	10.00
❏ DL 78262 [R]	When Irish Eyes Are Smiling	196?	2.50	5.00	10.00
❏ DL 78352 [R]	Songs I Wish I Had Sung…The First Time Around	196?	2.50	5.00	10.00
❏ DL 78419 [R]	A Christmas Sing with Bing Around the World	196?	2.50	5.00	10.00
❏ DL 78781 [R]	That Christmas Feeling	196?	2.50	5.00	10.00
❏ DL 79106 [R]	Ichabod/Rip Van Winkle	1962	2.50	5.00	10.00
ENCORE					
❏ E2E-201 [(2)]	The Bing Crosby Story, Volume 1	1968	3.75	7.50	15.00
❏ E2E-202 [(2)]	The Bing Crosby Story, Volume 2	1968	3.75	7.50	15.00
FOX AMERICAN					
❏ SMF 210	Bing Crosby Sings Christmas	1978	2.50	5.00	10.00
—Side 1 from radio show Dec. 19, 1951; Side 2 from radio show Dec. 14, 1949					
GNP CRESCENDO					
❏ GNP-9044	The Radio Years, Vol. 1	1985	2.00	4.00	8.00
❏ GNP-9046	The Radio Years, Vol. 2	1986	2.00	4.00	8.00
❏ GNP-9047	The Radio Years, Vol. 3	1986	2.00	4.00	8.00
❏ GNP-9048	The Radio Years, Vol. 4	1986	2.00	4.00	8.00
GOLDEN					
❏ A298:20 [M]	Ali Baba and the 40 Thieves	1957	6.25	12.50	25.00
❏ A298:21 [M]	How Lovely Is Christmas/A Christmas Story	195?	6.25	12.50	25.00
HARMONY					
❏ HL 7094 [M]	Crosby Classics	1958	3.75	7.50	15.00
❏ HS 11313 [R]	Crosby Classics	196?	2.50	5.00	10.00
LONDON					
❏ PS 679	Feels Good	1977	3.00	6.00	12.00
MARK 56					
❏ 762	Original Radio Broadcasts	197?	2.50	5.00	10.00
MCA					
❏ 177	Shillelaghs and Shamrocks	1973	2.50	5.00	10.00
❏ 519	When Irish Eyes Are Smiling	197?	2.50	5.00	10.00
❏ 915	Hey Bing!	198?	2.50	5.00	10.00
❏ 1502	Rare 1930-31 Brunswick Recordings	198?	2.50	5.00	10.00
❏ 3031	Bing Crosby's Greatest Hits	1977	2.50	5.00	10.00
❏ 2-4045 [(2)]	The Best of Bing	197?	2.50	5.00	10.00
—Blue labels with rainbow; regular cover					
❏ 2-4045 [(2)]	The Best of Bing	197?	3.00	6.00	12.00
—Black labels with rainbow; gatefold cover					
❏ 15017	Two Favorite Stories by Bing Crosby	197?	2.50	5.00	10.00
—Reissue of Decca DL 4283					
❏ 15018 [R]	A Christmas Sing with Bing Around the World	197?	2.00	4.00	8.00
—Reissue of Decca DL7-8419					
❏ 15019 [R]	That Christmas Feeling	1973	2.00	4.00	8.00
—Reissue of Decca DL7-8781					
❏ 15024 [R]	Merry Christmas	197?	2.00	4.00	8.00
—Reissue of Decca DL7-8128					
❏ 37076	Bing Crosby's Greatest Hits	198?	2.00	4.00	8.00
METRO					
❏ M-523 [M]	Bing Crosby	1965	3.00	6.00	12.00
❏ MS-523 [S]	Bing Crosby	1965	3.75	7.50	15.00
MGM					
❏ E-3890 [M]	Senor Bing	1961	3.75	7.50	15.00
❏ SE-3890 [S]	Senor Bing	1961	5.00	10.00	20.00
❏ E-4129 [M]	The Great Standards	1963	3.75	7.50	15.00
❏ SE-4129 [S]	The Great Standards	1963	5.00	10.00	20.00
❏ E-4203 [M]	The Very Best of Bing Crosby	1964	3.75	7.50	15.00
❏ SE-4203 [S]	The Very Best of Bing Crosby	1964	5.00	10.00	20.00
MOBILE FIDELITY					
❏ 1-260	Bing Sings Whilst Bregman Swings	1996	5.00	10.00	20.00
—Audiophile vinyl					
MURRAY HILL					
❏ 894637 [(4)]	Bing Crosby and His Friends	197?	6.25	12.50	25.00
P.I.P.					
❏ 6802	Thoroughly Modern Bing	1971	3.00	6.00	12.00
PHILCO					
❏ LP 436 [10]	Crosby Classics	195?	10.00	20.00	40.00
—Custom item for Philco (front cover has "Philco: Famous for Quality the World Over")					

Number	Title (A Side/B Side)	Yr	VG	VG+	NM
PICKWICK					
❏ SPC-3583	Thoroughly Modern Bing	1978	2.00	4.00	8.00
POLYDOR					
❏ PD-1-6128	Seasons: The Closing Chapter	1978	3.00	6.00	12.00
RCA VICTOR					
❏ LPM-1473 [M]	Bing with a Beat	1957	6.25	12.50	25.00
❏ AFL1-1854	Fancy Meeting You Here	1977	2.50	5.00	10.00
❏ LPM-1854 [M]	Fancy Meeting You Here	1958	5.00	10.00	20.00
❏ LSP-1854 [S]	Fancy Meeting You Here	1958	7.50	15.00	30.00
❏ LPM-2071 [M]	Young Bing Crosby	1959	5.00	10.00	20.00
❏ CPL1-2086(e)	A Legendary Performer	1976	2.50	5.00	10.00
READER'S DIGEST					
❏ RDA-175	Christmas with Bing	1980	2.50	5.00	10.00
—Repackage of Warner Bros.and Capitol recordings					
REPRISE					
❏ R-6106 [M]	Return to Paradise Islands	1964	3.75	7.50	15.00
❏ R9-6106 [S]	Return to Paradise Islands	1964	5.00	10.00	20.00
SPOKANE					
❏ 1	Bing Crosby On the Air, 1934 and 1938	197?	2.50	5.00	10.00
❏ 5	Der Bingle, Vol. 1	197?	2.50	5.00	10.00
❏ 10	Der Bingle, Vol. 2	197?	2.50	5.00	10.00
❏ 12	Bing in the 30's	197?	2.50	5.00	10.00
❏ 14	Bing in the 30s, Vol. 2	197?	2.50	5.00	10.00
❏ 15	Holiday Inn/The Bells of St. Mary's	197?	2.50	5.00	10.00
❏ 16	Kraft Music Hall Highlights	197?	2.50	5.00	10.00
❏ 19	Kraft Music Hall Highlights, Vol. 2	197?	2.50	5.00	10.00
❏ 20	Der Bingle, Vol. 3	197?	2.50	5.00	10.00
❏ 21	Bing Crosby & the Music Maids	197?	2.50	5.00	10.00
❏ 24	Bing in the 30s, Vol. 3	1986	2.00	4.00	8.00
❏ 25	Bing in the 30s, Vol. 4	1986	2.00	4.00	8.00
❏ 26	Bing in the 30s, Vol. 5	1986	2.00	4.00	8.00
❏ 27	Bing in the 30s, Vol. 6	1986	2.00	4.00	8.00
SUNBEAM					
❏ 502	Distinctively Bing, Vol. 1	197?	2.50	5.00	10.00
❏ 504	Distinctively Bing, Vol. 2	197?	2.50	5.00	10.00
TIME-LIFE					
❏ SLGD-06 [(2)]	Legendary Singers: Bing Crosby	1985	3.75	7.50	15.00
20TH CENTURY					
❏ T-551	A Holiday Toast	1977	3.00	6.00	12.00
UNITED ARTISTS					
❏ UA-LA554-G	That's What Life Is All About	1976	3.00	6.00	12.00
VERVE					
❏ MGV 2020 [M]	Bing Sings Whilst Bregman Swings	1956	12.50	25.00	50.00
❏ V-2020 [M]	Bing Sings Whilst Bregman Swings	1961	6.25	12.50	25.00
VOCALION					
❏ VL 3603 [M]	Bing Crosby Sings	195?	3.75	7.50	15.00
❏ VL 73603 [R]	Bing Crosby Sings	196?	2.50	5.00	10.00
WARNER BROS.					
❏ W 1363 [M]	Join with Bing and Sing Along	1960	3.75	7.50	15.00
❏ WS 1363 [S]	Join with Bing and Sing Along	1960	5.00	10.00	20.00
❏ 2W 1401 [(2)M]	101 Gang Songs	1961	5.00	10.00	20.00
❏ 2WS 1401 [(2)S]	101 Gang Songs	1961	6.25	12.50	25.00
❏ W 1422 [M]	Join Bing in a Gang Song Sing-Along	1961	3.75	7.50	15.00
❏ WS 1422 [S]	Join Bing in a Gang Song Sing-Along	1961	5.00	10.00	20.00
❏ W 1435 [M]	Join Bing and Sing Along	1962	3.75	7.50	15.00
❏ WS 1435 [S]	Join Bing and Sing Along	1962	5.00	10.00	20.00
❏ W 1482 [M]	On the Happy Side	1962	3.75	7.50	15.00
❏ WS 1482 [S]	On the Happy Side	1962	5.00	10.00	20.00
❏ W 1484 [M]	I Wish You a Merry Christmas	1962	3.75	7.50	15.00
❏ WS 1484 [S]	I Wish You a Merry Christmas	1962	5.00	10.00	20.00
"X"					
❏ XLVA-4250 [M]	Young Bing Crosby	1955	12.50	25.00	50.00

CROSBY, BING, AND LOUIS ARMSTRONG Also see each artist's individual listings.

45s

Number	Title (A Side/B Side)	Yr	VG	VG+	NM
DECCA					
❏ 27623	Gone Fishin'/We All Have a Song in My Heart	1951	3.75	7.50	15.00
MGM					
❏ SB 26 [S]	Muskrat Ramble/Way Down in New Orleans	1960	3.75	7.50	15.00
❏ SB 27 [S]	Dardanella/Brother Bill	1960	3.75	7.50	15.00
❏ SB 28 [S]	Preacher/Little Ol' Tune	1960	3.75	7.50	15.00
❏ SB 29 [S]	Let's Sing Like a Dixieland Band/At the Jazz Band Ball	1960	3.75	7.50	15.00
❏ SB 30 [S]	Rocky Mountain Moon/Bye Bye Blues	1960	3.75	7.50	15.00
—The above five are 33 1/3 rpm jukebox singles					
❏ 12961	Dardanella/Muskrat Ramble	1960	2.50	5.00	10.00
Albums					
CAPITOL					
❏ SM-11735	Bing Crosby and Louis Armstrong	1977	2.50	5.00	10.00
MGM					
❏ E-3882 [M]	Bing and Satchmo	1960	3.75	7.50	15.00
❏ SE-3882 [S]	Bing and Satchmo	1960	5.00	10.00	20.00

CROSBY, BING, AND FRED ASTAIRE

Albums

Number	Title (A Side/B Side)	Yr	VG	VG+	NM
UNITED ARTISTS					
❏ UA-LA588-G	A Couple of Song and Dance Men	1976	3.00	6.00	12.00

CROSBY, BING, AND PEGGY LEE Also see each artist's individual listings.

45s

Number	Title (A Side/B Side)	Yr	VG	VG+	NM
DECCA					
❏ 28238	Watermelon Weather/The Moon Came Up with a Great Idea Last Night	1952	3.00	6.00	12.00

CROSBY, DAVID Also see THE BYRDS; CROSBY, STILLS AND NASH; CROSBY, STILLS, NASH AND YOUNG; GRAHAM NASH AND DAVID CROSBY.

45s

Number	Title (A Side/B Side)	Yr	VG	VG+	NM
ATLANTIC					
❏ 2792	Laughing/Music Is Love	1971	—	2.50	5.00
❏ 2809	Orleans/Traction in the Rain	1971	—	2.50	5.00
❏ 87360	Hero/Coverage	1993	—	—	3.00
—A-side with Phil Collins					
Albums					
A&M					
❏ SP-5232	Oh Yes I Can	1989	2.50	5.00	10.00
ATLANTIC					
❏ SD 7203	If I Could Only Remember My Name…	1971	3.75	7.50	15.00
❏ SD 7203	If I Could Only Remember My Name…	2000	6.25	12.50	25.00
—Classic Records reissue on audiophile vinyl					

Number	Title (A Side/B Side)	Yr	VG	VG+	NM

CROSBY, DAVID, AND GRAHAM NASH See GRAHAM NASH AND DAVID CROSBY.

CROSBY, STILLS AND NASH Also see DAVID CROSBY; GRAHAM NASH; STEPHEN STILLS.

12-Inch Singles

ATLANTIC

Number	Title (A Side/B Side)	Yr	VG	VG+	NM
❏ PR (# unk) [DJ]	Southern Cross (LP Version)/Too Much Love to Hide	1982	3.75	7.50	15.00
❏ PR 445 [DJ]	Wasted on the Way/Daylight Again	1982	2.00	4.00	8.00
❏ PR 508 [DJ]	War Games/For What It's Worth/ Turn Your Back on Love	1983	2.00	4.00	8.00
❏ PR 3377 [DJ]	Live It Up (2 versions)	1990	2.50	5.00	10.00

45s

ATLANTIC

Number	Title (A Side/B Side)	Yr	VG	VG+	NM
❏ 2652	Marrakesh Express/Helplessly Hoping	1969	—	3.00	6.00
❏ 2676	Suite: Judy Blue Eyes/Long Time Gone	1969	—	3.00	6.00
❏ 3401	Just a Song Before I Go/Dark Star	1977	—	2.00	4.00
❏ 3401 [PS]	Just a Song Before I Go/Dark Star	1977	—	2.50	5.00
❏ 3432	Fair Game/Anything at All	1977	—	2.00	4.00
❏ 3453	I Give You Give Blind/Carried Away	1978	—	2.00	4.00
❏ 3784	Carry On/Shadow Captain	1980	—	2.50	5.00
❏ 4058	Wasted on the Way/Delta	1982	—	—	3.00
❏ 4058 [PS]	Wasted on the Way/Delta	1982	—	2.00	4.00
❏ 87909	Live It Up/Chuck's Lament	1990	—	2.00	4.00
❏ 89775	Raise a Voice/For What It's Worth	1983	—	—	3.00
❏ 89812	War Games/Shadow Captain	1983	—	—	3.00
❏ 89812 [PS]	War Games/Shadow Captain	1983	—	2.00	4.00
❏ 89888	Too Much Love to Hide/Song for Susan	1983	—	—	3.00
❏ 89969	Southern Cross/Into the Darkness	1982	—	—	3.00
❏ 89969 [PS]	Southern Cross/Into the Darkness	1982	—	2.00	4.00

Albums

ATLANTIC

Number	Title (A Side/B Side)	Yr	VG	VG+	NM
❏ SD 8229	Crosby, Stills & Nash	1969	5.00	10.00	20.00
❏ SD 8229	Crosby, Stills & Nash	2000	6.25	12.50	25.00
—Classic Records reissue on 180-gram vinyl					
❏ SD 16026	Replay	1980	3.00	6.00	12.00
—Also has solo cuts by Stephen Stills					
❏ SD 19104	CSN	1977	3.00	6.00	12.00
❏ SD 19117	Crosby, Stills & Nash	1977	2.50	5.00	10.00
—Reissue of 8229					
❏ SD 19360	Daylight Again	1982	3.00	6.00	12.00
❏ 80075	Allies	1983	3.00	6.00	12.00
❏ 82107	Live It Up	1990	3.75	7.50	15.00

NAUTILUS

Number	Title (A Side/B Side)	Yr	VG	VG+	NM
❏ NR-48	Crosby, Stills and Nash	1982	37.50	75.00	150.00
—Audiophile vinyl					

CROSBY, STILLS, NASH & YOUNG Also see DAVID CROSBY; GRAHAM NASH; STEPHEN STILLS; NEIL YOUNG.

12-Inch Singles

ATLANTIC

Number	Title (A Side/B Side)	Yr	VG	VG+	NM
❏ PR 2496 [DJ]	American Dream (same on both sides)	1988	3.75	7.50	15.00

45s

ATLANTIC

Number	Title (A Side/B Side)	Yr	VG	VG+	NM
❏ 2723	Woodstock/Helpless	1970	—	3.00	6.00
❏ 2735	Teach Your Children/Carry On	1970	—	3.00	6.00
❏ 2740	Ohio/Find the Cost of Freedom	1970	—	3.00	6.00
❏ 2740 [PS]	Ohio/Find the Cost of Freedom	1970	3.00	6.00	12.00
❏ 2760	Our House/Deja Vu	1970	—	3.00	6.00
❏ 88966	Got It Made/This Old House	1989	—	—	3.00
❏ 88966 [PS]	Got It Made/This Old House	1989	—	—	3.00
❏ 89003	American Dream/Compass	1988	—	—	3.00
❏ 89003 [PS]	American Dream/Compass	1988	—	—	3.00

Albums

ATLANTIC

Number	Title (A Side/B Side)	Yr	VG	VG+	NM
❏ PR 165 [M]	Celebration/CSNY Month	1974	25.00	50.00	100.00
—Promo-only LP in mono					
❏ PR 165 [S]	Celebration/CSNY Month	1974	12.50	25.00	50.00
—Promo-only LP in stereo					
❏ 2-902 [(2)M]	4 Way Street	1971	25.00	50.00	100.00
—White label promo; all stock copies are mono					
❏ SD 2-902 [(2)]	4 Way Street	1971	5.00	10.00	20.00
❏ SD 2-902 [(2)DJ]	4 Way Street	1971	12.50	25.00	50.00
—White label stereo promo					
❏ 7200 [M]	Deja Vu	1970	37.50	75.00	150.00
—White label promo; no stock copies are mono					
❏ SD 7200	Deja Vu	1970	3.75	7.50	15.00
—Pasted-on front cover photo must still be intact					
❏ SD 7200 [DJ]	Deja Vu	1970	15.00	30.00	60.00
—White label stereo promo					
❏ SD 18100	So Far	1974	3.00	6.00	12.00
❏ PR 18102 [DJ]	A Rap with C, S, N & Y	1974	12.50	25.00	50.00
—Promo-only interview album					
❏ SD 19118	Deja Vu	1977	2.50	5.00	10.00
—Reissue of 7200, this time with photo as part of the cover rather than as a paste-on					
❏ SD 19119	So Far	1977	2.50	5.00	10.00
—Reissue of 18100					
❏ 81888	American Dream	1988	2.50	5.00	10.00

MOBILE FIDELITY

Number	Title (A Side/B Side)	Yr	VG	VG+	NM
❏ 1-088	Deja Vu	198?	50.00	100.00	200.00
—Audiophile vinyl					

CROSS, JIMMY

45s

CHICKEN

Number	Title (A Side/B Side)	Yr	VG	VG+	NM
❏ 101	Hey Little Girl/Hey Little Girl (Part 2)	1966	3.00	6.00	12.00

RECORDO

Number	Title (A Side/B Side)	Yr	VG	VG+	NM
❏ 502	Pretty Girls Everywhere/Suntan Sally	1961	3.75	7.50	15.00

RED BIRD

Number	Title (A Side/B Side)	Yr	VG	VG+	NM
❏ 10-042	Hey Little Girl/Super Duper Man	1965	3.75	7.50	15.00

TOLLIE

Number	Title (A Side/B Side)	Yr	VG	VG+	NM
❏ 9039	I Want My Baby Back/Play the Other Side	1965	5.00	10.00	20.00
❏ 9044	The Ballad of James Bong/ Play the Other Side Again	1965	3.75	7.50	15.00

CROSS COUNTRY Includes three members of THE TOKENS.

45s

ATCO

Number	Title (A Side/B Side)	Yr	VG	VG+	NM
❏ 6932	Rock and Roll Music/Just a Thought	1973	2.00	4.00	8.00
❏ 6934	In the Midnight Hour/The Smile Song	1973	2.00	4.00	8.00
❏ 6947	Tastes So Good to Me/A Ball Song	1973	2.00	4.00	8.00

Albums

ATCO

Number	Title (A Side/B Side)	Yr	VG	VG+	NM
❏ SD 7024	Cross Country	1973	3.75	7.50	15.00

CROSSFIRES, THE (1) Group evolved into THE TURTLES.

45s

CAPCO

Number	Title (A Side/B Side)	Yr	VG	VG+	NM
❏ 104	Fiberglass Jungle/Dr. Jekyll and Mr. Hyde	1963	20.00	40.00	80.00

LUCKY TOKEN

Number	Title (A Side/B Side)	Yr	VG	VG+	NM
❏ 112	One Potato, Two Potato/That'll Be the Day	1965	12.50	25.00	50.00

Albums

RHINO

Number	Title (A Side/B Side)	Yr	VG	VG+	NM
❏ RNLP-019	Out of Control	1981	2.50	5.00	10.00

CROSSFIRES, THE (2)

45s

CUCA

Number	Title (A Side/B Side)	Yr	VG	VG+	NM
❏ 1027	Young Love/When My Blue Moon Turns to Gold Again	1961	3.00	6.00	12.00

CROSSFIRES, THE (3)

Albums

STRAND

Number	Title (A Side/B Side)	Yr	VG	VG+	NM
❏ SL-1083 [M]	Limbo Rock	1963	5.00	10.00	20.00
❏ SLS-1083 [S]	Limbo Rock	1963	6.25	12.50	25.00

CROSSFIRES, THE (4)

45s

TOWER

Number	Title (A Side/B Side)	Yr	VG	VG+	NM
❏ 278	Who'll Be the Next One/Making Love Is Fun	1966	5.00	10.00	20.00

CROW

45s

AMARET

Number	Title (A Side/B Side)	Yr	VG	VG+	NM
❏ 106	Busy Day/Time to Make a Turn	1969	—	3.00	6.00
❏ 112	Evil Woman Don't Play Your Games with Me/ Gonna Leave a Mark	1969	2.00	4.00	8.00
❏ 119	Cottage Cheese/Busy Day	1970	—	3.00	6.00
❏ 119	Cottage Cheese/Slow Down	1970	—	3.00	6.00
❏ 125	Don't Try to Lay No Boogie-Woogie on the "King of Rock 'n' Roll"/Satisfied	1970	—	3.00	6.00
❏ 129	Watching Can Waste Up the Time/Yellow Dawg	1971	—	2.50	5.00
❏ 133	Something in Your Blood/Yellow Dawg	1971	—	2.50	5.00
❏ 145	Everything Has Got to Be Free/Mobile Blues	1972	—	2.50	5.00
❏ 148	If It Feels Good, Do It/Cado Queen	1972	—	2.50	5.00

Albums

AMARET

Number	Title (A Side/B Side)	Yr	VG	VG+	NM
❏ ST-5002	Crow Music	1969	5.00	10.00	20.00
❏ ST-5006	Crow By Crow	1970	5.00	10.00	20.00
❏ ST-5009	Mosaic	1971	5.00	10.00	20.00
❏ AST-5012	Best of Crow	1972	3.75	7.50	15.00
❏ ST-5013	David Crow d/b/a Crow	1973	3.75	7.50	15.00

CROWN, BOBBY

45s

FELCO

Number	Title (A Side/B Side)	Yr	VG	VG+	NM
❏ 102	One Way Ticket/Your Conscience	1960	200.00	400.00	800.00

MANCO

Number	Title (A Side/B Side)	Yr	VG	VG+	NM
❏ 1005	I've Never Had a Broken Heart/Wait a Minute	1960	10.00	20.00	40.00

CROWN HEIGHTS AFFAIR

12-Inch Singles

DE-LITE

Number	Title (A Side/B Side)	Yr	VG	VG+	NM
❏ MK 79 [DJ]	Dance Lady Dance (6:25)/The Rock Is Hot (7:14)	1979	5.00	10.00	20.00
❏ MK 142 [DJ]	Sure Shot (6:20) (same on both sides)	1980	5.00	10.00	20.00
❏ PRO 225-1 [DJ]	Let Me Ride on the Wave of Your Love (5:44) (same on both sides)	1982	5.00	10.00	20.00
❏ DDS 582	Do It the French Way/Sexy Ways	1977	10.00	20.00	40.00
❏ DDS 588	Dancin' (6:13)/Love Me (6:01)	1977	10.00	20.00	40.00

SBK

Number	Title (A Side/B Side)	Yr	VG	VG+	NM
❏ V-19703	I'll Do Anything (Radio Edit 3:54) (Nineties Club Mix 6:53) (Red Zone Mix 6:04) (Marsha Mix 9:14)	1989	2.50	5.00	10.00

45s

DE-LITE

Number	Title (A Side/B Side)	Yr	VG	VG+	NM
❏ 803	You Gave Me Love/Tell Me You Love Me	1980	—	2.00	4.00
❏ 805	Sure Shot/I See the Light	1980	—	2.00	4.00
❏ 821	Somebody Tell Me What to Do/ You Gave Me Love	1982	—	2.00	4.00
❏ 823	Let Me Ride on the Wave of Your Love/ Wine and Dine You	1982	—	2.00	4.00
❏ 908	Say a Prayer for Two/Galaxy of Love	1978	—	2.00	4.00
❏ 911	I Love You/Dream World	1978	—	2.00	4.00
❏ 912	Dance Lady Dance/Come Fly with Me	1979	—	2.00	4.00
❏ 915	Empty Soul of Mine/Rock Is Hot	1979	—	2.00	4.00
❏ 1570	Dreaming a Dream/Dreaming a Dream (Part 2)	1975	—	2.00	4.00
❏ 1575	Every Beat of My Heart/Every Beat of My Heart (Disco Version)	1975	—	2.00	4.00
❏ 1581	Foxy Lady/Picture Show	1976	—	2.00	4.00
❏ 1588	Dancin'/Love Me	1976	—	2.00	4.00
❏ 1592	Do It the French Way/Sexy Ways	1977	—	2.00	4.00
❏ 1592 [PS]	Do It the French Way/Sexy Ways	1977	—	3.00	6.00

RCA VICTOR

Number	Title (A Side/B Side)	Yr	VG	VG+	NM
❏ APBO-0023	Super Rod (Part 1)/Super Rod (Part 2)	1973	—	2.50	5.00
❏ APBO-0243	Leave the Kids Alone/Rip-Off	1974	—	2.50	5.00
❏ PB-10018	Special Kind of Woman/Streaking	1974	—	2.50	5.00

Albums

DE-LITE

Number	Title (A Side/B Side)	Yr	VG	VG+	NM
❏ 2017	Dreaming a Dream	1975	2.50	5.00	10.00
❏ 2021	Foxy Lady	1976	2.50	5.00	10.00
❏ 2022	Do It	1977	2.50	5.00	10.00
❏ 8504	Think Positive	1982	2.50	5.00	10.00
❏ 9506	Dream World	1978	2.50	5.00	10.00

Number	Title (A Side/B Side)	Yr	VG	VG+	NM
❏ 9512	Dance Lady Dance	1979	2.50	5.00	10.00
❏ 9517	Sure Shot	1980	2.50	5.00	10.00
RCA VICTOR					
❏ APL1-0492	Crown Heights Affair	1974	3.00	6.00	12.00
❏ ANL1-2660	Crown Heights Affair	1977	2.00	4.00	8.00
—Reissue of above LP					

CROWNS, THE (1)
45s
CHORDETTE

Number	Title (A Side/B Side)	Yr	VG	VG+	NM
❏ 1001	Party Time/Amazon Basin Pop	1962	5.00	10.00	20.00

CROWNS, THE (2)
45s
OLD TOWN

Number	Title (A Side/B Side)	Yr	VG	VG+	NM
❏ 1171	Possibility/Watch Out	1964	3.75	7.50	15.00
—Black label with moon					
❏ 1171	Possibility/Watch Out	1964	10.00	20.00	40.00
—Old light blue Old Town label					

CROWNS, THE (3) Four members of THE FIVE CROWNS plus Benjamin Nelson (BEN E. KING). Also see THE DRIFTERS.
45s
R&B

Number	Title (A Side/B Side)	Yr	VG	VG+	NM
❏ 6901	Kiss and Make Up/I'll Forget About You	1958	20.00	40.00	80.00

CROWNS, THE (4)
45s
VEE JAY

Number	Title (A Side/B Side)	Yr	VG	VG+	NM
❏ 546	Better Luck Next Time/You Make Me Blue	1963	3.75	7.50	15.00

CROWS, THE
45s
RAMA

Number	Title (A Side/B Side)	Yr	VG	VG+	NM
❏ 3	Seven Lonely Days/No Help Wanted	1953	125.00	250.00	500.00
❏ 5	Gee/I Love You So	1953	17.50	35.00	70.00
—Blue label, black vinyl					
❏ 5	Gee/I Love You So	1953	100.00	200.00	400.00
—Blue label, red vinyl					
❏ 5	Gee/I Love You So	1955	7.50	15.00	30.00
—Red label, black vinyl					
❏ GG 8	Gee/Baby, Baby	196?	3.00	6.00	12.00
—"Golden Goodies Hits Series"; B-side is mistitled (the song is actually "Baby") and mis-credited to "The Teenagers"					
❏ 10	Heartbreaker/Call a Doctor	1953	100.00	200.00	400.00
—Black vinyl					
❏ 10	Heartbreaker/Call a Doctor	1953	150.00	300.00	600.00
—Black vinyl, label says "The Jewels"					
❏ 10	Heartbreaker/Call a Doctor	1953	150.00	300.00	600.00
—Black vinyl, label says "The Jewels" on one side, "The Crows" on the other					
❏ 10	Heartbreaker/Call a Doctor	1953	200.00	400.00	800.00
—Red vinyl					
❏ 10	Heartbreaker/Call a Doctor	1953	400.00	800.00	1200.
—Red vinyl; label says "The Jewels"					
❏ 29	Baby/Untrue	1954	50.00	100.00	200.00
❏ 30	Miss You/I Really, Really Love You So	1954	100.00	200.00	400.00
—Black vinyl					
❏ 30	Miss You/I Really, Really Love You So	1954	250.00	500.00	1000.
—Red vinyl					
❏ 50	Baby Doll/Sweet Sue (It's You)	1954	100.00	200.00	400.00
TICO					
❏ 1082	Mambo Shevitz/Mambo #5	1955	50.00	100.00	200.00
—B-side by Melino and Orchestra; black vinyl					
❏ 1082	Mambo Shevitz/Mambo #5	1955	75.00	150.00	300.00
—B-side by Melino and Orchestra; red vinyl					

CROWS, THE / THE HARPTONES
Albums
ROULETTE

Number	Title (A Side/B Side)	Yr	VG	VG+	NM
❏ RE-114 [(2)]	Echoes of a Rock Era: The Groups	1973	5.00	10.00	20.00

CRUDUP, ARTHUR
45s
ACE

Number	Title (A Side/B Side)	Yr	VG	VG+	NM
❏ 503	I Wonder/My Baby Boogies All the Time	1955	50.00	100.00	200.00
FIRE					
❏ 1501	Rock Me Mama/Mean Ole Frisco	1962	3.75	7.50	15.00
❏ 1502	Katie Mae/Dig Myself a Hole	1962	3.75	7.50	15.00
GROOVE					
❏ 0011	I Love My Baby/Fall on Your Knees and Pray	1954	10.00	20.00	40.00
❏ 0026	She's Got No Hair/If You Ever Been to Georgia	1954	10.00	20.00	40.00
RCA VICTOR					
❏ 47-4367	Love Me Mama/Where Did You Stay Last Night	1951	25.00	50.00	100.00
❏ 47-4572	Goin' Back to Georgia/Mr. So and So	1952	20.00	40.00	80.00
❏ 47-4753	Worried 'Bout You Baby/Late in the Evening	1952	20.00	40.00	80.00
❏ 47-4933	Second Man Blues/Do It If You Want	1952	20.00	40.00	80.00
❏ 47-5070	Lookin' for My Baby/Pearly Lee	1952	20.00	40.00	80.00
❏ 47-5167	Keep On Drinkin'/Nelvina	1953	20.00	40.00	80.00
❏ 47-5563	War Is Over/My Wife and Woman	1953	20.00	40.00	80.00
❏ 50-0000	That's All Right/Crudup's After Hours	1949	100.00	200.00	400.00
—Gray label, orange vinyl; the first R&B 45 rpm record!					
❏ 50-0001	Boy Friend Blues/Katie May	1949	25.00	50.00	100.00
—Gray label, orange vinyl					
❏ 50-0013	Shout Sister Shout/Crudup's Vicksburg Blues	1949	25.00	50.00	100.00
—Gray label, orange vinyl					
❏ 50-0032	Hoodoo Lady Blues/Tired of Worry	1949	25.00	50.00	100.00
—Gray label, orange vinyl					
❏ 50-0046	Come Back Baby/Mercy Blues	1949	25.00	50.00	100.00
—Gray label, orange vinyl					
❏ 50-0074	Dust My Broom/You Know That I Love You	1950	25.00	50.00	100.00
—Gray label, orange vinyl					
❏ 50-0092	Mean Old Santa Fe/Oo Wee Baby	1950	25.00	50.00	100.00
—Gray label, orange vinyl					
❏ 50-0100	Lonesome World to Me/Hand Me Down My Walking Cane	1950	25.00	50.00	100.00
—Gray label, orange vinyl					
❏ 50-0105	She's Just Like Caldonia/(B-side unknown)	1951	25.00	50.00	100.00
—Gray label, orange vinyl					

Number	Title (A Side/B Side)	Yr	VG	VG+	NM
❏ 50-0109	My Baby Left Me/Anytime Is the Right Time	1951	37.50	75.00	150.00
—Gray label, orange vinyl					
❏ 50-0117	Nobody Wants Me/Star Bootlegger	1951	25.00	50.00	100.00
—Gray label, black vinyl					
❏ 50-0123	Roberta Blues/Behind Closed Doors	1951	25.00	50.00	100.00
—Gray label, black vinyl					
❏ 50-0141	I'm Gonna Dig Myself a Hole/Too Much Competition	1951	25.00	50.00	100.00
—Gray label, black vinyl					

Albums
COLLECTABLES

Number	Title (A Side/B Side)	Yr	VG	VG+	NM
❏ COL-5130	Mean Ol' Frisco	1988	2.50	5.00	10.00
DELMARK					
❏ DS-614	Look on Yonder's Wall	1969	10.00	20.00	40.00
❏ DS-621	Crudup's Mood	1969	10.00	20.00	40.00
FIRE					
❏ 103 [M]	Mean Ol' Frisco	1960	300.00	600.00	900.00
RCA VICTOR					
❏ LVP-573	Father of Rock and Roll	1971	5.00	10.00	20.00
TRIP					
❏ 7501	Mean Ol' Frisco	1975	3.75	7.50	15.00

CRUM, SIMON See FERLIN HUSKY.

CRUSADERS, THE (1) Jazz and soul band. Originally recorded as "The Jazz Crusaders"; all releases on Pacific Jazz and World Pacific use that name.
12-Inch Singles
MCA

Number	Title (A Side/B Side)	Yr	VG	VG+	NM
❏ L33-1190 [DJ]	Dead End/Night Ladies	1984	2.50	5.00	10.00
❏ L33-1748 [DJ]	This Old World's Too Funky for Me/Standing Tall	1981	3.75	7.50	15.00
—A-side with Joe Cocker					
❏ L33-1833 [DJ]	Street Life (6:02) (same on both sides)	1979	5.00	10.00	20.00
❏ 13991	New Moves (Remixed Version 5:35) (Dub Version 6:26) (Single Mix 3:45)	1984	2.00	4.00	8.00

45s
ABC BLUE THUMB

Number	Title (A Side/B Side)	Yr	VG	VG+	NM
❏ 261	Stomp and Buck Dance/A Ballad for Joe (Louis)	1975	—	2.50	5.00
❏ 267	Creole/I Feel the Love	1975	—	2.50	5.00
❏ 269	Keep That Same Old Feeling/'Til the Sun Shines	1976	—	2.50	5.00
❏ 270	And Then There Was the Blues/Feeling Funky	1976	—	2.50	5.00
❏ 272	Feel It/The Way We Was	1977	—	2.50	5.00
❏ 273	Free as the Wind/The Way We Was	1977	—	2.50	5.00
❏ 278	Bayou Bottoms/Covert Action	1978	—	2.50	5.00
BLUE THUMB					
❏ 208	Put It Where You Want It/Mosadi	1972	—	2.50	5.00
❏ 217	So Far Away/That's How I Feel	1972	—	2.50	5.00
❏ 225	Don't Let It Get You Down/Journey from Within	1973	—	2.50	5.00
❏ 232	Take It or Leave It/That's How I Feel	1973	—	2.50	5.00
❏ 245	Lay It On the Line/Let's Boogie	1974	—	2.50	5.00
❏ 249	Scratch/Way Back Home	1974	—	2.50	5.00
CHISA					
❏ 8010	Way Back Home/Jackson	1970	—	3.00	6.00
—As "Jazz Crusaders"					
❏ 8013	Pass the Plate/Greasy Spoon	1971	—	3.00	6.00
MCA					
❏ 41054	Street Life/Hustler	1979	—	2.00	4.00
❏ 41295	Sweet Gentle Love/Soul Shadows	1980	—	2.00	4.00
❏ 51029	Last Call/Honky Tonk Struttin'	1980	—	2.00	4.00
❏ 51177	I'm So Glad I'm Standing Here Today/Standing Tall	1981	—	2.00	4.00
—A-side with Joe Cocker					
❏ 51222	This Old World's Too Funky for Me/Standing Tall	1981	—	2.00	4.00
—A-side with Joe Cocker					
❏ 51222 [PS]	This Old World's Too Funky for Me/Standing Tall	1981	2.50	5.00	10.00
—Promo-only sleeve with only the record number (neither title) and the following: "Happy Thanksgiving. If you're expecting a turkey ... this isn't it. We have a lot to be thankful for thanks to you. The Crusaders"					
❏ 52098	Street Life/Overture	1982	—	2.00	4.00
—With B.B. King and the London Symphony Orchestra					
❏ 52365	New Move/Mr. Cool	1984	—	2.00	4.00
❏ 52398	Dream Street/Dead End	1984	—	2.00	4.00
❏ 52454	Gotta Lotta Shakalada/Zalal 'E Mini	1984	—	2.00	4.00
❏ 52966	The Way It Goes/Good Times	1986	—	2.00	4.00
❏ 53330	A.C. (Alternating Currents)/Mulholland Nights	1988	—	—	3.00
MOWEST					
❏ 5028	Spanish Harlem/Papa Hooper's Barrelhouse Groove	1972	—	3.00	6.00
PACIFIC JAZZ					
❏ 340	Sinnin' Sam/Tonight	1962	3.00	6.00	12.00
❏ 342	Young Rabbits/(B-side unknown)	1962	3.00	6.00	12.00
❏ 371	No Name Samba/Tough Talk	1963	2.50	5.00	10.00
❏ 88125	Uptight (Everything's Alright)/Scratch	1966	2.00	4.00	8.00
❏ 88144	Eleanor Rigby/Ooga Boogaloo	1968	—	3.00	6.00
❏ 88146	Hey Jude/Love and Peace	1969	—	3.00	6.00
❏ 88153	Get Back/Willie and Laura Mae Jones	1969	—	3.00	6.00
WORLD PACIFIC					
❏ 388	Boopie/Turkish Black	1963	2.50	5.00	10.00
—As "Jazz Crusaders"					
❏ 401	Heat Wave/On Broadway	1964	2.50	5.00	10.00
❏ 412	I Remember Tomorrow/Long John	1964	2.50	5.00	10.00
❏ 77800	The Thing/Tough Talk	1965	2.00	4.00	8.00
❏ 77806	Aqua Dulce/Soul Bourgeoise	1966	2.00	4.00	8.00

Albums
ABC BLUE THUMB

Number	Title (A Side/B Side)	Yr	VG	VG+	NM
❏ SPMK-42 [DJ]	Crusaders In-Store Sampler Album	1978	5.00	10.00	20.00
—Promo-only issue					
❏ BT-6001 [(2)]	Crusaders 1	1975	3.00	6.00	12.00
❏ BT-6010	Scratch	1975	2.50	5.00	10.00
—Reissue					
❏ 6022	Chain Reaction	1975	2.50	5.00	10.00
❏ 6024	Those Southern Knights	1976	2.50	5.00	10.00
❏ 6027 [(2)]	The Best of the Crusaders	1976	3.00	6.00	12.00
❏ 6029	Free As the Wind	1977	2.50	5.00	10.00
❏ BA-6030	Images	1978	2.50	5.00	10.00
❏ BTSY-9002 [(2)]	Southern Comfort	1974	3.00	6.00	12.00

Number	Title (A Side/B Side)	Yr	VG	VG+	NM
APPLAUSE					
❑ APBL-2313	Powerhouse	197?	3.00	6.00	12.00
—Reissue of Pacific Jazz 20136					
BLUE NOTE					
❑ BN-LA170-G [(2)]	Tough Talk	1974	3.00	6.00	12.00
❑ BN-LA530-H2 [(2)]	Young Rabbits	1977	3.00	6.00	12.00
❑ LWB-530 [(2)]	Young Rabbits	1981	2.50	5.00	10.00
—Reissue of BN-LA530-H2					
❑ LT-1046	Live Sides	1980	2.50	5.00	10.00
BLUE THUMB					
❑ BTSA 1 [DJ]	The Crusaders Promotional Album	1973	5.00	10.00	20.00
—Promo-only album contains one side of material from "Crusaders 1" and one side from "The 2nd Crusade"					
❑ BT-6001 [(2)]	Crusaders 1	1972	3.75	7.50	15.00
❑ BT-6007	Unsung Heroes	1973	3.00	6.00	12.00
❑ BT-6010	Scratch	1974	3.00	6.00	12.00
❑ BT-7000 [(2)]	The 2nd Crusade	1973	3.75	7.50	15.00
CHISA					
❑ 804	Old Socks, New Shoes…New Socks, Old Shoes	1970	3.00	6.00	12.00
—As "Jazz Crusaders"					
❑ 807	Pass the Plate	1971	3.00	6.00	12.00
CRUSADERS					
❑ 16000	Street Life	1982	6.25	12.50	25.00
—Audiophile vinyl					
❑ 16002	Ongaku-Kai: Live in Japan	1982	6.25	12.50	25.00
—Audiophile vinyl					
LIBERTY					
❑ LST-11005	Give Peace a Chance	1970	3.75	7.50	15.00
—As "Jazz Crusaders"					
MCA					
❑ 3094	Street Life	1979	2.50	5.00	10.00
❑ 5124	Rhapsody and Blues	1980	2.50	5.00	10.00
❑ 5254	Standing Tall	1981	2.50	5.00	10.00
❑ 5429	Ghetto Blaster	1984	2.50	5.00	10.00
❑ 5781	The Good and Bad Times	1987	2.50	5.00	10.00
❑ 6006 [(2)]	The Best of the Crusaders	1980	2.50	5.00	10.00
—Reissue of Blue Thumb 6027					
❑ 6014 [(2)]	Crusaders 1	198?	2.50	5.00	10.00
—Reissue of Blue Thumb 6001					
❑ 6015 [(2)]	2nd Crusade	198?	2.50	5.00	10.00
—Reissue of Blue Thumb 7000					
❑ 6016 [(2)]	Southern Comfort	198?	2.50	5.00	10.00
—Reissue of Blue Thumb 9002					
❑ 8017 [(2)]	Royal Jam	1982	3.00	6.00	12.00
❑ 37072	Scratch	198?	2.00	4.00	8.00
—Reissue of Blue Thumb 6010					
❑ 37073	Free As the Wind	198?	2.00	4.00	8.00
—Reissue of Blue Thumb 6029					
❑ 37074	Images	198?	2.00	4.00	8.00
—Reissue of Blue Thumb 6030					
❑ 37146	Chain Reaction	198?	2.00	4.00	8.00
—Reissue of Blue Thumb 6022					
❑ 37147	Those Southern Knights	198?	2.00		8.00
—Reissue of Blue Thumb 6024					
❑ 37174	Rhapsody and Blues	198?	2.00	4.00	8.00
—Reissue of 5124					
❑ 37240	Standing Tall	1985	2.00	4.00	8.00
—Reissue of 5254					
❑ 42087	The Vocal Album	1988	2.50	5.00	10.00
❑ 42168	Life in the Modern World	1988	2.50	5.00	10.00
MOBILE FIDELITY					
❑ 1-010	Chain Reaction	1979	5.00	10.00	20.00
—Audiophile vinyl					
MOTOWN					
❑ M5-195V1	The Crusaders At Their Best	1981	2.50	5.00	10.00
❑ M 796	The Crusaders At Their Best	1973	3.00	6.00	12.00
MOWEST					
❑ 118	Hollywood	1972	3.00	6.00	12.00
PACIFIC JAZZ					
❑ PJ-27 [M]	Freedom Sound	1961	6.25	12.50	25.00
❑ ST-27 [S]	Freedom Sound	1961	7.50	15.00	30.00
❑ PJ-43 [M]	Lookin' Ahead	1962	6.25	12.50	25.00
❑ ST-43 [S]	Lookin' Ahead	1962	7.50	15.00	30.00
—Black vinyl					
❑ ST-43 [S]	Lookin' Ahead	1962	15.00	30.00	60.00
—Yellow vinyl					
❑ PJ-57 [M]	The Jazz Crusaders at the Lighthouse	1962	6.25	12.50	25.00
❑ ST-57 [S]	The Jazz Crusaders at the Lighthouse	1962	7.50	15.00	30.00
❑ PJ-68 [M]	Tough Talk	1963	6.25	12.50	25.00
❑ ST-68 [S]	Tough Talk	1963	7.50	15.00	30.00
❑ PJ-76 [M]	Heat Wave	1963	6.25	12.50	25.00
❑ ST-76 [S]	Heat Wave	1963	7.50	15.00	30.00
❑ PJ-83 [M]	Stretchin' Out	1964	6.25	12.50	25.00
❑ ST-83 [S]	Stretchin' Out	1964	7.50	15.00	30.00
❑ PJ-87 [M]	The Thing	1964	6.25	12.50	25.00
❑ ST-87 [S]	The Thing	1964	7.50	15.00	30.00
❑ PJ-10092 [M]	Chili Con Soul	1965	5.00	10.00	20.00
❑ PJ-10098 [M]	Live at the Lighthouse '66	1966	5.00	10.00	20.00
❑ PJ-10106 [M]	Talk That Talk	1966	5.00	10.00	20.00
❑ PJ-10115 [M]	The Festival Album	1967	6.25	12.50	25.00
❑ PJ-10124	Uh Huh	1967	6.25	12.50	25.00
❑ ST-20092 [S]	Chili Con Soul	1965	6.25	12.50	25.00
❑ ST-20098 [S]	Live at the Lighthouse '66	1966	6.25	12.50	25.00
❑ ST-20106 [S]	Talk That Talk	1966	6.25	12.50	25.00
❑ ST-20115 [S]	The Festival Album	1967	5.00	10.00	20.00
❑ ST-20124	Uh Huh	1967	5.00	10.00	20.00
❑ ST-20131	Lighthouse '68	1968	5.00	10.00	20.00
❑ ST-20136	Powerhouse	1968	5.00	10.00	20.00
❑ ST-20165	The Jazz Crusaders at the Lighthouse '69	1969	5.00	10.00	20.00
❑ ST-20175	The Best of the Jazz Crusaders	1969	5.00	10.00	20.00
❑ ST-90481 [S]	The Jazz Crusaders at the Lighthouse	1965	7.50	15.00	30.00
—Capitol Record Club edition					
❑ T-90598 [M]	Chili Con Soul	1965	6.25	12.50	25.00
—Capitol Record Club edition					
PAUSA					
❑ 9005	The Best of the Jazz Crusaders	1979	2.50	5.00	10.00
—As "Jazz Crusaders"					

Number	Title (A Side/B Side)	Yr	VG	VG+	NM
WORLD PACIFIC JAZZ					
❑ ST-20098 [S]	Live at the Lighthouse '66	1970	3.75	7.50	15.00
—Reissue with "Liberty/UA" on label					

CRUSADERS, THE (U) None of these are by group (1).

45s

Number	Title (A Side/B Side)	Yr	VG	VG+	NM
CAMEO					
❑ 285	Boogie Woogie/At the Club	1963	3.00	6.00	12.00
DKR					
❑ (no #)	Seminole/Busted Surfboard	1962	10.00	20.00	40.00
DOOTO					
❑ 472	Swinging Week-End/I Found Someone	1963	3.75	7.50	15.00
TOWER					
❑ 286	The Little Drummer Boy/Battle Hymn of the Republic	1966	2.50	5.00	10.00
❑ 328	Make a Joyful Noise/Praise We the Lord	1967	2.50	5.00	10.00

CRYAN' SHAMES, THE

45s

Number	Title (A Side/B Side)	Yr	VG	VG+	NM
COLUMBIA					
❑ 43836	I Wanna Meet You/We Could Be Happy	1966	2.50	5.00	10.00
❑ 44037	Mr. Unreliable/Georgia	1967	2.50	5.00	10.00
❑ 44191	It Could Be We're in Love/I Was Lonely When	1967	2.50	5.00	10.00
❑ 44191 [PS]	It Could Be We're in Love/I Was Lonely When	1967	5.00	10.00	20.00
❑ 44457	Up On the Roof/The Sailing Ship	1968	2.50	5.00	10.00
❑ 44545	Young Birds Fly/Sunshine Psalm	1968	2.00	4.00	8.00
❑ 44638	Greenburg, Blickstein, Charles, David Smith & Jones/The Warm	1968	2.00	4.00	8.00
❑ 44759	First Train to California/A Master's Fool	1969	2.00	4.00	8.00
❑ 45027	Rainmaker/Bits and Pieces	1969	2.00	4.00	8.00
DESTINATION					
❑ 624	Sugar and Spice/Ben Franklin's Almanac	1966	3.75	7.50	15.00
Albums					
COLUMBIA					
❑ CL 2589 [M]	Sugar & Spice	1967	5.00	10.00	20.00
❑ CL 2786 [M]	A Scratch in the Sky	1967	6.25	12.50	25.00
❑ CS 9389 [S]	Sugar & Spice	1967	6.25	12.50	25.00
❑ CS 9586 [S]	A Scratch in the Sky	1967	5.00	10.00	20.00
❑ CS 9719	Synthesis	1969	5.00	10.00	20.00

CRYIN' SHAMES, THE Not the same group as THE CRYAN' SHAMES.

45s

Number	Title (A Side/B Side)	Yr	VG	VG+	NM
LONDON					
❑ 1001	What's New Pussycat/Please Stay (Don't Go)	1966	2.50	5.00	10.00

CRYSTALS, THE (1) Well-known girl group.

45s

Number	Title (A Side/B Side)	Yr	VG	VG+	NM
GUSTO					
❑ 2090	Da Doo Ron Ron/Then He Kissed Me	1979	—	2.00	4.00
—Re-recordings					
MICHELLE					
❑ 4113	Ring-a-Ting-a-Ling/Should I Keep On Waiting	1967	2.50	5.00	10.00
PAVILLION					
❑ 03333	Rudolph the Red-Nosed Reindeer/I Saw Mommy Kissing Santa Claus	1982	—	2.50	5.00
—B-side by The Ronettes					
PHILLES					
❑ 100	There's No Other (Like My Baby)/Oh Yeah, Maybe Baby	1961	10.00	20.00	40.00
❑ 102	Uptown/What a Nice Way to Turn Seventeen	1962	10.00	20.00	40.00
❑ 105	He Hit Me (And It Felt Like a Kiss)/No One Ever Tells You	1962	25.00	50.00	100.00
❑ 106	He's a Rebel/I Love You Eddie	1962	10.00	20.00	40.00
—Light blue label					
❑ 106	He's a Rebel/I Love You Eddie	1962	15.00	30.00	60.00
—Orange label					
❑ 106	He's a Rebel/I Love You Eddie	1964	6.25	12.50	25.00
—Yellow and red label					
❑ 109	He's Sure the Boy I Love/Walkin' Along (La-La-La)	1962	7.50	15.00	30.00
❑ 111	(Let's Dance) The Screw — Part 1/(Let's Dance) The Screw — Part 2	1963	3000.	4500.	6000.
—Light blue label; no "D.J. Only Not for Sale" on label; "Audio Matrix" stamped in dead wax (counterfeits do not have this)					
❑ 111 [DJ]	(Let's Dance) The Screw — Part 1/(Let's Dance) The Screw — Part 2	1963	2000.	3000.	4000.
—White label; copies exist with the title as "Let's Dance The Screw" (no parentheses) also, with the same value as above					
❑ 112	Da Doo Ron Ron (When He Walked Me Home)/Git' It	1963	7.50	15.00	30.00
❑ 115	Then He Kissed Me/Brother Julius	1963	6.25	12.50	25.00
—Yellow and red label					
❑ 115	Then He Kissed Me/Brother Julius	1963	10.00	20.00	40.00
—Light blue label					
❑ 119	Little Boy/Harry (From West Virginia) and Milt	1964	6.25	12.50	25.00
❑ 119X	Little Boy/Harry (From West Virginia) and Milt	1964	5.00	10.00	20.00
❑ 122	All Grown Up/Irving (Jaggered Sixteenths)	1964	6.25	12.50	25.00
—Possible Rolling Stones involvement on instrumental B-side; "Jaggered" refers to Mick					
PHILLES/COLLECTABLES					
❑ 3200	He's a Rebel/He Hit Me (And It Felt Like a Kiss)	1985	—	3.00	6.00
—Red vinyl; part of box set "Phil Spector Wall of Sound Series Vol. 2"					
❑ 3200	He's a Rebel/He Hit Me (And It Felt Like a Kiss)	1986	—	2.50	5.00
—Black vinyl					
❑ 3201	Then He Kissed Me/Puddin' and Tain	1985	—	3.00	6.00
—Red vinyl; part of box set "Phil Spector Wall of Sound Series Vol. 2"; B-side by the Alley Cats					
❑ 3201	Then He Kissed Me/Puddin' and Tain	1986	—	2.50	5.00
—Black vinyl					
❑ 3202	Uptown/He's Sure the Boy I Love	1985	—	3.00	6.00
—Red vinyl; part of box set "Phil Spector Wall of Sound Series Vol. 2"					
❑ 3202	Uptown/He's Sure the Boy I Love	1986	—	2.50	5.00
—Black vinyl					
❑ 3204	There's No Other (Like My Baby)/Not Too Young to Get Married	1985	—	3.00	6.00
—Gold vinyl; part of box set "Phil Spector Wall of Sound Series Vol. 1"; B-side by Bob B. Soxx and the Blue Jeans					
❑ 3204	There's No Other (Like My Baby)/Not Too Young to Get Married	1986	—	2.50	5.00
—Black vinyl; B-side by Bob B. Soxx and the Blue Jeans					

Number	Title (A Side/B Side)	Yr	VG	VG+	NM
❑ 3206	Da Doo Ron Ron/All Grown Up	1985	—	3.00	6.00

—Gold vinyl; part of box set "Phil Spector Wall of Sound Series Vol. 1"

Number	Title (A Side/B Side)	Yr	VG	VG+	NM
❑ 3206	Da Doo Ron Ron/All Grown Up	1986	—	2.50	5.00

—Black vinyl
UNITED ARTISTS

Number	Title (A Side/B Side)	Yr	VG	VG+	NM
❑ 927	You Can't Tie a Good Girl Down/My Place	1965	3.75	7.50	15.00
❑ 994	I Got a Man/				
	Are You Trying to Get Rid of Me, Baby	1966	3.75	7.50	15.00

Albums
PHILLES

Number	Title	Yr	VG	VG+	NM
❑ PHLP-4000 [M]	Twist Uptown	1962	150.00	300.00	600.00
❑ PHLP-4001 [M]	He's a Rebel	1963	150.00	300.00	600.00
❑ PHLP-4003 [M]	The Crystals Sing the Greatest Hits, Vol. 1	1963	150.00	300.00	600.00
❑ DT-90722 [R]	Twist Uptown	1965	300.00	600.00	1200.

—Capitol Record Club edition

Number	Title	Yr	VG	VG+	NM
❑ T-90722 [M]	Twist Uptown	1965	150.00	300.00	600.00

—Capitol Record Club edition

CRYSTALS, THE (2)
45s
ALADDIN

Number	Title	Yr	VG	VG+	NM
❑ 3355	I Love My Baby/I Do Believe	1957	15.00	30.00	60.00

CRYSTALS, THE (3)
45s
BRENT

Number	Title	Yr	VG	VG+	NM
❑ 7011	Malaguena/Gypsy Ribbon	1960	3.75	7.50	15.00

CUB

| ❑ 9064 | Oh My You/Watching You | 1960 | 3.75 | 7.50 | 15.00 |

INDIGO

| ❑ 114 | Dreams and Wishes/Mr. Brush | 1961 | 5.00 | 10.00 | 20.00 |

METRO

| ❑ 20026 | Better Come Back to Me/That's Where I Belong | 1960 | 3.75 | 7.50 | 15.00 |

REGALIA

| ❑ 17 | Pony in Dixie/Espresso | 1961 | 3.75 | 7.50 | 15.00 |

CRYSTALS, THE (4)
45s
DELUXE

❑ 6013	Four Women/My Dear	1953	500.00	1000.	2000.
❑ 6037	Have Faith in Me/My Love	1954	500.00	1000.	2000.
❑ 6077	God Only Knows/My Girl	1955	50.00	100.00	200.00

LUNA

| ❑ 100 | Squeeze Me Baby/Come to Me, Darling | 1954 | 100.00 | 200.00 | 400.00 |
| ❑ 5001 | Squeeze Me Baby/Come to Me, Darling | 1954 | 50.00 | 100.00 | 200.00 |

ROCKIN'

| ❑ 518 | My Girl/Don't You Go | 1953 | 62.50 | 125.00 | 250.00 |

CRYSTALS, THE (5)
45s
FELSTED

| ❑ 8566 | Mary Ellen/Blind Date | 1959 | 5.00 | 10.00 | 20.00 |

MERCURY

| ❑ 71381 | Vampire/Tropical Illusion | 1958 | 3.75 | 7.50 | 15.00 |

SPECIALTY

| ❑ 657 | In the Deep/Love You So | 1959 | 3.75 | 7.50 | 15.00 |

CUBY AND THE BLIZZARDS
45s
PHILIPS

| ❑ 40685 | Thursday Night/Going Home | 1970 | 2.00 | 4.00 | 8.00 |

Albums
PHILIPS

| ❑ PHS 600307 | Cuby and the Blizzards Live | 1969 | 5.00 | 10.00 | 20.00 |
| ❑ PHS 600331 | King of the World | 1970 | 5.00 | 10.00 | 20.00 |

CUES, THE
45s
CAPITOL

❑ F3245	Burn That Candle/Oh My Darling	1955	5.00	10.00	20.00
❑ F3310	Charlie Brown/You're On My Mind	1956	5.00	10.00	20.00
❑ F3400	Destination 2100 and 65/Don't Make Believe	1956	5.00	10.00	20.00
❑ F3483	The Girl I Love/Crackerjack	1956	5.00	10.00	20.00
❑ F3582	Why/Prince or Pauper	1956	5.00	10.00	20.00

JUBILEE

| ❑ 5201 | Only You/I Feel for Your Loving | 1955 | 5.00 | 10.00 | 20.00 |

LAMP

| ❑ 8007 | Forty 'Leven Dozen Ways/Scoochie Scoochie | 1954 | 5.00 | 10.00 | 20.00 |

PREP

| ❑ 104 | I Pretend/Crazy, Crazy Party | 1957 | 5.00 | 10.00 | 20.00 |

CUFF LINKS, THE (1) Studio band with RON DANTE as lead singer.
45s
ATCO

| ❑ 6867 | Sandi/The Oke-Fen-Okee Electric Harmonica Band | 1972 | — | 2.50 | 5.00 |

DECCA

| ❑ 32533 | Tracy/Where Do You Go | 1969 | — | 3.00 | 6.00 |
| ❑ 32533 [PS] | Tracy/Where Do You Go | 1969 | 6.25 | 12.50 | 25.00 |

—Three-piece gatefold sleeve

❑ 32592	When Julie Comes Around/Sally Ann	1969	—	2.50	5.00
❑ 32639	Run, Sally, Run/I Remember	1970	—	2.50	5.00
❑ 32687	Lay a Little Love on Me/Robin's World	1970	—	2.50	5.00
❑ 32732	Thank You Pretty Baby/Kiss	1970	—	2.50	5.00
❑ 32791	All Because of You/Wake Up Judy	1971	—	2.50	5.00

Albums
DECCA

| ❑ DL 75160 | Tracy | 1969 | 5.00 | 10.00 | 20.00 |
| ❑ DL 75235 | The Cuff Links | 1970 | 5.00 | 10.00 | 20.00 |

CUFF LINKS, THE (2) Black vocal group.
45s
DOOTO

❑ 409	Guided Missiles/My Heart	1957	20.00	40.00	80.00
❑ 413	How You Lied/The Winner	1957	10.00	20.00	40.00
❑ 414	Twinkle/One Day Blues	1957	10.00	20.00	40.00
❑ 422	It's Too Late Now/Saxophone Rag	1957	12.50	25.00	50.00
❑ 474	Changing My Love/I Don't Want Nobody	1963	6.25	12.50	25.00

DOOTONE

| ❑ 409 | Guided Missiles/My Heart | 1956 | 50.00 | 100.00 | 200.00 |

CULLEY, FRANK "FLOORSHOW"
45s
BATON

| ❑ 226 | After Hours Express (Part 1)/(Part 2) | 1956 | 10.00 | 20.00 | 40.00 |

Albums
BATON

| ❑ BL 1201 [M] | Rock 'n Roll: Instrumentals for Dancing the Lindy Hop | 1955 | 150.00 | 300.00 | 600.00 |

—B-side tracks by Buddy Tate Orchestra

CULMER, LITTLE IRIS, AND THE MAJESTICS Also see THE MAJESTICS.
45s
MARLIN

| ❑ 803 | Frankie, My Eyes Are On You/(B-side unknown) | 1957 | 1000. | 1500. | 2500. |

CUNNINGHAM, BUDDY
45s
SUN

| ❑ 208 | Right or Wrong/Why Do I Care | 1954 | 500.00 | 1000. | 1500. |

CUPID'S INSPIRATION
45s
BELL

| ❑ 818 | Look at Me/Sad Thing | 1969 | 2.00 | 4.00 | 8.00 |

COLUMBIA

| ❑ 4-45049 | Yesterday Has Gone/Brown Eyed Woman | 1969 | 3.00 | 6.00 | 12.00 |

DATE

| ❑ 2-1665 | Yesterday Has Gone/Brown Eyed Woman | 1970 | 2.00 | 4.00 | 8.00 |

EPIC

| ❑ 5-10356 | Yesterday Has Gone/Dream | 1968 | 3.00 | 6.00 | 12.00 |

CUPIDS, THE (1)
45s
AANKO

| ❑ 1002 | Brenda/For You | 1963 | 25.00 | 50.00 | 100.00 |

KC

| ❑ 115 | Brenda/For You | 1963 | 12.50 | 25.00 | 50.00 |

CUPIDS, THE (2)
45s
ALADDIN

| ❑ 3404 | Now You Tell Me/Lillie Mae | 1957 | 15.00 | 30.00 | 60.00 |

—Maroon label

| ❑ 3404 | Now You Tell Me/Lillie Mae | 1958 | 6.25 | 12.50 | 25.00 |

—Black label

CUPIDS, THE (3)
45s
DECCA

| ❑ 30279 | The Answer to Your Prayer/My Dog Likes Your Dog | 1957 | 10.00 | 20.00 | 40.00 |

CUPIDS, THE (U) Some of these may be groups (1), (2) or (3), but more likely they aren't. It's also likely they aren't all the same.
45s
CHAN

| ❑ 107 | I Don't Know/Troubles Not At End | 1956 | 20.00 | 40.00 | 80.00 |

MUSICNOTE

| ❑ 119 | Lorraine/Little Girl of Mine | 1963 | 3.75 | 7.50 | 15.00 |

TIMES SQUARE

| ❑ 1 | Pretty Baby/Let's Rock | 1964 | 3.75 | 7.50 | 15.00 |

UWR

| ❑ 4241/2 | True Love, True Love/Let's Twist | 1962 | 10.00 | 20.00 | 40.00 |

CURB, MIKE Includes the Mike Curb Congregation.
45s
BUENA VISTA

❑ 492	Robin Hood March/Oo-De-Lally	1973	—	2.50	5.00
❑ 494	Winnie the Pooh/Zip-a-Dee-Doo-Dah	1973	—	2.50	5.00
❑ 499	Mickey Mouse March/Mickey Mouse Alma Mater	1974	—	2.50	5.00

—B-side by Jimmy Dodd and the Mouseketeers

| ❑ 499 [PS] | Mickey Mouse March/Mickey Mouse Alma Mater | 1974 | 2.00 | 4.00 | 8.00 |

CAPITOL

❑ 4054	Po'r Folk/You Were On My Mind	1975	—	2.00	4.00
❑ 4102	Mickey Mouse March/You Were On My Mind	1975	—	2.00	4.00
❑ 4166	Fools Rush In (Where Angels Fear to Tread)/Do You Wanna Dance	1975	—	2.00	4.00

FORWARD

| ❑ 124 | Bandstand Theme/Oh, Calcutta | 1970 | — | 2.50 | 5.00 |
| ❑ 124 [PS] | Bandstand Theme/Oh, Calcutta | 1970 | 2.50 | 5.00 | 10.00 |

—Called "The New Bandstand Theme" on sleeve
MGM

❑ 14110	Long Haired Lover from Liverpool/Sweet Gingerbread Man	1970	—	2.00	4.00
❑ 14151	Burning Bridges/We'll Sing in the Sunshine	1970	—	2.00	4.00
❑ 14243	I Was Born in Love with You/Sweet Gingerbread Man	1971	—	2.00	4.00
❑ 14265	Sweet Gingerbread Man/Fly Me a Place for the Summer	1971	—	2.00	4.00
❑ 14336	Softly Whispering I Love You/Forty Days and Forty Nights	1971	—	2.00	4.00
❑ 14366	I Saw the Light/Take Up the Hammer of Hope	1972	—	2.00	4.00
❑ 14391	The Very Same Time Next Year/See You in September	1972	—	2.00	4.00
❑ 14442	This Land Is Your Land/I Understand	1972	—	2.00	4.00
❑ 14494	It's a Small, Small World/Shinin' on Me	1973	—	2.00	4.00

REPRISE

| ❑ 0287 | Hot Dawg/Velocita | 1964 | 5.00 | 10.00 | 20.00 |

SMASH

| ❑ 1938 | The Rebel (Without a Cause)/Carole's Rebel | 1964 | 3.00 | 6.00 | 12.00 |

TOWER

| ❑ 202 | Sunshine/Suzie Darling | 1966 | 2.50 | 5.00 | 10.00 |
| ❑ 480 | Let's Go/Eight Young Me (The Devil's Theme) | 1969 | 2.00 | 4.00 | 8.00 |

WARNER BROS.

| ❑ 8463 | Cotton Fields/Dance On, Maria | 1977 | — | 2.00 | 4.00 |

Number	Title (A Side/B Side)	Yr	VG	VG+	NM
Albums					
COBURT					
❏ CO 1002	Come Together	1970	2.50	5.00	10.00
❏ CO 1003	Sweet Gingerbread Man	1970	2.50	5.00	10.00
MGM					
❏ SE-4761	Burning Bridges and Other Great Motion Picture Themes	1971	2.50	5.00	10.00
❏ SE-4785	Put Your Hand in the Hand	1971	2.50	5.00	10.00
❏ SE-4804	The Mike Curb Congregation Sing Their Hits from the Glen Campbell Show	1971	2.50	5.00	10.00
❏ SE-4821	Softly Whispering I Love You	1972	2.50	5.00	10.00
❏ SE-4844	Song for a Young Love	1972	2.50	5.00	10.00
WARNER BROS.					
❏ BS 3129	The Mike Curb Congregation	1977	2.50	5.00	10.00

CURLEY AND THE JADES
45s
MUSIC MAKERS

Number	Title (A Side/B Side)	Yr	VG	VG+	NM
❏ 109	Bullfighter/Boom Stix	1962	15.00	30.00	60.00
REPRISE					
❏ 20046	Bullfighter/Boom Stix	1962	7.50	15.00	30.00

CURRENTS, THE
45s
LAURIE

Number	Title (A Side/B Side)	Yr	VG	VG+	NM
❏ 3205	Night Run/Riff Raff	1963	7.50	15.00	30.00

CURTIS, EDDIE
45s
GEE

Number	Title (A Side/B Side)	Yr	VG	VG+	NM
❏ 7	Candy Man/The Girl I Left Behind	1954	10.00	20.00	40.00
—As "Eddie 'Tex' Curtis"					
❏ 9	Prayer to the Moon/Shake, Pretty Baby, Shake	1954	10.00	20.00	40.00
—As "Eddie 'Tex' Curtis"					
JOSIE					
❏ 957	Those Foxes and Pussycats (Part 1)/(Part 2)	1966	2.50	5.00	10.00
OKEH					
❏ 7063	Sweet Stuff/I Didn't Wanna Love You	1955	7.50	15.00	30.00
—As "Eddie 'Tex' Curtis"					

CURTIS, MAC
45s
DOT

Number	Title (A Side/B Side)	Yr	VG	VG+	NM
❏ 16315	You're the One/Dance Her By Me (One More Time)	1962	2.50	5.00	10.00
EPIC					
❏ 10257	Too Close to Home/Too Good to Be True	1967	—	3.00	6.00
❏ 10324	The Quiet Kind/Love's Been Good to Me	1968	—	3.00	6.00
❏ 10385	The Sunshine Man/It's My Way	1968	—	3.00	6.00
❏ 10438	Almost Persuaded/The Friendly City	1969	—	3.00	6.00
❏ 10468	Happiness Lives in This House/Little Ole Wine Drinker Me	1969	—	3.00	6.00
❏ 10530	Don't Make Love/Us	1969	—	3.00	6.00
❏ 10574	Honey Don't/Today's Teardrops	1970	—	3.00	6.00
FELSTED					
❏ 8592	Come Back Baby/No, Never Alone	1959	5.00	10.00	20.00
GRT					
❏ 26	Early in the Morning/When the Hurt Moves In	1970	—	2.50	5.00
❏ 41	Gulf Stream Line/I'd Run a Mile	1971	—	2.50	5.00
KING					
❏ 4927	If I Had Me a Woman/Just So You Call Me	1956	37.50	75.00	150.00
❏ 4949	Grandaddy's Rockin'/Half Hearted Love	1956	37.50	75.00	150.00
❏ 4965	You Ain't Treatin' Me Right/The Low Road	1956	37.50	75.00	150.00
❏ 4995	That Ain't Nothin' But Right/Don't You Love Me	1956	37.50	75.00	150.00
❏ 5007	What You Want/To Protect the Innocent	1957	25.00	50.00	100.00
❏ 5059	Say So/I'll Be Gentle	1957	10.00	20.00	40.00
❏ 5107	What You Want/You Are My Special Baby	1958	15.00	30.00	60.00
❏ 5121	Missy Ann/Little Miss Linda	1958	15.00	30.00	60.00
RANWOOD					
❏ 1017	Pistol Packin' Mama/Asphalt Cowboy, Parking Lot Lover	1975	—	2.50	5.00
❏ 1033	Keep Doin' What You're Doin' Now/She Knows All the Good Ways to Be Bad	1975	—	2.50	5.00
❏ 1041	More Like I Do Now/Nine Times Out of Ten	1975	—	2.50	5.00
❏ 1050	We Made It All the Way/West Texas Women	1976	—	2.50	5.00
TOWER					
❏ 319	Ties That Bind/Stepping Out on You	1967	—	3.00	6.00
Albums					
EPIC					
❏ BN 26419	The Sunshine Man	1969	5.00	10.00	20.00
HMG/HIGHTONE					
❏ HT 6601	Rockabilly Uprising: The Best of Mac Curtis	1997	2.50	5.00	10.00
ROLLIN' ROCK					
❏ LP-002	Ruffabilly	197?	2.50	5.00	10.00
❏ LP-007	Good Rockin' Tomorrow	197?	2.50	5.00	10.00

CURTIS, SONNY Also see THE CRICKETS (1).
45s
A&M

Number	Title (A Side/B Side)	Yr	VG	VG+	NM
❏ 1359	Lights of L.A./Sunny Mornin'	1972	7.50	15.00	30.00
❏ 1408	Love Is All Around/Last Days of Childhood	1973	—	—	—
—Unreleased?					
CAPITOL					
❏ 4158	Lovesick Blues/It's Only a Question of Time	1975	3.00	6.00	12.00
❏ 4227	It's Only a Question of Time/When It's Just You and Me	1976	3.00	6.00	12.00
❏ 4240	Where's Patricia Now/When It's Just You and Me	1976	3.00	6.00	12.00
CORAL					
❏ 60954	Someday You're Gonna Be Sorry/Forever Yours	1953	6.25	12.50	25.00
❏ 61023	No More Tears/The Best Way to Hold a Girl	1953	6.25	12.50	25.00
❏ 62207	Red Headed Stranger/Talk About My Baby	1960	10.00	20.00	40.00
DIMENSION					
❏ 1017	So Used to Loving You/The Last Song I'm Ever Gonna Sing	1963	5.00	10.00	20.00
❏ 1024	A Beatle I Want to Be/So Used to Loving You	1964	6.25	12.50	25.00
DOT					
❏ 15754	Wrong Again/Laughing Stock	1958	10.00	20.00	40.00
❏ 15799	A Pretty Girl/Willa May Jones	1958	7.50	15.00	30.00

Number	Title (A Side/B Side)	Yr	VG	VG+	NM
ELEKTRA					
❏ 46526	The Cowboy Singer/Cheatin' Clouds	1979	—	2.50	5.00
❏ 46568	Do You Remember Roll Over Beethoven/Walk Right Back	1979	—	2.50	5.00
❏ 46616	The Real Buddy Holly Story/Ain't Nobody Honest	1980	—	3.00	6.00
❏ 46643	Love Is All Around/The Clone Song	1980	—	2.50	5.00
❏ 47048	You Made My Life a Song/50 Ways to Leave Your Lover	1980	—	2.50	5.00
❏ 47129	Good Ol' Girls/So Used to Loving You	1981	—	2.50	5.00
❏ 47176	Married Woman/I Live Your Music	1981	—	2.50	5.00
❏ 47231 [DJ]	The Christmas Song/Little Drummer Boy	1981	2.00	4.00	8.00
—B-side by Hank Williams, Jr.					
❏ 69942	Together Alone/Dream Well All of You Children	1982	—	2.50	5.00
LIBERTY					
❏ 55710	Bo Diddley Bach/I Pledge My Love to You	1964	5.00	10.00	20.00
MERCURY					
❏ 73438	Rock and Rol (I Gave You the Best Years of My Life)/My Mama Sure Left Me Some Good Old Days	1973	3.75	7.50	15.00
OVATION					
❏ 1006	Love Is All Around/Here, There and Everywhere	1970	5.00	10.00	20.00
❏ 1023	Unsaintly Judy/You Don't Belong in This Place	1970	3.75	7.50	15.00
'STEEM					
❏ 110185	Now I've Got a Heart of Gold/(B-side unknown)	1985	—	3.00	6.00
VIVA					
❏ 602	My Way of Life/Last Call	1966	3.75	7.50	15.00
❏ 607	The Collection/Destiny's Child	1966	3.75	7.50	15.00
❏ 617	I'm a Gypsy Man/I Wanna Go Bummin' Around	1967	3.75	7.50	15.00
❏ 626	Day Drinker/Atlanta, Georgia Stray	1968	3.75	7.50	15.00
❏ 630	The Straight Life/How Little Men Care	1968	3.75	7.50	15.00
❏ 634	Holiday for Clowns/Day Gig	1969	3.75	7.50	15.00
❏ 636	Girl of the North/Hung Up in Your Eyes	1969	3.75	7.50	15.00
Albums					
ELEKTRA					
❏ 6E-227	Sonny Curtis	1979	2.50	5.00	10.00
❏ 6E-283	Love Is All Around	1980	2.50	5.00	10.00
❏ 6E-349	Rollin'	1981	2.50	5.00	10.00
IMPERIAL					
❏ LP-9276 [M]	Beatle Hits Flamenco Style	1964	10.00	20.00	40.00
❏ LP-12276 [S]	Beatle Hits Flamenco Style	1964	12.50	25.00	50.00
VIVA					
❏ V-36012	The First of Sonny Curtis	1968	6.25	12.50	25.00
❏ V-36021	The Sonny Curtis Style	1969	6.25	12.50	25.00

CUSTER AND THE SURVIVORS
45s
ASCOT

Number	Title (A Side/B Side)	Yr	VG	VG+	NM
❏ 2207	I Saw Her Walking/Flapjacks	1965	4.00	8.00	16.00
GOLDEN STATE					
❏ 1657	I Saw Her Walking/Flapjacks	1965	3.00	6.00	12.00
VARDAN					
❏ 202	I Saw Her Walking/Flapjacks	1965	5.00	10.00	20.00

CUTE-TEENS, THE
45s
ALADDIN

Number	Title (A Side/B Side)	Yr	VG	VG+	NM
❏ 3458	When My Teenage Days Are Over/From This Day Forward	1959	62.50	125.00	250.00

CYCLONE III
45s
PHILIPS

Number	Title (A Side/B Side)	Yr	VG	VG+	NM
❏ 40258	You've Got a Bomb/Surfnanny	1965	10.00	20.00	40.00

CYKLE, THE
45s
LABEL

Number	Title (A Side/B Side)	Yr	VG	VG+	NM
❏ 101	If You Can/(B-side unknown)	1969	7.50	15.00	30.00
❏ 101 [PS]	If You Can/(B-side unknown)	1969	15.00	30.00	60.00
Albums					
LABEL					
❏ 9-261	The Cykle	1969	125.00	250.00	500.00

CYMANDE
45s
JANUS

Number	Title (A Side/B Side)	Yr	VG	VG+	NM
❏ 203	The Message/Zion I	1972	—	2.50	5.00
❏ 215	Bra/Ras Tafarian Folk Song	1973	—	2.50	5.00
❏ 225	Anthracite/Fug	1973	—	2.50	5.00
Albums					
JANUS					
❏ 3044	Cymande	1972	2.50	5.00	10.00
❏ 3054	Second Time Round	1973	2.50	5.00	10.00

CYMARRON
45s
ENTRANCE

Number	Title (A Side/B Side)	Yr	VG	VG+	NM
❏ 7500	Rings/Like Children	1971	—	2.50	5.00
❏ 7502	Valerie/Across the Kansas Sky	1971	—	2.00	4.00
❏ 7506	Right Can Be Wrong/What's a Little Dirt	1972	—	2.00	4.00
❏ 7514	Keep Me Warm/Start Again	1972	—	2.00	4.00
Albums					
ENTRANCE					
❏ Z 30962	Rings	1971	3.00	6.00	12.00

CYMBAL, JOHNNY Includes releases as "Derek" on the Bang label. Also see CYMBAL AND CLINGER.
45s
AMARET

Number	Title (A Side/B Side)	Yr	VG	VG+	NM
❏ 110	Big River/Girl from Willow County	1969	2.00	4.00	8.00
❏ 111	Ode to Bubblegum/Save All Your Lovin' (Hold It for Me)	1969	2.00	4.00	8.00
BANG					
❏ 558	Cinnamon/This Is My Story	1968	2.00	4.00	8.00
❏ 566	Back Door Man/Tell Your Soul	1969	—	3.00	6.00
❏ 571	Inside Out-Outside In/Sell Your Soul	1969	—	3.00	6.00

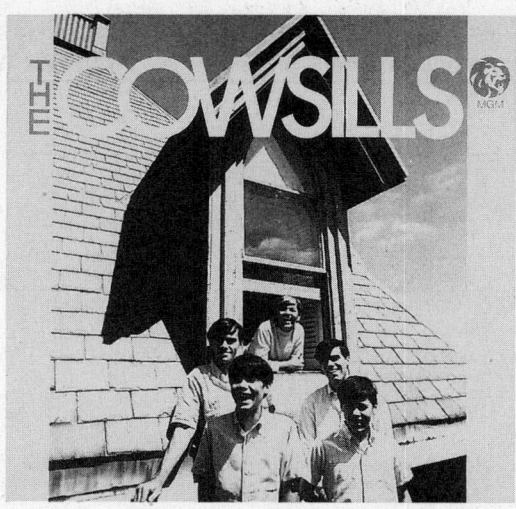

The Cowsills, *The Cowsills,* MGM SE-4498, stereo LP, black label, $7.50-$15.

Cream, *Disraeli Gears,* Atco 33-232, mono LP, $25-$50.

Creedence Clearwater Revival, *Cosmo's Factory,* Fantasy F-8402, stereo LP, dark blue label, $7.50-$15.

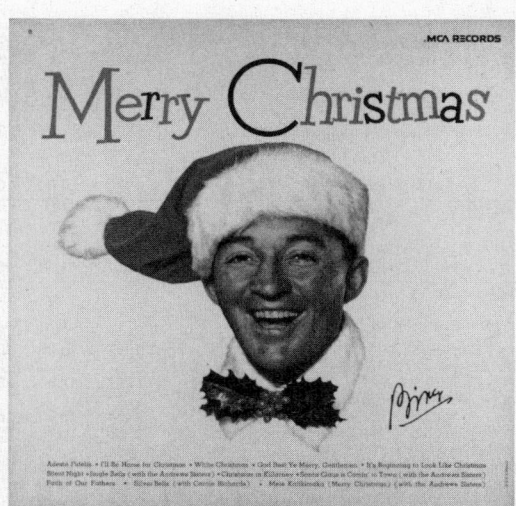

Bing Crosby, *Merry Christmas,* MCA 15024, rechanneled stereo LP, reissue, black label with rainbow, $4-$8 or less.

Crosby, Stills and Nash, *Crosby, Stills and Nash,* Atlantic SD 8229, stereo LP, $10-$20.

The Cyrkle, *Red Rubber Ball,* Columbia CL 2544, mono LP, $10-$20.

Number	Title (A Side/B Side)	Yr	VG	VG+	NM
COLUMBIA					
❑ 43842	Good Morning Blues/Jessica	1966	2.00	4.00	8.00
DCP					
❑ 1135	Go, VW, Go/Sorrow and Pain	1965	7.50	15.00	30.00
❑ 1146	My Last Day/Summertime's Here at Last	1965	3.75	7.50	15.00
KAPP					
❑ 503	Mr. Bass Man/Sacred Lovers' Vow	1963	5.00	10.00	20.00
❑ 524	Teenage Heaven/Cinderella Baby	1963	3.75	7.50	15.00
❑ 539	(Surfin' at) Tia Juana/Dum Dum Dee Dum	1963	3.75	7.50	15.00
❑ 556	Marshmallow/Hurdy Gurdy Man	1963	3.75	7.50	15.00
❑ 576	There Goes a Bad Girl/Refreshment Time	1964	3.75	7.50	15.00
❑ 594	Robinson Crusoe on Mars/Mitsu	1964	3.75	7.50	15.00
❑ 614	Connie/Little Miss Lonely	1964	3.75	7.50	15.00
❑ 634	Cheat, Cheat/16 Shades of Blue	1964	3.75	7.50	15.00
KEDLEN					
❑ 2001	Bachelor Man/Growing Up with You	1962	5.00	10.00	20.00
MGM					
❑ 12935	It'll Be Me/Always, Always	1960	5.00	10.00	20.00
❑ 12978	The Water Was Red/The Bunny	1961	5.00	10.00	20.00
MUSICOR					
❑ 1261	It Looks Like Love/May I Get to Know You	1967	3.00	6.00	12.00
❑ 1272	Breaking Your Balloon/The Marriage of Charlotte Brown	1967	3.00	6.00	12.00
VEE JAY					
❑ 495	Bachelor Man/Growing Up with You	1963	3.75	7.50	15.00
Albums					
KAPP					
❑ KL-1324 [M]	Mr. Bass Man	1963	12.50	25.00	50.00
❑ KS-3324 [S]	Mr. Bass Man	1963	17.50	35.00	70.00

CYMBAL & CLINGER Also see JOHNNY CYMBAL.
45s

Number	Title (A Side/B Side)	Yr	VG	VG+	NM
CHELSEA					
❑ 78-0106	God Bless You Rock & Roll/Forever and Forever	1972	—	2.50	5.00
❑ 78-0112	Dying River/Little Bit No, Little Bit Yes	1973	—	2.50	5.00
MARINA					
❑ 502	Pool Shooter/Mookie Mookie Man	1971	—	3.00	6.00
MGM					
❑ 14256	Pool Shooter/Mookie Mookie Man	1971	—	2.50	5.00
Albums					
CHELSEA					
❑ 1002	Cymbal & Clinger	1972	3.00	6.00	12.00

CYPRESS, BUDDY
45s

Number	Title (A Side/B Side)	Yr	VG	VG+	NM
FLASH					
❑ 118	I'm in Love with You/Don't Forsake Me	1957	12.50	25.00	50.00

CYRKLE, THE
45s

Number	Title (A Side/B Side)	Yr	VG	VG+	NM
COLUMBIA					
❑ CSM-466	Camaro/SS 396	1967	6.25	12.50	25.00
—B-side by Paul Revere and the Raiders					
❑ CSM-466 [PS]	Camaro/SS 396	1967	12.50	25.00	50.00
—B-side by Paul Revere and the Raiders					
❑ 43589	Red Rubber Ball/How Can I Leave Her	1966	3.00	6.00	12.00
❑ 43589 [DJ]	Red Rubber Ball (same on both sides)	1966	10.00	20.00	40.00
—Promo only on red vinyl					
❑ 43589 [PS]	Red Rubber Ball/How Can I Leave Her	1966	100.00	200.00	400.00
❑ 43729	Turn-Down Day/Big, Little Woman	1966	2.50	5.00	10.00
❑ 43729 [DJ]	Turn-Down Day (same on both sides)	1966	10.00	20.00	40.00
—Promo only on red vinyl					
❑ 43729 [PS]	Turn-Down Day/Big, Little Woman	1966	3.75	7.50	15.00
❑ 43871	Please Don't Ever Leave Me/Money to Burn	1966	2.00	4.00	8.00
❑ 43965	I Wish You Could Be Here/The Visit (She Was Here)	1967	2.00	4.00	8.00
❑ 43965 [PS]	I Wish You Could Be Here/The Visit (She Was Here)	1967	3.00	6.00	12.00
❑ 44108	We Had a Good Thing Goin'/Two Rooms	1967	2.00	4.00	8.00
❑ 44224	Penny Arcade/The Words	1967	2.00	4.00	8.00
❑ 44366	Turn of the Century/Don't Cry, No Fears, No Tears Comin'	1967	2.00	4.00	8.00
❑ 44426	Friends/Reading Her Papers	1968	2.00	4.00	8.00
❑ 44491	Red Chair Fade Away/Where Are You Going	1968	2.00	4.00	8.00
Albums					
COLUMBIA					
❑ CL 2544 [M]	Red Rubber Ball	1966	5.00	10.00	20.00
❑ CL 2632 [M]	Neon	1967	3.75	7.50	15.00
❑ CS 9344 [S]	Red Rubber Ball	1966	7.50	15.00	30.00
❑ CS 9432 [S]	Neon	1967	5.00	10.00	20.00

CYRUS ERIE Early ERIC CARMEN.
45s

Number	Title (A Side/B Side)	Yr	VG	VG+	NM
EPIC					
❑ 10451	Sparrow/Get the Message	1969	3.00	6.00	12.00

D

D-MEN, THE Early incarnation of THE FIFTH ESTATE.
45s

Number	Title (A Side/B Side)	Yr	VG	VG+	NM
KAPP					
❑ 691	So Little Time/Every Moment of Every Day	1965	3.00	6.00	12.00
VEEP					
❑ 1206	Don't You Know/No Hope for Me	1965	3.75	7.50	15.00
❑ 1209	Just Don't Care/Mousin' Around	1965	3.75	7.50	15.00

D'ABO, MIKE Lead singer of MANFRED MANN in the "Mighty Quinn" era.
45s

Number	Title (A Side/B Side)	Yr	VG	VG+	NM
A&M					
❑ 1374	Little Miss Understood/Belinda	1972	—	2.50	5.00
❑ 1628	Fuel to Burn/Hold On Sweet Darling	1974	—	2.00	4.00
BELL					
❑ 956	Miss Me in the Morning/Arabella Cinderella	1971	—	3.00	6.00
Albums					
A&M					
❑ SP-3634	Broken Rainbows	1974	3.00	6.00	12.00
❑ SP-4346	Down at Rachel's Place	1972	3.00	6.00	12.00

D.C. BLOSSOMS, THE
45s

Number	Title (A Side/B Side)	Yr	VG	VG+	NM
SHRINE					
❑ 107	I Know About Her/Hey Boy	1966	200.00	400.00	800.00

DA-PREES, THE
45s

Number	Title (A Side/B Side)	Yr	VG	VG+	NM
TWIST					
❑ 70913	Pay Day/Sometimes	1963	37.50	75.00	150.00

DACHE, BERTELL TONY ORLANDO with CAROLE KING on backing vocals.
45s

Number	Title (A Side/B Side)	Yr	VG	VG+	NM
DIAMOND					
❑ 201	Don't Stop the World for Me/Anchors Awaeigh Girl	1966	3.75	7.50	15.00
UNITED ARTISTS					
❑ 260	All the World Loves a Lover/You Gotta Have Chicks	1960	6.25	12.50	25.00
❑ 290	Not Just Tomorrow, But Today/Love Eyes	1961	6.25	12.50	25.00

DACRONS, THE
45s

Number	Title (A Side/B Side)	Yr	VG	VG+	NM
HIT					
❑ 38	Don't Hang Up/Limbo Rock	1962	2.00	4.00	8.00
—B-side by Bill Carmichael					
❑ 56	South Street/What Will My Mary Say	1963	2.00	4.00	8.00
—B-side by Tony Christopher					
❑ 57	He's So Fine/Follow the Boys	1963	2.00	4.00	8.00
—B-side by Connie Landers					
❑ 81	Then He Kissed Me/Surfer Girl	1963	2.00	4.00	8.00
—B-side by the Jalopy Five					

DADDY COOL
45s

Number	Title (A Side/B Side)	Yr	VG	VG+	NM
REPRISE					
❑ 1038	Eagle Rock/Bom Bom	1971	—	3.00	6.00
❑ 1064	Hi Honey Ho/Come Back Again	1972	—	3.00	6.00
❑ 1087	Teenage Blues/Donna Forgive Me	1972	—	3.00	6.00
❑ 1090	I'll Never Smile Again/Daddy Rocks Off	1972	—	3.00	6.00
Albums					
REPRISE					
❑ MS 2088	Teenage Heaven	1972	5.00	10.00	20.00
❑ RS 6471	Daddy Who? Daddy Cool!	1971	3.75	7.50	15.00

DADDY DEWDROP
12-Inch Singles

Number	Title (A Side/B Side)	Yr	VG	VG+	NM
T.K. DISCO					
❑ TKD 118	Nanu, Nanu (I Wanna Funky with You)/The Real Thing	1978	3.75	7.50	15.00
❑ TKD 153	The Real Thing (Vocal 7:40)/(Instrumental 6:13)	1979	3.75	7.50	15.00
45s					
CAPITOL					
❑ 4066	Dynamite Dyna/Goddaughter	1975	—	2.00	4.00
INPHASION					
❑ 7201	Nanu, Nanu (I Wanna Funky with You)/The Real Thing	1978	—	2.00	4.00
❑ 7203	The Real Thing/(Instrumental)	1978	—	2.00	4.00
❑ 7206	If You Wanna Wanna/Turn On the Motion	1979	—	2.00	4.00
SUNFLOWER					
❑ 105	Chick-a-Boom (Don't Ya Jes' Love It)/John Jacob Jingleheimer Smith	1971	—	2.50	5.00
❑ 111	Fox Huntin' (On a Weekend)/March of the White Corpuscles	1971	—	2.00	4.00
❑ 119	Chantilly Lace/Migraine Headaches	1972	—	2.00	4.00
Albums					
SUNFLOWER					
❑ SNF-5006	Daddy Dewdrop	1971	5.00	10.00	20.00

DAILEY, DON
Albums

Number	Title (A Side/B Side)	Yr	VG	VG+	NM
CROWN					
❑ CST-314 [R]	Surf Stompin'	1963	3.75	7.50	15.00
❑ CLP-5314 [M]	Surf Stompin'	1963	7.50	15.00	30.00

DAILY FLASH, THE
45s

Number	Title (A Side/B Side)	Yr	VG	VG+	NM
PARROT					
❑ 308	Jack of Diamonds/Queen Jane Approximately	1966	3.00	6.00	12.00
UNI					
❑ 55001	French Girl/Green Rocky Road	1967	3.00	6.00	12.00

DAISIES, THE
45s

Number	Title (A Side/B Side)	Yr	VG	VG+	NM
CAPITOL					
❏ 5667	Cold Wave/Put Your Arms Around Me	1966	6.25	12.50	25.00
ROULETTE					
❏ 4571	I Wanna Swim with Him/You Just Said You Loved Me	1964	3.00	6.00	12.00

DAKIL, FLOYD
45s

Number	Title (A Side/B Side)	Yr	VG	VG+	NM
EARTH					
❏ 402	Bad Boy/Stoppin' Traffic	1965	10.00	20.00	40.00
❏ 403	Kitty Kitty/It Takes a Lot to Hurt	1965	7.50	15.00	30.00
❏ 404	Stronger Than Dirt/You're the Kind of Girl	1965	7.50	15.00	30.00
GUYDEN					
❏ 2111	Dance, Franny, Dance/Look What You've Gone and Done	1964	7.50	15.00	30.00
JETSTAR					
❏ 103	Dance, Franny, Dance/Look What You've Gone and Done	1964	25.00	50.00	100.00
POMPEII					
❏ 66687	Merry Christmas, Baby/One Girl	1968	6.25	12.50	25.00

DAKOTAS, THE   Also see BILLY J. KRAMER AND THE DAKOTAS.
45s

Number	Title (A Side/B Side)	Yr	VG	VG+	NM
LIBERTY					
❏ 55618	The Cruel Surf/The Millionaire	1963	10.00	20.00	40.00

DAKUS, WES
45s

Number	Title (A Side/B Side)	Yr	VG	VG+	NM
KAPP					
❏ 806	Sad Souvenirs/Armful of Teddy Bears	1967	2.50	5.00	10.00

—As "Barry Allen with Wes Dakus' Rebels"

Number	Title (A Side/B Side)	Yr	VG	VG+	NM
❏ 815	Peggy Sue/See Saw	1967	2.50	5.00	10.00

—As "Dennis Paul with Wes Dakus' Rebels"

DALE, DICK, AND THE DEL-TONES
45s

Number	Title (A Side/B Side)	Yr	VG	VG+	NM
ACCENT					
❏ 1243	Eyes of a Child/Just a-Waitin'	1968	2.00	4.00	8.00
CAPITOL					
❏ 4963	King of the Surf Guitar/Havah Nagilah	1963	5.00	10.00	20.00
❏ 4963 [PS]	King of the Surf Guitar/Havah Nagilah	1963	20.00	40.00	80.00
❏ 5010	Secret Surfin' Spot/Surfin' and a-Swingin'	1963	5.00	10.00	20.00
❏ 5048	Wild Ideas/Scavenger	1963	5.00	10.00	20.00
❏ 5098	The Wedge/Night Rider	1963	5.00	10.00	20.00
❏ 5140	The Victor/Mr. Eliminator	1964	3.75	7.50	15.00
❏ 5187	Wild, Wild Mustang/Grunge Run	1964	3.75	7.50	15.00
❏ 5225	Never on Sunday/Glory Wave	1964	3.75	7.50	15.00
❏ 5290	Oh Marie/Who Can It Be	1964	3.75	7.50	15.00
❏ 5389	Let's Go Trippin' '65/Watusi Jo	1965	3.75	7.50	15.00
COLUMBIA					
❏ 38-07340	Pipeline/Love Struck Baby	1987	—	2.00	4.00

—B-side by Stevie Ray Vaughan

Number	Title (A Side/B Side)	Yr	VG	VG+	NM
❏ 38-07340 [PS]	Pipeline/Love Struck Baby	1987	—	3.00	6.00
CONCERT ROOM					
❏ 371	We'll Never Hear the End of It/Fairest of Them All	1963	6.25	12.50	25.00
COUGAR					
❏ 711	Ramblin' Man/You're Hurtin' Now	1967	3.75	7.50	15.00
❏ 712	Taco Wagon/Spanish Kiss	1967	3.75	7.50	15.00
CUPID					
❏ 106	We'll Never Hear the End of It/Fairest of Them All	1960	7.50	15.00	30.00

—Black vinyl

Number	Title (A Side/B Side)	Yr	VG	VG+	NM
❏ 106	We'll Never Hear the End of It/Fairest of Them All	1960	20.00	40.00	80.00

—Gold vinyl

Number	Title (A Side/B Side)	Yr	VG	VG+	NM
DELTONE					
❏ 4939	Misirlou/Eight Till Midnight	1963	5.00	10.00	20.00
❏ 4940	Surf Beat/Peppermint Man	1963	5.00	10.00	20.00

—Deltone 4939 and 4940 were part of the Capitol numbering system

Number	Title (A Side/B Side)	Yr	VG	VG+	NM
❏ 5012	Oh Whee Marie/Breaking Heart	1959	15.00	30.00	60.00
❏ 5013	Stop Teasin'/Without Your Love	1959	15.00	30.00	60.00
❏ 5014	Jessie Pearl/St. Louis Blues	1960	25.00	50.00	100.00
❏ 5017	Let's Go Trippin'/Del-Tone Rock	1961	7.50	15.00	30.00
❏ 5018	Shake and Stomp/Jungle Fever	1962	10.00	20.00	40.00
❏ 5019	Misirlou/Eight Till Midnight	1962	6.25	12.50	25.00
❏ 5020	Peppermint Man/Surf Beat	1962	6.25	12.50	25.00
❏ 5028	Run for Your Life/Lovin' on My Brain	1963	7.50	15.00	30.00
GNP CRESCENDO					
❏ 804	Let's Go Trippin'/Those Memories of You	1975	—	3.00	6.00
RENDEZVOUS					
❏ 204	Reincarnation (Part 1)/Reincarnation (Part 2)	1963	5.00	10.00	20.00
SATURN					
❏ 401	We'll Never Hear the End of It/Fairest of Them All	1963	7.50	15.00	30.00
U.S. ARMY					
❏ 1301 [DJ]	The Enlistment Twist/Dream Girl Waltz	1962	7.50	15.00	30.00

—B-side by Craig Adams and His Country Cousins; blue vinyl

Number	Title (A Side/B Side)	Yr	VG	VG+	NM
❏ 1301 [PS]	The Enlistment Twist/Dream Girl Waltz	1962	7.50	15.00	30.00
YES					
❏ 7014	We'll Never Hear the End of It/Fairest of Them All	1963	7.50	15.00	30.00
❏ 7014 [PS]	We'll Never Hear the End of It/Fairest of Them All	1963	10.00	20.00	40.00

Albums

Number	Title (A Side/B Side)	Yr	VG	VG+	NM
CAPITOL					
❏ ST 1930 [S]	King of the Surf Guitar	1963	25.00	50.00	100.00
❏ T 1930 [M]	King of the Surf Guitar	1963	15.00	30.00	60.00
❏ ST 2002 [S]	Checkered Flag	1963	20.00	40.00	80.00
❏ T 2002 [M]	Checkered Flag	1963	12.50	25.00	50.00
❏ ST 2053 [S]	Mr. Eliminator	1964	20.00	40.00	80.00
❏ T 2053 [M]	Mr. Eliminator	1964	12.50	25.00	50.00
❏ ST 2111 [S]	Summer Surf	1964	17.50	35.00	70.00

—Without bonus single

Number	Title (A Side/B Side)	Yr	VG	VG+	NM
❏ ST 2111 [S]	Summer Surf	1964	30.00	60.00	120.00

—With bonus single by Jerry Cole, "Racing Waves"/"Movin' Surf," in front cover pocket

Number	Title (A Side/B Side)	Yr	VG	VG+	NM
❏ T 2111 [M]	Summer Surf	1964	12.50	25.00	50.00

—Without bonus single

Number	Title (A Side/B Side)	Yr	VG	VG+	NM
❏ T 2111 [M]	Summer Surf	1964	25.00	50.00	100.00

—With bonus single by Jerry Cole, "Racing Waves"/"Movin' Surf," in front cover pocket

Number	Title (A Side/B Side)	Yr	VG	VG+	NM
❏ ST 2293 [S]	Rock Out — Live at Ciro's	1965	37.50	75.00	150.00
❏ T 2293 [M]	Rock Out — Live at Ciro's	1965	25.00	50.00	100.00
CLOISTER					
❏ CLP-6301 [M]	Silver Sounds of the Surf	1963	50.00	100.00	200.00

—With tracks by the Stompers

Number	Title (A Side/B Side)	Yr	VG	VG+	NM
DELTONE					
❏ LPM-1001 [M]	Surfer's Choice	1962	37.50	75.00	150.00
❏ DT 1886 [R]	Surfer's Choice	1962	10.00	20.00	40.00
❏ T 1886 [M]	Surfer's Choice	1962	15.00	30.00	60.00
DUB TONE					
❏ LP-1246 [M]	The Surf Family	1964	7.50	15.00	30.00

—With tracks by the Hollywood Surfers

Number	Title (A Side/B Side)	Yr	VG	VG+	NM
GNP CRESCENDO					
❏ GNPS-2095	Greatest Hits	1975	3.00	6.00	12.00
RHINO					
❏ RNLP-70074	King of the Surf Guitar: The Best of Dick Dale and the Del-Tones, 1961-1964	1986	3.00	6.00	12.00

DALE AND GRACE
45s

Number	Title (A Side/B Side)	Yr	VG	VG+	NM
GUYDEN					
❏ 6002	What's Happening to Me/Darling It's Wonderful	1972	—	2.50	5.00
HANNA-BARBERA					
❏ 472	Let Them Talk/I'd Rather Be Free	1966	2.00	4.00	8.00
MICHELLE					
❏ 921	I'm Leaving It Up to You/That's What I Like	1963	6.25	12.50	25.00
❏ 923	Stop and Think It Over/Bad Luck	1963	3.75	7.50	15.00
❏ 928	The Loneliest Night/I'm Not Free	1964	3.75	7.50	15.00
❏ 930	Darling It's Wonderful/What's Happening to Me	1964	3.75	7.50	15.00
❏ 936	Cool Water/Rules of Love	1964	3.75	7.50	15.00
MONTEL					
❏ 921	I'm Leaving It Up to You/That's What I Like About You	1963	3.00	6.00	12.00
❏ 922	Stop and Think It Over/Bad Luck	1963	3.00	6.00	12.00
❏ 928	The Loneliest Night/I'm Not Free	1964	3.00	6.00	12.00
❏ 930	Darling It's Wonderful/What's Happening to Me	1964	3.00	6.00	12.00
❏ 936	Cool Water/Rules of Love	1964	3.00	6.00	12.00
❏ 958	Make the World Go Away/Stranger	1965	3.00	6.00	12.00
❏ 989	It Keeps Right On a-Hurtin'/So Fine	1967	3.00	6.00	12.00
MONTEL/MICHELLE					
❏ 942	Something Special/What Am I Living For	1964	3.00	6.00	12.00

Albums

Number	Title (A Side/B Side)	Yr	VG	VG+	NM
MICHELLE					
❏ 100 [M]	I'm Leaving It Up to You	1964	37.50	75.00	150.00
MONTEL					
❏ 100 [M]	I'm Leaving It Up to You	1964	37.50	75.00	150.00

DALEY, JIMMY, AND THE DING-A-LINGS
45s

Number	Title (A Side/B Side)	Yr	VG	VG+	NM
DECCA					
❏ 30163	Rock, Pretty Baby/Can I Steal a Little Love	1956	10.00	20.00	40.00
❏ 30358	Red Lips and Green Eyes/How's About a Little Kiss?	1957	10.00	20.00	40.00
❏ 30532	Hole in the Wall/Bongo Rock	1957	10.00	20.00	40.00

7-Inch Extended Plays

Number	Title (A Side/B Side)	Yr	VG	VG+	NM
DECCA					
❏ ED 2480	Rock Pretty Baby/Dark Blue/Free & Easy//What's It Gonna Be/Rockin' the Boogie	1957	12.50	25.00	50.00
❏ ED 2480 [PS]	Rock Pretty Baby, Part 1	1957	12.50	25.00	50.00
❏ ED 2481	Rockabye Lullaby Blues/Teen Age Bop/The Most//Can I Steal a Little Love/Juke Box/The Saints Rock 'n' Roll	1957	12.50	25.00	50.00
❏ ED 2481 [PS]	Rock Pretty Baby, Part 2	1957	12.50	25.00	50.00
❏ ED 2482	Picnic by the Sea/Young Love//Happy Is a Boy Named Me/Hot Rod/Big Band Rock and Roll	1957	12.50	25.00	50.00
❏ ED 2482 [PS]	Rock Pretty Baby, Part 3	1957	12.50	25.00	50.00

DALLAS, MARIA
45s

Number	Title (A Side/B Side)	Yr	VG	VG+	NM
RCA VICTOR					
❏ 47-9279	Ambush/Lonely for You	1967	2.50	5.00	10.00
❏ 47-9386	Don't Love Me Too Much/It's Such a Pretty World Today	1967	2.50	5.00	10.00
❏ 47-9552	Everybody/Two Ships Passing in the Night	1968	2.50	5.00	10.00

DALTON, KATHY
45s

Number	Title (A Side/B Side)	Yr	VG	VG+	NM
DISCREET					
❏ 1191	At the Tropicana/Long Gone Charlie Hit & Run	1974	—	2.50	5.00
❏ 1210	Boogie Bands and One Night Stands/Pour Your Wine All Over Me	1974	—	2.50	5.00
❏ 1313	Midnight Creeper/Justine	1974	—	2.50	5.00

Albums

Number	Title (A Side/B Side)	Yr	VG	VG+	NM
DISCREET					
❏ MS 2168	Amazing	1973	4.50	9.00	18.00
❏ DS 2208	Boogie Bands and One Night Stands	1974	3.00	6.00	12.00

DALTON BOYS, THE
45s

Number	Title (A Side/B Side)	Yr	VG	VG+	NM
SKYLA					
❏ 1124	I'm Thinkin'/It's Much More Stronger	1962	7.50	15.00	30.00
TEEN					
❏ 505	Who's Gonna Hold Your Hand/Walkin'	1959	12.50	25.00	50.00
V.I.P.					
❏ 25025	I've Been Cheated/Something's Bothering You	1965	12.50	25.00	50.00
❏ 25025	I've Been Cheated/Take My Hand	1965	50.00	100.00	200.00

DALTREY, ROGER   Also see THE WHO.
12-Inch Singles

Number	Title (A Side/B Side)	Yr	VG	VG+	NM
ATLANTIC					
❏ PR 572 [DJ]	Walking in My Sleep (3:20) (same on both sides)	1984	—	3.50	7.00

—Label spells his last name "Daltry"

Number	Title (A Side/B Side)	Yr	VG	VG+	NM
❏ PR 832 [DJ]	Quicksilver Lightning (LP Version 4:46) (same on both sides)	1986	—	3.50	7.00
❏ PR 982 [DJ]	Move Better in the Night (LP Version 4:01) (same on both sides)	1986	2.00	4.00	8.00

Number	Title (A Side/B Side)	Yr	VG	VG+	NM
45s					
A&M					
❏ 1779	Love's Dream/Orpheus Song	1975	—	2.50	5.00
—With Rick Wakeman					
ATLANTIC					
❏ 89419	Under a Raging Moon/The Pride You Hide	1986	—	—	3.00
❏ 89457	Quicksilver Lightning/Love Me Like You Do	1986	—	—	3.00
❏ 89457 [PS]	Quicksilver Lightning/Love Me Like You Do	1986	—	2.50	5.00
❏ 89471	Let Me Down Easy/Fallen Angel	1985	—	—	3.00
❏ 89471 [PS]	Let Me Down Easy/Fallen Angel	1985	—	—	3.00
❏ 89491	After the Fire/Don't Satisfy Me	1985	—	—	3.00
❏ 89491 [PS]	After the Fire/Don't Satisfy Me	1985	—	—	3.00
❏ 89667	Parting Would Be Painless/Is There Anyone Out There?	1984	—	—	3.00
❏ 89704	Walking in My Sleep/Somebody Told Me	1984	—	—	3.00
❏ 89704 [PS]	Walking in My Sleep/Somebody Told Me	1984	—	—	3.00
MCA					
❏ 40453	Come and Get Your Love/Heart's Right	1975	—	2.50	5.00
❏ 40512	Oceans Away/Feeling	1976	—	2.50	5.00
❏ 40761	One of the Boys/Doing It All Again	1977	—	2.50	5.00
❏ 40765	Satin and Lace/Say It Ain't So, Joe	1977	—	2.00	4.00
❏ 40800	Avenging Annie/The Prisoner	1977	—	2.00	4.00
❏ 40862	Leon/The Prisoner	1978	—	2.00	4.00
❏ 52051	Martyrs and Madmen/Avenging Annie	1982	—	2.00	4.00
ODE					
❏ 66040	I'm Free/Underture	1973	—	2.50	5.00
POLYDOR					
❏ 2105	Free Me/McVicar	1980	—	2.00	4.00
❏ 2105 [PS]	Free Me/McVicar	1980	—	2.00	4.00
❏ 2121	Without Your Love/Escape (Part 1)	1980	—	2.00	4.00
❏ 2153	Waiting for a Friend/Bitter and Twisted	1981	—	2.00	4.00
❏ 2153 [DJ]	Waiting for a Friend (same on both sides)	1981	—	3.00	6.00
—One label has name misspelled as "Rodger Daltrey"					
❏ 15098	See Me, Feel Me-Listening to You/Overture from Tommy	1975	—	2.50	5.00
—B-side by Pete Townshend					
❏ 15098 [PS]	See Me, Feel Me-Listening to You/Overture from Tommy	1975	—	2.50	5.00
TRACK					
❏ 40053	Giving It All Away/Way of the World	1973	—	3.00	6.00
—B-side by Bryan Daly & the London Festival Orchestra					
❏ 40084	Thinking/There Is Love	1973	2.00	4.00	8.00
Albums					
ATLANTIC					
❏ 80128	Parting Should Be Painless	1984	2.50	5.00	10.00
❏ 81269	Under a Raging Moon	1985	2.50	5.00	10.00
❏ 81759	Can't Wait to See the Movie	1987	2.50	5.00	10.00
MCA					
❏ 2147	Ride a Rock Horse	1975	3.00	6.00	12.00
❏ 2271	One of the Boys	1977	3.00	6.00	12.00
❏ 2349	Daltrey	1977	2.50	5.00	10.00
—Reissue of Track 328					
❏ 5301	Best Bits	1982	2.50	5.00	10.00
❏ 37030	Ride a Rock Horse	1980	2.00	4.00	8.00
—Budget-line reissue					
❏ 37031	One of the Boys	1980	2.00	4.00	8.00
—Budget-line reissue					
❏ 37032	Daltrey	1980	2.00	4.00	8.00
—Budget-line reissue					
POLYDOR					
❏ PD-1-6284	McVicar	1980	2.50	5.00	10.00
TRACK					
❏ 328	Daltrey	1973	3.00	6.00	12.00

DAMIN EIH, A.L.K. AND BROTHER CLARK

Number	Title (A Side/B Side)	Yr	VG	VG+	NM
Albums					
DEMELOT					
❏ 7310	Never Mind	1973	37.50	75.00	150.00

DAMITA JO Also see BROOK BENTON AND DAMITA JO.

Number	Title (A Side/B Side)	Yr	VG	VG+	NM
45s					
ABC-PARAMOUNT					
❏ 9822	How Will I Know/I'll Never Cry	1957	3.75	7.50	15.00
❏ 9849	My Heart Is Home/Disillusioned Lovers	1957	3.75	7.50	15.00
❏ 10176	How Will I Know/Disillusioned Lovers	1961	2.50	5.00	10.00
BANG BANG					
❏ 4105	Why Love a Stranger/Whoa Now Boy	196?	3.00	6.00	12.00
EPIC					
❏ 9766	Tomorrow Night/Silver Dollar	1965	2.00	4.00	8.00
❏ 9797	Gotta Travel On/Something You Got	1965	2.00	4.00	8.00
❏ 9821	Nobody Knows You When You're Down and Out/Whispering Grass (Don't Tell the Trees)	1965	2.00	4.00	8.00
❏ 9860	Sweet Pussycat/Who Could Ask for More	1965	2.00	4.00	8.00
❏ 9887	That Special Way/Tossin' and Turnin'	1966	2.00	4.00	8.00
❏ 10061	If You Go Away/When the Fog Rolls In to San Francisco	1966	2.00	4.00	8.00
❏ 10061 [DJ]	If You Go Away (same on both sides)	1966	5.00	10.00	20.00
—Promo only on yellow vinyl					
❏ 10176	No Guilty Feelings/Yellow Days	1967	2.00	4.00	8.00
❏ 10235	Dinner For One/Please, James	1967	2.00	4.00	8.00
MERCURY					
❏ 71493	The Dance Was Over/Look at Yourself	1959	3.00	6.00	12.00
❏ 71568	What Would You Do/Widow Talk	1960	3.00	6.00	12.00
❏ 71608	Little Things Mean a Lot/I Burned Your Letter	1960	3.00	6.00	12.00
❏ 71690	I'll Save the Last Dance for You/Forgive	1960	3.75	7.50	15.00
❏ 71760	Keep Your Hands Off of Him/Hush, Somebody's Calling My Name	1961	3.00	6.00	12.00
❏ 71793	Sweet Georgia Brown/Do What You Want	1961	3.00	6.00	12.00
❏ 71840	I'll Be There/Love Laid Its Hands on Me	1962	3.75	7.50	15.00
❏ 71840 [PS]	I'll Be There/Love Laid Its Hands on Me	1962	6.25	12.50	25.00
❏ 71871	Dance with a Dolly (With a Hole in Her Stocking)/You're Nobody 'Til Somebody Loves You	1962	3.00	6.00	12.00
❏ 71929	I Didn't Know I Was Crying/I Built My World Around a Dream	1962	3.00	6.00	12.00
❏ 71946	You're Nobody 'Til Somebody Loves You/Joey	1962	3.00	6.00	12.00
❏ 71946 [PS]	You're Nobody 'Til Somebody Loves You/Joey	1962	5.00	10.00	20.00

Number	Title (A Side/B Side)	Yr	VG	VG+	NM
❏ 71984	Another Dancing Partner/Please Send Me Someone to Love	1962	3.00	6.00	12.00
❏ 72019	The Window Up Above/Tennessee Waltz	1962	3.00	6.00	12.00
❏ 72019 [PS]	The Window Up Above/Tennessee Waltz	1962	5.00	10.00	20.00
❏ 72056	Dance Him By Me/Las Vegas	1962	3.00	6.00	12.00
❏ 72056 [PS]	Dance Him By Me/Las Vegas	1962	5.00	10.00	20.00
❏ 72086	Little Things/Mr. Blues (Found a Home with Me)	1963	2.50	5.00	10.00
❏ 72086 [PS]	Little Things/Mr. Blues (Found a Home with Me)	1963	5.00	10.00	20.00
❏ 72121	Drama of Love/Hobo Flats	1963	2.50	5.00	10.00
❏ 72121 [PS]	Drama of Love/Hobo Flats	1963	6.25	12.50	25.00
❏ 72162	In the Dark/Melancholy Baby	1963	2.50	5.00	10.00
RANWOOD					
❏ 820	Loving You/Reason to Believe	1968	—	3.00	6.00
❏ 826	Grown-Up Games/Lonely Letters	1968	—	3.00	6.00
❏ 844	Brother Love's Traveling Salvation Show/I'll Save the Last Dance for You	1969	—	3.00	6.00
❏ 857	Lonely Teardrops/Ain't Misbehavin'	1969	—	3.00	6.00
❏ 869	Paint Me Loving You/Tomorrow Is the First Day of the Rest of My Life	1970	—	3.00	6.00
❏ 884	Mrs. Robinson/Two Worlds	1970	—	2.50	5.00
❏ 894	Hallelujah Baby/Two Worlds	1971	—	2.50	5.00
RCA VICTOR					
❏ 47-4685	Lonesome and Blue/I Need You	1952	3.75	7.50	15.00
—By John Greer, vocals by Damita Jo					
❏ 47-5022	I'd Do It Again/I Don't Care	1952	3.75	7.50	15.00
❏ 47-5120	Go 'Way From My Window/Let Me Share Your Name	1953	3.75	7.50	15.00
❏ 47-5253	Missing/The Widow Walk	1953	3.75	7.50	15.00
❏ 47-5328	Do Me a Favor/Don't You Care	1953	3.75	7.50	15.00
❏ 47-5570	Face to Face/Sadie Thompson's Song	1953	3.75	7.50	15.00
❏ 47-5987	Win or Lose/My Tzatskele	1955	3.75	7.50	15.00
❏ 47-6096	Feelin' Kinda Happy/Nuff of That Stuff	1955	3.75	7.50	15.00
—B-side by Steve Gibson and His Red Caps					
❏ 47-6185	In My Heart/Abracadabra	1955	3.75	7.50	15.00
❏ 47-6281	Always/Freehearted	1955	3.75	7.50	15.00
VEE JAY					
❏ 661	I'm Waiting for Ships That Never Come In/Hurt a Fool	1965	2.00	4.00	8.00
Albums					
ABC-PARAMOUNT					
❏ 378 [M]	The Big Fifteen	1961	20.00	40.00	80.00
❏ S-378 [S]	The Big Fifteen	1961	25.00	50.00	100.00
EPIC					
❏ LN 24131 [M]	This Is Damita Jo	1965	3.75	7.50	15.00
❏ LN 24164 [M]	One More Time with Feeling	1965	3.75	7.50	15.00
❏ LN 24202 [M]	Midnight Session	1966	3.75	7.50	15.00
❏ LN 24244 [M]	If You Go Away	1967	5.00	10.00	20.00
❏ BN 26131 [S]	This Is Damita Jo	1965	5.00	10.00	20.00
❏ BN 26164 [S]	One More Time with Feeling	1965	5.00	10.00	20.00
❏ BN 26202 [S]	Midnight Session	1966	5.00	10.00	20.00
❏ BN 26244 [S]	If You Go Away	1967	3.75	7.50	15.00
MERCURY					
❏ MG-20642 [M]	I'll Save the Last Dance for You	1961	7.50	15.00	30.00
❏ MG-20703 [M]	Damita Jo Live at the Diplomat	1962	6.25	12.50	25.00
❏ MG-20734 [M]	Sing a Country Song	1962	6.25	12.50	25.00
❏ MG-20818 [M]	This One's for Me	1963	5.00	10.00	20.00
❏ SR-60642 [S]	I'll Save the Last Dance for You	1961	10.00	20.00	40.00
❏ SR-60703 [S]	Damita Jo Live at the Diplomat	1962	7.50	15.00	30.00
❏ SR-60734 [S]	Sing a Country Song	1962	7.50	15.00	30.00
❏ SR-60818 [S]	This One's for Me	1963	6.25	12.50	25.00
RANWOOD					
❏ RLP.8037	Miss Damita Jo	1968	3.75	7.50	15.00
RCA CAMDEN					
❏ CAL-900 [M]	Go Go with Damita Jo	196?	3.75	7.50	15.00
❏ CAS-900(e) [R]	Go Go with Damita Jo	196?	3.00	6.00	12.00
SUNSET					
❏ SUS-5198	The Irresistible Damita Jo	1968	3.00	6.00	12.00
VEE JAY					
❏ LP-1137 [M]	Damita Jo Sings	1965	6.25	12.50	25.00
❏ LPS-1137 [S]	Damita Jo Sings	1965	12.50	25.00	50.00
WING					
❏ WC-16333	This One's for Me	196?	3.00	6.00	12.00

DAMNATION OF ADAM BLESSING, THE

Number	Title (A Side/B Side)	Yr	VG	VG+	NM
45s					
UNITED ARTISTS					
❏ 50609	Morning Dew/Cookbook	1969	2.00	4.00	8.00
❏ 50666	Last Train to Clarksville/Lonely	1970	2.00	4.00	8.00
❏ 50726	Back to the River/The Driver	1970	2.00	4.00	8.00
❏ 50819	Fingers on a Windmill/Leaving It Up to You	1971	—	3.00	6.00
❏ 50912	Cookbook/Leaving It Up to You	1972	—	3.00	6.00
Albums					
UNITED ARTISTS					
❏ UAS-5533	Which Is the Justice, Which Is the Thief	1971	5.00	10.00	20.00
❏ UAS-6738	The Damnation of Adam Blessing	1970	5.00	10.00	20.00
❏ UAS-6773	The Second Damnation	1970	5.00	10.00	20.00

DAMON

Number	Title (A Side/B Side)	Yr	VG	VG+	NM
Albums					
ANKH					
❏ 968	Song of a Gypsy	1970	500.00	1000.	1500.
—Regular cover					
❏ 968	Song of a Gypsy	1970	1500.00	2250.	3000.
—Gatefold cover					

DAMON, LIZ, 'S ORIENT EXPRESS

Number	Title (A Side/B Side)	Yr	VG	VG+	NM
45s					
ANTHEM					
❏ 51005	Loneliness Remembers/Quiet Sound	1971	2.50	5.00	10.00
❏ 51006	All in All/Walking Backwards Down the Road	1971	2.50	5.00	10.00
MAKAHA					
❏ 503	1900 Yesterday/You're Falling in Love	1970	3.00	6.00	12.00
WHITE WHALE					
❏ 368	1900 Yesterday/You're Falling in Love	1970	—	3.00	6.00
❏ 370	But For Love/You Make Me Feel Like Someone	1970	—	3.00	6.00

Number	Title (A Side/B Side)	Yr	VG	VG+	NM
Albums					
MAKAHA					
❏ MS-5003	Liz Damon's Orient Express	1970	5.00	10.00	20.00
WHITE WHALE					
❏ WWS 5003	Liz Damon's Orient Express	1971	3.00	6.00	12.00

DAMONE, VIC Also see JO STAFFORD AND VIC DAMONE.
45s

Number	Title (A Side/B Side)	Yr	VG	VG+	NM
CAPITOL					
❏ 4645	Something You Never Had Before/Tender Is the Night	1961	2.00	4.00	8.00
❏ 4718	No Strings/Once Upon a Time	1962	2.00	4.00	8.00
❏ 4756	Ebb Tide/My Heart Will Tell You So	1962	2.00	4.00	8.00
❏ 4799	Vieni, Vieni/Cathy	1962	2.00	4.00	8.00
❏ 4827	What Kind of Fool Am I/Charmaine	1962	2.00	4.00	8.00
❏ 4947	One Hand, One Heart/You're Just Another Pretty Face	1963	2.00	4.00	8.00
❏ 5039	Wives and Lovers/Oooh Looka There Ain't She Pretty	1963	2.00	4.00	8.00
❏ 5092	Again/Sweet Someone	1963	2.00	4.00	8.00
❏ 5138	Breaking Point/Who Are You Now	1964	2.00	4.00	8.00
❏ 5191	I'm Gonna Miss You/Where Did the Magic Go	1964	2.00	4.00	8.00
❏ 5252	On the Street Where You Live/Maria	1964	2.00	4.00	8.00
COLUMBIA					
❏ 40630	Help Me/Sure	1956	2.50	5.00	10.00
❏ 40654	On the Street Where You Live/We All Need Love	1956	2.50	5.00	10.00
❏ 40682	I Cried for You/To Love Again	1956	2.50	5.00	10.00
❏ 40733	War and Peace/Speak, My Love	1956	2.50	5.00	10.00
❏ 40783	When My Love Smiles/One Little Boy	1956	2.50	5.00	10.00
❏ 4-40807	You Stepped Out of a Dream/Long Before I Knew You	1956	2.50	5.00	10.00
❏ 40858	Do I Love You (Because You're Beautiful)/The Legend of the Bells	1957	2.50	5.00	10.00
❏ 40945	An Affair to Remember (Our Love Affair)/In the Eyes of the World	1957	2.50	5.00	10.00
❏ 41057	Junior Miss/I Can't Close the Book	1957	2.50	5.00	10.00
❏ 4-41085	Unafraid/The Gift of Love	1957	2.50	5.00	10.00
❏ 41122	Gigi/On the Street Where You Live	1958	2.50	5.00	10.00
❏ 41185	A Toujours/The Only Man on the Island	1958	2.50	5.00	10.00
❏ 41245	Forever New/Oooh, My Love	1958	2.50	5.00	10.00
❏ 41287	We Kiss in a Shadow/Separate Tables	1958	2.50	5.00	10.00
❏ 41333	Save a Kiss/Penny Serenade	1959	2.50	5.00	10.00
❏ 41407	My Heart Has Many Dreams/New Romance in Old Roma	1959	2.50	5.00	10.00
❏ 41510	The Night Has a Thousand Eyes/On a Sunday Afternoon	1959	2.50	5.00	10.00
❏ 41577	Your Smile/Very Warm	1959	2.50	5.00	10.00
❏ 41649	Christine/Never Will I Marry	1960	2.00	4.00	8.00
❏ 41783	Never Like This/What Fools We Mortals Be	1960	2.00	4.00	8.00
❏ 41915	If Ever I Would Love You/I'll Be Your Lover	1961	2.00	4.00	8.00
❏ 42006	Adrift on a Star/The Pleasure of Her Company	1961	2.00	4.00	8.00
❏ 42041	Theme from "By Love Possessed"/If It's the Last Thing I Do	1961	2.00	4.00	8.00
MERCURY					
❏ 5374	God's Country/Where I Belong	1950	3.75	7.50	15.00
—Mercury singles before 5374 are unconfirmed on 45					
❏ 5391	Don't Say Goodbye/This Is the Night	1950	3.75	7.50	15.00
❏ 5402	Where Can I Go/If We Could Be A-L-O-N-E	1950	3.75	7.50	15.00
❏ 5429	Vagabond Shoes/I Hadn't Anyone Till You	1950	3.75	7.50	15.00
❏ 5444	Mama/Operetta	1950	3.75	7.50	15.00
❏ 5454	Tzena, Tzena, Tzena/I Love That Girl	1950	3.75	7.50	15.00
❏ 5474	Just Say I Love Her/Can Anyone Explain (No! No! No!)	1950	3.75	7.50	15.00
❏ 5477	Cincinnati Dancing Pig/Forbidden Love	1950	3.75	7.50	15.00
❏ 5486	Take Me in Your Arms/Beloved, Be Faithful	1950	3.75	7.50	15.00
❏ 5496	A Marshmallow World/When the Lights Are Low	1950	3.75	7.50	15.00
❏ 5515	Silent Night/White Christmas	1950	3.75	7.50	15.00
❏ 5535	Ave Maria/Our Lady of Fatima	1950	3.75	7.50	15.00
❏ 5555	Possibilities/Use Your Imagination	1950	3.75	7.50	15.00
❏ 5563	My Heart Cries for You/Music by the Angels	1950	3.75	7.50	15.00
❏ 5565	If/You and Your Beautiful Eyes	1951	3.75	7.50	15.00
❏ 5566	Just For Tonight/The Night Is Young	1951	3.75	7.50	15.00
❏ 5572	Tell Me You Love Me/Little Café Paree	1951	3.75	7.50	15.00
❏ 5638	Someday/You Gotta Show Me	1951	3.75	7.50	15.00
❏ 5646	My Truly, Truly Fair/My Life's Desire	1951	3.75	7.50	15.00
❏ 5655	Longing for You/The Son of a Sailor	1951	3.75	7.50	15.00
❏ 5669	Wonder Why/I Can See You	1951	3.75	7.50	15.00
❏ 5670	In the Cool, Cool, Cool of the Evening/How D'Ya Like Your Eggs	1951	3.75	7.50	15.00
❏ 5698	Calla Calla/It's a Long Way	1951	3.75	7.50	15.00
❏ 5744	Don't Blame Me/I Remember You, Love	1951	3.75	7.50	15.00
❏ 5785	Jump Through the Ring/My Funny Valentine	1952	3.75	7.50	15.00
❏ 5831	Goodbye for Awhile/Good Morning, Morning Glory	1952	3.75	7.50	15.00
❏ 5855	Diane/Tenderly	1952	3.75	7.50	15.00
❏ 5858	Here in My Heart/Tomorrow Never Comes	1952	3.75	7.50	15.00
❏ 5865	A Message from Vic Damone to the Army Boys (Parts 1 & 2)	1952	6.25	12.50	25.00
❏ 5877	Roseanne/Take My Heart	1952	3.75	7.50	15.00
❏ 5878	Come Hell or High Water/Girls Are Marching	1952	3.75	7.50	15.00
❏ 5907	Nina Never Knew/Johnny with the Bandy Legs	1952	3.75	7.50	15.00
❏ 5909	Al-Lee-O! Al-Lee-Ay!/Roseanne	1952	3.75	7.50	15.00
❏ 70022	April in Paris/My Love Song	1953	3.00	6.00	12.00
❏ 70031	Greyhound/I Don't Care	1953	3.00	6.00	12.00
❏ 70054	Sugar/Amor	1953	3.00	6.00	12.00
❏ 70108	Afraid/Love Light	1953	3.00	6.00	12.00
❏ 70128	April in Portugal/I'm Walking Behind You	1953	3.00	6.00	12.00
❏ 70179	That Old Feeling/Serenade in Blue	1953	3.00	6.00	12.00
❏ 70186	Eternally (The Song from Limelight)/Simonetta	1953	3.00	6.00	12.00
❏ 70216	Ebb Tide/If I Could Make You Mine	1953	3.00	6.00	12.00
❏ 70257	Lover, Come Back to Me/I Just Love You	1953	3.00	6.00	12.00
❏ 70287	The Breeze and I/To Love You	1954	3.00	6.00	12.00
❏ 70326	Until You Came to Me/A Sparrow Sings	1954	3.00	6.00	12.00
❏ 70384	Sleeping Beauty/Don't Take Your Lips Away	1954	3.00	6.00	12.00
❏ 70436	Once and Only Once/In My Own Quiet Way	1954	3.00	6.00	12.00
❏ 70480	Wind Song/Silk Stockings	1954	3.00	6.00	12.00

Number	Title (A Side/B Side)	Yr	VG	VG+	NM
❏ 70507	Ave Maria/Our Lady of Fatima	1954	3.00	6.00	12.00
—With Kitty Kallen					
❏ 70545	Foolishly/Hello, Mrs. Jones, Is Mary There	1955	3.00	6.00	12.00
❏ 70577	My Symphony/Meet Me Halfway	1955	3.00	6.00	12.00
❏ 70624	Don't Keep It a Secret/A Man Doesn't Know	1955	3.00	6.00	12.00
❏ 70699	Por Favor/Born to Sing the Blues	1955	3.00	6.00	12.00
MGM					
❏ 14398	Tomorrow Belongs to the Children/Come Live Your Life with Me	1972	—	2.00	4.00
❏ 14498	Love Me As I Love You/This Time	1973	—	2.00	4.00
❏ 14576	Beautiful Land/Tell Her You Love Her	1973	—	2.00	4.00
RCA VICTOR					
❏ 47-8836	You Don't Have to Say You Love Me/Stay	1966	—	3.00	6.00
❏ 47-8982	Ciao Compare/What Is a Woman	1966	—	3.00	6.00
❏ 47-9046	Love Me Longer/Pretty Butterfly	1966	—	3.00	6.00
❏ 47-9145	A Quiet Tear/On the South Side of Chicago	1967	—	3.00	6.00
❏ 47-9250	I'll Sleep Tonight/It Makes No Difference	1967	—	3.00	6.00
❏ 47-9399	The Glory of Love/Come Live with Me	1967	—	3.00	6.00
❏ 47-9488	Goin' Out of My Head/Nothing to Lose	1968	—	2.50	5.00
❏ 47-9626	When You Laughed All Your Laughter/Why Can't I Walk Away	1968	—	2.50	5.00
❏ 74-0139	To Make a Big Man Cry/Take Me Walking in Your Mind	1969	—	2.50	5.00
REBECCA					
❏ 714	The Christmas Song/Silver Bells	1977	—	2.00	4.00
❏ 715	Christmas In San Francisco/(B-side unknown)	1977	—	2.00	4.00
WARNER BROS.					
❏ 5609	Bellisima/For Mama	1965	—	3.00	6.00
❏ 5616	You Were Only Fooling (While I Was Falling in Love)/Please Help Me, I'm Falling	1965	—	3.00	6.00
❏ 5644	The Thrill of Lovin' You/Why Don't You Believe Me	1965	—	3.00	6.00
❏ 5653	Lost and Found/Turn Around	1965	—	3.00	6.00
❏ 5668	Tears/Turn Around	1965	—	3.00	6.00
❏ 5801	Two of a Kind/Wonder	1966	—	3.00	6.00
7-Inch Extended Plays					
COLUMBIA					
❏ B-2565	*On the Street Where You Live/Smoke Gets In Your Eyes/An Affair to Remember/You Stepped Out of a Dream	1959	3.00	6.00	12.00
❏ B-2565 [PS]	Vic Damone (Hall of Fame Series)	1959	3.00	6.00	12.00
❏ B-9001	You Stepped Out of a Dream/Wait Till You See Her//Out of Nowhere/The Song Is You	195?	2.50	5.00	10.00
❏ B-9001 [PS]	That Towering Feeling!	195?	2.50	5.00	10.00
MERCURY					
❏ EP-1-3065	*Amor/The Breeze and I/Sugar/Love Light	195?	3.75	7.50	15.00
❏ EP-1-3065 [PS]	Amor	195?	3.75	7.50	15.00
❏ EP-1-3085	Serenade in Blue/That Old Feeling//There Is No You/This Love of Mine	195?	3.75	7.50	15.00
❏ EP-1-3085 [PS]	Sorority Serenade	195?	3.75	7.50	15.00
Albums					
APPLAUSE					
❏ 1018	Over the Rainbow	197?	2.50	5.00	10.00
CAPITOL					
❏ ST 1646 [S]	Linger Awhile with Vic Damone	1962	3.75	7.50	15.00
❏ T 1646 [M]	Linger Awhile with Vic Damone	1962	3.00	6.00	12.00
❏ ST 1691 [S]	Strange Enchantment	1962	3.75	7.50	15.00
❏ T 1691 [M]	Strange Enchantment	1962	3.00	6.00	12.00
❏ ST 1748 [S]	The Lively Ones	1962	3.75	7.50	15.00
❏ T 1748 [M]	The Lively Ones	1962	3.00	6.00	12.00
❏ ST 1811 [S]	My Baby Loves to Swing	1963	3.75	7.50	15.00
❏ T 1811 [M]	My Baby Loves to Swing	1963	3.00	6.00	12.00
❏ ST 1944 [S]	The Liveliest	1963	3.75	7.50	15.00
❏ T 1944 [M]	The Liveliest	1963	3.00	6.00	12.00
❏ ST 2123 [S]	On the Street Where You Live	1964	3.75	7.50	15.00
❏ T 2123 [M]	On the Street Where You Live	1964	3.00	6.00	12.00
COLUMBIA					
❏ CL 900 [M]	That Towering Feeling!	1956	6.25	12.50	25.00
❏ CL 1088 [M]	Angela Mia	1957	5.00	10.00	20.00
❏ CL 1174 [M]	Closer Than a Kiss	195?	5.00	10.00	20.00
❏ CL 1368 [M]	This Game of Love	1960	3.75	7.50	15.00
❏ CL 1573 [M]	On the Swingin' Side	1961	3.75	7.50	15.00
❏ CS 8019 [S]	Closer Than a Kiss	1959	7.50	15.00	30.00
❏ CS 8046 [S]	Angela Mia	1959	7.50	15.00	30.00
❏ CS 8169 [S]	This Game of Love	1960	5.00	10.00	20.00
❏ CS 8373 [S]	On the Swingin' Side	1961	5.00	10.00	20.00
HARMONY					
❏ HL 7328 [M]	The Best of Vic Damone	196?	3.00	6.00	12.00
❏ HL 7431 [M]	Vic Damone Sings	196?	3.00	6.00	12.00
❏ HS 11128 [S]	The Best of Vic Damone	196?	3.00	6.00	12.00
❏ HS 11231 [S]	Vic Damone Sings	196?	3.00	6.00	12.00
HOLIDAY					
❏ HDY 1936	Christmas with Vic Damone	1981	2.50	5.00	10.00
MERCURY					
❏ MG-20163 [M]	Yours for a Song	1957	6.25	12.50	25.00
❏ MG-20193 [M]	My Favorites	1957	6.25	12.50	25.00
❏ MG-25028 [10]	Vic Damone	1950	10.00	20.00	40.00
❏ MG-25029 [10]	Vic Damone	1950	10.00	20.00	40.00
❏ MG-25045 [10]	Vic Damone	1950	10.00	20.00	40.00
❏ MG-25054 [10]	Song Hits	1950	10.00	20.00	40.00
❏ MG-25092 [10]	Christmas Favorites	1951	10.00	20.00	40.00
❏ MG-25100 [10]	Vic Damone and Others	1952	10.00	20.00	40.00
❏ MG-25131 [10]	The Night Has a Thousand Eyes	1952	10.00	20.00	40.00
❏ MG-25132 [10]	Vocals by Vic	1952	10.00	20.00	40.00
❏ MG-25133 [10]	April in Paris	1952	10.00	20.00	40.00
❏ MG-25156 [10]	Vic Damone	1952	10.00	20.00	40.00
RANWOOD					
❏ 8204	The Best of Vic Damone — Live	198?	2.50	5.00	10.00
RCA VICTOR					
❏ ANL1-2462	The Best of Vic Damone	1977	2.50	5.00	10.00
❏ LPM-3671 [M]	Stay with Me	1966	3.00	6.00	12.00
❏ LSP-3671 [S]	Stay with Me	1966	3.75	7.50	15.00
❏ LPM-3765 [M]	On the South Side of Chicago	1967	3.00	6.00	12.00
❏ LSP-3765 [S]	On the South Side of Chicago	1967	3.75	7.50	15.00
❏ LPM-3916 [M]	A Damone Type of Thing	1968	3.75	7.50	15.00
❏ LSP-3916 [S]	A Damone Type of Thing	1968	3.75	7.50	15.00
❏ LSP-3984	Why Can't I Walk Away	1968	3.75	7.50	15.00

D

Number	Title (A Side/B Side)	Yr	VG	VG+	NM
REBECCA					
❏ 100 [(2)]	Let's Fall in Love Again	1981	3.00	6.00	12.00
❏ 1212	Feelings	1976	2.50	5.00	10.00
❏ 1213	Inspiration	19??	2.50	5.00	10.00
UNITED TALENT					
❏ 4501	Don't Let Me Go	1969	3.00	6.00	12.00
WARNER BROS.					
❏ W 1602 [M]	You Were Only Fooling	1965	3.00	6.00	12.00
❏ WS 1602 [S]	You Were Only Fooling	1965	3.75	7.50	15.00
❏ W 1607 [M]	Country Love Songs	1965	3.00	6.00	12.00
❏ WS 1607 [S]	Country Love Songs	1965	3.75	7.50	15.00
WING					
❏ MGW 12113 [M]	I'll Sing for You	196?	3.00	6.00	12.00
❏ MGW 12157 [M]	Tenderly	196?	3.00	6.00	12.00
❏ MGW 12182 [M]	Yours for a Song	196?	3.00	6.00	12.00
❏ SRW 16113 [R]	I'll Sing for You	196?	3.00	6.00	12.00
❏ SRW 16157 [R]	Tenderly	196?	3.00	6.00	12.00
❏ SRW 16182 [R]	Yours for a Song	196?	3.00	6.00	12.00

DAN AND DALE
45s
TIFTON

Number	Title (A Side/B Side)	Yr	VG	VG+	NM
❏ 125	Batman Theme/Robin's Theme	1966	2.50	5.00	10.00
❏ 125 [PS]	Batman Theme/Robin's Theme	1966	5.00	10.00	20.00

Albums
DIPLOMAT

Number	Title	Yr	VG	VG+	NM
❏ D-2390 [M]	The Nearness of You	196?	2.50	5.00	10.00
❏ DS-2390 [S]	The Nearness of You	196?	3.00	6.00	12.00
TIFTON					
❏ M-8002 [M]	Batman and Robin	1966	7.50	15.00	30.00
❏ S-78002 [S]	Batman and Robin	1966	10.00	20.00	40.00

DANA, BILL See JOSE JIMENEZ.

DANA, VIC
45s
CASINO

Number	Title (A Side/B Side)	Yr	VG	VG+	NM
❏ 093	Lay Me Down (Roll Me Out to Sea)/You Never Really Know	1976	—	2.00	4.00
COLUMBIA					
❏ 45261	You Gave Me a Reason (To Believe)/It Won't Hurt to Try It	1970	—	2.50	5.00
❏ 45342	If You Think I Love You Now (I;ve Just Started)/Angel She Was Love	1971	—	2.50	5.00
❏ 45439	Child of Mine/The Love in Your Eyes	1971	—	2.50	5.00
DOLTON					
❏ 34	The Girl of My Dreams/Someone New	1961	2.00	4.00	8.00
❏ 42	Golden Boy/The Story Behind My Tears	1961	2.00	4.00	8.00
❏ 48	Little Altar Boy/Hello Roomate	1961	2.00	4.00	8.00
❏ 51	I Will/Proud	1962	2.00	4.00	8.00
❏ 51 [PS]	I Will/Proud	1962	3.75	7.50	15.00
❏ 58	To Love and Be Loved/Time Can Change	1962	2.00	4.00	8.00
❏ 64	A Very Good Year for Girls/I Wanna Be There	1962	2.00	4.00	8.00
❏ 64	A Very Good Year for Girls/Looking for Me	1962	2.00	4.00	8.00
❏ 73	Danger/Heart, Hand and Teardrop	1963	2.00	4.00	8.00
❏ 73 [PS]	Danger/Heart, Hand and Teardrop	1963	3.75	7.50	15.00
❏ 81	More/That's Why I'm Sorry	1963	2.00	4.00	8.00
❏ 87	The Prisoner's Song/Voice in the Wind	1963	2.00	4.00	8.00
❏ 89	So Wide the World/Close Your Eyes	1964	2.00	4.00	8.00
❏ 92	Shangri-La/Warm and Tender	1964	2.00	4.00	8.00
❏ 95	Love Is All We Need/I Need You Now	1964	2.00	4.00	8.00
❏ 95 [PS]	Love Is All We Need/I Need You Now	1964	3.75	7.50	15.00
❏ 99	Garden in the Rain/Stairway to the Stars	1964	2.00	4.00	8.00
❏ 99 [PS]	Garden in the Rain/Stairway to the Stars	1964	3.75	7.50	15.00
❏ 301	Frenchy/It Was Night	1964	2.00	4.00	8.00
❏ 304	Red Roses for a Blue Lady/Blue Ribbons	1965	2.00	4.00	8.00
❏ 305	Bring a Little Sunshine (To My Heart)/That's All	1965	2.00	4.00	8.00
❏ 305 [PS]	Bring a Little Sunshine (To My Heart)/That's All	1965	3.00	6.00	12.00
❏ 309	Moonlight and Roses (Bring Mem'ries of You)/What'll I Do	1965	2.00	4.00	8.00
❏ 313	Crystal Chandelier/What Now My Love	1965	2.00	4.00	8.00
❏ 317	Lovely Kravezit/Hello Roomate	1966	2.00	4.00	8.00
❏ 319	I Love You Drops/Sunny Skies	1966	2.00	4.00	8.00
❏ 322	A Million and One/My Baby Wouldn't Leave Me	1966	2.00	4.00	8.00
❏ 324	Distant Drums/Love Me With All of Your Heart	1966	2.00	4.00	8.00
❏ 326	Grown Up Games/So What's New	1966	2.00	4.00	8.00
LIBERTY					
❏ 55950	Fraulein/A Little Bit Later on Down the Line	1967	—	3.00	6.00
❏ 55998	A Lifetime Lovin' You/Guess Who, You	1967	—	3.00	6.00
❏ 56023	Glory of Love/Let the Good Times In	1968	—	2.50	5.00
❏ 56050	Didn't We/Them	1968	—	2.50	5.00
❏ 56071	Little Arrows/Roses Are Red	1968	—	2.50	5.00
❏ 56098	You Are My Destiny/Where Has All the Love Gone	1969	—	2.50	5.00
❏ 56109	Loneliness (Is Messin' Up My Mind)/Look of Leavin'	1969	—	2.50	5.00
❏ 56137	Aren't We the Lucky Ones/I Tried to Love You Today	1969	—	3.00	6.00
❏ 56150	If I Never Knew Your Name/Sad Day Song	1969	—	3.00	6.00
❏ 56163	Red Red Wine/Another Dream Shot Down	1970	—	2.50	5.00
MGM					
❏ 14795	The Best I Ever Had/Memories Can't Make Love to Me	1975	—	2.00	4.00
UNITED ARTISTS					
❏ 0095	Red Roses for a Blue Lady/More	1973	—	2.00	4.00

—"Silver Spotlight Series" reissue

Albums
DOLTON

Number	Title	Yr	VG	VG+	NM
❏ BLP-2013 [M]	This Is Vic Dana	1961	5.00	10.00	20.00
❏ BLP-2015 [M]	Warm and Wild	1962	3.75	7.50	15.00
❏ BLP-2026 [M]	More	1963	3.75	7.50	15.00
❏ BLP-2028 [M]	Shangri-La	1964	3.75	7.50	15.00
❏ BLP-2032 [M]	Now	1964	3.75	7.50	15.00
❏ BLP-2034 [M]	Red Roses for a Blue Lady	1965	3.75	7.50	15.00
❏ BLP-2036 [M]	Moonlight and Roses	1965	3.75	7.50	15.00
❏ BLP-2041 [M]	Crystal Chandelier	1966	3.75	7.50	15.00
❏ BLP-2046 [M]	Town and Country	1966	3.75	7.50	15.00
❏ BLP-2048 [M]	Golden Greats	1966	3.75	7.50	15.00
❏ BLP-2049 [M]	Little Altar Boy and Other Christmas Songs	1966	3.75	7.50	15.00
❏ BST-8013 [S]	This Is Vic Dana	1961	7.50	15.00	30.00
❏ BST-8015 [S]	Warm and Wild	1962	5.00	10.00	20.00
❏ BST-8026 [S]	More	1963	5.00	10.00	20.00
❏ BST-8028 [S]	Shangri-La	1964	5.00	10.00	20.00
❏ BST-8032 [S]	Now	1964	5.00	10.00	20.00
❏ BST-8034 [S]	Red Roses for a Blue Lady	1965	5.00	10.00	20.00
❏ BST-8036 [S]	Moonlight and Roses	1965	5.00	10.00	20.00
❏ BST-8041 [S]	Crystal Chandelier	1966	5.00	10.00	20.00
❏ BST-8046 [S]	Town and Country	1966	5.00	10.00	20.00
❏ BST-8048 [S]	Golden Greats	1966	5.00	10.00	20.00
❏ BST-8049 [S]	Little Altar Boy and Other Christmas Songs	1966	5.00	10.00	20.00
LIBERTY					
❏ BST-8049 [S]	Little Altar Boy and Other Christmas Songs	1967	3.00	6.00	12.00

—Liberty record in Dolton cover

Number	Title	Yr	VG	VG+	NM
❏ LST-8063	If I Never Knew Your Name	1969	3.00	6.00	12.00
SUNSET					
❏ SUM-1130 [M]	Warm and Wonderful	196?	2.50	5.00	10.00
❏ SUM-1182 [M]	On the Country Side	1967	2.50	5.00	10.00
❏ SUS-5130 [S]	Warm and Wonderful	196?	3.00	6.00	12.00
❏ SUS-5182 [S]	On the Country Side	1967	3.00	6.00	12.00

DANCER, PRANCER, AND NERVOUS
45s
CAPITOL

Number	Title (A Side/B Side)	Yr	VG	VG+	NM
❏ 4300	The Happy Reindeer/Dancer's Waltz	1959	3.00	6.00	12.00
❏ 4300 [PS]	The Happy Reindeer/Dancer's Waltz	1959	6.25	12.50	25.00
❏ 4353	I Wanta Be an Easter Bunny/The Happy Birthday Song	1960	3.00	6.00	12.00

—As "The Singing Reindeer"

DANDERLIERS, THE
45s
B&F

Number	Title (A Side/B Side)	Yr	VG	VG+	NM
❏ 150	Shu-Wop/My Loving Partner	1960	6.25	12.50	25.00
❏ 160	My Love/She's Mine	1960	6.25	12.50	25.00
❏ 1344	Chop Chop Boom/My Autumn Love	1961	5.00	10.00	20.00
MIDAS					
❏ 9004	All the Way/Walk On with Your Nose Up	196?	5.00	10.00	20.00
STATES					
❏ 147	Chop Chop Boom/My Autumn Love	1955	100.00	200.00	400.00

—Black vinyl

Number	Title (A Side/B Side)	Yr	VG	VG+	NM
❏ 147	Chop Chop Boom/My Autumn Love	1955	300.00	600.00	1200.

—Red vinyl

Number	Title (A Side/B Side)	Yr	VG	VG+	NM
❏ 150	Shu-Wop/My Loving Partner	1955	50.00	100.00	200.00
❏ 152	May God Be With You/Little Man	1956	50.00	100.00	200.00
❏ 160	My Love/She's Mine	1956	62.50	125.00	250.00

DANDLEERS, THE See THE DANLEERS.

DANETTA AND THE STARLETS
45s
OKEH

Number	Title (A Side/B Side)	Yr	VG	VG+	NM
❏ 7155	You Belong to Me (We're Going Steady)/Impression	1962	25.00	50.00	100.00

DANIELS, CHARLIE, BAND
45s
EPIC

Number	Title (A Side/B Side)	Yr	VG	VG+	NM
❏ 02154	In America/The Legend of Wooley Swamp	1981	—	—	3.00

—Reissue

Number	Title (A Side/B Side)	Yr	VG	VG+	NM
❏ 02185	Sweet Home Alabama/Falling in Love for the Night	1981	—	2.00	4.00
❏ 02828	Still in Saigon/Blowing Along with the Wind	1982	—	2.00	4.00
❏ 02995	Ragin' Cajun/Universal Hand	1982	—	2.00	4.00
❏ 03251	We Had It All One Time/Makes You Want to Go Home	1982	—	2.00	4.00
❏ 03918	Stroker's Theme/(B-side unknown)	1983	—	2.00	4.00
❏ 38-05638	American Farmer/Runnin' with That Crowd	1985	—	—	3.00
❏ 38-05638 [PS]	American Farmer/Runnin' with That Crowd	1985	—	—	3.00
❏ 38-05699	Still Hurtin' Me/American Rock and Roll	1985	—	—	3.00
❏ 38-05699 [PS]	Still Hurtin' Me/American Rock and Roll	1985	—	—	3.00
❏ 05835	Drinkin' My Baby Goodbye/Ever Changing Lady	1986	—	—	3.00
❏ 08002	Boogie Woogie Fiddle Country Blues/Working Man You Got It All	1988	—	—	3.00
❏ 08519	Uneasy Rider '88/Boogie Woogie Fiddle	1988	—	2.00	4.00
❏ 50243	Wichita Jail/It's My Life	1976	—	2.00	4.00
❏ 50278	Sweet Louisiana/Sweetwater, Texas	1976	—	2.00	4.00
❏ 50322	Billy the Kid/Slow Song	1976	—	2.00	4.00
❏ 50456	Heaven Can Be Anywhere (Twin Pines Theme)/Good Ole Boy	1977	—	2.00	4.00
❏ 50516	Sugar Hill Saturday Night/Maria Teresa	1977	—	2.00	4.00
❏ 50637	Sweet Lousiana/Trudy	1978	—	2.00	4.00
❏ 50700	The Devil Went Down to Georgia/Rainbow Ride	1979	—	2.00	4.00
❏ 50768	Mississippi/Passing Lane	1979	—	2.00	4.00
❏ 50806	Behind Your Eyes/Blue Star	1979	—	2.00	4.00
❏ 50845	Long Haired Country Boy/Sweet Lousiana	1980	—	2.00	4.00
❏ 50888	In America/Blue Star	1980	—	2.00	4.00
❏ 50921	The Legend of Wooley Swamp/Money	1980	—	2.00	4.00
❏ 50955	Carolina (I Remember You)/South Sea Song	1980	—	2.00	4.00
❏ 19-50955 [DJ]	Carolina (I Remember You) (Long Version)/(Short Version)	1980	—	2.50	5.00
❏ 19-50955 [PS]	Carolina (I Remember You)	1980	—	2.50	5.00

—Sleeve may have been promo only

Number	Title (A Side/B Side)	Yr	VG	VG+	NM
❏ 68542	Cowboy Hat in Dallas/Easy Rider	1988	—	—	3.00
❏ 68738	Midnight Train/Back to Dixie	1989	—	—	3.00
❏ 73030	Simple Man/Ill Wind	1989	—	—	3.00
❏ 73236	Mister DJ/It's My Life	1990	—	—	3.00
❏ 73426	(What This World Needs Is) A Few More Rednecks/It's My Life	1990	—	—	3.00
❏ 73577	Oh Atlanta/What Is 26	1990	—	—	3.00
❏ 73768	Honky Tonk Life/Willie Jones	1991	—	—	3.00
❏ 74061	Little Folks/Let Freedom Ring	1991	—	—	3.00
❏ 74866	The Twang Factor/Old Rock 'n Roll	1991	—	2.00	4.00
HANOVER					
❏ 4541	Robot Bomp/Rover Had a Party	1959	7.50	15.00	30.00

Number	Title (A Side/B Side)	Yr	VG	VG+	NM
KAMA SUTRA					
❏ 553	Great Big Bunches of Love/(B-side unknown)	1972	—	3.00	6.00
❏ 576	Uneasy Rider/Funky Junky	1973	—	3.00	6.00
❏ 590	Whiskey//(B-side unknown)	1974	—	2.50	5.00
❏ 593	Way Down Yonder/I've Been Down	1974	—	2.50	5.00
❏ 595	Land of Opportunity//(B-side unknown)	1974	—	2.50	5.00
❏ 598	The South's Gonna Do It/King Size Rosewood Bed	1974		2.50	5.00
❏ 601	Long Haired Country Boy/I've Been Down	1975	—	2.50	5.00
❏ 606	Birmingham Blues/Damn Good Cowboy	1975	—	2.50	5.00
❏ 607	Texas/Everything Is Kinda Alright	1975	—	2.50	5.00
LIBERTY					
❏ S7-17398	All Night Long/America, I Believe in You	1993		2.50	5.00
PAULA					
❏ 246	The Middle of a Heartache/Skip It	1966	3.75	7.50	15.00
❏ 418	The Middle of a Heartache/Skip It	1976	—	2.00	4.00
Albums					
CAPITOL					
❏ ST-790	Charlie Daniels	1971	6.25	12.50	25.00
❏ ST-11414	Charlie Daniels	1975	3.00	6.00	12.00
—Reissue of ST-790					
❏ SN-16039	Charlie Daniels	1979	2.00	4.00	8.00
—Budget-line reissue					
EPIC					
❏ AS 586 [DJ]	Interchords	1979	3.75	7.50	15.00
—Music and interviews; promo only					
❏ EAS 1780 [DJ]	The Charlie Daniels Story	1990	3.75	7.50	15.00
—Promo-only interview/radio show					
❏ PE 34150	Saddle Tramp	1976	2.50	5.00	10.00
—Orange label, no bar code on cover					
❏ PE 34150	Saddle Tramp	198?	2.00	4.00	8.00
—With bar code on cover					
❏ JE 34365	Fire on the Mountain	1976	2.50	5.00	10.00
—Reissue of Kama Sutra 2603 without bonus EP; orange label, no bar code on cover					
❏ PE 34365	Fire on the Mountain	198?	2.00	4.00	8.00
—Budget-line reissue					
❏ JE 34369	Uneasy Rider	1976	2.50	5.00	10.00
—Reissue of Kama Sutra 2071 with new name; orange label, no bar code on cover					
❏ PE 34369	Uneasy Rider	198?	2.00	4.00	8.00
—Budget-line reissue					
❏ JE 34377	High Lonesome	1976	2.50	5.00	10.00
—Orange label, no bar code on cover					
❏ PE 34377	High Lonesome	198?	2.00	4.00	8.00
—Budget-line reissue					
❏ JE 34402	Nightrider	1977	2.50	5.00	10.00
—Reissue of Kama Sutra 2607; orange label, no bar code on cover					
❏ PE 34402	Nightrider	198?	2.00	4.00	8.00
—Budget-line reissue					
❏ JE 34664	Whiskey	1977	2.50	5.00	10.00
—Reissue of Kama Sutra 2076 with new name; orange label, no bar code on cover					
❏ PE 34664	Whiskey	198?	2.00	4.00	8.00
—Budget-line reissue					
❏ JE 34665	Te John, Grease and Wolfman	1977	2.50	5.00	10.00
—Reissue of Kama Sutra 2060; orange label, no bar code on cover					
❏ PE 34665	Te John, Grease and Wolfman	198?	2.00	4.00	8.00
—Budget-line reissue					
❏ JE 34970	Midnight Wind	1977	2.50	5.00	10.00
—Orange label, no bar code on cover					
❏ PE 34970	Midnight Wind	198?	2.00	4.00	8.00
—Budget-line reissue					
❏ JE 35751	Million Mile Reflections	1979	2.50	5.00	10.00
❏ PE 35751	Million Mile Reflections	198?	2.00	4.00	8.00
—Budget-line reissue					
❏ FE 36571	Full Moon	1980	2.50	5.00	10.00
❏ PE 36571	Full Moon	198?	2.00	4.00	8.00
—Budget-line reissue					
❏ FE 37694	Windows	1982	2.50	5.00	10.00
❏ PE 37694	Windows	198?	2.00	4.00	8.00
—Budget-line reissue					
❏ FE 38795	A Decade of Hits	1983	2.50	5.00	10.00
❏ FE 39878	Me and the Boys	1985	2.50	5.00	10.00
❏ PE 39878	Me and the Boys	198?	2.00	4.00	8.00
—Budget-line reissue					
❏ FE 40760	Powder Keg	1987	2.00	4.00	8.00
❏ FE 44324	Homesick Man	1988	2.00	4.00	8.00
❏ HE 44365	Fire on the Mountain	1982	10.00	20.00	40.00
—Half-speed mastered edition					
❏ FE 45316	Simple Man	1989	3.00	6.00	12.00
❏ HE 45751	Million Mile Reflections	1982	10.00	20.00	40.00
—Half-speed mastered edition					
KAMA SUTRA					
❏ KSBS 2060	Te John, Grease and Wolfman	1972	3.75	7.50	15.00
❏ KSBS 2071	Honey in the Rock	1973	3.75	7.50	15.00
❏ KSBS 2076	Way Down Yonder	1974	3.75	7.50	15.00
❏ KSBS 2603	Fire on the Mountain	1974	3.75	7.50	15.00
—Includes bonus EP, "Volunteer Jam" (deduct 20% if missing)					
❏ KSBS 2607	Nightrider	1975	3.75	7.50	15.00
MOBILE FIDELITY					
❏ 1-176	Million Mile Reflections	1984	7.50	15.00	30.00
—Audiophile vinyl					

DANIELS, JEFF
45s
Number	Title (A Side/B Side)	Yr	VG	VG+	NM
ASTRO					
❏ 108	Foxy Dan/Someday You'll Remember	1960	25.00	50.00	100.00
BIG HOWDY					
❏ 777	Switch Blade Sam/You're Still on My Mind	1959	25.00	50.00	100.00
❏ 8120	Uh-Huh/Table for Two	196?	25.00	50.00	100.00
❏ 8121	Foxy Dan/Someday You'll Remember	1961	25.00	50.00	100.00
MELADEE					
❏ 117	Daddy-O Rock/Hey Woman	1958	100.00	200.00	400.00

DANIELS, ROLY
45s
Number	Title (A Side/B Side)	Yr	VG	VG+	NM
COLUMBIA					
❏ 4-44793	Love Is a Symphony/Another Teardrop	1969	2.50	5.00	10.00

DANLEERS, THE
45s
Number	Title (A Side/B Side)	Yr	VG	VG+	NM
AMP 3					
❏ 2115	One Summer Night/Wheelin' and Dealin'	1958	10.00	20.00	40.00
—Corrected group name on label					
❏ 2115	One Summer Night/Wheelin' and Dealin'	1958	50.00	100.00	200.00
—By "Dandleers"					
EPIC					
❏ 9367	I Live Half a Block from an Angel/If You Don't Care	1960	7.50	15.00	30.00
❏ 9421	I'll Always Be in Love with You/Little Lover	1960	7.50	15.00	30.00
EVEREST					
❏ 19412	Foolish/I'm Looking Around	1961	7.50	15.00	30.00
LEMANS					
❏ 004	The Truth Hurts/Baby You've Got It	1963	2.50	5.00	10.00
❏ 008	I'm Sorry/This Thing Called Love	1963	2.50	5.00	10.00
MERCURY					
❏ 71322	One Summer Night/Wheelin' and a-Dealin'	1958	5.00	10.00	20.00
❏ 71356	I Really Love You/My Flaming Heart	1958	5.00	10.00	20.00
❏ 71401	A Picture of You/Prelude to Love	1959	5.00	10.00	20.00
❏ 71441	I Can't Sleep/Your Love	1959	5.00	10.00	20.00
SMASH					
❏ 1872	Were You There/If	1964	3.00	6.00	12.00
❏ 1895	Where Is Love/The Angels Sent You	1964	3.00	6.00	12.00

DANNY AND DEANIE
45s
Number	Title (A Side/B Side)	Yr	VG	VG+	NM
HIT					
❏ 137	Bread and Butter/House of the Rising Sun	1964	3.75	7.50	15.00
—B-side by the Spartas					

DANNY AND JERRY "Danny" is Danny Rapp of DANNY AND THE JUNIORS.
45s
Number	Title (A Side/B Side)	Yr	VG	VG+	NM
RONN					
❏ 5	We've Got a Groovy Thing Goin'/You Must Be Fooling	1966	3.00	6.00	12.00
❏ 12	I've Got Pride/Connection	1967	3.00	6.00	12.00
❏ 24	I Can't See Nobody/Mo'Reen	1967	3.00	6.00	12.00

DANNY AND THE JUNIORS
45s
Number	Title (A Side/B Side)	Yr	VG	VG+	NM
ABC-PARAMOUNT					
❏ 9871	At the Hop/Sometimes (When I'm All Alone)	1957	7.50	15.00	30.00
❏ 9888	Rock and Roll Is Here to Stay/School Boy Romance	1958	7.50	15.00	30.00
❏ 9926	Dottie/In the Meantime	1958	6.25	12.50	25.00
❏ 9953	A Thief/Crazy Cave	1958	6.25	12.50	25.00
❏ 9978	Sassy Fran/I Feel So Lonely	1958	12.50	25.00	50.00
❏ 10004	Do You Love Me/Somehow I Can't Forget	1959	6.25	12.50	25.00
❏ 10052	Playing Hard to Get/Of Love	1959	6.25	12.50	25.00
CRUNCH					
❏ 018001	At the Hop/Let the Good Times Roll	1973	—	2.50	5.00
GUYDEN					
❏ 2076	Oo-La-La-Limbo/Now and Then	1962	5.00	10.00	20.00
LUV					
❏ 252	Rock and Roll Is Here to Stay/Sometimes (When I'm All Alone)	1968	2.50	5.00	10.00
MCA					
❏ D-2411	At the Hop/Rock and Roll Is Here to Stay	1980	—	2.00	4.00
—Reissue					
MERCURY					
❏ 72240	Sad Girl/Let's Go Ski-ing	1964	5.00	10.00	20.00
ROULETTE					
❏ GG-121	At the Hop/Rock and Roll Is Here to Stay	1973	—	2.00	4.00
—"Golden Goodies Hit Series" issue					
SINGULAR					
❏ 711	At the Hop/Sometimes	1957	250.00	500.00	1000.
—Blue label, machine-stamped in dead wax, no mention of Artie Singer on label					
❏ 711	At the Hop/Sometimes	1957	250.00	500.00	1000.
—Blue label, machine-stamped in dead wax, with "Orchestra Directed by Artie Singer" credit. Both versions have a "count-in" before the song starts. Singular records on black labels or without the count-in are probably reproductions.					
SWAN					
❏ 4060	Twistin' U.S.A./A Thousand Miles Away	1960	5.00	10.00	20.00
❏ 4064	Candy Cane. Sugary Plum/Oh Holy Night	1960	6.25	12.50	25.00
❏ 4064 [PS]	Candy Cane. Sugary Plum/Oh Holy Night	1960	62.50	125.00	250.00
❏ 4068	Daydreamer/Pony Express	1961	5.00	10.00	20.00
❏ 4072	Cha Cha Go Go (Chicago Cha-Cha)/Mister Whisper	1961	5.00	10.00	20.00
❏ 4082	Back to the Hop/The Charleston Fish	1961	5.00	10.00	20.00
❏ 4082 [PS]	Back to the Hop/The Charleston Fish	1961	25.00	50.00	100.00
❏ 4084	Just Because/You Hair's Too Long	1961	—	—	—
—Unreleased?					
❏ 4092	Twistin' All Night Long/Some Kind of Nut	1962	5.00	10.00	20.00
❏ 4100	(Do the) Mashed Potatoes/Doin' the Continental Walk	1962	5.00	10.00	20.00
❏ 4113	We Got Soul/Funny	1962	5.00	10.00	20.00
7-Inch Extended Plays					
ABC-PARAMOUNT					
❏ EP-11	At The Hop/School Boy Romance//Rock And Roll Is Here To Stay/Sometimes (When I'm All Alone)	1958	150.00	300.00	600.00
❏ EP-11 [PS]	At the Hop	1958	225.00	450.00	900.00
Albums					
MCA					
❏ 1555	Rockin' with Danny and the Juniors	1987	2.50	5.00	10.00

DANNY AND THE MEMORIES "Danny" is Danny Whitten, later of CRAZY HORSE.
45s
Number	Title (A Side/B Side)	Yr	VG	VG+	NM
VALIANT					
❏ 705	Can't Help Lovin' That Girl of Mine/Don't Go	1965	6.25	12.50	25.00
❏ 6049	Can't Help Lovin' That Girl of Mine/Don't Go	1964	6.25	12.50	25.00

Number	Title (A Side/B Side)	Yr	VG	VG+	NM

DANNY AND THE OTHER GUYS
45s
CP

❑ (# unknown)	Hard Times/(B-side unknown)	196?	200.00	400.00	800.00

DANTE
45s
A&M

❑ 788	Speedoo/Sweet Lover	1966	2.50	5.00	10.00

DARROW

❑ 515	How Much I Care/Baby Baby	1960	10.00	20.00	40.00

DECCA

❑ 31178	If You Don't Know/Leave Your Tears Behind You	1960	3.75	7.50	15.00
❑ 31268	Bye Bye Baby/That's Why	1961	3.75	7.50	15.00
❑ 31319	Ring or Write or Call/Say It to Me	1961	3.75	7.50	15.00

IMPERIAL

❑ 5798	Something Happens/Are You Just My Friend	1961	3.75	7.50	15.00
❑ 5827	Miss America/Now I've Got You	1962	3.75	7.50	15.00
❑ 5867	Magic Ring/Am I the One	1962	3.75	7.50	15.00

—*Imperial titles as "Dante and His Friends"*

MADISON

❑ 130	Alley Oop/The Right Time	1960	5.00	10.00	20.00

—*As "Dante and the Evergreens"*

❑ 135	Time Machine/Dream Land	1960	3.75	7.50	15.00
❑ 143	What Are You Doing New Year's Eve/Yeah Baby	1960	3.75	7.50	15.00

—*As "Dante and the Evergreens"*

❑ 154	Think Sweet Thoughts/Da Doo	1961	3.75	7.50	15.00

MERCURY

❑ 71621	How Much I Care/Baby Baby	1960	5.00	10.00	20.00

TIDE

❑ 003	My Lament/Aching Heart	1960	5.00	10.00	20.00

Albums
MADISON

❑ MA-LP 1002 [M]	Dante and the Evergreens	1961	125.00	250.00	500.00

DANTE, RON Also see THE ARCHIES; THE CUFF LINKS (1); THE DETERGENTS.
45s
ALMONT

❑ 307	Little Lollypop/Funny	1963	3.75	7.50	15.00

BELL

❑ 45460	Christine/Don't Call It Love	1974	—	2.50	5.00

—*As "Bo Cooper"*

❑ 45610	Charmer/Yesterday Dreamin'	1974	—	2.00	4.00
❑ 45619	Midnight Show/The Christian	1974	—	2.00	4.00

COLUMBIA

❑ 43720	Think/221 East Maple	1966	2.50	5.00	10.00
❑ 43862	I Give You Things/Janie, Janie	1966	2.50	5.00	10.00

DOT

❑ 17023	Absence of Lisa/Gypsy Be Mine	1967	2.50	5.00	10.00

HANDSHAKE

❑ 02107	Show and Tell/God Bless Rock and Roll	1981	—	2.00	4.00
❑ 02552	Letter from Zowie/God Bless Rock and Roll	1981	—	2.00	4.00

INFINITY

❑ 50008	Ain't Misbehavin' (One Never Knows, Do One?)/'Round About Midnight	1979	—	2.50	5.00
❑ 50018	Fire Island/They're Playing Our Song	1979	—	2.50	5.00
❑ 50038	Brand New Key/They're Playing Our Song	1979	—	2.50	5.00

—*Infinity sides as "Dante's Inferno"*

KIRSHNER

❑ 63-1010	How Do You Know/Let Me Bring You Up	1970	—	3.00	6.00
❑ 63-1010 [PS]	How Do You Know/Let Me Bring You Up	1970	2.50	5.00	10.00
❑ 63-5007	Sweet Taste of Love/C'mon Girl	1970	—	3.00	6.00

MERCURY

❑ 72812	Follow a Dream/He's Raining in My Sunshine	1968	2.50	5.00	10.00

MUSIC VOICE

❑ 503	If You Love Me, Laurie/Don't Stand Up in a Canoe	1964	3.75	7.50	15.00

MUSICOR

❑ 1058	Look at Me/There's Love	1965	3.00	6.00	12.00
❑ 1090	In the Rain/Poor Boys	1965	3.00	6.00	12.00
❑ 1105	If You Love Me, Laurie/Don't Stand Up in a Canoe	1965	3.00	6.00	12.00
❑ 1134	Hey Mom, Hey Pop/(Heart) Stop Calling Her Name	1965	3.00	6.00	12.00

RCA

❑ PB-10898	How Am I to Know/Sky Rider	1977	—	2.00	4.00

RCA VICTOR

❑ PB-10340	Sugar, Sugar/Sugar, Sugar (Disco)	1975	—	2.50	5.00

SCEPTER

❑ 12333 [DJ]	That's What Life Is All About (mono/stereo)	1971	—	3.00	6.00

—*Stock copy may not exist*

Albums
HANDSHAKE

❑ JW 37341	Street Angel	1981	3.00	6.00	12.00

KIRSHNER

❑ KES-106	Ron Dante Brings You Up	1970	5.00	10.00	20.00

DAPPERS, THE
45s
EPIC

❑ 9423	My Love Is Real/Baby You Know You're Wrong	1960	6.25	12.50	25.00

FOXIE

❑ 7005	Chicken Twist/Lonely Street	1961	10.00	20.00	40.00

GROOVE

❑ 0156	Unwanted Love/That's All, That's All, That's All	1956	50.00	100.00	200.00

PEACOCK

❑ 1651	Come Back to Me/Mambo Oongh	1955	37.50	75.00	150.00

RAINBOW

❑ 373	Bop Bop Bu/How I Need You Baby	1956	10.00	20.00	40.00

STAR-X

❑ 505	We're in Love/Spellbound	1958	62.50	125.00	250.00

DAPPERS QUINTET, THE
45s
FLAYR

❑ 500	Look What I've Found/(B-side unknown)	1955	500.00	1000.	1500.

DAPS, THE
45s
MARTERRY

❑ 5429	When You're Alone/Down and Out	1956	15.00	30.00	60.00

DARBISHIRE, STEVE
45s
LONDON

❑ 1011	Trains Trains/Yum Yum	1966	2.00	4.00	8.00

DARCEL, DENISE
Albums
CAMEO

❑ C-1002 [M]	Banned in Boston	1958	10.00	20.00	40.00

DARIN, BOBBY
45s
ATCO

❑ (no #) [DJ]	She's Tanfastic!/Moments of Love	1960	10.00	20.00	40.00

—*Ferrion Inc. "Special Premium Record"*

❑ 6092	Million Dollar Baby/Talk to Me	1957	7.50	15.00	30.00
❑ 6103	Don't Call My Name/Pretty Betty	1957	7.50	15.00	30.00
❑ 6109	Just in Case You Change Your Mind/So Mean	1958	7.50	15.00	30.00
❑ 6117	Splish Splash/Judy, Don't Be Moody	1958	5.00	10.00	20.00
❑ 6121	Early in the Morning/Now We're One	1958	5.00	10.00	20.00
❑ 6121	Early in the Morning/Now We're One	1958	10.00	20.00	40.00

—*As "The Rinky Dinks"*

❑ 6127	Queen of the Hop/Lost Love	1958	5.00	10.00	20.00
❑ 6128	Mighty Mighty Man/You're Gone	1958	5.00	10.00	20.00
❑ 6128	Mighty Mighty Man/You're Gone	1958	10.00	20.00	40.00

—*As "The Rinky Dinks"*

❑ 6133 [M]	Plain Jane/While I'm Gone	1959	5.00	10.00	20.00
❑ 6133 [PS]	Plain Jane/While I'm Gone	1959	12.50	25.00	50.00
❑ SD-45-6133 [S]	Plain Jane/While I'm Gone	1959	10.00	20.00	40.00
❑ 6140	Dream Lover/Bullmoose	1959	5.00	10.00	20.00
❑ 6140 [PS]	Dream Lover/Bullmoose	1959	12.50	25.00	50.00
❑ 6147	Mack the Knife/Was There a Call for Me	1959	5.00	10.00	20.00
❑ 6147 [PS]	Mack the Knife/Was There a Call for Me	1959	10.00	20.00	40.00
❑ 6158	Beyond the Sea/That's the Way Love Is	1960	5.00	10.00	20.00
❑ 6158 [PS]	Beyond the Sea/That's the Way Love Is	1960	10.00	20.00	40.00
❑ 6161	Clementine/Tall Story	1960	5.00	10.00	20.00
❑ 6161 [PS]	Clementine/Tall Story	1960	10.00	20.00	40.00
❑ 6167	Won't You Come Home Bill Bailey/I'll Be There	1960	5.00	10.00	20.00
❑ 6167 [PS]	Won't You Come Home Bill Bailey/I'll Be There	1960	7.50	15.00	30.00
❑ 6173	Beachcomber/Autumn Blues	1960	5.00	10.00	20.00
❑ 6173 [PS]	Beachcomber/Autumn Blues	1960	7.50	15.00	30.00
❑ 6179	Artificial Flowers/Somebody to Love	1960	5.00	10.00	20.00
❑ 6179 [PS]	Artificial Flowers/Somebody to Love	1960	7.50	15.00	30.00
❑ 6183	Christmas Auld Lang Syne/Child of God	1960	6.25	12.50	25.00
❑ 6183 [PS]	Christmas Auld Lang Syne/Child of God	1960	10.00	20.00	40.00
❑ 6188	Lazy River/Oo-Ee Train	1961	3.00	6.00	12.00
❑ 6188 [PS]	Lazy River/Oo-Ee Train	1961	5.00	10.00	20.00
❑ 6196	Nature Boy/Look for My True Love	1961	3.00	6.00	12.00
❑ 6196 [PS]	Nature Boy/Look for My True Love	1961	5.00	10.00	20.00
❑ 6200	Come September/Walk Back to Me	1961	3.75	7.50	15.00
❑ 6200 [PS]	Come September/Walk Back to Me	1961	12.50	25.00	50.00
❑ 6206	You Must Have Been a Beautiful Baby/Sorrow Tomorrow	1961	3.00	6.00	12.00
❑ 6206 [PS]	You Must Have Been a Beautiful Baby/Sorrow Tomorrow	1961	5.00	10.00	20.00
❑ 6211	Ave Maria/O Come All Ye Faithful	1961	3.00	6.00	12.00
❑ 6211 [PS]	Ave Maria/O Come All Ye Faithful	1961	40.00	80.00	160.00
❑ 6214	Irresistible You/Multiplication	1961	3.00	6.00	12.00
❑ 6214 [PS]	Irresistible You/Multiplication	1961	5.00	10.00	20.00
❑ 6221	What'd I Say (Part 1)/What'd I Say (Part 2)	1962	3.00	6.00	12.00
❑ 6221 [PS]	What'd I Say (Part 1)/What'd I Say (Part 2)	1962	5.00	10.00	20.00
❑ 6229	Things/Jailer Bring Me Water	1962	3.00	6.00	12.00
❑ 6236	Baby Face/You Know How	1962	3.00	6.00	12.00
❑ 6244	I Found a New Baby/Keep a-Walkin'	1962	3.00	6.00	12.00
❑ 6297	Milord/Golden Earrings	1964	2.50	5.00	10.00
❑ 6316	Swing Low Sweet Chariot/Similau	1964	2.50	5.00	10.00
❑ 6334	Minnie the Moocher/Hard Hearted Hannah	1965	2.50	5.00	10.00

ATLANTIC

❑ 2305	Funny What Love Can Do/We Didn't Ask to Be Brought Here	1965	2.00	4.00	8.00
❑ 2317	Silver Dollar/The Breaking Point	1966	2.00	4.00	8.00
❑ 2329	Mame/Walking in the Shadow of Love	1966	2.00	4.00	8.00
❑ 2341	Who's Afraid of Virginia Woolf?/Merci, Cheri	1966	2.00	4.00	8.00
❑ 2350	If I Were a Carpenter/Rainin'	1966	2.50	5.00	10.00
❑ 2367	The Girl That Stood Beside Me/Reason to Believe	1966	2.00	4.00	8.00
❑ 2376	Lovin' You/Amy	1967	2.00	4.00	8.00
❑ 2395	The Lady Came from Baltimore/I Am	1967	2.00	4.00	8.00
❑ 2420	Darlin' Be Home Soon/Hello, Sunshine	1967	2.00	4.00	8.00
❑ 2433	Talk to the Animals/After Today	1967	2.00	4.00	8.00
❑ 2433	Talk to the Animals/She Knows	1967	2.00	4.00	8.00
❑ 89166	Beyond the Sea/Mack the Knife	1987	—	—	3.00
❑ 89166 [PS]	Beyond the Sea/Mack the Knife	1987	—	—	3.00

—*From the movie "Big Town"*

BRUNSWICK

❑ 55073	Early in the Morning/Now We're One	1958	20.00	40.00	80.00

—*As "The Ding Dongs"; also see Atco 6121*

CAPITOL

❑ 4837	If a Man Answers/True, True Love	1962	2.50	5.00	10.00
❑ 4837 [PS]	If a Man Answers/True, True Love	1962	3.75	7.50	15.00
❑ 4897	You're the Reason I'm Living/Now You're Gone	1962	2.50	5.00	10.00
❑ 4897 [PS]	You're the Reason I'm Living/Now You're Gone	1962	3.75	7.50	15.00
❑ 4970	18 Yellow Roses/Not for Me	1963	2.50	5.00	10.00
❑ 4970 [PS]	18 Yellow Roses/Not for Me	1963	3.75	7.50	15.00
❑ 5019	Treat My Baby Good/Down So Long	1963	2.50	5.00	10.00
❑ 5079	Be Mad Little Girl/Since You've Been Gone	1963	2.50	5.00	10.00

D

Number	Title (A Side/B Side)	Yr	VG	VG+	NM
❏ 5126	I Wonder Who's Kissing Her Now/ As Long As I'm Singing	1964	2.50	5.00	10.00
❏ 5257	The Things in This House/Wait by the Water	1964	2.50	5.00	10.00
❏ 5359	Hello, Dolly!/Golden Earrings	1965	2.50	5.00	10.00
❏ 5399	A World Without You/Venice Blue	1965	2.50	5.00	10.00
❏ 5443	When I Get Home/Lonely Road	1965	2.50	5.00	10.00
❏ 5443 [PS]	When I Get Home/Lonely Road	1965	6.25	12.50	25.00
❏ 5481	Gyp the Cat/That Funny Feeling	1965	2.50	5.00	10.00

DECCA

Number	Title (A Side/B Side)	Yr	VG	VG+	NM
❏ 29883	Rock Island Line/Timber	1956	10.00	20.00	40.00
❏ 29922	Silly Willy/Blue Eyed Mermaid	1956	12.50	25.00	50.00
❏ 30031	The Greatest Builder (Of Them All)/ Hear Them Bells	1956	10.00	20.00	40.00
❏ 30225	Dealer in Dreams/Help Me	1957	10.00	20.00	40.00
❏ 30737	Silly Willy/Dealer in Dreams	1958	7.50	15.00	30.00

DIRECTION

Number	Title (A Side/B Side)	Yr	VG	VG+	NM
❏ 350	Long Line Rider/Change	1968	2.00	4.00	8.00
❏ 351	Song for a Dollar/Mr. and Mrs. Hohner	1969	2.00	4.00	8.00
❏ 352	Distractions (Part 1)/Jive	1969	2.00	4.00	8.00
❏ 4000	Sugar Man/(9 to 5) Jive's Alive	1970	2.00	4.00	8.00
❏ 4001	Baby May/Sweet Reason	1970	2.00	4.00	8.00
❏ 4002	Maybe We Can Get It Together/Rx Pyro (Prescription: Fire)	1970	2.00	4.00	8.00

MOTOWN

Number	Title (A Side/B Side)	Yr	VG	VG+	NM
❏ 1183	Melodie/Someday We'll Be Together	1971	—	3.00	6.00
❏ 1193	Simple Song of Freedom/ I'll Be Your Baby Tonight	1971	—	3.00	6.00
❏ 1203	Sail Away/Something in Her Love	1972	—	3.00	6.00
❏ 1212	Average People/Something in Her Love	1972	—	3.00	6.00
❏ 1217	Happy/Something in Her Love	1973	—	3.00	6.00

7-Inch Extended Plays

ATCO

Number	Title (A Side/B Side)	Yr	VG	VG+	NM
❏ 4502	*Splish Splash/Judy, Don't Be Moody/I Found a Million Dollar Baby/(Since You're Gone) I Can't Go On	1959	12.50	25.00	50.00
❏ 4502 [PS]	Bobby Darin	1959	12.50	25.00	50.00
❏ 4504	Mack the Knife/That's the Way Love Is// Beyond the Sea/That's All	1959	12.50	25.00	50.00
❏ 4504 [PS]	That's All	1959	12.50	25.00	50.00
❏ 4505	Queen of the Hop/Lost Love//Plain Jane/While I'm Gone	1960	12.50	25.00	50.00
❏ 4505 [PS]	Bobby Darin	1960	12.50	25.00	50.00
❏ 4508	Clementine/My Gal Sal//Guys and Dolls/Down with Love	1960	12.50	25.00	50.00
❏ 4508 [PS]	This Is Darin	1960	12.50	25.00	50.00
❏ 4512	I Got A Woman/You'd Be So Nice To Come Home To//Medley: By Myself-When Your Lover Has Gone/Love For Sale	1960	12.50	25.00	50.00
❏ 4512 [PS]	Darin at the Copa	1960	12.50	25.00	50.00
❏ EP 4513-D	I Want You With Me/You Know How//Hush, Somebody's Calling My Name/Keep a-Walkin'	1960	17.50	35.00	70.00
❏ EP 4513-D [PS]	For Teenagers Only	1960	17.50	35.00	70.00

—Special promotional sleeve; has photo of LP 1001

CAPITOL CUSTOM

Number	Title (A Side/B Side)	Yr	VG	VG+	NM
❏ TB-2262/3	18 Yellow Roses/Not for Me/The Things in This House//You're the Reason I'm Living/Treat My Baby Good/Wait by the Water, Lillian	1963	7.50	15.00	30.00

—Small hole, plays at 33 1/3 rpm

| ❏ TB-2262/3 [PS] | Bobby Darin Presents | 1963 | 10.00 | 20.00 | 40.00 |

—"Manufactured by Capitol Records, Inc., Custom Services Department for Artistic Records"

| ❏ MB-2849/50 | If a Man Answers/True, True Love//Sermon of Samson/All By Myself | 1962 | 5.00 | 10.00 | 20.00 |
| ❏ MB-2849/50 [PS] | Scripto Inc. Presents Bobby Darin | 1962 | 7.50 | 15.00 | 30.00 |

—Value is for sleeve alone; the pen that came with the package is very rare

DECCA

Number	Title (A Side/B Side)	Yr	VG	VG+	NM
❏ ED 2676	(contents unknown)	1957	25.00	50.00	100.00
❏ ED 2676 [PS]	Hear Them Bells	1957	25.00	50.00	100.00

MOTOWN

Number	Title (A Side/B Side)	Yr	VG	VG+	NM
❏ PR-4 [DJ]	If I Were a Carpenter/Moritat (Mack the Knife)// Blue Monday/Happy	1973	3.75	7.50	15.00
❏ PR-4 [PS]	(title unknown)	1973	5.00	10.00	20.00

Albums

ATCO

Number	Title (A Side/B Side)	Yr	VG	VG+	NM
❏ 33-102 [M]	Bobby Darin	1958	25.00	50.00	100.00

—Yellow "harp" label

| ❏ 33-102 [M] | Bobby Darin | 1962 | 7.50 | 15.00 | 30.00 |

—Gold and dark blue label

| ❏ 33-104 [M] | That's All | 1959 | 10.00 | 20.00 | 40.00 |

—Yellow "harp" label

| ❏ 33-104 [M] | That's All | 1962 | 5.00 | 10.00 | 20.00 |

—Gold and dark blue label

| ❏ SD 33-104 [S] | That's All | 1959 | 25.00 | 50.00 | 100.00 |

—Yellow "harp" label

| ❏ SD 33-104 [S] | That's All | 1962 | 6.25 | 12.50 | 25.00 |

—Purple and brown label

| ❏ 33-115 [M] | This Is Darin | 1960 | 10.00 | 20.00 | 40.00 |

—Yellow "harp" label

| ❏ 33-115 [M] | This Is Darin | 1962 | 5.00 | 10.00 | 20.00 |

—Gold and dark blue label

| ❏ SD 33-115 [S] | This Is Darin | 1960 | 6.25 | 12.50 | 25.00 |

—Purple and brown label

| ❏ SD 33-115 [S] | This Is Darin | 1960 | 20.00 | 40.00 | 80.00 |

—Yellow "harp" label

| ❏ 33-122 [M] | Darin at the Copa | 1960 | 10.00 | 20.00 | 40.00 |

—Yellow "harp" label

| ❏ 33-122 [M] | Darin at the Copa | 1962 | 5.00 | 10.00 | 20.00 |

—Gold and dark blue label

| ❏ SD 33-122 [S] | Darin at the Copa | 1960 | 20.00 | 40.00 | 80.00 |

—Yellow "harp" label

| ❏ SD 33-122 [S] | Darin at the Copa | 1962 | 6.25 | 12.50 | 25.00 |

—Purple and brown label

| ❏ 33-124 [M] | It's You or No One | 1960 | 10.00 | 20.00 | 40.00 |

—Yellow "harp" label

| ❏ 33-124 [M] | It's You or No One | 1962 | 5.00 | 10.00 | 20.00 |

—Gold and dark blue label

Number	Title (A Side/B Side)	Yr	VG	VG+	NM
❏ SD 33-124 [S]	It's You or No One	1960	20.00	40.00	80.00
	—Yellow "harp" label				
❏ SD 33-124 [S]	It's You or No One	1962	6.25	12.50	25.00
	—Purple and brown label				
❏ 33-125 [M]	The 25th Day of December	1960	12.50	25.00	50.00
	—Yellow "harp" label				
❏ 33-125 [M]	The 25th Day of December	1962	5.00	10.00	20.00
	—Gold and dark blue label				
❏ SD 33-125 [S]	The 25th Day of December	1960	15.00	30.00	60.00
	—Yellow "harp" label				
❏ SD 33-125 [S]	The 25th Day of December	1962	6.25	12.50	25.00
	—Gold and dark blue label				
❏ 33-126 [M]	Two of a Kind	1961	10.00	20.00	40.00
	—Yellow "harp" label				
❏ 33-126 [M]	Two of a Kind	1962	5.00	10.00	20.00
	—Gold and dark blue label				
❏ SD 33-126 [S]	Two of a Kind	1961	12.50	25.00	50.00
	—Yellow "harp" label				
❏ SD 33-126 [S]	Two of a Kind	1962	6.25	12.50	25.00
	—Purple and brown label				
❏ 33-131 [M]	The Bobby Darin Story	1961	10.00	20.00	40.00
	—Yellow "harp" label; white cover				
❏ 33-131 [M]	The Bobby Darin Story	1962	5.00	10.00	20.00
	—Gold and dark blue label; black cover				
❏ SD 33-131 [S]	The Bobby Darin Story	1961	12.50	25.00	50.00
	—Yellow "harp" label; white cover				
❏ SD 33-131 [S]	The Bobby Darin Story	1962	6.25	12.50	25.00
	—Purple and brown label; black cover				
❏ SD 33-131	The Bobby Darin Story	1969	3.00	6.00	12.00
	—Yellow label, "Atco" on left				
❏ SD 33-131	The Bobby Darin Story	1978	2.00	4.00	8.00
	—Any later Atco label				
❏ 33-134 [M]	Love Swings	1961	10.00	20.00	40.00
	—Yellow "harp" label				
❏ 33-134 [M]	Love Swings	1962	5.00	10.00	20.00
	—Gold and dark blue label				
❏ SD 33-134 [S]	Love Swings	1961	12.50	25.00	50.00
	—Yellow "harp" label				
❏ SD 33-134 [S]	Love Swings	1962	6.25	12.50	25.00
	—Purple and brown label				
❏ 33-138 [M]	Twist with Bobby Darin	1961	10.00	20.00	40.00
	—Yellow "harp" label				
❏ 33-138 [M]	Twist with Bobby Darin	1962	5.00	10.00	20.00
	—Gold and dark blue label				
❏ SD 33-138 [S]	Twist with Bobby Darin	1961	12.50	25.00	50.00
	—Yellow "harp" label				
❏ SD 33-138 [S]	Twist with Bobby Darin	1962	6.25	12.50	25.00
	—Purple and brown label				
❏ 33-140 [M]	Bobby Darin Sings Ray Charles	1962	6.25	12.50	25.00
❏ SD 33-140 [S]	Bobby Darin Sings Ray Charles	1962	7.50	15.00	30.00
❏ 33-146 [M]	Things & Other Things	1962	6.25	12.50	25.00
❏ SD 33-146 [S]	Things & Other Things	1962	7.50	15.00	30.00
❏ 33-167 [M]	Winners	1964	6.25	12.50	25.00
❏ SD 33-167 [S]	Winners	1964	7.50	15.00	30.00
❏ SP 1001 [M]	For Teenagers Only	1960	18.75	37.50	75.00
	—With extras missing				
❏ SP 1001 [M]	For Teenagers Only	1960	37.50	75.00	150.00
	—Gatefold with fold-open poster and paper insert				
❏ 90484	Two of a Kind	1986	2.50	5.00	10.00

ATLANTIC

Number	Title (A Side/B Side)	Yr	VG	VG+	NM
❏ 8121 [M]	The Shadow of Your Smile	1966	3.75	7.50	15.00
❏ SD 8121 [S]	The Shadow of Your Smile	1966	5.00	10.00	20.00
❏ 8126 [M]	In a Broadway Bag	1966	3.75	7.50	15.00
❏ SD 8126 [S]	In a Broadway Bag	1966	5.00	10.00	20.00
❏ 8135 [M]	If I Were a Carpenter	1967	3.75	7.50	15.00
❏ SD 8135 [S]	If I Were a Carpenter	1967	12.50	25.00	50.00
	—Inexplicably rare in stereo				
❏ 8142 [M]	Inside Out	1967	3.75	7.50	15.00
❏ SD 8142 [S]	Inside Out	1967	7.50	15.00	30.00
❏ 8154 [M]	Bobby Darin Sings Doctor Dolittle	1967	3.75	7.50	15.00
❏ SD 8154 [S]	Bobby Darin Sings Doctor Dolittle	1967	3.75	7.50	15.00

BAINBRIDGE

Number	Title (A Side/B Side)	Yr	VG	VG+	NM
❏ 6220	Bobby Darin at the Copa	1981	2.50	5.00	10.00

CAPITOL

Number	Title (A Side/B Side)	Yr	VG	VG+	NM
❏ ST 1791 [S]	Oh! Look at Me Now	1962	5.00	10.00	20.00
❏ SW 1791 [S]	Oh! Look at Me Now	1962	6.25	12.50	25.00
❏ T 1791 [M]	Oh! Look at Me Now	1962	3.75	7.50	15.00
❏ W 1791 [M]	Oh! Look at Me Now	1962	5.00	10.00	20.00
❏ ST 1826 [S]	Earthy	1963	5.00	10.00	20.00
❏ T 1826 [M]	Earthy	1963	3.75	7.50	15.00
❏ ST 1866 [S]	You're the Reason I'm Living	1963	5.00	10.00	20.00
❏ T 1866 [M]	You're the Reason I'm Living	1963	3.75	7.50	15.00
❏ ST 1942 [S]	18 Yellow Roses	1963	5.00	10.00	20.00
❏ T 1942 [M]	18 Yellow Roses	1963	3.75	7.50	15.00
❏ ST 2007 [S]	Golden Folk Hits	1963	5.00	10.00	20.00
❏ T 2007 [M]	Golden Folk Hits	1963	3.75	7.50	15.00
❏ ST 2084 [S]	As Long As I'm Singing	1964	50.00	100.00	200.00
	—Canceled; price is for an acetate, which is known to exist				
❏ T 2084 [M]	As Long As I'm Singing	1964	—	—	—
	—Canceled				
❏ ST 2194 [S]	From Hello Dolly to Goodbye Charlie	1964	5.00	10.00	20.00
❏ T 2194 [M]	From Hello Dolly to Goodbye Charlie	1964	3.75	7.50	15.00
❏ ST 2322 [S]	Venice Blue	1965	5.00	10.00	20.00
❏ T 2322 [M]	Venice Blue	1965	3.75	7.50	15.00
❏ ST 2571 [S]	The Best of Bobby Darin	1966	3.75	7.50	15.00
❏ T 2571 [M]	The Best of Bobby Darin	1966	3.75	7.50	15.00

CLARION

Number	Title (A Side/B Side)	Yr	VG	VG+	NM
❏ 603 [M]	Clementine	1966	5.00	10.00	20.00
❏ SD 603 [S]	Clementine	1966	6.25	12.50	25.00

DIRECTION

Number	Title (A Side/B Side)	Yr	VG	VG+	NM
❏ 1936	Born Walden Robert Cassotto	1968	6.25	12.50	25.00
❏ 1937	Commitment	1969	6.25	12.50	25.00

MOTOWN

Number	Title (A Side/B Side)	Yr	VG	VG+	NM
❏ M5-185V1	Darin 1936-1973	1981	3.00	6.00	12.00
	—Reissue				
❏ MS-739	Finally	1972	125.00	250.00	500.00
	—Unreleased; value is for RCA test pressing				
❏ M 753L	Bobby Darin	1972	5.00	10.00	20.00
❏ M6-813L	Darin 1936-1973	1974	3.75	7.50	15.00

Number	Title (A Side/B Side)	Yr	VG	VG+	NM
DARIUS					
Albums					
CHARTMAKER					
❏ 1102	Darius	1969	62.50	125.00	250.00
DARLING, JOHNNY					
45s					
DELUXE					
❏ 6167	I Don't Want to Wind Up in Love/Baseball Baby	1956	37.50	75.00	150.00
DARNELL, LARRY					
45s					
ANNA					
❏ 1109	With Tears in My Eyes/I'll Get Along Somehow	1960	100.00	200.00	400.00
ARGO					
❏ 5372	With Tears in My Eyes/I'll Get Along Somehow	1960	6.25	12.50	25.00
DELUXE					
❏ 6123	Ramblin' Man/I Care	1957	7.50	15.00	30.00
❏ 6136	If You Go/Fing Fang Foy	1957	7.50	15.00	30.00
❏ 6141	Just Tell Me When/It Must Be Love	1957	7.50	15.00	30.00
OKEH					
❏ 6848	Work Baby Work/Left My Baby	1952	6.25	12.50	25.00
❏ 6869	Darlin'/Boogie-Oogie	1952	6.25	12.50	25.00
❏ 6902	What's On Your Mind/Better Be on My Way	1952	6.25	12.50	25.00
❏ 6916	No Time at All/Singin' My Blues	1952	6.25	12.50	25.00
❏ 6919	I'll Get Along Somehow (Part 1)/I'll Get Along Somehow (Part 2)	1952	6.25	12.50	25.00
❏ 6926	Christmas Blues/I Am the Sparrow	1952	6.25	12.50	25.00
❏ 6954	I'll Be Sittin', I'll Be Rockin'/Crazy She Calls Me	1953	6.25	12.50	25.00
❏ 7024	I'll Carry On/What More Do You Want Me to Do	1954	5.00	10.00	20.00
❏ 7039	I'm Gonna Change/Thank You, Darlin'	1954	5.00	10.00	20.00
❏ 7056	My Love for You/Feelin' Mighty Sad and Low	1955	5.00	10.00	20.00
REGAL					
❏ 3328	Do You Love Me Baby/Sad and Lonesome	1951	6.25	12.50	25.00
—Larry Darnell records on Regal before 3328 are unconfirmed on 45 rpm					
SAVOY					
❏ 1151	That's All I Want from You/Who Showed My Baby How to Love Me	1955	7.50	15.00	30.00
WARWICK					
❏ 506	If I Had You/Thankful	1959	5.00	10.00	20.00
7-Inch Extended Plays					
EPIC					
❏ 7072	(contents unknown)	1961	5.00	10.00	20.00
❏ 7072 [PS]	For You My Love	1961	5.00	10.00	20.00
DARNELLS, THE See THE MARVELETTES.					
DARRELL, JOHNNY					
45s					
CAPRICORN					
❏ 0207	Orange Blossom Special/Glendale, Arizona	1974	—	2.00	4.00
❏ 0223	Pieces of My Life/Glendale, Arizona	1975	—	2.00	4.00
❏ 0234	Rose Colored Gin/Glendale, Arizona	1975	—	2.00	4.00
CARTWHEEL					
❏ 203	Don't It Seem to Rain a Lot/I'll Never Get Up This Slow	1971	—	2.50	5.00
❏ 209	Mr. Tambourine Man/Let Me Stay Awhile	1972	—	2.50	5.00
GUSTO					
❏ 9001	Hard to Be Friends/These Days	1978	—	2.00	4.00
❏ 9011	Was Yesterday That Long Ago/Spanish Song	1978	—	2.00	4.00
MONUMENT					
❏ 8570	Crazy Daddy/Uncle Veneer	1973	—	2.50	5.00
❏ 8579	Dakota the Dancing Bear/Just a Memory	1973	—	2.50	5.00
UNITED ARTISTS					
❏ 869	Green, Green Grass of Home/Deepening Snow	1965	2.00	4.00	8.00
❏ 943	As Long As the Wind Blows/Beggars Can't Be Choosers	1965	2.00	4.00	8.00
❏ 50008	Johnny Lose It All/For Old Times' Sake	1966	2.00	4.00	8.00
❏ 50047	She's Mighty Gone/Baby Sitter	1966	2.00	4.00	8.00
❏ 50126	Ruby, Don't Take Your Love to Town/Little Things I Love	1967	2.00	4.00	8.00
❏ 50183	My Elusive Dreams/Pickin' with Gold	1967	2.00	4.00	8.00
❏ 50207	Come See What's Left of Your Man/Passin' Through	1967	2.00	4.00	8.00
❏ 50235	The Son of Hickory Holler's Tramp/But That's Alright	1967	2.00	4.00	8.00
❏ 50235 [PS]	The Son of Hickory Holler's Tramp/But That's Alright	1967	3.75	7.50	15.00
❏ 50292	With Pen in Hand/Poetry of Love	1968	—	3.00	6.00
❏ 50442	I Ain't Buying/Little Things	1968	—	3.00	6.00
❏ 50481	Woman Without Love/I Fought the Law	1968	—	3.00	6.00
❏ 50503	The Coming of the Roads/The Other Side of the Coin	1969	—	3.00	6.00
—With Anita Carter					
❏ 50518	Why You Been Gone So Long/You're Always the One	1969	—	3.00	6.00
❏ 50572	River Bottom/Ain't That Living	1969	—	3.00	6.00
❏ 50610	She's Headed for the Country/Trouble Maker	1969	—	3.00	6.00
❏ 50629	Mama Come'n Get Your Baby Boy/These Days	1970	—	3.00	6.00
❏ 50675	Brother River/Bed of Roses	1970	—	3.00	6.00
❏ 50716	They'll Never Take Her Love from Me/One Love, Two Hearts, Three Lives	1970	—	3.00	6.00
❏ 50739	Look Out Cleveland/Winter's Comin' On	1971	—	3.00	6.00
Albums					
CAPRICORN					
❏ CP 0154	Water Glass Full of Whiskey	1975	2.50	5.00	10.00
SUNSET					
❏ SUS-5232	The Johnny Darrell Sound	1969	2.50	5.00	10.00
UNITED ARTISTS					
❏ UAL 3594 [M]	Ruby, Don't Take Your Love to Town	1967	6.25	12.50	25.00
❏ UAS 6594 [S]	Ruby, Don't Take Your Love to Town	1967	5.00	10.00	20.00
❏ UAS 6634	The Son of Hickory Holler's Tramp	1968	5.00	10.00	20.00
❏ UAS 6660	With Pen in Hand	1968	5.00	10.00	20.00
❏ UAS 6707	Why You Been Gone So Long	1969	5.00	10.00	20.00
❏ UAS 6752	California Stop-Over	1970	5.00	10.00	20.00
❏ UAS 6759	The Best of Johnny Darrell, Volume 1	1970	3.75	7.50	15.00

Number	Title (A Side/B Side)	Yr	VG	VG+	NM
DARRELL AND THE OXFORDS See THE TOKENS.					
DARREN, JAMES					
45s					
BUDDAH					
❏ 177	That's My World/Wheeling, West Virginia	1970	—	2.50	5.00
COLPIX					
❏ 102	There's No Such Thing/Mighty Pretty Territory	1959	3.75	7.50	15.00
❏ 102 [PS]	There's No Such Thing/Mighty Pretty Territory	1959	7.50	15.00	30.00
❏ 113	Gidget/You	1959	3.75	7.50	15.00
❏ 119 [M]	Angel Face/I Don't Wanna Lose Ya	1959	3.75	7.50	15.00
❏ 119 [PS]	Angel Face/I Don't Wanna Lose Ya	1959	7.50	15.00	30.00
❏ SCP-119 [S]	Angel Face/I Don't Wanna Lose Ya	1959	10.00	20.00	40.00
❏ 128	I Ain't Sharin' Sharon/Love Among the Young	1959	3.75	7.50	15.00
❏ 130	Teenage Tears/Let There Be Love	1959	3.75	7.50	15.00
❏ 138	You Are My Dream/Your Smile	1960	3.75	7.50	15.00
❏ 142	Because They're Young/Tears in My Eyes	1960	3.75	7.50	15.00
❏ 142 [PS]	Because They're Young/Tears in My Eyes	1960	7.50	15.00	30.00
❏ 145	P.S. I Love You/Traveling Down a Lonesome Road	1960	3.75	7.50	15.00
❏ 155	How Sweet You Are/All the Young Men	1960	3.75	7.50	15.00
❏ 168	Man About Town/Come On My Love	1960	3.75	7.50	15.00
❏ 181	Walking My Baby Back Home/Goodbye My Lady	1960	3.75	7.50	15.00
—Colpix 102-181 by "Jimmy Darren"					
❏ 185	Fool's Paradise/Gotta Have Love	1961	3.75	7.50	15.00
❏ 189	Gidget Goes Hawaiian/Wild About the Girl	1961	3.75	7.50	15.00
❏ 194	Hand in Hand/Are My Dream	1961	3.75	7.50	15.00
❏ 609	Goodbye Cruel World/Valerie	1961	3.75	7.50	15.00
❏ 609 [PS]	Goodbye Cruel World/Valerie	1961	6.25	12.50	25.00
❏ 622	Her Royal Majesty/If I Could Only Tell You	1962	3.00	6.00	12.00
❏ 630	Conscience/Dream Big	1962	3.00	6.00	12.00
❏ 644	Mary's Little Lamb/The Life of the Party	1962	3.00	6.00	12.00
❏ 655	Hail to the Conquering Hero/Too Young to Go Steady	1962	3.00	6.00	12.00
❏ 664	Hear What I Want to Hear/I'll Be Loving You	1962	3.00	6.00	12.00
❏ 672	Pin a Medal on Joey/Diamond Head	1963	3.00	6.00	12.00
❏ 685	They Should Have Given You the Oscar/Blame It on My Youth	1963	3.00	6.00	12.00
❏ 696	Gegetta/Grande Luna, Italiana	1963	3.00	6.00	12.00
❏ 708	Under the Yum Yum Tree/Backstage	1963	3.00	6.00	12.00
❏ 758	Punch and Judy/Just Think of Tonight	1964	5.00	10.00	20.00
❏ 765	A Married Man/Baby, Talk to Me	1964	2.50	5.00	10.00
KIRSHNER					
❏ 63-1012	I Think Somebody Loves Me/Ain't Been Home in a Long Time	1970	—	2.50	5.00
❏ 63-5013	Bring Me Down Slow/More and More	1971	—	2.50	5.00
❏ 63-5015	Mammy Blue/As Long As You Love Me	1971	—	2.50	5.00
❏ 63-5025	Brian's Song/Thnak Heaven for Little Girls	1973	—	2.50	5.00
MGM					
❏ 14558	Let the Heartaches Begin/Sad Song	1973	—	2.00	4.00
❏ 14667	Sad-Eyed Romany Woman/Stay	1973	—	2.00	4.00
PRIVATE STOCK					
❏ 45,050	Love on the Screen/Losing You	1975	—	2.00	4.00
❏ 45,064	One Has My Name, The Other Has My Heart/Sleepin' in a Bed of Lies	1975	—	2.00	4.00
❏ 45,136	You Take My Heart Away/You Take My Heart Away (Disco)	1977	—	2.00	4.00
❏ 45,152 [DJ]	Only a Dream Away (mono/stereo)	1977	—	2.50	5.00
—Stock copies may not exist					
RCA					
❏ PB-11316	Let Me Take You in My Arms Again/California	1978	—	2.00	4.00
❏ PB-11419	Next Time/Something Like Nothing Before	1978	—	2.00	4.00
WARNER BROS.					
❏ 5648	Because You're Mine/Millions of Roses	1965	2.00	4.00	8.00
❏ 5689	I Want to Be Lonely/Tom Hawk	1966	2.00	4.00	8.00
❏ 5812	Where Did We Go Wrong/Counting the Cracks	1966	2.00	4.00	8.00
❏ 5838	Crazy Me/They Don't Know	1966	2.00	4.00	8.00
❏ 5856	Love Is Where You Find It/(Let's Worry About) Tomorrow Tomorrow	1966	2.00	4.00	8.00
❏ 5874	All/Misty Morning Eyes	1966	2.00	4.00	8.00
❏ 7013	I Miss You So/Since I Don't Have You	1967	2.00	4.00	8.00
❏ 7053	Didn't We/Counting the Cracks	1967	2.00	4.00	8.00
❏ 7071	The House Song/They Don't Know	1967	2.00	4.00	8.00
❏ 7152	Cherie/Wait Until Dark	1967	2.00	4.00	8.00
❏ 7206	A Little Bit of Heaven/Each and Every Part of Me	1968	2.00	4.00	8.00
Albums					
COLPIX					
❏ CP-406 [M]	James Darren (Album No. 1)	1960	10.00	20.00	40.00
—Black vinyl					
❏ CP-406 [M]	James Darren (Album No. 1)	1960	37.50	75.00	150.00
—Green vinyl					
❏ CP-418 [M]	Gidget Goes Hawaiian (James Darren Sings the Movies)	1961	7.50	15.00	30.00
❏ SCP-418 [S]	Gidget Goes Hawaiian (James Darren Sings the Movies)	1961	10.00	20.00	40.00
❏ CP-424 [M]	James Darren Sings for All Sizes	1962	7.50	15.00	30.00
❏ SCP-424 [S]	James Darren Sings for All Sizes	1962	10.00	20.00	40.00
❏ CP-428 [M]	Love Among the Young	1962	7.50	15.00	30.00
❏ SCP-428 [S]	Love Among the Young	1962	10.00	20.00	40.00
KIRSHNER					
❏ KES-115	Mammy Blue	1971	3.75	7.50	15.00
❏ KES-116	Love Songs from the Movies	1972	3.75	7.50	15.00
WARNER BROS.					
❏ W 1668 [M]	James Darren/All	1967	3.75	7.50	15.00
❏ WS 1668 [S]	James Darren/All	1967	5.00	10.00	20.00
DARREN, JAMES/ SHELLEY FABARES/PAUL PETERSEN					
Albums					
COLPIX					
❏ CP-444 [M]	Teenage Triangle	1963	10.00	20.00	40.00
❏ SCP-444 [R]	Teenage Triangle	1963	10.00	20.00	40.00
❏ CP-468 [M]	More Teenage Triangle	1964	10.00	20.00	40.00
❏ SCP-468 [P]	More Teenage Triangle	1964	15.00	30.00	60.00

Number	Title (A Side/B Side)	Yr	VG	VG+	NM
DARTELLS, THE					
45s					
ARLEN					
❑ 509	Hot Pastrami/Dartell Stomp	1963	6.25	12.50	25.00
❑ 513	Dance, Everybody, Dance/The Scoobie Song	1963	6.25	12.50	25.00
DOT					
❑ 16453	Hot Pastrami/Dartell Stomp	1963	5.00	10.00	20.00
❑ 16502	Dance, Everybody, Dance/The Scoobie Song	1963	5.00	10.00	20.00
❑ 16551	Convicted/Sweet Pea	1963	3.75	7.50	15.00
❑ 16646	Swiss Cheese/Dartell Stomp	1964	3.75	7.50	15.00
HANNA-BARBERA					
❑ 457	Clap Your Hands/Where Do We Stand	1965	3.75	7.50	15.00
SANDE					
❑ 103	The Girl Can't Help It/Stranger on the Shore	1964	7.50	15.00	30.00
Albums					
DOT					
❑ DLP-3522 [M]	Hot Pastrami	1963	7.50	15.00	30.00
❑ DLP-25522 [S]	Hot Pastrami	1963	10.00	20.00	40.00
DARTS, THE					
Albums					
DEL-FI					
❑ DFLP-1244 [M]	Hollywood Drag	1963	10.00	20.00	40.00
❑ DFST-1244 [S]	Hollywood Drag	1963	12.50	25.00	50.00
DARVELL, BARRY					
45s					
ATLANTIC					
❑ 2128	Lost Love/Silver Dollar	1961	5.00	10.00	20.00
❑ 2138	Adam and Eve/A King for Tonight	1962	5.00	10.00	20.00
COLT 45					
❑ 104	Teenage Love/(B-side unknown)	1959	5.00	10.00	20.00
❑ 107	Geronimo Stomp/How Will It End	1959	15.00	30.00	60.00
❑ 110	Butterfly Baby/Send Me Some Loving	1960	6.25	12.50	25.00
❑ 301	Run Little Billy/All I Need Is You	1961	5.00	10.00	20.00
COLUMBIA					
❑ 44197	My World of Make Believe/Beggar's Paradise	1967	2.00	4.00	8.00
CUB					
❑ 9088	Little Angel Lost/Fountain of Love	1961	5.00	10.00	20.00
PROVIDENCE					
❑ 404	When You're Alone/It's Rainin', It's Pourin'	1964	3.00	6.00	12.00
WORLD ARTISTS					
❑ 1042	I'll Remember/Where Is the Love for Me	1965	3.00	6.00	12.00
❑ 1058	I Found a Daisy (in the City)/Kissable Lips	1965	3.00	6.00	12.00
DASH, JULIAN					
45s					
VEE JAY					
❑ 144	Zero/Rhythm Punch	1955	12.50	25.00	50.00
DASHIEL, BUD, AND THE KINSMEN					
45s					
WARNER BROS.					
❑ 5231	Pom Pa Lum/I Talk to the Trees	1961	2.50	5.00	10.00
❑ 5276	In Tarrytown/Big Manuel	1962	2.50	5.00	10.00
Albums					
WARNER BROS.					
❑ W 1429 [M]	Folk Music in a Contemporary Manner	1961	6.25	12.50	25.00
❑ WS 1429 [S]	Folk Music in a Contemporary Manner	1961	7.50	15.00	30.00
❑ W 1432 [M]	Live Concert Extraordinaire — Bud Dashiel and the Kinsmen Sing Everybody's Hits	1961	6.25	12.50	25.00
❑ WS 1432 [S]	Live Concert Extraordinaire — Bud Dashiel and the Kinsmen Sing Everybody's Hits	1961	7.50	15.00	30.00
DATE WITH SOUL, A See HALE AND THE HUSHABYES.					
DAUGHTERS OF ALBION, THE					
45s					
FONTANA					
❑ 1619	Well Wired/The Story of Sad	1968	2.50	5.00	10.00
Albums					
FONTANA					
❑ SRF-67586	The Daughters of Albion	1968	5.00	10.00	20.00
DAVE AND THE CARDIGANS					
45s					
BAY					
❑ 216	My Falling Star/Cha Cha Baby	1963	50.00	100.00	200.00
DAVE AND THE MARKSMEN With Dave Marks, former member of THE BEACH BOYS.					
45s					
A&M					
❑ 730	Cruisin'/Kustom Kar Show	1964	12.50	25.00	50.00
WARNER BROS.					
❑ 5485	I Wanna Cry/I Could Make You Mine	1964	7.50	15.00	30.00
WESTCO					
❑ 10	Down the Tubes/Ooh Poo Pa Doo	1963	12.50	25.00	50.00
—Black vinyl					
❑ 10	Down the Tubes/Ooh Poo Pa Doo	1963	25.00	50.00	100.00
—Yellow vinyl					
DAVE DEE, DOZY, BEAKY, MICK & TICH					
45s					
ATLANTIC					
❑ 89757 [DJ]	Staying With It (same on both sides)	1983	—	2.50	5.00
—May be promo only					
BELL					
❑ 905	Kelly/Annabella	1970	—	3.00	6.00
—As "Dave Dee"					
❑ 942	Frisco Annie/Hey! Mr. President	1970	—	3.00	6.00
—As "D.B.M. & T."					
COTILLION					
❑ 44061	Bad News/Tonight-Today	1970	—	3.00	6.00
—As "Dozy, Beaky, Mick & Tich"					
❑ 44061 [PS]	Bad News/Tonight-Today	1970	2.50	5.00	10.00
—As "Dozy, Beaky, Mick & Tich"					

Number	Title (A Side/B Side)	Yr	VG	VG+	NM
FONTANA					
❑ 1537	You Make It Move/No Time	1965	2.50	5.00	10.00
❑ 1545	Hold Tight/You Know What I Want	1966	2.50	5.00	10.00
❑ 1553	Hideaway/Here's a Heart	1966	2.50	5.00	10.00
❑ 1559	Bend It/She's So Good	1966	3.00	6.00	12.00
—With "clean" lyrics that refer to a dance (starts "Bend it, bend it, show me you can move and do the dance that's really in the groove"); matrix number of "Bend It" is YW1-38890					
❑ 1559	Bend It/She's So Good	1966	5.00	10.00	20.00
—With "dirty" lyrics that don't mention a dance (starts "Bend it, bend it, just a little bit and take it easy, show you're likin' it"); matrix number of "Bend It" is YW1-39024					
❑ 1569	Save Me/Shame	1967	2.50	5.00	10.00
❑ 1591	Okay/Master Llewellyn	1967	2.50	5.00	10.00
IMPERIAL					
❑ 66270	Zabadak/The Sun Goes Down	1968	2.50	5.00	10.00
❑ 66287	Legend of Xanadu/Please	1968	2.00	4.00	8.00
❑ 66309	Break Out/Mrs. Thursday	1968	2.00	4.00	8.00
❑ 66325	Break Out/Mrs. Thursday	1968	2.00	4.00	8.00
❑ 66339	Wreck of the Antoinette/Margarita Linman	1968	2.00	4.00	8.00
Albums					
FONTANA					
❑ MGF-27567 [M]	Greatest Hits	1967	7.50	15.00	30.00
❑ SRF-67567 [P]	Greatest Hits	1967	10.00	20.00	40.00
—"Bend It" and "Hold Tight" are rechanneled.					
IMPERIAL					
❑ LP-12402 [P]	Time to Take Off	1968	10.00	20.00	40.00
—"Zabadak" is rechanneled.					
DAVENPORT SISTERS, THE					
45s					
TRI-PHI					
❑ 1008	You've Got Me Crying Again/Hoy Hoy	1962	15.00	30.00	60.00
DAVEY AND THE BADMEN					
Albums					
GOTHIC					
❑ KRW-054	Wanted	1963	50.00	100.00	200.00
DAVI					
45s					
SPARK					
❑ 110	Reason for Love/Go, Charley, Go	1962	75.00	150.00	300.00
DAVID, THE					
45s					
20TH CENTURY FOX					
❑ 6663	40 Miles/Bus Token	1966	7.50	15.00	30.00
V.M.C.					
❑ 716	I'm Not Alone/(B-side unknown)	1968	6.25	12.50	25.00
Albums					
V.M.C.					
❑ 124	Another Day, Another Lifetime	1968	25.00	50.00	100.00
DAVID AND JONATHAN					
45s					
AMY					
❑ 11012	Softly Whispering I Love You/Something's Gotten Hold of My Heart	1968	—	3.00	6.00
CAPITOL					
❑ 5563	Michelle/How Bitter the Taste of Love	1965	2.50	5.00	10.00
❑ 5625	I Know/Speak Her Name	1966	2.00	4.00	8.00
❑ 5625 [PS]	I Know/Speak Her Name	1966	3.00	6.00	12.00
❑ 5700	On My Word/Lovers of the World, Unite	1966	2.00	4.00	8.00
❑ 5777	The Magic Book/Time	1966	2.00	4.00	8.00
❑ 5870	Ten Stories High/Looking for My Life	1967	2.00	4.00	8.00
❑ 5934	She's Leaving Home/One Born Every Minute	1967	2.00	4.00	8.00
20TH FOX					
❑ 6641	Modesty/Willie Waltz	1966	2.00	4.00	8.00
Albums					
CAPITOL					
❑ ST 2473 [S]	Michelle	1966	5.00	10.00	20.00
❑ T 2473 [M]	Michelle	1966	3.75	7.50	15.00
DAVIDSON, JOHN					
45s					
COLUMBIA					
❑ 43531	I Can't Help This Feeling I Feel/I Still Send Her Flowers	1966	—	3.00	6.00
❑ 43635	Summer Love/I'll Try Lovin' You Less	1966	—	3.00	6.00
❑ 44005	Daydream/I'll Always Remember	1967	—	3.00	6.00
❑ 44005 [PS]	Daydream/I'll Always Remember	1967	2.00	4.00	8.00
❑ 44210	In the Sunshine Days/If You Can Put That in a Bottle	1967	—	3.00	6.00
❑ 44334	What Is a Woman/How Come You Love Me Like You Do	1967	—	3.00	6.00
❑ 44478	Visions of Sugarplums/Flame	1968	—	3.00	6.00
❑ 44770	Words/The Wonder of You	1969	—	3.00	6.00
❑ 44896	California Blood Lines/I Am Now	1969	—	3.00	6.00
❑ 45034	It's Such a Lovely Time of Year/What Makes a Woman Run	1969	—	3.00	6.00
❑ 45155	Five O'Clock Shadow/A Promise and a Lie	1970	—	2.50	5.00
❑ 45196	I Got Love/Politician	1970	—	2.50	5.00
❑ 45254	Let's Get Lost In Now/What You're Doing to Me	1970	—	2.50	5.00
❑ 45423	Say It Again/Just Magic	1971	—	2.50	5.00
❑ 45486	Good Times/A Clown Never Cries	1971	—	2.50	5.00
MERCURY					
❑ 73362	As Lonely As You/What She Left of Me	1973	—	2.50	5.00
20TH CENTURY					
❑ 2063	We Had It All/I Want to Spend My Life with You	1973	—	2.00	4.00
❑ 2121	Have a Nice Day/Less Than the Sun	1974	—	2.00	4.00
❑ 2175	The Other Woman/What Will I Tell the Kids	1975	—	2.00	4.00
❑ 2293	Everytime I Sing a Love Song/Love in the Shadows	1976	—	2.00	4.00
❑ 2313	I Let You Walk Away/Steal Her Away	1976	—	2.00	4.00
❑ 2326	Patch It Up/Save the Last Dance for Me	1976	—	2.00	4.00

Number	Title (A Side/B Side)	Yr	VG	VG+	NM

Albums
ACCORD

Number	Title (A Side/B Side)	Yr	VG	VG+	NM
❏ SN-7202	Closeup	1981	2.00	4.00	8.00

COLPIX

| ❏ CP-485 [M] | The Young Warm Sound of John Davidson | 1964 | 3.75 | 7.50 | 15.00 |
| ❏ SCP-485 [S] | The Young Warm Sound of John Davidson | 1964 | 5.00 | 10.00 | 20.00 |

COLUMBIA

❏ CL 2580 [M]	The Time of My Life	1966	2.50	5.00	10.00
❏ CL 2648 [M]	My Best to You	1967	2.50	5.00	10.00
❏ CL 2734 [M]	A Kind of Hush	1967	2.50	5.00	10.00
❏ CS 9380 [S]	The Time of My Life	1966	3.00	6.00	12.00
❏ CS 9448 [S]	My Best to You	1967	3.00	6.00	12.00
❏ CS 9534 [S]	A Kind of Hush	1967	3.00	6.00	12.00
❏ CS 9654	Goin' Places	1968	2.50	5.00	10.00
❏ CS 9795	John Davidson	1969	2.50	5.00	10.00
❏ CS 9859	My Cherie Amour	1969	2.50	5.00	10.00
❏ CS 9864	My Christmas Favorites	1969	3.00	6.00	12.00
❏ C 30098	Everything Is Beautiful	1970	2.50	5.00	10.00
❏ PC 36956	Incredible	1981	2.00	4.00	8.00

MERCURY

| ❏ SRM-1-658 | Well, Here I Am | 1973 | 2.50 | 5.00 | 10.00 |

20TH CENTURY

| ❏ T-429 | Touch Me | 1974 | 2.50 | 5.00 | 10.00 |
| ❏ T-512 | Every Time I Sing | 1976 | 2.50 | 5.00 | 10.00 |

DAVIE, HUTCH
45s
ATCO

❏ 6110	Woodchopper's Ball/Honky Tonk Train	1958	3.00	6.00	12.00
❏ 6123	In the Mood/Gwendolyn and the Werewolf	1958	3.00	6.00	12.00
❏ 6136	Begin the Beguine/The Dipsy Doodle	1959	3.00	6.00	12.00
❏ 6149	Sweet Georgia Brown/Heartaches	1959	3.00	6.00	12.00

CANADIAN AMERICAN

| ❏ 126 | The Glow Worm/Down Home | 1961 | 2.50 | 5.00 | 10.00 |

CLARIDGE

| ❏ 311 | East Is East (Part 1)/East Is East (Part 2) | 1966 | 2.00 | 4.00 | 8.00 |

CONGRESS

| ❏ 102 | But I Do/Time Was | 1962 | 2.50 | 5.00 | 10.00 |

DYNO VOICE

| ❏ 904 | Never My Love/A Lover's Concerto | 1968 | — | 3.00 | 6.00 |

NEW VOICE

| ❏ 823 | Swingin' Shepherd Blues/Salty | 1967 | — | 3.00 | 6.00 |

Albums
ATCO

| ❏ 33-105 [M] | Much Hutch | 1958 | 12.50 | 25.00 | 50.00 |

DAVIES, CYRIL
45s
DOT

| ❏ 16515 | Chicago Calling/Country Line Special | 1963 | 3.00 | 6.00 | 12.00 |

DAVIES, DAVE   Also see THE KINKS.
45s
RCA

❏ PB-12089	Imagination's Real/Wild Man	1980	2.50	5.00	10.00
❏ PB-12089 [PS]	Imagination's Real/Wild Man	1980	3.75	7.50	15.00
❏ PB-12147	Doing the Best for You/Got No More to Lose	1981	2.50	5.00	10.00

REPRISE

| ❏ 0614 | Death of a Clown/Love Me Till the Sun Shines | 1967 | 10.00 | 20.00 | 40.00 |
| ❏ 0660 | Suzannah's Still Alive/Funny Face | 1968 | 10.00 | 20.00 | 40.00 |

WARNER BROS.

❏ 29425	Mean Disposition/Cold Winter	1983	12.50	25.00	50.00
❏ 29425 [DJ]	Mean Disposition (same on both sides)	1983	2.50	5.00	10.00
❏ 29509	Love Gets You/One Night with You	1983	12.50	25.00	50.00
❏ 29509 [DJ]	Love Gets You (same on both sides)	1983	2.50	5.00	10.00

Albums
RCA VICTOR

| ❏ AFL1-3603 | AFL1-3603 | 1980 | 2.50 | 5.00 | 10.00 |
| ❏ AFL1-4036 | Glamour | 1981 | 2.50 | 5.00 | 10.00 |

WARNER BROS.

| ❏ 23917 | Chosen People | 1983 | 2.50 | 5.00 | 10.00 |

DAVIS, ANDREA   See MINNIE RIPERTON.

DAVIS, BILLIE
45s
JERDEN

| ❏ 758 | Last One to Be Loved/You Don't Know | 1965 | 2.50 | 5.00 | 10.00 |
| ❏ 772 | No Other Baby/Hands Off | 1965 | 2.50 | 5.00 | 10.00 |

LONDON

❏ 20041	I Want You to Be My Baby/Suffer	1968	—	3.00	6.00
❏ 20049	I Can Remember/I'll Come Home	1968	—	3.00	6.00
❏ 20062	There Must Be a Reason/Love	1971	—	2.50	5.00

DAVIS, BILLY
45s
COBBLESTONE

| ❏ 731 | Stanky (Get Funky)/I've Tried | 1969 | — | 3.00 | 6.00 |

HI

| ❏ 2146 | It's All Over/Once in a Lifetime | 1968 | — | 3.00 | 6.00 |

DAVIS, BILLY, JR.   Also see THE FIFTH DIMENSION.
45s
ABC

| ❏ 12106 | Three Steps from True Love/Light a Candle | 1975 | — | 2.50 | 5.00 |

DAVIS, BO
45s
CREST

| ❏ 1027 | Let's Coast Awhile/Drownin' All My Sorrows | 1956 | 37.50 | 75.00 | 150.00 |

—Eddie Cochran plays guitar on this record.

DAVIS, DANNY, AND THE NASHVILLE BRASS   Also includes Danny Davis credited alone. Also see HANK LOCKLIN.
45s
HICKORY

Number	Title (A Side/B Side)	Yr	VG	VG+	NM
❏ 1005	Can't You Feel It in Your Heart/Second Hand Dreams for Sale	1954	3.00	6.00	12.00

JAROCO

| ❏ 8742 | Green Eyes (Cryin' Those Blue Tears)/Little Pink Cloud | 1987 | — | 2.50 | 5.00 |

LIBERTY

| ❏ 55213 | Beauty and the Beast/Glory Bugle | 1959 | 2.50 | 5.00 | 10.00 |

MGM

❏ 11103	Crazy Heart/I'm Not Alone	1951	3.75	7.50	15.00
❏ 11175	Please Bring Back the Sunshine/Deep Water	1952	3.75	7.50	15.00
❏ 11244	Always/Do You Ever Think of Me	1952	3.75	7.50	15.00
❏ 11286	Forget/Love Came Out of the Night	1952	3.75	7.50	15.00
❏ 11443	I Don't Want Your Kisses/Come to the Wedding	1953	3.75	7.50	15.00
❏ 13077	Pots 'N' Pans/Travelin' Trumpets	1962	2.00	4.00	8.00
❏ 13106	Little Bandits of Juarez/Theme from "Kill Or Cure"	1962	2.00	4.00	8.00
❏ 13270	Circus World/There Goes My Heart	1964	—	3.00	6.00
❏ 13295	Night Train from Jamaica/Ska Dee Wah	1964	—	3.00	6.00

—With Byron Lee

| ❏ 13368 | Ballad of Cat Ballou/Theme from "The Saint" | 1965 | — | 3.00 | 6.00 |
| ❏ 13374 | I'm Henry VIII, I Am/The End of the World | 1965 | — | 3.00 | 6.00 |

RCA

❏ PB-10871	Country Disco/Disco Dante	1977	—	2.00	4.00
❏ PB-11073	How I Love Them Old Songs/Tara Jeanne	1977	—	2.00	4.00
❏ PB-11278	Old Fashioned Love Song/Falsely Accused	1978	—	2.00	4.00
❏ PB-11466	Sugarfoot Rag/Let Your Lovelight Shine	1979	—	2.00	4.00
❏ PB-11612	Ain't Misbehavin'/I'm Gonna Sit Right Down and Write Myself a Letter	1979	—	2.00	4.00
❏ PB-12070	Cotton Eyed Joe/Colinda	1980	—	2.00	4.00

RCA VICTOR

❏ 47-9785	Wabash Cannon Ball/Sweet Dreams	1969	—	2.00	4.00
❏ 47-9847	Columbus Stockade Blues/Wings of a Dove	1970	—	2.00	4.00
❏ 47-9905	Down Yonder/May the Circle Be Unbroken	1970	—	2.00	4.00
❏ 47-9936	Jingling Brass/Silent Night	1970	—	3.00	6.00
❏ 47-9936 [DJ]	Jingling Brass/Silent Night	1970	—	3.00	6.00

—Promos available on either yellow or green labels

❏ 74-0439	I Can't Stop Loving You/Rose Garden	1971	—	2.00	4.00
❏ 74-0506	Highland Brass/Ruby, Don't Take Your Love to Town	1971	—	2.00	4.00
❏ 74-0560	Wait for the Light to Shine/Blue Bayou	1971	—	2.00	4.00
❏ 74-0649	Java/Flowers on the Wall	1972	—	2.00	4.00
❏ 74-0760	From Dixie with Love/Under the Double Eagle	1972	—	2.00	4.00
❏ 74-0847	I'll Fly Away/Woman	1972	—	2.00	4.00
❏ 74-0858	White Christmas/Winter Wonderland	1972	—	2.50	5.00
❏ APBO-0019	Superstar/Come See Us	1973	—	2.00	4.00
❏ APBO-0301	Ruby, Are You Mad at Your Man/Rollin' in My Sweet Baby's Arms	1974	—	2.00	4.00
❏ PB-10232	Singing the Blues/Stay a Little Longer	1975	—	2.00	4.00
❏ PB-10255	Branigan/Peppy Time Tune	1975	—	2.00	4.00
❏ PB-10375	Running Bear/Nashville Brass Hoedown	1975	—	2.00	4.00
❏ PB-10570	Paloma Blanca/Nashville Express	1976	—	2.00	4.00
❏ PB-10814	Why Don't You Love Me/He'll Have to Go	1976	—	2.00	4.00

VERVE

| ❏ 10233 | Theme from "Carnival"/Stardust | 1961 | 2.50 | 5.00 | 10.00 |

WARTRACE

| ❏ 730 | I Dropped Your Name/(B-side unknown) | 1985 | — | 2.00 | 4.00 |

Albums
PICKWICK

| ❏ ACL-7034 | Down Yonder | 197? | 2.00 | 4.00 | 8.00 |
| ❏ ACL-7048 | Super Country | 1977 | 2.00 | 4.00 | 8.00 |

RCA SPECIAL PRODUCTS

| ❏ DPL1-0176 | America 200 Years Young | 1976 | 3.75 | 7.50 | 15.00 |

—Available only at Amana dealers

RCA VICTOR

❏ APD1-0034 [Q]	Travelin'	1973	3.00	6.00	12.00
❏ APD1-0232 [Q]	Caribbean Cruise	1973	3.75	7.50	15.00
❏ APL1-0232	Caribbean Cruise	1973	2.50	5.00	10.00
❏ APL1-0425	The Best of Danny Davis and the Nashville Brass	1973	2.50	5.00	10.00
❏ APD1-0565 [Q]	Bluegrass Country	1974	3.75	7.50	15.00
❏ APL1-0565	Bluegrass Country	1974	2.50	5.00	10.00
❏ APD1-0774 [Q]	The Latest and Greatest	1974	3.75	7.50	15.00
❏ APL1-0774	The Latest and Greatest	1974	2.50	5.00	10.00
❏ ANL1-0902	Orange Blossom Special	1974	2.50	5.00	10.00
❏ APD1-1043 [Q]	Dream Country	1975	3.00	6.00	12.00
❏ APL1-1043	Dream Country	1975	2.50	5.00	10.00
❏ APD1-1240 [Q]	Gold	1975	3.00	6.00	12.00
❏ APL1-1240	Gold	1975	2.50	5.00	10.00
❏ APD1-1578 [Q]	Texas	1976	3.00	6.00	12.00
❏ APL1-1578	Texas	1976	2.50	5.00	10.00
❏ ANL1-1930	Christmas with Danny Davis and the Nashville Brass	1976	2.00	4.00	8.00

—Reissue of LSP-4377

❏ APL1-1986	Super	1976	2.50	5.00	10.00
❏ APL1-2310	Live Vegas	1977	2.50	5.00	10.00
❏ APL1-2721	How I Love Them Ol' Songs	1977	2.50	5.00	10.00
❏ APL1-2980	Cookin' Country	1978	2.50	5.00	10.00
❏ AHL1-3415	Great Songs of the Big Band Era	1979	2.50	5.00	10.00
❏ AHL1-4022	Cotton Eyed Joe	1981	2.50	5.00	10.00
❏ LSP-4059	The Nashville Sound	1969	2.50	5.00	10.00
❏ LSP-4176	More Nashville Sounds	1969	2.50	5.00	10.00
❏ LSP-4232	Movin' On	1969	2.50	5.00	10.00
❏ LSP-4334	You Ain't Heard Nothin' Yet	1970	2.50	5.00	10.00
❏ LSP-4377	Christmas with Danny Davis and the Nashville Brass	1970	2.50	5.00	10.00
❏ LSP-4424	Down Homers	1970	2.50	5.00	10.00
❏ LSP-4475	Somethin' Else	1971	2.50	5.00	10.00
❏ LSP-4571	Super Country	1971	2.50	5.00	10.00
❏ LSP-4627	Turns to Gold	1972	2.50	5.00	10.00
❏ LSP-4720	Live — In Person	1972	2.50	5.00	10.00
❏ LSP-4803	Turn On Some Happy!	1972	2.50	5.00	10.00

Number	Title (A Side/B Side)	Yr	VG	VG+	NM
DAVIS, DANNY, AND WILLIE NELSON Also see each artist's individual listings.					
45s					
RCA					
❑ PB-11893	Night Life/December Day	1980	—	2.00	4.00
❑ PB-11999	Funny How Time Slips Away/The Local Memory	1980	—	2.00	4.00
DAVIS, EUNICE					
45s					
ATLANTIC					
❑ 992	Go to Work Pretty Daddy/My Beat Is 125th Street	1953	15.00	30.00	60.00
CORAL					
❑ 65075	Work Daddy Work/What Do You Want	1952	5.00	10.00	20.00
DELUXE					
❑ 6068	Get Your Enjoys/24 Hours a Day	1954	7.50	15.00	30.00
DERBY					
❑ 760	Evening Train/I'm a Wild West Woman	1951	7.50	15.00	30.00
❑ 768	Good News for You Baby/Tell Me I'm the Baby	1951	7.50	15.00	30.00
GRAND					
❑ 130	Let's Have a Party/Every Time Your Lips Meet Mine	1955	5.00	10.00	20.00
DAVIS, HAL					
45s					
ALDEN					
❑ 1301	My Young Heart/(B-side unknown)	1959	10.00	20.00	40.00
❑ 1303	King of Lovers/(B-side unknown)	1959	10.00	20.00	40.00
DEL-FI					
❑ 4146	You're Playing with Me/Read the Book of Love	1960	7.50	15.00	30.00
DYNAMITE					
❑ 1010	I Don't Want Nobody/(B-side unknown)	195?	50.00	100.00	200.00
FEDERAL					
❑ 12429	My Only Flower/You're the Girl	1961	3.00	6.00	12.00
GARDENA					
❑ 125	One More Chance/Show Me	1962	7.50	15.00	30.00
GSP					
❑ 2	I Don't Know/Lover's Plan	1963	7.50	15.00	30.00
KELLEY					
❑ 105	Way to My Heart/(B-side unknown)	196?	25.00	50.00	100.00
—Red vinyl					
MINASA					
❑ 6714	It's You/(B-side unknown)	196?	7.50	15.00	30.00
MJC					
❑ 104	You'll Find Love/(B-side unknown)	196?	7.50	15.00	30.00
VEE JAY					
❑ 387	Merchant of Love/What Do You Mean to Me	1961	5.00	10.00	20.00
WIZARD					
❑ 101	Merchant of Love/What Do You Mean to Me	1961	17.50	35.00	70.00
❑ 102	I Need Someone/(B-side unknown)	1961	7.50	15.00	30.00
DAVIS, JAN					
45s					
A&M					
❑ 733	Boss Machine/The Fugitive	1964	3.75	7.50	15.00
❑ 744	Guitar Star/The Unwanted	1964	3.75	7.50	15.00
ALJO					
❑ 104	The Surfin' Matador/Scramble	1964	7.50	15.00	30.00
BEAR					
❑ 1000	Hornet's Nest/Flamenco Funk (Mosaic)	1969	—	3.00	6.00
BIG BIRD					
❑ 128	International Love Process (Part 1)/International Love Process (Part 2)	1967	3.75	7.50	15.00
COLUMBIA					
❑ 43224	More (Theme from Mondo Cane)/Mystique	1965	3.75	7.50	15.00
DIRECT HIT					
❑ 1002	Raunchy 1970/Dark Blue	1970	—	3.00	6.00
HOLIDAY					
❑ 1213	Pooky/Watusi Zombie	1964	3.75	7.50	15.00
QUAD-ETT					
❑ 10039	Hot Sauce/Soul Mate	1974	—	2.50	5.00
RANWOOD					
❑ 1015	Hot Sauce/Soulmate	1974	—	2.50	5.00
❑ 1023	Gypsy Fox/Child of June (Danny's Theme)	1974	—	2.50	5.00
❑ 1035	El Lobo/Maiden Spain	1975	—	2.50	5.00
RCA VICTOR					
❑ 47-9018	Time Tunnel/Walkin' Back	1966	3.00	6.00	12.00
❑ 47-9923	Raunchy 1970/Dark Blue	1970	—	2.50	5.00
RENDEZVOUS					
❑ 131	Sleepless/Damascus	1960	5.00	10.00	20.00
—With the Ricco-Shays					
❑ 149	Sabre Dance/Hop, Skip and Jump	1961	5.00	10.00	20.00
❑ 205	Malaguena/Hop, Skip and Jump	1963	5.00	10.00	20.00
❑ 214	You're Not Welcome (Anymore)/Don't Walk Away	1963	7.50	15.00	30.00
❑ 218	Delicado/Sahara	1963	5.00	10.00	20.00
SHAMLEY					
❑ 44016	Hornet's Nest/Flamenco Funk (Mosaic)	1969	—	2.50	5.00
SMASH					
❑ 1863	The Snow Surfin' Matador/Scramble	1963	6.25	12.50	25.00
UNI					
❑ 55029	International Love Process (Part 1)/International Love Process (Part 2)	1967	2.00	4.00	8.00
❑ 55197	Walk Don't Run/Flamenco Funk	1970	—	2.50	5.00
WHITE WHALE					
❑ 226	Lost in Space/Run for Your Life	1966	3.00	6.00	12.00
DAVIS, JESSE ED					
45s					
ATCO					
❑ 6807	Every Night Is Saturday Night/Golden Sun Goddess	1971	—	2.50	5.00
❑ 6825	Reno Street Incident/Washita Love Child	1971	—	2.50	5.00
❑ 6873	Sue Me, Sue You Blues/My Captain	1972	2.00	4.00	8.00
❑ 6889	Ululu/Alcatraz	1972	—	2.50	5.00
EPIC					
❑ 11021	She's a Pain/Natural Anthem	1973	—	2.00	4.00
Albums					
ATCO					
❑ SD 33-346	Jesse Ed Davis	1970	3.75	7.50	15.00
❑ SD 33-382	Ululu	1972	3.75	7.50	15.00
EPIC					
❑ KE 32133	Keep On Comin'	1973	3.00	6.00	12.00
DAVIS, LEE					
45s					
CUB					
❑ 9026	Three Young Men/The Flower Song	1959	3.75	7.50	15.00
—B-side by the Naturals					
DAVIS, MAC					
45s					
CAPITOL					
❑ 5554	Bad Scene/I Protest	1965	2.00	4.00	8.00
CASABLANCA					
❑ 2244	It's Hard to Be Humble/Greatest Gift of All	1980	—	2.00	4.00
❑ 2286	Let's Keep It That Way/I Know You're Out There Somewhere	1980	—	—	3.00
❑ 2305	Texas in My Rear View Mirror/Sad Songs	1980	—	—	3.00
❑ 2327	Hooked On Music/Me and Fat Boy	1981	—	—	3.00
❑ 2336	Secrets/Remember When Beverly	1981	—	—	3.00
❑ 2341	You're My Bestest Friend/You Are So Lovely	1981	—	—	3.00
❑ 2346	Midnight Crazy/I Got the Hots for You	1981	—	—	3.00
❑ 2350	Rodeo Clown/Dammit Girl	1982	—	—	3.00
❑ 2355	The Beer Drinkin' Song/You Are So Lovely	1982	—	—	3.00
❑ 2363	Lying Here Lying/Quiet Times	1982	—	—	3.00
❑ 818168-7	Most of All/Springtime Down in Dixie	1984	—	—	3.00
❑ 818929-7	Caroline's Still in Georgia/I've Got a Dream	1984	—	—	3.00
COLUMBIA					
❑ 10018	Stop and Smell the Roses/Poor Boy Boogie	1974	—	2.00	4.00
❑ 10070	Rock 'n' Roll (I Gave You the Best Years of My Life)/Emily Suzanne	1974	—	2.00	4.00
❑ 10111	(If You Add) All the Love in the World/Smiley	1975	—	2.00	4.00
❑ 10148	Burnin' Thing/A Special Place in Heaven	1975	—	2.00	4.00
❑ 10187	I Still Love You (You Still Love Me)/The Hits Just Keep On Comin'	1975	—	2.00	4.00
❑ 10304	Forever Lovers/The Love Lamp	1976	—	2.00	4.00
❑ 10418	Every Now and Then/I'm Just in Love	1976	—	2.00	4.00
❑ 10535	Picking Up the Pieces of My Life/Do It (With Someone You Love)	1977	—	2.00	4.00
❑ 10745	Music in My Life/You Are	1978	—	2.00	4.00
❑ 45117	Whoever Finds This, I Love You/Half and Half	1970	—	2.50	5.00
❑ 45117 [PS]	Whoever Finds This, I Love You/Half and Half	1970	2.00	4.00	8.00
❑ 45192	I'll Paint You a Song/The Closest I Ever Came	1970	—	2.50	5.00
❑ 45245	I Believe in Music/Poor Man's Gold	1970	—	2.50	5.00
❑ 45302	Beginning to Feel the Pain/Butterfly Girl	1971	—	2.50	5.00
❑ 45355	Lucas Was a Red-Neck/Fall in Love with Your Wife	1971	—	2.50	5.00
❑ 45404	Sweet Dreams and Sarah/Poem for My Little Lady	1971	—	2.50	5.00
❑ 45456	I Believe in Music/Hollywood Humpty Dumpty	1971	—	2.50	5.00
❑ 45576	Beginning to Feel the Pain/Butterfly Girl	1972	—	2.00	4.00
❑ 45618	Baby Don't Get Hooked on Me/Poem for My Little Lady	1972	—	2.00	4.00
❑ 45727	Everybody Loves a Love Song/Friend, Lover, Woman, Wife	1972	—	2.00	4.00
❑ 45773	Dream Me Home/Spread Your Love on Me	1973	—	2.00	4.00
❑ 45839	Your Side of the Bed/(Hope You Didn't) Chop No Wood	1973	—	2.00	4.00
❑ 45911	Kiss It and Make It Better/Sunshine	1973	—	2.00	4.00
❑ 46004	One Hell of a Woman/A Poor Man's Gold	1974	—	2.00	4.00
JAMIE					
❑ 1227	I'm a Poor Loser/Let Him Try	1962	2.50	5.00	10.00
MCA					
❑ 52573	I Never Made Love (Till I Made Love to You)/I Think I'm Gonna Rain	1985	—	—	3.00
❑ 52669	I Feel the Country Callin' Me/Rainy Day Lovin'	1985	—	—	3.00
❑ 52765	Sexy Young Girl/Special Place in Heaven	1986	—	—	3.00
❑ 52826	Somewhere in America/I Need a Hug	1986	—	—	3.00
VEE JAY					
❑ 492	A Little Dutch Town/Looking at Linda	1963	2.50	5.00	10.00
Albums					
ACCORD					
❑ SN-7165	Little Touch of Love	1981	2.00	4.00	8.00
❑ SN-7189	With Love	1981	2.00	4.00	8.00
ALLEGIANCE					
❑ AV-5019	Volume XC	198?	2.00	4.00	8.00
❑ AV-5031	Losers	198?	2.00	4.00	8.00
CASABLANCA					
❑ NBLP 7207	It's Hard to Be Humble	1980	2.00	4.00	8.00
❑ NBLP 7239	Texas in My Rear View Mirror	1980	2.00	4.00	8.00
❑ NBLP 7257	Midnight Crazy	1981	2.00	4.00	8.00
❑ 822638-1	The Very Best and More	1984	2.00	4.00	8.00
COLUMBIA					
❑ CS 9969	Song Painter	1970	3.75	7.50	15.00
—Red "360 Sound" label					
❑ CS 9969	Song Painter	1974	2.50	5.00	10.00
—Orange label					
❑ C 30926	I Believe in Music	1971	2.50	5.00	10.00
❑ CQ 31770 [Q]	Baby Don't Get Hooked on Me	1972	3.75	7.50	15.00
❑ KC 31770	Baby Don't Get Hooked on Me	1972	2.50	5.00	10.00
❑ KC 32206	Mac Davis	1973	2.50	5.00	10.00
❑ CQ 32582 [Q]	Stop and Smell the Roses	1974	3.75	7.50	15.00
❑ KC 32582	Stop and Smell the Roses	1974	2.50	5.00	10.00
❑ PC 32582	Stop and Smell the Roses	1986	—	3.00	6.00
—Budget-line reissue					
❑ PC 32927	All the Love in the World	1975	2.50	5.00	10.00
❑ PCQ 32927 [Q]	All the Love in the World	1975	3.75	7.50	15.00
❑ PC 33551	Burnin' Thing	1975	2.50	5.00	10.00
❑ PC 34105	Forever Lovers	1976	2.50	5.00	10.00
❑ PCQ 34105 [Q]	Forever Lovers	1976	—	—	—
—Not released					
❑ PC 34313	Thunder in the Afternoon	1976	2.50	5.00	10.00
❑ PCQ 34313 [Q]	Thunder in the Afternoon	1976	3.75	7.50	15.00

D

Number	Title (A Side/B Side)	Yr	VG	VG+	NM
❑ JC 35284	Fantasy	1978	2.50	5.00	10.00
❑ JC 36317	Greatest Hits	1979	2.50	5.00	10.00
❑ PC 36317	Greatest Hits	198?	—	3.00	6.00
—Budget-line reissue					
❑ FC 38950	Who's Lovin' You	1983	2.00	4.00	8.00
❑ PC 38950	Who's Lovin' You	198?	—	3.00	6.00
—Budget-line reissue					
MCA					
❑ 5590	Till I Made It with You	1985	2.00	4.00	8.00
❑ 5718	Somewhere in America	1986	2.00	4.00	8.00
SPRINGBOARD					
❑ SPB-4024	Mac Davis	197?	2.00	4.00	8.00
TRIP					
❑ 9502	Mac Davis	1973	2.00	4.00	8.00

DAVIS, MAXWELL
Albums
ALADDIN

Number	Title (A Side/B Side)	Yr	VG	VG+	NM
❑ LP-709 [10]	Maxwell Davis	1955	100.00	200.00	400.00
❑ LP-804 [M]	Maxwell Davis	1956	50.00	100.00	200.00
SCORE					
❑ SLP-4106 [M]	Blue Tango	1957	50.00	100.00	200.00

DAVIS, MILES
12-Inch Singles
COLUMBIA/LEGACY

Number	Title (A Side/B Side)	Yr	VG	VG+	NM
❑ CAS 42193 [DJ]	Bitches Brew (Edit 11:32)/Spanish Key (Edit 11:50)	1999	3.75	7.50	15.00
—Red vinyl; entitled "Bitches Brew -- Singles"					

45s
BLUE NOTE

Number	Title (A Side/B Side)	Yr	VG	VG+	NM
❑ 1595	Dear Old Stockholm/Wouldn't You	195?	3.75	7.50	15.00
❑ 1596	Chance It/Yesterdays	195?	3.75	7.50	15.00
❑ 1597	Donna/The Squirrel 2nd Master	195?	3.75	7.50	15.00
❑ 1618	Enigma/Tempus Fugit	195?	3.75	7.50	15.00
❑ 1619	Ray's Idea/I Waited for You	195?	3.75	7.50	15.00
❑ 1620	Kelo/C.T.A.	195?	3.75	7.50	15.00
❑ 1633	Donna/Well You Needn't	195?	3.75	7.50	15.00
❑ 1649	Lazy Susan/Tempus Fugit	195?	3.75	7.50	15.00
❑ 1650	The Leap/Weirdo	195?	3.75	7.50	15.00
CAPITOL					
❑ F1221	Venus de Milo/Darn That Dream	1950	6.25	12.50	25.00
COLUMBIA					
❑ 38-02467	Shout/Fat Time	1981	—	2.50	5.00
❑ 38-04564	Code M.D./Decoy	1984	—	2.50	5.00
❑ 10110	Red China Blues/Maiysha	1975	—	3.00	6.00
❑ 30735 [S]	(contents unknown)	1960	3.75	7.50	15.00
❑ 30736 [S]	(contents unknown)	1960	3.75	7.50	15.00
❑ 30737 [S]	(contents unknown)	1960	3.75	7.50	15.00
❑ 30738 [S]	(contents unknown)	1960	3.75	7.50	15.00
❑ 30739 [S]	(contents unknown)	1960	3.75	7.50	15.00
❑ S7 31094 [S]	De Buzzard Song/Gone	1961	3.75	7.50	15.00
❑ S7 31095 [S]	Gone, Gone, Gone/Summertime	1961	3.75	7.50	15.00
❑ S7 31096 [S]	Bess, Oh Where's My Bess/Fishermen, Strawberries and Devil Crab	1961	3.75	7.50	15.00
❑ S7 31097 [S]	It Ain't Necessarily So/Here Comes De Honey Man	1961	3.75	7.50	15.00
❑ S7 31098 [S]	I Loves You Porgy/There's a Boat That's Leaving Soon for New York	1961	3.75	7.50	15.00
—The above five are "Stereo Seven" 33 1/3 rpm jukebox singles from set "JS 7-26" entitled "Porgy and Bess"					
❑ 31377 [S]	(contents unknown)	1962	3.75	7.50	15.00
❑ 31378 [S]	(contents unknown)	1962	3.75	7.50	15.00
❑ 31379 [S]	(contents unknown)	1962	3.75	7.50	15.00
❑ 31380 [S]	(contents unknown)	1962	3.75	7.50	15.00
❑ 31381 [S]	(contents unknown)	1962	3.75	7.50	15.00
—Anyone who can fill in these gaps -- the above 15 all are Columbia "Stereo 7" singles -- please let us know.					
❑ 42057	It Ain't Necessarily So/All Blues	1961	3.00	6.00	12.00
❑ 42069	I Loves You, Porgy/It Ain't Necessarily So	1961	3.00	6.00	12.00
❑ 42583	Slow Samba/New Rhumba	1962	3.00	6.00	12.00
❑ 42853	Seven Steps to Heaven/Devil May Care	1963	3.00	6.00	12.00
❑ 44652	Girls of Kilimanjaro/(B-side unknown)	1969	2.00	4.00	8.00
❑ 45090	Great Expectations/Little Blue Frog	1970	2.00	4.00	8.00
❑ 4-45171	Miles Runs the Voodoo Down/Spanish Key	1970	2.00	4.00	8.00
❑ 45327	Friday Miles/Saturday Miles	1971	2.00	4.00	8.00
❑ 45709	Molester/(B-side unknown)	1972	2.00	4.00	8.00
❑ 45822	Vote for Miles (Part 1)/Vote for Miles (Part 2)	1973	2.00	4.00	8.00
❑ 45946	Big Fun/Holly-Wood	1973	2.00	4.00	8.00
❑ 46074	Great Expectations/Go Ahead John	1974	2.00	4.00	8.00
PRESTIGE					
❑ 103	Green Haze (Part 1)/Green Haze (Part 2)	195?	3.75	7.50	15.00
❑ 114	A Night in Tunisia (Part 1)/ A Night in Tunisia (Part 2)	195?	3.75	7.50	15.00
❑ 123	If I Were a Bell (Part 1)/If I Were a Bell (Part 2)	195?	3.75	7.50	15.00
❑ 157	Walkin' (Part 1)/Walkin' (Part 2)	1957	3.75	7.50	15.00
❑ 165	It Never Entered My Mind (Part 1)/It Never Entered My Mind (Part 2)	1957	3.75	7.50	15.00
❑ 195	When I Fall in Love (Part 1)/ When I Fall in Love (Part 2)	195?	3.75	7.50	15.00
❑ 248	Surrey with the Fringe on Top/Diane	196?	3.75	7.50	15.00
❑ 268	S'posin'/Just Squeeze Me	196?	3.00	6.00	12.00
❑ 321	It's Only a Paper Moon/Dig	1964	3.00	6.00	12.00
❑ 353	Smooch/Valentine	196?	3.00	6.00	12.00
❑ 376	You Don't Know/That Old Devil Moon	196?	3.00	6.00	12.00
❑ 413	'Round Midnight/Airegin	196?	3.00	6.00	12.00
❑ 734	Morpheus/Blue Room	1952	5.00	10.00	20.00
❑ 742	Down/Whispering	195?	5.00	10.00	20.00
❑ 766	My Old Flame (Part 1)/My Old Flame (Part 2)	195?	5.00	10.00	20.00
❑ 777	Dig (Part 1)/Dig (Part 2)	1956	5.00	10.00	20.00
❑ 817	It's Only a Paper Moon (Part 1)/ It's Only a Paper Moon (Part 2)	195?	5.00	10.00	20.00
❑ 846	Bluing (Part 1)/Bluing (Part 2)	195?	5.00	10.00	20.00
❑ 868	Conception/Bluing 3	195?	5.00	10.00	20.00
❑ 876	Out of the Blue (Part 1)/Out of the Blue (Part 2)	195?	5.00	10.00	20.00
❑ 884	Tasty Pudding (Part 1)/Tasty Pudding (Part 2)	195?	5.00	10.00	20.00
❑ 893	Blue Haze (Part 1)/Blue Haze (Part 2)	1956	5.00	10.00	20.00
❑ 898	That Old Devil Moon/Four	195?	5.00	10.00	20.00
❑ 902	Miles Ahead/When Lights Are Low	195?	5.00	10.00	20.00
❑ 915	But Not for Me (Part 1)/But Not for Me (Part 2)	195?	5.00	10.00	20.00

7-Inch Extended Plays
CAPITOL

Number	Title (A Side/B Side)	Yr	VG	VG+	NM
❑ EAP 1-459	(contents unknown)	1954	10.00	20.00	40.00
❑ EAP 1-459	Classics in Jazz	1954	10.00	20.00	40.00

Albums
BLUE NOTE

Number	Title (A Side/B Side)	Yr	VG	VG+	NM
❑ BLP-1501 [M]	Miles Davis, Volume 1	1955	37.50	75.00	150.00
—Regular version with Lexington Ave. address on label					
❑ BLP-1501 [M]	Miles Davis, Volume 1	1955	50.00	100.00	200.00
—"Deep groove" version (deep indentation under label on both sides)					
❑ BLP-1501 [M]	Miles Davis, Volume 1	1958	12.50	25.00	50.00
—Regular version with W. 63rd St. address on label					
❑ BLP-1501 [M]	Miles Davis, Volume 1	1963	6.25	12.50	25.00
—With New York, USA address on label					
❑ BLP-1501 [M]	Miles Davis, Volume 1	1966	3.75	7.50	15.00
—With "A Division of Liberty Records" on label					
❑ BLP-1502 [M]	Miles Davis, Volume 2	1955	37.50	75.00	150.00
—Regular version with Lexington Ave. address on label					
❑ BLP-1502 [M]	Miles Davis, Volume 2	1955	50.00	100.00	200.00
—"Deep groove" version (deep indentation under label on both sides)					
❑ BLP-1502 [M]	Miles Davis, Volume 2	1958	12.50	25.00	50.00
—Regular version with W. 63rd St. address on label					
❑ BLP-1502 [M]	Miles Davis, Volume 2	1963	6.25	12.50	25.00
—With New York, USA address on label					
❑ BLP-1502 [M]	Miles Davis, Volume 2	1966	3.75	7.50	15.00
—With "A Division of Liberty Records" on label					
❑ BLP-5013 [10]	Miles Davis (Young Man with a Horn)	1952	75.00	150.00	300.00
❑ BLP-5022 [10]	Miles Davis, Vol. 2	1953	75.00	150.00	300.00
❑ BLP-5040 [10]	Miles Davis, Vol. 3	1954	75.00	150.00	300.00
❑ BLP-81501	Miles Davis, Volume 1	1968	3.00	6.00	12.00
❑ BST-81501	Miles Davis, Volume 1	1985	2.50	5.00	10.00
—Rechanneled stereo version of 1501					
❑ BLP-81502	Miles Davis, Volume 2	1968	3.00	6.00	12.00
—"The Finest in Jazz Since 1939" reissue label					
❑ BST-81502	Miles Davis, Volume 2	1985	2.50	5.00	10.00
—Rechanneled stereo version of 1502					
—"The Finest in Jazz Since 1939" reissue label					
CAPITOL					
❑ H 459 [10]	Classics in Jazz	1954	62.50	125.00	250.00
—First 33 1/3 rpm issue of some of the "Birth of the Cool" sessions					
❑ T 762 [M]	Birth of the Cool	1956	37.50	75.00	150.00
❑ DT 1974 [R]	Birth of the Cool	196?	3.00	6.00	12.00
❑ T 1974 [M]	Birth of the Cool	1963	7.50	15.00	30.00
—Reissue of 762					
❑ M-11026 [M]	The Complete Birth of the Cool	1972	3.00	6.00	12.00
❑ N-16168 [M]	Birth of the Cool	198?	2.00	4.00	8.00
—Budget-line reissue					
CHARLIE PARKER					
❑ PLP-824	Many Miles of Davis	196?	10.00	20.00	40.00
COLUMBIA					
❑ J 1	Facets	1973	3.00	6.00	12.00
❑ J 17	Miles Davis at Newport	1973	3.00	6.00	12.00
❑ C2L 20 [(2)M]	Miles Davis in Person (Friday & Saturday Nights at the Blackhawk, San Francisco)	1961	12.50	25.00	50.00
—Six "eye" logos on label					
❑ C2L 20 [(2)M]	Miles Davis in Person (Friday & Saturday Nights at the Blackhawk, San Francisco)	1963	7.50	15.00	30.00
—"Guaranteed High Fidelity" on label					
❑ C2L 20 [(2)M]	Miles Davis in Person (Friday & Saturday Nights at the Blackhawk, San Francisco)	1965	6.25	12.50	25.00
—"Mono" on label					
❑ GP 26 [(2)]	Bitches Brew	1970	3.75	7.50	15.00
—Orange labels					
❑ GP 26 [(2)]	Bitches Brew	1970	10.00	20.00	40.00
—"360 Sound Stereo" on red labels					
❑ PG 26 [(2)]	Bitches Brew	1977	3.00	6.00	12.00
—Orange labels, new prefix					
❑ C2S 820 [(2)S]	Miles Davis in Person (Friday & Saturday Nights at the Blackhawk, San Francisco)	1961	12.50	25.00	50.00
—Six "eye" logos on label					
❑ C2S 820 [(2)S]	Miles Davis in Person (Friday & Saturday Nights at the Blackhawk, San Francisco)	1963	7.50	15.00	30.00
—"360 Sound Stereo" in black on label					
❑ C2S 820 [(2)S]	Miles Davis in Person (Friday & Saturday Nights at the Blackhawk, San Francisco)	1965	6.25	12.50	25.00
—"360 Sound Stereo" in white on label					
❑ C2S 820 [(2)]	Miles Davis in Person (Friday & Saturday Nights at the Blackhawk, San Francisco)	1971	3.75	7.50	15.00
—Orange labels					
❑ CL 949 [M]	'Round About Midnight	1957	12.50	25.00	50.00
—Six "eye" logos on label					
❑ CL 949 [M]	'Round About Midnight	1963	6.25	12.50	25.00
—"Guaranteed High Fidelity" on label					
❑ CL 949 [M]	'Round About Midnight	1965	5.00	10.00	20.00
—"Mono" on label					
❑ CL 1041 [M]	Miles Ahead	1957	12.50	25.00	50.00
—Six "eye" logos on label; cover has Miles Davis blowing his trumpet					
❑ CL 1041 [M]	Miles Ahead	1957	20.00	40.00	80.00
—Six "eye" logos on label; cover has a while woman and her child on a sailboat					
❑ CL 1041 [M]	Miles Ahead	1963	6.25	12.50	25.00
—"Guaranteed High Fidelity" on label					
❑ CL 1041 [M]	Miles Ahead	1965	5.00	10.00	20.00
—"Mono" on label					
❑ CL 1193 [M]	Milestones	1958	12.50	25.00	50.00
—Six "eye" logos on label					
❑ CL 1193 [M]	Milestones	1963	6.25	12.50	25.00
—"Guaranteed High Fidelity" on label					
❑ CL 1193 [M]	Milestones	1965	5.00	10.00	20.00
—"Mono" on label					
❑ CL 1268 [M]	Jazz Track	1958	12.50	25.00	50.00
—Six "eye" logos on label; with Miles and a woman on cover					
❑ CL 1268 [M]	Jazz Track	1958	20.00	40.00	80.00
—Six "eye" logos on label; with abstract drawing on cover					

Number	Title (A Side/B Side)	Yr	VG	VG+	NM
❑ CL 1274 [M]	Porgy and Bess	1958	12.50	25.00	50.00
—Six "eye" logos on label					
❑ CL 1274 [M]	Porgy and Bess	1963	6.25	12.50	25.00
—"Guaranteed High Fidelity" on label					
❑ CL 1274 [M]	Porgy and Bess	1965	5.00	10.00	20.00
—"Mono" on label					
❑ CL 1355 [M]	Kind of Blue	1959	15.00	30.00	60.00
—Six "eye" logos on label					
❑ CL 1355 [M]	Kind of Blue	1963	6.25	12.50	25.00
—"Guaranteed High Fidelity" on label					
❑ CL 1355 [M]	Kind of Blue	1965	5.00	10.00	20.00
—"Mono" on label					
❑ CL 1480 [M]	Sketches of Spain	1960	12.50	25.00	50.00
—Six "eye" logos on label					
❑ CL 1480 [M]	Sketches of Spain	1963	6.25	12.50	25.00
—"Guaranteed High Fidelity" on label					
❑ CL 1480 [M]	Sketches of Spain	1965	5.00	10.00	20.00
—"Mono" on label					
❑ CL 1656 [M]	Someday My Prince Will Come	1961	10.00	20.00	40.00
—Six "eye" logos on label					
❑ CL 1656 [M]	Someday My Prince Will Come	1963	6.25	12.50	25.00
—"Guaranteed High Fidelity" on label					
❑ CL 1656 [M]	Someday My Prince Will Come	1965	5.00	10.00	20.00
—"Mono" on label					
❑ CL 1669 [M]	Miles Davis in Person, Vol. 1 (Friday Nights at the Blackhawk, San Francisco)	1961	7.50	15.00	30.00
—Six "eye" logos on label; later pressings may exist					
❑ CL 1670 [M]	Miles Davis in Person, Vol. 2 (Saturday Nights at the Blackhawk, San Francisco)	1961	7.50	15.00	30.00
—Six "eye" logos on label; later pressings may exist					
❑ CL 1812 [M]	Miles Davis at Carnegie Hall	1962	12.50	25.00	50.00
—Six "eye" logos on label					
❑ CL 1812 [M]	Miles Davis at Carnegie Hall	1963	6.25	12.50	25.00
—"Guaranteed High Fidelity" on label					
❑ CL 1812 [M]	Miles Davis at Carnegie Hall	1965	5.00	10.00	20.00
—"Mono" on label					
❑ CL 2051 [M]	Seven Steps to Heaven	1963	6.25	12.50	25.00
—"Guaranteed High Fidelity" on label					
❑ CL 2051 [M]	Seven Steps to Heaven	1965	5.00	10.00	20.00
—"Mono" on label					
❑ CL 2106 [M]	Quiet Nights	1964	6.25	12.50	25.00
—"Guaranteed High Fidelity" on label					
❑ CL 2106 [M]	Quiet Nights	1965	5.00	10.00	20.00
—"Mono" on label					
❑ CL 2183 [M]	Miles Davis in Europe	1964	6.25	12.50	25.00
—"Guaranteed High Fidelity" on label					
❑ CL 2183 [M]	Miles Davis in Europe	1965	5.00	10.00	20.00
—"Mono" on label					
❑ CL 2306 [M]	My Funny Valentine	1965	5.00	10.00	20.00
—"Mono" on label					
❑ CL 2306 [M]	My Funny Valentine	1965	6.25	12.50	25.00
—"Guaranteed High Fidelity" on label					
❑ CL 2350 [M]	E.S.P.	1965	5.00	10.00	20.00
—"Mono" on label					
❑ CL 2350 [M]	E.S.P.	1965	6.25	12.50	25.00
—"Guaranteed High Fidelity" on label					
❑ CL 2453 [M]	"Four" & More — Recorded Live in Concert	1966	5.00	10.00	20.00
❑ CL 2601 [M]	Miles Smiles	1966	5.00	10.00	20.00
❑ CL 2628 [M]	Milestones	1967	7.50	15.00	30.00
—Reissue of 1193?					
❑ CL 2732 [M]	Sorcerer	1967	7.50	15.00	30.00
❑ CL 2794 [M]	Nefertiti	1968	12.50	25.00	50.00
❑ CL 2828 [M]	Miles in the Sky	1968	20.00	40.00	80.00
❑ CS 8021 [S]	Milestones	1959	12.50	25.00	50.00
—Six "eye" logos on label					
❑ CS 8021 [S]	Milestones	1963	6.25	12.50	25.00
—"360 Sound Stereo" in black on label					
❑ CS 8021 [S]	Milestones	1965	5.00	10.00	20.00
—"360 Sound Stereo" in white on label					
❑ CS 8085 [S]	Porgy and Bess	1959	12.50	25.00	50.00
—Six "eye" logos on label					
❑ CS 8085 [S]	Porgy and Bess	1963	6.25	12.50	25.00
—"360 Sound Stereo" in black on label					
❑ CS 8085 [S]	Porgy and Bess	1965	5.00	10.00	20.00
—"360 Sound Stereo" in white on label					
❑ CS 8085	Porgy and Bess	1971	3.00	6.00	12.00
—Orange label					
❑ KCS 8085	Porgy and Bess	1974	2.50	5.00	10.00
—Orange label, new prefix					
❑ PC 8085	Porgy and Bess	1977	2.00	4.00	8.00
—Orange label, new prefix					
❑ CS 8163 [S]	Kind of Blue	1959	62.50	125.00	250.00
—Black and red label with "Stereo Fidelity" at top and "Columbia" in white at bottom; six white "eye" logos on label					
❑ CS 8163 [S]	Kind of Blue	1963	7.50	15.00	30.00
—"360 Sound Stereo" in black on label					
❑ CS 8163 [S]	Kind of Blue	1965	6.25	12.50	25.00
—"360 Sound Stereo" in white on label					
❑ CS 8163	Kind of Blue	1971	3.00	6.00	12.00
—Orange label					
❑ CS 8163 [(2)]	Kind of Blue	1997	17.50	35.00	70.00
—Reissue; contains both the original Side 1, which was mastered slightly fast, and the "correct" Side 1 (as Side 3); distributed by Classic Records					
❑ KCS 8163	Kind of Blue	1974	2.50	5.00	10.00
—Orange label, new prefix					
❑ PC 8163	Kind of Blue	1977	2.00	4.00	8.00
—Orange label, new prefix					
❑ CS 8271 [S]	Sketches of Spain	1960	20.00	40.00	80.00
—Six "eye" logos on label					
❑ CS 8271 [S]	Sketches of Spain	1963	6.25	12.50	25.00
—"360 Sound Stereo" in black on label					
❑ CS 8271 [S]	Sketches of Spain	1965	5.00	10.00	20.00
—"360 Sound Stereo" in white on label					
❑ CS 8271	Sketches of Spain	1971	3.00	6.00	12.00
—Orange label					
❑ CS 8271 [S]	Sketckes of Spain	1999	6.25	12.50	25.00
—Audiophile reissue; distributed by Classic Records					
❑ KCS 8271	Sketches of Spain	1974	2.50	5.00	10.00
—Orange label, new prefix					
❑ PC 8271	Sketches of Spain	1977	2.00	4.00	8.00
—Orange label, new prefix					
❑ CS 8456 [S]	Someday My Prince Will Come	1961	10.00	20.00	40.00
—Six "eye" logos on label					
❑ CS 8456 [S]	Someday My Prince Will Come	1963	6.25	12.50	25.00
—"360 Sound Stereo" in black on label					
❑ CS 8456 [S]	Someday My Prince Will Come	1965	5.00	10.00	20.00
—"360 Sound Stereo" in white on label					
❑ CS 8456	Someday My Prince Will Come	1971	3.00	6.00	12.00
—Orange label					
❑ KCS 8456	Someday My Prince Will Come	1974	2.50	5.00	10.00
—Orange label, new prefix					
❑ PC 8456	Someday My Prince Will Come	1977	2.00	4.00	8.00
—Orange label, new prefix					
❑ CS 8469 [S]	Miles Davis in Person, Vol. 1 (Friday Nights at the Blackhawk, San Francisco)	1961	7.50	15.00	30.00
—Six "eye" logos on label; later pressings may exist					
❑ CS 8470 [S]	Miles Davis in Person, Vol. 2 (Saturday Nights at the Blackhawk, San Francisco)	1961	7.50	15.00	30.00
—Six "eye" logos on label; later pressings may exist					
❑ CS 8612 [S]	Miles Davis at Carnegie Hall	1962	6.25	12.50	25.00
—"360 Sound Stereo" in black on label					
❑ CS 8612 [S]	Miles Davis at Carnegie Hall	1962	12.50	25.00	50.00
—Six "eye" logos on label					
❑ CS 8612 [S]	Miles Davis at Carnegie Hall	1965	5.00	10.00	20.00
—"360 Sound Stereo" in white on label					
❑ CS 8612	Miles Davis at Carnegie Hall	1971	3.00	6.00	12.00
—Orange label					
❑ KCS 8612	Miles Davis at Carnegie Hall	1974	2.50	5.00	10.00
—Orange label, new prefix					
❑ PC 8612	Miles Davis at Carnegie Hall	1977	2.00	4.00	8.00
—Orange label, new prefix					
❑ CS 8633 [R]	Miles Ahead	1963	3.00	6.00	12.00
—Rechanneled stereo version of 1041					
❑ CS 8633	Miles Ahead	1971	3.00	6.00	12.00
—Orange label					
❑ KCS 8633	Miles Ahead	1974	2.50	5.00	10.00
—Orange label, new prefix					
❑ PC 8633	Miles Ahead	1977	2.00	4.00	8.00
—Orange label, new prefix					
❑ CS 8649 [R]	'Round About Midnight	1963	3.00	6.00	12.00
—Rechanneled stereo version of 949					
❑ CS 8649	'Round About Midnight	1971	3.00	6.00	12.00
—Orange label					
❑ KCS 8649	'Round About Midnight	1974	2.50	5.00	10.00
—Orange label, new prefix					
❑ PC 8649	'Round About Midnight	1977	2.00	4.00	8.00
—Orange label, new prefix					
❑ CS 8851 [S]	Seven Steps to Heaven	1963	6.25	12.50	25.00
—"360 Sound Stereo" in black on label					
❑ CS 8851 [S]	Seven Steps to Heaven	1965	5.00	10.00	20.00
—"360 Sound Stereo" in white on label					
❑ CS 8851	Seven Steps to Heaven	1971	3.00	6.00	12.00
—Orange label					
❑ KCS 8851	Seven Steps to Heaven	1974	2.50	5.00	10.00
—Orange label, new prefix					
❑ PC 8851	Seven Steps to Heaven	1977	2.00	4.00	8.00
—Orange label, new prefix					
❑ CS 8906 [S]	Quiet Nights	1964	6.25	12.50	25.00
—"360 Sound Stereo" in black on label					
❑ CS 8906 [S]	Quiet Nights	1965	5.00	10.00	20.00
—"360 Sound Stereo" in white on label					
❑ CS 8906	Quiet Nights	1971	3.00	6.00	12.00
—Orange label					
❑ KCS 8906	Quiet Nights	1974	2.50	5.00	10.00
—Orange label, new prefix					
❑ PC 8906	Quiet Nights	1977	2.00	4.00	8.00
—Orange label, new prefix					
❑ CS 8983 [S]	Miles Davis in Europe	1964	6.25	12.50	25.00
—"360 Sound Stereo" in black on label					
❑ CS 8983 [S]	Miles Davis in Europe	1965	5.00	10.00	20.00
—"360 Sound Stereo" in white on label					
❑ CS 8983	Miles Davis in Europe	1971	3.00	6.00	12.00
—Orange label					
❑ KCS 8983	Miles Davis in Europe	1974	2.50	5.00	10.00
—Orange label, new prefix					
❑ PC 8983	Miles Davis in Europe	1977	2.00	4.00	8.00
—Orange label, new prefix					
❑ CS 9106 [S]	My Funny Valentine	1965	5.00	10.00	20.00
—"360 Sound Stereo" in white on label					
❑ CS 9106 [S]	My Funny Valentine	1965	6.25	12.50	25.00
—"360 Sound Stereo" in black on label					
❑ CS 9106	My Funny Valentine	1971	3.00	6.00	12.00
—Orange label					
❑ KCS 9106	My Funny Valentine	1974	2.50	5.00	10.00
—Orange label, new prefix					
❑ PC 9106	My Funny Valentine	1977	2.00	4.00	8.00
—Orange label, new prefix					
❑ CS 9150 [S]	E.S.P.	1965	5.00	10.00	20.00
—"360 Sound Stereo" in white on label					
❑ CS 9150 [S]	E.S.P.	1965	6.25	12.50	25.00
—"360 Sound Stereo" in black on label					
❑ CS 9150	E.S.P.	1971	3.00	6.00	12.00
—Orange label					
❑ KCS 9150	E.S.P.	1974	2.50	5.00	10.00
—Orange label, new prefix					
❑ PC 9150	E.S.P.	1977	2.00	4.00	8.00
—Orange label, new prefix					
❑ CS 9253 [S]	"Four" & More — Recorded Live in Concert	1966	5.00	10.00	20.00
—"360 Sound Stereo" on red label					
❑ CS 9253	"Four" and More — Recorded Live in Concert	1971	3.00	6.00	12.00
—Orange label					
❑ KCS 9253	"Four" and More — Recorded Live in Concert	1974	2.50	5.00	10.00
—Orange label, new prefix					

Number	Title (A Side/B Side)	Yr	VG	VG+	NM
PC 9253	"Four" and More — Recorded Live in Concert	1977	2.00	4.00	8.00
—Orange label, new prefix					
CS 9401 [S]	Miles Smiles	1966	5.00	10.00	20.00
—"360 Sound Stereo" on red label					
CS 9401	Miles Smiles	1971	3.00	6.00	12.00
—Orange label					
KCS 9401	Miles Smiles	1974	2.50	5.00	10.00
—Orange label, new prefix					
PC 9401	Miles Smiles	1977	2.00	4.00	8.00
—Orange label, new prefix					
CS 9428 [S]	Milestones	1967	5.00	10.00	20.00
—"360 Sound Stereo" on red label; reissue of 8021?					
KCS 9428	Milestones	1974	2.50	5.00	10.00
—Orange label, new prefix					
PC 9428	Milestones	1977	2.00	4.00	8.00
—Orange label, new prefix					
CS 9532 [S]	Sorcerer	1967	5.00	10.00	20.00
—"360 Sound Stereo" on red label					
CS 9532	Sorcerer	1971	3.00	6.00	12.00
—Orange label					
KCS 9532	Sorcerer	1974	2.50	5.00	10.00
—Orange label, new prefix					
PC 9532	Sorcerer	1977	2.00	4.00	8.00
—Orange label, new prefix					
CS 9594 [S]	Nefertiti	1968	5.00	10.00	20.00
—"360 Sound Stereo" on red label					
CS 9594	Nefertiti	1971	3.00	6.00	12.00
—Orange label					
KCS 9594	Nefertiti	1974	2.50	5.00	10.00
—Orange label, new prefix					
PC 9594	Nefertiti	1977	2.00	4.00	8.00
—Orange label, new prefix					
CS 9628 [S]	Miles in the Sky	1968	5.00	10.00	20.00
—"360 Sound Stereo" on red label					
CS 9628	Miles in the Sky	1971	3.00	6.00	12.00
—Orange label					
KCS 9628	Miles in the Sky	1974	2.50	5.00	10.00
—Orange label, new prefix					
PC 9628	Miles in the Sky	1977	2.00	4.00	8.00
—Orange label, new prefix					
CS 9750	Filles de Kilimanjaro	1969	5.00	10.00	20.00
—"360 Sound Stereo" on red label					
CS 9750	Filles de Kilimanjaro	1971	3.00	6.00	12.00
—Orange label					
KCS 9750	Filles de Kilimanjaro	1974	2.50	5.00	10.00
—Orange label, new prefix					
PC 9750	Filles de Kilimanjaro	1977	2.00	4.00	8.00
—Orange label, new prefix					
CS 9808	Miles Davis' Greatest Hits	1969	5.00	10.00	20.00
—"360 Sound Stereo" on red label					
CS 9808	Miles Davis' Greatest Hits	1971	3.00	6.00	12.00
—Orange label					
KCS 9808	Miles Davis' Greatest Hits	1974	2.50	5.00	10.00
—Orange label, new prefix					
PC 9808	Miles Davis' Greatest Hits	1977	2.00	4.00	8.00
—Orange label, new prefix					
CS 9875	In a Silent Way	1969	5.00	10.00	20.00
—"360 Sound Stereo" on red label					
CS 9875	In a Silent Way	1971	3.00	6.00	12.00
—Orange label					
KCS 9875	In a Silent Way	1974	2.50	5.00	10.00
—Orange label, new prefix					
PC 9875	In a Silent Way	1977	2.00	4.00	8.00
—Orange label, new prefix					
CG 30038 [(2)]	Miles Davis at Fillmore	1970	3.75	7.50	15.00
KC 30455	A Tribute to Jack Johnson	1971	3.00	6.00	12.00
PC 30455	A Tribute to Jack Johnson	1977	2.00	4.00	8.00
—Orange label, new prefix					
CG 30954 [(2)]	Live-Evil	1971	3.75	7.50	15.00
GQ 30954 [(2)Q]	Live-Evil	1973	7.50	15.00	30.00
GQ 30997 [(2)Q]	Bitches Brew	1972	10.00	20.00	40.00
KC 31906	On the Corner	1972	3.00	6.00	12.00
PC 31906	On the Corner	1977	2.00	4.00	8.00
—Orange label, new prefix					
KC 32025	Basic Miles — The Classic Performances of Miles Davis	1973	3.00	6.00	12.00
PC 32025	Basic Miles — The Classic Performances of Miles Davis	198?	2.00	4.00	8.00
—Budget-line reissue					
KG 32092 [(2)]	In Concert	1973	3.75	7.50	15.00
PG 32092 [(2)]	In Concert	1977	2.50	5.00	10.00
—Orange labels, new prefix					
C 32470	Jazz at the Plaza, Vol. 1	1973	3.00	6.00	12.00
CG 32866 [(2)]	Big Fun	1974	3.75	7.50	15.00
PG 32866 [(2)]	Big Fun	1977	3.00	6.00	12.00
—Orange labels, new prefix					
KG 33236 [(2)]	Get Up With It	1974	3.75	7.50	15.00
PG 33236 [(2)]	Get Up With It	1977	2.50	5.00	10.00
—Orange labels, new prefix					
PG 33967 [(2)]	Agharta	1976	3.75	7.50	15.00
PC 34396	Water Babies	1977	3.00	6.00	12.00
—Original has no bar code					
PC 34396	Water Babies	198?	2.00	4.00	8.00
—Reissue with bar code					
KC2 36278 [(2)]	Circle in the Round	1980	3.75	7.50	15.00
KC2 36472 [(2)]	Directions	1981	3.75	7.50	15.00
FC 36790	The Man with the Horn	1981	2.50	5.00	10.00
PC 36790	The Man with the Horn	198?	2.00	4.00	8.00
—Budget-line reissue					
C6X 36976 [(6)]	The Miles Davis Collection Vol. 1: 12 Sides of Miles	1980	12.50	25.00	50.00
C2 38005 [(2)]	We Want Miles	1982	3.00	6.00	12.00
C2 38266 [(2)]	Live at the Plugged Nickel	1982	3.00	6.00	12.00
C2 38506 [(2)]	Heard 'Round the World	1983	3.00	6.00	12.00
FC 38657	Star People	1983	2.50	5.00	10.00
FC 38991	Decoy	1984	2.50	5.00	10.00
FC 40023	You're Under Arrest	1985	2.50	5.00	10.00

Number	Title (A Side/B Side)	Yr	VG	VG+	NM
C2X 45332	Aura	1989	3.75	7.50	15.00
HC 46790	The Man with the Horn	1982	10.00	20.00	40.00
—Half-speed mastered edition					

COLUMBIA JAZZ MASTERPIECES

Number	Title (A Side/B Side)	Yr	VG	VG+	NM
CJ2 40577 [(2)]	Bitches Brew	1987	3.00	6.00	12.00
CJ 40578	Sketches of Spain	1987	2.50	5.00	10.00
CJ 40579	Kind of Blue	1987	2.50	5.00	10.00
CJ 40580	In a Silent Way	1987	2.50	5.00	10.00
CJ 40609	Live Miles: More Music from the Legendary Carnegie Hall Concert	1987	2.50	5.00	10.00
CJ 40610	'Round About Midnight	1987	2.50	5.00	10.00
CJ 40645	Cookin' at the Plugged Nickel	1987	2.50	5.00	10.00
CJ 40647	Porgy and Bess	1987	2.50	5.00	10.00
CJ 40784	Miles Ahead	1987	2.50	5.00	10.00
CJ 40837	Milestones	1987	2.50	5.00	10.00
CJ 40947	Someday My Prince Will Come	1987	2.50	5.00	10.00
CJ 44052	Miles and Coltrane	1988	2.50	5.00	10.00
CJ 44151	Ballads	1988	2.50	5.00	10.00
CJ 44257	Miles Davis in Person, Vol. 1 (Friday Nights at the Blackhawk, San Francisco)	1988	2.50	5.00	10.00
CJ 44425	Miles Davis in Person, Vol. 2 (Saturday Nights at the Blackhawk, San Francisco)	1989	2.50	5.00	10.00

COLUMBIA LIMITED EDITION

Number	Title (A Side/B Side)	Yr	VG	VG+	NM
LE 10018	Miles Davis in Person, Vol. 1 (Friday Nights at the Blackhawk, San Francisco)	197?	3.00	6.00	12.00

COLUMBIA SPECIAL PRODUCTS

Number	Title (A Side/B Side)	Yr	VG	VG+	NM
P 13811	Facets	1977	2.50	5.00	10.00

CONTEMPORARY

Number	Title (A Side/B Side)	Yr	VG	VG+	NM
7645	Miles Davis and the Lighthouse All-Stars At Last!	1985	3.00	6.00	12.00

DEBUT

Number	Title (A Side/B Side)	Yr	VG	VG+	NM
DEB 120 [M]	Blue Moods	1955	62.50	125.00	250.00

EVEREST ARCHIVE OF FOLK & JAZZ

Number	Title (A Side/B Side)	Yr	VG	VG+	NM
283	Miles Davis	197?	2.50	5.00	10.00

FANTASY

Number	Title (A Side/B Side)	Yr	VG	VG+	NM
OJC-004	The Musings of Miles	198?	2.50	5.00	10.00
—Reissue of Prestige 7007					
OJC-005	Dig Miles Davis/Sonny Rollins	198?	2.50	5.00	10.00
—Reissue of Prestige 7012					
OJC-006	Miles — The New Miles Davis Quintet	198?	2.50	5.00	10.00
—Reissue of Prestige 7014					
OJC-012	Miles Davis and the Milt Jackson Quintet/Sextet	198?	2.50	5.00	10.00
—Reissue of Prestige 7034					
OJC-043	Blue Moods	198?	2.50	5.00	10.00
—Reissue of Fantasy 6001					
OJC-053	Miles Davis and Horns	198?	2.50	5.00	10.00
—Reissue of Prestige 7025					
OJC-071	Collector's Item	198?	2.50	5.00	10.00
—Reissue of Prestige 7044					
OJC-093	Blue Haze	198?	2.50	5.00	10.00
—Reissue of Prestige 7054					
OJC-128	Cookin' with the Miles Davis Quintet	198?	2.50	5.00	10.00
—Reissue of Prestige 7094					
OJC-190	Relaxin' with the Miles Davis Quintet	1985	2.50	5.00	10.00
—Reissue of Prestige 7129					
OJC-213	Walkin'	1987	2.50	5.00	10.00
—Reissue of Prestige 7076					
OJC-245	Bags Groove	1987	2.50	5.00	10.00
—Reissue of Prestige 7109					
OJC-296	Workin' with the Miles Davis Quintet	1987	2.50	5.00	10.00
—Reissue of Prestige 7166					
OJC-347	Miles Davis and the Modern Jazz Giants	198?	2.50	5.00	10.00
—Reissue of Prestige 7150					
OJC-391	Steamin' with the Miles Davis Quintet	1989	2.50	5.00	10.00
—Reissue of Prestige 7200					
OJC-480	Miles Davis and the Lighthouse All-Stars At Last!	1991	2.50	5.00	10.00
—Reissue of Contemporary 7645					
6001 [M]	Blue Moods	1962	12.50	25.00	50.00
—Reissue of Debut album; red vinyl					
6001 [M]	Blue Moods	1963	7.50	15.00	30.00
—Black vinyl, red label					
86001 [R]	Blue Moods	1962	7.50	15.00	30.00
—Blue vinyl					
86001 [R]	Blue Moods	1963	3.75	7.50	15.00
—Black vinyl, blue label					

FONTANA

Number	Title (A Side/B Side)	Yr	VG	VG+	NM
MGF-27532 [M]	Jazz on the Screen	1965	6.25	12.50	25.00
—With Art Blakey and the Jazz Messengers					
SRF-67532 [S]	Jazz on the Screen	1965	7.50	15.00	30.00

MOBILE FIDELITY

Number	Title (A Side/B Side)	Yr	VG	VG+	NM
1-177	Someday My Prince Will Come	1985	20.00	40.00	80.00
—Audiophile vinyl					

MOSAIC

Number	Title (A Side/B Side)	Yr	VG	VG+	NM
MQ10-158 [(10)]	The Complete Plugged Nickel Sessions	1995	75.00	150.00	300.00
MQ11-164 [(11)]	Miles Davis & Gil Evans: The Complete Columbia Studio Recordings	1996	100.00	200.00	400.00
MQ10-177 [(10)]	The Complete Studio Recordings of the Miles Davis Quintet 1965-June 1968	1998	37.50	75.00	150.00
MQ6-183 [(6)]	The Complete Bitches Brew Sessions	1999	25.00	50.00	100.00
MQ9-191 [(9)]	The Complete Columbia Recordings of Miles Davis with John Coltrane	2000	42.50	85.00	170.00
MQ5-209 [(5)]	The Complete In a Silent Way Sessions (September 1968-February 1969)	2002	20.00	40.00	80.00
MQ6-220 [(6)]	The Complete Blackhawk Sessions	2003	25.00	50.00	100.00

PAIR

Number	Title (A Side/B Side)	Yr	VG	VG+	NM
PDL2-1095 [(2)]	Best of Miles Davis	1986	3.00	6.00	12.00

PHILIPS

Number	Title (A Side/B Side)	Yr	VG	VG+	NM
836305-1	Elevator to the Scaffold (L'Ancenseur Pour L'Echafaud)	198?	3.00	6.00	12.00
—Reissue of Columbia 1268					

PRESTIGE

Number	Title (A Side/B Side)	Yr	VG	VG+	NM
P-12 [(12)]	Chronicle: The Complete Prestige Recordings	1980	25.00	50.00	100.00
PRLP-124 [10]	The New Sounds of Miles Davis	1952	62.50	125.00	250.00
PRLP-140 [10]	Blue Period	1953	62.50	125.00	250.00
PRLP-154 [10]	Miles Davis Plays Al Cohn Compositions	1953	62.50	125.00	250.00
PRLP-161 [10]	Miles Davis Featuring Sonny Rollins	1953	62.50	125.00	250.00
PRLP-182 [10]	Miles Davis Sextet	1954	62.50	125.00	250.00

Number	Title (A Side/B Side)	Yr	VG	VG+	NM
❏ PRLP-185 [10] Miles Davis Quintet		1954	62.50	125.00	250.00
❏ PRLP-187 [10] Miles Davis Quintet Featuring Sonny Rollins		1954	62.50	125.00	250.00
❏ PRLP-196 [10] Miles Davis All Stars, Volume 1		1955	62.50	125.00	250.00
❏ PRLP-200 [10] Miles Davis All Stars, Volume 2		1955	62.50	125.00	250.00
❏ PRLP-7007 [M] The Musings of Miles		1955	37.50	75.00	150.00
❏ PRLP-7012 [M] Dig Miles Davis/Sonny Rollins		1956	37.50	75.00	150.00
—Gray cover					
❏ PRLP-7012 [M] Dig Miles Davis/Sonny Rollins		1957	30.00	60.00	120.00
—Color cover					
❏ PRLP-7014 [M] Miles — The New Miles Davis Quintet		1956	37.50	75.00	150.00
❏ PRLP-7025 [M] Miles Davis and Horns		1956	37.50	75.00	150.00
❏ PRLP-7034 [M] Miles Davis and the Milt Jackson Quintet/Sextet		1956	37.50	75.00	150.00
—With W. 50th St. address on yellow label					
❏ PRLP-7034 [M] Miles Davis and the Milt Jackson Quintet/Sextet		196?	7.50	15.00	30.00
—With trident on blue label					
❏ PRLP-7044 [M] Collectors' Item		1956	30.00	60.00	120.00
—With W. 50th St. address on yellow label					
❏ PRLP-7044 [M] Collectors' Item		196?	7.50	15.00	30.00
—With trident on blue label					
❏ PRLP-7054 [M] Blue Haze		1956	30.00	60.00	120.00
—With W. 50th St. address on yellow label					
❏ PRLP-7054 [M] Blue Haze		196?	7.50	15.00	30.00
—With trident on blue label					
❏ PRLP-7076 [M] All Stars		195?	17.50	35.00	70.00
—With Bergenfield, N.J. address on yellow label					
❏ PRLP-7076 [M] All Stars		1957	25.00	50.00	100.00
—With W. 50th St. address on yellow label					
❏ PRLP-7076 [M] All Stars		196?	7.50	15.00	30.00
—With trident on blue label					
❏ PRLP-7094 [M] Cookin' with the Miles Davis Quintet		195?	15.00	30.00	60.00
—With Bergenfield, N.J. address on yellow label					
❏ PRLP-7094 [M] Cookin' with the Miles Davis Quintet		1957	25.00	50.00	100.00
—With W. 50th St. address on yellow label					
❏ PRLP-7094 [M] Cookin' with the Miles Davis Quintet		196?	7.50	15.00	30.00
—With trident on blue label					
❏ PRLP-7109 [M] Bags Groove		1957	25.00	50.00	100.00
—With W. 50th St. address on yellow label					
❏ PRLP-7109 [M] Bags Groove		196?	7.50	15.00	30.00
—With trident on blue label					
❏ PRLP-7129 [M] Relaxin' with the Miles Davis Quintet		1957	15.00	30.00	60.00
—With Bergenfield, NJ address on yellow label					
❏ PRLP-7129 [M] Relaxin' with the Miles Davis Quintet		1957	25.00	50.00	100.00
—With W. 50th St. address on yellow label					
❏ PRLP-7129 [M] Relaxin' with the Miles Davis Quintet		196?	7.50	15.00	30.00
—With trident on blue label					
❏ PRLP-7150 [M] Miles Davis and the Modern Jazz Giants		1958	20.00	40.00	80.00
—With Bergenfield, NJ address on yellow label					
❏ PRLP-7150 [M] Miles Davis and the Modern Jazz Giants		196?	7.50	15.00	30.00
—With trident on blue label					
❏ PRLP-7166 [M] Workin' with the Miles Davis Quintet		1959	20.00	40.00	80.00
—With Bergenfield, NJ address on yellow label					
❏ PRLP-7166 [M] Workin' with the Miles Davis Quintet		196?	7.50	15.00	30.00
—With trident on blue label					
❏ PRLP-7168 [M] Early Miles		1959	20.00	40.00	80.00
—Reissue of 7025; with Bergenfield, NJ address on yellow label					
❏ PRLP-7168 [M] Early Miles		196?	7.50	15.00	30.00
—With trident on blue label					
❏ PRLP-7200 [M] Steamin' with the Miles Davis Quintet		196?	7.50	15.00	30.00
—With trident on blue label					
❏ PRLP-7200 [M] Steamin' with the Miles Davis Quintet		1961	20.00	40.00	80.00
—With Bergenfield, NJ address on yellow label					
❏ PRLP-7221 [M] The Beginning		196?	7.50	15.00	30.00
—With trident on blue label					
❏ PRLP-7221 [M] The Beginning		1962	12.50	25.00	50.00
—Reissue of 7007; with Bergenfield, NJ address on yellow label					
❏ PRLP-7254 [M] The Original Quintet		196?	7.50	15.00	30.00
—With trident on blue label					
❏ PRLP-7254 [M] The Original Quintet		1963	12.50	25.00	50.00
—Reissue of 7014; with Bergenfield, NJ address on yellow label					
❏ PRST-7254 [R] The Original Quintet		1963	5.00	10.00	20.00
❏ PRLP-7281 [M] Diggin'		196?	7.50	15.00	30.00
—With trident on blue label					
❏ PRLP-7281 [M] Diggin'		1963	12.50	25.00	50.00
—Reissue of 7012; with Bergenfield, NJ address on yellow label					
❏ PRST-7281 [R] Diggin'		1963	5.00	10.00	20.00
❏ PRLP-7322 [M] Miles Davis Plays Richard Rodgers		1964	7.50	15.00	30.00
❏ PRST-7322 [R] Miles Davis Plays Richard Rodgers		1964	5.00	10.00	20.00
❏ PRLP-7352 [M] Miles Davis Plays for Lovers		1965	7.50	15.00	30.00
❏ PRST-7352 [R] Miles Davis Plays for Lovers		1965	5.00	10.00	20.00
❏ PRLP-7373 [M] Jazz Classics		1965	7.50	15.00	30.00
❏ PRST-7373 [R] Jazz Classics		1965	5.00	10.00	20.00
❏ PRLP-7457 [M] Miles Davis' Greatest Hits		1967	5.00	10.00	20.00
❏ PRST-7457 [R] Miles Davis' Greatest Hits		1967	3.00	6.00	12.00
❏ PRST-7540 [R] Odyssey		1968	3.00	6.00	12.00
—Reissue of 7034					
❏ PRST-7580 [R] Steamin'		1968	3.00	6.00	12.00
—Reissue of 7200					
❏ PRST-7608 [R] Walkin'		1969	3.00	6.00	12.00
—Reissue of 7076					
❏ PRST-7650 [R] Miles Davis and the Modern Jazz Giants		1969	3.00	6.00	12.00
—Reissue of 7150					
❏ PRST-7674 [R] Early Miles		1969	3.00	6.00	12.00
—Reissue of 7168					
❏ PRST-7744 [R] Conception		1970	3.00	6.00	12.00
❏ PRST-7822 [R] Miles Ahead!		1971	3.00	6.00	12.00
❏ PRST-7847	Oleo	1972	3.00	6.00	12.00
❏ 24001 [(2)]	Miles Davis	1972	3.75	7.50	15.00
❏ 24012 [(2)]	The Tallest Trees	1972	3.75	7.50	15.00
❏ 24022 [(2)]	Collector's Items	1973	3.75	7.50	15.00
❏ 24034 [(2)]	Workin' and Steamin'	1973	3.75	7.50	15.00
❏ 24054 [(2)]	Dig	197?	3.00	6.00	12.00
❏ 24064 [(2)]	Green Haze	197?	3.00	6.00	12.00
❏ 24077 [(2)]	Tune Up	197?	3.00	6.00	12.00
SAVOY JAZZ					
❏ SJL-1196	First Miles	1989	2.50	5.00	10.00
TRIP					
❏ 5015	Miles of Jazz	1974	2.50	5.00	10.00

Number	Title (A Side/B Side)	Yr	VG	VG+	NM
UNITED ARTISTS					
❏ UAS-9952 [(2)] Miles Davis		1972	3.75	7.50	15.00
—Reissue of Blue Note material					
WARNER BROS.					
❏ 25490	Tutu	1986	2.50	5.00	10.00
❏ 25873	Amandla	1989	3.00	6.00	12.00
❏ 26938	Doo-Bop	1992	3.75	7.50	15.00

DAVIS, MILES, AND JOHN COLTRANE Also see each artist's individual listings.
Albums

Number	Title (A Side/B Side)	Yr	VG	VG+	NM
MOODSVILLE					
❏ MVLP-32 [M] Miles Davis and John Coltrane Play Richard Rodgers		1963	12.50	25.00	50.00
—Green label					
❏ MVLP-32 [M] Miles Davis and John Coltrane Play Richard Rodgers		1965	6.25	12.50	25.00
—Blue label, trident logo at right					
PRESTIGE					
❏ PRLP-7322 [M] Miles Davis and John Coltrane Play Rodgers and Hart		1964	10.00	20.00	40.00
❏ PRST-7322 [R] Miles Davis and John Coltrane Play Rodgers and Hart		1964	5.00	10.00	20.00

DAVIS, MILES, AND TADD DAMERON
Albums

Number	Title (A Side/B Side)	Yr	VG	VG+	NM
COLUMBIA					
❏ JC 34804	Paris Festival International, May 1949	1978	2.50	5.00	10.00

DAVIS, MILES, AND THELONIOUS MONK Also see each artist's individual listings.
Albums

Number	Title (A Side/B Side)	Yr	VG	VG+	NM
COLUMBIA					
❏ CL 2178 [M]	Miles and Monk at Newport	1964	6.25	12.50	25.00
—"Guaranteed High Fidelity" on label					
❏ CL 2178 [M]	Miles and Monk at Newport	1965	5.00	10.00	20.00
—"Mono" on label					
❏ CS 8978 [S]	Miles and Monk at Newport	1964	6.25	12.50	25.00
—"360 Sound Stereo" in black on label					
❏ CS 8978 [S]	Miles and Monk at Newport	1965	5.00	10.00	20.00
—"360 Sound Stereo" in white on label					
❏ KCS 8978	Miles and Monk at Newport	1974	2.50	5.00	10.00
—Orange label, new prefix					
❏ PC 8978	Miles and Monk at Newport	1977	2.00	4.00	8.00
—Orange label, new prefix					

DAVIS, PAUL Also see GRACIOUS.
45s

Number	Title (A Side/B Side)	Yr	VG	VG+	NM
ARISTA					
❏ 0645	Cool Night/One More Time for the Lonely	1981	—	2.00	4.00
❏ 0661	'65 Love Affair/We're Still Together	1982	—	2.00	4.00
❏ 0697	Love or Let Me Be Lonely/Oriental Eyes	1982	—	2.00	4.00
BANG					
❏ 568	If I Wuz a Magician/Mississippi River	1969	—	3.00	6.00
❏ 576	A Little Bit of Soap/Three Little Words	1970	—	3.00	6.00
❏ 579	I Just Wanna Keep It Together/Pollyanna	1970	2.00	4.00	8.00
❏ 581	Can't You/Gonna Keep On Loving You	1970	—	3.00	6.00
❏ 587	I Feel Better/When My Little Girl Is Smiling	1971	—	3.00	6.00
❏ 590	Got to Find My Way Back/I Can't Get Her Off My Mind	1971	—	3.00	6.00
❏ 593	Come On Honey/Livin' On Your Love	1972	—	2.50	5.00
❏ 597	Simple Man/What Would We Do Without Music	1972	—	2.50	5.00
❏ 599	Boogie Woogie Man/Johnny Poverty	1972	—	2.50	5.00
❏ 702	Broken Hearted and Free/Mississippi River	1973	—	2.50	5.00
❏ 705	Daydreamer/Love Don't Come Easy	1973	—	2.50	5.00
❏ 712	Ride 'Em Cowboy/I'm the Only Sinner (In Salt Lake City)	1974	—	2.50	5.00
❏ 717	Make Her My Baby/Can't Get Back to Alabama	1975	—	2.00	4.00
❏ 718	Keep Our Love Alive/I Got a Yearning	1975	—	2.00	4.00
❏ 724	Thinking of You/Karma Baby	1976	—	2.00	4.00
❏ 726	Superstar/Magnolia Blues	1976	—	2.00	4.00
❏ 729	Medicine Woman/Hallelujah, Thank You, Jesus	1976	—	2.00	4.00
❏ 733	I Go Crazy/Reggae Kinda Way	1977	—	2.00	4.00
❏ 736	Darlin'/You're Not Just a Rose	1978	—	2.00	4.00
❏ 738	Sweet Life/Bad Dream	1978	—	2.00	4.00
❏ 4808	Do Right/He Sang Our Love Songs	1980	—	2.00	4.00
❏ 4811	Cry Just a Little/Do You Believe in Love	1980	—	2.00	4.00
CAPITOL					
❏ B-5613	You're Still New to Me/New Love	1986	—	—	3.00
—With Marie Osmond					
❏ B-44100	I Won't Take Less Than Your Love/Heartbreaker	1986	—	—	3.00
—With Tanya Tucker and Paul Overstreet					
❏ B-44215	Sweet Life/My Home Town Boy	1988	—	—	3.00
—With Marie Osmond; B-side is Marie Osmond solo					
Albums					
ARISTA					
❏ AL 8376	Cool Night	198?	2.00	4.00	8.00
—Reissue of 9578					
❏ AL 9578	Cool Night	1981	2.50	5.00	10.00
BANG					
❏ BLPS-223	A Little Bit of Paul Davis	1970	10.00	20.00	40.00
❏ 401	Ride 'Em Cowboy	1974	3.00	6.00	12.00
❏ 405	Southern Tracks and Fantasies	1976	3.00	6.00	12.00
❏ 410	Singer of Songs — Teller of Tales	1977	3.00	6.00	12.00
❏ JZ 36094	Paul Davis	1980	2.50	5.00	10.00
❏ PZ 37973	The Best of Paul Davis	1982	2.50	5.00	10.00

DAVIS, SAMMY, JR.
45s

Number	Title (A Side/B Side)	Yr	VG	VG+	NM
APPLAUSE					
❏ 100	Smoke, Smoke, Smoke (That Cigarette)/We Could Have Been the Closest of Friends	1982	—	2.50	5.00
CAPITOL					
❏ F943	Inka Dinka Doo/Laura	1950	5.00	10.00	20.00
❏ F1050	I'm Sorry Dear/Dedicated to You	1950	3.75	7.50	15.00
DDR					
❏ 101/2	Who Needs Spring/(B-side unknown)	197?	2.00	4.00	8.00
—Red vinyl					

Number	Title (A Side/B Side)	Yr	VG	VG+	NM
DECCA					
29199	Hey There/And This Is My Beloved	1954	3.00	6.00	12.00
29200	Because of You (Part 1)/Because of You (Part 2)	1954	3.00	6.00	12.00
29310	Glad to Be Unhappy/Red Grapes	1954	3.00	6.00	12.00
29393	The Birth of the Blues/Love	1954	3.00	6.00	12.00
29402	All of You/Six Bridges to Cross	1955	3.00	6.00	12.00
29484	Love Me or Leave Me/Something's Gotta Give	1955	3.00	6.00	12.00
29541	That Old Black Magic/A Man with a Dream	1955	3.00	6.00	12.00
29620	I Go for You/A Fine Romance	1955	3.00	6.00	12.00
—With Carmen McRae					
29649	Back Track/It's Bigger Than You and Me	1955	3.00	6.00	12.00
29672	I'll Know/Adelaide	1955	3.00	6.00	12.00
29737	Ac-Cent-Tchu-Ate the Positive/Beat Me, Daddy, Eight to the Bar	1955	3.00	6.00	12.00
—With Gary Crosby					
29759	The Man with the Golden Arm/In a Persian Blanket	1955	3.00	6.00	12.00
29795	Frankie and Johnny/Circus	1956	3.00	6.00	12.00
29861	Too Close for Comfort/Jacques d'Iraque	1956	3.00	6.00	12.00
29929	Without You I'm Nothing/Get Out of the Car	1956	3.00	6.00	12.00
29976	Five/You're Sensational	1956	3.00	6.00	12.00
30035	Earthbound/Just One of Those Things	1956	3.00	6.00	12.00
30111	New York's My Home/Never Like This	1956	3.00	6.00	12.00
30158	All About Love/Dangerous	1956	3.00	6.00	12.00
30189	The Golden Key/Long Before I Knew You	1957	2.50	5.00	10.00
30300	Good Bye, So Long, I'm Gone/French Fried Potatoes and Ketchup	1957	2.50	5.00	10.00
30371	Doncha Go 'Way Mad/Specially for Little Girls	1957	2.50	5.00	10.00
30400	Baby It's Cold Outside/Happy to Make Your Acquaintance	1957	2.50	5.00	10.00
30441	Mad Ball/Cool Credo	1957	2.50	5.00	10.00
30479	All Dressed Up and No Place to Go/Moment of Madness	1957	2.50	5.00	10.00
30536	Hallelujah I Love Her So/I'm Comin' Home	1958	2.50	5.00	10.00
30611	No Fool Like an Old Fool/Unspoken	1958	2.50	5.00	10.00
30679	Song and Dance Man/I Ain't Gonna Change	1958	2.50	5.00	10.00
30769	That's Anna/I Never Got Out of Paris	1958	2.50	5.00	10.00
30898	Fair Warning/You'll Never Get Away from Me	1959	2.50	5.00	10.00
30915	I Got Plenty of Nothin'/There's a Boat Dat's Leaving Soon for New York	1959	2.50	5.00	10.00
31136	I Got a Woman/Mess Around	1960	2.50	5.00	10.00
31177	This Little Girl of Mine/Face to Face	1960	2.50	5.00	10.00
32470	Rhythm of Life/(B-side unknown)	1969	—	3.00	6.00
MGM					
14320	The Candy Man/I Want to Be Happy	1971	—	3.00	6.00
14426	Mr. Bojangles/The People Tree	1972	—	2.50	5.00
14513	(I'd Be) A Legend in My Time/I'm Not Anyone	1973	—	2.50	5.00
14685	Singin' in the Rain/Chattanooga Choo Choo	1973	—	2.50	5.00
14736	That's Entertainment/Singin' in the Rain	1974	—	2.00	4.00
14759	Sing/This Is the House of the People	1974	—	2.00	4.00
MOTOWN					
1738	Hello Detroit (Part 1)/Hello Detroit (Part 2)	1984	—	2.00	4.00
REPRISE					
(no #) [DJ]	Here's A Kiss For Christmas (The Christmas Seal Song)/What Kind Of Fool Am I	1963	3.75	7.50	15.00
OE-DJ-2 [DJ]	Open End Disc Jockey Interview	196?	10.00	20.00	40.00
—Small hole, plays at 33 1/3 rpm					
0248	What Kind of Fool Am I/Gonna Buila a Mountain	1963	2.00	4.00	8.00
0278	Choose/Bee Bom	1964	2.00	4.00	8.00
0289	Not for Me/Night Song	1964	2.00	4.00	8.00
0321	Hello, Dolly!/Take the Moment	1964	3.75	7.50	15.00
—Possibly released only outside the U.S.					
0322	Don't Shut Me Out/Disorderly Orderly	1964	2.00	4.00	8.00
0345	If I Ruled the World/Flash, Bang, Wallop	1965	2.00	4.00	8.00
0361	Hello, Dolly!/Take the Moment	1965	2.00	4.00	8.00
0370	Unforgettable/No One Can Live Forever	1965	2.00	4.00	8.00
0399	Love, At Last You Have Found Me/Courage	1965	2.00	4.00	8.00
0416	Yes I Can/Courage	1965	2.00	4.00	8.00
0425	If You Want This Love of Mine/Second-Best Secret Agent in the Whole Wide World	1965	2.00	4.00	8.00
0437	Lonely Weekends/More Than One Way	1965	2.00	4.00	8.00
0502	All That Jazz/Ev'ry Time We Say Goodbye	1966	—	3.00	6.00
0521	The Good Life/We'll Be Together Again	1966	—	3.00	6.00
0549	The Birth of the Blues/With a Song in My Heart	1967	—	3.00	6.00
0566	Don't Blame the Children/She Believes in Me	1967	—	3.00	6.00
0621	Talk to the Animals/Something in Your Smile	1967	—	3.00	6.00
0673	Lonely Is the Name/Flash, Bang, Wallop	1968	—	3.00	6.00
0720	What Kind of Fool Am I/Gonna Build a Mountain	1968	—	2.00	4.00
—"Back to Back Hits" series					
0733	I've Gotta Be Me/Lonely Is the Name	1970	—	2.00	4.00
—"Back to Back Hits" series					
0757	Break My Mind/Children, Children	1968	—	3.00	6.00
0779	I've Gotta Be Me/Bein' Natural Bein' Me	1968	2.00	4.00	8.00
0827	I Have But One Life to Live/The Goin's Great	1969	—	3.00	6.00
0989	She Is Today/Runaround	1971	—	2.50	5.00
20003	I'm a Fool to Want You/Back in Your Own Back Yard	1961	2.50	5.00	10.00
20018	One More Time (A Tribute to Ray Charles)/There Was a Tavern in the Town	1961	2.50	5.00	10.00
20048	What Kind of Fool Am I/Gonna Build a Mountain	1962	2.50	5.00	10.00
20079	The Fool I Used to Be/Everybody Calls Me Joe	1962	2.50	5.00	10.00
20087	Once in a Lifetime/Someone Nice Like You	1962	2.50	5.00	10.00
20128	Me and My Shadow/Sam's Song	1962	3.75	7.50	15.00
—A-side: With Frank Sinatra; B-side: With Dean Martin					
20128 [PS]	Me and My Shadow/Sam's Song	1962	7.50	15.00	30.00
20138	As Long As She Needs Me/Two for the Seesaw	1963	2.50	5.00	10.00
20212	We Kiss in a Shadow/Bye, Bye Blackbird	1963	2.50	5.00	10.00
20216	The Shelter of Your Arms/This Was My Love	1963	2.50	5.00	10.00
20227	The Shelter of Your Arms/Falling in Love with Love	1963	5.00	10.00	20.00
—Released only in England					
20TH CENTURY					
2236	Snap Your Fingers/Song and Dance Man	1975	—	2.00	4.00
2282	Chico and the Man (Main Theme)/(I'd Be) A Legend in My Time	1976	—	2.50	5.00
—May be promo only					
2292	Baretta's Theme (Keep Your Eye on the Sparrow)/I Heard a Song	1976	—	2.00	4.00
UNITED ARTISTS					
50334	Salt and Pepper/I Like the Way You Dance	1968	—	3.00	6.00
VERVE					
10219	Ain't That a Kick in the Head/Eee-O Eleven	1960	2.00	4.00	8.00
WARNER BROS.					
49047	Showtime/That Old Black Magic	1979	—	2.00	4.00
7-Inch Extended Plays					
DECCA					
ED 2214	Hey There/Glad to Be Unhappy//And This Is My Beloved/Easy to Love	195?	3.00	6.00	12.00
ED 2214 [PS]	Starring Sammy Davis, Jr., Part 1 (contents unknown)	195?	3.00	6.00	12.00
ED 2215 [PS]	Starring Sammy Davis, Jr., Part 2	195?	3.00	6.00	12.00
ED 2216	*Birth of the Blues (Remake)/Lonesome Road/Because of You (Part 1 and Part 2)	195?	3.00	6.00	12.00
ED 2216 [PS]	Starring Sammy Davis, Jr., Part 3	195?	3.00	6.00	12.00
ED 2508	*Begin the Beguine/By Myself/That Old Black Magic/Oo-Shoo-Be-Doo-Be	195?	3.00	6.00	12.00
ED 2508 [PS]	(title unknown)	195?	3.00	6.00	12.00
REPRISE					
SR 6214	Come Back to Me/What Now My Love/What The World Needs Now Is Love//What Kind of Fool Am I/I Know a Place/Please Don't Talk About Me When I'm Gone	197?	2.50	5.00	10.00
—Jukebox issue; small hole, plays at 33 1/3 rpm					
SR 6214 [PS]	The Sounds of '66	197?	2.50	5.00	10.00
—Part of "Little LP" series (LLP #211); paper envelope; this may also have been issued as a jukebox EP in 1966 with a cardboard cover, but we have no evidence of that at this time					
Albums					
DECCA					
DXB 192 [(2)M]	The Best of Sammy Davis, Jr.	1966	3.75	7.50	15.00
DL 4153 [M]	Mr. Entertainment	1961	3.75	7.50	15.00
DL 4381 [M]	Forget-Me-Nots for First Nighters	1963	3.75	7.50	15.00
DL 4582 [M]	Try a Little Tenderness	1965	3.00	6.00	12.00
DXSB 7192 [(2)S]	The Best of Sammy Davis, Jr.	1966	5.00	10.00	20.00
DL 8118 [M]	Starring Sammy Davis, Jr.	1955	7.50	15.00	30.00
DL 8170 [M]	Just for Lovers	1955	7.50	15.00	30.00
DL 8351 [M]	Here's Looking at You	1956	6.25	12.50	25.00
DL 8486 [M]	Sammy Swings	1957	6.25	12.50	25.00
DL 8641 [M]	It's All Over But the Swingin'	1957	6.25	12.50	25.00
DL 8676 [M]	Mood to Be Wooed	1958	6.25	12.50	25.00
DL 8779 [M]	All the Way And Then Some	1958	6.25	12.50	25.00
DL 8841 [M]	Sammy Davis, Jr., at Town Hall	1959	5.00	10.00	20.00
DL 8854 [M]	Porgy and Bess	1959	5.00	10.00	20.00
DL 8921 [M]	The Sammy Awards	1959	5.00	10.00	20.00
DL 8981 [M]	I Got a Right to Swing	1960	5.00	10.00	20.00
DL 74153 [S]	Mr. Entertainment	1961	5.00	10.00	20.00
DL 74381 [S]	Forget-Me-Nots for First Nighters	1963	5.00	10.00	20.00
DL 74582 [S]	Try a Little Tenderness	1965	3.75	7.50	15.00
DL 78841 [S]	Sammy Davis, Jr., at Town Hall	1959	6.25	12.50	25.00
DL 78854 [S]	Porgy and Bess	1959	6.25	12.50	25.00
DL 78921 [S]	The Sammy Awards	1960	6.25	12.50	25.00
DL 78981 [S]	I Got a Right to Swing	1960	6.25	12.50	25.00
HARMONY					
HS 11299	The Great Sammy Davis, Jr.	196?	3.00	6.00	12.00
HS 11365	Let There Be Love	1970	2.50	5.00	10.00
H 30568	What Kind of Fool Am I	1971	2.50	5.00	10.00
MCA					
4109 [(2)]	Sammy Davis Jr. At His Greatest	1975	3.00	6.00	12.00
MGM					
SE-4832	Sammy Davis Jr. Now	1972	2.50	5.00	10.00
SE-4852	Portrait of Sammy Davis, Jr.	1972	2.50	5.00	10.00
M3G-4965	That's Entertainment!	1974	2.50	5.00	10.00
MOTOWN					
MS 710	Something for Everyone	1970	3.00	6.00	12.00
4519 ML	Hello Detroit!	1984	2.50	5.00	10.00
PICKWICK					
SPC-3002	The Many Faces of Sammy Davis, Jr.	196?	2.50	5.00	10.00
REPRISE					
R-2003 [M]	The Wham of Sam	1961	3.75	7.50	15.00
R9-2003 [S]	The Wham of Sam	1961	5.00	10.00	20.00
R-2010 [M]	Sammy Davis, Jr., Belts the Best of Broadway	1962	3.75	7.50	15.00
R9-2010 [S]	Sammy Davis, Jr., Belts the Best of Broadway	1962	5.00	10.00	20.00
R-6033 [M]	All Star Spectacular	1962	3.75	7.50	15.00
R9-6033 [S]	All Star Spectacular	1962	5.00	10.00	20.00
R-6051 [M]	What Kind of Fool Am I and Other Show-Stoppers	1962	3.75	7.50	15.00
R9-6051 [S]	What Kind of Fool Am I and Other Show-Stoppers	1962	5.00	10.00	20.00
R-6063 [(2)M]	Sammy Davis Jr. at the Cocoanut Grove	1963	5.00	10.00	20.00
R9-6063 [(2)S]	Sammy Davis Jr. at the Cocoanut Grove	1963	6.25	12.50	25.00
R-6082 [M]	As Long As She Needs Me	1963	3.75	7.50	15.00
R9-6082 [S]	As Long As She Needs Me	1963	5.00	10.00	20.00
R-6095 [M]	Sammy Davis Jr. Salutes the Stars of the London Palladium	1964	3.75	7.50	15.00
RS-6095 [S]	Sammy Davis Jr. Salutes the Stars ❑ of the London Palladium	1964	5.00	10.00	20.00
R-6096 [M]	Treasury of Golden Hits	1964	3.75	7.50	15.00
RS-6096 [S]	Treasury of Golden Hits	1964	5.00	10.00	20.00
R-6114 [M]	The Shelter of Your Arms	1964	3.75	7.50	15.00
RS-6114 [S]	The Shelter of Your Arms	1964	5.00	10.00	20.00
R-6126 [M]	California Suite	1964	3.75	7.50	15.00
RS-6126 [S]	California Suite	1964	5.00	10.00	20.00
R-6131 [M]	Sammy Davis Jr. Sings the Big Ones for Young Lovers	1964	3.00	6.00	12.00
RS-6131 [S]	Sammy Davis Jr. Sings the Big Ones for Young Lovers	1964	3.75	7.50	15.00
R-6144 [M]	When the Feeling Hits You	1965	3.00	6.00	12.00
RS-6144 [S]	When the Feeling Hits You	1965	3.75	7.50	15.00
R-6159 [M]	If I Ruled the World	1965	3.00	6.00	12.00
RS-6159 [S]	If I Ruled the World	1965	3.75	7.50	15.00
R-6164 [M]	The Nat Cole Song Book	1965	3.00	6.00	12.00
RS-6164 [S]	The Nat Cole Song Book	1965	3.75	7.50	15.00
R-6169 [M]	Sammy's Back on Broadway	1965	3.00	6.00	12.00
RS-6169 [S]	Sammy's Back on Broadway	1965	3.75	7.50	15.00
R-6188 [M]	The Sammy Davis, Jr., Show	1965	3.00	6.00	12.00

Number	Title (A Side/B Side)	Yr	VG	VG+	NM
❏ RS-6188 [S]	The Sammy Davis, Jr., Show	1965	3.75	7.50	15.00
❏ R-6214 [M]	The Sounds of '66	1966	3.00	6.00	12.00
❏ RS-6214 [S]	The Sounds of '66	1966	3.75	7.50	15.00
❏ R-6236 [M]	Sammy Davis. Jr., Sings/ Laurindo Almeida Plays	1966	3.00	6.00	12.00
❏ RS-6236 [S]	Sammy Davis. Jr., Sings/ Laurindo Almeida Plays	1966	3.75	7.50	15.00
❏ R-6237 [(2)M]	That's All	1967	3.75	7.50	15.00
❏ RS-6237 [(2)S]	That's All	1967	5.00	10.00	20.00
❏ R-6264 [M]	Sammy Davis Jr. Sings the Complete Dr. Dolittle	1967	5.00	10.00	20.00
❏ RS-6264 [S]	Sammy Davis Jr. Sings the Complete Dr. Dolittle	1967	3.00	6.00	12.00
❏ RS-6291	Sammy Davis, Jr.'s Greatest Hits	1968	3.00	6.00	12.00
❏ RS-6308	Lonely Is the Name	1968	3.00	6.00	12.00
❏ RS-6324	I've Gotta Be Me	1969	3.00	6.00	12.00
❏ RS-6339	The Goin's Great	1969	3.00	6.00	12.00
❏ RS-6410	Sammy Davis, Jr., Steps Out	1970	3.00	6.00	12.00
WARNER BROS.					
❏ BSK 3128	Live Performance	1977	2.50	5.00	10.00
WARNER SPECIAL PRODUCTS					
❏ OP-1501	The Sound of Sammy	1978	2.50	5.00	10.00
—Special item for Alka-Seltzer					

DAVIS, SAMMY, JR., AND COUNT BASIE Also see each artist's individual listings.
Albums

Number	Title (A Side/B Side)	Yr	VG	VG+	NM
MGM					
❏ SE-4825	Sammy Davis Jr. and Count Basie	1972	2.50	5.00	10.00
—Reissue of Verve LP?					
VERVE					
❏ V-8605 [M]	Our Shining Hour	1965	3.00	6.00	12.00
❏ V6-8605 [S]	Our Shining Hour	1965	3.75	7.50	15.00

DAVIS, SAMMY, JR., AND CARMEN MCRAE
Albums

Number	Title (A Side/B Side)	Yr	VG	VG+	NM
DECCA					
❏ DL 8490 [M]	Boy Meets Girl	1957	7.50	15.00	30.00

DAVIS, SKEETER Also see THE DAVIS SISTERS.
45s

Number	Title (A Side/B Side)	Yr	VG	VG+	NM
MERCURY					
❏ 73818	I Love Us/It Feels So Good	1976	—	2.00	4.00
❏ 73898	If You Loved Me Now/It's Love That I Feel	1977	—	2.00	4.00
RCA VICTOR					
❏ 37-7863	The Hand You're Holding Now/ Someday Someday	1961	5.00	10.00	20.00
—"Compact Single 33" (small hole, plays at LP speed)					
❏ 47-7034	He Left His Heart for Me/ Don't Let Your Lips Say Yes	1957	3.75	7.50	15.00
❏ 47-7084	Lost to a Geisha Girl/I'm Going Steady with a Heartache	1957	3.75	7.50	15.00
❏ 47-7189	Walk Softly Darling/I Need You All the Time	1958	3.75	7.50	15.00
❏ 47-7293	Wave Bye Bye/ I Forgot More Than You'll Ever Know	1958	3.75	7.50	15.00
❏ 47-7401	I Ain't A-Talkin'/Slave	1958	3.75	7.50	15.00
❏ 47-7471	Set Him Free/The Devil's Doll	1959	3.00	6.00	12.00
❏ 47-7570	Homebreaker/Give Me Death	1959	3.00	6.00	12.00
❏ 47-7671	Am I That Easy to Forget/Wishful Thinking	1960	3.00	6.00	12.00
❏ 47-7767	(I Can't Help You) I'm Falling Too/No, Never	1960	3.00	6.00	12.00
❏ 47-7825	My Last Date (With You)/ Someone I'd Like to Forget	1960	3.00	6.00	12.00
❏ 47-7863	The Hand You're Holding Now/ Someday Someday	1961	3.00	6.00	12.00
❏ 47-7928	Optimistic/Blueberry Hill	1961	3.00	6.00	12.00
❏ 47-7979	Where I Ought to Be/Something Precious	1962	2.50	5.00	10.00
❏ 47-8055	The Little Music Box/The Final Stop	1962	2.50	5.00	10.00
❏ 47-8098	The End of the World/Somebody Loves You	1962	3.00	6.00	12.00
❏ 47-8176	I'm Saving My Love/ Somebody Else on Your Mind	1963	2.50	5.00	10.00
❏ 47-8219	I Can't Stay Mad at You/It Was Only a Heart	1963	2.50	5.00	10.00
❏ 47-8219 [PS]	I Can't Stay Mad at You/It Was Only a Heart	1963	5.00	10.00	20.00
❏ 47-8288	He Says the Same Things to Me/ How Much Can a Lonely Heart Stand	1963	2.50	5.00	10.00
❏ 47-8347	Gonna Get Along Without You Now/ Now You're Gone	1964	2.50	5.00	10.00
❏ 47-8397	Let Me Get Close to You/Face of a Clown	1964	2.50	5.00	10.00
❏ 47-8450	What Am I Going to Do with You/Don't Let Me Stand in Your Way	1964	2.50	5.00	10.00
❏ 47-8496	A Dear John Letter/Too Used to Being with You	1965	2.50	5.00	10.00
—With Bobby Bare					
❏ 47-8543	You Taught Me Everything I Know/I Can't Help It	1965	2.00	4.00	8.00
❏ 47-8642	Sun Glasses/He Loved Me Too Little	1965	2.00	4.00	8.00
❏ 47-8765	I Can't See Me Without You/ Don't Anybody Need My Love	1965	2.00	4.00	8.00
❏ 47-8837	If I Ever Get to Heaven/If I Had Wheels	1966	2.00	4.00	8.00
❏ 47-8932	Goin' Down the Road/ I Can't Stand the Sight of You	1966	2.00	4.00	8.00
❏ 47-9058	Fuel to the Flame/You Call This Love	1966	2.00	4.00	8.00
❏ 47-9242	What Does It Take (To Keep a Man Satisfied)/ What I Go Through	1967	—	3.00	6.00
❏ 47-9371	Set Him Free/Is It Worth It to You	1967	—	3.00	6.00
❏ 47-9459	How in the World/Instinct for Survival	1968	—	3.00	6.00
❏ 47-9543	There's a Fool Born Every Minute/I Can't See Past the Tears	1968	—	3.00	6.00
❏ 47-9625	I Look Up (And See You on My Mind)/Timothy	1968	—	3.00	6.00
❏ 47-9695	The Closest Thing to Love/ Mama Your Big Girl's About to Cry	1968	—	3.00	6.00
❏ 47-9789	Your Husband, My Wife/Before the Sunshine	1969	—	3.00	6.00
—With Bobby Bare					
❏ 47-9818	It's Hard to Be a Woman/ What a Little Girl Don't Know	1969	—	3.00	6.00
❏ 47-9871	We Need a Lot More Jesus/When You Gonna Bring Our Soldiers Home	1970	—	2.50	5.00
❏ 47-9893	Let's Get Together/Everything Is Beautiful	1970	—	3.00	6.00
—With George Hamilton IV					
❏ 47-9896	Bridge Over Troubled Water/How in the World Do You Kill a Memory	1970	—	2.50	5.00
❏ 47-9961	Bus Fare to Kentucky/From Her Arms Into Mine	1971	—	2.50	5.00
❏ 47-9997	Love Takes a Lot of Time/Love, Love, Love	1971	—	2.50	5.00

Number	Title (A Side/B Side)	Yr	VG	VG+	NM
❏ 74-0148	Baby Sweet Baby/Keep Baltimore Beautiful	1969	—	3.00	6.00
❏ 74-0203	Teach Me to Love You/Bobby Blows a Blue Note	1969	—	3.00	6.00
❏ 74-0292	I Didn't Cry Today/I'm a Lover (Not a Fighter)	1969	—	3.00	6.00
❏ 74-0608	One Tin Soldier/Rachel	1971	—	2.50	5.00
❏ 74-0681	Sad Situation/All I Ever Wanted Was Love	1972	—	2.00	4.00
❏ 74-0827	Hillbilly Song/Once	1972	—	2.00	4.00
❏ 74-0968	I Can't Believe That It's All Over/Try Jesus	1973	—	2.00	4.00
❏ APBO-0188	Don't Forget to Remember/Baby Get That Leavin' Off Your Mind	1973	—	2.00	4.00
❏ APBO-0277	One More Time/Stay Awhile with Me	1974	—	2.00	4.00
❏ VP-3-2668 [S]	Your Cheatin' Heart/El Paso	196?	3.75	7.50	15.00
—B-side by Sons of the Pioneers; jukebox issue; small hole, plays at 33 1/3 rpm					
❏ PB-10048	Come Mornin'/Lovin' Touch	1974	—	4.00	
Albums					
GUSTO					
❏ 0014	Best of the Best	1978	2.50	5.00	10.00
RCA CAMDEN					
❏ ACL1-0622	He Wakes Me with a Kiss	1974	2.50	5.00	10.00
❏ CAL-818 [M]	I Forgot More Than You'll Ever Know	196?	3.00	6.00	12.00
❏ CAS-818(e) [R]	I Forgot More Than You'll Ever Know	196?	3.75	7.50	15.00
❏ CAL-899 [M]	Blueberry Hill and Other Favorites	1965	3.00	6.00	12.00
❏ CAS-899 [S]	Blueberry Hill and Other Favorites	1965	3.75	7.50	15.00
❏ CAS-2367	Easy to Love	1970	3.00	6.00	12.00
❏ CAS-2517	Foggy Mountain Top	1971	3.00	6.00	12.00
❏ CAS-2607	The End of the World	1972	2.50	5.00	10.00
RCA VICTOR					
❏ APL1-0190	The Best of Skeeter Davis, Volume 2	1973	3.00	6.00	12.00
❏ APL1-0322	I Can't Believe That It's All Over	1974	3.00	6.00	12.00
❏ LPM-2197 [M]	I'll Sing You a Song and Harmonize, Too	1960	6.25	12.50	25.00
❏ LSP-2197 [S]	I'll Sing You a Song and Harmonize, Too	1960	7.50	15.00	30.00
❏ LPM-2327 [M]	Here's the Answer	1961	6.25	12.50	25.00
❏ LSP-2327 [S]	Here's the Answer	1961	7.50	15.00	30.00
❏ LPM-2699 [M]	The End of the World	1963	6.25	12.50	25.00
❏ LSP-2699 [S]	The End of the World	1963	7.50	15.00	30.00
❏ LPM-2736 [M]	Cloudy, With Occasional Tears	1963	6.25	12.50	25.00
❏ LSP-2736 [S]	Cloudy, With Occasional Tears	1963	7.50	15.00	30.00
❏ LPM-2980 [M]	Let Me Get Close to You	1964	5.00	10.00	20.00
❏ LSP-2980 [S]	Let Me Get Close to You	1964	6.25	12.50	25.00
❏ LPM-3374 [M]	The Best of Skeeter Davis	1965	6.25	12.50	25.00
❏ LSP-3374 [S]	The Best of Skeeter Davis	1965	6.25	12.50	25.00
❏ LPM-3382 [M]	Written by the Stars	1965	5.00	10.00	20.00
❏ LSP-3382 [S]	Written by the Stars	1965	6.25	12.50	25.00
❏ LPM-3463 [M]	Skeeter Sings Standards	1965	5.00	10.00	20.00
❏ LSP-3463 [S]	Skeeter Sings Standards	1965	6.25	12.50	25.00
❏ LPM-3567 [M]	Singin' in the Summer Sun	1966	5.00	10.00	20.00
❏ LSP-3567 [S]	Singin' in the Summer Sun	1966	6.25	12.50	25.00
❏ LPM-3667 [M]	My Heart's in the Country	1966	5.00	10.00	20.00
❏ LSP-3667 [S]	My Heart's in the Country	1966	6.25	12.50	25.00
❏ LPM-3763 [M]	Hand in Hand with Jesus	1967	7.50	15.00	30.00
❏ LSP-3763 [S]	Hand in Hand with Jesus	1967	5.00	10.00	20.00
❏ LPM-3790 [M]	Skeeter Davis Sings Buddy Holly	1967	12.50	25.00	50.00
❏ LSP-3790 [S]	Skeeter Davis Sings Buddy Holly	1967	10.00	20.00	40.00
❏ LPM-3876 [M]	What Does It Take (To Keep a Man Like You Satisfied)	1967	7.50	15.00	30.00
❏ LSP-3876 [S]	What Does It Take (To Keep a Man Like You Satisfied)	1967	5.00	10.00	20.00
❏ LPM-3960 [M]	Why So Lonely?	1968	12.50	25.00	50.00
❏ LSP-3960 [S]	Why So Lonely?	1968	5.00	10.00	20.00
❏ LSP-4055	I Love Flatt & Scruggs	1968	5.00	10.00	20.00
❏ LSP-4124	The Closest Thing to Love	1969	5.00	10.00	20.00
❏ LSP-4200	Maryfrances	1969	5.00	10.00	20.00
❏ LSP-4310	A Place in the Country	1970	3.75	7.50	15.00
❏ LSP-4382	It's Hard to Be a Woman	1970	3.75	7.50	15.00
❏ LSP-4486	Skeeter	1971	3.75	7.50	15.00
❏ LSP-4557	Love Takes a Lot	1971	3.75	7.50	15.00
❏ LSP-4642	Bring It on Home	1972	3.75	7.50	15.00
❏ LSP-4732	Skeeter Sings Dolly	1972	3.75	7.50	15.00
❏ LSP-4818	Hillbilly Singer	1972	3.75	7.50	15.00

DAVIS, SKEETER, AND DON BOWMAN
45s

Number	Title (A Side/B Side)	Yr	VG	VG+	NM
RCA VICTOR					
❏ 47-9415	For Loving You/Baby, It's Cold Outside	1967	2.00	4.00	8.00

DAVIS, SKEETER, AND NRBQ Also see each artist's individual listings.
Albums

Number	Title (A Side/B Side)	Yr	VG	VG+	NM
ROUNDER					
❏ 3092	She Sings, They Play	1986	3.00	6.00	12.00

DAVIS, SPENCER, GROUP Includes Spencer Davis solo. Also see STEVE WINWOOD.
45s

Number	Title (A Side/B Side)	Yr	VG	VG+	NM
ATCO					
❏ 6400	Keep On Running/High Time Baby	1966	3.75	7.50	15.00
❏ 6416	Somebody Help Me/Stevie's Blues	1966	3.75	7.50	15.00
FONTANA					
❏ 1960	I Can't Stand It/Midnight Train	1964	3.75	7.50	15.00
UNITED ARTISTS					
❏ SP 78 [DJ]	Voter Registration Promo Spot (:60 with music)/ (:30 without music)	1972	3.75	7.50	15.00
❏ 0115	Gimme Some Lovin'/Keep On Running	1973	—	2.00	4.00
—"Silver Spotlight Series" reissue					
❏ 0116	I'm a Man/Somebody Help Me	1973	—	2.00	4.00
—"Silver Spotlight Series" reissue					
❏ 1668	I'm a Man/I Can't Get Enough of It	196?	—	2.50	5.00
—Silver Spotlight Series					
❏ 50108	Gimme Some Lovin'/Blues in F	1966	3.00	6.00	12.00
❏ 50144	I'm a Man/Can't Get Enough of It	1967	3.00	6.00	12.00
❏ 50162	Somebody Help Me/On the Green Light	1967	2.50	5.00	10.00
❏ 50202	Time Seller/Don't Want You No More	1967	2.50	5.00	10.00
❏ 50202 [PS]	Time Seller/Don't Want You No More	1967	5.00	10.00	20.00
❏ 50286	Looking Back/After Tea	1968	2.50	5.00	10.00
❏ 50922	Listen to the Rhythm/Sunday Walk in the Rain	1972	—	3.00	6.00
—Spencer Davis solo					
❏ 50993	Rainy Season/Tumble-Down Tenement Row	1972	—	3.00	6.00
—Spencer Davis solo					

Number	Title (A Side/B Side)	Yr	VG	VG+	NM

VERTIGO

Number	Title (A Side/B Side)	Yr	VG	VG+	NM
❏ 110	Don't You Let It Bring You Down/				
	Today Gluggo, Tomorrow the World	1973	—	2.50	5.00
❏ 112	Living in a Back Street/Need a Helping Hand	1974	—	2.50	5.00

Albums

ALLEGIANCE

❏ AV-442	Crossfire	1983	2.50	5.00	10.00

DATE

❏ TES-4021	Funky	1971	37.50	75.00	150.00

—Deleted almost immediately upon release

MEDIARTS

❏ 41-11	It's Been So Long	1971	3.00	6.00	12.00

RHINO

❏ RNLP 117	The Best of the Spencer Davis Group	1983	2.00	4.00	8.00
❏ RNLP 70172	The Best of the Spencer Davis Group				
	(Golden Archive Series)	1987	3.00	6.00	12.00

UNITED ARTISTS

❏ UA-LA433-E	The Very Best of the Spencer Davis Group	1975	2.50	5.00	10.00
❏ UAL 3578 [M]	Gimme Some Lovin'	1967	12.50	25.00	50.00
❏ UAL 3589 [M]	I'm a Man	1967	10.00	20.00	40.00
❏ UAS 6578 [R]	Gimme Some Lovin'	1967	10.00	20.00	40.00
❏ UAS 6589 [P]	I'm a Man	1967	12.50	25.00	50.00
❏ UAS 6641 [P]	The Spencer Davis Group's Greatest Hits	1968	6.25	12.50	25.00
❏ UAS 6652	With Their New Face On	1968	5.00	10.00	20.00
❏ UAS 6691	Heavies	1969	5.00	10.00	20.00
❏ ST-91127 [R]	Gimme Some Lovin'	1967	12.50	25.00	50.00

—Capitol Record Club edition

VERTIGO

❏ VEL-1015	Gluggo	1973	3.00	6.00	12.00
❏ VEL-1021	Living in a Back Street	1974	3.00	6.00	12.00

DAVIS, TYRONE

45s

ABC

❏ 11030	Bet You Win/What If a Man	1967	3.00	6.00	12.00

COLUMBIA

❏ 02269	Just My Luck/Let's Be Closer Together	1981	—	2.00	4.00
❏ 02634	Leave Well Enough Alone/I Won't Let Go	1981	—	2.00	4.00
❏ 10388	Give It Up (Turn It Loose)/You're Too Much	1976	—	2.50	5.00
❏ 10457	Close to You/Wrong Doers	1976	—	2.50	5.00
❏ 10528	This I Swear/Givin' Myself to You	1977	—	2.50	5.00
❏ 10604	All You Got/I Got Carried Away	1977	—	2.50	5.00
❏ 10684	Get It Up (Disco)/It's You, It's You	1978	—	2.50	5.00
❏ 10773	Can't Help But Say/Bunky	1978	—	2.00	4.00
❏ 10904	In the Mood/I Can't Wait	1979	—	2.00	4.00
❏ 11035	Ain't Nothing I Can Do/The Love I Need	1979	—	2.00	4.00
❏ 11128	Be With Me/Love You Forever	1979	—	2.00	4.00
❏ 11199	Can't You Tell Me/				
	I Don't Think You Heard Me	1980	—	2.00	4.00
❏ 11246	Keep On Dancin'/Heart Failure	1980	—	2.00	4.00
❏ 11344	How Sweet It Is (To Be Loved By You)/				
	I Can't Wait	1980	—	2.00	4.00
❏ 11415	I Just Can't Keep On Going/				
	We Don't Need No Music	1980	—	2.00	4.00

DAKAR

❏ 602	Can I Change My Mind/				
	A Woman Needs to Be Loved	1968	2.50	5.00	10.00
❏ 605	Is It Something You've Got/Undying Love	1969	2.00	4.00	8.00
❏ 609	All the Waiting Is Not in Vain/				
	Need Your Lovin' Everybody	1969	2.00	4.00	8.00
❏ 611	If It's Love That You're After/				
	When I'm Not Around	1969	2.00	4.00	8.00
❏ 615	If I Didn't Love You/				
	You Can't Keep a Good Man Down	1969	2.00	4.00	8.00
❏ 616	Turn Back the Hands of Time/				
	I Keep Coming Back	1970	2.00	4.00	8.00
❏ 618	I'll Be Right Here/Just Because of You	1970	—	3.00	6.00
❏ 621	Let Me Back In/Love Bones	1970	—	3.00	6.00
❏ 623	Could I Forget You/Just My Way of Loving You	1971	—	3.00	6.00
❏ 624	One-Way Ticket/We Got a Love	1971	—	3.00	6.00
❏ 626	You Keep Me Holding On/				
	We Got a Love No One Can Deny	1971	—	3.00	6.00
❏ 1452	Can I Change My Mind/				
	A Woman Needs to Be Loved	1968	3.00	6.00	12.00
❏ 4501	I Had It All the Time/You Wouldn't Believe	1972	—	2.50	5.00
❏ 4507	Was I Just a Fool/After All This Time	1972	—	2.50	5.00
❏ 4510	Come and Get This Ring/After All This Time	1972	—	2.50	5.00
❏ 4513	If You Had a Change in Mind/Was It Just a Feelin'	1972	—	2.50	5.00
❏ 4519	Without You in My Life/How Could I Forget You	1973	—	2.50	5.00
❏ 4523	There It Is/You Wouldn't Believe	1973	—	2.50	5.00
❏ 4526	Wrapped Up in Your Warm and Tender Love/				
	True Love Is Hard to Find	1973	—	2.50	5.00
❏ 4529	I Wish It Was Me/				
	You Don't Have to Beg Me to Stay	1974	—	2.50	5.00
❏ 4532	What Goes Up (Must Come Down)/There's Got				
	to Be an Answer	1974	—	2.50	5.00
❏ 4536	Happiness Is Being with You/				
	Where Lovers Meet	1974	—	2.50	5.00
❏ 4538	I Can't Make It Without You/				
	You Wouldn't Believe	1974	—	2.50	5.00
❏ 4541	Homewreckers/This Time	1975	—	2.50	5.00
❏ 4545	A Woman Needs to Be Loved/Just Because of				
	You (I Can See My Way Through)	1975	—	2.50	5.00
❏ 4550	Turning Point/Don't Let It Be Too Late	1975	—	2.50	5.00
❏ 4553	So Good (To Be Home with You)/I Can't Bump	1976	—	2.50	5.00
❏ 4558	I Can't Bump, Part 2/Saving My Love for You	1976	—	2.50	5.00
❏ 4561	Ever Lovin' Girl/Forever	1976	—	2.50	5.00
❏ 4563	Where Lovers Meet (At the Dark End of the				
	Street)/It's All in the Game	1977	—	2.50	5.00

FUTURE

❏ 101	Sexy Thing/Save Me	1987	—	2.50	5.00
❏ 102	I'm in Love Again/Serious Love	1987	—	2.00	4.00
❏ 103	Do You Feel It/(Instrumental)	1988	—	2.00	4.00
❏ 104	It's a Miracle/Wrong Doers	1988	—	2.00	4.00
❏ 204	Flashin' Back/Flashin' Back (LP Version)	1988	—	2.00	4.00

HIGHRISE

❏ 2005	Are You Serious/Overdrive	1982	—	2.00	4.00
❏ 2009	A Little Bit of Loving (Goes a Long Way)/				
	Where Did We Lose	1983	—	2.00	4.00

ICHIBAN

❏ 139	Can I Change My Mind/Hey There Lonely Girl	1989	—	2.00	4.00

—B-side by Eddie Holman

❏ 226	I'll Always Love You/Can I Change My Mind	1991	—	—	3.00
❏ 237	Mom's Apple Pie/Do U Still Love Me	1991	—	—	3.00
❏ 255	Something's Mighty Wrong/Let Me Love You	1992	—	—	3.00
❏ 261	Running In and Out of My Life/				
	I've Gotta Get Over You	1992	—	—	3.00
❏ 273	Don't Make Me Choose/Ain't Gonna Get It	1992	—	—	3.00
❏ 285	It's a Miracle/Do You Feel It	1993	—	—	3.00
❏ 292	I Found Myself When I Lost You/Something				
	About a Woman	1993	—	—	3.00

OCEAN-FRONT

❏ 2001	I Found Myself When I Lost You/(Instrumental)	1983	—	2.00	4.00
❏ 2004	Let Me Be Your Pacifier/Turning Point	1984	—	2.00	4.00

Albums

COLUMBIA

❏ PC 34268	Love and Touch	1976	3.00	6.00	12.00
❏ PC 34654	Let's Be Closer Together	1977	3.00	6.00	12.00
❏ JC 35305	I Can't Go On This Way	1978	3.00	6.00	12.00
❏ JC 35723	In the Mood with Tyrone Davis	1979	3.00	6.00	12.00
❏ JC 36230	Can't You Tell It's Me	1979	3.00	6.00	12.00
❏ JC 36598	I Just Can't Keep On Going	1980	3.00	6.00	12.00
❏ FC 37366	Everything in Place	1981	3.00	6.00	12.00
❏ PC 37979	The Best of Tyrone Davis	1982	2.50	5.00	10.00

DAKAR

❏ DK-9005	Can I Change My Mind	1969	7.50	15.00	30.00
❏ DK-9027	Turn Back the Hands of Time	1970	7.50	15.00	30.00
❏ DK-76901	I Had It All the Time	1972	7.50	15.00	30.00
❏ DK-76902	Tyrone Davis' Greatest Hits	1972	6.25	12.50	25.00
❏ DK-76904	Without You in My Life	1973	6.25	12.50	25.00
❏ DK-76909	It's All in the Game	1974	5.00	10.00	20.00
❏ DK-76915	Homewrecker	1975	5.00	10.00	20.00
❏ DK-76918	Turning Point	1976	5.00	10.00	20.00

EPIC

❏ PE 38626	Tyrone Davis' Greatest Hits	1983	2.00	4.00	8.00

HIGHRISE

❏ 103	Tyrone Davis	1982	2.50	5.00	10.00

ICHIBAN

❏ ICH 1103	I'll Always Love You	1991	3.00	6.00	12.00

DAVIS SISTERS, THE SKEETER DAVIS and Betty Davis (replaced by Georgia Davis).

45s

FORTUNE

❏ 170	Jealous Love/Going Down the Road	1952	10.00	20.00	40.00

—B-side by Roy Hall

❏ 174	Kaw-Liga/Sorrow and Pain	1952	6.25	12.50	25.00
❏ 175	Heartbreak Ahead/Steelwood	1952	6.25	12.50	25.00

RCA VICTOR

❏ 47-5345	I Forgot More Than You'll Ever Know/Rock-a-				
	Bye Boogie	1953	6.25	12.50	25.00
❏ 47-5460	You're Gone/Sorrow and Pain	1953	3.75	7.50	15.00
❏ 47-5607	Takin' Time Out for Tears/Gotta Get a-Goin'	1954	3.75	7.50	15.00
❏ 47-5701	You Weren't Ashamed to Kiss Me Last Night/				
	Foggy Mountain Top	1954	3.75	7.50	15.00
❏ 47-5843	Show Me/Just Like Me	1954	3.75	7.50	15.00
❏ 47-5906	The Christmas Boogie/Tomorrow I'll Cry	1954	3.75	7.50	15.00
❏ 47-5966	Everlovin'/Tomorrow's Just Another Day to Cry	1954	3.75	7.50	15.00
❏ 47-6086	Fiddle Diddle Diddle/Come Back to Me	1955	3.75	7.50	15.00
❏ 47-6187	I'll Get Him Back/I've Closed the Door	1955	3.75	7.50	15.00
❏ 47-6291	Baby Be Mine/It's the Girl Who Gets the Blame	1955	3.75	7.50	15.00
❏ 47-6409	Don't Take Him for Granted/Blues for Company	1956	3.75	7.50	15.00
❏ 47-6490	Lonely and Blue/Lying Brown Eyes	1956	3.75	7.50	15.00

DAWE, TIM Also see IRON BUTTERFLY.

Albums

STRAIGHT

❏ STS-1058	Penrod	1969	7.50	15.00	30.00

WARNER BROS.

❏ WS 1841	Penrod	1970	3.75	7.50	15.00

DAWN (1) One-man, two-woman vocal group featuring TONY ORLANDO. Includes records issued as "Dawn Featuring Tony Orlando" and "Tony Orlando and Dawn."

45s

ARISTA

❏ 0105	Gimme a Good Old Mammy Song/Little Heads				
	in Bunk Beds	1975	—	2.00	4.00
❏ 0156	Skybird/That's the Way a Wallflower Grows	1975	—	2.00	4.00
❏ 0301	Tie a Yellow Ribbon Round the Ole Oak Tree/				
	Say, Has Anybody Seen My Sweet Gypsy				
	Rose	1978	—	2.00	4.00

BELL

❏ 903	Candida/Look At...	1970	—	3.00	6.00
❏ 938	Knock Three Times/Home	1970	—	3.00	6.00
❏ 970	I Play and Sing/Get Out from Where We Are	1971	—	2.50	5.00
❏ 45107	Summer Sand/The Sweet Soft Sounds of Love	1971	—	2.50	5.00
❏ 45141	What Are You Doing Sunday/				
	The Sweet Soft Sounds of Love	1971	—	2.50	5.00
❏ 45175	Runaway-Happy Together/				
	Don't Act Like a Baby	1972	—	2.50	5.00
❏ 45225	Vaya Con Dios/				
	I Can't Believe How Much I Love You	1972	—	2.50	5.00
❏ 45285	You're a Lady/In the Park	1972	—	2.00	4.00
❏ 45318	Tie a Yellow Ribbon Round the Ole Oak Tree/I				
	Can't Believe How Much I Love You	1973	—	2.50	5.00
❏ 45374	Say, Has Anybody Seen My Sweet Gypsy Rose/				
	The Spark of Love Is Kindlin'	1973	—	2.00	4.00
❏ 45424	Who's in the Strawberry Patch with Sally/				
	Ukulele Man	1973	—	2.00	4.00
❏ 45450	It Only Hurts When I Try to Smile/				
	Sweet Summer Days of My Life	1974	—	2.00	4.00
❏ 45601	Steppin' Out (Gonna Boogie Tonight)/She Can't				
	Hold a Candle to You	1974	—	2.00	4.00

D

Number	Title (A Side/B Side)	Yr	VG	VG+	NM
❑ 45620	Look in My Eyes Pretty Woman/				
	My Love Has No Pride	1974	—	2.00	4.00
ELEKTRA					
❑ 45240	He Don't Love You (Like I Love You)/Pick It Up	1975	—	2.00	4.00
❑ 45260	Mornin' Beautiful/Dance, Rosalie, Dance	1975	—	2.00	4.00
❑ 45275	You're All I Need to Get By/				
	Know You Like a Book	1975	—	2.00	4.00
❑ 45302	Cupid/You're Growin' on Me	1976	—	2.00	4.00
❑ 45319	Midnight Love Affair/The Selfish Ones	1976	—	2.00	4.00
❑ 45387	Sing/Sweet on Candy	1977	—	2.00	4.00
❑ 45432	Growin' on Me/You're All I Need to Get By	1977	—	2.00	4.00
❑ 45501	Bring It On Home to Me/Don't Let Go	1978	—	2.00	4.00
❑ 45542	I Count the Tears/A Lover's Question	1978	—	2.00	4.00
❑ 45542	I Count the Tears/This Is Rock and Roll	1978	—	2.00	4.00
Albums					
ARISTA					
❑ AL 4045	Greatest Hits	1975	2.50	5.00	10.00
❑ AQ 4045 [Q]	Greatest Hits	1975	3.75	7.50	15.00
❑ AL 4059	Skybird	1975	2.50	5.00	10.00
❑ A2L 9006 [(2)]	The World of Tony Orlando and Dawn	1977	3.00	6.00	12.00
BELL					
❑ 1112	Tuneweaving	1973	2.50	5.00	10.00
❑ 1130	Dawn's New Ragtime Follies	1973	2.50	5.00	10.00
❑ 1317	Prime Time	1974	2.50	5.00	10.00
❑ 1320	Candida & Knock Three Times	1974	2.50	5.00	10.00
—Reissue of 6052					
❑ 1322	Tony Orlando & Dawn II	1974	2.50	5.00	10.00
—Reissue of 6069					
❑ 6052	Candida	1970	3.00	6.00	12.00
❑ 6069	Dawn Featuring Tony Orlando	1971	3.00	6.00	12.00
ELEKTRA					
❑ 7E-1034	He Don't Love You (Like I Love You)	1975	2.50	5.00	10.00
❑ EQ-1034 [Q]	He Don't Love You (Like I Love You)	1975	3.75	7.50	15.00
❑ 7E-1049	To Be with You	1976	2.50	5.00	10.00
❑ EQ-1049 [Q]	To Be with You	1976	3.75	7.50	15.00

DAWN (2) Girl group.
45s

Number	Title (A Side/B Side)	Yr	VG	VG+	NM
ABC-PARAMOUNT					
❑ 10791	Baby's Gone Away/Gotta Get Away	1966	2.00	4.00	8.00
APT					
❑ 25088	Can't Get Him Off My Mind/Two of a Kind	1965	3.75	7.50	15.00

DAWN (3) Said to be THE FIVE DISCS in disguise.
45s

Number	Title (A Side/B Side)	Yr	VG	VG+	NM
LAURIE					
❑ 3388	I'm Afraid They're All Talking About Me/Lovers'				
	Melody	1967	3.00	6.00	12.00
❑ 3417	Sandy/For the Love of Money	1968	3.00	6.00	12.00
RUST					
❑ 5128	Baby I Love You/Bring It On Home	1968	3.00	6.00	12.00

DAWN (U) Definitely not groups (1) or (3), these may be by group (2), but we're not sure.
45s

Number	Title (A Side/B Side)	Yr	VG	VG+	NM
CADET					
❑ 5644	The Fifth Day of June/Ballad of Gene	1969	—	3.00	6.00
GAMBLE					
❑ 4002	Ba Ba Ba De Ba (on the Way Through My Mind)/				
	In Love Again	1969	—	3.00	6.00
❑ 4002 [PS]	Ba Ba Ba De Ba (on the Way Through My Mind)/				
	In Love Again	1969	3.00	6.00	12.00
UNITED ARTISTS					
❑ 50096	Love Is a Magic Word/How Can I Get Off This				
	Merry-Go-Round	1966	3.00	6.00	12.00

DAWSON, RON
45s

Number	Title (A Side/B Side)	Yr	VG	VG+	NM
COLUMBIA					
❑ 4-44757	If Baby's Still on My Mind/The Dark Side of Lovin'				
	You	1969	2.00	4.00	8.00
❑ 4-44978	She Cried/Steel Rail Blues	1969	2.00	4.00	8.00

DAWSON, RONNIE
45s

Number	Title (A Side/B Side)	Yr	VG	VG+	NM
BACK BEAT					
❑ 522	Action Packed/I Make the Love	1958	25.00	50.00	100.00
—As "Ronnie Dee"					
MAVERICK					
❑ 101	My Big Desire/How Can We Tell Her	1961	50.00	100.00	200.00
ROCKIN'					
❑ 1	Rockin' Bones/Congratulations to Me	1959	100.00	200.00	400.00
—Reproductions of this record exist					
SWAN					
❑ 4047	Ain't That a Kick in the Head/Hazel	1960	5.00	10.00	20.00
❑ 4054	Summer's Comin'/Decided by the Angels	1960	5.00	10.00	20.00

DAY, BING
45s

Number	Title (A Side/B Side)	Yr	VG	VG+	NM
FEDERAL					
❑ 12320	Pony Tail Partner/Since You Left Me	1958	17.50	35.00	70.00
MERCURY					
❑ 71446	I Can't Help It/Mama's Place	1959	15.00	30.00	60.00
❑ 71494	How Do I Do It/Mary's Place	1959	5.00	10.00	20.00

DAY, BOBBY
45s

Number	Title (A Side/B Side)	Yr	VG	VG+	NM
CASH					
❑ 1031	The Truth Hurts/Let's Live Together As One	1956	25.00	50.00	100.00
—As "Bobby Byrd and the Birds"					
CLASS					
❑ 207	Come Seven/So Long Baby	1957	5.00	10.00	20.00
❑ 211	Little Bitty Pretty One/When the Swallows Come				
	Back to Capistrano	1957	6.25	12.50	25.00
❑ 215	Beep-Beep-Beep/Darling, If I Had You	1957	5.00	10.00	20.00
❑ 225	Little Turtle Dove/Saving My Life for You	1958	5.00	10.00	20.00
❑ 229	Rock-N Robin/Over and Over	1958	7.50	15.00	30.00

Number	Title (A Side/B Side)	Yr	VG	VG+	NM
❑ 241	The Bluebird, the Buzzard, and the Oriole/				
	Alone Too Long	1959	5.00	10.00	20.00
❑ 245	That's All I Want/Say Yes	1959	3.75	7.50	15.00
❑ 252	Mr. and Mrs. Rock & Roll/Gotta New Girl	1959	3.75	7.50	15.00
❑ 255	Ain't Gonna Cry No More/				
	Love Is a One-Time Affair	1959	3.75	7.50	15.00
❑ 257	Unchained Melody/				
	Three Young Rebs from Georgia	1959	3.75	7.50	15.00
❑ 263	My Blue Heaven/I Don't Want To	1960	3.75	7.50	15.00
❑ 705	Don't Leave Me Hangin' on a String/				
	When I Started Dancin'	1965	3.00	6.00	12.00
CORVET					
❑ 1017	Why/Gotta Girl	1958	15.00	30.00	60.00
—As "Bobby Byrd and the Impalas"					
JAMIE					
❑ 1039	Bippin' and Boppin' Over You/Strawberry Stomp	1957	7.50	15.00	30.00
—As "Robert Byrd and His Birdies"					
RCA VICTOR					
❑ 47-8133	Another Country, Another World/Know-It-All	1963	2.50	5.00	10.00
❑ 47-8196	Buzz Buzz Buzz/Pretty Little Girl Next Door	1963	2.50	5.00	10.00
❑ 47-8230	Down on My Knees/Jole Blon, Little Darling	1963	2.50	5.00	10.00
❑ 47-8316	When I See My Baby Smile/				
	On the Street Where You Live	1964	2.50	5.00	10.00
RENDEZVOUS					
❑ 130	Teenage Philosopher/Undecided	1960	3.00	6.00	12.00
❑ 133	Rockin' Robin/Over and Over	1960	3.00	6.00	12.00
❑ 136	Gee Whiz/Over and Over	1960	3.00	6.00	12.00
❑ 146	I Need Help/Life Can Be Beautiful	1961	3.00	6.00	12.00
❑ 158	King's Highway/What Fools We Mortals Be	1961	3.00	6.00	12.00
❑ 167	Don't Worry 'Bout Me/Oop-E-Du-Pers Ball	1962	3.00	6.00	12.00
❑ 175	Undecided/Slow Pokey Joe	1962	3.00	6.00	12.00
SAGE AND SAND					
❑ 203	Please Don't Hurt Me/Delicious Are Your Kisses	1955	10.00	20.00	40.00
—As "Bobby Byrd"					
SPARK					
❑ 501	Bippin' and Boppin' Over You/Strawberry Stomp	1957	12.50	25.00	50.00
—As "Robert Byrd and His Birdies"					
SURE SHOT					
❑ 5036	So Lonely/Spicks and Specks	1967	2.00	4.00	8.00
ZEPHYR					
❑ 70-018	If We Should Meet Again/Looby Loo	1957	7.50	15.00	30.00
—As "Bobby Byrd"					
Albums					
CLASS					
❑ LP-5002 [M]	Rockin' with Robin	1959	100.00	200.00	400.00
COLLECTABLES					
❑ COL-5074	Golden Classics	198?	2.50	5.00	10.00
RENDEZVOUS					
❑ M-1312 [M]	Rockin' with Robin	196?	20.00	40.00	80.00
RHINO					
❑ RNDF-208	The Best of Bobby Day	1984	3.00	6.00	12.00

DAY, DARLENE
45s

Number	Title (A Side/B Side)	Yr	VG	VG+	NM
MUSIC MAKERS					
❑ 106	I Love You So/Will	1961	25.00	50.00	100.00

DAY, DAVE DIDDLE
45s

Number	Title (A Side/B Side)	Yr	VG	VG+	NM
FEE BEE					
❑ 212	Blue Moon Baby/Suzanne My Love	1958	6.25	12.50	25.00
❑ 215	Jelly Belly/Deep in My Heart	1958	6.25	12.50	25.00
❑ 219	Motorcycle Mike/Tired of Waiting	1958	3.75	7.50	15.00
MERCURY					
❑ 71114	Blue Moon Baby/Suzanne My Love	1957	37.50	75.00	150.00

DAY, DORIS
45s

Number	Title (A Side/B Side)	Yr	VG	VG+	NM
COLUMBIA					
❑ 1-108 (?)	If You Will Marry Me/You Was	1949	10.00	20.00	40.00
—Microgroove 7-inch, 33 1/3 rpm single					
❑ 1-113	Powder Your Face with Sunshine (Smile! Smile!				
	Smile!)/I'll String Along with You	1949	10.00	20.00	40.00
—Microgroove 7-inch, 33 1/3 rpm single					
❑ 1-125 (?)	Beginning to Miss You/Don't Gamble with				
	Romance	1949	10.00	20.00	40.00
—Microgroove 7-inch, 33 1/3 rpm single					
❑ 1-185 (?)	How It Lies, How It Lies/If I Could Be with You	1949	10.00	20.00	40.00
—Microgroove 7-inch, 33 1/3 rpm single					
❑ 1-211	Again/Everywhere You Go	1949	10.00	20.00	40.00
—Microgroove 7-inch, 33 1/3 rpm single					
❑ 1-251	(Where Are You) Now That I Need You/Blame				
	My Absent-Minded Heart	1949	10.00	20.00	40.00
—Microgroove 7-inch, 33 1/3 rpm single					
❑ 1-266 (?)	At the Café Rendezvous/It's a Great Feeling	1949	10.00	20.00	40.00
—Microgroove 7-inch, 33 1/3 rpm single					
❑ 1-353	Canadian Capers (Cuttin' Capers)/Better To				
	Conceal Than Reveal	1949	10.00	20.00	40.00
—Microgroove 7-inch, 33 1/3 rpm single					
❑ 1-376	(There's a) Bluebird on Your Windowsill/The				
	River Seine	1949	10.00	20.00	40.00
—Microgroove 7-inch, 33 1/3 rpm single					
❑ 1-381 (?)	The Three Rivers/Festival of Roses	1949	10.00	20.00	40.00
—Microgroove 7-inch, 33 1/3 rpm single					
❑ 1-406 (?)	The Game of Broken Hearts/I'll Never Slip				
	Around Again	1949	10.00	20.00	40.00
—Microgroove 7-inch, 33 1/3 rpm single					
❑ 1-407	Quicksilver/Crocodile Tears	1949	10.00	20.00	40.00
—Microgroove 7-inch, 33 1/3 rpm single					
❑ 1-454 (?)	Mama, What'll I Do/Save a Little Sunbeam	1950	10.00	20.00	40.00
—Microgroove 7-inch, 33 1/3 rpm single					
❑ 1-457 (?)	I Don't Wanna Be Kissed/With You Anywhere				
	You Are	1950	10.00	20.00	40.00
—Microgroove 7-inch, 33 1/3 rpm single					
❑ 1-480	Bewitched/Imagination	1950	10.00	20.00	40.00
—Microgroove 7-inch, 33 1/3 rpm single					

Number	Title (A Side/B Side)	Yr	VG	VG+	NM
❑ 1-497	I Said My Pajamas (And Put On My Prayers)/ Enjoy Yourself (It's Later Than You Think)	1950	10.00	20.00	40.00
—Microgroove 7-inch, 33 1/3 rpm single					
❑ 1-591	Hoop-Dee-Doo/Marriage Ties	1950	10.00	20.00	40.00
—Microgroove 7-inch, 33 1/3 rpm single					
❑ 1-637	I Didn't Slip — I Wasn't Pushed — I Fell/ Before I Loved You	1950	10.00	20.00	40.00
—Microgroove 7-inch, 33 1/3 rpm single					
❑ 1-708	Darn That Dream/I've Forgotten You	1950	10.00	20.00	40.00
—Microgroove 7-inch, 33 1/3 rpm single					
❑ 6-708	Darn That Dream/I've Forgotten You	1950	7.50	15.00	30.00
❑ 1-811	A Load of Hay/Orange Colored Sky	1950	10.00	20.00	40.00
—With the Paige Cavanaugh Trio; Microgroove 33 rpm 7-inch single, small hole					
❑ 6-811	A Load of Hay/Orange Colored Sky	1950	7.50	15.00	30.00
❑ 1-838 (?)	A Bushel and a Peck/The Best Thing for You	1950	10.00	20.00	40.00
—Microgroove 7-inch, 33 1/3 rpm single					
❑ 6-838 (?)	A Bushel and a Peck/The Best Thing for You	1950	7.50	15.00	30.00
❑ 1-859 (?)	If I Were a Bell/I've Never Been in Love Before	1950	10.00	20.00	40.00
—Microgroove 7-inch, 33 1/3 rpm single					
❑ 6-859 (?)	If I Were a Bell/I've Never Been in Love Before	1950	7.50	15.00	30.00
❑ 6-893	I Only Have Eyes for You/Do Do Do	1950	7.50	15.00	30.00
❑ 1-908 (?)	Nobody's Chasing Me/It's a Lovely Day Today	1950	10.00	20.00	40.00
—Microgroove 7-inch, 33 1/3 rpm single					
❑ 6-908 (?)	Nobody's Chasing Me/It's a Lovely Day Today	1950	7.50	15.00	30.00
❑ 31084 [S]	(contents unknown)	1961	2.50	5.00	10.00
❑ 31085 [S]	(contents unknown)	1961	2.50	5.00	10.00
❑ 31086 [S]	(contents unknown)	1961	2.50	5.00	10.00
❑ 31087 [S]	(contents unknown)	1961	2.50	5.00	10.00
❑ 31088 [S]	(contents unknown)	1961	2.50	5.00	10.00
—Anyone who can fill in these gaps -- the above 5 all are Columbia "Stereo 7" singles -- please let us know.					
❑ 4-38542	You're My Thrill/That Old Feeling	1950	3.75	7.50	15.00
—Alternate numbers are "B 189-1" and "B 189-2"					
❑ 4-38543	Bewitched/When Your Lover Has Gone	1950	3.75	7.50	15.00
—Alternate numbers are "B 189-3" and "B 189-4"					
❑ 4-38544	I'm Confessin'/I Didn't Know What Time It Was	1950	3.75	7.50	15.00
—Alternate numbers are "B 189-5" and "B 189-6"					
❑ 4-38545	You Go to My Head/Sometimes I'm Happy	1950	3.75	7.50	15.00
—Alternate numbers are "B 189-7" and "B 189-8"; the above four comprise box set B 189					
❑ 39008	A Bushel and a Peck/The Best Thing for You	1950	5.00	10.00	20.00
❑ 39031	If I Were a Bell/I've Never Been in Love Before	1950	5.00	10.00	20.00
❑ 39032	Christmas Story/Silver Bells	1950	3.00	6.00	12.00
❑ 39055	Nobody's Chasing Me/It's a Lovely Day Today	1950	5.00	10.00	20.00
❑ 39143	You Are My Sunshine/Comb and Paper Polka	1951	3.75	7.50	15.00
❑ 3-39143	You Are My Sunshine/Comb and Paper Polka	1951	7.50	15.00	30.00
—Microgroove 7-inch, 33 1/3 rpm single					
❑ 39159	Would I Love You (Love You, Love You)/ Lullaby of Broadway	1951	3.75	7.50	15.00
❑ 3-39159	Would I Love You (Love You, Love You)/Lullaby of Broadway	1951	7.50	15.00	30.00
—Microgroove 7-inch, 33 1/3 rpm single					
❑ 39191	I'll Be Around/I Love the Way You Say Goodnight	1951	3.75	7.50	15.00
❑ 39197	Lullaby of Broadway/Please Don't Talk About Me When I'm Gone	1951	3.00	6.00	12.00
❑ 39198	Fine and Dandy /I Love the Way You Say Goodnight	1951	3.00	6.00	12.00
❑ 39199	In a Shanty in Old Shanty Town/ You're Getting to Be a Habit with Me	1951	3.00	6.00	12.00
❑ 39200	Somebody Loves Me/Just One of Those Things	1951	3.00	6.00	12.00
—The above four comprise a box set					
❑ 39255	I Can't Get Over Pumpernickel/ You Are My Sunshine	1951	3.75	7.50	15.00
❑ 39293	We Kissed in a Shadow/Something Wonderful	1951	3.75	7.50	15.00
❑ 39295	It's So Laughable/Very Good Advice	1951	3.75	7.50	15.00
❑ 39423	(Why Did I Tell You I Was Going to) Shanghai/ My Life's Desire	1951	3.75	7.50	15.00
❑ 39450	Moonlight Bay/Tell Me (Tell Me Why)	1951	3.00	6.00	12.00
❑ 39451	Till We Meet Again/Every Little Movement	1951	3.00	6.00	12.00
❑ 39452	Love You/Cuddle Up a Little Closer	1951	3.00	6.00	12.00
❑ 39453	Christmas Story/I'm Forever Blowing Bubbles	1951	3.00	6.00	12.00
—The above four comprise a box set					
❑ 39490	Ask Me/Lonesome and Sorry	1951	3.75	7.50	15.00
❑ 39534	Kiss Me Goodbye/Got Him Offa My Hands	1951	3.75	7.50	15.00
❑ 39596	Domino/If That Doesn't Do It	1951	3.75	7.50	15.00
❑ 39622	I'll See You in My Dreams/Ain't We Got Fun	1951	3.00	6.00	12.00
❑ 39623	The One I Love/Makin' Whoopee	1951	3.00	6.00	12.00
❑ 39624	My Buddy/I Wish I Had a Girl	1951	3.00	6.00	12.00
❑ 39625	It Had to Be You/Nobody's Sweetheart	1951	3.00	6.00	12.00
—The above four comprise a box set					
❑ 39637	Oops/Baby Doll	1952	3.00	6.00	12.00
❑ 39673	A Guy Is a Guy/Who, Who, Who	1952	3.00	6.00	12.00
❑ 39693	Sugarbush/When I Look Into Your Eyes	1952	3.00	6.00	12.00
—A-side with Frankie Laine					
❑ 39714	Gentle Johnny/Little Kiss Goodnight	1952	3.00	6.00	12.00
❑ 39729	A Guy Is a Guy/What's the Use?	1952	2.50	5.00	10.00
—B-side by Johnnie Ray					
❑ 39738	It's Magic/Too Fat Polka	1952	2.50	5.00	10.00
—B-side by Arthur Godfrey					
❑ 39786	When I Fall in Love/Take Me in Your Arms	1952	3.00	6.00	12.00
❑ 39817	Make It Soon/My Love and Devotion	1952	3.00	6.00	12.00
❑ 39863	No Two People/You Can't Lose Me	1952	3.00	6.00	12.00
—A-side with Donald O'Connor					
❑ 39881	April in Paris/Cherries	1952	3.00	6.00	12.00
❑ 39906	Mister Tap Toe/Your Mother and Mine	1952	3.00	6.00	12.00
❑ 39913	You Have My Symphony/ Second Star to the Right	1953	3.00	6.00	12.00
❑ 39970	When the Red, Red Robin Comes Bob, Bob, Bobbin' Along/Beautiful Music to Love By	1953	2.00	4.00	8.00
❑ 39971	Little Silvery Moon/King Chant	1953	2.00	4.00	8.00
❑ 39972	Your Eyes Have Told Me So/I'll Forget You	1953	2.00	4.00	8.00
❑ 39973	Just One Girl/Be Bumble Bee	1953	2.00	4.00	8.00
❑ 39974	Ain't We Got Fun?/If You Were the Only Girl	1953	2.00	4.00	8.00
—The above five comprise a box set					
❑ 40020	Kiss Me Again Stranger/A Purple Cow	1953	2.50	5.00	10.00
❑ 40063	Choo Choo Train (Ch-Ch-Foo)/ This Too Shall Pass Away	1953	2.50	5.00	10.00
❑ 40094	The Deadwood Stage (Whip Crack Away!)/ I Can Do Without You	1953	2.00	4.00	8.00
❑ 40095	The Black Hills of Dakota/ Just Blew In from the Windy City	1953	2.00	4.00	8.00
❑ 40096	A Woman's Touch/Higher Than the Hawk	1953	2.00	4.00	8.00
❑ 40097	Secret Love/'Tis Harry I'm Planning to Marry	1953	2.00	4.00	8.00
—The above four comprise a box set					
❑ 40108	Secret Love/The Deadwood Stage (Whip Crack Away!)	1953	2.50	5.00	10.00
❑ 40168	Lost in Loveliness/What Every Girl Should Know	1954	2.50	5.00	10.00
❑ 40210	I Speak to the Stars/ The Blue Belles of Broadway	1954	2.50	5.00	10.00
❑ 40234	Someone Else's Roses/Kay-Muleta	1954	2.50	5.00	10.00
❑ 40300	If I Give My Heart to You/Anyone Can Fall in Love	1954	2.50	5.00	10.00
❑ 40371	Ready, Willing and Able/Hold Me In Your Arms	1954	2.50	5.00	10.00
❑ 40372	Till My Love Comes to Me/Ready and Able	1954	2.00	4.00	8.00
❑ 40373	Ready, Willing and Able/One for My Baby	1954	2.00	4.00	8.00
❑ 40374	Hold Me in Your Arms/There's a Rising Moon	1954	2.00	4.00	8.00
❑ 40375	Someone to Watch Over Me/ Just One of Those Things	1954	2.00	4.00	8.00
—The above four comprise a box set					
❑ 40408	There's a Rising Moon/ Till Your Love Comes to Me	1954	2.50	5.00	10.00
❑ 40483	Two Hearts, Two Kisses/Foolishly Yours	1955	2.50	5.00	10.00
❑ 40505	I'll Never Stop Loving You/Never Look Back	1955	2.50	5.00	10.00
❑ 40581	Ooh Bang Jiggily Bang/Jimmy Unknown	1955	2.50	5.00	10.00
❑ 40618	Let It Ring/Love's Little Island	1955	2.50	5.00	10.00
❑ 40673	We'll Love Again/Somebody Somewhere	1956	2.50	5.00	10.00
❑ 40704	Whatever Will Be, Will Me (Que Sera, Sera)/I've Gotta Sing Away the Blues	1956	2.50	5.00	10.00
❑ 40758	Julie/Love in a Home	1956	2.50	5.00	10.00
❑ 40798	The Party's Over/What'ya Put in That Kiss	1956	2.50	5.00	10.00
❑ 40870	Twelve O'Clock Tonight/Today Will Be Yesterday Tomorrow	1957	2.50	5.00	10.00
❑ 40952	Nothing in the World/Through the Eyes of Love	1957	2.50	5.00	10.00
❑ 41015	Rickety-Rackety Rendezvous/The Man Who Invented Love	1957	2.00	4.00	8.00
❑ 41071	Walk a Chalk Line/Soft As the Starlight	1957	2.00	4.00	8.00
❑ 41123	Teacher's Pet/A Very Precious Love	1958	2.00	4.00	8.00
❑ 41195	Everybody Loves a Lover/Instant Love	1958	2.00	4.00	8.00
❑ 41195 [PS]	Everybody Loves a Lover/Instant Love	1958	3.75	7.50	15.00
❑ 41252	Tunnel of Love/Run Away Skidaddle Skidoo	1958	2.00	4.00	8.00
❑ 41252 [PS]	Tunnel of Love/Run Away Skidaddle Skidoo	1958	3.75	7.50	15.00
❑ 41307	I Enjoy Being a Girl/Kissin' My Honey	1958	2.00	4.00	8.00
❑ 41354	Love Me in the Daytime/He's So Married	1959	2.00	4.00	8.00
❑ 41391	Be Prepared/It Happened to Jane	1959	2.00	4.00	8.00
❑ 41450	Roly Poly/Possess Me	1959	2.00	4.00	8.00
❑ 41463	Pillow Talk/Inspiration	1959	2.00	4.00	8.00
❑ 41463 [PS]	Pillow Talk/Inspiration	1959	3.75	7.50	15.00
❑ 41542	The Sound of Music/Heart Full of Love	1959	2.00	4.00	8.00
❑ 41569	Anyway the Wind Blows/Soft As the Starlight	1960	2.00	4.00	8.00
❑ 41630	Please Don't Eat the Daisies/Here We Go Again	1960	2.00	4.00	8.00
❑ 41630 [PS]	Please Don't Eat the Daisies/Here We Go Again	1960	3.75	7.50	15.00
❑ 41703	The Blue Train/A Perfect Understanding	1960	2.00	4.00	8.00
❑ 41791	What Does a Woman Do/Daffa Down Dilly	1960	2.00	4.00	8.00
❑ 41944	Make Someone Happy/Bright and Shiny	1961	2.00	4.00	8.00
❑ 41993	Twinkle and Shine/Gotta Feelin'	1961	2.00	4.00	8.00
❑ 42260	Should I Surrender/ Who Knows What Might Have Been	1962	2.00	4.00	8.00
❑ 42295	Lover Come Back/Falling	1962	2.00	4.00	8.00
❑ 42912	Move Over Darling/Twinkle Lullaby	1963	2.00	4.00	8.00
❑ 43153	Send Me No Flowers/Rainbow's End	1964	2.00	4.00	8.00
❑ 43174	Christmas Present/Be a Child at Christmas Time	1964	2.00	4.00	8.00
❑ 43278	How Insensitive/Meditation	1965	2.00	4.00	8.00
❑ 43314	Summer Has Gone/Catch the Bouquet	1965	2.00	4.00	8.00
❑ 43440	Another Go-Round/ Not Only Should You Love Him	1965	2.00	4.00	8.00
❑ 43459	Au Revoir Is Goodbye with a Smile/ Do Not Disturb	1965	2.00	4.00	8.00
❑ 43606	Every Now and Then/There They Are	1966	—	3.50	7.00
❑ 43688	Glass Bottom Boat/Soft As the Starlight	1966	—	3.50	7.00
❑ 44150	Caprice/Sorry	1967	—	3.50	7.00
❑ JZSP 55070/1 [DJ]	Let No Walls Divide/ God Rest Ye Merry, Gentlemen	1961	3.00	6.00	12.00
—B-side by Andre Previn					
❑ JZSP 79171/2 [DJ]	Silver Bells/Winter Wonderland	1963	2.50	5.00	10.00
—"Special Album Excerpt" promo					

7-Inch Extended Plays

COLUMBIA

Number	Title (A Side/B Side)	Yr	VG	VG+	NM
❑ B-189 [PS]	You're My Thrill	195?	3.75	7.50	15.00
—Gatefold sleeve for 2-EP set (5-1035 and 5-1036)					
❑ B-235 [PS]	Lullaby of Broadway	195?	3.75	7.50	15.00
—Gatefold sleeve for 2-EP set (5-1053 and 5-1054)					
❑ B-540 [PS]	Love Me or Leave Me	1955	2.50	5.00	10.00
—Gatefold sleeve for 3-EP set (5-2170, 5-2171, 5-2172)					
❑ 5-1035	You're My Thrill/Bewitched//When Your Lover Has Gone/That Old Feeling	195?	3.75	7.50	15.00
—Alternate numbers are "B-189-1" and "B-189-4"					
❑ 5-1036	I'm Confessin'/Sometimes I'm Happy//You Go to My Head/I Didn't Know What Time It Was	195?	3.75	7.50	15.00
—Alternate numbers are "B-189-2" and "B-189-3"					
❑ 5-1053	Lullaby of Broadway and Fine and Dandy//I Love the Way You Say Goodnight/Please Don't Talk About Me When I'm Gone	195?	3.75	7.50	15.00
—Alternate numbers are "B-235-1" and "B-235-4"					
❑ 5-1054	In a Shanty in Old Shanty Town/Somebody Loves Me//Just One of Those Things/You're Getting to Be a Habit with Me	195?	3.75	7.50	15.00
—Alternate numbers are "B-235-2" and "B-235-3"					
❑ 5-2170	It All Depends on You/You Made Me Love You/ /At Sundown/Love Me or Leave Me	1955	2.50	5.00	10.00
—Alternate numbers are "B-540-1" and "B-540-6"					
❑ 5-2171	Stay on the Right Side Sister/Mean to Me//I'll Never Stop Loving You/Never Look Back	1955	2.50	5.00	10.00
—Alternate numbers are "B-540-2" and "B-540-5"					

Number	Title (A Side/B Side)	Yr	VG	VG+	NM
❏ 5-2172	Everybody Loves My Baby/Sam the Old Accordion Man//Shaking the Blues Away/ Ten Cents a Dance	1955	2.50	5.00	10.00
—Alternate numbers are "B-540-3" and "B-540-4"					
❏ B-2522	It's Magic/A Guy Is a Guy//Secret Love/ Whatever Will Be, Will Be (Que Sera, Sera)	195?	3.75	7.50	15.00
❏ B-2522 [PS]	Doris Day (Hall of Fame Series)	195?	3.75	7.50	15.00
❏ B-2545	*Bewitched/Pretty Baby/My Dream Is Yours/ Canadian Capers	195?	3.75	7.50	15.00
❏ B-2545 [PS]	Doris Day (Hall of Fame Series)	195?	3.75	7.50	15.00
❏ B-2585	*A Bushel and a Peck/Hoop-Dee-Doo/If I Were a Bell/Lullaby of Broadway	1959	3.75	7.50	15.00
❏ B-2585 [PS]	Doris Day (Hall of Fame Series)	1959	3.75	7.50	15.00
❏ B-7491	(contents unknown)	1956	3.75	7.50	15.00
❏ B-7491 [PS]	Day in Hollywood, Vol. 1	1956	3.75	7.50	15.00
❏ B-7492	Secret Love/Be My Little Baby Bumble Bee// Makin' Whoopie!/Till We Meet Again	1956	3.75	7.50	15.00
❏ B-7492 [PS]	Day in Hollywood, Vol. II	1956	3.75	7.50	15.00
❏ B-7493	*Love Me or Leave Me/Just One of Those Things/It Had to Be You/Ain't We Got Fun	1956	3.75	7.50	15.00
❏ B-7493 [PS]	Day in Hollywood, Vol. 3	1956	3.75	7.50	15.00
❏ B-10533	Wrap Your Troubles in Dreams (And Dream Your Troubles Away)/Soft as the Starlight// Moonglow/Close Your Eyes	195?	3.00	6.00	12.00
❏ B-10533 [PS]	Day by Night, Vol. III	195?	3.00	6.00	12.00
Albums					
COLUMBIA					
❏ DD 1 [M]	Listen to Day	1960	5.00	10.00	20.00
❏ DDS 1 [S]	Listen to Day	1960	6.25	12.50	25.00
❏ C2L 5 [(2)M]	Hooray for Hollywood	1959	10.00	20.00	40.00
❏ CL 582 [M]	Young Man with a Horn	1954	10.00	20.00	40.00
—Reissue of 6106; red label, gold print					
❏ CL 624 [M]	Day Dreams	1955	10.00	20.00	40.00
—Red label, gold print					
❏ CL 624 [M]	Day Dreams	1956	6.25	12.50	25.00
—Six "eye" logos on label					
❏ CL 710 [M]	Love Me or Leave Me	1955	12.50	25.00	50.00
—Red label, gold print					
❏ CL 710 [M]	Love Me or Leave Me	1956	6.25	12.50	25.00
—Six "eye" logos on label					
❏ CL 710 [M]	Love Me or Leave Me	1962	3.75	7.50	15.00
—"Guaranteed High Fidelity" or "Mono" on label					
❏ CL 749 [M]	Day in Hollywood	1956	7.50	15.00	30.00
❏ C2S 805 [(2)S]	Hooray for Hollywood	1959	12.50	25.00	50.00
❏ CL 942 [M]	Day By Day	1957	7.50	15.00	30.00
❏ CL 1053 [M]	Day By Night	1958	5.00	10.00	20.00
❏ CL 1210 [M]	Doris Day's Greatest Hits	1958	7.50	15.00	30.00
—Six "eye" logos on label					
❏ CL 1210 [M]	Doris Day's Greatest Hits	1962	3.00	6.00	12.00
—"Guaranteed High Fidelity" or "Mono" on label					
❏ CL 1232 [M]	Cuttin' Capers	1959	5.00	10.00	20.00
❏ CL 1366 [M]	Hooray for Hollywood, Volume 1	1959	5.00	10.00	20.00
❏ CL 1367 [M]	Hooray for Hollywood, Volume 2	1959	5.00	10.00	20.00
❏ CL 1438 [M]	What Every Girl Should Know	1960	5.00	10.00	20.00
❏ CL 1470 [M]	Show Time	1960	5.00	10.00	20.00
❏ CL 1614 [M]	Bright and Shiny	1960	5.00	10.00	20.00
❏ CL 1660 [M]	I Have Dreamed	1961	5.00	10.00	20.00
❏ CL 1752 [M]	Duet	1962	5.00	10.00	20.00
—With Andre Previn					
❏ CL 1904 [M]	You'll Never Walk Alone	1962	3.75	7.50	15.00
❏ CL 2131 [M]	Love Him!	1964	3.75	7.50	15.00
❏ CL 2226 [M]	The Doris Day Christmas Album	1964	3.00	6.00	12.00
❏ CL 2266 [M]	With a Smile and a Song	1965	3.00	6.00	12.00
❏ CL 2310 [M]	Latin for Lovers	1965	3.00	6.00	12.00
❏ CL 2360 [M]	Sentimental Journey	1965	3.00	6.00	12.00
❏ CL 2518 [10]	Lights, Camera, Action	1955	12.50	25.00	50.00
❏ CL 6071 [10]	You're My Thrill	1949	15.00	30.00	60.00
❏ CL 6106 [10]	Young Man with a Horn	1950	25.00	50.00	100.00
❏ CL 6149 [10]	Tea for Two	1950	15.00	30.00	60.00
❏ CL 6168 [10]	Lullaby of Broadway	1951	15.00	30.00	60.00
❏ CL 6186 [10]	On Moonlight Bay	1951	15.00	30.00	60.00
❏ CL 6198 [10]	I'll See You in My Dreams	1951	15.00	30.00	60.00
❏ CL 6248 [10]	By the Light of the Silvery Moon	1953	15.00	30.00	60.00
❏ CL 6273 [10]	Calamity Jane	1953	15.00	30.00	60.00
❏ CL 6339 [10]	Young at Heart	1954	15.00	30.00	60.00
—Six songs by Doris Day, two by Frank Sinatra					
❏ CS 8066 [S]	Hooray for Hollywood, Volume 1	1959	6.25	12.50	25.00
❏ CS 8067 [S]	Hooray for Hollywood, Volume 2	1959	6.25	12.50	25.00
❏ CS 8078 [S]	Cuttin' Capers	1959	6.25	12.50	25.00
❏ CS 8089 [S]	Day By Night	1959	6.25	12.50	25.00
❏ CS 8234 [S]	What Every Girl Should Know	1960	6.25	12.50	25.00
❏ CS 8261 [S]	Show Time	1960	5.00	10.00	20.00
❏ CS 8414 [S]	Bright and Shiny	1960	6.25	12.50	25.00
❏ CS 8460 [S]	I Have Dreamed	1961	6.25	12.50	25.00
❏ CS 8552 [S]	Duet	1962	6.25	12.50	25.00
—With Andre Previn					
❏ CS 8635 [P]	Doris Day's Greatest Hits	1962	3.75	7.50	15.00
—"360 Sound Stereo" in black at bottom					
❏ PC 8635	Doris Day's Greatest Hits	198?	2.00	4.00	8.00
—Budget-line reissue					
❏ CS 8704 [S]	You'll Never Walk Alone	1962	5.00	10.00	20.00
❏ CS 8773 [R]	Love Me or Leave Me	1963	3.00	6.00	12.00
❏ CS 8931 [S]	Love Him!	1964	5.00	10.00	20.00
❏ CS 9026 [S]	The Doris Day Christmas Album	1964	3.75	7.50	15.00
❏ CS 9066 [S]	With a Smile and a Song	1965	3.75	7.50	15.00
❏ CS 9110 [S]	Latin for Lovers	1965	3.75	7.50	15.00
❏ CS 9160 [S]	Sentimental Journey	1965	3.75	7.50	15.00
COLUMBIA LIMITED EDITION					
❏ LE 10197	The Doris Day Christmas Album	197?	2.50	5.00	10.00
COLUMBIA SPECIAL PRODUCTS					
❏ C 10988	The Doris Day Christmas Album	197?	2.50	5.00	10.00
—Reissue of CS 9026					
❏ P2 13231 [(2)]	The Magic of Doris Day	1976	3.75	7.50	15.00
❏ P 13346	The Doris Day Christmas Album	197?	2.50	5.00	10.00
—Reissue of CS 9026					
❏ XTV 82021/2 [M]	Wonderful Day	1961	10.00	20.00	40.00

Number	Title (A Side/B Side)	Yr	VG	VG+	NM
HARMONY					
❏ HL 7392 [M]	Great Movie Hits	1966	3.00	6.00	12.00
❏ HL 9559 [M]	Do Re Mi (And Other Children's Favorites)	196?	3.00	6.00	12.00
❏ HS 11192 [R]	Great Movie Hits	1966	3.00	6.00	12.00
❏ HS 11282	Whatever Will Be, Will Be (Que Sera, Sera)	1968	3.00	6.00	12.00
❏ HS 11382	The Magic of Doris Day	1970	3.00	6.00	12.00
❏ HS 14559 [S]	Do Re Mi (And Other Children's Favorites)	196?	3.00	6.00	12.00
❏ KH 31498	Softly, As I Leave You	1972	2.50	5.00	10.00
HEARTLAND					
❏ HL 1102/3 [(2)]	The Best of Doris Day	1990	3.75	7.50	15.00
—Mail-order offer; alternate number is CBS Special Products P2 22031					
HINDSIGHT					
❏ HSR-200	Doris Day with Van Alexander's Orchestra	198?	2.50	5.00	10.00
DAY, DORIS, AND BUDDY CLARK					
7-Inch Extended Plays					
COLUMBIA					
❏ B-2541	Love Somebody/Confess//I'll String Along with You/Powder Your Face with Sunshine	195?	3.00	6.00	12.00
❏ B-2541 [PS]	Doris Day and Buddy Clark (Hall of Fame Series)	195?	3.00	6.00	12.00
DAY, DORIS/JOHNNIE RAY Also see each artist's individual listings.					
45s					
COLUMBIA					
❏ 39898	A Full Time Job/Ma Says, Pa Says	1952	3.00	6.00	12.00
❏ 40001	Candy Lips/Let's Walk That-A-Way	1953	2.50	5.00	10.00
DAY, LITTLE SUNNY, AND THE CLOUDS					
45s					
TANDEM					
❏ 7001	Lou Ann/Baby Doll	1961	100.00	200.00	400.00
DAY, TERRY See TERRY MELCHER.					
DAY BLINDNESS					
Albums					
STUDIO 10					
❏ DBX-101	Day Blindness	1969	15.00	30.00	60.00
DAYBREAKERS, THE (1)					
45s					
ALADDIN					
❏ 3434	I Wonder Why/Up, Up and Away	1958	10.00	20.00	40.00
LAMP					
❏ 2016	I Wonder Why/Up, Up and Away	1958	15.00	30.00	60.00
DAYBREAKERS, THE (2)					
45s					
DIAL					
❏ 4066	Psychedelic Siren/Afterthoughts	1967	7.50	15.00	30.00
DAYE, EDDIE, AND 4 BARS					
45s					
SHRINE					
❏ 112	Guess Who Loves You/What Am I Gonna Do	1966	250.00	500.00	1000.
DAYTONAS, THE Also see RONNY AND THE DATYONAS.					
45s					
AMY					
❏ 961	Hey Little Girl/Please Go Away	1966	5.00	10.00	20.00
DAYTONES, THE					
45s					
JUBILEE					
❏ 5452	Krambuli/Bless My Love	1963	5.00	10.00	20.00
DAYTONS, THE					
45s					
NORGOLDE					
❏ 101	King of Broken Hearts/Friday Better Come	1959	50.00	100.00	200.00
DE BONAIRS					
45s					
PING					
❏ 1000	Lanky Linda/Mother's Son	1956	75.00	150.00	300.00
❏ 1001	Say a Prayer for Me/Cracker-Jack Daddy	1956	100.00	200.00	400.00
DE-FENDERS, THE					
45s					
DEL-FI					
❏ 4226	Little Deuce Coupe/Hayburner	1963	7.50	15.00	30.00
—B-side by the Deuce Coupes					
WORLD PACIFIC					
❏ 382	(Dance to the) Yakety Sax/Wild One	1963	10.00	20.00	40.00
Albums					
DEL-FI					
❏ DFLP-1242 [M]	Drag Beat	1963	12.50	25.00	50.00
❏ DFST-1242 [S]	Drag Beat	1963	15.00	30.00	60.00
WORLD PACIFIC					
❏ ST-1810 [S]	The De-Fenders Play the Big Ones	1963	17.50	35.00	70.00
—Black vinyl					
❏ ST-1810 [S]	The De-Fenders Play the Big Ones	1963	37.50	75.00	150.00
—Green vinyl					
❏ ST-1810 [S]	The De-Fenders Play the Big Ones	1963	37.50	75.00	150.00
—Red vinyl					
❏ WP-1810 [M]	The De-Fenders Play the Big Ones	1963	12.50	25.00	50.00
DE VONS, THE					
45s					
KING					
❏ 6226	Someone to Treat Me (The Way You Used To)/Soul Party	1969	2.50	5.00	10.00
MR. G					
❏ 825	Groovin' with My Thing/Wise Up	1968	3.00	6.00	12.00
PARKWAY					
❏ 976	Put Me Down/Freddie	1966	7.50	15.00	30.00

Number	Title (A Side/B Side)	Yr	VG	VG+	NM

DEACON AND THE ROCK 'N' ROLLERS
45s
NAU-VOO

Number	Title (A Side/B Side)	Yr	VG	VG+	NM
❏ 804	Rockin' on the Moon/I Don't Wanna Leave	1959	500.00	1000.	1500.

DEADLY ONES, THE
Albums
VEE JAY

| ❏ LP-1090 [M] | It's Monster Surfing Time | 1964 | 25.00 | 50.00 | 100.00 |
| ❏ LPS-1090 [S] | It's Monster Surfing Time | 1964 | 30.00 | 60.00 | 120.00 |

DEAL, BILL, AND THE RHONDELS
45s
BUDDAH

| ❏ 318 | It's Too Late/So What If It Rains | 1972 | — | 3.00 | 6.00 |
| ❏ 330 | Everybody's Got Something to Hide/ I Live in the Night | 1972 | — | 3.00 | 6.00 |

GIG/WAY

| ❏ 902006 | Freak 'N' Freeze/(Instrumental) | 1978 | — | 2.50 | 5.00 |

HERITAGE

❏ 803	May I/Day By Day My Love Grows	1968	2.00	4.00	8.00
❏ 812	I've Been Hurt/I've Got My Seeds	1969	2.00	4.00	8.00
❏ 812 [PS]	I've Been Hurt/I've Got My Needs	1969	3.75	7.50	15.00
❏ 817	What Kind of Fool Do You Think I Am/Are You Ready for This	1969	2.00	4.00	8.00
❏ 818	Swingin' Tight/Tuck's Theme	1969	2.00	4.00	8.00
❏ 818 [PS]	Swingin' Tight/Tuck's Theme	1969	3.75	7.50	15.00
❏ 821	Nothing Succeeds Like Success/Swingin' Tight	1969	2.00	4.00	8.00
❏ 824	I'm Gonna Make You Love Me/Hey Bulldog	1970	—	3.00	6.00

MALA

| ❏ 502 | Big Toe in the Wind/Don't Put Me Down | 1965 | 7.50 | 15.00 | 30.00 |

—As "Bill Deal and the Big Deals"

POLYDOR

❏ 14042	Do I Love You/Won't You Set Me Free	1970	—	3.00	6.00
❏ 14061	19 Years (Everything I Do Is Wrong)/Sea of Life	1971	—	3.00	6.00
❏ 14103	Sea of Life/You Can Make It	1971	—	3.00	6.00

Albums
HERITAGE

| ❏ HTS 35003 | Vintage Rock | 1969 | 7.50 | 15.00 | 30.00 |
| ❏ HTS 35006 | The Best of Bill Deal and the Rhondels | 1970 | 7.50 | 15.00 | 30.00 |

RHINO

| ❏ RNLP-70129 | The Best of Bill Deal and the Rhondels (1969-1970) | 1986 | 2.50 | 5.00 | 10.00 |

DEAL, DON
45s
CAPITOL

| ❏ 4901 | How Do You Lie to a Heart/Ain't Gonna Try No More | 1963 | 2.50 | 5.00 | 10.00 |
| ❏ 5028 | You'll Get Used to Being Lonely/A-11 | 1963 | 2.50 | 5.00 | 10.00 |

CASH

| ❏ 1028 | Cryin' in One Eye/Broken Hearted Fellow | 1956 | 12.50 | 25.00 | 50.00 |

—Eddie Cochran plays guitar on this record

CHALLENGE

| ❏ 59389 | Love Touched Me/Piece at a Time | 1968 | 2.00 | 4.00 | 8.00 |

DONJIM

| ❏ 1007 | I Don't Change My Mind Overnight/ My Good Thing's Gone | 1979 | — | 3.50 | 7.00 |

ERA

❏ 1039	Unfaithful Diane/Devil of Deceit	1957	3.75	7.50	15.00
❏ 1051	My Blind Date/Even Then	1957	3.75	7.50	15.00
❏ 1060	She Was Here But She's Gone/You'd Look Good with a Tear in Your Eye	1957	3.75	7.50	15.00
❏ 1070	Sweet Love/The First Teenager	1958	3.75	7.50	15.00
❏ 1077	Just Thought I'd Call/A Chance Is All I Ask	1958	3.75	7.50	15.00

MGM

| ❏ K13235 | Lyin' Again/After the Boy Gets the Girl | 1964 | 2.50 | 5.00 | 10.00 |

SAND

| ❏ 432 | You Make It Summer All Winter Long/A Drop at a Time | 1969 | 2.00 | 4.00 | 8.00 |
| ❏ 438 | Our Last Night/So What | 1970 | 2.00 | 4.00 | 8.00 |

DEAN, BOBBY
45s
CHESS

| ❏ 1673 | Just Go Wild Over Rock and Roll/Dime Store Pony Tail | 1958 | 7.50 | 15.00 | 30.00 |
| ❏ 1710 | I'm Ready/Go Mr. Dillon | 1959 | 7.50 | 15.00 | 30.00 |

PROFILE

| ❏ 4006 | Just Between Tears/It's a Fad | 1959 | 10.00 | 20.00 | 40.00 |

DEAN, CHARLES
45s
BENTON

| ❏ 103 | Itchy/(B-side unknown) | 1958 | 62.50 | 125.00 | 250.00 |

DEAN, DEBBIE
45s
MOTOWN

❏ 1007	Don't Let Him Shop Around/A New Girl	1961	10.00	20.00	40.00
❏ 1014	Itty, Bitty, Pity Love/But I'm Afraid	1961	7.50	15.00	30.00
❏ 1025	Everybody's Talking About My Baby/I Cried All Night	1962	10.00	20.00	40.00
❏ 1025 [PS]	Everybody's Talking About My Baby/I Cried All Night	1962	20.00	40.00	80.00

V.I.P.

| ❏ 25044 | Why Am I Lovin' You/Stay My Love | 1967 | 75.00 | 150.00 | 300.00 |

DEAN, JIMMY
45s
CASINO

❏ 052	I.O.U./Let's Pick Up the Pieces	1976	—	2.00	4.00
❏ 074	To a Sleeping Beauty/I Didn't Have Time	1976	—	2.00	4.00
❏ 108	Where Is That Man/(B-side unknown)	1976	—	2.00	4.00

CHURCHILL

| ❏ 94024 | I.O.U./To a Sleeping Beauty | 1983 | — | 2.00 | 4.00 |

COLUMBIA

Number	Title (A Side/B Side)	Yr	VG	VG+	NM
❏ S7 31550 [S]	Basin Street Blues/Please Pass the Biscuits	1962	5.00	10.00	20.00
❏ S7 31551 [S]	Have You Ever Been Lonely/Nobody	1962	5.00	10.00	20.00
❏ S7 31552 [S]	I Was Just Walking Out the Door/The Dark Town Poker Club	1962	5.00	10.00	20.00
❏ S7 31553 [S]	You're Nobody Until Somebody Loves You/ Kentucky Means Paradise	1962	5.00	10.00	20.00
❏ S7 31554 [S]	Little Black Book/Old Pappy's New Banjo	1962	5.00	10.00	20.00

—The above five are "Stereo Seven" 33 1/3 rpm jukebox singles from set "JS7-63" entitled "Portrait of Jimmy Dean"

❏ 40995	Deep Blue Sea/Love Me So I'll Know	1957	3.00	6.00	12.00
❏ 41025	Little Sandy Sleighfoot/When They Ring the Golden Bells	1957	3.75	7.50	15.00
❏ 41025 [PS]	Little Sandy Sleighfoot/When They Ring the Golden Bells	1957	6.25	12.50	25.00
❏ 41118	Starlight, Starbright/Makin' My Mind Up	1958	3.00	6.00	12.00
❏ 41196	School of Love/You Should See Tennessee, Mam'selle	1958	3.00	6.00	12.00
❏ 41265	My Heart Is An Open Book/Shark in the Bathtub	1958	3.00	6.00	12.00
❏ 41395	Sing Along/Weekend Blues	1959	3.00	6.00	12.00
❏ 41395 [PS]	Sing Along/Weekend Blues	1959	6.25	12.50	25.00
❏ 41453	Stay a Little Longer/Counting Tears	1959	3.00	6.00	12.00
❏ 41543	Thanks for the Dream/There's Still Time, Brother	1959	3.00	6.00	12.00
❏ 41710	Little Boy Lost/There'll Be No Teardrops Tonight	1960	3.00	6.00	12.00
❏ 41956	Give Me Back My Heart/ It's Been a Long, Long Time	1961	2.50	5.00	10.00
❏ 42175	Big John/I Won't Go Huntin' with You Jake (But I'll Go Chasin' Wimmin)	1961	2.50	5.00	10.00

—Lyrics say: "At the bottom of this mine lies a big, big man." We think the song title was changed with the lyric, but we're not 100 percent sure. In other words, this title may exist with the "hell of a man" lyrics.

| ❏ 42175 | Big John/I Won't Go Huntin' with You Jake (But I'll Go Chasin' Wimmin) | 1961 | 5.00 | 10.00 | 20.00 |

—Lyrics say: "At the bottom of this mine lies one hell of a man."

❏ 42175 [PS]	Big Bad John/I Won't Go Huntin' with You Jake (But I'll Go Chasin' Wimmin)	1961	3.75	7.50	15.00
❏ 42248	Oklahoma Bill/To a Sleeping Beauty	1961	2.50	5.00	10.00
❏ 42259	Dear Ivan/ Smoke, Smoke, Smoke That Cigarette	1962	2.50	5.00	10.00
❏ 42259 [PS]	Dear Ivan/ Smoke, Smoke, Smoke That Cigarette	1962	3.75	7.50	15.00
❏ 42282	To a Sleeping Beauty/The Cajun Queen	1962	2.50	5.00	10.00
❏ 42282 [PS]	To a Sleeping Beauty/The Cajun Queen	1962	3.75	7.50	15.00
❏ 42338	P.T. 109/Walk On, Boy	1962	2.50	5.00	10.00
❏ 42338 [PS]	P.T. 109/Walk On, Boy	1962	3.75	7.50	15.00
❏ 42483	Steel Men/Little Bitty Big John	1962	2.50	5.00	10.00
❏ 42483 [PS]	Steel Men/Little Bitty Big John	1962	3.75	7.50	15.00
❏ 42529	Little Black Book/Please Pass the Biscuits	1962	2.50	5.00	10.00
❏ 42529 [PS]	Little Black Book/Please Pass the Biscuits	1962	3.75	7.50	15.00
❏ 42600	Gonna Raise a Rukus Tonight/ A Day That Changed the World	1962	2.50	5.00	10.00
❏ 42600 [PS]	Gonna Raise a Rukus Tonight/ A Day That Changed the World	1962	3.75	7.50	15.00
❏ 42738	Mile Long Train/This Ole House	1963	2.00	4.00	8.00
❏ 42861	The Funniest Thing I Ever Heard/ Thumb Pick Pete	1963	2.00	4.00	8.00
❏ 42861 [PS]	The Funniest Thing I Ever Heard/ Thumb Pick Pete	1963	3.00	6.00	12.00
❏ 42934	Mind Your Own Business/ I Really Don't Want to Know	1963	2.00	4.00	8.00
❏ 42934 [PS]	Mind Your Own Business/ I Really Don't Want to Know	1963	3.00	6.00	12.00
❏ 43021	Shenandoah/Waitin' for the Wagon	1964	2.00	4.00	8.00
❏ 43159	Sam Hill/When I Grow Too Old to Dream	1964	2.00	4.00	8.00
❏ 43172	Yes, Patricia, There Is a Santa Claus/Little Sandy Sleighfoot	1964	2.50	5.00	10.00
❏ 43263	The First Thing Ev'ry Morning (And the Last Thing Ev'ry Night)/Awkward Situation	1965	—	3.00	6.00
❏ 43382	Harvest of Sunshine/Under the Sun	1965	—	3.00	6.00
❏ 43457	Blue Christmas/ Yes, Patricia, There Is a Santa Claus	1965	2.00	4.00	8.00
❏ 43540	Things Have Gone to Pieces/Striker Bill	1966	—	3.00	6.00
❏ 43754	Once a Day/Let's Pretend	1966	—	3.00	6.00
❏ 45922	Your Sweet Love (Keeps Me Homeward Bound)/I'm Gonna Be Gone	1973	—	2.50	5.00
❏ 45981	Who's Gonna Love Me Tomorrow/The Days When Jim Liked Jimmy	1973	—	2.50	5.00
❏ 46039	I've Been Down Some Road/Your Sweet Love	1974	—	2.50	5.00
❏ JZSP 111915/6 [DJ]	Blue Christmas/ Yes, Patricia, There Is a Santa Claus	1965	5.00	10.00	20.00

—Promo only on green vinyl

4 STAR

❏ 1613	Bumming Around/Picking Sweethearts	1953	6.25	12.50	25.00
❏ 1640	Queen of Hearts/I'm Feeling For You	1953	5.00	10.00	20.00
❏ 1654	Release Me/Sweet Darling	1954	5.00	10.00	20.00
❏ 1732	Bumming Around/Release Me	1959	3.00	6.00	12.00

KING

| ❏ 5862 | There Stands the Glass/Bumming Around | 1964 | 2.00 | 4.00 | 8.00 |

MERCURY

❏ 70691	False Pride/Big Blue Diamonds	1955	3.75	7.50	15.00
❏ 70745	Find 'Em, Fool 'Em, and Leave 'Em Alone/My World Is You	1955	3.75	7.50	15.00
❏ 70786	Freight Train Blues/Glad Rags	1956	3.75	7.50	15.00
❏ 70855	Hello Mr. Blues/I Found Out	1956	3.75	7.50	15.00
❏ 71120	Losing Game/Happy Child	1957	3.75	7.50	15.00
❏ 71172	Look on the Good Side/Do You Love Me	1957	3.75	7.50	15.00
❏ 71240	Bumming Around/Nothing Can Stop My Love	1957	3.75	7.50	15.00
❏ 71313	What This Old World Needs/A Fool in Love	1958	3.75	7.50	15.00

RCA VICTOR

❏ 47-8971	Stand Beside Me/A Tiny Drop of Sadness	1966	2.00	4.00	8.00
❏ 47-9091	Sweet Misery/When Someone Mentions Your Name	1967	2.00	4.00	8.00
❏ 47-9241	Ninety Days/In the Same Old Way	1967	2.00	4.00	8.00
❏ 47-9350	I'm a Swinger/Your Country Boy	1967	2.00	4.00	8.00
❏ 47-9454	A Thing Called Love/One Last Time	1968	2.00	4.00	8.00
❏ 47-9567	Born to Be By Your Side/Read 'Em and Weep	1968	2.00	4.00	8.00

D

Number	Title (A Side/B Side)	Yr	VG	VG+	NM
❑ 47-9652	A Hammer and Nails/ I Taught Her Everything She Knows	1968	2.00	4.00	8.00
❑ 47-9800	When Judy Smiled/My Hometown Sweetheart	1969	—	3.00	6.00
❑ 47-9859	Down Comes the Rain/Us	1970	—	3.00	6.00
❑ 47-9915	Weakness in a Man/Aunt Maudie's Fun Garden	1970	—	3.00	6.00
❑ 47-9947	Slowly/Sweet Thang	1971	—	3.00	6.00

—With Dottie West

Number	Title (A Side/B Side)	Yr	VG	VG+	NM
❑ 47-9966	Everybody Knows/Ain't Life Sweet	1971	—	3.00	6.00
❑ 74-0122	A Rose Is a Rose Is a Rose/She's Mine	1969	—	3.00	6.00
❑ 74-0600	And I'm Still Missing You/ The One You Say Good Mornin' To	1971	—	3.00	6.00

7-Inch Extended Plays
COLUMBIA

Number	Title (A Side/B Side)	Yr	VG	VG+	NM
❑ B-10251	Sweet Hour of Prayer/The Farmer and the Lord/ /In the Garden/When They Ring the Golden Bells	195?	3.00	6.00	12.00
❑ B-10251 [PS]	Jimmy Dean's Hour of Prayer, Vol. I	195?	3.00	6.00	12.00

Albums
COLUMBIA

Number	Title (A Side/B Side)	Yr	VG	VG+	NM
❑ CL 1025 [M]	Jimmy Dean's Hour of Prayer	1957	10.00	20.00	40.00
❑ CL 1735 [M]	Big Bad John and Other Fabulous Songs and Tales	1961	5.00	10.00	20.00

—It's possible that two different editions exist, one with the "hell of a man" lyrics of "Big Bad John" and the other with the "big, big man" lyrics, but this has not been confirmed.

Number	Title (A Side/B Side)	Yr	VG	VG+	NM
❑ CL 1894 [M]	Portrait of Jimmy Dean	1962	5.00	10.00	20.00
❑ CL 2027 [M]	Everybody's Favorite	1963	3.75	7.50	15.00
❑ CL 2188 [M]	Songs We All Love Best	1964	3.75	7.50	15.00
❑ CL 2401 [M]	The First Thing Every Morning	1965	3.75	7.50	15.00
❑ CL 2404 [M]	Jimmy Dean's Christmas Card	1965	3.75	7.50	15.00
❑ CL 2485 [M]	Jimmy Dean's Greatest Hits	1966	3.75	7.50	15.00
❑ CL 2538 [M]	The Big Ones	1966	3.75	7.50	15.00
❑ CS 8535 [S]	Big Bad John and Other Fabulous Songs and Tales	1961	6.25	12.50	25.00

—It's possible that two different editions exist, one with the "hell of a man" lyrics of "Big Bad John" and the other with the "big, big man" lyrics, but this has not been confirmed.

Number	Title (A Side/B Side)	Yr	VG	VG+	NM
❑ CS 8694 [S]	Portrait of Jimmy Dean	1962	6.25	12.50	25.00
❑ CS 8827 [S]	Everybody's Favorite	1963	5.00	10.00	20.00
❑ CS 8988 [S]	Songs We All Love Best	1964	5.00	10.00	20.00
❑ CS 9201 [S]	The First Thing Every Morning	1965	5.00	10.00	20.00
❑ CS 9204 [S]	Jimmy Dean's Christmas Card	1965	3.00	6.00	12.00
❑ CS 9285 [S]	Jimmy Dean's Greatest Hits	1966	3.75	7.50	15.00
❑ PC 9285	Jimmy Dean's Greatest Hits	198?	2.00	4.00	8.00

—Budget-line reissue

Number	Title (A Side/B Side)	Yr	VG	VG+	NM
❑ CS 9338 [S]	The Big Ones	1966	3.75	7.50	15.00
❑ CS 9424 [R]	Jimmy Dean's Hour of Prayer	1966	3.00	6.00	12.00
❑ CS 9677 [M]	Dean's List	1968	7.50	15.00	30.00

—White label promo; "Special Mono Radio Station Copy" sticker on cover

Number	Title (A Side/B Side)	Yr	VG	VG+	NM
❑ CS 9677 [S]	Dean's List	1968	3.75	7.50	15.00
CROWN					
❑ 291	Jimmy Dean and the Western Gentlemen	196?	3.00	6.00	12.00
GRT					
❑ 8014	I.O.U.	1977	2.50	5.00	10.00
HARMONY					
❑ HL 7268 [M]	Hymns	1960	3.75	7.50	15.00
❑ HL 7408 [M]	Mr. Country Music	1967	3.00	6.00	12.00
❑ HS 11042 [R]	Hymns	1960	3.00	6.00	12.00
❑ HS 11208 [S]	Mr. Country Music	1967	3.00	6.00	12.00
❑ HS 11270	The Country's Favorite Son	1968	3.00	6.00	12.00
HILLTOP					
❑ 6004	Golden Favorites	196?	3.00	6.00	12.00
KING					
❑ 686 [M]	Favorites of Jimmy Dean	1961	15.00	30.00	60.00
MERCURY					
❑ MG-20319 [M]	Jimmy Dean Sings His Television Favorites	1957	10.00	20.00	40.00
RCA VICTOR					
❑ LPM-3727 [M]	Jimmy Dean Is Here	1967	3.75	7.50	15.00
❑ LSP-3727 [S]	Jimmy Dean Is Here	1967	3.75	7.50	15.00
❑ LPM-3824 [M]	Most Richly Blesed	1967	5.00	10.00	20.00
❑ LSP-3824 [S]	Most Richly Blesed	1967	3.75	7.50	15.00
❑ LPM-3890 [M]	The Jimmy Dean Show	1967	5.00	10.00	20.00
❑ LSP-3890 [S]	The Jimmy Dean Show	1967	3.75	7.50	15.00
❑ LPM-3999 [M]	A Thing Called Love	1968	7.50	15.00	30.00
❑ LSP-3999 [S]	A Thing Called Love	1968	3.75	7.50	15.00
❑ LSP-4035	Speaker of the House	1968	3.75	7.50	15.00
❑ LSP-4323	Dean of Country	1970	3.75	7.50	15.00
❑ LSP-4434	Country Boy and Country Girl	1970	3.75	7.50	15.00
❑ LSP-4511	Everybody Knows	1971	3.75	7.50	15.00
❑ LSP-4618	These Hands	1972	3.75	7.50	15.00
SEARS					
❑ 105	Jimmy Dean's Golden Favorites	196?	3.75	7.50	15.00
SPIN-O-RAMA					
❑ 108	Featuring the Coutnry Singing of Jimmy Dean	196?	3.00	6.00	12.00
❑ 137	Coutnry Round-Up Featuring Jimmy Dean	196?	3.00	6.00	12.00
WING					
❑ MGW-12292 [M]	Jimmy Dean Sings His Television Favorites	196?	3.75	7.50	15.00
❑ SRW-16292 [R]	Jimmy Dean Sings His Television Favorites	196?	3.00	6.00	12.00
WYNCOTE					
❑ 9032	Country Favorites	196?	3.00	6.00	12.00

DEAN, JIMMY / JOHNNY HORTON
Albums
LA BREA

Number	Title (A Side/B Side)	Yr	VG	VG+	NM
❑ L 8014 [M]	Bummin' Around with Jimmy Dean and Johnny Horton	1961	20.00	40.00	80.00
STARDAY					
❑ SLP-325 [M]	Bummin' Around with Jimmy Dean and Johnny Horton	1965	7.50	15.00	30.00

DEAN, JIMMY / MARVIN RAINWATER
Albums
PREMIER

Number	Title (A Side/B Side)	Yr	VG	VG+	NM
❑ 9054	Nashville Showtime	196?	3.00	6.00	12.00

DEAN, LENNY See THE ROCKIN' CHAIRS.

DEAN AND JEAN
45s
EMBER

Number	Title (A Side/B Side)	Yr	VG	VG+	NM
❑ 1048	We're Gonna Get Married/Too Young to Know	1958	3.00	6.00	12.00
❑ 1054	Turn It Off/Never Let Your Love Fade Away	1959	3.00	6.00	12.00
RUST					
❑ TR 1	Seven Day Wonder/ The Man Who Will Never Grow Old	196?	3.00	6.00	12.00
❑ 5044	Come Take a Walk with Me/Dance the Roach	1962	2.50	5.00	10.00
❑ 5046	Mack the Knife/You Can't Be Happy by Yourself	1962	2.50	5.00	10.00
❑ 5067	Tra La La La Suzy/I Love the Summertime	1963	2.50	5.00	10.00
❑ 5075	Hey Jean, Hey Dean/Please Don't Tell Me Now	1964	3.75	7.50	15.00
❑ 5081	I Wanna Be Loved/Thread Your Needle	1964	2.50	5.00	10.00
❑ 5085	Goddess of Love/ The Man Who Will Never Grow Old	1964	2.50	5.00	10.00
❑ 5089	Sticks and Stones/In My Way	1964	2.50	5.00	10.00
❑ 5100	Lovingly Yours/Goddess of Love	1965	2.50	5.00	10.00
❑ 5107	She's Too Respectable/I Love the Summertime	1965	2.50	5.00	10.00

DEAN AND MARC Also see THE NEWBEATS.
45s
BULLSEYE

Number	Title (A Side/B Side)	Yr	VG	VG+	NM
❑ 1025	Tell Him No/Change of Heart	1959	12.50	25.00	50.00
❑ 1026	Cry/The Beginning of Love	1959	6.25	12.50	25.00
CHECKMATE					
❑ 1008	Boogie Woogie Twist (Parts 1 & 2)	1962	3.75	7.50	15.00
HICKORY					
❑ 1227	With Tears in My Eyes/Kissin' Game	1963	2.50	5.00	10.00

—Hickory titles as "Dean and Mark" unless noted

Number	Title (A Side/B Side)	Yr	VG	VG+	NM
❑ 1249	When I Stop Dreaming/There Oughta Be a Law	1964	2.50	5.00	10.00
❑ 1294	Just a Step Away/A Falling Star	1965	2.50	5.00	10.00
❑ 1353	In the Middle of the Night/ You'll Never Really Know	1965	2.50	5.00	10.00
❑ 1414	When I Stop Dreaming/With Tears in My Eyes	1966	2.50	5.00	10.00

—As "The Mathis Brothers"

MAY

Number	Title (A Side/B Side)	Yr	VG	VG+	NM
❑ 135	Somebody's Smiling (While I'm Crying)/Pins and Needles (In My Heart)	1963	3.00	6.00	12.00

—As "Dean and Mark"

DEANS, THE
45s
LAURIE

Number	Title (A Side/B Side)	Yr	VG	VG+	NM
❑ 3114	I Don't Want to Wait/Little White Gardenia	1961	5.00	10.00	20.00
MOHAWK					
❑ 114	My Heart Is Low/I'll Love You Forever	1960	6.25	12.50	25.00
❑ 119	Humpty Dumpty/La Chiam	1960	6.25	12.50	25.00
❑ 126	It's You/I Don't Wanna Wait	1960	10.00	20.00	40.00
STAR MAKER					
❑ 1928	Oh Little Star/You Got Me Baby	1961	25.00	50.00	100.00
❑ 1931	Chills, Chills, Chills/(Lady of the) Caravan	1962	15.00	30.00	60.00

DEAUVILLE, RONNIE
45s
ERA

Number	Title (A Side/B Side)	Yr	VG	VG+	NM
❑ 1055	I Concentrate on You/As Children Do	1957	5.00	10.00	20.00
❑ 1055 [PS]	I Concentrate on You/As Children Do	1957	10.00	20.00	40.00
❑ 1056	Laura/It Wasn't Much of a Town	1957	5.00	10.00	20.00
❑ 1056 [PS]	Laura/It Wasn't Much of a Town	1957	15.00	30.00	60.00
❑ 1066	Hong Kong Affair/Crazy, Wonderful	1957	5.00	10.00	20.00
IMPERIAL					
❑ 5559	King of Fools/Blame Your Eyes	1959	3.75	7.50	15.00

Albums
ERA

Number	Title (A Side/B Side)	Yr	VG	VG+	NM
❑ 20002 [M]	Smoke Dreams	1957	10.00	20.00	40.00
IMPERIAL					
❑ LP-9060 [M]	Romance	1959	6.25	12.50	25.00
❑ LP-12009 [S]	Romance	1959	7.50	15.00	30.00

DEBBIE AND THE TEEN DREAMS
45s
VERNON

Number	Title (A Side/B Side)	Yr	VG	VG+	NM
❑ 101	Santa, Teach Me How To Dance/The Time	1962	6.25	12.50	25.00

DEBERRY, JIMMY
45s
SUN

Number	Title (A Side/B Side)	Yr	VG	VG+	NM
❑ 185	Take a Little Chance/Time Has Made a Change	1953	750.00	1500.	3000.

DEBONAIRES, THE (1)
45s
DORE

Number	Title (A Side/B Side)	Yr	VG	VG+	NM
❑ 526	Every Once in a While/Mama Don't Care	1959	20.00	40.00	80.00

—As "The Debonairs"

Number	Title (A Side/B Side)	Yr	VG	VG+	NM
❑ 592	Every Once in a While/Gert's Skirt	1961	7.50	15.00	30.00
❑ 654	Hold Back the Dawn/Mama Don't Care	1962	6.25	12.50	25.00
❑ 702	Every Once in a While/Gert's Skirt	1964	5.00	10.00	20.00
❑ 712	Everybody's Movin'/Mama Don't Care	1964	5.00	10.00	20.00
GEE					
❑ 1008	Won't You Tell Me/I'm Gone	1956	20.00	40.00	80.00
❑ 1054	We'll Wait/Make Believe Lover	1960	6.25	12.50	25.00
HERALD					
❑ 509	Darlin'/Whispering Blues	1957	15.00	30.00	60.00
❑ 509	Darlin'/Whispering Blues	1957	50.00	100.00	200.00

—As "The Five Debonaires"

LOST-NITE

Number	Title (A Side/B Side)	Yr	VG	VG+	NM
❑ 419	Darlin'/Whispering Blues	197?	—	2.50	5.00

—Reissue

DEBONAIRES, THE (2)
45s
ELMONT

Number	Title (A Side/B Side)	Yr	VG	VG+	NM
❑ 1004	This Must Be Paradise/I Need You Darling	1958	50.00	100.00	200.00

Number	Title (A Side/B Side)	Yr	VG	VG+	NM

DEBONAIRES, THE (3)
45s
GOLDEN WORLD

Number	Title (A Side/B Side)	Yr	VG	VG+	NM
❏ 17	A Little Too Long/				
	Please Don't Say We're Through	1964	5.00	10.00	20.00
❏ 26	Eenie Meenie Gypsaleenie/				
	Please Don't Say We're Through	1965	5.00	10.00	20.00
❏ 38	Big Time Fun/				
	How's Your New Love Treating You	1966	5.00	10.00	20.00
❏ 44	C.O.D./How's Your New Love Treating You	1966	5.00	10.00	20.00

DEBONAIRES, THE (U) This may be one of groups (1), (2) or (3), or it may be a completely different group.
45s
MASKE

Number	Title (A Side/B Side)	Yr	VG	VG+	NM
❏ 804	Every Other Day/Jivin' Guy	1959	10.00	20.00	40.00

DEBS, THE More than one group.
45s
BRUCE

Number	Title (A Side/B Side)	Yr	VG	VG+	NM
❏ 129	Shoo-Doo-De-Doo/Whadaya Want	1955	15.00	30.00	60.00

CROWN

Number	Title (A Side/B Side)	Yr	VG	VG+	NM
❏ 153	If You Were Here Tonight/				
	Look What You're Doin' to Me	1955	10.00	20.00	40.00

DOUBLE L

Number	Title (A Side/B Side)	Yr	VG	VG+	NM
❏ 727	Danger Ahead/Just Another Fool	1964	3.00	6.00	12.00

KEEN

Number	Title (A Side/B Side)	Yr	VG	VG+	NM
❏ 34003	Johnny Darling/Doom-a-Roca	1957	6.25	12.50	25.00

MERCURY

Number	Title (A Side/B Side)	Yr	VG	VG+	NM
❏ 72458	Give Him My Love/Goodbye Boy	1965	5.00	10.00	20.00
❏ 72566	My Best Friend/The Life and Soul of the Party	1966	3.75	7.50	15.00

DEBUTANTES, THE (1)
45s
KAYO

Number	Title (A Side/B Side)	Yr	VG	VG+	NM
❏ 928	Going Steady/Memories	1958	62.50	125.00	250.00

DEBUTANTES, THE (2)
45s
LUCKY ELEVEN

Number	Title (A Side/B Side)	Yr	VG	VG+	NM
❏ 237	Love Is Strange/A New Love Today	196?	3.75	7.50	15.00

DEBUTANTES, THE (3)
45s
SAVOY

Number	Title (A Side/B Side)	Yr	VG	VG+	NM
❏ 1191	Just Leave It to Me/Is It Too Soon	1956	7.50	15.00	30.00

DECARLO, YVONNE
45s
IMPERIAL

Number	Title (A Side/B Side)	Yr	VG	VG+	NM
❏ 5532	Rockin' in Orbit/I Would Give My Heart	1958	20.00	40.00	80.00

Albums
MASTERSEAL

Number	Title (A Side/B Side)	Yr	VG	VG+	NM
❏ 33-1869/70 [M]	Yvonne DeCarlo Sings	1957	20.00	40.00	80.00

DECARO, NICK
45s
A&M

Number	Title (A Side/B Side)	Yr	VG	VG+	NM
❏ 838	Amy's Theme/Spanish Flea	1967	—	3.00	6.00
❏ 1037	Happy Heart/Love Is All	1969	—	3.00	6.00
❏ 1109	I'm Gonna Make You Love Me/Amy's Theme	1969	—	3.00	6.00

Albums
A&M

Number	Title (A Side/B Side)	Yr	VG	VG+	NM
❏ SP-4176	Happy Heart	1969	2.50	5.00	10.00

DECASTRO SISTERS, THE
45s
ABBOTT

Number	Title (A Side/B Side)	Yr	VG	VG+	NM
❏ 3001	Teach Me Tonight/It's Love	1954	3.75	7.50	15.00
❏ 3002	I'm Bewildered/To Say You're Mine	1955	3.00	6.00	12.00
❏ 3003	Boom Boom Boomerang/Let Your Love Walk In	1955	3.00	6.00	12.00
❏ 3004	Cuckoo in the Clock/If I Ever Fall in Love	1955	3.00	6.00	12.00
❏ 3007	Cuban Love Song/I Can't Escape from You	1955	3.00	6.00	12.00
❏ 3008	Wedding Song/I'm Bewildered	1955	3.00	6.00	12.00
❏ 3011	Too Late Now/Give Me Time	1955	3.00	6.00	12.00
❏ 3012	Snowbound for Christmas/Christmas Is a-Comin'	1955	3.75	7.50	15.00
❏ 3014	Rockin' and Rollin' in Hawaii/Cry Baby Blues	1956	3.00	6.00	12.00
❏ 3019	No One to Blame But You/Cowboys Don't Cry	1956	3.00	6.00	12.00

ABC-PARAMOUNT

Number	Title (A Side/B Side)	Yr	VG	VG+	NM
❏ 9932	Who Are They to Say/When You Look at Me	1958	2.50	5.00	10.00
❏ 9988	Teach Me Tonight Cha Cha/The Things I Tell My Pillow	1958	2.50	5.00	10.00
❏ 10007	Close to You/With My Eyes Wide Open	1959	2.50	5.00	10.00

BOHA

Number	Title (A Side/B Side)	Yr	VG	VG+	NM
❏ 1001	Feliz Navidad/Santa Claus Is Coming To Town	197?	—	2.00	4.00

CAPITOL

Number	Title (A Side/B Side)	Yr	VG	VG+	NM
❏ 4537	The Bells/Red Sails in the Sunset	1961	2.00	4.00	8.00

RCA VICTOR

Number	Title (A Side/B Side)	Yr	VG	VG+	NM
❏ 47-6661	Don't Call Me Sweetie/It's Yours	1956	2.50	5.00	10.00
❏ 47-6774	I Never Meant to Hurt You/I Hear a Melody	1956	2.50	5.00	10.00
❏ 47-6862	Flowers on a Hillside/I Know Plenty	1957	2.50	5.00	10.00
❏ 47-7028	Where Have You Been All My Life/That Little Word Called Love	1957	2.50	5.00	10.00
❏ 47-7108	Old Timers' Tune/Blue and Broken Hearted	1957	2.50	5.00	10.00
❏ 47-7177	You Take Care of Me/What a Relief	1958	2.50	5.00	10.00

ZODIAC

Number	Title (A Side/B Side)	Yr	VG	VG+	NM
❏ 1016	Before the Next Teardrop Falls/ Teach Me Tonight	1977	—	2.00	4.00

Albums
ABBOTT

Number	Title (A Side/B Side)	Yr	VG	VG+	NM
❏ 5002 [M]	The DeCastro Sisters	1956	15.00	30.00	60.00

CAPITOL

Number	Title (A Side/B Side)	Yr	VG	VG+	NM
❏ ST 1402 [S]	The DeCastros Sing	1960	7.50	15.00	30.00
❏ T 1402 [M]	The DeCastros Sing	1960	6.25	12.50	25.00
❏ ST 1501 [S]	The Rockin' Beat	1961	7.50	15.00	30.00
❏ T 1501 [M]	The Rockin' Beat	1961	6.25	12.50	25.00

DECEMBER'S CHILDREN
45s
CAPITOL

Number	Title (A Side/B Side)	Yr	VG	VG+	NM
❏ 5883	A Girl Like You/Makin' Music	1967	3.00	6.00	12.00

LIBERTY

Number	Title (A Side/B Side)	Yr	VG	VG+	NM
❏ 56195	You're My Girl/Dirty City	1970	2.50	5.00	10.00

MAINSTREAM

Number	Title (A Side/B Side)	Yr	VG	VG+	NM
❏ 728	Sweet Talking Woman/(B-side unknown)	1970	3.75	7.50	15.00

WORLD PACIFIC

Number	Title (A Side/B Side)	Yr	VG	VG+	NM
❏ 77887	Backwards and Forwards/Kissin' Time	1968	2.50	5.00	10.00
❏ 77895	Lovin' Things/Extraordinary Man	1968	2.50	5.00	10.00
❏ 77910	I've Been Hurt/Good Time Boy	1969	2.50	5.00	10.00

Albums
MAINSTREAM

Number	Title (A Side/B Side)	Yr	VG	VG+	NM
❏ S-6128	December's Children	1970	12.50	25.00	50.00

DEE, CONNIE
45s
HIT

Number	Title (A Side/B Side)	Yr	VG	VG+	NM
❏ 12	Everybody Loves Me But You/Old Rivers	1962	2.00	4.00	8.00
—B-side by Charlie Jarrett					
❏ 14	Second Hand Love/I Can't Stop Loving You	1962	2.00	4.00	8.00
—B-side by Herbert Hunter					
❏ 85	Hello Heartache, Goodbye Love/Sugar Shack	1963	2.00	4.00	8.00
—B-side by Ricky Dickens					
❏ 90	She's a Fool/It's All Right	1963	2.00	4.00	8.00
—B-side by Leroy Jones					
❏ 108	Navy Blue/Stop and Think It Over	1964	2.00	4.00	8.00
—B-side by Dotty and Dan					
❏ 114	That's the Way Boys Are/The Shoop Shoop Song	1964	2.00	4.00	8.00
—B-side by Denny Dugan					
❏ 123	Be Anything (But Be Mine)/Tell Me Why	1964	2.00	4.00	8.00
—B-side by Bobby Brooks					
❏ 128	My Boy Lollipop/Tears and Roses	1964	2.00	4.00	8.00
—B-side by Marty Wood					
❏ 186	Ring Telephone/The Jolly Green Giant	1965	2.00	4.00	8.00
—B-side by the Chords (2)					
❏ 189	Look of Love/King of the Road	1965	2.00	4.00	8.00
—B-side by Charlie Bare					
❏ 197	Whisper Tell Me Sweetly/I've Got a Tiger by the Tail	1965	2.00	4.00	8.00
—B-side by Jack White					
❏ 202	Once a Cheater, Always a Cheater/I Must Be Seeing Things	1965	2.00	4.00	8.00
—B-side by Bobby Brooks					
❏ 274	Sugar Town/Single Girl	1966	2.00	4.00	8.00
—B-side by Sherry Young					

DEE, DONNA
45s
ABC-PARAMOUNT

Number	Title (A Side/B Side)	Yr	VG	VG+	NM
❏ 10296	Television/Nobody's Gonna Hurt You	1962	5.00	10.00	20.00

DEE, FRANKIE
45s
ABCO

Number	Title (A Side/B Side)	Yr	VG	VG+	NM
❏ 1002	Walking in the Rain/Everybody's Doin' It	195?	5.00	10.00	20.00

RCA VICTOR

Number	Title (A Side/B Side)	Yr	VG	VG+	NM
❏ 47-7276	Shake It Up Baby/After Graduation	1958	15.00	30.00	60.00

20TH FOX

Number	Title (A Side/B Side)	Yr	VG	VG+	NM
❏ 146	Swingin' in a Hammock/I Had the Craziest Dream	1959	7.50	15.00	30.00

DEE, JACKIE See JACKIE DeSHANNON.

DEE, JIMMY
45s
DOT

Number	Title (A Side/B Side)	Yr	VG	VG+	NM
❏ 15664	Henrietta/Don't Cry No More	1957	10.00	20.00	40.00
❏ 15721	Here I Come/You're Late, Miss Kate	1958	10.00	20.00	40.00

TNT

Number	Title (A Side/B Side)	Yr	VG	VG+	NM
❏ 148	Henrietta/Don't Cry No More	1957	20.00	40.00	80.00
❏ 152	Here I Come/You're Late, Miss Kate	1958	20.00	40.00	80.00
❏ 161	Feel Like Rockin'/Rock-Tick-Rock	1958	15.00	30.00	60.00

DEE, JOEY, AND THE STARLITERS
45s
BONUS

Number	Title (A Side/B Side)	Yr	VG	VG+	NM
❏ 7009	Lorraine/The Girl I Walk to School	1963	12.50	25.00	50.00
❏ 7009 [PS]	Lorraine/The Girl I Walk to School	1963	20.00	40.00	80.00

JUBILEE

Number	Title (A Side/B Side)	Yr	VG	VG+	NM
❏ 5532	Feel Good About It Part 1/Feel Good About It Part 2	1966	3.75	7.50	15.00
❏ 5539	Dancing on the Beach/Good Little You	1966	3.75	7.50	15.00
❏ 5554	She's So Exceptional/It's Got You	1966	3.75	7.50	15.00
❏ 5566	Can't Sit Down/Put Your Heart In It	1967	3.75	7.50	15.00
—Stock copy may not exist					

LITTLE

Number	Title (A Side/B Side)	Yr	VG	VG+	NM
❏ 813/4	Lorraine/The Girl I Walk to School	1958	100.00	200.00	400.00

MONUMENT

Number	Title (A Side/B Side)	Yr	VG	VG+	NM
❏ (# unknown) [DJ]	Ya Ya Twist/Runaround Sue	1962	6.25	12.50	25.00
—B-side by Dion					

ROULETTE

Number	Title (A Side/B Side)	Yr	VG	VG+	NM
❏ 4401	Peppermint Twist — Part 1/Peppermint Twist — Part 2	1961	4.00	8.00	16.00
❏ 4408	Hey, Let's Twist/Roly Poly	1962	3.75	7.50	15.00
❏ 4408 [PS]	Hey, Let's Twist/Roly Poly	1962	6.25	12.50	25.00
❏ 4416	Shout — Part 1/Shout — Part 2	1962	3.75	7.50	15.00
❏ 4416 [PS]	Shout — Part 1/Shout — Part 2	1962	6.25	12.50	25.00
❏ 4431	Every Time (I Think About You) Part 1/Every Time (I Think About You) Part 2	1962	3.00	6.00	12.00
❏ 4438	What Kind of Love Is This/Wing Ding	1962	2.50	5.00	10.00
—Pink label					
❏ 4438	What Kind of Love Is This/Wing Ding	1962	3.00	6.00	12.00
—White label with colored "spokes"					
❏ 4438 [PS]	What Kind of Love Is This/Wing Ding	1962	6.25	12.50	25.00

Number	Title (A Side/B Side)	Yr	VG	VG+	NM
❏ 4456	I Lost My Baby/				
	Keep Your Mind on What You're Doing	1962	3.00	6.00	12.00
❏ 4456 [PS]	I Lost My Baby/				
	Keep Your Mind on What You're Doing	1962	6.25	12.50	25.00
❏ 4467	Baby You're Driving Me Crazy/❏ Help Me Pick				
	Up the Pieces	1963	3.00	6.00	12.00
❏ 4488	Hot Pastrami with Mashed Potatoes — Part 1/				
	Hot Pastrami with Mashed Potatoes — Part 2	1963	3.00	6.00	12.00
❏ 4503	Dance, Dance, Dance/Let's Have a Party	1963	3.00	6.00	12.00
❏ 4523	Ya Ya/Fanny Mae	1963	3.00	6.00	12.00
❏ 4539	Down by the Riverside/Getting Nearer	1963	5.00	10.00	20.00
❏ 4617	Cry a Little Sometime/Wing Ding	1965	3.00	6.00	12.00

SCEPTER

Number	Title (A Side/B Side)	Yr	VG	VG+	NM
❏ 1210	Face of An Angel/Shimmy Baby	1960	7.50	15.00	30.00

—Originals have "Scepter" at top of label and are credited as "Joey Dee and the Starlights"

Number	Title (A Side/B Side)	Yr	VG	VG+	NM
❏ 1210	Face of An Angel/Shimmy Baby	1961	5.00	10.00	20.00

—Reissues have "Scepter Records" at side of label and are credited as listed

Number	Title (A Side/B Side)	Yr	VG	VG+	NM
❏ 1225	Three Memories/(Bad) Bulldog	1961	7.50	15.00	30.00

VASELINE HAIR TONIC

Number	Title (A Side/B Side)	Yr	VG	VG+	NM
❏ (no #)	Learn to Dance the Authentic Peppermint Twist				
	(Parts 1 & 2)	1962	3.75	7.50	15.00
❏ (no #) [PS]	Learn to Dance the Authentic Peppermint Twist				
	(Parts 1 & 2)	1962	3.75	7.50	15.00

Albums

FORUM

Number	Title (A Side/B Side)	Yr	VG	VG+	NM
❏ FC 9099 [M]	Joey Dee and the Starliters	1963	3.00	6.00	12.00
❏ FCS 9099 [S]	Joey Dee and the Starliters	1963	3.00	6.00	12.00

JUBILEE

Number	Title (A Side/B Side)	Yr	VG	VG+	NM
❏ JGM-8000 [M]	Hitsville	1966	5.00	10.00	20.00
❏ JGS-8000 [S]	Hitsville	1966	6.25	12.50	25.00

ROULETTE

Number	Title (A Side/B Side)	Yr	VG	VG+	NM
❏ R-25166 [M]	Doin' the Twist at the Peppermint Lounge	1961	10.00	20.00	40.00
❏ SR-25166 [S]	Doin' the Twist at the Peppermint Lounge	1961	12.50	25.00	50.00
❏ R-25171 [M]	All the World Is Twistin'	1962	7.50	15.00	30.00
❏ SR-25171 [S]	All the World Is Twistin'	1962	10.00	20.00	40.00
❏ R-25173 [M]	Back at the Peppermint Lounge — Twistin'	1962	7.50	15.00	30.00
❏ SR-25173 [S]	Back at the Peppermint Lounge — Twistin'	1962	10.00	20.00	40.00
❏ R-25197 [M]	Joey Dee	1963	6.25	12.50	25.00
❏ SR-25197 [S]	Joey Dee	1963	7.50	15.00	30.00
❏ R-25221 [M]	Dance, Dance, Dance	1963	6.25	12.50	25.00
❏ SR-25221 [S]	Dance, Dance, Dance	1963	7.50	15.00	30.00

SCEPTER

Number	Title (A Side/B Side)	Yr	VG	VG+	NM
❏ S 503 [M]	The Peppermint Twisters	1962	6.25	12.50	25.00
❏ SS 503 [S]	The Peppermint Twisters	1962	7.50	15.00	30.00

DEE, JOHNNY See JOHN D. LOUDERMILK.

DEE, KIKI Also see ELTON JOHN AND KIKI DEE.

45s

FONTANA

Number	Title (A Side/B Side)	Yr	VG	VG+	NM
❏ 1649	On a Magic Carpet Ride/Now the Flowers Die	1969	—	2.50	5.00

LIBERTY

Number	Title (A Side/B Side)	Yr	VG	VG+	NM
❏ 55994	Stop and Think/I	1967	—	3.00	6.00
❏ 56030	I'm Going Out/Patterns	1968	—	3.00	6.00
❏ 56089	On a Magic Carpet Ride/Now the Flowers Die	1969	—	3.00	6.00

POSSE

Number	Title (A Side/B Side)	Yr	VG	VG+	NM
❏ 5008	Nothing Can Stop Us Now/(B-side unknown)	1981	—	2.00	4.00

RARE EARTH

Number	Title (A Side/B Side)	Yr	VG	VG+	NM
❏ 5025	Love Makes the World Go Round/Jimmy	1970	—	2.50	5.00

RCA

Number	Title (A Side/B Side)	Yr	VG	VG+	NM
❏ PB-12347	Star/There's a Need	1981	—	2.00	4.00
❏ PB-13043	Loving You Is Sweeter Than Ever/Twenty-Four				
	Hours	1982	—	—	—

—Unreleased

ROCKET

Number	Title (A Side/B Side)	Yr	VG	VG+	NM
❏ YB-11413	One Step/Dark Side of Your Soul	1978	—	2.00	4.00
❏ YB-11490	Don't Stop Loving Me/One Step Ahead of the				
	Storm	1979	—	2.00	4.00
❏ 40095	The Last Good Man in My Life/Lonnie and Josie	1973	—	2.00	4.00
❏ 40157	Amoureuse/Rest My Head	1973	—	2.00	4.00
❏ 40256	Super Cool/Loving and Free	1974	—	2.00	4.00
❏ 40293	I've Got the Music in Me/Simple Melody	1974	—	2.50	5.00
❏ 40355	Step by Step/Amoureuse	1975	—	2.00	4.00
❏ 40401	How Glad I Am/Peter	1975	—	2.00	4.00
❏ 40506	Once a Fool/Someone to Me	1976	—	2.00	4.00
❏ 40730	Chicago/Bad Day Child	1977	—	2.00	4.00

TAMLA

Number	Title (A Side/B Side)	Yr	VG	VG+	NM
❏ 54193	The Day Will Come Between Sunday and				
	Monday/My Whole World Ended (The Moment				
	You Left Me)	1970	—	2.50	5.00
❏ 54193 [PS]	The Day Will Come Between Sunday and				
	Monday/My Whole World Ended (The Moment				
	You Left Me)	1970	3.75	7.50	15.00

WORLD PACIFIC

Number	Title (A Side/B Side)	Yr	VG	VG+	NM
❏ 77820	I Dig You Baby/Small Town	1966	2.00	4.00	8.00

Albums

LIBERTY

Number	Title (A Side/B Side)	Yr	VG	VG+	NM
❏ LST-7613	Patterns	1969	3.75	7.50	15.00
❏ LN-10148	Patterns	1981	2.00	4.00	8.00

—Budget-line reissue

RCA VICTOR

Number	Title (A Side/B Side)	Yr	VG	VG+	NM
❏ AFL1-4180	Perfect Timing	1981	2.50	5.00	10.00

ROCKET

Number	Title (A Side/B Side)	Yr	VG	VG+	NM
❏ PIG-395	Loving and Free	1973	2.50	5.00	10.00
❏ PIG-458	I've Got the Music In Me	1974	3.00	6.00	12.00
❏ BXL1-2257	Kiki Dee	1977	2.50	5.00	10.00
❏ BXL1-3011	Stay with Me	1979	2.50	5.00	10.00

TAMLA

Number	Title (A Side/B Side)	Yr	VG	VG+	NM
❏ TS 303	Great Expectations	1970	3.75	7.50	15.00

DEE, LENNY

45s

DECCA

Number	Title (A Side/B Side)	Yr	VG	VG+	NM
❏ 25531	Parade of the Wooden Soldiers/Twilight Time	1961	—	3.00	6.00
❏ 25563	Ain't She Sweet/Alabamy Bound	1962	—	3.00	6.00
❏ 25578	Baubles, Bangles and Beads/Blues in the Night	1962	—	3.00	6.00
❏ 25592	Moon Over Miami/Atlanta G.A.	1963	—	3.00	6.00
❏ 25613	Wagon Wheels/Hominy Grits	1963	—	3.00	6.00
❏ 25633	Devil Woman/San Antonio Rose	1964	—	3.00	6.00
❏ 25678	The Gang That Sang Heart of My Heart/				
	Down by the Old Mill Stream	1965	—	3.00	6.00
❏ 25696	Yakety Organ/A Walk in the Black Forest	1966	—	3.00	6.00
❏ 25702	Kerry Dancers/One of Those Songs	1966	—	3.00	6.00
❏ 25717	Cute/Daydream	1967	—	2.50	5.00
❏ 25725	There's a Kind of Hush/Exodus	1967	—	2.50	5.00
❏ 25735	Gentle on My Mind/Rossana's Theme	1968	—	2.50	5.00
❏ 25745	Folsom Prison Blues/Turn Around, Look at Me	1969	—	2.50	5.00
❏ 25750	Help Yourself/Try a Little Tenderness	1969	—	2.50	5.00
❏ 25755	Yesterday, When I Was Young/				
	Ruby, Don't Take Your Love to Town	1970	—	2.50	5.00
❏ 28500	Midnight/Bye Bye Blues	1952	2.50	5.00	10.00
❏ 28639	Oh Johnny Oh/Them There Eyes	1953	2.50	5.00	10.00
❏ 29360	Plantation Boogie/The Birth of the Blues	1954	2.50	5.00	10.00
❏ 29579	Crazy Organ Rag/Punxsutawney Boogie	1955	2.50	5.00	10.00
❏ 29596	Little Brown Jug/The World Is Waiting for the				
	Sunrise	1955	2.50	5.00	10.00
❏ 29689	Honeydripper/Flea Hop Boogie	1955	2.50	5.00	10.00
❏ 30032	Honky Tonk Train Blues/Yodelin' Organ	1956	2.00	4.00	8.00
❏ 30201	Stormy Weather/Goodnight Sweet Love	1957	2.00	4.00	8.00
❏ 30296	High Tide Boogie/Tara Lara	1957	2.00	4.00	8.00
❏ 30429	Big Boogie Dee/Cecelia	1957	2.00	4.00	8.00
❏ 30718	June Night/After You've Gone	1958	2.00	4.00	8.00
❏ 30801	Night Train/Chicken in the Rough	1959	2.00	4.00	8.00
❏ 31332	Mr. Santa/Auld Lang Syne	1961	2.50	5.00	10.00
❏ 32691	Rock Me Back to Little Rock/Sweet and Sassy	1970	—	2.50	5.00
❏ 32804	Help Me Make It Through the Night/				
	Remember Me	1971	—	2.00	4.00
❏ 33026	All I Ever Need Is You/Vaya Con Dios	1972	—	2.00	4.00

7-Inch Extended Plays

DECCA

Number	Title (A Side/B Side)	Yr	VG	VG+	NM
❏ ED 2266	(contents unknown)	195?	2.50	5.00	10.00
❏ ED 2266 [PS]	Dee-Lirious, Part 1	195?	2.50	5.00	10.00
❏ ED 2267	Five Foot Two, Eyes of Blue/Out of Nowhere//				
	Caravan/That's My Weakness Now	195?	2.50	5.00	10.00
❏ ED 2267 [PS]	Dee-Lirious, Part 2	195?	2.50	5.00	10.00
❏ ED 2345	Delicious/Fan Tango//Stompin' at the Savoy				
	(I'm in Heaven When I See You Smile) Diane	195?	2.50	5.00	10.00
❏ ED 2345 [PS]	(title unknown)	195?	2.50	5.00	10.00
❏ ED 2552	(contents unknown)	195?	2.50	5.00	10.00
❏ ED 2552 [PS]	Mr. Dee Goes to Town	195?	2.50	5.00	10.00
❏ ED 2613	(contents unknown)	195?	2.50	5.00	10.00
❏ ED 2613 [PS]	Dee-Day	195?	2.50	5.00	10.00
❏ ED 2628 [M]	(contents unknown)	195?	2.50	5.00	10.00
❏ ED 2628 [PS]	Mellow-Dee	1959	2.50	5.00	10.00
❏ ED 7-2628 [PS]	Mellow-Dee	1959	3.75	7.50	15.00
❏ ED 7-2628 [S]	(contents unknown)	1959	3.75	7.50	15.00
❏ ED 2645	(contents unknown)	195?	2.50	5.00	10.00
❏ ED 2645 [PS]	Lenny Dee Plays the Hits	195?	2.50	5.00	10.00
❏ 7-34111	Mississippi Mud/Georgia on My Mind/Carolina				
	in the Morning//When It's Sleepy Time Down				
	South/Way Down Yonder in New Orleans/				
	Beautiful Cypress Gardens	196?	2.50	5.00	10.00

—Jukebox issue; small hole, plays at 33 1/3 rpm

Number	Title (A Side/B Side)	Yr	VG	VG+	NM
❏ 7-34111 [PS]	Lenny Dee Down South	196?	2.50	5.00	10.00

Albums

DECCA

Number	Title (A Side/B Side)	Yr	VG	VG+	NM
❏ DL 4112 [M]	Golden Organ Favorites	1961	2.50	5.00	10.00
❏ DL 4146 [M]	Happy Holi-Dee	1961	2.50	5.00	10.00
❏ DL 4315 [M]	Lenny Dee In Hollywood	1962	2.50	5.00	10.00
❏ DL 4365 [M]	Lenny Dee Down South	1963	2.50	5.00	10.00
❏ DL 4429 [M]	By Popular Dee-Mand	1963	2.50	5.00	10.00
❏ DL 4498 [M]	Something Special	1964	2.50	5.00	10.00
❏ DL 4572 [M]	Most Requested	1964	2.50	5.00	10.00
❏ DL 4632 [M]	Sweethearts on Parade	1965	2.50	5.00	10.00
❏ DL 4654 [M]	The Lenny Dee Tour	1965	2.50	5.00	10.00
❏ DL 4706 [M]	My Favorite Things	1966	2.50	5.00	10.00
❏ DL 4818 [M]	In the Mood	1967	2.50	5.00	10.00
❏ DL 4880 [M]	Moving On	1967	3.00	6.00	12.00
❏ DL 4946 [M]	Relaxin'	1968	3.00	6.00	12.00
❏ DL 4994 [M]	Gentle on My Mind	1968	3.00	6.00	12.00
❏ DXS 7199 [(2)]	The Best of Lenny Dee	1968	3.00	6.00	12.00
❏ DL 8114 [M]	Dee-Lightful	1955	3.75	7.50	15.00
❏ DL 8165 [M]	Dee-Lirious	1956	3.00	6.00	12.00
❏ DL 8275 [M]	Dee-Licious	1956	3.00	6.00	12.00
❏ DL 8308 [M]	Dee-Most	1956	3.00	6.00	12.00
❏ DL 8406 [M]	Hi-Dee-Fi	1957	3.00	6.00	12.00
❏ DL 8497 [M]	Mr. Dee Goes to Town	1957	3.00	6.00	12.00
❏ DL 8628 [M]	Dee-Day	1957	3.00	6.00	12.00
❏ DL 8718 [M]	Dee-Latin Hi-Fi Organ	1958	3.00	6.00	12.00
❏ DL 8796 [M]	Mellow-Dee	1959	3.00	6.00	12.00
❏ DL 8857 [M]	Lenny Dee Plays the Hits	1959	3.00	6.00	12.00
❏ DL 8913 [M]	The Lenny Dee Show	1960	2.50	5.00	10.00
❏ DL 8978 [M]	Songs Everybody Knows	1960	2.50	5.00	10.00
❏ DL 74112 [S]	Golden Organ Favorites	1961	3.00	6.00	12.00
❏ DL 74146 [S]	Happy Holi-Dee	1961	3.00	6.00	12.00
❏ DL 74315 [S]	Lenny Dee In Hollywood	1962	3.00	6.00	12.00
❏ DL 74365 [S]	Lenny Dee Down South	1963	3.00	6.00	12.00
❏ DL 74429 [S]	By Popular Dee-Mand	1963	3.00	6.00	12.00
❏ DL 74498 [S]	Something Special	1964	3.00	6.00	12.00
❏ DL 74572 [S]	Most Requested	1964	3.00	6.00	12.00
❏ DL 74632 [S]	Sweethearts on Parade	1965	3.00	6.00	12.00
❏ DL 74654 [S]	The Lenny Dee Tour	1965	3.00	6.00	12.00
❏ DL 74706 [S]	My Favorite Things	1966	3.00	6.00	12.00
❏ DL 74818 [S]	In the Mood	1967	3.00	6.00	12.00
❏ DL 74946 [S]	Relaxin'	1968	2.50	5.00	10.00
❏ DL 74994 [S]	Gentle on My Mind	1968	2.50	5.00	10.00
❏ DL 75073	Turn Around, Look at Me	1969	2.50	5.00	10.00
❏ DL 75112	Little Green Apples	1969	2.50	5.00	10.00
❏ DL 75152	Spinning Wheel	1969	2.50	5.00	10.00
❏ DL 75196	Easy Come, Easy Go	1970	2.50	5.00	10.00
❏ DL 75255	Remember Me	1971	2.50	5.00	10.00
❏ DL 75320	Easy Lovin'	1972	2.50	5.00	10.00
❏ DL 75366	Where Is the Love	1972	2.50	5.00	10.00

Number	Title (A Side/B Side)	Yr	VG	VG+	NM
❑ DL 78796 [S]	Mellow-Dee	1959	3.75	7.50	15.00
❑ DL 78857 [S]	Lenny Dee Plays the Hits	1959	3.75	7.50	15.00
❑ DL 78880 [S]	Moving On	1967	2.50	5.00	10.00
❑ DL 78913 [S]	The Lenny Dee Show	1960	3.00	6.00	12.00
❑ DL 78978 [S]	Songs Everybody Knows	1960	3.00	6.00	12.00
MCA					
❑ 26	Remember Me	1971	2.00	4.00	8.00
—Reissue of Decca 75255					
❑ 172	In the Mood	1973	2.00	4.00	8.00
—Reissue of Decca 74818					
❑ 182	Golden Organ Favorites	1973	2.00	4.00	8.00
—Reissue of Decca 74112					
❑ 221	Something Special	1973	2.00	4.00	8.00
—Reissue of Decca 74498					
❑ 231	Most Requested	1973	2.00	4.00	8.00
—Reissue of Decca 74572					
❑ 241	My Favorite Things	1973	2.00	4.00	8.00
—Reissue of Decca 74706					
❑ 271	Gentle on My Mind	1973	2.00	4.00	8.00
—Reissue of Decca 74994					
❑ 279	Little Green Apples	1973	2.00	4.00	8.00
—Reissue of Decca 75112					
❑ 290	Easy Come, Easy Go	1973	2.00	4.00	8.00
—Reissue of Decca 75196					
❑ 297	Easy Lovin'	1973	2.00	4.00	8.00
—Reissue of Decca 75320					
❑ 334	"Sing" and Others	1973	2.00	4.00	8.00
❑ 334	Lenny Dee	1973	2.00	4.00	8.00
❑ 379	"Lenny"	1973	2.00	4.00	8.00
❑ 455	Steppin' Out with Lenny Dee	1974	2.00	4.00	8.00
❑ 476	City Lights	1974	2.00	4.00	8.00
❑ 504	Where Is the Love	1974	2.00	4.00	8.00
—Reissue of Decca 75366					
❑ 533	Songs Everybody Knows	1975	2.00	4.00	8.00
—Reissue of Decca 78978					
❑ 2162	I'll Play for You	1975	2.00	4.00	8.00
❑ 2200	Take It to the Limit	1976	2.00	4.00	8.00
❑ 2236	Misty Blue	1976	2.00	4.00	8.00
❑ 2301	Organ Magic	1977	2.00	4.00	8.00
❑ 2370	Organ Celebration	1978	2.00	4.00	8.00
❑ 4042 [(2)]	The Best of Lenny Dee	197?	2.50	5.00	10.00
—Reissue of Decca 7179					
❑ 4084 [(2)]	The Best of Lenny Dee, Volume II	1977	2.50	5.00	10.00
VOCALION					
❑ VL 3782 [M]	Here's Lenny Dee at the Organ	1967	2.50	5.00	10.00
❑ VL 73782 [S]	Here's Lenny Dee at the Organ	1967	2.50	5.00	10.00
❑ VL 73817	Organ Special	1968	2.50	5.00	10.00
❑ VL 73819	Varieties	1969	2.50	5.00	10.00

DEE, RONNIE See RONNIE DAWSON.

DEE, TOMMY
45s
CHALLENGE

Number	Title (A Side/B Side)	Yr	VG	VG+	NM
❑ 59083	The Hobo and the Puppy/There's a Star Spangled Banner Waving Somewhere	1960	5.00	10.00	20.00
❑ 59087	Ballad of a Drag Race/The Story of Susie	1960	5.00	10.00	20.00
CREST					
❑ 1057 [M]	Three Stars/I'll Never Change	1959	6.25	12.50	25.00
—With backing group and B-side credited to "Carol Kay and the Teen-Aires"					
❑ 1057 [M]	Three Stars/I'll Never Change	1959	7.50	15.00	30.00
—With backing group and B-side credited to "The Teen Tones and Orchestra"					
❑ 1057 [S]	Three Stars/I'll Never Change	1959	12.50	25.00	50.00
—With backing group and B-side credited to "Carol Kay and the Teen-Aires"					
❑ 1061	The Chair/Hello Lonesome	1959	5.00	10.00	20.00
❑ 1067	Merry Christmas, Mary/Angel of Love	1959	6.25	12.50	25.00
—With Carol Kay					
PIKE					
❑ 5906	Loving You (On Someone Else's Time)/Halfway to Hell	1961	5.00	10.00	20.00
❑ 5909	A Little Dog Cried/Look Homeward, Dear Angel	1961	5.00	10.00	20.00
❑ 5917	Missing on a Mountain/Look Homeward, Dear Angel	1962	5.00	10.00	20.00
SIMS					
❑ 260	Missing While Surfing/Goodbye High School	1966	5.00	10.00	20.00
❑ 308	How's Your Mama Em/Goodbye High School	1966	3.75	7.50	15.00
STARDAY					
❑ 802	Roger, Ed and Gus (America's Astronaut Heroes)/School for Fools	1967	2.00	4.00	8.00

DEE, WILLIE
45s
TUMBLEWEED

Number	Title (A Side/B Side)	Yr	VG	VG+	NM
❑ 100	Tear Filled Eyes/My Daddy's Not a Young Man Anymore	1968	5.00	10.00	20.00

DEEP, THE
Albums
PARKWAY

Number	Title (A Side/B Side)	Yr	VG	VG+	NM
❑ P 7051 [M]	Psychedelic Moods	1966	62.50	125.00	250.00
❑ SP 7051 [S]	Psychedelic Moods	1966	125.00	250.00	500.00

DEEP PURPLE
12-Inch Singles
MERCURY

Number	Title (A Side/B Side)	Yr	VG	VG+	NM
❑ PRO 332-1 [DJ]	Knocking at Your Back Door (AOR Edit Version) (Album Version)	1984	3.75	7.50	15.00
❑ PRO 334-1 [DJ]	Nobody's Home/Under the Gun	1984	7.50	15.00	30.00
❑ PRO 473-1 [DJ]	Bad Attitude (same on both sides)	1987	3.75	7.50	15.00
❑ PRO 485-1 [DJ]	Call of the Wild (same on both sides)	1987	2.50	5.00	10.00

45s
MERCURY

Number	Title (A Side/B Side)	Yr	VG	VG+	NM
❑ 880477-7	Knocking at Your Back Door/Wasted Sunset	1984	—	2.00	4.00
❑ 880477-7 [PS]	Knocking at Your Back Door/Wasted Sunset	1984	—	2.50	5.00
❑ 885617-7	Call of the Wild/Dead or Alive	1987	—	—	3.00
❑ 885617-7 [PS]	Call of the Wild/Dead or Alive	1987	—	—	3.00
❑ 885820-7	Bad Attitude/Black and White	1987	—	—	3.00

TETRAGRAMMATON

Number	Title (A Side/B Side)	Yr	VG	VG+	NM
❑ 1503	Hush/One More Rainy Day	1968	3.00	6.00	12.00
❑ 1503 [PS]	Hush/One More Rainy Day	1968	150.00	300.00	600.00
❑ 1508	Kentucky Woman/Hard Road	1968	3.00	6.00	12.00
❑ 1508 [PS]	Kentucky Woman/Hard Road	1968	7.50	15.00	30.00
❑ 1514	River Deep, Mountain High/Listen, Learn, Read On	1969	2.50	5.00	10.00
❑ 1519	The Bird Has Flown/Emmaretta	1969	2.50	5.00	10.00
❑ 1537	Hallelujah (I Am the Preacher)/April Part 1	1969	2.50	5.00	10.00
WARNER BROS.					
❑ PRO 402 [DJ]	Radio Spot for Concerto	1970	37.50	75.00	150.00
❑ 7405	Black Night/Into the Fire	1970	2.00	4.00	8.00
❑ 7493	Strange Kind of Woman/I'm Alone	1971	2.00	4.00	8.00
❑ 7528	Fire Ball/I'm Alone	1971	2.00	4.00	8.00
❑ 7572	Never Before/When a Blind Man Cries	1972	—	3.00	6.00
❑ 7595	Lazy/When a Blind Man Cries	1972	—	3.00	6.00
❑ 7634	Highway Star (Part 1)/Highway Star (Part 2)	1972	—	3.00	6.00
❑ 7654	Hush/Kentucky Woman	1972	—	3.00	6.00
❑ 7672	Woman from Tokyo/Super Trouper	1972	—	3.00	6.00
❑ 7710	Smoke on the Water (Edited Version) Studio/Smoke on the Water (Edited Version) Live	1973	—	2.50	5.00
❑ 7737	Woman from Tokyo/Super Trouper	1973	—	2.50	5.00
❑ 7784	Might Just Take Your Life/Coronarias Regid	1974	—	2.50	5.00
❑ 7784 [DJ]	Might Just Take Your Life (Mono 3:35/Stereo 4:36)	1974	2.00	4.00	8.00
❑ 7809	Burn/Coronarias Regid	1974	—	2.50	5.00
❑ 8049	High Ball Shooter/You Can't Do It Right	1974	—	2.50	5.00
❑ 8069	Stormbringer/Love Don't Mean a Thing	1975	—	2.50	5.00
❑ 8182	Gettin' Tighter/Love Child	1976	—	2.50	5.00

7-Inch Extended Plays
WARNER BROS.

Number	Title (A Side/B Side)	Yr	VG	VG+	NM
❑ S 2701	Smoke on the Water/Highway Star	1973	3.75	7.50	15.00
—Full-length versions; jukebox issue; small hole, plays at 33 1/3 rpm					
❑ S 2701 [PS]	Made in Japan	1973	3.75	7.50	15.00
—Part of "Little LP" series (LLP #214)					
❑ S 2766	Burn/Lay Down Stay Down/You Fool No One	1974	3.75	7.50	15.00
—Full-length versions; jukebox issue; small hole, plays at 33 1/3 rpm					
❑ S 2766 [PS]	Burn	1974	3.75	7.50	15.00
—Part of "Little LP" series (LLP #250)					

Albums
DCC COMPACT CLASSICS

Number	Title (A Side/B Side)	Yr	VG	VG+	NM
❑ LPZ-2052 [(2)]	Made in Japan	1998	10.00	20.00	40.00
—Audiophile vinyl					
MERCURY					
❑ 824003-1	Perfect Strangers	1984	2.50	5.00	10.00
❑ 831318-1	The House of Blue Light	1987	2.00	4.00	8.00
❑ 835897-1	Nobody's Perfect	1988	2.50	5.00	10.00
RCA					
❑ 2421-1-R	Slaves and Masters	1990	3.75	7.50	15.00
RHINO					
❑ R1-75622	Machine Head	2003	3.75	7.50	15.00
—180-gram reissue					
SCEPTER					
❑ CTN-18010	The Best of Deep Purple	1972	2.50	5.00	10.00
TETRAGRAMMATON					
❑ T-102	Shades of Deep Purple	1968	7.50	15.00	30.00
❑ T-107	The Book of Taliesyn	1968	7.50	15.00	30.00
❑ T-119	Deep Purple	1969	7.50	15.00	30.00
❑ T-131	Concerto for Group and Orchestra	1970	50.00	100.00	200.00
WARNER BROS.					
❑ WS 1860	Concerto for Group and Orchestra	1970	3.00	6.00	12.00
❑ WS 1877	Deep Purple in Rock	1970	3.00	6.00	12.00
❑ BS 2564	Fireball	1971	3.00	6.00	12.00
❑ BS 2607	Machine Head	1972	3.00	6.00	12.00
—Original copies have green "WB" labels					
❑ BS 2607	Machine Head	1973	2.50	5.00	10.00
—"Burbank" labels					
❑ BS4 2607 [Q]	Machine Head	1974	6.25	12.50	25.00
❑ 2LS 2644 [(2)]	(Purple Passages)	1972	3.75	7.50	15.00
❑ BS 2678	Who Do We Think We Are!	1973	2.50	5.00	10.00
—"Burbank" labels					
❑ BS 2678	Who Do We Think We Are!	1973	3.00	6.00	12.00
—Original copies have green "WB" labels					
❑ 2WS 2701 [(2)]	Made in Japan	1973	3.75	7.50	15.00
❑ 2WS 2701 [(2)]	Made in Japan	1979	2.00	6.00	12.00
—White labels					
❑ W 2766	Burn	1974	2.50	5.00	10.00
❑ BSK 3100	Machine Head	1976	2.00	4.00	8.00
WARNER BROS./PURPLE					
❑ PR 2832	Stormbringer	1974	2.50	5.00	10.00
❑ PR4 2832 [Q]	Stormbringer	1974	6.25	12.50	25.00
❑ PR 2895	Come Taste the Band	1975	2.50	5.00	10.00
❑ PR 2995	Made in Europe	1976	2.50	5.00	10.00
❑ PRK 3223	When We Rock, We Rock, and When We Roll, We Roll	1978	2.50	5.00	10.00
❑ PRK 3486	Deepest Purple: The Best of Deep Purple	1980	2.50	5.00	10.00

DEEP SIX, THE
45s
LIBERTY

Number	Title (A Side/B Side)	Yr	VG	VG+	NM
❑ 55838	Rising Sun/Strolling Blues	1965	2.00	4.00	8.00
❑ 55858	I Wanna Shout/Things We Say	1966	2.00	4.00	8.00
❑ 55882	When Morning Breaks/Counting	1966	2.00	4.00	8.00
❑ 55901	Why Say Goodbye/What Would You Wish from the Golden Fish	1966	2.00	4.00	8.00
❑ 55926	Image of a Girl/C'mon Baby	1966	2.00	4.00	8.00

Albums
LIBERTY

Number	Title (A Side/B Side)	Yr	VG	VG+	NM
❑ LRP-3475 [M]	The Deep Six	1966	3.75	7.50	15.00
❑ LST-7475 [S]	The Deep Six	1966	5.00	10.00	20.00

DEERFIELD
Albums
FLAT ROCK

Number	Title (A Side/B Side)	Yr	VG	VG+	NM
❑ FRS-1	Nil Desperandum	1971	30.00	60.00	120.00

D

Number	Title (A Side/B Side)	Yr	VG	VG+	NM

DEFENDERS, THE
45s
PARKWAY
❏ 926	Island of Love/I Laughed So Hard	1964	2.50	5.00	10.00

DEFRANCO FAMILY, THE
45s
20TH CENTURY
❏ 2030	Heartbeat — It's a Lovebeat/				
	Sweet, Sweet Loretta	1973	—	2.00	4.00
❏ 2030 [PS]	Heartbeat — It's a Lovebeat/				
	Sweet, Sweet Loretta	1973	—	3.00	6.00
❏ 2070	Abra-Ca-Dabra/Some Kind a' Love	1973	—	2.00	4.00
❏ 2070 [PS]	Abra-Ca-Dabra/Some Kind a' Love	1973	—	3.00	6.00
❏ 2088	Save the Last Dance for Me/				
	Because We Both Are Young	1974	—	2.00	4.00
❏ 2088 [PS]	Save the Last Dance for Me/Because We Both				
	Are Young	1974	—	3.00	6.00
❏ 2128	Baby Blue/Write Me a Letter	1974	—	2.00	4.00
❏ 2128 [PS]	Baby Blue/Write Me a Letter	1974	—	3.00	6.00
❏ 2214	We Belong Together/Time Enough for Love	1975	2.00	4.00	8.00
❏ 2214 [PS]	We Belong Together/Time Enough for Love	1975	2.50	5.00	10.00

Albums
20TH CENTURY
| ❏ T-422 | Heartbeat, It's a Lovebeat | 1973 | 2.50 | 5.00 | 10.00 |
| ❏ T-441 | Save the Last Dance for Me | 1974 | 2.50 | 5.00 | 10.00 |

DEJOHN SISTERS, THE
45s
COLUMBIA
❏ 40799	Mah Little Baby/Mu-Cha-Cha	1956	3.75	7.50	15.00
❏ 40843	Don't Promise Me (The Can Can Song)/He's Got				
	Time	1957	3.00	6.00	12.00
EPIC
❏ 9009	Should I Run/All Present But One	1953	3.75	7.50	15.00
❏ 9031	I Took Him from You/Juke-Box Polka	1954	3.75	7.50	15.00
❏ 9055	A Kiss and a Rose/Crazy Song of India	1954	3.75	7.50	15.00
❏ 9080	Lover's Slang/Mandolino	1954	3.75	7.50	15.00
❏ 9085	(My Baby Don't Love Me) No More/Theresa	1954	3.75	7.50	15.00
❏ 9097	D'Ja Hear What I Say/A Present for Bob	1955	3.00	6.00	12.00
❏ 9108	He Loves Me/				
	Pass the Plate of Happiness Around	1955	3.00	6.00	12.00
❏ 9124	(Love Is) The Tender Trap/				
	I'm Learning the Charleston	1955	—	—	—
—Canceled					
❏ 9131	C'est La Vie/Uninvited Love	1955	3.00	6.00	12.00
❏ 9133	The Only Thing I Want for Christmas/That's How				
	Santa Claus Will Look This Year	1955	3.75	7.50	15.00
❏ 9145	Hotta Chocolotta/The Man with the Blue Guitar	1956	3.00	6.00	12.00
❏ 9172	Big D/In My Innocence	1956	3.00	6.00	12.00
MERCURY
❏ 71131	Where Would I Be/Who Am I	1957	2.50	5.00	10.00
❏ 71203	Absence Makes the Heart Grow Fonder/That's				
	My Weakness Now	1957	2.50	5.00	10.00
OKEH
❏ 6989	The Angel Passed By/Never Since Then	1953	5.00	10.00	20.00
SUNBEAM
❏ 106	Straighten Up and Fly Right/Wrong Guy	1958	2.50	5.00	10.00
❏ 116	Do-Die/Wedding Postponed	1958	2.50	5.00	10.00
❏ 124	Watermelon Heart/Sorry for Myself	1959	2.50	5.00	10.00
❏ 126	Hoppity Moe Joe/Don't Forget to Remember	1959	2.50	5.00	10.00
UNITED ARTISTS
❏ 213	Be Anything (But Be Mine)/Yes Indeed	1960	2.00	4.00	8.00

Albums
EPIC
| ❏ LN 1116 [M] | The DeJohn Sisters | 195? | 7.50 | 15.00 | 30.00 |
UNITED ARTISTS
| ❏ UAL-3103 [M] | Yes Indeed | 1960 | 5.00 | 10.00 | 20.00 |
| ❏ UAS-6103 [S] | Yes Indeed | 1960 | 6.25 | 12.50 | 25.00 |

DEKKER, DESMOND, AND THE ACES
45s
UNI
❏ 55129	Israelites/My Precious World	1969	—	3.00	6.00
❏ 55150	It Mek/Problems	1969	—	3.00	6.00
❏ 55261	You Can Get It If You Really Want It/				
	Perseverance	1970	—	3.00	6.00

Albums
BULLDOG
| ❏ 1037 | The Israelites | 198? | 2.50 | 5.00 | 10.00 |
UNI
| ❏ 73059 | Israelites | 1969 | 7.50 | 15.00 | 30.00 |

DEL-AIRES, THE
45s
CORAL
❏ 62370	Elaine/Just Wigglin' and a-Wobblin'	1963	10.00	20.00	40.00
❏ 62404	The Drag/My Funny Valentine	1964	10.00	20.00	40.00
—As "Ronnie and the Del-Aires"					
❏ 62419	Arlene/I'm Yours Baby	1964	17.50	35.00	70.00

DEL AND THE ESCORTS
45s
ROME
| ❏ 103 | Baby Doll/Someone to Watch Over Me | 1961 | 12.50 | 25.00 | 50.00 |
SYMBOL
| ❏ 913 | You Don't Love Me/Skokiian | 1960 | — | — | — |
| —Unreleased? | | | | | |
TAURUS
| ❏ 350/1 | Happy/You're for Me (And I'm for You) | 1961 | 7.50 | 15.00 | 30.00 |

DEL-PHIS, THE Early incarnation of MARTHA AND THE VANDELLAS.
45s
CHECKMATE
| ❏ 1005 | I'll Let You Know/It Takes Two | 1961 | 50.00 | 100.00 | 200.00 |

DEL RAYS, THE
45s
CORD
| ❏ 1001 | Our Love Is True/ | | | | |
| | One Kiss, One Smile and a Dream | 1958 | 1000. | 2000. | 4000. |
MOON
| ❏ 110 | Have a Heart/Around the Corner | 1959 | 75.00 | 150.00 | 300.00 |
WARNER BROS.
| ❏ 5022 | My Darling/The One I Adore | 1958 | 20.00 | 40.00 | 80.00 |

DEL-RHYTHMETTES
45s
JVB
| ❏ 5000 | Chic-a-Boomer/I Need Your Love | 1959 | 15.00 | 30.00 | 60.00 |

DEL RIOS, THE Probably more than one group.
45s
BET-T
| ❏ 7001 | Heavenly Angel/Dangerous Lover | 1962 | 300.00 | 600.00 | 1200. |
METEOR
| ❏ 5038 | Lizzie/Alone on a Rainy Night | 1956 | 200.00 | 400.00 | 800.00 |
NEPTUNE
| ❏ 108 | Wait Wait Wait/I'm Crying | 1959 | 15.00 | 30.00 | 60.00 |
RUST
| ❏ 5066 | Valerie/Mystery | 1963 | 15.00 | 30.00 | 60.00 |
STAX
| ❏ 125 | There's a Love/Just Across the Street | 1962 | 12.50 | 25.00 | 50.00 |

DEL SATINS
45s
B.T. PUPPY
❏ 506	Hang Around/Candy Apple 'Vette	1965	3.75	7.50	15.00
❏ 509	Sweets for My Sweet/A Girl Named Arlene	1965	7.50	15.00	30.00
❏ 514	Relief/Throwaway Song	1966	3.75	7.50	15.00
❏ 563	I'll Do My Crying Tomorrow/A Girl Named Arlene	1970	3.00	6.00	12.00
COLUMBIA
❏ 42802	Feelin' No Pain/Who Cares	1963	6.25	12.50	25.00
❏ 42802 [PS]	Feelin' No Pain/Who Cares	1963	25.00	50.00	100.00
DIAMOND
❏ 216	A Little Rain Must Fall/Love, Hate, Revenge				
	(If I Want You to Cry)	1967	3.75	7.50	15.00
END
❏ 1096	I'll Pray for You/I Remember the Night	1961	50.00	100.00	200.00
LAURIE
❏ 3132	Teardrops Follow Me/				
	Best Wishes, Good Luck, Goodbye	1962	6.25	12.50	25.00
❏ 3149	Ballad of a Deejay/				
	Does My Love Stand a Chance	1962	6.25	12.50	25.00
MALA
❏ 475	Believe in Me/Two Broken Hearts	1964	5.00	10.00	20.00
WIN
❏ 702	Counting Teardrops/Remember	1961	15.00	30.00	60.00
—Orange label					
❏ 702	Counting Teardrops/Remember	1961	40.00	80.00	120.00
—Black label					

Albums
B.T. PUPPY
| ❏ BTS-1019 | Out to Lunch | 1972 | 75.00 | 150.00 | 300.00 |

DEL-VETTS, THE
45s
DUNWICH
❏ 125	Last Time Around/Everytime	1966	5.00	10.00	20.00
❏ 142	I Call My Baby STP/That's the Way It Is	1966	5.00	10.00	20.00
❏ 142 [PS]	I Call My Baby STP/That's the Way It Is	1966	7.50	15.00	30.00
—Some sleeves contain an STP decal.					
SEEBERG
❏ 3018 [M]	Ram Charger/Little Latin Lupe Lu	1965	7.50	15.00	30.00
❏ 3018 [S]	Little Latin Lupe Lu/Ram Charger	1965	10.00	20.00	40.00
—With "Stereo" on label					

7-Inch Extended Plays
SUNDAZED
❏ SEP 124	Last Time Around/Everytime//I Call My Baby				
	STP/That's the Way It Is	1997	—	—	3.00
—Gold vinyl					
❏ SEP 124 [PS]	The Del-Vetts	1997	—	—	3.00

DEL VIKINGS, THE Usually considered to be one group, but actually three: Two of them splintered from the original group, one featuring Kripp Johnson, the other featuring Gus Backus. For convenience's sake, all are listed together.
45s
ABC-PARAMOUNT
❏ 10208	I'll Never Stop Crying/Bring Back Your Heart	1961	6.25	12.50	25.00
❏ 10248	I Hear Bells (Wedding Bells)/Don't Get Slick on				
	Me	1961	12.50	25.00	50.00
❏ 10278	Kiss Me/Face the Music	1961	6.25	12.50	25.00
❏ 10304	Big Silence/One More River to Cross	1962	6.25	12.50	25.00
❏ 10341	Confession of Love/Kilimanjaro	1962	6.25	12.50	25.00
❏ 10385	An Angel Up in Heaven/Fishing Chant	1962	12.50	25.00	50.00
❏ 10425	Too Many Miles/Sorcerer's Apprentice	1963	6.25	12.50	25.00
ALPINE
❏ 66	Pistol Packin' Mama/The Sun	1960	20.00	40.00	80.00
❏ 66 [PS]	Pistol Packin' Mama/The Sun	1960	25.00	50.00	100.00
BIM BAM BOOM
❏ 111	Cold Feet/A Little Man Cried	1972	—	2.50	5.00
❏ 113	Watching the Moon/You Say You Love Me	1972	—	2.50	5.00
❏ 115	I'm Spinning/Girl Girl	1972	—	2.50	5.00
DOT
❏ 15538	Come Go with Me/How Can I Find True Love	1957	7.50	15.00	30.00
❏ 15571	What Made Maggie Run/Little Billy Boy	1957	7.50	15.00	30.00
❏ 15592	Whispering Bells/Don't Be a Fool	1957	7.50	15.00	30.00
❏ 15636	I'm Spinning/When I Come Home	1957	7.50	15.00	30.00
—As "Kripp Johnson with the Dell-Vikings"					
❏ 16092	Come Go with Me/How Can I Find True Love	1960	5.00	10.00	20.00
❏ 16236	Come Go with Me/Whispering Bells	1961	5.00	10.00	20.00

Number	Title (A Side/B Side)	Yr	VG	VG+	NM
16248	I Hear Bells (Wedding Bells)/Don't Get Slick on Me	1961	5.00	10.00	20.00
DRC					
101	Can't You See/Oh I	196?	10.00	20.00	40.00
FEE BEE					
173	Welfare Blues/Hollywood and Vine	1977	—	2.50	5.00
205	Come Go with Me/How Can I Find True Love	1957	62.50	125.00	250.00
—Orange label, one side has bee, the other side doesn't					
205	Come Go with Me/How Can I Find True Love	1957	125.00	250.00	500.00
—Orange label, bee on top					
205	Come Go with Me/How Can I Find True Love	1961	7.50	15.00	30.00
—Orange label, no bee					
205	Come Go with Me/Whispering Bells	1964	5.00	10.00	20.00
206	Down in Bermuda/Maggie	1964	20.00	40.00	80.00
210	What Made Maggie Run/Uh Uh Baby	1957	20.00	40.00	80.00
210	What Made Maggie Run/When I Come Home	1957	40.00	80.00	120.00
210	What Made Maggie Run/Down by the Stream	1964	7.50	15.00	30.00
214	Whispering Bells/Don't Be a Fool	1957	100.00	200.00	400.00
218	I'm Spinning/You Say You Love Me	1957	30.00	60.00	120.00
—Bee on label					
218	I'm Spinning/You Say You Love Me	1964	7.50	15.00	30.00
—No bee on label					
221	Willette/I Want to Marry You	1958	20.00	40.00	80.00
221	Willette/Woke Up This Morning	1958	25.00	50.00	100.00
227	Tell Me/Finger Poppin' Woman	1959	20.00	40.00	80.00
902	True Love/Baby, Let Me Know	1964	7.50	15.00	30.00
—As "The Original Dell Vikings"					
GATEWAY					
743	We Three/I've Got to Know	1964	7.50	15.00	30.00
JOJO					
108	Keep On Walkin'/My Body, Your Shadow	1976	—	2.50	5.00
LUNIVERSE					
106	Somewhere Over the Rainbow/Hey, Senorita	1957	25.00	50.00	100.00
110	Yours/Heaven and Paradise	1958	5.00	10.00	20.00
113	In the Still of the Night/The White Cliffs of Dover	1958	5.00	10.00	20.00
114	There I Go/Girl Girl	1958	5.00	10.00	20.00
—The above three Luniverse 45s are bootlegs, but they perversely do have collector's value!					
MERCURY					
71132	Cool Shake/Jitterbug Mary	1957	7.50	15.00	30.00
71180	Come Along with Me/Whatcha Gonna Lose	1957	7.50	15.00	30.00
71198	I'm Spinning/When I Come Home	1957	7.50	15.00	30.00
71241	Snowbound/Your Book of Life	1957	7.50	15.00	30.00
71266	The Voodoo Man/Can't Wait	1958	7.50	15.00	30.00
71345	You Cheated/Pretty Little Things Called Girls	1958	7.50	15.00	30.00
—Black label					
71345	You Cheated/Pretty Little Things Called Girls	1958	10.00	20.00	40.00
—Blue label					
71390	How Could You/Flat Tire	1958	7.50	15.00	30.00
SCEPTER					
12367	Come Go with Me/When You're Asleep	1973		2.50	5.00
SHIP					
214	Sunday Kind of Love/Over the Rainbow	197?	—	2.00	4.00
7-Inch Extended Plays					
DOT					
DEP-1058	Come Go with Me/Don't Be a Fool//Whispering Bells/What Made Maggie Run	1957	25.00	50.00	100.00
DEP-1058 [PS]	Come Go with Us	1957	50.00	100.00	200.00
MERCURY					
EP 1-3359	Come Along with Me/A Sunday Kind of Love//(There'll Be Blue Birds Over) The White Cliffs of Dover/Now Is the Hour	1957	25.00	50.00	100.00
EP 1-3359 [PS]	They Sing — They Swing, Vol. 1	1957	37.50	75.00	150.00
EP 1-3362	Heart and Soul/My Foolish Heart//Down in Bermuda/I'm Sitting on Top of the World	1957	25.00	50.00	100.00
EP 1-3362 [PS]	They Sing — They Swing, Vol. 2	1957	37.50	75.00	150.00
EP 1-3363	Somewhere Over the Rainbow/Is It Any Wonder//Yours/Summertime	1957	25.00	50.00	100.00
EP 1-3363 [PS]	They Sing — They Swing, Vol. 3	1957	37.50	75.00	150.00
Albums					
COLLECTABLES					
COL-5010	The Best of the Dell-Vikings	198?	3.00	6.00	12.00
DOT					
DLP-3685 [M]	Come Go with Me	1966	50.00	100.00	200.00
DLP-25685 [R]	Come Go with Me	1966	37.50	75.00	150.00
LUNIVERSE					
LP-1000 [M]	Come Go with the Del Vikings	1957	125.00	250.00	500.00
—Eight tracks, cover is composed of slicks. Counterfeits have more tracks and a preprinted cover (not slicks).					
MERCURY					
MG-20314 [M]	They Sing — They Swing	1957	75.00	150.00	300.00
MG-20353 [M]	A Swinging, Singing Record Session	1958	50.00	100.00	200.00

DEL VIKINGS, THE / THE SONNETS
Albums

Number	Title (A Side/B Side)	Yr	VG	VG+	NM
CROWN					
CLP-5368 [M]	The Del Vikings and the Sonnets	1963	10.00	20.00	40.00

DEL-VUES, THE
45s

Number	Title (A Side/B Side)	Yr	VG	VG+	NM
U-TOWN					
8008	After New Year's/My Confession	195?	150.00	300.00	600.00

DELACARDOS, THE (1)
45s

Number	Title (A Side/B Side)	Yr	VG	VG+	NM
ELGEY					
1001	A Letter to a School Girl/I'll Never Let You Down	1959	12.50	25.00	50.00
SHELL					
308	Dream Girl/I Just Want to Know	1961	5.00	10.00	20.00
311	Love Is the Greatest Thing/Girl-Girl	1962	5.00	10.00	20.00
UNITED ARTISTS					
276	I Got It/Thing-A-Ma-Jig	1960	3.75	7.50	15.00
310	Hold Back the Tears/Mr. Dillon	1961	5.00	10.00	20.00

DELACARDOS, THE (2)
45s

Number	Title (A Side/B Side)	Yr	VG	VG+	NM
ATLANTIC					
2368	Got No One/She's the One I Love	1966	2.50	5.00	10.00
2389	I Know I'm Not Much/You Don't Have to See Me	1967	2.50	5.00	10.00
2419	They Put a Spell on You/A Fool for You	1967	2.50	5.00	10.00

DELACARDOS, THE (U) These may be group (1) or (2), or they may be a completely different group or groups.
45s

Number	Title (A Side/B Side)	Yr	VG	VG+	NM
DIMENSION					
1040	Forget About the Guy/Dance, Gypsy, Dance	1964	5.00	10.00	20.00
IMPERIAL					
5992	On the Beach/Everybody's Rockin'	1963	3.75	7.50	15.00

DELANCEYS, THE
45s

Number	Title (A Side/B Side)	Yr	VG	VG+	NM
ABC-PARAMOUNT					
10353	High Voltage/The Scratch	1962	6.25	12.50	25.00

DELANEY AND BONNIE   Also see BONNIE BRAMLETT; DELANEY BRAMLETT.
45s

Number	Title (A Side/B Side)	Yr	VG	VG+	NM
ATCO					
6725	Groupie (Superstar)/Comin' Home	1969	2.00	4.00	8.00
6756	Soul Shake/Free the People	1970	2.00	4.00	8.00
6788	Miss Ann/They Call It Rock and Roll Music	1970	2.00	4.00	8.00
6804	Never Ending Song of Love/Don't Deceive Me	1971	2.00	4.00	8.00
6838	Only You Know and I Know/God Knows I Love You	1971	—	3.00	6.00
6866	Sing My Way Home/Move 'Em Out	1972	—	2.50	5.00
6883	Where There's a Will There's a Way/Lonesome and a Long Way from Home	1972	—	2.50	5.00
6904	Sing My Way Home/Will the Circle Be Unbroken	1972	—	2.50	5.00
COLUMBIA					
45608	Country Life/Walk in the River Jordan	1972	—	2.50	5.00
ELEKTRA					
45660	Soldiers of the Cross/Get Ourselves Together	1969	2.50	5.00	10.00
45662	When the Battle Is Over/Get Ourselves Together	1969	2.50	5.00	10.00
GARPAX					
44184	Cherry Pie/Hey Mr. Weatherman	1964	3.75	7.50	15.00
—As "Lani & Boni"					
INDEPENDENCE					
78	You've Lost That Lovin' Feelin'/Don't Let It (Be the Last Time)	1967	3.00	6.00	12.00
STAX					
0003	It's Been a Long Time Coming/We've Just Been Feeling Bad	1968	2.50	5.00	10.00
0057	Hard to Say Goodbye/Just Plain Beautiful	1969	2.50	5.00	10.00
Albums					
ATCO					
SD 33-326	Delaney & Bonnie & Friends On Tour with Eric Clapton	197?	2.50	5.00	10.00
—Later pressings on other labels					
SD 33-326	Delaney & Bonnie & Friends On Tour with Eric Clapton	1970	6.25	12.50	25.00
—Yellow label original					
33-341 [M]	To Bonnie from Delaney	1970	10.00	20.00	40.00
—White label promo; no stock copies were issued in mono					
SD 33-341 [S]	To Bonnie from Delaney	1970	6.25	12.50	25.00
SD 33-358	Motel Shot	1971	6.25	12.50	25.00
SD 33-383	Country Life	1972	5.00	10.00	20.00
SD 7014	The Best of Delaney and Bonnie	1972	5.00	10.00	20.00
COLUMBIA					
KC 31377	D&B Together	1972	5.00	10.00	20.00
ELEKTRA					
EKS-74039	Accept No Substitute — The Original Delaney & Bonnie & Friends	1969	7.50	15.00	30.00
GNP CRESCENDO					
GNPS-2054	Genesis	1970	5.00	10.00	20.00
STAX					
STS-2026	Home	1969	7.50	15.00	30.00

DELEGATES, THE (1)   Novelty group.
45s

Number	Title (A Side/B Side)	Yr	VG	VG+	NM
MAINSTREAM					
5525	Convention '72 (same on both sides)	1972	2.00	4.00	8.00
—Stock copy; "Funky Butt" deleted because of retailers' protests to the title					
5525	Convention '72/Funky Butt	1972	2.50	5.00	10.00
5530	Richard M. Nixon Faces the Issues (same on both sides)	1972	2.00	4.00	8.00
5530	Richard M. Nixon Faces the Issues/Touzie's Blues	1972	2.50	5.00	10.00
Albums					
MAINSTREAM					
100	The Delegates	1973	5.00	10.00	20.00

DELEGATES, THE (2)   See BILLY LARKIN.

DELEGATES, THE (3)   DEE CLARK was a member.
45s

Number	Title (A Side/B Side)	Yr	VG	VG+	NM
VEE JAY					
212	The Convention/Jay's Rock	1956	15.00	30.00	60.00
—B-side by Big Jay McNeely					
243	Mother's Son/I'm Gonna Be Glad	1957	15.00	30.00	60.00

DELFONICS, THE   Also see MAJOR HARRIS.
45s

Number	Title (A Side/B Side)	Yr	VG	VG+	NM
ARISTA					
0308	Don't Throw It All Away/I Don't Care What People Say	1978	—	2.00	4.00
CAMEO					
472	You've Been Untrue/I Was There	1967	3.75	7.50	15.00
MOON SHOT					
6703	He Don't Really Love You/Without You	1967	3.75	7.50	15.00

Number	Title (A Side/B Side)	Yr	VG	VG+	NM
PHILLY GROOVE					
❑ 150	La-La Means I Love You/				
	Can't Get Over Losing You	1968	2.50	5.00	10.00
❑ 151	I'm Sorry/You're Gone	1968	2.50	5.00	10.00
❑ 152	Break Your Promise/Alfie	1968	2.50	5.00	10.00
❑ 154	Ready Or Not Here I Come (Can't Hide from				
	Love)/Somebody Loves You	1968	2.50	5.00	10.00
❑ 156	Funny Feeling/My New Love	1969	2.50	5.00	10.00
❑ 157	You Got Yours and I'll Get Mine/Loving Him	1969	2.50	5.00	10.00
❑ 161	Didn't I (Blow Your Mind This Time)/				
	Down Is Up, Up Is Down	1970	2.50	5.00	10.00
❑ 162	Trying to Make a Fool of Me/Baby I Love You	1970	2.50	5.00	10.00
❑ 163	When You Get Right Down To It/I Gave to You	1970	2.50	5.00	10.00
❑ 166	Over and Over/Hey! Love	1971	2.00	4.00	8.00
❑ 169	Walk Right Up to the Sun/Round and Round	1971	2.00	4.00	8.00
❑ 172	Tell Me This Is a Dream/I'm a Man	1972	2.00	4.00	8.00
❑ 174	Think It Over/I'm a Man	1972	2.00	4.00	8.00
❑ 176	I Don't Want to Make You Wait/Baby I Miss You	1973	2.00	4.00	8.00
❑ 177	Alfie/Start All Over Again	1973	2.00	4.00	8.00
❑ 182	I Told You So/Seventeen and In Love	1973	2.00	4.00	8.00
❑ 184	Lying to Myself/Hey Baby	1974	2.00	4.00	8.00
❑ NS-1001/2	La-La Means I Love You/				
	Can't Get Over Losing You	1968	5.00	10.00	20.00
—Light blue label with no regular catalog number					
Albums					
ARISTA					
❑ AL 8333	The Best of the Delfonics	198?	2.50	5.00	10.00
COLLECTABLES					
❑ COL-5109	Golden Classics	198?	2.50	5.00	10.00
KORY					
❑ 1002	The Best of the Delfonics	1977	3.00	6.00	12.00
PHILLY GROOVE					
❑ 1150	La La Means I Love You	1968	20.00	40.00	80.00
❑ 1151	The Sexy Sound of Soul	1969	20.00	40.00	80.00
❑ 1152	The Delfonics Super Hits	1969	12.50	25.00	50.00
❑ 1153	The Delfonics	1970	12.50	25.00	50.00
❑ 1154	Tell Me This Is a Dream	1972	12.50	25.00	50.00
❑ 1501	Alive & Kicking	1974	12.50	25.00	50.00
POOGIE					
❑ 121680	The Delfonics Return	1981	3.00	6.00	12.00

DELICATES, THE More than one group?
45s

Number	Title (A Side/B Side)	Yr	VG	VG+	NM
CELESTE					
❑ 676	My Pillow/I Played 1,2,3,4	1961	7.50	15.00	30.00
CHALLENGE					
❑ 59232	I've Been Hurt/Come On Everybody	1964	3.75	7.50	15.00
❑ 59267	I Want to Get Married/Home from Camp	1965	3.75	7.50	15.00
❑ 59304	Stop Shovin' Me Around/Comin' Down with Love	1965	3.75	7.50	15.00
DEE DEE					
❑ 677	My Pillow/I Played 1,2,3,4	1961	7.50	15.00	30.00
ROULETTE					
❑ 4321	Little Ship/Not Tomorrow	1961	5.00	10.00	20.00
❑ 4360	Little Boy of Mine/Dickie Went and Did It	1961	5.00	10.00	20.00
❑ 4387	I Don't Know Why (I Just Do)/Strange Love	1961	5.00	10.00	20.00
UNART					
❑ 2017	Black and White Thunderbird/				
	Ronnie Is My Lover	1959	6.25	12.50	25.00
❑ 2024	Ringa Ding/Meusurry	1959	6.25	12.50	25.00
UNITED ARTISTS					
❑ 210	Flip Flip/Your Happiest Years	1960	5.00	10.00	20.00
❑ 228	The Kiss/Too Young to Date	1960	5.00	10.00	20.00

DELL, DICKEY, AND THE BING BONGS
45s

Number	Title (A Side/B Side)	Yr	VG	VG+	NM
DRAGON					
❑ 10205	Ding-a-Ling-a-Ling-Ding-Dong/The Cling	1958	37.50	75.00	150.00

DELL, EVELYN, AND THE VIBRATIONS
45s

Number	Title (A Side/B Side)	Yr	VG	VG+	NM
ABC-PARAMOUNT					
❑ 10218	Sincerely/Please Tell Me Why	1961	6.25	12.50	25.00

DELL, LENNY, AND THE DEMENSIONS See THE DEMENSIONS.

DELL, RICHIE
45s

Number	Title (A Side/B Side)	Yr	VG	VG+	NM
KING					
❑ 5888	Come On Let's Sing/King Lover	1964	5.00	10.00	20.00

DELL, TONY
45s

Number	Title (A Side/B Side)	Yr	VG	VG+	NM
KING					
❑ 5766	My Girl/Magic Wand	1963	12.50	25.00	50.00

DELL-COEDS, THE
45s

Number	Title (A Side/B Side)	Yr	VG	VG+	NM
DOT					
❑ 16314	Hey Mr. Banjo/Love in Return	1962	3.00	6.00	12.00

DELL VIKINGS, THE See THE DEL-VIKINGS.

DELLS, THE
45s

Number	Title (A Side/B Side)	Yr	VG	VG+	NM
ABC					
❑ 12386	Super Woman/My Life Is So Wonderful	1978	—	2.50	5.00
❑ 12422	(I Wanna) Testify/Don't Save Me	1978	—	2.50	5.00
❑ 12422	(I Wanna) Testify/Drowning for Your Love	1978	—	2.50	5.00
❑ 12440	(You Bring Out) The Best in Me/				
	Wrapped Up Tight	1978	—	2.50	5.00
ARGO					
❑ 5415	God Bless the Child/I'm Going Home	1962	3.00	6.00	12.00
❑ 5428	The (Bossa Nova) Bird/Eternally	1962	3.00	6.00	12.00
❑ 5442	Hi Diddle Dee Dum Dum (It's a Good Feelin')/If				
	It Ain't One Thing, It's Another	1963	3.00	6.00	12.00
❑ 5456	After You/Goodbye Mary Ann	1963	3.00	6.00	12.00

Number	Title (A Side/B Side)	Yr	VG	VG+	NM
CADET					
❑ 5538	Thinkin' About You/				
	The Change We Go Thru (For Love)	1966	—	3.00	6.00
❑ 5551	Over Again/Run for Cover	1967	—	3.00	6.00
❑ 5563	You Belong to Someone Else/Inspiration	1967	—	3.00	6.00
❑ 5574	O-O, I Love You/There Is	1967	—	3.00	6.00
❑ 5590	There Is/Show Me	1968	2.00	4.00	8.00
❑ 5599	Wear it On Our Face/				
	Please Don't Change Me Now	1968	—	3.00	6.00
❑ 5612	Stay in My Corner/Love Is So Simple	1969	—	3.00	6.00
❑ 5621	Always Together/I Want My Mama	1968	—	3.00	6.00
❑ 5631	Does Anybody Know I'm Here/Make Sure (You				
	Have Somebody to Love You)	1968	—	3.00	6.00
❑ 5636	I Can't Do Enough/Hallways of My Mind	1969	—	3.00	6.00
❑ 5641	I Can Sing a Rainbow-Love Is Blue/				
	Hallelujah Baby	1969	—	3.00	6.00
❑ 5649	Oh What a Night/Believe Me	1969	—	3.00	6.00
❑ 5658	On the Dock of the Bay/When I'm in Your Arms	1969	—	3.00	6.00
❑ 5663	Oh What a Day/				
	The Change We Go Thru (For Love)	1970	—	3.00	6.00
❑ 5667	Open Up My Heart/Nadine	1970	—	3.00	6.00
❑ 5672	Long Lonely Nights/A Little Understanding	1970	—	3.00	6.00
❑ 5679	The Glory of Love/A Whiter Shade of Pale	1970	—	3.00	6.00
❑ 5683	The Love We Had (Stays on My Mind)/				
	Freedom Means	1971	—	3.00	6.00
❑ 5689	It's All Up to You/Oh, My Dear	1972	—	3.00	6.00
❑ 5691	Walk On By/This Guy's in Love with You	1972	—	3.00	6.00
❑ 5694	Just As Long As We're in Love/				
	I'd Rather Be with You	1972	—	3.00	6.00
❑ 5696	Give Your Baby a Standing Ovation/Closer	1973	—	3.00	6.00
❑ 5698	My Pretending Days Are Over/Let's Make It Last	1973	—	3.00	6.00
❑ 5700	I Miss You/Don't Make Me a Storyteller	1973	—	3.00	6.00
❑ 5702	I Wish It Was Me You Loved/				
	Two Together Is Better Than One	1974	—	3.00	6.00
❑ 5703	Bring Back the Love of Yesterday/Learning to				
	Love You Was Easy				
	(It's So Hard Trying to Get Over You)	1974	—	3.00	6.00
❑ 5703	Sweeter as the Days Go By/				
	Learning to Love You Was Easy				
	(It's So Hard Trying to Get Over You)	1974	—	3.00	6.00
—A-side is the same song with a new title					
❑ 5707	The Glory of Love/You're the Greatest	1975	—	3.00	6.00
❑ 5711	We Got to Get Our Thing Together/				
	The Power of Love	1975	2.00	4.00	8.00
CHECKER					
❑ 794	Darling I Know/Christine	1954	400.00	800.00	1200.
—As "The El Rays"					
LOST-NITE					
❑ 264	Tell the World/Blues at Three	197?	—	2.50	5.00
—Reissue					
❑ 272	Dreams of Contentment/Zing, Zing, Zing	197?	—	2.50	5.00
—Reissue					
❑ 281	Why Do You Have to Go/Dance, Dance, Dance	197?	—	2.50	5.00
—Reissue					
❑ 290	Stay in My Corner/A Distant Love	197?	—	2.50	5.00
❑ 297	Pain in My Heart/Time Makes You Change	197?	—	2.50	5.00
—Reissue					
❑ 305	Oh What a Nite/Jo-Jo	197?	—	2.50	5.00
—Reissue					
MCA					
❑ 41051	Plastic People/What I Could	1979	—	2.50	5.00
MERCURY					
❑ 73723	We Got to Get Our Thing Together/Reminiscing	1975	—	2.50	5.00
❑ 73759	The Power of Love/Gotta Get Home to My Baby	1976	—	2.50	5.00
❑ 73807	Slow Motion/Ain't No Black and White in Music	1976	—	2.50	5.00
❑ 73842	No Way Back/Too Late for Love	1976	—	2.50	5.00
❑ 73901	Betcha Never Been Loved (Like This Before)/				
	Get On Down	1977	—	2.50	5.00
❑ 73909	Our Love/Could It Be	1977	—	2.50	5.00
❑ 73977	Private Property/Teaser	1977	—	2.50	5.00
PHILCO-FORD					
❑ HP-32	There Is/Show Me	1968	5.00	10.00	20.00
—4-inch plastic "Hip Pocket Record" with color sleeve					
PRIVATE I					
❑ 04343	Don't Want Nobody/You Can't Just Walk Away	1984	—	2.00	4.00
❑ 04448	One Step Closer/Come On Back to Me	1984	—	2.00	4.00
❑ 04540	Love On/Don't Want Nobody	1984	—	2.00	4.00
SKYLARK					
❑ 558	I Can't Help Myself/She's Just an Angel	198?	—	2.00	4.00
❑ 581	Someone to Call Me Darling/Now I Pray	198?	—	2.00	4.00
20TH CENTURY					
❑ 2463	I Touched a Dream/All About the Paper	1980	—	2.00	4.00
❑ 2475	Passionate Breezes/Your Song	1980	—	2.00	4.00
❑ 2504	Happy Song/Look at Us Now	1981	—	2.00	4.00
❑ 2602	Ain't It a Shame/Stay in My Corner	1982	—	2.00	4.00
VEE JAY					
❑ 134	Tell the World/Blues at Three	1955	500.00	1000.	2000.
❑ 134	Tell the World/Blues at Three	1955	2500.	3750.	5000.
—Red vinyl					
❑ 166	Dreams of Contentment/Zing, Zing, Zing	1955	50.00	100.00	200.00
❑ 204	Oh What a Nite/Jo-Jo	1956	30.00	60.00	120.00
❑ 230	Movin' On/I Wanna Go Home	1956	10.00	20.00	40.00
❑ 236	Why Do You Have to Go/Dance, Dance, Dance	1957	10.00	20.00	40.00
❑ 251	A Distant Love/O-Bop She-Bop	1957	10.00	20.00	40.00
❑ 258	Pain in My Heart/Time Makes You Change	1957	10.00	20.00	40.00
❑ 274	The Springer/What You Say Baby	1958	7.50	15.00	30.00
❑ 292	I'm Calling/Jeepers Creepers	1958	7.50	15.00	30.00
❑ 300	Wedding Day/My Best Girl	1958	25.00	50.00	100.00
❑ 324	Dry Your Eyes/Baby Open Up Your Heart	1959	10.00	20.00	40.00
❑ 338	Oh What a Nite/I Wanna Go Home	1960	5.00	10.00	20.00
❑ 376	Hold On to What You've Got/Swingin' Teens	1961	5.00	10.00	20.00
❑ 595	Shy Girl/What Do We Prove	1964	3.00	6.00	12.00
❑ 595 [PS]	Shy Girl/What Do We Prove	1964	12.50	25.00	50.00
—Promo-only sleeve					
❑ 615	Wait Till Tomorrow/Oh What a Good Night	1964	3.00	6.00	12.00
❑ 674	Stay in My Corner/It's Not Unusual	1965	3.00	6.00	12.00

Number	Title (A Side/B Side)	Yr	VG	VG+	NM
❏ 712	Poor Little Boy/Hey Sugar (Don't Get Serious)	1966	3.00	6.00	12.00
VETERAN					
❏ 7-101	Thought of You Just a Little Too Much/ (B-side unknown)	1989	—	2.50	5.00
Albums					
ABC					
❏ AA-1100	New Beginnings	1978	3.00	6.00	12.00
❏ AA-1113	Face to Face	1978	3.00	6.00	12.00
BUDDAH					
❏ BDS-5053	The Dells	1969	3.75	7.50	15.00
CADET					
❏ LPS-804	There Is	1968	12.50	25.00	50.00
❏ LPS-822	The Dells Musical Menu/Always Together	1969	12.50	25.00	50.00
❏ LPS-824	The Dells Greatest Hits	1969	12.50	25.00	50.00
❏ LPS-829	Love Is Blue	1969	12.50	25.00	50.00
❏ LPS-837	Like It Is, Like It Was	1970	12.50	25.00	50.00
❏ 50004	Freedom Means	1971	6.25	12.50	25.00
❏ 50017	The Dells Sing Dionne Warwicke's Greatest Hits	1972	6.25	12.50	25.00
❏ 50021	Sweet As Funk Can Be	1972	6.25	12.50	25.00
❏ 50037	Give Your Baby a Standing Ovation	1973	6.25	12.50	25.00
❏ 50046	The Dells	1973	6.25	12.50	25.00
❏ 60030	The Mighty Mighty Dells	1974	6.25	12.50	25.00
❏ 60036	The Dells' Greatest Hits, Vol. 2	1975	5.00	10.00	20.00
CHESS					
❏ CH-9103	The Dells	198?	2.50	5.00	10.00
—Reissue					
❏ CH-9288	There Is	1989	2.50	5.00	10.00
—Reissue of Cadet 804					
LOST-NITE					
❏ LLP-21 [10]	The Dells	1981	3.75	7.50	15.00
—Red vinyl, generic red cover					
MERCURY					
❏ SRM-1-1059	We Got to Get Our Thing Together	1975	3.75	7.50	15.00
❏ SRM-1-1084	No Way Back	1976	3.75	7.50	15.00
❏ SRM-1-1145	They Said It Couldn't Be Done	1977	3.75	7.50	15.00
❏ SRM-1-3711	Love Connection	1977	3.75	7.50	15.00
PRIVATE I					
❏ BFZ 39309	One Step Closer	1984	2.50	5.00	10.00
SOLID SMOKE					
❏ 8029	Breezy Ballads and Tender Tunes: The Best of the Early Years (1955-65)	1984	2.50	5.00	10.00
20TH CENTURY					
❏ T-618	I Touched a Dream	1980	3.00	6.00	12.00
❏ T-633	Whatever Turns You On	1981	3.00	6.00	12.00
UPFRONT					
❏ UPF-105	Stay In My Corner	1968	3.75	7.50	15.00
URGENT					
❏ URG-4108	The Second Time	1991	3.00	6.00	12.00
VEE JAY					
❏ LP 1010 [M]	Oh What a Nite	1959	200.00	400.00	800.00
—Maroon label					
❏ LP 1010 [M]	Oh What a Nite	1961	75.00	150.00	300.00
—Black label with colorband					
❏ VJLP-1010	Oh What a Nite	198?	2.50	5.00	10.00
—Late-80s reissue on reactivated Vee Jay label. "Trade Mark Reg." on label.					
❏ LP 1141 [M]	It's Not Unusual	1965	25.00	50.00	100.00
❏ LPS 1141 [S]	It's Not Unusual	1965	37.50	75.00	150.00
VJ INTERNATIONAL					
❏ 7305	The Dells In Concert	197?	3.00	6.00	12.00
ZOO					
❏ 11023	I Salute You	1992	3.75	7.50	15.00

DELLS, THE, AND THE DRAMATICS Also see each artist's individual listings.
45s
CADET

Number	Title (A Side/B Side)	Yr	VG	VG+	NM
❏ 5710	Love Is Missing from Our Lives/I'm in Love	1975	—	3.00	6.00

Albums
CADET

Number	Title (A Side/B Side)	Yr	VG	VG+	NM
❏ 60027	The Dells Vs. the Dramatics	1974	6.25	12.50	25.00

DELLTONES, THE
45s
BATON

Number	Title (A Side/B Side)	Yr	VG	VG+	NM
❏ 212	Don't Be Long/Baby Say You Love Me	1955	7.50	15.00	30.00
❏ 223	My Special Love/Believe It	1956	7.50	15.00	30.00
BRUNSWICK					
❏ 84015	My Heart's on Fire/Yours Alone	1953	50.00	100.00	200.00
RAINBOW					
❏ 244	I'm Not in Love with You/Little Short Daddy	1954	25.00	50.00	100.00

DELMIRAS, THE
45s
DADE

Number	Title (A Side/B Side)	Yr	VG	VG+	NM
❏ 1821	Dry Your Eyes/The Big Sound	1961	75.00	150.00	300.00

DELMONICOS, THE
45s
MUSICTONE

Number	Title (A Side/B Side)	Yr	VG	VG+	NM
❏ 6122	World's Biggest Fool/Until You	1963	7.50	15.00	30.00

DELPHS, JIMMY
45s
CARLA

Number	Title (A Side/B Side)	Yr	VG	VG+	NM
❏ 1904	Dancing a Hole in the World/(B-side unknown)	1968	300.00	600.00	1200.
❏ 2535	Almost/I've Been Fooled Before	1967	6.25	12.50	25.00
KAREN					
❏ 1538	Don't Sign the Paper Baby (I Want You Back)/ Almost	1968	3.00	6.00	12.00
❏ 1541	Feels Like Summer's Coming On/Mrs. Percy Please Have Mercy	1968	3.00	6.00	12.00
❏ 1550	Am I Losing You/Love, I Want You Back	1968	3.00	6.00	12.00

Number	Title (A Side/B Side)	Yr	VG	VG+	NM
DELRONS, THE See REPARATA AND THE DELRONS.					
DELROYS, THE					
45s					
APOLLO					
❏ 514	Bermuda Shorts/Time	1957	6.25	12.50	25.00
DELTAIRS, THE					
45s					
FELSTED					
❏ 8525	Who Would Have Thought It/You Won't Be Satisfied	1959	7.50	15.00	30.00
IVY					
❏ 101	Lullaby of the Bells/It's Only You Dear	1957	37.50	75.00	150.00
—Yellow label					
❏ 101	Lullaby of the Bells/It's Only You Dear	1958	7.50	15.00	30.00
❏ 105	Standing at the Altar/I Might Like It	1958	7.50	15.00	30.00
DELTAS, THE More than one group?					
45s					
CAMBRIDGE					
❏ 124	Goodnight My Love/Give My Love a Chance	1962	10.00	20.00	40.00
GONE					
❏ 5010	Let Me Share Your Dream/Lamplight	1957	20.00	40.00	80.00
—Multi-color label					
❏ 5010	Let Me Share Your Dream/Lamplight	1957	750.00	1500.	3000.
—Black label					
PHILIPS					
❏ 40023	My Own True Love/Hold Me, Thrill Me, Kiss Me	1962	3.75	7.50	15.00
❏ 40023	My Own True Love/Work Song	1962	5.00	10.00	20.00
DELTONES, THE					
45s					
JUBILEE					
❏ 5374	La La La/Bow-Legged Annie	1959	6.25	12.50	25.00
LANA					
❏ 113	Hey Little Girl/Love Potion No. 9	196?	2.00	4.00	8.00
—B-side by the Clovers					
❏ 114	Since I Met You/Devil or Angel	196?	2.00	4.00	8.00
—B-side by the Clovers					
VEE JAY					
❏ 288	I'm Coming Home/Early Morning Rock	1958	10.00	20.00	40.00
❏ 303	A Lover's Prayer/First Man to the Moon	1958	10.00	20.00	40.00
DELTOURS, THE					
45s					
STARVILLE					
❏ 1206	Sweet and Lovely/(B-side unknown)	196?	375.00	750.00	1500.
DELVETTS, THE					
45s					
END					
❏ 1106	I Want a Boy for Christmas/Repeat After Me	1961	7.50	15.00	30.00
❏ 1107	Will You Love Me in Heaven/Repeat After Me	1962	5.00	10.00	20.00
DEMARCO, RALPH					
45s					
GUARANTEED					
❏ 202	More Than Riches/Old Shep	1959	5.00	10.00	20.00
❏ 202 [PS]	More Than Riches/Old Shep	1959	10.00	20.00	40.00
SHELLEY					
❏ 1011	Donna/For All We Know	1960	10.00	20.00	40.00
20TH FOX					
❏ 309	Keep On Walkin'/Lonely for a Girl	1962	5.00	10.00	20.00
DEMENS, THE					
45s					
TEENAGE					
❏ 1006	Take Me As I Am/You Broke My Heart	1958	50.00	100.00	200.00
❏ 1007	I'm Not in Love with You/Short Daddy	1958	50.00	100.00	200.00
❏ 1008	The Greatest of Them All/Hey Young Girl	1958	50.00	100.00	200.00
DEMENSIONS, THE					
45s					
CORAL					
❏ 62277	Again/Count Your Blessings Instead of Sheep	1961	6.25	12.50	25.00
❏ 62293	As Time Goes By/Seven Days a Week	1961	6.25	12.50	25.00
❏ 62323	Young at Heart/Your Cheatin' Heart	1962	5.00	10.00	20.00
❏ 62344	My Foolish Heart/Just One More Chance	1963	7.50	15.00	30.00
❏ 62344 [PS]	My Foolish Heart/Just One More Chance	1963	25.00	50.00	100.00
❏ 62359	Fly Me to the Moon/You'll Never Know	1963	6.25	12.50	25.00
❏ 62382	Just a Shoulder to Cry On/ Don't Worry About Bobby	1963	6.25	12.50	25.00
❏ 62392	A Little White Gardenia/Don't Cry Pretty Baby	1964	5.00	10.00	20.00
❏ 62432	This Time Next Year/My Old Girlfriend	1964	5.00	10.00	20.00
—As "Lenny Dell and the Demensions"					
❏ 62444	Once a Day/Ting Along Ting Toy	1965	5.00	10.00	20.00
—As "Lenny Dell and the Demensions"					
❏ 65559	Over the Rainbow/Zing Went the Strings of My Heart	1962	5.00	10.00	20.00
❏ 65611	As Time Goes By/My Foolish Heart	1967	3.75	7.50	15.00
MOHAWK					
❏ 116	Over the Rainbow/Nursery Rhyme Rock	1960	6.25	12.50	25.00
—Red label					
❏ 116	Over the Rainbow/Nursery Rhyme Rock	1960	7.50	15.00	30.00
—Brown label					
❏ 116	Over the Rainbow/Nursery Rhyme Rock	1960	12.50	25.00	50.00
—Maroon label					
❏ 120	Zing Went the Strings of My Heart/ Don't Take Your Love from Me	1960	6.25	12.50	25.00
—As "The Dimensions"					
❏ 121	God's Christmas/Ave Maria	1960	15.00	30.00	60.00
❏ 123	A Tear Fell/Theresa	1961	15.00	30.00	60.00
Albums					
CORAL					
❏ CRL 57430 [M]	My Foolish Heart	1963	37.50	75.00	150.00
❏ CRL 757430 [S]	My Foolish Heart	1963	75.00	150.00	300.00

Number	Title (A Side/B Side)	Yr	VG	VG+	NM
DEMIAN Includes members of THE BUBBLE PUPPY.					
45s					
ABC					
❑ 11297	Face the Crowd/Love People	1970	5.00	10.00	20.00
Albums					
ABC					
❑ ABCS-718	Demian	1970	15.00	30.00	60.00
DEMILLES, THE					
45s					
LAURIE					
❑ 3230	Donna Lee/Um Ba Pa	1964	7.50	15.00	30.00
❑ 3247	Lazy Love/Cry and Be On Your Way	1964	12.50	25.00	50.00
DEMOLYRS, THE					
45s					
JASON SCOTT					
❑ 7	Rain/Hey Little Rosie	1978	—	3.00	6.00
U.W.R.					
❑ 900	Rain/Hey Little Rosie	1964	125.00	250.00	500.00
DEMOTRONS, THE					
45s					
ATLANTIC					
❑ 2589	I Want a Home in the Country/I Don't Want to Play No More	1969	2.50	5.00	10.00
CAMEO					
❑ 456	Beg, Borrow and Steal/Midnight in New York	1967	2.50	5.00	10.00
DORSET					
❑ 5010	Frisky/Steel Driving Man	196?	5.00	10.00	20.00
ENRICA					
❑ 1003	Rock-A-Way Special/Bugle Boy	1959	7.50	15.00	30.00
RADAR					
❑ 2615	Hombre/Swinging Soiree	1962	5.00	10.00	20.00
❑ 2616	Pretzel Twist/Meet Mister Callaghan	1962	5.00	10.00	20.00
❑ 2621	Sticks and Stones/Theme from "Adventures in Paradise"	1962	5.00	10.00	20.00
RUST					
❑ 5025	Rockin' with Mother Goose/Home on the Pad	1960	5.00	10.00	20.00
SCEPTER					
❑ 12148	Take This Love I Have/Sleep, Sleep, Sleep	1966	3.00	6.00	12.00
❑ 12174	Brother Where Are You/Take This Love I Have	1966	3.00	6.00	12.00
DEMURES, THE					
45s					
BRUNSWICK					
❑ 55284	Raining Teardrops/He's Got Your Number	1965	25.00	50.00	100.00
DENBY, JUNIOR					
45s					
KING					
❑ 4717	With This Ring/I'm Still Lonesome	1954	15.00	30.00	60.00
❑ 4725	This Fool Has Learned/If You Only Have Faith in Me	1954	15.00	30.00	60.00
❑ 5217	With This Ring/I'm Still Lonesome	1959	7.50	15.00	30.00
DENE, TERRY					
45s					
LONDON					
❑ 1802	Stairway of Love/Lover, Lover	1958	3.00	6.00	12.00
DENNIS, BILL					
45s					
SHRINE					
❑ 113	I'll Never Let You Get Away/Poor Little Fool	1966	250.00	500.00	1000.
DENNIS AND THE EXPLORERS See THE EXPLORERS.					
DENNY, MARTIN					
45s					
LIBERTY					
❑ 55089	Hong Kong Blues/Ah Me Furi	1957	2.50	5.00	10.00
❑ 55162	Quiet Village/Llama Serenade	1958	3.00	6.00	12.00
❑ 55199	Martinique/Sake Rock	1959	2.50	5.00	10.00
❑ 55212	The Enchanted Sea/Stranger in Paradise	1959	2.50	5.00	10.00
❑ 55230	Beyond the Reef/Forever	1959	2.50	5.00	10.00
❑ 55236	Frankie and Johnny/Banana Choo Choo	1960	2.50	5.00	10.00
❑ 55283	Volcano/Sugar Train	1960	2.50	5.00	10.00
❑ 55301	My Tane (My Man)/Volcano	1961	2.00	4.00	8.00
❑ 55331	Scimitar/My First Romance	1961	2.00	4.00	8.00
❑ 55384	Fandango/Bonsoir Dame	1961	2.00	4.00	8.00
❑ 55426	Paradise Cove/Secu Secu	1962	2.00	4.00	8.00
❑ 55470	A Taste of Honey/The Brighter Side	1962	2.00	4.00	8.00
❑ 55470 [PS]	A Taste of Honey/The Brighter Side	1962	3.75	7.50	15.00
❑ 55514	Cast Your Fate to the Wind/Pay Off	1962	2.00	4.00	8.00
❑ 55536	Blue Carousel/Anniversary Song	1963	2.00	4.00	8.00
❑ 55561	Quiet Village Bossa Nova/Strawberry Tree	1963	2.00	4.00	8.00
❑ 55571	More (Theme from Mondo Cane)/O Barquinho (Little Boat)	1963	2.00	4.00	8.00
❑ 55622	Theme from The V.I.P.'s/Cousin Ray	1963	2.00	4.00	8.00
❑ 55629	Something Latin/Once Is Enough	1963	2.00	4.00	8.00
❑ 55655	Sugar Cane/Everything Beautiful Happens	1963	2.00	4.00	8.00
❑ 55717	Latin Village/Angelito	1964	2.00	4.00	8.00
❑ 55754	Hawaii Tattoo/White Silver Sands	1964	2.00	4.00	8.00
❑ 55819	Hawaiian Village/Aloha Oe	1965	2.00	4.00	8.00
❑ 55851	Call Me/La Paloma	1965	2.00	4.00	8.00
❑ 55928	Tiny Bubbles/Hawaii	1967	—	3.00	6.00
❑ 56126	Midnight Cowboy/Quiet Village	1969	—	2.50	5.00
UNITED ARTISTS					
❑ 0069	Quiet Village/The Enchanted Sea	1973	—	2.00	4.00
—"Silver Spotlight Series" reissue					
7-Inch Extended Plays					
LIBERTY					
❑ LEP-1-3034	*Quiet Village/Return to Paradise/Stone God/Jungle Fever	1959	2.50	5.00	10.00
❑ LEP-1-3034 [PS]	Exotica Part 1	1959	2.50	5.00	10.00
❑ LEP-2-3034	(contents unknown)	1959	2.50	5.00	10.00

Number	Title (A Side/B Side)	Yr	VG	VG+	NM
❑ LEP-2-3034 [PS]	Exotica Part 2	1959	2.50	5.00	10.00
❑ LEP-3-3034	Lotus Land/Similau//Waipu/Love Dance	1959	2.50	5.00	10.00
❑ LEP-3-3034 [PS]	Exotica Part 3	1959	2.50	5.00	10.00
❑ LST 7237	A Taste of Honey/Take Five/Standing on This Shore//Route 66/Clair de Lune/Wild One	196?	2.50	5.00	10.00
—Jukebox issue; small hole, plays at 33 1/3 rpm					
❑ LST 7237 [PS]	A Taste of Honey	196?	2.50	5.00	10.00
Albums					
FIRST AMERICAN					
❑ 7743	From Hawaii With Love	1981	2.50	5.00	10.00
LIBERTY					
❑ LM-1009	Exotica Vol. 1	1982	2.00	4.00	8.00
—Reissue of United Artists 1009					
❑ LRP-3034 [M]	Exotica	1957	10.00	20.00	40.00
—Turquoise label					
❑ LRP-3034 [M]	Exotica	1960	6.25	12.50	25.00
—Black rainbow label					
❑ LRP-3077 [M]	Exotica, Volume II	1957	7.50	15.00	30.00
—Turquoise label					
❑ LRP-3077 [M]	Exotica, Volume II	1960	5.00	10.00	20.00
—Black rainbow label					
❑ LRP-3081 [M]	Forbidden Island	1958	7.50	15.00	30.00
—Turquoise label; woman in jungle on cover					
❑ LRP-3081 [M]	Forbidden Island	1960	5.00	10.00	20.00
—Black rainbow label; white foil on cover					
❑ LRP-3087 [M]	Primitiva	1958	7.50	15.00	30.00
—Turquoise label					
❑ LRP-3087 [M]	Primitiva	1960	5.00	10.00	20.00
—Black rainbow label					
❑ LRP-3102 [M]	Hypnotique	1958	7.50	15.00	30.00
—Turquoise label					
❑ LRP-3102 [M]	Hypnotique	1960	5.00	10.00	20.00
—Black rainbow label					
❑ LRP-3111 [M]	Afro-Desia	1959	7.50	15.00	30.00
—Turquoise label					
❑ LRP-3111 [M]	Afro-Desia	1960	5.00	10.00	20.00
—Black rainbow label					
❑ LRP-3116 [M]	Exotica, Vol. III	1959	7.50	15.00	30.00
—Turquoise label					
❑ LRP-3116 [M]	Exotica, Vol. III	1960	5.00	10.00	20.00
—Black rainbow label					
❑ LRP-3122 [M]	Quiet Village	1959	7.50	15.00	30.00
—Turquoise label					
❑ LRP-3122 [M]	Quiet Village	1960	5.00	10.00	20.00
—Black rainbow label					
❑ LRP-3141 [M]	The Enchanted Sea	1959	7.50	15.00	30.00
—Turquoise label					
❑ LRP-3141 [M]	The Enchanted Sea	1960	5.00	10.00	20.00
—Black rainbow label					
❑ LRP-3158 [M]	Exotic Sounds from the Silver Screen	1960	5.00	10.00	20.00
❑ LRP-3163 [M]	Exotic Sounds Visit Broadway	1960	5.00	10.00	20.00
❑ LRP-3168 [M]	Exotic Percussion	1961	5.00	10.00	20.00
❑ LRP-3224 [M]	The Exotic Sounds of Martin Denny In Person	1962	3.75	7.50	15.00
❑ LRP-3237 [M]	A Taste of Honey	1962	3.75	7.50	15.00
❑ LRP-3277 [M]	Another Taste of Honey	1963	3.75	7.50	15.00
❑ LRP-3307 [M]	The Versatile Martin Denny	1963	3.75	7.50	15.00
❑ LRP-3328 [M]	A Taste of Hits	1964	3.00	6.00	12.00
❑ LRP-3378 [M]	Latin Village	1964	3.00	6.00	12.00
❑ LRP-3394 [M]	Hawaii Tattoo	1964	3.00	6.00	12.00
❑ LRP-3415 [M]	20 Golden Hawaiian Hits	1965	3.00	6.00	12.00
❑ LRP-3438 [M]	Martin Denny	1965	3.00	6.00	12.00
❑ LRP-3445 [M]	Hawaiian A-Go-Go	1966	3.00	6.00	12.00
❑ LRP-3467 [M]	Golden Greats	1966	3.00	6.00	12.00
❑ LRP-3488 [M]	Hawaii	1967	3.00	6.00	12.00
❑ LRP-3513 [M]	Exotica Classica	1967	3.00	6.00	12.00
❑ L-5502 [M]	The Best of Martin Denny	1962	3.75	7.50	15.00
❑ S-6602 [S]	The Best of Martin Denny	1962	5.00	10.00	20.00
❑ LST-7001 [S]	Forbidden Island	1958	10.00	20.00	40.00
—All-black label; woman in jungle on cover					
❑ LST-7001 [S]	Forbidden Island	1960	6.25	12.50	25.00
—Black rainbow label; white foil on cover					
❑ LST-7006 [S]	Exotica, Volume II	1958	10.00	20.00	40.00
—All-black label					
❑ LST-7006 [S]	Exotica, Volume II	1960	6.25	12.50	25.00
—Black rainbow label					
❑ LST-7023 [S]	Primitiva	1958	10.00	20.00	40.00
—All-black label					
❑ LST-7023 [S]	Primitiva	1960	6.25	12.50	25.00
—Black rainbow label					
❑ LST-7034 [R]	Exotica	1958	6.25	12.50	25.00
—All-black label					
❑ LST-7034 [R]	Exotica	1960	5.00	10.00	20.00
—Black rainbow label					
❑ LST-7102 [S]	Hypnotique	1958	10.00	20.00	40.00
—All-black label					
❑ LST-7102 [S]	Hypnotique	1960	6.25	12.50	25.00
—Black rainbow label					
❑ LST-7111 [S]	Afro-Desia	1959	10.00	20.00	40.00
—All-black label					
❑ LST-7111 [S]	Afro-Desia	1960	6.25	12.50	25.00
—Black rainbow label					
❑ LST-7116 [S]	Exotica, Vol. III	1959	10.00	20.00	40.00
—All-black label					
❑ LST-7116 [S]	Exotica, Vol. III	1960	6.25	12.50	25.00
—Black rainbow label					
❑ LST-7122 [S]	Quiet Village	1959	10.00	20.00	40.00
—All-black label					
❑ LST-7122 [S]	Quiet Village	1960	6.25	12.50	25.00
—Black rainbow label					
❑ LST-7141 [S]	The Enchanted Sea	1959	10.00	20.00	40.00
—All-black label					
❑ LST-7141 [S]	The Enchanted Sea	1960	6.25	12.50	25.00
—Black rainbow label					
❑ LST-7158 [S]	Exotic Sounds from the Silver Screen	1960	6.25	12.50	25.00
❑ LST-7163 [S]	Exotic Sounds Visit Broadway	1960	6.25	12.50	25.00
❑ LST-7168 [S]	Exotic Percussion	1961	6.25	12.50	25.00
❑ LST-7224 [S]	The Exotic Sounds of Martin Denny In Person	1962	5.00	10.00	20.00

Number	Title (A Side/B Side)	Yr	VG	VG+	NM
❑ LST-7237 [S]	A Taste of Honey	1962	5.00	10.00	20.00
❑ LST-7277 [S]	Another Taste of Honey	1963	5.00	10.00	20.00
❑ LST-7307 [S]	The Versatile Martin Denny	1963	5.00	10.00	20.00
❑ LST-7328 [S]	A Taste of Hits	1964	3.75	7.50	15.00
❑ LST-7378 [S]	Latin Village	1964	3.75	7.50	15.00
❑ LST-7394 [S]	Hawaii Tattoo	1964	3.75	7.50	15.00
❑ LST-7415 [S]	20 Golden Hawaiian Hits	1965	3.75	7.50	15.00
❑ LST-7438 [S]	Martin Denny	1965	3.75	7.50	15.00
❑ LST-7445 [S]	Hawaiian A-Go-Go	1966	3.75	7.50	15.00
❑ LST-7467 [S]	Golden Greats	1966	3.75	7.50	15.00
❑ LST-7488 [S]	Hawaii	1967	3.75	7.50	15.00
❑ LST-7513 [S]	Exotica Classica	1967	3.75	7.50	15.00
❑ LST-7621	Exotic Moog	1969	10.00	20.00	40.00

SUNSET

Number	Title (A Side/B Side)	Yr	VG	VG+	NM
❑ SUM-1102 [M]	Paradise Moods	196?	3.00	6.00	12.00
❑ SUM-1169 [M]	Sayonara	1967	3.00	6.00	12.00
❑ SUS-5102 [S]	Paradise Moods	196?	3.00	6.00	12.00
❑ SUS-5169 [S]	Sayonara	1967	3.00	6.00	12.00
❑ SUS-5199	Exotic Night	1969	3.00	6.00	12.00

UNITED ARTISTS

Number	Title (A Side/B Side)	Yr	VG	VG+	NM
❑ UA-LA234-G	The Very Best of Martin Denny	1974	2.50	5.00	10.00
❑ UA-LA383-E	The Very Best of Martin Denny	1975	2.50	5.00	10.00
❑ LM-1009	Exotica Vol. 1	1980	2.50	5.00	10.00

—Reissue of Liberty 7034

DENNY, SANDY Also see FAIRPORT CONVENTION.
45s
A&M

Number	Title (A Side/B Side)	Yr	VG	VG+	NM
❑ 1331	Crazy Lady Blues/Let's Jump the Broomstick	1972	—	3.00	6.00
❑ 1410	Tomorrow Is a Long Time/Listen Listen	1973	—	3.00	6.00

Albums
A&M

Number	Title (A Side/B Side)	Yr	VG	VG+	NM
❑ SP-4317	The Northstar Grassman and the Ravens	1971	3.75	7.50	15.00
❑ SP-4371	Sandy	1972	3.75	7.50	15.00

CARTHAGE

Number	Title (A Side/B Side)	Yr	VG	VG+	NM
❑ CGLP-4423	Rendezvous	1985	2.50	5.00	10.00

—Reissue of Island 9433

Number	Title (A Side/B Side)	Yr	VG	VG+	NM
❑ CGLP-4425	Like an Old Fashioned Waltz	1985	2.50	5.00	10.00

—Reissue of Island 9340

Number	Title (A Side/B Side)	Yr	VG	VG+	NM
❑ CGLP-4429	The Northstar Grassman and the Ravens	1985	2.50	5.00	10.00

—Reissue of A&M 4317
HANNIBAL

Number	Title (A Side/B Side)	Yr	VG	VG+	NM
❑ HNBX-5301 [(3)]	Who Knows Where the Time Goes	198?	5.00	10.00	20.00

ISLAND

Number	Title (A Side/B Side)	Yr	VG	VG+	NM
❑ SW-9340	Like an Old Fashioned Waltz	1974	3.75	7.50	15.00
❑ ILPS 9433	Rendezvous	1977	3.75	7.50	15.00

DENSON, LEE
45s
ENTERPRISE

Number	Title (A Side/B Side)	Yr	VG	VG+	NM
❑ 9086	A Mom and Dad for Christmas/The Miracle of the Rosary	1973	—	2.50	5.00

KENT

Number	Title (A Side/B Side)	Yr	VG	VG+	NM
❑ 306	High School Hop/Devil Doll	1958	15.00	30.00	60.00

VIK

Number	Title (A Side/B Side)	Yr	VG	VG+	NM
❑ 0251	Heart of a Fool/The Pied Piper	1957	10.00	20.00	40.00
❑ 0281	New Shoes/Climb Love Mountain	1957	20.00	40.00	80.00

—With Eddie Cochran on guitar

DENTON, BOB
45s
CHANCELLOR

Number	Title (A Side/B Side)	Yr	VG	VG+	NM
❑ 1112	I Guess I'm Still in Love with You/Wrong Side of the Door	1962	3.00	6.00	12.00

DOT

Number	Title (A Side/B Side)	Yr	VG	VG+	NM
❑ 15622	Love Me, So I'll Know/I'm Sending You This Record	1957	5.00	10.00	20.00
❑ 15833	Playboy/Twenty-Four Hour Night	1958	5.00	10.00	20.00

JUDD

Number	Title (A Side/B Side)	Yr	VG	VG+	NM
❑ 1001	Sweet and Innocent/Back to School Again	1958	3.75	7.50	15.00
❑ 1013	I'll Always Be Yours/A Lover's Prayer	1959	3.75	7.50	15.00

DENTON, MICKEY
45s
AMY

Number	Title (A Side/B Side)	Yr	VG	VG+	NM
❑ 902	Top Ten/Now I'm Mr. Blue	1964	3.00	6.00	12.00

BIG TOP

Number	Title (A Side/B Side)	Yr	VG	VG+	NM
❑ 3078	Steady Kind/Now You Can't Give Them Away	1961	6.25	12.50	25.00
❑ 3094	Nature Boy/Ain't Nobody	1962	5.00	10.00	20.00
❑ 3114	Tell Her/How Mighty Hath Fallen	1962	5.00	10.00	20.00
❑ 3142	Dance With Me Mary/The Other Side of Betty	1963	5.00	10.00	20.00

IMPACT

Number	Title (A Side/B Side)	Yr	VG	VG+	NM
❑ 1002	Ain't Love Grand/Mi Amore	1965	5.00	10.00	20.00
❑ 1011	Heartache Is My Name/King Lonely the Blue	1966	5.00	10.00	20.00

WORLD ARTISTS

Number	Title (A Side/B Side)	Yr	VG	VG+	NM
❑ 1043	One More Time/Don't Throw My Toys Away	1965	3.00	6.00	12.00

DENVER, JOHN Also see DENVER, BOISE & JOHNSON; THE MITCHELL TRIO.
12-Inch Singles
RCA

Number	Title (A Side/B Side)	Yr	VG	VG+	NM
❑ JD-11189 [DJ]	Bet On the Blues (same on both sides)	1977	3.00	6.00	12.00

45s
CHERRY MOUNTAIN

Number	Title (A Side/B Side)	Yr	VG	VG+	NM
❑ 01/02	Let Us Begin (What Are We Making Weapons For)/Flying for Me	1986	—	2.00	4.00

COLUMBIA

Number	Title (A Side/B Side)	Yr	VG	VG+	NM
❑ 02679	Perhaps Love/Annie's Song	1982	—	2.00	4.00

—With Placido Domingo

Number	Title (A Side/B Side)	Yr	VG	VG+	NM
❑ 03148	Perhaps Love/Annie's Song	1982	—	—	3.00

—With Placido Domingo; reissue
LEGACY

Number	Title (A Side/B Side)	Yr	VG	VG+	NM
❑ 77993	For You/Rocky Mountain High (Live)	1995	—	—	2.00
❑ 77993 [PS]	For You/Rocky Mountain High (Live)	1995	—	—	3.00

RCA

Number	Title (A Side/B Side)	Yr	VG	VG+	NM
❑ 5086-7-R	Love Again/Let Us Begin (What Are We Making Weapons For)	1987	—	—	3.00

Number	Title (A Side/B Side)	Yr	VG	VG+	NM
❑ PB-10774	Like a Sad Song/Pegasus	1976	—	2.00	4.00
❑ PB-10854	Baby, You Look Good to Me Tonight/Wrangle Mountain Song	1976	—	2.00	4.00
❑ PB-10911	My Sweet Lady/Welcome to My Morning	1977	—	2.00	4.00
❑ GB-10940	I'm Sorry/Fly Away	1977	—	—	3.00

—Gold Standard Series

Number	Title (A Side/B Side)	Yr	VG	VG+	NM
❑ PB-11036	How Can I Leave You Again/To the Wild Country	1977	—	2.00	4.00
❑ PB-11214	It Amazes Me/Druthers	1978	—	2.00	4.00
❑ PB-11267	I Want to Live/Tradewinds	1978	—	2.00	4.00
❑ GB-11327	My Sweet Lady/Like a Sad Song	1978	—	—	3.00

—Gold Standard Series

Number	Title (A Side/B Side)	Yr	VG	VG+	NM
❑ PB-11479	Downhill Stuff/Life Is So Good	1979	—	2.00	4.00
❑ PB-11535	Sweet Melinda/What's On Your Mind	1979	—	2.00	4.00
❑ PB-11637	Garden Song/Berkeley Woman	1979	—	2.00	4.00
❑ PB-11915	Autograph/The Mountain Song	1980	—	2.00	4.00
❑ PB-11915 [PS]	Autograph/The Mountain Song	1980	—	2.00	4.00
❑ PB-12017	Dancing with the Mountains/American Child	1980	—	2.00	4.00
❑ PB-12246	Some Days Are Diamonds (Some Days Are Stone)/Country Love	1981	—	2.00	4.00
❑ PB-12345	The Cowboy and the Lady/Till You Opened My Eyes	1981	—	2.00	4.00
❑ PB-13071	Shanghai Breezes/What One Man Can Do	1982	—	2.00	4.00
❑ PB-13270	Seasons of the Heart/Islands	1982	—	2.00	4.00
❑ PB-13371	Opposite Tables/Relatively Speaking	1982	—	2.00	4.00
❑ PB-13562	Wild Montana Skies/I Remember Romance	1983	—	2.00	4.00

—A-side with Emmylou Harris

Number	Title (A Side/B Side)	Yr	VG	VG+	NM
❑ PB-13642	Flight (The Higher We Fly)/Hold On Tightly	1983	—	2.00	4.00
❑ PB-13740	World Games/It's About Time	1984	—	—	3.00
❑ PB-13782	The Way I Am/The Gold and Beyond	1984	—	—	3.00
❑ PB-13931	Love Again/It's About Time	1984	—	—	3.00

—A-side: With Sylvie Vartan

Number	Title (A Side/B Side)	Yr	VG	VG+	NM
❑ GB-14075	Calypso/Some Days Are Diamonds (Some Days Are Stone)	1985	—	—	3.00

—Gold Standard Series

Number	Title (A Side/B Side)	Yr	VG	VG+	NM
❑ PB-14115	Don't Close Your Eyes Tonight/A Wild Heart Looking for Home	1985	—	—	3.00
❑ PB-14227	Dreamland Express/African Sunrise	1985	—	—	3.00
❑ PB-14227 [PS]	Dreamland Express/African Sunrise	1985	—	2.00	4.00
❑ PB-14366 [DJ]	Flying for Me (same on both sides)	1986	—	2.00	4.00

—No stock copies were issued

Number	Title (A Side/B Side)	Yr	VG	VG+	NM
❑ PB-14406	Along for the Ride ('56 T-Bird)/Let Us Begin (What Are We Making Weapons For)	1986	—	—	3.00

RCA VICTOR

Number	Title (A Side/B Side)	Yr	VG	VG+	NM
❑ 74-0275	Daydream/I Wish I Knew How It Would Feel to Be Free	1969	2.50	5.00	10.00
❑ 74-0305	Anthem (Revelation)/Sticky Summer Weather	1970	2.50	5.00	10.00
❑ 74-0332	Follow Me/Isabel	1970	2.50	5.00	10.00
❑ 74-0376	Sail Away Home/I Wish I Could Have Been There	1970	2.50	5.00	10.00
❑ 74-0391	Whose Garden Is This/Mr. Bojangles	1970	2.50	5.00	10.00
❑ 74-0445	Take Me Home, Country Roads/Poems, Prayers and Promises	1971	2.00	4.00	8.00

—With Fat City

Number	Title (A Side/B Side)	Yr	VG	VG+	NM
❑ 74-0567	Friends with You/Starwood in Aspen	1971	—	3.00	6.00
❑ 74-0647	Everyday/City of New Orleans	1972	—	3.00	6.00
❑ 74-0737	Goodbye Again/The Eagle and the Hawk	1972	—	3.00	6.00
❑ 74-0801	Late Winter, Early Spring/Hard Life Hard Times	1972	—	3.00	6.00
❑ 74-0829	Rocky Mountain High/Spring	1972	—	2.50	5.00
❑ 74-0955	I'd Rather Be a Cowboy/Sunshine on My Shoulders	1973	—	2.00	4.00
❑ APBO-0067	Farewell Andromeda (Welcome to My Morning)/Whiskey Basin Blues	1973	—	2.00	4.00
❑ APBO-0182	Please, Daddy (Don't Get Drunk This Christmas)/Rocky Mountain High	1973	—	2.50	5.00
❑ APBO-0213	Sunshine on My Shoulders/Around and Around	1974	—	2.00	4.00
❑ APBO-0295	Annie's Song/Cool An' Green An' Shady	1974	—	2.00	4.00
❑ PB-10065	Back Home Again/It's Up to You	1974	—	2.00	4.00
❑ PB-10148	Sweet Surrender/Summer	1974	—	2.00	4.00
❑ PB-10239	Thank God I'm a Country Boy/My Sweet Lady	1975	—	2.00	4.00
❑ PB-10353	I'm Sorry/Calypso	1975	—	2.00	4.00
❑ PB-10464	Christmas for Cowboys/Silent Night, Holy Night	1975	—	2.00	4.00
❑ GB-10472	Annie's Song/Cool An' Green An' Shady	1975	—	—	3.00

—Gold Standard Series

Number	Title (A Side/B Side)	Yr	VG	VG+	NM
❑ GB-10473	Back Home Again/It's Up to You	1975	—	—	3.00

—Gold Standard Series

Number	Title (A Side/B Side)	Yr	VG	VG+	NM
❑ GB-10474	Sunshine on My Shoulders/Around and Around	1975	—	—	3.00

—Gold Standard Series

Number	Title (A Side/B Side)	Yr	VG	VG+	NM
❑ GB-10475	Farewell Andromeda (Welcome to My Morning)/Whiskey Basin Blues	1975	—	—	3.00

—Gold Standard Series

Number	Title (A Side/B Side)	Yr	VG	VG+	NM
❑ GB-10476	Thank God I'm a Country Boy/My Sweet Lady	1975	—	—	3.00

—Gold Standard Series

Number	Title (A Side/B Side)	Yr	VG	VG+	NM
❑ GB-10477	Rocky Mountain High/Spring	1975	—	—	3.00

—Gold Standard Series

Number	Title (A Side/B Side)	Yr	VG	VG+	NM
❑ GB-10478	Sweet Surrender/Summer	1975	—	—	3.00

—Gold Standard Series

Number	Title (A Side/B Side)	Yr	VG	VG+	NM
❑ PB-10517	Fly Away/Two Shots	1975	—	2.00	4.00
❑ PB-10586	Looking for Space/Windsong	1976	—	2.00	4.00
❑ PB-10687	It Makes Me Giggle/Spirit	1976	—	2.00	4.00

WINDSTAR

Number	Title (A Side/B Side)	Yr	VG	VG+	NM
❑ 75720	Country Girl in Paris/Bread and Roses	1988	—	2.50	5.00
❑ 75720 [PS]	Country Girl in Paris/Bread and Roses	1988	—	3.00	6.00

7-Inch Extended Plays
RCA

Number	Title (A Side/B Side)	Yr	VG	VG+	NM
❑ DTF0-2008 [PS]	Rocky Mountain High	1973	6.25	12.50	25.00
❑ DTF0-2008 [S]	Season Suite/Summer/Fall Goodbye Again//Mother Nature's Son/For Baby (For Bobbie)/Paradise	1973	6.25	12.50	25.00

—Jukebox issue; small hole, plays at 33 1/3 rpm
Albums
HJD

Number	Title (A Side/B Side)	Yr	VG	VG+	NM
❑ 66	John Denver Sings	1966	125.00	250.00	500.00

—Private issue of 300 or so, made by JD as Christmas gifts to friends.
MERCURY

Number	Title (A Side/B Side)	Yr	VG	VG+	NM
❑ SRM-1-704	Beginnings	1972	5.00	10.00	20.00

—With illustration on cover

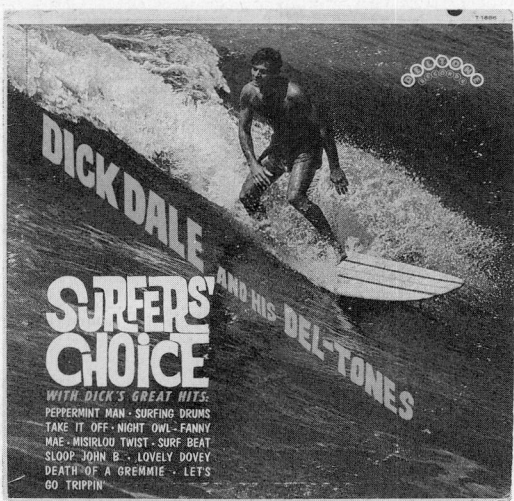

Dick Dale and the Del-Tones, *Surfers Choice*, Deltone T 1886, mono LP, $30-$60.

Dave Dee, Dozy, Beaky, Mick & Tich, *Time to Take Off,* Imperial LP-12402, stereo LP, $20-$40.

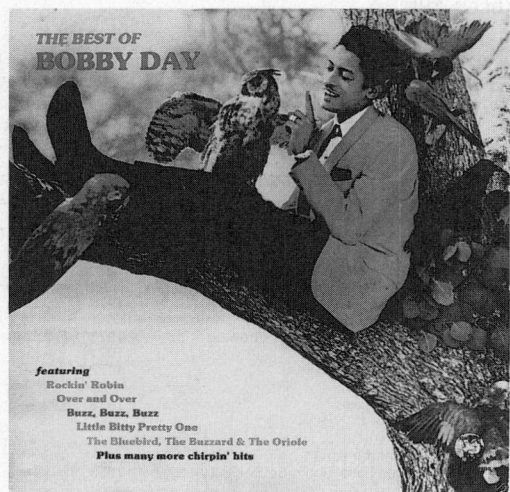

Bobby Day, *The Best of Bobby Day,* Rhino RNDF-208, mono LP, $6-$12.

Bobby Darin, *For Teenagers Only*, Atco EP 4513-D, 7-inch EP, $70-$140 (cover and record together).

Doris Day, *Wonderful Day*, Columbia Special Products XTV 82021 (side 1), XTV 82022 (side 2), mono LP, $20-$40.

John Denver, *Rhymes and Reasons,* RCA Victor LSP-4207, stereo LP, orange label, $7.50-$15.

Number	Title (A Side/B Side)	Yr	VG	VG+	NM
❑ SRM-1-704	Beginnings	1974	3.00	6.00	12.00
—With mountain scene on cover					
RCA					
❑ 7624-1-R	Back Home Again	1988	2.50	5.00	10.00
—Last vinyl reissue					
❑ 7631-1-R	Poems, Prayers and Promises	1988	2.50	5.00	10.00
—Last vinyl reissue					
❑ 7632-1-R	Rocky Mountain High	1988	2.50	5.00	10.00
—Last vinyl reissue					
RCA VICTOR					
❑ DJL1-0075 [DJ]	The John Denver Radio Show	1973	7.50	15.00	30.00
❑ APL1-0101	Farewell Andromeda	1973	3.00	6.00	12.00
—Orange label					
❑ APL1-0101	Farewell Andromeda	1975	2.50	5.00	10.00
—Tan label or black label, dog near top					
❑ APL1-0374	John Denver's Greatest Hits	197?	2.00	4.00	8.00
—Reissue					
❑ AQL1-0374	John Denver's Greatest Hits	197?	2.00	4.00	8.00
—Later reissue					
❑ CPL1-0374	John Denver's Greatest Hits	1974	2.50	5.00	10.00
—Orange label					
❑ CPL1-0374	John Denver's Greatest Hits	1975	2.00	4.00	8.00
—Tan label or black label, dog near top					
❑ AFL1-0548	Back Home Again	197?	2.00	4.00	8.00
—Reissue					
❑ AQL1-0548	Back Home Again	197?	2.00	4.00	8.00
—Later reissue					
❑ CPL1-0548	Back Home Again	1974	2.50	5.00	10.00
—Orange or tan label					
❑ CPL1-0548	Back Home Again	1976	2.00	4.00	8.00
—Black label, dog near top					
❑ DJL1-0683 [DJ]	The Second John Denver Radio Show	1974	7.50	15.00	30.00
❑ CPL2-0764 [(2)]	An Evening with John Denver	1975	3.00	6.00	12.00
—Orange or tan labels					
❑ CPL2-0764 [(2)]	An Evening with John Denver	1976	2.50	5.00	10.00
—Black label, dog near top					
❑ AFL1-1183	Windsong	197?	2.00	4.00	8.00
—Reissue					
❑ APL1-1183	Windsong	1975	2.50	5.00	10.00
—Tan label					
❑ APL1-1183	Windsong	1976	2.00	4.00	8.00
—Black label, dog near top					
❑ AQL1-1183	Windsong	197?	2.00	4.00	8.00
—Later reissue					
❑ AFL1-1201	Rocky Mountain Christmas	197?	2.00	4.00	8.00
—Reissue					
❑ APL1-1201	Rocky Mountain Christmas	1975	2.50	5.00	10.00
—Tan label					
❑ APL1-1201	Rocky Mountain Christmas	1976	2.00	4.00	8.00
—Black label, dog near top					
❑ APL2-1263 [(2)]	The John Denver Gift Pak	1974	7.50	15.00	30.00
—Contains "Rocky Mountain Christmas" and "Windsong" in a special Christmas sleeve.					
❑ AFL1-1694	Spirit	197?	2.00	4.00	8.00
—Reissue					
❑ APL1-1694	Spirit	1976	2.50	5.00	10.00
—Originals are black label, dog near top					
❑ AQL1-2195	John Denver's Greatest Hits, Volume 2	197?	2.00	4.00	8.00
—Reissue					
❑ CPL1-2195	John Denver's Greatest Hits, Volume 2	1977	2.50	5.00	10.00
❑ AFL1-2521	I Want to Live	1977	2.00	4.00	8.00
❑ AQL1-3075	John Denver	1979	2.00	4.00	8.00
❑ AQL1-3449	Autograph	1980	2.00	4.00	8.00
❑ AFL1-4055	Some Days Are Diamonds	1981	2.00	4.00	8.00
❑ LSP-4207	Rhymes & Reasons	1969	3.75	7.50	15.00
—Orange label, non-flexible vinyl					
❑ AFL1-4256	Seasons of the Heart	1982	2.00	4.00	8.00
❑ LSP-4278	Take Me to Tomorrow	1970	3.75	7.50	15.00
—Orange label, non-flexible vinyl					
❑ LSP-4414	Whose Garden Was This?	1970	3.75	7.50	15.00
—Orange label, non-flexible vinyl					
❑ AFL1-4499	Poems, Prayers and Promises	197?	2.00	4.00	8.00
—Reissue					
❑ LSP-4499	Poems, Prayers and Promises	1971	3.00	6.00	12.00
—Orange label					
❑ LSP-4499	Poems, Prayers and Promises	1975	2.50	5.00	10.00
—Tan label or black label, dog near top					
❑ AFL1-4607	Aerie	197?	2.00	4.00	8.00
—Reissue					
❑ LSP-4607	Aerie	1971	3.00	6.00	12.00
—Orange label					
❑ LSP-4607	Aerie	1975	2.50	5.00	10.00
—Tan label or black label, dog near top					
❑ AFL1-4683	It's About Time	1983	2.00	4.00	8.00
❑ AFL1-4731	Rocky Mountain High	197?	2.00	4.00	8.00
—Reissue					
❑ AQL1-4731	Rocky Mountain High	197?	2.00	4.00	8.00
—Later reissue					
❑ LSP-4731	Rocky Mountain High	1972	3.00	6.00	12.00
—Orange label					
❑ LSP-4731	Rocky Mountain High	1975	2.50	5.00	10.00
—Tan label or black label, dog near top					
❑ AYL1-5189	Poems, Prayers and Promises	198?	—	3.00	6.00
—"Best Buy Series" reissue					
❑ AYL1-5190	Rocky Mountain High	198?	—	3.00	6.00
—"Best Buy Series" reissue					
❑ AYL1-5191	Windsong	198?	—	3.00	6.00
—"Best Buy Series" reissue					
❑ AYL1-5192	I Want to Live	198?	—	3.00	6.00
—"Best Buy Series" reissue					
❑ AYL1-5193	Back Home Again	198?	—	3.00	6.00
—"Best Buy Series" reissue					
❑ AYL1-5194	Spirit	198?	—	3.00	6.00
—"Best Buy Series" reissue					
❑ AYL1-5195	Farewell Andromeda	198?	—	3.00	6.00
—"Best Buy Series" reissue					
❑ AJL1-5313	John Denver's Greatest Hits, Volume 3	1984	2.00	4.00	8.00
❑ DJL1-5398 [DJ]	The John Denver Holiday Radio Show	1984	5.00	10.00	20.00
❑ AFL1-5458	Dreamland Express	1985	2.00	4.00	8.00
❑ AFL1-5811	One World	1986	2.00	4.00	8.00

DENVER, JOHN, AND THE MUPPETS
45s
RCA

Number	Title (A Side/B Side)	Yr	VG	VG+	NM
❑ PB-11767	Have Yourself a Merry Little Christmas//We Wish You a Merry Christmas/ A Baby Just Like You	1979	—	2.50	5.00
❑ PB-11767 [PS]	Have Yourself a Merry Little Christmas//We Wish You a Merry Christmas/ A Baby Just Like You	1979	—	2.50	5.00

Albums
RCA VICTOR

Number	Title (A Side/B Side)	Yr	VG	VG+	NM
❑ AFL1-3451	A Christmas Together	1979	3.00	6.00	12.00

DENVER, JOHN, AND THE NITTY GRITTY DIRT BAND Also see each artist's individual listings.
45s
UNIVERSAL

Number	Title (A Side/B Side)	Yr	VG	VG+	NM
❑ UVL-66008	And So It Goes/Amazing Grace	1989	—	2.00	4.00

DENVER, KARL
45s
LONDON

Number	Title (A Side/B Side)	Yr	VG	VG+	NM
❑ 2020	Marcheta/Joe Sweeney	1961	3.75	7.50	15.00
❑ 9521	Wimoweh/Sleepy Lagoon	1962	3.00	6.00	12.00
❑ 9534	Zimba/Uska Dara	1962	3.00	6.00	12.00
❑ 9576	Blue Weekend/Pastures of Plenty	1963	3.00	6.00	12.00

DENVER, BOISE, & JOHNSON Also see JOHN DENVER.
45s
REPRISE

Number	Title (A Side/B Side)	Yr	VG	VG+	NM
❑ 0695	Take Me to Tomorrow/'68 Nixon (This Year's Model)	1968	3.00	6.00	12.00

DEPENDABLES, THE
Albums
UNITED ARTISTS

Number	Title (A Side/B Side)	Yr	VG	VG+	NM
❑ UAS-6799	Klaatu Berrada Niktu	1971	5.00	10.00	20.00

DERBY-HATVILLE
45s
SEA ELL

Number	Title (A Side/B Side)	Yr	VG	VG+	NM
❑ 102	You'll Forget Me/(B-side unknown)	1967	10.00	20.00	40.00
❑ 104	Instant Replay/(B-side unknown)	1967	10.00	20.00	40.00

DEREK See JOHNNY CYMBAL.

DEREK AND THE DOMINOS Also see ERIC CLAPTON.
45s
ATCO

Number	Title (A Side/B Side)	Yr	VG	VG+	NM
❑ 6780	Tell the Truth/Roll It Over	1970	12.50	25.00	50.00
—Yellow and white label stock copy; withdrawn shortly after release, this is much rarer than promos					
❑ 6780 [DJ]	Tell the Truth/Roll It Over	1970	6.25	12.50	25.00
—Produced by Phil Spector; all-white label					
❑ 6803	Bell Bottom Blues/Keep On Growing	1971	2.50	5.00	10.00
❑ 6809	Layla (2:43)/I Am Yours	1971	2.50	5.00	10.00
❑ 6809	Layla (7:10)/I Am Yours	1972	—	3.00	6.00
POLYDOR					
❑ 15040	Layla/I Am Yours	1972	—	—	—
—Unreleased?					
RSO					
❑ 400	Presence of the Lord/ Why Does Love Got to Be So Sad	1973	—	3.00	6.00

Albums
ATCO

Number	Title (A Side/B Side)	Yr	VG	VG+	NM
❑ 2-704 [(2)M]	Layla and Other Assorted Love Songs	1970	75.00	150.00	300.00
—White label promo only					
❑ SD 2-704 [(2)DJ]	Layla and Other Assorted Love Songs	1970	50.00	100.00	200.00
—White label promo					
❑ SD 2-704 [(2)S]	Layla and Other Assorted Love Songs	1970	7.50	15.00	30.00
DIRECT DISK					
❑ SD-16629 [(2)]	Layla and Other Assorted Love Songs	1981	37.50	75.00	150.00
—Audiophile vinyl					
MOBILE FIDELITY					
❑ 2-239 [(2)]	Derek and the Dominos in Concert	1996	12.50	25.00	50.00
—Audiophile vinyl					
POLYDOR					
❑ PD2-3501 [(2)]	Layla and Other Assorted Love Songs	1972	5.00	10.00	20.00
RSO					
❑ RS-2-3801 [(2)]	Layla and Other Assorted Love Songs	1977	3.75	7.50	15.00
❑ SO 2-8800 [(2)]	Derek and the Dominos in Concert	1973	5.00	10.00	20.00
❑ 823277-1 [(2)]	Layla and Other Assorted Love Songs	1985	3.00	6.00	12.00

DERRINGER, RICK Also see THE McCOYS.
45s
BLUE SKY

Number	Title (A Side/B Side)	Yr	VG	VG+	NM
❑ 2751	Rock and Roll Hoochie Koo/Time Warp	1974	—	2.50	5.00
❑ 2752	Teenage Love Affair/Slide Over Slinky	1974	—	2.00	4.00
❑ 2753	It's Raining/Cheqap Tequila	1974	—	2.00	4.00
❑ 2755	Hang On Sloopy/Skyscraper Blues	1975	—	2.00	4.00
❑ 2757	Don't Ever Say Goodbye/Gimme More	1975	—	2.00	4.00
❑ 2765	Let Me In/You Can Have Me	1976	—	2.00	4.00
❑ 2767	Don't Stop Loving Me/Let's Make It	1977	—	2.00	4.00
—As "Derringer"					
❑ 2770	Lawyers, Guns and Money/Sleepless	1977	—	2.00	4.00
—As "Derringer"					
❑ 2774	Midnight Road/Rocka-Rolla	1978	—	2.00	4.00
—As "Derringer"					
❑ 2783	Need a Little Girl (Just Like You)/ Something Warm	1979	—	2.00	4.00
❑ 2788	Don't Ever Say Goodbye/Timeless	1980	—	2.00	4.00
❑ 2793	Runaway/Teenage Love Affair	1980	—	2.00	4.00
❑ 2794	Let the Music Play/You'll Get Yours	1980	—	2.00	4.00
EPIC					
❑ 05830	The Real America/Grab Them Cakes	1986	—	—	3.00
—As "Derringer"					

Number	Title (A Side/B Side)	Yr	VG	VG+	NM
Albums					
BLUE SKY					
KZ 32481	All American Boy	1973	3.75	7.50	15.00
PZ 32481	All American Boy	197?	2.00	4.00	8.00
—Reissue with new prefix					
ZQ 32481 [Q]	All American Boy	1974	5.00	10.00	20.00
PZ 33423	Spring Fever	1975	3.00	6.00	12.00
PZQ 33423 [Q]	Spring Fever	1975	5.00	10.00	20.00
PZ 34181	Derringer	1976	3.00	6.00	12.00
PZ 34470	Sweet Evil	1977	3.00	6.00	12.00
PZ 34848	Derringer Live	1977	3.00	6.00	12.00
—Without bar code					
PZ 34848	Derringer Live	198?	2.00	4.00	8.00
—Reissue with bar code					
JZ 35075	If I Weren't So Romantic I'd Shoot You	1978	2.50	5.00	10.00
JZ 36092	Guitars and Women	1979	2.50	5.00	10.00
JZ 36551	Face to Face	1980	2.50	5.00	10.00
PASSPORT					
PB-6025	Good Dirty Fun	1983	2.50	5.00	10.00

DESHANNON, JACKIE
45s

Number	Title (A Side/B Side)	Yr	VG	VG+	NM
AMHERST					
725	I Don't Think I Can Wait/Don't Let the Flame Burn Out	1978	3.00	6.00	12.00
728	To Love Somebody/Just to Feel This Love from You	1978	3.00	6.00	12.00
733	You're the Only Dancer/Tonight You're Doin' It Right	1979	3.00	6.00	12.00
737	Things We Said Today/Way Above the Angels	1979	3.00	6.00	12.00
ATLANTIC					
2871	Only Love Can Break Your Heart/Vanilla Olay	1972	2.50	5.00	10.00
2895	I Wanna Roo You/Paradise	1972	2.50	5.00	10.00
2919	Sweet Sixteen/Speak Out to Me	1972	2.50	5.00	10.00
2924	Chains on My Soul/Peaceful in My Soul	1972	2.50	5.00	10.00
2994	Your Baby Is a Lady/(If You Never Have a Big Hit Record) You're Still Gonna Be My Star	1973	2.50	5.00	10.00
3041	You've Changed/Jimmie, Just Sing Me One More Song	1974	2.50	5.00	10.00
CAPITOL					
3130	Salinas/Keep Me Warm	1971	2.50	5.00	10.00
3185	Stone Cold Soul/West Virginia Mine	1971	2.50	5.00	10.00
COLUMBIA					
10221	Boat to Sail/Let the Sailors Dance	1975	3.75	7.50	15.00
—With Brian Wilson on backing vocal					
10340	Fire in the City/All Night Desire	1976	2.50	5.00	10.00
DOT					
15928	Cajun Blues/Just Another Lie	1959	6.25	12.50	25.00
—As "Jackie Shannon"					
15980	Trouble/Lies	1959	6.25	12.50	25.00
—As "Jackie Shannon"					
EDISON INTERNATIONAL					
416	I Wanna Go Home/So Warm	1960	25.00	50.00	100.00
418	Put My Baby Down/The Foolish One	1960	25.00	50.00	100.00
GONE					
5008	How Wrong I Was/I'll Be True	1957	7.50	15.00	30.00
—As "Jackie Dee"					
IMPERIAL					
66110	What the World Needs Now Is Love/I Remember the Boy	1965	2.00	4.00	8.00
66132	A Lifetime of Loneliness/Don't Turn Your Back on Me	1965	—	3.00	6.00
66171	Come and Get Me/Splendor in the Grass	1966	—	3.00	6.00
66194	Will You Love Me Tomorrow/Are You Ready for This	1966	—	3.00	6.00
66196	So Long Johnny/Windows and Doors	1966	—	3.00	6.00
66202	I Can Make It with You/To Be Myself	1966	—	3.00	6.00
66224	Come On Down/Find Me Love	1967	—	3.00	6.00
66236	Where Does the Sun Go/Wishing Doll	1967	—	3.00	6.00
66251	It's Late in the Game/Changin' My Mind	1967	—	3.00	6.00
66281	Me About You/I Keep Wanting You	1968	—	3.00	6.00
66301	Nobody's Home to Go Home To/Nicole	1968	—	3.00	6.00
66312	Didn't Want to Have to Do It/Splendor in the Grass	1968	—	3.00	6.00
66313	The Weight/Splendor in the Grass	1968	—	3.00	6.00
66342	Holly Would/My Heart's Been Marching	1968	—	3.00	6.00
66370	What Is This/Trust Me	1969	—	2.50	5.00
66385	Put a Little Love in Your Heart/Always Together	1969	—	3.00	6.00
66419	Love Will Find a Way/I Let Go Completely	1969	—	2.50	5.00
66430	One Christmas/Do You Know How Christmas Trees Are Grown	1969	—	3.00	6.00
66438	Brighton Hill/You Can Come to Me	1970	—	2.50	5.00
66452	You Keep Me Hangin' On-Hurt So Bad/What Was Your Day Like	1970	—	2.50	5.00
LIBERTY					
55148	Buddy/Strolypso Dance	1958	6.25	12.50	25.00
—As "Jackie Dee"					
55288	Lonely Girl/Teach Me	1960	3.75	7.50	15.00
55342	Think About You/Heaven Is Being with You	1961	3.75	7.50	15.00
55358	I Won't Turn You Down/Wish I Could Find a Boy	1961	3.75	7.50	15.00
55387	Baby (When You Kiss Me)/Ain't That Love	1961	3.75	7.50	15.00
55425	The Prince/I'll Drown in My Own Tears	1962	3.75	7.50	15.00
55425	The Prince/That's What Boys Are Made Of	1962	3.75	7.50	15.00
55484	Guess Who/Just Like in the Movies	1962	3.75	7.50	15.00
55497	You Won't Forget Me/I Don't Think So Much of Myself	1962	3.75	7.50	15.00
55526	Faded Love/Dancing Silhouettes	1962	3.75	7.50	15.00
55526 [PS]	Faded Love/Dancing Silhouettes	1962	10.00	20.00	40.00
55563	Needles and Pins/Did He Call Today, Mama?	1963	3.75	7.50	15.00
55602	Little Yellow Roses/500 Miles	1963	3.75	7.50	15.00
55602	Little Yellow Roses/Oh Sweet Chariot	1963	3.75	7.50	15.00
55602 [DJ]	Little Yellow Roses	1963	20.00	40.00	80.00
—Yellow vinyl promo					
55645	When You Walk in the Room/Til You Say You're Mine	1963	3.75	7.50	15.00
55673	I'm Gonna Be Strong/Should I Cry	1964	3.75	7.50	15.00
55678	Oh Boy/I'm Looking for Someone to Love	1964	3.75	7.50	15.00
55705	Hold Your Head High/She Don't Understand Him Like I Do	1964	3.75	7.50	15.00
55730	He's Got the Whole World in His Hands/It's Love Baby	1964	3.75	7.50	15.00
55735	When You Walk in the Room/Over You	1964	3.00	6.00	12.00
55787	What the World Needs Now Is Love/A Lifetime of Loneliness	1965	—	—	—
—Unreleased					
56187	Mediterranean Sky/It's So Nice	1970	—	3.00	6.00
PJ					
101	Trouble/Lies	1959	10.00	20.00	40.00
—As "Jackie Shannon"					
RCA					
PB-11902	I Don't Need You Anymore/Find Love	1980	—	2.50	5.00
SAGE AND SAND					
290	Just Another Lie/Cajun Blues	1960	6.25	12.50	25.00
330	Trouble/Lies	1960	6.25	12.50	25.00
UNITED ARTISTS					
0033	What the World Needs Now Is Love/Needles and Pins	1973	—	3.00	6.00
—"Silver Spotlight Series" reissue					
0034	Put a Little Love in Your Heart/When You Walk in the Room	1973	—	3.00	6.00
—"Silver Spotlight Series" reissue					
Albums					
AMHERST					
AMX 1010	You're the Only Dancer	1977	3.00	6.00	12.00
AMH 1016	Quick Touches	1978	3.00	6.00	12.00
ATLANTIC					
SD 7231	Jackie	1972	3.00	6.00	12.00
SD 7303	Your Baby Is a Lady	1974	3.00	6.00	12.00
CAPITOL					
ST-772	Songs	1971	3.00	6.00	12.00
COLUMBIA					
PC 33500	New Arrangement	1975	3.00	6.00	12.00
IMPERIAL					
LP-9286 [M]	This Is Jackie DeShannon	1965	5.00	10.00	20.00
—Black and pink label					
LP-9286 [M]	This Is Jackie DeShannon	1966	3.75	7.50	15.00
—Black and green label					
LP-9294 [M]	You Won't Forget Me	1965	5.00	10.00	20.00
—Black and pink label					
LP-9294 [M]	You Won't Forget Me	1966	3.75	7.50	15.00
—Black and green label					
LP-9296 [M]	In the Wind	1965	5.00	10.00	20.00
—Black and pink label					
LP-9296 [M]	In the Wind	1966	3.75	7.50	15.00
—Black and green label					
LP-9328 [M]	Are You Ready for This?	1966	3.75	7.50	15.00
LP-9344 [M]	New Image	1967	3.75	7.50	15.00
LP-9352 [M]	For You	1967	3.75	7.50	15.00
LP-12286 [S]	This Is Jackie DeShannon	1965	6.25	12.50	25.00
—Black and pink label					
LP-12286 [S]	This Is Jackie DeShannon	1966	5.00	10.00	20.00
—Black and green label					
LP-12294 [S]	You Won't Forget Me	1965	6.25	12.50	25.00
—Black and pink label					
LP-12294 [S]	You Won't Forget Me	1966	5.00	10.00	20.00
—Black and green label					
LP-12296 [S]	In the Wind	1965	6.25	12.50	25.00
—Black and pink label					
LP-12296 [S]	In the Wind	1966	5.00	10.00	20.00
—Black and green label					
LP-12328 [S]	Are You Ready for This?	1966	5.00	10.00	20.00
LP-12344 [S]	New Image	1967	5.00	10.00	20.00
LP-12352 [S]	For You	1967	5.00	10.00	20.00
LP-12386	Me About You	1968	3.75	7.50	15.00
LP-12404	What the World Needs Now Is Love	1968	3.75	7.50	15.00
LP-12415	Laurel Canyon	1969	3.75	7.50	15.00
LP-12442	Put a Little Love in Your Heart	1969	3.75	7.50	15.00
LP-12453	To Be Free	1970	3.75	7.50	15.00
LIBERTY					
LRP-3320 [M]	Jackie DeShannon	1963	10.00	20.00	40.00
LRP-3390 [M]	Breakin' It Up on the Beatles Tour!	1964	10.00	20.00	40.00
LST-7320 [S]	Jackie DeShannon	1963	12.50	25.00	50.00
LST-7390 [S]	Breakin' It Up on the Beatles Tour!	1964	12.50	25.00	50.00
LN-10179	The Very Best of Jackie DeShannon	1983	2.00	4.00	8.00
—Reissue of United Artists 434					
LN-10265	Jackie DeShannon	1985	2.00	4.00	8.00
SUNSET					
SUS-5225	Lonely Girl	1968	3.00	6.00	12.00
SUS-5322	Jackie DeShannon	1970	3.00	6.00	12.00
UNITED ARTISTS					
UA-LA434-E	The Very Best of Jackie DeShannon	1975	3.00	6.00	12.00

DESIRES, THE More than one group.
45s

Number	Title (A Side/B Side)	Yr	VG	VG+	NM
DASA					
102	Phyllis Beloved/The Girl for Me	1962	7.50	15.00	30.00
HERALD					
532	Bobby You/Cold Lonely Heart	1958	6.25	12.50	25.00
HULL					
730	Hey Lena/Let It Please Be You	1959	20.00	40.00	80.00
733	Set Me Free/Rendezvous with You	1960	20.00	40.00	80.00
SEVILLE					
118	The Story of Love/I Ask You	1962	7.50	15.00	30.00
SMASH					
1763	There I Go Again/I Never Loved Like This	1962	6.25	12.50	25.00
20TH FOX					
195	I Don't Know Why/Longing	1960	6.25	12.50	25.00

DESMOND, JOHNNY Also see DON CORNELL/JOHNNY DESMOND/ALAN DALE.
45s

Number	Title (A Side/B Side)	Yr	VG	VG+	NM
ARTISTS OF AMERICA					
119	Moonlight Serenade/(Instrumental)	1976	—	2.00	4.00

Number	Title (A Side/B Side)	Yr	VG	VG+	NM
ATCO					
❏ 6404	My Melancholy Baby/Common Touch	1966	—	3.00	6.00
❏ 6425	The Last of the Big Time Losers/				
	I Wanna Believe You	1966	—	3.00	6.00
COLUMBIA					
❏ 41343	Goodbye, My Love, Goodbye/Bye-Bye Barbara	1959	2.00	4.00	8.00
❏ 41414	Dancin' Man/Hey Little Dolly	1959	2.00	4.00	8.00
❏ 41525	Maria/Please	1959	2.00	4.00	8.00
❏ 41631	Eighth Wonder of the World/				
	Never Meant to Fall in Love	1960	2.00	4.00	8.00
❏ 41661	Hawk/Playing the Field	1960	2.00	4.00	8.00
❏ 41788	Lover Come Back to Me/				
	I Got a Right to Sing the Blues	1960	—	—	—
—Canceled					
❏ 41803	Lover Come Back to Me/No One Ever Tells You	1960	2.00	4.00	8.00
CORAL					
❏ 60629	Oh My Darlin'/Until	1952	3.00	6.00	12.00
❏ 60670	Festival/Confetti, I Stood and Threw	1952	3.00	6.00	12.00
❏ 60736	Battle Hymn of the Republic/				
	How Much Will I Miss You	1952	3.00	6.00	12.00
❏ 60798	One Way Heart/It's Meant to Be That Way	1952	3.00	6.00	12.00
❏ 60823	Trying/Wild Guitars	1952	3.00	6.00	12.00
❏ 60848	Nina Never Knew/Stay Where You Are	1952	3.00	6.00	12.00
❏ 60862	Christmas in the Air/Christmas Is a Time	1952	3.75	7.50	15.00
❏ 60929	The Gay Caballero/Thanks for Letting Me Know	1953	3.00	6.00	12.00
❏ 60978	The Japanese Sandman/Danger	1953	3.00	6.00	12.00
❏ 61031	It's So Nice to Be Your Neighbor/I'm a Love You	1953	3.00	6.00	12.00
❏ 61069	Woman/By the River Seine	1953	3.00	6.00	12.00
❏ 61153	Would You Let Me Hold Your Heart/The Zoo	1954	3.00	6.00	12.00
❏ 61198	Backward, Turn Backward/Forever Love	1954	3.75	7.50	15.00
—With Jane Russell					
❏ 61204	The High and the Mighty/In God We Trust	1954	3.00	6.00	12.00
❏ 61227	A Husband/A Wife	1954	3.00	6.00	12.00
—B-side by Eileen Barton					
❏ 61232	The High and the Mighty/Got No Time	1954	3.00	6.00	12.00
❏ 61255	Here I Go Walkin' Down the Road/Brooklyn				
	Bridge	1954	3.00	6.00	12.00
❏ 61301	My Own True Love/The Song from Desiree	1954	3.00	6.00	12.00
❏ 61379	Play Me Hearts and Flowers (I Wanna Cry)/I'm				
	So Ashamed	1955	2.50	5.00	10.00
❏ 61410	Togetherness/A Straw Hat and a Cane	1955	2.50	5.00	10.00
❏ 61436	It's a Sin to Tell a Lie/Learnin' the Blues	1955	2.50	5.00	10.00
❏ 61447	Land of the Pharaohs/This Too Shall Pass	1955	2.50	5.00	10.00
❏ 61476	The Yellow Rose of Texas/You're in Love with				
	Someone	1955	2.50	5.00	10.00
❏ 61505	Miss America/Gentlemen Marry Brunettes	1955	2.50	5.00	10.00
❏ 61529	Sixteen Tons/Ballo Italiano	1955	2.50	5.00	10.00
❏ 61543	Santo Natale/Happy Holidays to You	1955	3.00	6.00	12.00
❏ 61569	In My Diary/I'll Cry Tomorrow	1956	2.50	5.00	10.00
❏ 61570	Now Is the Time/Never Again	1956	2.50	5.00	10.00
❏ 61608	The Most Happy Fella/Without You	1956	2.50	5.00	10.00
❏ 61632	A Little Love Can Go a Long, Long Way/Please				
	Don't Forget Me Dear	1956	2.50	5.00	10.00
❏ 61663	The Proud Ones/I Only Know I Love You	1956	2.50	5.00	10.00
❏ 61729	A Girl Named Mary/Bueno	1956	2.50	5.00	10.00
❏ 61747	Old Fashioned Christmas/				
	Birthday Party of the King	1956	3.00	6.00	12.00
❏ 61768	Down Where the River Meets the Sea/				
	18th Century Music Box	1957	2.00	4.00	8.00
❏ 61797	I Just Want You to Want Me/				
	That's Where I Shine	1957	2.00	4.00	8.00
❏ 61835	A White Sport Coat (And a Pink Carnation)/Just				
	Lookin'	1957	2.00	4.00	8.00
❏ 61846	Shenandoah Rose/Consideration	1957	2.00	4.00	8.00
❏ 61880	Be Patient with Me/Missing	1957	2.00	4.00	8.00
❏ 61896	Rich Man, Poor Man/I Would Love You Still	1957	2.00	4.00	8.00
❏ 61910	Keep Me in Mind/Lonely Lament	1957	2.00	4.00	8.00
❏ 61934	Farewell to Naples/Temperamental You	1958	2.00	4.00	8.00
❏ 61952	The Sands of Time/The Jealous Boyfriend	1958	2.00	4.00	8.00
❏ 61968	Anniversary Song/First, Last and Always	1958	2.00	4.00	8.00
DIAMOND					
❏ 108	Twistin' Rose of Texas/Hello Honey	1962	2.00	4.00	8.00
MGM					
❏ 10703	The Picnic Song/I've Got a Heart	1950	3.75	7.50	15.00
—Earlier Johnny Desmond singles on MGM are unconfirmed on 45 rpm					
❏ 10736	Pagalle/Stars	1950	3.75	7.50	15.00
❏ 10758	Just Say I Love Her/If Anyone Desires	1950	3.75	7.50	15.00
❏ 10800	A Bushel and a Peck/So Long Sally	1950	3.75	7.50	15.00
❏ 10827	Sleigh Ride/Marshmallow World	1950	3.75	7.50	15.00
❏ 10850	C'est La Vie/You're for Me	1950	3.75	7.50	15.00
❏ 10920	Too Young/I Fell	1951	3.75	7.50	15.00
❏ 10930	The Chapel of the Roses/Forever and Always	1951	3.75	7.50	15.00
❏ 10939	Mama/My Yiddishe Momme	1951	3.75	7.50	15.00
❏ 10947	Because of You/Andiano	1951	3.75	7.50	15.00
❏ 10974	Mister and Mississippi/I Fall in Love	1951	3.75	7.50	15.00
❏ 10992	Out o' Breath/I'm Glad I Gave It Up for You	1951	3.75	7.50	15.00
❏ 11005	America's Prayer/I See God	1951	3.75	7.50	15.00
❏ 11027	I Want to Be Near You/I Will Never Change	1951	3.75	7.50	15.00
❏ 11049	So/More Love	1951	3.75	7.50	15.00
❏ 11078	True Love/Simple, Simple, Simple	1951	3.75	7.50	15.00
❏ 11122	My Lost Love/Hands Across the Table	1951	3.75	7.50	15.00
RCA VICTOR					
❏ 47-8233	I Can't Help Falling in Love/I Still Look at You				
	That Way	1963	—	3.00	6.00
20TH CENTURY FOX					
❏ 546	Fate Is the Hunter/Rio Conchos	1964	2.00	4.00	8.00
VIGOR					
❏ 710	Untouchable/Red Lips	1973	—	2.00	4.00
7-Inch Extended Plays					
CORAL					
❏ 83011	Christmas in the Air/Christmas Is a Time/The				
	Little Match Girl/The Night Before Christmas	195?	3.75	7.50	15.00
—B-side by Eileen Barton					
RCA CAMDEN					
❏ CAE-260	Guilty/I'll Close My Eyes//				
	Just Plain Love/If It's True	1955	3.00	6.00	12.00
❏ CAE-260 [PS]	Johnny Desmond Sings	1955	3.00	6.00	12.00

Number	Title (A Side/B Side)	Yr	VG	VG+	NM
Albums					
COLUMBIA					
❏ CL 1399 [M]	Once Upon a Time	1959	5.00	10.00	20.00
❏ CS 8194 [S]	Once Upon a Time	1959	6.25	12.50	25.00
MAYFAIR					
❏ 9635 [M]	Johnny Desmond Swings	196?	3.00	6.00	12.00
❏ 9635S [S]	Johnny Desmond Swings	196?	3.75	7.50	15.00
—Yellow vinyl					
MOVIETONE					
❏ 71011 [M]	Johnny Desmond On Location	1966	3.00	6.00	12.00
❏ S-72011 [S]	Johnny Desmond On Location	1966	3.75	7.50	15.00
VOCALION					
❏ VL 3773 [M]	Johnny Desmond	1966	3.00	6.00	12.00
❏ VL 73773 [R]	Johnny Desmond	1966	2.50	5.00	10.00

DESMOND, JOHNNY/JOHNNY KAY
Albums

Number	Title (A Side/B Side)	Yr	VG	VG+	NM
CORONET					
❏ CX-193 [M]	Johnny Desmond Sings	196?	3.00	6.00	12.00
❏ CXS-193 [R]	Johnny Desmond Sings	196?	2.50	5.00	10.00

DESMOND, PAUL
Also see DAVE BRUBECK (Desmond was the saxophone player on many of his LPs).
45s

Number	Title (A Side/B Side)	Yr	VG	VG+	NM
RCA VICTOR					
❏ 47-8035	Advise and Consent/Desmond Blue	1962	2.50	5.00	10.00
❏ 47-8264	Take Ten/Embarcadero	1963	2.50	5.00	10.00
Albums					
A&M					
❏ SP-3015	Summertime	1969	3.75	7.50	15.00
❏ SP-3024	From the Hot Afternoon	1969	3.75	7.50	15.00
❏ SP9-3024	From the Hot Afternoon	198?	5.00	10.00	20.00
—"Audio Master Plus" reissue					
❏ SP-3032	Bridge Over Troubled Water	1970	5.00	10.00	20.00
ARTISTS HOUSE					
❏ AH 2	Paul Desmond	1978	2.50	5.00	10.00
CTI					
❏ CTS-6039	Skylark	1974	2.50	5.00	10.00
❏ CTS-6059	Pure Desmond	1975	2.50	5.00	10.00
CTI/CBS ASSOCIATED					
❏ FZ 40806	Pure Desmond	1987	2.50	5.00	10.00
—Reissue of CTI 6059					
❏ FZ 44170	Skylark	1988	2.50	5.00	10.00
—Reissue of CTI 6039					
DISCOVERY					
❏ 840	East of the Sun	198?	2.50	5.00	10.00
FANTASY					
❏ 3-21 [10]	Paul Desmond	1955	25.00	50.00	100.00
❏ OJC-119	Paul Desmond Quartet Featuring Don Elliott	198?	2.50	5.00	10.00
—Reissue of Fantasy 3235					
❏ 3235 [M]	Paul Desmond Quartet Featuring Don Elliott	1956	20.00	40.00	80.00
—Red vinyl					
❏ 3235 [M]	Paul Desmond Quartet Featuring Don Elliott	1957	10.00	20.00	40.00
—Black vinyl, red label, non-flexible vinyl					
❏ 3235 [M]	Paul Desmond Quartet Featuring Don Elliott	1962	5.00	10.00	20.00
—Black vinyl, red label, flexible vinyl					
FINESSE					
❏ FW 37487	Paul Desmond and the Modern Jazz Quartet	1981	2.50	5.00	10.00
HORIZON					
❏ 850 [(2)]	Paul Desmond Live	1976	3.75	7.50	15.00
MOSAIC					
❏ MR6-120 [(6)]	The Complete Recordings of the Paul Desmond				
	Quartet with Jim Hall	199?	75.00	150.00	300.00
RCA CAMDEN					
❏ ACL1-0201	Samba de Orfeo	1973	2.50	5.00	10.00
RCA VICTOR					
❏ LPM-2438 [M]	Desmond Blue	1961	7.50	15.00	30.00
❏ LSP-2438 [S]	Desmond Blue	1961	7.50	15.00	30.00
❏ LPM-2569 [M]	Take Ten	1962	6.25	12.50	25.00
❏ LSP-2569 [S]	Take Ten	1962	7.50	15.00	30.00
❏ LPM-2654 [M]	Two of a Mind	1963	6.25	12.50	25.00
❏ LSP-2654 [S]	Two of a Mind	1963	7.50	15.00	30.00
❏ ANL1-2807	Pure Gold	1978	2.50	5.00	10.00
❏ LPM-3320 [M]	Boss Antigua	1965	5.00	10.00	20.00
❏ LSP-3320 [S]	Boss Antigua	1965	6.25	12.50	25.00
❏ LPM-3407 [M]	Glad to Be Unhappy	1965	5.00	10.00	20.00
❏ LSP-3407 [S]	Glad to Be Unhappy	1965	6.25	12.50	25.00
❏ LPM-3480 [M]	Easy Living	1965	5.00	10.00	20.00
❏ LSP-3480 [S]	Easy Living	1965	6.25	12.50	25.00
WARNER BROS.					
❏ W 1356 [M]	First Place Again	1960	7.50	15.00	30.00
❏ WS 1356 [S]	First Place Again	1960	7.50	15.00	30.00

DETERGENTS, THE
Also see RON DANTE.
45s

Number	Title (A Side/B Side)	Yr	VG	VG+	NM
KAPP					
❏ 735	I Can Never Eat Home Anymore/Igor's Cellar	1966	3.75	7.50	15.00
❏ 753	Pushin' the Panic Button/Some Sunday Morning	1966	3.75	7.50	15.00
ROULETTE					
❏ 4590	Leader of the Laundromat/Ulcers	1964	5.00	10.00	20.00
❏ 4590 [PS]	Leader of the Laundromat/Ulcers	1964	10.00	20.00	40.00
❏ 4603	Double-O-Seven/The Blue Kangaroo	1965	3.75	7.50	15.00
❏ 4616	Tea and Trumpets/Mrs. Jones (How "Bout It)	1965	3.75	7.50	15.00
❏ 4626	Little Dum-Dum/Soldier Girl	1965	3.75	7.50	15.00
❏ 4642	Bad Girl/Here She Comes	1965	3.75	7.50	15.00
Albums					
ROULETTE					
❏ R 25308 [M]	The Many Faces of the Detergents	1965	30.00	60.00	120.00
❏ SR 25308 [R]	The Many Faces of the Detergents	1965	25.00	50.00	100.00

DETOURS, THE
45s

Number	Title (A Side/B Side)	Yr	VG	VG+	NM
ATCO					
❏ 6448	Who Do You Love/Peace of Mind	1966	6.25	12.50	25.00
MCSHERRY					
❏ 1285	Bring Back My Beatles to Me/Money	1964	6.25	12.50	25.00
❏ 1285	Bring Back My Beatles/Money	1964	6.25	12.50	25.00

Number	Title (A Side/B Side)	Yr	VG	VG+	NM

DETROIT Mitch Ryder's post-Detroit Wheels band.
45s
PARAMOUNT
☐ 0094	It Ain't Easy/Long Neck Goose	1971	—	3.00	6.00
☐ 0133	Rock 'N Roll/Box of Old Roses	1971	—	3.00	6.00
☐ 0158	Gimmie Shelter/Oh Oh La La La Dee Da Doo	1972	—	3.00	6.00
Albums
PARAMOUNT
| ☐ PAS-6010 | Detroit | 1971 | 3.75 | 7.50 | 15.00 |

DETROIT CITY LIMITS, THE
45s
OKEH
| ☐ 7308 | 98c + Tax/Honey Chile | 1968 | 2.00 | 4.00 | 8.00 |
Albums
OKEH
| ☐ OKS 14127 | 98c + Tax | 1968 | 7.50 | 15.00 | 30.00 |

DETROIT EMERALDS
45s
RIC TIC
☐ 135	Show Time/(Instrumental)	1968	3.00	6.00	12.00
☐ 138	Shades Down/Ode to Billie Joe	1968	3.00	6.00	12.00
☐ 141	Take Me the Way I Am/I'll Keep On Coming Back	1968	3.00	6.00	12.00
WESTBOUND
☐ 147	Holding On/Things Are Looking Up	1969	2.00	4.00	8.00
☐ 156	If I Lose Your Love/I Bet You Get the One	1969	2.00	4.00	8.00
☐ 161	I Can't See Myself Doing Without You/ Just Now and Then	1970	2.00	4.00	8.00
☐ 172	Do Me Right/Just Now and Then	1970	2.00	4.00	8.00
☐ 181	Wear This Ring (With Love)/ Bet You Got the One Who Loves You	1971	—	3.00	6.00
☐ 192	You Want It, You Got It/ Till You Decide to Come Home	1971	—	3.00	6.00
☐ 203	Baby Let Me Take You (In My Arms)/I'll Never Sail the Sea Again	1972	—	3.00	6.00
☐ 209	Feel the Need in Me/ There's a Love for Me Somewhere	1972	—	3.00	6.00
☐ 213	You're Gettin' a Little Too Smart/Heaven Couldn't Be Like This	1973	—	3.00	6.00
☐ 220	Lee/Whatcha Gonna Wear Tomorrow	1973	—	3.00	6.00
☐ 226	I'm Qualified/Set It Out	1974	—	3.00	6.00
☐ 5005	Yes I Know I'm in Love/Rosetta Stone	1974	—	3.00	6.00
☐ 55401	Feel the Need/Love Has Come to Me	1977	—	2.50	5.00
☐ 55404	Set It Out (Part 1)/Set It Out (Part 2)	1977	—	2.50	5.00
☐ 55410	Turn On Lady/ Just Don't Know About This Girl of Mine	1977	—	2.50	5.00
Albums
WESTBOUND
☐ 302	Feel the Need	1977	3.75	7.50	15.00
☐ 2006	Do Me Right	1971	10.00	20.00	40.00
☐ 2013	You Want It, You Got It	1972	10.00	20.00	40.00
☐ 2018	I'm in Love with You	1973	10.00	20.00	40.00
☐ 6101	Let's Get Together	1978	3.75	7.50	15.00

DETROIT WHEELS, THE Mitch Ryder's band after he went solo.
45s
INFERNO
| ☐ 5002 | Linda Sue Dixon/Tally Ho | 1968 | 5.00 | 10.00 | 20.00 |
| ☐ 5003 | Think (Part 1)/Think (Part 2) | 1968 | 5.00 | 10.00 | 20.00 |

DEUCE COUPES, THE May be two different groups.
Albums
CROWN
| ☐ CST-393 [S] | The Shut Downs | 1963 | 6.25 | 12.50 | 25.00 |
| ☐ CLP-5393 [M] | The Shut Downs | 1963 | 5.00 | 10.00 | 20.00 |
DEL-FI
| ☐ DFLP-1243 [M] | Hotrodder's Choice | 1963 | 12.50 | 25.00 | 50.00 |
| ☐ DFST-1243 [S] | Hotrodder's Choice | 1963 | 15.00 | 30.00 | 60.00 |

DEUCES OF RHYTHM AND THE TEMPO TOPPERS, THE Also see LITTLE RICHARD.
45s
PEACOCK
| ☐ 1616 | Ain't That Good News/A Fool at the Wheel | 1953 | 20.00 | 40.00 | 80.00 |
| ☐ 1628 | Always/Rice, Red Beans and Turnip Greens | 1954 | 20.00 | 40.00 | 80.00 |

DEVAUGHN, WILLIAM
45s
ROXBURY
☐ BRBO-0236	Be Thankful for What You Got-Pt. 1/Be Thankful for What You Got-Pt. 2	1974	—	2.50	5.00
☐ 2001	Blood Is Thicker Than Water/Blood Is Thicker Than Water (Part 2)	1974	—	2.50	5.00
☐ 2005	Give the Little Man a Great Big Hand/Something Being Done	1974	—	2.50	5.00
☐ 2018	Kiss and Make Up/(B-side unknown)	1975	—	2.50	5.00
TEC
☐ 767	Figures Can't Calculate/(B-side unknown)	1980	—	2.00	4.00
Albums
ROXBURY
| ☐ RLX-100 | Be Thankful For What You Got | 1974 | 3.00 | 6.00 | 12.00 |

DEVAURS, THE
45s
D-TONE
| ☐ 3 | Baby Doll/Teenager | 1958 | 62.50 | 125.00 | 250.00 |
MOON
| ☐ 105 | Where Are You/Boy in Mexico | 1959 | 50.00 | 100.00 | 200.00 |
RED FOX
| ☐ 104 | Where Are You/Boy in Mexico | 1965 | 10.00 | 20.00 | 40.00 |

DEVIANTS, THE
Albums
SIRE
☐ SES-97001	Ptoof!	1968	15.00	30.00	60.00
☐ SES-97005	Disposable	1969	15.00	30.00	60.00
☐ SES-97016	No. 3	1969	15.00	30.00	60.00

DEVIL'S ANVIL, THE
Albums
COLUMBIA
| ☐ CL 2664 [M] | Hard Rock from the Middle East | 1967 | 6.25 | 12.50 | 25.00 |
| ☐ CS 9464 [S] | Hard Rock from the Middle East | 1967 | 7.50 | 15.00 | 30.00 |

DEVILED HAM
Albums
SUPER K
| ☐ SKS-6003 | I Had Too Much to Dream Last Night | 1968 | 6.25 | 12.50 | 25.00 |

DEVOL, FRANK
45s
ABC-PARAMOUNT
| ☐ 10608 | Theme from "Peyton Place"/ Hush, Hush, Sweet Charlotte | 1964 | 2.00 | 4.00 | 8.00 |
| ☐ 10628 | Combat/General Hospital | 1965 | 2.50 | 5.00 | 10.00 |
CAPITOL
☐ F835	Sing a Happy Song/Lady Play Your Mandolin	1950	3.75	7.50	15.00
☐ F1143	Dream a While/Powder and Paint	1950	3.75	7.50	15.00
☐ F1178	Love Letters in the Sand/This Year's Kisses	1950	3.75	7.50	15.00
☐ F1247	Jing-a-Ling/Sweethearts on Parade	1950	3.75	7.50	15.00
☐ F1297	One Finger Melody/You Can Marry Me	1950	3.75	7.50	15.00
☐ F1340	Teardrops/It's a Lonely Town	1950	3.75	7.50	15.00
☐ F1359	Lullaby of Broadway/Seven Wonders of the World	1951	3.00	6.00	12.00
☐ F1411	Ciribiribin on Mandolin/Chapel of Roses	1951	3.00	6.00	12.00
☐ F1460	Theme John & Marsha/Playball	1951	3.00	6.00	12.00
☐ F1503	Dear John/Lonely Acres	1951	3.00	6.00	12.00
☐ F1560	Hopalong Cassidy March/Circus Days	1951	3.00	6.00	12.00
☐ F3457	Toy Tiger/Three Fishermen	1956	2.50	5.00	10.00
COLGEMS
☐ 66-1015	Guess Who's Coming to Dinner/ The Glory of Love	1968	—	3.00	6.00
☐ 66-1015 [PS]	Guess Who's Coming to Dinner/ The Glory of Love	1968	5.00	10.00	20.00
COLUMBIA
☐ 40953	Love in the Afternoon/Venice	1957	2.50	5.00	10.00
☐ 41285	My Heart's in Portugal/How Can You Forget	1958	2.00	4.00	8.00
☐ 41366	House on Haunted Hill/Hadies	1959	2.00	4.00	8.00
☐ 41620	La Montana (If She Should Come to You)/ "The Key" Theme	1960	2.00	4.00	8.00
☐ 41620 [PS]	La Montana (If She Should Come to You)/ "The Key" Theme	1960	3.75	7.50	15.00
☐ 41702	Do You Think of Me/Same Old Summer	1960	2.00	4.00	8.00
☐ 41724	Same Old Summer/Do You Think of Me	1960	2.00	4.00	8.00
☐ 41987	David's Dream/Columbia	1961	2.00	4.00	8.00
☐ 42620	Whatever Happened to Baby Jane/I've Written a Letter to Daddy	1962	2.00	4.00	8.00
Albums
ABC-PARAMOUNT
☐ 513 [M]	Theme from "Peyton Place" and 11 Other Great Themes	1965	3.00	6.00	12.00
☐ S-513 [S]	Theme from "Peyton Place" and 11 Other Great Themes	1965	3.75	7.50	15.00
☐ 534 [M]	Italian Romance American Style	1966	3.00	6.00	12.00
☐ S-534 [S]	Italian Romance American Style	1966	3.75	7.50	15.00
COLUMBIA
☐ CS (# unk) [S]	Four Seasons of Love	1960	5.00	10.00	20.00
☐ C2L 12 [(2)M]	The Columbia Album of Irving Berlin	1958	7.50	15.00	30.00
☐ C2S 812 [(2)S]	The Columbia Album of Irving Berlin	1958	10.00	20.00	40.00
☐ CL 1108 [M]	Portraits	1957	3.75	7.50	15.00
☐ CL 1260 [M]	The Columbia Album of Irving Berlin, Volume 1	1958	3.75	7.50	15.00
☐ CL 1261 [M]	The Columbia Album of Irving Berlin, Volume 2	1958	3.75	7.50	15.00
☐ CL 1371 [M]	Fabulous Hollywood	1959	3.75	7.50	15.00
☐ CL 1413 [M]	The Old Sweet Songs	1960	3.75	7.50	15.00
☐ CL 1451 [M]	Four Seasons of Love	1960	3.75	7.50	15.00
☐ CL 1482 [M]	More Old Sweet Songs	1960	3.75	7.50	15.00
☐ CL 1543 [M]	The Old Sweet Songs of Christmas	1960	3.75	7.50	15.00
☐ CS 8044 [S]	The Columbia Album of Irving Berlin, Volume 1	1958	5.00	10.00	20.00
☐ CS 8045 [S]	The Columbia Album of Irving Berlin, Volume 2	1958	5.00	10.00	20.00
☐ CS 8172 [S]	Fabulous Hollywood	1959	5.00	10.00	20.00
☐ CS 8209 [S]	The Old Sweet Songs	1960	5.00	10.00	20.00
☐ CS 8273 [S]	More Old Sweet Songs	1960	5.00	10.00	20.00
☐ CS 8343 [S]	The Old Sweet Songs of Christmas	1960	3.75	7.50	15.00
COLUMBIA SPECIAL PRODUCTS
☐ EN2 16437 [(2)]	The Columbia Album of Irving Berlin	1983	3.00	6.00	12.00
HARMONY
☐ HL 7356 [M]	The Old Sweet Songs of Christmas	196?	3.00	6.00	12.00
☐ HS 11156 [S]	The Old Sweet Songs of Christmas	196?	3.75	7.50	15.00

DEVONS, THE (1)
45s
DECCA
☐ 31777	Honda Bike/Free Fall	1965	20.00	40.00	80.00
☐ 31822	Are You Really Real/It's All Over Now, Baby Blue	1965	10.00	20.00	40.00
☐ 31899	Come On/A Little Extra Effort	1966	10.00	20.00	40.00

DEVONS, THE (2) Also recorded as SIR DOUGLAS QUINTET.
45s
PIC ONE
| ☐ 111 | Wine, Wine, Wine/Joey's Guitar | 1965 | 20.00 | 40.00 | 80.00 |

DEVORZON, BARRY Also see BARRY AND THE TAMERLANES; BARRY DeVORZON AND PERRY BOTKIN, JR.
45s
A&M
| ☐ 2129 | Theme from "The Warriors"/ Baseball Furies' Chase | 1979 | — | 2.00 | 4.00 |
COLUMBIA
☐ 41464	Betty, Betty/Across the Street from Your House	1959	7.50	15.00	30.00
☐ 41612	Hey Little Darlin'/Rosemary	1960	6.25	12.50	25.00
☐ 41663	Love You Baby/Can-Can Ladies	1960	6.25	12.50	25.00
☐ 42031	Penny Moved Away/Lindy Lou	1961	6.25	12.50	25.00
☐ 3-42031	Penny Moved Away/Lindy Lou	1961	10.00	20.00	40.00
—"Compact 33" single with small hole

D

Number	Title (A Side/B Side)	Yr	VG	VG+	NM
RCA VICTOR					
❏ 47-7124	Barbara Jean/Baby Doll	1957	7.50	15.00	30.00
❏ 47-7226	False Love/Raindrops at My Window	1958	7.50	15.00	30.00
❏ 47-7406	Honey Bunny/Too Soon	1958	7.50	15.00	30.00
❏ 47-7510	Cora Lee/Blue, Green and Gold	1959	7.50	15.00	30.00
Albums					
ARISTA					
❏ AL 4104	Nadia's Theme	1976	2.50	5.00	10.00

DEVORZON, BARRY, AND PERRY BOTKIN, JR. Also see each artist's individual listings.
45s
A&M

Number	Title (A Side/B Side)	Yr	VG	VG+	NM
❏ 1856	Nadia's Theme (The Young and the Restless)/ Down the Line	1976	—	2.00	4.00
—Reissue; the original is listed under PERRY BOTKIN, JR.					
❏ 1856 [PS]	Nadia's Theme (The Young and the Restless)/ Down the Line	1976	—	2.00	4.00
—Green sleeve					
❏ 1856 [PS]	Nadia's Theme (The Young and the Restless)/ Down the Line	1976	—	3.00	6.00
—Black sleeve					
❏ 1856 [PS]	Nadia's Theme (The Young and the Restless)/ Down the Line	1976	—	3.00	6.00
—Blue sleeve					
❏ 1890	Bless the Beasts and Children/Down the Line	1976	—	2.00	4.00

DEVOTIONS, THE
45s
DELTA

Number	Title (A Side/B Side)	Yr	VG	VG+	NM
❏ 1001	Rip Van Winkle/ I Love You for Sentimental Reasons	1961	37.50	75.00	150.00
KAPE					
❏ 701	(How Do You Speak) To An Angel/ Teardrops Follow Me	1966	3.00	6.00	12.00
ROULETTE					
❏ 4406	Rip Van Winkle/ I Love You for Sentimental Reasons	1962	10.00	20.00	40.00
❏ 4541	Rip Van Winkle/ I Love You for Sentimental Reasons	1964	5.00	10.00	20.00
❏ 4556	A Sunday Kind of Love/ Tears from a Broken Heart	1964	7.50	5.00	30.00
❏ 4580	Snow White/Zindy Lou	1964	7.50	5.00	30.00

DEWEY, GEORGE AND JACK
45s
RAVEN

Number	Title (A Side/B Side)	Yr	VG	VG+	NM
❏ 700	The Flying Saucers Have Landed/The Flying Saucers Have Landed (Part 2)	195?	7.50	15.00	30.00

DEWITT, GEORGE
Albums
EPIC

Number	Title (A Side/B Side)	Yr	VG	VG+	NM
❏ BN 531 [S]	George DeWitt Sings That Tune	1959	7.50	15.00	30.00
❏ LN 3562 [M]	George DeWitt Sings That Tune	1959	5.00	10.00	20.00

DEXTER, LARRY
45s
HIT

Number	Title (A Side/B Side)	Yr	VG	VG+	NM
❏ 52	Ruby Baby/You're the Reason I'm Living	1963	2.00	4.00	8.00
—B-side by Rett Hardin					

DEY, TRACEY Also see DEY AND KNIGHT.
45s
AMY

Number	Title (A Side/B Side)	Yr	VG	VG+	NM
❏ 894	Teddy's the Boy I Love/Here Comes the Boy	1963	3.75	7.50	15.00
❏ 901	Gonna Get Along Without You Now/Go Away	1964	3.75	7.50	15.00
❏ 908	Hangin' On to My Baby/Ska-Doo-Dee-Yah	1964	3.75	7.50	15.00
❏ 912	I Won't Tell/Any Kind of Love	1964	3.75	7.50	15.00
❏ 917	Blue Turns to Grey/Didn't Ya	1964	5.00	10.00	20.00
❏ 928	Hanky Panky/Shakin' the Blues Away	1965	3.75	7.50	15.00
LIBERTY					
❏ 55604	Teenage Cleopatra/Who's That	1963	3.75	7.50	15.00
VEE JAY					
❏ 467	Jerry (I'm Your Sherry)/Once in a Blue Moon	1962	6.25	12.50	25.00
❏ 506	Jealous Eyes/Long Time, No See	1963	5.00	10.00	20.00

DEY AND KNIGHT Also see TRACEY DEY.
45s
COLUMBIA

Number	Title (A Side/B Side)	Yr	VG	VG+	NM
❏ 43466	Young Love/I'm Gonna Love You Tomorrow	1965	3.00	6.00	12.00
❏ 43693	Sayin' Somethin'/Ooh Da La Da Lay	1966	3.00	6.00	12.00

DEYOUNG, CLIFF Also see CLEAR LIGHT.
45s
MCA

Number	Title (A Side/B Side)	Yr	VG	VG+	NM
❏ 40156	My Sweet Lady/Sunshine on My Shoulders	1973	—	2.00	4.00
❏ 40156 [PS]	My Sweet Lady/Sunshine on My Shoulders	1973	—	2.50	5.00
❏ 40239	Escaping Reality/She Bent Me Straight Again	1974	—	2.00	4.00
❏ 40294	It Hurts a Little Even Now/Lives	1974	—	2.00	4.00
❏ 40388	If I Could Put You in My Song/ You Will Never Know	1975	—	2.00	4.00
Albums					
MCA					
❏ 387	Sunshine	1973	3.75	7.50	15.00
❏ 432	Cliff DeYoung	1974	2.50	5.00	10.00

DIABLITO
45s
PARKWAY

Number	Title (A Side/B Side)	Yr	VG	VG+	NM
❏ 850	The Jungle/Merengue Potatoes	1962	3.00	6.00	12.00

DIABLOS, THE (1) See NOLAN STRONG AND THE DIABLOS.

DIABLOS, THE (2)
45s
JUBILEE

Number	Title (A Side/B Side)	Yr	VG	VG+	NM
❏ 5553	Hombre/El Bandito	1966	5.00	10.00	20.00

DIABLOS, THE (3)
45s
PYRAMID

Number	Title (A Side/B Side)	Yr	VG	VG+	NM
❏ 159	White Christmas/Danny Boy	19??	5.00	10.00	20.00

DIALOGUE
Albums
COLD

Number	Title (A Side/B Side)	Yr	VG	VG+	NM
❏ (no #)	Dialogue	1968	25.00	50.00	100.00
—Orange cover with insert					
❏ (no #)	Dialogue	1968	75.00	150.00	300.00
—White cover with insert					

DIALS, THE
45s
HILLTOP

Number	Title (A Side/B Side)	Yr	VG	VG+	NM
❏ 219	No Hard Feelings/Win Yourself a Lover	1961	12.50	25.00	50.00
❏ 2009	Wondering About Your Love/Sorrento	1960	37.50	75.00	150.00
❏ 2010	School Bells Are Ringing/Ring Ting-a-Ling	1960	75.00	150.00	300.00
NORGOLDE					
❏ 105	Ring Ting-a Ling/All Kinds of Twistin'	1961	20.00	40.00	80.00
PHILIPS					
❏ 40040	These Foolish Things/At the Start of a New Romance	1962	10.00	20.00	40.00
TIME					
❏ 1068	Monkey Dance/Monkey Walk	1963	5.00	10.00	20.00
Albums					
TIME					
❏ S-2100 [S]	It's Monkey Time	1964	7.50	15.00	30.00
❏ 52100 [M]	It's Monkey Time	1964	6.25	12.50	25.00

DIALTONES, THE (1)
45s
DIAL

Number	Title (A Side/B Side)	Yr	VG	VG+	NM
❏ 4054	Don't Let the Sun Shine on Me/You Don't Know, You Just Don't Know	1967	5.00	10.00	20.00

DIALTONES, THE (2)
45s
GOLDISC

Number	Title (A Side/B Side)	Yr	VG	VG+	NM
❏ 3005	Till I Heard It from You/Johnny	1960	7.50	15.00	30.00
❏ 3020	Till I Heard It from You/Johnny	1961	5.00	10.00	20.00

DIALTONES, THE (U) Probably neither (1) nor (2), but we're not sure.
45s
LAWN

Number	Title (A Side/B Side)	Yr	VG	VG+	NM
❏ 203	So Young/Chicago Bird	1963	6.25	12.50	25.00

DIAMOND, BRIAN, AND THE CUTTERS
45s
HICKORY

Number	Title (A Side/B Side)	Yr	VG	VG+	NM
❏ 1321	Big Bad Wolf/See If I Care	1965	2.50	5.00	10.00

DIAMOND, LARRY
45s
ARGO

Number	Title (A Side/B Side)	Yr	VG	VG+	NM
❏ 5330	Bye Bye Doll/True Love, Come My Way	1959	3.00	6.00	12.00

DIAMOND, LEO
45s
AMBASSADOR

Number	Title (A Side/B Side)	Yr	VG	VG+	NM
❏ 1004	Easy Melody/Off Shore	1953	3.75	7.50	15.00
❏ 1006	On the Mall/Sadie Thompson's Song	195?	3.75	7.50	15.00
RCA VICTOR					
❏ 47-5765	China Nights/Hold On to Your Dreams	1954	3.00	6.00	12.00
❏ 47-5834	The High and the Mighty/Lisbon	1954	3.00	6.00	12.00
❏ 47-5973	Melody of Love/Phantom Gaucho	1955	3.00	6.00	12.00
❏ 47-6090	The One Rose/Land of the Pharaohs	1955	3.00	6.00	12.00
❏ 47-6194	Theme from "Female on the Beach"/Destiny	1955	3.00	6.00	12.00
❏ 47-6307	Mister X/Fantasia Mexicana	1955	3.00	6.00	12.00
❏ 47-6406	Lisbon Antigua/Music Box Tango	1956	3.00	6.00	12.00
❏ 47-6513	Polynesian/Du Bist Schoen Wie Musik	1956	3.00	6.00	12.00
❏ 47-6600	Go See Tony/Le Refifi	1956	3.00	6.00	12.00
❏ 47-6710	Sixth Finger Tune/I Remember When	1956	3.00	6.00	12.00
REPRISE					
❏ 20004	Bridge of Sighs/Choo Choo to Chihuahua	1961	—	—	—
—Canceled					
❏ 20016	Sweet and Lovely/Dream of Olwen	1961	2.00	4.00	8.00
❏ 20036	The 400 Blows/La Dolce Vita	1961	2.00	4.00	8.00
❏ 20074	Harbor Lights/Theme for a New Love	1962	2.00	4.00	8.00
❏ 20126	Born to Be With You/Miramor	1962	2.00	4.00	8.00
ROULETTE					
❏ 4025	Till/Sunrise in Texas	1957	2.50	5.00	10.00
❏ 4047	Flunky/Te Amo	1957	2.50	5.00	10.00
Albums					
ABC-PARAMOUNT					
❏ ABC-303 [M]	Subliminal Sounds	1960	7.50	15.00	30.00
❏ ABCS-303 [S]	Subliminal Sounds	1960	10.00	20.00	40.00
RCA VICTOR					
❏ LPM-1165 [M]	Skin Diver Suite and Other Selections	1955	15.00	30.00	60.00
REPRISE					
❏ R-6002 [M]	Exciting Sounds of the South Seas	1961	6.25	12.50	25.00
❏ R9-6002 [S]	Exciting Sounds of the South Seas	1961	7.50	15.00	30.00
❏ R-6009 [M]	Themes from Great Foreign Films	1961	6.25	12.50	25.00
❏ R9-6009 [S]	Themes from Great Foreign Films	1961	7.50	15.00	30.00
❏ R-6024 [M]	Off Shore	1962	6.25	12.50	25.00
❏ R9-6024 [S]	Off Shore	1962	7.50	15.00	30.00

DIAMOND, NEIL Also see BARBRA AND NEIL; NEIL AND JACK; TEN BROKEN HEARTS.
12-Inch Singles
CONTINUUM II

Number	Title (A Side/B Side)	Yr	VG	VG+	NM
❏ 001	We Wrote a Song Together/Beautiful Noise	1976	500.00	1000.	2000.
—Private pressing done for the grade school class of Jesse Diamond, Neil's son. All were autographed by Neil; the version of "Beautiful Noise" is an alternate take. Supposedly, between 30 and 40 copies were made.					

Number	Title (A Side/B Side)	Yr	VG	VG+	NM
45s					
BANG					
❏ 105	Cherry, Cherry/Girl, You'll Be a Woman Soon	1973	—	2.00	4.00
—Reissue					
❏ 108	Solitary Man/I'm a Believer	1973	—	2.00	4.00
—Reissue					
❏ 519	Solitary Man/Do It	1966	3.75	7.50	15.00
❏ 528	Cherry, Cherry/I'll Come Running	1966	3.00	6.00	12.00
❏ 536	I Got the Feelin' (Oh No No)/The Boat That I Row	1966	3.00	6.00	12.00
❏ 540	You Got to Me/Someday Baby	1967	3.00	6.00	12.00
❏ 542	Girl, You'll Be a Woman Soon/You'll Forget	1967	3.00	6.00	12.00
❏ 547	Thank the Lord for the Night Time/The Long Way Home	1967	2.50		10.00
—Title altered on second pressing					
❏ 547	I Thank the Lord for the Night Time/The Long Way Home	1967	3.75	7.50	15.00
❏ 551	Kentucky Woman/The Time Is Now	1967	2.50	5.00	10.00
❏ 554	New Orleans/Hanky Panky	1968	2.50	5.00	10.00
❏ 556	Red Red Wine/Red Rubber Ball	1968	2.00	4.00	8.00
❏ 561	Shilo/La Bamba	1968	2.00	4.00	8.00
❏ 575	Shilo/La Bamba	1970	—	3.00	6.00
❏ 578	Solitary Man/The Time Is Now	1970	—	3.00	6.00
❏ 580	Do It/Hanky Panky	1970	—	3.00	6.00
❏ 586	I'm a Believer/Crooked Street	1971	—	3.00	6.00
❏ 586	I'm a Believer/Crooked Street	1971	3.75	7.50	15.00
—Rare pressing with both sides in stereo					
❏ 703	The Long Way Home/Monday, Monday	1973	—	2.50	5.00
CAPITOL					
❏ 4939	Love on the Rocks/Acapulco	1980	—	2.00	4.00
❏ 4939 [PS]	Love on the Rocks/Acapulco	1980	—	2.00	4.00
❏ 4960	Hello Again/Amazed and Confused	1981	—	2.00	4.00
❏ 4960 [PS]	Hello Again/Amazed and Confused	1981	—	2.00	4.00
❏ 4994	America/Songs of Life	1981	—	2.00	4.00
❏ 4994 [PS]	America/Songs of Life	1981	—	2.00	4.00
COLUMBIA					
❏ AE7 1115 [DJ]	Song Sung Blue (mono/stereo)	1977	2.50	5.00	10.00
—Live version from "Love at the Greek"					
❏ 18-02604	Yesterday's Songs/Guitar Heaven	1981	—	—	3.00
❏ 18-02604 [PS]	Yesterday's Songs/Guitar Heaven	1981	—	—	3.00
❏ 18-02712	On the Way to the Sky/Save Me	1982	—	—	3.00
❏ 18-02712 [PS]	On the Way to the Sky/Save Me	1982	—	—	3.00
❏ 18-02928	Be Mine Tonight/Right By You	1982	—	—	3.00
❏ 38-03219	Heartlight/You Don't Know Me	1982	—	—	3.00
❏ 38-03219 [PS]	Heartlight/You Don't Know Me	1982	—	2.00	4.00
❏ CNR-03345	Heartlight/(B-side blank)	1982	—	3.00	6.00
—One-sided budget release					
❏ 38-03503	I'm Alive/Lost Among the Stars	1983	—	—	3.00
❏ CNR-03572	I'm Alive/(B-side blank)	1983	—	3.00	6.00
—One-sided budget release					
❏ 38-03801	Front Page Story/I'm Guilty	1983	—	—	3.00
❏ 38-03801 [PS]	Front Page Story/I'm Guilty	1983	—	—	3.00
❏ 38-04541	Turn Around/Brooklyn on a Saturday Night	1984	—	—	3.00
❏ 38-04541 [PS]	Turn Around/Brooklyn on a Saturday Night	1984	—	—	3.00
❏ 38-04646	Sleep with Me Tonight/One by One	1984	—	2.00	4.00
❏ 38-04719	You Make It Feel Like Christmas/Crazy	1984	—	3.00	6.00
❏ 38-05889	Headed for the Future/Angel	1986	—	—	3.00
❏ 38-05889 [PS]	Headed for the Future/Angel	1986	—	—	3.00
❏ 38-06136	The Story of My Life/Love Doesn't Live Here Anymore	1986			3.00
❏ 38-06136 [PS]	The Story of My Life/Love Doesn't Live Here Anymore	1986			3.00
❏ 38-07614	I Dreamed a Dream/Sweet Caroline	1987	—	—	3.00
❏ 38-07614 [PS]	I Dreamed a Dream/Sweet Caroline	1987	—	—	3.00
❏ 38-07751	Cherry, Cherry/America	1988	—	2.00	4.00
❏ 38-08514	This Time/If I Couldn't See You Again	1988	—	2.00	4.00
❏ 10043	Longfellow Serenade/Rosemary's Wine	1974	—	2.50	5.00
❏ 10084	I've Been This Way Before/Reggae Strut	1975	—	2.50	5.00
❏ 10138	The Last Picasso/The Gift of Song	1975	—	2.50	5.00
❏ 3-10366	If You Know What I Mean/Street Life	1976	—	2.50	5.00
❏ 3-10405	Don't Think...Feel/Home Is a Wounded Heart	1976	—	2.50	5.00
❏ 3-10452	Beautiful Noise/Signs	1976	—	2.50	5.00
❏ 3-10657	Desiree/Once in a While	1977	—	2.50	5.00
❏ 3-10897	Forever in Blue Jeans/Remember Me	1979	—	2.00	4.00
❏ 3-10945	Say Maybe/Diamond Girls	1979	—	2.00	4.00
❏ 1-11175	September Morn/I'm a Believer	1980	—	2.00	4.00
❏ 1-11232	The Good Lord Loves You/Jazz Time	1980	—	2.00	4.00
❏ 42809	Clown Town/At Night	1963	125.00	250.00	500.00
❏ 42809 [DJ]	Clown Town/At Night	1963	62.50	125.00	250.00
❏ 45942	Be/Flight of the Gull	1973	—	2.50	5.00
❏ 45998	Skybird/Lonely Looking Sky	1974	—	2.50	5.00
❏ 38-68741	The Best Years of Our Lives/Carmelita's Eyes	1989	—	2.00	4.00
❏ 38-78242	One Good Love/Kentucky Woman	1996	—	—	3.00
—A-side with Waylon Jennings					
MCA					
❏ 40017	Cherry, Cherry from Hot August Night/Morningside	1973	—	2.50	5.00
❏ 40092	The Last Thing on My Mind/Canta Libra	1973	—	2.50	5.00
PHILCO-FORD					
❏ HP-5	Girl, You'll Be a Woman Soon/Cherry, Cherry	1967	3.75	7.50	15.00
—4-inch plastic "Hip Pocket Record" with color sleeve					
❏ HP-17	Solitary Man/You Got to Me	1967	3.75	7.50	15.00
—4-inch plastic "Hip Pocket Record" with color sleeve					
UNI					
❏ 55065	Brooklyn Roads/Holiday Inn Blues	1968	2.00	4.00	8.00
❏ 55075	Two-Bit Manchild/Broad Old Woman	1968	2.00	4.00	8.00
❏ 55075 [DJ]	Two-Bit Manchild (same on both sides)	1968	20.00	40.00	80.00
—Red vinyl					
❏ 55075 [PS]	Two-Bit Manchild/Broad Old Woman	1968	6.25	12.50	25.00
❏ 55084	Sunday Sun/Honey-Drippin' Times	1968	2.00	4.00	8.00
❏ 55109	Brother Love's Travelling Salvation Show/A Modern-Day Version of Love	1969	—	3.00	6.00
❏ 55136	Sweet Caroline (Good Times Never Seemed So Good)/Dig In	1969	—	3.00	6.00
❏ 55175	Holly Holy/Hurtin' You Don't Come Easy	1969	—	3.00	6.00
❏ 55204	Until It's Time for You to Go/And the Singer Sings His Song	1970	—	3.00	6.00
❏ 55224	Soolaimon (African Trilogy II)/And the Grass Won't Pay No Mind	1970	—	3.00	6.00
❏ 55224 [PS]	Soolaimon (African Trilogy II)/And the Grass Won't Pay No Mind	1970	3.75	7.50	15.00
❏ 55250	Cracklin' Rosie/Lordy	1970	—	3.00	6.00
❏ 55264	He Ain't Heavy...He's My Brother/Free Life	1970	—	3.00	6.00
❏ 55278	I Am...I Said/Done Too Soon	1971	—	2.50	5.00
❏ 55310	Stones/Crunchy Granola Suite	1971	—	2.50	5.00
❏ 55326	Song Sung Blue/Gitchy Goomy	1972	—	2.50	5.00
❏ 55346	Play Me/Porcupine Pie	1972	—	2.50	5.00
❏ 55352	Walk on Water/High Rolling Man	1972	—	2.50	5.00
7-Inch Extended Plays					
UNI					
❏ 34818	Kentucky Woman/Solitary Man/Thank the Lord for the Night Time//Brother Love's Travelling Salvation Show/Sweet Caroline	1970	3.75	7.50	15.00
—Jukebox issue; small hole, plays at 33 1/3 rpm					
❏ 34818 [PS]	Gold	1970	3.75	7.50	15.00
—Part of "Little LP" series (LLP #127)					
❏ 34871	Suzanne/Husbands and Wives//I Am... I Said/Stones/Chelsea Morning	1971	3.75	7.50	15.00
—Jukebox issue; small hole, plays at 33 1/3 rpm					
❏ 34871 [PS]	Stones	1971	3.75	7.50	15.00
—Part of "Little LP" series (LLP #172)					
Albums					
BANG					
❏ BLP 214 [M]	The Feel of Neil Diamond	1966	15.00	30.00	60.00
—All tracks play mono					
❏ BLP 214 [P]	The Feel of Neil Diamond	1966	20.00	40.00	80.00
—Album is labeled mono, but plays in stereo					
❏ BLPS 214 [P]	The Feel of Neil Diamond	1966	25.00	50.00	100.00
—Album is labeled stereo and plays in stereo (except "Solitary Man," "Do It," "I'll Come Running" are rechanneled)					
❏ BLPS 214	The Feel of Neil Diamond	1974	3.00	6.00	12.00
—Later pressing on blue "clouds" label					
❏ BLP 217 [M]	Just for You	1967	10.00	20.00	40.00
—With blurb for "Thank the Lord for the Night Time" on cover					
❏ BLPS 217 [P]	Just for You	1967	12.50	25.00	50.00
—With blurb for "Thank the Lord for the Night Time" on cover					
❏ BLPS 217 [P]	Just for You	1968	10.00	20.00	40.00
—With blurb for "Shilo" pasted over "Thank the Lord for the Night Time" blurb					
❏ BLPS 217 [P]	Just for You	1970	5.00	10.00	20.00
—With blurb for "Shilo" imprinted on cover					
❏ BLPS 217	Just for You	1974	3.00	6.00	12.00
—Later pressing on blue "clouds" label					
❏ BLPS 219 [P]	Neil Diamond's Greatest Hits	196?	5.00	10.00	20.00
—Later editions have an alternate take of "Solitary Man" in true stereo					
❏ BLPS 219 [P]	Neil Diamond's Greatest Hits	1968	10.00	20.00	40.00
—First editions have the single version of "Solitary Man" in rechanneled stereo					
❏ BLPS 219	Neil Diamond's Greatest Hits	1974	3.00	6.00	12.00
—Later pressing on blue "clouds" label					
❏ BLPS 221 [S]	Shilo	1970	10.00	20.00	40.00
❏ BLPS 221	Shilo	1974	3.00	6.00	12.00
—Later pressing on blue "clouds" label					
❏ BLPS 224 [P]	Do It!	1971	7.50	15.00	30.00
❏ BLPS 224	Do It!	1974	3.00	6.00	12.00
—Later pressing on blue "clouds" label					
❏ BLPS 227 [(2)]	Double Gold	1974	3.75	7.50	15.00
—Later pressing on blue "clouds" label					
❏ BLPS-227 [(2)S]	Double Gold	1973	10.00	20.00	40.00
CAPITOL					
❏ SWAV-12120	The Jazz Singer	1980	2.50	5.00	10.00
COLUMBIA					
❏ AS 99-1586 [DJ]	Heartlight	1982	6.25	12.50	25.00
—Promo-only picture disc					
❏ KS 32550	Jonathan Livingston Seagull	1973	3.00	6.00	12.00
—With booklet					
❏ PC 32919	Serenade	1974	3.00	6.00	12.00
❏ PCQ 32919 [Q]	Serenade	1974	6.25	12.50	25.00
❏ PC 33965	Beautiful Noise	1976	3.00	6.00	12.00
—Originals have no bar code					
❏ KC2 34404 [(2)]	Love at the Greek	1977	3.75	7.50	15.00
❏ JC 34990	I'm Glad You're Here with Me Tonight	1977	3.00	6.00	12.00
❏ FC 35625	You Don't Bring Me Flowers	1978	3.00	6.00	12.00
❏ FC 36121	September Morn	1979	3.00	6.00	12.00
❏ TC 37628	On the Way to the Sky	1981	2.50	5.00	10.00
❏ TC 38068	12 Greatest Hits, Vol. II	1982	2.50	5.00	10.00
❏ TC 38359	Heartlight	1982	2.50	5.00	10.00
❏ PC 38792	Classics — The Early Years	1983	2.50	5.00	10.00
—Possibly a reissue of Frog King 1					
❏ QC 39199	Primitive	1984	2.50	5.00	10.00
❏ 9C9 39915 [PD]	Primitive	1984	5.00	10.00	20.00
❏ OC 40368	Headed for the Future	1986	2.00	4.00	8.00
❏ CG2 40990 [(2)]	Hot August Night II	1987	3.00	6.00	12.00
❏ HC 42550	Jonathan Livingston Seagull	1982	12.50	25.00	50.00
—Half-speed mastered edition					
❏ OC 45025	The Best Years of Our Lives	1988	2.00	4.00	8.00
❏ HC 45625	You Don't Bring Me Flowers	1982	10.00	20.00	40.00
—Half-speed mastered edition					
❏ HC 47628	On the Way to the Sky	1982	7.50	15.00	30.00
—Half-speed mastered edition					
❏ HC 48068	12 Greatest Hits, Vol. II	1982	25.00	50.00	100.00
—Half-speed mastered edition					
❏ HC 48359	Heartlight	1982	10.00	20.00	40.00
—Half-speed mastered edition					
❏ C 48610	Lovescape	1991	3.75	7.50	15.00
DIRECT DISK					
❏ SD 16612	His 12 Greatest Hits	1982	12.50	25.00	50.00
—Audiophile vinyl					
FROG KING					
❏ AAR-1	Early Classics	1972	10.00	20.00	40.00
—Compilation of Bang material for Columbia Record Club; includes songbook (deduct 25% if missing)					
MCA					
❏ 1489	Neil Diamond/His 12 Greatest Hits	1987	2.00	4.00	8.00
—Reissue of MCA 5219					

Number	Title (A Side/B Side)	Yr	VG	VG+	NM
❏ 2005	Moods	1973	2.50	5.00	10.00
❏ 2006	Touching You Touching Me	1973	2.50	5.00	10.00
❏ 2007	Neil Diamond/Gold	1973	2.50	5.00	10.00
❏ 2008	Stones	1973	2.50	5.00	10.00
❏ 2011	Sweet Caroline (Brother Love's Travelling Salvation Show)	1973	2.50	5.00	10.00
❏ 2013	Tap Root Manuscript	1973	2.50	5.00	10.00
❏ 2103	Rainbow	1973	3.75	7.50	15.00
—Compilation of Uni tracks					
❏ 2106	Neil Diamond/His 12 Greatest Hits	1974	3.75	7.50	15.00
❏ 2227	And the Singer Sings His Song	1976	3.75	7.50	15.00
❏ 5219	Neil Diamond/His 12 Greatest Hits	1981	2.50	5.00	10.00
—Reissue of MCA 2106					
❏ 5239	Love Songs	1981	2.50	5.00	10.00
❏ 6896 [(2)]	Hot August Night	1980	3.00	6.00	12.00
—Reissue of MCA 2-8000					
❏ 8000 [(2)]	Hot August Night	1972	5.00	10.00	20.00
❏ 37056	Velvet Gloves and Spit	1980	2.00	4.00	8.00
❏ 37057	Sweet Caroline/Brother Love's Travelling Salvation Show	1980	2.00	4.00	8.00
❏ 37058	Touching You Touching Me	1980	2.00	4.00	8.00
❏ 37059	Rainbow	1980	2.00	4.00	8.00
❏ 37060	And the Singer Sings His Song	1980	2.00	4.00	8.00
❏ 37194	Moods	1981	2.00	4.00	8.00
❏ 37195	Stones	1981	2.00	4.00	8.00
❏ 37196	Tap Root Manuscript	1981	2.00	4.00	8.00
❏ 37209	Gold	1981	2.00	4.00	8.00
❏ 37252	Neil Diamond/His 12 Greatest Hits	198?	2.00	4.00	8.00
—Reissue of MCA 5219					
MOBILE FIDELITY					
❏ 2-024 [(2)]	Hot August Night	1979	10.00	20.00	40.00
—Audiophile vinyl					
❏ 1-071	The Jazz Singer	1981	7.50	15.00	30.00
—Audiophile vinyl					
SILVER EAGLE					
❏ MSM-35151 [(3)]	The Neil Diamond Collection	1988	6.25	12.50	25.00
—Mail-order offer; contains material from his Uni period					
UNI					
❏ ND-11 [DJ]	Neil Diamond DJ Sampler	1970	50.00	100.00	200.00
❏ 1913 [DJ]	Open-End Interview with Neil Diamond	1971	75.00	150.00	300.00
❏ 73030	Velvet Gloves and Spit	1968	7.50	15.00	30.00
—First editions do not include "Shilo"					
❏ 73030-N	Velvet Gloves and Spit	1970	5.00	10.00	20.00
—Later editions add a new recording of "Shilo"					
❏ 73047	Brother Love's Travelling Salvation Show	1969	5.00	10.00	20.00
—Later editions add "Sweet Caroline"					
❏ 73047	Brother Love's Travelling Salvation Show	1969	7.50	15.00	30.00
—First editions do not include "Sweet Caroline"					
❏ 73071	Touching You Touching Me	1969	5.00	10.00	20.00
❏ 73084	Neil Diamond/Gold	1970	5.00	10.00	20.00
❏ 73092	Tap Root Manuscript	1970	5.00	10.00	20.00
❏ 93030-N	Velvet Gloves and Spit	1971	3.75	7.50	15.00
—Reissue of the version with "Shilo" added, with new number					
❏ 93047	Brother Love's Travelling Salvation Show	1971	3.75	7.50	15.00
—Reissue of the version with "Sweet Caroline," with new number					
❏ 93071	Touching You Touching Me	1971	3.75	7.50	15.00
—Reissue of 73071					
❏ 93106	Stones	1971	5.00	10.00	20.00
❏ 93136	Moods	1972	5.00	10.00	20.00
❏ ST-93501	Tap Root Manuscript	1970	6.25	12.50	25.00
—Capitol Record Club issue					

DIAMONDS, THE (1)

45s

Number	Title (A Side/B Side)	Yr	VG	VG+	NM
CORAL					
❏ 61502	Black Denim Trousers and Motorcycle Boots/ Nip Sip	1955	5.00	10.00	20.00
❏ 61577	Be My Lovin' Baby/Smooch Me	1956	5.00	10.00	20.00
GUSTO					
❏ 2019	Little Darlin'/The Stroll	1979	—	2.00	4.00
—Re-recordings					
MERCURY					
❏ 70790	Why Do Fools Fall in Love/You Baby You	1956	5.00	10.00	20.00
❏ 70835	The Church Bells May Ring/Little Girl of Mine	1956	5.00	10.00	20.00
❏ 70889	Love, Love, Love/Every Night About This Time	1956	5.00	10.00	20.00
❏ 70934	Ka-Ding-Dong/Soft Summer Breeze	1956	5.00	10.00	20.00
❏ 70983	My Judge and My Jury/Put Your House in Order	1956	5.00	10.00	20.00
❏ 71021	A Thousand Miles Away/Ev'ry Minute of the Day	1956	5.00	10.00	20.00
❏ 71060	Little Darlin'/Faithful and True	1957	10.00	20.00	40.00
—The only "cover version" generally considered a significant improvement over the original (by The Gladiolas)					
❏ 71128	Words of Love/Don't Say Goodbye	1957	5.00	10.00	20.00
❏ 71165	Zip Zip/Oh How I Wish	1957	5.00	10.00	20.00
❏ 71197	Silhouettes/Daddy Cool	1957	5.00	10.00	20.00
❏ 71242	The Stroll/Land of Beauty	1957	7.50	15.00	30.00
❏ 71291	High Sign/Chick-Lets (Don't Let Me Down)	1958	3.75	7.50	15.00
❏ 71291 [PS]	High Sign/Chick-Lets (Don't Let Me Down)	1958	25.00	50.00	100.00
❏ 71330	Kathy-O/Happy Years	1958	3.75	7.50	15.00
❏ 71366	Walking Along/Eternal Lovers	1958	3.75	7.50	15.00
❏ 71404	She Say (Oom Dooby Doom)/ From the Bottom of My Heart	1959	5.00	10.00	20.00
❏ 71449	A Mother's Love/Gretchen	1959	3.75	7.50	15.00
❏ 71468	Sneaky Alligator/Holding Your Hand	1959	3.75	7.50	15.00
❏ 71505	Young in Years/The Twenty-Second Day	1959	3.75	7.50	15.00
❏ 71534	Walking the Stroll/Batman, Wolfman, Frankenstein or Dracula	1959	5.00	10.00	20.00
❏ 71586	Real True Love/Tell the Truth	1960	3.75	7.50	15.00
❏ 71633	The Pencil Song/Slave Girl	1960	3.75	7.50	15.00
❏ 71734	The Crumble/You'd Be Mine	1960	3.75	7.50	15.00
❏ 71782	You Sure Changed Me/I Sure Lawd Will	1961	3.75	7.50	15.00
❏ 71818	The Munch/Woomai Ling	1961	3.75	7.50	15.00
❏ 71831	One Summer Night/It's a Doggone Shame	1961	3.75	7.50	15.00
❏ 71956	The Vanishing American/ The Horizontal Lieutenant	1962	3.75	7.50	15.00

7-Inch Extended Plays

Number	Title (A Side/B Side)	Yr	VG	VG+	NM
BRUNSWICK					
❏ EB 71031	(contents unknown)	1957	37.50	75.00	150.00
❏ EB 71031 [PS]	The Diamonds	1957	37.50	75.00	150.00

Number	Title (A Side/B Side)	Yr	VG	VG+	NM
MERCURY					
❏ EP 1-3356	(contents unknown)	1957	10.00	20.00	40.00
❏ EP 1-3356 [PS]	The Diamonds	1957	10.00	20.00	40.00
❏ EP 1-3357	Honey Bird/For You Alone//Zip Zip/Cool, Cool Baby	1957	10.00	20.00	40.00
❏ EP 1-3357 [PS]	The Diamonds	1957	10.00	20.00	40.00
❏ EP 1-3358	Till My Baby Comes Home/Girl of Mine//One and Only/Honey	1957	10.00	20.00	40.00
❏ EP 1-3358 [PS]	The Diamonds: America's Number One Singing Stylists	1957	10.00	20.00	40.00
❏ EP 1-3367	Silhouettes/Daddy Cool//Passion Flower/Sweet Wild Honey	1957	10.00	20.00	40.00
❏ EP 1-3367 [PS]	The Diamonds	1957	10.00	20.00	40.00
❏ EP 1-3390	(contents unknown)	1958	10.00	20.00	40.00
❏ EP 1-3390 [PS]	The Stroll	1958	10.00	20.00	40.00

Albums

Number	Title (A Side/B Side)	Yr	VG	VG+	NM
MERCURY					
❏ MG-20213 [M]	Collection of Golden Hits	1956	30.00	60.00	120.00
❏ MG-20309 [M]	The Diamonds	1957	30.00	60.00	120.00
❏ MG-20368 [M]	The Diamonds Meet Pete Rugolo	1958	20.00	40.00	80.00
❏ MG-20480 [M]	Songs from the Old West	1959	20.00	40.00	80.00
❏ SR-60076 [S]	The Diamonds Meet Pete Rugolo	1959	30.00	60.00	120.00
❏ SR-60159 [S]	Songs from the Old West	1959	30.00	60.00	120.00
RHINO					
❏ RNDF-209	The Best of the Diamonds	1984	3.00	6.00	12.00
WING					
❏ MGW-12114 [M]	The Diamonds: America's Famous Song Stylists	1959	7.50	15.00	30.00
❏ MGW-12178 [M]	Pop Hits by the Diamonds	1962	7.50	15.00	30.00

DIAMONDS, THE (2) Black vocal group. Also see SONNY WRIGHT (1).

45s

Number	Title (A Side/B Side)	Yr	VG	VG+	NM
ATLANTIC					
❏ 981	A Beggar for Your Kisses/Call, Baby, Call	1952	375.00	750.00	1500.
❏ 1003	I'll Live Again/Two Loves Have I	1953	150.00	300.00	600.00
❏ 1017	Romance in the Dark/Cherry	1954	150.00	300.00	600.00

DIANE AND THE DARLETTES

45s

Number	Title (A Side/B Side)	Yr	VG	VG+	NM
DUNES					
❏ 2016	Just You/The Wobble	1962	6.25	12.50	25.00
❏ 2026	Here She Comes/Just You	1963	3.75	7.50	15.00
—As "The Darlettes"					

DIBANGO, MANU

12-Inch Singles

Number	Title (A Side/B Side)	Yr	VG	VG+	NM
CELLULOID					
❏ CEL 171	Abele Dance/Abele Dance Dub	1984	2.00	4.00	8.00
❏ CEL 182	Makossa Rock (2 versions)/Gammatron	1985	2.00	4.00	8.00
ISLAND					
❏ 8680 [DJ]	Big Blow/Aloko Party	1976	2.00	4.00	8.00

45s

Number	Title (A Side/B Side)	Yr	VG	VG+	NM
ATLANTIC					
❏ 2971	Soul Makossa/Lily	1973	—	2.50	5.00
❏ 2983	Dangwa/Obaso	1973	—	2.50	5.00
❏ 3000	Weya/Moni	1974	—	2.00	4.00
❏ 3263	Super Kimba/Wasa N'Doto	1975	—	2.00	4.00
WARNER BROS.					
❏ 8680	Aloko Party/Big Blow	1978	—	2.00	4.00

Albums

Number	Title (A Side/B Side)	Yr	VG	VG+	NM
ATLANTIC					
❏ SD 7267	Soul Makossa	1973	2.50	5.00	10.00
❏ SD 7276	Makossa Man	1974	2.50	5.00	10.00
ISLAND					
❏ ILPS 9526	Afrovision	1976	3.00	6.00	12.00

DICK AND DEEDEE Also see DICK ST. JOHN.

45s

Number	Title (A Side/B Side)	Yr	VG	VG+	NM
DOT					
❏ 17145	Escape Suite/ I'm Not Gonna Get Hung-Up About It	1968	3.75	7.50	15.00
❏ 17261	We'll Sing in the Sunshine/ In the Season of Our Love	1969	2.50	5.00	10.00
❏ 17305	Do I Love You/You Came Back to Haunt Me	1970	2.50	5.00	10.00
LAMA					
❏ 7778	The Mountain's High/I Want Someone	1961	5.00	10.00	20.00
❏ 7780	Goodbye to Love/Swing Low	1961	4.00	8.00	16.00
❏ 7783	Tell Me/Will You Always Love Me	1961	4.00	8.00	16.00
LIBERTY					
❏ 55350	The Mountain's High/I Want Someone	1961	3.75	7.50	15.00
❏ 55382	Goodbye to Love/Swing Low	1961	3.00	6.00	12.00
❏ 55412	Tell Me/Will You Always Love Me	1962	3.00	6.00	12.00
❏ 55478	All I Want/Life's Just a Play	1962	3.00	6.00	12.00
UNITED ARTISTS					
❏ 0036	The Mountain's High/Tell Me	1973	—	2.50	5.00
—"Silver Spotlight Series" reissue					
WARNER BROS.					
❏ 5320	The River Took My Baby/My Lonely Self	1962	2.50	5.00	10.00
❏ 5320 [PS]	The River Took My Baby/My Lonely Self	1962	6.25	12.50	25.00
❏ 5342	Young and In Love/Say to Me	1963	3.00	6.00	12.00
❏ 5364	Love Is a Once in a Lifetime Thing/ Chug-a Chug-a Choo Choo	1963	2.50	5.00	10.00
❏ 5383	Where Did the Good Times Go/ Guess Our Love Must Show	1963	2.50	5.00	10.00
❏ 5396	Turn Around/Don't Leave Me	1963	2.50	5.00	10.00
❏ 5411	All My Trials/Don't Think Twice, It's All Right	1964	2.50	5.00	10.00
❏ 5426	Not Fade Away/The Gift	1964	2.50	5.00	10.00
❏ 5451	You Were Mine/Remember Then	1964	2.50	5.00	10.00
❏ 5470	The Riddle Song/Without Your Love	1964	2.50	5.00	10.00
❏ 5482	Thou Shalt Not Steal/Just 'Round the River Bend	1964	2.50	5.00	10.00
—Orange label					
❏ 5482	Thou Shalt Not Steal/Just 'Round the River Bend	1964	3.75	7.50	15.00
—Red label with arrows					
❏ 5482 [PS]	Thou Shalt Not Steal/Just 'Round the River Bend	1964	6.25	12.50	25.00
❏ 5608	Be My Baby/Room 404	1965	2.50	5.00	10.00

Number	Title (A Side/B Side)	Yr	VG	VG+	NM
❏ 5627	Blue Turns to Grey/				
	Some Things Just Stick in Your Mind	1965	5.00	10.00	20.00
—Both sides are Mick Jagger-Keith Richards songs produced by Andrew Loog Oldham					
❏ 5652	The World Is Waiting/Vini, Vini	1965	2.50	5.00	10.00
❏ 5671	P.S. 1402 (Your Local Charm School)/				
	Use What You've Got	1965	2.50	5.00	10.00
❏ 5680	New Orleans/Use What You've Got	1965	2.50	5.00	10.00
❏ 5699	Till/Sha-Ta	1966	2.50	5.00	10.00
❏ 5830	She Didn't Even Say Goodbye/				
	So Many Things We Didn't Know	1966	2.50	5.00	10.00
❏ 5860	Make Up Before We Break Up/				
	Can't Get Enough of Your Love	1966	2.50	5.00	10.00
❏ 7017	Long Lonely Nights/I'll Always Be Around	1967	2.50	5.00	10.00
❏ 7069	One in a Million/Baby, I Need You	1967	2.50	5.00	10.00
❏ 7109	Young and In Love/Thou Shalt Not Steal	1968	2.00	4.00	8.00
—"Back to Back Hits" series; originals have green labels with "W7" logo					
Albums					
LIBERTY					
❏ LRP-3236 [M]	Tell Me/The Mountain's High	1962	12.50	25.00	50.00
❏ LST-7236 [R]	Tell Me/The Mountain's High	1962	10.00	20.00	40.00
WARNER BROS.					
❏ W 1500 [M]	Young and In Love	1963	6.25	12.50	25.00
❏ WS 1500 [S]	Young and In Love	1963	7.50	15.00	30.00
❏ W 1538 [M]	Turn Around	1964	6.25	12.50	25.00
❏ WS 1538 [S]	Turn Around	1964	7.50	15.00	30.00
❏ W 1586 [M]	Thou Shalt Not Steal	1965	6.25	12.50	25.00
❏ WS 1586 [S]	Thou Shalt Not Steal	1965	7.50	15.00	30.00
❏ W 1623 [M]	Song We've Sung on "Shindig"	1966	6.25	12.50	25.00
❏ WS 1623 [S]	Song We've Sung on "Shindig"	1966	7.50	15.00	30.00

DICKENS, THE See NRBQ.

DICKENS, RICKY
45s
HIT
❏ 79	If I Had a Hammer/Hey Girl	1963	2.00	4.00	8.00
—B-side by Leroy Jones					
❏ 85	Sugar Shack/Hello Heartache, Goodbye Love	1963	2.00	4.00	8.00
—B-side by Connie Dee					
❏ 98	Midnight Mary/Drip Drop	1963	2.00	4.00	8.00
—B-side by Ed Hardin					
❏ 102	Daisy Petal Pickin'/Hey Little Cobra	1964	2.00	4.00	8.00
—B-side by the Roamers					
❏ 164	Ballad of Daniel Boone/Legend of Daniel Boone	1964	2.00	4.00	8.00
—B-side by Charlie Brown					

DICKIE G. AND THE DON'TS See DICKIE GOODMAN.

DICKY DOO AND THE DON'TS
45s
ASCOT
❏ 2178	Click Clack '65/Don't Count Me Out	1965	2.50	5.00	10.00
CASINO					
❏ 106	Click Clack/Lonely Hours Lady	196?	3.00	6.00	12.00
❏ 107	Flip Top Box/That's Life (That's Tough)	196?	3.00	6.00	12.00
DANNA					
❏ 4001	The Judge/Doo Plus Two	1967	2.50	5.00	10.00
SWAN					
❏ 4001	Click Clack/Did You Cry	1958	5.00	10.00	20.00
❏ 4006	Ne Ne Na Na Na Na Na Nu/Flip Top Box	1959	6.25	12.50	25.00
❏ 4014	Leave Me Alone (Let Me Cry)/Wild Party	1959	5.00	10.00	20.00
❏ 4025	Teardrops Will Fall/Come with Us	1959	5.00	10.00	20.00
❏ 4033	Ballad of a Train/Dear Heart, Don't Cry	1959	5.00	10.00	20.00
❏ 4046	Wabash Cannonball/The Drums of Richard A.				
	Doo	1960	5.00	10.00	20.00
UNITED ARTISTS					
❏ 238	Teen Scene/Pity, Pity	1960	5.00	10.00	20.00
❏ 362	The Judge/The Little Dog Cried	1961	5.00	10.00	20.00
Albums					
UNITED ARTISTS					
❏ UAL-3094 [M]	The Madison and Other Dances	1959	10.00	20.00	40.00
❏ UAL-3097 [M]	Teen Scene	1959	10.00	20.00	40.00
❏ UAS-6094 [S]	The Madison and Other Dances	1959	12.50	25.00	50.00
❏ UAS-6097 [S]	Teen Scene	1959	12.50	25.00	50.00

DIDDLEY, BO
45s
CHECKER
❏ 814	Bo Diddley/I'm a Man	1955	12.50	25.00	50.00
❏ 819	Diddley Daddy/She's Fine, She's Mine	1955	15.00	30.00	60.00
—A-side backing vocals: The Moonglows					
❏ 827	Pretty Thing/Bring It to Jerome	1955	12.50	25.00	50.00
❏ 832	Diddy Wah Diddy/I Am Looking for a Woman	1956	12.50	25.00	50.00
❏ 842	Who Do You Love?/I'm Bad	1956	10.00	20.00	40.00
—Note altered B-side title					
❏ 842	Who Do You Love?/In Bad	1956	15.00	30.00	60.00
❏ 850	Cops and Robbers/Down Home Special	1956	10.00	20.00	40.00
❏ 860	Hey! Bo Diddley/Mona	1957	12.50	25.00	50.00
—Originals of Checker 816-860 have "Checker" over a checkerboard on top of label					
❏ 878	Say! Boss Man/Before You Accuse Me	1957	6.25	12.50	25.00
❏ 896	Dearest Darling/Hush Your Mouth	1958	6.25	12.50	25.00
❏ 907	Bo Meets the Monster/Willie and Lillie	1958	7.50	15.00	30.00
❏ 914	I'm Sorry/Oh Yeah	1959	6.25	12.50	25.00
❏ 924	Crackin' Up/The Great Grandfather	1959	6.25	12.50	25.00
❏ 931	Say Man/Clock Strikes Twelve	1959	7.50	15.00	30.00
❏ 931 [PS]	Say Man/Clock Strikes Twelve	1959	100.00	200.00	400.00
❏ 936	Say Man, Back Again/She's Alright	1959	6.25	12.50	25.00
❏ 942	Road Runner/My Story	1960	5.00	10.00	20.00
❏ 951	Walkin' and Talkin'/Crawdad	1960	5.00	10.00	20.00
❏ 965	Gun Slinger/Signifying	1960	5.00	10.00	20.00
❏ 976	No Guilty/Aztec	1961	5.00	10.00	20.00
❏ 985	Pills/Call Me	1961	7.50	15.00	30.00
❏ 997	Bo Diddley/I'm a Man	1961	5.00	10.00	20.00
❏ 1019	You Can't Judge a Book By Its Cover/I Can Tell	1962	6.25	12.50	25.00
❏ 1045	Surfers' Love Call/Greatest Lover in the World	1963	5.00	10.00	20.00
❏ 1058	Memphis/Monkey Diddle	1963	5.00	10.00	20.00
❏ 1083	Jo Ann/Mama, Keep Your Big Mouth Shut	1964	5.00	10.00	20.00

Number	Title (A Side/B Side)	Yr	VG	VG+	NM
❏ 1089	Bo's Beat/Chuck's Beat	1964	5.00	10.00	20.00
—B-side by Chuck Berry					
❏ 1098	Hey, Good Lookin'/You Ain't Bad	1965	3.75	7.50	15.00
❏ 1123	500% More Man/Let the Kids Dance	1965	3.75	7.50	15.00
❏ 1142	We're Gonna Get Married/Do the Frog	1966	3.75	7.50	15.00
❏ 1158	Ooh Baby/Back to School	1966	3.75	7.50	15.00
❏ 1168	Bo-Ga-Loo Before You Go/				
	Wrecking My Love Life	1967	3.75	7.50	15.00
❏ 1200	Another Sugardaddy/I'm High Again	1968	3.75	7.50	15.00
❏ 1213	Bo Diddley 1969/Soul Train	1969	3.00	6.00	12.00
❏ 1238	The Shape I'm In/Pollution	1970	3.00	6.00	12.00
CHESS					
❏ 2117	I Love You More Than You'll Ever Know/I Said				
	Shut Up Woman	1971	2.50	5.00	10.00
❏ 2129	Bo Diddley-Itis/Infatuation	1972	2.50	5.00	10.00
❏ 2134	Bo-Jam/Husband-in-Law	1972	2.50	5.00	10.00
❏ 2142	I Don't Want No Lyin' Woman/Make a Hit Record	1973	2.50	5.00	10.00
PHILCO-FORD					
❏ HP-33	I'm a Man/Song of Bo Diddley	1968	7.50	15.00	30.00
—4-inch plastic "Hip Pocket Record" with color sleeve					
RCA VICTOR					
❏ PB-10618	Not Fade Away/Drag On	1976	2.50	5.00	10.00
7-Inch Extended Plays					
CHESS					
❏ 5125	Bo Diddley/I'm a Man//Willie and Lillie/Bo Meets				
	the Monster	1958	30.00	60.00	120.00
❏ 5125 [PS]	Bo Diddley	1958	45.00	90.00	180.00
Albums					
ACCORD					
❏ SN-7182	Toronto Rock and Roll Revival, Vol. 5	1982	5.00	10.00	20.00
CHECKER					
❏ LP 1431 [M]	Bo Diddley	1958	37.50	75.00	150.00
❏ LP 1436 [M]	Go Bo Diddley	1959	37.50	75.00	150.00
❏ LP 2974 [M]	Have Guitar, Will Travel	1960	37.50	75.00	150.00
❏ LP 2976 [M]	Spotlight on Bo Diddley	1960	37.50	75.00	150.00
❏ LP 2977 [M]	Bo Diddley Is a Gunslinger	1961	37.50	75.00	150.00
❏ LP 2980 [M]	Bo Diddley Is a Lover	1961	37.50	75.00	150.00
❏ LP 2982 [M]	Bo Diddley's a Twister	1962	25.00	50.00	100.00
❏ LP 2982 [M]	Road Runner	1967	20.00	40.00	80.00
—Reissue of "Bo Diddley's a Twister"					
❏ LP 2984 [M]	Bo Diddley	1962	25.00	50.00	100.00
❏ LP 2985 [M]	Bo Diddley and Company	1963	40.00	80.00	120.00
❏ LP 2987 [M]	Surfin' with Bo Diddley	1964	40.00	80.00	120.00
❏ LPS 2987 [R]	Surfin' with Bo Diddley	1964	7.50	15.00	30.00
❏ LP 2988 [M]	Bo Diddley's Beach Party	1963	25.00	50.00	100.00
❏ LP 2989 [M]	16 All Time Greatest Hits	1964	12.50	25.00	50.00
❏ LPS 2989 [R]	16 All Time Greatest Hits	1964	7.50	15.00	30.00
❏ LP 2992 [M]	Hey! Good Lookin'	1965	15.00	30.00	60.00
❏ LPS 2992 [R]	Hey! Good Lookin'	1965	7.50	15.00	30.00
❏ LP 2996 [M]	500% More Man	1965	15.00	30.00	60.00
❏ LPS 2996 [R]	500% More Man	1965	7.50	15.00	30.00
❏ LP 3001 [M]	The Originator	1966	7.50	15.00	30.00
❏ LPS 3001 [S]	The Originator	1966	10.00	20.00	40.00
❏ LP 3006 [M]	Go Bo Diddley	1967	12.50	25.00	50.00
—Reissue of 1436					
❏ LPS 3006 [R]	Go Bo Diddley	1967	10.00	20.00	40.00
❏ LP 3007 [M]	Boss Man	1967	20.00	40.00	80.00
—Reissue of Chess 1431					
❏ LPS 3007 [R]	Boss Man	1967	12.50	25.00	50.00
❏ LPS 3013	The Black Gladiator	1968	7.50	15.00	30.00
CHESS					
❏ LP 1431 [M]	Bo Diddley	1958	50.00	100.00	200.00
❏ CH-9106	His Greatest Sides, Vol. 1	1984	2.50	5.00	10.00
❏ CH-9187	Have Guitar, Will Travel	1985	2.50	5.00	10.00
—Reissue of Checker 2974					
❏ CH-9194	Bo Diddley	1986	2.50	5.00	10.00
—Reissue of 1431					
❏ CH-9196	Go Bo Diddley	1986	2.50	5.00	10.00
—Reissue of Checker 1436					
❏ CH-9264	Spotlight on Bo Diddley	1987	2.50	5.00	10.00
—Reissue of Checker 2976					
❏ CH-9285	Bo Diddley Is a Gunslinger	1989	2.50	5.00	10.00
—Reissue of Checker 2977					
❏ CH-9296	The London Bo Diddley Sessions	1989	2.50	5.00	10.00
—Reissue of 50029					
❏ CH3-19502 [(3)]	The Chess Box	1990	10.00	20.00	40.00
❏ CH 50001	Another Dimension	1971	10.00	20.00	40.00
❏ CH 50016	Where It All Began	1972	10.00	20.00	40.00
❏ CH 50029	The London Bo Diddley Sessions	1973	6.25	12.50	25.00
❏ CH 50047	Big Bad Bo	1974	6.25	12.50	25.00
❏ 2CH 60005 [(2)]	Got My Own Bag of Tricks	1972	6.25	12.50	25.00
RCA VICTOR					
❏ APL1-1229	The 20th Anniversary of Rock and Roll	1976	5.00	10.00	20.00

DIDDLEY, BO/CHUCK BERRY Also see each artist's individual listings.
Albums
CHECKER
❏ LP 2991 [M]	Two Great Guitars	1964	15.00	30.00	60.00
❏ LPS 2991 [R]	Two Great Guitars	1964	10.00	20.00	40.00
CHESS					
❏ CH-9170	Two Great Guitars	1985	2.50	5.00	10.00
—Reissue of Checker 2991					

DIDDLEY, BO/MUDDY WATERS/HOWLIN' WOLF Also see each artist's individual listings.
Albums
CHECKER
❏ LP 3010 [M]	Super, Super Blues Band	1968	12.50	25.00	50.00
❏ LPS 3010 [S]	Super, Super Blues Band	1968	10.00	20.00	40.00
CHESS					
❏ CH-9169	Super, Super Blues Band	1985	2.50	5.00	10.00
—Reissue of Checker 3010					

Number	Title (A Side/B Side)	Yr	VG	VG+	NM

DIDDLEY, BO/MUDDY WATERS/LITTLE WALTER Also see each artist's individual listings.
Albums
CHECKER
| ❑ LP 3008 [M] | Super Blues Band | 1968 | 12.50 | 25.00 | 50.00 |
| ❑ LPS 3008 [S] | Super Blues Band | 1968 | 10.00 | 20.00 | 40.00 |

CHESS
| ❑ CH-9168 | Super Blues Band | 1985 | 2.50 | 5.00 | 10.00 |
—Reissue of Checker 3008

DIFFERENT SHADES OF BROWN
45s
TAMLA
| ❑ 54219 | Label Me Love/Life's a Ball | 1972 | — | 2.50 | 5.00 |

DILEO, BOB
45s
COLUMBIA
| ❑ 4-44858 | Just Can't Help Believin'/Mind Excursion | 1969 | 2.00 | 4.00 | 8.00 |
| ❑ 4-44958 | Jessica/Sing to Me | 1969 | 2.00 | 4.00 | 8.00 |

DILL, DANNY
45s
ABC-PARAMOUNT
| ❑ 9681 | My Girl and His Girl/Geisha Sweetheart | 1956 | 7.50 | 15.00 | 30.00 |
| ❑ 9734 | I'm Hungry for Your Lovin'/The Stranger of Abilene | 1956 | 12.50 | 25.00 | 50.00 |

CUB
| ❑ 9045 | He's Biding His Time/He Ain't Gonna Study War | 1959 | 5.00 | 10.00 | 20.00 |

DILLARD, DOUG
Albums
TOGETHER
| ❑ STT-1003 | The Banjo Album | 1970 | 20.00 | 40.00 | 80.00 |

DILLARD, VARETTA
45s
CUB
❑ 9073	Teaser/I Know I'm Good for You	1960	3.00	6.00	12.00
❑ 9083	Little Bitty Tear/Mercy Mr. Percy	1961	3.00	6.00	12.00
❑ 9091	You Better Come Home/I Don't Know What It Is, But I Like It	1961	3.00	6.00	12.00

GROOVE
❑ 0139	Darling, Listen to the Words of This Song/Mama Don't Want (What Poppa Don't Want)	1956	10.00	20.00	40.00
❑ 0152	Gonna Tell My Daddy/Cherry Blossom	1956	6.25	12.50	25.00
❑ 0159	Got You On My Mind/Skinny Jimmy	1956	6.25	12.50	25.00
❑ 0167	I Miss You Jimmy/If You Want to Be My Baby	1956	6.25	12.50	25.00
❑ 0177	One More Time/I Can't Help Myself	1956	6.25	12.50	25.00

RCA VICTOR
❑ 47-6869	Pray for Me Mother/Leave a Happy Fool Alone	1957	5.00	10.00	20.00
❑ 47-6936	Time Was/I Got a Lot of Love	1957	5.00	10.00	20.00
❑ 47-7057	Undecided/That's Why I Cry	1957	5.00	10.00	20.00
❑ 47-7144	Star of Fortune/The Blues of Love	1958	5.00	10.00	20.00
❑ 47-7285	What'll I Do/Just Multiply	1958	5.00	10.00	20.00

SAVOY
❑ 822	Love and Wine/Please Come Back to Me	1951	12.50	25.00	50.00
❑ 839	Hurry Up/Please Tell Me Why	1952	10.00	20.00	40.00
❑ 847	Easy, Easy Baby/A Letter in Blue	1952	10.00	20.00	40.00
❑ 851	I'm Yours/Here in My Heart	1952	10.00	20.00	40.00
❑ 871	I Cried and Cried/Double Crossing Daddy	1952	10.00	20.00	40.00
❑ 884	Three Lies/Getting Ready for My Daddy	1953	10.00	20.00	40.00
❑ 897	Mercy, Mr. Percy/No Kinda Good No How	1953	10.00	20.00	40.00
❑ 1118	I Ain't Gonna Tell/(That's the Way) My Mind Is Working	1953	7.50	15.00	30.00
❑ 1137	Send Me Some Money/Love	1954	7.50	15.00	30.00
❑ 1153	Johnny Has Gone/So Many Ways	1955	7.50	15.00	30.00
❑ 1160	You're the Answer to My Prayer/Promise Mr. Thomas	1955	7.50	15.00	30.00
❑ 1166	I'll Never Forget You/I Can't Stop Now	1955	7.50	15.00	30.00

TRIUMPH
| ❑ 608 | Good Gravy Baby/Scorched | 1959 | 3.75 | 7.50 | 15.00 |

Albums
SAVOY JAZZ
| ❑ SJL-1203 | Mercy, Mr. Percy, Volume 1 | 1989 | 3.00 | 6.00 | 12.00 |

DILLARD AND CLARK
Albums
A&M
| ❑ SP-4158 | The Fantastic Expedition of Dillard and Clark | 1968 | 5.00 | 10.00 | 20.00 |
—Brown label

DILLARDS, THE
45s
ANTHEM
| ❑ 101 | It's About Time/One A.M. | 1971 | — | 2.50 | 5.00 |
| ❑ 51014 | Billy Jack/America | 1971 | — | 2.50 | 5.00 |

CAPITOL
| ❑ 5494 | Nobody Knows/Ebo Walker | 1965 | 2.00 | 4.00 | 8.00 |
| ❑ 5524 | Lemon Chimes/The Last Thing on My Mind | 1965 | 2.00 | 4.00 | 8.00 |

ELEKTRA
❑ 45003	Dooley/Dong's Love	1964	2.50	5.00	10.00
❑ 45006	Hootin' Banjo/Polly Vaughn	1964	2.50	5.00	10.00
❑ 45641	Reason to Believe/Nobody Knows	1968	2.00	4.00	8.00
❑ 45661	Listen to the Sound/The Biggest Whatever	1969	2.00	4.00	8.00
❑ 45679	Rain Maker/West Montana Hanna	1970	2.00	4.00	8.00
❑ 45681	Close the Door Lightly/Touch Her If You Can	1970	2.00	4.00	8.00

K-ARK
| ❑ 619 | My Only True Love/Doug's Breakdown | 196? | 5.00 | 10.00 | 20.00 |
—As "The Dillard Brothers"; recorded in 1958, but probably not issued until the Dillards were recording for Elektra
UNITED ARTISTS
| ❑ XW382 | Hot Rod Banjo/Love Has Gone Away | 1974 | — | 2.50 | 5.00 |

WHITE WHALE
| ❑ 351 | One Too Many Mornings/Turn It Around | 1970 | — | 3.00 | 6.00 |
| ❑ 359 | Comin' Home Again | 1970 | — | 3.00 | 6.00 |

Albums
ANTHEM
| ❑ ANS-5901 | Roots and Branches | 1972 | 3.75 | 7.50 | 15.00 |

CRYSTAL CLEAR
| ❑ CCS-5007 | Mountain Rock | 1979 | 6.25 | 12.50 | 25.00 |
—Direct-to-disc recording
ELEKTRA
❑ EKL-232 [M]	Back Porch Bluegrass	1963	6.25	12.50	25.00
❑ EKL-265 [M]	The Dillards, Live!!! Almost!!!	1964	5.00	10.00	20.00
❑ EKL-285 [M]	Pickin' and Fiddlin'	1965	5.00	10.00	20.00
❑ EKS-7232 [S]	Back Porch Bluegrass	1963	7.50	5.00	30.00
—Mandolin-player label
| ❑ EKS-7265 [S] | The Dillards, Live!!! Almost!!! | 1964 | 6.25 | 12.50 | 25.00 |
—Mandolin-player label
| ❑ EKS-7285 [S] | Pickin' and Fiddlin' | 1965 | 6.25 | 12.50 | 25.00 |
—Mandolin-player label
| ❑ EKS-74035 | Wheatstraw Suite | 1968 | 5.00 | 10.00 | 20.00 |
—Tan label with large stylized "E" on top
| ❑ EKS-74035 | Wheatstraw Suite | 1969 | 3.75 | 7.50 | 15.00 |
—Red label with large stylized "E" on top
| ❑ EKS-74054 | Copperfields | 1969 | 5.00 | 10.00 | 20.00 |
—Red label with large stylized "E" on top
FLYING FISH
❑ FF 040	The Dillards Vs. the Incredible L.A. Time Machine	1977	3.00	6.00	12.00
❑ FF 082	Decade Waltz	1979	3.00	6.00	12.00
❑ FF 215	Homecoming and Family Reunion	1979	3.00	6.00	12.00
POPPY
❑ PP-LA175-F	Tribute to the American Duck	1973	3.75	7.50	15.00

DING DONGS, THE See BOBBY DARIN.

DINNING, MARK
45s
CAMEO
| ❑ 299 | January/Joey | 1964 | 2.50 | 5.00 | 10.00 |
| ❑ 313 | Should We Do It/Call Her Your Sweetheart | 1964 | 2.50 | 5.00 | 10.00 |

HICKORY
❑ 1293	Dial AL1-4883/I'm Glad We Fell in Love	1965	2.00	4.00	8.00
❑ 1368	Last Rose/There Stands a Lady	1966	2.00	4.00	8.00
❑ 1404	Run, Opie, Run/He Reminds Me of Me	1966	2.00	4.00	8.00

MGM
❑ 12447	A Million Years Ago/Shameful Ways	1957	6.25	12.50	25.00
❑ 12553	School Fool/When You're Tired of Breaking Hearts	1957	6.25	12.50	25.00
❑ 12691	You Thrill Me/Do You Know	1958	6.25	12.50	25.00
❑ 12732	Blackeyed Gypsy/Secretly in Love with You	1958	6.25	12.50	25.00
❑ 12775	Cutie, Cutie/A Life of Love	1959	6.25	12.50	25.00
❑ 12845	Teen Angel/Bye Now Baby	1959	6.25	12.50	25.00
❑ 12888	A Star Is Born (A Love Has Died)/You Win Again	1960	5.00	10.00	20.00
❑ 12888 [PS]	A Star Is Born (A Love Has Died)/You Win Again	1960	6.25	12.50	25.00
❑ 12929	The Lovin' Touch/Come Back to Me (My Love)	1960	5.00	10.00	20.00
❑ 12929 [PS]	The Lovin' Touch/Come Back to Me (My Love)	1960	6.25	12.50	25.00
❑ 12958	She Cried On My Shoulder (When She Talked About You)/(Where Can You Hide Away) The World Is Getting Smaller	1960	5.00	10.00	20.00
❑ 12980	Top Forty, News, Weather and Sports/Suddenly (There's Only You)	1961	3.75	7.50	15.00
❑ 13007	Another Lonely Girl/Can't Forget	1961	3.75	7.50	15.00
❑ 13024	Lonely Island/Turn Me On	1961	3.75	7.50	15.00
❑ 13048	What Will My Mary Say/In a Matter of Moments	1961	3.75	7.50	15.00
❑ 13061	The Pickup/All of This for Sally	1962	3.75	7.50	15.00
❑ 13091	She's Changed/I Catch Myself Crying	1962	3.00	6.00	12.00
❑ 13150	The Twelfth of Never/Somebody Catch Me Kissin' Mary	1963	3.00	6.00	12.00

UNITED ARTISTS
❑ 50169	It's Such a Pretty World Today/Atlanta, Georgia Stray	1967	2.00	4.00	8.00
❑ 50225	Hangin' On/Maggie (I Wish We'd Never Met)	1967	2.00	4.00	8.00
❑ 50305	Throw a Little Love My Way/Dissatisfied Man	1968	2.00	4.00	8.00
❑ 50540	How Little Men Care/Lemon Yellow	1969	2.00	4.00	8.00

Albums
MGM
❑ E-3828 [M]	Teen Angel	1960	20.00	40.00	80.00
❑ SE-3828 [S]	Teen Angel	1960	37.50	75.00	150.00
❑ E-3855 [M]	Wanderin'	1960	20.00	40.00	80.00
❑ SE-3855 [S]	Wanderin'	1960	30.00	60.00	120.00

DINO, KENNY
45s
COLUMBIA
| ❑ 43062 | Betty Jean/Show Me | 1964 | 5.00 | 10.00 | 20.00 |

DOT
| ❑ 16207 | Just Wait and See/A Little Bit | 1961 | 3.00 | 6.00 | 12.00 |

MUSICOR
❑ 1013	You Ma Said You Cried in Your Sleep Last Night/Dream a Girl	1962	5.00	10.00	20.00
❑ 1015	Rosie, Why Do You Wear My Ring/What Did I Do	1962	3.75	7.50	15.00
❑ 1021	What Good Are Dreams/What Did I Do	1962	3.75	7.50	15.00
❑ 1027	Remembering Helps Me to Forget/Heartless Moon	1962	3.75	7.50	15.00

SMASH
| ❑ 1827 | Time Will Tell/I Wanna Know | 1963 | 3.00 | 6.00 | 12.00 |
| ❑ 1861 | You Had Your Chance/Danhoff's Theme | 1963 | 3.00 | 6.00 | 12.00 |

DINO AND SEMBELLO
45s
DATE
| ❑ 2-1667 | Imogene and Me/See the Light | 1970 | 2.00 | 4.00 | 8.00 |

DINO AND THE DIPLOMATS
45s
LAURIE
| ❑ 3103 | I Can't Believe/My Dream | 1961 | 7.50 | 15.00 | 30.00 |
VIDA
| ❑ 100/101 | Hushabye My Love/Homework | 1961 | 7.50 | 15.00 | 30.00 |
| ❑ 102/103 | Soft Wind/Such a Fool for You | 1961 | 7.50 | 15.00 | 30.00 |

Number	Title (A Side/B Side)	Yr	VG	VG+	NM
DINO, DESI AND BILLY					
45s					
COLUMBIA					
❑ 4-44975	Hawley/Let's Talk It Over	1969	3.00	6.00	12.00
REPRISE					
❑ 0324	We Know/Since You Broke My Heart	1964	3.75	7.50	15.00
❑ 0367	I'm a Fool/So Many Ways	1965	3.00	6.00	12.00
❑ 0367 [PS]	I'm a Fool/So Many Ways	1965	5.00	10.00	20.00
❑ 0401	Not the Lovin' Kind/Chimes of Freedom	1965	2.50	5.00	10.00
❑ 0401 [PS]	Not the Lovin' Kind/Chimes of Freedom	1965	5.00	10.00	20.00
❑ 0426	Please Don't Fight It/The Rebel Kind	1965	2.50	5.00	10.00
❑ 0426 [PS]	Please Don't Fight It/The Rebel Kind	1965	5.00	10.00	20.00
❑ 0444	Superman/I Can't Get Her Out of My Mind	1966	2.00	4.00	8.00
❑ 0462	It's Just the Way You Are/Tie Me Down	1966	2.00	4.00	8.00
❑ 0496	Look Out Girls/She's So Far Out She's In	1966	2.00	4.00	8.00
❑ 0529	I Hope She's There Tonight/Josephine	1966	2.00	4.00	8.00
❑ 0544	If You're Thinkin' What I'm Thinkin'/Pretty Flamingo	1966	2.00	4.00	8.00
❑ 0579	Two in the Afternoon/Good Luck, Best Wishes to You	1967	2.50	5.00	10.00
❑ 0619	Kitty Doyle/Without Hurtin' Some	1967	2.50	5.00	10.00
❑ 0653	My What a Shame/The Inside Outside Caspar Milquetoast Eskimo Flash	1967	3.00	6.00	12.00
❑ 0653 [PS]	My What a Shame/The Inside Outside Caspar Milquetoast Eskimo Flash	1967	5.00	10.00	20.00
❑ 0698	Tell Someone You Love Them/General Outline	1968	3.00	6.00	12.00
❑ 0716	I'm a Fool/Not the Lovin' Kind	1968	2.00	4.00	8.00
—"Back to Back Hits" series; originals have both "W7" and "r:" logos					
❑ 0965	Lady Love/A Certain Sound	1970	7.50	15.00	30.00
—A-side is a Brian Wilson composition					
UNI					
❑ 55127	Someday/Thru Spray Colored Glasses	1969	3.00	6.00	12.00
Albums					
REPRISE					
❑ R 6176 [M]	I'm a Fool	1965	5.00	10.00	20.00
❑ RS 6176 [S]	I'm a Fool	1965	6.25	12.50	25.00
❑ R 6194 [M]	Our Time's Coming	1966	5.00	10.00	20.00
❑ RS 6194 [S]	Our Time's Coming	1966	6.25	12.50	25.00
❑ R 6198 [M]	Memories Are Made of This	1966	5.00	10.00	20.00
❑ RS 6198 [S]	Memories Are Made of This	1966	6.25	12.50	25.00
❑ R 6224 [M]	Souvenir	1966	5.00	10.00	20.00
❑ R/RS 6224	Souvenir Bonus Photo Sheet	1966	—	2.50	5.00
❑ RS 6224 [S]	Souvenir	1966	6.25	12.50	25.00
DIO, ANDY					
45s					
CRUSADE					
❑ 1023	Bonnie Jean/Rough and Bold	1961	10.00	20.00	40.00
GONE					
❑ 5038	Daisy Belle/Hey Little Bluebird	1958	12.50	25.00	50.00
JOHNSON					
❑ 114	You Are My Sunshine/Satellite	1962	5.00	10.00	20.00
JOY					
❑ 283	Daisy Belle/Some of These Days	1964	10.00	20.00	40.00
MUSICOR					
❑ 1118	Sass-Afrass/Shout	1965	2.50	5.00	10.00
❑ 1162	Dancing Bull/Sorrento	1966	2.50	5.00	10.00
DIO, RONNIE Also see THE ELECTRIC ELVES; ELF; THE ELVES.					
45s					
ATLANTIC					
❑ 2145	The Ooh-Poo-Pah-Doo/Love Pains	1962	25.00	50.00	100.00
KAPP					
❑ 697	Say You're Mine Again/Where You Gonna Run To, Girl	1965	12.50	25.00	50.00
❑ 725	Smiling by Day (Crying by Night)/Dear Darlin' (I Won't Be Comin' Home)	1965	12.50	25.00	50.00
❑ 770	The Way of Love/Walking Alone	1966	12.50	25.00	50.00
LAWN					
❑ 218	Swingin' Street/Gonna Make It Alone	1963	37.50	75.00	150.00
PARKWAY					
❑ 143	Walking in Different Circles/Ten Days with Brenda	1967	10.00	20.00	40.00
SENECA					
❑ S 178-102	An Angel Is Missing/What'd I Say?	1959	50.00	100.00	200.00
—As "Ronnie Dio and the Red Caps"					
SWAN					
❑ 4165	Mr. Misery/Our Year	1963	20.00	40.00	80.00
VALEX					
❑ 001	Love Potion No. 9 (same on both sides)	1964	50.00	100.00	200.00
Albums					
JOVE					
❑ J-108	Dio at Domino's	1963	50.00	100.00	200.00
DION Also see DION AND THE BELMONTS; DION AND THE TIMBERLANES.					
45s					
ARISTA					
❑ 9797	And the Night Stood Still/Tower of Love	1989	—	2.00	4.00
❑ 9797 [PS]	And the Night Stood Still/Tower of Love	1989	—	2.00	4.00
BIG TREE/SPECTOR					
❑ 16063	Born to Be with You/Running Close Behind You	1976	3.75	7.50	15.00
—Produced by Phil Spector					
COLUMBIA					
❑ (no #) [PS]	"Dion Is Now on Columbia Records"	1962	12.50	25.00	50.00
—Promo-only sleeve issued with promos of Columbia 42662					
❑ 42662	Ruby Baby/He'll Only Hurt You	1962	5.00	10.00	20.00
❑ 42662 [PS]	Ruby Baby/He'll Only Hurt You	1962	10.00	20.00	40.00
❑ 42776	This Little Girl/The Loneliest Man in the World	1963	3.75	7.50	15.00
❑ 42810	Be Careful of Stones That You Throw/I Can't Believe (That You Don't Love Me Anymore)	1963	3.75	7.50	15.00
❑ 42810 [DJ]	Be Careful of Stones That You Throw (same on both sides)	1963	25.00	50.00	100.00
—Colored vinyl (some sources say blue, others red)					
❑ 42852	Donna the Prima Donna/You're Mine	1963	5.00	10.00	20.00
❑ 42852 [DJ]	Donna the Prima Donna (same on both sides)	1963	20.00	40.00	80.00
—Promo only on red vinyl					

Number	Title (A Side/B Side)	Yr	VG	VG+	NM
❑ 42917	Drip Drop/No One's Waiting for Me	1963	3.75	7.50	15.00
❑ 42977	I'm the Hoochie Coochie Man/The Road I'm On	1964	3.75	7.50	15.00
❑ 42977 [PS]	I'm the Hoochie Coochie Man/The Road I'm On	1964	10.00	20.00	40.00
❑ 43096	Johnny B. Goode/Chicago Blues	1964	3.75	7.50	15.00
❑ 43213	Sweet Sweet Baby/Unloved, Unwanted Me	1965	3.75	7.50	15.00
❑ 43293	Spoonful/Kickin' Child	1965	3.75	7.50	15.00
❑ 43423	Tomorrow Won't Bring the Rain/You Move Me Babe	1965	3.75	7.50	15.00
❑ 43423 [PS]	Tomorrow Won't Bring the Rain/You Move Me Babe	1965	37.50	75.00	150.00
❑ 43483	Time in My Heart for You/Wake Up Baby	1965	3.75	7.50	15.00
❑ 43692	So Much Younger/Two-Ton Feather	1966	3.75	7.50	15.00
❑ 44719	I Can't Help But Wonder Where I'm Bound/Southern Train	1968	2.50	5.00	10.00
DAYSPRING					
❑ 622 [DJ]	The Best (mono/stereo)	197?	—	2.50	5.00
LAURIE					
❑ 3070	Lonely Teenager/Little Miss Blue	1960	5.00	10.00	20.00
❑ 3070 [PS]	Lonely Teenager/Little Miss Blue	1960	12.50	25.00	50.00
❑ 3081	Havin' Fun/Northeast End of the Corner	1961	5.00	10.00	20.00
❑ 3081 [PS]	Havin' Fun/Northeast End of the Corner	1961	12.50	25.00	50.00
❑ 3090	Kissin Game/Heaven Help Me	1961	5.00	10.00	20.00
❑ 3090 [PS]	Kissin Game/Heaven Help Me	1961	12.50	25.00	50.00
❑ 3101	Somebody Nobody Wants/Could Somebody Take My Place Tonight	1961	5.00	10.00	20.00
❑ 3110 [M]	Runaround Sue/Runaway Girl	1961	6.25	12.50	25.00
❑ 3110 [PS]	Runaround Sue/Runaway Girl	1961	10.00	20.00	40.00
❑ 3110 [S]	Runaround Sue/Runaway Girl	1961	12.50	25.00	50.00
—"Stereo" in white area at right of label					
❑ 3115 [M]	The Wanderer/The Majestic	1961	6.25	12.50	25.00
❑ 3115 [PS]	The Wanderer/The Majestic	1961	10.00	20.00	40.00
❑ 3115 [S]	The Wanderer/The Majestic	1961	12.50	25.00	50.00
—"Stereo" in white area at right of label					
❑ 3115 [M]	The Wanderer/The Majestic	1979	2.50	5.00	10.00
—Reissue on regular Laurie label with "From the Orion Motion Picture 'The Wanderers'" on label					
❑ 3123	Lovers Who Wander/(I Was) Born to Cry	1962	5.00	10.00	20.00
❑ 3123 [PS]	Lovers Who Wander/(I Was) Born to Cry	1962	10.00	20.00	40.00
❑ 3134	Little Diane/Lost for Sure	1962	5.00	10.00	20.00
❑ 3134 [PS]	Little Diane/Lost for Sure	1962	10.00	20.00	40.00
❑ 3145	Love Came to Me/Little Girl	1962	5.00	10.00	20.00
❑ 3153	Sandy/Faith	1963	5.00	10.00	20.00
❑ 3171	Come Go with Me/King Without a Queen	1963	5.00	10.00	20.00
❑ 3187	Lonely World/Tag Along	1963	5.00	10.00	20.00
❑ 3225	After the Dance/Then I'll Be Tired of You	1964	5.00	10.00	20.00
❑ 3240	Shout/Little Girl	1964	5.00	10.00	20.00
❑ 3303	I Got the Blues/(I Was) Born to Cry	1965	5.00	10.00	20.00
❑ 3464	Abraham, Martin, and John/Daddy Rollin' (In Your Arms)	1968	3.00	6.00	12.00
❑ 3478	Purple Haze/The Dolphins	1969	3.00	6.00	12.00
❑ 3495	From Both Sides Now/Sun Fun Song	1969	3.00	6.00	12.00
❑ 3504	Loving You Is Sweeter Than Ever/He Looks a Lot Like Me	1969	3.00	6.00	12.00
LAURIE DOUBLE GOLD					
❑ 100	Runaround Sue/I Wonder Why	197?	—	2.00	4.00
—B-side by Dion and the Belmonts					
❑ 101	The Wanderer/No One Knows	197?	—	2.00	4.00
—B-side by Dion and the Belmonts					
❑ 103	Lonely Teenager/Little Diane	197?	—	2.00	4.00
❑ 104	Lovers Who Wander/Where or When	197?	—	2.00	4.00
—B-side by Dion and the Belmonts					
❑ 105	Love Came to Me/Sandy	197?	—	2.00	4.00
❑ 118	Abraham, Martin and John/From Both Sides Now	197?	—	2.00	4.00
LIFESONG					
❑ 1765	Heart of Saturday Night/You've Awakened Something in Me	1978	—	3.00	6.00
❑ 1770	Midtown American Main Street Gang/Guitar Queen	1978	—	3.00	6.00
❑ 1785	(I Used to Be a) Brooklyn Dodger/Streetheart Theme	1979	—	3.00	6.00
❑ 45082	Fire in the Night/Street Mama	1980	6.25	12.50	25.00
MONUMENT					
❑ (# unknown) [DJ]	Runaround Sue/Ya Ya Twist	1962	6.25	12.50	25.00
—B-side by Joey Dee and the Starliters					
THE RIGHT STUFF					
❑ S7-17651	Christmas (Baby Please Come Home)/Jingle Bell Rock	1993	—	2.50	5.00
—Red vinyl					
❑ S7-19769	Please Come Home for Christmas/Wintertime	1997	—	2.00	4.00
—B-side by the Belmonts on United Artists					
WARNER BROS.					
❑ PRO-537 [DJ]	Seagull/Soft Parade	1972	3.75	7.50	15.00
❑ PRO-814 [DJ]	The Wanderer (same on both sides)	1979	3.75	7.50	15.00
❑ 7356	Natural Man/If We Only Have Love	1969	2.50	5.00	10.00
❑ 7401	Your Own Back Yard/Sit Down Old Friend	1970	2.50	5.00	10.00
❑ 7469	Let It Be/Close to It All	1970	2.50	5.00	10.00
❑ 7491	Josie/Sunniland	1970	2.50	5.00	10.00
❑ 7537	Sanctuary/Brand New Morning	1971	2.50	5.00	10.00
❑ 7537 [PS]	Sanctuary/Brand New Morning	1971	5.00	10.00	20.00
❑ 7663	Seagull/Running Close Behind You	1972	2.50	5.00	10.00
❑ 7704	Doctor Rock and Roll/Sunshine Lady	1973	2.50	5.00	10.00
❑ 7793	New York City Song/Richer Than a Rich Man	1974	2.50	5.00	10.00
❑ 8234	Hey My Love/Lover Boy Supreme	1976	—	3.00	6.00
❑ 8258	The Way You Do the Things You Do/Lover Boy Supreme	1976	—	3.00	6.00
❑ 8293	Oh the Night/Queen of '59	1976	—	3.00	6.00
❑ 8406	Young Virgin Eyes (I'm All Wrapped Up)/Oh the Night	1977	—	3.00	6.00
WARNER/SPECTOR					
❑ 0403	Make the Woman Love Me/Running Close Behind You	1975	3.75	7.50	15.00
—Produced by Phil Spector					
Albums					
ARISTA					
❑ AL 8549	Yo Frankie	1989	2.50	5.00	10.00

Number	Title (A Side/B Side)	Yr	VG	VG+	NM
COLLECTABLES					
❑ 5027	Runaround Sue	198?	2.50	5.00	10.00
COLUMBIA					
❑ CL 2010 [M]	Ruby Baby	1963	7.50	15.00	30.00
❑ CL 2107 [M]	Donna the Prima Donna	1963	7.50	15.00	30.00
❑ CS 8810 [S]	Ruby Baby	1963	10.00	20.00	40.00
❑ CS 8907 [S]	Donna the Prima Donna	1963	10.00	20.00	40.00
❑ CS 9773	Wonder Where I'm Bound	1969	5.00	10.00	20.00
❑ KC 31942	Dion's Greatest Hits	1973	5.00	10.00	20.00
❑ PC 31942	Dion's Greatest Hits	198?	2.00	4.00	8.00
—Budget-line reissue					
DAYSPRING					
❑ DST-4022	Inside Job	1980	3.00	6.00	12.00
❑ DST-4027	Only Jesus	198?	3.00	6.00	12.00
❑ WR-8111	I Put Away My Idols	198?	3.00	6.00	12.00
❑ WR-8112	Seasons (The Best of Dion)	198?	3.00	6.00	12.00
LAURIE					
❑ LLP 2004 [M]	Alone with Dion	1960	50.00	100.00	200.00
—With three wallet-size photos on inside strip (deduct 50% if missing)					
❑ LLP 2009 [M]	Runaround Sue	1961	25.00	50.00	100.00
—Black vinyl					
❑ LLP 2009 [M]	Runaround Sue	1961	200.00	400.00	800.00
—Colored vinyl (gold, green or blue)					
❑ LLP 2009 [M]	Runaround Sue	1962	20.00	40.00	80.00
—Black vinyl; with sticker on front cover: "Includes the Hit Singles 'The Majestic'/'The Wanderer'"					
❑ LLP 2012 [M]	Lovers Who Wander	1962	17.50	35.00	70.00
❑ LLP 2013 [M]	Dion Sings His Greatest Hits	1962	17.50	35.00	70.00
❑ SLP 2013 [R]	Dion Sings His Greatest Hits	196?	12.50	25.00	50.00
❑ LLP 2015 [M]	Love Came to Me	1963	17.50	35.00	70.00
❑ LLP 2017 [M]	Dion Sings to Sandy (And All His Other Girls)	1963	12.50	25.00	50.00
❑ LLP 2019 [M]	Dion Sings the 15 Million Sellers	1963	12.50	25.00	50.00
❑ SLP 2019 [R]	Dion Sings the 15 Million Sellers	196?	7.50	15.00	30.00
❑ LLP 2022 [M]	More of Dion's Greatest Hits	1964	12.50	25.00	50.00
❑ SLP 2022 [R]	More of Dion's Greatest Hits	196?	7.50	15.00	30.00
❑ SLP 2047	Dion	1968	5.00	10.00	20.00
❑ LES-4004	Abraham, Martin and John	197?	3.00	6.00	12.00
—Reissue of SLP-2047					
❑ LES-4013	Dion Sings the Hits of the 50's and 60's	1978	3.00	6.00	12.00
❑ DT-90386 [R]	Dion Sings His Greatest Hits	1965	30.00	60.00	120.00
—Capitol Record Club edition					
❑ T-90386 [M]	Dion Sings His Greatest Hits	1965	30.00	60.00	120.00
—Capitol Record Club edition					
❑ DT-91027 [R]	Runaround Sue	196?	30.00	60.00	120.00
—Capitol Record Club edition					
❑ T-91027 [M]	Runaround Sue	196?	30.00	60.00	120.00
—Capitol Record Club edition					
❑ DT-91128 [R]	More of Dion's Greatest Hits	196?	30.00	60.00	120.00
—Capitol Record Club edition					
❑ T-91128 [M]	More of Dion's Greatest Hits	196?	30.00	60.00	120.00
—Capitol Record Club edition					
❑ ST-91577	Dion	1968	6.25	12.50	25.00
—Capitol Record Club edition					
LIFESONG					
❑ JZ 35356	Return of the Wanderer	1978	3.00	6.00	12.00
WARNER BROS.					
❑ WS 1826	Sit Down, Old Friend	1969	5.00	10.00	20.00
❑ WS 1872	You're Not Alone	1971	3.75	7.50	15.00
❑ WS 1945	Sanctuary	1971	3.75	7.50	15.00
❑ BS 2642	Suite for Late Summer	1972	3.75	7.50	15.00
❑ BS 2954	Streetheart	1976	3.75	7.50	15.00
WORD					
❑ WR-8285	Kingdom in the Streets	1985	3.00	6.00	12.00

DION AND THE BELMONTS Also see THE BELMONTS; CARLO; DION.
45s

Number	Title (A Side/B Side)	Yr	VG	VG+	NM
ABC					
❑ 10868	My Girl the Month of May/Berimbau	1966	3.00	6.00	12.00
❑ 10896	For Bobbie/Movin' Man	1967	3.00	6.00	12.00
LAURIE					
❑ ST-607 [S]	In the Still of the Night/All the Things You Are	196?	20.00	40.00	80.00
—Small hole, plays at 33 1/3 rpm					
❑ ST-608 [S]	Swinging on a Star/In Other Words	196?	20.00	40.00	80.00
—Small hole, plays at 33 1/3 rpm					
❑ ST-610 [S]	I've Cried Before/September Song	196?	20.00	40.00	80.00
—Small hole, plays at 33 1/3 rpm					
❑ 3013	I Wonder Why/Teen Angel	1958	5.00	10.00	20.00
—Black, red and white label					
❑ 3013	I Wonder Why/Teen Angel	1958	7.50	15.00	30.00
—Light blue label					
❑ 3013	I Wonder Why/Teen Angel	1958	15.00	30.00	60.00
—Gray label					
❑ 3015	No One Knows/I Can't Go On (Rosalie)	1958	5.00	10.00	20.00
—Black, red and white label					
❑ 3015	No One Knows/I Can't Go On (Rosalie)	1958	7.50	15.00	30.00
—Light blue label					
❑ 3015	No One Knows/I Can't Go On (Rosalie)	1958	12.50	25.00	50.00
—Gray label					
❑ 3021	Don't Pity Me/Just You	1958	6.25	12.50	25.00
❑ 3027 [M]	A Teenager in Love/I've Cried Before	1959	6.25	12.50	25.00
❑ S-3027 [S]	A Teenager in Love/I've Cried Before	1959	12.50	25.00	50.00
❑ 3035	Every Little Thing I Do/A Lover's Prayer	1959	6.25	12.50	25.00
❑ 3035 [PS]	Every Little Thing I Do/A Lover's Prayer	1959	12.50	25.00	50.00
❑ 3044	Where or When/That's My Desire	1959	6.25	12.50	25.00
❑ 3044 [PS]	Where or When/That's My Desire	1959	12.50	25.00	50.00
❑ 3052	When You Wish Upon a Star/Wonderful Girl	1960	6.25	12.50	25.00
❑ 3052 [PS]	When You Wish Upon a Star/Wonderful Girl	1960	12.50	25.00	50.00
❑ 3059	In the Still of the Night/A Funny Feeling	1960	6.25	12.50	25.00
❑ 3059 [PS]	In the Still of the Night/A Funny Feeling	1960	12.50	25.00	50.00
LAURIE DOUBLE GOLD					
❑ 100	I Wonder Why/Runaround Sue	197?	—	2.00	4.00
—B-side by Dion					
❑ 101	No One Knows/The Wanderer	197?	—	2.00	4.00
—B-side by Dion					
❑ 102	A Teenager in Love/A Lover's Prayer	197?	—	2.00	4.00
❑ 104	Where or When/Lovers Who Wander	197?	—	2.00	4.00
—B-side by Dion					

Number	Title (A Side/B Side)	Yr	VG	VG+	NM
MOHAWK					
❑ 106	Teenage Clementine/Santa Margarita	1957	15.00	30.00	60.00
—May be listed as "The Belmonts"					
❑ 107	Tag Along/We Went Away	1957	15.00	30.00	60.00
7-Inch Extended Plays					
LAURIE					
❑ EP-301	I Wonder Why/No One Knows//Don't Pity Me/A Teenager in Love	1959	30.00	60.00	120.00
❑ EP-301 [PS]	Dion and the Belmonts: Their Hits	1959	45.00	90.00	180.00
❑ 302	Where or When/You Better Not Do That// Wonderful Girl/That's My Desire	1959	25.00	50.00	100.00
❑ 302 [PS]	Where or When	1959	37.50	75.00	150.00
Albums					
ABC					
❑ 599 [M]	Together Again	1967	7.50	15.00	30.00
❑ S-599 [S]	Together Again	1967	10.00	20.00	40.00
ARISTA					
❑ A2L 8206 [(2)]	24 Original Classics	1984	3.00	6.00	12.00
COLLECTABLES					
❑ 5025	Presenting Dion & The Belmonts	198?	2.50	5.00	10.00
❑ 5026	Wish Upon a Star	198?	2.50	5.00	10.00
❑ 5041	20 Golden Classics	198?	2.50	5.00	10.00
LAURIE					
❑ LLP 1002 [M]	Presenting Dion & The Belmonts	1959	62.50	125.00	250.00
❑ LLP 2002 [M]	Presenting Dion & The Belmonts	1960	37.50	75.00	150.00
❑ SLP 2002 [R]	Presenting Dion & The Belmonts	196?	300.00	600.00	900.00
—Despite its rechanneled stereo sound, this record is collectible because of its utter rarity					
❑ LLP 2006 [M]	Wish Upon a Star	1960	37.50	75.00	150.00
❑ LLP 2016 [M]	"Together" On Records — By Special Request	1963	12.50	25.00	50.00
❑ LES 4002	Everything You Always Wanted to Hear by Dion and the Belmonts	197?	3.75	7.50	15.00
❑ SLP 6000 [(3)]	60 Greatest Hits	197?	5.00	10.00	20.00
—In regular cover					
❑ SLP 6000 [(3)]	60 Greatest Hits	197?	7.50	15.00	30.00
—In box					
PAIR					
❑ PDL2-1142 [(2)]	The Best of Dion and the Belmonts	1986	3.00	6.00	12.00
PICKWICK					
❑ SPC-3521	Doo Wop	1975	2.50	5.00	10.00
—Reissue of ABC tracks					
RHINO					
❑ RNLP 70228	Reunion — Live at Madison Square Garden — 1972	1987	2.50	5.00	10.00
—Reissue of ABC tracks					
WARNER BROS.					
❑ BS 2664	Reunion — Live at Madison Square Garden — 1972	1973	3.75	7.50	15.00

DION AND THE TIMBERLANES Early version of DION AND THE BELMONTS.
45s

Number	Title (A Side/B Side)	Yr	VG	VG+	NM
JUBILEE					
❑ 5294	The Chosen Few/Out in Colorado	1957	7.50	15.00	30.00
MOHAWK					
❑ 105	The Chosen Few/Out in Colorado	1957	15.00	30.00	60.00

DIPPERS QUINTET, THE
45s

Number	Title (A Side/B Side)	Yr	VG	VG+	NM
FLAYR					
❑ 500	It's Almost Christmas/Look What I've Found	1955	2000.	3000.	4000.

DIRKSEN, SENATOR EVERETT MCKINLEY
45s

Number	Title (A Side/B Side)	Yr	VG	VG+	NM
CAPITOL					
❑ 2034	The First Time the Christmas Story Was Told/I Heard the Bells on Christmas Day	1967	2.00	4.00	8.00
❑ 5805	Gallant Men/The New Colossus	1966	—	3.00	6.00
❑ 5805 [PS]	Gallant Men/The New Colossus	1966	2.00	4.00	8.00
❑ 5912	Man Is Not Alone/The Shepherd and His Flock	1967	—	2.50	5.00
Albums					
CAPITOL					
❑ ST 2643 [S]	Gallant Men	1966	3.75	7.50	15.00
❑ T 2643 [M]	Gallant Men	1966	3.75	7.50	15.00
❑ ST 2754 [S]	Man Is Not Alone	1967	3.75	7.50	15.00
❑ T 2754 [M]	Man Is Not Alone	1967	5.00	10.00	20.00
❑ ST 2792 [S]	Everett McKinley Dirksen at Christmas Time	1967	5.00	10.00	20.00
❑ T 2792 [M]	Everett McKinley Dirksen at Christmas Time	1967	7.50	15.00	30.00

DIRT BAND, THE See NITTY GRITTY DIRT BAND.

DIRTY BLUES BAND, THE
45s

Number	Title (A Side/B Side)	Yr	VG	VG+	NM
BLUESWAY					
❑ 61016	Hound Dog/New Orleans Woman	1968	2.00	4.00	8.00
Albums					
BLUESWAY					
❑ BLS-6010	The Dirty Blues Band	1968	5.00	10.00	20.00
❑ BLS-6020	Stone Dirt	1968	5.00	10.00	20.00

DISCO-TEX AND THE SEX-O-LETTES
45s

Number	Title (A Side/B Side)	Yr	VG	VG+	NM
CHELSEA					
❑ 3004	Get Dancin' (Part I)/Get Dancin' (Part II)	1974	—	2.00	4.00
❑ 3015	I Wanna Dance Wit'choo (Part I)/I Wanna Dance Wit'choo (Part II)	1975	—	2.00	4.00
❑ 3026	Jam Band/Jam Band Reprise	1975	—	2.00	4.00
❑ 3040	Hot Lava/Hot Lava 2	1976	—	2.00	4.00
❑ 3045	Dancin' Kid (Part I)/Dancin' Kid (Part II)	1976	—	2.00	4.00
❑ 3054	Strollin'/We're Havin' a Party (It's Gonna Be Alright)	1976	—	2.00	4.00
❑ 3070	Wooly Bully/On Broadway	1977	—	2.00	4.00
Albums					
CHELSEA					
❑ CHL 505	Disco-Tex and His Sex-O-Lettes	1975	2.50	5.00	10.00
❑ CHL 516	Manhattan Millionaire	1976	2.50	5.00	10.00
❑ CHL 555	A Piece of the Rock	1977	2.50	5.00	10.00

Rick Derringer, *All American Boy*, Blue Sky KZ 32481, stereo LP, $7.50-$15.

The Detergents, "Leader of the Laundromat," Roulette 4590, picture sleeve, $20-$40.

Neil Diamond, *The Feel of Neil Diamond,* Bang BLPS-214, stereo LP with red and white label, $50-$100.

Dion and the Belmonts, *Wish Upon a Star with Dion and the Belmonts,* Laurie LLP-2006, mono LP, $75-$150.

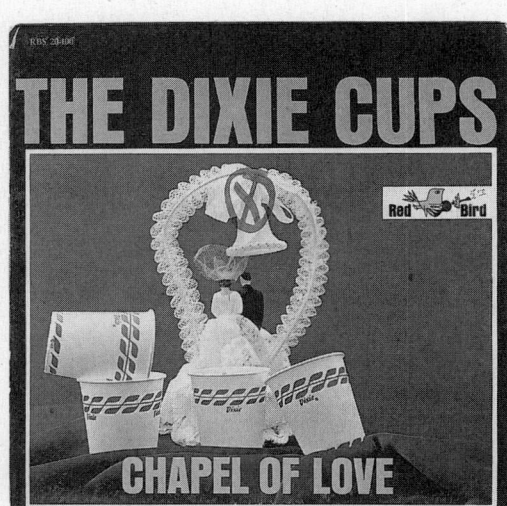

The Dixie Cups, *Chapel of Love,* Red Bird RB 20-100, mono LP, $30-$60.

The Doors, "Break On Through," Elektra 45611, picture sleeve, $60-$120.

Number	Title (A Side/B Side)	Yr	VG	VG+	NM

DISENTRI, TURNER Actually Bob Gaudio of THE ROYAL TEENS and THE FOUR SEASONS.
45s
TOPIX
| ❏ 6001 | 10,000,000 Tears/Spanish Lace | 1961 | 25.00 | 50.00 | 100.00 |

DISTANTS, THE
45s
NORTHERN
| ❏ 3732 | Come On/Always | 1960 | 150.00 | 300.00 | 600.00 |

WARWICK
| ❏ 546 | Come On/Always | 1960 | 25.00 | 50.00 | 100.00 |
| ❏ 577 | Always/Open Up Your Heart | 1960 | 25.00 | 50.00 | 100.00 |

DIXIE CUPS, THE
45s
ABC
| ❏ 10855 | Love Ain't So Bad (After All)/Daddy Said No | 1966 | 3.00 | 6.00 | 12.00 |

ABC-PARAMOUNT
❏ 10692	That's Where It's At/Two-Way-Poc-A-Way	1965	3.00	6.00	12.00
❏ 10715	I'm Not the Kind of Girl (To Marry)/				
	What Goes Up Must Come Down	1965	3.00	6.00	12.00
❏ 10755	A-B-C Song/That's What the Kids Said	1965	3.00	6.00	12.00

ANTILLES
| ❏ 707 | Iko Iko/Hey Hey (Indian's Coming) | 1987 | — | 2.00 | 4.00 |
| —B-side by The Wild Tchoupitoulas |
| ❏ 707 [PS] | Iko Iko/Hey Hey (Indian's Coming) | 1987 | — | 2.00 | 4.00 |

LANA
| ❏ 144 | Chapel of Love/Ain't That Nice | 196? | 2.00 | 4.00 | 8.00 |
| —Oldies reissue |

RED BIRD
❏ 10-001	Chapel of Love/Ain't That Nice	1964	7.50	15.00	30.00
❏ 10-006	People Say/Girls Can Tell	1964	5.00	10.00	20.00
❏ 10-012	You Should Have Seen the Way He				
	Looked at Me/No True Love	1964	5.00	10.00	20.00
❏ 10-017	Little Bell/Another Boy Like Me	1964	5.00	10.00	20.00
❏ 10-024	Iko Iko/Gee, Baby, Gee	1965	5.00	10.00	20.00
❏ 10-024	Iko Iko/I'm Gonna Get You Yet	1965	5.00	10.00	20.00
❏ 10-032	Gee, the Moon Is Shining Bright/				
	I'm Gonna Get You Yet	1965	5.00	10.00	20.00

Albums
ABC-PARAMOUNT
| ❏ 525 [M] | Riding High | 1965 | 15.00 | 30.00 | 60.00 |
| ❏ S-525 [S] | Riding High | 1965 | 20.00 | 40.00 | 80.00 |

RED BIRD
❏ RB 20-100 [M]	Chapel of Love	1964	15.00	30.00	60.00
❏ RBS 20-100 [S]	Chapel of Love	1964	20.00	40.00	80.00
❏ RB 20-103 [M]	Iko Iko	1965	37.50	75.00	150.00

DIXIEBELLES, THE
45s
SOUND STAGE 7
❏ 2507	(Down at) Papa Joe's/Rock, Rock, Rock	1963	2.50	5.00	10.00
❏ 2517	Southtown U.S.A./Why Don't You Set Me Free	1964	2.50	5.00	10.00
❏ 2521	New York Town/The Beale Street Dog	1964	2.50	5.00	10.00

Albums
SOUND STAGE 7
| ❏ SSM-5000 [M] | Down at Papa Joe's | 1963 | 10.00 | 20.00 | 40.00 |
| ❏ SSS-15000 [R] | Down at Papa Joe's | 1963 | 7.50 | 15.00 | 30.00 |

DIXIES, THE
45s
AUTUMN
| ❏ 12 | He's Got You/Geisha Girl | 1965 | 3.75 | 7.50 | 15.00 |

DIXON, BILLY, AND THE TOPICS See THE FOUR SEASONS.

DIXON, FLOYD
45s
ALADDIN
| ❏ 3101 | Do I Love You/Time and Place | 1951 | 50.00 | 100.00 | 200.00 |
| —Earlier Floyd Dixon 45s on Aladdin may exist |
❏ 3111	Too Much Jelly Roll/Baby, Let's Go to the Woods	1952	50.00	100.00	200.00
❏ 3121	Blues for Cuba/Bad Neighborhood	1952	50.00	100.00	200.00
❏ 3135	Wine, Wine, Wine/Call Operator 210	1952	50.00	100.00	200.00
❏ 3144	Red Cherries/The River	1952	75.00	150.00	300.00
—Black vinyl
❏ 3144	Red Cherries/The River	1952	175.00	350.00	700.00
—Red vinyl
❏ 3151	Tired, Broke and Busted/Come Back Baby	1952	37.50	75.00	150.00
❏ 3166	You Played Me for a Fool/Broken Hearted				
	Traveler	1953	37.50	75.00	150.00
❏ 3196	Lovin'/Married Woman	1953	37.50	75.00	150.00
❏ 3230	You Need Me Now/A Long Time Ago	1954	25.00	50.00	100.00

CASH
| ❏ 1057 | Oh Baby/Never Can Tell | 1957 | 12.50 | 25.00 | 50.00 |

CAT
| ❏ 106 | Moonshine/Roll Baby Roll | 1954 | 15.00 | 30.00 | 60.00 |
| ❏ 114 | Hey Bartender/It Is True | 1955 | 15.00 | 30.00 | 60.00 |

CHATTAHOOCHIE
| ❏ 652 | Tell Me, Tell Me/There Goes My Heart | 1964 | 2.50 | 5.00 | 10.00 |

CHECKER
| ❏ 857 | Alarm Clock Blues/I'm Ashamed of Myself | 1957 | 7.50 | 15.00 | 30.00 |

DODGE
| ❏ 807 | Opportunity Blues/Daisy | 1961 | 3.75 | 7.50 | 15.00 |

EBB
| ❏ 105 | What Is Life Without a Home/Oh-Ee Little Girl | 1957 | 7.50 | 15.00 | 30.00 |

IMPERIAL
| ❏ 5849 | Tired, Broke and Busted/Call Operator 210 | 1962 | 3.00 | 6.00 | 12.00 |

KENT
| ❏ 311 | Change Your Mind/Dance the Thing | 1958 | 5.00 | 10.00 | 20.00 |

SPECIALTY
| ❏ 468 | Hard Living Alone/Please Don't Go | 1953 | 20.00 | 40.00 | 80.00 |
| —Black vinyl |
| ❏ 468 | Hard Living Alone/Please Don't Go | 1953 | 50.00 | 100.00 | 200.00 |
| —Red vinyl |
| ❏ 477 | Hole in the Wall/Old Memories | 1953 | 20.00 | 40.00 | 80.00 |
| ❏ 486 | Ooh-Eee Ooh-Eee/Nose Job | 1954 | 20.00 | 40.00 | 80.00 |

SWINGIN'
| ❏ 626 | Tight Skirts/Wake Up and Live | 1960 | 5.00 | 10.00 | 20.00 |

DOBKINS, CARL, JR.
45s
ATCO
| ❏ 6283 | If Teardrops Were Diamonds/ | | | | |
| | I'm So Sorry Little Girl | 1964 | 3.00 | 6.00 | 12.00 |

CHALET
| ❏ 1053 | Days of Sand and Shovel/Linda the Motel Maid | 1969 | 2.50 | 5.00 | 10.00 |
| ❏ 1056 | My Heart Is an Open Book/Pictures | 1969 | 2.50 | 5.00 | 10.00 |

COLPIX
| ❏ 762 | His Loss Is My Gain/ | | | | |
| | A Little Bit Later On Down the Line | 1965 | 3.00 | 6.00 | 12.00 |

DECCA
❏ 30656	Love Is Everything/If You Don't Want My Lovin'	1958	5.00	10.00	20.00
❏ 30803	My Heart Is an Open Book/My Pledge to You	1959	6.25	12.50	25.00
❏ 31020	Lucky Devil/In My Heart	1959	5.00	10.00	20.00
❏ 31020 [PS]	Lucky Devil/In My Heart	1959	7.50	15.00	30.00
❏ 31088	Exclusively Yours/One Little Girl	1960	3.75	7.50	15.00
❏ 31088 [PS]	Exclusively Yours/One Little Girl	1960	7.50	15.00	30.00
❏ 31143	Different Kind of Love/Genie	1960	3.75	7.50	15.00
❏ 31182	Lovelight/Take Time Out	1960	3.75	7.50	15.00
❏ 31260	Pretty Little Girl in the Yellow Dress/That's What				
	I Call True Love	1961	3.75	7.50	15.00
❏ 31301	Sawdust Dolly/A Chance to Belong	1961	3.75	7.50	15.00
❏ 31353	Ask Me No Questions/Promise Me	1962	3.75	7.50	15.00

FRATERNITY
| ❏ 794 | That's Why I'm Asking/Take Hold of My Hand | 1958 | 7.50 | 15.00 | 30.00 |

7-Inch Extended Plays
DECCA
❏ ED 2664	My Heart Is An Open Book/My Pledge to You//				
	Love Is Everything/If You Don't Want My Lovin'	1959	10.00	20.00	40.00
❏ ED 2664 [PS]	My Heart Is An Open Book	1959	10.00	20.00	40.00

DOBRO, JIMMY See JAMES BURTON.

DOBRO, LON
45s
4 STAR
| ❏ 1754 | I Just Like You/All the Time | 1961 | 15.00 | 30.00 | 60.00 |

TROY
| ❏ 1003 | Undercurrent/Mid-Night Surf | 1963 | 12.50 | 25.00 | 50.00 |

DOC HOLLIDAY
45s
METROMEDIA
| ❏ 68-0114 | Whiskey Lady/Magga Blue | 1973 | 2.00 | 4.00 | 8.00 |

Albums
METROMEDIA
| ❏ 1017 | Doc Holliday | 1973 | 5.00 | 10.00 | 20.00 |

DR. FEELGOOD AND THE INTERNS Also see PIANO RED.
45s
COLUMBIA
| ❏ 43372 | Doctor of Love/Let the House Rock On | 1965 | 2.00 | 4.00 | 8.00 |
| ❏ 43615 | Where Did You Go/Don't Tell Me No Dirty | 1966 | 2.00 | 4.00 | 8.00 |

OKEH
❏ 7144	Mr. Moonlight/Dr. Feel-Good	1962	3.00	6.00	12.00
❏ 7153	Bald Headed Lena/What's Up Doc	1962	3.00	6.00	12.00
❏ 7156	The Right String But the Wrong Yo-Yo/				
	What's Up Doc	1962	3.00	6.00	12.00
❏ 7161	Let's Have a Good Time Tonight/				
	The Same Old Things Keep Happening	1962	3.00	6.00	12.00
❏ 7167	My Gal Jo/Bald Headed Lena	1963	3.00	6.00	12.00
❏ 7185	The Doctor's Boogie/Blang Dong	1963	3.00	6.00	12.00

Albums
OKEH
| ❏ OKM 12101 [M] | Dr. Feelgood and the Interns | 1962 | 25.00 | 50.00 | 100.00 |
| ❏ OKS 14101 [S] | Dr. Feelgood and the Interns | 1962 | 50.00 | 100.00 | 200.00 |

DR. HOOK Includes records as "Dr. Hook and the Medicine Show." Also see RAY SAWYER.
45s
CAPITOL
❏ 4081	Levitate/Cooky and Lila	1975	—	2.00	4.00
❏ 4104	The Millionaire/Cooky and Lila	1975	—	2.00	4.00
❏ 4171	Only You/Let Me Be Your Lover	1975	—	2.50	5.00
❏ 4280	A Little Bit More/A Couple More Years	1976	—	2.50	5.00
❏ 4364	If Not You/Bad Eye Bill	1976	—	2.00	4.00
❏ 4423	Walk Right In/Sexy Energy	1977	—	2.00	4.00
❏ 4534	Making Love and Music/Who Dat	1978	—	2.00	4.00
❏ 4615	I Don't Want to Be Alone Tonight/You Make My				
	Pants Want to Get Up and Dance	1978	—	2.00	4.00
❏ 4621	Sharing the Night Together/You Make My Pants				
	Want to Get Up and Dance	1978	—	2.00	4.00
❏ 4677	All the Time in the World/Dooley Jones	1979	—	2.00	4.00
❏ 4705	When You're in Love with a Beautiful Woman/				
	Knowing She's There	1979	—	2.00	4.00
❏ 4785	Better Love Next Time/Mountain Mary	1979	—	2.00	4.00
❏ 4831	Sexy Eyes/Help Me Mama	1980	—	2.00	4.00
❏ 4885	Years from Now/I Don't Feel Much Like Smilin'	1980	—	2.00	4.00
❏ 4885 [PS]	Years from Now/I Don't Feel Much Like Smilin'	1980	—	2.50	5.00
❏ SPRO-8220/1 [DJ]	Interview Record for Use in Promoting the				
	Album Release of "Bankrupt"	1975	2.00	4.00	8.00
❏ SPRO-8220/1 [PS]	The Stimu Dr. Hook	1975	3.00	6.00	12.00

CASABLANCA
❏ 2314	Girls Can Get It/Doin' It	1980	—	2.00	4.00
❏ 2325	S.O.S. For Love/99 and Me	1981	—	2.00	4.00
❏ 2347	Baby Makes Her Blue Jeans Talk/The Turn On	1981	—	2.00	4.00
❏ 2347 [PS]	Baby Makes Her Blue Jeans Talk/The Turn On	1981	—	2.50	5.00
❏ 2351	Loveline/Pity the Fool	1981	—	2.00	4.00

COLUMBIA
| ❏ 3-10032 | Make It Easy/Ballad of Lucy Jordan | 1974 | — | 3.00 | 6.00 |
| —All as "Dr. Hook and the Medicine Show" |
❏ 4-45392	Last Morning/One More Ride				
	(Lucille and Bunky)	1971	—	3.00	6.00
❏ 4-45562	Sylvia's Mother/Makin' It Natural	1972	—	2.50	5.00
—Gray label

Number	Title (A Side/B Side)	Yr	VG	VG+	NM
❑ 4-45562	Sylvia's Mother/Makin' It Natural	1972	—	3.00	6.00
—Orange label with "Columbia" background print					
❑ 4-45667	Carry Me, Carrie/Call That True Love	1972	—	2.50	5.00
❑ 4-45667 [PS]	Carry Me, Carrie/Call That True Love	1972	—	3.00	6.00
❑ 4-45732	The Cover of "Rolling Stone"/Queen of the Silver Dollar	1972		2.50	5.00
—Orange label					
❑ 4-45732	The Cover of "Rolling Stone"/Queen of the Silver Dollar	1972		3.00	6.00
—Gray label					
❑ 4-45878	Roland the Roadie and Gertrude the Groupie/ Put a Little Bit on Me	1973	—	2.50	5.00
❑ 4-45925	Life Ain't Easy/Wonderful Stone Soup	1973	—	2.50	5.00
❑ 4-46026	Monterey Jack/Cops and Robbers	1974	—	2.50	5.00
Albums					
CAPITOL					
❑ ST-11397	Bankrupt	1975	2.50	5.00	10.00
❑ ST-11522	A Little Bit More	1976	2.50	5.00	10.00
❑ ST-11632	Makin' Love and Music	1977	2.50	5.00	10.00
❑ SW-11859	Pleasure and Pain	1978	2.50	5.00	10.00
❑ ST-12018	Sometimes You Win...	1979	2.50	5.00	10.00
❑ SOO-12023	Sometimes You Win...	1979	2.50	5.00	10.00
—Other than the prefix and the number, we don't know if there are any differences between this and 12018, but both do exist					
❑ ST-12114	Live	1981	2.50	5.00	10.00
❑ SOO-12122	Dr. Hook/Greatest Hits	1980	2.50	5.00	10.00
❑ ST-12325	The Rest of Dr. Hook	1984	2.00	4.00	8.00
❑ SN-16179	Bankrupt	198?	2.00	4.00	8.00
—Budget-line reissue					
❑ SN-16180	A Little Bit More	198?	2.00	4.00	8.00
—Budget-line reissue					
❑ SN-16181	Pleasure and Pain	198?	2.00	4.00	8.00
—Budget-line reissue					
❑ SN-16228	Makin' Love and Music	198?	2.00	4.00	8.00
—Budget-line reissue					
❑ SN-16229	Sometimes You Win...	198?	2.00	4.00	8.00
—Budget-line reissue					
❑ SN-16325	Dr. Hook/Greatest Hits	198?	2.00	4.00	8.00
—Budget-line reissue					
CASABLANCA					
❑ NBLP-7251	Rising	1980	2.50	5.00	10.00
❑ NBLP-7264	Players in the Dark	1982	2.50	5.00	10.00
COLUMBIA					
❑ KC 30898	Dr. Hook & The Medicine Show	1972	3.75	7.50	15.00
❑ PC 30898	Dr. Hook & The Medicine Show	198?	2.00	4.00	8.00
—Budget-line reissue					
❑ KC 31622	Sloppy Seconds	1972	3.75	7.50	15.00
❑ PC 31622	Sloppy Seconds	198?	2.00	4.00	8.00
—Budget-line reissue					
❑ KC 32270	Belly Up!	1973	3.75	7.50	15.00
❑ C 34147	Dr. Hook and the Medicine Show Revisited	1976	2.50	5.00	10.00
❑ PC 34147	Dr. Hook and the Medicine Show Revisited	198?	2.00	4.00	8.00
—Budget-line reissue					
MERCURY					
❑ 800054-1	Players in the Dark	1983	2.00	4.00	8.00
—Reissue of Casablanca 7264					

DR. HOOK AND THE MEDICINE SHOW See DR. HOOK.

DR. JOHN Also see MIKE BLOOMFIELD/JOHN PAUL HAMMOND/DR. JOHN; HUEY "PIANO" SMITH.

45s

Number	Title (A Side/B Side)	Yr	VG	VG+	NM
A.F.O.					
❑ 309	The Point/One Naughty Flat	1962	6.25	12.50	25.00
—As "Mac Rebenack"					
ACE					
❑ 611	Good Times/Sahara	1961	6.25	12.50	25.00
—As "Mac Rebenack"					
ATCO					
❑ 6607	I Walk on Gilded Splinters (Part 1)/I Walk on Gilded Splinters (Part 2)	1968	3.00	6.00	12.00
❑ 6635	Jump Sturdy/Mama Roox	1968	3.00	6.00	12.00
❑ 6697	Patriotic Flag Waver (Long)/Patriotic Flag Waver (Short)	1969	2.00	4.00	8.00
❑ 6755	Wash, Mama, Wash/Loup Gardo	1970	3.00	6.00	12.00
❑ 6882	Iko Iko/The Huey Smith Medley	1972	2.50	5.00	10.00
❑ 6898	Wang Dang Doodle/Big Chief	1972	—	3.00	6.00
❑ 6900	Let the Good Times Roll/Stack-A-Lee	1972	—	3.00	6.00
❑ 6914	Right Place Wrong Time/I Been Hoodood	1973	—	3.00	6.00
❑ 6937	Such a Night/Cold, Cold, Cold	1973	—	3.00	6.00
❑ 6957	(Everybody Wanna Get Rich) Rite Away/ Mos'Scocious	1974	—	3.00	6.00
❑ 6971	Let's Make a Better World/Me Minus You Equals Loneliness	1974	—	3.00	6.00
HORIZON					
❑ 117	Wild Honey/Dance the Night Away with You	1979	—	2.00	4.00
❑ 125	Keep That Music Simple/I Thought I Heard New Orleans	1979	—	2.00	4.00
RCA					
❑ PB-11285	Take Me Higher/Sweet Rider	1978	—	2.00	4.00
REX					
❑ 1008	Storm Warning/Foolish Little Girl	1959	12.50	25.00	50.00
—As "Mac Rebenack"					
SCEPTER					
❑ 12393	One Night Late/She's Just a Square	1974	—	2.50	5.00
WARNER BROS.					
❑ 22976	Makin' Whoopee!/More Than You Know	1989	—	—	3.00
❑ 22976 [PS]	Makin' Whoopee!/More Than You Know	1989	—	—	3.00
❑ 49703	The Sailor and the Mermaid/One Good Turn	1981	—	2.00	4.00
—A-side with Libby Titus; B-side by Al Jarreau					
Albums					
ACCORD					
❑ SN-7118	Love Potion	1982	2.50	5.00	10.00
ALLIGATOR					
❑ AL-3901	Dr. John's Gumbo	1986	2.50	5.00	10.00
—Reissue of Atco 7006					

Number	Title (A Side/B Side)	Yr	VG	VG+	NM
❑ AL-3904	Gris-Gris	1987	2.50	5.00	10.00
—Reissue of Atco 33-234					
ATCO					
❑ SD 33-234	Gris-Gris	1968	3.75	7.50	15.00
—Yellow label					
❑ SD 33-234	Gris-Gris	1968	7.50	15.00	30.00
—Purple and brown label					
❑ SD 33-270	Babylon	1969	3.75	7.50	15.00
❑ SD 33-316	Remedies	1970	3.75	7.50	15.00
❑ SD 33-362	Dr. John, The Night Tripper (The Sun, Moon & Herbs)	1971	3.75	7.50	15.00
❑ SD 7006	Dr. John's Gumbo	1972	3.00	6.00	12.00
❑ SD 7018	In the Right Place	1973	3.00	6.00	12.00
❑ SD 7043	Desitively Bonaroo	1974	3.00	6.00	12.00
CLEAN CUTS					
❑ 705	Dr. John Plays Mac Rebennack	1982	2.50	5.00	10.00
❑ 707	The Brightest Smile in Town	1984	2.50	5.00	10.00
HORIZON					
❑ SP-732	City Lights	1978	2.50	5.00	10.00
❑ SP-740	Tango Palace	1979	2.50	5.00	10.00
KARATE					
❑ 5404	One Night Late	1978	2.50	5.00	10.00
TRIP					
❑ TLX-350 [(2)]	Superpak	1975	3.00	6.00	12.00
UNITED ARTISTS					
❑ UA-LA552-G	Hollywood Be Thy Name	1975	3.00	6.00	12.00
WARNER BROS.					
❑ 25889	In a Sentimental Mood	1989	3.00	6.00	12.00

DR. JOHN AND CHRIS BARBER Also see each artist's individual listings.

Albums

Number	Title (A Side/B Side)	Yr	VG	VG+	NM
GREAT SOUTHERN					
❑ GS-11024	On a Mardi Gras Day	1991	3.00	6.00	12.00

DOCTOR ROSS

45s

Number	Title (A Side/B Side)	Yr	VG	VG+	NM
HI-Q					
❑ 5027	Cannonball/Numbers Blues	1963	5.00	10.00	20.00
❑ 5033	Call the Doctor/New York Breakdown	1963	5.00	10.00	20.00
SUN					
❑ 193	Chicago Breakdown/Come Back Baby	1954	200.00	400.00	600.00
❑ 212	The Boogie Disease/Juke Box Boogie	1954	500.00	1000.	2000.
Albums					
FORTUNE					
❑ F-3011 [M]	Doctor Ross, The Harmonica Boss	1962	12.50	25.00	50.00
❑ FS-3011 [S]	Doctor Ross, The Harmonica Boss	1962	25.00	50.00	100.00
TESTAMENT					
❑ 2206 [M]	Doctor Ross	196?	5.00	10.00	20.00

DR. WEST'S MEDICINE SHOW AND JUG BAND Also see NORMAN GREENBAUM.

45s

Number	Title (A Side/B Side)	Yr	VG	VG+	NM
GO GO					
❑ 100	The Eggplant That Ate Chicago/You Can't Fight City Hall Blues	1966	3.00	6.00	12.00
❑ 102	Gondoliers, Shakespeares, Overseers, Playboys and Bums/Daddy, I Know	1967	2.50	5.00	10.00
❑ 102 [PS]	Gondoliers, Shakespeares, Overseers, Playboys and Bums/Daddy, I Know	1967	5.00	10.00	20.00
❑ 104	You Can Fly/The Circus Left Town Today	1967	2.50	5.00	10.00
GREGAR					
❑ 71-0100	Gondoliers, Shakespeares, Overseers, Playboys and Bums/Daddy, I Know	1969	2.50	5.00	10.00
❑ 106	Bullets Laverne/Jigsaw	1968	2.50	5.00	10.00
Albums					
GO GO					
❑ 22-17-002	The Eggplant That Ate Chicago	1967	6.25	12.50	25.00
GREGAR					
❑ GG-101	Norman Greenbaum with Dr. West's Medicine Show and Jug Band	1970	5.00	10.00	20.00

DODD, DICK Also see THE STANDELLS.

45s

Number	Title (A Side/B Side)	Yr	VG	VG+	NM
ATTARACK					
❑ 102	Guilty/Requiem 820	1970	2.50	5.00	10.00
TOWER					
❑ 447	Lonely Weekends/Little Sister	1968	3.00	6.00	12.00
❑ 447 [PS]	Lonely Weekends/Little Sister	1968	7.50	15.00	30.00
❑ 490	Fanny/Don't Be Ashamed to Call My Name	1969	3.00	6.00	12.00

DODD, JIMMIE

45s

Number	Title (A Side/B Side)	Yr	VG	VG+	NM
ABC-PARAMOUNT					
❑ 9665	Mouseketeer Theme/Hi to You	1956	5.00	10.00	20.00
❑ 9680	Mickey Mouse Mambo/Humphrey Hop-Pussy Cat	1956	5.00	10.00	20.00
❑ 9691	Zip-A-Dee-Doo-Dah/Song of the South	1956	5.00	10.00	20.00
—B-side by Jeanne Gayle					
7-Inch Extended Plays					
OFFICIAL MICKEY MOUSE CLUB					
❑ DBR 69	Annette/Hey! Cubby Boy!//Banjo Joe/Karen	195?	6.25	12.50	25.00
❑ DBR 69 [PS]	Walt Disney's Annette	195?	6.25	12.50	25.00
Albums					
DISNEYLAND					
❑ WDL-1014 [M]	Jimmie Dodd Sings His Favorite Hymns	1959	6.25	12.50	25.00
—Reissue of 3014 with new number					
❑ DQ-1235 [M]	Sing Along with Jimmie Dodd	1963	7.50	15.00	30.00
❑ DQ-1302 [M]	Favorite Hymns for Family Singing	1967	3.75	7.50	15.00
—Reissue of 1014					
❑ WDL-3014 [M]	Jimmie Dodd Sings His Favorite Hymns	1958	6.25	12.50	25.00
IMPERIAL					
❑ LP-9089 [M]	Lonely Guitar	1959	10.00	20.00	40.00
❑ LP-9121 [M]	Swing-A-Spell	1960	10.00	20.00	40.00
❑ LP-12058 [S]	Swing-A-Spell	1960	12.50	25.00	50.00

Number	Title (A Side/B Side)	Yr	VG	VG+	NM

DODD, KEN
45s
LIBERTY

Number	Title (A Side/B Side)	Yr	VG	VG+	NM
❏ 55733	All of My Life/Happiness	1964	3.00	6.00	12.00
❏ 55835	Tears (For Souvenirs)/You and I	1965	2.50	5.00	10.00
❏ 55859	The River/My Thanks to You	1966	2.50	5.00	10.00
❏ 55893	Promises/Thank You for Being You	1966	2.50	5.00	10.00

LONDON

Number	Title (A Side/B Side)	Yr	VG	VG+	NM
❏ 1942	Love Is Like a Violin/Treasure in My Heart	1960	3.00	6.00	12.00

Albums
LIBERTY

Number	Title (A Side/B Side)	Yr	VG	VG+	NM
❏ LRP-3442 [M]	Tears and The River	1966	3.75	7.50	15.00
❏ LST-7442 [S]	Tears and The River	1966	5.00	10.00	20.00

DODDS, MALCOLM
45s
AMY

Number	Title (A Side/B Side)	Yr	VG	VG+	NM
❏ 861	A Rendezvous with a Broken Heart/All My Wildest Dreams	1962	2.00	4.00	8.00

AURORA

Number	Title (A Side/B Side)	Yr	VG	VG+	NM
❏ 3250	Ich Bin Verry Happy (Merry, Merry Christmas)/Perfect Strangers	1962	2.50	5.00	10.00

DECCA

Number	Title (A Side/B Side)	Yr	VG	VG+	NM
❏ 30653	The Swingin' Platoon/Your Voice	1958	3.00	6.00	12.00
❏ 30766	I'll Always Be with You/This Is Real (This Is Love)	1958	3.00	6.00	12.00
❏ 30857	Deep Inside/Tremble	1959	3.00	6.00	12.00
❏ 30922	I've Waited So Long/Somehow	1959	3.00	6.00	12.00
❏ 30970	I Feel Peculiar/Only for You	1959	3.00	6.00	12.00

END

Number	Title (A Side/B Side)	Yr	VG	VG+	NM
❏ 1000	It Took a Long Time/Beauty and the Beast	1957	15.00	30.00	60.00
❏ 1004	Fools Rush In/Can't See You	1957	20.00	40.00	80.00
❏ 1010	Tonight/Unspoken Love	1958	15.00	30.00	60.00

MGM

Number	Title (A Side/B Side)	Yr	VG	VG+	NM
❏ 12975	All for the Love of a Woman/Come, Oh Come	1961	2.50	5.00	10.00
❏ 13029	Without a Song/Laugh My Heart	1961	2.50	5.00	10.00

PROJECT 3

Number	Title (A Side/B Side)	Yr	VG	VG+	NM
❏ 1319	Hey World/I Don't Want to Cry	196?	—	3.00	6.00
❏ 1338	I Love, I Live, I Love/Mr. Broadloom	196?	—	3.00	6.00

Albums
RCA CAMDEN

Number	Title (A Side/B Side)	Yr	VG	VG+	NM
❏ CAL-873 [M]	Happiness Is a Thing Called Love	196?	3.75	7.50	15.00
❏ CAS-873 [S]	Happiness Is a Thing Called Love	196?	3.00	6.00	12.00

DODDS, NELLA
45s
WAND

Number	Title (A Side/B Side)	Yr	VG	VG+	NM
❏ 167	Come See About Me/You Don't Love Me Anymore	1964	3.75	7.50	15.00
❏ 171	Finders Keepers Losers Weepers/A Girl's Life	1964	3.00	6.00	12.00
❏ 178	Your Love Back/P's and Q's	1965	3.00	6.00	12.00
❏ 187	Come Back Baby/Dream Boy	1965	3.00	6.00	12.00
❏ 1111	Gee Whiz/Maybe Baby	1966	3.75	7.50	15.00
❏ 1136	Honey Boy/I Just Gotta Have You	1966	20.00	40.00	80.00

DODO, JOE, AND THE GROOVERS
45s
RCA VICTOR

Number	Title (A Side/B Side)	Yr	VG	VG+	NM
❏ 47-7207	Groovy/Goin' Steady	1958	6.25	12.50	25.00

DOGGETT, BILL Also see EARL BOSTIC.
45s
ABC-PARAMOUNT

Number	Title (A Side/B Side)	Yr	VG	VG+	NM
❏ 10611	Mudcat/The Kicker	1965	—	3.00	6.00

CHUMLEY

Number	Title (A Side/B Side)	Yr	VG	VG+	NM
❏ 90001	Blue Point of View/Funky Feet	1974	—	2.00	4.00

COLUMBIA

Number	Title (A Side/B Side)	Yr	VG	VG+	NM
❏ 42384	Buster/Ladies Choice	1962	2.50	5.00	10.00
❏ 42531	Oops/Choo Choo	1962	2.50	5.00	10.00
❏ 42689	Soda Pop/Ham Fat	1963	2.50	5.00	10.00
❏ 42792	The Worm/Hot Fudge	1963	2.50	5.00	10.00

CORAL

Number	Title (A Side/B Side)	Yr	VG	VG+	NM
❏ 61739	A Pretty Girl Is Like a Melody/If I Should Lose You	1956	3.00	6.00	12.00

KING

Number	Title (A Side/B Side)	Yr	VG	VG+	NM
❏ S-7 1609 [S]	The Madison/After Hours	196?	6.25	12.50	25.00

—33 1/3 rpm jukebox single, small hole

Number	Title (A Side/B Side)	Yr	VG	VG+	NM
❏ S-7 1611 [S]	Mr. Ballard/The Eagle Speaks	196?	6.25	12.50	25.00

—33 1/3 rpm jukebox single, small hole

Number	Title (A Side/B Side)	Yr	VG	VG+	NM
❏ 4548	Please Don't Ever Let Me Go/Glo' Glug	1952	5.00	10.00	20.00
❏ 4702	It's a Dream/The Song Is Ended	1954	5.00	10.00	20.00
❏ 4711	There's No You/Easy	1954	5.00	10.00	20.00
❏ 4720	Sweet Lorraine/Tailor Made	1954	5.00	10.00	20.00
❏ 4732	Sweet Slumber/High Heels	1954	5.00	10.00	20.00
❏ 4738	The Nearness of You/Honey	1954	5.00	10.00	20.00
❏ 4742	The Christmas Song/Winter Wonderland	1954	5.00	10.00	20.00
❏ 4759	Tara's Theme/Gumbo	1955	3.75	7.50	15.00
❏ 4769	My Reverie/King Bee	1955	3.75	7.50	15.00
❏ 4784	Wild Oats/I'll Be Around	1955	3.75	7.50	15.00
❏ 4795	Oof/Street Scene	1955	3.75	7.50	15.00
❏ 4808	Quaker City/True Blue	1955	3.75	7.50	15.00
❏ 4825	You Don't Know What Love Is/Shove Off	1955	3.75	7.50	15.00
❏ 4838	Honey Boy/Misty Moon	1955	3.75	7.50	15.00
❏ 4888	In a Sentimental Mood/Who's Who	1956	3.75	7.50	15.00
❏ 4917	Squashy/We Found Love	1956	3.75	7.50	15.00
❏ 4936	What a Difference a Day Makes/Stella by Starlight	1956	3.75	7.50	15.00
❏ 4950	Honky Tonk (Part 1)/Honky Tonk (Part 2)	1956	5.00	10.00	20.00
❏ 5000	Slow Walk/Hand in Hand	1956	3.75	7.50	15.00
❏ 5001	Honky Tonk (Vocal)/Peacock Alley	1956	3.75	7.50	15.00

—Vocal by Tommy Brown

Number	Title (A Side/B Side)	Yr	VG	VG+	NM
❏ 5020	Ram-Bunk-Shush/Blue Largo	1957	3.00	6.00	12.00
❏ 5044	Chloe/Number Three	1957	3.00	6.00	12.00
❏ 5058	Ding Dong/Cling to Me	1957	3.00	6.00	12.00
❏ 5070	Hammer Head/Shindig	1957	3.00	6.00	12.00
❏ 5080	Hot Ginger/Soft	1957	3.00	6.00	12.00
❏ 5096	Hippy Dippy/Flying Home	1957	3.00	6.00	12.00

Number	Title (A Side/B Side)	Yr	VG	VG+	NM
❏ 5101	Leaps and Bounds (Part 1)/Leaps and Bounds (Part 2)	1958	3.00	6.00	12.00
❏ 5125	Boo Da Ba/Pimento	1958	3.00	6.00	12.00
❏ 5130	How Could You/Blues for Handy	1958	3.00	6.00	12.00
❏ 5138	Tanya/Blip Bop	1958	3.00	6.00	12.00
❏ 5149	Birdie/Hold It	1958	3.00	6.00	12.00
❏ 5159	Rainbow Riot (Part 1)/Rainbow Riot (Part 2)	1958	3.00	6.00	12.00
❏ 5176	Monster Party/Scott's Bluff	1959	3.00	6.00	12.00
❏ 5204	The Madison/Ocean Liner	1959	3.00	6.00	12.00
❏ 5227	After Hours/Big City Drag	1959	3.00	6.00	12.00
❏ 5256	Yucky Dock (Part 1)/Yucky Dock (Part 2)	1959	3.00	6.00	12.00
❏ 5281	The Goofy Organ/Zee	1959	3.00	6.00	12.00
❏ 5310	Smokie Part 2/Evening Dreams	1960	2.50	5.00	10.00
❏ 5319	Back Woods/Raw Turkey	1960	2.50	5.00	10.00
❏ 5339	Big Boy/Smoochie	1960	2.50	5.00	10.00
❏ 5364	Buttered Popcorn/The Slush	1960	2.50	5.00	10.00
❏ 5387	A Lover's Dream/Trav'lin' Light	1960	2.50	5.00	10.00
❏ 5419	Slidin'/Afternoon Jump	1960	2.50	5.00	10.00
❏ 5444	Honky Tonk (Part 2)/Floyd's Guitar Blues	1961	2.50	5.00	10.00
❏ 5482	Bugle Nose/The Doodle	1961	2.50	5.00	10.00
❏ 5561	High and Wide/In the Wee Hours	1961	2.50	5.00	10.00
❏ 5599	The Doodle Twist/Gene's Dream	1962	2.00	4.00	8.00
❏ 5642	George Washington Twist/Eleven O'Clock Twist	1962	2.00	4.00	8.00
❏ 5665	Teardrops/Moon Dust	1962	2.00	4.00	8.00
❏ 5684	Hometown Shout/For All We Know	1962	2.00	4.00	8.00
❏ 5718	Honky Tonk Bossa Nova (Part 2)/Ocean Liner Bossa Nova	1963	2.00	4.00	8.00
❏ 5740	Down Home Bossa Nova/Si Si Nova	1963	2.00	4.00	8.00
❏ 5788	The Fog/Groovy Movie	1963	2.00	4.00	8.00
❏ 5873	The Rail/Hey Big Boy, Hey Hey	1964	2.00	4.00	8.00
❏ 5878	Night Train (Part 1)/Night Train (Part 2)	1964	2.00	4.00	8.00
❏ 5948	Crackers/That's Enough, Lock 'Em Up	1964	2.00	4.00	8.00
❏ 5957	Snuff Box/Blood Pressure	1964	2.00	4.00	8.00
❏ 6019	Teardrops/Slidin'	1966	—	3.00	6.00
❏ 6217	Take Your Shot/Mad	1969	—	2.50	5.00
❏ 6225	Twenty-Five Miles/For Once in My Life	1969	—	2.50	5.00
❏ 6239	Honky Tonk Popcorn/Honky Tonk	1969	—	2.50	5.00
❏ 6312	The Nearness of You/Moon Dust	1970	—	2.00	4.00
❏ 6350	High Heels/Soft	1971	—	2.00	4.00
❏ 6356	In a Sentimental Mood/Eventide	1971	—	2.00	4.00

ROULETTE

Number	Title (A Side/B Side)	Yr	VG	VG+	NM
❏ 4732	Sapphire/Ko-Ko	1967	—	3.00	6.00
❏ 4749	Lovin' Mood/The Funky Wrestler	1967	—	3.00	6.00

SUE

Number	Title (A Side/B Side)	Yr	VG	VG+	NM
❏ 10-002	Fat Back/Si Si Cisco	1968	—	2.50	5.00

WARNER BROS.

Number	Title (A Side/B Side)	Yr	VG	VG+	NM
❏ 5181	Jack Rabbit/Let's Do the Hully Gully Twist	1960	3.00	6.00	12.00
❏ 5209	Let's Do the Continental/Pony Walk	1961	3.00	6.00	12.00
❏ 5223	You Can't Sit Down (Part 1)/You Can't Sit Down (Part 2)	1961	3.00	6.00	12.00

7-Inch Extended Plays
KING

Number	Title (A Side/B Side)	Yr	VG	VG+	NM
❏ EP-259	*Early Bird/Percy Speaks/Ready Mix/Moon Dust	1954	6.25	12.50	25.00
❏ EP-259 [PS]	Bill Doggett	1954	6.25	12.50	25.00
❏ EP-325	*The Song Is Ended/Eventide/And the Angels Sing/Tailor Made	1955	6.25	12.50	25.00
❏ EP-325 [PS]	Bill Doggett, Vol. 2	1955	6.25	12.50	25.00
❏ EP-334	*Honey/It's a Dream/High Heels/Real Gone Mambo	1955	6.25	12.50	25.00
❏ EP-334 [PS]	Bill Doggett, His Organ and Combo, Vol. 4	1955	6.25	12.50	25.00
❏ EP-346	White Christmas/Silent Ninght//Jingle Bells/I Saw Mommy Kissing Santa Claus	195?	6.25	12.50	25.00

—The label of the copy we examined has the listed typo on the song "Silent Night"

Number	Title (A Side/B Side)	Yr	VG	VG+	NM
❏ EP-346 [PS]	All-Time Christmas Favorites	195?	6.25	12.50	25.00

—The label of the copy we examined has the listed typo on the song "Silent Night"

Number	Title (A Side/B Side)	Yr	VG	VG+	NM
❏ EP-352	*Sweet Slumber/The Nearness of You/Gumbo/Tara's Theme	1955	6.25	12.50	25.00
❏ EP-352 [PS]	Bill Doggett, His Organ and Combo, Vol. 5	1955	6.25	12.50	25.00
❏ EP-382	*I'll Be Around/Street Scene/You Don't Know What Love Is/Misty Moon	1956	6.25	12.50	25.00
❏ EP-382 [PS]	Doggett Dreams	1956	6.25	12.50	25.00
❏ EP-388	*Quaker City/Oof!/Wild Oats/Shove Off	1956	6.25	12.50	25.00
❏ EP-388 [PS]	Doggett Jumps	1956	6.25	12.50	25.00
❏ EP-390	Honky Tonk (Part 1)/Honky Tonk (Part 2)//Squashy/Who's Who	1956	7.50	15.00	30.00
❏ EP-390 [PS]	Honky Tonk	1956	7.50	15.00	30.00
❏ EP-391	*Leaps and Bounds/On the Sunny Side of the Street/True Blue	1956	5.00	10.00	20.00
❏ EP-391 [PS]	Bill Doggett, Vol. 1	1956	5.00	10.00	20.00
❏ EP-392	*Honky Tonk Number Three/When Your Lover Has Gone/Big Boy/Nothin' Yet	1956	5.00	10.00	20.00
❏ EP-392 [PS]	Bill Doggett, Vol. 2	1956	5.00	10.00	20.00
❏ EP-393	*Slow Walk/Afternoon Jump/Peacock Alley/Honey Boy	1956	5.00	10.00	20.00
❏ EP-393 [PS]	Bill Doggett, Vol. 3	1956	5.00	10.00	20.00
❏ EP-394	*I Hadn't Anyone Till You/Yesterdays/A Cottage for Sale/As You Desire Me	1957	5.00	10.00	20.00
❏ EP-394 [PS]	As You Desire Me, Vol. 1	1957	5.00	10.00	20.00
❏ EP-395	*Alone/As Time Goes By/Dedicated to You/Sweet and Lovely	1957	5.00	10.00	20.00
❏ EP-395 [PS]	As You Desire Me, Vol. 2	1957	5.00	10.00	20.00
❏ EP-396	*Dream/Don't Blame Me/This Love of Mine/Fools Rush In	1957	5.00	10.00	20.00
❏ EP-396 [PS]	As You Desire Me, Vol. 3	1957	5.00	10.00	20.00
❏ EP-399	*Caravan/Solitude/I'm Just a Lucky So and So/Prelude to a Kiss	1958	3.75	7.50	15.00
❏ EP-399 [PS]	A Salute to Ellington, Vol. 1	1958	3.75	7.50	15.00
❏ EP-400	*I Let a Song Go Out of My Heart/Don't Get Around Much Anymore/I Got It Bad and That Ain't Good	1958	3.75	7.50	15.00
❏ EP-400 [PS]	A Salute to Ellington, Vol. 2	1958	3.75	7.50	15.00
❏ EP-401	*C Jam Blues/Sophisticated Lady/Perdido/Satin Doll	1958	3.75	7.50	15.00
❏ EP-401 [PS]	A Salute to Ellington, Vol. 3	1958	3.75	7.50	15.00
❏ EP-402	*Sweet Lorraine/Diane/Dinah/Cherry	1958	3.75	7.50	15.00
❏ EP-402 [PS]	Dame Dreaming, Vol. 1	1958	3.75	7.50	15.00
❏ EP-403	*Ramona/Cynthia/Tangerine/Nancy	1958	3.75	7.50	15.00

Number	Title (A Side/B Side)	Yr	VG	VG+	NM
❏ EP-403 [PS]	Dame Dreaming, Vol. 2	1958	3.75	7.50	15.00
❏ EP-404	*Marcheta/Laura/Jeannine/Estrellita	1958	3.75	7.50	15.00
❏ EP-404 [PS]	Dame Dreaming, Vol. 3	1958	3.75	7.50	15.00
❏ EP-407	*Ram-Bunk-Shus/Cling to Me/Ding Dong/Chloe	1958	3.75	7.50	15.00
❏ EP-407 [PS]	Hot Doggett	1958	3.75	7.50	15.00
❏ EP-408	*Soft/Hammer Head/Shindig/Hot Ginger	1958	3.75	7.50	15.00
❏ EP-408 [PS]	Soft	1958	3.75	7.50	15.00

Albums

ABC-PARAMOUNT

Number	Title (A Side/B Side)	Yr	VG	VG+	NM
❏ 507 [M]	Wow!	1965	5.00	10.00	20.00
❏ S-507 [S]	Wow!	1965	6.25	12.50	25.00

AFTER HOURS

| ❏ AFT-4112 | The Right Choice | 1991 | 3.75 | 7.50 | 15.00 |

COLUMBIA

❏ CL 1814 [M]	Oops!	1962	5.00	10.00	20.00
❏ CL 1942 [M]	Prelude to the Blues	1963	5.00	10.00	20.00
❏ CL 2082 [M]	Fingertips	1963	5.00	10.00	20.00
❏ CS 8614 [S]	Oops!	1962	6.25	12.50	25.00
❏ CS 8742 [S]	Prelude to the Blues	1963	6.25	12.50	25.00
❏ CS 8882 [S]	Fingertips	1963	6.25	12.50	25.00

KING

❏ 295-82 [10]	Bill Doggett — His Organ and Combo	1955	37.50	75.00	150.00
❏ 295-83 [10]	Bill Doggett — His Organ and Combo, Volume 2	1955	37.50	75.00	150.00
❏ 295-89 [10]	All-Time Christmas Favorites	1955	50.00	100.00	200.00
❏ 295-102 [10]	Sentimentally Yours	1956	37.50	75.00	150.00
❏ 395-502 [M]	Moondust	1957	15.00	30.00	60.00
❏ 395-514 [M]	Hot Doggett	1957	15.00	30.00	60.00
❏ 395-523 [M]	As You Desire	1957	15.00	30.00	60.00
❏ KLP-523 [M]	As You Desire	1987	2.50	5.00	10.00

—Reissue with "Highland Records" on label

❏ 395-531 [M]	Everybody Dance to the Honky Tonk	1958	15.00	30.00	60.00
❏ 395-532 [M]	Dame Dreaming	1958	15.00	30.00	60.00
❏ KLP-532 [M]	Dame Dreaming	1987	2.50	5.00	10.00

—Reissue with "Highland Records" on label

❏ 395-533 [M]	A Salute to Ellington	1958	15.00	30.00	60.00
❏ 395-557 [M]	The Doggett Beat for Dancing Feet	1958	15.00	30.00	60.00
❏ KLP-557 [M]	The Doggett Beat for Dancing Feet	1987	2.50	5.00	10.00

—Reissue with "Highland Records" on label

❏ 395-563 [M]	Candle Glow	1958	15.00	30.00	60.00
❏ 395-582 [M]	Swingin' Easy	1959	15.00	30.00	60.00
❏ 395-585 [M]	Dance Awhile	1959	15.00	30.00	60.00
❏ KLP-585 [M]	Dance Awhile	1987	2.50	5.00	10.00

—Reissue with "Highland Records" on label

❏ 395-600 [M]	A Bill Doggett Christmas	1959	10.00	20.00	40.00
❏ 395-609 [M]	Hold It	1959	15.00	30.00	60.00
❏ 633 [M]	High and Wide	1959	12.50	25.00	50.00
❏ 641 [M]	Big City Dance Party	1959	12.50	25.00	50.00
❏ 667 [M]	Bill Doggett On Tour	1959	12.50	25.00	50.00
❏ 706 [M]	For Reminiscent Lovers, Romantic Songs	1960	12.50	25.00	50.00
❏ 723 [M]	Back Again with More	1960	12.50	25.00	50.00
❏ 759 [M]	Bonanza of 24 Songs	1960	12.50	25.00	50.00
❏ 778 [M]	The Many Moods of Bill Doggett	1960	12.50	25.00	50.00
❏ KLP-778 [M]	The Many Moods of Bill Doggett	1987	2.50	5.00	10.00

—Reissue with "Highland Records" on label

❏ 830 [M]	American Songs in the Bossa Nova Style	1963	10.00	20.00	40.00
❏ 868 [M]	Impressions	1964	10.00	20.00	40.00
❏ 908 [M]	The Best of Bill Doggett	1964	10.00	20.00	40.00
❏ 959 [M]	Bonanza of 24 Hit Songs	1966	7.50	15.00	30.00
❏ KS-1078	Honky Tonk Popcorn	1969	12.50	25.00	50.00
❏ KS-1097	The Nearness of You	1970	6.25	12.50	25.00
❏ KS-1101	Ram-Bunk-Shush	1970	6.25	12.50	25.00
❏ KS-1104	Sentimental Journey	1970	6.25	12.50	25.00
❏ KS-1108	Soft	1970	6.25	12.50	25.00
❏ K-5009	14 Original Greatest Hits	1977	2.50	5.00	10.00

POWER PAK

| ❏ 269 | Hold It! | 197? | 2.50 | 5.00 | 10.00 |

ROULETTE

| ❏ R 25330 [M] | Honky Tonk A La Mod | 1966 | 5.00 | 10.00 | 20.00 |
| ❏ SR 25330 [S] | Honky Tonk A La Mod | 1966 | 6.25 | 12.50 | 25.00 |

STARDAY

| ❏ 3023 | 16 Bandstand Favorites | 197? | 2.50 | 5.00 | 10.00 |

WARNER BROS.

❏ W 1404 [M]	3,046 People Danced 'Til 4 AM	1960	5.00	10.00	20.00
❏ WS 1404 [S]	3,046 People Danced 'Til 4 AM	1960	6.25	12.50	25.00
❏ W 1421 [M]	The Band with the Beat	1961	5.00	10.00	20.00
❏ WS 1421 [S]	The Band with the Beat	1961	6.25	12.50	25.00
❏ W 1452 [M]	Bill Doggett Swings	1962	5.00	10.00	20.00
❏ WS 1452 [S]	Bill Doggett Swings	1962	6.25	12.50	25.00

WHO'S WHO IN JAZZ

| ❏ 21002 | Lionel Hampton Presents Bill Doggett | 1977 | 3.00 | 6.00 | 12.00 |

DOHENY, NED
45s

ASYLUM

| ❏ 11024 | On & On/I Know Sorrow | 1973 | — | 3.00 | 6.00 |

COLUMBIA

| ❏ 3-10438 | A Love of Your Own/Valentine | 1976 | — | 3.00 | 6.00 |
| ❏ 3-10476 | If You Should Fall/I've Got Your Number | 1977 | — | 3.00 | 6.00 |

Albums

ASYLUM

| ❏ SD 5059 | Ned Doheny | 1973 | 5.00 | 10.00 | 20.00 |

COLUMBIA

| ❏ PC 34259 | Hard Candy | 1976 | 3.75 | 7.50 | 15.00 |

DOHERTY, DENNY Also see THE MAMAS AND THE PAPAS; THE MUGWUMPS.
45s

ABC

| ❏ 11318 | To Claudia on Thursday/Tuesday Morning | 1972 | — | 3.00 | 6.00 |

COLUMBIA

❏ 45779	Indian Girl/Baby Catch the Moon	1973	—	2.50	5.00
❏ 45779 [PS]	Indian Girl/Baby Catch the Moon	1973	3.75	7.50	15.00
❏ 45866	My Song/Indian Girl	1973	—	2.50	5.00

PARAMOUNT

| ❏ 0286 | Good Night and Good Morning/You'll Never Know | 1974 | — | 2.50 | 5.00 |

PLAYBOY

Number	Title (A Side/B Side)	Yr	VG	VG+	NM
❏ 6066	Simone (mono/stereo)	1976	—	2.50	5.00

—May be promo only

Albums

ABC DUNHILL

| ❏ DS-50096 | Watcha' Gonna Do? | 1970 | 3.75 | 7.50 | 15.00 |

EMBER

| ❏ EMS-1036 | Waiting for a Song | 1975 | 3.00 | 6.00 | 12.00 |

DOJO
Albums

ECLIPSE

| ❏ ES-7309 | Down for the Last Time | 1971 | 6.25 | 12.50 | 25.00 |

DOLENZ, MICKEY Also see DOLENZ, JONES & TORK; DOLENZ, JONES, BOYCE & HART; THE MONKEES.
45s

BELL

| ❏ 986 | Do It in the Name of Love/Lady Jane | 1971 | 12.50 | 25.00 | 50.00 |

—With Davy Jones; value is for stock copy (promos worth about 50% of this)

CHALLENGE

❏ 59353	Don't Do It/Plastic Symphony III	1967	5.00	10.00	20.00
❏ 59353 [PS]	Don't Do It/Plastic Symphony III	1967	10.00	20.00	40.00
❏ 59372	Huff Puff/(The Obvious) Fate	1967	5.00	10.00	20.00
❏ 59372 [PS]	Huff Puff/(The Obvious) Fate	1967	15.00	30.00	60.00

CHRYSALIS

| ❏ 2297 | Alicia/Love Light | 1979 | — | 3.00 | 6.00 |

MGM

| ❏ 14309 | Easy on You/Oh Someone | 1971 | 5.00 | 10.00 | 20.00 |
| ❏ 14395 | A Lover's Prayer/Unattended in the Dungeon | 1972 | 5.00 | 10.00 | 20.00 |

ROMAR

| ❏ 710 | Daybreak/Love War | 1973 | 5.00 | 10.00 | 20.00 |
| ❏ 715 | Buddy Holly Tribute/Ooh, Se's So Young | 1974 | 5.00 | 10.00 | 20.00 |

DOLENZ, MICKEY, AND PETER TORK (OF THE MONKEES) See THE MONKEES.

DOLENZ, JONES & TORK Also see MICKEY DOLENZ; DAVY JONES; THE MONKEES.
45s

CHRISTMAS

| ❏ 700 | Christmas Is My Time of Year/White Christmas | 1976 | 5.00 | 10.00 | 20.00 |
| ❏ 700 [PS] | Christmas Is My Time of Year/White Christmas | 1976 | 10.00 | 20.00 | 40.00 |

DOLENZ, JONES, BOYCE & HART Also see TOMMY BOYCE; TOMMY BOYCE AND BOBBY HART; MICKEY DOLENZ; BOBBY HART; DAVY JONES; THE MONKEES.
45s

CAPITOL

| ❏ 4180 | You and I/I Remember the Feeling | 1975 | 2.50 | 5.00 | 10.00 |
| ❏ 4271 | Savin' My Love for You/I Love You (And I'm Glad I Said It) | 1976 | 2.50 | 5.00 | 10.00 |

Albums

CAPITOL

| ❏ ST-11513 | Dolenz, Jones, Boyce & Hart | 1976 | 3.75 | 7.50 | 15.00 |

DOLLS, THE
45s

LOMA

| ❏ 2036 | The Reason Why/And That Reminds Me | 1966 | 3.75 | 7.50 | 15.00 |

MALTESE

| ❏ 100 | This Is Our Day/What Next | 1965 | 15.00 | 30.00 | 60.00 |
| ❏ 107 | The Aeroplane Song/A Lover's Stand | 1965 | 300.00 | 600.00 | 1200. |

—As "Norma Jenkins and the Dolls"

OKEH

| ❏ 7122 | In Love/Please Come Home | 1959 | 3.00 | 6.00 | 12.00 |

TEENAGE

| ❏ 1010 | Just Before You Leave/I Love | 1958 | 250.00 | 500.00 | 1000. |

DOLLY AND THE FASHIONS
45s

TRI DISC

| ❏ 111 | Absence Made My Heart Grow Fonder/Waiting for My Man | 1963 | 3.00 | 6.00 | 12.00 |

DOMINO, FATS
45s

ABC

| ❏ 10902 | I Don't Want to Set the World on Fire/I'm Living Right | 1967 | 2.50 | 5.00 | 10.00 |

ABC-PARAMOUNT

❏ 10444	There Goes (My Heart Again)/Can't Go On Without You	1963	2.50	5.00	10.00
❏ 10475	When I'm Walking (Let Me Walk)/I've Got a Right to Cry	1963	2.50	5.00	10.00
❏ 10484	Red Sails in the Sunset/Song for Rosemary	1963	3.00	6.00	12.00
❏ 10512	Who Cares/Just a Lonely Man	1963	2.50	5.00	10.00
❏ 10531	Lazy Lady/I Don't Want to Set the World on Fire	1964	2.50	5.00	10.00
❏ 10545	If You Don't Know What Love Is/Something You Got, Baby	1964	2.50	5.00	10.00
❏ 10567	Mary, Oh Mary/Packin' Up	1964	2.50	5.00	10.00
❏ 10584	Sally Was a Good Old Girl/For You	1964	2.50	5.00	10.00
❏ 10596	Heartbreak Hill/Kansas City	1964	2.50	5.00	10.00
❏ 10631	Why Don't You Do Right/Wigs	1965	2.50	5.00	10.00
❏ 10644	Let Me Call You Sweetheart/Goodnight Sweetheart	1965	2.50	5.00	10.00

BROADMOOR

| ❏ 104 | The Lady in Black/Work My Way Up Steady | 1967 | 3.75 | 7.50 | 15.00 |
| ❏ 105 | Big Mouth/Wait 'Til It Happens to You | 1968 | 5.00 | 10.00 | 20.00 |

IMPERIAL

| ❏ 45-5058 | The Fat Man/Detroit City Blues | 1950 | 500.00 | 1000. | 2000. |

—Blue-label "script" logo; pressed in 1952 or so; counterfeits exist

| ❏ 45-5099 | Korea Blues/Every Night About This Time | 1950 | 200.00 | 400.00 | 800.00 |

—Blue-label "script" logo; pressed in 1952 or so

| ❏ 45-5167 | You Know I Miss You/I'll Be Gone | 1952 | 125.00 | 250.00 | 500.00 |

—Fats Domino records on Imperial before 5167 are unconfirmed on 45 rpm, except those listed above.

| ❏ 45-5180 | Goin' Home/Reeling and Rocking | 1952 | 75.00 | 150.00 | 300.00 |
| ❏ 45-5197 | Poor Poor Me/Trust in Me | 1952 | 50.00 | 100.00 | 200.00 |

Number	Title (A Side/B Side)	Yr	VG	VG+	NM
❏ 45-5209	How Long/Dreaming	1952	20.00	40.00	80.00
—Black vinyl					
❏ 45-5209	How Long/Dreaming	1952	75.00	150.00	300.00
—Red vinyl					
❏ 45-5220	Nobody Loves Me/Cheatin'	1953	20.00	40.00	80.00
—Black vinyl					
❏ 45-5220	Nobody Loves Me/Cheatin'	1953	75.00	150.00	300.00
—Red vinyl					
❏ 45-5231	Going to the River/Mardi Gras in New Orleans	1953	25.00	50.00	100.00
—Black vinyl					
❏ 45-5231	Going to the River/Mardi Gras in New Orleans	1953	125.00	250.00	500.00
—Red vinyl					
❏ 45-5240	Please Don't Leave Me/The Girl I Love	1953	15.00	30.00	60.00
—Black vinyl					
❏ 45-5240	Please Don't Leave Me/The Girl I Love	1953	75.00	150.00	300.00
—Red vinyl					
❏ 45-5251	You Said You Loved Me/Rose Mary	1953	15.00	30.00	60.00
❏ X5262	Something's Wrong/Don't Leave Me This Way	1954	12.50	25.00	50.00
—Black vinyl					
❏ X5262	Something's Wrong/Don't Leave Me This Way	1954	62.50	125.00	250.00
—Red vinyl					
❏ X5272	Little School Girl/You Done Me Wrong	1954	15.00	30.00	60.00
❏ X5283	Baby, Please/Where Did You Stay	1954	15.00	30.00	60.00
❏ X5301	You Can Pack Your Suitcase/I Lived My Life	1954	10.00	20.00	40.00
❏ X5313	Love Me/Don't You Hear Me Calling You	1954	10.00	20.00	40.00
❏ X5323	I Know/Thinking of You	1955	12.50	25.00	50.00
—Black vinyl					
❏ X5323	I Know/Thinking of You	1955	125.00	250.00	500.00
—Red vinyl					
❏ X5340	Don't You Know/Helping Hand	1955	10.00	20.00	40.00
❏ X5348	Ain't It a Shame/La La	1955	10.00	20.00	40.00
❏ X5357	All By Myself/Troubles of My Own	1955	6.25	12.50	25.00
—Red or maroon label, block logo					
❏ X5357	All By Myself/Troubles of My Own	1955	20.00	40.00	80.00
—Red label, script logo					
❏ X5369	Poor Me/I Can't Go On	1955	6.25	12.50	25.00
❏ X5375	Bo Weevil/Don't Blame It on Me	1956	6.25	12.50	25.00
❏ X5386	I'm in Love Again/My Blue Heaven	1956	6.25	12.50	25.00
❏ X5396	When My Dreamboat Comes Home/So-Long	1956	6.25	12.50	25.00
❏ X5407	Blueberry Hill/Honey Chile	1956	6.25	12.50	25.00
—Black vinyl, red label					
❏ X5407	Blueberry Hill/Honey Chile	1956	37.50	75.00	150.00
—Red vinyl					
❏ X5407	Blueberry Hill/Honey Chile	1957	3.75	7.50	15.00
—Black vinyl, black label					
❏ X5417	Blue Monday/What's the Reason I'm Not Pleasing You	1957	6.25	12.50	25.00
❏ X5428	I'm Walkin'/I'm in the Mood for Love	1957	6.25	12.50	25.00
—Maroon or red label					
❏ X5428 [PS]	I'm Walkin'/I'm in the Mood for Love	1957	12.50	25.00	50.00
❏ X5442	Valley of Tears/It's You I Love	1957	6.25	12.50	25.00
❏ X5454	When I See You/What Will I Tell My Heart	1957	6.25	12.50	25.00
❏ X5467	Wait and See/I Still Love You	1957	6.25	12.50	25.00
❏ X5477	The Big Beat/I Want You to Know	1957	6.25	12.50	25.00
❏ X5477 [PS]	The Big Beat/I Want You to Know	1957	15.00	30.00	60.00
❏ X5492	Yes, My Darling/Don't You Know I Love You	1958	6.25	12.50	25.00
—Black vinyl					
❏ X5492	Yes, My Darling/Don't You Know I Love You	1958	37.50	75.00	150.00
—Red vinyl					
❏ X5515	Sick and Tired/No, No	1958	6.25	12.50	25.00
❏ X5526	Little Mary/The Prisoner's Song	1958	6.25	12.50	25.00
❏ X5537	Young School Girl/It Must Be Love	1958	6.25	12.50	25.00
❏ X5553	Whole Lotta Loving/Coquette	1958	6.25	12.50	25.00
—Black label					
❏ X5553	Whole Lotta Loving/Coquette	1958	7.50	15.00	30.00
—Red label					
❏ X5553	Whole Lotta Loving/Coquette	1958	37.50	75.00	150.00
—Red vinyl (translucent)					
❏ 5569	Telling Lies/When the Saints Go Marching In	1959	3.75	7.50	15.00
❏ 5585	I'm Ready/Margie	1959	3.75	7.50	15.00
❏ 5606	I Want to Walk You Home/I'm Gonna Be a Wheel Some Day	1959	5.00	10.00	20.00
❏ 5606 [PS]	I Want to Walk You Home/I'm Gonna Be a Wheel Some Day	1959	—	—	—
—Rumored to exist, but without conclusive evidence, we will delete this from future editions					
❏ 5629	Be My Guest/I've Been Around	1959	3.75	7.50	15.00
❏ 5629 [PS]	Be My Guest/I've Been Around	1959	12.50	25.00	50.00
❏ 5645	Country Boy/If You Need Me	1960	3.75	7.50	15.00
❏ 5660	Tell Me That You Love Me/Before I Grow Too Old	1960	3.75	7.50	15.00
❏ 5675	Walking to New Orleans/Don't Come Knockin'	1960	5.00	10.00	20.00
❏ 5687	Three Nights a Week/Put Your Arms Around Me Honey	1960	3.75	7.50	15.00
❏ 5704	My Girl Josephine/Natural Born Lover	1960	5.00	10.00	20.00
❏ 5723	What a Price/Ain't That Just Like a Woman	1961	3.75	7.50	15.00
❏ 5734	Shu Rah/Fell in Love on Monday	1961	3.75	7.50	15.00
❏ 5753	It Keeps Rainin'/I Just Cry	1961	3.75	7.50	15.00
❏ 5764	Let the Four Winds Blow/Good Hearted Man	1961	3.75	7.50	15.00
❏ 5779	What a Party/Rockin' Bicycle	1961	3.75	7.50	15.00
❏ 5796	Jambalaya (On the Bayou)/I Hear You Knocking	1961	3.75	7.50	15.00
❏ 5816	You Win Again/Ida Jane	1962	3.75	7.50	15.00
❏ 5833	My Real Name/My Heart Is Bleeding	1962	3.75	7.50	15.00
❏ 5863	Nothing New (Same Old Thing)/Dance with Mr. Domino	1962	3.75	7.50	15.00
❏ 5875	Did You Ever See a Dream Walking/Stop the Clock	1962	3.75	7.50	15.00
❏ 5895	Won't You Come On Back/Hands Across the Table	1962	3.75	7.50	15.00
❏ 5895	Won't You Come On Back/Your Cheatin' Heart	1962	3.75	7.50	15.00
❏ 5909	Hum Diddy Doo/Those Eyes	1963	3.75	7.50	15.00
❏ 5937	You Always Hurt the One You Love/Trouble Blues	1963	3.75	7.50	15.00
❏ 5959	Isle of Capri/True Confession	1963	3.75	7.50	15.00
❏ 5980	One Night/I Can't Go On This Way	1963	3.75	7.50	15.00
❏ 5999	Your Cheatin' Heart/Goin' Home	1963	3.75	7.50	15.00
❏ 66005	I Can't Give You Anything But Love/Goin' Home	1963	3.00	6.00	12.00
❏ 66016	When I Was Young/Your Cheatin' Heart	1964	3.00	6.00	12.00

Number	Title (A Side/B Side)	Yr	VG	VG+	NM
MERCURY					
❏ 72463	I Left My Heart in San Francisco/I Done Got Over You	1965	2.50	5.00	10.00
❏ 72485	It's Never Too Late/What's That You Got	1965	2.50	5.00	10.00
❏ 72485 [PS]	It's Never Too Late/What's That You Got	1965	5.00	10.00	20.00
REPRISE					
❏ 0696	One for the Highway/Honest Papas Love Their Mamas Better	1968	3.75	7.50	15.00
❏ 0763	Lady Madonna/One for the Highway	1968	3.75	7.50	15.00
❏ 0775	Lovely Rita/Wait Till It Happens to You	1968	3.75	7.50	15.00
❏ 0810	Everybody's Got Someting to Hide (Except Me and My Monkey)/So Swell When You're Well	1969	3.75	7.50	15.00
❏ 0891	Have You Seen My Baby?/Make Me Belong to You	1970	3.75	7.50	15.00
❏ 0944	New Orleans Ain't the Same/Sweet Patootie	1970	3.75	7.50	15.00
THE RIGHT STUFF					
❏ S7-18216	Christmas Is a Special Day/Please Come Home for Christmas (Christmas Once Again)	1994	—	2.00	4.00
—Red vinyl					
❏ S7-19768	Frosty the Snowman/Every Heart Is Home at Christmas	1997	—	2.50	5.00
—B-side by the Five Keys on Aladdin					
TOOT TOOT					
❏ 001	My Toot Toot/My Toot Toot (Rock)	1985	—	2.50	5.00
—With Doug Kershaw					
❏ 002	Don't Mess with My Popeye's/My Toot Toot	1985	—	2.50	5.00
—With Doug Kershaw					
UNITED ARTISTS					
❏ 0001	Ain't That a Shame/Goin' Home	1973	—	2.00	4.00
❏ 0002	Blue Monday/I'm Gonna Be a Wheel Someday	1973	—	2.00	4.00
❏ 0003	I'm in Love Again/Whole Lotta Lovin'	1973	—	2.00	4.00
❏ 0004	Blueberry Hill/Bo Weevil	1973	—	2.00	4.00
❏ 0005	I'm Walkin'/One Night	1973	—	2.00	4.00
❏ 0006	I Hear You Knockin'/My Blue Heaven	1973	—	2.00	4.00
❏ 0007	Walkin' to New Orleans/Country Boy	1973	—	2.00	4.00
❏ 0008	I Want to Walk You Home/It's You I Love	1973	—	2.00	4.00
❏ 0009	I'm Ready/Wait and See	1973	—	2.00	4.00
❏ 0010	My Girl Josephine/When My Dreamboat Comes Home	1973	—	2.00	4.00
❏ 0011	Three Nights a Week/Let the Four Winds Blow	1973	—	2.00	4.00
—0001 through 0011 are "Silver Spotlight Series" reissues					
❏ XW 514	The Fat Man/Valley of Tears	1974	—	2.50	5.00
—Reissue					
WARNER BROS.					
❏ 49610	Whiskey Heaven/Beers to You	1980	—	2.00	4.00
—B-side by Texas Opera Company					
7-Inch Extended Plays					
IMPERIAL					
❏ IMP 127	Going to the River/Every Night About This Time//Going Home/Please Don't Leave Me	1955	25.00	50.00	100.00
—Maroon label, block-letter logo					
❏ IMP 127	Going to the River/Every Night About This Time//Going Home/Please Don't Leave Me	1955	37.50	75.00	150.00
—"Script" label					
❏ IMP 127 [PS]	Fats Domino	1955	12.50	25.00	50.00
❏ IMP 127	Going to the River/Every Night About This Time//Going Home/Please Don't Leave Me	1958	6.25	12.50	25.00
—Black label					
❏ IMP 138	Domino Stomp/The Girl I Love//Don't You Know/The Fat Man	1956	25.00	50.00	100.00
—Maroon label, block-letter logo					
❏ IMP 138 [PS]	Rock and Rollin' with Fats Domino	1956	12.50	25.00	50.00
❏ IMP 138	Domino Stomp/The Girl I Love//Don't You Know/The Fat Man	1958	6.25	12.50	25.00
—Black label					
❏ IMP 139	Rosemary/All By Myself//Tired of Crying/You Said You Loved Me	1956	25.00	50.00	100.00
—Maroon label, block-letter logo					
❏ IMP 139 [PS]	Rock and Rollin' with Fats Domino	1956	12.50	25.00	50.00
❏ IMP 139	Rosemary/All By Myself//Tired of Crying/You Said You Loved Me	1958	6.25	12.50	25.00
—Black label					
❏ IMP 140	Ain't It a Shame/Poor Me//Bo Weevil/Don't Blame It on Me	1956	25.00	50.00	100.00
—Maroon label, block-letter logo					
❏ IMP 140 [PS]	Rock and Rollin' with Fats Domino	1956	12.50	25.00	50.00
❏ IMP 140	Ain't It a Shame/Poor Me//Bo Weevil/Don't Blame It on Me	1958	6.25	12.50	25.00
—Black label					
❏ IMP 141	My Blue Heaven/Swanee River Hop//Second Line Jump/Goodbye	1956	25.00	50.00	100.00
—Maroon label, block-letter logo					
❏ IMP 141 [PS]	Rock and Rollin'	1956	12.50	25.00	50.00
❏ IMP 141	My Blue Heaven/Swanee River Hop//Second Line Jump/Goodbye	1958	6.25	12.50	25.00
—Black label					
❏ IMP 142	Careless Love/I Love Her//I'm in Love Again/When My Dreamboat Comes Home	1956	25.00	50.00	100.00
—Maroon label, block-letter logo					
❏ IMP 142 [PS]	Rock and Rollin'	1956	12.50	25.00	50.00
❏ IMP 142	Careless Love/I Love Her//I'm in Love Again/When My Dreamboat Comes Home	1958	6.25	12.50	25.00
—Black label					
❏ IMP 143	Are Your Going My Way/If You Need Me//My Heart Is In Your Hands/Fats Frenzy	1956	25.00	50.00	100.00
—Maroon label, block-letter logo					
❏ IMP 143 [PS]	Rock and Rollin'	1956	12.50	25.00	50.00
❏ IMP 143	Are Your Going My Way/If You Need Me//My Heart Is In Your Hands/Fats Frenzy	1958	6.25	12.50	25.00
—Black label					
❏ IMP 144	Blueberry Hill/Honey Chile//Troubles of My Own/You Done Me Wrong	1956	25.00	50.00	100.00
—Maroon label, block-letter logo					
❏ IMP 144 [PS]	This Is Fats Domino	1956	12.50	25.00	50.00

Number	Title (A Side/B Side)	Yr	VG	VG+	NM
❏ IMP 144	Blueberry Hill/Honey Chile//Troubles of My Own/ You Done Me Wrong	1958	6.25	12.50	25.00
—Black label					
❏ IMP 145	What's the Reason I'm Not Pleasing You/Blue Monday//Reeling and Rocking/ The Fat Man's Hop	1956	25.00	50.00	100.00
—Maroon label, block-letter logo					
❏ IMP 145 [PS]	This Is Fats Domino	1956	12.50	25.00	50.00
❏ IMP 145	What's the Reason I'm Not Pleasing You/Blue Monday//Reeling and Rocking/ The Fat Man's Hop	1958	6.25	12.50	25.00
—Black label					
❏ IMP 146	So Long/La La//Poor, Poor Me/Trust in Me	1956	25.00	50.00	100.00
—Maroon label, block-letter logo					
❏ IMP 146 [PS]	This Is Fats Domino	1956	12.50	25.00	50.00
❏ IMP 146	So Long/La La//Poor, Poor Me/Trust in Me	1958	6.25	12.50	25.00
—Black label					
❏ IMP 147	The Rooster Song/My Happiness//As Time Goes By/Hey La Bas	1956	25.00	50.00	100.00
—Maroon label, block-letter logo					
❏ IMP 147 [PS]	Here Comes Fats	1956	12.50	25.00	50.00
❏ IMP 147	The Rooster Song/My Happiness//As Time Goes By/Hey La Bas	1958	6.25	12.50	25.00
—Black label					
❏ IMP 148	Detroit City Blues/Hide Away Blues//She's My Baby/New Baby	1957	25.00	50.00	100.00
—Maroon label, block-letter logo					
❏ IMP 148 [PS]	Here Stands Fats Domino	1957	12.50	25.00	50.00
❏ IMP 148	Detroit City Blues/Hide Away Blues//She's My Baby/New Baby	1958	6.25	12.50	25.00
—Black label					
❏ IMP 149	Little Bee/Every Night About This Time// I'm Walkin'/Cheatin'	1957	25.00	50.00	100.00
—Maroon label, block-letter logo					
❏ IMP 149 [PS]	Here Stands Fats Domino	1957	12.50	25.00	50.00
❏ IMP 149	Little Bee/Every Night About This Time//I'm Walkin'/Cheatin'	1958	6.25	12.50	25.00
—Black label					
❏ IMP 150	I'm in the Mood for Love/You Can Pack Your Suitcase//Hey! Fat Man/I'll Be Gone	1957	25.00	50.00	100.00
—Maroon label, block-letter logo					
❏ IMP 150 [PS]	Here Stands Fats Domino	1957	12.50	25.00	50.00
❏ IMP 150	I'm in the Mood for Love/You Can Pack Your Suitcase//Hey! Fat Man/I'll Be Gone	1958	6.25	12.50	25.00
—Black label					
❏ IMP 151	Love Me/Don't You Hear Me Calling You//It's You I Love/Valley of Tears	1957	25.00	50.00	100.00
—Maroon label, block-letter logo					
❏ IMP 151 [PS]	Cookin' with Fats	1957	12.50	25.00	50.00
❏ IMP 151	Love Me/Don't You Hear Me Calling You//It's You I Love/Valley of Tears	1958	6.25	12.50	25.00
—Black label					
❏ IMP 152	Thinking of You/You Know I Miss You//Where Did You Stay/Baby Please	1957	25.00	50.00	100.00
—Maroon label, block-letter logo					
❏ IMP 152 [PS]	Rockin' with Fats	1957	12.50	25.00	50.00
❏ IMP 152	Thinking of You/You Know I Miss You//Where Did You Stay/Baby Please	1958	6.25	12.50	25.00
—Black label					
Albums					
ABC					
❏ S-455 [S]	Here Comes... Fats Domino	1967	3.75	7.50	15.00
❏ S-479 [S]	Fats on Fire	1967	3.75	7.50	15.00
❏ S-510 [S]	Get Away with Fats Domino	1967	3.75	7.50	15.00
❏ ST-90167 [S]	Get Away with Fats Domino	1969	6.25	12.50	25.00
—Capitol Record Club edition; reissue					
ABC-PARAMOUNT					
❏ 455 [M]	Here Comes... Fats Domino	1963	5.00	10.00	20.00
❏ S-455 [S]	Here Comes... Fats Domino	1963	6.25	12.50	25.00
❏ 479 [M]	Fats on Fire	1964	5.00	10.00	20.00
❏ S-479 [S]	Fats on Fire	1964	6.25	12.50	25.00
❏ 510 [M]	Get Away with Fats Domino	1965	5.00	10.00	20.00
❏ S-510 [S]	Get Away with Fats Domino	1965	6.25	12.50	25.00
❏ ST-90167 [S]	Get Away with Fats Domino	1965	7.50	15.00	30.00
—Capitol Record Club edition					
❏ T-90167 [M]	Get Away with Fats Domino	1965	6.25	12.50	25.00
—Capitol Record Club edition					
ATLANTIC					
❏ 81751	Live in Montreux	1987	3.00	6.00	12.00
COLUMBIA					
❏ C 35996	When I'm Walking	1979	2.50	5.00	10.00
—Reissue of Harmony LP					
❏ PC 35996	When I'm Walking	1986	2.00	4.00	8.00
—Budget-line reissue					
COLUMBIA SPECIAL PRODUCTS					
❏ P2 13197 [(2)]	The Legendary Music Man	1976	3.75	7.50	15.00
—Candelite Music TV offer					
EVEREST ARCHIVE OF FOLK & JAZZ					
❏ 280	Fats Domino	1974	2.50	5.00	10.00
❏ 330	Fats Domino, Vol. II	1975	2.50	5.00	10.00
GRAND AWARD					
❏ 267 [M]	Fats Domino	196?	5.00	10.00	20.00
❏ S-267 [R]	Fats Domino	196?	2.50	5.00	10.00
HARLEM HIT PARADE					
❏ 5005	Fats' Hits	197?	2.50	5.00	10.00
HARMONY					
❏ HS 11343	When I'm Walking	1969	3.00	6.00	12.00
IMPERIAL					
❏ LP-9004 [M]	Rock and Rollin' with Fats Domino	1956	37.50	75.00	150.00
—Maroon label					
❏ LP-9004 [M]	Rock and Rollin' with Fats Domino	1958	20.00	40.00	80.00
—Black label with stars on top					
❏ LP-9004 [M]	Rock and Rollin' with Fats Domino	1964	6.25	12.50	25.00
—Black and pink label					
❏ LP-9004 [M]	Rock and Rollin' with Fats Domino	1967	5.00	10.00	20.00
—Black and green label					
❏ LP-9009 [M]	Fats Domino Rock and Rollin'	1956	37.50	75.00	150.00
—Maroon label					
❏ LP-9009 [M]	Fats Domino Rock and Rollin'	1958	20.00	40.00	80.00
—Black label with stars on top					
❏ LP-9009 [M]	Fats Domino Rock and Rollin'	1964	6.25	12.50	25.00
—Black and pink label					
❏ LP-9009 [M]	Fats Domino Rock and Rollin'	1967	5.00	10.00	20.00
—Black and green label					
❏ LP-9028 [M]	This Is Fats Domino!	1957	37.50	75.00	150.00
—Maroon label					
❏ LP-9028 [M]	This Is Fats Domino!	1958	20.00	40.00	80.00
—Black label with stars on top					
❏ LP-9028 [M]	This Is Fats Domino!	1964	6.25	12.50	25.00
—Black and pink label					
❏ LP-9028 [M]	This Is Fats Domino!	1967	5.00	10.00	20.00
—Black and green label					
❏ LP-9038 [M]	Here Stands Fats Domino	1957	37.50	75.00	150.00
—Maroon label					
❏ LP-9038 [M]	Here Stands Fats Domino	1958	20.00	40.00	80.00
—Black label with stars on top					
❏ LP-9038 [M]	Here Stands Fats Domino	1964	6.25	12.50	25.00
—Black and pink label					
❏ LP-9038 [M]	Here Stands Fats Domino	1967	5.00	10.00	20.00
—Black and green label					
❏ LP-9040 [M]	This Is Fats	1957	37.50	75.00	150.00
—Maroon label					
❏ LP-9040 [M]	This Is Fats	1958	20.00	40.00	80.00
—Black label with stars on top					
❏ LP-9040 [M]	This Is Fats	1964	6.25	12.50	25.00
—Black and pink label					
❏ LP-9040 [M]	This Is Fats	1967	5.00	10.00	20.00
—Black and green label					
❏ LP-9055 [M]	The Fabulous Mr. D.	1958	25.00	50.00	100.00
—Black label with stars on top					
❏ LP-9055 [M]	The Fabulous Mr. D.	1964	7.50	15.00	30.00
—Black and pink label					
❏ LP-9055 [M]	The Fabulous Mr. D.	1967	5.00	10.00	20.00
—Black and green label					
❏ LP-9062 [M]	Fats Domino Swings	1959	25.00	50.00	100.00
—Black label with stars on top					
❏ LP-9062 [M]	Fats Domino Swings	1964	7.50	15.00	30.00
—Black and pink label					
❏ LP-9062 [M]	Fats Domino Swings	1967	5.00	10.00	20.00
—Black and green label					
❏ LP-9065 [M]	Let's Play Fats Domino	1959	25.00	50.00	100.00
—Black label with stars on top					
❏ LP-9065 [M]	Let's Play Fats Domino	1964	7.50	15.00	30.00
—Black and pink label					
❏ LP-9065 [M]	Let's Play Fats Domino	1967	5.00	10.00	20.00
—Black and green label					
❏ LP-9103 [M]	Million Record Hits	1960	25.00	50.00	100.00
—Black label with stars on top					
❏ LP-9103 [M]	Million Record Hits	1964	7.50	15.00	30.00
—Black and pink label					
❏ LP-9103 [M]	Million Record Hits	1967	5.00	10.00	20.00
—Black and green label					
❏ LP-9127 [M]	A Lot of Dominos	1960	25.00	50.00	100.00
—Black label with stars on top					
❏ LP-9127 [M]	A Lot of Dominos	1964	7.50	15.00	30.00
—Black and pink label					
❏ LP-9127 [M]	A Lot of Dominos	1967	5.00	10.00	20.00
—Black and green label					
❏ LP-9138 [M]	I Miss You So	1961	25.00	50.00	100.00
—Black label with stars on top					
❏ LP-9138 [M]	I Miss You So	1964	7.50	15.00	30.00
—Black and pink label					
❏ LP-9138 [M]	I Miss You So	1967	5.00	10.00	20.00
—Black and green label					
❏ LP-9153 [M]	Let the Four Winds Blow	1961	25.00	50.00	100.00
—Black label with stars on top					
❏ LP-9153 [M]	Let the Four Winds Blow	1964	7.50	15.00	30.00
—Black and pink label					
❏ LP-9153 [M]	Let the Four Winds Blow	1967	5.00	10.00	20.00
—Black and green label					
❏ LP-9164 [M]	What a Party	1962	15.00	30.00	60.00
—Black label with stars on top					
❏ LP-9164 [M]	What a Party	1964	7.50	15.00	30.00
—Black and pink label					
❏ LP-9164 [M]	What a Party	1967	5.00	10.00	20.00
—Black and green label					
❏ LP-9170 [M]	Twistin' the Stomp	1962	15.00	30.00	60.00
—Black label with stars on top					
❏ LP-9170 [M]	Twistin' the Stomp	1964	7.50	15.00	30.00
—Black and pink label					
❏ LP-9170 [M]	Twistin' the Stomp	1967	5.00	10.00	20.00
—Black and green label					
❏ LP-9195 [M]	Million Sellers by Fats	1962	12.50	25.00	50.00
—Black label with stars on top					
❏ LP-9195 [M]	Million Sellers by Fats	1964	7.50	15.00	30.00
—Black and pink label					
❏ LP-9195 [M]	Million Sellers by Fats	1967	5.00	10.00	20.00
—Black and green label					
❏ LP-9208 [M]	Just Domino	1962	12.50	25.00	50.00
—Black label with stars on top					
❏ LP-9208 [M]	Just Domino	1964	7.50	15.00	30.00
—Black and pink label					
❏ LP-9208 [M]	Just Domino	1967	5.00	10.00	20.00
—Black and green label					
❏ LP-9227 [M]	Walking to New Orleans	1963	12.50	25.00	50.00
—Black label with stars on top					
❏ LP-9227 [M]	Walking to New Orleans	1964	7.50	15.00	30.00
—Black and pink label					
❏ LP-9227 [M]	Walking to New Orleans	1967	5.00	10.00	20.00
—Black and green label					
❏ LP-9239 [M]	Let's Dance with Domino	1963	12.50	25.00	50.00
—Black label with stars on top					

Number	Title (A Side/B Side)	Yr	VG	VG+	NM
❑ LP-9239 [M]	Let's Dance with Domino	1964	7.50	15.00	30.00
—Black and pink label					
❑ LP-9239 [M]	Let's Dance with Domino	1967	5.00	10.00	20.00
—Black and green label					
❑ LP-9248 [M]	Here He Comes Again	1963	12.50	25.00	50.00
—Black label with stars on top					
❑ LP-9248 [M]	Here He Comes Again	1964	7.50	15.00	30.00
—Black and pink label					
❑ LP-9248 [M]	Here He Comes Again	1967	5.00	10.00	20.00
—Black and green label					
❑ LP-12066 [S]	A Lot of Dominos	1961	37.50	75.00	150.00
—Black label with silver top					
❑ LP-12066 [S]	A Lot of Dominos	1964	10.00	20.00	40.00
—Black and pink label					
❑ LP-12066 [S]	A Lot of Dominos	1967	6.25	12.50	25.00
—Black and green label					
❑ LP-12073 [S]	Let the Four Winds Blow	1961	37.50	75.00	150.00
—Black label with silver top					
❑ LP-12073 [S]	Let the Four Winds Blow	1964	10.00	20.00	40.00
—Black and pink label					
❑ LP-12073 [S]	Let the Four Winds Blow	1967	6.25	12.50	25.00
—Black and green label					
❑ LP-12091 [R]	Fats Domino Swings	1964	5.00	10.00	20.00
—Black and pink label					
❑ LP-12091 [R]	Fats Domino Swings	1967	3.75	7.50	15.00
—Black and green label					
❑ LP-12103 [R]	Million Record Hits	1964	5.00	10.00	20.00
—Black and pink label					
❑ LP-12103 [R]	Million Record Hits	1967	3.75	7.50	15.00
—Black and green label					
❑ LP-12195 [R]	Million Sellers by Fats	1964	5.00	10.00	20.00
—Black and pink label					
❑ LP-12195 [R]	Million Sellers by Fats	1967	3.75	7.50	15.00
—Black and green label					
❑ LP-12227 [R]	Walking to New Orleans	1964	5.00	10.00	20.00
—Black and pink label					
❑ LP-12227 [R]	Walking to New Orleans	1967	3.75	7.50	15.00
—Black and green label					
❑ LP-12248 [R]	Here He Comes Again	1964	5.00	10.00	20.00
—Black and pink label					
❑ LP-12248 [R]	Here He Comes Again	1967	3.75	7.50	15.00
—Black and green label					
❑ LP-12387 [R]	Rock and Rollin' with Fats Domino	1968	3.00	6.00	12.00
—Rechanneled reissue of 9004					
❑ LP-12388 [R]	Fats Domino Rock and Rollin'	1968	3.00	6.00	12.00
—Rechanneled reissue of 9009					
❑ LP-12389 [R]	This Is Fats Domino!	1968	3.00	6.00	12.00
—Rechanneled reissue of 9028					
❑ LP-12390 [R]	Here Stands Fats Domino	1968	3.00	6.00	12.00
—Rechanneled reissue of 9038					
❑ LP-12391 [R]	This Is Fats	1968	3.00	6.00	12.00
—Rechanneled reissue of 9040					
❑ LP-12394 [R]	The Fabulous Mr. D.	1968	3.00	6.00	12.00
—Rechanneled reissue of 9055					
❑ LP-12395 [R]	Let's Play Fats Domino	1968	3.00	6.00	12.00
—Rechanneled reissue of 9065					
❑ LP-12398 [R]	I Miss You So	1968	3.00	6.00	12.00
—Rechanneled reissue of 9138					
LIBERTY					
❑ LWB-122 [(2)]	Cookin' with Fats (Superpak)	1981	3.00	6.00	12.00
—Budget-line reissue of UA 122					
❑ LM-1027	Million Sellers by Fats	1981	2.00	4.00	8.00
—Budget-line reissue of UA 1027					
❑ LWB-9958 [(2)]	Legendary Masters	1981	2.50	5.00	10.00
—Budget-line reissue of UA 9958					
❑ LN-10135	Let's Play Fats Domino	1981	2.00	4.00	8.00
—Budget-line reissue					
❑ LN-10136	The Fabulous Mr. D.	1981	2.00	4.00	8.00
—Budget-line reissue					
MCA/SILVER EAGLE					
❑ 6170	Greatest Hits	198?	2.50	5.00	10.00
MERCURY					
❑ MG-21039 [M]	Fats Domino '65	1965	6.25	12.50	25.00
❑ 21065/61065	Southland U.S.A.	1966	—	—	—
—Canceled					
❑ SR-61039 [S]	Fats Domino '65	1965	10.00	20.00	40.00
PICKWICK					
❑ SPC-3111	Blueberry Hill	197?	2.50	5.00	10.00
❑ SPC-3165	When My Dreamboat Comes Home	197?	2.50	5.00	10.00
❑ SPC-3295	My Blue Heaven	1971	2.50	5.00	10.00
QUICKSILVER					
❑ QS-1016	Live Hits	198?	2.50	5.00	10.00
REPRISE					
❑ RS 6304	Fats Is Back	1968	7.50	15.00	30.00
❑ RS 6439	Fats	1970	125.00	250.00	500.00
—Officially unreleased, test pressings and coverless stock copies are known to exist					
SEARS					
❑ SPS-473	Blueberry Hill!	1970	6.25	12.50	25.00
SUNSET					
❑ SUM-1103 [M]	Fats Domino	1966	3.00	6.00	12.00
❑ SUM-1158 [M]	Stompin' Fats Domino	1967	3.00	6.00	12.00
❑ SUS-5103 [R]	Fats Domino	1966	3.00	6.00	12.00
❑ SUS-5158 [R]	Stompin' Fats Domino	1967	3.00	6.00	12.00
❑ SUS-5200 [P]	Trouble in Mind	1968	5.00	10.00	20.00
❑ SUS-5299 [R]	Ain't That a Shame	1970	3.00	6.00	12.00
UNITED ARTISTS					
❑ UAMG-104 [DJ]	The Fats Domino Sound	1973	10.00	20.00	40.00
—Promo compilation of 30 excerpts of Fats hits					
❑ UA-LA122-F2 [(2)]	Cookin' with Fats (Superpak)	1974	7.50	15.00	30.00
❑ UA-LA122-F2 [(2)DJ]	Cookin' with Fats (Superpak)	1974	75.00	150.00	300.00
—Promo with one black vinyl record and one colored vinyl record					
❑ UA-LA233-G	The Very Best of Fats Domino	1974	3.00	6.00	12.00
❑ LM-1027	Million Sellers by Fats	1980	2.50	5.00	10.00
❑ UAS-9958 [(2)]	Legendary Masters	1972	3.75	7.50	15.00

DOMINOES, THE See BILLY WARD AND THE DOMINOES.

DON AND DEWEY
45s

Number	Title (A Side/B Side)	Yr	VG	VG+	NM
FIDELITY					
❑ 3017	Jump Awhile/H.B. Boogie	1960	3.75	7.50	15.00
❑ 3018	Kill Me/Little Sally Walker	1960	3.75	7.50	15.00
RUSH					
❑ 1003	Don't Ever Leave Me (Don't Make Me Cry)/Heart Attack	196?	5.00	10.00	20.00
SHADE					
❑ 100	Miss Sue/My Heart Is Aching	195?	37.50	75.00	150.00
SPECIALTY					
❑ 599	Jungle Hop/A Little Love	1957	6.25	12.50	25.00
❑ 610	Leavin' It All Up to You/Jelly Bean	1957	7.50	15.00	30.00
❑ 617	Just a Little Lovin'/When the Sun Has Begun to Shine	1957	6.25	12.50	25.00
❑ 631	Justine/Bim Bam	1958	6.25	12.50	25.00
❑ 639	The Letter/Koko Joe	1958	6.25	12.50	25.00
❑ 659	Farmer John/Big Boy Pete	1959	6.25	12.50	25.00
❑ 691	Annie Lee/Get Your Hat	196?	3.00	6.00	12.00
Albums					
SPECIALTY					
❑ SPS-2131	They're Rockin' Til Midnight, Rollin' Til Dawn	1970	7.50	15.00	30.00
—Original labels are black and gold					

DON AND HIS ROSES
45s

Number	Title (A Side/B Side)	Yr	VG	VG+	NM
DOT					
❑ 15755	Since You Went Away to School/Right Now	1958	12.50	25.00	50.00
❑ 15874	Leave Those Cats Alone/Don't Try to Change Me	1958	37.50	75.00	150.00

DON AND JUAN
45s

Number	Title (A Side/B Side)	Yr	VG	VG+	NM
BIG TOP					
❑ 3079	What's Your Name/Chicken Necks	1961	6.25	12.50	25.00
❑ 3106	Two Fools Are We/Pot Luck	1962	5.00	10.00	20.00
❑ 3121	Magic Wand/What I Really Meant to Say	1962	10.00	20.00	40.00
❑ 3145	True Love Never Runs Smooth/Is It All Right If I Love You	1963	12.50	25.00	50.00
LANA					
❑ 150	What's Your Name/Chicken Necks	196?	2.00	4.00	8.00
—Oldies reissue					
LOST-NITE					
❑ 219	What's Your Name/Chicken Necks	196?	—	2.50	5.00
—Reissue					
MALA					
❑ 469	Lonely Man/Could This Be Love	1963	3.00	6.00	12.00
❑ 479	Pledging My Love/Molinda	1964	3.00	6.00	12.00
❑ 484	Sincerely/Maryana Cherie	1964	3.00	6.00	12.00
❑ 494	I Can't Help Myself/All That's Missing Is You	1964	3.00	6.00	12.00
❑ 509	The Heartbreaking Truth/Thank Goodness	1965	7.50	15.00	30.00
TWIRL					
❑ 2021	Because I Love You/Are You Putting Me on the Shelf	1966	7.50	15.00	30.00

DON AND THE CHEVELLS "Don" is Don Ciccone, later of THE CRITTERS and THE FOUR SEASONS.
45s

Number	Title (A Side/B Side)	Yr	VG	VG+	NM
SPEEDWAY					
❑ 1000	Inner Limits/The Only Girl	1964	20.00	40.00	80.00

DON AND THE GOODTIMES
45s

Number	Title (A Side/B Side)	Yr	VG	VG+	NM
BURDETTE					
❑ 3	Colors of Life/You Did It Before	196?	5.00	10.00	20.00
DUNHILL					
❑ 4008	Little Green Thing/Little Sally Tease	1965	2.50	5.00	10.00
❑ 4015	I'll Be Down Forever/Big Big Knight (On a Big White Horse)	1965	2.50	5.00	10.00
❑ 4022	Sweets for My Sweet/Hey There Mary Mae	1966	2.50	5.00	10.00
EPIC					
❑ 10145	I Could Be So Good to You/And It's So Good	1967	2.50	5.00	10.00
❑ 10145 [PS]	I Could Be So Good to You/And It's So Good	1967	3.75	7.50	15.00
❑ 10199	If You Love Her, Cherish Her and Such/Happy and Me	1967	2.50	5.00	10.00
❑ 10241	Bambi/Sally (Studio A at 6 O'Clock in the Morning)	1967	2.50	5.00	10.00
❑ 10280	Ball of Fire/May My Heart Be Cast Into Stone	1968	2.50	5.00	10.00
JERDEN					
❑ 762	You'll Never Walk Away/Little Sally Tease	1965	3.00	6.00	12.00
WAND					
❑ 165	Turn On/Make It	1964	2.50	5.00	10.00
❑ 184	Straight Scepter/There's Something on Your Mind	1965	2.50	5.00	10.00
Albums					
BEAT ROCKET					
❑ BR-130	The Original Northwest Sound of Don and the Goodtimes	2000	3.00	6.00	12.00
BURDETTE					
❑ 300 [M]	Don and the Goodtimes' Greatest Hits	1966	37.50	75.00	150.00
❑ 300S [R]	Don and the Goodtimes' Greatest Hits	1966	25.00	50.00	100.00
—LP plays rechanneled stereo					
❑ 300S [S]	Don and the Goodtimes' Greatest Hits	1966	75.00	150.00	300.00
—LP plays true stereo					
EPIC					
❑ LN 24311 [M]	So Good	1967	5.00	10.00	20.00
❑ BN 26311 [S]	So Good	1967	5.00	10.00	20.00
PICCADILLY					
❑ 3394	Goodtime Rock 'n' Roll	1980	6.25	12.50	25.00
WAND					
❑ WDS-679	Where the Action Is	1969	7.50	15.00	30.00

Number	Title (A Side/B Side)	Yr	VG	VG+	NM

DON, DICK & JIMMY
45s
CROWN

Number	Title (A Side/B Side)	Yr	VG	VG+	NM
❏ 113	The Old Gray Mare/It Shall Come to Pass	195?	3.75	7.50	15.00
❏ 116	Ol' Man River/Hawaiian War Chant	1954	3.75	7.50	15.00
❏ 125	That's What I Like/You Can't Have Your Cake and Eat It, Too	1954	3.75	7.50	15.00
❏ 131	The Touch of Your Lips/I Go to You	1954	3.75	7.50	15.00
❏ 138	Make Yourself Comfortable/Songs from Desiree	1955	3.75	7.50	15.00
❏ 147	Baby, You!/Nobody Likes to Cry	1955	3.75	7.50	15.00
❏ 152	This Little Piggie/Make Me a Present	1955	3.75	7.50	15.00
❏ 158	Love Is a Many-Splendored Thing/In Madrid	1955	3.75	7.50	15.00
❏ 162	Stolen Love/Adios My Madonna	1956	3.75	7.50	15.00

DOT

Number	Title (A Side/B Side)	Yr	VG	VG+	NM
❏ 15768	Too Young to Bop/This Was My Sin	1958	3.00	6.00	12.00

VERVE

Number	Title (A Side/B Side)	Yr	VG	VG+	NM
❏ 2020	That's the Way I Feel/Two Voices in the Night	1956	3.00	6.00	12.00
❏ 10043	A Man's Gotta Do/My Faith, My Hope, My Love	1957	3.00	6.00	12.00
❏ 10062	Be Sweet to Me/Building a Paradise	1957	3.00	6.00	12.00

Albums
CROWN

Number	Title (A Side/B Side)	Yr	VG	VG+	NM
❏ CLP-5005 [M]	Spring Fever	1958	10.00	20.00	40.00

DOT

Number	Title (A Side/B Side)	Yr	VG	VG+	NM
❏ DLP-3152 [M]	Don, Dick & Jimmy	1959	7.50	15.00	30.00

MODERN

Number	Title (A Side/B Side)	Yr	VG	VG+	NM
❏ MLP-1205 [M]	Spring Fever	1957	30.00	60.00	120.00

VERVE

Number	Title (A Side/B Side)	Yr	VG	VG+	NM
❏ MGV-2084 [M]	Medium Rare	1958	10.00	20.00	40.00
❏ MGV-2107 [M]	Songs for the Hearth	1959	10.00	20.00	40.00

DON JUANS, THE
45s
ONEZY

Number	Title (A Side/B Side)	Yr	VG	VG+	NM
❏ 101	The Girl of My Dreams/Dolores	1959	500.00	1000.	2000.

DONALDSON, BO, AND THE HEYWOODS
45s
ABC

Number	Title (A Side/B Side)	Yr	VG	VG+	NM
❏ 11402	Deeper and Deeper/Drive Me Crazy	1973	—	2.00	4.00
❏ 11402 [PS]	Deeper and Deeper/Drive Me Crazy	1973	2.00	4.00	8.00
❏ 11435	Billy, Don't Be a Hero/Don't Ever Look Back	1974	—	2.00	4.00
❏ 12006	Who Do You Think You Are/Fool's Way of Lovin'	1974	—	2.00	4.00
❏ 12011	Billy, Don't Be a Hero/Don't Ever Look Back	1974	—	2.50	5.00
❏ 12039	The Heartbreak Kid/Girl Don't Make Me Wait	1974	—	2.00	4.00
❏ 12039 [PS]	The Heartbreak Kid/Girl Don't Make Me Wait	1974	2.00	4.00	8.00
❏ 12072	Make the Most of This World/House on Telegraph Hill	1975	—	2.00	4.00
❏ 12108	Our Last Song Together/Make the Most of This World	1975	—	2.00	4.00

CAPITOL

Number	Title (A Side/B Side)	Yr	VG	VG+	NM
❏ 4237	Oh Boy/Tie Me Down	1976	—	2.00	4.00
❏ 4282	Teenage Rampage/Tie Me Down	1976	—	2.00	4.00

FAMILY PRODUCTIONS

Number	Title (A Side/B Side)	Yr	VG	VG+	NM
❏ 0917	Thank You Girl/You Don't Own Me	1972	—	2.50	5.00
❏ 0918	All Over the World/Just for You	1972	—	2.50	5.00
❏ 0918 [PS]	All Over the World/Just for You	1972	3.75	7.50	15.00
—Sleeve may be promo only					
❏ 0923	Da Doo Ron Ron/Just Because	1973	—	2.50	5.00

PLAYBOY

Number	Title (A Side/B Side)	Yr	VG	VG+	NM
❏ 5820	Are You Cuckoo/Gimmie Some Time	1977	—	2.00	4.00

Albums
ABC

Number	Title (A Side/B Side)	Yr	VG	VG+	NM
❏ D-824	Bo Donaldson and the Heywoods	1974	2.50	5.00	10.00

CAPITOL

Number	Title (A Side/B Side)	Yr	VG	VG+	NM
❏ ST-11501	Farther On	1976	3.75	7.50	15.00

FAMILY PRODUCTIONS

Number	Title (A Side/B Side)	Yr	VG	VG+	NM
❏ FPS-2711	Special Someone	1972	3.75	7.50	15.00

DONAYS, THE
45s
BRENT

Number	Title (A Side/B Side)	Yr	VG	VG+	NM
❏ 7033	Devil in His Heart/Bad Boy	1962	10.00	20.00	40.00

DONEGAN, LONNIE
45s
APT

Number	Title (A Side/B Side)	Yr	VG	VG+	NM
❏ 25067	Pick a Bale of Cotton/Ramblin' Round	1962	2.50	5.00	10.00

ATLANTIC

Number	Title (A Side/B Side)	Yr	VG	VG+	NM
❏ 2058	My Old Man's a Dustman/The Golden Vanity	1960	3.00	6.00	12.00
❏ 2063	Take This Hammer/Nobody Understands Me	1960	3.00	6.00	12.00
❏ 2081	Lorelei/Junco Partner	1960	3.00	6.00	12.00
❏ 2108	Have a Drink On Me/Beyond the Sunset	1961	3.00	6.00	12.00
❏ 2123	Wreck of the John B/Sorry, But I'm Gonna Have to Pass	1961	3.00	6.00	12.00

DOT

Number	Title (A Side/B Side)	Yr	VG	VG+	NM
❏ 15792	The Grand Coulee Dam/Nobody Loves Like an Irishman	1958	5.00	10.00	20.00
❏ 15873	Sally Don't You Grieve/Times Are Getting Hard, Boys	1958	5.00	10.00	20.00
❏ 15911	Does Your Chewing Gum Lose Its Flavor (On the Bedpost Overnight)/Aunt Rhody	1959	5.00	10.00	20.00
—Reissued in 1961 with the same number					
❏ 15953	Fort Worth Jail/Whoa, Back, Back	1959	5.00	10.00	20.00
❏ 16263	Whoa, Back, Back/Light from the Lighthouse	1961	3.75	7.50	15.00

FELSTED

Number	Title (A Side/B Side)	Yr	VG	VG+	NM
❏ 8630	Rock Island Line/John Henry	1961	3.00	6.00	12.00

HICKORY

Number	Title (A Side/B Side)	Yr	VG	VG+	NM
❏ 1247	Lemon Tree/A Very Good Year	1964	2.50	5.00	10.00
❏ 1267	Fisherman's Luck/There's a Big Wheel	1964	2.50	5.00	10.00
❏ 1274	Bad News/Interstate 40	1964	2.50	5.00	10.00
❏ 1299	Louisiana Man/Lovey Told Me Goodbye	1965	2.50	5.00	10.00
❏ 1345	Cajun Jo (Bully of the Bayou)/Nothing to Gain	1965	2.50	5.00	10.00

LONDON

Number	Title (A Side/B Side)	Yr	VG	VG+	NM
❏ 1650	Rock Island Line/John Henry	1956	7.50	15.00	30.00
❏ 20055	Juanita/Who Knows Where the Time Goes	1969	—	3.00	6.00

MERCURY

Number	Title (A Side/B Side)	Yr	VG	VG+	NM
❏ 70872	Lost John/Stewball	1956	6.25	12.50	25.00
❏ 70949	Bring a Little Water, Sylvie/Dead or Alive	1956	6.25	12.50	25.00
❏ 71026	Don't You Rock Me Daddy-O/How Long, How Long Blues	1957	6.25	12.50	25.00
❏ 71094	Cumberland Gap/Wabash Cannonball	1957	6.25	12.50	25.00
❏ 71181	Puttin' On the Style/Gamblin' Man	1957	6.25	12.50	25.00
❏ 71248	My Dixie Darling/I'm Just a Rolling Stone	1957	6.25	12.50	25.00

Albums
ABC-PARAMOUNT

Number	Title (A Side/B Side)	Yr	VG	VG+	NM
❏ 433 [M]	Sing Hallelujah	1963	5.00	10.00	20.00
❏ S-433 [S]	Sing Hallelujah	1963	6.25	12.50	25.00

ATLANTIC

Number	Title (A Side/B Side)	Yr	VG	VG+	NM
❏ 8038 [M]	Skiffle Folk Songs	1960	10.00	20.00	40.00
❏ SD 8038 [S]	Skiffle Folk Songs	1960	12.50	25.00	50.00

DOT

Number	Title (A Side/B Side)	Yr	VG	VG+	NM
❏ DLP-3159 [M]	Lonnie Donegan	1959	10.00	20.00	40.00

MERCURY

Number	Title (A Side/B Side)	Yr	VG	VG+	NM
❏ MG-20229 [M]	An Englishman Sings American Folk Songs	1957	12.50	25.00	50.00

UNITED ARTISTS

Number	Title (A Side/B Side)	Yr	VG	VG+	NM
❏ UA-LA827-?	Puttin' On the Style	1977	2.50	5.00	10.00

DONLEY, JIMMY
45s
CHESS

Number	Title (A Side/B Side)	Yr	VG	VG+	NM
❏ 1843	Santa, Don't Pass Me By/Think It Over	1962	3.00	6.00	12.00

CRAZY CAJUN

Number	Title (A Side/B Side)	Yr	VG	VG+	NM
❏ 9001	Santa, Don't Pass Me By/Think It Over	197?	—	2.50	5.00
❏ 9002	Forever Lillie Mae/I Still Care	197?	—	3.00	6.00
❏ 9003	Love Bug/I Still Care	197?	—	3.00	6.00
❏ 9004	I Really Got the Blues/Just a Game	197?	—	3.00	6.00
❏ 9005	You're Why I'm So Lonely/Let Me Hold You	197?	—	3.00	6.00
❏ 9006	Baby, Heaven Sent Me You/Door to My Heart	197?	—	3.00	6.00
❏ 9007	A Woman's Gotta Have Her Way/Hello, Remember Me	197?	—	3.00	6.00
❏ 9008	Please Mr. Sandman/Honey Stop	197?	—	3.00	6.00
❏ 9009	Lovin' Cajun Style/(B-side unknown)	197?	—	3.00	6.00
❏ 9010	Born to Be a Loser/Now I Know	197?	—	3.00	6.00

DECCA

Number	Title (A Side/B Side)	Yr	VG	VG+	NM
❏ 30308	Kickin' My Hound Around/Come Along	1957	20.00	40.00	80.00
❏ 30392	South of the Border/The Trail of the Lonesome Pine	1957	6.25	12.50	25.00
❏ 30519	Baby How Long/I Gotta Go	1957	6.25	12.50	25.00
❏ 30574	Please Baby Come Home/Born to Be a Loser	1958	6.25	12.50	25.00
❏ 30738	Radio, Jukebox and TV/I'm Alone	1958	6.25	12.50	25.00
❏ 30887	What Must I Do/The Shape You Left Me In	1959	6.25	12.50	25.00
❏ 31005	Now I Know/I Can't Love You	1959	6.25	12.50	25.00
❏ 31116	My Baby's Gone/Our Love	1960	10.00	20.00	40.00

TEARDROP

Number	Title (A Side/B Side)	Yr	VG	VG+	NM
❏ 3005	Honey Stop Twistin'/Hello, Remember Me	1962	3.75	7.50	15.00
❏ 3007	Santa, Don't Pass Me By/Forever Lillie Mae	1962	3.00	6.00	12.00
❏ 3007	Think It Over/Forever Lillie Mae	1962	3.00	6.00	12.00
❏ 3009	Baby, Heaven Sent Me You/Loving Cajun Style	1963	3.00	6.00	12.00
❏ 3017	You're Why I'm So Lonely/Let Me Hold You	1963	3.00	6.00	12.00
❏ 3021	Santa, Don't Pass Me By/Santa's Alley	1963	3.00	6.00	12.00
❏ 3026	I Really Got the Blues/Just a Game	1964	2.50	5.00	10.00
❏ 3034	I'm So Lonesome Without the Blues/Forget the Past	1964	2.50	5.00	10.00
❏ 3051	Love Bug/I'm to Blame	196?	2.50	5.00	10.00
❏ 3119	My Forbidden Love/Strange, Strange Feeling	196?	2.00	4.00	8.00

DONNER, RAL
45s
CHICAGO FIRE

Number	Title (A Side/B Side)	Yr	VG	VG+	NM
❏ 7402	The Wedding Song/Godfather Per Me	1974	2.00	4.00	8.00

END

Number	Title (A Side/B Side)	Yr	VG	VG+	NM
❏ GG-19	You Don't Know What You've Got (Until You Lose It)/She's Everything (I Wanted You to Be)	1963	7.50	15.00	30.00
—An early, and sought-after, reissue					

FONTANA

Number	Title (A Side/B Side)	Yr	VG	VG+	NM
❏ 1502	Poison Ivy League/A Tear in My Eye	1965	6.25	12.50	25.00
❏ 1502	Poison Ivy League/You Finally Said Something Good	1965	6.25	12.50	25.00
❏ 1515	Good Lovin'/The Other Side of Me	1965	6.25	12.50	25.00

GONE

Number	Title (A Side/B Side)	Yr	VG	VG+	NM
❏ 5102	Girl of My Best Friend/It's Been a Long, Long Time	1961	6.25	12.50	25.00
—Multi-color label					
❏ 5102	Girl of My Best Friend/It's Been a Long, Long Time	1961	10.00	20.00	40.00
—Black label					
❏ 5108	You Don't Know What You've Got (Until You Lose It)/So Close to Heaven	1961	7.50	15.00	30.00
❏ 5108	To Love/And Then	1961	10.00	20.00	40.00
—Deleted shortly after release					
❏ 5114	Please Don't Go/I Didn't Figure on Him	1961	6.25	12.50	25.00
❏ 5119	School of Heartbreakers/Because We're Young	1961	10.00	20.00	40.00
❏ 5121	She's Everything (I Wanted You to Be)/Because We're Young	1961	6.25	12.50	25.00
❏ 5121	She's Everything (I Wanted You to Be)/Will You Love Me in Heaven	1961	7.50	15.00	30.00
—B-side sung by a girl group, not Ral Donner.					
❏ 5125	To Love Someone/Will You Love Me in Heaven	1962	6.25	12.50	25.00
—B-side sung by Ral Donner as advertised					
❏ 5129	Loveless Life/Bells of Love	1962	6.25	12.50	25.00
❏ 5133	To Love/Sweetheart	1962	6.25	12.50	25.00

MID-EAGLE

Number	Title (A Side/B Side)	Yr	VG	VG+	NM
❏ 101	(If I Had My) Life to Live Over/Lost	1968	2.50	5.00	10.00
❏ 275	The Wedding Song/So Much Lovin'	1976	—	3.00	6.00

MJ

Number	Title (A Side/B Side)	Yr	VG	VG+	NM
❏ 222	(All of a Sudden) My Heart Sings/Lovin' Place	1970	—	3.00	6.00
❏ 222 [PS]	(All of a Sudden) My Heart Sings/Lovin' Place	1970	—	3.00	6.00

RED BIRD

Number	Title (A Side/B Side)	Yr	VG	VG+	NM
❏ 10-057	Love Isn't Like That/It Will Only Make You Love	1966	37.50	75.00	150.00

Number	Title (A Side/B Side)	Yr	VG	VG+	NM
REPRISE					
❑ 20135	(These Are the Things That Make Up) Christmas Day/Second Miracle (Of Christmas)	1962	10.00	20.00	40.00
❑ 20141	I Got Burned/A Tear in My Eye	1963	10.00	20.00	40.00
❑ 20141 [PS]	I Got Burned/A Tear in My Eye	1963	45.00	90.00	180.00
❑ 20176	I Wish This Night Would Never End/Don't Put Your Heart in His Hand	1963	12.50	25.00	50.00
❑ 20192	Beyond the Heartbreak/Run Little Linda	1963	15.00	30.00	60.00
RISING SONS					
❑ 714	Just a Little Sunshine (In the Rain)/If I Promise	1968	2.50	5.00	10.00
SCOTTIE					
❑ 1310	Tell Me Why/That's All Right with Me	1959	62.50	125.00	250.00
SMASH					
❑ 34774/5 [DJ]	Good Lovin'/The Other Side of Me	1964	10.00	20.00	40.00
—A Fontana promo using Smash labels in error and omitting the Fontana number?					
STARFIRE					
❑ 100	Don't Let It Slip Away/Wait a Minute Now	1978	—	5.00	10.00
—White vinyl					
❑ 100	Don't Let It Slip Away/Wait a Minute Now	1978	2.50	5.00	10.00
—Black vinyl					
❑ 100 [PS]	Don't Let It Slip Away/Wait a Minute Now	1978	2.50	5.00	10.00
❑ 103	(Things That Make Up) Christmas Day/Second Miracle (Of Christmas)	1978	2.50	5.00	10.00
—Green vinyl					
❑ 103 [PS]	(Things That Make Up) Christmas Day/Second Miracle (Of Christmas)	1978	2.50	5.00	10.00
❑ 114	Rip It Up/Don't Leave Me Now	1979	2.50	5.00	10.00
❑ 114	Rip It Up/Don't Leave Me Now	1979	6.25	12.50	25.00
—Picture disc					
❑ 114 [PS]	Rip It Up/Don't Leave Me Now	1979	2.50	5.00	10.00
SUNLIGHT					
❑ 1006	Don't Let It Slip Away/Wait a Minute Now	1972	3.00	6.00	12.00
TAU					
❑ 105	Loneliness of a Star/And Then	1963	7.50	15.00	30.00
—Yellow label					
❑ 105	Loneliness of a Star/And Then	1963	12.50	25.00	50.00
—Blue label					
THUNDER					
❑ 7801	The Day the Beat Stopped/Rock on Me	1978	—	3.00	6.00
Albums					
GONE					
❑ LP-5012 [M]	Takin' Care of Business	1961	75.00	150.00	300.00
STARFIRE					
❑ 1004	An Evening with Ral Donner	1982	3.75	7.50	15.00
—All copies on multi-color vinyl					

DONNER, RAL/RAY SMITH/BOBBY DALE
Albums

Number	Title (A Side/B Side)	Yr	VG	VG+	NM
CROWN					
❑ CST-335 [R]	Ral Donner, Ray Smith and Bobby Dale	1963	5.00	10.00	20.00
❑ CLP-5335 [M]	Ral Donner, Ray Smith and Bobby Dale	1963	10.00	20.00	40.00

DONNIE AND THE DARLINGTONS
45s

Number	Title (A Side/B Side)	Yr	VG	VG+	NM
ABC-PARAMOUNT					
❑ 10633	Poppin' My Clutch/Since Grandpa Got a Rail Job	1965	6.25	12.50	25.00

DONNIE AND THE DELCHORDS
45s

Number	Title (A Side/B Side)	Yr	VG	VG+	NM
EPIC					
❑ 9495	So Lonely/When You're Alone	1962	6.25	12.50	25.00
TAURUS					
❑ 352	So Lonely/When You're Alone	1962	10.00	20.00	40.00
❑ 357	I Don't Care/I'll Be With You in Apple Blossom Time	1963	6.25	12.50	25.00
❑ 361	Transylvania Mist/That Old Feeling	1963	6.25	12.50	25.00
❑ 363	Be with You/I Found Heaven	1963	6.25	12.50	25.00
❑ 364	I'm in the Mood for Love/I've Got a Woman	1964	6.25	12.50	25.00
Albums					
TAURUS					
❑ 1000	Sing with Triple Stereo	1967	75.00	150.00	300.00

DONNIE AND THE DREAMERS
45s

Number	Title (A Side/B Side)	Yr	VG	VG+	NM
DECCA					
❑ 31312	Carole/Ruby My Love	1961	12.50	25.00	50.00
WHALE					
❑ 500	Dorothy/Count Every Star	1961	6.25	12.50	25.00
❑ 505	Teenage Love/My Memories of You	1961	10.00	20.00	40.00

DONNYBROOKS, THE
45s

Number	Title (A Side/B Side)	Yr	VG	VG+	NM
CALICO					
❑ 108	Every Time We Kiss/Break the Glass	1959	5.00	10.00	20.00
❑ 112	Coming Home from School/Mandolins of Love	1959	5.00	10.00	20.00

DONOVAN
45s

Number	Title (A Side/B Side)	Yr	VG	VG+	NM
ALLEGIANCE					
❑ 3910	Lady of the Stars/(B-side unknown)	1983	—	2.00	4.00
ARISTA					
❑ 0280	Dare to Be Different/International Man	1977	—	2.00	4.00
EPIC					
❑ 10045	Sunshine Superman/The Trip	1966	2.50	5.00	10.00
❑ 10045 [DJ]	Sunshine Superman/The Trip	1966	10.00	20.00	40.00
—Promo only on red vinyl					
❑ 10045 [PS]	Sunshine Superman/The Trip	1966	3.75	7.50	15.00
❑ 10098	Mellow Yellow/Sunny South Kensington	1966	2.50	5.00	10.00
❑ 10098 [PS]	Mellow Yellow/Sunny South Kensington	1966	3.75	7.50	15.00
❑ 10127	Epistle to Dippy/Preachin' Love	1967	2.00	4.00	8.00
❑ 10127 [PS]	Epistle to Dippy/Preachin' Love	1967	3.00	6.00	12.00
❑ 10212	There Is a Mountain/Sand and Foam	1967	2.00	4.00	8.00
❑ 10253	Wear Your Love Like Heaven/Oh Gosh	1967	2.00	4.00	8.00
❑ 10253 [PS]	Wear Your Love Like Heaven/Oh Gosh	1967	3.00	6.00	12.00
❑ 10300	Jennifer Juniper/Poor Cow	1968	2.00	4.00	8.00
❑ 10300 [PS]	Jennifer Juniper/Poor Cow	1968	3.00	6.00	12.00

Number	Title (A Side/B Side)	Yr	VG	VG+	NM
❑ 10345	Hurdy Gurdy Man/Teen Angel	1968	2.00	4.00	8.00
—Features John Paul Jones, Jimmy Page, and possibly John Bonham, all later of Led Zeppelin					
❑ 10345 [PS]	Hurdy Gurdy Man/Teen Angel	1968	3.00	6.00	12.00
❑ 10393	Lalena/Aye My Love	1968	2.00	4.00	8.00
❑ 10393 [PS]	Lalena/Aye My Love	1968	3.00	6.00	12.00
❑ 10434	Atlantis/To Susan on the West Coast Waiting	1969	2.00	4.00	8.00
❑ 10434 [PS]	Atlantis/To Susan on the West Coast Waiting	1969	3.00	6.00	12.00
❑ 10510	Goo Goo Barabajagal (Love Is Hot)/Trust	1969	2.00	4.00	8.00
❑ 10510 [PS]	Goo Goo Barabajagal (Love Is Hot)/Trust	1969	3.00	6.00	12.00
—With the Jeff Beck Group					
❑ 10649	Riki Tiki Tavi/Roots of Oak	1970	2.00	4.00	8.00
❑ 10649 [PS]	Riki Tiki Tavi/Roots of Oak	1970	3.00	6.00	12.00
❑ 10694	Celia of the Seals/Song of the Wandering Aengus	1971	2.00	4.00	8.00
❑ 10694 [PS]	Celia of the Seals/Song of the Wandering Aengus	1971	3.00	6.00	12.00
❑ 10983	I Like You/Earth Sign Man	1973	—	2.50	5.00
❑ 11023	Maria Magenta/Intergalactic Laxative	1973	—	2.50	5.00
❑ 11108	Yellow Star/Sailing Homeward	1974	—	2.50	5.00
❑ 50016	Rock and Roll with Me/Divine Daze of Deathless Delight	1974	—	2.50	5.00
❑ 50077	Rock and Roll Souljer/How Silly	1975	—	2.50	5.00
❑ 50237	Dark Eyed Blue Jean Angel/Well Known Has-Been	1976	—	2.50	5.00
HICKORY					
❑ 1309	Catch the Wind/Why Do You Treat Me Like You Do	1965	3.75	7.50	15.00
❑ 1324	Colours/Josie	1965	3.00	6.00	12.00
❑ 1338	Universal Soldier/Do You Hear Me Now	1965	3.00	6.00	12.00
❑ 1375	You're Gonna Need Somebody on Your Mind/Little Tin Soldier	1966	3.00	6.00	12.00
❑ 1402	Turquoise/To Try for the Sun	1966	3.00	6.00	12.00
❑ 1417	Hey Gyp/The War Drags On	1966	3.00	6.00	12.00
❑ 1470	Sunny Goodge Street/Summer Day Reflection Song	1967	2.50	5.00	10.00
❑ 1492	Do You Hear Me Now/Why Do You Treat Me Like You Do	1968	2.50	5.00	10.00
JANUS					
❑ 138	Keep On Truckin'/Hey Gyp	1971	2.00	4.00	8.00
Albums					
ALLEGIANCE					
❑ AV-437	Lady of the Stars	1983	2.50	5.00	10.00
ARISTA					
❑ AB 4143	Donovan	1980	2.50	5.00	10.00
BELL					
❑ 1135	Early Treasures	1973	2.50	5.00	10.00
COLUMBIA LIMITED EDITION					
❑ LE 10184	Mellow Yellow	197?	2.50	5.00	10.00
EPIC					
❑ B2N 171 [(2)S]	A Gift from a Flower to a Garden	1967	6.25	12.50	25.00
—Boxed set of two LPs with portfolio of lyrics and drawings. The two records also were issued separately as Epic 26349 and 26350.					
❑ E2 171 [(2)]	A Gift from a Flower to a Garden	1979	3.75	7.50	15.00
—Blue label					
❑ L2N 6071 [(2)M]	A Gift from a Flower to a Garden	1967	12.50	25.00	50.00
—Boxed set of two LPs with portfolio of lyrics and drawings. The two records also were issued separately as Epic 24349 and 24350.					
❑ LN 24217 [M]	Sunshine Superman	1966	7.50	15.00	30.00
—Contains the single version of "Sunshine Superman"					
❑ LN 24239 [M]	Mellow Yellow	1967	7.50	15.00	30.00
❑ LN 24349 [M]	Wear Your Love Like Heaven	1967	3.00	6.00	12.00
—Part of Epic 6071, issued simultaneously					
❑ LN 24350 [M]	For Little Ones	1967	3.00	6.00	12.00
—Part of Epic 6071, issued simultaneously					
❑ BN 26217 [R]	Sunshine Superman	1966	3.75	7.50	15.00
—Contains the single version of "Sunshine Superman" (rechanneled)					
❑ BN 26239 [S]	Mellow Yellow	1967	3.75	7.50	15.00
❑ BN 26349 [S]	Wear Your Love Like Heaven	1967	3.75	7.50	15.00
—Part of Epic 171, issued simultaneously					
❑ BN 26350 [S]	For Little Ones	1967	3.75	7.50	15.00
—Part of Epic 171, issued simultaneously					
❑ BN 26386	Donovan in Concert	1968	3.00	6.00	12.00
❑ BN 26420	Hurdy Gurdy Man	1968	3.00	6.00	12.00
❑ PE 26420	Hurdy Gurdy Man	1986	2.00	4.00	8.00
—Blue label, new prefix					
❑ BXN 26439 [P]	Donovan's Greatest Hits	1969	3.00	6.00	12.00
—Yellow label; "Mellow Yellow" is rechanneled; "Sunshine Superman" is the full-length version in stereo; "Catch the Wind" and "Colours" were re-recorded					
❑ BXN 26439 [P]	Donovan's Greatest Hits	1973	2.50	5.00	10.00
—Orange label					
❑ PE 26439	Donovan's Greatest Hits	1979	2.00	4.00	8.00
—Blue label					
❑ BN 26481	Barabajagal	1969	3.00	6.00	12.00
❑ PE 26481	Barabajagal	1987	2.00	4.00	8.00
—Blue label, new prefix					
❑ E 30125	Open Road	1970	3.00	6.00	12.00
❑ KEG 31210 [(2)]	The World of Donovan	1972	3.00	6.00	12.00
❑ KE 32156	Cosmic Wheels	1973	3.75	7.50	15.00
—With enclosed poster					
❑ KE 32800	Essence to Essence	1974	3.00	6.00	12.00
❑ PE 33245	7-Tease	1974	3.00	6.00	12.00
❑ EG 33731 [(2)]	Hurdy Gurdy Man/Barabajagal	1975	3.75	7.50	15.00
❑ EG 33734 [(2)]	Donovan in Concert/Sunshine Superman	1975	3.75	7.50	15.00
❑ PE 33945	Slow Down World	1976	3.00	6.00	12.00
HICKORY					
❑ LPM-123 [M]	Catch the Wind	1965	6.25	12.50	25.00
—Most pressings have Donovan facing left, so he is correctly strumming his guitar with his right hand					
❑ LPM-123 [M]	Catch the Wind	1965	10.00	20.00	40.00
—First pressings have Donovan facing right, so it appears as if he's strumming his guitar with his left hand					
❑ LPS-123 [R]	Catch the Wind	1965	6.25	12.50	25.00
❑ LPM-127 [M]	Fairy Tale	1965	5.00	10.00	20.00
❑ LPS-127 [P]	Fairy Tale	1965	6.25	12.50	25.00
—"Colours" is rechanneled					
❑ LPM-135 [M]	The Real Donovan	1966	5.00	10.00	20.00

Number	Title (A Side/B Side)	Yr	VG	VG+	NM
❏ LPS-135 [P]	The Real Donovan	1966	6.25	12.50	25.00
—Half stereo, including "Colours," the rest rechanneled.					
❏ LPS-143 [P]	Like It Is, Was and Evermore Shall Be	1968	5.00	10.00	20.00
❏ LPS-149 [P]	The Best of Donovan	1969	5.00	10.00	20.00
JANUS					
❏ 3022	Donovan P. Leitch	1970	2.50	5.00	10.00
❏ 3025	Hear Me Now	1971	2.50	5.00	10.00
KORY					
❏ 3012	Early Treasures	1977	2.00	4.00	8.00
PYE					
❏ 502	Donovan	1975	2.50	5.00	10.00

DONTELS, THE
45s
BELTONE

Number	Title (A Side/B Side)	Yr	VG	VG+	NM
❏ 2040	Lover's Reunion/Make a Chance	1963	62.50	125.00	250.00

DOOBIE BROTHERS, THE Also see MICHAEL McDONALD.
45s
ASYLUM

Number	Title (A Side/B Side)	Yr	VG	VG+	NM
❏ 46630	Power/Cape Fear River	1980	—	2.50	5.00
—A-side: With John Hall and James Taylor; B-side by Sweet Honey in the Rock					
CAPITOL					
❏ B-44376	The Doctor/Too High a Price	1989	—	—	3.00
❏ B-44376 [PS]	The Doctor/Too High a Price	1989	—	—	3.00
❏ 7PRO-79723 [DJ]	Need a Little Taste of Love (same on both sides)	1989	—	3.00	6.00
—Vinyl is promo only					
SESAME STREET					
❏ 49642	Wynken, Blynken and Nod/In Harmony	1980	—	2.50	5.00
—B-side by Kate Taylor and the Simon-Taylor Family					
❏ 49642 [PS]	Wynken, Blynken and Nod/In Harmony	1980	—	2.50	5.00
WARNER BROS.					
❏ 7495	Nobody/Slippery St. Paul	1971	—	3.00	6.00
❏ 7527	Travelin' Man/Feelin' Down Partner	1971	—	3.00	6.00
❏ 7544	Beehive State/Closer Every Day	1971	—	3.00	6.00
❏ 7619	Listen to the Music/Toulouse Street	1972	—	2.50	5.00
❏ 7661	Jesus Is Just Alright/Rockin' Down the Highway	1972	—	2.50	5.00
❏ 7698	Long Train Runnin'/Without You	1973	—	2.00	4.00
❏ 7728	China Grove/Evil Woman	1973	—	2.00	4.00
❏ 7795	Another Park, Another Sunday/Black Water	1974	—	2.50	5.00
❏ 7832	Eyes of Silver/You Just Can't Stop It	1974	—	2.50	5.00
❏ 8011	Eyes of Silver/You Just Can't Stop It	1974	—	2.00	4.00
❏ 8041	Nobody/Flying Cloud	1974	—	2.00	4.00
❏ 8062	Black Water/Song to See You Through	1974	—	2.00	4.00
❏ 8092	Take Me in Your Arms (Rock Me)/Slat Key Soquel Rag	1975	—	2.00	4.00
❏ 8126	Sweet Maxine/Double Dealin' Four Flusher	1975	—	2.00	4.00
❏ 8161	I Cheat the Hangman/Music Man	1975	—	2.00	4.00
❏ 8196	Takin' It to the Streets/For Someone Special	1976	—	2.00	4.00
❏ 8233	Wheels of Fortune/Slat Key Soquel Rag	1976	—	2.00	4.00
❏ 8282	It Keeps You Runnin'/Turn It Loose	1976	—	2.00	4.00
❏ 8408	Little Darling (I Need You)/Losin' End	1977	—	2.00	4.00
❏ 8471	Echoes of Love/There's a Light	1977	—	2.00	4.00
❏ 8500	Livin' on the Fault Line/Nothin' but a Heartache	1977	—	2.00	4.00
❏ 8725	What a Fool Believes/Don't Stop to Watch the Wheels	1978	—	2.00	4.00
❏ 8725 [PS]	What a Fool Believes/Don't Stop to Watch the Wheels	1978	—	2.50	5.00
❏ 8828	Minute by Minute/Sweet Feelin'	1979	—	2.00	4.00
❏ 29552	You Belong to Me/South City Midnight Lady	1983	—	2.00	4.00
❏ 29552 [PS]	You Belong to Me/South City Midnight Lady	1983	—	2.50	5.00
❏ 49029	Dependin' on You/How Do the Fools Survive	1979	—	2.00	4.00
❏ 49503	Real Love/Thank You Love	1980	—	2.00	4.00
❏ 49503 [PS]	Real Love/Thank You Love	1980	—	2.50	5.00
❏ 49622	One Step Closer/South Bay Street	1980	—	2.00	4.00
❏ 49670	Keep This Train A-Rollin'/Just in Time	1981	—	2.00	4.00
❏ 50001	Here to Love You/Wynken, Bliinken and Nod	1982	—	2.00	4.00

7-Inch Extended Plays
WARNER BROS.

Number	Title (A Side/B Side)	Yr	VG	VG+	NM
❏ S 2694	China Grove/Busted Down Around O'Connelly Corners/Long Train Runnin'//Without You/Natural Thing	1973	2.00	4.00	8.00
—Jukebox issue, small hole, plays at 33 1/3 rpm					
❏ S 2694 [PS]	The Captain and Me	1973	2.00	4.00	8.00
—Part of "Little LP" series (LLP #221)					
❏ S 2750	Eyes of Silver/Pursuit on 53rd St./Spirit//Road Angel/Tell Me What You Want	1974	2.00	4.00	8.00
—Jukebox issue, small hole, plays at 33 1/3 rpm					
❏ S 2750 [PS]	What Were Once Vices Are Now Habits	1974	2.50	5.00	10.00
—Part of Little LP series (LLP #247)					

Albums
CAPITOL

Number	Title (A Side/B Side)	Yr	VG	VG+	NM
❏ C1-90371	Cycles	1989	3.00	6.00	12.00
❏ C1-594623	Brotherhood	1991	5.00	10.00	20.00
—U.S. vinyl version available only through Columbia House					
DCC COMPACT CLASSICS					
❏ LPZ-2053	Best of the Doobies	1998	10.00	20.00	40.00
—Audiophile vinyl					
MOBILE FIDELITY					
❏ 1-122	Takin' It to the Streets	1983	10.00	20.00	40.00
—Audiophile vinyl					
NAUTILUS					
❏ NR-5	The Captain and Me	1980	10.00	20.00	40.00
—Audiophile vinyl					
❏ NR-18	Minute by Minute	1981	7.50	15.00	30.00
—Audiophile vinyl					
PICKWICK					
❏ SPC-3721	Introducing the Doobie Brothers	1980	5.00	10.00	20.00
—Pre-Warner Bros. recordings; withdrawn shortly after release					
WARNER BROS.					
❏ WS 1919	The Doobie Brothers	1971	3.75	7.50	15.00
—Green label original					
❏ WS 1919	The Doobie Brothers	1973	2.50	5.00	10.00
—"Burbank" label					

Number	Title (A Side/B Side)	Yr	VG	VG+	NM
❏ BS 2634	Toulouse Street	1972	3.75	7.50	15.00
—Green label original					
❏ BS 2634	Toulouse Street	1973	2.50	5.00	10.00
—"Burbank" label					
❏ BS4 2634 [Q]	Toulouse Street	1975	6.25	12.50	25.00
❏ BS 2694	The Captain and Me	1973	3.00	6.00	12.00
—"Burbank" label					
❏ BS 2694	The Captain and Me	1973	5.00	10.00	20.00
—Green label					
❏ BS 2694	The Captain and Me	1979	2.00	4.00	8.00
—Cream label					
❏ BS4 2694 [Q]	The Captain and Me	1974	5.00	10.00	20.00
❏ W 2750	What Were Once Vices Are Now Habits	1974	2.50	5.00	10.00
—"Burbank" label					
❏ W 2750	What Were Once Vices Are Now Habits	1979	2.00	4.00	8.00
—Cream label					
❏ W4 2750 [Q]	What Were Once Vices Are Now Habits	1974	5.00	10.00	20.00
❏ BS 2835	Stampede	1975	2.50	5.00	10.00
—"Burbank" label					
❏ BS 2835	Stampede	1979	2.00	4.00	8.00
—Cream label					
❏ BS4 2835 [Q]	Stampede	1975	5.00	10.00	20.00
❏ BS 2899	Takin' It to the Streets	1976	2.50	5.00	10.00
—"Burbank" label					
❏ BS 2899	Takin' It to the Streets	1979	2.00	4.00	8.00
—Cream label					
❏ BS 2978	Best of the Doobies	1976	3.00	6.00	12.00
—Cream label					
❏ BSK 3045	Livin' on the Fault Line	1977	2.00	4.00	8.00
❏ BSK 3045	Livin' on the Fault Line	1977	2.50	5.00	10.00
—"Burbank" label					
❏ BSK 3112	Best of the Doobies	1978	2.50	5.00	10.00
—"Burbank" label					
❏ BSK 3112	Best of the Doobies	1979	2.00	4.00	8.00
—Cream label					
❏ BSK 3193	Minute by Minute	1978	2.50	5.00	10.00
❏ HS 3452	One Step Closer	1980	2.50	5.00	10.00
❏ BSK 3612	Best of the Doobies, Volume 2	1981	2.50	5.00	10.00
❏ 23772 [(2)]	Farewell Tour	1983	3.75	7.50	15.00

DOODLES, THE
45s
HIT

Number	Title (A Side/B Side)	Yr	VG	VG+	NM
❏ 104	I Want to Hold Your Hand/A Fool Never Learns	1964	3.00	6.00	12.00
—B-side by Fred York					

DOONICAN, VAL
45s
DECCA

Number	Title (A Side/B Side)	Yr	VG	VG+	NM
❏ 32252	I'd Rather Think of You/If the Whole World Stopped Lovin'	1968	—	2.50	5.00
❏ 32337	The Sun Always Shines When You're Young/Now	1968	—	2.50	5.00
LONDON					
❏ 1014	Two Streets/It Must Be You	1967	—	3.00	6.00
❏ 9717	Walk Talll/Only the Heartaches	1964	2.50	5.00	10.00
❏ 9735	The Special Years/Traveling Home	1965	2.50	5.00	10.00
❏ 9753	I'm Gonna Get There Somehow/How Can I Find Her	1965	2.50	5.00	10.00
PRESS					
❏ 5008	Gentle Mary/What Would I Be	1967	—	3.00	6.00

Albums
DECCA

Number	Title (A Side/B Side)	Yr	VG	VG+	NM
❏ DL 4962 [M]	If the Whole World Stopped Lovin'	1968	3.75	7.50	15.00
❏ DL 74962 [S]	If the Whole World Stopped Lovin'	1968	3.00	6.00	12.00
LONDON					
❏ PS 515 [S]	The Many Shades of Val Doonican	1967	3.75	7.50	15.00
❏ LL 3515 [M]	The Many Shades of Val Doonican	1967	3.00	6.00	12.00

DOORS, THE Also see BUTTS BAND; RAY MANZAREK.
12-Inch Singles
ELEKTRA

Number	Title (A Side/B Side)	Yr	VG	VG+	NM
❏ ED 4942 [DJ]	Gloria (clean edit)/Gloria (dirty LP)	1983	5.00	10.00	20.00
❏ ED 4955 [DJ]	Love Me Two Times/Moonlight Drive	1983	3.75	7.50	15.00
❏ ED 5245 [DJ]	Light My Fire (edit)/Light My Fire (live edit)	1987	3.75	7.50	15.00

45s
ELEKTRA

Number	Title (A Side/B Side)	Yr	VG	VG+	NM
❏ 45051	Light My Fire/Love Me Two Times	1972	—	3.00	6.00
—"Spun Gold" series; originals have a very dark gold label					
❏ 45051	Light My Fire/Love Me Two Times	1975	—	2.00	4.00
—"Spun Gold" series; reissues have a lighter gold label					
❏ 45052	Touch Me/Hello, I Love You	1972	—	3.00	6.00
—"Spun Gold" series; originals have a very dark gold label					
❏ 45052	Touch Me/Hello, I Love You	1975	—	2.00	4.00
—"Spun Gold" series; reissues have a lighter gold label					
❏ 45059	Riders on the Storm/Love Her Madly	1972	—	3.00	6.00
—"Spun Gold" series; originals have a very dark gold label					
❏ 45059	Riders on the Storm/Love Her Madly	1975	—	2.00	4.00
—"Spun Gold" series; reissues have a lighter gold label					
❏ 45122	L.A. Woman/Roadhouse Blues	1983	—	2.00	4.00
—"Spun Gold" series; lighter gold label					
❏ 45123	People Are Strange/Break On Through	1983	—	2.00	4.00
—"Spun Gold" series; lighter gold label					
❏ 45611	Break On Through (To the Other Side)/End of the Night	1966	7.50	15.00	30.00
—Originals have a yellow and black label with "ELEKTRA" in all capital letters and a woman's head above a white line at the top of the label					
❏ 45611 [PS]	Break On Through (To the Other Side)/End of the Night	1966	30.00	60.00	120.00
❏ 45611	Break On Through (To the Other Side)/End of the Night	1967	5.00	10.00	20.00
—Red, black and pink label					
❏ 45611	Break On Through (To the Other Side)/End of the Night	1967	5.00	10.00	20.00
—Red, black and white label					
❏ 45615	Light My Fire/The Crystal Ship	1967	3.00	6.00	12.00
—Second pressings have a red, black and white label					

Number	Title (A Side/B Side)	Yr	VG	VG+	NM
❑ 45615	Light My Fire/The Crystal Ship	1967	3.75	7.50	15.00

—Red, black and pink label

Number	Title (A Side/B Side)	Yr	VG	VG+	NM
❑ 45615	Light My Fire/The Crystal Ship	1967	7.50	15.00	30.00

—Originals have a yellow and black label with "ELEKTRA" in all capital letters and a woman's head above a white line at the top of the label

Number	Title (A Side/B Side)	Yr	VG	VG+	NM
❑ 45621	People Are Strange/Unhappy Girl	1967	3.00	6.00	12.00
❑ 45621 [PS]	People Are Strange/Unhappy Girl	1967	10.00	20.00	40.00
❑ 45624	Love Me Two Times/Moonlight Drive	1967	3.00	6.00	12.00

—Black, red and pink label

Number	Title (A Side/B Side)	Yr	VG	VG+	NM
❑ 45624	Love Me Two Times/Moonlight Drive	1967	3.00	6.00	12.00

—Black, red and white label

Number	Title (A Side/B Side)	Yr	VG	VG+	NM
❑ 45628	The Unknown Soldier/We Could Be So Good Together	1968	3.00	6.00	12.00

—Red, black and white label

Number	Title (A Side/B Side)	Yr	VG	VG+	NM
❑ 45628	The Unknown Soldier/We Could Be So Good Together	1968	3.75	7.50	15.00

—Red, black and pink label

Number	Title (A Side/B Side)	Yr	VG	VG+	NM
❑ 45628 [PS]	The Unknown Soldier/We Could Be So Good Together	1968	7.50	15.00	30.00
❑ 45635	Hello, I Love You/Love Street	1968	3.00	6.00	12.00
❑ 45635	Hello, I Love You, Won't You Tell Me Your Name?/Love Street	1968	5.00	10.00	20.00

—Original pressings have longer title

Number	Title (A Side/B Side)	Yr	VG	VG+	NM
❑ 45646	Touch Me/Wild Child	1968	3.00	6.00	12.00
❑ 45656	Wishful Sinful/Who Scared You?	1969	2.50	5.00	10.00
❑ 45663	Tell All the People/Easy Ride	1969	2.50	5.00	10.00
❑ 45663 [PS]	Tell All the People/Easy Ride	1969	6.25	12.50	25.00
❑ 45675	Runnin' Blue/Do It	1969	2.50	5.00	10.00
❑ 45685	You Make Me Real/Roadhouse Blues	1970	2.50	5.00	10.00
❑ 45726	Love Her Madly/(You Need Meat) Don't Go No Further	1971	2.00	4.00	8.00
❑ 45738	Riders on the Storm/Changeling	1971	2.00	4.00	8.00
❑ 45757	Tightrope Ride/Variety Is the Spice of Life	1971	2.00	4.00	8.00
❑ 45768	Ships w/ Sails/In the Eye of the Sun	1972	2.00	4.00	8.00
❑ 45793	Get Up and Dance/Treetrunk	1972	2.00	4.00	8.00
❑ 45807	The Mosquito/It Slipped My Mind	1972	2.00	4.00	8.00
❑ 45825	The Piano Bird/Good Rockin'	1972	2.00	4.00	8.00
❑ 46005	Roadhouse Blues (Live)/Albinoni/Adagio	1979	—	2.50	5.00
❑ 47097	People Are Strange/Not to Touch the Earth	1980	—	2.00	4.00
❑ 47097 [PS]	People Are Strange/Not to Touch the Earth	1980	2.00	4.00	8.00

—Also has an insert with photos of Doors albums

Number	Title (A Side/B Side)	Yr	VG	VG+	NM
❑ 69770	Gloria/Moonlight Drive	1983	—	2.00	4.00

—Contrary to prior reports, this was not issued with a picture sleeve

PHILCO-FORD

Number	Title (A Side/B Side)	Yr	VG	VG+	NM
❑ HP-9	Light My Fire/Break On Through	1968	10.00	20.00	40.00

—4-inch plastic "Hip Pocket Record" with color sleeve

Albums

DCC COMPACT CLASSICS

Number	Title (A Side/B Side)	Yr	VG	VG+	NM
❑ LPZ-2045	Strange Days	1997	20.00	40.00	80.00

—Audiophile vinyl

Number	Title (A Side/B Side)	Yr	VG	VG+	NM
❑ LPZ-2046	The Doors	1997	37.50	75.00	150.00

—Audiophile vinyl

Number	Title (A Side/B Side)	Yr	VG	VG+	NM
❑ LPZ-2049	Waiting for the Sun	1998	30.00	60.00	120.00

—Audiophile vinyl

Number	Title (A Side/B Side)	Yr	VG	VG+	NM
❑ LPZ-2050	L.A. Woman	1998	37.50	75.00	150.00

—Audiophile vinyl

ELEKTRA

Number	Title (A Side/B Side)	Yr	VG	VG+	NM
❑ 5E-502	An American Prayer	1978	3.00	6.00	12.00

—Butterfly labels

Number	Title (A Side/B Side)	Yr	VG	VG+	NM
❑ 5E-502	An American Prayer	1980	2.50	5.00	10.00

—Red labels with Warner Communications logo in lower right

Number	Title (A Side/B Side)	Yr	VG	VG+	NM
❑ 5E-502	An American Prayer	1983	2.00	4.00	8.00

—Red and black labels

Number	Title (A Side/B Side)	Yr	VG	VG+	NM
❑ 5E-502 SP DJ [DJ]	An American Prayer	1978	15.00	30.00	60.00

—White label; with sticker on cover "This album has been edited for broadcast from…"; only six tracks are on Side One rather than the eight on stock copies

Number	Title (A Side/B Side)	Yr	VG	VG+	NM
❑ 5E-515	Greatest Hits	1980	2.50	5.00	10.00

—Red labels with Warner Communications logo in lower right

Number	Title (A Side/B Side)	Yr	VG	VG+	NM
❑ 5E-515	Greatest Hits	1983	2.00	4.00	8.00

—Red and black labels

Number	Title (A Side/B Side)	Yr	VG	VG+	NM
❑ EKL-4007 [M]	The Doors	1967	50.00	100.00	200.00
❑ EKL-4014 [M]	Strange Days	1967	150.00	300.00	600.00

—Value assumes the record is mono. There are two different covers for this; some copies have mono numbers on the two covers and the stereo number on the spine, and others have the mono number on the spine and stereo number on front and back covers.

Number	Title (A Side/B Side)	Yr	VG	VG+	NM
❑ EKL-4024 [M]	Waiting for the Sun	1968	250.00	500.00	1000.
❑ 6E-5035 [S]	Best of the Doors	1977	5.00	10.00	20.00

—Columbia Record Club edition in stereo with the quad markings blacked out on the cover; note different prefix

Number	Title (A Side/B Side)	Yr	VG	VG+	NM
❑ EQ-5035 [Q]	Best of the Doors	1973	5.00	10.00	20.00

—Butterfly labels

Number	Title (A Side/B Side)	Yr	VG	VG+	NM
❑ EQ-5035 [Q]	Best of the Doors	1980	3.00	6.00	12.00

—Red labels with Warner Communications logo in lower right

Number	Title (A Side/B Side)	Yr	VG	VG+	NM
❑ EQ-5035 [Q]	Best of the Doors	1983	2.50	5.00	10.00

—Red and black labels

Number	Title (A Side/B Side)	Yr	VG	VG+	NM
❑ 8E-6001 [(2)]	Weird Scenes Inside the Gold Mine	1972	5.00	10.00	20.00

—Butterfly labels

Number	Title (A Side/B Side)	Yr	VG	VG+	NM
❑ 8E-6001 [(2)]	Weird Scenes Inside the Gold Mine	1980	3.00	6.00	12.00

—Red labels with Warner Communications logo in lower right

Number	Title (A Side/B Side)	Yr	VG	VG+	NM
❑ 8E-6001 [(2)]	Weird Scenes Inside the Gold Mine	1983	2.50	5.00	10.00

—Red and black labels

Number	Title (A Side/B Side)	Yr	VG	VG+	NM
❑ EKS-9002 [(2)]	Absolutely Live	1970	6.25	12.50	25.00

—Butterfly labels

Number	Title (A Side/B Side)	Yr	VG	VG+	NM
❑ EKS-9002 [(2)DJ]	Absolutely Live	1970	20.00	40.00	80.00

—White label promo

Number	Title (A Side/B Side)	Yr	VG	VG+	NM
❑ EKS-9002 [(2)]	Absolutely Live	1980	3.75	7.50	15.00

—Red labels with Warner Communications logo in lower right

Number	Title (A Side/B Side)	Yr	VG	VG+	NM
❑ EKS-9002 [(2)]	Absolutely Live	1983	3.00	6.00	12.00

—Red and black labels

Number	Title (A Side/B Side)	Yr	VG	VG+	NM
❑ 60269	Alive, She Cried	1984	3.00	6.00	12.00
❑ 60345 [(2)]	The Best of the Doors	1985	3.75	7.50	15.00
❑ 60345 [(2)]	The Best of the Doors	1985	10.00	20.00	40.00

—White label promo on audiophile vinyl

Number	Title (A Side/B Side)	Yr	VG	VG+	NM
❑ 60417	Classics	1986	3.00	6.00	12.00
❑ 60741 [EP]	Live at the Hollywood Bowl	1988	3.00	6.00	12.00
❑ E1-61047	The Doors	1991	25.00	50.00	100.00

—Soundtrack from the movie; only available on US vinyl from Columbia House

Number	Title (A Side/B Side)	Yr	VG	VG+	NM
❑ 61812	An American Prayer	1995	3.75	7.50	15.00

—Remastered and lengthened version of 5E-502

Number	Title (A Side/B Side)	Yr	VG	VG+	NM
❑ EKS-74007 [S]	The Doors	1967	12.50	25.00	50.00

—Brown labels

Number	Title (A Side/B Side)	Yr	VG	VG+	NM
❑ EKS-74007 [S]	The Doors	1969	3.75	7.50	15.00

—Red labels with large stylized "E"

Number	Title (A Side/B Side)	Yr	VG	VG+	NM
❑ EKS-74007 [S]	The Doors	1971	3.00	6.00	12.00

—Butterfly labels

Number	Title (A Side/B Side)	Yr	VG	VG+	NM
❑ EKS-74007 [S]	The Doors	1980	2.50	5.00	10.00

—Red labels with Warner Communications logo in lower right

Number	Title (A Side/B Side)	Yr	VG	VG+	NM
❑ EKS-74007 [S]	The Doors	1983	2.00	4.00	8.00

—Red and black labels

Number	Title (A Side/B Side)	Yr	VG	VG+	NM
❑ EKS-74014 [S]	Strange Days	1967	10.00	20.00	40.00

—Brown labels

Number	Title (A Side/B Side)	Yr	VG	VG+	NM
❑ EKS-74014 [S]	Strange Days	1969	3.75	7.50	15.00

—Red labels with large stylized "E"

Number	Title (A Side/B Side)	Yr	VG	VG+	NM
❑ EKS-74014 [S]	Strange Days	1971	3.00	6.00	12.00

—Butterfly labels

Number	Title (A Side/B Side)	Yr	VG	VG+	NM
❑ EKS-74014 [S]	Strange Days	1980	2.50	5.00	10.00

—Red labels with Warner Communications logo in lower right

Number	Title (A Side/B Side)	Yr	VG	VG+	NM
❑ EKS-74014 [S]	Strange Days	1983	2.00	4.00	8.00

—Red and black labels

Number	Title (A Side/B Side)	Yr	VG	VG+	NM
❑ EKS-74024 [S]	Waiting for the Sun	1968	7.50	15.00	30.00

—Brown labels

Number	Title (A Side/B Side)	Yr	VG	VG+	NM
❑ EKS-74024 [S]	Waiting for the Sun	1968	37.50	75.00	150.00

—White label promo

Number	Title (A Side/B Side)	Yr	VG	VG+	NM
❑ EKS-74024 [S]	Waiting for the Sun	1969	3.75	7.50	15.00

—Red labels with large stylized "E"

Number	Title (A Side/B Side)	Yr	VG	VG+	NM
❑ EKS-74024 [S]	Waiting for the Sun	1971	3.00	6.00	12.00

—Butterfly labels

Number	Title (A Side/B Side)	Yr	VG	VG+	NM
❑ EKS-74024 [S]	Waiting for the Sun	1980	2.50	5.00	10.00

—Red labels with Warner Communications logo in lower right

Number	Title (A Side/B Side)	Yr	VG	VG+	NM
❑ EKS-74024 [S]	Waiting for the Sun	1983	2.00	4.00	8.00

—Red and black labels

Number	Title (A Side/B Side)	Yr	VG	VG+	NM
❑ EKS-74079	13	1970	3.75	7.50	15.00

—Butterfly labels

Number	Title (A Side/B Side)	Yr	VG	VG+	NM
❑ EKS-74079 [DJ]	13	1970	10.00	20.00	40.00

—White label promo

Number	Title (A Side/B Side)	Yr	VG	VG+	NM
❑ EKS-74079	13	1980	2.50	5.00	10.00

—Red labels with Warner Communications logo in lower right

Number	Title (A Side/B Side)	Yr	VG	VG+	NM
❑ EKS-74079	13	1983	2.00	4.00	8.00

—Red and black labels

Number	Title (A Side/B Side)	Yr	VG	VG+	NM
❑ EKS-75005	The Soft Parade	1969	5.00	10.00	20.00

—Red labels with large stylized "E"

Number	Title (A Side/B Side)	Yr	VG	VG+	NM
❑ EKS-75005	The Soft Parade	1969	12.50	25.00	50.00

—Brown or tan labels

Number	Title (A Side/B Side)	Yr	VG	VG+	NM
❑ EKS-75005	The Soft Parade	1971	3.00	6.00	12.00

—Butterfly labels

Number	Title (A Side/B Side)	Yr	VG	VG+	NM
❑ EKS-75005	The Soft Parade	1980	2.50	5.00	10.00

—Red labels with Warner Communications logo in lower right

Number	Title (A Side/B Side)	Yr	VG	VG+	NM
❑ EKS-75005	The Soft Parade	1983	2.00	4.00	8.00

—Red and black labels

Number	Title (A Side/B Side)	Yr	VG	VG+	NM
❑ EKS-75007	Morrison Hotel	1970	6.25	12.50	25.00

—Red labels with large stylized "E"

Number	Title (A Side/B Side)	Yr	VG	VG+	NM
❑ EKS-75007	Morrison Hotel	1970	15.00	30.00	60.00

—Brown or tan labels

Number	Title (A Side/B Side)	Yr	VG	VG+	NM
❑ EKS-75007 [DJ]	Morrison Hotel	1970	25.00	50.00	100.00

—White label promo

Number	Title (A Side/B Side)	Yr	VG	VG+	NM
❑ EKS-75007	Morrison Hotel	1971	3.00	6.00	12.00

—Butterfly labels

Number	Title (A Side/B Side)	Yr	VG	VG+	NM
❑ EKS-75007	Morrison Hotel	1980	2.50	5.00	10.00

—Red labels with Warner Communications logo in lower right

Number	Title (A Side/B Side)	Yr	VG	VG+	NM
❑ EKS-75007	Morrison Hotel	1983	2.00	4.00	8.00

—Red and black labels

Number	Title (A Side/B Side)	Yr	VG	VG+	NM
❑ EKS-75011	L.A. Woman	197?	3.00	6.00	12.00

—Butterfly label, standard cover

Number	Title (A Side/B Side)	Yr	VG	VG+	NM
❑ EKS-75011	L.A. Woman	1971	12.50	25.00	50.00

—With see-through window on cover and yellow innersleeve with photo of Jim Morrison on a cross

Number	Title (A Side/B Side)	Yr	VG	VG+	NM
❑ EKS-75011 [DJ]	L.A. Woman	1971	25.00	50.00	100.00

—White label promo

Number	Title (A Side/B Side)	Yr	VG	VG+	NM
❑ EKS-75011	L.A. Woman	1980	2.50	5.00	10.00

—Red labels with Warner Communications logo in lower right

Number	Title (A Side/B Side)	Yr	VG	VG+	NM
❑ EKS-75011	L.A. Woman	1983	2.00	4.00	8.00

—Red and black labels

Number	Title (A Side/B Side)	Yr	VG	VG+	NM
❑ EKS-75017	Other Voices	1971	3.75	7.50	15.00
❑ EKS-75038	Full Circle	1972	3.75	7.50	15.00

MOBILE FIDELITY

Number	Title (A Side/B Side)	Yr	VG	VG+	NM
❑ 1-051	The Doors	1980	15.00	30.00	60.00

—Audiophile vinyl

DOOTONES, THE
45s
DOOTONE

Number	Title (A Side/B Side)	Yr	VG	VG+	NM
❑ 366	Teller of Fortune/Ay Si Si	1955	50.00	100.00	200.00
❑ 470	Strange Love Affair/The Day You Said Goodbye	1962	7.50	15.00	30.00
❑ 471	Sailor Boy/Down the Road	1962	7.50	15.00	30.00

DORELLS, THE
45s
ATLANTIC

Number	Title (A Side/B Side)	Yr	VG	VG+	NM
❑ 2244	Beating of My Heart/Maybe Baby	1964	3.75	7.50	15.00

GEI

Number	Title (A Side/B Side)	Yr	VG	VG+	NM
❑ 4401	Beating of My Heart/Maybe Baby	1963	7.50	15.00	30.00

DORMAN, HAROLD
45s
RITA

Number	Title (A Side/B Side)	Yr	VG	VG+	NM
❑ 1003	Mountain of Love/To Be with You	1960	6.25	12.50	25.00
❑ 1008	I'll Come Running/River of Tears	1960	5.00	10.00	20.00
❑ 1012	Moved to Kansas City/Take a Chance on Me	1960	5.00	10.00	20.00

SANTO

Number	Title (A Side/B Side)	Yr	VG	VG+	NM
❑ 9005	In an Instant/There on Yonder Hill	1962	3.75	7.50	15.00
❑ 9051	Ain't Gonna Change/What Comes Next	1962	3.75	7.50	15.00

SUN

Number	Title (A Side/B Side)	Yr	VG	VG+	NM
❑ 362	I'll Stick By You/There They Go	1961	5.00	10.00	20.00
❑ 370	Just One Step/Uncle Jonah's Place	1961	5.00	10.00	20.00
❑ 377	Wait 'Til Saturday Night/In the Beginning	1962	5.00	10.00	20.00

Number	Title (A Side/B Side)	Yr	VG	VG+	NM
DORN, JERRY					
45s					
ARWIN					
❏ 122	Brother, Can You Spare a Dime/ Disappointed Lover	1959	3.00	6.00	12.00
FLING					
❏ 711	Rocking Chair Rock/Prayer of Love	1959	12.50	25.00	50.00
KING					
❏ 4932	Wishing Well/Sentimental Heaven	1956	20.00	40.00	80.00
❏ 4968	I'm So in Love with You/Nightmare	1956	3.75	7.50	15.00
❏ 5029	Quicksand/The Key	1957	3.75	7.50	15.00
DORRELLES, THE					
45s					
RSVP					
❏ 1108	You Are/Good Luck to the Lucky Girl	1965	3.00	6.00	12.00
DORSAM, TOM					
45s					
LOREN					
❏ 5001	Baby of Mine/(B-side unknown)	1964	125.00	250.00	500.00
DORSEY, GERRY See ENGELBERT HUMPERDINCK.					
DORSEY, JACK					
45s					
PARKWAY					
❏ 938	Ringo's Dog/March of the Gonks	1965	3.00	6.00	12.00
DORSEY, LEE					
45s					
ABC					
❏ 12326	Night People/Can I Be the One	1978	—	2.00	4.00
❏ 12361	God Must Have Blessed America/Say It Again	1978	—	2.00	4.00
ABC-PARAMOUNT					
❏ 10192	Lottie Mo/Lover of Love	1961	3.75	7.50	15.00
ACE					
❏ 640	Lonely Evening/Rock	1961	3.75	7.50	15.00
AMY					
❏ 927	Ride Your Pony/The Kitty Cat Song	1965	2.00	4.00	8.00
❏ 939	Can You Hear Me/Work, Work, Work	1965	2.00	4.00	8.00
❏ 945	Get Out of My Life, Woman/So Long	1965	2.00	4.00	8.00
❏ 952	Confusion/The Neighbors' Daughter	1966	2.00	4.00	8.00
❏ 958	Working in the Coal Mine/Mexico	1966	2.50	5.00	10.00
❏ 965	Holy Cow/Operation Heartache	1966	2.00	4.00	8.00
❏ 974	Gotta Find a Job/Rain, Rain, Rain, Go Away	1967	—	3.00	6.00
❏ 987	My Old Car/Why Wait Until Tomorrow	1967	—	3.00	6.00
❏ 994	Can't Get Away/Vista Vista	1967	—	3.00	6.00
❏ 998	Go-Go Girl/I Can Hear You Callin'	1967	—	3.00	6.00
❏ 1010	I Can't Get Away/Cynthia	1968	—	3.00	6.00
❏ 1020	Wonder Woman/A Little Dab A Do Ya	1968	—	3.00	6.00
❏ 1031	Four Corners (Part 1)/Four Corners (Part 2)	1968	—	3.00	6.00
❏ 1048	I'm Gonna Sit Right Down/Little Ba-By	1968	—	3.00	6.00
❏ 1052	What Now My Love/A Lover Was Born	1969	—	3.00	6.00
❏ 1055	Everything I Do Gonna be Funky (From Now On)/There Should Be a Book	1969	—	3.00	6.00
❏ 1057	Give It Up/Candy Man	1969	—	3.00	6.00
BELL					
❏ 908	I Can Hear You Callin'/What You Want	1970	—	2.50	5.00
CONSTELLATION					
❏ 115	Organ Grinder's Swing/I Gotta Find a New Love	1964	5.00	10.00	20.00
❏ 135	You're Breaking Me Up/Messed Around and Fell in Love	1964	5.00	10.00	20.00
FURY					
❏ 1053	Ya Ya/Give Me You	1961	3.75	7.50	15.00
❏ 1056	Do-Re-Mi/People Gonna' Talk	1961	3.00	6.00	12.00
❏ 1061	Eenie Meenie Miny Moe/Behind the 8-Ball	1962	3.00	6.00	12.00
❏ 1066	You Are My Sunshine/Give Me Your Love	1962	3.00	6.00	12.00
❏ 1074	Hoodlum Joe/When I Met My Baby	1963	3.00	6.00	12.00
LOST-NITE					
❏ 385	Ya Ya/Give Me You	197?	—	2.50	5.00
—Reissue					
POLYDOR					
❏ 14038	Yes We Can — Part 1/O Me O, My O	1970	—	2.50	5.00
❏ 14055	Sneakin' Sally Through the Alley/Tears, Tears and More Tears	1971	—	2.50	5.00
❏ 14106	Freedom for the Stallion/If She Won't (Find Someone Who Will)	1971	—	2.50	5.00
❏ 14147	When Can I Come Home/Gator Tail	1972	—	2.50	5.00
❏ 14181	On Your Way Down/Freedom for the Stallion	1973	—	2.50	5.00
REX					
❏ 1005	Rock/Lonely Evening	1959	6.25	12.50	25.00
SANSU					
❏ 474	Love Lots of Lovin'/Take Care of Our Love	1967	3.00	6.00	12.00
—With Betty Harris					
SMASH					
❏ 1842	Hello Good Looking/Someday	1963	2.50	5.00	10.00
SPRING					
❏ 114	Occapella/Tears, Tears and More Tears	1971	—	2.50	5.00
VALIANT					
❏ 1001	Lottie Mo/Lover of Love	1958	10.00	20.00	40.00
Albums					
AMY					
❏ 8010 [M]	Ride Your Pony	1966	7.50	15.00	30.00
❏ 8010-S [S]	Ride Your Pony	1966	10.00	20.00	40.00
❏ 8011 [M]	The New Lee Dorsey/Working in the Coal Mine-Holy Cow	1966	6.25	12.50	25.00
❏ 8011-S [S]	The New Lee Dorsey/Working in the Coal Mine-Holy Cow	1966	7.50	15.00	30.00
ARISTA					
❏ AL 8387	Holy Cow! The Best of Lee Dorsey	1985	2.50	5.00	10.00
FURY					
❏ 1002 [M]	Ya Ya	1962	75.00	150.00	300.00
POLYDOR					
❏ 24-4024	Yes We Can	1970	3.00	6.00	12.00

Number	Title (A Side/B Side)	Yr	VG	VG+	NM
SPHERE SOUND					
❏ SR-7003 [M]	Ya Ya	196?	25.00	50.00	100.00
—Reissue of Fury 1002					
❏ SSR-7003 [R]	Ya Ya	196?	12.50	25.00	50.00
—Rechanneled reissue of Fury 1002					
DORSEY, TOMMY On albums with asterisks (*) after them, some of the tracks feature FRANK SINATRA as lead vocalist.					
45s					
DECCA					
❏ 27247	Music Maestro, Please/Strangers	1950	3.75	7.50	15.00
❏ 27248	Goofus/Ev'rybody Wants to Go to Heaven	1950	3.75	7.50	15.00
❏ 27396	As Time Goes By/Lullaby of Broadway	1951	3.00	6.00	12.00
❏ 27429	Alone Together/Dancing in the Dark	1951	3.00	6.00	12.00
❏ 27430	Louisiana Hayride/ Something to Remember You By	1951	3.00	6.00	12.00
❏ 27431	I Guess I'll Have to Change My Ways/I See Your Face Before Me	1951	3.00	6.00	12.00
❏ 27539	Sweet Adeline/Diane	1951	3.00	6.00	12.00
❏ 27690	My Magic Heart/If You Turn Me Down	1951	3.00	6.00	12.00
❏ 27691	I Fall in Love with You/Everything I Have Is Yours	1951	3.00	6.00	12.00
❏ 27709	September in the Rain/Black Strap Molasses	1951	3.00	6.00	12.00
❏ 27723	You Blew Out the Flame in My Heart/The Hula Hula Boo Boogie	1951	3.00	6.00	12.00
❏ 27733	Show Me You Love Me/Oh! Look at Me Now	1951	3.00	6.00	12.00
❏ 27759	My Love/Flower of Dawn	1951	3.00	6.00	12.00
❏ 27843	Solitaire/With All My Heart and Soul	1951	3.00	6.00	12.00
❏ 27973	May I/One Morning in May	1952	3.00	6.00	12.00
❏ 28035	There Are Such Things/What Is Time	1952	3.00	6.00	12.00
❏ 28057	Hambone/Come What May	1952	3.00	6.00	12.00
❏ 28064	Trouble in Mind/The Dirty Dozens	1952	3.00	6.00	12.00
❏ 28077	Keel Row/Love, Where Are You Now	1952	3.00	6.00	12.00
❏ 28152	Homing Pigeon/I Got Big Eyes	1952	3.00	6.00	12.00
❏ 28257	Your Daddy's Got the Gleeks/Deep in the Blue	1952	3.00	6.00	12.00
❏ 28328	They Didn't Believe Me/ Nobody Knows the Trouble I've Seen	1952	3.00	6.00	12.00
❏ 28366	This Is the Beginning of the End/ You Could Make Me Smile Again	1952	3.00	6.00	12.00
❏ 28425	Sentimental Serenade/I'm Going Home	1952	3.00	6.00	12.00
❏ 28451	This Love of Mine/Yours Is My Heart Alone	1952	3.00	6.00	12.00
❏ 28684	Sentimental Me and Romantic You/I'm Getting Sentimental Over You	1953	3.00	6.00	12.00
❏ 28766	The Most Beautiful Girl in the World/One Kiss	1953	3.00	6.00	12.00
❏ 28978	Island Queen/You're the Cause of It All	1953	3.00	6.00	12.00
❏ 29057	Liza Jane/Blue Moon	1954	2.50	5.00	10.00
RCA VICTOR					
❏ 47-2874	Royal Garden Blues/After You've Gone	1949	3.75	7.50	15.00
❏ 47-2875	Opus No. 1/On the Sunny Side of the Street	1949	3.75	7.50	15.00
❏ 47-2876	Marie/Song of India	1949	3.75	7.50	15.00
—The above three comprise a box set					
❏ 47-2900	Enjoy Yourself (It's Later Than You Think)/She's a Home Girl	1949	5.00	10.00	20.00
❏ 47-2917	The Continental/Ain'tcha Glad I Love Youq	1949	5.00	10.00	20.00
❏ 47-2958	Dream of You/Pussy Willow	1949	5.00	10.00	20.00
❏ 47-3002	Summertime/Dry Bones	1949	5.00	10.00	20.00
❏ 47-3028	The Huckle-Buck/Again	1949	5.00	10.00	20.00
❏ 47-3037	The Knock Song/Twilight	1949	5.00	10.00	20.00
❏ 47-3087	Shake That Tree/Hollywood Hat	1949	5.00	10.00	20.00
❏ 47-3132	Puddle Wump/Nice to Know You Care	1949	5.00	10.00	20.00
❏ 47-3159	Love for Sale/Just One of Those Things	1949	3.75	7.50	15.00
❏ 47-3160	You Do Something to Me/Why Shouldn't I	1949	3.75	7.50	15.00
❏ 47-3161	It's Delovely/I Get a Kick Out of You	1949	3.75	7.50	15.00
—The above three comprise a box set					
❏ 47-3210	When/Just for Old Times	1949	5.00	10.00	20.00
❏ 47-3712	I Oughta Know More About You/C'est Si Bon	1950	3.75	7.50	15.00
❏ 47-3715	Washboard Blues/Panama	1950	3.75	7.50	15.00
❏ 47-3716	Davenport Blues/Down Home Rag	1950	3.75	7.50	15.00
❏ 47-3717	Milenberg Joys (Part 1)/Milenberg Joys (Part 2)	1950	3.75	7.50	15.00
—The above three comprise a box set					
❏ 47-3791	Tiger Rag/'Way Down Yonder in New Orleans	1950	3.75	7.50	15.00
❏ 47-3840	Happy Feet/Birmingham Bounce	1950	3.75	7.50	15.00
❏ 47-3869	I've Forgotten You/No Other Love	1950	3.75	7.50	15.00
❏ 47-3910	It All Begins and Ends with You/Lullaby in Boogie	1950	3.75	7.50	15.00
❏ 47-3932	Nevada/Weary Blues	1950	3.75	7.50	15.00
❏ 447-0116	I'll Never Smile Again/I'll Be Seeing You	195?	2.50	5.00	10.00
—Black label, dog on top					
❏ 447-0117	Mississippi Mud/I'm Getting Sentimental Over You	195?	2.50	5.00	10.00
—Black label, dog on top					
❏ 447-0118	Marie/Song of India	195?	2.50	5.00	10.00
—Black label, dog on top					
❏ 447-0119	Opus #1/Boogie Woogie	195?	2.50	5.00	10.00
—Black label, dog on top					
❏ 447-0120	We'll Get It/Summertime	195?	2.50	5.00	10.00
—Black label, dog on top					
❏ 447-0121	On the Sunny Side of the Street/Who?	195?	2.50	5.00	10.00
—Black label, dog on top					
❏ 447-0122	The Huckle-Buck/Dry Bones	195?	2.50	5.00	10.00
—Black label, dog on top					
❏ 447-0123	There Are Such Things/Star Dust	195?	2.50	5.00	10.00
—Black label, dog on top					
❏ 447-0124	Chicago/Hawaiian War Chant	195?	2.50	5.00	10.00
—Black label, dog on top					
❏ 447-0445	Street of Dreams/East of the Sun	195?	2.50	5.00	10.00
7-Inch Extended Plays					
DECCA					
❏ ED 2016	*Diane/Opus Two/Marcheta/T.D.'s Boogie Woogie	195?	2.50	5.00	10.00
❏ ED 2016 [PS]	Tommy Dorsey, Vol. 1	195?	2.50	5.00	10.00
RCA CAMDEN					
❏ CAE 268	Original Dixieland One-Step/Bright Eyes//But He Can Dance/The Indian on the Nickel	1954	3.00	6.00	12.00
❏ CAE 268 [PS]	(title unknown)	1954	3.00	6.00	12.00

Number	Title (A Side/B Side)	Yr	VG	VG+	NM

RCA VICTOR
| ❏ LPC-102 | Boogie Woogie/There Are Such Things//Marie/ I'll Be Seeing You | 1961 | 2.50 | 5.00 | 10.00 |

—"Compact 33 Double"; small hole, plays at 33 1/3 rpm

❏ LPC-102 [PS]	Tommy Dorsey Originals	1961	2.50	5.00	10.00
❏ EPAT 408	Chinatown, My Chinatown/The Sheik of Araby/ /Twilight in Turkey/Rhythm Saved the World	1952	5.00	10.00	20.00
❏ EPAT 408 [PS]	Clambake Seven	1952	5.00	10.00	20.00
❏ 547-0933	I'm Getting Sentimental Over You/Marie//Who?/ Royal Garden Blues	195?	2.50	5.00	10.00

—Record 1 of 2-EP set EPB-1229

| ❏ 547-0934 | Star Dust/Yes Indeed!//Little White Lies/Song of India | 195? | 2.50 | 5.00 | 10.00 |

—Record 2 of 2-EP set EPB-1229

| ❏ EPB-1229 [PS] | Yes Indeed! | 195? | 3.75 | 7.50 | 15.00 |

—Cover for 2-EP set (547-0933, 547-0934)

❏ EPA-5007	Chicago/Dry Bones//Mississippi Mud/There Are Such Things	1958	2.50	5.00	10.00
❏ EPA-5007 [PS]	Tommy Dorsey (Gold Standard Series)	1958	2.50	5.00	10.00
❏ EPA-5045	I'm Getting Sentimental Over You/Who//The Huckle-Buck/Well, Git It!	1958	2.50	5.00	10.00
❏ EPA-5045 [PS]	I'm Getting Sentimental Over You (Gold Standard Series)	1958	2.50	5.00	10.00

Albums
BLUEBIRD
❏ AXM2-5521 [(2)]	The Complete Tommy Dorsey, Volume 1	197?	3.75	7.50	15.00
❏ AXM2-5549 [(2)]	The Complete Tommy Dorsey, Volume 2	197?	3.75	7.50	15.00
❏ AXM2-5560 [(2)]	The Complete Tommy Dorsey, Volume 3	197?	3.75	7.50	15.00
❏ AXM2-5564 [(2)]	The Complete Tommy Dorsey, Volume 4	197?	3.75	7.50	15.00
❏ AXM2-5573 [(2)]	The Complete Tommy Dorsey, Volume 5	197?	3.75	7.50	15.00
❏ AXM2-5578 [(2)]	The Complete Tommy Dorsey, Volume 6	197?	3.75	7.50	15.00
❏ AXM2-5582 [(2)]	The Complete Tommy Dorsey, Volume 7	197?	3.75	7.50	15.00
❏ AXM2-5586 [(2)]	The Complete Tommy Dorsey, Volume 8	197?	3.75	7.50	15.00
❏ 9987-1-RB	Yes, Indeed!	1990	3.75	7.50	15.00

COLPIX
❏ CP 401 [M]	The Great T.D.	1958	5.00	10.00	20.00
❏ CP 436 [M]	Tommy Dorsey & His Orchestra Volume 4	1962	5.00	10.00	20.00
❏ CP 498 [M]	Tommy Dorsey — A Man and His Trombone	196?	5.00	10.00	20.00

DECCA
❏ DL 5317 [10]	Tommy Dorsey Plays Howard Dietz	1951	12.50	25.00	50.00
❏ DL 5448 [10]	In a Sentimental Mood	1952	12.50	25.00	50.00
❏ DL 5449 [10]	Tenderly	1952	12.50	25.00	50.00
❏ DL 5452 [10]	Your Invitation to Dance	1952	12.50	25.00	50.00

HARMONY
| ❏ HL 7324 [M] | On the Sentimental Side | 196? | 3.75 | 7.50 | 15.00 |
| ❏ KH 32014 | The Beat of the Big Bands | 1972 | 2.50 | 5.00 | 10.00 |

MCA
| ❏ 732 | Sentimental | 198? | 2.00 | 4.00 | 8.00 |
| ❏ 4074 [(2)] | The Best of Tommy Dorsey | 197? | 3.00 | 6.00 | 12.00 |

MOVIETONE
❏ MTM-1004 [M]	Tommy Dorsey's Hullaballoo	196?	3.75	7.50	15.00
❏ MTM-1019 [M]	The Tommy Dorsey Years	1967	3.75	7.50	15.00
❏ MTS-72004 [R]	Tommy Dorsey's Hullaballoo	196?	3.00	6.00	12.00
❏ MTS-72019 [R]	The Tommy Dorsey Years	1967	3.00	6.00	12.00

PICKWICK
| ❏ PTP-2035 [(2)] | I'm Getting Sentimental* | 197? | 3.00 | 6.00 | 12.00 |

RCA CAMDEN
❏ ADL2-0178 [(2)]	I'll See You in My Dreams*	1973	3.75	7.50	15.00
❏ CAL-650 [M]	The One and Only Tommy Dorsey*	1961	3.75	7.50	15.00
❏ CAS-650(e) [R]	The One and Only Tommy Dorsey*	196?	2.50	5.00	10.00
❏ CAL-800 [M]	Dedicated to You*	1964	3.75	7.50	15.00
❏ CAS-800(e) [R]	Dedicated to You*	1964	2.50	5.00	10.00
❏ CXS-9027 [(2)]	I'm Getting Sentimental*	1972	3.75	7.50	15.00

RCA VICTOR
❏ LPT-10 [M]	Getting Sentimental with Tommy Dorsey*	1951	20.00	40.00	80.00
❏ ALPT-15 [M]	All Time Hits*	1951	20.00	40.00	80.00
❏ LPM-22 [10]	Tommy Dorsey Plays Cole Porter for Dancing	1951	12.50	25.00	50.00
❏ ANL1-1087	The Best of Tommy Dorsey	1976	2.50	5.00	10.00
❏ LPM-1229 [M]	Yes Indeed*	1956	12.50	25.00	50.00
❏ LPM-1425 [M]	Tommy Dorsey Plays Cole Porter and Jerome Kern	1956	6.25	12.50	25.00
❏ LPM-1432 [M]	Tribute to Dorsey, Volume 1*	1956	10.00	20.00	40.00
❏ LPM-1433 [M]	Tribute to Dorsey, Volume 2*	1956	10.00	20.00	40.00
❏ ANL1-1586	Pure Gold*	1976	2.50	5.00	10.00
❏ LPM-1643 [M]	Having a Wonderful Time*	1958	10.00	20.00	40.00
❏ ANL1-2162(e)	On the Sunny Side of the Street	1977	2.50	5.00	10.00
❏ LPT-3005 [M]	This Is Tommy Dorsey*	1952	20.00	40.00	80.00
❏ LPT-3018 [10]	This Is Tommy Dorsey	1952	12.50	25.00	50.00
❏ LPM-3674 [M]	The Best of Tommy Dorsey*	1966	5.00	10.00	20.00
❏ LSP-3674 [R]	The Best of Tommy Dorsey*	1966	3.00	6.00	12.00
❏ LPM-6003 [(2)M]	That Sentimental Gentleman*	1957	20.00	40.00	80.00

—Box set

❏ VPM-6038 [(2)]	This Is Tommy Dorsey*	197?	6.25	12.50	25.00
❏ VPM-6064 [(2)]	This Is Tommy Dorsey, Volume 2*	197?	6.25	12.50	25.00
❏ VPM-6087 [(2)]	This Is Tommy Dorsey and His Clambake Seven	1973	5.00	10.00	20.00

—Orange labels

| ❏ VPM-6087 [(2)] | This Is Tommy Dorsey and His Clambake Seven | 1977 | 3.75 | 7.50 | 15.00 |

—Black labels, dog near top

SUNBEAM
| ❏ 201 | Tommy Dorsey and His Orchestra 1935-39 | 197? | 2.50 | 5.00 | 10.00 |
| ❏ 220 | Tommy Dorsey and His Orchestra 1944-46 | 197? | 2.50 | 5.00 | 10.00 |

TIME-LIFE
| ❏ STBB-02 [(2)] | Big Bands: Tommy Dorsey* | 1983 | 5.00 | 10.00 | 20.00 |
| ❏ STBB-19 [(2)] | Big Bands: Sentimental Genrtleman* | 1985 | 5.00 | 10.00 | 20.00 |

20TH CENTURY FOX
| ❏ TCF 101/102 [(2)M] | Tommy Dorsey's Greatest Band | 1959 | 7.50 | 15.00 | 30.00 |
| ❏ FOX 1005 [M] | Tommy Dorsey and His Orchestra: His Greatest Arrangements — His Greatest Band | 196? | 3.75 | 7.50 | 15.00 |

—"Million Seller Hits" reissue series

❏ TFM-3157 [M]	This Is Tommy Dorsey and His Greatest Band, Vol. 1	196?	5.00	10.00	20.00
❏ TFM-3158 [M]	This Is Tommy Dorsey and His Greatest Band, Vol. 2	196?	5.00	10.00	20.00
❏ TFS-4157 [R]	This Is Tommy Dorsey and His Greatest Band, Vol. 1	196?	3.00	6.00	12.00
❏ TFS-4158 [R]	This Is Tommy Dorsey and His Greatest Band, Vol. 2	196?	3.00	6.00	12.00

VOCALION
| ❏ VL 3613 [M] | Dance Party | 196? | 3.75 | 7.50 | 15.00 |
| ❏ VL 73613 [R] | Dance Party | 196? | 2.50 | 5.00 | 10.00 |

DOTS, THE
45s
CADDY
❏ 101	I Confess/I Wish I Could Meet You	1956	20.00	40.00	80.00
❏ 107	I Lost You/Johnny	1957	20.00	40.00	80.00
❏ 111	Good Luck to You/Heartsick and Lonely	1957	20.00	40.00	80.00
REV
| ❏ 3512 | Ring Chimes/Wolf Call | 1958 | 375.00 | 750.00 | 1500. |

DOTTY AND DAN
45s
HIT
| ❏ 89 | I'm Leaving It Up to You/Down at Papa Joe's | 1963 | 2.00 | 4.00 | 8.00 |

—B-side by the Tennessee Six and Four More

| ❏ 108 | Stop and Think It Over/Navy Blue | 1964 | 2.00 | 4.00 | 8.00 |

—B-side by Connie Dee

DOUGLAS, CARL
45s
OKEH
| ❏ 7268 | Crazy Feeling/Keep It to Myself | 1966 | 3.00 | 6.00 | 12.00 |
| ❏ 7287 | Let the Birds Sing/Something for Nothing | 1967 | 3.00 | 6.00 | 12.00 |
20TH CENTURY
❏ 2140	Kung Fu Fighting/Gamblin' Man	1974	—	2.00	4.00
❏ 2168	Dance the Kung Fu/Changing Times	1975	—	2.00	4.00
❏ 2179	Blue Eyed Soul (Part 1)/Blue Eyed Soul (Part 2)	1975	—	2.00	4.00
❏ 2192	Witchfinder General/ Never Had This Dream Before	1975	—	2.00	4.00

Albums
20TH CENTURY
| ❏ T-464 | Kung Fu Fighting and Other Great Love Songs | 1974 | 3.00 | 6.00 | 12.00 |

DOUGLAS, CAROL
12-Inch Singles
MIDSONG INT'L.
| ❏ L33-1975 [DJ] | Night Fever (6:20) (same on both sides) | 1978 | 2.50 | 5.00 | 10.00 |
| ❏ 13905 | Night Fever/Let You Come Into My Life | 1978 | 3.00 | 6.00 | 12.00 |
45s
MIDLAND INT'L.
❏ MB-10113	Doctor's Orders/ Baby, Don't Let This Good Love Die	1974	—	2.00	4.00
❏ MB-10229	Hurricane Is Coming Tonight/ I Fell in Love with You	1975	—	2.00	4.00
❏ MB-10304	Will We Make It Tonight/ Take Me (Make Me Lose Control)	1975	—	2.00	4.00
❏ MB-10372	Headline News/ Boy, You Know Just What I'm After	1975	—	2.00	4.00
❏ MB-10753	Midnight Love Affair/ Midnight Love Affair (Long Version)	1976	—	2.00	4.00
❏ MB-10870	Dancing Queen/In the Morning	1976	—	2.00	4.00
❏ MB-10979	We Do It/Lie to Me	1977	—	2.00	4.00
MIDSONG INT'L.
| ❏ 1008 | I Got the Answer/We're Gonna Make It | 1979 | — | 2.00 | 4.00 |
| ❏ 40860 | Night Fever/Let You Come Into My Life | 1978 | — | 2.00 | 4.00 |

—A-side appeared in the movie Saturday Night Fever, but not on the soundtrack LP

| ❏ 40912 | So You Win Again/Let You Come Into My Life | 1978 | — | 2.00 | 4.00 |
| ❏ 40945 | Let's Get Down to Doin' It Tonight/Burnin' | 1978 | — | 2.00 | 4.00 |
RCA VICTOR
| ❏ GB-10479 | Doctor's Orders/ Baby, Don't Let This Good Love Die | 1975 | — | — | 3.00 |

—Gold Standard Series

20TH CENTURY
| ❏ 2484 | Slip Into Something Comfortable/ My Simple Heart | 1981 | — | — | 3.00 |

Albums
MIDLAND INT'L.
❏ BKL1-0931	The Carol Douglas Album	1975	2.50	5.00	10.00
❏ BKL1-1798	Midnight Love Affair	1976	2.50	5.00	10.00
❏ BKL1-2222	Full Bloom	1977	2.50	5.00	10.00
MIDSONG INT'L.
| ❏ 3048 | Burnin' | 1978 | 2.50 | 5.00 | 10.00 |
| ❏ W 36852 | The Best of Carol Douglas | 1980 | 2.50 | 5.00 | 10.00 |

DOUGLAS, CRAIG
45s
BETHLEHEM
| ❏ 3057 | When My Little Girl Is Smiling/Ring-a-Ding | 1963 | 3.00 | 6.00 | 12.00 |
EMBASSY
| ❏ 202 | No Greater Love/We'll Have a Lot to Tell | 1962 | 3.00 | 6.00 | 12.00 |
JARO
| ❏ 77016 | My First Love Affair/What Do You Want | 1960 | 3.00 | 6.00 | 12.00 |
| ❏ 77030 | Heart of a Teenage Girl/New Boy | 1960 | 3.00 | 6.00 | 12.00 |
LONDON
| ❏ 9611 | Danke Schoen/Love Her While She's Young | 1963 | 3.00 | 6.00 | 12.00 |
TCF HALL
| ❏ 107 | Around the Corner/Find the Girl | 1965 | 2.50 | 5.00 | 10.00 |

DOUGLAS, KELLIE
45s
RCA VICTOR
| ❏ 47-8005 | My Mama Don't Like Him/Big Hunky Baby | 1962 | 3.00 | 6.00 | 12.00 |

DOUGLAS, KIRK
45s
DECCA
| ❏ 29355 | A Whale of a Tale/ The Moon Grew Brighter and Brighter | 1954 | 6.25 | 12.50 | 25.00 |

Number	Title (A Side/B Side)	Yr	VG	VG+	NM

DOUGLAS, LEW
45s
CARLTON
| ❑ 533 | Theme from "The Angel Wore Red"/"From the Terrace" Love Theme | 1960 | 2.50 | 5.00 | 10.00 |

Albums
CARLTON
| ❑ LP 12-126 [M] | Themes from Motion Pictures and TV | 1960 | 6.25 | 12.50 | 25.00 |

DOUGLAS, MIKE
45s
ATLANTIC
| ❑ 3328 | Philadelphia/Smile, Smile, Smile | 1976 | — | 2.00 | 4.00 |
| ❑ 3344 | Loneliness/Dancin' Again | 1976 | — | 2.00 | 4.00 |

BLUE RIVER
| ❑ 220 | Tonight/High on a Hill | 196? | 2.00 | 4.00 | 8.00 |

DECCA
❑ 32495	The Day After Forever/Someday You'll Be Sorry	1969	—	2.50	5.00
❑ 32567	Jean/Rainbow of Love	1969	—	2.50	5.00
❑ 32618	That's a Woman/Tell Me Why, Why Don't You Cry	1970	—	2.50	5.00

EPIC
❑ 9876	The Men in My Little Girl's Life/Stranger on the Shore	1965	—	3.00	6.00
❑ 10002	Here's to My Jenny/While We're Young	1966	—	3.00	6.00
❑ 10041	The Parents of the Kids in Love/Real Love	1966	—	3.00	6.00
❑ 10041 [PS]	The Parents of the Kids in Love/Real Love	1966	2.00	4.00	8.00
❑ 10078	Cabaret/House of Love	1966	—	3.00	6.00
❑ 10089	Touch Hands on Christmas Morning/(The Story Of) The First Christmas Carol	1966	3.00	6.00	12.00
❑ 10126	What Is a Square/That's How Love Goes	1967	—	3.00	6.00
❑ 10132	Galway/A Little Town in Old County Down	1967	—	3.00	6.00
❑ 10170	Here Comes My Baby Back Again/Someone Took the Sweetness Out of Sweetheart	1967	—	3.00	6.00
❑ 10223	Father of the Bride/Hold Me	1967	—	3.00	6.00
❑ JZSP 135100/1 [DJ]	Silver Bells (mono/stereo)	1967	2.50	5.00	10.00

MGM
❑ 14337	For a Little While/Heaven Everyday	1971	—	2.00	4.00
❑ 14453	Ole Buttermilk Sky/Wonderful World	1972	—	2.00	4.00
❑ 14508	High Hopes/Song for Erik	1973	—	2.00	4.00

PROJECT 3
| ❑ 1335 | Do Unto Others/Young at Heart | 1968 | — | 3.00 | 6.00 |
—With Pearl Bailey

STAX
| ❑ 0211 | Birthday Song/Mother's Day | 1974 | — | 2.00 | 4.00 |

Albums
ATLANTIC
| ❑ SD 18168 | Mike Douglas Sings It All | 1976 | 2.50 | 5.00 | 10.00 |

EPIC
❑ LN 24169 [M]	It's Time for Mike Douglas	1965	3.00	6.00	12.00
❑ LN 24179 [M]	You Don't Have to Be Irish	1965	3.00	6.00	12.00
❑ LN 24186 [M]	The Men in My Little Girl's Life	1966	3.00	6.00	12.00
❑ LN 24205 [M]	Dear Mike, Please Sing	1966	3.00	6.00	12.00
❑ LN 24322 [M]	My Kind of Christmas	1967	3.00	6.00	12.00
❑ BN 26169 [S]	It's Time for Mike Douglas	1965	3.75	7.50	15.00
❑ BN 26179 [S]	You Don't Have to Be Irish	1965	3.75	7.50	15.00
❑ BN 26186 [S]	The Men in My Little Girl's Life	1966	3.75	7.50	15.00
❑ BN 26205 [S]	Dear Mike, Please Sing	1966	3.75	7.50	15.00
❑ BN 26322 [S]	My Kind of Christmas	1967	3.00	6.00	12.00

HARMONY
| ❑ HS 11263 | Young at Heart | 1968 | 3.00 | 6.00 | 12.00 |

WORD
| ❑ WR-8791 | I'll Sing This Song for You | 197? | 2.50 | 5.00 | 10.00 |
| ❑ 8815 | Christmas Album | 198? | 2.50 | 5.00 | 10.00 |

DOUGLAS, SCOTT, AND THE VENTURE QUINTET See THE VENTURES.

DOUGLAS, STEVE
45s
CAPITOL
| ❑ 5527 | Yesterday (Part 1)/Yesterday (Part 2) | 1965 | 3.00 | 6.00 | 12.00 |

GRAPEVINE
| ❑ 601 | Rockin' Green Sleeves/(B-side unknown) | 1961 | 5.00 | 10.00 | 20.00 |

MGM
| ❑ 13218 | Snowplows Schussing (Part 1)/Snowplows Schussing (Part 2) | 1964 | 3.00 | 6.00 | 12.00 |

PHILLES
| ❑ 104 | Yes Sir, That's My Baby/Lt. Col. Bogey's Parade | 1962 | 6.25 | 12.50 | 25.00 |

TANDEM
| ❑ 7000 | Magic Sound/There You Go | 1961 | 5.00 | 10.00 | 20.00 |

Albums
CROWN
| ❑ CLP-5251 [M] | Twist with Steve Douglas and the Rebel Rousers | 1962 | 5.00 | 10.00 | 20.00 |

MERCURY
| ❑ SR-61217 | Reflections in a Golden Horn | 1969 | 6.25 | 12.50 | 25.00 |

DOUGLAS, STEVE
45s
TEXAS OPRY
| ❑ 588 | Tyke (The Christmas Elf)/(Instrumental) | 198? | 2.00 | 4.00 | 8.00 |

DOUGLAS, WAYNE See DOUG SAHM.

DOVAL, JIM, AND THE GAUCHOS
45s
ABC-PARAMOUNT
| ❑ 10621 | Annie Ya Ya/Out of Sight | 1965 | 2.50 | 5.00 | 10.00 |
| ❑ 10637 | I Know You're Fooling Around/Uptown Caballero | 1965 | 2.50 | 5.00 | 10.00 |

DIPLOMACY
❑ 3	Donna/The Scrub	1964	5.00	10.00	20.00
❑ 5	Stranded in the Pool/Right Now	1964	5.00	10.00	20.00
❑ 6	Beatles Rule/Pink Elephant	1964	6.25	12.50	25.00
❑ 7	She's a Very Nice Girl/Bony Moronie	1964	25.00	50.00	100.00
❑ 8	The Good and the Bad/Fireballed	1965	5.00	10.00	20.00
❑ 17	She's So Fine/Mama, Keep Your Big Mouth Shut	1965	5.00	10.00	20.00

| ❑ 1000 | Love Me One More Time (Part 1)/Love Me One More Time (Part 2) | 1963 | 5.00 | 10.00 | 20.00 |
—As "Jim SanDoval and the Gauchos"

DOT
❑ 16468	Fire Ball/Good and Bad	1963	3.75	7.50	15.00
❑ 16548	Love Me One More Time (Part 1)/Love Me One More Time (Part 2)	1963	3.75	7.50	15.00
❑ 16571	Barracuda/The Scrub	1964	3.75	7.50	15.00

Albums
ABC-PARAMOUNT
| ❑ ABC-506 [M] | The Gauchos Featuring Jim Doval | 1965 | 7.50 | 15.00 | 30.00 |
| ❑ ABCS-506 [S] | The Gauchos Featuring Jim Doval | 1965 | 10.00 | 20.00 | 40.00 |

DOVE, RONNIE
45s
DECCA
| ❑ 31288 | Party Doll/Yes Darling, I'll Be Around | 1961 | 50.00 | 100.00 | 200.00 |
—Price is for stock copy; promos go for 20 to 25 percent of this value
❑ 32853	Just the Other Side of Nowhere/If I Cried	1971	—	3.00	6.00
❑ 32919	Kiss the Hurt Away/He Cries Like a Baby	1972	—	3.00	6.00
❑ 32997	It's No Sin/My World of Memories	1972	—	3.00	6.00
❑ 33038	Lilacs in Winter/Is It Wrong	1972	—	3.00	6.00

DIAMOND
❑ 163	Sweeter Than Sugar/I Believed in You	1964	2.50	5.00	10.00
❑ 167	Say You/Let Me Stay Today	1964	2.50	5.00	10.00
❑ 173	Right or Wrong/Baby Put Your Arms Around Me	1964	2.00	4.00	8.00
❑ 176	Hello Pretty Girl/Keep It a Secret	1965	2.00	4.00	8.00
❑ 179	One Kiss for Old Times' Sake/Bluebird	1965	2.00	4.00	8.00
❑ 179	One Kiss for Old Times' Sake/No Greater Love	1965	2.00	4.00	8.00
❑ 184	A Little Bit of Heaven/If I Live to Be a Hundred	1965	2.00	4.00	8.00
❑ 188	I'll Make All Your Dreams Come True/I Had to Lose You	1965	2.00	4.00	8.00
❑ 191	Kiss Away/Where in the World	1965	2.00	4.00	8.00
❑ 195	When Liking Turns to Loving/I'm Learning How to Smile Again	1965	2.00	4.00	8.00
❑ 198	Let's Start All Over Again/That Empty Feeling	1966	2.00	4.00	8.00
❑ 205	Happy Summer Days/Long After	1966	2.00	4.00	8.00
❑ 205 [PS]	Happy Summer Days/Long After	1966	3.75	7.50	15.00
❑ 208	I Really Don't Want to Know/Years of Tears	1966	2.00	4.00	8.00
❑ 214	Cry/Autumn Rhapsody	1966	2.00	4.00	8.00
❑ 217	One More Mountain to Climb/All	1967	2.00	4.00	8.00
❑ 221	My Babe/Put My Mind at Ease	1967	2.50	5.00	10.00
—A-side written and produced by Neil Diamond
| ❑ 227 | I Want to Love You for What You Are/I Thank You for Your Love | 1967 | 2.00 | 4.00 | 8.00 |
| ❑ 233 | Dancin' Out of My Heart/Back from Baltimore | 1967 | 5.00 | 10.00 | 20.00 |
—B-side written and produced by Neil Diamond, who also supplies backing vocals
❑ 240	In Some Time/Livin' for Your Lovin'	1968	2.00	4.00	8.00
❑ 244	Mountain of Love/Never Gonna Cry	1968	2.00	4.00	8.00
❑ 249	Tomboy/Tell Me Tomorrow	1968	2.00	4.00	8.00
❑ 256	What's Wrong with My World/That Empty Feeling	1969	—	3.00	6.00
❑ 260	I Need You Now/Bluebird	1969	—	3.00	6.00
❑ 271	Chains of Love/If I Live to Be a Hundred	1970	3.75	7.50	15.00
—Promos, with "Chains of Love" on both sides, go for about half this amount
| ❑ 378 | Heart (same on both sides) | 1987 | 2.50 | 5.00 | 10.00 |
| ❑ 378 | Heart/Old Time Rock and Roll | 1987 | 5.00 | 10.00 | 20.00 |
—The version with a B-side is much harder to find than the version with the same song on both sides; also, this version was not issued with a picture sleeve
| ❑ 378 [PS] | Heart (same on both sides) | 1987 | 5.00 | 10.00 | 20.00 |
| ❑ 379 | Rise and Shine/(B-side unknown) | 1987 | — | 2.50 | 5.00 |

DOVE
| ❑ 1021 | Lover Boy/I'll Be Around | 1959 | 1500. | 2750. | 4000. |
—As "Ronnie Dove and the Bell-Tones"

HITSVILLE
| ❑ 6038 | Tragedy/Songs We Sang As Children | 1976 | — | 2.50 | 5.00 |
| ❑ 6045 | The Morning After the Night Before/Why Daddy | 1976 | — | 2.50 | 5.00 |

JALO
| ❑ 1406 | No Greater Love/Saddest Hour | 1962 | 6.25 | 12.50 | 25.00 |

M.C.
| ❑ 5013 | The Angel in Your Eyes (Brings Out the Devil in Me)/Songs We Sang As Children | 1978 | — | 3.00 | 6.00 |

MCA
| ❑ 40106 | So Long Dixie/Take My Love | 1973 | — | 2.50 | 5.00 |

MELODYLAND
❑ 6004	Please Come to Nashville/Pictures on Paper	1975	—	2.50	5.00
❑ 6011	Things/Here We Go Again	1975	—	2.50	5.00
❑ 6021	Drina (Take Your Lady Off for Me)/Your Sweet Love	1975	—	2.50	5.00
❑ 6030	Right or Wrong/Guns	1976	—	2.50	5.00

Albums
DIAMOND
❑ D 5002 [M]	Right or Wrong	1964	5.00	10.00	20.00
❑ DS 5002 [S]	Right or Wrong	1964	6.25	12.50	25.00
❑ D 5003 [M]	One Kiss for Old Times' Sake	1965	5.00	10.00	20.00
❑ DS 5003 [S]	One Kiss for Old Times' Sake	1965	6.25	12.50	25.00
❑ D 5004 [M]	I'll Make All Your Dreams Come True	1965	5.00	10.00	20.00
❑ DS 5004 [S]	I'll Make All Your Dreams Come True	1965	6.25	12.50	25.00
❑ D 5005 [M]	The Best of Ronnie Dove	1966	3.75	7.50	15.00
❑ DS 5005 [S]	The Best of Ronnie Dove	1966	5.00	10.00	20.00
❑ D 5006 [M]	Ronnie Dove Sings the Hits for You	1966	3.75	7.50	15.00
❑ DS 5006 [S]	Ronnie Dove Sings the Hits for You	1966	5.00	10.00	20.00
❑ D 5007 [M]	Cry	1967	3.75	7.50	15.00
❑ DS 5007 [S]	Cry	1967	5.00	10.00	20.00
❑ D-5008 [M]	The Best of Ronnie Dove — Vol. 2	1968	7.50	15.00	30.00
❑ SD-5008 [S]	The Best of Ronnie Dove — Vol. 2	1968	3.75	7.50	15.00

POWER PAK
| ❑ 286 | Greatest Hits | 1975 | 3.00 | 6.00 | 12.00 |

DOVELLS, THE Also see LEN BARRY.
45s
ABKCO
❑ 4011	Bristol Stomp/You Can't Sit Down	1972	—	2.00	4.00
❑ 4029	Baby Workout/Hully Gully Baby	1973	2.50	5.00	10.00
❑ 4032	Bristol Twistin' Annie/Betty in Bermudas	1973	—	2.00	4.00

Number	Title (A Side/B Side)	Yr	VG	VG+	NM

EVENT
| ❏ 216 | Dancing in the Street/Back on the Road Again | 1974 | — | 2.50 | 5.00 |
| ❏ 3310 | Roll Over Beethoven/Something About You Boy | 1970 | — | 2.50 | 5.00 |

JAMIE
| ❏ 1369 | Our Winter Love/Blue | 1969 | 2.50 | 5.00 | 10.00 |

MGM
| ❏ 13628 | There's a Girl/Love Is Everywhere | 1966 | 2.50 | 5.00 | 10.00 |
| ❏ 14568 | Don't Vote for Luke McCabe/Mary's Magic Show | 1973 | — | 2.50 | 5.00 |

PARAMOUNT
| ❏ 0134 | L-O-V-E Love/We're All In This Together | 1971 | | 2.50 | 5.00 |

PARKWAY
❏ 819	No, No, No/Letters of Love	1961	5.00	10.00	20.00
❏ 827	Bristol Stomp/Letters of Love	1961	3.75	7.50	15.00
❏ 827	Bristol Stomp/Out in the Cold Again	1961	7.50	15.00	30.00
❏ 833	Do the New Continental/Mope-Itty Mope Stomp	1962	3.75	7.50	15.00
❏ 833 [PS]	Do the New Continental/Mope-Itty Mope Stomp	1962	7.50	15.00	30.00
❏ 838	Bristol Twistin' Annie/The Actor	1962	3.75	7.50	15.00
❏ 838 [PS]	Bristol Twistin' Annie/The Actor	1962	7.50	15.00	30.00
❏ 845	Hully Gully Baby/Your Last Chance	1962	3.75	7.50	15.00
❏ 845 [PS]	Hully Gully Baby/Your Last Chance	1962	7.50	15.00	30.00
❏ 855	The Jitterbug/Kissin' in the Kitchen	1962	3.75	7.50	15.00
❏ 855 [PS]	The Jitterbug/Kissin' in the Kitchen	1962	7.50	15.00	30.00
❏ 861	Save Me Baby/ You Can't Run Away from Yourself	1963	5.00	10.00	20.00
❏ 861 [PS]	Save Me Baby/ You Can't Run Away from Yourself	1963	7.50	15.00	30.00
❏ 867	You Can't Sit Down/Stompin' Everywhere	1963	3.00	6.00	12.00
❏ 867	You Can't Sit Down/Wildwood Days	1963	3.75	7.50	15.00
❏ 867 [PS]	You Can't Sit Down/Stompin' Everywhere	1963	10.00	20.00	40.00
❏ 867 [PS]	You Can't Sit Down/Wildwood Days	1963	10.00	20.00	40.00
❏ 882	Betty in Bermudas/Dance the Froog	1963	3.00	6.00	12.00
❏ 882 [PS]	Betty in Bermudas/Dance the Froog	1963	7.50	15.00	30.00
❏ 889	Stop Monkeyin' Aroun'/No, No, No	1963	3.00	6.00	12.00
❏ 889 [PS]	Stop Monkeyin' Aroun'/No, No, No	1963	7.50	15.00	30.00
❏ 901	Be My Girl/Dragster on the Prowl	1964	5.00	10.00	20.00
❏ 911	One Potato/Happy Birthday Just the Same	1964	3.75	7.50	15.00
❏ 925	Watusi with Lucy/ What in the World's Come Over You	1964	3.00	6.00	12.00
❏ 925 [PS]	Watusi with Lucy/ What in the World's Come Over You	1964	7.50	15.00	30.00

SWAN
| ❏ 4231 | Happy/(Hey, Hey, Hey) Alright | 1965 | 5.00 | 10.00 | 20.00 |

VERVE
| ❏ 10701 | Far Away/Sometimes | 1973 | — | 2.50 | 5.00 |

Albums
CAMEO
| ❏ C-1082 [M] | Len Barry Sings with the Dovells | 1965 | 7.50 | 15.00 | 30.00 |
| ❏ SC-1082 [S] | Len Barry Sings with the Dovells | 1965 | 12.50 | 25.00 | 50.00 |

PARKWAY
| ❏ P 7006 [M] | The Bristol Stomp | 1961 | 20.00 | 40.00 | 80.00 |
| —Light orange label |
| ❏ P 7006 [M] | The Bristol Stomp | 1962 | 12.50 | 25.00 | 50.00 |
| —Dark orange and yellow label |
❏ P 7010 [M]	All the Hits of the Teen Groups	1962	12.50	25.00	50.00
❏ P 7021 [M]	For Your Hully Gully Party	1962	12.50	25.00	50.00
❏ P 7025 [M]	You Can't Sit Down	1963	12.50	25.00	50.00

WYNCOTE
❏ SW 9052 [R]	Discotheque	1965	3.75	7.50	15.00
❏ W 9052 [M]	Discotheque	1965	5.00	10.00	20.00
❏ SW 9114 [R]	The Dovells' Biggest Hits	1965	3.75	7.50	15.00
❏ W 9114 [M]	The Dovells' Biggest Hits	1965	5.00	10.00	20.00

DOWD, LARRY
45s
SPINNING
| ❏ 6004 | Why, Oh Why/Forbidden Love | 1958 | 6.25 | 12.50 | 25.00 |
| ❏ 6009 | Blue Swinging Mama/Pink Cadillac | 1959 | 37.50 | 75.00 | 150.00 |

DOWELL, JOE
45s
JOURNEY
| ❏ 1238 [DJ] | Homeward on the Wind (mono/stereo) | 1973 | — | 3.00 | 6.00 |
| —Stock copy not known to exist |
| ❏ 1238 [PS] | Homeward on the Wind (mono/stereo) | 1973 | — | 3.00 | 6.00 |

MONUMENT
| ❏ 952 | If I Could Find Out What Is Wrong/
Indian Summer Days | 1966 | 2.00 | 4.00 | 8.00 |

SMASH
❏ 1708	Wooden Heart/Little Bo Peep	1961	3.75	7.50	15.00
❏ 1708 [PS]	Wooden Heart/Little Bo Peep	1961	6.25	12.50	25.00
❏ 1717	The Bridge of Love/Just Love Me	1961	3.00	6.00	12.00
❏ 1717 [PS]	The Bridge of Love/Just Love Me	1961	4.00	8.00	16.00
❏ 1728	(I Wonder) Who's Spending Christmas with You/ A Kiss for Christmas	1961	3.75	7.50	15.00
❏ 1730	The Sound of Sadness/The Thorn on the Rose	1962	3.00	6.00	12.00
❏ 1759	Little Red Rented Rowboat/ The One I Left for You	1962	3.00	6.00	12.00
❏ 1759 [PS]	Little Red Rented Rowboat/ The One I Left for You	1962	3.00	6.00	12.00
❏ 1786	Poor Little Cupid/No Secrets	1962	3.00	6.00	12.00
❏ 1786 [PS]	Poor Little Cupid/No Secrets	1962	4.00	8.00	16.00
❏ 1799	Our School Days/Bringa-Branga-Brought	1963	3.00	6.00	12.00
❏ 1799 [PS]	Our School Days/Bringa-Branga-Brought	1963	4.00	8.00	16.00
❏ 1816	Bobby Blue Loves Linda Lou/ My Darling Wears White Today	1963	3.00	6.00	12.00
❏ 1816 [PS]	Bobby Blue Loves Linda Lou/ My Darling Wears White Today	1963	4.00	8.00	16.00

Albums
SMASH
❏ MGS-27000 [M]	Wooden Heart	1961	10.00	20.00	40.00
❏ MGS-27011 [M]	German American Hits	1962	6.25	12.50	25.00
❏ SRS-67000 [S]	Wooden Heart	1961	12.50	25.00	50.00
❏ SRS-67011 [S]	German American Hits	1962	7.50	15.00	30.00

WING
| ❏ MGW-12328 [M] | Wooden Heart | 196? | 5.00 | 10.00 | 20.00 |
| ❏ SRW-16328 [S] | Wooden Heart | 196? | 5.00 | 10.00 | 20.00 |

Number	Title (A Side/B Side)	Yr	VG	VG+	NM

DOWLANDS, THE
45s
TOLLIE
| ❏ 9002 | All My Loving/Hey Sally | 1964 | 3.75 | 7.50 | 15.00 |

DOWNBEATS, THE (1)
45s
GEE
| ❏ 1019 | My Girl/China Girl | 1956 | 200.00 | 400.00 | 800.00 |
| —Red label |
| ❏ 1019 | My Girl/China Girl | 1958 | 7.50 | 15.00 | 30.00 |
| —Gray label |

PEACOCK
| ❏ 1689 | You're So Fine/Someday She'll Come Along | 1958 | 6.25 | 12.50 | 25.00 |

DOWNBEATS, THE (2)
45s
SARG
❏ 168	Darling of Mine/Come On Over	1959	10.00	20.00	40.00
❏ 173	Run to Me Baby/I Need Your Love	1959	10.00	20.00	40.00
❏ 197	Falling Stars/I Just Can't Understand	1960	10.00	20.00	40.00
—As "O.S. Grant and the Downbeats"
❏ 200	You Did Me Wrong/This Woman I Love	1960	10.00	20.00	40.00
❏ 223	Greyhound (Part 1)/Greyhound (Part 2)	196?	5.00	10.00	20.00
❏ 228	Grant's Soul Blues/Sock It Uptight	196?	5.00	10.00	20.00
❏ 233	Soul Bag/Darling Dear	196?	5.00	10.00	20.00
—As "O.S. Grant and the Downbeats"

DOWNBEATS, THE (3) If the record in question is on the TAMLA or V.I.P. label, see THE ELGINS.

DOWNBEATS, THE (4)
45s
WILCO
| ❏ 9 | Alfalfa/Red X | 1960 | 5.00 | 10.00 | 20.00 |
| ❏ 16 | Playin' Possum/One at a Time | 1960 | 5.00 | 10.00 | 20.00 |

DOWNEY, MORTON, JR.
45s
ARTISTS OF AMERICA
| ❏ 109 | He Played a Yo-Yo in Nashville/You'll Never
Have to Ask Me If I Love You | 1976 | — | 2.50 | 5.00 |
| —As "Sean Morton Downey" |
| ❏ 123 | He Played a Yo-Yo in Nashville/You'll Never
Have to Ask Me If I Love You | 1976 | — | 2.00 | 4.00 |
| —As "Sean Morton Downey" |
| ❏ 124 | You Made Me Love You/As Time Goes By | 1976 | — | 2.00 | 4.00 |
| —As "Sean Morton Downey" |

BULLDOG
| ❏ 105 | A Tear Fell in the Chapel/Tender Years | 1959 | 3.75 | 7.50 | 15.00 |
| —As "Sean Downey" |

CADENCE
| ❏ 1407 | The Ballad of Billy Brown/Flattery | 1961 | 2.50 | 5.00 | 10.00 |

CONTENDER
| ❏ 1317 | Love Bug/Rags to Riches | 1959 | 3.75 | 7.50 | 15.00 |

CUB
| ❏ 9004 | You Let Go/Hearts Are Wild | 1958 | 3.00 | 6.00 | 12.00 |
| —As "Sean Downey" |

ESO
| ❏ 932 | Green Eyed Girl/(B-side unknown) | 1981 | 2.00 | 4.00 | 8.00 |
| —As "Sean Morton Downey" |

IMPERIAL
| ❏ 5556 | Boulevard of Broken Dreams/Proud Possession | 1958 | 2.50 | 5.00 | 10.00 |

LAKE ERIE
| ❏ (# unknown) | Cleveland's Coming Back Again/(B-side
unknown) | 197? | 2.00 | 4.00 | 8.00 |

MAGIC LAMP
| ❏ 517 | The Ballad of Billy Brown/Flattery | 1964 | 2.00 | 4.00 | 8.00 |

NRLC
| ❏ 1977 | Got a Right to Live/Theme for Life | 197? | — | 3.00 | 6.00 |

PERSONALITY
| ❏ 3506 | Little Miss U.S.A./Football Freddy | 1959 | 3.00 | 6.00 | 12.00 |

PRIVATE STOCK
| ❏ 45,168 | Family Tree/Spanish Harlem | 1977 | — | 2.00 | 4.00 |

SCEPTER
| ❏ 12316 | Love Theme from Christine/Christine's a Lady | 1971 | — | 3.00 | 6.00 |
| —As "Sean Morton Downey, Jr." |
| ❏ 12360 | Break the Habit of Hate/Second Chance Lord | 1972 | — | 3.00 | 6.00 |
| —As "Sean Downey" |

STAX
| ❏ 0195 | I Believe in America/My Last Day on Earth | 1974 | — | 2.00 | 4.00 |
| —As "Sean Downey" |

WYE
| ❏ 1010 | I Beg Your Pardon/Three Steps to the Phone | 1961 | 3.00 | 6.00 | 12.00 |

Albums
ARTISTS OF AMERICA
| ❏ AOA-5005 | You'll Never Ask Me If I Love You | 1976 | 3.00 | 6.00 | 12.00 |

COMPOSE
| ❏ 9901 | Morton Downey Jr. Sings! | 1989 | 3.75 | 7.50 | 15.00 |

DOWNEY, PAUL
45s
HICKORY
| ❏ 1632 | Camp Meeting, U.S.A./Love | 1972 | — | 3.50 | 7.00 |

DOWNEY, SEAN; DOWNEY, SEAN MORTON See MORTON DOWNEY, JR.

DOWNING, BIG AL
45s
CARLTON
| ❏ 489 | Miss Lucy/Just Around the Corner | 1959 | 12.50 | 25.00 | 50.00 |
| ❏ 507 | It Must Be Love/
When My Blue Moon Turns to Gold Again | 1959 | 10.00 | 20.00 | 40.00 |

CHALLENGE
| ❏ 59006 | Down on the Farm/Oh Babe | 1958 | 12.50 | 25.00 | 50.00 |

Number	Title (A Side/B Side)	Yr	VG	VG+	NM
CHESS					
❏ 1817	The Story of My Life/I'd Love to Be Loved	1962	3.00	6.00	12.00
❏ 2158	I'll Be Holding On/Baby Let's Talk It Over	1974	—	2.50	5.00
COLUMBIA					
❏ 43028	I'm Just Nobody/All I Want Is You	1964	2.50	5.00	10.00
❏ 43185	I Feel Good/Georgia Slop	1964	2.50	5.00	10.00
DOOR KNOB					
❏ 328	I Guess By Now/(B-side unknown)	1989	—	2.50	5.00
❏ 340	Bound for Baltimore/(B-side unknown)	1989	—	2.50	5.00
❏ 345	Father #1/(B-side unknown)	1989	—	2.50	5.00
JANUS					
❏ 211	Thank You Baby//(B-side unknown)	1974	—	3.00	6.00
❏ 234	I'll Be Holding On/Hands	1974	—	3.00	6.00
LENOX					
❏ 5565	You Never Miss Your Water (Till the Well Runs Dry)/If You Want It (I Got It)	1963	3.00	6.00	12.00
—As "Little Esther Phillips and Big Al Downing"					
❏ 5572	Mr. Hurt Walked In/If I Had Our Love to Live Over	1963	3.00	6.00	12.00
POLYDOR					
❏ 14311	I Love to Love/I'm Just Nobody	1976	—	2.50	5.00
SILVER FOX					
❏ 3	Cornbread Row/The Saints	1969	2.00	4.00	8.00
❏ 11	Medley of Soul/These Arms You Push Away	1969	2.00	4.00	8.00
TEAM					
❏ 1001	I'll Be Loving You/Don't Mess with an Angel	1982	—	2.50	5.00
❏ 1002	Darlene/(B-side unknown)	1982	—	2.50	5.00
❏ 1003	Let's Sing About Love/We Can Only Say Goodbye	1983	—	2.50	5.00
❏ 1004	It Takes Love/If You're Leaving	1983	—	2.50	5.00
❏ 1007	The Best of Families/Fool of the Year	1983	—	2.50	5.00
❏ 1008	There'll Never Be a Better Night for Bein' Wrong/(B-side unknown)	1984	—	2.50	5.00
V-TONE					
❏ 215	Yes, I'm Loving You/Please Come Home	1960	3.00	6.00	12.00
❏ 220	If I Had Our Love to Live Over/Words of Love	1961	3.00	6.00	12.00
❏ 230	So Many Memories/There'll Come a Time	1961	3.00	6.00	12.00
VINE ST.					
❏ 103	How Beautiful You Are (To Me)/The Only Thing Missing Is You	1986	—	3.00	6.00
❏ 105	Just One Night Won't Do/How Beautiful You Are (To Me)	1987	—	3.00	6.00
❏ 106	How Ya Gonna Do It/The Only Thing Missing Is You	1987	—	3.00	6.00
WARNER BROS.					
❏ 8716	Mr. Jones/I Don't Cry (The Onion Song)	1978	—	2.50	5.00
❏ 8787	Touch Me (I'll Be Your Fool Once More)/I Ain't No Fool	1979	—	2.50	5.00
❏ 49034	Midnight Lace/Counting Highway Signs	1979	—	2.00	4.00
❏ 49141	I Ain't No Fool/Mr. Jones	1979	—	2.00	4.00
❏ 49161	The Story Behind the Story/Daddy Played the Banjo	1980	—	2.00	4.00
❏ 49270	Bring It On Home/Beer Drinking People	1980	—	2.00	4.00
WHITE ROCK					
❏ 1111	Down on the Farm/Oh Babe	1958	37.50	75.00	150.00
❏ 1113	Miss Lucy/Just Around the Corner	1958	37.50	75.00	150.00
Albums					
TEAM					
❏ 2001	Big Al Downing	1982	3.00	6.00	12.00

DOWNLINERS SECT, THE
45s

Number	Title (A Side/B Side)	Yr	VG	VG+	NM
SMASH					
❏ 1954	Little Egypt/I Feel Good	1965	3.00	6.00	12.00

DOWNS, HUGH
Albums

Number	Title (A Side/B Side)	Yr	VG	VG+	NM
EPIC					
❏ BN 541 [S]	An Evening with Hugh Downs	1961	7.50	15.00	30.00
❏ LN 3597 [M]	An Evening with Hugh Downs	1961	6.25	12.50	25.00

DOYLE, BOBBY, THREE KENNY ROGERS was in this group.
Albums

Number	Title (A Side/B Side)	Yr	VG	VG+	NM
COLUMBIA					
❏ CL 1858 [M]	In a Most Unusual Way	1962	10.00	20.00	40.00
❏ CS 8658 [S]	In a Most Unusual Way	1962	12.50	25.00	50.00

DOYLE, MIKE
Albums

Number	Title (A Side/B Side)	Yr	VG	VG+	NM
FLEETWOOD					
❏ FLP-3018 [M]	The Secrets of Surfing	1963	30.00	60.00	120.00

DOZIER, GENE, AND THE BROTHERHOOD
45s

Number	Title (A Side/B Side)	Yr	VG	VG+	NM
MINIT					
❏ 32026	House of Funk/One for Bess	1967	2.50	5.00	10.00
❏ 32031	I Wanna Testify/Mustang Sally	1967	2.50	5.00	10.00
❏ 32041	Funky Broadway/Soul Stroll	1968	2.50	5.00	10.00
Albums					
MINIT					
❏ 24010 [S]	Blues Power	1967	6.25	12.50	25.00
❏ 40010 [M]	Blues Power	1967	6.25	12.50	25.00

DOZIER, LAMONT Also see HOLLAND-DOZIER; THE VOICE MASTERS.
12-Inch Singles

Number	Title (A Side/B Side)	Yr	VG	VG+	NM
WARNER BROS.					
❏ 8802	Boogie Business/True Love Is Bittersweet	1979	2.50	5.00	10.00

45s

Number	Title (A Side/B Side)	Yr	VG	VG+	NM
ABC					
❏ 11407	Trying to Hold On to My Woman/We Don't Want Nobody to Come Between Us	1973	—	2.00	4.00
—Also see "Holland-Dozier."					
❏ 11438	Fish Ain't Bitin'/Breaking Out All Over	1974	—	2.00	4.00
❏ 12012	Fish Ain't Bitin'/Breaking Out All Over	1974	—	2.00	4.00
❏ 12044	Let Me Start Tonite/I Wanna Be with You	1974	—	2.00	4.00
❏ 12076	All Cried Out/Rose	1975	—	2.00	4.00
❏ 12234	Out Here on My Own/Take Off Your Make-Up	1976	—	2.00	4.00

Number	Title (A Side/B Side)	Yr	VG	VG+	NM
ANNA					
❏ 1125	Let's Talk It Over/Benny the Skinny Man	1960	6.25	12.50	25.00
—As "Lamont Anthony"					
❏ 1125	Let's Talk It Over/Popeye	1960	62.50	125.00	250.00
—As "Lamont Anthony"					
CHECKMATE					
❏ 1001	Just to Be Loved/I Didn't Know	1961	62.50	125.00	250.00
—As "Lamont Anthony"					
COLUMBIA					
❏ 02035	Cool Me Out/Starting Over (We've Made the Necessary Changes)	1981	—	2.00	4.00
❏ 02238	Too Little Too Long/Chained (To Your Love)	1981	—	2.00	4.00
M&M					
❏ 502	Shout About It/(Instrumental)	1982	—	2.50	5.00
MEL-O-DY					
❏ 102	Dearest One/Fortune Teller Please Tell Me	1962	25.00	50.00	100.00
WARNER BROS.					
❏ 8432	Sight for Sore Eyes/Tear Down the Walls	1977	—	2.00	4.00
❏ 8792	Boogie Business/True Love Is Bittersweet	1979	—	2.00	4.00
Albums					
ABC					
❏ D-804	Out Here on My Own	1973	2.50	5.00	10.00
❏ D-839	Black Bach	1974	2.50	5.00	10.00
INVICTUS					
❏ KZ 33134	Love and Beauty	1974	3.00	6.00	12.00
WARNER BROS.					
❏ BS 2929	Right There	1976	2.50	5.00	10.00
❏ BS 3039	Peddlin'	1977	2.50	5.00	10.00
❏ BSK 3282	Bittersweet	1979	2.50	5.00	10.00

DOZY, BEAKY, MICK & TICH See DAVE DEE, DOZY, BEAKY, MICK & TICH.

DRAG KINGS, THE
45s

Number	Title (A Side/B Side)	Yr	VG	VG+	NM
UNITED ARTISTS					
❏ 676	Bearing Burners/Nitro	1963	7.50	15.00	30.00

DRAGONFLY
Albums

Number	Title (A Side/B Side)	Yr	VG	VG+	NM
MEGAPHONE					
❏ MS-1202	Dragonfly	1968	75.00	150.00	300.00

DRAGONS, THE With Daryl Dragon, later of THE CAPTAIN AND TENNILLE.
45s

Number	Title (A Side/B Side)	Yr	VG	VG+	NM
CAPITOL					
❏ 5278	Elephant Stomp/Troll	1964	5.00	10.00	20.00

DRAGSTERS, THE
Albums

Number	Title (A Side/B Side)	Yr	VG	VG+	NM
WING					
❏ MGW-12269 [M]	Hey Little Cobra/Drag City	1964	20.00	40.00	80.00
❏ SRW-16269 [S]	Hey Little Cobra/Drag City	1964	25.00	50.00	100.00

DRAKE, CHARLIE
45s

Number	Title (A Side/B Side)	Yr	VG	VG+	NM
UNITED ARTISTS					
❏ 398	My Boomerang Won't Come Back/She's My Girl	1961	3.75	7.50	15.00
—With A-side lyric "Practiced 'til I was blue in the face."					
❏ 398	My Boomerang Won't Come Back/She's My Girl	1961	7.50	15.00	30.00
—With A-side lyric "Practiced 'til I was black in the face."					
❏ 437	Tanglefoot/Drake's Progress	1962	3.00	6.00	12.00
❏ 477	Sweet Freddie Green/Zulu Drake	1962	3.00	6.00	12.00

DRAKE, NICK
Albums

Number	Title (A Side/B Side)	Yr	VG	VG+	NM
ANTILLES					
❏ AN-7010	Five Leaves Left	1976	6.25	12.50	25.00
—Released in England in 1969					
❏ AN-7028	Bryter Layter	1977	6.25	12.50	25.00
—Released in England in 1970					
HANNIBAL					
❏ HNBL-1318	Time of No Reply	1987	10.00	20.00	40.00
❏ HNBX-5302 [(4)]	Fruit Tree	1986	37.50	75.00	150.00
ISLAND					
❏ SMAS-9307	Nick Drake	1971	20.00	40.00	80.00
—U.S.-only compilation of selected songs from his first two British LPs					
❏ SMAS-9318	Pink Moon	1972	12.50	25.00	50.00

DRAKE, PETE
45s

Number	Title (A Side/B Side)	Yr	VG	VG+	NM
SMASH					
❏ 1867	Forever/Sleepwalk	1964	2.00	4.00	8.00
❏ 1888	Midnight in Amarillo/Forever	1964	2.00	4.00	8.00
❏ 1910	I'm Sorry/I'm Just a Guitar (Everybody Picks On Me)	1964	2.00	4.00	8.00
❏ 1935	I'm Walkin'/Are You Sincere	1964	2.00	4.00	8.00
❏ 1978	Dream/Am I That Easy to Forget	1965	2.00	4.00	8.00
❏ 2046	I'm a Fool to Care/Mystic Dream	1966	2.00	4.00	8.00
STARDAY					
❏ 751	My Abilene/Y'All Come	1966	2.00	4.00	8.00
STOP					
❏ 222	Joggin'/Mama's Talkin' Guitar	1968	—	3.00	6.00
❏ 349	Lay Lady Lay/For Pete's Sake	1970	—	3.00	6.00
Albums					
CANAAN					
❏ 4640 [M]	Steel Away	1967	3.75	7.50	15.00
❏ 9640 [S]	Steel Away	1967	5.00	10.00	20.00
CUMBERLAND					
❏ MGC-29053 [M]	Country Steel Guitar	1963	5.00	10.00	20.00
❏ SRC-69053 [S]	Country Steel Guitar	1963	6.25	12.50	25.00
HILLTOP					
❏ 6052 [M]	Are You Sincere	1967	3.00	6.00	12.00
❏ S-6052 [S]	Are You Sincere	1967	3.00	6.00	12.00
SMASH					
❏ MGS-27053 [M]	Forever	1964	3.75	7.50	15.00
❏ MGS-27060 [M]	Talking Steel Guitar	1965	3.75	7.50	15.00
❏ MGS-27064 [M]	Talking Steel and Singing Strings	1965	3.75	7.50	15.00

Number	Title (A Side/B Side)	Yr	VG	VG+	NM
❏ SRS-67053 [S] Forever		1964	5.00	10.00	20.00
❏ SRS-67060 [S] Talking Steel Guitar		1965	5.00	10.00	20.00
❏ SRS-67064 [S] Talking Steel and Singing Strings		1965	5.00	10.00	20.00

STARDAY

Number	Title (A Side/B Side)	Yr	VG	VG+	NM
❏ SLP-180 [M]	The Fabulous Steel Guitar of Pete Drake	1962	10.00	20.00	40.00
❏ SLP-319 [M]	The Amazing Incredible Pete Drake	1964	7.50	15.00	30.00

STOP

Number	Title (A Side/B Side)	Yr	VG	VG+	NM
❏ 1011	The Pete Drake Show	1970	3.00	6.00	12.00

DRAKES, THE
45s
CONQUEST

Number	Title (A Side/B Side)	Yr	VG	VG+	NM
❏ 1001	Oo Wee So Good/Kitty	1958	150.00	300.00	600.00

OLIMPIC

Number	Title (A Side/B Side)	Yr	VG	VG+	NM
❏ 252	I Made a Wish/Ole King Cole	1965	30.00	60.00	120.00

DRAMATICS, THE Probably all the same group. Also see THE DELLS AND THE DRAMATICS.
45s
ABC

Number	Title (A Side/B Side)	Yr	VG	VG+	NM
❏ 12090	Mr. and Mrs. Jones/I Cried All the Way Home	1975	—	2.50	5.00
❏ 12125	(I'm Going By) The Stars in Your Eyes/ Trying to Get Over You	1975	—	2.50	5.00
❏ 12150	You're Fooling You/I'll Make It So Good	1975	—	2.50	5.00
❏ 12180	Treat Me Like a Man/I Was the Life of the Party	1976	—	2.50	5.00
❏ 12220	Finger Fever/Say the Word	1976	—	2.50	5.00
❏ 12235	Be My Girl/The Nicest Man Alive	1976	—	2.50	5.00
❏ 12258	I Can't Get Over You/Sundown Is Coming (Hold Back the Night)	1977	—	2.50	5.00
❏ 12299	Shake It Well/That Heaven Kind of Feeling	1977	—	2.50	5.00
❏ 12331	Ocean of Thoughts and Dreams/Come Inside	1978	—	2.50	5.00
❏ 12372	Stop Your Weeping/California Sunrise	1978	—	2.50	5.00
❏ 12400	Do What You Want to Do/Jane	1978	—	2.50	5.00
❏ 12429	Why Do You Wanna Do Me Wrong/Yo' Love (Can Only Bring Me Happiness)	1978	—	2.50	5.00
❏ 12460	I Just Wanna Dance with You/I've Got a Schoolboy Crush on You	1979	—	2.50	5.00

CADET

Number	Title (A Side/B Side)	Yr	VG	VG+	NM
❏ 5704	Door to Your Heart/Choosing Up on You	1974	—	3.00	6.00
❏ 5706	Don't Make Me No Promises/Tune Up	1974	—	3.00	6.00
❏ 5710	Love Is Missing from Our Lives/I'm in Love	1975	—	3.00	6.00

—With the Dells

CAPITOL

Number	Title (A Side/B Side)	Yr	VG	VG+	NM
❏ B-5103	Live It Up/She's My Kind of Girl	1982	—	2.00	4.00
❏ B-5140	Treat Me Right/Night Life	1982	—	2.00	4.00

CRACKERJACK

Number	Title (A Side/B Side)	Yr	VG	VG+	NM
❏ 4015	Toy Soldier/Hello Summer	1968	15.00	30.00	60.00

FANTASY

Number	Title (A Side/B Side)	Yr	VG	VG+	NM
❏ 966	Luv's Calling/Dream Lady	1985	—	—	3.00
❏ 967	One Love Ago/Dream Lady	1986	—	—	3.00

MAINSTREAM

Number	Title (A Side/B Side)	Yr	VG	VG+	NM
❏ 5571	No Rebate on Love/Feel It	1976	—	2.50	5.00

MCA

Number	Title (A Side/B Side)	Yr	VG	VG+	NM
❏ 12460	I Just Wanna Dance with You/I've Got a Schoolboy Crush on You	1979	—	2.00	4.00
❏ 41017	I Just Wanta Dance With You/I've Got a Schoolboy Crush on You	1979	—	2.00	4.00
❏ 41056	That's My Favorite Song/Bottom Line Woman	1979	—	2.00	4.00
❏ 41178	Welcome Back Home/Marriage on Paper Only	1980	—	2.00	4.00
❏ 41241	Be With the One You Love/If You Feel Like You Wanna Dance, Dance	1980	—	2.00	4.00
❏ 51004	Share Your Love with Me/Get It	1980	—	2.00	4.00
❏ 51041	(We Need More) Lovin' Time/ You're the Best Thing in My Life	1980	—	2.00	4.00

SPORT

Number	Title (A Side/B Side)	Yr	VG	VG+	NM
❏ 101	All Because of You/If You Haven't Got Love	1967	15.00	30.00	60.00

VOLT

Number	Title (A Side/B Side)	Yr	VG	VG+	NM
❏ 302	Bridge Over Troubled Water/(B-side unknown)	1989	—	2.00	4.00
❏ 4029	Since I've Been in Love/Your Love Was Strange	1969	2.00	4.00	8.00
❏ 4058	Whatcha See Is Whatcha Get/ Thankful for Your Love	1971	2.00	4.00	8.00
❏ 4071	Get Up and Get Down/Fall in Love, Lady Love	1971	2.00	4.00	8.00
❏ 4075	In the Rain/Good Soul Music	1972	2.00	4.00	8.00
❏ 4082	Toast to the Fool/Your Love Was Strange	1972	2.00	4.00	8.00
❏ 4090	Hey You! Get Off My Mountain/The Devil Is Dope	1973	2.00	4.00	8.00
❏ 4099	Fell for You/Now You Got Me Loving You	1973	2.00	4.00	8.00
❏ 4105	And I Panicked/Beware of the Man	1974	2.00	4.00	8.00
❏ 4108	I Made Myself Lonely/Highway to Heaven	1974	2.00	4.00	8.00

WINGATE

Number	Title (A Side/B Side)	Yr	VG	VG+	NM
❏ 18	Somewhere/Bingo!	1966	12.50	25.00	50.00

—As "The Dynamics"

Number	Title (A Side/B Side)	Yr	VG	VG+	NM
❏ 22	Baby I Need You/Inky Dinky Wang Dang Doo	1966	12.50	25.00	50.00

—As "The Dynamics"

Albums
ABC

Number	Title (A Side/B Side)	Yr	VG	VG+	NM
❏ D-867	The Dramatic Jackpot	1975	3.75	7.50	15.00
❏ D-916	Drama V	1975	3.75	7.50	15.00
❏ D-955	Joy Ride	1976	3.75	7.50	15.00
❏ AB-1010	Shake It Well	1977	3.75	7.50	15.00
❏ AA-1072	Do What You Wanna Do	1978	3.75	7.50	15.00
❏ AA-1125	Anytime, Anyplace	1979	3.75	7.50	15.00

CAPITOL

Number	Title (A Side/B Side)	Yr	VG	VG+	NM
❏ ST-12205	New Dimension	1982	2.50	5.00	10.00

FANTASY

Number	Title (A Side/B Side)	Yr	VG	VG+	NM
❏ 9642	Somewhere in Time: A Dramatic Reunion	1986	3.00	6.00	12.00

MCA

Number	Title (A Side/B Side)	Yr	VG	VG+	NM
❏ 761	Dramatic Way	198?	2.00	4.00	8.00

—Reissue of 5149

Number	Title (A Side/B Side)	Yr	VG	VG+	NM
❏ 762	10 1/2	198?	2.00	4.00	8.00

—Reissue of 3196

Number	Title (A Side/B Side)	Yr	VG	VG+	NM
❏ AA-1125	Anytime, Anyplace	1979	3.00	6.00	12.00

—Reissue of ABC 1125

Number	Title (A Side/B Side)	Yr	VG	VG+	NM
❏ 3196	10 1/2	1980	2.50	5.00	10.00
❏ 5149	Dramatic Way	1981	2.50	5.00	10.00

STAX

Number	Title (A Side/B Side)	Yr	VG	VG+	NM
❏ STX-4111	Whatcha See Is Whatcha Get	1978	3.00	6.00	12.00

—Reissue of Volt 6018

Number	Title (A Side/B Side)	Yr	VG	VG+	NM
❏ STX-4131	A Dramatic Experience	1979	3.00	6.00	12.00

—Reissue of Volt 6019

Number	Title (A Side/B Side)	Yr	VG	VG+	NM
❏ MPS-8523	Dramatically Yours	198?	2.00	4.00	8.00

—Reissue of Volt 9501

Number	Title (A Side/B Side)	Yr	VG	VG+	NM
❏ MPS-8526	The Best of the Dramatics	198?	2.50	5.00	10.00
❏ MPS-8545	The Dramatics Live	1988	2.50	5.00	10.00

VOLT

Number	Title (A Side/B Side)	Yr	VG	VG+	NM
❏ V-3402	Positive State of Mind	1989	2.50	5.00	10.00
❏ V-3407	Stone Cold	1990	2.50	5.00	10.00
❏ VOS-6018	Whatcha See Is Whatcha Get	1972	6.25	12.50	25.00
❏ VOS-6019	A Dramatic Experience	1973	6.25	12.50	25.00
❏ VOS-9501	Dramatically Yours	1974	6.25	12.50	25.00

DRAPER, RUSTY Also see PATTI PAGE.
45s
KL

Number	Title (A Side/B Side)	Yr	VG	VG+	NM
❏ 001	Harbor Lights/(B-side unknown)	1979	—	2.00	4.00

MERCURY

Number	Title (A Side/B Side)	Yr	VG	VG+	NM
❏ 5820	Just Because/How Could You (Blue Eyes)	1952	3.75	7.50	15.00
❏ 5851	Devil of a Woman/Bouncing on the Bayou	1952	3.75	7.50	15.00
❏ 5894	Sing Baby Sing/I Gotta Have My Baby Back	1952	3.75	7.50	15.00
❏ 70004	Angry/Blue Tears	1952	3.00	6.00	12.00
❏ 70077	No Help Wanted/Texarkana Baby	1953	3.00	6.00	12.00
❏ 70167	Gambler's Guitar/Free Home Demonstration	1953	3.00	6.00	12.00
❏ 70178	Lazy River/Bummin' Around	1953	3.00	6.00	12.00
❏ 70256	Native Dancer/Lonesome Song	1953	3.00	6.00	12.00
❏ 70300	Peter Rabbit/Easter Morning	1954	3.00	6.00	12.00
❏ 70327	The Train with a Rhumba Beat/Melancholy Baby	1954	3.00	6.00	12.00
❏ 70365	It Ain't Me Baby/Knock on Wood	1954	3.00	6.00	12.00
❏ 70415	Please, Please/Workshop of the Lord	1954	3.00	6.00	12.00
❏ 70446	Muskrat Ramble/The Magic Circle	1954	3.00	6.00	12.00
❏ 70526	Lookin' Back to See/Shame on You	1955	3.00	6.00	12.00
❏ 70555	The Ballad of Davy Crockett/I've Been Thinkin'	1955	3.75	7.50	15.00
❏ 70619	Eating Goober Peas/That's All I Need	1955	3.00	6.00	12.00
❏ 70651	Seventeen/Can't Live Without Them Anymore	1955	3.00	6.00	12.00
❏ 70696	The Shifting, Whispering Sands/Time	1955	2.50	5.00	10.00
❏ 70757	Are You Satisfied/Wabash Cannonball	1955	2.50	5.00	10.00
❏ 70818	Held for Questioning/Forty-Two	1956	2.50	5.00	10.00
❏ 70853	Sometimes You Win, Sometimes You Lose/The Gun of Billy the Kid	1956	2.50	5.00	10.00
❏ 70879	Rock and Roll Baby/House of Cards	1956	3.75	7.50	15.00
❏ 70921	In the Middle of the House/Pink Cadillac	1956	2.50	5.00	10.00
❏ 70938	Giant/Old Buttermilk Sky	1956	3.75	7.50	15.00
❏ 71039	Let's Go Calypso/Should I Ever Love Again	1957	2.50	5.00	10.00
❏ 71102	Freight Train/Seven Come Eleven	1957	2.50	5.00	10.00
❏ 71162	No Hu Hu/Good Golly	1957	2.50	5.00	10.00
❏ 71221	Buzz Buzz Buzz/I Get the Blues When It Rains	1957	2.50	5.00	10.00
❏ 71298	Gamblin' Gal/That's My Doll	1958	2.50	5.00	10.00
❏ 71336	June, July and August/Chicken-Pluckin' Hawk	1958	2.50	5.00	10.00
❏ 71351	Hip Monkey/Can You Depend on Me	1958	2.50	5.00	10.00
❏ 71388	With This Ring/Shopping Around	1958	2.50	5.00	10.00
❏ 71418	Hey Li Lee Li Lee Li/The Sun Will Always Shine	1959	2.50	5.00	10.00
❏ 71463	Next Stop Paradise/Don't Forget Your Shoes	1959	2.50	5.00	10.00
❏ 71545	I Get So Jealous/But For the Flow of Flo	1959	2.50	5.00	10.00
❏ 71564	Two of a Kind/If My Mother'd Only Let Me Cross the Street	1960	2.00	4.00	8.00
❏ 71581	That Lucky Old Sun/Any Time	1960	2.00	4.00	8.00
❏ 71634	Please Help Me, I'm Falling/Mule Skinner Blues	1960	2.00	4.00	8.00
❏ 71664	It's a Little More Like Heaven/Luck of the Irish	1960	2.00	4.00	8.00
❏ 71706	Jealous Heart/Ten Thousand Years Ago	1960	2.00	4.00	8.00
❏ 71784	Another/The Meadow	1961	2.00	4.00	8.00
❏ 71854	Signed, Sealed and Delivered/ Scared to Go Home	1961	2.00	4.00	8.00
❏ 71914	Well I've Learned/Tongue Tied Over You	1961	2.00	4.00	8.00
❏ 71976	Beggar to a King/Deep Roots	1962	2.00	4.00	8.00

MONUMENT

Number	Title (A Side/B Side)	Yr	VG	VG+	NM
❏ 823	Night Life/That's Why I Love You Like I Do	1963	—	3.50	7.00
❏ 832	It Should Be Easier Now/Lady of the House	1964	—	3.50	7.00
❏ 843	The Puppeteer/My Baby's Not Here (In Town Tonight)	1964	—	3.50	7.00
❏ 858	I'm Worried About Me/When I've Learned	1964	—	3.50	7.00
❏ 871	I Got What I Wanted/Love Don't Grow on Trees	1965	—	3.50	7.00
❏ 894	Folsom Prison Blues/You Can't Be True, Dear	1965	—	3.50	7.00
❏ 944	Mystery Train/The Shifting, Whispering Sands	1966	—	3.00	6.00
❏ 969	Love Is Gone for Good/ You Call Everybody Darling	1966	—	3.00	6.00
❏ 1019	My Elusive Dreams/Memory Lane	1967	—	3.00	6.00
❏ 1044	California Sunshine/The Gypsy	1968	—	3.00	6.00
❏ 1074	Buffalo Nickel/Make Believe I'm Him	1968	—	3.00	6.00
❏ 1116	Love Is Just a Game/ Something Old, Something New	1968	—	3.00	6.00
❏ 1137	Don't Build No Fences for Me/ Am I That Easy to Forget	1969	—	3.00	6.00
❏ 1157	I Walk Alone/Sunshine Man	1969	—	3.00	6.00
❏ 1188	Two Little Boys/It Don't Mean a Thing to Me	1970	—	2.50	5.00
❏ 1202	Every Man Has a Prison/ Tie Me to Your Apron Strings Again	1970	—	2.50	5.00
❏ 1223	There She Goes/Travelling Song	1970	—	2.50	5.00
❏ 8628	Walking on New Grass/You Were Right	1974	—	2.00	4.00

Albums
GOLDEN CREST

Number	Title (A Side/B Side)	Yr	VG	VG+	NM
❏ 31029	The Rusty Draper Show	1973	3.00	6.00	12.00
❏ 31030	Tour the USA	1973	3.00	6.00	12.00

MERCURY

Number	Title (A Side/B Side)	Yr	VG	VG+	NM
❏ MG-20068 [M]	Music for a Rainy Night	1956	7.50	15.00	30.00
❏ MG-20117 [M]	Encores	1957	7.50	15.00	30.00
❏ MG-20118 [M]	Rusty Draper Sings	1957	7.50	15.00	30.00
❏ MG-20173 [M]	Rusty Meets Hoagy	1957	7.50	15.00	30.00
❏ MG-20499 [M]	Hits That Sold a Million	1960	7.50	15.00	30.00
❏ MG-20657 [M]	Country and Western Golden Greats	1961	7.50	15.00	30.00
❏ SR-60176 [S]	Hits That Sold a Million	1960	10.00	20.00	40.00
❏ SR-60657 [S]	Country and Western Golden Greats	1961	10.00	20.00	40.00

MONUMENT

Number	Title (A Side/B Side)	Yr	VG	VG+	NM
❏ 6638	Greatest Hits	1977	3.00	6.00	12.00
❏ MLP-8005 [M]	Greatest Hits	1964	3.75	7.50	15.00
❏ MLP-8018 [M]	Night Life	1964	3.75	7.50	15.00
❏ MLP-8026 [M]	Rusty Draper Plays Guitar	1965	3.75	7.50	15.00
❏ SLP-18005 [S]	Greatest Hits	1964	5.00	10.00	20.00

Number	Title (A Side/B Side)	Yr	VG	VG+	NM
❏ SLP-18018 [S]	Night Life	1964	5.00	10.00	20.00
❏ SLP-18026 [S]	Rusty Draper Plays Guitar	1965	5.00	10.00	20.00
❏ SLP-18105	Something Old, Something New	1969	3.75	7.50	15.00
❏ ZG 33870 [(2)]	Swingin' Country/				
	Something Old, Something New	1976	3.75	7.50	15.00

WING

❏ MGW-12243 [M]	Hits That Sold a Million	196?	3.75	7.50	15.00
❏ MGW-12274 [M]	Country Classics	196?	3.75	7.50	15.00
❏ SRW-16243 [S]	Hits That Sold a Million	196?	3.75	7.50	15.00
❏ SRW-16274 [S]	Country Classics	196?	3.75	7.50	15.00

DREAM GIRLS, THE
45s
BIG TOP

❏ 3059	Don't Break My Heart/I Could Write a Book	1960	5.00	10.00	20.00
❏ 3085	Wanted/Mr. Fine	1961	5.00	10.00	20.00

—The rest of the Big Top singles as "Bobbie Smith and the Dream Girls"

❏ 3100	Duchess of Earl/Mine All Mine	1962	5.00	10.00	20.00
❏ 3111	Here Comes Baby/I Got a Feeling My Love	1962	5.00	10.00	20.00
❏ 3129	Your Lovey Dovey Ways/Now He's Gone	1962	5.00	10.00	20.00

CAMEO

❏ 165	Don't Break My Heart/Oh This Is Why	1959	6.25	12.50	25.00

METRO

❏ 20029	I'm in Love with You/Cryin' in the Night	1960	7.50	15.00	30.00
❏ 20034	Heartaches/Love Hen	1961	6.25	12.50	25.00

TWIRL

❏ 1002	Don't Break My Heart/Oh This Is Why	1959	12.50	25.00	50.00

DREAM KINGS, THE
45s
CHECKER

❏ 858	M.T.Y.L.T.T./Oh What a Baby	1957	37.50	75.00	150.00

DREAM TEAM, THE
45s
EPIC

❏ 9701	I'm Not Afraid/Inka Dinka Doo	1964	3.00	6.00	12.00

DREAM WEAVERS, THE
45s
DECCA

❏ 29683	It's Almost Tomorrow/You've Got Me Wondering	1955	3.75	7.50	15.00
❏ 29818	You're Mine/Into the Night	1956	3.00	6.00	12.00
❏ 29905	A Little Love Can Go a Long, Long Way/Is There Somebody Else	1956	3.00	6.00	12.00
❏ 29990	Give Us This Day/Why I Chose You	1956	3.00	6.00	12.00
❏ 30156	Till We Meet Again/All This Is Home	1956	3.00	6.00	12.00
❏ 30276	Fool's Gold/I'll Try, I'll Try	1957	3.00	6.00	12.00

DREAMERS, THE Several different groups.
45s
ABC-PARAMOUNT

❏ 9746	The Girl Down the Street/The Right Time for Love	1956	5.00	10.00	20.00

ALADDIN

❏ 3303	My Plea/Charles My Darling	1955	37.50	75.00	150.00

APT

❏ 25053	Mary's Little Lamb/I Sing This Song	1960	6.25	12.50	25.00

BLUE STAR

❏ 8001	I Really Love You/You Made Me Darling	1960	6.25	12.50	25.00

COUSINS

❏ 1005	Because of You/Little Girl	1961	25.00	50.00	100.00

EVENT

❏ 4270	Rock 'N Roll Baby/Ding Dong	1958	7.50	15.00	30.00

FAIRMOUNT

❏ 612	Daydreamin' of You/The Promise	1963	5.00	10.00	20.00

FLIP

❏ 319	Since You've Been Gone/Do Not Forget	1956	10.00	20.00	40.00
❏ 354	Since You've Been Gone/Do Not Forget	1961	5.00	10.00	20.00

GOLDISC

❏ 3015	Teenage Vows of Love/Natalie	1961	7.50	15.00	30.00

GRAND

❏ 131	Tears in My Eyes/535	1955	75.00	150.00	300.00

GUARANTEED

❏ 219	Mary, Mary/Canadian Sunset	1961	3.75	7.50	15.00

JUBILEE

❏ 5053	These Things I Miss/Can't Get You Off My Mind	1951	75.00	150.00	300.00

LOST-NITE

❏ 329	Tears in My Eyes/535	197?	—	2.50	5.00

—Reissue of Grand 131

MANHATTAN

❏ 503	Lips Were Meant for Kissing/No Obligation	1956	25.00	50.00	100.00

MAY

❏ 133	Because of You/Little Girl	1963	10.00	20.00	40.00

MERCURY

❏ 5843	I'm Gonna Hate Myself in the Morning/Ain't Gonna Worry No More	1952	37.50	75.00	150.00
❏ 70019	Please Don't Leave Me/Walkin' My Blues	1953	37.50	75.00	150.00

NUGGET

❏ 1000	Don't Cry/It's Gonna Be Alright	1959	7.50	15.00	30.00

ROLLIN'

❏ 1001	No Man Is an Island/Melba	1954	200.00	400.00	800.00

UNITED ARTISTS

❏ 841	Henry, Henry, Henry/Love, Love, Love	1965	3.00	6.00	12.00

DREAMETTES, THE
45s
UNITED ARTISTS

❏ 921	Gonna Make That Little Boy Mine/Run, Steven, Run	1965	5.00	10.00	20.00

DREAMLOVERS, THE
45s
CAMEO

❏ 326	These Will Be the Good Old Days/Oh Baby Mine (I Get So Lonely)	1964	3.75	7.50	15.00

CASINO

❏ 1308	Amazons and Coyotes/Together	1963	3.75	7.50	15.00

COLUMBIA

❏ 42698	Sad, Sad Boy/If I Were a Magician	1963	5.00	10.00	20.00
❏ 42752	Sad, Sad Boy/Black Bottom	1963	3.00	6.00	12.00
❏ 42842	Pretty Little Girl/I'm Through with You	1963	12.50	25.00	50.00

END

❏ 1114	If I Should Lose You/I Miss You	1962	5.00	10.00	20.00

HERITAGE

❏ 102	When We Get Married/Just Because	1961	5.00	10.00	20.00
❏ 104	Welcome Home/Let Them Love (And Be Loved)	1961	3.75	7.50	15.00
❏ 107	Zoom, Zoom, Zoom/While We Were Dancing	1962	3.75	7.50	15.00

LEN

❏ 1006	Take It from a Fool/For the First Time	1958	50.00	100.00	200.00

LOST-NITE

❏ 213	You Gave Me Someone to Love/Doin' Things Together with You	196?	—	2.50	5.00

—Reissue

❏ 214	When We Get Married/Just Because	196?	—	2.50	5.00

—Reissue

❏ 240	Amazons and Coyotes/Together	196?	—	2.50	5.00

—Reissue

MERCURY

❏ 72595	Bless Your Soul/ Bad Time Make the Good Times	1966	2.50	5.00	10.00
❏ 72630	Calling Jo-Ann/You Gave Me Someone to Love	1966	2.50	5.00	10.00

SWAN

❏ 4167	Amazons and Coyotes/Together	1963	3.00	6.00	12.00

—Black label

❏ 4167	Amazons and Coyotes/Together	1963	5.00	10.00	20.00

—White label

V-TONE

❏ 211	Annabelle Lee/Home Is Where the Heart Is	1960	5.00	10.00	20.00
❏ 229	May I Kiss the Bride/Time	1961	5.00	10.00	20.00

WARNER BROS.

❏ 5619	You Gave Me Someone to Love/Doin' Things Together with You	1965	6.25	12.50	25.00

Albums
COLLECTABLES

❏ COL-5004	The Best of the Dreamlovers	198?	3.00	6.00	12.00
❏ COL-5005	The Best of the Dreamlovers, Volume Two	198?	3.00	6.00	12.00

COLUMBIA

❏ CL 2020 [M]	The Bird and Other Golden Dancing Grooves	1963	10.00	20.00	40.00
❏ CS 8820 [S]	The Bird and Other Golden Dancing Grooves	1963	12.50	25.00	50.00

DREAMS
45s
COLUMBIA

❏ 45300	Devil Lady/Maryanne	1971	—	2.50	5.00
❏ 45369	Try Me/15 Miles to Provo	1971	—	2.50	5.00
❏ 45524	Medicated Goo/New York	1972	—	2.50	5.00

Albums
COLUMBIA

❏ C 30225	Dreams	1970	3.75	7.50	15.00
❏ C 30960	Imagine My Surprise	1971	3.75	7.50	15.00

DREAMS, THE
45s
SAVOY

❏ 1130	Darlene/A Letter to My Girl	1954	50.00	100.00	200.00
❏ 1140	Under the Willow/I'm Losing My Mind	1954	30.00	60.00	120.00

—A copy on gold vinyl with a blue Savoy label has shown up; its authenticity is unknown

❏ 1157	I'll Be Faithful/My Little Honeybun	1955	25.00	50.00	100.00

DREAMS AND ILLUSIONS
Albums
VERVE FORECAST

❏ FTS-3040	Dreams and Illusions	1968	5.00	10.00	20.00

DREW, PATTI Also see THE DREW-VELS.
45s
CAPITOL

❏ 2042	Where Is Daddy/Sufferer	1967	2.00	4.00	8.00
❏ 2121	Keep On Movin'/There'll Never Be Another	1968	2.00	4.00	8.00
❏ 2197	Workin' on a Groovy Thing/Without a Doubt	1968	2.00	4.00	8.00
❏ 2339	Hard to Handle/Just Can't Forget About You	1968	2.00	4.00	8.00
❏ 2389	I've Been Here All the Time/Welcome Back	1969	2.00	4.00	8.00
❏ 2473	The Love That a Woman Should Give to a Man/ Save the Last Dance for Me	1969	2.00	4.00	8.00
❏ 2575	He's the One/Which One Should I Choose	1969	2.00	4.00	8.00
❏ 2712	Wild Is Love/World of No Return	1969	2.00	4.00	8.00

—B-side by John Stewart

❏ 2713	The Pick-Up/Hundreds and Thousands of Guys	1970	2.00	4.00	8.00
❏ 2989	I'm Calling/It's Just a Dream	1970	2.00	4.00	8.00
❏ 5861	Tell Him/Turn Away from Me	1967	2.00	4.00	8.00
❏ 5969	Stop and Listen/Tired of Falling In and Out of Love	1967	2.00	4.00	8.00

QUILL

❏ 101	Where Is Daddy/Sufferer	1966	2.50	5.00	10.00

Albums
CAPITOL

❏ ST-156	I've Been Here All the Time	1969	5.00	10.00	20.00
❏ ST-408	Wild Is Love	1970	5.00	10.00	20.00
❏ ST 2804 [S]	Tell Him	1968	7.50	15.00	30.00
❏ T 2804 [M]	Tell Him	1968	7.50	15.00	30.00

DREW-VELS, THE Also see PATTI DREW.
45s
CAPITOL

❏ 5055	Tell Him/Just Because	1963	3.00	6.00	12.00
❏ 5145	It's My Time/Everybody Knows	1964	2.50	5.00	10.00
❏ 5244	Creepin'/I've Known	1964	2.50	5.00	10.00

QUILL

❏ 100	True Enough/Chilly Kisses	1966	2.50	5.00	10.00

Number	Title (A Side/B Side)	Yr	VG	VG+	NM

DRIFTERS, THE Several different groups with a common heritage, thus we list them together. Also see BEN E. KING; RUDY LEWIS; CLYDE McPHATTER; BILL PINKNEY.

45s

ATLANTIC

Number	Title (A Side/B Side)	Yr	VG	VG+	NM
❑ 1006	Money Honey/The Way I Feel	1953	20.00	40.00	80.00
❑ 1019	Such a Night/Lucille	1954	17.50	35.00	70.00
❑ 1029	Honey Love/Warm Your Heart	1954	12.50	25.00	50.00
❑ 1043	Bip Bam/Someday You'll Want Me to Want You	1954	10.00	20.00	40.00
❑ 1048	White Christmas/The Bells of St. Mary's	1954	15.00	30.00	60.00

—Yellow label, no spinner (original)

❑ 1048	White Christmas/The Bells of St. Mary's	1956	6.25	12.50	25.00

—Red label, no "fan" logo at lower left

❑ 1048 [DJ]	White Christmas/The Bells of St. Mary's	196?	6.25	12.50	25.00

—White/red label promo, no "fan" logo, with holly leaves encircling "45 R.P.M."

❑ 1048	White Christmas/The Bells of St. Mary's	1962	2.00	4.00	8.00

—Red label with "fan" logo at lower left

❑ 1048	White Christmas/The Bells of St. Mary's	197?	—	2.50	5.00

—Glossy yellow label with "fan" logo

❑ 1055	What'Cha Gonna Do/Gone	1955	12.50	25.00	50.00
❑ 1078	Adorable/Steamboat	1955	10.00	20.00	40.00
❑ 1089	Ruby Baby/Your Promise to Be Mine	1956	7.50	15.00	30.00
❑ 1101	Soldier of Fortune/I Got to Get Myself a Woman	1956	7.50	15.00	30.00
❑ 1123	Fools Fall in Love/It Was a Tear	1957	7.50	15.00	30.00
❑ 1141	Hypnotized/Drifting Away from You	1957	7.50	15.00	30.00
❑ 1161	I Know/Yodee Yakee	1957	7.50	15.00	30.00
❑ 1187	Drip Drop/Moonlight Bay	1958	7.50	15.00	30.00

—Last record by the "old" Drifters. The below Atlantic 45s are by a completely different group, although personnel changes resulted in at least one "old" Drifter (Johnny Moore) spending time with the "new" Drifters.

❑ 2025	There Goes My Baby/Oh My Love	1959	6.25	12.50	25.00
❑ 2040	Dance with Me/(If You Cry) True Love, True Love	1959	5.00	10.00	20.00
❑ 2050	This Magic Moment/Baltimore	1960	5.00	10.00	20.00
❑ 2062	Lonely Winds/Hey Senorita	1960	5.00	10.00	20.00
❑ 2071	Save the Last Dance for Me/Nobody But Me	1960	5.00	10.00	20.00
❑ 2087	I Count the Tears/Suddenly There's a Valley	1960	3.75	7.50	15.00
❑ 2096	Some Kind of Wonderful/Honey Bee	1961	3.75	7.50	15.00
❑ 2105	Please Stay/No Sweet Lovin'	1961	3.75	7.50	15.00
❑ 2117	Sweets for My Sweet/Loneliness or Happiness	1961	3.75	7.50	15.00
❑ 2127	Room Full of Tears/ Somebody New Dancin' with You	1961	3.75	7.50	15.00
❑ 2134	When My Little Girl Is Smiling/Mexican Divorce	1962	3.75	7.50	15.00
❑ 2143	Stranger on the Shore/What to Do	1962	3.75	7.50	15.00
❑ 2151	Sometimes I Wonder/Jackpot	1962	3.75	7.50	15.00
❑ 2162	Up On the Roof/Another Night with the Boys	1962	5.00	10.00	20.00
❑ 2182	On Broadway/Let the Music Play	1963	3.75	7.50	15.00
❑ 2191	Rat Race/If You Don't Come Back	1963	3.75	7.50	15.00
❑ 2201	I'll Take You Home/I Feel Good All Over	1963	3.75	7.50	15.00
❑ 2216	Vaya Con Dios/In the Land of Make Believe	1964	3.75	7.50	15.00
❑ 2225	One Way Love/Didn't It	1964	3.75	7.50	15.00
❑ 2237	Under the Boardwalk/ I Don't Want to Go On Without You	1964	3.75	7.50	15.00
❑ 2253	I've Got Sand in My Shoes/He's Just a Playboy	1964	3.00	6.00	12.00
❑ 2260	Saturday Night at the Movies/Spanish Lace	1964	3.00	6.00	12.00
❑ 2260 [PS]	Saturday Night at the Movies/Spanish Lace	1964	10.00	20.00	40.00
❑ 2261	The Christmas Song/I Remember Christmas	1964	3.00	6.00	12.00
❑ 2261 [PS]	The Christmas Song/I Remember Christmas	1964	7.50	15.00	30.00
❑ 2268	At the Club/Answer the Phone	1965	2.50	5.00	10.00
❑ 2285	Come On Over to My Place/Chains of Love	1965	2.50	5.00	10.00
❑ 2292	Follow Me/The Outside World	1965	2.50	5.00	10.00
❑ 2298	I'll Take You Where the Music's Playing/Far from the Maddening Crowd	1965	2.50	5.00	10.00
❑ 2310	Nylon Stockings/We Gotta Sing	1965	2.50	5.00	10.00
❑ 2325	Memories Are Made of This/My Islands in the Sun	1966	2.00	4.00	8.00
❑ 2336	Up in the Streets of Harlem/You Can't Love Them All	1966	2.00	4.00	8.00
❑ 2366	Aretha/Baby What I Mean	1966	2.00	4.00	8.00
❑ 2426	Up Jumped the Devil/Ain't It the Truth	1967	2.00	4.00	8.00
❑ 2471	I Need You Now/Still Burning in My Heart	1968	2.00	4.00	8.00
❑ 2624	Your Best Friend/Steal Away	1969	2.00	4.00	8.00
❑ 2746	You Got to Pay Your Dues/Black Silk	1970	2.50	5.00	10.00
❑ 2786	A Rose By Any Other Name/Be My Lady	1971	2.50	5.00	10.00
❑ 89189	Ruby Baby/Fever	1987	—	2.00	4.00

—B-side by Little Willie John

❑ 89189 [PS]	Ruby Baby/Fever	1987	—	2.00	4.00

—From the movie "Big Town"

BELL

❑ 45320	You've Got Your Troubles/I'm Feelin' Sad	1973	—	2.50	5.00
❑ 45387	The Songs We Used to Sing/Like Sister and Brother	1973	—	2.50	5.00
❑ 45600	Kissin' in the Back Row of the Movies/I'm Feelin' Sad	1974	—	2.50	5.00

CROWN

❑ 108	The World Is Changing/Sacroiliac Swing	1954	50.00	100.00	200.00

EMI-CAPITOL MUSIC

❑ S7-19351	Christmas Time Is Here/I'll Be Home for Christmas	1996	—	—	3.00

—As "The Drifters Featuring Rick Sheppard"

MUSICOR

❑ 1498	Midsummer Night in Harlem/Lonely Drifter, Don't Cry	1974	—	2.50	5.00

—As "Charlie Thomas and the Drifters"

S&J

❑ 800826	(More Than a Number in My) Little Red Book/I Count the Tears	196?	2.50	5.00	10.00

—As "Bill Pinkney and the Original Drifters"

7-Inch Extended Plays

ATLANTIC

❑ 534	(contents unknown)	1954	50.00	100.00	200.00
❑ 534 [PS]	Clyde McPhatter and the Drifters	1954	75.00	150.00	300.00
❑ 592	Fools Fall in Love/Adorable//Steamboat/ Ruby Baby	1957	25.00	50.00	100.00
❑ 592 [PS]	The Drifters	1957	50.00	100.00	200.00

Albums

ARISTA

❑ AB 4140	Every Night Is Saturday Night	1976	3.00	6.00	12.00

ATCO

❑ SD 33-375 [R]	Their Greatest Recordings — The Early Years	1971	3.00	6.00	12.00

ATLANTIC

❑ 8003 [M]	Clyde McPhatter and the Drifters	1956	125.00	250.00	500.00

—Black label

❑ 8003 [M]	Clyde McPhatter and the Drifters	1959	15.00	30.00	60.00

—Red and purple label, white "fan" logo at right

❑ 8003 [M]	Clyde McPhatter and the Drifters	1963	10.00	20.00	40.00

—Red and purple label, black "fan" logo at right

❑ 8022 [M]	Rockin' and Driftin'	1958	125.00	250.00	500.00

—White "bullseye" label

❑ 8022 [M]	Rockin' and Driftin'	1958	150.00	300.00	600.00

—Black label

❑ 8022 [M]	Rockin' and Driftin'	1959	15.00	30.00	60.00

—Red and purple label, white "fan" logo at right

❑ 8022 [M]	Rockin' and Driftin'	1963	10.00	20.00	40.00

—Red and purple label, black "fan" logo at right

❑ 8041 [M]	The Drifters' Greatest Hits	1960	25.00	50.00	100.00

—Red and purple label, white "fan" logo at right

❑ 8041 [M]	The Drifters' Greatest Hits	1960	150.00	300.00	600.00

—Black label

❑ 8041 [M]	The Drifters' Greatest Hits	1963	12.50	25.00	50.00

—Red and purple label, black "fan" logo at right

❑ 8059 [M]	Save the Last Dance for Me	1962	30.00	60.00	120.00

—Red and purple label, white "fan" logo at right

❑ 8059 [M]	Save the Last Dance for Me	1963	15.00	30.00	60.00

—Red and purple label, black "fan" logo at right

❑ SD 8059 [S]	Save the Last Dance for Me	1962	50.00	100.00	200.00

—Green and blue label, white "fan" logo at right

❑ SD 8059 [S]	Save the Last Dance for Me	1963	25.00	50.00	100.00

—Green and blue label, black "fan" logo at right

❑ SD 8059 [S]	Save the Last Dance for Me	1969	6.25	12.50	25.00

—Red and green label, white horizontal stripe through center hole

❑ 8073 [M]	Up on the Roof — The Best of the Drifters	1963	25.00	50.00	100.00

—Red and purple label, black "fan" logo at right

❑ SD 8073 [S]	Up on the Roof — The Best of the Drifters	1963	37.50	75.00	150.00

—Green and blue label, black "fan" logo at right

❑ 8093 [M]	Our Biggest Hits	1964	15.00	30.00	60.00

—Red and purple label, white "fan" logo at right

❑ SD 8093 [S]	Our Biggest Hits	1964	20.00	40.00	80.00

—Mostly red label, black "fan" logo

❑ 8099 [M]	Under the Boardwalk	1964	12.50	25.00	50.00

—Color photo of group on cover

❑ 8099 [M]	Under the Boardwalk	1964	20.00	40.00	80.00

—Black and white photo of group on cover

❑ SD 8099 [S]	Under the Boardwalk	1964	15.00	30.00	60.00

—Color photo of group on cover

❑ SD 8099 [S]	Under the Boardwalk	1964	30.00	60.00	120.00

—Black and white photo of group on cover

❑ 8103 [M]	The Good Life with the Drifters	1965	10.00	20.00	40.00
❑ SD 8103 [S]	The Good Life with the Drifters	1965	12.50	25.00	50.00
❑ 8113 [M]	I'll Take You Where the Music's Playing	1965	10.00	20.00	40.00
❑ SD 8113 [S]	I'll Take You Where the Music's Playing	1965	12.50	25.00	50.00
❑ 8153 [M]	The Drifters' Golden Hits	1968	7.50	15.00	30.00
❑ SD 8153 [P]	The Drifters' Golden Hits	1968	7.50	15.00	30.00

—Green and blue label

❑ SD 8153 [P]	The Drifters' Golden Hits	1969	3.75	7.50	15.00

—Red and green label

❑ 81927 [(2)]	Let the Boogie-Woogie Roll: Greatest Hits 1953-1958	1989	3.75	7.50	15.00
❑ 81931 [(2)]	All-Time Greatest Hits and More: 1959-1965	1989	3.75	7.50	15.00

CLARION

❑ 608 [M]	The Drifters	1964	5.00	10.00	20.00
❑ SD 608 [P]	The Drifters	1964	7.50	15.00	30.00

GUSTO

❑ 0063	Greatest Hits — The Drifters	1980	2.50	5.00	10.00

TRIP

❑ TOP-16-6	16 Greatest Hits — The Drifters	1976	2.50	5.00	10.00

DRIFTERS, THE (2) Instrumental group from England, and backing band for CLIFF RICHARD. They had one record in the US on Capitol; see THE SHADOWS, the name they adopted after the R&B Drifters became popular.

DRIFTERS, THE (3)

45s

CORAL

❑ 65037	Wine Head Woman/I'm the Caring Kind	1950	75.00	150.00	300.00
❑ 65040	And I Shook/I Had to Find Out for Myself	1951	75.00	150.00	300.00

DRIFTERS, THE (4)

45s

RAMA

❑ 22	Besame Mucho/Summertime	1953	50.00	100.00	200.00

DRIFTERS, THE (U) Definitely not group (2), (3) or (4), though it could be one of the many variants of group (1).

45s

STEELTOWN

❑ 671	Peace of Mind/The Struggler	1973	—	2.50	5.00

DRIFTIN' SLIM

Albums

MILESTONE

❑ MLS-93004 [(2)]	Driftin' Slim and His Blues Band	1968	6.25	12.50	25.00

DRIVERS, THE More than one group.

45s

COMET

❑ 2142	High Gear/Low Gear	1961	6.25	12.50	25.00

DELUXE

❑ 6094	Women/Smooth, Slow and Easy	1956	25.00	50.00	100.00
❑ 6104	My Lonely Prayer/Midnight Hours	1957	50.00	100.00	200.00
❑ 6117	Dangerous Lips/Oh Miss Nellie	1957	20.00	40.00	80.00

KING

❑ 5645	Mr. Astronaut/Dry Bones Twist	1962	3.00	6.00	12.00

LIN

❑ 1002	A Man's Glory/Teeter Totter	1954	100.00	200.00	400.00

RCA VICTOR

❑ 47-7023	Blue Moon/I Get Weak	1957	15.00	30.00	60.00

Number	Title (A Side/B Side)	Yr	VG	VG+	NM

DRONGOS, THE
45s
WHITE WHALE

| ❏ 235 | Under My Thumb/If You Wanna Know | 1966 | 5.00 | 10.00 | 20.00 |

DRUIDS OF STONEHENGE, THE
45s
UNI

| ❏ 55021 | A Garden Where Nothing Grows/Painted Woman | 1967 | 5.00 | 10.00 | 20.00 |

Albums
UNI

| ❏ 3004 [M] | Creation | 1967 | 15.00 | 30.00 | 60.00 |
| ❏ 73004 [S] | Creation | 1967 | 20.00 | 40.00 | 80.00 |

DRY CITY SCAT BAND, THE
Albums
ELEKTRA

| ❏ EKL-292 [M] | The Dry City Scat Band | 1965 | 6.25 | 12.50 | 25.00 |
| ❏ EKS-7292 [S] | The Dry City Scat Band | 1965 | 7.50 | 15.00 | 30.00 |

DRYSDALE, DON
45s
REPRISE

| ❏ 20162 | Give Her Love/Our Love | 1963 | 2.50 | 5.00 | 10.00 |
| ❏ 20162 [PS] | Give Her Love/Our Love | 1963 | 5.00 | 10.00 | 20.00 |

DU DROPPERS, THE
45s
GROOVE

❏ 0001	Speed King/Dead Broke	1954	20.00	40.00	80.00
❏ 0013	Just Whisper/How Much Longer	1954	25.00	50.00	100.00
❏ 0036	Boot 'Em Up/Let Nature Take Its Course	1955	12.50	25.00	50.00
❏ 0104	Talk That Talk/Give Me Some Consideration	1955	12.50	25.00	50.00
❏ 0120	I Wanna Love You/You're Mine Already	1955	12.50	25.00	50.00

RCA VICTOR

❏ 47-5229	I Wanna Know/Laughing Blues	1953	10.00	20.00	40.00
❏ 47-5321	I Found Out/Little Girl, Little Girl	1953	10.00	20.00	40.00
❏ 47-5425	Whatever You're Doin'/Somebody Work on My Baby's Mind	1953	10.00	20.00	40.00
❏ 47-5504	Don't Pass Me By/Get Lost	1953	10.00	20.00	40.00
❏ 47-5543	The Note in the Bottle/Mama's Gone Goodbye	1953	10.00	20.00	40.00

—*With Sunny Gale*
RED ROBIN

| ❏ 108 | Can't Do Sixty No More/Chain Me Baby (Blues of Desire) | 1952 | 50.00 | 100.00 | 200.00 |
| ❏ 108 | Can't Do Sixty No More/Chain Me Baby (Blues of Desire) | 1952 | 125.00 | 250.00 | 500.00 |

—*Red vinyl*

| ❏ 116 | Come On and Love Me Baby/Go Back | 1953 | 37.50 | 75.00 | 150.00 |

7-Inch Extended Plays
GROOVE

❏ 2	(contents unknown)	1955	50.00	100.00	200.00
❏ 2 [PS]	Talk That Talk	1955	50.00	100.00	200.00
❏ 5	(contents unknown)	1955	50.00	100.00	200.00
❏ 5 [PS]	Tops in Rhythm and Blues	1955	50.00	100.00	200.00

DUALS, THE
45s
ARC

| ❏ 4446 | Nearest to My Heart/Bye Bye | 1959 | 5.00 | 10.00 | 20.00 |

FURY

| ❏ 1013 | Wait Up Baby/Forever and Ever | 1958 | 10.00 | 20.00 | 40.00 |

INFINITY

| ❏ 032 | Oozy Groove/The Big Race | 1964 | 6.25 | 12.50 | 25.00 |

JUGGY

| ❏ 321 | Oozy Groove/The Big Race | 1964 | 12.50 | 25.00 | 50.00 |

STAR REVUE

| ❏ 1031 | Stick Shift/Cruising | 1961 | 200.00 | 400.00 | 800.00 |

SUE

| ❏ 745 | Stick Shift/Cruising | 1961 | 7.50 | 15.00 | 30.00 |
| ❏ 758 | Travelin' Guitar/Cha Cha Guitar | 1962 | 6.25 | 12.50 | 25.00 |

UNITED ARTISTS

| ❏ 0128 | Stick Shift/Keem-O-Sabe | 1973 | — | 2.00 | 4.00 |

—*"Silver Spotlight Series" reissue; B-side by The Electric Indian*
Albums
SUE

| ❏ LP-2002 [M] | Stick Shift | 1961 | 100.00 | 200.00 | 400.00 |

—*Cartoon cover*

| ❏ LP-2002 [M] | Stick Shift | 1964 | 50.00 | 100.00 | 200.00 |

—*Photo cover*

DU'AMBRA, JOEY
45s
ABC-PARAMOUNT

| ❏ 9917 | Baby Sue/Come Back-A Little Mama | 1958 | 7.50 | 15.00 | 30.00 |

DUANE, DICK
45s
ABC-PARAMOUNT

❏ 9656	Sobony/Now	1955	7.50	15.00	30.00
❏ 9677	To Make a Mistake/Blue Prelude	1956	7.50	15.00	30.00
❏ 9709	Fame and Fortune/Mean Don't Cry	1956	7.50	15.00	30.00

GNP

| ❏ 127 | What Good Does It Do/Savannah | 1957 | 5.00 | 10.00 | 20.00 |
| ❏ 130 | Eternally/I'll Never Make You Cry Again | 1957 | 5.00 | 10.00 | 20.00 |

DUBS, THE
45s
ABC-PARAMOUNT

❏ 10056	No One/Early in the Evening	1959	6.25	12.50	25.00
❏ 10100	Don't Laugh at Me/You Never Belong to Me	1960	12.50	25.00	50.00
❏ 10150	For the First Time/Ain't That So	1960	6.25	12.50	25.00
❏ 10198	If I Only Had Magic/Joogie Boogie	1961	7.50	15.00	30.00
❏ 10269	Lullaby/Down, Down, Down I Go	1961	7.50	15.00	30.00

Number	Title (A Side/B Side)	Yr	VG	VG+	NM

CLIFTON

| ❏ 2 | Where Do We Go from Here/I Only Have Eyes for You | 1973 | — | 3.00 | 6.00 |

END

| ❏ 1108 | Now That We Broke Up/This to Me Is Love | 1962 | 12.50 | 25.00 | 50.00 |

GONE

| ❏ 5002 | Don't Ask Me (To Be Lonely)/Darling | 1957 | 6.25 | 12.50 | 25.00 |

—*Multi-color label*

| ❏ 5002 | Don't Ask Me (To Be Lonely)/Darling | 1957 | 15.00 | 30.00 | 60.00 |

—*Black label, clown-face logo*

| ❏ 5002 | Don't Ask Me (To Be Lonely)/Darling | 1957 | 25.00 | 50.00 | 100.00 |

—*Black label, "shadow" logo*

| ❏ 5011 | Could This Be Magic/Such Lovin' | 1957 | 6.25 | 12.50 | 25.00 |

—*Multi-color label*

| ❏ 5011 | Could This Be Magic/Such Lovin' | 1957 | 12.50 | 25.00 | 50.00 |

—*Black label*

❏ 5020	Beside My Love/Gonna Make a Change	1957	15.00	30.00	60.00
❏ 5034	Song in My Heart/Be Sure (My Love)	1958	15.00	30.00	60.00
❏ 5046	Chapel of Dreams/Is There a Love for Me	1958	15.00	30.00	60.00
❏ 5069	Chapel of Dreams/Is There a Love for Me	1959	12.50	25.00	50.00
❏ 5138	You're Free to Go/Is There a Love for Me	1962	12.50	25.00	50.00

JOHNSON

❏ 097	Connie/Home Under My Hat	1973	—	3.00	6.00
❏ 098	Somebody Goofed/I Won't Have You Breaking My Heart	1973	—	3.00	6.00
❏ 102	Don't Ask Me (To Be Lonely)/Darling	1957	500.00	1000.	1500.

JOSIE

| ❏ 911 | Wisdom of a Fool/This I Swear | 1963 | 5.00 | 10.00 | 20.00 |

LANA

| ❏ 115 | Could This Be Magic/Blue Velvet | 1964 | 2.00 | 4.00 | 8.00 |

—*A-side is an alternate take of the hit version*

| ❏ 116 | Don't Ask Me (To Be Lonely)/Your Very First Love | 1964 | 2.00 | 4.00 | 8.00 |

—*A-side is an alternate take of the hit version*
MARK-X

| ❏ 8008 | Be Sure My Love/Song in My Heart | 1960 | 5.00 | 10.00 | 20.00 |

VICKIE

| ❏ 229 | I'm Downtown/Lost in the Wilderness | 1971 | 2.50 | 5.00 | 10.00 |

—*As "Richard Blandon and the Dubs"*
WILSHIRE

| ❏ 201 | Just You/Your Very First Love | 1963 | 10.00 | 20.00 | 40.00 |

Albums
CANDELITE

| ❏ 1003 | You've Got to Be Good to Make It in New York City | 197? | 3.00 | 6.00 | 12.00 |
| ❏ 1004 | The Best of the Dubs | 197? | 3.00 | 6.00 | 12.00 |

DUBS, THE / THE SHELLS Also see each artist's individual listings.
Albums
JOSIE

| ❏ JM-4001 [M] | The Dubs Meet the Shells | 1962 | 75.00 | 150.00 | 300.00 |
| ❏ JSS-4001 [S] | The Dubs Meet the Shells | 1962 | 150.00 | 300.00 | 600.00 |

DUCKS DELUXE
45s
RCA VICTOR

| ❏ APBO-0297 | Daddy Put the Bomp/Please, Please, Please | 1974 | 2.00 | 4.00 | 8.00 |

Albums
RCA VICTOR

| ❏ AFL1-3025 | Don't Mind Rockin' Tonight | 1978 | 2.50 | 5.00 | 10.00 |
| ❏ LPL1-5008 | Ducks Deluxe | 1973 | 3.75 | 7.50 | 15.00 |

DUDLEY, DAVE, AND TOM T. HALL
45s
MERCURY

| ❏ 73139 | Day Drinkin'/Get On with the Show | 1970 | — | 3.50 | 7.00 |

DUFFILL, TAM
45s
GROOVE

| ❏ 58-0004 | Cooly Dooly/You Put the Hurt on Me | 1963 | 15.00 | 30.00 | 60.00 |

DUGAN, DENNY
45s
HIT

| ❏ 114 | The Shoop Shoop Song/That's the Way Boys Are | 1964 | 2.00 | 4.00 | 8.00 |

—*B-side by Connie Dee*

DUKAYS, THE Also see GENE CHANDLER.
45s
NAT

| ❏ 4001 | The Big Lie/The Girl's a Devil | 1961 | 5.00 | 10.00 | 20.00 |
| ❏ 4002 | Nite Owl/Festival of Love | 1961 | 5.00 | 10.00 | 20.00 |

VEE JAY

❏ 430	Nite Owl/Festival of Love	1962	3.75	7.50	15.00
❏ 442	I'm Gonna Love You So/Please Help	1962	3.75	7.50	15.00
❏ 460	I Feel Good All Over/I Never Knew	1962	3.75	7.50	15.00
❏ 491	Combination/Every Step	1963	3.75	7.50	15.00

DUKE, BILLY
45s
ABC-PARAMOUNT

| ❏ 9816 | Chalypso/Fork in the Road | 1957 | 5.00 | 10.00 | 20.00 |
| ❏ 9826 | Ready to Go Steady/Let Me Know | 1957 | 5.00 | 10.00 | 20.00 |

CAPITOL

❏ 4784	New Orleans/Show Me the Way to Go Home	1962	3.00	6.00	12.00
❏ 4831	Summer at the Shore/Good Old Days	1962	3.00	6.00	12.00
❏ 4907	Goodbye Stranger/Millionaire	1963	3.00	6.00	12.00
❏ 5012	Echoes/The Best Man	1963	3.00	6.00	12.00

CASINO

| ❏ 138 | Flip, Flop and Fly/Fun Lovin' Mama | 1956 | 15.00 | 30.00 | 60.00 |

CORAL

| ❏ 9-61203 | I Cried/Love Ya, Love Ya, Love Ya | 1954 | 6.25 | 12.50 | 25.00 |

DATE

| ❏ 1005 | Roland/What You Told Me | 1958 | 5.00 | 10.00 | 20.00 |

Number	Title (A Side/B Side)	Yr	VG	VG+	NM

PEAK
| ❑ 104 | Chalypso/Fork in the Road | 1957 | 7.50 | 15.00 | 30.00 |

SEVILLE
❑ 132	I'm the Lonesomest Guy in Town/While the Bloom Is on the Roses	1964	3.00	6.00	12.00
❑ 134	Six-O-Nine/Ciumachella (Tender Flower)	1964	3.00	6.00	12.00
❑ 136	Prisoner of Love/Sugar and Spice	1965	3.00	6.00	12.00

TEEN
| ❑ 110 | Paradise Princess/I Know I Was Wrong | 1955 | 10.00 | 20.00 | 40.00 |
| ❑ 112 | Rocky Piano/Daddy Rock & Roll | 1955 | 10.00 | 20.00 | 40.00 |

20TH FOX
❑ 242	The River Flows On/This Is What I Ask	1961	3.00	6.00	12.00
❑ 276	Be a Dreamer/Where Is That Feeling	1961	3.00	6.00	12.00
❑ 296	Amen/Walking Cane	1962	3.00	6.00	12.00
❑ 301	(Oooh Looka There) Ain't She Pretty/Timbuctu	1962	3.00	6.00	12.00
❑ 301 [PS]	(Oooh Looka There) Ain't She Pretty/Timbuctu	1962	12.50	25.00	50.00

DUKE, DENVER, AND JEFFERY NULL
45s
BLUE HEN
| ❑ 127 | A Babe, A Star, A Manger/Christ, Who Came To Bethlehem | 19?? | 3.00 | 6.00 | 12.00 |

MERCURY
| ❑ 70970 | Hank Williams Isn't Dead/Rock and Roll Blues | 1956 | 15.00 | 30.00 | 60.00 |

DUKE, PATTY
45s
UNITED ARTISTS
❑ 0127	Don't Just Stand There/Say Something Funny	1973	—	2.00	4.00
—"Silver Spotlight Series" reissue					
❑ 875	Don't Just Stand There/Everything But Love	1965	2.50	5.00	10.00
❑ 875 [PS]	Don't Just Stand There/Everything But Love	1965	5.00	10.00	20.00
❑ 915	Funny Little Butterflies/Say Something Funny	1965	2.00	4.00	8.00
❑ 915 [PS]	Funny Little Butterflies/Say Something Funny	1965	5.00	10.00	20.00
❑ 958	Why Don't They Understand/Ribbons and Roses	1965	—	—	—
—Unreleased					
❑ 978	Whenever She Holds You/Nothing But Me	1966	2.00	4.00	8.00
❑ 50034	Little Things Mean a Lot/The World Is Watching Us	1966	2.00	4.00	8.00
❑ 50034 [PS]	Little Things Mean a Lot/The World Is Watching Us	1966	6.25	12.50	25.00
❑ 50057	The Wall Came Tumbling Down/What Makes You Special	1966	2.00	4.00	8.00
❑ 50073	Why Don't They Understand/Danke Schoen	1966	2.00	4.00	8.00
❑ 50216	Come Live with Me/My Own Little Place	1967	—	3.00	6.00
❑ 50299	Dona, Dona/And We Were Strangers	1968	—	3.00	6.00

Albums
UNART
| ❑ 20005 [M] | TV's Teen Star | 1967 | 3.00 | 6.00 | 12.00 |
| ❑ S 20005 [S] | TV's Teen Star | 1967 | 3.75 | 7.50 | 15.00 |

UNITED ARTISTS
❑ UAL-3452 [M]	Don't Just Stand There	1965	5.00	10.00	20.00
❑ UAL-3492 [M]	Patty	1966	5.00	10.00	20.00
❑ UAL-3535 [M]	Patty Duke's Greatest Hits	1966	3.75	7.50	15.00
❑ UAS-6452 [S]	Don't Just Stand There	1965	7.50	15.00	30.00
❑ UAS-6492 [S]	Patty	1966	7.50	15.00	30.00
❑ UAS-6535 [S]	Patty Duke's Greatest Hits	1966	6.25	12.50	25.00
❑ UAS-6623	Songs from the Valley of the Dolls	1968	6.25	12.50	25.00

DUKE, PATTY, WITH NORMAN VINCENT PEALE
Albums
GUIDEPOSTS
| ❑ GP-101 [M] | Guideposts for Christmas | 1963 | 20.00 | 40.00 | 80.00 |

DUKE OF EARL, THE See GENE CHANDLER.

DUKES, THE Possibly more than one group.
45s
FLIP
| ❑ 343 | Looking for You/Groceries Sir | 1959 | 7.50 | 15.00 | 30.00 |
| ❑ 345 | I Love You/Leap Year Cha Cha | 1959 | 10.00 | 20.00 | 40.00 |

IMPERIAL
| ❑ 5401 | Teardrop Eyes/Shimmies and Shakes | 1956 | 62.50 | 125.00 | 250.00 |
| ❑ 5415 | Wini Brown/Cotton Pickin' Hands | 1956 | 30.00 | 60.00 | 120.00 |

SPECIALTY
| ❑ 543 | Ooh Bop She Bop/Oh-Kay | 1954 | 18.75 | 37.50 | 75.00 |

DUKES OF DIXIELAND, THE
45s
COLUMBIA
❑ OP 50 [DJ]	If I Were a Bell/(B-side unknown)	195?	3.00	6.00	12.00
—"Special Coin-Operator Release"					
❑ 31356 [S]	(contents unknown)	1962	2.00	4.00	8.00
❑ 31357 [S]	(contents unknown)	1962	2.00	4.00	8.00
❑ 31358 [S]	(contents unknown)	1962	2.00	4.00	8.00
❑ 31359 [S]	(contents unknown)	1962	2.00	4.00	8.00
❑ 31360 [S]	(contents unknown)	1962	2.00	4.00	8.00
❑ 31575 [S]	(contents unknown)	1962	2.00	4.00	8.00
❑ 31576 [S]	(contents unknown)	1962	2.00	4.00	8.00
❑ 31577 [S]	(contents unknown)	1962	2.00	4.00	8.00
❑ 31578 [S]	(contents unknown)	1962	2.00	4.00	8.00
❑ 31579 [S]	(contents unknown)	1962	2.00	4.00	8.00
—Anyone who can fill in these gaps -- the above 10 all are Columbia "Stereo 7" singles -- please let us know.					
❑ 42416	What's the Time?/Too Bad	1962	2.00	4.00	8.00
❑ 42599	Bye and Bye/Deep River	1962	2.00	4.00	8.00
❑ 43013	Fair Is Fair/Big Parade	1964	2.00	4.00	8.00

DECCA
❑ 25693	Everybody Loves My Baby/Yvette	1966	—	2.50	5.00
❑ 25715	Baby Face/Rose of Washington Square	1967	—	2.50	5.00
❑ 25729	Smile/More and More	1968	—	2.50	5.00
❑ 31798	I Will Wait for You/Exactly Like You	1966	—	3.00	6.00

Albums
AUDIO FIDELITY
| ❑ AFLP-1823 [M] | You Have to Hear It to Believe It — The Dukes of Dixieland, Vol. 1 | 1956 | 3.75 | 7.50 | 15.00 |

Number	Title (A Side/B Side)	Yr	VG	VG+	NM

❑ AFLP-1840 [M]	You Have to Hear It to Believe It — The Dukes of Dixieland, Vol. 2	1957	3.75	7.50	15.00
❑ AFLP-1851 [M]	Marching Along with the Dukes of Dixieland, Vol. 3	1957	3.75	7.50	15.00
❑ AFLP-1860 [M]	The Dukes of Dixieland On Bourbon Street, Vol. 4	1958	3.75	7.50	15.00
❑ AFLP-1861 [M]	Minstrel Time with the Phenomenal Dukes of Dixieland, Volume 5	1957	3.75	7.50	15.00
❑ AFLP-1862 [M]	Mardi Gras Time	1958	3.75	7.50	15.00
❑ AFLP-1891 [M]	The Dukes of Dixieland On Campus	1959	3.75	7.50	15.00
❑ AFLP-1892 [M]	Up the Mississippi	1959	3.75	7.50	15.00
❑ AFLP-1918 [M]	Carnegie Hall Concert	1959	3.75	7.50	15.00
❑ AFLP-1924 [M]	Louie and the Dukes of Dixieland	1960	3.75	7.50	15.00
❑ AFLP-1928 [M]	Piano Ragtime (Vol. 11)	1960	3.75	7.50	15.00
❑ AFLP-1956 [M]	The Best of the Dukes of Dixieland	1961	3.75	7.50	15.00
❑ AFLP-1976 [M]	More of the Best of the Dukes of Dixieland	1962	3.75	7.50	15.00
❑ AFSD-5823 [S]	You Have to Hear It to Believe It — The Dukes of Dixieland, Vol. 1	196?	5.00	10.00	20.00
❑ AFSD-5840 [S]	You Have to Hear It to Believe It — The Dukes of Dixieland, Vol. 2	196?	5.00	10.00	20.00
❑ AFSD-5851 [S]	Marching Along with the Dukes of Dixieland, Vol. 3	1958	5.00	10.00	20.00
❑ AFSD-5860 [S]	The Dukes of Dixieland On Bourbon Street, Vol. 4	1958	5.00	10.00	20.00
❑ AFSD-5861 [S]	Minstrel Time with the Phenomenal Dukes of Dixieland, Volume 5	1958	5.00	10.00	20.00
❑ AFSD-5862 [S]	Mardi Gras Time	1958	5.00	10.00	20.00
❑ AFSD-5891 [S]	The Dukes of Dixieland On Campus	1959	5.00	10.00	20.00
❑ AFSD-5892 [S]	Up the Mississippi	1959	5.00	10.00	20.00
❑ AFSD-5918 [S]	Carnegie Hall Concert	1959	3.75	7.50	15.00
❑ AFSD-5924 [S]	Louie and the Dukes of Dixieland	1960	3.75	7.50	15.00
❑ AFSD-5928 [S]	Piano Ragtime (Vol. 11)	1960	3.75	7.50	15.00
❑ AFSD-5956 [S]	The Best of the Dukes of Dixieland	1961	3.75	7.50	15.00
❑ AFSD-5976 [S]	More of the Best of the Dukes of Dixieland	1962	3.75	7.50	15.00
❑ AFSD-6172	Tailgating	1967	3.00	6.00	12.00
❑ AFSD-6174	The Dukes of Dixieland On Parade	1967	3.00	6.00	12.00

COLUMBIA
❑ CL 1728 [M]	Breakin' It Up on Broadway	1962	3.00	6.00	12.00
❑ CL 1871 [M]	Dixieland Hootenanny!	1963	3.00	6.00	12.00
❑ CL 1966 [M]	The Dukes at Disneyland, Volume 1	1963	3.00	6.00	12.00
❑ CL 2194 [M]	Struttin' at the World's Fair	1964	3.00	6.00	12.00
❑ CS 8528 [S]	Breakin' It Up on Broadway	1962	3.75	7.50	15.00
❑ CS 8671 [S]	Dixieland Hootenanny!	1963	3.75	7.50	15.00
❑ CS 8766 [S]	The Dukes at Disneyland, Volume 1	1963	3.75	7.50	15.00
❑ CS 8994 [S]	Struttin' at the World's Fair	1964	3.75	7.50	15.00

DECCA
❑ DL 4653 [M]	"Live" At Bourbon Street, Chicago	1965	3.00	6.00	12.00
❑ DL 4708 [M]	Come On and Hear	1966	3.00	6.00	12.00
❑ DL 4807 [M]	Sunrise, Sunset	1966	3.00	6.00	12.00
❑ DL 4863 [M]	Come to the Cabaret	1967	3.75	7.50	15.00
❑ DL 4864 [M]	Thoroughly Modern Millie	1967	3.75	7.50	15.00
❑ DL 74653 [S]	"Live" At Bourbon Street, Chicago	1965	3.75	7.50	15.00
❑ DL 74708 [S]	Come On and Hear	1966	3.75	7.50	15.00
❑ DL 74807 [S]	Sunrise, Sunset	1966	3.75	7.50	15.00
❑ DL 74863 [S]	Come to the Cabaret	1967	3.00	6.00	12.00
❑ DL 74864 [S]	Thoroughly Modern Millie	1967	3.00	6.00	12.00
❑ DL 74975	Dixieland's Greatest Hits	1968	3.00	6.00	12.00

HARMONY
| ❑ HL 7349 [M] | Best of the Dukes of Dixieland | 1965 | 3.00 | 6.00 | 12.00 |
| ❑ HS 11149 [S] | Best of the Dukes of Dixieland | 1965 | 3.00 | 6.00 | 12.00 |

MCA
| ❑ 268 | Dixieland's Greatest Hits | 1973 | 2.50 | 5.00 | 10.00 |
| —Reissue of Decca 74975 | | | | | |

RCA VICTOR
| ❑ LPM-2097 [M] | The Dukes of Dixieland at the Jazz Band Ball | 1960 | 3.00 | 6.00 | 12.00 |
| ❑ LSP-2097(e) [R] | The Dukes of Dixieland at the Jazz Band Ball | 1960 | 3.75 | 7.50 | 15.00 |

ROULETTE
| ❑ R-25029 [M] | Curtain Going Up | 1958 | 5.00 | 10.00 | 20.00 |

VIK
| ❑ LX-1025 [M] | The Dukes of Dixieland at the Jazz Band Ball | 1956 | 7.50 | 15.00 | 30.00 |

VOCALION
| ❑ VL 73846 | Hello, Dolly! | 1968 | 2.50 | 5.00 | 10.00 |

DUMAURIERS, THE
45s
FURY
| ❑ 1011 | Baby I Love You/All Night Long | 1957 | 25.00 | 50.00 | 100.00 |

LOST-NITE
| ❑ 363 | Baby I Love You/All Night Long | 197? | — | 2.50 | 5.00 |
| —Reissue | | | | | |

DUNAVAN, TERRY
45s
FANFARE
| ❑ 727 | Rock It on Mars/Earthquake Boogie | 195? | 100.00 | 200.00 | 400.00 |

DUNBAR, AYNSLEY Also see JEFFERSON AIRPLANE; JOURNEY; JOHN MAYALL.
Albums
BLUE THUMB
❑ BTS-4	The Aynsley Dunbar Retaliation	1968	6.25	12.50	25.00
❑ BTS-6	Doctor Dunbar's Prescription	1969	6.25	12.50	25.00
❑ BTS-16	To Mum From Aynsley and the Boys	1970	6.25	12.50	25.00

DUNCAN, HERBIE
45s
GLENN
❑ 1400	Hot Lips Baby/Little Angel	1961	100.00	200.00	400.00
❑ 1401	Roll Along/Escape	1961	30.00	60.00	120.00
❑ 1402	That's All/End of the Rainbow	1961	20.00	40.00	80.00

MAR-VEL
| ❑ 1400 | Hot Lips Baby/Little Angel | 1960 | 25.00 | 50.00 | 100.00 |

DUNDEE, CARLYLE, AND THE DUNDEES
45s
SPACE
| ❑ 201 | Never/Evil One | 1954 | 100.00 | 200.00 | 400.00 |

DUNGAREE DARLINGS, THE
45s
KAREN
| ❑ 1005 | Boy of My Dreams/Little Wallflower | 1959 | 25.00 | 50.00 | 100.00 |

D

Number	Title (A Side/B Side)	Yr	VG	VG+	NM
REGO					
❑ 1003	Boy of My Dreams/Little Wallflower	1958	62.50	125.00	250.00
—As "The Dungaree Dolls"					

DUNGAREE DOLLS, THE See THE DUNGAREE DARLINGS.

DUNN, JOHN
45s

Number	Title (A Side/B Side)	Yr	VG	VG+	NM
HIT					
❑ 22	Ahab the Arab/Dancin' Party	1962	2.00	4.00	8.00
—B-side by Herbert Hunter					

DUPONTS, THE Little Anthony's group before joining the Imperials. They are NOT the same group as the Imperials.
45s

Number	Title (A Side/B Side)	Yr	VG	VG+	NM
ROULETTE					
❑ 4060	Half Past Nothing/A Screamin' Ball (At Dracula Hall)	1958	6.25	12.50	25.00
ROYAL ROOST					
❑ 627	Somebody/Prove It Tonight	1957	12.50	25.00	50.00
SAVOY					
❑ 1552	Must Be Falling in Love/You	1958	6.25	12.50	25.00
—As "Little Anthony Guardine and the Duponts"					
WINLEY					
❑ 212	Must Be Falling in Love/You	1957	20.00	40.00	80.00

DUPREE, CHAMPION JACK
45s

Number	Title (A Side/B Side)	Yr	VG	VG+	NM
ATLANTIC					
❑ 2032	Frankie and Johnny/Strollin'	1959	3.00	6.00	12.00
—As "Champion Jack"					
❑ 2095	My Mother-in-Law/Evil Woman	1961	2.50	5.00	10.00
EVERLAST					
❑ 5025	Shake Baby Shake/Walking Down the Highway	1963	2.50	5.00	10.00
❑ 5032	Highway Blues/Shake Baby Shake	1964	2.00	4.00	8.00
FEDERAL					
❑ 12408	Two Below Zero/Sharp Harp	1961	3.00	6.00	12.00
GROOVE					
❑ 0171	Lonely Road Blues/When I Get Married	1956	10.00	20.00	40.00
—With Mr. Bear					
KING					
❑ 4695	Hard Feeling/Walking Upside Your Head	1954	7.50	15.00	30.00
❑ 4706	Camille/Rub a Little Boogie	1954	7.50	15.00	30.00
❑ 4779	Blues for Everybody/Two Below Zero	1955	7.50	15.00	30.00
❑ 4797	Let the Doorbell Ring/Harelip Blues	1955	7.50	15.00	30.00
❑ 4812	Walking the Blues/Daybreak Rock	1955	7.50	15.00	30.00
—B-side by Mr. Bear and the Bearcats					
❑ 4827	That's My Pa/Stumbling Block	1955	7.50	15.00	30.00
❑ 4859	Silent Partner/She Cooks Me Cabbage	1955	7.50	15.00	30.00
❑ 4876	Me and My Mule/Failing Health Blues	1956	7.50	15.00	30.00
❑ 4906	So Sorry, So Sorry/Overhead	1956	7.50	15.00	30.00
❑ 4938	Big Leg Woman/Mail Order Woman	1956	7.50	15.00	30.00
❑ 6299	Blues for Everybody/Tongue-Tied Blues	1970	—	3.00	6.00
RED ROBIN					
❑ 109	Stumblin' Block Blues/Number Nine Blues	1952	100.00	200.00	400.00
❑ 112	Shake Baby Shake/Highway Blues	1952	50.00	100.00	200.00
❑ 130	Drunk Again/Shim Sham Shimmy	1954	50.00	100.00	200.00
VIK					
❑ 0260	Just Like a Woman/Dirty Woman	1957	10.00	20.00	40.00
❑ 0279	Old Time Rock and Roll/Rocky Mountain	1957	10.00	20.00	40.00
❑ 0304	Shake Baby Shake/Lollipop Baby	1957	10.00	20.00	40.00
Albums					
ATLANTIC					
❑ 8019 [M]	Blues from the Gutter	1959	37.50	75.00	150.00
—Black label					
❑ 8019 [M]	Blues from the Gutter	1960	12.50	25.00	50.00
—White "fan" logo at right of label					
❑ 8019 [M]	Blues from the Gutter	1963	5.00	10.00	20.00
—Black "fan" logo at right of label					
❑ SD 8019 [S]	Blues from the Gutter	1959	50.00	100.00	200.00
—Green label					
❑ SD 8019 [S]	Blues from the Gutter	1960	15.00	30.00	60.00
—Green and blue label, white "fan" logo at right of label					
❑ SD 8019 [S]	Blues from the Gutter	1963	6.25	12.50	25.00
—Green and blue label, black "fan" logo at right of label					
❑ 8045 [M]	Natural and Soulful Blues	1961	12.50	25.00	50.00
—White "fan" logo at right of label					
❑ 8045 [M]	Natural and Soulful Blues	1963	5.00	10.00	20.00
—Black "fan" logo at right of label					
❑ SD 8045 [S]	Natural and Soulful Blues	1961	15.00	30.00	60.00
—Green and blue label, white "fan" logo at right of label					
❑ SD 8045 [S]	Natural and Soulful Blues	1963	6.25	12.50	25.00
—Green and blue label, black "fan" logo at right of label					
❑ 8056 [M]	Champion of the Blues	1961	12.50	25.00	50.00
—White "fan" logo at right of label					
❑ 8056 [M]	Champion of the Blues	1963	5.00	10.00	20.00
—Black "fan" logo at right of label					
❑ SD 8056 [R]	Champion of the Blues	196?	3.75	7.50	15.00
❑ SD 8255	Blues from the Gutter	1970	3.75	7.50	15.00
BLUE HORIZON					
❑ 7702	When You Feel the Feeling	1969	6.25	12.50	25.00
BULLSEYE					
❑ BB-9502	Back Home In New Orleans	1990	3.00	6.00	12.00
CONTINENTAL					
❑ CLP-16002 [M]	Low Down Blues	1961	62.50	125.00	250.00
EVEREST ARCHIVE OF FOLK & JAZZ					
❑ 217	Champion Jack Dupree	197?	2.50	5.00	10.00
FOLKWAYS					
❑ FS-3825 [M]	Women Blues of Champion Jack Dupree	1961	6.25	12.50	25.00
GNP CRESCENDO					
❑ GNPS-10001	Tricks	1974	3.00	6.00	12.00
❑ GNPS-10005	Happy to Be Free	1974	3.00	6.00	12.00
❑ GNPS-10013	Legacy of Blues 3	197?	3.00	6.00	12.00
JAZZ MAN					
❑ BLZ-5501	Champion Jack Dupree	1982	2.50	5.00	10.00

Number	Title (A Side/B Side)	Yr	VG	VG+	NM
KING					
❑ 735 [M]	Champion Jack Dupree Sings the Blues	1961	75.00	150.00	300.00
❑ KS-1084	Walking the Blues	1970	3.75	7.50	15.00
LONDON					
❑ PS 553	From New Orleans to Chicago	1969	5.00	10.00	20.00
OKEH					
❑ OKM 12103 [M]	Cabbage Greens	1963	7.50	15.00	30.00
STORYVILLE					
❑ 4010	Best of the Blues	1982	2.50	5.00	10.00
❑ 4040	I'm Growing Older Every Day	198?	2.50	5.00	10.00

DUPREE, CHAMPION JACK, AND MICKEY BAKER Also see each artist's individual listings.
Albums

Number	Title (A Side/B Side)	Yr	VG	VG+	NM
SIRE					
❑ SES-97010	In Heavy Blues	1969	7.50	15.00	30.00

DUPREE, CHAMPION JACK, AND JIMMY RUSHING
Albums

Number	Title (A Side/B Side)	Yr	VG	VG+	NM
AUDIO LAB					
❑ AL-1512 [M]	Two Shades of Blue	1958	50.00	100.00	200.00

DUPREE, DAVE See DAVE BURGESS.

DUPREE, SIMON, AND THE BIG SOUND
45s

Number	Title (A Side/B Side)	Yr	VG	VG+	NM
TOWER					
❑ 427	Daytime, Night Time/I've Seen It All Before	1968	2.00	4.00	8.00
Albums					
TOWER					
❑ ST-5097 [S]	Without Reservations	1968	10.00	20.00	40.00
❑ T-5097 [M]	Without Reservations	1968	25.00	50.00	100.00

DUPREES, THE
45s

Number	Title (A Side/B Side)	Yr	VG	VG+	NM
COED					
❑ 569	You Belong to Me/Take Me As I Am	1962	5.00	10.00	20.00
❑ 571	My Own True Love/Ginny	1962	5.00	10.00	20.00
❑ 574	I'd Rather Be Here in Your Arms/I Wish I Could Believe You	1963	3.75	7.50	15.00
❑ 576	Gone with the Wind/Let's Make Love Again	1963	3.75	7.50	15.00
❑ 580	I Gotta Tell Her Now/Take Me As I Am	1963	3.75	7.50	15.00
❑ 584	Why Don't You Believe Me/My Dearest One	1963	3.75	7.50	15.00
❑ 584	Why Don't You Believe Me/The Things I Love	1963	7.50	15.00	30.00
❑ 585	Have You Heard/Love Eyes	1963	3.75	7.50	15.00
❑ 587	(It's No) Sin/The Sand and the Sea	1964	3.75	7.50	15.00
❑ 591	Please Let Her Know/Where Are You	1964	3.75	7.50	15.00
❑ 593	Unbelievable/So Many Have Told Me	1964	3.75	7.50	15.00
❑ 595	So Little Time/It Isn't Fair	1964	3.75	7.50	15.00
❑ 596	I'm Yours/Wishing Ring	1964	3.75	7.50	15.00
COLOSSUS					
❑ 110	Check Yourself/The Sky's the Limit	1970	—	3.00	6.00
—As "The Italian Asphalt and Pavement Company" or "The I.A.P. Co." for short					
❑ 110 [PS]	Check Yourself/The Sky's the Limit	1970	—	3.00	6.00
—As "The Italian Asphalt and Pavement Company" or "The I.A.P. Co." for short					
COLUMBIA					
❑ 43336	Around the Corner/They Said It Couldn't Be Done	1965	3.00	6.00	12.00
❑ 43464	Norma Jean/She Waits for Him	1965	3.00	6.00	12.00
❑ 43577	The Exodus Song/Let Them Talk	1966	3.00	6.00	12.00
❑ 43802	It's Not Time Now/Don't Want to Have to Do It	1966	2.50	5.00	10.00
❑ 44078	Be My Love/I Understand	1967	2.50	5.00	10.00
HERITAGE					
❑ 804	My Special Angel/Ring of Love	1968	2.50	5.00	10.00
❑ 805	Goodnight My Love/Ring of Love	1968	2.50	5.00	10.00
❑ 805 [PS]	Goodnight My Love/Ring of Love	1968	5.00	10.00	20.00
❑ 808	My Love, My Love/The Sky's the Limit	1968	2.50	5.00	10.00
❑ 808 [PS]	My Love, My Love/The Sky's the Limit	1968	5.00	10.00	20.00
❑ 811	Two Different Worlds/Hope	1969	2.50	5.00	10.00
❑ 811 [PS]	Two Different Worlds/Hope	1969	5.00	10.00	20.00
❑ 826	Have You Heard/My Love, My Love	1970	2.50	5.00	10.00
LOST-NITE					
❑ 165	You Belong to Me/Take Me As I Am	196?	—	3.00	6.00
—Reissue					
❑ 225	Why Don't You Believe Me/My Dearest One	196?	—	2.50	5.00
—Reissue					
❑ 228	Have You Heard/It Isn't Fair	196?	—	2.50	5.00
—Reissue					
❑ 232	Gone with the Wind/Let's Make Love Again	196?	—	2.50	5.00
—Reissue					
❑ 236	My Own True Love/Ginny	196?	—	2.50	5.00
—Reissue					
RCA VICTOR					
❑ PB-10407	The Sky's the Limit/Delicious	1975	2.50	5.00	10.00
Albums					
COED					
❑ LPC-905 [M]	You Belong to Me	1962	75.00	150.00	300.00
❑ LPC-906 [M]	Have You Heard	1963	50.00	100.00	200.00
COLLECTABLES					
❑ COL-5008	The Best of the Duprees	198?	3.00	6.00	12.00
COLOSSUS					
❑ 5000	Duprees Gold	1970	7.50	15.00	30.00
—As "The Italian Asphalt & Pavement Co."					
HERITAGE					
❑ HT-35002 [M]	Total Recall	1968	20.00	40.00	80.00
—Mono is promo only; in stereo cover with "DJ Monaural" sticker on front					
❑ HTS-35002 [S]	Total Recall	1968	7.50	15.00	30.00
POST					
❑ 1000	The Duprees Sing	196?	7.50	15.00	30.00

DURANTE, JIMMY
45s

Number	Title (A Side/B Side)	Yr	VG	VG+	NM
DECCA					
❑ 9-11046	Start Off Each Day with a Song/Inka Dinka Doo	195?	3.00	6.00	12.00
—"Collector's Classics" reissue; A-side with Eddie Jackson					
❑ 9-11046 [PS]	Start Off Each Day with a Song/Inka Dinka Doo	195?	3.75	7.50	15.00

Number	Title (A Side/B Side)	Yr	VG	VG+	NM
MGM					
❏ 30257	Frosty The Snowman/ Christmas Comes But Once A Year	1950	3.75	7.50	15.00
WARNER BROS.					
❏ 5382	September Song/Young at Heart	1963	2.00	4.00	8.00
❏ 5410	Hello Young Lovers/This Is All I Ask	1964	2.00	4.00	8.00
❏ 5456	This Train/When Love Flies Out the Window	1964	2.00	4.00	8.00
❏ 5483	Old Man Time/I Came Here to Swim	1964	2.00	4.00	8.00
❏ 5686	(I Wonder) What Became of Life/One of Those Songs	1965	2.00	4.00	8.00
❏ 5823	Mame/We're Going UFO'ing	1966	3.00	6.00	12.00
❏ 5843	Bill Bailey (Won't You Please Come Home)/ Margie	1966	2.00	4.00	8.00
❏ 7024	Hellzapoppin'/M.F. O'Brien	1967	—	3.00	6.00
❏ 7253	He Touched Me/Amen	1968	—	3.00	6.00
❏ 7367	He Ain't Heavy, He's My Brother/ Look Ahead Little Girl	1970	—	3.00	6.00
Albums					
DECCA					
❏ DL 5116 [10]	Jimmy Durante	195?	12.50	25.00	50.00
❏ DL 8884 [M]	Jimmy Durante at the Piano	1959	3.75	7.50	15.00
❏ DL 9049 [M]	Club Durant	195?	6.25	12.50	25.00
❏ DL 78884 [S]	Jimmy Durante at the Piano	1959	5.00	10.00	20.00
LION					
❏ L-70053 [M]	Jimmy Durante in Person	195?	7.50	15.00	30.00
MGM					
❏ E-3242 [M]	Jimmy Durante in Person	1955	7.50	15.00	30.00
❏ E-4207 [M]	The Very Best of Jimmy Durante	1964	3.00	6.00	12.00
❏ SE-4207 [S]	The Very Best of Jimmy Durante	1964	3.75	7.50	15.00
ROULETTE					
❏ R-25123 [M]	Jimmy Durante at the Copacabana	1961	5.00	10.00	20.00
❏ SR-25123 [S]	Jimmy Durante at the Copacabana	1961	6.25	12.50	25.00
WARNER BROS.					
❏ W 1506 [M]	September Song	1963	3.75	7.50	15.00
❏ WS 1506 [S]	September Song	1963	5.00	10.00	20.00
❏ W 1531 [M]	Hello Young Lovers	1964	3.75	7.50	15.00
❏ WS 1531 [S]	Hello Young Lovers	1964	5.00	10.00	20.00
❏ W 1577 [M]	Jimmy Durante's Way of Life	1965	3.75	7.50	15.00
❏ WS 1577 [S]	Jimmy Durante's Way of Life	1965	5.00	10.00	20.00
❏ W 1655 [M]	One of Those Songs	1966	3.75	7.50	15.00
❏ WS 1655 [S]	One of Those Songs	1966	5.00	10.00	20.00
❏ W 1713 [M]	Songs for Sunday	1967	3.75	7.50	15.00
❏ WS 1713 [S]	Songs for Sunday	1967	5.00	10.00	20.00

DUSK With Peggy Santaglia of THE ANGELS.
45s

Number	Title (A Side/B Side)	Yr	VG	VG+	NM
BELL					
❏ 961	Angel Baby/If We Just Leave Today	1971	—	3.00	6.00
❏ 961	Angel Baby/Reach Out and Speak My Name	1971	—	3.00	6.00
❏ 990	I Hear Those Church Bells Ringing/ I Cannot See to See You	1971	—	3.00	6.00
❏ 45148	Suburbia U.S.A./ Treat Me Like a Good Piece of Candy	1971	—	3.00	6.00
❏ 45207	Point of No Return/(B-side unknown)	1972	—	3.00	6.00

DUST
45s

Number	Title (A Side/B Side)	Yr	VG	VG+	NM
KAMA SUTRA					
❏ 534	Stone Woman/(B-side unknown)	1971	—	3.00	6.00
❏ 541	Love Me Hard/(B-side unknown)	1972	—	3.00	6.00
Albums					
KAMA SUTRA					
❏ KSBS-2041	Dust	1971	6.25	12.50	25.00
—Pink label					
❏ KSBS-2059	Hard Attack	1972	6.25	12.50	25.00
—Pink label					

DUSTERS, THE (1)
45s

Number	Title (A Side/B Side)	Yr	VG	VG+	NM
ABC-PARAMOUNT					
❏ 9887	Pretty Girl/Coolation	1958	7.50	15.00	30.00
CUPID					
❏ 5003	Rock at the Hop/She's Mine	1958	17.50	35.00	70.00
GLORY					
❏ 287	Darling Love/Teen-Age Jamboree	1958	12.50	25.00	50.00

DUSTERS, THE (2) TOMMY TUCKER was a member of this group.
45s

Number	Title (A Side/B Side)	Yr	VG	VG+	NM
ARC					
❏ 3000	Give Me Time/Sallie Mae	1956	75.00	150.00	300.00

DUVALL, HUELYN
45s

Number	Title (A Side/B Side)	Yr	VG	VG+	NM
CHALLENGE					
❏ 1012	Teen Queen/Comin' or Goin'	1957	7.50	15.00	30.00
—Maroon label					
❏ 1012	Teen Queen/Comin' or Goin'	1957	25.00	50.00	100.00
—Blue label					
❏ 59002	Hum-Dinger/You Knock Me Out	1958	7.50	15.00	30.00
❏ 59014	Little Boy Blue/Three Months to Kill	1958	10.00	20.00	40.00
❏ 59025	Friday Night on a Dollar Bill/Juliette	1958	7.50	15.00	30.00
❏ 59069	Pucker Paint/Boom Boom Baby	1960	7.50	15.00	30.00

DYKE AND THE BLAZERS
45s

Number	Title (A Side/B Side)	Yr	VG	VG+	NM
ARTCO					
❏ 45-101	Funky Broadway — Part 1/ Funky Broadway — Part 2	1966	25.00	50.00	100.00
ORIGINAL SOUND					
❏ 64	Funky Broadway — Part 1/ Funky Broadway — Part 2	1966	2.50	5.00	10.00
❏ 69	So Sharp/Don't Bug Me	1967	2.00	4.00	8.00
❏ 79	Funky Walk Part 1 — East/Funky Walk Part 2 — West	1967	2.00	4.00	8.00
❏ 83	Funky Bull — Part 1/Funky Bull — Part 2	1968	2.00	4.00	8.00
❏ 86	We Got More Soul/Shotgun Slim	1969	2.00	4.00	8.00
❏ 89	Let a Woman Be a Woman — Let a Man Be a Man/Uhh	1969	2.00	4.00	8.00
❏ 90	You Are My Sunshine/City Dump	1969	2.00	4.00	8.00
❏ 91	Uhh/My Sister's and My Brother's Day Is Coming	1970	2.00	4.00	8.00
❏ 96	Runaway People/I'm So All Alone	1970	2.00	4.00	8.00
Albums					
ORIGINAL SOUND					
❏ LP 8876 [M]	The Funky Broadway	1967	12.50	25.00	50.00
❏ LPS 8876 [S]	The Funky Broadway	1967	18.75	37.50	75.00
❏ LPS 8877	Dyke's Greatest Hits	1968	18.75	37.50	75.00

DYLAN, BOB Also see HARRY BELAFONTE; GEORGE HARRISON AND FRIENDS; CAROLYN HESTER.
12-Inch Singles

Number	Title (A Side/B Side)	Yr	VG	VG+	NM
COLUMBIA					
❏ CAS 2169 [DJ]	When the Night Comes Falling from the Sky (Edit) (same on both sides)	1985	2.50	5.00	10.00

45s

Number	Title (A Side/B Side)	Yr	VG	VG+	NM
ASYLUM					
❏ 11033	On a Night Like This/You Angel You	1974	—	3.00	6.00
❏ 11035	Something There Is About You/Going, Going, Gone	1974	—	3.00	6.00
❏ 11043	Most Likely You Go Your Way (And I'll Go Mine)/Stage Fright	1974	—	3.00	6.00
—With The Band					
❏ 45212	All Along the Watchtower/It Ain't Me Babe	1974	3.00	6.00	12.00
COLUMBIA					
❏ AE 25 [DJ]	All the Tired Horses (mono/stereo)	1970	10.00	20.00	40.00
❏ AE7 1039 [DJ]	If Not for You/Tomorrow Is a Long Time	1971	10.00	20.00	40.00
❏ 02510	Heart of Mine/ The Groom's Still Waiting at the Altar	1981	—	2.00	4.00
❏ 02510 [PS]	Heart of Mine/ The Groom's Still Waiting at the Altar	1981	—	2.50	5.00
❏ 04301	Sweetheart Like You/Union Sundown	1983	—	2.00	4.00
❏ 04301 [PS]	Sweetheart Like You/Union Sundown	1983	—	2.50	5.00
❏ 04425	Jokerman/Isis	1984	—	2.50	5.00
❏ 04933	Tight Connection to My Heart (Has Anybody Seen My Love)/We Better Talk This Over	1985	—	2.00	4.00
❏ 04933 [PS]	Tight Connection to My Heart (Has Anybody Seen My Love)/We Better Talk This Over	1985	—	2.00	4.00
❏ 05697	Emotionally Yours/When the Night Comes Falling from the Sky	1985	—	2.00	4.00
❏ 07970	Silvio/Too Far from Home	1988	—	2.50	5.00
❏ 10106	Tangled Up in Blue/If You See Her Say Hello	1975	—	3.00	6.00
❏ 10217	Million Dollar Bash/Tears of Rage	1975	2.50	5.00	10.00
❏ 10245	Hurricane (Part 1)/Hurricane (Part 2)	1975	—	3.00	6.00
❏ 10245 [DJ]	Hurricane (mono/stereo)	1975	3.75	7.50	15.00
—Plays at 33 1/3 rpm; has "Special Rush Reservice" on label					
❏ 10245 [DJ]	Hurricane (mono/stereo)	1975	5.00	10.00	20.00
—Plays at 33 1/3 rpm; does not have "Special Rush Reservice" on label					
❏ 10245 [PS]	Hurricane (Part 1)/Hurricane (Part 2)	1975	3.00	6.00	12.00
❏ 10245 [PS]	Hurricane (mono/stereo)	1975	3.75	7.50	15.00
—Special sleeve for above record					
❏ 10298	Mozambique/Oh, Sister	1976	—	3.00	6.00
❏ 10454	Stuck Inside of Mobile with the Memphis Blues Again/Rita Mae	1976	—	2.50	5.00
❏ 10454 [PS]	Stuck Inside of Mobile with the Memphis Blues Again/Rita Mae	1976	—	3.00	6.00
❏ 10805	Baby Stop Crying/New Pony	1978	—	2.50	5.00
❏ 10851	Changing of the Guards/Senor (Tales of Yankee Power)	1978	—	2.00	4.00
❏ 10851 [DJ]	Changing of the Guards (Short 3:39)/(Long 6:36)	1978	2.00	4.00	8.00
❏ 11072	Gotta Serve Somebody/Trouble in Mind	1979	—	2.00	4.00
❏ 11168	Man Gave Names to All the Animals/When You Gonna Wake Up	1979	—	2.00	4.00
❏ 11235	Slow Train/ Do Right to Me Baby (Do Unto Others)	1980	—	2.00	4.00
❏ 11235 [PS]	Slow Train/ Do Right to Me Baby (Do Unto Others)	1980	—	2.50	5.00
❏ 11318	Solid Rock/Covenant Woman	1980	—	2.00	4.00
❏ 11370	Saved/Are You Ready	1980	6.25	12.50	25.00
—Scarce on stock copy (promos worth about 20%)					
❏ CS7 32660 [DJ]	Tweedle Dee & Tweedle Dum/Bye & Bye	2001	2.50	5.00	10.00
—Promo only on red label with black cardboard sleeve					
❏ 4-33100	Like a Rolling Stone/ Rainy Day Women #12 and 35	196?	—	2.50	5.00
—"Hall of Fame" reissue; red and black label					
❏ 4-33178	Lay Lady Lay/I Threw It All Away	1970	—	2.50	5.00
—"Hall of Fame" reissue; red and black label					
❏ 13-33221	Positively 4th Street/Subterranean Home Sick Blues	198?	—	2.50	5.00
—Gray label; "Home Sick" is two words on label					
❏ 4-33221	Positively 4th Street/ Subterranean Home Sick Blues	197?	—	3.00	6.00
—"Hall of Fame" reissue; red and black label					
❏ 42656	Mixed-Up Confusion/Corrina, Corrina	1962	500.00	1000.	1500.
—Orange label					
❏ 42656 [DJ]	Mixed-Up Confusion/Corrina, Corrina	1962	125.00	250.00	500.00
—White label					
❏ 42856	Blowin' in the Wind/ Don't Think Twice, It's All Right	1963	125.00	250.00	500.00
❏ 42856 [DJ]	Blowin' in the Wind/ Don't Think Twice, It's All Right	1963	75.00	150.00	300.00
—Regular promo					
❏ 42856 [PS]	Blowin' in the Wind/ Don't Think Twice, It's All Right	1963	200.00	400.00	800.00
—"Rebel with a Cause" promotional flyer					
❏ 43242	Subterranean Homesick Blues/ She Belongs to Me	1965	5.00	10.00	20.00
❏ 43242 [DJ]	Subterranean Homesick Blues/ (same on both sides)	1965	62.50	125.00	250.00
—Promo only on red vinyl					
❏ 43242 [PS]	Subterranean Homesick Blues/ She Belongs to Me	1965	500.00	1000.	1500.
—Only issued with some promos					

Number	Title (A Side/B Side)	Yr	VG	VG+	NM
❏ 43242	Subterranean Homesick Blues/				
	She Belongs to Me	1972	7.50	15.00	30.00

—Briefly issued on gray label, which was used for about six months in 1972

Number	Title (A Side/B Side)	Yr	VG	VG+	NM
❏ 43346	Like a Rolling Stone/Gates of Eden	1965	5.00	10.00	20.00
❏ 43346 [DJ]	Like a Rolling Stone (same on both sides)	1965	50.00	100.00	200.00

—Promo only on red vinyl

| ❏ 43389 | Positively 4th Street/From a Buick 6 | 1965 | 5.00 | 10.00 | 20.00 |

—Standard version

| ❏ 43389 | Positively 4th Street/From a Buick 6 | 1965 | 7.50 | 15.00 | 30.00 |

—Odd version, possibly pressed for export, that plays at 45 but has a small center hole

| ❏ 43389 | Positively 4th Street/From a Buick 6 | 1965 | 37.50 | 75.00 | 150.00 |

—A-side contains alternate version of "Can You Please Crawl Out Your Window." Evidently must be heard to identify.

| ❏ 43389 [DJ] | Positively 4th Street/From a Buick 6 | 1965 | 30.00 | 60.00 | 120.00 |

—A-side contains alternate version of "Can You Please Crawl Out Your Window." Evidently must be heard to identify.

| ❏ 43389 | Positively 4th Street/From a Buick 6 | 1972 | 6.25 | 12.50 | 25.00 |

—Briefly issued on gray label, which was used for about six months in 1972

| ❏ 43389 [DJ] | Positively 4th Street (same on both sides) | 1965 | 37.50 | 75.00 | 150.00 |

—Promo only on red vinyl

❏ 43389 [PS]	Positively 4th Street/From a Buick 6	1965	17.50	35.00	70.00
❏ 43477	Can You Please Crawl Out Your Window?/				
	Highway 61 Revisited	1965	5.00	10.00	20.00
❏ 43541	One of Us Must Know (Sooner or Later)/				
	Queen Jane Approximately	1966	5.00	10.00	20.00
❏ 43592	Rainy Day Women #12 and 35/				
	Pledging My Time	1966	3.75	7.50	15.00
❏ 43592 [DJ]	Rainy Day Women #12 and 35				
	(same on both sides)	1966	37.50	75.00	150.00
❏ 43683	I Want You/Just Like Tom Thumb's Blues (Live)	1966	3.75	7.50	15.00
❏ 43683 [DJ]	I Want You (same on both sides)	1966	37.50	75.00	150.00

—Promo only on red vinyl

❏ 43683 [PS]	I Want You/Just Like Tom Thumb's Blues (Live)	1966	20.00	40.00	80.00
❏ 43792	Just Like a Woman/Obviously 5 Believers	1966	3.75	7.50	15.00
❏ 44069	Leopard-Skin Pill-Box Hat/Most Likely You'll Go				
	Your Way and I'll Go Mine	1967	5.00	10.00	20.00
❏ 44826	I Threw It All Away/Drifter's Escape	1969	2.00	4.00	8.00
❏ 44926	Lay Lady Lay/Peggy Day	1969	2.00	4.00	8.00
❏ 45004	Tonight I'll Be Staying Here with You/Country Pie	1969	2.50	5.00	10.00
❏ 45199	Wigwam/Copper Kettle (The Pale Moonlight)	1970	—	3.00	6.00

—Orange label with "Columbia" background print

| ❏ 45199 | Wigwam/Copper Kettle (The Pale Moonlight) | 1970 | — | 3.00 | 6.00 |

—Red label, "Columbia" repeated around outside of label

| ❏ 45199 | Wigwam/Copper Kettle (The Pale Moonlight) | 1970 | — | 3.00 | 6.00 |

—Red label, black print

❏ 45409	Watching the River Flow/Spanish Is the Loving				
	Tongue	1971	—	3.00	6.00
❏ 45516	George Jackson (Acoustic Version)/George				
	Jackson (Big Band Version)	1971	2.50	5.00	10.00
❏ 45913	Knockin' on Heaven's Door/Turkey Chase	1973	—	2.50	5.00
❏ 45982	A Fool Such As I/Lily of the West	1973	—	3.00	6.00
❏ 73042	Everything Is Broken/Dead Man, Dead Man	1989	2.00	4.00	8.00
❏ JZSP 75606/7 [DJ]	Blowin' in the Wind/Don't Think Twice, It's All				
	Right	1963	75.00	150.00	300.00

—"Special Album Excerpt" promo

❏ JZSP 110939/40 [DJ]	Like a Rolling Stone (Part 1)/Like a Rolling				
	Stone (Part 2)	1965	15.00	30.00	60.00
❏ JZSP 113096/147 [DJ]	One Of Us Must Know (Sooner or Later)				
	(4:49)/(3:07)	1966	25.00	50.00	100.00

—Promo only, long and short versions

MCA

| ❏ 52811 | Band of the Hand/Theme from Joe's Death | 1986 | — | — | 3.00 |

—By "Bob Dylan and the Heartbreakers"

| ❏ 52811 [PS] | Band of the Hand/Theme from Joe's Death | 1986 | — | — | 3.00 |

Albums

ASYLUM

| ❏ AB-201 [(2)] | Before the Flood | 1974 | 5.00 | 10.00 | 20.00 |
| ❏ AB-201 [(2)DJ] | Before the Flood | 1974 | 12.50 | 25.00 | 50.00 |

—White label promo

| ❏ 7E-1003 | Planet Waves | 1974 | 3.75 | 7.50 | 15.00 |

—Without wraparound (olive green) second cover

| ❏ 7E-1003 | Planet Waves | 1974 | 5.00 | 10.00 | 20.00 |

—With wraparound (olive green) second cover

| ❏ 7E-1003 [DJ] | Planet Waves | 1974 | 12.50 | 25.00 | 50.00 |

—White label promo

| ❏ 7E-1003 [DJ] | Ceremonies of the Horsemen | 1974 | 1500. | 2250. | 3000. |

—Original title of "Planet Waves"; no records were pressed with this title, but never-glued covers exist, of which 3 or 4 are known. Value is for one of these covers.

| ❏ EQ-1003 [Q] | Planet Waves | 1974 | 12.50 | 25.00 | 50.00 |

COLUMBIA

| ❏ C2L 41 [(2)M] | Blonde on Blonde | 1966 | 25.00 | 50.00 | 100.00 |

—"Female photos" inner gatefold with two women pictured

| ❏ C2L 41 [(2)M] | Blonde on Blonde | 1966 | 250.00 | 500.00 | 1000. |

—White label promo

| ❏ C2L 41 [(2)M] | Blonde on Blonde | 1968 | 75.00 | 150.00 | 300.00 |

—No photos of women inside gatefold

| ❏ AS 422 [DJ] | Renaldo and Clara | 1976 | 12.50 | 25.00 | 50.00 |

—Promo-only sampler from the movie. Authentic copies have a sticker on a white cover; counterfeits have the title printed on the cover

| ❏ AS 798 [DJ] | Saved | 1980 | 6.25 | 12.50 | 25.00 |

—Promo sampler from LP

| ❏ C2S 841 [(2)S] | Blonde on Blonde | 1966 | 15.00 | 30.00 | 60.00 |

—"Female photos" inner gatefold with two women pictured

| ❏ C2S 841 [(2)S] | Blonde on Blonde | 1968 | 7.50 | 15.00 | 30.00 |

—No photos of women inside gatefold; "360 Sound Stereo" on label

| ❏ C2S 841 [(2)S] | Blonde on Blonde | 1970 | 3.75 | 7.50 | 15.00 |

—Orange label

❏ CG 841 [(2)S]	Blonde on Blonde	198?	3.00	6.00	12.00
❏ AS 1259 [DJ]	The Dylan London Interview, July 1981	1981	6.25	12.50	25.00
❏ AS 1471 [DJ]	Electric Lunch	1982	6.25	12.50	25.00

—Promo-only sampler

| ❏ AS 1770 [DJ] | Infidels | 1983 | 5.00 | 10.00 | 20.00 |

—Promo-only sampler

| ❏ CL 1779 [M] | Bob Dylan | 1962 | 62.50 | 125.00 | 250.00 |

—Black and red (not orange) label with six white "eye" logos, three at 9 o'clock, three at 3 o'clock; stock copy

Number	Title (A Side/B Side)	Yr	VG	VG+	NM
❏ CL 1779 [M]	Bob Dylan	1962	125.00	250.00	500.00

—Six "eye" logos on label; "A New Star on Columbia" sticker on cover and promo stamp on label

| ❏ CL 1779 [M] | Bob Dylan | 1963 | 10.00 | 20.00 | 40.00 |

—"Guaranteed High Fidelity" on label

| ❏ CL 1779 [M] | Bob Dylan | 1966 | 7.50 | 15.00 | 30.00 |

—"Mono" on label

| ❏ CL 1986 [M] | The Freewheelin' Bob Dylan | 1963 | 10.00 | 20.00 | 40.00 |

—"Guaranteed High Fidelity" on label; corrected version (record plays what label says)

| ❏ CL 1986 [M] | The Freewheelin' Bob Dylan | 1963 | 125.00 | 250.00 | 500.00 |

—White label promo; label AND timing strip list, and record plays, "correct" tracks

| ❏ CL 1986 [M] | The Freewheelin' Bob Dylan | 1963 | 200.00 | 400.00 | 800.00 |

—White label promo; timing strip lists deleted tracks; label lists, and record plays, "correct" tracks

| ❏ CL 1986 [M] | The Freewheelin' Bob Dylan | 1963 | 500.00 | 1000. | 2000. |

—White label promo; label lists deleted tracks; timing strip lists, and record plays, "correct" tracks

| ❏ CL 1986 [M] | The Freewheelin' Bob Dylan | 1963 | 1000. | 2000. | 3000. |

—White label promo; label and timing strip list the deleted tracks but record plays the "correct" tracks

| ❏ CL 1986 [M] | The Freewheelin' Bob Dylan | 1963 | 4000. | 8000. | 12000. |

—"Guaranteed High Fidelity" on label; plays "Let Me Die in My Footsteps," "Rocks and Gravel," "Talkin' John Birch Blues" and "Gamblin' Willie's Dead Man's Hand." Label does NOT list these. In dead wax, matrix number ends in "--1" followed by a letter

| ❏ CL 1986 [M] | The Freewheelin' Bob Dylan | 1966 | 7.50 | 15.00 | 30.00 |

—"Mono" on label

| ❏ CL 2105 [M] | The Times They Are a-Changin' | 1964 | 10.00 | 20.00 | 40.00 |

—"Guaranteed High Fidelity" on label

| ❏ CL 2105 [M] | The Times They Are a-Changin' | 1964 | 100.00 | 200.00 | 400.00 |

—White label promo

| ❏ CL 2105 [M] | The Times They Are a-Changin' | 1965 | 7.50 | 15.00 | 30.00 |

—"Mono" on label

| ❏ CL 2193 [M] | Another Side of Bob Dylan | 1964 | 10.00 | 20.00 | 40.00 |

—"Guaranteed High Fidelity" on label

| ❏ CL 2193 [M] | Another Side of Bob Dylan | 1964 | 100.00 | 200.00 | 400.00 |

—White label promo

| ❏ CL 2193 [M] | Another Side of Bob Dylan | 1965 | 7.50 | 15.00 | 30.00 |

—"Mono" on label

| ❏ CAS 2222 [DJ] | Time Passes Slowly | 1985 | 6.25 | 12.50 | 25.00 |

—Promo-only sampler from Biograph box set

| ❏ CL 2302/CS 9102 | Bob Dylan In Concert | 1965 | 2000. | 3000. | 4000. |

—Never pressed; value is for a cover slick, some of which were printed

| ❏ CL 2328 [M] | Bringing It All Back Home | 1965 | 7.50 | 15.00 | 30.00 |

—"Mono" on label

| ❏ CL 2328 [M] | Bringing It All Back Home | 1965 | 12.50 | 25.00 | 50.00 |

—"Guaranteed High Fidelity" on label

| ❏ CL 2328 [M] | Bringing It All Back Home | 1965 | 75.00 | 150.00 | 300.00 |

—White label promo

| ❏ CL 2389 [M] | Highway 61 Revisited | 1965 | 20.00 | 40.00 | 80.00 |
| ❏ CL 2389 [M] | Highway 61 Revisited | 1965 | 100.00 | 200.00 | 400.00 |

—White label promo

| ❏ 2663/9463 | Bob Dylan's Greatest Hits Poster | 1967 | — | 2.00 | 4.00 |

—Almost every copy into the late 1970s came with a poster

❏ KCL 2663 [M]	Bob Dylan's Greatest Hits	1967	12.50	25.00	50.00
❏ CL 2804 [M]	John Wesley Harding	1968	37.50	75.00	150.00
❏ CS 8579 [S]	Bob Dylan	1962	100.00	200.00	400.00

—Red and black label with six white "eye" logos, three together at the left, three together at the right; stock copy

| ❏ CS 8579 [S] | Bob Dylan | 1962 | 150.00 | 300.00 | 600.00 |

—Six "eye" logos on label; "A New Star on Columbia" sticker on cover and promo stamp on label

| ❏ CS 8579 [S] | Bob Dylan | 1963 | 10.00 | 20.00 | 40.00 |

—"360 Sound Stereo" in black on label

| ❏ CS 8579 [S] | Bob Dylan | 1965 | 6.25 | 12.50 | 25.00 |

—"360 Sound Stereo" in white on label

| ❏ CS 8579 [S] | Bob Dylan | 1970 | 3.00 | 6.00 | 12.00 |

—Orange label

| ❏ JC 8579 [S] | Bob Dylan | 197? | 2.00 | 4.00 | 8.00 |

—Some copies of this pressing of the above album may have the song "You're No Good" listed on the label as "She's No Good." No extra premium has been attached to this error as yet.

| ❏ KCS 8579 [S] | Bob Dylan | 197? | 2.50 | 5.00 | 10.00 |
| ❏ PC 8579 [S] | Bob Dylan | 198? | 2.00 | 4.00 | 8.00 |

—Budget-line reissue

| ❏ PC 8579 [S] | Bob Dylan | 2001 | 3.00 | 6.00 | 12.00 |

—Reissue on 180-gram vinyl (sealed copies have a sticker indicating this)

| ❏ CS 8786 [S] | The Freewheelin' Bob Dylan | 1963 | 12.50 | 25.00 | 50.00 |

—"360 Sound Stereo" in black on label (no arrows)

| ❏ CS 8786 [S] | The Freewheelin' Bob Dylan | 1963 | 100.00 | 200.00 | 400.00 |

—Canadian pressing with the deleted tracks listed on the front cover. The label lists, and the record plays, the "correct" tracks.

| ❏ CS 8786 [S] | The Freewheelin' Bob Dylan | 1963 | 15000. | 22500. | 30000. |

—"360 Sound Stereo" in black on label (no arrows); record plays, and label lists, "Let Me Die in My Footsteps," "Rocks and Gravel," " Talkin' John Birch Blues" and "Gamblin' Willie's Dead Man's Hand." No known stereo copies play these without listing them, but just in case, check the trail-off for the numbers "XSM-58719-1A" and "XSM-58720-1A." If the number after the dash is "2" or higher, it's the standard version.

| ❏ CS 8786 [S] | The Freewheelin' Bob Dylan | 1964 | 10.00 | 20.00 | 40.00 |

—"360 Sound Stereo" in black on label (with arrows)

| ❏ CS 8786 [S] | The Freewheelin' Bob Dylan | 1965 | 6.25 | 12.50 | 25.00 |

—"360 Sound Stereo" in white on label

| ❏ CS 8786 [S] | The Freewheelin' Bob Dylan | 197? | 250.00 | 500.00 | 1000. |

—Orange label; unauthorized red vinyl pressing

| ❏ CS 8786 [S] | The Freewheelin' Bob Dylan | 1970 | 3.00 | 6.00 | 12.00 |

—Orange label

| ❏ KCS 8786 [S] | The Freewheelin' Bob Dylan | 197? | 2.50 | 5.00 | 10.00 |
| ❏ PC 8786 [S] | The Freewheelin' Bob Dylan | 198? | 2.00 | 4.00 | 8.00 |

—Budget-line reissue

| ❏ PC 8786 [S] | The Freewheelin' Bob Dylan | 2001 | 3.00 | 6.00 | 12.00 |

—Reissue on 180-gram vinyl (sealed copies have a sticker indicating this)

| ❏ CS 8905 [S] | The Times They Are a-Changin' | 1964 | 10.00 | 20.00 | 40.00 |

—"360 Sound Stereo" in black on label

| ❏ CS 8905 [S] | The Times They Are a-Changin' | 1965 | 6.25 | 12.50 | 25.00 |

—"360 Sound Stereo" in white on label

| ❏ CS 8905 [S] | The Times They Are a-Changin' | 1970 | 3.00 | 6.00 | 12.00 |

—Orange label

| ❏ KCS 8905 [S] | The Times They Are a-Changin' | 197? | 2.50 | 5.00 | 10.00 |
| ❏ PC 8905 [S] | The Times They Are a-Changin' | 198? | 2.00 | 4.00 | 8.00 |

—Budget-line reissue

| ❏ PC 8905 [S] | The Times They Are a-Changin' | 2001 | 3.00 | 6.00 | 12.00 |

—Reissue on 180-gram vinyl (sealed copies have a sticker indicating this)

| ❏ CS 8993 [S] | Another Side of Bob Dylan | 1964 | 10.00 | 20.00 | 40.00 |

—"360 Sound Stereo" in black on label

| ❏ CS 8993 [S] | Another Side of Bob Dylan | 1965 | 6.25 | 12.50 | 25.00 |

—"360 Sound Stereo" in white on label

Number	Title (A Side/B Side)	Yr	VG	VG+	NM
❑ CS 8993 [S]	Another Side of Bob Dylan	1970	3.00	6.00	12.00
—Orange label					
❑ KCS 8993 [S]	Another Side of Bob Dylan	197?	2.50	5.00	10.00
❑ PC 8993 [S]	Another Side of Bob Dylan	198?	2.00	4.00	8.00
—Budget-line reissue					
❑ PC 8993 [S]	Another Side of Bob Dylan	2001	3.00	6.00	12.00
—Reissue on 180-gram vinyl (sealed copies have a sticker indicating this)					
❑ CS 9128 [S]	Bringing It All Back Home	1965	6.25	12.50	25.00
—"360 Sound Stereo" in white on label					
❑ CS 9128 [S]	Bringing It All Back Home	1965	10.00	20.00	40.00
—"360 Sound Stereo" in black on label					
❑ CS 9128 [S]	Bringing It All Back Home	1970	3.00	6.00	12.00
—Orange label					
❑ JC 9128 [S]	Bringing It All Back Home	197?	2.50	5.00	10.00
❑ KCS 9128 [S]	Bringing It All Back Home	197?	2.50	5.00	10.00
❑ PC 9128 [S]	Bringing It All Back Home	198?	2.00	4.00	8.00
—Budget-line reissue					
❑ PC 9128 [S]	Bringing It All Back Home	2001	3.00	6.00	12.00
—Reissue on 180-gram vinyl (sealed copies have a sticker indicating this)					
❑ CS 9189 [S]	Highway 61 Revisited	1965	7.50	15.00	30.00
—With "regular" take of "From a Buick 6." Matrix number on Side 1 will end in "--2" or higher, plus a letter; "360 Sound Stereo" on label					
❑ CS 9189 [S]	Highway 61 Revisited	1965	62.50	125.00	250.00
—With alternate take of "From a Buick 6." Matrix number on Side 1 will end in "--1" plus a letter					
❑ CS 9189 [S]	Highway 61 Revisited	1970	3.00	6.00	12.00
—Orange label					
❑ JC 9189 [S]	Highway 61 Revisited	197?	2.50	5.00	10.00
❑ KCS 9189 [S]	Highway 61 Revisited	197?	2.50	5.00	10.00
❑ PC 9189 [S]	Highway 61 Revisited	198?	2.00	4.00	8.00
—Budget-line reissue					
❑ PC 9189 [S]	Highway 61 Revisited	2001	3.00	6.00	12.00
—Reissue on 180-gram vinyl (sealed copies have a sticker indicating this)					
❑ JC 9463 [S]	Bob Dylan's Greatest Hits	197?	2.50	5.00	10.00
❑ JC 9463 [S]	Bob Dylan's Greatest Hits	2001	3.00	6.00	12.00
—Reissue on 180-gram vinyl (sealed copies have a sticker indicating this)					
❑ KCS 9463 [S]	Bob Dylan's Greatest Hits	1967	3.75	7.50	15.00
—"360 Sound Stereo" label					
❑ KCS 9463 [S]	Bob Dylan's Greatest Hits	1970	3.00	6.00	12.00
—Orange label					
❑ CS 9604 [S]	John Wesley Harding	1968	5.00	10.00	20.00
—"360 Sound Stereo" label					
❑ CS 9604 [S]	John Wesley Harding	1970	3.00	6.00	12.00
—Orange label					
❑ JC 9604 [S]	John Wesley Harding	197?	2.50	5.00	10.00
❑ KCS 9604 [S]	John Wesley Harding	197?	2.50	5.00	10.00
❑ PC 9604 [S]	John Wesley Harding	198?	2.00	4.00	8.00
—Budget-line reissue					
❑ PC 9604 [S]	John Wesley Harding	2001	3.00	6.00	12.00
—Reissue on 180-gram vinyl (sealed copies have a sticker indicating this)					
❑ JC 9825	Nashville Skyline	197?	2.50	5.00	10.00
❑ KCS 9825	Nashville Skyline	1969	7.50	15.00	30.00
—"360 Sound Stereo" label					
❑ KCS 9825	Nashville Skyline	1970	3.00	6.00	12.00
—Orange label					
❑ PC 9825	Nashville Skyline	198?	2.00	4.00	8.00
—Budget-line reissue					
❑ C2X 30050 [(2)]	Self Portrait	1970	5.00	10.00	20.00
—Orange labels					
❑ C2X 30050 [(2)]	Self Portrait	1970	37.50	75.00	150.00
—"360 Sound Stereo" labels					
❑ CG 30050 [(2)]	Self Portrait	198?	3.00	6.00	12.00
❑ P2X 30050 [(2)]	Self Portrait	197?	3.75	7.50	15.00
❑ KC 30290	New Morning	1970	3.75	7.50	15.00
❑ PC 30290	New Morning	197?	2.00	4.00	8.00
❑ PC 30290	New Morning	2001	3.00	6.00	12.00
—Reissue on 180-gram vinyl (sealed copies have a sticker indicating this)					
❑ CG 31120 [(2)]	Bob Dylan's Greatest Hits, Vol. II	198?	2.50	5.00	10.00
❑ KG 31120 [(2)]	Bob Dylan's Greatest Hits, Vol. II	1971	3.75	7.50	15.00
❑ PG 31120 [(2)]	Bob Dylan's Greatest Hits, Vol. II	197?	3.00	6.00	12.00
❑ KC 32460	Pat Garrett and Billy the Kid	1973	3.75	7.50	15.00
❑ PC 32460	Pat Garrett and Billy the Kid	197?	2.00	4.00	8.00
❑ PC 32747	Dylan	1973	3.75	7.50	15.00
—No bar code on cover					
❑ PC 32747	Dylan	1979	2.00	4.00	8.00
—With bar code on back cover					
❑ KCQ 32825 [Q]	Nashville Skyline	1973	7.50	15.00	30.00
❑ PC 33235	Blood on the Tracks	1975	3.00	6.00	12.00
—With liner notes on back cover. Original pressings have them, then they were deleted, then restored after they won a Grammy Award! No bar code on cover.					
❑ PC 33235	Blood on the Tracks	1975	3.75	7.50	15.00
—With drawing on back cover and no liner notes. Actually a second pressing, but available only for a short time					
❑ PC 33235 [DJ]	Blood on the Tracks	1975	7.50	15.00	30.00
—Regular white label promo					
❑ PC 33235 [DJ]	Blood on the Tracks	1975	2500.	3750.	5000.
—Test pressing with radically different versions of five songs including "Idiot Wind" and "Tangled Up in Blue"					
❑ PC 33235	Blood on the Tracks	1979	2.00	4.00	8.00
—With bar code on back cover					
❑ PC 33235	Blood on the Tracks	2001	3.00	6.00	12.00
—Reissue on 180-gram vinyl (sealed copies have a sticker indicating this)					
❑ CG 33682 [(2)]	The Basement Tapes	198?	3.00	6.00	12.00
❑ PC2 33682 [(2)]	The Basement Tapes	1975	5.00	10.00	20.00
❑ PC2 33682 [(2)DJ]	The Basement Tapes	1975	10.00	20.00	40.00
—White label promo					
❑ JC 33893	Desire	1977	2.50	5.00	10.00
—No bar code on back cover					
❑ JC 33893	Desire	1979	2.00	4.00	8.00
—With bar code on back cover					
❑ PC 33893	Desire	1976	3.00	6.00	12.00
❑ PC 33893 [DJ]	Desire	1976	7.50	15.00	30.00
—White label promo					
❑ PCQ 33893 [Q]	Desire	1976	7.50	15.00	30.00
❑ JC 34349	Hard Rain	1977	2.50	5.00	10.00
❑ PC 34349	Hard Rain	1976	3.00	6.00	12.00
—No bar code on back cover					
❑ PC 34349 [DJ]	Hard Rain	1976	7.50	15.00	30.00
—White label promo					
❑ PC 34349	Hard Rain	198?	2.00	4.00	8.00
—With bar code on back cover					
❑ JC 35453	Street Legal	1978	3.00	6.00	12.00
❑ JC 35453 [DJ]	Street Legal	1978	6.25	12.50	25.00
—White label promo					
❑ PC 35453	Street Legal	198?	2.00	4.00	8.00
❑ CG 36067 [(2)]	Bob Dylan at Budokan	198?	3.00	6.00	12.00
❑ PC2 36067 [(2)]	Bob Dylan at Budokan	1979	3.75	7.50	15.00
❑ PC2 36067 [(2)DJ]	Bob Dylan at Budokan	1979	7.50	15.00	30.00
—White label promo					
❑ FC 36120	Slow Train Coming	1979	2.50	5.00	10.00
❑ FC 36120 [DJ]	Slow Train Coming	1979	6.25	12.50	25.00
—White label promo					
❑ PC 36120	Slow Train Coming	198?	2.00	4.00	8.00
—Budget-line reissue					
❑ FC 36553	Saved	1980	2.50	5.00	10.00
❑ PC 36553	Saved	198?	2.00	4.00	8.00
—Budget-line reissue with new cover					
❑ PC 37496	Shot of Love	198?	2.00	4.00	8.00
—Budget-line reissue					
❑ TC 37496	Shot of Love	1981	2.50	5.00	10.00
❑ PC 37637	Planet Waves	1981	2.50	5.00	10.00
—Reissue of Asylum 7E-1003					
❑ CG 37661 [(2)]	Before the Flood	1983	3.00	6.00	12.00
—Reissue of Asylum AB-201					
❑ PC 38819	Infidels	1986	2.00	4.00	8.00
—Budget-line reissue					
❑ QC 38819	Infidels	1983	2.50	5.00	10.00
❑ C5X 38830 [(5)]	Biograph	1985	7.50	15.00	30.00
❑ FC 39944	Real Live	1984	2.50	5.00	10.00
❑ FC 40110	Empire Burlesque	1985	2.50	5.00	10.00
❑ OC 40439	Knocked Out Loaded	1986	2.50	5.00	10.00
❑ OC 40957	Down in the Groove	1988	2.50	5.00	10.00
❑ HC 43235	Blood on the Tracks	198?	12.50	25.00	50.00
—Half-speed mastered edition					
❑ OC 45056	Dylan and the Dead	1989	3.00	6.00	12.00
—With backing by The Grateful Dead					
❑ OC 45281	Oh Mercy	1989	3.00	6.00	12.00
❑ C 46794	Under the Red Sky	1990	3.00	6.00	12.00
❑ HC 49825	Nashville Skyline	198?	15.00	30.00	60.00
—Half-speed mastered edition					
❑ C 53200	Good As I Been to You	1992	5.00	10.00	20.00
❑ CK2-65759-1 [(2)]	The Bootleg Series Vol. 4: Bob Dylan Live 1966, The "Royal Albert Hall" Concert	1999	25.00	50.00	100.00
—Classic Records box set with 12x12 booklet and two records individually packaged in cardboard jackets and sleeves					
❑ C2 67000 [(2)]	MTV Unplugged	1995	3.75	7.50	15.00
❑ C2 68556 [(2)]	Time Out of Mind	1998	3.75	7.50	15.00
❑ C2 85975 [(2)]	Love and Theft	2001	3.75	7.50	15.00
❑ C2K-87047-1 [(3)]	The Bootleg Series Vol. 5: Rolling Thunder Revue Starring Bob Dylan	2003	12.50	25.00	50.00
—Similar to the other package, but records are pressed on 140-gram vinyl and come in plain paper (rather than lined) sleeves					
❑ C2K-87047-1 [(3)]	The Bootleg Series Vol. 5: Rolling Thunder Revue Starring Bob Dylan	2003	25.00	50.00	100.00
—Classic Records box set with 12x12 booklet, three 200-gram 12-inch records individually packaged in cardboard jackets and sleeves, a blue vinyl 7-inch single in a picture sleeve, a poster, a souvenir handbill and facsimile tickets to the show					
❑ 474000 [(3)]	Bob Dylan — The 30th Anniversary Concert Celebration	1993	7.50	15.00	30.00
—Albums pressed in US for export to Europe; some stayed here					
ISLAND					
❑ AB-201 [(2)]	Before the Flood	1974	10.00	20.00	40.00
—Error pressing with wrong labels (should be Asylum)					
MOBILE FIDELITY					
❑ 1-114	The Times They Are a-Changin'	1982	12.50	25.00	50.00
—Audiophile vinyl					
SUNDAZED					
❑ LP 5070 [M]	Bringing It All Back Home	2001	3.75	7.50	15.00
—180-gram reissue of the original mono mix					
❑ LP 5071 [M]	Highway 61 Revisited	2001	3.75	7.50	15.00
—180-gram reissue of the original mono mix					
❑ LP 5108 [M]	The Times They Are a-Changin'	2001	3.75	7.50	15.00
—180-gram reissue of the original mono mix					
❑ LP 5110 [(2)M]	Blonde on Blonde	2002	6.25	12.50	25.00
—180-gram reissue of the original mono mix					
❑ LP 5115 [M]	The Freewheelin' Bob Dylan	2001	3.75	7.50	15.00
—180-gram reissue of the original mono mix					
❑ LP 5120 [M]	Bob Dylan	2004	3.75	7.50	15.00
—180-gram reissue of the original mono mix					
❑ LP 5121 [M]	Another Side of Bob Dylan	2002	3.75	7.50	15.00
—180-gram reissue of the original mono mix					
❑ LP 5123 [M]	John Wesley Harding	2003	3.75	7.50	15.00
—180-gram reissue of the original mono mix					
❑ LP 5156 [M]	Bob Dylan's Greatest Hits	2003	3.75	7.50	15.00
—180-gram reissue of the original mono mix					
WARNER BROS./7 ARTS MUSIC					
❑ XTV 221567 [DJ]	Bob Dylan	1969	375.00	750.00	1500.
—One-sided publisher's demo with 8 Dylan performances of then-unreleased songs from the "Basement Tapes" era					

DYLAN, BOB, AND ALAN J. WEBERMAN
Albums
FOLKWAYS

Number	Title (A Side/B Side)	Yr	VG	VG+	NM
❑ FB-5322 [M]	Bob Dylan Vs. A.J. Weberman	1977	75.00	150.00	300.00
—A tape-recorded phone conversation; quickly withdrawn from the market					

DYNA-SORES, THE
45s
RENDEZVOUS

Number	Title (A Side/B Side)	Yr	VG	VG+	NM
❑ 120	Alley-Oop/Jungle Walk	1960	6.25	12.50	25.00

D

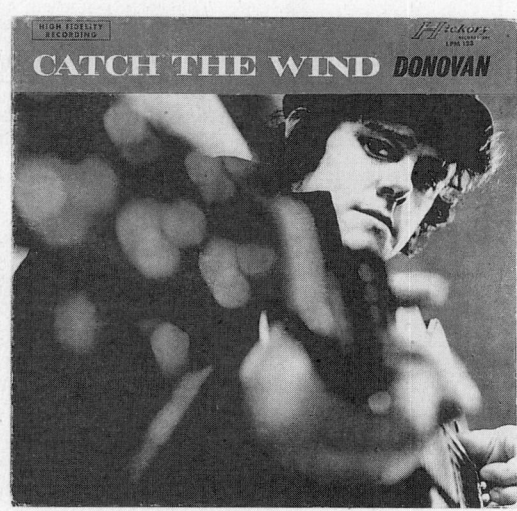

Donovan, *Catch the Wind,* Hickory LPM-123, mono LP, with Donovan facing to the right, $20-$40.

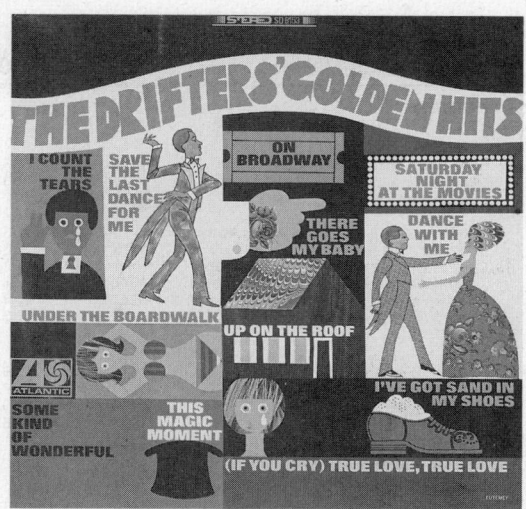

The Drifters, *The Drifters' Golden Hits,* Atlantic SD 8153, stereo LP, red and green label, $7.50-$15.

Bob Dylan, *Bob Dylan*, Columbia CL 1779, mono LP, red and black label with six white "eye" logos, three of them at 3 o'clock, three of them at 9 o'clock, $125-$250.

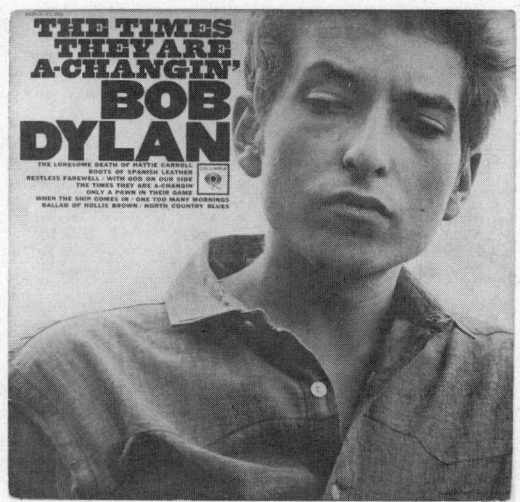

Bob Dylan, *The Times They Are a Changin'*, Columbia CL 2105, mono LP, "Guaranteed High Fidelity" on record label, $20-$40.

Bob Dylan, *John Wesley Harding,* Columbia CS 9604, stereo LP, "360 Sound Stereo" on red label, $10-$20.

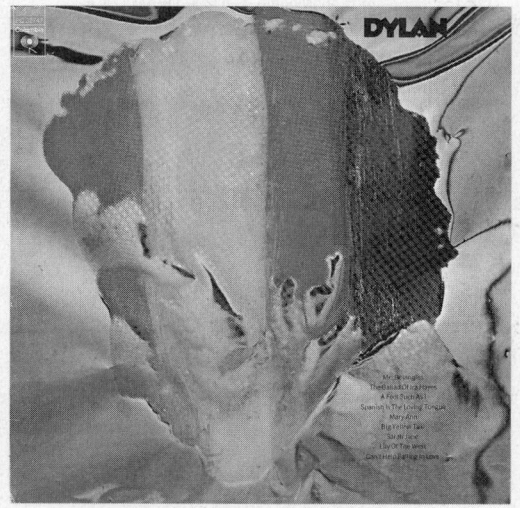

Bob Dylan, *Dylan,* Columbia PC 32747, stereo LP, no bar code on cover, $7.50-$15.

Number	Title (A Side/B Side)	Yr	VG	VG+	NM
DYNAMIC SUPERIORS					
45s					
MOTOWN					
❏ 1324	Shoe Shoe Shine/Release Me	1974	—	3.00	6.00
❏ 1342	Leave It Alone/One-Nighter	1975	—	3.00	6.00
❏ 1357	Romeo/I Got Away	1975	—	—	—
—Canceled?					
❏ 1359	Nobody's Gonna Change Me/I Got Away	1975	—	3.00	6.00
❏ 1365	Deception/One Nighter	1975	—	3.00	6.00
❏ 1413	Can't Stay Away (From the One I Love)/ Supersensuosensation (Try Some Love)	1977	—	3.00	6.00
❏ 1419	Nowhere to Run, Pt. 1/Nowhere to Run, Pt. 2	1977	—	3.00	6.00
❏ 1428	You're What I Need/Here Comes That Feeling	1977	—	3.00	6.00
Albums					
MOTOWN					
❏ M6-822	Dynamic Superiors	1974	3.00	6.00	12.00
❏ M6-841	Pure Pleasure	1975	3.00	6.00	12.00
❏ M6-875	You Name It	1976	3.00	6.00	12.00
❏ M6-879	Give and Take	1977	3.00	6.00	12.00
DYNAMICS, THE (1) Detroit R&B group with several charted hits.					
45s					
BIG TOP					
❏ 516	And That's a Natural Fact/I Wanna Know	1964	3.75	7.50	15.00
❏ 3161	Misery/I'm the Man	1963	3.75	7.50	15.00
BLACK GOLD					
❏ 8	What a Shame/Shucks, I Love You	1973	—	3.00	6.00
❏ 9	Funkey Key/Count Your Chips	1973	—	3.00	6.00
❏ 11	She's for Real (Bless You)/(B-side unknown)	1974	—	3.00	6.00
COTILLION					
❏ 44004	Ain't No Sun/Murder in the First Degree	1968	2.50	5.00	10.00
❏ 44021	Ice Cream Song/The Love That I Need	1969	2.50	5.00	10.00
❏ 44038	What Would I Do/Ain't No Love at All	1969	2.50	5.00	10.00
❏ 44045	Dum-De-Dum/I Want to Thank You	1969	2.50	5.00	10.00
Albums					
BLACK GOLD					
❏ 5001	What a Shame	1973	3.00	6.00	12.00
COTILLION					
❏ SD 9009	First Landing	1969	3.75	7.50	15.00
DYNAMICS, THE (2) Mostly an instrumental group.					
45s					
BOLO					
❏ 730	At the Mardi Gras/J.A.J.	1962	2.50	5.00	10.00
❏ 735	Wild Child/Spongy	1962	2.50	5.00	10.00
❏ 740	Tennessee Boy/Tough Talk	1963	2.50	5.00	10.00
❏ 751	Knee Poppin'/Who's Afraid of Virginia Woolf?	1964	2.50	5.00	10.00
GUARANTEED					
❏ 201	Aces Up/Baby	1959	5.00	10.00	20.00
PENGUIN					
❏ 1006	Aces Up/Baby	1959	12.50	25.00	50.00
SEAFAIR					
❏ 100	Onion Salad/Lonesome Llama	1960	5.00	10.00	20.00
❏ 107	At the Mardi Gras/J.A.J.	1961	5.00	10.00	20.00
Albums					
BOLO					
❏ BLP-8001 [M]	The Dynamics with Jimmy Hanna	1964	12.50	25.00	50.00
DYNAMICS, THE (3) Early version of ANTHONY AND THE SOPHOMORES.					
45s					
HERALD					
❏ 569	Forever Love/Betty My Own	1962	125.00	250.00	500.00
DYNAMICS, THE (4) Band from Chicago (probably).					
45s					
U.S.A.					
❏ 769	Summertime in the U.S.A./Coast to Coast	1964	6.25	12.50	25.00
DYNAMICS, THE (5) For records on Wingate, see THE DRAMATICS.					
DYNAMICS, THE (6) Vocal group from Pittsburgh, Pa.					
45s					
CINDY					
❏ 3005	When the Saints Come Marching In/ Gone Is My Love	1957	20.00	40.00	80.00
IMPALA					
❏ 501	Moonlight/Someone	1959	30.00	60.00	120.00
SEECO					
❏ 6008	Moonlight/Someone	1959	10.00	20.00	40.00
DYNAMICS, THE (U) Some of these may be groups (1) or (2). We're pretty sure that none of these are groups (3), (4), (5) or (6). It's possible that five more groups, if not more, are represented below. Any help in grouping these correctly will be appreciated.					
45s					
ARC					
❏ 4450	Enchanted Love/Happiness and Love	1959	10.00	20.00	40.00
CAPRI					
❏ 104	No One but You/Always, I Have Loved You	1959	100.00	200.00	400.00
COLUMBIA					
❏ 3-10666	We Found Love/You Can Make It If You Try	1978	—	2.50	5.00
DECCA					
❏ 31046	How Should I Feel/Seems Like Only Yesterday	1960	7.50	15.00	30.00
❏ 31129	At the End of Each Day/Girl by the Gate	1960	7.50	15.00	30.00
❏ 31450	How Should I Feel/Seems Like Only Yesterday	1962	3.75	7.50	15.00
DELTA					
❏ 1002	Blue Moon/Pigeon-Toed	1959	7.50	15.00	30.00

Number	Title (A Side/B Side)	Yr	VG	VG+	NM
DO-KAY-LO					
❏ 101	I Guess You Don't Love Me (No More)/ Oh Night of Nights	1963	7.50	15.00	30.00
DOUGLAS					
❏ 200	I Love to Be Loved/You Don't Seem to Realize	1961	7.50	15.00	30.00
DYNAMIC					
❏ 109	Don't Be Late/Eenie Meenie	1959	10.00	20.00	40.00
❏ 504	The Girl I Met Last Night/ Nobody's Going Out with Me	1959	10.00	20.00	40.00
❏ 578/9	Christmas Plea/Dream Girl	1962	17.50	35.00	70.00
❏ 1001	Don't Leave Me/Wasted	1959	12.50	25.00	50.00
❏ 1002	So Fine/Delsinia	1963	10.00	20.00	40.00
❏ 1008	If She Should Call/Dream Girl	1961	10.00	20.00	40.00
FARRALL					
❏ 964	Later On/Departure	196?	7.50	15.00	30.00
JERDEN					
❏ 800	I'll Be Standing There/All She Said	1966	2.50	5.00	10.00
LAVERE					
❏ 186	Wrap Your Troubles in Dreams/ I Can't Give You Anything But Love	1961	6.25	12.50	25.00
LIBAN					
❏ 1006	If I Give My Heart to You/Blind Date	1962	20.00	40.00	80.00
LIBERTY					
❏ 55628	Chapel on a Hill/Conquistador	1963	10.00	20.00	40.00
PANORAMA					
❏ 51	Stop and Take a Look Around/(B-side unknown)	1967	2.50	5.00	10.00
RCA VICTOR					
❏ 47-9084	Love Me/I Need Your Love	1967	10.00	20.00	40.00
❏ 47-9278	Lights Out/You Make Me Feel So Good	1967	15.00	30.00	60.00
—As "Zerben R. Hicks and the Dynamics"					
REPRISE					
❏ 20183	So Fine/Delsinia	1963	3.75	7.50	15.00
TOP TEN					
❏ 100	Yes I Love You Baby/Soul Sloopy	1965	20.00	40.00	80.00
❏ 927	Love to a Guy/Whenever I'm Without You	196?	15.00	30.00	60.00
WARNER					
❏ 1016	A Hundred Million Les/Ka Joom	1957	20.00	40.00	80.00
DYNAMO, SKINNY					
45s					
EXCELLO					
❏ 2097	So Long, So Long/Jingle Bell	1956	7.50	15.00	30.00
DYNATONES, THE (1)					
45s					
HANNA-BARBERA					
❏ 494	The Fife Piper/And I Always Will	1966	2.50	5.00	10.00
ST. CLAIR					
❏ 117	The Fife Piper/And I Always Will	1966	7.50	5.00	30.00
Albums					
HANNA-BARBERA					
❏ HLP-8509 [M]	The Fife Piper	1966	5.00	10.00	20.00
❏ HST-8509 [S]	The Fife Piper	1966	6.25	12.50	25.00
DYSON, RONNIE					
45s					
COLUMBIA					
❏ 10071	Captain of Your Soul/Life and Breath	1974	—	2.50	5.00
❏ 10211	Lady in Red/Cup (Runneth Over)	1975	—	2.50	5.00
❏ 10356	The More You Do It (The More I Like It Done to Me)/You and Me	1976	—	2.50	5.00
❏ 10441	(I Like Being) Close to You/Lovin' Feelin'	1976	—	2.50	5.00
❏ 10599	Don't Be Afraid/I Just Want to Be There	1977	—	2.50	5.00
❏ 10667	Ain't Nothing Wrong/Just As You Are	1978	—	2.50	5.00
❏ 10716	Sara Smile/No Way	1978	—	2.00	4.00
❏ 4-45025	Are We Ready for Love/God Bless the Children	1969	—	3.00	6.00
❏ 4-45110	(If You Let Me Make Love to You Then) Why Can't I Touch You?/Girl Don't Care	1970	—	2.50	5.00
❏ 4-45240	I Don't Wanna Cry/She's Gone	1970	—	2.50	5.00
❏ 4-45387	When You Get Right Down To It.../Sleeping Sun	1971	—	2.50	5.00
❏ 4-45599	Jesus Is Just Alright/Love Is Slipping Away	1972	—	3.00	6.00
❏ 4-45776	One Man Band (Plays All Alone)/ I Think I'll Tell Her	1973	—	2.50	5.00
❏ 4-45776 [PS]	One Man Band (Plays All Alone)/ I Think I'll Tell Her	1973	2.00	4.00	8.00
❏ 4-45867	Just Don't Want to Be Lonely/Point of No Return	1973	—	2.50	5.00
❏ 4-45974	Wednesday in Your Garden/I Think I'll Tell Her	1973	—	3.00	6.00
❏ 4-46021	We Can Make It Last Forever/ Just a Little Love from Me	1974	—	2.50	5.00
COTILLION					
❏ 47005	Heart to Heart/Bring It On Home	1982	—	—	3.00
❏ 99811	You Better Be Fierce/(B-side unknown)	1983	—	2.00	4.00
❏ 99841	All Over Your Face/Don't Need You Now	1983	—	—	3.00
RCA VICTOR					
❏ 74-0128	Aquarius/Hair	1969	2.50	5.00	10.00
—By "Ronald Dyson & Co."					
❏ GB-10658	Aquarius/Hair	1976	—	2.50	5.00
—"Gold Standard Series" reissue					
Albums					
COLUMBIA					
❏ C 30223	(If You Let Me Make Love to You Then) Why Can't You Touch You?	1970	3.00	6.00	12.00
❏ KC 31305	Back Home	1972	3.00	6.00	12.00
❏ KC 32211	One Man Band	1973	3.00	6.00	12.00
❏ PC 34350	The More You Do	1976	2.50	5.00	10.00
❏ PC 34866	Love in All Flavors	1977	2.50	5.00	10.00
COTILLION					
❏ 90119	Brand New Day	1982	2.50	5.00	10.00

Number	Title (A Side/B Side)	Yr	VG	VG+	NM

E

E-TYPES, THE
45s
DOT

Number	Title (A Side/B Side)	Yr	VG	VG+	NM
❑ 16864	I Can't Do It/Long Before	1966	3.00	6.00	12.00

LINK

Number	Title (A Side/B Side)	Yr	VG	VG+	NM
❑ 1	I Can't Do It/Long Before	1966	7.50	15.00	30.00
❑ 1 [PS]	I Can't Do It/Long Before	1966	7.50	15.00	30.00

SUNBURST

Number	Title (A Side/B Side)	Yr	VG	VG+	NM
❑ 001	Love of the Loved/She Moves Me	1966	6.25	12.50	25.00

SUNDAZED

Number	Title (A Side/B Side)	Yr	VG	VG+	NM
❑ 133	I Can't Do It/Long Before	199?	—	—	2.00
❑ 133 [PS]	I Can't Do It/Long Before	199?	—	—	2.00

TOWER

Number	Title (A Side/B Side)	Yr	VG	VG+	NM
❑ 325	Put the Clock Back On the Wall/14th Street	1967	6.25	12.50	25.00

UPTOWN

Number	Title (A Side/B Side)	Yr	VG	VG+	NM
❑ 754	Big City/Back to Me	1967	6.25	12.50	25.00

EADY, ERNESTINE
45s
JUNIOR

Number	Title (A Side/B Side)	Yr	VG	VG+	NM
❑ 1007	The Change/That's the Way It Goes	1963	7.50	15.00	30.00

SCEPTER

Number	Title (A Side/B Side)	Yr	VG	VG+	NM
❑ 12102	The Change/That's the Way It Goes	1965	3.00	6.00	12.00

EAGER, BRENDA LEE Also see JERRY BUTLER.
12-Inch Singles
PRIVATE I

Number	Title (A Side/B Side)	Yr	VG	VG+	NM
❑ 4Z9 05092	Watch My Body Talk (6:03) (Dub 5:45)	1984	2.50	5.00	10.00

45s
MERCURY

Number	Title (A Side/B Side)	Yr	VG	VG+	NM
❑ 73292	I'm a Lonely Woman/In My World	1972	—	3.00	6.00
❑ 73450	Let Me Be/When I'm With You	1974	—	2.50	5.00
❑ 73607	Ah, Sweet Mystery of Life/There Ain't No Way	1974	—	2.50	5.00
❑ 73627	You Gave Me Everything/When I'm With You	1974	—	2.50	5.00

PLAYBOY

Number	Title (A Side/B Side)	Yr	VG	VG+	NM
❑ 6047	Good Old Fashioned Lovin'/I'll Get By	1975	—	2.50	5.00

PRIVATE I

Number	Title (A Side/B Side)	Yr	VG	VG+	NM
❑ ZS4 04621	Watch My Body Talk/(Instrumental)	1984	—	2.00	4.00

EAGER, JIMMY
45s
SABRE

Number	Title (A Side/B Side)	Yr	VG	VG+	NM
❑ 100	Please Mr. Doctor/I Should Have Loved Her More	1953	50.00	100.00	200.00

EAGER, VINCE
45s
LONDON INT'L.

Number	Title (A Side/B Side)	Yr	VG	VG+	NM
❑ 10527	It's Only Make Believe/I Shall Not Be Moved	1964	3.00	6.00	12.00

EAGLE Also see THE BEACON STREET UNION.
45s
JANUS

Number	Title (A Side/B Side)	Yr	VG	VG+	NM
❑ 113	Kickin' It Back to You/Come In, It's All for Free	1970	2.00	4.00	8.00
❑ 135	Brown Hair/Working Man	1970	2.00	4.00	8.00

Albums
JANUS

Number	Title (A Side/B Side)	Yr	VG	VG+	NM
❑ JLS-3011	Come Under Nancy's Tent	1970	5.00	10.00	20.00

EAGLES Popular 1970s California band. Few of its records used the article "The" before the name. Its members had previously been in THE JAMES GANG; LONGBRANCH PENNYWHISTLE; POCO; and SHILOH, among others. Also see JOE WALSH.
12-Inch Singles
ASYLUM

Number	Title (A Side/B Side)	Yr	VG	VG+	NM
❑ AS 11402 [DJ]	Please Come Home for Christmas/Funky New Year (both stereo)//same (both mono)	1978	5.00	10.00	20.00

45s
ASYLUM

Number	Title (A Side/B Side)	Yr	VG	VG+	NM
❑ 11005	Take It Easy/Get You in the Mood	1972	—	2.50	5.00
❑ 11008	Witchy Woman/Early Bird	1972	—	2.00	4.00
❑ 11013	Peaceful Easy Feeling/Trying	1973	—	2.00	4.00
❑ 11017	Tequila Sunrise/21	1973	—	2.00	4.00
❑ 11025	Outlaw Man/Certain Kind of Fool	1973	—	2.00	4.00
❑ 11036	Already Gone/Is It True	1974	—	2.00	4.00
❑ 45202	James Dean/Good Day in Hell	1974	—	2.00	4.00
❑ 45218	Best of My Love/Ol' 55	1974	—	2.00	4.00
❑ 45257	One of These Nights/Visions	1975	—	2.00	4.00
❑ 45279	Lyin' Eyes/Too Many Hands	1975	—	2.00	4.00
❑ 45293	Take It to the Limit/After the Thrill Is Gone	1975	—	2.00	4.00
❑ 45373	New Kid in Town/Victim of Love	1976	—	2.00	4.00
❑ 45386	Hotel California/Pretty Maids All in a Row	1977	—	2.00	4.00
❑ 45403	Life in the Fast Lane/The Last Resort	1977	—	2.00	4.00
❑ 45555	Please Come Home for Christmas/Funky New Year	1978	—	2.00	4.00
—Original with "clouds" label					
❑ 45555 [PS]	Please Come Home for Christmas/Funky New Year	1978	—	2.00	4.00
—Sleeve was available with both original and reissue					
❑ 45555	Please Come Home for Christmas/Funky New Year	1984	—	—	3.00
—Reissue with black and yellow label					
❑ 46545	Heartache Tonight/Teenage Jail	1979	—	2.00	4.00
❑ 46569	The Long Run/The Disco Strangler	1979	—	2.00	4.00
❑ 46608	I Can't Tell You Why/The Greeks Don't Want No Freaks	1980	—	2.00	4.00
❑ 47100	Seven Bridges Road/The Long Run	1980	—	2.00	4.00

FULL MOON

Number	Title (A Side/B Side)	Yr	VG	VG+	NM
❑ 49654	I Can't Tell You Why/Outside	1981	—	2.50	5.00
—B-side by Ambrosia					

FULL MOON/ASYLUM

Number	Title (A Side/B Side)	Yr	VG	VG+	NM
❑ 47004	Lyin' Eyes/Looking for Love	1980	—	2.00	4.00
—B-side by Johnny Lee; contains the full-length version of "Lyin' Eyes"					
❑ 47004 [PS]	Lyin' Eyes/Looking for Love	1980	—	2.50	5.00
❑ 47073	Lyin' Eyes/Hello Texas	1980	—	2.50	5.00
—B-side by Jimmy Buffett					

GEFFEN

Number	Title (A Side/B Side)	Yr	VG	VG+	NM
❑ 19376	Get Over It/Get Over It (Live)	1994	—	2.50	5.00

Albums
ASYLUM

Number	Title (A Side/B Side)	Yr	VG	VG+	NM
❑ 6E-103	Hotel California	1977	2.00	4.00	8.00
❑ 6E-105	Eagles — Their Greatest Hits 1971-1975	1977	2.00	4.00	8.00
❑ 5E-508	The Long Run	1979	2.00	4.00	8.00
❑ BB-705 [(2)]	Eagles Live	1980	3.00	6.00	12.00
❑ 7E-1004	On the Border	1974	3.00	6.00	12.00
—Clouds label					
❑ EQ 1004 [Q]	On the Border	1974	5.00	10.00	20.00
❑ 7E-1039	One of These Nights	1975	2.50	5.00	10.00
—Clouds label					
❑ EQ 1039 [Q]	One of These Nights	1975	5.00	10.00	20.00
❑ 7E-1052	Eagles — Their Greatest Hits 1971-1975	1976	2.50	5.00	10.00
❑ 7E-1084	Hotel California	1976	2.50	5.00	10.00
❑ 5054 [M]	Eagles	1972	10.00	20.00	40.00
—Promo only; white label with "d/j copy monaural" sticker on cover					
❑ SD 5054	Eagles	1972	3.75	7.50	15.00
—Gatefold cover; white label with door-in-a-circle logo at top					
❑ SD 5054	Eagles	1973	3.00	6.00	12.00
—Regular cover; clouds label					
❑ SD 5068	Desperado	1973	3.00	6.00	12.00
—Clouds label					
❑ 60205	Eagles Greatest Hits, Volume 2	1982	2.50	5.00	10.00

DCC COMPACT CLASSICS

Number	Title (A Side/B Side)	Yr	VG	VG+	NM
❑ LPZ-2043	Hotel California	1997	30.00	60.00	120.00
—Audiophile vinyl					
❑ LPZ-2051	Eagles — Their Greatest Hits 1971-1975	1998	25.00	50.00	100.00
—Audiophile vinyl					

ELEKTRA

Number	Title (A Side/B Side)	Yr	VG	VG+	NM
❑ 60422	Anthology of the Eagles	1985	—	—	—
—Canceled					

MOBILE FIDELITY

Number	Title (A Side/B Side)	Yr	VG	VG+	NM
❑ 1-126	Hotel California	1984	25.00	50.00	100.00
—Audiophile vinyl					

EAGLES, THE (2)
45s
MERCURY

Number	Title (A Side/B Side)	Yr	VG	VG+	NM
❑ 70391	Tryin' to Get to You/Please, Please	1954	7.50	15.00	30.00
❑ 70464	Such a Fool/Don't You Wanna Be Mine	1954	7.50	15.00	30.00
❑ 70524	I Told Myself/What a Crazy Feeling	1955	7.50	15.00	30.00

EAGLES, THE (3) British group.
45s
SMASH

Number	Title (A Side/B Side)	Yr	VG	VG+	NM
❑ 1837	Christine/Stalactite	1963	3.00	6.00	12.00

EAGLES, THE (U) The record on Prep may be group (2); the record on Warner Bros. may be group (3). Then again, maybe not.
45s
PREP

Number	Title (A Side/B Side)	Yr	VG	VG+	NM
❑ 18	Kiss Them for Me/Ladies in the Sky	1957	5.00	10.00	20.00

WARNER BROS.

Number	Title (A Side/B Side)	Yr	VG	VG+	NM
❑ 5654	Ballad to a Lady/Eagle	1965	3.00	6.00	12.00

EAGLIN, SNOOKS
Albums
ARHOOLIE

Number	Title (A Side/B Side)	Yr	VG	VG+	NM
❑ 2014	Possum Up a Simmon Tree	198?	2.50	5.00	10.00

BLACK TOP

Number	Title (A Side/B Side)	Yr	VG	VG+	NM
❑ BT-1037	Baby, You Can Get Your Gun	1987	2.50	5.00	10.00
❑ BT-1046	Out of Nowhere	198?	2.50	5.00	10.00

BLUESVILLE

Number	Title (A Side/B Side)	Yr	VG	VG+	NM
❑ BVLP-1046 [M]	That's All Right	1962	15.00	30.00	60.00
—Blue label, silver print					
❑ BVLP-1046 [M]	That's All Right	1964	6.25	12.50	25.00
—Blue label, trident logo at right					

FOLKWAYS

Number	Title (A Side/B Side)	Yr	VG	VG+	NM
❑ FA-2476 [M]	New Orleans Street Singer	1959	10.00	20.00	40.00

GNP CRESCENDO

Number	Title (A Side/B Side)	Yr	VG	VG+	NM
❑ 10023	Down Yonder	1979	2.50	5.00	10.00

EARL-JEAN
45s
COLPIX

Number	Title (A Side/B Side)	Yr	VG	VG+	NM
❑ 729	I'm Into Somethin' Good/We Love and Learn	1964	3.00	6.00	12.00
❑ 748	Randy/They're Jealous of Me	1964	2.50	5.00	10.00

EARLAND, CHARLES
45s
COLUMBIA

Number	Title (A Side/B Side)	Yr	VG	VG+	NM
❑ 02710	The Only One/Never Knew Love Like This Before	1982	—	—	3.00
❑ 02881	Animal/Guilty	1982	—	—	3.00
❑ 11427	Coming to You (Live)/(B-side unknown)	1981	—	—	3.00

MERCURY

Number	Title (A Side/B Side)	Yr	VG	VG+	NM
❑ 73793	From My Heart to Yours/Intergalactic Love Song	1976	—	2.00	4.00
❑ 73869	Ahead of Your Time/Driftin'	1976	—	2.00	4.00

PRESTIGE

Number	Title (A Side/B Side)	Yr	VG	VG+	NM
❑ 731	Black Talk (Part 1)/Black Talk (Part 2)	1970	—	2.50	5.00
❑ 732	More Today Than Yesterday/Mighty Burner	197?	—	2.50	5.00
❑ 736	Raindrops Keep Falling on My Head/Sing a Simple Song	197?	—	2.50	5.00
❑ 741	Westbound No. 9 (Part 1)/Westbound No. 9 (Part 2)	197?	—	2.50	5.00
❑ 746	One for Scotty/I Was Made to Love Her	197?	—	2.50	5.00
❑ 755	Will You Still Love Me Tomorrow/Cause I Love Her	197?	—	2.50	5.00
❑ 761	Charles III/Girl You Need a Change of Mind	197?	—	2.50	5.00
❑ 763	Brown Eyes/Leaving This Planet	197?	—	2.50	5.00

Number	Title (A Side/B Side)	Yr	VG	VG+	NM
Albums					
COLUMBIA					
❏ JC 36449	Coming to You Live	1980	2.50	5.00	10.00
❏ FC 37573	Earland's Jam	1982	2.50	5.00	10.00
❏ FC 38547	Earland's Street Themes	1983	2.50	5.00	10.00
FANTASY					
❏ OJC-335	Black Talk!	1988	2.50	5.00	10.00
—Reissue of Prestige 7758					
MERCURY					
❏ SRM-1-1049	Odyssey	1976	2.50	5.00	10.00
❏ SRM-1-1139	The Great Pyramid	1976	2.50	5.00	10.00
❏ SRM-1-1149	Revelation	1977	2.50	5.00	10.00
❏ SRM-1-3720	Perception	1978	2.50	5.00	10.00
MILESTONE					
❏ M-9165	Front Burner	1988	2.50	5.00	10.00
❏ M-9175	Third Degree Burn	1989	2.50	5.00	10.00
MUSE					
❏ MR-5126	Smokin'	1978	2.50	5.00	10.00
❏ MR-5156	Mama Roots	1979	2.50	5.00	10.00
❏ MR-5181	Infant Eyes	1980	2.50	5.00	10.00
❏ MR-5201	Pleasant Afternoon	1981	2.50	5.00	10.00
❏ MR-5240	In the Pocket	1984	2.50	5.00	10.00
PRESTIGE					
❏ 2501	Burners	1982	2.50	5.00	10.00
❏ PRST-7758	Black Talk!	1970	5.00	10.00	20.00
❏ PRST-7815	Black Drops	1970	3.75	7.50	15.00
❏ 10009	Living Black!	1971	3.00	6.00	12.00
❏ 10018	Soul Story	1971	3.00	6.00	12.00
❏ 10024	Black Talk!	1971	2.50	5.00	10.00
—Reissue of 7758					
❏ 10029	Black Drops	1971	2.50	5.00	10.00
—Reissue of 7815					
❏ 10041	Intensity	1972	3.00	6.00	12.00
❏ 10051	Live at the Lighthouse	1972	3.00	6.00	12.00
❏ 10061	Charles III	1973	3.00	6.00	12.00
❏ 10095	Kharma	1975	3.00	6.00	12.00
❏ 66002 [(2)]	Leaving This Planet	1974	3.75	7.50	15.00
TRIP					
❏ 5004	Charles Earland	1974	2.50	5.00	10.00

EARLS, JACK, AND THE JIMBOS
45s
SUN

Number	Title (A Side/B Side)	Yr	VG	VG+	NM
❏ 240	Slow Down/A Fool for Loving You	1956	15.00	30.00	60.00

EARLS, THE (1) All of the below are by the same group or closely related.
45s
ABC

Number	Title (A Side/B Side)	Yr	VG	VG+	NM
❏ 11109	It's Been a Long Time Coming/My Lonely, Lonely Room	1968	3.75	7.50	15.00
BARRY					
❏ 1021	I Believe/Don't Forget	1963	10.00	20.00	40.00
CLIFTON					
❏ 39	Lookin' for My Baby/Cross My Heart	1974	—	2.50	5.00
❏ 43	Lost Love/My Heart's Desire	1974	—	2.50	5.00
❏ 47	Dreams Come True/My Heart's Desire	1974	—	2.50	5.00
COLUMBIA					
❏ 3-10225	Goin' Uptown/Mrs. Woman	1975	2.00	4.00	8.00
GONE					
❏ 5117	I'll Never Cry/My Heart's Desire	1961	15.00	30.00	60.00
HARVEY					
❏ 100	A Sunday Kind of Love/Teenage Dreams	1975	2.00	4.00	8.00
MR. G					
❏ 801	If I Could Do It Over Again/Papa	1967	3.75	7.50	15.00
OLD TOWN					
❏ 1130	Remember Then/Let's Waddle	1963	6.25	12.50	25.00
—Mostly black label with moon					
❏ 1130	Remember Then/Let's Waddle	1963	12.50	25.00	50.00
—Blue label					
❏ 1133	Never/I Keep a-Telling You	1963	5.00	10.00	20.00
—Mostly black label with moon					
❏ 1133	Never/I Keep a-Telling You	1963	10.00	20.00	40.00
—Blue label					
❏ 1141	Eyes/Look My Way	1963	5.00	10.00	20.00
❏ 1145	Cry, Cry, Cry/Kissin'	1963	5.00	10.00	20.00
❏ 1149	I Believe/Don't Forget	1963	5.00	10.00	20.00
—Mostly black label with moon					
❏ 1149	I Believe/Don't Forget	1963	10.00	20.00	40.00
—Blue label					
❏ 1169	Oh What a Time/Ask Anybody	1964	7.50	15.00	30.00
❏ 1181 [DJ]	Remember Me Baby/Amor	1965	12.50	25.00	50.00
—Assigned 1181 in error, as another record had been released with the number					
❏ 1182	Remember Me Baby/Amor	1965	5.00	10.00	20.00
—Error was corrected on stock copies					
POWER MARTIN					
❏ 1005	Stormy Weather/Could This Be Magic	1975	—	2.50	5.00
—B-side by the Pretenders					
ROME					
❏ 101	Life Is But a Dream/Without You	1961	10.00	20.00	40.00
❏ 101	Life Is But a Dream/It's You	1961	30.00	60.00	120.00
❏ 102	Lookin' for My Baby/Cross My Heart	1961	10.00	20.00	40.00
❏ 111	Stormy Weather/Could This Be Magic	1976	—	2.50	5.00
—B-side by the Pretenders					
❏ 112/3	Little Boy and Girl/Lost Love	1976	—	2.00	4.00
❏ 114/5	All Through Our Teens/Whoever You Are	1976	2.00	4.00	8.00
—Black vinyl					
❏ 114/5	All Through Our Teens/Whoever You Are	1976	3.00	6.00	12.00
—Colored vinyl					
WOODBURY					
❏ 101	Tonight (Could Be the Night)/Meditation	1977	2.00	4.00	8.00
Albums					
CHANCE					
❏ 1001	The Earls Today	1983	3.00	6.00	12.00

Number	Title (A Side/B Side)	Yr	VG	VG+	NM
OLD TOWN					
❏ LP-104 [M]	Remember Me Baby	1963	125.00	250.00	500.00
—Counterfeit identification: Counterfeits have more than 1-inch trailoffs or as little as 1/2 inch trailoffs; legitimate copies have 5/8- to 3/4-inch trailoff					
WOODBURY					
❏ 104	Remember Me Baby	1976	3.75	7.50	15.00

EARLS, THE (2)
45s
GEM

Number	Title (A Side/B Side)	Yr	VG	VG+	NM
❏ 221	Believe Me My Love/Spinnin'	1954	100.00	200.00	400.00
❏ 227	My Marie/Out of This World	197?	2.00	4.00	8.00
—There are differences of opinion on this record. Some claim that it was released in 1954 not long after Gem 221; others claim that it's a 1970s reproduction on a number that Gem never used. As no 78s are known to exist of this title, we lean toward the latter, but would appreciate positive evidence one way or the other.					

EARLY, SAM
45s
APT

Number	Title (A Side/B Side)	Yr	VG	VG+	NM
❏ 25041	Do You Love Me/You Are the Greatest of Them All	1960	6.25	12.50	25.00

EARTH AND FIRE Produced by members of GOLDEN EARRING.
45s
ATCO

Number	Title (A Side/B Side)	Yr	VG	VG+	NM
❏ 6744	Seasons/Hazy Paradise	1970	2.50	5.00	10.00
Albums					
RED BULLET					
❏ RBLP-3000	Earth and Fire	197?	3.75	7.50	15.00

EARTH ISLAND
45s
PHILIPS

Number	Title (A Side/B Side)	Yr	VG	VG+	NM
❏ 40673	Doomsday Afternoon/Tuesday Afternoon	1970	2.00	4.00	8.00
Albums					
PHILPS					
❏ PHS 600340	We Must Survive	1970	6.25	12.50	25.00

EARTH OPERA
45s
ELEKTRA

Number	Title (A Side/B Side)	Yr	VG	VG+	NM
❏ 45636	American Eagle Tragedy/When You Were Full of Wonder	1968	2.00	4.00	8.00
❏ 45650	Home to You/Alfie Finney	1969	2.00	4.00	8.00
Albums					
ELEKTRA					
❏ EKS-74016	Earth Opera	1968	5.00	10.00	20.00
❏ EKS-74038	The Great American Eagle Tragedy	1969	5.00	10.00	20.00

EARTH QUAKE
45s
A&M

Number	Title (A Side/B Side)	Yr	VG	VG+	NM
❏ 1301	Tickler/Guarding You	1971	2.00	4.00	8.00
❏ 1338	I Get the Sweetest Feeling/Live and Let Live	1972	2.00	4.00	8.00
❏ 1338 [PS]	I Get the Sweetest Feeling/Live and Let Live	1972	3.75	7.50	15.00
❏ 1365	Bright Lights/Live and Let Live	1972	2.00	4.00	8.00
BESERKLEY					
❏ 5701	Friday on My Mind/Roadrunner	1975	2.50	5.00	10.00
—B-side by Jonathan Richman and the Modern Lovers					
❏ 5701 [PS]	Friday on My Mind/Roadrunner	1975	2.50	5.00	10.00
❏ 5734/5	Mr. Security/Madness	1975	—	2.50	5.00
❏ 5736/7	Friday on My Mind/Tall Order for a Short Guy	1975	—	2.50	5.00
❏ 5742	Hit the Floor/Don't Want to Go Back	1976	—	2.50	5.00
❏ 5747	Kicks/Trainride	1977	—	2.50	5.00
Albums					
A&M					
❏ SP-4308	Earth Quake	1971	3.75	7.50	15.00
❏ SP-4337	Why Don't You Try Me?	1972	3.75	7.50	15.00
BESERKLEY					
❏ 0045	Rockin' the World	1975	3.00	6.00	12.00
❏ 0047	8.5	1976	3.00	6.00	12.00
❏ 0054	Leveled	1977	3.00	6.00	12.00
❏ BZ-10065	Two Years in a Padded Cell	1979	2.50	5.00	10.00
❏ PZ 34752	Rockin' the World	1977	2.50	5.00	10.00
—Reissue of 0045					
❏ PZ 34754	8.5	1977	2.50	5.00	10.00
—Reissue of 0047					
❏ PZ 34801	Leveled	1977	2.50	5.00	10.00
—Reissue of 0054					

EARTH, WIND, AND FIRE Also see WADE FLEMONS.
12-Inch Singles
ARC

Number	Title (A Side/B Side)	Yr	VG	VG+	NM
❏ AS 853 [DJ]	Let Me Talk (Remix)/(Instrumental)	1980	2.50	5.00	10.00
❏ AS 924 [DJ]	And Love Goes On (Single Version)/(LP Version)	1980	2.50	5.00	10.00
COLUMBIA					
❏ AS 1648 [DJ]	Side by Side/Something Special	1983	2.00	4.00	8.00
❏ AS 1842 [DJ]	Moonwalk/We're Living in Our Own Time	1983	2.00	4.00	8.00
❏ 44-04008	Spread Your Love/Freedom of Choice	1983	—	3.00	6.00
❏ 44-04211	Magnetic (Extended Dance Remix)/(Album Version)	1983	—	3.00	6.00
❏ 44-04211	Magnetic (Extended Dance Remix)/ (Instrumental)	1983	—	3.00	6.00
❏ 44-07475	System of Survival (4 versions)	1987	—	3.00	6.00
❏ 44-07562	Evil Roy (4 versions)	1987	—	3.00	6.00
❏ 44-08140	Turn On (The Beat Box) (4 versions)	1988	—	3.00	6.00
❏ 23-10512	Saturday Nite/On Your Face	1977	3.75	7.50	15.00
❏ 23-10786	Got to Get You Into My Life/I'll Write a Song for You	1978	2.50	5.00	10.00
❏ 73157	Heritage (Extended)/Heritage (Edit)	1990	—	3.00	6.00
❏ 73193	For the Love of You (6 versions)	1990	2.00	4.00	8.00
45s					
ARC					
❏ 02536	Let's Groove/(Instrumental)	1981	—	2.00	4.00
❏ 02688	Wanna Be with You/Kalimba Tree	1982	—	2.00	4.00

Number	Title (A Side/B Side)	Yr	VG	VG+	NM
❑ 10854	September/Love's Holiday	1978	—	2.50	5.00
❑ 11033	After the Love Has Gone/Rock That!	1979	—	2.50	5.00
❑ 11093	In the Stone/You and I	1979	—	2.00	4.00
❑ 11165	Star/You and I	1979	—	2.00	4.00
❑ 11366	Let Me Talk/(Instrumental)	1980	—	2.00	4.00
❑ 11366 [PS]	Let Me Talk/(Instrumental)	1980	—	2.50	5.00
❑ 11407	You/Share Your Love	1980	—	2.00	4.00
❑ 11434	And Love Goes On/Win or Lose	1981	—	2.00	4.00
COLUMBIA					
❑ 13-03136	Let's Groove/Sing a Song	1982	—	—	3.00
—Reissue					
❑ 38-03375	Fall in Love with Me/(Instrumental)	1982	—	2.00	4.00
❑ 38-03375 [PS]	Fall in Love with Me/(Instrumental)	1982	—	2.00	4.00
❑ CNR-03566	Fall in Love with Me	1983	—	3.00	6.00
—One-sided budget release					
❑ 38-03814	Side by Side/Something Special	1983	—	2.00	4.00
❑ 38-04002	Spread Your Love/Freedom of Choice	1983	—	2.00	4.00
❑ 38-04210	Magnetic/Speed of Love	1983	—	2.00	4.00
❑ 38-04210 [PS]	Magnetic/Speed of Love	1983	—	2.00	4.00
❑ 38-04329	Touch/Sweet Sassy Lady	1984	—	2.00	4.00
❑ 38-04329 [PS]	Touch/Sweet Sassy Lady	1984	—	2.00	4.00
❑ 38-04427	Moonwalk/We're Living in Our Own Time	1984	—	2.00	4.00
❑ 38-07608	System of Survival/Writing on the Wall	1987	—	—	3.00
❑ 38-07608 [PS]	System of Survival/Writing on the Wall	1987	—	—	3.00
❑ 38-07678	You and I/Musical Interlude: New Horizons	1988	—	—	3.00
❑ 38-07687	Evil Roy/(Instrumental)	1988	—	—	3.00
❑ 38-07687 [PS]	Evil Roy/(Instrumental)	1988	—	2.00	4.00
❑ 38-07695	Thinking of You/Money Tight	1988	—	—	3.00
❑ 38-07695 [PS]	Thinking of You/Money Tight	1988	—	—	3.00
❑ 38-08107	Turn On (The Beat Box)/(Instrumental)	1988	—	—	3.00
❑ 3-10026	Devotion/Fair But So Uncool	1974	—	3.00	6.00
❑ 3-10056	Hot Dawgit/R.L. Tambura	1974	—	2.50	5.00
—With Ramsey Lewis					
❑ 3-10090	Shining Star/Yearnin', Learnin'	1975	—	2.50	5.00
❑ 3-10090 [PS]	Shining Star/Yearnin', Learnin'	1975	2.50	5.00	10.00
❑ 3-10103	Sun Goddess/Jungle Strut	1975	—	2.50	5.00
—With Ramsey Lewis					
❑ 3-10172	That's the Way of the World/Africano	1975	—	2.50	5.00
❑ 3-10251	Sing a Song/(Instrumental)	1975	—	2.50	5.00
—Later pressings have title as three words					
❑ 3-10251	Singasong/(Instrumental)	1975	—	3.00	6.00
—Original pressings have title as one word					
❑ 3-10309	Can't Hide Love/Gratitude	1976	—	2.50	5.00
❑ 3-10373	Getaway/(Instrumental)	1976	—	2.50	5.00
❑ 3-10373 [PS]	Getaway/(Instrumental)	1976	2.50	5.00	10.00
❑ 3-10439	Saturday Nite/Departure	1976	—	2.50	5.00
❑ 3-10492	On Your Face/Biyo	1977	—	2.50	5.00
❑ 3-10625	Serpentine Fire/(Instrumental)	1977	—	2.50	5.00
❑ 3-10688	Fantasy/Runnin'	1978	—	2.50	5.00
❑ 3-10796	Got to Get You Into My Life/ I'll Write a Song for You	1978	—	2.50	5.00
❑ 4-45747	Power/M-O-M	1972	—	3.00	6.00
❑ 4-45800	Tims Is On Your Side/ Where Have All the Flowers Gone	1973	—	3.00	6.00
❑ 4-45888	Evil/Clover	1973	—	2.50	5.00
❑ 4-45888 [PS]	Evil/Clover	1973	2.50	5.00	10.00
❑ 4-45953	Keep Your Head to the Sky/Build Your Nest	1973	—	2.50	5.00
❑ 4-46007	Mighty Mighty/Drum Song	1974	—	2.50	5.00
❑ 4-46007 [PS]	Mighty Mighty/Drum Song	1974	2.50	5.00	10.00
❑ 4-46070	Kalimba Story/Tee Nine Chee Bit	1974	—	2.50	5.00
❑ 73205	Heritage/Gotta Find Out	1990	—	2.50	5.00
WARNER BROS.					
❑ 7480	Fan the Fire/This World Today	1971	—	3.00	6.00
❑ 7492	Love Is Life/This World Today	1971	—	3.00	6.00
❑ 7549	I Think About Lovin' You/C'mon Children	1972	—	3.00	6.00
Albums					
ARC					
❑ FC 35647	The Best of Earth, Wind & Fire, Vol. 1	1978	2.50	5.00	10.00
❑ FC 35730	I Am	1979	2.50	5.00	10.00
❑ PC 35730	I Am	1984	2.00	4.00	8.00
—Budget-line reissue					
❑ KC2 36795 [(2)]	Faces	1980	3.00	6.00	12.00
❑ PC 37548	Raise!	1984	2.00	4.00	8.00
—Budget-line reissue					
❑ TC 37548	Raise!	1981	2.50	5.00	10.00
❑ HC 45647	The Best of Earth, Wind & Fire, Vol. 1	1981	7.50	15.00	30.00
—Half-speed mastered edition					
❑ HC 45730	I Am	1981	7.50	15.00	30.00
—Half-speed mastered edition					
❑ HC 47548	Raise!	1982	7.50	15.00	30.00
—Half-speed mastered edition					
COLUMBIA					
❑ KC 31702	Last Days and Time	1972	3.75	7.50	15.00
❑ PC 31702	Last Days and Time	197?	2.00	4.00	8.00
—Reissue					
❑ CQ 32194 [Q]	Head to the Sky	1973	5.00	10.00	20.00
❑ KC 32194	Head to the Sky	1973	3.00	6.00	12.00
❑ PC 32194	Head to the Sky	197?	2.00	4.00	8.00
—Reissue					
❑ CQ 32712 [Q]	Open Our Eyes	1974	5.00	10.00	20.00
❑ KC 32712	Open Our Eyes	1974	3.00	6.00	12.00
❑ PC 32712	Open Our Eyes	197?	2.00	4.00	8.00
—Reissue					
❑ PC 33280	That's the Way of the World	1975	3.00	6.00	12.00
—No bar code					
❑ PC 33280	That's the Way of the World	198?	2.00	4.00	8.00
—Budget-line reissue with bar code					
❑ PCQ33280 [Q]	That's the Way of the World	1975	5.00	10.00	20.00
❑ PG 33694 [(2)]	Gratitude	1975	3.75	7.50	15.00
—No bar code					
❑ PG 33694 [(2)]	Gratitude	198?	2.50	5.00	10.00
—Budget-line reissue with bar code					
❑ PC 34241	Spirit	1976	3.00	6.00	12.00
—No bar code					
❑ PC 34241	Spirit	198?	2.00	4.00	8.00
—Budget-line reissue with bar code					
❑ PCQ 34241 [Q]	Spirit	1976	6.25	12.50	25.00

Number	Title (A Side/B Side)	Yr	VG	VG+	NM
❑ JC 34905	All 'N All	1977	3.00	6.00	12.00
❑ PC 34905	All 'N All	198?	2.00	4.00	8.00
—Budget-line reissue					
❑ PC 38367	Powerlight	1984	2.00	4.00	8.00
—Budget-line reissue					
❑ TC 38367	Powerlight	1983	2.50	5.00	10.00
❑ QC 38980	Electric Universe	1983	2.50	5.00	10.00
❑ FC 40596	Touch the World	1987	2.50	5.00	10.00
❑ OC 45013	The Best of Earth, Wind & Fire, Vol. II	1988	2.50	5.00	10.00
❑ C 45268	Heritage	1990	3.75	7.50	15.00
❑ HC 48367	Powerlight	1983	10.00	20.00	40.00
—Half-speed mastered edition					
MOBILE FIDELITY					
❑ 1-159	That's the Way of the World	198?	7.50	15.00	30.00
—Audiophile vinyl					
PAIR					
❑ PDL2-1064 [(2)]	Beat It to Life	1986	3.00	6.00	12.00
WARNER BROS.					
❑ WS 1905	Earth, Wind, and Fire	1971	—	10.00	20.00
—Green label					
❑ WS 1958	The Need of Love	1971	5.00	10.00	20.00
—Green label					
❑ 2WS 2798 [(2)]	Another Time	1974	5.00	10.00	20.00
—"Burbank" palm trees labels					

EARTH, WIND, AND FIRE WITH THE EMOTIONS

12-Inch Singles
ARC

Number	Title (A Side/B Side)	Yr	VG	VG+	NM
❑ 10950	Boogie Wonderland/(Instrumental)	1979	2.00	4.00	8.00

45s
ARC

Number	Title (A Side/B Side)	Yr	VG	VG+	NM
❑ 10956	Boogie Wonderland/(Instrumental)	1979	—	2.50	5.00

EAST

45s
CAPITOL

Number	Title (A Side/B Side)	Yr	VG	VG+	NM
❑ 3321	Some Sweet Day/Chanson D'Amour	1972	—	3.00	6.00
❑ 3400	Beautiful Morning/Black Hearted Woman	1972	—	3.00	6.00

Albums
CAPITOL

Number	Title (A Side/B Side)	Yr	VG	VG+	NM
❑ ST-11083	East	1972	6.25	12.50	25.00

EAST L.A. CAR POOL

45s
GRC

Number	Title (A Side/B Side)	Yr	VG	VG+	NM
❑ 2064	Like They Say in L.A./Linda Chicana	1975	2.00	4.00	8.00

EAST OF EDEN

45s
DERAM

Number	Title (A Side/B Side)	Yr	VG	VG+	NM
❑ 85042	Southern Hemisphere/Communion	1969	2.00	4.00	8.00
❑ 85075	Jig-a-Jig/Marcus Junior	1971	2.00	4.00	8.00

Albums
DERAM

Number	Title (A Side/B Side)	Yr	VG	VG+	NM
❑ DES 18023	Mercator Projected	1969	5.00	10.00	20.00
❑ DES 18043	Snafu	1970	5.00	10.00	20.00

HARVEST

Number	Title (A Side/B Side)	Yr	VG	VG+	NM
❑ SW-806	East of Eden	1971	5.00	10.00	20.00

EASTWOOD, CLINT

45s
CAMEO

Number	Title (A Side/B Side)	Yr	VG	VG+	NM
❑ 240	Rowdy/Cowboy Wedding Song	1963	5.00	10.00	20.00
❑ 240 [PS]	Rowdy/Cowboy Wedding Song	1963	12.50	25.00	50.00
CERTRON					
❑ 10010	Burning Bridges/When I Loved Her	1970	2.50	5.00	10.00
❑ 10010 [PS]	Burning Bridges/When I Loved Her	1970	6.25	12.50	25.00
GNP CRESCENDO					
❑ 177	Get Yourself Another Fool/For You, For Me, Forevermore	1962	10.00	20.00	40.00
❑ 177 [PS]	Get Yourself Another Fool/For You, For Me, Forevermore	1962	25.00	50.00	100.00
GOTHIC					
❑ 005	Unknown Girl of My Dreams/For All We Know	1961	6.25	12.50	25.00
❑ 005 [PS]	Unknown Girl of My Dreams/For All We Know	1961	15.00	30.00	60.00
PARAMOUNT					
❑ 0010	Best Things/Wand'rin' Star	1969	3.00	6.00	12.00
—B-side by Lee Marvin					
WARNER BROS.					
❑ 49760	Cowboy in a Three-Piece Business Suit/Dark Blue Feeling	1981	—	2.50	5.00

Albums
CAMEO

Number	Title (A Side/B Side)	Yr	VG	VG+	NM
❑ SC-1056 [S]	Clint Eastwood Sings Cowboy Favorites	1963	37.50	75.00	150.00

EASY RIDERS, THE See TERRY GILKYSON.

EASYBEATS, THE

45s
ASCOT

Number	Title (A Side/B Side)	Yr	VG	VG+	NM
❑ 2214	In My Book/Make You Feel Alright (Women)	1966	3.75	7.50	15.00
❑ 2214 [PS]	In My Book/Make You Feel Alright (Women)	1966	10.00	20.00	40.00
RARE EARTH					
❑ 5009	St. Louis/Can't Find Love	1969	3.75	7.50	15.00
UNITED ARTISTS					
❑ 0114	Friday on My Mind/Gonna Have a Good Time	1973	—	2.00	4.00
—"Silver Spotlight Series" reissue					
❑ 50106	Friday on My Mind/Made My Bed; Gonna Lie in It	1966	3.75	7.50	15.00
❑ 50187	Pretty Girl/Heaven and Hell	1967	2.50	5.00	10.00
❑ 50206	Falling Off the Edge of the World/ Remember Sam	1967	2.50	5.00	10.00
❑ 50289	Come In, You'll Get Pneumonia/ Hello, How Are You	1968	2.50	5.00	10.00
❑ 50488	Gonna Have a Good Time/Lay Me Down and Die	1969	2.50	5.00	10.00

E

Number	Title (A Side/B Side)	Yr	VG	VG+	NM

Albums
RARE EARTH
❏ 517　Easy Ridin'　1970　—　—　—
—Canceled
RHINO
❏ RNLP-124　The Best of the Easybeats　1985　2.00　4.00　8.00
UNITED ARTISTS
❏ UAL 3588 [M]　Friday on My Mind　1967　10.00　20.00　40.00
❏ UAS 6588 [P]　Friday on My Mind　1967　12.50　25.00　50.00
—"Make You Feel Alright" is rechanneled.
❏ UAS 6667 [P]　Falling Off the Edge of the World　1968　10.00　20.00　40.00
—"Women" is rechanneled.

EATON, HERB
45s
HIT
❏ 242　Ballad of the Green Berets/Listen People　1966　2.00　4.00　8.00
—B-side by the Chords (2)

EBB TIDES, THE　See NINO AND THE EBB TIDES.

EBBTIDES, THE　May be four different groups!
45s
DUANE
❏ 1022　Star of Love/First Love　1964　2000.　3000.　4000.
JAN-LAR
❏ 101　Love Doctor/Lonesome　1959　75.00　150.00　300.00
MONUMENTAL
❏ 520　Come On and Cry/Straightaway　1960　10.00　20.00　40.00
TEEN
❏ 121　What Is Your Name Dear/Only Be Mine　1957　2000.　3000.　4000.

EBBTONES, THE
45s
EBB
❏ 100　I've Got a Feeling/Danny's Blues　1957　37.50　75.00　150.00
PORT
❏ 70026　Rockin' on the Range/Ram Induction　1961　6.25　12.50　25.00

EBON-KNIGHTS, THE
45s
STEPHENY
❏ 1817　Poor Butterfly/The Way the Ball Bounces　1958　6.25　12.50　25.00
❏ 1822　First Date/Only Only You　1958　6.25　12.50　25.00
Albums
STEPHENY
❏ 4001 [M]　First Date　1959　375.00　750.00　1500.

EBONAIRES, THE
45s
ALADDIN
❏ 3211　3 O'Clock in the Morning/Baby, You're the One　1953　125.00　250.00　500.00
❏ 3212　You're Nobody 'Til Somebody Loves You/
　　　　　Lawd, Lawd, Lawd　1954　125.00　250.00　500.00
COLONIAL
❏ 117　We're in Love/Thinkin' and Thinkin'　1959　30.00　60.00　120.00
HOLLYWOOD
❏ 1046　Love For Christmas/Jingle Bell Hop　1955　100.00　200.00　400.00
❏ 1062　Let's Kiss and Say Hello Again/Jivarama Hop　1956　100.00　200.00　400.00
LENA
❏ 101　Love Call/Somewhere in My Heart　1959　50.00　100.00　200.00
LOST-NITE
❏ 118　Love Call/Somewhere in My Heart　196?　2.00　4.00　8.00
—Reissue
MONEY
❏ 220　The Very Best Luck in the World/Hey Baby Stop　1956　20.00　40.00　80.00
STARFIRE
❏ 116　Ooh Baby Baby/Most of the Pretty Young Girls　1979　—　2.50　5.00
❏ 116 [PS]　Ooh Baby Baby/Most of the Pretty Young Girls　1979　—　2.50　5.00

EBONYS, THE
45s
BUDDAH
❏ 537　Makin' Love Ain't No Fun (Without the One You
　　　　　Love) Part 1/Part 2　1976　—　3.00　6.00
PHILADELPHIA INT'L.
❏ 3503　You're the Reason Why/Sexy Ways　1971　2.00　4.00　8.00
❏ 3510　Determination/Do It　1971　2.00　4.00　8.00
❏ 3513 [DJ]　(Christmas Ain't Christmas, New Year's Ain't
　　　　　New Year's) Without The One You Love
　　　　　(mono/stereo)　1971　2.00　4.00　8.00
❏ 3514　Do You Like the Way I Love/I'm So Glad I'm Me　1972　2.00　4.00　8.00
❏ 3529　It's Forever/Sexy Ways　1973　—　3.50　7.00
❏ 3541　I Believe/Nation Time　1974　—　3.50　7.00
❏ 3548　Life in the Country/Hook Up and Get Down　1974　—　3.50　7.00
SOUL CLOCK
❏ 108　Don't Knock Me/Can't Get Enough　1969　3.75　7.50　15.00
Albums
BUDDAH
❏ BDS 5679　Sing About Life　1976　10.00　20.00　40.00
PHILADELPHIA INT'L.
❏ KZ 32419　The Ebonys　1973　3.00　6.00　12.00

ECHO VALLEY BOYS, THE
45s
ISLAND
❏ 1/2　Ramblin' Man/Wash Machine Boogie　195?　75.00　150.00　300.00

ECHOES, THE (1)
45s
SEG-WAY
❏ 103　Baby Blue/Boomerang　1961　6.25　12.50　25.00
❏ 106　Sad Eyes (Don't You Cry)/It's Raining　1961　6.25　12.50　25.00
❏ 1002　Angel of My Heart/Gee Oh Gee　1962　10.00　20.00　40.00

SMASH
❏ 1766　Bluebirds Over the Mountain/
　　　　　A Chicken Ain't Nothin' But a Bird　1962　3.75　7.50　15.00
❏ 1807　Keep an Eye on Her/
　　　　　A Million Miles from Nowhere　1963　3.75　7.50　15.00
❏ 1850　Annabelle Lee/If Love Is　1963　3.75　7.50　15.00
SRG
❏ 101　Baby Blue/Boomerang　1960　50.00　100.00　200.00

ECHOES, THE (2)　Early version of THE INNOCENTS.
45s
ANDEX
❏ 22102　Time/Dee Dee Di Oh　1958　7.50　15.00　30.00

ECHOES, THE (3)　Eddie Sulik was the singer of this group, which used Nashville professionals as backing musicians.
45s
COLUMBIA
❏ 4-41549　Bye-Bye My Baby/Do I Love You?　1960　3.75　7.50　15.00
❏ 4-41709　Loving and Losing/Ecstasy　1960　3.75　7.50　15.00
HARD ROCK HATTIE
❏ LS 1000-05　Bye-Bye My Baby/Do I Love You? ('Deed I Do)　2000　—　—　3.00
—Red vinyl; credited to "The Echoes - Eddie Sulik"; came as part of a 7x7 package called "Sweet Memories," which includes a CD, gatefold sleeve and poster
❏ LS 1000-06　Loving and Losing/Ecstasy　2000　—　—　3.00
—Blue vinyl

ECHOES, THE (4)
45s
COMBO
❏ 128　My Little Honey/Aye Senorita　1957　10.00　20.00　40.00

ECHOES, THE (5)　BONNIE GUITAR was in this group.
45s
DOLTON
❏ 18　Born to Be With You/My Guiding Light　1960　5.00　10.00　20.00

ECHOES, THE (6)
45s
ROCKIN'
❏ 523　All That Wine Is Gone/Please Say You're Mine　1953　100.00　200.00　400.00

ECHOES, THE (U)　Some of these may belong with the above groups. The record on Felsted is a reissue of the Hi Tide release.
45s
ASCOT
❏ 2188　I Love Candy/Paper Roses　1965　12.50　25.00　50.00
FELSTED
❏ 8614　Angel of Love/Twistin' Town　1961　12.50　25.00　50.00
GEE
❏ 1028　Ding Dong/My Heart Beats for You　1957　15.00　30.00　60.00
HI TIDE
❏ 106　Angel of Love/Twistin' Town　1961　50.00　100.00　200.00
—Black vinyl
❏ 106　Angel of Love/Twistin' Town　1961　100.00　200.00　400.00
—Colored vinyl
SPECIALTY
❏ 601　Over the Rainbow/Someone　1957　7.50　15.00　30.00
SWAN
❏ 4013　Scratch My Back/The Little Green Man　1959　3.00　6.00　12.00

ECKSTINE, BILLY　Also see SARAH VAUGHAN.
45s
A&M
❏ 1858　The Best Thing/
　　　　　Love Theme from "The Getaway"　1976　—　2.00　4.00
❏ 1858 [PS]　The Best Thing/
　　　　　Love Theme from "The Getaway"　1976　—　3.00　6.00
ENTERPRISE
❏ 9009　Stormy/When You Look in the Mirror　1970　—　3.00　6.00
❏ 9025　I Wanna Be Your Baby/The Name of My Sorrow　1970　—　3.00　6.00
❏ 9046　When Something Is Wrong with My Baby/Today
　　　　　Was Tomorrow Yesterday　1972　—　3.00　6.00
❏ 9076　I Didn't Mean to Love You/I Wanna Be Your Man　1973　—　2.50　5.00
❏ 9093　If She Walked Into My Life/Remembering　1974　—　2.50　5.00
MERCURY
❏ 71161　All of My Life/Poor Little Heart　1957　2.50　5.00　10.00
❏ 71217　Boulevard of Broken Dreams/If I Can Help
　　　　　Somebody　1957　2.50　5.00　10.00
❏ 71250　Gigi/Trust in Me　1957　2.50　5.00　10.00
❏ 71325　Vertigo/In the Rain　1958　2.50　5.00　10.00
❏ 71372　Prisoner of Love/Funny　1958　2.50　5.00　10.00
❏ 71861　Theme from Exodus/It Isn't Fair　1961　2.00　4.00　8.00
❏ 71907　Jeannie/Alright, Okay, You Win　1961　2.00　4.00　8.00
❏ 71967　Guilty/I Want to Talk About You　1962　2.00　4.00　8.00
❏ 72022　What Kind of Fool Am I/Till There Was You　1962　2.00　4.00　8.00
❏ 72050　You've Changed/The Beauty of True Love　1962　2.00　4.00　8.00
❏ 72128　Everything I Have Is Yours/Darling, Why Did You　1963　2.00　4.00　8.00
❏ 72264　People/Sweet Georgia Brown　1963　2.00　4.00　8.00
❏ 72302　Wanted/What Are You Afraid Of　1964　2.00　4.00　8.00
MGM
❏ K10525　O Come, All Ye Faithful/O, Holy Night　1949　3.75　7.50　15.00
❏ K10623　My Foolish Heart/Sure Thing　1950　5.00　10.00　20.00
❏ K10643　Free/Baby Won't You Say You Love Me　1950　5.00　10.00　20.00
❏ K10684　My Destiny/Roses　1950　5.00　10.00　20.00
❏ K10690　You're All I Need/Dedicated to You　1950　5.00　10.00　20.00
❏ K10716　I Wanna Be Loved/Stardust　1950　5.00　10.00　20.00
❏ K10778　The Show Must Go On/
　　　　　You've Got Me Cryin' Again　1950　5.00　10.00　20.00
❏ K10796　Blue Christmas/The Lonely Shepherd　1950　5.00　10.00　20.00
❏ K10799　Be My Love/Only a Moment Ago　1950　5.00　10.00　20.00
❏ K10825　I'll Know/I've Never Been in Love Before　1951　3.75　7.50　15.00
❏ K10856　I'm So Crazy for Love/Guess I'll Have to Dream　1951　3.75　7.50　15.00
❏ K10896　If/When You Return　1951　3.75　7.50　15.00
❏ K10903　I Apologize/Bring Back the Thrill　1951　3.75　7.50　15.00
❏ K10916　I Left My Hat/Here Come the Blues　1951　3.75　7.50　15.00
❏ K10944　I'm Yours to Command/What Will I Tell My Heart　1951　3.75　7.50　15.00

Number	Title (A Side/B Side)	Yr	VG	VG+	NM
❏ K10982	I'm a Fool/Lose Me	1951	3.75	7.50	15.00
❏ K10996	Pandora/Wonder Why	1951	3.75	7.50	15.00
❏ K11028	Enchanted Land/I've Got My Mind on You	1951	3.75	7.50	15.00
❏ K11073	Once/Out in the Cold	1951	3.75	7.50	15.00
❏ K11101	Taking a Chance/You're Driving Me Crazy	1951	3.75	7.50	15.00
❏ K11111	Jalousie/Strange Interlude	1951	3.75	7.50	15.00
❏ K11125	Take Me Back/Weaver of Dreams	1952	3.75	7.50	15.00
❏ K11144	Every Day/I Love You	1952	3.75	7.50	15.00
❏ K11177	Carnival/Room with a View	1952	3.75	7.50	15.00
❏ K11217	If They Ask Me/Hold Me Close to You	1952	3.75	7.50	15.00
❏ K11225	Kiss of Fire/Never Like This	1952	3.75	7.50	15.00
❏ K11291	Have a Good Time/Strange Sensation	1952	3.75	7.50	15.00
❏ K11301	Early Autumn/Because You're Mine	1952	3.75	7.50	15.00
❏ K11351	Be Fair/Come to the Mardi Gras	1952	3.75	7.50	15.00
❏ K11396	Until Eternity/Everything Depends on You	1953	3.75	7.50	15.00
❏ K11439	A Fool in Love/Until Today	1953	3.75	7.50	15.00
❏ K11511	Send My Baby Back to Me/ Laugh to Keep From Crying	1953	3.75	7.50	15.00
❏ K11550	It Can't Be Wrong/I Can Read Between the Lines	1953	3.75	7.50	15.00
❏ K11573	St. Louis Blues (Part 1)/St. Louis Blues (Part 2)	1953	3.75	7.50	15.00
❏ K11587	I'm Saving Dreams/Fortune Telling Cards	1953	3.75	7.50	15.00
❏ K11623	What Are You Doing New Year's Eve/ Christmas Eve	1953	5.00	10.00	20.00
❏ K11655	Rendezvous/I'm In a Mood	1954	3.75	7.50	15.00
❏ K11694	Don't Get Around Much Anymore/Lost in Loveliness	1954	3.75	7.50	15.00
❏ K11712	No One But You/Seabreeze	1954	3.75	7.50	15.00
❏ K11744	Beloved/Temporarily Blue	1954	3.75	7.50	15.00
❏ K11803	Olay, Olay/You Leave Me Breathless	1954	3.75	7.50	15.00
❏ K11845	Mood Indigo/Do Nothing 'Till You Hear from Me	1954	3.75	7.50	15.00
❏ K11855	Love Me/One Sweet Kiss	1954	3.75	7.50	15.00
❏ K11915	What More Is There to Say/Touching Shoulders	1955	3.00	6.00	12.00
❏ K11948	Give Me Another Chance/ More Than You'll Ever Know	1955	3.00	6.00	12.00
❏ K11984	Love Me or Leave Me/Only You	1955	3.00	6.00	12.00
❏ K11998	Careless Lips/A Man Doesn't Know	1955	3.00	6.00	12.00
❏ K12055	September Song/Pass the Word Around	1955	3.00	6.00	12.00
❏ K12105	La De Do De Do (The Honey Bug Song)/ Farewell to Romance	1955	3.00	6.00	12.00
❏ K12160	You'll Get Yours/Lonely Avenue	1955	3.00	6.00	12.00
❏ K12180	Good-Bye/The Show Must Go On	1956	3.00	6.00	12.00
❏ K12237	Out of My Mind/My Fickle Heart	1956	3.00	6.00	12.00
MOTOWN					
❏ 1077	Had You Been Around/Down to Earth	1965	3.00	6.00	12.00
❏ 1091	Wish You Were Here/Slender Thread	1966	3.00	6.00	12.00
❏ 1100	A Warmer World/And There You Were	1966	3.00	6.00	12.00
❏ 1105	I Wonder Why (Nobody Loves Me)/ I've Been Blessed	1967	3.00	6.00	12.00
❏ 1120	Is Anyone Here Going My Way/Thank You Love	1968	2.50	5.00	10.00
❏ 1131	For Love of Ivy/A Woman	1968	2.50	5.00	10.00
❏ 1143	My Cup Runneth Over/Ask the Lonely	1969	2.50	5.00	10.00
RCA VICTOR					
❏ 47-6436	The Bitter with the Sweet/Grapevine	1956	3.00	6.00	12.00
❏ 47-6488	My Heart Says No/Joey, Joey, Joey	1956	3.00	6.00	12.00
❏ 47-6524	Tennessee Rock 'n' Roll/Condemned for Life	1956	5.00	10.00	20.00
❏ 47-6691	The Chosen Few/Just Call Me Crazy	1956	3.00	6.00	12.00
❏ 47-6827	Blue Illusion/Oh My Pretty Pretty	1957	3.00	6.00	12.00
ROULETTE					
❏ 4199	Anything You Wanna Do/Like Wow	1959	3.00	6.00	12.00
❏ 4239	I Love You!/I Apologize	1960	3.00	6.00	12.00

7-Inch Extended Plays

Number	Title (A Side/B Side)	Yr	VG	VG+	NM
EMARCY					
❏ 16041	(contents unknown)	195?	5.00	10.00	20.00
❏ 16041 [PS]	Billy's Blues	195?	5.00	10.00	20.00
MGM					
❏ X1011	(contents unknown)	195?	5.00	10.00	20.00
❏ X1011 [PS]	My Foolish Heart	195?	5.00	10.00	20.00
❏ X1015	(contents unknown)	195?	3.75	7.50	15.00
❏ X1015 [PS]	I Apologize	195?	3.75	7.50	15.00
❏ X1041	(contents unknown)	195?	5.00	10.00	20.00
❏ X1041 [PS]	Songs by Billy Eckstine	195?	5.00	10.00	20.00
❏ X1052	Tenderly/If You Could See Me Now//Laura/One for My Baby (And One More for the Road)	1953	3.75	7.50	15.00
❏ X1052 [PS]	Billy Eckstine Sings "Tenderly"	1953	3.75	7.50	15.00
❏ X-1053	(contents unknown)	195?	3.75	7.50	15.00
❏ X-1053 [PS]	Smoke Gets In Your Eyes	195?	3.75	7.50	15.00
❏ X1078	St. Louis Blues — Parts 1 and 2/How High the Moon — Parts 1 and 2	195?	3.75	7.50	15.00
❏ X1078 [PS]	Billy Eckstine and the Metronome All-Stars	195?	3.75	7.50	15.00
❏ X-1084	(contents unknown)	195?	3.75	7.50	15.00
❏ X-1084 [PS]	A Fool in Love	195?	3.75	7.50	15.00
❏ X-1099	(contents unknown)	195?	3.75	7.50	15.00
❏ X-1099 [PS]	Love Songs, Vol. 1	195?	3.75	7.50	15.00
❏ X-1100	(contents unknown)	195?	3.75	7.50	15.00
❏ X-1100 [PS]	Love Songs, Vol. 2	195?	3.75	7.50	15.00
❏ X-1103	(contents unknown)	195?	3.75	7.50	15.00
❏ X-1103 [PS]	Billy Eckstine Favorites, Vol. 1	195?	3.75	7.50	15.00
❏ X-1104	*Bewildered/My Foolish Heart/Everything I Have Is Yours/Fool That I Am	195?	3.75	7.50	15.00
❏ X-1104 [PS]	Billy Eckstine Favorites, Vol. 2	195?	3.75	7.50	15.00
❏ X-1110	(contents unknown)	1955	3.75	7.50	15.00
❏ X-1110 [PS]	I Let a Song Go Out of My Heart, Vol. 1	1955	3.75	7.50	15.00
❏ X-1111	(contents unknown)	1955	3.75	7.50	15.00
❏ X-1111 [PS]	I Let a Song Go Out of My Heart, Vol. 2	1955	3.75	7.50	15.00
❏ X-1152	(contents unknown)	195?	3.00	6.00	12.00
❏ X-1152 [PS]	Early Autumn	195?	3.00	6.00	12.00

Albums

Number	Title (A Side/B Side)	Yr	VG	VG+	NM
AUDIO LAB					
❏ AL-1549 [M]	Mr. B	1960	30.00	60.00	120.00
DELUXE					
❏ FA-2010 [M]	Billy Eckstine and His Orchestra	195?	20.00	40.00	80.00
EMARCY					
❏ MG-26025 [10]	Blues for Sale	1954	30.00	60.00	120.00
❏ MG-26027 [10]	The Love Songs of Mr. B	1954	30.00	60.00	120.00
❏ MG-36010 [M]	I Surrender, Dear	1955	20.00	40.00	80.00
❏ MG-36029 [M]	Blues for Sale	1955	20.00	40.00	80.00

Number	Title (A Side/B Side)	Yr	VG	VG+	NM
❏ MG-36030 [M]	The Love Songs of Mr. B	1955	20.00	40.00	80.00
❏ MG-36129 [M]	Billy Eckstine's Imagination	1958	15.00	30.00	60.00
ENTERPRISE					
❏ ENS-1013	Stormy	1971	3.75	7.50	15.00
❏ ENS-1017	Feel the Warm	1971	3.75	7.50	15.00
❏ ENS-5004	Senior Soul	1972	3.75	7.50	15.00
FORUM					
❏ F-9027 [M]	Once More with Feeling	196?	3.75	7.50	15.00
❏ SF-9027 [S]	Once More with Feeling	196?	3.75	7.50	15.00
KING					
❏ 295-12 [10]	The Great Mr. B	1953	75.00	150.00	300.00
LION					
❏ L-70057 [M]	The Best of Billy Eckstine	1958	6.25	12.50	25.00
MERCURY					
❏ MG-20333 [M]	Billy's Best	1958	10.00	20.00	40.00
❏ MG-20637 [M]	Broadway, Bongos and Mr. B	1961	6.25	12.50	25.00
❏ MG-20674 [M]	Billy Eckstine and Quincy Jones at Basin St. East	1962	6.25	12.50	25.00
❏ MG-20736 [M]	Don't Worry 'Bout Me	1962	6.25	12.50	25.00
❏ MG-20796 [M]	The Golden Hits of Billy Eckstine	1963	3.75	7.50	15.00
❏ SR-60086 [S]	Billy's Best	1958	12.50	25.00	50.00
❏ SR-60637 [S]	Broadway, Bongos and Mr. B	1961	7.50	15.00	30.00
❏ SR-60674 [S]	Billy Eckstine and Quincy Jones at Basin St. East	1962	7.50	15.00	30.00
❏ SR-60736 [S]	Don't Worry 'Bout Me	1962	7.50	15.00	30.00
❏ SR-60796 [S]	The Golden Hits of Billy Eckstine	1963	5.00	10.00	20.00
METRO					
❏ M-537 [M]	Everything I Have Is Yours	1965	3.75	7.50	15.00
❏ MS-537 [R]	Everything I Have Is Yours	1965	3.00	6.00	12.00
MGM					
❏ E-153 [10]	Billy Eckstine Sings Rodgers & Hammerstein	1952	37.50	75.00	150.00
❏ E-219 [10]	Tenderly	1953	37.50	75.00	150.00
❏ E-257 [10]	I Let a Song Go Out of My Heart	1954	37.50	75.00	150.00
❏ E-523 [10]	Songs by Billy Eckstine	1951	40.00	80.00	160.00
❏ E-548 [10]	Favorites	1951	40.00	80.00	160.00
❏ E-3176 [M]	Mr. B with a Beat	1955	12.50	25.00	50.00
❏ E-3209 [M]	Rendezvous	1955	12.50	25.00	50.00
❏ E-3275 [M]	That Old Feeling	1956	12.50	25.00	50.00
MOTOWN					
❏ M 632 [M]	Prime of My Life	1965	5.00	10.00	20.00
❏ MS 632 [S]	Prime of My Life	1965	6.25	12.50	25.00
❏ M 646 [M]	My Way	1966	5.00	10.00	20.00
❏ MS 646 [S]	My Way	1966	6.25	12.50	25.00
❏ MS 677	For Love of Ivy	1969	6.25	12.50	25.00
NATIONAL					
❏ NLP-2001 [10]	Billy Eckstine Sings	1949	50.00	100.00	200.00
REGENT					
❏ MG-6052 [M]	Prisoner of Love	1957	12.50	25.00	50.00
❏ MG-6053 [M]	The Duke, the Blues and Me	1957	12.50	25.00	50.00
❏ MG-6054 [M]	My Deep Blue Dream	1957	12.50	25.00	50.00
❏ MG-6058 [M]	You Call It Madness	1957	12.50	25.00	50.00
ROULETTE					
❏ R-25052 [M]	No Cover, No Minimum	1961	6.25	12.50	25.00
❏ SR-25052 [S]	No Cover, No Minimum	1961	7.50	15.00	30.00
❏ R-25104 [M]	Once More with Feeling	1962	6.25	12.50	25.00
❏ SR-25104 [S]	Once More with Feeling	1962	7.50	15.00	30.00
SAVOY					
❏ 1127	Billy Eckstine Sings	1979	3.00	6.00	12.00
❏ SJL-2214 [(2)]	Mr. B and the Band/The Savoy Sessions	1976	3.75	7.50	15.00
TRIP					
❏ 5567	The Modern Sound of Mr. B	197?	2.50	5.00	10.00
VERVE					
❏ 819442-1 [(2)]	Everything I Have Is Yours: The MGM Years	1986	3.75	7.50	15.00
XANADU					
❏ 207	I Want to Talk About You	1987	2.50	5.00	10.00

ECKSTINE, BILLY, AND SARAH VAUGHAN See SARAH VAUGHAN AND BILLY ECKSTINE.

ECLECTION
Albums

Number	Title (A Side/B Side)	Yr	VG	VG+	NM
ELEKTRA					
❏ EKS-74023	Eclection	1968	3.75	7.50	15.00

ECSTASIES, THE
45s

Number	Title (A Side/B Side)	Yr	VG	VG+	NM
AMY					
❏ 853	That Lucky Old Sun/Time for Love	1962	12.50	25.00	50.00
CLIFTON					
❏ 40	White Christmas/Silent Night	19??	3.75	7.50	15.00

ECSTASY, PASSION AND PAIN
45s

Number	Title (A Side/B Side)	Yr	VG	VG+	NM
ROULETTE					
❏ 7151	I Wouldn't Give You Up/Don't Burn Your Bridges Behind You	1973	2.00	4.00	8.00
❏ 7156	Good Things Don't Last Forever/Born to Lose You	1974	2.00	4.00	8.00
❏ 7159	Ask Me/I'll Take the Blame	1974	2.00	4.00	8.00
❏ 7163	One Beautiful Day/Try to Believe Me	1975	2.00	4.00	8.00
❏ 7178	There's So Much Love All Around Me/(Long Version)	1975	2.00	4.00	8.00
❏ 7182	Touch and Go/I'll Do Anything for You	1976	—	3.00	6.00
	—As "Ecstasy, Passion and Pain Featuring Barbara Roy"				
❏ 7203	Passion/There's So Much Love All Around Me	1976	2.00	4.00	8.00
❏ 7209	Dance the Night Away/There's So Much Love All Around Me	1977	2.00	4.00	8.00

Albums

Number	Title (A Side/B Side)	Yr	VG	VG+	NM
ROULETTE					
❏ SR-3013	Ecstasy, Passion and Pain	1974	3.75	7.50	15.00

EDDIE AND BETTY
45s

Number	Title (A Side/B Side)	Yr	VG	VG+	NM
LARK					
❏ 4512	Sweet Someone/Saturday Night Fish Fry	1959	5.00	10.00	20.00
SIX THOUSAND					
❏ 601	Sweet Someone/Saturday Night Fish Fry	1957	6.25	12.50	25.00

E

Number	Title (A Side/B Side)	Yr	VG	VG+	NM

WARNER BROS.

Number	Title (A Side/B Side)	Yr	VG	VG+	NM
❑ 5054	Sweet Someone/Saturday Night Fish Fry	1959	3.75	7.50	15.00
❑ 5079	Embarcadeno Boogie/				
	Give Up Your Twin Pipe Mother	1959	3.75	7.50	15.00

EDDIE AND DUTCH
45s

IVANHOE

❑ 502	My Wife, the Dancer/Can't Help Lovin' That Girl	1970	—	3.00	6.00
❑ 505	My Mother-in-Law Came Out of Retirement/				
	Bambino	1970	—	3.00	6.00
❑ 507	Ah-Choo, Gesundheit/				
	Right in My Own Back Yard	1970	2.50	5.00	10.00

EDDIE AND ERNIE Also see EDDIE CAMPBELL; ERNIE JOHNSON.
45s

BUDDAH

❑ 250	Hiding in the Shadows/				
	Standing at the Crossroads	1971	7.50	15.00	30.00
CHECKER					
❑ 1057	Who's That Knocking at My Door/It's a Weak				
	Man That Cries	1963	6.25	12.50	25.00
—As "Ernie and Eddie"					
❑ 1086	Time Waits for No One/That's the Way It Is	1964	6.25	12.50	25.00
CHESS					
❑ 1984	We Try Harder/I Believe She Will	1967	5.00	10.00	20.00
COLUMBIA					
❑ 4-44276	Doggone It/Falling Tears (Indian Drums)	1967	5.00	10.00	20.00
EASTERN					
❑ 45-602	Time Waits for No One/That's the Way It Is	1965	3.75	7.50	15.00
❑ 45-603	Turn Here/I'm a Young Man	1965	3.75	7.50	15.00
❑ 45-606	I'm Goin' for Myself/The Cat	1965	3.75	7.50	15.00
❑ E 608	Outcast/I'm Gonna Always Love You	1966	5.00	10.00	20.00
❑ E 609	I Can't Do It (I Just Can't Leave You)/Lost Friends	1966	5.00	10.00	20.00
REVUE					
❑ R 11049	Thanks for Yesterday/				
	Woman, What Do You Be Doing	1969	3.75	7.50	15.00
❑ R 11063	You Give Me Love to Go On/Tell It Like It Is	1969	3.75	7.50	15.00
SHAZAM					
❑ 1004	We Try Harder/I Believe She Will	1967	37.50	75.00	150.00

EDDIE AND THE EVERGREENS See SHA NA NA.

EDDIE AND THE SHOWMEN
45s

LIBERTY

❑ 55566	Toes on the Nose/Border Town	1963	7.50	15.00	30.00
❑ 55608	Squad Car/Scratch	1963	7.50	15.00	30.00
❑ 55659	Movin'/Mr. Rebel	1963	7.50	15.00	30.00
❑ 55695	Faw Away Places/Lanky Bones	1964	7.50	15.00	30.00
❑ 55720	We Are the Young/Young and Lonely	1964	7.50	15.00	30.00

EDDIE AND THE STARLITES
45s

ALJON

❑ 1260	Come On Home/(B-side unknown)	1963	7.50	15.00	30.00
SCEPTER					
❑ 1202	To Make a Long Story Short/Pretty Little Girl	1958	7.50	15.00	30.00
—Red label					
❑ 1202	To Make a Long Story Short/Pretty Little Girl	1958	15.00	30.00	60.00
—White label					

EDDY, DUANE Also see AL CASEY; DUANE AND MIRRIAM EDDY.
45s

BIG TREE

❑ 157	Renegade/Nightly News	1972	2.00	4.00	8.00
CAPITOL					
❑ B-44018	Spies/Rockabilly Holiday	1987	—	2.50	5.00
❑ B-44018 [PS]	Spies/Rockabilly Holiday	1987	—	2.50	5.00
CHINA					
❑ 42986	Peter Gunn/Something Always Happens	1986	—	—	3.00
—With Art of Noise; B-side does not feature Eddy					
❑ 42986 [PS]	Peter Gunn/Something Always Happens	1986	—	—	3.00
COLPIX					
❑ 779	Trash/South Phoenix	1965	3.75	7.50	15.00
❑ 788	Don't Think Twice, It's All Right/House of the				
	Rising Sun	1965	3.75	7.50	15.00
❑ 788 [PS]	Don't Think Twice, It's All Right/House of the				
	Rising Sun	1965	12.50	25.00	50.00
❑ 795	El Rancho Grande/Poppa's Movin' On	1966	3.75	7.50	15.00
CONGRESS					
❑ 6010	Freight Train/Put a Little Love in Your Heart	1970	3.75	7.50	15.00
ELEKTRA					
❑ 45359	You Are My Sunshine/From 8 to 7	1977	—	2.50	5.00
FORD					
❑ 500	Ramrod/Caravan	1957	500.00	1000.	1500.
—As "Duane Eddy and His Rock-A-Billies"					
GREGMARK					
❑ 5	Caravan (Part 1)/Caravan (Part 2)	1961	3.75	7.50	15.00
—Credited to Duane Eddy, but is actually Al Casey					
GUSTO					
❑ 2047	Rebel Rouser/40 Miles of Bad Road	1979	—	2.00	4.00
—Re-recordings					
JAMIE					
❑ JLP-71 [S]	Lonesome Road/I Almost Lost My Mind	1960	6.25	12.50	25.00
❑ JLP-72 [S]	Loving You/Anything	1960	6.25	12.50	25.00
❑ JLP-73 [S]	Peter Gunn/Along the Navaho Trail	1960	6.25	12.50	25.00
❑ JLP-74 [S]	Hard Times/Along Came Linda	1960	6.25	12.50	25.00
❑ JLP-75 [S]	The Battle/You Are My Sunshine	1960	6.25	12.50	25.00
—The above five are 33 1/3 rpm singles with small holes					
❑ 1101	Moovin N' Groovin'/Up and Down	1958	6.25	12.50	25.00
—All-yellow label; "Jamie" at top					
❑ 1101	Moovin N' Groovin'/Up and Down	1958	12.50	25.00	50.00
—Originals have pink labels					
❑ 1104	Rebel-'Rouser/Stalkin'	1958	6.25	12.50	25.00
❑ 1109	Ramrod/The Walker	1958	6.25	12.50	25.00
❑ 1111	Cannonball/Mason Dixon Lion	1958	5.00	10.00	20.00

Number	Title (A Side/B Side)	Yr	VG	VG+	NM
❑ 1117 [M]	The Lonely One/Detour	1959	5.00	10.00	20.00
❑ 1117 [S]	The Lonely One/Detour	1959	12.50	25.00	50.00
❑ 1122	Yep!/Three-30-Blues	1959	5.00	10.00	20.00
❑ 1122 [PS]	Yep!/Three-30-Blues	1959	12.50	25.00	50.00
❑ 1126 [M]	Forty Miles of Bad Road/The Quiet Three	1959	5.00	10.00	20.00
❑ 1126 [PS]	Forty Miles of Bad Road/The Quiet Three	1959	12.50	25.00	50.00
❑ 1126 [S]	Forty Miles of Bad Road/The Quiet Three	1959	12.50	25.00	50.00
❑ 1130 [M]	Some Kind-a Earthquake/First Love, First Tears	1959	5.00	10.00	20.00
❑ 1130 [PS]	Some Kind-a Earthquake/First Love, First Tears	1959	10.00	20.00	40.00
❑ 1130 [S]	Some Kind-a Earthquake/First Love, First Tears	1959	12.50	25.00	50.00
❑ 1144	Bonnie Came Back/Lost Island	1959	5.00	10.00	20.00
❑ 1144 [PS]	Bonnie Came Back/Lost Island	1959	10.00	20.00	40.00
❑ 1151	Shazam!/The Secret Seven	1960	3.75	7.50	15.00
❑ 1151 [PS]	Shazam!/The Secret Seven	1960	7.50	15.00	30.00
❑ 1156	Because They're Young/Rebel Walk	1960	3.75	7.50	15.00
❑ 1156 [PS]	Because They're Young/Rebel Walk	1960	7.50	15.00	30.00
❑ 1163	Kommotion/Theme for Moon Children	1960	3.75	7.50	15.00
❑ 1163 [PS]	Kommotion/Theme for Moon Children	1960	7.50	15.00	30.00
❑ 1168	Peter Gunn/Along the Navaho Trail	1960	3.75	7.50	15.00
❑ 1168 [PS]	Peter Gunn/Along the Navaho Trail	1960	7.50	15.00	30.00
❑ 1175	"Pepe"/Lost Friend	1960	3.75	7.50	15.00
❑ 1175 [PS]	"Pepe"/Lost Friend	1960	7.50	15.00	30.00
—Yellow sleeve					
❑ 1175 [PS]	"Pepe"/Lost Friend	1960	10.00	20.00	40.00
—Red sleeve					
❑ 1183	Theme from Dixie/Gidget Goes Hawaiian	1961	3.75	7.50	15.00
❑ 1183 [PS]	Theme from Dixie/Gidget Goes Hawaiian	1961	7.50	15.00	30.00
❑ 1187	Ring of Fire/Bobbie	1961	3.75	7.50	15.00
❑ 1187 [PS]	Ring of Fire/Bobbie	1961	7.50	15.00	30.00
❑ 1195	Drivin' Home/Tammy	1961	3.75	7.50	15.00
❑ 1195 [PS]	Drivin' Home/Tammy	1961	7.50	15.00	30.00
❑ 1200	My Blue Heaven/Along Came Linda	1961	3.75	7.50	15.00
❑ 1200 [PS]	My Blue Heaven/Along Came Linda	1961	7.50	15.00	30.00
❑ 1206	The Avenger/Londonderry Air	1961	3.75	7.50	15.00
❑ 1209	The Battle/Trambone	1962	3.75	7.50	15.00
❑ 1224	Runaway Pony/Just Because	1962	3.75	7.50	15.00
❑ 1303	Rebel Rouser/Movin' N' Groovin'	1965	3.00	6.00	12.00
RCA VICTOR					
❑ 47-7999	Deep in the Heart of Texas/Saints and Sinners	1962	3.00	6.00	12.00
❑ 47-7999 [PS]	Deep in the Heart of Texas/Saints and Sinners	1962	6.25	12.50	25.00
❑ 47-8047	The Ballad of Paladin/The WIld Westerner	1962	3.00	6.00	12.00
❑ 47-8047 [PS]	The Ballad of Paladin/The WIld Westerner	1962	6.25	12.50	25.00
❑ 47-8087	(Dance with the) Guitar Man/Stretchin' Out	1962	3.75	7.50	15.00
❑ 47-8087 [PS]	(Dance with the) Guitar Man/Stretchin' Out	1962	7.50	15.00	30.00
❑ 47-8131	Boss Guitar/Desert Rat	1963	3.00	6.00	12.00
❑ 47-8131 [PS]	Boss Guitar/Desert Rat	1963	6.25	12.50	25.00
❑ 47-8180	Lonely Boy, Lonely Guitar/Joshin'	1963	3.00	6.00	12.00
❑ 47-8180 [PS]	Lonely Boy, Lonely Guitar/Joshin'	1963	6.25	12.50	25.00
❑ 47-8214	Your Baby's Gone Surfin'/Shuckin'	1963	3.75	7.50	15.00
❑ 47-8214 [PS]	Your Baby's Gone Surfin'/Shuckin'	1963	7.50	15.00	30.00
❑ 47-8276	The Son of Rebel Rouser/				
	The Story of Three Loves	1963	3.00	6.00	12.00
❑ 47-8276 [PS]	The Son of Rebel Rouser/				
	The Story of Three Loves	1963	6.25	12.50	25.00
❑ 47-8335	Guitar Child/Jerky Jalopy	1964	3.00	6.00	12.00
❑ 47-8376	Water Skiing/Theme from A Summer Place	1964	3.00	6.00	12.00
❑ 47-8442	Guitar Star/The Iguana	1964	3.00	6.00	12.00
❑ 47-8442 [PS]	Guitar Star/The Iguana	1964	7.50	15.00	30.00
❑ 47-8507	Moonshot/Roughneck	1965	3.00	6.00	12.00
❑ 47-8507 [PS]	Moonshot/Roughneck	1965	30.00	60.00	120.00
❑ 47-8335 [PS]	Guitar Child/Jerky Jalopy	1964	7.50	15.00	30.00
❑ 47-8376 [PS]	Water Skiing/Theme from A Summer Place	1964	15.00	30.00	60.00
REPRISE					
❑ 0504	Daydream/This Guitar Was Made for Twangin'	1966	2.50	5.00	10.00
❑ 0557	Roarin'/Monsoon	1967	2.50	5.00	10.00
❑ 0662	There Is a Mountain/This Town	1968	2.50	5.00	10.00
❑ 0690	Niki-Hoeky/Velvet Nights	1968	2.50	5.00	10.00
UNI					
❑ 55237	The Five-Seventeen/Something	1970	3.75	7.50	15.00
7-Inch Extended Plays					
JAMIE					
❑ JEP-100	Cannonball/Moovin' N' Groovin'//Mason-Dixon				
	Lion/The Lonely One	1958	12.50	25.00	50.00
❑ JEP-100 [PS]	Duane Eddy	1958	12.50	25.00	50.00
❑ JEP-301	Lonesome Road/I Almost Lost My Mind//				
	Detour/Loving You	1959	12.50	25.00	50.00
❑ JEP-301 [PS]	Detour	1959	12.50	25.00	50.00
❑ JEP-302	Yep/Three-30 Blues//Anytime/Stalkin'	1959	12.50	25.00	50.00
❑ JEP-302 [PS]	Yep!	1959	12.50	25.00	50.00
❑ JEP-303	Shazam/Tiger Love//My Blue Heaven/				
	Night Train To Memphis	1960	12.50	25.00	50.00
❑ JEP-303 [PS]	Shazam!	1960	12.50	25.00	50.00
❑ JEP-304	Because They're Young/Easy//Rebel Walk/				
	The Battle	1960	12.50	25.00	50.00
❑ JEP-304 [PS]	Because They're Young	1960	12.50	25.00	50.00
Albums					
CAPITOL					
❑ ST-12567	Duane Eddy	1987	3.00	6.00	12.00
COLPIX					
❑ CP-490 [M]	Duane A-Go-Go	1965	7.50	15.00	30.00
❑ CPS-490 [S]	Duane A-Go-Go	1965	10.00	20.00	40.00
❑ CPL-494 [M]	Duane Eddy Does Bob Dylan	1965	7.50	15.00	30.00
❑ CPS-494 [S]	Duane Eddy Does Bob Dylan	1965	10.00	20.00	40.00
JAMIE					
❑ JLP-3000 [M]	Have "Twangy" Guitar — Will Travel	1958	30.00	60.00	120.00
—Duane sitting with guitar case, title on cover in white (1st)					
❑ JLP-3000 [M]	Have "Twangy" Guitar — Will Travel	1959	12.50	25.00	50.00
—Duane standing with guitar (3rd)					
❑ JLP-3000 [M]	Have "Twangy" Guitar — Will Travel	1959	25.00	50.00	100.00
—Duane sitting with guitar case, title on cover in green and red (2nd)					
❑ JLPS-3000 [S]	Have "Twangy" Guitar — Will Travel	1958	100.00	200.00	400.00
—Duane sitting with guitar case, title on cover in white (1st)					
❑ JLPS-3000 [S]	Have "Twangy" Guitar — Will Travel	1959	25.00	50.00	100.00
—Duane standing with guitar (3rd), album plays true stereo					
❑ JLPS-3000 [S]	Have "Twangy" Guitar — Will Travel	1959	75.00	150.00	300.00
—Duane sitting with guitar case, title on cover in green and red (2nd)					

Number	Title (A Side/B Side)	Yr	VG	VG+	NM
❑ JLPS-3000 [R]	Have "Twangy" Guitar — Will Travel	196?	12.50	25.00	50.00
—Duane standing with guitar (3rd), album plays fake stereo					
❑ JLPM-3006 [M]	Especially for You…	1959	10.00	20.00	40.00
❑ JLPS-3006 [S]	Especially for You…	1959	15.00	30.00	60.00
❑ JLPM-3009 [M]	The "Twangs" The "Thang"	1959	10.00	20.00	40.00
❑ JLPS-3009 [S]	The "Twangs" The "Thang"	1959	15.00	30.00	60.00
❑ JLPM-3011 [M]	Songs of Our Heritage	196?	7.50	15.00	30.00
—Regular cover					
❑ JLPM-3011 [M]	Songs of Our Heritage	1960	20.00	40.00	80.00
—Gatefold cover					
❑ JLPS-3011 [S]	Songs of Our Heritage	196?	10.00	20.00	40.00
—Regular cover					
❑ JLPS-3011 [S]	Songs of Our Heritage	1960	25.00	50.00	100.00
—Gatefold cover					
❑ JLPS-3011 [S]	Songs of Our Heritage	1960	125.00	250.00	500.00
—Gatefold cover, blue vinyl					
❑ JLPS-3011 [S]	Songs of Our Heritage	1960	125.00	250.00	500.00
—Gatefold cover, red vinyl					
❑ JLPM-3014 [M]	$1,000,000.00 Worth of Twang	1960	10.00	20.00	40.00
❑ JLPS-3014 [S]	$1,000,000.00 Worth of Twang	1960	17.50	35.00	70.00
—All but one song -- "Up and Down" -- is in true stereo					
❑ JLPM-3019 [M]	Girls! Girls! Girls!	1961	10.00	20.00	40.00
❑ JLPS-3019 [R]	Girls! Girls! Girls!	1961	7.50	15.00	30.00
❑ JLPM-3021 [M]	$1,000,000.00 Worth of Twang, Volume 2	1962	10.00	20.00	40.00
❑ JLPS-3021 [R]	$1,000,000.00 Worth of Twang, Volume 2	1962	7.50	15.00	30.00
❑ JLPM-3022 [M]	Twistin' with Duane Eddy	1962	10.00	20.00	40.00
❑ JLPS-3022 [P]	Twistin' with Duane Eddy	1962	10.00	20.00	40.00
❑ JLPM-3024 [M]	Surfin'	1963	12.50	25.00	50.00
❑ JLPS-3024 [S]	Surfin'	1963	20.00	40.00	80.00
❑ JLPM-3025 [M]	Duane Eddy & The Rebels — In Person	1963	7.50	15.00	30.00
❑ JLPS-3025 [S]	Duane Eddy & The Rebels — In Person	1963	10.00	20.00	40.00
❑ JLPM-3026 [M]	16 Greatest Hits	1964	10.00	20.00	40.00
❑ JLPS-3026 [R]	16 Greatest Hits	1964	7.50	15.00	30.00
❑ ST-90663 [S]	Duane Eddy & The Rebels — In Person	1965	12.50	25.00	50.00
—Capitol Record Club edition					
❑ T-90663 [M]	Duane Eddy & The Rebels — In Person	1965	10.00	20.00	40.00
—Capitol Record Club edition					
❑ ST-90682 [S]	Have "Twangy" Guitar — Will Travel	1965	20.00	40.00	80.00
—Capitol Record Club edition					
❑ T-90682 [M]	Have "Twangy" Guitar — Will Travel	1965	15.00	30.00	60.00
—Capitol Record Club edition					
❑ ST-91301 [S]	The "Twangs" The "Thang"	1966	15.00	30.00	60.00
—Capitol Record Club edition					
❑ T-91301 [M]	The "Twangs" The "Thang"	1966	15.00	30.00	60.00
—Capitol Record Club edition					
RCA VICTOR					
❑ LPM-2525 [M]	Twistin' 'N' Twangin'	1962	6.25	12.50	25.00
❑ LSP-2525 [S]	Twistin' 'N' Twangin'	1962	10.00	20.00	40.00
❑ LPM-2576 [M]	Twangy Guitar — Silky Strings	1962	6.25	12.50	25.00
❑ LSP-2576 [S]	Twangy Guitar — Silky Strings	1962	10.00	20.00	40.00
❑ LPM-2648 [M]	Dance with the Guitar Man	1962	6.25	12.50	25.00
❑ LSP-2648 [S]	Dance with the Guitar Man	1962	10.00	20.00	40.00
❑ ANL1-2671	Pure Gold	1978	2.50	5.00	10.00
❑ LPM-2681 [M]	Twang a Country Song	1963	6.25	12.50	25.00
❑ LSP-2681 [S]	Twang a Country Song	1963	10.00	20.00	40.00
❑ LPM-2700 [M]	"Twangin' " Up a Storm!	1963	6.25	12.50	25.00
❑ LSP-2700 [S]	"Twangin' " Up a Storm!	1963	10.00	20.00	40.00
❑ LPM-2798 [M]	Lonely Guitar	1964	5.00	10.00	20.00
❑ LSP-2798 [S]	Lonely Guitar	1964	7.50	15.00	30.00
❑ LPM-2918 [M]	Water Skiing	1964	5.00	10.00	20.00
❑ LSP-2918 [S]	Water Skiing	1964	7.50	15.00	30.00
❑ LPM-2993 [M]	Twangin' the Golden Hits	1965	5.00	10.00	20.00
❑ LSP-2993 [S]	Twangin' the Golden Hits	1965	7.50	15.00	30.00
❑ LPM-3432 [M]	Twangsville	1965	5.00	10.00	20.00
❑ LSP-3432 [S]	Twangsville	1965	7.50	15.00	30.00
❑ LPM-3477 [M]	The Best of Duane Eddy	1965	5.00	10.00	20.00
❑ LSP-3477 [P]	The Best of Duane Eddy	1965	6.25	12.50	25.00
—Black "Stereo" label					
❑ LSP-3477 [P]	The Best of Duane Eddy	1969	3.75	7.50	15.00
—Orange label					
REPRISE					
❑ R-6218 [M]	The Biggest Twang of Them All	1966	7.50	15.00	30.00
❑ RS-6218 [S]	The Biggest Twang of Them All	1966	10.00	20.00	40.00
❑ R-6240 [M]	The Roaring Twangies	1967	7.50	15.00	30.00
❑ RS-6240 [S]	The Roaring Twangies	1967	10.00	20.00	40.00
SIRE					
❑ SASH-3707-2 [(2)]	The Vintage Years	1975	6.25	12.50	25.00

EDDY, DUANE AND MIRRIAM Also see JESSI COLTER, DUANE EDDY.
45s
REPRISE

Number	Title (A Side/B Side)	Yr	VG	VG+	NM
❑ 0622	Guitar on My Mind/Wicked Women from Wickenborg	1967	2.50	5.00	10.00

EDELMAN, RANDY
45s
ARISTA

Number	Title (A Side/B Side)	Yr	VG	VG+	NM
❑ 0268	Can't It All Be Love/Sentimental Fools	1977	—	3.00	6.00
❑ 0309	Take My Hand/Today (June Song)	1978	—	3.00	6.00
❑ 0347	Autumn Days with You/(B-side unknown)	1978	—	3.00	6.00
❑ 0434	You're the One/Don't Let Go of Me	1979	—	3.00	6.00
LION					
❑ 144	Mexico/(B-side unknown)	1972	2.00	4.00	8.00
❑ 153	The Laughter and the Tears/Lost	1973	2.00	4.00	8.00
MGM					
❑ 14599	Everybody Wants to Call You Sweetheart/Ball-Buster Circus	1973	2.00	4.00	8.00
SUNFLOWER					
❑ 108	Give a Little Laughter/Just Somebody	1971	2.00	4.00	8.00
❑ 121	My Cabin/T-Shirt 'n' Jeans	1972	2.00	4.00	8.00
20TH CENTURY					
❑ 2134	What Are You Going to Do When the Plumbing Goes/Pistol Packin' Melody	1974	—	3.00	6.00
❑ 2155	Everybody Wants to Find a Bluebird/Pistol Packin' Melody	1974	—	3.00	6.00
❑ 2196	Isn't It a Shame/Everybody Wants to Call You Sweetheart	1975	—	3.00	6.00

Number	Title (A Side/B Side)	Yr	VG	VG+	NM
❑ 2245	Fresh Out'a Love/Bring the Baby In with the Bacon	1975	2.00	4.00	8.00
❑ 2274	Concrete and Clay/Weekend in New England	1976	2.00	4.00	8.00
Albums					
ARISTA					
❑ AB 4139	If Love Is Real	1977	3.00	6.00	12.00
❑ AB 4210	You're the One	1979	3.00	6.00	12.00
LION					
❑ LN-1013	The Laughter and the Tears	1972	3.75	7.50	15.00
SUNFLOWER					
❑ SNF-5005	Randy Edelman	1971	3.75	7.50	15.00
20TH CENTURY					
❑ T-443	Prime Cuts	1974	3.75	7.50	15.00
❑ T-494	Farewell Fairbanks	1975	3.00	6.00	12.00

EDEN, BARBARA
45s
DOT

Number	Title (A Side/B Side)	Yr	VG	VG+	NM
❑ 16999	Bend It/I Wouldn't Be a Fool	1967	2.00	4.00	8.00
❑ 17022	Rebel/Heartaches	1967	2.00	4.00	8.00
❑ 17032	Pledge of Love/I'm a Fool to Care	1967	2.00	4.00	8.00
PLANTATION					
❑ 178	Widow Jones/We Tried	1978	—	2.50	5.00
Albums					
DOT					
❑ DLP-3795 [M]	Miss Barbara Eden	1967	10.00	20.00	40.00
❑ DLP-25795 [S]	Miss Barbara Eden	1967	12.50	25.00	50.00

EDEN'S CHILDREN
45s
ABC

Number	Title (A Side/B Side)	Yr	VG	VG+	NM
❑ 11053	Goodbye Girl/Just Let Go	1968	3.00	6.00	12.00
Albums					
ABC					
❑ 624 [M]	Eden's Children	1968	10.00	20.00	40.00
❑ S-624 [S]	Eden's Children	1968	6.25	12.50	25.00
❑ S-652	Sure Looks Real	1968	5.00	10.00	20.00

EDGE, GRAEME Of THE MOODY BLUES.
45s
LONDON

Number	Title (A Side/B Side)	Yr	VG	VG+	NM
❑ 1071	Everybody Needs Somebody/Be My Eyes	1977	—	2.50	5.00
—With Adrian Gurvitz					
THRESHOLD					
❑ 67018	We Like to Do It/Shotgun	1974	—	2.50	5.00
❑ 67022	The Tunnel/Bareback Rider	1975	—	2.50	5.00
Albums					
LONDON					
❑ PS 686	Paradise Ballroom	1977	3.00	6.00	12.00
THRESHOLD					
❑ THS 15	Kick Off Your Muddy Boots	1975	3.75	7.50	15.00

EDGE, THE
Albums
NOSE

Number	Title (A Side/B Side)	Yr	VG	VG+	NM
❑ NRS-48003	The Edge	1970	10.00	20.00	40.00

EDGEWOOD
45s
TMI

Number	Title (A Side/B Side)	Yr	VG	VG+	NM
❑ ZS7 9011	Ain't Had No Lovin'/Silent	1972	—	3.50	7.00

EDISON LIGHTHOUSE
45s
BELL

Number	Title (A Side/B Side)	Yr	VG	VG+	NM
❑ 858	Love Grows (Where My Rosemary Goes)/Every Lonely Day	1970	—	3.00	6.00
❑ 907	She Works in a Woman's Way/It's Gonna Be a Lonely Summer	1970	—	2.50	5.00
❑ 960	It's Up to You Petula/Let's Make It Up	1971	—	2.50	5.00
❑ 989	Take a Little Time/What's Happening	1971	—	2.50	5.00

EDMUNDS, DAVE Also see LOVE SCULPTURE.
12-Inch Singles
COLUMBIA

Number	Title (A Side/B Side)	Yr	VG	VG+	NM
❑ AS 1660 [DJ]	Slipping Away (same on both sides)	1982	2.00	4.00	8.00
❑ AS99-1725 [DJ]	Information	1983	6.25	12.50	25.00
—Promo-only picture disc					
❑ AS 1911 [DJ]	Something About You (same on both sides)	1984	—	3.00	6.00
❑ CAS 2077 [DJ]	Do You Want to Dance (same on both sides)	1985	—	3.00	6.00
❑ CAS 02598 [DJ]	The Wanderer/Dave Edmunds Mega-Mix	1986	—	3.00	6.00
45s					
CAPITOL					
❑ 7PRO-79973 [DJ]	Closer to the Flame (same on both sides)	1990	2.50	5.00	10.00
COLUMBIA					
❑ 02960	From Small Things (Big Things One Day Come)/Warmed Over Kisses (Left Over Love)	1982	—	2.00	4.00
—A-side is a Bruce Springsteen composition.					
❑ 03428	Run Rudolph Run/Deep in the Heart of Texas	1982	—	2.00	4.00
❑ 03428 [PS]	Run Rudolph Run/Deep in the Heart of Texas	1982	2.00	4.00	8.00
❑ 03877	Slipping Away/Don't Call Me Tonight	1983	—	—	3.00
❑ 04080	Information/What Have I Got to Do to Win	1983	—	—	3.00
❑ 04585	Something About You/Can't Get Enough	1984	—	—	3.00
❑ 04700	Breaking Out/How Could I Be So Wrong	1984	—	—	3.00
❑ 04762	High School Nights/Porky's Revenge	1985	—	—	2.50
❑ 04762 [PS]	High School Nights/Porky's Revenge	1985	—	—	2.50
❑ 04887	Queen of the Hop/I Don't Want to Do It	1985	5.00	10.00	20.00
—B-side by George Harrison, thus accounting for this 45's value					
❑ 04923	Do You Want to Dance/Don't Call Me Tonight	1985	—	—	3.00
❑ 05487	Run Rudolph Run/From Small Things (Big Things One Day Come)	198?	—	—	3.00
—"Golden Oldies" reissue					
❑ 06599	The Wanderer/Here Comes the Weekend	1987	—	—	3.00
❑ 06599	The Wanderer/Information	1987	—	—	3.00
❑ 07040	Paralyzed/Here Comes the Weekend	1987	—	—	3.00

Number	Title (A Side/B Side)	Yr	VG	VG+	NM
MAM					
❏ 3601	I Hear You Knocking/Black Bill	1970	2.00	4.00	8.00
❏ 3608	I'm Coming Home/Country Roll	1971	—	3.00	6.00
❏ 3611	Blue Monday/I'll Get Along	1971	—	3.00	6.00
MCA					
❏ 53256	Gonna Move/Red River Rock	1988	—	—	2.50
—B-side by Silicon Teens					
❏ 53256 [PS]	Gonna Move/Red River Rock	1988	—	—	2.50
—B-side by Silicon Teens					
RCA VICTOR					
❏ 74-0882	Baby I Love You/Maybe	1973	—	3.00	6.00
❏ LPBO-5000	Born to Be with You/Pick Axe Rag	1973	—	3.00	6.00
❏ PB-10118	Let It Be Me/Need a Shot of Rhythm and Blues	1974	—	2.50	5.00
SWAN SONG					
❏ 70113	I Knew the Bride/Little Darlin'	1978	—	2.00	4.00
❏ 70116	Get Out of Denver/Work Suits	1978	—	2.00	4.00
❏ 70118	Trouble Boys/What Looks Best on You	1978	—	2.00	4.00
❏ 71001	Girls Talk/Creature from the Black Lagoon	1979	—	2.50	5.00
❏ 71002	Crawling from the Wreckage/Queen of Hearts	1979	—	2.50	5.00
❏ 72000	Almost Saturday Night/You'll Never Get Me Up	1981	—	—	3.00
❏ 72000 [PS]	Almost Saturday Night/You'll Never Get Me Up	1981	—	—	3.00
❏ 72003	The Race Is On/Singin' the Blues	1981	—	2.50	5.00
—Backing group: Stray Cats					
Albums					
ATLANTIC					
❏ PR 320 [DJ]	College Network	1978	12.50	25.00	50.00
—Promo-only interview album					
CAPITOL					
❏ C1-90372	Closer to the Flame	1990	3.75	7.50	15.00
COLUMBIA					
❏ FC 37930	D.E. 7th	1982	3.00	6.00	12.00
❏ PC 37930	D.E. 7th	198?	2.00	4.00	8.00
—Budget-line reissue ("02" added to bar code on back cover)					
❏ FC 38651	Information	1983	3.00	6.00	12.00
❏ PC 38651	Information	198?	2.00	4.00	8.00
—Budget-line reissue ("02" added to bar code on back cover)					
❏ FC 39273	Riff Raff	1984	2.50	5.00	10.00
❏ FC 40603	I Hear You Rockin'	1987	2.50	5.00	10.00
❏ PC 40603	I Hear You Rockin'	198?	2.00	4.00	8.00
—Budget-line reissue ("02" added to bar code on back cover)					
MAM					
❏ 3	Rockpile	1972	10.00	20.00	40.00
RCA VICTOR					
❏ AYL1-4238	Subtle as a Flying Mallet	1982	2.50	5.00	10.00
—Reissue (black label, dog near top)					
❏ LPL1-5003	Subtle as a Flying Mallet	1975	3.00	6.00	12.00
SWAN SONG					
❏ SS 8418	Get It	1977	3.75	7.50	15.00
❏ SS 8505	Trax on Wax 4	1978	3.75	7.50	15.00
❏ SS 8507	Repeat When Necessary	1979	3.75	7.50	15.00
❏ SS 8510	The Best of Dave Edmunds	1981	3.00	6.00	12.00
❏ SD 16034	Twangin'	1981	3.00	6.00	12.00

EDMUNDS, DAVE, AND NICK LOWE
45s

Number	Title (A Side/B Side)	Yr	VG	VG+	NM
COLUMBIA					
❏ AE7-1219	Take a Message to Mary/Crying in the Rain// Poor Jenny/When Will I Be Loved	1980	—	3.00	6.00
—Bonus EP included in the Rockpile LP "Seconds of Pleasure"					
❏ AE7-1219 [PS]	Nick Lowe and Dave Edmunds Sing The Everly Brothers	1980	—	3.00	6.00

EDSELS, THE
45s

Number	Title (A Side/B Side)	Yr	VG	VG+	NM
CAPITOL					
❏ 4588	Bone Shaker Joe/My Jealous One	1961	5.00	10.00	20.00
❏ 4675	If Your Pillow Could Talk/Shake Shake Sherry	1961	5.00	10.00	20.00
❏ 4836	Shaddy Daddy Dip Dip/Don't You Feel	1962	5.00	10.00	20.00
DOT					
❏ 16311	My Whispering Heart/Could It Be	1962	6.25	12.50	25.00
DUB					
❏ 2843	Rama Lama Ding Dong/Bells	1958	12.50	25.00	50.00
—Repress with corrected title and the same recording as on Twin 700					
❏ 2843	Lama Rama Ding Dong/Bells	1958	17.50	35.00	70.00
—Originals have the wrong title and the same recording as on Twin 700					
❏ 2843	Rama Lama Ding Dong/Bells	197?	—	2.50	5.00
—Reproduction with an alternate take of the A-side; this has confused many who believe that the original Dub and Twin records are different.					
EMBER					
❏ 1078	Three Precious Words/Let's Go	1961	6.25	12.50	25.00
LOST-NITE					
❏ 206	Rama Lama Ding Dong/Bells	196?	2.00	4.00	8.00
—Reissue					
MUSICTONE					
❏ 1144	Rama Lama Ding Dong/Bells	1961	3.00	6.00	12.00
ROULETTE					
❏ 4151	Do You Love Me/Rink-a-Dink-a-Doo	1959	6.25	12.50	25.00
TAMMY					
❏ 1010	What Brought Us Together/ Don't Know What to Do	1960	12.50	25.00	50.00
❏ 1014	Three Precious Words/Let's Go	1960	12.50	25.00	50.00
❏ 1023	The Girl I Love/Got to Find Out About Love	1961	10.00	20.00	40.00
❏ 1027	Count the Tears/Twenty-Four Hours	1961	10.00	20.00	40.00
TWIN					
❏ 700	Rama Lama Ding Dong/Bells	1961	6.25	12.50	25.00

EDWARD BEAR
45s

Number	Title (A Side/B Side)	Yr	VG	VG+	NM
CAPITOL					
❏ 2801	You, Me and Mexico/Sinking Ship	1970	—	3.00	6.00
❏ 2955	You Can't Deny It/Toe Jam	1970	—	3.00	6.00
❏ 3351	Masquerade/The Pirate King	1972	—	2.00	4.00
❏ 3452	Last Song/Best Friend	1972	—	2.50	5.00
❏ 3452 [PS]	Last Song/Best Friend	1972	2.00	4.00	8.00
❏ 3581	Close Your Eyes/Cachet County	1973	—	2.00	4.00
❏ 3581 [PS]	Close Your Eyes/Cachet County	1973	2.50	5.00	10.00

Number	Title (A Side/B Side)	Yr	VG	VG+	NM
❏ 3683	I Love Her (You Love Me)/Walking On Back	1973	—	2.00	4.00
❏ 3683 [PS]	I Love Her (You Love Me)/Walking On Back	1973	2.50	5.00	10.00
❏ 3780	Coming Home Christmas/ Does Your Mother Know	1973	2.00	4.00	8.00
❏ 3804	Same Old Feeling/Fool	1973	—	2.00	4.00
❏ 3869	I Had Dreams/You, Me and Mexico	1974	—	2.00	4.00
❏ 3978	Freedom for the Stallion/ Why Don't You Marry Me	1974	—	2.00	4.00
Albums					
CAPITOL					
❏ SKAO-426	Bearings	1970	3.75	7.50	15.00
❏ ST-580	Eclipse	1971	3.75	7.50	15.00
❏ ST-11157	Edward Bear	1972	2.50	5.00	10.00
❏ ST-11192	Close Your Eyes	1973	2.50	5.00	10.00

EDWARDS, BOBBY
45s

Number	Title (A Side/B Side)	Yr	VG	VG+	NM
CAPITOL					
❏ 4674	What's the Reason/Walk Away Slowly	1961	2.00	4.00	8.00
❏ 4726	Singing the Blues/What'll I Do Without You	1962	2.00	4.00	8.00
❏ 4789	Someone New/Here's My Heart	1962	2.00	4.00	8.00
❏ 4874	Remember Who Brought You Here/ The Way I Am	1962	2.00	4.00	8.00
❏ 5006	Don't Pretend/Help Me	1963	2.00	4.00	8.00
CHART					
❏ 1020	I'm Sorry to See You Go/ Once a Fool (Always a Fool)	1968	—	2.50	5.00
❏ 1045	Each Time You Cross My Mind/Just Ain't My Day	1968	—	2.50	5.00
❏ 5016	Bring My Baby Home/Loving You Is Killing Me	1969	—	2.50	5.00
❏ 5061	You're the Reason/Don't Pretend	1970	—	2.50	5.00
CREST					
❏ 1075	You're the Reason/I'm a Fool for Loving You	1961	2.50	5.00	10.00
MANCO					
❏ 1026	Jealous Heart/I've Lost Everything But the Memories	1962	2.00	4.00	8.00
MUSICOR					
❏ 1101	A Little Less Heartache/Within Your Arms	1965	—	3.00	6.00

EDWARDS, DENNIS
45s

Number	Title (A Side/B Side)	Yr	VG	VG+	NM
INTERNATIONAL SOULVILLE					
❏ 100	Johnny on the Spot/I Didn't Have To But I Did	196?	375.00	750.00	1500.

EDWARDS, J.D.
45s

Number	Title (A Side/B Side)	Yr	VG	VG+	NM
IMPERIAL					
❏ 5245	Crying/Hobo	1953	30.00	60.00	120.00

EDWARDS, JIMMY
45s

Number	Title (A Side/B Side)	Yr	VG	VG+	NM
MERCURY					
❏ 71209	Love Bug Crawl/Honey Lovin'	1957	7.50	15.00	30.00
❏ 71272	My Honey/Golden Ruby Blue	1958	7.50	15.00	30.00
❏ 71348	Do That Again/Wedding Band	1958	7.50	15.00	30.00
RCA VICTOR					
❏ 47-7597	A Favor for a Friend/Your Love Is a Good Love	1959	6.25	12.50	25.00
❏ 47-7717	Rosie Lee/Live and Let Live	1960	5.00	10.00	20.00
❏ 47-7773	Silver Slippers/What Do You Want from Me	1960	5.00	10.00	20.00

EDWARDS, JOEY
45s

Number	Title (A Side/B Side)	Yr	VG	VG+	NM
COLUMBIA					
❏ 4-43620	Trapped/How Big Is Big	1966	3.00	6.00	12.00
❏ 4-43620 [PS]	Trapped/How Big Is Big	1966	5.00	10.00	20.00
LILLY					
❏ 501	This Little Girl/Shirley, Shirley	1960	50.00	100.00	200.00

EDWARDS, JOHNNY, AND THE WHITE CAPS
45s

Number	Title (A Side/B Side)	Yr	VG	VG+	NM
NORTHLAND					
❏ 90-7002	Rock 'n Roll Saddles/Why'd You Leave Me?	1957	50.00	100.00	200.00

EDWARDS, JONATHAN
45s

Number	Title (A Side/B Side)	Yr	VG	VG+	NM
ATCO					
❏ 6881	Train of Glory/Everybody Knows Her	1972	—	2.50	5.00
❏ 6911	That's What Our Life Is/Stop and Start It All Again	1972	—	2.50	5.00
❏ 6920	Honky-Tonk Stardust Cowboy/ (B-side unknown)	1973	—	2.50	5.00
❏ 6952	Rollin' Alone/The Place I've Been	1974	—	2.50	5.00
CAPRICORN					
❏ 8021	Sunshine/Emma	1971	—	2.50	5.00
CURB					
❏ NR-76829	Guitar Talk/Dime a Dance Romance	1990	—	2.00	4.00
MCA CURB					
❏ 53390	We Need to Be Locked Away/Back Up Grinnin'	1988	—	—	3.00
❏ 53467	Look What We Made (When We Made Love)/ Fewer Threads Than These	1988	—	—	3.00
❏ 53613	My Baby's a Country Song/It's a Natural Thing	1989	—	—	3.00
REPRISE					
❏ 1358	White Line/Favorite Song	1976	—	2.00	4.00
WARNER BROS.					
❏ 8364	Carolina Caroline/Never Together (But Close Sometimes)	1977	—	2.00	4.00
Albums					
ATCO					
❏ SD 36-104	Lucky Day	1974	3.00	6.00	12.00
❏ 7015 [M]	Honky-Tonk Stardust Cowboy	1972	7.50	15.00	30.00
—Mono is promo only; white label, "dj copy monaural" sticker on stereo cover					
❏ SD 7015 [S]	Honky-Tonk Stardust Cowboy	1972	3.00	6.00	12.00
❏ SD 7036	Have a Good Time for Me	1973	3.00	6.00	12.00
CAPRICORN					
❏ SD 862	Jonathan Edwards	1971	3.00	6.00	12.00
—Original has green label					
❏ SD 862	Jonathan Edwards	198?	2.00	4.00	8.00
—Reissue with tan label					

Number	Title (A Side/B Side)	Yr	VG	VG+	NM
CHRONIC					
❑ 1001	Live!	1982	3.00	6.00	12.00
MCA CURB					
❑ 42256	The Natural Thing	1989	2.50	5.00	10.00
REPRISE					
❑ MS 2238	Rockin' Chair	1976	2.50	5.00	10.00
SUGAR HILL					
❑ SH-3747	Blue Ridge	1985	2.50	5.00	10.00
—With the Seldom Scene					
WARNER BROS.					
❑ BS 3020	Sailboat	1977	2.50	5.00	10.00

EDWARDS, JONATHAN AND DARLENE Actually JO STAFFORD and PAUL WESTON as a comedy team.
45s

Number	Title (A Side/B Side)	Yr	VG	VG+	NM
DOT					
❑ 17012	Carioca/Who	1967	2.00	4.00	8.00

Albums

Number	Title (A Side/B Side)	Yr	VG	VG+	NM
COLUMBIA					
❑ CL 1024 [M]	The Piano Artistry of Jonathan Edwards	1955	12.50	25.00	50.00
❑ CL 1513 [M]	Jonathan and Darlene Edwards In Paris	1960	6.25	12.50	25.00
❑ CS 8313 [S]	Jonathan and Darlene Edwards In Paris	1960	7.50	15.00	30.00
CORINTHIAN					
❑ 103	Jonathan and Darlene Edwards In Paris	198?	2.50	5.00	10.00
❑ 104	The Original Piano Artistry of Jonathan Edwards	198?	2.50	5.00	10.00
❑ 120	Sing Along with Jonathan and Darlene	198?	2.50	5.00	10.00
❑ 122	Songs for Sheiks and Flappers	1986	2.50	5.00	10.00
DOT					
❑ DLP-3792 [M]	Songs for Sheiks and Flappers	1967	3.75	7.50	15.00
❑ DLP-25792 [S]	Songs for Sheiks and Flappers	1967	5.00	10.00	20.00
RCA VICTOR					
❑ LPM-2495 [M]	Sing Along with Jonathan and Darlene	1962	5.00	10.00	20.00
❑ LSP-2495 [S]	Sing Along with Jonathan and Darlene	1962	6.25	12.50	25.00

EDWARDS, SHIRLEY
45s

Number	Title (A Side/B Side)	Yr	VG	VG+	NM
SHRINE					
❑ 110	Dream My Heart/It Is Your Love	1966	200.00	400.00	800.00

EDWARDS, TOM
45s

Number	Title (A Side/B Side)	Yr	VG	VG+	NM
CORAL					
❑ 61773	What Is a Teen Age Boy/What Is a Teen Age Girl	1957	3.00	6.00	12.00
❑ 61826	The Story of Elvis Presley/What Is Rock 'n' Roll	1957	5.00	10.00	20.00
❑ 61938	Goodnight Rock 'n' Roll/The Spirit of Seventeen	1958	2.50	5.00	10.00
DOT					
❑ 15811	What Is a Boyfriend/All About Girls and Women	1958	2.50	5.00	10.00

EDWARDS, TOMMY
45s

Number	Title (A Side/B Side)	Yr	VG	VG+	NM
MGM					
❑ 10884	Once There Lived a Fool/A Friend of Johnny's	1951	5.00	10.00	20.00
❑ 10921	Gypsy Heart/Operetta	1951	5.00	10.00	20.00
❑ 10973	I'll Never Know Why/A Beggar in Love	1951	5.00	10.00	20.00
❑ 10989	The Morning Side of the Mountain/For Instance	1951	6.25	12.50	25.00
❑ 11035	It's All in the Game/All Over Again	1951	6.25	12.50	25.00
❑ 11077	Solitaire/My Concerto	1951	5.00	10.00	20.00
❑ 11097	Christmas Is for Children/Kris Kringle	1951	5.00	10.00	20.00
❑ 11134	Please Mr. Sun/I May Live with You	1952	6.25	12.50	25.00
❑ 11170	Forgive Me/The Bridge	1952	5.00	10.00	20.00
❑ 11209	My Girl/Piano, Bass and Drums	1952	5.00	10.00	20.00
❑ 11268	Easy to Say/The Greatest Sinner of Them All	1952	5.00	10.00	20.00
❑ 11326	You Win Again/Sinner and Saint	1952	5.00	10.00	20.00
❑ 11395	(Now and Then, There's) A Fool Such As I/I Can't Love Another	1953	5.00	10.00	20.00
❑ 11465	Au Revoir/I Lived When I Met You	1953	5.00	10.00	20.00
❑ 11485	Take These Chains from My Heart/Paging Mr. Jackson	1953	5.00	10.00	20.00
❑ 11541	Lover's Waltz/Baby, Baby, Baby	1953	5.00	10.00	20.00
❑ 11582	So Little Time/Blue Bird	1953	5.00	10.00	20.00
❑ 11604	That's All/Secret Love	1953	5.00	10.00	20.00
❑ 11624	Every Day Is Christmas/It's Christmas Once Again	1953	5.00	10.00	20.00
❑ 11668	There Was a Time/Wall of Ice	1954	5.00	10.00	20.00
❑ 11718	The Joker (In the Card Game of Life)/Within My Heart	1954	5.00	10.00	20.00
❑ 11763	Linger in My Arms/If You Would Love Me Again	1954	5.00	10.00	20.00
❑ 11821	You Walk By/I Have That Kind of Heart	1954	5.00	10.00	20.00
❑ 11932	Serenade to a Fool/It Could Have Been Me	1955	5.00	10.00	20.00
❑ 11993	Welcome to My Heart/Spring Never Came Around This Year	1955	5.00	10.00	20.00
❑ 12054	Teardrop on a Rose/To Those Who Wait	1955	5.00	10.00	20.00
❑ 12095	Baby, Let Me Take You Dreaming/My Sweetheart	1955	5.00	10.00	20.00
❑ 12248	Love Is a Child/There Must Be a Way to Your Heart	1956	5.00	10.00	20.00
❑ 12342	The Day That I Lost You/My Ship	1956	5.00	10.00	20.00
❑ 12514	We're Not Children Anymore/Any Place, Any Time	1957	5.00	10.00	20.00
❑ 12688	It's All in the Game/Please Love Me Forever	1958	3.75	7.50	15.00
❑ 12722	Love Is All We Need/Mr. Music Man	1958	3.75	7.50	15.00
❑ 12757 [M]	Please Mr. Sun/The Morning Side of the Mountain	1959	3.75	7.50	15.00
❑ 12794	My Melancholy Baby/It's Only the Good Times	1959	3.75	7.50	15.00
❑ 12814	I've Been There/I Looked at Heaven	1959	3.75	7.50	15.00
❑ 12837	Honestly and Truly/(New In) The Ways of Love	1959	3.75	7.50	15.00
❑ 12871	Don't Fence Me In/I'm Building Castles Again	1960	3.00	6.00	12.00
❑ 12890	I Really Don't Want to Know/Unloved	1960	3.00	6.00	12.00
❑ 12890 [PS]	I Really Don't Want to Know/Unloved	1960	7.50	15.00	30.00
❑ 12916	It's Not the End of Everything/Blue Heartaches	1960	3.00	6.00	12.00
❑ 12959	Suzie Wong/As You Desire Me	1960	3.00	6.00	12.00
❑ 12981	Vaya Con Dios/One and Twenty	1960	3.00	6.00	12.00
❑ 13002	The Golden Chain/That's the Way with Love	1961	3.00	6.00	12.00
❑ 13032	I'm So Lonesome I Could Cry/My Heart Would Know	1961	3.00	6.00	12.00
❑ 13057	I'll Cry You Out of My Heart/Tables Are Turning	1962	3.00	6.00	12.00
❑ 13100	Please Don't Tell Me/Tonight I Won't Be There	1962	3.00	6.00	12.00
❑ 13128	May I/Sometimes You Win, Sometimes You Lose	1963	2.50	5.00	10.00
❑ 13172	Country Boy/Love Is Best of All	1963	2.50	5.00	10.00
❑ 13317	Take These Chains from My Heart/You Win Again	1965	2.50	5.00	10.00
❑ SK 50112 [S]	Please Mr. Sun/The Morning Side of the Mountain	1959	6.25	12.50	25.00
MUSICOR					
❑ 1046	Left-Over Dreams/9 Chances Out of 10	1964	2.50	5.00	10.00
❑ 1159	I Must Be Doing Something Wrong/I Cried, I Cried	1966	2.50	5.00	10.00

7-Inch Extended Plays

Number	Title (A Side/B Side)	Yr	VG	VG+	NM
MGM					
❑ X-1003	*It's All in the Game/Solitaire/Forgive Me/You Win Again	1952	10.00	20.00	40.00
❑ X-1003 [PS]	It's All in the Game	1952	10.00	20.00	40.00
❑ X-1614	*It's All in the Game/My Sugar, My Sweet/I'll Always Be with You/That's All	1958	5.00	10.00	20.00
❑ X-1614 [PS]	It's All in the Game, Vol. 1	1958	5.00	10.00	20.00
❑ X1618	(contents unknown)	1958	5.00	10.00	20.00
❑ X1618 [PS]	It's All in the Game, Vol. 2	1958	5.00	10.00	20.00
❑ X1619	Please Love Me Forever/Love Is a Sacred Thing//Now and Then There's a Fool Such as I/Love Is All We Need	1958	5.00	10.00	20.00
❑ X1619 [PS]	It's All in the Game, Vol. 3	1958	5.00	10.00	20.00
❑ SX-1666 [PS]	For Young Lovers, Vol. 1	1959	6.25	12.50	25.00
❑ SX-1666 [S]	(contents unknown)	1959	6.25	12.50	25.00
❑ X-1666 [M]	(contents unknown)	1959	5.00	10.00	20.00
❑ X-1666 [PS]	For Young Lovers, Vol. 1	1959	5.00	10.00	20.00
❑ SX-1667 [PS]	For Young Lovers, Vol. 2	1959	6.25	12.50	25.00
❑ SX-1667 [S]	(contents unknown)	1959	6.25	12.50	25.00
❑ X-1667 [M]	(contents unknown)	1959	5.00	10.00	20.00
❑ X-1667 [PS]	For Young Lovers, Vol. 2	1959	5.00	10.00	20.00
❑ SX-1668 [PS]	For Young Lovers, Vol. 3	1959	6.25	12.50	25.00
❑ SX-1668 [S]	Once There Lived a Fool/Up in a Cloud//It's Only the Good Times/Welcome Me	1959	6.25	12.50	25.00
❑ X-1668 [M]	(contents unknown)	1959	5.00	10.00	20.00
❑ X-1668 [PS]	For Young Lovers, Vol. 3	1959	5.00	10.00	20.00

Albums

Number	Title (A Side/B Side)	Yr	VG	VG+	NM
LION					
❑ L-70120 [M]	Tommy Edwards	1959	7.50	15.00	30.00
METRO					
❑ M-511 [M]	Tommy Edwards	1965	3.00	6.00	12.00
❑ MS-511 [S]	Tommy Edwards	1965	3.75	7.50	15.00
MGM					
❑ E-3732 [M]	It's All in the Game	1958	7.50	15.00	30.00
—Yellow label					
❑ E-3732 [M]	It's All in the Game	1960	5.00	10.00	20.00
—Black label					
❑ SE-3732 [S]	It's All in the Game	1959	10.00	20.00	40.00
—Yellow label					
❑ SE-3732 [S]	It's All in the Game	1960	6.25	12.50	25.00
—Black label					
❑ E-3760 [M]	For Young Lovers	1959	7.50	15.00	30.00
—Yellow label					
❑ E-3760 [M]	For Young Lovers	1960	5.00	10.00	20.00
—Black label					
❑ SE-3760 [S]	For Young Lovers	1959	10.00	20.00	40.00
—Yellow label					
❑ SE-3760 [S]	For Young Lovers	1960	6.25	12.50	25.00
—Black label					
❑ E-3805 [M]	You Started Me Dreaming	1960	5.00	10.00	20.00
❑ SE-3805 [S]	You Started Me Dreaming	1960	6.25	12.50	25.00
❑ E-3822 [M]	Step Out Singing	1960	5.00	10.00	20.00
❑ SE-3822 [S]	Step Out Singing	1960	6.25	12.50	25.00
❑ E-3838 [M]	Tommy Edwards in Hawaii	1960	5.00	10.00	20.00
❑ SE-3838 [S]	Tommy Edwards in Hawaii	1960	6.25	12.50	25.00
❑ E-3884 [M]	Tommy Edwards' Greatest Hits	1961	5.00	10.00	20.00
❑ SE-3884 [S]	Tommy Edwards' Greatest Hits	1961	6.25	12.50	25.00
❑ E-3959 [M]	Golden Coutnry Hits	1961	5.00	10.00	20.00
❑ SE-3959 [S]	Golden Coutnry Hits	1961	6.25	12.50	25.00
❑ E-4020 [M]	Stardust	1962	5.00	10.00	20.00
❑ SE-4020 [S]	Stardust	1962	6.25	12.50	25.00
❑ E-4060 [M]	Soft Strings and Two Guitars	1962	5.00	10.00	20.00
❑ SE-4060 [S]	Soft Strings and Two Guitars	1962	6.25	12.50	25.00
❑ E-4141 [M]	The Very Best of Tommy Edwards	1963	3.75	7.50	15.00
❑ SE-4141 [S]	The Very Best of Tommy Edwards	1963	5.00	10.00	20.00
REGENT					
❑ MG-6096 [M]	Tommy Edwards Sings	1958	15.00	30.00	60.00

EDWARDS, VERN
45s

Number	Title (A Side/B Side)	Yr	VG	VG+	NM
PROBE					
❑ 100	Cool Baby, Cool/Glenda	1959	50.00	100.00	200.00

EDWARDS, VINCENT
45s

Number	Title (A Side/B Side)	Yr	VG	VG+	NM
CAPITOL					
❑ F3836	Lollipop/Wiget	1957	3.75	7.50	15.00
—As "Vince Edwards"					
❑ 4819	Lollipop/As You Desire Me	1962	2.50	5.00	10.00
COLPIX					
❑ 771	No, Not Much/See That Girl	1965	2.00	4.00	8.00
❑ 771 [PS]	No, Not Much/See That Girl	1965	2.50	5.00	10.00
DECCA					
❑ 31413	Don't Worry 'Bout Me/And Now	1962	2.00	4.00	8.00
❑ 31413 [PS]	Don't Worry 'Bout Me/And Now	1962	5.00	10.00	20.00
❑ 31426	I Got It Bad (And That Ain't Good)/Say It Isn't So	1962	2.00	4.00	8.00
❑ 31426 [PS]	I Got It Bad (And That Ain't Good)/Say It Isn't So	1962	3.00	6.00	12.00
❑ 31460	To Kill a Mockingbird/You'll Still Have Me	1963	2.00	4.00	8.00
❑ 31534	This Train/Looking for Someone	1963	2.00	4.00	8.00
❑ 31563	Does Goodnight Mean Goodbye/Per Te Per Me	1963	2.00	4.00	8.00
KAMA SUTRA					
❑ 221	Nylon Stockings/To Be with You	1967	—	3.00	6.00
❑ 221 [PS]	Nylon Stockings/To Be with You	1967	2.50	5.00	10.00

Number	Title (A Side/B Side)	Yr	VG	VG+	NM
MAGIC LAMP					
❑ 701	I'm Not the Marrying Kind/What Colors Are You	1964	2.00	4.00	8.00
RUSS-FI					
❑ 1	Oh Babe/Squealin' Parrot Twist	196?	3.00	6.00	12.00
❑ 7001	Why Did You Leave Me/Squealin' Parrot Twist	1962	2.50	5.00	10.00
Albums					
DECCA					
❑ DL 4311 [M]	Vincent Edwards Sings	1962	5.00	10.00	20.00
❑ DL 4336 [M]	Sometimes I'm Happy…Sometimes I'm Blue	1962	5.00	10.00	20.00
❑ DL 4399 [M]	In Person at the Riviera	1963	5.00	10.00	20.00
❑ DL 74311 [S]	Vincent Edwards Sings	1962	6.25	12.50	25.00
❑ DL 74336 [S]	Sometimes I'm Happy…Sometimes I'm Blue	1962	6.25	12.50	25.00
❑ DL 74399 [S]	In Person at the Riviera	1963	6.25	12.50	25.00
VOCALION					
❑ VL 3852 [M]	Here's Vincent Edwards	1967	3.00	6.00	12.00
❑ VL 73852 [S]	Here's Vincent Edwards	1967	3.00	6.00	12.00

EELY, JACK Sang lead on THE KINGSMEN's version of "Louie Louie."

45s

Number	Title (A Side/B Side)	Yr	VG	VG+	NM
BANG					
❑ 520	Louie Louie '66/David's Mood	1966	3.75	7.50	15.00
❑ 534	Louie Go Home/Ride Ride Baby	1966	3.75	7.50	15.00

EHRET, BOB

45s

Number	Title (A Side/B Side)	Yr	VG	VG+	NM
ALADDIN					
❑ 3377	Stop the Clock/So Lonely	1957	37.50	75.00	150.00

8TH DAY, THE Probably all the same group.

45s

Number	Title (A Side/B Side)	Yr	VG	VG+	NM
A&M					
❑ 2539	Call Me Up/I've Got My Heart in the Right Place	1983	—	2.00	4.00
❑ 2595 [DJ]	In the Valley (same on both sides)	1983	—	2.00	4.00
CADET					
❑ 5660	Hear the Grass Grow/Bring Your Love Back	1969	2.50	5.00	10.00
CRIB					
❑ 101	Let's Share the Miracle/It's Christmas Day	19??	—	2.00	4.00
INVICTUS					
❑ 9087	She's Not Just Another Woman/I Can't Fool Myself	1971	—	2.50	5.00
❑ 9098	You've Got to Crawl (Before You Walk)/It's Instrumental to Be Free	1971	—	2.50	5.00
❑ 9107	If I Could See the Light/If I Could See the Light (Part 2)	1971	—	2.50	5.00
❑ 9117	Eeny-Meeny-Miny-Mo (Three's a Crowd)/Rocks in My Head	1972	—	2.50	5.00
❑ 9124	Good Book/I Gotta Get Home	1972	—	2.50	5.00
KAPP					
❑ 862	Hey Boy (The Girl's in Love with You)/Million Lights	1967	2.00	4.00	8.00
❑ 862 [PS]	Hey Boy (The Girl's in Love with You)/Million Lights	1967	3.00	6.00	12.00
❑ 894	Raining Sunshine/That Good Old Fashioned Way	1968	2.00	4.00	8.00
❑ 916	Glory/Building with a Steeple	1968	2.00	4.00	8.00
Albums					
A&M					
❑ SP-4942	The 8th Day	1983	2.50	5.00	10.00
INVICTUS					
❑ ST-7306	The 8th Day	1971	3.00	6.00	12.00
❑ ST-9809	I Gotta Get Home	1973	3.00	6.00	12.00
KAPP					
❑ KS 3554	On the Eighth Day	1968	3.75	7.50	15.00

EIRE APPARENT, THE Produced by JIMI HENDRIX.

45s

Number	Title (A Side/B Side)	Yr	VG	VG+	NM
BUDDAH					
❑ 67	Yes I Need Someone/Let Me Stay	1968	3.75	7.50	15.00
Albums					
BUDDAH					
❑ BDS-5031	Sunrise	1969	10.00	20.00	40.00

EL CAPRIS

45s

Number	Title (A Side/B Side)	Yr	VG	VG+	NM
ARGYLE					
❑ 1010	Ooh But She Did/(Shimmy, Shimmy) Ko Ko Wop	1961	7.50	15.00	30.00
BULLSEYE					
❑ 102	Oh But She Did/(Shimmy Shimmy) Ko Ko Wop	1956	37.50	75.00	150.00
—Note slight difference in A-side title					
❑ 102	Ooh But She Did/(Shimmy Shimmy) Ko Ko Wop	1956	50.00	100.00	200.00
FEE BEE					
❑ 216	Your Star/To Live Again	1957	10.00	20.00	40.00
HI-Q					
❑ 5006	Girl of Mine/These Lonely Nights	1958	10.00	20.00	40.00
—Yellow label					
❑ 5006	Girl of Mine/These Lonely Nights	1958	25.00	50.00	100.00
—Blue label					
PARIS					
❑ 525	They're Always Laughing at Me/Ivy League Clean	1958	10.00	20.00	40.00
RING-O					
❑ 308	Safari/Quit Pulling My Woman	1960	7.50	15.00	30.00

EL CHICANO

45s

Number	Title (A Side/B Side)	Yr	VG	VG+	NM
GORDO					
❑ 703	Viva Tirado — Part I/Viva Tirado — Part II	1970	2.50	5.00	10.00
KAPP					
❑ 2085	Viva Tirado — Part I/Viva Tirado — Part II	1970	—	2.50	5.00
❑ 2129	Cuban Chant/Viva La Raza	1971	—	2.50	5.00
❑ 2150	Sugar, Sugar/Don't Put Me Down	1971	—	2.50	5.00
❑ 2173	Brown Eyed Girl/Mas Zacate	1972	—	2.50	5.00
❑ 2182	Senor Blues/Satisfy Me Woman	1972	—	2.50	5.00
MCA					
❑ 40021	Last Tango in Paris/In a Silent Way	1973	—	2.50	5.00
❑ 40104	Tell Her She's Lovely/Chachita	1973	—	2.50	5.00

Number	Title (A Side/B Side)	Yr	VG	VG+	NM
❑ 40240	El Cayuco/You've Been Wrong So Long	1974	—	2.00	4.00
❑ 40359	Follow the Apollo/You Can Have the Best of Everything	1975	—	2.00	4.00
❑ 40391	Put On a Show/Might As Well	1975	—	2.00	4.00
❑ 40422	Baretta's Theme (Keep Your Eyes on the Sparrow)/One More Night	1975	—	2.00	4.00
❑ 40457	Michael's Theme/When You Got a Heartache	1975	—	2.00	4.00
❑ 40520	All I Can Remember/Lake Aquabi	1976	—	2.00	4.00
Albums					
KAPP					
❑ KS-3632	Viva Tirado	1970	3.00	6.00	12.00
❑ KS-3640	Revolucion	1971	3.00	6.00	12.00
❑ KS-3663	Celebration	1972	3.00	6.00	12.00
MCA					
❑ 69	Revolucion	1973	2.50	5.00	10.00
—Reissue of Kapp 3640					
❑ 312	El Chicano	1973	2.50	5.00	10.00
❑ 401	Cinco	1974	2.50	5.00	10.00
❑ 437	The Best of Everything	1975	2.50	5.00	10.00
❑ 548	Viva Tirado	197?	2.50	5.00	10.00
—Reissue of Kapp 3632					
❑ 2150	Pyramid of Love	1975	2.50	5.00	10.00
SHADYBROOK					
❑ SB 33-005	This Is El Chicano	1977	3.75	7.50	15.00

EL CLOD

45s

Number	Title (A Side/B Side)	Yr	VG	VG+	NM
CHALLENGE					
❑ 9159	Tijuana Border (Wolverton Mountain)/Pedro's Piano Roll Twist	1962	5.00	10.00	20.00
MERCURY					
❑ 72082	He's Not a Rebel/Holiday in Havana	1963	3.75	7.50	15.00
VEE JAY					
❑ 647	Tijuana Watusi/Gringo	1965	3.75	7.50	15.00

EL DOMINGOS

45s

Number	Title (A Side/B Side)	Yr	VG	VG+	NM
CANDLELITE					
❑ 418	Made in Heaven/Lucky Me, I'm in Love	1963	6.25	12.50	25.00
CHELSEA					
❑ 1009	Made in Heaven/Lucky Me, I'm in Love	1962	50.00	100.00	200.00
KARMIN					
❑ 1001	Are You Ready to Say "I Do"/I Want to Know	1964	75.00	150.00	300.00

EL DORADOS

45s

Number	Title (A Side/B Side)	Yr	VG	VG+	NM
LOST-NITE					
❑ 263	One More Chance/Little Miss Love	197?	—	2.50	5.00
—Reissue					
❑ 270	Crazy Little Mama (At My Front Door)/What's Buggin' You Baby	197?	—	2.50	5.00
❑ 278	Now That You've Gone/Rock 'N' Roll's for Me	197?	—	2.50	5.00
—Reissue					
❑ 285	I'll Be Forever Lovin' You/I Began to Realize	197?	—	2.50	5.00
—Reissue					
❑ 293	Bim Bam Boom/There in the Night	197?	—	2.50	5.00
—Reissue					
❑ 300	Fallen Tear/Chop Ling Soon	197?	—	2.50	5.00
—Reissue					
❑ 308	Tears on My Pillow/A Rose for My Darling	197?	—	2.50	5.00
—Reissue					
OLDIES 45					
❑ 68	Baby, I Need You/Lovers Never Say Goodbye	1964	2.00	4.00	8.00
—B-side by the Flamingos					
PAULA					
❑ 347	Looking In from the Outside/Since You Came Into My Life	1971	2.50	5.00	10.00
❑ 369	Loose Booty (Part 1)/Loose Booty (Part 2)	1971	2.50	5.00	10.00
TORRID					
❑ 100	In Over My Head/You Make My Heart Sing	1970	3.75	7.50	15.00
VEE JAY					
❑ 115	Baby I Need You/My Loving Baby	1954	20.00	40.00	80.00
❑ 115	Baby I Need You/My Loving Baby	1954	100.00	200.00	400.00
—Red vinyl					
❑ 118	Annie's Answer/Living with Vivian	1954	20.00	40.00	80.00
❑ 118	Annie's Answer/Living with Vivian	1954	75.00	150.00	300.00
—Red vinyl					
❑ 127	One More Chance/Little Miss Love	1954	50.00	100.00	200.00
❑ 147	At My Front Door/What's Buggin' You Baby	1955	17.50	35.00	70.00
❑ 165	I'll Be Forever Lovin' You/I Began to Realize	1955	15.00	30.00	60.00
❑ 180	Now That You've Gone/Rock 'N' Roll's for Me	1956	12.50	25.00	50.00
❑ 197	Fallen Tear/Chop Ling Soon	1956	12.50	25.00	50.00
❑ 211	Bim Bam Boom/There in the Night	1956	20.00	40.00	80.00
❑ 250	Tears on My Pillow/A Rose for My Darling	1957	7.50	15.00	30.00
❑ 263	Three Reasons Why/Boom Diddle Boom	1958	37.50	75.00	150.00
❑ 302	Oh What a Girl/The Lights Are Low	1958	37.50	75.00	150.00
Albums					
LOST-NITE					
❑ LLP-20 [10]	The El Dorados	1981	3.00	6.00	12.00
—Red vinyl					
SOLID SMOKE					
❑ 8025	Low Mileage/High Octane	1984	2.50	5.00	10.00
VEE JAY					
❑ LP-1001 [M]	Crazy Little Mama	1959	200.00	400.00	800.00
—Maroon label, thick silver band					
❑ LP-1001 [M]	Crazy Little Mama	1960	100.00	200.00	400.00
—Maroon label, thin silver band					
❑ LP-1001 [M]	Crazy Little Mama	1962	62.50	125.00	250.00
—Black label with colorband					
❑ VJLP-1001 [M]	Crazy Little Mama	198?	2.50	5.00	10.00
—Authorized reissue					

Number	Title (A Side/B Side)	Yr	VG	VG+	NM
EL RAYS, THE See THE DELLS.					
EL VENOS, THE					
45s					
GROOVE					
❏ 0170	Now We're Together/Geraldine	1956	20.00	40.00	80.00
RCA VICTOR					
❏ 47-8303	My Heart Beats Faster/You Won't Be There	1963	6.25	12.50	25.00
VIK					
❏ 0305	My Heart Beats Faster/You Must Be True	1957	20.00	40.00	80.00
ELBERT, DONNIE					
45s					
ALL PLATINUM					
❏ 2330	Where Did Our Love Go/That's If You Love Me	1971	—	3.00	6.00
❏ 2333	Sweet Baby/Can't Get Over Losing You	1971	—	3.00	6.00
❏ 2336	If I Can't Have You/Can't Get Over Losing You	1972	—	3.00	6.00
❏ 2337	Little Piece of Leather/Sweet Baby	1972	—	3.00	6.00
❏ 2338	That's If You Love Me/Can't Get Over Losing You	1972	—	3.00	6.00
❏ 2346	This Feeling of Losing You/Can't Stand These Lonely Nights	1973	—	3.00	6.00
❏ 2351	Love Is Strange/(Instrumental)	1973	—	3.00	6.00
❏ 2367	What Do You Do/Will You Love Me Tomorrow	1974	—	2.50	5.00
❏ 2374	You Should Be Dancing/What Do You Do	1974	—	2.50	5.00
ATCO					
❏ 6550	Too Far Gone/In Between the Heartaches	1968	2.00	4.00	8.00
AVCO					
❏ 4587	I Can't Help Myself/Love Is Here and Now You're Gone	1972	—	3.00	6.00
❏ 4598	Ooh, Baby Baby/Tell Her for Me	1972	—	3.00	6.00
CUB					
❏ 9125	Don't Cry My Love/Love Stew	1963	3.00	6.00	12.00
DELUXE					
❏ 6125	What Can I Do/Hear My Plea	1957	5.00	10.00	20.00
❏ 6143	Believe It or Not/Tell Me So	1957	5.00	10.00	20.00
❏ 6148	Leona/Have I Sinned	1957	5.00	10.00	20.00
❏ 6156	Wild Child/Let's Do the Stroll	1958	5.00	10.00	20.00
❏ 6161	My Confession of Love/Peek-a-Boo	1958	5.00	10.00	20.00
❏ 6168	I Want to Be Near You/Come On Sugar	1958	5.00	10.00	20.00
❏ 6175	Just a Little Bit of Lovin'/When You're Near Me	1958	5.00	10.00	20.00
DERAM					
❏ 7526	Without You/Baby Please Come Home	1969	2.00	4.00	8.00
PARKWAY					
❏ 844	Set My Heart at Ease/Baby Cares	1962	3.75	7.50	15.00
RARE BULLET					
❏ 101	Can't Get Over Losing You/Got to Get Myself Together	1970	—	3.00	6.00
VEE JAY					
❏ 336	Hey Baby/Will You Ever Be Mine	1960	3.75	7.50	15.00
❏ 353	Baby Let Me Love You Tonight/Half as Old	1960	3.75	7.50	15.00
❏ 370	I've Loved You Baby/I Beg of You	1960	3.75	7.50	15.00
Albums					
ALL PLATINUM					
❏ 3007	Where Did Our Love Go	1971	6.25	12.50	25.00
❏ 3019	Dancin' the Night Away	1977	6.25	12.50	25.00
DELUXE					
❏ 12003	Have I Sinned	1971	6.25	12.50	25.00
KING					
❏ 629 [M]	The Sensational Donnie Elbert Sings	1959	100.00	200.00	400.00
SUGAR HILL					
❏ 256	From the Git Go	1981	3.00	6.00	12.00
TRIP					
❏ 9514	Donnie Elbert Sings	197?	3.75	7.50	15.00
❏ 9524	Stop in the Name of Love	197?	3.75	7.50	15.00
ELCHORDS, THE					
45s					
GOOD					
❏ 544	Peppermint Stick/Gee, I'm in Love	1958	20.00	40.00	80.00
—*Straight lines on label*					
❏ 544	Peppermint Stick/Gee, I'm in Love	1962	3.75	7.50	15.00
—*No lines on label*					
❏ 544	Peppermint Stick/Gee, I'm in Love	1962	5.00	10.00	20.00
—*Sawtooth lines on label*					
❏ 544	Peppermint Stick/Gee, I'm in Love	1962	15.00	30.00	60.00
—*Red vinyl*					
ELECTRIC ELVES, THE Also see RONNIE DIO.					
45s					
MGM					
❏ K 13839 [DJ]	Hey, Look Me Over/It Pays to Advertise	1967	12.50	25.00	50.00
—*Stock copy not known to exist; it would probably go for at least twice this amount*					
ELECTRIC EXPRESS, THE					
45s					
AVCO					
❏ 4607	I Can't Believe We Did (The Whole Thing)/Bee Pee	1972	3.75	7.50	15.00
KEY-VAC					
❏ 2930	Hearsay/(Instrumental)	197?	25.00	50.00	100.00
LINCO					
❏ 1001	It's the Real Thing - Pt. 1/Pt. 2	1971	2.50	5.00	10.00
❏ 1002	Where You Coming From - Pt. 1/Pt. 2	1972	5.00	10.00	20.00
❏ 1003	I Can't Believe We Did (The Whole Thing)/Bee Pee	1972	5.00	10.00	20.00
ELECTRIC FLAG, THE					
45s					
ATLANTIC					
❏ 3222	Sweet Soul Music/Every Now and Then	1974	—	2.00	4.00
❏ 3237	Doctor Oh Doctor/The Band Kept Playing	1975	—	2.00	4.00
COLUMBIA					
❏ 44307	Groovin' Is Easy/Over-Lovin' You	1967	2.00	4.00	8.00
❏ 44307 [PS]	Groovin' Is Easy/Over-Lovin' You	1967	5.00	10.00	20.00
❏ 44376	Soul Searchin'/Sunny	1967	2.00	4.00	8.00

Number	Title (A Side/B Side)	Yr	VG	VG+	NM
❏ 44765	Soul Searchin'/Sunny	1969	—	3.00	6.00
SIDEWALK					
❏ 929	Green and Gold/Peter's Trip	1967	3.75	7.50	15.00
Albums					
ATLANTIC					
❏ SD 18112	The Band Kept Playing	1974	2.50	5.00	10.00
COLUMBIA					
❏ CS 9597	A Long Time Comin'	1968	3.75	7.50	15.00
—*"360 Sound" label*					
❏ CS 9597	A Long Time Comin'	1970	2.50	5.00	10.00
—*Orange label*					
❏ PC 9597	A Long Time Comin'	198?	2.00	4.00	8.00
—*Budget-line reissue*					
❏ CS 9714	The Electric Flag	1968	3.75	7.50	15.00
—*"360 Sound" label*					
❏ CS 9714	The Electric Flag	1970	2.50	5.00	10.00
—*Orange label*					
❏ C 30422	The Best of the Electric Flag	1971	2.50	5.00	10.00
ELECTRIC INDIAN, THE					
45s					
MARMADUKE					
❏ 4001	Keem-O-Sabe/Broad Street	1969	5.00	10.00	20.00
UNITED ARTISTS					
❏ 0128	Keem-O-Sabe/Stick Shift	1973	—	2.00	4.00
—*"Silver Spotlight Series" reissue; B-side by The Duals*					
❏ 50563	Keem-O-Sabe/Broad Street	1969	—	3.00	6.00
❏ 50613	Geronimo/Land of 1,000 Dances	1969	—	2.50	5.00
❏ 50647	Rain Dance/Storm Warning	1970	—	2.50	5.00
❏ 50701	Apotchee/Chicago Hawk	1970	—	2.50	5.00
❏ 50744	Geronimo/My Cherie Amour	1971	—	2.50	5.00
Albums					
UNITED ARTISTS					
❏ UAS 6728	Keem-O-Sabe	1969	3.75	7.50	15.00
ELECTRIC LIGHT ORCHESTRA					
12-Inch Singles					
CBS ASSOCIATED					
❏ ZAS 2254 [DJ]	Calling America (3:29) (same on both sides)	1986	2.50	5.00	10.00
45s					
CBS ASSOCIATED					
❏ 05766	Calling America/Caught in a Trap	1986	—	—	3.00
❏ 05766 [PS]	Calling America/Caught in a Trap	1986	—	—	3.00
❏ 05892	So Serious/Endless Lies	1986	—	—	3.00
❏ 05892 [PS]	So Serious/Endless Lies	1986	—	—	3.00
JET					
❏ XW 1099	Turn to Stone/Mister Kingdom	1977	—	2.00	4.00
❏ XW 1099 [PS]	Turn to Stone/Mister Kingdom	1977	2.00	4.00	8.00
❏ XW 1145	Sweet Talkin' Woman/Fire on High	1978	—	2.00	4.00
❏ XW 1145	Sweet Talkin' Woman/Fire on High	1978	—	2.50	5.00
—*Purple vinyl*					
❏ XW 1145 [PS]	Sweet Talkin' Woman/Fire on High	1978	—	2.50	5.00
❏ 02408	Hold On Tight/When Time Stood Still	1981	—	2.00	4.00
❏ 02559	Twilight/Julie Don't Live Here	1981	—	2.00	4.00
❏ 02693	Rain Is Falling/Another Heart Broke	1982	—	2.00	4.00
❏ 03086	Hold On Tight/Mr. Blue Sky	1982	—	—	3.00
—*Reissue*					
❏ 03964	Rock and Roll Is King/After All	1983	—	2.00	4.00
❏ 04130	Four Little Diamonds/Letter from Spain	1983	—	2.00	4.00
❏ 04208	Stranger/Train of Gold	1983	—	2.00	4.00
❏ 5050	Mr. Blue Sky/One Summer Dream	1978	—	2.00	4.00
❏ 5052	It's Over/The Whale	1978	—	2.00	4.00
❏ 5057	Shine a Little Love/Jungle	1979	—	2.00	4.00
❏ 5057 [PS]	Shine a Little Love/Jungle	1979	2.00	4.00	8.00
❏ 5060	Don't Bring Me Down/Dreaming of 4000	1979	—	2.00	4.00
❏ 5064	Confusion/Poker	1979	—	2.00	4.00
❏ 5067	Last Train to London/Down Home Town	1979	—	2.00	4.00
MCA					
❏ 41246	I'm Alive/Drum Dreams	1980	—	2.00	4.00
❏ 41246 [PS]	I'm Alive/Drum Dreams	1980	—	2.50	5.00
❏ 41285	Xanadu/Whenever You're Away from Me	1980	—	2.00	4.00
—*A-side: Olivia Newton-John/Electric Light Orchestra*					
❏ 41289	All Over the World/Drum Dreams	1980	—	2.00	4.00
❏ 41289 [PS]	All Over the World/Drum Dreams	1980	—	2.50	5.00
UNITED ARTISTS					
❏ XW 173	Roll Over Beethoven/Queen of the Hours	1973	—	3.00	6.00
❏ XW 337	Showdown/In Old England Town	1973	—	3.00	6.00
❏ XW 405	Daybreaker/Ma-Ma-Ma-Belle	1974	—	3.00	6.00
❏ XW 513	Roll Over Beethoven/Showdown	1974	—	2.00	4.00
—*Reissue*					
❏ XW 573	Can't Get It Out of My Head/Illusions in G Major	1974	—	2.00	4.00
❏ XW 573 [PS]	Can't Get It Out of My Head/Illusions in G Major	1974	—	3.00	6.00
❏ XW 634	Boy Blue/Eldorado	1975	—	2.50	5.00
❏ XW 729	Evil Woman/10538 Overture (Live)	1975	—	2.00	4.00
❏ XW 770	Strange Magic/New World Rising	1976	—	2.00	4.00
❏ XW 770 [PS]	Strange Magic/New World Rising	1976	—	3.00	6.00
❏ XW 842	Showdown/Daybreaker (Live)	1976	—	2.50	5.00
❏ XW 888	Livin' Thing/Ma-Ma-Ma-Belle	1976	—	2.00	4.00
❏ XW 939	Do Ya/Nightrider	1977	—	2.00	4.00
❏ XW 1000	Telephone Line/Poorboy (The Greenwood)	1977	—	2.00	4.00
❏ XW 1000	Telephone Line/Poorboy (The Greenwood)	1977	—	2.50	5.00
—*Green vinyl*					
❏ XW 1000 [PS]	Telephone Line/Poorboy (The Greenwood)	1977	—	2.50	5.00
—*Picture sleeves were not issued with black vinyl versions*					
❏ XW 1176	Can't Get It Out of My Head/Strange Magic	1978	—	2.00	4.00
❏ XW 1177	Evil Woman/Livin' Thing	1978	—	2.00	4.00
❏ XW 1178	Do Ya/Nightrider	1978	—	2.00	4.00
❏ XW 1179	Boy Blue/Telephone Line	1978	—	2.00	4.00
❏ XW 1180	Ma-Ma-Ma-Belle/10538 Overture	1978	—	2.00	4.00
—*1176 through 1180 were available for a very short time just before ELO's rights transfered from UA to CBS.*					
❏ 50914	10538 Overture/(Battle of) Marston Moor	1972	2.00	4.00	8.00
Albums					
CBS ASSOCIATED					
❏ FZ 40048	Balance of Power	1986	2.50	5.00	10.00

E

Number	Title (A Side/B Side)	Yr	VG	VG+	NM
JET					
❏ JT-LA823-L2 [(2)]Out of the Blue		1977	3.75	7.50	15.00
—Originals include poster and die-cut cardboard "spaceship"					
❏ JT-LA823-L2 [(2)DJ]Out of the Blue		1977	6.25	12.50	25.00
—Promo only on blue vinyl					
❏ JZ 35524	No Answer	1978	2.50	5.00	10.00
❏ PZ 35524	No Answer	1981	2.00	4.00	8.00
❏ JZ 35525	On the Third Day	1978	2.50	5.00	10.00
❏ PZ 35525	On the Third Day	1981	2.00	4.00	8.00
❏ JZ 35526	Eldorado	1978	2.50	5.00	10.00
❏ PZ 35526	Eldorado	198?	2.00	4.00	8.00
❏ JZ 35527	Face the Music	1978	2.50	5.00	10.00
❏ PZ 35527	Face the Music	1981	2.00	4.00	8.00
❏ JZ 35528	Ole Elo	1978	2.50	5.00	10.00
❏ PZ 35528	Ole Elo	1981	2.00	4.00	8.00
❏ JZ 35529	A New World Record	1978	2.50	5.00	10.00
❏ PZ 35529	A New World Record	1981	2.00	4.00	8.00
❏ KZ2 35530 [(2)]Out of the Blue		1978	3.00	6.00	12.00
❏ JZ 35533	Electric Light Orchestra II	1978	2.50	5.00	10.00
❏ PZ 35533	Electric Light Orchestra II	1981	2.00	4.00	8.00
❏ FZ 35769	Discovery	1979	2.50	5.00	10.00
❏ PZ 35769	Discovery	1987	2.00	4.00	8.00
❏ FZ 36310	ELO's Greatest Hits	1979	2.50	5.00	10.00
❏ HZ 36310	ELO's Greatest Hits	1981	10.00	20.00	40.00
—Half-speed mastered edition					
❏ PZ 36310	ELO's Greatest Hits	1987	2.00	4.00	8.00
❏ Z4X 36966 [(4)]A Box of Their Best		1980	6.25	12.50	25.00
❏ FZ 37371	Time	1981	2.50	5.00	10.00
❏ PZ 37371	Time	1987	2.00	4.00	8.00
❏ PZ 38490	Secret Messages	1987	2.00	4.00	8.00
❏ QZ 38490	Secret Messages	1983	2.50	5.00	10.00
❏ HZ 45789	Discovery	1980	6.25	12.50	25.00
—Half-speed mastered edition					
❏ HZ 47371	Time	1982	6.25	12.50	25.00
—Half-speed mastered edition					
❏ HZ 48490	Secret Messages	1983	7.50	15.00	30.00
—Half-speed mastered edition					
UNITED ARTISTS					
❏ UA-LA040-F	Electric Light Orchestra II	1973	3.75	7.50	15.00
—Tan label					
❏ UA-LA040-F	Electric Light Orchestra II	1978	2.50	5.00	10.00
—Sunrise label					
❏ SP-123 [DJ]	Ole Elo	1976	12.50	25.00	50.00
—Gold vinyl promo with generic cover					
❏ SP-123 [DJ]	Ole Elo	1976	20.00	40.00	80.00
—Red, blue or white vinyl promos with generic cover					
❏ SP-123 [DJ]	Ole Elo	1976	25.00	50.00	100.00
—Gold vinyl, cover similar to the released version except for the single line "Ole Elo" (no "Electric Light Orchestra" underneath) at the top of the front cover					
❏ UA-LA188-F	On the Third Day	1973	3.75	7.50	15.00
—Tan label					
❏ UA-LA188-F	On the Third Day	1978	2.50	5.00	10.00
—Sunrise label					
❏ UA-LA318-F	The Night the Light Went On in Long Beach	1974	—	—	—
—Canceled					
❏ UA-LA339-G	Eldorado	1974	3.00	6.00	12.00
—Tan label					
❏ UA-LA339-G	Eldorado	1977	2.50	5.00	10.00
—Sunrise label					
❏ UA-LA546-DJ [DJ]Face the Music		1975	6.25	12.50	25.00
—Promo only, banded for airplay					
❏ UA-LA546-G	Face the Music	1975	3.00	6.00	12.00
—Tan label					
❏ UA-LA546-G	Face the Music	1978	2.50	5.00	10.00
—Sunrise label					
❏ UA-LA630-G	Ole Elo	1976	3.00	6.00	12.00
—Tan label					
❏ UA-LA630-G	Ole Elo	1978	2.50	5.00	10.00
—Sunrise label					
❏ UA-LA679-G	A New World Record	1976	3.00	6.00	12.00
—All copies have custom labels					
❏ UAS-5573	No Answer	1972	3.75	7.50	15.00
—Tan label					
❏ UAS-5573	No Answer	1978	2.50	5.00	10.00
—Sunrise label					

ELECTRIC PRUNES, THE
45s

Number	Title (A Side/B Side)	Yr	VG	VG+	NM
REPRISE					
❏ PRO 277 [DJ]	Sanctus/Credo	1968	12.50	25.00	50.00
❏ PRO 305 [DJ]	Help Us (Our Father, Our King)/The Adoration	1968	10.00	20.00	40.00
❏ 0473	Ain't It Hard/Little Olive	1966	10.00	20.00	40.00
❏ 0532	I Had Too Much to Dream (Last Night)/Lovin	1966	5.00	10.00	20.00
❏ 0564	Get Me to the World on Time/Are You Lovin' Me	1967	6.25	12.50	25.00
❏ 0594	Hideaway/Dr. Do-Good	1967	6.25	12.50	25.00
❏ 0607	The Great Banana Hoax/Wind-Up Toys	1967	6.25	12.50	25.00
❏ 0652	You Never Had It So Good/Everybody Knows You're Not in Love	1967	10.00	20.00	40.00
❏ 0704	I Had Too Much to Dream (Last Night)/Get Me to the World On Time	1968	—	2.50	5.00
—"Back to Back Hits" series -- originals have "W7" and "r:" logos					
❏ 0805	Hey, Mr. President/Flowing Smoothly	1969	6.25	12.50	25.00
❏ 0833	Violent Rose/Sell	1969	10.00	20.00	40.00
❏ 0858	Love Grows/Finders Keepers, Losers Weepers	1969	6.25	12.50	25.00
Albums					
REPRISE					
❏ R-6248 [M]	The Electric Prunes	1967	12.50	25.00	50.00
❏ RS-6248 [S]	The Electric Prunes	1967	10.00	20.00	40.00
❏ R-6262 [M]	Underground	1967	12.50	25.00	50.00
❏ RS-6262 [S]	Underground	1967	10.00	20.00	40.00
❏ R-6275 [M]	Mass in F Minor	1967	10.00	20.00	40.00
❏ RS-6275 [S]	Mass in F Minor	1967	7.50	15.00	30.00
❏ RS-6316	Release of an Oath	1968	7.50	15.00	30.00
❏ RS-6342	Just Good Rock 'n Roll	1969	7.50	15.00	30.00

Number	Title (A Side/B Side)	Yr	VG	VG+	NM
ELECTRIC TOILET, THE					
Albums					
NASCO					
❏ 9004	In the Hands of Karma	1970	50.00	100.00	200.00
ELECTRIC UNDERGROUND, THE					
Albums					
PREMIER					
❏ P-9060 [M]	Guitar Explosion	1967	12.50	25.00	50.00
❏ PS-9060 [S]	Guitar Explosion	1967	12.50	25.00	50.00
ELECTRONIC CONCEPT ORCHESTRA					
45s					
LIMELIGHT					
❏ 3090	Aquarius/Grazing in the Grass	1969	—	3.00	6.00
Albums					
LIMELIGHT					
❏ 86070	Moog Groove	1969	2.50	5.00	10.00
❏ 86072	Electric Love	1969	2.50	5.00	10.00
MERCURY					
❏ SR-61279	Cinemoog	1970	2.50	5.00	10.00
ELECTROSONICS, THE					
Albums					
PHILIPS					
❏ PHM 200047 [M]Electronic Music		1962	17.50	35.00	70.00
❏ PHS 600047 [S]Electronic Music		1962	22.50	45.00	90.00
ELEGANTS, THE Also see PAT CORDEL.					
45s					
ABC-PARAMOUNT					
❏ 10219	I've Seen Everything/Tiny Cloud	1961	10.00	20.00	40.00
APT					
❏ 25005	Little Star/Getting Dizzy	1958	10.00	20.00	40.00
—Black label with rainbow					
❏ 25005	Little Star/Getting Dizzy	1958	12.50	25.00	50.00
—All-black label					
❏ 25017	Goodnight/Please Believe Me	1958	7.50	15.00	30.00
❏ 25029	Pay Day/True Love Affair	1959	7.50	15.00	30.00
BANGAR					
❏ 613	Minor Chaos/Lost Souls	1964	7.50	15.00	30.00
BIM BAM BOOM					
❏ 121	It's Just a Matter of Time/Lonesome Weekends	1974	—	2.00	4.00
—Black vinyl					
❏ 121	It's Just a Matter of Time/Lonesome Weekends	1974	—	3.00	6.00
—Colored vinyl					
CRYSTAL BALL					
❏ 139	Maybe/Woo Woo Train	197?	—	2.50	5.00
HULL					
❏ 732	Little Boy Blue/Get Well Soon	1960	25.00	50.00	100.00
LAURIE					
❏ 3283	A Letter from Viet Nam/Barbara Beware	1965	7.50	15.00	30.00
❏ 3298	Wake Up/Bring Back Wendy	1965	12.50	25.00	50.00
❏ 3324	Belinda/Lazy Love	1965	6.25	12.50	25.00
—As "Vito and the Elegants"					
PHOTO					
❏ 2662	Dressin' Up/A Dream Can Come True	1963	12.50	25.00	50.00
❏ 2662 [PS]	Dressin' Up/A Dream Can Come True	1963	37.50	75.00	150.00
UNITED ARTISTS					
❏ 230	Speak Low/Let My Prayers Be With You	1960	10.00	20.00	40.00
❏ 295	Happiness/Spiritual	1961	12.50	25.00	50.00
Albums					
MURRAY HILL					
❏ 210	Little Star	1986	2.50	5.00	10.00
ELENA					
45s					
ROULETTE					
❏ 4605	Evening Time/Road of Love	1965	3.75	7.50	15.00
ELEPHANTS MEMORY					
45s					
APPLE					
❏ 1854	Liberation Special/Madness	1972	2.00	4.00	8.00
❏ 1854	Liberation Special/Power Boogie	1972	100.00	200.00	400.00
❏ 1854 [PS]	Liberation Special/Madness	1972	2.50	5.00	10.00
ATLANTIC					
❏ 3257	Shakedown/Brother Can You Spare Me a Dime	1975	—	2.50	5.00
BUDDAH					
❏ 98	Cross Roads of the Stepping Stones/Jungle Gym at the Zoo	1969	2.00	4.00	8.00
❏ 209	Don't Put Me on Trial No More/Hot Dog	1971	2.00	4.00	8.00
METROMEDIA					
❏ 182	Mongoose/I Couldn't Dream	1970	—	3.00	6.00
❏ 182 [PS]	Mongoose/I Couldn't Dream	1970	—	3.00	6.00
❏ 210	Skyscraper Commando/Power	1971	—	3.00	6.00
RCA VICTOR					
❏ APBO-0268	Rock and Roll Streaker/Angels Forever	1974	—	2.50	5.00
Albums					
APPLE					
❏ SMAS-3389	Elephants Memory	1972	6.25	12.50	25.00
BUDDAH					
❏ BDS-5033	Elephants Memory	1969	3.75	7.50	15.00
❏ BDS-5038	Songs from Midnight Cowboy	1970	3.75	7.50	15.00
METROMEDIA					
❏ MD-1035	Take It to the Streets	1970	5.00	10.00	20.00
RCA VICTOR					
❏ APL1-0569	Angela Forever	1974	3.75	7.50	15.00
ELEVENTH HOUR, THE					
45s					
BELL					
❏ 45153	Nothin' Comes Easy/Lori	1971	2.00	4.00	8.00
20TH CENTURY					
❏ 2076	So Good/My Bed	1974	—	3.00	6.00
❏ 2114	Far As We Felt Like Goin'/Volcano	1974	2.00	4.00	8.00

Number	Title (A Side/B Side)	Yr	VG	VG+	NM
❑ 2215	Hollywood Hot/Hollywood Hotter	1975	—	3.00	6.00
❑ 2278	Get On or Get Off/You'll Never Know Until You Try	1976	2.00	4.00	8.00

Albums
20TH CENTURY

Number	Title (A Side/B Side)	Yr	VG	VG+	NM
❑ T-435	Greatest Hits	1974	3.00	6.00	12.00
❑ T-511	Hollywood Hot	1975	3.75	7.50	15.00

ELF Also see RONNIE DIO.
45s
EASTERN ARTISTS

Number	Title (A Side/B Side)	Yr	VG	VG+	NM
❑ 5015	Sit Down Honey (Everything Will Be Alright)/ Gambler, Gambler	1972	12.50	25.00	50.00

EPIC

Number	Title (A Side/B Side)	Yr	VG	VG+	NM
❑ 5-10933	Hoochie Koochie Lady/First Avenue	1972	5.00	10.00	20.00

MGM

Number	Title (A Side/B Side)	Yr	VG	VG+	NM
❑ M 14752	L.A. 59/(B-side unknown)	1974	3.75	7.50	15.00

—*Stock copy may not exist*
Albums
EPIC

Number	Title (A Side/B Side)	Yr	VG	VG+	NM
❑ KE 31789	Elf	1972	7.50	15.00	30.00

—*Yellow label*

Number	Title (A Side/B Side)	Yr	VG	VG+	NM
❑ KE 31789	Elf	1973	5.00	10.00	20.00

—*Orange label*
MGM

Number	Title (A Side/B Side)	Yr	VG	VG+	NM
❑ M3G 4974	L.A. 59	1974	5.00	10.00	20.00
❑ M3G 4994	Trying to Burn the Sun	1975	5.00	10.00	20.00

ELGART, LARRY
12-Inch Singles
RCA

Number	Title (A Side/B Side)	Yr	VG	VG+	NM
❑ PD-13259	Hooked on Swing (7:07)/Hooked on Astaire (6:37)	1982	2.50	5.00	10.00
❑ PD-13627	La Cage Aux Folles (5:12)/The Best of Times	1983	2.50	5.00	10.00

45s
DECCA

Number	Title (A Side/B Side)	Yr	VG	VG+	NM
❑ 9-29043	More Than You Know/You're Driving Me Crazy (What Did I Do)	1954	3.00	6.00	12.00
❑ 9-29666	Spanish Lace/What the Thunder Said	1955	2.50	5.00	10.00

MGM

Number	Title (A Side/B Side)	Yr	VG	VG+	NM
❑ K12979	Arkansas Holler/This Heart of Mine	1961	2.00	4.00	8.00
❑ K13012	For the Soul/Green Valley	1961	2.00	4.00	8.00
❑ K13063	Elgart Twist/Cornelia	1962	2.00	4.00	8.00

RCA

Number	Title (A Side/B Side)	Yr	VG	VG+	NM
❑ PB-13219	Hooked on Swing/Hooked on the Big Bands	1982	—	2.50	5.00
❑ PB-13342	Hooked on Astaire/Hooked on the Blues	1982	—	2.50	5.00
❑ PB-13411	Hooked on Dixie/Swingin' the Classics	1982	—	2.50	5.00
❑ PB-13626	La Cage Aux Folles/The Best of Times	1983	—	2.50	5.00
❑ PB-13733	Caravan/The Best of Times	1984	—	3.00	6.00
❑ GB-14071	Hooked on Swing/Caravan	1985	—	—	3.00

—*"Gold Standard Series" reissue*
RCA VICTOR

Number	Title (A Side/B Side)	Yr	VG	VG+	NM
❑ 47-7461 [M]	Nola/Liza	1959	2.00	4.00	8.00
❑ 47-7575 [M]	Honeysuckle Rose/Mountain Greenery	1959	2.00	4.00	8.00
❑ 47-7651	Have You Heard/Duet from Saratoga-Game of Poker	1959	2.00	4.00	8.00
❑ 61-7575 [S]	Honeysuckle Rose/Mountain Greenery	1959	3.75	7.50	15.00

—*"Living Stereo" on label*
Albums
BRUNSWICK

Number	Title (A Side/B Side)	Yr	VG	VG+	NM
❑ BL 58054 [10]	Impressions of Outer Space	1954	15.00	30.00	60.00

DECCA

Number	Title (A Side/B Side)	Yr	VG	VG+	NM
❑ DL 5526 [10]	The Larry Elgart Band with Strings	1954	25.00	50.00	100.00
❑ DL 8034 [M]	Music for Barefoot Ballerinas	1955	10.00	20.00	40.00

MGM

Number	Title (A Side/B Side)	Yr	VG	VG+	NM
❑ E-3891 [M]	Sophisticated Sixties	1960	3.75	7.50	15.00
❑ SE-3891 [S]	Sophisticated Sixties	1960	5.00	10.00	20.00
❑ E-3896 [M]	The Shape of Sounds to Come	1961	3.75	7.50	15.00
❑ SE-3896 [S]	The Shape of Sounds to Come	1961	5.00	10.00	20.00
❑ E-3961 [M]	Visions	1961	3.75	7.50	15.00
❑ SE-3961 [S]	Visions	1961	5.00	10.00	20.00
❑ E-4007 [M]	The City	1961	3.75	7.50	15.00
❑ SE-4007 [S]	The City	1961	5.00	10.00	20.00
❑ E-4028 [M]	Music in Motion!	1962	3.75	7.50	15.00
❑ SE-4028 [S]	Music in Motion!	1962	5.00	10.00	20.00
❑ E-4080 [M]	More Music in Motion!	1962	3.75	7.50	15.00
❑ SE-4080 [S]	More Music in Motion!	1962	5.00	10.00	20.00

PROJECT 3

Number	Title (A Side/B Side)	Yr	VG	VG+	NM
❑ PR 5102	The Larry Elgart Dance Band	1979	2.50	5.00	10.00

RCA CAMDEN

Number	Title (A Side/B Side)	Yr	VG	VG+	NM
❑ CAL-575 [M]	Easy Goin' Swing	1960	3.00	6.00	12.00
❑ CAS-575 [S]	Easy Goin' Swing	1960	3.75	7.50	15.00
❑ CXS-9036 [(2)]	That Old Feeling	1972	3.00	6.00	12.00

RCA VICTOR

Number	Title (A Side/B Side)	Yr	VG	VG+	NM
❑ LPM-1961 [M]	Larry Elgart and His Orchestra	1959	3.75	7.50	15.00
❑ LSP-1961 [S]	Larry Elgart and His Orchestra	1959	5.00	10.00	20.00
❑ LPM-2045 [M]	New Sounds at the Roosevelt	1959	3.75	7.50	15.00
❑ LSP-2045 [S]	New Sounds at the Roosevelt	1959	5.00	10.00	20.00
❑ LPM-2166 [M]	Saratoga	1960	3.75	7.50	15.00
❑ LSP-2166 [S]	Saratoga	1960	5.00	10.00	20.00
❑ AFL1-4095	Flight of the Condor	1981	2.50	5.00	10.00
❑ AFL1-4343	Hooked on Swing	1982	2.50	5.00	10.00
❑ AFL1-4589	Hooked on Swing, Volume 2	1983	2.50	5.00	10.00
❑ AFL1-4850	Larry Elgart and His Manhattan Swing Orchestra	1984	2.50	5.00	10.00
❑ AYL1-5025	Hooked on Swing	1984	2.00	4.00	8.00

—*Budget-line reissue*

Number	Title (A Side/B Side)	Yr	VG	VG+	NM
❑ AYL1-5026	Hooked on Swing, Volume 2	1984	2.00	4.00	8.00

—*Budget-line reissue*

Number	Title (A Side/B Side)	Yr	VG	VG+	NM
❑ AYL1-7178	(The Theme from) La Cage Aux Folles	1986	2.00	4.00	8.00

ELGART, LES
45s
COLUMBIA

Number	Title (A Side/B Side)	Yr	VG	VG+	NM
❑ S7-30838 [S]	(titles unknown)	1960	2.00	4.00	8.00
❑ S7-30839 [S]	(titles unknown)	1960	2.00	4.00	8.00
❑ S7-30840 [S]	(titles unknown)	1960	2.00	4.00	8.00
❑ S7-30841 [S]	(titles unknown)	1960	2.00	4.00	8.00

Number	Title (A Side/B Side)	Yr	VG	VG+	NM
❑ S7-30842 [S]	(titles unknown)	1960	2.00	4.00	8.00

—*The above five are 33 1/3 rpm "Stereo Seven" jukebox singles with small center holes*

Number	Title (A Side/B Side)	Yr	VG	VG+	NM
❑ S7-31149 [S]	(titles unknown)	1961	2.00	4.00	8.00
❑ S7-31150 [S]	(titles unknown)	1961	2.00	4.00	8.00
❑ S7-31151 [S]	(titles unknown)	1961	2.00	4.00	8.00
❑ S7-31152 [S]	(titles unknown)	1961	2.00	4.00	8.00
❑ S7-31153 [S]	(titles unknown)	1961	2.00	4.00	8.00

—*The above five are 33 1/3 rpm "Stereo Seven" jukebox singles with small center holes*

Number	Title (A Side/B Side)	Yr	VG	VG+	NM
❑ S7-31267 [S]	(titles unknown)	1962	2.00	4.00	8.00
❑ S7-31268 [S]	(titles unknown)	1962	2.00	4.00	8.00
❑ S7-31269 [S]	(titles unknown)	1962	2.00	4.00	8.00
❑ S7-31270 [S]	(titles unknown)	1962	2.00	4.00	8.00
❑ S7-31271 [S]	(titles unknown)	1962	2.00	4.00	8.00

—*The above five are 33 1/3 rpm "Stereo Seven" jukebox singles with small center holes*

Number	Title (A Side/B Side)	Yr	VG	VG+	NM
❑ 4-40137	The Gang That Sang "Heart of My Heart"/ Geronimo	1953	2.50	5.00	10.00
❑ 4-40179	The Varsity Drag/Rocky's Prelude	1954	2.50	5.00	10.00
❑ 4-40180	Bandstand Boogie/When Yuba Plays the Rhumba on the Tuba	1954	6.25	12.50	25.00
❑ 4-40202	Flat Foot Floogie/Roo Roo (Kangaroo)	1954	2.50	5.00	10.00
❑ 4-40214	Charleston/Meet Me Tonight in Dreamland	1954	2.50	5.00	10.00
❑ 4-40215	Mango/East Is East	1954	2.50	5.00	10.00
❑ 4-40249	Wedding Bells (Are Breaking Up That Old Gang of Mine)/Spending the Summer in Love	1954	2.50	5.00	10.00
❑ 4-40294	Little White Duck/Zing Went the Strings of My Heart	1954	2.50	5.00	10.00
❑ 4-40326	One O'Clock Jump Mambo/I Don't Want to Set the World on Fire	1954	2.50	5.00	10.00
❑ 4-40353	It Ain't Necessarily So Pt. 1/Pt. 2	1954	2.50	5.00	10.00
❑ 4-40383	Mr. Sandman/Don't Let the Kiddy Geddin	1954	2.50	5.00	10.00
❑ 4-40388	Bazoom (I Need Your Lovin')/Charlie's Dream	1954	2.50	5.00	10.00
❑ 4-40414	Night Train/Ever Since You Went Away	1955	2.00	4.00	8.00
❑ 4-40458	Come to the Mardi Gras/Chattanooga Legion Band	1955	2.00	4.00	8.00
❑ 4-40500	At the Boppin' Stop/I Didn't Even Know Her Name	1955	2.00	4.00	8.00
❑ 4-40525	Love Me or Leave Me/When Yuba Plays the Rhumba on the Tuba	1955	2.00	4.00	8.00
❑ 4-40545	Start Dancin' with a Smile No. 1/No. 2	1955	2.00	4.00	8.00
❑ 4-40571	Honky Tonk Train Blues/Ain't She Sweet	1955	2.00	4.00	8.00
❑ 4-40617	The Trouble with Harry/Devil May Care	1955	2.00	4.00	8.00
❑ 4-40664	Main Title — Golden Arm/D.J. Jamboree	1956	2.50	5.00	10.00
❑ 4-40671	Saddle Shoe Boogie/La Chnouf	1956	2.00	4.00	8.00
❑ 4-40703	The Left Bank/The Poor Pianist of Paris	1956	2.00	4.00	8.00
❑ 4-40716	What'd Ya Know/While the City Sleeps	1956	2.00	4.00	8.00
❑ 4-40822	It Must Be True/I Ain't Foolin'	1957	2.00	4.00	8.00
❑ 4-41363	Strike Up the Band/Indian Summer	1959	2.00	4.00	8.00
❑ 4-41394	Moonlight Shuffle/When I Take My Sugar to Tea	1959	2.00	4.00	8.00
❑ 4-41566	Begin the Beguine/The Man I Love	1960	—	3.50	7.00
❑ 4-41778	Mar-Cha-Cha/Voo Doo Drums	1960	—	3.50	7.00
❑ 4-42622	All Alone Am I/Recado Bossa Nova	1962	—	3.50	7.00
❑ ZSP 56767/8 [DJ]	Bandstand Twist/Hawaiian War Chant	1962	3.75	7.50	15.00

—*"Special Album Excerpt" promotional item*

Number	Title (A Side/B Side)	Yr	VG	VG+	NM
❑ ZSP 56767/8 [PS]	Bandstand Twist/Hawaiian War Chant	1962	5.00	10.00	20.00

GOLD-MOR

Number	Title (A Side/B Side)	Yr	VG	VG+	NM
❑ 2	The Nearness of You/Out of Nowhere	1973	—	3.00	6.00

7-Inch Extended Plays
COLUMBIA

Number	Title (A Side/B Side)	Yr	VG	VG+	NM
❑ B-2562	Night Train/Street of Dreams//Harlem Nocturne/ Autumn Serenade	195?	2.50	5.00	10.00
❑ B-2562 [PS]	Les Elgart (Hall of Fame Series)	195?	2.50	5.00	10.00
❑ B-2581	*The Varsity Drag/Zing! Went the Strings of My Heart/The Gang That Sang "Heart of My Heart"/Wedding Bells	195?	2.50	5.00	10.00
❑ B-2581 [PS]	Les Elgart and His Orchestra (Hall of Fame Series)	195?	2.50	5.00	10.00
❑ B-8751	(contents unknown)	1956	2.50	5.00	10.00
❑ B-8751 [PS]	The Elgart Touch, Vol. 1	1956	2.50	5.00	10.00
❑ B-8752	*Stompin' at the Savoy/Street of Dreams/I Had the Craziest Dream/Three to Get Ready	1956	2.50	5.00	10.00
❑ B-8752 [PS]	The Elgart Touch, Vol. 2	1956	2.50	5.00	10.00
❑ B-8753	(contents unknown)	1956	2.50	5.00	10.00
❑ B-8753 [PS]	The Elgart Touch, Vol. 3	1956	2.50	5.00	10.00

Albums
CIRCLE

Number	Title (A Side/B Side)	Yr	VG	VG+	NM
❑ CLP-126	Les Elgart and His Orchestra	198?	2.50	5.00	10.00

COLUMBIA

Number	Title (A Side/B Side)	Yr	VG	VG+	NM
❑ CL 536 [M]	Sophisticated Swing	1953	7.50	15.00	30.00

—*Maroon label, gold print*

Number	Title (A Side/B Side)	Yr	VG	VG+	NM
❑ CL 594 [M]	Just One More Dance	1954	7.50	15.00	30.00

—*Maroon label, gold print*

Number	Title (A Side/B Side)	Yr	VG	VG+	NM
❑ CL 594 [M]	Just One More Dance	1955	5.00	10.00	20.00

—*Red and black label with six "eye" logos*

Number	Title (A Side/B Side)	Yr	VG	VG+	NM
❑ CL 619 [M]	The Band of the Year	1955	10.00	20.00	40.00

—*Maroon label, gold print; first LP appearance of "Bandstand Boogie"*

Number	Title (A Side/B Side)	Yr	VG	VG+	NM
❑ CL 684 [M]	The Dancing Sound	1955	7.50	15.00	30.00
❑ CL 803 [M]	For Dancers Only	1956	7.50	15.00	30.00
❑ CL 875 [M]	The Elgart Touch	1956	7.50	15.00	30.00

—*Red and black label, six "eye" logos*

Number	Title (A Side/B Side)	Yr	VG	VG+	NM
❑ CL 1008 [M]	For Dancers Also	1957	6.25	12.50	25.00
❑ CL 1052 [M]	Les and Larry Elgart and Their Orchestra	1957	5.00	10.00	20.00
❑ CL 1291 [M]	Les Elgart On Tour	1959	5.00	10.00	20.00
❑ CL 1350 [M]	The Great Sound of Les Elgart	1959	5.00	10.00	20.00
❑ CL 1450 [M]	The Band with That Sound	1960	5.00	10.00	20.00
❑ CL 1500 [M]	Designs for Dancing	1960	5.00	10.00	20.00
❑ CL 1567 [M]	Half Satin - Half Latin	1961	5.00	10.00	20.00
❑ CL 1659 [M]	It's De-Lovely	1961	5.00	10.00	20.00
❑ CL 1785 [M]	The Twist Goes to College	1962	5.00	10.00	20.00
❑ CL 1890 [M]	Best Band on Campus	1963	5.00	10.00	20.00
❑ CL 2503 [10]	Prom Date	1954	10.00	20.00	40.00
❑ CL 2578 [10]	Campus Hop	1955	10.00	20.00	40.00
❑ CL 2590 [10]	More of Les	1955	10.00	20.00	40.00
❑ CL 6287 [10]	Just One More Dance	195?	10.00	20.00	40.00
❑ CS 8002 [S]	Sound Ideas	1958	6.25	12.50	25.00
❑ CS 8092 [S]	Les and Larry Elgart and Their Orchestra	1959	6.25	12.50	25.00
❑ CS 8103 [S]	Les Elgart On Tour	1959	6.25	12.50	25.00
❑ CS 8159 [S]	The Great Sound of Les Elgart	1959	6.25	12.50	25.00

Number	Title (A Side/B Side)	Yr	VG	VG+	NM
❑ CS 8245 [S]	The Band with That Sound	1960	6.25	12.50	25.00
❑ CS 8291 [S]	Designs for Dancing	1960	6.25	12.50	25.00
❑ CS 8367 [S]	Half Satin - Half Latin	1961	6.25	12.50	25.00
❑ CS 8459 [S]	It's De-Lovely	1961	6.25	12.50	25.00
❑ CS 8585 [S]	The Twist Goes to College	1962	6.25	12.50	25.00
❑ CS 8690 [S]	Best Band on Campus	1963	6.25	12.50	25.00
COLUMBIA SPECIAL PRODUCTS					
❑ P 13168	The Greatest Dance Band in the Land	197?	2.50	5.00	10.00
HARMONY					
❑ HL 7374 [M]	The Greatest Dance Band in the Land	196?	3.00	6.00	12.00
❑ HS 11174 [R]	The Greatest Dance Band in the Land	196?	2.50	5.00	10.00
SUTTON					
❑ SU 283 [M]	Les Elgart and Blazing Brass	196?	2.50	5.00	10.00

ELGART, LES AND LARRY
45s
COLUMBIA

Number	Title (A Side/B Side)	Yr	VG	VG+	NM
❑ 4-42911	Walk Right In/Santy Anna	1963	—	3.50	7.00
❑ 4-43081	My Heart Belongs to Daddy/Blues in the Night	1964	—	3.50	7.00
❑ 4-43284	The First Man's Theme/Why Don't You Do Right	1965	—	3.50	7.00
❑ 4-43370	King of the Road/La Bostella	1965	—	3.50	7.00
❑ 4-43671	The Early Bird Catches the Bomb/ Brand New World	1966	—	3.50	7.00
❑ 4-43849	Soldier in the Rain/ Goodbye Is a Lonesome Sound	1966	—	3.50	7.00
❑ 4-43956	Music to Watch Girls By/Shine On Harvest Moon	1967	—	3.50	7.00
❑ 4-44030	Girl Talk/Bermuda Concerto	1967	—	3.50	7.00
❑ 4-44329	Ode to Billie Joe/Torino	1967	—	3.50	7.00
❑ 4-44467	The Sounds of Silence/ When I Look in Your Eyes	1968	—	3.50	7.00
❑ 4-44680	The Garbage/Soul Cakes	1968	—	3.50	7.00

Albums
COLUMBIA

Number	Title (A Side/B Side)	Yr	VG	VG+	NM
❑ CL 1123 [M]	Sound Ideas	1958	5.00	10.00	20.00
❑ CL 2112 [M]	Big Band Hootenanny	1963	3.75	7.50	15.00
❑ CL 2221 [M]	Command Performance! Les & Larry Elgart Play the Great Dance Hits	1964	3.75	7.50	15.00
❑ CL 2301 [M]	The New Elgart Touch	1965	3.75	7.50	15.00
❑ CL 2355 [M]	Elgart Au-Go-Go	1965	3.75	7.50	15.00
❑ CL 2511 [M]	Sound of the Times	1966	3.75	7.50	15.00
❑ CL 2591 [M]	Warm and Sensuous	1966	3.75	7.50	15.00
❑ CL 2633 [M]	Girl Watchers	1967	5.00	10.00	20.00
❑ CL 2780 [M]	The Wonderful World of Today's Hits	1968	6.25	12.50	25.00
❑ CS 8912 [S]	Big Band Hootenanny	1963	5.00	10.00	20.00
❑ CS 9021 [S]	Command Performance! Les & Larry Elgart Play the Great Dance Hits	1964	5.00	10.00	20.00
❑ CS 9101 [S]	The New Elgart Touch	1965	5.00	10.00	20.00
❑ CS 9155 [S]	Elgart Au-Go-Go	1965	5.00	10.00	20.00
❑ CS 9311 [S]	Sound of the Times	1966	5.00	10.00	20.00
❑ CS 9391 [S]	Warm and Sensuous	1966	5.00	10.00	20.00
❑ CS 9433 [S]	Girl Watchers	1967	3.75	7.50	15.00
❑ CS 9580 [S]	The Wonderful World of Today's Hits	1968	3.75	7.50	15.00
❑ CS 9722	Les & Larry Elgart's Greatest Hits	1968	3.75	7.50	15.00
❑ PC 38341	Swingtime	1982	2.50	5.00	10.00
HARMONY					
❑ KH 32053	Wonderful World	1972	2.50	5.00	10.00
SWAMPFIRE					
❑ 201	Nashville Country Piano	196?	3.00	6.00	12.00
❑ 202	Nashville Country Brass	196?	3.00	6.00	12.00
❑ 203	Nashville Country Guitars	196?	3.00	6.00	12.00
❑ 207	Bridge Over Troubled Water	1971	3.00	6.00	12.00

ELGINS, THE (1) Detroit R&B group.
45s
LUMMTONE

Number	Title (A Side/B Side)	Yr	VG	VG+	NM
❑ 113	Your Lovely Ways/Finding a Sweetheart	1963	6.25	12.50	25.00
TAMLA					
❑ 54056	Request of a Fool/Your Baby's Back	1962	7.50	15.00	30.00
—As "The Downbeats"; with "Tamla" in globe at top of label					
❑ 54056	Request of a Fool/Your Baby's Back	1962	75.00	150.00	300.00
—As "The Downbeats"; with "Tamla" circling globe at top of label					
V.I.P.					
❑ 25029	Darling Baby/Put Yourself in My Place	1965	5.00	10.00	20.00
❑ 25029	Darling Baby/Put Yourself in My Place	1965	50.00	100.00	200.00
—First pressings credited "The Downbeats"					
❑ 25037	Heaven Must Have Sent You/ Stay in My Lonely Arms	1965	5.00	10.00	20.00
❑ 25043	It's Been a Long, Long Time/ I Understand My Man	1966	5.00	10.00	20.00
❑ 25065	Heaven Must Have Sent You/ Stay in My Lonely Arms	1970	2.50	5.00	10.00

Albums
V.I.P.

Number	Title (A Side/B Side)	Yr	VG	VG+	NM
❑ 400 [M]	Darling Baby	1966	17.50	35.00	70.00
❑ S-400 [S]	Darling Baby	1966	25.00	50.00	100.00

ELGINS, THE (2)
45s
A.B.S.

Number	Title (A Side/B Side)	Yr	VG	VG+	NM
❑ 113	Pretending/Lonesome	1961	100.00	200.00	400.00

ELGINS, THE (3)
45s
CONGRESS

Number	Title (A Side/B Side)	Yr	VG	VG+	NM
❑ 214	The Times We've Wasted/Ritha Mae	1964	6.25	12.50	25.00
❑ 225	Here in Your Arms/We're Gonna Have a Good Time	1964	7.50	15.00	30.00

ELGINS, THE (4)
45s
LUMMTONE

Number	Title (A Side/B Side)	Yr	VG	VG+	NM
❑ 109	A Winner Never Quits/Johnny I'm Sorry	1962	6.25	12.50	25.00
❑ 110	You Got Your Magnet on Me Baby/ Johnny I'm Sorry	1962	6.25	12.50	25.00
❑ 112	Finally/I Lost My Love in the Big City	1963	6.25	12.50	25.00

ELGINS, THE (U) Some of these may be by group (3) or (4), but not all.
45s
DOT

Number	Title (A Side/B Side)	Yr	VG	VG+	NM
❑ 16563	Cheryl/Tell Gina	1963	15.00	30.00	60.00
FLIP					
❑ 353	Uncle Sam's Man/Casey Cop	1961	7.50	15.00	30.00
JOED					
❑ 716	Once Upon a Time/The Huddle	1964	175.00	350.00	700.00
MGM					
❑ 12670	A Picture of You/Mademoiselle	1958	15.00	30.00	60.00
TITAN					
❑ 1724	My Illness/Heartache Heartbreak	1962	50.00	100.00	200.00
❑ 1724	My Illness/Extra, Extra	1962	62.50	125.00	250.00
VALIANT					
❑ 712	Street Scene/You Found Yourself Another Fool	1965	5.00	10.00	20.00

ELIGIBLES, THE
45s
CAPITOL

Number	Title (A Side/B Side)	Yr	VG	VG+	NM
❑ 4203	Car Trouble/I Wrote a Song	1959	3.00	6.00	12.00
❑ 4265	Faker, Faker/24 Hours	1959	3.00	6.00	12.00
❑ 4304	My First Christmas with You/Little Engine	1959	3.75	7.50	15.00
❑ 4409	East of West Berlin/Young Is My Lover	1960	3.00	6.00	12.00
MERCURY					
❑ 72000	That Carmen Twist/Come Back, Music	1962	2.50	5.00	10.00
WARNER BROS.					
❑ 5344	Gabie/See What You Can Do For Me	1963	2.50	5.00	10.00

Albums
CAPITOL

Number	Title (A Side/B Side)	Yr	VG	VG+	NM
❑ ST 1310 [S]	Along the Trail	1960	7.50	15.00	30.00
❑ T 1310 [M]	Along the Trail	1960	6.25	12.50	25.00
❑ ST 1411 [S]	Love Is a Gamble	1960	7.50	15.00	30.00
❑ T 1411 [M]	Love Is a Gamble	1960	6.25	12.50	25.00

ELIMINATORS, THE
Albums
LIBERTY

Number	Title (A Side/B Side)	Yr	VG	VG+	NM
❑ LRP-3365 [M]	Liverpool! Dragsters! Cycles! Surfing!	1964	20.00	40.00	80.00
❑ LST-7365 [S]	Liverpool! Dragsters! Cycles! Surfing!	1964	25.00	50.00	100.00

ELIZABETH
45s
VANGUARD

Number	Title (A Side/B Side)	Yr	VG	VG+	NM
❑ 35070	Mary Anne/The World's For Free	1968	3.75	7.50	15.00

Albums
VANGUARD

Number	Title (A Side/B Side)	Yr	VG	VG+	NM
❑ VSD-6501	Elizabeth	1968	15.00	30.00	60.00

ELLEDGE, JIMMY
45s
4 STAR

Number	Title (A Side/B Side)	Yr	VG	VG+	NM
❑ 1003	One By One/After You	1975	—	2.00	4.00
❑ 1015	Lady Lover/(B-side unknown)	1976	—	2.00	4.00
HICKORY					
❑ 1313	Follow Every Rainbow/I Just Walked In (Your Heart Last Night)	1965	2.00	4.00	8.00
❑ 1341	A Good Woman's Love (Not Easy to Find)/World of Lavender Lace	1965	2.00	4.00	8.00
❑ 1363	A Legend in My Time/Pink Dally Rue	1966	2.00	4.00	8.00
❑ 1393	Time Is a Thief/I Just Walked In (Your Heart Last Night)	1966	2.00	4.00	8.00
❑ 1420	Let Me Love You a Little (So I Can Love You a Lot)/She Should Save Some Loving (For a Rainy Day)	1966	2.00	4.00	8.00
❑ 1452	The Darkest Part of Night (Is Dawn)/She Should Save Some Loving (For a Rainy Day)	1967	2.00	4.00	8.00
LITTLE DARLIN'					
❑ 0047	Florence Jean/No One Ever Lost More	1968	—	3.00	6.00
RCA VICTOR					
❑ 47-7910	Send Me a Letter/Swanee River Rocket	1961	3.00	6.00	12.00
❑ 47-7946	Funny How Time Slips Away/Hey Jimmy Joe John Jim Jack	1961	2.50	5.00	10.00
❑ 47-8012	Can't You See It in My Eyes/What a Laugh	1962	5.00	10.00	20.00
❑ 47-8042	Bo Diddley/Diamonds	1962	2.00	4.00	8.00
❑ 47-8081	A Golden Tear/I'll Get By (Don't Worry)	1962	2.00	4.00	8.00
❑ 47-8136	You Can Have Her/I Miss Her Already	1963	2.00	4.00	8.00
❑ 47-8191	Please Love Me Forever/A Penny's Worth of Happiness	1963	2.00	4.00	8.00
❑ 47-8241	I Had to Run Away/There's Nothing There for Me	1963	2.00	4.00	8.00
❑ 47-8355	Dream of the Year/Gonna Turn My Voodoo On	1964	2.00	4.00	8.00
❑ 47-8081 [PS]	A Golden Tear/I'll Get By (Don't Worry)	1962	6.25	12.50	25.00
❑ 47-8191 [PS]	Please Love Me Forever/ A Penny's Worth of Happiness	1963	6.25	12.50	25.00
SIMS					
❑ 204	I Gotta Live Here/Hold My Heart for Awhile	1964	2.00	4.00	8.00

ELLEN, IVY, & FAMILY
45s
FELSTED

Number	Title (A Side/B Side)	Yr	VG	VG+	NM
❑ 8609	Go Tell Santa/(Instrumental)	1960	3.75	7.50	15.00
—B-side by the Reindeers					
❑ 8609 [PS]	Go Tell Santa/(Instrumental)	1960	5.00	10.00	20.00

ELLIE POP
45s
MAINSTREAM

Number	Title (A Side/B Side)	Yr	VG	VG+	NM
❑ 686	Can't Be Love/Seven North Frederick	1968	5.00	10.00	20.00

Albums
MAINSTREAM

Number	Title (A Side/B Side)	Yr	VG	VG+	NM
❑ S-6115	Ellie Pop	1968	10.00	20.00	40.00

ELLIMAN, YVONNE
45s
DECCA

Number	Title (A Side/B Side)	Yr	VG	VG+	NM
❑ 32785	I Don't Know How to Love Him/Overture	1971	—	2.50	5.00
❑ 32870	Everything's Alright/Heaven on Their Minds	1971	—	2.50	5.00

Number	Title (A Side/B Side)	Yr	VG	VG+	NM
❑ 32949	Can't Find My Way Home/ I Would Have Had a Good Time	1972	—	2.00	4.00
❑ 32987	Nothing Rhymed/Speak Your Mind	1972	—	2.00	4.00
❑ 33018	Could We Start Again, Please/ Heaven on Their Minds	1972	—	2.50	5.00

—B-side by Ben Vereen

MCA

Number	Title (A Side/B Side)	Yr	VG	VG+	NM
❑ 40121	Hawaii/I Can't Explain	1973	—	2.00	4.00
❑ 40235	Casserole Me Over/ Come On Back Where You Belong	1974	—	2.00	4.00

RSO

Number	Title (A Side/B Side)	Yr	VG	VG+	NM
❑ 514	Somewhere in the Night/Who's Gonna Save the World	1975	—	2.00	4.00
❑ 517	Walk Right In/Small Town Talk	1975	—	2.00	4.00
❑ 858	Love Me/I Keep Hangin' On (I Don't Know Why)	1976	—	2.00	4.00
❑ 871	Hello Stranger/She'll Be the Home	1977	—	2.00	4.00
❑ 877	I Knew/I Can't Get You Out of My Mind	1977	—	2.00	4.00
❑ 884	If I Can't Have You/Good Sign	1977	—	2.00	4.00
❑ 905	Savannah/Up to the Man in You	1978	—	2.00	4.00
❑ 915	Moment by Moment/Sailing Ships	1978	—	2.00	4.00
❑ 915 [PS]	Moment by Moment/Sailing Ships	1978	—	2.00	4.00
❑ 1007	Love Pains/Rock Me Slowly	1979	—	2.00	4.00

Albums

DECCA

Number	Title (A Side/B Side)	Yr	VG	VG+	NM
❑ DL 75341	Yvonne Elliman	1972	3.75	7.50	15.00

MCA

Number	Title (A Side/B Side)	Yr	VG	VG+	NM
❑ 356	Food of Love	1973	3.00	6.00	12.00

RSO

Number	Title (A Side/B Side)	Yr	VG	VG+	NM
❑ RS-1-3018	Love Me	1977	2.50	5.00	10.00
❑ RS-1-3031	Night Flight	1978	2.50	5.00	10.00
❑ RS-1-3038	Yvonne	1979	2.50	5.00	10.00

ELLINGTON, DUKE   Also see LOUIS ARMSTRONG.

45s

BETHLEHEM

Number	Title (A Side/B Side)	Yr	VG	VG+	NM
❑ 11007	Indian Summer/The Jeep Is Jumpin'	1958	2.50	5.00	10.00
❑ 11016	The Blues (Part 1)/The Blues (Part 2)	1959	2.50	5.00	10.00
❑ 11066	In a Mellow Tone/Jack the Bear	1960	2.50	5.00	10.00

CAPITOL

Number	Title (A Side/B Side)	Yr	VG	VG+	NM
❑ F2458	Satin Doll/Without a Song	1953	3.00	6.00	12.00
❑ F2503	Ballin' the Blues/Nothin' Nothin' Baby	1953	3.00	6.00	12.00
❑ F2546	Blue Jean Beguine/Warm Vallen	1953	3.00	6.00	12.00
❑ F2598	Boo-Dar/Give Me the Right	1953	3.00	6.00	12.00
❑ F2723	Blue Moon/Ultra Deluxe	1954	3.00	6.00	12.00
❑ F2817	Isle of Capri/Band Call	1954	3.00	6.00	12.00
❑ F2875	Bunny Hop Mambo/Is It a Sin	1954	3.00	6.00	12.00
❑ F2930	Smile/If I Give My Heart to You	1954	3.00	6.00	12.00
❑ F2980	12th Street Rag Mambo/Chile Bowl	1954	3.00	6.00	12.00
❑ F3049	Echo Tango/All Day Long	1955	3.00	6.00	12.00

COLUMBIA

Number	Title (A Side/B Side)	Yr	VG	VG+	NM
❑ 31099 [S]	Three J's Blues/Smada	1961	3.00	6.00	12.00
❑ 31100 [S]	Pie Eye's Blues/Sweet and Pungent	1961	3.00	6.00	12.00
❑ 31101 [S]	(titles unknown)	1961	3.00	6.00	12.00
❑ 31102 [S]	(titles unknown)	1961	3.00	6.00	12.00
❑ 31103 [S]	(titles unknown)	1961	3.00	6.00	12.00
❑ S7 31433 [S]	I've Just Seen Her/Back to School	1962	3.00	6.00	12.00
❑ S7 31434 [S]	Which Way?/If I Were You	1962	3.00	6.00	12.00
❑ S7 31435 [S]	Once Upon a Time/Nightlife	1962	3.00	6.00	12.00
❑ S7 31436 [S]	(titles unknown)	1962	3.00	6.00	12.00
❑ S7 31437 [S]	What a Country!/We Speak the Same Language	1962	3.00	6.00	12.00

—The above five are "Stereo Seven" 33 1/3 rpm jukebox singles from set "JS 7-54" and the album "All American in Jazz"

Number	Title (A Side/B Side)	Yr	VG	VG+	NM
❑ S7 31478 [S]	(titles unknown)	1962	3.00	6.00	12.00
❑ S7 31479 [S]	B D B/Wild Man	1962	3.00	6.00	12.00
❑ S7 31480 [S]	To You/Jumpin' at the Woodside	1962	3.00	6.00	12.00
❑ S7 31481 [S]	Take the "A" Train/Until I Met You	1962	3.00	6.00	12.00
❑ S7 31482 [S]	Segue in C (Part I)/(Part II)	1962	3.00	6.00	12.00

—The above five are "Stereo Seven" 33 1/3 rpm jukebox singles from set "JS 7-59" and the album "First Time!"

Number	Title (A Side/B Side)	Yr	VG	VG+	NM
❑ 39110	Build That Railroad/Love You Madly	1950	3.75	7.50	15.00
❑ 39496	Monologue/8th Veil	1951	3.75	7.50	15.00
❑ 39545	Deep Night/Please Be Kind	1951	3.75	7.50	15.00
❑ 39670	Jam with Sam/V.I.P.'s Boogie	1952	3.75	7.50	15.00
❑ 39712	Blues at Sundown/Bensonality	1952	3.75	7.50	15.00
❑ 39942	Rock Skippin' at the Blue Note/The Vulture Song	1953	3.75	7.50	15.00
❑ 40903	Cop-Out/Rock City Rock	1957	2.50	5.00	10.00
❑ 41098	My Heart, My Mind, My Everything/Together	1958	2.50	5.00	10.00
❑ 41180	Duke's Place/Jones	1958	2.50	5.00	10.00
❑ 41362	Spank No. 1/Spank No. 2	1959	2.50	5.00	10.00
❑ 41401	Walkin' and Singin' the Blues/Hand Me Down Love	1959	2.50	5.00	10.00
❑ 41421	Anatomy of a Murder/Flirtbird	1959	2.50	5.00	10.00
❑ 41689	Blues in Orbit/Villes, Ville Is the Place, Man	1960	2.50	5.00	10.00
❑ 42144	Asphalt Jungle Theme (Part 1)/Asphalt Jungle Theme (Part 2)	1961	2.50	5.00	10.00
❑ 42237	Paris Blues (Part 1)/Paris Blues (Part 2)	1962	2.50	5.00	10.00
❑ 50014	Solitude/Mood Indigo	1954	3.00	6.00	12.00

—"Hall of Fame Series"

IMPULSE!

Number	Title (A Side/B Side)	Yr	VG	VG+	NM
❑ 210	Limbo Jazz (Part 1)/Limbo Jazz (Part 2)	196?	2.00	4.00	8.00

RCA VICTOR

Number	Title (A Side/B Side)	Yr	VG	VG+	NM
❑ 47-2955	The Sidewalks of New York/Don't Get Around Much Anymore	1949	5.00	10.00	20.00
❑ 47-3033	Frankie & Johnny/Royal Garden Blues	1949	3.00	6.00	12.00
❑ 47-3034	Drawing Room Blues/St. Louis Blues	1949	3.00	6.00	12.00
❑ 47-3035	Beale Street Blues/Pretty Woman	1949	3.00	6.00	12.00
❑ 47-4281	Jumping Room Only/A Gathering in a Clearing	1951	3.75	7.50	15.00
❑ 47-4711	Balcony Serenade/Strange Feeling	1952	3.75	7.50	15.00
❑ 47-4712	Dancers in Love/Coloratura	1952	3.75	7.50	15.00

REPRISE

Number	Title (A Side/B Side)	Yr	VG	VG+	NM
❑ 0545	Satin Doll/Don't Get Around Much Anymore	1967	—	3.00	6.00

7-Inch Extended Plays

CAPITOL

Number	Title (A Side/B Side)	Yr	VG	VG+	NM
❑ EAP 1-477	(contents unknown)	1954	3.75	7.50	15.00
❑ EAP 1-477 [PS]	The Duke Plays Ellington	1954	3.75	7.50	15.00
❑ EAP 1-521	Rockin' in Rhythm/Black and Tan Fantasy	1955	3.75	7.50	15.00

Number	Title (A Side/B Side)	Yr	VG	VG+	NM
❑ EAP 1-521 [PS]	Ellington '55, Part 1	1955	3.75	7.50	15.00
❑ EAP 2-521	Stompin' at the Savoy/In the Mood	1955	3.75	7.50	15.00
❑ EAP 2-521 [PS]	Ellington '55, Part 2	1955	3.75	7.50	15.00
❑ EAP 3-521	One O'Clock Jump/Honeysuckle Rose	1955	3.75	7.50	15.00
❑ EAP 3-521 [PS]	Ellington '55, Part 3	1955	3.75	7.50	15.00
❑ EAP 4-521	Happy Go Lucky Local/Flying Home	1955	3.75	7.50	15.00
❑ EAP 4-521 [PS]	Ellington '55, Part 4	1955	3.75	7.50	15.00
❑ EAP 1-679	Harlem Air Shaft/Serious Serenade//Don't Ever Say Goodbye/Big Drag	195?	3.00	6.00	12.00
❑ EAP 3-679	Blossom/Theme for Trambean//Gonna Tan Your Hide	195?	3.00	6.00	12.00
❑ EAP 3-679 [PS]	Ellington Showcase, Part 1	195?	3.00	6.00	12.00
❑ EAP 3-679 [PS]	Ellington Showcase, Part 3	195?	3.00	6.00	12.00

COLUMBIA

Number	Title (A Side/B Side)	Yr	VG	VG+	NM
❑ 5-1405	Skin Deep/The Mooche	195?	3.75	7.50	15.00

—Alternate numbers are "B 1629-1" and "B 1629-2"

Number	Title (A Side/B Side)	Yr	VG	VG+	NM
❑ B-1629 [PS]	Skin Deep/The Mooche	195?	3.75	7.50	15.00

—Contains record 5-1405

Number	Title (A Side/B Side)	Yr	VG	VG+	NM
❑ B-2514	*Solitude/Mood Indigo/Stormy Weather/Sophisticated Lady	195?	3.00	6.00	12.00
❑ B-2514 [PS]	Duke Ellington and His Orchestra (Hall of Fame Series)	195?	3.00	6.00	12.00
❑ B-2553	*The Hawk Talks/Monologue/Rock Skippin' at the Blue Note/Jam with Sam	195?	3.00	6.00	12.00
❑ B-2553 [PS]	Duke Ellington (Hall of Fame Series)	195?	3.00	6.00	12.00
❑ B-8301	(contents unknown)	1956	3.00	6.00	12.00
❑ B-8301 [PS]	Hi-Fi Ellington Uptown, Vol. 1	1956	3.00	6.00	12.00
❑ B-8302	Skin Deep/The Mooche	1956	3.00	6.00	12.00
❑ B-8302 [PS]	Hi-Fi Ellington Uptown, Vol. 2	1956	3.00	6.00	12.00
❑ B-8303	(contents unknown)	1956	3.00	6.00	12.00
❑ B-8303 [PS]	Hi-Fi Ellington Uptown, Vol. 3	1956	3.00	6.00	12.00

RCA VICTOR

Number	Title (A Side/B Side)	Yr	VG	VG+	NM
❑ EPA-5054	Caravan/Sophisticated Lady//Perdido/Mood Indigo	1958	3.75	7.50	15.00
❑ EPA-5054 [PS]	Caravan (Gold Standard Series)	1958	3.75	7.50	15.00

ROYALE

Number	Title (A Side/B Side)	Yr	VG	VG+	NM
❑ EP 203	Overture to Jam Session—Part 1/Overture to Jam Session—Part 2//Magenta Haze/Blue Skies	195?	2.50	5.00	10.00

—Red vinyl

Number	Title (A Side/B Side)	Yr	VG	VG+	NM
❑ EP 203 [PS]	Duke Ellington Plays	195?	2.50	5.00	10.00

Albums

AAMCO

Number	Title (A Side/B Side)	Yr	VG	VG+	NM
❑ ALP-301 [M]	The Royal Concert of Duke Ellington, Vol. 1	196?	7.50	15.00	30.00

—Reissue of Bethlehem material

Number	Title (A Side/B Side)	Yr	VG	VG+	NM
❑ ALP-313 [M]	The Royal Concert of Duke Ellington, Vol. 2	196?	7.50	15.00	30.00

—Reissue of Bethlehem material

ABC IMPULSE!

Number	Title (A Side/B Side)	Yr	VG	VG+	NM
❑ 9256 [(2)]	Ellingtonia: Reevaluations, The Impulse Years	1973	3.75	7.50	15.00
❑ 9285 [(2)]	Ellingtonia, Volume 2	1974	3.75	7.50	15.00
❑ IA-9350 [(2)]	Great Tenor Encounters	1978	3.75	7.50	15.00

AIRCHECK

Number	Title (A Side/B Side)	Yr	VG	VG+	NM
❑ 4	Duke on the Air	197?	2.50	5.00	10.00
❑ 29	Duke on the Air, Vol. 2	198?	2.50	5.00	10.00

ALLEGRO

Number	Title (A Side/B Side)	Yr	VG	VG+	NM
❑ 1591 [M]	Duke Ellington and His Orchestra Play	1955	12.50	25.00	50.00
❑ 3082 [M]	Duke Ellington	1953	12.50	25.00	50.00
❑ 4014 [10]	Duke Ellington and His Orchestra Play	1954	25.00	50.00	100.00
❑ 4038 [10]	Duke Ellington and His Orchestra Play	1954	25.00	50.00	100.00

ATLANTIC

Number	Title (A Side/B Side)	Yr	VG	VG+	NM
❑ SD 2-304 [(2)]	The Great Paris Concert	1972	3.75	7.50	15.00
❑ QD 1580 [Q]	New Orleans Suite	1974	6.25	12.50	25.00
❑ SD 1580	New Orleans Suite	1971	3.00	6.00	12.00
❑ SD 1665	Recollections of the Big Band Era	1974	3.00	6.00	12.00
❑ SD 1688	Jazz Violin Session	1976	3.00	6.00	12.00
❑ 90043	Recollections of the Big Band Era	1982	2.50	5.00	10.00

BASF

Number	Title (A Side/B Side)	Yr	VG	VG+	NM
❑ 21704	Collages	1973	3.00	6.00	12.00

BETHLEHEM

Number	Title (A Side/B Side)	Yr	VG	VG+	NM
❑ BCP-60 [M]	Historically Speaking, The Duke	1956	15.00	30.00	60.00
❑ BCP-6005 [M]	Duke Ellington Presents	1956	15.00	30.00	60.00
❑ 6013	The Bethlehem Years, Vol. 1	197?	2.50	5.00	10.00

BIOGRAPH

Number	Title (A Side/B Side)	Yr	VG	VG+	NM
❑ M-2	Band Shorts (1929-1935)	1978	2.50	5.00	10.00

BLUE NOTE

Number	Title (A Side/B Side)	Yr	VG	VG+	NM
❑ BT-85129	Money Jungle	1986	2.50	5.00	10.00

—Reissue of United Artists 15017

BLUEBIRD

Number	Title (A Side/B Side)	Yr	VG	VG+	NM
❑ 5659-1-RB [(4)]	Duke Ellington: The Blanton-Webster Band	1986	6.25	12.50	25.00
❑ 6287-1-RB	And His Mother Called Him Bill	1987	2.00	4.00	8.00

—Reissue of RCA Victor 3906

Number	Title (A Side/B Side)	Yr	VG	VG+	NM
❑ 6641-1-RB [(4)]	Black, Brown and Beige	1988	6.25	12.50	25.00
❑ 6852-1-RB	Early Ellington	1989	2.50	5.00	10.00

BOOK-OF-THE-MONTH

Number	Title (A Side/B Side)	Yr	VG	VG+	NM
❑ 30-5622 [(3)]	At Fargo, 1940	1978	5.00	10.00	20.00

BRIGHT ORANGE

Number	Title (A Side/B Side)	Yr	VG	VG+	NM
❑ 709	The Stereophonic Sound of Duke Ellington	1973	3.00	6.00	12.00

BRUNSWICK

Number	Title (A Side/B Side)	Yr	VG	VG+	NM
❑ BL 54007 [M]	Early Ellington	1954	12.50	25.00	50.00
❑ BL 58002 [10]	Ellingtonia, Volume 1	1950	25.00	50.00	100.00
❑ BL 58012 [10]	Ellingtonia, Volume 2	1950	25.00	50.00	100.00

BULLDOG

Number	Title (A Side/B Side)	Yr	VG	VG+	NM
❑ BDL-2021	20 Golden Pieces of Duke Ellington	198?	2.50	5.00	10.00

CAPITOL

Number	Title (A Side/B Side)	Yr	VG	VG+	NM
❑ H 440 [10]	Premiered by Ellington	1953	25.00	50.00	100.00
❑ H 477 [10]	The Duke Plays Ellington	1954	25.00	50.00	100.00
❑ T 477 [M]	The Duke Plays Ellington	1954	10.00	20.00	40.00

—Turquoise label

Number	Title (A Side/B Side)	Yr	VG	VG+	NM
❑ T 477 [M]	The Duke Plays Ellington	1958	5.00	10.00	20.00

—Black label with colorband, logo at left

Number	Title (A Side/B Side)	Yr	VG	VG+	NM
❑ T 521 [M]	Ellington '55	1955	10.00	20.00	40.00

—Turquoise label

Number	Title (A Side/B Side)	Yr	VG	VG+	NM
❑ T 521 [M]	Ellington '55	1958	5.00	10.00	20.00

—Black label with colorband, logo at left

Number	Title (A Side/B Side)	Yr	VG	VG+	NM
❑ T 637 [M]	Dance to the Duke	1955	10.00	20.00	40.00

—Turquoise label

Number	Title (A Side/B Side)	Yr	VG	VG+	NM
❏ T 637 [M]	Dance to the Duke	1958	5.00	10.00	20.00
—Black label with colorband, logo at left					
❏ T 679 [M]	Ellington Showcase	1956	10.00	20.00	40.00
—Turquoise label					
❏ T 679 [M]	Ellington Showcase	1958	5.00	10.00	20.00
—Black label with colorband, logo at left					
❏ DT 1602 [R]	The Best of Duke Ellington	1961	3.00	6.00	12.00
❏ SM-1602	The Best of Duke Ellington	197?	2.50	5.00	10.00
—Reissue with new prefix					
❏ T 1602 [M]	The Best of Duke Ellington	1961	5.00	10.00	20.00
❏ M-11058	Piano Reflections	1972	3.00	6.00	12.00
❏ M-11674	Ellington '55	1977	2.50	5.00	10.00
❏ N-16172	The Best of Duke Ellington	198?	2.00	4.00	8.00
—Budget-line reissue					
CIRCLE					
❏ CLP-101	Duke Ellington World Broadcasting Series, Vol. 1	1986	2.50	5.00	10.00
❏ CLP-102	Duke Ellington World Broadcasting Series, Vol. 2	1986	2.50	5.00	10.00
❏ CLP-103	Duke Ellington World Broadcasting Series, Vol. 3	1986	2.50	5.00	10.00
❏ CLP-104	Duke Ellington World Broadcasting Series, Vol. 4	199?	2.50	5.00	10.00
❏ CLP-105	Duke Ellington World Broadcasting Series, Vol. 5 (1943)	199?	2.50	5.00	10.00
❏ CLP-106	Duke Ellington World Broadcasting Series, Vol. 6 (1945)	1988	2.50	5.00	10.00
❏ CLP-108	Duke Ellington World Broadcasting Series, Vol. 8 (1945)	1988	2.50	5.00	10.00
❏ CLP-109	Duke Ellington World Broadcasting Series, Vol. 9 (1945)	1988	2.50	5.00	10.00
COLUMBIA					
❏ C3L 27 [(3)M]	The Ellington Era, Vol. 1	1963	10.00	20.00	40.00
❏ C3L 39 [(3)M]	The Ellington Era, Vol. 2	1964	10.00	20.00	40.00
❏ CL 558 [M]	The Music of Duke Ellington	1954	12.50	25.00	50.00
—Maroon label with gold print					
❏ CL 558 [M]	The Music of Duke Ellington	1956	10.00	20.00	40.00
—Red and black label with six "eye" logos					
❏ CL 558 [M]	The Music of Duke Ellington	1963	3.75	7.50	15.00
—Red label with "Guaranteed High Fidelity" or "360 Sound Mono"					
❏ CL 663 [M]	Blue Light	1955	10.00	20.00	40.00
❏ CL 825 [M]	Masterpieces by Ellington	1956	10.00	20.00	40.00
—Reissue of Columbia Masterworks 4418					
❏ CL 825 [M]	Masterpieces by Ellington	1963	3.75	7.50	15.00
—Red label with "Guaranteed High Fidelity" or "360 Sound Mono"					
❏ CL 830 [M]	Hi-Fi Ellington Uptown	1956	10.00	20.00	40.00
❏ CL 830 [M]	Hi-Fi Ellington Uptown	1963	3.75	7.50	15.00
—Red label with "Guaranteed High Fidelity" or "360 Sound Mono"					
❏ CL 848 [M]	Liberian Suite	1956	10.00	20.00	40.00
—Reissue of Columbia 6073					
❏ CL 934 [M]	Ellington at Newport '56	1957	10.00	20.00	40.00
—Red and black label with six "eye" logos					
❏ CL 934 [M]	Ellington at Newport '56	1963	3.75	7.50	15.00
—Red label with "Guaranteed High Fidelity" or "360 Sound Mono"					
❏ CL 951 [M]	A Drum Is a Woman	1957	10.00	20.00	40.00
❏ CL 1033 [M]	Such Sweet Thunder	1957	10.00	20.00	40.00
❏ CL 1085 [M]	Ellington Indigos	1958	6.25	12.50	25.00
❏ CL 1085 [M]	Ellington Indigos	1963	3.75	7.50	15.00
—Red label with "Guaranteed High Fidelity" or "360 Sound Mono"					
❏ CL 1162 [M]	Brown, Black and Beige	1958	6.25	12.50	25.00
❏ CL 1198 [M]	The Cosmic Scene	1959	20.00	40.00	80.00
❏ CL 1245 [M]	Newport 1958	1959	6.25	12.50	25.00
❏ CL 1282 [M]	Duke Ellington at the Bal Masque	1959	6.25	12.50	25.00
❏ CL 1323 [M]	Duke Ellington Jazz Party	1959	6.25	12.50	25.00
❏ CL 1400 [M]	Festival Session	1960	6.25	12.50	25.00
❏ CL 1445 [M]	Blues in Orbit	1960	6.25	12.50	25.00
❏ CL 1541 [M]	The Nutcracker Suite	1960	7.50	15.00	30.00
❏ CL 1546 [M]	Piano in the Background	1960	7.50	15.00	30.00
❏ CL 1546 [M]	Piano in the Background	1963	3.75	7.50	15.00
—Red label with "Guaranteed High Fidelity" or "360 Sound Mono"					
❏ CL 1597 [M]	Peer Gynt Suite/Suite Thursday	1961	6.25	12.50	25.00
❏ CL 1715 [M]	First Time	1962	6.25	12.50	25.00
❏ CL 1790 [M]	All American	1962	5.00	10.00	20.00
❏ CL 1907 [M]	Midnight in Paris	1963	5.00	10.00	20.00
❏ CL 2522 [10]	Duke's Mixture	1955	20.00	40.00	80.00
❏ CL 2562 [10]	Here's the Duke	1955	20.00	40.00	80.00
❏ CL 2593 [10]	Al Hibbler with the Duke	1956	20.00	40.00	80.00
❏ CL 6024 [10]	Mood Ellington	1949	25.00	50.00	100.00
❏ CL 6073 [10]	Liberian Suite	1949	25.00	50.00	100.00
❏ CS 8015 [S]	Brown, Black and Beige	1958	7.50	15.00	30.00
❏ CS 8053 [S]	Ellington Indigos	1958	7.50	15.00	30.00
❏ CS 8053 [S]	Ellington Indigos	1963	3.75	7.50	15.00
—Red label with "360 Sound Stereo"					
❏ PC 8053	Ellington Indigos	198?	2.00	4.00	8.00
—Budget-line reissue					
❏ CS 8072 [S]	Newport 1958	1959	7.50	15.00	30.00
❏ CS 8098 [S]	Duke Ellington at the Bal Masque	1959	7.50	15.00	30.00
❏ CS 8127 [S]	Duke Ellington Jazz Party	1959	7.50	15.00	30.00
❏ CS 8241 [S]	Blues in Orbit	1960	7.50	15.00	30.00
❏ CS 8341 [S]	The Nutcracker Suite	1960	10.00	20.00	40.00
❏ CS 8346 [S]	Piano in the Background	1960	10.00	20.00	40.00
❏ CS 8346 [S]	Piano in the Background	1963	3.75	7.50	15.00
—Red label with "360 Sound Stereo"					
❏ CS 8397 [S]	Peer Gynt Suite/Suite Thursday	1961	7.50	15.00	30.00
❏ CS 8515 [S]	First Time	1962	7.50	15.00	30.00
❏ CS 8590 [S]	All American	1962	6.25	12.50	25.00
❏ CS 8648 [R]	Ellington at Newport	1963	3.00	6.00	12.00
❏ PC 8648	Ellington at Newport	198?	2.00	4.00	8.00
—Budget-line reissue					
❏ CS 8829 [S]	Midnight in Paris	1963	6.25	12.50	25.00
❏ CS 9629	Duke Ellington's Greatest Hits	1969	3.75	7.50	15.00
❏ KG 32064 [(2)]	Duke Ellington Presents Ivie Anderson	1973	3.75	7.50	15.00
❏ C 32471	Jazz at the Plaza — Vol. II	1973	3.00	6.00	12.00
❏ G 32564 [(2)]	The World of Duke Ellington	1974	3.75	7.50	15.00
❏ KG 33341 [(2)]	The World of Duke Ellington, Volume 2	1975	3.75	7.50	15.00
❏ CG 33961 [(2)]	The World of Duke Ellington, Volume 3	1975	3.75	7.50	15.00
❏ PC 37340	It Don't Mean a Thing	1981	2.00	4.00	8.00
—Reissue					
❏ FC 38028	The Girl's Suite & Perfume Suite	1982	2.50	5.00	10.00
COLUMBIA JAZZ MASTERPIECES					
❏ CJ 40586	First Time	1987	2.50	5.00	10.00
—Reissue of Columbia 8515					
❏ CJ 40587	Ellington at Newport	1987	2.50	5.00	10.00
—Reissue of Columbia 934					
❏ CJ 40712	Duke Ellington Jazz Party	1987	2.50	5.00	10.00
—Reissue of Columbia 8127					
❏ CJ 40836	Uptown	1987	2.50	5.00	10.00
❏ CJ 44051	Blues in Orbit	1988	2.50	5.00	10.00
—Reissue of Columbia 8241					
❏ CJ 44444	Ellington Indigos	1989	2.50	5.00	10.00
—Reissue of Columbia 8053					
COLUMBIA JAZZ ODYSSEY					
❏ PC 36979	The Festival Session	1981	2.50	5.00	10.00
COLUMBIA MASTERWORKS					
❏ ML 4418 [M]	Masterpieces by Ellington	1951	25.00	50.00	100.00
❏ ML 4639 [M]	Ellington Uptown	195?	12.50	25.00	50.00
—Oddly, this exists as a reissue on the red and black "6 eye" label					
❏ ML 4639 [M]	Ellington Uptown	1951	25.00	50.00	100.00
—Blue or green label, gold print					
COLUMBIA SPECIAL PRODUCTS					
❏ P 13291	Duke Ellington's Greatest Hits (Recorded Live in Concert)	1976	2.50	5.00	10.00
❏ P 13500	Festival Session	1976	2.50	5.00	10.00
❏ P 14359	Suite Thursday/Controversial Suite/ Harlem Suite	198?	2.50	5.00	10.00
DAYBREAK					
❏ DR 2017	The Symphonic Ellington	1973	3.00	6.00	12.00
DECCA					
❏ DL 9224 [M]	Duke Ellington, Volume 1 — In the Beginning	1958	10.00	20.00	40.00
—Black label, silver print					
❏ DL 9224 [M]	Duke Ellington, Volume 1 — In the Beginning	1961	6.25	12.50	25.00
—Black label with color bars					
❏ DL 9241 [M]	Duke Ellington, Volume 2 — Hot in Harlem	1959	10.00	20.00	40.00
—Black label, silver print					
❏ DL 9241 [M]	Duke Ellington, Volume 2 — Hot in Harlem	1961	6.25	12.50	25.00
—Black label with color bars					
❏ DL 9247 [M]	Duke Ellington, Volume 3 — Rockin' in Rhythm	1959	10.00	20.00	40.00
—Black label, silver print					
❏ DL 9247 [M]	Duke Ellington, Volume 3 — Rockin' in Rhythm	1961	6.25	12.50	25.00
—Black label with color bars					
❏ DL 75069	Duke Ellington in Canada	1969	3.75	7.50	15.00
❏ DL 79224 [R]	Duke Ellington, Volume 1 — In the Beginning	1958	6.25	12.50	25.00
—Black label, silver print					
❏ DL 79224 [R]	Duke Ellington, Volume 1 — In the Beginning	1961	3.75	7.50	15.00
—Black label with color bars					
❏ DL 79241 [R]	Duke Ellington, Volume 2 — Hot in Harlem	1959	6.25	12.50	25.00
—Black label, silver print					
❏ DL 79241 [R]	Duke Ellington, Volume 2 — Hot in Harlem	1961	3.75	7.50	15.00
—Black label with color bars					
❏ DL 79247 [R]	Duke Ellington, Volume 3 — Rockin' in Rhythm	1959	6.25	12.50	25.00
—Black label, silver print					
❏ DL 79247 [R]	Duke Ellington, Volume 3 — Rockin' in Rhythm	1961	3.75	7.50	15.00
—Black label with color bars					
DISCOVERY					
❏ 841	Concert in the Virgin Islands	198?	2.50	5.00	10.00
—Reissue of Reprise 6185					
❏ 871	Afro Bossa	198?	2.50	5.00	10.00
—Reissue of Reprise 6069					
DO YOU LIKE JAZZ					
❏ P 13293	Monologue	1973	3.00	6.00	12.00
DOCTOR JAZZ					
❏ W2X 39137 [(2)]	All-Star Road Band	1984	3.00	6.00	12.00
❏ W2X 40012 [(2)]	All-Star Road Band, Vol. 2	1985	3.00	6.00	12.00
❏ FW 40030	Happy Reunion	1985	2.50	5.00	10.00
❏ FW 40359	New Mood Indigo	1986	2.50	5.00	10.00
EVEREST ARCHIVE OF FOLK & JAZZ					
❏ 221	Early Duke Ellington	1968	3.00	6.00	12.00
❏ 249	Early Duke Ellington Vol. 2	1970	3.00	6.00	12.00
❏ 266	Early Duke Ellington Vol. 3	1972	3.00	6.00	12.00
❏ 327	Duke Ellington at Carnegie Hall	197?	3.00	6.00	12.00
FANTASY					
❏ OJC-108	Great Times!	198?	2.50	5.00	10.00
—Reissue of Riverside 9475					
❏ OJC-446	The Ellington Suites	1990	2.50	5.00	10.00
—Reissue of Pablo 2310 762					
❏ OJC-469	Latin American Suite	1990	2.50	5.00	10.00
—Reissue of 8419					
❏ OJC-623	Duke Ellington Featuring Paul Gonsalves	1991	3.00	6.00	12.00
—Reissue of 9636					
❏ OJC-624	The Intimacy of the Blues	1991	3.00	6.00	12.00
—Reissue of 9640					
❏ OJC-633	Up in Duke's Workshop	1991	3.00	6.00	12.00
—Reissue of Pablo 2310 815					
❏ OJC-645	The Afro-Eurasian Eclipse	1991	3.00	6.00	12.00
—Reissue of 9498					
❏ F-8407/8 [(2)]	Duke Ellington's Second Sacred Concert	1971	3.75	7.50	15.00
❏ F-8419	Latin American Suite	1971	3.75	7.50	15.00
❏ F-9433	Yale Concert	1974	3.00	6.00	12.00
❏ F-9462	The Pianist	1974	3.00	6.00	12.00
❏ F-9498	Afro-American Eclipse	1976	3.00	6.00	12.00
❏ F-9636	Duke Ellington Featuring Paul Gonsalves	198?	2.50	5.00	10.00
❏ F-9640	The Intimacy of the Blues	1986	2.50	5.00	10.00
FLYING DUTCHMAN					
❏ BXL1-2832	It Don't Mean a Thing	198?	2.50	5.00	10.00
—Reissue					
❏ 10112	My People	1969	3.75	7.50	15.00
❏ 10166	It Don't Mean a Thing	1973	3.00	6.00	12.00
FOLKWAYS					
❏ FJ-2968	First Annual Tour of the Pacific Northwest, Spring, 1952	198?	2.50	5.00	10.00

Number	Title (A Side/B Side)	Yr	VG	VG+	NM
GALAXY					
❏ 4807	Duke Ellington and His Famous Orchestra and Soloists	197?	3.75	7.50	15.00
GNP CRESCENDO					
❏ GNP-9045	The 1953 Pasadena Concert	1986	2.50	5.00	10.00
❏ GNP-9049	The 1954 Los Angeles Concert	1987	2.50	5.00	10.00
HALL OF FAME					
❏ 625/6/7 [(3)]	The Immortal Duke Ellington	197?	5.00	10.00	20.00
HARMONY					
❏ HL 7436 [M]	Fantasies	1967	3.75	7.50	15.00
❏ HS 11236 [R]	Fantasies	1967	3.00	6.00	12.00
❏ HS 11323	In My Solitude	1969	3.00	6.00	12.00
❏ H 30566	Duke Ellington's Greatest Hits Live	1971	3.00	6.00	12.00
HINDSIGHT					
❏ HSR-125	Duke Ellington 1946	198?	2.50	5.00	10.00
❏ HSR-126	Duke Ellington 1946, Volume 2	198?	2.50	5.00	10.00
❏ HSR-127	Duke Ellington 1946, Volume 3	198?	2.50	5.00	10.00
❏ HSR-128	Duke Ellington 1947	198?	2.50	5.00	10.00
❏ HSR-129	Duke Ellington 1947, Volume 2	198?	2.50	5.00	10.00
IAJRC					
❏ LP-45	Fairfield, Connecticut Jazz Fest 1956	198?	2.00	4.00	8.00
INTERMEDIA					
❏ QS-5002	Sophisticated Duke	198?	2.50	5.00	10.00
❏ QS-5020	Lullaby of Birdland	198?	2.50	5.00	10.00
❏ QS-5021	Do Nothin' Till You Hear from Me	198?	2.50	5.00	10.00
❏ QS-5063	Satin Doll	198?	2.50	5.00	10.00
JAZZ ODYSSEY					
❏ 32160252	Nutcracker and Peer Gynt Suites	196?	3.00	6.00	12.00
JAZZ PANORAMA					
❏ 1802 [10]	Duke Ellington — Vol. 1	1951	25.00	50.00	100.00
❏ 1811 [10]	Duke Ellington — Vol. 2	1951	25.00	50.00	100.00
❏ 1816 [10]	Duke Ellington — Vol. 3	1951	25.00	50.00	100.00
JAZZBIRD					
❏ 2009	Meadowbrook to Manhattan	1980	2.50	5.00	10.00
LONDON					
❏ AL-3551 [10]	The Duke — 1926	195?	25.00	50.00	100.00
MCA					
❏ 1358	Duke Ellington, Volume 1 — In the Beginning	198?	2.00	4.00	8.00
—Reissue of 2075					
❏ 1359	Duke Ellington, Volume 2 — Hot in Harlem	198?	2.00	4.00	8.00
—Reissue of 2076					
❏ 1360	Duke Ellington, Volume 3 — Rockin' in Rhythm	198?	2.00	4.00	8.00
—Reissue of 2077					
❏ 1374	Brunswick-Vocalion Rarities	198?	2.50	5.00	10.00
❏ 2075	Duke Ellington, Volume 1 — In the Beginning	197?	2.50	5.00	10.00
—Reissue of Decca 79224					
❏ 2076	Duke Ellington, Volume 2 — Hot in Harlem	197?	2.50	5.00	10.00
—Reissue of Decca 79241					
❏ 2077	Duke Ellington, Volume 3 — Rockin' in Rhythm	197?	2.50	5.00	10.00
—Reissue of Decca 79247					
❏ 4142 [(2)]	Great Tenor Encounters	198?	3.00	6.00	12.00
—Reissue of Impulse! 9350					
❏ 42325	The Brunswick Era, Vol. 1	1990	3.00	6.00	12.00
MOBILE FIDELITY					
❏ 1-214	Anatomy of a Murder	1995	10.00	20.00	40.00
—Audiophile vinyl					
MOSAIC					
❏ MQ8-160 [(8)]	The Complete Capitol Recordings of Duke Ellington	199?	37.50	75.00	150.00
MUSICRAFT					
❏ 2002	Carnegie Hall Concert	1986	2.50	5.00	10.00
PABLO					
❏ 2310703	Duke's Big 4	1974	3.00	6.00	12.00
❏ 2310721	This One's for Blanton	197?	3.00	6.00	12.00
❏ 2310762	The Ellington Suites	197?	3.00	6.00	12.00
❏ 2310787	Intimate	197?	3.00	6.00	12.00
❏ 2310815	Up in Duke's Workshop	1980	2.50	5.00	10.00
❏ 2405401	The Best of Duke Ellington	198?	2.50	5.00	10.00
PABLO LIVE					
❏ 2308245	Harlem	198?	2.50	5.00	10.00
❏ 2308247	In the Uncommon Market	198?	2.50	5.00	10.00
PAIR					
❏ PDL2-1011 [(2)]	Original Recordings by Duke Ellington	1986	3.00	6.00	12.00
PICCADILLY					
❏ 3524	Classic Ellington	198?	2.50	5.00	10.00
PICKWICK					
❏ SPC-3390	We Love You Madly	197?	2.50	5.00	10.00
PRESTIGE					
❏ 24029 [(2)]	The Golden Duke	1973	3.75	7.50	15.00
❏ 24045 [(2)]	Duke Ellington's Second Sacred Concert	1974	3.00	6.00	12.00
—Reissue of Fantasy 8407/8					
❏ 24073 [(2)]	The Carnegie Hall Concerts: December 1944	1977	3.75	7.50	15.00
❏ 24074 [(2)]	The Carnegie Hall Concerts: January 1946	1977	3.75	7.50	15.00
❏ 24075 [(2)]	The Carnegie Hall Concerts: December 1947	1977	3.75	7.50	15.00
❏ 34003 [(3)]	The Carnegie Hall Concerts: January 1943	197?	5.00	10.00	20.00
RCA CAMDEN					
❏ ACL2-0152 [(2)]	Mood Indigo	1973	3.75	7.50	15.00
❏ CAL-394 [M]	Duke Ellington at Tanglewood	1958	5.00	10.00	20.00
❏ CAL-459 [M]	Duke Ellington at the Cotton Club	1959	5.00	10.00	20.00
❏ ACL-7052	The Duke at Tanglewood	197?	2.50	5.00	10.00
—Reissue of RCA Red Seal LSC-2857					
RCA VICTOR					
❏ WPT-11 [10]	Duke Ellington	1951	25.00	50.00	100.00
❏ SP-33-394 [M]	The Duke at Tanglewood	1966	6.25	12.50	25.00
—"Special Interview Recording for Radio Station Programming"					
❏ LPV-506 [M]	Daybreak Express	1964	5.00	10.00	20.00
❏ LPV-517 [M]	Jumpin' Punkins	1965	5.00	10.00	20.00
❏ LPV-541 [M]	Johnny Come Lately	1967	5.00	10.00	20.00
❏ LPV-553 [M]	Pretty Woman	1968	5.00	10.00	20.00
❏ LPV-568 [M]	Flaming Youth	1969	5.00	10.00	20.00
❏ LJM-1002 [M]	Seattle Concert	1954	12.50	25.00	50.00
❏ LPT-1004 [M]	Ellington's Greatest	1954	10.00	20.00	40.00
❏ APL1-1023	Eastbourne Performance	1974	3.00	6.00	12.00
❏ LPM-1092 [M]	Duke and His Men	1955	10.00	20.00	40.00
❏ LPM-1364 [M]	In a Mellotone	1957	10.00	20.00	40.00
—Black label, dog at top, "Long Play" at bottom					
❏ LPM-1364 [M]	In a Mellotone	196?	6.25	12.50	25.00
—Black label, dog at top, "Mono" at bottom					
❏ LPM-1364 [M]	In a Mellotone	1969	5.00	10.00	20.00
—Orange label					
❏ LPM-1715 [M]	Duke Ellington at His Very Best	1958	10.00	20.00	40.00
❏ ANL1-2811	Pure Gold	1978	2.50	5.00	10.00
❏ LPT-3017 [10]	This Is Duke Ellington and His Orchestra	1952	25.00	50.00	100.00
❏ LPT-3067 [10]	Duke Ellington Plays the Blues	1952	25.00	50.00	100.00
❏ LPM-3576 [M]	The Popular Duke Ellington	1966	3.75	7.50	15.00
❏ LSP-3576 [S]	The Popular Duke Ellington	1966	5.00	10.00	20.00
❏ LPM-3582 [M]	Concert of Sacred Music	1966	3.75	7.50	15.00
❏ LSP-3582 [S]	Concert of Sacred Music	1966	5.00	10.00	20.00
❏ LPM-3782 [M]	Far East Suite	1967	6.25	12.50	25.00
❏ LSP-3782 [S]	Far East Suite	1967	3.75	7.50	15.00
❏ LPM-3906 [M]	And His Mother Called Him Bill	1968	12.50	25.00	50.00
❏ LSP-3906 [S]	And His Mother Called Him Bill	1968	3.75	7.50	15.00
❏ CPL2-4098 [(2)]	Sophisticated Ellington	1983	3.00	6.00	12.00
❏ LPM-6009 [(2)]	The Indispensible Duke Ellington	1961	12.50	25.00	50.00
❏ VPM-6042 [(2)]	This Is Duke Ellington	1972	3.75	7.50	15.00
RCA VICTOR RED SEAL					
❏ LM-2857 [M]	The Duke at Tanglewood	1966	3.75	7.50	15.00
❏ LSC-2857 [S]	The Duke at Tanglewood	1966	5.00	10.00	20.00
REPRISE					
❏ R-6069 [M]	Afro-Bossa	1962	5.00	10.00	20.00
❏ R9-6069 [S]	Afro-Bossa	1962	5.00	10.00	20.00
❏ R-6097 [M]	The Symphonic Ellington	1963	5.00	10.00	20.00
❏ R9-6097 [S]	The Symphonic Ellington	1963	5.00	10.00	20.00
❏ R-6122 [M]	Ellington '65: Hits of the '60s/This Time by Ellington	1964		10.00	20.00
❏ RS-6122 [S]	Ellington '65: Hits of the '60s/This Time by Ellington	1964	5.00	10.00	20.00
❏ R-6141 [M]	Mary Poppins	1964	5.00	10.00	20.00
❏ RS-6141 [S]	Mary Poppins	1964	5.00	10.00	20.00
❏ R-6154 [M]	Ellington '66	1965	5.00	10.00	20.00
❏ RS-6154 [S]	Ellington '66	1965	3.75	7.50	15.00
❏ R-6168 [M]	Will Big Bands Ever Come Back?	1965	5.00	10.00	20.00
❏ RS-6168 [S]	Will Big Bands Ever Come Back?	1965	3.75	7.50	15.00
❏ R-6185 [M]	Concert in the Virgin Islands	1965	5.00	10.00	20.00
❏ RS-6185 [S]	Concert in the Virgin Islands	1965	3.75	7.50	15.00
❏ R-6234 [M]	Duke Ellington's Greatest Hits	1967	5.00	10.00	20.00
❏ RS-6234 [S]	Duke Ellington's Greatest Hits	1967	3.75	7.50	15.00
RIVERSIDE					
❏ RLP 12-129 [M]	Birth of Big Band Jazz	195?	7.50	15.00	30.00
—Blue label with mike logo					
❏ RLP 12-129 [M]	Birth of Big Band Jazz	1956	15.00	30.00	60.00
—White label, blue print					
❏ RLP-475 [M]	Great Times!	1963	6.25	12.50	25.00
❏ RS-9475 [S]	Great Times!	1963	6.25	12.50	25.00
RONDO-LETTE					
❏ A-7 [M]	Duke Ellington and Orchestra	1958	7.50	15.00	30.00
ROULETTE					
❏ 108 [(2)]	Echoes of an Era	1971	3.75	7.50	15.00
ROYALE					
❏ 18143 [10]	Duke Ellington and His Orchestra	195?	12.50	25.00	50.00
❏ 18152 [10]	Duke Ellington Plays Ellington	195?	12.50	25.00	50.00
SMITHSONIAN COLLECTION					
❏ P6-15079 [(6)]	An Explosion of Genius 1938-1940	1976	12.50	25.00	50.00
—"Produced in association with Columbia Special Products"					
SOLID STATE					
❏ SM-18022	Money Jungle	1968	3.75	7.50	15.00
—Reissue of United Artists 15017					
❏ SS-19000 [(2)]	75th Birthday	1970	5.00	10.00	20.00
STANYAN					
❏ 10105	For Always	197?	3.00	6.00	12.00
STARDUST					
❏ SD-124 [M]	Duke	196?	3.00	6.00	12.00
❏ SDS-124 [R]	Duke	196?	3.00	6.00	12.00
STORYVILLE					
❏ SLP-4003	Duke Ellington and His Orchestra	198?	2.50	5.00	10.00
SUPER MAJESTIC					
❏ 2000	Duke Ellington	197?	3.00	6.00	12.00
SUTTON					
❏ SU-276 [M]	Duke Meets Leonard Feather	196?	3.00	6.00	12.00
TIME-LIFE					
❏ STL-J-02 [(3)]	Giants of Jazz	1978	5.00	10.00	20.00
❏ STBB-05 [(2)]	Big Bands: Duke Ellington	1983	3.75	7.50	15.00
❏ STBB-16 [(2)]	Big Bands: Cotton Club Nights	1983	3.75	7.50	15.00
TREND					
❏ 529	The Symphonic Ellington	1982	5.00	10.00	20.00
❏ 2004	Carnegie Hall Concert	198?	2.50	5.00	10.00
UNITED ARTISTS					
❏ UXS-92 [(2)]	Togo Bravo Suite	1972	3.75	7.50	15.00
❏ UAS-5632	Money Jungle	1972	3.00	6.00	12.00
—Reissue					
❏ UAJ-14017 [M]	Money Jungle	1962	10.00	20.00	40.00
❏ UAJS-15017 [S]	Money Jungle	1962	10.00	20.00	40.00
VEE JAY					
❏ VJS-3061	Love You Madly	198?	2.50	5.00	10.00
VERVE					
❏ V-8701 [M]	Soul Call	1967	3.75	7.50	15.00
❏ V6-8701 [S]	Soul Call	1967	3.00	6.00	12.00
"X"					
❏ LVA-3037 [10]	Duke Ellington Plays	1955	25.00	50.00	100.00

ELLINGTON, HARVEY

Albums

Number	Title (A Side/B Side)	Yr	VG	VG+	NM
STEPHENY					
❏ MF-4010 [M]	I Can't Hide the Blues	1959	20.00	40.00	80.00

Number	Title (A Side/B Side)	Yr	VG	VG+	NM

ELLIOT, CASS Also see THE BIG THREE; THE MAMAS AND THE PAPAS; DAVE MASON; THE MUGWUMPS.

45s

ABC DUNHILL

Number	Title (A Side/B Side)	Yr	VG	VG+	NM
❑ 4145	Dream a Little Dream of Me/Midnight Voyage	1968	2.00	4.00	8.00
—Label credit: "Featuring Mama Cass with the Mamas and the Papas"					
❑ 4166	California Earthquake/Talkin' to Your Toothbrush	1968	—	3.00	6.00
❑ 4184	Move In a Little Closer, Baby/All for Me	1969	—	3.00	6.00
❑ 4195	It's Getting Better/Who's to Blame	1969	—	3.00	6.00
—The above three as "Mama Cass"					
❑ 4214	Make Your Own Kind of Music/Ladylove	1969	—	3.00	6.00
❑ 4225	New World Coming/Blow Me a Kiss	1970	—	3.00	6.00
❑ 4244	A Song That Never Comes/I Can Dream, Can't I?	1970	—	3.00	6.00
❑ 4253	Good Times Are Coming/Welcome to the World	1970	—	3.00	6.00
❑ 4264	Don't Let the Good Times Pass You By/A Song That Never Comes	1971	—	3.00	6.00
—The above five as "Mama Cass Elliott"					

DUNHILL

Number	Title (A Side/B Side)	Yr	VG	VG+	NM
❑ 4145	Dream a Little Dream of Me/Midnight Voyage	1968	6.25	12.50	25.00
—Label credit: "Featuring Mama Cass with the Mamas and the Papas"; no "ABC" at top of label					

RCA VICTOR

Number	Title (A Side/B Side)	Yr	VG	VG+	NM
❑ 74-0644	Baby, I'm Yours/Cherries Jubilee	1972	—	3.00	6.00
❑ 74-0693	That Song/When It Doesn't Work Out	1972	—	3.00	6.00
❑ 74-0764	Disney Girls/Break Another Heart	1972	—	3.00	6.00
❑ 74-0830	The Road Is No Place for a Lady/Does Anybody Love You	1972	—	3.00	6.00
❑ 74-0957	I Think a Lot About You/Listen to the World	1973	—	3.00	6.00

7-Inch Extended Plays

ABC DUNHILL

Number	Title (A Side/B Side)	Yr	VG	VG+	NM
❑ SP-DS-50040	California Earthquake/Talkin' to Your Toothbrush/Blues for Breakfast//Long Time Loving You/Jane the Insane Dog Lady/Burn Your Hatred	1968	3.00	6.00	12.00
—As "Mama Cass"; jukebox issue; small hole, plays at 33 1/3 rpm					
❑ SP-DS-50040 [PS]	Dream a Little Dream	1968	3.00	6.00	12.00

Albums

ABC DUNHILL

Number	Title (A Side/B Side)	Yr	VG	VG+	NM
❑ DS-50040	Dream a Little Dream	1968	5.00	10.00	20.00
❑ DS-50055	Bubble Gum, Lemonade &...Something for Mama	1969	5.00	10.00	20.00
❑ DS-50071	Make Your Own Kind of Music	1969	3.75	7.50	15.00
—Reissue of 50055 with new title and one added song					
❑ DS-50093	Mama's Big Ones	1970	3.75	7.50	15.00

MCA

Number	Title (A Side/B Side)	Yr	VG	VG+	NM
❑ 719	Mama's Big Ones	1980	2.00	4.00	8.00

RCA VICTOR

Number	Title (A Side/B Side)	Yr	VG	VG+	NM
❑ APL1-0303	Don't Call Me Mama Anymore	1973	3.75	7.50	15.00
❑ LSP-4619	Cass Elliot	1971	3.75	7.50	15.00
❑ LSP-4753	The Road Is No Place for a Lady	1972	3.75	7.50	15.00

ELLIOTT, BERN, AND THE FENMEN

45s

LONDON

Number	Title (A Side/B Side)	Yr	VG	VG+	NM
❑ 9670	New Orleans/Everybody Needs a Little Love	1964	3.00	6.00	12.00
❑ 9733	Money/Nobody But Me	1965	3.00	6.00	12.00

ELLIOTT, BILL, AND THE ELASTIC OZ BAND Also see JOHN LENNON; YOKO ONO.

45s

APPLE

Number	Title (A Side/B Side)	Yr	VG	VG+	NM
❑ 1835	God Save Us/Do the Oz	1971	2.00	4.00	8.00
❑ 1835 [PS]	God Save Us/Do the Oz	1971	2.50	5.00	10.00
❑ P-1835 [DJ]	God Save Us/Do the Oz	1971	6.25	12.50	25.00
—Has black star on A-side and unsliced apple on both sides					

ELLIOTT, RON Also see THE BEAU BRUMMELS.

Albums

WARNER BROS.

Number	Title (A Side/B Side)	Yr	VG	VG+	NM
❑ WS 1833	Candlestickmaker	1969	3.75	7.50	15.00

ELLIS, JIMMY Also see ORION.

45s

BOBLO

Number	Title (A Side/B Side)	Yr	VG	VG+	NM
❑ 526	Tupelo Woman/The Closer He Gets	1976	—	2.00	4.00
❑ 531	There You Go/Here Comes That Wonderful Feeling	1977	—	2.00	4.00
❑ 532	Movin' On/My Baby's Out of Sight	1977	—	2.00	4.00
❑ 536	I'm Not Trying to Be Like Elvis/Games You've Been Playing	1978	—	2.00	4.00
❑ 536 [PS]	I'm Not Trying to Be Like Elvis/Games You've Been Playing	1978	2.50	5.00	10.00

DRADCO

Number	Title (A Side/B Side)	Yr	VG	VG+	NM
❑ 1892	Don't Count Your Chickens/Love Is But Love	1964	3.75	7.50	15.00

GOLDBAND

Number	Title (A Side/B Side)	Yr	VG	VG+	NM
❑ 1191	Woman in the Picture/What Swinging Doors Did to Me	196?	2.50	5.00	10.00

KRIS

Number	Title (A Side/B Side)	Yr	VG	VG+	NM
❑ 8115	Outskirts of Town (Part 1)/Outskirts of Town (Part 2)	196?	2.00	4.00	8.00

MCA

Number	Title (A Side/B Side)	Yr	VG	VG+	NM
❑ 40060	There Ya Go/Here Comes That Feeling Again	1973	—	2.00	4.00

RIDE

Number	Title (A Side/B Side)	Yr	VG	VG+	NM
❑ 146	Baby I Love You/Kiddio	196?	2.00	4.00	8.00
—As "Jimmie Ellis"; may not be the same performer as the others					

SOUTHERN TRACKS

Number	Title (A Side/B Side)	Yr	VG	VG+	NM
❑ 1069	I Make the Livin' (You Make the Livin' Worthwhile)/Thank God for America	1986	—	2.00	4.00
❑ 1080	Sunday Fathers/Thank God for America	1987	—	2.00	4.00

SUN

Number	Title (A Side/B Side)	Yr	VG	VG+	NM
❑ 1129	That's All Right/Blue Moon of Kentucky	1973	—	2.00	4.00
—Second pressings credit Jimmy Ellis					
❑ 1129	That's All Right/Blue Moon of Kentucky	1973	—	2.50	5.00
—Originals have no artist on label in an attempt to make people believe these were lost Elvis Presley outtakes					
❑ 1131	I Use Her to Remind Me of You/Changing	1974	—	2.00	4.00
❑ 1136	D.O.A./Misty/That's All Right/Blue Moon of Kentucky	1977	—	2.00	4.00

Albums

BOBLO

Number	Title (A Side/B Side)	Yr	VG	VG+	NM
❑ 78-829	By Request Jimmy Sings Elvis	1978	25.00	50.00	100.00

ELLIS, JIMMY (2)

45s

ATLANTIC

Number	Title (A Side/B Side)	Yr	VG	VG+	NM
❑ 2572	I Don't Mind/Take the Lord With You	1968	2.00	4.00	8.00

ELLIS, LORRAINE

45s

BULLSEYE

Number	Title (A Side/B Side)	Yr	VG	VG+	NM
❑ 100	Perfidia/Piano Player Play a Tune	1955	15.00	30.00	60.00

GEE

Number	Title (A Side/B Side)	Yr	VG	VG+	NM
❑ 1	Perfidia/Piano Player Play a Tune	1953	75.00	150.00	300.00

ELLIS, MATTHEW

Albums

WARNER BROS.

Number	Title (A Side/B Side)	Yr	VG	VG+	NM
❑ BS 2610	Matthew Ellis	1972	3.75	7.50	15.00

ELLIS, RAY

45s

ASCOT

Number	Title (A Side/B Side)	Yr	VG	VG+	NM
❑ 2203	A Thousand Clowns/We'll Say Goodbye	1966	2.00	4.00	8.00

ATCO

Number	Title (A Side/B Side)	Yr	VG	VG+	NM
❑ 6389	I'll Never Be Lonely Again/Wait Till We're 65	1965	2.00	4.00	8.00
❑ 6396	I Got You Babe/King of the Road	1966	2.00	4.00	8.00

COLUMBIA

Number	Title (A Side/B Side)	Yr	VG	VG+	NM
❑ 4-40982	Fascination/Soft Sands	1957	3.00	6.00	12.00
❑ 4-41094	36-26-36/Come to Me	1958	3.00	6.00	12.00
❑ 4-41258	Ups 'n' Downs/Milk 'n' Honey	1958	3.00	6.00	12.00

MGM

Number	Title (A Side/B Side)	Yr	VG	VG+	NM
❑ K12770	Sweet Kentucky Belle/Lauralee	1959	2.50	5.00	10.00
❑ K12797	The Love That Used to Be/I Know the Place	1959	2.50	5.00	10.00
❑ K12874	Fallout/U.S. Marshal	1960	2.50	5.00	10.00
❑ K12926	Joey's Theme/Lonely Room	1960	2.50	5.00	10.00
❑ K12942	Midnight Lace/Theme from "Grand Jury"	1960	2.50	5.00	10.00

RCA VICTOR

Number	Title (A Side/B Side)	Yr	VG	VG+	NM
❑ 37-7888	La Dolce Vita (The Sweet Life)/Parlami Di Me (Speak to Me)	1961	5.00	10.00	20.00
—"Compact Single 33" (small hole, plays at LP speed)					
❑ 37-7888 [PS]	La Dolce Vita (The Sweet Life)/Parlami Di Me (Speak to Me)	1961	6.25	12.50	25.00
—Special picture sleeve for "Compact Single 33"					
❑ 47-7888	La Dolce Vita (The Sweet Life)/Parlami Di Me (Speak to Me)	1961	2.50	5.00	10.00
❑ 47-7888 [PS]	La Dolce Vita (The Sweet Life)/Parlami Di Me (Speak to Me)	1961	3.00	6.00	12.00
❑ 47-7953	Portofino/Shalom	1961	2.50	5.00	10.00
❑ 47-8023	The Sheik/Dumpy	1962	2.50	5.00	10.00
❑ 47-8150	Anything, Anywhere/Rubia	1963	2.50	5.00	10.00

20TH CENTURY FOX

Number	Title (A Side/B Side)	Yr	VG	VG+	NM
❑ 593	Theme from "Von Ryan's Express"/Theme from "Morituri"	1965	2.00	4.00	8.00

Albums

ATCO

Number	Title (A Side/B Side)	Yr	VG	VG+	NM
❑ 33-187 [M]	Big Hits for Swingers	1966	3.00	6.00	12.00
❑ SD 33-187 [S]	Big Hits for Swingers	1966	3.75	7.50	15.00

COLUMBIA

Number	Title (A Side/B Side)	Yr	VG	VG+	NM
❑ CL 993 [M]	Ellis in Wonderland	1957	3.75	7.50	15.00
❑ CL 1097 [M]	Let's Get Away from It All	1957	3.75	7.50	15.00
❑ CL 1122 [M]	Dancing with Gigi	1958	3.75	7.50	15.00

HARMONY

Number	Title (A Side/B Side)	Yr	VG	VG+	NM
❑ HL 7183 [M]	Gigi	1959	3.00	6.00	12.00
❑ HS 11003 [S]	Gigi	1959	3.75	7.50	15.00

MGM

Number	Title (A Side/B Side)	Yr	VG	VG+	NM
❑ E-3779 [M]	I'm in the Mood for Strings	1959	3.00	6.00	12.00
❑ SE-3779 [S]	I'm in the Mood for Strings	1959	3.75	7.50	15.00
❑ E-3813 [M]	The Best of Peter Gunn	1960	3.00	6.00	12.00
❑ E-3820 [M]	I'm in the Mood to Swing	1960	3.00	6.00	12.00
❑ SE-3820 [S]	I'm in the Mood to Swing	1960	3.75	7.50	15.00
❑ E-3842 [M]	The Big Voices, The Big Bands, The Big Songs, The Big Sounds	1960	3.00	6.00	12.00
❑ SE-3842 [S]	The Big Voices, The Big Bands, The Big Songs, The Big Sounds	1960	3.75	7.50	15.00
❑ E-3911 [M]	Carnival in Sound	1961	—	—	—
—Canceled					
❑ SE-3911 [M]	Carnival in Sound	1961	—	—	—
—Canceled					

RCA VICTOR

Number	Title (A Side/B Side)	Yr	VG	VG+	NM
❑ LPM-2400 [M]	Ray Ellis Plays the Top 20	1961	3.00	6.00	12.00
❑ LSP-2400 [S]	Ray Ellis Plays the Top 20	1961	3.75	7.50	15.00
❑ LPM-2410 [M]	La Dolce Vita	1961	3.00	6.00	12.00
❑ LSP-2410 [S]	La Dolce Vita	1961	3.75	7.50	15.00
❑ LPM-2493 [M]	How to Succeed in Business Without Really Trying	1961	3.00	6.00	12.00
❑ LSP-2493 [S]	How to Succeed in Business Without Really Trying	1961	3.75	7.50	15.00
❑ LPM-2615 [M]	Our Man on Broadway	1963	3.00	6.00	12.00
❑ LSP-2615 [S]	Our Man on Broadway	1963	3.75	7.50	15.00

ELLIS, SHIRLEY

45s

COLUMBIA

Number	Title (A Side/B Side)	Yr	VG	VG+	NM
❑ 43829	Truly, Truly, Truly/Birds, Bees, Cupids and Bows	1966	2.00	4.00	8.00
❑ 44021	Soul Time/Waitin'	1967	2.00	4.00	8.00
❑ 44137	Sugar Let's Shing-a-Ling/How Lonely Is Lonely	1967	2.00	4.00	8.00

CONGRESS

Number	Title (A Side/B Side)	Yr	VG	VG+	NM
❑ 202	The Nitty Gritty/Give Me a List	1963	3.75	7.50	15.00
❑ 208	(That's) What the Nitty Gritty Is/Get Out	1964	2.50	5.00	10.00
❑ 210	Shy One/Takin' Care of Business	1964	2.50	5.00	10.00
❑ 221	Such a Night/Bring It On Home to Me	1964	2.50	5.00	10.00
❑ 230	The Name Game/Whisper to the Wind	1964	3.00	6.00	12.00
❑ 230 [PS]	The Name Game/Whisper to the Wind	1964	5.00	10.00	20.00

E

Number	Title (A Side/B Side)	Yr	VG	VG+	NM
❑ 234	The Clapping Song (Clap Pat Clap Slap)/This Is Beautiful	1965	2.50	5.00	10.00
❑ 234 [PS]	The Clapping Song (Clap Pat Clap Slap)/This Is Beautiful	1965	5.00	10.00	20.00
❑ 238	The Puzzle Song (A Puzzle in Song)/I See It, I Like It, I Want It	1965	2.50	5.00	10.00
❑ 246	I Never Will Forget/I Told You So	1965	2.50	5.00	10.00
❑ 251	One Sour Note/You Better Be Good, World	1965	2.50	5.00	10.00
❑ 260	Ever See a Diver Kiss His Wife While the Bubbles Bounce About Above the Water/Stardust	1965	2.50	5.00	10.00

Albums
COLUMBIA

Number	Title (A Side/B Side)	Yr	VG	VG+	NM
❑ CL 2679 [M]	Sugar, Let's Shing-a-Ling	1967	5.00	10.00	20.00
❑ CS 9479 [S]	Sugar, Let's Shing-a-Ling	1967	6.25	12.50	25.00

CONGRESS

Number	Title (A Side/B Side)	Yr	VG	VG+	NM
❑ CGL-3002 [M]	Shirley Ellis In Action	1964	6.25	12.50	25.00
❑ CGS-3002 [S]	Shirley Ellis In Action	1964	7.50	15.00	30.00
❑ CGL-3003 [M]	The Name Game	1965	6.25	12.50	25.00
❑ CGS-3003 [S]	The Name Game	1965	7.50	15.00	30.00

ELLIS, STEVE, AND THE STARFIRES
Albums
I.G.L.

Number	Title (A Side/B Side)	Yr	VG	VG+	NM
❑ 105	The Steve Ellis Songbook	1967	125.00	250.00	500.00

ELLISON, LORRAINE
45s
LOMA

Number	Title (A Side/B Side)	Yr	VG	VG+	NM
❑ 2074	Heart Be Still/Cry Me a River	1967	2.50	5.00	10.00
❑ 2083	When Love Flies Away/I Want to Be Loved	1967	2.50	5.00	10.00
❑ 2094	Try (Just a Little Bit Harder)/In My Tomorrow	1968	2.50	5.00	10.00

MERCURY

Number	Title (A Side/B Side)	Yr	VG	VG+	NM
❑ 72472	Don't Let It Go to Your Head/I Dig You Baby	1965	3.75	7.50	15.00
❑ 72534	Call Me Anytime You Need Some Lovin'/Please Don't Teach Me to Love You	1966	3.75	7.50	15.00

SHARP

Number	Title (A Side/B Side)	Yr	VG	VG+	NM
❑ 635	Open Up Your Heart/This Is the Day	1963	5.00	10.00	20.00

WARNER BROS.

Number	Title (A Side/B Side)	Yr	VG	VG+	NM
❑ GWB 0324	Stay with Me/Heart Be Still	1975	—	3.00	6.00
—"Back to Back Hits" series; "Burbank" palm trees label					
❑ 5850	Stay with Me/I Got My Baby Back	1966	3.00	6.00	12.00
❑ 5879	Good Love/I'm Over You	1966	3.00	6.00	12.00
❑ 5895	If I Had a Hammer/Heart and Soul	1967	3.00	6.00	12.00
❑ 7042	He's My Guy/No Matter How It All Turns Out	1967	2.50	5.00	10.00
❑ 7302	Only Your Love/What Is a Woman	1969	2.00	4.00	8.00
❑ 7361	Stay with Me/Try (Just a Little Bit Harder)	1970	2.00	4.00	8.00
❑ 7394	You've Really Got a Hold on Me/You Don't Know Nothing About Love	1970	2.00	4.00	8.00
❑ 7700	Many Rivers to Cross/Stormy Weather	1973	2.00	4.00	8.00

Albums
WARNER BROS.

Number	Title (A Side/B Side)	Yr	VG	VG+	NM
❑ W 1674 [M]	Heart and Soul	1967	10.00	20.00	40.00
❑ WS 1674 [S]	Heart and Soul	1967	7.50	15.00	30.00
❑ WS 1821	Stay with Me	1969	6.25	12.50	25.00
❑ BS 2780 [S]	Lorraine Ellison	1974	3.75	7.50	15.00

ELMER GANTRY'S VELVET OPERA
Albums
EPIC

Number	Title (A Side/B Side)	Yr	VG	VG+	NM
❑ BN 26415	Elmer Gantry's Velvet Opera	1968	12.50	25.00	50.00

ELMO AND ALMO
45s
DADDY BEAT

Number	Title (A Side/B Side)	Yr	VG	VG+	NM
❑ 2501	When the Good Sun Shines/Part II	1967	2.00	4.00	8.00

ELVES, THE Also see RONNIE DIO.
45s
DECCA

Number	Title (A Side/B Side)	Yr	VG	VG+	NM
❑ 732507	Walking in Different Circles/She's Not the Same	1969	5.00	10.00	20.00
❑ 732617	Amber Velvet/West Virginia	1970	5.00	10.00	20.00

EMANONS, THE
45s
ABC-PARAMOUNT

Number	Title (A Side/B Side)	Yr	VG	VG+	NM
❑ 9913	Dear One/We Teenagers (Know What We Want)	1958	5.00	10.00	20.00

GEE

Number	Title (A Side/B Side)	Yr	VG	VG+	NM
❑ 1005	Change of Time/Hindu Baby	1956	30.00	60.00	120.00

JOSIE

Number	Title (A Side/B Side)	Yr	VG	VG+	NM
❑ 801	Blue Moon/Wish I Had My Baby	1956	25.00	50.00	100.00

WINLEY

Number	Title (A Side/B Side)	Yr	VG	VG+	NM
❑ 226	Dear One/We Teenagers (Know What We Want)	1958	10.00	20.00	40.00

EMBERS, THE Several different groups.
45s
ATLANTIC

Number	Title (A Side/B Side)	Yr	VG	VG+	NM
❑ 2627	Where Did I Go Wrong/You Got What You Want	1969	2.50	5.00	10.00

BELL

Number	Title (A Side/B Side)	Yr	VG	VG+	NM
❑ 664	It Ain't No Big Thing/It Ain't Necessary	1967	5.00	10.00	20.00

COLUMBIA

Number	Title (A Side/B Side)	Yr	VG	VG+	NM
❑ 40287	Sweet Lips/There'll Be No One Else But You	1954	10.00	20.00	40.00

DOT

Number	Title (A Side/B Side)	Yr	VG	VG+	NM
❑ 16101	Wait for Me/Couldn't Wait Any Longer	1960	3.75	7.50	15.00
❑ 16162	Please Mr. Sun/My Dearest Darling	1960	3.75	7.50	15.00

EMBER

Number	Title (A Side/B Side)	Yr	VG	VG+	NM
❑ 101	Sound of Love/Paradise Hill	1953	200.00	400.00	800.00

EMPRESS

Number	Title (A Side/B Side)	Yr	VG	VG+	NM
❑ 101	Solitaire/I'm Feeling All Right Again	1961	7.50	15.00	30.00
❑ 104	I Won't Cry Anymore/I Was Too Careful	1961	7.50	15.00	30.00
❑ 107	Abigail/I Was Too Careful	1962	7.50	15.00	30.00
❑ 108	What a Surprise/I Was Too Careful	1962	10.00	20.00	40.00

HERALD

Number	Title (A Side/B Side)	Yr	VG	VG+	NM
❑ 410	Sound of Love/Paradise Hill	1953	20.00	40.00	80.00
—Yellow label					
❑ 410	Sound of Love/Paradise Hill	1953	37.50	75.00	150.00
—Red vinyl					
❑ 410	Sound of Love/Paradise Hill	1953	50.00	100.00	200.00
—Black label					

JCP

Number	Title (A Side/B Side)	Yr	VG	VG+	NM
❑ 1008	In My Lonely Room/Good Good Lovin'	1964	15.00	30.00	60.00

LIBERTY

Number	Title (A Side/B Side)	Yr	VG	VG+	NM
❑ 55944	Evelyn/And Now I'm Blue	1967	2.50	5.00	10.00

MGM

Number	Title (A Side/B Side)	Yr	VG	VG+	NM
❑ 14167	Watch Out Girl/Far Away Places	1970	7.50	15.00	30.00

WYNNE

Number	Title (A Side/B Side)	Yr	VG	VG+	NM
❑ 101	Peter Gunn Cha Cha/Chinny Chin Cha Cha	1958	3.75	7.50	15.00

Albums
JCP

Number	Title (A Side/B Side)	Yr	VG	VG+	NM
❑ 2006 [M]	The Embers Roll Eleven	1965	50.00	100.00	200.00
❑ 2009 [M]	Just for the Birds	1966	37.50	75.00	150.00

EMBRY, TED
45s
ACCENT

Number	Title (A Side/B Side)	Yr	VG	VG+	NM
❑ 1057	New Shoes/Teen Age Confession	1958	15.00	30.00	60.00

EMERALDS, THE Several different groups.
45s
ABC-PARAMOUNT

Number	Title (A Side/B Side)	Yr	VG	VG+	NM
❑ 9889	You Belong to My Heart/The One I Adore	1958	6.25	12.50	25.00
❑ 9948	I'm Dreaming/Confess	1958	6.25	12.50	25.00

ALLIED

Number	Title (A Side/B Side)	Yr	VG	VG+	NM
❑ 10002	Sally Lou/Why Must I Wonder	1958	10.00	20.00	40.00

BOBBIN

Number	Title (A Side/B Side)	Yr	VG	VG+	NM
❑ 107	That's the Way It's Got to Be/Maria's Cha-Cha	1959	12.50	25.00	50.00
❑ 121	Lover's Cry/Rumblin' Tumblin' Baby	1960	10.00	20.00	40.00

JUBILEE

Number	Title (A Side/B Side)	Yr	VG	VG+	NM
❑ 5474	Dancing Alone/Wanna Make Him Mine	1964	3.00	6.00	12.00
❑ 5489	Did You Ever Love a Guy/I'm Gonna Ask That Boy to Dance	1964	3.00	6.00	12.00

KICKS

Number	Title (A Side/B Side)	Yr	VG	VG+	NM
❑ 3	Sally Lou/Why Must I Wonder	1954	175.00	350.00	700.00

KING

Number	Title (A Side/B Side)	Yr	VG	VG+	NM
❑ 6078	Baby You've Got Me/Promises	1967	6.25	12.50	25.00

MOONGLOW

Number	Title (A Side/B Side)	Yr	VG	VG+	NM
❑ 230	Ooh Poo Pah Doo/Sally's Snake	1964	7.50	15.00	30.00
❑ 232	Moonlight Surf/Little D Special	1964	7.50	15.00	30.00
—Black vinyl					
❑ 232	Moonlight Surf/Little D Special	1964	20.00	40.00	80.00
—Green vinyl					

REX

Number	Title (A Side/B Side)	Yr	VG	VG+	NM
❑ 1004	All the Time/Gotta Be on Time	1959	7.50	15.00	30.00
❑ 1013	I Kneel at Your Throne/Custer's Last Stand	1960	7.50	15.00	30.00

TOY

Number	Title (A Side/B Side)	Yr	VG	VG+	NM
❑ 7734	Silver/Roadrunner	1961	5.00	10.00	20.00

VENUS

Number	Title (A Side/B Side)	Yr	VG	VG+	NM
❑ 1002	Mademoiselle/The Lover	1959	25.00	50.00	100.00
❑ 1003	Marsha/You're Driving Me Crazy	1959	37.50	75.00	150.00

YALE

Number	Title (A Side/B Side)	Yr	VG	VG+	NM
❑ 232	The Web/Trapped	1960	5.00	10.00	20.00

EMERALS, THE
45s
TRIPLE X

Number	Title (A Side/B Side)	Yr	VG	VG+	NM
❑ 100/101	Please Don't Crush My Dreams/Jukebox Rock	1960	150.00	300.00	600.00

EMERSON, BILLY
45s
CHESS

Number	Title (A Side/B Side)	Yr	VG	VG+	NM
❑ 1711	Give Me a Little Love/Woodchuck	1959	5.00	10.00	20.00
❑ 1728	Holy Mackerel Baby/Believe Me	1959	5.00	10.00	20.00
❑ 1740	Uh Huh, My Baby/I'll Get to You	1959	5.00	10.00	20.00

CONSTELLATION

Number	Title (A Side/B Side)	Yr	VG	VG+	NM
❑ 148	Aunt Molly (Part 1)/Aunt Molly (Part 2)	1965	3.75	7.50	15.00

SUN

Number	Title (A Side/B Side)	Yr	VG	VG+	NM
❑ 195	No Teasin' Around/If Lovin' Is Believin'	1954	100.00	200.00	400.00
❑ 203	I'm Not Going Home/The Woodchuck	1954	200.00	400.00	600.00
❑ 214	Move, Baby, Move/When It Rains, It Pours	1955	12.50	25.00	50.00
❑ 219	Red Hot/No Greater Love	1955	25.00	50.00	100.00
❑ 233	Something for Nothing/Little Fine Healthy Thing	1956	12.50	25.00	50.00

VEE JAY

Number	Title (A Side/B Side)	Yr	VG	VG+	NM
❑ 219	Every Woman I Know/Tomorrow Never Comes	1956	7.50	15.00	30.00
❑ 247	Somebody Show Me/The Pleasure Is All Mine	1957	7.50	15.00	30.00
❑ 261	You Never Miss the Water/Do Yourself a Favor Billy	1957	7.50	15.00	30.00

EMERSON, LAKE AND PALMER
45s
ATLANTIC

Number	Title (A Side/B Side)	Yr	VG	VG+	NM
❑ 3398	Fanfare for the Common Man/Brain Salad Surgery	1977	—	2.50	5.00
❑ 3555	All I Want Is You/Tiger in a Spotlight	1979	—	2.50	5.00
❑ 3641	Peter Gunn Theme/Tiger in a Spotlight	1980	—	2.50	5.00

COTILLION

Number	Title (A Side/B Side)	Yr	VG	VG+	NM
❑ 44106	Lucky Man/Knife's Edge	1971	—	3.00	6.00
❑ 44131	A Time and a Place/Stone of Years	1971	—	2.50	5.00
❑ 44151	Nutrocker/The Great Gates of Kiev	1972	—	2.50	5.00
❑ 44158	From the Beginning/Living Sin	1972	—	2.50	5.00

MANTICORE

Number	Title (A Side/B Side)	Yr	VG	VG+	NM
❑ 2003	Still...You Turn Me On/Brain Salad Surgery	1973	—	2.50	5.00
❑ 2003 [PS]	Still...You Turn Me On/Brain Salad Surgery	1973	2.50	5.00	10.00

Albums
ATLANTIC

Number	Title (A Side/B Side)	Yr	VG	VG+	NM
❑ PR 277 [DJ]	Works Volume 1	1977	3.75	7.50	15.00
—Promo-only sampler					
❑ PR 281 [DJ]	On Tour with Emerson, Lake and Palmer	1977	10.00	20.00	40.00
❑ SD 7000 [(2)]	Works Volume 1	1977	3.75	7.50	15.00

Number	Title (A Side/B Side)	Yr	VG	VG+	NM
SD 19120	Emerson, Lake and Palmer	1977	2.00	4.00	8.00
SD 19121	Tarkus	1977	2.00	4.00	8.00
SD 19122	Pictures at an Exhibition	1977	2.00	4.00	8.00
SD 19123	Trilogy	1977	2.00	4.00	8.00
SD 19124	Brain Salad Surgery	1977	2.00	4.00	8.00
SD 19147	Works Volume 2	1977	2.50	5.00	10.00
SD 19211	Love Beach	1978	2.50	5.00	10.00
SD 19255	Emerson, Lake and Palmer In Concert	1979	2.50	5.00	10.00
SD 19283	The Best of Emerson, Lake and Palmer	1980	2.50	5.00	10.00

COTILLION

Number	Title (A Side/B Side)	Yr	VG	VG+	NM
SD 9040	Emerson, Lake and Palmer	1971	3.00	6.00	12.00
SD 9900	Tarkus	1971	3.00	6.00	12.00
SD 9903	Trilogy	1972	3.00	6.00	12.00
ELP 66666	Pictures at an Exhibition	1971	3.00	6.00	12.00
SMAS-94773	Trilogy	1972	3.75	7.50	15.00

—Capitol Record Club edition

MANTICORE

Number	Title (A Side/B Side)	Yr	VG	VG+	NM
SD 3-200 [(3)]	Welcome Back, My Friends, to the Show That Never Ends, Ladies and Gentlemen	1974	5.00	10.00	20.00
ELP 66669	Brain Salad Surgery	1973	3.00	6.00	12.00

MOBILE FIDELITY

Number	Title (A Side/B Side)	Yr	VG	VG+	NM
1-031	Pictures at an Exhibition	1980	7.50	15.00	30.00

—Audiophile vinyl

Number	Title (A Side/B Side)	Yr	VG	VG+	NM
1-203	Tarkus	1994	6.25	12.50	25.00

—Audiophile vinyl

Number	Title (A Side/B Side)	Yr	VG	VG+	NM
1-218	Trilogy	1994	10.00	20.00	40.00

—Audiophile vinyl

EMERSON'S OLD-TIMEY CUSTARD-SUCKIN' BAND
Albums
ESP-DISK'

Number	Title (A Side/B Side)	Yr	VG	VG+	NM
2006	Emerson's Old-Timey Custard-Suckin' Band	1970	7.50	15.00	30.00

EMOTIONS, THE (1) Female R&B vocal group. Also see EARTH, WIND AND FIRE WITH THE EMOTIONS.
45s
ARC

Number	Title (A Side/B Side)	Yr	VG	VG+	NM
18-02239	Turn It Out/When You Gonna Wake Up	1981	—	2.00	4.00
18-02535	Now That I Know/Here You Come Again	1981	—	2.00	4.00
11134	What's the Name of Your Love?/Layed Back	1979	—	2.50	5.00
11205	Where Is Your Love?/Layed Back	1980	—	2.50	5.00

COLUMBIA

Number	Title (A Side/B Side)	Yr	VG	VG+	NM
3-10347	Flowers/I Don't Wanna Lose Your Love	1976	—	2.50	5.00
3-10544	Best of My Love/A Feeling Is	1977	—	2.50	5.00
3-10622	Don't Ask My Neighbors/Love's What's Happenin'	1977	—	2.50	5.00
3-10791	Smile/Changes	1978	—	2.50	5.00
3-10828	Whole Lotta Shakin'/Time Is Passing By	1978	—	2.50	5.00
3-10874	Walking the Line/Ain't No Doubt About It	1978	—	2.50	5.00

MOTOWN

Number	Title (A Side/B Side)	Yr	VG	VG+	NM
1784	I Can't Wait to Make You Mine/I'm Gonna Miss Your Love	1985	—	2.00	4.00
1792	If I Only Knew Then (What I Know Now)/Eternally	1985	—	2.00	4.00

RED LABEL

Number	Title (A Side/B Side)	Yr	VG	VG+	NM
001-1	You're the One/I Can Do Anything	1984	—	2.50	5.00
001-2	You're the Best/(B-side unknown)	1984	—	2.50	5.00
001-3	Are You Through with My Heart/(B-side unknown)	1984	—	2.50	5.00

STAX

Number	Title (A Side/B Side)	Yr	VG	VG+	NM
1056	What Do The Lonely Do At Christmas?/Santa Claus Wants Some Lovin'	197?	—	3.00	6.00

—B-side by Albert King; reissue

Number	Title (A Side/B Side)	Yr	VG	VG+	NM
3200	Shouting Out Love/Baby, I'm Through	1977	—	2.50	5.00
3205	Baby, I'm Through/Any Way You Look at It	1978	—	2.50	5.00
3215	What Do the Lonely Do at Christmas/(Instrumental)	1978	—	2.50	5.00

TWIN STACKS

Number	Title (A Side/B Side)	Yr	VG	VG+	NM
126	Somebody New/Brushfire	1968	2.50	5.00	10.00
130	I Love You But I'll Leave You/Brushfire	1968	2.50	5.00	10.00

VOLT

Number	Title (A Side/B Side)	Yr	VG	VG+	NM
4010	So I Can Love You/Got to Be the Man	1969	2.00	4.00	8.00
4021	The Best Part of a Love Affair/I Like It	1969	2.00	4.00	8.00
4031	Stealing Love/When Tomorrow Comes	1970	2.00	4.00	8.00
4045	Heart Association/The Touch of Your Lips	1970	2.00	4.00	8.00
4053	Black Christmas/(Instrumental)	1970	2.50	5.00	10.00
4054	You Make Me Want to Love You/What You See Is What You Get	1971	—	3.50	7.00
4062	If You Think It/Love Ain't Easy One-Sided	1971	—	3.50	7.00
4066	Show Me How/Boss Love Maker	1971	—	3.50	7.00
4077	My Honey and Me/Blind Alley	1972	—	3.50	7.00
4083	I Could Never Be Happy/I've Fallen in Love	1972	—	3.50	7.00
4088	From Toys to Boys/I Call This Loving You	1972	—	3.50	7.00
4095	Runnin' Back (And Forth)/I Wanna Come Back	1973	—	3.50	7.00
4100	Peace Be Still/Runnin' Back (And Forth)	1973	—	3.50	7.00
4104	What Do the Lonely Do at Christmas/(Instrumental)	1973	2.00	4.00	8.00
4106	Put a Little Love Away/I Call This Loving You	1974	—	3.50	7.00
4110	Baby I'm Through/I Wanna Come Back	1974	—	3.50	7.00
4113	Any Way You Look At It/There Are More Questions Than Answers	1974	—	3.50	7.00

Albums
ARC

Number	Title (A Side/B Side)	Yr	VG	VG+	NM
JC 36149	Come Into Our World	1979	2.50	5.00	10.00
FC 37456	New Affair	1981	2.50	5.00	10.00

COLUMBIA

Number	Title (A Side/B Side)	Yr	VG	VG+	NM
PC 34163	Flowers	1976	2.50	5.00	10.00

—No bar code on cover

Number	Title (A Side/B Side)	Yr	VG	VG+	NM
PC 34163	Flowers	198?	2.00	4.00	8.00

—With bar code on cover

Number	Title (A Side/B Side)	Yr	VG	VG+	NM
PC 34762	Rejoice	1977	2.50	5.00	10.00

—No bar code on cover

Number	Title (A Side/B Side)	Yr	VG	VG+	NM
PC 34762	Rejoice	198?	2.00	4.00	8.00

—With bar code on cover

Number	Title (A Side/B Side)	Yr	VG	VG+	NM
JC 35385	Sunbeam	1978	2.50	5.00	10.00

MOTOWN

Number	Title (A Side/B Side)	Yr	VG	VG+	NM
6136 ML	If I Only Knew	1985	2.00	4.00	8.00

STAX

Number	Title (A Side/B Side)	Yr	VG	VG+	NM
STX-4100	Sunshine	1977	2.50	5.00	10.00
STX-4110	So I Can Love You	1978	2.50	5.00	10.00

—Reissue of Volt 6008

Number	Title (A Side/B Side)	Yr	VG	VG+	NM
STX-4112	Untouched	1978	2.50	5.00	10.00

—Reissue of Volt 6015

Number	Title (A Side/B Side)	Yr	VG	VG+	NM
STX-4121	Chronicle	1979	2.50	5.00	10.00

VOLT

Number	Title (A Side/B Side)	Yr	VG	VG+	NM
VOS-6008	So I Can Love You	1971	6.25	12.50	25.00
VOS-6015	Untouched	1972	6.25	12.50	25.00

EMOTIONS, THE (2) Brooklyn-based male vocal group.
45s
CALLA

Number	Title (A Side/B Side)	Yr	VG	VG+	NM
122	Baby I Need Your Lovin'/She's My Baby (I Just Can't Let Her Go)	1966	3.75	7.50	15.00

KAPP

Number	Title (A Side/B Side)	Yr	VG	VG+	NM
490	Echo/Come Dance Baby	1962	6.25	12.50	25.00
513	L-O-V-E/A Million Reasons	1963	6.25	12.50	25.00

20TH FOX

Number	Title (A Side/B Side)	Yr	VG	VG+	NM
430	A Story Untold/One Life. One Love, One You	1963	5.00	10.00	20.00
452	Rainbow/Little Miss Blue	1963	5.00	10.00	20.00
478	Boomerang/I Love You Madly	1964	5.00	10.00	20.00
6623	Heart Strings/Every Time	1966	3.75	7.50	15.00

EMOTIONS, THE (U) It's unlikely than any of these are group (1). Some of these may be group (2). Others are different.
45s
BRAINSTORM

Number	Title (A Side/B Side)	Yr	VG	VG+	NM
125	Can't Stand No More Heartaches/You'd Better Get Used to It	1968	2.00	4.00	8.00
129	Never Let Me Go/I Can't Control These Emotions	1968	2.00	4.00	8.00

CARD

Number	Title (A Side/B Side)	Yr	VG	VG+	NM
600	(By the Light of the) Silvery Moon/Do You Love Me	1962	37.50	75.00	150.00

FLIP

Number	Title (A Side/B Side)	Yr	VG	VG+	NM
356	I Ran to You/Keep Lookin' Your Way	1961	7.50	15.00	30.00

FURY

Number	Title (A Side/B Side)	Yr	VG	VG+	NM
1010	Candlelight/It's Love	1958	10.00	20.00	40.00

KARATE

Number	Title (A Side/B Side)	Yr	VG	VG+	NM
506	Hey Baby/I Wonder	1964	5.00	10.00	20.00

LAURIE

Number	Title (A Side/B Side)	Yr	VG	VG+	NM
3167	Fool's Paradise/Starlit Night	1963	5.00	10.00	20.00

VARDAN

Number	Title (A Side/B Side)	Yr	VG	VG+	NM
201	Love of a Girl/Do This for Me	1965	5.00	10.00	20.00

EMPERORS, THE (1) Band from Harrisburg, Pa.
45s
BRUNSWICK

Number	Title (A Side/B Side)	Yr	VG	VG+	NM
55333	Karate Boogaloo/Mumble Shing-a-Ling	1967	2.50	5.00	10.00

MALA

Number	Title (A Side/B Side)	Yr	VG	VG+	NM
543	Karate/I've Got to Have Her	1966	3.75	7.50	15.00
554	My Baby Likes to Boogaloo/You Got Me Where You Want Me	1967	3.00	6.00	12.00
561	Searchin'/Lookin' for My Baby	1967	3.00	6.00	12.00

EMPERORS, THE (2) Sometimes called "The Emperors with Rhythm."
45s
HAVEN

Number	Title (A Side/B Side)	Yr	VG	VG+	NM
511	I May Be Wrong/Come Back, Come Back	1954	2000.	3000.	4000.

EMPERORS, THE (3)
45s
OLIMPIC

Number	Title (A Side/B Side)	Yr	VG	VG+	NM
245	Darlin' in the Moonlight/Steve Allen	1964	10.00	20.00	40.00

EMPERORS, THE (4)
45s
SABRA

Number	Title (A Side/B Side)	Yr	VG	VG+	NM
5555	I Want My Woman/(B-side unknown)	196?	10.00	20.00	40.00

EMPIRES, THE (1) LES COOPER was a member of this group.
45s
AMP 3

Number	Title (A Side/B Side)	Yr	VG	VG+	NM
132	If I'm a Fool/Zippety Zip	1957	25.00	50.00	100.00

HARLEM

Number	Title (A Side/B Side)	Yr	VG	VG+	NM
2325	Corn Whiskey/My Baby, My Baby	1954	100.00	200.00	400.00
2333	Magic Mirror/Make Me or Break Me	1955	100.00	200.00	400.00

WHIRLIN' DISC

Number	Title (A Side/B Side)	Yr	VG	VG+	NM
104	Linda/Whispering Heart	1957	17.50	35.00	70.00

WING

Number	Title (A Side/B Side)	Yr	VG	VG+	NM
90023	I Want to Know/Shirley	1955	12.50	25.00	50.00
90050	By the Riverside/Tell My Baby	1956	10.00	20.00	40.00
90080	Don't Touch My Gal/My First Discovery	1956	10.00	20.00	40.00

EMPIRES, THE (2)
45s
CALICO

Number	Title (A Side/B Side)	Yr	VG	VG+	NM
121	Definition of Love/Only in My Dreams	1960	5.00	10.00	20.00

CANDI

Number	Title (A Side/B Side)	Yr	VG	VG+	NM
1026	Love You So Bad/Come Back Girl	1962	6.25	12.50	25.00
1033	You're on Top, Girl/Slide On By	1963	10.00	20.00	40.00

CHAVIS

Number	Title (A Side/B Side)	Yr	VG	VG+	NM
1026	Love You So Bad/Come Back Girl	1962	3.75	7.50	15.00

COLPIX

Number	Title (A Side/B Side)	Yr	VG	VG+	NM
680	Everyone Knew But Me/Three Little Fishes	1963	5.00	10.00	20.00

DCP

Number	Title (A Side/B Side)	Yr	VG	VG+	NM
1116	Have Mercy/Love Is Strange	1964	3.00	6.00	12.00

LAKE

Number	Title (A Side/B Side)	Yr	VG	VG+	NM
711	Over the Summer Vacation/You're So Popular	1961	5.00	10.00	20.00

EMPIRES, THE (3) Featuring David Blatt, later known as JAY BLACK of JAY AND THE AMERICANS.
45s
EPIC

Number	Title (A Side/B Side)	Yr	VG	VG+	NM
5-9527	A Time and a Place/Punch Your Nose	1962	10.00	20.00	40.00

Number	Title (A Side/B Side)	Yr	VG	VG+	NM

ENALOUISE AND THE HEARTS
45s
ARGYLE

| ❑ 1635 | From a Cap and a Gown/A Prisoner to You | 1959 | 12.50 | 25.00 | 50.00 |

ENCHANTERS, THE (1)
45s
BALD EAGLE

| ❑ 3001 | Come On Baby, Let's Do the Stroll/Rock Around | 1958 | 7.50 | 15.00 | 30.00 |

BAMBOO

| ❑ 513 | Touch of Love/Cafe Bohemian | 1961 | 6.25 | 12.50 | 25.00 |

CANDELITE

| ❑ 432 | Oh Rose Marie/Bewildered | 1964 | 3.00 | 6.00 | 12.00 |

EP-SOM

| ❑ 103 | I Need Your Love/Goddess of Love | 1962 | 100.00 | 200.00 | 400.00 |

J.J. & M.

| ❑ 1562 | Oh Rose Marie/Bewildered | 1962 | 50.00 | 100.00 | 200.00 |

MUSITRON

| ❑ 1072 | I Lied to My Heart/Talk While You Walk | 1961 | 10.00 | 20.00 | 40.00 |

ORBIT

| ❑ 532 | Touch of Love/Cafe Bohemian | 1959 | 12.50 | 25.00 | 50.00 |

SHARP

| ❑ 105 | We Make Mistakes/The Decision | 1960 | 6.25 | 12.50 | 25.00 |

STARDUST

| ❑ 102 | Spellbound by the Moon/Know It All | 1956 | 375.00 | 750.00 | 1500. |

ENCHANTERS, THE (2) Also see GARNET MIMMS AND THE ENCHANTERS.
45s
LOMA

❑ 2012	I Want to Be Loved/I Paid for the Party	1965	2.50	5.00	10.00
❑ 2035	You Were Meant to Be My Baby/God Bless the Girl, and Me	1966	2.50	5.00	10.00
❑ 2054	We Got Love/I've Lost All Communications	1966	2.50	5.00	10.00

WARNER BROS.

| ❑ 5460 | I Wanna Thank You/I'm a Good Man | 1964 | 3.75 | 7.50 | 15.00 |

ENCHANTERS, THE (3)
45s
CORAL

❑ 61756	True Love Gone/Wait a Minute Baby	1956	15.00	30.00	60.00
❑ 61832	There Goes (A Pretty Girl)/Fan Me Baby	1957	6.25	12.50	25.00
—Edited version of A-side; matrix number is "102,966"					
❑ 61832	There Goes (A Pretty Girl)/Fan Me Baby	1957	20.00	40.00	80.00
—Full-length version of A-side; matrix number is "100,974"					
❑ 61916	Mambo Santa Mambo/Bottle Up and Go	1957	10.00	20.00	40.00
❑ 62373	True Love Gone/The Day	1963	5.00	10.00	20.00
❑ 65610	True Love Gone/Today Is Your Birthday	1963	3.00	6.00	12.00

MERCER

| ❑ 992 | True Love Gone/Wait a Minute Baby | 1956 | 500.00 | 1000. | 2000. |

ENCHANTERS, THE (4)
45s
JUBILEE

| ❑ 5072 | Today Is Your Birthday/How Could You | 1952 | 62.50 | 125.00 | 250.00 |
| ❑ 5080 | I've Lost/Housewife Blues | 1952 | 50.00 | 100.00 | 200.00 |

ENCHANTERS, THE (U) May be group (1); may be a fifth different group also.
45s
TOM TOM

| ❑ 301 | Surf Blast/Tom Tiki | 1963 | 12.50 | 25.00 | 50.00 |

ENCHANTMENTS, THE
45s
FARO

| ❑ 620 | I'm in Love with Your Daughter/(B-side unknown) | 1964 | 25.00 | 50.00 | 100.00 |

GONE

| ❑ 5130 | (I Love You) Sherry/Come On Home | 1962 | 7.50 | 15.00 | 30.00 |

RITZ

| ❑ 17003 | I Love You Baby/Pains in My Heart | 1963 | 25.00 | 50.00 | 100.00 |

ENCHORDS, THE
45s
LAURIE

| ❑ 3089 | Zoom Zoom Zoom/I Need You Baby | 1961 | 12.50 | 25.00 | 50.00 |

ENCORES, THE More than one group.
45s
BOW

| ❑ 302 | Barbara/Thank You | 1958 | 25.00 | 50.00 | 100.00 |

CHECKER

| ❑ 760 | When I Look at You/Young Girls, Young Girls | 1952 | 2000. | 3000. | 4000. |

HOLLYWOOD

| ❑ 1034 | Time Is Moving On/Ha-Chi-Bi-Ri-Bi-Ri | 1955 | 20.00 | 40.00 | 80.00 |

LOOK

| ❑ 105 | Time Is Moving On/Ha-Chi-Bi-Ri-Bi-Ri | 1955 | 100.00 | 200.00 | 400.00 |

MGM

| ❑ 11947 | Chloe/Wa Va Ga Dot | 1955 | 3.00 | 6.00 | 12.00 |

ENCOUNTERS, THE
45s
LOST-NITE

| ❑ 235 | Don't Stop Now/Place in Your Heart | 196? | — | 2.50 | 5.00 |
| —Reissue | | | | | |

SWAN

| ❑ 4206 | Don't Stop Now/Place in Your Heart | 1964 | 37.50 | 75.00 | 150.00 |

END, THE
45s
LONDON

| ❑ 1016 | Shades of Orange/Loving, Sacred Loving | 1968 | 5.00 | 10.00 | 20.00 |

PHILIPS

| ❑ 40323 | Hey Little Girl/I Can't Get Any Joy | 1965 | 2.50 | 5.00 | 10.00 |

Albums
LONDON

| ❑ PS 560 | Introspection | 1969 | 12.50 | 25.00 | 50.00 |

ENDEAVORS, THE (1)
45s
J&S

| ❑ 254 | Suffering with My Heart/I Got the Feeling | 1960 | 300.00 | 600.00 | 1200. |

ENDEAVORS, THE (2) Country group.
45s
STOP

| ❑ 372 | Shattered Dreams/I Know You Don't Want Me | 1971 | 2.50 | 5.00 | 10.00 |

ENDORSERS, THE
45s
MOON

| ❑ 109 | Crying/Hold My Hand | 1959 | 500.00 | 1000. | 2000. |

ENEMYS, THE With Cory Wells, later of THREE DOG NIGHT.
45s
MGM

❑ 13485	Glitter and Gold/Too Much Monkey Business	1966	3.75	7.50	15.00
❑ 13525	Hey Joe/My Dues Have Been Paid	1966	3.75	7.50	15.00
❑ 13573	Mo-Jo Woman/My Dues Have Been Paid	1966	3.75	7.50	15.00

VALIANT

| ❑ 714 | Say Goodbye to Donna/Sinner Man | 1965 | 6.25 | 12.50 | 25.00 |
| —As "Corey Wells and the Enemys" | | | | | |

ENGEL, SCOTT Also see THE WALKER BROTHERS.
45s
CHALLENGE

| ❑ 9206 | Devil Surfer/Your Guess | 1963 | 5.00 | 10.00 | 20.00 |

LIBERTY

| ❑ 55312 | Mr. Jones/Anything Will Do | 1961 | 5.00 | 10.00 | 20.00 |
| ❑ 55428 | Anything Will Do/Forever More | 1962 | 5.00 | 10.00 | 20.00 |

MARTAY

| ❑ 2004 | Devil Surfer/Your Guess | 1963 | 10.00 | 20.00 | 40.00 |

ORBIT

❑ 506	The Livin' End/Good for Nothin'	1958	5.00	10.00	20.00
❑ 506 [PS]	The Livin' End/Good for Nothin'	1958	12.50	25.00	50.00
❑ 511	Charley Bop/All I Do Is Dream	1958	7.50	15.00	30.00
❑ 511 [PS]	Charley Bop/All I Do Is Dream	1958	15.00	30.00	60.00
❑ 512	Blue Bell/Paper Doll	1958	5.00	10.00	20.00
❑ 512 [PS]	Blue Bell/Paper Doll	1958	12.50	25.00	50.00
❑ 537	The Golden Rule/Sunday	1959	5.00	10.00	20.00
❑ 537 [PS]	The Golden Rule/Sunday	1959	12.50	25.00	50.00
❑ 545	Comin' Home/I Don't Wanna Know	1959	5.00	10.00	20.00

RKO UNIQUE

| ❑ 386 | Steady As a Rock/When Is a Boy a Man | 1957 | 6.25 | 12.50 | 25.00 |

ENGEL, SCOTT, AND JOHN STEWART See THE WALKER BROTHERS.

ENGLAND, BENNY
45s
SNAP

| ❑ 400 | Eloping/Some How | 1958 | 75.00 | 150.00 | 300.00 |

ENGLAND DAN AND JOHN FORD COLEY Also see SOUTHWEST F.O.B.
45s
A&M

❑ 1278	New Jersey/Tell Her Hello	1971	—	3.00	6.00
❑ 1354	Casey/Simone	1972	—	2.50	5.00
❑ 1369	Carolina/Free the People	1972	—	2.50	5.00
❑ 1465	I Hear the Music/Miss You Song	1973	—	2.50	5.00
❑ 1871	I Hear the Music/Simone	1976	—	2.00	4.00

BIG TREE

❑ 16069	I'd Really Love to See You Tonight/It's Not the Same	1976	—	2.00	4.00
❑ 16079	Nights Are Forever Without You/Showboat Gambler	1976	—	2.00	4.00
❑ 16088	It's Sad to Belong/The Time Has Come	1977	—	2.00	4.00
❑ 16102	Gone Too Far/Where Do I Go from Here	1977	—	2.00	4.00
❑ 16110	We'll Never Have to Say Goodbye Again/Calling for You Again	1978	—	2.00	4.00
❑ 16117	You Can't Dance/Wantin' You Desperately	1978	—	2.00	4.00
❑ 16125	If the World Ran Out of Love Tonight/Lovin' Somebody on a Rainy Night	1978	—	2.00	4.00
❑ 16130	Westward Wind/Some Things Don't Come Easy	1979	—	2.00	4.00
❑ 16131	Love Is the Answer/Running After You	1979	—	2.00	4.00
❑ 16135	Hollywood Heckle and Jive/Rolling Fever	1979	—	2.00	4.00
❑ 17000	What Can I Do with My Broken Heart/Caught Up in the Middle	1979	—	2.00	4.00
❑ 17002	In It for Love/Who's Lonely Now	1980	—	2.00	4.00

MCA

| ❑ 51027 | Part of Me, Part of You/Just Tell Me You Love Me | 1980 | — | 2.00 | 4.00 |

Albums
A&M

❑ SP-4305	England Dan and John Ford Coley	1971	3.75	7.50	15.00
❑ SP-4350	Fables	1972	3.75	7.50	15.00
❑ SP-4613	I Hear Music	1976	3.00	6.00	12.00

BIG TREE

❑ BT 76000	Dowdy Ferry Road	1977	2.50	5.00	10.00
❑ BT 76006	Some Things Don't Come Easy	1978	2.50	5.00	10.00
❑ BT 76015	Dr. Heckle & Mr. Jive	1979	2.50	5.00	10.00
❑ BT 76018	Best of England Dan & John Ford Coley	1980	2.50	5.00	10.00
❑ BT 89517	Nights Are Forever	1976	2.50	5.00	10.00

ENGLER, JERRY, AND THE FOUR EKKOS
45s
BRUNSWICK

| ❑ 55037 | Sputnik (Satellite Girl)/Unfaithful One | 1957 | 20.00 | 40.00 | 80.00 |
| —BUDDY HOLLY appears on this record | | | | | |

ENGLISH, BARBARA Also includes records as "Barbara Jean English." Also see THE FASHIONS (1).
45s
ALITHIA

❑ 6040	I'm Living a Lie/All This	1972	—	3.00	6.00
❑ 6041	So Many Ways to Die/(B-side unknown)	1972	—	3.00	6.00
❑ 6042	I'm Sorry/Lil' Baby	1972	—	3.00	6.00

E

Number	Title (A Side/B Side)	Yr	VG	VG+	NM
❏ 6046	Baby I'm-a Want You/Don't Make Me Over	1973	—	3.00	6.00
❏ 6053	You're Gonna Need Somebody to Love (While You're Looking for Someone to Love)/All This	1973	—	3.00	6.00
❏ 6059	Comin' or Goin'/Love's Arrangement	1973	—	3.00	6.00
❏ 6064	Breakin' Up a Happy Home/Guess Who	1974	—	3.00	6.00
AURORA					
❏ 155	Standin' on Tip-Toe/(You Got Me) Sittin' in the Corner	1965	20.00	40.00	80.00
MALA					
❏ 488	Easy Come, Easy Go/I Don't Deserve a Boy Like You	1964	6.25	12.50	25.00
REPRISE					
❏ 0290	I've Gotta Date/Shoo Fly	1964	6.25	12.50	25.00
❏ 0349	Small Town Girl/Tell It Like It Is	1965	6.25	12.50	25.00
ROULETTE					
❏ 4428	We Need Them/La-Ta-Tee-Ta-Ta	1962	7.50	15.00	30.00
❏ 4450	Fever/Bad News	1962	7.50	15.00	30.00
WARNER BROS.					
❏ 5685	All Because I Love Somebody/All the Good Times Are Gone	1965	5.00	10.00	20.00

ENGLISH, SCOTT
45s
DOT

Number	Title (A Side/B Side)	Yr	VG	VG+	NM
❏ 16099	White Cliffs of Dover/4000 Miles Away	1960	7.50	15.00	30.00
JANUS					
❏ 171	Brandy/Lead Me Back	1971	3.00	6.00	12.00

—A-side later recorded by Barry Manilow as "Mandy"

❏ 192	Woman in My Life/Ballad of the Unloved	1972	—	2.50	5.00
JOKER					
❏ 777	Ugly Pills (You're Takin')/When	1962	12.50	25.00	50.00
SPOKANE					
❏ 4003	High on a Hill/When	1964	6.25	12.50	25.00
❏ 4007	Here Comes the Pain/All I Want Is You	1964	10.00	20.00	40.00
SULTAN					
❏ 1003	High on a Hill/When	1963	12.50	25.00	50.00

ENGLISH CONGREGATION, THE
45s
ATCO

Number	Title (A Side/B Side)	Yr	VG	VG+	NM
❏ 6865	Softly Whispering I Love You/When Susie Takes the Plane	1972	—	3.00	6.00
SIGNPOST					
❏ 70002	Lovers of the World Unite/Love is the Sweetest Thing I Know	1972	—	3.00	6.00
❏ 70004	If I Could Have My Way/Jesahel	1972	—	3.00	6.00
Albums					
SIGNPOST					
❏ SP 7217	Softly Whispering I Love You	1972	3.00	6.00	12.00
❏ SP 8405	Jesahel	1972	3.00	6.00	12.00

ENJOYABLES, THE
45s
CAPITOL

Number	Title (A Side/B Side)	Yr	VG	VG+	NM
❏ 5321	Push a Little Harder/We'll Make Our Way	1964	7.50	15.00	30.00
SHRINE					
❏ 118	Shame/I'll Take You Back	1966	150.00	300.00	600.00

ENNIS, ETHEL
45s
JUBILEE

Number	Title (A Side/B Side)	Yr	VG	VG+	NM
❏ 5236	I've Got You Under My Skin/You Better Go Now	1956	3.00	6.00	12.00
RCA VICTOR					
❏ 47-8379	The Boy from Ipanema/When Will the Hurt Be Over	1964	2.00	4.00	8.00
❏ 47-8448	Matchmaker, Matchmaker/Now I Have Everything	1964	2.00	4.00	8.00
❏ 47-8491	For a Short While/San Juan	1964	2.00	4.00	8.00
Albums					
BASF					
❏ 25121	10 Sides of Ethel Ennis	1973	3.75	7.50	15.00
CAPITOL					
❏ T 941	Change of Scenery	1957	10.00	20.00	40.00
❏ T 1078 [M]	Have You Forgotten?	1959	10.00	20.00	40.00
JUBILEE					
❏ JLP-1021 [M]	Lullabies for Losers	1956	12.50	25.00	50.00
❏ JLP-5024 [M]	Ethel Ennis Sings	1963	5.00	10.00	20.00
❏ SJLP-5024 [S]	Ethel Ennis Sings	1963	6.25	12.50	25.00
PICKWICK					
❏ PC-3021 [M]	Ethel Ennis	196?	3.00	6.00	12.00
❏ SPC-3021 [S]	Ethel Ennis	196?	3.00	6.00	12.00
RCA CAMDEN					
❏ ACL1-0157	God Bless the Child	1973	2.50	5.00	10.00
RCA VICTOR					
❏ LPM-2786 [M]	This Is Ethel Ennis	1964	5.00	10.00	20.00
❏ LSP-2786 [S]	This Is Ethel Ennis	1964	6.25	12.50	25.00
❏ LPM-2862 [M]	Once Again, Ethel Ennis	1964	5.00	10.00	20.00
❏ LSP-2862 [S]	Once Again, Ethel Ennis	1964	6.25	12.50	25.00
❏ LPM-2984 [M]	Eyes for You	1964	5.00	10.00	20.00
❏ LSP-2984 [S]	Eyes for You	1964	6.25	12.50	25.00

ENO, BRIAN Also see ROXY MUSIC.
12-Inch Singles
OPAL

Number	Title (A Side/B Side)	Yr	VG	VG+	NM
❏ 40539	Fractal Zoom (6 versions)/The Roll, The Choke	1992	2.00	4.00	8.00
45s					
ISLAND					
❏ 036	The Lion Sleeps Tonight/I'll Come Running (To Tie Your Shoes)	1975	6.25	12.50	25.00
❏ 036 [DJ]	The Lion Sleeps Tonight (mono/stereo)	1975	3.75	7.50	15.00
Albums					
ANTILLES					
❏ AN-7001	No Pussyfooting	1973	3.75	7.50	15.00

—By Robert Fripp and Eno

Number	Title (A Side/B Side)	Yr	VG	VG+	NM
❏ AN-7018	Evening Star	1975	3.00	6.00	12.00

—By Robert Fripp and Eno

❏ AN-7030	Discreet Music	1975	3.00	6.00	12.00
❏ AN-7070	Music for Films	1978	3.75	7.50	15.00
EDITIONS EG					
❏ ENO-1	Here Come the Warm Jets	1982	2.50	5.00	10.00

—Reissue

| ❏ EGBS-2 [(11)] | Working Backwards: 1983-1973 | 1984 | 15.00 | 30.00 | 60.00 |

—Boxed set of nine albums plus Music For Films II and Rarities 12"

| ❏ ENO-2 | Taking Tiger Mountain (By Strategy) | 1982 | 2.50 | 5.00 | 10.00 |

—Reissue

| ❏ ENO-3 | Another Green World | 1982 | 2.50 | 5.00 | 10.00 |

—Reissue

| ❏ ENO-4 | Before and After Science | 1982 | 2.50 | 5.00 | 10.00 |

—Reissue

❏ ENO-5	Apollo: Atmospheres and Soundtracks	1983	2.50	5.00	10.00
❏ EGED-20	Ambient 4 — On Land	1982	2.50	5.00	10.00
❏ EGED-37	The Pearl	1984	3.00	6.00	12.00

—By Harold Budd and Brian Eno

| ❏ EGS-102 | No Pussyfooting | 1982 | 2.50 | 5.00 | 10.00 |

—By Robert Fripp and Eno; reissue

| ❏ EGS-103 | Evening Star | 1982 | 2.50 | 5.00 | 10.00 |

—By Robert Fripp and Eno; reissue

| ❏ EGS-105 | Music for Films | 1982 | 2.50 | 5.00 | 10.00 |

—Reissue

| ❏ EGS-107 | Fourth World Volume 1: Possible Musics | 1980 | 3.00 | 6.00 | 12.00 |

—With Jon Hassell

| ❏ EGS-201 | Ambient #1 — Music for Airports | 1982 | 3.00 | 6.00 | 12.00 |

—Reissue

| ❏ EGS-202 | Ambient 2 — The Plateaux of Mirrors | 1982 | 3.00 | 6.00 | 12.00 |

—By Harold Budd and Brian Eno

| ❏ EGS-301 | Pavilion of Dreams | 1982 | 3.00 | 6.00 | 12.00 |

—By Harold Budd and Brian Eno

| ❏ EGS-303 | Discreet Music | 1983 | 3.00 | 6.00 | 12.00 |

—Reissue

ISLAND					
❏ ILPS 9268	Here Come the Warm Jets	1973	3.00	6.00	12.00
❏ ILPS 9309	Taking Tiger Mountain (By Strategy)	1974	3.00	6.00	12.00
❏ ILPS 9351	Another Green World	1975	3.00	6.00	12.00
❏ ILPS 9478	Before and After Science	1977	3.00	6.00	12.00

—Double the value if four lithographs are included with the package.

| **JEM** | | | | | |
| ❏ ENO DJ [DJ] | Music for Airplay | 1981 | 12.50 | 25.00 | 50.00 |

—Promo-only 10-track sampler

OPAL/WARNER BROS.					
❏ 25769	Music for Films, Vol. III	1988	2.50	5.00	10.00
❏ 26421	Wrong Way Up	1990	2.50	5.00	10.00

—With John Cale

| **PVC** | | | | | |
| ❏ 7908 | Ambient #1 — Music for Airports | 1979 | 3.00 | 6.00 | 12.00 |

ENTWISTLE, JOHN Also see THE WHO.
45s
ATCO

Number	Title (A Side/B Side)	Yr	VG	VG+	NM
❏ 7337	Too Late the Hero/Dancin' Master	1981	—	2.00	4.00
❏ 7344	Talk Dirty/Try Me	1982	—	2.00	4.00
DECCA					
❏ 32896	I Believe in Everything/My Size	1971	—	3.00	6.00
❏ 33052	I Wonder/Who Cares	1973	—	3.00	6.00
TRACK					
❏ 40066	Made in Japan/Roller Skate Kate	1973	—	2.50	5.00
Albums					
ATCO					
❏ SD 38-142	Too Late the Hero	1981	2.50	5.00	10.00
DECCA					
❏ DL 79183	Smash Your Head Against the Wall	1971	6.25	12.50	25.00
MCA					
❏ 2024	Smash Your Head Against the Wall	1973	3.00	6.00	12.00

—Reissue of Decca 79183

TRACK					
❏ MCA-321	Rigor Mortis Sets In	1973	3.75	7.50	15.00
❏ L33-1926 [DJ]	Who's Ox	1975	12.50	25.00	50.00

—Promo-only sampler

| ❏ MCA-2129 | Mad Dog | 1975 | 3.75 | 7.50 | 15.00 |
| ❏ DL 79190 | Whistle Rymes | 1972 | 6.25 | 12.50 | 25.00 |

EPIC SPLENDOR, THE
45s
HOT BISCUIT

Number	Title (A Side/B Side)	Yr	VG	VG+	NM
❏ 1450	A Little Rain Must Fall/Cowboys and Indians	1967	2.00	4.00	8.00
❏ 1452	It Could Be Wonderful/She's High on Life	1968	2.00	4.00	8.00
❏ 1452 [PS]	It Could Be Wonderful/She's High on Life	1968	5.00	10.00	20.00

EPISODE SIX
45s
CHAPTER ONE

Number	Title (A Side/B Side)	Yr	VG	VG+	NM
❏ 2902	Lucky Sunday/Mr. Universe	1968	3.00	6.00	12.00
COMPASS					
❏ 7007	Morning Dew/Sunshine Girl	1967	3.75	7.50	15.00
ELEKTRA					
❏ 45617	Baby, Baby, Baby/Love-Hate-Revenge	1967	3.75	7.50	15.00
WARNER BROS.					
❏ 5851	Here, There and Everywhere/Mighty Morris Ten	1966	3.75	7.50	15.00

EPISODES, THE
45s
FOUR SEASONS

Number	Title (A Side/B Side)	Yr	VG	VG+	NM
❏ 1014	The Christmas Tree/Where Is My Love	1965	37.50	75.00	150.00

EPPS, PRESTON
45s
ADMIRAL

Number	Title (A Side/B Side)	Yr	VG	VG+	NM
❏ 901	Bongo Express/Flamenco Bongo	1963	3.75	7.50	15.00
DONNA					
❏ 1367	Mister Bongo/B'Wana Bongo	1962	3.75	7.50	15.00

Number	Title (A Side/B Side)	Yr	VG	VG+	NM
EMBASSY					
❑ 203	Rockin' in the Congo/Sing Donna Go	1961	3.75	7.50	15.00
JO JO					
❑ 106	Afro Mania/Love Is the Only Good Thing	1969	—	3.00	6.00
MAJESTY					
❑ 1300	Bongo Boogie/Flamenco Bongo	1962	3.75	7.50	15.00
ORIGINAL SOUND					
❑ 4 [M]	Bongo Rock/Bongo Party	1959	5.00	10.00	20.00
❑ 4 [S]	Bongo Rock/Bongo Party	1959	12.50	25.00	50.00
❑ 9	Bongo, Bongo, Bongo/Hully Gully Bongo	1960	5.00	10.00	20.00
❑ 14	Bongo Shuffle/Bongo in the Congo	1960	3.75	7.50	15.00
❑ 17	Bongo Rocket/Jungle Drums	1961	3.75	7.50	15.00
POLO					
❑ 218	Bongo Rock 1965/Bongo Waltz	1965	3.00	6.00	12.00
TOP RANK					
❑ 2067	Blue Bongo/Bongola	1960	3.75	7.50	15.00
❑ 2091	Bongo Hop/Caravan	1960	3.75	7.50	15.00
7-Inch Extended Plays					
ORIGINAL SOUND					
❑ EP 1001	Bongo Rock/Doin' the Cha Cha Cha//Bongos in Pastel/Bongo Party	1959	10.00	20.00	40.00
❑ EP 1001 [PS]	Bongo Rock	1959	10.00	20.00	40.00
Albums					
ORIGINAL SOUND					
❑ LPM-5002 [M]	Bongo, Bongo, Bongo	1960	12.50	25.00	50.00
❑ LPM-5009 [M]	Surfin' Bongos	1963	10.00	20.00	40.00
❑ LPS-8851 [S]	Bongo, Bongo, Bongo	1960	20.00	40.00	80.00
❑ LPS-8872 [S]	Surfin' Bongos	1963	12.50	25.00	50.00
TOP RANK					
❑ RM-349 [M]	Bongola	1961	10.00	20.00	40.00
❑ RS-349 [S]	Bongola	1961	12.50	25.00	50.00
EPSILONS, THE The Stax record may not be the same group as the others.					
45s					
HEM					
❑ 1003	Mind in a Bind/It's All Right	196?	37.50	75.00	150.00
SHRINE					
❑ 106	Mad at the World/I'm So Devoted	1966	62.50	125.00	250.00
STAX					
❑ 0021	The Echo/Really Rockin'	1969	15.00	30.00	60.00
EQUADORS, THE					
45s					
ARGO					
❑ 5353	Say You'll Be Mine/Let Me Sleep, Woman	1959	15.00	30.00	60.00
MIRACLE					
❑ 7	You're My Desire/Someone to Call My Own	1961	37.50	75.00	150.00
EQUALLOS, THE					
45s					
M&M					
❑ 1296	Beneath the Sun/In Between Tears	1962	375.00	750.00	1500.
EQUALS, THE					
45s					
BANG					
❑ 582	Ain't Got Nothing to Give You/ Black Skin, Blue Eyed Boys	1971	2.50	5.00	10.00
PRESIDENT					
❑ 103	Fire/I Won't Be There	1967	3.00	6.00	12.00
❑ 105	My Life Ain't Easy/You Got Too Many Boyfriends	1967	3.00	6.00	12.00
❑ 108	Giddy Up a Ding-Dong/I Get So Excited	1968	3.00	6.00	12.00
❑ 109	Lovely Rita/Softly, Softly	1968	3.00	6.00	12.00
❑ 110	Honey Gun/Michael and the Slipper Tree	1968	3.00	6.00	12.00
❑ 111	I Can't Let You Go/Viva Bobby Joe	1969	3.00	6.00	12.00
RCA VICTOR					
❑ 47-9186	Baby Come Back/Hold Me Closer	1967	3.75	7.50	15.00
❑ 47-9583	Baby Come Back/Hold Me Closer	1968	2.50	5.00	10.00
SHOUT					
❑ 247	Ain't Got Nothing to Give You/ Black Skin, Blue Eyed Boys	1970	3.00	6.00	12.00
Albums					
LAURIE					
❑ LLP-2045 [M]	Unequalled	1967	6.25	12.50	25.00
❑ SLP-2045 [S]	Unequalled	1967	7.50	15.00	30.00
PRESIDENT					
❑ PTL-1015	Equal Sensation	1968	6.25	12.50	25.00
❑ PTL-1020	The Sensational Equals	1968	6.25	12.50	25.00
❑ PTL-1025	Equals Supreme	1968	6.25	12.50	25.00
❑ PTL-1030	Strikeback	1969	6.25	12.50	25.00
RCA VICTOR					
❑ LSP-4078	Baby Come Back	1968	6.25	12.50	25.00
EQUIPE 84					
45s					
IMPERIAL					
❑ 66266	The Twenty-Ninth of September/Auschwitz	1967	5.00	10.00	20.00
ERICA					
Albums					
ESP-DISK'					
❑ 1099	You Used to Think	1968	15.00	30.00	60.00
ERLENE AND HER GIRLFRIENDS					
45s					
OLD TOWN					
❑ 1150	A Guy's a Guy/My Dada Say	1963	5.00	10.00	20.00
❑ 1152	Because of You/Casanova	1963	5.00	10.00	20.00

Number	Title (A Side/B Side)	Yr	VG	VG+	NM
ERMINES, THE See CORNEL GUNTER.					
ERNIE See JIM HENSON.					
ERNIE AND EDDIE See EDDIE AND ERNIE.					
ERNIE AND THE EMPERORS					
45s					
REPRISE					
❑ 0414	Got a Lot I Want to Say/Meet Me at the Corner	1965	7.50	15.00	30.00
ERVIN, SENATOR SAM					
45s					
COLUMBIA					
❑ 4-45956	Bridge Over Troubled Water/Zeke and the Snake	1973	—	3.00	6.00
Albums					
COLUMBIA					
❑ KC 32756	Senator Sam at Home	1973	6.25	12.50	25.00
ERVIN SISTERS, THE					
45s					
TRI PHI					
❑ 1014	Changing Baby/Do It Right	1962	15.00	30.00	60.00
❑ 1022	Every Day's a Holiday/Why I Love Him	1963	20.00	40.00	80.00
ERWIN, DEE See BIG DEE IRWIN.					
ESCORTS, THE (1) Group from Rahway State Prison in New Jersey.					
45s					
ALITHIA					
❑ 6048	All We Need (Is Another Chance) (Short)/All We Need (Is Another Chance) (Long)	1973	—	3.00	6.00
❑ 6052	Look Over Your Shoulder/ By the Time I Get to Phoenix	1973	—	2.50	5.00
❑ 6055	I'll Be Sweeter Tomorrow/I'm So Glad I Found You	1973	—	2.50	5.00
❑ 6062	Disrespect Can Wreck/All We Need	1974	—	2.50	5.00
❑ 6066	Let's Make Love (At Home Sometime)/Within Without	1974	—	2.50	5.00
Albums					
ALITHIA					
❑ 9104	All We Need Is One More Chance	1973	3.75	7.50	15.00
❑ 9106	Three Down and Four to Go	1974	3.75	7.50	15.00
ESCORTS, THE (2)					
45s					
CORAL					
❑ 62302	Gloria/Seven Wonders of the World	1961	10.00	20.00	40.00
❑ 62317	As I Love You/Gaudeamus	1962	10.00	20.00	40.00
❑ 62336	Somewhere/Submarine Race Watching	1962	6.25	12.50	25.00
❑ 62349	One Hand. One Heart/I Can't Be Free	1963	6.25	12.50	25.00
❑ 62372	Back Home Again/Something Has Changed Him	1963	6.25	12.50	25.00
—As "Goldie and the Escorts"					
❑ 62385	Give Me Tomorrow/My Heart Cries for You	1963	6.25	12.50	25.00
ESCORTS, THE (3) British group.					
45s					
FONTANA					
❑ 1512	Come On Home Baby/She Gets No Loving	1965	3.75	7.50	15.00
❑ 1912	Dizzy Miss Lizzy/All I Want Is You	1964	3.75	7.50	15.00
ESCORTS, THE (4)					
Albums					
TEO					
❑ LPM-5000 [M]	The Escorts Bring Down the House	1966	30.00	60.00	120.00
ESCORTS, THE (U) None of these are group (1) or (3). Some could be group (2) or (4). More likely, they are more than one other group.					
45s					
BOOMERANG					
❑ 621	Little Big Horn/Wiped Out	1962	10.00	20.00	40.00
JUDD					
❑ 1014	My First Year/Clap Happy	1959	3.75	7.50	15.00
RCA VICTOR					
❑ 47-6834	Bad Boy/Tore Up Over You	1957	3.75	7.50	15.00
❑ 47-6963	So Hard to Laugh, So Easy to Cry/Lonely Man	1957	3.75	7.50	15.00
❑ 47-8228	You Can't Even Be My Friend/Itchy Coo	1963	3.00	6.00	12.00
❑ 47-8327	The Hurt/No City Folks Allowed	1964	3.00	6.00	12.00
SCARLET					
❑ 4005	I Will Be Home Again/ Leaky Heart and His Red Go-Kart	1960	15.00	30.00	60.00
SCEPTER					
❑ 1201	Why Why Why/Ugly Duckling	1958	10.00	20.00	40.00
—With Don Crawford					
SOMA					
❑ 1144	Main Drag/Judy or Jo Ann	1961	6.25	12.50	25.00
ESQUERITA					
45s					
CAPITOL					
❑ F4007	Please Come On Home/Oh Baby	1958	7.50	15.00	30.00
❑ F4058	Rockin' the Joint/Esquerita and the Voola	1958	7.50	15.00	30.00
❑ F4145	Laid Off/Just Another Lie	1959	7.50	15.00	30.00
Albums					
CAPITOL					
❑ T 1186 [M]	Esquerita	1959	250.00	500.00	1000.
ESQUIRES, THE (1) Milwaukee-based R&B group.					
45s					
BUNKY					
❑ 7750	Get On Up/Listen to Me	1967	2.50	5.00	10.00
❑ 7752	And Get Away/Everybody's Laughin'	1967	2.50	5.00	10.00
❑ 7753	You Say/State Fair	1968	2.50	5.00	10.00
❑ 7755	Why Can't I Stop/The Feeling's Gone	1968	2.50	5.00	10.00
❑ 7756	How Could It Be/I Know I Can	1968	2.50	5.00	10.00

Number	Title (A Side/B Side)	Yr	VG	VG+	NM
CAPITOL					
❏ 2650	Reach Out/Listen to Me	1969	2.00	4.00	8.00
CIGAR MAN					
❏ 79880	The Show Ain't Over/What Good Is Music?	1980	—	3.00	6.00
JU-PAR					
❏ 104	Get On Up '76/Feeling's Gone (Also Known As Disco Dancing)	1976	—	3.00	6.00
LAMARR					
❏ 1001	Girls in the City/Ain't Gonna Give It Up	1971	2.00	4.00	8.00
SCEPTER					
❏ 12232	You've Got the Power/No Doubt About It	1968	—	—	—
—*Unreleased? (Possibly reassigned to Wand?)*					
WAND					
❏ 1193	You've Got the Power/No Doubt About It	1968	2.00	4.00	8.00
❏ 1195	I Don't Know/Part Angel	1969	2.00	4.00	8.00
❏ 11201	Whip It On Me/It Was Yesterday	1969	2.00	4.00	8.00
Albums					
BUNKY					
❏ 300	Get On Up and Get Away	1968	8.75	17.50	35.00

ESQUIRES, THE (2)
45s

Number	Title (A Side/B Side)	Yr	VG	VG+	NM
ARGO					
❏ 5435	Boat of Love/With a Feeling	1963	5.00	10.00	20.00

ESQUIRES, THE (3)
45s

Number	Title (A Side/B Side)	Yr	VG	VG+	NM
EPIC					
❏ 5-9024	If You Only Knew What a Three-Cent Stamp Can Do/Now, Now, Now	1954	375.00	750.00	1500.
—*This does exist on 45*					
HI-PO					
❏ 1003	Only the Angels Know/One Word for This	1955	500.00	1000.	2000.

ESQUIRES, THE (U) None of these are groups (1) or (3), but they may not all be the same group, either.
45s

Number	Title (A Side/B Side)	Yr	VG	VG+	NM
COLUMBIA					
❏ 4-43815	It's a Dirty Shame/Love Hides a Multitude of Sins	1966	5.00	10.00	20.00
DOT					
❏ 16954	Misfortune/She's My Woman	1966	3.75	7.50	15.00
DURCO					
❏ 1001	Flashin' Red/What a Burn	1964	10.00	20.00	40.00
TOWER					
❏ 174	Love's Made a Fool of You/Summertime	1965	3.75	7.50	15.00

ESQUIVEL
45s

Number	Title (A Side/B Side)	Yr	VG	VG+	NM
RCA VICTOR					
❏ 47-5969	Beasme Mucho/Vereda Tropical	1954	5.00	10.00	20.00
—*As "Juan Garcia Esquivel"*					
❏ 47-6008	Nocturnal/Amor	1955	5.00	10.00	20.00
❏ 47-6496	Nightingale/Jungle Drums	1956	3.75	7.50	15.00
❏ 47-6514	Port Au Prince/To Love Again	1956	3.75	7.50	15.00
❏ 47-7316	That Old Black Magic/Cielito Lindo	1958	3.75	7.50	15.00
❏ 47-7360	It Had to Be You/Begin the Beguine	1958	3.75	7.50	15.00
❏ 47-7361	Night and Day/Ballerina	1958	3.75	7.50	15.00
❏ 47-7462	I Feel Merely Marvelous/Whatchamacallit	1959	3.75	7.50	15.00
Albums					
BAR NONE					
❏ LP-043	Space Age Bachelor Pad Music	1994	3.00	6.00	12.00
❏ LP-056	Music for a Sparkling Planet	1995	3.00	6.00	12.00
RCA VICTOR					
❏ LPM-1345 [M]	To Love Again	1957	12.50	25.00	50.00
❏ LPM-1749 [M]	Four Corners of the World	1958	6.25	12.50	25.00
❏ LSP-1749 [S]	Four Corners of the World	1958	12.50	25.00	50.00
❏ LPM-1753 [M]	Other Worlds, Other Sounds	1959	6.25	12.50	25.00
❏ LSP-1753 [S]	Other Worlds, Other Sounds	1959	12.50	25.00	50.00
❏ LPM-1978 [M]	Exploring New Sounds in Hi-Fi	1959	7.50	15.00	30.00
❏ LSP-1978 [S]	Exploring New Sounds in Hi-Fi	1959	15.00	30.00	60.00
❏ LPM-1988 [M]	Strings Aflame	1959	6.25	12.50	25.00
❏ LSP-1988 [S]	Strings Aflame	1959	12.50	25.00	50.00
❏ LPM-2225 [M]	Infinity in Sound	1960	7.50	15.00	30.00
❏ LSP-2225 [S]	Infinity in Sound	1960	15.00	30.00	60.00
❏ LPM-2296 [M]	Infinity in Sound, Vol. 2	1961	7.50	15.00	30.00
❏ LSP-2296 [S]	Infinity in Sound, Vol. 2	1961	15.00	30.00	60.00
❏ LPM-2418 [M]	Latin-esque	1962	5.00	10.00	20.00
❏ LSP-2418 [S]	Latin-esque	1962	10.00	20.00	40.00
—*Standard cover*					
❏ LSP-2418 [S]	Latin-esque	1962	15.00	30.00	60.00
—*Die-cut cover that reveals inner sleeve*					
❏ LPM-3502 [M]	The Best of Esquivel	1966	5.00	10.00	20.00
❏ LSP-3502 [S]	The Best of Esquivel	1966	7.50	15.00	30.00
❏ LPM-3697 [M]	The Genius of Esquivel	1967	5.00	10.00	20.00
❏ LSP-3697 [S]	The Genius of Esquivel	1967	7.50	15.00	30.00
REPRISE					
❏ P9-6046 [S]	More of Other World, Other Sounds	1962	7.50	15.00	30.00
❏ R-6046 [M]	More of Other World, Other Sounds	1962	6.25	12.50	25.00

ESSEX, DAVID
45s

Number	Title (A Side/B Side)	Yr	VG	VG+	NM
COLUMBIA					
❏ 10005	America/Dance Little Girl	1974	—	2.50	5.00
❏ 10005 [PS]	America/Dance Little Girl	1974	2.00	4.00	8.00
❏ 10039	Gonna Make You a Star/Window	1974	—	2.50	5.00
❏ 10183	Rolling Stone/Coconut Ice	1975	—	2.50	5.00
❏ 10183 [PS]	Rolling Stone/Coconut Ice	1975	2.00	4.00	8.00
❏ 10256	Good Ol' Rock 'N' Roll/Hold Me Close	1975	—	2.50	5.00
❏ 45940	Rock On/On and On	1973	—	2.50	5.00
❏ 45940 [PS]	Rock On/On and On	1973	2.50	5.00	10.00
❏ 46041	Lamplight/We're All Insane	1974	—	2.50	5.00
❏ 46041 [PS]	Lamplight/We're All Insane	1974	2.50	5.00	10.00
RSO					
❏ 1006	Oh What a Circus (From Evita)/Ships That Pass in the Night	1979	—	2.00	4.00

Number	Title (A Side/B Side)	Yr	VG	VG+	NM
UNI					
❏ 55020	She's Leaving Home/He's a Better Man Than Me	1967	2.50	5.00	10.00
Albums					
COLUMBIA					
❏ CQ 32560 [Q]	Rock On	1974	7.50	15.00	30.00
❏ KC 32560	Rock On	1974	5.00	10.00	20.00
❏ KC 33289	David Essex	1974	3.75	7.50	15.00
❏ PC 33813	All the Fun of the Fair	1975	3.75	7.50	15.00
MERCURY					
❏ 812936-1	David Essex	1983	3.75	7.50	15.00

ESSEX, THE Also see ANITA HUMES.
45s

Number	Title (A Side/B Side)	Yr	VG	VG+	NM
BANG					
❏ 537	The Eagle/Moonlight, Music, and You	1966	2.00	4.00	8.00
ROULETTE					
❏ 4494	Easier Said Than Done/Are You Going My Way	1963	3.75	7.50	15.00
❏ 4515	A Walkin' Miracle/What I Don't Know Won't Hurt Me	1963	3.75	7.50	15.00
❏ 4530	She's Got Everything/Out of Sight, Out of Mind	1964	2.50	5.00	10.00
❏ 4542	What Did I Do/Curfew Lover	1964	2.50	5.00	10.00
Albums					
ROULETTE					
❏ R-25234 [M]	Easier Said Than Done	1963	10.00	20.00	40.00
❏ SR-25234 [S]	Easier Said Than Done	1963	12.50	25.00	50.00
❏ R-25235 [M]	A Walkin' Miracle	1963	10.00	20.00	40.00
❏ SR-25235 [S]	A Walkin' Miracle	1963	12.50	25.00	50.00
❏ R-25246 [M]	Young and Lively	1964	10.00	20.00	40.00
❏ SR-25246 [S]	Young and Lively	1964	12.50	25.00	50.00

ESTABLISHMENT, THE
45s

Number	Title (A Side/B Side)	Yr	VG	VG+	NM
KING					
❏ 6320	In My Heart I Am a Free Man/Stop Fightin' Start Lovin'	1970	—	3.00	6.00
❏ 6349	House of Jack/Why Is She All I See	1971	—	3.00	6.00
Albums					
KING					
❏ KS-1123	The Establishment	1971	3.00	6.00	12.00

ESTELLE Estelle Bennett, formerly of THE RONETTES.
45s

Number	Title (A Side/B Side)	Yr	VG	VG+	NM
LAURIE					
❏ 3449	The Year 2000/The Naked Boy	1968	25.00	50.00	100.00

ESTRADA, ROY, AND THE ROCKETEERS
45s

Number	Title (A Side/B Side)	Yr	VG	VG+	NM
KING					
❏ 5368	Jungle Dream (Part 1)/Jungle Dream (Part 2)	1960	12.50	25.00	50.00

ETERNALS, THE (1)
45s

Number	Title (A Side/B Side)	Yr	VG	VG+	NM
HOLLYWOOD					
❏ 68	Rockin' in the Jungle/Rock and Roll Cha Cha	1959	5.00	10.00	20.00
—*Yellow label*					
❏ 68	Rockin' in the Jungle/Rock and Roll Cha Cha	1959	10.00	20.00	40.00
—*Blue label*					
❏ 68	Rockin' in the Jungle/Rock and Roll Cha Cha	1959	15.00	30.00	60.00
—*White label*					
❏ 70	Babalu's Wedding Day/My Girl	1959	6.25	12.50	25.00
—*Blue label*					
❏ 70	Babalu's Wedding Day/My Girl	1959	12.50	25.00	50.00
—*Red label*					
LOST-NITE					
❏ 203	Rockin' in the Jungle/Rock and Roll Cha Cha	196?	—	2.50	5.00
—*Reissue*					
❏ 243	Babalu's Wedding Day/My Girl	196?	—	2.50	5.00
—*Reissue*					
WARWICK					
❏ 611	Blind Date/Today	1961	5.00	10.00	20.00

ETERNALS, THE (2)
45s

Number	Title (A Side/B Side)	Yr	VG	VG+	NM
QUALITY					
❏ 1902	Falling Tears/Sticks and Stones	1968	5.00	10.00	20.00

ETERNITY'S CHILDREN
45s

Number	Title (A Side/B Side)	Yr	VG	VG+	NM
A&M					
❏ 866	Rumors/Wait and See	1967	2.50	5.00	10.00
LIBERTY					
❏ 56162	Alone Again/From You Unto Us	1970	2.00	4.00	8.00
TOWER					
❏ 416	Mrs. Bluebird/Little Boy	1968	2.50	5.00	10.00
❏ 416 [PS]	Mrs. Bluebird/Little Boy	1968	6.25	12.50	25.00
❏ 439	Rupert White/Sunshine Among Us	1968	2.50	5.00	10.00
❏ 449	Till I Hear from You/I Wanna Be with You	1968	2.50	5.00	10.00
❏ 476	Sidewalks of the Ghetto/Look Away	1969	2.50	5.00	10.00
❏ 498	Blue Horizon/Lifetime Day	1969	2.50	5.00	10.00
Albums					
TOWER					
❏ ST-5123	Eternity's Children	1968	6.25	12.50	25.00
❏ ST-5144	Timeless	1969	7.50	15.00	30.00

ETRIS, BARRY
45s

Number	Title (A Side/B Side)	Yr	VG	VG+	NM
SIMS					
❏ 141	The Young Ones/It's Not Too Late	1963	2.50	5.00	10.00
❏ 141 [PS]	The Young Ones/It's Not Too Late	1963	3.75	7.50	15.00

ETTA AND HARVEY Also see HARVEY; ETTA JAMES.
45s

Number	Title (A Side/B Side)	Yr	VG	VG+	NM
CHESS					
❏ 1760	If I Can't Have You/My Heart Cries	1960	6.25	12.50	25.00
❏ 1771	Spoonful/It's a Crying Shame	1960	6.25	12.50	25.00

Number	Title (A Side/B Side)	Yr	VG	VG+	NM
ETZEL, ROY					
45s					
HICKORY					
❏ 1197	I Can't Stop Loving You/I Hate to Love You	1963	2.00	4.00	8.00
MGM					
❏ 13381	Melancholy/The Silence	1965	2.00	4.00	8.00
❏ 13801	Mexican Holiday/Vaya Con Dios	1967	2.00	4.00	8.00
PRESIDENT					
❏ 820	Tell Laura I Love Her/Reach for the Stars	1961	2.50	5.00	10.00
TIME					
❏ 1029	Jenny Oh Jenny/Apache Blues	1961	2.50	5.00	10.00
EUBANKS, JACK					
45s					
MONUMENT					
❏ 434	Chiricahua/What'd I Say	1961	2.50	5.00	10.00
❏ 451	Searching/Take a Message to Mary	1961	2.50	5.00	10.00
❏ 462	After the Rain/Since I Met You Baby	1962	2.50	5.00	10.00
❏ 809	Casino/Te Juana	1963	2.00	4.00	8.00
❏ 862	Action/Pickin' White Gold	1964	2.00	4.00	8.00
Albums					
MONUMENT					
❏ LP-8044 [M]	Guitar Sounds of the South	1966	3.75	7.50	15.00
❏ SLP-18044 [S]	Guitar Sounds of the South	1966	5.00	10.00	20.00
EUPHONIOUS WAIL					
Albums					
KAPP					
❏ KS-3668	Euphonious Wail	1973	10.00	20.00	40.00
EUPHORIA (1)					
45s					
BAND BOX					
❏ 393	Somebody Listen/Dedication of Sally and Cher	196?	7.50	15.00	30.00
MAINSTREAM					
❏ 655	Hungry Women/No Me Tomorrow	1967	5.00	10.00	20.00
EUPHORIA (2)					
45s					
HERITAGE					
❏ 831	You Must Forget/(B-side unknown)	1971	3.00	6.00	12.00
Albums					
HERITAGE					
❏ HTS 35005	Euphoria	1971	7.50	15.00	30.00
EUPHORIA (3)					
Albums					
CAPITOL					
❏ SKAO-363	A Gift from Euphoria	1969	30.00	60.00	120.00
EUPHORIA (4)					
Albums					
RAINBOW					
❏ 1003	Lost in a Trance	1973	75.00	150.00	300.00
EVANS, BARBARA					
45s					
RCA VICTOR					
❏ 47-7519	Souvenirs/Play for Me, Mother	1959	5.00	10.00	20.00
❏ 47-7576	Oo La La La La/The Little Girl Cried	1959	5.00	10.00	20.00
❏ 47-7634	Beatnik Daddy/A Game of Poker	1959	5.00	10.00	20.00
EVANS, MAUREEN					
45s					
COLUMBIA					
❏ 43189	Get Away/I've Often Wondered	1964	2.50	5.00	10.00
❏ 43354	Never Let Me Go/Poco Sole	1965	2.50	5.00	10.00
DOT					
❏ 16678	Time and Time Again/Tomorrow Is Another Day	1964	2.50	5.00	10.00
LITTLE DARLIN'					
❏ 0019	Touch My Heart/(B-side unknown)	1967	2.50	5.00	10.00
LONDON INT'L.					
❏ 10407	Like I Do/Starlight, Starbright	1963	3.00	6.00	12.00
❏ 10409	Melancholy Me/Pick the Petals	1963	3.00	6.00	12.00
EVANS, PAUL					
45s					
ATCO					
❏ 6138	At My Party/Beat Generation	1959	3.75	7.50	15.00
❏ 6170	Long Gone/Mickey, My Love	1960	3.75	7.50	15.00
BIG TREE					
❏ 16050	Happy Birthday, America/You Made Me Over	1975	—	2.50	5.00
CARLTON					
❏ 539	Show Folk/I Love to Make Love to You	1961	3.75	7.50	15.00
❏ 543	After the Hurricane/Not Me	1961	3.75	7.50	15.00
❏ 554	Just Because I Love You/This Pullover	1961	3.75	7.50	15.00
❏ 558	Over the Mountain, Across the Sea/Sisal Twine	1961	3.75	7.50	15.00
CINNAMON					
❏ 604	One Night Led to Two/Hangin' Out and Hangin' In	1980	—	2.50	5.00
COLUMBIA					
❏ 44472	One Red Rose/Bound to Silence	1968	—	3.00	6.00
DECCA					
❏ 30680	I Think About You All the Time/Oh No	1958	5.00	10.00	20.00
DOT					
❏ 17463	That's What Loving You Is All About/Do You Remember	1973	—	2.50	5.00
EPIC					
❏ 9726	Bewitched/I Think I'm Gonna Kill Myself	1962	2.50	5.00	10.00
—By Paul & Mimi Evans					
❏ 9751	Little Miss Tease/Gina Marina Petunia	1964	2.50	5.00	10.00
❏ 9842	I Wonder What to Do/Always Thinking of the Roses	1965	2.50	5.00	10.00
GUARANTEED					
❏ 200	Seven Little Girls Sitting in the Back Seat/Worshipping an Idol	1959	5.00	10.00	20.00
❏ 205	Midnite Special/Since I Met You Baby	1960	3.75	7.50	15.00

Number	Title (A Side/B Side)	Yr	VG	VG+	NM
❏ 208	Happy-Go-Lucky Me/Fish in the Ocean	1960	3.75	7.50	15.00
❏ 210	The Brigade of Broken Hearts/Twins	1960	3.75	7.50	15.00
❏ 213	Hushabye Little Guitar/Blind Boy	1960	3.75	7.50	15.00
KAPP					
❏ 473	A Picture of You/Feelin' No Pain	1962	3.00	6.00	12.00
❏ 486	D-Darling/Gonna Build a Mountain	1962	3.00	6.00	12.00
❏ 499	The Bell That Couldn't Jingle/Gilding the Lily	1962	3.00	6.00	12.00
❏ 520	(Mama and Papa) We've Got Something On You/What Are the Lips of Janet	1963	3.00	6.00	12.00
❏ 527	Ten Thousand Years/Evan Tan	1963	3.00	6.00	12.00
LAURIE					
❏ 3571	Think Summer/For Old Times Sake	1971	—	3.00	6.00
❏ 3581	The Man in a Row Boat/Here We Go Around Again	1971	—	3.00	6.00
MERCURY					
❏ 73499	But I Was Born in New York City/Just As Long As You Are There	1974	—	2.50	5.00
❏ 73650	All My Children/Move In with Me	1975	—	2.50	5.00
MUSICOR					
❏ 6305	Roses Are Red Medley/If I Had My Life to Live Over	1977	—	2.00	4.00
RANWOOD					
❏ 928	Try It, You'll Like It/We Liked It	1972	—	3.00	6.00
RCA VICTOR					
❏ 47-6806	What Do You Know/Dorothy	1957	5.00	10.00	20.00
❏ 47-6924	Looking for a Sweetie/Any Little Thing	1957	5.00	10.00	20.00
❏ 47-6992	Caught/Poor Broken Heart	1957	5.00	10.00	20.00
SPRING					
❏ 183	Hello, This Is Joanie (The Telephone Answering Machine Song)/Lullabye Tissue Paper Company	1978	—	2.00	4.00
❏ 187	Down at the Bluebird/I'm Givin' Up My Baby	1978	—	2.00	4.00
❏ 193	Disneyland Daddy/Build An Ark	1979	—	2.00	4.00
Albums					
CARLTON					
❏ STLP-129 [S]	Hear Paul Evans in Your Home Tonight	1961	15.00	30.00	60.00
❏ TLP-129 [M]	Hear Paul Evans in Your Home Tonight	1961	10.00	20.00	40.00
❏ STLP-130 [S]	Folk Songs of Many Lands	1961	15.00	30.00	60.00
❏ TLP-130 [M]	Folk Songs of Many Lands	1961	10.00	20.00	40.00
GUARANTEED					
❏ GUL-1000 [M]	Fabulous Teens	1960	17.50	35.00	70.00
❏ GUS-1000 [S]	Fabulous Teens	1960	20.00	40.00	80.00
KAPP					
❏ KL-1346 [M]	21 Years in a Tennessee Jail	1964	6.25	12.50	25.00
❏ KL-1475 [M]	Another Town, Another Jail	1966	6.25	12.50	25.00
❏ KS-3346 [S]	21 Years in a Tennessee Jail	1964	10.00	20.00	40.00
❏ KS-3475 [S]	Another Town, Another Jail	1966	7.50	15.00	30.00
EVELS, THE					
45s					
TRA-X					
❏ 14	The Magic of Love/Wonderful Guy	1960	15.00	30.00	60.00
EVENTUALS, THE					
45s					
OKEH					
❏ 4-7142	Charlie Chan/Just the Things That You Do	1961	3.75	7.50	15.00
❏ 4-7142 [PS]	Charlie Chan/Just the Things That You Do	1961	7.50	15.00	30.00
EVER-READY SINGERS, THE					
45s					
CAPITOL					
❏ F2763	I'm a Pilgrim and a Stranger/One Day While I Was Walking	1954	7.50	15.00	30.00
❏ F2867	This Heart of Mine/Two Wings	1954	7.50	15.00	30.00
❏ F2984	I Don't Care What the World May Do/Oh Mary Don't You Weep	1954	10.00	20.00	40.00
EVERETT, BETTY					
45s					
ABC					
❏ 10829	In Your Arms/Nothing I Wouldn't Do	1966	2.00	4.00	8.00
❏ 10861	Bye, Bye Baby/Your Love Is Important to Me	1966	2.00	4.00	8.00
❏ 10919	Love Comes Tumbling Down/People Around Me	1967	2.00	4.00	8.00
❏ 10978	I Can't Say/My Baby Loving My Best Friend	1967	2.00	4.00	8.00
CJ					
❏ 611	Why Did You Have to Go/Please Come Back	1961	5.00	10.00	20.00
—As "Bettie Everett & Daylighters"					
❏ 619	Your Lovin' Arms/Happy I Long to Be	1961	5.00	10.00	20.00
❏ 674	Days Gone By/Her New Love	1964	3.75	7.50	15.00
COBRA					
❏ 5019	My Love/My Life Depends on You	1957	7.50	15.00	30.00
❏ 5024	Ain't Gonna Cry/Killer Diller	1958	6.25	12.50	25.00
❏ 5031	Weep No More/Tell Me Darling	1959	6.25	12.50	25.00
FANTASY					
❏ 652	I Got to Tell Somebody/Why Are You Leaving Me	1970	—	2.50	5.00
❏ 658	Ain't Nothing Gonna Change Me/What Is It?	1971	—	2.50	5.00
❏ 667	I'm a Woman/Prove It	1971	—	2.50	5.00
❏ 687	Black Girl/Innocent Bystanders	1972	—	2.50	5.00
❏ 687	Black Girl/What Is It?	1972	—	2.50	5.00
❏ 696	Danger/Just a Matter of Time Till You're Gone	1973	—	2.50	5.00
❏ 714	Sweet Dan/Who Will Your Next Fool Be	1973	—	2.50	5.00
❏ 725	Try It, You'll Like It/Wondering	1974	—	2.50	5.00
❏ 738	Happy Endings/Keep It Up	1974	—	2.50	5.00
LOST-NITE					
❏ 313	The Shoop Shoop Song (It's In His Kiss)/Hands Off	197?	—	2.50	5.00
—Reissue					
ONE-DERFUL					
❏ 4806	I've Got a Claim on You/Your Love Is Important to Me	1962	3.75	7.50	15.00
❏ 4823	I'll Be There/Please Love Me	1964	3.00	6.00	12.00
UNI					
❏ 55100	Take Me/There'll Come a Time	1968	—	3.00	6.00
❏ 55122	I Can't Say No to You/Better Tomorrow Than Today	1969	—	3.00	6.00
❏ 55141	1900 Yesterday/Maybe	1969	—	3.00	6.00

Number	Title (A Side/B Side)	Yr	VG	VG+	NM
❏ 55174	Just a Man's Way/Been a Long Time	1969	—	3.00	6.00
❏ 55189	Sugar/Just Another Winter	1969	—	3.00	6.00
❏ 55219	Unlucky Girl/Better Tomorrow Than Today	1970	—	3.00	6.00
UNITED ARTISTS					
❏ XW1200	True Love (You Took My Heart)/You Can Do It	1978	—	2.00	4.00
VEE JAY					
❏ 513	By My Side/Prince of Players	1963	3.75	7.50	15.00
❏ 566	You're No Good/Chained to Your Love	1963	5.00	10.00	20.00
❏ 585	The Shoop Shoop Song (It's In His Kiss)/Hands Off	1964	5.00	10.00	20.00
❏ 599	I Can't Hear You/Can I Get to Know You	1964	3.75	7.50	15.00
❏ 610	It Hurts to Be in Love/Until You Were Gone	1964	3.75	7.50	15.00
❏ 628	Getting Mighty Crowded/Chained to a Memory	1964	3.75	7.50	15.00
❏ 683	The Real Thing/Gonna Be Ready	1965	3.75	7.50	15.00
❏ 699	I Don't Hurt Anymore/Too Hot to Hold	1965	3.75	7.50	15.00
❏ 716	Trouble Over the Weekend/My Shoe Won't Fly	1966	3.75	7.50	15.00
Albums					
FANTASY					
❏ 9447	Love Rhymes	1974	3.00	6.00	12.00
❏ 9480	Happy Endings	1975	3.00	6.00	12.00
SUNSET					
❏ SUS-5220	I Need You So	1968	3.75	7.50	15.00
UNI					
❏ 73048	There'll Come a Time	1969	6.25	12.50	25.00
VEE JAY					
❏ LP 1077 [M]	It's In His Kiss	1964	7.50	15.00	30.00
❏ LP 1077 [M]	You're No Good	1964	10.00	20.00	40.00
❏ SR 1077 [S]	It's In His Kiss	1964	12.50	25.00	50.00
❏ SR 1077 [S]	You're No Good	1964	17.50	35.00	70.00
❏ LP 1122 [M]	The Very Best of Betty Everett	1965	10.00	20.00	40.00
❏ VJLP 1122	The Very Best of Betty Everett	198?	2.50	5.00	10.00
—Authorized reissue					
❏ VJS 1122 [S]	The Very Best of Betty Everett	1965	12.50	25.00	50.00

EVERETT, BETTY, AND JERRY BUTLER Also see each artist's individual listings.
45s

Number	Title (A Side/B Side)	Yr	VG	VG+	NM
LOST-NITE					
❏ 299	Let It Be Me/Ain't That Loving You Baby	197?	—	2.50	5.00
—Reissue					
VEE JAY					
❏ 613	Let It Be Me/Ain't That Loving You Baby	1964	3.00	6.00	12.00
❏ 633	Smile/Love Is Strange	1964	3.00	6.00	12.00
❏ 676	Since I Don't Have You/Just Be True	1965	3.00	6.00	12.00
❏ 691	Fever/The Way You Do the Things You Do	1965	3.00	6.00	12.00
Albums					
BUDDAH					
❏ BDS-7505	Together	1969	3.75	7.50	15.00
TRADITION					
❏ 2073	Starring Betty Everett with Jerry Butler	197?	3.00	6.00	12.00
VEE JAY					
❏ LP 1099 [M]	Delicious Together	1964	5.00	10.00	20.00
❏ LP-1099 [M]	Delicious Together	1964	5.00	10.00	20.00
❏ VJLP 1099	Delicious Together	198?	3.00	6.00	12.00
—Authorized reissue					
❏ VJLP-1099	Delicious Together	198?	2.50	5.00	10.00
—Reissue of original 1099; has softer vinyl					
❏ VJS 1099 [S]	Delicious Together	1964	6.25	12.50	25.00
❏ VJS-1099 [S]	Delicious Together	1964	6.25	12.50	25.00

EVERETT, VINCE
45s

Number	Title (A Side/B Side)	Yr	VG	VG+	NM
ABC-PARAMOUNT					
❏ 10313	Such a Night/Don't Go	1962	15.00	30.00	60.00
❏ 10360	I Ain't Gonna Be Your Low Down Dog No More/Sugaree	1962	12.50	25.00	50.00
❏ 10472	Baby, Let's Play House/Livin' High	1963	20.00	40.00	80.00
❏ 10538	Sweet Flavors/Box Candy	1964	10.00	20.00	40.00
❏ 10624	Big Brother/To Have, to Hold and Let Go	1965	10.00	20.00	40.00
TOWN					
❏ 1964	Buttercup/Land of No Return	1960	10.00	20.00	40.00

EVERGREEN BLUES, THE
45s

Number	Title (A Side/B Side)	Yr	VG	VG+	NM
ABC					
❏ 11198	Funky Woman/Don't Mess Up My Mind	1969	—	3.00	6.00
❏ 11216	The Moon Is High/Girl I Got Wise	1969	—	3.00	6.00
MERCURY					
❏ 72756	Midnight Confessions/That's My Baby (Yes)	1967	2.50	5.00	10.00
❏ 72756 [PS]	Midnight Confessions/That's My Baby (Yes)	1967	5.00	10.00	20.00
❏ 72780	Laura (Keep Hangin' On)/Yesterday's Coming	1968	2.50	5.00	10.00
❏ 72780 [PS]	Laura (Keep Hangin' On)/Yesterday's Coming	1968	6.25	12.50	25.00
❏ 72826	Feelin' Your Love/Three's a Crowd	1968	2.50	5.00	10.00
Albums					
ABC					
❏ S-669	Comin' On	1969	3.75	7.50	15.00
MERCURY					
❏ SR-61157	7 Do 11	1968	5.00	10.00	20.00

EVERGREENS, THE
45s

Number	Title (A Side/B Side)	Yr	VG	VG+	NM
CHART					
❏ 605	Very Truly Yours/Guitar Player	1955	37.50	75.00	150.00

EVERLY, DON Also see THE EVERLY BROTHERS.
45s

Number	Title (A Side/B Side)	Yr	VG	VG+	NM
ABC HICKORY					
❏ 54002	Love at Last Sight/Oh I'd Like to Go Away	1976	—	3.00	6.00
❏ 54005	Since You Broke My Heart/Deep Water	1977	—	3.00	6.00
❏ 54012	Brother Juke-Box/Oh, What a Feeling	1977	—	3.00	6.00
HICKORY/MGM					
❏ 368	Yesterday Just Passed My Way Again/Never Like This	1976	—	3.00	6.00
ODE					
❏ 66009	Only Me/Tumbling Tumbleweeds	1970	2.00	4.00	8.00
❏ 66046	Warming Up the Band/Evelyn Swing	1974	2.00	4.00	8.00

Number	Title (A Side/B Side)	Yr	VG	VG+	NM
Albums					
ABC HICKORY					
❏ AH-44003	Brother Juke-Box	1977	3.00	6.00	12.00
ODE					
❏ SP-77005	Don Everly	1970	3.75	7.50	15.00
❏ SP-77023	Sunset Towers	1974	3.75	7.50	15.00

EVERLY, PHIL Also see THE EVERLY BROTHERS.
45s

Number	Title (A Side/B Side)	Yr	VG	VG+	NM
CAPITOL					
❏ B-5197	One Way Love/Who's Gonna Keep Me Warm	1983	2.50	5.00	10.00
CURB					
❏ 02116	Sweet Southern Love/In Your Eyes	1981	2.50	5.00	10.00
❏ 5401	Dare to Dream Again/Lonely Days, Lonely Nights	1980	2.50	5.00	10.00
ELEKTRA					
❏ 46007	Don't Say You Don't Love Me No More/I Seek the Night	1979	—	2.50	5.00
—A-side: With Sondra Locke; B-side: Sondra Locke solo					
❏ 46519	Living Alone/I Just Don't Feel Like Dancing	1979	—	2.50	5.00
❏ 46556	Buy Me a Beer/You Broke It	1979	—	2.50	5.00
PYE					
❏ 71014	Old Kentucky River/Summershine	1975	2.00	4.00	8.00
❏ 71036	New Old Song/Better Than Now	1975	2.00	4.00	8.00
❏ 71050	You and I Are a Song/Better Than Now	1975	2.00	4.00	8.00
❏ 71055	Words in Your Eyes/Back When the Bands Played in Rag Time	1976	2.00	4.00	8.00
❏ 71056	God Bless Older Ladies/Sweet Grass Country	1976	—	3.00	6.00
RCA VICTOR					
❏ APBO-0064	God Bless Older Ladies/Sweet Grass Country	1973	2.00	4.00	8.00
Albums					
ELEKTRA					
❏ 6E-213	Living Alone	1979	2.50	5.00	10.00
PYE					
❏ 12104	Phil's Diner	1975	3.00	6.00	12.00
❏ 12121	Mystic Line	1976	3.00	6.00	12.00
RCA VICTOR					
❏ APL1-0092	Star Spangled Springer	1973	3.75	7.50	15.00

EVERLY BROTHERS, THE Also see DON EVERLY; PHIL EVERLY.
12-Inch Singles

Number	Title (A Side/B Side)	Yr	VG	VG+	NM
MERCURY					
❏ PRO 312-1 [DJ]	On the Wings of a Nightingale (same on both sides)	1984	3.00	6.00	12.00

45s

Number	Title (A Side/B Side)	Yr	VG	VG+	NM
BARNABY					
❏ 500	('Til) I Kissed You/Oh, What a Feeling	197?	—	2.50	5.00
❏ 501	Wake Up Little Susie/Maybe Tomorrow	197?	—	2.50	5.00
❏ 502	Bye, Bye Love/I Wonder If I Care As Much	197?	—	2.50	5.00
❏ 503	This Little Girl of Mine/Should We Tell Him?	197?	—	2.50	5.00
❏ 504	Problems/Love of My Life	197?	—	2.50	5.00
❏ 505	Take a Message to Mary/Poor Jenny	197?	—	2.50	5.00
❏ 506	Let It Be Me/Since You Broke My Heart	197?	—	2.50	5.00
❏ 507	When Will I Be Loved/Be Bop A-Lula	197?	—	2.50	5.00
❏ 508	Like Strangers/Brand New Heartache	197?	—	2.50	5.00
❏ 509	All I Have to Do Is Dream/Claudette	197?	—	2.50	5.00
❏ 510	Bird Dog/Devoted to You	197?	—	2.50	5.00
❏ 511	I'm Here to Get My Baby Out of Jail/Lightning Express	197?	—	2.50	5.00
—All Barnaby records are reissues of original Cadence recordings					
CADENCE					
❏ 1315	Bye, Bye Love/I Wonder If I Care As Much	1957	6.25	12.50	25.00
❏ 1337	Wake Up Little Susie/Maybe Tomorrow	1957	7.50	15.00	30.00
❏ 1337 [PS]	Wake Up Little Susie/Maybe Tomorrow	1957	62.50	125.00	250.00
❏ 1342	This Little Girl of Mine/Should We Tell Him?	1958	6.25	12.50	25.00
❏ 1348	All I Have to Do Is Dream/Claudette	1958	6.25	12.50	25.00
❏ 1348	All I Have to Do Is Dream/Claudette	1961	5.00	10.00	20.00
—Reissue with red and black label; scarcer than original					
❏ 1350	Bird Dog/Devoted to You	1958	6.25	12.50	25.00
❏ 1355	Problems/Love of My Life	1958	6.25	12.50	25.00
❏ 1355 [PS]	Problems/Love of My Life	1958	12.50	25.00	50.00
❏ 1364	Take a Message to Mary/Poor Jenny	1959	6.25	12.50	25.00
❏ 1369	('Til) I Kissed You/Oh, What a Feeling	1959	6.25	12.50	25.00
❏ 1369 [PS]	('Til) I Kissed You/Oh, What a Feeling	1959	12.50	25.00	50.00
❏ 1376	Let It Be Me/Since You Broke My Heart	1959	6.25	12.50	25.00
❏ 1376 [PS]	Let It Be Me/Since You Broke My Heart	1959	12.50	25.00	50.00
❏ 1380	When Will I Be Loved/Be Bop A-Lula	1960	6.25	12.50	25.00
❏ 1388	Like Strangers/Brand New Heartache	1960	6.25	12.50	25.00
❏ 1429	I'm Here to Get My Baby Out of Jail/Lightning Express	1962	5.00	10.00	20.00
❏ 1429 [PS]	I'm Here to Get My Baby Out of Jail/Lightning Express	1962	10.00	20.00	40.00
CAPITOL					
❏ B-44297	Don't Worry Baby/Tequila Dreams	1989	—	2.00	4.00
—A-side with the Beach Boys; B-side by Dave Grusin					
❏ B-44297 [PS]	Don't Worry Baby/Tequila Dreams	1989	2.50	5.00	10.00
COLUMBIA					
❏ 4-21496	Keep A Lovin' Me/The Sun Keeps Shining	1956	150.00	300.00	600.00
—Maroon label					
❏ 4-21496 [DJ]	Keep A Lovin' Me/The Sun Keeps Shining	1956	62.50	125.00	250.00
—White label					
MERCURY					
❏ 872098-7	Ride the Wind/Don't Worry Baby	1988	—	—	3.00
❏ 872420-7	Ballad of a Teenage Queen/Get Rhythm	1988	—	—	3.00
—With Johnny Cash and Roseanne Cash					
❏ 880213-7	On the Wings of a Nightingale/Asleep	1984	—	2.50	5.00
—A-side written and produced by Paul McCartney					
❏ 880423-7	The Story of Me/First in Line	1984	—	2.00	4.00
❏ 884428-7	Don't Say Goodnight/Born Yesterday	1986	—	2.00	4.00
❏ 884694-7	I Know Love/These Shoes	1986	—	2.00	4.00
❏ 884694-7 [PS]	I Know Love/These Shoes	1986	—	2.00	4.00
RCA VICTOR					
❏ 74-0717	Stories We Could Tell/Ridin' High	1972	2.50	5.00	10.00
❏ 74-0849	Lay It Down/Paradise	1972	2.50	5.00	10.00
❏ 74-0901	Not Fade Away/Ladies Love Outlaws	1973	2.50	5.00	10.00
❏ SP-45-409 [DJ]	Pass the Chicken and Listen	1971	7.50	15.00	30.00
—Promo-only interview record					

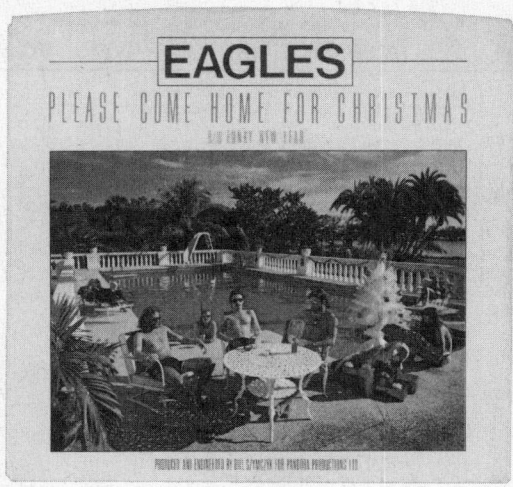

Eagles, "Please Come Home for Christmas," Asylum 45555, picture sleeve, $2-$4.

Duane Eddy, *Duane Eddy Does Bob Dylan*, Colpix SCP-494, stereo LP, $20-$40.

Shirley Ellis, *The Name Game,* Congress CGL-3003, mono LP, $12.50-$25.

Electric Light Orchestra, *Out of the Blue,* Jet JT-LA823-L2, stereo LP (2-record set), black vinyl, all inserts intact, $7.50-$15.

Emerson, Lake and Palmer, *Trilogy*, Cotillion SD 9903, stereo LP, $6-$12.

The Everly Brothers, *The Fabulous Style of the Everly Brothers,* Cadence CLP 3040, mono LP, maroon label with metronome, $40-$80.

Number	Title (A Side/B Side)	Yr	VG	VG+	NM
WARNER BROS.					
□ GWB 0311	That's Old Fashioned/Bowling Green	197?	—	2.00	4.00
—"Back to Back Hits" series; originals have palm-tree labels					
□ GWB 0314	Ebony Eyes/Walk Right Back	197?	—	2.00	4.00
—"Back to Back Hits" series; originals have palm-tree labels					
□ 5151 [DJ]	Cathy's Clown/Always It's You	1960	25.00	50.00	100.00
—Promo-only gold vinyl pressing					
□ 5151 [M]	Cathy's Clown/Always It's You	1960	3.75	7.50	15.00
—Second-pressing stock copies have red labels with arrows					
□ 5151 [M]	Cathy's Clown/Always It's You	1960	5.00	10.00	20.00
—Original stock copies have pink labels					
□ 5151 [PS]	Cathy's Clown/Always It's You	1960	12.50	25.00	50.00
□ S-5151 [S]	Cathy's Clown/Always It's You	1960	12.50	25.00	50.00
□ 5163	So Sad (To Watch Good Love Go Bad)/Lucille	1960	3.75	7.50	15.00
□ 5163 [DJ]	So Sad (To Watch Good Love Go Bad)/Lucille	1960	25.00	50.00	100.00
—Promo-only gold vinyl pressing					
□ 5163 [PS]	So Sad (To Watch Good Love Go Bad)/Lucille	1960	12.50	25.00	50.00
□ 5199	Ebony Eyes/Walk Right Back	1961	3.75	7.50	15.00
□ 5199 [DJ]	Ebony Eyes/Walk Right Back	1961	25.00	50.00	100.00
—Promo-only gold vinyl pressing					
□ 5199 [PS]	Ebony Eyes/Walk Right Back	1961	6.25	12.50	25.00
□ 5220	Temptation/Stick With Me, Baby	1961	3.75	7.50	15.00
□ 5220 [PS]	Temptation/Stick With Me, Baby	1961	7.50	15.00	30.00
□ 5250	Crying in the Rain/I'm Not Angry	1961	3.75	7.50	15.00
□ 5250 [PS]	Crying in the Rain/I'm Not Angry	1961	5.00	10.00	20.00
□ 5273	That's Old Fashioned (That's the Way Love Should Be)/How Can I Meet Her?	1962	3.75	7.50	15.00
□ 5273 [PS]	That's Old Fashioned (That's the Way Love Should Be)/How Can I Meet Her?	1962	7.50	15.00	30.00
□ 5297	Don't Ask Me to Be Friends/No One Can Make My Sunshine Smile	1962	5.00	10.00	20.00
□ 5297 [PS]	Don't Ask Me to Be Friends/No One Can Make My Sunshine Smile	1962	7.50	15.00	30.00
□ 5346	(So It Was...So It Is...) So It Always Will Be/Nancy's Minuet	1963	3.75	7.50	15.00
□ 5362	I'm Afraid/It's Been Nice	1963	3.75	7.50	15.00
□ 5389	Love Her/The Girl Sang the Blues	1963	3.75	7.50	15.00
□ 5422	Hello, Amy/Ain't That Loving You, Baby	1964	3.75	7.50	15.00
□ 5441	The Ferris Wheel/Don't Forget to Cry	1964	3.75	7.50	15.00
□ 5466	You're the One I Love/Ring Around My Rosie	1964	3.75	7.50	15.00
□ 5478	Gone, Gone, Gone/Torture	1964	3.75	7.50	15.00
□ 5501	Don't Blame Me/Walk Right Back//Muskrat/Lucille	1961	5.00	10.00	20.00
□ 5501 [PS]	Don't Blame Me/Walk Right Back//Muskrat/Lucille	1961	10.00	20.00	40.00
—Part of Warner Bros. "+2" series, with two new songs and excerpts of two prior hits					
□ 5600	You're My Girl/Don't Let the World Know	1965	3.00	6.00	12.00
□ 5611	That'll Be the Day/Give Me a Sweetheart	1965	3.00	6.00	12.00
□ 5628	The Price of Love/It Only Costs a Dime	1965	3.00	6.00	12.00
□ 5639	I'll Never Get Over You/Follow Me	1965	3.00	6.00	12.00
□ 5649	Love Is Strange/A Man with Money	1965	3.00	6.00	12.00
□ 5649 [PS]	Love Is Strange/A Man with Money	1965	37.50	75.00	150.00
□ 5682	It's All Over/I Used to Love You	1965	3.00	6.00	12.00
□ 5698	The Doll House Is Empty/Lovey Kravezit	1966	3.00	6.00	12.00
□ 5808	The Power of Love/Leave My Girl Alone	1966	3.00	6.00	12.00
□ 5833	Somebody Help Me/Hard, Hard Year	1966	3.00	6.00	12.00
□ 5857	Fifi the Flea/Like Every Time Before	1966	5.00	10.00	20.00
—A-side listed as "Don Everly Brother," B-side as "Phil Everly Brother"					
□ 5901	She Never Smiles Anymore/Devil Child	1967	3.00	6.00	12.00
□ 7020	Bowling Green/I Don't Want to Love You	1967	3.00	6.00	12.00
□ 7062	Mary Jane/Talking to the Flowers	1967	3.00	6.00	12.00
□ 7088	Love of the Common People/The Voice Within	1967	3.00	6.00	12.00
□ 7110	Cathy's Clown/So Sad	1968	2.00	4.00	8.00
—"Back to Back Hits" series; originals have green "W7" label					
□ 7111	Crying in the Rain/Lucille	1968	2.00	4.00	8.00
—"Back to Back Hits" series; originals have green "W7" label					
□ 7120	Wake Up Little Susie/Bird Dog	1969	2.00	4.00	8.00
—"Back to Back Hits" series; originals have green "W7" label; re-recordings					
□ 7121	Bye Bye Love/All I Have to Do Is Dream	1969	2.00	4.00	8.00
—"Back to Back Hits" series; originals have green "W7" label; re-recordings					
□ 7192	Empty Boxes/It's My Time	1968	3.00	6.00	12.00
□ 7226	Lord of the Manor/Milk Train	1968	3.00	6.00	12.00
□ 7262	T for Texas/I Wonder If I Care As Much	1969	3.00	6.00	12.00
□ 7290	I'm On My Way Home Again/Cuckoo Bird	1969	3.00	6.00	12.00
□ 7326	Carolina on My Mind/My Little Yellow Bird	1969	3.75	7.50	15.00
□ 7425	Yves/The Human Race	1970	3.75	7.50	15.00
7-Inch Extended Plays					
CADENCE					
□ CLLP 33-3	Bye Bye Love/('Til) I Kissed You/Bird Dog//Wake Up Little Susie/When Will I Be Loved/Problems	1961	10.00	20.00	40.00
—Jukebox issue; small hole, plays at 33 1/3 rpm					
□ CLLP 33-3 [PS]	Rockin' with the Everly Brothers	1961	15.00	30.00	60.00
—Cardboard insert in heavy vinyl envelope					
□ CLLP 33-4	All I Have to Do Is Dream/I Wonder If I Care As Much/Take a Message to Mary//Let It Be Me/Devoted to You/Maybe Tomorrow	1961	10.00	20.00	40.00
—Jukebox issue; small hole, plays at 33 1/3 rpm					
□ CLLP 33-4 [PS]	Dream with the Everly Brothers	1961	15.00	30.00	60.00
—Cardboard insert in heavy vinyl envelope					
□ CEP-104	Wake Up Little Susie/Maybe Tomorrow//Bye Bye Love/I Wonder If I Care As Much	1957	12.50	25.00	50.00
□ CEP-104 [PS]	The Everly Brothers	1957	12.50	25.00	50.00
□ CEP-105	This Little Girl of Mine/Leave My Woman Alone//Should We Tell Him/Be-Bop-a-Lula	1957	12.50	25.00	50.00
□ CEP-105 [PS]	The Everly Brothers	1957	12.50	25.00	50.00
□ CEP-107	Brand New Heartache/Keep a Knockin'//Rip It Up/Hey Doll Baby	1957	12.50	25.00	50.00
□ CEP-107 [PS]	The Everly Brothers	1957	12.50	25.00	50.00
□ CEP-108	Roving Gambler/Oh So Many Years//Put My Little Shoes Away/That Silver Haired Daddy Of Mine	1958	12.50	25.00	50.00
□ CEP-108 [PS]	Songs Our Daddy Taught Us, Vol. 1	1958	12.50	25.00	50.00
□ CEP-109	Barbara Allen/Long Time Gone//Lightning Express/Who's Gonna Shoe Your Pretty Little Feet	1958	12.50	25.00	50.00
□ CEP-109 [PS]	Songs Our Daddy Taught Us, Vol. 2	1958	12.50	25.00	50.00
□ CEP-110	*Down in the Willow Garden/Kentucky//I'm Here to Get My Baby Out of Jail/Rockin' Alone in My Old Rockin' Chair	1958	12.50	25.00	50.00
□ CEP-110 [PS]	Songs Our Daddy Taught Us, Vol. 3	1958	12.50	25.00	50.00
□ CEP-111	Bird Dog/Devoted to You//All I Have to Do Is Dream/Claudette	1959	12.50	25.00	50.00
□ CEP-111 [PS]	The Everly Brothers	1959	12.50	25.00	50.00
□ CEP-118	(contents unknown)	1959	12.50	25.00	50.00
□ CEP-118 [PS]	The Everly Brothers	1959	12.50	25.00	50.00
□ CEP-121	Let It Be Me/Since You Broke My Heart//'Til I Kissed You/Oh, What a Feeling	1960	6.25	12.50	25.00
□ CEP-121 [PS]	The Very Best of the Everly Brothers	1960	6.25	12.50	25.00
WARNER BROS.					
□ PRO 135 [DJ]	My Gal Sal/Grandfather's Clock/Bully of the Town/The Wayward Wind/Chlo-E//Hi-Lili, Hi-Lo/Don't Blame Me/Now Is the Hour/When I Grow Too Old to Dream/Love Is Where You Find It	1961	15.00	30.00	60.00
—7-inch record, large hole, with excerpts from each of the above songs					
□ PRO 135 [PS]	Souvenir Sampler	1961	25.00	50.00	100.00
—Back cover of sleeve has a coupon for LP W/WS 1418					
□ EA 1381	So Sad (To Watch Good Love Go Bad)/You Thrill Me (Through and Through)//Memories Are Made of This/Oh, True Love	1960	10.00	20.00	40.00
□ EA 1381 [PS]	Forever Yours	1960	10.00	20.00	40.00
□ EB 1381	Sleepless Nights/Carol Jane//Nashville Blues/That's What You Do to Me	1960	10.00	20.00	40.00
□ EB 1381 [PS]	Especially for You	1960	10.00	20.00	40.00
Albums					
ARISTA					
□ AL9-8207 [(2)]	24 Original Classics	1985	3.75	7.50	15.00
BARNABY					
□ BGP-350 [(2)]	The Everly Brothers' Original Golden Hits	1970	5.00	10.00	20.00
□ 4004	Greatest Hits, Vol. 1	1977	2.50	5.00	10.00
□ 4005	Greatest Hits, Vol. 2	1977	2.50	5.00	10.00
□ 4006	Greatest Hits, Vol. 3	1977	2.50	5.00	10.00
□ BR-6006 [(2)]	The Everly Brothers' Greatest Hits	1974	3.75	7.50	15.00
□ BR-15008 [(2)]	History of the Everly Brothers	1973	3.75	7.50	15.00
□ ZG 30260 [(2)]	End of an Era	1971	3.75	7.50	15.00
CADENCE					
□ CLP-3003 [M]	The Everly Brothers	1958	25.00	50.00	100.00
—Maroon label with metronome logo					
□ CLP-3003 [M]	The Everly Brothers	1962	15.00	30.00	60.00
—Red label with black border					
□ CLP-3016 [M]	Songs Our Daddy Taught Us	1958	25.00	50.00	100.00
—Maroon label with metronome logo					
□ CLP-3016 [M]	Songs Our Daddy Taught Us	1962	15.00	30.00	60.00
—Red label with black border					
□ CLP-3025 [M]	The Everly Brothers' Best	1959	22.50	45.00	90.00
—Maroon label with metronome logo					
□ CLP-3025 [M]	The Everly Brothers' Best	1962	15.00	30.00	60.00
—Red label with black border					
□ CLP-3040 [M]	The Fabulous Style of the Everly Brothers	1960	20.00	40.00	80.00
—Maroon label with metronome logo					
□ CLP-3040 [M]	The Fabulous Style of the Everly Brothers	1962	12.50	25.00	50.00
—Red label with black border					
□ CLP-3059 [M]	Folk Songs of the Everly Brothers	1963	12.50	25.00	50.00
—Reissue of 3016					
□ CLP-3062 [M]	15 Everly Hits 15	1963	10.00	20.00	40.00
□ CLP-25040 [P]	The Fabulous Style of the Everly Brothers	1960	30.00	60.00	120.00
—Maroon label with metronome logo					
□ CLP-25040 [P]	The Fabulous Style of the Everly Brothers	1962	15.00	30.00	60.00
—Red label with black border					
□ CLP-25059 [R]	Folk Songs of the Everly Brothers	1963	10.00	20.00	40.00
□ CLP-25062 [P]	15 Everly Hits 15	1963	12.50	25.00	50.00
HARMONY					
□ HS 11304	Wake Up Little Susie	1969	3.00	6.00	12.00
□ HS 11350	Christmas with the Everly Brothers and the Boys Town Choir	1969	5.00	10.00	20.00
□ KH 11388	Chained to a Memory	1970	3.00	6.00	12.00
MERCURY					
□ 822431-1	EB 84	1984	2.50	5.00	10.00
□ 826142-1	Born Yesterday	1986	2.50	5.00	10.00
□ 832520-1	Some Hearts	1989	3.00	6.00	12.00
PAIR					
□ PDL1-1063 [(2)]	Living Legends	1986	3.00	6.00	12.00
PASSPORT					
□ 11001 [(2)]	The Everly Brothers Reunion Concert	1984	3.75	7.50	15.00
RCA VICTOR					
□ LSP-4620	Stories We Could Tell	1972	3.75	7.50	15.00
□ LSP-4781	Pass the Chicken and Listen	1972	3.75	7.50	15.00
□ AFL1-5401	Home Again	1985	2.50	5.00	10.00
RHINO					
□ RNLP-211	The Everly Brothers	1985	2.50	5.00	10.00
□ RNLP-212	Songs Our Daddy Taught Us	1985	2.50	5.00	10.00
□ RNLP-213	The Fabulous Style of the Everly Brothers	1985	2.50	5.00	10.00
□ RNLP-214	All They Had to Do Was Dream	1985	2.50	5.00	10.00
□ RNDF-258 [PD]	Heartaches and Harmonies	1985	5.00	10.00	20.00
□ RNLP-70173	The Best of the Everly Brothers (Golden Archive Series)	1987	2.50	5.00	10.00
TIME-LIFE					
□ SRNR-09 [(2)]	The Everly Brothers: 1957-1962	1986	5.00	10.00	20.00
—Part of "The Rock 'n' Roll Era" series; box set with insert					
WARNER BROS.					
□ PRO 134 [10]	It's Everly Time!	1960	150.00	300.00	600.00
—Promo "souvenir sampler" from their debut on WB					
□ W 1381 [M]	It's Everly Time!	1960	7.50	15.00	30.00
□ WS 1381 [S]	It's Everly Time!	1960	10.00	20.00	40.00
□ W 1395 [M]	A Date with the Everly Brothers	1960	10.00	20.00	40.00
—Gatefold edition without poster or photos					
□ W 1395 [M]	A Date with the Everly Brothers	1960	12.50	25.00	50.00
—Gatefold edition with poster and wallet-size photos					
□ W 1395 [M]	A Date with the Everly Brothers	1961	7.50	15.00	30.00
—Regular edition					
□ WS 1395 [S]	A Date with the Everly Brothers	1960	12.50	25.00	50.00
—Gatefold edition without poster or photos					

Number	Title (A Side/B Side)	Yr	VG	VG+	NM
❑ WS 1395 [S]	A Date with the Everly Brothers	1960	18.75	37.50	75.00
—Gatefold edition with poster and wallet-size photos					
❑ WS 1395 [S]	A Date with the Everly Brothers	1961	10.00	20.00	40.00
—Regular edition					
❑ W 1418 [M]	Both Sides of an Evening	1961	7.50	15.00	30.00
❑ WS 1418 [S]	Both Sides of an Evening	1961	10.00	20.00	40.00
❑ W 1430 [M]	Instant Party!	1962	7.50	15.00	30.00
❑ WS 1430 [S]	Instant Party!	1962	10.00	20.00	40.00
❑ W 1471 [M]	The Golden Hits of the Everly Brothers	1962	7.50	15.00	30.00
❑ WS 1471 [S]	The Golden Hits of the Everly Brothers	1962	10.00	20.00	40.00
—Gold label					
❑ WS 1471	The Golden Hits of the Everly Brothers	1967	5.00	10.00	20.00
—Green "W7" label					
❑ WS 1471	The Golden Hits of the Everly Brothers	1970	3.75	7.50	15.00
—Green "WB" label					
❑ WS 1471	The Golden Hits of the Everly Brothers	1973	3.00	6.00	12.00
—"Burbank" palm-tree label					
❑ WS 1471	The Golden Hits of the Everly Brothers	1979	2.50	5.00	10.00
—White or tan label					
❑ W 1483 [M]	Christmas with the Everly Brothers and the Boys Town Choir	1962	10.00	20.00	40.00
❑ WS 1483 [S]	Christmas with the Everly Brothers and the Boys Town Choir	1962	12.50	25.00	50.00
❑ W 1513 [M]	Great Country Hits	1963	10.00	20.00	40.00
❑ WS 1513 [S]	Great Country Hits	1963	12.50	25.00	50.00
❑ W 1554 [M]	The Very Best of the Everly Brothers	1964	7.50	15.00	30.00
—Originals have yellow covers					
❑ W 1554 [M]	The Very Best of the Everly Brothers	1965	5.00	10.00	20.00
—Later pressings have white covers					
❑ WS 1554 [S]	The Very Best of the Everly Brothers	1964	10.00	20.00	40.00
—Originals have yellow covers					
❑ WS 1554 [S]	The Very Best of the Everly Brothers	1965	6.25	12.50	25.00
—White cover; gold label					
❑ WS 1554	The Very Best of the Everly Brothers	1967	5.00	10.00	20.00
—Green "W7" label					
❑ WS 1554	The Very Best of the Everly Brothers	1970	3.75	7.50	15.00
—Green "WB" label					
❑ WS 1554	The Very Best of the Everly Brothers	1973	3.00	6.00	12.00
—"Burbank" palm-tree label					
❑ WS 1554	The Very Best of the Everly Brothers	1979	2.50	5.00	10.00
—White or tan label					
❑ W 1578 [M]	Rock & Soul	1964	10.00	20.00	40.00
❑ WS 1578 [S]	Rock & Soul	1964	12.50	25.00	50.00
❑ W 1585 [M]	Gone, Gone, Gone	1965	10.00	20.00	40.00
❑ WS 1585 [S]	Gone, Gone, Gone	1965	12.50	25.00	50.00
❑ W 1605 [M]	Beat & Soul	1965	10.00	20.00	40.00
❑ WS 1605 [S]	Beat & Soul	1965	12.50	25.00	50.00
❑ W 1620 [M]	In Our Image	1966	10.00	20.00	40.00
❑ WS 1620 [S]	In Our Image	1966	12.50	25.00	50.00
❑ W 1646 [M]	Two Yanks in England	1966	10.00	20.00	40.00
❑ WS 1646 [S]	Two Yanks in England	1966	12.50	25.00	50.00
❑ W 1676 [M]	The Hit Sound of the Everly Brothers	1967	12.50	25.00	50.00
❑ WS 1676 [S]	The Hit Sound of the Everly Brothers	1967	10.00	20.00	40.00
❑ W 1708 [M]	The Everly Brothers Sing	1967	12.50	25.00	50.00
❑ WS 1708 [S]	The Everly Brothers Sing	1967	10.00	20.00	40.00
❑ WS 1752	Roots	1968	10.00	20.00	40.00
❑ WS 1858	The Everly Brothers Show	1970	7.50	15.00	30.00
❑ ST-91343 [S]	The Very Best of the Everly Brothers	1967	10.00	20.00	40.00
—Capitol Record Club edition					
❑ ST-91601	Roots	1968	12.50	25.00	50.00
—Capitol Record Club edition					
❑ STAO-93286	The Everly Brothers Show	1970	10.00	20.00	40.00
—Capitol Record Club edition					

EVERPRESENT FULLNESS, THE
45s
WHITE WHALE

Number	Title (A Side/B Side)	Yr	VG	VG+	NM
❑ 233	Wild About My Lovin'/Doin' a Number	1966	3.75	7.50	15.00
❑ 233	Wild About My Lovin'/Fine and Dandy	1966	3.75	7.50	15.00
❑ 248	Darlin' You Can Count On Me/Yeah	1967	3.75	7.50	15.00

Albums
WHITE WHALE

Number	Title	Yr	VG	VG+	NM
❑ 7132	The Everpresent Fullness	1970	6.25	12.50	25.00

EVERY FATHER'S TEENAGE SON
45s
BUDDAH

Number	Title (A Side/B Side)	Yr	VG	VG+	NM
❑ 25	A Letter to Dad/Josephine's Song	1968	2.00	4.00	8.00

EVERY MOTHERS' SON
45s
MGM

Number	Title (A Side/B Side)	Yr	VG	VG+	NM
❑ 13733	Come On Down to My Boat/I Believe in You	1967	2.50	5.00	10.00
❑ 13788	Put Your Mind at Ease/Proper Four Leaf Clover	1967	2.00	4.00	8.00
❑ 13788 [PS]	Put Your Mind at Ease/Proper Four Leaf Clover	1967	3.00	6.00	12.00
❑ 13844	Pony with the Golden Mane/Dolls in the Clock	1967	2.00	4.00	8.00
❑ 13887	No One Knows/What Became of Mary	1968	2.00	4.00	8.00
❑ 13987	Rainflowers/For Brandy	1968	2.00	4.00	8.00

Albums
MGM

Number	Title	Yr	VG	VG+	NM
❑ E-4471 [M]	Every Mothers' Son	1967	5.00	10.00	20.00
❑ SE-4471 [S]	Every Mothers' Son	1967	5.00	10.00	20.00
❑ E-4504 [M]	Every Mothers' Son's Back	1967	5.00	10.00	20.00
❑ SE-4504 [S]	Every Mothers' Son's Back	1967	5.00	10.00	20.00

EVERYTHING IS EVERYTHING
45s
VANGUARD APOSTOLIC

Number	Title (A Side/B Side)	Yr	VG	VG+	NM
❑ 35082	Witchi Tai To/Ooh Baby	1969	2.00	4.00	8.00
❑ 35097	Ya Hay Ho/You Don't Need No Music	1969	2.00	4.00	8.00

Albums
VANGUARD

Number	Title	Yr	VG	VG+	NM
❑ VSD-6512	Everything Is Everything	1969	6.25	12.50	25.00

EVIL, THE
45s
CAPITOL

Number	Title (A Side/B Side)	Yr	VG	VG+	NM
❑ 2038	Whatcha Gonna Do About It/Always Runnin' Around	1967	5.00	10.00	20.00

LIVING LEGEND

Number	Title (A Side/B Side)	Yr	VG	VG+	NM
❑ 108	Whatcha Gonna Do About It/Always Runnin' Around	1967	10.00	20.00	40.00

EVIL ENCORPORATED
45s
SCENE

Number	Title (A Side/B Side)	Yr	VG	VG+	NM
❑ 101	Hey You/The Thing Is...	1967	7.50	15.00	30.00
❑ 102	Baby It's You/All I Really Want to Do	1967	7.50	15.00	30.00

EXCALIBURS, THE
45s
TRENT TOWN

Number	Title (A Side/B Side)	Yr	VG	VG+	NM
❑ 1017	Christmas Dreaming/Peace On Earth	19??	25.00	50.00	100.00

EXCELLENTS, THE
45s
BLAST

Number	Title (A Side/B Side)	Yr	VG	VG+	NM
❑ 205	Coney Island Baby/You Baby You	1962	5.00	10.00	20.00
—Red and white label					
❑ 205	Coney Island Baby/You Baby You	1962	7.50	15.00	30.00
—All-red label					
❑ 205	Coney Island Baby/You Baby You	1965	6.25	12.50	25.00
—Purple label					
❑ 207	I Hear a Rhapsody/Why Did You Laugh	1963	15.00	30.00	60.00

MERMAID

Number	Title (A Side/B Side)	Yr	VG	VG+	NM
❑ 106	Love No One But You/Red Red Robin	1961	12.50	25.00	50.00
—No mermaid on label					
❑ 106	Love No One But You/Red Red Robin	1961	50.00	100.00	200.00
—With mermaid on label					

EXCELS, THE (1)
45s
GONE

Number	Title (A Side/B Side)	Yr	VG	VG+	NM
❑ 5094	My Foolish Heart/Just You and I Together	1960	6.25	12.50	25.00

RSVP

Number	Title (A Side/B Side)	Yr	VG	VG+	NM
❑ 111	Can't Help Lovin' That Girl of Mine/Till You	1961	12.50	25.00	50.00

EXCELS, THE (2)
45s
CARLA

Number	Title (A Side/B Side)	Yr	VG	VG+	NM
❑ 1901	Little Innocent Girl/Some Kind of Fun	1968	5.00	10.00	20.00
❑ 2529	Gonna Make You Mine Girl/Goodbye Poor Boy	1966	5.00	10.00	20.00
❑ 2534	I Wanna Be Free/Too Much Too Soon	1967	5.00	10.00	20.00
❑ 2536	California on My Mind/Arrival of Mary	1967	5.00	10.00	20.00

EXCELS, THE (3)
45s
CENTRAL

Number	Title (A Side/B Side)	Yr	VG	VG+	NM
❑ 2601	You're Mine Forever/Baby Doll	1957	12.50	25.00	50.00

RELIC

Number	Title (A Side/B Side)	Yr	VG	VG+	NM
❑ 1007	You're Mine Forever/Baby Doll	1965	2.50	5.00	10.00

EXCEPTION, THE   Peter Cetera (later of CHICAGO) was a member of this group.
45s
CAPITOL

Number	Title (A Side/B Side)	Yr	VG	VG+	NM
❑ 2046	Business As Usual/My Mind Goes Traveling	1967	3.00	6.00	12.00
❑ 2120	You Always Hurt Me/You Don't Know Like I Know	1968	3.00	6.00	12.00
❑ 5982	The Girl from New York City/As Far As I Can See	1967	3.00	6.00	12.00

EXCITERS, THE
45s
BANG

Number	Title (A Side/B Side)	Yr	VG	VG+	NM
❑ 515	A Little Bit of Soap/I'm Gonna Get Him Someday	1966	3.00	6.00	12.00
❑ 518	You Better Come Home/Weddings Make Me Cry	1966	7.50	15.00	30.00

FARGO

Number	Title (A Side/B Side)	Yr	VG	VG+	NM
❑ 1400	Alone Again, Naturally/(B-side unknown)	1972	2.00	4.00	8.00

RCA VICTOR

Number	Title (A Side/B Side)	Yr	VG	VG+	NM
❑ 47-9633	Take One Step (I'll Take Two)/If You Want My Love	1968	7.50	15.00	30.00
❑ 47-9723	You Don't Know What You're Missing ('Til It's Gone!)/Blowing Up My Mind	1969	7.50	15.00	30.00
❑ 48-1035	You Don't Know What You're Missing ('Til It's Gone!)/Blowing Up My Mind	1972	3.75	7.50	15.00

ROULETTE

Number	Title (A Side/B Side)	Yr	VG	VG+	NM
❑ 4591	I Want You to Be My Boy/Tonight, Tonight	1965	3.00	6.00	12.00
❑ 4591 [PS]	I Want You to Be My Boy/Tonight, Tonight	1965	12.50	25.00	50.00
❑ 4594	Are You Satisfied/Just Not Ready	1965	3.00	6.00	12.00
❑ 4614	My Father/Run Mascara	1965	3.00	6.00	12.00
❑ 4632	I Knew You Would/There They Go	1965	3.00	6.00	12.00

SHOUT

Number	Title (A Side/B Side)	Yr	VG	VG+	NM
❑ 205	Number One/You Got Love	1966	2.50	5.00	10.00
❑ 214	Soulmotion/You Know It Ain't Right	1967	2.50	5.00	10.00

TODAY

Number	Title (A Side/B Side)	Yr	VG	VG+	NM
❑ 1002	Learning How to Fly/Life, Love and Peace	1970	2.00	4.00	8.00

UNITED ARTISTS

Number	Title (A Side/B Side)	Yr	VG	VG+	NM
❑ 0029	Tell Him/Do Wah Diddy	1973	—	2.00	4.00
—"Silver Spotlight Series" reissue					
❑ 544	Tell Him/Hard Way to Go	1963	3.75	7.50	15.00
❑ 572	Drama of Love/He's Got the Power	1963	3.00	6.00	12.00
❑ 604	Get Him/It's So Exciting	1963	3.00	6.00	12.00
❑ 662	Do-Wah-Diddy/If Love Came Your Way	1963	3.00	6.00	12.00
❑ 721	Having My Fun/We Were Lovers (When the Party Began)	1964	3.00	6.00	12.00
❑ 830	Having My Fun/We Were Lovers (When the Party Began)	1965	2.50	5.00	10.00

Albums
ROULETTE

Number	Title	Yr	VG	VG+	NM
❑ R 25326 [M]	The Exciters	1966	7.50	15.00	30.00
❑ SR 25326 [S]	The Exciters	1966	10.00	20.00	40.00

E

Number	Title (A Side/B Side)	Yr	VG	VG+	NM
TODAY					
❏ 1001	Black Beauty	1971	5.00	10.00	20.00
UNITED ARTISTS					
❏ UAL-3264 [M]	Tell Him	1963	17.50	35.00	70.00
❏ UAS-6264 [S]	Tell Him	1963	37.50	75.00	150.00
EXILE					
45s					
ARISTA					
❏ 2009	Nobody's Talking/Don't Hang Up (Girl)	1990	—	—	3.00
❏ 2075	Yet/Show Me	1990	—	—	3.00
❏ 2139	There You Go/I'm Still Standing	1990	—	—	3.00
❏ 2228	Even Now/One Too Many Times	1991	—	—	3.00
❏ 9911	Keep It in the Middle of the Road/Yet	1989	—	—	3.00
❏ 12351	Nothing at All/What You See	1991	—	—	3.00
ATCO					
❏ 7072	Try It On/Show Me What You Got	1977	—	2.50	5.00
COLUMBIA					
❏ 4-44972	Church Street Soul Revival/Your Day Is Comin'	1969	2.00	4.00	8.00
—As "The Exiles"					
❏ 4-45210	Put Your Hands Together/Your Day Is Comin'	1970	2.00	4.00	8.00
—As "The Exiles"					
EPIC					
❏ 34-04041	High Cost of Leaving/Like a Fool's Supposed to Do	1983	—	—	3.00
❏ 34-04247	Woke Up in Love/First Things First	1983	—	2.00	4.00
❏ 34-04421	I Don't Want to Be a Memory/After All These Years (I'm Still Chasing You)	1984	—	—	3.00
❏ 34-04567	Give Me One More Chance/Ain't That a Pity	1984	—	—	3.00
❏ 34-04567 [PS]	Give Me One More Chance/Ain't That a Pity	1984	—	2.00	4.00
❏ 34-04722	Crazy for Your Love/Just in Case	1984	—	—	3.00
❏ 34-04864	She's a Miracle/I've Never Seen Anything	1985	—	—	3.00
❏ 34-05580	Hang On to Your Heart/She Loves Her Lovin'	1985	—	—	3.00
❏ 34-05723	I Could Get Used to You/Practice Makes Perfect	1985	—	—	3.00
❏ 34-05860	Super Love/Proud to Be Your Man	1986	—	—	3.00
❏ 34-06229	It'll Be Me/Music	1986	—	—	3.00
❏ 34-07135	She's Too Good to Be True/Promises, Promises	1987	—	—	3.00
❏ 34-07597	I Can't Get Close Enough/As Long As I Have Your Memory	1987	—	—	3.00
❏ 34-07710	Feel Like Foolin' Around/Showdown	1988	—	—	3.00
❏ 34-0 7775	Just One Kiss/As Long As I Have Your Memory	1988	—	—	3.00
❏ 34-08020	It's You Again/The Girl Can't Help It	1988	—	—	3.00
MCA CURB					
❏ 52551	Stay with Me/Kiss You All Over	1985	—	—	3.00
❏ 52596	Dixie Girl/Someone Like You	1985	—	—	3.00
SSS INTERNATIONAL					
❏ 848	Got to Be All Right/Second Hand Lady	197?	2.00	4.00	8.00
—As "The Exiles"					
WARNER BROS.					
❏ 8589	Kiss You All Over/Don't Do It	1978	—	2.00	4.00
❏ 8711	You Thrill Me/One Step at a Time	1978	—	2.00	4.00
❏ 8796	How Could This Go Wrong/Being in Love with You Is Easy	1979	—	2.00	4.00
❏ 8848	Part of Me That Needs You Most/Let's Do It All Over Again	1979	—	2.00	4.00
❏ 49048	Too Proud to Cry/Destiny	1979	—	2.00	4.00
❏ 49245	You're Gone for Me/Let's Do It All Over Again	1980	—	2.00	4.00
❏ 49548	Take Me Down/It Takes Love to Make Love	1980	—	3.00	6.00
—A-side was later a hit for Alabama					
❏ 49794	Heart and Soul/Your Love Is Everything	1981	—	2.00	4.00
❏ 49863	Till the Very End/What Kind of Love Is This	1981	—	2.00	4.00
WOODEN NICKEL					
❏ BWBO-0006	Do What You Think You Should/Hold Tight Sweet Woman	1973	—	3.50	7.00
❏ 65-0115	Devil's Rite/Mabel	1973	—	3.50	7.00
Albums					
ARISTA					
❏ AL-9624	Still Standing	1990	3.75	7.50	15.00
EPIC					
❏ B6E 39154	Exile	1983	2.00	4.00	8.00
❏ FE 39424	Kentucky Hearts	1984	2.00	4.00	8.00
❏ BFE 40000	Hang On to Your Heart	1985	2.00	4.00	8.00
❏ FE 40401	Greatest Hits	1986	2.00	4.00	8.00
❏ FE 40901	Shelter from the Night	1987	2.00	4.00	8.00
MCA CURB					
❏ 946	All There Is	1986	2.00	4.00	8.00
❏ 947	Heart and Soul	1986	2.00	4.00	8.00
❏ 963	Mixed Emotions	1986	2.00	4.00	8.00
❏ 964	Don't Leave Me This Way	1986	2.00	4.00	8.00
❏ 1456	More of the Best of Exile	1986	2.00	4.00	8.00
❏ 5581	Best of Exile	1985	2.00	4.00	8.00
RCA VICTOR					
❏ AFL1-3086	Exile	1978	3.00	6.00	12.00
❏ AFL1-3087	Stage Pass	1978	3.00	6.00	12.00
WARNER BROS.					
❏ BSK 3205	Mixed Emotions	1978	2.50	5.00	10.00
❏ BSK 3323	All There Is	1979	2.50	5.00	10.00
❏ BSK 3437	Don't Leave Me This Way	1980	2.50	5.00	10.00
❏ BSK 3588	Heart and Soul	1981	2.50	5.00	10.00
WOODEN NICKEL					
❏ BWL1-0120	Exile	1973	3.75	7.50	15.00
EXODUS					
45s					
JAMIE					
❏ 1442	Four Seasons Medley (mono/stereo)	1981	—	2.50	5.00
—As "Exodus II"					
WAND					
❏ 11248	M&M/Silhouettes-You Cheated	1972	7.50	15.00	30.00
—Multi-colored label					
❏ 11248	M&M/Silhouettes-You Cheated	1972	25.00	50.00	100.00
—Black and white label					
EXOTIC GUITARS AL CASEY was guitarist for this studio group.					
45s					
RANWOOD					
❏ 804	Spanish Eyes/C'est Si Bon	1968	—	2.50	5.00
❏ 811	I Will Wait for You/Blueberry Hill	1968	—	2.50	5.00
❏ 830	I Walk Alone/Twilight Time	1969	—	2.50	5.00
❏ 843	Indian Love Call/Trying	1969	—	2.50	5.00

Number	Title (A Side/B Side)	Yr	VG	VG+	NM
❏ 856	To Rome with Love/Peg o' My Heart	1969	—	2.50	5.00
❏ 863	I Was Kaiser Bill's Batman/Now Is the Hour	1970	—	2.50	5.00
❏ 871	Holly Holy/High Noon	1970	—	2.50	5.00
❏ 882	Orange Blossom Special/San Antonio Rose	1970	—	2.50	5.00
❏ 898	Till Love Touches Your Life/I Can't Stop Loving You	1971	—	2.00	4.00
❏ 914	Memphis/Maria Elena	1971	—	2.00	4.00
❏ 936	Crusing Down the River/You Can't Be True Dear	1971	—	2.00	4.00
Albums					
RANWOOD					
❏ 8002	The Exotic Guitars	1968	3.00	6.00	12.00
❏ 8040	Those Were the Days	1968	3.00	6.00	12.00
❏ 8051	Indian Love Call	1969	3.00	6.00	12.00
❏ 8061	Everybody's Talkin'	1970	2.50	5.00	10.00
❏ 8073	Holly Holy	1970	2.50	5.00	10.00
❏ 8080	Country Music	1970	2.50	5.00	10.00
❏ 8085	I Can't Stop Loving You	1971	2.50	5.00	10.00
❏ 8090	All the Guitar Hits	1971	2.50	5.00	10.00
❏ 8171	300 Watt Music Box	1975	2.50	5.00	10.00
EXOTICS, THE More than one group.					
45s					
BOLO					
❏ 722	Oasis/Chattanooga Choo Choo	1962	3.00	6.00	12.00
CORAL					
❏ 62268	That's My Desire/Darking, I Want to Get Married	1961	5.00	10.00	20.00
❏ 62289	The Gang That Sang (Heart of My Heart)/Hotcha Mighty Knows	1961	5.00	10.00	20.00
❏ 62310	Fortune Hunter/Manpower	1962	5.00	10.00	20.00
❏ 62343	My Life's Desire (Part 1)/My Life's Desire (Part 2)	1963	3.75	7.50	15.00
❏ 62399	Let's Get Together/Sad, Sad Song	1964	3.75	7.50	15.00
❏ 62439	Like You Hurt Me/Big Time Charlie	1964	5.00	10.00	20.00
EXCELLO					
❏ 2284	Boogaloo Investigator/I Won't Ever Stop Loving You	1967	2.00	4.00	8.00
❏ 2292	Let Me Be a Part of You/Let's Try to Build a Love Affair	1968	2.00	4.00	8.00
JERDEN					
❏ 106	Four Banger/Cat Hairs	1960	3.75	7.50	15.00
MONUMENT					
❏ 984	Fire Engine Red/Morning Sun	1966	3.00	6.00	12.00
SEAFAIR					
❏ 108	Ginger Snap/(B-side unknown)	1962	2.50	5.00	10.00
❏ 113	Jerk Time/For the Winds	1965	2.50	5.00	10.00
SPRINGBOARD					
❏ 101	Gee/Lorraine	1963	5.00	10.00	20.00
❏ 101 [PS]	Gee/Lorraine	1963	10.00	20.00	40.00
EXPLORERS, THE					
45s					
CORAL					
❏ 62147	Vision of Love/On a Clear Night	1959	15.00	30.00	60.00
❏ 62175	Don't Be a Fool/In the Wee Small Hours of the Morning	1960	25.00	50.00	100.00
❏ 62295	Remember/Every Road (I Walk Along)	1961	15.00	30.00	60.00
—As "Dennis and the Explorers"					
❏ 65575	Don't Be a Fool/Vision of Love	196?	7.50	15.00	30.00
—Was listed in the last edition under "The Visions"					
EXPORTS, THE					
45s					
KING					
❏ 5917	Car Hop/Seat Belts Please	1964	6.25	12.50	25.00
❏ 5985	Mustang '65/Always It's You	1965	6.25	12.50	25.00
EXPRESSIONS, THE					
45s					
ARLISS					
❏ 1012	My Love, My Love/The Sign of Happiness	1962	12.50	25.00	50.00
FEDERAL					
❏ 12533	You Better Know It/Out of My Life	1964	2.50	5.00	10.00
GUYDEN					
❏ 2122	Be-Bop-a-Lula/Skinnie Minnie	1965	3.75	7.50	15.00
—As "J-D and the Expressions"					
PARKWAY					
❏ 892	On the Corner/To Cry	1963	3.75	7.50	15.00
REPRISE					
❏ 0360	Playboy/One Plus One	1965	5.00	10.00	20.00
SMASH					
❏ 1848	Karen/Thrill	1963	3.75	7.50	15.00
TEEN					
❏ 101	Now That You've Gone/Crazy	1957	50.00	100.00	200.00
EXTERMINATORS, THE					
45s					
CHANCELLOR					
❏ 1143	The Beetle Bomb/Stomp 'Em Out	1963	6.25	12.50	25.00
❏ 1148	Beatle Stomp/Stomp 'Em Out	1964	3.75	7.50	15.00
—A-sides are the same song with different titles					
GOLDEN WEST					
❏ 1002	Beatle Stomp/Stomp 'Em Out	1964	5.00	10.00	20.00
EXTREMES, THE					
45s					
EVERLAST					
❏ 5013	Come Next Spring/Let's Elope	1958	37.50	75.00	150.00
PARO					
❏ 733	The Bells/That's All I Want	1962	75.00	150.00	300.00
EYES OF BLUE					
45s					
DERAM					
❏ 85001	Heart Trouble/Up and Down	1967	2.00	4.00	8.00
❏ 85003	Don't Ask Me to Mend Your Broken Heart/Supermarket Full of Cans	1967	2.00	4.00	8.00
MERCURY					
❏ 72911	Apache '69/QIII	1969	2.00	4.00	8.00
Albums					
MERCURY					
❏ SR-61184	Crossroads of Time	1968	7.50	15.00	30.00
❏ SR-61220	In Fields of Ardath	1969	7.50	15.00	30.00

F

FABARES, SHELLEY

45s

COLPIX

Number	Title (A Side/B Side)	Yr	VG	VG+	NM
❏ 621	Johnny Angel/Where's It Gonna Get Me	1962	5.00	10.00	20.00
❏ 621 [PS]	Johnny Angel/Where's It Gonna Get Me	1962	125.00	250.00	500.00
❏ 631	What Did They Do Before Rock and Roll/Very Unlikely	1962	5.00	10.00	20.00

—With Paul Petersen

Number	Title (A Side/B Side)	Yr	VG	VG+	NM
❏ 631 [PS]	What Did They Do Before Rock and Roll/Very Unlikely	1962	100.00	200.00	400.00
❏ 636	Johnny Loves Me/I'm Growing Up	1962	5.00	10.00	20.00
❏ 636 [PS]	Johnny Loves Me/I'm Growing Up	1962	30.00	60.00	120.00
❏ 654	The Things We Did Last Summer/Breaking Up Is Hard to Do	1962	5.00	10.00	20.00
❏ 667	Big Star/Telephone (Don't You Ring)	1962	5.00	10.00	20.00
❏ 682	Ronnie, Call Me When You Get a Chance/I Left a Note to Say Goodbye	1963	5.00	10.00	20.00
❏ 705	Welcome Home/Billy Boy	1963	5.00	10.00	20.00
❏ 721	Football Season's Over/He Don't Love Me	1963	25.00	50.00	100.00

—Produced by Jan Berry of Jan and Dean

DUNHILL

Number	Title (A Side/B Side)	Yr	VG	VG+	NM
❏ 4001	My Prayer/Pretty Please	1965	7.50	15.00	30.00
❏ 4041	See Ya 'Round on the Rebound/Pretty Please	1966	7.50	15.00	30.00

VEE JAY

Number	Title (A Side/B Side)	Yr	VG	VG+	NM
❏ 632	I Know You'll Be There/Lost Summer Love	1964	10.00	20.00	40.00

Albums

COLPIX

Number	Title (A Side/B Side)	Yr	VG	VG+	NM
❏ CP-426 [M]	Shelley!	1962	37.50	75.00	150.00
❏ SCP-426 [S]	Shelley!	1962	150.00	300.00	600.00
❏ CP-431 [M]	The Things We Did Last Summer	1962	25.00	50.00	100.00
❏ SCP-431 [S]	The Things We Did Last Summer	1962	100.00	200.00	400.00

FABIAN

45s

CHANCELLOR

Number	Title (A Side/B Side)	Yr	VG	VG+	NM
❏ 1020	I'm in Love/Shivers	1958	6.25	12.50	25.00
❏ 1024	Be My Steady Date/Lilly Lou	1958	6.25	12.50	25.00
❏ 1029 [M]	I'm a Man/Hypnotized	1959	5.00	10.00	20.00
❏ 1029 [PS]	I'm a Man/Hypnotized	1959	10.00	20.00	40.00
❏ 1029 [PS]	I Am a Man/Hypnotized	1959	12.50	25.00	50.00

—Incorrect title on A-side of sleeve

Number	Title (A Side/B Side)	Yr	VG	VG+	NM
❏ S-1029 [S]	I'm a Man/Hypnotized	1959	12.50	25.00	50.00
❏ 1033 [M]	Turn Me Loose/Stop Thief!	1959	5.00	10.00	20.00
❏ 1033 [PS]	Turn Me Loose/Stop Thief!	1959	10.00	20.00	40.00
❏ S-1033 [S]	Turn Me Loose/Stop Thief!	1959	12.50	25.00	50.00
❏ 1037 [M]	Tiger/Mighty Cold (To a Warm, Warm Heart)	1959	5.00	10.00	20.00
❏ 1037 [PS]	Tiger/Mighty Cold (To a Warm, Warm Heart)	1959	10.00	20.00	40.00
❏ S-1037 [S]	Tiger/Mighty Cold (To a Warm, Warm Heart)	1959	12.50	25.00	50.00
❏ 1041 [M]	Come On and Get Me/Got the Feeling	1959	5.00	10.00	20.00
❏ 1041 [PS]	Come On and Get Me/Got the Feeling	1959	10.00	20.00	40.00
❏ S-1041 [S]	Come On and Get Me/Got the Feeling	1959	12.50	25.00	50.00
❏ 1044 [M]	Hound Dog Man/Friendly World	1959	6.25	12.50	25.00
❏ 1044 [M]	Hound Dog Man/This Friendly World	1959	5.00	10.00	20.00

—Note difference in B-side title

Number	Title (A Side/B Side)	Yr	VG	VG+	NM
❏ 1044 [PS]	Hound Dog Man/This Friendly World	1959	10.00	20.00	40.00
❏ S-1044 [S]	Hound Dog Man/This Friendly World	1959	12.50	25.00	50.00
❏ 1047 [M]	About This Thing Called Love/String Along	1960	3.00	6.00	12.00
❏ 1047 [PS]	About This Thing Called Love/String Along	1960	7.50	15.00	30.00
❏ S-1047 [S]	About This Thing Called Love/String Along	1960	12.50	25.00	50.00
❏ 1051	I'm Gonna Sit Right Down and Write Myself a Letter/Strollin' in the Springtime	1960	3.00	6.00	12.00
❏ 1051 [PS]	I'm Gonna Sit Right Down and Write Myself a Letter/Strollin' in the Springtime	1960	7.50	15.00	30.00
❏ 1055	Tomorrow/King of Love	1960	3.00	6.00	12.00
❏ 1055 [PS]	Tomorrow/King of Love	1960	7.50	15.00	30.00
❏ 1061	Kissin' and Twistin'/Long Before	1960	3.00	6.00	12.00
❏ 1061 [PS]	Kissin' and Twistin'/Long Before	1960	7.50	15.00	30.00
❏ 1067	You Know You Belong to Someone Else/Hold On	1961	3.00	6.00	12.00
❏ 1067 [PS]	You Know You Belong to Someone Else/Hold On	1961	7.50	15.00	30.00
❏ 1072	Grapevine/David and Goliath	1961	3.00	6.00	12.00
❏ 1079	The Love That I'm Giving to You/You're Only Young Once	1961	3.75	7.50	15.00
❏ 1079 [PS]	The Love That I'm Giving to You/You're Only Young Once	1961	10.00	20.00	40.00
❏ 1084	A Girl Like You/Dream Factory	1961	3.00	6.00	12.00
❏ 1084 [PS]	A Girl Like You/Dream Factory	1961	7.50	15.00	30.00
❏ 1086	Tongue-Tied/Kansas City	1961	5.00	10.00	20.00
❏ 1092	Wild Party/Made You	1961	5.00	10.00	20.00
❏ 1092	Wild Party/The Gospel Truth	1961	6.25	12.50	25.00
❏ 1092 [PS]	Wild Party/Made You	1961	10.00	20.00	40.00

CREAM

Number	Title (A Side/B Side)	Yr	VG	VG+	NM
❏ 7717	Ease On (Into My Life)/The American East	1977	—	2.50	5.00
❏ 7717 [PS]	Ease On (Into My Life)/The American East	1977	—	2.50	5.00

DOT

Number	Title (A Side/B Side)	Yr	VG	VG+	NM
❏ 16413	Break Down and Cry/She's Staying Inside with Me	1963	2.50	5.00	10.00

7-Inch Extended Plays

CHANCELLOR

Number	Title (A Side/B Side)	Yr	VG	VG+	NM
❏ A-301	*Hound Dog Man/This Friendly World/Pretty Little Girl/I'm Growin' Up/Single	1960	12.50	25.00	50.00
❏ A-301 [PS]	5 Songs from Hound Dog Man	1960	12.50	25.00	50.00
❏ A-5003	*Hold Me (In Your Arms)/Just One More Time/Please Don't Stop/Ooh, What You Do!	1959	15.00	30.00	60.00
❏ A-5003 [PS]	Hold That Tiger! Volume 1	1959	15.00	30.00	60.00
❏ B-5003	(contents unknown)	1959	15.00	30.00	60.00
❏ B-5003 [PS]	Hold That Tiger! Volume 2	1959	15.00	30.00	60.00
❏ C-5003	Turn Me Loose/Steady Date//Don't You Think It's Time?/Cuddle Up a Little Closer	1959	15.00	30.00	60.00
❏ C-5003 [PS]	Hold That Tiger! Volume 3	1959	15.00	30.00	60.00
❏ A-5005	Remember Me/I'm Sincere//Everything Is Just Right/You'll Never Tame Me	1959	15.00	30.00	60.00
❏ A-5005 [PS]	The Fabulous Fabian, Volume 1	1959	15.00	30.00	60.00
❏ B-5005	(contents unknown)	1959	15.00	30.00	60.00
❏ B-5005 [PS]	The Fabulous Fabian, Volume 2	1959	15.00	30.00	60.00
❏ C-5005	(contents unknown)	1959	15.00	30.00	60.00
❏ C-5005 [PS]	The Fabulous Fabian, Volume 3	1959	15.00	30.00	60.00
❏ A-9802	Young and Wonderful/Think of Me//Take Me/Exactly Like You	1960	12.50	25.00	50.00
❏ A-9802 [PS]	Young and Wonderful	1960	12.50	25.00	50.00

Albums

ABC

Number	Title (A Side/B Side)	Yr	VG	VG+	NM
❏ X-806	16 Greatest Hits	1973	3.00	6.00	12.00

CHANCELLOR

Number	Title (A Side/B Side)	Yr	VG	VG+	NM
❏ CHL-5003 [M]	Hold That Tiger!	1959	12.50	25.00	50.00

—Black label

Number	Title (A Side/B Side)	Yr	VG	VG+	NM
❏ CHL-5003 [M]	Hold That Tiger!	1959	25.00	50.00	100.00

—Pink label

Number	Title (A Side/B Side)	Yr	VG	VG+	NM
❏ CHLS-5003 [S]	Hold That Tiger!	1959	18.75	37.50	75.00

—Black label

Number	Title (A Side/B Side)	Yr	VG	VG+	NM
❏ CHLS-5003 [S]	Hold That Tiger!	1959	37.50	75.00	150.00

—Pink label

Number	Title (A Side/B Side)	Yr	VG	VG+	NM
❏ CHL-5005 [M]	Fabulous Fabian	1959	12.50	25.00	50.00
❏ CHLS-5005 [S]	Fabulous Fabian	1959	18.75	37.50	75.00
❏ CHL-5012 [M]	The Good Old Summertime	1960	12.50	25.00	50.00
❏ CHLS-5012 [S]	The Good Old Summertime	1960	18.75	37.50	75.00
❏ CHL-5019 [M]	Rockin' Hot	1961	18.75	37.50	75.00
❏ CHL-5024 [M]	Fabian's 16 Fabulous Hits	1962	18.75	37.50	75.00
❏ CHL-69802 [M]	The Fabian Facade: Young and Wonderful	1960	20.00	40.00	80.00

—Felt gatefold cover with die-cut window

MCA

Number	Title (A Side/B Side)	Yr	VG	VG+	NM
❏ 27095	The Best of Fabian	1985	2.00	4.00	8.00

UNITED ARTISTS

Number	Title (A Side/B Side)	Yr	VG	VG+	NM
❏ UA-LA449-E	The Very Best of Fabian	1975	3.00	6.00	12.00

FABIAN / FRANKIE AVALON

Albums

CHANCELLOR

Number	Title (A Side/B Side)	Yr	VG	VG+	NM
❏ CHL-5009 [M]	The Hit Makers	1960	25.00	50.00	100.00

FABRIC, BENT   Also see ACKER BILK.

45s

ATCO

Number	Title (A Side/B Side)	Yr	VG	VG+	NM
❏ 6226	Alley Cat/Marking Time	1962	2.00	4.00	8.00
❏ 6245	Chicken Feed/That Certain Party	1962	2.00	4.00	8.00
❏ 6271	The Happy Puppy/Sermonette	1963	2.00	4.00	8.00
❏ 6304	The Organ Grinder's Swing/Goofus	1964	2.00	4.00	8.00
❏ 6333	The Old Piano Roll Blues/Titena	1964	2.00	4.00	8.00
❏ 6363	The Drunken Penguin/Alley Cat	1965	2.00	4.00	8.00
❏ 6401	Sweet Charity Theme/Can't You See	1966	2.00	4.00	8.00

Albums

ATCO

Number	Title (A Side/B Side)	Yr	VG	VG+	NM
❏ 33-148 [M]	Alley Cat	1962	3.75	7.50	15.00
❏ SD 33-148 [S]	Alley Cat	1962	5.00	10.00	20.00
❏ 33-155 [M]	The Happy Puppy	1963	3.00	6.00	12.00
❏ SD 33-155 [S]	The Happy Puppy	1963	3.75	7.50	15.00
❏ 33-164 [M]	Organ Grinder's Swing	1964	3.00	6.00	12.00
❏ SD 33-164 [S]	Organ Grinder's Swing	1964	3.75	7.50	15.00
❏ 33-173 [M]	The Drunken Penguin	1965	3.00	6.00	12.00
❏ SD 33-173 [S]	The Drunken Penguin	1965	3.75	7.50	15.00
❏ 33-185 [M]	Never Tease Tigers	1966	3.00	6.00	12.00
❏ SD 33-185 [S]	Never Tease Tigers	1966	3.75	7.50	15.00
❏ 33-202 [M]	Operation Lovebirds	1967	3.00	6.00	12.00
❏ SD 33-202 [S]	Operation Lovebirds	1967	3.75	7.50	15.00
❏ 33-221 [M]	Relax	1967	3.75	7.50	15.00
❏ SD 33-221 [S]	Relax	1967	3.00	6.00	12.00

FABS, THE

45s

COTTON BALL

Number	Title (A Side/B Side)	Yr	VG	VG+	NM
❏ 1005	That's the Bag I'm In/Dinah Wants Religion	1966	37.50	75.00	150.00

FABULAIRES, THE

45s

EASTWEST

Number	Title (A Side/B Side)	Yr	VG	VG+	NM
❏ 103	While Walking/No No	1957	75.00	150.00	300.00

LOST-NITE

Number	Title (A Side/B Side)	Yr	VG	VG+	NM
❏ 184	While Walking/No No	196?	—	3.00	6.00

—Reissue

MAIN LINE

Number	Title (A Side/B Side)	Yr	VG	VG+	NM
❏ 103	While Walking/No No	1958	50.00	100.00	200.00

FABULONS, THE (1)

45s

EMBER

Number	Title (A Side/B Side)	Yr	VG	VG+	NM
❏ 1069	Smoke From Your Cigarette/Give Me Back My Ring	1960	6.25	12.50	25.00

—Black label

Number	Title (A Side/B Side)	Yr	VG	VG+	NM
❏ 1069	Smoke From Your Cigarette/Give Me Back My Ring	1960	12.50	25.00	50.00

—White label

FABULONS, THE (2)   Also see THE TIKIS AND THE FABULONS.

45s

TOWER

Number	Title (A Side/B Side)	Yr	VG	VG+	NM
❏ 259	Since You've Been Gone/Don't Ask Me	1966	3.75	7.50	15.00

FABULOUS COUNTS, THE

45s

MOIRA

Number	Title (A Side/B Side)	Yr	VG	VG+	NM
❏ 103	Jan Jan/Girl from Kenya	1969	2.50	5.00	10.00
❏ 105	Dirty Red/Scrambled Eggs	1970	3.75	7.50	15.00
❏ 108	Get Down People/Lunar Funk	1970	2.50	5.00	10.00

Albums

COTILLION

Number	Title (A Side/B Side)	Yr	VG	VG+	NM
❏ SD 9011	Jan Jan	1969	25.00	50.00	100.00
❏ SD 9011	Jan Jan	199?	3.00	6.00	12.00

—Reissue; superficially almost identical to original

F

Number	Title (A Side/B Side)	Yr	VG	VG+	NM

FABULOUS FARQUAHR See FARQUAHR.

FABULOUS FIVE, THE
45s
KING
| ❏ 5220 | Janie Made a Monster/Gettin' Old | 1959 | 3.75 | 7.50 | 15.00 |

FABULOUS FLAMES, THE (1)
45s
BAY-TONE
| ❏ 102 | Do You Remember/Get to Stepping | 1961 | 10.00 | 20.00 | 40.00 |
| ❏ 105 | Lover/I'm So All Alone | 1961 | 12.50 | 25.00 | 50.00 |
REX
| ❏ 3000 | Josephine/My Joan | 1958 | 30.00 | 60.00 | 120.00 |

FABULOUS FLAMES, THE (2) For records on Harlem, see THE FLAMES.

FABULOUS FOUR, THE
45s
BRASS
❏ 311	Now You Cry/Got to Get Her Back	1964	5.00	10.00	20.00
❏ 314	Who Could It Be/Happy	1964	5.00	10.00	20.00
❏ 316	I'm Always Doing Something Wrong/Young Blood	1964	5.00	10.00	20.00
CHANCELLOR
❏ 1062	In the Chapel in the Moonlight/Mr. Twist	1960	6.25	12.50	25.00
❏ 1068	Let's Try Again/Precious Moments	1961	6.25	12.50	25.00
❏ 1078	Why Do Fools Fall in Love/Sounds of Summer	1961	10.00	20.00	40.00
❏ 1085	Prisoner of Love/Betty Ann	1961	20.00	40.00	80.00
❏ 1090	Everybody Knows/I'm Coming Home	1961	5.00	10.00	20.00
❏ 1098	Mr. Twist/Everybody Knows	1961	5.00	10.00	20.00
❏ 1102	Forever/(It's No) Sin	1962	6.25	12.50	25.00
CORAL
❏ 62479	Now You Cry/Got to Get Her Back	1966	3.75	7.50	15.00
MELIC
❏ 4114	Welcome Me Home/Oop Shoobee Doop	1962	12.50	25.00	50.00

FABULOUS JOKERS, THE
Albums
MONUMENT
| ❏ MLP-8059 [M] | Guitars Extraordinaire | 1966 | 25.00 | 50.00 | 100.00 |
| ❏ SLP-18059 [S] | Guitars Extraordinaire | 1966 | 37.50 | 75.00 | 150.00 |

FABULOUS PACK, THE See TERRY KNIGHT AND THE PACK.

FABULOUS PEARL DEVINES, THE
45s
ALCO
| ❏ 101 | You've Been Gone/So Lonely | 1963 | 100.00 | 200.00 | 400.00 |

FABULOUS PEPS, THE
45s
D-TOWN
| ❏ 1049 | You Never Had It So Good/Detroit, Michigan | 1965 | 10.00 | 20.00 | 40.00 |
—As "The Peps"
| ❏ 1060 | Thinking About You/This I Pray | 1965 | 10.00 | 20.00 | 40.00 |
—As "The Peps"
| ❏ 1065 | My Love Looks Good on You/Speak Your Peace | 1966 | 12.50 | 25.00 | 50.00 |
GE GE
| ❏ 503 | This Love I Have for You/She's Going to Leave You | 1965 | 10.00 | 20.00 | 40.00 |
PREMIUM STUFF
❏ 1	Why Are You Blowing My Mind/I Can't Get Right	1967	10.00	20.00	40.00
❏ 3	So Fine/I'll Never Be the Same Again	1967	10.00	20.00	40.00
❏ 7	Gypsy Woman/Why Are You Blowing My Mind	1967	10.00	20.00	40.00
WEE-3
❏ 233	With These Eyes/I've Been Trying	1967	7.50	15.00	30.00
WHEELSVILLE
❏ 109	With These Eyes/Light of My Life	1968	3.00	6.00	12.00

FABULOUS RHINESTONES, THE
45s
JUST SUNSHINE
❏ 500	What a Wonderful Thing We Have/Nothing New	1972	—	2.50	5.00
❏ 500 [PS]	What a Wonderful Thing We Have/Nothing New	1972	—	3.00	6.00
❏ 501	Free/Live It Out to the End	1972	—	2.50	5.00
❏ 509	Freewheelin'/Whitecaps	1973	—	2.50	5.00
Albums
JUST SUNSHINE
❏ 1	The Fabulous Rhinestones	1972	3.00	6.00	12.00
❏ 9	Freewheelin'	1973	3.00	6.00	12.00

FABULOUS UPTONES, THE
45s
TULIP
| ❏ 100 | New Love I've Found/Turtle | 1962 | 75.00 | 150.00 | 300.00 |

FABULOUS VALIENTS, THE
45s
HOLIDAY
| ❏ 61005 | Your Golden Teardrops/Carmelita | 1962 | 62.50 | 125.00 | 250.00 |

FACENDA, JOHN (NARRATOR)
Albums
MANUSCRIPT
| ❏ MLP-571 [M] | The Nativity | 1957 | 10.00 | 20.00 | 40.00 |
—Original Philadelphia-area issue; gatefold with 12-page booklet
RCA VICTOR
| ❏ LOP-1504 [M] | The Nativity | 1958 | 7.50 | 15.00 | 30.00 |
—National reissue of Manuscript LP; very similar to original issue

FACENDA, TOMMY
45s
ATLANTIC
❏ 45-51	High School U.S.A.-Virginia/Plea of Love	1959	10.00	20.00	40.00
❏ 45-52	High School U.S.A.-New York City/Plea of Love	1959	10.00	20.00	40.00
❏ 45-53	High School U.S.A.-North & South Carolina/Plea of Love	1959	10.00	20.00	40.00
❏ 45-54	High School U.S.A.-Washington, D.C./Plea of Love	1959	10.00	20.00	40.00
❏ 45-55	High School U.S.A.-Philadelphia/Plea of Love	1959	10.00	20.00	40.00
❏ 45-56	High School U.S.A.-Detroit/Plea of Love	1959	10.00	20.00	40.00
❏ 45-57	High School U.S.A.-Pittsburgh/Plea of Love	1959	10.00	20.00	40.00
❏ 45-58	High School U.S.A.-Minneapolis-St. Paul/Plea of Love	1959	10.00	20.00	40.00
❏ 45-59	High School U.S.A.-Florida/Plea of Love	1959	10.00	20.00	40.00
❏ 45-60	High School U.S.A.-Newark, N.J./Plea of Love	1959	10.00	20.00	40.00
❏ 45-61	High School U.S.A.-Boston/Plea of Love	1959	10.00	20.00	40.00
❏ 45-62	High School U.S.A.-Cleveland/Plea of Love	1959	10.00	20.00	40.00
❏ 45-63	High School U.S.A.-Buffalo/Plea of Love	1959	10.00	20.00	40.00
❏ 45-64	High School U.S.A.-Hartford, Conn./Plea of Love	1959	10.00	20.00	40.00
❏ 45-65	High School U.S.A.-Nashville/Plea of Love	1959	10.00	20.00	40.00
❏ 45-66	High School U.S.A.-Indianapolis/Plea of Love	1959	10.00	20.00	40.00
❏ 45-67	High School U.S.A.-Chicago/Plea of Love	1959	10.00	20.00	40.00
❏ 45-68	High School U.S.A.-New Orleans/Plea of Love	1959	10.00	20.00	40.00
❏ 45-69	High School U.S.A.-St. Louis & Kansas City/Plea of Love	1959	10.00	20.00	40.00
❏ 45-70	High School U.S.A.-Georgia, Alabama/Plea of Love	1959	10.00	20.00	40.00
❏ 45-71	High School U.S.A.-Cincinnati/Plea of Love	1959	10.00	20.00	40.00
❏ 45-72	High School U.S.A.-Memphis/Plea of Love	1959	10.00	20.00	40.00
❏ 45-73	High School U.S.A.-Los Angeles/Plea of Love	1959	10.00	20.00	40.00
❏ 45-74	High School U.S.A.-San Francisco/Plea of Love	1959	10.00	20.00	40.00
❏ 45-75	High School U.S.A.-Texas/Plea of Love	1959	10.00	20.00	40.00
❏ 45-76	High School U.S.A.-Seattle, Portland/Plea of Love	1959	10.00	20.00	40.00
❏ 45-77	High School U.S.A.-Denver/Plea of Love	1959	10.00	20.00	40.00
❏ 45-78	High School U.S.A.-Oklahoma/Plea of Love	1959	10.00	20.00	40.00
❏ 2057	Bubba Ditty/I Don't Know	1960	5.00	10.00	20.00
LEGRAND
❏ 1001	High School U.S.A./Give Me Another Chance	1959	6.25	12.50	25.00
—Original pressings have purple labels
| ❏ 1001 | High School U.S.A./Give Me Another Chance | 196? | 3.75 | 7.50 | 15.00 |
—Later pressings have red and gold labels
NASCO
| ❏ 6018 | Little Baby/You Are My Everything | 1958 | 6.25 | 12.50 | 25.00 |

FACES Also see SMALL FACES; ROD STEWART; RONNIE WOOD.
45s
WARNER BROS.
| ❏ 7393 | Around the Phynth/Wicked Messenger | 1970 | 2.50 | 5.00 | 10.00 |
—As "Small Faces"
❏ 7442	Real Good Time/Real Wheel Skid	1970	2.50	5.00	10.00
❏ 7483	Maybe I'm Amazed/Oh Lord I'm Browned Off	1971	2.00	4.00	8.00
❏ 7545	Stay with Me/You're So Rude	1971	—	3.00	6.00
❏ 7681	Cindy Incidentally/Skewiff (Mend the Fuse)	1973	—	2.50	5.00
❏ 7681 [PS]	Cindy Incidentally/Skewiff (Mend the Fuse)	1973	—	3.00	6.00
❏ 7711	Ooh-La-La/Borstal Boys	1973	—	2.50	5.00
Albums
WARNER BROS.
❏ WS 1851	First Step	197?	3.00	6.00	12.00
—Later pressings have "faces." on front cover
| ❏ WS 1851 | First Step | 1970 | 5.00 | 10.00 | 20.00 |
—First pressings have "small faces." on front cover
| ❏ WS 1892 | Long Player | 1971 | 3.75 | 7.50 | 15.00 |
| ❏ BS 2574 | A Nod Is As Good As a Wink...To a Blind Horse | 1971 | 3.75 | 7.50 | 15.00 |
—Green label
| ❏ BS 2574 | A Nod Is As Good As a Wink...To a Blind Horse | 1973 | 3.00 | 6.00 | 12.00 |
—"Burbank" palm trees label
| ❏ BS 2665 | Ooh La La | 1973 | 3.00 | 6.00 | 12.00 |
—"Burbank" palm trees label
| ❏ BS 2665 | Ooh La La | 1973 | 3.75 | 7.50 | 15.00 |
—Green label
| ❏ BS 2897 | Snakes and Ladders: The Best of Faces | 1976 | 3.00 | 6.00 | 12.00 |
| ❏ ST-93718 | Long Player | 1971 | 5.00 | 10.00 | 20.00 |
—Capitol Record Club edition

FACES, THE
45s
IGUANA
| ❏ 601 | Christmas/New Year's Resolution | 1965 | 25.00 | 50.00 | 100.00 |
REGINA
| ❏ 326 | Skier Jones/What Is This Dream (I Have) | 1965 | 6.25 | 12.50 | 25.00 |
| ❏ 328 | I'll Walk Alone/I Didn't Want Her | 1965 | 6.25 | 12.50 | 25.00 |

FACTORY, THE Lowell George was in this group before LITTLE FEAT.
45s
UNI
| ❏ 55005 | Smile, Let Your Life Begin/When I Was An Apple | 1967 | 3.00 | 6.00 | 12.00 |

FAHEY, JOHN
45s
VANGUARD
| ❏ 35076 | A March for Martin Luther King/Singing Bridge | 1968 | 3.00 | 6.00 | 12.00 |
Albums
REPRISE
| ❏ MS 2089 | Of Rivers and Religions | 1972 | 5.00 | 10.00 | 20.00 |
| ❏ MS 2145 | After the Ball | 1973 | 5.00 | 10.00 | 20.00 |
RIVERBOAT
| ❏ RB-1 [M] | The Transfiguration of Blind Joe Death | 1965 | 50.00 | 100.00 | 200.00 |
—Original issue of 50 copies with booklet, hand-written labels and no "Volume 5" anywhere on the cover
| ❏ RB-1 [M] | The Transfiguration of Blind Joe Death | 1967 | 15.00 | 30.00 | 60.00 |
—Green cover with booklet; "Volume 5" added to back cover
SHANACHIE
| ❏ 97006 | God, Time and Causality | 1990 | 3.75 | 7.50 | 15.00 |
TABLE OF THE ELEMENTS
| ❏ 38 [(2)] | Georgia Stomps, Atlanta Struts, and Other Contemporary Dance Favorites | 1999 | 5.00 | 10.00 | 20.00 |
TAKOMA
| ❏ (# unknown) | Blind Joe Death | 1959 | 50.00 | 100.00 | 200.00 |
—Original edition of 1,000 has a white cover with "Blind Joe Death" on one side and "John Fahey" on the other; possibly pressed by RCA Victor Custom Division; no Berkeley, California address on cover

Number	Title (A Side/B Side)	Yr	VG	VG+	NM
❏ C-1002	Blind Joe Death	1964	12.50	25.00	50.00

—White cover, similar to first edition, except it has a Berkeley, California address on cover; six tracks were re-recorded for this edition

❏ C-1002	Volume 1: Blind Joe Death	1967	10.00	20.00	40.00

—Psychedelic gold and blue cover; the entire album was re-recorded for this edition, including the six songs re-recorded for the first Berkeley edition and one song not on the white-cover editions, "I'm Gonna Do All I Can For My Lord"

❏ C-1002	Volume 1: Blind Joe Death	1968	3.75	7.50	15.00

—Blue and white cover with "Stereo" added to upper left

❏ C-1003	Death Chants, Break Downs & Military Waltzes	1964	15.00	30.00	60.00

—First cover is white with block print with title on cover as above

❏ C-1003	Death Chants, Breakdowns and Military Waltzes Vol. II	1965	12.50	25.00	50.00

—Second cover is white with what looks like handwritten print; title is as listed above and "Vol. II" is added to the lower left corner

❏ C-1003	Volume 2: Death Chants, Breakdowns & Military Waltzes	1967	10.00	20.00	40.00

—Psychedelic gold and orange cover; most of the album was re-recorded for this edition

❏ C-1003	Volume 2: Death Chants, Breakdowns & Military Waltzes	1968	3.75	7.50	15.00

—Orange and white cover with orange lettering

❏ C-1004	Dance of Death & Other Plantation Favorites/ John Fahey Vol. 3	1964	15.00	30.00	60.00

—White cover with block lettering

❏ C-1004	Volume 3: The Dance of Death & Other Plantation Favorites	1967	10.00	20.00	40.00

—Psychedelic gold and brown cover

❏ C-1004	Volume 3: The Dance of Death & Other Plantation Favorites	1968	3.75	7.50	15.00

—Brown and white cover

❏ C-1008	Vol. 4: The Great San Bernardino Birthday Party	1966	7.50	15.00	30.00

—First pressings have a discography on the back cover

❏ C-1008	Vol. 4: The Great San Bernardino Birthday Party	1968	3.00	6.00	12.00

—Without discography on back cover

❏ C-1014	Days Have Gone By Volume 6	1967	7.50	15.00	30.00

—With booklet

❏ C-1014	Days Have Gone By Volume 6	1968	3.00	6.00	12.00

—Without booklet

❏ C-1019	The Voice of the Turtle	197?	3.75	7.50	15.00

—Later pressings with no gatefold

❏ C-1019	The Voice of the Turtle	1971	7.50	15.00	30.00

—With gatefold jacket and booklet

❏ C-1020	The New Possibility: John Fahey's Guitar Soli Christmas Album	1968	6.25	12.50	25.00

—Originals with back cover liner notes

❏ C-1020	The New Possibility: John Fahey's Guitar Soli Christmas Album	197?	3.75	7.50	15.00

—Later pressings with no liner notes

❏ C-1030	America	197?	3.75	7.50	15.00

—Later pressings with no gatefold

❏ C-1030	America	1972	6.25	12.50	25.00

—With gatefold jacket and booklet

❏ C-1035	Fare Forward Voyagers	1973	5.00	10.00	20.00
❏ C-1043	Old Fashioned Love	1975	3.75	7.50	15.00
❏ C-1045	Christmas with John Fahey, Vol. 2	1975	3.75	7.50	15.00
❏ C-1058	The Best of John Fahey 1959-1977	1977	3.75	7.50	15.00
❏ TAK-7002	Blind Joe Death	1979	3.00	6.00	12.00

—Reissue of 1002

❏ TAK-7003	Death Chants, Breakdowns and Military Waltzes	198?	3.00	6.00	12.00

—Reissue of 1003

❏ TAK-7004	Dance of Death and Other Plantation Favorites	198?	3.00	6.00	12.00

—Reissue of 1004

❏ TAK-7015	The Transfiguration of Blind Joe Death	198?	3.00	6.00	12.00

—Reissue of 9015

❏ TAK-7020	The New Possibility: John Fahey's Guitar Soli Christmas Album	198?	3.00	6.00	12.00

—Reissue of 1020

❏ TAK-7035	Fare Forward Voyagers	198?	3.00	6.00	12.00

—Reissue of 1035

❏ TAK-7043	Old Fashioned Love	198?	3.00	6.00	12.00

—Reissue of 1043

❏ TAK-7045	Christmas with John Fahey, Vol. 2	198?	3.00	6.00	12.00

—Reissue of 1045

❏ TAK-7058	The Best of John Fahey 1959-1977	198?	3.00	6.00	12.00

—Reissue of 1058

❏ TAK-7069	John Fahey Visits Washington, D.C.	1979	3.00	6.00	12.00
❏ TAK-7085	Yes! Jesus Loves Me	1980	3.00	6.00	12.00
❏ TAK-7089	Live in Tasmania	198?	3.00	6.00	12.00
❏ TAK-7102	Railroads I	1981	3.00	6.00	12.00
❏ R-9015	The Transfiguration of Blind Joe Death	1969	5.00	10.00	20.00

—Reissue of Riverboat RB-1; logo added to lower right front cover, and the drawing in the center is much more green than on 1967 Riverboat covers

TERRA
❏ T-2	Requia	1985	2.50	5.00	10.00

—Reissue of Vanguard 79259

VANGUARD
❏ VSD 55/56 [(2)]	Essential John Fahey	1974	5.00	10.00	20.00
❏ VRS-9259 [M]	Requia	1968	6.25	12.50	25.00
❏ VSD-79259 [S]	Requia	1968	5.00	10.00	20.00
❏ VSD-79293	The Yellow Princess	1969	5.00	10.00	20.00

VARRICK
❏ VR-002	John Fahey Christmas Guitar, Volume 1	1982	3.75	7.50	15.00
❏ VR-008	Let Go	1983	3.75	7.50	15.00
❏ VR-012	Popular Songs of Christmas and New Year's	1983	3.75	7.50	15.00
❏ VR-019	Rain Forests, Oceans & Other Themes	1985	3.00	6.00	12.00
❏ VR-028	I Remember Blind Joe Death	1987	3.00	6.00	12.00

FAIR, YVONNE
45s
DADE
❏ 1851	Straighten Up/Say Yeah Yeah	1963	3.00	6.00	12.00
❏ 5006	Straighten Up/Say Yeah Yeah	1963	5.00	10.00	20.00

KING
❏ 5594	I Found You/If I Knew	1962	3.75	7.50	15.00

—With the James Brown Band

❏ 5654	Tell Me Why/Say So Long	1962	3.75	7.50	15.00

—With James Brown

Number	Title (A Side/B Side)	Yr	VG	VG+	NM
❏ 5687	It Hurts to Be in Love/You Can Make It If You Try	1962	3.75	7.50	15.00

—With James Brown

❏ 6017	Tell Me Why/You Can Make It If You Try	1966	2.00	4.00	8.00

MOTOWN
❏ 1306	Funky Music Sho Nuff Turns Me On/ Let Your Hair Down	1974	—	3.50	7.00
❏ 1323	Walk Out the Door If You Wanna/ It Should Have Been Me	1974	—	3.50	7.00
❏ 1323 [PS]	Walk Out the Door If You Wanna/ It Should Have Been Me	1974	2.50	5.00	10.00
❏ 1344	It's Bad for Me to See You/You Can't Judge a Book By Its Cover	1975	—	3.50	7.00
❏ 1354 [PS]	Love Ain't No Toy/It's Bad for Me to See You	1975	—	3.50	7.00
❏ 1384	It Should Have Been Me/ Tell Me Something Good	1976	—	3.00	6.00

SMASH
❏ 2030	Just As Sure (As You Play, You Must Pay)/ Baby, Baby, Baby	1966	2.50	5.00	10.00

SOUL
❏ 35075	Stay a Little Longer/ We Should Never Be Lonely My Love	1970	2.00	4.00	8.00

Albums
MOTOWN
❏ M6-832S1	The Bitch Is Black	1975	7.50	15.00	30.00

FAIRLANES, THE
45s
ARGO
❏ 5357	Little Girl, Little Girl/Comin' After You	1960	7.50	15.00	30.00

CONTINENTAL
❏ 1001	Writing This Letter/Playboy	1961	75.00	150.00	300.00

DART
❏ 109	Just for Me/Bullseye	1959	20.00	40.00	80.00

LUCKY SEVEN
❏ 102	Seventeen Steps/Johnny Rhythm	1959	15.00	30.00	60.00

MINARET
❏ 103	The Dagwood/I'm Not the Kind of Guy	1962	5.00	10.00	20.00

RADIANT
❏ 101	Baby Baby/Tell Me	1964	62.50	125.00	250.00

REPRISE
❏ 20213	Surf Train/Lonely Weekends	1963	7.50	15.00	30.00

FAIRPORT CONVENTION Also see SANDY DENNY; RICHARD THOMPSON.
45s
A&M
❏ 1108	Fotheringay/I'll Keep It with Me	1969	3.00	6.00	12.00
❏ 1155	Genesis Hall/Si Tu Dois Partie	1969	3.00	6.00	12.00
❏ 1333	Journeyman's Grace/ The World Has Surely Lost Its Head	1972	2.00	4.00	8.00
❏ 1348	John Lee/The Time Is Near	1972	2.00	4.00	8.00

Albums
A&M
❏ SP-3530 [(2)]	The Fairport Chronicles	1976	3.75	7.50	15.00
❏ SP-3603	Fairport Nine	1974	3.00	6.00	12.00

—Early reissue of 4407

❏ SP-4185	Fairport Convention	1969	3.75	7.50	15.00

—Not a reissue of Cotillion LP, but the US issue of the second UK LP "What We Did On Our Holidays"

❏ SP-4206	Unhalfbricking	1969	3.75	7.50	15.00
❏ SP-4257	Liege and Lief	1970	3.75	7.50	15.00
❏ SP-4265	Full House	1970	3.75	7.50	15.00
❏ SP-4316	Angel Delight	1971	3.75	7.50	15.00
❏ SP-4333	"Babbacombe" Lee	1972	3.75	7.50	15.00
❏ SP-4383	Rosie	1973	3.75	7.50	15.00
❏ SP-4407	Fairport Nine	1973	3.75	7.50	15.00
❏ SP-6016 [(2)]	The Fairport Chronicles	198?	3.00	6.00	12.00

—Reissue of 3530

ANTILLES
❏ 7054	Gottle O' Geer	1976	3.00	6.00	12.00

CARTHAGE
❏ CGLP-4417	Full House	198?	2.50	5.00	10.00

—Reissue of A&M 4265

❏ CGLP-4418	Unhalfbricking	198?	2.50	5.00	10.00

—Reissue of A&M 4206

❏ CGLP-4430	What We Did on Our Holidays	198?	2.50	5.00	10.00

—Reissue of A&M 4185 with UK title restored

COTILLION
❏ 9024 [M]	Fairport Convention	1968	20.00	40.00	80.00

—Mono is white label promo only; "DJ Copy Monaural" sticker on front cover

❏ SD 9024 [S]	Fairport Convention	1968	7.50	15.00	30.00

HANNIBAL
❏ HNBL-1319	House Full	1986	2.50	5.00	10.00
❏ HNBL-1329	Heyday	1987	2.50	5.00	10.00

ISLAND
❏ ILPS-9285	Fairport Live/A Movable Feast	1974	3.00	6.00	12.00
❏ ILPS-9313	Rising for the Moon	1975	3.00	6.00	12.00
❏ 90678	In Real Time — Live '87	1987	2.50	5.00	10.00

VARRICK
❏ VR-023	Gladys' Leap	1986	2.50	5.00	10.00
❏ VR-029	Expletive Delighted!	1987	2.50	5.00	10.00

FAITH, ADAM
45s
AMY
❏ 895	The First Time/So Long Baby	1964	3.75	7.50	15.00
❏ 899	We Are in Love/What Now	1964	3.75	7.50	15.00
❏ 913	It's Alright/I Just Don't Know	1964	3.75	7.50	15.00
❏ 922	Talk About Love/Stop Feeling Sorry for Yourself	1965	3.75	7.50	15.00
❏ 936	Don't You Know/Someone's Taken Marie Away	1965	3.75	7.50	15.00

CAPITOL
❏ 5543	I'm Used to Losing You/ I Don't Need That Kind of Lovin'	1965	2.50	5.00	10.00
❏ 5699	To Make a Big Man Cry/Here's Another Day	1966	2.50	5.00	10.00

CUB
❏ 9061	What Do You Want/From Now Until September	1960	5.00	10.00	20.00
❏ 9068	Poor Me/The Reason	1960	5.00	10.00	20.00

F

Number	Title (A Side/B Side)	Yr	VG	VG+	NM
❑ 9074	I Did What You Told Me/ When Johnny Comes Marching Home	1960	5.00	10.00	20.00
DOT					
❑ 16405	Don't That Beat All/Mix Me a Person	1962	3.75	7.50	15.00
LAURIE					
❑ 3455	Daddy, What'll Happen to Me/ Cowman, Milk Your Cow	1968	2.00	4.00	8.00
Albums					
AMY					
❑ 8005 [M]	Adam Faith	1965	6.25	12.50	25.00
❑ S-8005 [S]	Adam Faith	1965	0.50	15.00	30.00
MGM					
❑ E-3951 [M]	England's Top Singer	1961	10.00	20.00	40.00
❑ SE-3951 [S]	England's Top Singer	1961	12.50	25.00	50.00

FAITH, PERCY
45s
COLUMBIA

Number	Title (A Side/B Side)	Yr	VG	VG+	NM
❑ 1-607	I Cross My Fingers/Valencia	1950	5.00	10.00	20.00
—*Microgroove 33 1/3 rpm 7-inch single*					
❑ 1-619 (?)	Violins from Nowhere/Tzin-Tzun-Tzan	1950	5.00	10.00	20.00
—*Microgroove 33 1/3 rpm 7-inch single*					
❑ 1-681 (?)	They Can't Take That Away from Me/If I Had a Magic Carpet	1950	5.00	10.00	20.00
—*Microgroove 33 1/3 rpm 7-inch single*					
❑ 1-699 (?)	I Was Dancing with Someone/Friendly Star	1950	5.00	10.00	20.00
—*Microgroove 33 1/3 rpm 7-inch single*					
❑ 1-752	All My Love/This Is the Time	1950	4.50	9.00	18.00
—*Microgroove 33 1/3 rpm 7-inch single*					
❑ 6-752	All My Love/This Is the Time	1950	3.75	7.50	15.00
❑ 1-812 (?)	Brazilian Sleighride/What Is This Thing Called Love	1950	5.00	10.00	20.00
—*Microgroove 33 1/3 rpm 7-inch single*					
❑ 6-812 (?)	Brazilian Sleighride/What Is This Thing Called Love	1950	3.75	7.50	15.00
❑ 1-830 (?)	Green Grass/I'm in the Middle of a Riddle	1950	4.50	9.00	18.00
—*Microgroove 33 1/3 rpm 7-inch single*					
❑ 6-830 (?)	Green Grass/I'm in the Middle of a Riddle	1950	3.75	7.50	15.00
❑ 1-841 (?)	Christmas in My Heart/Sleigh Ride	1950	5.00	10.00	20.00
—*Microgroove 33 1/3 rpm 7-inch single*					
❑ 6-841 (?)	Christmas in My Heart/Sleigh Ride	1950	3.75	7.50	15.00
❑ 1-899	Christmas In Killarney/Norah	1950	5.00	10.00	20.00
—*Microgroove 33 1/3 rpm 7-inch single*					
❑ 6-899	Christmas In Killarney/Norah	1950	3.75	7.50	15.00
❑ 10010	Theme from "Chinatown"/Tubular Bells	1974	—	2.00	4.00
❑ 10098	Orange Blossom Special/1,2,3,4	1975	—	2.00	4.00
❑ 10165	El Bimbo/Cherry Cherry	1975	—	2.00	4.00
❑ 10233	Summer Place '76/Chompin'	1975	—	2.00	4.00
❑ 10301	Emmanuelle-The Joys of a Woman/Ding Dong	1976	—	2.00	4.00
❑ 31500 [S]	Non Dimenticar/Tropical Merengue	1962	2.00	4.00	8.00
❑ 31501 [S]	The Syncopated Clock/Delicado	1962	2.00	4.00	8.00
❑ 31502 [S]	The Rain in Spain/Till	1962	2.00	4.00	8.00
❑ 31503 [S]	Jamaican Rhumba/ They Can't Take That Away from Me	1962	2.00	4.00	8.00
❑ 31504 [S]	Swedish Rhapsody/All My Love	1962	2.00	4.00	8.00
❑ 31536 [S]	(contents unknown)	1962	2.00	4.00	8.00
❑ 31537 [S]	(contents unknown)	1962	2.00	4.00	8.00
❑ 31538 [S]	(contents unknown)	1962	2.00	4.00	8.00
❑ 31539 [S]	Maxine/The Minute Samba	1962	2.00	4.00	8.00
❑ 31540 [S]	(contents unknown)	1962	2.00	4.00	8.00
—*The above 10 are Columbia "Stereo 7" singles*					
❑ 39155	Zing Zing/Kiss and Promise	1951	3.75	7.50	15.00
❑ 39192	The Loveliest Night of the Year/You Are the One	1951	3.75	7.50	15.00
❑ 39257	No One But You/Goodbye John	1951	3.75	7.50	15.00
❑ 39329	Nervous Gavotte/Hot Canary	1951	3.75	7.50	15.00
❑ 39356	Carousel Waltz/ When I'm Not Near the Girl I Love	1951	3.00	6.00	12.00
❑ 39357	While We're Young/The Girl that I Marry	1951	3.00	6.00	12.00
❑ 39358	A Kiss in the Dark/Valse Huguette	1951	3.00	6.00	12.00
❑ 39359	Waltz in Swingtown/I'll Take Romance	1951	3.00	6.00	12.00
—*The above four comprise a box set*					
❑ 39426	Black Ball Perry Line/Wondrous Word	1951	3.75	7.50	15.00
❑ 39491	Fiddle Derby/March of the Siamese Children	1951	3.75	7.50	15.00
❑ 39528	When the Saints Go Marching In/I Want to Be Near You	1951	3.75	7.50	15.00
❑ 39559	Sleigh Ride/Christmas in Killarney	1951	3.75	7.50	15.00
❑ 39613	If I Loved You/Dizzy Fingers	1951	3.75	7.50	15.00
❑ 39638	Would You/I Talk to the Trees	1952	3.00	6.00	12.00
❑ 39640	Flight 33 1/3/Ba-Tu-Ca-Da	1952	2.50	5.00	10.00
❑ 39641	One Night of Love/My Shawl	1952	2.50	5.00	10.00
❑ 39642	Brazilian Sleighride/ What Is This Thing Called Love	1952	2.50	5.00	10.00
❑ 39643	Beautiful Love/Nightingale	1952	2.50	5.00	10.00
—*The above four comprise a box set*					
❑ 39664	Carefree/Invitation	1952	3.00	6.00	12.00
❑ 39708	Delicado/Festival	1952	3.00	6.00	12.00
❑ 39732	Delicado/The Gandy Dancers' Ball	1952	2.50	5.00	10.00
—*B-side by Frankie Laine; this is part of a various-artists box set*					
❑ 39781	Enlloro/Jungle Fantasy	1952	2.50	5.00	10.00
❑ 39782	Caribbean Night/Cu-Tu-Gu-Ru	1952	2.50	5.00	10.00
❑ 39783	Minute Samba/The Girl with the Spanish Drawl	1952	2.50	5.00	10.00
❑ 39784	Oye Negra/Jamaican Rhumba	1952	2.50	5.00	10.00
—*The above four comprise a box set*					
❑ 39790	Jamaican Rhumba/Dadu	1952	3.00	6.00	12.00
❑ 39874	Amorada/Funny Fellow	1952	3.00	6.00	12.00
❑ 39907	Over the Mountain/Caress	1952	3.00	6.00	12.00
❑ 39944	The Song from Moulin Rouge (Where Is Your Heart)/Swedish Rhapsody	1953	2.50	5.00	10.00
—*Vocal on A-side by Felicia Sanders*					
❑ 39998	Return to Paradise (Part 1)/ Return to Paradise (Part 2)	1953	2.50	5.00	10.00
❑ 40029	Tropic Holiday/Gaviotta	1953	2.50	5.00	10.00
❑ 40076	Many Times/In Love	1953	2.50	5.00	10.00
❑ 40115	Ev'rybody Loves Saturday Night/True or False	1953	2.50	5.00	10.00
❑ 40155	Non Dimenticar (Don't Forget)/They Can't Take That Away from Me	1954	2.50	5.00	10.00

Number	Title (A Side/B Side)	Yr	VG	VG+	NM
❑ 40174	Baubles, Bangles and Beads/ And This Is My Beloved	1954	2.50	5.00	10.00
❑ 40185	Eleanora/Dream, Dream, Dream	1954	2.50	5.00	10.00
❑ 4-40277	Song for Sweethearts/Bubbling Over	1954	2.50	5.00	10.00
❑ 40323	Rainfall/The Bandit	1954	2.50	5.00	10.00
❑ 40390	Ching-Ching-a-Ling/Petite	1954	2.50	5.00	10.00
❑ 40428	If Hearts Could Talk/Blue Mirage	1955	2.50	5.00	10.00
❑ 40482	Land of the Pharaohs/The World Is Mine	1955	2.50	5.00	10.00
❑ 40512	The Fiddling Bullfighter/Not As a Stranger	1955	2.50	5.00	10.00
❑ 40543	Tropical Merengue/We Won't Say Goodbye	1955	2.50	5.00	10.00
❑ 40588	The Rose Tattoo/Tambora	1955	2.50	5.00	10.00
❑ 40633	Valley Valparaiso/Bluebell	1956	2.50	5.00	10.00
❑ 40644	We All Need Love/Carmelita	1956	2.50	5.00	10.00
❑ 40696	With a Little Bit of Luck/The Rain in Spain	1956	2.50	5.00	10.00
❑ 40719	Wouldn't It Be Lovely/Sierra Madre	1956	2.50	5.00	10.00
❑ 40764	Baby Doll/Vagabond Waltz King	1956	2.50	5.00	10.00
❑ 40826	Till/The Last Dance	1957	2.50	5.00	10.00
❑ 40900	Italiano!/Bahama Lullaby	1957	2.50	5.00	10.00
❑ 40949	Hey Jose/What's It Like in Paree?	1957	2.50	5.00	10.00
❑ 41024	Never Till Now/Katsumi Love Theme	1957	2.50	5.00	10.00
❑ 41095	Maria/The Stars	1958	2.00	4.00	8.00
❑ 41126	The Impala Theme/Pizzicato Polka	1958	2.00	4.00	8.00
❑ 41181	Same Old Moon/Indiscreet	1958	2.00	4.00	8.00
❑ 41271	The Pyramid Dance/Quia Quia	1958	2.00	4.00	8.00
❑ 41328	Goin' Home Train/Isle of Paradise	1959	2.00	4.00	8.00
❑ 41490	Theme from "A Summer Place"/Go-Go-Po-Go	1959	2.00	4.00	8.00
❑ 41490 [PS]	Theme from "A Summer Place"/Go-Go-Po-Go	1959	3.75	7.50	15.00
❑ 41655	Theme for Young Lovers/Bimini Goombay	1960	2.00	4.00	8.00
❑ 41731	Sons and Lovers/Hawaiian Lullaby	1960	2.00	4.00	8.00
❑ 41796	Theme from "The Dark at the Top of the Stairs"/ Our Language of Love	1960	2.00	4.00	8.00
❑ 41978	The Bilbao Song/Lover's Prelude	1961	2.00	4.00	8.00
❑ 42011	At Last-Angel Face/Tammy Tell Me True	1961	2.00	4.00	8.00
❑ 42239	Brass Ring/I Just Can't Wait	1961	2.00	4.00	8.00
❑ 42333	Love Theme from "The Four Horsemen of the Apocalypse"/Theme from "Light in the Piazza"	1962	—	3.00	6.00
❑ 42423	Advise and Consent/Jacqueline's Journey	1962	—	3.00	6.00
❑ 42844	The Sound of Surf/Our Love	1963	—	3.00	6.00
❑ 42979	The Virginian/Melody from "Mahogany"	1964	—	3.00	6.00
❑ 42991	Sloop John B/This Train	1964	—	3.00	6.00
❑ 43116	Judy/Love Goddess	1964	—	3.00	6.00
❑ 43208	Kahlua/Insensatez	1965	—	3.00	6.00
❑ 43326	Love Me/We're Gonna Be Alright	1965	—	3.00	6.00
❑ 43555	Song from "The Oscar"/Glass Mountain	1966	—	3.00	6.00
❑ 43642	Cheryl/Swingin' Village	1966	—	3.00	6.00
❑ 43746	Tropic Holiday/Reza	1966	—	3.00	6.00
❑ 43846	Christmas Is.../Silver Bells	1966	—	3.00	6.00
❑ 44086	A Man and a Woman/This Hotel	1967	—	2.50	5.00
❑ 44166	Kahlua/Yellow Days	1967	—	2.50	5.00
❑ 44319	Can't Take My Eyes Off You/Windy	1967	—	2.50	5.00
❑ 44412	Theme from "The Dark at the Top of the Stairs"/ Tara's Theme (From "Gone with the Wind")	1967	—	2.50	5.00
❑ 44446	For Those in Love/There Was a Time	1968	—	2.50	5.00
❑ 44585	MacArthur Park/Elvira Madigan Theme	1968	—	2.50	5.00
❑ 44734	Zorba/A Quiet Day	1969	—	2.50	5.00
❑ 44876	The Windmills of Your Mind/Theme from "The Fox"	1969	—	2.00	4.00
❑ 44932	Theme from "A Summer Place"/Hello Tomorrow	1969	—	2.50	5.00
❑ 44987	Spinning Wheel/April Fools	1969	—	2.00	4.00
❑ 45051	Peppermint Hill and Strawberry Lane/The Time for Love Is Anytime	1969	—	2.00	4.00
❑ 45114	Airport Love Theme/Theme for Young Lovers	1970	—	2.00	4.00
❑ 45297	I Don't Know How to Love Him/Everything's Alright	1971	—	2.00	4.00
❑ 45374	Anytime of the Year/I Can Hear the Music	1971	—	2.00	4.00
❑ 45401	Theme from "Summer of '42"/Tres	1971	—	2.00	4.00
❑ 45525	Diamonds Are Forever/ Love Theme from "Mary Queen of Scots"	1972	—	2.00	4.00
❑ 45563	Love Theme from "The Godfather"/ Godfather Waltz	1972	—	2.50	5.00
❑ 45619	Theme from "Kotch"/Back's Lunch	1972	—	2.00	4.00
❑ 45868	Viva Vivaldi/We Were Having Some Fun at the Conservatory, When ...	1973	—	2.00	4.00
❑ 45945	Corazon/Crunchy Granola Suite	1973	—	2.00	4.00
❑ 46013	Euterpe/Hill Where the Lord Hides	1974	—	2.00	4.00
❑ JZSP 75661/2 [DJ]	I Will Follow You/Theme for Young Lovers	1963	3.00	6.00	12.00
—*Promo-only "Special Album Excerpt"*					
❑ JZSP 111903/4 [DJ]	Away In A Manger/We Three Kings Of Orient Are	1965	3.00	6.00	12.00
—*Promo only on green vinyl*					
❑ JZSP 119961/2 [DJ]	Christmas Is . . ./Happy Holiday	1966	2.50	5.00	10.00
—*Yellow label*					
❑ JZSP 119961/2 [DJ]	Christmas Is . . ./Happy Holiday	1967	2.50	5.00	10.00
—*White label*					
❑ JZSP 119961/2 [PS]	Christmas Is . . ./Happy Holiday	1967	3.75	7.50	15.00
—*Sleeve announces this as the 1967 Christmas Seals Record*					
DECCA					
❑ 27542	I Love You/Long Ago (and Far Away)	1951	3.00	6.00	12.00
❑ 27543	I'll Close My Eyes/There's No Holding Me	1951	3.00	6.00	12.00
—*With Hildegarde*					
❑ 27544	Amor/Spring Will Be a Little Late This Year	1951	3.00	6.00	12.00
RCA VICTOR					
❑ 47-3004	Deep Purple/Oodles of Noodles	1949	3.75	7.50	15.00
❑ 47-3063	Whirlwind/My Dream Concerto	1949	3.75	7.50	15.00
❑ 47-4001	Perpetual Motion/Solitude	1950	3.75	7.50	15.00
❑ 47-4002	Body and Soul/Cumana	1950	3.75	7.50	15.00
❑ 47-4003	Beyond the Sea/El Cumbanchero	1950	3.75	7.50	15.00
7-Inch Extended Plays					
COLUMBIA					
❑ B-1610	Would You/I Talk to the Trees//If I Loved You/ Easy to Love	195?	2.50	5.00	10.00
❑ B-1610 [PS]	Percy Faith's Magic Voices	195?	2.50	5.00	10.00
❑ B-2529	"The Song from Moulin Rouge/Swedish Rhapsody/Delicado/Invitation	1958	2.50	5.00	10.00
❑ B-2529 [PS]	Percy Faith (Hall of Fame Series)	1958	2.50	5.00	10.00
❑ B-2623	Mademoiselle De Paree/Under the Bridges of Paris//Non Dimenticar/April in Portugal	195?	2.50	5.00	10.00

Number	Title (A Side/B Side)	Yr	VG	VG+	NM
❏ B-2623 [PS]	(title unknown)	195?	2.50	5.00	10.00
❏ B-9553	If I Had My Druthers/Oh Happy Day//Matrimonial Stomp/Namely You	195?	2.50	5.00	10.00
❏ B-9553 [PS]	Li'l Abner, Vol. 3	195?	2.50	5.00	10.00
❏ B-11871	Hallelujah Chorus/Carol of the Bells//I Wonder As I Wander/What Child Is This (Greensleeves)	195?	2.50	5.00	10.00
❏ B-11871 [PS]	Hallelujah!	195?	2.50	5.00	10.00

Albums

COLUMBIA

Number	Title (A Side/B Side)	Yr	VG	VG+	NM
❏ GP 1 [(2)]	Forever Young	1968	3.75	7.50	15.00
❏ C2L 15 [(2)M]	The Columbia Album of Christmas Music	1958	7.50	15.00	30.00
—Combines CL 588 and CL 1187 into one gatefold package					
❏ CL 525 [M]	Continental Music	1955	5.00	10.00	20.00
❏ CL 550 [M]	Kismet	1955	5.00	10.00	20.00
❏ CL 577 [M]	Music from Hollywood	1955	5.00	10.00	20.00
❏ CL 588 [M]	Music of Christmas	1955	6.25	12.50	25.00
❏ CL 640 [M]	House of Flowers	1956	5.00	10.00	20.00
❏ CL 681 [M]	Delicado	1956	5.00	10.00	20.00
❏ CL 705 [M]	Music for Her	1956	5.00	10.00	20.00
❏ CL 880 [M]	Passport to Romance	1956	5.00	10.00	20.00
❏ CL 895 [M]	My Fair Lady	1957	5.00	10.00	20.00
❏ CL 955 [M]	L'il Abner	1957	5.00	10.00	20.00
❏ CL 1010 [M]	Adventure in the Sun	1957	5.00	10.00	20.00
❏ CS 1019	Held Over! Today's Great Movie Themes	1970	3.00	6.00	12.00
❏ CL 1075 [M]	Viva!	1957	5.00	10.00	20.00
❏ CL 1105 [M]	South Pacific	1957	3.75	7.50	15.00
❏ CL 1182 [M]	Touchdown!	1957	5.00	10.00	20.00
❏ CL 1187 [M]	Hallelujah!	1957	5.00	10.00	20.00
❏ CL 1188 [M]	Jubliation!	1957	5.00	10.00	20.00
❏ CL 1267 [M]	Malaguena	1958	5.00	10.00	20.00
❏ CL 1298 [M]	Porgy and Bess	1958	3.75	7.50	15.00
❏ CL 1302 [M]	A Night with Sigmund Romberg	1959	3.75	7.50	15.00
❏ CL 1322 [M]	Bouquet	1959	3.75	7.50	15.00
❏ CL 1381 [M]	Music of Christmas	1959	5.00	10.00	20.00
—Re-recorded version of CL 588 with same track order					
❏ CL 1386 [M]	A Night with Jerome Kern	1959	3.75	7.50	15.00
❏ CL 1417 [M]	Bon Voyage!	1960	3.75	7.50	15.00
❏ CL 1418 [M]	The Sound of Music	1960	3.75	7.50	15.00
❏ CL 1493 [M]	Percy Faith's Greatest Hits	1960	3.75	7.50	15.00
❏ CL 1501 [M]	Jealousy	1960	3.00	6.00	12.00
❏ CL 1570 [M]	Camelot	1960	3.00	6.00	12.00
❏ CL 1627 [M]	Tara's Theme from "Gone with the Wind" and Other Themes	1961	3.00	6.00	12.00
❏ CL 1639 [M]	Mucho Gusto! More Music of Brazil	1961	3.00	6.00	12.00
❏ CL 1681 [M]	Bouquet of Love	1962	3.00	6.00	12.00
❏ CL 1783 [M]	Hollywood's Great Themes	1962	3.00	6.00	12.00
❏ CL 1822 [M]	The Music of Brazil!	1962	3.00	6.00	12.00
❏ CL 1902 [M]	Exotic Strings	1963	3.00	6.00	12.00
❏ CL 1957 [M]	American Serenade	1963	3.00	6.00	12.00
❏ CL 2023 [M]	Themes for Young Lovers	1963	3.00	6.00	12.00
❏ CL 2024 [M]	Shangri-La!	1963	3.00	6.00	12.00
❏ CL 2108 [M]	Great Folk Themes	1964	3.00	6.00	12.00
❏ CL 2167 [M]	More Themes for Young Lovers	1964	3.00	6.00	12.00
❏ CL 2209 [M]	Love Goddess	1966	3.00	6.00	12.00
❏ CL 2279 [M]	Latin Themes for Young Lovers	1966	3.00	6.00	12.00
❏ CL 2317 [M]	Do I Hear a Waltz	1965	3.00	6.00	12.00
❏ CL 2356 [M]	Broadway Bouquet	1965	3.00	6.00	12.00
❏ CL 2405 [M]	Music of Christmas, Volume 2	1965	3.00	6.00	12.00
❏ CL 2441 [M]	Themes for the "In" Crowd	1966	3.00	6.00	12.00
❏ CL 2529 [M]	Bim Bam Boom	1966	3.00	6.00	12.00
❏ CL 2577 [M]	Christmas Is…	1966	3.00	6.00	12.00
❏ CL 2650 [M]	The Academy Award Winner and Other Great Movie Themes	1967	3.75	7.50	15.00
❏ CL 2704 [M]	Today's Themes for Young Lovers	1967	3.75	7.50	15.00
❏ CL 2810 [M]	For Those in Love	1968	5.00	10.00	20.00
❏ CL 2906 [M]	Angel of the Morning (Hit Themes for Young Lovers)	1968	5.00	10.00	20.00
❏ CL 6148 [10]	Football Songs	1950	10.00	20.00	40.00
❏ CS 8005 [S]	South Pacific	1958	6.25	12.50	25.00
❏ CS 8033 [S]	Hallelujah!	1958	6.25	12.50	25.00
❏ CS 8038 [S]	Viva!	1958	6.25	12.50	25.00
❏ CS 8081 [S]	Malaguena	1958	6.25	12.50	25.00
❏ CS 8105 [S]	Porgy and Bess	1959	5.00	10.00	20.00
❏ CS 8108 [S]	A Night with Sigmund Romberg	1959	5.00	10.00	20.00
❏ CS 8124 [S]	Bouquet	1959	3.75	7.50	15.00
❏ CS 8176 [S]	Music of Christmas	1959	3.75	7.50	15.00
❏ CS 8181 [S]	A Night with Jerome Kern	1959	5.00	10.00	20.00
❏ CS 8214 [S]	Bon Voyage!	1960	3.75	7.50	15.00
❏ CS 8215 [S]	The Sound of Music	1960	3.75	7.50	15.00
❏ CS 8292 [S]	Jealousy	1960	3.75	7.50	15.00
❏ CS 8370 [S]	Camelot	1960	3.75	7.50	15.00
❏ CS 8427 [S]	Tara's Theme from "Gone with the Wind" and Other Themes	1961	3.75	7.50	15.00
❏ CS 8439 [S]	Mucho Gusto! More Music of Brazil	1961	3.75	7.50	15.00
❏ CS 8481 [S]	Bouquet of Love	1962	3.75	7.50	15.00
❏ CS 8583 [S]	Hollywood's Great Themes	1962	3.75	7.50	15.00
❏ CS 8622 [S]	The Music of Brazil!	1962	3.75	7.50	15.00
❏ CS 8637 [R]	Percy Faith's Greatest Hits	1963	2.50	5.00	10.00
❏ PC 8637 [R]	Percy Faith's Greatest Hits	198?	2.00	4.00	8.00
—Budget-line reissue					
❏ CS 8642 [R]	Kismet	1963	2.50	5.00	10.00
❏ CS 8702 [S]	Exotic Strings	1963	3.00	6.00	12.00
❏ CS 8757 [S]	American Serenade	1963	3.00	6.00	12.00
❏ CS 8823 [S]	Themes for Young Lovers	1963	3.00	6.00	12.00
❏ CS 8824 [S]	Shangri-La!	1963	3.00	6.00	12.00
❏ CS 8908 [S]	Great Folk Themes	1964	3.00	6.00	12.00
❏ CS 8967 [S]	More Themes for Young Lovers	1964	3.00	6.00	12.00
❏ CS 9004 [R]	My Fair Lady	1964	3.00	6.00	12.00
❏ CS 9009 [S]	Love Goddess	1964	3.00	6.00	12.00
❏ CS 9079 [S]	Latin Themes for Young Lovers	1965	3.00	6.00	12.00
❏ CS 9117 [S]	Do I Hear a Waltz	1965	3.00	6.00	12.00
❏ CS 9156 [S]	Broadway Bouquet	1965	3.00	6.00	12.00
❏ CS 9205 [S]	Music of Christmas, Volume 2	1965	3.00	6.00	12.00
❏ CS 9241 [S]	Themes for the "In" Crowd	1966	3.00	6.00	12.00
❏ CS 9329 [S]	Bim Bam Boom	1966	3.00	6.00	12.00
❏ 3C 9377	Christmas Is…	198?	2.00	4.00	8.00
—Budget-line reissue					
❏ CS 9377 [S]	Christmas Is…	1966	3.00	6.00	12.00
❏ CS 9450 [S]	The Academy Award Winner and Other Great Movie Themes	1967	3.00	6.00	12.00
❏ CS 9504 [S]	Today's Themes for Young Lovers	1967	3.00	6.00	12.00
❏ CS 9610 [S]	For Those in Love	1968	3.00	6.00	12.00
❏ CS 9706 [S]	Angel of the Morning (Hit Themes for Young Lovers)	1968	3.00	6.00	12.00
❏ CS 9762	Those Were the Days	1969	3.00	6.00	12.00
❏ CS 9835	Windmills of Your Mind	1969	3.00	6.00	12.00
❏ CS 9906	Love Theme from "Romeo & Juliet"	1969	3.00	6.00	12.00
❏ CS 9983	Leaving on a Jet Plane	1970	3.00	6.00	12.00
❏ C 30097	The Beatles Album	1970	3.00	6.00	12.00
❏ G 30330 [(2)]	A Time for Love	1971	3.75	7.50	15.00
❏ C 30502	I Think I Love You	1971	2.50	5.00	10.00
❏ CQ 30502 [Q]	I Think I Love You	1971	3.75	7.50	15.00
❏ C 30800	Black Magic Woman	1971	2.50	5.00	10.00
❏ CQ 31004 [Q]	Love Theme from "Romeo & Juliet"	1971	3.75	7.50	15.00
❏ C 31042	Jesus Christ Superstar	1971	2.50	5.00	10.00
❏ C 31301	Joy	1972	2.50	5.00	10.00
❏ CQ 31301 [Q]	Joy	1972	3.75	7.50	15.00
❏ KG 31588 [(2)]	All-Time Greatest Hits	1972	3.00	6.00	12.00
❏ PG 31588 [(2)]	All-Time Greatest Hits	198?	2.50	5.00	10.00
—Budget-line reissue					
❏ CQ 31627 [Q]	Day By Day	1972	3.75	7.50	15.00
❏ KC 31627	Day By Day	1972	2.50	5.00	10.00
❏ CQ 32164 [Q]	Clair	1973	3.75	7.50	15.00
❏ KC 32164	Clair	1973	2.50	5.00	10.00
❏ KC 32380	My Love	1973	2.50	5.00	10.00
❏ C 32585	Remembering the Hits of the 60's	1973	2.50	5.00	10.00
❏ KC 32714	Corazon	1974	2.50	5.00	10.00
❏ CQ 32803 [Q]	A New Thing	1974	3.75	7.50	15.00
❏ KC 32803	A New Thing	1974	2.50	5.00	10.00
❏ PCQ 33006 [Q]	The Entertainer	1974	3.75	7.50	15.00
❏ KC 33142	Country Bouquet	1975	2.50	5.00	10.00
❏ CQ 33244 [Q]	Chinatown (Featuring "The Entertainer")	1974	3.75	7.50	15.00
❏ KC 33244	Chinatown (Featuring "The Entertainer")	1974	2.50	5.00	10.00
❏ KC 33549	Disco Party	1975	2.50	5.00	10.00
❏ CG 33606 [(2)]	Viva!/Mucho Gusto!	1975	3.00	6.00	12.00
❏ CG 33895 [(2)]	Great Moments of Percy Faith	1976	3.00	6.00	12.00
❏ KC 33915	Summer of '76	1976	2.50	5.00	10.00
❏ PC 38302	Music of Christmas	1983	2.00	4.00	8.00
❏ PC 39471	Christmas Melodies	1984	2.00	4.00	8.00
—Repackage of previously released material					

COLUMBIA LIMITED EDITION

Number	Title (A Side/B Side)	Yr	VG	VG+	NM
❏ LE 10004	Tara's Theme from "Gone with the Wind" and Other Themes	197?	2.50	5.00	10.00
❏ LE 10015	Windmills of Your Mind	197?	2.50	5.00	10.00
❏ LE 10041	Themes for the "In" Crowd	197?	2.50	5.00	10.00
❏ LE 10042	Bouquet	197?	2.50	5.00	10.00
❏ LE 10082	Music of Christmas	197?	2.50	5.00	10.00
—Brown label "Limited Edition" series; same contents as CS 8176					
❏ LE 10088	Music of Christmas, Volume 2	197?	2.50	5.00	10.00
❏ LE 10095	Great Folk Themes	197?	2.50	5.00	10.00
❏ LE 10131	Jealousy	197?	2.50	5.00	10.00
❏ LE 10185	Those Were the Days	197?	2.50	5.00	10.00
❏ LE 10350	Hallelujah!	197?	2.50	5.00	10.00

COLUMBIA SPECIAL PRODUCTS

Number	Title (A Side/B Side)	Yr	VG	VG+	NM
❏ P 13091	Broadway Bouquet	197?	2.00	4.00	8.00
❏ P 13277	Leaving on a Jet Plane	197?	2.00	4.00	8.00
❏ P2 13719 [(2)]	The Columbia Album of George Gershwin	197?	3.00	6.00	12.00
❏ P 13827	American Serenade	197?	2.00	4.00	8.00

HARMONY

Number	Title (A Side/B Side)	Yr	VG	VG+	NM
❏ HS 11348	Sounds of Music	1969	2.50	5.00	10.00
❏ H 30020	Younger Than Springtime	1970	2.50	5.00	10.00
❏ KH 30607	A Summer Place	1971	2.50	5.00	10.00
❏ KH 30977	Raindrops Keep Fallin'	1971	2.50	5.00	10.00
❏ KH 31777	Every Night at the Movies	1972	2.50	5.00	10.00

VOCALION

Number	Title (A Side/B Side)	Yr	VG	VG+	NM
❏ VL 3600 [M]	North and South of the Border	1958	3.75	7.50	15.00

FAITH HOPE & CHARITY

45s

MAXWELL

Number	Title (A Side/B Side)	Yr	VG	VG+	NM
❏ 805	So Much Love/Let's Try It Over	1970	—	3.00	6.00
❏ 808	Baby Don't Take Your Love/Make Love to Me	1970	—	3.00	6.00

RCA

Number	Title (A Side/B Side)	Yr	VG	VG+	NM
❏ PB-10749	You're My Peace of Mind/Rescue Me	1976	—	2.50	5.00
❏ PB-10865	Life Goes On/You've Gotta Tell Her	1976	—	2.50	5.00

RCA VICTOR

Number	Title (A Side/B Side)	Yr	VG	VG+	NM
❏ PB-10343	To Each His Own/Find a Way	1975	—	2.50	5.00
❏ PB-10542	Don't Go Looking for Love/Disco Dan	1976	—	2.50	5.00

SUSSEX

Number	Title (A Side/B Side)	Yr	VG	VG+	NM
❏ 216	Come Back and Finish What You Started/I Worship the Very Ground You Walk On	1971	—	2.50	5.00
❏ 224	No Trespassing/Ghosts Keep Haunting Me	1971	—	2.50	5.00
❏ 231	We Can Change the World/God Bless the World	1972	—	2.50	5.00
❏ 243	I Was There/Who Could Love You More Than I	1972	—	2.50	5.00
❏ 252	Who Made You Go/Heavy Love	1973	—	2.50	5.00

20TH CENTURY

Number	Title (A Side/B Side)	Yr	VG	VG+	NM
❏ 2370	Don't Pity Me/Find What You Need	1978	—	2.00	4.00
❏ 2391	How Can I Help But Love You/Keep Me Baby	1978	—	2.00	4.00

Albums

RCA VICTOR

Number	Title (A Side/B Side)	Yr	VG	VG+	NM
❏ APL1-1100	Faith, Hope & Charity	1975	3.00	6.00	12.00
❏ APL1-1827	Life Goes	1976	3.00	6.00	12.00

SUSSEX

Number	Title (A Side/B Side)	Yr	VG	VG+	NM
❏ SXSB-7019	Heavy Love	1972	3.75	7.50	15.00

FAITHFULL, MARIANNE

12-Inch Singles

ANTILLES

Number	Title (A Side/B Side)	Yr	VG	VG+	NM
❏ AN 801	Broken English (5:59)/Why D'Ya Do It	1979	2.50	5.00	10.00

ISLAND

Number	Title (A Side/B Side)	Yr	VG	VG+	NM
❏ DMD 627 [DJ]	Blue Millionaire (Long)/Blue Millionaire (Short)	1983	2.00	4.00	8.00

F

Number	Title (A Side/B Side)	Yr	VG	VG+	NM

45s
COLLECTABLES

❑ 2605	Broken English/Why D'Ya Do It	199?	—	—	3.00
—Reissue					
❑ 4238	As Tears Go By/Gloria	199?	—	—	3.00
—Reissue; B-side by Them					

ISLAND

❑ 49121	Broken English/Brain Drain	1979	—	2.50	5.00
❑ 49873	Sweetheart/For Beauty's Sake	1981	—	2.00	4.00
❑ 94997	Broken English/Why D'Ya Do It?	198?	2.50	5.00	10.00
—Gold label "Revival of the Fittest" series					
❑ 99888	Running for Our Lives/(B-side unknown)	1983	—	2.00	4.00

LONDON

❑ 1022	Sister Morphine/Something Better	1969	25.00	50.00	100.00
—Promo worth about 50% of these values.					
❑ 9697	As Tears Go By/Greensleeves	1964	3.00	6.00	12.00
❑ 9731	Come and Stay with Me/				
	What Have I Done Wrong	1965	2.50	5.00	10.00
❑ 9759	This Little Bird/Morning Sun	1965	2.50	5.00	10.00
❑ 9780	Summer Nights/The Sha-La-La Song	1965	2.50	5.00	10.00
❑ 9802	Go Away from My World/Oh Look Around You	1965	2.50	5.00	10.00
❑ 9802 [PS]	Go Away from My World/Oh Look Around You	1965	5.00	10.00	20.00
❑ 20012	Counting/Tomorrow's Calling	1966	2.50	5.00	10.00
❑ 20012 [PS]	Counting/Tomorrow's Calling	1966	5.00	10.00	20.00
❑ 20020	Is This What I Get for Loving You/				
	Tomorrow's Calling	1966	2.50	5.00	10.00

Albums
ABKCO

❑ 75471	Greatest Hits	1988	2.50	5.00	10.00
—Reissue of London PS 547					

ISLAND

❑ PRO 794 [EP]	Blazing Away Sampler	1990	5.00	10.00	20.00
—Promo-only sampler for radio					
❑ ILPS 9570	Broken English	1979	2.50	5.00	10.00
❑ ILPS 9648	Dangerous Acquaintances	1981	2.50	5.00	10.00
❑ 90039	Broken English	1983	2.00	4.00	8.00
—Reissue					
❑ 90066	A Child's Adventure	1983	2.50	5.00	10.00
❑ 90066 [DJ]	A Child's Adventure	1983	3.75	7.50	15.00
—Promo-only Quiex II audiophile pressing					
❑ 90613	Strange Weather	1987	2.50	5.00	10.00

LONDON

❑ PS 423 [R]	Marianne Faithfull	1965	3.75	7.50	15.00
❑ PS 452 [S]	Go Away from My World	1965	5.00	10.00	20.00
❑ PS 482 [S]	Faithfull Forever	1966	5.00	10.00	20.00
❑ PS 547	Greatest Hits	1969	3.75	7.50	15.00
❑ LL 3423 [M]	Marianne Faithfull	1965	5.00	10.00	20.00
❑ LL 3452 [M]	Go Away from My World	1965	3.75	7.50	15.00
❑ LL 3482 [M]	Faithfull Forever	1966	3.75	7.50	15.00

MOBILE FIDELITY

❑ 1-235	Broken English	1995	6.25	12.50	25.00
—Audiophile vinyl					

FALCONS, THE (1) Detroit R&B group. Also see EDDIE FLOYD; WILSON PICKETT.

45s
ANNA

❑ 1110	Just for Your Love/This Heart of Mine	1959	25.00	50.00	100.00

ATLANTIC

❑ 2153	Darling/Lah-Tee-Lah-Tah	1962	5.00	10.00	20.00
❑ 2179	Let's Kiss and Make Up/Take This Love I've Got	1963	5.00	10.00	20.00
❑ 2207	Oh Baby/Fine, Fine, Fine	1963	5.00	10.00	20.00

BIG WHEEL

❑ 321	I Must Love You/Love, Love, Love	1966	5.00	10.00	20.00
❑ 323/4	I Can't Help It/Standing on Guard	1966	5.00	10.00	20.00
❑ 1967	Standing On Guard/I Can't Help It	1966	5.00	10.00	20.00
❑ 1972	Good Good Feeling/You Like You Never Been				
	Loved	1966	5.00	10.00	20.00

CHESS

❑ 1743	Just for Your Love/This Heart of Mine	1959	6.25	12.50	25.00

FALCON

❑ 1006	Now That It's Over/My Only Love	1957	50.00	100.00	200.00

FLICK

❑ 001	You're So Fine/Goddess of Angels	1959	100.00	200.00	400.00
❑ 008	You Must Know I Love You/That's What I Aim to Do	1960	30.00	60.00	120.00

KUDO

❑ 661	This Heart of Mine/Romanita	1958	100.00	200.00	400.00

LUPINE

❑ 103	I Found a Love/Swim	1962	12.50	25.00	50.00
❑ 124	Lonely Nights/Has It Happened to You	1962	25.00	50.00	100.00
❑ 1003	I Found a Love/Swim	1962	12.50	25.00	50.00
❑ 1024	Lonely Nights/Has It Happened to You	1962	10.00	20.00	40.00

UNART

❑ 2013 [M]	You're So Fine/Goddess of Angels	1959	7.50	15.00	30.00
❑ 2013-S [S]	You're So Fine/Goddess of Angels	1959	25.00	50.00	100.00
—Though labeled as stereo, this seems to be rechanneled					
❑ 2022	You're Mine/Country Shack	1959	6.25	12.50	25.00

UNITED ARTISTS

❑ 0108	You're So Fine/Showtime	1973	—	2.00	4.00
—"Silver Spotlight Series" reissue					
❑ 229	The Teacher/Waiting for You	1960	5.00	10.00	20.00
❑ 255	I Plus Love Plus You/Wonderful Love	1960	5.00	10.00	20.00
❑ 289	Pow! You're in Love/Workin' Man's Song	1961	5.00	10.00	20.00
❑ 420	You're So Fine/Goddess of Angels	1962	5.00	10.00	20.00
❑ 1624	You're So Fine/Goddess of Angels	196?	2.00	4.00	8.00
—"Silver Spotlight Series" issue					

7-Inch Extended Plays
UNITED ARTISTS

❑ 10010	*The Teacher/Waiting for You/You're So Fine/				
	Goddess of Angels	1960	75.00	150.00	300.00
❑ 10010 [PS]	The Falcons	1960	75.00	150.00	300.00

Number	Title (A Side/B Side)	Yr	VG	VG+	NM

Albums
RELIC

❑ 8005	You're So Fine (The Falcons' Story				
	Part One: 1956-1959)	1987	3.00	6.00	12.00
❑ 8006	I Found a Love (The Falcons' Story				
	Part Two: 1960-1964)	1987	3.00	6.00	12.00

FALCONS, THE (2)
45s
CASH

❑ 1002	Tell Me Why/I Miss You Darling	1955	125.00	250.00	500.00

FLIP

❑ 301	Stay Mine/Du-Bi-A-Do	1954	50.00	100.00	200.00
❑ 302	You Are the Only One/Mambo Baby Tonight	1954	50.00	100.00	200.00

FALCONS, THE (U) These may be by group (1) or by group (2) or by neither.
45s
MERCURY

❑ 70940	Baby That's It/This Day	1956	15.00	30.00	60.00

SILHOUETTE

❑ 522	Can This Be Christmas/Sent Up	1957	75.00	150.00	300.00

FALLEN ANGELS, THE
45s
LAURIE

❑ 3343	Eveytime I Fall in Love/I Have Found	1966	6.25	12.50	25.00
❑ 3369	Have You Ever Lost a Love/A Little Love from				
	You Will Do	1966	6.25	12.50	25.00

PHILCO-FORD

❑ HP-23	Room at the Top/Most Children Do	1968	5.00	10.00	20.00
—4-inch plastic "Hip Pocket Record" with color sleeve					

ROULETTE

❑ 4770	Room at the Top/Your Friends Here in				
	Dunderville	1967	5.00	10.00	20.00
❑ 4785	Most Children Do/Hello Girl	1967	5.00	10.00	20.00

TOLLIE

❑ 9049	Up on the Mountain/So Young, So Fine	1965	6.25	12.50	25.00

Albums
ROULETTE

❑ R 25358 [M]	The Fallen Angels	1967	7.50	15.00	30.00
❑ SR 25358 [S]	The Fallen Angels	1967	10.00	20.00	40.00
❑ SR 42011	It's a Long Way Down	1968	25.00	50.00	100.00

FALLENROCK
45s
CAPRICORN

❑ 0211	Sayin' It's So Don't Make It So/She's a Mystery	1974	—	2.50	5.00
❑ 0227	Mary Anne/My World Begins and Ends with You	1975	—	2.50	5.00

Albums
CAPRICORN

❑ CP 0143	Watch for Fallenrock	1974	2.50	5.00	10.00

FALLING PEBBLES, THE Early version of THE BUCKINGHAMS.
45s
ALLEY CAT

❑ 201	Lawdy Miss Clawdy/Virginia Wolf	1964	6.25	12.50	25.00

FALLOWS, SCOTT, AND THE EBBTONES
45s
DOT

❑ 16577	Surfing Boop-Boop-A-Do/King of Lovers	1964	5.00	10.00	20.00

FAME, GEORGIE
45s
EPIC

❑ 10166	Because I Love You/Bidin' My Time				
	('Cos I Love You)	1967	2.00	4.00	8.00
❑ 10283	The Ballad of Bonnie and Clyde/				
	Beware of the Dog	1968	2.50	5.00	10.00
❑ 10347	Hideaway/Runaway Child	1968	—	3.00	6.00
❑ 10402	Someone to Watch Over Me/For Your Pleasure	1968	—	3.00	6.00
❑ 10477	I'll Be Your Baby Tonight/Down Along the Cove	1969	—	3.00	6.00
❑ 10546	Peaceful/Hideaway	1969	—	3.00	6.00
❑ 10640	Fire and Rain/The Movie Star Song	1970	—	3.00	6.00

IMPERIAL

❑ 66086	Yeh, Yeh/Preach and Teach	1965	3.00	6.00	12.00
❑ 66104	Let the Sunshine In/In the Meantime	1965	2.50	5.00	10.00
❑ 66125	Blue Monday/Like We Used to Be	1965	2.50	5.00	10.00
❑ 66189	El Bandido/Get Away	1966	2.50	5.00	10.00
❑ 66220	Last Night/Sitting in the Park	1966	2.50	5.00	10.00
❑ 66299	Funny How Time Slips Away/Last Night	1968	2.00	4.00	8.00

ISLAND

❑ 035	Everlovin' Woman/Ozone	1975	—	2.50	5.00

7-Inch Extended Plays
EPIC

❑ 5-26368	The Ballad of Bonnie & Clyde/Ask Me Nice/				
	Exactly Like You//Someone to Watch Over Me/				
	Blue Prelude/Side by Side	1968	5.00	10.00	20.00
—Jukebox issue; small hole, plays at 33 1/3 rpm					
❑ 5-26368 [PS]	The Ballad of Bonnie & Clyde	1968	5.00	10.00	20.00

Albums
EPIC

❑ BN 26368	The Ballad of Bonnie and Clyde	1968	6.25	12.50	25.00

IMPERIAL

❑ LP-9282 [M]	Yeh, Yeh	1965	6.25	12.50	25.00
❑ LP-9331 [M]	Get Away	1966	6.25	12.50	25.00
❑ LP-12282 [P]	Yeh, Yeh	1965	7.50	15.00	30.00
—Entire album is stereo except "Yeh, Yeh" (rechanneled)					
❑ LP-12331 [R]	Get Away	1966	6.25	12.50	25.00

ISLAND

❑ ILPS 9293	Georgie Fame	1975	2.50	5.00	10.00

Number	Title (A Side/B Side)	Yr	VG	VG+	NM
FAME, GEORGIE, AND ANNIE ROSS					
Albums					
DRG					
☐ 5197	Georgie Fame and Annie Ross in Hoagland	198?	3.00	6.00	12.00
FAME & PRICE — PRICE & FAME TOGETHER GEORGIE FAME and ALAN PRICE.					
45s					
REPRISE					
☐ 1014	John and Mary/Rosetta	1971	—	2.50	5.00
FAMILY					
45s					
REPRISE					
☐ 0786	Hey Mr. Policeman/Old Songs, New Songs	1968	2.00	4.00	8.00
☐ 0809	Second Generation Woman/Hometown	1969	2.00	4.00	8.00
☐ 0881	Good Friend of Mine/No Mule Fool	1969	2.00	4.00	8.00
UNITED ARTISTS					
☐ XW171	My Friend the Sun/Glove	1973	—	2.50	5.00
☐ XW416	Suspicion/It's Only a Movie	1974	—	2.50	5.00
☐ 50832	Seasons/In My Own Time	1971	—	3.00	6.00
☐ 50882	Between Blue and Me/Laff and Sing	1972	—	2.50	5.00
Albums					
REPRISE					
☐ RS-6313	Music in a Doll's House	1968	5.00	10.00	20.00
☐ RS-6340	Family Entertainment	1969	3.75	7.50	15.00
☐ RS-6384	A Song for Me	1970	3.75	7.50	15.00
UNITED ARTISTS					
☐ UA-LA181-F	It's Only a Movie	1974	3.00	6.00	12.00
☐ UAS-5527	Anyway	1971	3.75	7.50	15.00
☐ UAS-5562	Fearless	1972	3.75	7.50	15.00
☐ UAS-5644	Bandstand	1972	3.75	7.50	15.00
FAMILY DOGG					
45s					
BELL					
☐ 848	Arizona/The House and the Heather	1969	—	3.00	6.00
☐ 863	Moonshine Mary/Sympathy	1970	—	3.00	6.00
☐ 885	This Unhappy Heart of Mine/When Tomorrow Becomes Tomorrow	1970	—	3.00	6.00
☐ 939	This Unhappy Heart of Mine/(B-side unknown)	1970	—	2.50	5.00
Albums					
BUDDAH					
☐ BDS-5100	The View from Rowland's Head	1972	6.25	12.50	25.00
FAMILY TREE, THE					
45s					
MIRA					
☐ 228	Prince of Dreams/Live Your Own Life	1966	2.50	5.00	10.00
PAULA					
☐ 329	Electric Kangaroo/Terry Tommy	1970	—	3.00	6.00
RCA VICTOR					
☐ 47-9184	Do You Have the Time/Keepin' a Secret	1967	2.00	4.00	8.00
Albums					
RCA VICTOR					
☐ LSP-3955	Miss Butters	1968	3.75	7.50	15.00
FAMOUS FLAMES, THE Backing group for JAMES BROWN.					
45s					
KING					
☐ 6341	Nobody Knows But My Baby and Me/Who Am I	1970	2.00	4.00	8.00
FANADOS, THE					
45s					
CARTER					
☐ 2050	The One I Love/She Must Be from a Different Planet	195?	200.00	400.00	800.00
FANCY (1) British pop group.					
45s					
BIG TREE					
☐ 15004	Wild Thing/Fancy	1974	—	2.50	5.00
☐ 16026	Touch Me/I Don't Need Your Love	1974	—	2.50	5.00
Albums					
BIG TREE					
☐ BT 89502	Wild Thing	1974	3.00	6.00	12.00
RCA VICTOR					
☐ APL1-1482	Fancy Turns You On	1976	3.00	6.00	12.00
FANCY (2) Rock band from Connecticut.					
45s					
POISON RING					
☐ PR-716	All My Best (Sweet Mary)/Goin' Down to the Sea	1971	5.00	10.00	20.00
Albums					
POISON RING					
☐ PRR-2238	Meeting You Here	1971	20.00	40.00	80.00
FANCY (3)					
12-Inch Singles					
PERSONAL					
☐ P 49812	Come Inside (Long Version 9:00) (Short Version 4:10)/Chinese Eyes (5:58)	1985	2.00	4.00	8.00
☐ P 49818	Check It Out (6:00)//Get Lost Tonight (5:38)/Burnin' Out the Light (5:08)	1985	2.00	4.00	8.00
FANNY					
45s					
CASABLANCA					
☐ 0009	I've Had It/First Time	1974	—	2.50	5.00
☐ 814	Butter Boy/Beggar Man	1974	—	2.50	5.00
REPRISE					
☐ 0901	Ladies' Choice/New Day	1970	—	3.00	6.00
☐ 0938	One Step at a Time/Nowhere to Run	1970	—	3.00	6.00
☐ 0963	Changing Horses/Conversation with a Copy	1970	—	3.00	6.00
☐ 1033	Charity Ball/Place in the Country	1971	—	3.00	6.00
☐ 1080	Ain't That Peculiar/Think About the Children	1972	—	3.00	6.00
☐ 1097	Rock Bottom Blues/Wonderful Feeling	1972	—	3.00	6.00

Number	Title (A Side/B Side)	Yr	VG	VG+	NM
☐ 1119	Knock on My Door/Young and Dumb	1972	—	3.00	6.00
☐ 1148	All Mine/I Need You Need Me	1972	—	3.00	6.00
☐ 1162	Last Night I Had a Dream/Beside Myself	1973	—	3.00	6.00
Albums					
CASABLANCA					
☐ NBLP 7007	Rock & Roll Survivors	1974	3.00	6.00	12.00
REPRISE					
☐ MS-2058	Fanny Hill	1972	3.75	7.50	15.00
☐ MS-2137	Mother's Pride	1973	3.75	7.50	15.00
☐ RS-6416	Fanny	1970	3.75	7.50	15.00
☐ RS-6456	Charity Ball	1971	3.75	7.50	15.00
FANS, THE					
45s					
DOT					
☐ 16688	I Want a Beatle for Christmas/How Far Should I Let My Heart Go Tonight	1964	3.75	7.50	15.00
FANTASIES, THE					
45s					
HIT					
☐ 84	Mickey's Monkey/Cry Baby	1963	2.00	4.00	8.00
FANTASTIC BAGGYS, THE Also see STEVE BARRI; P.F. SLOAN.					
45s					
IMPERIAL					
☐ 66047	Tell 'Em I'm Surfin'/Surfer Boy's Dream	1964	17.50	35.00	70.00
☐ 66072	Anywhere the Girls Are/Debbie Be True	1964	12.50	25.00	50.00
☐ 66092	Alone on the Beach/It Was I	1965	12.50	25.00	50.00
Albums					
IMPERIAL					
☐ LP-9270 [M]	Tell 'Em I'm Surfin'	1964	37.50	75.00	150.00
☐ LP-12270 [S]	Tell 'Em I'm Surfin'	1964	75.00	150.00	300.00
LIBERTY					
☐ LN-10192	Tell 'Em I'm Surfin'	1982	2.50	5.00	10.00
FANTASTIC DEE JAYS, THE					
Albums					
STONE					
☐ SLP-4003	The Fantastic Dee Jays	1966	250.00	500.00	1000.
FANTASTIC FOUR, THE					
12-Inch Singles					
WESTBOUND					
☐ DSKO 136	Sexy Lady (Vocal 7:04) (same on both sides)	1978	5.00	10.00	20.00
☐ DSKO 152	BYOF (Bring Your Own Funk) (6:06) (same on both sides)	1978	3.75	7.50	15.00
45s					
EASTBOUND					
☐ 609	I Had the Whole World to Choose From/If You Need Me	1973	2.00	4.00	8.00
☐ 620	I'm Falling in Love (I Feel Good All Over)/I Believe in Miracles	1974	2.50	5.00	10.00
RIC-TIC					
☐ 113	Can't Stop Looking for My Baby/Can't Stop Looking for My Baby (Part 2)	1966	50.00	100.00	200.00
☐ 119	Girl Have Pity/Live Up to What She Thinks	1967	5.00	10.00	20.00
☐ 121	Can't Stop Looking for My Baby/Just the Lonely	1967	25.00	50.00	100.00
☐ 122	The Whole World Is a Stage/Ain't Love Wonderful	1967	3.75	7.50	15.00
☐ 128	You Gave Me Something (And Everything's Alright)/I Don't Wanna Live Without You	1967	3.75	7.50	15.00
☐ 130	To Share Your Love/As Long As I Live (I Live for You)	1967	3.75	7.50	15.00
☐ 134	Goddess of Love/As Long As the Feeling Is There	1968	3.75	7.50	15.00
☐ 136	Love Is a Many-Splendored Thing/Goddess of Love	1968	3.75	7.50	15.00
☐ 137	No Love Like Your Love/A Man in Love	1968	3.75	7.50	15.00
☐ 139	I've Got to Have You/Win or Lose	1968	3.75	7.50	15.00
☐ 144	I Love You Madly/(Instrumental)	1968	5.00	10.00	20.00
SOUL					
☐ 35052	I Love You Madly/(Instrumental)	1968	3.00	6.00	12.00
☐ 35058	I Feel Like I'm Falling in Love/Pin Point It Out	1969	3.75	7.50	15.00
☐ 35065	Just Another Lonely Night/I Don't Care Why You Want Me	1969	3.75	7.50	15.00
☐ 35072	On the Brighter Side of a Blue World/I'm Gonna Hurry On	1970	3.00	6.00	12.00
WESTBOUND					
☐ 5009	Alvin Stone (The Birth & Death of a Gangster)/I Believe in Miracles, I Believe in You	1975	—	3.50	7.00
☐ 5017	Have a Little Mercy/County Line	1975	—	2.50	5.00
☐ 5030	Don't Risk Your Happiness On Foolish Things/They Took the Show on the Road	1976	—	2.50	5.00
☐ 5032	Hideaway/They Took the Show on the Road	1976	—	2.50	5.00
☐ 55403	I Got to Have Your Love/Ain't I Been Good to You	1977	—	2.50	5.00
☐ 55408	Mixed Up Moods and Attitudes/Disco Fool Blues	1978	—	2.50	5.00
☐ 55417	Sexy Lady/If This Is Love	1979	—	2.50	5.00
☐ 55419	BYOF (Bring Your Own Funk)/If This Is Love	1979	—	2.50	5.00
Albums					
SOUL					
☐ SS-717	The Best of the Fantastic Four	1969	10.00	20.00	40.00
☐ SS-722	How Sweet He Is	1970	—	—	—
—Canceled					
WESTBOUND					
☐ W 201	Alvin Stone (The Birth and Death of a Gangster)	1975	3.75	7.50	15.00
☐ W 226	Night People	1976	3.75	7.50	15.00
☐ WT 306	Got to Have Your Love	1977	3.75	7.50	15.00
☐ WT 6108	BYOF (Bring Your Own Funk)	1978	3.75	7.50	15.00
FANTASTIC JOHNNY C, THE					
45s					
KAMA SUTRA					
☐ 511	Let's Do It Together/Peace Treaty	1970	—	2.50	5.00
☐ 515	Good Love/You Got Your Hooks in Me	1970	—	2.50	5.00

F

Number	Title (A Side/B Side)	Yr	VG	VG+	NM
PHIL.-LA OF SOUL					
❑ 305	Boogaloo Down Broadway/				
	Look What Love Can Make You Do	1967	2.00	4.00	8.00
❑ 309	Got What You Need/New Love	1968	—	3.00	6.00
❑ 315	Hitch It to the Horse/Cool Broadway	1968	—	3.00	6.00
❑ 320	Baby I Need You/Some Kind of Wonderful	1968	—	3.00	6.00
❑ 327	Is There Anything Better Than Making Love/				
	New Love	1969	—	3.00	6.00
❑ 361	Don't Depend on Me/Waitin' for the Rain	1973	—	2.00	4.00
❑ 363	Just Say the Word/I'm a Man	1973	—	2.00	4.00
PHILCO-FORD					
❑ HP-39	Boogaloo Down Broadway/Got What You Need	1969	5.00	10.00	20.00
—4-inch plastic "Hip Pocket Record" with color sleeve					
Albums					
PHIL-LA OF SOUL					
❑ 4000	Boogaloo Down Broadway	1968	20.00	40.00	80.00

FANTASTICS, THE (1) Male R&B group.
45s

Number	Title (A Side/B Side)	Yr	VG	VG+	NM
BELL					
❑ 977	Something Old, Something New/High and Dry	1971	5.00	10.00	20.00
❑ 45157	(Love Me) Love the Life I Lead/Old Rags and				
	Tatters	1971	3.75	7.50	15.00
DERAM					
❑ 7528	Face to Face with Heartache/This Must Be My				
	Rainy Day	1970	3.75	7.50	15.00

FANTASTICS, THE (2)
45s

Number	Title (A Side/B Side)	Yr	VG	VG+	NM
RCA VICTOR					
❑ 47-7572	There Goes My Love/Millionaire Hobo	1959	10.00	20.00	40.00
—Black label, dog on top					
❑ 47-7572	There Goes My Love/I Wanna Be a Millionaire				
	Hobo	1965	3.75	7.50	15.00
—Evidently, a reissue with the same number, but the dog on side of label rather than on top, exists					
❑ 47-7664	This Is My Wedding Day/I Got a Zero	1960	10.00	20.00	40.00
UNITED ARTISTS					
❑ 309	Dancing Doll/I Told You Once	1961	12.50	25.00	50.00

FANTASTICS, THE (3) Nashville studio group.
45s

Number	Title (A Side/B Side)	Yr	VG	VG+	NM
HIT					
❑ 289	Bernadette/I Never Loved a Man				
	the Way I Love You	1967	2.00	4.00	8.00
—B-side by Odessa Crawford					
❑ 293	Here Comes My Baby/I Got Rhythm	1967	2.00	4.00	8.00
—B-side by the Jalopy Five					
❑ 297	A Whiter Shade of Pale/San Francisco				
	(Be Sure to Wear Flowers in Your Hair)	1967	2.00	4.00	8.00
—B-side by Bobby Sims					
❑ 302	Light My Fire./Mercy, Mercy, Mercy	1967	2.00	4.00	8.00
—B-side by the Chords (2)					
❑ 309	People Are Strange/Please Love Me Forever	1967	2.00	4.00	8.00
—B-side by Bobby Sims					
❑ 314	Pata Pata/Massachusetts	1967	2.00	4.00	8.00
—B-side by the Chords (2)					
❑ 324	Cowboys to Girls/Tighten Up	1968	2.00	4.00	8.00
—B-side by the Classmates					
❑ 329	Mony Mony/I Wanna Live	1968	2.00	4.00	8.00
—B-side by Ed Hardin					
❑ 336	Stoned Soul Picnic/Hurdy Gurdy Man	1968	2.00	4.00	8.00
—B-side by the Jalopy Five					
❑ 340	1-2-3, Red Light/The House That Jack Built	1968	2.00	4.00	8.00
—B-side by Kathy Shannon					
❑ 344	Over You/My Special Angel	1968	2.00	4.00	8.00
—B-side by the Chords (2)					
❑ 348	White Room/Who's Making Love	1968	2.00	4.00	8.00
—B-side by Bobby Sims					
❑ 352	Touch Me/Everyday People	1969	2.00	4.00	8.00
—B-side by the Jalopy Five					
❑ 355	You Showed Me/Soulful Strut	1969	2.00	4.00	8.00
—B-side by the New Society Group					

FANTASTICS, THE (U) Neither group (1) nor group (2), but are they both the same?
45s

Number	Title (A Side/B Side)	Yr	VG	VG+	NM
SCORPIO					
❑ 407	Malaguena/Dance for an Unnamed				
	Gypsy Queen	1966	6.25	12.50	25.00
SOUND STAGE 7					
❑ 2565	Have a Little You/Me and You	1966	3.00	6.00	12.00

FANTASY
45s

Number	Title (A Side/B Side)	Yr	VG	VG+	NM
IMPERIAL					
❑ 66394	Painted Horse/I Got the Fever	1969	2.50	5.00	10.00
LIBERTY					
❑ 56190	Stoned Cowboy/Understand	1970	2.00	4.00	8.00
Albums					
LIBERTY					
❑ LSP-7643	Fantasy	1970	5.00	10.00	20.00

FAPARDOKLY
Albums

Number	Title (A Side/B Side)	Yr	VG	VG+	NM
U.I.P.					
❑ 2250	Fapardokly	1967	250.00	500.00	1000.

FAR CRY
45s

Number	Title (A Side/B Side)	Yr	VG	VG+	NM
VANGUARD					
❑ 35085	Shapes/Hellhound	1969	2.50	5.00	10.00
Albums					
VANGUARD					
❑ VSD-6510	Far Cry	1969	6.25	12.50	25.00

FARDON, DON
CAPITOL

Number	Title (A Side/B Side)	Yr	VG	VG+	NM
❑ 3929	St. Matthew, St. Mark, St. Luke and St. John/Lola	1974	—	2.50	5.00
CHELSEA					
❑ 78-0115	Delta Queen/Home Town Baby	1973	—	3.00	6.00
DECCA					
❑ 32696	Belfast Boy/Echoes of the Cheers	1970	—	3.00	6.00
GNP CRESCENDO					
❑ 405	(The Lament of the Cherokee) Indian				
	Reservation/Dreaming Room	1968	2.00	4.00	8.00
❑ 418	Take a Heart/How Do You Break a Broken Heart	1968	—	3.00	6.00
❑ 421	Sally Goes 'Round the Moon/How Do You Break				
	a Broken Heart	1969	—	3.00	6.00
❑ 424	Running Bear/Ruby's Picture	1969	—	3.00	6.00
ROXBURY					
❑ BRBO-0159	Louisiana/Lady Zelda	1973	—	2.50	5.00
Albums					
DECCA					
❑ DL 75225	I've Paid My Dues	1970	3.75	7.50	15.00
GNP CRESCENDO					
❑ GNPS-2044	Indian Reservation	1968	5.00	10.00	20.00

FARGO, DONNA
45s

Number	Title (A Side/B Side)	Yr	VG	VG+	NM
ABC/DOT					
❑ 17523	U.S. of A./A Woman's Prayer	1974	—	2.50	5.00
❑ 17541	If Do Feel Good/Only the Strong	1974	—	2.50	5.00
❑ 17557	Hello Little Bluebird/2 Sweet 2 Be 4 Gotten	1975	—	2.50	5.00
❑ 17579	Whatever I Say/Rain Song	1975	—	2.50	5.00
❑ 17586	What Will the New Year Bring/				
	A Woman's Prayer	1975	—	2.50	5.00
❑ 17609	You're Not Charlie Brown				
	(And I'm Not Raggedy Ann)/Sing, Sing, Sing	1976	—	2.00	4.00
❑ 17660	Don't Be Angry/You Don't Mess Around with Jim	1976	—	2.00	4.00
❑ 17692	I'd Love You to Want Me/How Close You Came				
	(To Being Gone)	1977	—	2.00	4.00
CHALLENGE					
❑ 59387	Daddy/Sticks and Stones	1968	2.50	5.00	10.00
❑ 59391	Wishful Thinking/All That's Keeping Me Alive	1968	2.50	5.00	10.00
CLEVELAND INTERNATIONAL					
❑ 1	My Heart Will Always Belong to You/				
	Reasons to Be	1984	—	2.00	4.00
❑ 10	Soldier Boy/Stand Tall	1991	—	2.50	5.00
COLUMBIA					
❑ 04097	The Sign of the Times/Reasons to Be	1983	—	2.00	4.00
COUNTRY HEARTS					
❑ CH-001 [DJ]	My Side of the Bed/Country Singer's Wife	1970	7.50	15.00	30.00
—Promo-only release					
DECCA					
❑ 33001	Daddy/Sticks and Stones	1972	2.00	4.00	8.00
DOT					
❑ 17409	The Happiest Girl in the Whole U.S.A./				
	The Awareness of Nothing	1972	—	3.00	6.00
❑ 17409 [PS]	The Happiest Girl in the Whole U.S.A.				
	/The Awareness of Nothing	1972	2.00	4.00	8.00
❑ 17429	Funny Face/How Close You Came				
	(To Being Gone)	1972	—	3.00	6.00
❑ 17444	Superman/Forever Is As Far As I Could Go	1973	—	2.50	5.00
❑ 17460	You Were Always There/He Can Have All He				
	Wants	1973	—	2.50	5.00
❑ 17476	Little Girl Gone/Just Call Me	1973	—	2.50	5.00
❑ 17476 [PS]	Little Girl Gone/Just Call Me	1973	2.00	4.00	8.00
❑ 17491	I'll Try a Little Bit Harder/All About a Feeling	1973	—	2.50	5.00
❑ 17506	You Can't Be a Beacon (If Your Light Don't				
	Shine)/Just a Friend of Mine	1974	—	2.50	5.00
MCA					
❑ 51209	Say "I Do"/All About a Feeling	1981	—	2.00	4.00
MERCURY					
❑ 884712-7	Woman of the 80's/You Were Always There	1986	—	—	3.00
❑ 888043-7	Winners/I've Laid Too Many Eggs	1986	—	—	3.00
❑ 888093-7	Me and You/I've Laid Too Many Eggs	1986	—	—	3.00
❑ 888680-7	Members Only/Funny Face	1987	—	—	3.00
—A-side: With Billy Joe Royal					
RAMCO					
❑ 1982	You Make Me Feel Like a Woman/Would You				
	Believe a Lifetime	1967	3.75	7.50	15.00
❑ 1988	Who's Been Playin' House/You Reach for the				
	Bottle	1967	3.75	7.50	15.00
❑ 1991	Kind of Glad I'm Me/Then You Haven't Lied	1967	3.75	7.50	15.00
RCA					
❑ PB-13264	It's Hard to Be the Dreamer/I Just Saw My				
	Reflection in You	1982	—	2.00	4.00
❑ PB-13329	Did We Have to Go This Far (To Say Goodbye)/				
	All I Need to Know	1982	—	2.00	4.00
WARNER BROS.					
❑ 8186	Mr. Doodles/If You Can't Love All of Me	1976	—	2.50	5.00
❑ 8227	I've Loved You All the Way/				
	One of God's Children	1976	—	2.50	5.00
❑ 8305	Mockingbird Hill/Second Chance	1976	—	2.50	5.00
❑ 8375	That Was Yesterday/Cricket Song	1977	—	2.50	5.00
❑ 8431	Shame on Me/Hey, Mister Music Man	1977	—	2.50	5.00
❑ 8509	Do I Love You (Yes in Every Way)/Dee Dee	1977	—	2.50	5.00
❑ 8578	Ragamuffin Girl/Everybody's Girl	1978	—	2.00	4.00
❑ 8643	Another Goodbye/Changes in My Life	1978	—	2.00	4.00
❑ 8722	Somebody Special/Changes in My Life	1978	—	2.00	4.00
❑ 8867	Daddy/For the Rest of My Life	1979	—	2.00	4.00
❑ 49093	Preacher Berry/I Don't Know What to Do	1979	—	2.00	4.00
❑ 49183	Walk On By/I Wrote This Song Just for You	1980	—	2.00	4.00
❑ 49514	Land of Cotton/I Still Believe in You	1980	—	2.00	4.00
❑ 49575	Seeing Is Believing/Look What You've Done	1980	—	2.00	4.00
❑ 49757	Lonestar Cowboy/Utah Song	1981	—	2.00	4.00
❑ 49757 [PS]	Lonestar Cowboy/Utah Song	1981	—	3.00	6.00
❑ 49852	Jacamo/Song to Celebrate Life	1981	—	2.00	4.00

Number	Title (A Side/B Side)	Yr	VG	VG+	NM
Albums					
ABC/DOT					
❑ DOSD-2002	Miss Donna Fargo	1974	3.00	6.00	12.00
❑ DOSD-2029	Whatever I Say Means I Love You	1975	3.00	6.00	12.00
❑ DO-2075	The Best of Donna Fargo	1977	3.00	6.00	12.00
DOT					
❑ DOS-26000	The Happiest Girl in the Whole U.S.A.	1972	3.00	6.00	12.00
❑ DOS-26006	My Second Album	1973	3.00	6.00	12.00
❑ DOS-26019	All About a Feeling	1973	3.00	6.00	12.00
MCA					
❑ 667	The Happiest Girl in the Whole U.S.A.	198?	2.00	4.00	8.00
—*Budget-line reissue*					
❑ 37108	The Best of Donna Fargo	198?	2.00	4.00	8.00
—*Budget-line reissue*					
MERCURY					
❑ 830236-1	Winners	1986	3.00	6.00	12.00
❑ 832507-1	Winners	1987	2.00	4.00	8.00
—*Reissue with two songs deleted and one added from above*					
PICKWICK					
❑ SPC-6187	Superman	197?	2.00	4.00	8.00
SONGBIRD					
❑ 5203	Brotherly Love	1982	2.50	5.00	10.00
WARNER BROS.					
❑ BS 2926	On the Move	1976	2.50	5.00	10.00
❑ BS 2996	Donna Fargo Country	1977	2.50	5.00	10.00
❑ BS 3099	Shame on Me	1977	2.50	5.00	10.00
❑ BSK 3191	Dark Eyed Lady	1978	2.50	5.00	10.00
❑ BSK 3377	Just for You	1979	2.50	5.00	10.00
❑ BSK 3470	Fargo	1980	2.50	5.00	10.00

FARLOWE, CHRIS

45s					
GENERAL AMERICAN					
❑ 718	What You Gonna Do/Just a Dream	1964	3.75	7.50	15.00
IMMEDIATE					
❑ 5002	Paint It Black/You're So Good to Me	1967	2.50	5.00	10.00
❑ 5005	Handbags and Gladrags/Everyone Makes a Mistake	1968	2.50	5.00	10.00
❑ 5011	What Have I Been Doing/Paint It Black	1968	2.50	5.00	10.00
MGM					
❑ 13567	Out of Time/Baby Make It Soon	1966	5.00	10.00	20.00
—*A-side is a Mick Jagger-Keith Richards composition only later recorded by the Rolling Stones.*					
POLYDOR					
❑ 14008	Circles 'Round the Sun/Save Your Tears	1969	2.00	4.00	8.00
❑ 14013	Medicated Goo/Betty Lou	1970	2.00	4.00	8.00
Albums					
COLUMBIA					
❑ CL 2593 [M]	The Fabulous Chris Farlowe	1966	10.00	20.00	40.00
❑ CS 9393 [R]	The Fabulous Chris Farlowe	1966	6.25	12.50	25.00
IMMEDIATE					
❑ Z12 52010	Paint It Farlowe	1968	5.00	10.00	20.00
POLYDOR					
❑ 24-4041	From Here to Mama Rosa with the Hill	1970	3.00	6.00	12.00

FARM BAND, THE

Albums					
MANTRA					
❑ 777 [(2)]	The Farm Band	1972	7.50	15.00	30.00
—*With poster*					

FARNER, MARK Of GRAND FUNK RAILROAD.

45s					
ATLANTIC					
❑ 3448	You and Me Baby/Second Chance to Dance	1977	—	2.00	4.00
❑ 3510	When a Man Loves a Woman/If It Took All Day	1978	—	2.00	4.00
❑ 3529	Just One Look/Crystal Eyes	1978	—	2.00	4.00
LUCKY ELEVEN					
❑ 352	Down in the Valley/I Got News for You	1968	2.50	5.00	10.00
Albums					
ATLANTIC					
❑ SD 18232	Mark Farner	1977	2.50	5.00	10.00
❑ SD 19196	No Frills	1978	2.50	5.00	10.00

FARNER, MARK, AND DON BREWER Both later of GRAND FUNK RAILROAD.

45s					
LUCKY ELEVEN					
❑ 366	Does It Matter to You Girl/We Gotta Have Love	1968	3.00	6.00	12.00
❑ 366 [PS]	Does It Matter to You Girl/We Gotta Have Love	1968	10.00	20.00	40.00
Albums					
QUADICO					
❑ 7401	Monumental Funk	1977	2.50	5.00	10.00
❑ 7401 [PD]	Monumental Funk	1977	5.00	10.00	20.00
—*Picture disc*					

FARNHAM, JOHN

12-Inch Singles					
MCA CURB					
❑ L33-1206 [DJ]	Justice for One/Innocent Hearts	1984	3.00	6.00	12.00
45s					
CAPITOL					
❑ 2128	Sadie the Cleaning Lady/In My Room	1968	2.50	5.00	10.00
—*As "Johnny Farnham"*					
❑ 3522	Don't You Know It's Magic/Sweet Cherry Wine	1973	2.50	5.00	10.00
—*As "Johnny Farnham"*					
MCA					
❑ 52798	Break the Ice/Thunder in Your Heart	1986	—	2.00	4.00
MCA CURB					
❑ 52580	Love (It's Just the Way It Goes)/Ragtop Day	1984	—	2.50	5.00
—*A-side with Sarah M. Taylor*					
RCA					
❑ 5146-7-R	You're the Voice/Going, Going, Gone	1986	—	2.00	4.00
❑ 5264-7-R	Pressure Down/Trouble	1986	—	2.00	4.00
❑ 8915-7-R	Two Strong Hearts/Some Do, Some Don't	1988	—	2.00	4.00

Number	Title (A Side/B Side)	Yr	VG	VG+	NM
Albums					
RCA					
❑ 6300-1-R	Whispering Jack	1986	2.50	5.00	10.00

FARON'S FLAMINGOS

45s					
COLUMBIA					
❑ 43018	Let's Stomp/I Can Tell	1964	6.25	12.50	25.00
—*B-side by Rory Storm and the Hurricanes*					

FARQUAHR

45s					
ELEKTRA					
❑ 45735	Holy Moses/My Island	1971	—	3.00	6.00
VERVE FORECAST					
❑ 5077	My Eggs Don't Taste the Same Without You/ Sister Theresa's East River Orphanage	1968	2.00	4.00	8.00
❑ 5085	Teddy Bear Days/My Island	1968	2.00	4.00	8.00
WARNER BROS.					
❑ 7354	Kiss the Wind Goodbye/Neither Here Nor There	1969	—	3.00	6.00
Albums					
ELEKTRA					
❑ EKS-74083	Farquahr	1970	3.00	6.00	12.00
VERVE FORECAST					
❑ FTS-3053	Fabulous Farquahr	1969	3.00	6.00	12.00

FARR, GARY, AND THE T-BONES

45s					
EPIC					
❑ 9832	Don't Stop and Stare/Give All She's Got	1965	3.00	6.00	12.00

FARR, LITTLE JOEY

45s					
BAND BOX					
❑ 286	Rock & Roll Santa/Big White Cadillac	196?	12.50	25.00	50.00

FARRELL AND THE FLAMES

45s					
FRANSIL					
❑ 14	Dreams and Memories/You'll Be Sorry	1961	100.00	200.00	400.00

FASCINATIONS, THE (1) Female vocal group.

45s					
ABC-PARAMOUNT					
❑ 10387	Mama Didn't Lie/Someone Like You	1962	5.00	10.00	20.00
—*Some of the ABC-Paramount pressings are misspelled "Fasinations"*					
❑ 10443	Tears In My Eyes/You're Gonna Be Sorry	1963	6.25	12.50	25.00
MAYFIELD					
❑ 7711	(Say It Isn't So) Say You'd Never Go/I'm So Lucky	1966	2.50	5.00	10.00
❑ 7714	Girls Are Out to Get You/You'll Be Sorry	1966	2.50	5.00	10.00
❑ 7716	I Can't Stay Away from You/(B-side unknown)	1967	2.50	5.00	10.00

FASCINATIONS, THE (2)

45s					
DORE					
❑ 593	If I Had Your Love/Why	1961	12.50	25.00	50.00
PAXLEY					
❑ 750	If I Had Your Love/Why	1960	37.50	75.00	150.00

FASCINATIONS, THE (U) It's doubtful that any of these are group (1), but they could be group (2).

45s					
A&G					
❑ 101	I'm Gonna Cry/Since You Went Away	1972	5.00	10.00	20.00
SURE					
❑ 106	It's Midnight/Boom Bada Boom	1960	20.00	40.00	80.00
❑ 106	Midnight/Boom Bada Boom	1960	30.00	60.00	120.00

FASCINATORS, THE (1)

45s					
BIM BAM BOOM					
❑ 110	Oh, Rose Marie/Forgive Me, My Darling	1974	2.50	5.00	10.00
CAPITOL					
❑ F-4053	Chapel Bells/I Wonder Who	1958	37.50	75.00	150.00
❑ F-4137	Come to Paradise/Who Do You Think You Are	1959	50.00	100.00	200.00
❑ F-4247	Oh Rose Marie/Fried Chicken and Macaroni	1959	50.00	100.00	200.00
❑ 4544	Chapel Bells/I Wonder Who	1961	20.00	40.00	80.00

FASCINATORS, THE (2)

45s					
BLUE LAKE					
❑ 112	Can't Stop/Don't Give My Love Away	1953	500.00	1000.	2000.

FASCINATORS, THE (3)

45s					
BURN					
❑ 845	I'll Be Gone/Can't You See I'm Lonely	1965	5.00	10.00	20.00

FASCINATORS, THE (4)

45s					
DOOTO					
❑ 441	Teardrop Eyes/Shivers and Shakes	1958	15.00	30.00	60.00

FASCINATORS, THE (5)

45s					
YOUR COPY					
❑ 1135	The Bells of My Heart/Sweet Baby	1954	250.00	500.00	1000.
—*Black vinyl*					
❑ 1135	The Bells of My Heart/Sweet Baby	1954	500.00	1000.	2000.
—*Red vinyl*					
❑ 1136	My Beauty, My Own/Don't Give It Away	1954	250.00	500.00	1000.

FASCINATORS, THE (U) If these are not completely different groups, these are most likely by group (3) or (4).

45s					
KING					
❑ 5119	Cuddle Up with Carolyn/Tee Hee	1958	12.50	25.00	50.00
TRANS ATLAS					
❑ 688	You're to Blame/Revived	196?	7.50	15.00	30.00

F

Number	Title (A Side/B Side)	Yr	VG	VG+	NM

FASHIONS, THE (1) BARBARA ENGLISH was a member of this group.
45s
CAMEO

Number	Title (A Side/B Side)	Yr	VG	VG+	NM
❑ 331	Baby That's Me/Nick and Joe Callin'	1964	2.50	5.00	10.00

ELMOR

❑ 301	Please Let It Be Me/Fairy Tales	1961	6.25	12.50	25.00

EMBER

❑ 1084	I Just Got a Letter/Try My Love	1962	3.00	6.00	12.00

V-TONE

❑ 202	I'm Dreaming of You/I Love You So	1959	5.00	10.00	20.00
—Blue label					
❑ 202	I'm Dreaming of You/I Love You So	1959	7.50	15.00	30.00
—Orange label					
❑ 202	I'm Dreaming of You/Lonesome Road	1959	12.50	25.00	50.00

WARWICK

❑ 646	All I Want/Dearest One	1961	5.00	10.00	20.00

FASHIONS, THE (2)
45s
FELSTED

❑ 8689	Surfer's Memories/Surfin' Back to School	1964	7.50	15.00	30.00

FASHIONS, THE (3)
45s
PHIL-L.A. OF SOUL

❑ 354	I Don't Mind Doin' It/What Goes Up (Must Come Down)	1972	—	3.00	6.00

FASHIONS, THE (4)
45s
20TH CENTURY FOX

❑ 6710	Lover's Stand/Only Those in Love	1968	2.00	4.00	8.00

FASTEST GROUP ALIVE, THE
45s
TEEN

❑ 100	The Bears/Beside	1966	7.50	15.00	30.00

VALIANT

❑ 754	The Bears/Beside	1966	5.00	10.00	20.00
❑ 759	Lullabye/5:15 Sports	1967	5.00	10.00	20.00

FAT CITY Also see JOHN DENVER.
45s
ABC PROBE

❑ 469	Wall Street/City Cat	1969	—	3.00	6.00

PARAMOUNT

❑ 0162	I Guess He'd Rather Be in Colorado/ Morning Go Away	1972	—	3.00	6.00
❑ 0176	Workingman's Day/Hey, Loretta	1972	—	2.50	5.00

Albums
ABC PROBE

❑ 4508	Reincarnation	1969	5.00	10.00	20.00

PARAMOUNT

❑ PAS-6028	Welcome to Fat City	1972	3.75	7.50	15.00

FAT MATTRESS
Albums
ATCO

❑ 33-309 [M]	Fat Mattress	1969	10.00	20.00	40.00
—White label promo only; "DJ Copy Monaural" sticker on cover					
❑ SD 33-309 [S]	Fat Mattress	1969	5.00	10.00	20.00
❑ SD 33-347	Fat Mattress II	1970	3.75	7.50	15.00

FATBACK Includes records as "Fatback Band."
12-Inch Singles
COTILLION

❑ PR 763 [DJ]	You've Got That Magic (6:43)/ You've Got That Magic (3:55)	1984	2.00	4.00	8.00

SPRING

❑ PRO 184 [DJ]	On the Floor (same on both sides)	1982	2.00	4.00	8.00
❑ 402	King Tim III (Personalty Jock)/ You're My Candy Sweet	1979	2.50	5.00	10.00
❑ 409	The Girl Is Fine (So Fine)/(B-side unknown)	1983	2.00	4.00	8.00
❑ 414	Spread Love/(B-side unknown)	1984	—	3.00	6.00

45s
COTILLION

❑ 99642	Lover Undercover/(B-side unknown)	1985	—	—	3.00
❑ 99665	Girls on My Mind/Osiris (There's a Party Goin' On)	1985	—	—	3.00
❑ 99730	You've Got That Magic/(B-side unknown)	1984	—	—	3.00
❑ 99749	Call Out My Name/I Love You So	1984	—	—	3.00

EVENT

❑ 217	Keep On Steppin'/Breakin' Up Is Hard to Do	1974	—	2.50	5.00
❑ 219	Wicki-Wacky/Can't Fight the Flame	1974	—	2.50	5.00
❑ 224	(Hey I) Feel Real Good (Part 1)/(Hey I) Feel Real Good (Part 2)	1975	—	2.50	5.00
❑ 226	Yum Yum (Gimme Some)/Let the Drums Speak	1975	—	2.50	5.00
❑ 227	(Are You Ready) Do the Bus Stop/ Gotta Learn to Dance	1975	—	2.50	5.00
❑ 229	Spanish Hustle/Put Your Love (In My Tender Care)	1976	—	2.50	5.00

PERCEPTION

❑ 520	Soul March/To Be with You	1973	—	2.50	5.00
❑ 526	Street Dance/Goin' to See My Baby	1973	—	2.50	5.00
❑ 540	Nija (Nija) Walk (Street Walk)/Soul Man	1973	—	2.50	5.00

SPRING

❑ 165	Party Time/Groovy Kind of Day	1976	—	2.50	5.00
❑ 168	The Booty/If That's the Way You Want It	1976	—	2.50	5.00
❑ 171	Double Dutch/Spank the Baby	1977	—	2.50	5.00
❑ 174	NYCNY USA (Nik-Ne-Yoo-Sa)/Soulfinger	1977	—	2.50	5.00
❑ 177	Master Booty/Zodiac Man	1977	—	2.50	5.00
❑ 180	Mile High/Midnight Freak	1978	—	2.50	5.00
❑ 181	I Like Girls/Get Out on the Dance Floor	1978	—	2.50	5.00
❑ 188	Boogie Freak/I'm Fired Up	1978	—	2.50	5.00
❑ 191	Freak the Freak the Funk (Rock)/Wild Dreams	1979	—	2.50	5.00
❑ 195	(Do the) Boogie Woogie/Hesitation	1979	—	2.50	5.00
❑ 199	King Tim III (Personality Jock)/ You're My Candy Sweet	1979	—	3.00	6.00
❑ 3005	Love in Perfect Harmony/Disco Bass	1979	—	2.00	4.00
❑ 3008	Gotta Get My Hands on Some (Money)/Street Band	1980	—	2.00	4.00
❑ 3012	Backstrokin'/Love Spell	1980	—	2.00	4.00
❑ 3015	Let's Do It Again/Come and Get the Love	1980	—	2.00	4.00
❑ 3016	Angel/Concrete Jungle	1981	—	2.00	4.00
❑ 3018	Take It Any Way You Want It/Lady Groove	1981	—	2.00	4.00
❑ 3020	Kool Whip/Keep Your Fingers Out of the Jam	1981	—	2.00	4.00
❑ 3022	Rockin' to the Beat/Wanna Dance	1981	—	2.00	4.00
❑ 3023	Na Na Hey Hey Kiss Her Goodbye/I'm So in Love	1982	—	2.00	4.00
❑ 3025	On the Floor/Chillin' Out	1982	—	2.00	4.00
❑ 3026	She's My Shining Star/UFO (Unidentified Funk Object)	1982	—	2.00	4.00
❑ 3030	The Girl Is Fine (So Fine)/(B-side unknown)	1983	—	2.00	4.00
❑ 3032	Is This the Future/Double Love Affair	1983	—	2.00	4.00
❑ 3033	Up Against the Wall/With Love	1983	—	2.00	4.00
❑ 3037	I Wanna Be Your Lover/(B-side unknown)	1984	—	2.00	4.00

Albums
COTILLION

❑ 90168	Phoenix	1984	2.00	4.00	8.00
❑ 90253	So Delicious	1985	2.00	4.00	8.00

EVENT

❑ 6902	Keep On Steppin'	1974	3.75	7.50	15.00
—As "The Fatback Band"					
❑ 6904	Yum Yum	1975	3.75	7.50	15.00
—As "The Fatback Band"					
❑ 6905	Raising Hell	1976	3.75	7.50	15.00
—As "The Fatback Band"					

SPRING

❑ 6711	Night Fever	1976	3.00	6.00	12.00
—As "The Fatback Band"					
❑ 6714	NYCNYUSA	1977	3.00	6.00	12.00
—As "The Fatback Band"					
❑ 6717	Man with a Plan	1978	3.00	6.00	12.00
—As "The Fatback Band"					
❑ 6718	Fired Up 'N' Kickin'	1978	2.50	5.00	10.00
❑ 6721	Bright Lites, Big City	1979	2.50	5.00	10.00
❑ 6723	Fatback XII	1979	2.50	5.00	10.00
❑ 6726	Hot Box	1980	2.50	5.00	10.00
❑ 6729	14 Karat	1980	2.50	5.00	10.00
❑ 6731	Tasty Jam	1981	2.50	5.00	10.00
❑ 6734	Gigolo	1981	2.50	5.00	10.00
❑ 6736	On the Floor	1982	2.50	5.00	10.00

FATBACK BAND, THE See FATBACK.

FATHER YOD AND THE SPIRIT OF '76 See YA HO WA 13.

FAUN
45s
GREGAR

❑ 7000	Better Dig What You Find/I Asked My Mother	1969	5.00	10.00	20.00
❑ 7001	Son of a Literate Man/Yes I'm Really Lonely	1969	5.00	10.00	20.00

Albums
GREGAR

❑ 7000	Faun	1969	12.50	25.00	50.00

FAWNS, THE
45s
APT

❑ 25015	Come On/Until I Die	1958	6.25	12.50	25.00

FEAR ITSELF
45s
DOT

❑ 17278	The Letter/Born Under a Bad Sign	1969	2.00	4.00	8.00

Albums
DOT

❑ DLP-25942	Fear Itself	1969	5.00	10.00	20.00

FEATHER
45s
COLUMBIA

❑ 4-45231	The Fifth Stone/No Time for Sorrow	1970	2.00	4.00	8.00
❑ 4-45405	Choo Choo Nairobi/Down to the Wire	1971	2.00	4.00	8.00

VIVA

❑ 635	Kiss of Fire/Moccasin	1969	2.50	5.00	10.00

WHITE WHALE

❑ 353	Friends/Salli	1970	—	3.00	6.00

Albums
COLUMBIA

❑ C 30137	Friends by Feather	1970	3.75	7.50	15.00

FEATHERBED Early BARRY MANILOW.
45s
BELL

❑ 971	Amy/Morning	1971	15.00	30.00	60.00
—Stock copies are much scarcer than promo copies					
❑ 45133 [DJ]	Could It Be Magic (mono/stereo)	1971	25.00	50.00	100.00
—Stock copy may not exist					

FEATHERS, CHARLIE
45s
FLIP

❑ 503	I've Been Deceived/Peeping Eyes	1955	125.00	250.00	500.00

HOLIDAY INN

❑ 114	Deep Elm Blues/Nobody's Darling	1962	50.00	100.00	200.00

KAY

❑ 1001	Jungle Fever/Why Don't You	1960	50.00	100.00	200.00

KING

❑ 4971	Can't Hardly Stand It/ Everybody's Lovin' My Baby	1956	150.00	300.00	600.00
❑ 4997	One Hand Loose/Bottle to the Baby	1956	125.00	250.00	500.00
❑ 5022	Nobody's Woman/When You Decide	1957	100.00	200.00	400.00
❑ 5043	When You Come Around/Too Much Alike	1957	100.00	200.00	400.00

Number	Title (A Side/B Side)	Yr	VG	VG+	NM
MEMPHIS					
❑ 103	Wild, Wild Party/Today and Tomorrow	1961	25.00	50.00	100.00
METEOR					
❑ 5032	Tongue-Tied Jill/Get With It	1956	100.00	200.00	400.00
—Blue label					
❑ 5032	Tongue-Tied Jill/Get With It	1956	500.00	1000.	1500.
—Maroon label					
PHILWOOD					
❑ 223	Tear It Up/Stutterin' Cindy	197?	2.00	4.00	8.00
POMPADOUR					
❑ 231	Uh-Huh Honey/A Wedding Gown of White	1974	2.00	4.00	8.00
ROLLIN' ROCK					
❑ 45-025	That Certain Female/She Set Me Free	1978	2.00	4.00	8.00
SUN					
❑ 231	Defrost Your Heart/Wedding Gown of White	1956	200.00	400.00	600.00
❑ 503	I've Been Deceived/Peeping Eyes	1956	200.00	400.00	600.00
WAL-MAY					
❑ 101	Dinky John/South of Chicago	1960	50.00	100.00	200.00

FEATHERS, THE (1)
45s

Number	Title (A Side/B Side)	Yr	VG	VG+	NM
ALADDIN					
❑ 3267	Johnny Darling/Shake 'Em Up	1954	50.00	100.00	200.00
❑ 3277	I Need a Girl/Standing Right There	1955	50.00	100.00	200.00
HOLLYWOOD					
❑ 1051	Dear One/Lonesome Tonight	1956	1000.	2000.	3000.
SHOW TIME					
❑ 1104	Nona/Johnny Darling	1954	75.00	150.00	300.00
❑ 1105	Why Don't You Write Me/Where Did Caledonia Go	1954	37.50	75.00	150.00
❑ 1105	Why Don't You Write Me/Busy as a Bee	1954	50.00	100.00	200.00
❑ 1106	Love Only You/Crashing the Party	1955	50.00	100.00	200.00

FEATHERS, THE (2)
45s

Number	Title (A Side/B Side)	Yr	VG	VG+	NM
KAPP					
❑ 887	Give Him Love/To Be Loved by You	1968	2.00	4.00	8.00

FEATHERS, THE (U) May or may not be by group (2).
45s

Number	Title (A Side/B Side)	Yr	VG	VG+	NM
VEEP					
❑ 1200	The Dummy/Them Onions	1964	2.00	4.00	8.00

FEDERALS, THE (1) British group.
45s

Number	Title (A Side/B Side)	Yr	VG	VG+	NM
CAPITOL					
❑ 5526	Bucketful of Love/Leah	1965	2.50	5.00	10.00

FEDERALS, THE (2)
45s

Number	Title (A Side/B Side)	Yr	VG	VG+	NM
DELUXE					
❑ 6112	Come Go with Me/Cold Cash	1957	20.00	40.00	80.00
FURY					
❑ 1005	While Our Hearts Are Young/You're the One I Love	1957	25.00	50.00	100.00
❑ 1009	Dear Lorraine/She's My Girl	1958	25.00	50.00	100.00

FELDERS ORIOLES
45s

Number	Title (A Side/B Side)	Yr	VG	VG+	NM
MERCURY					
❑ 72480	Down Home Girl/Misty	1965	2.50	5.00	10.00

FELDMAN, VICTOR
45s

Number	Title (A Side/B Side)	Yr	VG	VG+	NM
AVA					
❑ 123	Theme from "Lawrence of Arabia"/Theme from "David & Lisa"	1963	2.50	5.00	10.00
INFINITY					
❑ 020	A Taste of Honey/Valerie	1962	2.50	5.00	10.00
❑ 025	New Dell High/John Brown's Battle Hymn	1962	2.50	5.00	10.00
❑ 030	Moon River/Theme from 9073	1963	2.50	5.00	10.00
PACIFIC JAZZ					
❑ 88127	Do the Jake/Have a Heart	1966	2.00	4.00	8.00
VEE JAY					
❑ 630	Hard to Find/Make Me a Present of You	1964	2.50	5.00	10.00
❑ 662	Green Dolphin Street/Overfat Cat	1965	2.50	5.00	10.00

Albums

Number	Title (A Side/B Side)	Yr	VG	VG+	NM
AVA					
❑ A-19 [M]	Soviet Jazz Themes	1963	6.25	12.00	25.00
❑ AS-19 [S]	Soviet Jazz Themes	1963	6.25	12.00	25.00
CHOICE					
❑ CRS 1005 [M]	Your Smile	1974	3.75	7.50	15.00
COHEARANT					
❑ CSR 1001	In My Pocket	1977	10.00	20.00	40.00
CONCORD JAZZ					
❑ CJ-38	The Artful Dodger	1977	3.00	6.00	12.00
CONTEMPORARY					
❑ C-3541 [M]	Suite Sixteen	1957	10.00	20.00	40.00
❑ C-3549 [M]	The Arrival of Victor Feldman	1958	10.00	20.00	40.00
❑ M-5005 [M]	Latinsville	1960	37.50	75.00	150.00
❑ S-7541 [S]	Suite Sixteen	1959	7.50	15.00	30.00
❑ S-7549 [S]	The Arrival of Victor Feldman	1959	7.50	15.00	30.00
❑ S-9005 [S]	Latinsville	1960	25.00	50.00	100.00
FANTASY					
❑ OJC-268	The Arrival of Victor Feldman	1987	2.50	5.00	10.00
❑ OJC-402	Merry Olde Soul	1989	3.00	6.00	12.00
INFINITY					
❑ 5000 [M]	A Taste of Honey and a Taste of Bossa Nova	1962	6.25	12.50	25.00
INTERLUDE					
❑ MO-510 [M]	With Mallets Aforethought	1959	10.00	20.00	40.00
—Reissue of Mode LP					
MODE					
❑ LP-120 [M]	Victor Feldman on Vibes	1957	15.00	30.00	60.00
NAUTILUS					
❑ NR-50	The Secret of the Andes	1982	5.00	10.00	20.00
—Audiophile vinyl					

Number	Title (A Side/B Side)	Yr	VG	VG+	NM
PACIFIC JAZZ					
❑ PJ-10121 [M]	Victor Feldman Plays Everything in Sight	196?	5.00	10.00	20.00
❑ ST-20121 [S]	Victor Feldman Plays Everything in Sight	196?	6.25	12.50	25.00
❑ PJ-20128 [M]	Venezuela Joropo	196?	6.25	12.50	25.00
❑ ST-20128 [S]	Venezuela Joropo	196?	6.25	12.50	25.00
PALO ALTO					
❑ PA-8053	The Secret of the Andes	1982	2.50	5.00	10.00
❑ PA-8056	To Chopin with Love	1983	2.50	5.00	10.00
❑ PA-8066	Fiesta	1984	2.50	5.00	10.00
RIVERSIDE					
❑ RLP-366 [M]	Merry Ole Soul	1961	6.25	12.00	25.00
❑ RS-9366 [S]	Merry Ole Soul	1961	6.25	12.00	25.00
VEE JAY					
❑ LP-1096 [M]	Love Me with All Your Heart	1964	7.50	15.00	30.00
❑ LP-2507 [M]	It's a Wonderful World	1965	5.00	10.00	20.00
WORLD PACIFIC					
❑ ST-1807 [S]	Stop the World, I Want to Get Off	1962	5.00	10.00	20.00
—Black vinyl					
❑ ST-1807 [S]	Stop the World, I Want to Get Off	1962	12.50	25.00	50.00
—Yellow vinyl					

FELICIANO, JOSE
45s

Number	Title (A Side/B Side)	Yr	VG	VG+	NM
EMI LATIN					
❑ S7-18214	Feliz Navidad/Blue Christmas	1994	—	2.00	4.00
—B-side on Liberty by Glen Campbell; red vinyl					
MOTOWN					
❑ 1517	The Drought Is Over/Everybody Loves Me	1981	—	2.00	4.00
❑ 1524	I Second That Emotion/Let's Make Love Over the Telephone	1981	—	2.00	4.00
❑ 1530	I Wanna Be Where You Are/Let's Make Love Over the Telephone	1981	—	2.00	4.00
❑ 1618	Free Me from My Freedom/I Second That Emotion	1982	—	2.00	4.00
❑ 1647	Samba Pa Ti (Long)/Samba Pa Ti (Short)	1982	—	2.00	4.00
❑ 1673 [DJ]	Balada Del Pianista (same on both sides)	1983	—	2.00	4.00
—May be promo only					
❑ 1674	Let's Find Each Other Tonight/Cuidado	1983	—	2.00	4.00
❑ 1679	Lonely Teardrops/Cuidado	1983	—	2.00	4.00
PRIVATE STOCK					
❑ 45,062	Angela/Willful Strut	1975	—	2.00	4.00
❑ 45,085	Angela (Spanish)/(B-side unknown)	1976	—	2.00	4.00
❑ 45,103	Why/(B-side unknown)	1976	—	2.00	4.00
❑ 45,143	Marguerita/(B-side unknown)	1977	—	2.00	4.00
❑ 45,151	The Air That I Breathe/I Love Making Love to You	1977	—	2.00	4.00
RCA					
❑ 447-0936	Feliz Navidad/The Little Drummer Boy	197?	—	—	3.00
—Black label, dog near top					
RCA VICTOR					
❑ 47-8425	Everybody Do the Click/Ginny's Garden	1964	2.00	4.00	8.00
❑ 47-8683	Where I'm Goin'/A Woman, a Lover, a Friend	1965	2.00	4.00	8.00
❑ 47-8884	(I Love You) For Sentimental Reasons/Quit While You're Ahead	1966	2.00	4.00	8.00
❑ 47-9085	A Man and a Woman/And We Were Lovers (Theme from The Sand Pebbles)	1967	2.00	4.00	8.00
❑ 47-9550	Light My Fire/California Dreamin'	1968	2.00	4.00	8.00
❑ 47-9641	Hi-Heel Sneakers/Hitchcock Railway	1968	—	3.00	6.00
❑ 47-9665	The Star Spangled Banner/And I Love Her	1968	2.50	5.00	10.00
❑ 47-9714	Hey Baby/My World Is Empty Without You	1969	—	3.00	6.00
❑ 47-9739	Marley Purt Drive/The Old Turkey Buzzard	1969	—	3.00	6.00
❑ 47-9757	Rain/She's a Woman	1969	—	3.00	6.00
❑ 47-9807	Wichita Lineman/Point of View	1969	—	3.00	6.00
❑ 47-9912	Pegao/Life Is That Way	1970	—	3.00	6.00
❑ 74-0290	So Long, Paul/Here Comes Werbley	1969	2.50	5.00	10.00
—As "Werbley Finster"					
❑ 74-0341	Girl (You'll Never Get Away from Me)/Younger Generation	1970	—	3.00	6.00
❑ 74-0358	Susie Q/Destiny	1970	—	3.00	6.00
❑ 74-0404	Feliz Navidad/The Little Drummer Boy	1970	2.50	5.00	10.00
❑ 74-0451	Que Sera/There's No One About	1971	—	2.50	5.00
❑ 74-0452	Shake a Hand/There's No One About	1971	—	2.50	5.00
❑ 74-0476	I Only Want to Say/Watch It With My Heart	1971	—	2.50	5.00
❑ 74-0545	Come Down Jesus/Only Once	1971	—	2.50	5.00
❑ 74-0586	Daytime Dreams/Fireworks	1971	—	2.50	5.00
❑ 74-0768	Magnolia/It Doesn't Matter Anyhow	1972	—	2.50	5.00
❑ 74-0841	Where Is My Woman/One More Mile	1972	—	2.50	5.00
❑ 74-0975	Hey Look at the Sun/Compartments	1973	—	2.50	5.00
❑ 447-0936	Feliz Navidad/The Little Drummer Boy	197?	—	2.00	4.00
—Red label reissue					
❑ APBO-0051	Yes We Can Can/I'm Leavin'	1973	—	2.50	5.00
❑ APBO-0140	I Want to Learn a Love Song/Find Somebody	1973	—	2.50	5.00
❑ APBO-0206	The Gypsy/I Like What You Give	1974	—	2.00	4.00
❑ PB-10094	Golden Lady/Virgo	1974	—	2.00	4.00
❑ PB-10145	Chico and the Man/Hard Times in El Barrio	1974	—	2.00	4.00
❑ PB-10306	Twilight Time/Stay with Me	1975	—	2.00	4.00

Albums

Number	Title (A Side/B Side)	Yr	VG	VG+	NM
MOTOWN					
❑ M8-953	Jose Feliciano	1981	2.50	5.00	10.00
❑ 6018 ML	Escenas de Amor	1982	2.50	5.00	10.00
❑ 6035 ML	Romance in the Night	1983	2.50	5.00	10.00
PAIR					
❑ PDL2-1091 [(2)]	His Hits and Other Classics	1986	3.00	6.00	12.00
PRIVATE STOCK					
❑ PS-2010	Angela	1976	2.50	5.00	10.00
❑ PS-2022	Sweet Soul	1977	2.50	5.00	10.00
RCA CAMDEN					
❑ CAS-2563	Jose Feliciano Sings	1972	2.50	5.00	10.00
RCA VICTOR					
❑ APD1-0141 [Q]	Compartments	1973	3.75	7.50	15.00
—All copies are quadraphonic					
❑ FSP-253	Fantastico	1970	4.50	9.00	18.00
❑ AFL1-0266	For My Love...Mother Music	1977	2.00	4.00	8.00
—Reissue with new prefix					
❑ APL1-0266	For My Love...Mother Music	1974	2.50	5.00	10.00
❑ FSP-277	En Mi Soledad	1971	4.50	9.00	18.00

F

Number	Title (A Side/B Side)	Yr	VG	VG+	NM
❑ AFL1-0407	And the Feeling's Good	1977	2.00	4.00	8.00
—Reissue with new prefix					
❑ CPL1-0407	And the Feeling's Good	1974	2.50	5.00	10.00
❑ AFL1-1005	Just Wanna Rock 'n' Roll	1977	2.00	4.00	8.00
—Reissue with new prefix					
❑ APL1-1005	Just Wanna Rock 'n' Roll	1975	2.50	5.00	10.00
❑ LSPX-1005	Encore! Jose Feliciano's Finest Performances	1971	3.00	6.00	12.00
❑ AFL1-2824	Encore! Jose Feliciano's Finest Performances	1978	2.50	5.00	10.00
—Reissue of LSPX-1005					
❑ LPM-3358 [M]	The Voice and Guitar of Jose Feliciano	1965	3.75	7.50	15.00
❑ LSP-3358 [S]	The Voice and Guitar of Jose Feliciano	1965	5.00	10.00	20.00
❑ LPM-3503 [M]	Bag Full of Soul (Folk, Rock and Blues)	1966	3.75	7.50	15.00
❑ LSP-3503 [S]	Bag Full of Soul (Folk, Rock and Blues)	1966	5.00	10.00	20.00
❑ LPM-3581 [M]	Fantastic Feliciano	1966	3.75	7.50	15.00
❑ LSP-3581 [S]	Fantastic Feliciano	1966	5.00	10.00	20.00
❑ AFL1-3957	Feliciano!	1977	2.00	4.00	8.00
—Reissue with new prefix					
❑ LPM-3957 [M]	Feliciano!	1968	6.25	12.50	25.00
❑ LSP-3957 [S]	Feliciano!	1968	3.75	7.50	15.00
❑ LSP-4045	Souled	1968	3.75	7.50	15.00
❑ AFL1-4185	Feliciano/10 to 23	1977	2.00	4.00	8.00
—Reissue with new prefix					
❑ LSP-4185	Feliciano/10 to 23	1969	3.75	7.50	15.00
❑ AFL1-4370	Fireworks	1977	2.00	4.00	8.00
—Reissue with new prefix					
❑ LSP-4370	Fireworks	1970	3.00	6.00	12.00
❑ LSP-4421	Jose Feliciano	1970	3.75	7.50	15.00
❑ LSP-4573	That the Spirit Needs	1971	3.00	6.00	12.00
❑ LSP-4656	Memphis Menu	1972	3.00	6.00	12.00
❑ LSP-6021 [(2)]	Alive Alive-O!	1969	3.75	7.50	15.00

FELICITY Either Don Henley or Glenn Frey was a member of this group (sources conflict).
45s
WILSON

❑ 101	Hurtin'/I'll Try It	1965	7.50	15.00	30.00

FELIX AND THE ESCORTS An early version of THE (YOUNG) RASCALS. "Felix" is FELIX CAVALIERE.
45s
JAG

❑ 685	The Syracuse/Save	1964	37.50	75.00	150.00

FELT
Albums
NASCO

❑ 9006	Felt	1971	50.00	100.00	200.00

FEMALE BEATLES, THE
45s
20TH FOX

❑ 531	I Don't Want to Cry/I Want You	1964	5.00	10.00	20.00

FEMININE COMPLEX, THE
45s
ATHENA

❑ 5003	Six O'Clock in the Morning/I've Been Workin' on You	1969	3.00	6.00	12.00
❑ 5006	I Won't Run/Forgetting	1969	3.00	6.00	12.00
❑ 5008	Are You Lonesome Like Me/Run That Through Your Mind	1969	3.00	6.00	12.00

Albums
ATHENA

❑ 600	The Feminine Complex	1969	7.50	15.00	30.00

FENDER, FREDDY
45s
ABC

❑ 12339	Louisiana Woman/If You're Looking for a Fool	1978	—	2.00	4.00
❑ 12370	Talk to Me/Please Mr. Sun	1978	—	2.00	4.00
❑ 12415	I'm Leaving It All Up to You/Whe It Rains It Really Pours	1978	—	2.00	4.00
❑ 12453	Sweet Summer Day/Walking Piece of Heaven	1979	—	2.00	4.00

ABC/DOT

❑ 17540	Before the Next Teardrop Falls/Waiting for Your Love	1974	—	2.50	5.00
❑ 17558	Wasted Days and Wasted Nights/I Love My Rancho Grande	1975	—	2.50	5.00
❑ 17585	Secret Love/Loving Cajun Style	1975	—	2.00	4.00
❑ 17607	You'll Lose a Good Thing/I'm to Blame	1976	—	2.00	4.00
❑ 17627	Vaya Con Dios/My Happiness	1976	—	2.00	4.00
❑ 17652	Living It Down/Take Her a Message, I'm Lonely	1976	—	2.00	4.00
❑ 17686	The Rains Came/Sugar Coated Love	1977	—	2.00	4.00
❑ 17713	If You Don't Love Me (Why Don't You Just Leave Me Alone)/Thank You, My Love	1977	—	2.00	4.00
❑ 17730	Think About Me/If That's the Way You Want It	1977	—	2.00	4.00
❑ 17734	Christmas Time in the Valley/Please Come Home for Christmas	1977	—	2.50	5.00

ARGO

❑ 5375	A Man Can Cry/You're Something Else for Me	1960	3.75	7.50	15.00

ARV INTERNATIONAL

❑ 5083	Crazy Arms/She Thinks I Still Care	196?	2.50	5.00	10.00
❑ 5102	Un Dia de Sol/La Costumbre	196?	2.50	5.00	10.00
❑ 5146	El Rock de la Carcel/No Seasa Cruel	196?	2.50	5.00	10.00
❑ 5216	Crazy Arms/She Thinks I Still Care	198?	—	2.50	5.00

COLLECTABLES

❑ 90152	Please Come Home for Christmas/Christmas to Christmas (Loving You)	199?	—	—	3.00

—B-side by Lee Greenwood
CRAZY CAJUN

❑ 2002	Before the Next Teardrop Falls/Crazy, Crazy Baby	198?	—	2.50	5.00
❑ 2002	Before the Next Teardrop Falls/Waiting for Your Love	198?	—	2.50	5.00
❑ 2006	Esta Noche Mia Sera/(B-side unknown)	198?	—	2.50	5.00
❑ 2014	No Toquen Ya/I Love My Rancho Grande	198?	—	2.50	5.00
❑ 2019	Vaya Con Dios/No Say El Mismo	198?	—	2.50	5.00

Number	Title (A Side/B Side)	Yr	VG	VG+	NM
❑ 2037	Fannie Mae/Going Out with the Tide	198?	—	2.50	5.00
—With Tommy McLain					
❑ 2060	My Confession/Goin' Honky Tonkin'	198?	—	2.00	4.00
DUNCAN					
❑ 1000	Mean Woman/Holy One	1959	10.00	20.00	40.00
❑ 1001	Wasted Days and Wasted Nights/San Antonio Walk	1959	6.25	12.50	25.00
❑ 1002	Wild Side of Life/Crazy Baby	1959	6.25	12.50	25.00
❑ 1004	Since I Met You Baby/Little Mama	1959	6.25	12.50	25.00
GOLDBAND					
❑ 1214	My Tears of Love/Carmelia	197?	2.50	5.00	10.00
❑ 1264	Bye, Bye, Little Angel/Oh My Love	1975	—	2.50	5.00
❑ 1272	Three Wishes/Me and My Bottle of Rum	1975	—	2.50	5.00
GRT					
❑ 031	Since I Met You Baby/Little Mama	1975	—	2.50	5.00
❑ 039	Wild Side of Life/Go On Baby	1975	—	2.50	5.00
IMPERIAL					
❑ 5659	Mean Woman/Holy One	1960	5.00	10.00	20.00
❑ 5670	Wasted Days and Wasted Nights/I Can't Remember When I Didn't Love You	1960	5.00	10.00	20.00
INSTANT					
❑ 3332	Some People Say/Today's Your Wedding Day	1972	2.00	4.00	8.00
MCA					
❑ 12453	Sweet Summer Day/Walking Piece of Heaven	1979	—	2.00	4.00
❑ 52003	Across the Borderline/Before the Next Teardrop Falls	1982	—	2.00	4.00
NORCO					
❑ 100	Love's Light Is an Ember/The New Stroll	1963	2.50	5.00	10.00
❑ 102	You Made Me Cry/Never Trust a Cheating Woman	1963	2.50	5.00	10.00
❑ 103	Coming Home Soon/Going Out with the Tide	1964	2.50	5.00	10.00
❑ 104	Just a Little Bit/You Made Me a Fool	1964	2.50	5.00	10.00
❑ 106	Ooh Poo Pah Doo/Three Wishes	1964	2.50	5.00	10.00
❑ 107	Magic of Love/Bony Moronie	1965	2.50	5.00	10.00
—With Noel Vill					
❑ 108	In the Still of the Night/You Don't Have to Go	1965	2.50	5.00	10.00
❑ 111	Donna/Lover's Quarrel	1965	2.50	5.00	10.00
PA GO GO					
❑ 115	Cool Mary Lou/You Are My Sunshine	1967	2.50	5.00	10.00
PACEMAKER					
❑ 1973	Wasted Days and Wasted Nights/Bidin' My Time	197?	—	2.50	5.00
REPRISE					
❑ 19143	It's All in the Game/Before the Next Teardrop Falls	1992	—	—	3.00
STARFLITE					
❑ 4900	Yours/Rock Down in My Shoe	1979	—	2.00	4.00
❑ 4904	Squeeze Box/Turn Around	1979	—	2.00	4.00
❑ 4906	My Special Prayer/(B-side unknown)	1979	—	2.00	4.00
❑ 4908	Please Talk to My Heart/(B-side unknown)	1980	—	2.00	4.00
WARNER BROS.					
❑ 29794	Chokin' Kind/I Might As Well Forget You	1983	—	2.00	4.00
Albums					
ABC					
❑ AA-1062	Swamp Gold	1978	2.50	5.00	10.00
❑ AA-1132	Tex-Mex	1979	3.00	6.00	12.00
ABC/DOT					
❑ DOSD-2020	Before the Next Teardrop Falls	1975	3.00	6.00	12.00
❑ DOSD-2044	Are You Ready for Freddy	1975	3.00	6.00	12.00
❑ DOSD-2050	Rock 'n Country	1976	3.00	6.00	12.00
❑ DOSD-2061	If You're Ever in Texas	1976	3.00	6.00	12.00
❑ DO-2079	The Best of Freddy Fender	1977	3.00	6.00	12.00
❑ DP-2090	If You Don't Love Me	1977	3.00	6.00	12.00
❑ DO-2101	Merry Christmas — Feliz Navidad	1977	3.00	6.00	12.00
ACCORD					
❑ SN-7121	Since I Met You Baby	1981	2.50	5.00	10.00
GRT					
❑ 8005	Since I Met You Baby	1975	3.00	6.00	12.00
INTERMEDIA					
❑ QS-5035	Before the Next Teardrop Falls	198?	2.00	4.00	8.00
MCA					
❑ 639	Are You Ready for Freddy	1980	2.00	4.00	8.00
—Reissue of ABC/Dot 2044					
❑ 668	Swamp Gold	1980	2.00	4.00	8.00
—Reissue of ABC 1062					
❑ 669	If You Don't Love Me	1980	2.00	4.00	8.00
—Reissue of ABC/Dot 2090					
❑ 835	The Best of Freddy Fender	198?	2.00	4.00	8.00
—Reissue of MCA 3285					
❑ AA-1132	Tex-Mex	1979	2.50	5.00	10.00
—Reissue of ABC 1132					
❑ 3285	The Best of Freddy Fender	1979	2.50	5.00	10.00
—Reissue of ABC/Dot 2079					
❑ 15025	Merry Christmas	198?	2.00	4.00	8.00
❑ 15037	Christmas Time in the Valley	198?	2.50	5.00	10.00
❑ 37109	Tex-Mex	1980	2.00	4.00	8.00
—Reissue of MCA 1132					
❑ 37110	Before the Next Teardrop Falls	1980	2.00	4.00	8.00
—Reissue of ABC/Dot 2020					
PICCADILLY					
❑ 3589	Enter My Heart	1981	2.50	5.00	10.00
PICKWICK					
❑ JS-6178	Freddy Fender	1975	2.50	5.00	10.00
POWER PAK					
❑ PO-280	Recorded Inside Louisiana State Prison	1975	2.50	5.00	10.00
STARFLITE					
❑ JZ 36073	Balladeer	1980	2.50	5.00	10.00
❑ JZ 36284	Together We Drifted Apart	1980	2.50	5.00	10.00

FENDER IV
45s
IMPERIAL

❑ 66061	Mar-Gaya/You Better Tell Me Now	1964	12.50	25.00	50.00
❑ 66098	Malibu Run/Everybody Up	1965	12.50	25.00	50.00

Number	Title (A Side/B Side)	Yr	VG	VG+	NM

FENDERMEN, THE
45s
CUCA
| ❏ 1003 | Mule Skinner Blues/Torture | 1960 | 50.00 | 100.00 | 200.00 |

SOMA
❏ 1137	Mule Skinner Blues/Torture	1960	6.25	12.50	25.00
❏ 1142	Don't You Just Know It/Beach Party	1960	5.00	10.00	20.00
❏ 1155	Heartbreakin' Special/Can't You Wait	1960	5.00	10.00	20.00

Albums
BEAT ROCKET
| ❏ BR 116 | Mule Skinner Blues | 199? | 3.00 | 6.00 | 12.00 |

SOMA
❏ MG-1240 [M]	Mule Skinner Blues	1960	300.00	600.00	1200.
—Black vinyl					
❏ MG-1240 [M]	Mule Skinner Blues	1960	2000.	3000.	4000.
—Blue vinyl					

FENTON, SHANE, AND THE FENTONES
45s
LAURIE
| ❏ 3287 | Don't Do That/I'll Know | 1965 | 2.50 | 5.00 | 10.00 |

20TH FOX
| ❏ 439 | Don't Do That/I'll Know | 1963 | 3.75 | 7.50 | 15.00 |

FERG, JOHNNY May be the same person as JOHNNY FERGUSON.
45s
DECCA
| ❏ 30572 | Candy Love/Sad, Sad Day | 1958 | 7.50 | 15.00 | 30.00 |

FERGUSON, HELEN
45s
20TH CENTURY-FOX
| ❏ 485 | One Last Chance/Forgetfulness | 1964 | 2.00 | 4.00 | 8.00 |

FERGUSON, HELENA
45s
COMPASS
| ❏ 7009 | Where Is the Party/My Terms | 1967 | 5.00 | 10.00 | 20.00 |
| ❏ 7017 | Don't Spoil Our Good Thing/The Loneliness | 1968 | 5.00 | 10.00 | 20.00 |

CONGRESS
| ❏ 6009 | I'm So Glad/I'd Rather Go Blind | 1970 | 15.00 | 30.00 | 60.00 |

FERGUSON, JOHNNY Also see JOHNNY FERG.
45s
DECCA
| ❏ 30731 | Last Date/'Til School Starts Again | 1959 | 5.00 | 10.00 | 20.00 |

MGM
❏ 12789	Afterglow/Waitin' for the Sandman	1959	7.50	15.00	30.00
❏ 12855	Angela Jones/Blue Serge and White Lace	1959	5.00	10.00	20.00
❏ 12905	I Understand Just How You Feel/Flutter Flutter	1960	7.50	15.00	30.00
❏ 12960	No One Can Love You (Like I Do)/Valley of Love	1960	3.75	7.50	15.00

FERGUSON, SHEILA
45s
LANDA
| ❏ 706 | How Did That Happen/Little Red Riding Hood | 1965 | 7.50 | 15.00 | 30.00 |

SWAN
❏ 4217	I Weep for You/Don't (Leave Me Lover)	1965	10.00	20.00	40.00
❏ 4225	And In Return/Are You Satisfied	1965	7.50	15.00	30.00
❏ 4234	Signs of Love/Heartbroken Memories	1965	10.00	20.00	40.00

FERKO STRING BAND The below discography for the Philadelphia Mummers Parade institution, one of the least likely charted artists ever, is almost certainly incomplete.
45s
ARGO
| ❏ 5451 | Ferko's Monkey/Golden Slipper Strut | 1963 | 2.50 | 5.00 | 10.00 |

FERKO
❏ 4501	Golden Slippers/Hello	195?	3.00	6.00	12.00
❏ 4502	I'm Looking Over a Four Leaf Clover/ Heart of My Heart	195?	3.00	6.00	12.00
❏ 4503	Sweet Georgia Brown/Red Wing	195?	3.00	6.00	12.00
❏ 4504	Do You Ever Think of Me/When You're Smiling	195?	3.00	6.00	12.00
❏ 4505	Auld Lang Syne/When You Wore a Tulip	195?	3.00	6.00	12.00
❏ 4505	Heartbreaker/I Want a Girl	195?	3.00	6.00	12.00
❏ 4507	Kelley/Two Eyes in Dixie	195?	3.00	6.00	12.00
❏ 4508	Baby Face/Underneath the Arches	195?	3.00	6.00	12.00

MEDIA
❏ 1010	Alabama Jubilee/Sing a Little Melody	1955	2.50	5.00	10.00
❏ 1013	You Are My Sunshine/ Ma (She's Makin' Eyes at Me)	1955	2.50	5.00	10.00
❏ 1016	Happy Days Are Here Again/ Deep in the Heart of Texas	1955	2.50	5.00	10.00

PALDA
❏ 100	Golden Slippers/Hello	195?	3.75	7.50	15.00
❏ 200	Four Leaf Clover/Heart Breaker	195?	3.75	7.50	15.00
❏ 300	Lili Marlene/Red Wing	195?	3.75	7.50	15.00
❏ 400	Baby Face/Take Me Out to the Ball Game	195?	3.75	7.50	15.00
❏ 700	Alexander's Ragtime Band/Old Gang of Mine	195?	3.75	7.50	15.00
❏ 1000	You Darlin'/Two-Timer	195?	3.75	7.50	15.00

SAVOY
| ❏ 1169 | Smiles/There Are Two "I"s in Dixie | 1955 | 3.75 | 7.50 | 15.00 |

SURE
| ❏ 1032 | Medley/Bill Bailey | 195? | 2.50 | 5.00 | 10.00 |

Albums
ABC-PARAMOUNT
| ❏ ABC 440 [M] | The World Renowned Ferko String Band | 1963 | 3.00 | 6.00 | 12.00 |
| ❏ ABC 440 [S] | The World Renowned Ferko String Band | 1963 | 3.75 | 7.50 | 15.00 |

ESSEX
| ❏ ESLP-209 [M] | Happy Days Are Here Again! | 1956 | 5.00 | 10.00 | 20.00 |

FERKO
| ❏ LP 3301 [10] | Favorites | 195? | 5.00 | 10.00 | 20.00 |

REGENT
| ❏ MG-6007 [M] | Ferko String Band | 195? | 3.75 | 7.50 | 15.00 |
| ❏ MG-6008 [M] | Ferko String Band, Vol. 2 | 195? | 3.75 | 7.50 | 15.00 |

SOMERSET
| ❏ P 3700 [M] | The Happiest Music in the World | 196? | 2.50 | 5.00 | 10.00 |
| ❏ P 12700 [M] | Happy Days Are Here Again! | 196? | 2.50 | 5.00 | 10.00 |

STEREO-FIDELITY
| ❏ SF 12700 [S] | Happy Days Are Here Again! | 196? | 3.00 | 6.00 | 12.00 |

SURE
❏ SM-7 [M]	The World Renowned Ferko String Band	1963	3.75	7.50	15.00
❏ Vol. 8	Ferko String Band On Broadway	196?	2.50	5.00	10.00
❏ Vol. 42	Before the Parade Passes By	197?	2.50	5.00	10.00

TRANS-WORLD
| ❏ TWLP-209 [M] | Happy Days Are Here Again! | 1956 | 3.75 | 7.50 | 15.00 |

FERLINGHETTI, LAWRENCE
Albums
FANTASY
❏ 7004 [M]	The Impeachment of Eisenhower	1958	25.00	50.00	100.00
—Black vinyl					
❏ 7004 [M]	The Impeachment of Eisenhower	1958	50.00	100.00	200.00
—Red vinyl					

FERRANTE AND TEICHER
45s
ABC-PARAMOUNT
❏ 9957	Che Si Dice/How High the Moon	1958	3.00	6.00	12.00
❏ 9975	Aflame/How High the Moon	1958	3.00	6.00	12.00
❏ 10017	Prairie Blues/Side Saddle	1959	3.00	6.00	12.00
❏ 10165	Take Me Along/Lida Rose	1960	3.00	6.00	12.00
❏ 10347	Till There Was You/Lida Rose	1962	3.00	6.00	12.00

COLUMBIA
| ❏ 40088 | Taboo/Semper Fideles | 1953 | 3.75 | 7.50 | 15.00 |

UNITED ARTISTS
❏ 0111	Exodus/Tonight	1973	—	2.00	4.00
❏ 0112	Midnight Cowboy/Theme from "The Apartment"	1973	—	2.00	4.00
❏ 0113	Rudolph, the Red-Nosed Reindeer/Silent Night	1973	—	2.00	4.00
—0111, 0112 and 0113 are "Silver Spotlight Series" reissues					
❏ XW168	Song Sung Blue/American Pie	1973	—	2.00	4.00
❏ 196	Lover's Symphony/Dream Concerto	1960	2.50	5.00	10.00
❏ XW205 [DJ]	Last Tango in Paris (mono/stereo)	1973	—	2.00	4.00
❏ 231	Theme from "The Apartment"/Lonely Room	1960	2.50	5.00	10.00
❏ 231 [PS]	Theme from "The Apartment"/Lonely Room	1960	3.75	7.50	15.00
❏ 274	Exodus/Twilight	1960	3.00	6.00	12.00
❏ 274 [PS]	Exodus/Twilight	1960	3.75	7.50	15.00
❏ XW295	Love Theme from "Lady Sings the Blues"/ Summer Is Coming	1973	—	2.00	4.00
❏ 300	Love Theme from One-Eyed Jacks/Tara's Theme	1961	2.50	5.00	10.00
❏ 300 [PS]	Love Theme from One-Eyed Jacks/Tara's Theme	1961	3.75	7.50	15.00
❏ 319	Theme from "Goodbye Again"/Possessed	1961	2.50	5.00	10.00
❏ XW367	When Heaven Smiles/I Want to Spend My Life with You	1973	—	2.00	4.00
❏ 373	Tonight/Dream of Love	1961	2.50	5.00	10.00
❏ 431	Smile/Streets of Paris	1962	2.50	5.00	10.00
❏ XW433	Freedom/Early Morning	1974	—	2.00	4.00
❏ XW448	I'm Stone in Love with You/Cristo Redentor	1974	—	2.00	4.00
❏ 470	Lisa/Negligee	1962	2.50	5.00	10.00
❏ 537	Theme from "The Eleventh Hour"/Wishing Star	1963	2.00	4.00	8.00
❏ 563	Lawrence of Arabia/Paris Joy Ride	1963	2.00	4.00	8.00
❏ 607	(Love Theme from) Cleopatra/Caesar and Cleopatra Theme	1963	2.00	4.00	8.00
❏ 631	Sands of Time/Devotion	1963	2.00	4.00	8.00
❏ 654	Japanese Garden/April in Portugal	1963	2.00	4.00	8.00
❏ 660	Crystal Fingers/Greensleeves	1963	2.00	4.00	8.00
❏ 700	It's Alright/Corn Pone	1964	2.00	4.00	8.00
❏ 735	The Seventh Dawn/You're Too Much	1964	2.00	4.00	8.00
❏ 735 [PS]	The Seventh Dawn/You're Too Much	1964	3.00	6.00	12.00
❏ XW759	Theme from "Breakheart Pass"/Mandy	1976	—	2.00	4.00
❏ 770	What More Can I Say/I've Grown Accustomed to Her Face	1964	2.00	4.00	8.00
❏ XW779	Theme from "Mahogany"/Theme from "Breakheart Pass"	1976	—	2.00	4.00
❏ 816	The Greatest Story Ever Told/To Spring	1965	—	3.00	6.00
❏ XW821	Theme from "The Missouri Breaks"/Serendipity	1976	—	2.00	4.00
❏ 903	Country Boy/The Knack	1965	—	3.00	6.00
❏ XW915	Gonna Fly Now (Theme from "Rocky")/You Take My Heart Away	1976	—	2.00	4.00
❏ 925	Race to Live/Debutante Waltz	1965	—	3.00	6.00
❏ 977	Ol' Man River/Judith	1966	—	3.00	6.00
❏ XW1034	A Bridge Too Far/ Theme from "New York, New York"	1977	—	2.00	4.00
❏ XW1173	Theme from "Star Trek"/Swinging on a Star	1978	—	2.00	4.00
❏ XW1224	Theme from "The Last Waltz"/Finger Painting	1978	—	2.00	4.00
❏ XW1272	Can You Read My Mind/Ski Fever	1979	—	2.00	4.00
❏ 50038	Theme from "Khartoum"/Firebird	1966	—	3.00	6.00
❏ 50038 [PS]	Theme from "Khartoum"/Firebird	1966	2.50	5.00	10.00
❏ 50084	Theme from "The Bible"/Three Over Four	1966	—	3.00	6.00
❏ 50101	A Man and a Woman/Dark Eyes	1966	—	3.00	6.00
❏ 50188	Rage to Live/Exodus	1967	—	3.00	6.00
❏ 50228	Live for Life/Pavanne	1967	—	3.00	6.00
❏ 50257	In the Heat of the Night/You Only Live Twice	1968	—	2.50	5.00
❏ 50259	Rock-a-Bye Baby/Here Is Where I Belong	1968	—	2.50	5.00
❏ 50468	Prelude to Love/A Boy and a Girl	1969	—	2.50	5.00
❏ 50501	Chitty Chitty Bang Bang/ Buona Sera, Mrs. Campbell	1969	—	2.50	5.00
❏ 50512	Joanna/Andrea	1969	—	2.50	5.00
❏ 50554	Midnight Cowboy/Rock-a-Bye Baby	1969	—	2.50	5.00
❏ 50646	Lay Lady Lay/Theme from "Z"	1970	—	2.00	4.00
❏ 50711	Pieces of Dreams/Magical Connection	1970	—	2.00	4.00
❏ 50747	Music Lovers/Love Is Now	1971	—	2.00	4.00
❏ 50869	Diamonds Are Forever/ There's a New Day Coming	1971	—	2.00	4.00

Number	Title (A Side/B Side)	Yr	VG	VG+	NM
❏ 50895	Love Theme from "The Godfather"/There's a New Day Coming	1972	—	2.00	4.00
❏ 50963	Everything You Always Wanted to Know But Were Afraid to Ask/Tranquillo	1972	—	2.00	4.00

7-Inch Extended Plays
UNITED ARTISTS

Number	Title (A Side/B Side)	Yr	VG	VG+	NM
❏ UALP 9-6526	The More I See You/Three Over Four/Work Song//You Don't Have to Say You Love Me/Lara's Theme from "Dr. Zhivago"	1966	2.50	5.00	10.00

—Jukebox issue; small hole, plays at 33 1/3 rpm

❏ UALP 9-6526 [PS]	You Asked For It	1966	2.50	5.00	10.00

Albums
ABC

Number	Title (A Side/B Side)	Yr	VG	VG+	NM
❏ 553 [M]	World's Greatest Semi-Classical Favorites	1966	2.50	5.00	10.00
❏ S-553 [S]	World's Greatest Semi-Classical Favorites	1966	3.00	6.00	12.00
❏ 554 [M]	Memories	1966	2.50	5.00	10.00
❏ S-554 [S]	Memories	1966	3.00	6.00	12.00
❏ 555 [M]	Heaven Sounds	1966	2.50	5.00	10.00
❏ S-555 [S]	Heaven Sounds	1966	3.00	6.00	12.00
❏ 556 [M]	We've Got Rhythm	1966	2.50	5.00	10.00
❏ S-556 [S]	We've Got Rhythm	1966	3.00	6.00	12.00
❏ 557 [M]	Twin Piano Magic, Vol. 1	1966	2.50	5.00	10.00
❏ S-557 [S]	Twin Piano Magic, Vol. 1	1966	3.00	6.00	12.00
❏ 558 [M]	Autumn Leaves	1966	2.50	5.00	10.00
❏ S-558 [S]	Autumn Leaves	1966	3.00	6.00	12.00
❏ 559 [M]	Twin Piano Magic, Vol. 2	1966	2.50	5.00	10.00
❏ S-559 [S]	Twin Piano Magic, Vol. 2	1966	3.00	6.00	12.00
❏ 560 [M]	Bolero	1966	2.50	5.00	10.00
❏ S-560 [S]	Bolero	1966	3.00	6.00	12.00
❏ 561 [M]	Temptation	1966	2.50	5.00	10.00
❏ S-561 [S]	Temptation	1966	3.00	6.00	12.00

ABC-PARAMOUNT

Number	Title (A Side/B Side)	Yr	VG	VG+	NM
❏ 221 [M]	Heavenly Sounds in Hi-Fi	1958	3.75	7.50	15.00
❏ S-221 [S]	Heavenly Sounds in Hi-Fi	1958	5.00	10.00	20.00
❏ 248 [M]	Ferrante and Teicher with Percussion	1958	3.75	7.50	15.00
❏ S-248 [S]	Ferrante and Teicher with Percussion	1958	5.00	10.00	20.00
❏ 285 [M]	Ferrante and Teicher Blast Off	1959	3.75	7.50	15.00
❏ S-285 [S]	Ferrante and Teicher Blast Off	1959	5.00	10.00	20.00
❏ 313 [M]	Ferrante and Teicher Play Light Classics	1960	3.75	7.50	15.00
❏ S-313 [S]	Ferrante and Teicher Play Light Classics	1960	5.00	10.00	20.00
❏ 336 [M]	Themes from Broadway Shows	1960	3.75	7.50	15.00
❏ S-336 [S]	Themes from Broadway Shows	1960	5.00	10.00	20.00
❏ 430 [M]	Postcards from Paris	1962	3.00	6.00	12.00
❏ S-430 [S]	Postcards from Paris	1962	3.75	7.50	15.00
❏ 437 [M]	Popular Classics	1962	3.00	6.00	12.00
❏ S-437 [S]	Popular Classics	1962	3.75	7.50	15.00
❏ 454 [M]	The Artistry of Ferrante and Teicher	1963	3.00	6.00	12.00
❏ S-454 [S]	The Artistry of Ferrante and Teicher	1963	3.75	7.50	15.00
❏ ST-90467 [S]	Postcards from Paris	196?	3.75	7.50	15.00

—Capitol Record Club edition

BAINBRIDGE

Number	Title (A Side/B Side)	Yr	VG	VG+	NM
❏ BT-6263	A Few of Our Favorites on Stage	1986	2.50	5.00	10.00
❏ BT-6266	American Fantasy	1987	2.50	5.00	10.00

COLUMBIA

❏ CL 573 [M]	Hi-Fire Works	1955	6.25	12.50	25.00

GRAND AWARD

❏ GA-263	Themes from Broadway Shows	1962	3.00	6.00	12.00

HARMONY

❏ HL 7325 [M]	Twin Piano Magic	1965	3.00	6.00	12.00
❏ HL 7427 [M]	Fireworks	1967	3.00	6.00	12.00
❏ HS 11125 [R]	Twin Piano Magic	1965	2.50	5.00	10.00
❏ HS 11227 [R]	Fireworks	1967	2.50	5.00	10.00
❏ HS 11411	Encore	1970	2.50	5.00	10.00

LIBERTY

❏ LWB-70 [(2)]	10th Anniversary — Golden Piano Hits	198?	2.50	5.00	10.00

—Reissue of United Artists 70

❏ LWB-73 [(2)]	The Best of Ferrante and Teicher	198?	2.50	5.00	10.00

—Reissue of United Artists 73

❏ LW-662	Feelings	198?	2.00	4.00	8.00

—Reissue of United Artists 662

❏ LT-782	Rocky and Other Knockouts	198?	2.00	4.00	8.00

—Reissue of United Artists 782

❏ LKDL-831 [(4)]	For You with Love	198?	4.50	9.00	18.00

—Reissue of United Artists 831

❏ LT-908	You Light Up My Life	198?	2.00	4.00	8.00

—Reissue of United Artists 908

❏ LT-980	Classical Disco	198?	2.00	4.00	8.00

—Reissue of United Artists 980

❏ LM-1016	Midnight Cowboy	1981	2.00	4.00	8.00

—Reissue of United Artists 1016

❏ LN-10112	Supermen	198?	2.00	4.00	8.00

—Reissue of United Artists 941

❏ LN-10113	Star Wars	198?	2.00	4.00	8.00

—Reissue of United Artists 855

❏ LN-10141	The People's Choice	1981	2.00	4.00	8.00

—Budget-line reissue of United Artists 6385

❏ LN-10142	Snowbound	1981	2.00	4.00	8.00

—Budget-line reissue of United Artists 6233

❏ LN-10158	Concert for Lovers	1981	2.00	4.00	8.00

—Budget-line reissue of United Artists 6315

❏ LN-10175	Showstoppers	1983	2.00	4.00	8.00
❏ LN-10176	The Movie Theme Team	1983	2.00	4.00	8.00
❏ LN-10198	Classic Lites	1983	2.00	4.00	8.00
❏ LN-10210	The Movie Theme Team II	1984	2.00	4.00	8.00
❏ LN-10242 [(2)]	Ferrante and Teicher Superpak	1984	2.50	5.00	10.00

PICKWICK

❏ PC-3003 [M]	Excitement	196?	2.50	5.00	10.00
❏ SPC-3003 [S]	Excitement	196?	2.50	5.00	10.00
❏ PC-3077 [M]	In Love	196?	2.50	5.00	10.00
❏ SPC-3077 [S]	In Love	196?	2.50	5.00	10.00
❏ SPC-3397	How High the Moon	197?	2.00	4.00	8.00
❏ SPC-3586	Getting Together	1978	2.00	4.00	8.00
❏ SPC-3612	Fabulous Favorites	197?	2.00	4.00	8.00

SUNSET

❏ SUS-5235	Incomparable Piano	1969	2.00	4.00	8.00
❏ SUS-5277	Midnight Memories	1970	2.00	4.00	8.00

Number	Title (A Side/B Side)	Yr	VG	VG+	NM
❏ SUS-5313	Love Is a Rainbow	1971	2.00	4.00	8.00

UNITED ARTISTS

Number	Title (A Side/B Side)	Yr	VG	VG+	NM
❏ UA-LA018-F	Hear & Now	1972	2.50	5.00	10.00
❏ UXS-70 [(2)]	10th Anniversary — Golden Piano Hits	1969	3.00	6.00	12.00
❏ UA-LA072-G	The Roaring 20's	1973	2.50	5.00	10.00
❏ UXS-73 [(2)]	The Best of Ferrante and Teicher	1971	3.00	6.00	12.00
❏ UXS-77 [(2)]	Ferrante and Teicher Superpak	1972	3.00	6.00	12.00
❏ UA-LA101-G2 [(2)]	Greatest Love Themes of the Twentieth Century	1973	3.00	6.00	12.00
❏ UA-LA118-G	Killing Me Softly	1973	2.50	5.00	10.00
❏ UA-LA195-G	Dial M for Music	1974	2.50	5.00	10.00
❏ UA-LA227-G	In a Soulful Mood	1974	2.50	5.00	10.00
❏ UA-LA236-G	The Very Best of Ferrante and Teicher	1974	2.50	5.00	10.00
❏ UA-LA490-G	The Carpenters Songbook	1975	2.50	5.00	10.00
❏ UA-LA573-G	Spirit of 1976	1975	2.50	5.00	10.00
❏ UA-LA585-G	Piano Portraits	1976	2.50	5.00	10.00
❏ UA-LA662-G	Feelings	1976	2.50	5.00	10.00
❏ UA-LA681-G	Around	1977	2.50	5.00	10.00
❏ UA-LA782-G	Rocky and Other Knockouts	1977	2.50	5.00	10.00
❏ UA-LA831-P [(4)]	For You with Love	1978	5.00	10.00	20.00
❏ UA-LA855-G	Star Wars	1978	3.00	6.00	12.00
❏ UA-LA908-H	You Light Up My Life	1978	2.50	5.00	10.00
❏ UA-LA941-H	Supermen	1979	2.50	5.00	10.00
❏ LT-980	Classical Disco	1979	2.50	5.00	10.00
❏ LM-1016	Midnight Cowboy	1980	2.00	4.00	8.00

—Reissue of 6725

❏ UAL 3121 [M]	The World's Greatest Themes	1960	3.00	6.00	12.00
❏ UAL 3135 [M]	Latin Pianos	1960	3.00	6.00	12.00
❏ UAL 3166 [M]	West Side Story & Other Motion Picture & Broadway Hits	1961	3.00	6.00	12.00
❏ UAL 3171 [M]	Tonight	1962	3.00	6.00	12.00
❏ UAL 3210 [M]	Golden Themes from Motion Pictures	1962	3.00	6.00	12.00
❏ UAL 3211 [M]	The Many Moods of Ferrante & Teicher	1962	3.00	6.00	12.00
❏ UAL 3230 [M]	Pianos in Paradise	1962	3.00	6.00	12.00
❏ UAL 3233 [M]	Snowbound	1962	3.00	6.00	12.00
❏ UAL 3247 [M]	Keys to Her Apartment	1963	3.00	6.00	12.00
❏ UAL 3269 [M]	Golden Piano Hits	1963	2.50	5.00	10.00

—Reissue of 7505

❏ UAL 3282 [M]	Love Themes	1963	2.50	5.00	10.00

—Reissue of 7514

❏ UAL 3284 [M]	Keyboard Kapers	1963	2.50	5.00	10.00
❏ UAL 3290 [M]	Love Themes from Cleopatra	1963	3.00	6.00	12.00
❏ UAL 3298 [M]	Holiday for Pianos	1963	2.50	5.00	10.00
❏ UAL 3315 [M]	Concert for Lovers	1964	3.00	6.00	12.00
❏ UAL 3340 [M]	Exotic Love Themes	1964	3.00	6.00	12.00
❏ UAL 3343 [M]	50 Fabulous Piano Favorites	1964	3.00	6.00	12.00
❏ UAL 3361 [M]	My Fair Lady	1964	2.50	5.00	10.00
❏ UAL 3375 [M]	The Enchanted World of Ferrante and Teicher	1964	3.00	6.00	12.00
❏ UAL 3385 [M]	The People's Choice	1964	2.50	5.00	10.00
❏ UAL 3406 [M]	Springtime	1965	2.50	5.00	10.00
❏ UAL 3416 [M]	By Popular Demand	1965	2.50	5.00	10.00
❏ UAL 3434 [M]	Only the Best	1965	2.50	5.00	10.00
❏ UAL 3444 [M]	The Ferrante and Teicher Concert	1965	2.50	5.00	10.00
❏ UAL 3475 [M]	The Ferrante and Teicher Concert, Part 2	1966	2.50	5.00	10.00
❏ UAL 3483 [M]	For Lovers of All Ages	1966	2.50	5.00	10.00
❏ UAL 3526 [M]	You Asked For It!	1966	2.50	5.00	10.00
❏ UAL 3536 [M]	We Wish You a Merry Christmas	1966	3.75	7.50	15.00
❏ UAL 3556 [M]	Our Golden Favorites	1967	3.00	6.00	12.00
❏ UAL 3572 [M]	A Man and a Woman & Other Motion Picture Themes	1967	2.50	5.00	10.00
❏ UAS 5501	Getting Together	1970	2.50	5.00	10.00
❏ UAS 5531	It's Too Late	1971	2.50	5.00	10.00
❏ UAS 5552	Fiddler on the Roof	1971	2.50	5.00	10.00
❏ UAS 5588	Ferrante and Teicher Play Hit Themes	1972	2.50	5.00	10.00
❏ UAS 5645	Ferrante and Teicher Salute Nashville	1972	2.50	5.00	10.00
❏ UAS 6121 [S]	The World's Greatest Themes	1960	3.75	7.50	15.00
❏ UAS 6135 [S]	Latin Pianos	1960	3.75	7.50	15.00
❏ UAS 6166 [S]	West Side Story & Other Motion Picture & Broadway Hits	1961	3.75	7.50	15.00
❏ UAS 6171 [S]	Tonight	1962	3.75	7.50	15.00
❏ UAS 6210 [S]	Golden Themes from Motion Pictures	1962	3.75	7.50	15.00
❏ UAS 6211 [S]	The Many Moods of Ferrante & Teicher	1962	3.75	7.50	15.00
❏ UAS 6230 [S]	Pianos in Paradise	1962	3.75	7.50	15.00
❏ UAS 6233 [S]	Snowbound	1962	3.75	7.50	15.00
❏ UAS 6247 [S]	Keys to Her Apartment	1963	3.75	7.50	15.00
❏ UAS 6269 [S]	Golden Piano Hits	1963	3.00	6.00	12.00

—Reissue of 8505

❏ UAS 6282 [S]	Love Themes	1963	3.00	6.00	12.00

—Reissue of 8514

❏ UAS 6284 [S]	Keyboard Kapers	1963	3.00	6.00	12.00
❏ UAS 6290 [S]	Love Themes from Cleopatra	1963	3.75	7.50	15.00
❏ UAS 6298 [S]	Holiday for Pianos	1963	3.00	6.00	12.00
❏ UAS 6315 [S]	Concert for Lovers	1964	3.75	7.50	15.00
❏ UAS 6340 [S]	Exotic Love Themes	1964	3.75	7.50	15.00
❏ UAS 6343 [S]	50 Fabulous Piano Favorites	1964	3.75	7.50	15.00
❏ UAS 6361 [S]	My Fair Lady	1964	3.00	6.00	12.00
❏ UAS 6375 [S]	The Enchanted World of Ferrante and Teicher	1964	3.75	7.50	15.00
❏ UAS 6385 [S]	The People's Choice	1964	3.00	6.00	12.00
❏ UAS 6406 [S]	Springtime	1965	3.00	6.00	12.00
❏ UAS 6416 [S]	By Popular Demand	1965	3.00	6.00	12.00
❏ UAS 6434 [S]	Only the Best	1965	3.00	6.00	12.00
❏ UAS 6444 [S]	The Ferrante and Teicher Concert	1965	3.00	6.00	12.00
❏ UAS 6475 [S]	The Ferrante and Teicher Concert, Part 2	1966	3.00	6.00	12.00
❏ UAS 6483 [S]	For Lovers of All Ages	1966	3.00	6.00	12.00
❏ UAS 6526 [S]	You Asked For It!	1966	3.00	6.00	12.00
❏ UAS 6536 [S]	We Wish You a Merry Christmas	1966	3.00	6.00	12.00
❏ UAS 6536 [S]	We Wish You a Merry Christmas	1972	2.00	4.00	8.00

—Tan label (may also exist on late-1960s UA labels)

❏ UAS 6556 [S]	Our Golden Favorites	1967	2.50	5.00	10.00
❏ UAS 6572 [S]	A Man and a Woman & Other Motion Picture Themes	1967	3.00	6.00	12.00
❏ UAS 6659	A Bouquet of Hits	1968	2.50	5.00	10.00
❏ UAS 6701	Listen to the Movies	1969	2.50	5.00	10.00
❏ UAS 6725	Midnight Cowboy	1969	2.50	5.00	10.00
❏ UAS 6771	Love Is a Soft Touch	1970	2.50	5.00	10.00
❏ UAS 6792	The Music Lovers	1971	2.50	5.00	10.00
❏ WW 7504 [M]	Dynamic Twin Pianos	1961	3.00	6.00	12.00

Number	Title (A Side/B Side)	Yr	VG	VG+	NM
☐ WW 7505 [M]	Golden Piano Hits	1961	3.00	6.00	12.00
☐ WW 7514 [M]	Love Themes	1961	3.00	6.00	12.00
☐ WWS 8505 [S]	Golden Piano Hits	1961	3.75	7.50	15.00
☐ WWS 8514 [S]	Love Themes	1961	3.75	7.50	15.00
☐ ST-90931 [S]	You Asked For It!	1966	3.75	7.50	15.00
—Capitol Record Club edition					
URANIA					
☐ 8011	Rhapsody	196?	3.00	6.00	12.00
WESTMINSTER					
☐ SW 1045 [S]	Soundproof	195?	6.25	12.50	25.00
☐ SW 1048 [S]	Latin American Adventure	195?	6.25	12.50	25.00
☐ WL 3044 [M]	Christmas Hi-Fi Favorites	195?	5.00	10.00	20.00
☐ WP 6001 [M]	Postcards from Paris	195?	5.00	10.00	20.00
☐ WP 6021 [M]	Adventure in Carols	195?	5.00	10.00	20.00

FERRIER, GARRY
45s
ACADEMY

Number	Title (A Side/B Side)	Yr	VG	VG+	NM
☐ 112	Ringo-Deer/Just My Luck	1964	5.00	10.00	20.00

FERRIS AND THE WHEELS
45s
BAMBI

Number	Title (A Side/B Side)	Yr	VG	VG+	NM
☐ 801	I Want to Dance (Every Night)/Chop Chop	1961	6.25	12.50	25.00
UNITED ARTISTS					
☐ 458	Moments Like This/He Was a Fortune Teller	1962	25.00	50.00	100.00

FERRY, BRYAN   Also see ROXY MUSIC.
12-Inch Singles
MCA

Number	Title (A Side/B Side)	Yr	VG	VG+	NM
☐ 23620	Is Your Love Strong Enough (2 versions)/ Windswept	1986	2.00	4.00	8.00
REPRISE					
☐ PRO-A-2852 [DJ]	The Right Stuff (same on both sides)	1987	—	3.00	6.00
☐ 20799	The Right Stuff (3 mixes)	1987	—	3.00	6.00
☐ 20841	Kiss and Tell (3 versions)/Zamba	1988	2.50	5.00	10.00
—With picture cover; deduct 40% if cover is missing					
☐ 20846	Limbo (2 versions)/Bete Noire	1989	2.50	5.00	10.00
WARNER BROS.					
☐ PRO-A-2304 [DJ]	Slave to Love (Long)/Slave to Love (Short)	1985	2.00	4.00	8.00
☐ PRO-A-2352 [DJ]	Don't Stop the Dance/ Don't Stop the Dance (Edit)	1985	2.00	4.00	8.00
☐ PRO-A-2577 [DJ]	Help Me (same on both sides)	1986	3.00	6.00	12.00
☐ 20385	Don't Stop the Dance/Slave to Love	1985	—	3.00	6.00

45s
ATLANTIC

Number	Title (A Side/B Side)	Yr	VG	VG+	NM
☐ 3017	A Hard Rain's Gonna Fall/2 HB	1974	—	2.50	5.00
☐ 3351	Let's Stick Together (Let's Work Together)/Sea Breezes	1976	—	2.00	4.00
☐ 3364	Heart on My Sleeve/Re-Make, Re-Model	1976	—	2.00	4.00
☐ 3399	Tokyo Joe/As the World Turns	1977	—	2.00	4.00
☐ 3539	Sign of the Times/Can't Let Go	1978	—	2.00	4.00
MCA					
☐ 52788	Is Your Love Strong Enough/Windswept	1986	—	—	3.00
☐ 52788 [PS]	Is Your Love Strong Enough/Windswept	1986	—	—	3.00
REPRISE					
☐ 28116	Limbo (Brooklyn Version)/Limbo (Latin Version)	1988	—	—	3.00
☐ 28116 [PS]	Limbo (Brooklyn Version)/Limbo (Latin Version)	1988	—	—	3.00
☐ 28117	Kiss and Tell/Zamba	1988	—	—	3.00
☐ 28117 [PS]	Kiss and Tell/Zamba	1988	—	—	3.00
☐ 28172	The Right Stuff/The Right Stuff (Brooklyn Mix)	1987	—	—	3.00
VIRGIN					
☐ S7-18133	Mamouna/Don't Stop the Dance (Live)	1994	—	2.00	4.00
☐ 38684	As Time Goes By/Falling in Love Again	1999	—	—	3.00
WARNER BROS.					
☐ 28582	Help Me/Broken Wings	1986	—	—	3.00
☐ 28582 [PS]	Help Me/Broken Wings	1986	—	—	3.00
☐ 28887	Don't Stop the Dance/Nocturne	1985	—	—	3.00
☐ 28887 [PS]	Don't Stop the Dance/Nocturne	1985	—	—	3.00
☐ 28990	Slave to Love/Valentine	1985	—	—	3.00
☐ 28990 [PS]	Slave to Love/Valentine	1985	—	—	3.00

Albums
ATLANTIC

Number	Title (A Side/B Side)	Yr	VG	VG+	NM
☐ SD 7304	These Foolish Things	1973	3.75	7.50	15.00
☐ SD 18113	Another Time, Another Place	1974	3.75	7.50	15.00
☐ SD 18187	Let's Stick Together	1976	3.00	6.00	12.00
☐ SD 18216	In Your Mind	1977	3.00	6.00	12.00
☐ SD 19205	The Bride Stripped Bare	1978	3.00	6.00	12.00
REPRISE					
☐ 25598	Bete Noire	1988	3.00	6.00	12.00
WARNER BROS.					
☐ 25082	Boys and Girls	1985	3.00	6.00	12.00

FESTIVALS, THE
45s
BLUE ROCK

Number	Title (A Side/B Side)	Yr	VG	VG+	NM
☐ 4076	Hey Girl/Checkin' Out	1969	2.00	4.00	8.00
COLOSSUS					
☐ 122	You're Gonna Make It/So in Love	1970	—	3.50	7.00
☐ 136	Baby Show It/Take Your Time	1971	—	3.50	7.00
☐ 146	Gee Baby/Give Her Up	1971	—	3.50	7.00
GORDY					
☐ 7120	Green Grows the Lilacs/So in Love	1972	—	3.00	6.00
SMASH					
☐ 2056	I'll Always Love You/Music	1966	2.00	4.00	8.00
☐ 2196	Hey Girl/Not Gonna Let Her	1968	2.00	4.00	8.00

FEVER TREE
45s
AMPEX

Number	Title (A Side/B Side)	Yr	VG	VG+	NM
☐ 11013	She Comes in Colors/You're Not the Same Baby	1970	3.75	7.50	15.00
☐ 11028	I Put a Spell on You/ Hey Joe, Where You Gonna Go	1970	3.75	7.50	15.00
MAINSTREAM					
☐ 661	Hey Mister/I Can Beat Your Drum	1967	3.00	6.00	12.00
☐ 665	Girl, Oh Girl (Don't Push Me)/Steve Lenore	1967	3.00	6.00	12.00

F

UNI

Number	Title (A Side/B Side)	Yr	VG	VG+	NM
☐ 55060	San Fransisco Girls (Return of the Native)/Come with Me	1968	3.00	6.00	12.00
☐ 55060 [DJ]	San Fransisco Girls (Return of the Native) (same on both sides)	1968	10.00	20.00	40.00
—Promo only on blue vinyl					
☐ 55095	What Time Did You Say It Is in Salt Lake City/ Where Do You Go	1968	3.75	7.50	15.00
☐ 55146	Love Makes the Sun Rise/Filigree and Shadow	1969	3.75	7.50	15.00
☐ 55172	The Sun Also Rises/Clancey	1969	3.75	7.50	15.00
☐ 55202	Catcher in the Rye/What Time Did You Say It Is in Salt Lake City?	1970	5.00	10.00	20.00
☐ 55228	I Am/Grand Candy Young Sweet	1970	5.00	10.00	20.00

Albums
AMPEX

Number	Title (A Side/B Side)	Yr	VG	VG+	NM
☐ A-10113	For Sale	1970	6.25	12.50	25.00
MCA					
☐ 551	Fever Tree	197?	2.50	5.00	10.00
UNI					
☐ 73024	Fever Tree	1968	6.25	12.50	25.00
☐ 73040	Another Time, Another Place	1968	6.25	12.50	25.00
☐ 73067	Creation	1970	6.25	12.50	25.00

FI-TONES, THE
45s
ANGLE TONE

Number	Title (A Side/B Side)	Yr	VG	VG+	NM
☐ 525	You'll Be the Last/Wake Up	1958	25.00	50.00	100.00
☐ 530	It Wasn't a Lie/What Am I Goin' to Do	1958	20.00	40.00	80.00
☐ 536	Deep In My Heart/Minnie	1959	15.00	30.00	60.00
ATLAS					
☐ 1050	Foolish Dreams/Let's Fall in Love	1955	25.00	50.00	100.00
—Second pressings identify label as "Atlas Records" and have Atlas logo at left side					
☐ 1050	Foolish Dreams/Let's Fall in Love	1955	100.00	200.00	400.00
—Originals identify label as "Atlas Record Company" and have Atlas logo at far upper left					
☐ 1051	It Wasn't a Lie/Lots and Lots of Love	1955	25.00	50.00	100.00
☐ 1052	I Call to You/Love You Baby	1955	25.00	50.00	100.00
☐ 1055	I Belong to You/Silly and Happy	1956	25.00	50.00	100.00
☐ 1056	Waiting for Your Call/My Tired Feet	1956	25.00	50.00	100.00
OLD TOWN					
☐ 1042	My Faith/My Heart	1957	100.00	200.00	400.00

FIDELITY'S, THE   BUDDY MILES was in this group.
45s
BATON

Number	Title (A Side/B Side)	Yr	VG	VG+	NM
☐ 252	The Things I Love/Hold On to Whatcha Got	1958	6.25	12.50	25.00
☐ 256	Memories of You/Can't You Come Out	1958	6.25	12.50	25.00
☐ 261	Captain of My Ship/My Greatest Thrill	1958	6.25	12.50	25.00
SIR					
☐ 271	Marie/The Invitation	1959	5.00	10.00	20.00
☐ 274	Walk with the Wind/Only to You	1959	5.00	10.00	20.00
☐ 276	Where in the World/This Girl of Mine	1960	5.00	10.00	20.00
☐ 277	Wishing Star/Broken Love	1960	7.50	15.00	30.00

FIELD, JERRY, AND THE LAWYERS
45s
PARKWAY

Number	Title (A Side/B Side)	Yr	VG	VG+	NM
☐ 801	The Trial/Easy Steppin'	1958	5.00	10.00	20.00
—White label. This is actually a cover of a break-in record (for the original, see HERB B. LOU AND THE LEGAL EAGLES).					
☐ 801	The Trial/Easy Steppin'	1958	7.50	15.00	30.00
—Blue label					

FIELD, SALLY
45s
COLGEMS

Number	Title (A Side/B Side)	Yr	VG	VG+	NM
☐ 66-1008	Felicidad/Find Yourself a Rainbow	1967	2.50	5.00	10.00
☐ 66-1008 [PS]	Felicidad/Find Yourself a Rainbow	1967	3.75	7.50	15.00
☐ 66-1014	Golden Days/You're a Grand Old Flag	1967	2.00	4.00	8.00

Albums
COLGEMS

Number	Title (A Side/B Side)	Yr	VG	VG+	NM
☐ COM-106 [M]	The Flying Nun	1967	7.50	15.00	30.00
☐ COS-106 [S]	The Flying Nun	1967	6.25	12.50	25.00

FIELDS, BOBBY
45s
ACE

Number	Title (A Side/B Side)	Yr	VG	VG+	NM
☐ 504	Pity Poor Me/Give Me a Helping Hand	1955	15.00	30.00	60.00

FIELDS, ERNIE
45s
CAPITOL

Number	Title (A Side/B Side)	Yr	VG	VG+	NM
☐ 5161	St. Louis Blues/Lilies of the Field	1964	2.00	4.00	8.00
☐ 5326	Swanne River/Chloe	1964	2.00	4.00	8.00
RENDEZVOUS					
☐ 110	In the Mood/Christopher Columbus	1959	3.00	6.00	12.00
☐ 117	Chattanooga Choo Choo/Workin' Out	1960	2.50	5.00	10.00
☐ 122	Begin the Beguine/Things Ain't What They Used to Be	1960	2.50	5.00	10.00
☐ 129	Teen Flip/Sweet Slumber	1960	2.50	5.00	10.00
☐ 138	The Honeydripper/Monkey	1960	2.50	5.00	10.00
☐ 142	The Happy Whistler/Honky Tonk	1961	2.50	5.00	10.00
☐ 148	Be Anything (But Be Mine)/Fallin'	1961	2.50	5.00	10.00
☐ 150	The Charleston/12th Street Rag	1961	2.50	5.00	10.00
☐ 161	A String of Pearls/Castle Rock	1961	2.50	5.00	10.00
☐ 170	Hucklebuck (Twist)/Ernie's Tune	1962	2.00	4.00	8.00
☐ 181	Theme from Perry Mason/Me and My Shadow	1962	2.50	5.00	10.00

Albums
RENDEZVOUS

Number	Title (A Side/B Side)	Yr	VG	VG+	NM
☐ 1309 [M]	In the Mood	1960	15.00	30.00	60.00

FIELDS, GRACIE
Albums
LIBERTY

Number	Title (A Side/B Side)	Yr	VG	VG+	NM
☐ LRP-3059 [M]	Our Gracie	1957	10.00	20.00	40.00

Number	Title (A Side/B Side)	Yr	VG	VG+	NM

FIELDS, THE
45s
UNI

Number	Title (A Side/B Side)	Yr	VG	VG+	NM
❏ 55106	Bide My Time/Take You Home	1969	2.50	5.00	10.00

Albums
UNI

| ❏ 73050 | Fields | 1969 | 12.50 | 25.00 | 50.00 |

FIESTAS, THE
45s
CHIMNEYVILLE

| ❏ 10216 | Tina, the Disco Queen/I'm No Better Than You | 1977 | 3.00 | 6.00 | 12.00 |
| ❏ 10221 | Is That Long Enough for You/
I'm Gonna Make Myself | 1977 | 3.00 | 6.00 | 12.00 |

COTILLION

| ❏ 44117 | So Fine/Broken Heart | 1971 | 6.25 | 12.50 | 25.00 |

OLD TOWN

| ❏ 1062 | So Fine/Last Night I Dreamed | 1958 | 7.50 | 15.00 | 30.00 |

—Standard version; no "ZTSP" on label

| ❏ 1062 | So Fine/Last Night I Dreamed | 1958 | 12.50 | 25.00 | 50.00 |

—Versions pressed by Columbia have a piano intro not available elsewhere. Look for "ZTSP" on label

❏ 1067	Grandma Gave a Party/I'm Your Slave	1959	6.25	12.50	25.00
❏ 1069	Our Anniversary/I'm Your Slave	1959	6.25	12.50	25.00
❏ 1074	Good News/That Was Me	1959	6.25	12.50	25.00
❏ 1080	Dollar Bill/It Don't Make Sense	1960	6.25	12.50	25.00
❏ 1090	So Nice/You Could Be My Girlfriend	1960	6.25	12.50	25.00
❏ 1104	Look at That Girl/Mr. Dillon, Mr. Dillon	1961	6.25	12.50	25.00
❏ 1111	Hobo's Prayer/She's Mine	1961	10.00	20.00	40.00
❏ 1122	Broken Heart/Railroad Song	1962	5.00	10.00	20.00
❏ 1127	I Feel Good All Over/Look at That Girl	1962	5.00	10.00	20.00
❏ 1134	The Gypsy Said/Mama Put the Law Down	1963	5.00	10.00	20.00
❏ 1140	The Party's Over/Try It One More Time	1963	5.00	10.00	20.00
❏ 1148	Foolish Dreamer/Rock-a-By Baby	1963	5.00	10.00	20.00
❏ 1166	All That's Good/Rock-a-By Baby	1964	5.00	10.00	20.00
❏ 1178	Think Smart/Anna	1965	20.00	40.00	80.00
❏ 1187	Love Is Strange/Love Is Good to Me	1965	3.75	7.50	15.00
❏ 1189	Ain't She Sweet/I Gotta Have Your Lovin'	1965	3.75	7.50	15.00

RESPECT

| ❏ 2509 | I Can't Shake Your Love (Can't Shake You
Loose)/A Sometimes Storm | 1972 | 2.00 | 4.00 | 8.00 |

STRAND

| ❏ 25046 | Come On Everybody/Julia | 1961 | 10.00 | 20.00 | 40.00 |

VIGOR

| ❏ 712 | So Fine/Darling You've Changed | 1974 | 2.00 | 4.00 | 8.00 |

FIFTH DIMENSION, THE   Also see BILLY DAVIS.
45s
ABC

❏ 12136	Magic in My Life/Lean On Me Always	1975	—	2.00	4.00
❏ 12168	Walk Your Feet in the Sunshine/Speaking with My Heart	1976	—	2.00	4.00
❏ 12181	Love Hangover/Will You Be There	1976	—	2.00	4.00

ARISTA

| ❏ 0101 | No Love in the Room/I Don't Know How to Look
for Love | 1975 | — | 2.00 | 4.00 |

BELL

❏ 860	Medley: A Change Is Gonna Come & People Gotta Be Free/The Declaration	1970	—	2.50	5.00
❏ 880	Puppet Man/A Love Like Ours	1970	—	2.50	5.00
❏ 895	Save the Country/Dimension 5	1970	—	2.50	5.00
❏ 913	On the Beach (In the Summertime)/ This Is Your Life	1970	—	2.50	5.00
❏ 940	One Less Bell to Answer/Feelin' Alright?	1970	—	2.50	5.00
❏ 965	Love's Lines, Angles and Rhymes/The Singer	1971	—	2.50	5.00
❏ 999	Light Sings/Viva Tirado	1971	—	2.50	5.00
❏ 45134	Never My Love/A Love Like Ours	1971	—	2.50	5.00
❏ 45170	Together Let's Find Love/ I Just Wanta Be Your Friend	1972	—	2.50	5.00
❏ 45195	(Last Night) I Didn't Get to Sleep at All/ The River Witch	1972	—	2.50	5.00
❏ 45261	If I Could Reach You/ Tomorrow Belongs to the Children	1972	—	2.50	5.00
❏ 45310	Living Together, Growing Together/ What Do I Need to Be Me	1973	—	2.00	4.00
❏ 45338	Everything's Been Changed/ There Never Was a Day	1973	—	2.00	4.00
❏ 45380	Ashes to Ashes/The Singer	1973	—	2.00	4.00
❏ 45425	Flashback/Diggin' for a Livin'	1973	—	2.00	4.00
❏ 45612	Harlem/My Song	1974	—	2.00	4.00

MOTOWN

| ❏ 1437 | You Are the Reason (I Feel Like Dancing)/
Slipping Into Something New | 1978 | — | 2.00 | 4.00 |
| ❏ 1453 | Everybody's Got to Give It Up/You're My Star | 1978 | — | 2.00 | 4.00 |

SOUL CITY

❏ 752	I'll Be Loving You Forever/ Train, Keep On Moving	1966	15.00	30.00	60.00
❏ 753	Go Where You Wanna Go/Too Poor to Die	1967	2.00	4.00	8.00
❏ 753 [PS]	Go Where You Wanna Go/Too Poor to Die	1967	5.00	10.00	20.00
❏ 755	Another Day, Another Heartache/ Rosecrans Blvd.	1967	2.50	5.00	10.00
❏ 755 [PS]	Another Day, Another Heartache/ Rosecrans Blvd.	1967	5.00	10.00	20.00
❏ 756	Up-Up and Away/Which Way to Nowhere	1967	2.00	4.00	8.00
❏ 760	Paper Cup/Poor Side of Town	1967	2.00	4.00	8.00
❏ 762	Carpet Man/Magic Garden	1968	2.00	4.00	8.00
❏ 766	Stoned Soul Picnic/The Sailboat Song	1968	2.00	4.00	8.00
❏ 766 [PS]	Stoned Soul Picnic/The Sailboat Song	1968	3.75	7.50	15.00
❏ 768	Sweet Blindness/Bobby's Blues	1968	2.00	4.00	8.00
❏ 768 [PS]	Sweet Blindness/Bobby's Blues	1968	3.75	7.50	15.00
❏ 770	California Soul/It'll Never Be the Same	1968	2.00	4.00	8.00
❏ 772	Aquarius/Let the Sunshine In (The Flesh Failures)//Don'tcha Hear Me Callin' To Ya	1969	2.00	4.00	8.00
❏ 772 [DJ]	Aquarius/Let the Sunshine In (The Flesh Failures) (same on both sides?)	1969	3.75	7.50	15.00

—Promo only on yellow vinyl

❏ 772 [PS]	Aquarius/Let the Sunshine In (The Flesh Failures)//Don'tcha Hear Me Callin' To Ya	1969	3.75	7.50	15.00
❏ 776	Workin' on a Groovy Thing/Broken Wing Bird	1969	2.00	4.00	8.00
❏ 779	Wedding Bell Blues/Lovin' Stew	1969	2.00	4.00	8.00
❏ 780	Blowing Away/Skinny Man	1970	—	3.00	6.00
❏ 781	The Girls' Song/It'll Never Be the Same Again	1970	—	3.00	6.00

SUTRA

| ❏ 122 | Surrender/Fantasy | 1983 | — | 2.00 | 4.00 |

Albums
ABC

| ❏ D-897 | Earthbound | 1975 | 2.50 | 5.00 | 10.00 |

ARISTA

| ❏ ABM-1106 | Greatest Hits on Earth | 1975 | 2.00 | 4.00 | 8.00 |

—Reissue of Bell 1106

| ❏ AL 8335 | Greatest Hits on Earth | 198? | 2.00 | 4.00 | 8.00 |

—Reissue of Arista 1106

BELL

❏ 1106	Greatest Hits on Earth	1972	2.50	5.00	10.00
❏ 1116	Living Together, Growing Together	1973	2.50	5.00	10.00
❏ 1315	Soul and Inspiration	1974	2.50	5.00	10.00
❏ 6045	Portrait	1970	3.00	6.00	12.00
❏ 6060	Love's Lines, Angles and Rhymes	1971	3.00	6.00	12.00
❏ 6065	Reflections	1971	2.50	5.00	10.00
❏ 6073	Individually & Collectively	1972	2.50	5.00	10.00
❏ 9000 [(2)]	The 5th Dimension/Live!!	1971	3.00	6.00	12.00

MOTOWN

| ❏ M7-896 | Star | 1978 | 2.50 | 5.00 | 10.00 |

PAIR

| ❏ PDL2-1108 [(2)] | The Glory Days | 1986 | 3.00 | 6.00 | 12.00 |

RHINO

| ❏ RNDA-71104 [(2)] | The 5th Dimension Anthology | 1986 | 3.00 | 6.00 | 12.00 |

SOUL CITY

❏ SCS-33900	The 5th Dimension/Greatest Hits	1970	3.00	6.00	12.00
❏ SCS-33901	The July 5th Album	1970	3.00	6.00	12.00
❏ SCM-91000 [M]	Up, Up and Away	1967	5.00	10.00	20.00
❏ SCM-91001 [M]	The Magic Garden	1967	5.00	10.00	20.00
❏ SCS-92000 [S]	Up, Up and Away	1967	3.75	7.50	15.00
❏ SCS-92001 [S]	The Magic Garden	1967	3.75	7.50	15.00
❏ SCS-92002	Stoned Soul Picnic	1968	3.75	7.50	15.00
❏ SCS-92005	The Age of Aquarius	1969	3.75	7.50	15.00

FIFTH ESTATE, THE   Also see THE D-MEN.
45s
JUBILEE

❏ 5573	Ding! Dong! The Witch Is Dead/The Rub-a-Dub	1967	3.00	6.00	12.00
❏ 5588	Lost Generation/The Goofin' Song	1967	2.00	4.00	8.00
❏ 5595	Heigh-Ho/It's Waiting There for You	1967	2.00	4.00	8.00
❏ 5607	Morning, Morning/Tomorrow Is My Turn	1967	2.00	4.00	8.00
❏ 5617	Do Drop Inn/That's Love	1968	2.00	4.00	8.00
❏ 5627	Coney Island Sally/Tomorrow Is My Turn	1968	2.00	4.00	8.00
❏ 5655	Mickey Mouse Club March/ I Knew You Before I Met You	1969	2.00	4.00	8.00
❏ 5683 [DJ]	Parade of the Wooden Soldiers (mono/stereo)	1969	2.50	5.00	10.00

—Stock copies may not exist ("I Knew You Before I Met You" was listed as B-side)

RED BIRD

| ❏ 10-064 | Love Is All a Game/Like I Love You | 1966 | 3.75 | 7.50 | 15.00 |

Albums
JUBILEE

| ❏ JGM-8005 [M] | Ding Dong! The Witch Is Dead | 1967 | 6.25 | 12.50 | 25.00 |
| ❏ JGS-8005 [S] | Ding Dong! The Witch Is Dead | 1967 | 7.50 | 15.00 | 30.00 |

FIFTY FOOT HOSE
Albums
LIMELIGHT

| ❏ 86062 | Cauldron | 1968 | 25.00 | 50.00 | 100.00 |

FILETS OF SOUL
45s
SAVOY

| ❏ 1630 | Since I Fell for You/C'mon Let's Dance | 1968 | 6.25 | 12.50 | 25.00 |

Albums
SQUID

| ❏ 4857 | Freedom | 1968 | 25.00 | 50.00 | 100.00 |

FINCHLEY BOYS, THE
Albums
GOLDEN THROAT

| ❏ 200-19 | Everlasting Tribute | 1971 | 50.00 | 100.00 | 200.00 |

FINDERS KEEPERS
45s
CHALLENGE

| ❏ 59338 | Lavender Blue/Raggedy Ann | 1966 | 3.75 | 7.50 | 15.00 |
| ❏ 59364 | Don't Give In to Him/I've Done All I Can | 1967 | 3.75 | 7.50 | 15.00 |

FONTANA

| ❏ 1609 | Friday Kind of Monday/On the Beach | 1968 | 3.00 | 6.00 | 12.00 |

FINN, MICKY
45s
CHATTAHOOCHIE

| ❏ 663 | I Still Want You/Reelin' and Rockin' | 1965 | 3.00 | 6.00 | 12.00 |

WORLD ARTISTS

| ❏ 1048 | Night Comes Down/This Sporting Life | 1965 | 3.00 | 6.00 | 12.00 |

FINNEGAN, LARRY
45s
CORAL

| ❏ 62313 | I'll Be Back, Jack/There Ain't Nothin' in This
World | 1962 | 2.50 | 5.00 | 10.00 |

OLD TOWN

❏ 1113	Dear One/Candy Lips	1961	3.00	6.00	12.00
❏ 1120	Pretty Susie Sunshine/It's Walkin' Talkin' Time	1962	2.50	5.00	10.00
❏ 1136	A Kiss and a Dozen Roses/Pick Up the Pieces	1963	2.50	5.00	10.00

RIC

| ❏ 146 | The Other Ringo (A Tribute to Ringo Starr)/
When My Love Passes By | 1964 | 3.75 | 7.50 | 15.00 |

Number	Title (A Side/B Side)	Yr	VG	VG+	NM

FINNEGAN, MIKE, AND THE SERFS
45s
PARKWAY

❏ 113	Help Me Somebody/Bread and Water	1966	5.00	10.00	20.00

FINSTER, WERBLEY See JOSE FELICIANO.

FIRE
Albums
ABC

❏ ABCS-661	Fire	1969	5.00	10.00	20.00

FIRE & ICE LTD.
45s
CAPITOL

❏ 2587	Music Man/For the Money	1969	2.00	4.00	8.00

—As "Fire & Ice"
Albums
CAPITOL

❏ ST 2577 [S]	The Happening	1966	10.00	20.00	40.00
❏ T 2577 [M]	The Happening	1966	7.50	15.00	30.00

FIRE AND RAIN
45s
MERCURY

❏ 73358	Alright Tonight/Home to You	1973	2.50	5.00	10.00
❏ 73373	Hello Stranger/Somebody to Love	1973	10.00	20.00	40.00
❏ 73420	Take Me for a Little While/Touch Me	1973	2.50	5.00	10.00

20TH CENTURY

❏ 2240	Don't Throw It All Away/Layin' in Your Arms (Before Daybreak)	1975	—	3.00	6.00
❏ 2280	Dance for Me/Make Love to Me	1976	—	3.00	6.00

Albums
MERCURY

❏ SRM-1-654	Fire and Rain	1973	3.75	7.50	15.00

FIRE ESCAPE, THE
45s
GNP CRESCENDO

❏ 384	Blood Beat/Love Special Delivery	1967	3.00	6.00	12.00

Albums
GNP CRESCENDO

❏ GNP-2034 [M]	Psychotic Reaction	1967	10.00	20.00	40.00
❏ GNPS-2034 [S]	Psychotic Reaction	1967	7.50	15.00	30.00

FIREBALLET
45s
PASSPORT

❏ 7908	Desiree/Carrollon	1975	—	2.50	5.00

Albums
PASSPORT

❏ 98010	Night on Bald Mountain	1975	3.00	6.00	12.00
❏ 98016	Two, Too…	1976	3.00	6.00	12.00

FIREBALLS, THE Includes records credited to "Jimmy Gilmer and the Fireballs." Also see JIMMY GILMER.
45s
ASTRA

❏ 1021	Torquay/Sweet Walk	1966	2.50	5.00	10.00

ATCO

❏ 6491	Bottle of Wine/Can't You See I'm Tryin'	1967	2.50	5.00	10.00
❏ 6569	Goin' Away/Groovy Motions	1968	2.00	4.00	8.00
❏ 6595	Chicken Little/Three Minutes' Time	1968	2.00	4.00	8.00
❏ 6614	Come On, React!/Woman Help Me	1968	2.00	4.00	8.00
❏ 6651	Long Green/Light in the Window	1969	2.00	4.00	8.00
❏ 6678	Watch Her Walk/Good Morning Shame	1969	2.00	4.00	8.00

DOT

❏ 16487	Sugar Shack/My Heart Is Free	1963	3.75	7.50	15.00
—Jimmy Gilmer and the Fireballs					
❏ 16493	Torquay Two/Peg Leg	1963	3.75	7.50	15.00
❏ 16539	Daisy Petal Pickin'/When My Tears Have Dried	1963	3.00	6.00	12.00
—Jimmy Gilmer and the Fireballs					
❏ 16583	Ain't Gonna Tell Anybody/Young Am I	1964	3.00	6.00	12.00
—Jimmy Gilmer and the Fireballs					
❏ 16591	Daytona Drag/Gently, Gently	1964	3.75	7.50	15.00
❏ 16609	I'll Send for You/Look at Me	1964	2.50	5.00	10.00
—Jimmy Gilmer and the Fireballs					
❏ 16642	Wishing/What Kinda Love	1964	2.50	5.00	10.00
—Jimmy Gilmer and the Fireballs					
❏ 16661	Dumbo/Mr. Reed	1964	3.75	7.50	15.00
❏ 16666	Cry Baby/Thunder 'N' Lightnin'	1964	2.50	5.00	10.00
—Jimmy Gilmer and the Fireballs					
❏ 16687	Break His Heart for Me/Cinnamon Cindy	1965	2.50	5.00	10.00
—Jimmy Gilmer and the Fireballs					
❏ 16692	Yummie Yama Papa/Baby, What's Wrong	1965	3.75	7.50	15.00
❏ 16714	Born to Be with You/Lonesome Tears	1965	2.50	5.00	10.00
—Jimmy Gilmer and the Fireballs					
❏ 16715	More Than I Can Say/Beating of My Heart	1965	3.75	7.50	15.00
❏ 16743	The Fool/Somebody Stole My Watermelon	1965	2.50	5.00	10.00
❏ 16745	Ahhh, Soul/Campusology	1965	3.75	7.50	15.00
❏ 16768	Codine/Come to Me	1965	2.50	5.00	10.00
—Jimmy Gilmer and the Fireballs					
❏ 16786	She Belongs to Me/Rambler's Blues	1965	2.50	5.00	10.00
—Jimmy Gilmer and the Fireballs					
❏ 16833	Hungry, Hungry, Hungry/Wild Roses	1966	2.50	5.00	10.00
—Jimmy Gilmer and the Fireballs					
❏ 16834	Jada/What I Am	1966	3.75	7.50	15.00
❏ 16881	All I Do Is Dream of You/Ain't That Rain	1966	2.50	5.00	10.00
—Jimmy Gilmer and the Fireballs					
❏ 16918	Torquay Two/Say I Am	1966	3.75	7.50	15.00
❏ 16979	Sugar Shack/Daisy Petal Pickin'	1966	2.50	5.00	10.00
❏ 16992	Shy Girl/I Think I'll Catch a Bus	1967	2.50	5.00	10.00
—Jimmy Gilmer and the Fireballs					

HAMILTON

❏ 50036	Blacksmith Blues/Tuff-a-Nuff	1960	5.00	10.00	20.00

JARO

❏ 77029	Long, Long Ponytail/Let There Be Love	1960	20.00	40.00	80.00

—Chuck Tharp and the Fireballs
KAPP

❏ 248	Fireball/I Don't Know	1958	25.00	50.00	100.00

—Chuck Tharp and the Fireballs
7 ARTS

❏ 714	Callin' the Sheriff/Don't Stop	1961	—		

—Evidently, record was never released, though its picture sleeve exists

❏ 714 [PS]	Callin' the Sheriff/Don't Stop	1961	12.50	25.00	50.00

TOP RANK

❏ 2008	Torquay/Cry Baby	1959	5.00	10.00	20.00
❏ 2026 [M]	Bulldog/Nearly Sunrise	1959	5.00	10.00	20.00
❏ 2026ST [S]	Bulldog/Nearly Sunrise	1959	12.50	25.00	50.00
❏ 2038 [M]	Foot Patter/Kissin'	1959	5.00	10.00	20.00
❏ 2038ST [S]	Foot Patter/Kissin'	1959	12.50	25.00	50.00
❏ 2054	Vaquero/Chief Whoopin'-Koff	1960	5.00	10.00	20.00
❏ 2081	Almost Paradise/Sweet Talk	1960	5.00	10.00	20.00
❏ 3003	Rick-a-Tic/Tacky Doo	1961	5.00	10.00	20.00

WARWICK

❏ 630	Rik-A-Tik/Yackey-Doo	1961	4.00	8.00	16.00
❏ 644	Quite a Party/Gunshot	1961	4.00	8.00	16.00

7-Inch Extended Plays
TOP RANK

❏ REX 1000	Bulldog/Torquay//Kissin'/Foot Patter	196?	37.50	75.00	150.00
❏ REX 1000 [PS]	The Fireballs	196?	37.50	75.00	150.00

Albums
ATCO

❏ 33-239 [M]	Bottle of Wine	1968	10.00	20.00	40.00
❏ SD 33-239 [S]	Bottle of Wine	1968	6.25	12.50	25.00
❏ SD 33-275	Come On, React!	1969	6.25	12.50	25.00

CROWN

❏ CST-376 [R]	Jimmy Gilmer and the Fireballs & The Sugar Shackers	1963	6.25	12.50	25.00
❏ CST-387 [R]	The Sensational Jimmy Gilmer & The Fireballs	1964	6.25	12.50	25.00
❏ CLP-5376 [M]	Jimmy Gilmer and the Fireballs & The Sugar Shackers	1963	6.25	12.50	25.00
❏ CLP-5387 [M]	The Sensational Jimmy Gilmer & The Fireballs	1964	6.25	12.50	25.00

DOT

❏ DLP-3512 [M]	Torquay	1963	12.50	25.00	50.00
❏ DLP-3545 [M]	Sugar Shack	1963	10.00	20.00	40.00
—Jimmy Gilmer and the Fireballs					
❏ DLP-3577 [M]	Buddy's Buddy	1964	12.50	25.00	50.00
—Jimmy Gilmer and the Fireballs					
❏ DLP-3643 [M]	Lucky 'Leven	1965	7.50	15.00	30.00
❏ DLP-3668 [M]	Folkbeat	1965	7.50	15.00	30.00
❏ DLP-3709 [M]	Campusology	1966	7.50	15.00	30.00
❏ DLP-3856 [M]	Firewater	1968	12.50	25.00	50.00

—Stereo cover with "Monaural" and "Promotional Copy Not for Sale" stickers, but the record is stock mono

❏ DLP-25512 [S]	Torquay	1963	20.00	40.00	80.00
❏ DLP-25545 [S]	Sugar Shack	1963	15.00	30.00	60.00
—Jimmy Gilmer and the Fireballs					
❏ DLP-25577 [S]	Buddy's Buddy	1964	20.00	40.00	80.00
—Jimmy Gilmer and the Fireballs					
❏ DLP-25643 [S]	Lucky 'Leven	1965	10.00	20.00	40.00
❏ DLP-25668 [S]	Folkbeat	1965	10.00	20.00	40.00
❏ DLP-25709 [S]	Campusology	1966	10.00	20.00	40.00
❏ DLP-25856 [S]	Firewater	1968	6.25	12.50	25.00

SUNDAZED

❏ LP-5016	The Fireballs	1995	2.50	5.00	10.00
❏ LP-5017	Torquay	1995	2.50	5.00	10.00
❏ LP-5018	Gunshot!	1995	2.50	5.00	10.00

TOP RANK

❏ RM-324 [M]	The Fireballs	1960	37.50	75.00	150.00
❏ RM-343 [M]	Vaquero	1960	37.50	75.00	150.00
❏ RS-643 [S]	Vaquero	1960	50.00	100.00	200.00

WARWICK

❏ W-2042 [M]	Here Are the Fireballs	1961	37.50	75.00	150.00
❏ WST-2042 [S]	Here Are the Fireballs	1961	62.50	125.00	250.00

FIREBIRDS, THE
Albums
CROWN

❏ CST-589	Light My Fire	1968	17.50	35.00	70.00

FIREFLIES, THE
45s
CANADIAN AMERICAN

❏ 117	Marianne/Give All Your Love to Me	1960	5.00	10.00	20.00

RIBBON

❏ 6901	You Were Mine/Stella Got a Fella	1959	6.25	12.50	25.00
—With "Ribbon" encased in a ribbon on label					
❏ 6901	You Were Mine/Stella Got a Fella	1959	7.50	15.00	30.00
—With "Ribbon" standing alone on label					
❏ 6904	I Can't Say Goodbye/What Did I Do Wrong	1959	5.00	10.00	20.00
❏ 6906	My Girl/Because of My Pride	1960	5.00	10.00	20.00

TAURUS

❏ 355	One O'Clock Twist/You Were Mine for Awhile	1962	5.00	10.00	20.00
❏ 366	Good Friends/My Prayer for You	1964	5.00	10.00	20.00
❏ 376	Runaround/Could You Mean More	1965	5.00	10.00	20.00
❏ 380	Tonight/A Time for Us	1965	5.00	10.00	20.00

Albums
TAURUS

❏ 1002 [M]	You Were Mine	196?	25.00	50.00	100.00
❏ S-1002 [S]	You Were Mine	196?	75.00	150.00	300.00

FIREFLY (1)
45s
A&M

❏ 1736	Hey There Little Firefly Part I/Part II	1975	—	2.50	5.00
❏ 1798	If You Ever Stopped Callin' Me Baby Part I/Part II	1976	—	3.00	6.00

POLYDOR

❏ 14496	My Jole Part I/Part II	1978	2.50	5.00	10.00

F

Number	Title (A Side/B Side)	Yr	VG	VG+	NM

FIRESIGN THEATRE, THE

45s

COLUMBIA

Number	Title (A Side/B Side)	Yr	VG	VG+	NM
❑ 45052	Forward Into the Past/Station Break	1969	2.50	5.00	10.00
❑ 45052 [PS]	Forward Into the Past/Station Break	1969	10.00	20.00	40.00

Albums

BUTTERFLY

❑ 001	Jost Folks...A Firesign Chat	1977	2.50	5.00	10.00

COLUMBIA

❑ CL 2718 [M]	Waiting for the Electrician or Someone Like Him	1968	6.25	12.50	25.00
❑ CS 9518 [S]	Waiting for the Electrician or Someone Like Him	1968	3.75	7.50	15.00
❑ CS 9884	How Can You Be in Two Places at Once When You're Not Anywhere at All	1969	3.75	7.50	15.00

—"360 Sound" label

❑ C 30102	Don't Crush That Dwarf, Hand Me the Pliers	1970	3.75	7.50	15.00
❑ C 30737	I Think We're All Bozos on This Bus	1971	3.75	7.50	15.00
❑ CQ 30737 [Q]	I Think We're All Bozos on This Bus	1972	5.00	10.00	20.00
❑ KG 31099 [(2)]	Dear Friends	1972	5.00	10.00	20.00
❑ KC 31585	Not Insane or Anything You Want To	1972	3.75	7.50	15.00
❑ KC 32411	David Ossman's How Time Flys	1973	3.00	6.00	12.00
❑ KC 32730	The Tale of the Giant Rat of Sumatra	1974	3.00	6.00	12.00
❑ CQ 33141 [Q]	Everything You Know Is Wrong	1974	5.00	10.00	20.00
❑ KC 33141	Everything You Know Is Wrong	1974	3.00	6.00	12.00
❑ PC 33475	In the Next World You're On Your Own	1975	3.00	6.00	12.00
❑ PG 34391 [(2)]	Forward Into the Past (An Anthology)	1977	3.75	7.50	15.00

MERCURY

❑ 826452-1	Eat or Be Eaten	1985	2.50	5.00	10.00

RHINO

❑ RNLP-018	Fighting Clowns	1979	3.00	6.00	12.00
❑ RNEP-506 [EP]	Nick Danger, Third Eye	1983	2.50	5.00	10.00
❑ RNLP-806	Lawyer's Hospital	1981	3.00	6.00	12.00
❑ RNLP-807	Shakespeare's Lost Comedie	1982	3.00	6.00	12.00
❑ RNLP-812	Nick Danger In: The Three Faces of Al	1984	3.00	6.00	12.00
❑ RNLP-904	Reagan/Carter	1980	3.00	6.00	12.00

FIRST CHOICE

12-Inch Singles

GOLD MIND

❑ GG-401	Hold Your Horses (5:50) (2:44)	1978	5.00	10.00	20.00
❑ GG-405	Double Cross (6:59) (B-side unknown)	1979	5.00	10.00	20.00
❑ GG-502	Love Thang (8:04)/Great Expectations	1980	5.00	10.00	20.00
❑ GG-504	Breakaway (6:56) (Instrumental 6:56)	1980	5.00	10.00	20.00
❑ 12G-4004	Doctor Love (7:35) (2:38)	1977	6.25	12.50	25.00

SALSOUL

❑ SG 397	Let No Man Put Asunder (Vocal 7:25) (Instrumental) (Vocal 7:00)	1982	12.50	25.00	50.00

—A-side remixed by Shep Pettibone; B-side remixed by Frankie Knuckles

❑ SG 404	Double Cross (unknown versions)	1983	12.50	25.00	50.00
❑ SG 419	Doctor Love (7:47) (Mega Dub Remix 8:15)	1983	10.00	20.00	40.00

—Remixed by Shep Pettibone

❑ 2571-1	Let No Man Put Asunder (Vocal Dub 6:57) (90's Dub 6:59) (Masters at Work Remix 5:54) (90's Mix 6:56) (Vocal 6:59)	1993	3.75	7.50	15.00
❑ 2573-1	Doctor Love (Love Mix 12:14) (Radio Edit 3:38) (David's Jam 11:55) (David's Theme 4:38)	1993	3.75	7.50	15.00
❑ 2574-1 [(2)]	Doctor Love (Love Mix 12:14) (Robapella Mix 5:52) (David's Jam 11:55) (C & C Theme 6:40) (Dr. Dub 8:37) (Acapella Mix 5:54) (LP Version 7:25) (Radio Version 3:38) (David's Theme 4:38)	1993	6.25	12.50	25.00
❑ 5599-1	Double Cross (Club Mix 6:06) (Swing Mix 8:27) (Techno Mix 5:55) (Flute Dub 6:04) (Percapella Mix 5:59) (Traxx Mix 5:50)	1993	3.75	7.50	15.00

—Remixes of the original version

45s

GOLD MIND

❑ 4004	Doctor Love/I Love You More Than Before	1977	—	2.50	5.00
❑ 4009	Love Having You Around/Indian Giver	1977	—	2.50	5.00
❑ 4017	Hold Your Horses/Now I've Thrown It All Away	1978	—	2.50	5.00
❑ 4019	Double Cross/Game of Love	1979	—	2.50	5.00
❑ 4022	Love Thang/Great Expectations	1980	—	2.50	5.00
❑ 4023	Breakaway/House for Sale	1980	—	2.50	5.00

PHILLY GROOVE

❑ 175	Armed and Extremely Dangerous/Gonna Keep On Lovin' Him	1973	—	2.50	5.00
❑ 179	Smarty Pants/One Step Away	1973	—	3.00	6.00
❑ 183	Newsy Neighbors/This Little Woman	1974	—	3.00	6.00
❑ 200	The Player — Part 1/The Player — Part 2	1974	—	3.00	6.00
❑ 202	Guilty/Wake Up to Me	1974	—	3.00	6.00
❑ 204	Love Freeze/A Boy Named Junior	1975	2.50	5.00	10.00

SCEPTER

❑ 12347	This Is the House (Where Love Died)/One Step Away	1972	12.50	25.00	50.00

WARNER BROS.

❑ 8214	Gotta Get Away (From You Baby)/Yes, Maybe Not	1976	2.00	4.00	8.00
❑ 8251	First Choice Theme/Let Him Go	1976	2.00	4.00	8.00

Albums

GOLD MIND

❑ 7501	Delusions	1977	3.75	7.50	15.00
❑ GA 9502	Hold Your Horses	1979	5.00	10.00	20.00
❑ GA 9505	Breakaway	1980	7.50	15.00	30.00

PHILLY GROOVE

❑ 1400	Armed and Extremely Dangerous	1973	3.75	7.50	15.00
❑ 1502	The Player	1974	5.00	10.00	20.00

WARNER BROS.

❑ BS 2934	So Let Us Entertain You	1976	3.75	7.50	15.00

FIRST CLASS (1) British studio group featuring Tony Burrows on vocals.

45s

UK

❑ 49022	Beach Baby/Both Sides of the Story	1974	—	2.50	5.00

—Most stock copies have the full-length (4:59) version of the A-side

❑ 49022	Beach Baby/Both Sides of the Story	1974	—	3.00	6.00

—Some stock copies have a short version of the A-side

❑ 49028	Dreams Are Ten a Penny/Lavender Man	1974	—	2.00	4.00
❑ 49033	Funny How Love Can Be/Surfer Queen	1975	—	2.00	4.00

Albums

UK

❑ 53108	The First Class	1974	3.75	7.50	15.00

FIRST CLASS (2) U.S. R&B group.

45s

ALL PLATINUM

❑ 2365	Me and My Gemini/Me and My Gemini (Part 2)	1976	—	2.50	5.00
❑ 2368	This Is It/Filled with Desire	1977	—	2.50	5.00
❑ 2372	Coming Back to You/This Is It	1977	—	2.50	5.00

EBONY SOUNDS

❑ 187	The Beginning of My End/(B-side unknown)	1975	—	2.50	5.00

TODAY

❑ 1528	What About Me/Outside Your World	1974	—	2.50	5.00

FIRST CLASS (U) This is either group (1) or group (2).

45s

PRIVATE STOCK

❑ 45,093	Ain't No Love/Long Time Gone	1976	—	2.00	4.00

FIRST EDITION, THE Includes "Kenny Rogers and the First Edition." Also see KENNY ROGERS.

45s

JOLLY ROGERS

❑ 1001	Lady, Play Your Symphony/There's An Old Man in Our Town	1973	—	2.50	5.00
❑ 1003	(Do You Remember) The First Time/Indian Joe	1973	—	2.50	5.00
❑ 1004	Today I Started Loving You Again/She Thinks I Still Care	1973	—	2.50	5.00
❑ 1006	Whatcha Gonna Do/Something About Your Song	1973	—	2.50	5.00
❑ 1007	A Stranger in My Place/Makin' Music for Money	1974	—	2.50	5.00

—All of the above as "Kenny Rogers and the First Edition"

REPRISE

❑ 0628	Ticket to Nowhere/I Found a Reason	1967	2.00	4.00	8.00
❑ 0655	Just Dropped In (To See What Condition My Condition Was In)/Shadow in the Corner of Your Mind	1967	2.50	5.00	10.00

—Second pressing has lighter orange "steamboat" Reprise/W7 label

❑ 0655	Just Dropped In (To See What Condition My Condition Was In)/Shadow in the Corner of Your Mind	1967	3.00	6.00	12.00

—Original pressing has orange and brown label

❑ 0683	Dream On/Only Me	1968	—	3.00	6.00
❑ 0693	Look Around, I'll Be There/Charlie the Fer-De-Lance	1968	—	3.00	6.00
❑ 0737	Just Dropped In (To See What Condition My Condition Was In)/But You Know I Love You	1971	—	2.00	4.00

—As "Kenny Rogers and the First Edition"; "Back to Back Hits" series

❑ 0738	Ruby, Don't Take Your Love to Town/Reuben James	1971	—	2.00	4.00

—As "Kenny Rogers and the First Edition"; "Back to Back Hits" series

❑ 0747	Something's Burning/Someone Who Cares	1972	—	2.00	4.00

—As "Kenny Rogers and the First Edition"; "Back to Back Hits" series

❑ 0748	Tell It All Brother/Heed the Call	1972	—	2.00	4.00

—As "Kenny Rogers and the First Edition"; "Back to Back Hits" series

❑ 0773	If I Could Only Change Your Mind/Are My Thoughts With You	1968	—	3.00	6.00
❑ 0799	But You Know I Love You/Homemade Lies	1968	—	3.00	6.00
❑ 0822	Good Time Liberator/Once Again She's All Alone	1969	—	2.50	5.00

—Starting above, by "Kenny Rogers and the First Edition"

❑ 0829	Ruby, Don't Take Your Love to Town/Girl Get a Hold of Yourself	1969	—	2.50	5.00
❑ 0854	Reuben James/Sunshine	1969	—	2.50	5.00
❑ 0854	Ruben James/Sunshine	1969	—	2.50	5.00
❑ 0888	Something's Burning/Mama's Waiting	1970	—	2.50	5.00
❑ 0923	Tell It All Brother/Just Remember You're My Sunshine	1970	—	2.50	5.00
❑ 0953	Heed the Call/A Stranger in My Place	1970	—	2.50	5.00
❑ 0999	Someone Who Cares/Mission of San Mohera	1971	—	2.50	5.00
❑ 1018	Take My Hand/All God's Lonely Children	1971	—	2.50	5.00
❑ 1053	Where Does Rosie Go/What Am I Gonna Do	1971	—	2.50	5.00
❑ 1069	School Teacher/Trigger Happy Kid	1972	—	2.50	5.00

Albums

JOLLY ROGERS

❑ 5001	Backroads	1973	3.75	7.50	15.00
❑ 5003	Rollin'	1974	3.75	7.50	15.00
❑ 5004	Monumental	1974	3.75	7.50	15.00

—All the above as "Kenny Rogers and the First Edition"

MCA

❑ 912	Love Songs	1984	2.00	4.00	8.00
❑ 913	Country Songs	1984	2.00	4.00	8.00
❑ 942	Hits and Pieces	1985	2.00	4.00	8.00
❑ 943	The 60's Revisited	1985	2.00	4.00	8.00
❑ 944	Pieces of Calico Silver	1985	2.00	4.00	8.00
❑ 1460	Greatest Hits	1985	2.00	4.00	8.00

—Reissue of Reprise 6437

REPRISE

❑ MS 2039	Transition	1971	5.00	10.00	20.00

—As "Kenny Rogers and the First Edition"

❑ R-6276 [M]	The First Edition	1967	7.50	15.00	30.00
❑ RS-6276 [S]	The First Edition	1967	6.25	12.50	25.00
❑ RS-6302	The First Edition's Second	1968	6.25	12.50	25.00
❑ RS-6328	The First Edition '69	1969	6.25	12.50	25.00
❑ RS-6352	Ruby, Don't Take Your Love to Town	1969	5.00	10.00	20.00

—Starting above, as "Kenny Rogers and the First Edition"

❑ RS-6385	Something's Burning	1970	5.00	10.00	20.00
❑ RS-6412	Tell It All Brother	1970	5.00	10.00	20.00
❑ RS-6437	Greatest Hits	1971	5.00	10.00	20.00
❑ 2XS 6476 [(2)]	The Ballad of Calico	1972	6.25	12.50	25.00
❑ ST-92060	Ruby, Don't Take Your Love to Town	1969	6.25	12.50	25.00

—Capitol Record Club edition

Number	Title (A Side/B Side)	Yr	VG	VG+	NM
WARNER SPECIAL PRODUCTS					
❏ OP-2514 [(2)]	Kenny Rogers and the First Edition	1979	3.75	7.50	15.00
—Manufactured for Lakeshore Music					

FISCHER, WILD MAN
45s
REPRISE

| ❏ 0781 | Merry-Go-Round/The Circle | 1968 | 5.00 | 10.00 | 20.00 |

Albums
REPRISE

| ❏ 2XS 6332 [(2)] | An Evening with Wild Man Fischer | 1969 | 12.50 | 25.00 | 50.00 |

RHINO

❏ RNLP-001	Wildmania	1978	3.75	7.50	15.00
❏ RNLP-021	Pronounced Normal	1981	2.50	5.00	10.00
❏ RNLP-022	Nothing Scary	1981	2.50	5.00	10.00

FISCHER, WILLIAM S.
Albums
EMBRYO

| ❏ 529 | Circles | 1970 | 3.75 | 7.50 | 15.00 |

FISCHOFF, GEORGE
12-Inch Singles
COLUMBIA

| ❏ AS 339 [DJ] | Piano Dancing (stereo/mono) | 1977 | 6.25 | 12.50 | 25.00 |

45s
AVALANCHE

| ❏ XW231 | That Summer Night/For Gladys | 1973 | — | 3.00 | 6.00 |

DRIVE

| ❏ 6273 | The Piano Picker/Love Dust | 1979 | — | 2.50 | 5.00 |

GNP CRESCENDO

| ❏ 491 | That Great Old Song/Blue Night | 1975 | — | 2.50 | 5.00 |

HERITAGE

| ❏ 300 | Little Ballerina Blue/Foxy | 197? | — | 3.00 | 6.00 |

LISA

| ❏ 1 | That Great Old Song/Blue Night | 1975 | — | 3.50 | 7.00 |
| ❏ 17315 | Starry Night/(B-side unknown) | 198? | — | 2.50 | 5.00 |

MMG

| ❏ 006 | Carnival Island/(B-side unknown) | 198? | — | 2.50 | 5.00 |
| ❏ 13365 | Summer Love/(B-side unknown) | 198? | — | 2.50 | 5.00 |

P.I.P.

| ❏ 6503 | New Kingston/Waterflower | 1975 | — | 3.00 | 6.00 |

RANWOOD

| ❏ 1053 | Funky Doodle/Quiet Time | 1976 | — | 2.50 | 5.00 |

REWARD

| ❏ WS4-04354 | Boogie Piano Man/Blues for the Boogie Man | 1984 | — | 2.00 | 4.00 |

Albums
MMG

| ❏ 1140 | Pretty Kitty: The Piano Magic of George Fischoff | 1982 | 5.00 | 10.00 | 20.00 |

FISHER, EDDIE
45s
ABC-PARAMOUNT

❏ 10264	Milk and Honey/Shalom	1961	2.00	4.00	8.00
❏ 10326	Arrivederci, Roma/A Camminare	1962	2.00	4.00	8.00
❏ 10371	Back in Your Back Yard/The Sweetest Sounds	1962	2.00	4.00	8.00

DOT

❏ 16732	Sunrise, Sunset/Walking in the Footsteps of a Fool	1965	—	3.00	6.00
❏ 16753	Any Time/When I Was Wrong	1965	—	3.00	6.00
❏ 16779	I Don't Care If the Sun Don't Shine/Young and Foolish	1965	—	3.00	6.00
❏ 16792	White Christmas/Mary Christmas	1965	5.00	10.00	20.00
❏ 16824	They Call the Wind Maria/Great Day	1966	—	3.00	6.00
❏ 16938	Unchained Melody/Old Devil Moon	1966	—	3.00	6.00

MUSICOR

| ❏ 1354 | I'll Pick a Rose for My Rose/Lady Mae | 1969 | — | 2.50 | 5.00 |

RAMROD

❏ (# unknown)	Scent of Mystery/The Chase	1960	2.00	4.00	8.00
❏ (# unknown) [PS]	Scent of Mystery/The Chase	1960	2.50	5.00	10.00
❏ 100	This Nearly Was Mine/Don't Let It Get You Down	1960	2.00	4.00	8.00
❏ 100 [PS]	This Nearly Was Mine/Don't Let It Get You Down	1960	2.50	5.00	10.00

RCA VICTOR

❏ 47-3764	Where in the World/A Little Bit Independent	1950	5.00	10.00	20.00
❏ 47-3792	Nightwind/Warm Kisses in the Cool of Night	1950	5.00	10.00	20.00
❏ 47-3829	Just Say I Love Her/Give a Broken Heart a Chance to Cry	1950	5.00	10.00	20.00
❏ 47-3901	Thinking of You/If You Should Leave Me	1950	3.75	7.50	15.00
❏ 47-3955	When You Kiss a Stranger/You Love Me	1950	3.75	7.50	15.00
❏ 47-4016	Bring Back the Thrill/If It Hadn't Been for You	1951	3.75	7.50	15.00
❏ 47-4036	My Mammy/My Blue Heaven	1951	3.75	7.50	15.00
❏ 47-4037	What Can I Say After I Say I'm Sorry/My Mom	1951	3.75	7.50	15.00
❏ 47-4038	My Buddy/At Sundown	1951	3.75	7.50	15.00
—The above three comprise a box set					
❏ 47-4100	Goodbye, G.I. Al/Get Your Paper	1951	3.75	7.50	15.00
❏ 47-4120	Unless/I Have No Heart	1951	3.75	7.50	15.00
❏ 47-4191	I'll Hold You in My Heart ('Til I Can Hold You in My Arms)/I Heard a Song	1951	3.75	7.50	15.00
❏ 47-4257	Turn Back the Hands of Time/I Can't Go On Without You	1951	3.75	7.50	15.00
❏ 47-4359	Any Time/Never Before	1951	3.75	7.50	15.00
❏ 47-4444	Tell Me Why/Trust in Me	1951	3.75	7.50	15.00
❏ 47-4574	Forgive Me/That's the Chance You Take	1952	3.75	7.50	15.00
❏ 47-4616	Just Say I Love Her/Sorry	1952	3.00	6.00	12.00
❏ 47-4617	A Little Bit Independent/If You Should Love Me	1952	3.00	6.00	12.00
❏ 47-4618	I Remember When/Am I Wasting My Time on You	1952	3.00	6.00	12.00
❏ 47-4619	I Love You Because/Thinking of You	1952	3.00	6.00	12.00
—The above four comprise a box set					
❏ 47-4680	I'm Yours/Just a Little Lovin' (Will Go a Long Way)	1952	3.75	7.50	15.00
❏ 47-4744	Maybe/Watermelon Weather	1952	3.00	6.00	12.00
—With Perry Como					
❏ 47-4830	Wish You Were Here/The Hand of Fate	1952	3.00	6.00	12.00
❏ 47-4840	I'm in the Mood for Love/You'll Never Know	1952	3.00	6.00	12.00
❏ 47-4841	Hold Me/Everything I Have Is Yours	1952	3.00	6.00	12.00
❏ 47-4842	That Old Feeling/Full Moon and Empty Arms	1952	3.00	6.00	12.00
❏ 47-4843	Paradise/I've Got You Under My Skin	1952	3.00	6.00	12.00
—The above four comprise a box set					
❏ 47-4910	Silent Night/White Christmas	1952	3.75	7.50	15.00
❏ 47-4911	Christmas Baby/You're All I Want for Christmas	1952	3.75	7.50	15.00
❏ 47-4912	Here Comes Santa/Christmas Means	1952	3.75	7.50	15.00
❏ 47-4913	Jingle Bells/O Come All Ye Faithful	1952	3.75	7.50	15.00
—The above four comprise a box set					
❏ 47-4953	Lady of Spain/Outside of Heaven	1952	3.00	6.00	12.00
❏ 47-5038	Christmas Day/That's What Christmas Means to Me	1952	3.75	7.50	15.00
❏ 47-5137	Downhearted/How Do You Speak to an Angel	1953	3.00	6.00	12.00
❏ 47-5293	I'm Walking Behind You/Just Another Polka	1953	3.00	6.00	12.00
❏ 47-5365	With These Hands/When I Was Young	1953	3.00	6.00	12.00
❏ 47-5365 [PS]	With These Hands/When I Was Young	1953	6.25	12.50	25.00
❏ 47-5453	Many Times/Just to Be with You	1953	3.00	6.00	12.00
❏ 47-5552	Oh My Papa (O Mein Papa)/Until You Said Goodbye	1953	3.00	6.00	12.00
—The above exists with both punctuated and unpunctuated A-side					
❏ 47-5552	Oh! My Pa-Pa (O Mein Papa)/Until You Said Goodbye	1953	3.00	6.00	12.00
❏ 47-5552 [PS]	Oh My Papa (O Mein Papa)/Until You Said Goodbye	1953	6.25	12.50	25.00
❏ 47-5675	A Girl, A Girl (Zoom-Ba Di Alli Nella)/Anema E Core (With All My Heart and Soul)	1954	3.00	6.00	12.00
❏ 47-5748	Green Years/My Friend	1954	3.00	6.00	12.00
❏ 47-5830	I Need You Now/Heaven Was Never Like This	1954	3.00	6.00	12.00
❏ 47-5871	Count Your Blessings (Instead of Sheep)/Fanny	1954	3.75	7.50	15.00
❏ 47-5871	Count Your Blessings/Fanny	1954	3.75	7.50	15.00
—Some pressings do not list the subtitle					
❏ 47-6015	A Man Chases a Girl (Until She Catches Him)/(I'm Always Hearing) Wedding Bells	1955	3.00	6.00	12.00
❏ 47-6015 [PS]	A Man Chases a Girl (Until She Catches Him)/(I'm Always Hearing) Wedding Bells	1955	6.25	12.50	25.00
—"This Is His Life" picture sleeve (possibly promo only)					
❏ 47-6071	Just One More Time/Take My Love	1955	3.00	6.00	12.00
❏ 47-6097	Heart/Near to You	1955	3.00	6.00	12.00
❏ 47-6196	Song of the Dreamer/Don't Stay Away Too Long	1955	3.00	6.00	12.00
❏ 47-6264	Magic Fingers/I Wanna Go Where You Go, Do What You Do (Then I'll Be Happy)	1955	3.00	6.00	12.00
❏ 47-6337	Dungaree Doll/Everybody's Got a Home But Me	1955	2.50	5.00	10.00
❏ 47-6470	Without You/No Other One	1956	2.50	5.00	10.00
❏ 47-6470 [PS]	Without You/No Other One	1956	—	—	—
—Rumored to exist, but without conclusive evidence, we will delete this from future editions					
❏ 47-6529	On the Street Where You Live/Sweet Heartaches	1956	2.50	5.00	10.00
❏ 47-6615	Oh My Maria/If I'm Elected	1956	2.50	5.00	10.00
❏ 47-6677	Cindy, Oh Cindy/Around the World	1956	2.50	5.00	10.00
❏ 47-6746	Some Day Soon/All About Love	1956	2.50	5.00	10.00
❏ 47-6849	Tonight My Heart Will Be Crying/Blues for Me	1957	2.50	5.00	10.00
❏ 47-6913	Sunshine Girl/Did You Close Your Eyes	1957	2.50	5.00	10.00
❏ 47-6947	Around the World/Slow Burning Love	1957	2.50	5.00	10.00
❏ 47-7051	Sayonara/That's the Way It Goes	1957	2.50	5.00	10.00
❏ 47-7135	I Don't Hurt Anymore/What's the Use of Cryin'	1958	2.50	5.00	10.00
❏ 47-7230	Pick a Partner/Kari Waits for Me	1958	2.50	5.00	10.00
❏ 47-7352	Take Me/The Best Thing for You	1958	2.50	5.00	10.00
❏ 47-9070	People Like You/Come Love	1967	—	3.00	6.00
❏ 47-9204	Now I Know/I Haven't Got Anything Better to Do	1967	—	3.00	6.00
❏ 47-9311	Jerusalem, Jerusalem/There's a World Full of Girls	1967	—	3.00	6.00
❏ 47-9430	Fool on the Hill/Sunny	1968	—	3.00	6.00
❏ 47-9574	Rain in My Heart/Eyes of a Child	1968	—	3.00	6.00
❏ 47-5106	Even Now/If It Were Up to Me	1952	3.00	6.00	12.00
❏ 47-5106 [PS]	Even Now/If It Were Up to Me	1952	6.25	12.50	25.00
❏ 47-8956	Games That Lovers Play/Mame	1966	—	3.00	6.00
❏ AMAO-0121	Dungaree Doll/Anytime	1973	—	2.00	4.00
—Gold Standard Series					

7 ARTS

| ❏ 719 | Tonight/Breezin' Along with the Breeze | 1961 | 2.00 | 4.00 | 8.00 |

7-Inch Extended Plays
DOT

❏ DLP 631	Red Roses for a Blue Lady/Who Can I Turn To/Hello, Dolly!//Once Upon a Time/Downtown/Dear Heart	196?	2.50	5.00	10.00
—Jukebox issue; small hole, plays at 33 1/3 rpm					
❏ DLP 631 [PS]	Eddie Fisher Today!	196?	2.50	5.00	10.00

RCA VICTOR

❏ 547-0009	I'm in the Mood for Love/You'll Never Know//Hold Me/Everything I Have Is Yours	1952	3.00	6.00	12.00
—Record 1 of 2-EP set EPB 3058					
❏ 547-0010	That Old Feeling/Full Moon and Empty Arms//Paradise/I've Got You Under My Skin	1952	3.00	6.00	12.00
—Record 2 of 2-EP set EPB 3058					
❏ 547-0095	Just Say I Love Her/Sorry//A Little Bit Independent/If You Should Leave Me	195?	3.00	6.00	12.00
—Record 1 of 2-EP set EPB 3025					
❏ 547-0096	I Remember When/Am I Wasting My Time on You//I Love You Because/Thinking of You	195?	3.00	6.00	12.00
—Record 2 of 2-EP set EPB 3025					
❏ 547-0137	Silent Night/White Christmas//You're All I Want for Christmas/Christmas Day	195?	3.00	6.00	12.00
—Record 1 of 2-EP set EPB 3065					
❏ 547-0138	That's What Christmas Means to Me/Here Comes Santa Claus//Jingle Bells/O Come All Ye Faithful	195?	3.00	6.00	12.00
—Record 2 of 2-EP set EPB 3065					
❏ 547-0326	April Showers/I'm Just a Vagabond Lover//You Call It Madness But I Call It Love/Where the Blue of the Night Meets the Gold of the Day	1953	3.00	6.00	12.00
—Record 2 of 2-EP set EPB 3185					
❏ 547-0327	Night and Day/Nature Boy//Begin the Beguine/May I Sing to You	1953	3.00	6.00	12.00
—Record 1 of 2-EP set EPB 3185					
❏ EPA-426	Cheek to Cheek/They Say It's Wonderful//All By Myself/Remember	1953	3.75	7.50	15.00
❏ EPA-426 [PS]	Cheek to Cheek: Irving Berlin Songs	1953	3.75	7.50	15.00

F

FISHER, EDDIE, AND DEBBIE REYNOLDS

Number	Title (A Side/B Side)	Yr	VG	VG+	NM
❑ EPA-448	*With You/How About Me?/How Deep Is the Ocean/When I Leave the World Behind	195?	3.75	7.50	15.00
❑ EPA-448 [PS]	Eddie Fisher Sings Irving Berlin Favorites	195?	3.75	7.50	15.00
❑ 547-0539	So in Love/Pretty Baby//What Is This Thing Called Love?/Let's Fall in Love	195?	3.00	6.00	12.00
—Record 1 of 2-EP set EPB 1097					
❑ 547-0540	My One and Only Love/I Can't Give You Anything But Love//The Girl That I Marry/I Surrender Dear	195?	3.00	6.00	12.00
—Record 2 of 2-EP set EPB 1097					
❑ EPA-561	(contents unknown)	195?	3.75	7.50	15.00
❑ EPA-561 [PS]	Broadway Classics	195?	3.75	7.50	15.00
❑ EPA-718	Dungaree Doll/Everybody Has a Home But Me//Magic Fingers/I Wanna Go Where You Go	1956	3.75	7.50	15.00
❑ EPA-718 [PS]	Dungaree Doll	1956	3.75	7.50	15.00
❑ EPA-720	The Continental/Lullaby of Broadway/The Way You Look Tonight//Sweet Leilani/Thanks for the Memory/Over the Rainbow/When You Wish Upon a Star	1956	3.75	7.50	15.00
❑ EPA-720 [PS]	Eddie Fisher Sings Academy Award Winning Songs Volume 1	1956	3.75	7.50	15.00
❑ EPA-742	(contents unknown)	1956	3.75	7.50	15.00
❑ EPA-742 [PS]	I'm in the Mood for Love	1956	3.75	7.50	15.00
❑ EPB-1097 [PS]	I Love You	195?	3.00	6.00	12.00
—Two-pocket jacket for two-EP set (547-0539, 547-0540)					
❑ EPB 3025 [PS]	Eddie Fisher Sings	195?		6.00	12.00
—Two-pocket jacket for two-EP set (547-0095, 547-0096)					
❑ EPB-3058 [PS]	I'm in the Mood for Love	1952	3.00	6.00	12.00
—Two-pocket jacket for two-EP set (547-0009, 547-0010)					
❑ EPB 3065 [PS]	Christmas with Eddie Fisher	195?	3.00	6.00	12.00
—Two-pocket jacket for two-EP set (547-0137, 547-0138)					
❑ EPB-3185 [PS]	May I Sing to You	1953	3.00	6.00	12.00
—Two-pocket jacket for two-EP set (547-0325, 547-0326)					
❑ EPA-4018	Worry About Tomorrow - Tomorrow/What's So Good About Good Morning; Worry About Tomorrow - Tomorrow (reprise)/Lullaby in Blue//I Never Felt This Way Before/Bundle of Joy and All About Love	1957	3.75	7.50	15.00
❑ EPA-4018 [PS]	Bundle of Joy	1957	3.75	7.50	15.00
❑ EPA-4047	Thinking of You/Wish You Were Here//My Blue Heaven/I Need You Now	1957	3.00	6.00	12.00
❑ EPA-4047 [PS]	Thinking of You	1957	3.00	6.00	12.00
❑ CEP-6144X	Wish You Were Here/I'll Hold You in My Heart (Till I Can Hold You in My Arms)/Lady of Spain//I'm Walking Behind You/Downhearted/Outside of Heaven	1956	3.00	6.00	12.00
—Coca-Cola logo on label					
❑ CEP-6144X [PS]	Souvenir Record from Coke Time with Eddie Fisher	1956	5.00	10.00	20.00

Albums

DOT
Number	Title (A Side/B Side)	Yr	VG	VG+	NM
❑ DLP-3631 [M]	Eddie Fisher Today!	1965	3.00	6.00	12.00
❑ DLP-3648 [M]	When I Was Young	1965	3.00	6.00	12.00
❑ DLP-3658 [M]	Mary Christmas	1965	3.75	7.50	15.00
❑ DLP-3670 [M]	Young and Foolish	1966	3.00	6.00	12.00
❑ DLP-3785 [M]	His Greatest Hits	1967	3.00	6.00	12.00
❑ DLP-25361 [S]	Eddie Fisher Today!	1965	3.75	7.50	15.00
❑ DLP-25648 [S]	When I Was Young	1965	3.75	7.50	15.00
❑ DLP-25658 [S]	Mary Christmas	1965	5.00	10.00	20.00
❑ DLP-25670 [S]	Young and Foolish	1966	3.75	7.50	15.00
❑ DLP-25785 [S]	His Greatest Hits	1967	3.75	7.50	15.00

MCA
Number	Title (A Side/B Side)	Yr	VG	VG+	NM
❑ 1549	The Best of Eddie Fisher	1983	2.00	4.00	8.00

PICKWICK
Number	Title (A Side/B Side)	Yr	VG	VG+	NM
❑ SPC-3141	Oh My Papa	196?	3.00	6.00	12.00

RAMROD
Number	Title (A Side/B Side)	Yr	VG	VG+	NM
❑ RR-1 [(2)M]	Eddie Fisher at the Winter Garden	1963	3.75	7.50	15.00
❑ RRS-1 [(2)S]	Eddie Fisher at the Winter Garden	1963	5.00	10.00	20.00

RCA CAMDEN
Number	Title (A Side/B Side)	Yr	VG	VG+	NM
❑ CAL-789 [M]	Bring Back the Thrill	196?	3.00	6.00	12.00
❑ CAS-789 [R]	Bring Back the Thrill	196?	2.50	5.00	10.00

RCA VICTOR
Number	Title (A Side/B Side)	Yr	VG	VG+	NM
❑ LOC-1024 [M]	Academy Award Winners	1955	10.00	20.00	40.00
❑ LPM-1097 [M]	I Love You	1955	7.50	15.00	30.00
❑ ANL1-1138	Eddie Fisher's Greatest Hits	1975	2.00	4.00	8.00
❑ LPM-1180 [M]	I'm in the Mood for Love	1955	7.50	15.00	30.00
❑ LPM-1181 [M]	May I Sing to You?	1955	7.50	15.00	30.00
❑ LPM-1399 [M]	Bundle of Joy	1957	7.50	15.00	30.00
❑ LPM-1548 [M]	Thinking of You	1957	7.50	15.00	30.00
❑ LPM-1647 [M]	As Long As There's Music	1958	7.50	15.00	30.00
❑ LSP-1647 [S]	As Long As There's Music	1958	12.50	25.00	50.00
❑ LPM-2504 [M]	Eddie Fisher's Greatest Hits	1962	3.75	7.50	15.00
❑ LSP-2504 [S]	Eddie Fisher's Greatest Hits	1962	5.00	10.00	20.00
❑ LPM-3025 [10]	Fisher Sings	1952	12.50	25.00	50.00
❑ LPM-3058 [10]	I'm in the Mood for Love	1952	12.50	25.00	50.00
❑ LPM-3065 [10]	Christmas with Eddie Fisher	1952	12.50	25.00	50.00
❑ LPM-3122 [10]	Irving Berlin Favorites	1953	12.50	25.00	50.00
❑ LPM-3185 [10]	May I Sing to You?	1953	12.50	25.00	50.00
❑ LPM-3375 [M]	The Best of Eddie Fisher	1965	3.75	7.50	15.00
❑ LSP-3375 [R]	The Best of Eddie Fisher	1965	3.00	6.00	12.00
❑ LPM-3726 [M]	Games That Lovers Play	1966	3.75	7.50	15.00
❑ LSP-3726 [S]	Games That Lovers Play	1966	3.75	7.50	15.00
❑ LPM-3820 [M]	People Like You	1967	5.00	10.00	20.00
❑ LSP-3820 [S]	People Like You	1967	3.00	6.00	12.00
❑ LSP-3914	You Ain't Heard Nothin' Yet	1968	3.00	6.00	12.00

FISHER, EDDIE, AND DEBBIE REYNOLDS

45s

RCA VICTOR
Number	Title (A Side/B Side)	Yr	VG	VG+	NM
❑ 47-6820	Lullaby in Love/I Never Felt This Way Before	1957	2.50	5.00	10.00

FISHER, JERRY

45s

NEW DESIGN
Number	Title (A Side/B Side)	Yr	VG	VG+	NM
❑ ZS7 1003	A New Day's Comin'/Do It If You Want To	1971	2.00	4.00	8.00
❑ ZS7 1007	I Never Had It So Good/Yonder Stands Little Maggie	1972	2.00	4.00	8.00

FISHER, MARY ANN

45s

FIRE
Number	Title (A Side/B Side)	Yr	VG	VG+	NM
❑ 1002	Put On My Shoes/Wild As You Can Be	1959	6.25	12.50	25.00
❑ 1010	Only Yesterday/Wild As You Can Be	1960	6.25	12.50	25.00

IMPERIAL
Number	Title (A Side/B Side)	Yr	VG	VG+	NM
❑ 5853	I Keep Comin' Back for More/It's a Man's World	1962	5.00	10.00	20.00

SEG-WAY
Number	Title (A Side/B Side)	Yr	VG	VG+	NM
❑ 1001	I Can't Take It/Forever More	1961	5.00	10.00	20.00
❑ 1007	Can't Take the Heartbreak/Give	1961	5.00	10.00	20.00

FISHER, TONI

45s

BIG TOP
Number	Title (A Side/B Side)	Yr	VG	VG+	NM
❑ 3097	West of the Wall/What Did I Do	1962	3.00	6.00	12.00
❑ 3124	The Music from the House Next Door/Quickly My Love	1962	3.00	6.00	12.00

CAPITOL
Number	Title (A Side/B Side)	Yr	VG	VG+	NM
❑ 5901	Train of Love/A Million Heartbeats from Now	1967	2.00	4.00	8.00

COLUMBIA
Number	Title (A Side/B Side)	Yr	VG	VG+	NM
❑ 42066	If I Loved You/Love Big	1961	3.00	6.00	12.00

SIGNET
Number	Title (A Side/B Side)	Yr	VG	VG+	NM
❑ 275	The Big Hurt/Memphis Belle	1959	3.75	7.50	15.00
❑ 276	How Deep Is the Ocean/Blue, Blue, Blue	1960	3.00	6.00	12.00
❑ 279	Everlasting Love/The Red Sea of Mars	1960	3.00	6.00	12.00
❑ 364	You Never Told Me/Toot Toot Amore	1964	2.00	4.00	8.00
❑ 400	A Man That's Steady/You Never Told Me	196?	2.00	4.00	8.00
❑ 664	Springtime of Love/Train of Love	1964	2.00	4.00	8.00

SMASH
Number	Title (A Side/B Side)	Yr	VG	VG+	NM
❑ 1797	Hold Me/Laugh or Cry	1963	2.50	5.00	10.00
❑ 1820	Cry a Little for Me/365 Disappointments	1963	2.50	5.00	10.00
❑ 1832	Lovers, Dreamers, Fools/You Won't Forget Me	1963	2.50	5.00	10.00
❑ 1847	Your Royal Majesty/Billy, Marry Me	1963	2.50	5.00	10.00

Albums

SIGNET
Number	Title (A Side/B Side)	Yr	VG	VG+	NM
❑ WP-509 [S]	The Big Hurt	1960	12.50	25.00	50.00
—Issued in "Stereomonic"					

FITZGERALD, ELLA

45s

CAPITOL
Number	Title (A Side/B Side)	Yr	VG	VG+	NM
❑ 2099	Born to Lose/I Taught Him Everything He Knows	1968	2.00	4.00	8.00
❑ 2212	Brighten the Corner/It's Up to Me and You	1968	2.00	4.00	8.00
❑ 2267	Hawaiian War Chant/It's Only Love	1968	2.00	4.00	8.00
❑ 5946	Just a Closer Walk with Thee/I Shall Not Be Moved	1967	2.00	4.00	8.00

DECCA
Number	Title (A Side/B Side)	Yr	VG	VG+	NM
❑ 27061	Mississippi/I Don't Want the World (With a Fence Around It)	1950	5.00	10.00	20.00
❑ 27120	I've Got the World on a String/Peas and Rice	1950	5.00	10.00	20.00
❑ 27200	Ain't Nobody's Business If I Do/I'll Never Be Free	1950	5.00	10.00	20.00
—With Louis Jordan					
❑ 27255	Santa Claus Got Stuck (In My Chimney)/Molasses, Molasses (It's Icky Sticky Goo)	1950	5.00	10.00	20.00
❑ 27368	My One and Only/Someone to Watch Over Me	1951	3.75	7.50	15.00
❑ 27369	But Not for Me/Looking for a Boy	1951	3.75	7.50	15.00
❑ 27370	I've Got a Crush on You/How Long Has This Been Going On	1951	3.75	7.50	15.00
❑ 27371	Soon/Maybe	1951	3.75	7.50	15.00
—The above four comprise a box set					
❑ 27419	Little Small Town/I Still Feel the Same About You	1951	5.00	10.00	20.00
—With the Ink Spots					
❑ 27453	The Beanbag Song/Lonesome Gal	1951	5.00	10.00	20.00
❑ 27578	The Hot Canary/Two Little Men	1951	5.00	10.00	20.00
❑ 27602	The Chesapeke and Ohio/Because of Rain	1951	5.00	10.00	20.00
❑ 27634	Do You Really Love Me/Even As You and I	1951	5.00	10.00	20.00
❑ 27680	Come On-a My House/Mixed Emotions	1951	5.00	10.00	20.00
❑ 27693	Smooth Sailing/Love You Madly	1951	5.00	10.00	20.00
❑ 27724	Give a Little — Get a Little/There Never Was a Baby (Like My Baby)	1951	5.00	10.00	20.00
❑ 27900	Baby Doll/Lady Bug	1951	5.00	10.00	20.00
❑ 27901	Oops!/Necessary Evil	1951	5.00	10.00	20.00
❑ 27948	I Don't Want to Take a Chance/Rough Ridin'	1952	3.75	7.50	15.00
❑ 28034	Lazy Day/What Does It Take	1952	3.75	7.50	15.00
❑ 28049	A Guy Is a Guy/That Old Feeling	1952	3.75	7.50	15.00
❑ 28126	Goody Goody/Air Mail Special	1952	3.75	7.50	15.00
❑ 28181	I Hadn't Anyone Till You/Gee, But I'm Glad to Know You Love Me	1952	3.75	7.50	15.00
❑ 28321	Ding-Dong Boogie/Preview	1952	3.75	7.50	15.00
❑ 28375	Trying/My Bonnie Lies Over the Ocean	1952	3.75	7.50	15.00
❑ 28433	My Favorite Song/Walkin' by the River	1952	3.75	7.50	15.00
❑ 28589	I Can't Lie to Myself/Don't Wake Me Up	1953	3.75	7.50	15.00
❑ 28671	Careless/Blue Lou	1953	3.75	7.50	15.00
❑ 28707	Angel Eyes/Nowhere Guy	1953	3.75	7.50	15.00
❑ 28762	Crying in the Chapel/When the Hands of the Clock Pray at Midnite	1953	3.75	7.50	15.00
❑ 28774	You'll Have to Swing It (Part 1)/You'll Have to Swing It (Part 2)	1953	3.75	7.50	15.00
❑ 28930	The Greatest There Is/I Wonder What Kind of Guy You'd Be	1953	3.75	7.50	15.00
❑ 28993	A Sunday Kind of Love/That's My Desire	1954	3.75	7.50	15.00
❑ 29008	Somebody Bad Stole De Wedding Bell/Melancholy Me	1954	3.75	7.50	15.00
❑ 29108	Baby/I Need	1954	3.75	7.50	15.00
❑ 29136	(I Love You) For Sentimental Reasons/It's Only a Paper Moon	1954	3.75	7.50	15.00
—With the Delta Rhythm Boys					
❑ 29137	Who's Afraid/I Wished on the Moon	1954	3.75	7.50	15.00
❑ 29198	Lullaby of Birdland/Later	1954	3.75	7.50	15.00
❑ 29259	Empty Ballroom/If You Don't, I Know Who Will	1954	3.75	7.50	15.00
❑ 29475	Moanin' Low/Take a Chance on Love	1955	3.00	6.00	12.00
❑ 29580	Old Devil Moon/Lover, Come Back to Me	1955	3.00	6.00	12.00
❑ 29609	Pete Kelly's Blues/Hard Hearted Hannah	1955	3.00	6.00	12.00
❑ 29648	Soldier Boy/A Satisfied Mind	1955	3.00	6.00	12.00
❑ 29665	The Impatient Years/But Not Like Mine	1955	3.00	6.00	12.00

Number	Title (A Side/B Side)	Yr	VG	VG+	NM
❑ 29746	(Love Is) The Tender Trap/				
	My One and Only Love	1955	3.00	6.00	12.00
❑ 29810	Early Autumn/Ella's Contribution to the Blues	1956	3.00	6.00	12.00
❑ 30222	Stone Cold Dead in the Market/Peas and Rice	1957	3.00	6.00	12.00
❑ 30405	Goody Goody/It's Too Soon to Know	1957	6.25	12.50	25.00
—Reissued to compete with Frankie Lymon's remake, this is scarcer than the original on 28126					
❑ 31142	How High the Moon/Smooth Sailing	1960	2.50	5.00	10.00
PRESTIGE					
❑ 715	Hey Jude/Sunshine of Your Love	1969	2.00	4.00	8.00
REPRISE					
❑ 0850	Get Ready/Open Your Window	1969	—	3.00	6.00
❑ 0875	I'll Never Fall in Love Again/Savoy Truffle	1969	—	3.00	6.00
❑ 0922	Yellow Man/Try a Little Bit	1970	—	3.00	6.00
❑ 0995	I Wonder Why/Ooo Baby Baby	1971	—	3.00	6.00
VERVE					
❑ 2002	It's Only a Man/Too Young for the Blues	1956	3.00	6.00	12.00
❑ 2012	A Beautiful Friendship/Stay There	1956	3.00	6.00	12.00
❑ 2021	The Silent Treatment/The Sun Forgot to Shine				
	This Morning	1956	3.00	6.00	12.00
❑ 10031	Hotta Chocolatta/Hear My Heart	1957	3.00	6.00	12.00
❑ 10050	Let's Do It (Let's Fall in Love)/Manhattan	1957	3.00	6.00	12.00
❑ 10077	All of Me/It's All Right with Me	1957	3.00	6.00	12.00
❑ 10111	What Will I Tell My Heart/Midnight Sun	1958	2.50	5.00	10.00
❑ 10130	Beale Street Blues/St. Louis Blues	1958	2.50	5.00	10.00
❑ 10132	Swingin' Shepherd Blues/Teach Me How to Cry	1958	2.50	5.00	10.00
❑ 10143	Trav'lin' Light/Your Red Wagon	1958	2.50	5.00	10.00
❑ 10158	Oh What a Night for Love/				
	Dreams Are Made for Children	1959	2.50	5.00	10.00
❑ 10166	Teardrops from My Eyes/A Little Jazz	1959	2.50	5.00	10.00
❑ 10171	Stairway to the Stars/I'm Through with Love	1959	2.50	5.00	10.00
❑ 10180	But Not for Me/You Make Me Feel So Young	1959	2.50	5.00	10.00
❑ 10186	The Christmas Song/The Secret of Christmas	1959	3.75	7.50	15.00
❑ 10189	Like Young/Beat Me Daddy, Eight to the Bar	1959	2.50	5.00	10.00
❑ 10209	Mack the Knife/Lorelei	1960	2.50	5.00	10.00
❑ 10220	How High the Moon (Part 1)/				
	How High the Moon (Part 2)	1960	2.50	5.00	10.00
❑ 10222	I Can't Give You Anything But Love/				
	Reach for Tomorrow	1960	2.50	5.00	10.00
❑ 10224	Jingle Bells/Good Morning Blues	1960	3.75	7.50	15.00
❑ 10237	(You'll Have to Swing It) Mr. Paganini/				
	You're Driving Me Crazy	1961	2.50	5.00	10.00
❑ 10237 [DJ]	(You'll Have to Swing It) Mr. Paganini/				
	You're Driving Me Crazy	1961	6.25	12.50	25.00
—Promo copy on gold vinyl					
❑ 10237 [PS]	(You'll Have to Swing It) Mr. Paganini/				
	You're Driving Me Crazy	1961	7.50	15.00	30.00
—Sleeve may be promo only					
❑ 10241	Clap Hands (Here Come Charlie!)/				
	Cry Me a River	1961	2.50	5.00	10.00
❑ 10241 [PS]	Clap Hands (Here Come Charlie!)				
	/Cry Me a River	1961	5.00	10.00	20.00
❑ 10248	What Is This Thing Called Love/Call Me Darling	1962	2.00	4.00	8.00
❑ 10274	Desafinado (Slightly Out of Tune)/				
	Stardust Bossa Nova	1962	2.00	4.00	8.00
❑ 10288	Bill Bailey, Won't You Please Come Home/				
	Ol' Man Mose	1963	2.00	4.00	8.00
❑ 10305	Shiny Stockings				
	/Into Each Love Some Rain Must Fall	1963	2.00	4.00	8.00
❑ 10319	See See Rider/Trouble in Mind	1964	2.00	4.00	8.00
❑ 10324	Can't Buy Me Love/Hello, Dolly!	1964	2.50	5.00	10.00
❑ 10337	I've Grown Accustomed to Your Face/I Could				
	Have Danced All Night	1964	2.00	4.00	8.00
❑ 10340	Ringo Beat/I'm Falling in Love	1964	3.75	7.50	15.00
❑ 10341	All the Livelong Day/(B-side unknown)	1965	2.00	4.00	8.00
❑ 10359	Mae (She's Just a Quiet Girl)/We Three	1965	2.00	4.00	8.00
❑ 10368	A Hard Day's Night/And the Angels Sing	1965	2.50	5.00	10.00
❑ 10379	Imagine My Frustration (Part 1)/Imagine My				
	Frustration (Part 2)	1966	2.00	4.00	8.00
❑ 10408	Love Theme from "The Sandpiper"/				
	Duke's Place	1966	2.00	4.00	8.00

7-Inch Extended Plays
DECCA

Number	Title (A Side/B Side)	Yr	VG	VG+	NM
❑ ED 2014	It's Only a Paper Moon/(I Love You) For				
	Sentimental Reasons//Guilty/Stairway to the				
	Stars	195?	5.00	10.00	20.00
❑ ED 2014 [PS]	Ella Fitzgerald Sings — Volume 1	195?	5.00	10.00	20.00
❑ ED 2028	Smooth Sailing/Flying Home//Oh, Lady Be				
	Good/How High the Moon	195?	5.00	10.00	20.00
❑ ED 2028 [PS]	Smooth Sailing	195?	5.00	10.00	20.00
❑ ED 2049	(contents unknown)	195?	5.00	10.00	20.00
❑ ED 2049 [PS]	Ella Fitzgerald Sings — Volume 2	195?	5.00	10.00	20.00
❑ ED 2253	Moanin' Low/Taking a Chance on Love//(If You				
	Can't Sing It) You'll Have to Swing It (Part 1)				
	(Part 2)	195?	5.00	10.00	20.00
❑ ED 2253 [PS]	Sweet and Hot, Part 3	195?	5.00	10.00	20.00
❑ ED 2269	(contents unknown)	1955	5.00	10.00	20.00
❑ ED 2269 [PS]	Pete Kelly's Blues	1955	5.00	10.00	20.00
❑ 34244 [PS]	Early Ella	196?	3.00	6.00	12.00
❑ 34244 [S]	Mixed Emotions/It's Too Soon to Know/Walkin'				
	by the River//Baby Doll/I Hadn't Anyone Till				
	You/So Long	196?	3.00	6.00	12.00
—33 1/3 rpm, small hole					

VERVE

Number	Title (A Side/B Side)	Yr	VG	VG+	NM
❑ SLV 4055	Sweet and Slow/Street of Dreams/The Very				
	Thought of You//It's a Blue World/I Wished on				
	the Moon/Body and Soul	196?	5.00	10.00	20.00
—Jukebox issue; small hole, plays at 33 1/3 rpm					
❑ SLV 4055 [PS]	Ella Fitzgerald Swings Gently with Nelson Riddle	196?	5.00	10.00	20.00

Albums
AMERICAN RECORDING SOCIETY

Number	Title (A Side/B Side)	Yr	VG	VG+	NM
❑ G-433 [M]	Ella Fitzgerald At Newport	195?	10.00	20.00	40.00

ATLANTIC

Number	Title (A Side/B Side)	Yr	VG	VG+	NM
❑ SD 1631	Ella Loves Cole	1972	3.00	6.00	12.00

BAINBRIDGE

Number	Title (A Side/B Side)	Yr	VG	VG+	NM
❑ 6223	Things Ain't What They Used to Be	1982	2.50	5.00	10.00
—Reissue of Reprise 6432					

BASF

Number	Title (A Side/B Side)	Yr	VG	VG+	NM
❑ 20712	Watch What Happens	1972	3.00	6.00	12.00

CAPITOL

Number	Title (A Side/B Side)	Yr	VG	VG+	NM
❑ ST 2685 [S]	Brighten the Corner	1967	3.75	7.50	15.00
❑ T 2685 [M]	Brighten the Corner	1967	5.00	10.00	20.00
❑ ST 2805 [S]	Ella Fitzgerald's Christmas	1967	3.00	6.00	12.00
—Same as above, but in stereo					
❑ T 2805 [M]	Ella Fitzgerald's Christmas	1967	5.00	10.00	20.00
❑ ST 2888	Misty Blue	1968	3.75	7.50	15.00
❑ ST 2960	Thirty by Ella	1968	3.75	7.50	15.00
❑ SM-11793	Brighten the Corner	1978	2.50	5.00	10.00
❑ SN-16276	Thirty by Ella	1983	2.50	5.00	10.00
—Budget-line reissue					

CLASSICS RECORD LIBRARY/VERVE

Number	Title (A Side/B Side)	Yr	VG	VG+	NM
❑ 80-55713 [(4)]	Ella Fitzgerald Sings the George and Ira				
	Gershwin Songbook	1978	10.00	20.00	40.00
—Reissue of the entire set for Book-of-the-Month Club					

COLUMBIA

Number	Title (A Side/B Side)	Yr	VG	VG+	NM
❑ KG 32557 [(2)]	Carnegie Hall & Newport Jazz Festival 1973	1973	3.75	7.50	15.00

DECCA

Number	Title (A Side/B Side)	Yr	VG	VG+	NM
❑ DXB 156 [(2)M]	The Best of Ella	1959	10.00	20.00	40.00
—Black labels, silver print					
❑ DXB 156 [(2)M]	The Best of Ella	1961	6.25	12.50	25.00
—Black labels with color bars					
❑ DL 4129 [M]	Golden Favorites	1961	5.00	10.00	20.00
❑ DL 4446 [M]	Stairway to the Stars	1964	3.75	7.50	15.00
❑ DL 4447 [M]	Early Ella	1964	3.75	7.50	15.00
❑ DL 4451 [M]	Ella Sings Gershwin	1964	3.75	7.50	15.00
❑ DL 4887 [M]	Smooth Sailing	1967	3.75	7.50	15.00
❑ DL 5084 [10]	Souvenir Album	1950	30.00	60.00	120.00
❑ DL 5300 [10]	Ella Fitzgerald Sings Gershwin Songs	1951	30.00	60.00	120.00
❑ DXSB 7156 [(2)R]	The Best of Ella	196?	5.00	10.00	20.00
❑ DL 8068 [M]	Songs in a Mellow Mood	1954	12.50	25.00	50.00
❑ DL 8149 [M]	Lullabies of Birdland	1955	12.50	25.00	50.00
❑ DL 8155 [M]	Sweet and Hot	1955	12.50	25.00	50.00
❑ DL 8378 [M]	Ella Sings Gershwin	1957	10.00	20.00	40.00
❑ DL 8477 [M]	Ella and Her Fellas	1957	10.00	20.00	40.00
❑ DL 8695 [M]	The First Lady of Song	1958	10.00	20.00	40.00
❑ DL 8696 [M]	Miss Ella Fitzgerald and Mr. Nelson Riddle Invite				
	You to Listen and Relax	1958	10.00	20.00	40.00
❑ DL 8832 [M]	For Sentimental Reasons	1958	10.00	20.00	40.00
❑ DL 74129 [R]	Golden Favorites	1961	3.00	6.00	12.00
❑ DL 74446 [R]	Stairway to the Stars	1964	3.00	6.00	12.00
❑ DL 74447 [R]	Early Ella	1964	3.00	6.00	12.00
❑ DL 74451 [R]	Ella Sings Gershwin	1964	3.00	6.00	12.00
❑ DL 74887 [R]	Smooth Sailing	1967	3.00	6.00	12.00

EVEREST ARCHIVE OF FOLK & JAZZ

Number	Title (A Side/B Side)	Yr	VG	VG+	NM
❑ 276	Ella Fitzgerald	1973	3.00	6.00	12.00

FANTASY

Number	Title (A Side/B Side)	Yr	VG	VG+	NM
❑ OJC-376	Montreux '77	1989	3.00	6.00	12.00
—Reissue of Pablo Live 2308 206					
❑ OJC-442	Ella & Nice	1990	3.00	6.00	12.00
—Reissue of Pablo Live 2308 234					

INTERMEDIA

Number	Title (A Side/B Side)	Yr	VG	VG+	NM
❑ QS-5049	Ella by Starlight	198?	2.50	5.00	10.00

MCA

Number	Title (A Side/B Side)	Yr	VG	VG+	NM
❑ 215	Ella Sings Gershwin	1973	2.50	5.00	10.00
❑ 734	Memories	198?	2.50	5.00	10.00
❑ 4016 [(2)]	The Best of Ella, Vol. 2	1973	3.75	7.50	15.00
❑ 4047 [(2)]	The Best of Ella	197?	3.75	7.50	15.00

METRO

Number	Title (A Side/B Side)	Yr	VG	VG+	NM
❑ M-500 [M]	Ella Fitzgerald	1965	3.00	6.00	12.00
❑ MS-500 [S]	Ella Fitzgerald	1965	3.00	6.00	12.00
❑ M-567 [M]	The World of Ella Fitzgerald	1966	3.00	6.00	12.00
❑ MS-567 [S]	The World of Ella Fitzgerald	1966	3.00	6.00	12.00

MGM

Number	Title (A Side/B Side)	Yr	VG	VG+	NM
❑ GAS-130	Ella Fitzgerald (Golden Archive Series)	1970	3.75	7.50	15.00

PABLO

Number	Title (A Side/B Side)	Yr	VG	VG+	NM
❑ 2310702	Take Love Easy	1974	3.00	6.00	12.00
❑ 2310711	Ella in London	1974	3.00	6.00	12.00
❑ 2310751	Montreux '75	1976	3.00	6.00	12.00
❑ 2310759	Ella and Oscar	1976	3.00	6.00	12.00
❑ 2310772	Again	1977	3.00	6.00	12.00
❑ 2310814	Dream Dancing	1978	3.00	6.00	12.00
❑ 2310825	Lady Time	1978	3.00	6.00	12.00
❑ 2310829	Fine and Mellow	1979	3.00	6.00	12.00
❑ 2310888	Speak Love	1983	2.50	5.00	10.00
❑ 2310921	Easy Living	1987	2.50	5.00	10.00
❑ 2310938	All That Jazz	1990	3.00	6.00	12.00
❑ 2405421	The Best of Ella Fitzgerald	198?	2.50	5.00	10.00

PABLO LIVE

Number	Title (A Side/B Side)	Yr	VG	VG+	NM
❑ 2308206	Montreux '77	1978	3.00	6.00	12.00
❑ 2308234	Ella & Nice	197?	3.75	7.50	15.00

PABLO TODAY

Number	Title (A Side/B Side)	Yr	VG	VG+	NM
❑ 2312132	A Classy Pair	1983	2.50	5.00	10.00
❑ 2312138	The Best Is Yet to Come	1982	2.50	5.00	10.00
❑ 2312140	Nice Work If You Can Get It	198?	2.50	5.00	10.00
❑ 2630201 [(2)]	Ella Abraca Jobim: Ella Fitzgerald Sings the				
	Antonio Carlos Jobim Song Book	1981	3.75	7.50	15.00

PAUSA

Number	Title (A Side/B Side)	Yr	VG	VG+	NM
❑ 7130	Love You Madly	198?	2.50	5.00	10.00

PICKWICK

Number	Title (A Side/B Side)	Yr	VG	VG+	NM
❑ SPC-3259	Misty Blues	1974	2.50	5.00	10.00

PRESTIGE

Number	Title (A Side/B Side)	Yr	VG	VG+	NM
❑ PRLP-7685	Sunshine of Your Love	1970	3.75	7.50	15.00

REPRISE

Number	Title (A Side/B Side)	Yr	VG	VG+	NM
❑ RS-6354	Ella	1969	3.75	7.50	15.00
❑ RS-6432	Things Ain't What They Used to Be	1971	3.00	6.00	12.00

SUNBEAM

Number	Title (A Side/B Side)	Yr	VG	VG+	NM
❑ 205	Ella Fitzgerald and Her Orchestra, 1940	197?	2.50	5.00	10.00

TIME-LIFE

Number	Title (A Side/B Side)	Yr	VG	VG+	NM
❑ SLGD-03 [(2)]	Legendary Singers: Ella Fitzgerald	1985	3.75	7.50	15.00

VERVE

Number	Title (A Side/B Side)	Yr	VG	VG+	NM
❑ V-10-4 [(4)M]	Ella Fitzgerald Sings the				
	Duke Ellington Song Book	196?	12.50	25.00	50.00

Number	Title (A Side/B Side)	Yr	VG	VG+	NM
❑ V-29-5 [(5)M]	Ella Fitzgerald Sings the George and Ira Gershwin Song Book	196?	25.00	50.00	100.00
—Reissue of MGV-4029					
❑ V6-29-5 [(5)S]	Ella Fitzgerald Sings the George and Ira Gershwin Song Book	196?	25.00	50.00	100.00
—Reissue of MGVS-6082					
❑ VE-2-2511 [(2)]	The Cole Porter Song Book	197?	3.75	7.50	15.00
❑ VE-2-2519 [(2)]	The Rodgers and Hart Song Book	197?	3.75	7.50	15.00
❑ VE-2-2525 [(2)]	The George Gershwin Song Book	1978	3.75	7.50	15.00
❑ VE-2-2535 [(2)]	The Duke Ellington Song Book	1979	3.75	7.50	15.00
❑ VE-1-2539	Ella Wishes You a Swinging Christmas	198?	3.00	6.00	12.00
—Reissue					
❑ VE-2-2540 [(2)]	The Duke Ellington Song Book, Vol. 2	1982	3.75	7.50	15.00
❑ MGV-4001-2 [(2)M]	Ella Fitzgerald Sings the Cole Porter Song Book	1956	20.00	40.00	80.00
❑ V-4001-2 [(2)M]	Ella Fitzgerald Sings the Cole Porter Song Book	1961	6.25	12.50	25.00
❑ MGV-4002-2 [(2)M]	Ella Fitzgerald Sings the Rodgers & Hart Song Book	1956	20.00	40.00	80.00
❑ V-4002-2 [(2)M]	Ella Fitzgerald Sings the Rodgers and Hart Song Book	1961	6.25	12.50	25.00
❑ MGV-4004 [M]	Like Someone in Love	1957	12.50	25.00	50.00
❑ V-4004 [M]	Like Someone in Love	1961	5.00	10.00	20.00
❑ V6-4004 [S]	Like Someone in Love	1961	5.00	10.00	20.00
❑ MGV-4008-2 [(2)M]	Ella Fitzgerald Sings the Duke Ellington Song Book, Vol. 1	1957	20.00	40.00	80.00
❑ V-4008-2 [(2)M]	Ella Fitzgerald Sings the Duke Ellington Song Book, Vol. 1	1961	6.25	12.50	25.00
❑ MGV-4009-2 [(2)M]	Ella Fitzgerald Sings the Duke Ellington Song Book, Vol. 2	1957	20.00	40.00	80.00
❑ V-4009-2 [(2)M]	Ella Fitzgerald Sings the Duke Ellington Song Book, Vol. 2	1961	6.25	12.50	25.00
❑ MGV-4010-4 [(4)M]	Ella Fitzgerald Sings the Duke Ellington Song Book	1957	37.50	75.00	150.00
—Combines 4008 and 4009 into one package					
❑ MGV-4013 [M]	Ella Fitzgerald Sings the Gershwin Song Book	1957	12.50	25.00	50.00
❑ MGV-4019-2 [(2)M]	Ella Fitzgerald Sings the Irving Berlin Song Book	1958	20.00	40.00	80.00
❑ V-4019-2 [(2)M]	Ella Fitzgerald Sings the Irving Berlin Song Book	1961	6.25	12.50	25.00
❑ V6-4019-2 [(2)S]	Ella Fitzgerald Sings the Irving Berlin Song Book	1961	6.25	12.50	25.00
❑ MGV-4021 [M]	Ella Swings Lightly	1958	12.50	25.00	50.00
❑ V-4021 [M]	Ella Swings Lightly	1961	5.00	10.00	20.00
❑ V6-4021 [S]	Ella Swings Lightly	1961	5.00	10.00	20.00
❑ MGV-4022 [M]	Ella Fitzgerald Sings the Rodgers & Hart Song Book, Vol. 1	1959	12.50	25.00	50.00
❑ V-4022 [M]	Ella Fitzgerald Sings the Rodgers & Hart Song Book, Vol. 1	1961	5.00	10.00	20.00
❑ V6-4022 [S]	Ella Fitzgerald Sings the Rodgers & Hart Song Book, Vol. 1	1961	5.00	10.00	20.00
❑ MGV-4023 [M]	Ella Fitzgerald Sings the Rodgers & Hart Song Book, Vol. 2	1959	12.50	25.00	50.00
❑ V-4023 [M]	Ella Fitzgerald Sings the Rodgers & Hart Song Book, Vol. 2	1961	5.00	10.00	20.00
❑ V6-4023 [S]	Ella Fitzgerald Sings the Rodgers & Hart Song Book, Vol. 2	1961	5.00	10.00	20.00
❑ MGV-4024 [M]	Ella Fitzgerald Sings the George and Ira Gershwin Song Book, Vol. 1	1959	12.50	25.00	50.00
❑ V-4024 [M]	Ella Fitzgerald Sings the George and Ira Gershwin Song Book, Vol. 1	1961	5.00	10.00	20.00
❑ V6-4024 [S]	Ella Fitzgerald Sings the George and Ira Gershwin Song Book, Vol. 1	1961	5.00	10.00	20.00
❑ MGV-4025 [M]	Ella Fitzgerald Sings the George and Ira Gershwin Song Book, Vol. 2	1959	12.50	25.00	50.00
❑ V-4025 [M]	Ella Fitzgerald Sings the George and Ira Gershwin Song Book, Vol. 2	1961	5.00	10.00	20.00
❑ V6-4025 [S]	Ella Fitzgerald Sings the George and Ira Gershwin Song Book, Vol. 2	1961	5.00	10.00	20.00
❑ MGV-4026 [M]	Ella Fitzgerald Sings the George and Ira Gershwin Song Book, Vol. 3	1959	12.50	25.00	50.00
❑ V-4026 [M]	Ella Fitzgerald Sings the George and Ira Gershwin Song Book, Vol. 3	1961	5.00	10.00	20.00
❑ V6-4026 [S]	Ella Fitzgerald Sings the George and Ira Gershwin Song Book, Vol. 3	1961	5.00	10.00	20.00
❑ MGV-4027 [M]	Ella Fitzgerald Sings the George and Ira Gershwin Song Book, Vol. 4	1959	12.50	25.00	50.00
❑ V-4027 [M]	Ella Fitzgerald Sings the George and Ira Gershwin Song Book, Vol. 4	1961	5.00	10.00	20.00
❑ V6-4027 [S]	Ella Fitzgerald Sings the George and Ira Gershwin Song Book, Vol. 4	1961	5.00	10.00	20.00
❑ MGV-4028 [M]	Ella Fitzgerald Sings the George and Ira Gershwin Song Book, Vol. 5	1959	12.50	25.00	50.00
❑ V-4028 [M]	Ella Fitzgerald Sings the George and Ira Gershwin Song Book, Vol. 5	1961	5.00	10.00	20.00
❑ V6-4028 [S]	Ella Fitzgerald Sings the George and Ira Gershwin Song Book, Vol. 5	1961	5.00	10.00	20.00
❑ MGV-4029-5 [(5)M]	Ella Fitzgerald Sings the George and Ira Gershwin Song Book	1959	62.50	125.00	250.00
—Box set with 4024 through 4028 plus bonus 10-inch LP					
❑ MGV-4029-5 [(5)M]	Ella Fitzgerald Sings the George and Ira Gershwin Song Book	1959	125.00	250.00	500.00
—Box set with 4024 through 4028 plus bonus 10-inch LP, all in walnut box with leather pockets					
❑ MGV-4030 [M]	Ella Fitzgerald Sings the Irving Berlin Song Book, Vol. 1	1959	12.50	25.00	50.00
❑ V-4030 [M]	Ella Fitzgerald Sings the Irving Berlin Song Book, Vol. 1	1961	5.00	10.00	20.00
❑ V6-4030 [S]	Ella Fitzgerald Sings the Irving Berlin Song Book, Vol. 1	1961	5.00	10.00	20.00
❑ MGV-4031 [M]	Ella Fitzgerald Sings the Irving Berlin Song Book, Vol. 2	1959	12.50	25.00	50.00
❑ V-4031 [M]	Ella Fitzgerald Sings the Irving Berlin Song Book, Vol. 2	1961	5.00	10.00	20.00
❑ V6-4031 [S]	Ella Fitzgerald Sings the Irving Berlin Song Book, Vol. 2	1961	5.00	10.00	20.00
❑ MGV-4032 [M]	Sweet Songs for Swingers	1959	12.50	25.00	50.00
❑ V-4032 [M]	Sweet Songs for Swingers	1961	5.00	10.00	20.00
❑ V6-4032 [S]	Sweet Songs for Swingers	1961	5.00	10.00	20.00
❑ MGV-4034 [M]	Hello, Love	1959	12.50	25.00	50.00
❑ V-4034 [M]	Hello, Love	1961	5.00	10.00	20.00
❑ V6-4034 [S]	Hello, Love	1961	5.00	10.00	20.00
❑ MGV-4036 [M]	Get Happy!	1960	10.00	20.00	40.00
❑ V-4036 [M]	Get Happy!	1961	5.00	10.00	20.00
❑ V6-4036 [S]	Get Happy!	1961	5.00	10.00	20.00
❑ MGV-4041 [M]	Mack the Knife — Ella in Berlin	1960	10.00	20.00	40.00
❑ V-4041 [M]	Mack the Knife — Ella in Berlin	1961	5.00	10.00	20.00
❑ V6-4041 [M]	Mack the Knife — Ella in Berlin	1961	5.00	10.00	20.00
❑ MGV-4042 [M]	Ella Wishes You a Swinging Christmas	1960	12.50	25.00	50.00
❑ V-4042 [M]	Ella Wishes You a Swinging Christmas	1961	10.00	20.00	40.00
❑ V6-4042 [S]	Ella Wishes You a Swinging Christmas	1961	12.50	25.00	50.00
❑ MGV-4043 [M]	Let No Man Write My Epitaph	1961	10.00	20.00	40.00
❑ V-4043 [M]	Let No Man Write My Epitaph	1961	5.00	10.00	20.00
❑ V6-4043 [S]	Let No Man Write My Epitaph	1961	5.00	10.00	20.00
❑ MGV-4046-2 [(2)M]	Ella Fitzgerald Sings the Harold Arlen Song Book	1961	15.00	30.00	60.00
❑ MGV-4049 [M]	Ella Fitzgerald Sings Cole Porter	1961	10.00	20.00	40.00
❑ V-4049 [M]	Ella Fitzgerald Sings Cole Porter	1961	5.00	10.00	20.00
❑ MGV-4050 [M]	Ella Fitzgerald Sings More Cole Porter	1961	10.00	20.00	40.00
❑ V-4050 [M]	Ella Fitzgerald Sings More Cole Porter	1961	5.00	10.00	20.00
❑ MGV-4052 [M]	Ella in Hollywood	1961	10.00	20.00	40.00
❑ V-4052 [M]	Ella in Hollywood	1961	5.00	10.00	20.00
❑ V-4053 [M]	Clap Hands, Here Comes Charley	1962	10.00	20.00	40.00
❑ V6-4053 [S]	Clap Hands, Here Comes Charley	1962	37.50	75.00	150.00
❑ V-4054 [M]	Ella Swings Brightly with Nelson	1962	7.50	15.00	30.00
❑ V6-4054 [M]	Ella Swings Brightly with Nelson	1962	7.50	15.00	30.00
❑ V-4055 [M]	Ella Swings Gently with Nelson	1962	7.50	15.00	30.00
❑ V6-4055 [S]	Ella Swings Gently with Nelson	1962	7.50	15.00	30.00
❑ V-4056 [M]	Rhythm Is My Business	1962	7.50	15.00	30.00
❑ V6-4056 [S]	Rhythm Is My Business	1962	7.50	15.00	30.00
❑ V-4057 [M]	Ella Fitzgerald Sings the Harold Arlen Song Book, Vol. 1	1962	7.50	15.00	30.00
❑ V6-4057 [S]	Ella Fitzgerald Sings the Harold Arlen Song Book, Vol. 1	1962	7.50	15.00	30.00
❑ V-4058 [M]	Ella Fitzgerald Sings the Harold Arlen Song Book, Vol. 2	1962	7.50	15.00	30.00
❑ V6-4058 [S]	Ella Fitzgerald Sings the Harold Arlen Song Book, Vol. 2	1962	7.50	15.00	30.00
❑ V-4059 [M]	Ella Sings Broadway	1963	6.25	12.50	25.00
❑ V6-4059 [S]	Ella Sings Broadway	1963	6.25	12.50	25.00
❑ V-4060 [M]	Ella Fitzgerald Sings the Jerome Kern Song Book	1963	6.25	12.50	25.00
❑ V6-4060 [S]	Ella Fitzgerald Sings the Jerome Kern Song Book	1963	6.25	12.50	25.00
❑ V-4062 [M]	These Are the Blues	1963	6.25	12.50	25.00
❑ V6-4062 [S]	These Are the Blues	1963	6.25	12.50	25.00
❑ V-4063 [M]	The Best of Ella Fitzgerald	1964	3.75	7.50	15.00
❑ V6-4063 [S]	The Best of Ella Fitzgerald	1964	3.75	7.50	15.00
❑ V-4064 [M]	Hello, Dolly!	1964	6.25	12.50	25.00
❑ V6-4064 [S]	Hello, Dolly!	1964	6.25	12.50	25.00
❑ V-4065 [M]	Ella at Juan Les Pins	1964	6.25	12.50	25.00
❑ V6-4065 [S]	Ella at Juan Les Pins	1964	6.25	12.50	25.00
❑ V-4066 [M]	A Tribute to Cole Porter	1964	6.25	12.50	25.00
❑ V6-4066 [S]	A Tribute to Cole Porter	1964	6.25	12.50	25.00
❑ V-4067 [M]	Ella Fitzgerald Sings the Johnny Mercer Song Book	1965	5.00	10.00	20.00
❑ V6-4067 [S]	Ella Fitzgerald Sings the Johnny Mercer Song Book	1965	5.00	10.00	20.00
❑ V-4068 [M]	Porgy & Bess	1965	5.00	10.00	20.00
❑ V6-4068 [S]	Porgy & Bess	1965	5.00	10.00	20.00
❑ V-4069 [M]	Ella in Hamburg	1966	5.00	10.00	20.00
❑ V6-4069 [S]	Ella in Hamburg	1966	5.00	10.00	20.00
❑ V-4070 [M]	Ella at Duke's Place	1966	5.00	10.00	20.00
❑ V6-4070 [S]	Ella at Duke's Place	1966	5.00	10.00	20.00
❑ V-4071 [M]	Whisper Not	1966	5.00	10.00	20.00
❑ V6-4071 [S]	Whisper Not	1966	5.00	10.00	20.00
❑ V-4072 [M]	Ella & Duke at Cote d'Azur	1967	6.25	12.50	25.00
❑ V6-4072 [S]	Ella & Duke at Cote d'Azur	1967	3.75	7.50	15.00
❑ MGVS-6000 [S]	Like Someone in Love	1960	10.00	20.00	40.00
❑ MGVS-6005-2 [(2)S]	Ella Fitzgerald Sings the Irving Berlin Song Book	1960	15.00	30.00	60.00
❑ MGVS-6009 [S]	Ella Fitzgerald Sings the Rodgers & Hart Song Book, Vol. 1	1960	10.00	20.00	40.00
❑ MGVS-6010 [S]	Ella Fitzgerald Sings the Rodgers & Hart Song Book, Vol. 2	1960	10.00	20.00	40.00
❑ MGVS-6019 [S]	Ella Swings Lightly	1960	10.00	20.00	40.00
❑ MGVS-6026 [S]	Ella Fitzgerald at the Opera House	1960	10.00	20.00	40.00
❑ MGVS-6052 [S]	Ella Fitzgerald Sings the Irving Berlin Song Book, Vol. 1	1960	10.00	20.00	40.00
❑ MGVS-6053 [S]	Ella Fitzgerald Sings the Irving Berlin Song Book, Vol. 2	1960	10.00	20.00	40.00
❑ MGVS-6072 [S]	Sweet Songs for Swingers	1960	10.00	20.00	40.00
❑ MGVS-6077 [S]	Ella Fitzgerald Sings the George and Ira Gershwin Song Book, Vol. 1	1960	10.00	20.00	40.00
❑ MGVS-6078 [S]	Ella Fitzgerald Sings the George and Ira Gershwin Song Book, Vol. 2	1960	10.00	20.00	40.00
❑ MGVS-6079 [S]	Ella Fitzgerald Sings the George and Ira Gershwin Song Book, Vol. 3	1960	10.00	20.00	40.00
❑ MGVS-6080 [S]	Ella Fitzgerald Sings the George and Ira Gershwin Song Book, Vol. 4	1960	10.00	20.00	40.00
❑ MGVS-6081 [S]	Ella Fitzgerald Sings the George and Ira Gershwin Song Book, Vol. 5	1960	10.00	20.00	40.00
❑ MGVS-6082-5 [(5)S]	Ella Fitzgerald Sings the George and Ira Gershwin Song Book	1960	50.00	100.00	200.00
—Box set with 6077 through 6081 plus bonus 10-inch LP					
❑ MGVS-6100 [S]	Hello, Love	1960	10.00	20.00	40.00
❑ MGVS-6102 [S]	Get Happy!	1960	10.00	20.00	40.00
❑ MGVS-6163 [S]	Mack the Knife — Ella in Berlin	1960	10.00	20.00	40.00
❑ MGVS-7000 [S]	Ella Fitzgerald Sings the Gershwin Song Book	1959	12.50	25.00	50.00
❑ MGV-8264 [M]	Ella Fitzgerald at the Opera House	1958	12.50	25.00	50.00
❑ V-8264 [M]	Ella Fitzgerald at the Opera House	1961	5.00	10.00	20.00
❑ V6-8264 [S]	Ella Fitzgerald at the Opera House	1961	5.00	10.00	20.00
❑ MGV-8288 [M]	One O'Clock Jump	1958	12.50	25.00	50.00
❑ V-8288 [M]	One O'Clock Jump	1961	5.00	10.00	20.00
❑ V-8670 [M]	Ella Fitzgerald Sings the Jerome Kern Song Book	1967	—	—	—
—Canceled reissue					

Number	Title (A Side/B Side)	Yr	VG	VG+	NM
❏ V-8720 [M]	The Best of Ella Fitzgerald	1967	3.75	7.50	15.00
❏ V6-8720 [S]	The Best of Ella Fitzgerald	1967	3.00	6.00	12.00
❏ V-8745 [M]	Ella "Live"	1968	7.50	15.00	30.00
❏ V6-8745 [S]	Ella "Live"	1968	3.75	7.50	15.00
❏ V6-8795	The Best of Ella Fitzgerald, Vol. 2	1969	3.00	6.00	12.00
❏ V6-8817 [(2)]	History	1973	3.75	7.50	15.00
❏ MGVS-64042	[S]Ella Wishes You a Swinging Christmas	1960	15.00	30.00	60.00
❏ SMAS-90644	[S]Ella at Duke's Place	1966	6.25	12.50	25.00
—Capitol Record Club edition					
❏ 817526-1 [(2)]	The Harold Arlen Song Book	1984	3.75	7.50	15.00
❏ 821693-1 [(2)]	The Rodgers and Hart Song Book	198?	3.00	6.00	12.00
❏ 823247-1	The Johnny Mercer Song Book	1985	2.50	5.00	10.00
❏ 823278-1 [(2)]	The Cole Porter Song Book	198?	3.00	6.00	12.00
❏ 823279-1 [(2)]	The George and Ira Gershwin Songbook (Highlights)	198?	3.00	6.00	12.00
❏ 825024-1 [(5)]	The George and Ira Gershwin Songbook (Complete)	198?	6.25	12.50	25.00
❏ 825098-1	Lady Be Good	1985	2.50	5.00	10.00
❏ 825669-1	The Jerome Kern Song Book	1985	2.50	5.00	10.00
❏ 825670-1	Mack the Knife — Ella in Berlin	1985	2.50	5.00	10.00
❏ 827150-1	Ella Wishes You a Swinging Christmas	198?	2.50	5.00	10.00
❏ 827163-1 [(2)]	The Duke Ellington Song Book, Vol. 1	198?	3.00	6.00	12.00
❏ 827169-1 [(2)]	The Duke Ellington Song Book, Vol. 2	198?	3.00	6.00	12.00
❏ 829533-1 [(2)]	The Irving Berlin Song Book	1988	3.00	6.00	12.00
❏ 835454-1	Ella in Rome: The Birthday Concert	1988	2.50	5.00	10.00
VOCALION					
❏ VL 3797 [M]	Ella Fitzgerald	1967	3.00	6.00	12.00
❏ VL 73797 [R]	Ella Fitzgerald	1967	3.00	6.00	12.00

FITZGERALD, ELLA, AND LOUIS ARMSTRONG Also see each artist's individual listings.
45s
DECCA

Number	Title (A Side/B Side)	Yr	VG	VG+	NM
❏ 27209	Can Anyone Explain? (No, No, No)/Dream a Little Dream of Me	1950	5.00	10.00	20.00
❏ 28552	Who Walks In When I Walk Out/Would You Like to Take a Walk	1953	3.75	7.50	15.00
VERVE					
❏ 2023	Stars Fell on Alabama/Can't We Be Friends	1956	3.00	6.00	12.00
❏ 10079	Goody Goody/A-Tisket, A-Tasket	1957	5.00	10.00	20.00

7-Inch Extended Plays
DECCA

Number	Title (A Side/B Side)	Yr	VG	VG+	NM
❏ ED 2027	You Won't Be Satisfied/Dream a Little Dream of Me//Would You Like to Take a Walk/The Frim-Fram Sauce	195?	3.75	7.50	15.00
❏ ED 2027 [PS]	Ella Fitzgerald and Louis Armstrong, Vol. 1	195?	3.75	7.50	15.00

Albums
METRO

Number	Title (A Side/B Side)	Yr	VG	VG+	NM
❏ M-601 [M]	Louis and Ella	1967	3.00	6.00	12.00
❏ MS-601 [S]	Louis and Ella	1967	3.00	6.00	12.00
MOBILE FIDELITY					
❏ 2-248 [(2)]	Ella and Louis Again	1996	37.50	75.00	150.00
—Audiophile vinyl					
VERVE					
❏ VE-1-2507	Porgy and Bess	197?	2.50	5.00	10.00
❏ MGV-4003 [M]	Ella and Louis	1956	12.50	25.00	50.00
❏ V-4003 [M]	Ella and Louis	1961	5.00	10.00	20.00
❏ MGV-4006-2 [(2)M]Ella and Louis Again		1956	20.00	40.00	80.00
❏ V-4006-2 [(2)M]Ella and Louis Again		1961	6.25	12.50	25.00
❏ MGV-4011-2 [(2)M]Porgy and Bess		1957	20.00	40.00	80.00
❏ V-4011-2 [(2)M]Porgy and Bess		1961	6.25	12.50	25.00
❏ V6-4011-2 [(2)S]Porgy and Bess		1961	6.25	12.50	25.00
❏ MGV-4017 [M]	Ella and Louis Again, Vol. 1	1958	12.50	25.00	50.00
❏ V-4017 [M]	Ella and Louis Again, Vol. 1	1961	5.00	10.00	20.00
❏ MGV-4018 [M]	Ella and Louis Again, Vol. 2	1958	12.50	25.00	50.00
❏ V-4018 [M]	Ella and Louis Again, Vol. 2	1961	5.00	10.00	20.00
❏ MGVS-6040-2 [(2)S]Porgy and Bess		1960	15.00	30.00	60.00
❏ V6-8811 [(2)]	Ella and Louis	1972	3.75	7.50	15.00
❏ 827475-1 [(2)]	Porgy and Bess	198?	3.00	6.00	12.00

FITZGERALD, ELLA, AND COUNT BASIE
Albums
PABLO TODAY

Number	Title (A Side/B Side)	Yr	VG	VG+	NM
❏ 2312110	A Perfect Match	1980	3.00	6.00	12.00
—Red vinyl					
VERVE					
❏ V-4061 [M]	Ella and Basie!	1963	6.25	12.50	25.00
❏ V6-4061 [S]	Ella and Basie!	1963	6.25	12.50	25.00
❏ ST-90028 [S]	Ella and Basie!	1964	7.50	15.00	30.00
—Capitol Record Club edition					
❏ T-90028 [M]	Ella and Basie!	1964	7.50	15.00	30.00
—Capitol Record Club edition					

FITZGERALD, ELLA, AND DUKE ELLINGTON
Albums
PABLO LIVE

Number	Title (A Side/B Side)	Yr	VG	VG+	NM
❏ 2308242	The Stockholm Concert 1966	1984	2.50	5.00	10.00

FITZGERALD, ELLA, AND BILLIE HOLIDAY Also see each artist's individual listings.
Albums
AMERICAN RECORDING SOCIETY

Number	Title (A Side/B Side)	Yr	VG	VG+	NM
❏ G-433 [M]	Ella Fitzgerald and Billie Holiday at Newport	1957	10.00	20.00	40.00
VERVE					
❏ MGVS-6022 [S]Ella Fitzgerald and Billie Holiday at Newport		1960	10.00	20.00	40.00
❏ MGV-8234 [M]	Ella Fitzgerald and Billie Holiday at Newport	1958	12.50	25.00	50.00
❏ V-8234 [M]	Ella Fitzgerald and Billie Holiday at Newport	1961	5.00	10.00	20.00
❏ V6-8234 [S]	Ella Fitzgerald and Billie Holiday at Newport	1961	5.00	10.00	20.00
❏ V-8826	Newport Years	1973	3.00	6.00	12.00

FI-DELLS, THE
45s
IMPERIAL

Number	Title (A Side/B Side)	Yr	VG	VG+	NM
❏ 5780	What Is Love/Don't Let Me Love You	1961	6.25	12.50	25.00
WARNER					
❏ 1014	No Other Love/Come Back to Me	1957	5.00	10.00	20.00

FIVE AMERICANS, THE
45s
ABC-PARAMOUNT

Number	Title (A Side/B Side)	Yr	VG	VG+	NM
❏ 10686	Show Me/Love, Love, Love	1965	3.75	7.50	15.00
ABNAK					
❏ 106	Say That You Love Me/Without You	1965	2.50	5.00	10.00
❏ 106 [DJ]	Say That You Love Me/Without You	1965	6.25	12.50	25.00
—Promo only on yellow vinyl					
❏ 109	I See the Light/The Outcast	1965	5.00	10.00	20.00
❏ 109 [DJ]	I See the Light/The Outcast	1965	6.25	12.50	25.00
—Promo only on yellow vinyl					
❏ 114	Reality/Sympathy	1966	2.50	5.00	10.00
❏ 114 [DJ]	Reality/Sympathy	1966	6.25	12.50	25.00
—Promo only on yellow vinyl					
❏ 116	If I Could/Now That It's Over	1966	2.50	5.00	10.00
❏ 116 [DJ]	If I Could/Now That It's Over	1966	6.25	12.50	25.00
—Promo only on yellow vinyl					
❏ 118	Western Union/Now That It's Over	1967	3.00	6.00	12.00
❏ 118 [DJ]	Western Union/Now That It's Over	1967	6.25	12.50	25.00
—Promo only on yellow vinyl					
❏ 120	Sound of Love/Sympathy	1967	2.00	4.00	8.00
❏ 120 [DJ]	Sound of Love/Sympathy	1967	6.25	12.50	25.00
—Promo only on yellow vinyl					
❏ 123	Zip Code/Sweet Bird of Youth	1967	2.00	4.00	8.00
❏ 123 [DJ]	Zip Code/Sweet Bird of Youth	1967	6.25	12.50	25.00
—Promo only on yellow vinyl					
❏ 125	Stop Light/Tell Ann I Love Her	1967	2.00	4.00	8.00
❏ 125 [DJ]	Stop Light/Tell Ann I Love Her	1967	6.25	12.50	25.00
—Promo only on yellow vinyl					
❏ 125 [PS]	Stop Light/Tell Ann I Love Her	1967	3.75	7.50	15.00
❏ 126	7:30 Guided Tour/See Saw Baby	1967	2.00	4.00	8.00
❏ 126 [DJ]	7:30 Guided Tour/See Saw Baby	1967	6.25	12.50	25.00
—Promo only on yellow vinyl					
❏ 126 [PS]	7:30 Guided Tour/See Saw Baby	1967	3.75	7.50	15.00
❏ 128	The Rain Maker/No Communication	1968	2.00	4.00	8.00
❏ 128 [DJ]	The Rain Maker/No Communication	1968	6.25	12.50	25.00
—Promo only on yellow vinyl					
❏ 131	Con Man/Lovin' Is Lovin'	1968	2.00	4.00	8.00
❏ 131 [DJ]	Con Man/Lovin' Is Lovin'	1968	6.25	12.50	25.00
—Promo only on yellow vinyl					
❏ 132	Generation Gap/The Source	1968	2.00	4.00	8.00
❏ 132 [DJ]	Generation Gap/The Source	1968	6.25	12.50	25.00
—Promo only on yellow vinyl					
❏ 134	Virginia Girl/Call on Me	1969	2.00	4.00	8.00
❏ 134 [DJ]	Virginia Girl/Call on Me	1969	6.25	12.50	25.00
—Promo only on yellow vinyl					
❏ 137	Scrooge/Ignert Woman	1969	2.00	4.00	8.00
❏ 137 [DJ]	Scrooge/Ignert Woman	1969	6.25	12.50	25.00
—Promo only on yellow vinyl					
❏ 139	I See the Light '69/Red Cape	1969	2.00	4.00	8.00
—As "Michael Rabon and the Five Americans"					
❏ 139 [DJ]	I See the Light '69/Red Cape	1969	6.25	12.50	25.00
—As "Michael Rabon and the Five Americans"; promo only on yellow vinyl					
❏ 142	She's Too Good to Me/Molly Black	1969	2.00	4.00	8.00
❏ 142 [DJ]	She's Too Good to Me/Molly Black	1969	6.25	12.50	25.00
—Promo only on yellow vinyl					
HANNA-BARBERA					
❏ 454	I See the Light/The Outcast	1965	3.00	6.00	12.00
❏ 468	Evol-Not Love/Don't Blame Me	1966	3.00	6.00	12.00
❏ 468 [PS]	Evol-Not Love/Don't Blame Me	1966	3.75	7.50	15.00
❏ 483	Good Times/The Losing Game	1966	3.00	6.00	12.00
JETSTAR					
❏ 104	It's You Girl/I'm Gonna Leave You	1966	6.25	12.50	25.00
❏ 105	I'm Feeling OK/Slippin' and Slidin'	1966	7.50	15.00	30.00
PHILCO-FORD					
❏ HP-10	Western Union/Sounds of Love	1968	5.00	10.00	20.00
—4-inch plastic "Hip Pocket Record" with color sleeve					
Albums					
ABNAK					
❏ AB-1967 [M]	Western Union/Sound of Love	1967	5.00	10.00	20.00
❏ AB-1969 [M]	Progressions	1967	5.00	10.00	20.00
❏ ABST-2067 [S]	Western Union/Sound of Love	1967	7.50	15.00	30.00
❏ ABST-2069 [S]	Progressions	1967	7.50	15.00	30.00
❏ ABST-2071 [(2)]Now and Then		1968	6.25	12.50	25.00
HANNA-BARBERA					
❏ HLP-8503 [M]	I See the Light	1966	10.00	20.00	40.00
❏ HST-9503 [S]	I See the Light	1966	15.00	30.00	60.00

FIVE BARS, THE
45s
MONEY

Number	Title (A Side/B Side)	Yr	VG	VG+	NM
❏ 224	Stormy Weather/Somebody Else's Fool	1957	15.00	30.00	60.00

FIVE BELLS, THE
45s
BRUNSWICK

Number	Title (A Side/B Side)	Yr	VG	VG+	NM
❏ 84002	Till I Waltz Again with You/Can't Wait for Tomorrow	1952	125.00	250.00	500.00
❏ 84004	Till Dawn and Tomorrow/Waiting, Waiting	1952	125.00	250.00	500.00

FIVE BLOBS, THE
45s
COLUMBIA

Number	Title (A Side/B Side)	Yr	VG	VG+	NM
❏ 4-41250	The Blob/Saturday Night in Tiajuana	1958	6.25	12.50	25.00
JOY					
❏ 226	Rockin' Pow Wow/From the Top of Your Guggle	1959	5.00	10.00	20.00
❏ 230	Juliet/Young and Wild	1959	5.00	10.00	20.00

FIVE BLUE FLAMES, THE See CHRIS POWELL AND THE FIVE BLUE FLAMES.

FIVE BLUE NOTES, THE
45s
SABRE

Number	Title (A Side/B Side)	Yr	VG	VG+	NM
❏ 103	My Gal Is Gone/Ooh Baby	1953	250.00	500.00	1000.
❏ 108	The Beat of Our Hearts/You Gotta Go Baby	1954	625.00	1250.	2500.

F

Number	Title (A Side/B Side)	Yr	VG	VG+	NM
FIVE BUDDS, THE					
45s					
RAMA					
❏ 1	I Was Such a Fool (To Fall in Love with You)/Midnight	1953	125.00	250.00	500.00
❏ 2	I Guess It's All Over Now/I Want Her Back	1953	125.00	250.00	500.00
FIVE BY FIVE					
45s					
PAULA					
❏ 261	Shake a Tail Feather/Tell Me What to Do	1967	3.00	6.00	12.00
❏ 283	Harlem Shuffle/You Really Got a Hold on Me	1967	3.00	6.00	12.00
❏ 302	Fire/Hang Up	1968	3.75	7.50	15.00
❏ 311	Ain't Gonna Be Your Fool No More/ She Digs My Love	1968	3.00	6.00	12.00
❏ 319	Apple Cider/Fruitstand Man	1970	2.50	5.00	10.00
❏ 322	Too Much Tomorrow/ Ain't Gonna Be Your Fool No More	1970	2.50	5.00	10.00
❏ 326	15 Going on 20/Penthouse Pauper	1970	2.50	5.00	10.00
❏ 328	Never/Good Connection	1970	2.50	5.00	10.00
FIVE CAMPBELLS, THE					
45s					
MUSIC CITY					
❏ 794	Hey Baby/Morrine	1956	125.00	250.00	500.00
FIVE CARD STUD					
45s					
RED BIRD					
❏ 10-082	Be-Bop-A-Lula/Everybody Needs Somebody	1967	3.75	7.50	15.00
SMASH					
❏ 2080	Bag Me/Once	1967	3.75	7.50	15.00
FIVE CATS, THE					
45s					
RCA VICTOR					
❏ 47-5885	He Follows She/Santa Lucia	1954	6.25	12.50	25.00
❏ 47-6012	Rockin' Chair/Mine, Mine, Mine	1955	7.50	15.00	30.00
❏ 47-6181	I Was So Wrong/Someone's Gonna Cry	1955	10.00	20.00	40.00
FIVE CHANCES, THE					
45s					
ATOMIC					
❏ 2494	Make Love to Me/California	1977	3.00	6.00	12.00
BLUE LAKE					
❏ 115	All I Want/Shake-a-Link	1955	200.00	400.00	800.00
CHANCE					
❏ 1157	I May Be Small/Nagasaki	1954	250.00	500.00	1000.
FEDERAL					
❏ 12303	My Days Are Blue/Tell Me Why	1957	125.00	250.00	500.00
P.S.					
❏ 1510	Is This Love/Need Your Love	1960	75.00	150.00	300.00
STATES					
❏ 156	Gloria/Sugar Lips	1956	200.00	400.00	800.00
—Black vinyl					
❏ 156	Gloria/Sugar Lips	1956	300.00	600.00	1200.
—Red vinyl					
FIVE CHANELS, THE					
45s					
DEB					
❏ 500	The Reason/Skiddily Doo	1958	10.00	20.00	40.00
—As "The Five Chanels"					
❏ 500	The Reason/Skiddily Doo	1958	20.00	40.00	80.00
—As "The Chanels"					
FIVE DEBONAIRES, THE See THE DEBONAIRES.					
FIVE DELIGHTS, THE					
45s					
ABEL					
❏ 228	The Thought of Losing You/That Love Affair	1959	75.00	150.00	300.00
NEWPORT					
❏ 7002	There'll Be No Goodbye/Okey Dokey Mama	1958	37.50	75.00	150.00
UNART					
❏ 2003	There'll Be No Goodbye/Okey Dokey Mama	1958	7.50	15.00	30.00
FIVE DISCS, THE Evidently these are all the same group or closely related. Also see DAWN (3).					
45s					
CALO					
❏ 202	Adios/My Baby Loves Me	1961	37.50	75.00	150.00
—Green label					
❏ 202	Adios/My Baby Loves Me	1962	25.00	50.00	100.00
—White label					
CHEER					
❏ 1000	Never Let You Go/That Was the Time	1962	12.50	25.00	50.00
—Red label					
❏ 1000	Never Let You Go/That Was the Time	1962	25.00	50.00	100.00
—Black label					
❏ 1000 [DJ]	Never Let You Go/That Was the Time	1962	75.00	150.00	300.00
—White label, promo only					
CRYSTAL BALL					
❏ 114	Mirror Mirror/Most of All I Wonder Why	1978	2.50	5.00	10.00
❏ 120	Unchained Melody/The Shrine of St. Cecelia	1978	2.50	5.00	10.00
❏ 136	Playing a Game of Love/Bells	1979	2.00	4.00	8.00
❏ 141	This Love of Ours/To the Fair	1979	2.00	4.00	8.00
DWAIN					
❏ 803	My Chinese Girl/Roses	1959	37.50	75.00	150.00
❏ 803	My Chinese Girl/Roses	1959	50.00	100.00	200.00
—As "Mario and the Five Discs"					
❏ 6072	My Chinese Girl/Roses	1959	500.00	1000.	2000.
EMGE					
❏ 1004	I Remember/The World Is a Beautiful Place	1958	100.00	200.00	400.00
LAURIE					
❏ 3601	Rock and Roll Revival/Gypsy Women	1973	3.75	7.50	15.00
MELLO MOOD					
❏ 1002	My Chinese Girl/Roses	1964	3.75	7.50	15.00

Number	Title (A Side/B Side)	Yr	VG	VG+	NM
PYRAMID					
❏ 166	Let's Fall in Love/That Was the Time	197?	—	3.00	6.00
RUST					
❏ 5027	I Remember/The World Is a Beautiful Place	1961	6.25	12.50	25.00
VIK					
❏ 0327	I Remember/The World Is a Beautiful Place	1958	20.00	40.00	80.00
YALE					
❏ 240	When Love Comes Knocking/Go-Go	1961	100.00	200.00	400.00
❏ 243/4	Come On Baby/I Don't Know What to Do	1961	100.00	200.00	400.00
Albums					
CRYSTAL BALL					
❏ 119	Unchained	1978	3.75	7.50	15.00
MAGIC CARPET					
❏ 1002	The Five Discs Sing Again	1991	5.00	10.00	20.00
—Dark blue cover					
FIVE DOLLARS, THE					
45s					
FORTUNE					
❏ 821	Harmony of Love/Doctor Baby	1955	25.00	50.00	100.00
❏ 826	So Strange/You Know I Can't Refuse	1956	25.00	50.00	100.00
❏ 830	I Will Wait/Hard Working Mama	1956	25.00	50.00	100.00
❏ 833	You Fool/How Do You Do the Bacon Fat	1957	20.00	40.00	80.00
❏ 854	That's the Way It Goes/My Baby-O	1960	12.50	25.00	50.00
FRATERNITY					
❏ 821	Harmony of Love/Doctor Baby	1958	10.00	20.00	40.00
FIVE DU-TONES, THE					
45s					
LOST-NITE					
❏ 196	Shake a Tail Feather/Divorce Court	196?	—	3.00	6.00
—Reissue of One-derful 4815					
ONE-DERFUL					
❏ 4811	The Flea/Please Change Your Mind	1963	3.75	7.50	15.00
❏ 4814	Dry Your Eyes/Come Back Baby	1963	3.75	7.50	15.00
❏ 4815	Shake a Tail Feather/Divorce Court	1963	3.75	7.50	15.00
❏ 4818	The Gouster/Monkey See-Monkey Do	1963	3.75	7.50	15.00
❏ 4821	Nobody But (My Baby)/That's How I Love You	1964	3.75	7.50	15.00
❏ 4824	The Cool Bird/The Chicken Astronaut	1964	3.75	7.50	15.00
❏ 4828	Sweet Lips/Let Me Love You	1964	7.50	15.00	30.00
❏ 4831	We Want More/The Woodbine Twine	1965	3.75	7.50	15.00
❏ 4836	Mountain of Love/Outside the Record Hop	1965	3.75	7.50	15.00
FIVE ECHOES, THE					
45s					
SABRE					
❏ 102	Baby Come Back to Me/Lonely Mood	1953	150.00	300.00	600.00
—Black vinyl					
❏ 102	Baby Come Back to Me/Lonely Mood	1953	750.00	1125.	1500.
—Red vinyl					
❏ 105	So Lonesome/Broke	1954	150.00	300.00	600.00
—Black vinyl					
❏ 105	So Lonesome/Broke	1954	750.00	1125.	1500.
—Red vinyl					
VEE JAY					
❏ 129	I Really Do/Tell Me Baby	1954	75.00	150.00	300.00
❏ 156	Fool's Prayer/Tastee Freeze	1955	250.00	500.00	1000.
❏ 190	Soldier Boy/Pledging to You	1956	50.00	100.00	200.00
FIVE EMBERS, THE					
45s					
GEM					
❏ 224	Please Come Home/(B-side unknown)	1954	200.00	400.00	800.00
FIVE EMERALDS, THE					
45s					
S.R.C.					
❏ 106	I'll Beg/Let Me Take You Out Tonight	1953	250.00	500.00	1000.
—Label spells out "Five" in group name, and "S-R-C" has hyphens in it					
❏ 106	I'll Beg/Let Me Take You Out Tonight	1953	250.00	500.00	1000.
—Label uses numeral "5" in group name, and "S.R.C." has periods in it					
❏ 107	Darling/Pleasure Me	1954	300.00	600.00	1200.
FIVE EMPREES, THE					
45s					
FREEPORT					
❏ 1001	Little Miss Sad/Hey Lover	1965	3.00	6.00	12.00
❏ 1001	Little Miss Sad/Hey Lover	1965	6.25	12.50	25.00
—Originally released as "The Five Empressions"					
❏ 1002	Hey Baby/Why	1965	3.00	6.00	12.00
❏ 1007	Little Miss Happiness/Over the Mountain	1966	3.00	6.00	12.00
❏ 1009	Pretty Face (Part 1)/Pretty Face (Part 2)	1966	3.00	6.00	12.00
❏ 1010	Johnny B. Goode/Hey Lover	1966	3.00	6.00	12.00
SMASH					
❏ 2065	Gone from My Mind/Hey Diddle Diddle	1966	2.50	5.00	10.00
Albums					
FREEPORT					
❏ 3001 [M]	The Five Emprees	1965	12.50	25.00	50.00
❏ 3001 [M]	Little Miss Sad	1966	7.50	15.00	30.00
—Same LP, new title					
❏ 4001 [S]	The Five Emprees	1965	15.00	30.00	60.00
❏ 4001 [S]	Little Miss Sad	1966	10.00	20.00	40.00
—Same LP, new title					
FIVE EMPRESSIONS, THE See THE FIVE EMPREES.					
FIVE FLIGHTS UP					
45s					
T-A					
❏ 202	Do What You Wanna Do/Black Cat	1970	2.00	4.00	8.00
❏ 207	After the Feeling Is Gone/ Where Are You Going, Girl?	1970	2.00	4.00	8.00
❏ 212	Like Monday Follows Sunday/California Girl	1971	2.00	4.00	8.00

Number	Title (A Side/B Side)	Yr	VG	VG+	NM

FIVE FORTUNES, THE
45s
RANSOM
| ☐ 103 | You Are My Only Love/Time Out for Love | 1958 | 250.00 | 500.00 | 1000. |

FIVE JETS, THE
45s
DELUXE
☐ 6018	I Am in Love/Not a Hand to Shake	1953	37.50	75.00	150.00
☐ 6053	I'm Stuck/I Want a Woman	1954	37.50	75.00	150.00
☐ 6058	Tell Me You're Mine/Give In	1954	50.00	100.00	200.00
☐ 6064	Crazy Chicken/Everybody Do the Chicken	1954	15.00	30.00	60.00
☐ 6071	Down Slow/Please Love Me Baby	1955	20.00	60.00	120.00
KING
☐ 6058	Tell Me You're Mine/Give In	1966	5.00	10.00	20.00

FIVE KEYS, THE
45s
ALADDIN
| ☐ 3085 | With a Broken Heart/Too Late | 1951 | — | — | — |
—Unconfirmed on 45 rpm
☐ 3099	The Glory of Love/Hucklebuck with Jimmy	1951	250.00	500.00	1000.
☐ 3113	It's Christmas Time/Old Mac Donald	1951	250.00	500.00	1000.
☐ 3118	Yes Sir That's My Baby/Old Mac Donald	1952	250.00	500.00	1000.
☐ 3119	Darling/Goin' Downtown	1952	250.00	500.00	1000.
☐ 3127	Red Sails in the Sunset/Be Anything, But Be Mine	1952	3000.	4500.	6000.
☐ 3131	How Long/Mistakes	1952	300.00	600.00	1200.
☐ 3136	Hold Me/I Hadn't Anyone Till You	1952	200.00	400.00	800.00
☐ 3158	I Cried for You/Serve Another Round	1953	225.00	450.00	900.00
☐ 3167	Can't Keep From Crying/Come Go My Bail, Louise	1953	200.00	400.00	800.00
☐ 3175	There Ought to Be a Law/Mama (Your Daughter Told a Lie on Me)	1953	200.00	400.00	800.00
☐ 3182	I'll Always Be in Love with You/Rocking and Crying Blues	1953	200.00	400.00	800.00
☐ 3190	These Foolish Things/Lonesome Old Story	1953	1000.	2000.	4000.
☐ 3204	Teardrops in Your Eyes/I'm So High	1953	200.00	400.00	800.00
☐ 3214	My Saddest Hour/Oh! Babe!	1953	200.00	400.00	800.00
☐ 3228	Someday Sweetheart/Love My Loving	1954	200.00	400.00	800.00
☐ 3245	Deep in My Heart/How Do You Expect Me to Get It	1954	200.00	400.00	800.00
☐ 3263	My Love/Why, Oh Why	1954	75.00	150.00	300.00
☐ 3312	Story of Love/Serve Another Round	1956	75.00	150.00	300.00
☐ S7-19768	Every Heart Is Home at Christmas/Frosty the Snowman	1997	—	2.50	5.00
—B-side by Fats Domino on The Right Stuff
BANGAR
| ☐ 661 | Run-Around/I Tell My Heart | 1965 | 3.75 | 7.50 | 15.00 |
CAPITOL
☐ F-2945	Ling, Ting, Tong/I'm Alone	1954	10.00	20.00	40.00
☐ F-3032	Close Your Eyes/Doggone It, You Did It	1955	10.00	20.00	40.00
☐ F-3127	The Verdict/Me Make Um Pow Wow	1955	10.00	20.00	40.00
☐ F-3185	Don't You Know I Love You/I Wish I'd Never Learned to Read	1955	10.00	20.00	40.00
☐ F-3267	'Cause You're My Lover/Gee Whittakers	1955	10.00	20.00	40.00
☐ F-3318	You Broke the Rules of Love/What Goes On	1956	10.00	20.00	40.00
☐ F-3392	She's the Most/I Dreamt I Dwelt in Heaven	1956	10.00	20.00	40.00
—Regular large hole
| ☐ F-3392 | She's the Most/I Dreamt I Dwelt in Heaven | 1956 | 17.50 | 35.00 | 70.00 |
—Small hole
☐ F-3455	My Pigeon's Gone/Peace and Love	1956	10.00	20.00	40.00
☐ F-3502	Out of Sight, Out of Mind/That's Right	1956	7.50	15.00	30.00
☐ F-3597	Wisdom of a Fool/Now Don't That Prove I Love You	1956	7.50	15.00	30.00
☐ F-3660	Tiger Lily/Let There Be You	1957	6.25	12.50	25.00
☐ F-3710	Four Walls/It's a Groove	1957	6.25	12.50	25.00
☐ F-3738	This I Promise You/The Blues Don't Care	1957	6.25	12.50	25.00
☐ F-3786	Boom Boom/Face of An Angel	1957	6.25	12.50	25.00
☐ F-3830	Do Anything/It's a Cryin' Shame	1957	6.25	12.50	25.00
☐ F-3861	From Me to You/Whippety Whirl	1957	6.25	12.50	25.00
☐ F-3948	You're for Me/With All My Love	1958	6.25	12.50	25.00
☐ F-4009	Emily Please/Handy Andy	1958	6.25	12.50	25.00
☐ F-4092	One Great Love/Really-O, Truly-O	1958	6.25	12.50	25.00
☐ 4828	Out of Sight, Out of Mind/From the Bottom of My Heart	1962	5.00	10.00	20.00
CLASSIC ARTISTS
☐ 115	I Want You For Christmas/Express Yourself Back Home	1989	—	2.50	5.00
—As "Rudy West and the Five Keys"
GROOVE
| ☐ 0031 | I'll Follow You/Lawdy Miss Mary | 1954 | 2000. | 3000. | 4000. |
—There is some debate about whether this record actually exists on 45.
INFERNO
| ☐ 4500 | Hey Girl/No Matter | 1967 | 5.00 | 10.00 | 20.00 |
KING
☐ 5251	I Took Your Love for a Toy/Ziggus	1959	7.50	15.00	30.00
☐ 5273	Dancing Senorita/Dream On	1959	5.00	10.00	20.00
☐ 5302	How Can I Forget You/I Burned Your Letter	1960	5.00	10.00	20.00
☐ 5330	Gonna Be Too Late/Rosetta	1960	5.00	10.00	20.00
☐ 5358	I Didn't Know/No, Says My Heart	1960	5.00	10.00	20.00
☐ 5398	Bimbo/Valley of Love	1960	5.00	10.00	20.00
☐ 5446	You Broke the Only Heart/That's What You're Doing to Me	1961	5.00	10.00	20.00
☐ 5496	Do Something for Me/Stop Your Crying	1961	5.00	10.00	20.00
☐ 5877	I'll Never Stop Loving You/I Can't Escape from You	1964	3.00	6.00	12.00
LIBERTY
☐ 1394	It's Christmas Time/It's Christmas	1980	2.00	4.00	8.00
—B-side by Marvin and Johnny
OWL
| ☐ 321 | A Dreamer/Your Teeth and Your Tongue | 1973 | 2.00 | 4.00 | 8.00 |
SEG-WAY
| ☐ 1008 | Out of Sight, Out of Mind/You're the One | 1962 | 3.75 | 7.50 | 15.00 |

UNITED ARTISTS
| ☐ 0150 | The Glory of Love/My Saddest Hour | 1973 | — | 2.00 | 4.00 |
—"Silver Spotlight Series" reissue
7-Inch Extended Plays
CAPITOL
☐ EAP 1-572	Ling Ting Tong/I'm Alone//Close Your Eyes/Doggone It, You Did It	1955	25.00	50.00	100.00
☐ EAP 1-572 [PS]	The Five Keys	1955	25.00	50.00	100.00
☐ EAP 1-828	(contents unknown)	1957	25.00	50.00	100.00
☐ EAP 1-828 [PS]	The Five Keys On Stage! Volume 1	1957	25.00	50.00	100.00
—On cover, the far left singer's "offending" thumb is airbrushed out
| ☐ EAP 1-828 [PS] | The Five Keys On Stage! Volume 1 | 1957 | 37.50 | 75.00 | 150.00 |
—On cover, the far left singer has his thumb sticking out (inadvertently?) in a phallic way
| ☐ EAP 2-828 | (contents unknown) | 1957 | 25.00 | 50.00 | 100.00 |
| ☐ EAP 2-828 [PS] | The Five Keys On Stage! Volume 2 | 1957 | 25.00 | 50.00 | 100.00 |
—On cover, the far left singer's "offending" thumb is airbrushed out
| ☐ EAP 2-828 [PS] | The Five Keys On Stage! Volume 2 | 1957 | 37.50 | 75.00 | 150.00 |
—On cover, the far left singer has his thumb sticking out (inadvertently?) in a phallic way
| ☐ EAP 3-828 | C'est La Vie/Dream//Let There Be You/All I Need Is You | 1957 | 25.00 | 50.00 | 100.00 |
| ☐ EAP 3-828 [PS] | The Five Keys On Stage! Volume 3 | 1957 | 25.00 | 50.00 | 100.00 |
—On cover, the far left singer's "offending" thumb is airbrushed out
| ☐ EAP 3-828 [PS] | The Five Keys On Stage! Volume 3 | 1957 | 37.50 | 75.00 | 150.00 |
—On cover, the far left singer has his thumb sticking out (inadvertently?) in a phallic way
Albums
ALADDIN
| ☐ LP-806 [M] | The Best of the Five Keys | 1956 | 1000. | 1500. | 2000. |
—Copies of Aladdin 806 entitled "On the Town" are bootlegs made in the 1970s.
CAPITOL
| ☐ T 828 [M] | The Five Keys On Stage! | 1957 | 75.00 | 150.00 | 300.00 |
—On cover, the far left singer has his thumb sticking out (inadvertently?) in a phallic way
| ☐ T 828 [M] | The Five Keys On Stage! | 1957 | 125.00 | 250.00 | 500.00 |
—On cover, the far left singer's "offending" thumb is airbrushed out
| ☐ M-1769 | The Fantastic Five Keys | 1977 | 5.00 | 10.00 | 20.00 |
—Reissue with new prefix
| ☐ T 1769 [M] | The Fantastic Five Keys | 1962 | 75.00 | 150.00 | 300.00 |
HARLEM HIT PARADE
| ☐ 5004 | The Five Keys | 1972 | 3.75 | 7.50 | 15.00 |
KING
☐ 688 [M]	The Five Keys	1960	200.00	400.00	800.00
☐ 692 [M]	Rhythm and Blues Hits, Past and Present	1960	150.00	300.00	600.00
☐ 5013	14 Hits	1978	3.00	6.00	12.00
SCORE
☐ LP-4003 [M]	The Five Keys On the Town	1957	200.00	400.00	800.00
—Reissue of Aladdin 806.

FIVE KIDS, THE
45s
MAXWELL
| ☐ 101 | Carolyn/Oh Baby | 1955 | 1000. | 2000. | 3000. |

FIVE LYRICS, THE
45s
MUSIC CITY
| ☐ 799 | I'm Traveling Light/My Honeysweet Pea | 1956 | 375.00 | 750.00 | 1500. |

FIVE MAN ELECTRICAL BAND
45s
CAPITOL
☐ 2368	It Never Rains on Maple Lane/Private Train	1968	—	3.00	6.00
☐ 2517	Baby/Lovin' Look	1969	—	3.00	6.00
☐ 2562	Sunrise to Sunset/Little Bit of Love	1969	—	3.00	6.00
☐ 2628	Riverboat/Good	1969	—	3.00	6.00
LION
☐ 112	Coming of Age/The Devil and Miss Lucy	1972	—	2.50	5.00
☐ 127	Money Back Guarantee/Find the One	1972	—	2.50	5.00
☐ 149	I'm a Stranger Here/Doin' The Best We Can Rag	1973	—	2.50	5.00
☐ 160	Sweet Paradise/Baby Wanna Boogie	1973	—	2.50	5.00
LIONEL
☐ 3213	Signs/Hello Melinda Goodbye	1971	—	3.00	6.00
—Lists no A and B sides and contains an edited version (3:20) of "Signs"
| ☐ 3213 | Signs/Hello Melinda Goodbye | 1971 | 2.00 | 4.00 | 8.00 |
—Lists "Hello Melinda Goodbye" as the A-side and contains the full-length version of "Signs"
| ☐ 3220 | Absolutely Right/Butterfly | 1971 | — | 2.50 | 5.00 |
| ☐ 3224 | Friends and Family/Julianna | 1971 | — | 2.50 | 5.00 |
MGM
| ☐ 14149 | Moonshine/Forever Together | 1970 | — | 3.00 | 6.00 |
| ☐ 14182 [DJ] | Hello Melinda Goodbye/Signs | 1970 | 2.50 | 5.00 | 10.00 |
—Evidently only exists as a promo
POLYDOR
| ☐ 14221 | Werewolf/Country Angel | 1974 | — | 2.00 | 4.00 |
| ☐ 14263 | Johnnie Get a Gun/And the World Goes Round | 1974 | — | 3.00 | 6.00 |
Albums
CAPITOL
| ☐ ST-165 | Five Man Electrical Band | 1969 | 5.00 | 10.00 | 20.00 |
LION
| ☐ LN-1009 | Sweet Paradise | 1973 | 5.00 | 10.00 | 20.00 |
LIONEL
| ☐ LRS-1100 | Good-Byes & Butterflies | 1970 | 7.50 | 15.00 | 30.00 |
| ☐ LRS-1101 | Coming of Age | 1971 | 5.00 | 10.00 | 20.00 |
MGM
| ☐ SE-4725 | Good-Byes & Butterflies | 1970 | 12.50 | 25.00 | 50.00 |
PICKWICK
| ☐ SPC-3289 | Five Man Electrical Band | 1973 | 2.50 | 5.00 | 10.00 |
—Reissue of Capitol material

FIVE NOTES, THE
45s
CHESS
| ☐ 1614 | Show Me the Way/Park Your Lover | 1955 | 37.50 | 75.00 | 150.00 |
JEN D
| ☐ 4185 | You Are So Beautiful/Broken Hearted Baby | 1955 | 125.00 | 250.00 | 500.00 |
JOSIE
| ☐ 784 | You Are So Beautiful/Broken Hearted Baby | 1955 | 20.00 | 40.00 | 80.00 |

F

Number	Title (A Side/B Side)	Yr	VG	VG+	NM

FIVE PLAYBOYS, THE
45s
DOT
| ❑ 15605 | When We Were Young/Pages of My Scrapbook | 1957 | 6.25 | 12.50 | 25.00 |

FEE BEE
| ❑ 213 | When We Were Young/Pages of My Scrapbook | 1958 | 12.50 | 25.00 | 50.00 |
| ❑ 232 | Angel Mine/She's My Baby | 1959 | 25.00 | 50.00 | 100.00 |

MERCURY
| ❑ 71269 | Time Will Allow/Why Be a Fool | 1958 | 6.25 | 12.50 | 25.00 |

PETITE
| ❑ 504 | She's My Baby/Mr. Echo | 1959 | 10.00 | 20.00 | 40.00 |

FIVE ROVERS, THE
45s
MUSIC CITY
| ❑ 798 | Down to the Sea/Change Your Mind | 1956 | 30.00 | 60.00 | 120.00 |

FIVE ROYALES, THE   Also includes "The Five Royals" and "The '5' Royales."
45s
ABC-PARAMOUNT
| ❑ 10348 | Catch That Teardrop/Goof Ball | 1962 | 2.50 | 5.00 | 10.00 |
| ❑ 10368 | What's In Your Heart/I Want It Like That | 1962 | 2.50 | 5.00 | 10.00 |

APOLLO
❑ 441	Courage to Love/You Know I Know	1952	25.00	50.00	100.00
—Black vinyl					
❑ 441	Courage to Love/You Know I Know	1952	100.00	200.00	400.00
—Red vinyl					
❑ 443	Baby Don't Do It/Take All of Me	1952	25.00	50.00	100.00
—Black vinyl					
❑ 443	Baby Don't Do It/Take All of Me	1952	100.00	200.00	400.00
—Red vinyl					
❑ 446	Help Me, Somebody/Crazy, Crazy, Crazy	1953	25.00	50.00	100.00
❑ 448	Too Much Lovin' (Much Too Much)/Laundromat Blues	1953	30.00	60.00	120.00
❑ 449	I Want to Thank You/All Righty	1953	20.00	40.00	80.00
❑ 452	I Do/Good Things	1954	20.00	40.00	80.00
❑ 454	Cry Some More/I Like It Like That	1954	20.00	40.00	80.00
❑ 458	What's That/Let Me Come Back Home	1954	17.50	35.00	70.00
❑ 467	With All Your Heart/6 O'Clock in the Morning	1955	17.50	35.00	70.00

HOME OF THE BLUES
❑ 112	Please, Please, Please/I Got to Know	1960	3.75	7.50	15.00
❑ 218	If You Don't Need Me/I'm Gonna Tell Them	1961	3.75	7.50	15.00
❑ 232	Take Me With You Baby/Not Going to Cry	1961	3.75	7.50	15.00
❑ 234	Nuch in Need/They Don't Know	1962	3.75	7.50	15.00
❑ 243	Catch That Teardrop/Goof Ball	1962	3.75	7.50	15.00

KING
❑ 4740	I'm Gonna Run It Down/Behave Yourself	1954	20.00	40.00	80.00
❑ 4744	Monkey Hips and Rice/Devil with the Rest	1954	20.00	40.00	80.00
❑ 4762	School Girl/One Mistake	1955	20.00	40.00	80.00
❑ 4770	Every Dog Has His Day/You Didn't Learn It at Home	1955	20.00	40.00	80.00
❑ 4785	How I Wonder/Mohawk Squaw	1955	20.00	40.00	80.00
❑ 4806	I Need Your Lovin'/When I Get Like This	1955	12.50	25.00	50.00
❑ 4819	Women About to Make Me Go Crazy/Do Unto You	1955	12.50	25.00	50.00
❑ 4830	I Ain't Gettin' Caught/Someone Made You for Me	1955	12.50	25.00	50.00
❑ 4869	When You Walked Through the Door/Right Around the Corner	1956	12.50	25.00	50.00
❑ 4901	I Could Love You/My Wants for Love	1956	12.50	25.00	50.00
❑ 4952	Get Something Out of It/Come On and Save Me	1956	12.50	25.00	50.00
❑ 4973	Just As I Am/Mine Forevermore	1956	12.50	25.00	50.00
❑ 5032	Tears of Joy/Thirty Second Lover	1957	10.00	20.00	40.00
❑ 5053	Think/I'd Better Make a Move	1957	10.00	20.00	40.00
❑ 5082	Messin' Up/Say It	1957	10.00	20.00	40.00
❑ 5098	Dedicated to the One I Love/Don't Be Ashamed	1958	10.00	20.00	40.00
❑ 5131	Do the Cha Cha Cherry/The Feeling Is Real	1958	6.25	12.50	25.00
❑ 5141	Tell the Truth/Double or Nothing	1958	6.25	12.50	25.00
❑ 5153	The Slummer the Slum/Don't Let It Be in Vain	1958	6.25	12.50	25.00
❑ 5162	Your Only Love/The Real Thing	1958	6.25	12.50	25.00
❑ 5191	Miracle of Love/I Know It's Hard, But It's Fair	1959	6.25	12.50	25.00
❑ 5237	Tell Me You Care/Wonder Where Your Love Has Gone	1959	6.25	12.50	25.00
❑ 5266	My Sugar Sugar/It Hurts Inside	1959	6.25	12.50	25.00
❑ 5329	Don't Give No More Than You Can Take/I'm with You	1960	6.25	12.50	25.00
❑ 5357	Why/Within My Heart	1960	6.25	12.50	25.00
❑ 5453	Dedicated to the One I Love/Miracle of Love	1961	3.75	7.50	15.00
❑ 5756	Dedicated to the One I Love/Tears of Joy	1963	3.75	7.50	15.00
❑ 5892	I Wonder Where Your Love Has Gone/I Need Your Lovin' Baby	1964	3.75	7.50	15.00

—The Five Royals
SMASH
| ❑ 1936 | Baby Don't Do It/I Like It Like That | 1964 | 2.50 | 5.00 | 10.00 |
| ❑ 1963 | Never Turn Your Back/Faith | 1965 | 2.50 | 5.00 | 10.00 |

TODD
| ❑ 1086 | I'm Standing in the Shadows/Doin' Everything | 1963 | 2.50 | 5.00 | 10.00 |
| ❑ 1088 | Baby Don't Do It/There's Somebody Over There | 1963 | 2.50 | 5.00 | 10.00 |

VEE JAY
| ❑ 412 | Much in Need/They Don't Know | 1961 | 3.75 | 7.50 | 15.00 |
| ❑ 431 | Help Me Somebody/Talk About My Woman | 1962 | 3.75 | 7.50 | 15.00 |

Albums
APOLLO
❑ LP-488 [M]	The Rockin' 5 Royales	1956	250.00	500.00	1000.
—Yellow label					
❑ LP-488 [M]	The Rockin' 5 Royales	1956	1000.	1500.	2000.
—Green label					
❑ LP-488 [M]	The Rockin' 5 Royales	1956	2000.	3000.	4000.
—Purple label					

KING
❑ 580 [M]	Dedicated to You	1957	125.00	250.00	500.00
❑ 616 [M]	The 5 Royales Sing for You	1959	100.00	200.00	400.00
❑ 678 [M]	The Five Royales	1960	62.50	125.00	250.00
❑ 955 [M]	24 All Time Hits	1966	25.00	50.00	100.00
❑ 5014	17 Hits	197?	3.00	6.00	12.00

Number	Title (A Side/B Side)	Yr	VG	VG+	NM

FIVE SATINS, THE   Also see FRED PARRIS; THE WILDWOODS.
45s
BUDDAH
| ❑ 477 | Everybody Stand and Clap Your Hands/Hey There Pretty Lady | 1975 | — | 2.50 | 5.00 |
| —As "Black Satin" | | | | | |

CANDELITE
| ❑ 411 | She's Gone (With the Wind)/Somewhere a Voice Is Calling | 1974 | — | 3.00 | 6.00 |

CHANCELLOR
| ❑ 1110 | The Masquerade Is Over/Raining in My Heart | 1962 | 5.00 | 10.00 | 20.00 |
| ❑ 1121 | Do You Remember/Downtown | 1962 | 5.00 | 10.00 | 20.00 |

CUB
❑ 9071	Your Memory/I Didn't Know	1960	6.25	12.50	25.00
❑ 9077	These Foolish Things/A Beggar with a Dream	1960	6.25	12.50	25.00
❑ 9090	Golden Earrings/Can I Come Over Tonight	1961	6.25	12.50	25.00

ELEKTRA
❑ 47411	Memories of Days Gone By Medley/Loving You (Would Be the Sweetest Thing)	1982	5.00	10.00	20.00
—As "Fred Parris and the Five Satins"					
❑ 69888	Didn't I (Blow Your Mind)/Loving You (Would Be the Sweetest Thing)	1982	—	2.50	5.00
❑ 69938	Breaking Up/Loving You (Would Be the Sweetest Thing)	1982	—	2.50	5.00
❑ 69984	I'll Be Seeing You/Loving You (Would Be the Sweetest Thing)	1982	—	2.50	5.00

EMBER
❑ 1005	I'll Remember (In the Still of the Nite)/The Jones Girl	1956	7.50	15.00	30.00
—Red label					
❑ 1005	In the Still of the Nite/The Jones Girl	1956	7.50	15.00	30.00
—Red label; has "E-1005" in the trail-off vinyl					
❑ 1005	In the Still of the Nite/The Jones Girl	1956	12.50	25.00	50.00
—Red label; has "E-2105-45" in the trail-off vinyl					
❑ 1005	In the Still of the Nite/The Jones Girl	1956	50.00	100.00	200.00
—Red label; has "6106A" in the trail-off vinyl					
❑ 1005	I'll Remember (In the Still of the Nite)/The Jones Girl	1959	7.50	15.00	30.00
—Multi-color "logs" label; no "Special Demand Release"					
❑ 1005	In the Still of the Nite/The Jones Girl	1959	10.00	20.00	40.00
—Multi-color "logs" label with original A-side title					
❑ 1005	I'll Remember (In the Still of the Nite)/The Jones Girl	1959	12.50	25.00	50.00
—Multi-color "logs" label; reads "Special Demand Release"					
❑ 1005	In the Still of the Night "I'll Remember"/The Jones Girl	1961	7.50	15.00	30.00
—Black label, white logo and red flames at left; A-side title revised yet again					
❑ 1008	Weeping Willow/Wonderful Girl	1956	10.00	20.00	40.00
❑ 1014	Our Love Is Forever/Oh Happy Day	1957	10.00	20.00	40.00
❑ 1019	To the Aisle/Wish I Had My Baby	1957	10.00	20.00	40.00
—Red label					
❑ 1019	To the Aisle/Wish I Had My Baby	1960	7.50	15.00	30.00
—Multi-color "logs" label					
❑ 1019	To the Aisle/Wish I Had My Baby	1961	5.00	10.00	20.00
—Black label					
❑ 1025	Our Anniversary/Pretty Baby	1957	5.00	10.00	20.00
—Black label					
❑ 1025	Our Anniversary/Pretty Baby	1957	10.00	20.00	40.00
—Red label					
❑ 1028	A Million to One/Love with No Love in Return	1957	10.00	20.00	40.00
❑ 1038	A Night to Remember/Senorita Lolita	1958	7.50	15.00	30.00
—As "Fred Parris and the Satins"					
❑ 1056	Shadows/Toni My Love	1959	7.50	15.00	30.00
❑ 1061	I'll Be Seeing You/A Night Like This	1960	7.50	15.00	30.00
❑ 1066	Candlelight/The Time	1960	6.25	12.50	25.00
❑ 1070	Wishing Ring/Tell Me Dear	1961	6.25	12.50	25.00

FIRST
❑ 104	When Your Love Comes Along/Skippity Doo	1959	6.25	12.50	25.00
—Green label					
❑ 104	When Your Love Comes Along/Skippity Doo	1959	10.00	20.00	40.00
—Orange label					

GLENVILLE MUSIC
| ❑ 106 | (I'll Remember) In the Still of the Night/The Jones Girl | 196? | 2.00 | 4.00 | 8.00 |
| —Reissue | | | | | |

KIRSHNER
| ❑ 4251 | Very Precious Oldies/You Are Love | 1974 | 2.50 | 5.00 | 10.00 |
| ❑ 4252 | Two Different Worlds/Love Is Such a Beautiful Thing | 1974 | 2.50 | 5.00 | 10.00 |

KLIK
| ❑ 1020 | I Love You So/Story to You | 1973 | 2.50 | 5.00 | 10.00 |

LANA
| ❑ 106 | In the Still of the Nite/The Jones Girl | 196? | 2.00 | 4.00 | 8.00 |
| —Oldies reissue | | | | | |

LOST-NITE
❑ 151	All Mine/Rose Mary	196?	—	3.00	6.00
—Reissue					
❑ 202	To the Aisle/Just to Be Near You	196?	—	2.50	5.00
—Reissue					
❑ 411	In the Still of the Nite/The Jones Girl	197?	—	2.50	5.00
—Reissue					
❑ 423	Our Love Is Forever/Oh Happy Day	197?	—	2.50	5.00
—Reissue					
❑ 426	To the Aisle/Wish I Had My Baby	197?	—	2.50	5.00
—Reissue					
❑ 428	Our Anniversary/Pretty Baby	197?	—	2.50	5.00
—Reissue					
❑ 431	Weeping Willow/Wonderful Girl	197?	—	2.50	5.00
—Reissue					
❑ 434	Shadows/Toni My Love	197?	—	2.50	5.00
—Reissue					

MAMA SADIE
| ❑ 1001 | In the Still of the Night "67"/Heck No (Instrumental) | 1967 | 3.00 | 6.00 | 12.00 |

MUSICTONE
| ❑ 1108 | To the Aisle/Just to Be Near You | 1961 | 6.25 | 12.50 | 25.00 |

Number	Title (A Side/B Side)	Yr	VG	VG+	NM
NIGHTRAIN					
❑ 901	All Mine/The Voice	1970	2.50	5.00	10.00
RCA					
❑ 6989-7-R	In the Still of the Night/Yes	1988	—	—	3.00
—B-side by Merry Clayton					
RCA VICTOR					
❑ 74-0478	Summer in New York/Dark at the Top of My Heart	1971	2.50	5.00	10.00
ROULETTE					
❑ 4563	Ain't Gonna Cry/You Can Count on Me	1964	2.50	5.00	10.00
SAMMY					
❑ 103	No One Knows/Musical Chairs	196?	7.50	15.00	30.00
SIGNATURE					
❑ 001	Everybody's Got a Home But Me/Heartache	1990	—	2.50	5.00
STANDORD					
❑ 100	All Mine/Rose Mary	1956	175.00	350.00	700.00
—Red label					
❑ 100	All Mine/Rose Mary	1962	50.00	100.00	200.00
—Maroon label					
❑ 200	In the Still of the Nite/The Jones Girl	1956	300.00	600.00	900.00
❑ 200	In the Still of the Nite/The Jones Girl	1956	1000.00	1500.	2000.
—With "Produced by Martin Kuegell" credit					
TIME MACHINE					
❑ 570	Wonder Why/No One Knows	1962	2.00	4.00	8.00
❑ 571	The Masquerade Is Over/Lonely Hearts	1962	2.00	4.00	8.00
TIMES SQUARE					
❑ 4	All Mine/Rose Mary	1962	5.00	10.00	20.00
—Blue vinyl					
❑ 21	Paradise on Earth/Monkey Business	1963	5.00	10.00	20.00
❑ 94	Paradise on Earth/Monkey Business	1964	3.75	7.50	15.00
UNITED ARTISTS					
❑ 368	On a Lover's Island/Till the End	1961	6.25	12.50	25.00
WARNER BROS.					
❑ 5367	Remember Me/Kangaroo	1963	3.00	6.00	12.00
X-BAT					
❑ 1000	When the Swallows Come Back to Capistrano/Dance Girl Dance	1995	—	2.50	5.00
—Red vinyl					
❑ 1000 [PS]	When the Swallows Come Back to Capistrano/Dance Girl Dance	1995	—	2.50	5.00
7-Inch Extended Plays					
EMBER					
❑ EEP-100	I'll Remember/The Jones Girl//Wonderful Girl/Pretty Baby	1957	50.00	100.00	200.00
❑ EEP-100 [PS]	The Five Satins Sing (Vol. 1)	1957	50.00	100.00	200.00
❑ EEP-101	To the Aisle/Sugar//Our Love Is Forever/Weeping Willow	1957	50.00	100.00	200.00
❑ EEP-101 [PS]	The Five Satins Sing (Vol. 2)	1957	50.00	100.00	200.00
❑ EEP-102	Our Anniversary/I'll Get Along//Wish I Had My Baby/Moonlight and I	1957	50.00	100.00	200.00
❑ EEP-102 [PS]	The Five Satins Sing (Vol. 3)	1957	50.00	100.00	200.00
Albums					
BUDDAH					
❑ BDS-5654	Black Satin	1976	3.75	7.50	15.00
—As "Black Satin"					
CELEBRITY SHOWCASE					
❑ JB-7671	The Best of the Five Satins	1970	5.00	10.00	20.00
COLLECTABLES					
❑ COL-5017	The Five Satins Sing Their Greatest Hits	198?	2.50	5.00	10.00
EMBER					
❑ ELP-100 [M]	The Five Satins Sing	1957	150.00	300.00	600.00
—Red label; group pictured on front cover; black vinyl					
❑ ELP-100 [M]	The Five Satins Sing	1957	1000.	1500.	2000.
—Red label; group pictured on front cover; blue vinyl					
❑ ELP-100 [M]	The Five Satins Sing	1959	50.00	100.00	200.00
—Mostly white "logs" label; no picture on cover					
❑ ELP-100 [M]	The Five Satins Sing	1959	75.00	150.00	300.00
—Mostly white "logs" label; group pictured on front cover					
❑ ELP-100 [M]	The Five Satins Sing	1961	25.00	50.00	100.00
—Black label; no picture on cover					
❑ ELP-401 [M]	The Five Satins Encore	1960	50.00	100.00	200.00
—Mostly white "logs" label					
❑ ELP-401 [M]	The Five Satins Encore	1961	25.00	50.00	100.00
—Black label					
LOST-NITE					
❑ LLP-8 [10]	The Five Satins	1981	2.50	5.00	10.00
—Red vinyl					
❑ LLP-9 [10]	The Five Satins	1981	2.50	5.00	10.00
—Red vinyl					
MOUNT VERNON					
❑ 108	The Five Satins Sing	196?	7.50	15.00	30.00
RELIC					
❑ 5008	The Five Satins' Greatest Hits (1956-1959), Volume 1	198?	2.50	5.00	10.00
❑ 5013	The Five Satins' Greatest Hits (1956-1959), Volume 2	198?	2.50	5.00	10.00
❑ 5024	The Five Satins' Greatest Hits (1956-1959), Volume 3	198?	2.50	5.00	10.00

FIVE SCALDERS, THE
45s

Number	Title (A Side/B Side)	Yr	VG	VG+	NM
DRUMMOND					
❑ 3000	If Only You Were Mine/There Will Come a Time	1956	250.00	500.00	1000.
❑ 3001	Girl Friend/Willow Blues	1956	250.00	500.00	1000.
—Maroon label					
❑ 3001	Girl Friend/Willow Blues	1956	500.00	1000.	1500.
—Blue label					
SUGAR HILL					
❑ 3000	If Only You Were Mine/There Will Come a Time	1956	500.00	1000.	2000.

FIVE SECRETS, THE
45s

Number	Title (A Side/B Side)	Yr	VG	VG+	NM
DECCA					
❑ 30350	See You Next Year/Queen Bee	1957	10.00	20.00	40.00
—As "The Secrets"					
❑ 30350	See You Next Year/Queen Bee	1957	20.00	40.00	80.00

FIVE SHARKS, THE
45s

Number	Title (A Side/B Side)	Yr	VG	VG+	NM
AMBER					
❑ 852	The Lion Sleeps Tonight/Land of 1000 Dances	1966	2.50	5.00	10.00
LOST-NITE					
❑ 404	Stormy Weather/If You Love Me	197?	—	3.00	6.00
—Reissue					
OLD TIMER					
❑ 604	Gloria/Flames	1964	5.00	10.00	20.00
❑ 605	Stand By Me/I'll Never Let You Go	1964	4.00	8.00	16.00
—Blue vinyl					
❑ 605	Stand By Me/I'll Never Let You Go	1964	5.00	10.00	20.00
—Gold vinyl					
❑ 611	Gloria/Flames	1965	3.75	7.50	15.00
—Black vinyl					
❑ 611	Gloria/Flames	1965	5.00	10.00	20.00
—Red vinyl					
RELIC					
❑ 525	Stormy Weather (2:45)/If You Love Me	1965	2.50	5.00	10.00
SIAMESE					
❑ 404	Gloria/Flames	1965	3.00	6.00	12.00
TIMES SQUARE					
❑ 35	Stormy Weather (2:45)/If You Love Me	1964	7.50	15.00	30.00
❑ 35	Stormy Weather (3:45)/If You Love Me	1964	10.00	20.00	40.00
—Black vinyl					
❑ 35	Stormy Weather (3:45)/If You Love Me	1964	15.00	30.00	60.00
—Blue vinyl					

FIVE SHARPS, THE (1)
45s

Number	Title (A Side/B Side)	Yr	VG	VG+	NM
BIM BAM BOOM					
❑ 103	Stormy Weather/Sleepy Cowboy	1972	2.00	4.00	8.00
—Reissue mastered off the cracked Jubilee 78 (see below); the original master has long since disappeared					
JUBILEE					
❑ 5104	Stormy Weather/Sleepy Cowboy	1952	—	—	—
—Unknown on 45 RPM (3 known copies, one of which is cracked, exist on 78; all known 45s are counterfeits. Known counterfeits do not match the proper typeface of the era for the label, and the blue labels are too bright compared to authentic Jubilee 45s of the early 1950s. If a legitimate 45 would be confirmed, it could sell for more than any record ever made!					

FIVE SHARPS, THE (2)
A completely different group than (1), they were assembled by Jubilee to record a new version of "Stormy Weather" in the midst of the hubbub about the first Five Sharps version. (For the full story, see The Complete Book of Doo-Wop by Gribin and Schiff, Krause Publications, 2000.)

45s

Number	Title (A Side/B Side)	Yr	VG	VG+	NM
JUBILEE					
❑ 5478	Stormy Weather/Mammy Jammy	1964	3.00	6.00	12.00

FIVE SHITS
45s

Number	Title (A Side/B Side)	Yr	VG	VG+	NM
CHANCE					
❑ 1163	My Pretty Little Girl/Stormy Weather	1974	5.00	10.00	20.00
—This was not released in the 1950s; this used the classic 1950s label, either as a lark or an attempt to fool gullible collectors. (Come on; would a group called the Five Shits ever made it onto record in the 1950s?)					
LOST-CAUSE					
❑ 100	Dreaming of You/Let Me Tell You	1974	5.00	10.00	20.00
—Blue vinyl					

FIVE STAIRSTEPS, THE
Includes records by "Five Stairsteps and Cubie" and "Stairsteps."

45s

Number	Title (A Side/B Side)	Yr	VG	VG+	NM
BUDDAH					
❑ 20	Something's Missing/Tell Me Who	1967	2.00	4.00	8.00
—As "Five Stairsteps and Cubie"					
❑ 20 [PS]	Something's Missing/Tell Me Who	1967	3.75	7.50	15.00
❑ 26	A Million to One/You Make Me So Mad	1968	2.00	4.00	8.00
—As "Five Stairsteps and Cubie"					
❑ 26 [PS]	A Million to One/You Make Me So Mad	1968	3.75	7.50	15.00
❑ 35	The Shadow of Your Love/Bad News	1968	2.00	4.00	8.00
❑ 165	O-o-h Child/Who Do You Belong To	1970	—	3.00	6.00
❑ 165	Dear Prudence/O-o-h Child	1970	2.00	4.00	8.00
❑ 188	Because I Love You/America Standing	1970	—	2.50	5.00
❑ 213	Didn't It Look So Easy/Peace Is Gonna Come	1971	—	2.50	5.00
—Starting with the above, as "Stairsteps"					
❑ 222	Snow/Look Out	1971	—	2.50	5.00
❑ 277	I Love You-Stop/I Feel a Song (In My Heart Again)	1972	—	2.50	5.00
❑ 291	Hush Child/The Easy Way	1972	—	2.50	5.00
❑ 320	Every Single Way/Two Weeks' Notice	1972	—	2.50	5.00
CURTOM					
❑ 1931	Don't Change Your Love/New Dance Craze	1968	—	3.00	6.00
—Curtom releases as "Five Stairsteps and Cubie"					
❑ 1933	I Made a Mistake/Stay Close to Me	1968	—	3.00	6.00
❑ 1936	Baby Make Me Feel So Good/Little Young Lover	1969	—	3.00	6.00
❑ 1944	Madame Mary/Little Boy Blue	1969	—	3.00	6.00
❑ 1945	We Must Be in Love/Little Young Lover	1969	—	3.00	6.00
DARK HORSE					
❑ 10005	From Us to You/Time	1975	—	2.50	5.00
❑ 10005 [PS]	From Us to You/Time	1975	—	3.00	6.00
❑ 10009	Tell Me Why/Salaam	1976	—	2.50	5.00
WINDY "C"					
❑ 601	You Waited Too Long/Don't Waste Your Time	1966	2.50	5.00	10.00
❑ 602	World of Fantasy/Playgirl's Love	1966	2.50	5.00	10.00
❑ 603	Come Back/You Don't Love Me	1966	2.50	5.00	10.00
❑ 604	Danger, She's a Stranger/Behind Curtains	1967	2.50	5.00	10.00
❑ 605	Ain't Gonna Rest (Till I Get You)/You Can't See	1967	2.50	5.00	10.00
❑ 607	Oooh, Baby Baby/The Girl I Love	1967	2.50	5.00	10.00
❑ 608	The Touch of You/Change of Face	1967	2.50	5.00	10.00
Albums					
BUDDAH					
❑ BDS-5008	Our Family Portrait	1967	5.00	10.00	20.00
❑ BDS-5061	Stairsteps	1970	3.75	7.50	15.00
—As "Stairsteps"					
❑ BDS-5068	Step by Step by Step	1970	3.75	7.50	15.00
—As "Stairsteps"					

F

Number	Title (A Side/B Side)	Yr	VG	VG+	NM
COLLECTABLES					
❑ COL-5023	Greatest Hits	1985	2.50	5.00	10.00
CURTOM					
❑ 8002	Love's Happening	1969	5.00	10.00	20.00
WINDY C					
❑ 6000 [M]	The Five Stairsteps	1967	6.25	12.50	25.00
❑ S-6000 [S]	The Five Stairsteps	1967	6.25	12.50	25.00
FIVE STARS, THE (1)					
45s					
ABC-PARAMOUNT					
❑ 9911	Pickin' on the Wrong Chicken/Dreaming	1958	6.25	12.50	25.00
HUNT					
❑ 318	Pickin' on the Wrong Chicken/Dreaming	1959	5.00	10.00	20.00
NOTE					
❑ 10011	Pickin' on the Wrong Chicken/Dreaming	1958	7.50	15.00	30.00
❑ 10016	My Paradise/Friction	1958	10.00	20.00	40.00
❑ 10031	Am I Wasting My Time/Gamblin' Man	1959	7.50	15.00	30.00
FIVE STARS, THE (2)					
45s					
SHOW TIME					
❑ 1102	Where Did Caledonia Go?/Walkin' An' Talkin'	1954	62.50	125.00	250.00
FIVE STARS, THE (U) Many of these are probably group (1); the Treat release may be group (2).					
45s					
ATCO					
❑ 6065	Take Five/Humpty Dump	1956	7.50	15.00	30.00
BLUES BOYS KINGDOM					
❑ 106	So Lonely, Baby/Hey Juanita	1957	50.00	100.00	200.00
COLUMBIA					
❑ 4-42056	Baby Baby/Blabber Mouth	1961	15.00	30.00	60.00
END					
❑ 1028	Baby Baby/Blabber Mouth	1958	20.00	40.00	80.00
KERNEL					
❑ 3195	Atom Bomb Baby/You Sweet Little Thing	1957	25.00	50.00	100.00
MARK-X					
❑ 7006	Dead Wrong/Ooh Shucks	1957	25.00	50.00	100.00
TREAT					
❑ 505	Let's Fall in Love/We Danced in the Moonlight	1955	500.00	1000.	2000.
FIVE SUPERIORS, THE					
45s					
GARPAX					
❑ 44170	There's a Fool Born Every Day/Big Shot	1962	37.50	75.00	150.00
FIVE SWANS, THE					
45s					
MUSIC CITY					
❑ 795	Little Girl of My Dreams/Little Tipa Tins	1956	75.00	150.00	300.00
5000 VOLTS					
45s					
PHILIPS					
❑ 40801	I'm on Fire/Still on Fire	1975	—	3.00	6.00
❑ 40804	Bye Love/Look Out I'm Coming	1976	—	3.00	6.00
PRIVATE STOCK					
❑ 45,114	Doctor Kiss-Kiss/Thunderfire	1976	2.00	4.00	8.00
FIVE THRILLS, THE					
45s					
LOST-NITE					
❑ 152	My Baby's Gone/Feel So Good	196?	—	3.00	6.00
—Reissue					
❑ 157	Gloria/Wee Wee Baby	196?	—	3.00	6.00
—Reissue					
PARROT					
❑ 796	My Baby's Gone/Feel So Good	1954	200.00	400.00	800.00
❑ 800	Gloria/Wee Wee Baby	1954	1000.	1500.	2000.
—Black vinyl					
❑ 800	Gloria/Wee Wee Baby	1954	2000.	3000.	4000.
—Red vinyl					
FIVE TINOS, THE					
45s					
SUN					
❑ 222	Sitting By My Window/Don't Do That	1955	300.00	600.00	1200.
FIVE TRUMPETS, THE					
45s					
GOTHAM					
❑ 681	Stand By Me/Jesus Is Here Today	1951	15.00	30.00	60.00
❑ 693	My Chains Fell Off/The Lord Knows What I Need	1952	15.00	30.00	60.00
❑ 696	No Not One/A Hand I Can See	1952	15.00	30.00	60.00
RCA VICTOR					
❑ 50-0014	Oh Lord/Don't Let Nobody Turn You Around	1949	17.50	35.00	70.00
—Orange vinyl					
❑ 50-0034	Swing Low Sweet Chariot/Sign of the Judgment	1949	17.50	35.00	70.00
—Orange vinyl					
❑ 50-0080	When the Saints Go Marching In/Preach My Word	1950	17.50	35.00	70.00
—Orange vinyl					
SAVOY					
❑ 4060	Amazing Grace/Lord I Want to Be a Christian	1955	6.25	12.50	25.00
❑ 4072	I've Got Jesus/I Shall Not Be Moved	1956	6.25	12.50	25.00
FIVE WHISPERS, THE					
45s					
DOLTON					
❑ 61	Awake or Asleep/Especially for You	1962	3.75	7.50	15.00
❑ 69	Awake or Asleep/Especially for You	1963	3.75	7.50	15.00
❑ 90	Can't Face the Crowd/Sleep Walker	1964	3.75	7.50	15.00
FIVE WILLOWS, THE					
45s					
ALLEN					
❑ 1000	My Dear, Dearest Darling/Rock, Little Francis	1953	75.00	150.00	300.00
❑ 1002	Delores/All Night Long	1953	150.00	300.00	600.00
❑ 1003	The White Cliffs of Dover/With These Hands	1953	175.00	350.00	700.00

Number	Title (A Side/B Side)	Yr	VG	VG+	NM
HERALD					
❑ 433	Baby Come a Little Closer/Lay Your Head on My Shoulder	1954	75.00	150.00	300.00
❑ 442	Look Me in the Eyes/So Help Me	1954	100.00	200.00	400.00
LOST-NITE					
❑ 174	My Dear, Dearest Darling/Rock, Little Francis	196?	—	3.00	6.00
❑ 183	Delores/All Night Long	196?	—	3.00	6.00
❑ 187	The White Cliffs of Dover/With These Hands	196?	—	3.00	6.00
—Lost-Nite records are reissues					
❑ 192	Love Bells/Please Baby	196?	—	3.00	6.00
PEE DEE					
❑ 290	Love Bells/Please, Baby	1953	375.00	750.00	1500.
FIVE WINGS, THE					
45s					
KING					
❑ 4778	Johnny Has Gone/Johnny's Still Singing	1955	50.00	100.00	200.00
❑ 4781	Teardrops Are Falling/Rock-A-Locka	1955	100.00	200.00	400.00
—Later released on King 5199 as The Checkers.					
FLACK, ROBERTA					
12-Inch Singles					
ATLANTIC					
❑ 85501	Killing Me Softly with His Song (unknown versions)	1996	3.75	7.50	15.00
❑ 86414	Shock to My System (Extended) (Dub)	1989	2.00	4.00	8.00
❑ 86453	Uh-Uh Ooh-Ooh Look Out (Here It Comes) (Arthur Baker's Dance Mix) (Arthur Baker's Dub) (Steve Hurley's House Mix)	1989	2.00	4.00	8.00
❑ 86502	Oasis (LP Version) (Radio Version)/You Know What It's Like (LP Version)	1988	2.00	4.00	8.00
45s					
ANGEL					
❑ S7-19773	The Christmas Song (Chestnuts Roasting on an Open Fire)/25th of Last December	1997	—	2.00	4.00
ATLANTIC					
❑ 2665	Compared to What/That's No Way to Say Goodbye	1969	2.00	4.00	8.00
❑ 2730	How Many Broken Wings/Baby Baby	1970	—	3.00	6.00
—With Les McCann					
❑ 2758	Reverend Lee/Business Goes On As Usual	1970	—	3.00	6.00
❑ 2785	Let It Be Me/Do What Cha Gotta Do	1971	—	3.00	6.00
❑ 2851	Will You Still Love Me Tomorrow/Go Up Moses	1972	—	2.50	5.00
❑ 2864	The First Time Ever I Saw Your Face/Trade Winds	1972	—	2.50	5.00
❑ 2940	Killing Me Softly with His Song/Just Like a Woman	1973	—	2.50	5.00
❑ 2982	Jesse/No Tears	1973	—	2.50	5.00
❑ 3025	Feel Like Makin' Love/When You Smile	1974	—	2.50	5.00
❑ 3203	Feel Like Makin' Love/When You Smile	1974	—	2.00	4.00
❑ 3271	Feelin' That Glow/Some Gospel According to Matthew	1975	—	2.00	4.00
❑ 3441	The 25th of Last December/Move In with Me	1977	—	2.00	4.00
❑ 3483	If Ever I See You Again/I'd Like to Be a Baby to You	1978	—	2.00	4.00
❑ 3521	When It's Over/Come Share My Love	1978	—	2.00	4.00
❑ 3560	You Are Everything/Knowing That We're Made for Each Other	1979	—	2.00	4.00
❑ 3627	You Are My Heaven/I'll Love You Forever and Ever	1979	—	2.00	4.00
❑ 3753	Don't Make Me Wait Too Long/Only Heaven Can Wait (For Love)	1980	—	2.00	4.00
❑ 4005	Making Love/Jesse	1982	—	2.00	4.00
❑ 4005 [PS]	Making Love/Jesse	1982	—	3.00	6.00
❑ 4068	I'm the One/'Til the Morning Comes	1982	—	2.00	4.00
❑ 87607	Set the Night to Music/Natural Thing	1991	—	2.00	4.00
—A-side: With Maxi Priest					
❑ 88898	Shock to My System/You Know What It's Like	1989	—	—	3.00
❑ 88941	Uh-Uh Ooh-Ooh Look Out (Here It Comes)/You Know What It's Like	1989	—	—	3.00
❑ 88941 [PS]	Uh-Uh Ooh-Ooh Look Out (Here It Comes)/You Know What It's Like	1989	—	—	3.00
❑ 88996	Oasis/You Know What It's Like	1988	—	—	3.00
❑ 88996 [PS]	Oasis/You Know What It's Like	1988	—	—	3.00
❑ 89295	We Shall Overcome/We Shall Overcome	1987	—	—	3.00
❑ 89440	Let Me Be a Light to Shine/We Shall Overcome	1986	—	—	3.00
—With Howard Hewett					
❑ 89931	Our Love Will Stop the World/Only Heaven Can Wait (For Love)	1982	—	2.00	4.00
—A-side: With Eric Mercury					
❑ 89932	In the Name of Love/Happiness	1982	—	2.00	4.00
COLUMBIA					
❑ 44050	Si, Si, Senor/This Year	1967	2.50	5.00	10.00
❑ 44448	Cold, Cold Winter/If You Ever Leave Me Now	1968	2.50	5.00	10.00
MCA					
❑ 51126	You Stopped Loving Me/Qual E Maundrinio	1981	—	2.00	4.00
❑ 51173	Lovin' You/Hittin' Me Where It Hurts	1981	—	2.00	4.00
VIVA					
❑ 29401	This Side of Forever/Robbery Suspects	1983	—	2.00	4.00
—B-side by The Enforcers					
7-Inch Extended Plays					
ATLANTIC					
❑ SD 7-7271	I'm the Girl/Conversation Love//River/When You Smile	1973	2.00	4.00	8.00
—Jukebox issue; small hole, plays at 33 1/3 rpm					
❑ SD 7-7271 [PS]	Killing Me Softly	1973	2.00	4.00	8.00
Albums					
ATLANTIC					
❑ SD 1569	Chapter Two	1970	2.50	5.00	10.00
❑ SD 1594	Quiet Fire	1971	2.50	5.00	10.00
❑ QD 7271 [Q]	Killing Me Softly	1973	3.75	7.50	15.00
❑ SD 7271	Killing Me Softly	1973	2.50	5.00	10.00
❑ SD 8230	First Take	1969	2.50	5.00	10.00
—Red and green label (second edition)					
❑ SD 8230	First Take	1969	5.00	10.00	20.00
—Brown and purple label (first edition)					

Number	Title (A Side/B Side)	Yr	VG	VG+	NM
☐ SD 16013	Roberta Flack Featuring Donny Hathaway	1980	2.50	5.00	10.00
—Only two tracks feature Mr. Hathaway					
☐ SD 18131	Feel Like Makin' Love	1974	2.50	5.00	10.00
☐ SD 19149	Blue Lights in the Basement	1977	2.50	5.00	10.00
☐ SD 19154	Killing Me Softly	1978	2.00	4.00	8.00
—Reissue of 7271					
☐ SD 19186	Roberta Flack	1978	2.50	5.00	10.00
☐ SD 19317	The Best of Roberta Flack	1981	2.50	5.00	10.00
☐ SD 19354	I'm the One	1982	2.50	5.00	10.00
☐ 81916	Oasis	1988	2.50	5.00	10.00
☐ SW-94346	First Take	1972	3.75	7.50	15.00
—Capitol Record Club edition					
MCA					
☐ 5141	Bustin' Loose	1981	2.50	5.00	10.00

FLACK, ROBERTA, AND DONNY HATHAWAY Also see each artist's individual listings.
45s
ATLANTIC

Number	Title (A Side/B Side)	Yr	VG	VG+	NM
☐ 2808	You've Got a Friend/Gone Away	1971	—	2.50	5.00
☐ 2837	You've Lost That Lovin' Feeling/Be Real Black for Me	1971	—	2.50	5.00
☐ 2879	Where Is the Love/Mood	1972	—	2.50	5.00
☐ 3463	The Closer I Get to You/Love Is the Healing	1978	—	2.00	4.00
—B-side by Flack alone					
☐ 3661	Back Together Again/God Don't Like Ugly	1980	—	2.00	4.00

Albums
ATLANTIC

Number	Title	Yr	VG	VG+	NM
☐ SD 7216	Roberta Flack and Donny Hathaway	1972	2.50	5.00	10.00

FLAGG, BILL
45s
MGM

Number	Title (A Side/B Side)	Yr	VG	VG+	NM
☐ 12637	Doin' My Time/I Will Always Love You	1958	25.00	50.00	100.00
TETRA					
☐ 4445	Go Cat, Go/A Good Woman's Leaving	1956	37.50	75.00	150.00
☐ 4448	Guitar Rock/I'm So Lonely	1957	37.50	75.00	150.00

FLAGG, FANNIE
Albums
RCA VICTOR

Number	Title	Yr	VG	VG+	NM
☐ LPM-3856 [M]	Rally 'Round the Flagg	1967	5.00	10.00	20.00
☐ LSP-3856 [S]	Rally 'Round the Flagg	1967	3.75	7.50	15.00

FLAIRS, THE (1) Also see CORNEL GUNTER; SHIRLEY GUNTER.
45s
ABC-PARAMOUNT

Number	Title (A Side/B Side)	Yr	VG	VG+	NM
☐ 9740	Aladdin's Lamp/Steppin' Out	1956	10.00	20.00	40.00
FLAIR					
☐ 1012	I Had a Love/She Wants to Rock	1953	100.00	200.00	400.00
☐ 1019	Tell Me You Love Me/You Should Care for Me	1953	100.00	200.00	400.00
☐ 1028	Love Me Girl/Gettin' High	1954	100.00	200.00	400.00
☐ 1041	Baby Wants/You Were Untrue	1954	100.00	200.00	400.00
☐ 1044	This Is the Night for Love/Let's Make with Some Love	1954	100.00	200.00	400.00
☐ 1051	Love Me, Love Me, Love Me/My Heart's Crying for You	1954	100.00	200.00	400.00
—As "The Chimes"					
☐ 1056	I'll Never Let You Go/Hold Me, Thrill Me, Chill Me	1955	100.00	200.00	400.00
☐ 1067	She Loves to Dance/My Darling, My Sweet	1955	100.00	200.00	400.00

Albums
CROWN

Number	Title	Yr	VG	VG+	NM
☐ CLP-5356 [M]	The Flairs	1963	20.00	40.00	80.00

FLAIRS, THE (2) For records on Epic, see THE REDWOODS.

FLAIRS, THE (3) For records on Jamie and Palms, see THE VELAIRES.

FLAME, THE With Rikki Fataar and Blondie Chaplin, who later spent time in THE BEACH BOYS. (Fataar also was with The Rutles in the studio.)
45s
BROTHER

Number	Title (A Side/B Side)	Yr	VG	VG+	NM
☐ 3501	See the Light/Got Your Mind Made Up	1970	3.75	7.50	15.00
☐ 3502	Another Day Like Heaven/I'm So Happy	1970	3.75	7.50	15.00

Albums
BROTHER

Number	Title	Yr	VG	VG+	NM
☐ BR-2500	The Flame	1970	7.50	15.00	30.00
—Deduct 1/3 if poster is missing					

FLAMES, THE More than one group. Also see THE HOLLYWOOD FLAMES.
45s
HARLEM

Number	Title (A Side/B Side)	Yr	VG	VG+	NM
☐ 114	So Long My Darling/I'm Going to Try to Live My Life All Over	1960	200.00	400.00	800.00
—As "The Flames"					
☐ 114	So Long My Darling/I'm Going to Try to Live My Life All Over	1960	1500.00	2250.00	3000.
—As "The Fabulous Flames"					

FLAMIN' GROOVIES, THE
45s
BOMP!

Number	Title (A Side/B Side)	Yr	VG	VG+	NM
☐ 101	You Tore Me Down/Him or Me (What's It Gonna Be?)	1975	2.00	4.00	8.00
EPIC					
☐ 10507	Rockin' Pneumonia & The Boogie Woogie Flu/The First One's Free	1969	2.50	5.00	10.00
☐ 10564	Somethin' Else/Laurie Did It	1969	2.50	5.00	10.00
KAMA SUTRA					
☐ 527	Have You Seen My Baby/Yesterday's Numbers	1971	2.50	5.00	10.00
RCA					
☐ PB-11266	Too Many Cooks/Watch Me Run	1978	—	3.00	6.00
SIRE					
☐ 731	I Can't Hide/Teenage Confidential	1976	—	3.00	6.00

Albums
BUDDAH

Number	Title	Yr	VG	VG+	NM
☐ BDS-5683	Shill Shakin'	1977	3.75	7.50	15.00

Number	Title (A Side/B Side)	Yr	VG	VG+	NM
EPIC					
☐ BN 26487	Supersnazz	1969	12.50	25.00	50.00
KAMA SUTRA					
☐ KSBS-2021	Flamingo	1970	7.50	15.00	30.00
—Pink label					
☐ KSBS-2021	Flamingo	1972	3.75	7.50	15.00
—Blue label					
☐ KSBS-2031	Teenage Head	1971	7.50	15.00	30.00
—Pink label					
☐ KSBS-2031	Teenage Head	1972	3.75	7.50	15.00
—Blue label					
SIRE					
☐ SRK 6059	The Flamin' Groovies Now	1978	3.00	6.00	12.00
—Reissues have 14 tracks					
☐ SRK 6059	The Flamin' Groovies Now	1978	3.75	7.50	15.00
—Originals have 12 tracks					
☐ SRK 6067	Jumpin' in the Night	1979	3.00	6.00	12.00
☐ SASD-7521	Shake Some Action	1976	3.75	7.50	15.00
SNAZZ					
☐ R-2371 [10]	Sneakers	1969	25.00	50.00	100.00
—This album has been counterfeited					

FLAMING EMBER, THE
45s
FORTUNE

Number	Title (A Side/B Side)	Yr	VG	VG+	NM
☐ 869	Gone, Gone, Gone/You Can Count on Me	1965	15.00	30.00	60.00
HOT WAX					
☐ 6902	Mind, Body and Soul/Filet de Soul	1969	—	3.00	6.00
☐ 6907	Shades of Green/Don't You Wanna Wanna	1969	—	3.00	6.00
☐ 7003	Westbound #9/Why Don't You Stay	1970	—	3.00	6.00
☐ 7006	I'm Not My Brothers Keeper/Deserted Village	1970	—	3.00	6.00
☐ 7010	Stop the World and Let Me Off/Robot in a Robot's World	1970	—	3.00	6.00
☐ 7103	Sunshine/1200 Miles	1971	—	3.00	6.00
☐ 7109	If It's Good to You (Part 1)/If It's Good to You (Part 2)	1971		3.00	6.00
RIC-TIC					
☐ 129	Let's Have a Love-In (Vocal)/Let's Have a Love-In (Instrumental)	1967	5.00	10.00	20.00
—B-side credited to Wingate's Love-In Strings					
☐ 131	She's a Real Live Wire/Let's Have a Love-In (Instrumental)	1967	5.00	10.00	20.00
—B-side credited to Wingate's Love-In Strings					
☐ 132	Hey Mama/Let's Have a Love-In	1967	5.00	10.00	20.00
☐ 140	Bless You (My Love) (Instrumental)/Bless You (My Love) (Vocal)	1968	3.75	7.50	15.00
—B-side by Al Kent					
☐ 143	Children (Vocal)/Children (Instrumental)	1968	3.75	7.50	15.00
☐ 145	Tell It Like It Is/Just Like Children	1968	3.75	7.50	15.00

Albums
HOT WAX

Number	Title	Yr	VG	VG+	NM
☐ HA-702	Westbound #9	1970	3.75	7.50	15.00
☐ HA-705	Sunshine	1971	3.75	7.50	15.00

FLAMING YOUTH Phil Collins was in this group.
Albums
UNI

Number	Title	Yr	VG	VG+	NM
☐ 73075	Ark 2	1969	10.00	20.00	40.00

FLAMINGOS, THE
45s
CHANCE

Number	Title (A Side/B Side)	Yr	VG	VG+	NM
☐ 1133	If I Can't Have You/Someday, Somehow	1953	200.00	400.00	800.00
—Black vinyl					
☐ 1133	If I Can't Have You/Someday, Somehow	1953	1000.	1500.	2000.
—Red vinyl					
☐ 1140	That's My Desire/Hurry Home Baby	1953	150.00	300.00	600.00
—Black vinyl					
☐ 1140	That's My Desire/Hurry Home Baby	1953	375.00	750.00	1500.
—Red vinyl					
☐ 1145	Golden Teardrops/Carried Away	1953	250.00	500.00	1000.
—Black vinyl					
☐ 1145	Golden Teardrops/Carried Away	1953	750.00	1500.	3000.
—Red vinyl					
☐ 1149	Plan for Love/You Ain't Ready	1953	200.00	400.00	800.00
—Blue and silver label					
☐ 1149	Plan for Love/You Ain't Ready	1953	500.00	1000.	2000.
—Yellow and black label					
☐ 1154	Cross Over the Bridge/Listen to My Plea	1954	250.00	500.00	1000.
☐ 1162	Jump Children/Blues in the Letter	1954	150.00	300.00	600.00
CHECKER					
☐ 815	That's My Baby (Chick-a-Boom)/When	1955	20.00	40.00	80.00
☐ 821	I Want to Love You/Please Come Back Home	1955	20.00	40.00	80.00
☐ 830	I'll Be Home/Need Your Love	1956	20.00	40.00	80.00
☐ 837	A Kiss from Your Lips/Get With It	1956	20.00	40.00	80.00
☐ 846	The Vow/Shilly Dilly	1956	20.00	40.00	80.00
☐ 853	Just for a Kick/Would I Be Crying	1957	20.00	40.00	80.00
—Originals of above Checker singles are maroon with a checkerboard at top of label					
☐ 915	Whispering Stars/Dream of a Lifetime	1959	12.50	25.00	50.00
☐ 1084	Lover Come Back to Me/Your Little Guy	1964	3.75	7.50	15.00
☐ 1091	Goodnight Sweetheart/Does It Really Matter	1964	3.75	7.50	15.00
DECCA					
☐ 30335	The Ladder of Love/Let's Make Up	1957	7.50	15.00	30.00
☐ 30454	Helpless/My Faith in You	1957	7.50	15.00	30.00
☐ 30687	Rock and Roll March/Where Mary Go	1958	7.50	15.00	30.00
☐ 30880	Kiss-A Me/Ever Since I Met Lucy	1959	7.50	15.00	30.00
☐ 30948	Jerri-Lee/Hey Now	1959	7.50	15.00	30.00
END					
☐ 1035	Lovers Never Say Goodbye/That Love Is You	1958	10.00	20.00	40.00
—A-sides of End 1035 are the same song, the titles were changed					
☐ 1035	Please Wait for Me/That Love Is You	1958	15.00	30.00	60.00
☐ 1040	I Shed a Tear at Your Wedding/But Not for Me	1959	7.50	15.00	30.00
☐ 1044	At the Prom/Love Walked In	1959	10.00	20.00	40.00
☐ 1046 [M]	I Only Have Eyes for You/At the Prom	1959	6.25	12.50	25.00
☐ 1046 [M]	I Only Have Eyes for You/Love Walked In	1959	6.25	12.50	25.00
☐ 1046 [M]	I Only Have Eyes for You/Goodnight Sweetheart	1959	7.50	15.00	30.00

F

Number	Title (A Side/B Side)	Yr	VG	VG+	NM
❑ 1046 [S]	I Only Have Eyes for You/At the Prom	1959	12.50	25.00	50.00
—This B-side has been confirmed for the stereo version; others are not yet known					
❑ 1055 [M]	Yours/Love Walked In	1959	6.25	12.50	25.00
❑ 1055 [S]	Yours/Love Walked In	1959	12.50	25.00	50.00
❑ 1062	I Was Such a Fool/Heavenly Angel	1959	6.25	12.50	25.00
❑ 1065	Mio Amore/You, Me and the Sea	1960	6.25	12.50	25.00
❑ 1068	Nobody Loves Me Like You/You, Me and the Sea	1960	6.25	12.50	25.00
❑ 1068	Nobody Loves Me Like You/Besame Mucho	1960	7.50	15.00	30.00
❑ 1070	Besame Mucho/You, Me and the Sea	1960	6.25	12.50	25.00
❑ 1073	Mio Amore/At Night	1960	5.00	10.00	20.00
❑ 1079	Beside You/When I Fall in Love	1960	5.00	10.00	20.00
❑ 1081	Your Other Love/Lovers Gotta Cry	1960	5.00	10.00	20.00
❑ 1085	That's Why I Love You/Ko Ko Mo	1961	5.00	10.00	20.00
❑ 1092	Time Was/Dream Girl	1961	5.00	10.00	20.00
❑ 1099	My Memories of You/I Want to Love You	1961	5.00	10.00	20.00
❑ 1111	It Must Be Love/I'm No Fool Anymore	1962	5.00	10.00	20.00
❑ 1116	For All We Know/Near You	1962	5.00	10.00	20.00
❑ 1121	I Know Better/Flame of Love	1963	5.00	10.00	20.00
❑ 1124	(Talk About) True Love/Come to My Party	1963	5.00	10.00	20.00
JULMAR					
❑ 506	Dealin' All the Way/Dealin' (Groovin' with Feelin')	1969	2.50	5.00	10.00
LOST-NITE					
❑ 149	Dream of a Lifetime/On My Merry Way	196?	—	3.00	6.00
—Reissue					
❑ 154	I'm Yours/Ko Ko Mo	196?	—	3.00	6.00
—Reissue					
❑ 161	I Really Don't Want to Know/Get With It	196?	—	3.00	6.00
—Reissue					
❑ 269	If I Can't Have You/Plan for Love	197?	—	2.50	5.00
❑ 287	That's My Desire/Cross Over the Bridge	197?	—	2.50	5.00
❑ 294	Golden Teardrops/Secret Love	197?	—	2.50	5.00
—B-side by the Moonglows; reissue					
❑ 316	September Song/Vooit Vooit	197?	—	2.50	5.00
MERCURY					
❑ 72455	Temptation/Call Her on the Phone	1965	—	—	—
—Cancelled					
OLDIES 45					
❑ 35	Golden Teardrops/Carried Away	1963	2.00	4.00	8.00
❑ 43	I Only Have Eyes for You/At the Prom	1963	2.00	4.00	8.00
❑ 68	Lovers Never Say Goodbye/Baby, I Need You	1964	2.00	4.00	8.00
—B-side by the El Dorados					
PARROT					
❑ 808	Dream of a Lifetime/On My Merry Way	1954	200.00	400.00	800.00
—Black vinyl					
❑ 808	Dream of a Lifetime/On My Merry Way	1954	400.00	800.00	1600.
—Red vinyl					
❑ 811	I Really Don't Want to Know/Get With It	1955	2500.	2750.	5000.
—Black vinyl					
❑ 811	I Really Don't Want to Know/Get With It	1955	4000.	6000.	8000.
—Red vinyl					
❑ 812	I'm Yours/Ko Ko Mo	1955	200.00	400.00	800.00
—Black vinyl					
❑ 812	I'm Yours/Ko Ko Mo	1955	400.00	800.00	1600.
—Red vinyl					
PHILIPS					
❑ 40308	Temptation/Call Her on the Phone	1965	3.75	7.50	15.00
❑ 40347	The Boogaloo Party/The Nearness of You	1965	3.75	7.50	15.00
❑ 40378	Brooklyn Boogaloo/Since My Baby Put Me Down	1966	3.75	7.50	15.00
❑ 40413	Itty Bitty Baby/She Shook My World	1966	3.75	7.50	15.00
❑ 40452	Koo Koo/It Keeps the Doctor Away	1967	3.75	7.50	15.00
❑ 40496	Oh Mary Don't You Worry/Do It, Do It	1967	3.75	7.50	15.00
POLYDOR					
❑ 14019	Buffalo Soldier (Long)/Buffalo Soldier (Short)	1970	2.50	5.00	10.00
❑ 14044	Straighten It Up (Get It Together)/Lover Come Back to Me	1970	2.50	5.00	10.00
RONZE					
❑ 111	Welcome Home/Gotta Have All Your Lovin'	1971	—	2.50	5.00
❑ 115	Someone to Watch Over Me/Heavy Hips	1972	—	2.50	5.00
❑ 116	Love Keeps the Doctor Away (Long)/Love Keeps the Doctor Away (Short)	1972	—	2.50	5.00
ROULETTE					
❑ 4524	Ol' Man River (Part 1)/Ol' Man River (Part 2)	1963	5.00	10.00	20.00
SKYLARK					
❑ 541	If I Could Love You/I Found a New Baby	197?	—	2.50	5.00
TIMES SQUARE					
❑ 102	A Lovely Way to Spend an Evening/Walking My Baby Back Home	1964	3.75	7.50	15.00
VEE JAY					
❑ 384	Golden Teardrops/Carried Away	1961	6.25	12.50	25.00
WORLDS					
❑ 103	Think About Me/(Instrumental)	1974	—	2.50	5.00
7-Inch Extended Plays					
END					
❑ 205	Goodnight Sweetheart/Music Maestro Please//I Only Have Eyes for You/I'm in the Mood for Love	1959	50.00	100.00	200.00
❑ 205 [PS]	The Flamingos	1959	50.00	100.00	200.00
Albums					
CHECKER					
❑ LP-1433 [M]	The Flamingos	1959	100.00	200.00	400.00
—Black label					
❑ LP-1433 [M]	The Flamingos	196?	37.50	75.00	150.00
—Blue label					
❑ LPS-3005 [R]	The Flamingos	1966	6.25	12.50	25.00
—Rechanneled reissue of 1433					
CONSTELLATION					
❑ CS-3 [M]	Collectors Showcase: The Flamingos	1964	12.50	25.00	50.00
—With more restrained pink lettering on cover					
❑ CS-3 [M]	Collectors Showcase: The Flamingos	1964	25.00	50.00	100.00
—With hot pink lettering on cover					
END					
❑ LP-304 [M]	Flamingo Serenade	1959	50.00	100.00	200.00
—Gray label with dog					

Number	Title (A Side/B Side)	Yr	VG	VG+	NM
❑ LP-304 [M]	Flamingo Serenade	1959	100.00	200.00	400.00
—Black label with shadow print logo					
❑ LPS-304 [S]	Flamingo Serenade	1959	125.00	250.00	500.00
—Cover says "Stereo"					
❑ LPS-304 [S]	Flamingo Serenade	196?	50.00	100.00	200.00
—Cover says "Rechanneled Stereo" (only one track is)					
❑ LP-307 [M]	Flamingo Favorites	1960	25.00	50.00	100.00
❑ LPS-307 [R]	Flamingo Favorites	1960	17.50	35.00	70.00
❑ LP-308 [M]	Requestfully Yours	1960	25.00	50.00	100.00
❑ LPS-308 [R]	Requestfully Yours	1960	17.50	35.00	70.00
❑ LP-316 [M]	The Sound of the Flamingos	1962	25.00	50.00	100.00
❑ LPS-316 [R]	The Sound of the Flamingos	1962	17.50	35.00	70.00
❑ LPS-316 [S]	The Sound of the Flamingos	1962	50.00	100.00	200.00
—"Stereo" at upper right corner of front cover					
LOST-NITE					
❑ LLP-7 [10]	The Flamingos	1981	2.50	5.00	10.00
—Red vinyl					
PHILIPS					
❑ PHM 200206 [M]	Their Hits — Then and Now	1966	6.25	12.50	25.00
❑ PHS 600206 [S]	Their Hits — Then and Now	1966	7.50	15.00	30.00
RONZE					
❑ RLP-1001	The Flamingos Today	1972	3.75	7.50	15.00
SOLID SMOKE					
❑ 8018	Golden Teardrops	198?	2.50	5.00	10.00

FLAMINGOS, THE, AND THE MOONGLOWS
Albums

Number	Title (A Side/B Side)	Yr	VG	VG+	NM
VEE JAY					
❑ LP-1052 [M]	The Flamingos Meet the Moonglows on the Dusty Road of Hits	1962	37.50	75.00	150.00
❑ VJLP-1052 [M]	The Flamingos Meet the Moonglows on the Dusty Road of Hits	198?	3.00	6.00	12.00
—Authorized reissue					

FLARES, THE
45s

Number	Title (A Side/B Side)	Yr	VG	VG+	NM
FELSTED					
❑ 8604	Loving You/Hotcha Cha-Cha Brown	1960	5.00	10.00	20.00
❑ 8607	What Do You Want If You Don't Want Love/Jump and Hump	1960	5.00	10.00	20.00
❑ 8624	Foot Stomping — Part 1/Foot Stomping — Part 2	1961	5.00	10.00	20.00
PRESS					
❑ 2800	Rock and Roll Heaven — Part 1/Rock and Roll Heaven — Part 2	1962	3.75	7.50	15.00
❑ 2802	Doing the Hully Gully/Truck and Trailer	1962	3.75	7.50	15.00
❑ 2803	Madhouse/Make It Be Me	1962	3.75	7.50	15.00
❑ 2807	Do It with Me/Yon He Go	1963	3.75	7.50	15.00
❑ 2808	Hand Clappin'/Shimmy and Stomp	1963	3.75	7.50	15.00
❑ 2810	Monkey Walk/Do It If You Wanna	1963	3.75	7.50	15.00
❑ 2814	I Didn't Lose a Doggone Thing/Write a Song About Me	1964	3.75	7.50	15.00
Albums					
PRESS					
❑ PR 73001 [M]	Encore of Foot Stompin' Hits	196?	20.00	40.00	80.00
❑ PRS 83001 [S]	Encore of Foot Stompin' Hits	196?	30.00	60.00	120.00

FLASH
45s

Number	Title (A Side/B Side)	Yr	VG	VG+	NM
CAPITOL					
❑ 3345	Small Beginnings/Morning Haze	1972	—	2.50	5.00
Albums					
SOVEREIGN/CAPITOL					
❑ SMAS-11040	Flash	1972	3.00	6.00	12.00
❑ SMAS-11115	Flash in the Can	1972	3.00	6.00	12.00
❑ SMAS-11218	Out of Our Hands	1973	3.00	6.00	12.00

FLASH CADILLAC AND THE CONTINENTAL KIDS
45s

Number	Title (A Side/B Side)	Yr	VG	VG+	NM
EPIC					
❑ 10930	Muleskinner Blues/Teenage Eyes	1972	—	2.50	5.00
❑ 11043	At the Hop/She's So Fine	1973	—	2.50	5.00
❑ 11102	The Way I Feel Tonight/Dancin'	1974	—	2.50	5.00
PRIVATE STOCK					
❑ 45,006	Good Times, Rock and Roll/It's Hard	1974	—	2.00	4.00
❑ 45,026	Hot Summer Girls/Time Will Tell	1975	—	2.00	4.00
❑ 45,079	Did You Boogie (With Your Baby)/Maybe It's All in My Mind	1976	—	2.00	4.00
❑ 45,134	See My Baby Jive/Brown Water	1977	—	2.00	4.00
Albums					
EPIC					
❑ KE 31787	Flash Cadillac and the Continental Kids	1972	3.75	7.50	15.00
—Yellow label					
❑ KE 31787	Flash Cadillac and the Continental Kids	1973	3.00	6.00	12.00
—Orange label					
❑ KE 32488	There's No Face Like Chrome	1974	3.00	6.00	12.00
PRIVATE STOCK					
❑ PS 2003	Sons of Beaches	1975	3.00	6.00	12.00

FLAT EARTH SOCIETY, THE
Albums

Number	Title (A Side/B Side)	Yr	VG	VG+	NM
FLEETWOOD					
❑ 3027	Waleeco	1968	75.00	150.00	300.00

FLATT AND SCRUGGS Also includes records credited to "Lester Flatt and Earl Scruggs."
45s

Number	Title (A Side/B Side)	Yr	VG	VG+	NM
COLUMBIA					
❑ 20777	Come Back Darling/I'm Waiting to Hear You Call Me Darling	1951	5.00	10.00	20.00
❑ 20805	We Can't Be Darlings/I'm Head Over Heels in Love	1951	5.00	10.00	20.00
❑ 20830	Jimmy Brown the Newsboy/Somehow Tonight	1951	5.00	10.00	20.00
❑ 20854	Don't Get Above Your Raisin'/I've Lost You	1951	5.00	10.00	20.00
❑ 20886	'Tis Sweet to Be Remembered/Earl's Breakdown	1952	5.00	10.00	20.00
❑ 20915	Brother I'm Getting Ready to Go/Get in Line Brother	1952	5.00	10.00	20.00
❑ 20957	I'll Stay Around/Old Home Town	1952	5.00	10.00	20.00

Number	Title (A Side/B Side)	Yr	VG	VG+	NM
❏ 21002	Over the Hills to the Poorhouse/My Darling's Last Goodbye	1952	5.00	10.00	20.00
❏ 21043	I'm Gonna Settle Down/I'm Lonesome and Blue	1952	5.00	10.00	20.00
❏ 21054	Dim Lights Thick Smoke/Flint Hill Special	1952	5.00	10.00	20.00
❏ 21091	Why Did You Wander/Thinking About You	1953	5.00	10.00	20.00
❏ 21125	Dear Old Dixie/If I Should Wander Back	1953	5.00	10.00	20.00
❏ 21147	I'm Workin' on a Road/He Took Your Place	1953	5.00	10.00	20.00
❏ 21179	Foggy Mountain Chimes/I'll Go Steppin' Now	1953	5.00	10.00	20.00
❏ 21209	Be Ready/Mother Prays Loud	1954	5.00	10.00	20.00
❏ 21248	Somebody Took My Place with You/I'd Rather Be Alone	1954	5.00	10.00	20.00
❏ 21295	Foggy Mountain Breakdown/You're Not a Drop in the Bucket	1954	5.00	10.00	20.00
❏ 21334	Till the End of the World Rolls Around/Don't This Road Look Rough	1954	5.00	10.00	20.00
❏ 21370	You Can Feel It in Your Soul/Old Fashioned Preacher	1955	3.75	7.50	15.00
❏ 21412	I'm Gonna Sleep with One Eye Open/Before I Met You	1955	3.75	7.50	15.00
❏ 21460	Gone Home/Bubbling in My Soul	1955	3.75	7.50	15.00
❏ 21501	Randy Lynn Rag/On My Mind	1956	3.75	7.50	15.00
❏ 21536	Joy Bells/Give Mother My Crown	1956	3.75	7.50	15.00
❏ 21561	No Doubt About It/What's Good for You	1956	3.75	7.50	15.00
❏ S7 30904 [S]	Ground Speed/Home Sweet Home	1960	3.75	7.50	15.00
❏ S7 30905 [S]	Sally Ann/Reuben	1960	3.75	7.50	15.00
❏ S7 30906 [S]	Cripple Creek/Lonesome Road Blues	1960	3.75	7.50	15.00
❏ S7 30907 [S]	John Henry/Fire Ball Mail	1960	3.75	7.50	15.00
❏ S7 30908 [S]	Bugle Call Rag/Cumberland Gap	1960	3.75	7.50	15.00
—The above five are "Stereo Seven" 33 1/3 rpm jukebox singles from "JS7-19"					
❏ 40853	Shuckin' the Corn/Six White Horses	1957	3.75	7.50	15.00
❏ 40928	Give Me Flowers While I'm Living/Is There Room for Me?	1957	3.75	7.50	15.00
❏ 40990	Don't Let Your Deal Go Down/Let Those Brown Eyes Smile at Me	1957	3.75	7.50	15.00
❏ 41064	A Hundred Years from Now/I Won't Be Hanging Around	1957	3.75	7.50	15.00
❏ 41125	Big Black Train/Crying Alone	1958	3.75	7.50	15.00
❏ 41184	Building on Sand/Heaven	1958	3.75	7.50	15.00
❏ 41244	Mama's and Daddy's Little Girl/I Don't Care Anymore	1958	3.75	7.50	15.00
❏ 41336	A Million Years in Glory/Jesus Savior, Pilot Me	1959	3.75	7.50	15.00
❏ 41389	Cabin in the Hills/Someone You Have Forgotten	1959	3.75	7.50	15.00
❏ 41518	Crying My Heart Out Over You/Foggy Mountain Rock	1959	3.75	7.50	15.00
❏ 41708	The Great Historical Bum/All I Want Is You	1960	3.75	7.50	15.00
❏ 41786	Polka on a Banjo/Shuckin' the Corn	1960	3.75	7.50	15.00
❏ 41983	I Ain't Going to Work Tomorrow/I Should Wander Back Tonight	1961	3.75	7.50	15.00
❏ 42141	Go Home/Where Will I Shelter My Sheep	1961	3.00	6.00	12.00
❏ 42280	Just Ain't/Cold, Cold Loving	1962	3.00	6.00	12.00
❏ 42413	The Legend of the Johnson Boys/Hear the Whistle Blow a Hundred Miles	1962	3.00	6.00	12.00
❏ 42606	The Ballad of Jed Clampett/Coal Loadin' Johnny	1962	3.75	7.50	15.00
❏ 42606 [PS]	The Ballad of Jed Clampett/Coal Loadin' Johnny	1962	5.00	10.00	20.00
❏ 4-42606 [DJ]	The Ballad of Jed Clampett (same on both sides)	1962	7.50	15.00	30.00
—Promo only on red vinyl					
❏ 42755	Pearl Pearl Pearl/Hard Travelin'	1963	3.00	6.00	12.00
❏ 42755 [PS]	Pearl Pearl Pearl/Hard Travelin'	1963	3.75	7.50	15.00
❏ 42840	New York Town/Mama Don't Allow It	1963	3.00	6.00	12.00
❏ 42954	You Are My Flower/My Saro Jane	1964	2.50	5.00	10.00
❏ 42982	Petticoat Junction/Have You Seen My Dear Companion	1964	3.75	7.50	15.00
❏ 43080	Workin' It Out/Fireball	1964	2.50	5.00	10.00
❏ 43135	Sally Don't You Grieve/Little Birdie	1964	2.50	5.00	10.00
❏ 43204	I Still Miss Someone/Father's Table Grace	1964	2.50	5.00	10.00
❏ 43259	Rock Salt and Nails/Gonna Have Myself a Ball	1965	2.50	5.00	10.00
❏ 43412	Memphis/Foggy Mountain Breakdown	1965	2.50	5.00	10.00
❏ 43497	Green Acres/I Had a Dream	1965	3.75	7.50	15.00
—With June Carter					
❏ 43627	For Lovin' Me/Colours	1966	2.50	5.00	10.00
❏ 43803	The Last Thing on My Mind/Mama You Been on My Mind	1966	2.50	5.00	10.00
❏ 43973	It Was Only the Wind/Why Can't I Find Myself with You	1967	2.50	5.00	10.00
❏ 44040	Nashville Cats/Roust-A-Bout	1967	2.50	5.00	10.00
❏ 44194	California Up Tight Band/Last Train to Clarksville	1967	2.50	5.00	10.00
❏ 44194 [PS]	California Up Tight Band/Last Train to Clarksville	1967	3.75	7.50	15.00
❏ 44380	Foggy Mountain Breakdown/Down in the Flood	1967	3.00	6.00	12.00
❏ 44380 [PS]	Foggy Mountain Breakdown/Down in the Flood	1967	3.00	6.00	12.00
❏ 44623	Like a Rolling Stone/I'd Like to Say a Word About Texas	1968	2.50	5.00	10.00
❏ 44731	I'll Be Your Baby Tonight/Universal Soldier	1969	2.50	5.00	10.00
❏ 45030	Maggie's Farm/Tonight We'll Be Fine	1969	2.50	5.00	10.00
MERCURY					
❏ 6161	God Loves His Children/I'm Going to Make Heaven My Home	1950	7.50	15.00	30.00
—Note: Earlier Mercury 45s by Flatt and Scruggs may exist					
❏ 6211	Down the Road/Why Don't You Tell Me So	1950	7.50	15.00	30.00
❏ 6268	Is It Too Late Now/So Happy I'll Be	1950	7.50	15.00	30.00
❏ 6287	I'll Never Love Another/My Little Girl in Tennessee	1950	7.50	15.00	30.00
❏ 6302	That Little Old Country Church House/Cora Is Gone	1951	6.25	12.50	25.00
❏ 6317	Pain in My Heart/Take Me in a Lifeboat	1951	6.25	12.50	25.00
❏ 6333	Doin' My Time/Farewell Blues	1951	6.25	12.50	25.00
❏ 6372	Roll in My Sweet Baby's Arms/I'll Just Pretend	1952	6.25	12.50	25.00
❏ 6396	Pike County Breakdown/Old Salty Dog Blues	1952	6.25	12.50	25.00
❏ 70016	Preachin', Prayin', Singin'/Will Roses Bloom	1952	5.00	10.00	20.00
❏ 70064	God Loves His Children/Back to the Cross	1953	5.00	10.00	20.00
❏ 72739	Theme from Bonnie & Clyde (Foggy Mountain Breakdown)/My Cabin in Caroline	1967	2.50	5.00	10.00
❏ 72739 [PS]	Theme from Bonnie & Clyde (Foggy Mountain Breakdown)/My Cabin in Caroline	1967	3.75	7.50	15.00

Number	Title (A Side/B Side)	Yr	VG	VG+	NM
7-Inch Extended Plays					
COLUMBIA					
❏ B-2823	Jimmy Brown, The Newsboy/Mother Prays Loud in Her Sleep//I'll Go Stepping Too/Randy Lynn Rag	195?	6.25	12.50	25.00
❏ B-2823 [PS]	(title unknown)	195?	6.25	12.50	25.00
Albums					
COLUMBIA					
❏ GP 30 [(2)]	20 All-Time Great Recordings	1970	5.00	10.00	20.00
❏ CL 1019 [M]	Foggy Mountain Jamboree	1957	12.50	25.00	50.00
❏ CL 1424 [M]	Songs of Glory	1960	5.00	10.00	20.00
❏ CL 1564 [M]	Foggy Mountain Banjo	1961	5.00	10.00	20.00
❏ CL 1664 [M]	Songs of the Famous Carter Family	1961	5.00	10.00	20.00
❏ CL 1830 [M]	Folk Songs of Our Land	1962	5.00	10.00	20.00
❏ CL 1951 [M]	Hard Travelin' Featuring The Ballad of Jed Clampett	1963	5.00	10.00	20.00
❏ CL 2045 [M]	Flatt and Scruggs at Carnegie Hall	1963	5.00	10.00	20.00
❏ CL 2134 [M]	Recorded Live at Vanderbilt University	1964	5.00	10.00	20.00
❏ CL 2255 [M]	The Fabulous Sound of Flatt & Scruggs	1964	5.00	10.00	20.00
❏ CL 2354 [M]	Pickin' Strummin' and Singin'	1965	3.75	7.50	15.00
❏ CL 2443 [M]	Town and Country	1966	3.75	7.50	15.00
❏ CL 2513 [M]	When the Saints Go Marching In	1966	3.75	7.50	15.00
❏ CL 2570 [M]	Flatt and Scruggs' Greatest Hits	1966	3.75	7.50	15.00
❏ CL 2643 [M]	Strictly Instrumental	1967	5.00	10.00	20.00
❏ CL 2686 [M]	Hear the Whistle Blow	1967	5.00	10.00	20.00
❏ CL 2796 [M]	Changin' Times Featuring Foggy Mountain Breakdown	1968	10.00	20.00	40.00
❏ CS 8221 [S]	Songs of Glory	1960	6.25	12.50	25.00
❏ CS 8364 [S]	Foggy Mountain Banjo	1961	6.25	12.50	25.00
❏ CS 8464 [S]	Songs of the Famous Carter Family	1961	6.25	12.50	25.00
❏ CS 8630 [S]	Folk Songs of Our Land	1962	6.25	12.50	25.00
❏ CS 8751 [S]	Hard Travelin' Featuring The Ballad of Jed Clampett	1963	6.25	12.50	25.00
❏ CS 8845 [S]	Flatt and Scruggs at Carnegie Hall	1963	6.25	12.50	25.00
❏ PC 8845	Flatt and Scruggs at Carnegie Hall	198?	2.00	4.00	8.00
—Budget-line reissue					
❏ CS 8934 [S]	Recorded Live at Vanderbilt University	1964	6.25	12.50	25.00
❏ CS 9055 [S]	The Fabulous Sound of Flatt & Scruggs	1964	6.25	12.50	25.00
❏ CS 9154 [S]	Pickin' Strummin' and Singin'	1965	5.00	10.00	20.00
❏ CS 9243 [S]	Town and Country	1966	5.00	10.00	20.00
❏ CS 9313 [S]	When the Saints Go Marching In	1966	5.00	10.00	20.00
❏ CS 9370 [S]	Flatt and Scruggs' Greatest Hits	1966	5.00	10.00	20.00
❏ PC 9370	Flatt and Scruggs' Greatest Hits	198?	2.00	4.00	8.00
—Budget-line reissue					
❏ CS 9443 [S]	Strictly Instrumental	1967	5.00	10.00	20.00
❏ CS 9486 [S]	Hear the Whistle Blow	1967	5.00	10.00	20.00
❏ CS 9596 [S]	Changin' Times Featuring Foggy Mountain Breakdown	1968	5.00	10.00	20.00
—Red "360 Sound" label					
❏ CS 9596	Changin' Times Featuring Foggy Mountain Breakdown	1970	3.00	6.00	12.00
—Orange label with six "Columbia"s along edge					
❏ CS 9649	The Story of Bonnie & Clyde	1968	5.00	10.00	20.00
❏ CS 9741	Nashville Airplane	1969	5.00	10.00	20.00
❏ CS 9945	Final Fling	1970	3.75	7.50	15.00
❏ C 30347	Breaking Out	1971	3.00	6.00	12.00
❏ CG 31964 [(2)]	The World of Flatt and Scruggs	1972	3.75	7.50	15.00
❏ C 32244	A Boy Named Sue	1973	3.00	6.00	12.00
❏ FC 37469	Lester Flatt & Earl Scruggs	1981	2.50	5.00	10.00
COLUMBIA LIMITED EDITION					
❏ LE 10149	Breaking Out	197?	2.50	5.00	10.00
COLUMBIA MUSICAL TREASURY					
❏ DS 493	Detroit City	1969	3.75	7.50	15.00
COUNTY					
❏ CCS-111	You Can Feel It in Your Soul	1988	2.50	5.00	10.00
EVEREST ARCHIVE OF FOLK & JAZZ					
❏ 259	Lester Flatt & Earl Scruggs	197?	2.50	5.00	10.00
HARMONY					
❏ HL 7250 [M]	Lester Flatt & Earl Scruggs	1960	3.75	7.50	15.00
❏ HL 7340 [M]	Great Original Recordings	1965	3.75	7.50	15.00
❏ HL 7402 [M]	Sacred Songs	1967	3.75	7.50	15.00
❏ HL 7465 [M]	Songs to Cherish	1968	3.75	7.50	15.00
❏ HS 11202 [S]	Sacred Songs	1967	3.00	6.00	12.00
❏ HS 11265 [S]	Songs to Cherish	1968	3.00	6.00	12.00
❏ HS 11401	Foggy Mountain Chimes	1970	3.00	6.00	12.00
❏ H 30932	Wabash Cannonball	197?	2.50	5.00	10.00
MERCURY					
❏ MG-20358 [M]	Country Music	1958	10.00	20.00	40.00
❏ MG-20542 [M]	Lester Flatt & Earl Scruggs	1959	10.00	20.00	40.00
❏ MG-20773 [M]	The Original Sound of Flatt & Scruggs	1963	6.25	12.50	25.00
❏ SR-60773 [R]	The Original Sound of Flatt & Scruggs	1963	3.75	7.50	15.00
❏ SR-61162	Original Theme from Bonnie & Clyde	1968	5.00	10.00	20.00
NASHVILLE					
❏ 2087	The Best of Flatt and Scruggs	1970	3.00	6.00	12.00
PICKWICK					
❏ 6093	Foggy Mountain Breakdown	197?	3.00	6.00	12.00
❏ 6140	Blue Grass Banjos	197?	2.50	5.00	10.00
POWER PAK					
❏ 297	Golden Hits	197?	2.50	5.00	10.00
ROUNDER					
❏ SS-05	The Golden Era	198?	2.50	5.00	10.00
❏ SS-08	Don't Get Above Your Raisin'	198?	2.50	5.00	10.00
❏ SS-18	The Mercury Sessions, Volume 1	1985	2.50	5.00	10.00
❏ SS-19	The Mercury Sessions, Volume 2	1985	2.50	5.00	10.00
STARDAY					
❏ SLP-365 [M]	Stars of the Grand Ol' Opry	1966	6.25	12.50	25.00
—With Jim and Jesse					
WING					
❏ SRW-16376	The Original Foggy Mountain Breakdown	1968	3.00	6.00	12.00

FLAVOR May be two different groups.
45s
BUNKY

Number	Title (A Side/B Side)	Yr	VG	VG+	NM
❏ 711	Don't Freeze Up/(Instrumental)	1976	2.50	5.00	10.00
COLUMBIA					
❏ 4-44521	Sally Had a Party/Shop Around	1968	2.00	4.00	8.00
❏ 4-44673	Heart Teaser/Yeah, I'm Hip	1968	2.00	4.00	8.00
❏ 4-44881	Comin' On Home/Dancing in the Streets	1969	3.00	6.00	12.00

F

Number	Title (A Side/B Side)	Yr	VG	VG+	NM

JU-PAR
| ❑ 8001 | Don't Freeze Up/(Instrumental) | 1976 | 2.00 | 4.00 | 8.00 |

Albums
JU-PAR
| ❑ JP6-1002S1 | In Good Taste | 1976 | 5.00 | 10.00 | 20.00 |

FLEAS, THE All-star studio group supposedly with DAVE BURGESS, GLEN CAMPBELL, JERRY FULLER and RICK NELSON!
45s
CHALLENGE
| ❑ 9115 | Scratchin'/Tears | 1961 | 10.00 | 20.00 | 40.00 |

FLEETWOOD MAC Also see BUCKINGHAM NICKS; PETER GREEN; CHRISTINE McVIE; JEREMY SPENCER.
12-Inch Singles
REPRISE
| ❑ 44540 | Landslide (Remix) (String Mix) (Analog Mix) (Live LP Version) | 1998 | 2.50 | 5.00 | 10.00 |

WARNER BROS.
❑ PRO-A-652 [DJ]	Go Your Own Way/Silver Springs	1977	3.75	7.50	15.00
❑ PRO-A-831 [DJ]	Tusk/Never Make Me Cry	1979	3.00	6.00	12.00
❑ PRO-A-845 [DJ]	Sara (Edit) (same on both sides)	1979	2.50	5.00	10.00
❑ PRO-A-853 [DJ]	Think About Me (Remix)/Save Me a Place	1980	5.00	10.00	20.00
❑ PRO-A-932 [DJ]	Fireflies (Remix Long Version 4:05)(Remix Edit 3:22)	1981	3.75	7.50	15.00
❑ PRO-A-1040 [DJ]	Hold Me (same on both sides)	1982	2.50	5.00	10.00
❑ PRO-A-2688 [DJ]	Big Love (same on both sides)	1987	2.00	4.00	8.00
❑ PRO-A-2723 [DJ]	Big Love (Extended Remix)/(Remix Edit)	1987	2.50	5.00	10.00
❑ PRO-A-2728 [DJ]	Tango in the Night (same on both sides)	1987	2.50	5.00	10.00
❑ PRO-A-2773 [DJ]	Isn't It Midnight (same on both sides)	1987	2.50	5.00	10.00
❑ PRO-A-2884 [DJ]	Everywhere (same on both sides)	1987	2.00	4.00	8.00
❑ 20683	Big Love (Extended Remix)/(House on the Hill Dub)//(Piano Dub)/You and I, Part I	1987	2.50	5.00	10.00
—Record is labeled "You and I, Part I" but actually plays the LP version of "You and I, Part II"					
❑ 20746	Seven Wonders (Extended Version)//(Dub)/Book of Miracles	1987	2.50	5.00	10.00
❑ 20761	Little Lies (Extended Version)//(Dub)/Ricky	1987	2.50	5.00	10.00
❑ 20842	Family Man (Extended Vocal Remix)/(I'm a Jazz Man Dub)//(Extended Guitar Remix)/Family Party (Bonus Beats)/Down Endless Street	1988	2.50	5.00	10.00

45s
BLUE HORIZON
| ❑ 304 | Hungry Country Woman/Walkin' | 1970 | 3.00 | 6.00 | 12.00 |
| —A-side by Otis Spann with Fleetwood Mac; B-side by Otis Spann | | | | | |

DJM
| ❑ 1007 | Man of the World/Best Girl in the World | 1976 | 2.50 | 5.00 | 10.00 |
| —B-side by Danny Kirwan | | | | | |

EPIC
❑ 5-10351	Black Magic Woman/Long Grey Mare	1968	3.75	7.50	15.00
❑ 5-10368	Stop Messin' Around/Need Your Love So Bad	1968	3.00	6.00	12.00
❑ 5-10436	Albatross/Jigsaw Puzzle Blues	1969	3.00	6.00	12.00
❑ 5-11029	Albatross/Black Magic Woman	1973	2.00	4.00	8.00

REPRISE
❑ GRE 0108	Oh Well, Part 1/The Green Manalishi (With the Two-Prong Crown)	1972	—	2.50	5.00
—"Back to Back Hits" reissue					
❑ GRE 0119	Rhiannon (Will You Ever Win)/Over My Head	1978	—	—	3.00
—"Back to Back Hits" series					
❑ 0860	Rattlesnake Shake/Coming Your Way	1969	6.25	12.50	25.00
❑ 0860 [DJ]	Rattlesnake Shake/Coming Your Way	1969	2.50	5.00	10.00
❑ 0883	Oh Well, Part 1/Part 2	1970	5.00	10.00	20.00
❑ 0883 [DJ]	Oh Well, Part 1/Part 2	1970	2.50	5.00	10.00
❑ 0925	The Green Manalishi (With the Two-Prong Crown)/World In Harmony	1970	5.00	10.00	20.00
❑ 0925 [DJ]	The Green Manalishi (With the Two-Prong Crown)/World In Harmony	1970	2.50	5.00	10.00
❑ 0984	Jewel-Eyed Judy/Station Man	1971	3.75	7.50	15.00
❑ 0984 [DJ]	Jewel-Eyed Judy/Station Man	1971	2.50	5.00	10.00
❑ 1057	Sands of Time/Lay It All Down	1971	2.50	5.00	10.00
❑ 1077	Oh Well, Part 1/The Green Manalishi (With the Two-Prong Crown)	1971	2.00	4.00	8.00
—"Back to Back Hits" reissue					
❑ 1093	Sentimental Lady/Sunny Side of Heaven	1972	5.00	10.00	20.00
❑ 1093 [DJ]	Sentimental Lady/Sunny Side of Heaven	1972	3.00	6.00	12.00
❑ 1159	Remember Me/Dissatisfied	1973	2.50	5.00	10.00
❑ 1172	Did You Ever Love Me/Revelation	1973	3.00	6.00	12.00
❑ 1172 [DJ]	Did You Ever Love Me (stereo/mono)	1973	2.00	4.00	8.00
❑ 1188	For Your Love/Hypnotized	1973	3.75	7.50	15.00
❑ 1188 [DJ]	For Your Love (stereo/mono)	1973	2.50	5.00	10.00
❑ 1317	Heroes Are Hard to Find/Born Enchanter	1974	2.00	4.00	8.00
❑ 1339	Over My Head/I'm So Afraid	1975	—	2.50	5.00
❑ 1345	Rhiannon (Will You Ever Win)/Sugar Daddy	1976	—	2.50	5.00
❑ 1356	Say You Love Me (Edited)/Monday Morning	1976	—	2.50	5.00
—The A-sides of Reprise 1339, 1345 and 1356 feature significantly different mixes than those on their parent album, "Fleetwood Mac."					
❑ 17300	Silver Springs/Go Your Own Way	1997	—	2.00	4.00
❑ 17300 [PS]	Silver Springs/Go Your Own Way	1997	—	2.00	4.00

WARNER BROS.
❑ GWB 0348	Go Your Own Way/Dreams	1979	—	—	3.00
—"Back to Back Hits" series					
❑ GWB 0388	Tusk/Sara	1981	—	—	3.00
—"Back to Back Hits" series					
❑ GWB 0439	Hold Me/Gypsy	1984	—	—	3.00
—"Back to Back Hits" series					
❑ 8304	Go Your Own Way/Silver Springs	1976	2.00	4.00	8.00
—Sought-after because of its non-LP B-side					
❑ 8371	Dreams/Songbird	1977	—	2.00	4.00
❑ 8413	Don't Stop/Never Going Back Again	1977	—	2.00	4.00
❑ 8413 [PS]	Don't Stop/Never Going Back Again	1977	—	2.50	5.00
❑ 8483	You Make Loving You/Gold Dust Woman	1977	—	2.00	4.00
❑ 18661	Paper Doll/The Chain	1993	—	2.00	4.00
❑ 19866	Save Me/Another Woman	1990	—	2.00	4.00
❑ 19867	Skies the Limit/The Second Time	1990	—	2.00	4.00
❑ 21888	Little Lies/Everywhere	1989	—	—	3.00
—"Back to Back Hits" series					
❑ 21943	Big Love/Seven Wonders	1988	—	—	3.00
—"Back to Back Hits" series					
❑ 21990	Don't Stop/Silver Springs	1988	—	—	3.00
—"Back to Back Hits" series					
❑ 21991	You Make Loving Fun/Say You Love Me	1988	—	—	3.00
—"Back to Back Hits" series					
❑ 27644	As Long As You Follow/Oh Well (Live)	1988	—	—	3.00
❑ 27644 [PS]	As Long As You Follow/Oh Well (Live)	1988	—	—	3.00
❑ 28114	Family Man/Down Endless Street	1988	—	—	3.00
❑ 28114 [PS]	Family Man/Down Endless Street	1988	—	—	3.00
❑ 28143	Everywhere/When I See You Again	1987	—	—	3.00
❑ 28143 [PS]	Everywhere/When I See You Again	1987	—	—	3.00
❑ 28291	Little Lies/Ricky	1987	—	—	3.00
❑ 28291 [PS]	Little Lies/Ricky	1987	—	—	3.00
❑ 28317	Seven Wonders/Book of Miracles	1987	—	—	3.00
❑ 28317 [PS]	Seven Wonders/Book of Miracles	1987	—	—	3.00
❑ 28398	Big Love/You and I, Part 1	1987	—	—	3.00
❑ 28398 [PS]	Big Love/You and I, Part 1	1987	—	—	3.00
❑ 29698	Oh Diane/That's Alright	1983	—	—	3.00
❑ 29848	Love in Store/Can't Go Back	1983	—	—	3.00
❑ 29918	Gypsy/Cool Water	1982	—	—	3.00
❑ 29918 [PS]	Gypsy/Cool Water	1982	—	—	3.00
❑ 29966	Hold Me/Eyes of the World	1982	—	—	3.00
❑ 29966 [PS]	Hold Me/Eyes of the World	1982	—	—	3.00
❑ 49077	Tusk/Never Make Me Cry	1979	—	2.00	4.00
❑ 49077 [PS]	Tusk/Never Make Me Cry	1979	—	2.00	4.00
—Version 2: Black print, large dog photo					
❑ 49077 [PS]	Tusk/Never Make Me Cry	1979	—	2.50	5.00
—Version 1: Brown print, small dog photo					
❑ 49150	Sara/That's Enough for Me	1979	—	2.00	4.00
❑ 49150 [PS]	Sara/That's Enough for Me	1979	—	3.00	6.00
❑ 49196	Think About Me/Save Me a Place	1980	—	2.00	4.00
❑ 49196 [PS]	Think About Me/Save Me a Place	1980	—	3.00	6.00
❑ 49500	Sisters of the Moon/Walk a Thin Line	1980	2.50	5.00	10.00
—Scarce on stock copy; A-side is a different mix than the LP version					
❑ 49660	Fireflies/Over My Head (Live)	1981	—	2.00	4.00
❑ 49660 [PS]	Fireflies/Over My Head (Live)	1981	—	2.00	4.00
❑ 49700	The Farmer's Daughter/Monday Morning (Live)	1982	—	3.00	6.00
❑ 49700 [PS]	The Farmer's Daughter/Monday Morning (Live)	1982	—	3.00	6.00

Albums
BLUE HORIZON
❑ BH-3801 [(2)]	Fleetwood Mac in Chicago	1970	7.50	15.00	30.00
❑ BH-4802	Blues Jam in Chicago, Vol. 1	1970	3.75	7.50	15.00
❑ BH-4803	Blues Jam in Chicago, Vol. 2	1970	3.75	7.50	15.00

EPIC
❑ LN 24402 [M]	Fleetwood Mac	1968	25.00	50.00	100.00
—White label promo only					
❑ LN 24446 [M]	English Rose	1969	25.00	50.00	100.00
—White label promo only					
❑ BN 26402 [S]	Fleetwood Mac	1968	7.50	15.00	30.00
❑ BN 26446 [S]	English Rose	1969	7.50	15.00	30.00
❑ KE 30632 [(2)]	Black Magic Woman	1971	5.00	10.00	20.00
❑ KE 33740 [(2)]	Fleetwood Mac/English Rose	1974	3.75	7.50	15.00

MOBILE FIDELITY
❑ 1-012	Fleetwood Mac	1980	10.00	20.00	40.00
—Audiophile vinyl					
❑ 1-119	Mirage	1984	10.00	20.00	40.00
—Audiophile vinyl					

NAUTILUS
| ❑ NR-8 | Rumours | 1980 | 10.00 | 20.00 | 40.00 |
| —Audiophile vinyl | | | | | |

REPRISE
❑ MS 2080	Bare Trees	197?	3.75	7.50	15.00
—Without brown line on front cover; uncommon with the MS 2080 number					
❑ MS 2080	Bare Trees	1972	3.00	6.00	12.00
—With brown line near all four edges of the front cover					
❑ MS 2138	Penguin	1973	3.75	7.50	15.00
❑ MS 2158	Mystery to Me	1973	3.00	6.00	12.00
—With "For Your Love" listed correctly on the back cover					
❑ MS 2158	Mystery to Me	1973	5.00	10.00	20.00
—With "Good Things (Come to Those Who Wait)" listed on the album cover; it was replaced at the last minute by "For Your Love"					
❑ MS 2196	Heroes Are Hard to Find	1974	3.00	6.00	12.00
❑ MS 2225	Fleetwood Mac	1975	2.50	5.00	10.00
❑ MSK 2278	Bare Trees	1977	2.00	4.00	8.00
—Reissue; no brown line on the front cover					
❑ MSK 2279	Mystery to Me	1977	2.00	4.00	8.00
❑ MSK 2281	Fleetwood Mac	1977	2.00	4.00	8.00
❑ RS 6368	Then Play On	1969	6.25	12.50	25.00
—First pressings include "When You Say" and "My Dream"					
❑ RS 6368	Then Play On	1970	3.75	7.50	15.00
—Later pressings replace above two tracks with "Oh Well (Parts 1 and 2)."					
❑ RS 6408	Kiln House	1970	3.75	7.50	15.00
❑ RS 6465	Future Games	1971	6.25	12.50	25.00
—Originals have a pale yellow cover					
❑ RS 6465	Future Games	1972	3.75	7.50	15.00
—Later pressings have a pale green cover					

SIRE
❑ SASH-3706 [(2)]	Vintage Years	1975	3.75	7.50	15.00
❑ SASH-3715 [(2)]	Fleetwood Mac in Chicago	1975	3.75	7.50	15.00
—Reissue of Blue Horizon 3801					
❑ 2XS-6006 [(2)]	Vintage Years	1977	3.00	6.00	12.00
❑ 2XS-6009 [(2)]	Fleetwood Mac in Chicago	1977	3.00	6.00	12.00
❑ 2XS-6045 [(2)]	The Original Fleetwood Mac	1977	3.00	6.00	12.00

VARRICK
| ❑ VR-020 | Jumping at Shadows | 1985 | 3.00 | 6.00 | 12.00 |

WARNER BROS.
❑ PRO-A-866 [DJ]	Tusk Remix	1979	5.00	10.00	20.00
—Promo-only EP					
❑ BSK 3010	Rumours	1977	2.00	4.00	8.00
—With long version (2:16) of "Never Going Back Again"; we do not yet know how to identify these without playing them					
❑ BSK 3010	Rumours	1977	2.50	5.00	10.00
—With short version (2:02) of "Never Going Back Again"; we do not yet know how to identify these without playing them					
❑ BSK3010	Rumours	1979	—	3.00	6.00
—White label reissue					
❑ 2HS 3350 [(2)]	Tusk	1979	3.75	7.50	15.00

Fabian, *Hold That Tiger!,* Chancellor CHL-5003, mono LP, pink label, $50-$100.

The Falcons, *The Falcons,* United Artists UAS 10,010, 7-inch EP, $300-$600 (cover and record together).

The Fifth Dimension, "Go Where You Wanna Go," Soul City 753, picture sleeve, $10-$20.

Eddie Fisher, *Christmas with Eddie Fisher,* RCA Victor LPM-3065, 10-inch LP, $25-$50.

The Five Satins, "In the Still of the Nite," Standord 200, 45 rpm record, $600-$900.

Fleetwood Mac, "Sara," Warner Bros. WBS 49150, picture sleeve, $3-$6.

FLEETWOODS, THE

Number	Title (A Side/B Side)	Yr	VG	VG+	NM
❏ 2WB 3500 [(2)]	Fleetwood Mac Live	1980	3.00	6.00	12.00
❏ 23607	Mirage	1982	2.50	5.00	10.00
❏ 23607 [DJ]	Mirage	1982	5.00	10.00	20.00
—Promo on Quiex II vinyl					
❏ 25471	Tango in the Night	1987	2.50	5.00	10.00
❏ 25801	Greatest Hits	1989	2.50	5.00	10.00
❏ 26111	Behind the Mask	1990	3.75	7.50	15.00

FLEETWOODS, THE
45s
DOLPHIN

Number	Title (A Side/B Side)	Yr	VG	VG+	NM
❏ 1	Come Softly to Me/I Care So Much	1959	6.25	12.50	25.00
DOLTON					
❏ 3	Graduation's Here/Oh Lord, Let It Be	1959	5.00	10.00	20.00
❏ S-3 [S]	Graduation's Here/Oh Lord, Let It Be	1959	12.50	25.00	50.00
❏ 5	Mr. Blue/You Mean Everything to Me	1959	5.00	10.00	20.00
❏ 15	Outside My Window/Magic Star	1960	5.00	10.00	20.00
❏ 22	Runaround/Truly Do	1960	5.00	10.00	20.00
❏ 22 [PS]	Runaround/Truly Do	1960	12.50	25.00	50.00
❏ 27	The Last One to Know/Dormilona	1960	3.75	7.50	15.00
❏ 30	Confidential/I Love You So	1960	3.75	7.50	15.00
❏ 40	Tragedy/Little Miss Sad One	1961	3.75	7.50	15.00
❏ 45	(He's) The Great Impostor/Poor Little Girl	1961	3.75	7.50	15.00
❏ 49	Billy Old Buddy/Trouble	1962	3.75	7.50	15.00
❏ 62	They Tell Me It's Summer/Lovers by Night, Strangers by Day	1962	3.75	7.50	15.00
❏ 74	You Should Have Been There/Sure Is Lonesome Downtown	1963	3.75	7.50	15.00
❏ 75	Goodnight My Love/Jimmy Beware	1963	3.75	7.50	15.00
❏ 86	Baby Bye-O/What'll I Do	1963	2.50	5.00	10.00
❏ 93	Lonesome Town/Ruby Red Baby Blue	1964	2.50	5.00	10.00
❏ 97	Ten Times Blue/Ska Light Ska Bright	1964	2.50	5.00	10.00
❏ 98	Mr. Sandman/This Is My Prayer	1964	2.50	5.00	10.00
❏ 302	Before and After (Losing You)/Lonely Is As Lonely Does	1964	2.50	5.00	10.00
❏ 307	Come Softly to Me/I'm Not Jimmy	1965	2.50	5.00	10.00
❏ 310	Rainbow/Just As I Need You	1965	2.50	5.00	10.00
❏ 315	For Lovin' Me/This Is Where I See Her	1965	2.50	5.00	10.00
LIBERTY					
❏ 62	They Tell Me It's Summer/Lovers by Night, Strangers by Day	1970	3.75	7.50	15.00
—Odd reissue keeping the Dolton number					
❏ 55188 [M]	Come Softly to Me/I Care So Much	1959	6.25	12.50	25.00
❏ 77188 [S]	Come Softly to Me/I Care So Much	1959	12.50	25.00	50.00
UNITED ARTISTS					
❏ 0038	Come Softly to Me/Runaround	1973	—	2.00	4.00
❏ 0039	Mr. Blue/Tragedy	1973	—	2.00	4.00
❏ 0040	He's the Great Impostor/Goodnight My Love	1973	—	2.00	4.00
—0038, 0039 and 0040 are "Silver Spotlight Series" reissues					
❏ XW515	(He's) The Great Impostor/Goodnight My Love	1974	—	2.00	4.00
—Reissue					

7-Inch Extended Plays
DOLTON

Number	Title (A Side/B Side)	Yr	VG	VG+	NM
❏ BEP-502	Runaround/Mr. Blue//Outside My Window/Come Softly to Me	1960	15.00	30.00	60.00
❏ BEP-502 [PS]	The Fleetwoods	1960	22.50	45.00	90.00

Albums
DOLTON

Number	Title (A Side/B Side)	Yr	VG	VG+	NM
❏ BLP-2001 [M]	Mr. Blue	1959	20.00	40.00	80.00
—Pale blue label with dolphins on top					
❏ BLP-2001 [M]	Mr. Blue	1963	5.00	10.00	20.00
—Dark label, logo on left					
❏ BLP-2002 [M]	The Fleetwoods	1960	12.50	25.00	50.00
—Pale blue label with dolphins on top					
❏ BLP-2002 [M]	The Fleetwoods	1963	5.00	10.00	20.00
—Dark label, logo on left					
❏ BLP-2005 [M]	Softly	1961	12.50	25.00	50.00
—Pale blue label with dolphins on top					
❏ BLP-2005 [M]	Softly	1963	5.00	10.00	20.00
—Dark label, logo on left					
❏ BLP-2007 [M]	Deep in a Dream	1961	10.00	20.00	40.00
—Pale blue label with dolphins on top					
❏ BLP-2007 [M]	Deep in a Dream	1963	5.00	10.00	20.00
—Dark label, logo on left					
❏ BLP-2011 [M]	The Best of the Oldies	1962	10.00	20.00	40.00
—Pale blue label with dolphins on top					
❏ BLP-2011 [M]	The Best of the Oldies	1963	5.00	10.00	20.00
—Dark label, logo on left					
❏ BLP-2018 [M]	The Fleetwoods' Greatest Hits	1962	6.25	12.50	25.00
❏ BLP-2020 [M]	The Fleetwoods Sings for Lovers by Night	1963	7.50	15.00	30.00
❏ BLP-2025 [M]	Goodnight My Love	1963	7.50	15.00	30.00
❏ BLP-2030 [M]	Before and After	1965	7.50	15.00	30.00
❏ BLP-2039 [M]	Folk Rock	1965	7.50	15.00	30.00
❏ BST-8001 [S]	Mr. Blue	1959	25.00	50.00	100.00
—Pale blue label with dolphins on top					
❏ BST-8001 [S]	Mr. Blue	1963	6.25	12.50	25.00
—Dark label, logo on left					
❏ BST-8002 [S]	The Fleetwoods	1960	17.50	35.00	70.00
—Pale blue label with dolphins on top					
❏ BST-8002 [S]	The Fleetwoods	1963	6.25	12.50	25.00
—Dark label, logo on left					
❏ BST-8005 [S]	Softly	1961	17.50	35.00	70.00
—Pale blue label with dolphins on top					
❏ BST-8005 [S]	Softly	1963	6.25	12.50	25.00
—Dark label, logo on left					
❏ BST-8007 [S]	Deep in a Dream	1961	12.50	25.00	50.00
—Pale blue label with dolphins on top					
❏ BST-8007 [S]	Deep in a Dream	1963	6.25	12.50	25.00
—Dark label, logo on left					
❏ BST-8011 [S]	The Best of the Oldies	1962	12.50	25.00	50.00
—Pale blue label with dolphins on top					
❏ BST-8011 [S]	The Best of the Oldies	1963	6.25	12.50	25.00
—Dark label, logo on left					
❏ BST-8018 [S]	The Fleetwoods' Greatest Hits	1962	7.50	15.00	30.00
❏ BST-8020 [S]	The Fleetwoods Sings for Lovers by Night	1963	10.00	20.00	40.00
❏ BST-8025 [S]	Goodnight My Love	1963	10.00	20.00	40.00
❏ BST-8030 [S]	Before and After	1965	10.00	20.00	40.00

Number	Title (A Side/B Side)	Yr	VG	VG+	NM
❏ BST-8039 [S]	Folk Rock	1965	10.00	20.00	40.00
LIBERTY					
❏ LN-10159	The Fleetwoods' Greatest Hits	1982	2.00	4.00	8.00
❏ LN-10160	The Best Goodies of the Oldies	1982	2.00	4.00	8.00
❏ LN-10199	Buried Treasure	1983	2.00	4.00	8.00
SUNSET					
❏ SUM-1131 [M]	In a Mellow Mood	1966	3.00	6.00	12.00
❏ SUS-5131 [S]	In a Mellow Mood	1966	3.75	7.50	15.00
UNITED ARTISTS					
❏ UA-LA334-E	The Very Best of the Fleetwoods	1975	3.00	6.00	12.00

FLEMONS, WADE   Also see EARTH, WIND AND FIRE.
45s
VEE JAY

Number	Title (A Side/B Side)	Yr	VG	VG+	NM
❏ 295	Here I Stand/My Baby Likes to Rock	1958	7.50	15.00	30.00
❏ 309	Hold Me Close/You'll Remain Forever	1959	7.50	15.00	30.00
❏ 321	Slow Motion/Wailing by the River	1959	7.50	15.00	30.00
❏ 335	Goodnite, It's Time To Go/What's Happening	1959	7.50	15.00	30.00
❏ 344	Easy Lovin'/Woops Now	1960	7.50	15.00	30.00
❏ 368	Ain't That Lovin' You Baby/I'll Come Runnin'	1960	5.00	10.00	20.00
❏ 377	At the Party/Devil in Your Soul	1961	5.00	10.00	20.00
❏ 389	Please Send Me Someone to Love/Keep On Loving Me	1961	5.00	10.00	20.00
❏ 427	Half a Love/Welcome Stranger	1962	5.00	10.00	20.00
❏ 471	Ain't These Tears/I Hope, I Think, I Wish	1962	5.00	10.00	20.00
❏ 533	That Time of the Year/I Came Running	1963	3.75	7.50	15.00
❏ 578	When It Rains, It Pours/Watch Over Her	1964	3.75	7.50	15.00
—The Four Seasons sing backup on this record					
❏ 614	I Knew You When/That Other Place	1964	3.75	7.50	15.00
❏ 668	Where Did You Go Last Night/Empty Balcony	1965	3.00	6.00	12.00

Albums
VEE JAY

Number	Title (A Side/B Side)	Yr	VG	VG+	NM
❏ LP-1011 [M]	Wade Flemons	1959	37.50	75.00	150.00
—Maroon label					
❏ LP-1011 [M]	Wade Flemons	196?	20.00	40.00	80.00
—Black label					

FLESH GORDON AND THE NUDE HOLLYWOOD ARGYLES   Also see THE HOLLYWOOD ARGYLES.
45s
PARAMOUNT

Number	Title (A Side/B Side)	Yr	VG	VG+	NM
❏ 0289	Superstreaker/Naked	1974	3.00	6.00	12.00

FLETCHER, DARROW
45s
ATCO

Number	Title (A Side/B Side)	Yr	VG	VG+	NM
❏ 7083	Improve/Let's Get Together	1977	5.00	10.00	20.00
ATLANTIC					
❏ 3600	The Rising Cost of Love/Honey Can I	1979	2.50	5.00	10.00
CONGRESS					
❏ 6011	I Think I'm Gonna Write a Song/Sitting There That Night	1970	3.75	7.50	15.00
CROSSOVER					
❏ 980	It's No Mistake/Try Something New	1975	10.00	20.00	40.00
❏ 983	We've Got to Get an Understanding/This Time (I'll Be the Fool)	1976	2.50	5.00	10.00
GROOVY					
❏ 3001	The Pain Gets a Little Deeper/My Judgement Day	1965	6.25	12.50	25.00
❏ 3004	My Young Misery/I've Gotta Know Why	1966	5.00	10.00	20.00
❏ 3007	Gotta Draw the Line/I've Gotta Know Why	1966	5.00	10.00	20.00
❏ 3009	That Certain Little Something/My Judgement Day	1966	5.00	10.00	20.00
JACKLYN					
❏ 1002	What Have I Got Now/Sitting There That Night	1966	12.50	25.00	50.00
❏ 1003	Infatuation/Little Girl	1966	5.00	10.00	20.00
❏ 1006	What Good Am I Without You/Little Girl	1967	5.00	10.00	20.00
REVUE					
❏ 11008	I Like the Way I Feel/The Way of a Man	1967	3.75	7.50	15.00
❏ 11023	Gonna Keep Loving You/We Can't Go On This Way	1967	3.75	7.50	15.00
❏ 11035	Those Hanging Heartaches/Sitting There That Night	1968	5.00	10.00	20.00
UNI					
❏ 55244	Changing by the Minute/When Love Calls	1970	3.00	6.00	12.00
❏ 55270	Dolly Baby/What Is This	1971	3.00	6.00	12.00

FLETCHER, LOIS
45s
COLUMBIA

Number	Title (A Side/B Side)	Yr	VG	VG+	NM
❏ 4-43633	Winken, Blinken and Nod/Until I Get Over You	1966	2.50	5.00	10.00
PLAYBOY					
❏ 6003	Ever Lovin' Sunshine/Man Smart, Woman Smarter	1974	—	3.00	6.00
❏ 50049	I Am What I Am/One More Time	1974	—	3.00	6.00

FLETCHER, SAM
45s
CUB

Number	Title (A Side/B Side)	Yr	VG	VG+	NM
❏ 9032	No Such Luck/Time Has a Way	1959	7.50	15.00	30.00
❏ 9048	Only Heaven Knows/Beyond My Wildest Dreams	1959	7.50	15.00	30.00
METRO					
❏ 20013	Before/Torn Between Two Loves	1959	6.25	12.50	25.00
❏ 20022	Out in the Cold Again/If You Love Me	1959	6.25	12.50	25.00
RCA VICTOR					
❏ 47-7676	Take Me in Your Arms/I Just Had to Tell Someone	1960	6.25	12.50	25.00
❏ 47-7817	Tall Hope/Far Away from Home	1960	5.00	10.00	20.00
❏ 47-7872	Hold Me/You Did It	1961	3.75	7.50	15.00
❏ 47-7972	I Believe in You/Sweet Slumber	1961	3.75	7.50	15.00
❏ 47-8027	My Girl/This One Night	1962	5.00	10.00	20.00
❏ 47-8076	The Answer to Everything/Me and the One I Love	1962	5.00	10.00	20.00
TOLLIE					
❏ 9012	I'd Think It Over/Friday Night	1964	50.00	100.00	200.00

Number	Title (A Side/B Side)	Yr	VG	VG+	NM
VAULT					
❑ 502	More Today Than Yesterday/What'll I Do	197?	6.25	12.50	25.00
❑ 934	The Look of Love/You Better Come Home	1967	3.75	7.50	15.00
VEE JAY					
❑ 623	Guess Who/The Sinner	1964	3.00	6.00	12.00
WARNER BROS.					
❑ 5384	As Time Goes By/My Wish	1963	3.75	7.50	15.00

FLINT, SHELBY
45s
CADENCE

Number	Title (A Side/B Side)	Yr	VG	VG+	NM
❑ 1352	Oh, I Miss Him So/I Will Love You	1958	3.75	7.50	15.00
VALIANT					
❑ 701	Angel on My Shoulder/I Will Love You	1965	2.00	4.00	8.00
❑ 716	Joy in the Morning/Lonely Cinderella	1965	2.00	4.00	8.00
❑ 743	Cast Your Fate to the Wind/The Lily	1966	2.00	4.00	8.00
❑ 6001	Angel on My Shoulder/Someday	1960	3.00	6.00	12.00
❑ 6010	I Will Love You/Every Night	1961	2.50	5.00	10.00
❑ 6014	A Broken Vow/Magic Wand	1961	2.50	5.00	10.00
❑ 6017	The Riddle Song/I Love a Wanderer	1962	2.50	5.00	10.00
❑ 6022	The Boy I Love/Ugly Duckling	1962	2.50	5.00	10.00
❑ 6031	Little Dancing Doll/It Really Wouldn't Matter	1963	2.50	5.00	10.00
❑ 6052	Wonderland/Pipes of Keith	1964	2.50	5.00	10.00
❑ 6060	I've Grown Accustomed to Her (Your) Face/ Our Town	1964	2.50	5.00	10.00
Albums					
MAD SATYR					
❑ MSR-101	You've Been On My Mind	1982	6.25	12.50	25.00
VALIANT					
❑ LP-401 [M]	Shelby Flint — The Quiet Girl	1961	10.00	20.00	40.00
❑ LP-403 [M]	Shelby Flint Sings Folk	1962	10.00	20.00	40.00
❑ LPS-403 [S]	Shelby Flint Sings Folk	1962	12.50	25.00	50.00
❑ VL-5003 [M]	Cast Your Fate to the Wind	1966	6.25	12.50	25.00
❑ VLS-25003 [S]	Cast Your Fate to the Wind	1966	7.50	15.00	30.00

FLINTSTONE, FRED
45s
EPIC

Number	Title (A Side/B Side)	Yr	VG	VG+	NM
❑ 9475	Bedrock Beat/Stone Age Roll	1961	5.00	10.00	20.00

FLIRTATIONS, THE (1) Female vocal group.
45s
DERAM

Number	Title (A Side/B Side)	Yr	VG	VG+	NM
❑ 7531	Give Me Love, Love, Love/This Must Be the End	1970	2.00	4.00	8.00
❑ 85036	Christmas Time Is Here Again/Nothing But a Heartache	1968	2.00	4.00	8.00
❑ 85038	Nothing But a Heartache/How Can You Tell Me	1969	—	3.00	6.00
❑ 85048	Need Your Loving/South Caroline	1969	—	3.00	6.00
❑ 85057	I Wanna Be There/Keep On Searching	1970	—	3.00	6.00
❑ 85062	Can't Stop Lovin' You/ Everybody Needs Somebody	1970	—	3.00	6.00
PARROT					
❑ 40028	Somewhere Out There/How Can You Tell Me	1968	3.00	6.00	12.00
Albums					
DERAM					
❑ DES-18028	Nothing But a Heartache	1969	5.00	10.00	20.00

FLIRTATIONS, THE (2) Male vocal group.
45s
FESTIVAL

Number	Title (A Side/B Side)	Yr	VG	VG+	NM
❑ 705	Stronger Than Her Love/Settle Down	1967	15.00	30.00	60.00

FLIRTATIONS, THE (U) May be group (2), or perhaps a completely different group.
45s
JOSIE

Number	Title (A Side/B Side)	Yr	VG	VG+	NM
❑ 956	Natural Born Lover/ Change My Darkness Into Light	1965	3.75	7.50	15.00

FLO AND EDDIE Also see THE TURTLES.
45s
COLUMBIA

Number	Title (A Side/B Side)	Yr	VG	VG+	NM
❑ 10028	Come to My Rescue, Webelos/Let Me Make Love to You	1974	—	3.00	6.00
❑ 10204	Come to My Rescue, Webelos/Let Me Make Love to You	1975	—	2.50	5.00
❑ 10264	Illegal, Immoral and Fattening/Rebecca	1975	—	2.50	5.00
❑ 10425	Elenore/The Love You Gave Away	1976	—	2.50	5.00
❑ 10458	Keep It Warm/Hot	1976	—	2.50	5.00
REPRISE					
❑ 1113	Nikki Hoi/Godbye Surprise	1972	—	2.50	5.00
❑ 1142	Afterglow/Original Soundtract from "Carlos & De Bull"	1972	—	2.50	5.00
❑ 1160	If We Only Had the Time/You're a Lady	1973	—	2.50	5.00
Albums					
COLUMBIA					
❑ PC 33554	Illegal, Immoral and Fattening	1975	3.00	6.00	12.00
❑ PC 34262	Moving Targets	1976	3.00	6.00	12.00
EPIPHANY					
❑ ELP-4010	Rock Steady with Flo & Eddie	1981	2.50	5.00	10.00
REPRISE					
❑ MS 2099	The Phlorescent Leech and Eddie	1972	5.00	10.00	20.00
❑ MS 2141	Flo and Eddie	1973	5.00	10.00	20.00
RHINO					
❑ RNTA-1999 [(3)]	History of Flo & Eddie	198?	5.00	10.00	20.00

FLOATING BRIDGE, THE
45s
VAULT

Number	Title (A Side/B Side)	Yr	VG	VG+	NM
❑ 947	Watch Your Step/Brought Up Wrong	1969	2.50	5.00	10.00
❑ 953	Don't Mean a Thing/Mr. Jaybird	1969	2.50	5.00	10.00
Albums					
VAULT					
❑ VS-124	The Floating Bridge	1969	7.50	15.00	30.00

FLOCK, THE
45s
COLUMBIA

Number	Title (A Side/B Side)	Yr	VG	VG+	NM
❑ 45021	Tired of Waiting/Store Bought Store Thought	1969	2.00	4.00	8.00
❑ 45295	Mermaid/Crabfoot	1971	2.00	4.00	8.00
DESTINATION					
❑ 628	Can't You See/Hold On to My Mind	1966	2.50	5.00	10.00
❑ 631	Are You the Kind/I Like You	1966	2.50	5.00	10.00
❑ 635	Take Me Back/Each Day Is a Lonely Night	1967	2.50	5.00	10.00
U.S.A.					
❑ 910	Magical Winds/ What Would You Do If the Sun Died?	1968	2.00	4.00	8.00
Albums					
COLUMBIA					
❑ CS 9911	The Flock	1969	5.00	10.00	20.00
—"360 Sound" label					
❑ CS 9911	The Flock	1970	3.75	7.50	15.00
—Orange label					
❑ C 30007	Dinosaur Swamps	1970	3.75	7.50	15.00
—Orange label					
❑ C 30007	Dinosaur Swamps	1970	5.00	10.00	20.00
—"360 Sound" label					
MERCURY					
❑ SRM-1-1035	Inside Out	1975	3.75	7.50	15.00

FLOOD, DICK
45s
EPIC

Number	Title (A Side/B Side)	Yr	VG	VG+	NM
❑ 5-9479	Hellbound Train/Judy Lynn	1961	3.00	6.00	12.00
❑ 5-9500	King or Clown/Never Has So Much Been Lost	1962	3.00	6.00	12.00
❑ 5-9556	Another Stretch of Track/Outside Your Door (Someone Was Standing)	1962	3.00	6.00	12.00
KAPP					
❑ 640	These Things Make a Heartache/I Need All the Friends	1965	2.50	5.00	10.00
❑ 681	Between Two Worlds/ From Warm to Cool to Cold	1965	2.50	5.00	10.00
❑ 754	Don't Sweetheart Me/Trouble's Back in Town	1966	2.50	5.00	10.00
MONUMENT					
❑ 45-408	The Three Bells (The Jimmy Brown Story)/ Far Away	1959	3.75	7.50	15.00
❑ 45-414	It's My Way/It Only Costs a Dime	1960	3.75	7.50	15.00
❑ 45-427	Carita/Cowpoke	1960	3.75	7.50	15.00
NASCO					
❑ 025	Slow It Down/Speak My Name	1971	2.00	4.00	8.00
NUGGET					
❑ 1026	Home Was Never Like This/ Woman Leave Me Alone	1968	2.00	4.00	8.00
TOTEM					
❑ 7	Sure Gets Dark/(B-side unknown)	1967	2.00	4.00	8.00

FLORIDIANS, THE
45s
ABC-PARAMOUNT

Number	Title (A Side/B Side)	Yr	VG	VG+	NM
❑ 10185	That Lucky Old Sun/I Love Marie	1961	12.50	25.00	50.00

FLOW
45s
CTI

Number	Title (A Side/B Side)	Yr	VG	VG+	NM
❑ 503	Mr. Invisible/Daddy	1970	—	3.00	6.00
Albums					
CTI					
❑ 1003	Flow	1970	5.00	10.00	20.00

FLOWER SISTERS, THE
45s
HIT

Number	Title (A Side/B Side)	Yr	VG	VG+	NM
❑ 120	Chapel of Love/A World Without Love	1964	2.00	4.00	8.00
—B-side by Bobby Brooks					
❑ 136	People Say/C'Mon and Swim	1964	2.00	4.00	8.00
—B-side by Leroy Jones					

FLOWERPOT MEN, THE
45s
DERAM

Number	Title (A Side/B Side)	Yr	VG	VG+	NM
❑ 7513	Let's Go to San Francisco/Let's Go to San Francisco, Part 2	1967	3.75	7.50	15.00
—As "The Flower Pots"					
❑ 7516	Am I Losing You/A Walk in the Sky	1968	3.75	7.50	15.00
❑ 85051	A Moment of Madness/Young Birds Fly	1969	3.00	6.00	12.00

FLOWERS, THE
45s
HIT

Number	Title (A Side/B Side)	Yr	VG	VG+	NM
❑ 310	The Rain, the Park, and Other Things/It Must Be Him	1967	2.00	4.00	8.00
—B-side by Kathy Shannon					

FLOYD, EDDIE Also see THE FALCONS.
45s
ATLANTIC

Number	Title (A Side/B Side)	Yr	VG	VG+	NM
❑ 2275	Hush Hush/Drive On	1965	3.00	6.00	12.00
LUPINE					
❑ 115	Set My Soul on Fire/Will I Be the One	1963	3.75	7.50	15.00
MALACO					
❑ 1032	Somebody Touch Me/Never Too Old	1976	—	2.50	5.00
❑ 1035	Chi-Town Hustler/In Paradise	1976	—	2.50	5.00
❑ 1039	Special Christmas Day/Mother, My Dear Mother	1976	—	2.50	5.00
❑ 1040	We Should Really Be in Love/I'll Never Be Loved	1977	—	2.50	5.00
—With Dorothy Moore					
❑ 1043	You're Gonna Walk Out on Me/Prove It to Me	1977	—	2.50	5.00
MERCURY					
❑ 73964	If You Really Love Me/It's Me	1977	—	2.00	4.00
❑ 74003	Disco Summer/Do It in the Water	1978	—	2.00	4.00

F

Number	Title (A Side/B Side)	Yr	VG	VG+	NM

SAFICE
| ❏ 336 | Can This Be Christmas/ | | | | |
| | I'll Be Home For Christmas | 1964 | 3.00 | 6.00 | 12.00 |

STAX
❏ 0002	I've Never Found a Girl (To Love Me Like You				
	Do)/I'm Just the Kind of Fool	1968	—	3.00	6.00
❏ 0012	Bring It On Home to Me/				
	The Sweet Things You Do	1968	—	3.00	6.00
❏ 0025	I've Got to Have Your Love/Girl I Love You	1969	—	3.00	6.00
❏ 0036	Don't Tell Your Mama (Where You've Been)/				
	Consider Me	1969	—	3.00	6.00
❏ 0041	Never Never Let You Go/Ain't That Good	1969	—	3.00	6.00
—With Mavis Staples					
❏ 0051	Why Is the Wine Sweeter (On the Other Side)/				
	People Get It Together	1969	—	3.00	6.00
❏ 0060	California Girl/The Woodman	1970	—	3.00	6.00
❏ 0072	My Girl/Laurie	1970	—	3.00	6.00
❏ 0077	The Best Years of My Life/My Little Girl	1970	—	3.00	6.00
❏ 0087	Oh How It Rained/When My Baby Said Goodbye	1971	—	3.00	6.00
❏ 0095	Blood Is Thicker Than Water/Have You Heard				
	the Word	1971	—	3.00	6.00
❏ 0109	Yum Yum Yum (I Want Some)/Tears of Joy	1971	—	3.00	6.00
❏ 0134	You're Good Enough (To Be My Baby)/Spend				
	All You Have on Love	1972	—	3.00	6.00
❏ 0158	Knock on Wood/Lay Your Loving on Me	1973	—	3.00	6.00
❏ 0171	Baby Lay Your Head Down (Gently on My Bed)/				
	Check Me Out	1973	—	3.00	6.00
❏ 187	Things Get Better/Good Love, Bad Love	1966	3.00	6.00	12.00
❏ 0188	I Wanna Do Things for You/We've Been Through				
	Too Much Together	1973	—	3.00	6.00
❏ 194	Knock on Wood/Got to Make a Comeback	1966	3.75	7.50	15.00
❏ 208	Raise Your Hand/I've Just Been Feeling Bad	1967	2.50	5.00	10.00
❏ 0209	Guess Who/Something to Write Home About	1974	—	3.00	6.00
❏ 0216	Soul Street/Highway Man	1974	—	3.00	6.00
❏ 219	Don't Rock the Boat/This House	1967	2.50	5.00	10.00
❏ 223	Love Is a Doggone Good Thing/Hey Now	1967	2.50	5.00	10.00
❏ 0232	Stealing Love/I Got a Reason to Smile	1974	—	3.00	6.00
❏ 233	On a Saturday Night/Under My Nose	1967	2.50	5.00	10.00
❏ 0239	Talk to the Man/I Got a Reason to Smile	1975	—	3.00	6.00
❏ 246	Holding On with Both Hands/Big Bird	1968	2.50	5.00	10.00
❏ 0251	I'm So Glad I Met You/I'm So Grateful	1975	—	3.00	6.00

Albums
MALACO
| ❏ 6352 | Experience | 1977 | 3.00 | 6.00 | 12.00 |

STAX
❏ 714 [M]	Knock on Wood	1967	17.50	35.00	70.00
❏ ST 714 [S]	Knock on Wood	1967	17.50	35.00	70.00
❏ STS-2002	I've Never Found a Girl	1968	7.50	15.00	30.00
❏ STS-2011	Rare Stamps	1969	6.25	12.50	25.00
❏ STS-2017	You've Got to Have Eddie	1969	6.25	12.50	25.00
❏ STS-2029	California Girl	1970	6.25	12.50	25.00
❏ STS-2041	Down to Earth	1971	6.25	12.50	25.00
❏ STS-3016	Baby Lay Your Head Down	1973	6.25	12.50	25.00
❏ STX-4122	Chronicle	1979	3.00	6.00	12.00
❏ STS-5512	Soul Street	1974	6.25	12.50	25.00
❏ MPS-8527	Soul Street	198?	2.50	5.00	10.00

FLOYD, KING
45s
CHIMNEYVILLE
❏ 435	Groove Me/What Our Love Needs	1970	—	3.00	6.00
❏ 437	Baby Let Me Kiss You/				
	Please Don't Leave Me Lonely	1971	—	2.50	5.00
❏ 437 [PS]	Baby Let Me Kiss You/				
	Please Don't Leave Me Lonely	1971	2.00	4.00	8.00
❏ 439	Got to Have Your Lovin'/Let Us Be	1971	—	2.50	5.00
❏ 442	It's Wonderful/Let Me See You Do That Thing	1971	—	2.50	5.00
❏ 443	Woman Don't Go Astray/				
	Everybody Needs Somebody	1972	—	2.50	5.00
❏ 446	Think About It/Here It Is	1973	—	2.50	5.00
❏ 1779	So Much Confusion/So Much Confusion (Part 2)	1973	—	2.50	5.00
❏ 10202	I Feel Like Dynamite/Handle with Care	1974	—	2.50	5.00
❏ 10205	Don't Cry No More/I'm Missing You	1974	—	2.50	5.00
❏ 10206	Can't Give It Up/I'm Gonna Fall in Love with You	1975	—	2.50	5.00
❏ 10207	We Can Love/Making Love	1975	—	3.00	6.00
—With Dorothy Moore					
❏ 10209	Hey Baby/I Really Love You	1976	—	2.50	5.00
❏ 10212	Body English/I Really Love You	1976	—	2.50	5.00
❏ 10218	Stop, Look and Listen/Trouble	1977	—	2.50	5.00
❏ 10222	So True/Doing That No More	197?	—	2.50	5.00
❏ 10224	I Wanna Slow Dance Wit 'Cha/				
	Stop, Look and Listen	197?	—	2.50	5.00

DIAL
| ❏ 1027 | Can You Dig It/Learning to Forget You | 1974 | — | 3.00 | 6.00 |

ORIGINAL SOUND
| ❏ 52 | Why Did She Leave Me/Walkin' and Thinkin' | 1964 | 3.75 | 7.50 | 15.00 |

PULSAR
❏ 2401	Times Have Changed/Groov-a-Ling	1969	2.50	5.00	10.00
—With the Three Queens					
❏ 2406	Together We Can Do It/You Got the Love I Need	1969	2.50	5.00	10.00

UPTOWN
❏ 719	Love Makes the World Go Round/				
	Walkin' and Thinkin'	1965	3.00	6.00	12.00
❏ 733	Come On Home (Where You Belong)/				
	I Don't Care (No More)	1966	3.00	6.00	12.00

V.I.P.
| ❏ 25061 | Heartaches/Together We Can Do Anything | 1970 | 5.00 | 10.00 | 20.00 |

Albums
CHIMNEYVILLE
| ❏ SD 9047 | King Floyd | 1971 | 3.75 | 7.50 | 15.00 |

PULSAR
| ❏ 10602 | A Man in Love | 1969 | 5.00 | 10.00 | 20.00 |

V.I.P.
| ❏ 407 | The Heart of the Matter | 1970 | 10.00 | 20.00 | 40.00 |

Number	Title (A Side/B Side)	Yr	VG	VG+	NM

FLYERS, THE
45s
ATCO
| ❏ 6088 | On Bended Knee/My Only Desire | 1957 | 10.00 | 20.00 | 40.00 |

FLYING BURRITO BROTHERS, THE Also includes records as "Burrito Brothers." Also see GRAM PARSONS; EARL SCRUGGS.
45s
A&M
❏ 1067	Train Song/Hot Burrito #1	1969	2.00	4.00	8.00
❏ 1166	If You Gotta Go, Go Now/Cody, Cody	1970	2.00	4.00	8.00
❏ 1189	Down in the Churchyard/Older Guys	1970	2.00	4.00	8.00
❏ 1277	White Line Fever/Colorado	1971	2.00	4.00	8.00
❏ 1277 [PS]	White Line Fever/Colorado	1971	3.75	7.50	15.00

COLUMBIA
❏ 10229	Building Fires/Hot Burrito No. 3	1975	—	2.50	5.00
❏ 10287	Bon Soir Blues/Hot Burrito No. 3	1976	—	2.50	5.00
❏ 10389	Big Bayou/Waiting for Love to Begin	1976	—	2.50	5.00

CURB
❏ 01011	Does She Wish She Was Single Again/				
	Oh Lonesome Me	1981	—	2.00	4.00
—As "Burrito Brothers"					
❏ 02243	She Belongs to Everyone But Me/Why Must the				
	Ending Always Be So Sad	1981	—	2.00	4.00
—As "Burrito Brothers"					
❏ 02641	If Something Should Come Between Us/				
	Damned If I'll Be Lonely Tonight	1981	—	2.00	4.00
—As "Burrito Brothers"					
❏ 02667	If Something Should Come Between Us	1982	—	2.00	4.00
—As "Burrito Brothers"					
❏ 02835	Closer to You/Coast to Coast	1982	—	2.00	4.00
—As "Burrito Brothers"					
❏ 03023	I'm Drinkin' Canada Dry/				
	How'd We Ever Get This Way	1982	—	2.00	4.00
—As "Burrito Brothers"					
❏ 03314	Blue and Broken Hearted Me/				
	Our Roots Are Country Music	1982	—	2.00	4.00
—As "Burrito Brothers"					
❏ 5402	She's a Friend of a Friend/(B-side unknown)	1981	—	2.00	4.00
—As "Burrito Brothers"					

MCA CURB
❏ 52329	Almost Saturday Night/Juke Box Kind of Night	1983	—	—	3.00
—As "Burrito Brothers"					
❏ 52379	My Kind of Lady/Dream Chaser	1984	—	—	3.00
—As "Burrito Brothers"					

REGENCY
| ❏ 45001 | White Line Fever/(B-side unknown) | 1980 | — | 3.00 | 6.00 |

Albums
A&M
❏ SP-3122	The Gilded Palace of Sin	198?	2.00	4.00	8.00
—Budget-line reissue					
❏ SP-3631 [(2)]	Close Up the Honky-Tonks	1974	3.75	7.50	15.00
❏ SP-4175	The Gilded Palace of Sin	1969	5.00	10.00	20.00
—Brown label					
❏ SP-4175	The Gilded Palace of Sin	1974	3.00	6.00	12.00
—Silvery label					
❏ SP-4258	Burrito Deluxe	1970	3.75	7.50	15.00
—Brown label					
❏ SP-4258	Burrito Deluxe	1974	3.00	6.00	12.00
—Silvery label					
❏ SP-4295	The Flying Burrito Bros.	1971	3.75	7.50	15.00
—Brown label					
❏ SP-4295	The Flying Burrito Bros.	1974	3.00	6.00	12.00
—Silvery label					
❏ SP-4343	Last of the Red Hot Burritos	1972	3.75	7.50	15.00
—Brown label					
❏ SP-4343	Last of the Red Hot Burritos	1974	3.00	6.00	12.00
—Silvery label					
❏ SP-4578	Sleepless Nights	1976	3.00	6.00	12.00
—As "Gram Parsons/The Flying Burrito Bros."					
❏ SP-6510 [(2)]	Close Up the Honky-Tonks	198?	3.00	6.00	12.00
—Reissue of 3631					
❏ SP-8070 [DJ]	Hot Burrito	1975	10.00	20.00	40.00
—Promo-only issue with poster					

COLUMBIA
| ❏ PC 33817 | Flying Again | 1975 | 3.00 | 6.00 | 12.00 |
| ❏ PC 34222 | Airborne | 1976 | 3.00 | 6.00 | 12.00 |

CURB
❏ JZ 37004	Hearts on the Line	1981	2.50	5.00	10.00
—As "Burrito Brothers"					
❏ FZ 37705	Sunset Sundown	1982	2.50	5.00	10.00
—As "Burrito Brothers"					

REGENCY
| ❏ REG-79001 | Live from Tokyo | 1980 | 2.50 | 5.00 | 10.00 |

FLYING MACHINE, THE This is a British group, no relation to the American group that featured JAMES TAYLOR.
45s
CONGRESS
❏ 6000	Smile a Little Smile for Me/				
	Maybe We've Been Loving Too Long	1969	2.00	4.00	8.00
❏ 6012	There She Goes/Baby Make It Soon	1970	—	3.00	6.00

JANUS
❏ 121	Hanging on the Edge of Sadness/				
	My Baby's Coming Home	1970	—	3.00	6.00
❏ 137	Hey Little Girl/				
	The Devil Has Possession of My Mind	1971	—	3.00	6.00

Albums
JANUS
| ❏ JLS-3007 | The Flying Machine | 1969 | 5.00 | 10.00 | 20.00 |

FOCUS Also see JAN AKKERMAN. The "Focus" that appeared on EMI America in the mid-1980s was an R&B group from the United States and not this group.
45s
ATCO
| ❏ 7002 | Harem Scarem/Birth | 1974 | — | 3.00 | 6.00 |

Number	Title (A Side/B Side)	Yr	VG	VG+	NM
SIRE					
❑ 352	House of the King/Black Beauty	1971	2.00	4.00	8.00
❑ 704	Hocus Pocus/Hocus Pocus II	1973	—	3.00	6.00
❑ 708	Sylvia/Love Remembered	1973	—	2.50	5.00
Albums					
ATCO					
❑ SD 36-100	Hamburger Concerto	1974	3.00	6.00	12.00
❑ SD 36-117	Mother Focus	1975	3.00	6.00	12.00
HARVEST					
❑ ST-11721	Focus Con Proby	1978	3.00	6.00	12.00
—With P.J. Proby					
MERCURY					
❑ 824524-1	Focus: Jan Akkerman and Thijs Van Leer	1986	3.00	6.00	12.00
SIRE					
❑ SAS-3901 [(2)]	Focus 3	1973	3.75	7.50	15.00
❑ SAS-7401	Moving Waves	1972	3.00	6.00	12.00
❑ SAS-7404	In and Out of Focus	1973	3.00	6.00	12.00
—Reissue of 97027					
❑ SAS-7408	Live at the Rainbow	1973	3.00	6.00	12.00
❑ SASD-7505	Dutch Masters — A Selection of Their Finest Recordings 1969-1973	1975	3.00	6.00	12.00
❑ SASD-7531	Ship of Memories	1977	3.00	6.00	12.00
❑ SES-97027	In and Out of Focus	1970	5.00	10.00	20.00
—Original issue					
FOGELBERG, DAN					
12-Inch Singles					
FULL MOON/EPIC					
❑ AS 392 [DJ]	Nether Lands (Stereo) (Mono)	1977	7.50	15.00	30.00
❑ AS 703 [DJ]	Longer//Face the Fire/Phoenix	1979	6.25	12.50	25.00
❑ AS 1812 [DJ]	The Language of Love (same on both sides)	1984	—	3.50	7.00
❑ EAS 2039 [DJ]	Go Down Easy (same on both sides)	1985	—	3.00	6.00
45s					
COLUMBIA					
❑ 4-45764	Anyway I Love You/Looking for a Lady	1973	2.00	4.00	8.00
FULL MOON/EPIC					
❑ ES7 2142 [DJ]	High Country Snows (same on both sides)	1985	—	2.50	5.00
❑ 15-02155	Longer/Heart Hotels	1981	—	2.00	4.00
—Reissue					
❑ 14-02488	Hard to Say/The Innocent Age	1981	—	2.00	4.00
❑ 14-02647	Leader of the Band/Times Like These	1981	—	2.00	4.00
❑ 14-02821	Run for the Roses/The Sand and the Foam	1982	—	2.00	4.00
❑ 15-03087	Same Old Lang Syne/Hard to Say	1982	—	—	3.00
—Reissue					
❑ 34-03289	Missing You/Hearts and Crafts	1982	—	2.00	4.00
❑ ENR-03323	Missing You/(B-side blank)	1982	2.00	4.00	8.00
—One-sided budget release					
❑ 34-03525	Make Love Stay/Hearts and Crafts	1983	—	2.00	4.00
❑ ENR-03570	Make Love Stay/(B-side blank)	1983	—	3.00	6.00
—One-sided budget release					
❑ 15-03843	Leader of the Band/Run for the Roses	1983	—	—	3.00
—Reissue					
❑ 34-04314	The Language of Love/Windows and Walls	1984	—	—	3.00
❑ 34-04314 [PS]	The Language of Love/Windows and Walls	1984	—	—	3.00
❑ 34-04447	Believe in Me/Windows and Walls	1984	—	2.00	4.00
❑ 34-04660	Sweet Magnolia and the Traveling Salesman/The Loving Cup	1984	—	2.00	4.00
❑ 34-04835	Go Down Easy/High Country Snows	1985	—	2.00	4.00
❑ 34-05446	Down the Road-Mountain Pass/High Country Snows	1985	—	2.00	4.00
❑ 15-05498	Missing You/Make Love Stay	1985	—	—	3.00
—Reissue					
❑ 34-07044	She Don't Look Back/It Doesn't Matter	1987	—	—	3.00
❑ 34-07044 [PS]	She Don't Look Back/It Doesn't Matter	1987	—	—	3.00
❑ 34-07275	Lonely in Love/Beyond the Edge	1987	—	2.00	4.00
❑ 34-07275 [PS]	Lonely in Love/Beyond the Edge	1987	—	2.00	4.00
❑ 34-07640	Seeing You Again/Hearts in Decline	1987	—	2.00	4.00
❑ 34-07756	The Way It Must Be/What You're Doing	1988	—	2.00	4.00
❑ 8-50055	Part of the Plan/Song from Half Mountain	1974	—	2.50	5.00
❑ 8-50108	Changing Horses/Morning Sky	1975	—	3.00	6.00
❑ 8-50165	Captured Angel/Next Time	1975	—	3.00	6.00
❑ 8-50189	Below the Surface/Comes and Goes	1976	—	3.00	6.00
❑ 8-50234	Old Tennessee/The Crow	1976	—	3.00	6.00
❑ 8-50412	Love Gone By/Scarecrow's Dream	1977	—	3.00	6.00
❑ 8-50462	Nether Lands/False Faces	1977	—	2.50	5.00
❑ 8-50462 [PS]	Nether Lands/False Faces	1977	2.00	4.00	8.00
❑ 8-50536	Sketches/Promises Made	1978	—	3.00	6.00
❑ 8-50577	There's a Place in the World for a Gambler/Souvenirs	1978	—	3.00	6.00
❑ 9-50824	Longer/Along the Road	1980	—	2.00	4.00
❑ 9-50862	Heart Hotels/Beggar's Game	1980	—	2.50	5.00
❑ 19-50961	Same Old Lang Syne/Hearts and Crafts	1980	—	2.00	4.00
❑ 19-50961 [PS]	Same Old Lang Syne/Hearts and Crafts	1980	—	3.00	6.00
❑ 34-73513	Rhythm of the Rain-Rain/Ever On	1990	—	2.50	5.00
Albums					
COLUMBIA					
❑ KC 31751	Home Free	1972	3.00	6.00	12.00
❑ PC 31751	Home Free	197?	2.00	4.00	8.00
—Reissue with new prefix					
FULL MOON/EPIC					
❑ AS 1284 [DJ]	The Innocent Age Sampler	1982	3.00	6.00	12.00
—Promo only; 6 songs					
❑ A2S 1335 [(2)DJ]	Interchords	1982	6.25	12.50	25.00
—Promo-only release					
❑ KE 33137	Souvenirs	1974	3.00	6.00	12.00
—First pressings have orange Epic label with small Full-Moon logo					
❑ KE 33137	Souvenirs	1975	2.50	5.00	10.00
—Second pressings have dark blue/black Full Moon label					
❑ PE 33137	Souvenirs	197?	2.00	4.00	8.00
—Reissue with new prefix					
❑ PE 33499	Captured Angel	1975	2.50	5.00	10.00
—No bar code on cover					
❑ PE 33499	Captured Angel	198?	2.00	4.00	8.00
—With bar code on cover					
❑ PEQ 33499 [Q]	Captured Angel	1975	5.00	10.00	20.00

Number	Title (A Side/B Side)	Yr	VG	VG+	NM
❑ PE 34185	Nether Lands	1977	2.50	5.00	10.00
—No bar code on cover					
❑ PE 34185	Nether Lands	198?	2.00	4.00	8.00
—With bar code on cover					
❑ PE 35364	Phoenix	198?	2.00	4.00	8.00
—Budget-line reissue					
❑ FE 35634	Phoenix	1979	2.50	5.00	10.00
❑ KE2 37393 [(2)]	The Innocent Age	1981	3.00	6.00	12.00
❑ QE 38308	Dan Fogelberg/Greatest Hits	1982	2.50	5.00	10.00
❑ QE 39004	Windows and Walls	1984	2.50	5.00	10.00
❑ FE 39616	High Country Snows	1985	2.50	5.00	10.00
❑ OE 40271	Exiles	1987	2.50	5.00	10.00
❑ HE 45634	Phoenix	1981	7.50	15.00	30.00
—Half-speed mastered edition					
❑ HE 48308	Dan Fogelberg/Greatest Hits	1983	7.50	15.00	30.00
—Half-speed mastered edition					
FOGELBERG, DAN, AND TIM WEISBERG					
12-Inch Singles					
FULL MOON/EPIC					
❑ AS 550 [DJ]	Tell Me to My Face (7:15) (4:09)	1978	6.25	12.50	25.00
45s					
FULL MOON/EPIC					
❑ 8-50605	Tell Me to My Face/Hurtwood Alley	1978	—	3.00	6.00
❑ 8-50606	The Power of Gold/Lahaina Luna	1978	—	2.00	4.00
Albums					
FULL MOON/EPIC					
❑ JE 35339	Twin Sons of Different Mothers	1978	2.50	5.00	10.00
❑ PE 35339	Twin Sons of Different Mothers	198?	2.00	4.00	8.00
—Budget-line reissue					
❑ HE 45339	Twin Sons of Different Mothers	198?	7.50	15.00	30.00
—Half-speed mastered edition					
FOGERTY, JOHN Includes records as "The Blue Ridge Rangers." Also see CREEDENCE CLEARWATER REVIVAL; TOMMY FOGERTY AND THE BLUE VELVETS; THE GOLLIWOGS.					
12-Inch Singles					
WARNER BROS.					
❑ PRO-A-2234 [DJ]	The Old Man Down the Road (same on both sides)	1984	2.00	4.00	8.00
❑ PRO-A-2267 [DJ]	Rock and Roll Girls/Centerfield	1985	2.00	4.00	8.00
❑ PRO-A-2337 [DJ]	I Can't Help Myself (same on both sides)	1985	2.00	4.00	8.00
❑ PRO-A-2362 [DJ]	Vanz Kant Danz (edit)/(LP)	1985	2.00	4.00	8.00
❑ PRO-A-2514 [DJ]	Eye of the Zombie (same on both sides)	1986	2.00	4.00	8.00
❑ PRO-A-2595 [DJ]	Change in the Weather (edit)/(LP)	1986	2.00	4.00	8.00
❑ PRO-A-2637 [DJ]	Knockin' on Your Door (same on both sides)	1986	2.00	4.00	8.00
45s					
ASYLUM					
❑ 45274	Rockin' All Over the World/The Wall	1975	—	3.00	6.00
❑ 45293	Almost Saturday Night/Sea Cruise	1975	—	3.00	6.00
❑ 45309	You Got the Magic/Evil Thing	1976	3.75	7.50	15.00
❑ 45309 [DJ]	You Got the Magic (stereo/mono)	1976	2.50	5.00	10.00
ELEKTRA					
❑ 45309 [DJ]	You Got the Magic (stereo/mono)	1976	5.00	10.00	20.00
—Promo-only version with wrong label (promos also exist on Asylum)					
FANTASY					
❑ 683	Blue Ridge Mountain Blues/Have Thine Own Way, Lord	1972	—	2.50	5.00
—As "The Blue Ridge Rangers"					
❑ 683 [PS]	Blue Ridge Mountain Blues/Have Thine Own Way, Lord	1972	3.75	7.50	15.00
—As "The Blue Ridge Rangers"					
❑ 689	Jambalaya (On the Bayou)/Workin' on a Building	1972	—	3.00	6.00
—As "The Blue Ridge Rangers"; green, red and orange label					
❑ 689	Jambalaya (On the Bayou)/Workin' on a Building	1973	—	2.50	5.00
—As "The Blue Ridge Rangers"; brown label					
❑ 700	Hearts of Stone/Somewhere Listening	1973	—	2.50	5.00
—As "The Blue Ridge Rangers"					
❑ 710	Back in the Hills/You Don't Own Me	1973	—	2.50	5.00
—As "The Blue Ridge Rangers"					
❑ 717	Coming Down the Road/Ricochet	1973	—	2.50	5.00
REPRISE					
❑ 17191	Premonition/Born on the Bayou	1998	—	—	3.00
❑ 17192	Almost Saturday Night/Who'll Stop the Rain	1998	—	—	3.00
WARNER BROS.					
❑ PRO-S-2363 [DJ]	Vanz Kant Danz (edit)/(LP)	1985	2.50	5.00	10.00
❑ 17283	Blueboy/Bad Bad Boy	1997	—	—	3.00
❑ 28535	Change in the Weather/My Toot Toot	1986	—	2.00	4.00
❑ 28535 [PS]	Change in the Weather/My Toot Toot	1986	—	2.00	4.00
❑ 28657	Eye of the Zombie/I Confess	1986	—	2.00	4.00
❑ 28657 [PS]	Eye of the Zombie/I Confess	1986	—	2.00	4.00
❑ 29053	Rock and Roll Girls/Centerfield	1985	—	2.00	4.00
❑ 29053 [PS]	Rock and Roll Girls/Centerfield	1985	—	2.00	4.00
❑ 29100	The Old Man Down the Road/Big Train (From Memphis)	1985	—	2.00	4.00
❑ 29100 [PS]	The Old Man Down the Road/Big Train (From Memphis)	1985	—	2.00	4.00
Albums					
ASYLUM					
❑ 7E-1046	John Fogerty	1975	3.00	6.00	12.00
❑ 7E-1081	Hoodoo	1976	—	—	—
—Canceled; poor quality bootleg cassettes exist					
FANTASY					
❑ MPF-4502	John Fogerty: The Blue Ridge Rangers	1981	2.50	5.00	10.00
—Reissues prominently place John Fogerty's name on the cover					
❑ F-9415	The Blue Ridge Rangers	1973	3.75	7.50	15.00
—As "The Blue Ridge Rangers"					
WARNER BROS.					
❑ 25203	Centerfield	1985	3.75	7.50	15.00
—Originals have the last song on side 2 as "Zanz Kant Danz"					
❑ 25203 [DJ]	Centerfield	1985	7.50	15.00	30.00
—Promo versions on Quiex II audiophile vinyl					
❑ 25203	Centerfield	1986	2.50	5.00	10.00
—Later editions have the last song on side 2 re-recorded and listed as "Vanz Kant Danz"					
❑ 25449	Eye of the Zombie	1986	2.50	5.00	10.00

F

Number	Title (A Side/B Side)	Yr	VG	VG+	NM

FOGERTY, TOM Also see CREEDENCE CLEARWATER REVIVAL; TOMMY FOGERTY AND THE BLUE VELVETS; THE GOLLIWOGS.
45s
FANTASY

Number	Title (A Side/B Side)	Yr	VG	VG+	NM
❏ 661	Goodbye, Media Man/Goodbye, Media Man (Part 2)	1971	—	2.50	5.00
❏ 661 [PS]	Goodbye, Media Man/Goodbye, Media Man (Part 2)	1971	2.50	5.00	10.00
❏ 680	Cast the First Stone/Lady of Fatima	1972	—	2.50	5.00
❏ 691	Forty Years/Faces, Places, People	1972	—	2.50	5.00
❏ 702	Heartbeat/Joyful Resurrection	1973	—	2.50	5.00
❏ 715	Mystic Island Avalon/Reggie	1973	—	2.50	5.00
❏ 726	It's Been a Good Day/Money	1974	—	2.50	5.00
❏ 737	Sweet Things to Come/There Was a Time	1974	—	2.50	5.00

Albums
FANTASY

Number	Title (A Side/B Side)	Yr	VG	VG+	NM
❏ 9407	Tom Fogerty	1972	3.75	7.50	15.00
❏ 9413	Excalibur	1972	3.75	7.50	15.00
❏ 9448	Zephyr National	1974	3.00	6.00	12.00
❏ 9469	Myopia	1974	3.00	6.00	12.00
❏ 9611	Deal It Out	1981	2.50	5.00	10.00

FOGERTY, TOMMY, AND THE BLUE VELVETS Early version of THE GOLLIWOGS, which was an early version of CREEDENCE CLEARWATER REVIVAL.
45s
ORCHESTRA

Number	Title (A Side/B Side)	Yr	VG	VG+	NM
❏ (# unknown)	Yes, You Did/Now You're Not Mine	1962			

—This record may not exist; when the "complete" Creedence Clearwater Revival box set was compiled in 2001, no copy could be found

Number	Title (A Side/B Side)	Yr	VG	VG+	NM
❏ 1010	Have You Ever Been Lonely/Bonita	1961	20.00	40.00	80.00
❏ 6177	Come On Baby/Oh! My Love	1961	20.00	40.00	80.00

FOGHAT
12-Inch Singles
BEARSVILLE

Number	Title (A Side/B Side)	Yr	VG	VG+	NM
❏ PRO-A-725 [DJ]	Stone Blue (Edit) (LP Version)	1978	3.75	7.50	15.00

—Blue vinyl
45s
BEARSVILLE

Number	Title (A Side/B Side)	Yr	VG	VG+	NM
❏ 0008	I Just Want to Make Love to You/Hole to Hide In	1973	—	2.50	5.00
❏ 0014	What a Shame/Helping Hand	1973	—	2.50	5.00
❏ 0019	That'll Be the Day/Wild Cherry	1974	—	2.50	5.00
❏ 0021	Maybelline/Step Outside	1974	—	2.50	5.00
❏ 0306	Slow Ride/Save Your Loving	1975	—	2.50	5.00
❏ 0307	Fool for the City/Take It or Leave It	1976	—	2.50	5.00
❏ 0313	Drivin' Wheel/Night Shift	1976	—	2.00	4.00
❏ 0315	I'll Be Standing By/Take Me to the River	1977	—	2.00	4.00
❏ 0319	I Just Want to Make Love to You (Live)/Fool for the City (Live)	1977	—	2.00	4.00
❏ 0325	Stone Blue/Chevrolet	1978	—	2.00	4.00
❏ 0329	High on Love/Sweet Home Chicago	1978	—	2.00	4.00
❏ PRO-S-780 [DJ]	Run, Run, Rudolph (same on both sides)	1978	2.50	5.00	10.00
❏ PRO-S-1002 [DJ]	All I Want for Christmas Is You (same on both sides)	1981	2.50	5.00	10.00
❏ 29612	Seven Day Weekend/That's What Love Can Do	1983	—	2.00	4.00
❏ 29860	Slipped, Tripped, Fell in Love/And I Do Just What I Want	1982	—	2.00	4.00
❏ 49125	Third Time Lucky (First Time I Was a Fool)/Love in Motion	1979	—	2.00	4.00
❏ 49125 [PS]	Third Time Lucky (First Time I Was a Fool)/Love in Motion	1979	—	2.50	5.00
❏ 49510	Stranger in My Home Town/Be My Woman	1980	—	2.00	4.00
❏ 49779	Wide Boy/Love Zone	1981	—	2.00	4.00
❏ 49779 [PS]	Wide Boy/Love Zone	1981	—	3.00	6.00

FOGHAT

Number	Title (A Side/B Side)	Yr	VG	VG+	NM
❏ 1069	Goin' Home For Christmas/Santa Claus Is Back In Town	1986	—	3.00	6.00
❏ 1069 [PS]	Goin' Home For Christmas/Santa Claus Is Back In Town	1986	—	3.00	6.00

Albums
BEARSVILLE

Number	Title (A Side/B Side)	Yr	VG	VG+	NM
❏ BR 2077	Foghat	1972	3.00	6.00	12.00
❏ BR 2136	Foghat	1973	3.00	6.00	12.00
❏ BSK 3578	Girls to Chat & Boys to Bounce	1981	2.50	5.00	10.00
❏ BR 6950	Energized	1974	2.50	5.00	10.00
❏ BR 6956	Rock and Roll Outlaws	1974	2.50	5.00	10.00
❏ BR 6959	Fool for the City	1975	2.50	5.00	10.00
❏ BR 6962	Night Shift	1976	2.50	5.00	10.00
❏ BRK 6971	Foghat Live	1977	2.50	5.00	10.00
❏ BRK 6977	Stone Blue	1978	2.50	5.00	10.00
❏ BRK 6980	Fool for the City	1978	2.00	4.00	8.00

—Reissue of 6959

Number	Title (A Side/B Side)	Yr	VG	VG+	NM
❏ BHS 6990	Boogie Motel	1979	2.50	5.00	10.00
❏ HS 6999	Tight Shoes	1980	2.50	5.00	10.00
❏ 23747	In the Mood for Something Rude	1982	2.50	5.00	10.00
❏ 23888	Zig-Zag Walk	1983	2.50	5.00	10.00

RHINO

Number	Title (A Side/B Side)	Yr	VG	VG+	NM
❏ R1-70088	The Best of Foghat	1989	2.50	5.00	10.00
❏ RNLP-70881	Stone Blue	1987	2.00	4.00	8.00

—Reissue of Bearsville 6977

Number	Title (A Side/B Side)	Yr	VG	VG+	NM
❏ RNLP-70882	Fool for the City	1987	2.00	4.00	8.00

—Reissue of Bearsville 6980

Number	Title (A Side/B Side)	Yr	VG	VG+	NM
❏ RNLP-70883	Energized	1988	2.00	4.00	8.00

—Reissue of Bearsville 6950

Number	Title (A Side/B Side)	Yr	VG	VG+	NM
❏ RNLP-70884	Foghat Live	1988	2.00	4.00	8.00

—Reissue of Bearsville 6971

Number	Title (A Side/B Side)	Yr	VG	VG+	NM
❏ RNLP-70887	Foghat	1988	2.00	4.00	8.00

—Reissue of Bearsville 2077

Number	Title (A Side/B Side)	Yr	VG	VG+	NM
❏ RNLP-70888	Night Shift	1988	2.00	4.00	8.00

—Reissue of Bearsville 6962

Number	Title (A Side/B Side)	Yr	VG	VG+	NM
❏ R1-70889	Rock and Roll Outlaws	1988	2.00	4.00	8.00

—Reissue of Bearsville 6956

Number	Title (A Side/B Side)	Yr	VG	VG+	NM
❏ R1-70890	Foghat	1988	2.00	4.00	8.00

—Reissue of Bearsville 2136

FOLEY, BRIAN
45s
DOT

Number	Title (A Side/B Side)	Yr	VG	VG+	NM
❏ 16889	Where Are We Going in Such a Hurry/Time and Tide	1966	2.50	5.00	10.00

KAPP

Number	Title (A Side/B Side)	Yr	VG	VG+	NM
❏ 861	Love Was Here Before the Stars/Love Me, Please Love Me	1967	2.00	4.00	8.00
❏ 861 [PS]	Love Was Here Before the Stars/Love Me, Please Love Me	1967	3.00	6.00	12.00
❏ 885	Love Never Changes/Once There Was a Time	1968	2.00	4.00	8.00
❏ 924	Elvira Madigan Theme/Let's Go	1968	2.00	4.00	8.00

FOLEY, RED Also see RED FOLEY AND ERNEST TUBB; KITTY WELLS AND RED FOLEY.
45s
DECCA

Number	Title (A Side/B Side)	Yr	VG	VG+	NM
❏ 25514	I Want a Girl/It's a Sin to Tell a Lie	196?	3.00	6.00	12.00
❏ 25539	Beyond the Sunset/Should You Go First//He	196?	3.00	6.00	12.00
❏ 25634	Pack Up Your Troubles/When You're Smiling	1964	3.00	6.00	12.00
❏ 25652	Moonlight Bay/Smiles	196?	3.00	6.00	12.00
❏ 25689	Goodnight Irene/Sleepy Time Gal	196?	3.00	6.00	12.00
❏ 25720	I Really Don't Want to Know/No One to Cry To	196?	3.00	6.00	12.00
❏ 25762	Peace in the Valley/Where Could I Go But to the Lord	196?	3.00	6.00	12.00
❏ 9-27378	My Heart Cries for You/'Tater Pie	1951	6.25	12.50	25.00

—With Evelyn Knight

Number	Title (A Side/B Side)	Yr	VG	VG+	NM
❏ 9-27763	Night Train to Memphis/If I Had-a Knowed, You Could-a Goed	1950	7.50	15.00	30.00

—With Roberta Lee

Number	Title (A Side/B Side)	Yr	VG	VG+	NM
❏ 9-27812	Alabama Jubilee/Dixie	1951	6.25	12.50	25.00
❏ 9-27856	Say a Little Prayer/Peace in the Valley	1951	6.25	12.50	25.00
❏ 9-27929	Whistle While You Work/Who's Afraid of the Big Bad Wolf	1952	7.50	15.00	30.00
❏ 9-27981	Milk Bucket Boogie/Salty Dog Rag	1952	6.25	12.50	25.00
❏ 9-28147	I'm Bound For Christmas/I'd Rather Have Jesus	1952	6.25	12.50	25.00
❏ 9-28252	Somebody Bigger Than You and I/God's Little Candle	1952	6.25	12.50	25.00
❏ 9-28288	Are You Trying to Tell Me Goodbye/Kisses on Paper	1952	6.25	12.50	25.00
❏ 9-28420	Midnight/Deep Blues	1952	6.25	12.50	25.00
❏ 9-28447	My God Is Real/The Mocking Bird	1952	6.25	12.50	25.00
❏ 9-28460	Don't Let the Stars Get In Your Eyes/Sally	1952	5.00	10.00	20.00
❏ 9-28567	Slaves of a Hopeless Love Affair/Blue Letter	1953	5.00	10.00	20.00
❏ 9-28587	Hot Toddy/Playin' Dominoes and Shootin' Dice	1953	5.00	10.00	20.00
❏ 9-28694	I Believe/Mansion Over the Hilltop	1953	5.00	10.00	20.00
❏ 9-28695	I'm Sorry We Met/Treasure Untold	1953	5.00	10.00	20.00
❏ 9-28759	Hot Dog Rag/That Old River Line	1953	5.00	10.00	20.00
❏ 9-28767	Unless You're Free/Baby Blues	1953	5.00	10.00	20.00

—With Patti Andrews

Number	Title (A Side/B Side)	Yr	VG	VG+	NM
❏ 9-28796	The Keys to the Kingdom/Last Mile of the Way	1953	6.25	12.50	25.00
❏ 9-28839	Shake a Hand/Stranded in Deep Water	1953	5.00	10.00	20.00
❏ 9-28940	Put Christ Back in Christmas/The Gentle Carpenter of Bethlehem	1953	5.00	10.00	20.00
❏ 9-28944	Goodbye, Bobby Boy/Peace of Mind	1953	5.00	10.00	20.00
❏ 9-29044	The Rose of Calvary/Consideration	1954	5.00	10.00	20.00
❏ 9-29100	Jilted/Pin Ball Boogie	1954	5.00	10.00	20.00
❏ 9-29159	My Friend/Lady of Guadaloupe	1954	5.00	10.00	20.00
❏ 9-29222	She'll Never Know/Bury Me Beneath the Willow	1954	5.00	10.00	20.00

—With the Andrews Sisters

Number	Title (A Side/B Side)	Yr	VG	VG+	NM
❏ 9-29339	Lookin' Glass/Walkin' in the Cold, Cold Rain	1954	5.00	10.00	20.00
❏ 9-29375	Hearts of Stone/Never	1954	5.00	10.00	20.00
❏ 9-29494	Nobody/Hominy Grits	1955	5.00	10.00	20.00
❏ 9-29505	Have a Little Talk with Jesus/Strange Things Happen	1955	5.00	10.00	20.00

—With Sister Rosetta Tharpe

Number	Title (A Side/B Side)	Yr	VG	VG+	NM
❏ 9-29517	Plantation Boogie/You Little So-and-So	1955	5.00	10.00	20.00
❏ 9-29626	Just Call Me Lonesome/Blue Guitar	1955	5.00	10.00	20.00
❏ 9-29667	When You Come to the End of the Day/The Night Watch	1955	5.00	10.00	20.00
❏ 9-29775	I See God/Someone to Care	1956	5.00	10.00	20.00
❏ 9-29894	The Hoot Owl Boogie/A Handful of Love	1956	5.00	10.00	20.00
❏ 9-30010	Take My Hand, Precious Lord/Someday, Somewhere	1956	5.00	10.00	20.00
❏ 9-30067	Rock 'n Reelin'/Don't Blame It on the Girl	1956	7.50	15.00	30.00
❏ 9-30080	(There'll Be) Peace in the Valley/A Servant	1956	5.00	10.00	20.00
❏ 9-30177	Passing By (Just Passing By)/His Arms	1957	5.00	10.00	20.00
❏ 9-30249	Come a Little Closer/One Life, Two Loves	1957	5.00	10.00	20.00
❏ 9-30334	Sweet Innocence/Why Ask for the Moon	1957	5.00	10.00	20.00
❏ 9-30452	This Could Very Well Be It/Strike While the Iron Is Hot	1957	5.00	10.00	20.00
❏ 9-30470	Steal Away/Just a Closer Walk with Thee	1957	5.00	10.00	20.00
❏ 9-30639	Strolling the Blues/With You Beside Me	1958	5.00	10.00	20.00
❏ 9-30674	Crazy Little Guitar Man/Fate	1958	7.50	15.00	30.00
❏ 9-30710	Good Night, Dear Lord/If I Can Help Somebody	1958	5.00	10.00	20.00
❏ 9-30802	Love Is Love/Smiles	1959	5.00	10.00	20.00
❏ 9-30882	Travelin' Man/Just This Side of Memphis	1959	5.00	10.00	20.00
❏ 9-30924	God Walks These Hills with Me/God Forgive Me When I Whine	1959	5.00	10.00	20.00
❏ 9-30975	Crazy 'Bout Banjos/Living Is a Lonesome Thing	1959	3.75	7.50	15.00
❏ 31056	Rockin' Chair/Blues in My Red Wagon Blues	1960	3.75	7.50	15.00
❏ 31194	End of the World/Georgia Town Blues	1961	3.75	7.50	15.00
❏ 31254	Another Heartache (For Me)/Just Before Dawn	1961	3.75	7.50	15.00
❏ 31302	The South/Dear Young Lovers	1961	3.75	7.50	15.00
❏ 31369	A Wasted Year/Happy Song	1962	3.75	7.50	15.00
❏ 31408	Mountain Boy/Polka on a Banjo	1962	3.75	7.50	15.00
❏ 31437	Hang Your Head in Shame/That's What's Wrong with Me	1962	3.75	7.50	15.00
❏ 31482	Lights Across the Bay/One True Love	1963	3.00	6.00	12.00
❏ 31530	Goodnight Mama, Goodnight Papa/Poor Jack	1963	3.00	6.00	12.00
❏ 31727	Chained to a Memory/Shame on You	1965	2.50	5.00	10.00
❏ 31776	(Remember Me) I'm the One Who Loves You/Sugar Moon	1965	2.50	5.00	10.00
❏ 31831	River of Regret/So Long Baby	1965	2.50	5.00	10.00
❏ 32044	My Gal Country Style/How's the World Treating You	1966	2.50	5.00	10.00
❏ 32063	Is There Really a Santa Claus/From Our House to Your House	1966	3.00	6.00	12.00

Number	Title (A Side/B Side)	Yr	VG	VG+	NM
❑ 7-38115 [S]	I Want a Girl/It's a Sin to Tell a Lie	196?	3.75	7.50	15.00
—Jukebox issue; small hole, plays at 33 1/3 rpm					
❑ 7-38117 [S]	When You're Smiling/Smiles	196?	3.75	7.50	15.00
—Jukebox issue; small hole, plays at 33 1/3 rpm					
❑ 7-38119 [S]	Moonlight Bay/Sleepy Time Girl	196?	3.75	7.50	15.00
—Jukebox issue; small hole, plays at 33 1/3 rpm					
❑ 7-38268 [S]	Tennessee Border/You're Nobody Till Somebody Loves You	196?	3.75	7.50	15.00
—Jukebox issue; small hole, plays at 33 1/3 rpm					
❑ 9-46052	Old Shep/Honey Be My Honey Bee	1950	10.00	20.00	40.00
—Lines on either side of "Decca"					
❑ 9-46052	Old Shep/Honey Be My Honey Bee	1955	5.00	10.00	20.00
—Star under "Decca"					
❑ 9-46136	Tennessee Saturday Night/Blues in My Heart	1950	10.00	20.00	40.00
—Reissue of 78 originally issued in 1948; lines on either side of "Decca"					
❑ 9-46185	Our Christmas Waltz/Here Comes Santa Claus	1950	10.00	20.00	40.00
—With Judy Martin					
❑ 9-46205	Chattanoogie Shoe Shine Boy/Sugarfoot Rag	1950	10.00	20.00	40.00
—The 45 was released later than the 78 by a few months					
❑ 9-46234	Birmingham Bounce/Choc'late Ice Cream Cone	1950	7.50	15.00	30.00
❑ 9-46235	Let's Go to Church/Remember Me	1950	7.50	15.00	30.00
❑ 9-46241	Mississippi/Old Kentucky Fox Chase	1950	7.50	15.00	30.00
❑ 9-46261	Cincinnati Dancing Pig/Somebody's Cryin'	1950	7.50	15.00	30.00
❑ 9-46267	Frosty the Snowman/Rudolph the Red-Nosed Reindeer	1950	7.50	15.00	30.00
❑ 9-46277	I Won't Be Home/Dear Little Girls	1950	7.50	15.00	30.00
❑ 9-46285	Someone Else Not Me/Music by the Angels (Lyrics by the Lord)	1951	7.50	15.00	30.00
❑ 9-46286	Hot Rod Race/Smoke on the Water No. 2	1951	7.50	15.00	30.00
❑ 9-46291	Old Shep/Just a Man and His Dog	1951	6.25	12.50	25.00
❑ 9-46292	Tennessee Polka/Tennessee Saturday Night	1951	6.25	12.50	25.00
❑ 9-46293	Back to Tennessee/Sunday Down in Tennessee	1951	6.25	12.50	25.00
❑ 9-46294	That Little Boy of Mine/Don't Make Me Go to Bed	1951	6.25	12.50	25.00
—The above four comprise a box set					
❑ 9-46297	The Chicken Song/So Long	1951	6.25	12.50	25.00
❑ 9-46304	Hobo Boogie/Heska Holka	1951	6.25	12.50	25.00
❑ 9-46317	Tennessee Hillbilly Ghost/Giles County Pulaski Post Office	1951	6.25	12.50	25.00
❑ 9-46319	There'll Be Peace in the Valley for Me/Old Soldiers Never Die	1951	6.25	12.50	25.00
❑ 9-46349	Cock-a-Doodle-Doo/Sugar Foot Rag Square Dance	1951	6.25	12.50	25.00
❑ 9-46357	Jesus and the Atheist/The Weapon of Prayer	1951	6.25	12.50	25.00
❑ 9-46411	When the Saints Go Marching In/Lonely Mile	1952	6.25	12.50	25.00
❑ 9-88030	The Prettiest Song in the World/(B-side unknown)	1950	10.00	20.00	40.00
—Yellow label "Chidren's Series" issue					
❑ 9-88060	Frosty the Snowman/Rudolph the Red-Nosed Reindeer	1950	10.00	20.00	40.00
—Yellow label "Chidren's Series" issue					
❑ 9-88137	Jesus Loves Me/I'll Be a Sunbeam	195?	7.50	15.00	30.00
—Yellow label "Chidren's Series" issue					
DECCA FAITH SERIES					
❑ 9-14505	Steal Away/Just a Closer Walk with Thee	1950	10.00	20.00	40.00
❑ 9-14526	Our Lady of Fatima/The Rosary	1950	10.00	20.00	40.00
❑ 9-14537	I Hear a Choir/The Place Where I Worship	1951	7.50	15.00	30.00
❑ 9-14553	He'll Understand and Say Well Done/Milky White Way	1951	7.50	15.00	30.00
❑ 9-14566	He Bought My Soul at Calvary/It Is No Secret (What God Can Do)	1951	7.50	15.00	30.00
❑ 9-14573	Peace in the Valley/Where Could I Go But to the Lord	1951	7.50	15.00	30.00
7-Inch Extended Plays					
DECCA					
❑ ED 2025	Chattanoogie Shoe Shine Boy/Sugarfoot Rag// Alabama Jubilee/Mississippi	195?	6.25	12.50	25.00
❑ ED 2025 [PS]	(title unknown)	195?	6.25	12.50	25.00
❑ ED 2090	(contents unknown)	195?	6.25	12.50	25.00
❑ ED 2090 [PS]	Sing a Song of Christmas	195?	6.25	12.50	25.00
❑ ED 2184	Our Lady of Fatima/The Rosary//The Place Where I Worship (Is the Wide Open Spaces)/ I Hear a Choir	195?	3.75	7.50	15.00
❑ ED 2184 [PS]	Lift Up Your Voice, Vol. 1	195?	3.75	7.50	15.00
❑ ED 2207	Beyond the Sunset-Should You Go First/ (There'll Be) Peace in the Valley (For Me)//Old Pappy's New Banjo/Someone to Care	1955	6.25	12.50	25.00
❑ ED 2207 [PS]	Beyond the Sunset	1955	6.25	12.50	25.00
❑ ED 2363	A Satisfied Mind/As Far As I'm Concerned//Pin Ball Boogie/Hearts of Stone	195?	3.75	7.50	15.00
—A-side tracks with Betty Foley					
❑ ED 2363 [PS]	Souvenir Album	195?	3.75	7.50	15.00
❑ ED 2644	It's a Sin to Tell a Lie/Smiles//When You're Smiling (The Whole World Smiles with You)/ Moonlight Bay	195?	3.75	7.50	15.00
❑ ED 2644 [PS]	Let's All Sing with Red Foley	195?	3.75	7.50	15.00
Albums					
DECCA					
❑ DXB 177 [(2)M]	The Red Foley Story	1964	6.25	12.50	25.00
❑ DL 4107 [M]	Red Foley's Golden Favorites	1961	5.00	10.00	20.00
❑ DL 4140 [M]	Company's Comin'	1961	5.00	10.00	20.00
❑ DL 4198 [M]	Songs of Devotion	1961	5.00	10.00	20.00
❑ DL 4290 [M]	Dear Hearts and Gentle People	1962	5.00	10.00	20.00
❑ DL 4341 [M]	The Red Foley Show	1963	5.00	10.00	20.00
❑ DL 4603 [M]	Songs Everybody Knows	1965	5.00	10.00	20.00
❑ DL 4849 [M]	Songs for the Soul	1967	6.25	12.50	25.00
❑ DL 5003 [M]	Red Foley's Greatest Hits	1968	12.50	25.00	50.00
—White label promo; mono copies may only exist as promos					
❑ DL 5303 [10]	Red Foley Souvenir Album	1951	20.00	40.00	80.00
❑ DL 5338 [10]	Lift Up Your Voice	1952	20.00	40.00	80.00
❑ DXSB 7177 [(2)S]	The Red Foley Story	1964	7.50	15.00	30.00
❑ DL 8294 [M]	Red Foley Souvenir Album	1956	12.50	25.00	50.00
❑ DL 8296 [M]	Beyond the Sunset	1956	12.50	25.00	50.00
❑ DL 8767 [M]	He Walks with Thee	1958	12.50	25.00	50.00
❑ DL 8806 [M]	My Keepsake Album	1958	12.50	25.00	50.00
❑ DL 8847 [M]	Let's All Sing with Red Foley	1959	10.00	20.00	40.00
❑ DL 8903 [M]	Let's All Sing to Him	1959	10.00	20.00	40.00

Number	Title (A Side/B Side)	Yr	VG	VG+	NM
❑ DL 38068 [M]	Gratefully	1958	25.00	50.00	100.00
—Special-products issue for Dickies clothing					
❑ DL 74107 [S]	Red Foley's Golden Favorites	1961	6.25	12.50	25.00
❑ DL 74140 [S]	Company's Comin'	1961	6.25	12.50	25.00
❑ DL 74198 [S]	Songs of Devotion	1961	6.25	12.50	25.00
❑ DL 74290 [S]	Dear Hearts and Gentle People	1962	6.25	12.50	25.00
❑ DL 74341 [S]	The Red Foley Show	1963	6.25	12.50	25.00
❑ DL 74603 [S]	Songs Everybody Knows	1965	6.25	12.50	25.00
❑ DL 74849 [S]	Songs for the Soul	1967	5.00	10.00	20.00
❑ DL 75003 [S]	Red Foley's Greatest Hits	1968	3.75	7.50	15.00
❑ DL 78847 [S]	Let's All Sing with Red Foley	1959	12.50	25.00	50.00
❑ DL 78903 [S]	Let's All Sing to Him	1959	12.50	25.00	50.00

FOLEY, RED AND BETTY
45s
DECCA

Number	Title (A Side/B Side)	Yr	VG	VG+	NM
❑ 9-29000	As Far As I'm Concerned/Tennessee Whistling Man	1954	5.00	10.00	20.00
❑ 9-29526	Satisfied Mind/How About Me	1955	5.00	10.00	20.00
❑ 9-29704	Croce di Oro (Cross of Gold)/Sweet Kentucky Rose	1955	5.00	10.00	20.00

FOLEY, RED, AND GRADY MARTIN
45s
DECCA

Number	Title (A Side/B Side)	Yr	VG	VG+	NM
❑ 9-29059	My Window Faces South/Pork Chop Stomp	1954	5.00	10.00	20.00

FOLEY, RED, AND ERNEST TUBB Also see each artist's individual listings.
45s
DECCA

Number	Title (A Side/B Side)	Yr	VG	VG+	NM
❑ 9-28634	No Help Wanted #2/You're a Real Good Friend	1953	5.00	10.00	20.00
❑ 9-28911	Too Old to Tango/Doctor Ketchum	1953	5.00	10.00	20.00
❑ 9-29195	Double-Datin'/It's the Mileage That's Slowin' Us Down	1954	5.00	10.00	20.00
❑ 9-46255	Goodnight Irene/Hillbilly Fever No. 2	1950	10.00	20.00	40.00
❑ 9-46278	The Lovebug Itch/Texas vs. Kentucky	1950	7.50	15.00	30.00
❑ 9-46311	The Strange Little Girl/Kentucky Waltz	1951	6.25	12.50	25.00
❑ 9-46387	Too Old to Cut the Mustard/I'm in Love with Molly	1952	6.25	12.50	25.00

7-Inch Extended Plays
DECCA

Number	Title (A Side/B Side)	Yr	VG	VG+	NM
❑ ED 2059	When Jimmie Rodgers Said Good-Bye/Jimmie Rodgers' Last Thoughts//Treasure Untold/I'm Sorry We Met	195?	6.25	12.50	25.00
—A-side by Ernest Tubb; B-side by Red Foley					
❑ ED 2059 [PS]	A Tribute to Jimmie Rodgers	195?	6.25	12.50	25.00
❑ ED 2368	Tennessee Border No. 2/Double-Datin'//It's the Mileage That's Slowin' Us Down/You're a Real Good Friend	195?	5.00	10.00	20.00
❑ ED 2368 [PS]	Red and Ernie, Part 2	195?	5.00	10.00	20.00

FOLKSWINGERS, THE
45s
WORLD PACIFIC

Number	Title (A Side/B Side)	Yr	VG	VG+	NM
❑ 391	This Train/Black Mountain Rag	1963	2.50	5.00	10.00
❑ 396	12 String Special/Amor A Todos	1963	2.50	5.00	10.00
❑ 77831	Norwegian Wood/Raga Rock	1966	2.00	4.00	8.00

Albums
WORLD PACIFIC

Number	Title (A Side/B Side)	Yr	VG	VG+	NM
❑ ST-1812 [S]	12 String Guitar!	1963	7.50	15.00	30.00
—Black vinyl					
❑ ST-1812 [S]	12 String Guitar!	1963	15.00	30.00	60.00
—Red vinyl					
❑ WP-1812 [M]	12 String Guitar!	1963	6.25	12.50	25.00
❑ ST-1814 [S]	12 String Guitar, Volume 2	1963	7.50	15.00	30.00
❑ WP-1814 [M]	12 String Guitar, Volume 2	1963	6.25	12.50	25.00
❑ ST-1846 [S]	Raga Rock	1966	7.50	15.00	30.00
❑ WP-1846 [M]	Raga Rock	1966	6.25	12.50	25.00

FONTAINE, EDDIE
45s
ARGO

Number	Title (A Side/B Side)	Yr	VG	VG+	NM
❑ 5309	Nothin' Shakin'/Don't Ya Know	1958	6.25	12.50	25.00
CHANCELLOR					
❑ 1018	Goodness, It's Gladys/Middle of the Road	1958	5.00	10.00	20.00
DECCA					
❑ 30042	Cool It Baby/Into Each Life Some Rain Must Fall	1956	6.25	12.50	25.00
❑ 30108	A Rose and a Baby Ruth/The Years Before	1956	6.25	12.50	25.00
❑ 30121	As Far As I'm Concerned/'Til Tonight	1956	6.25	12.50	25.00
—With Karen Chandler					
❑ 30202	I'll Be There/East of Mississippi	1957	6.25	12.50	25.00
❑ 30256	Money/Homesick Blues	1957	6.25	12.50	25.00
❑ 30338	Hey Marie, Rock with Me/The One and Only	1957	6.25	12.50	25.00
❑ 30446	Fun Lovin'/Honky Tonk Man	1957	6.25	12.50	25.00
JALO					
❑ 102	Where Is Da Woman/ It Ain't Gonna Happen No More	1956	20.00	40.00	80.00
LIBERTY					
❑ 55776	Blue Roses/Way Down Home	1965	2.50	5.00	10.00
❑ 55823	I Need You/It Can Happen to You	1965	2.50	5.00	10.00
SUNBEAM					
❑ 105	Nothin' Shakin'/Oh, Wonderful Night	1958	10.00	20.00	40.00
❑ 112	Nobody Can Handle This Job/I'm Ready As I'll Ever Be	1958	6.25	12.50	25.00
—B-side by Gerry Granahan					
❑ 118	Love Eyes/Something Cha Cha	1958	6.25	12.50	25.00
VIK					
❑ 0184	Turn the Light On/Boom-De-De-Boom	1955	6.25	12.50	25.00
❑ 0193	Here 'Tis/I Look at You	1956	6.25	12.50	25.00
❑ 0203	Stand On That Rock/Baby You Did This to Me	1956	6.25	12.50	25.00
WARNER BROS.					
❑ 5313	My Heart Belongs to You/I'm Gonna Settle Down	1962	3.75	7.50	15.00
❑ 5345	(It's No) Sin/All I Want Is You	1963	3.75	7.50	15.00
"X"					
❑ 0096	Rock Love/All My Love Belongs to You	1955	7.50	15.00	30.00
❑ 0108	On Bended Knees/I Miss You So	1955	7.50	15.00	30.00
❑ 0128	Rollin' Stone/I'm Through Chasin' After You	1955	7.50	15.00	30.00
❑ 0151	Poor Little Monday/The Rain Song	1955	7.50	15.00	30.00

Number	Title (A Side/B Side)	Yr	VG	VG+	NM
❏ 0184	Turn the Light On/Boom-De-De-Boom	1955	7.50	15.00	30.00
❏ 0193	Here 'Tis/I Look at You	1956	7.50	15.00	30.00
❏ 0203	Stand On That Rock/Baby You Did This to Me	1956	7.50	15.00	30.00

FONTAINE, FRANK
45s
ABC-PARAMOUNT

Number	Title (A Side/B Side)	Yr	VG	VG+	NM
❏ 10384	When Your Hair Has Turned to Silver/ Here in My Heart	1962	2.00	4.00	8.00
❏ 10384 [PS]	When Your Hair Has Turned to Silver/ Here in My Heart	1962	3.00	6.00	12.00
❏ 10430	Easter Parade/Always	1963	2.00	4.00	8.00
❏ 10491	Daddy's Little Girl/Oh How I Miss You Tonight	1963	2.00	4.00	8.00
❏ 10517	RSVP/Alouette, Sweet Alouette	1964	2.00	4.00	8.00
❏ 10574	Any Man Who Loves His Mother/When Your Old Wedding Ring Was New	1964	2.00	4.00	8.00
❏ 10618	Mexicali Rose/I'm Counting on You	1965	2.00	4.00	8.00
❏ 10662	I Ain't Got Nobody/Someday	1965	2.00	4.00	8.00

CAPITOL

Number	Title (A Side/B Side)	Yr	VG	VG+	NM
❏ 4929	John L.C. Savoney The Sweepstakes Winner/ The Maharajah	1963	2.00	4.00	8.00

—B-side by Lou Holtz

Number	Title (A Side/B Side)	Yr	VG	VG+	NM
❏ 4929 [PS]	John L.C. Savoney The Sweepstakes Winner/ The Maharajah	1963	3.00	6.00	12.00

MGM

Number	Title (A Side/B Side)	Yr	VG	VG+	NM
❏ 12129	Everybody Rocks/Livin' It Up	1955	15.00	30.00	60.00

Albums
ABC-PARAMOUNT

Number	Title (A Side/B Side)	Yr	VG	VG+	NM
❏ 442 [M]	Songs I Sing on the Jackie Gleason Show	1963	3.75	7.50	15.00
❏ S-442 [S]	Songs I Sing on the Jackie Gleason Show	1963	5.00	10.00	20.00
❏ 460 [M]	Sings Like Crazy	1963	3.75	7.50	15.00
❏ S-460 [S]	Sings Like Crazy	1963	5.00	10.00	20.00
❏ 470 [M]	How Sweet It Is	1964	3.75	7.50	15.00
❏ S-470 [S]	How Sweet It Is	1964	5.00	10.00	20.00
❏ 490 [M]	More Songs I Sing on the Jackie Gleason Show	1964	3.75	7.50	15.00
❏ S-490 [S]	More Songs I Sing on the Jackie Gleason Show	1964	5.00	10.00	20.00
❏ 514 [M]	I'm Counting on You	1965	3.75	7.50	15.00
❏ S-514 [S]	I'm Counting on You	1965	5.00	10.00	20.00
❏ 541 [M]	All Time Great Hits	1966	3.75	7.50	15.00
❏ S-541 [S]	All Time Great Hits	1966	5.00	10.00	20.00
❏ T-90121 [M]	Songs I Sing on the Jackie Gleason Show	1964	5.00	10.00	20.00

—Capitol Record Club edition
MGM

Number	Title (A Side/B Side)	Yr	VG	VG+	NM
❏ E-4470 [M]	Frank Fontaine's Ireland	1967	3.00	6.00	12.00
❏ SE-4470 [S]	Frank Fontaine's Ireland	1967	3.75	7.50	15.00

FONTANA, WAYNE Also see WAYNE FONTANA AND THE MINDBENDERS.
45s
BRUT

Number	Title (A Side/B Side)	Yr	VG	VG+	NM
❏ 812	Sweet America/Interested	1973	—	2.50	5.00

METROMEDIA

Number	Title (A Side/B Side)	Yr	VG	VG+	NM
❏ 133	Say Goodbye to Yesterday/Dayton, Ohio	1969	—	3.00	6.00

MGM

Number	Title (A Side/B Side)	Yr	VG	VG+	NM
❏ 13456	It Was Easier to Hurt Her/ You Made Me What I Am Today	1966	2.00	4.00	8.00
❏ 13516	Come On Home/My Eyes	1966	2.00	4.00	8.00
❏ 13661	Pamela, Pamela, Something Keeps Calling Me Back	1967	—	3.00	6.00
❏ 13762	From a Boy to a Girl/24 Sycamore	1967	—	3.00	6.00

Albums
MGM

Number	Title (A Side/B Side)	Yr	VG	VG+	NM
❏ E-4459 [M]	Wayne Fontana	1967	5.00	10.00	20.00
❏ SE-4459 [S]	Wayne Fontana	1967	6.25	12.50	25.00

FONTANA, WAYNE, AND THE MINDBENDERS Also see WAYNE FONTANA; THE MINDBENDERS.
45s
A&M

Number	Title (A Side/B Side)	Yr	VG	VG+	NM
❏ 3010	Game of Love/What a Wonderful World	1988	—	2.00	4.00

—B-side by Louis Armstrong

Number	Title (A Side/B Side)	Yr	VG	VG+	NM
❏ 3010 [PS]	Game of Love/What a Wonderful World	1988	—	2.00	4.00

—"Good Morning Vietnam" sleeve
FONTANA

Number	Title (A Side/B Side)	Yr	VG	VG+	NM
❏ 1503	Game of Love/Since You've Been Gone	1965	3.75	7.50	15.00
❏ 1509	Game of Love/One More Time	1965	3.00	6.00	12.00
❏ 1514	It's Just a Little Bit Too Late/Long Time Comin'	1965	2.50	5.00	10.00
❏ 1524	She Needs Love/Like I Do	1965	2.50	5.00	10.00
❏ 1917	Stop, Look, Listen/Road Runner	1964	3.00	6.00	12.00
❏ 1945	Um, Um, Um, Um, Um, Um/First Taste of Love	1964	3.00	6.00	12.00

Albums
FONTANA

Number	Title (A Side/B Side)	Yr	VG	VG+	NM
❏ MGF-27542 [M]	The Game of Love	1965	7.50	15.00	30.00
❏ SRF-67542 [R]	The Game of Love	1965	6.25	12.50	25.00

FONTANE SISTERS, THE Also see PERRY COMO.
45s
DOT

Number	Title (A Side/B Side)	Yr	VG	VG+	NM
❏ 15171	Happy Days and Lonely Nights/If I Didn't Have You	1954	3.00	6.00	12.00
❏ 15248	Willow Weep for Me/A Love Like You	1954	3.00	6.00	12.00
❏ 15265	Hearts of Stone/Bless Your Heart	1954	3.75	7.50	15.00
❏ 15333	Rock Love/You're Mine	1955	3.00	6.00	12.00
❏ 15352	Most of All/Put Me in the Mood	1955	3.00	6.00	12.00
❏ 15370	Rollin' Stone/Playmates	1955	3.00	6.00	12.00
❏ 15386	Seventeen/If I Could Be with You	1955	3.00	6.00	12.00
❏ 15428	Daddy-O/Adorable	1955	3.00	6.00	12.00
❏ 15434	Nuttin' for Christmas/Silver Bells	1955	3.00	6.00	12.00
❏ 15450	Eddie My Love/Yum, Yum	1956	3.00	6.00	12.00
❏ 15462	I'm in Love Again/ You Always Hurt the One You Love	1956	3.00	6.00	12.00
❏ 15480	Voices/Lonesome Lover Blues	1956	3.00	6.00	12.00
❏ 15501	Please Don't Leave Me/Still	1956	3.00	6.00	12.00
❏ 15527	The Banana Boat Song/Honolulu Moon	1957	2.50	5.00	10.00
❏ 15547	Dancing to the Rock and Roll/I'm the One Who Loves You	1957	2.50	5.00	10.00
❏ 15555	I'm Stickin' with You/ Let the Rest of the World Go By	1957	2.50	5.00	10.00

Number	Title (A Side/B Side)	Yr	VG	VG+	NM
❏ 15581	Fool Around/Which Way to Your Heart	1957	2.50	5.00	10.00
❏ 15682	Ain't It the Truth/Love Like a Fool	1957	2.50	5.00	10.00
❏ 15736	Chanson D'Amour/Coconut Grove	1958	2.50	5.00	10.00
❏ 15782	Buttermilk/Take a Step	1958	2.50	5.00	10.00
❏ 15853	Encore D'Amour/Jealous Heart	1958	2.50	5.00	10.00
❏ 15908	Billy Boy/Third Man Theme	1959	2.50	5.00	10.00
❏ 15943	You Are My Sunshine/A Lover's Hymn	1959	2.50	5.00	10.00
❏ 16014	Listen to Your Heart/Please Be Kind	1959	2.50	5.00	10.00
❏ 16027	Hearts of Stone/Seventeen	1960	2.00	4.00	8.00
❏ 16059	Theme from "A Summer Place"/Darling, It's Wonderful	1960	2.00	4.00	8.00
❏ 16086	Come Home Eddie/Lover's Leap	1960	2.00	4.00	8.00
❏ 16499	The Tip of My Fingers/Summertime Love	1963	—	3.00	6.00

RCA VICTOR

Number	Title (A Side/B Side)	Yr	VG	VG+	NM
❏ 47-2926	I'm a Little Cuckoo/Turtle Song	1949	3.00	6.00	12.00

—With the Cavanaugh Trio

Number	Title (A Side/B Side)	Yr	VG	VG+	NM
❏ 47-2976	The Bumpity Bus/24 Hours of Sunshine	1949	3.00	6.00	12.00
❏ 47-3127	Fairy Tales/The Cinderella Work Song	1949	3.00	6.00	12.00
❏ 47-3713	(If I Knew You Were Comin') I'd've Baked a Cake/Mississippi Mud	1950	3.00	6.00	12.00
❏ 47-3772	I Wanna Be Loved/I Didn't Know What Time It Was	1950	3.00	6.00	12.00
❏ 47-3814	Three Little Rings/Down Home Rag	1950	3.00	6.00	12.00
❏ 47-3940	Sleigh Bells/Jing-a-Ling, Jing-a-Ling	1950	3.00	6.00	12.00

—With Dick Contino

Number	Title (A Side/B Side)	Yr	VG	VG+	NM
❏ 47-3979	Tennessee Waltz/I Guess I'll Have to Dream the Rest	1950	3.00	6.00	12.00
❏ 47-4009	Bouncy Bouncy Bally/What Did I Do	1950	3.00	6.00	12.00
❏ 47-4077	Let Me In/Hurry Home to Me	1951	3.75	7.50	15.00

—With Texas Jim Robertson

Number	Title (A Side/B Side)	Yr	VG	VG+	NM
❏ 47-4106	The Fortune Teller Song/The Fifth Wheel on the Wagon	1951	3.00	6.00	12.00
❏ 47-4168	Rhumba Boogie/Moon-June-Spoon	1951	3.00	6.00	12.00
❏ 47-4233	Castle Rock/Makin' Like a Train	1951	3.00	6.00	12.00
❏ 47-4274	Cold, Cold Heart/I Get the Blues When It Rains	1951	3.00	6.00	12.00
❏ 47-4322	A Howdy Doody Christmas/The Popcorn Song	1951	5.00	10.00	20.00

—With Howdy Doody

Number	Title (A Side/B Side)	Yr	VG	VG+	NM
❏ 47-4387	Alabama Jubilee/Grand Central Station	1951	3.00	6.00	12.00
❏ 47-4449	Snowflakes/River in Moonlight	1952	3.00	6.00	12.00

—With Merv Griffin and Freddie Martin

Number	Title (A Side/B Side)	Yr	VG	VG+	NM
❏ 47-4667	When I Dream/I Grabbed for the Ending	1952	3.00	6.00	12.00
❏ 47-4776	If You Would Only Be Mine/There's Doubt in My Mind	1952	3.00	6.00	12.00
❏ 47-5049	Winter's Here Again/Lonesome Road	1952	3.00	6.00	12.00
❏ 47-5162	Walkin' the Floor Over You/The Price I Paid for Loving You	1953	3.00	6.00	12.00
❏ 47-5266	Mexican Joe/He Who Has Love	1953	3.00	6.00	12.00
❏ 47-5383	Please Play Our Song/Falling	1953	3.00	6.00	12.00
❏ 47-5612	Till Then/Baion	1954	3.00	6.00	12.00

7-Inch Extended Plays
DOT

Number	Title (A Side/B Side)	Yr	VG	VG+	NM
❏ DEP-1020	Does Your Heart Beat for Me/Playmates//Royal Garden Blues/If I Didn't Have You	195?	3.75	7.50	15.00

—Maroon label

Number	Title (A Side/B Side)	Yr	VG	VG+	NM
❏ DEP-1020 [PS]	(title unknown)	195?	3.75	7.50	15.00

Albums
DOT

Number	Title (A Side/B Side)	Yr	VG	VG+	NM
❏ DLP-104 [10]	The Fontane Sisters	1955	12.50	25.00	50.00
❏ DLP-3004 [M]	The Fontanes Sing	1956	10.00	20.00	40.00

—Maroon label

Number	Title (A Side/B Side)	Yr	VG	VG+	NM
❏ DLP-3004 [M]	The Fontanes Sing	1957	6.25	12.50	25.00

—Black label

Number	Title (A Side/B Side)	Yr	VG	VG+	NM
❏ DLP-3042 [M]	A Visit with the Fontane Sisters	1957	7.50	15.00	30.00
❏ DLP-3531 [M]	The Tips of My Fingers	1963	3.75	7.50	15.00
❏ DLP-25531 [S]	The Tips of My Fingers	1963	5.00	10.00	20.00

FOOD
Albums
CAPITOL

Number	Title (A Side/B Side)	Yr	VG	VG+	NM
❏ ST-304	Forever Is a Dream	1969	15.00	30.00	60.00

FOOL, THE
45s
MERCURY

Number	Title (A Side/B Side)	Yr	VG	VG+	NM
❏ 72896	Lay It Down/Rainbow Man	1969	2.00	4.00	8.00
❏ 72918	We Are One/Shining Light	1969	2.00	4.00	8.00

Albums
MERCURY

Number	Title (A Side/B Side)	Yr	VG	VG+	NM
❏ SR-61178	The Fool	1968	7.50	15.00	30.00

FOOTPRINTS
45s
CAPITOL

Number	Title (A Side/B Side)	Yr	VG	VG+	NM
❏ 2052	Never Say Die/Mama Rand's	1967	3.75	7.50	15.00

FORBES, GRAHAM
Albums
PHILLIPS INTERNATIONAL

Number	Title (A Side/B Side)	Yr	VG	VG+	NM
❏ PLP-1955 [M]	The Martini Set	1959	200.00	400.00	800.00

FORCE FIVE, THE
45s
ASCOT

Number	Title (A Side/B Side)	Yr	VG	VG+	NM
❏ 2206	Gee Too Tiger/I Want You Babe	1966	12.50	25.00	50.00

FORD, BILLY Of BILLY AND LILLIE.
45s
JOSIE

Number	Title (A Side/B Side)	Yr	VG	VG+	NM
❏ 775	String of Pearls/Stop Lyin' on Me	1955	10.00	20.00	40.00

REPRISE

Number	Title (A Side/B Side)	Yr	VG	VG+	NM
❏ 0265	This Is Worth Fighting For/My Girl	1964	3.00	6.00	12.00

UNITED

Number	Title (A Side/B Side)	Yr	VG	VG+	NM
❏ 142	Smooth Rocking/You Foxie Thing	1954	7.50	15.00	30.00
❏ 167	Confessing/Old Age	1955	7.50	15.00	30.00

VIK

Number	Title (A Side/B Side)	Yr	VG	VG+	NM
❏ 0263	How Can I Be Sure/Billy Boy Blow	1957	6.25	12.50	25.00

F

FORD, DEE DEE Also see DON GARDNER AND DEE DEE FORD.

45s

Number	Title (A Side/B Side)	Yr	VG	VG+	NM
ABC-PARAMOUNT					
❏ 10503	Just Like a Fool (I Keep Hopin')/Shoo-Fly Pie	1963	3.00	6.00	12.00
BRIAR					
❏ 142	Good Morning Blues/I Just Can't Believe	1962	3.00	6.00	12.00
TODD					
❏ 1049	Good Morning Blues/I Just Can't Believe	1959	3.75	7.50	15.00

FORD, EMILE, AND THE CHECKMATES

45s

Number	Title (A Side/B Side)	Yr	VG	VG+	NM
ANDIE					
❏ 5018	Don't Tell Me Your Troubles/What Do You Want to Make Those Eyes at Me For	1960	3.75	7.50	15.00

FORD, FRANKIE

45s

Number	Title (A Side/B Side)	Yr	VG	VG+	NM
ABC					
❏ 11431	All Alone Am I/Blue Monday	1974	—	2.50	5.00
ACE					
❏ 549	The Last One to Cry/Cheatin' Woman	1958	6.25	12.50	25.00
❏ 554	Sea Cruise/Roberta	1959	7.50	15.00	30.00
❏ 566	Alimony/Can't Tell My Heart (What to Do)	1959	6.25	12.50	25.00
❏ 580	Time After Time/Want to Be Your Man	1960	6.25	12.50	25.00
❏ 592	Chinatown/What's Goin' On	1960	6.25	12.50	25.00
❏ 592 [PS]	Chinatown/What's Goin' On	1960	12.50	25.00	50.00
❏ 8009	Ocean Full of Tears/Hour of Need	1963	3.75	7.50	15.00
BRIARMEADE					
❏ 7600	I've Found Someone of My Own/Battle Hymn of the Republic	1976	—	2.50	5.00
❏ 7701	Desperado/Mardi Gras in New Orleans	1977	—	2.50	5.00
❏ 7901	Halfway to Paradise/I'm Proud of What I Am	1979	—	2.50	5.00
CINNAMON					
❏ 752	When I Stop Dreamin'/I'm Proud of What I Am	1972	—	2.50	5.00
❏ 767	Talk to a Carpenter/When I Stop Dreamin'	1973	—	2.50	5.00
CONSTELLATION					
❏ 101	Chinatown/Ocean Full of Tears	1963	3.75	7.50	15.00
DOUBLOON					
❏ 101	Half a Crown/I Can't Face Tomorrow	1967	2.50	5.00	10.00
IMPERIAL					
❏ 5686	You Talk Too Much/If You've Got Troubles	1960	3.75	7.50	15.00
❏ 5706	My Southern Belle/The Groom	1960	3.75	7.50	15.00
❏ 5735	Seventeen/Doghouse	1961	3.75	7.50	15.00
❏ 5749	Saturday Night Fish Fry/Love Don't Love Nobody	1961	3.75	7.50	15.00
❏ 5776	Let 'Em Talk/What Happened to You	1961	3.75	7.50	15.00
❏ 5819	They Said It Couldn't Be Done/A Man Only Does	1962	3.75	7.50	15.00
PAULA					
❏ 351	Peace of Mind/I'm Proud of What I Am	1971	2.00	4.00	8.00
STARFIRE					
❏ 119	Time After Time/Cheatin' Woman	1979	—	2.50	5.00
SYC					
❏ 1227	Growing Pains/Ups and Downs	1982	—	2.00	4.00
❏ 1228	My Prayer/Gospel Ship	1983	—	2.00	4.00

▶ 7-Inch Extended Plays

Number	Title (A Side/B Side)	Yr	VG	VG+	NM
ACE					
❏ 105	(contents unknown)	1959	37.50	75.00	150.00
❏ 105 [PS]	The Best of Frankie Ford	1959	37.50	75.00	150.00

Albums

Number	Title (A Side/B Side)	Yr	VG	VG+	NM
ACE					
❏ LP 1005 [M]	Let's Take a Sea Cruise	1959	75.00	150.00	300.00
BRIARMEADE					
❏ BR-5002	Frankie Ford	1976	3.00	6.00	12.00

FORD, ROCKY BILLY

Albums

Number	Title (A Side/B Side)	Yr	VG	VG+	NM
AUDIO LAB					
❏ AL-1561 [M]	A New Singing Star	1960	37.50	75.00	150.00

FORD, TENNESSEE ERNIE Includes records issued as "Tennessee Ernie."

45s

Number	Title (A Side/B Side)	Yr	VG	VG+	NM
CANADA DRY					
❏ 72-6596 [DJ]	The Real Story Of Christmas from St. Luke, Chapter 2	1972	—	2.50	5.00
—Special promo for his 1972 Christmas TV special					
❏ 72-6596 [PS]	The Real Story Of Christmas from St. Luke, Chapter 2	1972	—	2.50	5.00
—Special promo for his 1972 Christmas TV special					
CAPITOL					
❏ F985	I've Got to Feed 'Em in the Morning/My Hobby	1950	3.75	7.50	15.00
❏ F1124	I'll Never Be Free/Ain't Nobody's Business But My Own	1950	3.75	7.50	15.00
—With Kay Starr					
❏ F1159	What This Country Needs/The Lord's Lariat	1950	3.75	7.50	15.00
❏ F1174	Bright Lights/The Cincinnati Dancing Pig	1950	3.75	7.50	15.00
❏ F1205	Mama Goes Everywhere Papa Goes/Please Love Me	1950	3.75	7.50	15.00
❏ F1275	Bryant's Boogie/Little Juan Pedro	1950	5.00	10.00	20.00
❏ F1295	The Shot Gun Boogie/I Ain't Gonna Let It Happen No More	1950	5.00	10.00	20.00
❏ F1349	Tailor Made Woman/Stack-O-Lee	1951	3.75	7.50	15.00
❏ F1470	Kentucky Waltz/Strange Little Girl	1951	3.75	7.50	15.00
❏ F1521	Mr. and Mississippi/She's My Baby	1951	3.75	7.50	15.00
❏ F1567	Oceans of Tears/You're My Sugar	1951	3.75	7.50	15.00
—With Kay Starr					
❏ F1623	I'll Never Be Free/Ain't Nobody's Business But My Own	1951	3.00	6.00	12.00
—With Kay Starr; reissue					
❏ F1626	The Shot Gun Boogie/Anticipation Blues	1951	3.00	6.00	12.00
❏ F1695	Mule Train/The Cry of the Wild Goose	1951	3.00	6.00	12.00
❏ F1775	Kissin' Bug Boogie/Woman Is a Five-Letter Word	1951	5.00	10.00	20.00
❏ F1809	Hey, Good Lookin'/Cool, Cool Kisses	1951	3.75	7.50	15.00
❏ F1830	A Rootin' Tootin' Santa Claus/Christmas Dinner	1951	3.75	7.50	15.00

Number	Title (A Side/B Side)	Yr	VG	VG+	NM
❏ F1911	Rock City Boogie/Streamline Cannonball	1951	5.00	10.00	20.00
—With the Dinning Sisters					
❏ F2017	Hambone/Candy Dancers' Ball	1952	3.75	7.50	15.00
❏ F2042	Put Your Arms Around Me/Everybody's Got a Girl But Me	1952	3.75	7.50	15.00
❏ F2066	Snowshoe Thompson/Fatback Louisiana USA	1952	3.75	7.50	15.00
❏ 2145	Talk to the Animals/What a Wonderful World	1968	—	3.00	6.00
❏ F2170	Blackberry Boogie/Tennessee Local	1952	5.00	10.00	20.00
❏ F2179	Smokey Mountain Boogie/Country Junction	1952	5.00	10.00	20.00
❏ F2215	I'm Hog Tied Over You/False Hearted Girl	1952	3.75	7.50	15.00
—With Ella Mae Morse					
❏ 2334	The Little Boy King/Bring a Torch, Jeanette, Isabella	1968	—	3.00	6.00
❏ F2338	Sweet Temptation/I Don't Know	1953	3.75	7.50	15.00
❏ F2443	Hey, Mr. Cotton Picker/Three Things (A Man Must Do)	1953	3.75	7.50	15.00
❏ 2522	Honey-Eyed Girl (That's You That's You)/Good Morning, Dear	1969	—	3.00	6.00
❏ F2602	Catfish Boogie/Kiss Me Big	1953	5.00	10.00	20.00
❏ F2809	The Honeymoon's Over/This Must Be the Place	1954	3.00	6.00	12.00
—With Betty Hutton					
❏ F2810	River of No Return/Give Me Your Word	1954	3.00	6.00	12.00
❏ F2876	Losing You/Eins, Zwei, Drei	1954	3.00	6.00	12.00
❏ 2918	Rainy Night in Georgia/Let the Lovelight in Your Eyes Lead Me On	1970	—	2.50	5.00
❏ F2939	Somebody Bigger Than You and I/There Is Beauty in Everything	1954	3.00	6.00	12.00
❏ F3058	Ballad of Davy Crockett/Farewell	1955	3.75	7.50	15.00
❏ 3079	Happy Songs of Love/Don't Let the Good Life Pass You By	1971	—	2.50	5.00
❏ F3135	I Am a Pilgrim/His Hands	1955	3.00	6.00	12.00
❏ F3262	Sixteen Tons/You Don't Have to Be a Baby to Cry	1955	3.75	7.50	15.00
❏ F3343	Bright Lights and Blonde Haired Women/That's All	1956	5.00	10.00	20.00
❏ F3421	John Henry/Rovin' Gambler	1956	3.00	6.00	12.00
❏ 3422	Pea-Pickin' Cook/The Song	1972	—	2.50	5.00
❏ F3474	Rock Roll Boogie/Call Me Darling, Call Me Sweetheart	1956	5.00	10.00	20.00
❏ F3553	First Born/Have You Seen Her	1956	3.00	6.00	12.00
❏ 3556	Printers' Alley Stars/Baby	1973	—	2.00	4.00
❏ 3631	Farther Down the River (Where the Fishin's Good)/You've Still Got Love All Over You	1973	—	2.00	4.00
❏ F3649	The Watermelon Song/One Suit	1957	3.00	6.00	12.00
❏ F3700	Lonely Man/False Hearted Girl	1957	3.00	6.00	12.00
❏ 3704	Colorado Country Morning/Daddy Usta Say	1973	—	2.00	4.00
❏ F3762	In the Middle of An Island/Ivy League	1957	3.00	6.00	12.00
❏ 3783	She Picked Up the Pieces/Sweet Child of Sunshine	1973	—	2.00	4.00
❏ 3848	I've Got Confidence/I'd Like to Be	1974	—	2.00	4.00
❏ F3868	Bless Your Pea Pickin' Heart/Down Deep	1957	3.00	6.00	12.00
❏ 3916	Come On Down/Bits and Pieces of Life	1974	—	2.00	4.00
❏ F3997	Love Makes the World Go Round/Sunday Barbecue	1958	2.50	5.00	10.00
❏ 4044	Baby/I'd Like to Be	1975	—	2.00	4.00
—With Andra Willis					
❏ F4107	Sleepin' at the Foot of the Bed/Glad Rags	1958	2.50	5.00	10.00
❏ 4160	The Devil Ain't a Lonely Woman's Friend/Smokey Taverns, Bar Room Girls	1975	—	2.00	4.00
❏ F4173	Code of the Mountains/Black-Eyed Susie	1959	2.50	5.00	10.00
❏ 4285	I Been to Georgia on a Fast Train/Baby's Home	1976	—	2.00	4.00
❏ 4302	Love Is the Only Thing/Sunny Side of Heaven	1959	2.00	4.00	8.00
❏ 4333	Sweet Feelin's/Dogs and Sheriff John	1976	—	2.00	4.00
❏ 4416	Joshua Fit De Battle/Oh Mary, Don't You Weep	1960	2.00	4.00	8.00
❏ 4446	Little Klinker/Jingle-O-The-Brownie	1960	3.00	6.00	12.00
❏ 4446 [PS]	Little Klinker/Jingle-O-The-Brownie	1960	5.00	10.00	20.00
❏ 4468	Bless This Land/Lord of All Creation	1960	2.00	4.00	8.00
❏ 4531	Dark As a Dungeon/His Love (Makes the World Go Round)	1961	2.00	4.00	8.00
❏ 4577	Litttle Red Rockin' Hood/I Gotta Have My Baby Back	1961	2.00	4.00	8.00
❏ 4734	Take Your Girlie to the Movies/There'll Be No New Tunes	1962	2.00	4.00	8.00
❏ 4793	The Work Song/Rags and Old Iron	1962	2.00	4.00	8.00
❏ 4838	How Great Thou Art/Eternal Life	1962	2.00	4.00	8.00
❏ 5425	Sixteen Tons/Hicktown	1965	—	3.00	6.00
❏ 5520	Girl Don't You Know/Now It's All Over	1965	—	3.00	6.00
❏ 5534	Sing We Now of Christmas/The Little Drummer Boy	1965	2.00	4.00	8.00
❏ 5757	God Lives/How Great Thou Art	1966	—	3.00	6.00
❏ 5900	Pearly Shells/Lahaina Luna	1967	—	3.00	6.00
❏ 5996	The Road/Hand Me Down Things	1967	—	3.00	6.00
❏ F40280	The Cry of the Wild Goose/The Donkey Serenade	1950	5.00	10.00	20.00

7-Inch Extended Plays

Number	Title (A Side/B Side)	Yr	VG	VG+	NM
CAPITOL					
❏ EAP 1-413	*Shot Gun Boogie/Smokey Mountain Boogie/Blackberry Boogie/Anticipation Blues	1953	5.00	10.00	20.00
❏ EAP 1-413 [PS]	Backwoods Boogie and Blues	1953	5.00	10.00	20.00
❏ EAP 1-639	His Hands/Somebody Bigger Than You and I/I Am a Pilgrim/There Is Beauty in Everything	195?	3.75	7.50	15.00
❏ EAP 1-639 [PS]	Tennessee Ernie Ford	195?	3.75	7.50	15.00
❏ EAP 1-693	Sixteen Tons/River of No Return//You Don't Have to Be a Baby to Cry/Give Me Your Word	1956	3.75	7.50	15.00
❏ EAP 1-693 [PS]	16 Tons	1956	3.75	7.50	15.00
❏ EAP 1-700	John Henry/Trouble in Mind//Gaily the Troubadour/The Lost Letter	1956	3.75	7.50	15.00
❏ EAP 1-700 [PS]	This Lusty Land! Part 1	1956	3.75	7.50	15.00
❏ EAP 2-700	Dark as a Dungeon/False Hearted Girl//I Gave My Love a Cherry/Nine Pound Hammer	1956	3.75	7.50	15.00
❏ EAP 2-700 [PS]	This Lusty Land! Part 2	1956	3.75	7.50	15.00
❏ EAP 3-700	Chicken Road/Who Will Shoe Your Pretty Little Foot//The Rovin' Gambler/In the Pines	1956	3.75	7.50	15.00
❏ EAP 3-700 [PS]	This Lusty Land! Part 3	1956	3.75	7.50	15.00
❏ EAP 1-756	The Ninety and Nine/Softly and Tenderly//Who at My Door Is Standing/Rock of Ages	1956	3.75	7.50	15.00
❏ EAP 1-756 [PS]	Hymns, Part 1	1956	3.75	7.50	15.00

Number	Title (A Side/B Side)	Yr	VG	VG+	NM
❏ EAP 2-756	When They Ring the Golden Bells/In the Garden//Sweet Hour of Prayer/The Old Rugged Cross	1956	3.75	7.50	15.00
❏ EAP 2-756 [PS]	Hymns, Part 2	1956	3.75	7.50	15.00
❏ EAP 3-756	Let the Lower Lights Be Burning/Others//My Task/Ivory Palaces	1956	3.75	7.50	15.00
❏ EAP 3-756 [PS]	Hymns, Part 3	1956	3.75	7.50	15.00
❏ EAP 1-818	Just a Closer Walk with Thee/Peace in the Valley//Wayfaring Pilgrim/Were You There	195?	3.75	7.50	15.00
❏ EAP 1-818 [PS]	Spirituals, Part 1	195?	3.75	7.50	15.00
❏ EAP 2-818	He'll Understand and Say "Well Done"/I Know the Lord Laid His Hands on Me//Noah Found Grace in the Eyes of the Lord/I Want to Be Ready	195?	3.75	7.50	15.00
❏ EAP 2-818 [PS]	Spirituals, Part 2	195?	3.75	7.50	15.00
❏ EAP 3-818	Take My Hand, Precious Lord/Stand By Me//When God Dips His Love in My Heart/Get On Board, Little Children	195?	3.75	7.50	15.00
❏ EAP 3-818 [PS]	Spirituals, Part 3	195?	3.75	7.50	15.00
❏ EAP 1-888	Country Junction/Milk 'Em in the Mornin' Blues/Anticipation Blues/Catfish Boogie	1956	3.75	7.50	15.00
❏ EAP 1-888 [PS]	Ol' Rockin' Ern, Part 1	1956	3.75	7.50	15.00
❏ EAP 2-888	*The Shot-Gun Boogie/She's My Baby/Blackberry Boogie/Kiss Me Big	1956	3.75	7.50	15.00
❏ EAP 2-888 [PS]	Ol' Rockin' Ern, Part 2	1956	3.75	7.50	15.00
❏ EAP 3-888	Smokey Mountain Boogie/Ain't Nobody's Business But My Own/I Ain't a-Gonna Let It Happen No More/The Lord's Lariat	1956	3.75	7.50	15.00
❏ EAP 3-888 [PS]	Ol' Rockin' Ern, Part 3	1956	3.75	7.50	15.00
❏ EAP 1-1005	What a Friend We Have in Jesus/Jesus, Savior, Pilot Me//His Eye Is on the Sparrow/Beautiful Isle of Somewhere	1958	2.50	5.00	10.00
❏ EAP 1-1005 [PS]	Nearer the Cross, Part 1	1958	2.50	5.00	10.00
❏ EAP 2-1005	Now the Day Is Over/Nearer My God to Thee//Sweet Peace the Gift of God's Love/Whispering Hope	1958	2.50	5.00	10.00
❏ EAP 2-1005 [PS]	Nearer the Cross, Part 2	1958	2.50	5.00	10.00
❏ EAP 3-1005	Lord, I'm Coming Home/I Need Thee Every Hour//Take Time to Be Holy/God Be With You	1958	2.50	5.00	10.00
❏ EAP 3-1005 [PS]	Nearer the Cross, Part 3	1958	2.50	5.00	10.00
❏ EAP 1-1071	*Joy to the World/O Little Town of Bethlehem/The Star Carol/Hark! The Herald Angels Sing	1958	3.00	6.00	12.00
❏ EAP 1-1071 [PS]	The Star Carol, Part 1	1958	3.00	6.00	12.00
❏ EAP 2-1071	(contents unknown)	1958	3.00	6.00	12.00
❏ EAP 2-1071 [PS]	The Star Carol, Part 2	1958	3.00	6.00	12.00
❏ EAP 3-1071	(contents unknown)	1958	3.00	6.00	12.00
❏ EAP 3-1071 [PS]	The Star Carol, Part 3	1958	3.00	6.00	12.00
❏ EAP 1-1227	Brown's Ferry Blues/Black Is the Color of My True Love's Hair//Old Blue/Freight Train Blues	1959	3.00	6.00	12.00
❏ EAP 1-1227 [PS]	Gather 'Round, Part 1	1959	3.00	6.00	12.00
❏ EAP 2-1227	The Night Herding Song/Darby's Ram//Prety Little Pink/Barbara Allen	1959	3.00	6.00	12.00
❏ EAP 2-1227 [PS]	Gather 'Round, Part 2	1959	3.00	6.00	12.00
❏ EAP 3-1227	Look Down/My Grandfather's Clock//Twenty-One Years/Left My Gal in the Mountains	1959	3.00	6.00	12.00
❏ EAP 3-1227 [PS]	Gather 'Round, Part 3	1959	3.00	6.00	12.00
❏ EAP 1-1272	No Tears in Heaven/Precious Memories//When I Reach That City/An Empty Mansion	1959	3.00	6.00	12.00
❏ EAP 1-1272 [PS]	A Friend We Have, Part 1	1959	3.00	6.00	12.00
❏ EAP 2-1272	Where Could I Go/O Come Angel Band//Hold To God's Unchanging Hand/Wondrous Love	1959	3.00	6.00	12.00
❏ EAP 2-1272 [PS]	A Friend We Have, Part 2	1959	3.00	6.00	12.00
❏ EAP 3-1272	Life's Railway to Heaven/Good Night And Good Morning//Drifting Too Far from the Shore/My Jesus As Thou Wilt	1959	3.00	6.00	12.00
❏ EAP 3-1272 [PS]	A Friend We Have, Part 3	1959	3.00	6.00	12.00
❏ EAP 1-1332	*There Is Power in the Blood/When the Roll Is Called Up Yonder/Shall We Gather at the River/Brighten The Corner Where You Are/What a Friend	1960	3.00	6.00	12.00
❏ EAP 1-1332 [PS]	Sing a Hymn with Me, Part 1	1960	3.00	6.00	12.00
❏ EAP 2-1332	Onward Christian Soldiers/Oh How I Love Jesus//I Love to Tell the Story/The Church in the Wilderness	1960	3.00	6.00	12.00
❏ EAP 2-1332 [PS]	Sing a Hymn with Me, Part 2	1960	3.00	6.00	12.00
❏ EAP 3-1332	*Bring In the Sheaves/Jesus Loves Me/All Hail the Power/The Home Over There/Count Your Blessings	1960	3.00	6.00	12.00
❏ EAP 3-1332 [PS]	Sing a Hymn with Me, Part 3	1960	3.00	6.00	12.00
❏ MA1-1380	*Sixteen Tons/Mule Train/Shot-Gun Boogie/The Cry of the Wild Goose	196?	3.75	7.50	15.00
—"Compact Double 33" single, small hole					
❏ MA1-1380 [PS]	Tennessee Ernie Ford	196?	3.75	7.50	15.00
❏ EAP 3-1434	Ain't Gonna Study War No More/Joshua Fit the Battle//Were You There/Nobody Knows the Trouble I've Seen	196?	3.00	6.00	12.00
❏ EAP 3-1434 [PS]	Sing a Spiritual with Me, Part 3	196?	3.00	6.00	12.00
GREEN GIANT					
❏ PB-2565 [DJ]	Down in the Valley/Medley: The More We Get Together-Dear Evalina-Keep on the Sunny Side of Life-How Many Biscuits Can We Eat-For He's a Jolly Green Giant/How the Green Giant Found His Song (And Almost Lost His Ho-Ho-Ho)/Good Things from the Garden	1963	2.50	5.00	10.00
—Promotional item for the Green Giant Company/Le Sueur Peas					
❏ PB-2565 [PS]	When Pea-Pickers Get Together	1963	2.50	5.00	10.00
—Promotional item for the Green Giant Company/Le Sueur Peas					

Albums

CAPITOL

Number	Title (A Side/B Side)	Yr	VG	VG+	NM
❏ ST-127	Songs I Like to Sing	1969	3.00	6.00	12.00
❏ ST-334	Holy, Holy, Holy	1969	3.00	6.00	12.00
❏ SM-412	America the Beautiful	197?	2.00	4.00	8.00
—Reissue with new prefix					
❏ STAO-412	America the Beautiful	1970	3.00	6.00	12.00
❏ STBB-485 [(2)]	Christmas Special	1970	3.75	7.50	15.00
❏ STBB-506 [(2)]	Sweet Hour of Prayer/Let Me Walk with Thee	1971	3.75	7.50	15.00
❏ SF-8-0507	Sweet Hour of Prayer	1970	3.75	7.50	15.00
—Capitol Record Club edition					
❏ SF-8-0508	Let Me Walk with Thee	1970	3.75	7.50	15.00
—Capitol Record Club edition					
❏ ST-583	Everything Is Beautiful	1971	3.00	6.00	12.00
❏ DT 700 [R]	This Lusty Land!	196?	3.00	6.00	12.00
❏ T 700 [M]	This Lusty Land	1956	6.25	12.50	25.00
—Turquoise label					
❏ T 700 [M]	This Lusty Land	1959	5.00	10.00	20.00
—Black label with colorband, logo at left					
❏ T 700 [M]	This Lusty Land!	1963	3.75	7.50	15.00
—Black label with colorband, logo at top					
❏ ST-730	Abide with Me	1971	3.00	6.00	12.00
❏ ST 756 [S]	Hymns	1962	3.75	7.50	15.00
—Re-recording of the original mono LP					
❏ T 756 [M]	Hymns	1956	6.25	12.50	25.00
—Turquoise label					
❏ T 756 [M]	Hymns	1959	5.00	10.00	20.00
—Black label with colorband, logo at left					
❏ T 756 [M]	Hymns	1962	3.75	7.50	15.00
—Black label with colorband, logo at top					
❏ ST 818 [S]	Spirituals	1962	3.75	7.50	15.00
—Re-recording of the original mono LP					
❏ T 818 [M]	Spirituals	1957	6.25	12.50	25.00
—Turquoise label					
❏ T 818 [M]	Spirituals	1959	5.00	10.00	20.00
—Black label with colorband, logo at left					
❏ T 818 [M]	Spirituals	1962	3.75	7.50	15.00
—Black label with colorband, logo at top					
❏ ST-831 [S]	C-H-R-I-S-T-M-A-S	1971	3.00	6.00	12.00
❏ ST-833	The Folk Album	1971	3.00	6.00	12.00
❏ DT 841 [R]	Tennessee Ernie Ford Favorites	196?	3.00	6.00	12.00
❏ T 841 [M]	Tennessee Ernie Ford Favorites	1957	7.50	15.00	30.00
—Turquoise label					
❏ T 841 [M]	Tennessee Ernie Ford Favorites	1958	5.00	10.00	20.00
—Black label with colorband, logo at left					
❏ T 841 [M]	Tennessee Ernie Ford Favorites	1962	3.75	7.50	15.00
—Black label with colorband, logo at top					
❏ T 888 [M]	Ol' Rockin' Ern	1957	12.50	25.00	50.00
—Turquoise or gray label					
❏ ST 1005 [S]	Nearer the Cross	1959	6.25	12.50	25.00
—Black label with colorband, logo at left					
❏ ST 1005 [S]	Nearer the Cross	1962	5.00	10.00	20.00
—Black label with colorband, logo at top					
❏ T 1005 [M]	Nearer the Cross	1958	5.00	10.00	20.00
—Black label with colorband, logo at left					
❏ T 1005 [M]	Nearer the Cross	1962	3.75	7.50	15.00
—Black label with colorband, logo at top					
❏ ST 1071 [S]	The Star Carol	1958	7.50	15.00	30.00
—Black labels with colorband, Capitol logo on left					
❏ ST 1071 [S]	The Star Carol	1962	5.00	10.00	20.00
—Black label with colorband, "Capitol" logo on top. This was also reissued on later Capitol labels into the 1970s with values no more than half the above.					
❏ T 1071 [M]	The Star Carol	1958	6.25	12.50	25.00
—Black labels with colorband, "Capitol" logo on left					
❏ T 1071 [M]	The Star Carol	1962	3.75	7.50	15.00
—Black label with colorband, logo on top					
❏ ST 1227 [S]	Gather 'Round	1959	5.00	10.00	20.00
❏ T 1227 [M]	Gather 'Round	1959	3.75	7.50	15.00
❏ ST 1272 [S]	A Friend We Have	1959	5.00	10.00	20.00
❏ T 1272 [M]	A Friend We Have	1959	3.75	7.50	15.00
❏ STAO 1332 [S]	Sing a Hymn with Me	1960	6.25	12.50	25.00
—With hymnal					
❏ TAO 1332 [M]	Sing a Hymn with Me	1960	5.00	10.00	20.00
—With hymnal					
❏ DT 1380 [R]	Sixteen Tons	196?	3.00	6.00	12.00
❏ T 1380 [M]	Sixteen Tons	1960	3.75	7.50	15.00
❏ ST 1539 [S]	Civil War Songs of the North	1961	5.00	10.00	20.00
❏ T 1539 [M]	Civil War Songs of the North	1961	3.75	7.50	15.00
❏ ST 1540 [S]	Civil War Songs of the South	1961	5.00	10.00	20.00
❏ T 1540 [M]	Civil War Songs of the South	1961	3.75	7.50	15.00
❏ ST 1679 [S]	Sing a Hymn with Me	1962	3.75	7.50	15.00
—Reissue of 1332 with standard cover?					
❏ T 1679 [M]	Sing a Hymn with Me	1962	3.00	6.00	12.00
—Reissue of 1332 with standard cover?					
❏ ST 1680 [S]	Sing a Spiritual with Me	1962	3.75	7.50	15.00
❏ T 1680 [M]	Sing a Spiritual with Me	1962	3.00	6.00	12.00
❏ ST 1684 [S]	Here Comes the Mississippi Showboat	1962	3.75	7.50	15.00
❏ T 1684 [M]	Here Comes the Mississippi Showboat	1962	3.00	6.00	12.00
❏ ST 1694 [S]	Hymns at Home	1962	3.75	7.50	15.00
❏ T 1694 [M]	Hymns at Home	1962	3.00	6.00	12.00
❏ ST 1751 [S]	I Love to Tell the Story	1962	3.75	7.50	15.00
❏ T 1751 [M]	I Love to Tell the Story	1962	3.00	6.00	12.00
❏ ST 1794 [S]	Book of Favorite Hymns	1962	5.00	10.00	20.00
❏ T 1794 [M]	Book of Favorite Hymns	1962	3.75	7.50	15.00
❏ ST 1875 [S]	Long Long Ago	1963	3.75	7.50	15.00
❏ T 1875 [M]	Long Long Ago	1963	3.00	6.00	12.00
❏ ST 1937 [S]	We Gather Together	1963	3.75	7.50	15.00
❏ T 1937 [M]	We Gather Together	1963	3.00	6.00	12.00
❏ ST 1994 [S]	The Story of Christmas	1963	5.00	10.00	20.00
❏ T 1994 [M]	The Story of Christmas	1963	3.75	7.50	15.00
—With the Roger Wagner Chorale					
❏ SM-2026	Great Gospel Songs	197?	2.00	4.00	8.00
—Reissue with new prefix					
❏ ST 2026 [S]	Great Gospel Songs	1964	3.75	7.50	15.00
❏ T 2026 [M]	Great Gospel Songs	1964	3.00	6.00	12.00
❏ SM-2097	Country Hits…Feelin' Blue	197?	2.00	4.00	8.00
—Reissue with new prefix					
❏ ST 2097 [S]	Country Hits…Feelin' Blue	1964	3.75	7.50	15.00
❏ T 2097 [M]	Country Hits…Feelin' Blue	1964	3.00	6.00	12.00
❏ STBL 2183 [(2)S]	The World's Best Loved Hymns	1964	6.25	12.50	25.00
❏ TBL 2183 [(2)M]	The World's Best Loved Hymns	1964	5.00	10.00	20.00
❏ ST 2296 [S]	Let Me Walk with Thee	1965	3.75	7.50	15.00
❏ T 2296 [M]	Let Me Walk with Thee	1965	3.00	6.00	12.00
❏ ST 2394 [S]	Sing We Now of Christmas	1965	3.75	7.50	15.00
—Same as above, but in stereo					
❏ T 2394 [M]	Sing We Now of Christmas	1965	3.00	6.00	12.00
❏ ST 2444 [S]	My Favorite Things	1966	3.75	7.50	15.00
❏ T 2444 [M]	My Favorite Things	1966	3.00	6.00	12.00

Number	Title (A Side/B Side)	Yr	VG	VG+	NM
❑ ST 2557 [S]	Wonderful Peace	1966	3.75	7.50	15.00
❑ T 2557 [M]	Wonderful Peace	1966	3.00	6.00	12.00
❑ ST 2618 [S]	God Lives	1966	3.75	7.50	15.00
❑ T 2618 [M]	God Lives	1966	3.00	6.00	12.00
❑ ST 2681 [S]	Aloha from Tennessee Ernie Ford	1967	3.00	6.00	12.00
❑ T 2681 [M]	Aloha from Tennessee Ernie Ford	1967	3.75	7.50	15.00
❑ SM-2761	Faith of Our Fathers	197?	2.00	4.00	8.00
—Reissue with new prefix					
❑ ST 2761 [S]	Faith of Our Fathers	1967	3.00	6.00	12.00
❑ T 2761 [M]	Faith of Our Fathers	1967	3.75	7.50	15.00
❑ ST 2845 [S]	Our Garden of Hymns	1968	3.00	6.00	12.00
❑ T 2845 [M]	Our Garden of Hymns	1968	5.00	10.00	20.00
❑ ST 2896	The World of Pop and Country Hits	1968	3.00	6.00	12.00
❑ STCL 2942 [(3)]	The Tennessee Ernie Ford Deluxe Set	1968	5.00	10.00	20.00
❑ SKAO 2949	Best Hymns	1968	3.00	6.00	12.00
❑ ST 2968	O Come All Ye Faithful	1968	3.00	6.00	12.00
❑ ST-11001	Mr. Words and Music	1972	2.50	5.00	10.00
❑ ST-11092	It's Tennessee Ernie Ford	1973	2.50	5.00	10.00
❑ ST-11232	Tennessee Ernie Ford Sings About Jesus	1973	2.50	5.00	10.00
❑ ST-11290	Make a Joyful Noise	1974	2.50	5.00	10.00
❑ SVBB-11325 [(2)]	25th Anniversary/Yesterday and Today	1974	3.00	6.00	12.00
❑ SVBB-11326 [(2)]	25th Anniversary/Hymns & Gospel	1974	3.00	6.00	12.00
❑ SVBB-11382 [(2)]	Precious Memories	1975	3.00	6.00	12.00
❑ ST-11495	Tennessee Ernie Ford Sings His Great Love Songs	1975	2.50	5.00	10.00
❑ SM-12033	Book of Favorite Hymns	1980	2.50	5.00	10.00
❑ SN-16040	Yesterday	1981	2.00	4.00	8.00
❑ SN-16042	Gospel	1981	2.00	4.00	8.00
❑ SN-16043	Hymns	1981	2.00	4.00	8.00
❑ SN-16173	Hymns	1981	2.00	4.00	8.00
❑ SN-16174	Spirituals	1981	2.00	4.00	8.00
❑ SN-16289	The Star Carol	1982	2.00	4.00	8.00
—Budget-line reissue					
EVEREST ARCHIVE OF FOLK & JAZZ					
❑ 279	Tennessee Ernie Ford	197?	2.50	5.00	10.00
PICKWICK					
❑ PTP-2016 [(2)]	Tennessee Ernie Ford	197?	3.00	6.00	12.00
❑ PTP-2050 [(2)]	Hymns	197?	3.00	6.00	12.00
❑ SPC-3047	Bless Your Pea-Pickin' Heart	196?	3.00	6.00	12.00
❑ SPC-3066	I Love You So Much	196?	3.00	6.00	12.00
❑ SPC-3222	The Need for Prayer	197?	2.50	5.00	10.00
❑ SPC-3268	Sixteen Tons	197?	2.50	5.00	10.00
❑ SPC-3273	Jesus Loves Me	197?	2.50	5.00	10.00
❑ SPC-3308	Amazing Grace	197?	2.50	5.00	10.00
❑ SPC-3353	Rock of Ages	197?	2.50	5.00	10.00
RANWOOD					
❑ RLP-7026 [(2)]	Tennessee Ernie Ford Sings 22 Favorite Hymns	198?	3.00	6.00	12.00
WORD					
❑ 8764	He Touched Me	1978	2.50	5.00	10.00
❑ 8798	Swing Wide Your Golden Gate	198?	2.50	5.00	10.00
❑ 8841	Tell Me the Old Story	1979	2.50	5.00	10.00
❑ 8841	Tell Me the Old Story	198?	2.50	5.00	10.00
❑ 8858	There's a Song in My Heart	198?	2.50	5.00	10.00

FORD, TENNESSEE ERNIE, AND MOLLY BEE
45s
CAPITOL

Number	Title (A Side/B Side)	Yr	VG	VG+	NM
❑ F2473	Don't Start Courtin' in a Hot Rod/We're a-Growin' Up	1953	5.00	10.00	20.00

FORD THEATRE, THE
45s
ABC

Number	Title (A Side/B Side)	Yr	VG	VG+	NM
❑ 11118	Theme for the Masses/I Can't Help It Baby	1968	2.50	5.00	10.00
❑ 11227	I've Got the Fever/Jefferson Airplane	1969	2.50	5.00	10.00

Albums
ABC

Number	Title (A Side/B Side)	Yr	VG	VG+	NM
❑ S-658	Trilogy	1968	6.25	12.50	25.00
❑ S-681	Time Changes	1969	5.00	10.00	20.00

FOREST
Albums
HARVEST

Number	Title (A Side/B Side)	Yr	VG	VG+	NM
❑ SKAO-419	Forest	1970	12.50	25.00	50.00

FOREVER MORE
45s
RCA VICTOR

Number	Title (A Side/B Side)	Yr	VG	VG+	NM
❑ 74-0277	Home Country Blues/Back in the States Again	1969	2.00	4.00	8.00
❑ 74-0335	Beautiful Afternoon/One O'Clock and All's Well	1970	2.00	4.00	8.00

Albums
RCA VICTOR

Number	Title (A Side/B Side)	Yr	VG	VG+	NM
❑ LSP-4272	Yours Forever More	1970	3.75	7.50	15.00
❑ LSP-4425	Words on Black Plastic	1971	3.75	7.50	15.00

FORMATIONS, THE
45s
BANK

Number	Title (A Side/B Side)	Yr	VG	VG+	NM
❑ 1007	At the Top of the Stairs/Magic Melody	1968	7.50	15.00	30.00

MGM

Number	Title (A Side/B Side)	Yr	VG	VG+	NM
❑ 13899	At the Top of the Stairs/Magic Melody	1968	2.50	5.00	10.00
❑ 13963	Love's Not Only for the Heart/Lonely Voice of Love	1968	5.00	10.00	20.00
❑ 14009	Don't Get Close/There's No Room	1968	3.00	6.00	12.00

FORTUNE
Group of studio musicians who appear to have specialized in recording "song poems," lyrics sent in by unwitting members of the public in reply to ads in the backs of magazines.
45s
SONGUILD

Number	Title (A Side/B Side)	Yr	VG	VG+	NM
❑ 926	Christmas Without You/For One Moment in Time You Were Mine	197?	—	2.50	5.00
❑ 931	Astrologer/A Poet	197?	—	2.50	5.00
—B-side by Dick Charles					
❑ 932	Ho Chi Minh Trail/You're Coming Back to Me	197?	—	2.50	5.00
❑ 935	Be Good to Your Baby/To My Beloved Myrtle	197?	—	2.50	5.00
❑ 936	Traffic Lights/Spring	197?	—	2.50	5.00
❑ 937	Your Song/Race Horses Have Funny Names	197?	—	2.50	5.00

Number	Title (A Side/B Side)	Yr	VG	VG+	NM
❑ 938	A Little Bit North and Way Out West/Mary Jane	197?	—	2.50	5.00
❑ 942	Blue Bird Blues/Jakey Stuff	197?	—	2.50	5.00
❑ 945	Red Headed Baby Doll/That Gray Haired Sweetheart of Mine	197?	—	2.50	5.00
❑ 946	One and Only/Them Wailin' Blues	197?	—	2.50	5.00
❑ 947	I Saw The Light/Grapes Born of Vine	197?	—	2.50	5.00
❑ 956	Last Bus To Memphis/A Place in Your Memory	197?	—	2.50	5.00
❑ 957	Walk a Tight Rope/Luxury of Lies	197?	—	2.50	5.00
❑ 969	Something of Value/The Key Is Still There	197?	—	2.50	5.00
—B-side by Bobbi Blake					

FORTUNE, JOHNNY
45s
ARENA

Number	Title (A Side/B Side)	Yr	VG	VG+	NM
❑ 102	I'm a Fool for You/Gee But I Miss You	1963	5.00	10.00	20.00

ARHAVEN

Number	Title (A Side/B Side)	Yr	VG	VG+	NM
❑ 1001	I'm a Fool for You/Gee But I Miss You	1962	6.25	12.50	25.00

BEAVER

Number	Title (A Side/B Side)	Yr	VG	VG+	NM
❑ 111	I'm Requesting a Love Song/Stay Just One More Day	1966	3.75	7.50	15.00

CRUSADER

Number	Title (A Side/B Side)	Yr	VG	VG+	NM
❑ 104	If You Love Me/Gee But I Miss You	1964	3.75	7.50	15.00

CURRENT

Number	Title (A Side/B Side)	Yr	VG	VG+	NM
❑ 101	Say You Will/Come On and Love Me	1965	3.75	7.50	15.00
❑ 104	Dan Stole My Girl/You Want Me to Be Your Baby	1965	3.75	7.50	15.00
❑ 105	I Am Lonely for You/I'll Never Let You Go	1965	3.75	7.50	15.00

EMMY

Number	Title (A Side/B Side)	Yr	VG	VG+	NM
❑ 1001	If You Love Me/Alone and Crying	1960	7.50	15.00	30.00
❑ 1002	I'm in Heaven (When You Kiss Me)/Gee But I Miss You	1960	7.50	15.00	30.00

PARK AVENUE

Number	Title (A Side/B Side)	Yr	VG	VG+	NM
❑ 104	Need You/One Less Angel	1963	3.75	7.50	15.00
❑ 110	Midnight Surf/Soul Surfer	1963	3.75	7.50	15.00
❑ 126	Surfer's Trip/Soul Traveler	1963	3.75	7.50	15.00
❑ 130	Dragster/Siboney	1963	3.75	7.50	15.00
❑ 4905	I'm Talkin' About You/My Wandering Love	1963	3.75	7.50	15.00

UNITED ARTISTS

Number	Title (A Side/B Side)	Yr	VG	VG+	NM
❑ 720	Juarez/It Ain't Necessarily So	1964	3.75	7.50	15.00
❑ 780	Don't You Lie to Me/Don't Stay Out After Midnight	1964	3.75	7.50	15.00

VAULT

Number	Title (A Side/B Side)	Yr	VG	VG+	NM
❑ 954	Your True Love/Tell me You Love Me	1969	2.50	5.00	10.00

FORTUNES, THE (1) British band.
45s
CAPITOL

Number	Title (A Side/B Side)	Yr	VG	VG+	NM
❑ 3086	Here Comes That Rainy Day Feeling Again/I Gotta Dream	1971	—	3.00	6.00
❑ 3086	Here Comes That Rainy Day Feeling Again/Bad Side of Town	1971	2.50	5.00	10.00
❑ 3179	Freedom Comes, Freedom Goes/There's a Man	1971	—	2.50	5.00
❑ 3248	Storm in a Teacup/I'm Not Following You	1971	—	2.50	5.00
❑ 3445	Wait Until September/Don't Sing to Me	1972	—	2.50	5.00
❑ 3514	I Can't Remember When the Sun Went In/Secret Love	1973	—	2.50	5.00
❑ 3626	Give Me Some Room/Whenever It's a Sunday	1973	—	2.50	5.00

PRESS

Number	Title (A Side/B Side)	Yr	VG	VG+	NM
❑ 9773	You've Got Your Troubles/I've Gotta Go	1965	3.00	6.00	12.00
—Purple label					
❑ 9773	You've Got Your Troubles/I've Gotta Go	1965	4.00	8.00	16.00
—White label stock copy					
❑ 9798	Here It Comes Again/Things I Should Have Known	1965	2.50	5.00	10.00
—Purple label					
❑ 9798	Here It Comes Again/Things I Should Have Known	1965	3.75	7.50	15.00
—White label stock copy					
❑ 9811	This Golden Ring/Someone to Care	1966	2.50	5.00	10.00
❑ 60001	Gone from My Mind/Silent Street	1966	2.50	5.00	10.00

UNITED ARTISTS

Number	Title (A Side/B Side)	Yr	VG	VG+	NM
❑ 50211	The Idol/His Smile Was a Lie	1967	2.50	5.00	10.00
❑ 50280	Painting a Shadow/Fire Brigade	1968	2.50	5.00	10.00

WORLD PACIFIC

Number	Title (A Side/B Side)	Yr	VG	VG+	NM
❑ 77937	That Same Old Feeling/Lifetime of Love	1970	2.00	4.00	8.00

Albums
CAPITOL

Number	Title (A Side/B Side)	Yr	VG	VG+	NM
❑ ST-647	Freedom	1971	—	—	—
—Canceled					
❑ ST-809	Here Comes That Rainy Day Feeling Again	1971	5.00	10.00	20.00
❑ ST-11041	Storm in a Teacup	1972	3.75	7.50	15.00
—Contains the canceled "Freedom" LP with one track deleted, plus the title song added					

COCA-COLA

Number	Title (A Side/B Side)	Yr	VG	VG+	NM
❑ (no #) [DJ]	It's the Real Thing	1969	15.00	30.00	60.00

PRESS

Number	Title (A Side/B Side)	Yr	VG	VG+	NM
❑ PR 73002 [M]	The Fortunes	1965	8.75	17.50	35.00
❑ PRS 83002 [S]	The Fortunes	1965	12.50	25.00	50.00

WORLD PACIFIC

Number	Title (A Side/B Side)	Yr	VG	VG+	NM
❑ WPS-21904	That Same Old Feeling	1970	3.75	7.50	15.00

FORTUNES, THE (U) None of these are by group (1), but exactly which ones are by the same group as others, we have not yet determined.
45s
ARGO

Number	Title (A Side/B Side)	Yr	VG	VG+	NM
❑ 5364	Congratulations/Look at Me, Look at You	1960	15.00	30.00	60.00

CHECKER

Number	Title (A Side/B Side)	Yr	VG	VG+	NM
❑ 818	Believe in Me/My Baby Is Fine	1955	15.00	30.00	60.00

CUB

Number	Title (A Side/B Side)	Yr	VG	VG+	NM
❑ 9123	The Ghoul in School/You Don't Know (What I've Been Through)	1963	3.75	7.50	15.00

DECCA

Number	Title (A Side/B Side)	Yr	VG	VG+	NM
❑ 30541	Tarnished Angel/Who Cares?	1958	15.00	30.00	60.00
❑ 30688	How Clever of You/Trees	1958	12.50	25.00	50.00

DRA

Number	Title (A Side/B Side)	Yr	VG	VG+	NM
❑ 320	Tell Me/Running Away from Love	1962	75.00	150.00	300.00

LAKE

Number	Title (A Side/B Side)	Yr	VG	VG+	NM
❑ 704	St. John's Cha Cha/Runnin'	196?	3.75	7.50	15.00

F

Number	Title (A Side/B Side)	Yr	VG	VG+	NM
QUEEN					
❑ 24010	Nothing Matters Anymore/Ugly Duckling	1962	6.25	12.50	25.00
TOP RANK					
❑ 2019	Steady Vows/In the Night	1959	10.00	20.00	40.00
YUCCA					
❑ 168	Laugh of the Train/Chi Wawa	1964	7.50	15.00	30.00
❑ 170	Lonely Teardrops/This Is Love	1964	10.00	20.00	40.00

49TH PARALLEL, THE
45s
MAVERICK

Number	Title (A Side/B Side)	Yr	VG	VG+	NM
❑ 1004	Close the Barn Door/Twilight Woman	1968	5.00	10.00	20.00
❑ 1011	(Come On Little Child and) Talk to Me/Now That I'm a Man	1968	5.00	10.00	20.00

Albums
MAVERICK

Number	Title	Yr	VG	VG+	NM
❑ MAS-7001	The 49th Parallel	1969	62.50	125.00	250.00

FORUM, THE
45s
MIRA

Number	Title (A Side/B Side)	Yr	VG	VG+	NM
❑ 232	The River Is Wide/I Fall in Love	1967	3.00	6.00	12.00
❑ 243	Trip on Me/It's Sunday	1967	3.00	6.00	12.00
❑ 248	A Girl Without a Boy/Go Try to Put Out the Sun	1968	3.00	6.00	12.00
PENTHOUSE					
❑ 504	The River Is Wide/(B-side unknown)	1966	5.00	10.00	20.00

Albums
MIRA

Number	Title	Yr	VG	VG+	NM
❑ MLP-301 [M]	The River Is Wide	1967	3.75	7.50	15.00
❑ MLPS-301 [S]	The River Is Wide	1967	5.00	10.00	20.00

FOSTER, CELL, AND THE AUDIOS
45s
ULTRA

Number	Title (A Side/B Side)	Yr	VG	VG+	NM
❑ 105	Honest I Do/I Prayed for You	1956	62.50	125.00	250.00
—Maroon label					
❑ 105	Honest I Do/I Prayed for You	1956	100.00	200.00	400.00
—Yellow label					

FOSTER, JOHN, AND SONS BLACK DYKE MILLS BAND
45s
APPLE

Number	Title (A Side/B Side)	Yr	VG	VG+	NM
❑ 1800	Thingumybob/Yellow Submarine	1968	25.00	50.00	100.00
—With "Thingumybob" on uncut apple side					
❑ 1800	Thingumybob/Yellow Submarine	1968	25.00	50.00	100.00
—With "Yellow Submarine" on uncut apple side					
❑ 1800	Thingumybob/Yellow Submarine	1968	30.00	60.00	120.00
—With black star on uncut apple side					

FOTHERINGAY Also see SANDY DENNY.
Albums
A&M

Number	Title	Yr	VG	VG+	NM
❑ SP-4289	Faotheringay	1970	3.75	7.50	15.00

FOTO-FI FOUR, THE Some sources say Harry NILSSON is on this recording.
45s
FOTO-FI

Number	Title (A Side/B Side)	Yr	VG	VG+	NM
❑ 107	Stand Up and Holler!/Ismael	1964	6.25	12.50	25.00
❑ 107 [PS]	Stand Up and Holler!/Ismael	1964	12.50	25.00	50.00

—Sleeve states: "The Beatles arrive in America! Have fun running the film with this specially scored recording." Price does not include film.

FOUL DOGS, THE
Albums
RHYTHM SOUND

Number	Title	Yr	VG	VG+	NM
❑ GA-481	No. 1	1968	75.00	150.00	300.00

FOUNDATIONS, THE
45s
UNI

Number	Title (A Side/B Side)	Yr	VG	VG+	NM
❑ 55038	Baby, Now That I've Found You/Come On Back to Me	1967	2.00	4.00	8.00
❑ 55058	Back on My Feet Again/I Can Take or Leave Your Loving	1968	—	3.00	6.00
❑ 55073	We Are Happy People/Any Old Time	1968	—	3.00	6.00
❑ 55101	Build Me Up Buttercup/New Direction	1968	2.00	4.00	8.00
❑ 55117	In the Bad, Bad Old Days (Before You Loved Me)/Give Me Love	1969	—	3.00	6.00
❑ 55137	My Little Chickadee/Solomon Grundy	1969	—	3.00	6.00
❑ 55162	Why Did You Cry/Born to Live, Born to Die	1969	—	3.00	6.00
❑ 55210	Take a Girl Like You/I'm Gonna Be a Rich Man	1970	—	3.00	6.00
❑ 55315	I'll Give You Love/Stoney Ground	1972	—	3.00	6.00

Albums
UNI

Number	Title	Yr	VG	VG+	NM
❑ 73016	Baby Now That I've Found You	1968	7.50	15.00	30.00
❑ 73043	Build Me Up Buttercup	1969	7.50	15.00	30.00
❑ 73058	Digging the Foundations	1969	7.50	15.00	30.00

FOUNTAIN, PETE
45s
CORAL

Number	Title (A Side/B Side)	Yr	VG	VG+	NM
❑ 62107	My Inspiration/Japansy	1959	2.00	4.00	8.00
❑ 62154	A Closer Walk/Do You Know What It Means to Miss New Orleans	1959	2.00	4.00	8.00
❑ 62211	Sentimental Journey/Columbus Stockade Blues	1960	2.00	4.00	8.00
❑ 62243	Alone Together/Forbidden Love	1961	2.00	4.00	8.00
❑ 62266	Oh, Didn't He Ramble/Allison's Theme from Parrish	1962	2.00	4.00	8.00
❑ 62350	The Grasshopper/Lonely Little Tune	1963	—	3.00	6.00
❑ 62365	Casablanca/Lost Love	1963	—	3.00	6.00
❑ 62376	China Nights/Theme from "Women of the World"	1963	—	3.00	6.00
❑ 62413	Licorice Stick/Estrellita	1964	—	3.00	6.00
❑ 62427	The Horny Wind Blows/Humbug	1964	—	3.00	6.00
❑ 62441	Mr. Stick Man/Amazon	1965	—	3.00	6.00
❑ 62446	Whipped Cream/Midnight Pete	1965	—	3.00	6.00
❑ 62454	Mae/Gotta Travel On	1965	—	3.00	6.00
❑ 62460	Rave On/The Whippenpoof Song	1965	—	3.00	6.00

Number	Title (A Side/B Side)	Yr	VG	VG+	NM
❑ 62474	Juliet's Theme/Walking the Floor Over You	1965	—	3.00	6.00
❑ 62496	Mood Indigo/Sleepy Serenade	1966	—	2.50	5.00
❑ 62516	Thoroughly Modern Millie/Jimmy	1967	—	2.50	5.00
❑ 62527	Music to Turn You On/(Carol's Theme) The Eyes of Love	1967	—	2.50	5.00
❑ 62545	For Pete's Sake/Danke Schoen	1967	—	2.50	5.00
❑ 62557	Les Bicyclettes De Belsize/Puddin	1969	—	2.50	5.00
❑ 62561	Aquarius/The Flesh Failures	1969	—	2.50	5.00
❑ 62564	Sunday in the Country/Applause	1970	—	2.00	4.00
❑ 62565	Night Train to Memphis/San Antonio Rose	1970	—	2.00	4.00
❑ 65545	San Antonio Rose/Dixie	1961	2.00	4.00	8.00
❑ 65549	Yes Indeed/While We Danced at the Mardi Gras	1962	2.00	4.00	8.00
❑ 65563	Corrine, Corrina/Talkin' 'Bout You	196?	—	3.00	6.00
❑ 65566	Shine/Mighty Like the Blues	196?	—	3.00	6.00
❑ 65577	Sugar Bowl Parade/Marching 'Round the Mountain	196?	—	3.00	6.00
❑ 65579	Birth of the Blues/Begin the Beguine	196?	—	3.00	6.00
❑ 65586	Hello, Dolly!/Tippin' In	1964	—	3.00	6.00
❑ 65601	Born to Lose/I Love You So Much It Hurts	196?	—	2.50	5.00
❑ 65602	Tiger Rag/I Love You So Much It Hurts	196?	—	2.50	5.00
❑ 65605	The Christmas Song (Merry Christmas To You)/Santa Claus Medley	1966	2.00	4.00	8.00
❑ 65606	Fountain in the Rain/Over the Waves	196?	—	2.50	5.00
❑ 65612	My Blue Heaven/Tiger Rag	196?	—	2.50	5.00
❑ 65614	Swing Low, Sweet Chariot/Walking Through New Orleans	196?	—	2.50	5.00
❑ 65616	Maria Elena/Put On Your Old Grey Bonnet	196?	—	2.50	5.00
❑ 65617	When the Saints Go Marching In March/Mardi Gras Walking Club	196?	—	2.50	5.00
❑ 65619	Make Your Own Kind of Music/Early in the Morning	1970	—	2.00	4.00

7-Inch Extended Plays
CORAL

Number	Title	Yr	VG	VG+	NM
❑ EC 81190	Yes Indeed/Dis Ol' Train//Nobody Knows the Trouble I've Seen/Sing You Sinners	195?	2.50	5.00	10.00
❑ EC 81190 [PS]	Yes Indeed	195?	2.50	5.00	10.00

Albums
CAPITOL

Number	Title	Yr	VG	VG+	NM
❑ SN-16224	Pete Fountain and Friends	1982	2.00	4.00	8.00
❑ SN-16225	Way Down Yonder in New Orleans	1982	2.00	4.00	8.00
CORAL					
❑ CXS-710 [(2)]	The Best of Pete Fountain	1969	3.75	7.50	15.00
❑ CRL 57200 [M]	Lawrence Welk Presents Pete Fountain	1958	5.00	10.00	20.00
❑ CRL 57282 [M]	Pete Fountain's New Orleans	1959	3.75	7.50	15.00
❑ CRL 57284 [M]	The Blues	1959	3.75	7.50	15.00
❑ CRL 57313 [M]	Pete Fountain Day	1960	3.75	7.50	15.00
❑ CRL 57314 [M]	Pete Fountain at the Bateau Lounge	1960	3.75	7.50	15.00
❑ CRL 57333 [M]	Pete Fountain Salutes the Great Clarinetists	1960	3.75	7.50	15.00
❑ CRL 57357 [M]	Pete Fountain On Tour	1961	3.75	7.50	15.00
❑ CRL 57359 [M]	Pete Fountain's French Quarter	1961	3.75	7.50	15.00
❑ CRL 57378 [M]	I Love Paris	1961	3.75	7.50	15.00
❑ CRL 57394 [M]	Swing Low Sweet Chariot	1962	3.75	7.50	15.00
❑ CRL 57401 [M]	Pete Fountain's Music from Dixie	1962	3.75	7.50	15.00
❑ CRL 57419 [M]	New Orleans Scene	1963	3.75	7.50	15.00
❑ CRL 57424 [M]	Plenty of Pete	1963	3.00	6.00	12.00
❑ CRL 57429 [M]	New Orleans at Midnight	1964	3.00	6.00	12.00
❑ CRL 57440 [M]	South Rampart Street Parade	1963	3.00	6.00	12.00
❑ CRL 57453 [M]	Pete's Place	1964	3.00	6.00	12.00
❑ CRL 57460 [M]	Licorice Stick	1964	3.00	6.00	12.00
❑ CRL 57473 [M]	Mr. Stick Man	1965	3.00	6.00	12.00
❑ CRL 57474 [M]	Standing Room Only	1965	3.00	6.00	12.00
❑ CRL 57484 [M]	Mood Indigo	1966	3.00	6.00	12.00
❑ CRL 57486 [M]	A Taste of Honey	1966	3.00	6.00	12.00
❑ CRL 57487 [M]	Candy Clarinet — Merry Christmas from Pete Fountain	1966	3.00	6.00	12.00
❑ CRL 57488 [M]	I've Got You Under My Skin	1967	3.00	6.00	12.00
❑ CRL 57496 [M]	Music to Turn You On	1967	3.75	7.50	15.00
❑ CRL 57499 [M]	Pete Fountain Plays Bert Kaempfert	1968	3.75	7.50	15.00
❑ CRL 757282 [S]	Pete Fountain's New Orleans	1959	5.00	10.00	20.00
❑ CRL 757284 [S]	The Blues	1959	5.00	10.00	20.00
❑ CRL 757313 [S]	Pete Fountain Day	1960	5.00	10.00	20.00
❑ CRL 757314 [S]	Pete Fountain at the Bateau Lounge	1960	5.00	10.00	20.00
❑ CRL 757333 [S]	Pete Fountain Salutes the Great Clarinetists	1960	5.00	10.00	20.00
❑ CRL 757357 [S]	Pete Fountain On Tour	1961	5.00	10.00	20.00
❑ CRL 757359 [S]	Pete Fountain's French Quarter	1961	5.00	10.00	20.00
❑ CRL 757378 [S]	I Love Paris	1961	5.00	10.00	20.00
❑ CRL 757394 [S]	Swing Low Sweet Chariot	1962	5.00	10.00	20.00
❑ CRL 757401 [S]	Pete Fountain's Music from Dixie	1962	5.00	10.00	20.00
❑ CRL 757419 [S]	New Orleans Scene	1963	5.00	10.00	20.00
❑ CRL 757424 [S]	Plenty of Pete	1963	3.75	7.50	15.00
❑ CRL 757429 [S]	New Orleans at Midnight	1964	3.75	7.50	15.00
❑ CRL 757440 [S]	South Rampart Street Parade	1963	3.75	7.50	15.00
❑ CRL 757453 [S]	Pete's Place	1964	3.75	7.50	15.00
❑ CRL 757460 [S]	Licorice Stick	1964	3.75	7.50	15.00
❑ CRL 757473 [S]	Mr. Stick Man	1965	3.75	7.50	15.00
❑ CRL 757474 [S]	Standing Room Only	1965	3.75	7.50	15.00
❑ CRL 757484 [S]	Mood Indigo	1966	3.75	7.50	15.00
❑ CRL 757486 [S]	A Taste of Honey	1966	3.75	7.50	15.00
❑ CRL 757487 [S]	Candy Clarinet — Merry Christmas from Pete Fountain	1966	3.75	7.50	15.00
❑ CRL 757488 [S]	I've Got You Under My Skin	1967	3.75	7.50	15.00
❑ CRL 757496 [S]	Music to Turn You On	1967	3.00	6.00	12.00
❑ CRL 757499 [S]	Pete Fountain Plays Bert Kaempfert	1968	3.00	6.00	12.00
❑ CRL 757503	Walking Through New Orleans	1968	3.00	6.00	12.00
❑ CRL 757505	Those Were the Days	1969	3.00	6.00	12.00
❑ CRL 757507	Both Sides Now	1969	3.00	6.00	12.00
❑ CRL 757510	Make Your Own Kind of Music	1970	3.00	6.00	12.00
❑ CRL 757511	Golden Favorites	1970	3.00	6.00	12.00
❑ CRL 757513	Dr. Fountain's Magical Licorice Stick	1971	3.00	6.00	12.00
❑ CRL 757516	Something/Misty	1971	3.00	6.00	12.00
❑ CRL 757517	New Orleans Tennessee	1971	3.00	6.00	12.00
DECCA					
❑ DL 75374	Pete Fountain's New Orleans	1972	3.00	6.00	12.00
—Reissue of Coral 757282					
❑ DL 75375	The Blues	1972	3.00	6.00	12.00
—Reissue of Coral 757284					
❑ DL 75377	Mr. New Orleans	1972	3.00	6.00	12.00

Number	Title (A Side/B Side)	Yr	VG	VG+	NM
❏ DL 75378	Dr. Fountain's Magical Licorice Stick	1972	2.50	5.00	10.00
—Reissue of Coral 757513					
❏ DL 75379	Something/Misty	1972	2.50	5.00	10.00
—Reissue of Coral 757516					
❏ DL 75380	New Orleans Tennessee	1972	3.00	6.00	12.00
—Reissue of Coral 757517					

EVEREST ARCHIVE OF FOLK & JAZZ

Number	Title (A Side/B Side)	Yr	VG	VG+	NM
❏ 257	New Orleans All-Stars	197?	2.50	5.00	10.00

FIRST AMERICAN

Number	Title (A Side/B Side)	Yr	VG	VG+	NM
❏ 7706	New Orleans Jazz	1978	2.50	5.00	10.00

INTERMEDIA

Number	Title (A Side/B Side)	Yr	VG	VG+	NM
❏ QS-5038	Down on Rampart Street	198?	2.00	4.00	8.00

JUCU

Number	Title (A Side/B Side)	Yr	VG	VG+	NM
❏ JMK-12S	Pete Fountain's Jazz Reunion	1976	3.00	6.00	12.00

MCA

Number	Title (A Side/B Side)	Yr	VG	VG+	NM
❏ 165	Mr. New Orleans	1973	2.50	5.00	10.00
—Reissue of Decca 75377					
❏ 176	Something/Misty	1973	2.50	5.00	10.00
—Reissue of Decca 75379					
❏ 336	Crescent City	1974	2.50	5.00	10.00
❏ 505	Pete Fountain's New Orleans	1974	2.50	5.00	10.00
—Reissue of Decca 75374					
❏ 506	The Blues	1974	2.50	5.00	10.00
—Reissue of Decca 75375					
❏ 507	Dr. Fountain's Magical Licorice Stick	1974	2.50	5.00	10.00
—Reissue of Decca 75378					
❏ 508	New Orleans Tennessee	1974	2.50	5.00	10.00
—Reissue of Decca 75380					
❏ 4032 [(2)]	The Best of Pete Fountain	1974	3.00	6.00	12.00
—Reissue of Coral 710					
❏ 4095 [(2)]	The Best of Pete Fountain, Vol. 2	1974	3.00	6.00	12.00

PICKWICK

Number	Title (A Side/B Side)	Yr	VG	VG+	NM
❏ SPC-3024	Pete Fountain	196?	3.00	6.00	12.00
❏ SPC-3201	High Society	1971	2.50	5.00	10.00

RCA CAMDEN

Number	Title (A Side/B Side)	Yr	VG	VG+	NM
❏ CAL-727 [M]	Dixieland	1962	3.00	6.00	12.00
❏ CAS-727 [R]	Dixieland	1962	2.50	5.00	10.00

RCA VICTOR

Number	Title (A Side/B Side)	Yr	VG	VG+	NM
❏ LPM-2097 [M]	Pete Fountain at the Jazz Band Ball	1960	3.75	7.50	15.00
❏ LSP-2097 [S]	Pete Fountain at the Jazz Band Ball	1960	5.00	10.00	20.00

VOCALION

Number	Title (A Side/B Side)	Yr	VG	VG+	NM
❏ VL 3803 [M]	And the Angels Sing	1967	3.00	6.00	12.00
❏ VL 73803 [S]	And the Angels Sing	1967	3.00	6.00	12.00

FOUNTAIN, PETE, AND AL HIRT Also see each artist's individual listings.
45s
CORAL

Number	Title (A Side/B Side)	Yr	VG	VG+	NM
❏ 65544	March of the Bob Cats/Farewell Blues	1962	2.00	4.00	8.00

Albums
CORAL

Number	Title (A Side/B Side)	Yr	VG	VG+	NM
❏ CRL 57389 [M]	Bourbon Street	1962	3.75	7.50	15.00
❏ CRL 757389 [S]	Bourbon Street	1962	5.00	10.00	20.00

MGM

Number	Title (A Side/B Side)	Yr	VG	VG+	NM
❏ E-4216 [M]	The Very Best of Al Hirt and Pete Fountain	1964	3.00	6.00	12.00
❏ SE-4216 [S]	The Very Best of Al Hirt and Pete Fountain	1964	3.75	7.50	15.00

MONUMENT

Number	Title (A Side/B Side)	Yr	VG	VG+	NM
❏ 8602 [(2)]	Super I	1975	2.50	5.00	10.00

FOUNTAIN, PETE, AND "BIG" TINY LITTLE
45s
CORAL

Number	Title (A Side/B Side)	Yr	VG	VG+	NM
❏ 65557	Ain't Misbehavin'/American Patrol	196?	—	3.00	6.00
❏ 65598	Honeysuckle Rose/Darktown Strutters' Ball	196?	—	2.50	5.00

Albums
CORAL

Number	Title (A Side/B Side)	Yr	VG	VG+	NM
❏ CRL 57334 [M]	Mr. New Orleans Meets Mr. Honky Tonk	1961	3.75	7.50	15.00
❏ CRL 757334 [S]	Mr. New Orleans Meets Mr. Honky Tonk	1961	5.00	10.00	20.00

FOUNTAIN, ROOSEVELT, AND PENS OF RHYTHM
45s
M&M

Number	Title (A Side/B Side)	Yr	VG	VG+	NM
❏ 331	I'm Gonna Be with You/One Night	196?	25.00	50.00	100.00

PRINCE-ADAMS

Number	Title (A Side/B Side)	Yr	VG	VG+	NM
❏ 45-447	Red Pepper I/Red Pepper II	1962	5.00	10.00	20.00

FOUNTAIN OF YOUTH
45s
COLGEMS

Number	Title (A Side/B Side)	Yr	VG	VG+	NM
❏ 66-1020	Livin' Too Fast/(Angie, Love Me) Make the Hurt Go Away	1968	5.00	10.00	20.00
❏ 66-1024	Take a Giant Step/Don't Blame Me (For Trying)	1968	5.00	10.00	20.00
❏ 66-1032	The Day Don't Come/Sunshine on a Cold Morning	1969	3.75	7.50	15.00
❏ 66-5003	Liza Jane/Mistress People	1969	3.75	7.50	15.00

FOUR ACES Also see AL ALBERTS.
45s
ABC-PARAMOUNT

Number	Title (A Side/B Side)	Yr	VG	VG+	NM
❏ 10166	Searching/Dolce Par Niente	1960	2.50	5.00	10.00
❏ 10183	Me Without You/The Ballad of Patrick Henry	1961	2.50	5.00	10.00

DECCA

Number	Title (A Side/B Side)	Yr	VG	VG+	NM
❏ 27860	Tell Me Why/A Garden in the Rain	1951	5.00	10.00	20.00
❏ 27937	Perfidia/You Brought Me Love	1952	5.00	10.00	20.00
❏ 28073	My Hero/Spring Is a Wonderful Thing	1952	5.00	10.00	20.00
❏ 28162	I'm Yours/I Understand	1952	5.00	10.00	20.00
❏ 28323	Should I/There's Only Tonight	1952	5.00	10.00	20.00
❏ 28390	Heart and Soul/Just Squeeze Me	1952	5.00	10.00	20.00
❏ 28391	I'll Never Smile Again/My Devotion	1952	5.00	10.00	20.00
❏ 28392	Tip-Pi-Tin/Heaven Can Wait	1952	5.00	10.00	20.00
❏ 28393	La Rosita/Take Me in Your Arms	1952	5.00	10.00	20.00
❏ 28560	You Fooled Me/If You Take My Heart Away	1953	3.75	7.50	15.00
❏ 28691	Organ Grinder's Swing/Honey in the Horn	1953	3.75	7.50	15.00
❏ 28744	Don't Forget Me/False Love	1953	3.75	7.50	15.00
❏ 28843	Laughing on the Outisde (Crying on the Inside)/I've Been Waiting a Lifetime	1953	3.75	7.50	15.00
❏ 28927	The Gang That Sang "Heart of My Heart"/Stranger in Paradise	1953	3.75	7.50	15.00
❏ 28979	Bandera (Texas Polka)/What More Is There	1954	3.75	7.50	15.00
❏ 29036	Amor/So Long	1954	3.75	7.50	15.00
❏ 29123	Three Coins in the Fountain/Wedding Bells (Are Breaking Up That Old Gang of Mine)	1954	3.75	7.50	15.00
❏ 29217	Dream/It Shall Come to Pass	1954	3.75	7.50	15.00
❏ 29269	It's a Woman's World/The Cuckoo Bird in the Pickle Tree	1954	3.75	7.50	15.00
❏ 29344	Mister Sandman/(I'll Be With You) In Apple Blossom Time	1954	3.75	7.50	15.00
❏ 29395	Melody of Love/There Is a Tavern in the Town	1954	3.75	7.50	15.00
❏ 29435	There Goes My Heart/You'll Always Be the One	1955	3.00	6.00	12.00
❏ 29476	Heart/Sluefoot	1955	3.00	6.00	12.00
❏ 29625	Love is a Many-Splendored Thing/Shine On Harvest Moon	1955	3.00	6.00	12.00
❏ 29702	The Christmas Song (Merry Christmas to You)/Jingle Bells	1955	3.00	6.00	12.00
❏ 29712	O Holy Night/Silent Night	1955	3.00	6.00	12.00
❏ 29725	A Woman in Love/Of This I'm Sure	1955	3.00	6.00	12.00
❏ 29809	If You Can Dream/The Gal with the Yaller Shoes	1956	3.00	6.00	12.00
❏ 29889	To Love Again/Charlie Was a Boxer	1956	3.00	6.00	12.00
❏ 29989	I Only Know I Love You/Dreamer	1956	3.00	6.00	12.00
❏ 30041	Friendly Persuasion (Thee I Love)/You Can't Run Away from It	1956	3.00	6.00	12.00
❏ 30123	Someone to Love/Written on the Wind	1956	3.00	6.00	12.00
❏ 30242	Bahama Mama/You're Mine	1957	3.00	6.00	12.00
❏ 30348	Three Sheets to the Wind/Yes Sir, That's My Baby	1957	3.00	6.00	12.00
❏ 30384	Half of My Heart/When My Sugar Walks Down the Street	1957	3.00	6.00	12.00
❏ 30466	How Do You Say Goodbye?/I Would Love You Still	1957	3.00	6.00	12.00
❏ 30575	Rock and Roll Rhapsody/I Wish I May, I Wish I Might	1958	3.00	6.00	12.00
❏ 30649	Saturday Swing-Out/Take My Heart	1958	3.00	6.00	12.00
❏ 30695	Two Arms, Two Lips, One Heart/Heartache in Costume	1958	3.00	6.00	12.00
❏ 30721	Roses of Rio/Hangin' Up a Horseshoe	1958	3.00	6.00	12.00
❏ 30764	The World Outside/How Can You Forget	1958	3.00	6.00	12.00
❏ 30775	Ol' Fatso/Christmas Tree	1958	3.00	6.00	12.00
❏ 30822	No Other Arms, No Other Lips/The Inn of the Sixth Happiness	1959	2.50	5.00	10.00
❏ 30874	Ciao, Ciao Bambino/Paradise Island	1959	2.50	5.00	10.00
❏ 30897	The Five Pennies/Anyone Would Love You	1959	2.50	5.00	10.00
❏ 30989	Waltzing Matilda/The Wonder of It All	1959	2.50	5.00	10.00
❏ 31027	I Love Paris/Till Tomorrow	1959	2.50	5.00	10.00
❏ 31081	Poor Butterfly/You Are Music	1960	2.50	5.00	10.00

FLASH

Number	Title (A Side/B Side)	Yr	VG	VG+	NM
❏ 103	Who's to Blame/Two Little Kisses	1950	7.50	15.00	30.00

JUBILEE

Number	Title (A Side/B Side)	Yr	VG	VG+	NM
❏ 5416	It's All Over But the Crying/Lonely Hill	1962	2.00	4.00	8.00

RADNOR

Number	Title (A Side/B Side)	Yr	VG	VG+	NM
❏ 301	Always Keep Me in Your Heart/Didn't We	1968	—	2.50	5.00
❏ 302	I Started a Joke/Summer Won't Be Summer	1969	—	2.50	5.00

VICTORIA

Number	Title (A Side/B Side)	Yr	VG	VG+	NM
❏ 101	Sin/Arizona Moon	1951	6.25	12.50	25.00
—Black vinyl					
❏ 101	Sin/Arizona Moon	1951	15.00	30.00	60.00
—Red vinyl					
❏ 102	There's a Christmas Tree in Heaven/There's a Small Hotel	1951	7.50	15.00	30.00

7-Inch Extended Plays
DECCA

Number	Title (A Side/B Side)	Yr	VG	VG+	NM
❏ ED 2004	Tell Me Why/Perfidia//I Understand/My Hero	195?	3.75	7.50	15.00
❏ ED 2004 [PS]	The Four Aces, Vol. 1	195?	3.75	7.50	15.00
❏ ED 2170	*I Don't Know Why/(I'll Be With You) In Apple Blossom Time/Dream/Among My Souvenirs	195?	3.75	7.50	15.00
❏ ED 2170 [PS]	Dream	195?	3.75	7.50	15.00
❏ ED 2211	I'm in the Mood for Love/What a Difference a Day Makes//Stars Fell on Alabama/Pennies from Heaven	195?	3.00	6.00	12.00
❏ ED 2211 [PS]	Mood for Love, Volume 1	195?	3.00	6.00	12.00
❏ ED 2212	Let's Fall in Love/Don't Take Your Love from Me//It's the Talk of the Town/I'm Sitting on Top of the World	195?	3.00	6.00	12.00
❏ ED 2212 [PS]	Mood for Love, Volume 2	195?	3.00	6.00	12.00
❏ ED 2213	There Goes My Heart/Melody of Love//Three Coins in the Fountain/Stranger in Paradise	195?	3.00	6.00	12.00
❏ ED 2213 [PS]	Mood for Love, Volume 3	195?	3.00	6.00	12.00
❏ ED 2309	White Christmas/The Christmas Song//Silent Night/O Little Town of Bethlehem/Joy to the World	1956	3.00	6.00	12.00
❏ ED 2309 [PS]	A Merry Christmas with the Four Aces, Part 1	1956	3.00	6.00	12.00
❏ ED 2310	Silver Bells/Jingle Bells//O Come All Ye Faithful/Hark! The Herald Angels Sing/We Three Kings of Orient Are	1956	3.00	6.00	12.00
❏ ED 2310 [PS]	A Merry Christmas with the Four Aces, Part 2	1956	3.00	6.00	12.00
❏ ED 2311	Santa Claus Is Comin' to Town/Rudolph the Red-Nosed Reindeer///O Holy Night (Cantique de Noel)/The First Nowell/Deck the Hall	1956	3.00	6.00	12.00
❏ ED 2311 [PS]	A Merry Christmas with the Four Aces, Part 3	1956	3.00	6.00	12.00
❏ ED 2323	The Gang That Sang "Heart of My Heart"/Wedding Bells (Are Breaking Up That Old Gang of Mine)//Mister Sandman/There Is a Tavern in the Town	195?	3.00	6.00	12.00
❏ ED 2323 [PS]	Heart of My Heart	195?	3.00	6.00	12.00
❏ ED 2324	Amor/I'm Yours//Organ Grinder's Swing/So Long	195?	3.00	6.00	12.00
❏ ED 2324 [PS]	Amor	195?	3.00	6.00	12.00
❏ ED 2529	(contents unknown)	195?	3.00	6.00	12.00
❏ ED 2529 [PS]	Shufflin' Along, Volume 1	195?	3.00	6.00	12.00
❏ ED 2565	(contents unknown)	195?	3.00	6.00	12.00
❏ ED 2565 [PS]	Hits from Hollywood	195?	3.00	6.00	12.00
❏ ED 2675	(contents unknown)	1959	3.00	6.00	12.00
❏ ED 2675 [PS]	Beyond the Blue Horizon	1959	3.00	6.00	12.00

Number	Title (A Side/B Side)	Yr	VG	VG+	NM
Albums					
DECCA					
☐ DL 4013 [M]	The Golden Hits of the Four Aces	1960	5.00	10.00	20.00
☐ DL 5429 [10]	The Four Aces	1952	20.00	40.00	80.00
☐ DL 8122 [M]	The Mood for Love	1955	12.50	25.00	50.00
—All-black label, silver print					
☐ DL 8122 [M]	The Mood for Love	196?	5.00	10.00	20.00
—Black label with color bars					
☐ DL 8191 [M]	Merry Christmas	1956	12.50	25.00	50.00
☐ DL 8227 [M]	Sentimental Souvenirs	1956	12.50	25.00	50.00
—All-black label, silver print					
☐ DL 8227 [M]	Sentimental Souvenirs	196?	5.00	10.00	20.00
—Black label with color bars					
☐ DL 8228 [M]	Heart and Soul	1956	12.50	25.00	50.00
—All-black label, silver print					
☐ DL 8228 [M]	Heart and Soul	196?	5.00	10.00	20.00
—Black label with color bars					
☐ DL 8312 [M]	She Sees All the Hollywood Hits	1957	12.50	25.00	50.00
☐ DL 8567 [M]	Shuffling Along	1957	12.50	25.00	50.00
—All-black label, silver print					
☐ DL 8567 [M]	Shuffling Along	196?	5.00	10.00	20.00
—Black label with color bars					
☐ DL 8693 [M]	Hits from Hollywood	1958	12.50	25.00	50.00
—All-black label, silver print					
☐ DL 8693 [M]	Hits from Hollywood	196?	5.00	10.00	20.00
—Black label with color bars					
☐ DL 8766 [M]	The Swingin' Aces	1958	10.00	20.00	40.00
—All-black label, silver print					
☐ DL 8766 [M]	The Swingin' Aces	196?	5.00	10.00	20.00
—Black label with color bars					
☐ DL 8855 [M]	Hits from Broadway	1959	10.00	20.00	40.00
—All-black label, silver print					
☐ DL 8855 [M]	Hits from Broadway	196?	5.00	10.00	20.00
—Black label with color bars					
☐ DL 8944 [M]	Beyond the Blue Horizon	1959	10.00	20.00	40.00
—All-black label, silver print					
☐ DL 8944 [M]	Beyond the Blue Horizon	196?	5.00	10.00	20.00
—Black label with color bars					
☐ DL 74013 [S]	The Golden Hits of the Four Aces	1960	6.25	12.50	25.00
☐ DL 78766 [S]	The Swingin' Aces	1958	12.50	25.00	50.00
—All-black label, silver print					
☐ DL 78766 [S]	The Swingin' Aces	196?	6.25	12.50	25.00
—Black label with color bars					
☐ DL 78855 [S]	Hits from Broadway	1959	12.50	25.00	50.00
—All-black label, silver print					
☐ DL 78855 [S]	Hits from Broadway	196?	6.25	12.50	25.00
—Black label with color bars					
☐ DL 78944 [S]	Beyond the Blue Horizon	1959	12.50	25.00	50.00
—All-black label, silver print					
☐ DL 78944 [S]	Beyond the Blue Horizon	196?	6.25	12.50	25.00
—Black label with color bars					
MCA					
☐ 4033 [(2)]	The Best of the Four Aces	197?	3.75	7.50	15.00
PICKWICK					
☐ SPC-3527	Love Is a Many-Splendored Thing	197?	2.50	5.00	10.00
UNITED ARTISTS					
☐ UAL-3337 [M]	Record Oldies	1963	5.00	10.00	20.00
☐ UAS-6337 [S]	Record Oldies	1963	6.25	12.50	25.00
VOCALION					
☐ VL 3604 [M]	The Four Aces Sing	196?	3.75	7.50	15.00
☐ VL 73881	There Goes My Heart	1969	3.00	6.00	12.00
☐ VL 73902	Written on the Wind	1970	3.00	6.00	12.00

FOUR AIMS, THE See FOUR TOPS.

FOUR BARS, THE
45s

Number	Title (A Side/B Side)	Yr	VG	VG+	NM
JOSIE					
☐ 762	Grief by Day, Grief by Night/Hey Baby	1954	75.00	150.00	300.00
☐ 768	If I Give My Heart to You/Stop It! Quit It!	1954	75.00	150.00	300.00
☐ 783	Let Me Live/Why Do You Treat Me This Way	1955	150.00	300.00	600.00
REPUBLIC					
☐ 7101	Memories of You/When Did You Leave Heaven	1954	150.00	300.00	600.00

FOUR BELLS, THE
45s

Number	Title (A Side/B Side)	Yr	VG	VG+	NM
GEM					
☐ 207	Please Tell It to Me/Long Way to Go	1953	200.00	400.00	800.00
☐ 220	Only a Miracle/My Tree	1954	200.00	400.00	800.00

FOUR BROTHERS AND A COUSIN
45s

Number	Title (A Side/B Side)	Yr	VG	VG+	NM
JAGUAR					
☐ 3003	Trust in Me/Whistle Stop Blues	1954	100.00	200.00	400.00
☐ 3005	Whispeing Wind/Can It Be	1954	125.00	250.00	500.00

FOUR BUDDIES, THE (1) Vocal group from Baltimore.
45s

Number	Title (A Side/B Side)	Yr	VG	VG+	NM
SAVOY					
☐ 769	I Will Wait/Just to See You Smile Again	1951	100.00	200.00	400.00
☐ 769	I Will Wait/Just to See You Smile Again	1951	125.00	250.00	500.00
—As "The Four Buds"					
☐ 779	Don't Leave Me Now/Sweet Slumber	1951	100.00	200.00	400.00
☐ 789	My Summer's Gone/Why at a Time Like This	1951	75.00	150.00	300.00
☐ 817	Heart and Soul/Sin	1951	75.00	150.00	300.00
☐ 823	Window Eyes/Simply Say Goodbye	1951	75.00	150.00	300.00
☐ 845	You're Part of Me/Story Blues	1952	75.00	150.00	300.00
☐ 866	What's the Matter with Me/Sweet Tooth for My Baby	1952	75.00	150.00	300.00
☐ 888	My Mother's Eyes/Ooh Ow	1953	75.00	150.00	300.00
☐ 891	I'd Climb the Highest Mountain/I Wanna Know	1953	75.00	150.00	300.00
—B-side by Dolly Cooper					

FOUR BUDDIES, THE (2) Vocal group from Chicago.
45s

Number	Title (A Side/B Side)	Yr	VG	VG+	NM
CLUB 51					
☐ 105	Delores/Look Out	1956	50.00	100.00	200.00
—Black vinyl					
☐ 105	Delores/Look Out	1956	1000.	2000.	4000.
—Red vinyl					

FOUR BUDDIES, THE (3)
45s

Number	Title (A Side/B Side)	Yr	VG	VG+	NM
CORAL					
☐ 62217	Hurt/Moonglow & Theme from Picnic	1960	5.00	10.00	20.00
☐ 62325	The Light/Cin Cin (Che Bell)	1962	5.00	10.00	20.00
IMPERIAL					
☐ 66018	I Want to Be the Boy You Love/Just Enough of Your Love	1964	15.00	30.00	60.00
PHILIPS					
☐ 40122	Lonely Summer/Slow Locomotion	1963	5.00	10.00	20.00

FOUR CAL-QUETTES, THE
45s

Number	Title (A Side/B Side)	Yr	VG	VG+	NM
CAPITOL					
☐ 4534	Sparkle and Shine/In This World	1961	7.50	15.00	30.00
—As "The Four Coquettes"					
☐ 4574	Billy, My Billy/Star Bright	1961	7.50	15.00	30.00
☐ 4657	Most of All/I'm Gonna Love Him Anyway	1961	7.50	15.00	30.00
☐ 4725	I'll Never Come Back (Silly Boy)/Again	1962	7.50	15.00	30.00
LIBERTY					
☐ 55549	I Cried/Movie Magazines	1963	3.75	7.50	15.00

FOUR CASTS, THE
45s

Number	Title (A Side/B Side)	Yr	VG	VG+	NM
ATLANTIC					
☐ 2228	Stormy Weather/Workin' at the Factory	1964	3.00	6.00	12.00

FOUR CHEERS, THE
45s

Number	Title (A Side/B Side)	Yr	VG	VG+	NM
END					
☐ 1034	Fatal Charms of Love/Periwinkle Blue	1958	50.00	100.00	200.00

FOUR CHELLOWS, THE See THE CHELLOWS.

FOUR CHEVELLES, THE
45s

Number	Title (A Side/B Side)	Yr	VG	VG+	NM
BAND BOX					
☐ 357	This Is Our Wedding Day/Darling Forever	1957	5.00	10.00	20.00
☐ 358	I Can't Believe/I Know	1957	5.00	10.00	20.00
DELFT					
☐ 357	This Is Our Wedding Day/Darling Forever	1957	150.00	300.00	600.00

FOUR CHICADEES, THE
45s

Number	Title (A Side/B Side)	Yr	VG	VG+	NM
CHECKER					
☐ 849	Ding Dong/Teenage Blues	1956	15.00	30.00	60.00

FOUR COINS, THE
45s

Number	Title (A Side/B Side)	Yr	VG	VG+	NM
COLUMBIA					
☐ 44006	If You Love Me (Really Love Me)/Learning to Live Without Your Love	1967	—	3.00	6.00
EPIC					
☐ 9074	Once More/We'll Be Married...	1954	3.75	7.50	15.00
☐ 9082	I Love You Madly/Maybe	1954	3.75	7.50	15.00
☐ 9091	My Anxious Heart/Oh Mother Dear	1955	3.75	7.50	15.00
☐ 9104	Promises, Promises/That's the Way	1955	3.75	7.50	15.00
☐ 9107	A Story Untold/Magnolia	1955	3.75	7.50	15.00
☐ 9116	The Song That Brought Us Together/Need You	1955	3.75	7.50	15.00
☐ 9129	Memories of You/Tear Down the Fence	1955	3.75	7.50	15.00
☐ 9148	The Song That God Sings/The Old Professor	1956	3.00	6.00	12.00
☐ 9164	Cherry Lips/All My Tomorrows	1956	3.00	6.00	12.00
☐ 9171	This I Offer You/One Kiss (Is Worth a Thousand Words)	1956	3.00	6.00	12.00
☐ 9183	Manhattan Serenade/Too Late	1956	3.00	6.00	12.00
☐ 9192	Destination Love/The Time of the Year	1956	3.00	6.00	12.00
☐ 9200	Falling Star/My Love Is a Little Kitten	1957	3.00	6.00	12.00
☐ 9213	Shangri-La/First in Line	1957	3.00	6.00	12.00
☐ 9229	My One Sin/This Life	1957	3.00	6.00	12.00
☐ 9253	Follow Your Heart/A Broken Promise	1957	3.00	6.00	12.00
☐ 9258	My Love Loves Me/New World	1957	3.00	6.00	12.00
☐ 9276	Dream World/One Life, One Love	1958	2.50	5.00	10.00
☐ 9286	Wendy, Wendy/Be Still My Heart	1958	2.50	5.00	10.00
☐ 9295	The World Outside/Roselle	1958	2.50	5.00	10.00
☐ 9306	Angel of Love/Who Are You	1959	2.50	5.00	10.00
☐ 9314	My First Love/One Love, One Heart	1959	2.50	5.00	10.00
☐ 9337	Angel in the Rain/First Signs of Love	1959	2.50	5.00	10.00
☐ 9348	Buon Natale/Serenade of the Bells	1959	2.50	5.00	10.00
☐ 9383	My Only Love/You're Breaking My Heart	1960	2.50	5.00	10.00
JOY					
☐ 287	Answer Me, My Love/Joanna	1964	2.00	4.00	8.00
JUBILEE					
☐ 5411	Gee, Officer Krupki/The Miracle of St. Marie	1961	2.00	4.00	8.00
☐ 5419	Come a Little Closer/Windows of Heaven	1962	2.00	4.00	8.00
☐ 5429	One Red Rose/I Wish You Were Here	1962	2.00	4.00	8.00
LAURIE					
☐ 3331	I'll Never Love Again/Try Your Luck	1966	—	3.00	6.00
☐ 3360	Shout Shout (Knock Yourself Out)/People Get Jealous	1966	—	3.00	6.00
MGM					
☐ 12951	Pledging My Love/I Want a Little Girl	1960	2.00	4.00	8.00
☐ 12977	Love Is Where You Find It/Beat on Your Drum Little Susan	1961	2.00	4.00	8.00
☐ 13003	To Love/From Your Very Own Lips	1961	2.00	4.00	8.00
☐ 13031	Pretty Nina/Moon of Manakoora	1961	2.00	4.00	8.00
VEE JAY					
☐ 474	They Say/Jimmy San	1962	2.00	4.00	8.00
☐ 551	Take a Bow (Little Darlin')/Nina	1963	2.00	4.00	8.00

Number	Title (A Side/B Side)	Yr	VG	VG+	NM
7-Inch Extended Plays					
EPIC					
❑ EG-7121	(contents unknown)	195?	3.00	6.00	12.00
❑ EG-7121 [PS]	The Four Coins	195?	3.00	6.00	12.00
❑ EG-7186	(contents unknown)	195?	3.00	6.00	12.00
❑ EG-7186 [PS]	The Four Coins in Shangri-La	195?	3.00	6.00	12.00
❑ EG-7196	(contents unknown)	195?	2.50	5.00	10.00
❑ EG-7196 [PS]	The Four Coins Sing	195?	2.50	5.00	10.00
❑ EG-7197	(contents unknown)	195?	2.50	5.00	10.00
❑ EG-7197 [PS]	The Four Coins Sing	195?	2.50	5.00	10.00
Albums					
EPIC					
❑ LN 1104 [M]	The Four Coins	1955	12.50	25.00	50.00
❑ LN 3445 [M]	The Four Coins in Shangri-La	1958	7.50	15.00	30.00
MGM					
❑ E-3944 [M]	Greek Songs	1961	3.75	7.50	15.00
❑ SE-3944 [S]	Greek Songs	1961	5.00	10.00	20.00
ROULETTE					
❑ R-25288 [M]	Greek Songs Mama Never Taught Me	1965	3.75	7.50	15.00
❑ SR-25288 [S]	Greek Songs Mama Never Taught Me	1965	5.00	10.00	20.00

FOUR COQUETTES, THE See THE FOUR CAL-QUETTES.

FOUR DATES, THE
45s

Number	Title (A Side/B Side)	Yr	VG	VG+	NM
CHANCELLOR					
❑ 1014	I'm Happy/Eloise	1958	5.00	10.00	20.00
❑ 1019	I say babe/Hey Roly Poly	1958	5.00	10.00	20.00
❑ 1027	Feel Good/Teenage Neighbor	1958	6.25	12.50	25.00

FOUR DEALS, THE
45s

Number	Title (A Side/B Side)	Yr	VG	VG+	NM
CAPITOL					
❑ F1313	It's Too Late Now/There Ain't No Bears	1950	25.00	50.00	100.00

FOUR DEEP TONES, THE
45s

Number	Title (A Side/B Side)	Yr	VG	VG+	NM
CORAL					
❑ 65061	Just in Case You Change Your Mind/Castle Rock	1951	50.00	100.00	200.00
❑ 65062	The Night You Said Goodbye/When the Saints Go Marching In	1951	50.00	100.00	200.00

FOUR DEUCES, THE
45s

Number	Title (A Side/B Side)	Yr	VG	VG+	NM
EVEREST					
❑ 19311	Polly/Yella Shoes	1959	7.50	15.00	30.00
MUSIC CITY					
❑ 790	W-P-L-J/Here Lies My Love	1955	10.00	20.00	40.00
—Black label					
❑ 790	W-P-L-J/Here Lies My Love	1955	37.50	75.00	150.00
—Maroon label					
❑ 796	Down It Went/Goose Is Gone	1955	15.00	30.00	60.00

FOUR DIRECTIONS, THE
45s

Number	Title (A Side/B Side)	Yr	VG	VG+	NM
CORAL					
❑ 62456	(Doin' the) Arthur/Tonight We Love	1965	7.50	15.00	30.00

FOUR DUKES, THE (1)
45s

Number	Title (A Side/B Side)	Yr	VG	VG+	NM
DUKE					
❑ 116	Crying in the Chapel/I Done Done It	1953	200.00	400.00	800.00

FOUR DUKES, THE (2)
45s

Number	Title (A Side/B Side)	Yr	VG	VG+	NM
IMPERIAL					
❑ 5653	Baby Won't You Please Come Home/John Henry	1960	7.50	15.00	30.00

FOUR EPICS, THE
45s

Number	Title (A Side/B Side)	Yr	VG	VG+	NM
HERITAGE					
❑ 109	I'm On My Way to Love/When the Music Ends	1962	25.00	50.00	100.00
LAURIE					
❑ 3155	Again/I Love You Diane	1963	6.25	12.50	25.00
❑ 3183	How I Wish I Was Single Again/Dance Joanne	1963	6.25	12.50	25.00

FOUR ESQUIRES, THE
45s

Number	Title (A Side/B Side)	Yr	VG	VG+	NM
CADENCE					
❑ 1260	Three Things/The Sphinx Won't Tell	1955	5.00	10.00	20.00
❑ 1277	Adorable/Thunderbolt	1955	5.00	10.00	20.00
LONDON					
❑ 1652	Look Homeward Angel/Santo Domingo	1956	6.25	12.50	25.00
PARIS					
❑ 501	Song of April/Everyone's Sweet on My Sugar	1957	5.00	10.00	20.00
❑ 505	The Chopstick Rock/Never Look for Love	1957	5.00	10.00	20.00
❑ 509	Love Me Forever/I Ain't Been Right Since You Left	1957	5.00	10.00	20.00
❑ 512	Always and Forever/I Walk Down the Street	1958	5.00	10.00	20.00
❑ 515	All Around the Clock/The Big Dance	1958	5.00	10.00	20.00
❑ 520	Hideaway/Repeat After Me	1958	5.00	10.00	20.00
—With Rosemary June					
❑ 526	Follow Me/The Land of You and Me	1958	5.00	10.00	20.00
❑ 531	Lucky Old Sun/Non E Cosi	1959	5.00	10.00	20.00
❑ 535	Act Your Age/So Ends the Night	1959	5.00	10.00	20.00
❑ 539	Wonderful One/Wouldn't It Be Wonderful	1959	5.00	10.00	20.00
❑ 544	Make Them Mine/Peg O' My Heart	1960	5.00	10.00	20.00
❑ 549	Sweet Sixteen She'll Never Be/The Chopstick Rock	1960	5.00	10.00	20.00
PILGRIM					
❑ 717	Follow Me/Summer Vacation	1956	6.25	12.50	25.00
TERRACE					
❑ 7502	Can't Help Falling in Love/Merry-Go-Round of Love	1961	3.75	7.50	15.00

Number	Title (A Side/B Side)	Yr	VG	VG+	NM
❑ 7516	The James Bond Theme (Double-O-Seven)/Summer Vacation	1963	6.25	12.50	25.00
—Betcha didn't know this had lyrics...					

FOUR-EVERS, THE
45s

Number	Title (A Side/B Side)	Yr	VG	VG+	NM
CHATTAHOOCHIE					
❑ 630	Colors/Come Up in the World	1963	3.75	7.50	15.00
COLUMBIA					
❑ 42303	You Belong to Me/Such a Good Night for Dreaming	1962	15.00	30.00	60.00
❑ 43886	A Lovely Way to Say Goodnight/The Girl I Wanna Bring Home	1966	5.00	10.00	20.00
CONSTELLATION					
❑ 151	Stormy/Out of the Crowd	1965	7.50	15.00	30.00
JAMIE					
❑ 1247	Everybody South Street/One More Time	1963	3.75	7.50	15.00
RED BIRD					
❑ 10-078	You Never Had It So Good/What a Scene	1966	6.25	12.50	25.00
SMASH					
❑ 1853	Lover Come Back to Me/It's Love	1963	3.75	7.50	15.00
❑ 1887	Be My Girl/If I Were a Magician	1964	3.75	7.50	15.00
—Same A-side, different title					
❑ 1887	Please Be Mine/If I Were a Magician	1964	7.50	15.00	30.00
❑ 1921	(Say I Love You) Doo Bee Dum/Everlasting	1964	3.75	7.50	15.00

FOUR EXCEPTIONS, THE
45s

Number	Title (A Side/B Side)	Yr	VG	VG+	NM
PARKWAY					
❑ 986	You Got the Power/A Sad Goodbye	1966	12.50	25.00	50.00

FOUR FELLOWS, THE
45s

Number	Title (A Side/B Side)	Yr	VG	VG+	NM
DERBY					
❑ 862	I Tried/Bend of the River	1954	100.00	200.00	400.00
GLORY					
❑ 231	I Wish I Didn't Know You/I Know Love	1955	20.00	40.00	80.00
❑ 234	Soldier Boy/Take Me Back Baby	1955	15.00	30.00	60.00
❑ 236	Angels Say/In the Rain	1955	15.00	30.00	60.00
❑ 238	Fallen Angel/Hold 'Em Joe	1956	15.00	30.00	60.00
❑ 242	Darling You/Please Don't Deprive Me of My Love	1956	20.00	40.00	80.00
❑ 244	I Sit in My Window/Please Play My Song	1956	15.00	30.00	60.00
❑ 248	You Don't Know Me/Sweet Girl	1956	15.00	30.00	60.00
❑ 250	Loving You, Darling/Give Me Back My Broken Heart	1957	15.00	30.00	60.00
NESTOR					
❑ 27	Remember/That Kiss You Gave Me	1958	75.00	150.00	300.00

FOUR FIFTHS, THE
45s

Number	Title (A Side/B Side)	Yr	VG	VG+	NM
COLUMBIA					
❑ 43913	If You Still Want Me/Have You Ever Loved a Girl	1966	3.00	6.00	12.00
HUDSON					
❑ 8101	After Graduation/Come On Girl	1963	37.50	75.00	150.00
—Black vinyl					
❑ 8101	After Graduation/Come On Girl	1963	100.00	200.00	400.00
—Blue vinyl					

FOUR FRESHMEN, THE
45s

Number	Title (A Side/B Side)	Yr	VG	VG+	NM
CAPITOL					
❑ F1293	Mr. B's Blues/Then I'll Be Happy	1950	3.75	7.50	15.00
❑ F1377	Now You Know/Pick Up Tears	1951	3.75	7.50	15.00
❑ F2152	It's a Blue World/Tuxedo Junction	1952	3.00	6.00	12.00
❑ F2286	Stormy Weather/The Day Isn't Long Enough	1952	3.00	6.00	12.00
❑ F2398	Baltimore Oriole/Poinciana	1953	3.00	6.00	12.00
❑ F2564	Holiday/It Happened Once Before	1953	3.00	6.00	12.00
❑ F2745	Seems Like Old Times/Crazy Bones	1954	3.00	6.00	12.00
❑ F2832	I'll Be Seeing You/Please Remember	1954	3.00	6.00	12.00
❑ F2898	We'll Be Together Again/My Heart Stood Still	1954	3.00	6.00	12.00
❑ F2961	Mood Indigo/Love Turns Winter to Spring	1954	3.00	6.00	12.00
❑ F3070	It Never Occurred to Me/Malaya	1955	2.50	5.00	10.00
❑ F3154	Day by Day/How Can I Tell Her	1955	2.50	5.00	10.00
❑ F3292	Charmaine/In This Whole Wide World	1955	2.50	5.00	10.00
❑ F3359	Angel Eyes/Love Is Just Around the Corner	1956	2.50	5.00	10.00
❑ F3410	Graduation Day/Lonely Night in Paris	1956	3.75	7.50	15.00
❑ F3532	You're So Far Above Me/He Who Loves and Runs Away	1956	2.50	5.00	10.00
❑ F3652	That's the Way I Feel/What's It Gonna Be	1957	2.50	5.00	10.00
❑ F3779	Julie Is Her Name/Sometimes I'm Happy	1957	2.50	5.00	10.00
❑ F3832	Grenada/How Can I Begin to Tell	1957	2.50	5.00	10.00
❑ F3930	Whistle Me Some Blues/Nights Are Longer	1958	2.50	5.00	10.00
❑ 4341	Candy/Route 66	1960	2.00	4.00	8.00
❑ 4749	Shangri-La/Teach Me Tonight	1962	2.00	4.00	8.00
❑ 4824	I'm Gonna Go Fishin'/Taps Miller	1962	2.00	4.00	8.00
❑ 5007	Summertime/Baby Won't You Please Come Home	1963	2.00	4.00	8.00
❑ 5007 [PS]	Summertime/Baby Won't You Please Come Home	1963	3.75	7.50	15.00
❑ 5083	Charade/Funny How Time Slips Away	1963	2.00	4.00	8.00
❑ 5151	Don't Make Me Sorry/My Baby's Gone	1964	2.00	4.00	8.00
❑ 5401	When I Stop Lovin' You/Nights Are Long	1965	2.00	4.00	8.00
❑ 5471	Those Magnificent Men in Their Flying Machines/Old Cape Cod	1965	2.50	5.00	10.00
DECCA					
❑ 32070	Cry/Nowhere to Go	1966	—	3.00	6.00
LIBERTY					
❑ 56047	Cherish-Windy/Come Fly with Me-Up Up and Away	1968	—	3.00	6.00
❑ 56099	By the Time I Get to Phoenix-My Special Angel/It's a Blue World	1969	—	3.00	6.00
7-Inch Extended Plays					
CAPITOL					
❑ EAP 1-433	It's a Blue World/Stormy Weather//Tuxedo Junction/Mr. B's Blues	195?	3.75	7.50	15.00
❑ EAP 1-433 [PS]	The Four Freshmen	195?	3.75	7.50	15.00

F

Number	Title (A Side/B Side)	Yr	VG	VG+	NM
❏ EAP 1-522	After You/Over the Rainbow//My Heart Stood Still/The Nearness of You	195?	3.75	7.50	15.00
❏ EAP 1-522 [PS]	Voices in Modern, Part 1	195?	3.75	7.50	15.00
❏ EAP 2-522	Street of Dreams/We'll Be Together Again//Circus/Mood Indigo	195?	3.75	7.50	15.00
❏ EAP 2-522 [PS]	Voices in Modern, Part 2	195?	3.75	7.50	15.00
❏ EAP 1-683	(contents unknown)	1956	3.00	6.00	12.00
❏ EAP 1-683 [PS]	Four Freshmen and Five Trombones, Part 1	1956	3.00	6.00	12.00
❏ EAP 2-683	Mam'selle/Speak Low//Love/Love Is Here to Stay	1956	3.00	6.00	12.00
❏ EAP 2-683 [PS]	Four Freshmen and Five Trombones, Part 2	1956	3.00	6.00	12.00
❏ EAP 3-683	(contents unknown)	1956	3.00	6.00	12.00
❏ EAP 3-683 [PS]	Four Freshmen and Five Trombones, Part 3	1956	3.00	6.00	12.00
❏ EAP 1-743	(contents unknown)	1957	2.50	5.00	10.00
❏ EAP 1-743 [PS]	Freshmen Favorites, Part 1	1957	2.50	5.00	10.00
❏ EAP 2-743	Graduation Day/Poinciana//Lonely Night in Paris/Seems Like Old Times	1957	2.50	5.00	10.00
❏ EAP 2-743 [PS]	Freshmen Favorites, Part 2	1957	2.50	5.00	10.00
❏ EAP 3-743	(contents unknown)	1957	2.50	5.00	10.00
❏ EAP 3-743 [PS]	Freshmen Favorites, Part 3	1957	2.50	5.00	10.00
❏ EAP 1-763	After You've Gone/Ev'ry Time We Say Goodbye//Easy Street/Good Night Sweetheart	1957	2.50	5.00	10.00
❏ EAP 1-763 [PS]	4 Freshmen and 5 Trumpets, Part 1	1957	2.50	5.00	10.00
❏ EAP 2-763	(contents unknown)	1957	2.50	5.00	10.00
❏ EAP 2-763 [PS]	4 Freshmen and 5 Trumpets, Part 2	1957	2.50	5.00	10.00
❏ EAP 3-763	(contents unknown)	1957	2.50	5.00	10.00
❏ EAP 3-763 [PS]	4 Freshmen and 5 Trumpets, Part 3	1957	2.50	5.00	10.00
❏ EAP 1-844	*Liza/You've Got Me Cryin' Again/This Love of Mine/I Get Along Without You Very Well	1957	2.50	5.00	10.00
❏ EAP 1-844 [PS]	Four Freshmen and Five Saxes, Part 1	1957	2.50	5.00	10.00
❏ EAP 2-844	(contents unknown)	1957	2.50	5.00	10.00
❏ EAP 2-844 [PS]	Four Freshmen and Five Saxes, Part 2	1957	2.50	5.00	10.00
❏ EAP 3-844	(contents unknown)	1957	2.50	5.00	10.00
❏ EAP 3-844 [PS]	Four Freshmen and Five Saxes, Part 3	1957	2.50	5.00	10.00
❏ EAP 1-922	(contents unknown)	1958	2.50	5.00	10.00
❏ EAP 1-922 [PS]	Voices in Latin, Part 1	1958	2.50	5.00	10.00
❏ EAP 2-922	(contents unknown)	1958	2.50	5.00	10.00
❏ EAP 2-922 [PS]	Voices in Latin, Part 2	1958	2.50	5.00	10.00
❏ EAP 3-922	What's New/Chelsea Bridge//Tangerine/Brazil	1958	2.50	5.00	10.00
❏ EAP 3-922 [PS]	Voices in Latin, Part 3	1958	2.50	5.00	10.00
❏ EAP 1-1255	(contents unknown)	1959	2.50	5.00	10.00
❏ EAP 1-1255 [PS]	The Four Freshmen and Five Guitars, Part 1	1959	2.50	5.00	10.00
❏ EAP 2-1255	(contents unknown)	1959	2.50	5.00	10.00
❏ EAP 2-1255 [PS]	The Four Freshmen and Five Guitars, Part 2	1959	2.50	5.00	10.00
❏ EAP 3-1255	(contents unknown)	1959	2.50	5.00	10.00
❏ EAP 3-1255 [PS]	The Four Freshmen and Five Guitars, Part 3	1959	2.50	5.00	10.00

Albums

CAPITOL

Number	Title (A Side/B Side)	Yr	VG	VG+	NM
❏ H 522 [10]	Voices in Modern	1955	12.50	25.00	50.00
❏ T 522 [M]	Voices in Modern	1955	10.00	20.00	40.00
❏ T 683 [M]	Four Freshmen and Five Trombones	1956	10.00	20.00	40.00
❏ DT 743 [R]	Freshmen Favorites	196?	3.00	6.00	12.00
❏ SM-743	Freshmen Favorites	197?	2.50	5.00	10.00
❏ T 743 [M]	Freshmen Favorites	1956	10.00	20.00	40.00
❏ T 763 [M]	4 Freshmen and 5 Trumpets	1957	10.00	20.00	40.00
❏ T 844 [M]	Four Freshmen and Five Saxes	1957	10.00	20.00	40.00
❏ T 992 [M]	Voices in Latin	1958	7.50	15.00	30.00
❏ ST 1008 [S]	The Four Freshmen In Person	1958	10.00	20.00	40.00
❏ T 1008 [M]	The Four Freshmen In Person	1958	7.50	15.00	30.00
❏ ST 1074 [S]	Voices in Love	1958	7.50	15.00	30.00
❏ T 1074 [M]	Voices in Love	1958	5.00	10.00	20.00
❏ ST 1103 [S]	Freshmen Favorites, Vol. 2	1959	7.50	15.00	30.00
❏ T 1103 [M]	Freshmen Favorites, Vol. 2	1959	5.00	10.00	20.00
❏ ST 1189 [S]	Love Lost	1959	7.50	15.00	30.00
❏ T 1189 [M]	Love Lost	1959	5.00	10.00	20.00
❏ ST 1255 [S]	The Four Freshmen and Five Guitars	1959	7.50	15.00	30.00
❏ T 1255 [M]	The Four Freshmen and Five Guitars	1959	5.00	10.00	20.00
❏ ST 1295 [S]	Voices and Brass	1960	7.50	15.00	30.00
❏ T 1295 [M]	Voices and Brass	1960	5.00	10.00	20.00
❏ ST 1378 [S]	First Affair	1960	7.50	15.00	30.00
❏ T 1378 [M]	First Affair	1960	5.00	10.00	20.00
❏ ST 1485 [S]	Freshmen Year	1961	6.25	12.50	25.00
❏ T 1485 [M]	Freshmen Year	1961	5.00	10.00	20.00
❏ ST 1543 [S]	Voices in Fun	1961	6.25	12.50	25.00
❏ T 1543 [M]	Voices in Fun	1961	5.00	10.00	20.00
❏ ST 1640 [S]	The Best of the Four Freshmen	1962	6.25	12.50	25.00
❏ T 1640 [M]	The Best of the Four Freshmen	1962	5.00	10.00	20.00
❏ ST 1682 [S]	Stars in Our Eyes	1962	6.25	12.50	25.00
❏ T 1682 [M]	Stars in Our Eyes	1962	5.00	10.00	20.00
❏ ST 1753 [S]	Swingers	1963	5.00	10.00	20.00
❏ T 1753 [M]	Swingers	1963	3.75	7.50	15.00
❏ ST 1860 [S]	The Four Freshmen In Person, Volume 2	1963	5.00	10.00	20.00
❏ T 1860 [M]	The Four Freshmen In Person, Volume 2	1963	3.75	7.50	15.00
❏ ST 1950 [S]	Got That Feelin'	1963	5.00	10.00	20.00
❏ T 1950 [M]	Got That Feelin'	1963	3.75	7.50	15.00
❏ ST 2067 [S]	Funny How Time Slips Away	1964	5.00	10.00	20.00
❏ T 2067 [M]	Funny How Time Slips Away	1964	3.75	7.50	15.00
❏ ST 2168 [S]	More Four Freshmen and Five Trombones	1964	5.00	10.00	20.00
❏ T 2168 [M]	More Four Freshmen and Five Trombones	1964	3.75	7.50	15.00
❏ SM-11639	Four Freshmen and Five Trombones	1977	2.50	5.00	10.00
❏ SM-11965	Best of the Four Freshmen	1978	2.50	5.00	10.00

CREATIVE WORLD

Number	Title (A Side/B Side)	Yr	VG	VG+	NM
❏ ST-1059 [(2)]	Stan Kenton and the Four Freshmen at Butler University	1972	5.00	10.00	20.00

LIBERTY

Number	Title (A Side/B Side)	Yr	VG	VG+	NM
❏ LST-7563	Today Is Tomorrow	1968	3.75	7.50	15.00
❏ LST-7590	In a Class By Themselves	1969	3.75	7.50	15.00
❏ LST-7630	Different Strokes	1969	3.75	7.50	15.00
❏ LN-10181	In a Class By Themselves	198?	2.00	4.00	8.00

PAUSA

Number	Title (A Side/B Side)	Yr	VG	VG+	NM
❏ PR-7193	Fresh!	1986	2.50	5.00	10.00
❏ PR-9029	The Four Freshmen and Five Guitars	198?	2.50	5.00	10.00
❏ PR-9040	4 Freshmen and 5 Trumpets	1985	2.50	5.00	10.00

PICKWICK

Number	Title (A Side/B Side)	Yr	VG	VG+	NM
❏ SPC-3080	The Fabulous Four Freshmen	196?	3.00	6.00	12.00
❏ SPC-3563	A Taste of Honey	1977	2.50	5.00	10.00

SUNSET

Number	Title (A Side/B Side)	Yr	VG	VG+	NM
❏ SUS-5289	My Special Angel	1970	3.00	6.00	12.00

FOUR GRADUATES, THE

45s

CRYSTAL BALL

Number	Title (A Side/B Side)	Yr	VG	VG+	NM
❏ 116	May I Have This Dance/Caught in a Lie	1978	—	2.00	4.00
❏ 119	Your Initials/Every Year About This Time	1978	—	2.00	4.00

RUST

Number	Title (A Side/B Side)	Yr	VG	VG+	NM
❏ 5062	Picture of An Angel/A Lovely Way to Spend An Evening	1963	25.00	50.00	100.00
❏ 5084	Candy Queen/A Girl in Love	1964	45.00	90.00	180.00

FOUR HAVEN KNIGHTS, THE

45s

ANGLETONE

Number	Title (A Side/B Side)	Yr	VG	VG+	NM
❏ 1066	In My Lonely Room/I'm Just a Dreamer	1958	12.50	25.00	50.00
❏ 1092	Just to Be in Love/Why Go On Pretending	1958	12.50	25.00	50.00

ATLAS

Number	Title (A Side/B Side)	Yr	VG	VG+	NM
❏ 1066	In My Lonely Room/I'm Just a Dreamer	1957	37.50	75.00	150.00
❏ 1092	Just to Be in Love/Why Go On Pretending	1957	37.50	75.00	150.00

JOSIE

Number	Title (A Side/B Side)	Yr	VG	VG+	NM
❏ 824	In My Lonely Room/I'm Just a Dreamer	1957	7.50	15.00	30.00

FOUR HOLIDAYS, THE

45s

UNITED ARTISTS

Number	Title (A Side/B Side)	Yr	VG	VG+	NM
❏ 163	Who Can Say/Nobody Loves You Like-a Me	1959	7.50	15.00	30.00

VERVE

Number	Title (A Side/B Side)	Yr	VG	VG+	NM
❏ 10204	I Don't Wanna Go to School/Love Ya' Baby	1960	3.75	7.50	15.00

FOUR HUES, THE

45s

CORAL

Number	Title (A Side/B Side)	Yr	VG	VG+	NM
❏ 61617	Ivory Tower/Sister Jenny	1956	7.50	15.00	30.00

CROWN

Number	Title (A Side/B Side)	Yr	VG	VG+	NM
❏ 159	Rock-a-Bye/Take Me Out of Your Heart	1955	10.00	20.00	40.00

FOUR IMPERIALS, THE

45s

CHANT

Number	Title (A Side/B Side)	Yr	VG	VG+	NM
❏ 10067	My Girl/Teen Age Fool	1958	12.50	25.00	50.00

DIAL

Number	Title (A Side/B Side)	Yr	VG	VG+	NM
❏ 101	Valley of Tears/Time Out	1959	37.50	75.00	150.00

DOT

Number	Title (A Side/B Side)	Yr	VG	VG+	NM
❏ 15737	Lazy Bonnie/Let's Make a Scene	1958	6.25	12.50	25.00

FOX

Number	Title (A Side/B Side)	Yr	VG	VG+	NM
❏ 102	Give Me One More Chance/Look Up and Live	1958	20.00	40.00	80.00

LORELEI

Number	Title (A Side/B Side)	Yr	VG	VG+	NM
❏ 4444	Lazy Bonnie/Let's Make a Scene	1958	25.00	50.00	100.00

TWIRL

Number	Title (A Side/B Side)	Yr	VG	VG+	NM
❏ 2005	Santa's Got a Coupe de Ville/Seven Lonely Days	1960	6.25	12.50	25.00

FOUR J'S, THE

45s

CONGRESS

Number	Title (A Side/B Side)	Yr	VG	VG+	NM
❏ 6003	Dreamin'/Love My Life	1969	2.50	5.00	10.00

4-J

Number	Title (A Side/B Side)	Yr	VG	VG+	NM
❏ 506	Will You Be My Love/Nursery	1963	3.75	7.50	15.00

HERALD

Number	Title (A Side/B Side)	Yr	VG	VG+	NM
❏ 528	Kissin' at the Drive-In/Dreams Are a Dime a Dozen	1958	7.50	15.00	30.00

JAMIE

Number	Title (A Side/B Side)	Yr	VG	VG+	NM
❏ 1267	Here I Am Broken-Hearted/She Said That She Loved Me	1964	6.25	12.50	25.00
❏ 1274	By Love Possessed/My Love, My Love	1964	6.25	12.50	25.00

UNITED ARTISTS

Number	Title (A Side/B Side)	Yr	VG	VG+	NM
❏ 125	Rock and Roll Age/Be Nice, Don't Fight	1958	10.00	20.00	40.00

FOUR J'S, THE, AND THE FABULOUS IMPERIALS

45s

MGM

Number	Title (A Side/B Side)	Yr	VG	VG+	NM
❏ 12687	Class Ring/Weird	1958	20.00	40.00	80.00

FOUR JACKS, THE

45s

FEDERAL

Number	Title (A Side/B Side)	Yr	VG	VG+	NM
❏ 12075	You Met a Fool/Goodbye Baby	1952	200.00	400.00	800.00
❏ 12087	The Last of the Good Rockin' Men/I'll Be Home Again	1952	125.00	250.00	500.00

MGM

Number	Title (A Side/B Side)	Yr	VG	VG+	NM
❏ 11179	You're in Love with Someone Else/Darling, Lonesome for You	1952	5.00	10.00	20.00

FOUR JACKS AND A JILL (1)

45s

RCA VICTOR

Number	Title (A Side/B Side)	Yr	VG	VG+	NM
❏ 47-9473	Master Jack/I Looked Back	1968	2.00	4.00	8.00
❏ 47-9572	Mister Nico/Hamba Liliwam	1968	—	3.00	6.00
❏ 47-9655	Hey Mister/Sad Little Pigeon	1968	—	3.00	6.00
❏ 47-9728	Stone in My Shoe/Grandfather Dugan	1969	—	3.00	6.00

Albums

RCA VICTOR

Number	Title (A Side/B Side)	Yr	VG	VG+	NM
❏ LPM-4019 [M]	Master Jack	1968	7.50	15.00	30.00
❏ LSP-4019 [S]	Master Jack	1968	3.75	7.50	15.00
❏ LSP-4103	Fables	1968	3.75	7.50	15.00

FOUR JACKS AND A JILL (2)

45s

FORTUNE

Number	Title (A Side/B Side)	Yr	VG	VG+	NM
❏ 507	Love's Not Love Without You/I'm in Love with Someone	1955	7.50	15.00	30.00

FOUR JACKS AND A JILL (U)

45s

HEART SONG

Number	Title (A Side/B Side)	Yr	VG	VG+	NM
❏ 103	It's Christmas Time Again/(B-side unknown)	19??	2.50	5.00	10.00

Number	Title (A Side/B Side)	Yr	VG	VG+	NM

FOUR JETS, THE See THE SHADOWS.

FOUR JEWELS, THE
45s
CHECKER

Number	Title (A Side/B Side)	Yr	VG	VG+	NM
❏ 1039	Dapper Dan/Loaded with Goodies	1963	5.00	10.00	20.00
❏ 1069	Time for Love/That's What They Put Erasers on Pencils For	1964	5.00	10.00	20.00

START

Number	Title	Yr	VG	VG+	NM
❏ 638	Johnny Jealousy/Someone Special	1963	7.50	15.00	30.00
❏ 638	Loaded with Goodies/Fire	1963	10.00	20.00	40.00
❏ 641	All That's Good/I Love Me Some You	1963	7.50	15.00	30.00

TEC

Number	Title	Yr	VG	VG+	NM
❏ 3007	Baby It's You/She's Wrong for You Baby	1964	6.25	12.50	25.00

FOUR JOKERS, THE (1)
45s
AMY

Number	Title	Yr	VG	VG+	NM
❏ 832	She's a Flirt/Uggaboo	1961	5.00	10.00	20.00

FOUR JOKERS, THE (2)
45s
CRYSTALLETTE

Number	Title	Yr	VG	VG+	NM
❏ 730	Your Decision/We Met in Catalina	1959	3.75	7.50	15.00
❏ 733	Beyond the Reef/That's the Way	1959	3.75	7.50	15.00

FOUR JOKERS, THE (3) Jimmy Drake, a.k.a. NERVOUS NORVUS, was in this group.
45s
DIAMOND

Number	Title	Yr	VG	VG+	NM
❏ 3004	Transfusion/You Dig	1956	7.50	15.00	30.00

FOUR JOKERS, THE (4)
45s
MGM

Number	Title	Yr	VG	VG+	NM
❏ 11815	Tell Me Now/Caring	1954	7.50	15.00	30.00

FOUR JOKERS, THE (5)
45s
SUE

Number	Title	Yr	VG	VG+	NM
❏ 703	Written in the Stars/The Run-Around	1958	15.00	30.00	60.00

FOUR JUST MEN Also see FREDDIE AND THE DREAMERS.
45s
TOWER

Number	Title	Yr	VG	VG+	NM
❏ 118	That's My Baby/Things Will Never Be the Same	1965	3.00	6.00	12.00

FOUR KNIGHTS, THE
45s
CAPITOL

Number	Title	Yr	VG	VG+	NM
❏ F1587	I Love the Sunshine of Your Smile/Sentimental Fool	1951	12.50	25.00	50.00
❏ F1707	Walkin' and Whistlin' Blues/Who Am I	1951	10.00	20.00	40.00
❏ F1787	I Go Crazy/Get Her Off My Hands	1951	10.00	20.00	40.00
❏ F1806	It's No Sin/The Glory of Love	1951	10.00	20.00	40.00
❏ F1875	Cry/Charmaine	1951	10.00	20.00	40.00
❏ F1914	Marshmallow Moon/Five Foot Two, Eyes of Blue	1951	7.50	15.00	30.00
❏ F1930	The Way I Feel/I Wish I Had a Girl	1952	7.50	15.00	30.00
❏ F1971	There Are Two Sides to Every Heartache/Walkin' in Sunshine	1952	7.50	15.00	30.00
❏ F1998	The More I Go Out with Somebody Else/The Doll with the Sawdust Heart	1952	7.50	15.00	30.00
❏ F2087	I'm the World's Biggest Fool/It's a Sin to Tell a Lie	1952	7.50	15.00	30.00
❏ F2127	Win or Lose/Do-Wacka-Do	1952	7.50	15.00	30.00
❏ F2195	Say No More/That's the Way It's Gonna Be	1952	7.50	15.00	30.00
❏ F2234	Lies/One Way Kisses	1952	7.50	15.00	30.00
❏ F2315	Oh Happy Day/A Million Tears	1953	6.25	12.50	25.00
❏ F2403	Anniversary Song/A Few Kind Words	1953	6.25	12.50	25.00
❏ F2517	Baby Doll/Tennessee Train	1953	6.25	12.50	25.00
❏ F2654	I Get So Lonely (When I Dream About You)/I Couldn't Stay Away from You	1953	5.00	10.00	20.00
❏ F2654	Oh Baby Mine/I Couldn't Stay Away from You	1953	10.00	20.00	40.00
❏ F2782	I Was Meant for You/They Tell Me	1954	5.00	10.00	20.00
❏ F2847	How Wrong Can You Be/Period	1954	5.00	10.00	20.00
❏ F2894	In the Chapel in the Moonlight/Easy Street	1954	5.00	10.00	20.00
❏ F2938	I Don't Wanna See You Cryin'/Saw Your Eyes	1954	5.00	10.00	20.00
❏ F3024	Write Me Baby/Honey Bunch	1955	5.00	10.00	20.00
❏ F3093	Foolishly Yours/Inside You	1955	5.00	10.00	20.00
❏ F3155	Gratefully Yours/Me	1955	5.00	10.00	20.00
❏ F3192	Don't Sit Under the Apple Tree/Believing You	1955	5.00	10.00	20.00
❏ F3250	Perdido/After	1955	5.00	10.00	20.00
❏ F3279	Guilty/You	1955	5.00	10.00	20.00
❏ F3339	I Love You Still/Happy Birthday Baby	1956	3.75	7.50	15.00
❏ F3386	Bottle Up the Moonlight/Mistaken	1956	3.75	7.50	15.00
❏ F3494	Don't Depend on Me/You're a Honey	1956	3.75	7.50	15.00
❏ F3689	It Doesn't Cost Money/How Can You Not Believe	1957	3.75	7.50	15.00
❏ F3730	Walkin' and Whistlin' Blues/I Love That Song	1957	3.75	7.50	15.00
❏ F15895	I Ain't Got Nobody/When My Baby Smiles at Me	1952	7.50	15.00	30.00
❏ F15896	Easy Street/Ida, Sweet As Apple Cider	1952	7.50	15.00	30.00
❏ F15897	Georgia on My Mind/Sentimental Journey	1952	7.50	15.00	30.00

CORAL

Number	Title	Yr	VG	VG+	NM
❏ 61936	The Four Minute Mile/When Your Lover Has Gone	1958	3.00	6.00	12.00
❏ 61981	Yes I Do/If You Ever Change Your Mind	1958	3.00	6.00	12.00
❏ 62045	O Falling Star/Foolish Tears	1959	3.00	6.00	12.00
❏ 62110	Where Is the Love/Things to Do Today	1959	3.00	6.00	12.00

DECCA

Number	Title	Yr	VG	VG+	NM
❏ 9-48018	He'll Understand and Say Well Done/Lead Me to That Rock	1952	25.00	50.00	100.00

—Reissue of original 78 from 1947 (Decca 48014 and 48026 are known to exist only on 78s)

DECCA FAITH SERIES

Number	Title	Yr	VG	VG+	NM
❏ 9-14524	He'll Understand and Say Well Done/Lead Me to That Rock	195?	12.50	25.00	50.00

—Later pressing; black Decca label with the words "Faith Series" where the star would normally be on the label

Number	Title	Yr	VG	VG+	NM
❏ 9-14524	He'll Understand and Say Well Done/Lead Me to That Rock	1950	30.00	60.00	120.00

—Purple label

7-Inch Extended Plays
CAPITOL

Number	Title	Yr	VG	VG+	NM
❏ EAP 1-414	*(It's No) Sin/The Glory of Love/Cry/Charmaine	1953	10.00	20.00	40.00
❏ EAP 1-414 [PS]	The Four Knights Sing	1953	10.00	20.00	40.00
❏ EAP 1-506	I Get So Lonely/Tennessee Train//Till Then/Anniversary Song	1954	10.00	20.00	40.00
❏ EAP 1-506 [PS]	I Get So Lonely	1954	10.00	20.00	40.00

MONOGRAM

Number	Title	Yr	VG	VG+	NM
❏ 2	Speaking of Angels/What Are You Doing New Year's Eve// + 2	19??	2.50	5.00	10.00

Albums
CAPITOL

Number	Title	Yr	VG	VG+	NM
❏ H 346 [10]	Spotlight Songs	1953	50.00	100.00	200.00
❏ T 346 [M]	Spotlight Songs	1956	37.50	75.00	150.00

CORAL

Number	Title	Yr	VG	VG+	NM
❏ CRL 57221 [M]	The Four Knights	1959	25.00	50.00	100.00
❏ CRL 57309 [M]	Million Dollar Baby	1960	15.00	30.00	60.00
❏ CRL 757309 [S]	Million Dollar Baby	1960	20.00	40.00	80.00

FOUR LADS, THE
45s
COLUMBIA

Number	Title	Yr	VG	VG+	NM
❏ 39865	Somebody Loves Me/Thanks to You	1952	3.75	7.50	15.00
❏ 39902	Blackberry Boogie/Girl on the Shore	1952	3.75	7.50	15.00
❏ 39958	He Who Has Love/I Wonder, I Wonder, I Wonder	1953	3.75	7.50	15.00
❏ 40005	Down By the Riverside/Take Me Back	1953	3.75	7.50	15.00
❏ 40082	Istanbul (Not Constantinople)/I Should Have Told You Long Ago	1953	3.75	7.50	15.00
❏ 40140	Harmony Brown/Gotta Go to the Fais Do Do	1953	3.75	7.50	15.00
❏ 40204	Long John/The Place Where I Worship	1954	3.75	7.50	15.00
❏ 40220	What Can I Lose by Letting You Know/Oh That'll Be Joyful	1954	3.75	7.50	15.00
❏ 40236	Gilly Gilly Ossenfeffer Katzenelle Bogen by the Sea/I Hear It Everywhere	1954	3.75	7.50	15.00
❏ 40306	Skokiaan (South African Song)/Why Should I Love You So	1954	3.75	7.50	15.00
❏ 40402	Two Ladies in De Shade of De Banana Tree/Dance Calinda	1954	3.75	7.50	15.00
❏ 40436	Pledging My Love/I've Been Thinking	1955	3.00	6.00	12.00
❏ 40490	Too Much! Baby, Baby/The Average Giraffe	1955	3.00	6.00	12.00
❏ 40539	Moments to Remember/Dream On, My Love, Dream On	1955	3.00	6.00	12.00
❏ 40629	No, Not Much!/I'll Never Know	1955	3.00	6.00	12.00
❏ 40674	Standing on the Corner/My Little Angel	1956	3.00	6.00	12.00
❏ 40736	The Bus Stop Song (A Paper of Pins)/A House with Love In It	1956	3.00	6.00	12.00
❏ 40788	Mary's Little Boy Child/The Stingiest Man in Town	1956	3.00	6.00	12.00
❏ 40811	Who Needs You/It's So Easy to Forget	1956	3.00	6.00	12.00
❏ 40811 [PS]	Who Needs You/It's So Easy to Forget	1956	5.00	10.00	20.00
❏ 40914	I Just Don't Know/Golly	1957	3.00	6.00	12.00
❏ 40974	The Eyes of God/His Invisible Hand	1957	3.00	6.00	12.00
❏ 41058	Put a Light in the Window/The Things We Did Last Summer	1957	2.50	5.00	10.00
❏ 41136	There's Only One of You/Blue Tattoo	1958	2.50	5.00	10.00
❏ 41194	Enchanted Island/Guess What the Neighbors'll Say	1958	2.50	5.00	10.00
❏ 41194 [PS]	Enchanted Island/Guess What the Neighbors'll Say	1958	3.75	7.50	15.00
❏ 41266	The Mocking Bird/I May Hate Myself in the Morning	1958	2.50	5.00	10.00
❏ 41310	The Girl on Page 44/Sunday	1958	2.50	5.00	10.00
❏ 41365	The Fountain of Youth/Meet Me Tonight in Dreamland	1959	2.50	5.00	10.00
❏ 41409	The Chosen Few/Together Wherever We Go	1959	2.50	5.00	10.00
❏ 41443	Got a Locket in My Pocket/Real Thing	1959	2.50	5.00	10.00
❏ 41497	Happy Anniversary/Who Do You Think You Are	1959	2.50	5.00	10.00
❏ 41497 [PS]	Happy Anniversary/Who Do You Think You Are	1959	3.75	7.50	15.00
❏ 41629	You're Nobody 'Til Somebody Loves You/Goona Goona	1960	2.50	5.00	10.00
❏ 41682	Our Lady of Fatima (Vocal)/Our Lady of Fatima (Recitation)	1960	2.50	5.00	10.00
❏ 41733	Two Other People/The Sheik of Chicago (Mustafa)	1960	2.50	5.00	10.00

DOT

Number	Title	Yr	VG	VG+	NM
❏ 16328	Don't Fly Away, Flamingo/Winter Snow	1962	2.00	4.00	8.00
❏ 16373	The Exodus Song/Never on Sunday	1962	2.00	4.00	8.00
❏ 16390	That's What I Like/Sweet Mama Tree-Top Tall	1962	2.00	4.00	8.00
❏ 16412	Beyond My Heart/Not That I Care	1962	2.00	4.00	8.00

EPIC

Number	Title	Yr	VG	VG+	NM
❏ 9150	The Mocking Bird/I May Hate Myself in the Morning	1956	3.00	6.00	12.00

FONA

Number	Title	Yr	VG	VG+	NM
❏ 1000	You'll Never Know/(B-side unknown)	1977	—	2.00	4.00
❏ 1001	Moments to Remember/Skokiaan	1977	—	2.00	4.00

KAPP

Number	Title	Yr	VG	VG+	NM
❏ 359	Just Young/Goodbye Mr. Love	1960	2.00	4.00	8.00
❏ 359 [PS]	Just Young/Goodbye Mr. Love	1960	2.50	5.00	10.00
❏ 404	555 Times/I Should Know Better	1961	2.00	4.00	8.00
❏ 412	Giuggigla/Oceans of Love	1961	2.00	4.00	8.00

OKEH

Number	Title	Yr	VG	VG+	NM
❏ 6885	The Mocking Bird/I May Hate Myself in the Morning	1952	5.00	10.00	20.00

REPRISE

Number	Title	Yr	VG	VG+	NM
❏ 20163	My Home Town/Cornflower Blue	1963	2.00	4.00	8.00

UNITED ARTISTS

Number	Title	Yr	VG	VG+	NM
❏ 653	It's a Mad, Mad, Mad, Mad World/Stolen Hours	1963	—	3.00	6.00
❏ 702	Love Theme from "Tom Jones"/Theme from "Lilies of the Field"	1964	—	3.00	6.00
❏ 760	Memories of You/Always Thinking of the Roses	1964	—	3.00	6.00
❏ 852	Thanks, Mr. Florist/Barabanchik	1965	—	3.00	6.00
❏ 893	With My Eyes Wide Open/I'm Not a Run-Around	1965	—	3.00	6.00
❏ 962	Give Her My Love/All the Winds	1965	—	3.00	6.00
❏ 50006	No, Not Much/Standing on the Corner	1966	—	2.50	5.00
❏ 50339	Where Do I Go/A Woman	1968	—	2.50	5.00
❏ 50517	My Heart's Symphony/Pardon Me Kiss	1969	—	2.50	5.00
❏ 50585	Moments to Remember/Free Again	1969	—	2.50	5.00

F

Number	Title (A Side/B Side)	Yr	VG	VG+	NM
7-Inch Extended Plays					
COLUMBIA					
❏ B-2538	*Moments to Remember/No, Not Much!/Istanbul (Not Constantinople)/Down by the River Side	195?	3.75	7.50	15.00
❏ B-2538 [PS]	The Four Lads (Hall of Fame Series)	195?	3.75	7.50	15.00
❏ B-2557	*Standing on the Corner/Take Me Back/ Skokiaan/Who Needs You	1958	3.75	7.50	15.00
❏ B-2557 [PS]	The Four Lads (Hall of Fame Series)	1958	3.75	7.50	15.00
❏ B-9121	On the Sunny Side of the Street/The Things We Did Last Summer//Taking a Chance on Love/ Bidin' My Time	1956	3.00	6.00	12.00
❏ B-9121 [PS]	On the Sunny Side, Vol. 1	1956	3.00	6.00	12.00
❏ B-9122	(contents unknown)	1956	3.00	6.00	12.00
❏ B-9122 [PS]	On the Sunny Side, Vol. 2	1956	3.00	6.00	12.00
❏ B-9123	(contents unknown)	1956	3.00	6.00	12.00
❏ B-9123 [PS]	On the Sunny Side, Vol. 3	1956	3.00	6.00	12.00
Albums					
COLUMBIA					
❏ CL 861 [M]	The Four Lads with Frankie Laine	1956	10.00	20.00	40.00
❏ CL 912 [M]	On the Sunny Side	1956	10.00	20.00	40.00
❏ CL 1045 [M]	The Four Lads Sing Frank Loesser	1957	10.00	20.00	40.00
❏ CL 1111 [M]	Four on the Aisle	1958	6.25	12.50	25.00
❏ CL 1223 [M]	Breezin' Along	1958	6.25	12.50	25.00
❏ CL 1235 [M]	The Four Lads' Greatest Hits	1958	6.25	12.50	25.00
❏ CL 1299 [M]	The Four Lads Swing Along	1959	6.25	12.50	25.00
❏ CL 1407 [M]	High Spirits!	1959	6.25	12.50	25.00
❏ CL 1502 [M]	Love Affair	1960	3.75	7.50	15.00
❏ CL 1550 [M]	Everything Goes	1960	3.75	7.50	15.00
❏ CL 2545 [10]	The Four Lads Sing Frank Loesser	1956	12.50	25.00	50.00
❏ CL 2577 [10]	Stage Show	1956	12.50	25.00	50.00
❏ CL 6329 [10]	Stage Show	1954	12.50	25.00	50.00
❏ CS 8035 [S]	Breezin' Along	1958	7.50	15.00	30.00
❏ CS 8047 [S]	Four on the Aisle	1958	7.50	15.00	30.00
❏ CS 8106 [S]	The Four Lads Swing Along	1959	7.50	15.00	30.00
❏ CS 8203 [S]	High Spirits!	1959	7.50	15.00	30.00
❏ CS 8293 [S]	Love Affair	1960	5.00	10.00	20.00
❏ CS 8350 [S]	Everything Goes	1960	5.00	10.00	20.00
DOT					
❏ DLP-3438 [M]	Hits of the 60's	1962	3.75	7.50	15.00
❏ DLP-3533 [M]	Oh Happy Day	1963	3.75	7.50	15.00
❏ DLP-25438 [S]	Hits of the 60's	1962	5.00	10.00	20.00
❏ DLP-25533 [S]	Oh Happy Day	1963	5.00	10.00	20.00
HARMONY					
❏ HS 11369	Moments to Remember	1970	3.00	6.00	12.00
KAPP					
❏ KL-1224 [M]	Twelve Hits	1961	3.75	7.50	15.00
❏ KL-1254 [M]	Dixieland Doin's	1961	3.75	7.50	15.00
❏ KS-3224 [S]	Twelve Hits	1961	5.00	10.00	20.00
❏ KS-3254 [S]	Dixieland Doin's	1961	5.00	10.00	20.00
UNITED ARTISTS					
❏ UAL-3356 [M]	This Year's Top Movie Hits	1964	3.75	7.50	15.00
❏ UAL-3399 [M]	Songs of World War I	1964	3.75	7.50	15.00
❏ UAS-6356 [S]	This Year's Top Movie Hits	1964	5.00	10.00	20.00
❏ UAS-6399 [S]	Songs of World War I	1964	5.00	10.00	20.00

FOUR LARKS, THE

45s

Number	Title (A Side/B Side)	Yr	VG	VG+	NM
TOWER					
❏ 364	Rain/Another Chance	1967	7.50	15.00	30.00
❏ 402	I Still Love You (From the Bottom of My Heart)/ Groovin' at the Go-Go	1968	10.00	20.00	40.00
❏ 450	Can I Have Another Helping, Please/ I've Got Plenty	1968	2.50	5.00	10.00
UPTOWN					
❏ 748	You and Me/That's All That Counts	1967	10.00	20.00	40.00

FOUR LOVERS, THE Also see THE FOUR SEASONS; FRANKIE VALLI.

45s

Number	Title (A Side/B Side)	Yr	VG	VG+	NM
EPIC					
❏ 9255	My Life for Your Love/Pucker Up	1957	500.00	1000.	2000.
RCA VICTOR					
❏ 47-6518	You're the Apple of My Eye/ The Girl of My Dreams	1956	10.00	20.00	40.00
❏ 47-6519	Honey Love/Please Don't Leave Me	1956	10.00	20.00	40.00
❏ 47-6646	Be Lovey Dovey/Jambalaya	1956	7.50	15.00	30.00
❏ 47-6768	Happy Am I/Never Never	1956	7.50	15.00	30.00
❏ 47-6812	Shake a Hand/The Stranger	1957	10.00	20.00	40.00
❏ 47-6819	Night Train/The Stranger	1957	10.00	20.00	40.00
7-Inch Extended Plays					
RCA VICTOR					
❏ EPA-869	Diddley Diddley Babe/Shake a Hand//The Stranger/Night Train	1956	37.50	75.00	150.00
❏ EPA-869 [PS]	The Four Lovers	1956	37.50	75.00	150.00
❏ EPA-871	I Want a Girl Just Like the Girl That Married Dear Old Dad/(I Love You) For Sentimental Reasons//This Is My Story/Memories of You	1956	37.50	75.00	150.00
❏ EPA-871 [PS]	Joyride	1956	37.50	75.00	150.00
Albums					
RCA VICTOR					
❏ LPM-1317 [M]	Joyride	1956	175.00	350.00	700.00

FOUR NATURALS, THE

45s

Number	Title (A Side/B Side)	Yr	VG	VG+	NM
RED TOP					
❏ 113	How Strange/Blue Moon	1958	12.50	25.00	50.00
—As "The Naturals"					
❏ 119	I Hear a Rhapsody/When I'm In Your Arms	1959	12.50	25.00	50.00
❏ 125	The Thought of You Darling/Long Long Ago	1959	20.00	40.00	80.00

FOUR OF A KIND More than one group.

45s

Number	Title (A Side/B Side)	Yr	VG	VG+	NM
BOMARC					
❏ 302	It's Better That Way/I Care for You	1959	5.00	10.00	20.00
CAMEO					
❏ 154	You Were Made T'Love/ Love Every Moment You Love	1958	5.00	10.00	20.00

Number	Title (A Side/B Side)	Yr	VG	VG+	NM
LAURIE					
❏ 3309	Chippies' Playground/Prance Around	1965	2.50	5.00	10.00
MELBA					
❏ 110	I'm Gonna Rock My Heart/ Our Song Dedicated to You	1957	6.25	12.50	25.00
❏ 117	Dreamy Eyes/Fools Fall in Love	1957	6.25	12.50	25.00

FOUR PEARLS, THE

45s

Number	Title (A Side/B Side)	Yr	VG	VG+	NM
DOLTON					
❏ 26	Look at Me/It's Almost Tomorrow	1960	50.00	100.00	200.00

FOUR PENNIES, THE (1) See THE CHIFFONS.

FOUR PENNIES, THE (2) British group.

45s

Number	Title (A Side/B Side)	Yr	VG	VG+	NM
PHILIPS					
❏ 40202	Juliet/Tell Me Girl, What Are You Gonna Do	1964	3.75	7.50	15.00
❏ 40333	Until It's Time for You to Go/Till Another Day	1965	3.75	7.50	15.00

FOUR PENNIES, THE (U) May also be by group (2), but we're not sure.

45s

Number	Title (A Side/B Side)	Yr	VG	VG+	NM
BRUNSWICK					
❏ 55304	You Have No Time to Lose/You're a Gas with Your Trash	1966	2.50	5.00	10.00
❏ 55324	Shake a Hand/'Tis the Season	1967	5.00	10.00	20.00

FOUR PREPS, THE

45s

Number	Title (A Side/B Side)	Yr	VG	VG+	NM
CAPITOL					
❏ F3576	Dreamy Eyes/Fools Will Be Fools	1956	5.00	10.00	20.00
❏ F3621	Moonstruck in Madrid/I Cried a Million Tears	1957	5.00	10.00	20.00
❏ F3699	Falling Star/Where Wuzz You	1957	5.00	10.00	20.00
❏ F3761	Promise Me Baby/Again 'N Again 'N Again	1957	5.00	10.00	20.00
❏ F3775	Band of Angels/How About That	1957	5.00	10.00	20.00
❏ F3845	26 Miles (Santa Catalina)/It's You	1957	5.00	10.00	20.00
❏ F3960	Big Man/Stop Baby	1958	5.00	10.00	20.00
❏ F4023	Lazy Summer Night/Summertime Lies	1958	5.00	10.00	20.00
❏ F4078	Cinderella/Gidget	1959	5.00	10.00	20.00
❏ F4126	She Was Five and He Was Ten/Riddle of Love	1959	5.00	10.00	20.00
❏ F4218	Big Surprise/Try My Arms	1959	5.00	10.00	20.00
❏ F4256	I Ain't Never/Memories, Memories	1959	5.00	10.00	20.00
❏ 4312	Down by the Station/Listen Honey	1959	3.00	6.00	12.00
❏ 4362	Got a Girl/Wait Till You Hear It from Me	1960	3.00	6.00	12.00
❏ 4400	Sentimental Kid/Madelina	1960	3.00	6.00	12.00
❏ 4435	The Sand and the Sea/Kaw-Liga	1960	3.00	6.00	12.00
❏ 4478	Balboa/I've Already Started In	1960	3.00	6.00	12.00
❏ 4508	Calcutta/Gone Are the Days	1961	3.00	6.00	12.00
❏ 4568	Dream, Boy, Dream/Grounded	1961	7.50	15.00	30.00
❏ 4599	More Money for You and Me/ Swing Down Chariot	1961	3.00	6.00	12.00
—With edited version of A-side					
❏ 4599	More Money for You and Me/ Swing Down Chariot	1961	3.75	7.50	15.00
—With full-length version of A-side					
❏ 4599 [PS]	More Money for You and Me/Swing Down Chariot	1961	5.00	10.00	20.00
❏ 4641	Smoke Gets In Your Eyes/Swing Down Chariot	1961	3.00	6.00	12.00
❏ 4659	Once Around the Block/The Seine	1961	3.00	6.00	12.00
❏ 4716	The Big Draft/Suzy Cockroach	1962	2.50	5.00	10.00
❏ 4716 [PS]	The Big Draft/Suzy Cockroach	1962	2.50	5.00	10.00
❏ 4792	Alice/Goodnight Sweetheart	1962	2.50	5.00	10.00
❏ 4974	Charmaine/Hi-Ho Anybody Home	1963	2.50	5.00	10.00
❏ 5020	Oh Where, Oh Where/Demons and Witches	1963	2.50	5.00	10.00
❏ 5074	The Greatest Surfer Couple/ I'm Falling in Love with a Girl	1963	2.50	5.00	10.00
❏ 5143	A Letter to the Beatles/College Cannonball	1964	6.25	12.50	25.00
❏ 5178	I've Known You All My Life/ What Kind of Bird Is That	1964	2.00	4.00	8.00
❏ 5236	A Girl Without a Top/ Two Wrongs Don't Make a Right	1964	2.00	4.00	8.00
❏ 5274	How to Succeed in Love/My Love, My Love	1964	2.00	4.00	8.00
❏ 5351	Everlasting/I'll Set My Love to Music	1965	2.00	4.00	8.00
❏ 5450	Now I'll Never Be the Same/ Our First American Dance	1965	2.00	4.00	8.00
❏ 5609	Annie in Her Granny/ Something to Remember You By	1966	2.00	4.00	8.00
❏ 5687	Let's Call It a Day, Girl/The Girl in the Shade of a Striped Umbrella	1966	2.00	4.00	8.00
❏ 5819	Love of the Common People/ What I Don't Know Won't Hurt Me	1967	2.00	4.00	8.00
❏ 5921	Draft Dodger Rag/The Hitchhiker	1967	2.00	4.00	8.00
7-Inch Extended Plays					
CAPITOL					
❏ EAP 1-1015	26 Miles/It's You//Moonstruck in Madrid/How About That	1958	6.25	12.50	25.00
❏ EAP 1-1015 [PS]	Twenty-Six Miles	1958	6.25	12.50	25.00
❏ EAP 1-1064	Big Man/Too Young for Love//Stop, Baby/ Humble Pie	1958	6.25	12.50	25.00
❏ EAP 1-1064 [PS]	Big Man	1958	6.25	12.50	25.00
❏ EAP 1-1090	(contents unknown)	1959	6.25	12.50	25.00
❏ EAP 1-1090 [PS]	Things We Did Last Summer	1959	6.25	12.50	25.00
❏ EAP 1-1139	(contents unknown)	1959	6.25	12.50	25.00
❏ EAP 1-1139 [PS]	Lazy Summer Night	1959	6.25	12.50	25.00
Albums					
CAPITOL					
❏ T 994 [M]	The Four Preps	1958	7.50	15.00	30.00
❏ T 1090 [M]	The Things We Did Last Summer	1958	6.25	12.50	25.00
❏ ST 1216 [S]	Dancing and Dreaming	1959	6.25	12.50	25.00
❏ T 1216 [M]	Dancing and Dreaming	1959	5.00	10.00	20.00
❏ DT 1291 [R]	Early in the Morning	1960	3.00	6.00	12.00
❏ T 1291 [M]	Early in the Morning	1960	6.25	12.50	25.00
❏ ST 1566 [S]	The Four Preps on Campus	1961	6.25	12.50	25.00
❏ T 1566 [M]	The Four Preps on Campus	1961	5.00	10.00	20.00
❏ ST 1647 [S]	Campus Encore	1962	6.25	12.50	25.00
❏ T 1647 [M]	Campus Encore	1962	5.00	10.00	20.00
❏ ST 1814 [S]	Campus Confidential	1963	5.00	10.00	20.00
❏ T 1814 [M]	Campus Confidential	1963	3.75	7.50	15.00

Number	Title (A Side/B Side)	Yr	VG	VG+	NM
❏ ST 1976 [S]	Songs for a Campus Party	1963	5.00	10.00	20.00
❏ T 1976 [M]	Songs for a Campus Party	1963	3.75	7.50	15.00
❏ ST 2169 [S]	How to Succeed in Love	1964	5.00	10.00	20.00
❏ T 2169 [M]	How to Succeed in Love	1964	3.75	7.50	15.00
❏ ST 2708 [S]	The Best of the Four Preps	1967	3.00	6.00	12.00
❏ T 2708 [M]	The Best of the Four Preps	1967	3.75	7.50	15.00

FOUR REPUTATIONS, THE
45s
MILLAGE

Number	Title (A Side/B Side)	Yr	VG	VG+	NM
❏ 105	Call on Me/(B-side unknown)	196?	200.00	400.00	800.00

FOUR SEASONS, THE Also see THE FOUR LOVERS; FRANKIE VALLI.
45s
COLUMBIA

Number	Title (A Side/B Side)	Yr	VG	VG+	NM
❏ (# unknown)	Big Man's World	1964	7.50	15.00	30.00

—One-sided cardboard soundsheet, a promo for the Columbia Record Club. Number has been reported as both 6675 and 6724.

CREWE

Number	Title (A Side/B Side)	Yr	VG	VG+	NM
❏ 333	And That Reminds Me (My Heart Reminds Me)/ The Singles Game	1969	2.00	4.00	8.00
❏ 333 [PS]	And That Reminds Me (My Heart Reminds Me)/ The Singles Game	1969	2.50	5.00	10.00

—No shadow behind Frankie Valli's and Joe Long's heads

Number	Title (A Side/B Side)	Yr	VG	VG+	NM
❏ 333 [PS]	And That Reminds Me (My Heart Reminds Me)/ The Singles Game	1969	3.00	6.00	12.00

—With shadow behind Frankie Valli's and Joe Long's heads

FBI

Number	Title (A Side/B Side)	Yr	VG	VG+	NM
❏ 7701	East Meets West/Rhapsody	1986	5.00	10.00	20.00

—With the Beach Boys

FOUR SEASONS

Number	Title (A Side/B Side)	Yr	VG	VG+	NM
❏ 0019	I Saw Mommy Kissing Santa Claus/ Santa Claus Is Coming to Town	198?	—	2.00	4.00

GONE

Number	Title (A Side/B Side)	Yr	VG	VG+	NM
❏ 5122	Bermuda/Spanish Lace	1961	20.00	40.00	80.00
❏ 5122 [DJ]	Bermuda/Spanish Lace	1961	15.00	30.00	60.00

MCA/CURB

Number	Title (A Side/B Side)	Yr	VG	VG+	NM
❏ 52618	Streetfighter/Deep Inside Your Love	1985	—	2.00	4.00
❏ 52724	Moonlight Memories/What About Tomorrow	1985	—	2.00	4.00
❏ 52871	Book of Love/What About Tomorrow	1986	—	2.00	4.00
❏ 53440	Big Girls Don't Cry (Enhanced Original Mix)/Big Girls Don't Cry (Dirty Dancing Rap)	1988	—	2.00	4.00

MOTOWN

Number	Title (A Side/B Side)	Yr	VG	VG+	NM
❏ 1255	How Come/Life and Breath	1973	2.50	5.00	10.00
❏ 1288	Hickory/Charisma	1973	2.50	5.00	10.00

MOWEST

Number	Title (A Side/B Side)	Yr	VG	VG+	NM
❏ 5026	Walk On, Don't Look Back/Sun Country	1972	2.50	5.00	10.00

OLDIES 45

Number	Title (A Side/B Side)	Yr	VG	VG+	NM
❏ 18	Sherry/I've Cried Before	1964	2.00	4.00	8.00
❏ 47	Big Girls Don't Cry/Connie-O	1964	2.00	4.00	8.00
❏ 60	Walk Like a Man/Lucky Ladybug	1964	2.00	4.00	8.00
❏ 116	Candy Girl/Marlena	1964	2.00	4.00	8.00
❏ 319	Stay/Goodnight My Love	1965	2.00	4.00	8.00

PHILIPS

Number	Title (A Side/B Side)	Yr	VG	VG+	NM
❏ 40166	Dawn (Go Away)/No Surfin' Today	1964	3.75	7.50	15.00

—Black label

Number	Title (A Side/B Side)	Yr	VG	VG+	NM
❏ 40166	Dawn (Go Away)/No Surfin' Today	1967	2.00	4.00	8.00

—Light blue label with "S" stamp

Number	Title (A Side/B Side)	Yr	VG	VG+	NM
❏ 40185	Ronnie/Born to Wander	1964	3.00	6.00	12.00
❏ 40185 [PS]	Ronnie/Born to Wander	1964	7.50	15.00	30.00
❏ 40211	Rag Doll/Silence Is Golden	1964	3.75	7.50	15.00

—Black label

Number	Title (A Side/B Side)	Yr	VG	VG+	NM
❏ 40211 [PS]	Rag Doll/Silence Is Golden	1964	7.50	15.00	30.00

—Green sleeve

Number	Title (A Side/B Side)	Yr	VG	VG+	NM
❏ 40211 [PS]	Rag Doll/Silence Is Golden	1964	7.50	15.00	30.00

—Yellow sleeve

Number	Title (A Side/B Side)	Yr	VG	VG+	NM
❏ 40211	Rag Doll/Silence Is Golden	1967	2.00	4.00	8.00

—Light blue label with "S" stamp

Number	Title (A Side/B Side)	Yr	VG	VG+	NM
❏ 40225	Save It for Me/Funny Face	1964	2.50	5.00	10.00
❏ 40238	Big Man in Town/Little Angel	1964	2.50	5.00	10.00
❏ 40238 [PS]	Big Man in Town/Little Angel	1964	6.25	12.50	25.00
❏ 40260	Bye, Bye Baby (Baby Goodbye)/Searching Wind	1965	2.50	5.00	10.00
❏ 40260 [PS]	Bye, Bye Baby (Baby Goodbye)/Searching Wind	1965	6.25	12.50	25.00
❏ 40278	Toy Soldier/Betrayed	1965	2.50	5.00	10.00
❏ 40278 [PS]	Toy Soldier/Betrayed	1965	6.25	12.50	25.00
❏ 40305	Girl Come Running/Cry Myself to Sleep	1965	2.50	5.00	10.00
❏ 40305 [PS]	Girl Come Running/Cry Myself to Sleep	1965	6.25	12.50	25.00
❏ 40317	Let's Hang On!/On Broadway Tonight	1965	2.50	5.00	10.00

—Black label

Number	Title (A Side/B Side)	Yr	VG	VG+	NM
❏ 40317	Let's Hang On!/On Broadway Tonight	1967	2.00	4.00	8.00

—Light blue label with "S" stamp

Number	Title (A Side/B Side)	Yr	VG	VG+	NM
❏ 40324	Don't Think Twice/Sassy	1965	2.50	5.00	10.00
❏ 40324 [PS]	Don't Think Twice/Sassy	1965	6.25	12.50	25.00

—Philips 40324 by "The Wonder Who?"

Number	Title (A Side/B Side)	Yr	VG	VG+	NM
❏ 40350	Working My Way Back to You/Too Many Memories	1966	2.50	5.00	10.00
❏ 40370	Opus 17 (Don't You Worry 'Bout Me)/Beggar's Paradise	1966	2.50	5.00	10.00
❏ 40370 [PS]	Opus 17 (Don't You Worry 'Bout Me)/Beggar's Paradise	1966	6.25	12.50	25.00
❏ 40380	On the Good Ship Lollipop/You're Nobody Until Somebody Loves You	1966	2.50	5.00	10.00
❏ 40380 [PS]	On the Good Ship Lollipop/You're Nobody Until Somebody Loves You	1966	6.25	12.50	25.00

—Philips 40380 by "The Wonder Who?"

Number	Title (A Side/B Side)	Yr	VG	VG+	NM
❏ 40393	I've Got You Under My Skin/Huggin' My Pillow	1966	2.50	5.00	10.00
❏ 40393 [PS]	I've Got You Under My Skin/Huggin' My Pillow	1966	6.25	12.50	25.00
❏ 40412	Tell It to the Rain/Show Girl	1966	2.50	5.00	10.00
❏ 40412 [PS]	Tell It to the Rain/Show Girl	1966	6.25	12.50	25.00
❏ 40433	Beggin'/Dody	1967	2.00	4.00	8.00

—Light blue label

Number	Title (A Side/B Side)	Yr	VG	VG+	NM
❏ 40433	Beggin'/Dody	1967	2.50	5.00	10.00

—Black label

Number	Title (A Side/B Side)	Yr	VG	VG+	NM
❏ 40433 [PS]	Beggin'/Dody	1967	6.25	12.50	25.00
❏ 40460	C'mon Marianne/Let's Ride Again	1967	2.50	5.00	10.00

—Black label

Number	Title (A Side/B Side)	Yr	VG	VG+	NM
❏ 40460	C'mon Marianne/Let's Ride Again	1967	3.00	6.00	12.00

—Blue label; contains a noticeably different, slowed-down mix of A-side

Number	Title (A Side/B Side)	Yr	VG	VG+	NM
❏ 40460 [PS]	C'mon Marianne/Let's Ride Again	1967	6.25	12.50	25.00
❏ 40471	Lonesome Road/Around and Around	1967	2.50	5.00	10.00
❏ 40471 [PS]	Lonesome Road/Around and Around	1967	6.25	12.50	25.00

—Philips 40471 by "The Wonder Who?"; B-side listed as The Four Seasons

Number	Title (A Side/B Side)	Yr	VG	VG+	NM
❏ 40490	Watch the Flowers Grow/Raven	1967	2.50	5.00	10.00
❏ 40490 [PS]	Watch the Flowers Grow/Raven	1967	6.25	12.50	25.00
❏ 40500	Donneybrook/Around and Around	1968	5.00	10.00	20.00

—Only released in Canada

Number	Title (A Side/B Side)	Yr	VG	VG+	NM
❏ 40523	Will You Love Me Tomorrow/Around and Around	1968	2.50	5.00	10.00

—Blue label

Number	Title (A Side/B Side)	Yr	VG	VG+	NM
❏ 40523	Will You Love Me Tomorrow/Around and Around	1968	3.00	6.00	12.00

—Black label

Number	Title (A Side/B Side)	Yr	VG	VG+	NM
❏ 40542	Saturday's Father/Good-Bye Girl	1968	—	3.00	6.00
❏ 40542 [PS]	Saturday's Father/Good-Bye Girl	1968	2.50	5.00	10.00

—Standard sleeve

Number	Title (A Side/B Side)	Yr	VG	VG+	NM
❏ 40542 [PS]	Saturday's Father/Good-Bye Girl	1968	3.75	7.50	15.00

—Fold-open sleeve

Number	Title (A Side/B Side)	Yr	VG	VG+	NM
❏ 40577	Electric Stories/Pity	1968	—	3.00	6.00
❏ 40597	Something's On Her Mind/Idaho	1969	—	3.00	6.00
❏ 40597 [PS]	Something's On Her Mind/Idaho	1969	2.50	5.00	10.00
❏ 40662	Patch of Blue/She Gives Me Light	1970	2.00	4.00	8.00

—As "Frankie Valli & THE 4 SEASONS"

Number	Title (A Side/B Side)	Yr	VG	VG+	NM
❏ 40662 [PS]	Patch of Blue/She Gives Me Light	1970	2.50	5.00	10.00
❏ 40688	Lay Me Down (Wake Me Up)/ Heartaches and Rainbows	1970	6.25	12.50	25.00
❏ 40688 [DJ]	Lay Me Down (Wake Me Up) (mono/stereo)	1970	3.75	7.50	15.00
❏ 40694	Where Are My Dreams?/ Any Day Now-Oh Happy Day	1971	6.25	12.50	25.00
❏ 40694 [DJ]	Where Are My Dreams? (mono/stereo)	1971	3.75	7.50	15.00

SEASONS 4-EVER

Number	Title (A Side/B Side)	Yr	VG	VG+	NM
❏ 777	Trance/I Am All Alone	1971	2.00	4.00	8.00

—As "Billy Dixon and the Topics"; green vinyl

Number	Title (A Side/B Side)	Yr	VG	VG+	NM
❏ 777	Trance/I Am All Alone	1971	3.75	7.50	15.00

—As "Billy Dixon and the Topics"; blue vinyl

TOPIX

Number	Title (A Side/B Side)	Yr	VG	VG+	NM
❏ 6000	Too Young to Start/Red Lips	1960	25.00	50.00	100.00

—As "The Village Voices"; yellow, black and white label

Number	Title (A Side/B Side)	Yr	VG	VG+	NM
❏ 6000	Too Young to Start/Red Lips	1960	37.50	75.00	150.00

—As "The Village Voices"; yellow and black label

Number	Title (A Side/B Side)	Yr	VG	VG+	NM
❏ 6002	I Am All Alone/Trance	1961	37.50	75.00	150.00

—As "Billy Dixon and the Topics"

Number	Title (A Side/B Side)	Yr	VG	VG+	NM
❏ 6008	Lost Lullaby/Trance	1961	50.00	100.00	200.00

—As "Billy Dixon and the Topics"

VEE JAY

Number	Title (A Side/B Side)	Yr	VG	VG+	NM
❏ 456	Sherry/I've Cried Before	1962	6.25	12.50	25.00

—A later pressing has an all-black label

Number	Title (A Side/B Side)	Yr	VG	VG+	NM
❏ 456	Sherry/I've Cried Before	1962	6.25	12.50	25.00

—First pressings have black rainbow labels with oval logo

Number	Title (A Side/B Side)	Yr	VG	VG+	NM
❏ 465	Big Girls Don't Cry/Connie-O	1962	5.00	10.00	20.00

—First pressings have black rainbow labels with oval logo

Number	Title (A Side/B Side)	Yr	VG	VG+	NM
❏ 465	Big Girls Don't Cry/Connie-O	1962	6.25	12.50	25.00

—A later pressing has an all-black label

Number	Title (A Side/B Side)	Yr	VG	VG+	NM
❏ 478	Santa Claus Is Coming to Town/ Christmas Tears	1962	6.25	12.50	25.00
❏ 485	Walk Like a Man/Lucky Ladybug	1963	3.75	7.50	15.00
❏ 512	Ain't That a Shame!/Soon (I'll Be Home Again)	1963	5.00	10.00	20.00
❏ 539	Candy Girl/Marlena	1963	3.75	7.50	15.00
❏ 539 [PS]	Candy Girl/Marlena	1963	—	—	—

—Rumored to exist, but without conclusive evidence, we will delete this from future editions

Number	Title (A Side/B Side)	Yr	VG	VG+	NM
❏ 562	New Mexican Rose/That's the Only Way	1963	3.75	7.50	15.00
❏ 562	New Mexican Rose/That's the Way It Goes	1963	15.00	30.00	60.00

—Wrong title on B-side; stock copy

Number	Title (A Side/B Side)	Yr	VG	VG+	NM
❏ 562 [DJ]	New Mexican Rose/That's the Way It Goes	1963	7.50	15.00	30.00

—Wrong title on B-side; white label promo

Number	Title (A Side/B Side)	Yr	VG	VG+	NM
❏ 576	Peanuts/Stay	1963	25.00	50.00	100.00
❏ 576 [DJ]	Peanuts/Stay	1963	15.00	30.00	60.00
❏ 582	Stay/Goodnight My Love	1964	3.75	7.50	15.00
❏ 597	Alone/Long, Lonely Nights	1964	3.75	7.50	15.00

—Black rainbow label

Number	Title (A Side/B Side)	Yr	VG	VG+	NM
❏ 597	Alone/Long, Lonely Nights	1964	6.25	12.50	25.00

—Plain black label

Number	Title (A Side/B Side)	Yr	VG	VG+	NM
❏ 597	Alone/Long, Lonely Nights	1964	7.50	15.00	30.00

—Yellow label

Number	Title (A Side/B Side)	Yr	VG	VG+	NM
❏ 597 [PS]	Alone/Long, Lonely Nights	1964	12.50	25.00	50.00
❏ 608	Sincerely/One Song	1964	5.00	10.00	20.00
❏ 618	Happy, Happy Birthday Baby/You're the Apple of My Eye	1964	5.00	10.00	20.00
❏ 626	I Saw Mommy Kissing Santa Claus/ Christmas Tears	1964	5.00	10.00	20.00
❏ 626 [PS]	I Saw Mommy Kissing Santa Claus/ Christmas Tears	1964	12.50	25.00	50.00
❏ 639	Never on Sunday/Connie-O	1965	5.00	10.00	20.00
❏ 664	Since I Don't Have You/Tonite, Tonite	1965	7.50	15.00	30.00
❏ 713	Little Boy (In Grown Up Clothes)/Silver Wings	1965	5.00	10.00	20.00

—Maroon label

Number	Title (A Side/B Side)	Yr	VG	VG+	NM
❏ 713	Little Boy (In Grown Up Clothes)/Silver Wings	1965	7.50	15.00	30.00

—Black label

Number	Title (A Side/B Side)	Yr	VG	VG+	NM
❏ 717	Peanuts/My Sugar	1966	7.50	15.00	30.00

—As "The Wonder Who"

Number	Title (A Side/B Side)	Yr	VG	VG+	NM
❏ 719	My Mother's Eyes/Stay	1966	3.75	7.50	15.00
❏ 901 [DJ]	Peanuts	1963	25.00	50.00	100.00

—One-sided promo from EP 901

WABC RADIO

Number	Title (A Side/B Side)	Yr	VG	VG+	NM
❏ 77	Cousin Brucie Go Go	1964	37.50	75.00	150.00

—One-sided yellow vinyl; theme song for Cousin Brucie's radio show

WARNER BROS.

Number	Title (A Side/B Side)	Yr	VG	VG+	NM
❏ 8122	Who Loves You/Who Loves You (Disco Version)	1975	—	2.50	5.00
❏ 8168	December, 1963 (Oh, What a Night)/Slip Away	1975	—	2.50	5.00
❏ 8203	Silver Star/Mystic Mr. Sam	1976	—	2.50	5.00
❏ 8407	Down the Hall/I Believe in You	1977	2.00	4.00	8.00
❏ 49585	Heaven Must Have Sent You (Here in the Night)/ Silver Star	1981	2.00	4.00	8.00
❏ 49597	Spend the Night in Love/Slip Away	1980	2.00	4.00	8.00

F

Number	Title (A Side/B Side)	Yr	VG	VG+	NM
WIBBAGE					
❑ WIBG-	Joey Reynolds Theme/Rats in My Room	1965	25.00	50.00	100.00
—Custom pressing for Philadelphia radio station; B-side by Joey and Danny					
WXYZ DETROIT					
❑ 121003	Joey Reynolds Theme (same on both sides)	1965	25.00	50.00	100.00
—Custom pressing for Detroit radio station					
7-Inch Extended Plays					
PHILIPS					
❑ PHS 810-C	Dawn/Rag Doll/Bye Bye Baby//Let's Hang On!/ Big Man in Town/Save It for Me	1966	3.75	7.50	15.00
—Jukebox issue; small hole, plays at 33 1/3 rpm					
❑ PHS 810-C [PS]	The 4 Seasons' Gold Vault of Hits	1966	3.75	7.50	15.00
VEE JAY					
❑ EP 1-901	Never on Sunday/Peanuts//I Can't Give You Anything But Love/La Dee Dah	1962	6.25	12.50	25.00
❑ EP 1-901 [PS]	The Four Seasons Sing	1962	6.25	12.50	25.00
❑ EP 1-902	Why Do Fools Fall in Love/Silhouettes//Since I Don't Have You/Alone	1963	6.25	12.50	25.00
❑ EP 1-902 [PS]	The Four Seasons Sing	1963	6.25	12.50	25.00
Albums					
MCA/CURB					
❑ 5632	Starfighter	1985	2.50	5.00	10.00
MOTOWN					
❑ 788	Inside Out	1973	—	—	—
—Canceled					
MOWEST					
❑ MW 108L	Chameleon	1972	3.00	6.00	12.00
PHILIPS					
❑ PHS-2-6501 [(2)]	Edizione d'Oro	1968	6.25	12.50	25.00
—Number "4" on cover is red on gold foil					
❑ PHS-2-6501 [(2)]	Edizione d'Oro	1968	7.50	15.00	30.00
—Number "4" on cover is white on gold foil					
❑ PHS-2-6501 [(2)]	Edizione d'Oro	1969	6.25	12.50	25.00
—Number "4" on cover is white on gold board					
❑ PHM 200124 [M]	Dawn (Go Away) and 11 Other Great Songs	1964	5.00	10.00	20.00
❑ PHM 200129 [M]	Born to Wander	1964	5.00	10.00	20.00
❑ PHM 200146 [M]	Rag Doll	1964	5.00	10.00	20.00
—With yellow seal noting presence of "Save It For Me"					
❑ PHM 200146 [M]	Rag Doll	1964	5.00	10.00	20.00
—Without yellow seal noting presence of "Save It For Me"					
❑ PHM 200150 [M]	All the Song Hits of the Four Seasons	1964	5.00	10.00	20.00
❑ PHM 200164 [M]	The 4 Seasons Entertain You	1964	3.75	7.50	15.00
—With blue seal noting presence of "Bye Bye Baby" and "Toy Soldier"					
❑ PHM 200164 [M]	The 4 Seasons Entertain You	1965	5.00	10.00	20.00
—With orange seal noting presence of "Bye Bye Baby" and "Toy Soldier"					
❑ PHM 200164 [M]	The 4 Seasons Entertain You	1965	5.00	10.00	20.00
—With orange seal noting presence of "Bye Bye Baby"					
❑ PHM 200193 [M]	Big Hits by Burt Bacharach...Hal David...Bob Dylan	1965	5.00	10.00	20.00
—"Open book" cover					
❑ PHM 200193 [M]	Big Hits by Burt Bacharach...Hal David...Bob Dylan	1966	7.50	15.00	30.00
—Group photos on cover					
❑ PHM 200196 [M]	The 4 Seasons' Gold Vault of Hits	196?	3.00	6.00	12.00
—Title in all-black print					
❑ PHM 200196 [M]	The 4 Seasons' Gold Vault of Hits	1965	3.75	7.50	15.00
—Title in red print with black border					
❑ PHM 200196 [M]	The 4 Seasons' Gold Vault of Hits	1965	5.00	10.00	20.00
—Title in red print with no border					
❑ PHM 200201 [M]	Working My Way Back to You	1966	5.00	10.00	20.00
❑ PHM 200221 [M]	2nd Vault of Golden Hits	1966	3.75	7.50	15.00
❑ PHM 200222 [M]	Lookin' Back	1966	5.00	10.00	20.00
❑ PHM 200223 [M]	The Four Seasons' Christmas Album	1966	6.25	12.50	25.00
—Reissue of Vee Jay album (same contents and order) with new cover					
❑ PHM 200243 [M]	New Gold Hits	1967	5.00	10.00	20.00
❑ PHS 600124 [S]	Dawn (Go Away) and 11 Other Great Songs	1964	6.25	12.50	25.00
❑ PHS 600129 [S]	Born to Wander	1964	6.25	12.50	25.00
❑ PHS 600146 [S]	Rag Doll	1964	6.25	12.50	25.00
—With yellow seal noting presence of "Save It For Me"					
❑ PHS 600146 [S]	Rag Doll	1964	6.25	12.50	25.00
—Without yellow seal noting presence of "Save It For Me"					
❑ PHS 600150 [S]	All the Song Hits of the Four Seasons	1964	6.25	12.50	25.00
❑ PHS 600164 [S]	The 4 Seasons Entertain You	1965	5.00	10.00	20.00
—With blue seal noting presence of "Bye Bye Baby" and "Toy Soldier"					
❑ PHS 600164 [S]	The 4 Seasons Entertain You	1965	6.25	12.50	25.00
—With orange seal noting presence of "Bye Bye Baby" and "Toy Soldier"					
❑ PHS 600164 [S]	The 4 Seasons Entertain You	1965	6.25	12.50	25.00
—With orange seal noting presence of "Bye Bye Baby"					
❑ PHS 600193 [S]	Big Hits by Burt Bacharach...Hal David...Bob Dylan	1965	6.25	12.50	25.00
—"Open book" cover					
❑ PHS 600193 [S]	Big Hits by Burt Bacharach...Hal David...Bob Dylan	1966	10.00	20.00	40.00
—Group photos on cover					
❑ PHS 600196 [S]	The 4 Seasons' Gold Vault of Hits	196?	3.75	7.50	15.00
—Title in all-black print					
❑ PHS 600196 [S]	The 4 Seasons' Gold Vault of Hits	1965	5.00	10.00	20.00
—Title in red print with black border					
❑ PHS 600196 [S]	The 4 Seasons' Gold Vault of Hits	1965	6.25	12.50	25.00
—Title in red print with no border					
❑ PHS 600201 [S]	Working My Way Back to You	1966	6.25	12.50	25.00
❑ PHS 600221 [S]	2nd Vault of Golden Hits	1966	5.00	10.00	20.00
❑ PHS 600222 [S]	Lookin' Back	1966	6.25	12.50	25.00
❑ PHS 600223 [S]	The Four Seasons' Christmas Album	1966	7.50	15.00	30.00
❑ PHS 600243 [S]	New Gold Hits	1967	6.25	12.50	25.00
❑ PHS 600290	The Genuine Imitation Life Gazette	1969	3.75	7.50	15.00
—White newspaper					
❑ PHS 600290	The Genuine Imitation Life Gazette	1969	6.25	12.50	25.00
—Yellow newspaper					
❑ PHS 600341	Half & Half	1970	5.00	10.00	20.00
PICKWICK					
❑ SPC-3223	Brotherhood of Man	1970	3.00	6.00	12.00
—Mass-market version of Sears 609					
PRIVATE STOCK					
❑ PS-7000 [(2)]	The Four Seasons Story	1975	3.75	7.50	15.00

Number	Title (A Side/B Side)	Yr	VG	VG+	NM
RHINO					
❑ RNLP 70234	The Four Seasons' Christmas Album	1987	3.00	6.00	12.00
—Reissue of Philips album (same contents and order)					
❑ R1-70247	Working My Way Back to You	1988	2.50	5.00	10.00
—Reissue of Philips 600-201					
❑ R1-70249	The Genuine Imitation Life Gazette	1988	2.50	5.00	10.00
—Reissue of Philips 600-290					
❑ R1-71248	Big Hits by Burt Bacharach...Hal David...Bob Dylan	1988	2.50	5.00	10.00
—Reissue of Philips 600-193					
❑ R1-71490 [(2)]	Anthology	1988	3.00	6.00	12.00
❑ RNRP-72998 [(4)]	25th Anniversary Collection	1987	6.25	12.50	25.00
SEARS					
❑ SPS-609	Brotherhood of Man	1970	6.25	12.50	25.00
VEE JAY					
❑ LP-1053 [M]	Sherry & 11 Others	1962	10.00	20.00	40.00
❑ SR-1053 [S]	Sherry & 11 Others	1962	15.00	30.00	60.00
❑ LP 1055 [M]	The Four Seasons Greetings	1962	7.50	15.00	30.00
❑ SR 1055 [S]	The Four Seasons Greetings	1962	10.00	20.00	40.00
❑ LP-1056 [M]	Big Girls Don't Cry and Twelve Others	1963	7.50	15.00	30.00
❑ SR-1056 [S]	Big Girls Don't Cry and Twelve Others	1963	10.00	20.00	40.00
❑ LP-1059 [M]	Ain't That a Shame and 11 Others	1963	7.50	15.00	30.00
❑ SR-1059 [S]	Ain't That a Shame and 11 Others	1963	10.00	20.00	40.00
❑ LP 1065 [M]	Golden Hits of the Four Seasons	1963	7.50	15.00	30.00
❑ SR-1065 [S]	Golden Hits of the Four Seasons	1963	10.00	20.00	40.00
❑ LP-1082 [M]	Stay & Other Great Hits	1964	6.25	12.50	25.00
—Retitled version of Folk-Nanny					
❑ LP-1082 [M]	Folk-Nanny	1964	7.50	15.00	30.00
❑ SR-1082 [S]	Stay & Other Great Hits	1964	7.50	15.00	30.00
—Retitled version of Folk-Nanny					
❑ SR-1082 [S]	Folk-Nanny	1964	10.00	20.00	40.00
❑ LP-1088 [M]	More Golden Hits by the Four Seasons	1964	5.00	10.00	20.00
—With "Apple of My Eye" on record					
❑ LP-1088 [M]	More Golden Hits by the Four Seasons	1964	7.50	15.00	30.00
—With "Long Lonely Nights" on record					
❑ SR-1088 [S]	More Golden Hits by the Four Seasons	1964	6.25	12.50	25.00
—With "Apple of My Eye" on record					
❑ SR-1088 [S]	More Golden Hits by the Four Seasons	1964	10.00	20.00	40.00
—With "Long Lonely Nights" on record					
❑ LP-1121 [M]	We Love Girls	1965	7.50	15.00	30.00
❑ LPS-1121 [S]	We Love Girls	1965	10.00	20.00	40.00
❑ LP-1154 [M]	Recorded Live on Stage	1965	7.50	15.00	30.00
❑ LPS-1154 [S]	Recorded Live on Stage	1965	10.00	20.00	40.00
WARNER BROS.					
❑ BS 2900	Who Loves You	1975	3.00	6.00	12.00
❑ BS 3016	Helicon	1977	3.00	6.00	12.00
❑ 2WB 3497 [(2)]	Reunited Live	1980	3.75	7.50	15.00

FOUR SEASONS, THE (2) Not the same as the better-known group.
45s

Number	Title (A Side/B Side)	Yr	VG	VG+	NM
ALANNA					
❑ 555	Don't Sweat It Baby/That's the Way the Ball Bounces	1959	10.00	20.00	40.00
❑ 555	I'm Still in Love with You, Baby/That's the Way the Ball Bounces	1959	15.00	30.00	60.00
❑ 558	Love Knows No Season/Hot Water Bottle	1959	7.50	15.00	30.00
ROBBEE					
❑ 106	Mirage/Nancy's Trampoline	1960	37.50	75.00	150.00

FOUR SONICS, THE
45s

Number	Title (A Side/B Side)	Yr	VG	VG+	NM
JMC					
❑ 141	If It Wasn't for My Baby/There's No Love	197?	3.75	7.50	15.00
SEPIA					
❑ 1	Tell Me You're Mine/Lost Without You	196?	10.00	20.00	40.00
—As "The Four Sonics Plus One"					
SPORT					
❑ 110	You Don't Have to Say You Love Me/It Takes Two	1968	3.75	7.50	15.00
❑ 111	Easier Said Than Done/The Greatest Love	1968	5.00	10.00	20.00
TRIPLE B					
❑ 0002	Where Are You/Blue Velvet	196?	15.00	30.00	60.00

FOUR SPARKS, THE
45s

Number	Title (A Side/B Side)	Yr	VG	VG+	NM
ABC-PARAMOUNT					
❑ 9906	My Sweet Juanita/Out of This World	1958	5.00	10.00	20.00

FOUR SPEEDS, THE
45s

Number	Title (A Side/B Side)	Yr	VG	VG+	NM
CHALLENGE					
❑ 9187	R.P.M./My Sting Ray	1963	10.00	20.00	40.00
❑ 9202	Four on the Floor/Cheater Slicks	1963	10.00	20.00	40.00
FEDERAL					
❑ 6070	I Need You Baby/The Girls Back Home	1954	20.00	40.00	80.00

FOUR SPORTSMEN, THE
45s

Number	Title (A Side/B Side)	Yr	VG	VG+	NM
SUNNYBROOK					
❑ 1	Surrender/Franklin Delano Brown	1960	15.00	30.00	60.00
❑ 2	Lucille/Mother-in-Law	1961	7.50	15.00	30.00
❑ 4	Pitter-Patter/Git Up Paint	1961	7.50	15.00	30.00
❑ 5	Sixty Minute Man/Jellyroll Brown	1961	7.50	15.00	30.00
❑ 6	If Your Heart Can Take It/Records, Records, Records	1961	10.00	20.00	40.00

FOUR STUDENTS, THE
45s

Number	Title (A Side/B Side)	Yr	VG	VG+	NM
GROOVE					
❑ 0110	So Near and Yet So Far/Hot Rotten Soda Pop	1955	12.50	25.00	50.00

FOUR TEENS, THE
45s

Number	Title (A Side/B Side)	Yr	VG	VG+	NM
CHALLENGE					
❑ 59021	Go Little Go Cat/Spark Plug	1958	15.00	30.00	60.00

Number	Title (A Side/B Side)	Yr	VG	VG+	NM

FOUR TEMPTATIONS, THE
45s
ABC-PARAMOUNT

Number	Title (A Side/B Side)	Yr	VG	VG+	NM
❏ 9920	Cathy/Rock and Roll Baby	1958	7.50	15.00	30.00

FOUR TOPS, THE   Also see DELORES CARROLL AND THE FOUR TOPS.
12-Inch Singles
ABC

Number	Title (A Side/B Side)	Yr	VG	VG+	NM
❏ DM-21 [DJ]	H.E.L.P. (stereo/mono)	1978	2.50	5.00	10.00
ARISTA					
❏ AD1-9705	Indestructible (4 versions)/Are You With Me	1988	2.00	4.00	8.00
CASABLANCA					
❏ NBD 20239	Let Me Set You Free (4:24) (same on both sides)	1981	2.50	5.00	10.00
RELIANT					
❏ REG 3691	I'm Here Again (2 versions)	1983	2.00	4.00	8.00

45s
ABC

Number	Title (A Side/B Side)	Yr	VG	VG+	NM
❏ 12096	Seven Lonely Nights/ I Can't Hold Out Much Longer	1975	—	2.00	4.00
❏ 12123	We All Gotta Stick Together/(It Would Almost) Drive Me Out of My Mind	1975	—	2.00	4.00
❏ 12155	I'm Glad You Walked Into My Life/ Mama, You're All Right with Me	1975	—	2.00	4.00
❏ 12214	Catfish/Look at My Baby	1976	—	2.00	4.00
❏ 12223	Look at My Baby/Catfish	1976	—	2.00	4.00
❏ 12236	Feel Free/I Know You Like It	1976	—	2.00	4.00
❏ 12267	Strung Out for Your Love/ You Can't Hold Back on Love	1977	—	2.00	4.00
❏ 12315	Runnin' From Your Love/The Show Must Go On	1977	—	2.00	4.00
❏ 12427	Inside a Brokenhearted Man/H.E.L.P.	1977	—	2.00	4.00
❏ 12457	Just in Time/This House	1978	—	2.00	4.00
ABC DUNHILL					
❏ 4330	Keeper of the Castle/Jubilee with Soul	1972	—	2.50	5.00
❏ 4334	Guardian De Tu Castle/Jubilee with Soul	1972	—	2.50	5.00
❏ 4339	Ain't No Woman (Like the One I've Got)/The Good Lord Knows	1973	—	2.50	5.00
❏ 4354	Are You Man Enough/Peace of Mind	1973	—	2.50	5.00
❏ 4366	Sweet Understanding Love/Main Street People	1973	—	2.50	5.00
❏ 4377	I Just Can't Get You Out of My Mind/Am I My Brother's Keeper?	1973	—	2.50	5.00
❏ 4386	One Chain Don't Make No Prison/❏ Light of Your Love	1974	—	2.50	5.00
❏ 15005	Midnight Flower/All My Love	1974	—	2.50	5.00
ARISTA					
❏ 9706	Indestructible/Are You With Me	1988	—	—	3.00
❏ 9706 [PS]	Indestructible/Are You With Me	1988	—	—	3.00
❏ 9766	If Ever a Love There Was/Indestructible	1988	—	—	3.00
—A-side with Aretha Franklin					
❏ 9766 [PS]	If Ever a Love There Was/Indestructible	1988	—	—	3.00
❏ 9801	Change of Heart/Loco in Acapulco	1989	—	—	3.00
CASABLANCA					
❏ 2338	When She Was My Girl/Something to Remember	1981	—	2.00	4.00
❏ 2344	Let Me Set You Free/From a Distance	1981	—	2.00	4.00
❏ 2345	Tonight I'm Gonna Love You All Over/I'll Never Leave Again	1981	—	2.00	4.00
❏ 2353	Sad Hearts/I Believe in You and Me	1982	—	2.00	4.00
CHESS					
❏ 1623	Could It Be You?/Kiss Me, Baby	1956	50.00	100.00	200.00
COLUMBIA					
❏ 41755	Ain't That Love/Lonely Summer	1960	15.00	30.00	60.00
❏ 43356	Ain't That Love/Lonely Summer	1965	6.25	12.50	25.00
GRADY					
❏ 012	If Only I Had Known/(B-side unknown)	1956	150.00	300.00	600.00
—As "The Four Aims"					
MOTOWN					
❏ 1062	Baby I Need Your Loving/Call On Me	1964	3.75	7.50	15.00
❏ 1069	Without the One You Love (Life's Not Worth While)/Love Has Gone	1964	3.00	6.00	12.00
❏ 1073	Ask the Lonely/Where Did You Go	1965	3.75	7.50	15.00
❏ 1073 [PS]	Ask the Lonely/Where Did You Go	1965	20.00	40.00	80.00
❏ 1076	I Can't Help Myself/Sad Souvenirs	1965	3.75	7.50	15.00
❏ 1081	It's the Same Old Song/Your Love Is Amazing	1965	3.75	7.50	15.00
❏ 1084	Something About You/Darling, I Hum Our Song	1965	3.75	7.50	15.00
❏ 1090	Shake Me, Wake Me (When It's Over)/ Just As Long As You Need Me	1966	3.75	7.50	15.00
❏ 1096	Loving You Is Sweeter Than Ever/ I Like Everything About You	1966	3.75	7.50	15.00
❏ 1098	Reach Out I'll Be There/Until You Love Someone	1966	3.75	7.50	15.00
❏ 1098 [PS]	Reach Out I'll Be There/Until You Love Someone	1966	20.00	40.00	80.00
❏ 1102	Standing in the Shadows of Love/Since You've Been Gone	1966	3.75	7.50	15.00
❏ 1104	Bernadette/I Got a Feeling	1967	3.00	6.00	12.00
❏ 1110	7-Rooms of Gloom/I'll Turn to Stone	1967	3.00	6.00	12.00
❏ 1113	You Keep Running Away/ If You Don't Want My Love	1967	3.00	6.00	12.00
❏ 1119	Walk Away Renee/Your Love Is Wonderful	1968	3.00	6.00	12.00
❏ 1124	If I Were a Carpenter/Wonderful Baby	1968	3.00	6.00	12.00
❏ 1127	Yesterday's Dreams/For Once in My Life	1968	2.00	4.00	8.00
❏ 1132	I'm in a Different World/Remember When	1968	2.00	4.00	8.00
❏ 1147	What Is a Man/Don't Bring Back Memories	1969	2.00	4.00	8.00
❏ 1159	Don't Let Him Take Your Love from Me/The Key	1969	2.00	4.00	8.00
❏ 1164	It's All in the Game/Love (Is the Answer)	1970	2.00	4.00	8.00
❏ 1164 [PS]	It's All in the Game/Love (Is the Answer)	1970	5.00	10.00	20.00
❏ 1170	Still Water (Love)/Still Water (Peace)	1970	—	3.00	6.00
❏ 1175	Just Seven Numbers (Can Straighten Out My Life)/I Wish I Were Your Mirror	1971	—	3.00	6.00
❏ 1175 [PS]	Just Seven Numbers (Can Straighten Out My Life)/I Wish I Were Your Mirror	1971	5.00	10.00	20.00
❏ 1185	In These Changing Times/Right Before My Eyes	1971	—	3.00	6.00
❏ 1189	MacArthur Park (Part 2)/MacArthur Park (Part 1)	1971	—	3.00	6.00
❏ 1196	A Simple Game/L.A. My Town	1972	—	3.00	6.00
❏ 1198	I Can't Quit Your Love/Happy (Is a Bumpy Road)	1972	—	3.00	6.00
❏ 1210	(It's the Way) Nature Planned It/I'll Never Change	1972	—	3.00	6.00

Number	Title (A Side/B Side)	Yr	VG	VG+	NM
❏ 1254	Hey Man-We Gotta Get You a Woman/ How Can I Forget You	1973	—	—	—
—Unreleased					
❏ 1706	I Just Can't Walk Away/Hang	1983	—	—	3.00
❏ 1718	Make Yourself Right at Home/Sing a Song of Yesterday	1984	—	—	3.00
❏ 1790	Sexy Ways/Body and Soul	1985	—	—	3.00
❏ 1811	Don't Tell Me That It's Over/I'm Ready for Love	1985	—	—	3.00
❏ 1854	Hot Nights/Again	1986	—	—	3.00
RELIANT					
❏ 1691	I'm Here Again/(Instrumental)	1983	—	2.00	4.00
RIVERSIDE					
❏ 4534	Pennies from Heaven/Where Are You?	1962	18.75	37.50	75.00
RSO					
❏ 1069	Back to School Again/Rock-a-Hula Luau	1982	—	—	3.00
❏ 1069 [PS]	Back to School Again/Rock-a-Hula Luau	1982	—	—	3.00
—B-side: by The Cast (from the movie Grease 2)					
TOPPS/MOTOWN					
❏ 5	I Can't Help Myself	1967	18.75	37.50	75.00
❏ 9	Baby I Need Your Loving	1967	18.75	37.50	75.00
—These are cardboard discs					

Albums
ABC

Number	Title (A Side/B Side)	Yr	VG	VG+	NM
❏ D-862	Night Lights Harmony	1975	3.00	6.00	12.00
❏ D-968	Catfish	1976	3.00	6.00	12.00
❏ D-1014	The Show Must Go On	1977	3.00	6.00	12.00
❏ AA-1092	At the Top	1978	3.00	6.00	12.00
ABC DUNHILL					
❏ DSX-50129	Keeper of the Castle	1972	3.00	6.00	12.00
❏ DSX-50144	Main Street People	1973	3.00	6.00	12.00
❏ DSX-50166	Meeting of the Minds	1974	3.00	6.00	12.00
❏ DSX-50188	Live & In Concert	1974	3.00	6.00	12.00
ARISTA					
❏ AL-8492	Indestructible	1988	2.00	4.00	8.00
CASABLANCA					
❏ NBLP 7258	Tonight!	1981	2.50	5.00	10.00
❏ NBLP 7266	One More Mountain	1982	2.50	5.00	10.00
COMMAND					
❏ CQD-40011 [Q]	Keeper of the Castle	1974	5.00	10.00	20.00
❏ CQD-40012 [Q]	Main Street People	1974	5.00	10.00	20.00
MCA					
❏ 27019	Greatest Hits	198?	2.50	5.00	10.00
MOTOWN					
❏ M5-114V1	Superstar Series, Vol. 14	1981	2.50	5.00	10.00
❏ M5-122V1	Four Tops	1981	2.00	4.00	8.00
—Reissue of 622					
❏ M5-149V1	Four Tops Reach Out	1981	—	4.00	8.00
—Reissue of 660					
❏ M5-209V1	The Four Tops' Greatest Hits	1981	2.00	4.00	8.00
—Reissue of 662					
❏ 622 [M]	Four Tops	1964	7.50	15.00	30.00
❏ MS-622 [S]	Four Tops	1964	10.00	20.00	40.00
❏ 634 [M]	Four Tops Second Album	1965	6.25	12.50	25.00
❏ MS-634 [S]	Four Tops Second Album	1965	7.50	15.00	30.00
❏ 647 [M]	4 Tops On Top	1966	6.25	12.50	25.00
❏ MS-647 [S]	4 Tops On Top	1966	7.50	15.00	30.00
❏ 654 [M]	Four Tops Live!	1966	6.25	12.50	25.00
❏ MS-654 [S]	Four Tops Live!	1966	7.50	15.00	30.00
❏ 657 [M]	4 Tops on Broadway	1967	6.25	12.50	25.00
❏ MS-657 [S]	4 Tops on Broadway	1967	7.50	15.00	30.00
❏ 660 [M]	Four Tops Reach Out	1967	6.25	12.50	25.00
❏ MS-660 [S]	Four Tops Reach Out	1967	7.50	15.00	30.00
❏ 662 [M]	The Four Tops Greatest Hits	1967	5.00	10.00	20.00
❏ MS-662 [S]	The Four Tops Greatest Hits	1967	7.50	15.00	30.00
❏ 669 [M]	Yesterday's Dreams	1968	7.50	15.00	30.00
❏ MS-669 [S]	Yesterday's Dreams	1968	5.00	10.00	20.00
❏ MS-675	Four Tops Now!	1969	5.00	10.00	20.00
❏ MS-695	Soul Spin	1969	5.00	10.00	20.00
❏ MS-704	Still Waters Run Deep	1970	5.00	10.00	20.00
❏ MS-721	Changing Times	1970	5.00	10.00	20.00
❏ M-740L	Four Tops Greatest Hits, Vol. 2	1971	5.00	10.00	20.00
❏ M-748L	Nature Planned It	1972	5.00	10.00	20.00
❏ M-764D [(2)]	The Best of the 4 Tops	1973	3.75	7.50	15.00
❏ M9-809A3 [(3)]	Anthology	1974	5.00	10.00	20.00
❏ 5224 ML	Still Waters Run Deep	1982	2.00	4.00	8.00
—Reissue of 704					
❏ 5258 ML	Four Tops Live!	1983	2.00	4.00	8.00
—Reissue of 654					
❏ 5314 ML	Great Songs	1983	2.50	5.00	10.00
❏ 6066 ML	Back Where I Belong	1983	2.50	5.00	10.00
❏ 6130 ML	Magic	1985	2.50	5.00	10.00
WORKSHOP JAZZ					
❏ 217 [M]	Breakin' Through	1962	—	—	—
—This album is pictured on some early Motown inner sleeves, but is not known to exist					

FOUR TUNES, THE
45s
JUBILEE

Number	Title (A Side/B Side)	Yr	VG	VG+	NM
❏ 5128	Marie/I Gambled with Love	1953	10.00	20.00	40.00
❏ 5132	I Understand Just How You Feel/Sugar Lump	1953	7.50	15.00	30.00
❏ 5135	My Wild Irish Rose/Do-Do-Do It Again	1954	7.50	15.00	30.00
❏ 5152	Lonesome/The Greatest Feeling in the World	1954	7.50	15.00	30.00
❏ 5165	Don't Cry Darling/L'Amour Toujours, L'Amour	1954	7.50	15.00	30.00
❏ 5174	I Sold My Heart to the Junkman/Good News	1954	7.50	15.00	30.00
❏ 5174	I Sold My Heart to the Junkman/Let Me Go Lover	1954	7.50	15.00	30.00
❏ 5183	I Hope/I Close My Eyes	1955	6.25	12.50	25.00
❏ 5200	Tired of Waitin'/Time Out for Texas	1955	6.25	12.50	25.00
❏ 5212	Brooklyn Bridge/Three Little Chickens	1955	6.25	12.50	25.00
❏ 5218	You Are My Love/At the Steamboat River Ball	1955	6.25	12.50	25.00
❏ 5232	Rock and Roll Call/Our Love	1956	5.00	10.00	20.00
❏ 5239	I Gotta Go/Hold Me Closer	1956	5.00	10.00	20.00
❏ 5245	Far Away Places/Dancing with Tears in My Eyes	1956	5.00	10.00	20.00
❏ 5255	The Ballad of James Dean/Japanses Farewell	1956	5.00	10.00	20.00
❏ 5276	Cool Water/A Little on the Lonely Side	1957	5.00	10.00	20.00
❏ 6000	I Understand/Marie	196?	2.50	5.00	10.00

F

Number	Title (A Side/B Side)	Yr	VG	VG+	NM

KAY-RON

Number	Title (A Side/B Side)	Yr	VG	VG+	NM
❑ 1000	I Want to Be Loved/Savannah Sings the Blues	1953	10.00	20.00	40.00
❑ 1005	I Understand/				
	Just in Case You Change Your Mind	1953	10.00	20.00	40.00

RCA VICTOR

Number	Title (A Side/B Side)	Yr	VG	VG+	NM
❑ 47-3881	Say When/Do I Worry?	1950	12.50	25.00	50.00
❑ 47-3967	How Can You Say That I Don't Care/Cool Water	1950	10.00	20.00	40.00
❑ 47-4102	Wishing You Were Here Tonight/				
	The Last Roundup	1951	10.00	20.00	40.00
❑ 47-4198	Cool Water/Carry Me Back to the Lone Prairie	1951	10.00	20.00	40.00
❑ 47-4241	The Prisoner's Song/I Married an Angel	1951	7.50	15.00	30.00
❑ 47-4305	My Buddy/Early in the Morning	1951	7.50	15.00	30.00
❑ 47-4427	Tell Me Why/I'll See You in My Dreams	1951	10.00	20.00	40.00
❑ 47-4489	Greatest Song I Ever Heard/Come What May	1952	6.25	12.50	25.00
❑ 47-4663	I Wonder/Can I Say Any More?	1952	6.25	12.50	25.00
❑ 47-4828	They Don't Understand/Why Did You Do This	1952	6.25	12.50	25.00
❑ 47-4968	I Don't Want to Set the World On Fire/Let's Give				
	Love Another Chance	1952	10.00	20.00	40.00
❑ 47-5532	Don't Get Around Much Anymore/Water Boy	1953	7.50	15.00	30.00
❑ 50-0008	You're Heartless/Careless Love	1949	50.00	100.00	200.00
—Gray label, orange vinyl					
❑ 50-0016	My Last Affair/I'm the Guy	1949	50.00	100.00	200.00
—Gray label, orange vinyl					
❑ 50-0042	I'm Just a Fool in Love/The Lonesome Road	1949	50.00	100.00	200.00
—Gray label, orange vinyl					
❑ 50-0072	There Goes My Heart/Am I Blue	1950	37.50	75.00	150.00
—Gray label, orange vinyl					
❑ 50-0085	Old Fashioned Love/Kentucky Babe	1950	37.50	75.00	150.00
—Gray label, orange vinyl					
❑ 50-0131	May That Day Never Come/Carry Me Back to				
	the Lone Prairie	1951	37.50	75.00	150.00
—Gray label, orange vinyl					

7-Inch Extended Plays

RCA VICTOR

Number	Title (A Side/B Side)	Yr	VG	VG+	NM
❑ EPA-586	(contents unknown)	1954	10.00	20.00	40.00
❑ EPA-586 [PS]	The Four Tunes	1954	10.00	20.00	40.00

FOUR UPSETTERS, THE
45s

SUN

Number	Title (A Side/B Side)	Yr	VG	VG+	NM
❑ 381	Crazy Arms/Midnight Soiree	1962	5.00	10.00	20.00
❑ 386	Surfin' Calliope/Wabash Cannonball	1963	7.50	15.00	30.00

FOUR WINDS, THE (1) Also see THE TOKENS, to which they are related.
45s

B.T. PUPPY

Number	Title (A Side/B Side)	Yr	VG	VG+	NM
❑ 555	Let It Ride/One Face in the Crowd	1970	2.50	5.00	10.00

CRYSTAL BALL

Number	Title (A Side/B Side)	Yr	VG	VG+	NM
❑ 102	Come Softly to Me/Judy	1978	—	2.50	5.00
❑ 105	Arlene/Goodbye, Maureen	1978	—	2.50	5.00
—Black vinyl					
❑ 105	Arlene/Goodbye, Maureen	1978	2.50	5.00	10.00
—Red vinyl					

SWING

Number	Title (A Side/B Side)	Yr	VG	VG+	NM
❑ 100	Remember Last Summer/Strange, Strange				
	Feeling	1964	5.00	10.00	20.00

FOUR WINDS, THE (U) None of these are group (1), but they aren't all the same group, either.
45s

CHATTAHOOCHIE

Number	Title (A Side/B Side)	Yr	VG	VG+	NM
❑ 655	Down and Out/To Love or Not to Love	1964	3.75	7.50	15.00

DECOR

Number	Title (A Side/B Side)	Yr	VG	VG+	NM
❑ 175	Short Shorts/Five Minutes More	1961	5.00	10.00	20.00

DERBY

Number	Title (A Side/B Side)	Yr	VG	VG+	NM
❑ 10022	Playgirl/Jennifer	1964	7.50	15.00	30.00

DIAL

Number	Title (A Side/B Side)	Yr	VG	VG+	NM
❑ 3006	Woe Is Me/Promised Land	1962	3.75	7.50	15.00

FELSTED

Number	Title (A Side/B Side)	Yr	VG	VG+	NM
❑ 8703	Playgirl/Jennifer	1964	5.00	10.00	20.00

HIDE-A-WAY

Number	Title (A Side/B Side)	Yr	VG	VG+	NM
❑ 101	Mission by the Sea/These Hearts Were Mine	1958	5.00	10.00	20.00

VIK

Number	Title (A Side/B Side)	Yr	VG	VG+	NM
❑ 0221	Colorado Moon/Find Someone New	1956	5.00	10.00	20.00

WARWICK

Number	Title (A Side/B Side)	Yr	VG	VG+	NM
❑ 633	Daddy's Home/Bull-Moose Stomp	1961	10.00	20.00	40.00

FOURMOST, THE
45s

ATCO

Number	Title (A Side/B Side)	Yr	VG	VG+	NM
❑ 6280	Hello Little Girl/Just in Case	1963	5.00	10.00	20.00
❑ 6285	I'm in Love/Respectable	1964	3.75	7.50	15.00
❑ 6307	If You Cry/Little Bit of Loving	1964	3.75	7.50	15.00
❑ 6317	How Can I Tell Her/You Got That Way	1964	3.75	7.50	15.00

CAPITOL

Number	Title (A Side/B Side)	Yr	VG	VG+	NM
❑ 5591	Girls, Girls, Girls/Why Do Fools Fall in Love	1966	3.00	6.00	12.00
❑ 5738	Here, There and Everywhere/You've Changed	1966	5.00	10.00	20.00

FOURTH CEKCION, THE
Albums

SOLAR

Number	Title (A Side/B Side)	Yr	VG	VG+	NM
❑ 110	The Fourth Cekcion	1970	15.00	30.00	60.00

FOURTH WAY, THE
45s

CAPITOL

Number	Title (A Side/B Side)	Yr	VG	VG+	NM
❑ 2619	Bucklehuggin'/Clouds	1969	2.00	4.00	8.00

SOUL CITY

Number	Title (A Side/B Side)	Yr	VG	VG+	NM
❑ 765	Far Side of Your Moon/Pink Cloud	1968	2.00	4.00	8.00

Albums

CAPITOL

Number	Title (A Side/B Side)	Yr	VG	VG+	NM
❑ ST-317	The Fourth Way	1969	6.25	12.50	25.00

HARVEST

Number	Title (A Side/B Side)	Yr	VG	VG+	NM
❑ SKAO-423	The Sun and Moon Have Come Together	1970	5.00	10.00	20.00
❑ ST-666	Werewolf	1971	5.00	10.00	20.00

FOWLER, RAY

Number	Title (A Side/B Side)	Yr	VG	VG+	NM

45s

HIT

Number	Title (A Side/B Side)	Yr	VG	VG+	NM
❑ 09	What'd I Say/Soul Twist	1962	2.00	4.00	8.00
—B-side by the Hit Combo					

FOWLEY, KIM
45s

CAPITOL

Number	Title (A Side/B Side)	Yr	VG	VG+	NM
❑ 3403	Forbidden Love/I'm Bad	1972	—	3.00	6.00
❑ 3534	International Heroes/E.S.P. Reader	1973	—	3.00	6.00
❑ 3662	A Born Dancer/Something New	1973	—	3.00	6.00

IMPERIAL

Number	Title (A Side/B Side)	Yr	VG	VG+	NM
❑ 66326	Born to Be Wild/Space Odyssey	1968	2.50	5.00	10.00
❑ 66349	Bubble Gum/Wildfire	1969	2.50	5.00	10.00

LIVING LEGEND

Number	Title (A Side/B Side)	Yr	VG	VG+	NM
❑ 721	Mr. Responsibility/My Foolish Heart	1965	3.75	7.50	15.00
❑ 725	Underground Lady/Pop Art '66	1966	3.75	7.50	15.00

LOMA

Number	Title (A Side/B Side)	Yr	VG	VG+	NM
❑ 2064	Lights/Something New and Different	1966	2.50	5.00	10.00

MIRA

Number	Title (A Side/B Side)	Yr	VG	VG+	NM
❑ 209	American Dream/The Statue	1965	2.50	5.00	10.00

ORIGINAL SOUND

Number	Title (A Side/B Side)	Yr	VG	VG+	NM
❑ 98	Thunder Road/Born to Make You Cry	1970	2.50	5.00	10.00

RCA VICTOR

Number	Title (A Side/B Side)	Yr	VG	VG+	NM
❑ 74-0511	Citizen Kane/The Sky Is On Fire	1971	—	—	—
—Canceled					

REPRISE

Number	Title (A Side/B Side)	Yr	VG	VG+	NM
❑ 0569	Don't Be Cruel/Strangers from the Sky	1967	2.50	5.00	10.00

TOWER

Number	Title (A Side/B Side)	Yr	VG	VG+	NM
❑ 342	Love Is Alive and Well/Reincarnation	1967	2.50	5.00	10.00

Albums

ANTILLES

Number	Title (A Side/B Side)	Yr	VG	VG+	NM
❑ AN-7075	Snake Document Masquerade	1979	3.00	6.00	12.00

CAPITOL

Number	Title (A Side/B Side)	Yr	VG	VG+	NM
❑ ST-11075	I'm Bad	1972	5.00	10.00	20.00
❑ ST-11159	International Heroes	1973	5.00	10.00	20.00
❑ ST-11248	Automatic	1974	5.00	10.00	20.00

GNP CRESCENDO

Number	Title (A Side/B Side)	Yr	VG	VG+	NM
❑ GNPS-2132	Hollywood Confidential	197?	3.00	6.00	12.00

IMPERIAL

Number	Title (A Side/B Side)	Yr	VG	VG+	NM
❑ LP-12413	Born to Be Wild	1968	10.00	20.00	40.00
❑ LP-12423	Outrageous	1969	10.00	20.00	40.00
❑ LP-12443	Good Clean Fun	1969	10.00	20.00	40.00

PVC

Number	Title (A Side/B Side)	Yr	VG	VG+	NM
❑ 7906	Sunset Boulevard	1978	3.00	6.00	12.00

TOWER

Number	Title (A Side/B Side)	Yr	VG	VG+	NM
❑ ST 5080 [S]	Love Is Alive and Well	1967	10.00	20.00	40.00
❑ T 5080 [M]	Love Is Alive and Well	1967	7.50	15.00	30.00

FOX

45s

ARIOLA AMERICA

Number	Title (A Side/B Side)	Yr	VG	VG+	NM
❑ 7601	Only You Can/Out of My Body	1975	—	3.00	6.00
❑ 7608	Imagine Me Imagine You/If I Point at the Moon	1975	—	3.00	6.00

GTO

Number	Title (A Side/B Side)	Yr	VG	VG+	NM
❑ 1003	Only You Can/Out of My Body	1975	2.50	5.00	10.00
—Original issue					

Albums

ARIOLA AMERICA

Number	Title (A Side/B Side)	Yr	VG	VG+	NM
❑ ST-50001	Fox	1975	3.00	6.00	12.00

FOX, BARNEY
45s

HIT

Number	Title (A Side/B Side)	Yr	VG	VG+	NM
❑ 30	Teenage Idol/Sherry	1962	2.00	4.00	8.00
—B-side by the Four Chellows					

FOX, NORMAN, AND THE ROB ROYS
45s

BACK BEAT

Number	Title (A Side/B Side)	Yr	VG	VG+	NM
❑ 499	Lover Doll/Little Star	197?	—	2.00	4.00
—Bootleg					
❑ 501	Tell Me Why/Audry	1957	10.00	20.00	40.00
—Red label					
❑ 501	Tell Me Why/Audry	1957	20.00	40.00	80.00
—White label					
❑ 508	Dance Girl Dance/My Dearest One	1958	20.00	40.00	80.00

CAPITOL

Number	Title (A Side/B Side)	Yr	VG	VG+	NM
❑ F4128	Dream Girl/Pizza Pie	1959	175.00	350.00	700.00

HAMMER

Number	Title (A Side/B Side)	Yr	VG	VG+	NM
❑ 544	Dream Girl/Pizza Pie	1958	7.50	15.00	30.00

FOX, SAMMY
45s

HIT

Number	Title (A Side/B Side)	Yr	VG	VG+	NM
❑ 80	The Monkey Time/My Boyfriend's Back	1963	2.00	4.00	8.00
—B-side by Dot Hester					

FOXX, INEZ (AND CHARLIE)
45s

DYNAMO

Number	Title (A Side/B Side)	Yr	VG	VG+	NM
❑ 102	Baby Take It All/Tightrope	1967	2.00	4.00	8.00
❑ 104	I Stand Accused/Guilty	1967	2.00	4.00	8.00
❑ 109	You Are the Man/Hard to Get	1967	2.00	4.00	8.00
❑ 112	(1-2-3-4-5-6-7) Count the Days/				
	A Stranger I Don't Know	1967	2.00	4.00	8.00
❑ 117	Undecided/I Ain't Goin' for That	1968	2.00	4.00	8.00
❑ 119	Vaya Con Dios/Fellows in Vietnam	1968	2.00	4.00	8.00
❑ 126	Come On In/Baby Drop a Dime	1968	2.00	4.00	8.00
❑ 127	Baby Give It to Me/You Fixed My Heartache	1968	2.00	4.00	8.00
❑ 134	We Got a Chance to Be Free/Speed Ticket	1969	2.00	4.00	8.00
❑ 138	North Carolina (South Carolina)/I Got It	1970	2.00	4.00	8.00
❑ 144	You Shouldn't Have Set My Soul on Fire/				
	Live for Today	1970	2.00	4.00	8.00

Number	Title (A Side/B Side)	Yr	VG	VG+	NM
LANA					
❑ 148	Mockingbird/Jaybirds	196?	2.00	4.00	8.00
—Oldies reissue					
MUSICOR					
❑ 1201	No Stranger to Love/Come By Here	1966	2.50	5.00	10.00
SYMBOL					
❑ 20-001	Hurt by Love/Confusion	1964	3.00	6.00	12.00
❑ 201	La De Da, I Love You/Yankee Doodle Dandy	1964	3.00	6.00	12.00
❑ 204	Don't Do It No More/I Fancy You	1964	3.00	6.00	12.00
❑ 206	I Feel Alright/My Mama Told Me	1965	3.00	6.00	12.00
❑ 208	I've Come to One Conclusion/Down by the Seashore	1965	3.00	6.00	12.00
❑ 213	Hummingbird/If I Need Anyone	1966	3.00	6.00	12.00
❑ 919	Mockingbird/Jaybirds	1963	6.25	12.50	25.00
❑ 922	Broken Hearted Fool/He's the One You Love	1963	3.75	7.50	15.00
❑ 924	Hi Diddle Diddle/Talk with Me	1963	3.75	7.50	15.00
❑ 926	Ask Me/I See You My Love	1963	3.75	7.50	15.00
UNITED ARTISTS					
❑ XW516	Mockingbird/I Know (You Don't Love Me No More)	1974	—	2.00	4.00
—Reissue; B-side by Barbara George					
VOLT					
❑ 4087	Watch the Dog/You Hurt Me for the Last Time	1972	—	3.00	6.00
❑ 4093	One Woman's Man/The Time	1973	—	3.00	6.00
❑ 4096	Crossing Over That Bridge/You're Saving Me for a Rainy Day	1973	—	3.00	6.00
❑ 4101	I Had a Talk with My Man/The Lady, The Doctor and the Prescription	1973	—	3.00	6.00
❑ 4107	Circuit's Overloaded/There's a Hand That's Reading Out	1974	—	3.00	6.00
Albums					
DYNAMO					
❑ DM-7000 [M]	Come By Here	1967	7.50	15.00	30.00
❑ DM-7002 [M]	Inez and Charlie Foxx's Greatest Hits	1967	7.50	15.00	30.00
❑ DS-8000 [S]	Come By Here	1967	10.00	20.00	40.00
❑ DS-8002 [S]	Inez and Charlie Foxx's Greatest Hits	1967	10.00	20.00	40.00
❑ DS-8003	Swingin' Mockin' Band	1968	7.50	15.00	30.00
SUE					
❑ LP-1027 [M]	Mockingbird	1966	25.00	50.00	100.00
SYMBOL					
❑ SYM-4400 [M]	Mockingbird	1963	37.50	75.00	150.00
VOLT					
❑ VOS-6022	Inez Foxx at Memphis	1973	3.75	7.50	15.00
FRACTION					
45s					
ANGELUS					
❑ 5005	Sanc Divided/(B-side unknown)	1971	25.00	50.00	100.00
Albums					
ANGELUS					
❑ 571	Moon Blood	1971	1000.	1500.	2000.
FRAMPTON, PETER Also see THE HERD; HUMBLE PIE; THE TAGES.					
12-Inch Singles					
ATLANTIC					
❑ PR 826 [DJ]	Lying (Edit 4:11) (LP Version 5:40)	1985	2.50	5.00	10.00
45s					
A&M					
❑ 1379	Jumping Jack Flash/Oh for Another Day	1972	2.50	5.00	10.00
❑ 1456	All Night Long/Don't Fade Away	1973	—	3.00	6.00
—As "Frampton's Camel"					
❑ 1470	I Believe (When I Fall in Love It Will Be Forever)/Which Way the Wind Blows	1973	2.00	4.00	8.00
—As "Frampton's Camel"					
❑ 1506	Somethin's Happening/I Wanna Go to the Sun	1974	—	3.00	6.00
❑ 1693	Show Me the Way/Crying Clown	1975	2.00	4.00	8.00
❑ 1738	Baby I Love Your Way/(I'll Give You) Money	1975	2.00	4.00	8.00
❑ 1763	(I'll Give You) Money/Nowhere's Too Far (For My Baby)	1975	—	3.00	6.00
❑ 1795	Show Me the Way/Shine On	1976	—	2.00	4.00
❑ 1795 [PS]	Show Me the Way/Shine On	1976	—	3.00	6.00
❑ 1832	Baby, I Love Your Way/It's a Plain Shame	1976	—	2.00	4.00
❑ 1832 [PS]	Baby, I Love Your Way/It's a Plain Shame	1976	—	3.00	6.00
❑ 1867	Do You Feel Like We Do/Penny for Your Thoughts	1976	—	2.00	4.00
❑ 1941	I'm in You/St. Thomas (Don't You Know How I Feel)	1977	—	2.00	4.00
❑ 1941	I'm in You/St. Thomas (Know How I Feel)	1977	—	2.50	5.00
❑ 1941 [PS]	I'm in You/St. Thomas (Don't You Know How I Feel)	1977	—	3.00	6.00
❑ 1941 [PS]	I'm in You/St. Thomas (Know How I Feel)	1977	—	3.50	7.00
❑ 1972	Signed, Sealed, Delivered (I'm Yours)/Rocky's Hot Club	1977	—	2.00	4.00
❑ 1972 [PS]	Signed, Sealed, Delivered (I'm Yours)/Rocky's Hot Club	1977	—	3.00	6.00
❑ 1988	Tried to Love/You Don't Have to Worry	1977	—	2.00	4.00
❑ 1988 [PS]	Tried to Love/You Don't Have to Worry	1977	—	3.00	6.00
❑ 2070	The Long and Winding Road/Tried to Love	1978	—	3.00	6.00
❑ 2148	I Can't Stand It No More/Where Should I Be	1979	—	2.00	4.00
❑ 2148 [PS]	I Can't Stand It No More/Where Should I Be	1979	—	2.50	5.00
❑ 2174	She Don't Reply/St. Thomas (Don't You Know How I Feel)	1979	—	2.00	4.00
❑ 2350	Breaking All the Rules/Night Town	1981	—	2.00	4.00
❑ 2350 [PS]	Breaking All the Rules/Night Town	1981	—	3.00	6.00
❑ 2362	You Kill Me/Wasting the Night Away	1981	—	3.00	6.00
❑ 2442	Sleepwalk/Theme from Night	1982	2.00	4.00	8.00
❑ 8595	Show Me the Way/Baby, I Love Your Way	1977	—	2.00	4.00
—"Forget Me Nots" reissue; green and gold label					
❑ 8595 [PS]	Show Me the Way/Baby, I Love Your Way	1977	2.50	5.00	10.00
❑ 8604	I'm in You/Do You Feel Like We Do	1978	—	2.00	4.00
—"Forget Me Nots" reissue; green and gold label					
ATLANTIC					
❑ 88820	Holding On to You/Give Me a Love That's Real	1990	—	—	3.00
❑ 89395	Hiding from a Heartache/Into View	1986	—	—	3.00
❑ 89426	All Eyes on You/So Far Away	1986	—	—	3.00
❑ 89426 [PS]	All Eyes on You/So Far Away	1986	—	—	3.00
❑ 89463	Lying/Into View	1985	—	—	3.00
❑ 89463 [PS]	Lying/Into View	1985	—	—	3.00
Albums					
A&M					
❑ SP-3133	Wind of Change	198?	2.00	4.00	8.00
—Budget-line reissue					
❑ SP-3619	Somethin's Happening	1974	3.00	6.00	12.00
❑ PR-3703	Frampton Comes Alive!	1976	5.00	10.00	20.00
—Single-record picture disc of highlights					
❑ SP-3703 [(2)]	Frampton Comes Alive!	1976	3.00	6.00	12.00
❑ SP-3710	Where I Should Be	1979	2.50	5.00	10.00
❑ SP-3722	Breaking All the Rules	1981	2.50	5.00	10.00
❑ SP-4348	Wind of Change	1972	3.00	6.00	12.00
—Brown label					
❑ SP-4348	Wind of Change	1974	2.50	5.00	10.00
—Silvery label					
❑ SP-4389	Frampton's Camel	1973	3.00	6.00	12.00
—Brown label					
❑ SP-4389	Frampton's Camel	1974	2.50	5.00	10.00
—Silvery label					
❑ SP-4512	Frampton	1975	2.50	5.00	10.00
❑ SP-4704	I'm In You	1977	2.50	5.00	10.00
❑ SP-4704 [DJ]	I'm In You	1977	10.00	20.00	40.00
—Promo-only picture disc					
❑ SP-4905	The Art of Control	1982	2.50	5.00	10.00
❑ SP-6505 [(2)]	Frampton Comes Alive!	198?	2.50	5.00	10.00
—Budget-line reissue					
❑ SP-17100 [DJ]	Peter Frampton Radio Special	1979	5.00	10.00	20.00
—Promo-only interview record					
ATLANTIC					
❑ PR 848 [DJ]	Frampton Is Alive!	1986	5.00	10.00	20.00
—Promo-only interview record					
❑ PR 3093 [DJ]	Perfect Fit: A Candid Interview	1989	5.00	10.00	20.00
—Promo-only album					
❑ 81290	Premonition	1986	2.00	4.00	8.00
❑ 82030	Where All the Pieces Fit	1989	2.00	4.00	8.00
MOBILE FIDELITY					
❑ 2-262 [(2)]	Frampton Comes Alive!	1996	10.00	20.00	40.00
—Audiophile vinyl					
SWEET THUNDER					
❑ 6 [(2)]	Frampton Comes Alive!	198?	25.00	50.00	100.00
—Audiophile edition					
FRANCESCO					
45s					
DATE					
❑ 2-1625	You Want to Be Americano (Tu Vuo' Da L'Americano)/Taxi, Taxi Italiano	1968	2.00	4.00	8.00
FRANCHI, SERGIO					
12-Inch Singles					
LAX					
❑ L33-1836 [DJ]	Laugh You Silly Clown/More (Theme from Mondo Cane)	1979	2.50	5.00	10.00
45s					
LAX					
❑ 41164	Laugh You Silly Clown/(B-side unknown)	1979	—	2.00	4.00
METROMEDIA					
❑ 238	If/Somehow	1971	—	2.00	4.00
RCA VICTOR					
❑ 47-8103	I Mustn't Say I Love You/Once	1962	2.00	4.00	8.00
❑ 47-8103	I Mustn't Say I Love Her/Once	1962	2.50	5.00	10.00
—Some copies have this incorrect title					
❑ 47-8103 [PS]	I Mustn't Say I Love You/Once	1962	3.75	7.50	15.00
❑ 47-8149	The Good Life/Bella Nina	1963	2.00	4.00	8.00
❑ 47-8315	Cuando Caliente El Sol/Chicago	1964	—	3.00	6.00
❑ 47-8409	No Arms Can Ever Hold You/Seventh Dawn	1964	—	3.00	6.00
❑ 47-8552	Someone Like You/Take the Moment	1965	—	3.00	6.00
❑ 47-8686	Ciao, Ciao (So Long for Now)/Moon Over Naples	1965	—	3.00	6.00
❑ 47-9124	What Will Tomorrow Bring/Maybe It's Time for Me	1967	—	3.00	6.00
❑ 47-9277	I Should Care/No One Else	1967	—	3.00	6.00
❑ 47-9471	Time Alone Will Tell/I'm a Fool to Want You	1968	—	3.00	6.00
UNITED ARTISTS					
❑ 50612	Hold Me/Song of Santa Vittoria	1969	—	2.50	5.00
❑ 50630	Granada/Within Me	1970	—	2.50	5.00
❑ 50664	More Than Strangers/Buona Fortuna, Addio Bambino	1970	—	2.50	5.00
❑ 50681	Here We Go Again/Love Is All	1970	—	2.50	5.00
Albums					
4 CORNERS OF THE WORLD					
❑ FCL-4221 [M]	La Bella Italia	196?	3.00	6.00	12.00
❑ FCS-4221 [S]	La Bella Italia	196?	3.75	7.50	15.00
❑ FCL 4223 [M]	Buon Natale	196?	3.00	6.00	12.00
❑ FCS 4223 [S]	Buon Natale	196?	3.75	7.50	15.00
❑ FCL-4228 [M]	Il Fantastico	196?	3.00	6.00	12.00
❑ FCS-4228 [S]	Il Fantastico	196?	3.75	7.50	15.00
METROMEDIA					
❑ MD 1047	Sergio Franchi	1971	2.50	5.00	10.00
RCA VICTOR					
❑ ANL1-1070	The Best of Sergio Franchi	1975	2.50	5.00	10.00
❑ APL1-2132	Volare	1976	2.50	5.00	10.00
❑ ANL1-2643	Songs of Richard Rodgers	1977	2.00	4.00	8.00
—Reissue of LSP-3365					
❑ LPM-2943 [M]	The Exciting Voice of Sergio Franchi	1964	3.00	6.00	12.00
❑ LSP-2943 [S]	The Exciting Voice of Sergio Franchi	1964	3.75	7.50	15.00
❑ LPM-3310 [M]	Live at the Cocoanut Grove	1965	2.50	5.00	10.00
❑ LSP-3310 [S]	Live at the Cocoanut Grove	1965	3.00	6.00	12.00
❑ LPM-3365 [M]	Songs of Richard Rodgers	1965	2.50	5.00	10.00
❑ LSP-3365 [S]	Songs of Richard Rodgers	1965	3.00	6.00	12.00
❑ LPM-3437 [M]	The Heart of Christmas (Cuor' di Natale)	1965	3.00	6.00	12.00
❑ LSP-3437 [S]	The Heart of Christmas (Cuor' di Natale)	1965	3.75	7.50	15.00
❑ LPM-3500 [M]	La Dolce Italy	1966	2.50	5.00	10.00
❑ LSP-3500 [S]	La Dolce Italy	1966	3.00	6.00	12.00
❑ LPM-3654 [M]	From Sergio — With Love	1966	2.50	5.00	10.00
❑ LSP-3654 [S]	From Sergio — With Love	1966	3.00	6.00	12.00

F

Number	Title (A Side/B Side)	Yr	VG	VG+	NM
❑ LPM-3810 [M]	There Goes My Heart	1967	2.50	5.00	10.00
❑ LSP-3810 [S]	There Goes My Heart	1967	3.00	6.00	12.00
❑ LPM-3933 [M]	I'm a Fool to Want You	1968	3.75	7.50	15.00
❑ LSP-3933 [S]	I'm a Fool to Want You	1968	3.00	6.00	12.00
❑ AFL1-4018	Wine and Song	1977	2.00	4.00	8.00
—Reissue of LSP-4018					
❑ LPM-4018 [M]	Wine and Song	1968	5.00	10.00	20.00
❑ LSP-4018 [S]	Wine and Song	1968	3.00	6.00	12.00
❑ VPS-6082 [(2)]	This Is Sergio Franchi	1972	3.00	6.00	12.00
RCA VICTOR RED SEAL					
❑ LM-2640 [M]	Romantic Italian Songs	1962	3.00	6.00	12.00
❑ LSC-2640 [S]	Romantic Italian Songs	1962	3.75	7.50	15.00
❑ LM-2657 [M]	Our Man from Italy	1963	3.00	6.00	12.00
❑ LSC-2657 [S]	Our Man from Italy	1963	3.75	7.50	15.00
❑ LM-2674 [M]	Broadway...I Love You	1963	3.00	6.00	12.00
❑ LSC-2674 [S]	Broadway...I Love You	1963	3.75	7.50	15.00
❑ LM-2675 [M]	The Dream Duet	1963	3.00	6.00	12.00
—With Anna Moffo					
❑ LSC-2675 [S]	The Dream Duet	1963	3.75	7.50	15.00
—With Anna Moffo					
❑ LM-2696 [M]	The Women in My Life	1964	3.00	6.00	12.00
❑ LSC-2696 [S]	The Women in My Life	1964	3.75	7.50	15.00
UNITED ARTISTS					
❑ UAS-6727	Within Me	1970	2.50	5.00	10.00

FRANCIS, CONNIE
45s

GSF

Number	Title (A Side/B Side)	Yr	VG	VG+	NM
❑ 6901	The Answer (Should I Tie a Yellow Ribbon Round the Ole Oak Tree?)/Paint the Rain	1973	—	2.50	5.00
IVANHOE					
❑ 508	I Don't Wanna Walk Without You/Don't Turn Around	197?	—	2.50	5.00
MGM					
❑ CS6-5	Celebrity Scene: Connie Francis	1967	15.00	30.00	60.00

—Box set of five singles (13708-13712). Price includes box, all 5 singles, jukebox title strips, bio. Records are sometimes found by themselves, so they are also listed separately.

Number	Title (A Side/B Side)	Yr	VG	VG+	NM
❑ SB-9 [S]	Rock-A-Bye Your Baby with a Dixie Melody/Ciao Ciao Bambino	1960	12.50	25.00	50.00
❑ SB-10 [S]	I Almost Lost My Mind/Come Back to Sorrento	1960	12.50	25.00	50.00
❑ 126	Stupid Cupid/I'm Sorry I Made You Cry	196?	2.00	4.00	8.00
—Reissue					
❑ 129	Who's Sorry Now/You Were Only Fooling	196?	2.00	4.00	8.00
—Reissue					
❑ 135	Mama/You're Gonna Miss Me	196?	2.00	4.00	8.00
—Reissue					
❑ 136	Among My Souvenirs/God Bless America	196?	2.00	4.00	8.00
—Reissue					
❑ 139	Lipstick on Your Collar/Frankie	196?	2.00	4.00	8.00
—Reissue					
❑ 141	My Happiness/If I Didn't Care	196?	2.00	4.00	8.00
—Reissue					
❑ 148	My Heart Has a Mind of Its Own/Malaguena	196?	2.00	4.00	8.00
—Reissue					
❑ 150	Where the Boys Are/No One	196?	2.00	4.00	8.00
—Reissue					
❑ 153	Breakin' In a Brand New Broken Heart/Somebody Else's Boy	196?	2.00	4.00	8.00
—Reissue					
❑ 155	Together/Too Many Rules	196?	2.00	4.00	8.00
—Reissue					
❑ 156	Many Tears Ago/Senza Mama E Numerata	196?	2.00	4.00	8.00
—Reissue					
❑ 157	Don't Break the Heart That Loves You/Second Hand Love	196?	2.00	4.00	8.00
—Reissue					
❑ 165	Everybody's Somebody's Fool/Al Di La	196?	2.00	4.00	8.00
—Reissue					
❑ 169	Jealous Heart/Forget Domani	196?	2.00	4.00	8.00
—Reissue					
❑ 511	Who's Sorry Now/Stupid Cupid	197?	—	2.50	5.00
—Reissue					
❑ 512	Lipstick on Your Collar/Mama	197?	—	2.50	5.00
—Reissue					
❑ 513	Everybody's Somebody's Fool/Al Di La	197?	—	2.50	5.00
—Reissue					
❑ 524	My Happiness/If I Didn't Care	197?	—	2.50	5.00
—Reissue					
❑ 12015	Freddy/Didn't I Love You Enough	1955	12.50	25.00	50.00
❑ 12056	Oh Please Make Him Jealous/Goody Goodbye	1955	12.50	25.00	50.00
❑ 12122	Are You Satisfied/My Treasure	1956	6.25	12.50	25.00
❑ 12191	My First Real Love/Believe in Me	1956	15.00	30.00	60.00
❑ 12251	Send for My Baby/Forgetting	1956	6.25	12.50	25.00
❑ 12335	My Sailor Boy/Everyone Needs Someone	1956	6.25	12.50	25.00
❑ 12375	I Never Had a Sweetheart/Little Blue Wren	1957	6.25	12.50	25.00
❑ 12440	No Other One/I Leaned on a Man	1957	6.25	12.50	25.00
❑ 12490	Eighteen/Faded Orchid	1957	6.25	12.50	25.00
❑ 12588	Who's Sorry Now?/You Were Only Fooling	1958	5.00	10.00	20.00
❑ 12647	I'm Sorry I Made You Cry/Lock Up Your Heart	1958	5.00	10.00	20.00
❑ 12669	Heartaches/I Miss You So	1958	12.50	25.00	50.00
❑ 12683	Stupid Cupid/Carolina Moon	1958	5.00	10.00	20.00
❑ 12713	Fallin'/Happy Days and Lonely Nights	1958	5.00	10.00	20.00
❑ 12738 [M]	My Happiness/Never Before	1958	5.00	10.00	20.00
❑ 12738 [PS]	My Happiness/Never Before	1958	7.50	15.00	30.00
—Pink sleeve					
❑ 12738 [PS]	My Happiness/Never Before	1958	10.00	20.00	40.00
—White sleeve					
❑ 12769	If I Didn't Care/Toward the End of the Day	1959	5.00	10.00	20.00
❑ 12769 [PS]	If I Didn't Care/Toward the End of the Day	1959	7.50	15.00	30.00
❑ 12793 [M]	Lipstick on Your Collar/Frankie	1959	5.00	10.00	20.00
❑ 12824 [M]	You're Gonna Miss Me/Plenty Good Lovin'	1959	5.00	10.00	20.00
❑ 12841 [M]	Among My Souvenirs/God Bless America	1959	5.00	10.00	20.00
—Second pressing has a black label					
❑ 12841 [M]	Among My Souvenirs/God Bless America	1959	7.50	15.00	30.00
—First pressing has a yellow label					
❑ 12878	Mama/Teddy	1960	3.75	7.50	15.00
❑ 12899	Everybody's Somebody's Fool/Jealous of You	1960	3.75	7.50	15.00

Number	Title (A Side/B Side)	Yr	VG	VG+	NM
❑ 12899 [PS]	Everybody's Somebody's Fool/Jealous of You	1960	5.00	10.00	20.00
❑ 12923	My Heart Has a Mind of Its Own/Malaguena	1960	3.75	7.50	15.00
❑ 12923 [PS]	My Heart Has a Mind of Its Own/Malaguena	1960	5.00	10.00	20.00
❑ 12964	Many Tears Ago/Senza Mama (With No One)	1960	3.75	7.50	15.00
❑ 12964 [PS]	Many Tears Ago/Senza Mama (With No One)	1960	5.00	10.00	20.00
❑ 12971	Where the Boys Are/No One	1961	3.75	7.50	15.00
❑ 12971 [PS]	Where the Boys Are/No One	1961	5.00	10.00	20.00
❑ 12995	Breakin' In a Brand New Broken Heart/Someone Else's Boy	1961	3.75	7.50	15.00
❑ 12995 [PS]	Breakin' In a Brand New Broken Heart/Someone Else's Boy	1961	5.00	10.00	20.00
❑ 13005	Atashi-No/Swanee	1961	7.50	15.00	30.00
❑ 13019	Together/Too Many Rules	1961	3.75	7.50	15.00
❑ 13019 [PS]	Together/Too Many Rules	1961	5.00	10.00	20.00
❑ 13039	(He's My) Dreamboat/Hollywood	1961	3.75	7.50	15.00
❑ 13039 [PS]	(He's My) Dreamboat/Hollywood	1961	5.00	10.00	20.00
❑ 13051	When the Boy in Your Arms (Is the Boy in Your Heart)/Baby's First Christmas	1961	3.75	7.50	15.00
❑ 13051 [PS]	When the Boy in Your Arms (Is the Boy in Your Heart)/Baby's First Christmas	1961	5.00	10.00	20.00
❑ 13059	Don't Break the Heart That Loves You/Drop It, Joe	1962	3.75	7.50	15.00
❑ 13059 [PS]	Don't Break the Heart That Loves You/Drop It, Joe	1962	5.00	10.00	20.00
❑ 13074	Second Hand Love/Gonna Git That Man	1962	5.00	10.00	20.00
—A-side is said to have been produced by Phil Spector, though Connie Francis disputes this; regardless, Spector did co-write the song					
❑ 13074 [PS]	Second Hand Love/Gonna Git That Man	1962	6.25	12.50	25.00
❑ 13087	Vacation/The Biggest Sin of All	1962	3.75	7.50	15.00
❑ 13087 [PS]	Vacation/The Biggest Sin of All	1962	5.00	10.00	20.00
❑ 13096	I Was Such a Fool (To Fall in Love with You)/He Thinks I Still Care	1962	3.00	6.00	12.00
❑ 13096 [PS]	I Was Such a Fool (To Fall in Love with You)/He Thinks I Still Care	1962	4.00	8.00	16.00
❑ 13116	I'm Gonna' Be Warm This Winter/Al Di La	1962	3.00	6.00	12.00
❑ 13116 [PS]	I'm Gonna' Be Warm This Winter/Al Di La	1962	4.00	8.00	16.00
❑ 13127	Follow the Boys/Waiting for Billy	1962	3.00	6.00	12.00
❑ 13127 [PS]	Follow the Boys/Waiting for Billy	1962	4.00	8.00	16.00
❑ 13143	If My Pillow Could Talk/You're the Only One Can Hurt Me	1963	3.00	6.00	12.00
❑ 13143 [PS]	If My Pillow Could Talk/You're the Only One Can Hurt Me	1963	4.00	8.00	16.00
❑ 13160	Drownin' My Sorrows/Mala Femmena	1963	3.00	6.00	12.00
❑ 13160 [PS]	Drownin' My Sorrows/Mala Femmena	1963	4.00	8.00	16.00
❑ 13176	Your Other Love/Whatever Happened to Rosemarie?	1963	3.00	6.00	12.00
❑ 13176 [PS]	Your Other Love/Whatever Happened to Rosemarie?	1963	4.00	8.00	16.00
❑ 13203	In the Summer of His Years/My Buddy	1963	3.00	6.00	12.00
❑ 13203 [PS]	In the Summer of His Years/My Buddy	1963	10.00	20.00	40.00
❑ 13214	Blue Winter/You Know You Don't Want Me (So Why Don't You Leave Me Alone)	1964	3.00	6.00	12.00
❑ 13214 [PS]	Blue Winter/You Know You Don't Want Me (So Why Don't You Leave Me Alone)	1964	4.00	8.00	16.00
❑ 13237	Be Anything (But Be Mine)/Tommy	1964	3.00	6.00	12.00
❑ 13237 [PS]	Be Anything (But Be Mine)/Tommy	1964	4.00	8.00	16.00
❑ 13256	Looking for Love/This Is My Happiest Moment	1964	3.00	6.00	12.00
❑ 13256 [PS]	Looking for Love/This Is My Happiest Moment	1964	4.00	8.00	16.00
❑ 13287	Don't Ever Leave Me/We Have Something More (Than a Summer Love)	1964	3.00	6.00	12.00
❑ 13287 [PS]	Don't Ever Leave Me/We Have Something More (Than a Summer Love)	1964	4.00	8.00	16.00
❑ 13303	Whose Heart Are You Breaking Tonight/Come On Jerry	1965	2.50	5.00	10.00
❑ 13303 [PS]	Whose Heart Are You Breaking Tonight/Come On Jerry	1965	3.00	6.00	12.00
❑ 13325	For Mama (La Mamma)/She'll Be Coming 'Round the Mountain	1965	3.00	6.00	12.00
❑ 13331	Wishing It Was You/You're Mine (Just When You're Lonely)	1965	2.50	5.00	10.00
❑ 13331 [PS]	Wishing It Was You/You're Mine (Just When You're Lonely)	1965	3.00	6.00	12.00
❑ 13363	Forget Domani/No One Sends Me Roses	1965	2.50	5.00	10.00
❑ 13389	Roundabout/Bossa Nova Hand Dance	1965	2.50	5.00	10.00
❑ 13420	Jealous Heart/Can I Rely on You	1965	2.50	5.00	10.00
❑ 13470	Love Is Me, Love Is You/I'd Let You Break My Heart All Over Again	1966	2.50	5.00	10.00
❑ 13470 [PS]	Love Is Me, Love Is You/I'd Let You Break My Heart All Over Again	1966	3.00	6.00	12.00
❑ 13505	It's a Different World/Empty Chapel	1966	2.50	5.00	10.00
❑ 13505 [PS]	It's a Different World/Empty Chapel	1966	5.00	10.00	20.00
❑ 13545	A Letter from a Soldier (Dear Mama)/Somewhere, My Love	1966	2.50	5.00	10.00
❑ 13550 [DJ]	A Nurse in the U.S. Army (same on both sides)	1966	7.50	15.00	30.00
—Promotional item for the U.S. Army					
❑ 13578	All the Love in the World/So Nice	1966	2.50	5.00	10.00
❑ 13610	Spanish Nights and You/Games That Lovers Play	1966	2.50	5.00	10.00
❑ 13610 [PS]	Spanish Nights and You/Games That Lovers Play	1966	5.00	10.00	20.00
❑ 13665	Another Page/Souvenir d'Italie	1967	2.50	5.00	10.00
❑ 13708	Mama/Never on Sunday	1967	2.50	5.00	10.00
—Part of Celebrity Series CS-5					
❑ 13709	My Happiness/Al Di La	1967	2.50	5.00	10.00
—Part of Celebrity Series CS-5					
❑ 13710	Malaguena/I Love You Much Too Much	1967	2.50	5.00	10.00
—Part of Celebrity Series CS-5					
❑ 13711	Once in a Lifetime/Oh Lonesome Me	1967	2.50	5.00	10.00
—Part of Celebrity Series CS-5					
❑ 13712	Jealous Heart/Will You Still Be Mine	1967	2.50	5.00	10.00
—Part of Celebrity Series CS-5					
❑ 13718	Time Alone Will Tell/Born Free	1967	2.50	5.00	10.00
❑ 13773	My Heart Cries for You/Someone Took the Sweetness Out of Sweetheart	1967	2.50	5.00	10.00
❑ 13773 [PS]	My Heart Cries for You/Someone Took the Sweetness Out of Sweetheart	1967	5.00	10.00	20.00
❑ 13814	Lonely Again/When You Care a Lot for Someone	1967	2.50	5.00	10.00

Number	Title (A Side/B Side)	Yr	VG	VG+	NM
13876	My World Is Slipping Away/Till We're Together	1967	2.50	5.00	10.00
13923	Why Say Goodbye/Adios, Me Amore	1968	2.00	4.00	8.00
13948	Somebody Else Is Taking My Place/Brother, Can You Spare a Dime?	1968	2.00	4.00	8.00
14004	I Don't Wanna Play House/The Welfare Check	1968	2.00	4.00	8.00
14034	The Wedding Cake/Over Hill, Under Ground	1969	2.00	4.00	8.00
14058	Gone Like the Wind/Am I Blue?	1969	2.00	4.00	8.00
14058 [PS]	Gone Like the Wind/Am I Blue?	1969	5.00	10.00	20.00
14089	Invierno Trieste/Noches Espanolas Y Tu	1969	—	—	—
—Not known to exist					
14091	Mr. Love/Zingara	1969	2.00	4.00	8.00
14091 [PS]	Mr. Love/Zingara	1969	5.00	10.00	20.00
14853	I'm Me Again/Comme Si, Comme Sa	1976	—	3.00	6.00
SK-50117 [S]	My Happiness/Never Before	1958	12.50	25.00	50.00
SK-50121 [S]	Lipstick on Your Collar/Frankie	1959	15.00	30.00	60.00
SK-50129 [S]	You're Gonna Miss Me/Plenty Good Lovin'	1959	12.50	25.00	50.00
SK-50133 [S]	Among My Souvenirs/God Bless America	1959	12.50	25.00	50.00
POLYDOR					
2143	I'm Me Again/Comme Si, Comme Sa	1981	—	2.50	5.00
810087-7	There's Still a Few Good Love Songs Left in Me/Let's Make It Love Tonight	1983	—	2.50	5.00

7-Inch Extended Plays

MGM

Number	Title (A Side/B Side)	Yr	VG	VG+	NM
HC5-6 [DJ]	Heart Circuit Interview	1959	25.00	50.00	100.00
X-1599	Who's Sorry Now/You Were Only Fooling (While I Was Falling in Love)//Eighteen/Faded Orchid	1958	10.00	20.00	40.00
X-1599 [PS]	Connie Francis	1958	10.00	20.00	40.00
X-1603	(contents unknown)	1958	10.00	20.00	40.00
X-1603 [PS]	Who's Sorry Now Vol. I	1958	10.00	20.00	40.00
X-1604	(contents unknown)	1958	10.00	20.00	40.00
X-1604 [PS]	Who's Sorry Now Vol. II	1958	10.00	20.00	40.00
X-1605	*You Always Hurt the One You Love/If I Had You/How Deep Is the Ocean?/I'll Get By	1958	10.00	20.00	40.00
X-1605 [PS]	Who's Sorry Now Vol. III	1958	10.00	20.00	40.00
X-1655	My Happiness/No Other One//You're My Everything/Never Before	1958	10.00	20.00	40.00
X-1655 [PS]	My Happiness	1958	10.00	20.00	40.00
X-1662	If I Didn't Care/Toward the End of the Day//Don't Speak of Love/If You Loved Me Tonight	1959	10.00	20.00	40.00
X-1662 [PS]	If I Didn't Care	1959	10.00	20.00	40.00
SX-1663 [PS]	The Exciting Connie Francis Vol. 1	1959	20.00	40.00	80.00
—A stereo copy of the above has recently emerged. We presume that Vol. 2 and Vol. 3 of the same title also were made in stereo, but we don't have concrete proof, so we don't list them yet.					
SX-1663 [S]	*Come Rain or Come Shine/Time After Time//Hallelujah, I Love Him So/How Did He Look	1959	20.00	40.00	80.00
X-1663	*Come Rain or Come Shine/Time After Time//Hallelujah, I Love Him So/How Did He Look	1959	10.00	20.00	40.00
X-1663 [PS]	The Exciting Connie Francis Vol. 1	1959	10.00	20.00	40.00
X-1664	(contents unknown)	1959	10.00	20.00	40.00
X-1664 [PS]	The Exciting Connie Francis Vol. 2	1959	10.00	20.00	40.00
X-1665	(contents unknown)	1959	10.00	20.00	40.00
X-1665 [PS]	The Exciting Connie Francis Vol. 3	1959	10.00	20.00	40.00
X-1687	You're Gonna Miss Me/Plenty Good Lovin'//Frankie/Lipstick on Your Collar	1959	7.50	15.00	30.00
X-1687 [PS]	Connie Francis	1959	7.50	15.00	30.00
X-1688	Who's Sorry Now/Fallin'//Happy Days and Lonely Nights/Stupid Cupid	1960	7.50	15.00	30.00
X-1688 [PS]	Connie's Greatest Hits (Part 1)	1960	7.50	15.00	30.00
X-1689	(contents unknown)	1960	7.50	15.00	30.00
X-1689 [PS]	Connie's Greatest Hits (Part 2)	1960	7.50	15.00	30.00
X-1690	(contents unknown)	1960	7.50	15.00	30.00
X-1690 [PS]	Connie's Greatest Hits (Part 3)	1960	7.50	15.00	30.00
X-1691	(contents unknown)	1960	7.50	15.00	30.00
X-1691 [PS]	Rock 'N Roll Million Sellers (Part 1)	1960	7.50	15.00	30.00
X-1692	(contents unknown)	1960	7.50	15.00	30.00
X-1692 [PS]	Rock 'N Roll Million Sellers (Part 2)	1960	7.50	15.00	30.00
X-1693	(contents unknown)	1960	7.50	15.00	30.00
X-1693 [PS]	Rock 'N Roll Million Sellers (Part 3)	1960	7.50	15.00	30.00
X-1694	(contents unknown)	1960	7.50	15.00	30.00
X-1694 [PS]	Country & Western Golden Hits (Part 1)	1960	7.50	15.00	30.00
X-1695	(contents unknown)	1960	7.50	15.00	30.00
X-1695 [PS]	Country & Western Golden Hits (Part 2)	1960	7.50	15.00	30.00
X-1696	(contents unknown)	1960	7.50	15.00	30.00
X-1696 [PS]	Country & Western Golden Hits (Part 3)	1960	7.50	15.00	30.00
X-1703	Valentino/You Made Me Love You//Because of You/Young at Heart	1961	7.50	15.00	30.00
X-1703 [PS]	Connie Francis	1961	7.50	15.00	30.00
—Has paper sleeve rather than a cardboard sleeve					
X-1706	Don't Break the Heart That Loves You/It Happened Last Night//Too Many Rules/Kiss 'N' Twist	1962	10.00	20.00	40.00
X-1706 [PS]	Connie Francis	1962	10.00	20.00	40.00
—Paper sleeve rather than the typical cardboard EP sleeve					
SLM-4079	I'm Movin' On/She'll Have to Go/I'm a Fool to Care//I Really Don't Want to Know/Someday (You'll Want Me to Want You)/He Thinks I Still Care	196?	6.25	12.50	25.00
—Jukebox issue; small hole, plays at 33 1/3 rpm					
SLM-4079 [PS] Country Music Connie Style		196?	6.25	12.50	25.00

Albums

LEO

Number	Title (A Side/B Side)	Yr	VG	VG+	NM
LE-903 [M]	Connie Francis and the Kids Next Door	1967	12.50	25.00	50.00
LES-903 [S]	Connie Francis and the Kids Next Door	1967	15.00	30.00	60.00
MATI-MOR					
8002 [M]	Sing Along wth Connie Francis	1961	10.00	20.00	40.00
—Made for Brylcreem					
METRO					
M-519 [M]	Connie Francis	1964	5.00	10.00	20.00
MS-519 [S]	Connie Francis	1964	6.25	12.50	25.00
M-538 [M]	Folk Favorites	1965	5.00	10.00	20.00
MS-538 [S]	Folk Favorites	1965	6.25	12.50	25.00
M-571 [M]	Songs of Love	1966	5.00	10.00	20.00
MS-571 [S]	Songs of Love	1966	6.25	12.50	25.00
M-603 [M]	The Incomparable Connie Francis	1967	5.00	10.00	20.00
MS-603 [S]	The Incomparable Connie Francis	1967	6.25	12.50	25.00

MGM

Number	Title (A Side/B Side)	Yr	VG	VG+	NM
GAS-109	Greatest Golden Groovie Goodies (Golden Archive Series)	1970	6.25	12.50	25.00
E-3686 [M]	Who's Sorry Now?	1958	25.00	50.00	100.00
—Yellow label					
E-3686 [M]	Who's Sorry Now?	1960	10.00	20.00	40.00
—Black label					
E-3761 [M]	The Exciting Connie Francis	1959	7.50	15.00	30.00
—Black label					
E-3761 [M]	The Exciting Connie Francis	1959	20.00	40.00	80.00
—Yellow label					
SE-3761 [S]	The Exciting Connie Francis	1959	10.00	20.00	40.00
—Black label					
SE-3761 [S]	The Exciting Connie Francis	1959	25.00	50.00	100.00
—Yellow label					
E-3776 [M]	My Thanks to You	1959	7.50	15.00	30.00
SE-3776 [S]	My Thanks to You	1959	10.00	20.00	40.00
E-3791 [M]	Italian Favorites	1959	7.50	15.00	30.00
SE-3791 [S]	Italian Favorites	1959	10.00	20.00	40.00
E-3792 [M]	Christmas in My Heart	1959	7.50	15.00	30.00
SE-3792 [S]	Christmas in My Heart	1959	10.00	20.00	40.00
—Same as above, but in stereo					
E-3793 [M]	Connie's Greatest Hits	1960	7.50	15.00	30.00
E-3794 [M]	Rock 'N' Roll Million Sellers	1960	7.50	15.00	30.00
SE-3794 [S]	Rock 'N' Roll Million Sellers	1960	10.00	20.00	40.00
E-3795 [M]	Country and Western Golden Hits	1960	7.50	15.00	30.00
SE-3795 [S]	Country and Western Golden Hits	1960	10.00	20.00	40.00
E-3853 [M]	Spanish and Latin American Favorites	1960	7.50	15.00	30.00
SE-3853 [S]	Spanish and Latin American Favorites	1960	10.00	20.00	40.00
E-3869 [M]	Jewish Favorites	1961	7.50	15.00	30.00
SE-3869 [S]	Jewish Favorites	1961	10.00	20.00	40.00
E-3871 [M]	More Italian Favorites	1960	7.50	15.00	30.00
SE-3871 [S]	More Italian Favorites	1960	10.00	20.00	40.00
E-3893 [M]	Songs to a Swinging Band	1961	7.50	15.00	30.00
SE-3893 [S]	Songs to a Swinging Band	1961	10.00	20.00	40.00
E-3913 [M]	Connie Francis at the Copa	1961	7.50	15.00	30.00
SE-3913 [S]	Connie Francis at the Copa	1961	10.00	20.00	40.00
E-3942 [M]	More Greatest Hits	1961	7.50	15.00	30.00
SE-3942 [S]	More Greatest Hits	1961	10.00	20.00	40.00
E-3965 [M]	Never on Sunday and Other Title Songs from Motion Pictures	1961	7.50	15.00	30.00
SE-3965 [S]	Never on Sunday and Other Title Songs from Motion Pictures	1961	10.00	20.00	40.00
E-3969 [M]	Folk Song Favorites	1961	7.50	15.00	30.00
SE-3969 [S]	Folk Song Favorites	1961	10.00	20.00	40.00
E-4013 [M]	Irish Favorites	1962	7.50	15.00	30.00
SE-4013 [S]	Irish Favorites	1962	10.00	20.00	40.00
E-4022 [M]	Dance Party	196?	6.25	12.50	25.00
—Retitled version of "Do the Twist"					
E-4022 [M]	Do the Twist	1962	7.50	15.00	30.00
SE-4022 [S]	Dance Party	196?	7.50	15.00	30.00
—Retitled version of "Do the Twist"					
SE-4022 [S]	Do the Twist	1962	10.00	20.00	40.00
E-4023 [M]	Fun Songs for Children	1962	12.50	25.00	50.00
E-4048 [M]	Award Winning Motion Picture Hits	1963	6.25	12.50	25.00
SE-4048 [S]	Award Winning Motion Picture Hits	1963	7.50	15.00	30.00
E-4049 [M]	Connie Francis Sings Second Hand Love and Other Hits	1962	6.25	12.50	25.00
SE-4049 [S]	Connie Francis Sings Second Hand Love and Other Hits	1962	7.50	15.00	30.00
E-4079 [M]	Country Music Connie Style	1962	6.25	12.50	25.00
SE-4079 [S]	Country Music Connie Style	1962	7.50	15.00	30.00
E-4102 [M]	Modern Italian Hits	1963	6.25	12.50	25.00
SE-4102 [S]	Modern Italian Hits	1963	7.50	15.00	30.00
E-4123 [M]	Follow the Boys	1963	6.25	12.50	25.00
SE-4123 [S]	Follow the Boys	1963	7.50	15.00	30.00
E-4124 [M]	German Favorites	1963	6.25	12.50	25.00
SE-4124 [S]	German Favorites	1963	7.50	15.00	30.00
E-4145 [M]	Greatest American Waltzes	1963	6.25	12.50	25.00
SE-4145 [S]	Greatest American Waltzes	1963	7.50	15.00	30.00
E-4161 [M]	Mala Femmena & Connie's Big Hits from Italy	1963	6.25	12.50	25.00
SE-4161 [S]	Mala Femmena & Connie's Big Hits from Italy	1963	7.50	15.00	30.00
E-4167 [M]	The Very Best of Connie Francis	1963	6.25	12.50	25.00
SE-4167 [S]	The Very Best of Connie Francis	1963	7.50	15.00	30.00
E-4210 [M]	In the Summer of His Years	1964	6.25	12.50	25.00
SE-4210 [S]	In the Summer of His Years	1964	7.50	15.00	30.00
E-4229 [M]	Looking for Love	1964	6.25	12.50	25.00
SE-4229 [S]	Looking for Love	1964	7.50	15.00	30.00
E-4253 [M]	A New Kind of Connie	1964	6.25	12.50	25.00
SE-4253 [S]	A New Kind of Connie	1964	7.50	15.00	30.00
E-4294 [M]	Connie Francis Sings For Mama	1965	6.25	12.50	25.00
SE-4294 [S]	Connie Francis Sings For Mama	1965	7.50	15.00	30.00
E-4298 [M]	All Time International Hits	1965	6.25	12.50	25.00
SE-4298 [S]	All Time International Hits	1965	7.50	15.00	30.00
E-4355 [M]	Jealous Heart	1966	6.25	12.50	25.00
SE-4355 [S]	Jealous Heart	1966	7.50	15.00	30.00
E-4382 [M]	Movie Greats of the 60's	1966	6.25	12.50	25.00
SE-4382 [S]	Movie Greats of the 60's	1966	7.50	15.00	30.00
E-4399 [M]	Connie's Christmas	1966	6.25	12.50	25.00
SE-4399 [S]	Connie's Christmas	1966	7.50	15.00	30.00
E-4411 [M]	Live at the Sahara in Las Vegas	1967	6.25	12.50	25.00
SE-4411 [S]	Live at the Sahara in Las Vegas	1967	7.50	15.00	30.00
E-4448 [M]	Love, Italian Style	1967	6.25	12.50	25.00
SE-4448 [S]	Love, Italian Style	1967	7.50	15.00	30.00
E-4472 [M]	Connie Francis On Broadway Today	1967	6.25	12.50	25.00
SE-4472 [S]	Connie Francis On Broadway Today	1967	7.50	15.00	30.00
E-4474 [M]	Grandes Exitos del Cine de los Anos 60	1967	6.25	12.50	25.00
SE-4474 [S]	Grandes Exitos del Cine de los Anos 60	1967	7.50	15.00	30.00
E-4487 [M]	My Heart Cries for You	1967	7.50	15.00	30.00
SE-4487 [S]	My Heart Cries for You	1967	6.25	12.50	25.00
E-4522 [M]	Hawaii: Connie	1968	25.00	50.00	100.00
SE-4522 [S]	Hawaii: Connie	1968	6.25	12.50	25.00
SE-4573	Connie & Clyde	1968	6.25	12.50	25.00
SE-4585	Connie Francis Sings Bacharach & David	1968	6.25	12.50	25.00
SE-4637	The Wedding Cake	1969	6.25	12.50	25.00
SE-4655	The Songs of Les Reed	1969	6.25	12.50	25.00
MG-1-5406	I'm Me Again	198?	3.00	6.00	12.00

Number	Title (A Side/B Side)	Yr	VG	VG+	NM
❑ MG-1-5410	Greatest Hits	198?	3.00	6.00	12.00
❑ MG-1-5411	Greatest Jewish Hits	198?	3.00	6.00	12.00
❑ T-90027 [M]	Award Winning Motion Picture Hits	196?	7.50	15.00	30.00
—Capitol Record Club edition					
❑ ST-90068 [S]	A New Kind of Connie	1964	8.75	17.50	35.00
—Capitol Record Club issue					
❑ T-90068 [M]	A New Kind of Connie	1964	7.50	15.00	30.00
—Capitol Record Club issue					
❑ ST 90510 [S]	The Very Best of Connie Francis	1965	10.00	20.00	40.00
—Capitol Record Club edition					
❑ T 90510 [M]	The Very Best of Connie Francis	1965	10.00	20.00	40.00
—Capitol Record Club edition					
❑ ST-91145	My Best to You	1968	7.50	15.00	30.00
—Capitol Record Club					
POLYDOR					
❑ 827569-1	The Very Best of Connie Francis	1985	2.50	5.00	10.00
❑ 827582-1	Greatest Hits	1985	2.50	5.00	10.00
❑ 827584-1	Greatest Jewish Hits	1985	2.50	5.00	10.00
❑ 839922-1	Lo Mejor De Su Repertorio	198?	2.50	5.00	10.00
❑ 839923-1	12 Exitos De Connie Francis	198?	2.50	5.00	10.00

FRANCIS, CONNIE, AND MARVIN RAINWATER Also see each artist's individual listings.
45s
MGM

Number	Title (A Side/B Side)	Yr	VG	VG+	NM
❑ 12555	You, My Darlin', You/The Majesty of Love	1957	6.25	12.50	25.00

FRANCIS, CONNIE, AND HANK WILLIAMS, JR. Also see each artist's individual listings.
Albums
MGM

Number	Title (A Side/B Side)	Yr	VG	VG+	NM
❑ E-4251 [M]	Connie Francis & Hank Williams, Jr. Sing Great Country Favorites	1964	7.50	15.00	30.00
❑ SE-4251 [S]	Connie Francis & Hank Williams, Jr. Sing Great Country Favorites	1964	10.00	20.00	40.00

FRANCISCUS, JAMES
45s
MGM

Number	Title (A Side/B Side)	Yr	VG	VG+	NM
❑ K 13319	Droppity Dropouts/On Friday Day	1965	2.50	5.00	10.00
—B-side by Vince Howard					
❑ K 13319 [PS]	Droppity Dropouts/On Friday Day	1965	6.25	12.50	25.00

FRANK, JOE, AND THE KNIGHTS
45s
ABC-PARAMOUNT

Number	Title (A Side/B Side)	Yr	VG	VG+	NM
❑ 10782	Can't Find a Way/Won't You Come Home	1966	5.00	10.00	20.00

FRANK AND JACK
45s
BERGEN

Number	Title (A Side/B Side)	Yr	VG	VG+	NM
❑ 100	'Twas The Night Before Christmas/Jingle Bells	1957	5.00	10.00	20.00
JOSIE					
❑ 827	Twas the Night Before Christmas (Breaking Thru the Sound Barrier)/Jingle Bells (From the Sound Track)	1957	3.75	7.50	15.00

FRANKIE AND THE C-NOTES
45s
RICHIE

Number	Title (A Side/B Side)	Yr	VG	VG+	NM
❑ 2	Forever and Ever/Fade Out	1959	100.00	200.00	400.00

FRANKLIN, ALAN, EXPLOSION
Albums
ALADDIN

Number	Title (A Side/B Side)	Yr	VG	VG+	NM
❑ 104049	Come Home Baby	1969	20.00	40.00	80.00
HORNE					
❑ JC-888	The Blues Climax	1970	20.00	40.00	80.00

FRANKLIN, ARETHA
12-Inch Singles
ARISTA

Number	Title (A Side/B Side)	Yr	VG	VG+	NM
❑ SP-103 [DJ]	What a Fool Believes (Long Version) (Short Version)	1980	3.00	6.00	12.00
❑ SP-138 [DJ]	Jump To It (6:40) (3:58)/Just My Daydream	1982	2.50	5.00	10.00
❑ SP-147 [DJ]	Love Me Right (Dance Version) (Short Version)	1982	3.75	7.50	15.00
❑ CP 718	Jump to It (Extended Version 6:40) (Single Version 3:58)/Just My Daydream	1982	5.00	10.00	20.00
❑ 2240	Everyday People (People Remix) (Bonus Beats)/(Everyday Remix) (People Dub)	1991	2.50	5.00	10.00
❑ ADP 2651 [(3)DJ]	A Deeper Love (9 versions)	1994	5.00	10.00	20.00
❑ ADP 2703 [DJ]	Jump To It (CJ's Masta Mix) (Gorda Dub) (Original Extended Version)	1994	3.75	7.50	15.00
❑ ADP 3455 [DJ]	A Rose Is Still a Rose (Without Intro) (With Intro)	1998	2.50	5.00	10.00
❑ ADP 3484 [(2)DJ]	A Rose Is Still a Rose (Hex Hector Club Mix 8:55) (Album Version 4:29)/(Johnny Vicious Dub 9:28) (Love to Infinity Kick Mix 7:11)//(Johnny Vicious Club Mix 10:44) (HEx Hector Drums 3:50)/(Love to Infinity Club Mix) (Love to Infinity Rhythm Radio Mix) (Album Version Instrumental)	1998	3.75	7.50	15.00
—Promo version of 13484					
❑ ADP 3486 [DJ]	A Rose Is Still a Rose (Yogi's Bystorm Remix) (Yogi's Bystorm Remix Instrumental) (Yogi's Bystorm Remix Acappella) (Desert Eagle Remix) (Desert Eagle Remix Instrumental) (Original Radio Edit)	1998	5.00	10.00	20.00
❑ ADP 3493 [DJ]	Here We Go Again (LP Version) (Instrumental) (Acappella)	1998	2.50	5.00	10.00
❑ ADP 3513 [(2)DJ]	Here We Go Again (Morales Classic Mix) (Razor-N-Guido Mix) (Morales Rascal Dub) (Razor-N-Guido Key Line) (Morales Def Zone Dub) (Mixologist Bass Mix) (Morales Bass Dub) (Album Version)	1998	6.25	12.50	25.00
❑ ADP 3514 [DJ]	Here We Go Again (Bump Mix) (Mixologist Bass Rap) (Acappella) (Bass Mix) (Instrumental)	1998	3.75	7.50	15.00
❑ AD1-9043	Get It Right (Long Version 6:22)/(Instrumental 6:31)	1983	2.50	5.00	10.00
❑ AD1-9355	Freeway of Love (Rock Mix)/(Radio Mix) (Extended Remix)	1985	2.00	4.00	8.00

Number	Title (A Side/B Side)	Yr	VG	VG+	NM
❑ AD1-9411	Who's Zoomin' Who (Dance Mix) (Dub Mix)/(Radio Mix) (Acappella Mix)	1985	2.00	4.00	8.00
❑ AD1-9454	Another Night (Dance Mix 6:40) (Dub 6:57)/(Radio Mix 5:02) (7" Edit 4:03)	1985	2.00	4.00	8.00
❑ AD1-9473	Ain't Nobody Ever Loved You (Remix 6:22) (Dub 6:59) (Single Edit 4:16) (Percapella)	1986	2.00	4.00	8.00
❑ AD1-9529	Jumpin' Jack Flash (LP Mix) (Street Mix)/(Street Mix Radio Edit) (Master Dub Mix) (Beat Dub)	1986	2.50	5.00	10.00
❑ AD1-9547	Jimmy Lee (Extended Remix 7:16) (Single Version 5:47) (Dub Mix 6:14)/Aretha Megamix	1986	2.00	4.00	8.00
❑ AD1-9560	I Knew You Were Waiting (For Me) (Edited Remix) (Percapella)/(LP Version) (Extended Remix)	1987	2.00	4.00	8.00
—With George Michael					
❑ AD1-9575	Rock-a-Lott (Street Mix) (Single Version) (Street Mix Radio Edit) (Dub Mix) (Acappella)	1987	2.00	4.00	8.00
❑ ADP 9682 [DJ]	Oh Happy Day/The Lord's Prayer//I've Been in the Storm Too Long/Packing Up, Getting Ready to Go	1988	3.75	7.50	15.00
❑ AD1-9851	It Isn't, It Wasn't, It Ain't Never Gonna Be (Extended Radio) (House Radio Mix)/(Hip Hop Radio) (New Jack Swing Dub)/Think '89	1989	2.00	4.00	8.00
—With Whitney Houston					
❑ ADP 9877 [DJ]	It Isn't, It Wasn't, It Ain't Never Gonna Be (Extended Radio Mix 6:12) (Dub Mix 6:20)/(After Hours Club Mix 7:35) (1989 Vogue Dub Mix 5:36)	1989	3.75	7.50	15.00
—With Whitney Houston					
❑ AD1-9885	Gimme Your Love (Single Edit) (Extended Remix)/Think '89	1989	2.00	4.00	8.00
—With James Brown					
❑ ADP 9906 [DJ]	Gimme Your Love (Single Edit) (Extended Remix)/Interview	1989	3.75	7.50	15.00
—With James Brown					
❑ 12702	Willing to Forgive/Jump to It (2 versions)	1994	2.50	5.00	10.00
❑ 13484 [(2)]	A Rose Is still a Rose (Hex Hector Club Mix 8:55) (Album Version 4:29)/(Johnny Vicious Dub 9:28)/(Love to Infinity Kick Mix 7:11)//(Johnny Vicious Club Mix 10:44) (HEx Hector Drums 3:50)/(Love to Infinity Club Mix) (Love to Infinity Rhythm Radio Mix) (Album Version Instrumental)	1998	3.00	6.00	12.00
❑ 13503	Here We Go Again (Morales Classic Mix 9:25) (Album Version 3:30) (Razor-N-Guide Key Line 1:31) (Razor-N-Guido Mix 9:41) (Mixologist Bass Mix 3:26)	1999	2.50	5.00	10.00

45s
ARISTA

Number	Title (A Side/B Side)	Yr	VG	VG+	NM
❑ 0569	United Together/Take Me With You	1980	—	2.00	4.00
❑ 0591	What a Fool Believes/Love Me Forever	1980	—	2.00	4.00
❑ 0600	Come to Me/School Days	1981	—	2.00	4.00
❑ 0624	Love All the Hurt Away/Whole Lotta Me	1981	—	2.00	4.00
—Aretha Franklin and George Benson					
❑ 0646	It's My Turn/Kind of Man	1981	—	2.00	4.00
❑ 0665	Livin' in the Streets/There's a Star for Everyone	1982	—	2.00	4.00
❑ 0699	Jump To It/Just My Daydream	1982	—	2.00	4.00
❑ 1023	Love Me Right/(It's Just) Your Love	1982	—	2.00	4.00
❑ 1043	This Is for Real/I Just Want to Make It Up to You	1983	—	2.00	4.00
❑ 2239	Everyday People/You Can't Take Me for Granted	1991	—	2.50	5.00
❑ 9034	Get It Right/Giving In	1983	—	2.00	4.00
❑ 9095	Every Girl (Wants My Guy)/I Got Your Love	1983	—	2.00	4.00
❑ 9354	Freeway of Love/Until You Say You Love Me	1985	—	—	3.00
❑ 9354 [DJ]	Freeway of Love (Short) (Long)	1985	5.00	10.00	20.00
—Promo only on pink vinyl					
❑ 9354 [PS]	Freeway of Love/Until You Say You Love Me	1985	—	—	3.00
❑ 9410	Who's Zoomin' Who/Sweet Bitter Love	1985	—	—	3.00
❑ 9410 [PS]	Who's Zoomin' Who/Sweet Bitter Love	1985	—	—	3.00
❑ 9453	Another Night/Kind of Man	1986	—	—	3.00
❑ 9474	Ain't Nobody Ever Loved You/Push	1986	—	—	3.00
—B-side with Peter Wolf					
❑ 9528	Jumpin' Jack Flash/Integrity	1986	—	—	3.00
—Second pressing on black vinyl					
❑ 9528	Jumpin' Jack Flash/Integrity	1986	—	2.50	5.00
—Original stock pressings on clear vinyl					
❑ 9528 [DJ]	Jumpin' Jack Flash (Long Version) (Short Version)	1986	2.50	5.00	10.00
—Promo on clear vinyl					
❑ 9528 [PS]	Jumpin' Jack Flash/Integrity	1986	—	—	3.00
—Picture sleeve with black vinyl pressing lists catalog number as AL-9528					
❑ 9528 [PS]	Jumpin' Jack Flash/Integrity	1986	—	2.50	5.00
—Picture sleeve with clear vinyl pressing lists catalog number as ALC-9528					
❑ 9541	Jumpin' Jack Flash/(Street Mix Radio Edit)	1986	—	2.00	4.00
❑ 9541 [PS]	Jumpin' Jack Flash/(Street Mix Radio Edit)	1986	—	2.50	5.00
❑ 9546	Jimmy Lee/If You Need My Love Tonight	1986	—	2.00	4.00
❑ 9546 [DJ]	Jimmy Lee (Short Version 4:10)/(Long Version 5:47)	1986	—	2.00	4.00
❑ 9546 [PS]	Jimmy Lee/If You Need My Love Tonight	1986	—	2.00	4.00
—B-side by Larry Graham					
❑ 9557	Jimmy Lee/An Angel Cries	1986	—	—	3.00
❑ 9557 [PS]	Jimmy Lee/An Angel Cries	1986	—	—	3.00
❑ 9559	I Knew You Were Waiting (For Me)/(Instrumental)	1987	—	—	3.00
—With George Michael					
❑ 9559 [PS]	I Knew You Were Waiting (For Me)/(Instrumental)	1987	—	—	3.00
—With George Michael					
❑ 9574	Rock-A-Lott/Look to the Rainbow	1987	—	—	3.00
❑ 9574 [PS]	Rock-A-Lott/Look to the Rainbow	1987	—	—	3.00
❑ 9623	If You Need My Love Tonight/He'll Come Along	1987	—	—	3.00
—A-side with Larry Graham					
❑ 9672	Oh Happy Day/The Lord's Prayer	1988	—	2.50	5.00
❑ 9672 [PS]	Oh Happy Day/The Lord's Prayer	1988	—	2.50	5.00
❑ 9809	Through the Storm/Come to Me	1989	—	—	3.00
—A-side with Elton John					
❑ 9809 [PS]	Through the Storm/Come to Me	1989	—	—	3.00

Number	Title (A Side/B Side)	Yr	VG	VG+	NM
9850	It Isn't, It Wasn't, It Ain't Never Gonna Be/If Ever a Love There Was	1989	—	—	3.00
—A-side with Whitney Houston; B-side with the Four Tops					
9850 [PS]	It Isn't, It Wasn't, It Ain't Never Gonna Be/If Ever a Love There Was	1989	—	—	3.00
—A-side with Whitney Houston; B-side with the Four Tops					
9884	Gimme Your Love/Think	1989	—	—	3.00
—With James Brown					
9884 [PS]	Gimme Your Love/Think	1989	—	—	3.00
—With James Brown					
55977	The Only Thing Missin'/Wonderful	2003	—	—	3.00

ATLANTIC

Number	Title (A Side/B Side)	Yr	VG	VG+	NM
2386	I Never Loved a Man (The Way I Love You)/Do Right Woman, Do Right Man	1967	2.50	5.00	10.00
2403	Respect/Dr. Feelgood	1967	2.50	5.00	10.00
2427	Baby I Love You/Going Down Now	1967	2.50	5.00	10.00
2441	(You Make Me Feel Like) A Natural Woman/Baby, Baby, Baby	1967	2.50	5.00	10.00
2464	Chain of Fools/Prove It	1967	2.50	5.00	10.00
2486	(Sweet Sweet Baby) Since You've Been Gone/Ain't No Way	1968	2.50	5.00	10.00
2518	Think/You Send Me	1968	2.50	5.00	10.00
2546	I Say a Little Prayer/The House That Jack Built	1968	2.50	5.00	10.00
2574	See Saw/My Song	1968	2.00	4.00	8.00
2603	The Weight/Tracks of My Tears	1969	2.00	4.00	8.00
2619	I Can't See Myself Leaving You/Gentle On My Mind	1969	2.00	4.00	8.00
2650	Share Your Love with Me/Pledging My Love-The Clock	1969	2.00	4.00	8.00
2683	Eleanor Rigby/It Ain't Fair	1969	2.00	4.00	8.00
2706	Call Me/Son of a Preacher Man	1970	2.00	4.00	8.00
2731	Spirit in the Dark/The Thrill Is Gone	1970	2.00	4.00	8.00
2751	Don't Play That Song/Let It Be	1970	2.00	4.00	8.00
2772	Border Song (Holy Moses)/You and Me	1970	2.00	4.00	8.00
2787	You're All I Need to Get By/Pullin'	1971	—	3.00	6.00
2796	Bridge Over Troubled Water/Brand New Me	1971	—	3.00	6.00
2817	Spanish Harlem/Lean On Me	1971	—	3.00	6.00
2838	Rock Steady/Oh Me Oh My (I'm a Fool for You Baby)	1971	—	3.00	6.00
2866	Day Dreaming/I've Been Loving You Too Long	1972	—	3.00	6.00
2883	All the King's Horses/April Fools	1972	—	3.00	6.00
2901	Wholy Holy/Give Yourself to Jesus	1972	—	3.00	6.00
2941	Master of Eyes (The Deepness of Your Eyes)/Moody's Mood for You	1973	—	3.00	6.00
2969	Angel/Hey Now Hey (Sister from Texas)	1973	—	3.00	6.00
2995	Until You Come Back to Me (That's What I'm Gonna Do)/If You Don't Think	1973	—	3.00	6.00
2999	I'm in Love/Oh Baby	1974	—	3.00	6.00
3200	Ain't Nothing Like the Real Thing/Eight Days on the Road	1974	—	3.00	6.00
3224	Without Love/Don't Go Breaking My Heart	1974	—	3.00	6.00
3249	With Everything I Feel in Me/Sing It Again, Say It Again	1975	—	3.00	6.00
3289	Mr. D.J. (5 for the D.J.)/As Long As You Are There	1975	—	3.00	6.00
3311	You/Without You	1975	—	3.00	6.00
3326	Something He Can Feel/Loving You, Baby	1976	—	3.00	6.00
3358	Jump/Hooked on Your Love	1976	—	3.00	6.00
3373	Look Into Your Heart/Rock with Me	1977	—	3.00	6.00
3393	Break It To Me Gently/Meadows of Springtime	1977	—	3.00	6.00
3418	When I Think About You/Touch Me Up	1978	—	3.00	6.00
3468	Almighty Fire (Woman of the Future)/I'm Your Speed	1978	—	3.00	6.00
3495	More Than Just a Joy/This You Can Believe	1979	—	3.00	6.00
3605	Ladies Only/What If I Should Ever Need You	1979	—	2.50	5.00
3632	Half a Love/Only Star	1979	—	2.50	5.00

CHECKER

Number	Title (A Side/B Side)	Yr	VG	VG+	NM
861	Never Grow Old/You Grow Closer	1957	5.00	10.00	20.00
941	Precious Lord, Part 1/Precious Lord, Part 2	1960	3.75	7.50	15.00

COLUMBIA

Number	Title (A Side/B Side)	Yr	VG	VG+	NM
S7 31202 [S]	Won't Be Long/Love Is the Only Thing	1961	3.00	6.00	12.00
S7 31203 [S]	Sweet Lover/All Night Long	1961	3.00	6.00	12.00
S7 31204 [S]	Who Needs You?/Right Now	1961	3.00	6.00	12.00
S7 31205 [S]	Maybe I'm a Fool/It Ain't Necessarily So	1961	3.00	6.00	12.00
S7 31206 [S]	(Blue) By Myself/Today I Sing the Blues	1961	3.00	6.00	12.00
—The above five are "Stereo Seven" 33 1/3 rpm jukebox singles from set "JS 7-38" entitled "Aretha (with the Ray Bryant Combo)"					
41793	Today I Sing the Blues/Love Is the Only Thing	1960	3.00	6.00	12.00
41923	Won't Be Long/Right Now	1961	3.00	6.00	12.00
41965	Are You Sure/Maybe I'm a Fool	1961	3.00	6.00	12.00
42157	Rock-A-Bye Your Baby with a Dixie Melody/Operation Heartbreak	1961	3.00	6.00	12.00
42266	I Surrender, Dear/Rough Lover	1962	2.50	5.00	10.00
42266 [PS]	I Surrender, Dear/Rough Lover	1962	7.50	15.00	30.00
42456	Don't Cry, Baby/Without the One You Love	1962	2.50	5.00	10.00
42456 [PS]	Don't Cry, Baby/Without the One You Love	1962	7.50	15.00	30.00
42520	Try a Little Tenderness/Just for a Thrill	1962	2.50	5.00	10.00
42520 [PS]	Try a Little Tenderness/Just for a Thrill	1962	6.25	12.50	25.00
42625	Trouble in Mind/God Bless the Child	1962	2.50	5.00	10.00
42796	Here's Where I Came In/Say It Isn't So	1963	2.50	5.00	10.00
42796 [PS]	Here's Where I Came In/Say It Isn't So	1963	7.50	15.00	30.00
42874	Skylark/You've Got Her	1963	2.50	5.00	10.00
42933	Johnny/Kissin' by the Mistletoe	1963	2.50	5.00	10.00
43009	Soulville/Evil Gal Blues	1964	2.50	5.00	10.00
43113	Runnin' Out of Fools/It's Just a Matter of Time	1964	2.50	5.00	10.00
43177	Winter Wonderland/The Christmas Song (Chestnuts Roasting on an Open Fire)	1964	2.50	5.00	10.00
43203	Can't You Just See Me/Little Miss Raggedy Ann	1965	2.50	5.00	10.00
43241	One Step Ahead/I Can't Wait Until I See My Baby's Face	1965	2.50	5.00	10.00
43333	(No, No) I'm Losing You/Sweet Bitter Love	1965	2.50	5.00	10.00
43442	You Made Me Love You/There Is No Greater Love	1966	2.50	5.00	10.00
43515	Hands Off/Tighten Up Your Tie, Button Up Your Jacket	1966	2.50	5.00	10.00
43637	Until You Were Gone/Swanee	1966	2.50	5.00	10.00
43827	Cry Like a Baby/Swanee	1966	2.50	5.00	10.00
44181	Until You Were Gone/Lee Cross	1967	2.50	5.00	10.00
44270	Take a Look/Follow Your Heart	1967	2.50	5.00	10.00
44381	Mockingbird/A Mother's Love	1967	2.00	4.00	8.00
44441	Soulville/If Ever I Would Leave You	1968	2.00	4.00	8.00
44851	Friendly Persuasion/Jim	1969	2.00	4.00	8.00
44951	Today I Sing the Blues/People	1969	2.00	4.00	8.00

JVB

Number	Title (A Side/B Side)	Yr	VG	VG+	NM
47	Never Grow Old/You Grow Closer	1957	7.50	15.00	30.00
75	Precious Lord, Part 1/Precious Lord, Part 2	1959	7.50	15.00	30.00

PHILCO-FORD

Number	Title (A Side/B Side)	Yr	VG	VG+	NM
HP-24	Respect/Soul Serenade	1968	6.25	12.50	25.00
—4-inch plastic "Hip Pocket Record" with color sleeve					

7-Inch Extended Plays

ATLANTIC

Number	Title (A Side/B Side)	Yr	VG	VG+	NM
A 1025 [DJ]	Precious Lord, Take My Hand/You've Got a Friend/Precious Memories//Wholy Holy/Mary, Don't You Weep	1972	3.75	7.50	15.00
—Mono; white label promo sampler					
A 1025 [PS]	Amazing Grace	1972	5.00	10.00	20.00
SD 7-7265	Somewhere/Moody's Mood//Hey Now Hey/So Swell When You're Well	1973	2.50	5.00	10.00
—Jukebox issue; small hole, plays at 33 1/3 rpm					
SD 7-7265 [PS]	Hey Now Hey	1973	2.50	5.00	10.00
SD 7-8207	Satisfaction/Baby, I Love You/Groovin'//Soul Serenade/Dr. Feelgood	196?	3.75	7.50	15.00
—Jukebox issue; small hole, plays at 33 1/3 rpm					
SD 7-8207 [PS]	Aretha in Paris	196?	3.75	7.50	15.00
SD 7-8248	Let It Be/The Weight/Eleanor Rigby//This Girl's in Love with You/Share Your Love with Me	1970	3.00	6.00	12.00
—Jukebox issue; small hole, plays at 33 1/3 rpm					
SD 7-8248 [PS]	This Girl's in Love with You	1970	3.00	6.00	12.00

Albums

ARISTA

Number	Title (A Side/B Side)	Yr	VG	VG+	NM
AL8-8019	Get It Right	1983	2.50	5.00	10.00
AL8-8286	Who's Zoomin' Who	1985	2.50	5.00	10.00
AL-8344	Jump To It	1985	2.00	4.00	8.00
—Budget-line reissue					
AL-8368	Love All the Hurt Away	1985	2.00	4.00	8.00
—Budget-line reissue					
AL-8442	Aretha	1986	2.50	5.00	10.00
—Different album than 9538					
A2L-8497 [(2)]	One Lord, One Faith, One Baptism	1987	5.00	10.00	20.00
AL-8572	Through the Storm	1989	2.50	5.00	10.00
AL-9538	Aretha	1980	2.50	5.00	10.00
AL-9552	Love All the Hurt Away	1981	2.50	5.00	10.00
AL-9602	Jump To It	1982	2.50	5.00	10.00

ATLANTIC

Number	Title (A Side/B Side)	Yr	VG	VG+	NM
SD 2-906 [(2)]	Amazing Grace	1972	5.00	10.00	20.00
QD 7205 [Q]	Aretha Live at Fillmore West	1973	6.25	12.50	25.00
SD 7205	Aretha Live at Fillmore West	1971	3.75	7.50	15.00
7213 [M]	Yoing, Gifted & Black	1972	10.00	20.00	40.00
—Mono is promo only; "d/j copy monaural" sticker on front cover					
SD 7213 [S]	Yoing, Gifted & Black	1972	3.75	7.50	15.00
SD 7265	Hey Now Hey (The Other Side of the Sky)	1973	3.00	6.00	12.00
SD 7292	Let Me in Your Life	1974	3.00	6.00	12.00
8139 [M]	I Never Loved a Man the Way I Love You	1967	6.25	12.50	25.00
SD 8139 [S]	I Never Loved a Man the Way I Love You	1967	5.00	10.00	20.00
—Green and blue label					
SD 8139	I Never Loved a Man the Way I Love You	1969	3.00	6.00	12.00
—Green and red label					
8150 [M]	Aretha Arrives	1967	6.25	12.50	25.00
SD 8150 [S]	Aretha Arrives	1967	5.00	10.00	20.00
—Green and blue label					
SD 8150	Aretha Arrives	1969	3.00	6.00	12.00
—Green and red label					
8176 [M]	Aretha: Lady Soul	1968	7.50	15.00	30.00
SD 8176 [S]	Aretha: Lady Soul	1968	5.00	10.00	20.00
—Green and blue label					
SD 8176	Aretha: Lady Soul	1969	3.00	6.00	12.00
—Green and red label					
SD 8186	Aretha Now	1968	5.00	10.00	20.00
—Green and blue label					
SD 8186	Aretha Now	1969?	3.00	6.00	12.00
—Green and red label					
SD 8207	Aretha in Paris	1968	3.75	7.50	15.00
8212 [M]	Aretha Franklin: Soul '69	1969	12.50	25.00	50.00
—White label promo; no stock copies in mono					
SD 8212 [S]	Aretha Franklin: Soul '69	1969	3.75	7.50	15.00
SD 8227	Aretha's Gold	1969	3.75	7.50	15.00
SD 8248	This Girl's in Love with You	1970	3.75	7.50	15.00
SD 8265	Spirit in the Dark	1970	3.75	7.50	15.00
8295 [M]	Aretha's Greatest Hits	1971	10.00	20.00	40.00
—Mono is white label promo only in stereo cover with "d/j monaural" sticker					
SD 8295 [S]	Aretha's Greatest Hits	1971	—	7.50	15.00
QD 8305 [Q]	The Best of Aretha Franklin	1974	5.00	10.00	20.00
SD 18116	With Everything I Feel in Me	1974	3.00	6.00	12.00
SD 18151	You	1975	3.00	6.00	12.00
SD 18176	Sparkle	1976	3.00	6.00	12.00
SD 18204	Ten Years of Gold	1976	3.00	6.00	12.00
SD 19102	Sweet Passion	1977	3.00	6.00	12.00
SD 19161	Almighty Fire	1978	3.00	6.00	12.00
SD 19248	La Diva	1979	3.00	6.00	12.00
81230	Aretha's Jazz	1984	2.50	5.00	10.00
81280	The Best of Aretha Franklin	1985	2.50	5.00	10.00
81668 [(2)]	30 Greatest Hits	1986	3.75	7.50	15.00
STAO-95151	Hey Now Hey (The Other Side of the Sky)	1973	3.75	7.50	15.00
—Capitol Record Club edition					

CHECKER

Number	Title (A Side/B Side)	Yr	VG	VG+	NM
10009 [M]	Songs of Faith	1965	125.00	250.00	500.00
—Original issue of this album; cover has Aretha sitting at a piano					
10009 [M]	Gospel Soul	1967	5.00	10.00	20.00
—Reissue with new title and cover					

COLUMBIA

Number	Title (A Side/B Side)	Yr	VG	VG+	NM
GP 4 [(2)]	Two All-Time Great Albums in One Great Package	196?	6.25	12.50	25.00
—Contains CS 9081 and CS 9429					

F

Number	Title (A Side/B Side)	Yr	VG	VG+	NM
❏ CL 1612 [M]	Aretha	1961	12.50	25.00	50.00
—Red and black label with six "eye" logos					
❏ CL 1612 [M]	Aretha	1963	5.00	10.00	20.00
—"Guaranteed High Fidelity" on label					
❏ CL 1612 [M]	Aretha	1965	3.75	7.50	15.00
—"360 Sound Mono" on label					
❏ CL 1761 [M]	The Electrifying Aretha Franklin	1962	10.00	20.00	40.00
—Red and black label with six "eye" logos					
❏ CL 1761 [M]	The Electrifying Aretha Franklin	1963	5.00	10.00	20.00
—"Guaranteed High Fidelity" on label					
❏ CL 1761 [M]	The Electrifying Aretha Franklin	1965	3.75	7.50	15.00
—"360 Sound Mono" on label					
❏ CL 1876 [M]	The Tender, The Moving, The Swinging Aretha Franklin	1962	10.00	20.00	40.00
—Red and black label with six "eye" logos					
❏ CL 1876 [M]	The Tender, The Moving, The Swinging Aretha Franklin	1963	5.00	10.00	20.00
—"Guaranteed High Fidelity" on label					
❏ CL 1876 [M]	The Tender, The Moving, The Swinging Aretha Franklin	1965	3.75	7.50	15.00
—"360 Sound Mono" on label					
❏ CL 2079 [M]	Laughing on the Outside	1963	5.00	10.00	20.00
—"Guaranteed High Fidelity" on label					
❏ CL 2079 [M]	Laughing on the Outside	1965	3.75	7.50	15.00
—"360 Sound Mono" on label					
❏ CL 2163 [M]	Unforgettable	1964	5.00	10.00	20.00
—"Guaranteed High Fidelity" on label					
❏ CL 2163 [M]	Unforgettable	1965	3.75	7.50	15.00
—"360 Sound Mono" on label					
❏ CL 2281 [M]	Runnin' Out of Fools	1964	5.00	10.00	20.00
—"Guaranteed High Fidelity" on label					
❏ CL 2281 [M]	Runnin' Out of Fools	1965	3.75	7.50	15.00
—"360 Sound Mono" on label					
❏ CL 2351 [M]	Yeah!!!	1965	5.00	10.00	20.00
—"Guaranteed High Fidelity" on label					
❏ CL 2351 [M]	Yeah!!!	1966	3.75	7.50	15.00
—"360 Sound Mono" on label					
❏ CL 2521 [M]	Soul Sister	1966	5.00	10.00	20.00
❏ CL 2629 [M]	Take It Like You Give It	1967	6.25	12.50	25.00
❏ CL 2673 [M]	Aretha Franklin's Greatest Hits	1967	6.25	12.50	25.00
❏ CL 2754 [M]	Take a Look	1967	7.50	15.00	30.00
❏ CS 8412 [S]	Aretha	1961	20.00	40.00	80.00
—Red and black label with six "eye" logos					
❏ CS 8412 [S]	Aretha	1963	6.25	12.50	25.00
—"360 Sound Stereo" on label					
❏ CS 8561 [S]	The Electrifying Aretha Franklin	1962	12.50	25.00	50.00
—Red and black label with six "eye" logos					
❏ CS 8561 [S]	The Electrifying Aretha Franklin	1963	6.25	12.50	25.00
—"360 Sound Stereo" on label					
❏ CS 8676 [S]	The Tender, The Moving, The Swinging Aretha Franklin	1962	12.50	25.00	50.00
—Red and black label with six "eye" logos					
❏ CS 8676 [S]	The Tender, The Moving, The Swinging Aretha Franklin	1963	6.25	12.50	25.00
—"360 Sound Stereo" on label					
❏ CS 8879 [S]	Laughing on the Outside	1963	6.25	12.50	25.00
—"360 Sound Stereo" on label					
❏ CS 8963 [S]	Unforgettable	1964	6.25	12.50	25.00
—"360 Sound Stereo" on label					
❏ CS 9081 [S]	Runnin' Out of Fools	1964	6.25	12.50	25.00
—"360 Sound Stereo" on label					
❏ CS 9151 [S]	Yeah!!!	1965	6.25	12.50	25.00
—"360 Sound Stereo" on label					
❏ CS 9321 [S]	Soul Sister	1966	6.25	12.50	25.00
—"360 Sound Stereo" on label					
❏ CS 9429 [S]	Take It Like You Give It	1967	5.00	10.00	20.00
—"360 Sound Stereo" on label					
❏ CS 9473 [S]	Aretha Franklin's Greatest Hits	1967	5.00	10.00	20.00
—"360 Sound Stereo" on label					
❏ CS 9554 [S]	Take a Look	1967	5.00	10.00	20.00
—"360 Sound Stereo" on label					
❏ CS 9601	Aretha Franklin's Greatest Hits, Volume 2	1968	5.00	10.00	20.00
—"360 Sound Stereo" on label					
❏ CS 9776	Soft and Beautiful	1969	5.00	10.00	20.00
—"360 Sound Stereo" on label					
❏ CS 9956	Today I Sing the Blues	1970	3.75	7.50	15.00
—"360 Sound Stereo" on label					
❏ KG 31355 [(2)]	In the Beginning/The World of Aretha Franklin 1960-1967	1972	5.00	10.00	20.00
❏ KC 31953	The First 12 Sides	1973	3.00	6.00	12.00
❏ C2 37377 [(2)]	The Legendary Queen of Soul	1981	3.00	6.00	12.00
❏ PC 38042	Sweet Bitter Love	1982	2.50	5.00	10.00
❏ FC 40105	Aretha Franklin Sings the Blues	1985	2.50	5.00	10.00
❏ FC 40708	Aretha After Hours	1987	2.50	5.00	10.00
COLUMBIA SPECIAL PRODUCTS					
❏ C 10589	Take a Look	1971	3.00	6.00	12.00
HARMONY					
❏ HS 11349	Once in a Lifetime	1969	3.00	6.00	12.00
❏ HS 11418	Two Sides of Love	1970	3.00	6.00	12.00
❏ KH 30606	Greatest Hits 1960-1965	1971	3.00	6.00	12.00
❏ KH 30606	Greatest Hits 1960-1966	1972	3.00	6.00	12.00

FRANKLIN, CAROLYN

45s

RCA VICTOR

Number	Title (A Side/B Side)	Yr	VG	VG+	NM
❏ 47-9734	The Boxer/I Don't Want to Lose You	1969	—	3.00	6.00
❏ 74-0188	Reality/It's True I'm Gonna Miss You	1969	—	3.00	6.00
❏ 74-0289	Ain't That Groovy/All I Want Is to Be Your Woman	1969	—	3.00	6.00
❏ 74-0314	Everybody's Talkin'/Chain Reaction	1970	—	2.50	5.00
❏ 74-0373	You Really Didn't Mean It/All I Want Is to Be Your Woman	1970	—	2.50	5.00
❏ 74-0783	As Long As You're There/I Want to Be With You	1972	—	2.50	5.00
❏ APBO-0022	You Are Everything/If You Want Me	1973	—	2.50	5.00
❏ PB-10688	I Can't Help My Feeling So Blue/If You Want Me	1976	—	2.00	4.00

Albums

RCA VICTOR

Number	Title (A Side/B Side)	Yr	VG	VG+	NM
❏ LSP-4160	Baby Dynamite	1969	5.00	10.00	20.00
❏ LSP-4317	Chain Reaction	1970	5.00	10.00	20.00
❏ LSP-4411	I'd Rather Be Lonely	1973	5.00	10.00	20.00

FRANKLIN, DOUG, AND THE BLUENOTES

45s

COLONIAL

Number	Title (A Side/B Side)	Yr	VG	VG+	NM
❏ 7777	My Lucky Love/Drizzlin' Rain	1958	5.00	10.00	20.00
❏ 7779	Christmas Chimes/Let Her Know	1958	6.25	12.50	25.00
❏ 8888	I Used to Wonder/I Wonder Who's Kissing Her Now	1959	5.00	10.00	20.00
❏ 9999	Darling of Mine/Never Never Land	1959	5.00	10.00	20.00

FRANKLIN, ERMA

45s

BRUNSWICK

Number	Title (A Side/B Side)	Yr	VG	VG+	NM
❏ 55403	Change My Thoughts from You/Gotta Find Me a Lover	1969	2.00	4.00	8.00
❏ 55415	Saving My Love/You've Been Cancelled	1969	2.00	4.00	8.00
❏ 55424	I Just Don't Need You (At All)/It Could've Been Me	1969	2.00	4.00	8.00
❏ 55430	Whispers (Gettin' Louder)/(I Get the) Sweetest Feeling	1970	2.00	4.00	8.00
EPIC					
❏ 5-9468	Don't Blame Me/What Kind of Girl (Do You Think I Am)	1961	5.00	10.00	20.00
❏ 5-9488	Hello Again/It's Over	1962	5.00	10.00	20.00
❏ 5-9511	Each Night I Cry/Time After Time	1962	5.00	10.00	20.00
❏ 5-9516	Dear Mama/Never Again	1962	5.00	10.00	20.00
❏ 5-9559	Don't Wait Too Long/Time After Time	1962	5.00	10.00	20.00
❏ 5-9594	Have You Ever Had the Blues/I Don't Want No Mama's Boy	1963	3.75	7.50	15.00
❏ 5-9610	Abracadabra/Love Is Blind	1963	3.75	7.50	15.00
SHOUT					
❏ 218	Big Boss Man/Didn't Catch the Dog's Bone	1967	2.50	5.00	10.00
❏ 221	Piece of My Heart/Baby What You Want Me to Do	1967	3.00	6.00	12.00
❏ 230	Open Up Your Soul/I'm Just Not Ready for Love	1967	2.50	5.00	10.00
❏ 234	Right to Cry/I'm Just Not Ready for Love	1968	2.50	5.00	10.00

Albums

BRUNSWICK

Number	Title (A Side/B Side)	Yr	VG	VG+	NM
❏ BL 754147	Soul Sister	1969	5.00	10.00	20.00
EPIC					
❏ BN 619 [S]	Her Name Is Erma	1962	10.00	20.00	40.00
❏ LN 3824 [M]	Her Name Is Erma	1962	7.50	15.00	30.00

FRANKS, MICHAEL

12-Inch Singles

REPRISE

Number	Title (A Side/B Side)	Yr	VG	VG+	NM
❏ PRO-A-4084 [DJ]	The Art of Love (same on both sides)	1990	2.00	4.00	8.00
❏ PRO-A-4564 [DJ]	Speak to Me (4 versions)	1990	3.75	7.50	15.00
❏ PRO-A-6175 [DJ]	Practice Makes Perfect (4 versions)	1993	—	3.50	7.00
WARNER BROS.					
❏ PRO-A-2834 [DJ]	Doctor Sax/Face to Face	1987	—	3.00	6.00

45s

BRUT

Number	Title (A Side/B Side)	Yr	VG	VG+	NM
❏ 809	Can't Seem to Shake This Rock 'n' Roll/King of Oklahoma	1973	3.75	7.50	15.00
JOHN HAMMOND					
❏ WS4 03794	Can't Seem to Shake This Rock 'n' Roll/Just Like Key Largo	1983	—	2.50	5.00
❏ WS4 03794 [PS]	Can't Seem to Shake This Rock 'n' Roll/Just Like Key Largo	1983	—	2.50	5.00
REPRISE					
❏ 1360	Popsicle Toes/I Don't Know Why I'm So Happy I'm Sad	1976	—	2.50	5.00
WARNER BROS.					
❏ 8583	When the Cookie Jar Is Empty/Burchfield Nines	1978	—	2.50	5.00
❏ 8811	When It's Over/(B-side unknown)	1979	—	2.50	5.00
❏ 27997	The Camera Never Lies/Innuendo	1988	—	2.50	5.00
❏ 28184	Face to Face/Innuendo	1987	—	2.50	5.00
❏ 28285	Island Life/Innuendo	1987	—	2.50	5.00
❏ 28819	When I Give My Love to You/When She Is Mine	1986	—	2.00	4.00
—With Brenda Russell					
❏ 28819 [PS]	When I Give My Love to You/When She Is Mine	1986	—	2.00	4.00
❏ 28928	Your Secret's Safe with Me/Please Don't Say Goodnight	1985	—	2.00	4.00
❏ 29004	Queen of the Underground/Now I Know Why	1985	—	2.50	5.00
❏ 29400	When Sly Calls/Never Satisfied	1983	2.00	4.00	8.00
❏ 29989	Jealousy/Wonderland	1982	—	2.50	5.00
❏ 49271	One Bad Habit/Still Lifes	1980	—	2.50	5.00
❏ 49556	Baseball/Loving You More and More	1980	—	2.00	4.00
❏ 50025	Love Duet/No One But You	1982	—	2.50	5.00
—With S. Renee Diggs					

Albums

BRUT

Number	Title (A Side/B Side)	Yr	VG	VG+	NM
❏ 6005	Michael Franks	1973	5.00	10.00	20.00
DIRECT DISK					
❏ SD-16611	Tiger in the Rain	1980	7.50	15.00	30.00
—Audiophile vinyl					
DRG					
❏ SL-5210	Previously Unavailable	1989	3.00	6.00	12.00
—Reissue of John Hammond LP					
JOHN HAMMOND					
❏ BFW 38664	Previously Unavailable	1983	3.75	7.50	15.00
REPRISE					
❏ MS 2230	The Art of Tea	1975	2.50	5.00	10.00
WARNER BROS.					
❏ BS 3004	Sleeping Gypsy	1977	2.50	5.00	10.00
❏ BSK 3167	Burchfield Nines	1978	2.50	5.00	10.00
❏ BSK 3294	Tiger in the Rain	1979	2.50	5.00	10.00
❏ BSK 3427	One Bad Habit	1980	2.50	5.00	10.00
❏ BSK 3648	Objects of Desire	1981	2.50	5.00	10.00
❏ 23962	Passion Fruit	1983	2.00	4.00	8.00

Number	Title (A Side/B Side)	Yr	VG	VG+	NM
❏ 25275	Skin Dive	1985	2.00	4.00	8.00
❏ 25570	The Camera Never Lies	1987	2.00	4.00	8.00

FRANLKIN, DOUG, WITH THE BLUENOTES
45s
COLONIAL

Number	Title (A Side/B Side)	Yr	VG	VG+	NM
❏ 7777	My Lucky Love/Drizzin' Rain	1958	5.00	10.00	20.00

FRANTIC
45s
LIZARD

Number	Title (A Side/B Side)	Yr	VG	VG+	NM
❏ 20002	Shady Sam/(B-side unknown)	1970	3.75	7.50	15.00

Albums
LIZARD

Number	Title (A Side/B Side)	Yr	VG	VG+	NM
❏ 20103	Conception	1971	6.25	12.50	25.00

FRANTICS, THE
45s
BOLO

Number	Title (A Side/B Side)	Yr	VG	VG+	NM
❏ 728	Pony Moronie/Meet Me in Seattle Twist	1962	2.50	5.00	10.00
❏ 736	Oh Yeah/Let Our Love Roll On	1962	2.50	5.00	10.00
DOLTON					
❏ 2	Straight Flush/Young Blues	1959	5.00	10.00	20.00
❏ 6	Fog Cutter/Black Sapphire	1959	5.00	10.00	20.00
❏ 13	Checkerboard/Werewolf	1959	5.00	10.00	20.00
❏ 16	Werewolf/No Werewolf	1960	3.75	7.50	15.00
❏ 24	The Whip/Delilah	1960	3.75	7.50	15.00
❏ 31	Yankee Doodlin'/One Minute of Flamenco	1961	3.75	7.50	15.00
❏ 33	San Antonio Rose/Trees	1961	3.75	7.50	15.00
SEAFAIR					
❏ 111	San Francisco Swim/Blue Day	1964	2.50	5.00	10.00

FRATERNITY OF MAN, THE
45s
ABC

Number	Title (A Side/B Side)	Yr	VG	VG+	NM
❏ 11106	Don't Bogart Me/Wispy Paisley Skies	1968	2.00	4.00	8.00

Albums
ABC

Number	Title (A Side/B Side)	Yr	VG	VG+	NM
❏ S-647	The Fraternity of Man	1968	7.50	15.00	30.00
DOT					
❏ DLP-25955	Get It On	1969	6.25	12.50	25.00

FRAWLEY, WILLIAM
Albums
DOT

Number	Title (A Side/B Side)	Yr	VG	VG+	NM
❏ DLP-3061 [M]	William Frawley Sings the Old Ones	1958	10.00	20.00	40.00

FRAZIER, DALLAS
45s
CAPITOL

Number	Title (A Side/B Side)	Yr	VG	VG+	NM
❏ 2011	Everybody Oughta Sing a Song/Only a Fool	1967	2.50	5.00	10.00
❏ 2133	The Sunshine of My World/Lonelier and More in Love	1968	2.50	5.00	10.00
❏ 2257	I Hope I Like Mexico Blues/I Just Thought That I Love Her ('Till I Lost You)	1968	2.50	5.00	10.00
❏ 2402	The Conspiracy of Homer Jones/Sundown of My Mind	1969	2.50	5.00	10.00
❏ F2813	Space Command/Ain't You Had No Bringin' Up at All	1954	5.00	10.00	20.00
❏ F2895	Love Life at 14/I'm Gonna Move Over Yonder	1954	5.00	10.00	20.00
❏ F2956	My Birthday Comes on Christmas/Jingle o' the Brownie	1954	5.00	10.00	20.00
—With Joe "Fingers" Carr					
❏ 5444	King of the Jungle/Make Believe You're Here with Me	1965	3.00	6.00	12.00
❏ 5560	Elvira/That Ain't No Stuff	1966	3.75	7.50	15.00
❏ 5670	Walkin' Wonder/Just a Little Bit of You	1966	3.00	6.00	12.00
❏ 5728	Tennessee Sue/Especially for You	1966	3.00	6.00	12.00
❏ 5862	My Woman Up't and Gone/Clawhammer Clyde	1967	3.00	6.00	12.00
JAMIE					
❏ 1135	Can't Go On/Without Your Love	1959	5.00	10.00	20.00
MERCURY					
❏ 72279	My Little Swing Broke Down/Money Greases the Wheels	1964	3.00	6.00	12.00
RCA VICTOR					
❏ 47-9881	The Birthmark Henry Thompson Talks About/If My Heart Had Windows	1970	2.00	4.00	8.00
❏ 47-9950	Big Mable Murphy/White Fences and Evergreen Trees	1971	2.00	4.00	8.00
❏ 47-9991	My Baby Packed Up My Mind and Left Me/I'm Finally Over You	1971	2.00	4.00	8.00
❏ 74-0259	California Cotton Fields/Sweetheart Don't Throw Yourself Away	1969	2.00	4.00	8.00
❏ 74-0569	Common, Broke Elastic, Rotten Cotton, Hound Dog Snoopin', Ankle Droopin', Funky Fuzzy, White Sock Blues No. 2/High Steppin' Mama	1971	2.00	4.00	8.00
❏ 74-0748	North Carolina/The Last Time I Called Somebody Darlin'	1972	2.00	4.00	8.00
❏ 74-0903	This Time the Hurtin's on Me/Lonesome Fiddle Man	1973	2.00	4.00	8.00
20TH CENTURY					
❏ 2171	Cash on Delivery/Watching My World Walk Away	1975	—	3.00	6.00
❏ 2199	Liberal Acres/Heaven Hangin' Over My Head	1975	—	3.00	6.00

Albums
CAPITOL

Number	Title (A Side/B Side)	Yr	VG	VG+	NM
❏ ST 2552 [S]	Elvira	1966	6.25	12.50	25.00
❏ T 2552 [M]	Elvira	1966	5.00	10.00	20.00
❏ ST 2764 [S]	Tell It Like It Is	1967	5.00	10.00	20.00
❏ T 2764 [M]	Tell It Like It Is	1967	6.25	12.50	25.00

FREAK SCENE, THE
45s
COLUMBIA

Number	Title (A Side/B Side)	Yr	VG	VG+	NM
❏ 4-44056	A Million Grains of Sand/Behind the Mind	1967	6.25	12.50	25.00

Albums
COLUMBIA

Number	Title (A Side/B Side)	Yr	VG	VG+	NM
❏ CL 2656 [M]	Psychedelic Psoul	1967	17.50	35.00	70.00
❏ CS 9456 [S]	Psychedelic Psoul	1967	25.00	50.00	100.00

FREBERG, STAN
45s
CAPITOL

Number	Title (A Side/B Side)	Yr	VG	VG+	NM
❏ F1356	John & Marsha/Ragtime Dan	1951	7.50	15.00	30.00
❏ F1697	St. George and the Dragonet/Little Blue Riding Hood	1954	5.00	10.00	20.00
—Reissue (despite the lower number)					
❏ F1711	That's My Boy/I've Got You Under My Skin	1951	7.50	15.00	30.00
❏ F1962	Maggie/Tele-Vee-Shun	1951	7.50	15.00	30.00
❏ F2029	Try/Pass the Udder Udder	1952	7.50	15.00	30.00
❏ F2125	Abe Snake for President/Ba Ba Ball and Chain	1952	12.50	25.00	50.00
❏ F2279	The World Is Waiting for the Sunrise/Boogie Woogie Banjo Man from Birmingham	1952	6.25	12.50	25.00
❏ F2596	St. George and the Dragonet/Little Blue Riding Hood	1953	7.50	15.00	30.00
❏ F2671	Christmas Dragnet Part 1/Christmas Dragnet Part 2	1953	7.50	15.00	30.00
❏ F2677	C'est Si Bon (It's So Good)/A Dear John & Marsha Letter	1953	6.25	12.50	25.00
❏ F2838	Point of Order/Person to Pearson	1954	6.25	12.50	25.00
❏ F2929	Sh-Boom/Widescreen Mama Blues	1954	6.25	12.50	25.00
❏ F2986	Yulenet (Part 1)/Yulenet (Part 2)	1954	6.25	12.50	25.00
—Same recording as "Christmas Dragnet" (Capitol 2671)					
❏ F3138	The Honey Earthers/The Lone Psychiatrist	1955	7.50	15.00	30.00
—With Daws Butler					
❏ F3249	The Yellow Rose of Texas/Rock Around Stephen Foster	1955	6.25	12.50	25.00
❏ F3280	Nuttin' for Christmas/The Night Before Christmas	1955	6.25	12.50	25.00
❏ 3355	Try/John and Marsha	1972	2.50	5.00	10.00
❏ F3396	The Great Pretender/The Quest for Bridey Hammerschlaugen	1956	6.25	12.50	25.00
❏ F3480	Heartbreak Hotel/Rock Island Line	1956	6.25	12.50	25.00
❏ 3503	Green Chritma (Part 1)/Green Chritma (Part 2)	1972	2.50	5.00	10.00
❏ F3687	Banana Boat (Day-O)/Tele-Vee-Shun	1957	6.25	12.50	25.00
❏ F3815	Wun'erful, Wun'erful! (Part uh-one)/Wun'erful, Wun'erful! (Part uh-two)	1957	6.25	12.50	25.00
❏ F3892	Ya Got Trouble/Gary Indiana	1958	5.00	10.00	20.00
❏ F4097	Green Chritma/The Meaning of Christmas	1958	5.00	10.00	20.00
❏ F4097 [PS]	Green Chritma/The Meaning of Christmas	1958	7.50	15.00	30.00
❏ 4329	The Old Payola Roll Blues Part 1/The Old Payola Roll Blues Part 2	1960	5.00	10.00	20.00
❏ 4329 [PS]	The Old Payola Roll Blues Part 1/The Old Payola Roll Blues Part 2	1960	7.50	15.00	30.00
❏ 4433	Comments for Our Time Part 1/Comments for Our TIme Part 2	1960	5.00	10.00	20.00
❏ 5726	Flackman and Reagan Part 1/Flackman and Reagan Part 2	1966	5.00	10.00	20.00
❏ 5726 [PS]	Flackman and Reagan Part 1/Flackman and Reagan Part 2	1966	7.50	15.00	30.00
❏ S7-19761	Green Chritma/The Meaning of Christmas	1997	—	—	3.00
❏ S7-57891	Nuttin' for Christmas/I Yust Go Nuts at Christmas	1992	—	2.00	4.00
—B-side by Yogi Yorgesson					

7-Inch Extended Plays
CAPITOL

Number	Title (A Side/B Side)	Yr	VG	VG+	NM
❏ EAP 1-496	John and Marsha/The World Is Waiting for the Sunrise//Try/I've Got You Under My Skin	1954	7.50	15.00	30.00
❏ EAP 1-496 [PS]	Any Requests?	1954	7.50	15.00	30.00
❏ EAP 1-628	St. George and the Dragonet/C'est Si Bon (It's So Good)//Sh-Boom/That's My Boy	1955	7.50	15.00	30.00
❏ EAP 1-628 [PS]	Real St. George	1955	7.50	15.00	30.00
❏ EAP 1-1101	Overture/Whatta They Got in Omaha?/Omaha Moon/I Look in Your Face (And I See Omaha)/Reprise	195?	7.50	15.00	30.00
❏ EAP 1-1101 [PS]	Omaha!	195?	7.50	15.00	30.00
❏ MA 1-1589	St. George and the Dragonet/Banana Boat//John and Marsha/The Yellow Rose of Texas	196?	7.50	15.00	30.00
—Jukebox issue; small hole, plays at 33 1/3 rpm					
❏ MA 1-1589 [PS]	Stan Freberg	196?	7.50	15.00	30.00

Albums
CAPITOL

Number	Title (A Side/B Side)	Yr	VG	VG+	NM
❏ T 777 [M]	A Child's Garden of Freberg	1957	12.50	25.00	50.00
—Turquoise label					
❏ WBO 1035 [(2)M]	The Best of the Stan Freberg Shows	1958	15.00	30.00	60.00
❏ SM-1242 [R]	Stan Freberg with the Original Cast	197?	2.50	5.00	10.00
❏ T 1242 [M]	Stan Freberg with the Original Cast	1959	7.50	15.00	30.00
❏ SW 1573 [S]	Stan Freberg Presents the United States of America	1961	7.50	15.00	30.00
❏ W 1573 [M]	Stan Freberg Presents the United States of America	1961	6.25	12.50	25.00
❏ T 1694 [M]	Face the Funnies	1962	6.25	12.50	25.00
❏ T 1816 [M]	Madison Ave. Werewolf	1962	6.25	12.50	25.00
❏ SM-2020 [R]	The Best of Stan Freberg	197?	2.50	5.00	10.00
❏ T 2020 [M]	The Best of Stan Freberg	1964	6.25	12.50	25.00
❏ SM-2551 [S]	The Stan Freberg Underground Show #1	197?	2.50	5.00	10.00
❏ ST 2551 [S]	The Stan Freberg Underground Show #1	1966	6.25	12.50	25.00
❏ T 2551 [M]	The Stan Freberg Underground Show #1	1966	5.00	10.00	20.00
❏ SM-11765	The Best of the Stan Freberg Shows	197?	3.00	6.00	12.00

FRED, JOHN, AND HIS PLAYBOY BAND
45s
BELL

Number	Title (A Side/B Side)	Yr	VG	VG+	NM
❏ 45382	I'm in Love Again/In the Mood	1973	—	2.50	5.00
—As "John Fred and the Creepers"					
JEWEL					
❏ 730	The Fool/There'll Be No Teardrops Tonight	1964	2.50	5.00	10.00
❏ 736	Lenne/You're Mad at Me	1964	2.50	5.00	10.00
❏ 737	Boogie Children/My First Love	1964	2.50	5.00	10.00
—As "The Playboys"					
❏ 743	Wrong to Me/How Can I Prove	1965	2.50	5.00	10.00

F

Number	Title (A Side/B Side)	Yr	VG	VG+	NM
MONTEL					
❏ 904	Down in New Orleans/I Love You	1959	3.75	7.50	15.00
❏ 1002	Shirley/My Love for You	1959	3.75	7.50	15.00
❏ 1007	Good Lovin'/You Know You Made Me Cry	1961	2.50	5.00	10.00
❏ 2001	Mirror Mirror (On the Wall)/To Have and to Hold	1962	2.50	5.00	10.00
N-JOY					
❏ 1005	Boogie Children/My First Love	1965	2.50	5.00	10.00
PAULA					
❏ 225	Fortune Teller/Making Love to You	1965	2.00	4.00	8.00
❏ 234	Can't I Get a Word In/Sun City	1966	2.00	4.00	8.00
❏ 244	Doin' the Best I Can/Leave Her Never	1966	2.00	4.00	8.00
❏ 247	Outta My Head/Love Comes in Time	1966	2.00	4.00	8.00
❏ 259	Up and Down/Wind-Up Doll	1967	2.00	4.00	8.00
❏ 273	Agnes English/Sad Story	1967	2.00	4.00	8.00
❏ 282	Judy in Disguise (With Glasses)/When the Lights Go Out	1967	2.00	4.00	8.00
—Pink label					
❏ 282	Judy in Disguise (With Glasses)/When the Lights Go Out	1967	2.50	5.00	10.00
—Yellow label					
❏ 282	Judy in Disguise (With Glasses)/When the Lights Go Out	1967	3.00	6.00	12.00
—White label					
❏ 294	Hey Hey Bunny/No Letter Today	1968	2.00	4.00	8.00
❏ 303	Lonely Are the Lonely/We Played Games	1968	2.00	4.00	8.00
❏ 310	Tissue Paper/Little Dum Dum	1968	2.00	4.00	8.00
❏ 315	What Is Happiness/Sometimes You Just Can't Win	1968	2.00	4.00	8.00
PHILCO-FORD					
❏ HP-25	Judy in Disguise/No Letter Today	1968	5.00	10.00	20.00
—4-inch plastic "Hip Pocket Record" with color sleeve					
SUGARCANE					
❏ 1001	Keep It Hid/You Had to Be a Woman	1975	—	2.00	4.00
❏ 1002	Jukebox Shirley/Hey, Good Lookin'	1975	—	2.00	4.00
UNI					
❏ 55135	Back in the U.S.S.R./Silly Sarah Carter	1969	—	3.00	6.00
❏ 55160	Open Doors/Three Deep Is a Feeling	1969	—	3.00	6.00
❏ 55187	Love My Soul/Julia Julia	1969	—	3.00	6.00
❏ 55220	Come with Me/Where's Everybody Going	1970	—	3.00	6.00
Albums					
JIN					
❏ 9027	The Best of John Fred and His Playboys	198?	2.50	5.00	10.00
PAULA					
❏ LP-2191 [M]	John Fred and His Playboys	1966	5.00	10.00	20.00
❏ LPS-2191 [S]	John Fred and His Playboys	1966	6.25	12.50	25.00
❏ LP-2193 [M]	34:40 of John Fred and His Playboys	1967	5.00	10.00	20.00
❏ LPS-2193 [S]	34:40 of John Fred and His Playboys	1967	6.25	12.50	25.00
❏ LP-2197 [M]	Agnes English	1967	6.25	12.50	25.00
❏ LPS-2197 [S]	Agnes English	1967	5.00	10.00	20.00
❏ LPS-2197 [S]	Judy in Disguise with Glasses	1968	5.00	10.00	20.00
—Retitled version of "Agnes English".					
❏ LPS-2201	Permanently Stated	1969	5.00	10.00	20.00
UNI					
❏ 73077	Love in My Soul	1970	10.00	20.00	40.00

FREDDIE AND THE DREAMERS
45s

Number	Title (A Side/B Side)	Yr	VG	VG+	NM
CAPITOL					
❏ 5053	I'm Telling You Now/What Have I Done to You	1963	5.00	10.00	20.00
❏ 5137	You Were Made for Me/Send a Letter to Me	1964	5.00	10.00	20.00
MERCURY					
❏ 72285	I Love You Baby/Don't Make Me Cry	1965	2.50	5.00	10.00
❏ 72285 [PS]	I Love You Baby/Don't Make Me Cry	1965	5.00	10.00	20.00
❏ 72327	Don't Do That to Me/Just for You	1965	2.50	5.00	10.00
❏ 72377	I Understand (Just How You Feel)/I Will	1965	2.50	5.00	10.00
❏ 72428	Do the Freddie/Tell Me When	1965	2.50	5.00	10.00
❏ 72428	Do the Freddie/A Love Like You	1965	3.00	6.00	12.00
❏ 72462	A Little You/Things I'd Like to Say	1965	2.50	5.00	10.00
❏ 72487	I Don't Know/Windmill in Old Amsterdam	1965	2.50	5.00	10.00
❏ 72487 [PS]	I Don't Know/Windmill in Old Amsterdam	1965	5.00	10.00	20.00
❏ 72548	When I'm Home with You/If You Got a Minute Baby	1966	2.50	5.00	10.00
❏ 72604	Some Day/Short Shorts	1966	2.50	5.00	10.00
SUPER K					
❏ 146	She Needs Me/Susan's Tuba	1970	2.00	4.00	8.00
TOWER					
❏ 125	I'm Telling You Now/What Have I Done to You	1964	3.75	7.50	15.00
❏ 127	You Were Made for Me/So Fine	1965	3.75	7.50	15.00
—B-side: "Introducing the Beat Merchants"					
❏ 127	You Were Made for Me/Send a Letter to Me	1965	5.00	10.00	20.00
❏ 163	Send a Letter to Me/There's Not One Thing	1965	3.75	7.50	15.00
—B-side by 4 Just Men					
UNITED ARTISTS					
❏ 50239	Come Back When You Grow Up/Oh What a Lovely Day	1967	—	—	—
—Unreleased					

7-Inch Extended Plays

Number	Title (A Side/B Side)	Yr	VG	VG+	NM
MERCURY					
❏ SRC 661-C	Thou Shalt Not Steal/Funny Over You/He Got What He Wanted//I Fell in Love with Your Picture/I Think of You/Some Other Guy	1965	5.00	10.00	20.00
—Jukebox mini-LP					
❏ SRC 661-C [PS]	Fun Lovin' Freddie	1965	5.00	10.00	20.00
Albums					
CAPITOL					
❏ SM-11896 [B]	The Best of Freddie and the Dreamers	1976	2.50	5.00	10.00
—"I'm Telling You Now," "You Were Made for Me," "I Just Don't Understand," "A Little You" and "Over You" are in stereo, the rest are mono.					
MERCURY					
❏ MG-21017 [M]	Freddie and the Dreamers	1965	6.25	12.50	25.00
❏ MG-21026 [M]	Do the Freddie	1965	5.00	10.00	20.00
❏ MG-21031 [M]	Seaside Swingers	1965	5.00	10.00	20.00
❏ MG-21053 [M]	Frantic Freddie	1965	3.75	7.50	15.00
❏ MG-21061 [M]	Fun Lovin' Freddie	1966	3.75	7.50	15.00
❏ SR-61017 [R]	Freddie and the Dreamers	1965	5.00	10.00	20.00

Number	Title (A Side/B Side)	Yr	VG	VG+	NM
❏ SR-61026 [S]	Do the Freddie	1965	6.25	12.50	25.00
❏ SR-61031 [S]	Seaside Swingers	1965	6.25	12.50	25.00
❏ SR-61053 [S]	Frantic Freddie	1965	5.00	10.00	20.00
❏ SR-61061 [S]	Fun Lovin' Freddie	1966	5.00	10.00	20.00
TOWER					
❏ DT 5003 [R]	I'm Telling You Now	1965	5.00	10.00	20.00
—Contains only two Freddie and the Dreamers songs, but the group's picture is on the cover. Also includes Four Just Men (2), Heinz (2), Linda Laine and the Sinners (2), Mike Rabin and the Demons (2) and The Toggery Five (2)					
❏ T 5003 [M]	I'm Telling You Now	1965	6.25	12.50	25.00
—Contains only two Freddie and the Dreamers songs, but the group's picture is on the cover. Also includes Four Just Men (2), Heinz (2), Linda Laine and the Sinners (2), Mike Rabin and the Demons (2) and The Toggery Five (2)					

FREDDIE AND THE PARLIAMENTS
45s

Number	Title (A Side/B Side)	Yr	VG	VG+	NM
TWIRL					
❏ 1003	Darlene/That Girl	1959	25.00	50.00	100.00

FREDRIC
45s

Number	Title (A Side/B Side)	Yr	VG	VG+	NM
EVOLUTION					
❏ 1001	Five O'Clock Traffic/Red Pier	1968	6.25	12.50	25.00
FORTE					
❏ 3001	Five O'Clock Traffic/Red Pier	1968	10.00	20.00	40.00
Albums					
FORTE					
❏ 80461	Phases and Faces	1968	200.00	400.00	800.00

FREE Also see PAUL KOSSOFF.
45s

Number	Title (A Side/B Side)	Yr	VG	VG+	NM
A&M					
❏ 1099	I'm a Mover/Worry	1969	—	2.00	4.00
❏ 1172	I'll Be Creepin'/Mouthful of Grass	1970	—	2.00	4.00
❏ 1206	All Right Now/Mouthful of Grass	1970	—	2.50	5.00
❏ 1230	Stealer/Broad Daylight	1970	—	2.00	4.00
❏ 1230 [PS]	Stealer/Lying in the Sunshine	1970	2.50	5.00	10.00
—Picture sleeve lists a different B-side than is on the record					
❏ 1248	Highway Song/Love You So	1971	—	2.00	4.00
❏ 1266	Mr. Big/I'll Be Creepin'	1971	—	2.00	4.00
❏ 1276	My Brother Jake/Only My Soul	1971	—	2.00	4.00
❏ 1352	Little Bit of Love/Sail On	1972	—	2.00	4.00
❏ 1720	All Right Now/Stealer	1975	—	2.00	4.00
ISLAND					
❏ 1212	Wishing Well/Let Me Show You	1972	—	2.00	4.00
Albums					
A&M					
❏ SP-3126	Fire and Water	198?	2.00	4.00	8.00
—Budget-line reissue					
❏ SP-3663	Best of Free	1975	3.00	6.00	12.00
❏ SP-4198	Tons of Sobs	1969	3.75	7.50	15.00
❏ SP-4204	Free	1969	3.75	7.50	15.00
❏ SP-4268	Fire and Water	1970	3.75	7.50	15.00
❏ SP-4287	Highway	1971	3.75	7.50	15.00
❏ SP-4306	Free Live!	1971	3.75	7.50	15.00
❏ SP-4349	Free at Last	1972	3.75	7.50	15.00
ISLAND					
❏ ILSD 4 [(2)]	The Free Story	1975	3.75	7.50	15.00
❏ ILPS 9217	Heartbreaker	1975	2.50	5.00	10.00
—U.S. reissue with same number as original U.K. issue					
❏ SW-9324	Heartbreaker	1973	3.00	6.00	12.00
—Original U.S. number, distributed by Capitol					
PICKWICK					
❏ SPC-3706	Free at Last	197?	2.50	5.00	10.00

FREE BAND, THE
Albums

Number	Title (A Side/B Side)	Yr	VG	VG+	NM
VANGUARD					
❏ VSD-6507	The Free Band	1969	5.00	10.00	20.00

FREE DESIGN, THE
45s

Number	Title (A Side/B Side)	Yr	VG	VG+	NM
PROJECT 3					
❏ 1324	Kites Are Fun/Proper Ornaments	1967	2.00	4.00	8.00
❏ 1331	You Be You and I'll Be Me/Never Tell the World	1967	2.00	4.00	8.00
❏ 1336	I Found Love/Umbrellas	1968	2.00	4.00	8.00
❏ 1345	Eleanor Rigby/Make the Madness Stop	1968	2.00	4.00	8.00
❏ 1347 [DJ]	Close Your Mouth (It's Christmas)/Christmas Is The Day	1968	2.50	5.00	10.00
—Stock copy may not exist					
❏ 1350	You Could Be Born Again/A Leaf Has Veins	1968	2.00	4.00	8.00
❏ 1356	Where Do I Go/Girls Alone	1969	2.00	4.00	8.00
❏ 1358	Summertime/Dorian Benediction	1969	2.00	4.00	8.00
❏ 1360	If I Were a Carpenter/Now Is the Time	1969	2.00	4.00	8.00
❏ 1366	2002: A Hit Song/Hurry Sundown	1969	2.00	4.00	8.00
❏ 1370	Butterflies Are Free/(B-side unknown)	1970	2.00	4.00	8.00
❏ 1375	I'm a Yogi/Bubbles	1970	2.00	4.00	8.00
❏ 1383	Tomorrow Is the First Day of the Rest of My Life/Kije's Ouija	1970	2.00	4.00	8.00
❏ 1393	Felt So Good/You Are My Sunshine	1971	2.00	4.00	8.00
❏ 1404	Stay Off of Your Frown/Friendly Man	1971	2.00	4.00	8.00
Albums					
AMBROTYPE					
❏ 1016	There Is a Song	1972	12.50	25.00	50.00
PROJECT 3					
❏ PR 4006 SD	The Free Design Sing for Very Important People	1970	6.25	12.50	25.00
❏ PR-5019 QD [Q]	Kites Are Fun	197?	10.00	20.00	40.00
❏ PR-5019 SD	Kites Are Fun	1967	6.25	12.50	25.00
❏ PR-5031 SD	You Could Be Born Again	1968	6.25	12.50	25.00
❏ PR-5037 SD	Heaven/Earth	1969	6.25	12.50	25.00
❏ PR-5045 SD	Stars/Times/Bubbles/Love	1971	6.25	12.50	25.00
❏ PR-5061 SD	One By One	1971	6.25	12.50	25.00

FREE MOVEMENT, THE
45s

Number	Title (A Side/B Side)	Yr	VG	VG+	NM
COLUMBIA					
❏ 45512	The Harder I Try (The Bluer I Get)/Comin' Home	1972	—	2.50	5.00
❏ 45567	Could You Believe in a Dream/Love the One You're With	1972	—	2.50	5.00

Dan Fogelberg, *Home Free,* Columbia KC 31751, stereo LP, $6-$12.

Wayne Fontana and the Mindbenders, *The Game of Love,* Fontana MGF-27542, mono LP, $15-$30.

The Four Seasons, *Born to Wander,* Philips PHS 600-129, stereo LP, $12.50-$25.

Connie Francis, *Rock n' Roll Million Sellers,* MGM E-3794, mono LP, $15-$30.

John Fred and His Playboy Band, *Agnes English,* Paula LPS-2197, stereo LP, $10-$20.

Freddie and the Dreamers, *Do the Freddie,* Mercury MG 21026, mono LP, $10-$20.

Number	Title (A Side/B Side)	Yr	VG	VG+	NM
❏ 45778	Every Step of the Way/I Can't Move No Mountains	1973	—	2.50	5.00

DECCA

Number	Title (A Side/B Side)	Yr	VG	VG+	NM
❏ 32818	I've Found Someone of My Own/I Can't Convince My Heart	1971	—	3.00	6.00

Albums

COLUMBIA

Number	Title (A Side/B Side)	Yr	VG	VG+	NM
❏ KC 31136	I've Found Someone of My Own	1972	3.75	7.50	15.00

FREEBORNE
Albums

MONITOR

Number	Title (A Side/B Side)	Yr	VG	VG+	NM
❏ MPS-607	Peak Impressions	1967	25.00	50.00	100.00

FREED, ALAN Also see VARIOUS ARTISTS COLLECTIONS.
45s

CORAL

Number	Title (A Side/B Side)	Yr	VG	VG+	NM
❏ 61626	Right Now, Right Now/Tina's Cantine	1956	7.50	15.00	30.00
❏ 61660	THe Camel Rock/I Don't Need Lotsa Money	1956	7.50	15.00	30.00
❏ 61693	The Space Man/Jazzbo's Theory	1956	7.50	15.00	30.00

—With Al "Jazzbo" Collins and the Modernaires

Number	Title (A Side/B Side)	Yr	VG	VG+	NM
❏ 61749	Rock 'N' Roll Boogie/The Grey Bear	1956	10.00	20.00	40.00
❏ 61818	Sentimental Journey/Stop! Look! and Run!	1957	10.00	20.00	40.00

Albums

BRUNSWICK

Number	Title (A Side/B Side)	Yr	VG	VG+	NM
❏ BL 54043 [M]	The Alan Freed Rock 'n' Roll Show	1959	37.50	75.00	150.00

CORAL

Number	Title (A Side/B Side)	Yr	VG	VG+	NM
❏ CRL 57063 [M]	Alan Freed's Rock 'n' Roll Dance Party, Vol. 1	1956	37.50	75.00	150.00
❏ CRL 57115 [M]	Alan Freed's Rock 'n' Roll Dance Party, Vol. 2	1957	37.50	75.00	150.00
❏ CRL 57177 [M]	Go Go Go — Alan Freed's TV Record Hop	1957	37.50	75.00	150.00
❏ CRL 57213 [M]	Rock Around the Block	1958	37.50	75.00	150.00
❏ CRL 57216 [M]	Alan Freed Presents the King's Henchmen	1958	37.50	75.00	150.00

MGM

Number	Title (A Side/B Side)	Yr	VG	VG+	NM
❏ E-293 [10]	The Big Beat	195?	50.00	100.00	200.00

FREEMAN, ART
45s

FAME

Number	Title (A Side/B Side)	Yr	VG	VG+	NM
❏ 1008	I Can't Get You Out of My Mind/Slippin' Around with You	1966	12.50	25.00	50.00
❏ 1012	A Piece of My Heart/Everybody's Got to Cry Sometime	1966	7.50	15.00	30.00

FREEMAN, ARTHUR
45s

EXCELLO

Number	Title (A Side/B Side)	Yr	VG	VG+	NM
❏ 2322	Here I Am/Played Out Play Girl	1971	5.00	10.00	20.00

FREEMAN, BOBBY
45s

AUTUMN

Number	Title (A Side/B Side)	Yr	VG	VG+	NM
❏ 1	Come to Me/Let's Surf Again	1964	5.00	10.00	20.00
❏ 2	C'mon and Swim/C'mon and Swim — Part 2	1964	2.50	5.00	10.00

—Tan label

Number	Title (A Side/B Side)	Yr	VG	VG+	NM
❏ 2	C'mon and Swim/C'mon and Swim — Part 2	1964	3.00	6.00	12.00

—White label, red print

Number	Title (A Side/B Side)	Yr	VG	VG+	NM
❏ 5	S-W-I-M/That Little Old Heartbreaker	1964	2.50	5.00	10.00
❏ 9	I'll Never Fall in Love Again/Friends	1965	2.50	5.00	10.00
❏ 25	Cross My Heart/The Duck	1965	2.50	5.00	10.00

DOUBLE SHOT

Number	Title (A Side/B Side)	Yr	VG	VG+	NM
❏ 139	There Oughta Be a Law/Everybody's Got a Hang-Up	1969	—	3.00	6.00
❏ 144	Susie Sunshine/Four Piece Funky Nitty Gritty Junky Band	1969	—	3.00	6.00
❏ 148	Can You Stand the Pressure/Put Another Dime in the Parking Meter	1970	—	3.00	6.00
❏ 152	Do You Wanna Dance 1970/Society for the Prevention of Cruelty to People	1970	—	3.00	6.00

JOSIE

Number	Title (A Side/B Side)	Yr	VG	VG+	NM
❏ 835	Do You Want to Dance/Big Fat Woman	1958	5.00	10.00	20.00
❏ 841	Betty Lou Got a New Pair of Shoes/Starlight	1958	5.00	10.00	20.00
❏ 844	Need Your Love/Shame On You, Miss Johnson	1958	3.75	7.50	15.00
❏ 855	A Love to Last a Lifetime/When You're Smiling	1959	3.75	7.50	15.00
❏ 863	Love Me/Mary Ann Thomas	1959	3.75	7.50	15.00
❏ 867	My Guardian Angel/Where Did My Baby Go	1959	3.75	7.50	15.00
❏ 872	Ebb Tide/Sinbad	1959	3.75	7.50	15.00
❏ 879	I Need Someone/First Day of Spring	1960	3.00	6.00	12.00
❏ 886	Miss You So/Baby What Would You Do	1961	3.00	6.00	12.00
❏ 887	The Mess Around/So Much to Do	1961	3.00	6.00	12.00
❏ 889	Put You Down/She Said She Wants to Dance	1961	3.00	6.00	12.00
❏ 896	Love Me/Little Girl Don't You Understand	1962	3.00	6.00	12.00
❏ 928	The Mess Around/Little Girl Don't You Understand	1965	2.50	5.00	10.00

KING

Number	Title (A Side/B Side)	Yr	VG	VG+	NM
❏ 5373	Shimmy Shimmy/You Don't Understand	1960	3.00	6.00	12.00
❏ 5953	Fever/What Can I Do	1964	2.50	5.00	10.00
❏ 5962	Somebody, Somewhere/Be My Little Chick-A-Dee	1964	2.50	5.00	10.00
❏ 5975	Come to Me/There's Gonna Be a Change	1965	2.50	5.00	10.00

LOMA

Number	Title (A Side/B Side)	Yr	VG	VG+	NM
❏ 2056	Shadow of Your Love/Soulful Sound of Music	1966	2.00	4.00	8.00
❏ 2080	I Got a Good Thing/Lies	1967	2.00	4.00	8.00

PARKWAY

Number	Title (A Side/B Side)	Yr	VG	VG+	NM
❏ 875	She's a Hippy/Whip It Up Baby	1963	3.00	6.00	12.00

RHINO

Number	Title (A Side/B Side)	Yr	VG	VG+	NM
❏ 4508	S-W-I-M/C'mon and Swim	198?	—	2.00	4.00
❏ 4508 [PS]	S-W-I-M/C'mon and Swim	198?	—	2.00	4.00

Albums

AUTUMN

Number	Title (A Side/B Side)	Yr	VG	VG+	NM
❏ LP 102 [M]	C'mon and S-W-I-M	1964	12.50	25.00	50.00

JOSIE

Number	Title (A Side/B Side)	Yr	VG	VG+	NM
❏ JM-4007 [M]	Get In the Swim with Bobby Freeman	1965	7.50	15.00	30.00
❏ JS-4007 [R]	Get In the Swim with Bobby Freeman	1965	6.25	12.50	25.00

JUBILEE

Number	Title (A Side/B Side)	Yr	VG	VG+	NM
❏ JLP-1086 [M]	Do You Wanna Dance?	1959	35.00	70.00	140.00
❏ JLPS-1086 [S]	Do You Wanna Dance?	1959	50.00	100.00	200.00
❏ JGM-5010 [M]	Twist with Bobby Freeman	1962	25.00	50.00	100.00

KING

Number	Title (A Side/B Side)	Yr	VG	VG+	NM
❏ 930 [M]	The Lovable Style of Bobby Freeman	1965	62.50	125.00	250.00

FREEMAN, ERNIE
45s

AVA

Number	Title (A Side/B Side)	Yr	VG	VG+	NM
❏ 176	Raunchy '65/Jivin' Around	1965	2.00	4.00	8.00

CASH

Number	Title (A Side/B Side)	Yr	VG	VG+	NM
❏ 1017	Jivin' Around (Part 1)/Jivin' Around (Part 2)	1955	3.75	7.50	15.00

IMPERIAL

Number	Title (A Side/B Side)	Yr	VG	VG+	NM
❏ 5381	Rockin' Around/Lost Dreams	1956	3.75	7.50	15.00
❏ 5391	Rainy Day/Funny Face	1956	3.75	7.50	15.00
❏ 5403	Spring Fever/Walking the Beat	1956	3.75	7.50	15.00
❏ 5419	Return to Me/A Touch of the Blues	1957	3.75	7.50	15.00
❏ 5430	Without Love/Night Life	1957	3.75	7.50	15.00
❏ 5444	Swing It/River Boat	1957	3.75	7.50	15.00
❏ 5461	Dumplin's/Beautiful Weekend	1957	3.75	7.50	15.00
❏ 5474	Raunchy/Puddin'	1957	6.25	12.50	25.00
❏ 5486	The Tuttle/Leaps and Bounds	1958	3.00	6.00	12.00
❏ 5518	Indian Love Call/Summer Serenade	1958	3.00	6.00	12.00
❏ 5527	Rose Marie/After Sunset	1958	3.00	6.00	12.00
❏ 5541	Jamboree/Junior Jive	1958	3.00	6.00	12.00
❏ 5551	School Room Rock/Blues After Hours	1958	3.00	6.00	12.00
❏ 5566	Live It Up/Whispering Hope (Freedom and Land)	1959	2.50	5.00	10.00
❏ 5574	Marshmallows, Popcorn & Soda Pop/Honey Dripper	1959	2.50	5.00	10.00
❏ 5612	A Summer Love/Always with You	1959	2.50	5.00	10.00
❏ 5621	Lost Dreams/One More Time Around	1959	2.50	5.00	10.00
❏ 5633	Big River/Night Sounds	1959	2.50	5.00	10.00
❏ 5656	Rockin' Red Wing/Dark Eyes	1960	2.00	4.00	8.00
❏ 5677	Autumn and Eve/Prayer	1960	2.00	4.00	8.00
❏ 5693	Theme from "The Dark at the Top of the Stairs"/Come On Home	1960	2.00	4.00	8.00
❏ 5716	Hawaiian Eye/Heartbreak Hotel	1960	2.00	4.00	8.00
❏ 5732	Swamp Meeting/That's All	1961	2.00	4.00	8.00
❏ 5752	Theme from "Return to Peyton Place"/Warsaw Concerto	1961	2.00	4.00	8.00
❏ 5769	Conquest/Swingin' Preacher	1961	2.00	4.00	8.00
❏ 5793	The Twist/Shine On Harvest Moon	1961	2.00	4.00	8.00
❏ 5815	What Am I Living For/I Didn't Want to Do It	1962	2.00	4.00	8.00
❏ 5841	The Stripper/I Hear You Knocking	1962	2.00	4.00	8.00
❏ 5883	The Freeloader/Say It Isn't So	1962	2.00	4.00	8.00

LIBERTY

Number	Title (A Side/B Side)	Yr	VG	VG+	NM
❏ 55515	Half as Much/I'm Sorry for You My Friend	1962	2.00	4.00	8.00

Albums

DUNHILL

Number	Title (A Side/B Side)	Yr	VG	VG+	NM
❏ D 50026 [M]	Hitmaker	1967	3.00	6.00	12.00
❏ DS 50026 [S]	Hitmaker	1967	3.75	7.50	15.00

IMPERIAL

Number	Title (A Side/B Side)	Yr	VG	VG+	NM
❏ LP-9022 [M]	Ernie Freeman Plays Irving Berlin	1957	12.50	25.00	50.00
❏ LP-9030 [M]	Jivin' Around	1957	12.50	25.00	50.00
❏ LP-9057 [M]	Ernie Freeman	1958	12.50	25.00	50.00
❏ LP-9133 [M]	Dark at the Top of the Stairs	1959	7.50	15.00	30.00
❏ LP-9148 [M]	Raunchy	1960	12.50	25.00	50.00
❏ LP-9157 [M]	Twistin' Time	1961	7.50	15.00	30.00
❏ LP-9193 [M]	The Stripper	1962	5.00	10.00	20.00
❏ LP-12067 [S]	Dark at the Top of the Stairs	1959	10.00	20.00	40.00
❏ LP-12081 [S]	Twistin' Time	1961	10.00	20.00	40.00
❏ LP-12193 [S]	The Stripper	1962	6.25	12.50	25.00

LIBERTY

Number	Title (A Side/B Side)	Yr	VG	VG+	NM
❏ LRP-3264 [M]	Ernie Freeman's Soulful Sounds of Country Classics	1962	5.00	10.00	20.00
❏ LRP-3283 [M]	Limbo Dance Party	1962	5.00	10.00	20.00
❏ LRP-3331 [M]	Comin' Home Baby	1963	5.00	10.00	20.00
❏ LST-7264 [S]	Ernie Freeman's Soulful Sounds of Country Classics	1962	6.25	12.50	25.00
❏ LST-7283 [S]	Limbo Dance Party	1962	6.25	12.50	25.00
❏ LST-7331 [S]	Comin' Home Baby	1963	6.25	12.50	25.00

FREEMAN, GEORGE
45s

EPIC

Number	Title (A Side/B Side)	Yr	VG	VG+	NM
❏ 5-10668	I'll Be Long Gone (Make My Life Shine)/Stop Now (There's Still Time)	1971	3.00	6.00	12.00

GARDENA

Number	Title (A Side/B Side)	Yr	VG	VG+	NM
❏ 129	Sugar Lips/If I Told You	1962	5.00	10.00	20.00

GROOVE MERCHANT

Number	Title (A Side/B Side)	Yr	VG	VG+	NM
❏ 1016	Guitar Lover Man/(B-side unknown)	197?	3.00	6.00	12.00

OKEH

Number	Title (A Side/B Side)	Yr	VG	VG+	NM
❏ 4-7333	All Right Now/You Lied, I Cried, Love Died	1969	6.25	12.50	25.00

SHOUT

Number	Title (A Side/B Side)	Yr	VG	VG+	NM
❏ 201	Why Are You Doing This to Me/I'm Like a Fish	1966	6.25	12.50	25.00

VALIANT

Number	Title (A Side/B Side)	Yr	VG	VG+	NM
❏ 6035	Come to Me/You Guessed It	1963	5.00	10.00	20.00
❏ 6039	Down and Out/The Quiver	1963	62.50	125.00	250.00
❏ 6057	One Last Dance/You're Guilty	1964	6.25	12.50	25.00

FREEMAN BROTHERS, THE
45s

MALA

Number	Title (A Side/B Side)	Yr	VG	VG+	NM
❏ 553	I'm Counting on You/Everyday It's You	1966	6.25	12.50	25.00

SOUL

Number	Title (A Side/B Side)	Yr	VG	VG+	NM
❏ 35011	My Baby/Beautiful Brown Eyes	1965	10.00	20.00	40.00

FREEPORT
45s

MAINSTREAM

Number	Title (A Side/B Side)	Yr	VG	VG+	NM
❏ 730	I Need Your Lovin'/(B-side unknown)	1970	2.50	5.00	10.00
❏ 732	Now That She's Gone/Misunderstood	1970	2.50	5.00	10.00

Albums

MAINSTREAM

Number	Title (A Side/B Side)	Yr	VG	VG+	NM
❏ S-6130	Freeport	1970	12.50	25.00	50.00

Number	Title (A Side/B Side)	Yr	VG	VG+	NM
FREEWHEELERS, THE					
45s					
EPIC					
❑ 9664	Walk, Walk/The Best of It	1964	5.00	10.00	20.00
❑ 9700	San Francisco Bay Blues/Susu	1964	5.00	10.00	20.00
❑ 9725	Beach Boy/Annie	1964	3.75	7.50	15.00
FRENCH, DON					
45s					
LANCER					
❑ 104	Lonely Saturday Night/Goldilocks	1959	6.25	12.50	25.00
❑ 105	Little Blonde Girl/I Look Into My Heart	1959	7.50	15.00	30.00
FRENCH, LISA					
45s					
HIT					
❑ 181	The Name Game/You Don't Want My Love	1965	2.00	4.00	8.00
—B-side by Leroy Jones					
❑ 200	You Can't Trust a Friend/Send Me the Pillow You Dream On	1965	2.00	4.00	8.00
—B-side by Marty Wood					
FRIAR TUCK Curt Boetcher was in the group.					
45s					
BANSHEE					
❑ 100	The Return of Robin Hood/(B-side unknown)	196?	3.75	7.50	15.00
MERCURY					
❑ 72684	Alley-Oop/Sweet Pea	1967	2.50	5.00	10.00
Albums					
MERCURY					
❑ MG-21111 [M]	Friar Tuck and His Psychedelic Guitar	1967	10.00	20.00	40.00
❑ SR-61111 [S]	Friar Tuck and His Psychedelic Guitar	1967	12.50	25.00	50.00
FRIEDMAN, KINKY					
45s					
ABC					
❑ 12073	Lover Please/Autograph	1975	—	3.00	6.00
❑ 12107	Wild Man from Borneo/Popeye the Sailor Man	1975	—	3.00	6.00
EPIC					
❑ 50299	Catfish/Dear Abby	1976	—	2.50	5.00
SUNRISE					
❑ 41932	Twirl/Hello, Good Mornin'	1983	—	3.00	6.00
—B-side with Ronee Blakely					
VANGUARD					
❑ 35173	Sold American/Western Union Wire	1973	2.00	4.00	8.00
Albums					
ABC					
❑ X-829	Kinky Friedman	1974	2.50	5.00	10.00
EPIC					
❑ PE 34304	Lasso from El Paso	1976	2.50	5.00	10.00
VANGUARD					
❑ VSD-79333	Sold American	1973	3.00	6.00	12.00
FRIEND AND LOVER					
45s					
ABC					
❑ 10910	Town Called Love/If Tomorrow	1967	3.00	6.00	12.00
CADET CONCEPT					
❑ 7019	Hard Lovin'/Colorado Exile	1970	—	3.00	6.00
❑ 7019 [PS]	Hard Lovin'/Colorado Exile	1970	3.75	7.50	15.00
VERVE FORECAST					
❑ 5069	Reach Out of the Darkness/Time on Your Side (You're Only 15 Years Old)	1967	2.50	5.00	10.00
❑ 5091	If Love Is In Your Heart/Zig Zag	1968	2.00	4.00	8.00
❑ 5100	I Want to Be Free/Circus	1968	2.00	4.00	8.00
❑ 5106	Ode to a Dandelion/A Wise Man Changes His Mind	1969	—	3.00	6.00
Albums					
VERVE FORECAST					
❑ FTS-3055	Reach Out of the Darkness	1968	5.00	10.00	20.00
FRIENDLY TORPEDOES, THE					
45s					
ORIGINAL SOUND					
❑ 95	Nothing's Too Good for My Car/So Long Ago	1970	6.25	12.50	25.00
FRIENDS, THE					
45s					
MGM					
❑ 14646	Gonna Have a Good Time/Would You Laugh	1973	—	3.00	6.00
❑ 14646 [PS]	Gonna Have a Good Time/Would You Laugh	1973	3.00	6.00	12.00
Albums					
MGM					
❑ SE-4901	The Friends	1973	3.00	6.00	12.00
FRIENDS OF DISTINCTION, THE					
45s					
RCA VICTOR					
❑ 74-0107	Grazing in the Grass/I Really Hope You Do	1969	—	3.00	6.00
❑ 74-0204	Going in Circles/Let Yourself Go	1969	—	3.00	6.00
❑ 74-0319	Love Or Let Me Be Lonely/This Generation	1970	—	3.00	6.00
❑ 74-0385	Time Waits for No One/Mother Nature	1970	—	2.50	5.00
❑ 74-0416	Check It Out/I Need You	1971	—	2.50	5.00
❑ 74-0516	It Don't Matter to Me/Down I Go	1971	—	2.50	5.00
❑ 74-0562	Let Me Be/Long Time Comin' My Way	1971	—	2.50	5.00
❑ 74-0679	Love Is the Way of Life/Jenny Wants to Know	1972	—	2.50	5.00
❑ 74-0787	Now Is the Time/Thumb Tripping	1972	—	2.50	5.00
❑ 74-0888	Ain't No Woman (Like the One I've Got)/Easy Evil	1973	—	2.50	5.00
❑ 74-0956	Check It Out/Love Can Make It Easier	1973	—	2.50	5.00
❑ PB-10197	Honey Baby Theme Part 1/Honey Baby Theme Part 2	1975	—	2.00	4.00
❑ PB-10220	Love Shack Part 1/Love Shack Part 2	1975	—	2.00	4.00

Number	Title (A Side/B Side)	Yr	VG	VG+	NM
Albums					
RCA VICTOR					
❑ APD1-0276 [Q]	Greatest Hits	1973	5.00	10.00	20.00
❑ LSP-4149	Grazin'	1969	3.75	7.50	15.00
❑ LSP-4212	Highly Distinct	1969	3.75	7.50	15.00
❑ LSP-4313	Real Friends	1970	3.75	7.50	15.00
❑ LSP-4408	Whatever	1970	3.75	7.50	15.00
❑ LSP-4492	Friends & People	1971	3.75	7.50	15.00
❑ LSP-4819	Greatest Hits	1972	3.00	6.00	12.00
❑ LSP-4829	Love Can Make It Easier	1973	3.00	6.00	12.00
FRIJID PINK					
45s					
LION					
❑ 115	Earth Omen/Lazy Day	1972	2.00	4.00	8.00
❑ 136	Go Now/Lazy Day	1972	2.00	4.00	8.00
❑ 158	Big Betty/Shady Lady	1973	—	3.00	6.00
PARROT					
❑ 334	Tell Me Why/Cryin' Shame	1969	—	3.00	6.00
❑ 340	God Gave Me You/Drivin' Blues	1970	—	3.00	6.00
❑ 341	House of the Rising Sun/Drivin' Blues	1970	2.00	4.00	8.00
❑ 349	Sing a Song for Freedom/End of the Line	1970	—	3.00	6.00
❑ 352	Heartbreak Hotel/Bye Bye Blues	1970	—	3.00	6.00
❑ 355	Music for the People/Sloony	1971	—	3.00	6.00
❑ 358	We're Gonna Be There/Shorty Kline	1971	—	3.00	6.00
❑ 360	Lost Son/I Love Her	1971	—	3.00	6.00
Albums					
FANTASY					
❑ 9464	All Pink Inside	1974	3.75	7.50	15.00
LION					
❑ LN-1004	Earth Omen	1972	5.00	10.00	20.00
PARROT					
❑ PAS 71033	Frijid Pink	1970	6.25	12.50	25.00
❑ PAS 71041	Defrosted	1970	6.25	12.50	25.00
FRIZZELL, LEFTY					
45s					
ABC					
❑ 11350	I Buy the Wine/Let Me Give Her the Flowers	1973	2.00	4.00	8.00
❑ 11387	I Can't Get Over You to Save My Life/Somebody's Words	1973	—	3.50	7.00
❑ 11416	I Never Go Around Mirrors/That's the Way It Goes	1974	—	3.50	7.00
❑ 11442	Railroad Lady/If I Had Half the Sense (A Fool Was Born With)	1974	—	3.50	7.00
❑ 12023	Lucky Arms/If She Just Helps Me Get Over You	1974	—	3.50	7.00
❑ 12061	Life's Like Poetry/Sittin' and Thinkin'	1975	—	3.50	7.00
❑ 12103	Falling/I Love You a Thousand Ways	1975	—	3.50	7.00
COLUMBIA					
❑ 38-04264	Get This Stranger Out of Me/This Just Ain't No Good Day for Leaving	1983	—	2.50	5.00
❑ 38-04480	Watermelon Time in Georgia/Everything Keeps Coming Back to You	1984	—	2.50	5.00
❑ 4-20739	If You've Got the Money, I've Got the Time/I Love You a Thousand Ways	1950	10.00	20.00	40.00
❑ 4-20772	Look What Thoughts Will Do/Shine, Shave, Shower (It's Saturday)	1951	6.25	12.50	25.00
❑ 4-20799	I Want to Be With You Always/My Baby's Just Like Money	1951	6.25	12.50	25.00
❑ 4-20837	Always Late (With Your Kisses)/Mom and Dad's Waltz	1951	6.25	12.50	25.00
❑ 4-20840	Blue Yodel #2/Treasures Untold	1951	5.00	10.00	20.00
❑ 4-20841	Brakeman's Blues/My Old Pal	1951	5.00	10.00	20.00
❑ 4-20842	Travellin' Blues/Blue Yodel #6	1951	6.25	12.50	25.00
❑ 4-20843	My Rough and Rowdy Ways/Lullaby Yodel	1951	5.00	10.00	20.00
—The above four comprise a box set (20842 was also available separately)					
❑ 4-20885	Give Me More, More, More (Of Your Kisses)/How Long Will It Take (To Stop Loving You)	1951	6.25	12.50	25.00
❑ 4-20911	Don't Stay Away (Till Love Grows Cold)/You're Here, So Everything's All Right	1952	6.25	12.50	25.00
❑ 4-20941	Don't Stay Away (Till Love Grows Cold)/Sad Singin', Slow Ridin'	1952	5.00	10.00	20.00
—B-side by Polly Possum; part of a 4-record various-artists box set					
❑ 4-20950	If You Can Spare the Time/It's Just You	1952	6.25	12.50	25.00
❑ 4-20958	If You've Got the Money, I've Got the Time/Look What Thoughts Will Do	1952	5.00	10.00	20.00
❑ 4-20959	I Love You a Thousand Ways/I Want to Be with You Always	1952	5.00	10.00	20.00
❑ 4-20960	Always Late (With Your Kisses)/Mom and Dad's Waltz	1952	5.00	10.00	20.00
❑ 4-20961	Don't Stay Away (Till Love Grows Cold)/If You Can Spare the Time	1952	5.00	10.00	20.00
—The above four comprise a box set					
❑ 4-20997	Forever (And Always)/I Know You're Lonesome While Waiting for Me	1952	6.25	12.50	25.00
❑ 4-21034	I'm an Old, Old Man (Tryin' to Live While I Can)/You're Just Mine (Only in My Dreams)	1952	6.25	12.50	25.00
❑ 4-21084	(Honey, Baby, Hurry) Bring Your Sweet Self Back to Me/Time Changes Things	1953	6.25	12.50	25.00
❑ 4-21100	Never No More Blues/Sleep Baby Sleep	1953	6.25	12.50	25.00
❑ 4-21101	California Blues/I'm Lonely and Blue	1953	6.25	12.50	25.00
❑ 4-21118	We Crucified Our Jesus/When It Comes to Measuring Love	1953	6.25	12.50	25.00
❑ 4-21142	Two Friends of Mine/Before You Go	1953	6.25	12.50	25.00
❑ 4-21169	Hopeless Love/Then I'll Come Back to You	1953	6.25	12.50	25.00
❑ 4-21194	Run 'Em Off/Darkest Moment	1953	6.25	12.50	25.00
❑ 4-21208	My Little Her and Him/I've Been Away Way Too Long	1954	6.25	12.50	25.00
❑ 4-21241	King Without a Queen/You Can Always Count on Me	1954	6.25	12.50	25.00
❑ 4-21284	You're Too Late/Two Hearts Broken Now	1954	6.25	12.50	25.00
❑ 4-21328	I Love You Mostly/Mama	1954	6.25	12.50	25.00
❑ 4-21366	Making Believe/A Forest Fire	1955	6.25	12.50	25.00
❑ 4-21393	I'll Sit Alone and Cry/Moonlight Darling and You	1955	6.25	12.50	25.00
❑ 4-21433	Sweet Lies/I'm Lost Between Right and Wrong	1955	6.25	12.50	25.00

F

Number	Title (A Side/B Side)	Yr	VG	VG+	NM
❑ 4-21458	It Gets Late So Early/				
	Your Tomorrows Will Never Come	1955	6.25	12.50	25.00
❑ 4-21488	First to Have a Second Chance/These Hands	1956	6.25	12.50	25.00
❑ 4-21506	Promises Promises/Today Is That Tomorrow	1956	6.25	12.50	25.00
❑ 4-21530	Just Can't Live That Fast/Waltz of the Angels	1956	6.25	12.50	25.00
❑ 4-21554	Heart's Highway/I'm a Boy Left Alone	1956	6.25	12.50	25.00
❑ 4-40818	Glad I Found You/Lullaby Waltz	1957	5.00	10.00	20.00
❑ 4-40867	From an Angel to a Devil/				
	Now That You Are Gone	1957	5.00	10.00	20.00
❑ 4-40938	Is It Only That You're Lonely/No One to Talk To	1957	5.00	10.00	20.00
❑ 4-41080	Time Out for the Blues/Tell Me Dear	1957	5.00	10.00	20.00
❑ 4-41161	Silence/The Torch Within My Heart	1958	5.00	10.00	20.00
❑ 4-41268	Cigarettes and Coffee Blues/				
	You're Humbuggin' Me	1958	5.00	10.00	20.00
❑ 4-41384	The Long Black Veil/Knock Again, True Love	1959	5.00	10.00	20.00
❑ 4-41455	Farther Than My Eyes Can See/Ballad of the				
	Blue and Gray	1959	5.00	10.00	20.00
❑ 4-41635	She's Gone/My Blues Will Pass	1960	3.75	7.50	15.00
❑ 4-41751	What You Gonna Do Leroy/				
	That's All I Can Remember	1960	3.75	7.50	15.00
❑ 4-41984	Looking for You/Heaven's Plan	1961	3.75	7.50	15.00
❑ 4-42253	I Feel Sorry for Me/So What, Let It Rain	1961	3.75	7.50	15.00
❑ 4-42521	Stranger/Just Passing Through	1962	3.75	7.50	15.00
❑ 4-42676	Forbidden Lovers/A Few Steps Away	1963	3.00	6.00	12.00
❑ 4-42839	Don't Let Her See Me Cry/James River	1963	3.00	6.00	12.00
❑ 4-42924	Saginaw, Michigan/When It Rains the Blues	1963	3.00	6.00	12.00
❑ 4-42924 [DJ]	Saginaw, Michigan (same on both sides)	1963	7.50	15.00	30.00
—Promo only on blue vinyl					
❑ 4-43051	The Nester/The Rider	1964	3.00	6.00	12.00
❑ 4-43169	'Gator Hollow/				
	Make That One for the Road a Cup of Coffee	1964	3.00	6.00	12.00
❑ 4-43256	She's Gone Gone Gone/Confused	1965	2.50	5.00	10.00
❑ 4-43364	A Little Unfair/Love Looks Good on You	1965	2.50	5.00	10.00
❑ 4-43590	Writing on the Wall/Mama	1966	2.50	5.00	10.00
❑ 4-43747	I Just Couldn't See the Forest (For the Trees)/				
	Everything Keeps Coming Back (But You)	1966	2.50	5.00	10.00
❑ 4-44023	You Gotta Be Puttin' Me On/A Song from a				
	Lonely Heart	1967	2.50	5.00	10.00
❑ 4-44205	Get This Stranger Out of Me/Hobo's Pride	1967	2.50	5.00	10.00
❑ 4-44390	Anything You Can Spare/A Prayer on Your Lips	1967	2.50	5.00	10.00
❑ 4-44563	The Marriage Bit/				
	When the Grass Grows Green Again	1968	2.50	5.00	10.00
❑ 4-44692	Wasted Way of Life/Keep the Flowers Watered				
	When I'm Gone	1968	2.50	5.00	10.00
❑ 4-44738	An Article from Life/Only Way to Fly	1969	2.50	5.00	10.00
❑ 4-44984	Honky Tonk Hill/Wasted Way of Life	1969	2.50	5.00	10.00
❑ 4-45145	My Baby Is a Tramp/				
	She Brought Love, Sweet Love	1970	2.50	5.00	10.00
❑ 4-45197	Watermelon Time in Georgia/Out of You	1970	2.50	5.00	10.00
❑ 4-45310	Three Cheers for the Good Guys/				
	I Must Be Getting Over You	1971	2.50	5.00	10.00
❑ 4-45347	Honky Tonk Stardust Cowboy/				
	What Am I Gonna Do	1971	2.50	5.00	10.00
❑ 4-45652	You, Babe/When It Rains the Blues	1972	2.50	5.00	10.00
❑ 4-52019	If You've Got the Money, I've Got the Time/I Love				
	You a Thousand Ways	195?	3.75	7.50	15.00
—Early "Hall of Fame Series" issue with maroon label					

7-Inch Extended Plays
COLUMBIA

Number	Title (A Side/B Side)	Yr	VG	VG+	NM
❑ B-2802	*Always Late (With Your Kisses)/Mom and Dad's				
	Waltz/If You've Got the Money, I've Got the				
	Time/I Love You a Thousand Ways	195?	5.00	10.00	20.00
❑ B-2802 [PS]	Lefty Frizzell (Hall of Fame Series)	195?	5.00	10.00	20.00

Albums
ABC

Number	Title	Yr	VG	VG+	NM
❑ ABCX-799	The Legendary Lefty Frizzell	1974	5.00	10.00	20.00
—Revised title					
❑ ABCX-799	Lefty	1974	7.50	15.00	30.00
—Original title					
❑ AC-30035	The ABC Collection	1976	5.00	10.00	20.00
COLUMBIA					
❑ CL 1342 [M]	The One and Only Lefty Frizzell	1959	30.00	60.00	120.00
❑ CL 2169 [M]	Saginaw, Michigan	1964	7.50	15.00	30.00
❑ CL 2386 [M]	The Sad Side of Love	1965	7.50	15.00	30.00
❑ CL 2488 [M]	Lefty Frizzell's Greatest Hits	1966	7.50	15.00	30.00
❑ CL 2772 [M]	Puttin' On	1967	12.50	25.00	50.00
❑ CS 8969 [S]	Saginaw, Michigan	1964	10.00	20.00	40.00
❑ CL 9019 [10]	Lefty Frizzell Sings the Songs of Jimmie				
	Rodgers	1951	62.50	125.00	250.00
❑ CL 9021 [10]	Listen to Lefty	1952	62.50	125.00	250.00
❑ CS 9186 [S]	The Sad Side of Love	1965	10.00	20.00	40.00
❑ CS 9288 [S]	Lefty Frizzell's Greatest Hits	1966	10.00	20.00	40.00
—Red label, "360 Sound Stereo" at bottom					
❑ CS 9572 [S]	Puttin' On	1967	10.00	20.00	40.00
❑ C 32249	Lefty Frizzell Sings the Songs of Jimmie				
	Rodgers	1973	5.00	10.00	20.00
❑ PC 33882	Remembering…The Greatest Hits of Lefty				
	Frizzell	1975	5.00	10.00	20.00
COLUMBIA LIMITED EDITION					
❑ LE 10027	Saginaw, Michigan	197?	2.50	5.00	10.00
HARMONY					
❑ HL 7241 [M]	Lefty Frizzell Sings the Songs of				
	Jimmie Rodgers	1960	7.50	15.00	30.00

FROGGIE BEAVER
Albums
FROGGIE BEAVER

Number	Title	Yr	VG	VG+	NM
❑ 7301	From the Pond	1973	12.50	25.00	50.00

FROGMEN, THE
45s
ASTRA

Number	Title (A Side/B Side)	Yr	VG	VG+	NM
❑ 1009	Underwater/The Mad Rush	196?	12.50	25.00	50.00
❑ 1010	Beware Below/Tioga	196?	12.50	25.00	50.00
—The above two are East Coast reissues					
CANDIX					
❑ 314	Underwater/The Mad Rush	1961	6.25	12.50	25.00

Number	Title (A Side/B Side)	Yr	VG	VG+	NM
❑ 326	Beware Below/Tioga	1961	6.25	12.50	25.00
SCOTT					
❑ 101	Seahorse Flats/Tioga	1961	12.50	25.00	50.00
❑ 102	Underwater/Beware Below	1961	12.50	25.00	50.00
TEE JAY					
❑ 131	Sea Haunt/Diamond Back	1964	20.00	40.00	80.00
—Blue vinyl					

FROLIC, HARVEY
45s
HIT

Number	Title (A Side/B Side)	Yr	VG	VG+	NM
❑ 23	Things/Heart in Hand	1962	2.00	4.00	8.00
—B-side by Connie Landers					
❑ 74	Ring of Fire/On Top of Spaghetti	1963	2.00	4.00	8.00
❑ 91	The Matador/Maria Elena	1963	2.00	4.00	8.00
—B-side by the Music City Five					
❑ 105	Talking About My Baby/You Don't Know Me	1964	2.00	4.00	8.00
—B-side by Bill Austin					
❑ 131	Dang Me/The Girl from Ipanema	1964	2.00	4.00	8.00
—B-side by Betty Coleson					
❑ 148	Chug-a-Lug/Lonesome Fool	1964	2.00	4.00	8.00
—B-side by Joanne Kay					
❑ 181	Midnight Special/Sha La La	1965	3.00	6.00	12.00
—B-side by the Spartas					

FROLIC, ROGER
45s
HIT

Number	Title (A Side/B Side)	Yr	VG	VG+	NM
❑ 267	My Uncle Used to Love Me But She Died/Almost				
	Persuaded	1966	2.00	4.00	8.00
—B-side by Leroy Jones					

FROLK HEAVEN
Albums
LRS

Number	Title	Yr	VG	VG+	NM
❑ RF-6023	At the Apex of High	197?	100.00	200.00	400.00

FRONT PAGE NEWS
45s
DIAL

Number	Title (A Side/B Side)	Yr	VG	VG+	NM
❑ 4052	Thoughts/You Better Behave	1967	6.25	12.50	25.00

FROST, FRANK
45s
JEWEL

Number	Title (A Side/B Side)	Yr	VG	VG+	NM
❑ 765	My Back Scratcher/Harp and Soul	1966	3.75	7.50	15.00
❑ 771	Things You Do/Harpin' On It	1966	3.75	7.50	15.00
❑ 778	Pocketful of Money/Ride with Your Daddy				
	Tonight	1967	5.00	10.00	20.00
PHILLIPS INTERNATIONAL					
❑ 3578	Jelly Roll King/Crawlback	1962	5.00	10.00	20.00
Albums					
EARWIG					
❑ 4901	Rockin' the Juke Joint Down	1986	2.50	5.00	10.00
❑ 4914	Midnight Prowler	1990	2.50	5.00	10.00
JEWEL					
❑ LPS-5013	Frank Frost	1973	3.75	7.50	15.00
PHILLIPS INTERNATIONAL					
❑ PLP-1975 [M]	Hey Boss Man!	1962	1500.	2250.	3000.

FROST, MAX, AND THE TROOPERS
45s
SIDEWALK

Number	Title (A Side/B Side)	Yr	VG	VG+	NM
❑ 938	There Is a Party Going On/Stomper's Ride	1968	3.75	7.50	15.00
TOWER					
❑ 419	Shape of Things to Come/Free Lovin'	1968	3.75	7.50	15.00
❑ 419 [PS]	Shape of Things to Come/Free Lovin'	1968	12.50	25.00	50.00
—Promo-only sleeve with message to DJs on back					
❑ 452	52%/Max Frost Theme	1968	3.75	7.50	15.00
❑ 452 [PS]	52%/Max Frost Theme	1968	5.00	10.00	20.00
❑ 478	Paxton Quigley's Had the Course/				
	Sittin' in Circles	1969	3.75	7.50	15.00
❑ 478 [PS]	Paxton Quigley's Had the Course/				
	Sittin' in Circles	1969	5.00	10.00	20.00
Albums					
TOWER					
❑ ST-5147	Shape of Things to Come	1968	12.50	25.00	50.00

FROST, THE
45s
DATE

Number	Title (A Side/B Side)	Yr	VG	VG+	NM
❑ 1577	Bad Girl/Rainy Day	1967	3.00	6.00	12.00
—As "Dick Wagner and the Frosts"					
❑ 1596	Little Girl/Sunshine	1968	3.00	6.00	12.00
—As "Dick Wagner and the Frosts"					
VANGUARD					
❑ 35099	Linda/Sweet Lady Love	1969	2.00	4.00	8.00
❑ 35111	Rock and Roll Music/Donny's Blues	1969	2.00	4.00	8.00
❑ 35115	A Long Way from Home/Black As Night	1970	2.00	4.00	8.00
Albums					
VANGUARD					
❑ VSD-6520	Frost Music	1969	5.00	10.00	20.00
❑ VSD-6541	Rock and Roll Music	1969	5.00	10.00	20.00
❑ VSD-6556	Through the Eyes of Love	1970	5.00	10.00	20.00
❑ VSD-79392	Early Frost	1978	3.75	7.50	15.00

FROST, THOMAS AND RICHARD
45s
IMPERIAL

Number	Title (A Side/B Side)	Yr	VG	VG+	NM
❑ 66405	She's Got Love/The Word Is Love	1969	2.00	4.00	8.00
❑ 66426	With Me My Love/Gotta Find a New Place to Stay	1969	2.50	5.00	10.00
❑ 66451	Hello Stranger/Fairy Tale Affair	1970	2.50	5.00	10.00
UNI					
❑ 55320	Got to Find the Light/St. Petersburg	1972	2.50	5.00	10.00
❑ 55320	Mona Lisas and Mad Hatters/Kentucky Moon	1972	2.50	5.00	10.00

Number	Title (A Side/B Side)	Yr	VG	VG+	NM
Albums					
UNI					
❑ 73124	Thomas and Richard Frost	1972	3.75	7.50	15.00
FRUMIOUS BANDERSNATCH					
7-Inch Extended Plays					
MUGGLES GRAMOPHONE WORKS					
❑ (no #)	Hearts to Cry/Misty Cloudy//Cheshire	1967	62.50	125.00	250.00
—Legitimate copies show purple vinyl when held to a light; all others are counterfeits					
❑ (no #) [PS]	Frumious Bandersnatch	1967	62.50	125.00	250.00
FRUMMOX					
45s					
PROBE					
❑ 470	Mary Martin/There You Go	1970	2.00	4.00	8.00
Albums					
PROBE					
❑ 4511	From Here to There	1970	3.75	7.50	15.00
FRUT					
45s					
WESTBOUND					
❑ 189	Prison of Love/Send Me Down	1972	2.50	5.00	10.00
Albums					
TRASH					
❑ (# unknown)	Keep On Truckin'	1971	20.00	40.00	80.00
—Originals on yellow vinyl					
WESTBOUND					
❑ WB-2005	Keep On Truckin'	1971	7.50	15.00	30.00
—Reissue of Trash LP					
❑ WB-2008	Spoiled Rotten	1972	7.50	15.00	30.00
FRYE, DAVID					
45s					
BUDDAH					
❑ 378 [DJ]	Nixon Meets the Godfather (mono/stereo)	1973	2.50	5.00	10.00
—Promo only?					
ELEKTRA					
❑ 45722	My Way/Farm Report	1971	2.50	5.00	10.00
Albums					
BUDDAH					
❑ 1600	Richard Nixon: A Fantasy	1973	3.00	6.00	12.00
❑ BDS-5097	Richard Nixon: Superstar	1971	3.00	6.00	12.00
ELEKTRA					
❑ EKS-74085	Radio Free Nixon	1971	3.00	6.00	12.00
❑ EKS-75006	I Am the President	1969	3.00	6.00	12.00
FRYE					
❑ DFP-80	The Great Debate	1980	3.75	7.50	15.00
FUGS, THE					
45s					
ESP-DISK'					
❑ 4507	Frenzy/I Want to Know	1966	3.75	7.50	15.00
Albums					
BROADSIDE					
❑ 304 [M]	The Village Fugs Sing Ballads of Contemporary Protest, Point of View, and General Dissatisfaction	1965	100.00	200.00	400.00
—Without insert					
❑ 304 [M]	The Village Fugs Sing Ballads of Contemporary Protest, Point of View, and General Dissatisfaction	1965	125.00	250.00	500.00
—With insert					
ESP-DISK					
❑ 1018 [M]	The Fugs First Album	1966	10.00	20.00	40.00
—"Reissue of Broadside 304" on cover					
❑ 1018 [M]	The Fugs First Album	1966	37.50	75.00	150.00
—Turquoise and black cover, different from all other versions					
❑ 1018 [M]	The Fugs First Album	1967	7.50	15.00	30.00
—No reference to reissue on cover					
❑ 1028 [S]	The Fugs	1966	7.50	5.00	30.00
—Black and white cover, back cover photos aligned					
❑ 1028 [S]	The Fugs	1966	12.50	25.00	50.00
—Black and white cover, back cover photos staggered					
❑ 1028 [S]	The Fugs	1966	20.00	40.00	80.00
—Psychedelic color shield on cover					
❑ 1038 [S]	Virgin Fugs	1967	7.50	15.00	30.00
—"For Adult Minds" printed on cover					
❑ 1038 [S]	Virgin Fugs	1967	12.50	25.00	50.00
—"For Adult Minds" stamped on cover					
❑ 1038 [S]	Virgin Fugs	1967	12.50	25.00	50.00
—"For Adult Minds" sticker, no inserts					
❑ 1038 [S]	Virgin Fugs	1967	25.00	50.00	100.00
—"For Adult Minds" sticker on cover; with poster, book and stickers					
❑ 2018	Fugs 4, Rounders Score	196?	20.00	40.00	80.00
PVC					
❑ 8914	Proto Punk: The Fugs Greatest Hits, Vol. 1	1982	3.75	7.50	15.00
REPRISE					
❑ R-6280 [M]	Tenderness Junction	1968	10.00	20.00	40.00
❑ RS-6280 [S]	Tenderness Junction	1968	7.50	15.00	30.00
❑ RS-6305	It Crawled Into My Hand, Honest	1968	6.25	12.50	25.00
❑ RS-6359	Belle of Avenue A	1969	6.25	12.50	25.00
❑ RS-6396	Golden Fifth	1970	6.25	12.50	25.00
FULL MOON					
45s					
DOUGLAS					
❑ ZS7 6506	To Know//(B-side unknown)	1972	2.00	4.00	8.00
Albums					
DOUGLAS					
❑ KZ 31904	Full Moon	1972	3.75	7.50	15.00
FULLER, BOBBY, FOUR					
45s					
CAPITOL					
❑ 3038	The Only God I Know/A Name Like Watermelon	1971	5.00	10.00	20.00

Number	Title (A Side/B Side)	Yr	VG	VG+	NM
DONNA					
❑ 1403	Those Memories of You/Our Favorite Martian	1965	50.00	100.00	200.00
—As "Bobby Fuller and the Fantastics"					
EASTWOOD					
❑ 345	Not Fade Away/Nervous Breakdown	1962	25.00	50.00	100.00
EXETER					
❑ 122	King of the Beach/Wine, Wine, Wine	1964	50.00	100.00	200.00
❑ 124	I Fought the Law/She's My Girl	1964	87.50	175.00	350.00
❑ 126	Fool of Love/Shakedown	1964	30.00	60.00	120.00
LIBERTY					
❑ 55812	Let Her Dance/Another Sad and Lonely Night	1965	7.50	15.00	30.00
LOST-NITE					
❑ 257	I Fought the Law/Little Annie Lou	196?	—	2.50	5.00
—Reissue					
MUSTANG					
❑ 3004	She's My Girl/Take My Hand	1965	6.25	12.50	25.00
❑ 3006	Let Her Dance/Another Sad and Lonely Night	1965	3.75	7.50	15.00
❑ 3011	Never to Be Forgotten/You Kissed Me	1965	6.25	12.50	25.00
❑ 3012	Let Her Dance/Another Sad and Lonely Night	1965	3.75	7.50	15.00
❑ 3014	I Fought the Law/Little Annie Lou	1966	3.75	7.50	15.00
❑ 3016	Love's Made a Fool of You/Don't Ever Let Me Know	1966	3.75	7.50	15.00
❑ 3018	Magic Touch/My True Love	1966	3.00	6.00	12.00
TODD					
❑ 1090	Saturday Night/The Stinger	1963	25.00	50.00	100.00
YUCCA					
❑ 140	You're in Love/Guess We'll Fall in Love	1961	10.00	20.00	40.00
—Fast version					
❑ 140	You're in Love/Guess We'll Fall in Love	1961	20.00	40.00	80.00
—Slow version					
❑ 144	My Heart Jumped/Gently My Love	1961	20.00	40.00	80.00
Albums					
MUSTANG					
❑ M-900 [M]	KRLA King of the Wheels	1965	37.50	75.00	150.00
❑ MS-900 [S]	KRLA King of the Wheels	1965	50.00	100.00	200.00
❑ M-901 [M]	I Fought the Law	1966	20.00	40.00	80.00
❑ MS-901 [S]	I Fought the Law	1966	37.50	75.00	150.00
RHINO					
❑ RNLP-057	The Bobby Fuller Tapes, Vol. 1	1983	2.50	5.00	10.00
❑ RNDF-201	The Best of the Bobby Fuller Four	1981	3.00	6.00	12.00
❑ RNLP 70174	The Best of the Bobby Fuller Four (Golden Archive Series)	1987	2.50	5.00	10.00
VOXX					
❑ VXS 200028	The Bobby Fuller Tapes, Vol. 2	1984	2.50	5.00	10.00
FULLER, JERRY Also see THE FLEAS; THE FULLER BROTHERS.					
45s					
ABC					
❑ 12436	Salt on the Wound/No Time	1978	—	2.00	4.00
BELL					
❑ 45233	Rhyme/Thumb Tripping	1972	—	2.50	5.00
❑ 45295	Bookends/(B-side unknown)	1972	—	2.50	5.00
❑ 45349	Lazy Susan/How Do We Stand	1973	—	2.50	5.00
❑ 45433	Arianne/(B-side unknown)	1974	—	2.50	5.00
CHALLENGE					
❑ 9120	Guilty of Loving You/First Love Never Dies	1961	5.00	10.00	20.00
❑ 9128	The Place Where I Cry/Poor Little Heart	1961	5.00	10.00	20.00
❑ 9132	Wake Up Sleeping Beauty/Trust Me	1962	5.00	10.00	20.00
❑ 9148	Too Many People/Willingly, I'll Let You Go	1962	5.00	10.00	20.00
❑ 9161	Why Do They Say Goodbye/Let Me Be with You	1962	5.00	10.00	20.00
❑ 9184	Give My Love to Christy/Dear Teresa	1963	5.00	10.00	20.00
❑ 59052	Betty My Angel/Memories of You	1959	7.50	15.00	30.00
❑ 59057	Tennessee Waltz/Charlene	1959	5.00	10.00	20.00
❑ 59068	Two Loves Have I/I Dreamed About My Lover	1960	5.00	10.00	20.00
❑ 59074	Above and Beyond/One Heart	1960	5.00	10.00	20.00
—With Diane Maxwell					
❑ 59085	Gone for the Summer/Anna from Louisiana	1960	5.00	10.00	20.00
❑ 59104	Shy Away/Heavenly	1961	5.00	10.00	20.00
❑ 59217	I Only Came to Dance with You/Young Land	1963	5.00	10.00	20.00
❑ 59235	Footprints in the Snow/Hollywood Star	1964	3.75	7.50	15.00
❑ 59252	Don't Let Go/Roses Love Sunshine	1964	3.75	7.50	15.00
❑ 59269	The Killer/Mi Amora Mi Vidor	1965	3.75	7.50	15.00
❑ 59279	I Get Carried Away/Am I That Easy to Forget	1965	7.50	15.00	30.00
❑ 59307	Don't Look at Me Like That/What Happened to the Music	1965	3.75	7.50	15.00
❑ 59315	Man in Black/Master Plan	1965	3.75	7.50	15.00
❑ 59329	Double Life/Turn to Me	1966	6.25	12.50	25.00
COLUMBIA					
❑ 4-45131	Could It Be/I Know We Can Make It	1970	2.00	4.00	8.00
❑ 4-45209	Go/If I Had a Mind To	1970	2.00	4.00	8.00
LIN					
❑ 5011	Blue Memories/I Found a New Love	1958	7.50	15.00	30.00
❑ 5012	Do You Love Me/Teenage Love	1958	7.50	15.00	30.00
❑ 5015	A Certain Smile/Angel from Above	1958	7.50	15.00	30.00
❑ 5016	The Door Is Open/Through Eternity	1958	7.50	15.00	30.00
❑ 5019	Lipstick and Rouge/Mother Goose at the Bandstand	1959	7.50	15.00	30.00
MCA					
❑ 41022	Lines/Over You	1979	—	2.00	4.00
❑ 41114	Don't Do Anything/Don't Tell Me	1979	—	2.00	4.00
Albums					
LIN					
❑ 100 [M]	Teenage Love	1960	62.50	125.00	250.00
MCA					
❑ 3170	My Turn Now	1979	3.00	6.00	12.00
FULLER, JOHNNY					
45s					
ALADDIN					
❑ 3278	Johnny Ace's Last Letter/Fools Paradise	1955	20.00	40.00	80.00
❑ 3286	Cruel, Cruel World/My Heart Beats for You	1955	15.00	30.00	60.00
ART TONE					
❑ 828	No More/The Power	1962	5.00	10.00	20.00
CHECKER					
❑ 899	You Got Me Whistling/All Night Long	1958	6.25	12.50	25.00

Number	Title (A Side/B Side)	Yr	VG	VG+	NM
FLAIR					
❑ 1054	Buddy/Hard Times	1955	37.50	75.00	150.00
HOLLYWOOD					
❑ 1043	Train Train Blues/Bad Luck Overtook Me	1955	20.00	40.00	80.00
❑ 1057	Mean Old World/How Long	1956	20.00	40.00	80.00
❑ 1063	Comin' Round the Corner/Roughest Place in Town	1956	20.00	40.00	80.00
❑ 1077	My Mama Told Me/Too Late to Change My Mind	1956	20.00	40.00	80.00
❑ 1084	Sunny Road/I Can't Succeed	1957	20.00	40.00	80.00
IMPERIAL					
❑ 5580	Heavenly Love/Whispering Wind	1959	5.00	10.00	20.00
❑ 5697	Miss You/Stop, Look and Listen	1960	5.00	10.00	20.00
IRMA					
❑ 106	Weeping and Mourning/Strange Land	1958	20.00	40.00	80.00
❑ 110	First Stage of the Blues/No More, No More	1958	20.00	40.00	80.00
❑ 112	You Got Me Whistling/All Night Long	1958	15.00	30.00	60.00
MONEY					
❑ 206	I Walk All Night/These Young Girls	1955	15.00	30.00	60.00
SPECIALTY					
❑ 655	Haunted House/The Mighty Hand	1959	5.00	10.00	20.00
❑ 671	Swingin' at the Creek/Many Rivers, Mighty Seas	1959	5.00	10.00	20.00

FULLER BROTHERS, THE Also see JERRY FULLER.
45s

Number	Title (A Side/B Side)	Yr	VG	VG+	NM
CHALLENGE					
❑ 9119	Moon River/Framed, Convicted and Condemned	1961	5.00	10.00	20.00
❑ 9145	Ballad of the Midnight Special/The Gallows Tree	1962	5.00	10.00	20.00

FULSON, LOWELL Also recorded as "Lowell Folsom" and "Lowell Fulsum," both included below.
45s

Number	Title (A Side/B Side)	Yr	VG	VG+	NM
ALADDIN					
❑ 3088	Double Trouble/Good Woman Blues	1951	37.50	75.00	150.00
❑ 3104	Night and Day/Stormin' and Rainin'	1951	25.00	50.00	100.00
—Black vinyl					
❑ 3104	Night and Day/Stormin' and Rainin'	1951	250.00	500.00	1000.
—Green vinyl					
❑ 3217	Don't Leave Me Baby/Check with the Boys	1954	20.00	40.00	80.00
❑ 3233	Blues Never Fail/You've Gotta Reap	1954	20.00	40.00	80.00
CASH					
❑ 1051	Love Society Blues/Blue Shadows	1957	10.00	20.00	40.00
CHECKER					
❑ 804	Reconsider Baby/I Believe I'll Give It Up	1954	10.00	20.00	40.00
❑ 812	Loving You (Is All I Crave)/Check Yourself	1955	10.00	20.00	40.00
❑ 820	Lonely Hours/Do Me Right	1955	7.50	15.00	30.00
❑ 829	Trouble, Trouble/I Still Love You Baby	1955	7.50	15.00	30.00
❑ 841	It's Your Fault, Baby/Tollin' Bells	1956	7.50	15.00	30.00
❑ 854	Blues Rhumba/Please Don't Go	1957	6.25	12.50	25.00
❑ 865	Don't Drive Me, Baby/You're Gonna Miss Me	1957	6.25	12.50	25.00
❑ 882	I Want to Make Love to You/Rock This Morning	1958	6.25	12.50	25.00
❑ 937	It Took a Long Time/That's Alright	1960	5.00	10.00	20.00
❑ 952	Comin' Home/Have You Changed Your Mind	1960	5.00	10.00	20.00
❑ 959	I'm Glad You Reconsidered/Blue Shadows	1960	5.00	10.00	20.00
❑ 972	I Want to Know (Part 1)/I Want to Know (Part 2)	1961	3.75	7.50	15.00
❑ 992	So Many Tears/Hung Down Head	1961	3.75	7.50	15.00
❑ 1027	Shed No Tears/Can She	1962	3.75	7.50	15.00
❑ 1046	Trouble with the Blues/Love Grows Cold	1963	3.75	7.50	15.00
GRANITE					
❑ 533	Do You Love Me/A Step at a Time	1975	—	2.50	5.00
❑ 538	The Old Blues Singer/Monday Morning Blues	1976	—	2.50	5.00
HOLLYWOOD					
❑ 567-242	The Original Lonesome Christmas Part 1/The Original Lonesome Christmas Part 2	196?	2.50	5.00	10.00
❑ 1022	The Original Lonesome Christmas Part 1/The Original Lonesome Christmas Part 2	1955	5.00	10.00	20.00
❑ 1029	Everyday I Have the Blues/Guitar Shuffle	1955	12.50	25.00	50.00
❑ 1103	Everyday I Have the Blues/Guitar Shuffle	1962	3.75	7.50	15.00
JEWEL					
❑ 801	Letter Home/Lady in the Rain	1969	2.00	4.00	8.00
❑ 802	Why Don't We Do It in the Road/Too Soon	1969	2.50	5.00	10.00
❑ 805	How Do You Want Your Man/Sleeper	1969	2.00	4.00	8.00
❑ 808	Don't Leave Me/Thug	1970	2.00	4.00	8.00
❑ 811	Do You Feel It/Don't Destroy Me	1970	2.00	4.00	8.00
❑ 813	Lonesome Christmas (Part 1)/Lonesome Christmas (Part 2)	1970	—	3.00	6.00
❑ 818	My Baby/Bluesway	1971	—	3.00	6.00
❑ 820	Teach Me/Man of Motion	1971	—	3.00	6.00
❑ 827	Change of Heart/Every Second a Fool Is Born	1972	—	3.00	6.00
❑ 832	Look at You Baby/Fed Up	1972	—	3.00	6.00
KENT					
❑ 395	Every Time It Rains/Just One More Time	1964	3.00	6.00	12.00
❑ 395	Every Time It Rains/My Heart Belongs to You	1964	3.00	6.00	12.00
❑ 401	Key to My Heart/Too Many Drivers	1964	3.00	6.00	12.00
❑ 410	Strange Feeling/What's Gonna Be	1965	3.00	6.00	12.00
❑ 422	No More (Part 1)/No More (Part 2)	1965	3.00	6.00	12.00
❑ 431	Black Nights/Little Angel	1965	2.50	5.00	10.00
❑ 440	Sittin' Here Thinkin'/Shattered Dreams	1966	2.50	5.00	10.00
❑ 443	Blues Around Midnight/Talkin' Woman	1966	2.50	5.00	10.00
❑ 448	Change Your Ways/My Aching Back	1966	2.50	5.00	10.00
❑ 452	The Trouble I'm In/Ask at Any Door in Town	1966	2.50	5.00	10.00
❑ 456	Tramp/Pico	1966	2.50	5.00	10.00
❑ 463	Make a Little Love/I'm Sinking	1967	2.50	5.00	10.00
❑ 463 [PS]	Make a Little Love/I'm Sinking	1967	5.00	10.00	20.00
❑ 466	Everyday I Have the Blues/No Hard Feelings	1967	2.50	5.00	10.00
❑ 471	I Cried/The Thing	1967	2.50	5.00	10.00
❑ 474	I'm a Drifter/Hobo Meetin'	1967	2.50	5.00	10.00
❑ 477	I Wanna Spend Christmas with You Part 1/I Wanna Spend Christmas with You Part 2	1967	3.00	6.00	12.00
❑ 479	Tomorrow/Push Me	1968	2.50	5.00	10.00
❑ 486	The Letter/Let's Go Get Stoned	1968	2.50	5.00	10.00
❑ 489	Blues Pain/Mellow Together	1968	2.50	5.00	10.00
❑ 497	Sweetest Thing/What the Heck	1968	2.50	5.00	10.00
❑ 505	Lovin' Touch/Price for Love	1969	2.50	5.00	10.00
❑ 4535	Let's Go Get Stoned/Funky Broadway	1970	2.00	4.00	8.00
MOVIN'					
❑ 128	Stop and Think/Baby	1964	3.00	6.00	12.00

Number	Title (A Side/B Side)	Yr	VG	VG+	NM
PARROT					
❑ 787	I've Been Mistreated/Juke Box Shuffle	1953	25.00	50.00	100.00
—Black vinyl					
❑ 787	I've Been Mistreated/Juke Box Shuffle	1953	50.00	100.00	200.00
—Red vinyl					
SWING TIME					
❑ 242	Lonesome Christmas (Part 1)/Lonesome Christmas (Part 2)	1951	15.00	30.00	60.00
—78 released in 1950; 45 released in 1951					
❑ 243	I'm a Night Owl (Part 1)/I'm a Night Owl (Part 2)	1951	25.00	50.00	100.00
❑ 272	Why Can't You Cry for Me/Blues with a Feeling	1951	—	—	—
—Unreleased on 45 rpm?					
❑ 289	Let's Live Right/Best Wishes	1952	12.50	25.00	50.00
❑ 290	Three O'Clock in the Morning Blues/I'm Wild About You Baby	1952	—	—	—
—Unreleased on 45 rpm?					
❑ 295	Guitar Shuffle/Mean Old Lonesome Song	1952	12.50	25.00	50.00
❑ 308	Black Widow Spider/Midnight Showers of Rain	1953	12.50	25.00	50.00
❑ 315	Raggedy Daddy Blues/Goodbye	1953	12.50	25.00	50.00
❑ 320	Ride Until the Sun Goes Down/Good Party Shuffle	1953	12.50	25.00	50.00
❑ 325	Upstairs/Let Me Ride Your Automobile	1953	12.50	25.00	50.00
❑ 330	The Blues Come Rollin' In/I Love My Baby	1954	12.50	25.00	50.00
❑ 335	Cash Box Boogie/My Daily Prayer	1954	12.50	25.00	50.00
❑ 338	I've Been Mistreated/Juke Box Shuffle	1954	12.50	25.00	50.00
Albums					
ARHOOLIE					
❑ R-2003	Early Recordings	1962	7.50	15.00	30.00
BIG TOWN					
❑ 1008	Lovemaker	1978	3.00	6.00	12.00
CHESS					
❑ 408	Hung Down Head	197?	3.75	7.50	15.00
GRANITE					
❑ 1006	Ol' Blues Singer	1976	3.75	7.50	15.00
JEWEL					
❑ LPS-5003	In a Heavy Bag	1970	3.75	7.50	15.00
❑ LPS-5009	I've Got the Blues	1973	3.75	7.50	15.00
KENT					
❑ KST-516 [S]	Lowell Fulsom	1965	10.00	20.00	40.00
❑ KST-520 [S]	Tramp	1967	10.00	20.00	40.00
❑ KST-531	Lowell Fulsom Now	1969	7.50	15.00	30.00
❑ KLP-5016 [M]	Lowell Fulsom	1965	7.50	15.00	30.00
❑ KLP-5020 [M]	Tramp	1967	7.50	15.00	30.00
ROUNDER					
❑ 2088	It's a Good Day	198?	3.00	6.00	12.00

FUN AND GAMES
45s

Number	Title (A Side/B Side)	Yr	VG	VG+	NM
UNI					
❑ 55086	Elephant Candy/The Way She Smiles	1968	3.00	6.00	12.00
❑ 55098	The Grooviest Girl in the World/It Must Have Been the Wind	1968	3.00	6.00	12.00
❑ 55128	Gotta Say Goodbye/We	1969	3.00	6.00	12.00
Albums					
UNI					
❑ 73042	Elephant Candy	1968	6.25	12.50	25.00

FUNK INC.
45s

Number	Title (A Side/B Side)	Yr	VG	VG+	NM
PRESTIGE					
❑ 752	Whipper (Part 1)/Whipper (Part 2)	1972	—	3.00	6.00
❑ 754	The Thrill Is Gone/Bowlegs	1973	—	3.00	6.00
❑ 759	Dirty Red (Part 1)/Dirty Red (Part 2)	197?	—	3.00	6.00
❑ 762	Goodbye, So Long/Just Don't Mean a Thing	197?	—	3.00	6.00
Albums					
PRESTIGE					
❑ 10031	Funk Inc.	1971	3.75	7.50	15.00
❑ 10043	Chicken Lickin'	1972	3.75	7.50	15.00
❑ 10059	Hangin' Out	1973	3.75	7.50	15.00
❑ 10071	Superfunk	1973	3.75	7.50	15.00
❑ 10087	Priced to Sell	1974	3.75	7.50	15.00

FUNKADELIC Also see GEORGE CLINTON; FUNKADELIC (2); PARLIAMENT; THE PARLIAMENTS.
12-Inch Singles

Number	Title (A Side/B Side)	Yr	VG	VG+	NM
MCA					
❑ L33-17955 [DJ]	By Way of the Drum (Extended Version 9:15) (Acappella 5:50) (Radio Edit 6:00) (Basstrumental 6:10) (Dub 6:55) (Drum Beats 3:59)	1989	2.50	5.00	10.00
❑ 23953	By Way of the Drum (Extended Version) (Dub) (Basstrumental)	1989	2.00	4.00	8.00
WARNER BROS.					
❑ PRO-A-766 [DJ]	One Nation Under a Groove (11:26) (Instrumental 5:26)	1978	37.50	75.00	150.00
❑ PRO-A-829 [DJ]	(Not Just) Knee Deep (unknown versions)	1979	25.00	50.00	100.00
❑ WBSD 8803	One Nation Under a Groove (Part 1) (Part 2)	1979	6.25	12.50	25.00
45s					
MCA					
❑ 53654	By Way of the Drum/(Instrumental)	1989	—	—	3.00
WARNER BROS.					
❑ 8618	One Nation Under a Groove (Part 1)/One Nation Under a Groove (Part 2)	1978	—	2.50	5.00
❑ 8618 [PS]	One Nation Under a Groove (Part 1)/One Nation Under a Groove (Part 2)	1978	—	2.50	5.00
❑ 8735	Cholly (Funk Getting Ready to Roll)/Into You	1979	—	2.50	5.00
❑ 49040	(Not Just) Knee Deep — Part 1/(Not Just) Knee Deep — Part 2	1979	—	2.50	5.00
❑ 49117	Uncle Jam (Part 1)/Uncle Jam (Part 2)	1979	—	2.50	5.00
❑ 49667	The Electric Spanking of War Babies/The Electric Spanking of War Babies (Part 2)	1981	—	2.00	4.00
❑ 49667 [PS]	The Electric Spanking of War Babies/The Electric Spanking of War Babies (Part 2)	1981	—	2.50	5.00
❑ 49807	Shockwaves/Bullino's Bounce	1981	—	2.00	4.00
WESTBOUND					
❑ 148	Music for My Mother/(Instrumental)	1969	2.50	5.00	10.00
❑ 150	I'll Bet You/Open Your Eyes	1969	2.50	5.00	10.00

Number	Title (A Side/B Side)	Yr	VG	VG+	NM
❏ 158	I Got a Thing, You Got a Thing, Everybody's Got a Thing/Fish, Chips and Sweat	1970	2.50	5.00	10.00
❏ 167	I Wanna Know If It's Good to You?/I Wanna Know If It's Good to You? (Part 2)	1970	2.50	5.00	10.00
❏ 175	You and Your Folks, Me and My Folks/Funky Dollar Bill	1971	2.50	5.00	10.00
❏ 185	Can You Get to That/Back in Our Minds	1971	2.50	5.00	10.00
❏ 197	I Miss My Baby/Baby I Owe You Something Good	1972	2.50	5.00	10.00

—As "U.S. Music with Funkadelic"

Number	Title (A Side/B Side)	Yr	VG	VG+	NM
❏ 198	Hit It and Quit It/A Whole Lot of B.S.	1972	2.50	5.00	10.00
❏ 205	A Joyful Process/Loose Booty	1972	2.50	5.00	10.00
❏ 218	Cosmic Slop/If You Don't Like the Effects, Don't Produce the Cause	1973	2.50	5.00	10.00
❏ 224	Standing on the Verge of Getting It On/Jimmy's Got a Little Bit of Bitch in Him	1974	2.50	5.00	10.00
❏ 5000	Red Hot Momma/Vital Juices	1975	2.00	4.00	8.00
❏ 5014	Better by the Pound/Stuffs and Things	1975	2.00	4.00	8.00
❏ 5026	Let's Take It to the Stage/Bilogical Speculation	1976	2.00	4.00	8.00
❏ 5029	Undisco Kidd/How Do Yeau View You	1976	2.00	4.00	8.00

Albums

SCARFACE/PRIORITY

Number	Title (A Side/B Side)	Yr	VG	VG+	NM
❏ 53872	One Nation Under a Groove	1993	3.75	7.50	15.00

—Limited-edition reissue of Warner Bros. 3209

Number	Title	Yr	VG	VG+	NM
❏ 53873	Hardcore Jollies	1993	3.75	7.50	15.00

—Limited-edition reissue of Warner Bros. 2973

Number	Title	Yr	VG	VG+	NM
❏ 53874	The Electric Spanking of War Babies	1993	3.75	7.50	15.00

—Limited-edition reissue of Warner Bros. 3482

Number	Title	Yr	VG	VG+	NM
❏ 53875	Uncle Jam Wants You	1993	3.75	7.50	15.00

—Limited-edition reissue of Warner Bros. 3371

WARNER BROS.

Number	Title	Yr	VG	VG+	NM
❏ BS 2973	Hardcore Jollies	1976	6.25	12.50	25.00
❏ BS 3209	One Nation Under a Groove	1978	6.25	12.50	25.00

—Includes bonus 7-inch single with small hole (deduct 20% if missing)

Number	Title	Yr	VG	VG+	NM
❏ BSK 3371	Uncle Jam Wants You	1979	6.25	12.50	25.00
❏ BSK 3482	The Electric Spanking of War Babies	1981	6.25	12.50	25.00

WESTBOUND

Number	Title	Yr	VG	VG+	NM
❏ 208	Standing on the Verge of Getting It On	1975	6.25	12.50	25.00

—Reissue of Westbound 1001

Number	Title	Yr	VG	VG+	NM
❏ 215	Let's Take It to the Stage	1975	12.50	25.00	50.00
❏ 215	Let's Take It to the Stage	1992	3.75	7.50	15.00

—Reissue with bar code

Number	Title	Yr	VG	VG+	NM
❏ 216	Funkadelic	1975	7.50	15.00	30.00

—Reissue of Westbound 2000

Number	Title	Yr	VG	VG+	NM
❏ 217	Free Your Mind…And Your Ass Will Follow	1975	6.25	12.50	25.00

—Reissue of Westbound 2001

Number	Title	Yr	VG	VG+	NM
❏ 218	Maggot Brain	1975	6.25	12.50	25.00

—Reissue of Westbound 2007

Number	Title	Yr	VG	VG+	NM
❏ 221 [(2)]	America Eats Its Young	1976	6.25	12.50	25.00

—Reissue of Westbound 2020

Number	Title	Yr	VG	VG+	NM
❏ 223	Cosmic Slop	1976	6.25	12.50	25.00

—Reissue of Westbound 2022

Number	Title	Yr	VG	VG+	NM
❏ 227	Tales of Kidd Funkadelic	1976	12.50	25.00	50.00
❏ 227	Tales of Kidd Funkadelic	1992	3.75	7.50	15.00

—Reissue with bar code

Number	Title	Yr	VG	VG+	NM
❏ 303	Best of the Early Years	197?	10.00	20.00	40.00
❏ 1001	Standing on the Verge of Getting It On	1974	12.50	25.00	50.00
❏ 1001	Standing on the Verge of Getting It On	1991	3.75	7.50	15.00

—Reissue with bar code

Number	Title	Yr	VG	VG+	NM
❏ 1004	Funkadelic's Greatest Hits	1975	12.50	25.00	50.00
❏ 2000	Funkadelic	1970	12.50	25.00	50.00
❏ 2000	Funkadelic	1990	3.75	7.50	15.00

—Reissue with bar code

Number	Title	Yr	VG	VG+	NM
❏ 2001	Free Your Mind…And Your Ass Will Follow	1970	12.50	25.00	50.00
❏ 2001	Free Your Mind…And Your Ass Will Follow	1990	3.75	7.50	15.00

—Reissue with bar code

Number	Title	Yr	VG	VG+	NM
❏ 2007	Maggot Brain	1971	12.50	25.00	50.00
❏ 2007	Maggot Brain	1990	3.75	7.50	15.00

—Reissue with bar code

Number	Title	Yr	VG	VG+	NM
❏ 2020 [(2)]	America Eats Its Young	1972	15.00	30.00	60.00
❏ 2020 [(2)]	America Eats Its Young	1991	5.00	10.00	20.00

—Reissue with bar code

Number	Title	Yr	VG	VG+	NM
❏ 2022	Cosmic Slop	1973	12.50	25.00	50.00
❏ 2022	Cosmic Slop	1991	3.75	7.50	15.00

—Reissue with bar code

FUNKADELIC (2) Splinter group from the original band, listed separately because GEORGE CLINTON is not involved.

45s

LAX

Number	Title (A Side/B Side)	Yr	VG	VG+	NM
❏ 70055	Connections and Disconnections/The Witch	1981	—	2.00	4.00

Albums

LAX

Number	Title	Yr	VG	VG+	NM
❏ FW 37087	Connections and Disconnections	1981	2.50	5.00	10.00

FURY, BILLY

45s

LONDON

Number	Title (A Side/B Side)	Yr	VG	VG+	NM
❏ 1857	Maybe Tomorrow/Gonna Type a Letter	1959	5.00	10.00	20.00
❏ 1925	Colette/Baby How I Cried	1960	5.00	10.00	20.00
❏ 1991	Halfway to Paradise/Cross My Heart	1961	5.00	10.00	20.00
❏ 2004	Stick Around/Coming Up in the World	1961	5.00	10.00	20.00
❏ 9515	I'll Never Find Another You/Don't Jump	1962	3.75	7.50	15.00
❏ 9548	Once Upon a Dream/Running Around	1962	3.75	7.50	15.00
❏ 9594	Because of Love/Like I've Never Loved Before	1963	3.75	7.50	15.00
❏ 9615	Don't Walk Away/When Will I Say I Love You	1963	3.75	7.50	15.00
❏ 9662	Hippy Hippy Shake/Glad All Over	1964	3.75	7.50	15.00
❏ 9675	I Will/What Am I Living For	1964	3.75	7.50	15.00
❏ 9740	I'm Lost Without You/Go Ahead and Ask Her	1965	3.75	7.50	15.00

MALA

Number	Title	Yr	VG	VG+	NM
❏ 569	Loving You/I'll Go Along With It	1967	2.50	5.00	10.00
❏ 583	Suzanne in the Mirror/It Just Don't Matter Now	1968	2.50	5.00	10.00

Number	Title (A Side/B Side)	Yr	VG	VG+	NM
❏ 595	Beyond the Shadow of a Doubt/Baby Do You Love Me	1968	2.50	5.00	10.00
❏ 12018	Silly Boy Blue/One Minute Woman	1968	2.50	5.00	10.00

PARROT

Number	Title	Yr	VG	VG+	NM
❏ 9692	Baby What You Want Me to Do/It's Only Make Believe	1964	3.75	7.50	15.00

UNITED ARTISTS

Number	Title	Yr	VG	VG+	NM
❏ 968	In Thoughts of You/Away from You	1966	3.00	6.00	12.00
❏ 50061	She's So Far Out She's In/Give Me Your Word	1966	3.00	6.00	12.00

FURYS (1), THE Doo-wop/R&B group. These were the only Furys to have a chart hit.

45s

EDSEL

Number	Title	Yr	VG	VG+	NM
❏ 786	So Tough/I've Got a Pain in My Head (Over You)	1961	15.00	30.00	60.00

LIBERTY

Number	Title	Yr	VG	VG+	NM
❏ 55692	Baby You Can Bet Your Boots/The Man Who Has Everything	1964	12.50	25.00	50.00
❏ 55719	If I Didn't Have a Dime/Dream	1964	12.50	25.00	50.00

MACK IV

Number	Title	Yr	VG	VG+	NM
❏ 112	Zing! Went the Strings of My Heart/Never More	1962	7.50	15.00	30.00
❏ 114	If There's a Next Time/Another Fella	1963	7.50	15.00	30.00
❏ 115	I Really Feel So Good/Always	1963	10.00	20.00	40.00
❏ 118	What Is Soul/I Lost My Baby	1963	10.00	20.00	40.00

WORLD PACIFIC

Number	Title	Yr	VG	VG+	NM
❏ 386	Cat 'n Mouse/Anything for You	1964	7.50	15.00	30.00

FURYS (2), THE Rock band, probably from Wisconsin.

45s

CUCA

Number	Title	Yr	VG	VG+	NM
❏ 1010	This Way Out/St. Louis Blues	1960	7.50	15.00	30.00
❏ 1097	Run to Him/Jenny	1962	6.25	12.50	25.00

FURYS (3), THE Band probably from the Boston, Massachusetts area.

45s

FLEETWOOD

Number	Title	Yr	VG	VG+	NM
❏ 4569	I Walk Away/Gone in the Night	1966	7.50	15.00	30.00

LAURIE

Number	Title	Yr	VG	VG+	NM
❏ 3382	I Walk Away/Gone in the Night	1967	3.00	6.00	12.00

FURYS (4), THE Pacific Northwest band from Springfield, Oregon.

45s

LAVENDER

Number	Title	Yr	VG	VG+	NM
❏ 1806	Parchman Farm/Beachin'	1962	5.00	10.00	20.00
❏ 1926	Merryman/Sand Flea	1963	5.00	10.00	20.00

FURYS (5), THE Band from Rochester, Minnesota.

45s

STUDIO CITY

Number	Title	Yr	VG	VG+	NM
❏ 1026	Baby What's Wrong/Little Queenie	1965	7.50	15.00	30.00

FURYS (U), THE

45s

AURA

Number	Title	Yr	VG	VG+	NM
❏ 395	Cover Girl/Where My Money Goes	196?	12.50	25.00	50.00

DIAMOND

Number	Title	Yr	VG	VG+	NM
❏ 242	That's All Right You're in Love/You're My Little Baby	1968	3.00	6.00	12.00

FUSE Early version of Cheap Trick.

45s

EPIC

Number	Title	Yr	VG	VG+	NM
❏ 10514	Cruisin' for Burgers/Hound Dog	1969	6.25	12.50	25.00

Albums

EPIC

Number	Title	Yr	VG	VG+	NM
❏ BN 26502	Fuse	1970	20.00	40.00	80.00

FUT, THE Maurice Gibb was in this group, whose single often was bootlegged as a "lost" Beatles track. It has no Beatles involvement whatsoever.

45s

BEACON

Number	Title	Yr	VG	VG+	NM
❏ 160	Have You Heard the Word/Futting	1970	2.50	5.00	10.00

FUT

Number	Title	Yr	VG	VG+	NM
❏ 160	Have You Heard the Word/Futting	1976	—	2.50	5.00

FUTURE, FREDDY

45s

PARKWAY

Number	Title	Yr	VG	VG+	NM
❏ 832	Don't Forget Me/Like Soiree	1961	3.00	6.00	12.00

FUTURE, THE

45s

UNI

Number	Title	Yr	VG	VG+	NM
❏ 55082	The Shape of Things to Come/52%	1968	2.00	4.00	8.00

Albums

SHAMLEY

Number	Title	Yr	VG	VG+	NM
❏ 703	Down the Country Road	1969	5.00	10.00	20.00

FUZZ, THE

45s

CALLA

Number	Title	Yr	VG	VG+	NM
❏ 174	I Love You for All Seasons/I Love You for All Seasons (Part 2)	1970	—	3.00	6.00
❏ 177	Like an Open Door/Leave It All Behind Me	1971	—	3.00	6.00
❏ 179	I'm So Glad/All About Love	1971	—	3.00	6.00
❏ 183	Mr. Heartache and Miss Tears/Do Just What You Can	1971	—	3.00	6.00

Albums

CALLA

Number	Title	Yr	VG	VG+	NM
❏ SD 2001	The Fuzz	1971	3.75	7.50	15.00

Number	Title (A Side/B Side)	Yr	VG	VG+	NM

G

G-CLEFS, THE
45s
LOMA

Number	Title (A Side/B Side)	Yr	VG	VG+	NM
❏ 2034	Party '66/Little Lonely Boy	1966	2.50	5.00	10.00
❏ 2048	I Can't Stand It/Whirlwind	1966	2.50	5.00	10.00

PARIS

❏ 502	Symbol of Love/Love Her in the Mornin'	1957	7.50	15.00	30.00
❏ 506	Zing Zang Zoo/Is This the Way	1957	6.25	12.50	25.00

PILGRIM

❏ 715	Ka-Ding-Dong/Darla My Darlin'	1956	5.00	10.00	20.00
—Red label					
❏ 715	Ka-Ding-Dong/Darla My Darlin'	1956	7.50	15.00	30.00
—Purple label					
❏ 720	'Cause You're Mine/ Please Write While I'm Away	1956	7.50	15.00	30.00

REGINA

❏ 1314	To the Winner Goes the Prize/ I Believe in All I Feel	1964	3.75	7.50	15.00
❏ 1319	Angel Listen to Me/Nobody But Betty	1964	5.00	10.00	20.00

TERRACE

❏ 7500	I Understand (Just How You Feel)/ Little Girl I Love You	1961	5.00	10.00	20.00
❏ 7503	Girl Has to Know/Lad (There Never Was a Dog Like You)	1962	5.00	10.00	20.00
❏ 7507	Make Up Your Mind/They'll Call Me Away	1962	5.00	10.00	20.00
❏ 7510	A Lover's Prayer/Sitting in the Moonlight	1962	6.25	12.50	25.00
❏ 7514	All My Trials/Big Train	1963	6.25	12.50	25.00

VEEP

❏ 1218	I Have/On the Other Side of Town	1965	3.75	7.50	15.00
❏ 1226	This Time/On the Other Side of Town	1965	3.75	7.50	15.00

G.T.O.'S, THE (1) Also see JOEY AND THE CONTINENTALS.
45s
CLARIDGE

❏ 312	She Rides with Me/Rudy Vahoo	1966	5.00	10.00	20.00
—Reissue of Claridge 304 by "Joey and the Continentals"					

PARKWAY

❏ 108	Girl from New York City/Missing Out on the Fun	1966	3.75	7.50	15.00

G.T.O.'S, THE (2) Short for "Girls Together Outrageously."
Albums
REPRISE

❏ RS 6390	Permanent Damage	1970	12.50	25.00	50.00
—Without booklet					
❏ RS 6390	Permanent Damage	1970	17.50	35.00	70.00
—With booklet					

STRAIGHT

❏ STS-1059	Permanent Damage	1969	20.00	40.00	80.00
—Without booklet					
❏ STS-1059	Permanent Damage	1969	25.00	50.00	100.00
—With booklet					

GABRIEL AND THE ANGELS
45s
AMY

❏ 802	Chumba/Hey	1960	5.00	10.00	20.00
❏ 823	Zing Went the Strings of My Heart/The Rooster	1961	10.00	20.00	40.00

APRIL

❏ 1102	Chumba/Hey	1960	12.50	25.00	50.00

NORMAN

❏ 506	I'm Gabriel/Ginza	1961	3.75	7.50	15.00
❏ 510	Gabriel, Blow Your Horn (Part 1)/Gabriel, Blow Your Horn (Part 2)	1961	3.75	7.50	15.00
❏ 514	Miss You So/See See Rider	1962	3.75	7.50	15.00
—As "Gabriel and His Trumpet"					

SWAN

❏ 4118	That's Life (That's Tough)/ Don't Wanna Twist No More	1962	3.00	6.00	12.00
❏ 4118	That's Life/Don't Wanna Twist No More	1962	3.75	7.50	15.00
—No subtitle on A-side					
❏ 4133	The Peanut Butter Song/All Work and No Play	1963	3.00	6.00	12.00

GABRIEL BONDAGE
Albums
DHARMA

❏ D-804	Angel Dust	1975	12.50	25.00	50.00
❏ D-808	Another Trip to Earth	1977	5.00	10.00	20.00
—Exists on white, red, or blue vinyl; each of similar value					

GADABOUTS, THE
45s
JARO

❏ 77022	Caress Me/Deep Are the Roots of a Happy Home	1960	3.75	7.50	15.00

MERCURY

❏ 70495	By the Waters of the Minnetonka/Giuseppe Mandolino	1954	6.25	12.50	25.00
❏ 70581	Go Boom Boom/Oochi Pachi	1955	6.25	12.50	25.00
❏ 70823	Busy Body Rock/All My Love Belongs to You	1956	6.25	12.50	25.00
❏ 70898	Stranded in the Jungle/Blues Train	1956	6.25	12.50	25.00
❏ 70978	Too Much Monkey Business/To Be with You	1956	6.25	12.50	25.00

WING

❏ 90008	Two Things I Love/Glass Heart	1955	6.25	12.50	25.00
❏ 90043	Teenage Rock/If You Only Had a Heart	1955	6.25	12.50	25.00
❏ 90062	Busy Body Rock/All My Love Belongs to You	1956	5.00	10.00	20.00

GADDY, BOB
45s
DOT

❏ 1185	Honey Stealin' Blues/Hold That Train, Conductor	1954	25.00	50.00	100.00
—As "Doctor Gaddy and His Orchestra"					

HARLEM

Number	Title (A Side/B Side)	Yr	VG	VG+	NM
❏ 2330	The Blues Has Walked in My Room/ Slow Down Baby	1954	37.50	75.00	150.00

JAX

❏ 308	No Help Wanted/Little Girls Boogie	1952	75.00	150.00	300.00

OLD TOWN

❏ 1031	I Love My Baby/Operator	1956	6.25	12.50	25.00
❏ 1039	Paper Lady/Out of My Name	1957	6.25	12.50	25.00
❏ 1050	Woe, Woe Is Me/Rip and Run	1958	6.25	12.50	25.00
❏ 1057	You Are the One/Take My Advice	1958	6.25	12.50	25.00
❏ 1064	What Would I Do/Paper Lady	1959	5.00	10.00	20.00
❏ 1070	Till the Day I Die/I'll Go My Way	1959	5.00	10.00	20.00
❏ 1077	Early One Morning/What Wrong Did I Do	1960	5.00	10.00	20.00
❏ 1085	Don't Tell Her/Could I	1960	5.00	10.00	20.00
❏ 1162	I Love My Baby/Operator	1964	3.00	6.00	12.00

GADDY, DOCTOR See BOB GADDY.

GADSON, MEL
45s
BIG TOP

❏ 3034	Comin' Down with Love/I'm Getting Sentimental Over You	1959	6.25	12.50	25.00

GAILTONES, THE
45s
DECCA

❏ 30726	Lover Boy/Please Don't Go	1958	10.00	20.00	40.00

GAINES, PEGGY
45s
HIT

❏ 17	Playboy/A Steel Guitar and a Glass of Wine	1962	2.00	4.00	8.00
—B-side by Joe Cash					
❏ 19	Gravy (For My Mashed Potatoes)/Roses Are Red (My Love)	1962	2.00	4.00	8.00
—B-side by Jimmy Lucas					
❏ 24	The Loco-Motion/Bring It On Home to Me	1962	2.00	4.00	8.00
—B-side by Herbert Hunter					
❏ 40	Ride!/Bobby's Girl	1962	2.00	4.00	8.00
—B-side by Connie Landers					
❏ 45	Tell Him/It's Up to You	1962	2.00	4.00	8.00
—B-side by Bill Carmichael					
❏ 124	Every Little Bit Hurts/What'd I Say	1964	2.00	4.00	8.00
—B-side by Jerry Poncher					

GAINES, ROY
45s
CHART

❏ 606	Loud Mouth Lucy/I'm Setting You Free	1955	15.00	30.00	60.00

DEL-FI

❏ 4169	What Is This Thing Called Love/Lizzie	1961	3.75	7.50	15.00

DELUXE

❏ 6119	Isabella/Gainesville	1957	6.25	12.50	25.00
❏ 6132	You're Right, I'm Left/Stolen Moments	1957	6.25	12.50	25.00
❏ 6147	Annabelle/Night Beat	1957	6.25	12.50	25.00

GROOVE

❏ 0146	Right Now Baby/De Dat De Dum Dum	1956	7.50	15.00	30.00
❏ 0161	Worried 'Bout You Baby/All My Life	1956	7.50	15.00	30.00

RCA VICTOR

❏ 47-7243	Skippy Is a Sissy/Weeping Willow	1958	15.00	30.00	60.00

GALAHADS, THE
Albums
LIBERTY

❏ LRP-3371 [M]	Hello, Galahads	1964	5.00	10.00	20.00
❏ LST-7371 [S]	Hello, Galahads	1964	6.25	12.50	25.00

GALAXYS, THE
45s
CARTHAY

❏ 103	A Lover's Prayer/Jelly Bean	1959	375.00	750.00	1500.

GALBRAITH, ROB
45s
COLUMBIA

❏ 4-44997	Willie Was a Honkie/Maggie McGhee, the Preacher's Daughter	1969	2.00	4.00	8.00
❏ 4-45156	Jezebel of the Morning/Mudflap Cadillac	1970	2.00	4.00	8.00

RCA

❏ PB-11051	No Pride/One on One with You	1977	—	2.50	5.00

Albums
COLUMBIA

❏ CS 1057	Nashville Dirt	1970	5.00	10.00	20.00

GALE, BARBARA
45s
LLOYDS

❏ 107	Lonely Weather/So Long, Good-Bye Joe	1953	30.00	60.00	120.00
❏ 109	Once Again/Fool Fool Me	1953	30.00	60.00	120.00
❏ 111	When You're Near/Who Walks In	1954	75.00	150.00	300.00
—With the Larks					
❏ 115	Johnny Darlin'/You're Gonna Lose That Gal	1954	75.00	150.00	300.00
—With the Larks					

GALE, SUNNY
45s
BLAINE

❏ 4002	Stay/Once in Every Lifetime	1965	—	3.00	6.00
❏ 4003	March of the Angels/ Let the Rest of the World Go By	1965	—	3.00	6.00

CANADIAN AMERICAN

❏ 163	Too Bad for You/I'm Telling My Heart	1963	2.00	4.00	8.00
❏ 171	I Wish I Didn't Love You So/I'm Not Sorry	1964	2.00	4.00	8.00
❏ 176	I Really Loved Him So/I'm Telling My Heart	1964	2.00	4.00	8.00

DECCA

❏ 9-30063	One Kiss Led to Another/Two Hearts	1956	2.50	5.00	10.00

Number	Title (A Side/B Side)	Yr	VG	VG+	NM
❏ 9-30125	Hot Dog! That Made Him Mad/				
	Welcome to My Heart	1956	2.50	5.00	10.00
❏ 9-30157	I Have You/Maybe You'll Be There	1956	2.50	5.00	10.00
❏ 9-30231	Come Go with Me/Please Go	1957	2.50	5.00	10.00
❏ 9-30319	Let's Be Friendly/Mirror	1957	2.50	5.00	10.00
❏ 9-30391	My Arms Are a House/Don't Worry 'Bout Me	1957	2.50	5.00	10.00
❏ 9-30518	A Meeting of the Eyes/Who Are We to Say?	1957	2.50	5.00	10.00
❏ 9-30597	For Crying Out Loud/I Don't Want Your				
	Greenback Dollars	1958	2.50	5.00	10.00
❏ 9-30670	A Certain Smile/Just Friends	1958	2.50	5.00	10.00
❏ 9-30791	Wheel of Fortune/Three O'Clock	1958	2.50	5.00	10.00
❏ 9-30837	The Gypsy Told Me So/Oh What It Seemed to Be	1959	2.50	5.00	10.00
RCA VICTOR					
❏ 47-4789	I Laughed at Love/Father Time	1952	3.00	6.00	12.00
❏ 47-4901	Tossin' and Turnin'/				
	You Could Make Me Smile Again	1952	3.00	6.00	12.00
❏ 47-5103	Teardrops on My Pillow/A Stolen Waltz	1952	3.00	6.00	12.00
❏ 47-5216	How Could You/				
	I Feel Like I'm Gonna Live Forever	1953	3.00	6.00	12.00
❏ 47-5306	Send My Baby Back to Me/Meanwhile	1953	3.00	6.00	12.00
❏ 47-5424	Love Me Again/Before It's Too Late	1953	3.00	6.00	12.00
❏ 47-5543	The Note in the Bottle/Mama's Gone Goodbye	1953	10.00	20.00	40.00
—With the Du Droppers					
❏ 47-5609	Close to Me/Just in Case You Change Your Mind	1954	3.00	6.00	12.00
❏ 47-5677	Dream, Dream, Dream/Don't Cry Mama	1954	3.00	6.00	12.00
❏ 47-5746	Goodnight, Sweetheart, Goodnight/Call Off the				
	Wedding	1954	3.00	6.00	12.00
❏ 47-5836	Smile/An Old Familiar Love Song	1954	3.00	6.00	12.00
❏ 47-5952	Let Me Go, Lover!/Unsuspecting Heart	1954	3.00	6.00	12.00
❏ 47-6160	Constantly/A Little You	1955	2.50	5.00	10.00
❏ 47-6227	Soldier Boy/Certainly Baby	1955	2.50	5.00	10.00
❏ 47-6286	C'est La Vie/Looking Glass	1955	2.50	5.00	10.00
❏ 47-6398	On the Way to Your Heart/Devotion	1956	2.50	5.00	10.00
❏ 47-6479	Rock and Roll Wedding/Winner Take All	1956	2.50	5.00	10.00
❏ 47-6588	If You Really Want to Know/Try a Little Prayer	1956	2.50	5.00	10.00
❏ 47-9580	Our Love Is a Sad Song/Georgie Porgie	1968	—	3.50	7.00
TERRACE					
❏ 7505	Crying in the Chapel/Love Me Again	1962	2.00	4.00	8.00
THIMBLE					
❏ THS 009	Birningham Rag/Sunshine State	1974	—	3.00	6.00
WARWICK					
❏ 526	Falling Star/What Do You Want to Make Those				
	Eyes at Me For	1960	2.00	4.00	8.00
❏ 540	Church Bells May Ring/My Foolish Heart	1960	2.00	4.00	8.00
❏ 578	It's Your Turn/Where Have You Been All My Life	1960	2.00	4.00	8.00
❏ 626	Please Love Me Forever/Sunny	1961	2.50	5.00	10.00
❏ 648	Near You/Please Don't Tell Him I Love Him	1961	2.00	4.00	8.00
Albums					
ROYALE					
❏ 18123 [10]	Sunny Gale and Jazz Orchestra	1954	12.50	25.00	50.00
THIMBLE					
❏ TLP-10	Sunny Sings Dixieland and Blues	1974	5.00	10.00	20.00

GALENS, THE
45s

Number	Title (A Side/B Side)	Yr	VG	VG+	NM
CHALLENGE					
❏ 59212	Baby I Do Love You/Love Bells	1963	3.75	7.50	15.00
❏ 59253	Stranger in Paradise/Chinese Lanterns	1964	3.75	7.50	15.00
❏ 59302	Young Dreams/I Love You More Than You Know	1965	3.75	7.50	15.00

GALES, THE
45s

Number	Title (A Side/B Side)	Yr	VG	VG+	NM
DEBRA					
❏ 1002	Tommy/Around the Clock with You	1963	10.00	20.00	40.00
J.O.B.					
❏ 3001	Darling Patricia/All Is Well, All Is Well	1956	50.00	100.00	200.00
JVB					
❏ 34	His Eyes Keep Me in Trouble/Don't Let the Sun				
	Catch You Cryin'	1955	1000.	2000.	3000.
❏ 35	Darling Patricia/All Is Well, All Is Well	1955	125.00	250.00	500.00
MEL-O					
❏ 111	Guiding Angel/Boy Come Home	1958	62.50	125.00	250.00
❏ 113	Josephine/If I Could Forget	1958	62.50	125.00	250.00
WINN					
❏ 916	I Love You/Squeeze Me	1960	125.00	250.00	500.00

GALLAGHER, JAMES
45s

Number	Title (A Side/B Side)	Yr	VG	VG+	NM
DECCA					
❏ 29984	Crazy Chicken/Just for You	1956	30.00	60.00	120.00

GALLAGHER, RORY
Albums

Number	Title (A Side/B Side)	Yr	VG	VG+	NM
ATCO					
❏ SD 33-368	Rory Gallagher	1971	3.75	7.50	15.00
❏ SD 7004	Deuce	1971	3.75	7.50	15.00
CHRYSALIS					
❏ CHR 1098	Against the Grain	1975	2.50	5.00	10.00
❏ CHR 1124	Calling Card	1976	2.50	5.00	10.00
❏ CHR 1170	Photo-Finish	1978	2.50	5.00	10.00
❏ CHR 1235	Top Priority	1979	2.50	5.00	10.00
❏ CHR 1280	Stage Struck	1980	2.50	5.00	10.00
MERCURY					
❏ SRM-1-4051	Jinx	1982	2.50	5.00	10.00
POLYDOR					
❏ PD-5513	Rory Gallagher/Live!	1972	3.00	6.00	12.00
❏ PD-5522	Blueprint	1973	3.00	6.00	12.00
❏ PD-5539	Tattoo	1973	3.00	6.00	12.00
❏ PD-1-6510	Sinner...And Saint	1975	3.00	6.00	12.00
❏ PD-1-6519	The Story So Far	1975	3.00	6.00	12.00
❏ PD-9501 [(2)]	Irish Tour '74	1974	3.00	6.00	12.00
SPRINGBOARD					
❏ 4056	In the Beginning	1976	2.50	5.00	10.00

GALLAHADS, THE (1)
45s

Number	Title (A Side/B Side)	Yr	VG	VG+	NM
CAPITOL					
❏ F-3060	Ooh Ah/Careless	1955	6.25	12.50	25.00
❏ F-3175	Do You Believe Me/If It Wasn't for You	1955	6.25	12.50	25.00
JUBILEE					
❏ 5252	The Fool/The Morning Mail	1956	7.50	15.00	30.00
❏ 5259	Take My Love/I Give You My Word	1956	6.25	12.50	25.00

GALLAHADS, THE (2)
45s

Number	Title (A Side/B Side)	Yr	VG	VG+	NM
DEL-FI					
❏ 4137	Lonely Guy/Jo Jo the Big Wheel	1960	5.00	10.00	20.00
—Black label					
❏ 4137	Lonely Guy/Jo Jo the Big Wheel	1960	10.00	20.00	40.00
—Green label					
❏ 4148	Be Fair/I'm Without a Girl Friend	1960	5.00	10.00	20.00
—Black label					
❏ 4148	Be Fair/I'm Without a Girl Friend	1960	10.00	20.00	40.00
—Green label					
DONNA					
❏ 1322	Lonely Guy/Jo Jo the Big Wheel	1960	10.00	20.00	40.00
❏ 1361	This Letter to You/The Answer to Love	1962	12.50	25.00	50.00
LOST-NITE					
❏ 205	Be Fair/I'm Without a Girl Friend	196?	—	2.50	5.00
—Reissue					

GALLAHADS, THE (U) It's unlikely any of these are group (1). Some of these are probably group (2). Others could be by different groups.
45s

Number	Title (A Side/B Side)	Yr	VG	VG+	NM
BEECHWOOD					
❏ 3001	Keeper of Dreams/Sad Girl	1960	30.00	60.00	120.00
—More than one group.					
NITE OWL					
❏ 20	Gone/So Long	1961	15.00	30.00	60.00
RENDEZVOUS					
❏ 153	Gone/Why Do Fools Fall in Love	1961	10.00	20.00	40.00
SEA CREST					
❏ 6005	Have Love, Will Travel/My Offering	1964	10.00	20.00	40.00
STARLA					
❏ 15	Keeper of Dreams/Sad Girl	1960	5.00	10.00	20.00

GALLALADS, THE
45s

Number	Title (A Side/B Side)	Yr	VG	VG+	NM
VIK					
❏ 4X-0291	Take Back My Ring/One Love Alone	1957	6.25	12.50	25.00
❏ 4X-0316	Best Wishes/Steady Man	1958	6.25	12.50	25.00
❏ 4X-0332	Silently/Barracuda	1958	6.25	12.50	25.00

GALLANT, RONNIE
45s

Number	Title (A Side/B Side)	Yr	VG	VG+	NM
ATLANTIC					
❏ 2169	Shake Shake Baby/Shadows	1962	3.00	6.00	12.00
WARNER BROS.					
❏ 5251	Hole in the Wall/In the Night	1962	3.00	6.00	12.00

GALLERY
45s

Number	Title (A Side/B Side)	Yr	VG	VG+	NM
SUSSEX					
❏ 232	Nice to Be with You/Ginger Haired Man	1972	—	2.50	5.00
❏ 239	I Believe in Music/Someone	1972	—	2.50	5.00
❏ 239 [PS]	I Believe in Music/Someone	1972	2.00	4.00	8.00
❏ 248	Big City Miss Ruth Ann/Lover's Hideaway	1972	—	2.50	5.00
❏ 255	Rest in Peace/Riverboat Captain	1973	—	2.50	5.00
❏ 259	Maybe Baby/Lady Luck	1973	—	2.50	5.00
❏ 512	Friends/I Love Every Little Thing About You	1974	—	2.00	4.00
❏ 630	Living Next Door to Alice/Captain Sam	1975	—	2.00	4.00
❏ 639	Power to All Our Friends/(B-side unknown)	1975	—	2.00	4.00
Albums					
SUSSEX					
❏ SUX-7017	Nice to Be with You	1972	3.00	6.00	12.00
❏ SUX-7026	Jim Gold and Gallery	1973	3.00	6.00	12.00

GALLERY (2)
Albums

Number	Title (A Side/B Side)	Yr	VG	VG+	NM
ECM					
❏ 1206	Gallery	1982	3.00	6.00	12.00

GALLICOS, THE
45s

Number	Title (A Side/B Side)	Yr	VG	VG+	NM
HIT					
❏ 260	Hungry/Hanky Panky	1966	2.50	5.00	10.00
—B-side by the McCalls					

GALLOP, FRANK
45s

Number	Title (A Side/B Side)	Yr	VG	VG+	NM
ABC-PARAMOUNT					
❏ 9931	Got a Match?/I Beg Your Pardon	1958	3.00	6.00	12.00
KAPP					
❏ 745	The Ballad of Irving/Would You Believe It	1966	2.50	5.00	10.00
—B-side by Phil Leeds					
MUSICOR					
❏ 1191	Son of Irving/One Love I'll Never Forget	1966	2.00	4.00	8.00
❏ 1191 [PS]	Son of Irving/One Love I'll Never Forget	1966	3.00	6.00	12.00
Albums					
MUSICOR					
❏ MM-2110 [M]	Frank Gallop Sings	1966	3.75	7.50	15.00
❏ MS-3110 [S]	Frank Gallop Sings	1966	5.00	10.00	20.00

GALS & PALS
Albums

Number	Title (A Side/B Side)	Yr	VG	VG+	NM
FONTANA					
❏ MGF-27538 [M]	Gals & Pals (The Exciting Vocal Sounds of				
	Europe's Newest "In" Group)	1965	3.75	7.50	15.00
❏ MGF-27557 [M]	Gals & Pals Sing Something for Everybody	1966	3.75	7.50	15.00
❏ SRF-67538 [S]	Gals & Pals (The Exciting Vocal Sounds of				
	Europe's Newest "In" Group)	1965	5.00	10.00	20.00
❏ SRF-67557 [S]	Gals & Pals Sing Something for Everybody	1966	5.00	10.00	20.00

G

Number	Title (A Side/B Side)	Yr	VG	VG+	NM

GALT, JAMES
45s
AURORA
| ❏ 158 | With My Baby/Most Unusual Feeling | 1966 | 7.50 | 15.00 | 30.00 |

GAMBLE, DEE DEE SHARP See DEE DEE SHARP.

GAMBLE, KENNY
45s
ARCTIC
❏ 107	Down by the Seashore (Part 1)/Down by the Seashore (Part 2)	1965	50.00	100.00	200.00
❏ 114	Ain't It Baby (Part 1)/Ain't It Baby (Part 2)	1965	50.00	100.00	200.00
❏ 123	The Joke's on You/Don't Stop Loving Me	1966	50.00	100.00	200.00

COLUMBIA
| ❏ 43132 | Our Love/You Don't Know What You Got Until You Lose It | 1964 | 7.50 | 15.00 | 30.00 |

EPIC
| ❏ 9636 | Standing in the Shadows/No Mail on Monday | 1963 | 7.50 | 15.00 | 30.00 |

GAMBLERS, THE (1) BRUCE JOHNSTON and SANDY NELSON were in this group.
45s
LAST CHANCE
| ❏ 2 | Teen Machine/Tonky | 1961 | 10.00 | 20.00 | 40.00 |
| ❏ 108 | Teen Machine/Tonky | 1962 | 6.25 | 12.50 | 25.00 |
WORLD PACIFIC
| ❏ 815 | Moon Dawg/LSD-25 | 1960 | 15.00 | 30.00 | 60.00 |

GAMBLERS, THE (2) British group.
45s
CORAL
| ❏ 62525 | Cry Me a River/Who Will Buy | 1967 | 2.00 | 4.00 | 8.00 |
PRESS
| ❏ 9739 | Now I'm All Alone/Find Out What's Happening | 1965 | 3.00 | 6.00 | 12.00 |

GAME
45s
EVOLUTION
| ❏ 1042 | Fat Mama/The Girl Next Door | 1970 | — | 3.00 | 6.00 |
| ❏ 1053 | Two Songs for the Senorita/(B-side unknown) | 1971 | — | 3.00 | 6.00 |
Albums
EVOLUTION
| ❏ 2021 | Game | 1970 | 3.00 | 6.00 | 12.00 |
| ❏ 3008 | Long Hot Summer | 1971 | 3.00 | 6.00 | 12.00 |
FAITHFUL VIRTUE
| ❏ 2003 | Game | 1969 | 5.00 | 10.00 | 20.00 |

GAMMA GOOCHEE
45s
COLPIX
| ❏ 786 | I'm Gonna Buy Me a Dog/(You Got the) Gamma Goochee | 1965 | 5.00 | 10.00 | 20.00 |
| ❏ 804 | I'm So Glad/Sweet Violets | 1966 | 3.75 | 7.50 | 15.00 |
MGM
| ❏ 13874 | Booga-Loo/Everybody's Somebody's Fool | 1967 | 3.75 | 7.50 | 15.00 |

GANDALF
45s
CAPITOL
| ❏ 2400 | Golden Earrings/Never Too Far | 1969 | 6.25 | 12.50 | 25.00 |
Albums
CAPITOL
| ❏ ST-121 | Gandalf | 1969 | 50.00 | 100.00 | 200.00 |

GANDALF THE GREY
Albums
G.W.R.
| ❏ 7 | The Grey Wizard Am I | 1972 | 75.00 | 150.00 | 300.00 |

GANEY, JERRY
45s
MGM
| ❏ 13697 | Hi-Heel Sneakers/You Don't Love Me | 1967 | 5.00 | 10.00 | 20.00 |
VERVE
| ❏ 10454 | Who Am I/Just a Fool | 1966 | 25.00 | 50.00 | 100.00 |

GANT, CECIL
45s
DECCA
| ❏ 9-30320 | I Wonder/Cecil's Boogie | 1957 | 7.50 | 15.00 | 30.00 |
| ❏ 9-48167 | Goodnight Irene/My House Fell Down | 1950 | 12.50 | 25.00 | 50.00 |
—As "Gunter Lee Carr"
| ❏ 9-48170 | We're Gonna Rock/Yesterday | 1950 | 12.50 | 25.00 | 50.00 |
—As "Gunter Lee Carr"
❏ 9-48171	Someday You'll Be Sorry (Part 1)/Someday You'll Be Sorry (Part 2)	1950	10.00	20.00	40.00
❏ 9-48185	It's Christmas Time Again/Hello Santa Claus	1950	10.00	20.00	40.00
❏ 9-48191	Train Time Blues No. 2/It Ain't Gonna Be Like That	1951	10.00	20.00	40.00
❏ 9-48200	Shot Gun Boogie/Rock Little Baby	1951	12.50	25.00	50.00
❏ 9-48212	Don't You Worry/My Little Baby	1951	10.00	20.00	40.00
❏ 9-48231	Owl Stew/Playin' Myself the Blues	1951	10.00	20.00	40.00
❏ 9-48249	God Bless My Daddy/The Grass Is Gettin' Greener	1951	10.00	20.00	40.00
DOT
❏ 1112	All By Myself/It Hurts Me Too	1952	10.00	20.00	40.00
—Earlier singles on Dot may not exist on 45s
| ❏ 1121 | Sloppy Joes/Train Time Blues | 1952 | 10.00 | 20.00 | 40.00 |
GILT EDGE
| ❏ 5090 | I Wonder/Cecil's Boogie | 1955 | 10.00 | 20.00 | 40.00 |
—Reissue of 78 first released in 1944
Albums
KING
| ❏ 671 [M] | Cecil Gant | 1960 | 20.00 | 40.00 | 80.00 |
RED MILL
| ❏ (no #) [M] | Cecil Gant | 1956 | 125.00 | 250.00 | 500.00 |
—Red vinyl

SOUND
| ❏ 601 [M] | The Incomparable Cecil Gant | 1958 | 25.00 | 50.00 | 100.00 |

GANTS, THE
45s
ALADDIN
| ❏ 3387 | My Unfaithful Love/Happening After School | 1957 | 15.00 | 30.00 | 60.00 |
LIBERTY
❏ 55829	Road Runner/My Baby Don't Care	1965	3.75	7.50	15.00
❏ 55853	Smoke Rings/Little Boy Sad	1966	2.50	5.00	10.00
❏ 55884	Dr. Feelgood/Crackin' Up	1966	2.50	5.00	10.00
❏ 55903	I Want Your Lovin'/A Spoonful of Sugar	1966	2.50	5.00	10.00
❏ 55940	Greener Days/I Wonder	1967	2.50	5.00	10.00
❏ 55965	Drifter's Sunrise/Just a Good Show	1967	2.50	5.00	10.00
STATUE
❏ 605	Road Runner/My Baby Don't Care	1965	12.50	25.00	50.00
❏ 608	What's Happening/Careless Hands	1965	6.25	12.50	25.00
—B-side by the Niteliters
Albums
LIBERTY
❏ LRP-3432 [M]	Road Runner	1965	7.50	15.00	30.00
❏ LRP-3455 [M]	The Gants Galore	1966	7.50	15.00	30.00
❏ LRP-3473 [M]	The Gants Again	1966	7.50	15.00	30.00
❏ LST-7432 [S]	Road Runner	1965	10.00	20.00	40.00
❏ LST-7455 [S]	The Gants Galore	1966	10.00	20.00	40.00
❏ LST-7473 [S]	The Gants Again	1966	10.00	20.00	40.00

GAP BAND, THE
12-Inch Singles
ARISTA
| ❏ AD1-9777 | I'm Gonna Git Ya Sucka (Extended Version 6:13) (Sugar Shack Version 6:00)/(Single Version 3:34) (Extended Edit 3:58) (Tripped Out Dub Version 6:00) | 1988 | — | 3.50 | 7.00 |
CAPITOL
| ❏ V-15493 | All of My Love (Extended Mix) (Instrumental) (Just Coolin' Mix) (Radio Mix) (Percussapella) (Bonus Beats) | 1989 | — | 3.50 | 7.00 |
| ❏ V-15534 | Addicted to Your Love (Extended Mix) (Instrumental) (Silly Stoopid Crazy Over You Mix)/(I'll Groove 4 U Remix) (I'll Groove 4 U Rap) (I'll Groove 4 U Instrumental) | 1990 | 2.00 | 4.00 | 8.00 |
MERCURY
❏ MK 86 [DJ]	Baby Baba Boogie (7:32)/Shake	1979	3.00	6.00	12.00
❏ MK 124 [DJ]	Steppin' (Out) (same on both sides)	1979	2.00	4.00	8.00
❏ MK 138 [DJ]	Party Lights (2 versions)	1980	3.00	6.00	12.00
❏ MK 175 [DJ]	Yearning for Your Love/Humpin'	1980	2.00	4.00	8.00
❏ MDS 4006	Shake/Baby Baba Boogie	1979	2.50	5.00	10.00
❏ 884662-1	You Dropped a Bomb on Me/Party Train	1986	3.00	6.00	12.00
—Reissue in conjunction with 'The 12" Collection' LP
PASSPORT
| ❏ PB-4005 | Not Guilty/Knucklehead Funkin'/Listen to the Music | 1983 | 2.00 | 4.00 | 8.00 |
RAGING BULL
| ❏ RB 5023 | Got It Goin' On (Extended BATT Edit) (Radio Edit) | 1995 | 2.00 | 4.00 | 8.00 |
| ❏ RB 8013 | First Lover (4 versions) | 1995 | 2.00 | 4.00 | 8.00 |
TOTAL EXPERIENCE
❏ TK 214 [DJ]	You Dropped a Bomb on Me (Long Version 13:05)/(LP Version 5:12)	1982	3.00	6.00	12.00
❏ TED-701	Early in the Morning (Short Version 6:30) (Long Version 7:33)	1982	2.00	4.00	8.00
❏ TED-702	You Dropped a Bomb on Me (13:05)/Humpin' (5:06)	1982	3.75	7.50	15.00
❏ TED-704	Outstanding (unknown versions)	1982	2.00	4.00	8.00
❏ TED-706	Party Train (5:55) (6:10)	1983	2.50	5.00	10.00
❏ TED-707	I'm Ready (If You're Ready) (5:51)/Shake a Leg	1983	—	3.50	7.00
❏ TED 1003	Straight from the Heart (Cardiac Mix) (Pump the Heart Dub Mix) (Thump Thump Instrumental)	1988	—	3.00	6.00
❏ TED 1005	All the Way Yours (unknown versions)	1988	—	3.00	6.00
❏ TED1-2606	Beep a Freak (Short Version, To Be LP Mix 5:10) (Dance Mix 7:47) (Instrumental)	1984	2.00	4.00	8.00
❏ TED1-2615	Disrespect (Extended LP Version with Breakdown) (LP Version) (Club Mix)	1985	2.00	4.00	8.00
❏ TED1-2624	Desire (Special Remix) (LP Version) (Dub Version)	1985	2.00	4.00	8.00
❏ TED1-2632	Going in Circles (4:31)/I Believe (4:28)	1985	—	3.50	7.00
❏ TED1-2636	Automatic Brain (Main Radio and Club Mix Vocal 7:40) (Acapella 5:10) (Dub Version 5:55) (Rap Version)	1986	2.00	4.00	8.00
❏ 2701-1-TD	Big Fun (Radio Mix) (Serious Dub Mix) (Acapella Mix) (Mega Mix) (Bandolero Mix)	1986	—	3.50	7.00
❏ 2705-1-TD	Zibble, Zibble (Get the Money) (aka: Get Loose Get Funky) (Album Mix 5:27) (Radio Short Mix 4:04) (Dub-Zibble Money Mix 5:37)	1986	2.00	4.00	8.00
45s
A&M
| ❏ 1788 | Hard Time Charlie/This Place Called Heaven | 1976 | — | 2.50 | 5.00 |
ARISTA
| ❏ 9788 | I'm Gonna Git Ya Sucka/Clean Up Your Act | 1988 | — | — | 3.00 |
—B-side by Jermaine Jackson
| ❏ 9788 [PS] | I'm Gonna Git Ya Sucka/Clean Up Your Act | 1988 | — | — | 3.00 |
CAPITOL
| ❏ B-44418 | All of My Love (7" Version)/(Radio Mix) | 1989 | — | 2.00 | 4.00 |
| ❏ 7PRO-79045 [DJ] | We Can Make It Alright (same on both sides) | 1990 | — | 3.00 | 6.00 |
—Vinyl is promo only
COLLECTABLES
| ❏ 4391 | Early in the Morning/Open Your Mind (Wide) | 199? | — | — | 3.00 |
| ❏ 4478 | Steppin' (Out)/Shake | 199? | — | — | 3.00 |
MEGA
| ❏ 4005 | Not Guilty/(B-side unknown) | 1984 | — | 2.50 | 5.00 |
MERCURY
❏ DJ-568 [DJ]	The Boys Are Back in Town (stereo/mono?)	1980	2.00	4.00	8.00
❏ 74053	Shake/Got to Get Away	1979	—	2.00	4.00
❏ 74080	Open Up Your Mind (Wide)/I Can Sing	1979	—	2.00	4.00
❏ 76021	Steppin' (Out)/You Are My High	1979	—	2.00	4.00

Number	Title (A Side/B Side)	Yr	VG	VG+	NM
❏ 76037	I Don't Believe You Want to Get Up and Dance (Oops, Up Side Your Head)/Who Do You Call	1980	—	2.00	4.00
❏ 76062	Party Lights/The Boys Are Back in Town	1980	—	2.00	4.00
❏ 76091	Burn Rubber (Why You Wanna Hurt Me)/Nothin' Comes to a Sleeper	1980	—	2.00	4.00
❏ 76101	Yearning for Your Love/When I Look in Your Eyes	1981	—	2.00	4.00
❏ 76114	Humpin'/No Hiding Place	1981	—	2.00	4.00
❏ 811357-7	Burn Rubber/Yearning for Your Love	1983	—	—	3.00

—Reissue

| ❏ 884662-7 | You Dropped a Bomb on Me/Party Train | 1986 | — | 2.50 | 5.00 |

—Reissue in conjunction with 'The 12" Collection' LP

RCA

| ❏ 5035-7-R | Sweeter Than Candy (Penitentiary III)/(Instrumental) | 1986 | — | 2.00 | 4.00 |

SHELTER

| ❏ 40228 | Backbone/Loving You Is Everything | 1974 | — | 3.00 | 6.00 |
| ❏ 40295 | I-Yike-It/Tommy's Groove | 1974 | — | 3.00 | 6.00 |

TATTOO

| ❏ TB-10884 | Out of the Blue (Can You Feel It)/Silly Grin | 1977 | — | 2.50 | 5.00 |
| ❏ TB-10990 | Little Bit of Love/Knucklehead Sunckin' | 1977 | — | 2.50 | 5.00 |

TOTAL EXPERIENCE

❏ 101	Straight from the Heart/(Dub Mix)	1988	—	—	3.00
❏ 101 [PS]	Straight from the Heart/(Dub Mix)	1988	—	2.00	4.00
❏ 2405	Beep a Freak/(Dub Version)	1984	—	—	3.00
❏ 2405 [PS]	Beep a Freak/(Dub Version)	1984	—	2.00	4.00
❏ 2412	I Found My Baby/(Instrumental)	1985	—	—	3.00
❏ 2418	Disrespect/(Instrumental)	1985	—	—	3.00
❏ 2427	Desire/(Album Version)	1985	—	—	3.00
❏ 2428	Automatic Brain/(Instrumental)	1986	—	2.00	4.00
❏ 2435	The Christmas Song (Chestnuts Roasting on an Open Fire)/Joy to the World	1985	—	2.50	5.00

—B-side by Oliver Scott

❏ 2436	Going in Circles/I Believe	1986	—	—	3.00
❏ 2436 [DJ]	Going in Circles (Remix 3:59)/(Remix Instrumental with Harmonica 5:15)	1986	—	3.00	6.00
❏ 2440	Automatic Brain/(With Rap)	1986	—	—	3.00
❏ 2700	Big Fun/(Ooh Ah Dub)	1986	—	—	3.00
❏ 2703	Zibble, Zibble (Get the Money) (aka: Get Loose, Get Funky)/(Instrumental)	1987	—	—	3.00
❏ 8201	Early in the Morning/I'm in Love	1982	—	2.00	4.00
❏ 8201 [PS]	Early in the Morning/I'm in Love	1982	—	2.50	5.00
❏ 8203	You Dropped a Bomb on Me/Lonely Like Me	1982	—	2.00	4.00
❏ 8205	Outstanding/The Blues Are Back in Town	1982	—	2.00	4.00
❏ 8209	Party Train/The Special Party Train Dance Mix	1983	—	2.00	4.00
❏ 8210	Jam the Motha' (Party Mix)/(Munchkin People)	1983	—	2.00	4.00
❏ 8211	I'm Ready (If You're Ready)/Shake a Leg	1984	—	2.00	4.00

Albums

CAPITOL

| ❏ C1-90799 | Round Trip | 1989 | 2.50 | 5.00 | 10.00 |

MERCURY

❏ SRM-1-3758	The Gap Band	1979	2.50	5.00	10.00
❏ SRM-1-3804	The Gap Band II	1979	2.50	5.00	10.00
❏ SRM-1-4003	The Gap Band III	1980	2.50	5.00	10.00
❏ 822788-1	The Gap Band III	198?	2.00	4.00	8.00

—Reissue

| ❏ 826808-1 | The 12" Collection | 1986 | 2.00 | 4.00 | 8.00 |

PASSPORT

| ❏ PB-6026 | Strike a Groove | 1983 | 2.50 | 5.00 | 10.00 |

SHELTER

| ❏ 2111 | Magicians' Holiday | 1974 | 3.75 | 7.50 | 15.00 |

TATTOO

| ❏ BJL1-2168 | The Gap Band | 1977 | 3.75 | 7.50 | 15.00 |

TOTAL EXPERIENCE

❏ 2700-1-T	Gap Band 8	1986	2.00	4.00	8.00
❏ 2710-1-T	Straight from the Heart	1987	2.00	4.00	8.00
❏ TE-1-3001	Gap Band IV	1982	2.00	4.00	8.00
❏ TE-1-3004	Gap Band V — Jammin'	1983	2.00	4.00	8.00
❏ TEL8-5705	Gap Band VI	1984	2.00	4.00	8.00
❏ TEL8-5714	Gap Band VII	1986	2.00	4.00	8.00
❏ 812186-1	Gap Band V — Jammin'	198?	—	3.00	6.00

—Reissue

| ❏ 822794-1 | Gap Band IV | 198? | — | 3.00 | 6.00 |

—Reissue

| ❏ 824343-1 | Gap Gold/Best of the Gap Band | 1985 | 2.00 | 4.00 | 8.00 |

GARAGIOLA, JOE

Albums

UNITED ARTISTS

| ❏ UAL-3032 [M] | That Holler Guy! | 1959 | 10.00 | 20.00 | 40.00 |
| ❏ UAS-6032 [S] | That Holler Guy! | 1959 | 12.50 | 25.00 | 50.00 |

GARCIA, JERRY Also see THE GRATEFUL DEAD; NEW RIDERS OF THE PURPLE SAGE; OLD & IN THE WAY.

45s

ROUND

| ❏ 4504 | Let It Rock/Midnight Town | 1974 | — | 3.00 | 6.00 |

WARNER BROS.

| ❏ PRO 514 [DJ] | Deal/The Wheel | 1972 | 3.75 | 7.50 | 15.00 |

—White label, small hole, plays at 33 1/3 rpm

| ❏ PRO 514 [PS] | Deal/The Wheel | 1972 | 6.25 | 12.50 | 25.00 |

—Title sleeve with the above promo

| ❏ 7551 | Deal/The Wheel | 1972 | — | 3.00 | 6.00 |
| ❏ 7569 | Deep Hour/Sugaree | 1972 | — | 3.00 | 6.00 |

Albums

ARISTA

| ❏ AB 4160 | Cats Under the Stars | 1978 | 3.00 | 6.00 | 12.00 |
| ❏ AL 8364 | Run for the Roses | 198? | 2.00 | 4.00 | 8.00 |

—Reissue of 9603

| ❏ AL 9603 | Run for the Roses | 1982 | 3.00 | 6.00 | 12.00 |

ROUND

❏ RX-102	Garcia	1974	6.25	12.50	25.00
❏ RX-107	Reflections	1975	7.50	15.00	30.00
❏ RN-LA565-G	Reflections	1976	5.00	10.00	20.00

—Reissue of Round 107 with United Artists distribution

Number	Title (A Side/B Side)	Yr	VG	VG+	NM

WARNER BROS.

| ❏ BS 2582 | Garcia | 1972 | 10.00 | 20.00 | 40.00 |

—Green label with "WB" logo

GARDENIAS, THE (1)

45s

FEDERAL

| ❏ 12284 | Flaming Love/My Baby's Tops | 1956 | 30.00 | 60.00 | 120.00 |

GARDENIAS, THE (2)

45s

FAIRLANE

| ❏ 21019 | Darling It's You, You, You/What's the Matter with Me | 1962 | 6.25 | 12.50 | 25.00 |

GARDNER, BROTHER DAVE Includes records as "Dave Gardner."

45s

DECCA

| ❏ 30548 | Hop Along Rock/All By Myself | 1958 | 5.00 | 10.00 | 20.00 |
| ❏ 30627 | Slick Slacks/Wild Streak | 1958 | 10.00 | 20.00 | 40.00 |

OJ

| ❏ 1002 | White Silver Sands/Fat Charlie | 1957 | 3.75 | 7.50 | 15.00 |
| ❏ 1006 | Love Is My Business/Mad Witch | 1958 | 3.75 | 7.50 | 15.00 |

RCA VICTOR

| ❏ 47-7876 | Coward at the Alamo/You Are My Love | 1961 | 2.50 | 5.00 | 10.00 |

Albums

CAPITOL

❏ ST 1867 [S]	It Don't Make No Difference	1963	6.25	12.50	25.00
❏ T 1867 [M]	It Don't Make No Difference	1963	5.00	10.00	20.00
❏ ST 2055 [S]	It's All in How You Look at It	1964	6.25	12.50	25.00
❏ T 2055 [M]	It's All in How You Look at It	1964	5.00	10.00	20.00

4 STAR

| ❏ 4S 75003 | Brother Dave Gardner's New Comedy Album | 1976 | 5.00 | 10.00 | 20.00 |

RCA VICTOR

❏ LPM-2083 [M]	Rejoice, Dear Hearts!	1960	5.00	10.00	20.00
❏ LSP-2083(e) [S]	Rejoice, Dear Hearts!	196?	6.25	12.50	25.00
❏ LPM-2239 [M]	Kick Thy Own Self	1960	5.00	10.00	20.00
❏ LSP-2239(e) [S]	Kick Thy Own Self	196?	6.25	12.50	25.00
❏ LPM-2335 [M]	Ain't That Weird?	1961	5.00	10.00	20.00
❏ LSP-2335 [S]	Ain't That Weird?	1961	6.25	12.50	25.00
❏ LPM-2498 [M]	Did You Ever?	1962	5.00	10.00	20.00
❏ LSP-2498 [S]	Did You Ever?	1962	6.25	12.50	25.00
❏ LPM-2628 [M]	All Seriousness Aside	1963	5.00	10.00	20.00
❏ LSP-2628 [S]	All Seriousness Aside	1963	6.25	12.50	25.00
❏ LPM-2761 [M]	It's Bigger Than Both of Us	1963	5.00	10.00	20.00
❏ LSP-2761 [S]	It's Bigger Than Both of Us	1963	6.25	12.50	25.00
❏ LPM-2852 [M]	Best of Dave Gardner	1964	5.00	10.00	20.00
❏ LSP-2852 [S]	Best of Dave Gardner	1964	6.25	12.50	25.00

TONKA

| ❏ TLP 713 | Out Front | 1969 | 5.00 | 10.00 | 20.00 |

TOWER

❏ ST 5050 [S]	Hip-ocracy	1966	5.00	10.00	20.00
❏ T 5050 [M]	Hip-ocracy	1966	3.75	7.50	15.00
❏ ST 5075 [S]	It Don't Make No Difference	1967	5.00	10.00	20.00
❏ T 5075 [M]	It Don't Make No Difference	1967	3.75	7.50	15.00

GARDNER, DON Also see DON GARDNER AND DEE DEE FORD.

45s

BRUCE

❏ 105	How Do You Speak to an Angel/Sonotone Bounce	1954	15.00	30.00	60.00
❏ 108	I'll Walk Alone/Going Down Mary	1954	12.50	25.00	50.00
❏ 127	It's a Sin to Tell a Lie/I Hear a Rhapsody	1955	12.50	25.00	50.00

CAMEO

| ❏ 102 | Love Only Brings Happiness/Sneakin' In | 1957 | 10.00 | 20.00 | 40.00 |

DELUXE

| ❏ 6133 | This Nearly Was Mine/A Dagger in My Chest | 1957 | 6.25 | 12.50 | 25.00 |
| ❏ 6155 | There! I've Said It Again/I Don't Want to Go Home | 1958 | 6.25 | 12.50 | 25.00 |

JUBILEE

❏ 5482	I Really Love You Baby/Talking About You	1964	2.50	5.00	10.00
❏ 5484	The Bitter with the Sweet/I Don't Know What I'm Gonna Do	1964	2.50	5.00	10.00
❏ 5493	Little Girl Blue/I'm In Such Misery	1964	2.50	5.00	10.00

JUNIOR

| ❏ 393 | High School Baby/Crying All Alone | 1957 | 10.00 | 20.00 | 40.00 |
| ❏ 394 | Dark Alley/Up the Street | 1957 | 7.50 | 15.00 | 30.00 |

KAISER

| ❏ 399 | Ask Anything/Humility | 1958 | 6.25 | 12.50 | 25.00 |
| ❏ 402 | At Last/The Hump | 1959 | 6.25 | 12.50 | 25.00 |

MR. G

| ❏ 824 | Your Love Is Driving Me Crazy/There Ain't Gonna Be No Loving | 1969 | 2.00 | 4.00 | 8.00 |

SEDGRICK

| ❏ 3001 | Cheatin' Kind/(B-side unknown) | 196? | 2000. | 3000. | 4000. |

VERVE

| ❏ 10582 | You Babe/I'm a Practical Guy | 1967 | 3.00 | 6.00 | 12.00 |

GARDNER, DON, AND DEE DEE FORD Also see each artist's individual listings.

45s

FIRE

| ❏ 508 | I Need Your Loving/Tell Me | 1962 | 3.75 | 7.50 | 15.00 |

—Multicolor label

| ❏ 508 | I Need Your Loving/Tell Me | 1962 | 5.00 | 10.00 | 20.00 |

—Red label

| ❏ 513 | Don't You Worry/I'm Coming Home to Stay | 1962 | 3.75 | 7.50 | 15.00 |
| ❏ 517 | Lead Me On/TCB (Taking Care of Business) | 1962 | 3.75 | 7.50 | 15.00 |

KC

| ❏ 196 | Glory of Love/'Deed I Do | 1963 | 3.00 | 6.00 | 12.00 |

LOST-NITE

| ❏ 384 | I Need Your Loving/Tell Me | 197? | — | 2.50 | 5.00 |

—Reissue

LUDIX

| ❏ 104 | You Upset My Soul/Son My Son | 1963 | 3.00 | 6.00 | 12.00 |

G

Number	Title (A Side/B Side)	Yr	VG	VG+	NM

Albums
COLLECTABLES

| ❏ COL-5155 | Golden Classics: Need Your Lovin' | 198? | 3.00 | 6.00 | 12.00 |

FIRE

| ❏ LP-105 [M] | Need Your Lovin' | 1962 | 100.00 | 200.00 | 400.00 |

SUE

| ❏ LP-1044 [M] | Don Gardner and Dee Dee Ford In Sweden | 1965 | 30.00 | 60.00 | 120.00 |

GARDNERS, THE
Albums
PRESTIGE INT'L.

| ❏ PRLP-13062 [M] | Folk Songs Far and Near | 1962 | 7.50 | 15.00 | 30.00 |

GARFUNKEL, ART Also see SIMON AND GARFUNKEL; TOM AND JERRY (1).
45s
COLUMBIA

❏ 02307	A Heart in New York/Is This Love	1981	—	2.00	4.00
❏ 02307 [PS]	A Heart in New York/Is This Love	1981	—	2.00	4.00
❏ 02627	Bright Eyes/The Romance	1981	—	2.00	4.00
❏ 06590	Carol of the Birds/The Decree	1986	—	—	3.00
—With Amy Grant
❏ 06590 [PS]	Carol of the Birds/The Decree	1986	—	—	3.00
❏ 07711	So Much in Love/King of Tonga	1988	—	—	3.00
❏ 07949	This Is the Moment/Slow Breakup	1988	—	—	3.00
❏ 08511	When a Man Loves a Woman/I Have a Love	1988	—	—	3.00
❏ 10020	Second Avenue/Woyaya	1974	—	2.50	5.00
—As "Garfunkel"
❏ 10190	I Only Have Eyes for You/Looking for the Right One	1975	—	2.50	5.00
❏ 10274	Breakaway/Disney Girls	1975	—	2.50	5.00
❏ 10608	Crying in My Sleep/Mr. Shuck 'N' Jive	1977	—	2.50	5.00
❏ 10676	(What a) Wonderful World/Wooden Planes	1978	—	3.00	6.00
—A-side: Art Garfunkel with Paul Simon and James Taylor
❏ 10933	In a Little While (I'll Be On My Way)/And I Know	1979	—	2.00	4.00
❏ 10999	Since I Don't Have You/When Someone Doesn't Want You	1979	—	2.00	4.00
❏ 11050	Bright Eyes/Sail on a Rainbow	1979	—	2.00	4.00
❏ 45926	All I Know/Mary Was An Only Child	1973	—	2.50	5.00
—As "Art Garfunkel"
❏ 45926	All I Know/Mary Was An Only Child	1973	—	2.50	5.00
—As "Garfunkel"
❏ 45926 [DJ]	All I Know (mono/stereo)	1973	2.00	4.00	8.00
—As "Garfunkel"; mono version is about 10 seconds longer than any other version of this song (longer piano fade at the end)
❏ 45926	All I Know/Mary Was An Only Child	1973	2.50	5.00	10.00
—As "Garfunkel"; promo-only quadraphonic pressing
❏ 45983	I Shall Sing/Feuilles-Oh: Do Space Men Pass Dead Souls on Their Way to the Moon	1973	—	2.50	5.00
—As "Garfunkel"
❏ 46030	Traveling Boy/Old Men	1974	—	2.50	5.00
—As "Garfunkel"

OCTAVIA

| ❏ 8002 | Forgive Me/Private World | 1960 | 10.00 | 20.00 | 40.00 |
| —As "Artie Garr" |

WARWICK

| ❏ 515 | Beat Love/Dream Alone | 1959 | 10.00 | 20.00 | 40.00 |
| —As "Artie Garr" |

Albums
COLUMBIA

❏ CQ 31474 [Q]	Angel Clare	1973	5.00	10.00	20.00
❏ KC 31474	Angel Clare	1973	3.00	6.00	12.00
❏ PC 31474	Angel Clare	197?	2.00	4.00	8.00
—Reissue
❏ PC 33700	Breakaway	197?	2.00	4.00	8.00
—With bar code on cover
❏ PC 33700	Breakaway	1975	3.00	6.00	12.00
—Originals have no bar code
❏ PCQ 33700 [Q]	Breakaway	1975	5.00	10.00	20.00
❏ JC 34975	Watermark	1978	3.00	6.00	12.00
—Stock copy with "(What a) Wonderful World" on side 2
❏ JC 34975	Watermark	1978	25.00	50.00	100.00
—Stock copy with "Fingerpaint" on side 2
❏ JC 34975 [DJ]	Watermark	1978	15.00	30.00	60.00
—Test pressing or white label promo with "Fingerpaint" on side 2
❏ PC 34975	Watermark	198?	2.00	4.00	8.00
—Reissue
❏ JC 35780	Fate for Breakfast	1979	3.00	6.00	12.00
—With six different covers, each illustrating Art Garfunkel at a different stage of eating breakfast. No difference in value.
❏ FC 37392	Scissors Cut	1981	2.50	5.00	10.00
❏ FC 40212	The Animals' Christmas By Jimmy Webb	1986	2.50	5.00	10.00
—With Amy Grant
❏ FC 40942	Lefty	1988	2.00	4.00	8.00
❏ OC 45008	Garfunkel	1989	2.50	5.00	10.00

GARI, FRANK
45s
ATLANTIC

| ❏ 2171 | Ain't That Fun/You Make Me Wanna Dance | 1962 | 3.00 | 6.00 | 12.00 |

CAPITOL

| ❏ 2101 | April/Love That's Where It's At | 1968 | 2.00 | 4.00 | 8.00 |

CRUSADE

❏ 1020	Utopia/I Ain't Got a Girl	1960	3.75	7.50	15.00
❏ 1021	Lullaby of Love/Tonight Is Our Last Night	1961	3.75	7.50	15.00
❏ 1021 [PS]	Lullaby of Love/Tonight Is Our Last Night	1961	6.25	12.50	25.00
❏ 1022	Princess/The Last Bus Left at Midnight	1961	3.75	7.50	15.00
❏ 1022 [PS]	Princess/The Last Bus Left at Midnight	1961	6.25	12.50	25.00
❏ 1024	You Better Keep Runnin'/There's Lots More Where This Came From	1962	3.75	7.50	15.00
❏ 1024 [PS]	You Better Keep Runnin'/There's Lots More Where This Came From	1962	7.50	15.00	30.00

RIBBON

| ❏ 6903 | Lil' Girl/Your Only Love | 1958 | 3.75 | 7.50 | 15.00 |

Number	Title (A Side/B Side)	Yr	VG	VG+	NM

GARLAND, JUDY
45s
ABC

| ❏ 10973 | I Feel a Song Coming On/What Now My Love | 1967 | 2.00 | 4.00 | 8.00 |

CAPITOL

❏ 4624	Rock-a-Bye Your Baby with a Dixie Melody/Zing Went the Strings of My Heart	1961	2.50	5.00	10.00
❏ 4656	Sweet Danger/Comes Once in a Lifetime	1961	2.50	5.00	10.00
❏ 4938	Hello Bluebird/I Could Go On Singing	1963	2.50	5.00	10.00

CAPITOL STARLINE

| ❏ 6125 | San Francisco/Chicago | 1968 | 2.00 | 4.00 | 8.00 |
| —Originals have red and white "target" labels |
| ❏ 6126 | The Man That Got Away/April Showers | 1968 | 2.00 | 4.00 | 8.00 |
| —Originals have red and white "target" labels |
| ❏ 6127 | Rock-a-Bye Your Baby with a Dixie Melody/ Come Rain or Come Shine | 1968 | 2.00 | 4.00 | 8.00 |
| —Originals have red and white "target" labels |
| ❏ 6128 | Over the Rainbow/Maybe I'll Come Back | 1968 | 2.00 | 4.00 | 8.00 |
| —Originals have red and white "target" labels |
| ❏ 6129 | That's Entertainment/Swanee | 1968 | 2.00 | 4.00 | 8.00 |
| —Originals have red and white "target" labels |

COLUMBIA

❏ 40010	Send My Baby Back to Me/Without a Memory	1953	3.75	7.50	15.00
❏ 40023	Go Home Joe/Heartbroken	1953	3.75	7.50	15.00
❏ 40270	The Man That Got Away/Here's What I'm Here For	1954	3.75	7.50	15.00

DECCA

| ❏ 23658 | The Birthday of a King/The Star of the East | 195? | 3.75 | 7.50 | 15.00 |
| ❏ 29295 | Have Yourself a Merry Little Christmas/You'll Never Walk Alone | 1954 | 3.75 | 7.50 | 15.00 |

MGM

| ❏ 166 | Over the Rainbow/You Made Me Love You | 196? | 2.00 | 4.00 | 8.00 |
| ❏ 505 | Over the Rainbow/You Made Me Love You | 1969 | 2.00 | 4.00 | 8.00 |

WARNER BROS.

| ❏ 5310 | Little Drops of Rain/Paris Is a Lonely Town | 1962 | 2.50 | 5.00 | 10.00 |

7-Inch Extended Plays
CAPITOL

❏ EAP 1-676	This Is the Time of the Evening/While We're Young//Over the Rainbow	195?	3.00	6.00	12.00
❏ EAP 1-676 [PS]	Miss Show Business, Part 1	195?	3.00	6.00	12.00
❏ EAP 2-676	Medley: You Made Me Love You/For Me and My Gal/The Boy Next Door/The Trolley Song// Danny Boy/After You've Gone	195?	3.00	6.00	12.00
❏ EAP 2-676 [PS]	Miss Show Business, Part 2	195?	3.00	6.00	12.00
❏ EAP 3-676	A Pretty Girl Milking Her Cow/Rock-a-Bye Your Baby with a Dixie Melody//Carolina in the Morning	195?	3.00	6.00	12.00
❏ EAP 3-676 [PS]	Miss Show Business, Part 3	195?	3.00	6.00	12.00
❏ EAP 4-676	Happiness Is a Thing Called Joe//Judy at the Palace — Shine On Harvest Moon/Some of These Days/My Man/I Don't Care	195?	3.00	6.00	12.00
❏ EAP 4-676 [PS]	Miss Show Business, Part 4	195?	3.00	6.00	12.00
❏ EDM-676 [PS]	Miss Show Business	195?	3.75	7.50	15.00
—Box only; used for some editions of all four 676 records

DECCA

❏ ED 2022	Embraceable You/Bidin' My Time//But Not for Me/I Got Rhythm	195?	3.75	7.50	15.00
❏ ED 2022 [PS]	Judy Garland	195?	3.75	7.50	15.00
❏ ED 2050	Smilin' Through/You'll Never Walk Alone//The Boy Next Door/I'm Always Chasing Rainbows	195?	3.75	7.50	15.00
❏ ED 2050 [PS]	Judy Garland Vol. 2	195?	3.75	7.50	15.00

MGM

| ❏ X1038 | Get Happy/Love of My Life//Johnny One Note/ Who? | 1953 | 6.25 | 12.50 | 25.00 |
| ❏ X1038 [PS] | Get Happy | 1953 | 6.25 | 12.50 | 25.00 |

Albums
A.E.I.

❏ 2108	Judy Garland Vol. 1: Born in a Trunk	198?	2.50	5.00	10.00
❏ 2109	Judy Garland Vol. 2: 1940-45	198?	2.50	5.00	10.00
❏ 2110	Judy Garland Vol. 3: Superstar 1945-50	198?	2.50	5.00	10.00

ABC

❏ 620 [M]	Judy Garland At Home at the Palace — Opening Night	1967	5.00	10.00	20.00
❏ S-620 [S]	Judy Garland At Home at the Palace — Opening Night	1967	6.25	12.50	25.00
❏ AC-30007	The ABC Collection	1976	3.75	7.50	15.00

CAPITOL

❏ DW 676 [R]	Miss Show Business	1963	3.00	6.00	12.00
❏ W 676 [M]	Miss Show Business	1955	10.00	20.00	40.00
❏ DT 734 [R]	Judy	1963	3.75	7.50	15.00
❏ T 734 [M]	Judy	1956	10.00	20.00	40.00
❏ DT 835 [R]	Alone	1963	3.75	7.50	15.00
❏ T 835 [M]	Alone	1957	10.00	20.00	40.00
❏ ST 1036 [S]	Judy in Love	1959	10.00	20.00	40.00
❏ T 1036 [M]	Judy in Love	1958	6.25	12.50	25.00
❏ ST 1118 [S]	Garland at the Grove	1959	10.00	20.00	40.00
❏ T 1118 [M]	Garland at the Grove	1959	6.25	12.50	25.00
❏ ST 1188 [S]	The Letter	1959	10.00	20.00	40.00
—Add 80% if letter is on cover
❏ T 1188 [M]	The Letter	1959	6.25	12.50	25.00
—Add 80% if letter is on cover
❏ ST 1467 [S]	Judy — That's Entertainment	196?	5.00	10.00	20.00
—Black rainbow label, Capitol logo at top
❏ ST 1467 [S]	Judy — That's Entertainment	1960	10.00	20.00	40.00
—Black rainbow label, Capitol logo at left
❏ T 1467 [M]	Judy — That's Entertainment	196?	3.75	7.50	15.00
—Black rainbow label, Capitol logo at top
❏ T 1467 [M]	Judy — That's Entertainment	1960	6.25	12.50	25.00
—Black rainbow label, Capitol logo at left
❏ SWBO 1569 [(2)S]	Judy at Carnegie Hall	1961	12.50	25.00	50.00
❏ WBO 1569 [(2)M]	Judy at Carnegie Hall	1961	10.00	20.00	40.00
❏ SW 1710 [S]	The Garland Touch	1962	7.50	15.00	30.00
❏ W 1710 [M]	The Garland Touch	1962	5.00	10.00	20.00
❏ SW 1861 [P]	I Could Go On Singing	1963	15.00	30.00	60.00
—"I Am the Monarch of the Sea" and "It Never Was You" are rechanneled
❏ W 1861 [M]	I Could Go On Singing	1963	10.00	20.00	40.00

Number	Title (A Side/B Side)	Yr	VG	VG+	NM
❏ ST 1941 [S]	Our Love Letter	1963	7.50	15.00	30.00
—Reissue of ST 1188					
❏ T 1941 [M]	Our Love Letter	1963	5.00	10.00	20.00
—Reissue of T 1188					
❏ SM-1999	The Hits of Judy Garland	197?	2.50	5.00	10.00
—Reissue					
❏ ST 1999 [P]	The Hits of Judy Garland	1964	7.50	15.00	30.00
—"Over the Rainbow," "Come Rain or Come Shine" and "April Showers" are rechanneled					
❏ T 1999 [M]	The Hits of Judy Garland	1964	5.00	10.00	20.00
❏ DW 2062 [R]	Just for Openers	1964	3.75	7.50	15.00
❏ W 2062 [M]	Just for Openers	1964	5.00	10.00	20.00
❏ STCL 2988 [(3)]	The Judy Garland Deluxe Set	1968	10.00	20.00	40.00
❏ DNFR-7632 [(6)]	The Magic of Judy Garland	196?	10.00	20.00	40.00
—Box set with 4-page insert; 20 of the 60 tracks are rechanneled					
❏ SM-11763	Alone	1978	2.50	5.00	10.00
—Edited reissue of 835					
❏ SM-11876	Judy — That's Entertainment	1978	2.50	5.00	10.00
—Edited reissue					
❏ M-12034	Just for Openers	1979	2.50	5.00	10.00
—Edited reissue					
❏ SN-16175	The Hits of Judy Garland	198?	2.00	4.00	8.00
—Budget-line reissue					
DECCA					
❏ DXB 172 [(2)M]	The Best of Judy Garland	1963	5.00	10.00	20.00
❏ DL 4199 [M]	The Magic of Judy Garland	1961	7.50	15.00	30.00
❏ DL 6020 [10]	Judy at the Palace	1952	25.00	50.00	100.00
❏ DXSB 7172 [(2)R]	The Best of Judy Garland	1963	5.00	10.00	20.00
❏ DL 8190 [M]	Judy Garland's Greatest Performances	1955	10.00	20.00	40.00
—Black label, silver print					
❏ DL 8190 [M]	Judy Garland's Greatest Performances	196?	6.25	12.50	25.00
—Black label with color bars					
❏ DL 75150 [R]	Judy Garland's Greatest Hits	1969	3.00	6.00	12.00
DRG					
❏ SL 5179	The Wit and the Wonder of Judy Garland	1977	3.75	7.50	15.00
❏ SL-5187	The Beginning	1979	3.75	7.50	15.00
LONGINES SYMPHONETTE					
❏ SY 5217 [(5)]	The Magic of Judy Garland	197?	7.50	15.00	30.00
MARK 56					
❏ 632 [PD]	In Concert: San Francisco	1978	15.00	30.00	60.00
MCA					
❏ 907	From the Decca Vaults	1984	2.50	5.00	10.00
❏ 4003 [(2)]	The Best of Judy Garland	1973	3.75	7.50	15.00
—Black label with rainbow					
❏ 4003 [(2)]	The Best of Judy Garland	1980	2.50	5.00	10.00
—Blue label with rainbow					
❏ 4046 [(2)]	Collector's Items (1936-45)	197?	3.00	6.00	12.00
❏ 25165	The Best of Judy Garland from MGM Classic Films	1988	3.00	6.00	12.00
METRO					
❏ M-505 [M]	Judy Garland	1965	3.75	7.50	15.00
❏ MS-505 [S]	Judy Garland	1965	5.00	10.00	20.00
❏ M-581 [M]	Judy Garland in Song	1966	3.75	7.50	15.00
❏ MS-581 [S]	Judy Garland in Song	1966	5.00	10.00	20.00
MGM					
❏ SDP-1 [(2)]	Golden Years at MGM	1969	7.50	15.00	30.00
❏ E-82 [10]	Judy Garland Sings	1951	25.00	50.00	100.00
❏ PX 102	Forever Judy	1969	6.25	12.50	25.00
—White label "Limited Edition" with poster					
❏ E-3149 [M]	If You Feel Like Singing, Sing	1955	15.00	30.00	60.00
❏ E-3989 [M]	The Judy Garland Story Vol. 1: The Star Years	1961	7.50	15.00	30.00
❏ E-4005 [M]	The Judy Garland Story Vol. 2: The Hollywood Years	1962	7.50	15.00	30.00
❏ E-4204 [M]	The Very Best of Judy Garland	1964	7.50	15.00	30.00
❏ SE-4204 [R]	The Very Best of Judy Garland	1964	2.50	5.00	10.00
—Blue and gold label					
❏ SE-4204 [R]	The Very Best of Judy Garland	1964	3.75	7.50	15.00
—Black label					
MINERVA					
❏ LP-6JG-FNJ	Judy Garland and Friends	1982	2.50	5.00	10.00
❏ LP-6JG-FST	The Judy Garland Show: Mutual Admiration Society	1982	2.50	5.00	10.00
PAIR					
❏ PDL2-1030 [(2)]	Golden Memories	1986	3.00	6.00	12.00
❏ PDL2-1127 [(2)]	The Legendary Judy Garland	1986	3.00	6.00	12.00
PICKWICK					
❏ PTP-2010 [(2)]	Her Greatest Hits	197?	3.00	6.00	12.00
❏ SPC-3053	I Feel a Song Coming On	197?	3.00	6.00	12.00
SPRINGBOARD					
❏ SPB-4054	Over the Rainbow	197?	2.00	4.00	8.00
STANYAN					
❏ POW-3001	More Than a Memory	198?	2.50	5.00	10.00
—Reissue of 10095					
❏ 10095	More Than a Memory	1974	2.50	5.00	10.00
TIME-LIFE					
❏ SLGD-12 [(2)]	Legendary Singers: Judy Garland	1986	5.00	10.00	20.00
TROPHY					
❏ TR-7-2145 [(2)]	Judy Garland Concert	1974	3.75	7.50	15.00

GARLAND, JUDY, AND LIZA MINNELLI Also see each artist's individual listings.
45s

Number	Title (A Side/B Side)	Yr	VG	VG+	NM
CAPITOL					
❏ 5497	Hello Dolly/ He's Got the Whole World In His Hands	1965	2.00	4.00	8.00

Albums

Number	Title (A Side/B Side)	Yr	VG	VG+	NM
CAPITOL					
❏ SWBO 2295 [(2)S]	"Live" at the London Palladium	1965	7.50	15.00	30.00
❏ WBO 2295 [(2)M]	"Live" at the London Palladium	1965	6.25	12.50	25.00
❏ ST-11191	"Live" at the London Palladium	1973	3.00	6.00	12.00
—Condensation of above 2-record set					
MOBILE FIDELITY					
❏ 1-048	"Live" at the London Palladium	1981	6.25	12.50	25.00
—Audiophile vinyl					

GARNER, JOHNNY
45s

Number	Title (A Side/B Side)	Yr	VG	VG+	NM
IMPERIAL					
❏ 5536	Kiss Me Sweet/Little Starry Eyes	1958	6.25	12.50	25.00
❏ 5548	Didi Didi/The Fool	1958	12.50	25.00	50.00

GARNETT, GALE
45s

Number	Title (A Side/B Side)	Yr	VG	VG+	NM
COLUMBIA					
❏ 44479	Breaking Through/Fall in Love Again	1968	—	2.50	5.00
RCA VICTOR					
❏ 47-8388	We'll Sing in the Sunshine/Prism Song	1964	2.50	5.00	10.00
❏ 47-8472	Lovin' Place/I Used to Live Here	1964	2.00	4.00	8.00
❏ 47-8472 [PS]	Lovin' Place/I Used to Live Here	1964	2.00	4.00	8.00
❏ 47-8549	I'll Cry Alone/Where Do You Go to Go Away	1965	2.00	4.00	8.00
❏ 47-8668	I'm Gonna Sit Right Down and Write Myself a Letter/Why Am I Standing in the Window	1965	2.00	4.00	8.00
❏ 47-8824	This Kind of Love/Oh There'll Be Laughter	1966	—	3.00	6.00
❏ 47-8961	It's Been a Lonely Summer/You've Got to Fall in Love Again	1966	—	3.00	6.00
❏ 47-9020	The Sun Is Gray/I Make Him Fly	1966	—	3.00	6.00
❏ 47-9196	Over the Rainbow/The Cats I Know	1967	—	3.00	6.00
Albums					
COLUMBIA					
❏ CL 2825 [M]	An Audience with the King of Wands	1968	5.00	10.00	20.00
❏ CS 9625 [S]	An Audience with the King of Wands	1968	3.75	7.50	15.00
❏ CS 9760	Sausalito Heliport	1969	3.75	7.50	15.00
RCA VICTOR					
❏ LPM-2833 [M]	My Kind of Folk Songs	1964	10.00	20.00	40.00
—Black and white/blueish cover					
❏ LPM-2833 [M]	My Kind of Folk Songs	1965	3.75	7.50	15.00
—Color photo on cover					
❏ LSP-2833 [S]	My Kind of Folk Songs	1964	12.50	25.00	50.00
—Black and white/blueish cover					
❏ LSP-2833 [S]	My Kind of Folk Songs	1965	5.00	10.00	20.00
—Color photo on cover					
❏ LPM-3305 [M]	Lovin' Place	1965	3.75	7.50	15.00
❏ LSP-3305 [S]	Lovin' Place	1965	5.00	10.00	20.00
❏ LPM-3325 [M]	The Many Faces of Gale Garnett	1965	3.75	7.50	15.00
❏ LSP-3325 [S]	The Many Faces of Gale Garnett	1965	5.00	10.00	20.00
❏ LPM-3493 [M]	Variety Is the Spice of Gale Garnett	1966	3.75	7.50	15.00
❏ LSP-3493 [S]	Variety Is the Spice of Gale Garnett	1966	5.00	10.00	20.00
❏ LPM-3586 [M]	New Adventures	1966	3.75	7.50	15.00
❏ LSP-3586 [S]	New Adventures	1966	5.00	10.00	20.00
❏ LPM-3747 [M]	Gale Garnett Sings About Flying & Rainbows & Love & Other Groovy Things	1967	6.25	12.50	25.00
❏ LSP-3747 [S]	Gale Garnett Sings About Flying & Rainbows & Love & Other Groovy Things	1967	5.00	10.00	20.00

GARR, ARTIE   See ART GARFUNKEL.

GARRETT, SCOTT
45s

Number	Title (A Side/B Side)	Yr	VG	VG+	NM
LAURIE					
❏ 3023	House of Love/So Far So Good	1959	5.00	10.00	20.00
❏ 3029	Love Story/Graduation Souvenir	1959	12.50	25.00	50.00
—With vocal backing by the Mystics					
❏ 3034	Where Are You/Jumpin' Blue Blazes	1959	5.00	10.00	20.00
OKEH					
❏ 7104	In My Heart/The Day I Died	1960	5.00	10.00	20.00

GARRETT, TOMMY, 50 GUITARS OF
45s

Number	Title (A Side/B Side)	Yr	VG	VG+	NM
LIBERTY					
❏ 55731	Stranger from Durango/Juarez	1964	—	3.00	6.00
❏ 55797	Corcovado/La Violettra	1965	—	3.00	6.00
❏ 55868	Our Man Flint/Tender Moments	1966	—	3.00	6.00
❏ 55888	La Cucaracha/Spanish Lights	1966	—	3.00	6.00
❏ 55969	Theme for Someone in Love/Courtin'	1967	—	3.00	6.00
❏ 56046	Hang 'Em High/Spanish Pearls	1968	—	2.50	5.00
❏ 56129	Flamenco Funk/Mexican Standoff	1969	—	2.50	5.00
Albums					
LIBERTY					
❏ L-5507 [M]	Limited Edition	196?	3.00	6.00	12.00
❏ S-6607 [S]	Limited Edition	196?	3.75	7.50	15.00
❏ LMM-13005 [M]	50 Guitars Go South of the Border	1961	3.00	6.00	12.00
❏ LMM-13016 [M]	50 Guitars Go South of the Border, Volume 2	1962	3.00	6.00	12.00
❏ LMM-13022 [M]	50 Guitars Visit Hawaii	1962	3.00	6.00	12.00
❏ LMM-13025 [M]	50 Guitars Go Country	1963	3.00	6.00	12.00
❏ LMM-13028 [M]	50 Guitars Go Italiano	1964	3.00	6.00	12.00
❏ LMM-13030 [M]	Maria Elena	1963	3.00	6.00	12.00
❏ LMM-13031 [M]	Bordertown Bandito	1964	3.00	6.00	12.00
❏ LMM-13032 [M]	Espana	1964	3.00	6.00	12.00
❏ LMM-13033 [M]	Return to Paradise	1965	3.00	6.00	12.00
❏ LMM-13035 [M]	Love Songs from South of the Border	1965	3.00	6.00	12.00
❏ LMM-13036 [M]	Viva Mexico	1966	3.00	6.00	12.00
❏ LMM-13037 [M]	50 Guitars in Love	1966	3.00	6.00	12.00
❏ LMM-13039 [M]	More 50 Guitars in Love	1967	3.00	6.00	12.00
❏ LSS-14005 [S]	50 Guitars Go South of the Border	1961	3.75	7.50	15.00
❏ LSS-14016 [S]	50 Guitars Go South of the Border, Volume 2	1962	3.75	7.50	15.00
❏ LSS-14022 [S]	50 Guitars Visit Hawaii	1962	3.75	7.50	15.00
❏ LSS-14025 [S]	50 Guitars Go Country	1963	3.75	7.50	15.00
❏ LSS-14028 [S]	50 Guitars Go Italiano	1964	3.75	7.50	15.00
❏ LSS-14030 [S]	Maria Elena	1963	3.75	7.50	15.00
❏ LSS-14031 [S]	Bordertown Bandito	1964	3.75	7.50	15.00
❏ LSS-14032 [S]	Espana	1964	3.75	7.50	15.00
❏ LSS-14033 [S]	Return to Paradise	1965	3.75	7.50	15.00
❏ LSS-14035 [S]	Love Songs from South of the Border	1965	3.75	7.50	15.00
❏ LSS-14036 [S]	Viva Mexico	1966	3.75	7.50	15.00
❏ LSS-14037 [S]	50 Guitars in Love	1966	3.75	7.50	15.00
❏ LSS-14039 [S]	More 50 Guitars in Love	1967	3.00	6.00	12.00
❏ LSS-14045	The Best of the 50 Guitars of Tommy Garrett	1969	3.00	6.00	12.00
❏ LSS-14046	Mexican Leather	1969	3.00	6.00	12.00
❏ LSS-14047	For Midnight Lovers	1970	3.00	6.00	12.00
❏ LSS-35001 [(2)]	The Best of the 50 Guitars of Tommy Garrett, Volumes 2 & 3	1970	3.75	7.50	15.00

Number	Title (A Side/B Side)	Yr	VG	VG+	NM
MUSICOR					
❏ 4606 [(2)]	The Best of the 50 Guitars of Tommy Garrett	1976	3.00	6.00	12.00
PICKWICK					
❏ SPC-3585	In Love	197?	2.00	4.00	8.00
❏ SPC-3615	Brazilian Mood	197?	2.00	4.00	8.00
SUNSET					
❏ SUS-5282	The Fabulous 50 Guitars of Tommy Garrett	197?	2.50	5.00	10.00
UNITED ARTISTS					
❏ UA-LA039-F	You're a Lady	1973	2.50	5.00	10.00
❏ UXS-79 [(2)]	Tommy Garrett Superpak	1972	3.00	6.00	12.00
❏ UAS-5528	50 Guitars Go South of the Border, Volume 3	1971	2.50	5.00	10.00
❏ UAS-5569	The Way of Love	1972	2.50	5.00	10.00

GARRIGAN, EDDIE
45s
FONTANA					
❏ 1575	I Wish I Was/Mail Call	1966	10.00	20.00	40.00

GARRISON, GLEN
45s
CREST					
❏ 1047	Lovin' Lorene/You're My Darling	1958	15.00	30.00	60.00
IMPERIAL					
❏ 66191	Green to Blue/You Can't Win 'Em All	1966	2.50	5.00	10.00
❏ 66215	Where Do I Go from Here/Strong and Handsome, Sweet and Simple Side	1966	2.50	5.00	10.00
❏ 66230	Listen, They're Playing My Song/My New Creation	1967	2.50	5.00	10.00
❏ 66257	Goodbye Swingers/Hello Mama	1967	2.50	5.00	10.00
❏ 66279	Your Side of Me/If I Lived Here (I'd Be Home Now)	1968	2.00	4.00	8.00
❏ 66300	I'll Be Your Baby Tonight/You Know I Love You	1968	2.00	4.00	8.00
❏ 66333	That Lucky Old Sun/She Thinks I Still Care	1968	2.00	4.00	8.00
❏ 66401	Goodnight Irene/Change Me	1969	2.00	4.00	8.00
LODE					
❏ 106	Pony Tail Girl/Ballad of Hank Gordon	1959	15.00	30.00	60.00

GARROWAY, DAVE
Albums
CAMEO					
❏ C-1001 [M]	An Adventure in Hi-Fi Music	1958	10.00	20.00	40.00
—Black label, brown print, cameo figure at top					

GARY, JOHN
45s
ACE					
❏ 861	First Lady Waltz/A River of Silver	1962	3.00	6.00	12.00
FRATERNITY					
❏ 844	Let Them Talk/Tell My Love	1959	3.75	7.50	15.00
❏ 858	Little Things Mean a Lot/Ever Since I Met Lucy	1959	3.75	7.50	15.00
❏ 860	Thank the Lord (For This Thanksgiving Day)/The Rest of My Days	1959	3.75	7.50	15.00
❏ 864	The Shrine of St. Cecelia/When I'm Alone	1960	3.00	6.00	12.00
❏ 870	The Bell Rings/Forget It	1960	3.00	6.00	12.00
❏ 958	Let Them Talk/Tell My Love	1966	—	3.00	6.00
RCA VICTOR					
❏ 47-8292	That's Life/Ciumanchella	1963	2.00	4.00	8.00
❏ 47-8386	Warm and Willing/Friend and Lover	1964	2.00	4.00	8.00
❏ 47-8413	Soon I'll Wed My Love/The Young Lovers	1964	2.00	4.00	8.00
❏ 47-8475	Do You Hear What I Hear/Little Snow Girl	1964	3.00	6.00	12.00
❏ 47-8479	Sunrise, Sunset/The Bell Rings	1964	2.00	4.00	8.00
❏ 47-8526	Color of Love/My First Love Song	1965	—	3.00	6.00
❏ 47-8617	Joy in the Morning/Linger Awhile	1965	—	3.00	6.00
❏ 47-8677	Don't Throw Those Roses Away/Give Me This Moment	1965	—	3.00	6.00
❏ 47-8731	Ashamed/She Wasn't You	1965	—	3.00	6.00
❏ 47-8806	You Don't Know Me/Don't Let the Music Play	1966	—	3.00	6.00
❏ 47-8890	Sunrise, Sunset/The Bell Rings	1966	—	3.00	6.00
❏ 47-8993	Mine/You've Never Kissed Her	1966	—	3.00	6.00
❏ 47-9119	Hang On to Me/Sleeping Beauty	1967	—	3.00	6.00
❏ 47-9213	Everybody Say Peace/Spanish Moonlight	1967	—	3.00	6.00
❏ 47-9361	Cold/Imagine	1967	—	3.00	6.00
❏ 47-9456	A Certain Girl/The End of Time	1968	—	2.50	5.00
❏ 47-9540	Let There Be Peace on Earth/Give Some Time to Be Happy	1968	—	2.50	5.00
❏ 47-9868	In the Morning/In the Wind	1970	—	2.50	5.00
❏ 74-0149	The Windmills of Your Mind/Then She's a Lover	1969	—	2.50	5.00
❏ 74-0218	Natalie/Summer Me, Winter Me	1969	—	2.50	5.00
TAP					
❏ 7033	I Thought I Had You/The Bell Rings	197?	—	2.50	5.00
❏ 7033 [PS]	I Thought I Had You/The Bell Rings	197?	—	2.50	5.00
Albums					
CHURCHILL					
❏ 67236	In a Class By Himself	1977	2.50	5.00	10.00
LA BREA					
❏ 8010 [M]	John Gary	1961	6.25	12.50	25.00
❏ S-8010 [S]	John Gary	1961	7.50	15.00	30.00
METRO					
❏ M-522 [M]	John Gary	1966	2.50	5.00	10.00
❏ MS-522 [S]	John Gary	1966	3.00	6.00	12.00
PICKWICK					
❏ SPC-3025	John Gary	197?	2.50	5.00	10.00
RCA CAMDEN					
❏ CAL-983 [M]	The One and Only John Gary	1966	2.50	5.00	10.00
❏ CAS-983 [S]	The One and Only John Gary	1966	3.00	6.00	12.00
RCA VICTOR					
❏ LOC-1139 [M]	The John Gary Carnegie Hall Concert	1967	5.00	10.00	20.00
❏ LSO-1139 [S]	The John Gary Carnegie Hall Concert	1967	3.00	6.00	12.00
❏ ANL1-2342	Pure Gold	1977	2.50	5.00	10.00
❏ ANL1-2672	A Little Bit of Heaven	1978	2.50	5.00	10.00
—Reissue of LSP-2994					
❏ LPM-2745 [M]	Catch a Rising Star	1963	3.75	7.50	15.00
❏ LSP-2745 [S]	Catch a Rising Star	1963	5.00	10.00	20.00
❏ LPM-2804 [M]	Encore	1964	3.75	7.50	15.00
❏ LSP-2804 [S]	Encore	1964	5.00	10.00	20.00
❏ LPM-2922 [M]	So Tenderly	1964	3.75	7.50	15.00

Number	Title (A Side/B Side)	Yr	VG	VG+	NM
❏ LSP-2922 [S]	So Tenderly	1964	5.00	10.00	20.00
❏ LPM-2940 [M]	The John Gary Christmas Album	1964	3.75	7.50	15.00
❏ LSP-2940 [S]	The John Gary Christmas Album	1964	5.00	10.00	20.00
❏ LPM-2994 [M]	A Little Bit of Heaven	1965	3.00	6.00	12.00
❏ LSP-2994 [S]	A Little Bit of Heaven	1965	3.75	7.50	15.00
❏ LPM-3349 [M]	The Nearness of You	1965	3.00	6.00	12.00
❏ LSP-3349 [S]	The Nearness of You	1965	3.75	7.50	15.00
❏ LPM-3411 [M]	Your All-Time Favorite Songs	1965	3.00	6.00	12.00
❏ LSP-3411 [S]	Your All-Time Favorite Songs	1965	3.75	7.50	15.00
❏ LPM-3501 [M]	Choice	1966	3.00	6.00	12.00
❏ LSP-3501 [S]	Choice	1966	3.75	7.50	15.00
❏ LPM-3570 [M]	Your All-Time Country Favorites	1966	3.00	6.00	12.00
❏ LSP-3570 [S]	Your All-Time Country Favorites	1966	3.75	7.50	15.00
❏ LPM-3666 [M]	A Heart Filled with Song	1966	3.00	6.00	12.00
❏ LSP-3666 [S]	A Heart Filled with Song	1966	3.75	7.50	15.00
❏ LPM-3695 [M]	Especially for You	1967	3.75	7.50	15.00
❏ LSP-3695 [S]	Especially for You	1967	3.00	6.00	12.00
❏ LPM-3730 [M]	The Best of John Gary	1967	3.75	7.50	15.00
❏ LSP-3730 [S]	The Best of John Gary	1967	3.00	6.00	12.00
❏ LPM-3785 [M]	Spanish Moonlight	1967	3.75	7.50	15.00
❏ LSP-3785 [S]	Spanish Moonlight	1967	3.00	6.00	12.00
❏ LPM-3928 [M]	John Gary On Broadway	1968	5.00	10.00	20.00
❏ LSP-3928 [S]	John Gary On Broadway	1968	3.00	6.00	12.00
❏ LPM-3992 [M]	John Gary Sings/John Gary Swings	1968	5.00	10.00	20.00
❏ LSP-3992 [S]	John Gary Sings/John Gary Swings	1968	3.00	6.00	12.00
❏ LSP-4075	Holding Your Mind	1969	3.00	6.00	12.00
❏ LSP-4134	Love of a Gentle Woman	1970	3.00	6.00	12.00
❏ LSP-4233	That's the Way It Was	1971	3.00	6.00	12.00
❏ VPS-6041 [(2)]	This Is John Gary	1971	3.75	7.50	15.00

GARY AND CLYDE   See SKIP AND FLIP.

GARY AND DAVE
45s
LONDON					
❏ 200	Could You Ever Love Me Again/Where Do We Go from Here	1973	—	3.00	6.00
❏ 204	I Fell in Love with You Sometime/For You	1974	—	3.00	6.00
❏ 207	It Might As Well Rain Until September/(B-side unknown)	1974	5.00	10.00	20.00

GARY AND THE CASUALS
45s
VANDAN					
❏ 609	My Own Desire/Someone Like You	1959	15.00	30.00	60.00

GARY AND THE HORNETS
45s
SMASH					
❏ 2061	Hi, Hi, Hazel/Patty Girl	1966	3.75	7.50	15.00
❏ 2061 [PS]	Hi, Hi, Hazel/Patty Girl	1966	6.25	12.50	25.00
❏ 2078	A Kind of Hush/That's All for Now Sugar Baby	1967	3.00	6.00	12.00
❏ 2078 [PS]	A Kind of Hush/That's All for Now Sugar Baby	1967	3.75	7.50	15.00
❏ 2090	Baby It's You/Tell Tale	1967	3.00	6.00	12.00
❏ 2145	Turn the World On/Holdin' Back	1968	3.00	6.00	12.00

GARY AND THE KNIGHT-LITES   Evolved into THE AMERICAN BREED.
45s
BELL					
❏ 643	Lonely Soldier's Pledge/So Far Away from Home	1966	3.75	7.50	15.00
NIKE					
❏ 1020	I'm Glad She's Mine/How Can I Forget Her	1963	10.00	20.00	40.00
PRIMA					
❏ 1016	I Can't Love You Anymore/Will You Go Steady	1963	25.00	50.00	100.00
SEEBURG					
❏ 3016	Sweet Little Sixteen/Take Me Back	1965	6.25	12.50	25.00
❏ 3017	Bony Moronie/Glad You're Mine	1965	6.25	12.50	25.00
U.S.A.					
❏ 833	Bid Bad Wolf/I Don't Need Your Help	1966	5.00	10.00	20.00

GAS AND FUNK FACTORY, THE
45s
BRUNSWICK					
❏ 55434	Goodnight Song/Everybody Get Some Love	1970	7.50	15.00	30.00

GAS MASK
Albums
TONSIL					
❏ 4001	Gas Mask	1970	5.00	10.00	20.00

GASSAWAY, SENATOR BOLLIVAR E.
45s
RCA VICTOR					
❏ 47-7743	Senator Bolivar E. Gassaway for President/Senator Bolivar E. Gassaway Visits Russia	1960	3.00	6.00	12.00
❏ 47-7743 [PS]	Senator Bolivar E. Gassaway for President/Senator Bolivar E. Gassaway Visits Russia	1960	5.00	10.00	20.00

GATEMEN, THE
45s
COLPIX					
❏ 671	Silent Night/White Christmas	1962	5.00	10.00	20.00
MAY					
❏ 141	Goodnight Irene/The Klan	1963	5.00	10.00	20.00

GATES, DAVID   Also see BREAD; THE MANCHESTERS.
45s
ARISTA					
❏ 0615	Take Me Now/It's What You Say	1981	—	2.00	4.00
❏ 0653	Come Home for Christmas/Lady Valentine	1981	2.00	4.00	8.00
DEL-FI					
❏ 4206	No One Really Loves a Clown/You Had It Comin' To Ya	1963	6.25	12.50	25.00
EASTWEST					
❏ 123	Walkin' and Talkin'/Swingin' Baby Doll	1959	37.50	75.00	150.00
ELEKTRA					
❏ 45223	Never Let Her Go/Watch Out	1974	—	2.00	4.00

Number	Title (A Side/B Side)	Yr	VG	VG+	NM
❑ 45245	Part-Time Love/Chain Me	1975	—	2.00	4.00
❑ 45450	Goodbye Girl/Sunday Rider	1977	—	2.00	4.00
❑ 45450 [PS]	Goodbye Girl/Sunday Rider	1977	—	2.50	5.00
—Version 1: Titles on both sides, no photo					
❑ 45450 [PS]	Goodbye Girl/Sunday Rider	1977	—	2.50	5.00
—Version 2: Titles on one side, photo on other side					
❑ 45500	Took the Last Train/Ann	1978	—	2.00	4.00
❑ 45857	Clouds/I Use the Soap	1973	—	2.00	4.00
❑ 45857 [PS]	Clouds/I Use the Soap	1973	—	3.00	6.00
❑ 45868	Sail Around the World/Help Is On the Way	1973	—	2.00	4.00
❑ 46588	Where Does the Lovin' Go/Starship Ride	1980	—	2.00	4.00
❑ 46646	Can I Call You/Chingo	1980	—	2.00	4.00
❑ 47011	Falling in Love Again/Sweet Desire	1980	—	2.00	4.00
MALA					
❑ 413	You'll Be My Baby/What's This I Hear	1960	12.50	25.00	50.00
❑ 418	The Happiest Man Alive/				
	A Road That Leads to Love	1960	12.50	25.00	50.00
❑ 427	Jo-Baby/Teardrops in My Heart	1961	12.50	25.00	50.00
MANCHESTER					
❑ 101	There's a Heaven/She Don't Cry	196?	10.00	20.00	40.00
—As "Del Ashley"					
PERSPECTIVE					
❑ (no #)	Jo-Baby/Lovin' at Night	1961	37.50	75.00	150.00
PLANETARY					
❑ 103	Little Miss Stuck-Up/The Brighter Side	1965	6.25	12.50	25.00
—As "Del Ashley"					
❑ 108	Let You Go/Once Upon a Time	1965	5.00	10.00	20.00
ROBBINS					
❑ 1008	Jo-Baby/Lovin' at Night	1961	25.00	50.00	100.00
Albums					
ARISTA					
❑ AL 9563	Take Me Now	1981	2.50	5.00	10.00
ELEKTRA					
❑ 6E-148	Goodbye Girl	1978	3.00	6.00	12.00
❑ 6E-251	Falling in Love Again	1980	2.50	5.00	10.00
❑ 7E-1028	Never Let Her Go	1975	3.00	6.00	12.00
❑ EQ-1028 [Q]	Never Let Her Go	1975	5.00	10.00	20.00
❑ EQ-5066 [Q]	First	1973	5.00	10.00	20.00
❑ EKS-75066	First	1973	3.00	6.00	12.00

GATES, HEN

Albums

MASTERSEAL

Number	Title (A Side/B Side)	Yr	VG	VG+	NM
❑ MLP-700 [M]	Let's All Dance to Rock and Roll	1956	25.00	50.00	100.00
PALACE					
❑ P-700 [M]	Let's All Dance to Rock and Roll	1958	15.00	30.00	60.00
—Reissue of Masterseal 700					
❑ PST-700 [S]	Let's All Dance to Rock and Roll	1958	20.00	40.00	80.00
—Labeled stereo, but plays in mono					
PARIS					
❑ 101 [M]	Rock and Roll Festival	1957	15.00	30.00	60.00
PLYMOUTH					
❑ R12-144 [M]	Rock and Roll	1956	15.00	30.00	60.00
❑ R12-149 [M]	Rock and Roll, No. 2	1957	15.00	30.00	60.00

GATEWAY SINGERS, THE

45s

DECCA

Number	Title (A Side/B Side)	Yr	VG	VG+	NM
❑ 29972	The Midnight Special/Puttin' On the Style	1956	3.00	6.00	12.00
❑ 30088	Bury Me in My Overalls/Monaco	1956	3.00	6.00	12.00
❑ 30630	Hey Li Lee/Come to the Dance	1958	2.50	5.00	10.00
MGM					
❑ 12927	Billy Boy/Goin' Down the Road	1960	2.00	4.00	8.00
❑ 12939	Wait for the Wagon/Kingston Market	1960	2.00	4.00	8.00
WARNER BROS.					
❑ 5073	The M.T.A./Keep a-Movin'	1959	2.50	5.00	10.00
Albums					
DECCA					
❑ DL 8413 [M]	Puttin' On the Style	1956	10.00	20.00	40.00
❑ DL 8671 [M]	The Gateway Singers at the Hungry I	1958	7.50	15.00	30.00
❑ DL 8742 [M]	The Gateway Singers in Hi-Fi	1958	7.50	15.00	30.00
MGM					
❑ E-3905 [M]	Down in the Valley	1961	5.00	10.00	20.00
❑ SE-3905 [S]	Down in the Valley	1961	6.25	12.50	25.00
❑ E-4154 [M]	Hootenanny	1963	5.00	10.00	20.00
❑ SE-4154 [S]	Hootenanny	1963	6.25	12.50	25.00
WARNER BROS.					
❑ W 1295 [M]	The Gateway Singers on the Lot	1959	6.25	12.50	25.00
❑ WS 1295 [S]	The Gateway Singers on the Lot	1959	7.50	15.00	30.00
❑ W 1334 [M]	Wagons West	1960	6.25	12.50	25.00
❑ WS 1334 [S]	Wagons West	1960	7.50	15.00	30.00

GATEWAY TRIO, THE

45s

CAPITOL

Number	Title (A Side/B Side)	Yr	VG	VG+	NM
❑ 5045	Soldiers Who Want to Be Heroes/Poor Man's				
	Travellin' Blues	1963	3.75	7.50	15.00
❑ 5286	Coney Island/All the Good Times	1964	3.75	7.50	15.00
Albums					
CAPITOL					
❑ ST 1868 [S]	The Mad, Mad, Mad Gateway Trio	1963	5.00	10.00	20.00
❑ T 1868 [M]	The Mad, Mad, Mad Gateway Trio	1963	3.75	7.50	15.00
❑ ST 2184 [S]	The Gateway Trio	1964	5.00	10.00	20.00
❑ T 2184 [M]	The Gateway Trio	1964	3.75	7.50	15.00

GATLIN, LARRY, AND THE GATLIN BROTHERS BAND
Includes records issued as "Larry Gatlin"; "Larry Gatlin with Family and Friends"; "The Gatlins: Larry, Steve, Rudy"; "The Gatlin Quartet."

45s

CAPITOL

Number	Title (A Side/B Side)	Yr	VG	VG+	NM
❑ 7PRO-79053	Boogie and Beethoven (same on both sides)	1990	—	2.50	5.00
—Vinyl is promo only					
❑ 7PRO-79378	Country Girl Heart (same on both sides)	1991	—	2.50	5.00
—Vinyl is promo only					
COLUMBIA					
❑ 02123	Wind Is Bound to Change/Help Yourself to Me	1981	—	—	3.00
❑ 02522	What Are We Doin' Lonesome/				
	You Wouldn't Know Love	1981	—	—	3.00

Number	Title (A Side/B Side)	Yr	VG	VG+	NM
❑ 02698	In Like With Each Other/Hard Workin' Hands	1982	—	—	3.00
❑ 02910	She Used to Sing on Sunday/				
	Can't Take It With You	1982	—	—	3.00
❑ 03159	Sure Feels Like Love/				
	Home Is Where the Healin' Is	1982	—	—	3.00
❑ 03356	Steps/Sweet Baby Jesus	1982	—	2.00	4.00
❑ CNR-03364	Sure Feels Like Love	1982	—	2.50	5.00
—One-sided budget release					
❑ 03517	Almost Called Her Baby By Mistake/Somethin'				
	Like Each Other's Arms	1983	—	—	3.00
❑ 03885	Easy on the Eye/Anything But Leavin'	1983	—	—	3.00
❑ 04105	Houston (Means I'm One Day Closer to You)/				
	The Whole Wide World Stood Still	1983	—	—	3.00
❑ 04395	Denver/A Dream That Got Out of Hand	1984	—	—	3.00
❑ 04533	The Lady Takes the Cowboy Everytime/It's Me	1984	—	—	3.00
❑ 05632	Runaway Go Home/				
	Nothing But Your Love Matters	1985	—	—	3.00
❑ 05764	Nothing But Your Love Matters/				
	When the Night Closes In	1985	—	—	3.00
❑ 06252	She Used to Be Somebody's Baby/Being Alone	1986	—	—	3.00
❑ 06592	Talkin' to the Moon/Give Me a Chance	1986	—	—	3.00
❑ 07088	From Time to Time (It Feels Like Love Again)/				
	Texas (Is What Life Is All About)	1987	—	—	3.00
—With Janie Frickie					
❑ 07320	Changin' Partners/				
	Got a Lot of Women on His Hands	1987	—	—	3.00
❑ 07747	Love of a Lifetime/Don't Blame Me for Colorado	1988	—	—	3.00
❑ 07998	Alive and Well/One on One	1988	—	—	3.00
❑ 11066	All the Gold in California/How Much Is Man				
	Supposed to Take	1979	—	2.00	4.00
❑ 11169	The Midnight Choir/Hold Me Closer	1980	—	2.00	4.00
❑ 11219	Taking Somebody With Me When I Fall/				
	Piece by Piece	1980	—	2.00	4.00
❑ 11282	We're Number One/Can't Cry Anymore	1980	—	2.00	4.00
❑ 11369	Take Me to Your Lovin' Place/				
	Straight to My Heart	1980	—	2.00	4.00
❑ 11438	It Don't Get No Better Than This/				
	Straight to My Heart	1981	—	2.00	4.00
MONUMENT					
❑ 45-201	Statues Without Hearts/What Will I Do Now	1976	—	2.00	4.00
❑ 45-212	Anything But Leavin'/Take Back "It's Over"	1977	—	2.00	4.00
❑ 45-221	I Don't Wanna Cry/Mercy River	1977	—	2.00	4.00
❑ 45-226	Love Is Just a Game/Everytime a Plane Flies				
	Over Our House	1977	—	2.00	4.00
❑ 45-234	I Just Wish You Were Someone I Love/Kiss It				
	All Goodbye	1977	—	2.00	4.00
❑ 45-249	Night Time Magic/It's Love at Last	1978	—	2.00	4.00
❑ 45-259	Do It Again Tonight/Cold Day in Hell	1978	—	2.00	4.00
❑ 45-270	I've Done Enough Dyin' Today/Nothin' You Do	1978	—	2.00	4.00
❑ 8550	Look to the Sunrise/N.Y.C.	1972	—	3.50	7.00
—As "The Gatlins"					
❑ 8568	Come On In/The Way I Did Before	1973	—	3.00	6.00
—As "The Gatlins"					
❑ 8569	My Mind's Gone to Memphis/Try to Win a Friend	1973	—	2.50	5.00
❑ 8584	Sweet Becky Walker/You've Been Handed				
	Down to Me	1973	—	2.50	5.00
❑ 8602	Bitter They Are Harder They Fall/Silver Threads				
	and Golden Needles	1974	—	2.50	5.00
❑ 8622	Delta Dirt/Those Also Love	1974	—	2.50	5.00
❑ 8643	Jannie/Penny Annie	1975	—	2.50	5.00
❑ 8657	Let's Turn the Lights On/Takin' a Chance on You	1975	—	2.50	5.00
❑ 8680	Broken Lady/Heart	1975	—	2.50	5.00
❑ 8696	Warm and Tender/				
	The Heart Is Quicker Than the Eye	1976	—	2.50	5.00
UNIVERSAL					
❑ 53501	When She Holds Me/Go or Stay	1989	—	—	3.00
❑ UVL-66005	I Might Be What You're Looking For/Rain	1989	—	—	3.00
❑ UVL-66021	#1 Heartache Place/Your Door	1989	—	—	3.00
7-Inch Extended Plays					
SWORD AND SHIELD					
❑ EP 601	I'm Feeling Fine/He's Already Done//He's				
	Everywhere/I Wonder What My New Address				
	Will Be	1959	25.00	50.00	100.00
—As "The Gatlin Family: La Donna - age 5, Rudy - age 7, Stevie - age 8, Larry - age 11"					
❑ EP 601 [PS]	(title unknown)	1959	25.00	50.00	100.00
Albums					
COLUMBIA					
❑ JC 36250	Straight Ahead	1979	2.50	5.00	10.00
❑ JC 36488	Larry Gatlin's Greatest Hits, Volume 1	1980	2.00	4.00	8.00
—Reissue of Monument 7628					
❑ PC 36541	The Pilgrim	1980	2.00	4.00	8.00
—Reissue of Monument 6632					
❑ JC 36582	Help Yourself.	1980	2.50	5.00	10.00
❑ PC 36582	Help Yourself.	198?	2.00	4.00	8.00
—Budget-line reissue					
❑ FC 37464	Not Guilty.	1981	2.50	5.00	10.00
❑ PC 37464	Not Guilty.	198?	2.00	4.00	8.00
—Budget-line reissue					
❑ FC 38135	Sure Feels Like Love.	1982	2.50	5.00	10.00
❑ PC 38135	Sure Feels Like Love.	198?	2.00	4.00	8.00
—Budget-line reissue					
❑ FC 38183	A Gatlin Family Christmas.	1982	3.00	6.00	12.00
❑ PC 38183	A Gatlin Family Christmas.	198?	2.00	4.00	8.00
—Budget-line reissue					
❑ PC 38336	Love Is Just a Game.	1982	2.00	4.00	8.00
—Reissue of Monument 7616					
❑ PC 38337	Larry Gatlin with Family and Friends.	1982	2.00	4.00	8.00
—Reissue of Monument 6634					
❑ PC 38338	High Time.	1982	2.00	4.00	8.00
—Reissue of Monument 6644					
❑ PC 38339	Rain-Rainbow.	1982	2.00	4.00	8.00
—Reissue of Monumnet 6633					
❑ PC 38340	Oh! Brother.	1982	2.00	4.00	8.00
—Reissue of Monumnet 7626					
❑ FC 38923	Larry Gatlin's Greatest Hits, Volume 2.	1983	2.50	5.00	10.00
❑ FC 39291	Houston to Denver.	1984	2.50	5.00	10.00
❑ FC 40068	Smile!	1985	2.50	5.00	10.00
❑ FC 40431	Partners	1986	2.50	5.00	10.00

G

Number	Title (A Side/B Side)	Yr	VG	VG+	NM
❑ FC 40905	Alive and Well…Living in the Land of Dreams	1988	2.50	5.00	10.00
❑ FC 44471	The Gatlin Brothers' Biggest Hits (1984-88)	1989	2.50	5.00	10.00
❑ HC 48135	Sure Feels Like Love	1982	62.50	125.00	250.00
—Half-speed mastered edition					

MONUMENT

Number	Title (A Side/B Side)	Yr	VG	VG+	NM
❑ 6632	The Pilgrim	1976	3.00	6.00	12.00
—Reissue of KZ 32571					
❑ 6633	Rain-Rainbow	1976	3.00	6.00	12.00
—Reissue of KZ 33069					
❑ 6634	Larry Gatlin with Family and Friends	1976	3.00	6.00	12.00
—Reissue of KZ 34042					
❑ 6644	High Time	1977	3.00	6.00	12.00
❑ MG 7616	Love Is Just a Game	1978	3.00	6.00	12.00
❑ MG 7626	Oh! Brother	1978	3.00	6.00	12.00
❑ MG 7628	Larry Gatlin's Greatest Hits	1978	3.00	6.00	12.00
❑ KZ 32571	The Pilgrim	1974	3.75	7.50	15.00
❑ KZ 33069	Rain-Rainbow	1974	3.75	7.50	15.00
❑ KZ 34042	Larry Gatlin with Family & Friends	1975	3.75	7.50	15.00

SWORD & SHIELD

Number	Title (A Side/B Side)	Yr	VG	VG+	NM
❑ 9009 [M]	The Old Country Church	1961	25.00	50.00	100.00
—As "The Gatlin Quartet" (with sister La Donna joining Larry, Rudy and Steve)					

GATORCREEK
Albums
MERCURY

Number	Title (A Side/B Side)	Yr	VG	VG+	NM
❑ SR-61311	Gatorcreek	1970	3.00	6.00	12.00

GAUCHOS, THE See JIM DOVAL AND THE GAUCHOS.

GAUDET, JOHN, AND THE LAURELS
45s
MARY GLEN

Number	Title (A Side/B Side)	Yr	VG	VG+	NM
❑ 1001/2	Christmas Will Soon Be Here/Your Name Shall Be Remembered	1961	6.25	12.50	25.00

GAVIN, TONY
45s
20TH FOX

Number	Title (A Side/B Side)	Yr	VG	VG+	NM
❑ 228	Ever Lovin' Baby/I Just Don't Know	1960	10.00	20.00	40.00

GAY KNIGHTS, THE
45s
PET

Number	Title (A Side/B Side)	Yr	VG	VG+	NM
❑ 801	The Loudness of My Heart/Angel	1958	10.00	20.00	40.00

GAY NOTES, THE
45s
DREXEL

Number	Title (A Side/B Side)	Yr	VG	VG+	NM
❑ 905	For Only a Moment/Pu-Pu-Pa-Doo	1955	150.00	300.00	600.00

POST

Number	Title (A Side/B Side)	Yr	VG	VG+	NM
❑ 2006	Crossroads/Hear My Plea	1955	15.00	30.00	60.00

VIM

Number	Title (A Side/B Side)	Yr	VG	VG+	NM
❑ 501	Something Special/Cherie	1959	15.00	30.00	60.00

GAYE, ELLIE May be ELLIE GREENWICH.
45s
RCA VICTOR

Number	Title (A Side/B Side)	Yr	VG	VG+	NM
❑ 47-7231	Silly Isn't It/Cha Cha Charming	1958	10.00	20.00	40.00

GAYE, MARVIN Also see THE MARQUEES (5); DIANA ROSS AND MARVIN GAYE.
12-Inch Singles
COLUMBIA

Number	Title (A Side/B Side)	Yr	VG	VG+	NM
❑ AS 1566 [DJ]	Sexual Healing (Long Version 5:10) (Short Version 3:52)	1982	15.00	30.00	60.00
❑ CAS 2124 [DJ]	Masochistic Beauty (Vocal 4:39) (Instrumental 4:39)	1985	2.00	4.00	8.00
❑ 44-03934	Joy (2 versions?)	1983	2.00	4.00	8.00
❑ 44-05188	Sanctified Lady/(Instrumental)	1985	2.00	4.00	8.00
❑ 44H-69170	Sexual Healing/The Groove	1989	2.00	4.00	8.00
—"Mixed Masters" reissue; B-side by Rodney Franklin					

MOTOWN

Number	Title (A Side/B Side)	Yr	VG	VG+	NM
❑ M 00014D1	A Funky Space Reincarnation (8:15) (Instrumental 8:19)	1978	5.00	10.00	20.00
❑ PR-129 [DJ]	I Heard It Through the Grapevine (5:03)//The Tracks of My Tears/I Second That Emotion	1983	2.50	5.00	10.00
—B-side by Smokey Robinson and the Miracles; promo-only item issued in conjunction with the movie "The Big Chill"					

REPRISE

Number	Title (A Side/B Side)	Yr	VG	VG+	NM
❑ PRO-A-8343 [DJ]	Piece of Clay (Edit) (LP Version)	1996	2.50	5.00	10.00

TAMLA

Number	Title (A Side/B Side)	Yr	VG	VG+	NM
❑ PR-16 [DJ]	I Want You (Vocal 4:33) (Instrumental 4:36)/Love Hangover (7:49)	1976	50.00	100.00	200.00
—B-side by Diana Ross on Motown label					
❑ PR-46 [DJ]	A Funky Space Reincarnation (8:15) (same on both sides)	1979	7.50	15.00	30.00
❑ PR-178 [DJ]	The World Is Rated X (12-Inch Version 6:28)//(Single Version 3:58)/Dark Side of the World/Lonely Lover/I'm Going Home	1986	3.75	7.50	15.00

45s
COLUMBIA

Number	Title (A Side/B Side)	Yr	VG	VG+	NM
❑ 38-03302	Sexual Healing/(Instrumental)	1982	—	2.00	4.00
❑ CNR-03344	Sexual Healing/(B-side blank)	1982	—	3.00	6.00
—One-sided budget release					
❑ 13-03585	Sexual Healing/(Instrumental)	1983	—	—	3.00
—Reissue					
❑ 38-03589	'Til Tomorrow/Rockin' After Midnight	1983	—	2.00	4.00
❑ 38-03860	Joy/(Instrumental)	1983	—	—	—
—Canceled? (Replaced by 38-03935?)					
❑ 38-03870	Star Spangled Banner/Turn On Some Music	1983	—	—	—
—Canceled?					
❑ 38-03935	Joy/Turn On Some Music	1983	—	2.00	4.00
❑ 38-04861	Sanctified Lady/(Instrumental)	1985	—	2.00	4.00
❑ 38-05442	It's Madness/Ain't It Funny (How Things Turn Around)	1985	—	2.00	4.00
❑ 38-05791	Just Like/More	1986	—	2.00	4.00

DETROIT FREE PRESS

Number	Title (A Side/B Side)	Yr	VG	VG+	NM
❑ (no #) [DJ]	The Teen Beat Song/Loraine Alterman Interviews Marvin Gaye	1966	37.50	75.00	150.00

TAMLA

Number	Title (A Side/B Side)	Yr	VG	VG+	NM
❑ (no #) [DJ]	Masquerade (Is Over)/Witchcraft	1962	150.00	300.00	600.00
—As "Marvin Gay"; label states "Single Not Available extracted from Album (TM-221)"					
❑ S4KM 0741/2 [DJ]	This Is the Life/My Way	1965	12.50	25.00	50.00
❑ 1836	The World Is Rated X/No Greater Love	1986	—	2.50	5.00
❑ 1836 [PS]	The World Is Rated X/No Greater Love	1986	—	2.50	5.00
❑ 54041	Let Your Conscience Be Your Guide/Never Let You Go	1961	100.00	200.00	400.00
❑ 54055	Sandman/I'm Yours, You're Mine	1962	15.00	30.00	60.00
❑ 54062	Masquerade (Is Over)/Witchcraft	1962	—	—	—
—Unreleased					
❑ 54063	Soldier's Plea/Taking My Time	1962	10.00	20.00	40.00
—With label credit "Marvin Gaye Love Tones"					
❑ 54063	Soldier's Plea/Taking My Time	1962	12.50	25.00	50.00
—With label credit "Marvin Gaye"					
❑ 54068	Stubborn Kind of Fellow/It Hurts Me Too	1962	7.50	15.00	30.00
❑ 54075	Hitch Hike/Hello There Angel	1963	5.00	10.00	20.00
❑ 54079	Pride and Joy/One of These Days	1963	5.00	10.00	20.00
❑ 54087	Can I Get a Witness/I'm Crazy 'Bout My Baby	1963	5.00	10.00	20.00
❑ 54093	You're a Wonderful One/When I'm Alone I Cry	1964	3.75	7.50	15.00
❑ 54095	Try It Baby/If My Heart Could Sing	1964	3.75	7.50	15.00
❑ 54095 [PS]	Try It Baby/If My Heart Could Sing	1964	15.00	30.00	60.00
❑ 54101	Baby Don't You Do It/Walk on the Wild Side	1964	3.75	7.50	15.00
❑ 54101 [PS]	Baby Don't You Do It/Walk on the Wild Side	1964	15.00	30.00	60.00
❑ 54107	How Sweet It Is To Be Loved By You/Forever	1964	3.75	7.50	15.00
❑ 54112	I'll Be Doggone/You've Been a Long Time Coming	1965	3.75	7.50	15.00
❑ 54117	Pretty Little Baby/Now That You've Won Me	1965	3.75	7.50	15.00
❑ 54122	Ain't That Peculiar/She's Got to Be Real	1965	3.75	7.50	15.00
❑ 54129	One More Heartache/When I Had Your Love	1966	3.00	6.00	12.00
❑ 54132	Take This Heart of Mine/Need Your Lovin' (Want You Back)	1966	3.00	6.00	12.00
❑ 54138	Little Darling, I Need You/Hey Diddle Diddle	1966	3.00	6.00	12.00
❑ 54153	Your Unchanging Love/I'll Take Care of You	1967	2.50	5.00	10.00
❑ 54160	You/Change What You Can	1967	2.50	5.00	10.00
❑ 54170	Chained/At Last I Found a Love	1968	2.50	5.00	10.00
❑ 54176	I Heard It Through the Grapevine/You're What's Happening (In the World Today)	1968	2.50	5.00	10.00
❑ 54181	Too Busy Thinking About My Baby/Wherever I Lay My Hat (That's My Home)	1969	2.00	4.00	8.00
❑ 54185	That's the Way Love Is/Gonna Keep On Tryin' Till I Win Your Love	1969	2.00	4.00	8.00
❑ 54190	Gonna Give Her All the Love I've Got/How Can I Forget You	1970	2.00	4.00	8.00
❑ 54195	The End of Our Road/Me and My Lonely Room	1970	2.00	4.00	8.00
❑ 54201	What's Going On/God Is Love	1971	—	3.00	6.00
❑ 54207	Mercy Mercy Me (The Ecology)/Sad Tomorrows	1971	—	3.00	6.00
❑ 54209	Inner City Blues (Make Me Wanna Holler)/Wholly Holy	1971	—	3.00	6.00
❑ 54221	You're the Man (Part 1)/You're the Man (Part 2)	1972	—	3.00	6.00
❑ 54228	Trouble Man/Don't Mess With Mister "T"	1972	—	3.00	6.00
❑ 54229	Christmas in the City/I Want to Come Home for Christmas	1972	—	—	—
—Canceled					
❑ 54234	Let's Get It On/I Wish It Would Rain	1973	—	2.00	4.00
❑ 54241	Come Get to This/Distant Lover	1973	—	2.00	4.00
❑ 54244	You Sure Love to Ball/Just to Keep You Satisfied	1974	—	2.00	4.00
❑ 54253	Distant Lover/Trouble Man	1974	—	2.00	4.00
❑ 54264	I Want You/I Want You (Instrumental)	1975	—	2.00	4.00
❑ 54273	After the Dance/Feel All My Love Inside	1976	—	2.00	4.00
❑ 54280	Got to Give It Up — Pt. 1/Got to Give It Up — Pt. 2	1977	—	2.00	4.00
❑ 54280 [PS]	Got to Give It Up — Pt. 1/Got to Give It Up — Pt. 2	1977	2.50	5.00	10.00
❑ 54298	Funky Space Reincarnation — Pt. 1/Funky Space Reincarnation — Pt. 2	1979	—	2.00	4.00
❑ 54300	Time to Get It Together/Anger	1979	2.50	5.00	10.00
—Only released in Canada					
❑ 54305	Ego Tripping Out/(Instrumental)	1979	—	2.00	4.00
❑ 54322	Funk Me/Praise	1981	—	2.00	4.00
❑ 54326	Heavy Love Affair/Far Cry	1981	—	2.00	4.00

TOPPS/MOTOWN

Number	Title (A Side/B Side)	Yr	VG	VG+	NM
❑ 6	How Sweet It Is	1967	18.75	37.50	75.00
—Cardboard record					

Albums
COLUMBIA

Number	Title (A Side/B Side)	Yr	VG	VG+	NM
❑ FC 38197	Midnight Love	1982	2.50	5.00	10.00
❑ PC 38197	Midnight Love	1986	2.00	4.00	8.00
—Budget-line reissue					
❑ FC 39916	Dream of a Lifetime	1985	2.50	5.00	10.00
❑ 9C9 40133 [PD]	Dream of a Lifetime	1985	5.00	10.00	20.00
❑ FC 40208	Romantically Yours	1986	2.50	5.00	10.00
❑ HC 48197	Midnight Love	1984	10.00	20.00	40.00
—Half-speed mastered edition					

MOTOWN

Number	Title (A Side/B Side)	Yr	VG	VG+	NM
❑ M5-115V1	Motown Superstar Series, Vol. 15	1981	2.50	5.00	10.00
❑ M5-125V1	M.P.G.	1981	2.50	5.00	10.00
—Reissue of Tamla 292					
❑ M5-181V1	Marvin Gaye Live!	1981	2.50	5.00	10.00
—Reissue of Tamla 333					
❑ M5-191V1	Marvin Gaye's Greatest Hits	1981	2.50	5.00	10.00
—Reissue of Tamla 348					
❑ M5-192V1	Let's Get It On	1981	2.50	5.00	10.00
—Reissue of Tamla 329					
❑ M5-216V1	A Tribute to the Great Nat King Cole	1981	2.50	5.00	10.00
—Reissue of Tamla 261					
❑ M5-218V1	That Stubborn Kinda' Fellow	1981	2.50	5.00	10.00
—Reissue of Tamla 239					
❑ M9-791A3 [(3)]	Anthology	1974	5.00	10.00	20.00
❑ 37463 1296-1 [DJ]	The Master 1961-1984	1995	5.00	10.00	20.00
—Vinyl is promo only; 8-song sampler from box set					
❑ 5259 ML [(2)]	Marvin Gaye Live at the London Palladium	1983	3.00	6.00	12.00
—Reissue of Tamla 352					
❑ 5306 ML	Super Hits	198?	2.50	5.00	10.00
❑ 5339 ML	What's Going On	198?	2.50	5.00	10.00
—Reissue of Tamla 322					

Number	Title (A Side/B Side)	Yr	VG	VG+	NM
❑ 6058 ML	Every Great Motown Hit of Marvin Gaye	1983	2.50	5.00	10.00
❑ 6255 ML [(2)]	A Musical Testament 1964-1984	1988	3.00	6.00	12.00
NATURAL RESOURCES					
❑ NR 4007T1	The Soulful Moods of Marvin Gaye	1978	3.00	6.00	12.00
—Reissue of Tamla 221					
TAMLA					
❑ TM 221 [M]	The Soulful Moods of Marvin Gaye	1961	250.00	500.00	1000.
❑ T 239 [M]	That Stubborn Kinda' Fella	1963	150.00	300.00	600.00
❑ T 242 [M]	Recorded Live — Marvin Gaye on Stage	1963	75.00	150.00	300.00
❑ T 251 [M]	When I'm Alone I Cry	1964	62.50	125.00	250.00
❑ T 252 [M]	Marvin Gaye/Greatest Hits	1964	7.50	15.00	30.00
❑ TS 252 [S]	Marvin Gaye/Greatest Hits	1964	10.00	20.00	40.00
❑ T 258 [M]	How Sweet It Is to Be Loved by You	1965	10.00	20.00	40.00
❑ TS 258 [S]	How Sweet It Is to Be Loved by You	1965	12.50	25.00	50.00
❑ T 259 [M]	Hello Broadway, This Is Marvin	1965	10.00	20.00	40.00
❑ TS 259 [S]	Hello Broadway, This Is Marvin	1965	12.50	25.00	50.00
❑ T 261 [M]	A Tribute to the Great Nat King Cole	1965	10.00	20.00	40.00
❑ TS 261 [S]	A Tribute to the Great Nat King Cole	1965	12.50	25.00	50.00
❑ T 266 [M]	Moods of Marvin Gaye	1966	10.00	20.00	40.00
❑ TS 266 [S]	Moods of Marvin Gaye	1966	12.50	25.00	50.00
❑ T 278 [M]	Marvin Gaye/Greatest Hits, Vol. 2	1967	6.25	12.50	25.00
❑ TS 278 [S]	Marvin Gaye/Greatest Hits, Vol. 2	1967	5.00	10.00	20.00
❑ T 285 [M]	In the Groove	1968	12.50	25.00	50.00
❑ TS 285 [S]	In the Groove	1968	6.25	12.50	25.00
❑ TS 285 [S]	I Heard It Through the Grapevine	1969	5.00	10.00	20.00
—Retitled version of "In the Groove"					
❑ TS 292	M.P.G.	1969	5.00	10.00	20.00
❑ TS 293	Marvin Gaye and His Girls	1969	5.00	10.00	20.00
—Includes duets with Tammi Terrell, Mary Wells, Kim Weston					
❑ TS 299	That's the Way Love Is	1969	5.00	10.00	20.00
❑ TS 300	Marvin Gaye Super Hits	1970	5.00	10.00	20.00
❑ T5-310	What's Going On	1971	3.75	7.50	15.00
❑ T5-322	Trouble Man	1972	3.75	7.50	15.00
❑ T6-329	Let's Get It On	1973	3.75	7.50	15.00
❑ T6-333	Marvin Gaye Live!	1974	3.75	7.50	15.00
❑ T6-342	I Want You	1976	3.75	7.50	15.00
❑ T6-348	Marvin Gaye's Greatest Hits	1976	3.75	7.50	15.00
❑ T7-352 [(2)]	Marvin Gaye Live at the London Palladium	1977	3.75	7.50	15.00
❑ T13-364 [(2)]	Here, My Dear	1978	3.75	7.50	15.00
❑ T8-374	In Our Lifetime	1981	2.50	5.00	10.00
❑ 6172 TL	Motown Remembers Marvin Gaye	1986	2.50	5.00	10.00

GAYE, MARVIN, AND TAMMI TERRELL Also see each artist's individual listings.
45s
TAMLA

Number	Title (A Side/B Side)	Yr	VG	VG+	NM
❑ 54149	Ain't No Mountain High Enough/Give a Little Love	1967	2.00	4.00	8.00
❑ 54156	Your Precious Love/Hold Me Oh My Darling	1967	2.00	4.00	8.00
❑ 54161	If I Could Build My Whole World Around You/If This World Were Mine	1967	2.00	4.00	8.00
❑ 54163	Ain't Nothing Like the Real Thing/Little Ole Boy, Little Ole Girl	1968	2.00	4.00	8.00
❑ 54169	You're All I Need to Get By/Two Can Have a Party	1968	2.00	4.00	8.00
❑ 54173	You Ain't Livin' 'Till You're Lovin'/Keep On Lovin' Me Honey	1968	—	3.00	6.00
❑ 54179	Good Lovin' Ain't Easy to Come By/Satisfied Feelin'	1969	—	3.00	6.00
❑ 54179 [PS]	Good Lovin' Ain't Easy to Come By/Satisfied Feelin'	1969	5.00	10.00	20.00
❑ 54187	What You Gave Me/How You Gonna Keep It	1969	—	3.00	6.00
❑ 54192	The Onion Song/California Soul	1970	—	3.00	6.00
Albums					
MOTOWN					
❑ M5-102V1	Motown Superstar Series, Vol. 2	1981	2.50	5.00	10.00
❑ M5-142V1	You're All I Need	1981	2.50	5.00	10.00
—Reissue of Tamla 284					
❑ M5-200V1	United	1981	2.50	5.00	10.00
—Reissue of Tamla 277					
TAMLA					
❑ T 277 [M]	United	1967	7.50	15.00	30.00
❑ TS 277 [S]	United	1967	6.25	12.50	25.00
❑ T 284 [M]	You're All I Need	1968	12.50	25.00	50.00
❑ TS 284 [S]	You're All I Need	1968	5.00	10.00	20.00
❑ TS 294	Easy	1969	5.00	10.00	20.00
❑ TS 302	Marvin Gaye & Tammi Terrell/Greatest Hits	1970	5.00	10.00	20.00

GAYE, MARVIN, AND MARY WELLS Also see each artist's individual listings.
45s
MOTOWN

Number	Title (A Side/B Side)	Yr	VG	VG+	NM
❑ 1057	Once Upon a Time/What's the Matter with You Baby	1964	3.75	7.50	15.00
❑ 1057 [PS]	Once Upon a Time/What's the Matter with You Baby	1964	15.00	30.00	60.00
Albums					
MOTOWN					
❑ M 613 [M]	Together	1964	12.50	25.00	50.00
❑ 5260 ML	Together	1982	2.50	5.00	10.00

GAYE, MARVIN, AND KIM WESTON Also see each artist's individual listings.
45s
TAMLA

Number	Title (A Side/B Side)	Yr	VG	VG+	NM
❑ 54104	What Good Am I Without You/I Want You 'Round	1964	3.75	7.50	15.00
❑ 54141	It Takes Two/It's Got to Be a Miracle	1966	3.00	6.00	12.00
Albums					
TAMLA					
❑ T/TS 260	Side by Side	1965	—	—	—
—Canceled					
❑ T 270 [M]	Take Two	1966	7.50	15.00	30.00
❑ TS 270 [S]	Take Two	1966	10.00	20.00	40.00

GAYLARKS, THE
45s
MUSIC CITY

Number	Title (A Side/B Side)	Yr	VG	VG+	NM
❑ 792	Tell Me Darling/Whole Lot of Love	1956	30.00	60.00	120.00
—B-side by the Rovers					
❑ 793	Romantic Memories/Li'l Dream Girl	1956	30.00	60.00	120.00

Number	Title (A Side/B Side)	Yr	VG	VG+	NM
❑ 805	My Greatest Sin/Teenage Mambo	1957	25.00	50.00	100.00
❑ 809	Church on the Hill/Mr. Rock-n-Roll	1957	30.00	60.00	120.00
❑ 812	Just One More Chance/Somewhere in This World	1957	15.00	30.00	60.00
❑ 819	Ivy League Clothes/Rockin' Satellite	1958	12.50	25.00	50.00

GAYLE, CRYSTAL
45s
CAPITOL NASHVILLE

Number	Title (A Side/B Side)	Yr	VG	VG+	NM
❑ 7PRO-79054	Everybody's Reaching Out for Someone (same on both sides)	1990	—	2.50	5.00
—Vinyl is promo only					
❑ 7PRO-79256	Never Ending Song of Love (same on both sides)	1990	—	2.50	5.00
—Vinyl is promo only					
❑ 7PRO-79421	Just an Old Love (same on both sides)	1990	—	3.00	6.00
—Vinyl is promo only					
COLUMBIA					
❑ 02078	Too Many Lovers/Help Yourself to Each Other	1981	—	2.00	4.00
❑ 02523	The Woman in Me/Crying in the Rain	1981	—	2.00	4.00
❑ 02718	You Never Gave Up on Me/Tennessee	1982	—	2.00	4.00
❑ 03048	Livin' in These Troubled Times/Ain't No Sunshine	1982	—	2.00	4.00
❑ 04093	Keepin' Power/Half the Way	1983	—	2.00	4.00
❑ 11087	Half the Way/Room for One More	1979	—	2.00	4.00
❑ 11198	It's Like We Never Said Goodbye/Don't Go My Love	1980	—	2.00	4.00
❑ 11270	The Blue Side/The Danger Zone	1980	—	2.00	4.00
❑ 11359	If You Ever Change Your Mind/I Just Can't Leave Your Love Alone	1980	—	2.00	4.00
❑ 11436	Take It Easy/Ain't No Love in the Heart of the City	1981	—	2.00	4.00
DECCA					
❑ 32721	I've Cried (The Blue Right Out of My Eyes)/Sparkling Look of Love	1970	2.00	4.00	8.00
❑ 32925	Everybody Oughta Cry/MRS Degree	1972	2.00	4.00	8.00
❑ 32969	I Hope You're Havin' Better Luck Than Me/Too Far	1972	2.00	4.00	8.00
ELEKTRA					
❑ 69893	'Til I Gain Control Again/Easier Said Than Done	1982	—	2.00	4.00
❑ 69893 [PS]	'Til I Gain Control Again/Easier Said Than Done	1982	—	2.00	4.00
❑ 69936	You and I/All My Life, All My Love	1982	—	2.00	4.00
—A-side with Eddie Rabbitt; B-side by Eddie Rabbitt solo					
MCA					
❑ 40016	Clock on the Wall/Show Me How	1973	—	3.00	6.00
❑ 40837	I've Cried (The Blue Right Out of My Eyes)/Sparklin' Look of Love	1977	—	3.00	6.00
UNITED ARTISTS					
❑ XW428	Restless/Layback Lover	1974	—	2.50	5.00
❑ XW555	Wrong Road Again/They Come Out at Night	1974	—	2.50	5.00
❑ XW600	Beyond You/Loving You So Long Now	1975	—	2.50	5.00
❑ XW680	This Is My Year for Mexico/When I Dream	1975	—	2.50	5.00
❑ XW740	Somebody Loves You/Coming Closer	1975	—	2.50	5.00
❑ XW781	I'll Get Over You/High Time	1976	—	2.50	5.00
❑ XW838	One More Time/Oh My Soul	1976	—	2.50	5.00
❑ XW883	You Never Miss a Real Good Thing (Till He Says Goodbye)/Forgetting About You	1976	—	2.50	5.00
❑ XW948	I'll Do It All Over Again/I'm Not So Far Away	1977	—	2.50	5.00
❑ XW1016	Don't It Make My Brown Eyes Blue/It's All Right with Me	1977	—	2.00	4.00
❑ XW1136	Ready for the Times to Get Better/Beyond You	1978	—	2.00	4.00
❑ XW1146	I'll Get Over You/The Wrong Road Again	1978	—	2.00	4.00
—Reissue					
❑ XW1147	Somebody Loves You/You Never Miss a Real Good Thing (Till He Says Goodbye)	1978	—	2.00	4.00
—Reissue					
❑ XW1148	Don't It Make My Brown Eyes Blue/The Green Door	1978	—	2.00	4.00
—Reissue					
❑ XW1149	I Wanna Come Back to You/One More Time	1978	—	2.00	4.00
—Reissue					
❑ XW1150	I'll Do It All Over Again/This Is My Year for Mexico	1978	—	2.00	4.00
—Reissue					
❑ XW1214	Talking in Your Sleep/Paintin' This Old Town Blue	1978	—	2.00	4.00
❑ XW1259	Why Have You Left the One You Left Me For/Cry Me a River	1978	—	2.00	4.00
❑ XW1288	When I Dream/Hello I Love You	1979	—	2.00	4.00
❑ XW1306	Your Kisses Will/Time Will Prove I'm Right	1979	—	2.00	4.00
❑ 1329	Your Old Cold Shoulder/We Should Be Together	1979	—	2.00	4.00
❑ 1347	Come Home Daddy/River Road	1980	—	2.00	4.00
❑ 1362	Heart Mender/This Is My Year for Mexico	1980	—	2.00	4.00
WARNER BROS.					
❑ 27682	Tennessee Nights/When Love Is New	1988	—	—	3.00
❑ 27811	Nobody's Angel/When Love Is New	1988	—	—	3.00
❑ 28209	Only Love Can Save Me Now/Till I Gain Control Again	1987	—	—	3.00
❑ 28210	Oh Holy Night/I'll Be Home for Christmas	1987	—	2.00	4.00
❑ 28409	Nobody Should Have to Love You This Way/A Little Bit Closer	1987	—	—	3.00
❑ 28499	I Still Hear the Music of Nashville/I Still Hear the Music of Nashville (Part 2)	1987	—	—	3.00
❑ 28518	Straight to the Heart/Do I Have to Say Goodbye	1986	—	—	3.00
❑ 28555	Have Yourself a Merry Little Christmas/Silver Bells	1986	—	2.00	4.00
❑ 28689	Cry/Crazy in the Heart	1986	—	—	3.00
❑ 28963	A Long and Lasting Love/Someone Like You	1985	—	—	3.00
❑ 29050	Nobody Wants to Be Alone/Coming to the Dance	1985	—	—	3.00
❑ 29151	Me Against the Night/You Made a Fool of Me	1984	—	2.00	4.00
❑ 29254	Turning Away/On Our Way to Love	1984	—	2.00	4.00
❑ 29356	I Don't Wanna Lose Your Love/Victim or a Fool	1984	—	2.00	4.00
❑ 29452	The Sound of Goodbye/Take Me Home	1983	—	2.00	4.00
❑ 29582	Baby, What About You/He Is Beautiful to Me	1983	—	2.00	4.00
❑ 29719	Our Love Is On the Faultline/Deeper in the Fire	1983	—	2.00	4.00
Albums					
COLUMBIA					
❑ JC 36203	Miss the Mississippi	1979	2.50	5.00	10.00
❑ PC 36203	Miss the Mississippi	198?	2.00	4.00	8.00
—Budget-line reissue					

G

Number	Title (A Side/B Side)	Yr	VG	VG+	NM
❑ JC 36512	These Days	1980	2.50	5.00	10.00
❑ PC 36512	These Days	198?	2.00	4.00	8.00
—Budget-line reissue					
❑ FC 37438	Hollywood, Tennessee	1981	2.50	5.00	10.00
❑ PC 37438	Hollywood, Tennessee	198?	2.00	4.00	8.00
—Budget-line reissue					
❑ FC 38803	Crystal Gayle's Greatest Hits	1983	2.50	5.00	10.00
ELEKTRA					
❑ 60200	True Love	1982	2.50	5.00	10.00
LIBERTY					
❑ LMAS-858	When I Dream	1981	2.00	4.00	8.00
—Reissue of UA 858					
❑ LOO-1034	Favorites	1981	2.00	4.00	8.00
—Reissue of UA 1034					
❑ LOO-1080	A Woman's Heart	1981	2.50	5.00	10.00
❑ LN-10002	Crystal Gayle	1981	2.00	4.00	8.00
❑ LN-10003	Somebody Loves You	1981	2.00	4.00	8.00
—Budget-line reissue of UA 543					
❑ LN-10004	Crystal	1981	2.00	4.00	8.00
—Budget-line reissue of UA 614					
❑ LN-10005	We Must Believe in Magic	1981	2.00	4.00	8.00
—Budget-line reissue of UA 771					
❑ LN-10006	We Should Be Together	1980	2.00	4.00	
—Budget-line reissue					
❑ LN-10150	Classic Crystal	1982	2.00	4.00	8.00
—Budget-line reissue of UA 982					
❑ LN-10227	When I Dream	1984	2.00	4.00	8.00
—Budget-line reissue					
❑ LN-10229	Favorites	1984	2.00	4.00	8.00
—Budget-line reissue					
MCA					
❑ 2334	I've Cried the Blue Right Out of My Eyes	1977	2.50	5.00	10.00
—Reissue of Decca material					
❑ 37077	I've Cried the Blue Right Out of My Eyes	198?	2.00	4.00	8.00
—Budget-line reissue					
MOBILE FIDELITY					
❑ 1-043	We Must Believe in Magic	1981	5.00	10.00	20.00
—Audiophile vinyl					
NAUTILUS					
❑ NR-36	When I Dream	198?	7.50	15.00	30.00
—Audiophile vinyl					
PAIR					
❑ PDL2-1083 [(2)]	Country Pure	1986	3.00	6.00	12.00
❑ PDL2-1126 [(2)]	Musical Jewels	1986	3.00	6.00	12.00
UNITED ARTISTS					
❑ UA-LA543-G	Somebody Loves You	1975	3.00	6.00	12.00
❑ UA-LA614-G	Crystal	1976	3.00	6.00	12.00
❑ UA-LA771-G	We Must Believe in Magic	1977	2.50	5.00	10.00
❑ UA-LA858-H	When I Dream	1978	2.50	5.00	10.00
❑ UA-LA969-H	We Should Be Together	1979	2.50	5.00	10.00
❑ LOO-982	Classic Crystal	1979	2.50	5.00	10.00
❑ LOO-1034	Favorites	1980	2.50	5.00	10.00
WARNER BROS.					
❑ 23958	Cage the Songbird	1983	2.50	5.00	10.00
❑ 25154	Nobody Wants to Be Alone	1984	2.50	5.00	10.00
❑ 25405	Straight to the Heart	1986	2.50	5.00	10.00
❑ 25508	A Crystal Christmas	1986	3.75	7.50	15.00
—Original cover has decorated Christmas tree on front					
❑ 25508	A Crystal Christmas	1987	2.50	5.00	10.00
—Reissue cover has photo of Crystal Gayle on front					
❑ 25622	The Best of Crystal Gayle	1987	2.50	5.00	10.00
❑ 25706	Nobody's Angel	1988	2.50	5.00	10.00
❑ 60200	True Love	1983	2.00	4.00	8.00
—Reissue of Elektra 60200					

GAYLE, CRYSTAL, AND GARY MORRIS Also see CRYSTAL GAYLE.

45s

WARNER BROS.

Number	Title (A Side/B Side)	Yr	VG	VG+	NM
❑ 28106	All of This And More/Makin' Up for Lost Time	1988	—	—	3.00
❑ 28373	Another World/Makin' Up for Lost Time	1987	—	—	3.00
❑ 28856	Makin' Up for Lost Time (The Dallas Lovers' Song)/A Few Good Men	1985	—	—	3.00
❑ 28856 [PS]	Makin' Up for Lost Time (The Dallas Lovers' Song)/A Few Good Men	1985	—	—	3.00

Albums

WARNER BROS.

Number	Title (A Side/B Side)	Yr	VG	VG+	NM
❑ 25507	What If We Fell in Love?	1987	2.50	5.00	10.00

GAYLES, BILLY, WITH IKE TURNER'S RHYTHM ROCKERS

45s

FEDERAL

Number	Title (A Side/B Side)	Yr	VG	VG+	NM
❑ 12265	I'm Tore Up/If I Had Never Known You	1956	10.00	20.00	40.00
❑ 12272	Let's Call It a Day/Take Your Fine Frame Home	1956	10.00	20.00	40.00
❑ 12282	No Coming Back/Do Right Baby	1956	10.00	20.00	40.00
❑ 12287	Just One More Time/Sad as a Man Can Be	1957	10.00	20.00	40.00

GAYLES, THE

45s

ABC-PARAMOUNT

Number	Title (A Side/B Side)	Yr	VG	VG+	NM
❑ 9707	Shortnin' Bread Rock/You Fool	1956	6.25	12.50	25.00

KING

Number	Title (A Side/B Side)	Yr	VG	VG+	NM
❑ 4846	My Boy, Flat Top/I Get So Happy	1955	5.00	10.00	20.00
❑ 4860	I Had to Love You/Too Late I Learned	1955	5.00	10.00	20.00

GAYLORDS, THE

45s

MERCURY

Number	Title (A Side/B Side)	Yr	VG	VG+	NM
❑ 70030	Tell Me You're Mine/Cuban Love Song	1952	3.75	7.50	15.00
❑ 70067	Tell Me You're Mine/Aye Aye Aye	1952	3.00	6.00	12.00
❑ 70112	Ramona/Spinning a Web	1953	3.00	6.00	12.00
❑ 70170	Tell Me That You Love Me/Coquette	1953	3.00	6.00	12.00
❑ 70235	Wonderin'/Sweet Sue	1953	3.00	6.00	12.00
❑ 70286	Stolen Moments/Patzo for Pizza	1954	3.00	6.00	12.00
❑ 70296	From the Vine Came the Grape/Stolen Moments	1954	3.00	6.00	12.00
❑ 70308	From the Vine Came the Grape/Patzo for Pizza	1954	2.50	5.00	10.00
❑ 70350	Isle of Capri/Love I You	1954	3.00	6.00	12.00
❑ 70403	The Little Shoemaker/Masque, Masque	1954	3.00	6.00	12.00

Number	Title (A Side/B Side)	Yr	VG	VG+	NM
❑ 70427	Veni, Vida, Vida/A Kiss to Call My Own	1954	3.00	6.00	12.00
❑ 70543	Chow Mein/Poppa Poppadopolis	1955	2.50	5.00	10.00
❑ 70586	The Woodpecker Song/My Babe	1955	2.50	5.00	10.00
❑ 70589	Mambo Rock/Plantation Boogie	1955	2.50	5.00	10.00
❑ 70630	Chee Chee O-Chee/Who's Got the Pain	1955	2.50	5.00	10.00
❑ 70660	Happy Time Medley (1. Minnie the Mermaid; 2. The Man Who Broke the Bank at Monte Carlo; 3. Goodbye My Coney Island Baby; 4. If You Knew Susie)/Madalaina	1955	2.50	5.00	10.00
❑ 70706	No Arms Can Ever Hold You/Bring Me a Bluebird	1955	2.50	5.00	10.00
❑ 70778	Molly-O/Vino Vino	1956	2.50	5.00	10.00
❑ 70834	Bella Bambinella/Who's Gonna Take You to the Prom	1956	2.50	5.00	10.00
❑ 70891	First Row Balcony/One Night Only	1956	2.50	5.00	10.00
❑ 70979	A Little Love, A Little Kiss/The Mountain Climber	1956	2.50	5.00	10.00
❑ 71051	The Dum-De-Dum Song/Open the Letter	1957	2.50	5.00	10.00
❑ 71186	Satin Doll/Wandering Heart	1957	2.50	5.00	10.00
❑ 71236	O Mari/Magic Song	1957	2.50	5.00	10.00
❑ 71265	Love/Each Time I Love You More	1958	2.00	4.00	8.00
❑ 71337	Ma Ma Ma Marie/Buona Sera	1958	2.00	4.00	8.00
❑ 71369	Flamingo L'Amore/I'm Longing for Love	1958	2.00	4.00	8.00
❑ 71399	Again/How About Me	1959	2.00	4.00	8.00
❑ 71450	Sweeter Than You/Homin' Pigeon	1959	2.00	4.00	8.00
❑ 71503	Jesse James/The Shovel	1959	2.00	4.00	8.00
❑ 71569	She's Gone/Please Consider	1960	2.00	4.00	8.00
❑ 71601	Love Me Now and Forever/Whip of the Wind	1960	2.00	4.00	8.00
❑ 71625	Sensation/Carina	1960	2.00	4.00	8.00
❑ 71762	Daisy, You're Driving Me Crazy/Born to Be Loved	1961	2.00	4.00	8.00
❑ 71832	Oh Lonesome Me/Yakety Yak	1961	2.00	4.00	8.00
❑ 71902	It Hurts Me More (The Second Time Around)/American 100%	1961	2.00	4.00	8.00
❑ 71970	How About Me/Two-Ton Tessie	1962	2.00	4.00	8.00

7-Inch Extended Plays

MERCURY

Number	Title (A Side/B Side)	Yr	VG	VG+	NM
❑ EP-1-3210	Wonderin'/Coquette//Cuban Love Song/The Strings of My Heart	195?	5.00	10.00	20.00
❑ EP-1-3210 [PS]	(title unknown)	195?	5.00	10.00	20.00
❑ EP-1-3263	A Kiss to Call My Own/It//Serenade in the Night/Frivolette	195?	5.00	10.00	20.00
❑ EP-1-3263 [PS]	(title unknown)	195?	5.00	10.00	20.00
❑ EP-1-3288	Pupalina/Wonderful Lips//The Little Shoemaker/Mecque, Mecque	195?	5.00	10.00	20.00
❑ EP-1-3288 [PS]	(title unknown)	195?	5.00	10.00	20.00

Albums

MERCURY

Number	Title (A Side/B Side)	Yr	VG	VG+	NM
❑ MG-20186 [M]	Italia	1957	7.50	15.00	30.00
❑ MG-20213 [M]	Collection of Golden Hits	1957	7.50	15.00	30.00
❑ MG-20356 [M]	Let's Have a Pizza Party	1958	5.00	10.00	20.00
❑ MG-20430 [M]	That's Amore	1959	5.00	10.00	20.00
❑ MG-20620 [M]	American Hits in Italian	1961	5.00	10.00	20.00
❑ MG-20695 [M]	The Gaylords at the Shamrock	1962	5.00	10.00	20.00
❑ MG-20742 [M]	Party Style	1963	5.00	10.00	20.00
❑ MG-25198 [10]	By Request	1955	12.50	25.00	50.00
❑ SR-60075 [S]	Let's Have a Pizza Party	1959	7.50	15.00	30.00
❑ SR-60102 [S]	That's Amore	1959	7.50	15.00	30.00
❑ SR-60620 [S]	American Hits in Italian	1961	7.50	15.00	30.00
❑ SR-60695 [S]	The Gaylords at the Shamrock	1962	6.25	12.50	25.00
❑ SR-60742 [S]	Party Style	1963	6.25	12.50	25.00

TIME

Number	Title (A Side/B Side)	Yr	VG	VG+	NM
❑ S-2109 [S]	Live at Lake Tahoe	196?	5.00	10.00	20.00
❑ S-2127 [S]	Bella Italia	196?	5.00	10.00	20.00
❑ 52109 [M]	Live at Lake Tahoe	196?	3.75	7.50	15.00
❑ 52127 [M]	Bella Italia	196?	3.75	7.50	15.00

WING

Number	Title (A Side/B Side)	Yr	VG	VG+	NM
❑ MGW-12139 [M]	Italiano Favorites	196?	3.00	6.00	12.00
❑ MGW-12278 [M]	Let's Have a Pizza Party	196?	3.00	6.00	12.00
❑ SRW-16139 [S]	Italiano Favorites	196?	3.00	6.00	12.00
❑ SRW-16278 [S]	Let's Have a Pizza Party	196?	3.00	6.00	12.00

GAYNOR, GLORIA

12-Inch Singles

ATLANTIC

Number	Title (A Side/B Side)	Yr	VG	VG+	NM
❑ 369	Tease Me (2 versions)	1982	—	3.00	6.00
❑ 633	America/Runaround Love	1982	—	3.00	6.00

MCA

Number	Title (A Side/B Side)	Yr	VG	VG+	NM
❑ L33-1847 [DJ]	Love Is a Heartbeat Away (2 versions)	1979	2.50	5.00	10.00

POLYDOR

Number	Title (A Side/B Side)	Yr	VG	VG+	NM
❑ PRO 107 [DJ]	Most of All/As Time Goes By	1977	2.50	5.00	10.00
❑ PRO 111 [DJ]	Let Me Know (I Have a Right) (2 versions)	1979	2.00	4.00	8.00
❑ PD-D-504 [DJ]	Substitute (same on both sides)	1978	2.00	4.00	8.00
❑ PD-D-507 [DJ]	Anybody Wanna Party (same on both sides)	1978	2.00	4.00	8.00
❑ PD-D-517 [DJ]	Let's Mend What's Been Broken (same on both sides)	1981	2.00	4.00	8.00

SILVER BLUE

Number	Title (A Side/B Side)	Yr	VG	VG+	NM
❑ 220	I Am What I Am (From La Cage Aux Folles)/(Dub Mix)	198?	2.00	4.00	8.00
❑ 05018	Bullseye/Chain of Whispers	1984	—	3.00	6.00

45s

ATLANTIC

Number	Title (A Side/B Side)	Yr	VG	VG+	NM
❑ 89824 [DJ]	America (same on both sides)	1983	—	2.00	4.00
—May be promo only					
❑ 89887	Stop in the Name of Love/For You, My Love	1982	—	2.00	4.00
❑ 89947	Tease Me/Mack Side	1982	—	2.00	4.00

COLUMBIA

Number	Title (A Side/B Side)	Yr	VG	VG+	NM
❑ 45909	Honey Bee/All It Took, Boy, Was Losing You	1973	—	3.00	6.00

MGM

Number	Title (A Side/B Side)	Yr	VG	VG+	NM
❑ 14706	Honey Bee/Come Tonight	1974	—	2.50	5.00
❑ 14748	Never Can Say Goodbye/We Can Just Make It	1974	—	2.00	4.00
❑ 14790	Reach Out, I'll Be There/Searchin'	1975	—	2.00	4.00
❑ 14808	Walk On By/Real Good People	1975	—	2.00	4.00
❑ 14823	(If You Want It) Do It Yourself/I'm Still Yours	1975	—	2.00	4.00
❑ 14838	How High the Moon/My Man's Gone	1975	—	2.00	

POLYDOR

Number	Title (A Side/B Side)	Yr	VG	VG+	NM
❑ 2021	Let Me Know (I Have a Right)/One Plus One	1979	—	2.00	4.00
❑ 2056	Midnight Rocker/Can't Fight This Feelin'	1980	—	2.00	4.00

Number	Title (A Side/B Side)	Yr	VG	VG+	NM
❏ 2089	The Luckiest Girl in the World/Ain't No Bigger Fool	1980	—	2.00	4.00
❏ 2173	Let's Mend What's Been Broken/I Love You Because	1981	—	2.00	4.00
❏ 2179	I Kinda Like Me/Fingers in the Rain	1981	—	2.00	4.00
❏ 14342	Do It Right/Touch of Lightning	1976	—	2.00	4.00
❏ 14357	Let's Make a Deal/Let's Make Love	1976	—	2.00	4.00
❏ 14391	Most of All/So Much Love	1977	—	2.00	4.00
❏ 14443	After the Lovin'/You're All I Need to Get By	1977	—	2.00	4.00
❏ 14472	This Love Affair/For the First Time in My Life	1978	—	2.00	4.00
❏ 14508	I Will Survive/Substitute	1978	—	2.00	4.00
❏ 14558	Anybody Wanna Party?/Please Be There	1979	—	2.00	4.00

SILVER BLUE

Number	Title (A Side/B Side)	Yr	VG	VG+	NM
❏ 720	I Am What I Am/More Than Enough	1983	—	2.50	5.00
❏ 04294	I Am What I Am/More Than Enough	1983	—	2.00	4.00
❏ 04422	Strive/I've Been Watching You	1984	—	2.00	4.00

Albums

ATLANTIC

Number	Title (A Side/B Side)	Yr	VG	VG+	NM
❏ 80033	Gloria Gaynor	1982	2.50	5.00	10.00

MGM

Number	Title (A Side/B Side)	Yr	VG	VG+	NM
❏ M3G-4982	Never Can Say Goodbye	1975	2.50	5.00	10.00
❏ M3G-4997	Experience Gloria Gaynor	1975	2.50	5.00	10.00

POLYDOR

Number	Title (A Side/B Side)	Yr	VG	VG+	NM
❏ PD-1-6063	I've Got You	1976	2.50	5.00	10.00
❏ PD-1-6095	Glorious	1977	2.50	5.00	10.00
❏ PD-1-6139	Gloria Gaynor's Park Avenue Sound	1978	2.50	5.00	10.00
❏ PD-1-6184	Love Tracks	1978	2.50	5.00	10.00
❏ PD-1-6231	I Have a Right	1979	2.50	5.00	10.00
❏ PD-1-6274	Stories	1980	2.50	5.00	10.00

GAYTEN, PAUL Also see THE TUNE WEAVERS.
45s

ANNA

Number	Title (A Side/B Side)	Yr	VG	VG+	NM
❏ 1106	The Hunch/Hot Cross Buns	1959	5.00	10.00	20.00
❏ 1112	Beatnick Beat/Scratch Back	1960	5.00	10.00	20.00

ARGO

Number	Title (A Side/B Side)	Yr	VG	VG+	NM
❏ 5257	The Music Goes Round and Round/Be My Baby	1957	6.25	12.50	25.00
❏ 5263	Driving Home Part 1/Driving Home Part 2	1957	6.25	12.50	25.00
❏ 5267	Old Buttermilk Sky/The Sweeper	1957	6.25	12.50	25.00
❏ 5277	Nervous Boogie/Flatfoot Sam	1957	6.25	12.50	25.00
—B-side by Oscar Wiles					
❏ 5300	Windy/Tickle Toe	1958	6.25	12.50	25.00

CHECKER

Number	Title (A Side/B Side)	Yr	VG	VG+	NM
❏ 801	I'm Tired/Get It	1954	6.25	12.50	25.00
❏ 836	You Better Believe It/Mother Roux	1956	6.25	12.50	25.00

OKEH

Number	Title (A Side/B Side)	Yr	VG	VG+	NM
❏ 6847	Lonesome for My Baby/All Alone and Lonely	1952	7.50	15.00	30.00
❏ 6870	Give Me Liberty or Give Me Death/Happy Days	1952	7.50	15.00	30.00
❏ 6908	True (You Don't Love Me)/They All Ask for You	1952	7.50	15.00	30.00
❏ 6934	Yes You Do, Yes You Do/Don't Worry Me	1953	7.50	15.00	30.00
❏ 6972	Time Is a-Passin'/Ain't Nothin' Happenin'	1953	7.50	15.00	30.00
❏ 6982	Cow Cow Blues/Ooh-Boo	1953	7.50	15.00	30.00
❏ 7003	Hurry Home/Sugar Baby	1953	7.50	15.00	30.00
❏ 7019	Mule Face/It's Over	1954	7.50	15.00	30.00
❏ 7068	True (You Don't Love Me)/Cow Cow Blues	1956	6.25	12.50	25.00

GAYTUNES, THE
45s

JOYCE

Number	Title (A Side/B Side)	Yr	VG	VG+	NM
❏ 101	I Love You/You Left Me	1957	50.00	100.00	200.00
❏ 106	Pen Pal/Plea in the Moonlight	199?	2.00	4.00	8.00
—Black vinyl					
❏ 106	Pen Pal/Plea in the Moonlight	199?	2.50	5.00	10.00
—Red vinyl					

LOST-NITE

Number	Title (A Side/B Side)	Yr	VG	VG+	NM
❏ 244	I Love You/You Left Me	196?	—	2.50	5.00
—Reissue					

GAZELLES, THE
45s

GOTHAM

Number	Title (A Side/B Side)	Yr	VG	VG+	NM
❏ 315	Honest/Pretty Baby, Baby	1956	75.00	150.00	300.00

GEDDES, DAVID
45s

ATCO

Number	Title (A Side/B Side)	Yr	VG	VG+	NM
❏ 7028	Run Joey Run/Honey Don't Blow It	1975	—	—	—
—Canceled?					

BIG TREE

Number	Title (A Side/B Side)	Yr	VG	VG+	NM
❏ 16044	Run Joey Run/Honey Don't Blow It	1975	—	2.00	4.00
❏ 16052	The Last Game of the Season (A Blind Man in the Bleachers)/Wake Up Girl	1975	—	2.00	4.00
❏ 16059	Stephanie/Changing Colours	1976	—	2.00	4.00
❏ 16067	Trouble/Wait for Me	1976	—	2.00	4.00

H&L

Number	Title (A Side/B Side)	Yr	VG	VG+	NM
❏ 4684	Rocky's Girl/Changing Colours	1977	—	2.00	4.00

ZODIAC

Number	Title (A Side/B Side)	Yr	VG	VG+	NM
❏ 1019	Rocky's Girl/Changing Colours	1977	—	2.00	4.00

Albums

BIG TREE

Number	Title (A Side/B Side)	Yr	VG	VG+	NM
❏ BT 89511	Run Joey Run	1975	3.00	6.00	12.00

GEE, ELLIE See ELLIE GREENWICH.

GEE, JOEY
45s

ABC-PARAMOUNT

Number	Title (A Side/B Side)	Yr	VG	VG+	NM
❏ 10781	Don't Blow Your Cool/It's More Than I Deserve	1966	6.25	12.50	25.00

SARA

Number	Title (A Side/B Side)	Yr	VG	VG+	NM
❏ 2599	She's Mean/(B-side unknown)	1966	3.75	7.50	15.00

GEE CEES, THE Also see THE KELLY FOUR.
45s

CREST

Number	Title (A Side/B Side)	Yr	VG	VG+	NM
❏ 1088	Buzz Saw/Annie Had a Party	1961	10.00	20.00	40.00
—Glen Campbell is on A-side; Eddie Cochran is on B-side					
❏ 1088	Buzz Saw Twist/Annie Had a Party	1962	7.50	5.00	30.00

GEILS, J., BAND
45s

ATLANTIC

Number	Title (A Side/B Side)	Yr	VG	VG+	NM
❏ 2784	First I Look at the Purse/Homework	1971	2.00	4.00	8.00
❏ 2802	Cruisin' for a Love/Wait	1971	—	3.00	6.00
❏ 2843	Dead Presidents/I Don't Need You No More	1971	—	3.00	6.00
❏ 2844	Looking for a Love/What's Your Whammer Jammer	1971	—	3.00	6.00
❏ 2929	Hard Drivin' Man/Whammer Jammer	1972	—	3.00	6.00
❏ 2953	Give It To Me/Hold Your Loving	1973	—	2.50	5.00
❏ 2974	Make Up Your Mind/Southside Shuffle	1973	—	2.50	5.00
❏ 2974 [PS]	Make Up Your Mind/Southside Shuffle	1973	2.50	5.00	10.00
❏ 3007	Did You No Wrong/That's Why I'm Thinking of You	1974	—	2.50	5.00
❏ 3214	Must of Got Lost/Funky Judge	1974	—	2.50	5.00
❏ 3251	Givin' It All Up/Gettin' Out	1975	—	2.50	5.00
❏ 3301	Think It Over/Love-Itis	1975	—	2.50	5.00
❏ 3320	Where Did Our Love Go/What's Your Hurry	1976	—	2.50	5.00
❏ 3350	(Ain't Nothing But a) House Party/Give It To Me	1976	—	2.50	5.00
❏ 3378	Peanut Buuter/Magic's Mood	1976	—	2.50	5.00
❏ 3411	You're the Only One/Wreckage	1977	—	2.50	5.00
—As "Geils"					
❏ 3438	Monkey Island (Part 1)/Surrender	1977	—	2.50	5.00
—As "Geils"					
❏ 3454	I Do/Trying to Live My Life Without You	1978	—	2.50	5.00
—As "Geils"					
❏ 3454 [PS]	I Do/Trying to Live My Life Without You	1978	2.00	4.00	8.00
—As "Geils"					

EMI AMERICA

Number	Title (A Side/B Side)	Yr	VG	VG+	NM
❏ 8007	One Last Kiss/Revenge	1978	—	2.00	4.00
❏ 8007 [PS]	One Last Kiss/Revenge	1978	—	3.00	6.00
❏ 8012	Take It Back/I Can't Believe You	1979	—	2.00	4.00
❏ 8016	Wild Man/Just Can't Stop Me	1979	—	2.00	4.00
❏ 8016 [PS]	Wild Man/Just Can't Stop Me	1979	2.50	5.00	10.00
❏ 8032	Come Back/Takin' You Down	1980	—	2.00	4.00
❏ 8032 [DJ]	Come Back (Long)/Come Back (Edit)	1980	—	2.50	5.00
❏ 8039	Love Stinks/Till the Walls Come Tumblin' Down	1980	—	2.00	4.00
❏ 8039 [PS]	Love Stinks/Till the Walls Come Tumblin' Down	1980	—	2.50	5.00
❏ 8047	Just Can't Wait/No Anchovies, Please	1980	—	2.00	4.00
❏ 8100	Angel in Blue/Rage in the Cage	1982	—	—	3.00
❏ 8100 [PS]	Angel in Blue/Rage in the Cage	1982	—	2.00	4.00
❏ 8102	Centerfold/Rage in the Cage	1981	—	—	3.00
—Custom pink label					
❏ 8102	Centerfold/Rage in the Cage	1981	—	2.50	5.00
—Regular gray EMI America label					
❏ 8102 [PS]	Centerfold/Rage in the Cage	1981	2.50	5.00	10.00
❏ 8108	Freeze-Frame/Flamethrower	1982	—	—	3.00
❏ 8108 [PS]	Freeze-Frame/Flamethrower	1982	—	3.00	6.00
❏ 8148	I Do/Sanctuary	1982	—	—	3.00
❏ 8148 [PS]	I Do/Sanctuary	1982	—	2.00	4.00
❏ 8156	Land of 1000 Dances/Jus' Can't Stop Me	1983	—	—	3.00
❏ 8242	Concealed Weapons/Tell 'Em Jonsey	1984	—	—	3.00
❏ 8242 [PS]	Concealed Weapons/Tell 'Em Jonsey	1984	—	2.00	4.00
❏ 8260	Eenie Meenie Miney Mo/I Will Carry You Home	1985	—	—	3.00

PRIVATE I

Number	Title (A Side/B Side)	Yr	VG	VG+	NM
❏ 05462	Fright Night/Boppin' Tonight	1985	—	—	3.00
—B-side by The Fabulous Fontaines					
❏ 05462 [PS]	Fright Night/Boppin' Tonight	1985	—	2.00	4.00

SILVER SPOTLIGHT SERIES

Number	Title (A Side/B Side)	Yr	VG	VG+	NM
❏ X-7106	Centerfold/I Do (Live Version)	198?	—	2.50	5.00
—Unusual reissue					

7-Inch Extended Plays

ATLANTIC

Number	Title (A Side/B Side)	Yr	VG	VG+	NM
❏ SD 7-7260	House Party/Give It to Me//Start All Over Again/Make Up Your Mind	1973	3.75	7.50	15.00
—Jukebox issue; small hole, plays at 33 1/3 rpm					
❏ SD 7-7260 [PS]	Bloodshot	1973	3.75	7.50	15.00
—Part of "Little LP" series (LLP #219)					

Albums

ATLANTIC

Number	Title (A Side/B Side)	Yr	VG	VG+	NM
❏ SD 2-507 [(2)]	Live — Blow Your Face Out	1976	3.75	7.50	15.00
❏ SD 7241	"Live" — Full House	1972	3.00	6.00	12.00
❏ QD 7260 [Q]	Bloodshot	1973	5.00	10.00	20.00
❏ SD 7260	Bloodshot	1973	3.00	6.00	12.00
—Black vinyl					
❏ SD 7260	Bloodshot	1973	5.00	10.00	20.00
—Red vinyl					
❏ QD 7286 [Q]	Ladies Invited	1973	—	—	—
—Not released					
❏ SD 7286	Ladies Invited	1973	3.00	6.00	12.00
❏ 8275 [M]	The J. Geils Band	1970	10.00	20.00	40.00
—Mono is white label promo only; stereo cover with "dj copy monaural" sticker					
❏ SD 8275 [S]	The J. Geils Band	1970	3.75	7.50	15.00
❏ SD 8297	The Morning After	1971	3.00	6.00	12.00
❏ QD 18107 [Q]	Nightmares and Other Tales from the Vinyl Jungle	1974	5.00	10.00	20.00
❏ SD 18107	Nightmares and Other Tales from the Vinyl Jungle	1974	3.00	6.00	12.00
❏ SD 18147	Hotline	1975	3.00	6.00	12.00
❏ SD 19103	Monkey Island	1977	3.00	6.00	12.00
—As "Geils"					
❏ SD 19234	Best of the J. Geils Band	1979	2.50	5.00	10.00
❏ SD 19284	Best of the J. Geils Band — 2	1980	2.50	5.00	10.00

EMI AMERICA

Number	Title (A Side/B Side)	Yr	VG	VG+	NM
❏ SN-16316	Sanctuary	1985	2.00	4.00	8.00
—Reissue					
❏ SN-16373	Showtime!	1986	2.00	4.00	8.00
—Reissue					
❏ SN-16374	Freeze-Frame	1986	2.00	4.00	8.00
—Reissue					
❏ SN-16375	Love Stinks	1986	2.00	4.00	8.00
—Reissue					
❏ SO-17006	Sanctuary	1978	2.50	5.00	10.00
❏ SOO-17016	Love Stinks	1980	2.50	5.00	10.00
❏ SOO-17062	Freeze-Frame	1981	2.50	5.00	10.00
❏ SO-17087	Showtime!	1982	2.50	5.00	10.00

G

Number	Title (A Side/B Side)	Yr	VG	VG+	NM
❑ SJ-17137	You're Gettin' Even While I'm Gettin' Odd	1984	2.00	4.00	8.00
❑ ST-17174	Flashback — The Best of the J. Geils Band	1985	2.00	4.00	8.00

NAUTILUS

Number	Title (A Side/B Side)	Yr	VG	VG+	NM
❑ NR-25	Love Stinks	1982	5.00	10.00	20.00

—Audiophile vinyl

GEMS, THE (1)
45s
CHESS

Number	Title (A Side/B Side)	Yr	VG	VG+	NM
❑ 1863	One More Year/Let Your Hair Down	1963	3.00	6.00	12.00
❑ 1875	If It's the Last Thing I Do/A Girl's Impression	1963	3.00	6.00	12.00
❑ 1882	A Love of Mine/That's Why They Put Erasers On	1964	3.00	6.00	12.00
❑ 1908	I Can't Help Myself/Can't You Take a Hint	1964	3.00	6.00	12.00
❑ 1917	Love For Christmas/All Of It	1964	3.00	6.00	12.00
❑ 1930	He Makes Me Feel So Good/Happy New Love	1965	2.50	5.00	10.00
❑ 2104	Girls Can Do It/Ain't That Loving You	1971	—	3.00	6.00

GEMS, THE (2)
45s
DREXEL

Number	Title (A Side/B Side)	Yr	VG	VG+	NM
❑ 901	Deed I Do/Talk About the Weather	1954	100.00	200.00	400.00
—Black vinyl					
❑ 901	Deed I Do/Talk About the Weather	1954	625.00	1250.	2500.
—Red vinyl					
❑ 903	I Thought You'd Care/Kitty from New York City	1954	75.00	150.00	300.00
—Black vinyl					
❑ 903	I Thought You'd Care/Kitty from New York City	1954	150.00	300.00	600.00
—Red vinyl					
❑ 904	You're Tired of Love/Ol' Man River	1954	75.00	150.00	300.00
—Black vinyl					
❑ 904	You're Tired of Love/Ol' Man River	1954	150.00	300.00	600.00
—Red vinyl					
❑ 909	One Woman Man/The Darkest Night	1955	100.00	200.00	400.00
❑ 915	Till the Day I Die/Monkey Face Baby	1956	100.00	200.00	400.00

GEMS, THE (U) These probably are neither group (1) nor (2).
45s
MERCURY

Number	Title (A Side/B Side)	Yr	VG	VG+	NM
❑ 71819	Crazy Chicken/Hippy Dippy	1961	2.50	5.00	10.00

PAT

Number	Title (A Side/B Side)	Yr	VG	VG+	NM
❑ 101	There's No One Like My Love/School Rock	1961	7.50	15.00	30.00

RECORTE

Number	Title (A Side/B Side)	Yr	VG	VG+	NM
❑ 407	Waiting/Please Change Your Mind	1959	12.50	25.00	50.00

RIVERSIDE

Number	Title (A Side/B Side)	Yr	VG	VG+	NM
❑ 4590	I'll Be There/I Miss Him	1967	7.50	15.00	30.00

WIN

Number	Title (A Side/B Side)	Yr	VG	VG+	NM
❑ 701	Nursery Rhymes/The Night Is Over	1958	75.00	150.00	300.00

GENE AND DEBBE Also see GENE THOMAS.
45s
HICKORY

Number	Title (A Side/B Side)	Yr	VG	VG+	NM
❑ 1643	Lovin' Season/Then You Can Tell Me Goodbye	1972	—	3.50	7.00

SAN

Number	Title (A Side/B Side)	Yr	VG	VG+	NM
❑ 1519	Go with Me/The Torch I Carry	1967	5.00	10.00	20.00

TRX

Number	Title (A Side/B Side)	Yr	VG	VG+	NM
❑ 5002	Go with Me/The Torch I Carry	1967	2.00	4.00	8.00
❑ 5006	Playboy/I'll Come Running	1967	2.50	5.00	10.00
❑ 5010	Lovin' Season/Love Will Give Us Wings	1968	2.00	4.00	8.00
❑ 5014	Rings of Gold/Make a Noise Like Love	1968	2.00	4.00	8.00
❑ 5017	Memories Are Made of This/The Sun Won't Shine Again	1969	2.00	4.00	8.00
❑ 5021	I'm Only Human/Loan Some	1969	2.00	4.00	8.00

Albums
TRX

Number	Title (A Side/B Side)	Yr	VG	VG+	NM
❑ 1001	Here and Now	1968	6.25	12.50	25.00

GENE AND EUNICE
45s
ALADDIN

Number	Title (A Side/B Side)	Yr	VG	VG+	NM
❑ 3276	Ko Ko Mo (I Need You So)/You and Me	1954	6.25	12.50	25.00
❑ 3282	This Is My Story/Move It Over Baby	1954	6.25	12.50	25.00
❑ 3292	Flim Flam/Can We Forget It	1954	6.25	12.50	25.00
❑ 3305	I Gotta Go Home/Have You Changed Your Mind	1954	6.25	12.50	25.00
❑ 3315	Hootchy Kootchy/I'll Never Believe in You	1955	5.00	10.00	20.00
❑ 3321	Let's Get Together/I'm So in Love with You	1955	5.00	10.00	20.00
❑ 3351	Bom Bom Lulu/Hi Diddle Diddle	1956	5.00	10.00	20.00
❑ 3374	The Vow/Strange World	1957	5.00	10.00	20.00
❑ 3376	Doodle Doodle Doo/Don't Treat Me This Way	1957	5.00	10.00	20.00
❑ 3414	I Mean Love/The Angels Gave You to Me	1958	5.00	10.00	20.00

CASE

Number	Title (A Side/B Side)	Yr	VG	VG+	NM
❑ 1001	Poco-Loco/Go-On Kokomo	1959	7.50	15.00	30.00
❑ 1002	Ah! Ah!/You Think I'm Not Thinking	1959	7.50	15.00	30.00
❑ 1005	Without Love/(B-side unknown)	1959	6.25	12.50	25.00
❑ 1007	Sugar Babe/Let's Play the Game	1960	6.25	12.50	25.00

COMBO

Number	Title (A Side/B Side)	Yr	VG	VG+	NM
❑ 64	Ko Ko Mo (I Need You So)/You and Me	1954	7.50	15.00	30.00

LILLY

Number	Title (A Side/B Side)	Yr	VG	VG+	NM
❑ 512	Everlovin' Baby/Got a Right to Know	1962	3.75	7.50	15.00

UNITED ARTISTS

Number	Title (A Side/B Side)	Yr	VG	VG+	NM
❑ 0151	Ko Ko Mo (I Love You So)/This Is My Story	1973	—	2.00	4.00

—"Silver Spotlight Series" reissue

GENE AND TOMMY Real names: TERRY CASHMAN; TOMMY WEST.
45s
ABC

Number	Title (A Side/B Side)	Yr	VG	VG+	NM
❑ 10981	Richard and Me/Can't Get to Stopping	1967	2.00	4.00	8.00

GENESIS Popular British group with Phil Collins, Peter Gabriel, Tony Banks and Mike Rutherford, among others.
12-Inch Singles
ATLANTIC

Number	Title (A Side/B Side)	Yr	VG	VG+	NM
❑ PR 311 [DJ]	Go West Young Man (same on both sides)	1978	5.00	10.00	20.00
❑ PR 404 [DJ]	No Reply at All (4:37) (4:00)	1981	2.50	5.00	10.00
❑ PR 416 [DJ]	Abacab (same on both sides)	1981	2.50	5.00	10.00
❑ PR 425 [DJ]	Man on the Corner (same on both sides)	1981	2.00	4.00	8.00
❑ PR 535 [DJ]	Mama (same on both sides)	1983	2.00	4.00	8.00

Number	Title (A Side/B Side)	Yr	VG	VG+	NM
❑ PR 581 [DJ]	Illegal Alien//Home by the Sea/ Second Home by the Sea	1983	2.00	4.00	8.00
❑ PR 897 [DJ]	Invisible Touch (same on both sides)	1986	—	3.00	6.00
❑ PR 924 [DJ]	Invisible Touch (Special Remix) (same on both sides)	1986	3.00	6.00	12.00
❑ 86722	Tonight, Tonight, Tonight (Remix) (12" Remix)/ /In the Glow of the Night/Paperlate	1987	—	3.00	6.00
❑ 86812	Invisible Touch (Special Remix)/ The Last Domino	1986	—	3.00	6.00

45s
ATCO

Number	Title (A Side/B Side)	Yr	VG	VG+	NM
❑ 7013	The Lamb Lies Down on Broadway/ Counting Out Time	1975	5.00	10.00	20.00
❑ 7050	Entangled/Ripples	1976	2.50	5.00	10.00
❑ 7076	Your Own Special Way/In That Quiet Earth	1977	2.50	5.00	10.00

ATLANTIC

Number	Title (A Side/B Side)	Yr	VG	VG+	NM
❑ 3474	Follow You Follow Me/Inside and Out	1978	—	2.00	4.00
—A radically different mix than the LP version of A-side					
❑ 3511	Go West Young Man (In the Motherlode)/Scene from a Night's Dream	1978	—	2.00	4.00
❑ 3662	Misunderstanding/Behind the Lines	1980	—	2.00	4.00
❑ 3662 [PS]	Misunderstanding/Behind the Lines	1980	—	2.50	5.00
❑ 3751	Turn It On Again/Evidence of Autumn	1980	—	2.00	4.00
❑ 3858	No Reply At All/Heaven Love My Life	1981	—	2.00	4.00
❑ 3891	Abacab/Who Dunnit?	1982	—	2.00	4.00
❑ 3891 [PS]	Abacab/Who Dunnit?	1982	—	2.00	4.00
❑ 4025	Man on the Corner/Submarine	1982	—	2.00	4.00
❑ 4025 [PS]	Man on the Corner/Submarine	1982	—	2.00	4.00
❑ 4053	Paperlate/You Might Recall	1982	—	2.00	4.00
❑ 4053 [PS]	Paperlate/You Might Recall	1982	—	2.50	5.00
❑ 84043	Not About Us/Turn It On Again (Live)	1997	—	—	3.00
❑ 87481	Hold On My Heart/Way of the World	1992	—	2.00	4.00
❑ 87532	I Can't Dance/On the Shoreline	1992	—	2.00	4.00
❑ 87571	No Son of Mine/Living Forever	1991	—	2.00	4.00
❑ 89290	Tonight, Tonight, Tonight/ In the Glow of the Night	1987	—	—	3.00
❑ 89290 [PS]	Tonight, Tonight, Tonight/ In the Glow of the Night	1987	—	2.00	4.00
—Color sleeve					
❑ 89290 [PS]	Tonight, Tonight, Tonight/ In the Glow of the Night	1987	—	2.50	5.00
—Black and white sleeve					
❑ 89316	In Too Deep/I'd Rather Be You	1987	—	—	3.00
❑ 89316 [PS]	In Too Deep/I'd Rather Be You	1987	—	2.00	4.00
❑ 89336	Land of Confusion/Feeding the Fire	1986	—	—	3.00
—Regular Atlantic red and black label					
❑ 89336	Land of Confusion/Feeding the Fire	1986	2.50	5.00	10.00
—Black label with different Atlantic logo					
❑ 89336 [PS]	Land of Confusion/Feeding the Fire	1986	2.50	5.00	10.00
—Sleeve came only with black-label versions					
❑ 89372	Throwing It All Away/Do the Neurotic	1986	—	—	3.00
❑ 89372 [PS]	Throwing It All Away/Do the Neurotic	1986	—	—	3.00
❑ 89407	Invisible Touch/The Last Domino	1986	—	—	3.00
❑ 89407 [PS]	Invisible Touch/The Last Domino	1986	—	—	3.00
❑ 89656	Taking It All Too Hard/Silver Rainbow	1984	—	—	3.00
❑ 89656 [PS]	Taking It All Too Hard/Silver Rainbow	1984	—	—	3.00
❑ 89698	Illegal Alien/Turn It On Again (Live in Philadelphia)	1984	—	—	3.00
❑ 89698 [PS]	Illegal Alien/Turn It On Again (Live in Philadelphia)	1984	—	—	3.00
❑ 89724	That's All/Second Home by the Sea	1983	—	—	3.00
❑ 89724 [PS]	That's All/Second Home by the Sea	1983	—	2.00	4.00
—Brown title sleeve with center cut-out					
❑ 89724 [PS]	That's All/Second Home by the Sea	1983	—	2.50	5.00
—Brown title sleeve with no center cut-out					
❑ 89770	Mama/It's Gonna Get Better	1983	—	—	3.00
❑ 89770 [PS]	Mama/It's Gonna Get Better	1983	—	2.00	4.00

CHARISMA

Number	Title (A Side/B Side)	Yr	VG	VG+	NM
❑ 103	Watcher of the Skies/Willow Farm	1973	12.50	25.00	50.00
❑ 26002	I Know What I Like/Twilight Ale House	1973	10.00	20.00	40.00

PARROT

Number	Title (A Side/B Side)	Yr	VG	VG+	NM
❑ 3018	Silent Sun/That's Me	1968	100.00	200.00	400.00
—Stock copy with black label and green and yellow bird. This has been proven to exist.					
❑ 3018 [DJ]	Silent Sun/That's Me	1968	25.00	50.00	100.00
—Promotional copy; orangeish label with black bird					

Albums
ABC

Number	Title (A Side/B Side)	Yr	VG	VG+	NM
❑ X-816	Trespass	1971	3.00	6.00	12.00
—Reissue of Impulse album					

ABC IMPULSE!

Number	Title (A Side/B Side)	Yr	VG	VG+	NM
❑ ASD-9205	Trespass	1971	7.50	15.00	30.00

ATCO

Number	Title (A Side/B Side)	Yr	VG	VG+	NM
❑ SD 38-100	Wind & Wuthering	1978	2.50	5.00	10.00
❑ SD 38-101	A Trick of the Tail	1978	2.50	5.00	10.00
❑ SD 36-129	A Trick of the Tail	1976	3.00	6.00	12.00
❑ SD 36-144	Wind & Wuthering	1977	3.00	6.00	12.00
❑ SD 2-401 [(2)]	The Lamb Lies Down on Broadway	1974	3.75	7.50	15.00
—Originals have yellow labels (other labels worth less)					

ATLANTIC

Number	Title (A Side/B Side)	Yr	VG	VG+	NM
❑ SD 2-2000 [(2)]	Three Sides Live	1982	3.00	6.00	12.00
❑ SD 2-9002 [(2)]	Seconds Out	1977	3.00	6.00	12.00
❑ SD 16014	Duke	1980	2.50	5.00	10.00
❑ SD 19173	...And Then There Were Three	1978	2.50	5.00	10.00
❑ SD 19277	Selling England by the Pound	1981	2.00	4.00	8.00
—Reissue of Charisma LP of same name					
❑ SD 19313	Abacab	1981	2.50	5.00	10.00
—Released with four different covers, lettered "A" through "D" on spine; no difference in value					
❑ 80030	Nursery Cryme	1982	2.00	4.00	8.00
—Reissue of Charisma LP of same name					
❑ 80116	Genesis	1983	2.00	4.00	8.00
❑ 81641	Invisible Touch	1986	2.00	4.00	8.00
❑ 81848	Foxtrot	1988	2.50	5.00	10.00
—Reissue of Charisma LP of the same name					
❑ 81855	Genesis Live	1988	2.50	5.00	10.00
—Reissue of Charisma LP of same name					

Number	Title (A Side/B Side)	Yr	VG	VG+	NM
BUDDAH					
❏ BDS-5659	The Best of Genesis	1976	3.75	7.50	15.00
CHARISMA					
❏ CAS-1052	Nursery Cryme	1971	3.75	7.50	15.00
❏ CAS-1052	Nursery Cryme	2000	6.25	12.50	25.00
—Classic Records reissue on 180-gram vinyl					
❏ CAS-1058	Foxtrot	1972	3.75	7.50	15.00
❏ CAS-1058	Foxtrot	2001	6.25	12.50	25.00
—Classic Records reissue on 180-gram vinyl					
❏ CAS-1666	Genesis Live	1974	3.75	7.50	15.00
❏ CAS-1666	Genesis Live	2001	6.25	12.50	25.00
—Classic Records reissue on 180-gram vinyl					
❏ CA-2701 [(2)]	Nursery Cryme/Foxtrot	1976	3.75	7.50	15.00
—Repackage of the individual albums of these names					
❏ CAS-6060	Selling England by the Pound	1973	3.75	7.50	15.00
❏ FC-6060	Selling England by the Pound	2001	6.25	12.50	25.00
—Classic Records reissue on 180-gram vinyl					
LONDON					
❏ PS 643	From Genesis to Revelation	1974	5.00	10.00	20.00
—First US release of debut album					
❏ LC-50006	In the Beginning	1977	3.00	6.00	12.00
❏ 820322-1	In the Beginning	198?	2.00	4.00	8.00
—Reissue of London 50006					
MCA					
❏ 816	Trespass	1979	2.50	5.00	10.00
—Reissue of ABC album					
❏ 37151	Trespass	198?	2.00	4.00	8.00
—Reissue of MCA 816					
MOBILE FIDELITY					
❏ 1-062	A Trick of the Tail	1981	12.50	25.00	50.00
—Audiophile vinyl					
GENESIS (2)					
45s					
BUDDAH					
❏ 132	Journey to the Moon (Part 1)/Journey to the Moon (Part 2)	1969	2.50	5.00	10.00
GENESIS (3)					
45s					
MERCURY					
❏ 72806	Angeline/Suzanne	1968	2.50	5.00	10.00
❏ 72869	Gloomy Sunday/What's It All About	1968	2.50	5.00	10.00
Albums					
MERCURY					
❏ SR 61175	In the Beginning	1968	10.00	20.00	40.00
GENESIS (4)					
45s					
RIPCHORD					
❏ 004	Window of Sand/Would You Like To	1967	6.25	12.50	25.00
GENESIS (5)					
45s					
SCEPTER					
❏ 12341	Second Coming/Double Bubble	1972	—	2.50	5.00
GENIES, THE (1)					
45s					
HOLLYWOOD					
❏ 69	No More Knockin'/On the Edge of Town	1959	5.00	10.00	20.00
SHAD					
❏ 5002	Who's That Knocking/The First Time	1959	3.75	7.50	15.00
—Blue label					
❏ 5002	Who's That Knocking/The First Time	1959	6.25	12.50	25.00
—Pink label					
WARWICK					
❏ 573	Crazy Love/There Goes That Rain	1960	3.75	7.50	15.00
❏ 607	Just Like the Bluebird/Twistin' Pneumonia	1960	3.75	7.50	15.00
❏ 643	Little Young Girl/Crazy Feeling	1961	3.75	7.50	15.00
GENIES, THE (2)					
45s					
RONN					
❏ 50	Anybody Here Know How to Pray/Take Me There	1971	—	3.00	6.00
❏ 56	No News Is Good News/Sunday Morning People	1971	—	3.00	6.00
❏ 68	Know Whatr to Do When You Get It/Prove It	197?	—	3.00	6.00
GENTEELS, THE					
45s					
CAPITOL					
❏ 4798	Take It Off/Hitchhiker	1962	6.25	12.50	25.00
STAG					
❏ 2930/1	Take It Off/Hitch Hiker	1962	12.50	25.00	50.00
❏ 4949/50	The Force of Gravity/Springboard	1962	12.50	25.00	50.00
GENTLE GIANT					
45s					
CAPITOL					
❏ 4484	Cogs in Cogs/I'm Turning Around	1977	—	2.50	5.00
❏ 4652	Spooky Boogie/Words from the Wise	1978	—	2.50	5.00
Albums					
CAPITOL					
❏ ST-11337	The Power and the Glory	1974	2.50	5.00	10.00
❏ ST-11428	Free Hand	1975	2.50	5.00	10.00
❏ ST-11532	Interview	1976	2.50	5.00	10.00
❏ SKBB-11592 [(2)]	The Official "Live" Gentle Giant — Playing the Fool	1977	3.00	6.00	12.00
❏ ST-11696	The Missing Piece	1977	2.50	5.00	10.00
❏ SW-11813	Giant for a Day	1978	2.50	5.00	10.00
❏ SN-16044	The Power and the Glory	1980	2.00	4.00	8.00
—Budget-line reissue					
❏ SN-16045	Giant for a Day	1980	2.00	4.00	8.00
—Budget-line reissue					
❏ SN-16046	The Missing Piece	1980	2.00	4.00	8.00
—Budget-line reissue					
❏ SN-16047	Interview	1980	2.00	4.00	8.00
—Budget-line reissue					
❏ SN-16048	Free Hand	1980	2.00	4.00	8.00
—Budget-line reissue					
COLUMBIA					
❏ KC 31649	Three Friends	1972	3.00	6.00	12.00
❏ PC 31649	Three Friends	197?	2.00	4.00	8.00
—Reissue					
❏ KC 32022	Octopus	1973	3.00	6.00	12.00
❏ PC 32022	Octopus	197?	2.00	4.00	8.00
—Reissue					
❏ JC 36341	Civilian	1980	2.50	5.00	10.00
VERTIGO					
❏ VE-1005	Acquiring the Taste	1971	3.75	7.50	15.00
GENTLE SOUL					
45s					
EPIC					
❏ 10448	Reelin'/2:30 Train	1969	3.00	6.00	12.00
Albums					
EPIC					
❏ BN 26374	Gentle Soul	1969	25.00	50.00	100.00
GENTLEMEN FOUR, THE					
45s					
WAND					
❏ 1184	It Won't Hurt Baby/You Can't Keep a Good Man Down	1968	20.00	40.00	80.00
GENTONES, THE					
45s					
CASINO					
❏ 52261	City Lights/Counting Stars	1961	125.00	250.00	500.00
GENTRY, BOBBIE					
45s					
BRUNSWICK					
❏ 55517	Another Place — Another Time/I Think I'll Cry Out Loud	1975	—	3.00	6.00
CAPITOL					
❏ 2044	Okolona River Bottom Band/Penduli Pendulum	1967	2.00	4.00	8.00
❏ 2044 [PS]	Okolona River Bottom Band/Penduli Pendulum	1967	3.75	7.50	15.00
❏ 2147	Louisiana Man/Courtyard	1968	2.00	4.00	8.00
❏ 2295	Hushabye Mountain/Sweet Peony	1968	2.00	4.00	8.00
❏ 2501	Touch 'Em With Love/Casket Vignette	1969	—	3.00	6.00
❏ 2675	Fancy/Courtyard	1969	—	3.00	6.00
❏ 2788	He Made a Woman Out of Me/Billy the Kid	1970	—	3.00	6.00
❏ 2849	Apartment 21/Seasons Come, Seasons Go	1970	—	3.00	6.00
❏ 3071	But I Can't Get Back/Marigolds and Tangerines	1971	—	3.00	6.00
❏ 3413	Girl from Cincinnati/You and Me Together	1972	—	3.00	6.00
❏ 3413 [PS]	Girl from Cincinnati/You and Me Together	1972	2.00	4.00	8.00
❏ 4294	Ode to Billie Joe/Mississippi Delta	1976	—	2.50	5.00
❏ 5950	Ode to Billie Joe/Mississippi Delta	1967	2.50	5.00	10.00
❏ 5992	I Saw An Angel Die/Poppa, Won'tcha Let Me Go to Town with You	1967	2.00	4.00	8.00
TITAN					
❏ 1736	Requiem for Love/Stranger in the Mirror	1963	3.75	7.50	15.00
—With Jody Reynolds					
WARNER BROS.					
❏ 8210	Ode to Billie Joe/There'll Be a Time	1976	—	2.50	5.00
—B-side by Michel Legrand					
❏ 8210 [PS]	Ode to Billie Joe/There'll Be a Time	1976	2.50	5.00	10.00
❏ 8532	Steal Away/He Did Me Wrong But He Did It Right	1978	—	2.00	4.00
Albums					
CAPITOL					
❏ ST-155	Touch 'Em with Love	1969	3.75	7.50	15.00
❏ SKAO-381	Bobbie Gentry's Greatest!	1969	3.75	7.50	15.00
❏ SM-381	Bobbie Gentry's Greatest!	197?	2.00	4.00	8.00
❏ ST-428	Fancy	1970	3.75	7.50	15.00
❏ ST-494	Patchwork	1970	3.75	7.50	15.00
❏ STBB-704 [(2)]	Sittin' Pretty/Tobacco Road	1971	3.75	7.50	15.00
❏ SM-2830	Ode to Billie Joe	197?	2.00	4.00	8.00
❏ ST 2830 [S]	Ode to Billie Joe	1967	3.75	7.50	15.00
❏ T 2830 [M]	Ode to Billie Joe	1967	5.00	10.00	20.00
❏ ST 2842 [S]	The Delta Sweete	1968	3.75	7.50	15.00
❏ T 2842 [M]	The Delta Sweete	1968	6.25	12.50	25.00
❏ ST 2964	The Local Gentry	1968	3.75	7.50	15.00
GENTRY, BOBBIE, AND GLEN CAMPBELL See GLEN CAMPBELL AND BOBBIE GENTRY.					
GENTRY, RAY					
45s					
MAVERICK					
❏ 614	Willie Was a Bad Boy/Do the Fly	1958	100.00	200.00	400.00
GENTRYS, THE					
45s					
BELL					
❏ 720	You Better Come Home/I Can't Go Back to Denver	1968	—	3.00	6.00
❏ 740	Thinking Like a Child/Silky	1968	—	3.00	6.00
❏ 753	Midnight Train/You Tell Me You Care	1968	—	3.00	6.00
CAPITOL					
❏ 3459	Changin'/Let Me Put This Ring Upon Your Finger	1972	—	2.50	5.00
HIT					
❏ 229	Keep On Dancing/A Lover's Concerto	1965	5.00	10.00	20.00
—B-side by Alpha Zoe					
MGM					
❏ 13379	Keep On Dancing/Make Up Your Mind	1965	3.75	7.50	15.00
❏ 13432	Spread It On Thick/Brown Paper Sack	1965	3.00	6.00	12.00
❏ 13432 [PS]	Spread It On Thick/Brown Paper Sack	1965	4.00	8.00	16.00
❏ 13495	Everyday I Have to Cry/Don't Let It Be (This Time)	1966	3.00	6.00	12.00
❏ 13561	There Are Two Sides to Every Story/Woman of the World	1966	3.00	6.00	12.00
❏ 13690	There's a Love/You Make Me Feel So Good	1967	6.25	12.50	25.00

Number	Title (A Side/B Side)	Yr	VG	VG+	NM
❏ 13749	I Can See/90 Pound Weakling	1967	2.50	5.00	10.00
STAX					
❏ 0223	All Hung Up on You/Little Gold Band	1974	—	2.00	4.00
❏ 0242	High Flyer/Little Gold Band	1975	—	2.00	4.00
SUN					
❏ 1108	I Need Love/Why Should I Cry	1969	—	2.50	5.00
❏ 1114	Cinnamon Girl/I Just Got the News	1970	—	2.50	5.00
❏ 1114 [DJ]	Cinnamon Girl/I Just Got the News	1970	2.50	5.00	10.00
—Promo only on blue vinyl					
❏ 1118	I Hate to See You Go/He'll Never Love Me	1970	—	2.50	5.00
❏ 1120	Friends/Goddess of Love	1970	—	2.50	5.00
❏ 1122	Wild World/Sunshine	1971	—	2.50	5.00
❏ 1126	God Save Our Country/Love You All My Life	1971	—	2.50	5.00
YOUNGSTOWN					
❏ 600	Sometimes/Little Drops of Water	1965	6.25	12.50	25.00
❏ 601	Keep On Dancing/Make Up Your Mind	1965	7.50	15.00	30.00
Albums					
MGM					
❏ GAS-127	The Gentrys (Golden Archive Series)	1970	5.00	10.00	20.00
❏ E-4336 [M]	Keep On Dancing	1965	6.25	12.50	25.00
❏ SE-4336 [P]	Keep On Dancing	1965	7.50	15.00	30.00
❏ E-4346 [M]	Gentry Time	1966	5.00	10.00	20.00
❏ SE-4346 [S]	Gentry Time	1966	6.25	12.50	25.00
SUN					
❏ LP-117	The Gentrys	1970	7.50	15.00	30.00

GEORDIE
45s

Number	Title (A Side/B Side)	Yr	VG	VG+	NM
MGM					
❏ 14539	Ain't It Just Like a Woman/All Because of You	1973	—	3.00	6.00
Albums					
MGM					
❏ SE-4903	Hope You Like It	1973	7.50	15.00	30.00

GEORGE, BARBARA
45s

Number	Title (A Side/B Side)	Yr	VG	VG+	NM
A.F.O.					
❏ 302	I Know (You Don't Love Me No More)/Love	1961	3.00	6.00	12.00
—Orange and black label					
❏ 302	I Know (You Don't Love Me No More)/Love	1961	3.75	7.50	15.00
—All-orange label					
❏ 304	You Talk About Love/Whip-O-Will	1962	2.50	5.00	10.00
LANA					
❏ 147	I Know (You Don't Love Me No More)/Love	196?	—	3.00	6.00
—Oldies reissue					
SUE					
❏ 763	If You Think/If When You've Done the Best You Can	1962	2.00	4.00	8.00
❏ 766	Send for Me (If You Need Some Lovin')/Bless You	1962	2.00	4.00	8.00
❏ 773	Recipe (For Perfect Fools)/Try Again	1962	2.00	4.00	8.00
❏ 796	Something's Definitely Wrong/I Need Something Different	1963	2.50	5.00	10.00
UNITED ARTISTS					
❏ XW516	I Know (You Don't Love Me No More)/Mockingbird	1974	—	2.00	4.00
—Reissue; B-side by Charles and Inez Foxx					
Albums					
A.F.O.					
❏ LP 5001 [M]	I Know (You Don't Love Me No More)	1962	62.50	125.00	250.00

GEORGE, LLOYD
45s

Number	Title (A Side/B Side)	Yr	VG	VG+	NM
IMPERIAL					
❏ 5837	Twistville/Young Date	1962	3.75	7.50	15.00
❏ 5896	Come On Train/Frog Hunt	1962	3.75	7.50	15.00

GEORGE AND EARL
45s

Number	Title (A Side/B Side)	Yr	VG	VG+	NM
MERCURY					
❏ 70605	Got Anything Good/Can I?	1955	6.25	12.50	25.00
❏ 70632	Goin' Steady with the Blues/Sweet Little Miss Blue Eyes	1955	6.25	12.50	25.00
❏ 70683	Heartaches/Don't, Don't, Don't	1955	6.25	12.50	25.00
❏ 70773	Cry, Baby, Cry/Take a Look at My Darlin'	1956	6.25	12.50	25.00
❏ 70852	Done Gone/Better Stop, Look and Listen	1956	15.00	30.00	60.00
❏ 70935	Eleven Roses/Remember and Regret	1956	6.25	12.50	25.00

GEORGE AND GREER
45s

Number	Title (A Side/B Side)	Yr	VG	VG+	NM
GOLDWAX					
❏ 313	You Don't Know It, But You Had Me/Good Times	1966	7.50	15.00	30.00
—Reissue as "George Jackson and Dan Greer"					
❏ 313	You Don't Know It, But You Had Me/Good Times	1966	10.00	20.00	40.00

GEORGE AND LOUIS
45s

Number	Title (A Side/B Side)	Yr	VG	VG+	NM
SUN					
❏ 301	The Return of Jerry Lee/The Return of Jerry Lee, Part 2	1958	6.25	12.50	25.00
❏ 301	The Return of Jerry Lee/Lewis Boogie	1958	7.50	15.00	30.00
—B-side by Jerry Lee Lewis					

GEORGETTES, THE See GERRY AND THE GEORGETTES.

GERARD, DANYEL
45s

Number	Title (A Side/B Side)	Yr	VG	VG+	NM
COLUMBIA					
❏ 4-45468	Butterfly/One White Rose	1971	2.00	4.00	8.00
MGM VERVE					
❏ 10670	Butterfly/Let's Love	1972	—	3.00	6.00
❏ 10670 [PS]	Butterfly/Let's Love	1972	2.50	5.00	10.00
❏ 10685	Elie Lama Sabacthani/The Gun	1972	—	3.00	6.00
Albums					
MGM VERVE					
❏ MV 5081	Danyel Gerard	1972	3.00	6.00	12.00

GERMZ, THE
45s

Number	Title (A Side/B Side)	Yr	VG	VG+	NM
VERTIGO					
❏ 8001	Boy-Girl Love/No Easy Way Down	1967	3.75	7.50	15.00

GERONIMO BLACK
45s

Number	Title (A Side/B Side)	Yr	VG	VG+	NM
UNI					
❏ 55339	Let Us Live/'59 Chevy	1972	2.50	5.00	10.00
Albums					
UNI					
❏ 73132	Geronimo Black	1972	6.25	12.50	25.00

GERRY AND THE GEORGETTES
45s

Number	Title (A Side/B Side)	Yr	VG	VG+	NM
HIT					
❏ 83	Be My Baby/Sally Go 'Round the Roses	1963	2.00	4.00	8.00
—As "The Georgettes"; B-side by the Belles					
❏ 97	Quicksand/Loddy Lo	1963	2.00	4.00	8.00
—B-side by Leroy Jones					

GERRY AND THE PACEMAKERS
45s

Number	Title (A Side/B Side)	Yr	VG	VG+	NM
LAURIE					
❏ 3162	How Do You Do It/Away From You	1963	5.00	10.00	20.00
❏ 3196	I Like It/It Happened to Me	1963	5.00	10.00	20.00
❏ 3218	You'll Never Walk Alone/It's All Right	1964	5.00	10.00	20.00
❏ 3233	I'm the One/How Do You Do It	1964	3.75	7.50	15.00
❏ 3233	I'm the One/It's All Right	1964	3.75	7.50	15.00
❏ 3233	I'm the One/You've Got What I Like	1964	5.00	10.00	20.00
❏ 3251	Don't Let the Sun Catch You Crying/Away from You	1964	3.75	7.50	15.00
❏ 3261	How Do You Do It/You'll Never Walk Alone	1964	3.00	6.00	12.00
❏ 3271	I Like It/Jambalaya	1964	3.00	6.00	12.00
❏ 3279	I'll Be There/You, You, You	1964	3.00	6.00	12.00
❏ 3284	Ferry Across the Mersey/Pretend	1965	3.00	6.00	12.00
❏ 3293	It's Gonna Be Alright/Skinny Minnie	1965	2.50	5.00	10.00
❏ 3302	You'll Never Walk Alone/Away from You	1965	2.50	5.00	10.00
❏ 3313	Give All Your Love to Me/You're the Reason	1965	2.50	5.00	10.00
❏ 3323	Dreams/Walk Hand in Hand	1965	2.50	5.00	10.00
❏ 3337	La La La/Without You	1966	2.50	5.00	10.00
❏ 3354	Girl on a Swing/The Way You Look Tonight	1966	2.50	5.00	10.00
❏ 3370	The Big Bright Green Pleasure Machine/Looking for My Life	1966	3.00	6.00	12.00
Albums					
CAPITOL					
❏ SM-11898 [B]	The Best of Gerry and the Pacemakers	1979	2.00	4.00	8.00
—All stereo except "I Like It," "Away from You" and "I'm the One," which are mono.					
LAURIE					
❏ LLP-2024 [M]	Don't Let the Sun Catch You Crying	1964	7.50	15.00	30.00
❏ SLP-2024 [R]	Don't Let the Sun Catch You Crying	1964	6.25	12.50	25.00
❏ LLP-2027 [M]	Gerry and the Pacemakers' Second Album	1964	7.50	15.00	30.00
❏ SLP-2027 [R]	Gerry and the Pacemakers' Second Album	1964	6.25	12.50	25.00
❏ LLP-2030 [M]	I'll Be There	1964	7.50	15.00	30.00
❏ SLP-2030 [R]	I'll Be There	1964	6.25	12.50	25.00
❏ LLP-2031 [M]	Greatest Hits	1965	6.25	12.50	25.00
❏ SLP-2031 [R]	Greatest Hits	1965	3.75	7.50	15.00
❏ LLP-2037 [M]	Girl on a Swing	1966	6.25	12.50	25.00
❏ SLP-2037 [S]	Girl on a Swing	1966	5.00	10.00	20.00
❏ DT 90384 [R]	Greatest Hits	1965	6.25	12.50	25.00
—Capitol Record Club edition					
❏ T 90384 [M]	Greatest Hits	1965	6.25	12.50	25.00
—Capitol Record Club edition					
❏ DT 90555 [R]	Don't Let the Sun Catch You Crying	1964	7.50	15.00	30.00
—Capitol Record Club edition					
❏ T 90555 [M]	Don't Let the Sun Catch You Crying	1964	10.00	20.00	40.00
—Capitol Record Club edition					
UNITED ARTISTS					
❏ UAL 3387 [M]	Ferry Cross the Mersey	1965	6.25	12.50	25.00
—Also contains incidental music by George Martin					
❏ UAS 6387 [S]	Ferry Cross the Mersey	1965	10.00	20.00	40.00
❏ ST 90812 [S]	Ferry Cross the Mersey	1965	12.50	25.00	50.00
—Capitol Record Club edition					
❏ T 90812 [M]	Ferry Cross the Mersey	1965	10.00	20.00	40.00
—Capitol Record Club edition					

GESTURES, THE
45s

Number	Title (A Side/B Side)	Yr	VG	VG+	NM
SOMA					
❏ 1417	Run, Run, Run/It Seems to Me	1964	3.75	7.50	15.00
❏ 1426	Don't Mess Around/Candlelight	1965	6.25	12.50	25.00

GHOULS, THE
Albums

Number	Title (A Side/B Side)	Yr	VG	VG+	NM
CAPITOL					
❏ ST 2215 [S]	Dracula's Deuce	1965	37.50	75.00	150.00
❏ T 2215 [M]	Dracula's Deuce	1965	30.00	60.00	120.00

GIANT CRAB, THE
45s

Number	Title (A Side/B Side)	Yr	VG	VG+	NM
UNI					
❏ 55094	Hi Ho Silver Lining/Hot Line Conversation	1968	2.00	4.00	8.00
❏ 55103	Believe It or Not/The Color Purple	1968	2.00	4.00	8.00
❏ 55134	Cool It/Intensify My Soul	1969	2.00	4.00	8.00
❏ 55155	ESP/Hot Line Conversation	1969	2.00	4.00	8.00
Albums					
UNI					
❏ 73037	A Giant Crab Comes Forth	1968	6.25	12.50	25.00
❏ 73057	Cool It, Helios	1969	6.25	12.50	25.00

GIBB, BARRY Also see BEE GEES; BARBRA STREISAND.
45s

Number	Title (A Side/B Side)	Yr	VG	VG+	NM
ATCO					
❏ 6786	One Bad Thing/The Day Your Eyes Met Mine	1970	—	—	—
—May not exist as a US pressing					
MCA					
❏ 52443	Shine Shine/She Says	1984	—	—	3.00
❏ 52443 [PS]	Shine Shine/She Says	1984	—	—	3.00

Number	Title (A Side/B Side)	Yr	VG	VG+	NM
❑ 52501	Fine Line/Stay Alone	1984	—	—	3.00
❑ 52501 [PS]	Fine Line/Stay Alone	1984	—	2.00	4.00

GIBB, MAURICE Also see BEE GEES; THE FUT.
45s
ATCO

Number	Title (A Side/B Side)	Yr	VG	VG+	NM
❑ 6757	Railroad/I've Come Back	1970	7.50	15.00	30.00

—Possibly only issued in Canada

GIBB, ROBIN Also see BEE GEES.
12-Inch Singles
MIRAGE

Number	Title (A Side/B Side)	Yr	VG	VG+	NM
❑ DMD 740 [DJ]	Boys Do Fall in Love (same on both sides?)	1984	2.50	5.00	10.00
❑ PR 775 [DJ]	Secret Agent/Robot	1984	2.50	5.00	10.00

45s
ATCO

Number	Title (A Side/B Side)	Yr	VG	VG+	NM
❑ 6698	Saved by the Bell/Mother and Jack	1969	2.00	4.00	8.00
❑ 6727	Weekend/One Million Years	1969	2.00	4.00	8.00
❑ 6737	Give Me a Smile/August October	1970	2.00	4.00	8.00

EMI AMERICA

Number	Title (A Side/B Side)	Yr	VG	VG+	NM
❑ 8291	Like a Fool/Possession	1985	—	—	3.00
❑ 8291 [PS]	Like a Fool/Possession	1985	—	2.00	4.00
❑ 8304	Toys/Do You Love Her	1986	—	—	3.00
❑ 8304 [PS]	Toys/Do You Love Her	1986	—	2.00	4.00

MIRAGE

Number	Title (A Side/B Side)	Yr	VG	VG+	NM
❑ 99688 [DJ]	In Your Diary (same on both sides)	1984	—	2.00	4.00

—Stock copy unknown

Number	Title (A Side/B Side)	Yr	VG	VG+	NM
❑ 99712	Secret Agent/Robot	1984	—	—	3.00
❑ 99743	Boys Do Fall in Love/Diamonds	1984	—	—	3.00
❑ 99743 [PS]	Boys Do Fall in Love/Diamonds	1984	—	—	3.00

POLYDOR

Number	Title (A Side/B Side)	Yr	VG	VG+	NM
❑ 810895-7	Juliet/Hearts on Fire	1983	—	—	3.00
❑ 810895-7 [PS]	Juliet/Hearts on Fire	1983	—	2.00	4.00

RSO

Number	Title (A Side/B Side)	Yr	VG	VG+	NM
❑ 907	Oh Darling/She's Leaving Home	1978	—	2.00	4.00

—B-side by The Bee Gees

Number	Title (A Side/B Side)	Yr	VG	VG+	NM
❑ 1047	Help Me/(Instrumental)	1980	—	2.00	4.00

—With Marcy Levy

Number	Title (A Side/B Side)	Yr	VG	VG+	NM
❑ 1047 [PS]	Help Me/(Instrumental)	1980	—	2.00	4.00

SESAME STREET

Number	Title (A Side/B Side)	Yr	VG	VG+	NM
❑ 99070	Sesame Street Fever/Trash	1978	—	2.50	5.00
❑ 99070 [PS]	Sesame Street Fever/Trash	1978	—	3.00	6.00

Albums
ATCO

Number	Title (A Side/B Side)	Yr	VG	VG+	NM
❑ SD 33-323	Robin's Reign	1969	5.00	10.00	20.00

MIRAGE

Number	Title (A Side/B Side)	Yr	VG	VG+	NM
❑ 90170	Secret Agent	1984	2.00	4.00	8.00

POLYDOR

Number	Title (A Side/B Side)	Yr	VG	VG+	NM
❑ 810896-1	How Old Are You?	1983	2.50	5.00	10.00

GIBBS, GEORGIA
45s
BELL

Number	Title (A Side/B Side)	Yr	VG	VG+	NM
❑ 608	I Wouldn't Have It Any Other Way/You Can Never Get Away from Me	1965	—	3.00	6.00
❑ 615	Let Me Cry on Your Shoulder/Venice Blue	1965	—	3.00	6.00
❑ 626	Call Me/Don't Cry Joe	1965	—	3.00	6.00
❑ 635	In Time/Let Me Dream	1965	—	3.00	6.00
❑ 641	Kiss of Fire/Blue Grass	1966	—	3.00	6.00

CORAL

Number	Title (A Side/B Side)	Yr	VG	VG+	NM
❑ 60210	I Don't Care If the Sun Don't Shine/I'll Get Myself a Choo-Choo Train (And Go Far, Far Away)	1950	3.75	7.50	15.00
❑ 60227	Simple Melody/A Little Bit Independent	1950	3.75	7.50	15.00

—With Bob Crosby

Number	Title (A Side/B Side)	Yr	VG	VG+	NM
❑ 60234	Red Hot Mama/Razz-A-Ma-Tazz	1950	3.75	7.50	15.00
❑ 60255	I Was Dancing with Someone/Then I'll Be Happy	1950	3.75	7.50	15.00
❑ 60310	If I Were a Bell/I'll Know	1950	3.75	7.50	15.00
❑ 60315	Ballin' the Jack/Looks Like a Cold Cold Winter	1950	3.75	7.50	15.00
❑ 60353	I Still Feel the Same About You/Get Out Those Old Records	1951	3.75	7.50	15.00
❑ 60406	Shoo Shoo Baby/Once Upon a Nickel	1951	3.75	7.50	15.00
❑ 60462	Ballin' the Jack/Then I'll Be Happy	1951	3.75	7.50	15.00
❑ 60463	Get Out Those Old Records/I'll Get Myself a Choo-Choo Train (And Go Far, Far Away)	1951	3.75	7.50	15.00
❑ 61525	If I Were a Bell/I'll Know	1955	2.50	5.00	10.00

EPIC

Number	Title (A Side/B Side)	Yr	VG	VG+	NM
❑ 9573	Candy Kisses/Nobody's Asking Questions	1963	—	—	—

—Unreleased?

Number	Title (A Side/B Side)	Yr	VG	VG+	NM
❑ 9585	I Will Follow Him (You)/Candy Kisses	1963	2.00	4.00	8.00
❑ 9606	Tater Poon/Nine Girls Out of Ten Girls	1963	5.00	10.00	20.00

IMPERIAL

Number	Title (A Side/B Side)	Yr	VG	VG+	NM
❑ 5652	Seven Lonely Days/The Stroll That Stole My Heart	1960	2.50	5.00	10.00
❑ 5688	So in Love/Loch Lomond	1960	2.50	5.00	10.00

KAPP

Number	Title (A Side/B Side)	Yr	VG	VG+	NM
❑ 286	Pretend/Hamburgers, Frankfurters and Potato Chips	1959	2.50	5.00	10.00

MERCURY

Number	Title (A Side/B Side)	Yr	VG	VG+	NM
❑ 5644	Tom's Tune/I Wish, I Wish	1951	3.75	7.50	15.00
❑ 5662	Good Morning Mister Echo/Be Doggone Sure You Call	1951	3.75	7.50	15.00
❑ 5681	While You Danced, Danced, Danced/While We're Young	1951	3.75	7.50	15.00
❑ 5687	Got Him Offa My Hands/Cherry Pink	1951	3.75	7.50	15.00
❑ 5718	What You Do to Me/While We Danced	1951	3.75	7.50	15.00
❑ 5749	Cry/My Old Flame	1951	3.75	7.50	15.00
❑ 5758	Be My Life's Companion/The Oklahoma Polka	1951	3.75	7.50	15.00
❑ 5823	Kiss of Fire/A Lasting Thing	1952	3.00	6.00	12.00
❑ 5874	So Madly in Love/Make Me Love You	1952	3.00	6.00	12.00
❑ 5912	My Favorite Song/Sinner or Saint	1952	3.00	6.00	12.00
❑ 70034	A Moth and a Flame/Photograph on the Piano	1953	3.00	6.00	12.00
❑ 70057	What Does It Mean/Winter's Here Again	1953	3.00	6.00	12.00
❑ 70095	Seven Lonely Days/If You Take My Heart Away	1953	3.00	6.00	12.00
❑ 70172	For Me, For Me/Thunder and Lightning	1953	3.00	6.00	12.00
❑ 70218	Say It Isn't So/He's Funny That Way	1953	3.00	6.00	12.00
❑ 70238	Bridge of Sighs/Hard Lovin' Man	1953	3.00	6.00	12.00

Number	Title (A Side/B Side)	Yr	VG	VG+	NM
❑ 70274	I Love Paris/Under Paris Skies	1953	3.00	6.00	12.00
❑ 70298	Somebody Bad Stole De Wedding Bell (Who's Got de Ding Dong)/Baubles, Bangles and Beads	1954	3.00	6.00	12.00
❑ 70339	My Sin/I'll Always Be Happy with You	1954	3.00	6.00	12.00
❑ 70386	Wait for Me Darling/Whistle and I'll Wait	1954	3.00	6.00	12.00
❑ 70430	The Man That Got Away/More Than Ever	1954	3.00	6.00	12.00
❑ 70473	Mambo Baby/Love Me	1954	3.00	6.00	12.00
❑ 70517	Tweedle Dee/You're Wrong, All Wrong	1954	3.75	7.50	15.00
❑ 70572	Dance with Me Henry (Wallflower)/Every Road Must Have a Turning	1955	3.75	7.50	15.00
❑ 70647	Sweet and Gentle/Blueberries	1955	3.00	6.00	12.00
❑ 70685	I Want You to Be My Baby/Come Rain or Come Shine	1955	3.00	6.00	12.00
❑ 70743	Goodbye to Rome (Arrividerci Roma)/24 Hours a Day (365 a Year)	1955	3.00	6.00	12.00
❑ 70811	Rock Right/The Greatest Thing	1956	3.00	6.00	12.00
❑ 70850	Kiss Me Another/Fool of the Year	1956	3.00	6.00	12.00
❑ 70920	Happiness Street/Happiness Is a Thing Called Joe	1956	3.00	6.00	12.00
❑ 70998	Tra La La/Morning, Noon and Night	1956	3.00	6.00	12.00
❑ 71058	Silent Lips/Pretty Pretty	1957	3.00	6.00	12.00
❑ 71103	The Sheik of Araby/I Am a Heart, a Heart, a Heart	1957	3.00	6.00	12.00

RCA VICTOR

Number	Title (A Side/B Side)	Yr	VG	VG+	NM
❑ 47-6922	I'm Walking the Floor Over You/Sugar Candy	1957	3.00	6.00	12.00
❑ 47-7047	Fun Lovin' Baby/I Never Had the Blues	1957	3.00	6.00	12.00
❑ 47-7098	Great Balls of Fire/I Miss You	1957	3.00	6.00	12.00
❑ 47-7166	You're Doin' It/Way Way Down	1958	3.00	6.00	12.00
❑ 47-7239	Hello Happiness, Goodbye Blues/It's My Pleasure	1958	3.00	6.00	12.00
❑ 47-9173	Time Will Tell/Where's the Music Coming From	1967	—	3.00	6.00

ROULETTE

Number	Title (A Side/B Side)	Yr	VG	VG+	NM
❑ 4106	The Hula Hoop Song/Keep in Touch	1958	2.50	5.00	10.00
❑ 4126	Ther Huckelbuck/Better Loved You'll Never Be	1959	2.50	5.00	10.00

7-Inch Extended Plays
MERCURY

Number	Title (A Side/B Side)	Yr	VG	VG+	NM
❑ EP1-3061	Say It Isn't So/It Had to Be You//I'll Always Be in Love with You/How Long Has This Been Going On	195?	3.00	6.00	12.00
❑ EP1-3061 [PS]	Georgia Sings Oldies	195?	3.00	6.00	12.00
❑ EP1-3062	(contents unknown)	195?	3.00	6.00	12.00
❑ EP1-3062 [PS]	Her Nibs, Miss Georgia Gibbs	195?	3.00	6.00	12.00
❑ EP1-3082	(contents unknown)	195?	3.00	6.00	12.00
❑ EP1-3082 [PS]	Encores	195?	3.00	6.00	12.00
❑ EP1-3130	My Favorite Song/A Moth and a Flame//Seven Lonely Days/Sinner or Saint	195?	3.00	6.00	12.00
❑ EP1-3130 [PS]	For Gentlemen Only	195?	3.00	6.00	12.00
❑ EP-1-3176	Under Paris Skies/I Love Paris//Autumn Leaves/Comme Ci, Comme Ca	195?	3.00	6.00	12.00
❑ EP-1-3176 [PS]	(title unknown)	195?	3.00	6.00	12.00
❑ EP1-3214	(contents unknown)	195?	3.00	6.00	12.00
❑ EP1-3214 [PS]	Bridge of Sighs	195?	3.00	6.00	12.00
❑ EP1-3226	(contents unknown)	195?	3.00	6.00	12.00
❑ EP1-3226 [PS]	Somebody Bad Stole De Wedding Bell	195?	3.00	6.00	12.00
❑ EP1-3241	Whistle and I'll Dance/Thunder and Lightning//What Does It Mean/A Lasting Thing	195?	3.00	6.00	12.00
❑ EP1-3241 [PS]	Thunder and Lightning	195?	3.00	6.00	12.00
❑ EP1-3242	(contents unknown)	195?	3.00	6.00	12.00
❑ EP1-3242 [PS]	Kiss of Fire	195?	3.00	6.00	12.00
❑ EP1-3243	(contents unknown)	195?	3.00	6.00	12.00
❑ EP1-3243 [PS]	So Madly in Love	195?	3.00	6.00	12.00
❑ EP-1-3266	*After You've Gone/What'll I Do/It's the Talk of the Town/All Alone	195?	3.00	6.00	12.00
❑ EP-1-3266 [PS]	After You've Gone	195?	3.00	6.00	12.00
❑ EP-1-4002	Tweedle Dee/You're Wrong, All Wrong//Melancholy Baby/Ballin' the Jack	195?	3.00	6.00	12.00
❑ EP-1-4002 [PS]	Tops in Pops	195?	3.00	6.00	12.00

ROYALE

Number	Title (A Side/B Side)	Yr	VG	VG+	NM
❑ EP 259	Ballin' the Jack/Old Man Mose//Wrap Your Troubles in Dreams/The One I Love	195?	5.00	10.00	20.00

—Red vinyl

Number	Title (A Side/B Side)	Yr	VG	VG+	NM
❑ EP 259 [PS]	Georgia Gibbs Sings	195?	5.00	10.00	20.00

Albums
BELL

Number	Title (A Side/B Side)	Yr	VG	VG+	NM
❑ 6000 [M]	Call Me Georgia Gibbs	1966	3.75	7.50	15.00
❑ 6000S [S]	Call Me Georgia Gibbs	1966	5.00	10.00	20.00

CORAL

Number	Title (A Side/B Side)	Yr	VG	VG+	NM
❑ CRL 56037 [10]	Ballin' the Jack	1951	12.50	25.00	50.00
❑ CRL 57183 [M]	Her Nibs	1957	10.00	20.00	40.00

EMARCY

Number	Title (A Side/B Side)	Yr	VG	VG+	NM
❑ MG-36103 [M]	Swingin' with Gibbs	1957	7.50	15.00	30.00

EPIC

Number	Title (A Side/B Side)	Yr	VG	VG+	NM
❑ LN 24059 [M]	Georgia Gibbs' Greatest Hits	1963	3.75	7.50	15.00
❑ BN 26059 [S]	Georgia Gibbs' Greatest Hits	1963	5.00	10.00	20.00

GOLDEN TONE

Number	Title (A Side/B Side)	Yr	VG	VG+	NM
❑ 4093 [M]	Her Nibs!! Miss Georgia Gibbs	1962	3.00	6.00	12.00
❑ 14093 [R]	Her Nibs!! Miss Georgia Gibbs	1962	2.50	5.00	10.00

—Cover misspells it "Nibbs"

IMPERIAL

Number	Title (A Side/B Side)	Yr	VG	VG+	NM
❑ LP-9107 [M]	Something's Gotta Give	1960	5.00	10.00	20.00
❑ LP-12064 [S]	Something's Gotta Give	1960	6.25	12.50	25.00

MERCURY

Number	Title (A Side/B Side)	Yr	VG	VG+	NM
❑ MG-20071 [M]	Music and Memories	1955	10.00	20.00	40.00
❑ MG-20114 [M]	Song Favorites	1956	10.00	20.00	40.00
❑ MG-20170 [M]	Swingin' with Her Nibs	1956	10.00	20.00	40.00
❑ MG-25175 [10]	Georgia Gibbs Sings Oldies	1953	12.50	25.00	50.00
❑ MG-25199 [10]	The Man That Got Away	1954	12.50	25.00	50.00

ROYALE

Number	Title (A Side/B Side)	Yr	VG	VG+	NM
❑ 18126 [10]	Georgia Gibbs and Orchestra	195?	10.00	20.00	40.00

SUNSET

Number	Title (A Side/B Side)	Yr	VG	VG+	NM
❑ SUM-1113 [M]	Her Nibs, Miss Georgia Gibbs	196?	3.75	7.50	15.00
❑ SUS-5113 [S]	Her Nibs, Miss Georgia Gibbs	196?	3.75	7.50	15.00

Number	Title (A Side/B Side)	Yr	VG	VG+	NM
GIBSON, ALTHEA					
Albums					
DOT					
❏ DLP-3105 [M]	Althea Gibson Sings	1959	10.00	20.00	40.00
❏ DLP-25105 [S]	Althea Gibson Sings	1959	12.50	25.00	50.00
GIBSON, BOBBY, AND THE VOYAGERS					
45s					
GIBSON					
❏ 6003	B-52/Samoa	1959	12.50	25.00	50.00
GIBSON, DAVE					
45s					
HIT					
❏ 50	I Saw Linda Yesterday/Hey Paula	1963	2.00	4.00	8.00
—B-side by Bob and Bobbie					
GIBSON, DON Also see DOTTIE WEST.					
45s					
ABC HICKORY					
❏ 54001	I'm All Wrapped Up in You/We Live in Two Different Worlds	1976	—	2.50	5.00
❏ 54010	Fan the Flame, Feed the Fire/Bringin' In the Georgia Mail	1977	—	2.50	5.00
❏ 54014	If You Ever Get to Houston (Look Me Down)/It's All Over	1977	—	2.50	5.00
❏ 54019	When Do We Stop Starting Over/Love Is Not the Way (You Told Me)	1977	—	2.50	5.00
❏ 54024	Starting All Over Again/I'd Rather Die Young (Than Grow Old Without You)	1978	—	2.50	5.00
❏ 54029	The Fool/Every Song I Sang Would Be Blue	1978	—	2.50	5.00
❏ 54036	Oh, Such a Stranger/I Love You Because	1978	—	2.50	5.00
❏ 54039	Any Day Now/Baby's Not Home	1978	—	2.50	5.00
COLUMBIA					
❏ 20999	No Shoulder to Cry On/We're Stepping Out	1952	5.00	10.00	20.00
❏ 21060	Sample Kisses/Let Me Stay in Your Arms	1952	5.00	10.00	20.00
❏ 21109	Just Walkin' in the Moonlight/I Just Love the Way You Tell a Lie	1953	5.00	10.00	20.00
❏ 21156	You Cast Me Out/Waitin' Down the Road	1953	5.00	10.00	20.00
❏ 21231	Symptoms of Love/Many Times I've Waited	1954	5.00	10.00	20.00
❏ 21281	Selfish with Your Kisses/Ice Cold Heart	1954	5.00	10.00	20.00
HICKORY					
❏ 1559	Don't Take All Your Loving/Pretending Every Day	1970	—	2.50	5.00
❏ 1571	A Perfect Mountain/Would You Believe	1970	—	2.50	5.00
❏ 1579	Someway/Comfort for Your Mind	1970	—	2.50	5.00
❏ 1588	Guess Away the Blues/I Wanna Live	1970	—	2.50	5.00
❏ 1598	(I Heard That) Lonesome Whistle/Window Shopping	1971	2.00	4.00	8.00
❏ 1614	Country Green/Move It On Over	1971	2.00	4.00	8.00
❏ 1623	Far, Far Away/What's Happened to Me	1972	2.00	4.00	8.00
❏ 1638	Woman (Sensuous Woman)/If You Want Me To I'll Go	1972	2.00	4.00	8.00
❏ 1651	Is This the Best I'm Gonna Feel/Watching It Go	1972	2.00	4.00	8.00
❏ 1661	If You're Goin' Girl/Lonesome Number One	1973	2.00	4.00	8.00
❏ 1671	Touch the Morning/Too Much to Know	1973	2.00	4.00	8.00
HICKORY/MGM					
❏ 301	Touch the Morning/Too Much to Know	1973	—	3.00	6.00
❏ 306	That's What I'll Do/Sweet Dreams	1973	—	3.00	6.00
❏ 312	Snap Your Fingers/Love Is a Lonesome Thing	1973	—	3.00	6.00
❏ 318	One Day at a Time/Rainbow Love	1974	—	3.00	6.00
❏ 327	Bring Back Your Love to Me/Drinking Champagne	1974	—	3.00	6.00
❏ 338	I'll Sing for You/Pocatello	1974	—	3.00	6.00
❏ 345	(There She Goes) I Wish Her Well/Funny Familiar Forgotten Feelings	1975	—	3.00	6.00
❏ 353	Don't Stop Loving Me/Somebody's Words	1975	—	3.00	6.00
❏ 361	I Don't Think I'll Ever (Get Over You)/It Can't Last Always	1975	—	3.00	6.00
❏ 365	You've Got to Stop Hurting Me, Darling/Blues in My Mind	1976	—	3.00	6.00
❏ 372	Doing My Time/The World Is Waiting for the Sunrise	1976	—	3.00	6.00
MCA					
❏ 41031	Forever One Day at a Time/Look Who's Blue	1979	—	2.00	4.00
MGM					
❏ 12109	Run Boy/I Must Forget You	1955	7.50	15.00	30.00
❏ 12194	Sweet Dreams/The Road of Life Alone	1956	7.50	15.00	30.00
❏ 12290	I Ain't Gonna Waste My Time/Ah-Ha	1956	10.00	20.00	40.00
❏ 12331	I Believed in You/What a Fool I Was to Fall	1956	7.50	15.00	30.00
❏ 12494	I Ain't a-Studying You Baby/It's Hoppin'	1957	10.00	20.00	40.00
RCA VICTOR					
❏ 37-7841	What About Me/The World Is Waiting for the Sunrise	1961	5.00	10.00	20.00
—"Compact Single 33" (small hole, plays at LP speed)					
❏ 47-4364	Red Lips, White Lies and Blue Hours/Just Let Me Love You	1951	6.25	12.50	25.00
❏ 47-4473	Dark Future/Blue Million Tears	1952	6.25	12.50	25.00
❏ 47-6860	I Can't Leave/I Love You Still	1957	5.00	10.00	20.00
❏ 47-6942	Everything Turns Out for the Best/Sittin' Here Cryin'	1957	5.00	10.00	20.00
❏ 47-7010	Blue Blue Day/Too Soon to Know	1957	3.75	7.50	15.00
❏ 47-7133	Oh Lonesome Me/I Can't Stop Lovin' You	1958	3.75	7.50	15.00
❏ 47-7330	Give Myself a Party/Look Who's Blue	1958	3.75	7.50	15.00
❏ 47-7437	Who Cares/A Stranger to Me	1959	3.75	7.50	15.00
❏ 47-7505	Lonesome Old House/I Couldn't Care Less	1959	3.75	7.50	15.00
❏ 47-7566	Don't Tell Me Your Troubles/Heartbreak Avenue	1959	3.75	7.50	15.00
❏ 47-7629	I'm Movin' On/Big Hearted Man	1959	3.75	7.50	15.00
❏ 47-7690	Just One Time/I May Never Get to Heaven	1960	3.00	6.00	12.00
❏ 47-7762	Far, Far Away/A Legend in My Time	1960	3.00	6.00	12.00
❏ 47-7805	Sweet Dreams/The Same Street	1960	3.00	6.00	12.00
❏ 47-7841	What About Me/The World Is Waiting for the Sunrise	1961	3.00	6.00	12.00
❏ 47-7890	Sea of Heartbreak/I Think It's Best (To Forget Me)	1961	3.00	6.00	12.00
❏ 47-7959	Lonesome Number One/Same Old Trouble	1961	3.00	6.00	12.00
❏ 47-8017	I Can Mend Your Broken Heart/I Let Her Get Lonely	1962	2.50	5.00	10.00
❏ 47-8085	So How Come (No One Loves Me)/Baby We're Really in Love	1962	2.50	5.00	10.00
❏ 47-8085 [PS]	So How Come (No One Loves Me)/Baby We're Really in Love	1962	3.75	7.50	15.00
❏ 47-8144	Head Over Heels in Love with You/It Was Worth It All	1963	2.50	5.00	10.00
❏ 47-8144 [PS]	Head Over Heels in Love with You/It Was Worth It All	1963	3.75	7.50	15.00
❏ 47-8192	Anything New Gets Old (Except My Love for You)/After the Heartache	1963	2.50	5.00	10.00
❏ 47-8192 [PS]	Anything New Gets Old (Except My Love for You)/After the Heartache	1963	3.75	7.50	15.00
❏ 47-8367	Fireball Mail/Oh, Such a Stranger	1964	2.50	5.00	10.00
❏ 47-8456	Cause I Believe in You/A Love That Can't Be	1964	2.50	5.00	10.00
❏ 47-8589	Again/You're Going Away	1965	2.00	4.00	8.00
❏ 47-8678	Watch Where You're Going/There's a Big Wheel	1965	2.00	4.00	8.00
❏ 47-8732	A Born Loser/All the World Is Lonely Now	1965	2.00	4.00	8.00
❏ 47-8812	(Yes) I'm Hurting/My Whole World Is Hurt	1966	2.00	4.00	8.00
❏ 47-8975	Funny, Familiar, Forgotten, Feelings/Forget Me	1966	2.00	4.00	8.00
❏ 47-9177	Lost Highway/Around the Town	1967	2.00	4.00	8.00
❏ 47-9266	All My Love/No Doubt About It	1967	2.00	4.00	8.00
❏ 47-9395	Satisfied/Where No Man Stands Alone	1967	2.00	4.00	8.00
❏ 47-9460	Ashes of Love/Good Morning, Dear	1968	—	3.00	6.00
❏ 47-9563	It's a Long, Long Way to Georgia/Low and Lonely	1968	—	3.00	6.00
❏ 47-9663	Ever Changing Mind/Thoughts	1968	—	3.00	6.00
❏ 47-9906	Montego Bay/If My Heart Had Windows	1970	—	3.00	6.00
❏ 48-0424	I Love No One But You/Carolina Breakdown	1951	6.25	12.50	25.00
❏ 48-0460	Roses Are Red/Wiggle Wag	1951	6.25	12.50	25.00
❏ 61-7762 [S]	Far, Far Away/A Legend in My Time	1960	6.25	12.50	25.00
—"Living Stereo" (large hole, plays at 45 rpm)					
❏ 74-0143	Solitary/I Just Said Goodbye to My Dreams	1969	—	3.00	6.00
❏ 74-0219	I Will Always/Half As Much	1969	—	3.00	6.00
WARNER BROS.					
❏ 49193	Sweet Sensuous Sensations/Stranger to Me	1980	—	2.00	4.00
❏ 49504	I'd Be Crazy Over You/Somewhere Between Yesterday	1980	—	2.00	4.00
❏ 49602	Love Fires/Come Back and Love Me	1980	—	2.00	4.00
7-Inch Extended Plays					
COLUMBIA					
❏ B-2146	(contents unknown)	1957	5.00	10.00	20.00
❏ B-2146 [PS]	Don Gibson	1957	5.00	10.00	20.00
RCA VICTOR					
❏ EPA-4323	(contents unknown)	1958	3.75	7.50	15.00
❏ EPA-4323 [PS]	Blue, Blue Day	1958	3.75	7.50	15.00
❏ EPA-4335	(contents unknown)	1958	3.75	7.50	15.00
❏ EPA-4335 [PS]	That Lonesome Valley	1958	3.75	7.50	15.00
❏ EPA-5114	Oh Lonesome Me/Look Who's Blue//Who Cares/Blue, Blue Day	1959	3.75	7.50	15.00
❏ EPA-5114 [PS]	Blue and Lonesome	1959	3.75	7.50	15.00
Albums					
ABC HICKORY					
❏ AH-44001	I'm All Wrapped Up in You	1976	3.00	6.00	12.00
❏ AH-44007	If You Ever	1977	3.00	6.00	12.00
❏ AH-44010	Starting All Over	1978	3.00	6.00	12.00
❏ AH-44014	Look Who's Blue	1978	3.00	6.00	12.00
HARMONY					
❏ HL 7358 [M]	The Fabulous Don Gibson Sings	196?	3.75	7.50	15.00
❏ HS 11158 [R]	The Fabulous Don Gibson Sings	196?	3.00	6.00	12.00
❏ KH 31765	Sample Kisses	1972	2.50	5.00	10.00
HICKORY					
❏ LPS-153	Hits, The Don Gibson Way	1970	3.75	7.50	15.00
❏ LPS-155	Perfect Mountain	1971	3.75	7.50	15.00
❏ LPS-157	Don Gibson Sings Hank Williams	1971	3.75	7.50	15.00
❏ LPS-160	Country Green	1971	3.75	7.50	15.00
❏ LPS-166	Woman (Sensuous Woman)	1972	3.75	7.50	15.00
❏ ST-94817	Woman (Sensuous Woman)	1972	5.00	10.00	20.00
—Capitol Record Club edition					
HICKORY/MGM					
❏ HR-4501	Touch the Morning/That's What I'll Do	1973	3.75	7.50	15.00
❏ H3G-4502	The Very Best of Don Gibson	1974	3.75	7.50	15.00
❏ H3F-4509	Snap Your Fingers	1974	3.75	7.50	15.00
❏ H3G-4516	Bring Back Your Love to Me	1974	3.00	6.00	12.00
❏ H3G-4519	I'm the Loneliest Man	1975	3.00	6.00	12.00
LION					
❏ L-70069 [M]	Songs by Don Gibson	1958	20.00	40.00	80.00
METRO					
❏ M-529 [M]	Don Gibson	1965	3.00	6.00	12.00
❏ MS-529 [R]	Don Gibson	1965	2.50	5.00	10.00
MGM					
❏ GAS-138	Don Gibson (Golden Archive Series)	1970	3.75	7.50	15.00
RCA CAMDEN					
❏ ACL1-0328	Just Call Me Lonesome	1973	2.50	5.00	10.00
❏ ACL1-0758	Just One Time	1974	2.50	5.00	10.00
❏ CAL-852 [M]	A Blue Million Tears	196?	3.00	6.00	12.00
❏ CAS-852 [P]	A Blue Million Tears	196?	3.00	6.00	12.00
—All tracks are rechanneled except "I Let Her Get Lonely" and "I May Never Get to Heaven," which are true stereo					
❏ CAL-2101 [M]	Hurtin' Inside	1966	3.00	6.00	12.00
❏ CAS-2101 [S]	Hurtin' Inside	1966	3.75	7.50	15.00
❏ CAS-2246	I Love You So Much	1968	3.00	6.00	12.00
❏ CAS-2317	My God Is Real	1969	3.00	6.00	12.00
❏ CAS-2392	Lovin' Lies	1970	3.00	6.00	12.00
❏ CAS-2502	I Walk Alone	1971	3.00	6.00	12.00
❏ CAS-2592	Am I That Easy to Forget	1972	3.00	6.00	12.00
RCA VICTOR					
❏ LPM-1743 [M]	Oh Lonesome Me	1958	12.50	25.00	50.00
❏ LPM-1918 [M]	No One Stands Alone	1959	7.50	15.00	30.00
❏ LSP-1918 [S]	No One Stands Alone	1959	10.00	20.00	40.00
❏ LPM-2038 [M]	That Gibson Boy	1959	7.50	15.00	30.00
❏ LSP-2038 [S]	That Gibson Boy	1959	10.00	20.00	40.00
❏ LPM-2184 [M]	Look Who's Blue	1960	7.50	15.00	30.00
❏ LSP-2184 [S]	Look Who's Blue	1960	10.00	20.00	40.00
❏ LPM-2269 [M]	Sweet Dreams	1960	7.50	15.00	30.00
❏ LSP-2269 [S]	Sweet Dreams	1960	10.00	20.00	40.00

Number	Title (A Side/B Side)	Yr	VG	VG+	NM
LPM-2361 [M]	Girls, Guitars and Gibson	1961	7.50	15.00	30.00
LSP-2361 [S]	Girls, Guitars and Gibson	1961	10.00	20.00	40.00
LPM-2448 [M]	Some Favorites of Mine	1962	7.50	15.00	30.00
LSP-2448 [S]	Some Favorites of Mine	1962	10.00	20.00	40.00
LPM-2702 [M]	I Wrote a Song	1963	7.50	15.00	30.00
LSP-2702 [S]	I Wrote a Song	1963	10.00	20.00	40.00
LPM-2878 [M]	God Walks These Hills	1964	5.00	10.00	20.00
LSP-2878 [S]	God Walks These Hills	1964	6.25	12.50	25.00
LPM-3376 [M]	The Best of Don Gibson	1965	5.00	10.00	20.00
LSP-3376 [S]	The Best of Don Gibson	1965	6.25	12.50	25.00
LPM-3470 [M]	Too Much Hurt	1965	5.00	10.00	20.00
LSP-3470 [S]	Too Much Hurt	1965	6.25	12.50	25.00
LPM-3594 [M]	Don Gibson with Spanish Guitars	1966	5.00	10.00	20.00
LSP-3594 [S]	Don Gibson with Spanish Guitars	1966	6.25	12.50	25.00
LPM-3680 [M]	Great Country Songs	1966	5.00	10.00	20.00
LSP-3680 [S]	Great Country Songs	1966	6.25	12.50	25.00
LPM-3843 [M]	All My Love	1967	5.00	10.00	20.00
LSP-3843 [S]	All My Love	1967	6.25	12.50	25.00
LPM-3974 [M]	The King of Country Soul	1968	12.50	25.00	50.00
LSP-3974 [S]	The King of Country Soul	1968	5.00	10.00	20.00
LSP-4053	More Country Soul	1968	5.00	10.00	20.00
LSP-4169	All-Time Country Gold	1969	3.75	7.50	15.00
LSP-4281	The Best of Don Gibson, Vol. 2	1970	3.75	7.50	15.00
CPL1-7052	Collector's Series	1985	2.50	5.00	10.00

GIBSON, DON (2) Pianist; not to be confused with the country singer of the same name.
Albums
JAZZOLOGY

Number	Title (A Side/B Side)	Yr	VG	VG+	NM
J-40	The Al Capone Memorial Jazz Band	197?	3.00	6.00	12.00

GIBSON, DON, AND SUE THOMPSON Also see each artist's individual listings.
45s
HICKORY

Number	Title (A Side/B Side)	Yr	VG	VG+	NM
1607	The Two of Us Together/Oh Yes, I Love You	1971	2.00	4.00	8.00
1629	Did You Ever Think/Love Garden	1972	2.00	4.00	8.00
1646	I Think They Call It Love/Over There's the Door	1972	2.00	4.00	8.00
1654	Cause I Love You/My Tears Don't Show	1972	2.00	4.00	8.00
1665	Go with Me/Two of Us Together	1973	2.00	4.00	8.00

HICKORY/MGM

Number	Title (A Side/B Side)	Yr	VG	VG+	NM
303	Warm Love/Fly the Friendly Skies with Jesus	1973	—	3.00	6.00
324	Good Old Fashioned Country Love/Ages and Ages Ago	1974	—	3.00	6.00
342	No One Will Ever Know/Put It Off Till Tomorrow	1975	—	3.00	6.00
350	Oh, How Love Changes/Sweet and Tender Times	1975	—	3.00	6.00
360	Maybe Tomorrow/I Can't Tell My Heart That	1975	—	3.00	6.00
367	Get Ready, Here I Come/Once More	1976	—	3.00	6.00
373	You've Still Got a Place in My Heart/Let's Get Together	1976	—	3.00	6.00

Albums
HICKORY/MGM

Number	Title (A Side/B Side)	Yr	VG	VG+	NM
H3G-4520	Oh How Love Changes	1975	3.00	6.00	12.00

GIBSON, GINNY
45s
ABC-PARAMOUNT

Number	Title (A Side/B Side)	Yr	VG	VG+	NM
9739	Miracle of Love/Two Innocent Hearts	1956	3.75	7.50	15.00
9786	I Pledge Allegiance to Your Heart/Pair of Fools	1957	3.75	7.50	15.00
9872	Homing Pigeon/September Till June	1957	3.75	7.50	15.00

DAVIS

Number	Title (A Side/B Side)	Yr	VG	VG+	NM
442	Mommy's Little Angel/Wanting You	1955	3.75	7.50	15.00

DERBY

Number	Title (A Side/B Side)	Yr	VG	VG+	NM
810	Mommy's Little Angel/Wanting You	195?	5.00	10.00	20.00

KAMA

Number	Title (A Side/B Side)	Yr	VG	VG+	NM
500	You Pass This Way (Only Once)/Bluesville	1962	2.50	5.00	10.00

MGM

Number	Title (A Side/B Side)	Yr	VG	VG+	NM
K10661	Where in the World/You're Finding Out How Much I Love You	1950	6.25	12.50	25.00
K11383	You Blew Me a Kiss/Too Far Between Kisses	1952	5.00	10.00	20.00
K11435	Condemned Without a Trial/Kiss	1953	5.00	10.00	20.00
K11499	Lonely Lover/Unless You're Really Mine	1953	5.00	10.00	20.00
K11571	Dansero/No More Tears	1953	5.00	10.00	20.00
K11672	Baton Rouge/Don't Stop Kissing Me Goodnight	1954	5.00	10.00	20.00
K11736	Aye, Aye, Aye, Aye/Serenade to Spring	1954	5.00	10.00	20.00
K11814	There's a Small Hotel/The Song That Broke My Heart	1954	5.00	10.00	20.00
K11913	Like M-A-D/Once There Was a Little Girl	1955	5.00	10.00	20.00
K11961	Whatever Lola Wants/If Anything Should Happen to You	1955	5.00	10.00	20.00
K12019	Am I Asking Too Much/Chihuahua Choo-Choo	1955	5.00	10.00	20.00
K12113	Ooh (How I Love Ya)/If You Want to Make Me Happy	1955	5.00	10.00	20.00

GIBSON, JILL For a very brief time in late 1966, she was a member of THE MAMAS AND THE PAPAS.
45s
IMPERIAL

Number	Title (A Side/B Side)	Yr	VG	VG+	NM
66068	It's as Easy as 1,2,3/Jilly's Flip Side	1964	15.00	30.00	60.00

—Produced by Jan Berry

GIBSON, JOHNNY
45s
BIG TOP

Number	Title (A Side/B Side)	Yr	VG	VG+	NM
3088	Midnight/Chuck-a-Luck	1961	5.00	10.00	20.00
3118	After Midnight/Walking On Down	1962	5.00	10.00	20.00
3149	Summer Holiday/Ooh Poo Pa Doo	1963	5.00	10.00	20.00

LAURIE

Number	Title (A Side/B Side)	Yr	VG	VG+	NM
3256	Beachcomber/Swanky	1964	6.25	12.50	25.00

—As "The Johnny Gibson Trio"
TWIRL

Number	Title (A Side/B Side)	Yr	VG	VG+	NM
2012	Beachcomber/Swanky	1964	10.00	20.00	40.00

—As "The Johnny Gibson Trio"

GIBSON, STEVE, AND THE RED CAPS
45s
ABC-PARAMOUNT

Number	Title (A Side/B Side)	Yr	VG	VG+	NM
9702	Love Me Tenderly/Rock and Roll Stomp	1956	5.00	10.00	20.00
9750	Write to Me/Cuacho Serenade	1956	5.00	10.00	20.00

Number	Title (A Side/B Side)	Yr	VG	VG+	NM
9796	You've Got Me Dizzy/You May Not Love Me	1957	5.00	10.00	20.00
9856	Silhouettes/Flamingo	1957	5.00	10.00	20.00
10105	I Went to Your Wedding/Together	1960	3.75	7.50	15.00

BAND BOX

Number	Title (A Side/B Side)	Yr	VG	VG+	NM
325	No More/Peppermint Baby	1962	3.00	6.00	12.00

HUNT

Number	Title (A Side/B Side)	Yr	VG	VG+	NM
326	Bless You/Cheryl Lee	1959	3.75	7.50	15.00
330	Where Are You/San Antonio Rose	1959	3.75	7.50	15.00

JAY DEE

Number	Title (A Side/B Side)	Yr	VG	VG+	NM
796	It Hurts Me But I Like It/Ouch!	1954	10.00	20.00	40.00

MERCURY

Number	Title (A Side/B Side)	Yr	VG	VG+	NM
5380	I'll Never Love Anyone Else/(B-side unknown)	1950	37.50	75.00	150.00
8146	Blueberry Hill/I Love You	1951	20.00	40.00	80.00

—78 released in 1949

Number	Title (A Side/B Side)	Yr	VG	VG+	NM
70389	Wedding Bells (Are Breaking Up That Old Gang of Mine)/Second Hand Romance	1954	12.50	25.00	50.00

RCA VICTOR

Number	Title (A Side/B Side)	Yr	VG	VG+	NM
47-3986	The Thing/Am I To Blame?	1950	15.00	30.00	60.00
47-4076	Did Ya Eat Yet, Joe/$3.98	1951	12.50	25.00	50.00
47-4294	Shame/Boogie Woogie on Saturday Night	1951	12.50	25.00	50.00
47-4670	Two Little Kisses/I May Hate Myself in the Morning	1952	10.00	20.00	40.00
47-4835	I Went to Your Wedding/Wait	1952	10.00	20.00	40.00
47-5013	Why Don't You Love Me/Truthfully	1952	10.00	20.00	40.00
47-5130	Big Game Hunter/Do I, Do I, Do I	1953	10.00	20.00	40.00
47-6096	Nuff of That Stuff/Feelin' Kinda Happy	1955	5.00	10.00	20.00
	—B-side by Damita Jo				
47-6345	How I Cry/Bobbin'	1955	5.00	10.00	20.00
50-0127	I'm to Blame/Sidewalk Shuffle	1951	15.00	30.00	60.00
50-0138	Would I Mind/When You Come Back to Me	1951	15.00	30.00	60.00

7-Inch Extended Plays
MERCURY

Number	Title (A Side/B Side)	Yr	VG	VG+	NM
EP1-3215	(contents unknown)	1952	50.00	100.00	200.00
EP1-3215 [PS]	Blueberry Hill	1952	50.00	100.00	200.00

Albums
MERCURY

Number	Title (A Side/B Side)	Yr	VG	VG+	NM
MG-25115 [10]	You're Driving Me Crazy (Harmony Time)	1952	100.00	200.00	400.00
MG-25116 [10]	Blueberry Hill (Singing & Swinging)	1952	100.00	200.00	400.00

GIGOLOS, THE
45s
BROADWAY

Number	Title (A Side/B Side)	Yr	VG	VG+	NM
1000	Movin' Out/Black and Blue	1961	7.50	15.00	30.00

CHESS

Number	Title (A Side/B Side)	Yr	VG	VG+	NM
1715	Luna Rock/La Companola	1959	7.50	15.00	30.00

DAYNITE

Number	Title (A Side/B Side)	Yr	VG	VG+	NM
1	Sqingin' Saints/Night Crawlers	1960	12.50	25.00	50.00

ENTERPRISE

Number	Title (A Side/B Side)	Yr	VG	VG+	NM
5000	Don't You Just Know It/Movin' Out	1965	3.75	7.50	15.00

GILBERTO, ASTRUD
45s
PERCEPTION

Number	Title (A Side/B Side)	Yr	VG	VG+	NM
524	Make Love to Me/General Da Banda	1973	—	2.50	5.00

VERVE

Number	Title (A Side/B Side)	Yr	VG	VG+	NM
CS?-5	Celebrity Scene: Astrud Gilberto	1967	12.50	25.00	50.00

—Box set of five singles (10531-10535). Price includes box, all 5 singles, jukebox title strips, bio. Records are sometimes found by themselves, so they are also listed separately.

Number	Title (A Side/B Side)	Yr	VG	VG+	NM
10339	Who Can I Turn To/Funny World	1965	2.00	4.00	8.00
10347	Day by Day/Ecco Homo	1965	2.00	4.00	8.00
10358	The Shadow of Your Smile/O Gauso	1965	2.00	4.00	8.00
10414	Don't Go Breaking My Heart/Wish Me a Rainbow	1966	—	3.00	6.00
10457	Who Needs Forever/Main Theme "The Deadly Affair"	1966	—	3.00	6.00
10480	A Certain Smile/A Certain Sadness	1967	—	3.00	6.00
	—With Walter Wanderley				
10531 [DJ]	Once Upon a Summertime/Once I Loved	1967	2.00	4.00	8.00
10532 [DJ]	Aruanda/Dindi	1967	2.00	4.00	8.00
10533 [DJ]	Manha De Carnival/Berimbau	1967	2.00	4.00	8.00
10534 [DJ]	Look to the Rainbow/Lugar Bonita	1967	2.00	4.00	8.00
10535 [DJ]	So Nice/Wish Me a Rainbow	1967	2.00	4.00	8.00
10548	Stay/I Had the Craziest Dream	1967	—	3.00	6.00
10554	A Banda/You Didn't Have to Be So Nice	1967	—	3.00	6.00
10580	Come Softly to Me-Hushabye/Lilies by Monet	1968	—	3.00	6.00
10638	I Haven't Got Anything Better to Do/The Sea Is My Soul	1969	—	2.50	5.00
10643	Love Theme from "Romeo and Juliet"/The Thought of Loving You	1969	—	2.50	5.00
10651	Holiday/Let's Have the Morning After	1970	—	2.50	5.00

Albums
CTI

Number	Title (A Side/B Side)	Yr	VG	VG+	NM
CTS-6008	Astrud Gilberto with Stanley Turrentine	1970	3.00	6.00	12.00

ELEKTRA/MUSICIAN

Number	Title (A Side/B Side)	Yr	VG	VG+	NM
60760	Live in Montreux	1988	2.50	5.00	10.00

PERCEPTION

Number	Title (A Side/B Side)	Yr	VG	VG+	NM
29	Now	1973	2.50	5.00	10.00

VERVE

Number	Title (A Side/B Side)	Yr	VG	VG+	NM
V-8608 [M]	The Astrud Gilberto Album	1965	3.00	6.00	12.00
V6-8608 [S]	The Astrud Gilberto Album	1965	3.75	7.50	15.00
V-8629 [M]	The Shadow of Your Smile	1965	3.00	6.00	12.00
V6-8629 [S]	The Shadow of Your Smile	1965	3.75	7.50	15.00
V-8643 [M]	Look to the Rainbow	1966	3.00	6.00	12.00
V6-8643 [S]	Look to the Rainbow	1966	3.75	7.50	15.00
V-8673 [M]	A Certain Smile, A Certain Sadness	1966	3.00	6.00	12.00
V6-8673 [S]	A Certain Smile, A Certain Sadness	1966	3.75	7.50	15.00
V-8708 [M]	Beach Samba	1967	3.00	6.00	12.00
V6-8708 [S]	Beach Samba	1967	3.75	7.50	15.00
V6-8754	Windy	1968	3.00	6.00	12.00
V6-8776	I Haven't Got Anything Better to Do	1969	3.00	6.00	12.00
V6-8793	September 17, 1969	1969	3.00	6.00	12.00
821566-1	Look to the Rainbow	1986	2.50	5.00	10.00

—Reissue of V6-8643

G

Number	Title (A Side/B Side)	Yr	VG	VG+	NM
GILES, GILES & FRIPP					
Albums					
DERAM					
❑ DES 18019	The Cheerful Insanity of Giles, Giles & Fripp	1968	15.00	30.00	60.00
GILKYSON, TERRY Also includes records credited to "The Easy Riders." Also see THE WEAVERS.					
45s					
COLUMBIA					
❑ 40189	Tall Timber/Come Home Zelda	1954	3.00	6.00	12.00
❑ 40742	The Sky Is High/Yearmo's Nightmare and Yearmo's Red	1956	3.00	6.00	12.00
❑ 40817	Marianne/Goodbye Chiquita	1957	3.00	6.00	12.00
❑ 40817 [PS]	Marianne/Goodbye Chiquita	1957	3.75	7.50	15.00
❑ 40860	True Love and Tender Care/ Don't Hurry Worry Me	1957	2.50	5.00	10.00
❑ 40910	Tina/Strollin' Blues	1957	2.50	5.00	10.00
❑ 41016	The Times/South Coast	1957	2.50	5.00	10.00
❑ 41088	Blue Mountain/Shorty Joe	1958	2.50	5.00	10.00
❑ 41147	Windjammer/Kari Waits for Me	1958	2.50	5.00	10.00
❑ 41284	Wanderin' Blues/Sweet Sugar Cane	1958	2.50	5.00	10.00
❑ 41347	John Henry/East Virginia	1959	2.50	5.00	10.00
DECCA					
❑ 27068	I Know Where I'm Going/Black Is the Color (Of My True Love's Hair)	1950	3.75	7.50	15.00
❑ 27069	Jennie Jenkins/Rovin' Gambler	1950	3.75	7.50	15.00
❑ 27070	The Story of the Creation//Cotton Eyed Joe/Billy Boy	1950	3.75	7.50	15.00
❑ 27071	Black Eyed Susie/Boll Weevil	1950	3.75	7.50	15.00
—The above four comprise a box set					
❑ 27337	A Solitary Singer/Runnin' Away	1950	3.75	7.50	15.00
❑ 27338	Fast Freight/The Secret	1950	3.75	7.50	15.00
❑ 27339	Nellie Lou/The Tick Tock Song	1950	3.75	7.50	15.00
❑ 27340	Mr. Buzzard/Everyone's Crazy 'Ceptin' Me	1950	3.75	7.50	15.00
—The above four comprise a box set					
❑ 27586	Hoofbeat Serenade/Fast Freight	1951	3.75	7.50	15.00
❑ 27708	The Girl in the Wood/Mr. Buzzard	1951	3.75	7.50	15.00
❑ 27793	Stay Awhile/Rollin' Stone	1951	3.75	7.50	15.00
❑ 28258	Fond Affection/ The Man You Don't Meet Everyday	1952	3.75	7.50	15.00
KAPP					
❑ 350	Saturday's Child/Young In Love	1960	2.00	4.00	8.00
❑ 355	Ballad of the Alamo/ The Green Leaves of Summer	1960	2.00	4.00	8.00
Albums					
COLUMBIA					
❑ CL 990 [M]	Marianne and Other Songs	1957	12.50	25.00	50.00
❑ CL 1302 [M]	Wanderin' Folk Songs	1959	7.50	15.00	30.00
DECCA					
❑ DL 5263 [10]	Folk Songs	1950	12.50	25.00	50.00
❑ DL 5457 [10]	Golden Minutes of Folk Music	1952	12.50	25.00	50.00
KAPP					
❑ KL 1196 [M]	Rollin'	1960	3.75	7.50	15.00
❑ KL 1327 [M]	The Cry of the Wild Goose	1963	3.75	7.50	15.00
❑ KS 3196 [S]	Rollin'	1960	5.00	10.00	20.00
❑ KS 3327 [S]	The Cry of the Wild Goose	1963	5.00	10.00	20.00
GILLESPIE, DANA					
45s					
JERDEN					
❑ 764	Donna Donna/It's No Use Saying If	1965	3.00	6.00	12.00
Albums					
LONDON					
❑ PS 540	Foolish Seasons	1968	5.00	10.00	20.00
GILLESPIE, DARLENE					
45s					
CORAL					
❑ 62178	I Loved, I Laughed, I Cried/Ring the Bell, Beat the Drum	1960	3.75	7.50	15.00
DISNEYLAND					
❑ F-050	Sittin' in the Balcony/Too Much	1957	7.50	15.00	30.00
❑ F-051	Butterfly/Seven Days	1957	7.50	15.00	30.00
❑ F-052	I've Never Been in Love/Rock-a-Billy	1957	7.50	15.00	30.00
❑ F-060	Together Time/Now to Sleep	1957	6.25	12.50	25.00
—A-side with Jimmie Dodd					
❑ F-061	Break of Day/Perri	1957	6.25	12.50	25.00
—With Jimmie Dodd					
Albums					
DISNEYLAND					
❑ WDL-1010 [M]	Top Tunes of the '50's — Darlene Gillespie Sings TV Favorites	1959	10.00	20.00	40.00
❑ DQ-1228 [M]	Sleeping Beauty	1962	5.00	10.00	20.00
—Cover is black and white; later pressings, which go for less, are shaded blue on the back					
❑ WDL-3010 [M]	Darlene of the Teens	1957	20.00	40.00	80.00
❑ WDL-3010 [M]	Top Tunes of the '50's — Darlene Gillespie Sings TV Favorites	1958	12.50	25.00	50.00
—Reissue with new title and cover					
MICKEY MOUSE CLUB					
❑ MM-32 [M]	Sleeping Beauty	1959	10.00	20.00	40.00
GILLEY, MICKEY Also see RAY CHARLES.					
45s					
ACT 1					
❑ 101	Say No More/Make Me Believe	1966	2.50	5.00	10.00
AIRBORNE					
❑ 10002	I'm Your Puppet/Don't Show Me Your Memories (And I Won't Show You Mine)	1988	—	2.00	4.00
❑ 10008	She Reminded Me of You/Easy Climb	1988	—	2.00	4.00
❑ 10016	You Still Got a Way with Love Die/It's Killing Me to Watch Love Die	1989	—	2.00	4.00
❑ 75740	There I've Said It Again/ It's Killing Me to Watch Love Die	1989	—	2.00	4.00
ASTRO					
❑ 102	Down the Line/Lonely Wine	196?	25.00	50.00	100.00
❑ 103	Is It Wrong/Turn Around	196?	6.25	12.50	25.00
❑ 104	Night After Night/Susie Q	196?	6.25	12.50	25.00
❑ 106	Lotta Lovin'/I Miss You So	196?	6.25	12.50	25.00
❑ 110	A Certain Smile/If I Didn't Have a Dime	196?	6.25	12.50	25.00
❑ 112	Little Egypt/If I Didn't Have a Dime	196?	6.25	12.50	25.00
❑ 5002	Everything Is Yours That Once Was Mine/Don't Throw a Good Love Away	1971	2.00	4.00	8.00
❑ 5003	You Touch My Life/Toast to Mary Ann	1971	2.00	4.00	8.00
❑ 10003	Room Full of Roses/She Called Me Baby	1973	2.50	5.00	10.00
DARYL					
❑ 101	What Have I Done/Three's a Crowd	1963	2.50	5.00	10.00
DOT					
❑ 15706	Call Me Shorty/Come On Baby	1958	50.00	100.00	200.00
EPIC					
❑ AE7 1356 [DJ]	Mickey Gilley's Christmas Medley (2:51)/Mickey Gilley's Christmas Medley (3:34)	1981	2.50	5.00	10.00
❑ AE7 1774	Home to Texas for Christmas/I'm Spending Christmas with You	1982	—	2.50	5.00
❑ 02172	You Don't Know Me/Juke Box Argument	1981	—	—	3.00
❑ 02578	Lonely Nights/We've Watched Another Evening Waste Away	1981	—	—	3.00
❑ 02774	Tears of the Lonely/Ladies Night	1982	—	—	3.00
❑ 03055	Put Your Dreams Away/If I Can't Hold Her on the Outside	1982	—	—	3.00
❑ 03326	Talk to Me/Honky Tonkin' (I Guess I Done Some)	1982	—	—	3.00
❑ 03332	Blue Christmas/Jingle Bell Rock	1982	—	2.00	4.00
❑ 03783	Fool for Your Love/Shakin' a Heartache	1983	—	—	3.00
❑ 04018	Your Love Shines Through/ Wish You Were Mine Again	1983	—	—	3.00
❑ 04269	You've Really Got a Hold on Me/ Giving Up Getting Over You	1983	—	—	3.00
❑ 04563	Too Good to Stop Now/A Shoulder to Cry On	1984	—	—	3.00
❑ 04746	I'm the One Mama Warned You About/You Can Lie to Me Tonight	1985	—	—	3.00
❑ 05460	You've Got Something on Your Mind/I Feel Good About Lovin' You	1985	—	—	3.00
❑ 05744	Your Memory Ain't What It Used to Be/Lonely Nights, Lonely Heartaches	1985	—	—	3.00
❑ 05895	Play, Ruby, Play/After She's Gone	1986	—	—	3.00
❑ 06184	Doo-Wah Days/After She's Gone	1986	—	—	3.00
❑ 07009	Full Grown Fool/To My One and Only	1987	—	—	3.00
❑ 50580	Here Comes the Hurt Again/ I Hate It, But I Drink It Anyway	1978	—	2.00	4.00
❑ 50631	The Song We Made Love To/ Memphis Memories	1978	—	2.00	4.00
❑ 50672	Just Long Enough to Say Goodbye/ Tying One On	1979	—	2.00	4.00
❑ 50740	My Silver Lining/Picture of Our Love	1979	—	2.00	4.00
❑ 50801	A Little Getting Used To/Can't Nobody Love You	1979	—	2.00	4.00
❑ 50876	True Love Ways/The More I Turn the Bottle	1980	—	2.00	4.00
❑ 50940	That's All That Matters/ The Blues Don't Care Who's Got 'Em	1980	—	2.00	4.00
❑ 50973	A Headache Tomorrow (Or a Heartache Tonight)/Million Dollar Memories	1981	—	2.00	4.00
❑ 51003	Mamas Don't Let Your Babies Grow Up to Be Cowboys/Cotton-Eyed Joe	1981	—	2.00	4.00
—A-side with Johnny Lee; B-side by Bayou City Beats					
ERIC					
❑ 7021	Whole Lot of Twistin' Going On/Fraulein	1962	5.00	10.00	20.00
FULL MOON/ASYLUM					
❑ 46640	Stand By Me/Cotton Eyed Joe	1980	—	2.00	4.00
—B-side by the Unstrung Heroes					
❑ 46640 [PS]	Stand By Me/Cotton Eyed Joe	1980	—	2.50	5.00
—"Urban Cowboy" sleeve (John Travolta pictured)					
GOLDBAND					
❑ 1223	I Ain't Goin' Home/No Greater Love	1964	2.50	5.00	10.00
GRT					
❑ 27	I'm Nobody Today (But I Was Somebody Last Night)/She's Not Yours Anymore	1970	2.00	4.00	8.00
❑ 45	Time to Tell Another Lie/Because I Love You	1970	2.00	4.00	8.00
KHOURY'S					
❑ 712	Drive In Movie/Give Me a Chance	1959	75.00	150.00	300.00
LYNN					
❑ 503	Your Selfish Pride/Everything Turned to Love	1960	6.25	12.50	25.00
❑ 508	My Baby's Been Cheating Again/Turn Around	1960	6.25	12.50	25.00
❑ 512	Slippin' and Slidin'/End of the Line	1961	6.25	12.50	25.00
❑ 515	Long Lonely Nights/My Babe	1961	6.25	12.50	25.00
MINOR					
❑ 106	Oo-Ee Baby/Tell Me Why	1957	150.00	300.00	600.00
PAULA					
❑ 256	Make Me Believe/Say No to You	1966	2.50	5.00	10.00
❑ 269	A World of My Own/Love in the Want Ads	1967	2.00	4.00	8.00
❑ 280	Blame It on the Moon/Sounds Like Trouble	1967	2.00	4.00	8.00
❑ 281	One Way Street/Tears in My Eyes	1967	2.00	4.00	8.00
❑ 301	A New Way to Live/That Heart Belongs to Me	1968	2.00	4.00	8.00
❑ 402	Night After Night/I'm to Blame	1974	—	2.50	5.00
❑ 441	She Cheats on Me/You Can Count Me Missing	1983	—	2.00	4.00
❑ 1200	Now I Can Live Again/Without You	1968	2.00	4.00	8.00
❑ 1208	She's Still Got a Hold on You/There's No One Like You	1969	2.00	4.00	8.00
❑ 1215	Watching the Way/It's Just a Matter of Making Up My Mind	1969	2.00	4.00	8.00
PLAYBOY					
❑ 5807	Honky Tonk Memories/ Five Foot Two, Eyes of Blue	1977	—	2.00	4.00
❑ 5818	Chains of Love/ No. 1 Rock 'n Roll C & W Boogie Blues Man	1977	—	2.00	4.00
❑ 5826	The Power of Positive Drinkin'/ Playing My Old Piano	1978	—	2.00	4.00
❑ 6004	I Overlooked an Orchid/Swinging Doors	1974	—	2.50	5.00
❑ 6015	City Lights/Fraulein	1974	—	2.50	5.00
❑ 6031	Window Up Above/I'm Movin' On	1975	—	2.50	5.00
❑ 6041	Bouquet of Roses/If You Were Mine to Lose	1975	—	2.50	5.00
❑ 6045	Roll You Like a Wheel/ Let's Sing a Song Together	1975	—	2.50	5.00
—With Barbi Benton					

Number	Title (A Side/B Side)	Yr	VG	VG+	NM
❑ 6045 [PS]	Roll You Like a Wheel/				
	Let's Sing a Song Together	1975	—	3.00	6.00
—With Barbi Benton					
❑ 6055	Overnight Sensation/I'll Sail My Ship Alone	1975	—	2.50	5.00
❑ 6063	Don't All the Girls Get Prettier at Closing Time/	1976	—	2.50	5.00
	Where Do You Go to Lose a Heartache				
❑ 6075	Bring It On Home to Me/	1976	—	2.50	5.00
	How's My Ex Treating You				
❑ 6089	Lawdy Miss Clawdy/What Is It	1976	—	2.50	5.00
❑ 6095	Pretty Paper/Lonely Christmas Call	1976	—	2.50	5.00
❑ 6100	She's Pulling Me Back Again/	1977	—	2.50	5.00
	Sweet Mama Goodtime				
❑ 50056	Room Full of Roses/She Called Me Baby	1974	—	2.50	5.00
POTOMAC					
❑ 901	Is It Wrong/No Greater Love	1960	3.75	7.50	15.00
PRINCESS					
❑ 4004	Drive-In Movie/Your First Time	1962	10.00	20.00	40.00
❑ 4006	Wild Side of Life/Caught in the Middle	1962	10.00	20.00	40.00
❑ 4011	I'll Keep On Dancing/I'll Keep On Searching	196?	3.75	7.50	15.00
❑ 4015	A World of My Own/I Still Care	196?	3.75	7.50	15.00
RESCO					
❑ 617	You Touch My Life/Toast to Mary Ann	1974	—	3.00	6.00
❑ 622	She Gives Me Love/Quittin' Time	1974	—	3.00	6.00
REX					
❑ 1007	Grapevine/That's How It's Got to Be	1959	7.50	15.00	30.00
SABRA					
❑ 518	Valley of Tears/I Need Your Love	1961	5.00	10.00	20.00
SAN					
❑ 1513	I Ain't No Bo Diddley/I'm to Blame	1966	2.50	5.00	10.00
SUPREME					
❑ 101	Now That I Have You/Happy Birthday	1962	3.75	7.50	15.00
❑ 102	Everything Turned to Love/	1962	3.75	7.50	15.00
	No One Will Ever Know				
TCF HALL					
❑ 126	When Two Worlds Collide/Let's Hurt Together	1965	2.00	4.00	8.00
Albums					
ACCORD					
❑ SN-7151	Suburban Cowboy	1981	2.50	5.00	10.00
ASTRO					
❑ 101 [M]	Lonely Wine	1964	75.00	150.00	300.00
COLUMBIA SPECIAL PRODUCTS					
❑ P 16198	All My Best	1982	2.50	5.00	10.00
EPIC					
❑ PE 34736	Room Full of Roses	198?	2.00	4.00	8.00
—Budget-line reissue					
❑ PE 34749	Smokin'	198?	2.00	4.00	8.00
—Budget-line reissue					
❑ PE 34776	First Class	198?	2.00	4.00	8.00
—Budget-line reissue					
❑ KE 35174	Songs We Made Love To	1979	2.50	5.00	10.00
❑ JE 36201	Mickey Gilley	1980	2.50	5.00	10.00
❑ JE 36492	That's All That Matters to Me	1980	2.50	5.00	10.00
❑ PE 36492	That's All That Matters to Me	198?	2.00	4.00	8.00
—Budget-line reissue					
❑ JE 36851	Encore	1981	2.50	5.00	10.00
❑ FE 37416	You Don't Know Me	1981	2.50	5.00	10.00
❑ PE 37416	You Don't Know Me	198?	2.00	4.00	8.00
—Budget-line reissue					
❑ PE 37595	Christmas at Gilley's	1981	2.50	5.00	10.00
—Some labels have "FE" prefix					
❑ FE 38082	Put Your Dreams Away	1982	2.50	5.00	10.00
❑ PE 38082	Put Your Dreams Away	198?	2.00	4.00	8.00
—Budget-line reissue					
❑ FE 38320	Mickey Gilley's Biggest Hits	1982	2.50	5.00	10.00
❑ FE 38583	Fool for Your Love	1983	2.50	5.00	10.00
❑ PE 38583	Fool for Your Love	1985	2.00	4.00	8.00
—Budget-line reissue					
❑ FE 39000	You've Really Got a Hold on Me	1983	2.50	5.00	10.00
❑ FE 39324	Too Good to Stop Now	1983	2.50	5.00	10.00
❑ KE2 39867 [(2)]	Ten Years of Hits	1984	3.00	6.00	12.00
❑ FE 39900	Live at Gilley's	1984	2.50	5.00	10.00
❑ FE 40115	I Feel Good (About Lovin' You)	1985	2.50	5.00	10.00
❑ FE 40353	The One and Only	1986	2.50	5.00	10.00
INTERMEDIA					
❑ QS-5024	With Love from Pasadena, Texas	198?	2.50	5.00	10.00
J.M.					
❑ 8127	Norwegian Wood	1981	3.00	6.00	12.00
PAIR					
❑ PDL2-1072 [(2)]	The Best of Mickey Gilley	1986	3.00	6.00	12.00
PAULA					
❑ LP-2195 [M]	Down the Line	1967	10.00	20.00	40.00
❑ LPS-2195 [S]	Down the Line	1967	10.00	20.00	40.00
❑ LPS-2224	Mickey Gilley at His Best	1974	3.75	7.50	15.00
❑ LPS-2234	Mickey Gilley	1978	3.00	6.00	12.00
PICKWICK					
❑ SPC-6180	Wild Side of Life	1975	2.50	5.00	10.00
PLAYBOY					
❑ PB-128	Room Full of Roses	1974	5.00	10.00	20.00
❑ PB-403	City Lights	1974	5.00	10.00	20.00
❑ PB-405	Mickey's Movin' On	1975	3.75	7.50	15.00
❑ PB-408	Overnight Sensation	1976	3.75	7.50	15.00
❑ PB-409	Gilley's Greatest Hits Vol. 1	1976	3.75	7.50	15.00
❑ PB-415	Gilley's Smokin'	1976	3.75	7.50	15.00
❑ PZ 34736	Room Full of Roses	1977	2.50	5.00	10.00
—Reissue of 128					
❑ PZ 34742	Overnight Sensation	1977	2.50	5.00	10.00
—Reissue of 408					
❑ PZ 34743	Gilley's Greatest Hits Vol. 1	1977	2.50	5.00	10.00
—Reissue of 409					
❑ PZ 34749	Gilley's Smokin'	1977	3.00	6.00	12.00
—Reissue of 415					
❑ PZ 34776	First Class	1977	3.00	6.00	12.00
❑ KZ 34881	Gilley's Greatest Hits, Vol. 2	1977	3.00	6.00	12.00
❑ KZ 35099	Flyin' High	1978	3.00	6.00	12.00

G

GILMER, JIMMY Also see THE FIREBALLS.
45s
ATCO

Number	Title (A Side/B Side)	Yr	VG	VG+	NM
❑ 6583	Three Squares (And a Place to Lay Your Head)/	1968	2.00	4.00	8.00
	Baby				
❑ 6716	Sugar in the Woods/Model Child	1969	2.00	4.00	8.00
DECCA					
❑ 30942	Look Alive/Because I Need You	1959	6.25	12.50	25.00
HAMILTON					
❑ 50037	Won't Be Long/I'm Gonna Go Walkin'	1960	3.75	7.50	15.00
WARWICK					
❑ 592	Good Good Lovin'/Do You Think	1960	5.00	10.00	20.00

GILMER, JIMMY, AND THE FIREBALLS See THE FIREBALLS.

GILREATH, JAMES
45s
JOY

Number	Title (A Side/B Side)	Yr	VG	VG+	NM
❑ 274	Little Band of Gold/I'll Walk with You	1963	3.00	6.00	12.00
❑ 278	Lollipops, Lace and Lipstick/Mean Ole River	1963	3.75	7.50	15.00
❑ 286	Blue Is My Color/Keep Her Out of Sight	1964	2.50	5.00	10.00

GILSTRAP, JIM
45s
BELL

Number	Title (A Side/B Side)	Yr	VG	VG+	NM
❑ 45435	Airport/(B-side unknown)	1974	—	2.50	5.00
❑ 45474	When You Come Back Down/(B-side unknown)	1974	—	2.50	5.00
ROXBURY					
❑ 2006	Swing Your Daddy/Swing Your Daddy (Part 2)	1975	—	2.00	4.00
❑ 2013	House of Strangers/Take Your Daddy for a Ride	1975	—	2.00	4.00
❑ 2016	I'm on Fire/I'm on Fire (Part 2)	1975	—	2.00	4.00
❑ 2026	Move Me/Move Me (Part 2)	1976	—	2.00	4.00
❑ 2029	Love Talk/Love Talk (Part 2)	1976	—	2.00	4.00
❑ 2032	Hello It's Me/Never Stop Your Loving Me	1976	—	2.00	4.00
Albums					
ROXBURY					
❑ 102	Swing Your Daddy	1975	2.50	5.00	10.00
❑ 105	Love Talk	1976	2.50	5.00	10.00

GINGER Also see GINGER AND THE SNAPS; THE HONEYS.
45s
TITAN

Number	Title (A Side/B Side)	Yr	VG	VG+	NM
❑ 1717	Dry Tears/Spare Time	1961	25.00	50.00	100.00

GINGER AND THE CHIFFONS
45s
GROOVE

Number	Title (A Side/B Side)	Yr	VG	VG+	NM
❑ 58-0003	She/Where Were You Last Night	1963	7.50	15.00	30.00

GINGER AND THE SNAPS Also see GINGER.
45s
MGM

Number	Title (A Side/B Side)	Yr	VG	VG+	NM
❑ 13413	Growing Up Is Hard to Do/Seven Days in	1965	37.50	75.00	150.00
	September				
TORE					
❑ 1008	Love Me the Way That I Love You/Truly	1961	18.75	37.50	75.00

GINGER-SNAPS, THE
45s
DUNHILL

Number	Title (A Side/B Side)	Yr	VG	VG+	NM
❑ 4003	The Sh-Down-Down Song/I've Got Faith in Him	1965	5.00	10.00	20.00

GINGOLEERS, THE
45s
BRUNSWICK

Number	Title (A Side/B Side)	Yr	VG	VG+	NM
❑ 55108	Jingle Bell Rock/Christmas Morn	1958	3.75	7.50	15.00

GINNY AND THE GALLIONS
45s
DOWNEY

Number	Title (A Side/B Side)	Yr	VG	VG+	NM
❑ 110	Hava Nagila/Hava Nagila Part 2	1963	3.00	6.00	12.00
❑ 112	Wheel of Fortune/Hava Nagila	1963	3.00	6.00	12.00
Albums					
DOWNEY					
❑ D-1003 [M]	Two Sides of Ginny and the Gallions	1964	7.50	15.00	30.00
❑ DS-1003 [S]	Two Sides of Ginny and the Gallions	1964	10.00	20.00	40.00

GINO AND GINA
45s
BRUNSWICK

Number	Title (A Side/B Side)	Yr	VG	VG+	NM
❑ 55215	I Hope You're Satisfied/Why Do You Make	1961	5.00	10.00	20.00
	Believe				
MERCURY					
❑ 71283X45	Pretty Baby/Love's a Carousel	1958	3.75	7.50	15.00
❑ 71283X45	(It's Been a Long Time) Pretty Baby/Love's a	1958	5.00	10.00	20.00
	Carousel				
❑ 71346X45	She Belongs to Me/Rainin' and Rainin'	1958	5.00	10.00	20.00
❑ 71370X45	Brand New Penny/I Don't Love You	1958	5.00	10.00	20.00
❑ 71398X45	Kooka Dong/You're Mine Alone	1959	6.25	12.50	25.00
❑ 71483X45	I Don't Need a Ring Around Your Finger/Charlie	1959	6.25	12.50	25.00
WARWICK					
❑ 554	I'm Bugged Over You/Come On Legs	1960	5.00	10.00	20.00

GINO AND THE DELLS
45s
GOLDEN CREST

Number	Title (A Side/B Side)	Yr	VG	VG+	NM
❑ 567	Altar of Dreams/Baby Don't Go Now	1962	75.00	150.00	300.00
❑ 576	We'll Make It Someday/I'm a Boy in Love	1963	10.00	20.00	40.00
❑ 581	It's Only a Paper Moon/Home Sweet Home	1963	10.00	20.00	40.00

GINSBERG, ALLEN
Albums
ATLANTIC

Number	Title (A Side/B Side)	Yr	VG	VG+	NM
❑ 4001 [M]	Allen Ginsburg Reads Kaddish	1966	7.50	15.00	30.00
FANTASY					
❑ F-7006 [M]	Howl and Other Poems	1959	50.00	100.00	200.00
—Black non-flexible vinyl					

Number	Title (A Side/B Side)	Yr	VG	VG+	NM
❏ F-7006 [M]	Howl and Other Poems	1959	100.00	200.00	400.00
—Red vinyl					

GIORDANO, LOU
45s
BRUNSWICK

Number	Title (A Side/B Side)	Yr	VG	VG+	NM
❏ 55115	Stay Close to Me/Don'Cha Know	1959	400.00	800.00	1200.
—With Buddy Holly on guitar					

GIOVANNI, NIKKI
Albums
NIKTOM

Number	Title (A Side/B Side)	Yr	VG	VG+	NM
❏ NK 4200	Like a Ripple on a Pond	1973	2.50	5.00	10.00
❏ NK 4201	The Way I Feel	1975	2.50	5.00	10.00

RIGHT-ON

Number	Title (A Side/B Side)	Yr	VG	VG+	NM
❏ 5001	Truth Is On Its Way	1971	2.50	5.00	10.00

GIRLFRIENDS, THE
45s
COLPIX

Number	Title (A Side/B Side)	Yr	VG	VG+	NM
❏ 712	My One and Only Jimmy Boy/For My Sake	1963	5.00	10.00	20.00
❏ 744	Baby Don't Cry/I Don't Believe in You	1964	5.00	10.00	20.00

MELIC

Number	Title (A Side/B Side)	Yr	VG	VG+	NM
❏ 4125	No More Tears/I Want to Be Happy	1963	3.75	7.50	15.00

PIONEER

Number	Title (A Side/B Side)	Yr	VG	VG+	NM
❏ 71833	Four Shy Girls (In Their Itsy Bitsy Teeny Weeny Yellow Polka Dot Bikinis)/Jackie	1961	5.00	10.00	20.00

GIRLS, THE
45s
CAPITOL

Number	Title (A Side/B Side)	Yr	VG	VG+	NM
❏ 5528	My Baby/My Love	1965	5.00	10.00	20.00
❏ 5675	Chico's Girl/The Dumb Song	1966	5.00	10.00	20.00

SCEPTER

Number	Title (A Side/B Side)	Yr	VG	VG+	NM
❏ 12242	Perfect Love/Mr. Poster	1969	2.00	4.00	8.00

20TH CENTURY FOX

Number	Title (A Side/B Side)	Yr	VG	VG+	NM
❏ 6651	Way, Way Out/Modesty Blaise	1966	5.00	10.00	20.00

GLACIERS, THE
Albums
MERCURY

Number	Title (A Side/B Side)	Yr	VG	VG+	NM
❏ MG-20895 [M]	From Sea to Ski	1964	12.50	25.00	50.00
❏ SR-60895 [S]	From Sea to Ski	1964	15.00	30.00	60.00

GLAD, THE Timothy Schmit, later of POCO and EAGLES, was in this group.
45s
ABC

Number	Title (A Side/B Side)	Yr	VG	VG+	NM
❏ 11163	Johnny Silver's Ride/Love Needs the World	1969	3.00	6.00	12.00

EQUINOX

Number	Title (A Side/B Side)	Yr	VG	VG+	NM
❏ 70004	See What You Mean/(B-side unknown)	1968	5.00	10.00	20.00
❏ 70006	A New Tomorrow/Pickin' Up the Pieces	1968	5.00	10.00	20.00

Albums
ABC

Number	Title (A Side/B Side)	Yr	VG	VG+	NM
❏ S-655	Feelin' Glad	1969	6.25	12.50	25.00

GLADIATORS, THE
45s
DIG

Number	Title (A Side/B Side)	Yr	VG	VG+	NM
❏ 135	Girl of My Heart/My Baby Doll	1957	75.00	150.00	300.00

GLADIOLAS, THE Evolved into MAURICE WILLIAMS AND THE ZODIACS.
45s
EXCELLO

Number	Title (A Side/B Side)	Yr	VG	VG+	NM
❏ 2101	Little Darlin'/Sweetheart, Please Don't Go	1957	18.75	37.50	75.00
❏ 2110	Run, Run, Little Joe/Comin' Home to You	1957	12.50	25.00	50.00
❏ 2120	Hey Little Girl/I Wanta Know	1957	12.50	25.00	50.00
❏ 2136	Shoop Shoop/Say You'll Be Mine	1958	12.50	25.00	50.00

GLADSTONE
45s
ABC

Number	Title (A Side/B Side)	Yr	VG	VG+	NM
❏ 11327	A Piece of Paper/Livin' in the Country	1972	—	3.00	6.00
❏ 11340	Marietta Station/Lady Eyes	1972	—	3.00	6.00
❏ 11361	Natural Inclination/Here Comes That Feeling	1973	—	3.00	6.00

Albums
ABC

Number	Title (A Side/B Side)	Yr	VG	VG+	NM
❏ ABCX-751	From Down Home in Tyler, Texas, U.S.A.	1972	3.00	6.00	12.00
❏ ABCX-778	Lookin' for a Smile	1973	3.00	6.00	12.00

GLAHE, WILL
45s
LONDON

Number	Title (A Side/B Side)	Yr	VG	VG+	NM
❏ 1523	Came the Morning/Rose of the Wildwood	1954	2.50	5.00	10.00
❏ 1673	The March Hare/The Peanut Polka	1956	2.50	5.00	10.00
❏ 1693	Beer Barrel Polka/Hearts and Heartaches	1957	2.50	5.00	10.00
❏ 1755	Liechtensteiner Polka/Schweizer Kanton Polka	1957	2.50	5.00	10.00
❏ 1788	Sweet Elizabeth/Tavern in the Town	1958	2.50	5.00	10.00
❏ 1818	Duschka/The Pretzel Waltz	1958	2.50	5.00	10.00
❏ 1859	In Einen Weindorf/The 30th of May	1959	2.50	5.00	10.00
❏ 1900	Flower on Your Hat/Swedish Punch	196?	2.00	4.00	8.00
❏ 1915	Ei, Ei, Wat Hat Du Da/In Pfaffenhofen	196?	2.00	4.00	8.00
❏ 10037	I Want to Marry a Cowboy/America	196?	3.00	6.00	12.00

LONDON INT'L.

Number	Title (A Side/B Side)	Yr	VG	VG+	NM
❏ 10023	Just Because/Seven Roses	196?	2.50	5.00	10.00
❏ 10029	I'd Rather Buy Myself a Tyrolean Hat/(Instrumental)	196?	2.50	5.00	10.00

Albums
LONDON

Number	Title (A Side/B Side)	Yr	VG	VG+	NM
❏ PS 146 [S]	Christmas Greetings from Germany	195?	5.00	10.00	20.00
❏ PS 150 [S]	Old Heidelberg	196?	3.75	7.50	15.00
❏ LB 311 [10]	Beer Garden Rhythms	195?	6.25	12.50	25.00
❏ PS 344 [S]	Big Polka Band Hits	196?	3.75	7.50	15.00
❏ PS 397 [S]	Happy Days Are Here Again	196?	3.75	7.50	15.00
❏ LL 1710 [M]	Beer Garden Music	195?	5.00	10.00	20.00
❏ LL 3021 [M]	Beer Garden Musik	195?	3.75	7.50	15.00
❏ LL 3046 [M]	The Polka King	195?	3.75	7.50	15.00
❏ LL 3099 [M]	Old Heidelberg	196?	3.75	7.50	15.00
❏ LL 3344 [M]	Big Polka Band Hits	196?	3.00	6.00	12.00
❏ LL 3397 [M]	Happy Days Are Here Again	196?	3.75	7.50	15.00
❏ TW 91223 [M]	Christmas Greetings from Germany	195?	3.75	7.50	15.00
❏ TW 91225 [M]	Cafe International	195?	3.75	7.50	15.00
❏ TW 91227 [M]	Old Heidelberg	196?	3.00	6.00	12.00
❏ SW 99009 [S]	German Sing-a-Long	195?	3.75	7.50	15.00
❏ SW 99227 [S]	Old Heidelberg	196?	3.00	6.00	12.00
❏ SW 99419 [S]	More German Sing-a-Long	196?	3.00	6.00	12.00

LONDON PHASE 4

Number	Title (A Side/B Side)	Yr	VG	VG+	NM
❏ SP-44069	New Beer Barrel Polka	196?	3.75	7.50	15.00
❏ SP-44122	Strictly Oompah	1969	3.75	7.50	15.00
❏ SP-44145	Oktoberfest!	1970	3.75	7.50	15.00
❏ SP-44224	The Polka King, Volume 1	197?	3.75	7.50	15.00
❏ SP-44226	The Polka King, Volume 2	197?	3.75	7.50	15.00
❏ SP-44257	Bavarian Merry-Go-Round	1976	3.75	7.50	15.00

RICHMOND

Number	Title (A Side/B Side)	Yr	VG	VG+	NM
❏ B 20016 [M]	Polka Hits	196?	3.00	6.00	12.00

GLASS BOTTLE, THE
45s
AVCO

Number	Title (A Side/B Side)	Yr	VG	VG+	NM
❏ 4584	The Girl Who Loved Me When/Because She's Mine Again	1971	—	3.00	6.00
❏ 4592	Don't It Make You Feel So Good/(B-side unknown)	1972	—	2.50	5.00
❏ 4597	Pretty Thing/(B-side unknown)	1972	—	2.50	5.00
—Both of the above credit lead singer Gary Criss					

AVCO EMBASSY

Number	Title (A Side/B Side)	Yr	VG	VG+	NM
❏ 4575	I Ain't Got Time Anymore/The First Time	1971	—	3.00	6.00

Albums
AVCO

Number	Title (A Side/B Side)	Yr	VG	VG+	NM
❏ 33012	The Glass Bottle	1971	3.75	7.50	15.00

GLASS HARP Christian rock pioneer Phil Keaggy was in this group.
45s
DECCA

Number	Title (A Side/B Side)	Yr	VG	VG+	NM
❏ 32830	Children's Fantasy/Village Queen	1971	2.50	5.00	10.00
❏ 32915	The Answer/Just Always	1972	2.50	5.00	10.00
❏ 32995	La De Da/(B-side unknown)	1972	2.50	5.00	10.00

Albums
DECCA

Number	Title (A Side/B Side)	Yr	VG	VG+	NM
❏ DL 75261	Glass Harp	1971	6.25	12.50	25.00
❏ DL 75306	Synergy	1971	6.25	12.50	25.00
❏ DL 75358	It Makes Me Glad	1972	6.25	12.50	25.00

MCA

Number	Title (A Side/B Side)	Yr	VG	VG+	NM
❏ 293	Glass Harp	1974	2.50	5.00	10.00
—Reissue of Decca 75261					

GLASS HOUSE, THE
45s
INVICTUS

Number	Title (A Side/B Side)	Yr	VG	VG+	NM
❏ 9071	Crumbs Off the Table/Bad Bill of Goods	1969	—	3.00	6.00
❏ 9076	I Can't Be You (You Can't Be Me)/He's In My Life	1970	—	3.00	6.00
❏ 9082	Stealing Moments From Another Woman's Life/If It Ain't Love, It Don't Matter	1970	—	3.00	6.00
❏ 9090	Touch Me Jesus/If It Ain't Love, It Don't Matter	1971	—	3.00	6.00
❏ 9097	Look What We've Done to Love/Heaven's There to Guide Us	1971	—	3.00	6.00
❏ 9111	Let It Flow/Playing Games	1972	—	3.00	6.00
❏ 9129	Thanks I Needed That/I Don't See Me in Your Eyes Anymore	1972	—	3.00	6.00

Albums
INVICTUS

Number	Title (A Side/B Side)	Yr	VG	VG+	NM
❏ ST-7305	Inside the Glass House	1971	3.00	6.00	12.00
❏ ST-9810	Thanks I Needed That	1972	3.00	6.00	12.00

GLASS PRISM, THE
45s
RCA VICTOR

Number	Title (A Side/B Side)	Yr	VG	VG+	NM
❏ 74-0205	The Raven/El Dorado	1969	—	3.00	6.00

Albums
RCA VICTOR

Number	Title (A Side/B Side)	Yr	VG	VG+	NM
❏ LSP-4201	Poe Through the Glass Prism	1969	3.75	7.50	15.00
❏ LSP-4270	On Joy and Sorrow	1970	3.75	7.50	15.00

GLEAMS, THE
45s
HIT

Number	Title (A Side/B Side)	Yr	VG	VG+	NM
❏ 36	He's a Rebel/Next Door to an Angel	1962	2.50	5.00	10.00
—B-side by Ward Oliver					

J-V

Number	Title (A Side/B Side)	Yr	VG	VG+	NM
❏ 101	Bad Boy/Give Me a Chance	1961	75.00	150.00	300.00

GLEASON, JACKIE
45s
CAPITOL

Number	Title (A Side/B Side)	Yr	VG	VG+	NM
❏ F2361	Melancholy Serenade/You're Getting to Be a Habit	1953	3.75	7.50	15.00
❏ F2437	Alone Together/Body & Soul	1953	2.50	5.00	10.00
❏ F2438	My Funny Valentine/Love Is Here to Stay	1953	2.50	5.00	10.00
❏ F2439	But Not for Me/Love	1953	2.50	5.00	10.00
❏ F2440	I'm in the Mood for Love/I Only Have Eyes for You	1953	2.50	5.00	10.00
—The above four comprise a box set					
❏ F2507	Terry's Theme from "Limelight"/Peg o' My Heart	1953	3.75	7.50	15.00
❏ F2515	White House Serenade/The President's Lady	1953	3.75	7.50	15.00
❏ F2659	Mystery Street/Golden Violins	1954	3.75	7.50	15.00
❏ F3092	Rain/I'll Never Be the Same	1955	3.00	6.00	12.00
❏ F3144	The Band Played On/In the Good Old Summertime	1955	3.00	6.00	12.00
❏ F3223	Autumn Leaves/Oo! What You Do to Me	1955	3.00	6.00	12.00
❏ F4062	Where Is She Now/Just One Yesterday	1958	2.50	5.00	10.00
❏ 4704	Melancholy Serenade/Apology at Bedtime	1962	2.00	4.00	8.00
❏ 4800	'Allo 'Allo 'Allo/Joi De Vivre	1962	2.00	4.00	8.00
❏ 4933	It's Such a Happy Day/La La La La La La La	1963	2.00	4.00	8.00
❏ 5131	Bird Brain/Soldier in the Rain	1964	2.00	4.00	8.00

Number	Title (A Side/B Side)	Yr	VG	VG+	NM
❏ 5584	Love Theme from "Madame X"/ One of Those Songs	1966	—	3.50	7.00
DECCA					
❏ 27684	What Is a Girl?/What Is a Boy?	1951	3.75	7.50	15.00
7-Inch Extended Plays					
CAPITOL					
❏ EAP 1-352	Alone Together/My Funny Valentine//I Only Have Eyes for You/Body and Soul	195?	2.50	5.00	10.00
❏ EAP 1-352 [PS]	Music for Lovers Only, Part 1	195?	2.50	5.00	10.00
❏ EAP 2-352	But Not for Me/Love (Your Spell Is Everywhere)/ /I'm in the Mood for Love/Love Is Here to Stay	195?	2.50	5.00	10.00
❏ EAP 2-352 [PS]	Music for Lovers Only, Part 2	195?	2.50	5.00	10.00
❏ EBF-352 [PS]	Music for Lovers Only	195?	6.25	12.50	25.00
—Gatefold sleeve for some editions of EAP 1-352 and 2-352					
❏ EAP 1-366	Desire/Flirtation//Temptation/Enchantment	195?	2.50	5.00	10.00
❏ EAP 1-366 [PS]	Songs from Lover's Rhapsody, Part 1	195?	2.50	5.00	10.00
❏ EAP 2-366	When Your Lover Has Gone/Tenderly//I'm Thru with Love/Dark Is the Night (C'est Fini)	195?	2.50	5.00	10.00
❏ EAP 2-366 [PS]	Songs from Lover's Rhapsody, Part 2	195?	2.50	5.00	10.00
❏ EAP 1-455	Say It Isn't So/I Guess I'll Have to Change My Plan//It Happened in Monterey/It All Depends on You	195?	2.50	5.00	10.00
❏ EAP 1-455 [PS]	Music to Make You Misty, Part 1	195?	2.50	5.00	10.00
❏ EAP 2-455	The Man I Love/Mickey//I Hadn't Anyone Till You/You Were Meant for Me	195?	2.50	5.00	10.00
❏ EAP 2-455 [PS]	Music to Make You Misty, Part 2	195?	2.50	5.00	10.00
❏ EBF-455 [PS]	Music to Make You Misty	195?	6.25	12.50	25.00
—Gatefold sleeve for some editions of EAP 1-455 and 2-455					
❏ EAP 1-509	Once in a While/I Can't Get Started//I Got It Bad and That Ain't Good/My Ideal	195?	2.50	5.00	10.00
❏ EAP 1-509 [PS]	Music, Martinis, and Memories, Part 1	195?	2.50	5.00	10.00
❏ EAP 1-568	Don't Blame Me/You Can't Pull the Wool Over My Eyes//Soon/My Blue Heaven	1955	2.50	5.00	10.00
❏ EAP 1-568 [PS]	Jackie Gleason Plays Romantic Jazz, Part 1	1955	2.50	5.00	10.00
❏ EAP 2-568	There'll Be Some Changes Made/How About You//The World Is Waiting for the Sunrise/The Love Nest	1955	2.50	5.00	10.00
❏ EAP 2-568 [PS]	Jackie Gleason Plays Romantic Jazz, Part 2	1955	2.50	5.00	10.00
❏ EBF-568 [PS]	Jackie Gleason Plays Romantic Jazz	1955	6.25	12.50	25.00
—Gatefold sleeve for some editions of EAP 1-570 and 2-570					
❏ EAP 1-570	Louise/Ruby//Dinah/Laura	195?	2.50	5.00	10.00
❏ EAP 1-570 [PS]	Music to Remember Her, Part 1	195?	2.50	5.00	10.00
❏ EAP 2-570	(contents unknown)	195?	2.50	5.00	10.00
❏ EAP 2-570 [PS]	Music to Remember Her, Part 2	195?	2.50	5.00	10.00
❏ EBF-570 [PS]	Music to Remember Her	195?	6.25	12.50	25.00
—Gatefold sleeve for some editions of EAP 1-570 and 2-570					
❏ EAP 1-627	There Must Be a Way/Come Rain or Come Shine//Darling, Je Vous Aime Beaucoup/I'm Always Chasing Rainbows	1955	2.50	5.00	10.00
❏ EAP 1-627 [PS]	Lonesome Echo, Part 1	1955	3.00	6.00	12.00
❏ EAP 2-627	*Remember/Speak Low/The Thrill Is Gone/I Wished on the Moon	1955	2.50	5.00	10.00
❏ EAP 2-627 [PS]	Lonesome Echo, Part 2	1955	3.00	6.00	12.00
❏ EAP 3-627	Deep Purple/I Still Get a Thrill//I Don't Know Why/A Garden in the Rain	1955	2.50	5.00	10.00
❏ EAP 3-627 [PS]	Lonesome Echo, Part 3	1955	3.00	6.00	12.00
❏ EAP 4-627	*Mad About the Boy/Dancing on the Ceiling/How Deep Is the Ocean/Someday I'll Find You	1955	2.50	5.00	10.00
❏ EAP 4-627 [PS]	Lonesome Echo, Part 4	1955	3.00	6.00	12.00
❏ EBF 1-627 [PS]	Lonesome Echo, Parts 1 & 2	1955	6.25	12.50	25.00
—Gatefold sleeve with some editions of 1-627 and 2-627					
❏ EBF 2-627 [PS]	Lonesome Echo, Parts 3 & 4	1955	6.25	12.50	25.00
—Gatefold sleeve with some editions of 3-627 and 4-627					
❏ EAP 1-674	Autumn Leaves/Can This Be Love//Oo! What You Do to Me/After My Laughter Came Tears	195?	2.50	5.00	10.00
❏ EAP 1-674 [PS]	Autumn Leaves	195?	2.50	5.00	10.00
❏ EAP 1-717	When You're Away/What Can I Say Afer I Say I'm Sorry//Dancing with Tears in My Eyes/A Thousand Goodnights	195?	2.50	5.00	10.00
❏ EAP 1-717 [PS]	Night Winds, Part 1	195?	2.50	5.00	10.00
❏ EAP 2-717	Alone/Love Letters in the Sand//I Apologize/ Close as Pages in a Book	195?	2.50	5.00	10.00
❏ EAP 2-717 [PS]	Night Winds, Part 2	195?	2.50	5.00	10.00
❏ EAP 3-717	You Are Too Beautiful/If I Should Lose You// Love Locked Out/Are You Lonesome Tonight	195?	2.50	5.00	10.00
❏ EAP 3-717 [PS]	Night Winds, Part 3	195?	2.50	5.00	10.00
❏ EAP 4-717	The Touch of Your Lips/Sleepy Time Gal//Good Night, Sweet Nightingale/Memories of You	195?	2.50	5.00	10.00
❏ EAP 4-717 [PS]	Night Winds, Part 4	195?	2.50	5.00	10.00
❏ EBF 1-717 [PS]	Night Winds, Parts 1 and 2	195?	3.00	6.00	12.00
—Gatefold sleeve with some copies of 1-717 and 2-717					
❏ EBF 2-717 [PS]	Night Winds, Parts 3 and 4	195?	2.50	5.00	10.00
—Gatefold sleeve for some editions of 3-717 and 4-717					
❏ EAP 1-758	(contents unknown)	1956	2.50	5.00	10.00
❏ EAP 1-758 [PS]	Merry Christmas	1956	3.00	6.00	12.00
❏ EAP 1-859	You're Driving Me Crazy/Skyliner//Out of Nowhere/Chinatown, My Chinatown	195?	2.50	5.00	10.00
❏ EAP 1-859 [PS]	Velvet Brass, Part 1	195?	2.50	5.00	10.00
❏ EAP 1-871	To a Sleeping Beauty//Apology at Bedtime	1957	3.75	7.50	15.00
❏ EAP 1-871 [PS]	To a Sleeping Beauty	1957	3.75	7.50	15.00
Albums					
CAPITOL					
❏ SW-106	Irving Berlin's Music	1968	3.00	6.00	12.00
❏ SKAO-146	The Best of Jackie Gleason (Vol. 2)	1968	3.00	6.00	12.00
❏ SWBB-256 [(2)]	Close-Up	1969	3.75	7.50	15.00
—Reissue of Capitol DW 352 and DW 509 in one package					
❏ STBB-346 [(2)]	All I Want for Christmas	1969	3.75	7.50	15.00
❏ H 352 [10]	Music for Lovers Only	1952	7.50	15.00	30.00
❏ SM-352	Music for Lovers Only	197?	2.50	5.00	10.00
—Reissue					
❏ SW 352 [S]	Music for Lovers Only	1959	3.75	7.50	15.00
—Re-recorded version of W 352; black rainbow label, Capitol logo at left					
❏ SW 352 [S]	Music for Lovers Only	1963	2.50	5.00	10.00
—Re-recorded version; black rainbow label, Capitol logo at top					
❏ W 352 [M]	Music for Lovers Only	1953	6.25	12.50	25.00
❏ H 366 [10]	Lover's Rhapsody	1953	7.50	15.00	30.00
❏ ST-398	Romeo and Juliet	1970	3.00	6.00	12.00

Number	Title (A Side/B Side)	Yr	VG	VG+	NM
❏ DW 455 [R]	Music to Make You Misty	196?	2.50	5.00	10.00
❏ H 455 [10]	Music to Make You Misty	1954	7.50	15.00	30.00
❏ SM-455	Music to Make You Misty	197?	2.50	5.00	10.00
—Reissue					
❏ W 455 [M]	Music to Make You Misty	1954	6.25	12.50	25.00
❏ L 471 [10]	Tawny	1954	7.50	15.00	30.00
❏ W 471 [M]	Tawny	1954	6.25	12.50	25.00
❏ WAO 475 [(2)M]	Music for Lovers Only/Music to Make You Misty	1954	10.00	20.00	40.00
❏ ST-480	Come Saturday Morning	1970	3.00	6.00	12.00
❏ DW 509 [R]	Music, Martini and Memories	196?	2.50	5.00	10.00
❏ SM-509	Music, Martini and Memories	197?	2.50	5.00	10.00
—Reissue					
❏ W 509 [M]	Music, Martini and Memories	1954	6.25	12.50	25.00
❏ STBB-510 [(2)]	Tenderly/Laura	1971	3.75	7.50	15.00
❏ H 511 [10]	And Awaaay We Go!	1954	20.00	40.00	80.00
❏ W 511 [M]	And Awaaay We Go!	1955	10.00	20.00	40.00
❏ W 568 [M]	Jackie Gleason Plays Romantic Jazz	1955	6.25	12.50	25.00
❏ DW 570 [R]	Music to Remember Her	196?	2.50	5.00	10.00
❏ W 570 [M]	Music to Remember Her	1955	6.25	12.50	25.00
❏ DW 627 [R]	Lonesome Echo	196?	2.50	5.00	10.00
❏ H 627 [10]	Lonesome Echo	1955	7.50	15.00	30.00
❏ W 627 [M]	Lonesome Echo	1955	6.25	12.50	25.00
❏ DW 632 [R]	Music to Change Her Mind	196?	2.50	5.00	10.00
❏ W 632 [M]	Music to Change Her Mind	1956	6.25	12.50	25.00
❏ ST-693	Words of Love	1971	3.00	6.00	12.00
❏ DW 717 [R]	Night Winds	196?	2.50	5.00	10.00
❏ W 717 [M]	Night Winds	1956	6.25	12.50	25.00
❏ DW 758 [R]	Merry Christmas	196?	2.50	5.00	10.00
❏ W 758 [M]	Merry Christmas	1956	6.25	12.50	25.00
❏ DW 816 [R]	Music for the Love Hours	196?	2.50	5.00	10.00
❏ W 816 [M]	Music for the Love Hours	1957	6.25	12.50	25.00
❏ SM-859	Velvet Brass	197?	2.50	5.00	10.00
—Reissue					
❏ SW 859 [S]	Velvet Brass	1959	6.25	12.50	25.00
—We haven't confirmed if this is in true stereo or not.					
❏ W 859 [M]	Velvet Brass	1957	6.25	12.50	25.00
❏ SW 905 [S]	Jackie Gleason Presents "Oooo!"	1959	6.25	12.50	25.00
—We haven't confirmed if this is in true stereo or not.					
❏ W 905 [M]	Jackie Gleason Presents "Oooo!"	1957	6.25	12.50	25.00
❏ SW 961 [S]	The Torch with Blue Flame	1959	6.25	12.50	25.00
❏ W 961 [M]	The Torch with Blue Flame	1958	5.00	10.00	20.00
❏ SW 1020 [S]	Riff Jazz	1959	6.25	12.50	25.00
❏ W 1020 [M]	Riff Jazz	1958	5.00	10.00	20.00
❏ SW 1075 [S]	Rebound	1959	6.25	12.50	25.00
❏ W 1075 [M]	Rebound	1959	5.00	10.00	20.00
❏ SW 1147 [S]	That Moment	1959	6.25	12.50	25.00
❏ W 1147 [M]	That Moment	1959	5.00	10.00	20.00
❏ SW 1250 [S]	Aphrodisia	1960	6.25	12.50	25.00
❏ W 1250 [M]	Aphrodisia	1960	5.00	10.00	20.00
❏ SW 1315 [S]	Opiate D'Amour	1960	5.00	10.00	20.00
❏ W 1315 [M]	Opiate D'Amour	1960	3.75	7.50	15.00
❏ SW 1439 [S]	Lazy Lively Love	1961	6.25	12.50	25.00
❏ W 1439 [M]	Lazy Lively Love	1961	5.00	10.00	20.00
❏ SW 1519 [S]	The Gentle Touch	1961	6.25	12.50	25.00
❏ W 1519 [M]	The Gentle Touch	1961	5.00	10.00	20.00
❏ SWBO 1619 [(2)S]	A Lover's Portfolio	1962	6.25	12.50	25.00
❏ WBO 1619 [(2)M]	A Lover's Portfolio	1962	5.00	10.00	20.00
❏ SW 1689 [S]	Love, Embers and Flame	1962	5.00	10.00	20.00
❏ W 1689 [M]	Love, Embers and Flame	1962	3.75	7.50	15.00
❏ SW 1830 [S]	Champagne, Candlelight & Kisses	1963	3.75	7.50	15.00
❏ W 1830 [M]	Champagne, Candlelight & Kisses	1963	3.00	6.00	12.00
❏ SW 1877 [S]	Movie Themes — For Lovers Only	1963	3.75	7.50	15.00
❏ W 1877 [M]	Movie Themes — For Lovers Only	1963	3.00	6.00	12.00
❏ SW 1978 [S]	Today's Romantic Hits/For Lovers Only	1963	3.75	7.50	15.00
❏ W 1978 [M]	Today's Romantic Hits/For Lovers Only	1963	3.00	6.00	12.00
❏ SW 1979 [S]	A Lover's Portfolio, Vol. 1 (Music for Sippin' and Dancin')	1963	3.75	7.50	15.00
❏ W 1979 [M]	A Lover's Portfolio, Vol. 1 (Music for Sippin' and Dancin')	1963	3.00	6.00	12.00
❏ SW 1980 [S]	A Lover's Portfolio, Vol. 2 (Music for Listenin' and Lovin')	1963	3.75	7.50	15.00
❏ W 1980 [M]	A Lover's Portfolio, Vol. 2 (Music for Listenin' and Lovin')	1963	3.00	6.00	12.00
❏ SW 2056 [S]	Today's Romantic Hits/For Lovers Only, Vol. 2	1964	3.75	7.50	15.00
❏ W 2056 [M]	Today's Romantic Hits/For Lovers Only, Vol. 2	1964	3.00	6.00	12.00
❏ SW 2144 [S]	Last Dance For Lovers Only	1964	3.75	7.50	15.00
❏ W 2144 [M]	Last Dance For Lovers Only	1964	3.00	6.00	12.00
❏ SW 2409 [S]	Silk 'N' Brass	1966	3.75	7.50	15.00
❏ W 2409 [M]	Silk 'N' Brass	1966	3.00	6.00	12.00
❏ SW 2471 [S]	Music Around the World — For Lovers Only	1966	3.75	7.50	15.00
❏ W 2471 [M]	Music Around the World — For Lovers Only	1966	3.00	6.00	12.00
❏ SW 2582 [S]	How Sweet It Is For Lovers Only	1966	3.75	7.50	15.00
❏ W 2582 [M]	How Sweet It Is For Lovers Only	1966	3.00	6.00	12.00
❏ SW 2684 [S]	A Taste of Brass For Lovers Only	1967	3.75	7.50	15.00
❏ W 2684 [M]	A Taste of Brass For Lovers Only	1967	3.00	6.00	12.00
❏ ST 2791 [S]	'Tis the Season	1967	3.75	7.50	15.00
❏ T 2791 [M]	'Tis the Season	1967	5.00	10.00	20.00
❏ SM-2796	The Best of Jackie Gleason	197?	2.50	5.00	10.00
—Reissue					
❏ SW 2796 [S]	The Best of Jackie Gleason	1967	3.75	7.50	15.00
❏ W 2796 [M]	The Best of Jackie Gleason	1967	3.75	7.50	15.00
❏ STCL 2816 [(3)S]	The Jackie Gleason Deluxe Set	1968	6.25	12.50	25.00
—Reissue of three complete LPs (titles unknown)					
❏ TCL 2816 [(3)M]	The Jackie Gleason Deluxe Set	1968	6.25	12.50	25.00
❏ SW 2880	Doublin' in Brass	1968	3.75	7.50	15.00
❏ SW 2935	The Now Sound ... For Today's Lovers	1968	3.75	7.50	15.00
PAIR					
❏ PDL2-1069 [(2)]	Lush Moods	1986	3.00	6.00	12.00
PICKWICK					
❏ SPC-1008	White Christmas	197?	2.50	5.00	10.00
—Abridged version of Capitol ST 2791					
❏ SPC-2004	Romantic Moods	197?	2.50	5.00	10.00
❏ SPC-2029	The More I See You	197?	2.50	5.00	10.00
❏ SPC-3064	Plays Pretty for the People	196?	2.50	5.00	10.00
❏ SPC-3218	Shangri-La	197?	2.50	5.00	10.00

G

Number	Title (A Side/B Side)	Yr	VG	VG+	NM
GLEEMS, THE					
45s					
PARKWAY					
❏ 893	Sandra Baby/You Are the One	1964	5.00	10.00	20.00
GLENCOVES, THE					
45s					
SELECT					
❏ 724	Hootenanny/It's Sister Ginny's Turn to Throw the Bomb	1963	2.50	5.00	10.00
❏ 726	Don't Knock/Ginny's Come Home	1963	2.50	5.00	10.00
❏ 727	Devil's Waitin'/Better Think Twice	1963	2.50	5.00	10.00
❏ 729	Keep Away from My Gal/Keep On Truckin' Mama	1964	3.00	6.00	12.00
GLENN, GLEN					
45s					
DORE					
❏ 523	Goofin' Around/Susie Green from Abilene	1959	3.75	7.50	15.00
ERA					
❏ 1061	Everybody's Movin'/I'm Glad My Baby's Gone	1957	15.00	30.00	60.00
❏ 1074	One Cup of Coffee/Laurie Ann	1958	12.50	25.00	50.00
GLENN, LLOYD					
45s					
ALADDIN					
❏ 3268	Nite Flite/Still Waters	1954	6.25	12.50	25.00
❏ 3288	Footloose/Glen's Glide	1955	6.25	12.50	25.00
❏ 3307	Sunrise/Tiddly Winks	1955	6.25	12.50	25.00
❏ 3327	Southbound Special/Blue Ivories	1956	5.00	10.00	20.00
❏ 3346	After Hours (Part 1)/After Hours (Part 2)	1956	5.00	10.00	20.00
❏ 3353	Chica-Boo/Old Time Shuffle	1957	5.00	10.00	20.00
❏ 3378	The Vamp/Ballroom Shuffle	1957	5.00	10.00	20.00
❏ 3400	Hyde Park/Love for Sale	1957	5.00	10.00	20.00
❏ 3407	Cute-Tee/Black Fantasy	1958	5.00	10.00	20.00
❏ 3446	Petite Fleur/Honky Tonk Train	1959	3.75	7.50	15.00
❏ 3459	Long Gone (Part 1)/Long Gone (Part 2)	1959	3.75	7.50	15.00
HOLLYWOOD					
❏ 1021	Merry Christmas Baby/Sleigh Ride	1954	5.00	10.00	20.00
—B-side by Charles Brown; red label					
❏ 1021	Merry Christmas Baby/Sleigh Ride	196?	2.00	4.00	8.00
—B-side by Charles Brown; color label					
❏ 1021	Merry Christmas Baby/Sleigh Ride	197?	—	2.50	5.00
—B-side by Charles Brown; black label					
❏ 1028	Chica-Boo/Old Time Shuffle	1954	6.25	12.50	25.00
❏ 1033	Sleigh Ride/China Doll	1954	6.25	12.50	25.00
IMPERIAL					
❏ 5839	Twistville/Young Date	1962	3.00	6.00	12.00
SWING TIME					
❏ 254	Chica-Boo/Jungle Town Jubilee	1951	7.50	15.00	30.00
❏ 271	Sleigh Ride/Savage Boy	1951	7.50	15.00	30.00
❏ 277	Day Break Stomp/Jungle Twilight	1952	7.50	15.00	30.00
❏ 278	Cute-Tee/Rhumba	1952	7.50	15.00	30.00
❏ 292	After Hours/Yancey Special	1952	7.50	15.00	30.00
❏ 293	Honky Tonk Train/Pine Top Boogie Woogie	1952	7.50	15.00	30.00
❏ 296	Angora/Cuba Doll	1952	7.50	15.00	30.00
❏ 311	Boogie Woogie on St. Louis Blues/Ugh	1953	7.50	15.00	30.00
❏ 324	Night Time/It Moves Me	1953	7.50	15.00	30.00
❏ 336	Not the Girl for Me/Black Fantasy	1954	7.50	15.00	30.00
Albums					
ALADDIN					
❏ LP-808 [M]	Chica-Boo	1956	250.00	500.00	1000.
—Black vinyl					
❏ LP-808 [M]	Chica-Boo	1956	1000.	1500.	2000.
—Red vinyl					
BLACK & BLUE					
❏ 33077	Old Time Shuffle	1977	3.00	6.00	12.00
IMPERIAL					
❏ LP-9174 [M]	Chica-Boo	1962	37.50	75.00	150.00
❏ LP-9175 [M]	After Hours	1962	37.50	75.00	150.00
❏ LP-12174 [S]	Chica-Boo	1962	50.00	100.00	200.00
❏ LP-12175 [S]	After Hours	1962	50.00	100.00	200.00
SCORE					
❏ SLP-4006 [M]	Lloyd Glenn	1957	250.00	500.00	1000.
❏ SLP-4020 [M]	After Hours	1958	250.00	500.00	1000.
SWING TIME					
❏ 1901 [10]	Lloyd Glenn Presents All Time Favorites	1954	1500.	2250.	3000.
GLITTER, GARY					
45s					
ARISTA					
❏ 0173	I Love You Love Me Love/Hands Up! It's a Stick-Up	1976	—	2.50	5.00
BELL					
❏ 45237	Rock and Roll, Part 2/Rock and Roll, Part 1	1972	—	3.00	6.00
❏ 45276	I Didn't Know I Loved You (Till I Saw You Rock and Roll)/Shakey Sue	1972	—	2.50	5.00
❏ 45326	Do You Wanna Touch Me (Oh Yeah)/I Would If I Could But I Can't	1973	—	2.50	5.00
❏ 45345	Baby Please Don't Go/I.O.U.	1973	—	2.50	5.00
❏ 45375	Come On, Come In/Happy Birthday	1973	—	2.50	5.00
❏ 45398	(I'm the) Leader of the Gang (I Am)/(B-side unknown)	1973	—	2.50	5.00
❏ 45438	I Love You Love Me Love/(B-side unknown)	1974	—	2.50	5.00
DECCA					
❏ 32714	Goodbye Seattle/Wait for Me	1970	3.75	7.50	15.00
—As "Paul Raven"					
TOMMY BOY					
❏ 639	Rock 'N' Roll Part 2...The Hey Song (same on both sides)	1995	—	—	3.00
—Original recording with overdubbed crowd sounds					
Albums					
BELL					
❏ 1108	Glitter	1972	3.75	7.50	15.00
❏ 6082	Gary Glitter	1973	3.75	7.50	15.00
EPIC					
❏ PE 39299	The Leader	1984	3.75	7.50	15.00
EPIC/NU-DISK					
❏ 3E 36848 [10]	Glitter & Gold	1981	3.00	6.00	12.00
GLITTERHOUSE					
45s					
DYNOVOICE					
❏ 925	I Lost Me a Friend/Tinkerbell's Mind	1968	2.50	5.00	10.00
❏ 927	Barbarella/Love Drags Me Down	1968	3.00	6.00	12.00
Albums					
DYNOVOICE					
❏ 31905	Color Bland	1968	5.00	10.00	20.00
GLOBETROTTERS, THE					
45s					
BUDDAH					
❏ 309	Don't Rock the Boat/Hatfield Small	1972	2.50	5.00	10.00
KIRSHNER					
❏ 63-5006	Cheer Me Up/Gravy	1970	3.00	6.00	12.00
❏ 63-5006 [PS]	Cheer Me Up/Gravy	1970	3.75	7.50	15.00
❏ 63-5008	Rainy Day Bells/Meadowlark	1970	3.75	7.50	15.00
❏ 63-5012	Duke of Earl/Everybody's Got Hot Pants	1971	3.00	6.00	12.00
❏ 63-5016	Everybody Needs Love/ESP	1971	3.00	6.00	12.00
Albums					
KIRSHNER					
❏ KES-108	The Globetrotters	1970	5.00	10.00	20.00
GLORIES, THE					
45s					
DATE					
❏ 1553	I Stand Accused (Of Loving You)/Wish They Could Write a Song	1967	2.50	5.00	10.00
❏ 1571	Give Me My Freedom/Security	1967	6.25	12.50	25.00
❏ 1579	Sing Me a Love Song/Ooh, That's Love, Baby	1967	6.25	12.50	25.00
❏ 1593	Stand By (I'm Coming Home)/My Sweet, Sweet Baby	1968	6.25	12.50	25.00
❏ 1593 [PS]	Stand By (I'm Coming Home)/My Sweet, Sweet Baby	1968	12.50	25.00	50.00
❏ 1615	I Worship You Baby/Don't Dial My Number	1968	12.50	25.00	50.00
❏ 1622	No News/Oh Baby That's Love	1968	6.25	12.50	25.00
❏ 1636	Try a Little Tenderness/There He Is	1969	6.25	12.50	25.00
❏ 1647	Don't Make the Good Girls Go Bad/The Dark End of the Street	1969	5.00	10.00	20.00
GLORY (1)					
45s					
AVALANCHE					
❏ XW-289	Find Out Lover/Mrs. Walter	1973	—	3.00	6.00
Albums					
AVALANCHE					
❏ AV-LA148-F	Glory	1973	3.75	7.50	15.00
GLORY (2)					
Albums					
TEXAS REVOLUTION					
❏ CFS-2531	A Meat Music Sampler	1969	25.00	50.00	100.00
GLORYTONES, THE					
45s					
EPIC					
❏ 9243	You Only Came Back to Hurt Me/Was That the Right Thing to Do	1957	10.00	20.00	40.00
GLOWTONES, THE					
45s					
ATLANTIC					
❏ 1156	The Girl I Love/Ping Pong	1957	—	—	—
—Only known on 78 rpm; 45 rpm release was on EastWest 101					
EASTWEST					
❏ 101	The Girl I Love/Ping Pong	1957	7.50	15.00	30.00
GO-GO'S, THE No relation to the 1980s girl group.					
45s					
RCA VICTOR					
❏ 47-8370	Lonely Girl/Chicken of the Sea	1964	3.75	7.50	15.00
❏ 47-8435	The Wild One/Saturday's Hero	1964	7.50	15.00	30.00
Albums					
RCA VICTOR					
❏ LPM-2930 [M]	Swim with the Go-Go's	1964	6.25	12.50	25.00
❏ LSP-2930 [S]	Swim with the Go-Go's	1964	7.50	15.00	30.00
GODCHAUX, KEITH AND DONNA See KEITH AND DONNA.					
GODDARD, GEOFF					
45s					
LAWN					
❏ 235	Walk With My Angel/Sky Men	1964	3.00	6.00	12.00
GODFREY, RAY					
45s					
ABC					
❏ 10999	I Can't Go On Living Like This/Right Straight in the Eye	1967	2.50	5.00	10.00
COLUMBIA					
❏ 4-43398	Old Love/There's Always Room (For One More Fool Like Me)	1965	2.50	5.00	10.00
❏ 4-43618	I Can Live It Down/Keep Your Chin Up, Soldier	1966	2.50	5.00	10.00
❏ 4-43618 [PS]	I Can Live It Down/Keep Your Chin Up, Soldier	1966	3.00	6.00	12.00
❏ 4-43785	Winner Take All/Please Don't Mention My Name	1966	2.50	5.00	10.00
❏ 4-44071	Three Little Words from You/The Difference in Me	1967	2.50	5.00	10.00
J&J					
❏ 001	The Picture/The Overall Song	1960	10.00	20.00	40.00
PEACH					
❏ 757	Let's Move to the City/Wait, Weep and Wonder	1961	5.00	10.00	20.00

Number	Title (A Side/B Side)	Yr	VG	VG+	NM
SAVOY					
❏ 3021	The Picture/The Overall Song	1960	6.25	12.50	25.00
SIMS					
❏ 130	Better Times a-Comin'/Ten Silver Dollars	1962	5.00	10.00	20.00
SPRING					
❏ 104	I Gotta Get Away/Sherry Washington	1970	2.00	4.00	8.00
❏ 135	Candy Clown/I Want to Be Your Only Love	1973	—	3.00	6.00

GODSPELL
45s
Number	Title (A Side/B Side)	Yr	VG	VG+	NM
BELL					
❏ 45147	By My Side/Crucifixion, Resurrection	1971	—	2.50	5.00
❏ 45210	Day By Day/Bless the Lord	1972	—	2.00	4.00
❏ 45240	We Beseech Thee/On the Willows	1972	—	2.50	5.00
❏ 45275	By My Side/(B-side unknown)	1972	—	2.50	5.00
❏ 45351	Beautiful City/Bless the Lord	1973	—	2.50	5.00

GODZ, THE No relation to the late-1970s punk/metal band of the same name.
45s
Number	Title (A Side/B Side)	Yr	VG	VG+	NM
ESP-DISK'					
❏ 4503	Lay in the Sun/I Want a Word with You	1966	2.50	5.00	10.00
Albums					
ESP-DISK'					
❏ 1037 [M]	Contact High with the Godz	1967	15.00	30.00	60.00
❏ S-1037 [S]	Contact High with the Godz	1967	12.50	25.00	50.00
❏ 1047	Godz 2	1968	12.50	25.00	50.00
❏ 1077	Third Testament	1969	12.50	25.00	50.00
❏ 2017	Godzundheit	1970	12.50	25.00	50.00

GOGGLES, THE
45s
Number	Title (A Side/B Side)	Yr	VG	VG+	NM
AUDIO FIDELITY					
❏ 168	Don't Say You Don't Remember/We All Live on a Rainbow	1971	—	2.50	5.00
Albums					
AUDIO FIDELITY					
❏ AFSD-6244	The Goggles	1971	3.75	7.50	15.00

GOINS, HERBIE, AND THE NIGHT-RIDERS
45s
Number	Title (A Side/B Side)	Yr	VG	VG+	NM
CAPITOL					
❏ 5978	Coming Home to You/The Incredible Miss Brown	1967	2.50	5.00	10.00

GOLD, ANDREW Also see BRYNDLE.
45s
Number	Title (A Side/B Side)	Yr	VG	VG+	NM
ASYLUM					
❏ 45286	That's Why I Love You/A Note from You	1975	—	2.00	4.00
❏ 45339	Stay/Firefly	1976	—	2.00	4.00
❏ 45378	Angel Woman/Do Wah Diddy	1976	—	2.00	4.00
❏ 45384	Lonely Boy/Must Be Crazy	1977	—	2.00	4.00
❏ 45384 [PS]	Lonely Boy/Must Be Crazy	1977	—	2.50	5.00
❏ 45417	One of Them Is Me/Passing Thing	1977	—	2.00	4.00
❏ 45439	Go Back Home Again/Firefly	1977	—	2.00	4.00
❏ 45456	Thank You for Being a Friend/Still You Linger On	1978	—	2.00	4.00
❏ 45489	Never Let Her Slip Away/Genevieve	1978	—	2.00	4.00
❏ 45489 [PS]	Never Let Her Slip Away/Genevieve	1978	—	2.50	5.00
❏ 45521	Looking for My Love/How Can This Be Love	1978	—	2.00	4.00
❏ 45522	I'm On My Way/Always for You	1978	—	2.00	4.00
❏ 46626	Kiss This One Goodbye/Make Up Your Mind	1980	—	2.00	4.00
Albums					
ASYLUM					
❏ 6E-116	All This and Heaven Too	1978	2.50	5.00	10.00
❏ 6E-264	Whirlwind	1979	2.50	5.00	10.00
❏ 7E-1047	Andrew Gold	1975	2.50	5.00	10.00
❏ 7E-1086	What's Wrong with This Picture?	1977	2.50	5.00	10.00

GOLD, MARTY
45s
Number	Title (A Side/B Side)	Yr	VG	VG+	NM
KAPP					
❏ 244	Hey! Paesano Cha Cha Cha/I'm Not Afraid Anymore	1958	2.50	5.00	10.00
RCA VICTOR					
❏ 47-7696	Lissabon/Music of Home	1960	2.00	4.00	8.00
❏ 47-7722	Lonely Guitar/Home from the Hill	1960	2.00	4.00	8.00
❏ 47-7822	The Breeze and I/Cry Like the Wind	1960	2.00	4.00	8.00
❏ 47-7856	Carnival in Rome/My Romance	1961	2.00	4.00	8.00
Albums					
KAPP					
❏ KL-1125 [M]	By the Waters of the Minnetonka	1959	3.75	7.50	15.00
PICKWICK					
❏ ACL-9003	Songs from "How the Grinch Stole Christmas" and Other Children's Christmas Songs	197?	2.00	4.00	8.00
RCA VICTOR					
❏ LPM-2290 [M]	It's Magic	1961	3.00	6.00	12.00
❏ LSP-2290 [S]	It's Magic	1961	3.75	7.50	15.00
❏ LSP-2381 [S]	Stereo Action Goes Hollywood	1962	3.00	6.00	12.00
❏ LPM-2620 [M]	Soundpower!	1963	3.00	6.00	12.00
❏ LSP-2620 [S]	Soundpower!	1963	3.75	7.50	15.00
❏ LSP-3599 [S]	Soundaroundus	1966	3.00	6.00	12.00
VIK					
❏ LX-1069 [M]	Organized for Hi-Fi	1957	3.75	7.50	15.00

GOLD, SANDY
45s
Number	Title (A Side/B Side)	Yr	VG	VG+	NM
HIT					
❏ 27	Sheila/She's Not You	1962	2.00	4.00	8.00
—B-side by George Killebrew					

GOLD BUGS, THE
45s
Number	Title (A Side/B Side)	Yr	VG	VG+	NM
CORAL					
❏ 62453	Stop That Wedding/It's So Nice	1965	10.00	20.00	40.00

GOLDBERG, BARRY Also see GOLDBERG-MILLER BLUES BAND.
45s
Number	Title (A Side/B Side)	Yr	VG	VG+	NM
ATCO					
❏ 6946	(I've Got to Use My) Imagination/Dusty Country	1973	2.50	5.00	10.00
—A-side co-produced by Bob Dylan					
BUDDAH					
❏ 59	Sittin' in Circles/Hole in My Pocket	1968	2.50	5.00	10.00
❏ 103	Jimi the Fox/On the Road Again	1969	2.50	5.00	10.00
EPIC					
❏ 10007	Blowing My Mind/Think	1966	3.75	7.50	15.00
❏ 10033	Ginger Man/Whole Lotta Shakin' Goin' On	1966	3.75	7.50	15.00
Albums					
ATCO					
❏ SD 7040	Barry Goldberg	1974	3.00	6.00	12.00
BUDDAH					
❏ BDM-1012 [M]	The Barry Goldberg Reunion	1968	12.50	25.00	50.00
—White-label promo in stereo cover with "mono" sticker					
❏ BDS-5012 [S]	The Barry Goldberg Reunion	1968	6.25	12.50	25.00
❏ BDS-5029	Two Jews Blues	1969	6.25	12.50	25.00
❏ BDS-5051	Street Man	1970	3.75	7.50	15.00
❏ BDS-5081	Blast from My Past	1974	3.75	7.50	15.00
EPIC					
❏ LN 24199 [M]	Blowing My Mind	1966	7.50	15.00	30.00
❏ BN 26199 [S]	Blowing My Mind	1966	10.00	20.00	40.00
RECORD MAN					
❏ CR 5015	Barry Goldberg and Friends	1972	3.75	7.50	15.00

GOLDBERG-MILLER BLUES BAND Also see BARRY GOLDBERG; STEVE MILLER.
45s
Number	Title (A Side/B Side)	Yr	VG	VG+	NM
EPIC					
❏ 9865	More Soul Than Soulful/Mother Song	1965	3.75	7.50	15.00
❏ 9865 [DJ]	More Soul Than Soulful/Mother Song	1965	6.25	12.50	25.00
—Promo only on blue vinyl					
❏ 9865 [PS]	More Soul Than Soulful/Mother Song	1965	12.50	25.00	50.00
—Promo only					

GOLDDIGGERS, THE DEAN MARTIN's girl group from his TV show.
45s
Number	Title (A Side/B Side)	Yr	VG	VG+	NM
METROMEDIA					
❏ 141	I Wanna Be Loved/It's Fun to Be Young	1969	—	2.50	5.00
❏ 156	We Need A Little Christmas/I Just Want You For Christmas	1969	—	3.00	6.00
RCA VICTOR					
❏ 74-0670	A-Flat Cricket and B-Flat Frog/Nobody Else But You	1972	—	2.50	5.00
Albums					
METROMEDIA					
❏ MD 1009	The Golddiggers	1969	3.00	6.00	12.00
❏ MD 1012	We Need a Little Christmas	1969	3.75	7.50	15.00
RCA VICTOR					
❏ LSP-4643	The Golddiggers Today!	1972	3.00	6.00	12.00

GOLDEBRIARS, THE Curt Boettcher was a member of this group.
45s
Number	Title (A Side/B Side)	Yr	VG	VG+	NM
EPIC					
❏ 9673	Pretty Girls and Rolling Stones/Shenandoah	1964	3.00	6.00	12.00
❏ 9719	The Castle in the Corner/I've Got to Love Somebody	1964	3.00	6.00	12.00
❏ 9806	Don't Want Your Love/Give Me Lovin'	1965	3.00	6.00	12.00
Albums					
EPIC					
❏ LN 24087 [M]	The Goldebriars	1964	3.75	7.50	15.00
❏ LN 24114 [M]	Straight Ahead	1964	3.75	7.50	15.00
❏ BN 26087 [S]	The Goldebriars	1964	5.00	10.00	20.00
❏ BN 26114 [S]	Straight Ahead	1964	5.00	10.00	20.00

GOLDEN DAWN
Albums
Number	Title (A Side/B Side)	Yr	VG	VG+	NM
INTERNATIONAL ARTISTS					
❏ 4	Power Plant	1968	25.00	50.00	100.00
❏ 4	Power Plant	1979	3.75	7.50	15.00
—Reissue with "Masterfonics" in trail-off wax					

GOLDEN EARRING
45s
Number	Title (A Side/B Side)	Yr	VG	VG+	NM
ATLANTIC					
❏ 2710	Eight Miles High/One Huge Road	1970	—	3.00	6.00
DWARF					
❏ 2001	Back Home/As Long As the Wind Blows	1969	2.50	5.00	10.00
❏ 2001 [PS]	Back Home/As Long As the Wind Blows	1969	5.00	10.00	20.00
MCA					
❏ 40513	Babylon/Sleep Walkin'	1976	—	2.00	4.00
❏ 40802	Radar Love (Live)/Radar Love (Studio)	1977	—	2.00	4.00
POLYDOR					
❏ 2004	Weekend Love/Tiger Bay	1979	—	2.00	4.00
❏ 14001	It's Alright, But I Admit It Could Be Better/Song of a Devil's Servant	1969	2.50	5.00	10.00
❏ 14581	Weekend Love/Tiger Bay	1979	—	—	—
—Unreleased					
TRACK					
❏ 40202	Radar Love/Just Like Vince Taylor	1974	—	3.00	6.00
❏ 40309	Candy's Going Bad/She Flies on Strange Wings	1974	—	2.50	5.00
❏ 40369	Ce Soir/Lucky Numbers	1975	—	2.50	5.00
❏ 40412	The Switch/Lonesome D.J.	1975	—	2.50	5.00
21 RECORDS					
❏ 103	Twilight Zone/King Dark	1982	—	2.00	4.00
❏ 108	The Devil Made Me Do It/Chargin' Batteries	1983	—	2.00	4.00
❏ 112	When the Lady Smiles/Orwell's Ear	1984	—	—	3.00
❏ 112 [PS]	When the Lady Smiles/Orwell's Ear	1984	—	2.50	5.00
❏ 113	Fist in Glove/One Night Moonlight	1984	—	—	3.00
❏ 99515	Love in Motion/Why Do I	1986	—	—	3.00
❏ 99533	Quiet Eyes/Love in Motion	1986	—	—	3.00
❏ 99533 [PS]	Quiet Eyes/Love in Motion	1986	—	2.00	4.00
❏ 881415-7	Something Heavy Going Down/Enough Is Enough	1984	—	—	3.00

G

Number	Title (A Side/B Side)	Yr	VG	VG+	NM
Albums					
ATLANTIC					
❏ SD 8244	Eight Miles High	1970	6.25	12.50	25.00
CAPITOL					
❏ ST-164	Miracle Mirror	1969	10.00	20.00	40.00
❏ ST 2823 [S]	Winter Harvest	1967	6.25	12.50	25.00
❏ T 2823 [M]	Winter Harvest	1967	12.50	25.00	50.00
❏ ST-11315	The Golden Earring	1974	3.00	6.00	12.00
DWARF					
❏ 2000	Golden Earring	1971	6.25	12.50	25.00
MCA					
❏ 703	Grab It For a Second	198?	2.00	4.00	8.00
—Reissue of 3057					
❏ 827	Switch	198?	2.00	4.00	8.00
—Reissue of 2139					
❏ 2139	Switch	197?	2.50	5.00	10.00
—Reissue of Track 2139					
❏ 2183	To the Hilt	1976	3.00	6.00	12.00
❏ 2254	Mad Love	1977	3.00	6.00	12.00
❏ 2352	Moontan	1978	2.50	5.00	10.00
—Reissue of Track 396					
❏ 3057	Grab It For a Second	1978	3.00	6.00	12.00
❏ 6004 [(2)]	Golden Earring Live!	198?	2.50	5.00	10.00
—Reissue of 8009					
❏ 8009 [(2)]	Golden Earring Live!	1977	3.75	7.50	15.00
❏ 37172	Moontan	198?	2.00	4.00	8.00
—Reissue of 2352					
POLYDOR					
❏ PD-1-6223	No Promises...No Debts	1979	3.00	6.00	12.00
❏ PD-1-6303	Long Blond Animal	1980	3.00	6.00	12.00
TRACK					
❏ 396	Moontan	1974	3.75	7.50	15.00
—Reissue cover with close-up of earring in ear					
❏ 396	Moontan	1974	6.25	12.50	25.00
—Original cover with nude dancer					
❏ 2139	Switch	1975	3.75	7.50	15.00
21 RECORDS					
❏ T1-1-9004	Cut	1982	2.50	5.00	10.00
❏ T1-1-9008	N.E.W.S.	1984	2.50	5.00	10.00
❏ 90514	The Hole	1986	2.50	5.00	10.00
❏ 817585-1	Cut	1985	2.00	4.00	8.00
—Reissue					
❏ 823717-1	Something Heavy Going Down — Live from the Twilight Zone	1984	2.50	5.00	10.00

GOLDEN GATE STRINGS, THE
Albums

Number	Title (A Side/B Side)	Yr	VG	VG+	NM
EPIC					
❏ LN 24158 [M]	The Bob Dylan Song Book	1965	3.00	6.00	12.00
❏ LN 24160 [M]	A String of Hits	1965	3.00	6.00	12.00
❏ LN 24248 [M]	The Monkees Song Book	1967	3.00	6.00	12.00
❏ BN 26158 [S]	The Bob Dylan Song Book	1965	3.75	7.50	15.00
❏ BN 26160 [S]	A String of Hits	1965	3.75	7.50	15.00
❏ BN 26248 [S]	The Monkees Song Book	1967	3.75	7.50	15.00

GOLDEN NUGGETS, THE
45s

Number	Title (A Side/B Side)	Yr	VG	VG+	NM
FUTURA					
❏ 1691	I Was a Fool/Teenage Josephine	1959	150.00	300.00	600.00
HAWK					
❏ 107/8	Surf Everybody/Everybody Bird	1963	10.00	20.00	40.00

GOLDENROD
Albums

Number	Title (A Side/B Side)	Yr	VG	VG+	NM
CHARTMAKER					
❏ CSG-1101	Goldenrod	1968	50.00	100.00	200.00

GOLDENRODS, THE
45s

Number	Title (A Side/B Side)	Yr	VG	VG+	NM
VEE JAY					
❏ 307	Wish I Was Back in School/Color Cartoons	1959	62.50	125.00	250.00

GOLDIE, DAN
45s

Number	Title (A Side/B Side)	Yr	VG	VG+	NM
TEARDROP					
❏ 3070	Take Our Last Walk Tonight/Walking the Streets	1966	6.25	12.50	25.00
—The Sir Douglas Quintet is the backing band					

GOLDSBORO, BOBBY
45s

Number	Title (A Side/B Side)	Yr	VG	VG+	NM
BUENA VISTA					
❏ 561	These Are the Best Times/(B-side unknown)	1979	—	2.50	5.00
CURB					
❏ 02117	Love Ain't Never Hurt Nobody/Wings of an Angel	1981	—	2.00	4.00
❏ 02583	The Round-Up Saloon/Green-Eyed Woman, Nashville Blues	1981	—	2.00	4.00
❏ 02726	Lucy and the Stranger/Outrun the Sun	1982	—	2.00	4.00
❏ 5400	Goodbye Marie/Love Has Made a Woman Out of You	1980	—	2.00	4.00
❏ 70052	Alice Doesn't Love Here Anymore/Green-Eyed Woman, Nashville Blues	1981	—	2.00	4.00
EPIC					
❏ 50342	Me and the Elephants/I Love Music	1977	—	2.00	4.00
❏ 50413	The Cowboy and the Lady/Me and Millie	1977	—	2.00	4.00
❏ 50480	He'll Have to Go/Too Hot to Handle	1977	—	2.00	4.00
❏ 50535	Life Gets Hard on Easy Street/Black Fool's Gold	1978	—	2.00	4.00
LAURIE					
❏ 3130	Lonely Traveler/You Better Go Home	1962	3.75	7.50	15.00
❏ 3148	Molly/Honey Baby	1962	3.75	7.50	15.00
❏ 3159	The Letter/The Runaround	1963	3.75	7.50	15.00
❏ 3168	Light the Candles/That's What Love Will Do	1963	3.75	7.50	15.00
UNITED ARTISTS					
❏ 0044	See the Funny Little Clown/Little Things	1973	—	2.00	4.00
❏ 0045	It's Too Late/Voodoo Woman	1973	—	2.00	4.00
❏ 0046	Honey/Autumn of My Life	1973	—	2.00	4.00
❏ 0047	Watching Scotty Grow/I'm a Drifter	1973	—	2.00	4.00
—0044 through 0047 are "Silver Spotlight Series" reissues					

Number	Title (A Side/B Side)	Yr	VG	VG+	NM
❏ XW251	Summer (The First Time)/Childhood 1949	1973	—	2.50	5.00
❏ XW251 [PS]	Summer (The First Time)/Childhood 1949	1973	—	3.00	6.00
❏ XW371	Marlena/Sing Me a Smile	1973	—	2.50	5.00
❏ XW422	I Believe the South Is Gonna Rise Again/She	1974	—	2.00	4.00
❏ XW451	And Then There Was Gina/Quicksand	1974	—	2.00	4.00
❏ XW517	Summer (The First Time)/Marlena	1974	—	2.00	4.00
—Reissue					
❏ XW529	Hello Summertime/And Then There Was Gina	1974	—	2.00	4.00
❏ XW633	And Then There Was Gina/You Pull Me Down (Into Sweet, Sweet Love)	1975	—	2.00	4.00
❏ 672	See the Funny Little Clown/Hello Loser	1963	2.50	5.00	10.00
❏ XW681	I Wrote a Song (Sing Along)/You Pull Me Down (Into Sweet, Sweet Love)	1975	—	2.00	4.00
❏ 710	Whenever He Holds You/If She Was Mine	1964	2.00	4.00	8.00
❏ 710 [PS]	Whenever He Holds You/If She Was Mine	1964	3.75	7.50	15.00
❏ 742	Me Japanese Boy, I Love You/Everyone But Me	1964	2.00	4.00	8.00
❏ 781	I Don't Know You Anymore/Little Drops of Water	1964	2.00	4.00	8.00
❏ XW793	A Butterfly for Bucky/Another Night Alone	1976	—	2.00	4.00
❏ 810	Little Things/I Can't Go On Pretending	1965	2.50	5.00	10.00
❏ 862	Voodoo Woman/It Breaks My Heart	1965	2.00	4.00	8.00
❏ XW866	She Taught Me How to Live Again/Reunion	1976	—	2.00	4.00
❏ 908	If You Wait for Love/If You've Got a Heart	1965	2.00	4.00	8.00
❏ 952	Broomstick Cowboy/Ain't Got Time for Happy	1965	2.00	4.00	8.00
❏ 980	It's Too Late/I'm Goin' Home	1966	2.00	4.00	8.00
❏ 50018	I Know You Better Than That/When Your Love Has Gone	1966	2.00	4.00	8.00
❏ 50018 [PS]	I Know You Better Than That/When Your Love Has Gone	1966	3.75	7.50	15.00
❏ 50044	Longer Than Forever/Take Your Love	1966	2.00	2.00	8.00
❏ 50056	It Hurts Me/Pity the Fool	1966	2.00	2.00	8.00
❏ 50087	Blue Autumn/I Just Don't Love You Anymore	1966	2.00	2.00	8.00
❏ 50138	Love Is/Goodbye to All You Women	1967	2.00	4.00	8.00
❏ 50186	Three in the Morning/Trusty Little Herbert	1967	2.00	4.00	8.00
❏ 50224	Pledge of Love/Jo-Jo's Place	1967	2.00	2.00	8.00
❏ 50283	Honey/Danny	1968	2.00	4.00	8.00
—Orange and pink label					
❏ 50283	Honey/Danny	1968	2.50	5.00	10.00
—Black label					
❏ 50318	Autumn of My Life/She Chased Me	1968	—	3.00	6.00
❏ 50318 [PS]	Autumn of My Life/She Chased Me	1968	3.75	7.50	15.00
❏ 50321	Autumn of My Life/She Chased Me	1968	—	—	—
—Unreleased; these were edits of the versions on UA 50318					
❏ 50461	The Straight Life/Tomorrow Is Forgotten	1968	—	3.00	6.00
❏ 50470	A Christmas Wish/Look Around You (It's Christmas Time)	1968	2.50	5.00	10.00
❏ 50497	Glad She's a Woman/Letter to Emily	1969	—	3.00	6.00
❏ 50525	I'm a Drifter/Hobos and Kings	1969	—	3.00	6.00
❏ 50565	Muddy Mississippi Line/A Richer Man Than I	1969	—	3.00	6.00
❏ 50614	Mornin' Mornin'/Requiem	1969	—	3.00	6.00
❏ 50650	Can You Feel It/Time Good, Time Bad	1970	—	2.50	5.00
❏ 50696	Down on the Bayou/It's Gonna Change	1970	—	2.50	5.00
❏ 50715	My God and I/The World Beyond	1970	—	2.50	5.00
❏ 50727	Watching Scotty Grow/Water Color Days	1970	—	2.50	5.00
❏ 50776	And I Love You So/Gentle of a Man	1971	—	2.50	5.00
❏ 50807	I'll Remember You/Come Back Home	1971	—	2.50	5.00
❏ 50846	Poem for the Little Lady/Danny Is a Mirror to Me	1971	—	2.50	5.00
❏ 50891	California Wine/To Be with You	1972	—	2.50	5.00
❏ 50938	With Pen in Hand/Southern Fried Singin' Sunday Mornin'	1972	—	2.50	5.00
❏ 51107	Country Feelin's/Brand New Kind of Love	1973	—	2.50	5.00
Albums					
CURB					
❏ JZ 36822	Bobby Goldsboro	1980	3.00	6.00	12.00
❏ FZ 37734	Round-Up Saloon	1982	2.50	5.00	10.00
EPIC					
❏ PE 34703	Goldsboro	1977	3.00	6.00	12.00
LIBERTY					
❏ LMAS-5502	Bobby Goldsboro's Greatest Hits	1981	2.00	4.00	8.00
—Reissue of United Artists 5502					
❏ LN-10007	Bobby Goldsboro's 10th Anniversary Album, Volume 1	1981	2.00	4.00	8.00
❏ LN-10047	Bobby Goldsboro's 10th Anniversary Album, Volume 2	1981	2.00	4.00	8.00
❏ LN-10114	The Best of Bobby Goldsboro	1981	2.00	4.00	8.00
SUNSET					
❏ SUS-5236	This Is Bobby Goldsboro	1969	3.00	6.00	12.00
❏ SUS-5284	Pledge of Love	1970	3.00	6.00	12.00
❏ SUS-5313	Autumn of My Life	1971	3.00	6.00	12.00
UNITED ARTISTS					
❏ UA-LA019-F	Brand New Kind of Love	1972	3.75	7.50	15.00
❏ SP-58 [DJ]	The Bobby Goldsboro Family Album	1971	12.50	25.00	50.00
—Promo-only compilation					
❏ UA-LA124-F	Summer (The First Time)	1973	3.75	7.50	15.00
❏ UA-LA311-H2 [(2)]	Bobby Goldsboro's 10th Anniversary Album	1974	5.00	10.00	20.00
❏ UA-LA424-G	Through the Eyes of a Man	1975	3.00	6.00	12.00
❏ UA-LA639-G	Butterfly for Bucky	1976	3.00	6.00	12.00
❏ UAL 3358 [M]	The Bobby Goldsbob Album	1964	5.00	10.00	20.00
❏ UAL 3381 [M]	I Can't Stop Loving You	1964	5.00	10.00	20.00
❏ UAL 3425 [M]	Little Things	1965	5.00	10.00	20.00
❏ UAL 3471 [M]	Broomstick Cowboy	1966	5.00	10.00	20.00
❏ UAL 3486 [M]	It's Too Late	1966	5.00	10.00	20.00
❏ UAL 3552 [M]	Blue Autumn	1967	5.00	10.00	20.00
❏ UAL 3561 [M]	Solid Goldsboro/Bobby Goldsboro's Greatest Hits	1967	5.00	10.00	20.00
❏ UAL 3599 [M]	Romantic, Soulful, Wacky	1967	5.00	10.00	20.00
❏ UAL 3642 [M]	Honey	1968	10.00	20.00	40.00
—Some, if not all, copies of this have the title "Pledge of Love" on the label					
❏ UAS 5502	Bobby Goldsboro's Greatest Hits	1970	5.00	10.00	20.00
❏ UAS 5516	Come Back Home	1971	3.75	7.50	15.00
❏ UAS-5578	California Wine	1972	3.75	7.50	15.00
❏ UAS 6358 [S]	I Can't Stop Loving You	1964	6.25	12.50	25.00
❏ UAS 6358 [S]	The Bobby Goldsbob Album	1964	6.25	12.50	25.00
❏ UAS 6425 [S]	Little Things	1965	6.25	12.50	25.00
❏ UAS 6471 [S]	Broomstick Cowboy	1966	6.25	12.50	25.00
❏ UAS 6486 [S]	It's Too Late	1966	6.25	12.50	25.00
❏ UAS 6552 [S]	Blue Autumn	1967	6.25	12.50	25.00

Number	Title (A Side/B Side)	Yr	VG	VG+	NM
❏ UAS 6561 [S]	Sold Goldsboro/				
	Bobby Goldsboro's Greatest Hits	1967	5.00	10.00	20.00
❏ UAS 6599 [S]	Romantic, Soulful, Wacky	1967	5.00	10.00	20.00
❏ UAS 6642 [S]	Honey	1968	5.00	10.00	20.00
❏ UAS 6657	Word Pictures Featuring Autumn of My Life	1968	5.00	10.00	20.00
❏ UAS 6704	Today	1969	5.00	10.00	20.00
❏ UAS 6735	Muddy Mississippi Line	1969	5.00	10.00	20.00
❏ UAS 6777	We Gotta Start Lovin'	1970	5.00	10.00	20.00
❏ UAS 6777	Watching Scotty Grow	1971	3.75	7.50	15.00
—Retitled version of above					
❏ ST-91460	Honey	1968	6.25	12.50	25.00
—Capitol Record Club edition					
❏ SKAO-91543	Word Pictures Featuring Autumn of My Life	1968	6.25	12.50	25.00
—Capitol Record Club edition					

GOLDTONES, THE Two different groups?
45s
A&R

❏ 714	Strike/Gutterball	1963	7.50	15.00	30.00
❏ 714 [PS]	Strike/Gutterball	1963	12.50	25.00	50.00
Albums					
LABREA					
❏ L-8011 [M]	The Goldtones	1961	10.00	20.00	40.00
❏ LS-8011 [S]	The Goldtones	1961	12.50	25.00	50.00

GOLLIWOGS, THE Early CREEDENCE CLEARWATER REVIVAL. Also see TOMMY FOGERTY AND THE BLUE VELVETS.
45s
FANTASY

❏ 590	Don't Tell Me No Lies/Little Girl, Does Your Mama Know	1964	15.00	30.00	60.00
❏ 597	Where You Been/You Came Walking	1965	15.00	30.00	60.00
❏ 599	You Got Nothin' on Me/You Can't Be True	1965	12.50	25.00	50.00
SCORPIO					
❏ 404	Brown Eyed Girl/You Better Be Careful	1967	12.50	25.00	50.00
❏ 405	Fragile Child/Fight Fire	1967	12.50	25.00	50.00
❏ 408	Walking on the Water/You Better Get It Before It Gets You	1967	12.50	25.00	50.00
❏ 412 [DJ]	Porterville/Call It Pretending	1968	15.00	30.00	60.00
—Only promos credit the Golliwogs; all known stock copies credit Creedence Clearwater Revival.					
Albums					
FANTASY					
❏ F-9474	Pre-Creedence	1975	7.50	15.00	30.00
—Reissue of Fantasy and Scorpio sides					

GONE ALL STARS
45s
GONE

❏ 5016	7-11/Down Yonder Rock	1957	6.25	12.50	25.00

GONKS, THE
45s
LONDON

❏ 9696	The Gonk Song/Take Care	1964	3.00	6.00	12.00

GONN
45s
EMIR

❏ SS-9217-01	Blackout of Gretley/Pain in My Heart	1966	200.00	400.00	800.00
EMIR/MCCM					
❏ 88-9217	Blackout of Gretley/Pain in My Heart	1988	—	2.50	5.00
—Black vinyl					
❏ 88-9217	Blackout of Gretley/Pain in My Heart	1988	3.75	7.50	15.00
—Red vinyl					
❏ 88-9217 [PS]	Blackout of Gretley/Pain in My Heart	1988	2.50	5.00	10.00
MERRY JAINE					
❏ IT-2316	Come with Me (To the Stars)/You're Looking Fine	1967	25.00	50.00	100.00

GONZALES, FRANK
45s
F-G

❏ 1001	Sweet Surfing Little Girl/Let's Make Up	1961	62.50	125.00	250.00

GONZALES, NITOY
Albums
CAPITOL

❏ ST 10305 [S]	Christmas in the Philippines	196?	3.75	7.50	15.00
❏ T 10305 [M]	Christmas in the Philippines	196?	3.00	6.00	12.00

GOOBERS, THE
45s
SURF

❏ 1001	Hawaiian Holiday/Buyer Beware	1963	12.50	25.00	50.00

GOOD, TOMMY
45s
GORDY

❏ 7034	Baby I Miss You/Leaving Here	1964	10.00	20.00	40.00

GOOD AND PLENTY
45s
SENATE

❏ 2105	Living in a World of Make Believe/I Played My Part Well	1967	2.50	5.00	10.00
❏ 2106	Sunny and Me/Children Dreamin'	1967	2.50	5.00	10.00
Albums					
SENATE					
❏ LP-21001 [M]	The World of Good and Plenty	1967	7.50	15.00	30.00
❏ LPS-21001 [S]	The World of Good and Plenty	1967	7.50	15.00	30.00

GOOD GUYS, THE
45s
GNP CRESCENDO

❏ 326	Asphalt Wipe Out/Scratch	1964	5.00	10.00	20.00

Number	Title (A Side/B Side)	Yr	VG	VG+	NM
Albums					
GNP CRESCENDO					
❏ GNP-2001 [M]	Sidewalk Surfing	1964	7.50	15.00	30.00
❏ GNPS-2001 [S]	Sidewalk Surfing	1964	10.00	20.00	40.00
UNITED ARTISTS					
❏ UAL-3370 [M]	The Good Guys Sing	1964	3.75	7.50	15.00
❏ UAS-6370 [S]	The Good Guys Sing	1964	5.00	10.00	20.00

GOOD RATS, THE
45s
KAPP

❏ 946	The Hobo/Truth Is Gone	1968	3.00	6.00	12.00
PASSPORT					
❏ 7912	Just Found a Lady/Coo Coo Coo Blues	1978	—	2.50	5.00
Albums					
KAPP					
❏ KS-3580	The Good Rats	1969	10.00	20.00	40.00
PASSPORT					
❏ SP-20 [DJ]	Rats the Way You Like It (Live)	1978	15.00	30.00	60.00
❏ PB-9825	From Rats to Riches	1978	3.00	6.00	12.00
❏ PB-9830	Birth Comes to Us All	1978	3.00	6.00	12.00
RAT CITY					
❏ 998 [(2)]	Live at Last	1979	3.75	7.50	15.00
❏ RCR-8001	Rat City in Blue	1975	5.00	10.00	20.00
❏ RCR-8002	Tasty	1978	3.00	6.00	12.00
❏ RCR-8003	Great American Music	1981	3.00	6.00	12.00
WARNER BROS.					
❏ BS 2813	Tasty	1974	7.50	15.00	30.00

GOOD ROCKIN' SAM
45s
EXCELLO

❏ 2059	Baby I'm Fool Proof/Thing-a-Ma-Jig	1955	12.50	25.00	50.00

GOOD TIMES, THE
45s
KAMA SUTRA

❏ 215	That's When Your Heartaches Begin/Good Life	1966	2.00	4.00	8.00
❏ 247	You Got the Fever/Mr. & Mrs. Arthur Thompson Request (Your Presence at the Marriage of Their Daughter Lorna Beth)	1968	2.00	4.00	8.00
Albums					
KAMA SUTRA					
❏ KLP-8052 [M]	The Good Times	1966	3.75	7.50	15.00
❏ KSLP-8052 [S]	The Good Times	1966	5.00	10.00	20.00

GOODEES, THE
45s
HIP

❏ 109	For a Little While/Would You, Could You	1968	2.00	4.00	8.00
❏ 8005	Condition Red/Didn't Know Love Was So Good	1968	2.50	5.00	10.00
❏ 8010	Jilted/Love Is Here	1969	2.00	4.00	8.00
❏ 8016	He's a Rebel/Goodies	1969	2.00	4.00	8.00
Albums					
HIP					
❏ HIS-7002	Candy Coated Goodees	1969	7.50	15.00	30.00

GOODIES, THE
45s
20TH CENTURY

❏ 2189	The Funky Gibbon/The Inbetweenies	1975	—	3.50	7.00

GOODMAN, BENNY
45s
CAPITOL

❏ F828	Spin a Record/Little Girl Don't Cry	1950	5.00	10.00	20.00
❏ F860	It Isn't Fair/You're Always There	1950	5.00	10.00	20.00
❏ F1646	Chicago/Back in Your Own Backyard	1951	3.00	6.00	12.00
—Reissue					
❏ F3043	Let's Dance/Jumpin' at the Woodside	1954	3.00	6.00	12.00
❏ F3331	Goody Goody/Sometimes I'm Happy	1956	3.00	6.00	12.00
CHESS					
❏ 1742	Mission to Moscow/You Do Something to Me	1959	2.50	5.00	10.00
COLUMBIA					
❏ 1-889	Oh Babe/Walkin' with the Blues	1950	7.50	15.00	30.00
—Microgroove 33 1/3 rpm 7-inch small hole single					
❏ 6-889	Oh Babe/Walkin' with the Blues	1950	6.25	12.50	25.00
❏ 39121	Lullaby of the Leaves/Temptation Rag	1950	5.00	10.00	20.00
❏ 3-39121	Lullaby of the Leaves/Temptation Rag	1950	7.50	15.00	30.00
—Microgroove 7-inch, 33 1/3 rpm, small hole single					
❏ 39277	Don't Be That Way/The Man I Love	1951	3.00	6.00	12.00
❏ 39278	One O'Clock Jump/Avalon	1951	3.00	6.00	12.00
❏ 39279	One O'Clock Jump/Body and Soul	1951	3.00	6.00	12.00
❏ 39280	Dixieland One Step/Jam Session	1951	3.00	6.00	12.00
❏ 39281	Shine/Blue Reverie	1951	3.00	6.00	12.00
❏ 39282	Life Goes to a Party (Beginning)/Life Goes to a Party (Conclusion)	1951	3.00	6.00	12.00
❏ 39284	Blue Skies/Sing, Sing, Sing (Conclusion)	1951	3.00	6.00	12.00
❏ 39285	Loch Lomond/Sing, Sing, Sing (Beginning)	1951	3.00	6.00	12.00
❏ 39286	Swingtime in the Rockies/Dizzy Spells (Conclusion)	1951	3.00	6.00	12.00
❏ 39287	Bei Mir Bist Du Schoen/Stompin' at the Savoy (Conclusion)-Dizzy Spells (Beginning)	1951	3.00	6.00	12.00
❏ 39288	China Boy/Stompin' at the Savoy	1951	3.00	6.00	12.00
❏ 39304	Don't Be That Way/Sing, Sing, Sing (Conclusion)	1951	3.00	6.00	12.00
❏ 39305	One O'Clock Jump (Beginning)/Sing, Sing, Sing (Continuation)	1951	3.00	6.00	12.00
❏ 39306	One O'Clock Jump (Conclusion)/Sing, Sing, Sing (Beginning)	1951	3.00	6.00	12.00
❏ 39307	Dixieland One Step-I'm Coming Virginia-When My Baby Smiles at Me/Dizzy Spells (Conclusion)-Big John's Special	1951	3.00	6.00	12.00
❏ 39308	Shine-Blue Reverie/Stompin' at the Savoy (Conclusion)-Dizzy Spells (Beginning)	1951	3.00	6.00	12.00

G

Number	Title (A Side/B Side)	Yr	VG	VG+	NM
❏ 39309	Life Goes to a Parrty/Stompin' at the Savoy (Beginning)	1951	3.00	6.00	12.00
❏ 39310	Jam Session (Beginning)/China Boy	1951	3.00	6.00	12.00
❏ 39311	Jam Session (Continuation)/ Bei Mir Bist Du Schoen	1951	3.00	6.00	12.00
❏ 39312	Blue Moon/Swingtime in the Rockies	1951	3.00	6.00	12.00
❏ 39313	Body and Soul/Loch Lomond	1951	3.00	6.00	12.00
❏ 39314	Avalon/Blue Skies	1951	3.00	6.00	12.00
❏ 39315	The Man I Love/I Got Rhythm	1951	3.00	6.00	12.00
❏ 39416	South of the Border/Down South CampMeeting'	1951	3.75	7.50	15.00
❏ 39478	The Wang-Wang Blues/ It Never Entered My Mind	1951	3.75	7.50	15.00
❏ 39564	Farewell Blues/King Porter Stomp	1951	3.75	7.50	15.00
❏ 39741	Jersey Bounce/You'll Never Walk Alone	1952	5.00	10.00	20.00

—B-side by Frank Sinatra

Number	Title (A Side/B Side)	Yr	VG	VG+	NM
❏ 39976	I'll Never Say "Never Again" Again/What a Little Moonlight Can Do	1952	3.75	7.50	15.00
❏ 40616	Memories of You/It's Bad for Me	1955	3.00	6.00	12.00

—With Rosemary Clooney

Number	Title (A Side/B Side)	Yr	VG	VG+	NM
❏ 40625	A Fine Romance/Goodbye	1955	3.00	6.00	12.00

—With Rosemary Clooney

COMMAND

Number	Title (A Side/B Side)	Yr	VG	VG+	NM
❏ 4104	Peace/Hava Nagila	1967	—	3.00	6.00
❏ 4108	Mimi/Petite Fleur	1967	—	3.00	6.00

DECCA

Number	Title (A Side/B Side)	Yr	VG	VG+	NM
❏ 25548	Don't Be That Way/Jersey Bounce	1962	2.50	5.00	10.00

RCA VICTOR

Number	Title (A Side/B Side)	Yr	VG	VG+	NM
❏ 27-0117	After You've Gone/Someday Sweetheart	195?	3.75	7.50	15.00
❏ 27-0118	Body and Soul/Nobody's Sweetheart	195?	3.75	7.50	15.00
❏ 27-0119	Oh Lady Be Good/Tiger Rag	195?	3.75	7.50	15.00

—The above three records comprise box set WPT 26, "Benny Goodman Trio"

Number	Title (A Side/B Side)	Yr	VG	VG+	NM
❏ 47-2953	Don't Be That Way/My Melancholy Baby	1949	3.75	7.50	15.00
❏ 47-2954	Tiger Rag/Alexander's Ragtime Band	1949	3.75	7.50	15.00
❏ 47-2973	Jingle Bells/Santa Claus Is Coming to Town	1949	5.00	10.00	20.00
❏ WPT 26 [PS]	Benny Goodman Trio	195?	3.75	7.50	15.00

—Empty box for 27-0117, 27-0118 and 27-0119 with inserts

7-Inch Extended Plays

CAPITOL

Number	Title (A Side/B Side)	Yr	VG	VG+	NM
❏ EAP 1-409	(contents unknown)	195?	3.00	6.00	12.00
❏ EAP 1-409 [PS]	The Benny Goodman Band, Part 1	195?	3.00	6.00	12.00
❏ EAP 2-409	Chicago/Whistle Blues//Tattletale/Muskrat Ramble	195?	3.00	6.00	12.00
❏ EAP 2-409 [PS]	The Benny Goodman Band, Part 2	195?	3.00	6.00	12.00
❏ EAP 1-479	(contents unknown)	1954	3.75	7.50	15.00
❏ EAP 1-479	Classics in Jazz, Part 1	1954	3.75	7.50	15.00
❏ EAP 1-479	Classics in Jazz, Part 2	1954	3.75	7.50	15.00
❏ EAP 2-479	Love Is Just Around the Corner/I'll Never Be the Same//Cherokee/Music, Maestro, Please	1954	3.75	7.50	15.00
❏ EAP 1-519	All the Cats Join In//After You've Gone/There'll Be Some Changes Made	195?	3.00	6.00	12.00
❏ EAP 1-519 [PS]	2 for the Record	195?	3.00	6.00	12.00

COLUMBIA

Number	Title (A Side/B Side)	Yr	VG	VG+	NM
❏ B-2523	*Jersey Bounce/A String of Pearls/Six Flats Unfurnished/The World Is Waiting for the Sunrise	195?	3.75	7.50	15.00
❏ B-2523 [PS]	Benny Goodman and His Orchestra (Hall of Fame Series)	195?	3.75	7.50	15.00
❏ B-2556	On the Sunny Side of the Street/Where or When/ /Blues in the Night/The Way You Look Tonight	195?	3.75	7.50	15.00
❏ B-2556 [PS]	Benny Goodman Sextet with Peggy Lee	195?	3.75	7.50	15.00
❏ B-2587	Why Don't You Do It Right/Flying Home// Someday Sweetheart/Down South Camp Meeting	195?	3.00	6.00	12.00
❏ B-2587 [PS]	Benny Goodman (Hall of Fame Series)	195?	3.00	6.00	12.00
❏ B-8201	Sing Sing Sing (With a Swing) (Beginning)/Sing Sing Sing (With a Swing) (Conclusion)	195?	3.75	7.50	15.00
❏ ZTEP 27372/3	Swing Into Spring/Blue Skies//Have You Met Miss Jones/Swingtime in the Rockies	1956	3.75	7.50	15.00

—Purple label; has Texaco star at right and "Prepared Expressly for Texaco" at left

Number	Title (A Side/B Side)	Yr	VG	VG+	NM
❏ ZTEP 27372/3 [PS]	Swing Into Spring	1956	5.00	10.00	20.00

—Texaco premium

RCA VICTOR

Number	Title (A Side/B Side)	Yr	VG	VG+	NM
❏ 947-0134	Swingtime in the Rockies/Sugarfoot Stomp// Changes/Big John Special	1954	3.75	7.50	15.00

—Record 1 of 2-EP set EPBT 3056

Number	Title (A Side/B Side)	Yr	VG	VG+	NM
❏ 947-0135	Camel Hop/Riffin' at the Ritz//Wrappin' It Up/Life Goes to a Party	1954	3.75	7.50	15.00

—Record 2 of 2-EP set EPBT 3056

Number	Title (A Side/B Side)	Yr	VG	VG+	NM
❏ EPBT 3056 [PS]	This Is Benny Goodman	1954	3.75	7.50	15.00

—Two-pocket jacket for 2-EP set (947-0134 and 947-0135)

Albums

ABC

Number	Title (A Side/B Side)	Yr	VG	VG+	NM
❏ AC-30014	The ABC Collection	1976	3.00	6.00	12.00

AIRCHECK

Number	Title (A Side/B Side)	Yr	VG	VG+	NM
❏ 16	Benny Goodman and His Orchestra	197?	3.00	6.00	12.00
❏ 16	Benny Goodman and His Orchestra On the Air, Vol. 1	1986	2.50	5.00	10.00

—Reissue of above with revised title

Number	Title (A Side/B Side)	Yr	VG	VG+	NM
❏ 32	Benny Goodman and His Orchestra On the Air, Vol. 2	1986	2.50	5.00	10.00
❏ 34	Benny Goodman and His Orchestra On the Air, Vol. 3	1986	2.50	5.00	10.00

BIOGRAPH

Number	Title (A Side/B Side)	Yr	VG	VG+	NM
❏ C-1	Great Soloists 1929-33	1972	2.50	5.00	10.00

BLUEBIRD

Number	Title (A Side/B Side)	Yr	VG	VG+	NM
❏ AXM2-5505 [(2)]	The Complete Benny Goodman, Vol. 1 (1935)	197?	3.00	6.00	12.00
❏ AXM2-5515 [(2)]	The Complete Benny Goodman, Vol. 2 (1935-36)	197?	3.00	6.00	12.00
❏ AXM2-5532 [(2)]	The Complete Benny Goodman, Vol. 3 (1936)	197?	3.00	6.00	12.00
❏ AXM2-5537 [(2)]	The Complete Benny Goodman, Vol. 4 (1936-37)	197?	3.00	6.00	12.00
❏ AXM2-5557 [(2)]	The Complete Benny Goodman, Vol. 5 (1937-38)	197?	3.00	6.00	12.00
❏ AXM2-5566 [(2)]	The Complete Benny Goodman, Vol. 6 (1938)	197?	3.00	6.00	12.00
❏ AXM2-5567 [(2)]	The Complete Benny Goodman, Vol. 7 (1938-39)	197?	3.00	6.00	12.00
❏ AXM2-5568 [(2)]	The Complete Benny Goodman, Vol. 8 (1936-39)	197?	3.00	6.00	12.00

BRUNSWICK

Number	Title (A Side/B Side)	Yr	VG	VG+	NM
❏ BL 54010 [M]	Benny Goodman 1927-34	1954	7.50	15.00	30.00
❏ BL 58015 [10]	Chicago Jazz Classics	1950	12.50	25.00	50.00

CAPITOL

Number	Title (A Side/B Side)	Yr	VG	VG+	NM
❏ H 202 [10]	Session for Six	1950	12.50	25.00	50.00
❏ H 295 [10]	Easy Does It	1952	12.50	25.00	50.00
❏ H 343 [10]	The Benny Goodman Trio	1952	12.50	25.00	50.00
❏ T 395 [M]	Session for Six	1953	10.00	20.00	40.00

—Turquoise label

Number	Title (A Side/B Side)	Yr	VG	VG+	NM
❏ T 395 [M]	Session for Six	1958	5.00	10.00	20.00

—Black label with colorband, Capitol logo on left

Number	Title (A Side/B Side)	Yr	VG	VG+	NM
❏ H 409 [10]	The Benny Goodman Band	1953	12.50	25.00	50.00
❏ T 409 [M]	The Benny Goodman Band	1953	10.00	20.00	40.00

—Turquoise label

Number	Title (A Side/B Side)	Yr	VG	VG+	NM
❏ T 409 [M]	The Benny Goodman Band	1958	5.00	10.00	20.00

—Black label with colorband, Capitol logo on left

Number	Title (A Side/B Side)	Yr	VG	VG+	NM
❏ H 441 [10]	The Goodman Touch	1953	12.50	25.00	50.00
❏ T 441 [M]	The Goodman Touch	1953	10.00	20.00	40.00

—Turquoise label

Number	Title (A Side/B Side)	Yr	VG	VG+	NM
❏ T 441 [M]	The Goodman Touch	1958	5.00	10.00	20.00

—Black label with colorband, Capitol logo on left

Number	Title (A Side/B Side)	Yr	VG	VG+	NM
❏ H 479 [10]	Small Combo 1947	1954	12.50	25.00	50.00
❏ H1-565 [10]	B.G. in Hi-Fi (Volume 1)	1955	7.50	15.00	30.00
❏ H2-565 [10]	B.G. in Hi-Fi (Volume 2)	1955	7.50	15.00	30.00
❏ W 565 [M]	B.G. in Hi-Fi	1955	10.00	20.00	40.00

—Gray label

Number	Title (A Side/B Side)	Yr	VG	VG+	NM
❏ W 565 [M]	B.G. in Hi-Fi	1958	5.00	10.00	20.00

—Black label with colorband, Capitol logo on left

Number	Title (A Side/B Side)	Yr	VG	VG+	NM
❏ T 668 [M]	Mostly Sextets	1956	7.50	15.00	30.00

—Turquoise label

Number	Title (A Side/B Side)	Yr	VG	VG+	NM
❏ T 668 [M]	Mostly Sextets	1958	5.00	10.00	20.00

—Black label with colorband, Capitol logo on left

Number	Title (A Side/B Side)	Yr	VG	VG+	NM
❏ T 669 [M]	Benny Goodman Combos	1956	7.50	15.00	30.00

—Turquoise label

Number	Title (A Side/B Side)	Yr	VG	VG+	NM
❏ T 669 [M]	Benny Goodman Combos	1958	5.00	10.00	20.00

—Black label with colorband, Capitol logo on left

Number	Title (A Side/B Side)	Yr	VG	VG+	NM
❏ S 706 [M]	Selections Featured in "The Benny Goodman Story"	1956	7.50	15.00	30.00

—Turquoise label

Number	Title (A Side/B Side)	Yr	VG	VG+	NM
❏ S 706 [M]	Selections Featured in "The Benny Goodman Story"	1958	5.00	10.00	20.00

—Black label with colorband, Capitol logo on left

Number	Title (A Side/B Side)	Yr	VG	VG+	NM
❏ SM-706	Selections Featured in "The Benny Goodman Story"	197?	2.50	5.00	10.00

—Reissue of S 706

Number	Title (A Side/B Side)	Yr	VG	VG+	NM
❏ DT 1514 [R]	The Hits of Benny Goodman	1961	3.00	6.00	12.00
❏ SM-1514	The Hits of Benny Goodman	197?	2.50	5.00	10.00

—Reissue of DT 1514

Number	Title (A Side/B Side)	Yr	VG	VG+	NM
❏ T 1514 [M]	The Hits of Benny Goodman	1961	5.00	10.00	20.00

—Black label with colorband, Capitol logo on left

Number	Title (A Side/B Side)	Yr	VG	VG+	NM
❏ T 1514 [M]	The Hits of Benny Goodman	1963	3.75	7.50	15.00

—Black label with colorband, Capitol logo on top

Number	Title (A Side/B Side)	Yr	VG	VG+	NM
❏ ST 2157 [S]	Hello Benny!	1964	3.75	7.50	15.00
❏ T 2157 [M]	Hello Benny!	1964	3.00	6.00	12.00
❏ ST 2282 [S]	Made in Japan	1965	3.75	7.50	15.00
❏ T 2282 [M]	Made in Japan	1965	3.00	6.00	12.00

CENTURY

Number	Title (A Side/B Side)	Yr	VG	VG+	NM
❏ 1150	The King of Swing Direct to Disc	1979	7.50	15.00	30.00

—Direct-to-disc audiophile recording

CHESS

Number	Title (A Side/B Side)	Yr	VG	VG+	NM
❏ LP-1440 [DJ]	Benny Rides Again	1960	25.00	50.00	100.00

—Multi-color swirl vinyl

Number	Title (A Side/B Side)	Yr	VG	VG+	NM
❏ LP-1440 [M]	Benny Rides Again	1960	12.50	25.00	50.00
❏ LPS-1440 [S]	Benny Rides Again	1960	7.50	15.00	30.00
❏ CH-9161	Benny Rides Again	1984	2.50	5.00	10.00

—Reissue

CLASSICS RECORD LIBRARY

Number	Title (A Side/B Side)	Yr	VG	VG+	NM
❏ RL-7673 [(3)M]	An Album of Swing Classics	1967	12.50	25.00	50.00
❏ SRL-7673 [(3)S]	An Album of Swing Classics	1967	10.00	20.00	40.00

—Above two were compiled for Book-of-the-Month Club

COLUMBIA

Number	Title (A Side/B Side)	Yr	VG	VG+	NM
❏ C2L 16 [(2)M]	Benny in Brussels	195?	10.00	20.00	40.00

—Red and black label with six white "eye" logos

Number	Title (A Side/B Side)	Yr	VG	VG+	NM
❏ GL 102 [10]	Let's Hear the Melody	1950	15.00	30.00	60.00
❏ CL 500 [M]	Combos	1952	10.00	20.00	40.00

—Maroon label with gold print

Number	Title (A Side/B Side)	Yr	VG	VG+	NM
❏ CL 500 [M]	Combos	1955	7.50	15.00	30.00

—Red and black label with six "eye" logos

Number	Title (A Side/B Side)	Yr	VG	VG+	NM
❏ GL 500 [M]	Combos	1951	12.50	25.00	50.00

—Black label, silver print

Number	Title (A Side/B Side)	Yr	VG	VG+	NM
❏ CL 501 [M]	The Golden Era Series Presents Benny Goodman and His Orchestra	1952	10.00	20.00	40.00

—Maroon label with gold print

Number	Title (A Side/B Side)	Yr	VG	VG+	NM
❏ CL 501 [M]	The Golden Era Series Presents Benny Goodman and His Orchestra	1955	7.50	15.00	30.00

—Red and black label with six "eye" logos

Number	Title (A Side/B Side)	Yr	VG	VG+	NM
❏ GL 501 [M]	The Golden Era Series Presents Benny Goodman and His Orchestra	1951	12.50	25.00	50.00

—Black label, silver print

Number	Title (A Side/B Side)	Yr	VG	VG+	NM
❏ CL 516 [M]	The Benny Goodman Trio Plays for the Fletcher Henderson Fund	1953	10.00	20.00	40.00

—Maroon label with gold print

Number	Title (A Side/B Side)	Yr	VG	VG+	NM
❏ CL 516 [M]	The Benny Goodman Trio Plays for the Fletcher Henderson Fund	1955	7.50	15.00	30.00

—Red and black label with six "eye" logos

Number	Title (A Side/B Side)	Yr	VG	VG+	NM
❏ GL 516 [M]	The Benny Goodman Trio Plays for the Fletcher Henderson Fund	1952	12.50	25.00	50.00

—Reissue of Martin Block 1000; black label, silver print

Number	Title (A Side/B Side)	Yr	VG	VG+	NM
❏ CL 523 [M]	Benny Goodman Presents Eddie Sauter Arrangements	1953	10.00	20.00	40.00

—Maroon label with gold print

Number	Title (A Side/B Side)	Yr	VG	VG+	NM
❏ CL 523 [M]	Benny Goodman Presents Eddie Sauter Arrangements	1955	7.50	15.00	30.00

—Red and black label with six "eye" logos

Number	Title (A Side/B Side)	Yr	VG	VG+	NM
GL 523 [M]	Benny Goodman Presents Eddie Sauter Arrangements	1953	12.50	25.00	50.00
—Black label, silver print					
CL 524 [M]	Benny Goodman Presents Fletcher Henderson Arrangements	1953	7.50	15.00	30.00
—Red and black label with six "eye" logos					
CL 524 [M]	Benny Goodman Presents Fletcher Henderson Arrangements	1954	10.00	20.00	40.00
—Maroon label with gold print					
GL 524 [M]	Benny Goodman Presents Fletcher Henderson Arrangements	1953	12.50	25.00	50.00
—Black label, silver print					
CL 534 [M]	Benny Goodman and His Orchestra	1953	10.00	20.00	40.00
—Maroon label with gold print					
CL 534 [M]	Benny Goodman and His Orchestra	1955	7.50	15.00	30.00
—Red and black label with six "eye" logos					
CL 552 [M]	The New Benny Goodman Sextet	1954	10.00	20.00	40.00
—Maroon label with gold print					
CL 552 [M]	The New Benny Goodman Sextet	1955	7.50	15.00	30.00
—Red and black label with six "eye" logos					
CL 652 [M]	The Benny Goodman Sextet and Orchestra with Charlie Christian	1955	7.50	15.00	30.00
—Red and black label with six "eye" logos					
CL 652 [M]	The Benny Goodman Sextet and Orchestra with Charlie Christian	1963	5.00	10.00	20.00
—Red label with "Guaranteed High Fidelity" or "Mono" at bottom					
CL 814 [M]	Carnegie Hall Jazz Concert, Volume 1	1956	7.50	15.00	30.00
—Red and black label with six "eye" logos					
CL 814 [M]	Carnegie Hall Jazz Concert, Volume 1	1963	5.00	10.00	20.00
—Red label with "Guaranteed High Fidelity" or "Mono" at bottom					
CL 815 [M]	Carnegie Hall Jazz Concert, Volume 2	1956	7.50	15.00	30.00
—Red and black label with six "eye" logos					
CL 815 [M]	Carnegie Hall Jazz Concert, Volume 2	1963	5.00	10.00	20.00
—Red label with "Guaranteed High Fidelity" or "Mono" at bottom					
CL 815 [M]	Carnegie Hall Jazz Concert, Volume 2	197?	3.00	6.00	12.00
—Orange label with "Mono" under "CL 815" at left					
CL 816 [M]	Carnegie Hall Jazz Concert, Volume 3	1956	7.50	15.00	30.00
—Red and black label with six "eye" logos					
CL 816 [M]	Carnegie Hall Jazz Concert, Volume 3	1963	5.00	10.00	20.00
—Red label with "Guaranteed High Fidelity" or "Mono" at bottom					
CL 817 [M]	The King of Swing, Volume 1	1956	7.50	15.00	30.00
CL 818 [M]	The King of Swing, Volume 2	1956	7.50	15.00	30.00
CL 819 [M]	The King of Swing, Volume 3	1956	7.50	15.00	30.00
CL 820 [M]	The Great Benny Goodman	1956	7.50	15.00	30.00
—Red and black label with six "eye" logos					
CL 820 [M]	The Great Benny Goodman	1963	5.00	10.00	20.00
—Red label with "Guaranteed High Fidelity" or "Mono" at bottom					
CL 821 [M]	Vintage Goodman	1956	7.50	15.00	30.00
CL 1247 [M]	Benny in Brussels, Vol. I	1958	7.50	15.00	30.00
CL 1248 [M]	Benny in Brussels, Vol. II	1958	7.50	15.00	30.00
CL 1324 [M]	The Happy Session	1959	7.50	15.00	30.00
CL 1579 [M]	Benny Goodman Swings Again	1960	7.50	15.00	30.00
CL 2483 [M]	Benny Goodman's Greatest Hits	1966	3.75	7.50	15.00
CL 2533 [10]	Benny at the Ballroom	1955	10.00	20.00	40.00
—Retitled reissue of 6100					
CL 2564 [10]	The B.G. Six	1955	10.00	20.00	40.00
—Retitled reissue of 6052					
CL 6033 [10]	Benny Goodman and Peggy Lee	1949	20.00	40.00	80.00
CL 6048 [10]	Dance Parade	1949	12.50	25.00	50.00
CL 6052 [10]	Goodman Sextet Session	1949	12.50	25.00	50.00
CL 6100 [10]	Dance Parade, Volume 2	1950	12.50	25.00	50.00
CL 6302 [10]	Let's Hear the Melody	1951	12.50	25.00	50.00
—Reissue of GL 102					
CS 8075 [S]	Benny in Brussels, Vol. I	1959	10.00	20.00	40.00
CS 8076 [S]	Benny in Brussels, Vol. II	1959	10.00	20.00	40.00
CS 8129 [S]	The Happy Session	1959	6.25	12.50	25.00
CS 8379 [S]	Benny Goodman Swings Again	1960	6.25	12.50	25.00
CS 8643 [R]	The Great Benny Goodman	1962	3.00	6.00	12.00
—Red label, "360 Sound Stereo" at bottom					
CS 8643 [R]	The Great Benny Goodman	1970	2.50	5.00	10.00
—Orange label					
PC 8643	The Great Benny Goodman	198?	2.00	4.00	8.00
—Reissue					
CS 9283 [S]	Benny Goodman's Greatest Hits	1966	3.00	6.00	12.00
—"360 Sound Stereo" on label					
PC 9283	Benny Goodman's Greatest Hits	198?	2.00	4.00	8.00
—Reissue					
XTV 28995/6 [M]	Swing Into Spring	1959	5.00	10.00	20.00
—Special item made for Texaco service stations					
KG 31547 [(2)]	The All-Time Greatest Hits of Benny Goodman	1972	3.75	7.50	15.00
PG 31547 [(2)]	The All-Time Greatest Hits of Benny Goodman	197?	3.00	6.00	12.00
—Reissue					
PG 33405 [(2)]	Solid Gold Instrumental Hits	1975	3.00	6.00	12.00
FC 38265	Seven Come Eleven	1983	2.50	5.00	10.00
COLUMBIA JAZZ MASTERPIECES					
CJ 44292	Slipped Disc, 1945-1946	1988	2.50	5.00	10.00
COLUMBIA MASTERWORKS					
OSL 160 [(2)M]	The Famous 1938 Carnegie Hall Jazz Concert	1956	18.75	37.50	75.00
—Gray and black labels with six "eye" logos					
OSL 160 [(2)M]	The Famous 1938 Carnegie Hall Jazz Concert	1963	10.00	20.00	40.00
—Gray labels with "Columbia" at top					
OSL 160 [(2)M]	The Famous 1938 Carnegie Hall Jazz Concert	1970	5.00	10.00	20.00
—Olive labels with "Columbia" circling edge					
SL 160 [(2)M]	The Famous 1938 Carnegie Hall Jazz Concert	1950	25.00	50.00	100.00
—Green labels					
SL 176 [(6)M]	King of Swing	1950	37.50	75.00	150.00
OSL 180 [(2)M]	The King of Swing	1956	18.75	37.50	75.00
—Gray and black labels with six "eye" logos					
OSL 180 [(2)M]	The King of Swing	1963	10.00	20.00	40.00
—Gray labels with "Columbia" at top					
SL 180 [(2)M]	1937-38 Jazz Concert No. 2	1950	18.75	37.50	75.00
ML 4358 [M]	Carnegie Hall Jazz Concert, Volume 1	1950	10.00	20.00	40.00
ML 4359 [M]	Carnegie Hall Jazz Concert, Volume 2	1950	10.00	20.00	40.00
ML 4590 [M]	1937-38 Jazz Concert No. 2, Volume 1	1950	10.00	20.00	40.00
ML 4591 [M]	1937-38 Jazz Concert No. 2, Volume 2	1950	10.00	20.00	40.00
ML 4613 [M]	King of Swing, Volume 1	1950	10.00	20.00	40.00
ML 4614 [M]	King of Swing, Volume 2	1950	10.00	20.00	40.00
ML 6205 [M]	Meeting at the Summit	1961	3.75	7.50	15.00
—With the Columbia Jazz Combo and the Columbia Orchestra					
MS 6805 [S]	Meeting at the Summit	1961	5.00	10.00	20.00
—With the Columbia Jazz Combo and the Columbia Orchestra					
COLUMBIA MUSICAL TREASURY					
P4M 5678 [(4)]	The Best of Benny Goodman	197?	7.50	15.00	30.00
—Issued by Columbia House					
COMMAND					
RS-921	Benny Goodman & Paris: Listen to the Magic	1967	3.75	7.50	15.00
DECCA					
DXB 188 [(2)M]	The Benny Goodman Story	1956	15.00	30.00	60.00
—Black label, silver print					
DXB 188 [(2)M]	The Benny Goodman Story	1961	10.00	20.00	40.00
—Black label with color bars					
DXSB 7188 [(2)R]	The Benny Goodman Story	196?	3.75	7.50	15.00
DL 8252 [M]	The Benny Goodman Story, Volume 1	1956	7.50	15.00	30.00
—Black label, silver print					
DL 8252 [M]	The Benny Goodman Story, Volume 1	1961	5.00	10.00	20.00
—Black label with color bars					
DL 8253 [M]	The Benny Goodman Story, Volume 2	1956	7.50	15.00	30.00
—Black label, silver print					
DL 8253 [M]	The Benny Goodman Story, Volume 2	1961	5.00	10.00	20.00
—Black label with color bars					
DL 78252 [R]	The Benny Goodman Story, Volume 1	1961	2.50	5.00	10.00
DL 78253 [R]	The Benny Goodman Story, Volume 2	1961	2.50	5.00	10.00
DOCTOR JAZZ					
W2X 40350 [(2)]	Airplay	1986	3.00	6.00	12.00
EVEREST ARCHIVE OF FOLK & JAZZ					
277	Benny Goodman	1973	3.00	6.00	12.00
GIANTS OF JAZZ					
1030	The Benny Goodman Caravans — Big Band Broadcasts Vol. 1: Ciribiribin	1983	2.50	5.00	10.00
1033	The Benny Goodman Caravans — Big Band Broadcasts Vol. 2: Swingin' Down the Lane	1985	2.50	5.00	10.00
1034	The Benny Goodman Caravans — The Small Groups, Vol. 1	1985	2.50	5.00	10.00
1036	The Benny Goodman Caravans — Big Band Broadcasts Vol. 3: One O'Clock Jump	1985	2.50	5.00	10.00
1039	The Benny Goodman Caravans — Big Band Broadcasts Vol. 4: Sing, Sing, Sing	1985	2.50	5.00	10.00
HARMONY					
HL 7005 [M]	Peggy Lee Sings with Benny Goodman	1957	5.00	10.00	20.00
HL 7190 [M]	Swing with Benny Goodman in High Fidelity	196?	3.75	7.50	15.00
HL 7225 [M]	Swing Time	196?	3.75	7.50	15.00
HL 7278 [M]	Swingin' Benny Goodman Sextet	196?	3.75	7.50	15.00
HS 11090 [R]	Swing with Benny Goodman in High Fidelity	196?	2.50	5.00	10.00
HS 11271 [R]	Sing, Sing, Sing	1968	2.50	5.00	10.00
INTERMEDIA					
QS-5046	All the Cats Join In	198?	2.50	5.00	10.00
LONDON					
PS 918/9 [(2)]	Live at Carnegie Hall 1978	1979	3.75	7.50	15.00
LONDON PHASE 4					
SPB-21 [(2)]	Benny Goodman Today	1971	3.75	7.50	15.00
SP-44182/83 [(2)]	Benny Goodman On Stage	1972	3.75	7.50	15.00
MARTIN BLOCK					
MB-1000 [M]	The Benny Goodman Trio Plays for the Fletcher Henderson Fund	1951	15.00	30.00	60.00
MCA					
4018 [(2)]	Jazz Holiday	197?	3.00	6.00	12.00
MEGA					
606	Let's Dance Again	1974	2.50	5.00	10.00
—Reissue of 51-5002					
51-5002	Let's Dance Again	1971	3.00	6.00	12.00
MGM					
3E-9 [(3)M]	The Benny Goodman Treasure Chest	1959	37.50	75.00	150.00
E-3788 [M]	Performance Recordings, Volume 1	1959	6.25	12.50	25.00
E-3788 [M]	The Benny Goodman Treasure Chest, Volume 1	198?	2.00	4.00	8.00
—Reissue on blue and gold label					
E-3789 [M]	Performance Recordings, Volume 2	1959	6.25	12.50	25.00
E-3789 [M]	The Benny Goodman Treasure Chest, Volume 2	198?	2.00	4.00	8.00
—Reissue on blue and gold label					
E-3790 [M]	Performance Recordings, Volume 3	1959	6.25	12.50	25.00
E-3790 [M]	The Benny Goodman Treasure Chest, Volume 3	198?	2.00	4.00	8.00
—Reissue on blue and gold label					
E-3810 [M]	The Sound of Music	1960	5.00	10.00	20.00
SE-3810 [S]	The Sound of Music	1960	6.25	12.50	25.00
MOSAIC					
MQ6-148 [(6)]	The Complete Capitol Small Group Recordings of Benny Goodman 1944-1955	199?	25.00	50.00	100.00
MUSICMASTERS					
MM-20112 Z	Let's Dance	1986	2.50	5.00	10.00
—From the PBS TV special of 1985					
PAIR					
PDL2-1014 [(2)]	Original Recordings by Benny Goodman	1986	3.00	6.00	12.00
PDL2-1054 [(2)]	Original Recordings by Benny Goodman, Volume 2	1986	3.00	6.00	12.00
PDL2-1093 [(2)]	Original Recordings by Benny Goodman, Volume 3	1986	3.00	6.00	12.00
PAUSA					
9031	The Benny Goodman Trios (and One Duet)	198?	2.50	5.00	10.00
PICKWICK					
SPC-3270	Let's Dance	197?	2.50	5.00	10.00
SPC-3529	Francaise	197?	2.50	5.00	10.00
PRESTIGE					
PRST-7644	Benny Goodman and the Giants of Swing	1969	3.75	7.50	15.00
RCA CAMDEN					
CAL-624 [M]	Swing, Swing, Swing	1960	3.75	7.50	15.00
CAS-624(e) [R]	Swing, Swing, Swing	1960	2.50	5.00	10.00
CAL-872 [M]	Benny Goodman and His Orchestra Featuring Great Vocalists of Our Times	1965	3.75	7.50	15.00
CAS-872 [S]	Benny Goodman and His Orchestra Featuring Great Vocalists of Our Times	1965	3.00	6.00	12.00
RCA VICTOR					
WPT 12 [10]	Benny Goodman	1951	12.50	25.00	50.00
LPT-17 [10]	A Treasury of Immortal Performances	1951	12.50	25.00	50.00

G

Number	Title (A Side/B Side)	Yr	VG	VG+	NM
❑ WPT 26 [10]	Immortal Performances	1952	12.50	25.00	50.00
❑ LPV-521 [M]	B.G. The Small Groups	1965	3.75	7.50	15.00
❑ ANL1-0973(e)	Pure Gold	1974	2.50	5.00	10.00
—Reissue of LSP-4005(e)					
❑ LPT-1005 [M]	Benny Goodman	1954	10.00	20.00	40.00
❑ LPM-1099 [M]	The Golden Age of Benny Goodman	1956	10.00	20.00	40.00
❑ LPM-1226 [M]	The Benny Goodman Trio/Quartet/Quintet	1956	10.00	20.00	40.00
❑ LPM-1239 [M]	This Is Benny Goodman	1956	10.00	20.00	40.00
❑ LPM-2247 [M]	The Kingdom of Swing	1960	5.00	10.00	20.00
❑ LSP-2247 [S]	The Kingdom of Swing	1960	6.25	12.50	25.00
❑ CPL1-2470	A Legendary Performer	1977	2.50	5.00	10.00
❑ LPM-2698 [M]	Together Again	1964	3.75	7.50	15.00
❑ LSP-2698 [S]	Together Again	1964	5.00	10.00	20.00
❑ LPT-3004 [10]	Benny Goodman Quartet	1952	12.50	25.00	50.00
❑ LPT-3056 [10]	This Is Benny Goodman and His Orchestra	1954	12.50	25.00	50.00
❑ AFL1-4005(e)	The Best of Benny Goodman	1977	2.50	5.00	10.00
—Reissue of LSP-4005					
❑ LSP-4005(e)	The Best of Benny Goodman	1968	3.75	7.50	15.00
❑ LOC-6008 [(2)M]	Benny Goodman in Moscow	1962	5.00	10.00	20.00
❑ LSO-6008 [(2)S]	Benny Goodman in Moscow	1962	6.25	12.50	25.00
❑ VPM-6040 [(2)PS]	This Is Benny Goodman	1971	3.75	7.50	15.00
❑ VPM-6063 [(2)]	This Is Benny Goodman, Vol. 2	1972	3.75	7.50	15.00
❑ LPT-6703 [(5)M]	The Golden Age of Swing	1956	150.00	300.00	600.00
—Five-record set in white vinyl binder with bound-in booklet					
SUNBEAM					
❑ 100	The Let's Dance Broadcasts 1934-35, Volume 1	197?	2.50	5.00	10.00
❑ 104	The Let's Dance Broadcasts 1934-35, Volume 2	197?	2.50	5.00	10.00
❑ 105	Benny Goodman On the Air 1935-36, Volume 1	197?	2.50	5.00	10.00
❑ 106	Benny Goodman In a Mellotone Manner 1930-31	197?	2.50	5.00	10.00
❑ 107	Benny Goodman On the Side 1929-31	197?	2.50	5.00	10.00
❑ 111	Benny Goodman Accompanies Girls 1931-33	197?	2.50	5.00	10.00
❑ 112	Rare Benny Goodman 1927-29	197?	2.50	5.00	10.00
❑ 113	The Hotsy Totsy Gang 1928-29	197?	2.50	5.00	10.00
❑ 114	Whoopee Makers 1928-29	197?	2.50	5.00	10.00
❑ 116/27 [(12)]	Manhattan Room 1937	197?	15.00	30.00	60.00
❑ 128/32 [(5)]	From the Congress Hotel, Chicago, 1935-36	197?	6.25	12.50	25.00
❑ 133	Benny Goodman 1933	197?	2.50	5.00	10.00
❑ 135	Benny Goodman and the Modernists 1934-35	197?	2.50	5.00	10.00
❑ 138	Benny Goodman and His Orchestra 1931-33, Volume 1	197?	2.50	5.00	10.00
❑ 139	Benny Goodman and His Orchestra 1931-33, Volume 2	197?	2.50	5.00	10.00
❑ 140	Benny Goodman and His Orchestra 1931-33, Volume 3	197?	2.50	5.00	10.00
❑ 141	The Benny Goodman Boys 1928-29	197?	2.50	5.00	10.00
❑ 142	Benny Goodman On V-Disc 1939-48, Volume 1	197?	2.50	5.00	10.00
❑ 143	Benny Goodman On V-Disc 1939-48, Volume 2	197?	2.50	5.00	10.00
❑ 144	Benny Goodman On V-Disc 1939-48, Volume 3	197?	2.50	5.00	10.00
❑ 145	Fitch Bandwagon 1945	197?	2.50	5.00	10.00
❑ 146	Camel Caravan 1937, Volume 1	197?	2.50	5.00	10.00
❑ 147	Camel Caravan 1937, Volume 2	197?	2.50	5.00	10.00
❑ 148	Benny Goodman 1934	197?	2.50	5.00	10.00
❑ 149	Jam Session 1935-37	197?	2.50	5.00	10.00
❑ 150	The Let's Dance Broadcasts 1934-35, Volume 3	197?	2.50	5.00	10.00
❑ 151	The Benny Goodman Show 1946	197?	2.50	5.00	10.00
❑ 152 [(2)]	Benny Goodman and His Orchestra 1937-38	197?	3.00	6.00	12.00
❑ 153	Benny Goodman On the Air 1935-36, Volume 2	197?	2.50	5.00	10.00
❑ 154	Benny Goodman 1946	197?	2.50	5.00	10.00
❑ 156	Broadcasts from Hollywood 1946-47	197?	2.50	5.00	10.00
❑ 158	Benny Goodman 1941-42	1984	2.50	5.00	10.00
TIME-LIFE					
❑ STBB-03 [(2)]	Big Bands: Benny Goodman	1983	3.75	7.50	15.00
❑ STL-J-01 [(3)]	Giants of Jazz	1979	5.00	10.00	20.00
❑ STBB-23 [(2)]	Benny Goodman: King of Swing	1986	3.75	7.50	15.00
❑ STBB-23 [(2)]	Big Bands: King of Swing	1986	3.75	7.50	15.00
VERVE					
❑ MGV-4013 [M]	The Superlative Goodman, Volume 1	1958	—	—	—
—Canceled					
❑ MGV-4014 [M]	The Superlative Goodman, Volume 2	1958	—	—	—
—Canceled					
❑ MGV-4015-2 [(2)M]	The Superlative Goodman	1958	—	—	—
—Canceled					
❑ V-8582 [M]	The Essential Benny Goodman	1964	3.75	7.50	15.00
❑ V6-8582 [S]	The Essential Benny Goodman	1964	3.75	7.50	15.00
WESTINGHOUSE					
❑ (no #) [(5)M]	Benny in Brussels	1958	25.00	50.00	100.00
❑ XTV 27713/4 [M]	Benny Goodman Plays World Favorites in High Fidelity	1958	7.50	15.00	30.00
—No number on cover or label; these numbers come from the trail-off wax					

GOODMAN, BENNY/CHARLIE BARNET
Albums
CAPITOL

Number	Title (A Side/B Side)	Yr	VG	VG+	NM
❑ M-11061	BeBop Spoken Here	197?	3.00	6.00	12.00

GOODMAN, DICKIE Also see BUCHANAN AND GOODMAN; JOHN AND ERNEST; SPENCER AND SPENCER.
45s
ASI

Number	Title (A Side/B Side)	Yr	VG	VG+	NM
❑ 1013	Rocky and the Angel/Pug Rock	1977	—	3.00	6.00
—As "Dickie G. and the Don'ts"					
AUDIO SPECTRUM					
❑ 75	Presidential Interview (Flying Saucer '64)/Paul Revere	1964	10.00	20.00	40.00
CASH					
❑ 451	Mr. Jaws/Irv's Theme	1975	—	2.50	5.00
❑ 451	Mr. Jaws/Irv's Theme	1975	12.50	25.00	50.00
—Clear purple vinyl, possibly an "after-hours" edition; at least two, and probably more, exist					
COTIQUE					
❑ 158	On Campus/Mombo Suzie	1969	—	3.00	6.00
—B-side by Johnny Colo					
❑ 173	Luna Trip/My Victrola	1969	—	3.00	6.00
—B-side by Joey Pastrana					
DAVY JONES					
❑ 663	White House Happening/President Johnson	1967	6.25	12.50	25.00
❑ 663 [PS]	White House Happening/President Johnson	1967	10.00	20.00	40.00

Number	Title (A Side/B Side)	Yr	VG	VG+	NM
DIAMOND					
❑ 119	Ben Crazy/Flip Side	1962	3.75	7.50	15.00
EXTRAN					
❑ 601	Hey, E.T./Get a Job	1982	—	2.50	5.00
GOODNAME					
❑ 7100	Safe Sex Report/Safety First	1987	3.75	7.50	15.00
—His last record					
HOT LINE					
❑ 1017	Energy Crisis '79/Pain	1979	—	3.00	6.00
J.M.D.					
❑ 001	Ben Crazy/Flip Side	1962	6.25	12.50	25.00
JANUS					
❑ 271	Star Warts/The Boys Tune	1977	—	2.50	5.00
M.D.					
❑ 101	Schmonanza/Backwards Theme	1961	5.00	10.00	20.00
MARK-X					
❑ 8009	The Touchables/Martian Melody	1961	5.00	10.00	20.00
—Black label					
❑ 8009	The Touchables/Martian Melody	1961	7.50	15.00	30.00
—Yellow label					
❑ 8010	The Touchables in Brooklyn/Mystery	1961	5.00	10.00	20.00
MONTAGE					
❑ 1220	Hey, E.T./The Ride of Paul Revere	1982	3.75	7.50	15.00
❑ 1220 [DJ]	Hey, E.T. (same on both sides)	1982	—	2.50	5.00
ORON					
❑ 101	Washington Uptight/The Cat	1967	6.25	12.50	25.00
—As "The Pennsylvania Players"					
PRELUDE					
❑ 8018	Election '80 (same on both sides)	1980	—	2.50	5.00
RAINY WEDNESDAY					
❑ 202	Watergrate/Friends	1973	—	3.00	6.00
❑ 204	Purple People Eater/Ruthie's Theme	1973	—	3.00	6.00
❑ 205	The Constitution/The End	1973	—	3.00	6.00
❑ 206	Energy Crisis '74/The Mistake	1974	—	3.00	6.00
❑ 206	Energy Crisis '74/Ruthie's Theme	1974	2.00	4.00	8.00
❑ 207	Mr. President/Popularity	1974	—	3.00	6.00
❑ 208	Gerry Ford, A Special Report/Robert	1974	—	3.00	6.00
❑ 209	Inflation in the Nation/Jon and Jed's Theme	1975	—	3.00	6.00
RAMGO					
❑ 501	Speaking of Ecology/Dayton's Theme	1970	6.25	12.50	25.00
RED BIRD					
❑ 10-058	Batman & His Grandmother/Suspense	1966	5.00	10.00	20.00
RHINO					
❑ 019	Radio Russia/Washington Inside Out	1984	—	2.00	4.00
RORI					
❑ 601	Horror Movies/Whoa, Mule	1961	6.25	12.50	25.00
❑ 602	The Berlin Top Ten/Little Tiger	1961	6.25	12.50	25.00
❑ 701	Santa and the Touchables/North Pole Rock	1961	6.25	12.50	25.00
SCEPTER					
❑ 12339	Speaking of Ecology/Dayton's Theme	1971	3.00	6.00	12.00
SHARK					
❑ 1001	Mrs. Jaws/(B-side unknown)	1979	5.00	10.00	20.00
❑ 1002	Super Superman/Chomp Chomp	1979	3.75	7.50	15.00
SHELL					
❑ 711	Election '84/Herb's Theme	1984	—	2.00	4.00
SHOCK					
❑ 6	Kong/Ed's Tune	1977	—	2.50	5.00
20TH FOX					
❑ 443	Senate Hearing/Lock-Up	1963	3.75	7.50	15.00
TWIRL					
❑ 2015	James Bomb/Seventh Theme	1966	3.75	7.50	15.00
WACKO					
❑ 1001	Mr. President/Dancin' U.S.A.	1981	—	2.50	5.00
❑ 1002	Super-Duper Man/Robert's Tune	1981	—	2.50	5.00
❑ 1381	America '81 (two different versions)	1981	2.00	4.00	8.00
Z-100					
❑ 100 [DJ]	Attack of the Z Monster/Mystery	1984	2.50	5.00	10.00
—Promo item for New York radio station					
Albums					
CASH					
❑ CR 6000	Mr. Jaws and Other Fables	1975	6.25	12.50	25.00
COMET					
❑ 69	My Son, the Joke	1963	10.00	20.00	40.00
IX CHAINS					
❑ NCS 9000	The Original Flying Saucers	1973	10.00	20.00	40.00
RHINO					
❑ RNLP-811	Dickie Goodman's Greatest Hits	1983	3.75	7.50	15.00
RORI					
❑ 3301	The Many Heads of Dickie Goodman	1962	20.00	40.00	80.00

GOODMAN, JERRY, AND JAN HAMMER
Albums
NEMPEROR

Number	Title (A Side/B Side)	Yr	VG	VG+	NM
❑ SD 430	Like Children	1975	2.50	5.00	10.00

GOODMAN, SHIRLEY Of SHIRLEY AND LEE; also of SHIRLEY (AND COMPANY).
45s
IMPERIAL

Number	Title (A Side/B Side)	Yr	VG	VG+	NM
❑ 5944	When a Boy Meets a Girl/Don't Marry Too Soon	1963	3.00	6.00	12.00

GOODMAN, STEVE
45s
ASYLUM

Number	Title (A Side/B Side)	Yr	VG	VG+	NM
❑ 45284	Jessie's Jig (Rob's Romp, Beth's Bounce)/It's a Sin to Tell a Lie	1975	—	3.00	6.00
❑ 45331	Between the Lines/Can't Go Back	1976	—	3.00	6.00
❑ 45481	Video Tape/My Old Man	1978	—	3.00	6.00
❑ 46012	Men Who Love Women Who Love Men/The One That Got Away	1979	—	3.00	6.00
❑ 46522	Men Who Love Women Who Love Men/The One That Got Away	1979	—	2.50	5.00
❑ 47107	Bobby Don't Stop/Trust Me	1981	—	2.50	5.00
BUDDAH					
❑ 270	City of New Orleans/(B-side unknown)	1971	3.00	6.00	12.00
❑ 326	Election Year Rag/Someone Else's Troubles	1972	2.50	5.00	10.00
❑ 348	The Dutchman/Song for David	1973	2.50	5.00	10.00

Number	Title (A Side/B Side)	Yr	VG	VG+	NM
RED PAJAMA					
❏ 1001	A Dying Cub Fan's Last Request/				
	Take Me Out to the Ball Game	1981	3.75	7.50	15.00
WGN					
❏ 784	Go Cubs Go (WGN Radio Cubs Theme)				
	(same on both sides)	1984	3.00	6.00	12.00
Albums					
ASYLUM					
❏ 6E-174	High and Outside	1979	3.00	6.00	12.00
❏ 6E-297	Hot Spot	1980	3.00	6.00	12.00
❏ 7E-1037	Jessie's Jig & Other Favorites	1975	3.00	6.00	12.00
❏ 7E-1061	Words We Can Dance To	1976	3.00	6.00	12.00
❏ 7E-1118	Say It in Private	1977	3.00	6.00	12.00
BUDDAH					
❏ BDS 5096	Steve Goodman	1971	3.75	7.50	15.00
❏ BDS 5121	Somebody Else's Troubles	1972	3.75	7.50	15.00
❏ BDS 5665 [(2)]	The Essential Steve Goodman	1976	3.75	7.50	15.00
RED PAJAMAS					
❏ RPJ-001	Artistic Hair	1982	3.00	6.00	12.00
❏ RPJ-002	Affordable Art	1983	3.00	6.00	12.00
❏ RPJ-003	Santa Ana Winds	1984	3.00	6.00	12.00
❏ RPJ-005	Unfinished Business	1985	3.00	6.00	12.00
❏ RPJ-006	Best of the Asylum Years, Vol. 1	198?	3.00	6.00	12.00
❏ RPJ-007	Best of the Asylum Years, Vol. 2	198?	3.00	6.00	12.00

GOODMAN, STEVE, AND PHOEBE SNOW Also see each artist's individual listings.
45s
ASYLUM

Number	Title (A Side/B Side)	Yr	VG	VG+	NM
❏ 47069	Sometimes Love Forgets/Can't Find My Heart	1980	—	2.50	5.00

GOODTIMERS, THE See DON COVAY.

GOODWIN, DON
45s
SILVER BLUE

Number	Title (A Side/B Side)	Yr	VG	VG+	NM
❏ 806	This Is Your Song/Help It Along	1973	—	3.50	7.00
❏ 808	Time to Cry/Good Good Lovin'	1974	—	3.50	7.00
❏ 821	Diana/I'll Never Be Away from You	1974	—	3.50	7.00
❏ 822	Baby, Baby Do It/(B-side unknown)	1974	2.00	4.00	8.00

GOODWIN, RON
45s
CAPITOL

Number	Title (A Side/B Side)	Yr	VG	VG+	NM
❏ F3708	The Headless Horseman/When I Fall in Love	1957	2.50	5.00	10.00
❏ F3748	Swinging Sweethearts/I'll Find You	1957	2.50	5.00	10.00
❏ F3834	Lingering Lovers/Swedish Polka	1957	2.50	5.00	10.00
❏ F3927	Red Cloak/Laughing Sailor	1958	2.50	5.00	10.00
❏ F4139	Wagon Train/Latin Lovers	1959	2.50	5.00	10.00
❏ F4201	The Venus Waltz/Martians on Parade	1959	2.50	5.00	10.00
KING					
❏ 45-5509	Romanoff and Juliet/El Morocco Tea Rooms	1961	3.00	6.00	12.00
Albums					
CAPITOL					
❏ T 10078 [M]	It Can't Be Wrong	1957	5.00	10.00	20.00
❏ T 10177 [M]	Swinging Sweethearts	1958	5.00	10.00	20.00
❏ ST 10188 [S]	Music in Orbit	1958	10.00	20.00	40.00
❏ T 10188 [M]	Music in Orbit	1958	7.50	15.00	30.00
❏ ST 10251 [S]	Music for an Arabian Night	1959	7.50	15.00	30.00
❏ T 10251 [M]	Music for an Arabian Night	1959	6.25	12.50	25.00
❏ SP-10560	Jet Flight to Beirut	196?	5.00	10.00	20.00
❏ ST-11012	Ron Goodwin Plays Someone Named				
	Burt Bacharach	1972	2.50	5.00	10.00

GOONS, THE
45s
LONDON

Number	Title (A Side/B Side)	Yr	VG	VG+	NM
❏ 1684	I'm Walking Backwards for Christmas/Bluebottle				
	Blues	1956	6.25	12.50	25.00

GOOSE CREEK SYMPHONY
45s
CAPITOL

Number	Title (A Side/B Side)	Yr	VG	VG+	NM
❏ 2729	Big Time Saturday Nite/Beautiful Bertha	1970	—	3.00	6.00
❏ 2853	Charlie's Tune/No News Is Good News	1970	—	3.00	6.00
❏ 3246	(Oh Lord Won't You Buy Me a) Mercedes Benz/				
	Rich on Love	1971	—	2.50	5.00
❏ 3371	Guitars Pickin', Fiddles Playin'/				
	Broken Creek Goose Down	1972	—	2.50	5.00
COLUMBIA					
❏ 10062	Hot Dog Daddy/Plans of the Lord	1974	—	2.50	5.00
Albums					
CAPITOL					
❏ SM-444	Goose Creek Symphony	197?	2.50	5.00	10.00
—Reissue					
❏ ST-444	Goose Creek Symphony	1970	3.75	7.50	15.00
❏ ST-690	Welcome to Goose Creek	1971	3.75	7.50	15.00
❏ ST-11044	Words of Earnest	1972	3.75	7.50	15.00
COLUMBIA					
❏ KC 32918	Do Your Thing But Don't Touch Mine	1974	3.00	6.00	12.00

GORDIAN KNOT, THE JIM WEATHERLY was in this group.
45s
VERVE

Number	Title (A Side/B Side)	Yr	VG	VG+	NM
❏ 10595	Year of the Sun/If Only I Could Cry	1968	2.50	5.00	10.00
❏ 10612	Broken Down Old Merry-Go-Round/We Must Be				
	Doin' Something Right	1968	2.50	5.00	10.00
Albums					
VERVE					
❏ V-5062 [M]	Tones	1968	7.50	15.00	30.00
—White label promo only (no stock copies were issued in mono)					
❏ V6-5062 [S]	Tones	1968	3.75	7.50	15.00

GORDON, BARRY
45s
ABC

Number	Title (A Side/B Side)	Yr	VG	VG+	NM
❏ 11113	The Girl I Left Behind/A House Built on Sand	1968	2.00	4.00	8.00

Number	Title (A Side/B Side)	Yr	VG	VG+	NM
ABC DUNHILL					
❏ 4126	Days of Pearly Spencer/Ramshackle Guy	1968	2.00	4.00	8.00
❏ 4141	The Girl I Left Behind/A House Built on Sand	1968	2.00	4.00	8.00
❏ 4188	You Can't Love a Child Like a Woman/				
	Take Off the Veil	1969	—	3.50	7.00
CADENCE					
❏ 1431	You Can't Lie to a Liar/You Can't See the Trees	1962	2.50	5.00	10.00
DUNHILL					
❏ 4110	Angelica/Take Off the Veil	1967	2.00	4.00	8.00
❏ 4126	Days of Pearly Spencer/Ramshackle Guy	1968	3.75	7.50	15.00
—No "ABC" logo next to "Dunhill" at top of label					
ERA					
❏ 1084	Katy/They	1958	3.00	6.00	12.00
❏ 1092	Bluebird Song/Rabbit Habit	1959	3.00	6.00	12.00
MERCURY					
❏ 71878	Sad Little Girl/She's Got Soul	1961	3.00	6.00	12.00
MGM					
❏ K12166	Rock Around Mother Goose/Seven	1956	5.00	10.00	20.00
❏ K12222	I Can't Whistle/The Milkman's Polka	1956	5.00	10.00	20.00
❏ K12276	How Do We Look to the Monkeys/				
	Ten Years to Go	1956	5.00	10.00	20.00
❏ K12373	Rock Little Chillun/				
	That Pretty Little Girl Next Door	1956	5.00	10.00	20.00
❏ K12468	The Thief/Yes, We Have No Bananas	1957	3.75	7.50	15.00
UNITED ARTISTS					
❏ 730	Go Back Little Tear/Susan	1964	2.50	5.00	10.00
❏ 795	True Love Can Never Die/The Two of Them	1964	2.50	5.00	10.00
❏ 876	Sealed with a Kiss/Talk, Talk, Talk	1965	2.50	5.00	10.00
❏ 950	Let Me Try/The World Is Mine	1965	2.50	5.00	10.00
❏ 50019	Yes Sir, That's My Baby/				
	True Love Can Never Die	1966	2.50	5.00	10.00
Albums					
CAPITOL					
❏ ST-805	Pieces of Time	1971	3.00	6.00	12.00
UNITED ARTISTS					
❏ UAL 3491 [M]	Yes Sir, That's My Baby	1966	3.75	7.50	15.00
❏ UAS 6491 [S]	Yes Sir, That's My Baby	1966	5.00	10.00	20.00

GORDON, JUSTIN
Albums
DOT

Number	Title (A Side/B Side)	Yr	VG	VG+	NM
❏ DLP-3214 [M]	Justin Gordon Swings	1959	10.00	20.00	40.00

GORDON, MIKE, AND THE AGATES
45s
DORE

Number	Title (A Side/B Side)	Yr	VG	VG+	NM
❏ 681	Rumble at Newport Beach/Last Call for Dinner	1963	7.50	15.00	30.00
❏ 780	Curfew on the Strip/Last Call for Dinner	1966	3.75	7.50	15.00

GORDON, MIKE, AND THE EL TEMPOS
45s
CAT

Number	Title (A Side/B Side)	Yr	VG	VG+	NM
❏ 101	Why Don't You Do Right/You Got to Give	1954	12.50	25.00	50.00

GORDON, ROSCOE
45s
ABC-PARAMOUNT

Number	Title (A Side/B Side)	Yr	VG	VG+	NM
❏ 10351	A Girl to Love/As You Walk Away	1962	3.00	6.00	12.00
❏ 10407	A Little Bit of Magic/I Want Revenge	1963	3.00	6.00	12.00
❏ 10501	I Don't Stand a Chance/That's What You Did	1963	3.00	6.00	12.00
—As "Barbara & Roscoe Gordon"					
CALLA					
❏ 145	Just a Little Bit/I Really Love You	1968	2.00	4.00	8.00
CHESS					
❏ 1487	Booted/I Love You Till the Day I Die	1951	375.00	750.00	1500.
DUKE					
❏ 101	Tell Daddy/Hey Fat Girl	1952	25.00	50.00	100.00
❏ 106	T-Model Boogie/New Orleans Woman	1953	12.50	25.00	50.00
❏ 109	Too Many Women/Wise to You, Baby	1953	12.50	25.00	50.00
❏ 114	Ain't No Use/Roscoe's Mambo	1953	12.50	25.00	50.00
❏ 129	Three Can't Love/You Figure It Out	1954	12.50	25.00	50.00
❏ 165	Keep On Doggin'/Bad Dream	1957	7.50	15.00	30.00
❏ 173	I've Loved and Lost/Tummer Tee	1957	7.50	15.00	30.00
❏ 320	Dilly Bop/You'll Never Know	1960	3.75	7.50	15.00
FLIP					
❏ 227	Weeping Blues/Just Love Me, Baby	1956	75.00	150.00	300.00
❏ 237	The Chicken (Dance with You)/				
	Love for You Baby	1956	12.50	25.00	50.00
OLD TOWN					
❏ 1167	Gotta Keep Rollin'/Just a Little at a Time	1964	2.50	5.00	10.00
❏ 1175	It Ain't Right/Could This Be Love	1965	2.50	5.00	10.00
—As "Roscoe and Barbara"					
RPM					
❏ 324	Saddled the Cow/Ouch, Pretty Baby	1951	100.00	200.00	400.00
❏ 336	Dime a Dozen/A New Remedy for Love	1951	62.50	125.00	250.00
❏ 344	Booted/Cold, Cold Winter	1952	50.00	100.00	200.00
❏ 350	No More Doggin'/Maria	1952	50.00	100.00	200.00
❏ 358	New Orleans Woman/I Remember Your Kisses	1952	25.00	50.00	100.00
❏ 365	What You Got on Your Mind/				
	Two Kinds of Women	1952	25.00	50.00	100.00
❏ 369	Trying/Dream Baby	1952	15.00	30.00	60.00
❏ 373	Lucille/Blues for My Baby	1953	15.00	30.00	60.00
❏ 379	I'm in Love/Just In from Texas	1953	15.00	30.00	60.00
❏ 384	We're All Loaded/Tomorrow May Be Too Late	1953	15.00	30.00	60.00
SUN					
❏ 227	Weeping Blues/Just Love Me, Baby	1956	125.00	250.00	500.00
❏ 237	The Chicken (Dance with You)/				
	Love for You Baby	1956	50.00	100.00	200.00
❏ 257	Shoobie Oobie/Cheese and Crackers	1956	12.50	25.00	50.00
❏ 305	Sally Jo/Torro	1958	6.25	12.50	25.00
VEE JAY					
❏ 316	A Fool in Love/No More Doggin'	1959	3.75	7.50	15.00
❏ 332	Just a Little Bit/Goin' Home	1959	3.75	7.50	15.00
❏ 348	Surely I Love You/What You Do to Me	1960	3.75	7.50	15.00
❏ 385	What I Wouldn't Do/Let 'Em Try	1961	3.00	6.00	12.00

G

Number	Title (A Side/B Side)	Yr	VG	VG+	NM

GORDON 'N ROGERS' INTER-URBAN ELECTRIC A&E PIT CREW & RHYTHM BAND
Albums
CAPITOL

Number	Title (A Side/B Side)	Yr	VG	VG+	NM
❏ STAO-276	Bug In!	1969	5.00	10.00	20.00

GORE, LESLEY
45s
A&M

❏ 1710	Give It to Me, Sweet Thing/Immortality	1975	—	2.50	5.00
❏ 1710 [PS]	Give It to Me, Sweet Thing/Immortality	1975	—	3.00	6.00
❏ 1830	Sometimes/Give It To Me, Sweet Thing	1976	—	2.50	5.00

CREWE

❏ 338	Why Doesn't Love Make Me Happy/ Tomorrow's Children	1970	2.50	5.00	10.00
❏ 344	When Yesterday Was Tomorrow/ Why Me, Why You	1970	2.50	5.00	10.00
❏ 601	Back Together/Quiet Love	1971	2.50	5.00	10.00

MANHATTAN

| ❏ 50039 | Since I Don't Have You-It's Only Make Believe/ Our Love Was Meant to Be | 1986 | 2.00 | 4.00 | 8.00 |

—With Lou Christie
MERCURY

❏ 72119	It's My Party/Danny	1963	3.75	7.50	15.00
❏ 72119 [PS]	It's My Party/Danny	1963	7.50	15.00	30.00
❏ 72143	Judy's Turn to Cry/Just Let Me Cry	1963	3.75	7.50	15.00
❏ 72143 [PS]	Judy's Turn to Cry/Just Let Me Cry	1963	6.25	12.50	25.00
❏ 72180	She's a Fool/The Old Crowd	1963	3.75	7.50	15.00
❏ 72180 [PS]	She's a Fool/The Old Crowd	1963	6.25	12.50	25.00
❏ 72206	You Don't Own Me/Run, Bobby, Run	1963	3.75	7.50	15.00
❏ 72206 [PS]	You Don't Own Me/Run, Bobby, Run	1963	10.00	20.00	40.00

—With insert (deduct 25% if missing)

❏ 72245	Je Ne Sais Plus/Je N'ose Pas	1964	5.00	10.00	20.00
❏ 72259	That's the Way Boys Are/That's the Way the Ball Bounces	1964	2.50	5.00	10.00
❏ 72259 [PS]	That's the Way Boys Are/That's the Way the Ball Bounces	1964	5.00	10.00	20.00
❏ 72270	I Don't Wanna Be a Loser/It's Gotta Be You	1964	2.50	5.00	10.00
❏ 72270 [PS]	I Don't Wanna Be a Loser/It's Gotta Be You	1964	5.00	10.00	20.00
❏ 72309	Maybe I Know/Wonder Boy	1964	2.50	5.00	10.00
❏ 72309 [PS]	Maybe I Know/Wonder Boy	1964	5.00	10.00	20.00
❏ 72352	Hey Now/Sometimes I Wish I Were a Boy	1964	2.50	5.00	10.00
❏ 72352 [PS]	Hey Now/Sometimes I Wish I Were a Boy	1964	5.00	10.00	20.00
❏ 72372	Look of Love/Little Girl Gone Home	1964	2.50	5.00	10.00
❏ 72372 [PS]	Look of Love/Little Girl Gone Home	1964	5.00	10.00	20.00
❏ 72412	All of My Life/I Cannot Hope for Anything	1965	2.50	5.00	10.00
❏ 72412 [PS]	All of My Life/I Cannot Hope for Anything	1965	5.00	10.00	20.00
❏ 72433	Sunshine, Lollipops and Rainbows/ You've Come Back	1965	2.50	5.00	10.00
❏ 72433 [PS]	Sunshine, Lollipops and Rainbows/ You've Come Back	1965	5.00	10.00	20.00
❏ 72475	My Town, My Guy and Me/Girl in Love	1965	2.50	5.00	10.00
❏ 72475 [PS]	My Town, My Guy and Me/Girl in Love	1965	5.00	10.00	20.00
❏ 72513	I Won't Love You Anymore (Sorry)/ No Matter What You Do	1966	2.50	5.00	10.00
❏ 72513 [PS]	I Won't Love You Anymore (Sorry)/ No Matter What You Do	1966	5.00	10.00	20.00
❏ 72530	We Know We're in Love/That's What We'll Do	1966	2.50	5.00	10.00
❏ 72553	Young Love/I Just Don't Know If I Can	1966	2.50	5.00	10.00
❏ 72580	Off and Running/I Don't Care	1966	2.50	5.00	10.00
❏ 72611	Maybe Now/Treat Me Like a Lady	1966	2.50	5.00	10.00
❏ 72649	California Nights/I'm Goin' Out	1967	2.50	5.00	10.00
❏ 72649 [PS]	California Nights/I'm Goin' Out		—	—	—

—Rumored to exist, but without conclusive evidence, we will delete this from future editions

❏ 72683	Summer and Sandy/I'm Fallin' Down	1967	2.50	5.00	10.00
❏ 72683 [PS]	Summer and Sandy/I'm Fallin' Down	1967	5.00	10.00	20.00
❏ 72726	Brink of Disaster/On a Day Like This	1967	2.50	5.00	10.00
❏ 72759	It's a Happening/Magic Colors	1967	2.50	5.00	10.00
❏ 72787	Small Talk/Say What You See	1968	3.00	6.00	12.00
❏ 72819	He Gives Me Love (La, La, La)/Brand New Me	1968	3.00	6.00	12.00
❏ 72842	Where Can I Go/I Can't Make It Without You	1968	3.00	6.00	12.00
❏ 72867	Look the Other Way/I'll Be Standing By	1968	3.00	6.00	12.00
❏ 72892	Take Good Care (Of My Heart)/I Can't Make It Without You	1969	3.00	6.00	12.00
❏ 72892	Take Good Care (Of My Heart)/ You Sent Me Silver Bells	1969	3.00	6.00	12.00
❏ 72931	Summer Symphony/98.6-Lazy Day	1969	3.75	7.50	15.00
❏ 72969	Wedding Bell Blues/One by One	1969	3.75	7.50	15.00

MOWEST

| ❏ 5029 | The Road I Walk/She Said That | 1972 | 2.50 | 5.00 | 10.00 |
| ❏ 5042 | Give It to Me, Sweet Thing/Don't Want to Be One | 1973 | — | — | — |

—Unreleased
PHILCO-FORD

| ❏ HP-21 | You Don't Own Me/That's the Way Boys Are | 1968 | 3.75 | 7.50 | 15.00 |

—4-inch plastic "Hip Pocket Record" with color sleeve
Albums
A&M

| ❏ SP-4564 | Love Me by Name | 1975 | 3.75 | 7.50 | 15.00 |

MERCURY

| ❏ ML-8016 | I'll Cry If I Want To | 1980 | 2.50 | 5.00 | 10.00 |

—Reissue of 60805

| ❏ MG 20805 [M] | I'll Cry If I Want To | 1963 | 7.50 | 15.00 | 30.00 |

—With no blurb for "It's My Party"

| ❏ MG 20805 [M] | I'll Cry If I Want To | 1964 | 5.00 | 10.00 | 20.00 |

—With blurb for "It's My Party"

❏ MG 20849 [M]	Lesley Gore Sings of Mixed-Up Hearts	1963	7.50	15.00	30.00
❏ MG 20901 [M]	Boys, Boys, Boys	1964	7.50	15.00	30.00
❏ MG 20943 [M]	Girl Talk	1964	7.50	15.00	30.00
❏ MG 21024 [M]	The Golden Hits of Lesley Gore	1965	7.50	15.00	30.00
❏ MG 21042 [M]	My Town, My Guy & Me	1965	7.50	15.00	30.00
❏ MG 21066 [M]	All About Love	1966	7.50	15.00	30.00
❏ MG 21120 [M]	California Nights	1967	7.50	15.00	30.00
❏ SR 60805 [S]	I'll Cry If I Want To	1963	10.00	20.00	40.00

—With no blurb for "It's My Party"

| ❏ SR 60805 [S] | I'll Cry If I Want To | 1964 | 7.50 | 15.00 | 30.00 |

—With blurb for "It's My Party"

❏ SR 60849 [S]	Lesley Gore Sings of Mixed-Up Hearts	1963	10.00	20.00	40.00
❏ SR 60901 [S]	Boys, Boys, Boys	1964	10.00	20.00	40.00
❏ SR 60943 [S]	Girl Talk	1964	10.00	20.00	40.00
❏ SR 61024 [S]	The Golden Hits of Lesley Gore	196?	3.75	7.50	15.00

—Reissues have 10 tracks

| ❏ SR 61024 [S] | The Golden Hits of Lesley Gore | 1965 | 10.00 | 20.00 | 40.00 |

—Originals have 12 tracks

| ❏ SR 61042 [S] | My Town, My Guy & Me | 1965 | 10.00 | 20.00 | 40.00 |
| ❏ SR 61066 [S] | All About Love | 1966 | 10.00 | 20.00 | 40.00 |

—Stereo version has a different cover and liner notes than the mono version

❏ SR 61120 [S]	California Nights	1967	10.00	20.00	40.00
❏ SR 61185	Golden Hits Vol. 2	1968	10.00	20.00	40.00
❏ 810370-1	The Golden Hits of Lesley Gore	1983	2.50	5.00	10.00

—Reissue of 61024
MOWEST

| ❏ MW 117L | Someplace Else Now | 1972 | 3.75 | 7.50 | 15.00 |

RHINO

| ❏ RNFP-71496 [(2)] | The Lesley Gore Anthology (1963-1968) | 1986 | 3.75 | 7.50 | 15.00 |

WING

❏ PRW-2-119 [(2)]	The Sound of Young Love	1969	5.00	10.00	20.00
❏ SRW-16350	Girl Talk	1968	3.75	7.50	15.00
❏ SRW-16382	Love, Love, Love	1968	3.75	7.50	15.00

GORMAN, FREDDIE
45s
MIRACLE

| ❏ 11 | The Day Will Come/Just for You | 1962 | 17.50 | 35.00 | 70.00 |

RIC-TIC

| ❏ 101 | In a Bad Way/There Can Be Too Much | 1964 | 7.50 | 15.00 | 30.00 |
| ❏ 102 | Take Me Back/Can't Get It Out of My Mind | 1965 | 7.50 | 15.00 | 30.00 |

GORME, EYDIE Also see STEVE LAWRENCE AND EYDIE GORME.
45s
ABC-PARAMOUNT

| ❏ 9655 | Sincerely Yours/Come Home | 1955 | 3.75 | 7.50 | 15.00 |

—The first 45 (numerically) on ABC-Paramount

❏ 9684	Too Close for Comfort/That's How	1956	2.50	5.00	10.00
❏ 9722	Mama, Teach Me to Dance/You Bring Out the Lover in Me	1956	2.50	5.00	10.00
❏ 9758	Soda Pop Hop/I've Got a Right to Cry	1956	2.50	5.00	10.00
❏ 9780	I'll Take Romance/First Impression	1957	2.50	5.00	10.00
❏ 9817	Your Kisses Kill Me/Kiss in Your Eyes	1957	2.50	5.00	10.00
❏ 9852	When Your Lover Has Gone/Until They Sail	1957	2.50	5.00	10.00
❏ 9863	Love Me Forever/Let Me Be Loved	1957	2.50	5.00	10.00
❏ 9925	You Need Hands/Dormi, Dormi	1958	2.50	5.00	10.00
❏ 9944	Gotta Have Rain/To You From Me	1958	2.50	5.00	10.00
❏ 9971	The Voice in My Heart/Separate Tables	1958	2.50	5.00	10.00
❏ 10006	I'm Yours/Don't Take Your Love from Me	1959	2.50	5.00	10.00
❏ 10041	Taking a Chance on Love/The Years Between	1959	2.50	5.00	10.00
❏ 10061	Happiness/Fool Around	1959	2.50	5.00	10.00
❏ 10111	The Dance Is Over/Too Young to Know	1960	2.50	5.00	10.00
❏ 10155	Be Sure My Love/I Will Follow You	1960	2.50	5.00	10.00
❏ 10383	Fly Me to the Moon/I'm Yours	1962	2.50	5.00	10.00

CALENDAR

| ❏ 63-1002 | He Needs Me/How Could I Be So Wrong | 1968 | — | 2.50 | 5.00 |
| ❏ 63-1004 | This Guy's (Girl's) in Love with You/ It's You Again | 1968 | — | 2.50 | 5.00 |

COLUMBIA

❏ 42424	Yes My Darling Daughter/Sonny Boy	1962	2.00	4.00	8.00
❏ 42424 [PS]	Yes My Darling Daughter/Sonny Boy	1962	2.50	5.00	10.00
❏ 42607	Where Is Love/Before Your Time	1962	2.00	4.00	8.00
❏ 42661	Blame It on the Bossa Nova/Guess I Should Have Loved Him More	1963	2.00	4.00	8.00
❏ 42661 [PS]	Blame It on the Bossa Nova/Guess I Should Have Loved Him More	1963	2.50	5.00	10.00
❏ 42790	Don't Try to Fight It, Baby/Theme from Light Fantastic (My Secret World)	1963	—	3.00	6.00
❏ 42854	Everybody Go Home/The Message	1963	—	3.00	6.00
❏ 42953	The Friendliest Thing/Something to Live For	1963	—	3.00	6.00
❏ 4-43082	I Want You to Meet My Baby/Can't Get Over (The Bossa Nova)	1964	—	3.00	6.00
❏ 4-43082 [DJ]	I Want You to Meet My Baby (same on both sides)	1964	3.75	7.50	15.00

—Promo only on red vinyl

❏ 43191	The Moon and the Stars and a Little Bit of Wine/ Piel Canela	1964	—	3.00	6.00
❏ 43225	Do I Hear a Waltz/After You've Gone	1965	—	3.00	6.00
❏ 43302	Just Dance On By/Where Are You Now	1965	—	3.00	6.00
❏ 43444	Don't Go to Strangers/Mas Amor (More Love)	1965	—	3.00	6.00
❏ 43542	What Did I Have That I Didn't Have/Tell Him I Said Hello	1966	—	3.00	6.00
❏ 43660	If He Walked Into My Life/Tell Him I Said Hello	1966	—	3.00	6.00
❏ 43856	Allegre Navidad/Navidad Y Ano Nuevo	1966	2.00	4.00	8.00
❏ 43906	Guess I Should Have Loved Him More/ What Is a Woman	1966	—	3.00	6.00
❏ 43971	Softly, As I Leave You/ What's Good About Goodbye	1967	—	3.00	6.00
❏ 44299	Life Is But a Moment/What Makes Me Love Him	1967	—	3.00	6.00
❏ JZSP 116419/20 [DJ]	Alegre Navidad/Blanca Navidad	1966	2.50	5.00	10.00

—With Trio Los Panchos
CORAL

❏ 60879	That Night of Heaven/Tell Me More	1952	3.75	7.50	15.00
❏ 60921	Don't Tell Lies/Love Me Not Just a Little	1953	3.00	6.00	12.00
❏ 60977	Frenesi/All Night Long	1953	3.00	6.00	12.00
❏ 60999	Uska Dara/Coconuts	1953	3.00	6.00	12.00
❏ 61036	I Danced with My Darling/I'd Be Forgotten	1953	3.00	6.00	12.00
❏ 61093	Gimme Gimme John/Fini	1953	3.00	6.00	12.00
❏ 61138	Crocodile Tears/Fallen Apples	1954	3.00	6.00	12.00
❏ 61189	Tea for Two/Climb Up the Wall	1954	3.00	6.00	12.00
❏ 61347	Give a Fool a Chance/A Girl Can't Say	1955	3.00	6.00	12.00
❏ 61481	Soldier Boy/What Is the Secret to Success	1955	3.00	6.00	12.00

MGM

❏ 14213	Mem'ries and Souvenirs/Rosy's Theme	1971	—	2.50	5.00
❏ 14276	Sal and Sally/Somebody Waiting	1971	—	2.50	5.00
❏ 14397	Mr. Number One/Butterfly	1972	—	2.50	5.00
❏ 14563	Take One Step/The Garden	1973	—	2.50	5.00

Number	Title (A Side/B Side)	Yr	VG	VG+	NM
❏ 14681	Touch the Wind (Eres Tu)/It Takes Too Long to Learn to Live Alone	1973	—	2.50	5.00

RCA VICTOR

Number	Title (A Side/B Side)	Yr	VG	VG+	NM
❏ 74-0206	Runaway/Girl with a Suitcase	1969	—	2.50	5.00
❏ 74-0250	Wild One/Tonight I'll Say a Prayer	1969	—	2.50	5.00
❏ 74-0360	Ladies Who Lunch/My World Keeps Getting Smaller Every Day	1970	—	2.50	5.00

UNITED ARTISTS

❏ 283	Let Me Be the First to Wish You a Merry Christmas/I Love to Dance (But Never on Sunday)	1960	3.00	6.00	12.00
❏ 292	What Happened to Our Love/Yours Tonight	1961	2.00	4.00	8.00
❏ 325	Mem'ries and Souvenirs/My Heart	1961	2.00	4.00	8.00
❏ 414	Frenesi/Granada	1962	2.00	4.00	8.00
❏ XW852	What I Did for Love/Can It Ever Be the Same	1976	—	2.00	4.00

7-Inch Extended Plays
ABC-PARAMOUNT

❏ C-218	Chicago/Button Up Your Overcoat//Tip Toe Through the Tulips with Me/Back in Your Own Backyard	195?	2.50	5.00	10.00
❏ C-218 [PS]	Eydie Gorme Vamps the Roaring 20's, Volume 3	195?	2.50	5.00	10.00
❏ C-246	Why Try to Change Me Now/Idle Conversation//It Could Happen to You/In the Wee Small Hours of the Morning	195?	2.50	5.00	10.00
❏ C-246 [PS]	Eydie in Love, Volume 3	195?	2.50	5.00	10.00

Albums
ABC-PARAMOUNT

❏ 150 [M]	Eydie Gorme	1957	7.50	15.00	30.00
❏ 192 [M]	Eydie Swings the Blues	1957	7.50	15.00	30.00
❏ 218 [M]	Eydie Gorme Vamps the Roaring 20's	1958	7.50	15.00	30.00
❏ S-218 [S]	Eydie Gorme Vamps the Roaring 20's	196?	3.00	6.00	12.00
❏ 246 [M]	Eydie in Love	1958	7.50	15.00	30.00
❏ S-246 [S]	Eydie in Love	196?	3.00	6.00	12.00
❏ 254 [M]	Show Stoppers	1959	6.25	12.50	25.00
❏ S-254 [S]	Show Stoppers	1959	7.50	15.00	30.00
❏ 273 [M]	Love Is a Season	1959	6.25	12.50	25.00
❏ S-273 [S]	Love Is a Season	1959	7.50	15.00	30.00
❏ 307 [M]	On Stage	1959	6.25	12.50	25.00
❏ S-307 [S]	On Stage	1959	7.50	15.00	30.00
❏ 343 [M]	Eydie in Dixieland	1960	6.25	12.50	25.00
❏ S-343 [S]	Eydie in Dixieland	1960	7.50	15.00	30.00
❏ 512 [M]	The Best of Romance, Ballads, Blues, Dixieland, Roaring 20's, Showstoppers	1965	3.75	7.50	15.00
❏ S-512 [S]	The Best of Romance, Ballads, Blues, Dixieland, Roaring 20's, Showstoppers	1965	5.00	10.00	20.00

COLUMBIA

❏ CL 2012 [M]	Blame It on the Bossa Nova	1963	3.75	7.50	15.00
❏ CL 2065 [M]	Let the Good Times Roll	1963	3.75	7.50	15.00
❏ CL 2120 [M]	Gorme Country Style	1964	3.75	7.50	15.00
❏ CL 2203 [M]	Amor	1964	3.75	7.50	15.00
❏ CL 2300 [M]	The Sound of Music (And Other Broadway Hits)	1965	3.75	7.50	15.00
❏ CL 2376 [M]	More Amor	1965	3.75	7.50	15.00
❏ CL 2476 [M]	Don't Go to Strangers	1966	3.75	7.50	15.00
❏ CL 2557 [M]	Navidad Means Christmas	1966	3.75	7.50	15.00

—With Trio Los Panchos

❏ CL 2594 [M]	Softly, As I Leave You	1967	3.75	7.50	15.00
❏ CL 2764 [M]	Eydie Gorme's Greatest Hits	1967	5.00	10.00	20.00
❏ CS 8812 [S]	Blame It on the Bossa Nova	1963	5.00	10.00	20.00
❏ CS 8865 [S]	Let the Good Times Roll	1963	5.00	10.00	20.00
❏ CS 8920 [S]	Gorme Country Style	1964	5.00	10.00	20.00
❏ CS 9003 [S]	Amor	1964	5.00	10.00	20.00
❏ PC 9003	Amor	198?	2.00	4.00	8.00

—Budget-line reissue

❏ CS 9100 [S]	The Sound of Music (And Other Broadway Hits)	1965	5.00	10.00	20.00
❏ CS 9176 [S]	More Amor	1965	5.00	10.00	20.00
❏ CS 9276 [S]	Don't Go to Strangers	1966	5.00	10.00	20.00
❏ CS 9357 [S]	Navidad Means Christmas	1966	5.00	10.00	20.00

—With Trio Los Panchos

❏ CS 9394 [S]	Softly, As I Leave You	1967	5.00	10.00	20.00
❏ CS 9564 [S]	Eydie Gorme's Greatest Hits	1967	3.75	7.50	15.00
❏ PC 9564	Eydie Gorme's Greatest Hits	198?	2.00	4.00	8.00

—Budget-line reissue

❏ CS 9652 [M]	The Look of Love	1968	7.50	15.00	30.00

—White label promo; "Special Mono Radio Station Copy" sticker on front of stereo jacket

❏ CS 9652 [S]	The Look of Love	1968	3.75	7.50	15.00

CORAL

❏ CRL 57109 [M]	Delight	1957	10.00	20.00	40.00

HARMONY

❏ HS 11361	Yes Indeed!	1970	2.50	5.00	10.00
❏ KH 30319	If He Walked Into My Life	1971	2.50	5.00	10.00

MGM

❏ SE-4780	It Was a Good Time	1971	3.00	6.00	12.00

RCA VICTOR

❏ LSP-4093	Eydie	1968	3.00	6.00	12.00
❏ LSP-4303	Tonight I'll Say a Prayer	1970	3.00	6.00	12.00

UNITED ARTISTS

❏ UAL 3143 [M]	Come Sing with Me	1961	5.00	10.00	20.00
❏ UAL 3152 [M]	I Feel So Spanish	1961	5.00	10.00	20.00
❏ UAL 3189 [M]	The Very Best of Eydie	1962	5.00	10.00	20.00
❏ UAS 6143 [S]	Come Sing with Me	1961	6.25	12.50	25.00
❏ UAS 6152 [S]	I Feel So Spanish	1961	6.25	12.50	25.00
❏ UAS 6189 [S]	The Very Best of Eydie	1962	6.25	12.50	25.00

VOCALION

❏ VL 3708 [M]	Here's Eydie Gorme	196?	3.75	7.50	15.00
❏ VL 73708 [R]	Here's Eydie Gorme	196?	3.00	6.00	12.00

GOSPEL STARS, THE
45s
TAMLA

❏ 54037	He Lifted Me/Behold the Saints of God	1961	15.00	30.00	60.00

—Globe logo

❏ 54037	He Lifted Me/Behold the Saints of God	1961	37.50	75.00	150.00

—Horizontal lines logo

Albums
TAMLA

❏ TM-222 [M]	The Great Gospel Stars	1961	1000.	2000.	3000.

GOTHAM CITY CRIME FIGHTERS, THE
45s
BATWING

❏ 1001	Who Stole the Batmobile/That's Life	1966	7.50	15.00	30.00

GOULDMAN, GRAHAM Also see THE MOCKINGBIRDS; 10CC.
45s
A&M

❏ 2251	Away from It All/Bionic Boar	1980	—	2.00	4.00

RCA VICTOR

❏ 47-9453	Impossible Years/No Milk Today	1968	3.00	6.00	12.00
❏ 47-9584	For Your Love/Pamela, Pamela	1968	3.00	6.00	12.00

Albums
RCA VICTOR

❏ LPM-3954 [M]	The Graham Gouldman Thing	1968	12.50	25.00	50.00
❏ LSP-3954 [S]	The Graham Gouldman Thing	1968	12.50	25.00	50.00

GOULET, ROBERT
45s
ABC

❏ 12049	The Little Prince: Title/Mack and Mable: I Won't Send Roses	1974	—	2.00	4.00
❏ 12049 [PS]	The Little Prince: Title/Mack and Mable: I Won't Send Roses	1974	—	2.50	5.00

ARTISTS OF AMERICA

❏ 103	Someone to Give My Love To/Something to Believe In	1975	—	2.00	4.00
❏ 118	After All Is Said and Done/(B-side unknown)	1976	—	2.00	4.00

COLUMBIA

❏ 42249	One Life/I'm Just Taking My Time	1961	2.00	4.00	8.00
❏ 42369	Too Soon/Two Different Worlds	1962	—	3.00	6.00
❏ 42369 [PS]	Too Soon/Two Different Worlds	1962	2.00	4.00	8.00
❏ 42519	What Kind of Fool Am I/Where Do I Go from Here	1962	—	3.00	6.00
❏ 42519 [PS]	What Kind of Fool Am I/Where Do I Go from Here	1962	2.00	4.00	8.00
❏ 42612	Young at Love/Don't Be Afraid of Romance	1962	—	3.00	6.00
❏ 42740	These Are the Closing Credits/Two of Us	1963	—	3.00	6.00
❏ 42740 [PS]	These Are the Closing Credits/Two of Us	1963	2.00	4.00	8.00
❏ 42835	Believe in Me/How Very Special You Are	1963	—	3.00	6.00
❏ 42885	Under the Yum Yum Tree/If You Go	1963	—	3.00	6.00
❏ 43029	The Name of the Game/Choose	1964	—	3.00	6.00
❏ 4-43063	Seventh Dawn/Too Good	1964	—	3.00	6.00
❏ 43131	My Love, Forgive Me (Amore, Scusami)/I'd Rather Be Rich	1964	—	3.00	6.00
❏ 43224	I Never Got to Paris/Begin to Love	1965	—	2.50	5.00
❏ 43301	Summer Sounds/The More I See of Mimi	1965	—	2.50	5.00
❏ 43394	On a Clear Day You Can See Forever/Come Back to Me, My Love	1965	—	2.50	5.00
❏ 43481	Crazy Heart of Love/Everlasting	1965	—	2.50	5.00
❏ 43558	Young Only Yesterday/Why Be Ashamed	1966	—	2.50	5.00
❏ 43668	Daydreamer/My Best Girl	1966	—	2.50	5.00
❏ 43760	Once I Had a Heart/I Heard a Different Drummer	1966	—	2.50	5.00
❏ 43865	There But for You Go I/Fortissimo	1966	—	2.50	5.00
❏ 44019	Ciao Compare/World of Clowns	1967	—	2.50	5.00
❏ 44100	One Life, One Dream/If There's a Way	1967	—	2.50	5.00
❏ 44186	The Sinner/How Can I Leave You	1967	—	2.50	5.00
❏ 44305	Mon Amour, Mon Amour/This Year	1967	—	2.50	5.00
❏ 44368	Follow Me/If Ever I Would Leave You	1967	—	2.50	5.00
❏ 44466	Happy Time/I Don't Remember You	1968	—	2.50	5.00
❏ 44548	What a Wonderful World/I Don't Want to Hurt You Anymore	1968	—	2.50	5.00
❏ 44618	Thirty Days Hath September/A Chance to Live in Camelot	1968	—	2.50	5.00
❏ 44710	Hurry Home for Christmas/Wonderful World of Christmas	1968	2.00	4.00	8.00
❏ 44710 [PS]	Hurry Home for Christmas/Wonderful World of Christmas	1968	3.00	6.00	12.00
❏ 44754	Wait for Me/I'll Catch the Sun	1969	—	2.50	5.00
❏ 44847	Didn't We/Bon Soir Dame	1969	—	2.50	5.00
❏ 44935	One Life to Live/Only Yesterday	1969	—	2.50	5.00
❏ 45054	One Night/I Can't Live Without You	1969	—	2.50	5.00
❏ 45165	My Woman, My Woman, My Wife/Come Saturday	1970	—	2.50	5.00
❏ 45250	Heaing River/One at a Time	1970	—	2.50	5.00
❏ JZSP 58174/203 [DJ]	What Kind of Fool Am I?/Where Do I Go from Here?	1962	2.50	5.00	10.00

—Custom silver label with portrait of Goulet; promo only on yellow vinyl

❏ JZSP 58174/203 [PS]	What Kind of Fool Am I?/Where Do I Go from Here?	1962	3.75	7.50	15.00

—"Special Presentation Record" on full-color sleeve

❏ JZSP 58877/59227 [DJ]	You Stepped Out of a Dream/The Moon Was Yellow	1963	3.00	6.00	12.00

—Custom silver label with portrait of Goulet; promo only on yellow vinyl

❏ JZSP 58877/59227 [PS]	Opening Night Souvenir: The Fabulous Flamingo Prsents Columbia Record Star Robert Goulet, February 11th, 1963, Las Vegas, Nevada	1963	6.25	12.50	25.00

—Sleeve for above promotional record

❏ JZSP 76415/6 [DJ]	December Time/Silver Bells	1963	2.50	5.00	10.00
❏ JZSP 111805/6 [DJ]	This Christmas I Spend With You/White Christmas	1965	2.50	5.00	10.00

—Promotional record for Christmas Seals

❏ JZSP 111805/6 [PS]	This Christmas I Spend With You/White Christmas	1965	3.00	6.00	12.00

MGM

❏ 14487	God Is at Work Within You/One Solitary Life	1973	—	2.00	4.00

PARAMOUNT

❏ 0271	Pages of Life/Summer Green, Autumn Gold	1974	—	2.00	4.00

7-Inch Extended Plays
COLUMBIA

❏ 7-9096	My Love, Forgive Me/Softly, As I Leave You/What Kind of Fool Am I//Just Say I Love Her/Welcome Home Angelina/Too Good	1964	2.50	5.00	10.00

—33 1/3 rpm, small hole, "Special Coin Operator Release"

❏ 7-9096 [PS]	My Love, Forgive Me	1964	2.50	5.00	10.00

G

Number	Title (A Side/B Side)	Yr	VG	VG+	NM
Albums					
COLUMBIA					
❏ C 1051	Today's Greatest Hits	1970	3.00	6.00	12.00
❏ CS 1051	Today's Greatest Hits	1970	3.00	6.00	12.00
❏ PC 1051	Today's Greatest Hits	198?	2.00	4.00	8.00
—Budget-line reissue					
❏ CL 1676 [M]	Always You	1962	3.00	6.00	12.00
❏ CL 1826 [M]	Two of Us	1962	3.00	6.00	12.00
❏ CL 1931 [M]	Sincerely Yours	1962	3.00	6.00	12.00
❏ CL 1993 [M]	The Wonderful World of Love	1963	3.00	6.00	12.00
❏ CL 2076 [M]	This Christmas I Spend with You	1963	3.00	6.00	12.00
❏ CL 2088 [M]	Robert Goulet in Person	1963	3.00	6.00	12.00
❏ CL 2200 [M]	Without You	1964	3.00	6.00	12.00
❏ CL 2296 [M]	My Love Forgive Me	1964	3.00	6.00	12.00
❏ CL 2342 [M]	Begin to Love	1965	3.00	6.00	12.00
❏ CL 2380 [M]	Summer Sounds	1965	3.00	6.00	12.00
❏ CL 2418 [M]	Robert Goulet on Broadway	1965	3.00	6.00	12.00
❏ CL 2482 [M]	I Remember You	1966	3.00	6.00	12.00
❏ CL 2541 [M]	Traveling On	1966	3.00	6.00	12.00
❏ CL 2586 [M]	Robert Goulet on Broadway, Volume 2	1967	3.00	6.00	12.00
❏ CL 2727 [M]	Hollywood Mon Amour (Great Songs from the Movies)	1967	3.75	7.50	15.00
❏ CS 8476 [S]	Always You	1962	3.75	7.50	15.00
❏ CS 8626 [S]	Two of Us	1962	3.75	7.50	15.00
❏ CS 8731 [S]	Sincerely Yours	1962	3.75	7.50	15.00
❏ CS 8793 [S]	The Wonderful World of Love	1963	3.75	7.50	15.00
❏ CS 8876 [S]	This Christmas I Spend with You	1963	3.75	7.50	15.00
❏ CS 8888 [S]	Robert Goulet in Person	1963	3.75	7.50	15.00
❏ CS 9000 [S]	Without You	1964	3.75	7.50	15.00
❏ CS 9096 [S]	My Love, Forgive Me	1964	3.75	7.50	15.00
❏ CS 9142 [S]	Begin to Love	1965	3.75	7.50	15.00
❏ CS 9180 [S]	Summer Sounds	1965	3.75	7.50	15.00
❏ CS 9218 [S]	Robert Goulet on Broadway	1965	3.75	7.50	15.00
❏ CS 9282 [S]	I Remember You	1966	3.75	7.50	15.00
❏ CS 9341 [S]	Traveling On	1966	3.75	7.50	15.00
❏ CS 9386 [S]	Robert Goulet on Broadway, Volume 2	1967	3.75	7.50	15.00
❏ CS 9527 [S]	Hollywood Mon Amour (Great Songs from the Movies)	1967	3.00	6.00	12.00
❏ CS 9695	Woman, Woman	1968	3.00	6.00	12.00
❏ CS 9734	Robert Goulet's Wonderful World of Christmas	1968	3.00	6.00	12.00
❏ CS 9763	Both Sides Now	1969	3.00	6.00	12.00
❏ CS 9815	Robert Goulet's Greatest Hits	1969	3.00	6.00	12.00
❏ PC 9815	Robert Goulet's Greatest Hits	197?	2.00	4.00	8.00
—Reissue with new prefix					
❏ CS 9874	Souvenir d'Italie	1969	3.00	6.00	12.00
❏ CG 30011 [(2)]	I Wish You Love	1970	3.75	7.50	15.00
COLUMBIA SPECIAL PRODUCTS					
❏ P 13345	Robert Goulet's Wonderful World of Christmas	1976	3.00	6.00	12.00
—Same as CS 9734, but "Exclusively distributed by Sutton Distributors, Inc."					
HARMONY					
❏ KH 30507	Raindrops Keep Fallin' on My Head	1971	2.50	5.00	10.00
❏ KH 31107	Bridge Over Troubled Water	1972	2.50	5.00	10.00
MERLIN					
❏ 2001	I Never Did As I Was Told	1971	3.00	6.00	12.00

GOWENS, SAMMY
45s

Number	Title (A Side/B Side)	Yr	VG	VG+	NM
UNITED ARTISTS					
❏ 114	Kissin' at the Drive-In/Rockin' By Myself	1958	25.00	50.00	100.00

GRACIE, CHARLIE
45s

Number	Title (A Side/B Side)	Yr	VG	VG+	NM
CADILLAC					
❏ 141	Boogie Boogie Blues/I'm Gonna Sit Right Down and Write Myself a Letter	1953	37.50	75.00	150.00
❏ 144	Rockin' and Rollin'/(B-side unknown)	1954	37.50	75.00	150.00
CAMEO					
❏ 105	Butterfly/Ninety-Nine Ways	1957	6.25	12.50	25.00
❏ 107	Fabulous/Just Lookin'	1957	5.00	10.00	20.00
❏ 111	I Love You So Much It Hurts/Wandering Eyes	1957	5.00	10.00	20.00
❏ 118	Cool Baby/You've Got a Heart Like a Rock	1957	5.00	10.00	20.00
❏ 127	Crazy Girl/Dressin' Up	1958	5.00	10.00	20.00
❏ 141	Love Bird/Trying	1958	5.00	10.00	20.00
CORAL					
❏ 62073	Hurry Up Buttercup/Doodlebug	1959	3.75	7.50	15.00
❏ 62115	Angel of Love/I'm a Fool, That's Why	1959	3.75	7.50	15.00
❏ 62141	Oh-Well-a/Because I Love You So	1959	3.75	7.50	15.00
DIAMOND					
❏ 178	He'll Never Love You Like I Do/Keep My Love Next to Your Heart	1965	6.25	12.50	25.00
FELSTED					
❏ 8629	W-Wow/Makin' Whoopee	1961	3.75	7.50	15.00
PRESIDENT					
❏ 825	Pretty Baby/Night and Day U.S.A.	1962	3.75	7.50	15.00
❏ 828	Count to Three/Just Like Us	1963	3.75	7.50	15.00
ROULETTE					
❏ 4255	I Look for You/The Race	1960	3.75	7.50	15.00
❏ 4312	Sorry for You/Scenery	1960	3.75	7.50	15.00
20TH CENTURY					
❏ 5033	Head Home, Honey/My Baby Loves Me	1955	12.50	25.00	50.00
❏ 5035	Honey Honey/Wildwood Boogie	1955	15.00	30.00	60.00

GRACIOUS PAUL DAVIS was in this group.
Albums

Number	Title (A Side/B Side)	Yr	VG	VG+	NM
CAPITOL					
❏ ST-602	Gracious	1970	10.00	20.00	40.00

GRADS, THE
45s

Number	Title (A Side/B Side)	Yr	VG	VG+	NM
A&M					
❏ 797	Everything in the Garden/Stage Door	1966	2.50	5.00	10.00
MERCURY					
❏ 72346	Cool One/Wild One	1964	5.00	10.00	20.00
MGM					
❏ 13216	Their Hearts Were Full of Spring/It Happened Once Before	1964	2.50	5.00	10.00
VALIANT					
❏ 6023	Once Again/White Steeple	1962	3.75	7.50	15.00

GRADUATES, THE (1)
45s

Number	Title (A Side/B Side)	Yr	VG	VG+	NM
CORSICAN					
❏ 0058	What Good Is Graduation/Lonely	1959	10.00	20.00	40.00
LAWN					
❏ 208	Ballad of a Girl and Boy/Goodbye My Love	1963	5.00	10.00	20.00
SHAN-TODD					
❏ 0055	Ballad of a Girl and Boy/Care	1959	7.50	15.00	30.00

GRADUATES, THE (2)
45s

Number	Title (A Side/B Side)	Yr	VG	VG+	NM
GNP CRESCENDO					
❏ 404	(The Shape of) Things to Come/Listen to the Music	1968	2.50	5.00	10.00

GRADUATES, THE (U) Definitely not group (1); might not be group (2), either.
45s

Number	Title (A Side/B Side)	Yr	VG	VG+	NM
RISING SONS					
❏ 712	If Ever I Get Out of This Mess I'm In/Seventh Generation Breakthrough	1968	7.50	15.00	30.00

GRADY, DON
45s

Number	Title (A Side/B Side)	Yr	VG	VG+	NM
CANTERBURY					
❏ 501	The Children of St. Monica/A Good Man to Have Around the House	1967	3.00	6.00	12.00
❏ 501 [PS]	The Children of St. Monica/A Good Man to Have Around the House	1967	3.75	7.50	15.00
❏ 507	Impressions with Syvonne/Leaving It Up to You	1967	3.00	6.00	12.00
CAPITOL					
❏ 5181	I Think You're Through/A Broken Heart Knows Better	1964	3.00	6.00	12.00
❏ 5362	It's Better This Way/One Good Turn Deserves Another	1965	3.00	6.00	12.00
CHALLENGE					
❏ 59328	Don't Let It Happen/Out	1966	3.00	6.00	12.00
ELEKTRA					
❏ 45846	One Man Woman/Story	1973	—	3.00	6.00
—As "Don Agrati"					
❏ 45860	Bloodstream/Two-Bit Afternoon	1973	—	3.00	6.00
—As "Don Agrati"					
ORANGE EMPIRE					
❏ 91647	Summertime Game/Little People	1965	5.00	10.00	20.00
Albums					
ELEKTRA					
❏ EKS-75057	Homegrown	1973	3.75	7.50	15.00
—As "Don Agrati"					

GRAFFITI
45s

Number	Title (A Side/B Side)	Yr	VG	VG+	NM
ABC					
❏ 11123	He's Got the Knack/Love In Spite	1968	7.50	15.00	30.00
Albums					
ABC					
❏ S-663	Graffiti	1968	15.00	30.00	60.00

GRAHAM, DAVY
Albums

Number	Title (A Side/B Side)	Yr	VG	VG+	NM
LONDON					
❏ PS 552	Large As Life and Twice As Natural	1968	3.75	7.50	15.00

GRAHAM, LARRY Also see GRAHAM CENTRAL STATION; SLY AND THE FAMILY STONE.
12-Inch Singles

Number	Title (A Side/B Side)	Yr	VG	VG+	NM
WARNER BROS.					
❏ PRO-A-1027 [DJ]	Don't Stop When You're Hot (edit)/(LP version)	1982	2.00	4.00	8.00
❏ PRO-A-1046 [DJ]	Sooner or Later/(Instrumental)	1982	2.00	4.00	8.00
❏ PRO-A-2065 [DJ]	I'm Sick and Tired (same on both sides)	1983	2.00	4.00	8.00

45s

Number	Title (A Side/B Side)	Yr	VG	VG+	NM
WARNER BROS.					
❏ 29003	What We All Need Is More Love/Tearing Out My Heart	1985	—	—	3.00
❏ 29529	I'm Sick and Tired/I'd Rather Be Loving You	1983	—	2.00	4.00
❏ 29620	I Never Forgot Your Eyes/Movin' Inside Your Love	1983	—	2.00	4.00
❏ 29884	Let Me Come Into Your Life/What You Are Inside	1982	—	2.00	4.00
❏ 29956	Sooner or Later/I Feel Good	1982	—	2.00	4.00
❏ 29956 [PS]	Sooner or Later/I Feel Good	1982	—	2.50	5.00
❏ 49221	One in a Million You/The Entertainer	1980	—	2.00	4.00
❏ 49221 [PS]	One in a Million You/The Entertainer	1980	—	2.50	5.00
❏ 49581	When We Get Married/Tonight	1980	—	2.00	4.00
❏ 49744	Just Be My Lady/Feels Like Love	1981	—	2.00	4.00
❏ 49833	Guess Who/Sweetheart	1981	—	2.00	4.00
❏ 50068	Don't Stop When You're Hot/I Love Loving You	1982	—	2.00	4.00
❏ 50068 [PS]	Don't Stop When You're Hot/I Love Loving You	1982	—	2.50	5.00
Albums					
WARNER BROS.					
❏ BSK 3447	One in a Million You	1980	2.00	4.00	8.00
❏ BSK 3554	Just Be My Lady	1981	2.00	4.00	8.00
❏ BSK 3668	Sooner or Later	1982	2.00	4.00	8.00
❏ 23878	Victory	1983	2.00	4.00	8.00
❏ 25307	Fired Up	1985	2.00	4.00	8.00

GRAHAM, LOU
45s

Number	Title (A Side/B Side)	Yr	VG	VG+	NM
CLYMAX					
❏ 318	Wee Willie Brown/You Were Mean Baby	1957	75.00	150.00	300.00
CORAL					
❏ 61931	Wee Willie Brown/You Were Mean Baby	1958	25.00	50.00	100.00

GRAHAM CENTRAL STATION Also see LARRY GRAHAM.
12-Inch Singles

Number	Title (A Side/B Side)	Yr	VG	VG+	NM
WARNER BROS.					
❏ PRO-A-639 [DJ]	Entrow (2 versions)	1976	3.75	7.50	15.00
❏ PRO-A-673 [DJ]	Now Do U Wanta Dance (same on both sides)	1977	3.75	7.50	15.00

Number	Title (A Side/B Side)	Yr	VG	VG+	NM

45s
WARNER BROS.

Number	Title (A Side/B Side)	Yr	VG	VG+	NM
❏ 7782	Can You Handle It/Ghetto	1974	—	2.50	5.00
❏ 8025	Release Yourself/'Tis Your Kind of Music	1974	—	2.50	5.00
❏ 8061	Feel the Need/We Be's Gettin' Down	1974	—	2.50	5.00
❏ 8105	Your Love/I Believe in You	1975	—	2.00	4.00
❏ 8148	It's Alright/Luckiest People	1975	—	2.00	4.00
❏ 8175	The Jam/The Jam (Disco Version)	1975	—	2.00	4.00
❏ 8205	Love/Why	1976	—	2.00	4.00
❏ 8235	Entrow — Part 1/Entrow — Part 2	1976	—	2.00	4.00
❏ 8288	Do Yah/I Got a Reason	1976	—	2.00	4.00
❏ 8378	Now Do-U-Wanta Dance/(B-side unknown)	1977	—	2.00	4.00
❏ 8417	Stomped Beat-Up and Whooped/Ole Smokey	1977	—	2.00	4.00
❏ 8464	Crazy Chicken/Saving My Love for You	1977	—	2.00	4.00
❏ 8602	My Radio Sure Sounds Good to Me/Turn It Out	1978	—	2.00	4.00
❏ 8665	Is It Love?/Are You Happy?	1978	—	2.00	4.00
❏ 8816	(You're a) Foxy Lady/Tonight	1979	—	2.00	4.00
❏ 49011	Star Walk/Boogie Baby	1979	—	2.00	4.00
❏ 49067	Sneaky Freak/Boogie Baby	1979	—	2.00	4.00

Albums
WARNER BROS.

Number	Title (A Side/B Side)	Yr	VG	VG+	NM
❏ BS 2763	Graham Central Station	1974	2.50	5.00	10.00
❏ BS4 2763 [Q]	Graham Central Station	1974	3.75	7.50	15.00
❏ BS 2814	Release Yourself	1974	2.50	5.00	10.00
❏ BS 2876	Ain't No 'Bout-a-Doubt It	1975	2.50	5.00	10.00
❏ BS4 2876 [Q]	Ain't No 'Bout-a-Doubt It	1975	3.75	7.50	15.00
❏ BS 2937	Mirror	1976	2.50	5.00	10.00
❏ BS 3041	Now Do U Wanta Dance	1977	2.50	5.00	10.00
❏ BSK 3175	My Radio Sure Sounds Good to Me	1978	2.50	5.00	10.00

—As "Larry Graham and Graham Central Station"

| ❏ BSK 3322 | Star Walk | 1979 | 2.50 | 5.00 | 10.00 |

—As "Larry Graham and Graham Central Station"

GRAMMER, BILLY
45s
DECCA

Number	Title (A Side/B Side)	Yr	VG	VG+	NM
❏ 31226	Columbus Stockade Blues/There's a Rainbow 'Round My Shoulder	1961	2.50	5.00	10.00
❏ 31274	Have a Drink on Me/Finger	1961	2.50	5.00	10.00
❏ 31321	Save Your Tears/I'd Like to Know You	1961	2.50	5.00	10.00
❏ 31396	He Ain't My Buddy No More/Blue Roller Rink	1962	2.50	5.00	10.00
❏ 31449	I Wanna Go Home (Detroit City)/Bottom of the Glass	1962	2.50	5.00	10.00
❏ 31514	Love Gets Better with Time/Lonesome Life	1963	2.50	5.00	10.00
❏ 31562	Old Foolish Me/I'll Leave the Porch Lights a-Burning	1963	2.50	5.00	10.00
❏ 31618	Don't Drop It/I Saw Your Face in the Moon	1964	2.00	4.00	8.00
❏ 31669	Wabash Cannonball/Gonna Lay Down My Old Guitar	1964	2.00	4.00	8.00
❏ 31757	Little Bit of Happiness/I'm Letting You Go (Goodbye)	1965	2.00	4.00	8.00
❏ 31892	Brown's Ferry Blues/Souvenirs of Sorrow	1966	2.00	4.00	8.00

EPIC

❏ 10052	Bottles/Temporarily	1966	2.00	4.00	8.00
❏ 10103	Heaven Help This Heart of Mine/The Real Thing	1966	2.00	4.00	8.00
❏ 10169	I've Seen That Look on Me (A Thousand Times)/Written on a Jailhouse	1967	2.00	4.00	8.00

EVEREST

| ❏ 19353 | Unknown Soldier/Princess of Persia | 1960 | 2.50 | 5.00 | 10.00 |
| ❏ 19384 | Big Big Dream/River of Regret | 1960 | 2.50 | 5.00 | 10.00 |

JMI

| ❏ 9 | Nobody's Listening to the Preacher Anymore/(B-side unknown) | 1972 | 2.00 | 4.00 | 8.00 |

MERCURY

❏ 72785	Money, Love and War/Last of My Future	1968	2.00	4.00	8.00
❏ 72836	The Ballad of John Dillinger/Do You Still Believe	1968	2.00	4.00	8.00
❏ 72893	The Hour of Separation/The Changing Scene	1969	—	3.00	6.00

MONUMENT

❏ 400	Gotta Travel On/Chasing a Dream	1958	3.75	7.50	15.00
❏ 403	Bonaparte's Retreat/The Kissing Tree	1959	3.00	6.00	12.00
❏ 407	It Takes You/Willie, Quit Your Playing	1959	3.00	6.00	12.00
❏ 413	Loveland/On the Job Too Long	1960	3.00	6.00	12.00
❏ 8653	Family Man/What We Have in Common Is Love	1975	—	2.00	4.00
❏ 8665	Steppin' Out/Mom and Dad's Waltz	1975	—	2.00	4.00
❏ 8685	That's Life/Who's Gonna Buy You the Ribbons	1976	—	2.00	4.00

RICE

| ❏ 5025 | Mabel (You Have Been a Friend to Me)/Papa and Mama | 1967 | 2.00 | 4.00 | 8.00 |

STONEWAY

| ❏ 1129 | Tie Me to Your Apron Strings Again/Blue Jay Rag | 197? | — | 3.00 | 6.00 |

STOP

| ❏ 321 | Jesus Is a Soul Man/Peace on Earth Begins Today | 1969 | — | 3.00 | 6.00 |

TAP

| ❏ 7031 | Wabash Cannonball/Take Me Down South | 197? | 2.00 | 4.00 | 8.00 |
| ❏ 7031 [PS] | Wabash Cannonball/Take Me Down South | 197? | 3.00 | 6.00 | 12.00 |

7-Inch Extended Plays
DECCA

| ❏ ED 2767 | Detroit City/Old Foolish Me//Love Gets Better with Time/Have a Drink on Me | 196? | 3.00 | 6.00 | 12.00 |
| ❏ ED 2767 [PS] | Billy Grammer | 196? | 3.00 | 6.00 | 12.00 |

Albums
DECCA

❏ DL 4212 [M]	Gospel Guitar	1962	3.75	7.50	15.00
❏ DL 4460 [M]	Golden Gospel Favorites	1964	3.00	6.00	12.00
❏ DL 4542 [M]	Gotta Travel On	1965	3.00	6.00	12.00
❏ DL 4642 [M]	Country Guitar	1965	3.00	6.00	12.00
❏ DL 74212 [S]	Gospel Guitar	1962	5.00	10.00	20.00
❏ DL 74460 [S]	Golden Gospel Favorites	1964	3.75	7.50	15.00
❏ DL 74542 [S]	Gotta Travel On	1965	3.75	7.50	15.00
❏ DL 74642 [S]	Country Guitar	1965	3.75	7.50	15.00

EPIC

| ❏ LN 24233 [M] | Sunday Guitar | 1967 | 3.75 | 7.50 | 15.00 |
| ❏ BN 26233 [S] | Sunday Guitar | 1967 | 3.75 | 7.50 | 15.00 |

MONUMENT

Number	Title (A Side/B Side)	Yr	VG	VG+	NM
❏ MLP-4000 [M]	Travelin' On	1959	10.00	20.00	40.00
❏ MLP-8039 [M]	Travelin' On	1965	6.25	12.50	25.00
❏ SLP-18039 [P]	Travelin' On	1965	7.50	15.00	30.00

VOCALION

| ❏ VL 73826 | Favorites | 1968 | 3.00 | 6.00 | 12.00 |

GRANAHAN, GERRY Also see JERRY GRANT.
45s
ATCO

| ❏ 6122 | Sweet Affection/Confess It to Your Heart | 1958 | 7.50 | 15.00 | 30.00 |

CANADIAN AMERICAN

❏ 116	When Irish Eyes Are Smiling/In My Heart	1960	5.00	10.00	20.00
❏ 119	You'll Never Walk Alone/Where's the Girl	1960	5.00	10.00	20.00
❏ 121	Short Skirts/I'm Afraid You'll Never Know	1960	5.00	10.00	20.00

CAPRICE

| ❏ 106 | Unchained Melody/Dancing Man | 1961 | 5.00 | 10.00 | 20.00 |
| ❏ 108 | Too Big for Her Bikini/Dance, Girl, Dance | 1961 | 25.00 | 50.00 | 100.00 |

—With backing by the Belmonts or the Five Satins (sources disagree)

GONE

❏ 5065	Let the Rumors Fly/Put Me Anywhere	1959	5.00	10.00	20.00
❏ 5081	It Hurts/Look for Me	1959	5.00	10.00	20.00
❏ 5081 [PS]	It Hurts/Look for Me	1959	15.00	30.00	60.00

MARK

| ❏ 121 | Love's Young Dream/Oh Well-A Watch-A Gonna Do | 1957 | 8.75 | 17.50 | 35.00 |

SUNBEAM

❏ 102	No Chemise, Please/Girl of My Dreams	1958	7.50	15.00	30.00
❏ 108	Baby Wait/Completely	1958	6.25	12.50	25.00
❏ 112	I'm Ready As I'll Ever Be/Nobody Can Handle This Job	1958	6.25	12.50	25.00

—B-side by Eddie Fontaine

| ❏ 122 | King Size/I'm Afraid You'll Never Know | 1958 | 6.25 | 12.50 | 25.00 |
| ❏ 127 | A Ring, a Bracelet, a Heart/You're Adorable | 1959 | 6.25 | 12.50 | 25.00 |

20TH CENTURY FOX

| ❏ 425 | Hang Up the Phone/Too Weak to Win | 1963 | 3.75 | 7.50 | 15.00 |
| ❏ 541 | Racing Fever: Title/Racing Fever: Mainstream | 1964 | 3.75 | 7.50 | 15.00 |

—B-side by Arnold Goland and His Orchestra

VEEP

| ❏ 1205 | All the Live-Long Day/Sophia | 1965 | 3.00 | 6.00 | 12.00 |

GRANATA, ROCCO
45s
EPIC

| ❏ 5-9401 | E Primavera/Oh Oh Rose | 1960 | 2.50 | 5.00 | 10.00 |

LAURIE

| ❏ 3041 | Marina/Manuela | 1959 | 3.00 | 6.00 | 12.00 |
| ❏ 3041 [PS] | Marina/Manuela | 1959 | 3.75 | 7.50 | 15.00 |

—All black and white sleeve

| ❏ 3041 [PS] | Marina/Manuela | 1959 | 5.00 | 10.00 | 20.00 |

—Pink title strip on otherwise black and white sleeve

| ❏ 3048 | Lo Bella/Torna A Sorriento | 1960 | 3.00 | 6.00 | 12.00 |

GRAND CANYON
45s
BANG

| ❏ 713 | Evil Boll-Weevil/Got to Find My Way Back | 1974 | 2.00 | 4.00 | 8.00 |

GRAND FUNK RAILROAD Includes records as "Grand Funk." Also see MARK FARNER; MARK FARNER AND DON BREWER; TERRY KNIGHT AND THE PACK.
45s
CAPITOL

Number	Title (A Side/B Side)	Yr	VG	VG+	NM
❏ 2567	Time Machine/High on a Horse	1969	—	3.00	6.00
❏ 2691	Mr. Limousine Driver/High Falootin' Woman	1969	—	3.00	6.00
❏ 2732	Heartbreaker/Please Don't Worry	1970	—	3.00	6.00
❏ 2816	Nothing Is the Same/Sin's a Good Man's Brother	1970	—	3.00	6.00
❏ 2877	Closer to Home/Aimless Lady	1970	—	3.00	6.00
❏ 2996	Mean Mistreater/Mark Says Alright	1970	—	3.00	6.00
❏ 3095	Feelin' Alright/I Want Freedom	1971	—	3.00	6.00
❏ 3160	Gimme Shelter/I Can Feel Him in the Morning	1971	—	3.00	6.00
❏ 3160 [PS]	Gimme Shelter/I Can Feel Him in the Morning	1971	2.50	5.00	10.00
❏ 3217	People, Let's Stop the War/Save the Land	1971	—	3.00	6.00
❏ 3255	Footstompin' Music/I Come Tumblin	1972	—	3.00	6.00
❏ 3316	Upsetter/No Lies	1972	—	3.00	6.00
❏ 3363	Rock 'N Roll Soul/Flight of the Phoenix	1972	—	3.00	6.00
❏ 3660	We're An American Band/Creepin'	1973	—	2.00	4.00
❏ 3660	We're An American Band/Creepin'	1973	—	3.00	6.00

—Originals on gold vinyl

❏ 3660 [PS]	We're An American Band/Creepin'	1973	—	2.50	5.00
❏ 3760	Walk Like a Man/The Railroad	1973	—	2.00	4.00
❏ 3760 [PS]	Walk Like a Man/The Railroad	1973	—	2.50	5.00
❏ 3840	The Loco-Motion/Destitute and Losin'	1974	—	2.00	4.00
❏ 3840 [PS]	The Loco-Motion/Destitute and Losin'	1974	—	2.50	5.00
❏ 3917	Shinin' On/Mr. Pretty Boy	1974	—	2.00	4.00
❏ 3917 [PS]	Shinin' On/Mr. Pretty Boy	1974	—	2.50	5.00
❏ 4002	Some Kind of Wonderful/Wild	1974	—	2.00	4.00
❏ 4002 [PS]	Some Kind of Wonderful/Wild	1974	—	2.50	5.00
❏ 4046	Bad Time/Good and Evil	1975	—	2.00	4.00
❏ 4199	Take Me/Genevieve	1975	—	2.00	4.00
❏ 4199 [PS]	Take Me/Genevieve	1975	—	2.50	5.00
❏ 4235	Sally/Love Is Dyin'	1976	—	2.00	4.00
❏ 4235 [PS]	Sally/Love Is Dyin'	1976	—	2.50	5.00

FULL MOON

❏ 49823	Y.O.U./Testify	1981	—	2.00	4.00
❏ 49823 [PS]	Y.O.U./Testify	1981	—	3.00	6.00
❏ 49866	No Reason Why/Stuck in the Middle	1981	—	2.00	4.00

MCA

❏ 40590	Can You Do It/1976	1976	—	2.50	5.00
❏ 40590 [PS]	Can You Do It/1976	1976	—	3.00	6.00
❏ 40641	Out to Get You/Just Couldn't Wait	1976	—	2.50	5.00

—The MCA sides were produced by Frank Zappa

Albums
CAPITOL

❏ ST-307	On Time	1969	3.75	7.50	15.00
❏ SKAO-406	Grand Funk	1970	3.75	7.50	15.00
❏ SKAO-471	Closer to Home	1970	3.75	7.50	15.00

G

Number	Title (A Side/B Side)	Yr	VG	VG+	NM
❏ SWBB-633 [(2)]Live Album		1970	3.75	7.50	15.00
—Includes poster					
❏ SW-764	Survival	1971	3.75	7.50	15.00
❏ SW-853	E Pluribus Funk	1971	3.75	7.50	15.00
—Round cover designed like a coin					
❏ SABB-11042 [(2)]Mark, Don and Mel 1969-71		1972	3.75	7.50	15.00
❏ SMAS-11099	Phoenix	1972	3.00	6.00	12.00
❏ SMAS-11207	We're An American Band	1973	2.50	5.00	10.00
—Black vinyl					
❏ SMAS-11207	We're An American Band	1973	5.00	10.00	20.00
—Gold vinyl without sheet of four stickers					
❏ SMAS-11207	We're An American Band	1973	7.50	15.00	30.00
—Gold vinyl with sheet of four stickers					
❏ SWAE-11278	Shinin' On	1974	2.00	4.00	8.00
—With 3-D glasses missing and no poster					
❏ SWAE-11278	Shinin' On	1974	3.00	6.00	12.00
—With 3-D glasses attached to cover and with 3-D poster					
❏ SO-11356	All the Girls in the World Beware!!!	1974	3.75	7.50	15.00
—With poster (deduct 33% if missing)					
❏ SABB-11445	Caught in the Act	1975	2.50	5.00	10.00
❏ ST-11482	Born to Die	1976	2.50	5.00	10.00
❏ ST-11579	Grand Funk Hits	1976	2.50	5.00	10.00
❏ SN-16138	Grand Funk Hits	1981	2.00	4.00	8.00
❏ SN-16176	Closer to Home	1981	2.00	4.00	8.00
❏ SN-16177	Grand Funk	1981	2.00	4.00	8.00
❏ SN-16178	On Time	1981	2.00	4.00	8.00
❏ 21692	We're An American Band	1999	6.25	12.50	25.00
—Limited-edition reissue on 180-gram gold vinyl with original 1973 packaging					
FULL MOON					
❏ HS 3625	Grand Funk Lives	1981	2.50	5.00	10.00
❏ 23750	What's Funk	1983	2.50	5.00	10.00
MCA					
❏ 2216	Good Singin' Good Playin'	1976	3.00	6.00	12.00
—Produced by Frank Zappa					

GRANDMA'S ROCKERS
Albums
FREDLO
| ❏ 6727 | Homemade Apple Pie | 1967 | 500.00 | 1000. | 1500. |

GRANT, CARY
45s
COLUMBIA
| ❏ 4-44377 | Christmas Lullaby/Here's to You | 1967 | 7.50 | 15.00 | 30.00 |

GRANT, EARL
45s
DECCA
❏ 25526	Ebb Tide/Deep Purple	1962	2.00	4.00	8.00
❏ 25560	Swingin' Gently/Beyond the Roof	1962	2.00	4.00	8.00
❏ 25574	Sweet Sixteen Bars/Learnin' the Blues	1962	2.00	4.00	8.00
❏ 25601	Caravan/I'll Build a Stairway to Paradise	1963	2.00	4.00	8.00
❏ 25607	More (Theme from "Mondo Cane")/Sukiyaki	1963	2.00	4.00	8.00
❏ 25626	Black Coffee/I'm Just a Lucky So-and-So	1964	2.00	4.00	8.00
❏ 25638	Satin Doll/Just One More Time	1964	2.00	4.00	8.00
❏ 25659	Without a Song/Meditation	1965	2.00	4.00	8.00
❏ 25674	Stand By Me/After Hours	1965	2.00	4.00	8.00
❏ 25683	Rudolph the Red-Nosed Reindeer/Santa Claus Is Comin' to Town	1965	2.00	4.00	8.00
❏ 25697	Blue Velvet/The Sweetest Sounds	1966	—	3.00	6.00
❏ 25703	Jingle Bells/Silver Bells	1966	—	3.00	6.00
❏ 25704	The Lonesome Road/When I Grow Too Old to Dream	1966	—	3.00	6.00
❏ 25713	Summertime/September in the Rain	1967	—	3.00	6.00
❏ 25721	Without a Song/I'm in the Mood for Love	1967	—	3.00	6.00
❏ 25730	I Miss You So/Stormy Weather	1967	—	3.00	6.00
❏ 25737	My Foolish Heart/One Note Samba	1968	—	3.00	6.00
❏ 25743	Bewitched/In Motion	1968	—	3.00	6.00
❏ 30150	Goodnight My Love, Pleasant Dreams/My Consolation	1956	3.75	7.50	15.00
❏ 30244	Thanks for You/Through the Eyes of a Boy and Girl	1956	3.75	7.50	15.00
❏ 30475	Fever/Malaguena	1957	3.75	7.50	15.00
❏ 30561	Honky Tonk/The Next Time You See Me	1958	3.00	6.00	12.00
❏ 30640	Ol' Man River/Kathy-O	1958	3.00	6.00	12.00
❏ 30719	(At) The End (Of a Rainbow)/Hunky Dunky Doo	1958	3.00	6.00	12.00
—Same song, altered title on A-side					
❏ 30719	The End/Hunky Dunky Doo	1958	3.75	7.50	15.00
❏ 30819	Evening Rain/Evening Rain (Instrumental)	1959	2.50	5.00	10.00
❏ 30856	Last Night/Imitation of Life	1959	2.50	5.00	10.00
❏ 30908	The Wish/Don't Point Your Finger at Anyone Else	1959	2.50	5.00	10.00
❏ 30983	All for the Best/Not One Minute More	1959	2.50	5.00	10.00
❏ 31022	Christmas Card/Swingin' Christmas	1959	2.50	5.00	10.00
❏ 31044	House of Bamboo/Two Loves Have I	1960	2.50	5.00	10.00
❏ 31110	Dreamy/Building Castles	1960	2.50	5.00	10.00
❏ 31203	You Thrill Me/Quando La Luna	1961	2.00	4.00	8.00
❏ 31222	Ebb Tide/Next Time	1961	2.00	4.00	8.00
❏ 31263	My Foolish Heart/Sermonette	1961	2.00	4.00	8.00
❏ 31328	Honey/Tender Is the Night	1961	2.00	4.00	8.00
❏ 31468	Steve's Theme (From "Forty Pounds of Trouble")/Yes Sirree	1963	2.00	4.00	8.00
❏ 31716	This Little Girl of Mine/Come to Me (Pretty Baby)	1964	2.00	4.00	8.00
❏ 31902	I'll Drown in My Own Tears/I Can't Stop Loving You	1966	—	3.00	6.00
❏ 32093	I Love You, Yes I Do/Hide Nor Hair	1967	—	3.00	6.00
❏ 32443	It Was a Very Good Year/If I Only Had Time	1969	—	—	2.50
❏ 32499	I Wonder/The Importance of the Rose	1969	—	—	2.50
❏ 32667	Grant's Pass/Elizabethan Reggae	1970	—	—	2.50
MCA					
❏ 65023	Silver Bells/Jingle Bells	1973	—	2.00	4.00
—Black label with rainbow					
❏ 65023	Silver Bells/Jingle Bells	1980	—	—	3.00
—Blue label with rainbow					
PRINCE					
❏ 1201	One Way Street/(B-side unknown)	1956	3.75	7.50	15.00
—Black vinyl					
❏ 1201	One Way Street/(B-side unknown)	1956	6.25	12.50	25.00
—Colored vinyl					

Number	Title (A Side/B Side)	Yr	VG	VG+	NM
7-Inch Extended Plays					
DECCA					
❏ ED 2591	(contents unknown)	195?	2.50	5.00	10.00
❏ ED 2591 [PS]	The Versatile Earl Grant	195?	2.50	5.00	10.00
❏ ED 2634	(contents unknown)	195?	2.50	5.00	10.00
❏ ED 2634 [PS]	The Versatile Earl Grant	195?	2.50	5.00	10.00
❏ ED 2635	(contents unknown)	195?	2.50	5.00	10.00
❏ ED 2635 [PS]	The Versatile Earl Grant	195?	2.50	5.00	10.00
❏ ED 2639 [M]	(contents unknown)	1959	2.50	5.00	10.00
❏ ED 2639 [PS]	The End	1959	2.50	5.00	10.00
❏ ED 7-2639 [PS]The End		1959	3.75	7.50	15.00
❏ ED 7-2639 [S]	(contents unknown)	1959	3.75	7.50	15.00
❏ ED 2705	Ebb Tide/My Foolish Heart//Exodus Theme/I'm in the Mood for Love	196?	2.50	5.00	10.00
❏ ED 2705 [PS]	Earl Grant	196?.	2.50	5.00	10.00
❏ ED 2722	Swingin' Gently/Beyond the Reef//Yellow Bird/Make Someone Happy	196?	2.50	5.00	10.00
❏ ED 2722 [PS]	Swingin' Gently	196?	2.50	5.00	10.00
❏ ED 2736	Sweet Sixteen Bars/Learnin' the Blues//Because of Rain/Too Close for Comfort	196?	2.50	5.00	10.00
❏ ED 2736 [PS]	Earl Grant	196?	2.50	5.00	10.00
Albums					
DECCA					
❏ DL 4044 [M]	The Magic of Earl Grant	1960	3.00	6.00	12.00
❏ DL 4165 [M]	Ebb Tide	1961	3.00	6.00	12.00
❏ DL 4188 [M]	Earl After Dark	1961	3.00	6.00	12.00
❏ DL 4231 [M]	Beyond the Reef	1962	3.00	6.00	12.00
❏ DL 4299 [M]	Earl Grant at Basin Street East	1962	3.00	6.00	12.00
❏ DL 4338 [M]	Midnight Sun	1963	3.00	6.00	12.00
❏ DL 4405 [M]	Yes Sirree	1963	3.00	6.00	12.00
❏ DL 4454 [M]	Fly Me to the Moon	1963	3.00	6.00	12.00
❏ DL 4506 [M]	Just for a Thrill	1964	3.00	6.00	12.00
❏ DL 4576 [M]	Just One More Time	1964	3.00	6.00	12.00
❏ DL 4623 [M]	Trade Winds	1965	3.00	6.00	12.00
❏ DL 4624 [M]	Spotlight on Earl Grant	1965	3.00	6.00	12.00
❏ DL 4677 [M]	Winter Wonderland	1965	3.00	6.00	12.00
❏ DL 4729 [M]	Songs Made Famous by Nat Cole	1966	3.00	6.00	12.00
❏ DL 4738 [M]	Stand By Me	1966	3.00	6.00	12.00
❏ DL 4806 [M]	Bali Ha'l	1967	3.00	6.00	12.00
❏ DL 4811 [M]	Just a Closer Walk with Thee	1967	3.75	7.50	15.00
❏ DL 4813 [M]	Earl Grant's Greatest Hits	1967	3.75	7.50	15.00
❏ DL 4937 [M]	Gently Swingin'	1968	5.00	10.00	20.00
❏ DL 4974 [M]	Spanish Eyes	1968	6.25	12.50	25.00
❏ DXS 7204 [(2)]	The Best of Earl Grant	1969	5.00	10.00	20.00
❏ DL 8672 [M]	The Versatile Earl Grant	1958	5.00	10.00	20.00
❏ DL 8830 [M]	The End	1959	3.75	7.50	15.00
❏ DL 8905 [M]	Grant Takes Rhythm	1959	3.75	7.50	15.00
❏ DL 8916 [M]	Nothing But the Blues	1960	3.75	7.50	15.00
❏ DL 8935 [M]	Paris Is My Beat	1960	3.75	7.50	15.00
❏ DL 74044 [S]	The Magic of Earl Grant	1960	3.75	7.50	15.00
❏ DL 74165 [S]	Ebb Tide	1961	3.75	7.50	15.00
❏ DL 74188 [S]	Earl After Dark	1961	3.75	7.50	15.00
❏ DL 74231 [S]	Beyond the Reef	1962	3.75	7.50	15.00
❏ DL 74299 [S]	Earl Grant at Basin Street East	1962	3.75	7.50	15.00
❏ DL 74338 [S]	Midnight Sun	1963	3.75	7.50	15.00
❏ DL 74405 [S]	Yes Sirree	1963	3.75	7.50	15.00
❏ DL 74454 [S]	Fly Me to the Moon	1963	3.75	7.50	15.00
❏ DL 74506 [S]	Just for a Thrill	1964	3.75	7.50	15.00
❏ DL 74576 [S]	Just One More Time	1964	3.75	7.50	15.00
❏ DL 74623 [S]	Trade Winds	1965	3.75	7.50	15.00
❏ DL 74624 [S]	Spotlight on Earl Grant	1965	3.75	7.50	15.00
❏ DL 74677 [S]	Winter Wonderland	1965	3.75	7.50	15.00
❏ DL 74729 [S]	Songs Made Famous by Nat Cole	1966	3.75	7.50	15.00
❏ DL 74738 [S]	Stand By Me	1966	3.75	7.50	15.00
❏ DL 74806 [S]	Bali Ha'l	1967	3.75	7.50	15.00
❏ DL 74811 [S]	Just a Closer Walk with Thee	1967	3.75	7.50	15.00
❏ DL 74813 [S]	Earl Grant's Greatest Hits	1967	3.75	7.50	15.00
❏ DL 74937 [S]	Gently Swingin'	1968	3.75	7.50	15.00
❏ DL 74974 [S]	Spanish Eyes	1968	3.75	7.50	15.00
❏ DL 75052	In Motion	1969	3.75	7.50	15.00
❏ DL 75108	This Magic Moment	1970	3.75	7.50	15.00
❏ DL 75158	A Time for Us	1970	3.00	6.00	12.00
❏ DL 75223	Earl Grant	1970	3.00	6.00	12.00
❏ DL 78830 [S]	The End	1959	5.00	10.00	20.00
❏ DL 78905 [S]	Grant Takes Rhythm	1959	5.00	10.00	20.00
❏ DL 78916 [S]	Nothing But the Blues	1960	5.00	10.00	20.00
❏ DL 78935 [S]	Paris Is My Beat	1960	5.00	10.00	20.00
VOCALION					
❏ VL 3793 [M]	It's So Good	1967	3.00	6.00	12.00
❏ VL 73793 [S]	It's So Good	1967	3.00	6.00	12.00
❏ VL 73860	Send for Me	1969	3.00	6.00	12.00
❏ VL 73893	One for My Baby	1969	3.00	6.00	12.00

GRANT, ESTHER
45s
WILSTONE
| ❏ 001 | Let's Make the Most Out of Love/(B-side unknown) | 196? | 250.00 | 500.00 | 1000. |

GRANT, GEORGE, AND THE CASTELLES See THE CASTELLES.

GRANT, GOGI
45s
ERA
❏ 1003	Suddenly There's a Valley/Love Is	1955	3.75	7.50	15.00
❏ 1008	Who Are We/We Believe in Love	1955	3.75	7.50	15.00
❏ 1013	The Wayward Wind/No More Than Forever	1956	4.00	8.00	16.00
❏ 1019	You're in Love/When the Tide Is High	1956	3.75	7.50	15.00
❏ 1053	The Golden Ladder/All of Me	1957	3.00	6.00	12.00
❏ 1062	I Gave You My Heart/I Don't Want to Walk Without You	1957	3.00	6.00	12.00
❏ 3046	The Wayward Wind/The Tide Is High	1961	2.00	4.00	8.00
❏ 3205	The Wayward Wind/Suddenly There's a Valley	1969	—	—	2.50	5.00
LIBERTY					
❏ 55214	If and When/I'll Never Smile Again	1959	2.50	5.00	10.00
❏ 55229	Goin' Home/All God's Children Got Shoes	1959	2.50	5.00	10.00
❏ 55252	I Never Meant to Fall in Love/Stay Here with Me	1960	2.50	5.00	10.00

Lesley Gore, *I'll Cry If I Want To*, Mercury MG-20805, mono LP, no blurb for "It's My Party," $15-$30.

Grateful Dead, *History of the Grateful Dead, Vol. I (Bear's Choice)*, Warner Bros. BS 2721, stereo LP, "Burbank" palm-trees label, $10-$20.

Al Green, *I'm Still in Love with You,* Hi SHL-32074, stereo LP, $7.50-$15.

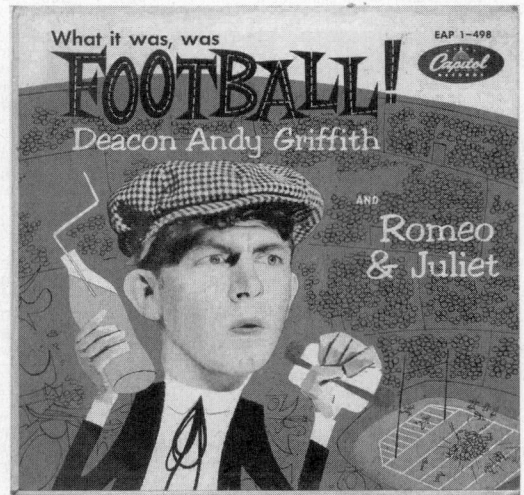

Andy Griffith, *What It Was, Was Football,* Capitol EAP 1-498, 7-inch EP, $40-$80 (cover and record together).

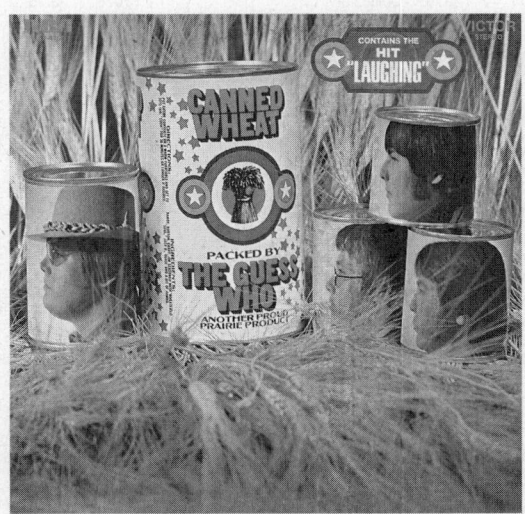

The Guess Who, *Canned Wheat,* RCA Victor LSP-4157, stereo LP, orange label with rigid vinyl, $10-$20.

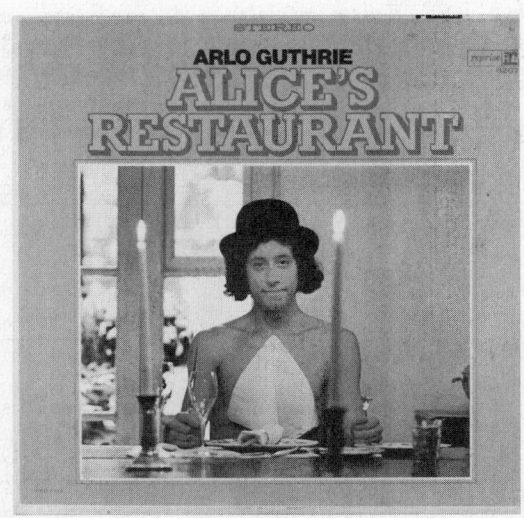

Arlo Guthrie, *Alice's Restaurant,* Reprise RS-6267, stereo LP, pink, gold and green label, $7.50-$15.

Number	Title (A Side/B Side)	Yr	VG	VG+	NM
☐ 55286	Two Lovers by the Sea/In a Sentimental Mood	1960	2.50	5.00	10.00
☐ 55316	That One Kiss/Adrift on a Star	1961	2.50	5.00	10.00
MONUMENT					
☐ 986	Don't Touch Me/Pathfinder	1966	—	3.00	6.00
☐ 1005	The Sea/How Much Will I Love You	1967	—	3.00	6.00
PETE					
☐ 701	Down Here on the Ground/The Magic of People	1968	—	2.50	5.00
☐ 708	Buy Me Penny Candy/Paradise	1968	—	2.50	5.00
☐ 717	Yesterday, When I Was Young/ (B-side unknown)	1969	—	2.50	5.00
☐ 718	On the Mountain/Faure	1969	—	2.50	5.00
RCA VICTOR					
☐ 47-4994	Forget Me Not/ Where There's Smoke, There's Fire	1952	5.00	10.00	20.00
☐ 47-5053	Mommy's Little Angel/My Tormented Heart	1952	5.00	10.00	20.00
—B-side by the Three Suns					
☐ 47-5436	Everyone Knows I Love You/Ricochet	1953	5.00	10.00	20.00
☐ 47-5512	Secret Love/Ricochet	1953	5.00	10.00	20.00
☐ 47-6996	That's the Life for Me/ It's a Wonderful Thing to Be Loved	1957	2.50	5.00	10.00
☐ 47-7082	Johnny's Dream/What a Beautiful Combination	1957	2.50	5.00	10.00
☐ 47-7146	Chinese Nightingale/Bonjour Tristesse	1958	2.50	5.00	10.00
☐ 47-7215	My Secret Prayer/How Do We Know We're in Love	1958	2.50	5.00	10.00
☐ 47-7294	Strange Are the Ways of Love/Marjolaino	1958	2.50	5.00	10.00
☐ 47-7438	Two Dreams/(Kiss Me) Honey Honey (Kiss Me)	1959	2.50	5.00	10.00
☐ 47-7492	The Ride Back from Boot Hill/A Restless Pair	1959	2.50	5.00	10.00
20TH FOX					
☐ 284	Johnny, I Hardly Knew Ye/ The Second Time Around	1961	2.50	5.00	10.00
☐ 297	Magic Music/Tender Is the Night	1962	2.50	5.00	10.00
☐ 403	Magic Music/Tender Is the Night	1963	2.00	4.00	8.00
Albums					
ERA					
☐ EL-106 [M]	The Wayward Wind	196?	6.25	12.50	25.00
☐ 20001 [M]	Suddenly There's Gogi Grant	1956	15.00	30.00	60.00
—Black vinyl					
☐ 20001 [M]	Suddenly There's Gogi Grant	1956	25.00	50.00	100.00
—Red vinyl					
LIBERTY					
☐ LRP-3144 [M]	If You Want to Get to Heaven, Shout	1960	7.50	15.00	30.00
☐ LST-7144 [S]	If You Want to Get to Heaven, Shout	1960	10.00	20.00	40.00
PETE					
☐ S-1101	Gogi Grant	1968	3.75	7.50	15.00
☐ S-1111	The Way a Woman Feels	1970	3.75	7.50	15.00
RCA VICTOR					
☐ LOC-1030 [M]	The Helen Morgan Story	1957	15.00	30.00	60.00
☐ LPM-1717 [M]	Welcome to My Heart	1958	10.00	20.00	40.00
☐ LPM-1940 [M]	Torch Time	1959	7.50	15.00	30.00
☐ LSP-1940 [S]	Torch Time	1959	10.00	20.00	40.00
☐ LPM-2000 [M]	Granted… It's Gogi	1960	7.50	15.00	30.00
☐ LSP-2000 [S]	Granted… It's Gogi	1960	10.00	20.00	40.00

GRANT, JANIE
45s
CAPRICE

Number	Title (A Side/B Side)	Yr	VG	VG+	NM
☐ 104	Triangle/She's Going Steady with You	1961	3.75	7.50	15.00
☐ 109	Romeo/Roller Coaster	1961	3.75	7.50	15.00
☐ 111	I Wonder Who's Kissing You Now/Unhappy	1961	3.75	7.50	15.00
☐ 113	Oh Johnny/Oh My Love	1962	3.75	7.50	15.00
☐ 115	That Greasy Kid Stuff/Trying to Forget You	1962	3.75	7.50	15.00
☐ 119	Peggy Got Engaged/Two Is Company and Three's a Crowd	1962	3.75	7.50	15.00
PARKWAY					
☐ 982	My Heart, Your Heart/ And That Reminds Me of You	1966	7.50	15.00	30.00
UNITED ARTISTS					
☐ 616	Tell Me Mama/ Whose Heart Are You Breaking Now	1963	3.00	6.00	12.00
☐ 649	That Kind of Boy/Priceless Persuasion	1963	3.00	6.00	12.00
☐ 731	Ribbons and Roses/Too Young for Me	1964	3.00	6.00	12.00
☐ 775	After Last Night/All I Did Was Fall in Love	1964	3.00	6.00	12.00
☐ 843	I Shouldn't Care (If You're Using Me)/There Ain't No Party Tonight	1965	3.00	6.00	12.00

GRANT, JERRY
Probably the artist who later recorded as GERRY GRANAHAN.
45s
ATCO

Number	Title (A Side/B Side)	Yr	VG	VG+	NM
☐ 6100	Talkin' About Love/Some Day, Maybe Tonight	1957	10.00	20.00	40.00

GRANT, JULIE
45s
HICKORY

Number	Title (A Side/B Side)	Yr	VG	VG+	NM
☐ 1260	Every Day I Have to Cry/Watch What You Do with Your Baby	1964	3.00	6.00	12.00
☐ 1288	You're Nobody 'Til Somebody Loves You/Come to Me	1964	3.00	6.00	12.00

GRAPEFRUIT
45s
ABC DUNHILL

Number	Title (A Side/B Side)	Yr	VG	VG+	NM
☐ 4178	This Little Man/Round Going Round	1968	2.50	5.00	10.00
EQUINOX					
☐ 70000	Dear Delilah/Dead Boot	1967	3.75	7.50	15.00
☐ 70005	Elevator/Yes	1968	3.75	7.50	15.00
☐ 70008	C'mon Marianne/Ain't It Good	1968	3.75	7.50	15.00
RCA VICTOR					
☐ 74-0241	Thunder and Lightning/Blues in Your Head	1969	3.75	7.50	15.00
Albums					
ABC DUNHILL					
☐ DS-50050	Around Grapefruit	1968	10.00	20.00	40.00
RCA VICTOR					
☐ LSP-4215	Deep Water	1969	7.50	15.00	30.00

GRASS ROOTS, THE
Originally a studio group produced by STEVE BARRI and P.F. SLOAN; the touring group, completely different from those who recorded "Where Were You When I Needed You," featured Rob Grill on vocals.
45s
ABC DUNHILL

Number	Title (A Side/B Side)	Yr	VG	VG+	NM
☐ 4144	Midnight Confessions/ Who Will You Be Tomorrow	1968	2.00	4.00	8.00
☐ 4162	Bella Linda/Hot Bright Blues	1968	2.00	4.00	8.00
☐ 4162	Della Linda/Hot Bright Blues	1968	3.00	6.00	12.00
—Some labels have A-side typographical error as shown					
☐ 4180	Lovin' Things/You and Love Are the Same	1969	2.00	4.00	8.00
☐ 4187	The River Is Wide/(You Gotta) Live for Love	1969	2.00	4.00	8.00
☐ 4198	I'd Wait a Million Years/Fly Me to Havana	1969	—	3.00	6.00
☐ 4217	Heaven Knows/Don't Remind Me	1969	—	3.00	6.00
☐ 4227	Walking Through the Country/Truck Drivin' Man	1970	—	3.00	6.00
☐ 4237	Baby Hold On/Get It Together	1970	—	3.00	6.00
☐ 4237 [PS]	Baby Hold On/Get It Together	1970	2.50	5.00	10.00
☐ 4249	Come On and Say It/ Something's Comin' Over Me	1970	—	3.00	6.00
☐ 4249 [PS]	Come On and Say It/ Something's Comin' Over Me	1970	2.50	5.00	10.00
☐ 4263	Temptation Eyes/Keepin' Me Down	1971	—	2.50	5.00
☐ 4279	Sooner or Later/I Can Turn Off the Rain	1971	—	2.50	5.00
☐ 4289	Two Divided by Love/Let It Go	1971	—	2.50	5.00
☐ 4302	Glory Bound/The Only One	1972	—	2.50	5.00
☐ 4316	The Runway/Move Along	1972	—	2.50	5.00
☐ 4325	Any Way the Wind Blows/Monday Love	1972	—	2.50	5.00
☐ 4335	Love Is What You Make It/Someone to Love	1973	—	3.00	6.00
☐ 4345	Where There's Smoke There's Fire/Look but Don't Touch	1973	2.50	5.00	10.00
☐ 4371	We Can't Dance to Your Music/ Look but Don't Touch	1973	2.50	5.00	10.00
☐ 15006	Stealin' Love (In the Night)/ We Almost Made It Together	1974	3.75	7.50	15.00
DUNHILL					
☐ 4013	Mr. Jones (A Ballad of a Thin Man)/ You're a Lonely Girl	1965	5.00	10.00	20.00
☐ 4029	Where Were You When I Needed You/ (These Are) Bad Times	1966	5.00	10.00	20.00
☐ 4043	Only When You're Lonely/ This Is What I Was Made For	1966	5.00	10.00	20.00
☐ 4053	Tip of My Tongue/Look Out, Girl	1966	6.25	12.50	25.00
☐ 4084	Let's Live for Today/Depressed Feeling	1967	3.00	6.00	12.00
☐ 4094	Things I Should Have Said/Tip of My Tongue	1967	2.50	5.00	10.00
☐ 4094 [PS]	Things I Should Have Said/Tip of My Tongue	1967	3.75	7.50	15.00
☐ 4105	Wake Up, Wake Up/No Exit	1967	2.50	5.00	10.00
☐ 4122	A Melody for You/Hey Friend	1968	2.50	5.00	10.00
☐ 4129	Feelings/Here's Where You Belong	1968	2.50	5.00	10.00
☐ 4144	Midnight Confessions/ Who Will You Be Tomorrow	1968	7.50	15.00	30.00
—Original label has no "ABC" logo next to "Dunhill"					
HAVEN					
☐ 802	Out in the Open/Optical Illusion	1976	2.00	4.00	8.00
☐ 7015	Mamacita/Last Time Around	1975	—	2.50	5.00
☐ 7021	Naked Man/Nothing Good Comes Easy	1975	—	2.50	5.00
MCA					
☐ 52058	Here Comes That Feeling Again/ Temptation Eyes	1982	2.50	5.00	10.00
☐ 52104	She Don't Know Me/Keep On Burning	1982	2.50	5.00	10.00

7-Inch Extended Plays
ABC DUNHILL

Number	Title (A Side/B Side)	Yr	VG	VG+	NM
☐ PRO-50107	Midnight Confessions/Sooner or Later/Where Were You When I Needed You//Temptation Eyes/Wait a Million Years/Heaven Knows	1971	3.75	7.50	15.00
—Jukebox issue; small hole, plays at 33 1/3 rpm					
☐ PRO-50107 [PS]	Their 16 Greatest Hits	1971	3.75	7.50	15.00
—Part of "Little LP" series (LLP #165)					

Albums
ABC

Number	Title (A Side/B Side)	Yr	VG	VG+	NM
☐ AC-30003	The ABC Collection	1976	3.75	7.50	15.00
ABC DUNHILL					
☐ DS-50027	Feelings	1968	3.75	7.50	15.00
—Reissue with ABC logo					
☐ DS-50047	Golden Grass	1968	5.00	10.00	20.00
☐ DS-50052	Lovin' Things	1969	5.00	10.00	20.00
☐ DS-50067	Leaving It All Behind	1969	5.00	10.00	20.00
☐ DS-50087	More Golden Grass	1970	5.00	10.00	20.00
☐ DSX-50107	Their 16 Greatest Hits	1971	5.00	10.00	20.00
☐ DSX-50112	Move Along	1972	3.75	7.50	15.00
☐ DSX-50137	A Lotta Mileage	1973	3.75	7.50	15.00
COMMAND					
☐ QD-40013 [Q]	Their 16 Greatest Hits	1974	7.50	15.00	30.00
DUNHILL					
☐ D-50011 [M]	Where Were You When I Needed You	1966	37.50	75.00	150.00
☐ DS-50011 [S]	Where Were You When I Needed You	1966	25.00	50.00	100.00
☐ D-50020 [M]	Let's Live for Today	1967	6.25	12.50	25.00
☐ DS-50020 [S]	Let's Live for Today	1967	7.50	15.00	30.00
☐ D-50027 [M]	Feelings	1968	7.50	15.00	30.00
☐ DS-50027 [S]	Feelings	1968	5.00	10.00	20.00
HAVEN					
☐ ST-9204	The Grass Roots	1975	3.75	7.50	15.00
MCA					
☐ 5331	Powers of the Night	1982	3.00	6.00	12.00
☐ 37154	Their 16 Greatest Hits	198?	2.00	4.00	8.00
—Budget-line reissue of ABC Dunhill 50107					

GRATEFUL DEAD, THE
Also see JERRY GARCIA; MICKEY HART; BOB WEIR.
12-Inch Singles
ARISTA

Number	Title (A Side/B Side)	Yr	VG	VG+	NM
☐ ADP 9757 [DJ]	Throwing Stones (Ashes Ashes) (LP version)/(Edit Remix)	1987	3.00	6.00	12.00

45s
ARISTA

Number	Title (A Side/B Side)	Yr	VG	VG+	NM
☐ 0276	Dancin' in the Streets/Terrapin Station	1977	—	3.00	6.00
☐ 0291	Passenger/Terrapin Station	1977	—	3.00	6.00

Number	Title (A Side/B Side)	Yr	VG	VG+	NM
❏ 0383	Good Lovin'/Stagger Lee	1978	—	3.00	6.00
❏ 0383 [PS]	Good Lovin'/Stagger Lee	1978	150.00	300.00	600.00
❏ 0410	France/Shakedown Street	1979	—	3.00	6.00
❏ 0519	Alabama Getaway/Far from Me	1980	—	2.50	5.00
❏ 0519 [PS]	Alabama Getaway/Far from Me	1980	—	2.50	5.00
❏ 0546	Don't Ease Me In/Far from Me	1980	—	2.50	5.00
❏ 9606	Touch of Grey/My Brother Esau	1987	—	—	3.00

—Black vinyl (not issued with picture sleeve)

Number	Title (A Side/B Side)	Yr	VG	VG+	NM
❏ 9606	Touch of Grey/My Brother Esau	1987	—	2.50	5.00

—Grey vinyl

Number	Title (A Side/B Side)	Yr	VG	VG+	NM
❏ 9606 [PS]	Touch of Grey/My Brother Esau	1987	—	2.50	5.00

—Fold-open poster sleeve (add $2 for sticker attached to original shrink wrap)

Number	Title (A Side/B Side)	Yr	VG	VG+	NM
❏ 9643	Throwing Stones (Ashes Ashes) Edit/Throwing Stones (Ashes Ashes) LP Version	1987	—	—	3.00
❏ 9643 [PS]	Throwing Stones (Ashes Ashes) Edit/Throwing Stones (Ashes Ashes) LP Version	1987	—	—	3.00
❏ 9899	Foolish Heart/We Can Run	1989	—	2.00	4.00
❏ 9899 [PS]	Foolish Heart/We Can Run	1989	—	2.00	4.00

GRATEFUL DEAD

Number	Title (A Side/B Side)	Yr	VG	VG+	NM
❏ 01	Here Comes Sunshine/ Let Me Sing Your Blues Away	1973	3.00	6.00	12.00
❏ 02	Eyes of the World/Weather Report (Part 1)	1974	3.00	6.00	12.00
❏ 03	U.S. Blues/Loose Lucy	1974	2.50	5.00	10.00
❏ 03 [PS]	U.S. Blues/Loose Lucy	1974	6.25	12.50	25.00
❏ XW-718	The Music Never Stopped/Help on the Way	1975	3.75	7.50	15.00
❏ XW-762	Franklin's Tower/Help on the Way	1976	6.25	12.50	25.00

SCORPIO

Number	Title (A Side/B Side)	Yr	VG	VG+	NM
❏ 201	Stealin'/Don't Ease Me In	1966	250.00	500.00	1000.

WARNER BROS.

Number	Title (A Side/B Side)	Yr	VG	VG+	NM
❏ 7016	The Golden Road (To Unlimited Devotion)/ Cream Puff War	1967	6.25	12.50	25.00
❏ 7186	Dark Star/Born Cross-Eyed	1968	6.25	12.50	25.00
❏ 7186 [PS]	Dark Star/Born Cross-Eyed	1968	125.00	250.00	500.00
❏ 7324	Dupree's Diamond Blues/Cosmic Charlie	1969	6.25	12.50	25.00
❏ 7410	Uncle John's Band/New Speedway Boogie	1970	3.75	7.50	15.00

—A picture sleeve for this is rumored to exist

Number	Title (A Side/B Side)	Yr	VG	VG+	NM
❏ 7464	Truckin'/Ripple	1971	3.75	7.50	15.00
❏ 7627	Johnny B. Goode/So Fine	1972	5.00	10.00	20.00

—B-side by Elvin Bishop Group

Number	Title (A Side/B Side)	Yr	VG	VG+	NM
❏ 7653	Truckin'/Johnny B. Goode	1973	2.00	4.00	8.00

—"Back to Back Hits" series

Number	Title (A Side/B Side)	Yr	VG	VG+	NM
❏ 7667	Sugar Magnolia/Mr. Charlie	1972	3.75	7.50	15.00

7-Inch Extended Plays
WARNER BROS.

Number	Title (A Side/B Side)	Yr	VG	VG+	NM
❏ S 1893	Sugar Magnolia/Operator/Till the Morning Comes//Truckin'/Friend of the Devil	1973	5.00	10.00	20.00

—Jukebox issue, small hole, plays at 33 1/3 rpm

Number	Title (A Side/B Side)	Yr	VG	VG+	NM
❏ S 1893 [PS]	American Beauty	1973	7.50	15.00	30.00

—Part of Little LP series (LLP #226)

Albums
ARISTA

Number	Title (A Side/B Side)	Yr	VG	VG+	NM
❏ SP-35 [DJ]	Grateful Dead Sampler	1978	7.50	15.00	30.00
❏ AB 4198	Shakedown Street	1978	3.00	6.00	12.00
❏ AL 7001	Terrapin Station	1977	3.75	7.50	15.00
❏ AL 7001 [DJ]	Terrapin Station	1977	12.50	25.00	50.00

—Radio station promos are banded for airplay

Number	Title (A Side/B Side)	Yr	VG	VG+	NM
❏ AL 8112 [(2)]	Dead Set	198?	2.50	5.00	10.00

—Budget-line reissue of 8606

Number	Title (A Side/B Side)	Yr	VG	VG+	NM
❏ AL 8321	Shakedown Street	198?	2.00	4.00	8.00

—Budget-line reissue of 4198

Number	Title (A Side/B Side)	Yr	VG	VG+	NM
❏ AL 8329	Terrapin Station	198?	2.00	4.00	8.00

—Budget-line reissue of 7001

Number	Title (A Side/B Side)	Yr	VG	VG+	NM
❏ AL 8332	Go to Heaven	198?	2.00	4.00	8.00

—Budget-line reissue of 9508

Number	Title (A Side/B Side)	Yr	VG	VG+	NM
❏ AL 8452	In the Dark	1987	2.50	5.00	10.00
❏ AL 8575	Built to Last	1989	2.50	5.00	10.00
❏ A2L 8604 [(2)]	Reckoning	1981	3.75	7.50	15.00
❏ A2L 8606 [(2)]	Dead Set	1981	3.75	7.50	15.00
❏ AL3 8634 [(3)]	Without a Net	1990	6.25	12.50	25.00
❏ AL 9508	Go to Heaven	1980	3.00	6.00	12.00

DIRECT DISK

Number	Title (A Side/B Side)	Yr	VG	VG+	NM
❏ SD-16619	Terrapin Station	1980	25.00	50.00	100.00

—Audiophile vinyl

GRATEFUL DEAD

Number	Title (A Side/B Side)	Yr	VG	VG+	NM
❏ GD-01	Wake of the Flood	1973	5.00	10.00	20.00

—With no contributing artists on back cover

Number	Title (A Side/B Side)	Yr	VG	VG+	NM
❏ GD-01 [DJ]	Wake of the Flood	1973	100.00	200.00	400.00

—Green vinyl meant for fan-club members; ironically, most copies were damaged in a flood before distribution

Number	Title (A Side/B Side)	Yr	VG	VG+	NM
❏ GD-01	Wake of the Flood	1975	3.75	7.50	15.00

—With contributing artists on back cover and United Artists distribution

Number	Title (A Side/B Side)	Yr	VG	VG+	NM
❏ GD-102	Grateful Dead from the Mars Hotel	1974	5.00	10.00	20.00

—Without United Artists distribution

Number	Title (A Side/B Side)	Yr	VG	VG+	NM
❏ GD-102	Grateful Dead from the Mars Hotel	1975	3.75	7.50	15.00

—With United Artists distribution

Number	Title (A Side/B Side)	Yr	VG	VG+	NM
❏ GD-LA494-G	Blues for Allah	1975	5.00	10.00	20.00
❏ GD-LA620-J2 [(2)]	Steal Your Face	1976	6.25	12.50	25.00

MOBILE FIDELITY

Number	Title (A Side/B Side)	Yr	VG	VG+	NM
❏ 1-014	American Beauty	1980	12.50	25.00	50.00

—Audiophile vinyl

Number	Title (A Side/B Side)	Yr	VG	VG+	NM
❏ 1-172	Grateful Dead from the Mars Hotel	1984	10.00	20.00	40.00

—Audiophile vinyl

PAIR

Number	Title (A Side/B Side)	Yr	VG	VG+	NM
❏ PDL2-1053 [(2)]	For the Faithful...	1986	3.00	6.00	12.00

RHINO

Number	Title (A Side/B Side)	Yr	VG	VG+	NM
❏ R1-74395 [(2)]	Live/Dead	2003	6.25	12.50	25.00

—Reissue on 180-gram vinyl

Number	Title (A Side/B Side)	Yr	VG	VG+	NM
❏ R1-74396	Workingman's Dead	2003	3.75	7.50	15.00

—Reissue on 180-gram vinyl

Number	Title (A Side/B Side)	Yr	VG	VG+	NM
❏ R1-74397	American Beauty	2003	3.75	7.50	15.00

—Reissue on 180-gram vinyl

SUNFLOWER

Number	Title (A Side/B Side)	Yr	VG	VG+	NM
❏ SUN-5001	Vintage Dead	1970	10.00	20.00	40.00

—Album has been counterfeited, but bogus covers are 1/4" shorter than normal LP cover

Number	Title (A Side/B Side)	Yr	VG	VG+	NM
❏ SNF-5004	Historic Dead	1971	10.00	20.00	40.00

WARNER BROS.

Number	Title (A Side/B Side)	Yr	VG	VG+	NM
❏ W 1689 [M]	The Grateful Dead	1967	50.00	100.00	200.00
❏ WS 1689 [S]	The Grateful Dead	1967	20.00	40.00	80.00

—Gold label

Number	Title (A Side/B Side)	Yr	VG	VG+	NM
❏ WS 1689 [S]	The Grateful Dead	1968	6.25	12.50	25.00

—Green label with "W7" logo

Number	Title (A Side/B Side)	Yr	VG	VG+	NM
❏ WS 1689 [S]	The Grateful Dead	1970	3.75	7.50	15.00

—Green label with "WB" logo

Number	Title (A Side/B Side)	Yr	VG	VG+	NM
❏ WS 1689 [S]	The Grateful Dead	1973	3.00	6.00	12.00

—"Burbank" palm-trees label

Number	Title (A Side/B Side)	Yr	VG	VG+	NM
❏ WS 1689 [S]	The Grateful Dead	1979	2.00	4.00	8.00

—White or tan label

Number	Title (A Side/B Side)	Yr	VG	VG+	NM
❏ WS 1749	Anthem of the Sun	1968	7.50	15.00	30.00

—Green label with "W7" logo

Number	Title (A Side/B Side)	Yr	VG	VG+	NM
❏ WS 1749	Anthem of the Sun	197?	12.50	25.00	50.00

—Green label with "WB" logo, white background on cover with radically remixed version of LP

Number	Title (A Side/B Side)	Yr	VG	VG+	NM
❏ WS 1749	Anthem of the Sun	1970	3.75	7.50	15.00

—Green label with "WB" logo, purple cover

Number	Title (A Side/B Side)	Yr	VG	VG+	NM
❏ WS 1749	Anthem of the Sun	1973	3.00	6.00	12.00

—"Burbank" palm-trees label

Number	Title (A Side/B Side)	Yr	VG	VG+	NM
❏ WS 1749	Anthem of the Sun	1979	2.00	4.00	8.00

—White or tan label

Number	Title (A Side/B Side)	Yr	VG	VG+	NM
❏ WS 1790	Aoxomoxoa	1969	7.50	15.00	30.00

—Green label with "W7" logo

Number	Title (A Side/B Side)	Yr	VG	VG+	NM
❏ WS 1790	Aoxomoxoa	1970	3.75	7.50	15.00

—Green label with "WB" logo

Number	Title (A Side/B Side)	Yr	VG	VG+	NM
❏ WS 1790	Aoxomoxoa	1973	3.00	6.00	12.00

—"Burbank" palm-trees label

Number	Title (A Side/B Side)	Yr	VG	VG+	NM
❏ WS 1790	Aoxomoxoa	1979	2.00	4.00	8.00

—White or tan label

Number	Title (A Side/B Side)	Yr	VG	VG+	NM
❏ 2WS 1830 [(2)]	Live/Dead	1969	10.00	20.00	40.00

—Green labels with "W7" logo

Number	Title (A Side/B Side)	Yr	VG	VG+	NM
❏ 2WS 1830 [(2)]	Live/Dead	1970	5.00	10.00	20.00

—Green labels with "WB" logo

Number	Title (A Side/B Side)	Yr	VG	VG+	NM
❏ 2WS 1830 [(2)]	Live/Dead	1973	3.75	7.50	15.00

—"Burbank" palm-trees labels

Number	Title (A Side/B Side)	Yr	VG	VG+	NM
❏ 2WS 1830 [(2)]	Live/Dead	1979	2.50	5.00	10.00

—White or tan label

Number	Title (A Side/B Side)	Yr	VG	VG+	NM
❏ WS 1869	Workingman's Dead	1970	6.25	12.50	25.00

—Green label with "WB" logo; textured cover with back cover slick upside down

Number	Title (A Side/B Side)	Yr	VG	VG+	NM
❏ WS 1869	Workingman's Dead	1973	3.00	6.00	12.00

—"Burbank" palm-trees label; standard cover with back cover right side up

Number	Title (A Side/B Side)	Yr	VG	VG+	NM
❏ WS 1869	Workingman's Dead	1979	2.00	4.00	8.00

—White or tan label

Number	Title (A Side/B Side)	Yr	VG	VG+	NM
❏ WS 1893	American Beauty	1970	6.25	12.50	25.00

—Green label with "WB" logo

Number	Title (A Side/B Side)	Yr	VG	VG+	NM
❏ WS 1893	American Beauty	1973	3.00	6.00	12.00

—"Burbank" palm-trees label

Number	Title (A Side/B Side)	Yr	VG	VG+	NM
❏ WS 1893	American Beauty	1979	2.00	4.00	8.00

—White or tan label

Number	Title (A Side/B Side)	Yr	VG	VG+	NM
❏ 2WS 1935 [(2)]	Grateful Dead	1971	7.50	15.00	30.00

—Green labels with "WB" logo

Number	Title (A Side/B Side)	Yr	VG	VG+	NM
❏ 2WS 1935 [(2)]	Grateful Dead	1973	3.75	7.50	15.00

—"Burbank" palm-trees labels

Number	Title (A Side/B Side)	Yr	VG	VG+	NM
❏ 2WS 1935 [(2)]	Grateful Dead	1979	2.50	5.00	10.00

—White or tan labels

Number	Title (A Side/B Side)	Yr	VG	VG+	NM
❏ 3WX 2668 [(3)]	Europe '72	1972	10.00	20.00	40.00

—Green labels with "WB" logo

Number	Title (A Side/B Side)	Yr	VG	VG+	NM
❏ 3WX 2668 [(3)]	Europe '72	1973	5.00	10.00	20.00

—"Burbank" palm-trees labels

Number	Title (A Side/B Side)	Yr	VG	VG+	NM
❏ 3WX 2668 [(3)]	Europe '72	1979	3.00	6.00	12.00

—White or tan labels

Number	Title (A Side/B Side)	Yr	VG	VG+	NM
❏ BS 2721	History of the Grateful Dead, Vol. 1 (Bear's Choice)	1973	2.00	4.00	8.00

—White or tan labels

Number	Title (A Side/B Side)	Yr	VG	VG+	NM
❏ BS 2721	History of the Grateful Dead, Vol. 1 (Bear's Choice)	1973	5.00	10.00	20.00

—"Burbank" palm-trees labels

Number	Title (A Side/B Side)	Yr	VG	VG+	NM
❏ W 2764	The Best of/Skeletons from the Closet	1974	5.00	10.00	20.00

—"Burbank" palm-trees labels

Number	Title (A Side/B Side)	Yr	VG	VG+	NM
❏ W 2764	The Best of/Skeletons from the Closet	1979	2.00	4.00	8.00

—White or tan labels

Number	Title (A Side/B Side)	Yr	VG	VG+	NM
❏ 2WS 3091 [(2)]	What a Long Strange Trip It's Been: The Best of the Grateful Dead	1977	5.00	10.00	20.00

—"Burbank" palm-trees labels

Number	Title (A Side/B Side)	Yr	VG	VG+	NM
❏ 2WS 3091 [(2)]	What a Long Strange Trip It's Been: The Best of the Grateful Dead	1979	2.50	5.00	10.00

—White or tan labels

Number	Title (A Side/B Side)	Yr	VG	VG+	NM
❏ ST-93416	American Beauty	1970	12.50	25.00	50.00

—Capitol Record Club edition; green label with "W7" logo

GRAVENITES, NICK
Albums
COLUMBIA

Number	Title (A Side/B Side)	Yr	VG	VG+	NM
❏ CS 9899	My Labors	1969	3.75	7.50	15.00

GRAVES, BILLY
45s
MONUMENT

Number	Title (A Side/B Side)	Yr	VG	VG+	NM
❏ 401	The Shag (Is Totally Cool)/Uncertain	1958	5.00	10.00	20.00
❏ 404	Long Journey Home/Midnight Bus	1959	3.75	7.50	15.00
❏ 418	Right or Wrong (I'll Be With You)/ Mount Fujiyama	1960	3.00	6.00	12.00
❏ 992	The Lonesome Ape/I've Got a Feeling	1966	2.00	4.00	8.00

GRAVES, CARL
45s
A&M

Number	Title (A Side/B Side)	Yr	VG	VG+	NM
❏ 1620	Baby, Hang Up the Phone/Walk Softly	1974	2.50	5.00	10.00
❏ 1673	The Next Best Thing/Brown Skin Love	1975	2.50	5.00	10.00
❏ 1716	Hey Radio/Something's Telling Me	1975	2.50	5.00	10.00
❏ 1757	Heart Be Still/Breaking Up Is Hard to Do	1975	2.50	5.00	10.00
❏ 1799	My Whole World Ended (The Moment You Left Me)/Baby Don't Knock	1976	2.50	5.00	10.00

ARIOLA AMERICA

Number	Title (A Side/B Side)	Yr	VG	VG+	NM
❏ 7660	Sad Girl/Walk in Love	1977	2.50	5.00	10.00

Number	Title (A Side/B Side)	Yr	VG	VG+	NM

GRAVES, JOE
45s
PARKWAY

Number	Title (A Side/B Side)	Yr	VG	VG+	NM
❏ 103	Debbie/A Boy and a Girl Fall in Love	1966	3.75	7.50	15.00
❏ 964	See Saw/Beautiful Girl	1965	3.75	7.50	15.00

GRAVITY ADJUSTERS EXPANSION BAND
Albums
NOCTURNE

❏ NRS-302	One	1973	75.00	150.00	300.00

GRAY, BARRY, AND THE SPACEMAKERS
45s
ABC-PARAMOUNT

❏ 10424	Fireball/XL 5	1963	3.00	6.00	12.00

GRAY, BILLY
45s
DECCA

❏ 29489	Okie Blondie/I've Had At My Heart	1955	7.50	15.00	30.00
❏ 29678	Harbor of Love/Girls, Girls, Girls	1955	7.50	15.00	30.00
❏ 29800	Tennessee Toddy/It Could Have Been Me	1956	10.00	20.00	40.00

LIBERTY

❏ 55599	I'll Never Live Long Enough/ I Left My Heart in San Francisco	1963	3.00	6.00	12.00
❏ 55712	Last Call for Alcohol/Late Last Night	1964	2.50	5.00	10.00

GRAY, CLAUDE
45s
COLUMBIA

❏ 4-43150	Too Many Rivers/House of Tears	1964	2.50	5.00	10.00
❏ 4-43294	Thank You Neighbor/Kinderhook Bill	1965	2.50	5.00	10.00
❏ 4-43443	For Losing You/Thank You for the Ride	1965	2.50	5.00	10.00
❏ 4-43614	Mean Old Woman/Then Cry You Away	1966	2.50	5.00	10.00

COUNTRY INT'L.

❏ 158	Every Night Sensation/(B-side unknown)	1980	—	3.00	6.00
❏ 164	Pride Goes Before a Fall/Every Night Sensation	1980	—	3.00	6.00
❏ 169	He's Just an Illusion/Every Night Sensation	1981	—	3.00	6.00
❏ 208	Sweet Caroline/Half a Mind	1986	—	3.00	6.00

D

❏ 1059	Letter Overdue/I'm Not Supposed	1959	6.25	12.50	25.00
❏ 1093	Best Part of Me/Loneliness	1959	6.25	12.50	25.00
❏ 1118	Family Bible/Crying in the Night	1960	6.25	12.50	25.00
❏ 1144	My Party's Over/Leave Alone	1960	5.00	10.00	20.00
❏ 1154	When the Light Shines in the Valley/ Homecoming in Heaven	1960	5.00	10.00	20.00

DECCA

❏ 32039	I Never Had the One I Wanted/Effects Your Leaving Had on Me	1966	2.00	4.00	8.00
❏ 32122	Because of Him/If I Ever Need a Lady (I'll Call You)	1967	—	3.50	7.00
❏ 32180	How Fast Them Trucks Can Go/ Next Time You See Me	1967	—	3.50	7.00
❏ 32266	Easy Way Out/Your Devil Memory	1968	—	3.00	6.00
❏ 32312	Night Life/Just Between Us Tears	1968	—	3.00	6.00
❏ 32393	The Love of a Woman/The Kind You Find Tonight Forget Tomorrow	1968	—	3.00	6.00
❏ 32456	Don't Give Me a Chance/Once in Every Lifetime	1969	—	3.00	6.00
❏ 32566	Take Off Time/Sherry Ann	1969	—	3.00	6.00
❏ 32648	The Cleanest Man in Cincinnati/Crazy Arms	1970	—	3.00	6.00
❏ 32697	Everything Will Be Alright/Apartment No. 9	1970	—	3.00	6.00
❏ 32786	Angel/Save My Mind	1971	—	3.00	6.00
❏ 32852	Baton Rouge/Your Devil Memory	1971	—	3.00	6.00

GRANNY WHITE

❏ 10001	Rockin' My Memories (To Sleep)/But That's All Right	1976	—	3.50	7.00
❏ 10002	We Fell in Love That Way/That's My Baby	1976	—	3.50	7.00
❏ 10003	It'll Do/Vin Rose	1977	—	3.50	7.00
❏ 10005	Slow Dancing/Late Cup of Coffee	1977	—	3.50	7.00
❏ 10006	If I Ever Need a Lady/The Bar	1978	—	3.50	7.00
❏ 10007	I Never Had the One I Wanted/ Late Cup of Coffee	1978	—	3.50	7.00
❏ 10009	Let's Go All the Way/ We Climbed a Mountain Last Night	1982	—	3.50	7.00

—With Norma Jean

❏ 10010	So Sad (To Watch Good Love Go Bad)/ Who Sent My Ex to Texas	1982	—	3.50	7.00
❏ 10011	Old Flames Can't Hold a Candle to You/ How Fast Them Trucks Can Go	198?	—	3.50	7.00

LITTLE DARLIN'

❏ 7924	It Ain't the Wakin' Up/The Effects Your Leaving Had on Me	1979	—	3.50	7.00

MERCURY

❏ 71732	I'll Just Have a Cup of Coffee (Then I'll Go)/ I Just Want to Be Alone	1960	3.00	6.00	12.00
❏ 71826	My Ears Should Burn (When Fools Are Talked About)/Crying in the Night	1961	3.00	6.00	12.00
❏ 71898	Let's End It Before It Begins/Talk to Me Old Lonesome Heart	1961	3.00	6.00	12.00
❏ 71936	You Take the Table (I'll Take the Chairs)/ Stone Heart	1962	3.00	6.00	12.00
❏ 72001	Daddy Stopped In/Three Times	1962	3.00	6.00	12.00
❏ 72063	Knock Again, True Love/Call of the Wild	1962	3.00	6.00	12.00
❏ 72088	First Love Never Dies/Heartbreak Eve	1963	3.00	6.00	12.00
❏ 72156	Go Home Cheater//I'm Gonna Lie Again	1963	3.00	6.00	12.00
❏ 72236	Eight Years (And Two Children Later)/ Lonesome	1964	3.00	6.00	12.00

MILLION

❏ 3	Straight Down to Heaven/Jeannie	1972	2.00	4.00	8.00
❏ 18	What Every Woman Wants to Hear/There's You	1972	2.00	4.00	8.00
❏ 31	Woman Ease My Mind/Don't Fight the Feeling	1972	2.00	4.00	8.00
❏ 36	Loving You Is a Habit I Can't Break/We Could	1973	2.00	4.00	8.00

Albums
DECCA

❏ DL 4882 [M]	Claude Gray Sings	1967	6.25	12.50	25.00
❏ DL 74882 [S]	Claude Gray Sings	1967	5.00	10.00	20.00
❏ DL 74963	The Easy Way of Claude Gray	1968	5.00	10.00	20.00

Number	Title (A Side/B Side)	Yr	VG	VG+	NM

HILLTOP

❏ JM-6051 [M]	Treasure of Love	1967	3.75	7.50	15.00
❏ JS-6051 [S]	Treasure of Love	1967	3.00	6.00	12.00

MERCURY

❏ MG-20658 [M]	Songs of Broken Love Affairs	1962	5.00	10.00	20.00
❏ MG-20718 [M]	Country Goes to Town	1962	5.00	10.00	20.00
❏ SR-60658 [S]	Songs of Broken Love Affairs	1962	6.25	12.50	25.00
❏ SR-60718 [S]	Country Goes to Town	1962	6.25	12.50	25.00

GRAY, DOBIE
12-Inch Singles
INFINITY

❏ INF-16001	You Can Do It/Thank You for Tonight	1979	3.00	6.00	12.00

45s
ANTHEM

❏ 200	Guess Who?/Bits and Pieces	1972	—	2.50	5.00

ARISTA

❏ 1047	One Can Fake It!/(B-side unknown)	1983	—	2.00	4.00

CAPITOL

❏ 2241	We the People/Funny and Groovy	1968	2.50	5.00	10.00
❏ B-5562	Gonna Be a Long Night/That's One to Grown On	1986	—	—	3.00
❏ B-5596	The Dark Side of Life/ A Night in the Life of a Country Boy	1986	—	—	3.00
❏ B-5647	From Where I Stand/So Far So Good	1986	—	—	3.00
❏ 5853	River Deep, Mountain High/Tennessee Waltz	1967	3.75	7.50	15.00
❏ B-44087	Take It Real Easy/You Must Have Been Reading My Heart	1987	—	—	3.00
❏ B-44126	Love Letters/Steady As She Goes	1988	—	—	3.00

CAPRICORN

❏ 0249	If Love Must Go/Lover's Sweat	1975	—	2.00	4.00
❏ 0259	Find 'Em, Fool 'Em and Forget 'Em/Mellow Man	1976	—	2.00	4.00
❏ 0267	Let Go/Mellow Man	1976	—	2.00	4.00

CHARGER

❏ 105	The "In" Crowd/Be a Man	1964	3.00	6.00	12.00
❏ 107	See You at the "Go-Go"/Walk with Love	1965	2.50	5.00	10.00
❏ 109	In Hollywood/Mr. Engineer	1965	2.50	5.00	10.00
❏ 113	Monkey Jerk/My Baby	1965	2.50	5.00	10.00
❏ 115	No Room to Cry/Out on the Floor	1966	2.50	5.00	10.00

CORDAK

❏ 1602	Look at Me/Walkin' and Whistlin'	1962	3.75	7.50	15.00

DECCA

❏ 33057	Drift Away/City Stars	1973	—	2.50	5.00

INFINITY

❏ 50003	You Can Do It/Sharing the Night Together	1978	—	2.00	4.00
❏ 50010	Who's Lovin' You/Thank You for Tonight	1979	—	2.00	4.00
❏ 50020	Spending Time, Making Love, and Going Crazy/ Let This Man Take Hold of Your Life	1979	—	2.00	4.00
❏ 50043	The In Crowd/ Let This Man Take Hold of Your Life	1979	—	2.00	4.00

LANA

❏ 138	The "In" Crowd/Be a Man	196?	—	3.00	6.00

—Oldies reissue

MCA

❏ 40100	Loving Arms/Now That I'm Without You	1973	—	2.00	4.00
❏ 40153	Good Old Song/Reachin' for the Feelin'	1973	—	2.00	4.00
❏ 40188	Rose/Lovin' the Easy Way	1974	—	2.00	4.00
❏ 40201	There's a Honky Tonk Angel (Who'll Take Me Back In)/Lovin' the Easy Way	1974	—	2.00	4.00
❏ 40268	Watch Out for Lucy/Turning On You	1974	—	2.00	4.00
❏ 40315	The Music's Real/Roll On Sweet Mississippi	1974	—	2.00	4.00

ROBOX

❏ RRS-117	Decorate the Night (same on both sides)	1979	—	2.50	5.00

WHITE WHALE

❏ 300	Rose Garden/Where's the Girl Gone	1969	2.50	5.00	10.00
❏ 330	What a Way to Go/Do You Really Have a Heart	1969	50.00	100.00	200.00
❏ 342	Honey, You Can't Take It Back	1970	15.00	30.00	60.00

Albums
CAPITOL

❏ ST-12489	From Where I Stand	1986	2.50	5.00	10.00

CAPRICORN

❏ CP 0163	New Ray of Sunshine	1976	2.50	5.00	10.00

CHARGER

❏ CHR-M-2002 [M]	Dobie Gray Sings for "In" Crowders That Go "Go Go"	1965	10.00	20.00	40.00
❏ CHR-S-2002 [S]	Dobie Gray Sings for "In" Crowders That Go "Go Go"	1965	30.00	60.00	120.00

DECCA

❏ DL 75397	Drift Away	1973	3.00	6.00	12.00

INFINITY

❏ INF-9001	Midnight Diamond	1979	2.50	5.00	10.00

MCA

❏ 371	Loving Arms	1973	2.50	5.00	10.00
❏ 449	Hey Dixie	1974	2.50	5.00	10.00
❏ 515	Drift Away	1974	2.50	5.00	10.00

—Reissue of Decca 75397

ROBOX

❏ RBX 8102	Welcome Home	1981	2.50	5.00	10.00

STRIPE

❏ LPM 2001 [M]	Look — Dobie Gray	1963	25.00	50.00	100.00

GRAY, GENE, AND THE STINGRAYS
45s
DOT

❏ 16478	Surf Bunny/Surfer's Mood	1963	5.00	10.00	20.00

LINDA

❏ 110	Surf Bunny/Surfer's Mood	1963	10.00	20.00	40.00

GRAY, GLEN
7-Inch Extended Plays
CAPITOL

❏ EAP 1-747	No Name Jive//Black Jazz/Smoke Rings	1956	2.50	5.00	10.00

—Sides 1 and 8 of "Album 747"

❏ EAP 1-747 [PS]	Casa Loma in Hi-Fi! Part 1	1956	2.50	5.00	10.00

Number	Title (A Side/B Side)	Yr	VG	VG+	NM
❑ EAP 2-747	Memories of You/White Jazz// Dance of the Lame Duck/For You	1956	2.50	5.00	10.00
—Sides 2 and 7 of "Album 747"					
❑ EAP 2-747 [PS]	Casa Loma in Hi-Fi! Part 2	1956	2.50	5.00	10.00
❑ EAP 3-747	(contents unknown)	1956	2.50	5.00	10.00
—Sides 3 and 6 of "Album 747"					
❑ EAP 3-747 [PS]	Casa Loma in Hi-Fi! Part 3	1956	2.50	5.00	10.00
❑ EAP 4-747	Sunrise Serenade/Maniac's Ball//Casa Loma Stomp/Just an Old Manuscript	1956	2.50	5.00	10.00
—Sides 4 and 5 of "Album 747"					
❑ EAP 4-747 [PS]	Casa Loma in Hi-Fi! Part 4	1956	2.50	5.00	10.00
❑ EAP 1-856	Drifting Apart/The World Is Waiting for the Sunrise//Out of Space/Under a Blanket of Blue	195?	2.50	5.00	10.00
❑ EAP 1-856 [PS]	Casa Loma Caravan, Part 1	195?	2.50	5.00	10.00
❑ EAP 2-856	(contents unknown)	195?	2.50	5.00	10.00
❑ EAP 2-856 [PS]	Casa Loma Caravan, Part 2	195?	2.50	5.00	10.00
❑ EAP 3-856	(contents unknown)	195?	2.50	5.00	10.00
❑ EAP 3-856 [PS]	Casa Loma Caravan, Part 3	195?	2.50	5.00	10.00
❑ EAP 1-1022	(contents unknown)	195?	2.50	5.00	10.00
❑ EAP 1-1022 [PS]	Sounds of the Great Bands, Part 1	195?	2.50	5.00	10.00
❑ EAP 2-1022	One O'Clock Jump/Contrasts//Boogie Woogie on St. Louis Blues/String of Pearls	195?	2.50	5.00	10.00
❑ EAP 2-1022 [PS]	Sounds of the Great Bands, Part 2	195?	2.50	5.00	10.00
DECCA					
❑ 7-34556	Smoke Rings/Casa Loma Stomp/It's the Talk of the Town//No Name Jive (Part 1 & 2)	1968	2.50	5.00	10.00
—Jukebox issue; small hole, plays at 33 1/3 rpm					
❑ 7-34556 [PS]	Glen Gray and the Original Casa Loma Orchestra's Greatest Hits	1968	2.50	5.00	10.00
Albums					
CAPITOL					
❑ W 747 [M]	Casa Loma in Hi-Fi!	1956	6.25	12.50	25.00
❑ T 856 [M]	Casa Loma Caravan	1957	5.00	10.00	20.00
—Turquoise label					
❑ SM-1022	Sounds of the Great Bands!	197?	2.50	5.00	10.00
—Reissue					
❑ SW 1022 [S]	Sounds of the Great Bands!	1959	3.75	7.50	15.00
❑ W 1022 [M]	Sounds of the Great Bands!	1959	3.00	6.00	12.00
❑ SM-1067	Sounds of the Great Bands Volume 2	197?	2.50	5.00	10.00
—Reissue					
❑ ST 1067 [S]	Sounds of the Great Bands Volume 2	1959	3.75	7.50	15.00
❑ T 1067 [M]	Sounds of the Great Bands Volume 2	1959	3.00	6.00	12.00
❑ ST 1234 [S]	Solo Spotlight	1960	3.75	7.50	15.00
❑ T 1234 [M]	Solo Spotlight	1960	3.00	6.00	12.00
❑ ST 1289 [S]	Swingin' Decade	1960	3.75	7.50	15.00
❑ T 1289 [M]	Swingin' Decade	1960	3.00	6.00	12.00
❑ ST 1400 [S]	Swingin' Southern Style	1961	3.75	7.50	15.00
❑ T 1400 [M]	Swingin' Southern Style	1961	3.00	6.00	12.00
❑ ST 1506 [S]	Please Mr. Gray… More Sounds of the Great Bands	1961	3.75	7.50	15.00
❑ T 1506 [M]	Please Mr. Gray… More Sounds of the Great Bands	1961	3.00	6.00	12.00
❑ DT 1588 [R]	Sounds of the Great Casa Loma Band	1961	3.00	6.00	12.00
❑ SM-1588	Sounds of the Great Casa Loma Band	197?	2.50	5.00	10.00
—Reissue					
❑ T 1588 [M]	Sounds of the Great Casa Loma Band	1961	3.75	7.50	15.00
❑ ST 1615 [S]	Shall We Swing?	1961	3.75	7.50	15.00
❑ T 1615 [M]	Shall We Swing?	1961	3.00	6.00	12.00
❑ ST 1739 [S]	Sounds of the Great Bands Volume 5: They All Swung the Blues	1962	3.75	7.50	15.00
❑ T 1739 [M]	Sounds of the Great Bands Volume 5: They All Swung the Blues	1962	3.00	6.00	12.00
❑ SM-1812	Themes of the Great Bands	197?	2.50	5.00	10.00
—Reissue					
❑ ST 1812 [S]	Themes of the Great Bands	1963	3.75	7.50	15.00
❑ T 1812 [M]	Themes of the Great Bands	1963	3.00	6.00	12.00
❑ ST 1938 [S]	Sounds of the Great Bands Volume 7: Today's Best	1963	3.00	6.00	12.00
❑ T 1938 [M]	Sounds of the Great Bands Volume 7: Today's Best	1963	2.50	5.00	10.00
❑ ST 2014 [S]	Sounds of the Great Bands Volume 8: More of Today's Best	1964	3.00	6.00	12.00
❑ T 2014 [M]	Sounds of the Great Bands Volume 8: More of Today's Best	1964	2.50	5.00	10.00
❑ ST 2131 [S]	Sounds of the Great Bands in Latin	1964	3.00	6.00	12.00
❑ T 2131 [M]	Sounds of the Great Bands in Latin	1964	2.50	5.00	10.00
CIRCLE					
❑ 16	Glen Gray and the Casa Loma Orchestra	198?	2.50	5.00	10.00
CORAL					
❑ CRL 56006 [10]	Hoagy Carmichael Songs	1950	12.50	25.00	50.00
❑ CRL 56009 [10]	Glen Gray Souvenirs	1950	12.50	25.00	50.00
CREATIVE WORLD					
❑ ST-1055	Shall We Swing?	197?	2.50	5.00	10.00
DECCA					
❑ DL 5089 [10]	Musical Smoke Rings	1950	12.50	25.00	50.00
❑ DL 5397 [10]	No-Name Jive	1953	12.50	25.00	50.00
❑ DL 8570 [M]	Smoke Rings	1957	5.00	10.00	20.00
❑ DL 75016 [R]	Greatest Hits	1968	3.00	6.00	12.00
HARMONY					
❑ HL 7045 [M]	The Great Recordings of Glen Gray	1957	5.00	10.00	20.00
HINDSIGHT					
❑ HSR-104	Glen Gray and the Casa Loma Orchestra, 1939-1940	198?	2.50	5.00	10.00
❑ HSR-120	Glen Gray and the Casa Loma Orchestra, 1943-1946	198?	2.50	5.00	10.00
INSIGHT					
❑ 214	Glen Gray and the Casa Loma Orchestra, 1939-1946	198?	2.50	5.00	10.00
MCA					
❑ 122	Greatest Hits	1973	2.50	5.00	10.00
—Reissue of Decca 75016					
❑ 4076 [(2)]	The Best of Glen Gray	197?	3.00	6.00	12.00
❑ 20199	Smoke Rings	198?	2.00	4.00	8.00

Number	Title (A Side/B Side)	Yr	VG	VG+	NM
GRAY, MAUREEN					
45s					
CHANCELLOR					
❑ 1082	Crazy Over You/Today's the Day	1961	6.25	12.50	25.00
❑ 1091	Come On and Dance/I Don't Want to Cry	1961	6.25	12.50	25.00
❑ 1100	I'm So Young/There's a Boy	1962	6.25	12.50	25.00
LANDA					
❑ 689	Dancin' the Strand/Oh My	1962	3.75	7.50	15.00
❑ 692	People Are Talking/Oh My	1962	3.75	7.50	15.00
MERCURY					
❑ 72131	Story of My Love/Summertime Is Near	1963	3.00	6.00	12.00
❑ 72227	I'm a Happy Girl (Tra La La)/Goodbye Baby	1964	3.00	6.00	12.00
GRAY, RUDY See RUDY GRAYZELL.					
GRAYZELL, RUDY					
45s					
ABBOTT					
❑ 147	Bonita Chiquita/I'm Gone Again	1953	20.00	40.00	80.00
❑ 157	Ocean Paradise/It Ain't My Baby	1954	20.00	40.00	80.00
CAPITOL					
❑ F2946	Hearts Made of Stone/There's Gonna Be a Ball	1954	10.00	20.00	40.00
❑ F3044	You Better Believe It/Ca-Razy	1955	10.00	20.00	40.00
❑ F3149	Please Big Mama/My Heart Is Willing	1955	10.00	20.00	40.00
—Capitol titles as "Rudy Gray"					
MERCURY					
❑ 71138	Let's Get Wild/I Love You So	1957	20.00	40.00	80.00
STARDAY					
❑ 229	The Moon Is Up/Day by Day	1956	20.00	40.00	80.00
❑ 241	Duck Dail/You're Gone	1956	20.00	40.00	80.00
❑ 270	You Hurt Me So/Jig-Ga-Lee-Ga	1956	20.00	40.00	80.00
❑ 321	Let's Get Wild/I Love You So	1957	25.00	50.00	100.00
SUN					
❑ 290	Judy/I Think of You	1958	12.50	25.00	50.00
GREAN, CHARLES RANDOLPH					
45s					
RANWOOD					
❑ 840	Quentin's Theme/#1 at the Blue Whale	1969	—	3.50	7.00
❑ 858	Josette's Music Box/Back at the Blue Whale	1969	—	2.50	5.00
❑ 864	Peter and the Wolf/Georgy	1970	—	2.50	5.00
❑ 872	Marcus Welby, M.D. Theme/ Come Touch the Sun	1970	—	3.00	6.00
❑ 880	The Odd Couple/ Theme from "Borsalino"	1970	—	3.00	6.00
❑ 891	Bullfrog/Singalong Junk	1970	—	2.50	5.00
❑ 901	Any Time of the Year/ Although You Make Me Cry	1971	—	2.50	5.00
❑ 907	Johnny, Harvey, Charlie, Herbie, Etc. (Part 1 & 2)	1971	—	2.50	5.00
❑ 918	Concerto for Knives, Forks, Spoons and Soup Ladle/Gymnopedie	1971	—	2.50	5.00
❑ 938	Theme from Star Trek/Rayo de Sol	1972	—	2.50	5.00
❑ 952	The Old Piano Roll Blues/Rag-a-Muffin	1972	—	2.50	5.00
❑ 973	Karamoja Krackerjack/Two Men of Karamoja	1973	—	2.50	5.00
❑ 1010	Very, Very Blue Danube/Now	1974	—	2.00	4.00
❑ 1044	Star Trek/Love Theme from "Hustle"	1975	—	2.00	4.00
❑ 1064	The $128,000 Question/Sentimentale	1976	—	2.00	4.00
❑ 1088	The Masterpiece/Solitary Joe	197?	—	2.00	4.00
Albums					
HARMONY					
❑ KH 31389	Volume 2	1972	2.50	5.00	10.00
RANWOOD					
❑ 8055	Quentin's Theme	1969	3.00	6.00	12.00
❑ 8075	The Charles Randolph Grean Sounde	1970	3.00	6.00	12.00
❑ 8105	Masterpiece	1972	3.00	6.00	12.00
GREASE BAND					
45s					
SHELTER					
❑ 7304	Let It Be Gone/Laughed at the Judge	1971	—	3.00	6.00
❑ 7310	All I Wanna Do/Jesse James	1971	—	3.00	6.00
Albums					
SHELTER					
❑ SW-8904	Grease Band	1971	3.00	6.00	12.00
GREAT LOVE TRIP, THE					
45s					
UNI					
❑ 55163	Why Can't We Be/Noah	1969	25.00	5.00	10.00
GREAT SCOTTS, THE					
45s					
EPIC					
❑ 9805	Don't Want Your Love/Give Me Lovin'	1965	5.00	10.00	20.00
❑ 9866	That's My Girl (Rotten to the Core)/ Lost in Conversation	1965	10.00	20.00	40.00
TRIUMPH					
❑ 66	Ball and Chain/Run, Run for Your Life	1966	7.50	15.00	30.00
❑ 67	Light Hurts My Eyes/ You Know What You Can Do	1966	7.50	15.00	30.00
GREAT SOCIETY, THE Also see GRACE SLICK.					
45s					
COLUMBIA					
❑ 44583	Sally Go 'Round the Roses/Didn't Think So	1968	5.00	10.00	20.00
NORTH BEACH					
❑ 1001	Someone to Love/Free Advice	1966	62.50	125.00	250.00
—As "The Great!! Society!!"					
Albums					
COLUMBIA					
❑ CS 9627 [M]	Conspicuous Only In Its Absence	1968	12.50	25.00	50.00
—White label promo only; "Special Mono Radio Station Copy" sticker on front; same number as stereo version					
❑ CS 9627 [S]	Conspicuous Only In Its Absence	1968	6.25	12.50	25.00
—Red label, "360 Sound Stereo"					

G

Number	Title (A Side/B Side)	Yr	VG	VG+	NM
❏ CS 9702	How It Was	1968	6.25	12.50	25.00
—Red label, "360 Sound Stereo"					
❏ G 30459 [(2)]	The Great Society Collectors Item	1971	3.75	7.50	15.00
HARMONY					
❏ KH 30391	Somebody to Love	1970	3.00	6.00	12.00

GREAT SPECKLED BIRD
45s
AMPEX

Number	Title (A Side/B Side)	Yr	VG	VG+	NM
❏ 11003	We Sail/Disappearing Woman	1970	2.00	4.00	8.00
❏ 11006	Trucker's Café/Smiling Wine	1970	2.00	4.00	8.00
Albums					
AMPEX					
❏ A-10103	Great Speckled Bird	1970	5.00	10.00	20.00

GREATS, THE
45s
EBB

Number	Title (A Side/B Side)	Yr	VG	VG+	NM
❏ 145	Marching Elvis/Fiddler's Rock	1958	12.50	25.00	50.00

GREAVES, R.B.
45s
ATCO

Number	Title (A Side/B Side)	Yr	VG	VG+	NM
❏ 6714	Take a Letter Maria/Big Bad City	1969	2.00	4.00	8.00
❏ 6726	Always Something There to Remind Me/Oh, When I Was a Boy	1969	—	3.00	6.00
❏ 6745	Fire and Rain/The Ballad of Leroy	1970	—	3.00	6.00
❏ 6778	Oh When I Was a Boy/Georgia Took Her Back	1970	—	3.00	6.00
❏ 6789	Whiter Shade of Pale/Show Me the Way to Go	1970	—	3.00	6.00
❏ 6839	Paperback Writer/Over You Now	1971	—	2.50	5.00
BAREBACK					
❏ 523	Margie, Who's Watching the Baby/(B-side unknown)	1977	—	3.00	6.00
MGM					
❏ 14483	Margie, Who's Watching the Baby/Area Code 213	1973	—	2.50	5.00
❏ 14567	All I Want to Do/Long Live the King	1973	—	2.50	5.00
MIDSONG INT'L.					
❏ 72006	Let Me Be the One Tonight/Please Mister Mailman	1980	—	2.00	4.00
SUNFLOWER					
❏ 128	Margie, Who's Watching the Baby/Area Code 213	1972	—	3.00	6.00
20TH CENTURY					
❏ 2147	Rock and Roll/I'm Married, You're Married	1974	—	2.00	4.00
❏ 2203	Let's Try It Again/My Place or Yours	1975	—	2.00	4.00
Albums					
ATCO					
❏ SD 33-311	R.B. Greaves	1969	5.00	10.00	20.00
INTERMEDIA					
❏ QS-5032	Rock and Roll	198?	2.50	5.00	10.00

GRECH, RICH
Albums
RSO

Number	Title (A Side/B Side)	Yr	VG	VG+	NM
❏ SO 876	The Last Five Years	1973	3.00	6.00	12.00

—Compiles his work with such groups as Family, Traffic, Blind Faith, Ginger Baker's Air Force and KGB

GRECO, BUDDY
45s
CORAL

Number	Title (A Side/B Side)	Yr	VG	VG+	NM
❏ 9-60573	I Ran All the Way Home/The Glory of Love	1951	3.75	7.50	15.00
❏ 9-60623	Take Me Back/'Till the Stars Fall	1952	3.00	6.00	12.00
❏ 9-60672	It's a Sin to Tell a Lie/Never Leave Your Sugar	1952	3.00	6.00	12.00
❏ 9-60904	I'll Always Love You Some/And So Goodbye	1953	3.00	6.00	12.00
❏ 9-60979	You're Driving Me Crazy (What Did I Do)/I Predict	1953	3.00	6.00	12.00
❏ 9-61038	Don't Say Goodbye/How Do You Think I Feel	1953	3.00	6.00	12.00
❏ 9-61128	Up the Chimney in Smoke/The Sheik of Araby	1954	3.00	6.00	12.00
❏ 9-61190	What Word Is Sweeter Than Sweetheart/Lulu's Back in Town	1954	3.00	6.00	12.00
❏ 9-61236	If I Give My Heart to You/Cold Glass of Water	1954	3.00	6.00	12.00
❏ 9-61265	Paris Loves Lovers/Ain't No In-Between	1954	3.00	6.00	12.00
❏ 9-61409	Tonight/Truly	1955	2.50	5.00	10.00
❏ 9-61483	Why Don't You Write Me/Pennies from Heaven	1955	3.00	6.00	12.00
EPIC					
❏ 5-9377	The Lady Is a Tramp/The More I See You	1960	2.00	4.00	8.00
❏ 5-9378	Like Young/Something's Gotta Give	1960	2.00	4.00	8.00
❏ 5-9379	Cheek to Cheek/How About You	1960	2.00	4.00	8.00
❏ 5-9380	(I Don't Care) Only Love Me/Misty	1960	2.00	4.00	8.00
❏ 5-9381	Just in Time/I Laughed at Love	1960	2.00	4.00	8.00
—The above five presumably are stereo jukebox singles from the album "My Buddy"					
❏ 5-9387	The Lady Is a Tramp/Like Young	1960	2.00	4.00	8.00
❏ 5-9387 [PS]	The Lady Is a Tramp/Like Young	1960	2.50	5.00	10.00
❏ 5-9404	Oooh Look-a-There, Ain't She Pretty/This Could Be the Start of Something	1960	2.00	4.00	8.00
❏ 5-9404 [PS]	Oooh Look-a-There, Ain't She Pretty/This Could Be the Start of Something	1960	2.50	5.00	10.00
❏ 5-9408	(titles unknown)	1960	2.00	4.00	8.00
❏ 5-9409	(titles unknown)	1960	2.00	4.00	8.00
❏ 5-9410	(titles unknown)	1960	2.00	4.00	8.00
❏ 5-9411	(titles unknown)	1960	2.00	4.00	8.00
❏ 5-9412	(titles unknown)	1960	2.00	4.00	8.00
—The above five presumably are stereo jukebox singles from the album "Songs for Swinging Losers"					
❏ 5-9439	I Could Write a Book/They Took John Away	1961	2.00	4.00	8.00
❏ 5-9451	Around the World/Hey There	1961	2.00	4.00	8.00
❏ 5-9455	(titles unknown)	1961	2.00	4.00	8.00
❏ 5-9456	(titles unknown)	1961	2.00	4.00	8.00
❏ 5-9457	(titles unknown)	1961	2.00	4.00	8.00
❏ 5-9458	(titles unknown)	1961	2.00	4.00	8.00
❏ 5-9459	(titles unknown)	1961	2.00	4.00	8.00
—The above five presumably are stereo jukebox singles from the album "I Like It Swinging"					
❏ 5-9472	Roses of Picardy/Hallelujah! I Love Her So	1961	2.00	4.00	8.00
❏ 5-9499	Let Me Love You/Twistin' to the Blues	1962	2.00	4.00	8.00
❏ 5-9499 [PS]	Let Me Love You/Twistin' to the Blues	1962	2.50	5.00	10.00

Number	Title (A Side/B Side)	Yr	VG	VG+	NM
❏ 5-9536	Mr. Lonely/Sentimental Fool	1962	2.00	4.00	8.00
—A-side has the same backing track as Bobby Vinton's 1964 hit version of the song					
❏ 5-9563	Stranger/Just Walk Away	1962	2.00	4.00	8.00
❏ 5-9563 [PS]	Stranger/Just Walk Away	1962	2.50	5.00	10.00
❏ 5-9588	Make Up Your Mind/What Now My Love	1963	2.00	4.00	8.00
❏ 5-9588 [PS]	Make Up Your Mind/What Now My Love	1963	2.50	5.00	10.00
❏ 5-9627	The Magic of a Girl/Miss Kiss and Run	1963	2.00	4.00	8.00
❏ 5-9657	Ciumachella (Tender Flower)/I'll Be a Fool	1964	2.00	4.00	8.00
❏ 5-9666	More/It Had Better Be Tonight	1964	2.00	4.00	8.00
❏ 5-9713	It's Such a Happy Day/Zip-a-Dee-Doo-Dah	1964	2.00	4.00	8.00
❏ 5-9750	I Can't Help It (If I'm Still in Love with You)/Jambalaya	1965	2.00	4.00	8.00
❏ 5-9786	The Most Beautiful Girl in the World/You Win Again	1965	2.00	4.00	8.00
❏ 5-9817	I Can't Begin to Tell You/When the Subject Was Roses	1965	2.00	4.00	8.00
❏ 5-9834	The Best Is Yet to Come/Time's a-Wastin' While You're Gone	1965	2.00	4.00	8.00
❏ 5-9864	That Darn Cat/I'm Gonna Laugh You Out of My Life	1965	2.00	4.00	8.00
❏ 5-9864 [PS]	That Darn Cat/I'm Gonna Laugh You Out of My Life	1965	2.50	5.00	10.00
HERALD					
❏ 545	Ooh Baby/Ask Her	1959	3.00	6.00	12.00
KAPP					
❏ 155	In Time to Come/Love Don't Be a Stranger	1956	2.50	5.00	10.00
❏ 165	Holiday Romance/You're the Love of My Love	1956	2.50	5.00	10.00
❏ 170	Wow/Pink Flamingo and Dancing Crane	1957	2.50	5.00	10.00
❏ 183	Game of Love/With All My Heart	1957	2.50	5.00	10.00
❏ 192	You Are Mine/Leona	1957	2.50	5.00	10.00
MGM					
❏ 14235	How Can I Live Without Your Love/Mountain Girl	1971	—	2.50	5.00
❏ 14269	Days of Icy Fingers/You Can Close Your Eyes	1971	—	2.50	5.00
❏ 14325	Keep the Customer Satisfied/Your Love's Return	1972	—	2.50	5.00
REPRISE					
❏ 0474	Keep the Lovin' Feelin'/You Don't Have to Say You Love Me	1966	—	3.50	7.00
❏ 0495	Put Yourself in My Place/Be Anything (But Be Mine)	1966	—	3.50	7.00
❏ 0515	Walking on New Grass/What Am I	1966	—	3.50	7.00
❏ 0551	Dani/Where's the Girl	1967	—	3.00	6.00
❏ 0562	There She Goes/Your Name	1967	—	3.00	6.00
❏ 0584	Love's Gonna Live Here Again/Bonita	1967	—	3.00	6.00
❏ 0605	I Will Wait for You/She's a Carioca	1967	—	3.00	6.00
❏ 0638	Good Times/Is All That Bright and Beautiful	1967	—	3.00	6.00
❏ 0657	Girl Talk/This Is Your Life	1968	—	3.00	6.00
SCEPTER					
❏ 12260	From Atlanta to Goodbye/Love Is a Hurtin' Thing	1969	—	3.00	6.00
❏ 12270	Distant Carolina/Double Life	1970	—	3.00	6.00
❏ 12278	Let It Be/Walking Backwards Down the Road	1970	—	3.00	6.00
❏ 12287	My God and I/Walking Backwards Down the Road	1970	—	3.00	6.00
Albums					
APPLAUSE					
❏ APLP-1004	Hot Nights	1982	2.50	5.00	10.00
BAINBRIDGE					
❏ 8004 [(2)]	Greatest Hits	198?	3.75	7.50	15.00
EPIC					
❏ BN 557 [S]	My Buddy	1960	3.75	7.50	15.00
❏ BN 585 [S]	Songs for Swinging Losers	1960	3.75	7.50	15.00
❏ BN 593 [S]	Buddy's Back in Town	1961	3.75	7.50	15.00
❏ BN 602 [S]	I Like It Swinging	1961	3.75	7.50	15.00
❏ BN 615 [S]	Let's Love	1961	3.75	7.50	15.00
❏ LN 3660 [M]	My Buddy	1960	3.00	6.00	12.00
❏ LN 3746 [M]	Songs for Swinging Losers	1960	3.00	6.00	12.00
❏ LN 3771 [M]	Buddy's Back in Town	1961	3.00	6.00	12.00
❏ LN 3793 [M]	I Like It Swinging	1961	3.00	6.00	12.00
❏ LN 3820 [M]	Let's Love	1961	3.00	6.00	12.00
❏ LN 24010 [M]	Buddy and Soul	1962	3.00	6.00	12.00
❏ LN 24032 [M]	Soft and Gentle	1962	3.00	6.00	12.00
❏ LN 24043 [M]	Buddy Greco's Greatest Hits	1963	3.00	6.00	12.00
❏ LN 24057 [M]	Buddy Greco Sings for Intimate Moments	1963	3.00	6.00	12.00
❏ LN 24088 [M]	My Last Night in Rome	1964	3.00	6.00	12.00
❏ LN 24116 [M]	On Stage	1964	3.00	6.00	12.00
❏ LN 24130 [M]	Modern Sounds of Hank Williams	1965	3.00	6.00	12.00
❏ LN 24181 [M]	From the Wrists Down	1965	3.00	6.00	12.00
❏ BN 26010 [S]	Buddy and Soul	1962	3.75	7.50	15.00
❏ BN 26032 [S]	Soft and Gentle	1962	3.75	7.50	15.00
❏ BN 26043 [S]	Buddy Greco's Greatest Hits	1963	3.75	7.50	15.00
❏ BN 26057 [S]	Buddy Greco Sings for Intimate Moments	1963	3.75	7.50	15.00
❏ BN 26088 [S]	My Last Night in Rome	1964	3.75	7.50	15.00
❏ BN 26116 [S]	On Stage	1964	3.75	7.50	15.00
❏ BN 26130 [S]	Modern Sounds of Hank Williams	1965	3.75	7.50	15.00
❏ BN 26181 [S]	From the Wrists Down	1965	3.75	7.50	15.00
HARMONY					
❏ HL 7448 [M]	You're Something Else	196?	2.50	5.00	10.00
❏ HS 11248 [S]	You're Something Else	196?	3.00	6.00	12.00
KAPP					
❏ KL-1033 [M]	Broadway Melodies	1956	5.00	10.00	20.00
❏ KL-1107 [M]	Buddy	1958	5.00	10.00	20.00
❏ KL-1231 [M]	The Best of Buddy Greco	1961	3.75	7.50	15.00
PROJECT 3					
❏ PR 5105	For Once in My Life: In Concert	1980	2.50	5.00	10.00
REPRISE					
❏ R-6220 [M]	Big Band and Ballads	1966	3.00	6.00	12.00
❏ RS-6220 [S]	Big Band and Ballads	1966	3.75	7.50	15.00
❏ R-6230 [M]	Buddy's in a Brand New Bag	1966	3.00	6.00	12.00
❏ RS-6230 [S]	Buddy's in a Brand New Bag	1966	3.75	7.50	15.00
❏ R-6256 [M]	Away We Go!	1967	3.75	7.50	15.00
❏ RS-6256 [S]	Away We Go!	1967	3.00	6.00	12.00
SCEPTER					
❏ SPS-579	Let the Sunshine In	1969	3.00	6.00	12.00
SUTTON					
❏ SSU 282 [M]	All Time Favorites Featuring Buddy Greco	196?	2.50	5.00	10.00

Number	Title (A Side/B Side)	Yr	VG	VG+	NM
VOCALION					
☐ VL 3706 [M]	Here's Buddy Greco	1964	3.00	6.00	12.00
☐ VL 73706 [R]	Here's Buddy Greco	1964	2.50	5.00	10.00
GRECO, JOHNNY					
45s					
PAGEANT					
☐ 602	Rocket Ride/(B-side unknown)	1963	37.50	75.00	150.00
GREELEY, GEORGE					
45s					
REPRISE					
☐ 0490	Who's Afraid/Jungle Fantasy	1966	—	3.00	6.00
WARNER BROS.					
☐ 5100	Malaguena/My Love	1959	2.50	5.00	10.00
☐ 5175	Love Music from Tristan & Isolde/My Love	1960	2.00	4.00	8.00
☐ 5175 [PS]	Love Music from Tristan & Isolde/My Love	1960	3.00	6.00	12.00
☐ 5188	Come Back to Sorrento/Guinevere	1960	2.00	4.00	8.00
☐ 5207	Main Theme from "Gone with the Wind"/Tara's Theme	1961	2.00	4.00	8.00
☐ 5210	Unchained Melody/Anniversary Song	1961	2.00	4.00	8.00
☐ 5218	Lucy's Theme from Parrish/Allison's Theme from Parrish	1961	2.00	4.00	8.00
☐ 5218 [PS]	Lucy's Theme from Parrish/Allison's Theme from Parrish	1961	3.00	6.00	12.00
☐ 5239	Tonight/Tender Is the Night	1961	2.00	4.00	8.00
☐ 5264	What Now My Love/11th Hour Melody	1962	2.00	4.00	8.00
☐ 5293	Ride the High Country/Being in Love	1962	2.00	4.00	8.00
☐ 5311	Theme from Mutiny on the Bounty/Love Song from Mutiny on the Bounty	1962	2.00	4.00	8.00
☐ 5511	Tonight/Tender Is The Night//Polonaise/Mattinata	1961	3.00	6.00	12.00
☐ 5511 [PS]	Tonight/Tender Is The Night//Polonaise/Mattinata	1961	3.00	6.00	12.00

—Part of Warner Bros. "+2" series, with two new songs and excerpts of two prior hits

Number	Title (A Side/B Side)	Yr	VG	VG+	NM
Albums					
CAPITOL					
☐ H 438 [10]	Piano Demitasse	1954	7.50	15.00	30.00
REPRISE					
☐ R 6092 [M]	Piano Rhapsodies of Love	1964	2.50	5.00	10.00
☐ RS 6092 [S]	Piano Rhapsodies of Love	1964	3.00	6.00	12.00
WARNER BROS.					
☐ W 1249 [M]	The World's Greatest Popular Piano Concertos	1958	3.75	7.50	15.00
☐ WS 1249 [S]	The World's Greatest Popular Piano Concertos	1959	5.00	10.00	20.00
☐ W 1291 [M]	World Renowned Popular Piano Concertos	1959	3.75	7.50	15.00
☐ WS 1291 [S]	World Renowned Popular Piano Concertos	1959	5.00	10.00	20.00
☐ W 1319 [M]	The Greatest Motion Picture Piano Concertos	1959	3.75	7.50	15.00
☐ WS 1319 [S]	The Greatest Motion Picture Piano Concertos	1959	5.00	10.00	20.00
☐ WS 1338 [S]	22 Best Loved Christmas Piano Concertos	1959	5.00	10.00	20.00
☐ W 1366 [M]	The Most Beautiful Music of Hawaii	1960	3.00	6.00	12.00
☐ WS 1366 [S]	The Most Beautiful Music of Hawaii	1960	3.75	7.50	15.00
☐ W 1387 [M]	The World's Greatest Love Themes	1960	3.00	6.00	12.00
☐ WS 1387 [S]	The World's Greatest Love Themes	1960	3.75	7.50	15.00
☐ W 1402 [M]	Piano Italiano	1961	3.00	6.00	12.00
☐ WS 1402 [S]	Piano Italiano	1961	3.75	7.50	15.00
☐ W 1410 [M]	The Best of the Popular Piano Concertos	1961	3.00	6.00	12.00
☐ WS 1410 [S]	The Best of the Popular Piano Concertos	1961	3.75	7.50	15.00
☐ W 1415 [M]	Great Broadway Musicals	1961	3.00	6.00	12.00
☐ WS 1415 [S]	Great Broadway Musicals	1961	3.75	7.50	15.00
☐ W 1427 [M]	Famous Film Themes	1961	3.00	6.00	12.00
☐ WS 1427 [S]	Famous Film Themes	1961	3.75	7.50	15.00
☐ W 1451 [M]	George Greeley Plays George Gershwin	1962	3.00	6.00	12.00
☐ WS 1451 [S]	George Greeley Plays George Gershwin	1962	3.75	7.50	15.00
☐ W 1476 [M]	Themes from Mutiny on the Bounty and Other Great Films	1962	3.00	6.00	12.00
☐ WS 1476 [S]	Themes from Mutiny on the Bounty and Other Great Films	1962	3.75	7.50	15.00
☐ W 1503 [M]	A Classic Affair	1963	3.00	6.00	12.00
☐ WS 1503 [S]	A Classic Affair	1963	3.75	7.50	15.00
☐ W 1560 [M]	Best Loved Christmas Piano Concertos	1965	3.00	6.00	12.00
☐ WS 1560 [S]	Best Loved Christmas Piano Concertos	1965	3.75	7.50	15.00
GREEN					
45s					
ATCO					
☐ 6833	Big Dipper/All My Bells	1971	—	2.50	5.00
Albums					
ATCO					
☐ SD 33-282	Green	1969	3.75	7.50	15.00
☐ SD 33-366	To Help Somebody	1971	3.00	6.00	12.00
GREEN, AL					
12-Inch Singles					
A&M					
☐ 12311	As Long As We're Together (4 versions)	1989	—	3.00	6.00
☐ 12323	The Message Is Love (6 versions)	1989	—	3.00	6.00
HI					
☐ 78510	I Feel Good (7:30)/I Feel Good (3:17)	1978	3.75	7.50	15.00
45s					
A&M					
☐ 1427	As Long As We're Together/Blessed	1989	—	—	3.00
☐ 2786	Going Away/Building Up	1985	—	2.00	4.00
☐ 2807	True Love/He Is the Light	1986	—	2.00	4.00
☐ 2919	Everything's Gonna Be Alright/So Real to Me	1987	—	—	3.00
☐ 2952	You Know and I Know/True Love	1987	—	—	3.00
☐ 2962	Soul Survivor/Jesus Will Fix It	1987	—	—	3.00
BELL					
☐ 45258	Guilty/Let Me Help You	1972	—	2.50	5.00
☐ 45305	Hot Wire/Don't Leave Me	1973	—	2.50	5.00
CAPITOL					
☐ S7-18869	Tired of Being Alone/Walk On By	1995	—	—	3.00
—B-side by Isaac Hayes					
HI					
☐ 2159	I Want to Hold Your Hand/What Am I Gonna Do with Myself	1969	2.00	4.00	8.00
☐ 2164	One Woman/Tomorrow's Dream	1969	2.00	4.00	8.00

Number	Title (A Side/B Side)	Yr	VG	VG+	NM
☐ 2172	You Say It/Gotta Find a New World	1969	—	3.00	6.00
☐ 2177	Right Now, Right Now/All Because I'm a Foolish One	1970	—	3.00	6.00
☐ 2182	I Can't Get Next to You/Ride Sally Ride	1970	—	3.00	6.00
☐ 2188	Driving Wheel/True Love	1971	—	3.00	6.00
☐ 2194	Tired of Being Alone/Get Back Baby	1971	—	2.50	5.00
☐ 2202	Let's Stay Together/Tomorrow's Dream	1971	—	2.50	5.00
☐ 2211	Look What You Done for Me/La La for You	1972	—	2.50	5.00
☐ 2216	I'm Still in Love with You/Old Time Lovin'	1972	—	2.50	5.00
☐ 2227	You Ought to Be with Me/What Is This Feeling	1972	—	2.50	5.00
☐ 2235	Call Me (Come Back Home)/What a Wonderful Thing Love Is	1973	—	2.50	5.00
☐ 2247	Here I Am (Come and Take Me)/I'm Glad You're Mine	1973	—	2.50	5.00
☐ 2257	Livin' for You/It Ain't No Fun to Me	1973	—	2.50	5.00
☐ 2262	Let's Get Married/So Good to Be Here	1974	—	2.50	5.00
☐ 2274	Sha-La-La (Make Me Happy)/School Days	1974	—	2.50	5.00
☐ 2282	L-O-V-E (Love)/I Wish You Were Here	1975	—	2.50	5.00
☐ 2288	Oh Me, Oh My (Dreams in My Arms)/Strong As Death (Sweet As Love)	1975	—	2.50	5.00
☐ 2300	Full of Fire/Could I Be the One	1975	—	2.50	5.00
☐ 2306	Let It Shine/There's No Way	1976	—	2.50	5.00
☐ 2319	Keep Me Cryin'/There Is Love	1976	—	2.50	5.00
☐ 2322	I Tried to Tell Myself/Something	1977	—	2.50	5.00
☐ 2324	Love and Happiness/Glory Glory	1977	—	2.50	5.00
☐ 77505	Belle/Chariots of Fire	1977	—	2.00	4.00
☐ 77505 [PS]	Belle/Chariots of Fire	1977	—	3.00	6.00
☐ 77680	White Christmas/Winter Wonderland	2001	—	2.50	5.00
—Clear vinyl					
☐ 78511	I Feel Good/Feels Like Summer	1978	—	2.00	4.00
☐ 78522	Wait Here/To Sir with Love	1978	—	2.00	4.00
☐ 78522 [PS]	Wait Here/To Sir with Love	1978	—	3.00	6.00
HOT LINE JOURNAL					
☐ 15000	Back Up Train/Don't Leave Me	1967	6.25	12.50	25.00
☐ 15001	Don't Hurt Me No More/Get Yourself Together	1967	7.50	15.00	30.00
☐ 15002	I'll Be Good to You/Lover's Hideaway	1967	7.50	15.00	30.00
THE RIGHT STUFF					
☐ S7-17524	Let's Stay Together/I'm Still in Love with You	1993	—	—	3.00
☐ S7-18217	I'll Be Home for Christmas/It Feels Like Christmas	1994	—	2.50	5.00
7-Inch Extended Plays					
HI					
☐ SBG 81	How Can You Mend a Broken Heart/So You're Leaving//I've Never Found a Girl/What Is This Feeling/It Ain't No Fun to Me	1972	2.50	5.00	10.00
—Jukebox issue; small hole, plays at 33 1/3 rpm					
☐ SBG 81 [PS]	Let's Stay Together	1972	2.50	5.00	10.00
☐ SBG 87	Funny How Time Slips Away/Love Is like the Morning Sun//Have You Been Making Out O.K./Stand Up	1973	2.50	5.00	10.00
—Jukebox issue; small hole, plays at 33 1/3 rpm					
☐ SBG 87 [PS]	Call Me	1973	2.50	5.00	10.00
Albums					
A&M					
☐ SP-5150	Soul Survivor	1987	2.50	5.00	10.00
☐ SP-5228	I Get Joy	1989	2.50	5.00	10.00
BELL					
☐ 6076	Al Green	1972	5.00	10.00	20.00
—Reissue of Hot Line LP					
DCC COMPACT CLASSICS					
☐ LPZ-2058	Greatest Hits	1998	7.50	15.00	30.00
—Audiophile vinyl					
HI					
☐ 6004	The Belle Album	1977	3.00	6.00	12.00
☐ 6009	Truth 'N' Time	1978	3.00	6.00	12.00
☐ 8000	Tired of Being Alone	1977	3.00	6.00	12.00
☐ 8001	Al Green Gets Next to You	1977	3.00	6.00	12.00
☐ 8007	Let's Stay Together	1977	3.00	6.00	12.00
☐ SHL-32055	Green Is Blues	1969	3.75	7.50	15.00
☐ SHL-32062	Al Green Gets Next to You	1971	3.75	7.50	15.00
☐ SHL-32070	Let's Stay Together	1972	3.75	7.50	15.00
☐ SHL-32074	I'm Still in Love with You	1972	3.75	7.50	15.00
☐ SHL-32077	Call Me	1973	3.75	7.50	15.00
☐ SHL-32082	Livin' for You	1973	3.75	7.50	15.00
☐ SHL-32087	Al Green Explores Your Mind	1974	3.75	7.50	15.00
☐ SHL-32089	Al Green/Greatest Hits	1975	3.75	7.50	15.00
☐ SHL-32092	Al Green Is Love	1975	3.75	7.50	15.00
☐ SHL-32097	Full of Fire	1976	3.75	7.50	15.00
☐ SHL-32103	Have a Good Time	1976	3.75	7.50	15.00
☐ SHL-32105	Al Green's Greatest Hits, Volume II	1977	3.75	7.50	15.00
HOT LINE					
☐ 1500 [M]	Back Up Train	1967	12.50	25.00	50.00
—As "Al Greene"					
☐ S-1500 [S]	Back Up Train	1967	20.00	40.00	80.00
—As "Al Greene"					
KORY					
☐ 1005	Al Green	1977	2.50	5.00	10.00
—Reissue of Bell LP					
MCA					
☐ 42308	Love Ritual	1988	2.50	5.00	10.00
MOTOWN					
☐ 5283 ML	Al Green/Greatest Hits	198?	2.50	5.00	10.00
—Reissue of Hi 32089					
☐ 5284 ML	I'm Still in Love with You	198?	2.50	5.00	10.00
—Reissue of Hi 32074					
☐ 5290 ML	Let's Stay Together	198?	2.50	5.00	10.00
—Reissue of Hi 32070					
☐ 5291 ML	Al Green's Greatest Hits, Volume II	198?	2.50	5.00	10.00
—Reissue of Hi 32105					
☐ 5317 ML	Truth N' Time	198?	2.50	5.00	10.00
MYRRH					
☐ MSB-6661	The Lord Will Make a Way	1980	2.50	5.00	10.00
☐ MSB-6671	Higher Plane	1981	2.50	5.00	10.00
☐ MSB-6702	Precious Lord	1981	2.50	5.00	10.00
☐ MSB-6747	I'll Rise Again	1982	2.50	5.00	10.00
☐ MSB-6774	Al Green and the Full Gospel Tabernacle Choir	1984	2.50	5.00	10.00

G

Number	Title (A Side/B Side)	Yr	VG	VG+	NM
❏ WR-8113	The Lord Will Make a Way	1985	2.00	4.00	8.00
—Reissue with new number and A&M logo					
❏ WR-8114	Higher Plane	1985	2.00	4.00	8.00
—Reissue with new number and A&M logo					
❏ WR-8115	Precious Lord	1985	2.00	4.00	8.00
—Reissue with new number and A&M logo					
❏ WR-8116	I'll Rise Again	1985	2.00	4.00	8.00
—Reissue with new number and A&M logo					
❏ WR-8117	White Christmas	1985	2.50	5.00	10.00
—Reissue with new number and A&M logo					
❏ WR-8118	Trust in God	1985	2.00	4.00	8.00
—Reissue with new number and A&M logo					
❏ WR-8209	Al Green and the Full Gospel Tabernacle Choir	1986	2.00	4.00	8.00
—Reissue with new number and A&M logo					
❏ 7-01-678006-6	White Christmas	1984	3.00	6.00	12.00
❏ 7-01-678306-?	Trust in God	1984	2.50	5.00	10.00
THE RIGHT STUFF					
❏ T1-27121	Let's Stay Together	1995	3.75	7.50	15.00
—Green vinyl reissue					
❏ T1-27627	I'm Still in Love with You	1995	3.75	7.50	15.00
—Green vinyl reissue					
WORD					
❏ E 77000	One in a Million	1991	3.00	6.00	12.00

GREEN, BARBARA See BARBARA GREENE.

GREEN, BERNIE, WITH THE STEREO MAD-MEN
Albums
RCA VICTOR

Number	Title (A Side/B Side)	Yr	VG	VG+	NM
❏ LPM-1929 [M]	Musically Mad	1959	15.00	30.00	60.00
❏ LSP-1929 [S]	Musically Mad	1959	30.00	60.00	120.00

GREEN, FRED
45s
BOBBIN

Number	Title (A Side/B Side)	Yr	VG	VG+	NM
❏ 111	Wham Slam Baby/It's Funny	1959	25.00	50.00	100.00
❏ 123	Don't Make a Fool Out of Me/If You Ever Try to Leave Me	1960	25.00	50.00	100.00

GREEN, FRED, AND THE MELLARDS
45s
BALLAD

Number	Title (A Side/B Side)	Yr	VG	VG+	NM
❏ 1012	My Sweetheart/You Can't Keep Love in a Broken Heart	1955	75.00	150.00	300.00
❏ 1016	Love Me Crazy/That's Life	1955	50.00	100.00	200.00

GREEN, GARLAND
45s
CASINO

Number	Title (A Side/B Side)	Yr	VG	VG+	NM
❏ 056	I.O.U./It's a Backdoor World	1976	—	2.50	5.00
COTILLION					
❏ 44098	Plain and Simple Girl/Hey Cloud	1971	—	3.00	6.00
OCEAN-FRONT					
❏ 2000	Tryin' to Hold On/(B-side unknown)	1983	—	2.00	4.00
RCA					
❏ PB-10889	Don't Let Love Walk Out on Us/Ask Me for What You Want	1977	—	3.00	6.00
❏ PB-11023	Shake Your Shaker/Lovin' You Baby	1977	—	2.50	5.00
❏ PB-11126	Let's Celebrate/Let Me Be Your Pacifier	1977	—	2.50	5.00
REVUE					
❏ 11001	Girl I Love You/It Rained Forty Days and Nights	1967	3.75	7.50	15.00
❏ 11020	Mr. Misery/You Played on a Prayer	196?	3.00	6.00	12.00
❏ 11030	Love Now, Pay Later/Ain't That Good Enough	196?	3.00	6.00	12.00
SPRING					
❏ 142	He Didn't Know (He Kept On Talkin')/Please Come Home	1973	—	2.50	5.00
❏ 146	Sweet Loving Woman/Sending My Best Friend	1974	—	2.50	5.00
❏ 151	Let the Good Times Roll/You and I Go Good Together	1974	—	2.50	5.00
❏ 158	Bumpin' and Stompin'/Nothing Can Take You from Me	1975	—	2.50	5.00
❏ 160	Just Loving You/Nothing Can Take You from Me	1975	—	2.50	5.00
UNI					
❏ 55143	Jealous Kind of Fella/I Can't Believe You Quit Me	1969	2.00	4.00	8.00
❏ 55188	Don't Think That I Am a Violent Guy/All She Said (Was Goodbye to Me)	1969	2.00	4.00	8.00
❏ 55213	Angel Baby/You Played On a Player	1970	2.00	4.00	8.00
Albums					
RCA VICTOR					
❏ APL1-2351	Love Is What We Came Here For	1977	3.00	6.00	12.00
UNI					
❏ 73073	Jealous Kind of Fellow	1969	5.00	10.00	20.00

GREEN, JANICE (THE "OH JULIE" GIRL)
45s
NASCO

Number	Title (A Side/B Side)	Yr	VG	VG+	NM
❏ 6013	With All My Heart/Jackie	1958	5.00	10.00	20.00

GREEN, KEITH
45s
DECCA

Number	Title (A Side/B Side)	Yr	VG	VG+	NM
❏ 31799	A Go-Go Letter/The Way I Used to Be	1965	5.00	10.00	20.00
❏ 31859	Girl Don't Tell Me/How to Be Your Guy	1965	6.25	12.50	25.00
❏ 31973	Home Town Girls/Hear What's Happening, Baby	1966	5.00	10.00	20.00
ERA					
❏ 108	Sgt. Pepper's Epitaph/Country Store	1970	2.50	5.00	10.00
❏ 3210	Fantastic/L.A. City Smog Blues	1969	2.50	5.00	10.00
Albums					
PRETTY GOOD					
❏ PGR-1	So You Wanna Go Back to Egypt	1980	3.00	6.00	12.00
SPARROW					
❏ SPR-1015	For Him Who Has Ears to Hear	1977	3.00	6.00	12.00
❏ SPR-1024	No Compromise	1978	3.00	6.00	12.00
❏ SP-9901	For Him Who Has Ears to Hear	198?	2.00	4.00	8.00
—Reissue of 1015					
❏ SP-9904	No Compromise	198?	2.00	4.00	8.00
—Reissue of 1024					
❏ SP-9927	The Collection	198?	2.50	5.00	10.00

GREEN, LIL
45s
ATLANTIC

Number	Title (A Side/B Side)	Yr	VG	VG+	NM
❏ 951	Every Time/I've Got That Feeling	1952	25.00	50.00	100.00

GREEN, LLOYD
45s
MONUMENT

Number	Title (A Side/B Side)	Yr	VG	VG+	NM
❏ 8648	I Can Help/Theme from A Summer Place	1975	—	2.50	5.00
—With Charlie McCoy					

GREEN, PETER Also see FLEETWOOD MAC.
45s
SAIL

Number	Title (A Side/B Side)	Yr	VG	VG+	NM
❏ 116	In the Skies/(B-side unknown)	1979	2.50	5.00	10.00
Albums					
REPRISE					
❏ RS 6436	The End of the Game	1970	5.00	10.00	20.00
SAIL					
❏ 0110	In the Skies	1979	2.50	5.00	10.00
❏ 0112	Little Dreamer	1980	2.50	5.00	10.00

GREEN, RUDY See RUDY GREENE.

GREEN, VERNON, AND THE MEDALLIONS See THE MEDALLIONS.

GREEN BULLFROG
Albums
DECCA

Number	Title (A Side/B Side)	Yr	VG	VG+	NM
❏ DL 75269	Green Bullfrog	1971	6.25	12.50	25.00

GREEN SLIME, THE
45s
MGM

Number	Title (A Side/B Side)	Yr	VG	VG+	NM
❏ K14052	The Green Slime/Far Beyond the Stars	1969	2.50	5.00	10.00
❏ K14052 [PS]	The Green Slime/Far Beyond the Stars	1969	12.50	25.00	50.00

GREENBAUM, NORMAN Also see DR. WEST'S MEDICINE SHOW AND JUG BAND.
45s
GREGAR

Number	Title (A Side/B Side)	Yr	VG	VG+	NM
❏ 71-0107	Nancy Whiskey/Twentieth Century Fox	1969	2.50	5.00	10.00
REPRISE					
❏ 0739	Spirit in the Sky/Canned Ham	1971	—	2.00	4.00
—"Back to Back Hits" series					
❏ 0752	Children of Paradise/School for Sweet Talk	1968	2.50	5.00	10.00
❏ 0818	Marcy/Children of Paradise	1969	2.50	5.00	10.00
❏ 0846	Jubilee/Skyline	1969	2.50	5.00	10.00
❏ 0885	Spirit in the Sky/Milk Cow	1969	2.00	4.00	8.00
❏ 0919	Canned Ham/Junior Cadillac	1970	—	3.00	6.00
❏ 0956	Rhode Island Red/I.J. Foxx	1970	—	3.00	6.00
❏ 0956 [PS]	Rhode Island Red/I.J. Foxx	1970	7.50	15.00	30.00
❏ 1008	California Earthquake/Rhode Island Red	1971	—	3.00	6.00
❏ 1134	Dairy Queen/Petaluma	1972	—	3.00	6.00
Albums					
REPRISE					
❏ MS 2048	Petaluma	1972	3.75	7.50	15.00
❏ RS 6365	Spirit in the Sky	1969	5.00	10.00	20.00
❏ RS 6422	Back Home Again	1970	3.75	7.50	15.00

GREENBEATS, THE
45s
JERDEN

Number	Title (A Side/B Side)	Yr	VG	VG+	NM
❏ 757	You Must Be the One/If This World Were Mine	1965	3.00	6.00	12.00
❏ 763	So Sad/I'm on Fire	1965	3.00	6.00	12.00
PARKWAY					
❏ 939	You Must Be the One/If This World Were Mine	1965	3.75	7.50	15.00

GREENBERG, STEVE
45s
TRIP

Number	Title (A Side/B Side)	Yr	VG	VG+	NM
❏ 3000	Big Bruce/Run to You	1969	2.50	5.00	10.00

GREENE, BARBARA
45s
ATCO

Number	Title (A Side/B Side)	Yr	VG	VG+	NM
❏ 6250	Long Tall Sally/Slippin' and Slidin'	1963	12.50	25.00	50.00
RENEE					
❏ 5001	Young Boy/I Should Have Treated You Right	1968	3.75	7.50	15.00
❏ 5004	A Lover's Plea/Our Love Is No Secret Now	1968	3.75	7.50	15.00
VIVID					
❏ 105	Young Boy/I Should Have Treated You Right	1968	6.25	12.50	25.00
—As "Barbara Green"					

GREENE, JACK
45s
DECCA

Number	Title (A Side/B Side)	Yr	VG	VG+	NM
❏ 31768	Don't You Ever Get Tired/The Hurt's On Me	1965	2.50	5.00	10.00
❏ 31856	Ever Since My Baby Went Away/Room for One More Heartache	1965	2.00	4.00	8.00
❏ 32023	There Goes My Everything/The Hardest Easy Thing	1966	2.00	4.00	8.00
❏ 32123	All the Time/Wanting You But Never Having You	1967	2.00	4.00	8.00
❏ 32190	What Locks the Door/Left Over Feelings	1967	2.00	4.00	8.00
❏ 32261	You Are My Treasure/If God Can Forgive You, So Can I	1968	2.00	4.00	8.00
❏ 32352	Love Takes Care of Me/Your Favorite Fool	1968	2.00	4.00	8.00
❏ 32423	Until My Dreams Come True/We'll Try a Little Bit Harder	1968	2.00	4.00	8.00
❏ 32490	Statue of a Fool/There's More to Love	1969	2.00	4.00	8.00
❏ 32558	Back in the Arms of Love/The Key That Fits Her Door	1969	2.00	4.00	8.00
❏ 32631	Lord Is That Me/Just a Little While Ago	1970	—	3.50	7.00
❏ 32699	The Whole World Comes to Me/If This Is Love	1970	—	3.50	7.00
❏ 32755	Something Unseen/What's the Use	1970	—	3.50	7.00
❏ 32823	There's a Whole Lot About a Woman (A Man Don't Know)/Makin' Up His Mind	1971	—	3.50	7.00
❏ 32863	Hanging Over Me/The Birth of Our Love	1971	—	3.50	7.00
❏ 32939	If You Ever Need My Love/Ask Me to Stay	1972	—	3.50	7.00

Number	Title (A Side/B Side)	Yr	VG	VG+	NM
❑ 33008	Satisfaction/From Here On Out	1972	—	3.50	7.00

EMH

Number	Title (A Side/B Side)	Yr	VG	VG+	NM
❑ 0015	I'd Be Home On Christmas Day//(B-side unknown)	1982	—	3.00	6.00
❑ 0016	The Jukebox Never Plays Home Sweet Home/I Don't Want to Be Alone Tonight	1983	—	2.50	5.00
❑ 0019	From Cotton to Satin/I'd Be Home on Christmas Day	1983	—	2.50	5.00
❑ 0025	Midnight Tennessee Woman/Goin' Through Hell for an Angel	1983	—	2.50	5.00
❑ 0028	I'd Do As Much for You/Singing My Heart Out for You	1984	—	2.50	5.00
❑ 0031	Dying to Believe/There Goes My Everything	1984	—	2.50	5.00
❑ 0035	If It's Love (Then Bet It All)/Statue of a Fool	1984	—	2.50	5.00

FIRSTLINE

Number	Title (A Side/B Side)	Yr	VG	VG+	NM
❑ 709	Devil's Den/It's Not the End of the World	1980	—	2.50	5.00

FRONTLINE

Number	Title (A Side/B Side)	Yr	VG	VG+	NM
❑ 704	Yours for the Taking/Sixty Days	1979	—	2.50	5.00
❑ 706	The Rock I'm Leaning On/I'll Do It Better Next Time	1980	—	2.50	5.00

MCA

Number	Title (A Side/B Side)	Yr	VG	VG+	NM
❑ 40035	The Fool I've Been Today/You Left Me	1973	—	2.50	5.00
❑ 40108	I Need Somebody Bad/Joyride	1973	—	2.50	5.00
❑ 40179	It's Time to Cross That Bridge/Half That Much	1974	—	2.50	5.00
❑ 40263	Sing for the Good Times/Something Seems to Fall Apart Inside	1974	—	2.50	5.00
❑ 40354	This Time The Hurtin's On Me/Sawmill Depot	1974	—	2.50	5.00
❑ 40415	Cheatin' River/On the Way Home	1975	—	2.50	5.00
❑ 40481	He Little Thing'd Her Out of His Arms/Let Me Love You Back Together Again	1975	—	2.50	5.00
❑ 40526	Birmingham/My Long Gone Reason	1976	—	2.50	5.00

STEP ONE

Number	Title (A Side/B Side)	Yr	VG	VG+	NM
❑ 456	I'd Be Home on Christmas Day/My Favorite Time of Year	199?	—	2.50	5.00

—B-side by Jack Robertson; red vinyl

Albums

DECCA

Number	Title (A Side/B Side)	Yr	VG	VG+	NM
❑ DL 4845 [M]	There Goes My Everything	1967	5.00	10.00	20.00
❑ DL 4904 [M]	All the Time	1967	5.00	10.00	20.00
❑ DL 4939 [M]	What Locks the Door	1968	6.25	12.50	25.00
❑ DL 4979 [M]	You Are My Treasure	1968	7.50	15.00	30.00
❑ DL 74845 [S]	There Goes My Everything	1967	3.75	7.50	15.00
❑ DL 74904 [S]	All the Time	1967	3.75	7.50	15.00
❑ DL 74939 [S]	What Locks the Door	1968	3.75	7.50	15.00
❑ DL 74979 [S]	You Are My Treasure	1968	3.75	7.50	15.00
❑ DL 75080	I Am Not Alone	1969	3.75	7.50	15.00
❑ DL 75124	Statue of a Fool	1969	3.75	7.50	15.00
❑ DL 75156	Back in the Arms of Love	1969	3.75	7.50	15.00
❑ DL 75188	Lord Is That Me	1970	3.75	7.50	15.00
❑ DL 75208	Greatest Hits	1970	3.75	7.50	15.00
❑ DL 75283	There's a Whole Lot About a Woman	1971	3.75	7.50	15.00
❑ DL 75308	Greene Country	1972	3.75	7.50	15.00
❑ ST-91433 [S]	What Locks the Door	1968	5.00	10.00	20.00

—Capitol Record Club edition

Number	Title (A Side/B Side)	Yr	VG	VG+	NM
❑ T-91433 [M]	What Locks the Door	1968	10.00	20.00	40.00

—Capitol Record Club edition

MCA

Number	Title (A Side/B Side)	Yr	VG	VG+	NM
❑ 291	Greatest Hits	1973	3.00	6.00	12.00

—Reissue of Decca 75208

Number	Title (A Side/B Side)	Yr	VG	VG+	NM
❑ 295	Greene Country	1973	3.00	6.00	12.00

—Reissue of Decca 75308

PICKWICK

Number	Title (A Side/B Side)	Yr	VG	VG+	NM
❑ SPC-6173	I Never Had It So Good	197?	2.50	5.00	10.00

GREENE, JACK, AND JEANNIE SEELY

45s

DECCA

Number	Title (A Side/B Side)	Yr	VG	VG+	NM
❑ 32580	Wish I Didn't Have to Miss You/My Tears Don't Show	1969	—	3.50	7.00
❑ 32898	Much Oblige/First Day	1971	—	3.50	7.00
❑ 32991	What in the World Has Gone Wrong with Our Love/Willingly	1972	—	3.00	6.00

Albums

DECCA

Number	Title (A Side/B Side)	Yr	VG	VG+	NM
❑ DL 75171	Jack Greene and Jeannie Seely	1970	3.75	7.50	15.00
❑ DL 75392	Two for the Show	1972	3.75	7.50	15.00

MCA

Number	Title (A Side/B Side)	Yr	VG	VG+	NM
❑ 77	Two for the Show	1973	3.00	6.00	12.00

—Reissue of Decca 75392

GREENE, LORNE

45s

ARTISTS OF AMERICA

Number	Title (A Side/B Side)	Yr	VG	VG+	NM
❑ 1776	National Glass Casket Company/Spirit of America	1976	2.00	4.00	8.00

COLUMBIA

Number	Title (A Side/B Side)	Yr	VG	VG+	NM
❑ 4-44971	The Perfect Woman/It's All in the Game	1969	—	3.00	6.00

GRT

Number	Title (A Side/B Side)	Yr	VG	VG+	NM
❑ 32	Daddy (I'm Proud to Be Your Son)/I Love a Rainbow	1969		3.00	6.00
❑ 37	The First Word/I Love a Rainbow	1970	—	3.00	6.00

RCA VICTOR

Number	Title (A Side/B Side)	Yr	VG	VG+	NM
❑ 47-8113	My Sons, My Sons/The Place Where I Worship	1962	2.50	5.00	10.00
❑ 47-8229	I'm the Same Old Me/Love Finds a Way	1963	2.50	5.00	10.00
❑ 47-8444	Ringo/Bonanza	1964	2.00	4.00	8.00
❑ 47-8490	The Man/Pop Goes the Hammer	1964	2.00	4.00	8.00
❑ 47-8554	An Ol' Tin Cup/Sand	1965	2.00	4.00	8.00
❑ 47-8757	Five Card Stud/Shadow of the Cactus	1965	2.00	4.00	8.00
❑ 47-8819	Daddy's Little Girl/I Love a Rainbow	1966	2.00	4.00	8.00
❑ 47-8901	Waco/All But the Remembering	1966	2.00	4.00	8.00
❑ 47-9037	Must Be Santa/One Solitary Life	1966	2.50	5.00	10.00
❑ 47-8554 [PS]	An Ol' Tin Cup/Sand	1965	3.75	7.50	15.00

Albums

RCA CAMDEN

Number	Title (A Side/B Side)	Yr	VG	VG+	NM
❑ CAS-2391	Five Card Stud	1970	6.25	12.50	25.00

RCA VICTOR

Number	Title (A Side/B Side)	Yr	VG	VG+	NM
❑ SP-33-327 [DJ]	Palaver with The Man	1965	12.50	25.00	50.00

—Promo-only interview record with script

Number	Title (A Side/B Side)	Yr	VG	VG+	NM
❑ LPM-2661 [M]	Young at Heart	1963	6.25	12.50	25.00
❑ LSP-2661 [S]	Young at Heart	1963	7.50	15.00	30.00
❑ LPM-2843 [M]	Welcome to the Ponderosa	1964	6.25	12.50	25.00
❑ LSP-2843 [S]	Welcome to the Ponderosa	1964	7.50	15.00	30.00
❑ LPM-3302 [M]	The Man	1965	6.25	12.50	25.00
❑ LSP-3302 [S]	The Man	1965	7.50	15.00	30.00
❑ LPM-3409 [M]	Lorne Greene's American West	1965	6.25	12.50	25.00
❑ LSP-3409 [S]	Lorne Greene's American West	1965	7.50	15.00	30.00
❑ LPM-3410 [M]	Have a Happy Holiday	1965	6.25	12.50	25.00
❑ LSP-3410 [S]	Have a Happy Holiday	1965	7.50	15.00	30.00
❑ LPM-3678 [M]	Portrait of the West	1966	6.25	12.50	25.00
❑ LSP-3678 [S]	Portrait of the West	1966	7.50	15.00	30.00

RCA VICTOR RED SEAL

Number	Title (A Side/B Side)	Yr	VG	VG+	NM
❑ LM-2783 [M]	Peter and the Wolf	1964	6.25	12.50	25.00
❑ LSC-2783 [S]	Peter and the Wolf	1964	7.50	15.00	30.00

—Above with the London Symphony Orchestra

GREENE, LORNE; MICHAEL LANDON; DAN BLOCKER

Albums

RCA VICTOR

Number	Title (A Side/B Side)	Yr	VG	VG+	NM
❑ LPM-2583 [M]	Bonanza — Ponderosa Party Time!	1962	7.50	15.00	30.00
❑ LSP-2583 [S]	Bonanza — Ponderosa Party Time!	1962	10.00	20.00	40.00
❑ LPM-2757 [M]	Christmas on the Ponderosa	1963	6.25	12.50	25.00
❑ LSP-2757 [S]	Christmas on the Ponderosa	1963	7.50	15.00	30.00

GREENE, RUDY

45s

CHANCE

Number	Title (A Side/B Side)	Yr	VG	VG+	NM
❑ 1139	Love Is a Pain/No Need of Your Crying	1953	37.50	75.00	150.00
❑ 1146	The Letter/It's You I Love	1953	37.50	75.00	150.00
❑ 1151	I Had a Feeling/Meet Me Baby	1954	37.50	75.00	150.00

—Black vinyl

Number	Title (A Side/B Side)	Yr	VG	VG+	NM
❑ 1151	I Had a Feeling/Meet Me Baby	1954	100.00	200.00	400.00

—Red vinyl

CLUB 51

Number	Title (A Side/B Side)	Yr	VG	VG+	NM
❑ 103	Highway No. 1/You Mean Everything to Me	1956	50.00	100.00	200.00

—With the Four Buddies

EMBER

Number	Title (A Side/B Side)	Yr	VG	VG+	NM
❑ 1012	Juicy Fruit/You're the One for Me	1957	10.00	20.00	40.00
❑ 1020	Lonesome/Wild Life	1957	10.00	20.00	40.00

EXCELLO

Number	Title (A Side/B Side)	Yr	VG	VG+	NM
❑ 2074	Cool Lovin' Mama/My Mumblin' Baby	1955	12.50	25.00	50.00
❑ 2090	Teeny Weeny Baby/Queer Feeling	1956	12.50	25.00	50.00

GREENSLADE

Albums

MERCURY

Number	Title (A Side/B Side)	Yr	VG	VG+	NM
❑ SRM-1-1015	Spy Guest	1974	3.00	6.00	12.00
❑ SRM-1-1025	Time and Tide	1975	3.00	6.00	12.00

WARNER BROS.

Number	Title (A Side/B Side)	Yr	VG	VG+	NM
❑ BS 2698	Greenslade	1973	3.00	6.00	12.00

GREENWICH, ELLIE   Also see THE RAINDROPS.

45s

BELL

Number	Title (A Side/B Side)	Yr	VG	VG+	NM
❑ 855	Ain't That Peculiar/I Don't Want to Be Left Outside	1970	2.50	5.00	10.00
❑ 933	That Certain Someone/It's Like a Sad Old Kind of Movie	1970	2.50	5.00	10.00

MADISON

Number	Title (A Side/B Side)	Yr	VG	VG+	NM
❑ 160	Red Corvette/I Go, You Go	1961	7.50	15.00	30.00

—As "Ellie Gee"

RED BIRD

Number	Title (A Side/B Side)	Yr	VG	VG+	NM
❑ 10-034	You Don't Know/Baby	1965	10.00	20.00	40.00

UNITED ARTISTS

Number	Title (A Side/B Side)	Yr	VG	VG+	NM
❑ 50151	I Want You to Be My Baby/Goodnight, Goodnight	1967	3.75	7.50	15.00
❑ 50278	A Long Time Comin'/Niki-Hoeky	1968	3.75	7.50	15.00

VERVE

Number	Title (A Side/B Side)	Yr	VG	VG+	NM
❑ 10719	Today I Met the Boy I'm Gonna Marry/Maybe I Know	1973	2.50	5.00	10.00
❑ 10724	Chapel of Love/River Deep, Mountain High	1973	2.50	5.00	10.00

Albums

UNITED ARTISTS

Number	Title (A Side/B Side)	Yr	VG	VG+	NM
❑ UAS-6648	Ellie Greenwich Composes, Produces and Sings	1968	12.50	25.00	50.00

VERVE

Number	Title (A Side/B Side)	Yr	VG	VG+	NM
❑ V6-5091	Let It Be Written, Let It Be Sung	1973	6.25	12.50	25.00

GREENWOOD COUNTY SINGERS, THE   Includes "The Greenwood Singers" and "The Greenwoods," though we're not sure if "The Greenwoods" on Decca were the same group. VAN DYKE PARKS was a member of this group on the Kapp records.

45s

KAPP

Number	Title (A Side/B Side)	Yr	VG	VG+	NM
❑ KJB-47	Seven Daffodils/Old Home Place	1965	2.00	4.00	8.00
❑ 591	Frankie and Johnny/Climb Up Sunshine Mountain	1964	2.00	4.00	8.00
❑ 591	The New Frankie and Johnny Song/Climb Up Sunshine Mountain	1964	2.50	5.00	10.00
❑ 623	Anne/Cake Walking Babies from Home	1964	2.00	4.00	8.00
❑ 660	Easter Rebellion/Trombone Cholly	1965	2.00	4.00	8.00
❑ 675	The Bridge Washed Out/Nobody Waved Goodbye	1965	2.00	4.00	8.00
❑ 688	Ballad of Cat Ballou/Blue Is the Wind	1965	2.00	4.00	8.00
❑ 742	Please Don't Sell My Daddy No More Wine/Southbound	1966	2.00	4.00	8.00

—As "The Greenwoods"

Number	Title (A Side/B Side)	Yr	VG	VG+	NM
❑ 760	Tear Down the Walls/Friends I Used to Know	1966	2.00	4.00	8.00

—As "The Greenwood Singers"

Number	Title (A Side/B Side)	Yr	VG	VG+	NM
❑ 774	The Eagle and Me/Eternal Love, Eternal Spring	1966	2.00	4.00	8.00

—As "The Greenwood Singers"

G

Number	Title (A Side/B Side)	Yr	VG	VG+	NM
Albums					
KAPP					
❑ KL 1362 [M]	The New Frankie and Johnny Song	1964	3.00	6.00	12.00
❑ KL 1362 [M]	The First Recordings by the Joyful Greenwood County Singers	1964	3.75	7.50	15.00
—Original title					
❑ KL 1422 [M]	Have You Heard	1965	3.00	6.00	12.00
❑ KL 1448 [M]	Ballad of Cat Ballou	1965	3.00	6.00	12.00
❑ KL 1487 [M]	Tear Down the Walls	1966	3.00	6.00	12.00
—As "The Greenwood Singers"					
❑ KS 3362 [S]	The New Frankie and Johnny Song	1964	3.75	7.50	15.00
❑ KS 3362 [S]	The First Recordings by the Joyful Greenwood County Singers	1964	5.00	10.00	20.00
—Original title					
❑ KS 3422 [S]	Have You Heard	1965	3.75	7.50	15.00
❑ KS 3448 [S]	Ballad of Cat Ballou	1965	3.75	7.50	15.00
❑ KS 3487 [S]	Tear Down the Walls	1966	3.75	7.50	15.00
—As "The Greenwood Singers"					
RCA VICTOR					
❑ LSP-4384	Return to Greenwood County	1970	3.75	7.50	15.00

GREENWOODS, THE Probably not the same group as THE GREENWOOD COUNTY SINGERS.

Number	Title (A Side/B Side)	Yr	VG	VG+	NM
45s					
DECCA					
❑ 31651	The Riddle/All My Trials	1964	2.00	4.00	8.00
❑ 31953	Silver Dagger/Harlan Breakdown	1965	2.00	4.00	8.00
Albums					
DECCA					
❑ DL 4496 [M]	Folk Instrumentals	1964	3.00	6.00	12.00
❑ DL 74496 [S]	Folk Instrumentals	1964	3.75	7.50	15.00

GREER, BIG JOHN

Number	Title (A Side/B Side)	Yr	VG	VG+	NM
45s					
GROOVE					
❑ 0002	Bottle It Up and Go/You'll Never Be Mine	1954	10.00	20.00	40.00
❑ 0016	When the Roses Bloom in Lover's Lane/Too Long	1954	10.00	20.00	40.00
❑ 0038	We Wanna See Santa Do the Mambo/Wait Till After Christmas	1954	10.00	20.00	40.00
❑ 0108	Soon, Soon, Soon/I'm Glad for Your Sake	1955	10.00	20.00	40.00
❑ 0119	Come Back Maybellene/Night Crawlin'	1955	12.50	25.00	50.00
❑ 0131	A Man and a Woman/Blam	1955	15.00	30.00	60.00
—With the Four Students					
KING					
❑ 4878	Record Hop/Keep On Loving Me	1956	5.00	10.00	20.00
❑ 4941	Let Me Come Home/Come Back, Uncle John	1956	5.00	10.00	20.00
❑ 5006	Midnight Ramble/Sweet Slumber	1957	5.00	10.00	20.00
❑ 5057	Duck Walk/I Still Love You So	1957	5.00	10.00	20.00
RCA VICTOR					
❑ 47-4293	Have Another Drink/I'm Savin' All My Lovin'	1951	10.00	20.00	40.00
❑ 47-4348	Got You on My Mind/Woman Is a Five-Letter Word	1951	10.00	20.00	40.00
❑ 47-4484	Strong Red Whiskey/If You Let Me	1952	10.00	20.00	40.00
❑ 47-5037	I'm the Fat Man/Since You Went Away from Me	1952	10.00	20.00	40.00
❑ 47-5170	I'll Never Let You Go/You Played on My Piano	1953	10.00	20.00	40.00
❑ 47-5259	Ride Pretty Baby/Don't Worry 'Bout Me	1953	10.00	20.00	40.00
❑ 47-5531	Drinkin' Fool/Gettin' Mighty Lonesome for You	1953	10.00	20.00	40.00
❑ 50-0007	Drinkin' Wine Spo-Dee-O-Dee/Long Tall Gal	1949	17.50	35.00	70.00
—Orange vinyl					
❑ 50-0029	If I Told You Once/I Found a Dream	1949	17.50	35.00	70.00
—Orange vinyl					
❑ 50-0051	Rockin' Jenny Jones/I've Just Found Love	1950	17.50	35.00	70.00
—Orange vinyl					
❑ 50-0076	I'll Never Do That Again/A Fool Hasn't Got a Chance	1950	15.00	30.00	60.00
—Orange vinyl					
❑ 50-0096	Cheatin'/It's Better to Have Been Taken for Granted	1950	15.00	30.00	60.00
—Orange vinyl					
❑ 50-0104	Red Juice/Big John's a-Blowin'	1950	15.00	30.00	60.00
—Orange vinyl					
❑ 50-0108	Once There Lived a Fool/I Want Ya, I Need Ya	1951	12.50	25.00	50.00
❑ 50-0113	Why Did You Go/Our Wedding Time	1951	12.50	25.00	50.00
❑ 50-0125	Clambake Boogie/When You Love	1951	12.50	25.00	50.00
❑ 50-0137	Big Rock/How Can You Forget?	1951	12.50	25.00	50.00

GREER, DAN

Number	Title (A Side/B Side)	Yr	VG	VG+	NM
45s					
BIG BEAT					
❑ 149	My Baby's Got a New Way/Wait for Me	196?	10.00	20.00	40.00
MGM					
❑ 14653	Hell Paso (Part I)/(Part II)	1973	2.50	5.00	10.00
❑ 14653 [PS]	Hell Paso (Part I)/(Part II)	1973	3.75	7.50	15.00
ODE					
❑ 66002	Curiosity Killed the Cat/I Remember Mama	1970	12.50	25.00	50.00
SOUNDS OF MEMPHIS					
❑ 702	Masquerade/Thanks to You	1972	3.00	6.00	12.00

GREGG, BOBBY

Number	Title (A Side/B Side)	Yr	VG	VG+	NM
45s					
COTTON					
❑ 1003	The Jam Part 1/Part 2	1962	3.75	7.50	15.00
❑ 1006	Potato Peeler/Sweet Georgia Brown	1962	3.75	7.50	15.00
EPIC					
❑ 5-9541	Let's Jam Again Part 1/Part 2	1962	3.00	6.00	12.00
❑ 5-9579	Drummer Man/Walk On	1962	3.00	6.00	12.00
❑ 5-9601	Scarlet O'Hara/Take Me Out to the Ball Game	1963	3.00	6.00	12.00
❑ 5-9616	Kootanda/Kangaroo Part 2 (Tie Me Kangaroo Down, Sport)	1963	3.00	6.00	12.00
LAURIE					
❑ 3358	Theme from The Other Side/If You Wanna Be Happy	1966	2.50	5.00	10.00
VEEP					
❑ 1207	Hullabaloo/Charly Ba-Ba	1965	2.50	5.00	10.00

GREGORY, DICK

Number	Title (A Side/B Side)	Yr	VG	VG+	NM
45s					
VEE JAY					
❑ 469	They Won't Hire Me/Benefit	1962	3.00	6.00	12.00
Albums					
COLPIX					
❑ CP 417 [M]	In Living Black and White	1961	6.25	12.50	25.00
❑ CP 420 [M]	East and West	1961	6.25	12.50	25.00
❑ CP 480 [M]	We All Have Problems	1964	6.25	12.50	25.00
GATEWAY					
❑ GLP 9007 [M]	My Brother's Keeper	1963	10.00	20.00	40.00
POPPY					
❑ PP-LA176-G2 [(2)]	Caught in the Act	1973	3.75	7.50	15.00
❑ PYS 40008	Dick Gregory On...	1970	3.75	7.50	15.00
❑ PYS 40011	Dick Gregory at the Village Gate	1972	3.75	7.50	15.00
❑ PYS 60001 [(2)]	The Light Side: The Dark Side	1969	5.00	10.00	20.00
❑ PYS 60004 [(2)]	Frankenstein	1970	3.75	7.50	15.00
❑ PYS 60005 [(2)]	Dick Gregory at Kent State	1971	3.75	7.50	15.00
TOMATO					
❑ 9001 [(3)]	The Best of Dick Gregory	1978	5.00	10.00	20.00
VEE JAY					
❑ LP 1093 [M]	Running for President	1964	6.25	12.50	25.00
❑ LP 4001 [M]	Dick Gregory Talks Turkey	1962	6.25	12.50	25.00
❑ LP 4005 [M]	Two Sides of Dick Gregory	1963	6.25	12.50	25.00

GREGORY, IVAN, AND THE BLUE NOTES

Number	Title (A Side/B Side)	Yr	VG	VG+	NM
45s					
G&G					
❑ 110	Elvis Presley Blues/Kathy	1956	62.50	125.00	250.00

GRENFELL, JOYCE

Number	Title (A Side/B Side)	Yr	VG	VG+	NM
Albums					
ELEKTRA					
❑ EKL-184 [M]	Presenting Joyce Grenfell	1960	7.50	15.00	30.00

GRIER, FRANKIE, QUARTET

Number	Title (A Side/B Side)	Yr	VG	VG+	NM
45s					
SWAN					
❑ 4019	Oh, Gloria/Lonesome for You	1958	100.00	200.00	400.00

GRIER, ROOSEVELT Most of his 1970s records, and scattered earlier ones, were as "Rosey Grier."

Number	Title (A Side/B Side)	Yr	VG	VG+	NM
45s					
A					
❑ 105	Sincerely/Why Don't You Do Me Right	1959	6.25	12.50	25.00
❑ 110	Moonlight in Vermont/Smoky Morning	1960	6.25	12.50	25.00
A&M					
❑ 1457	Beautiful People/I'll Be Back Tomorrow	1973	—	2.50	5.00
❑ 1500	If You Hit a Good Lick, Lay On It/You're the Violin	1974	—	2.50	5.00
ABC					
❑ 11275	Rat Race/I Don't Want Nobody (To Lead Me On)	1970	—	3.00	6.00
AGP					
❑ 109	Bad News/Ring Around the World	1969	2.00	4.00	8.00
AMY					
❑ 11004	Who's Got the Ball (Y'All)/Halftime	1967	3.00	6.00	12.00
❑ 11015	High Society Woman/C'mon Cupid	1968	3.00	6.00	12.00
❑ 11029	Hard to Forget/People Make the World	1968	3.00	6.00	12.00
BATTLE					
❑ 45911	Why/Lover Set Me Free	1963	6.25	12.50	25.00
BELL					
❑ 45459	It's All Right to Cry/(B-side unknown)	1974	2.00	4.00	8.00
D-TOWN					
❑ 1058	Pizza Pie Man/Welcome to the Club	1965	10.00	20.00	40.00
LIBERTY					
❑ 55413	Struttin' 'n Twistin'/Let the Cool Wind Blow	1962	3.75	7.50	15.00
❑ 55453	The Mail Must Go Thru/Your Has Been	1962	3.75	7.50	15.00
MGM					
❑ 13698	Slow Drag/Yesterday	1967	3.00	6.00	12.00
❑ 13840	Spanish Harlem/I'm Living Good	1967	3.00	6.00	12.00
RIC					
❑ 102	Fool, Fool, Fool/Since You've Been Gone	1964	5.00	10.00	20.00
❑ 112	Down So Long/In My Tenement	1964	5.00	10.00	20.00
SPINDLE TOP					
❑ 102	I'm Going Home/Jinny	1961	5.00	10.00	20.00
20TH CENTURY					
❑ 2212	Take the Time to Love Somebody/Your Love Is Right Up My Alley	1975	2.00	4.00	8.00
UNITED ARTISTS					
❑ 50893	Bring Back the Time/Oh How I Miss You Baby	1972	—	3.00	6.00
YOUNGSTOWN					
❑ 609	Deputy Dog/(B-side unknown)	1966	7.50	15.00	30.00
Albums					
RIC					
❑ M-1008 [M]	Soul City	1964	5.00	10.00	20.00
❑ S-1008 [S]	Soul City	1964	6.25	12.50	25.00
WORD					
❑ WR-8342	Committed	1986	—	6.00	12.00

GRIEVES, GRANT

Number	Title (A Side/B Side)	Yr	VG	VG+	NM
45s					
BIG K					
❑ 1002	Four in the Floor/Married Woman	196?	15.00	30.00	60.00

GRIFFIN, BUCK

Number	Title (A Side/B Side)	Yr	VG	VG+	NM
45s					
HOLIDAY INN					
❑ 109	Pretty Lou/The Girl in Room 1209	1963	10.00	20.00	40.00
LIN					
❑ 1005	Meadowlark Boogie/It Don't Make No Never Mind	1954	15.00	30.00	60.00
❑ 1007	Rollin' Tears/One Day After Pay Day	1955	15.00	30.00	60.00
❑ 1008	Going Home, All Alone/Lookin' for the Green	1955	15.00	30.00	60.00
❑ 1014	Next to Mine/Lord, Give Me Strength	1955	15.00	30.00	60.00
❑ 1015	Bawlin' and Squallin'/Let's Elope, Baby	1955	18.75	37.50	75.00
❑ 1016	Go-Stop-O/Cochise	1955	25.00	50.00	100.00
❑ 1018	Little Dan/Neither Do I	1956	15.00	30.00	60.00

Number	Title (A Side/B Side)	Yr	VG	VG+	NM
METRO					
❑ 20007	The Party/Every Night	1958	7.50	15.00	30.00
MGM					
❑ 12284	Stutterin' Papa/Watchin' the 7:10 Roll By	1956	25.00	50.00	100.00
❑ 12439	Bow My Back/Old Bee Tree	1957	20.00	40.00	80.00
❑ 12597	Jessie Lee/You'll Never Come Back	1957	20.00	40.00	80.00

GRIFFIN, JIMMY Some of these were credited to "James Griffin." Also see BREAD.
45s

Number	Title (A Side/B Side)	Yr	VG	VG+	NM
IMPERIAL					
❑ 66108	These Are the Times/Walking to New Orleans	1965	3.00	6.00	12.00
❑ 66152	He Will Break Your Heart/Hard Row to Hoe	1965	3.00	6.00	12.00
POLYDOR					
❑ 14213	Breakin' Up Is Easy/Melody Maker	1973	—	2.50	5.00
❑ 14236	She Knows/Beachwood Band	1974	—	2.50	5.00
❑ 14282	Treat Her Right/How Do You Say Goodbye	1975	—	2.50	5.00
REPRISE					
❑ 0268	All My Loving/My Baby Made Me Cry	1964	3.75	7.50	15.00
❑ 0280	Gotta Lotta Love/Running to You	1964	3.75	7.50	15.00
❑ 0304	You're Nobody Till Somebody Loves You/Try	1964	3.75	7.50	15.00
❑ 20114	Girls Grow Up Faster Than Boys/It's a Free Country	1962	5.00	10.00	20.00
❑ 20161	What Kind of Girl Are You/A Little Like Lovin' You	1963	5.00	10.00	20.00
❑ 20178	Love Letters in the Sand/Summer Holiday	1963	5.00	10.00	20.00
❑ 20221	Little Miss Cool/Marie Is Moving	1963	5.00	10.00	20.00
VIVA					
❑ 611	Miracle Worker/Looking So Much Better	1967	2.50	5.00	10.00
❑ 627	Thank You Love/Light of Your Mind	1968	2.50	5.00	10.00
❑ 642	Miracle Worker/Thank You Love	1970	2.50	5.00	10.00
Albums					
POLYDOR					
❑ PD 6018	James Griffin and Co.	1973	3.75	7.50	15.00
REPRISE					
❑ R-6091 [M]	Summer Holiday	1963	12.50	25.00	50.00
❑ R9-6091 [S]	Summer Holiday	1963	15.00	30.00	60.00

GRIFFIN, MERV
45s

Number	Title (A Side/B Side)	Yr	VG	VG+	NM
CAMEO					
❑ 266	Always/Hey Pretty Baby	1963	2.50	5.00	10.00
❑ 298	Have I Told You Lately That I Love You/I'm Sorry I Made You Cry	1964	2.50	5.00	10.00
CARLTON					
❑ 540	Banned in Boston/The World We Love In	1961	3.75	7.50	15.00
❑ 545	The Charanga/Along Came Joe	1961	2.50	5.00	10.00
❑ 552	Would You/You Came a Long Way from St. Louis	1961	2.50	5.00	10.00
❑ 562	Screamin' Memories from Planet X/I've Got a Lovely Bunch of Coconuts	1961	2.50	5.00	10.00
COLUMBIA					
❑ 4-40026	I'll Be There/I Kiss Your Hand, Madame	1953	3.75	7.50	15.00
❑ 4-40141	Hey Garcon!/All the Live Long Day	1953	3.75	7.50	15.00
❑ 4-40274	Much Too Young to Die/A Girl with a Figure Like an Hour Glass	1954	3.00	6.00	12.00
❑ 4-40328	Do You Remember Me?/The Story of Tina	1954	3.00	6.00	12.00
❑ 4-40424	I Never Has Seen Snow/Hot-Cha-Cha	1955	3.00	6.00	12.00
❑ 4-40530	Sweet and Gentle/That's Hot-Cha-Cha with Me	1955	3.00	6.00	12.00
❑ 4-40557	Five Cups of Coffee (Five Cups of Tea)/(I Couldn't Get the Hang of) The Merengue	1955	3.00	6.00	12.00
❑ 4-40624	Call Out the Engines/A Handful of Dreams	1955	3.00	6.00	12.00
❑ 4-40685	Ginny/Joey, Joey, Joey	1956	3.00	6.00	12.00
❑ 4-40765	Prunes/We Ain't Goin' Nowhere	1956	3.00	6.00	12.00
—With Rita Farrell					
CORAL					
❑ 62480	I Keep Running Away from You/Think of All the Nice Things He's Done	1966	2.50	5.00	10.00
DECCA					
❑ 9-30131	Wringle, Wrangle/It Was My Father's Habit	1957	3.00	6.00	12.00
❑ 9-30240	Love Story/I'll Be Thinking of You	1957	3.00	6.00	12.00
❑ 9-30380	I Keep Running Away from You/Will I Find My Love Today	1957	3.00	6.00	12.00
❑ 9-30525	Homing Bird/Think of All the Nice Things He's Done	1957	3.00	6.00	12.00
❑ 9-30562	Introduce Me to the Gal/You're the Prettiest Thing	1958	3.00	6.00	12.00
DOT					
❑ 17184	And I'll Forget You/Have a Nice Trip	1968	2.00	4.00	8.00
GRIFFIN					
❑ 501	Happy to Know You/A Man Who Sings	1973	—	3.50	7.00
MERCURY					
❑ 72069	Count Your Blessings (Every Day)/Casanova Bossa Nova	1962	2.00	4.00	8.00
METROMEDIA					
❑ 167	Theme from Minnie's Boys/Time for Tony	1970	—	3.00	6.00
MGM					
❑ K13638	Santa Claus Is Coming to Town/Sleep My Little Child	1966	2.50	5.00	10.00
❑ K13826	Keep It in the Family/Tell Us Papa	1967	2.50	5.00	10.00
RCA VICTOR					
❑ 47-4181	The Morningside of the Mountain/I Love the Sunshine of Your Smile	1951	5.00	10.00	20.00
❑ 47-4217	Belle, Belle, My Liberty Belle/I Fall in Love with You Ev'ry Day	1951	5.00	10.00	20.00
❑ 47-4270	Twenty Three Starlets (And Me)/The Lord's Ridin' with Me Tonight	1951	5.00	10.00	20.00
❑ 47-4511	Neither Am I/They Say You Cry	1952	3.75	7.50	15.00
❑ 47-4512	The Hills of County Clare/The Isle of Innisfree	1952	3.75	7.50	15.00
❑ 47-4644	Heart of a Clown/With No One to Love Tonight	1952	3.75	7.50	15.00
❑ 47-4746	The Young Maine Moon/(B-side unknown)	1952	3.75	7.50	15.00
❑ 47-4747	Mush-Mush-Mush-Tural-I-Addy/The Humour Is On Me Now	1952	3.75	7.50	15.00
❑ 47-4748	Galway Bay/The Kerry Dance	1952	3.75	7.50	15.00
❑ 47-4749	The Wild Colonial Boy/I'll Take You Home Again, Kathleen	1952	3.75	7.50	15.00
—The above four comprise a box set					
❑ 47-4778	Mama's Gone, Goodbye/Love Me, Love Me	1952	3.75	7.50	15.00

Number	Title (A Side/B Side)	Yr	VG	VG+	NM
ZOO YORK					
❑ WS4 03949	Changing Keys/Nightwalk	1983	—	3.00	6.00
—As "The Merv Griffin Orchestra"; "Changing Keys" is the second (and most familiar) theme song to the game show "Wheel of Fortune"					
Albums					
51 WEST					
❑ Q 16281	P.S. I Love You	198?	2.00	4.00	8.00
GRIFFIN					
❑ G3G-1501	As Time Goes By	1973	3.00	6.00	12.00
METROMEDIA					
❑ MD 1023	Appearing Nightly	1969	3.00	6.00	12.00
MGM					
❑ E-4326 [M]	A Tinkling Piano in the Next Apartment	1965	3.00	6.00	12.00
❑ SE-4326 [S]	A Tinkling Piano in the Next Apartment	1965	3.75	7.50	15.00
❑ E-4381 [M]	'Alf and 'Alf: Songs of the British Music Hall	1966	3.75	7.50	15.00
—With Arthur Treacher					
❑ SE-4381 [S]	'Alf and 'Alf: Songs of the British Music Hall	1966	5.00	10.00	20.00
—With Arthur Treacher					
❑ E-4401 [M]	And a Sled .... And a Catcher's Mitt ... And a Puppy ... And a Popgun ... And a Big Christmas Album from Merv Griffin and His TV Family	1966	5.00	10.00	20.00
❑ SE-4401 [S]	And a Sled .... And a Catcher's Mitt ... And a Puppy ... And a Popgun ... And a Big Christmas Album from Merv Griffin and His TV Family	1966	6.25	12.50	25.00
❑ SE-4562 [S]	Irving Berlin Songs	1968	—	—	—
—Canceled					

GRIFFINS, THE
45s

Number	Title (A Side/B Side)	Yr	VG	VG+	NM
MERCURY					
❑ 70558	I Swear By All the Stars Above/Sing to Me	1955	30.00	60.00	120.00
❑ 70650	Bad Little Girl/Scheming	1955	30.00	60.00	120.00
❑ 70913	My Baby's Gone/Why Must You Go	1956	10.00	20.00	40.00
WING					
❑ 90067	Forever More/Leave It to Me	1956	50.00	100.00	200.00

GRIFFITH, ANDY
45s

Number	Title (A Side/B Side)	Yr	VG	VG+	NM
CAPITOL					
❑ 2571	Romeo and Juliet (Part 1)/Romeo and Juliet (Part 2)	1969	2.00	4.00	8.00
❑ F2693	What It Was, Was Football (Part 1)/What It Was, Was Football (Part 2)	195?	6.25	12.50	25.00
—Later pressings (purple Capitol label, large logo at top) as "Andy Griffith"					
❑ F2693	What It Was, Was Football (Part 1)/What It Was, Was Football (Part 2)	1953	7.50	15.00	30.00
—Original pressings as "Deacon Andy Griffith"					
❑ F2696	Romeo and Juliet (Part 1)/Romeo and Juliet (Part 2)	195?	6.25	12.50	25.00
—Later pressings (purple label, large Capitol logo at top) as "Andy Griffith"					
❑ F2696	Romeo and Juliet (Part 1)/Romeo and Juliet (Part 2)	1954	7.50	15.00	30.00
—Original pressings as "Deacon Andy Griffith"					
❑ F2855	Swan Lake (Part 1)/Swan Lake (Part 2)	1954	6.25	12.50	25.00
❑ F3057	Make Yourself Comfortable/Ko Ko Mo (I Love You So)	1955	5.00	10.00	20.00
❑ F3402	Opera Carmen (Part 1)/Opera Carmen (Part 2)	1956	6.25	12.50	25.00
❑ F3498	Standing on the Corner/No Time for Sergeants	1956	5.00	10.00	20.00
❑ F3705	Mama Guitar/A Face in the Crowd	1957	5.00	10.00	20.00
❑ F3706	Free Man in the Morning/Just a Closer Walk with Thee	1957	5.00	10.00	20.00
❑ F3872	Silhouettes/Conversation with a Mule	1958	5.00	10.00	20.00
❑ F3938	Andy's Lament/Thank Heaven for Little Girls	1958	5.00	10.00	20.00
❑ F3990	Love Poems: To the Lovely Juanita Beasley/Togetherness	1958	5.00	10.00	20.00
❑ F4052	Midnight Special/She's Bad, Bad Business	1958	5.00	10.00	20.00
❑ F4157	Hamlet (Part 1)/Hamlet (Part 2)	1959	5.00	10.00	20.00
❑ F4204	Once Knew a Fella/Don't Look Back	1959	3.75	7.50	15.00
❑ 4236	Look at the Son-Shine/My Dog Underdog	1976	—	3.00	6.00
❑ 4539	New River Train/(B-side unknown)	1961	3.75	7.50	15.00
❑ 4684	Flop Eared Mule/A Good Man Is Hard to Find	1962	3.75	7.50	15.00
❑ 4848	The Pool Table/Whistling Ping Pong Game	1962	3.75	7.50	15.00
❑ 5073	Andy and Cleopatra (Part 1)/Andy and Cleopatra (Part 2)	1963	3.75	7.50	15.00
COLONIAL					
❑ E3	What It Was, Was Football (Part 1)/What It Was, Was Football (Part 2)	1953	15.00	30.00	60.00
COLUMBIA					
❑ 4-45711	Lead Me to That Rock/Somebody Bigger Than You and I	1972	2.00	4.00	8.00
7-Inch Extended Plays					
CAPITOL					
❑ EAP 1-498	What It Was, Was Football/Romeo and Juliet	1954	10.00	20.00	40.00
❑ EAP 1-498 [PS]	What It Was, Was Football!	1954	10.00	20.00	40.00
❑ EAP 1-630	Make Yourself Comfortable/Ko Ko Mo//Swan Lake	1955	7.50	15.00	30.00
❑ EAP 1-630 [PS]	Make Yourself Comfortable	1955	7.50	15.00	30.00
Albums					
CAPITOL					
❑ T 962 [M]	Just for Laughs	1958	10.00	20.00	40.00
❑ ST 1105 [S]	Andy Griffith Shouts the Blues and Old Timey Songs	1959	12.50	25.00	50.00
❑ T 1105 [M]	Andy Griffith Shouts the Blues and Old Timey Songs	1959	10.00	20.00	40.00
❑ ST 1215 [S]	This Here Andy Griffith	1959	10.00	20.00	40.00
❑ T 1215 [M]	This Here Andy Griffith	1959	7.50	15.00	30.00
❑ ST 1611 [S]	Songs, Themes and Laughs from The Andy Griffith Show	1961	30.00	60.00	120.00
❑ T 1611 [M]	Songs, Themes and Laughs from The Andy Griffith Show	1961	20.00	40.00	80.00
❑ ST 2066 [S]	Andy and Cleopatra	1964	6.25	12.50	25.00
❑ T 2066 [M]	Andy and Cleopatra	1964	5.00	10.00	20.00

G

Number	Title (A Side/B Side)	Yr	VG	VG+	NM
GRIFFITH, PEGGI					
45s					
DOLTON					
❏ 35	Lovely Girl/You're In My Dreams to Stay	1961	5.00	10.00	20.00
GRIN Also see NILS LOFGREN.					
45s					
A&M					
❏ 1502	Beggar's Day/You're the Weight	1974	—	2.00	4.00
SPINDIZZY					
❏ ZS7 4001	If I Were a Song/See What a Love Can Do	1971	—	3.00	6.00
❏ ZS7 4002	Everybody's Missing the Sun/				
	Eighteen-Faced Lover	1971	—	3.00	6.00
❏ ZS7 4005	White Lies/Just to Have You	1972	—	3.00	6.00
❏ ZS7 4006	End Unkind/Slippery Fingers	1972	—	3.00	6.00
THUNDER					
❏ 4000	We All Sung Together/See What a Love Can Do	1970	2.00	4.00	8.00
Albums					
A&M					
❏ SP-4405	Gone Crazy	1973	2.50	5.00	10.00
COLUMBIA LIMITED EDITION					
❏ LE 10265	All Out	197?	2.50	5.00	10.00
—Remixed version on Columbia's brown-label "Limited Edition" series					
EPIC					
❏ PE 34247	The Best of Grin	1976	2.50	5.00	10.00
—Without bar code on back					
❏ PE 34247	The Best of Grin	198?	2.00	4.00	8.00
—With bar code on back					
SPINDIZZY					
❏ Z 30321	Grin	1971	3.00	6.00	12.00
❏ Z 31038	1 + 1	1972	3.00	6.00	12.00
❏ KZ 31701	All Out	1973	3.00	6.00	12.00
GRINER, LINDA					
45s					
MOTOWN					
❏ 1037	Good-By Cruel Love/Envious	1963	50.00	100.00	200.00
—With corrected A-side title					
❏ 1037	Good-By Cruel World/Envious	1963	87.50	175.00	350.00
—With incorrect A-side title					
GROCE, LARRY					
45s					
DISNEYLAND					
❏ 564	Winnie the Pooh for President (Campaign				
	Song)/(B-side unknown)	1976	5.00	10.00	20.00
MGM					
❏ 14621	Muddy Boggy Banjo Man/Sweet Sweet Love	1973	—	2.50	5.00
PEACEABLE					
❏ 3	Junk Food Junkie/Muddy Boggy Banjo Man	1975	2.50	5.00	10.00
❏ 3 [PS]	Junk Food Junkie/Muddy Boggy Banjo Man	1975	2.50	5.00	10.00
WARNER BROS.					
❏ 8165	Junk Food Junkie/Muddy Boggy Banjo Man	1975	—	2.50	5.00
❏ 8221	We've Been Malled/Old Fashioned Girl	1976	—	2.00	4.00
❏ 8327	The Ballad of Billy Don Rice				
	/Big White House in Indiana	1977	—	2.00	4.00
❏ 8442	Turn On Your TV/Hog and Dog Factory	1977	—	2.00	4.00
Albums					
DAYBREAK					
❏ 2000	The Wheat Lies Low	1971	3.00	6.00	12.00
❏ 2010	Crescentville	1972	3.00	6.00	12.00
WARNER BROS.					
❏ BS 2933	Junkfood Junkie	1976	2.50	5.00	10.00
GRODECK WHIPPERJENNY					
Albums					
PEOPLE					
❏ 3000	Grodeck Whipperjenny	1969	50.00	100.00	200.00
GROGAN, TOBY					
45s					
VEE JAY					
❏ 560	Angel/Just a Friend	1963	7.50	15.00	30.00
—The Four Seasons sing on this record.					
GROOTNA					
45s					
COLUMBIA					
❏ 45461	Full Time Woman/Is It All Over	1971	—	3.00	6.00
❏ 45538	Waitin' for My Ship/That's What You Get	1972	—	3.00	6.00
Albums					
COLUMBIA					
❏ C 31033	Grootna	1971	3.75	7.50	15.00
GROOV-U					
Albums					
GATEWAY					
❏ GLP-3010	Groov-U On Campus	196?	10.00	20.00	40.00
GROOVIE GOOLIES, THE					
45s					
RCA VICTOR					
❏ 74-0383	The First Annual Semi-Formal Combination				
	Celebration Meet-the-Monster Population				
	Party/Save Your Good Lovin' for Me	1970	2.50	5.00	10.00
Albums					
RCA VICTOR					
❏ LSP-4420	The Groovie Goolies	1970	6.25	12.50	25.00
GROSS, HENRY					
45s					
A&M					
❏ 1494	Fly Away/Simone	1974	—	2.00	4.00
❏ 1534	Come On Say It/Ever Lovin' Days	1974	—	2.00	4.00
❏ 1613	Meet Me on the Corner/				
	With the Sleep in My Eyes	1974	—	2.00	4.00

Number	Title (A Side/B Side)	Yr	VG	VG+	NM
❏ 1682	One More Tomorrow/Evergreen	1975	—	2.00	4.00
❏ 1701	Travelin' Time/All My Love	1975	—	2.00	4.00
ABC					
❏ 11322	New York City/My Sunshine	1972	—	3.00	6.00
❏ 11334	Close My Eyes/Prayer for All	1972	—	3.00	6.00
CAPITOL					
❏ 4946	Better Now We're Friends/You're My Ride Home	1980	—	2.00	4.00
❏ 4980	How Long Is Forever/I Love You Now	1981	—	2.00	4.00
LIFESONG					
❏ 1761	Only the Beautiful/Creepin' Jenny	1978	—	2.00	4.00
❏ 1769	Love Is the Stuff/Shake Down Your Love	1978	—	2.00	4.00
❏ 45002	Shannon/Pokey	1976	—	2.50	5.00
❏ 45008	Springtime Mama/Overton Square	1976	—	2.00	4.00
❏ 45014	Someday (I Didn't Want to Have to Be the One)/				
	Lincoln Road	1976	—	2.00	4.00
❏ 45023	String of Hearts/Painting My Love Song	1977	—	2.00	4.00
❏ 45024	What a Sound/Painting My Love Song	1977	—	2.00	4.00
Albums					
A&M					
❏ SP-4416	Henry Gross	1973	3.00	6.00	12.00
❏ SP-4502	Plug Me Into Something	1974	3.00	6.00	12.00
ABC					
❏ X-747	Henry Gross	1971	3.75	7.50	15.00
CAPITOL					
❏ ST 12113	What's in a Name	1980	2.50	5.00	10.00
LIFESONG					
❏ LS 6002	Release	1976	2.50	5.00	10.00
❏ LS 6010	Show Me to the Stage	1977	2.50	5.00	10.00
❏ PZ 34995	Release	1978	2.00	4.00	8.00
—Reissue of 6002					
❏ PZ 35002	Show Me to the Stage	1978	2.00	4.00	8.00
—Reissue of 6010					
❏ JZ 35280	Love Is the Stuff	1978	2.50	5.00	10.00
GROSS SISTERS, THE					
45s					
CHECKER					
❏ 932	Oom Baby!/My Baby Ain't Nothin' But Bad	1959	10.00	20.00	40.00
GROUNDHOGS, THE					
45s					
INTERPHON					
❏ 7715	Rock Me/Shake It	1965	3.00	6.00	12.00
LIBERTY					
❏ 56205	Ship on the Ocean/Sailor	1970	2.00	4.00	8.00
Albums					
CLEVE					
❏ CH-82871	The Groundhogs with John Lee Hooker and				
	John Mayall	196?	25.00	50.00	100.00
IMPERIAL					
❏ LP-12452	Blues Obituary	1969	10.00	20.00	40.00
LIBERTY					
❏ LST-7644	Thank Christ for the Bomb	1970	7.50	15.00	30.00
UNITED ARTISTS					
❏ UA-LA008-F	Hogwash	1973	5.00	10.00	20.00
❏ UA-LA603-G	Crosscut Saw	1976	5.00	10.00	20.00
❏ UA-LA680-G	Black Diamond	1976	5.00	10.00	20.00
❏ UAS-5513	The Groundhogs Split	1971	5.00	10.00	20.00
❏ UAS-5570	Who Will Save the World	1972	5.00	10.00	20.00
WORLD PACIFIC					
❏ WPS-21892	Scratching the Surface	1968	10.00	20.00	40.00
GROUNDSPEED					
45s					
DECCA					
❏ 32344	In a Dream/L-12 East	1968	6.25	12.50	25.00
GROUP, THE Probably more than one group.					
45s					
WARNER BROS.					
❏ 5840	Baby, Baby It's You/Can't Get Enough of Your				
	Love	1966	3.00	6.00	12.00
Albums					
BELL					
❏ 6038	The Group	1970	5.00	10.00	20.00
RCA VICTOR					
❏ LPM-2663 [M]	The Group	1963	5.00	10.00	20.00
❏ LSP-2663 [S]	The Group	1963	6.25	12.50	25.00
GROUP "B" Early incarnation of BLUE CHEER.					
45s					
SCORPIO					
❏ 402	Stop Calling Me/She's Gone	1967	6.25	12.50	25.00
❏ 406	I Know Your Name Girl/I Never Really Knew	1967	6.25	12.50	25.00
GROUP IMAGE, THE					
Albums					
COMMUNITY					
❏ A-101	A Mouth in the Clouds	1968	7.50	15.00	30.00
GROUP ONE					
Albums					
RCA VICTOR					
❏ LPM-3524 [M]	Brothers Go to Mothers and Others	1966	3.75	7.50	15.00
❏ LSP-3524 [S]	Brothers Go to Mothers and Others	1966	5.00	10.00	20.00
GROUP THERAPY					
45s					
CANTERBURY					
❏ 517	Magic in the Air/Bad News	1967	3.00	6.00	12.00
MERCURY					
❏ 72702	Thoughts/Come On	1967	3.00	6.00	12.00
PHILIPS					
❏ 40598	Can't Stop Lovin' You Baby/I Must Go	1969	2.00	4.00	8.00
RCA VICTOR					
❏ 47-9527	People Get Ready/Who'll Be Next	1968	2.00	4.00	8.00

Number	Title (A Side/B Side)	Yr	VG	VG+	NM
Albums					
PHILIPS					
❏ PHS 600303	37 Minutes of Group Therapy	1969	3.75	7.50	15.00
RCA VICTOR					
❏ LPM-3976 [M]	People Get Ready for Group Therapy	1968	10.00	20.00	40.00
❏ LSP-3976 [S]	People Get Ready for Group Therapy	1968	5.00	10.00	20.00

GROUPIES, THE
45s
ATCO

Number	Title (A Side/B Side)	Yr	VG	VG+	NM
❏ 6393	I'm a Hog for You/Primitive	1966	7.50	15.00	30.00

GROWING CONCERN, THE
45s
MAINSTREAM

Number	Title (A Side/B Side)	Yr	VG	VG+	NM
❏ 685	Tomorrow Has Been Canceled/A Boy I Once Knew Well	1968	7.50	15.00	30.00
Albums					
MAINSTREAM					
❏ S-6108 [S]	The Growing Concern	1968	30.00	60.00	120.00
❏ 56108 [M]	The Growing Concern	1968	20.00	40.00	80.00

GROWL
Albums
DISCREET

Number	Title (A Side/B Side)	Yr	VG	VG+	NM
❏ DS 2209	Growl	1974	5.00	10.00	20.00

GRUNDY, DAVE, COMBO
45s
HIT

Number	Title (A Side/B Side)	Yr	VG	VG+	NM
❏ 32	Green Onions/I Remember You	1962	2.00	4.00	8.00
—B-side by Ed Mendel					

GRUNION HUNTERS, THE
45s
HIGHLAND

Number	Title (A Side/B Side)	Yr	VG	VG+	NM
❏ 1035	The Four-Eyed, Tongue-Tied, Swimmin' Surfer Biter/Sing Along to the Swimmin' Surfer Biter	1963	10.00	20.00	40.00

GRUNIONS, THE
45s
JOCKO

Number	Title (A Side/B Side)	Yr	VG	VG+	NM
❏ 505	Surfin' Psycho/Big Noise from Winnetka	1963	12.50	25.00	50.00

GRYPHON
Albums
(NO LABEL)

Number	Title (A Side/B Side)	Yr	VG	VG+	NM
❏ 12497	Gryphon	197?	20.00	40.00	80.00
BELL					
❏ 1316	Red Queen to Gryphon Three	1974	3.75	7.50	15.00

GUARALDI, VINCE
45s
FANTASY

Number	Title (A Side/B Side)	Yr	VG	VG+	NM
❏ 563	Cast Your Fate to the Wind/Samba de Orpheus	1962	2.50	5.00	10.00
❏ 567	Zalas/Jitterbug Waltz	1963	2.50	5.00	10.00
❏ 571	Mr. Lucky/Treat Street	1963	2.50	5.00	10.00
❏ 580	Days of Wine and Roses/(B-side unknown)	1963	2.50	5.00	10.00
❏ 593	Linus & Lucy/Oh, Good Grief	1964	5.00	10.00	20.00
❏ 606	Humbly I Adore Thee/Theme to Grace	1965	2.50	5.00	10.00
❏ 608	Christmas Time Is Here/What Child Is This	1966	5.00	10.00	20.00
❏ 613	I'm a Loser/Favela	1966	2.50		5.00	10.00
ORIGINAL JAZZ CLASSICS					
❏ 18001	Cast Your Fate to the Wind/Mr. Lucky	1984	—	2.50	5.00
—Stereo reissue					
Albums					
FANTASY					
❏ OJC-149	Vince Guaraldi Trio	198?	2.50	5.00	10.00
—Reissue of 3225					
❏ OJC-235	A Flower Is a Lovesome Thing	198?	2.50	5.00	10.00
—Reissue of 3257					
❏ OJC-272	Modern Music from San Francisco	1987	2.50	5.00	10.00
—Reissue of 3213					
❏ OJC-287	Jazz Impressions	1987	2.50	5.00	10.00
—Reissue of 8359					
❏ OJC-289	Live at the El Matador	1987	2.50	5.00	10.00
—Reissue of 8371					
❏ OJC-437	Jazz Impressions of Black Orpheus (Cast Your Fate to the Wind)	198?	2.50	5.00	10.00
—Reissue of 8089					
❏ 3213 [M]	Modern Music from San Francisco	195?	6.25	12.50	25.00
—Black vinyl, red label, non-flexible vinyl					
❏ 3213 [M]	Modern Music from San Francisco	1956	12.50	25.00	50.00
—Red vinyl					
❏ 3225 [M]	Vince Guaraldi Trio	195?	6.25	12.50	25.00
—Black vinyl, red label, non-flexible vinyl					
❏ 3225 [M]	Vince Guaraldi Trio	1956	12.50	25.00	50.00
—Red vinyl					
❏ 3225 [M]	Vince Guaraldi Trio	196?	3.75	7.50	15.00
—Black vinyl, red label, flexible vinyl					
❏ 3257 [M]	A Flower Is a Lovesome Thing	195?	6.25	12.50	25.00
—Black vinyl, red label, non-flexible vinyl					
❏ 3257 [M]	A Flower Is a Lovesome Thing	1958	10.00	20.00	40.00
—Red vinyl					
❏ 3257 [M]	A Flower Is a Lovesome Thing	196?	3.75	7.50	15.00
—Black vinyl, red label, flexible vinyl					
❏ 3337 [M]	Jazz Impressions of Black Orpheus (Cast Your Fate to the Wind)	1962	3.75	7.50	15.00
—Black vinyl, red label, flexible vinyl					
❏ 3337 [M]	Jazz Impressions of Black Orpheus (Cast Your Fate to the Wind)	1962	6.25	12.50	25.00
—Black vinyl, red label, non-flexible vinyl					
❏ 3337 [M]	Jazz Impressions of Black Orpheus (Cast Your Fate to the Wind)	1962	10.00	20.00	40.00
—Red vinyl					
❏ 3352 [M]	Vince Guaraldi in Person	1963	6.25	12.50	25.00
❏ 3356 [M]	Vince Guaraldi and Bola Sete and Friends	1964	6.25	12.50	25.00

Number	Title (A Side/B Side)	Yr	VG	VG+	NM
❏ 3358 [M]	Tour de Force	1964	6.25	12.50	25.00
❏ 3359 [M]	Jazz Impressions	1965	6.25	12.50	25.00
❏ 3360 [M]	The Latin Side of Vince Guaraldi	1965	6.25	12.50	25.00
❏ 3362 [M]	From All Sides	1966	5.00	10.00	20.00
❏ 3367 [M]	Vince Guaraldi at Grace Cathedral	1967	5.00	10.00	20.00
❏ 3371 [M]	Live at the El Matador	1967	5.00	10.00	20.00
❏ MPF-4505	Vince Guaraldi's Greatest Hits	1981	3.00	6.00	12.00
❏ 5019 [M]	A Charlie Brown Christmas	1964	7.50	15.00	30.00
❏ 8089 [S]	Jazz Impressions of Black Orpheus (Cast Your Fate to the Wind)	1962	3.75	7.50	15.00
—Black vinyl, blue label, flexible vinyl					
❏ 8089 [S]	Jazz Impressions of Black Orpheus (Cast Your Fate to the Wind)	1962	6.25	12.50	25.00
—Black vinyl, blue label, non-flexible vinyl					
❏ 8089 [S]	Jazz Impressions of Black Orpheus (Cast Your Fate to the Wind)	1962	10.00	20.00	40.00
—Blue vinyl					
❏ 8352 [S]	Vince Guaraldi in Person	1963	6.25	12.50	25.00
❏ 8356 [S]	Vince Guaraldi and Bola Sete and Friends	1964	6.25	12.50	25.00
❏ 8358 [S]	Tour de Force	1964	6.25	12.50	25.00
❏ 8359 [S]	Jazz Impressions	1965	6.25	12.50	25.00
❏ 8360 [S]	The Latin Side of Vince Guaraldi	1965	6.25	12.50	25.00
❏ 8362 [S]	From All Sides	1966	5.00	10.00	20.00
❏ 8367 [S]	Vince Guaraldi at Grace Cathedral	1967	5.00	10.00	20.00
❏ 8371 [S]	Live at the El Matador	1967	5.00	10.00	20.00
❏ 8377	Live-Live-Live	1968	5.00	10.00	20.00
❏ 8430	A Boy Named Charlie Brown — Jazz Impressions	1971	5.00	10.00	20.00
—Reissue of 85017					
❏ 8431	A Charlie Brown Christmas	1971	6.25	12.50	25.00
—Reissue of 85019; dark blue label					
❏ 8431	A Charlie Brown Christmas	1988	3.75	7.50	15.00
—Remastered version with "1988" on back cover. Lighter blue label. Also has a bonus track!					
❏ 85017	A Boy Named Charlie Brown — Jazz Impressions	196?	6.25	12.50	25.00
❏ 85019 [S]	A Charlie Brown Christmas	1964	10.00	20.00	40.00
MOBILE FIDELITY					
❏ 1-112	Jazz Impressions of Black Orpheus (Cast Your Fate to the Wind)	1983	12.50	25.00	50.00
—Audiophile vinyl					
WARNER BROS.					
❏ WS 1747	Oh Good Grief!	1968	5.00	10.00	20.00
❏ WS 1775	Eclectic	1969	3.75	7.50	15.00
❏ WS 1828	Alma-Ville	1970	3.75	7.50	15.00

GUARALDI, VINCE/CONTE CANDOLI
Albums
CROWN

Number	Title (A Side/B Side)	Yr	VG	VG+	NM
❏ CST-417 [R]	Vince Guaraldi and the Conte Candoli All Stars	1963	2.50	5.00	10.00
❏ CLP-5417 [M]	Vince Guaraldi and the Conte Candoli All Stars	1963	3.00	6.00	12.00
PREMIER					
❏ PM-2009 [M]	Vince Guaraldi-Conte Candoli Quartet	1963	3.00	6.00	12.00
❏ PS-2009 [R]	Vince Guaraldi-Conte Candoli Quartet	1963	2.50	5.00	10.00

GUARALDI, VINCE/FRANK ROSOLINO
Albums
PREMIER

Number	Title (A Side/B Side)	Yr	VG	VG+	NM
❏ PM-2014 [M]	Vince Guaraldi-Frank Rosolino Quintet	1963	3.00	6.00	12.00
❏ PS-2014 [R]	Vince Guaraldi-Frank Rosolino Quintet	1963	2.50	5.00	10.00

GUARD, DAVE, AND THE WHISKEYHILL SINGERS
Dave Guard had split from THE KINGSTON TRIO.
45s
CAPITOL

Number	Title (A Side/B Side)	Yr	VG	VG+	NM
❏ 4787	Plane Wreck at Los Gatos/Ride On, Railroad Bill	1962	2.50	5.00	10.00
Albums					
CAPITOL					
❏ ST 1728 [S]	Dave Guard and the Whiskeyhill Singers	1962	6.25	12.50	25.00
❏ T 1728 [M]	Dave Guard and the Whiskeyhill Singers	1962	5.00	10.00	20.00

GUESS WHO, THE
45s
AMY

Number	Title (A Side/B Side)	Yr	VG	VG+	NM
❏ 967	And She's Mine/All Right	1966	5.00	10.00	20.00
—The existence of stock copies of this record has been questioned					
❏ 976	His Girl/It's My Pride	1967	7.50	15.00	30.00
—Price is for stock copy; promos go for less					
FONTANA					
❏ 1597	This Time Long Ago/There's No Getting Away from It	1967	7.50	15.00	30.00
HILLTAK					
❏ 7803	C'mon Little Mama/Moon Wave Maker	1979	—	3.00	6.00
❏ 7807	Sweet Young Thing/It's Getting Pretty Bad	1979	—	3.00	6.00
RCA VICTOR					
❏ 74-0102	These Eyes/Lightfoot	1969	—	3.00	6.00
❏ 74-0195	Laughing/Undun	1969	—	3.00	6.00
❏ 74-0300	No Time/Proper Stranger	1969	—	3.00	6.00
❏ 74-0325	American Woman/No Sugar Tonight	1970	—	2.50	5.00
❏ 74-0367	Hand Me Down World/Runnin' Down the Street	1970	—	2.50	5.00
❏ 74-0388	Share the Land/Bus Rider	1970	—	2.50	5.00
❏ 74-0388 [PS]	Share the Land/Bus Rider	1970	2.50	5.00	10.00
❏ 74-0414	Hang On to Your Life/Do You Miss Me, Darlin'?	1970	—	2.50	5.00
❏ 74-0414 [PS]	Hang On to Your Life/Do You Miss Me, Darlin'?	1970	6.25	12.50	25.00
❏ 74-0458	Albert Flasher/Broken	1971	—	2.50	5.00
❏ 74-0522	Rain Dance/One Divided	1971	—	2.50	5.00
❏ 74-0578	Sour Suite/Life in the Bloodstream	1971	—	2.50	5.00
❏ 74-0659	Heartbroken Bopper/Arrivederci Girl	1972	—	2.50	5.00
❏ 74-0708	Guns, Guns, Guns/Heaven Only Moved Once Yesterday	1972	—	2.50	5.00
❏ 74-0803	Runnin' Back to Saskatoon/New Mother Nature	1972	—	2.50	5.00
❏ 74-0880	Follow Your Daughter Home/Bye Bye Babe	1973	—	2.50	5.00
❏ 74-0926	The Watcher/Orly	1973	—	2.50	5.00
❏ 74-0977	Lie Down/Glamour Boy	1973	—	2.50	5.00
❏ SPS-45-223 [DJ]	Friends of Mine (Part 1)/Friends of Mine (Part 2)	1969	3.00	6.00	12.00
❏ APBO-0217	Star Baby/Musicione	1974	—	2.50	5.00
❏ APBO-0324	Clap for the Wolfman/Road Food	1974	—	2.50	5.00

G

Number	Title (A Side/B Side)	Yr	VG	VG+	NM
❏ PB-10075	Dancin' Fool/Seems Like I Can't Live With You, But I Can't Live Without You	1974	—	2.50	5.00
❏ GB-10161	Clap for the Wolfman/Star Baby	1975	—	2.00	4.00
—Gold Standard Series					
❏ PB-10216	Loves Me Like a Brother/Hoe Down Time	1975	—	2.50	5.00
❏ PB-10360	Dreams/Rosanne	1975	—	2.50	5.00
❏ PB-10410	When the Band Was Singin' (Shakin' All Over)/Women	1975	—	3.00	6.00
❏ PB-10716	Silver Bird/Runnin' Down the Street	1976	3.00	6.00	12.00
SCEPTER					
❏ 1295	Shakin' All Over/Till We Kissed	1965	3.75	7.50	15.00
❏ 1295	Shakin' All Over/Monkey in a Cage	1965	7.50	15.00	30.00
—B-side by the Discotays					
❏ 12108	Hey Ho What You Do to Me/Goodnight Goodnight	1965	3.75	7.50	15.00
❏ 12118	Hurting Each Other/Baby's Birthday	1965	5.00	10.00	20.00
❏ 12131	Believe Me/Baby Feelin'	1966	5.00	10.00	20.00
❏ 12144	One Day/Clock on the Wall	1966	5.00	10.00	20.00
Albums					
COMPLEAT					
❏ 672012-1 [(2)]	The Best of the Gues Who, Live	1986	5.00	10.00	20.00
HILLTAK					
❏ HT 19227	All This for a Song	1979	3.00	6.00	12.00
MGM					
❏ SE-4645	The Guess Who	1969	3.75	7.50	15.00
—Compilation of pre-RCA Victor recordings					
P.I.P.					
❏ 6806	The Guess Who Play Pure Guess Who	197?	3.00	6.00	12.00
PICKWICK					
❏ SPC-3246	The Guess Who	1970	2.50	5.00	10.00
PRIDE					
❏ PRD 0012	The History of the Guess Who	197?	3.00	6.00	12.00
RCA					
❏ 7622-1-R	The Greatest of the Guess Who	1987	2.50	5.00	10.00
—Late reissue					
RCA VICTOR					
❏ APD1-0130 [Q]	#10	1974	6.25	12.50	25.00
❏ APL1-0130	#10	1973	3.75	7.50	15.00
❏ AFL1-0269	The Best of the Guess Who, Volume II	1977	2.50	5.00	10.00
—Reissue with new prefix					
❏ APD1-0269 [Q]	The Best of the Guess Who, Volume II	1974	6.25	12.50	25.00
❏ APL1-0269	The Best of the Guess Who, Volume II	1973	3.75	7.50	15.00
❏ APD1-0405 [Q]	Road Food	1974	6.25	12.50	25.00
❏ APL1-0405	Road Food	1974	3.75	7.50	15.00
❏ CPD1-0636 [Q]	Flavours	1975	6.25	12.50	25.00
❏ CPL1-0636	Flavours	1975	3.75	7.50	15.00
❏ ANL1-0983	Canned Wheat Packed By the Guess Who	1975	2.50	5.00	10.00
—Reissue of LSP-4157					
❏ APD1-0995 [Q]	Power in the Music	1975	6.25	12.50	25.00
❏ APL1-0995	Power in the Music	1975	3.75	7.50	15.00
❏ LSPX-1004	The Best of the Guess Who	1971	3.75	7.50	15.00
❏ ANL1-1117	Wheatfield Soul	1975	2.50	5.00	10.00
—Reissue of LSP-4141					
❏ APL1-1778	The Way They Were	1976	3.75	7.50	15.00
❏ APL1-2253	The Greatest of the Guess Who	1977	3.75	7.50	15.00
❏ AFL1-2594	The Best of the Guess Who	1978	2.50	5.00	10.00
—Reissue of LSPX-1004					
❏ AYL1-3662	The Best of the Guess Who	1979	2.00	4.00	8.00
—"Best Buy Series" reissue					
❏ AYL1-3673	American Woman	1979	2.00	4.00	8.00
—"Best Buy Series" reissue					
❏ AYL1-3746	The Greatest of the Guess Who	1980	2.00	4.00	8.00
—"Best Buy Series" reissue					
❏ LSP-4141	Wheatfield Soul	1969	5.00	10.00	20.00
—Orange label, non-flexible vinyl					
❏ LSP-4141	Wheatfield Soul	1971	3.00	6.00	12.00
—Orange label, flexible vinyl					
❏ LSP-4157	Canned Wheat Packed By the Guess Who	1969	5.00	10.00	20.00
—Orange label, non-flexible vinyl					
❏ LSP-4157	Canned Wheat Packed By the Guess Who	1971	3.00	6.00	12.00
—Orange label, flexible vinyl					
❏ AFL1-4266	American Woman	1977	2.50	5.00	10.00
—Reissue with new prefix					
❏ LSP-4266	American Woman	1970	5.00	10.00	20.00
—Orange label, non-flexible vinyl					
❏ LSP-4266	American Woman	1971	3.00	6.00	12.00
—Orange label, flexible vinyl					
❏ LSP-4359	Share the Land	1970	5.00	10.00	20.00
—Orange label, non-flexible vinyl					
❏ LSP-4359	Share the Land	1971	3.00	6.00	12.00
—Orange label, flexible vinyl					
❏ LSP-4574	So Long, Bannatyne	1971	3.75	7.50	15.00
❏ LSP-4602	Rockin'	1972	3.75	7.50	15.00
❏ LSP-4779	Live at the Paramount (Seattle)	1972	6.25	12.50	25.00
❏ LSP-4830	Artificial Paradise	1973	3.75	7.50	15.00
—Add 1/3 if paper bag is with package					
SCEPTER					
❏ SP-533 [M]	Shakin' All Over	1966	10.00	20.00	40.00
❏ SPS-533 [P]	Shakin' All Over	1966	6.25	12.50	25.00
—The above lists the artist as "The Guess Who's Chad Allan & The Expressions" on the cover					
SPRINGBOARD					
❏ SPB-4022	Shakin' All Over	1972	2.50	5.00	10.00
SUNDAZED					
❏ LP 5113 [(2)]	Shakin' All Over	2001	3.75	7.50	15.00
WAND					
❏ WDS-691 [P]	Born in Canada	1969	3.75	7.50	15.00
—Reissue of Scepter LP; three tracks are rechanneled					

GUIDES, THE
45s
GUYDEN

Number	Title (A Side/B Side)	Yr	VG	VG+	NM
❏ 2023	How Long Must a Fool Go On/You Must Try	1959	7.50	15.00	30.00
—Originally released under the name "The Swallows"					

GUILLOTEENS, THE
45s
COLUMBIA

Number	Title (A Side/B Side)	Yr	VG	VG+	NM
❏ 43852	Wild Child/You Think You're Happy	1966	3.75	7.50	15.00
❏ 43852 [PS]	Wild Child/You Think You're Happy	1966	10.00	20.00	40.00
—Sleeve is promo only					
❏ 44089	I Love That Girl/Dear Mrs. Applebee	1967	3.00	6.00	12.00
HANNA-BARBERA					
❏ 446	I Don't Believe/Hey You	1965	3.75	7.50	15.00
❏ 451	Don't Let the Rain Get You Down/For My Own	1965	3.75	7.50	15.00
❏ 451 [PS]	Don't Let the Rain Get You Down/For My Own	1965	7.50	15.00	30.00
❏ 486	I Sit and Cry/Crying All Over My Time	1966	5.00	10.00	20.00

GUITAR, BILLY
45s
DECCA

Number	Title (A Side/B Side)	Yr	VG	VG+	NM
❏ 30634	Here Comes the Night/You Should Have Loved Her More	1958	17.50	35.00	70.00

GUITAR, BONNIE
45s
COLUMBIA

Number	Title (A Side/B Side)	Yr	VG	VG+	NM
❏ 4-45643	Just As Soon As I Get Over Loving You/Happy Everything	1972	—	2.50	5.00
DOLTON					
❏ 10	Candy Apple Red/Come to Me, I Love You	1959	3.00	6.00	12.00
❏ 19	Candy Apple Red/Come to Me, I Love You	1960	2.50	5.00	10.00
DOT					
❏ 15550	Dark Moon/Big Mile	1957	3.75	7.50	15.00
❏ 15587	Half Your Heart/If You See My Love Dancing	1957	3.00	6.00	12.00
❏ 15612	There's a New Moon Over My Shoulder/Mister Fire Eyes	1957	3.00	6.00	12.00
❏ 15678	Making Believe/I Saw Your Face in the Moon	1957	3.00	6.00	12.00
❏ 15708	A Very Precious Love/Johnny Vagabond	1958	3.00	6.00	12.00
❏ 15776	I Found You Out/If You'll Be the Teacher	1958	3.00	6.00	12.00
❏ 15862	Rocky Mountain Moon/Whispering Hope	1958	3.00	6.00	12.00
❏ 15894	Baby Moon/Solitude	1959	3.00	6.00	12.00
❏ 16811	I'm Living in Two Worlds/Goodtime Charlie	1965	—	3.00	6.00
❏ 16872	Would You Believe/Get Your Life the Way You Want It	1966	—	3.00	6.00
❏ 16919	Are You Sincere/The Tallest Tree	1966	—	3.00	6.00
❏ 16968	I'll Be Missing You (Under the Mistletoe)/Blue Christmas	1966	5.00	10.00	20.00
❏ 16987	The Kickin' Tree/Only I	1967	—	3.00	6.00
❏ 17007	You Can Steal Me/Ramblin' Man	1967	—	3.00	6.00
❏ 17029	I Want My Baby/Woman in Love	1967	—	3.00	6.00
❏ 17057	Wings of a Dove/Stop the Sun	1967	—	3.00	6.00
❏ 17097	Faded Love/I Believe in Love	1968	—	2.50	5.00
❏ 17150	Almost Like Being with You/Leaves Are the Tears of Autumn	1968	—	2.50	5.00
❏ 17249	Perfect Strangers/I'll Meet You in Denver	1969	—	2.50	5.00
❏ 17276	I'll Pick Up My Heart/That See Me Later Look	1969	—	2.50	5.00
FABOR					
❏ 138	Ra Ta Ta Ta/Leave Weeping to the Willow Tree	1964	2.00	4.00	8.00
❏ 4013	If You See My Love Dancing/Hello, Hello, Please Answer	1956	6.25	12.50	25.00
❏ 4017	Clinging VIne/Dream Dreamers	1956	6.25	12.50	25.00
❏ 4018	Dark Moon/Big Mile	1957	10.00	20.00	40.00
4 STAR					
❏ 1006	I Wanna Spend My Life with You/Maggie	1975	—	2.50	5.00
❏ 1041	Honey on the Moon/Lonely Eyes	1980	—	2.50	5.00
—Number also listed as 1003. Which is correct? Or are both?					
JERDEN					
❏ 707	There'll Be No Teardrops Tonight/The Fool	1963	2.50	5.00	10.00
MCA					
❏ 40192	The Bed I Love In/Wishing Star	1974	—	2.00	4.00
❏ 40306	From This Moment On/Shine	1974	—	2.00	4.00
PARAMOUNT					
❏ 0004	A Truer Love You'll Never Find (Than Mine)/That's When	1969	—	3.50	7.00
—As "Bonnie and Buddy"					
❏ 0045	Allegheny/Red Checkered Blazer	1970	—	3.50	7.00
PLAYBACK					
❏ 1304	Things Songs Are Made Of/Here We Lie	1988	—	3.00	6.00
❏ 1309	Paradise/Wine from My Table	1988	—	3.00	6.00
❏ 1326	What Can I Say/What's In It for Me	1989	—	3.00	6.00
❏ 1341	Lonely Eyes/Honey on the Moon	1989	—	3.00	6.00
❏ 75714	Still the Same/If You Were Here	1989	—	2.50	5.00
RADIO					
❏ 101	Please, My Love/Love Is Over, Love Is Done	1958	3.00	6.00	12.00
❏ 110	Shanty Boat/Only the Moon Man Knows	1958	3.00	6.00	12.00
RCA VICTOR					
❏ 37-7951	I'll Step Down/Tell Her Bye	1961	5.00	10.00	20.00
—"Compact Single 33"; small hole, plays at 33 1/3 rpm					
❏ 47-7951	I'll Step Down/Tell Her Bye	1961	2.50	5.00	10.00
❏ 47-8063	Broken Hearted Girl/Who Is She	1962	2.50	5.00	10.00
Albums					
DOT					
❏ DLP-3069 [M]	Moonlight and Shadows	1957	12.50	25.00	50.00
❏ DLP-3151 [M]	Whispering Hope	1958	10.00	20.00	40.00
❏ DLP-3335 [M]	Dark Moon	1961	6.25	12.50	25.00
❏ DLP-3696 [M]	Two Worlds	1966	5.00	10.00	20.00
❏ DLP-3737 [M]	Miss Bonnie Guitar	1966	5.00	10.00	20.00
❏ DLP-3746 [M]	Merry Christmas from Bonnie Guitar	1966	5.00	10.00	20.00
❏ DLP-3793 [M]	Award Winner	1967	5.00	10.00	20.00
❏ DLP-25069 [R]	Moonlight and Shadows	196?	3.75	7.50	15.00
❏ DLP-25151 [S]	Whispering Hope	1958	12.50	25.00	50.00
❏ DLP-25335 [R]	Dark Moon	196?	3.75	7.50	15.00
❏ DLP-25696 [S]	Two Worlds	1966	6.25	12.50	25.00
❏ DLP-25737 [S]	Miss Bonnie Guitar	1966	6.25	12.50	25.00
❏ DLP-25746 [S]	Merry Christmas from Bonnie Guitar	1966	6.25	12.50	25.00
❏ DLP-25793 [S]	Award Winner	1967	5.00	10.00	20.00
❏ DLP-25840	Bonnie Guitar	1968	5.00	10.00	20.00
❏ DLP-25892	Leaves Are the Tears of Autumn	1968	5.00	10.00	20.00
❏ DLP-25947	Affair!	1969	5.00	10.00	20.00

Number	Title (A Side/B Side)	Yr	VG	VG+	NM
PARAMOUNT					
❑ PAS-5018	Allegheny	1970	3.75	7.50	15.00
PICKWICK					
❑ SPC-3086	Favorite Lady of Song	196?	3.00	6.00	12.00
❑ SPC-3144	Green, Green Grass of Home	196?	3.00	6.00	12.00
RCA CAMDEN					
❑ CAS-2339	Night Train to Memphis	1969	3.75	7.50	15.00

GUITAR SLIM
45s

Number	Title (A Side/B Side)	Yr	VG	VG+	NM
ATCO					
❑ 6072	Oh Yeah/Down Through the Years	1956	10.00	20.00	40.00
❑ 6097	It Hurts to Love Someone/If I Should Lose You	1957	7.50	15.00	30.00
❑ 6108	I Won't Mind at All/Hello, How Ya' Been, Goodbye	1958	7.50	15.00	30.00
❑ 6120	If I Had My Life to Live Over/When There's No Way Out	1958	7.50	15.00	30.00
IMPERIAL					
❑ 5278	Woman Troubles/Cryin' in the Mornin'	1954	15.00	30.00	60.00
❑ 5310	New Arrival/Standing at the Station	1954	15.00	30.00	60.00
SPECIALTY					
❑ 482	The Things That I Used to Do/Well, I Done Get Over It	1954	12.50	25.00	50.00
❑ 490	Story of My Life/A Letter to My Girl Friend	1954	10.00	20.00	40.00
❑ 527	Later for You Baby/Troubles Don't Last	1954	6.25	12.50	25.00
❑ 536	Sufferin' Mind/Twenty-Five Lies	1955	6.25	12.50	25.00
❑ 542	Stand By Me/Our Only Child	1955	6.25	12.50	25.00
❑ 551	You're Gonna Miss Me/I Got Sumpin' for You	1955	6.25	12.50	25.00
❑ 557	Think It Over/Quicksand	1955	6.25	12.50	25.00
❑ 569	Sumthin' to Remember Me By/You Give Me Nothin' But the Blues	1956	6.25	12.50	25.00
Albums					
ATLANTIC					
❑ 81760	The Atco Sessions	1987	2.50	5.00	10.00
SPECIALTY					
❑ SP-2130	Things That I Used to Do	1969	5.00	10.00	20.00

GUITARS, INC. Pseudonym for THE FIREBALLS.
45s

Number	Title (A Side/B Side)	Yr	VG	VG+	NM
HAMILTON					
❑ 50035	Little Toy/Holiday Love	1960	6.25	12.50	25.00

GULLIVER With Daryl Hall. John Oates joined later, but is not on these records.
45s

Number	Title (A Side/B Side)	Yr	VG	VG+	NM
ELEKTRA					
❑ 45689	Angelina/Every Day's a Lovely Day	1970	2.00	4.00	8.00
❑ 45698	A Truly Good Song/Every Day's a Lovely Day	1970	2.00	4.00	8.00
Albums					
ELEKTRA					
❑ EKS-74070	Gulliver	1970	5.00	10.00	20.00

GUM DROPS, THE

Number	Title (A Side/B Side)	Yr	VG	VG+	NM
CORAL					
❑ 62003	My Own True Love/On the Wings of the Wind	1958	3.75	7.50	15.00
❑ 62102	I Spoke Too Soon/Sie Tu (It's You, It's You)	1959	3.75	7.50	15.00
❑ 62138	It Happens Every Day/They Wake Me	1959	3.75	7.50	15.00
DECCA					
❑ 30584	You're the One/Gum Drop Shoes and Bells in Her Hair	1958	5.00	10.00	20.00
KING					
❑ 1496	Gum Drop/Don't Take It So Hard	1955	5.00	10.00	20.00
❑ 1499	I'll Wait for One More Train/Don't Take It So Hard	1955	5.00	10.00	20.00
❑ 4913	I Wonder and Wonder/I'll Follow You	1956	6.25	12.50	25.00
❑ 4963	Natural Born Lover/Chapel of Hearts	1956	6.25	12.50	25.00
❑ 5051	Ba-Bee Da Boat Is Leaving/Pigeon	1957	5.00	10.00	20.00

GUN
45s

Number	Title (A Side/B Side)	Yr	VG	VG+	NM
EPIC					
❑ 10413	Race with the Devil/Sunshine	1968	2.50	5.00	10.00
❑ 10537	Don't Look Back/Hobo	1969	2.50	5.00	10.00
❑ 10593	Drown Yourself in the River/Long Hair Wildman	1970	2.50	5.00	10.00
Albums					
EPIC					
❑ BN 26468	Gun	1969	5.00	10.00	20.00
❑ BN 26551	Gunsight	1970	6.25	12.50	25.00

GUNHILL ROAD
45s

Number	Title (A Side/B Side)	Yr	VG	VG+	NM
KAMA SUTRA					
❑ 562	Ford, De Soto, Cadillac/(B-side unknown)	1972	—	2.50	5.00
❑ 569	Back When My Hair Was Short/We Can't Ride the Roller Coaster Anymore	1973	—	3.00	6.00
❑ 582	Ford, De Soto, Cadillac/Sailing	1973	—	2.50	5.00
❑ 591	She Made a Man Out of Me/(B-side unknown)	1974	—	2.50	5.00
MERCURY					
❑ 73232	42nd Street/(B-side unknown)	1971	—	3.00	6.00
Albums					
KAMA SUTRA					
❑ KLS-2061	Gunhill Road	1972	3.00	6.00	12.00
MERCURY					
❑ SR-61341	Gun Hill Road	1971	3.00	6.00	12.00

GUNS & BUTTER
Albums

Number	Title (A Side/B Side)	Yr	VG	VG+	NM
COTILLION					
❑ SD 9901	Guns & Butter	1972	5.00	10.00	20.00

GUNTER, ARTHUR
45s

Number	Title (A Side/B Side)	Yr	VG	VG+	NM
EXCELLO					
❑ 2047	Baby Let's Play House/Blues After Hours	1954	30.00	60.00	120.00
❑ 2053	She's Mine, All Mine/You Are Doin' Me Wrong	1955	15.00	30.00	60.00
❑ 2058	Honey Babe/No Happy Home	1955	15.00	30.00	60.00
❑ 2073	Baby You Better Listen/Trouble with My Baby	1955	7.50	15.00	30.00

Number	Title (A Side/B Side)	Yr	VG	VG+	NM
❑ 2084	Hear My Plea Baby/Love Has Got Me	1956	7.50	15.00	30.00
❑ 2125	Baby Can't You See/You're Always on My Mind	1958	6.25	12.50	25.00
❑ 2137	Ludella/We're Gonna Shake	1959	6.25	12.50	25.00
❑ 2147	Crazy Me/Don't Leave Me Now	1959	6.25	12.50	25.00
❑ 2164	No Naggin' No Draggin'/I Want Her Back	1959	6.25	12.50	25.00
❑ 2191	Little Blue Jeans/Mind Your Own Business Babe	1960	5.00	10.00	20.00
❑ 2201	My Heart's Always Lonesome/I'm Fallin', Love's Got Me	1961	5.00	10.00	20.00
Albums					
EXCELLO					
❑ LPS-8017	Black and Blues	1971	6.25	12.50	25.00

GUNTER, CORNEL
45s

Number	Title (A Side/B Side)	Yr	VG	VG+	NM
ABC-PARAMOUNT					
❑ 9698	She Loves to Rock/In Self Defense	1956	10.00	20.00	40.00
—As "Cornel Gunter and the Flairs"					
CHALLENGE					
❑ 59281	If I Had the Key to Your Heart/Wishful	1965	2.50	5.00	10.00
DOT					
❑ 15654	You Send Me/Call Me a Fool	1957	5.00	10.00	20.00
EAGLE					
❑ 301	Baby Come Home/I Want You Madly	1957	7.50	15.00	30.00
LIBERTY					
❑ 55096	If We Should Meet Again/Neighborhood Dance	1957	5.00	10.00	20.00
LOMA					
❑ 701	True Love/Peek, Peek-a-Boo	1955	25.00	50.00	100.00
❑ 703	You Broke My Heart/(Pretty Baby) I'm Used to You Now	1956	37.50	75.00	150.00
❑ 704	Keep Me Alive/Muchacha, Muchacha	1956	20.00	40.00	80.00
❑ 705	I'm Sad/One Thing	1956	25.00	50.00	100.00
—The Loma singles credit "The Ermines," and may or may not mention Gunter.					
WARNER BROS.					
❑ 5266	Lieft Me Up Angel/Hope of Sand	1962	3.00	6.00	12.00
❑ 5292	It Ain't No Use/In a Dream of Love	1962	3.00	6.00	12.00

GUNTER, HARDROCK
45s

Number	Title (A Side/B Side)	Yr	VG	VG+	NM
DECCA					
❑ 9-46300	Boogie Woogie on a Saturday Night/Honky Tonk	1951	10.00	20.00	40.00
❑ 9-46350	I've Done Gone Hog Wild/I Believe That Mountain Music	1951	6.25	12.50	25.00
❑ 9-46363	Sixty Minute Man/Tennessee Blues	1951	6.25	12.50	25.00
❑ 9-46367	Dixieland Boogie/If I Could Only Live My Dreams	1951	6.25	12.50	25.00
❑ 9-46383	Hesitation Boogie/Don't You Argue	1951	6.25	12.50	25.00
❑ 9-46401	Silver and Gold/Senator from Tennessee	1952	6.25	12.50	25.00
KING					
❑ 4858	Turn the Other Cheek/Before My Time	1955	5.00	10.00	20.00
MGM					
❑ K-11520	Like the Lovers Do/Naptown, Indiana	1953	6.25	12.50	25.00
❑ K-11596	Sunday Angel/Where Have You Been	1953	6.25	12.50	25.00
SUN					
❑ 201	Fallen Angel/Gonna Dance All Night	1954	500.00	1000.	2000.

GUNTER, SHIRLEY
45s

Number	Title (A Side/B Side)	Yr	VG	VG+	NM
FLAIR					
❑ 1020	Send Him Back/Since I Fell for You	1953	10.00	20.00	40.00
❑ 1027	Found Some Good Lovin'/Strange Romance	1954	7.50	15.00	30.00
❑ 1050	Oop Shoop/It's You	1955	7.50	15.00	30.00
❑ 1060	You're Mine/Why	1955	7.50	15.00	30.00
❑ 1065	What Difference Does It Make/Baby I Love You So	1955	7.50	15.00	30.00
❑ 1070	That's the Way I Like It/Gimme, Gimme, Gimme	1955	7.50	15.00	30.00
❑ 1076	How Can I Tell You/Ipsy Gypsy Ooh	1955	15.00	30.00	60.00
—With the Flairs					
MODERN					
❑ 979	Please Tell Me/Come On	1956	6.25	12.50	25.00
❑ 1001	Fortune in Love/Just Got Rid of a Heartache	1956	6.25	12.50	25.00
—With the Flairs					
❑ 1011	I'm So Sorry/I've Been Searching	1956	6.25	12.50	25.00
TANGERINE					
❑ 949	Stuck Up/You Let My Love Grow Cold	1965	2.50	5.00	10.00
TENDER					
❑ 503	Believe Me/Crazy Little Baby	1958	10.00	20.00	40.00

GURUS, THE
45s

Number	Title (A Side/B Side)	Yr	VG	VG+	NM
UNITED ARTISTS					
❑ 50089	Come Girl/Blue Snow Night	1966	3.00	6.00	12.00
❑ 50089 [PS]	Come Girl/Blue Snow Night	1966	6.25	12.50	25.00
❑ 50140	It Just Won't Be That Way/Everybody's Got to Be Alone Sometime	1967	3.00	6.00	12.00

GUTHRIE, ARLO
45s

Number	Title (A Side/B Side)	Yr	VG	VG+	NM
REPRISE					
❑ PRO 304 [DJ]	Motorcycle Song/The Pause of Mr. Claus	1970	5.00	10.00	20.00
❑ 0644	Motorcycle Song/Now and Then	1967	3.00	6.00	12.00
❑ 0793	Motorcycle Song (Part 1)/Motorcycle Song (Part 2)	1968	3.00	6.00	12.00
❑ 0877	Alice's Rock & Roll Restaurant/Coming Into Los Angeles	1969	3.00	6.00	12.00
❑ 0951	Gabriel's Mother's Hiway/Ballad #16 Blues	1970	2.00	4.00	8.00
❑ 0994	The Ballad of Tricky Fred/Shackles and Chains	1971	—	3.00	6.00
❑ 1103	The City of New Orleans/Days Are Short	1972	—	3.00	6.00
❑ 1137	Ukulele Lady/Cooper's Lament	1972	—	2.50	5.00
❑ 1158	A Week on the Rag/Gypsy Dave	1973	—	2.50	5.00
❑ 1211	Nostalgia Rag/Presidential Rag	1974	—	2.00	4.00
❑ 1363	Patriot's Dream/Ocean Crossing	1976	—	2.00	4.00
❑ 1376	Grocery Blues/Guabi, Guabi	1976	—	2.00	4.00
❑ 1388	Massachusetts/My Love	1977	—	2.00	4.00
WARNER BROS.					
❑ 49037	Wedding Song/Prologue	1979	—	2.00	4.00
❑ 49796	Slow Boat/If I Could Only Touch Your Life	1981	—	2.00	4.00
❑ 49889	Oklahoma Nights/Power of Love	1981	—	2.00	4.00

G

Number	Title (A Side/B Side)	Yr	VG	VG+	NM
Albums					
REPRISE					
❏ MS 2060	Hobo's Lullabye	1972	3.00	6.00	12.00
❏ MS 2142	Last of the Brooklyn Cowboys	1973	3.00	6.00	12.00
❏ MS4 2142 [Q]	Last of the Brooklyn Cowboys	1973	5.00	10.00	20.00
❏ MS 2183	Arlo Guthrie	1974	3.00	6.00	12.00
❏ MS 2239	Amigo	1976	3.00	6.00	12.00
❏ R 6267 [M]	Alice's Restaurant	1967	5.00	10.00	20.00
❏ RS 6267 [S]	Alice's Restaurant	1967	3.75	7.50	15.00
—Pink, green and gold label					
❏ RS 6267 [S]	Alice's Restaurant	1968	3.00	6.00	12.00
—With "W7" and "r:" logos on two-tone orange label					
❏ RS 6267 [S]	Alice's Restaurant	1970	2.50	5.00	10.00
—With only "r:" logo on all-orange (tan) label					
❏ RS 6299	Arlo	1968	3.75	7.50	15.00
—With "W7" and "r:" logos on two-tone orange label					
❏ RS 6299	Arlo	1970	2.50	5.00	10.00
—With only "r:" logo on all-orange (tan) label					
❏ RS 6346	Running Down the Road	1969	3.75	7.50	15.00
—With "W7" and "r:" logos on two-tone orange label					
❏ RS 6346	Running Down the Road	1970	2.50	5.00	10.00
—With only "r:" logo on all-orange (tan) label					
❏ RS 6411	Washington County	1970	3.00	6.00	12.00
WARNER BROS.					
❏ BSK 3117	The Best of Arlo Guthrie	1977	2.50	5.00	10.00
—"Burbank" palm trees label					
❏ BSK 3117	The Best of Arlo Guthrie	1979	2.00	4.00	8.00
—White or tan label					
❏ BSK 3232	One Night	1978	2.50	5.00	10.00
❏ BSK 3336	Outlasting the Blues	1979	2.50	5.00	10.00
❏ BSK 3558	Power of Love	1981	2.50	5.00	10.00

GUTHRIE, WOODY

Number	Title (A Side/B Side)	Yr	VG	VG+	NM
Albums					
COLLECTABLES					
❏ COL-5095	Golden Classics Vol. 1: Worried Man Blues	198?	3.00	6.00	12.00
❏ COL-5098	Golden Classics Vol. 2: Immortal	198?	3.00	6.00	12.00
ELEKTRA					
❏ EKL-271/2 [(3)M]	The Library of Congress Recordings	1964	10.00	20.00	40.00
—Original pressing has "guitar player" labels					
EVEREST ARCHIVE OF FOLK & JAZZ					
❏ 204	Woody Guthrie	1966	3.00	6.00	12.00
FOLKWAYS					
❏ FP-11 [10]	Dust Bowl Ballads	1950	150.00	300.00	600.00
❏ FP-715 [10]	Songs to Grow On For Mother and Child	195?	150.00	30.00	600.00
❏ FA-2011 [10]	Dust Bowl Ballads	195?	125.00	250.00	500.00
—Reissue of FP-11					
❏ FA-2481 [M]	Bound for Glory: Songs and Stories of Woody Guthrie	1956	37.50	75.00	150.00
❏ FA-2483 [M]	Woody Guthrie Sings Folk Songs	1964	12.50	25.00	50.00
❏ FA-2484 [M]	Woody Guthrie Sings Folk Songs, Vol. 2	1964	12.50	25.00	50.00
❏ FA-2485 [M]	Struggle	1964	12.50	25.00	50.00
❏ FH-5212 [M]	Dust Bowl Ballads	1964	7.50	15.00	30.00
❏ FH-5485 [M]	Ballds of Sacco and Vanzetti	196?	7.50	15.00	30.00
❏ FC-7005 [10]	Songs to Grow On	1950	125.00	250.00	500.00
❏ FC-7015 [10]	Songs to Grow On For Mother and Child	1953	125.00	250.00	500.00
—Reissue of FP-715					
❏ FC-7027 [10]	Songs to Grow On Vol. 3	1951	125.00	250.00	500.00
❏ 31001 [R]	This Land Is Your Land	196?	3.00	6.00	12.00
RCA VICTOR					
❏ LPV-502 [M]	Dust Bowl Ballads	1964	6.25	12.50	25.00
ROUNDER					
❏ 1036	Columbia River Collection	1987	2.50	5.00	10.00
❏ 1040	Dust Bowl Ballads	1988	2.50	5.00	10.00
❏ 1041/2/3 [(3)]	The Library of Congress Recordings	1988	5.00	10.00	20.00
SMITHSONIAN FOLKWAYS					
❏ SF-40007	Woody Guthrie Sings Folk Songs	1989	3.00	6.00	12.00
❏ SF-40025	Struggle	1989	3.00	6.00	12.00
VERVE FOLKWAYS					
❏ FV-9007 [M]	Bed on the Floor	1965	7.50	15.00	30.00
❏ FVS-9007 [R]	Bed on the Floor	1965	5.00	10.00	20.00
❏ FV-9036 [M]	Bonneville Dam & Other Columbia River Songs	1965	7.50	15.00	30.00
❏ FVS-9036 [R]	Bonneville Dam & Other Columbia River Songs	1965	5.00	10.00	20.00

GUTHRIE, WOODY, AND CISCO HOUSTON

Number	Title (A Side/B Side)	Yr	VG	VG+	NM
Albums					
STINSON					
❏ SLP-32 [10]	Cowboy Songs	195?	50.00	100.00	200.00
❏ SLP-44 [10]	Folk Songs, Vol. 1	195?	50.00	100.00	200.00
❏ SLP-53 [10]	More Songs	195?	50.00	100.00	200.00

GUTHRIE, WOODY; SONNY TERRY; ALEX STEWART

Number	Title (A Side/B Side)	Yr	VG	VG+	NM
Albums					
STINSON					
❏ SLP-7 [10]	Chain Gang, Vol. 1	195?	50.00	100.00	200.00
❏ SLP-8 [10]	Chain Gang, Vol. 2	195?	50.00	100.00	200.00

GUY, ART

Number	Title (A Side/B Side)	Yr	VG	VG+	NM
45s					
VALIANT					
❏ 762	Where You Gonna Go/Teenage Millionaire	1967	7.50	15.00	30.00

GUY, BOB Pseudonym for FRANK ZAPPA.

Number	Title (A Side/B Side)	Yr	VG	VG+	NM
45s					
DONNA					
❏ 1380	Letter from Jeepers/Dear Jeepers	1963	25.00	50.00	100.00

GUY, BOBBY

Number	Title (A Side/B Side)	Yr	VG	VG+	NM
45s					
APT					
❏ 25052	A Vow/Good Enough	1960	7.50	15.00	30.00

GUY, BROWLEY, AND THE SKYSCRAPERS

Number	Title (A Side/B Side)	Yr	VG	VG+	NM
45s					
CHECKER					
❏ 779	Watermelon Man/You Look Good to Me	1954	75.00	150.00	300.00
—Black vinyl					
❏ 779	Watermelon Man/You Look Good to Me	1954	187.50	375.00	750.00
—Red vinyl					

GUY, BUDDY

Number	Title (A Side/B Side)	Yr	VG	VG+	NM
45s					
ARTISTIC					
❏ 1501	Sit and Cry/Try to Quit You Baby	1958	10.00	20.00	40.00
❏ 1503	You Sure Can't Do/This Is the End	1958	10.00	20.00	40.00
CHESS					
❏ 1753	I Got My Eyes on You/The First Time I Met the Blues	1960	7.50	15.00	30.00
❏ 1759	Stop Around/Broken Hearted Blues	1960	6.25	12.50	25.00
❏ 1784	Let Me Love You Baby/Ten Years Ago	1961	6.25	12.50	25.00
❏ 1812	Stone Crazy/Skippin'	1962	6.25	12.50	25.00
❏ 1838	When My Left Eye Jumps/My Treasure Untold	1962	6.25	12.50	25.00
❏ 1878	No Lie/Hard But It's Fair	1963	5.00	10.00	20.00
❏ 1899	My Time After a While/I Dig Your Wig	1964	5.00	10.00	20.00
❏ 1936	Leave My Girl Alone/Crazy Music	1965	5.00	10.00	20.00
❏ 1974	My Mother/Mother-in-Law Blues	1966	5.00	10.00	20.00
❏ 2022	Gonna Keep It to Myself/Suffer	1967	3.75	7.50	15.00
❏ 2067	She Suits Me to a Tee/Buddy's Groove	1969	3.75	7.50	15.00
VANGUARD					
❏ 35060	Sweet Little Angel/Mary Had a Little Lamb	1968	3.00	6.00	12.00
Albums					
BLUE THUMB					
❏ BTS 20	Buddy and the Juniors	1970	6.25	12.50	25.00
CHESS					
❏ LP-409	I Was Walking Through the Woods	1970	5.00	10.00	20.00
❏ LP-1527 [M]	I Left My Blues in San Francisco	1968	7.50	15.00	30.00
❏ CH-9115	Buddy Guy	1984	2.00	4.00	8.00
MCA					
❏ 11165	I Was Walking Through the Woods	1995	6.25	12.50	25.00
—"Heavy Vinyl" audiophile reissue					
VANGUARD					
❏ VSD-79272	A Man and the Blues	1968	6.25	12.50	25.00
❏ VSD-79290	This Is Buddy Guy	1969	6.25	12.50	25.00
❏ VSD-79323	Hold That Plane!	1972	5.00	10.00	20.00

GUYTON, HOWARD

Number	Title (A Side/B Side)	Yr	VG	VG+	NM
45s					
VERVE					
❏ 10386	I Watched You Slowly Slip Away/I Got My Own Thing Going	1966	25.00	50.00	100.00

GUYTONES, THE

Number	Title (A Side/B Side)	Yr	VG	VG+	NM
45s					
DELUXE					
❏ 6144	You Won't Let Me Go/Ooh Bop Sha Boo (Give All Your Love to Me)	1957	20.00	40.00	80.00
❏ 6152	She's Mine/Not Wanted	1957	20.00	40.00	80.00
❏ 6159	Hunky Dory/This Is Love	1958	20.00	40.00	80.00
❏ 6163	Baby, I Don't Care/Young Dreamer	1958	15.00	30.00	60.00
❏ 6169	Tell Me (How Was I to Know)/Your Heart's Bigger Than Mine	1958	15.00	30.00	60.00

GYPSIES, THE

Number	Title (A Side/B Side)	Yr	VG	VG+	NM
45s					
ATLAS					
❏ 1073	Why/Young Girl to Calypso	1957	20.00	40.00	80.00
GROOVE					
❏ 0117	One, Two, Three, Go/I'm Good to You Baby	1955	5.00	10.00	20.00
❏ 0129	Rock Around the Christmas Tree/You've Been Away Too Long	1955	5.00	10.00	20.00
OLD TOWN					
❏ 1168	Blue Bird/Hey There Hey There	1964	5.00	10.00	20.00
❏ 1180	Jerk It/Diamonds, Rubies, Gold and Fame	1965	5.00	10.00	20.00
❏ 1184	It's a Woman's World/They're Having a Party	1965	20.00	40.00	80.00
❏ 1193	Oh I Wonder Why/Diamonds, Rubies, Gold and Fame	1966	6.25	12.50	25.00

GYPSY

Number	Title (A Side/B Side)	Yr	VG	VG+	NM
45s					
METROMEDIA					
❏ 202	Gypsy Queen/Dead and Gone	1970	—	3.00	6.00
RCA VICTOR					
❏ 74-0862	Lean On Me/Day After Day	1973	—	2.50	5.00
❏ 74-0933	Make Peace with Jesus/Don't Bother Me	1973	—	2.50	5.00
❏ APBO-0036	Need You Baby/Precious One	1973	—	2.50	5.00
Albums					
METROMEDIA					
❏ MD-1031 [(2)]	Gypsy	1970	5.00	10.00	20.00
❏ MD 1044	In the Garden	1971	3.75	7.50	15.00
RCA VICTOR					
❏ APL1-0093	Unlock the Gates	1973	3.75	7.50	15.00
❏ LSP-4775	Antithesis	1972	3.75	7.50	15.00

GYPSY TRIPS, THE

Number	Title (A Side/B Side)	Yr	VG	VG+	NM
45s					
WORLD PACIFIC					
❏ 77809	Rock 'n Roll Gypsies/Ain't It Hard	1966	7.50	15.00	30.00

Number	Title (A Side/B Side)	Yr	VG	VG+	NM

H

H.P. LOVECRAFT
45s
MERCURY
| 73698 | Flight/I Feel Better | 1975 | — | 3.00 | 6.00 |

—As "Lovecraft"
| 73707 | We Love You (Whoever You Are)/ | | | | |
| | Ain't Gettin' Home | 1975 | — | 3.00 | 6.00 |

—As "Lovecraft"
PHILIPS
40464	Anyway That You Want Me/It's All Over for You	1967	3.00	6.00	12.00
40491	Wayfaring Stranger/The Time Machine	1967	3.00	6.00	12.00
40491 [PS]	Wayfaring Stranger/The Time Machine	1967	6.25	12.50	25.00
40506	The White Ship (Part 1)/The White Ship (Part 2)	1967	3.00	6.00	12.00
40578	Blue Jack of Diamonds/Keeper of the Keys	1968	3.00	6.00	12.00
REPRISE
0996	We Can All Have It Together/				
	Will I Know When My Time Comes	1971	2.00	4.00	8.00

—As "Lovecraft"
Albums
MERCURY
| SRM-1-1041 | We Love You | 1975 | 3.75 | 7.50 | 15.00 |
PHILIPS
PHM 200252 [M]	H.P. Lovecraft	1967	5.00	10.00	20.00
PHS 600252 [S]	H.P. Lovecraft	1967	6.25	12.50	25.00
PHS 600279	Lovecraft II	1968	6.25	12.50	25.00
REPRISE
RS 6419	Valley of the Moon	1970	5.00	10.00	20.00
SUNDAZED
LP-5004	Live May 11, 1968	199?	2.50	5.00	10.00

H.Y. SLEDGE
Albums
SSS INTERNATIONAL
| 22 | Bootleg Music | 1971 | 5.00 | 10.00 | 20.00 |

HA'PENNYS, THE
Albums
FERSCH
| FL-1110 | Love Is Not the Same | 1968 | 50.00 | 100.00 | 200.00 |

HACKAMORE BRICK
45s
KAMA SUTRA
| 521 | Searchin'/Radio | 1971 | — | 3.00 | 6.00 |
Albums
KAMA SUTRA
| KSBS-2025 | One Kiss Leads to Another | 1971 | 3.00 | 6.00 | 12.00 |

HACKERT, VALINE
45s
BRUNSWICK
| 55151 | Billy Boy/Show Me How | 1959 | 50.00 | 100.00 | 200.00 |

HADLEY, RED
45s
METEOR
| 5017 | Ring Out Those Bells/Brother, That's All | 1955 | 27.50 | 75.00 | 150.00 |

HAGAN, SAMMY, AND THE VISCOUNTS
45s
CAPITOL
F-3772	Out of Your Heart/Shoochie Poochie	1957	10.00	20.00	40.00
F-3818	Wild Bird/Don't Cry	1957	10.00	20.00	40.00
F-3885	Tail Light/Snuggle Bunny	1958	7.50	15.00	30.00

HAGGARD, MERLE Also see PAYCHECK AND HAGGARD.
45s
CAPITOL
2017	Sing Me Back Home/Good Times	1967	2.00	4.00	8.00
2017 [PS]	Sing Me Back Home/Good Times	1967	2.00	4.00	8.00
2123	The Legend of Bonnie and Clyde/I Started				
	Loving You Again	1968	2.00	4.00	8.00
2219	Mama Tried/You'll Never Love Me Now	1968	2.00	4.00	8.00
2219 [PS]	Mama Tried/You'll Never Love Me Now	1968	2.00	4.00	8.00
2289	I Take a Lot of Pride in What I Am/				
	Keep Me from Cryin' Today	1968	2.00	4.00	8.00
2289 [PS]	I Take a Lot of Pride in What I Am/				
	Keep Me from Cryin' Today	1968	2.00	4.00	8.00
2383	Hungry Eyes/California Blues	1969	2.00	4.00	8.00
2383 [PS]	Hungry Eyes/California Blues	1969	2.00	4.00	8.00
2503	Workin' Man Blues/Silver Wings	1969	2.00	4.00	8.00
2503 [PS]	Workin' Man Blues/Silver Wings	1969	2.00	4.00	8.00
2626	Okie from Muskogee/If I Had Left It Up to You	1969	2.00	4.00	8.00
2626 [PS]	Okie from Muskogee/If I Had Left It Up to You	1969	2.00	4.00	8.00
2719	The Fightin' Side of Me/E				
	very Fool Has a Rainbow	1970	2.00	4.00	8.00
2719 [PS]	The Fightin' Side of Me/				
	Every Fool Has a Rainbow	1970	2.00	4.00	8.00
2778	Street Singer/Mexican Rose	1970	2.00	4.00	8.00
2838	Jesus, Take a Hold/No Reason to Quit	1970	2.00	4.00	8.00
2891	I Can't Be Myself/Sidewalks of Chicago	1970	2.00	4.00	8.00
2891 [PS]	I Can't Be Myself/Sidewalks of Chicago	1970	2.00	4.00	8.00
3024	Soldier's Last Letter/The Farmer's Daughter	1971	—	3.00	6.00
3024 [PS]	Soldier's Last Letter/The Farmer's Daughter	1971	2.00	4.00	8.00
3112	Someday We'll Look Back/It's Great to Be Alive	1971	—	3.00	6.00
3198	Daddy Frank (The Guitar Man)/				
	My Heart Would Know	1971	—	3.00	6.00
3222	Carolyn/When the Feelin' Goes Away	1971	—	3.00	6.00
3294	Grandma Harp/Turnin' Off a Memory	1972	—	3.00	6.00
3419	It's Not Love (But It's Not Bad)/				
	My Woman Keeps Lovin' Her Man	1972	—	3.00	6.00
3488	I Wonder If They Ever Think of Me/				
	I Forget You Every Day	1972	—	3.00	6.00

Number	Title (A Side/B Side)	Yr	VG	VG+	NM
3552	The Emptiest Arms in the World/				
	Radiator Man from Waco	1973	—	2.50	5.00
3641	Everybody's Had the Blues/				
	Nobody Knows I'm Hurtin'	1973	—	2.50	5.00
3746	If We Make It Through December/				
	Bobby Wants a Puppy Dog for Christmas	1973	—	2.50	5.00
3830	Things Aren't Funny Anymore/				
	Honky Tonk Night Time Man	1974	—	2.50	5.00
3900	Old Man from the Mountain/				
	Holding Things Together	1974		2.50	5.00
3974	Kentucky Gambler/I've Got a Darlin' (For a Wife)	1974		2.50	5.00
3989	Santa Claus and Popcorn/				
	If We Make It Through December	1974		2.50	5.00
4027	Always Wanting You/I've Got a Yearning	1975		2.50	5.00
4085	Movin' On/Here in Frisco	1975		2.50	5.00
4141	It's All in the Movies/				
	Living with the Shades Pulled Down	1975		2.50	5.00
4204	The Roots of My Raising/The Way It Was in '51	1975		2.50	5.00
4267	Here Comes the Freedom Train/				
	I Won't Give Up My Train	1976		2.50	5.00
4326	Cherokee Maiden/				
	What Have You Got Planned Tonight Diana	1976		2.50	5.00
4477	A Workin' Man Can't Get Nowhere Today/				
	Blues Stay Away from Me	1977	—	2.50	5.00
4525	Running Kind/Making Believe	1978	—	2.50	5.00
4636	The Way It Was in '51/Moanin' the Blues	1978	—	2.50	5.00
5460	I'm Gonna Break Every Heart I Can/				
	Falling for You	1965	2.50	5.00	10.00
5523	This Town's Not Big Enough/Shade Tree	1965	2.50	5.00	10.00
5600	Swinging Doors/The Girl Turned Ripe	1966	2.50	5.00	10.00
5704	The Bottle Let Me Down/The Longer You Wait	1966	2.50	5.00	10.00
5803	The Fugitive/Someone Told My Story	1966	3.00	6.00	12.00
5803	I'm a Lonesome Fugitive/				
	Someone Told My Story	1967	2.00	4.00	8.00

—Retitled A-side
5844	I Threw Away the Rose/				
	Loneliness Is Eating Me Alive	1967	2.00	4.00	8.00
5844 [PS]	I Threw Away the Rose/				
	Loneliness Is Eating Me Alive	1967	2.00	4.00	8.00
5931	Branded Man/You Don't Have Very Far to Go	1967	2.00	4.00	8.00
5931 [PS]	Branded Man/You Don't Have Very Far to Go	1967	2.00	4.00	8.00

CAPITOL NASHVILLE
| S7-19346 | White Christmas/Silver Bells | 1996 | — | 2.00 | 4.00 |
CURB
76832	When It Rains It Pours/Me and Crippled Soldiers	1990	—	2.00	4.00
76846	Blue Jungle/Me and Crippled Soldiers	1990	—	2.00	4.00
76854	A Bar in Bakersfield/Lucky Old Colorado	1991	—	2.00	4.00
ELEKTRA
46634	Bar Room Buddies/				
	The Not So Great Train Robbery	1980	—	2.00	4.00

—With Clint Eastwood
| 46634 [PS] | Bar Room Buddies/ | | | | |
| | The Not So Great Train Robbery | 1980 | — | 2.50 | 5.00 |
EPIC
AE7 1777 [DJ]	Santa Claus and Popcorn/Grandma's				
	Homemade Christmas Card	1982	—	2.50	5.00
02504	My Favorite Memory/Texas Fiddle Song	1981	—	—	3.00
02686	Big City/I Think I'm Gonna Live Forever	1981	—	—	3.00
02894	Are the Good Times Really Over (I Wish a Buck				
	Was Still Silver)/I Always Get Lucky with You	1982	—	—	3.00
03315	Going Where the Lonely Go/Someday You're				
	Gonna Need Your Friends Again	1982	—	—	3.00
03365	Going Where the Lonely Go	1982	2.00	4.00	8.00

—One-sided budget release
03406	Goin' Home for Christmas/				
	If We Make It Through December	1982	—	2.00	4.00
03723	You Take Me for Granted/				
	I Won't Give Up My Train	1983	—	—	3.00
04006	What Am I Gonna Do (With the Rest of My Life)/				
	I Think I'll Stay	1983	—	—	3.00
04226	That's the Way Love Goes/Don't Seem Like				
	We've Been Together All Our Lives	1983	—	—	3.00
04402	Someday When Things Are Good/				
	If You Hated Me	1984	—	—	3.00
04512	Let's Chase Each Other Around the Room/All I				
	Want to Do Is Sing My Song	1984	—	—	3.00
04830	Natural High/I Never Go Home Anymore	1985	—	—	3.00
05426	Kern River/The Old Water Mill	1985	—	—	3.00
05659	Amber Waves of Grain/I Wish Things Were				
	Simple Again	1985	—	—	3.00
05734	American Waltz/The Farmer's Daughter	1985	—	—	3.00
05782	I Had a Beautiful Time/This Time I Really Do	1986	—	—	3.00
06097	A Friend in California/Mama's Prayers	1986	—	—	3.00
06344	Out Among the Stars/Suzie	1986	—	—	3.00
07036	Almost Persuaded/Love Don't Hurt Everytime	1987	—	—	3.00
07631	Twinkle, Twinkle, Lucky Star/I Don't Have Any				
	Love Around	1987	—	—	3.00
07754	Chill Factor/Thanking the Good Lord	1988	—	—	3.00
07944	We Never Touch at All/Man from Another Time	1988	—	—	3.00
08111	You Babe/Thirty Again	1988	—	—	3.00
68598	5:01 Blues/Man from Another Time	1989	—	—	3.00
68979	A Better Love Next Time/Losin' in Las Vegas	1989	—	—	3.00
73076	If You Want to Be My Woman/				
	Someday We'll Know	1989	—	—	3.00
73303	Broken Friend/Wouldn't That Be Something	1990	—	2.00	4.00
MCA
40700	If We're Not Back in Love By Monday/				
	I Think It's Gone Forever	1977	—	2.00	4.00
40743	Ramblin' Fever/				
	When My Blue Moon Turns to Gold Again	1977	—	2.00	4.00
40804	From Graceland to the Promised Land/				
	Are You Lonesome Tonight	1977	—	3.00	6.00
40869	I'm Always on a Mountain When I Fall/				
	The Life of a Rodeo Cowboy	1978	—	2.00	4.00
40936	It's Been a Great Afternoon/				
	Love Me When You Can	1978	—	2.00	4.00
41007	Red Bandana/I Must Have Done Something Bad	1979	—	2.00	4.00

Number	Title (A Side/B Side)	Yr	VG	VG+	NM
❏ 41112	My Own Kind of Hat/Heaven Was a Drink of Wine	1979	—	2.00	4.00
❏ 41168	If We Make It Through December/				
	The Fightin' Side of Me	1979	—	2.50	5.00
❏ 41200	The Way I Am/Wake Up	1980	—	2.00	4.00
❏ 41255	Misery and Gin/No One to Sing For	1980	—	2.00	4.00
❏ 41255 [PS]	Misery and Gin/No One to Sing For	1980	—	2.50	5.00
❏ 51014	I Think I'll Just Stay Here and Drink/				
	Back to the Barrooms	1980	—	2.00	4.00
❏ 51048	Leonard/Our Paths May Never Cross	1981	—	2.00	4.00
❏ 51120	Rainbow Stew/Blue Yodel No. 9	1981	—	2.00	4.00
❏ 52020	Dealing with the Devil/Fiddle Breakdown	1982	—	2.00	4.00
❏ 52276	It's All in the Game/New Cocaine Blues	1983	—	—	3.00
❏ 52595	Make-Up and Faded Blue Jeans/				
	Love Me When You Can	1985	—	—	3.00

TALLY

Number	Title (A Side/B Side)	Yr	VG	VG+	NM
❏ 152	Singin' My Heart Out/Skid Row	1963	5.00	10.00	20.00
❏ 155	Sing a Sad Song/You Don't Even Try	1963	3.75	7.50	15.00
❏ 178	Sam Hill/You Don't Have Far to Go	1964	3.75	7.50	15.00
❏ 179	(My Friends Are Gonna Be) Strangers/				
	Please Mr. D.J.	1964	3.75	7.50	15.00

Albums

CAPITOL

Number	Title (A Side/B Side)	Yr	VG	VG+	NM
❏ SKAO-168	Pride In What I Am	1969	6.25	12.50	25.00
❏ SM-168	Pride In What I Am	197?	2.50	5.00	10.00
—Reissue with new prefix					
❏ SWBB-223 [(2)]	Same Train, A Different Time	1969	7.50	15.00	30.00
❏ SWBB-259 [(2)]	Close-Up	1969	7.50	15.00	30.00
—Reissue in one package of "Strangers" and "Swinging Doors"					
❏ ST-319	A Portrait of Merle Haggard	1969	5.00	10.00	20.00
❏ ST-384	Okie from Muskogee	1970	5.00	10.00	20.00
❏ ST-451	The Fightin' Side of Me	1970	5.00	10.00	20.00
❏ ST-638	A Tribute to the Best Damn Fiddle Player in the				
	World (Or, My Salute to Bob Wills)	1970	6.25	12.50	25.00
❏ STBB-707 [(2)]	Sing a Sad Song/High on a Hilltop	1971	7.50	15.00	30.00
❏ ST-735	Hag	1971	3.75	7.50	15.00
❏ SWBO-803 [(2)]	The Land of Many Churches	1971	15.00	30.00	60.00
❏ ST-823	Truly the Best of Merle Haggard	1971	10.00	20.00	40.00
❏ ST-835	Someday We'll Look Back	1971	5.00	10.00	20.00
❏ ST-882	Let Me Tell You About a Song	1972	5.00	10.00	20.00
❏ ST 2373 [S]	Strangers	1965	7.50	15.00	30.00
❏ T 2373 [M]	Strangers	1965	6.25	12.50	25.00
❏ SM-2585	Swinging Doors	197?	2.50	5.00	10.00
—Reissue with new prefix					
❏ ST 2585 [S]	Swinging Doors	1966	7.50	15.00	30.00
❏ T 2585 [M]	Swinging Doors	1966	6.25	12.50	25.00
❏ SM-2702	I'm a Lonesome Fugitive	197?	2.50	5.00	10.00
—Reissue with new prefix					
❏ ST 2702 [S]	I'm a Lonesome Fugitive	1967	7.50	15.00	30.00
❏ T 2702 [M]	I'm a Lonesome Fugitive	1967	6.25	12.50	25.00
❏ ST 2789 [S]	Branded Man	1967	7.50	15.00	30.00
❏ T 2789 [M]	Branded Man	1967	6.25	12.50	25.00
❏ ST 2848 [S]	Sing Me Back Home	1968	6.25	12.50	25.00
❏ T 2848 [M]	Sing Me Back Home	1968	7.50	15.00	30.00
❏ ST 2912	The Legend of Bonnie and Clyde	1968	6.25	12.50	25.00
❏ SKAO 2951	The Best of Merle Haggard	1968	6.25	12.50	25.00
❏ ST 2972	Mama Tried	1968	6.25	12.50	25.00
❏ ST-11082	The Best of the Best of Merle Haggard	1972	3.75	7.50	15.00
❏ ST-11127	It's Not Love	1972	3.00	6.00	12.00
❏ ST-11141	Totally Instrumental with One Exception	1973	3.75	7.50	15.00
❏ ST-11200	I Love Dixie Blues...				
	So I Recorded "Live" in New Orleans	1973	3.00	6.00	12.00
❏ ST-11230	Merle Haggard's Christmas Present (Something				
	Old, Something New)	1973	3.00	6.00	12.00
❏ ST-11276	If We Make It Through December	1974	3.00	6.00	12.00
❏ ST-11331	Merle Haggard Presents His 30th Album	1974	3.00	6.00	12.00
❏ ST-11365	Keep Movin' On	1975	3.00	6.00	12.00
❏ ST-11483	It's All in the Movies	1975	3.00	6.00	12.00
❏ SABB-11531 [(2)]	Songs I'll Always Sing	1976	3.75	7.50	15.00
❏ ST-11544	My Love Affair with Trains	1976	3.00	6.00	12.00
❏ ST-11586	The Roots of My Raising	1976	3.00	6.00	12.00
❏ ST-11693	A Working Man Can't Get Nowhere Today	1977	3.00	6.00	12.00
❏ ST-11745	Eleven Winners	1977	3.00	6.00	12.00
❏ SM-11823	My Love Affair with Trains	1978	2.50	5.00	10.00
—Reissue					
❏ SW-11839	The Way It Was	1978	3.00	6.00	12.00
❏ SM-12036	It's All in the Movies	1979	2.50	5.00	10.00
—Reissue					
❏ SN-16052	Sing a Sad Song	1979	2.00	4.00	8.00
—Budget-line reissue					
❏ SN-16053	High on a Hilltop	1979	2.00	4.00	8.00
—Budget-line reissue					
❏ SN-16054	The Best of Merle Haggard	1979	2.00	4.00	8.00
—Budget-line reissue					
❏ SN-16277	Okie from Muskogee	1982	2.00	4.00	8.00
—Budget-line reissue					
❏ SN-16278	The Fightin' Side of Me	1982	2.00	4.00	8.00
—Budget-line reissue					
❏ SN-16279	A Tribute to the Best Damn Fiddle Player in the				
	World (Or, My Salute to Bob Wills)	1982	2.00	4.00	8.00
—Budget-line reissue					
❏ SN-16303	Eleven Winners	1984	2.00	4.00	8.00
—Budget-line reissue					

CAPITOL SPECIAL MARKETS

Number	Title (A Side/B Side)	Yr	VG	VG+	NM
❏ SL-8086 [(2)]	Songs I'll Always Sing	1977	5.00	10.00	20.00
❏ SLB-8137 [(2)]	Merle Haggard Salutes the Greats	1980	3.75	7.50	15.00

EPIC

Number	Title (A Side/B Side)	Yr	VG	VG+	NM
❏ FE 37593	Big City	1981	2.50	5.00	10.00
❏ PE 37593	Big City	1985	2.00	4.00	8.00
—Budget-line reissue					
❏ FE 38092	Going Where the Lonely Go	1982	2.50	5.00	10.00
❏ PE 38092	Going Where the Lonely Go	1985	2.00	4.00	8.00
—Budget-line reissue					
❏ PE 38307	Goin' Home for Christmas	1982	2.50	5.00	10.00
❏ FE 38815	That's the Way Love Goes	1983	2.50	5.00	10.00
❏ FE 39159	The Epic Collection	1983	2.50	5.00	10.00
❏ PE 39159	The Epic Collection	1985	2.00	4.00	8.00
—Budget-line reissue					

Number	Title (A Side/B Side)	Yr	VG	VG+	NM
❏ FE 39364	It's All in the Game	1984	2.50	5.00	10.00
❏ FE 39545	His Epic Hits: The First 11	1985	2.50	5.00	10.00
❏ FE 39602	Kern River	1985	2.50	5.00	10.00
❏ FE 40107	Out Among the Stars	1986	2.50	5.00	10.00
❏ PE 40107	Out Among the Stars	1986	2.00	4.00	8.00
—Budget-line reissue					
❏ FE 40224	Amber Waves of Grain	1985	2.50	5.00	10.00
❏ FE 40286	A Friend in California	1986	2.50	5.00	10.00
❏ FE 40986	Chill Factor	1988	2.50	5.00	10.00
❏ FE 44283	5:01 Blues	1989	2.50	5.00	10.00

MCA

Number	Title (A Side/B Side)	Yr	VG	VG+	NM
❏ 2267	Ramblin' Fever	1977	3.00	6.00	12.00
❏ 2314	My Farewell to Elvis	1977	3.75	7.50	15.00
❏ 2375	I'm Always on a Mountain	1978	3.00	6.00	12.00
❏ 3089	Serving 190 Proof	1979	3.00	6.00	12.00
❏ 3229	The Way I Am	1980	3.00	6.00	12.00
❏ 5139	Back to the Barrooms	1980	3.00	6.00	12.00
❏ 5250	Songs for the Mamma	1981	3.00	6.00	12.00
❏ 5386	Greatest Hits	1982	3.00	6.00	12.00
❏ 5573	His Best	1985	2.50	5.00	10.00
❏ 37138	Ramblin' Fever	1980	2.00	4.00	8.00
—Budget-line reissue					
❏ 37139	My Farewell to Elvis	1980	2.00	4.00	8.00
—Budget-line reissue					
❏ 37140	I'm Always on a Mountain	1980	2.00	4.00	8.00
—Budget-line reissue					
❏ 37141	Serving 190 Proof	1980	2.00	4.00	8.00
—Budget-line reissue					
❏ 37207	The Way I Am	1982	2.00	4.00	8.00
—Budget-line reissue					

HAGGARD, MERLE, AND JANIE FRICKE

45s

EPIC

Number	Title (A Side/B Side)	Yr	VG	VG+	NM
❏ 04663	A Place to Fall Apart/All I Want to Do Is Sing My				
	Song	1984	—	—	3.00

HAGGARD, MERLE, AND JEWEL

45s

BNA

Number	Title (A Side/B Side)	Yr	VG	VG+	NM
❏ 65895	That's the Way Love Goes/Silver Wings	1999	—	—	3.00

HAGGARD, MERLE, AND GEORGE JONES Also see each artist's individual listings.

45s

EPIC

Number	Title (A Side/B Side)	Yr	VG	VG+	NM
❏ 03072	Yesterday's Wine/I Haven't Found Her Yet	1982	—	—	3.00
❏ 03405	C.C. Waterback/After I Sing All My Songs	1982	—	—	3.00

Albums

EPIC

Number	Title (A Side/B Side)	Yr	VG	VG+	NM
❏ FE 38203	A Taste of Yesterday's Wine	1982	2.50	5.00	10.00

HAGGARD, MERLE, AND WILLIE NELSON Also see each artist's individual listings.

45s

EPIC

Number	Title (A Side/B Side)	Yr	VG	VG+	NM
❏ 03494	Reasons to Quit/Half a Man	1983	—	2.00	4.00
❏ ENR-03495	Reasons to Quit	1983	2.00	4.00	8.00
—One-sided budget release					
❏ 03842	Pancho and Lefty/Opportunity to Cry	1983	—	2.00	4.00
—As "Willie Nelson and Merle Haggard"					
❏ 34-07400	If I Could Only Fly/Without You on My Side	1987	—	—	3.00

Albums

EPIC

Number	Title (A Side/B Side)	Yr	VG	VG+	NM
❏ FE 37958	Pancho and Lefty	1983	2.50	5.00	10.00
—Reissue corrects spelling of LP title					
❏ FE 37958	Poncho and Lefty	1983	3.75	7.50	15.00
—Note misspelled LP title					
❏ FE 40293	Seashores of Old Mexico	1987	2.50	5.00	10.00

HAGGARD, MERLE, AND BONNIE OWENS Also see each artist's individual listings.

45s

TALLY

Number	Title (A Side/B Side)	Yr	VG	VG+	NM
❏ 181	Just Between the Two of Us/Slowly But Sure	1964	5.00	10.00	20.00

Albums

CAPITOL

Number	Title (A Side/B Side)	Yr	VG	VG+	NM
❏ ST 2453 [S]	Just Between the Two of Us	1966	7.50	15.00	30.00
❏ T 2453 [M]	Just Between the Two of Us	1966	6.25	12.50	25.00

HAGGARD, MERLE, AND LEONA WILLIAMS Also see each artist's individual listings.

45s

MCA

Number	Title (A Side/B Side)	Yr	VG	VG+	NM
❏ 40962	The Bull and the Beaver/I'm Gettin' High	1978	—	2.00	4.00

MERCURY

Number	Title (A Side/B Side)	Yr	VG	VG+	NM
❏ 812214-7	We're Strangers Again/				
	Sally Let Your Bangs Hang Down	1983	—	—	3.00
❏ 814359-7	Waltz Across Texas/				
	Waitin' on the Good Life to Come	1983	—	—	3.00
❏ 880139-7	Don't Ever Let Your Lover Sleep Alone/				
	It's Cold in California	1984	—	2.00	4.00

Albums

MERCURY

Number	Title (A Side/B Side)	Yr	VG	VG+	NM
❏ 812183-1	Heart to Heart	1983	2.50	5.00	10.00

HAGGETT, JIMMY

45s

CAPROCK

Number	Title (A Side/B Side)	Yr	VG	VG+	NM
❏ 107	All I Have Is You/Without You	1958	10.00	20.00	40.00

METEOR

Number	Title (A Side/B Side)	Yr	VG	VG+	NM
❏ 5043	Gonna Shut You Off Baby/Tell Her True	1957	50.00	100.00	200.00

SUN

Number	Title (A Side/B Side)	Yr	VG	VG+	NM
❏ 236	No More/They Call Our Love a Sin	1956	150.00	300.00	600.00

HAIG, RONNIE

45s

ABC-PARAMOUNT

Number	Title (A Side/B Side)	Yr	VG	VG+	NM
❏ 9912	Don't You Hear Me Calling, Baby/				
	Traveler of Love	1958	7.50	15.00	30.00

Number	Title (A Side/B Side)	Yr	VG	VG+	NM
☐ 10209	Don't You Hear Me Calling, Baby/ Traveler of Love	1961	20.00	40.00	80.00

NOTE

Number	Title (A Side/B Side)	Yr	VG	VG+	NM
☐ 10010	Don't You Hear Me Calling, Baby/ Traveler of Love	1958	7.50	15.00	30.00
☐ 10014	Rockin' with Rhythm and Blues/ Money Is a Thing of the Past	1958	25.00	50.00	100.00

HAINES, CONNIE
45s
MOTOWN

Number	Title (A Side/B Side)	Yr	VG	VG+	NM
☐ 1092	What's Easy for Two Is Hard for One/ Walk in Silence	1966	7.50	15.00	30.00

HAIRCUTS, THE
45s
PARKWAY

Number	Title (A Side/B Side)	Yr	VG	VG+	NM
☐ 899	She Loves You/Love Me Do	1964	5.00	10.00	20.00
☐ 899 [PS]	She Loves You/Love Me Do	1964	10.00	20.00	40.00

HAIRSTON, BROTHER WILL
45s
JVB

Number	Title (A Side/B Side)	Yr	VG	VG+	NM
☐ 44	The Alabama Bus (Part 1)/The Alabama Bus (Part 2)	1956	75.00	150.00	300.00

HAIRSTON, JACKIE
45s
ATCO

Number	Title (A Side/B Side)	Yr	VG	VG+	NM
☐ 6464	Monkey on My Back/Hijack	1967	5.00	10.00	20.00

HALE AND THE HUSHABYES All-star group including BRIAN WILSON, JACKIE DeSHANNON, and SONNY AND CHER.
45s
APOGEE

Number	Title (A Side/B Side)	Yr	VG	VG+	NM
☐ 104	Yes Sir, That's My Baby/900 Quetzals	1964	75.00	150.00	300.00

REPRISE

Number	Title (A Side/B Side)	Yr	VG	VG+	NM
☐ 0299	Yes Sir, That's My Baby/Jack's Theme	1964	50.00	100.00	200.00

—Reissued in 1967 by "A Date With Soul"
YORK

Number	Title (A Side/B Side)	Yr	VG	VG+	NM
☐ 408	Yes Sir, That's My Baby/Bee Side Soul	1967	12.50	25.00	50.00

—As "A Date with Soul"

HALEE'S COMET Roy Halee, later producer for SIMON AND GARFUNKEL.
45s
EPIC

Number	Title (A Side/B Side)	Yr	VG	VG+	NM
☐ 10207	All I Want Is What's Real/From a Parachute	1967	3.00	6.00	12.00

HALEY, BILL, AND HIS COMETS
45s
APT

Number	Title (A Side/B Side)	Yr	VG	VG+	NM
☐ 25081	Stop, Look, and Listen/Burn That Candle	1965	5.00	10.00	20.00
☐ 25087	Haley A-Go-Go/Tongue Tied Tony	1965	6.25	12.50	25.00

ARZEE

Number	Title (A Side/B Side)	Yr	VG	VG+	NM
☐ 4677	Yodel Your Blues Away/Within This Broken Heart of Mine	1978	6.25	12.50	25.00
☐ 4677 [PS]	Yodel Your Blues Away/Within This Broken Heart of Mine	1978	6.25	12.50	25.00

BUDDAH

Number	Title (A Side/B Side)	Yr	VG	VG+	NM
☐ 169	Rock Around the Clock/Framed	1970	3.75	7.50	15.00

DECCA

Number	Title (A Side/B Side)	Yr	VG	VG+	NM
☐ 29124	(We're Gonna) Rock Around the Clock/Thirteen Women (And Only One Man in Town)	196?	2.50	5.00	10.00

—Black label with color bars

Number	Title (A Side/B Side)	Yr	VG	VG+	NM
☐ 9-29124	(We're Gonna) Rock Around the Clock/Thirteen Women (And Only One Man in Town)	1954	15.00	30.00	60.00

—With lines on either side of "Decca"

Number	Title (A Side/B Side)	Yr	VG	VG+	NM
☐ 9-29124	(We're Gonna) Rock Around the Clock/Thirteen Women (And Only One Man in Town)	1955	5.00	10.00	20.00

—With star under "Decca"

Number	Title (A Side/B Side)	Yr	VG	VG+	NM
☐ 29204	Shake, Rattle and Roll/A.B.C. Boogie	1954	5.00	10.00	20.00

—With star under "Decca"

Number	Title (A Side/B Side)	Yr	VG	VG+	NM
☐ 29204	Shake, Rattle and Roll/A.B.C. Boogie	1954	10.00	20.00	40.00

—With lines on either side of "Decca"

Number	Title (A Side/B Side)	Yr	VG	VG+	NM
☐ 29317	Dim, Dim the Lights (I Want Some Atmosphere)/ Happy Baby	1954	5.00	10.00	20.00

—With star under "Decca"

Number	Title (A Side/B Side)	Yr	VG	VG+	NM
☐ 29317	Dim, Dim the Lights (I Want Some Atmosphere)/ Happy Baby	1954	10.00	20.00	40.00

—With lines on either side of "Decca"

Number	Title (A Side/B Side)	Yr	VG	VG+	NM
☐ 29418	Mambo Rock/Birth of the Boogie	1955	6.25	12.50	25.00
☐ 29552	Razzle-Dazzle/Two Hound Dogs	1955	6.25	12.50	25.00
☐ 29713	Burn That Candle/Rock-a-Beatin' Boogie	1955	6.25	12.50	25.00
☐ 29791	See You Later, Alligator/The Paper Boy (On Main Street, U.S.A.)	1956	6.25	12.50	25.00
☐ 29870	R-O-C-K/The Saints Rock 'N' Roll	1956	6.25	12.50	25.00
☐ 29948	Hot Dog Buddy Buddy/Rockin' Through the Rye	1956	6.25	12.50	25.00
☐ 30028	Rip It Up/Teenager's Mother (Are You Right?)	1956	6.25	12.50	25.00
☐ 30085	Rudy's Rock/Blue Comet Blues	1956	6.25	12.50	25.00
☐ 30148	Don't Knock the Rock/Choo Choo Ch'Boogie	1956	6.25	12.50	25.00
☐ 30214	Forty Cups of Coffee/Hook, Line and Sinker	1957	6.25	12.50	25.00
☐ 30314	(You Hit the Wrong Note) Billy Goat/ Rockin' Rollin' Rover	1957	6.25	12.50	25.00
☐ 30314 [PS]	(You Hit the Wrong Note) Billy Goat/ Rockin' Rollin' Rover	1957	30.00	60.00	120.00
☐ 30394	The Dipsy Doodle/Miss You	1957	6.25	12.50	25.00
☐ 30461	Rock the Joint/How Many	1957	6.25	12.50	25.00
☐ 30530	It's a Sin/Mary, Mary Lou	1957	6.25	12.50	25.00
☐ 30530 [PS]	It's a Sin/Mary, Mary Lou	1957	20.00	40.00	80.00
☐ 30592	Skinny Minnie/Sway with Me	1958	7.50	15.00	30.00
☐ 30681	Lean Jean/Don't Nobody Move	1958	6.25	12.50	25.00
☐ 30741	Chiquita Linda/Whoa Mabel	1958	6.25	12.50	25.00
☐ 30781	Corrine, Corrina/B.B. Betty	1958	6.25	12.50	25.00
☐ 30844	Charmaine/I Got a Woman	1959	6.25	12.50	25.00
☐ 30873	(Now and Then, There's) A Fool Such As I/ Where Did You Go Last Night	1959	6.25	12.50	25.00
☐ 30926	Caldonia/Shakey	1959	6.25	12.50	25.00

Number	Title (A Side/B Side)	Yr	VG	VG+	NM
☐ 30956	Joey's Song/Ooh, Look-a-There, Ain't She Pretty	1959	6.25	12.50	25.00
☐ 31030	Skokiaan (South African Song)/ Puerto Rican Peddler	1959	6.25	12.50	25.00
☐ 31080	Music, Music, Music/Strictly Instrumental	1960	6.25	12.50	25.00
☐ 31649	The Green Door/Yeah, She's Evil	1964	3.00	6.00	12.00

ESSEX

Number	Title (A Side/B Side)	Yr	VG	VG+	NM
☐ 102	Rock Around the Clock/Crazy Man, Crazy	1955	12.50	25.00	50.00

—Actually a bootleg, but highly sought-after nonetheless

Number	Title (A Side/B Side)	Yr	VG	VG+	NM
☐ 303	Rock the Joint/Icy Heart	1952	15.00	30.00	60.00

—Black vinyl, script logo ("Essex" not in all caps)

Number	Title (A Side/B Side)	Yr	VG	VG+	NM
☐ 303	Rock the Joint/Icy Heart	1952	25.00	50.00	100.00

—Black vinyl, block logo ("ESSEX" in all caps)

Number	Title (A Side/B Side)	Yr	VG	VG+	NM
☐ 303	Rock the Joint/Icy Heart	1952	900.00	1350.	1800.

—Red vinyl

Number	Title (A Side/B Side)	Yr	VG	VG+	NM
☐ 305	Rocking Chair on the Moon/Dance with a Dolly (With a Hole in Her Stocking)	1952	25.00	50.00	100.00

—Essex 303 and 305 credit "Bill Haley and the Saddlemen"

Number	Title (A Side/B Side)	Yr	VG	VG+	NM
☐ 310	Real Rock Drive/ Stop Beatin' Round the Mulberry Bush	1952	20.00	40.00	80.00

—Orange label

Number	Title (A Side/B Side)	Yr	VG	VG+	NM
☐ 310	Real Rock Drive/ Stop Beatin' Round the Mulberry Bush	1952	37.50	75.00	150.00

—Blue label

Number	Title (A Side/B Side)	Yr	VG	VG+	NM
☐ 321	Crazy Man, Crazy/Whatcha Gonna Do	1953	15.00	30.00	60.00
☐ 327	Pat-a-Cake/Fractured	1953	10.00	20.00	40.00
☐ 332	Live It Up/Farewell, So Long, Goodbye	1953	10.00	20.00	40.00
☐ 340	Ten Little Indians/I'll Be True	1953	10.00	20.00	40.00
☐ 348	Chattanooga Choo Choo/Straight Jacket	1954	10.00	20.00	40.00
☐ 374	Sundown Boogie/Jukebox Cannonball	1954	18.75	37.50	75.00
☐ 381	Rocket 88/Green Tree Boogie	1955	31.25	62.50	125.00
☐ 399	Rock the Joint/Farewell, So Long, Goodbye	1955	18.75	37.50	75.00

GNP CRESCENDO

Number	Title (A Side/B Side)	Yr	VG	VG+	NM
☐ 475	I'm Walkin'/Crazy Man, Crazy	1974	3.00	6.00	12.00

GONE

Number	Title (A Side/B Side)	Yr	VG	VG+	NM
☐ 5111	Spanish Twist/My Kind of Woman	1961	6.25	12.50	25.00
☐ 5116	Riviera/War Paint	1961	6.25	12.50	25.00

HOLIDAY

Number	Title (A Side/B Side)	Yr	VG	VG+	NM
☐ 113	Sundown Boogie/Jukebox Cannonball	1951	125.00	250.00	500.00

—As "Bill Haley and the Saddlemen"; the only Holiday single known to exist on a 45. Earlier Holiday singles only exist on 78s.
JANUS

Number	Title (A Side/B Side)	Yr	VG	VG+	NM
☐ 162	Travelin' Band/A Little Piece at a Time	1971	3.00	6.00	12.00

KAMA SUTRA

Number	Title (A Side/B Side)	Yr	VG	VG+	NM
☐ 508	Rock Around the Clock/Framed	1970	5.00	10.00	20.00

KASEY

Number	Title (A Side/B Side)	Yr	VG	VG+	NM
☐ 7006	A.B.C. Boogie/Rock Around the Clock	1961	5.00	10.00	20.00

—B-side by Phil Flowers
MCA

Number	Title (A Side/B Side)	Yr	VG	VG+	NM
☐ 60025	(We're Gonna) Rock Around the Clock/Thirteen Women (And Only One Man in Town)	1973	—	2.50	5.00

—Reissue on black label with rainbow; made the Top 40 in 1974
NEWTOWN

Number	Title (A Side/B Side)	Yr	VG	VG+	NM
☐ 5013	Tenor Man/Up Goes My Love	1962	5.00	10.00	20.00
☐ 5024	Dance Around the Clock/ What Can I Say After I Say I'm Sorry	1963	5.00	10.00	20.00

NICETOWN

Number	Title (A Side/B Side)	Yr	VG	VG+	NM
☐ 5025	You Call Everybody Darling/Tandy	1963	5.00	10.00	20.00

TRANS WORLD

Number	Title (A Side/B Side)	Yr	VG	VG+	NM
☐ 718	Real Rock Drive/Yes, Indeed	1954	50.00	100.00	200.00

UNITED ARTISTS

Number	Title (A Side/B Side)	Yr	VG	VG+	NM
☐ 50483	Ain't Love Funny, Ha Ha Ha/That's How I Got to Memphis	1969	3.00	6.00	12.00

WARNER BROS.

Number	Title (A Side/B Side)	Yr	VG	VG+	NM
☐ 5145	Candy Kisses/Tamiami	1960	6.25	12.50	25.00
☐ 5145 [DJ]	Candy Kisses/Tamiami	1960	12.50	25.00	50.00

—Promo only on yellow vinyl

Number	Title (A Side/B Side)	Yr	VG	VG+	NM
☐ 5154	Hawk/Chick Safari	1960	6.25	12.50	25.00
☐ 5171	Let the Good Times Roll, Creole/So Right Tonight	1960	6.25	12.50	25.00
☐ 5228	Flip, Flop and Fly/Honky Tonk	1961	6.25	12.50	25.00
☐ 7124	Rock Around the Clock/Shake, Rattle and Roll	1969	3.75	7.50	15.00

7-Inch Extended Plays
CLAIRE

Number	Title (A Side/B Side)	Yr	VG	VG+	NM
☐ 4779	*All I Need Is Some More Lovin'/Trouble in Mind/ Life of the Party/ I Should Write a Song About You	1978	3.75	7.50	15.00
☐ 4779 [PS]	Bill Haley and the Comets	1978	3.75	7.50	15.00

DECCA

Number	Title (A Side/B Side)	Yr	VG	VG+	NM
☐ ED 2168	Shake, Rattle and Roll/A.B.C. Boogie//(We're Gonna) Rock Around the Clock/Thirteen Women (And Only One Man in Town)	1954	15.00	30.00	60.00
☐ ED 2168 [PS]	Shake, Rattle and Roll	1954	15.00	30.00	60.00
☐ ED 2209	Dim, Dim the Lights/Happy Baby//Birth of the Boogie/Mambo Rock	1955	15.00	30.00	60.00
☐ ED 2209 [PS]	Dim, Dim the Lights	1955	15.00	30.00	60.00
☐ ED 2322	Razzle-Dazzle/Two Hound Dogs//Burn That Candle/Rock-a-Beatin' Boogie	1956	15.00	30.00	60.00
☐ ED 2322 [PS]	Rock and Roll	1956	15.00	30.00	60.00
☐ ED 2398	See You Later Alligator/R-O-C-K//The Saints Rock 'n Roll/Burn That Candle	1956	12.50	25.00	50.00
☐ ED 2398 [PS]	He Digs RnR (Music for the Boyfriend)	1956	12.50	25.00	50.00
☐ ED 2416	Calling All Comets/Rockin' Through the Rye// Hook, Line and Sinker/Rudy's Rock	1956	12.50	25.00	50.00
☐ ED 2416 [PS]	Rock 'n' Roll Stage Show, Part 1	1956	12.50	25.00	50.00
☐ ED 2417	A Rockin' Little Tune/Hide and Seek//Choo Choo Ch' Boogie/Blue Comet Blues	1956	12.50	25.00	50.00
☐ ED 2417 [PS]	Rock 'n' Roll Stage Show, Part 2	1956	12.50	25.00	50.00
☐ ED 2418	Hey Then, There Now/Goofin' Around//Hot Dog Buddy Buddy/Tonight's the Night	1956	12.50	25.00	50.00
☐ ED 2418 [PS]	Rock 'n' Roll Stage Show, Part 3	1956	12.50	25.00	50.00
☐ ED 2532	The Dipsy Doodle/Miss You//Is It True What They Say About Dixie?/Carolina in the Morning	1957	12.50	25.00	50.00
☐ ED 2532 [PS]	Rockin' the Oldies	1957	12.50	25.00	50.00

H

HALFNELSON

Number	Title (A Side/B Side)	Yr	VG	VG+	NM
☐ ED 2533	*One Sweet Letter from You/Please Don't Talk About Me When I'm Gone/Apple Blossom Time/Somebody Else Is Taking My Place	1957	12.50	25.00	50.00
☐ ED 2533 [PS]	Rock 'n' Roll Party	1957	12.50	25.00	50.00
☐ ED 2534	*Moon Over Miami/Ain't Misbehavin'/You Can't Stop Me from Dreaming/I'm Gonna Sit Right Down and Write Myself a Letter	1957	12.50	25.00	50.00
☐ ED 2534 [PS]	Rockin' & Rollin'	1957	12.50	25.00	50.00
☐ ED 2564	*Me Rock-a-Hula/Wooden Shoe Rock/Oriental Rock/Rockin' Matilda	1957	12.50	25.00	50.00
☐ ED 2564 [PS]	Rockin' Around the World	1957	12.50	25.00	50.00
☐ ED 2576	*Piccadilly Rock/Vive La Rock & Roll/Rockin' Rollin' Schnitzlebank/Come Rock with Me	1957	12.50	25.00	50.00
☐ ED 2576 [PS]	Rockin' Around Europe	1957	12.50	25.00	50.00
☐ ED 2577	*Pretty Alouette/El Rocko/Rockin' Rita/Jamaican DJ	1957	12.50	25.00	50.00
☐ ED 2577 [PS]	Rockin' Around the Americas	1957	12.50	25.00	50.00
☐ ED 2615	Rock Lomond/It's a Sin//Move It On Over/New Rock the Joint	1958	10.00	20.00	40.00
☐ ED 2615 [PS]	Rockin' the Joint, Part 1	1958	10.00	20.00	40.00
☐ ED 2616	Rip It Up/The Beak (Speaks)//Sway with Me/Forty Cups of Coffee	1958	10.00	20.00	40.00
☐ ED 2616 [PS]	Rockin' the Joint, Part 2	1958	10.00	20.00	40.00
☐ ED 2638 [M]	*Whoa Mabel!/Ida Sweet as Apple Cider/Eloise/Dinah	1958	10.00	20.00	40.00
☐ ED 2638 [PS]	Bill Haley's Chicks	1958	10.00	20.00	40.00
☐ ED 7-2638 [PS]	Bill Haley's Chicks	1959	20.00	40.00	80.00
☐ ED 7-2638 [S]	*Whoa Mabel!/Ida Sweet as Apple Cider/Eloise/Dinah	1959	20.00	40.00	80.00
☐ ED 2670 [M]	Joe's Song/Ooh Look-a There Ain't She Pretty//Shakey/Caledonia	1959	10.00	20.00	40.00
☐ ED 2670 [PS]	Bill Haley and His Comets	1959	10.00	20.00	40.00
☐ ED 7-2670 [PS]	Bill Haley and His Comets	1959	20.00	40.00	80.00
☐ ED 7-2670 [S]	Joe's Song/Ooh Look-a There Ain't She Pretty//Shakey/Caledonia	1959	20.00	40.00	80.00
☐ ED 2671 [M]	Strictly Instrumental/South Africa Song//Mack the Knife/In a Little Spanish Town	1959	10.00	20.00	40.00
☐ ED 2671 [PS]	Strictly Instrumental	1959	10.00	20.00	40.00
☐ ED 7-2671 [PS]	Strictly Instrumental	1959	20.00	40.00	80.00
☐ ED 7-2671 [S]	Strictly Instrumental/South Africa Song//Mack the Knife/In a Little Spanish Town	1959	20.00	40.00	80.00

ESSEX

Number	Title (A Side/B Side)	Yr	VG	VG+	NM
☐ TWEP-102	Rock the Joint/Rockin' Chair on the Moon//Crazy Man, Crazy/Pat-a-Cake	1954	25.00	50.00	100.00
☐ TWEP-102 [PS]	For Your Dance Party	1954	30.00	60.00	120.00
☐ EP-117	*Live It Up/Farewell, So Long, Goodbye/Real Rock Drive/Fractured	1954	25.00	50.00	100.00
☐ EP-117 [PS]	Rock with Bill Haley and His Comets, Volume 1	1954	30.00	60.00	120.00
☐ EP-118	*Stop Beatin' Round the Mulberry Bush/Watcha Gonna Do/I'll Be True/Juke Box Cannon Ball	1954	25.00	50.00	100.00
☐ EP-118 [PS]	Rock with Bill Haley and His Comets, Volume 2	1954	30.00	60.00	120.00
☐ EP-119	(contents unknown)	1954	25.00	50.00	100.00
☐ EP-119 [PS]	Rock with Bill Haley and His Comets, Volume 3	1954	30.00	60.00	120.00

SOMERSET

Number	Title (A Side/B Side)	Yr	VG	VG+	NM
☐ 460	(contents unknown)	1955	20.00	40.00	80.00
☐ 460 [PS]	Rock with Bill Haley and His Comets	1955	20.00	40.00	80.00

TRANS WORLD

Number	Title (A Side/B Side)	Yr	VG	VG+	NM
☐ TWEP-117	(contents unknown)	1955	20.00	40.00	80.00
☐ TWEP-117 [PS]	Rock with Bill Haley and His Comets, Volume 1	1955	20.00	40.00	80.00
☐ TWEP-118	(contents unknown)	1955	20.00	40.00	80.00
☐ TWEP-118 [PS]	Rock with Bill Haley and His Comets, Volume 2	1955	20.00	40.00	80.00
☐ TWEP-119	(contents unknown)	1955	20.00	40.00	80.00
☐ TWEP-119 [PS]	Rock with Bill Haley and His Comets, Volume 3	1955	20.00	40.00	80.00

Albums
ACCORD

Number	Title (A Side/B Side)	Yr	VG	VG+	NM
☐ SN-7125	Rockin' and Rollin'	1981	2.50	5.00	10.00

DECCA

Number	Title (A Side/B Side)	Yr	VG	VG+	NM
☐ DL 5560 [10]	Shake, Rattle and Roll	1955	200.00	400.00	800.00
☐ DXSE-7211 [(2)]	Bill Haley's Golden Hits	1972	3.75	7.50	15.00
☐ DL 8225 [M]	Rock Around the Clock	1955	37.50	75.00	150.00
—All-black label with silver print					
☐ DL 8225 [M]	Rock Around the Clock	1960	12.50	25.00	50.00
—Black label with colorband, no mention of MCA on label					
☐ DL 8225 [M]	Rock Around the Clock	1967	7.50	15.00	30.00
—Black label with colorband, "A Division of MCA" on label					
☐ DL 8315 [M]	Music for the Boyfriend	1956	37.50	75.00	150.00
☐ DL 8345 [M]	Rock 'n Roll Stage Show	1956	37.50	75.00	150.00
☐ DL 8569 [M]	Rockin' the Oldies	1957	37.50	75.00	150.00
☐ DL 8692 [M]	Rockin' Around the World	1958	37.50	75.00	150.00
☐ DL 8775 [M]	Rockin' the Joint	1958	37.50	75.00	150.00
☐ DL 8821 [M]	Bill Haley's Chicks	1959	25.00	50.00	100.00
☐ DL 8964 [M]	Strictly Instrumental	1960	25.00	50.00	100.00
☐ DL 75027	Bill Haley's Greatest Hits	1968	3.75	7.50	15.00
☐ DL 78225 [R]	Rock Around the Clock	1959	18.75	37.50	75.00
—All-black label with silver print					
☐ DL 78225 [R]	Rock Around the Clock	1960	6.25	12.50	25.00
—Black label with colorband, no mention of MCA on label					
☐ DL 78225 [R]	Rock Around the Clock	1967	3.75	7.50	15.00
—Black label with colorband, "A Division of MCA" on label					
☐ DL 78821 [S]	Bill Haley's Chicks	1959	37.50	75.00	150.00
☐ DL 78964 [S]	Strictly Instrumental	1960	37.50	75.00	150.00

ESSEX

Number	Title (A Side/B Side)	Yr	VG	VG+	NM
☐ LP 202 [M]	Rock with Bill Haley and the Comets	1955	125.00	250.00	500.00

51 WEST

Number	Title (A Side/B Side)	Yr	VG	VG+	NM
☐ Q 16120	Live in New York/Greatest Hits	1981	2.50	5.00	10.00
—"All selections under license from Buddah Records"					

GNP CRESCENDO

Number	Title (A Side/B Side)	Yr	VG	VG+	NM
☐ GNPS-2077	Rock 'N' Roll	1973	3.00	6.00	12.00
☐ GNPS-2097	Rock Around the Country	1976	3.00	6.00	12.00

GREAT NORTHWEST

Number	Title (A Side/B Side)	Yr	VG	VG+	NM
☐ GNW 4015	Interviewed by Red Robinson	1981	3.00	6.00	12.00

JANUS

Number	Title (A Side/B Side)	Yr	VG	VG+	NM
☐ 3035	Travelin' Band	1972	6.25	12.50	25.00
☐ 7003 [(2)]	Razzle-Dazzle	1972	3.75	7.50	15.00

KAMA SUTRA

Number	Title (A Side/B Side)	Yr	VG	VG+	NM
☐ KLPS-2014	Scrapbook	1970	7.50	15.00	30.00

MCA

Number	Title (A Side/B Side)	Yr	VG	VG+	NM
☐ 161	Bill Haley's Greatest Hits	1973	2.50	5.00	10.00
—Reissue of Decca 75027					
☐ 4010 [(2)]	Bill Haley's Golden Hits	1973	3.00	6.00	12.00
—Reissue of Decca 7211					
☐ 5539 [(2)]	From the Original Master Tapes	1987	3.00	6.00	12.00

PAIR

Number	Title (A Side/B Side)	Yr	VG	VG+	NM
☐ MSM2-35069 [(2)]	Rock and Roll Giant	1986	3.00	6.00	12.00

PICCADILLY

Number	Title (A Side/B Side)	Yr	VG	VG+	NM
☐ PIC-3408	Greatest Hits	1980	2.50	5.00	10.00

PICKWICK

Number	Title (A Side/B Side)	Yr	VG	VG+	NM
☐ PTP-2077 [(2)]	Rock 'N' Roll	197?	3.00	6.00	12.00
☐ SPC-3256	Bill Haley and the Comets	1970	2.50	5.00	10.00
☐ SPC-3280	Rock 'N' Roll Revival	197?	2.50	5.00	10.00

ROULETTE

Number	Title (A Side/B Side)	Yr	VG	VG+	NM
☐ R 25174 [M]	Twistin' Knights at the Roundtable	1962	20.00	40.00	80.00
☐ SR 25174 [S]	Twistin' Knights at the Roundtable	1962	25.00	50.00	100.00

SOMERSET

Number	Title (A Side/B Side)	Yr	VG	VG+	NM
☐ P-4600 [M]	Rock with Bill Haley and the Comets	1958	37.50	75.00	150.00

TRANS WORLD

Number	Title (A Side/B Side)	Yr	VG	VG+	NM
☐ LP 202	Rock with Bill Haley and the Comets	1956	75.00	150.00	300.00

VOCALION

Number	Title (A Side/B Side)	Yr	VG	VG+	NM
☐ VL 3696 [M]	Bill Haley and the Comets	1963	6.25	12.50	25.00

WARNER BROS.

Number	Title (A Side/B Side)	Yr	VG	VG+	NM
☐ W 1378 [M]	Bill Haley and His Comets	1959	12.50	25.00	50.00
☐ WS 1378 [S]	Bill Haley and His Comets	1959	17.50	35.00	70.00
☐ W 1391 [M]	Bill Haley's Jukebox	1960	12.50	25.00	50.00
☐ WS 1391 [S]	Bill Haley's Jukebox	1960	17.50	35.00	70.00
☐ WS 1831	Rock 'N' Roll Revival	1970	3.75	7.50	15.00
☐ ST-93103	Rock 'N' Roll Revival	1970	6.25	12.50	25.00
—Capitol Record Club edition					

HALFNELSON See SPARKS.

HALL, DARYL Also see GULLIVER; DARYL HALL AND JOHN OATES; THE TEMPTONES.

12-Inch Singles
RCA

Number	Title (A Side/B Side)	Yr	VG	VG+	NM
☐ 5714-1-RD	Dreamtime (Extended)/(Dub)	1986	2.00	4.00	8.00
☐ 5745-1-RD	Foolish Pride/Let It Out	1986	2.00	4.00	8.00
☐ 5748-1-RD	Foolish Pride (Extended Version) (Edit Remix) (Dub)/What's Gonna Happen to Us	1986	2.00	4.00	8.00
☐ PD-14386 [DJ]	Dreamtime (same on both sides)	1986	2.00	4.00	8.00

45s
AMY

Number	Title (A Side/B Side)	Yr	VG	VG+	NM
☐ 11049	The Princess and the Soldier (Part 1)/The Princess and the Soldier (Part 2)	1969	—	3.00	6.00

EPIC

Number	Title (A Side/B Side)	Yr	VG	VG+	NM
☐ 34-77139	I'm in a Philly Mood/Money Changes Everything	1993	—	—	3.00
☐ 34-77258	Stop Lovin' Me, Stop Lovin' You/(Churban Remix)	1993	—	—	3.00

PARALLAX

Number	Title (A Side/B Side)	Yr	VG	VG+	NM
☐ 404	A Lonely Girl/Vicky - Vicky	196?	7.50	15.00	30.00

RCA

Number	Title (A Side/B Side)	Yr	VG	VG+	NM
☐ 5038-7-R	Foolish Pride/What's Gonna Happen to Us	1986	—	—	3.00
☐ 5038-7-R [PS]	Foolish Pride/What's Gonna Happen to Us	1986	—	—	3.00
☐ 5105-7-R	Someone Like You (The Guitar Solo)/Someone Like You (The Sax Solo)	1987	—	—	3.00
☐ 5105-7-R [PS]	Someone Like You (The Guitar Solo)/Someone Like You (The Sax Solo)	1987	—	—	3.00
☐ PB-12001	Something in 4/4 Time/Sacred Songs	1980	—	2.00	4.00
☐ PB-12001 [PS]	Something in 4/4 Time/Sacred Songs	1980	—	2.50	5.00
☐ PB-14387	Dreamtime/Let It Out	1986	—	—	3.00
☐ PB-14387 [PS]	Dreamtime/Let It Out	1986	—	—	3.00

Albums
RCA VICTOR

Number	Title (A Side/B Side)	Yr	VG	VG+	NM
☐ AFL1-3573	Sacred Songs	1980	2.50	5.00	10.00
☐ AJL1-7196	Three Hearts in the Happy Ending Machine	1986	2.00	4.00	8.00

HALL, DARYL, AND JOHN OATES

12-Inch Singles
ARISTA

Number	Title (A Side/B Side)	Yr	VG	VG+	NM
☐ AD1-9685	Everything Your Heart Desires (If You Want the World Mix 7:53) (54th Street Remix 9:12) (No Words Can Help Dub Mix 5:57) (7th Avenue Remix 4:26)/Realove	1988	2.50	5.00	10.00
☐ AD1-9728	Missed Opportunity (Unlimited Mix 6:58) (Smooth Mix 8:57) (Radio Mix 4:39)/Soul Love	1988	2.00	4.00	8.00
☐ AD1-9768	Downtown Life (5 versions)	1989	2.00	4.00	8.00
☐ ADP-9779 [DJ]	Talking All Night (Extended Remix 6:08) (Dub Mix) (A Cappella) (LP Version) (Radio Remix)	1989	3.75	7.50	15.00

PUSH

Number	Title (A Side/B Side)	Yr	VG	VG+	NM
☐ 90405-1 [(2)DJ]	Hold On to Yourself (Tommy Musto's Club Mix 5:54) (Rachid Wehbi's Extended Mix 6:07) (Tribal Path Mix 4:37) (Naughty G's Rubber Mix 6:10) (Tommy Musto's Dub Mix 5:21) (Tommy Musto's Club Instrumental 5:57) (Tribal Path Hip-Hop Mix 4:39) (Tommy Musto's Radio Mix 4:18)	1998	10.00	20.00	40.00

RCA

Number	Title (A Side/B Side)	Yr	VG	VG+	NM
☐ JT-11022 [DJ]	Back Together Again/Kerry	1977	5.00	10.00	20.00
—B-side by Stephen Dees					
☐ JD-11302 [DJ]	Do What You Want, Be What You Are (Long Version) (Short Version)	1977	5.00	10.00	20.00
☐ JD-11431 [DJ]	I Don't Wanna Lose You/August Day	1977	5.00	10.00	20.00
☐ JD-11770 [DJ]	Running from Paradise (6:29)/Portable Radio	1979	3.75	7.50	15.00
☐ JD-12053 [DJ]	How Does It Feel to Be Back (same on both sides)	1980	5.00	10.00	20.00
☐ PD-12297	Private Eyes/Tell Me What You Want	1981	3.00	6.00	12.00
☐ PD-12358	I Can't Go for That (No Can Do)/Unguarded Minute	1981	3.00	6.00	12.00
☐ PD-13080	Did It in a Minute/Head Above Water	1982	3.00	6.00	12.00
☐ PD-13253	Your Imagination (Extended Remix 5:41)/Sara Smile (3:07)	1982	3.00	6.00	12.00
☐ JD-13403 [DJ]	Maneater (Special Extended Club Mix)/I Can't Go for That (Club Mix)	1982	3.75	7.50	15.00

Number	Title (A Side/B Side)	Yr	VG	VG+	NM
❏ PD-13428	One on One (Club Mix 5:30)/I Can't Go for That (Long)	1983	3.00	6.00	12.00
❏ PD-13508	Family Man (Extended Dance Remix)/Maneater	1983	2.50	5.00	10.00
❏ JD-13659 [DJ]	Say It Isn't So/Wait for Me (Live)	1983	3.00	6.00	12.00
❏ PW-13679	Say It Isn't So (Special Extended Dance Mix 6:49)//(Dub Version 4:47)/Kiss on My List	1983	2.50	5.00	10.00
❏ JM-13705 [DJ]	Jingle Bell Rock from Daryl/Jingle Bell Rock from John	1983	7.50	15.00	30.00
—Promo-only picture disc in plastic sleeve					
❏ PD-13715	Adult Eduation (Special Club Mix 6:04)/Maneater	1984	2.00	4.00	8.00
❏ JD-13736 [DJ]	Adult Education (Special Extended Mix Long)/(Special Extended Mix Short)	1984	3.00	6.00	12.00
❏ PW-13917	Out of Touch (Extended Remix 7:37)//(Dub Version 7:24)/Cold, Dark and Yesterday	1984	2.50	5.00	10.00
❏ JR-13927 [DJ]	Out of Touch (4:24) (same on both sides)	1984	3.00	6.00	12.00
❏ PW-13971	Method of Modern Love (7:50)//(Dub)/Bank On Your Love	1984	2.50	5.00	10.00
❏ JD-13972 [DJ]	Method of Modern Love (5:27)/Bank On Your Love	1984	3.00	6.00	12.00
❏ JD-13983 [DJ]	Jingle Bell Rock from Daryl/Jingle Bell Rock from John	1984	3.00	6.00	12.00
—Promo-only reissue, not a picture disc					
❏ PW-14036	Some Things Are Better Left Unsaid (Special New Mix 5:24)//All American Girl/Some Things Are Better Left Unsaid (Instrumental 5:25)	1985	2.00	4.00	8.00
❏ JD-14038 [DJ]	Some Things Are Better Left Unsaid (Special New Mix 5:24) (same on both sides)	1985	3.00	6.00	12.00
❏ PW-14099	Possession Obsession//Dance on Your Knees/Everytime You Go Away	1985	2.00	4.00	8.00
❏ JR-14100 [DJ]	Possession Obsession (Special New Mix) (same on both sides)	1985	2.50	5.00	10.00
❏ PW-14179	A Nite at the Apollo Live! The Way You Do the Things You Do-My Girl//Everytime You Go Away/Adult Education	1985	2.00	4.00	8.00
❏ JR-14180 [DJ]	A Nite at the Apollo Live! The Way You Do the Things You Do-My Girl (same on both sides)	1985	2.50	5.00	10.00
❏ PD-14250	Jingle Bell Rock from Daryl/Jingle Bell Rock from John//Everytime You Go Away/When Something Is Wrong with My Baby	1985	—	—	—
—Canceled					

45s

ARISTA

Number	Title (A Side/B Side)	Yr	VG	VG+	NM
❏ 2085	So Close/So Close (Unplugged)	1990	—	—	3.00
❏ 2157	Don't Hold Back Your Love/Change of Season	1990	—	—	3.00
❏ 9684	Everything Your Heart Desires/Real Love	1988	—	—	3.00
❏ 9684 [PS]	Everything Your Heart Desires/Real Love	1988	—	—	3.00
❏ 9727	Missed Opportunity/Soul Love	1988	—	—	3.00
❏ 9727 [PS]	Missed Opportunity/Soul Love	1988	—	—	3.00
❏ 9753	Downtown Life (LP Version)/Downtown Life (Urban Mix)	1988	—	—	3.00
❏ 9753 [PS]	Downtown Life (LP Version)/Downtown Life (Urban Mix)	1988	—	—	3.00

ATLANTIC

Number	Title (A Side/B Side)	Yr	VG	VG+	NM
❏ 2922	Goodnight & Good Morning/All Our Love	1972	2.50	5.00	10.00
—As "Whole Oats"					
❏ 2939	Lilly (Are You Happy)/I'm Sorry	1973	2.00	4.00	8.00
❏ 2993	She's Gone/I'm Just a Kid (Don't Make Me Feel Like a Man)	1973	2.00	4.00	8.00
❏ 3026	Lady Rain/When the Morning Comes	1974	—	2.50	5.00
❏ 3239	Can't Stop the Music/70's Scenario	1975	—	2.50	5.00
❏ 3332	She's Gone/I'm Just a Kid (Don't Make Me Feel Like a Man)	1976	—	2.00	4.00
❏ 3332 [DJ]	She's Gone (Long Version)/She's Gone	1976	—	3.00	6.00
❏ 3397	It's Uncanny/Lilly (Are You Happy)	1977	—	2.00	4.00

CHELSEA

Number	Title (A Side/B Side)	Yr	VG	VG+	NM
❏ 3063	If That's What Makes You Happy/The Reason Why	1977	—	2.50	5.00
—B-side by "Daryl Hall and Gulliver"					
❏ 3065	Red River Blues/(B-side unknown)	1977	—	2.50	5.00
❏ 3069	Perkiomen/The Provider	1977	—	2.50	5.00

RCA

Number	Title (A Side/B Side)	Yr	VG	VG+	NM
❏ PB-10808	Do What You Want, Be What You Are/You'll Never Learn	1976	—	2.00	4.00
❏ PB-10860	Rich Girl/London Luck, & Love	1976	—	2.00	4.00
❏ PB-10860 [PS]	Rich Girl/London Luck, & Love	1976	2.00	4.00	8.00
❏ GB-10942	Sara Smile/Do What You Want, Be What You Are	1977	—	—	3.00
—Gold Standard Series					
❏ PB-10970	Back Together Again/Room to Breathe	1977	—	2.00	4.00
❏ PB-11132	Why Do Lovers (Break Each Other's Heart?)/A Girl Who Used to Be	1977	—	2.00	4.00
❏ PB-11181	Don't Change/The Emptiness	1977	—	2.00	4.00
❏ GB-11324	Rich Girl/Back Together Again	1978	—	—	3.00
—Gold Standard Series					
❏ PB-11371	It's a Laugh/Serious Music	1978	—	2.00	4.00
❏ PB-11424	I Don't Wanna Lose You/August Day	1978	—	2.00	4.00
❏ PB-11747	Wait for Me/No Brain No Pain	1979	—	2.00	4.00
❏ PB-11920	All You Want Is Heaven/Who Said the World Was Fair	1980	—	2.00	4.00
❏ GB-11970	It's a Laugh/I Don't Wanna Lose You	1980	—	—	3.00
—Gold Standard Series					
❏ PB-12048	How Does It Feel to Be Back/United State	1980	—	2.00	4.00
❏ PB-12103	You've Lost That Lovin' Feeling/Diddy Doo Wap (I Hear the Voices)	1980	—	2.00	4.00
❏ PB-12142	Kiss on My List/Africa	1981	—	2.00	4.00
❏ PB-12217	You Make My Dreams/Gotta Lotta Love	1981	—	2.00	4.00
❏ PB-12296	Private Eyes/Tell Me What You Want	1981	—	2.00	4.00
❏ GB-12318	Kiss on My List/You've Lost That Lovin' Feeling	1981	—	—	3.00
—Gold Standard Series					
❏ PB-12357	I Can't Go for That (No Can Do)/Unguarded Minute	1981	—	2.00	4.00
❏ JB-12361 [DJ]	I Can't Go for That (No Can Do)/(Club Mix)	1981	2.50	5.00	10.00
—Promo only					
❏ PB-13065	Did It in a Minute/Head Above Water	1982	—	2.00	4.00
❏ PB-13252	Your Imagination/Sara Smile	1982	—	2.00	4.00
❏ PB-13354	Maneater/Delayed Reaction	1982	—	—	3.00
❏ PB-13354 [PS]	Maneater/Delayed Reaction	1982	—	2.00	4.00
❏ PB-13421	One on One/Art of Heartbreak	1983	—	—	3.00
❏ PB-13421 [PS]	One on One/Art of Heartbreak	1983	—	2.00	4.00
❏ GB-13480	Private Eyes/I Can't Go for That (No Can Do)	1983	—	—	3.00
—Gold Standard Series					
❏ GB-13481	You Make My Dreams/Did It in a Minute	1983	—	—	3.00
—Gold Standard Series					
❏ PB-13507	Family Man/Open All Night	1983	—	—	3.00
❏ PB-13654	Say It Isn't So/Kiss on My List	1983	—	—	3.00
❏ PB-13654 [PS]	Say It Isn't So/Kiss on My List	1983	—	2.00	4.00
❏ PB-13714	Adult Education/Maneater	1984	—	—	3.00
❏ PB-13714 [PS]	Adult Education/Maneater	1984	—	2.00	4.00
❏ GB-13796	Maneater/One on One	1984	—	—	3.00
—Gold Standard Series					
❏ GB-13797	Family Man/Say It Isn't So	1984	—	—	3.00
—Gold Standard Series					
❏ PB-13916	Out of Touch/Cold, Dark, and Yesterday	1984	—	—	3.00
❏ PB-13916 [PS]	Out of Touch/Cold, Dark, and Yesterday	1984	—	—	3.00
❏ PB-13970	Method of Modern Love (Remix Edit)/Method of Modern Love	1984	—	—	3.00
❏ PB-13970 [PS]	Method of Modern Love (Remix Edit)/Method of Modern Love	1984	—	—	3.00
❏ PB-14035	Some Things Are Better Left Unsaid/All American Girl	1985	—	—	3.00
❏ PB-14035 [PS]	Some Things Are Better Left Unsaid/All American Girl	1985	—	—	3.00
❏ GB-14064	Out of Touch/Adult Education	1985	—	—	3.00
—Gold Standard Series					
❏ PB-14098	Possession Obsession/Dance on Your Knees	1985	—	—	3.00
❏ PB-14098 [PS]	Possession Obsession/Dance on Your Knees	1985	—	—	3.00
❏ PB-14178	A Nite at the Apollo Live! The Way You Do the Things You Do-My Girl/Everytime You Go Away	1985	—	—	3.00
—A-side: With David Ruffin and Eddie Kendrick (sic)					
❏ PB-14178 [PS]	A Nite at the Apollo Live! The Way You Do the Things You Do-My Girl/Everytime You Go Away	1985	—	—	3.00
—A-side: With David Ruffin and Eddie Kendrick (sic)					
❏ JR-14259 [DJ]	Jingle Bell Rock from Daryl/Jingle Bell Rock from John	1985	2.50	5.00	10.00
—Promo only on green vinyl					
❏ JR-14259 [DJ]	Jingle Bell Rock from Daryl/Jingle Bell Rock from John	1985	2.50	5.00	10.00
—Promo only on red vinyl					
❏ JR-14259 [PS]	Jingle Bell Rock from Daryl/Jingle Bell Rock from John	1985	2.50	5.00	10.00
❏ GB-14340	Method of Modern Love/Possession Obsession	1986	—	—	3.00
—Gold Standard Series					
❏ GB-14341	Some Things Are Better Left Unsaid/A Nite at the Apollo Live! The Way You Do the Things You Do-My Girl	1986	—	—	3.00
—Gold Standard Series					

RCA VICTOR

Number	Title (A Side/B Side)	Yr	VG	VG+	NM
❏ PB-10373	Camellia/Ennui on the Mountain	1975	—	2.50	5.00
❏ PB-10436	Nothing at All/Alone Too Long	1975	—	2.50	5.00
❏ PB-10530	Sara Smile/Soldering	1975	—	2.50	5.00

SIRE

Number	Title (A Side/B Side)	Yr	VG	VG+	NM
❏ 22967	Love Train/"Earth Girls Are Easy" Theme	1989	—	—	3.00
❏ 22967 [PS]	Love Train/"Earth Girls Are Easy" Theme	1989	—	—	3.00

Albums

ALLEGIANCE

Number	Title (A Side/B Side)	Yr	VG	VG+	NM
❏ AV-5014	Nucleus	198?	2.00	4.00	8.00

ARISTA

Number	Title (A Side/B Side)	Yr	VG	VG+	NM
❏ AL-8539	Ooh Yeah!	1988	2.50	5.00	10.00
❏ AL-8614	Change of Season	1989	3.00	6.00	12.00

ATLANTIC

Number	Title (A Side/B Side)	Yr	VG	VG+	NM
❏ SD 7242	Whole Oats	1972	3.00	6.00	12.00
❏ SD 7269	Abandoned Luncheonette	1973	3.00	6.00	12.00
❏ SD 18109	War Babies	1974	3.00	6.00	12.00
❏ SD 18213	No Goodbyes	1977	2.50	5.00	10.00
❏ SD 19139	Abandoned Luncheonette	1977	2.00	4.00	8.00

CHELSEA

Number	Title (A Side/B Side)	Yr	VG	VG+	NM
❏ CHL-547	Past Times Behind	1976	3.00	6.00	12.00

INTERMEDIA

Number	Title (A Side/B Side)	Yr	VG	VG+	NM
❏ QS-5040	The Early Years	198?	2.00	4.00	8.00

JEM

Number	Title (A Side/B Side)	Yr	VG	VG+	NM
❏ 55002	Early Years	198?	2.00	4.00	8.00

MOBILE FIDELITY

Number	Title (A Side/B Side)	Yr	VG	VG+	NM
❏ 1-069	Abandoned Luncheonette	1982	5.00	10.00	20.00
—Audiophile vinyl					

RCA VICTOR

Number	Title (A Side/B Side)	Yr	VG	VG+	NM
❏ APL1-1144	Daryl Hall & John Oates	1976	2.50	5.00	10.00
❏ APL1-1467	Bigger Than Both of Us	1976	2.50	5.00	10.00
❏ AFL1-2300	Beauty on a Back Street	1977	2.50	5.00	10.00
❏ AFL1-2802	Livetime!	1978	2.50	5.00	10.00
❏ AFL1-2804	Along the Red Ledge	1978	2.50	5.00	10.00
❏ AFL1-2804	Along the Red Ledge	1978	3.75	7.50	15.00
—Red vinyl					
❏ ANL1-3463	Daryl Hall & John Oates	1979	2.00	4.00	8.00
❏ AFL1-3494	X-Static	1979	2.50	5.00	10.00
❏ DJL1-3512 [DJ]	Post Static	1979	5.00	10.00	20.00
—Promo-only one-sided 4-song sampler					
❏ AQL1-3646	Voices	1980	2.00	4.00	8.00
—"RE 4" on back cover: Color photo of Hall and Oates on each side					
❏ AQL1-3646	Voices	1980	2.50	5.00	10.00
—"RE 2" on back cover: Cover not embossed; Hall's head 3 inches-plus below "Voices" on front cover					
❏ AQL1-3646	Voices	1980	3.00	6.00	12.00
—No "RE" of any type on back cover: Embossed lettering and sound waves, Hall's head almost touches the word "Voices" on front					
❏ AQL1-3646	Voices	1980	3.00	6.00	12.00
—"RE 3" on back cover: Cover lettering in black					
❏ AQL1-3646	Voices	1980	3.00	6.00	12.00
—"RE" on back cover: Variation unknown					
❏ AQL1-3646	Voices	1981	2.00	4.00	8.00
—"RE 5" on back cover: Variation unknown					

H

Number	Title (A Side/B Side)	Yr	VG	VG+	NM
❑ AQL1-3646	Voices	1981	2.00	4.00	8.00

—"RE 6" on back cover: Bar code on upper left back cover

Number	Title (A Side/B Side)	Yr	VG	VG+	NM
❑ DJL1-3832	RCA Radio Special Interview Series	1980	3.75	7.50	15.00
❑ AYL1-3836	Daryl Hall & John Oates	1980	2.00	4.00	8.00
❑ AYL1-3866	Bigger Than Both of Us	1980	2.00	4.00	8.00
❑ AFL1-4028	Private Eyes	1981	2.50	5.00	10.00
❑ DJL1-4179	Special Radio Series	1981	3.75	7.50	15.00
❑ AYL1-4230	Beauty on a Back Street	1981	2.00	4.00	8.00
❑ AYL1-4231	Along the Red Ledge	1981	2.00	4.00	8.00
❑ AYL1-4303	X-Static	1982	2.00	4.00	8.00
❑ AFL1-4383	H2O	1982	2.50	5.00	10.00
❑ AYL1-4722	Livetime!	1983	2.00	4.00	8.00
❑ CPL1-4858	Rock 'n Soul Part 1	1983	2.00	4.00	8.00

—"RE 2" on lower left back: Variation unknown

❑ CPL1-4858	Rock 'n Soul Part 1	1983	2.50	5.00	10.00

—"RE" on lower left back: back cover says "Plus Two New Songs (Recorded September 1983)," then mentions "Say It Isn't So" and "Adult Education"

❑ CPL1-4858	Rock 'n Soul Part 1	1983	3.00	6.00	12.00

—Original cover: back cover says "Plus Two New Songs (Recorded September 1983)" WITHOUT mentioning what the songs are

❑ AFL1-5309	Big Bam Boom	1984	3.00	6.00	12.00
❑ AJL1-5336	Big Bam Boom	1984	2.50	5.00	10.00
❑ AFL1-7035	Live at the Apollo	1985	2.50	5.00	10.00

HALL, DICKSON
45s
EPIC

Number	Title (A Side/B Side)	Yr	VG	VG+	NM
❑ 9262	Cowboy/It's a Long Walk Home	1958	3.75	7.50	15.00
❑ 9262 [PS]	Cowboy/It's a Long Walk Home	1958	6.25	12.50	25.00

Albums
EPIC

❑ LN 3427 [M]	25 All-Time Country and Western Hits	1958	6.25	12.50	25.00

KAPP

❑ KL-1067 [M]	Fabulous Country Hits Way Out West	1957	7.50	15.00	30.00
❑ KL-1464 [M]	24 Fabulous Country Hits	1966	5.00	10.00	20.00
❑ KS-3464 [S]	24 Fabulous Country Hits	1966	6.25	12.50	25.00

MGM

❑ E-329 [10]	Outlaws of the Old West	1954	15.00	30.00	60.00
❑ E-3263 [M]	Outlaws of the Old West	1956	10.00	20.00	40.00

PERFECT

❑ P-14016 [M]	Country & Western Million Sellers	1960	5.00	10.00	20.00
❑ PS-14016 [S]	Country & Western Million Sellers	1960	6.25	12.50	25.00

HALL, LARRY
45s
HOT

Number	Title (A Side/B Side)	Yr	VG	VG+	NM
❑ 1	Sandy/Lovin' Tree	1959	12.50	25.00	50.00

STRAND

❑ 25007	Sandy/Lovin' Tree	1959	6.25	12.50	25.00
❑ 25013	A Girl Like You/Rosemary	1960	5.00	10.00	20.00
❑ 25016	For Every Boy/I'll Stay Single	1960	5.00	10.00	20.00
❑ 25025	The Girl I Left Behind/Kool Love	1961	5.00	10.00	20.00
❑ 25029	Lips of Wine/Rebel Heart	1961	5.00	10.00	20.00
❑ 25048	Ladder of Love/The One You Left Behind	1961	5.00	10.00	20.00

Albums
STRAND

❑ SL-1005 [M]	Sandy	1960	37.50	75.00	150.00
❑ SLS-1005 [S]	Sandy	1960	50.00	100.00	200.00

HALL, ROY (1) Rockabilly and country singer-pianist; wrote "Whole Lot of Shakin' Goin' On." Not to be confused with the pre-World War II country singer of the same name.
45s
DECCA

Number	Title (A Side/B Side)	Yr	VG	VG+	NM
❑ 29697	Whole Lotta Shakin' Goin' On/All By Myself	1955	20.00	40.00	80.00
❑ 29786	See You Later, Alligator/Don't Stop Now	1956	12.50	25.00	50.00
❑ 29880	Blue Suede Shoes/Luscious	1956	12.50	25.00	50.00
❑ 30060	Three Alley Cats/Diggin' the Boogie	1956	12.50	25.00	50.00

FORTUNE

❑ 170	Going Down the Road/Jealous Love	1952	10.00	20.00	40.00

—B-side by the Davis Sisters

❑ 521	Corrine, Corrina/Don't Ask Me No Questions	1956	12.50	25.00	50.00

HI-Q

❑ 5045	Three Alley Cats/Bedspring Motel	196?	15.00	30.00	60.00
❑ 5050	Go Go Little Queenie/Everybody Dig That Boogie	196?	15.00	30.00	60.00

HALL, SIDNEY
45s
SHRINE

Number	Title (A Side/B Side)	Yr	VG	VG+	NM
❑ 109	The Weekend/I'm a Lover	1966	250.00	500.00	1000.

HALL, TOM T. Also see PATTI PAGE.
45s
MERCURY

Number	Title (A Side/B Side)	Yr	VG	VG+	NM
❑ DJ-111 [DJ]	Ballad of Forty Dollars//Memphis Morning/Since They Fired the Band Director (At Murphy High)/ Please Let Me Prove (My Love for You)	1968	3.75	7.50	15.00

—Promo only; the B-side contains 60-second excerpts of the three songs performed by Roy Drusky, Linda Manning and Dave Dudley, respectively

❑ 55001	It's All in the Game/The Little Green Flower with the Yellow on Top	1977	—	2.00	4.00
❑ 72700	I Washed My Face in the Morning Dew/ A Picture of Your Mother	1967	2.00	4.00	8.00
❑ 72749	Beauty Is a Fading Flower/ Your Love Is Mine Again	1967	2.00	4.00	8.00
❑ 72786	The World the Way I Want It/Shame on the Rain	1968	2.00	4.00	8.00
❑ 72835	Ain't Got the Time/Hope	1968	2.00	4.00	8.00
❑ 72863	Ballad of Forty Dollars/Highways	1968	—	3.00	6.00
❑ 72913	Strawberry Farms/3	1969	—	3.00	6.00
❑ 72951	Homecoming/Myra	1969	—	3.00	6.00
❑ 72998	A Week in a Country Jail/Flat-Footin' It	1969	—	3.00	6.00
❑ 73039	Shoeshine Man/Kentucky in the Morning	1970	—	3.00	6.00
❑ 73078	Salute to a Switchblade/That'll Be Alright with Me	1970	—	3.00	6.00
❑ 73140	One Hundred Children/ I Took a Memory to Lunch	1970	—	3.00	6.00
❑ 73189	Ode to a Half Pound of Ground Round/Pinto the Wonder Horse Is Dead	1971	—	3.00	6.00

Number	Title (A Side/B Side)	Yr	VG	VG+	NM
❑ 73221	The Year That Clayton Delaney Died/Second Handed Flowers	1971	—	2.50	5.00
❑ 73278	Me and Jesus/Coot Marseilles Blues	1972	—	2.50	5.00
❑ 73297	The Monkey That Became President/She Gave Her Heart to Jethro	1972	—	2.50	5.00
❑ 73327	More About John Henry/Windy City Anne	1972	—	2.50	5.00
❑ 73346	(Old Dogs-Children and) Watermelon Wine/ Grandma Whistled	1972	—	2.50	5.00
❑ 73377	Ravishing Ruby /I Flew Over Our House Last Night	1973	—	2.50	5.00
❑ 73394	Watergate Blues/Spokane Motel Blues	1973	—	2.50	5.00
❑ 73436	I Love/Back When We Were Young	1973	—	2.00	4.00
❑ 73488	That Song Is Driving Me Crazy/Forget It	1974	—	2.00	4.00
❑ 73617	Country Is/God Came Through Bellville, Ga.	1974	—	2.00	4.00
❑ 73641	I Care/Sneaky Snake	1974	—	2.00	4.00
❑ 73686	Deal/It Rained in Every Town Except Paducah	1975	—	2.00	4.00
❑ 73704	I Like Beer/From a Mansion to a Honky Tonk	1975	—	2.00	4.00
❑ 73755	Faster Horses (The Cowboy and the Poet)/No New Friends Please	1975	—	2.00	4.00
❑ 73795	Negatory Romance/ It's Got to Be Kentucky for Me	1976	—	2.00	4.00
❑ 73850	Fox on the Run/Bluegrass Festival in the Sky	1976	—	2.00	4.00
❑ 73899	Your Man Loves You Honey/ One of the Mysteries of Life	1977	—	2.00	4.00
❑ 76147	Little Lady Preacher/Ramona's Revenge	1982	—	2.00	4.00
❑ 812835-7	Everything from Jesus to Jack Daniels/(Old Dogs-Children and) Watermelon Wine	1983	—	—	3.00
❑ 814560-7	How'd You Get Home So Soon/The Year That Clayton Delaney Died	1983	—	—	3.00
❑ 870669-7	Let's Play Remember/Fox Hollow's Animal Train	1988	—	—	3.00
❑ 872180-7	Let's Spend Christmas at My House/ Let's Go Shopping Today	1988	—	—	3.00
❑ 880030-7	Famous in Missouri/ I Only Think About You When I'm Drunk	1984	—	—	3.00
❑ 880216-7	P.S. I Love You/ My Heroes Have Always Been Cowboys	1984	—	—	3.00
❑ 880690-7	A Bar with No Beer/Red Sails in the Sunset	1985	—	—	3.00
❑ 884017-7	Down in the Florida Keys/Song in a Seashell	1985	—	—	3.00
❑ 884850-7	Susie's Beauty Shop/Love Letters in the Sand	1986	—	—	3.00
❑ 888155-7	Dowm at the Mall/We're All Through Dancing	1986	—	—	3.00

RCA

❑ PB-11158	May the Force Be With You Always/ No One Feels My Heart	1977	—	2.50	5.00
❑ PB-11253	I Wish I Loved Somebody Else/Whiskey	1978	—	2.00	4.00
❑ PB-11376	What Have You Got to Lose/ The Three Sofa Story	1978	—	2.00	4.00
❑ PB-11453	Son of Clayton Delaney/The Great East Breadway Onion Championship of 1978	1978	—	2.00	4.00
❑ PB-11568	There Is a Miracle in You/ Saturday Morning Show	1979	—	2.00	4.00
❑ PB-11713	You Show Me Your Heart (And I'll Show You Mine)/Old Habits Die Hard	1979	—	2.00	4.00
❑ PB-11765	Christmas Is/Thanksgiving Is	1979	—	2.00	4.00
❑ PB-11888	The Old Side of Town/Jesus on the Radio (Daddy on the Phone)	1979	—	—	3.00
❑ PB-12005	Soldier of Fortune/ The World According to Raymond	1980	—	—	3.00
❑ PB-12066	Back When Gas Was Thirty Cents a Gallon/ Texas Never Fell in Love with Me	1980	—	—	3.00
❑ PB-12219	The All New Me/Pour Me (Pour Me Another Drink)	1981	—	—	3.00

Albums
MERCURY

❑ SRM-1-500	Songs of Fox Hollow	1975	3.00	6.00	12.00
❑ SRM-1-668	The Rhymer and Other Five and Dimers	1973	3.00	6.00	12.00
❑ SRM-1-687	For the People in the Last Hard Town	1974	3.00	6.00	12.00
❑ SRM-1-1009	Country Is	1974	3.00	6.00	12.00
❑ SRM-1-1033	I Wrote	1975	3.00	6.00	12.00
❑ SRM-1-1044	Greatest Hits, Volume 2	1975	3.00	6.00	12.00
❑ SRM-1-1076	Faster Horses	1976	3.00	6.00	12.00
❑ SRM-1-1111	Magnificent Music	1977	3.00	6.00	12.00
❑ SRM-1-1139	About Love	1977	3.00	6.00	12.00
❑ SRM-1-5008	Greatest Hits, Volume 3	1978	3.00	6.00	12.00
❑ SR-61211	Ballad of Forty Dollars and His Other Great Songs	1969	5.00	10.00	20.00
❑ SR-61247	Homecoming	1969	5.00	10.00	20.00
❑ SR-61277	Witness Life	1970	5.00	10.00	20.00
❑ SR-61307	100 Children	1970	5.00	10.00	20.00
❑ SR-61350	In Search of a Song	1971	3.75	7.50	15.00
❑ SR-61362	We All Got Together And…	1972	3.75	7.50	15.00
❑ SR-61369	Greatest Hits	1972	3.75	7.50	15.00
❑ 814025-1	Jesus to Jack Daniels	1983	2.00	4.00	8.00
❑ 822425-1	Natural Dreams	1984	2.00	4.00	8.00
❑ 822500-1	In Search of a Song	1987	2.00	4.00	8.00
❑ 824143-1	Greatest Hits	1985	2.00	4.00	8.00

—Reissue

❑ 824144-1	Greatest Hits, Volume 2	1985	2.00	4.00	8.00

—Reissue

❑ 824145-1	Greatest Hits, Volume 3	1985	2.00	4.00	8.00

—Reissue

❑ 824508-1	Song in a Seashell	1985	2.00	4.00	8.00
❑ 832350-1	Songs of Fox Hollow	1987	2.00	4.00	8.00

—Reissue

❑ 834779-1	Country Songs for Children	1988	2.00	4.00	8.00

—Reissue

PICCADILLY

❑ 3558	I Like Beer	198?	2.00	4.00	8.00

RCA VICTOR

❑ AHL1-2622	New Train	1978	2.50	5.00	10.00
❑ AHL1-3018	Places I've Been	1979	2.50	5.00	10.00
❑ AHL1-3495	T's in Town	1979	2.50	5.00	10.00
❑ AHL1-3685	Soldier of Fortune	1980	2.50	5.00	10.00
❑ AHL1-4749	In Concert: Recorded Live at the Grand Ole Opry	1983	2.50	5.00	10.00
❑ AYL1-5432	In Concert: Recorded Live at the Grand Ole Opry	1985	2.00	4.00	8.00

—"Best Buy Series" reissue

Number	Title (A Side/B Side)	Yr	VG	VG+	NM
HALLMARKS, THE					
45s					
DOT					
❏ 16418	My Little Sailor Boy/Congratulations	1963	5.00	10.00	20.00
EPIC					
❏ 9681	Let There Be You/Royal King	1964	3.00	6.00	12.00
SMASH					
❏ 2115	Soul Shakin' Psychedelic Sally/ Girl of My Dreams	1967	7.50	15.00	30.00
HALLOWAY, LARRY					
45s					
PARKWAY					
❏ 903	Beatle Teen Beat/Going Up	1964	5.00	10.00	20.00
HALLYDAY, JOHNNY					
45s					
PHILIPS					
❏ 40024	I Got a Woman/Be-Bop-a-Lula	1962	6.25	12.50	25.00
❏ 40043	Hey Little Girl/Caravan of Lonely Men	1962	6.25	12.50	25.00
Albums					
PHILIPS					
❏ PHM 200019 [M]	America's Rockin' Hits	1962	20.00	40.00	80.00
❏ PHS 600019 [S]	America's Rockin' Hits	1962	25.00	50.00	100.00
HALOS, THE					
45s					
CONGRESS					
❏ 244	Do I/Just Keep On Loving Me	1965	3.00	6.00	12.00
❏ 249	Since I Fell for You/You're Never Gonna Find	1965	3.00	6.00	12.00
❏ 253	Baby What You Want Me to Do/Hey, Hey, Love Me	1965	3.00	6.00	12.00
❏ 262 [DJ]	Come Softly to Me/(B-side unknown)	1966	3.00	6.00	12.00
—May be promo-only					
7 ARTS					
❏ 709	Nag/Copy Cat	1961	5.00	10.00	20.00
❏ 720	Come On/What'd I Say	1962	5.00	10.00	20.00
Albums					
WARWICK					
❏ W-2046 [M]	The Halos	1962	100.00	200.00	400.00
HAMILTON, GEORGE					
45s					
ABC-PARAMOUNT					
❏ 10734	Loneliness/So Small	1965	2.50	5.00	10.00
❏ 10734 [PS]	Loneliness/So Small	1965	5.00	10.00	20.00
MGM					
❏ 13178	Don't Envy Me/Little Betty Falling Star	1963	3.00	6.00	12.00
❏ 13178 [PS]	Don't Envy Me/Little Betty Falling Star	1963	5.00	10.00	20.00
❏ 13215	Does Goodnight Mean Goodbye/ Errand of Mercy	1964	3.00	6.00	12.00
UNI					
❏ 55303	Evel Knievel/Boy from the Country	1971	2.50	5.00	10.00
Albums					
ABC-PARAMOUNT					
❏ 535 [M]	By George	1966	5.00	10.00	20.00
❏ S-535 [S]	By George	1966	6.25	12.50	25.00
HAMILTON, GEORGE, IV					
45s					
ABC					
❏ 12342	Only the Best/My Ship Will Sail	1978	—	2.50	5.00
❏ 12376	One Day at a Time/Take This Heart	1978	—	2.00	4.00
ABC-PARAMOUNT					
❏ 9765	A Rose and a Baby Ruth/If You Don't Know	1956	7.50	15.00	30.00
❏ 9782	Only One Love/If I Possessed a Printing Press	1957	7.50	15.00	30.00
❏ 9838	High School Romance/Everybody's Baby	1957	7.50	15.00	30.00
❏ 9862	Why Don't They Understand/Even Tho'	1957	7.50	15.00	30.00
❏ 9898	Now and For Always/One Heart	1958	6.25	12.50	25.00
❏ 9924	I Know Where I'm Goin'/ Who's Taking You to the Prom	1958	6.25	12.50	25.00
❏ 9946	When Will I Know/Your Cheatin' Heart	1958	6.25	12.50	25.00
❏ 9966	Lucy, Lucy/The Two of Us	1958	6.25	12.50	25.00
❏ 10009	The Steady Game/Can You Blame Us	1959	5.00	10.00	20.00
❏ 10028	Gee/I Know Your Sweetheart	1959	5.00	10.00	20.00
❏ 10059	One Little Acre/Little Tom	1959	5.00	10.00	20.00
❏ 10090	Why I'm Walkin'/Tremble	1960	5.00	10.00	20.00
❏ 10125	Before This Day Ends/Loneliness All Around Me	1960	5.00	10.00	20.00
❏ 10167	A Walk on the Wild Side of Life/It's Just the Idea	1960	5.00	10.00	20.00
ABC/DOT					
❏ 17687	I Wonder Who's Kissing Her Now/ In the Palm of Her Hand	1977	—	2.00	4.00
❏ 17708	Cornbread, Beans and Sweet Potato Pie/May the Wind Be Always at Your Back	1977	—	2.00	4.00
❏ 17723	Everlasting (Everlasting Love)/ In the Palm of Your Hand	1977	—	2.00	4.00
COLONIAL					
❏ 420	A Rose and a Baby Ruth/If You Don't Know	1956	20.00	40.00	80.00
❏ 451	I've Got a Secret/Sam	1956	10.00	20.00	40.00
GRT					
❏ 063	Blue Jeans, Ice Cream and Saturday Shoes/ Bad Romancer	1976	—	2.50	5.00
MCA					
❏ 41149	Forever Young/'Rangement Blues	1979	—	2.00	4.00
❏ 41215	I'll Be Here in the Morning/Spin Spin	1980	—	2.00	4.00
❏ 41282	Catfish Bates/Mose Rankin	1980	—	2.00	4.00
RCA					
❏ 2722-7-R	Abilene/Oh So Many Tears	1990	—	2.00	4.00
RCA VICTOR					
❏ 47-7881	Three Steps to the Phone (Millions of Miles)/ The Ballad of Widder Jones	1961	3.75	7.50	15.00
❏ 47-7934	To You and Yours (From Me and Mine)/ I Want a Girl	1961	3.75	7.50	15.00
❏ 47-8001	China Doll/ Commerce Street and Sixth Avenue North	1962	3.75	7.50	15.00

Number	Title (A Side/B Side)	Yr	VG	VG+	NM
❏ 47-8062	If You Don't Know, I Ain't Gonna Tell You/ Where Nobody Knows Me	1962	3.75	7.50	15.00
❏ 47-8118	In This Very Same Room/If You Want Me To	1962	3.75	7.50	15.00
❏ 47-8181	Abilene/Oh So Many Years	1963	3.00	6.00	12.00
❏ 47-8250	There's More Pretty Girls Than One/ If You Don't, Somebody Else Will	1963	3.00	6.00	12.00
❏ 47-8304	Linda with the Lonely Eyes/ Fair and Tender Ladies	1963	3.00	6.00	12.00
❏ 47-8392	Fort Worth, Dallas or Houston /Life's Railway to Heaven	1964	3.00	6.00	12.00
❏ 47-8462	Truck Driving Man/The Little Grave	1964	3.00	6.00	12.00
❏ 47-8537	The Last Mister Jones/Anymore	1965	2.50	5.00	10.00
❏ 47-8608	Walking the Floor Over You/ Driftwood on the River	1965	2.50	5.00	10.00
❏ 47-8690	Write Me a Picture/Twist of the Wrist	1965	2.50	5.00	10.00
❏ 47-8797	Steel Rail Blues/Tobacco	1966	2.50	5.00	10.00
❏ 47-8924	Early Morning Rain/Slightly Used	1966	2.50	5.00	10.00
❏ 47-9059	Urge for Going/Changes	1966	2.50	5.00	10.00
❏ 47-9239	Break My Mind/Something Special to Me	1967	2.00	4.00	8.00
❏ 47-9385	Little World Girl/Song for a Winter's Night	1967	2.00	4.00	8.00
❏ 47-9519	It's My Time/Canadian Railroad Trilogy	1968	2.00	4.00	8.00
❏ 47-9637	Take My Hand for Awhile/ Wonderful World of My Dreams	1968	2.00	4.00	8.00
❏ 47-9775	Natividad (The Nativity)/The Little Grave	1969	2.00	4.00	8.00
❏ 47-9829	She's a Little Bit Country/My Nova Scotia Home	1970	—	3.00	6.00
❏ 47-9886	Back Where It's At/Then I Miss You	1970	—	3.00	6.00
❏ 47-9893	Let's Get Together/Everything Is Beautiful	1970	—	3.00	6.00
—With Skeeter Davis					
❏ 47-9937	Natividad (The Nativity)/The Little Grave	1970	—	3.00	6.00
❏ 47-9945	Anyway/The Best That I Can Do	1971	—	3.00	6.00
❏ 74-0100	Back to Denver/Suzanne	1969	2.00	4.00	8.00
❏ 74-0171	Canadian Pacific/Sisters of Mercy	1969	2.00	4.00	8.00
❏ 74-0256	Carolina in My Mind/ I'm Gonna Be a Country Boy Again	1969	2.00	4.00	8.00
❏ 74-0469	Countryfied/My North Country Home	1971	—	3.00	6.00
❏ 74-0531	West Texas Highway/ There's No Room in This Rat Race	1971	—	3.00	6.00
❏ 74-0622	10 Degrees and Getting Colder/Tumbleweed	1971	—	3.00	6.00
❏ 74-0697	Country Music in My Soul/Child's Song	1972	—	2.50	5.00
❏ 74-0776	Travelin' Light/Alberta Bound	1972	—	2.50	5.00
❏ 74-0854	Blue Train (Of the Heartbreak Line)/ Maritime Farewell	1972	—	2.50	5.00
❏ 74-0948	Dirty Old Man/Abilene	1973	—	2.50	5.00
❏ APBO-0084	Second Cup of Coffee/Farmer's Song	1973	—	2.00	4.00
❏ APBO-0203	Claim on Me/Early Mornin' Rain	1973	—	2.00	4.00
❏ APBO-0314	The Ways of a Country Girl/Pictou County Jail	1974	—	2.00	4.00
7-Inch Extended Plays					
ABC-PARAMOUNT					
❏ A-220	Clementine/When I Grow Too Old to Dream//Tell Me Why/Let Me Call You Sweetheart	1958	5.00	10.00	20.00
❏ A-220 [PS]	On Campus	1958	5.00	10.00	20.00
Albums					
ABC					
❏ X-750	16 Greatest Hits	1972	2.50	5.00	10.00
❏ AC-30032	The ABC Collection	1975	3.00	6.00	12.00
ABC-PARAMOUNT					
❏ 220 [M]	On Campus	1958	10.00	20.00	40.00
❏ S-220 [S]	On Campus	1958	12.50	25.00	50.00
❏ 251 [M]	Sing Me a Sad Song (A Tribute to Hank Williams)	1958	10.00	20.00	40.00
❏ S-251 [S]	Sing Me a Sad Song (A Tribute to Hank Williams)	1958	12.50	25.00	50.00
❏ 461 [M]	George Hamilton IV's Big 15	1963	7.50	15.00	30.00
❏ S-461 [P]	George Hamilton IV's Big 15	1963	10.00	20.00	40.00
ABC/DOT					
❏ DO-2081	Fine Lace	1977	2.50	5.00	10.00
DOT					
❏ 39033	George Hamilton IV	1985	2.50	5.00	10.00
HARMONY					
❏ HS 11379	Your Cheatin' Heart	1970	2.50	5.00	10.00
LAMB AND LION					
❏ 1015	Bluegrass Gospel	1974	3.00	6.00	12.00
MCA					
❏ 705	Forever Young	198?	2.00	4.00	8.00
—Reissue of 3206					
❏ 3206	Forever Young	1980	2.50	5.00	10.00
RCA CAMDEN					
❏ ACL1-0242	Singin' on the Mountains	1973	2.50	5.00	10.00
❏ CAL-2200 [M]	A Rose and a Baby Ruth	1967	3.75	7.50	15.00
❏ CAS-2200 [S]	A Rose and a Baby Ruth	1967	2.50	5.00	10.00
❏ CAS-2468	Early Morning Rain	1971	2.50	5.00	10.00
RCA VICTOR					
❏ APL1-0455	Greatest Hits	1974	3.00	6.00	12.00
❏ LPM-2373 [M]	To You and Yours from Me and Mine	1961	6.25	12.50	25.00
❏ LSP-2373 [S]	To You and Yours from Me and Mine	1961	7.50	15.00	30.00
❏ LPM-2778 [M]	Abilene	1963	6.25	12.50	25.00
❏ LSP-2778 [S]	Abilene	1963	7.50	15.00	30.00
❏ LPM-2972 [M]	Fort Worth, Dallas or Houston	1964	6.25	12.50	25.00
❏ LSP-2972 [S]	Fort Worth, Dallas or Houston	1964	7.50	15.00	30.00
❏ LPM-3371 [M]	Mister Sincerity... A Tribute to Ernest Tubb	1965	6.25	12.50	25.00
❏ LSP-3371 [S]	Mister Sincerity... A Tribute to Ernest Tubb	1965	7.50	15.00	30.00
❏ LPM-3510 [M]	Coast Country	1966	6.25	12.50	25.00
❏ LSP-3510 [S]	Coast Country	1966	7.50	15.00	30.00
❏ LPM-3601 [M]	Steel Rail Blues	1966	5.00	10.00	20.00
❏ LSP-3601 [S]	Steel Rail Blues	1966	5.00	10.00	20.00
❏ LPM-3752 [M]	Folk Country Classics	1967	6.25	12.50	25.00
❏ LSP-3752 [S]	Folk Country Classics	1967	5.00	10.00	20.00
❏ LPM-3854 [M]	Folksy	1967	6.25	12.50	25.00
❏ LSP-3854 [S]	Folksy	1967	5.00	10.00	20.00
❏ LPM-3962 [M]	The Gentle Country Sound of George Hamilton IV	1968	10.00	20.00	40.00
❏ LSP-3962 [S]	The Gentle Country Sound of George Hamilton IV	1968	5.00	10.00	20.00
❏ LSP-4066	In the 4th Dimension	1968	5.00	10.00	20.00
❏ LSP-4164	Canadian Pacific	1969	3.75	7.50	15.00
❏ LSP-4265	The Best of George Hamilton IV	1970	3.75	7.50	15.00
❏ LSP-4342	Back Where It's At	1970	3.75	7.50	15.00
❏ LSP-4435	Down Home in the Country	1971	3.75	7.50	15.00

Number	Title (A Side/B Side)	Yr	VG	VG+	NM
❑ LSP-4517	North Country	1971	3.75	7.50	15.00
❑ LSP-4609	West Texas Highway	1971	3.75	7.50	15.00
❑ LSP-4700	Country Music in My Soul	1972	3.00	6.00	12.00
❑ LSP-4772	Travelin' Light	1972	3.00	6.00	12.00
❑ LSP-4826	International Ambassador	1973	3.00	6.00	12.00

HAMILTON, JUDD
45s
AMERICAN INT'L.

Number	Title (A Side/B Side)	Yr	VG	VG+	NM
❑ 151	Rules/Someday Morning	1970	2.00	4.00	8.00
❑ 163	Baltimore/Sunshine Man	1970	2.00	4.00	8.00

DOLTON

Number	Title (A Side/B Side)	Yr	VG	VG+	NM
❑ 80	Dream/Your Only Boy	1963	7.50	15.00	30.00

HAMILTON, LITTLE JOHNNY
45s
DORE

Number	Title (A Side/B Side)	Yr	VG	VG+	NM
❑ 754	Oh How I Love You/Go	1966	20.00	40.00	80.00
❑ 760	Keep On Movin'/Mudpie	1966	300.00	600.00	1200.

HAMILTON, ROY
45s
AGP

Number	Title (A Side/B Side)	Yr	VG	VG+	NM
❑ 113	The Dark End of the Street/100 Years	1969	2.00	4.00	8.00
❑ 116	Angelica/Hang Ups	1969	2.00	4.00	8.00
❑ 125	It's Only Make Believe/100 Years	1969	2.00	4.00	8.00

CAPITOL

Number	Title (A Side/B Side)	Yr	VG	VG+	NM
❑ 2057	Let This World Be Free/Wait Until Dark	1967	2.00	4.00	8.00

EPIC

Number	Title (A Side/B Side)	Yr	VG	VG+	NM
❑ 9015	You'll Never Walk Alone/ I'm Gonna Sit Right Down and Cry	1954	6.25	12.50	25.00
❑ 9047	So Let There Be Love/If You Loved Me	1954	6.25	12.50	25.00
❑ 9068	Ebb Tide/Beware	1954	6.25	12.50	25.00
❑ 9086	Hurt/Star of Love	1954	6.25	12.50	25.00
❑ 9092	I Believe/If You Are But a Dream	1955	5.00	10.00	20.00
❑ 9102	Unchained Melody/From Here to Eternity	1955	6.25	12.50	25.00
❑ 9111	Forgive This Fool/You Wanted to Change Me	1955	5.00	10.00	20.00
❑ 9118	A Little Voice/All This Is Mine	1955	5.00	10.00	20.00
❑ 9125	Without a Song/Cuban Love Song	1955	5.00	10.00	20.00
❑ 9132	Everybody's Got a Home/Take Me with You	1955	5.00	10.00	20.00
❑ 9147	There Goes My Heart/Walk Along with Kings	1956	5.00	10.00	20.00
❑ 9160	Somebody, Somewhere/Since I Fell for You	1956	5.00	10.00	20.00
❑ 9180	I Took My Grief to Him/Chained	1956	5.00	10.00	20.00
❑ 9203	The Simple Prayer/A Mother's Love	1957	5.00	10.00	20.00
❑ 9212	My Faith, My Hope, My Love/So Long	1957	5.00	10.00	20.00
❑ 9224	The Aisle/That Old Feeling	1957	5.00	10.00	20.00
❑ 9232	(All of a Sudden) My Heart Sings/I'm Gonna Lock You in My Heart	1957	5.00	10.00	20.00
❑ 9257	Don't Let Go/The Night to Love	1957	5.00	10.00	20.00
❑ 9268	Crazy Feelin'/In a Dream	1958	3.75	7.50	15.00
❑ 9274	Lips/Jungle Fever	1958	3.75	7.50	15.00
❑ 9282	Wait for Me/Everything	1958	3.75	7.50	15.00
❑ 9294	Pledging My Love/My One and Only Love	1958	3.75	7.50	15.00
❑ 9301	It's Never Too Late/Somewhere Along the Way	1959	3.75	7.50	15.00
❑ 9307	I Need Your Lovin'/Blue Prelude	1959	3.75	7.50	15.00
❑ 9323	Time Marches On/Take It Easy, Joe	1959	3.75	7.50	15.00
❑ 9342	Great Romance/On My Way Back Home	1959	3.75	7.50	15.00
❑ 9354	The Ten Commandments/Dowm by the Riverside	1959	3.75	7.50	15.00
❑ 9354	The Ten Commandments/Nobody Knows the Trouble I've Seen	1959	5.00	10.00	20.00
❑ 9372	Down by the Riverside/Nobody Knows the Trouble I've Seen	1960	3.75	7.50	15.00
❑ 9373	I Let a Song Go Out of My Heart/I Get the Blues When It Rains	1960	3.75	7.50	15.00
❑ 9374	My Story/Please Send Me Someone to Love	1960	3.75	7.50	15.00
❑ 9375	Something's Gotta Give/Cheek to Cheek	1960	—	—	—

—Unreleased?

Number	Title (A Side/B Side)	Yr	VG	VG+	NM
❑ 9376	Sing You Sinners/Blow, Gabriel, Blow	1960	3.75	7.50	15.00
❑ 9386	Having Myself a Ball/Slowly	1960	3.75	7.50	15.00

—B-side by Bobby Sykes

Number	Title (A Side/B Side)	Yr	VG	VG+	NM
❑ 9388	Never Let Me Go/I Get the Blues When It Rains	1960	—	—	—

—Unreleased?

Number	Title (A Side/B Side)	Yr	VG	VG+	NM
❑ 9390	The Clock/I Get the Blues When It Rains	1960	3.75	7.50	15.00
❑ 9398	A Lover's Prayer/Never Let Me Go	1960	3.75	7.50	15.00
❑ 9407	Lonely Hands/Your Love	1960	3.75	7.50	15.00
❑ 9434	You Can Have Her/Abide With Me	1961	3.75	7.50	15.00
❑ 9434 [PS]	You Can Have Her/Abide With Me	1961	7.50	15.00	30.00
❑ 9443	You're Gonna Need Magic/To the One I Love	1961	3.75	7.50	15.00
❑ 9443 [PS]	You're Gonna Need Magic/To the One I Love	1961	7.50	15.00	30.00
❑ 9449	No Substitute for Love/Please Louise	1961	3.75	7.50	15.00
❑ 9449 [PS]	No Substitute for Love/Please Louise	1961	7.50	15.00	30.00
❑ 9460	Excerpts from "You Can Have Her"	1961	3.75	7.50	15.00
❑ 9461	Excerpts from "You Can Have Her"	1961	3.75	7.50	15.00
❑ 9462	Excerpts from "You Can Have Her"	1961	3.75	7.50	15.00
❑ 9463	Excerpts from "You Can Have Her"	1961	3.75	7.50	15.00
❑ 9464	Excerpts from "You Can Have Her"	1961	3.75	7.50	15.00
❑ 9466	There We Were/If	1961	3.00	6.00	12.00
❑ 9492	Don't Come Cryin' to Me/If Only I Had Known	1962	3.00	6.00	12.00
❑ 9520	Climb Ev'ry Mountain/ I'll Come Running Back to You	1962	3.00	6.00	12.00
❑ 9538	I Am/Earthquake	1962	3.00	6.00	12.00
❑ 10559	You'll Never Walk Alone/The Golden Boy	1969	2.00	4.00	8.00

MGM

Number	Title (A Side/B Side)	Yr	VG	VG+	NM
❑ 13138	Let Go/You Still Love Him	1963	2.50	5.00	10.00
❑ 13157	Midnight Town–Daybreak City/Intermezzo	1963	2.50	5.00	10.00
❑ 13175	Theme from "The V.I.P.'s" (The Willow)/The Sinner	1963	2.50	5.00	10.00
❑ 13217	The Panic Is On/There She Is	1964	6.25	12.50	25.00
❑ 13247	Answer Me, My Love/Unchained Melody	1964	2.50	5.00	10.00
❑ 13291	You Can Count on Me/ She Makes Me Wanna Dance	1964	6.25	12.50	25.00
❑ 13315	Sweet Violets/A Thousand Years Ago	1965	2.50	5.00	10.00

RCA VICTOR

Number	Title (A Side/B Side)	Yr	VG	VG+	NM
❑ 47-8641	Heartache/Ain't It the Truth	1965	2.50	5.00	10.00
❑ 47-8705	And I Love Her/Tore Up Over You	1965	2.50	5.00	10.00
❑ 47-8813	The Impossible Dream/She's Got a Heart	1966	2.50	5.00	10.00
❑ 47-8960	Walk Hand in Hand/Crackin' Up Over You	1966	6.25	12.50	25.00
❑ 47-9061	I Taught Her Everything She Knows/Lament	1967	2.50	5.00	10.00
❑ 47-9171	So High My Love/You Shook Me Up	1967	12.50	25.00	50.00
❑ 48-1034	Walk Hand in Hand/Crackin' Up Over You	1972	2.50	5.00	10.00

7-Inch Extended Plays
EPIC

Number	Title (A Side/B Side)	Yr	VG	VG+	NM
❑ EG-7065	You'll Never Walk Alone/I'm Gonna Sit Right Down and Cry (Over You)//If I Loved You/So Let There Be Love	195?	5.00	10.00	20.00
❑ EG-7065 [PS]	You'll Never Walk Alone	195?	5.00	10.00	20.00
❑ EG-7079	Ebb Tide/Beware//If You Are But a Dream/From Here to Eternity	195?	5.00	10.00	20.00
❑ EG-7079 [PS]	Ebb Tide	195?	5.00	10.00	20.00
❑ EG-7080	(contents unknown)	195?	5.00	10.00	20.00
❑ EG-7080 [PS]	Faith, Hope and Hamilton	195?	5.00	10.00	20.00
❑ EG-7133	Unchained Melody/Star of God//Hurt/One God	195?	5.00	10.00	20.00
❑ EG-7133 [PS]	Roy Hamilton Sings Unchained Melodies	195?	5.00	10.00	20.00
❑ EG-7158	(contents unknown)	195?	3.75	7.50	15.00
❑ EG-7158 [PS]	Roy Hamilton	195?	3.75	7.50	15.00
❑ EG-7159	(contents unknown)	195?	3.75	7.50	15.00
❑ EG-7159 [PS]	Roy Hamilton	195?	3.75	7.50	15.00
❑ EG-7200	(contents unknown)	1958	3.75	7.50	15.00
❑ EG-7200 [PS]	Don't Let Go	1958	3.75	7.50	15.00
❑ EG-7205	(contents unknown)	1958	3.75	7.50	15.00
❑ EG-7205 [PS]	Lips	1958	3.75	7.50	15.00
❑ EG-7210	(contents unknown)	195?	3.75	7.50	15.00
❑ EG-7210 [PS]	With All My Love	195?	3.75	7.50	15.00
❑ EG-7214	(contents unknown)	195?	3.75	7.50	15.00
❑ EG-7214 [PS]	You Belong to My Heart	195?	3.75	7.50	15.00

Albums
EPIC

Number	Title (A Side/B Side)	Yr	VG	VG+	NM
❑ BN 518 [S]	With All My Love	1958	10.00	20.00	40.00
❑ BN 525 [S]	Why Fight The Feeling?	1959	7.50	15.00	30.00
❑ BN 530 [S]	Come Out Swingin'	1959	7.50	15.00	30.00
❑ BN 535 [S]	Have Blues, Must Travel	1959	7.50	15.00	30.00
❑ BN 551 [S]	Spirituals	1960	7.50	15.00	30.00
❑ BN 578 [S]	Soft 'n Warm	1960	7.50	15.00	30.00
❑ BN 595 [S]	You Can Have Her	1961	10.00	20.00	40.00
❑ BN 610 [S]	Only You	1961	7.50	15.00	30.00
❑ BN 632 [R]	You'll Never Walk Alone	1962	5.00	10.00	20.00
❑ LN 1023 [10]	You'll Never Walk Alone	1954	50.00	100.00	200.00
❑ LN 1103 [10]	The Voice of Roy Hamilton	1954	50.00	100.00	200.00
❑ LN 3176 [M]	Roy Hamilton	1955	15.00	30.00	60.00
❑ LN 3294 [M]	You'll Never Walk Alone	1956	17.50	35.00	70.00
❑ LN 3364 [M]	Golden Boy	1957	12.50	25.00	50.00
❑ LN 3519 [M]	With All My Love	1958	7.50	15.00	30.00
❑ LN 3545 [M]	Why Fight The Feeling?	1959	6.25	12.50	25.00
❑ LN 3561 [M]	Come Out Swingin'	1959	6.25	12.50	25.00
❑ LN 3580 [M]	Have Blues, Must Travel	1959	6.25	12.50	25.00
❑ LN 3628 [M]	Roy Hamilton At His Best	1960	10.00	20.00	40.00
❑ LN 3654 [M]	Spirituals	1960	6.25	12.50	25.00
❑ LN 3717 [M]	Soft 'n Warm	1960	6.25	12.50	25.00
❑ LN 3775 [M]	You Can Have Her	1961	7.50	15.00	30.00
❑ LN 3807 [M]	Only You	1961	6.25	12.50	25.00
❑ LN 24000 [M]	Mr. Rock and Soul	1962	6.25	12.50	25.00
❑ LN 24009 [M]	Roy Hamilton's Greatest Hits	1962	5.00	10.00	20.00
❑ LN 24316 [M]	Roy Hamilton's Greatest Hits, Vol. 2	1967	5.00	10.00	20.00
❑ BN 26000 [S]	Mr. Rock and Soul	1962	7.50	15.00	30.00
❑ BN 26009 [S]	Roy Hamilton's Greatest Hits	1962	6.25	12.50	25.00
❑ BN 26316 [S]	Roy Hamilton's Greatest Hits, Vol. 2	1967	6.25	12.50	25.00

MGM

Number	Title (A Side/B Side)	Yr	VG	VG+	NM
❑ E-4139 [M]	Warm and Soul	1963	3.75	7.50	15.00
❑ SE-4139 [S]	Warm and Soul	1963	5.00	10.00	20.00
❑ E-4233 [M]	Sentimental, Lonely & Blue	1964	3.75	7.50	15.00
❑ SE-4233 [S]	Sentimental, Lonely & Blue	1964	5.00	10.00	20.00

RCA VICTOR

Number	Title (A Side/B Side)	Yr	VG	VG+	NM
❑ LPM-3552 [M]	The Impossible Dream	1966	3.75	7.50	15.00
❑ LSP-3552 [S]	The Impossible Dream	1966	5.00	10.00	20.00

HAMILTON, RUSS
45s
KAPP

Number	Title (A Side/B Side)	Yr	VG	VG+	NM
❑ 184	Rainbow/We Will Make Love	1957	3.75	7.50	15.00
❑ 194	Wedding Ring/I Still Belong to You	1957	3.00	6.00	12.00
❑ 204	My Mother's Eyes/I Had a Dream	1957	3.00	6.00	12.00
❑ 219	Drifting and Dreaming/ Tip Toe Through the Tulips	1958	3.00	6.00	12.00
❑ 250	All Alone/The Things I Didn't Say	1958	3.00	6.00	12.00
❑ 281	I Found Out/My Unbreakable Heart	1959	3.00	6.00	12.00
❑ 612	Valley of Love/The Loneliest Boy in Town	1964	2.50	5.00	10.00

MGM

Number	Title (A Side/B Side)	Yr	VG	VG+	NM
❑ 12947	Gonna Find Me a Bluebird/Choir Girl	1960	3.00	6.00	12.00

Albums
KAPP

Number	Title (A Side/B Side)	Yr	VG	VG+	NM
❑ KL-1076 [M]	Rainbow	1957	20.00	40.00	80.00

HAMILTON, JOE FRANK & DENNISON See HAMILTON, JOE FRANK & REYNOLDS.

HAMILTON, JOE FRANK & REYNOLDS Includes records as "Hamilton, Joe Frank & Dennison." Also see THE T-BONES.
45s
ABC DUNHILL

Number	Title (A Side/B Side)	Yr	VG	VG+	NM
❑ 4276	Don't Pull Your Love/Funk-In-Wagnall	1971	—	3.00	6.00
❑ 4287	Annabelle/Goin' Down	1971	—	2.50	5.00
❑ 4296	Daisy Mae/It Takes the Best	1971	—	2.50	5.00
❑ 4305	Don't Refuse My Love/One Good Woman	1972	—	2.50	5.00

PLAYBOY

Number	Title (A Side/B Side)	Yr	VG	VG+	NM
❑ 5801	Now That I've Got You/Get On the Bus	1977	—	2.00	4.00

—As "Hamilton, Joe Frank & Dennison"

Number	Title (A Side/B Side)	Yr	VG	VG+	NM
❑ 6024	Fallin' in Love/So Good at Lovin' You	1975	—	2.50	5.00
❑ 6054	Winners and Losers/Barroom Blues	1975	—	2.00	4.00
❑ 6068	Everyday Without You/Badman	1976	—	2.00	4.00
❑ 6077	Light Up the World with Sunshine/Houdini	1976	—	2.00	4.00

—As "Hamilton, Joe Frank & Dennison"

Number	Title (A Side/B Side)	Yr	VG	VG+	NM
❑ 6077 [PS]	Light Up the World with Sunshine/Houdini	1976	—	2.50	5.00

—As "Hamilton, Joe Frank & Dennison"

Number	Title (A Side/B Side)	Yr	VG	VG+	NM
❑ 6088	Don't Fight the Hands (That Need You)/Get On the Bus	1976	—	2.00	4.00

—As "Hamilton, Joe Frank & Dennison"

Number	Title (A Side/B Side)	Yr	VG	VG+	NM
❑ 6088 [PS]	Don't Fight the Hands (That Need You)/Get On the Bus	1976	—	2.50	5.00

—As "Hamilton, Joe Frank & Dennison"

Albums
ABC DUNHILL

Number	Title (A Side/B Side)	Yr	VG	VG+	NM
❑ DS-50103	Hamilton, Joe Frank & Reynolds	1971	2.50	5.00	10.00
❑ DSX-50113	Hallway Symphony	1972	2.50	5.00	10.00

PLAYBOY

Number	Title (A Side/B Side)	Yr	VG	VG+	NM
❑ PB-407	Fallin' in Love	1975	2.50	5.00	10.00
❑ PZ 34741	Fallin' in Love	1977	2.00	4.00	8.00

—Reissue of 107

HAMILTON STREETCAR
45s
DOT

Number	Title (A Side/B Side)	Yr	VG	VG+	NM
❑ 17253	Silver Wings/I See I Am	1969	3.00	6.00	12.00
❑ 17279	Brother Speed/Wasn't It You	1969	3.00	6.00	12.00
❑ 17306	Honey and Wine/Now I Taste the Tears	1969	3.00	6.00	12.00

LHI

Number	Title (A Side/B Side)	Yr	VG	VG+	NM
❑ 1206	Confusion/Your Own Come Down	1968	3.75	7.50	15.00
❑ 17016	Invisible People/Flash	1967	3.75	7.50	15.00

Albums
DOT

Number	Title (A Side/B Side)	Yr	VG	VG+	NM
❑ DLP-25939	Hamilton Streetcar	1969	6.25	12.50	25.00

HAMLISCH, MARVIN
45s
A&M

Number	Title (A Side/B Side)	Yr	VG	VG+	NM
❑ 1775	All I Needed Was the Laughter/ If You Hadn't Left Me Crying	1975	—	2.00	4.00

ARISTA

Number	Title (A Side/B Side)	Yr	VG	VG+	NM
❑ 0392	Theme from "Ice Castles"/Touch	1979	—	2.00	4.00

MCA

Number	Title (A Side/B Side)	Yr	VG	VG+	NM
❑ 40174	The Entertainer/Solace	1974	—	2.50	5.00
❑ 40307	Maple Leaf Rag/Mexican Dreams	1974	—	2.00	4.00
❑ 52175	The Entertainer/Heliotrope Bouquet	1983	—	2.00	4.00

—B-side by Lalo Schifrin
PLANET

Number	Title (A Side/B Side)	Yr	VG	VG+	NM
❑ 45922 [DJ]	Theme from "Ordinary People" (same on both sides)	1980	—	2.00	4.00

UNITED ARTISTS

Number	Title (A Side/B Side)	Yr	VG	VG+	NM
❑ XW1082	Bond '77 — James Bond Theme (Part 1)/Bond '77 — James Bond Theme (Part 2)	1977	—	2.00	4.00
❑ 50798	Bananas/'Cause I Believe in Loving	1971	—	2.50	5.00

Albums
MCA

Number	Title (A Side/B Side)	Yr	VG	VG+	NM
❑ 390	The Sting	1973	2.50	5.00	10.00
❑ 2115	The Entertainer	1974	2.50	5.00	10.00
❑ 37091	The Sting	198?	2.00	4.00	8.00

—Budget-line reissue

HAMMER
Albums
SAN FRANCISCO

Number	Title (A Side/B Side)	Yr	VG	VG+	NM
❑ SD 203	Hammer	1970	5.00	10.00	20.00

HAMMILL, PETER Also see VAN DER GRAAF GENERATOR.
Albums
CHARISMA

Number	Title (A Side/B Side)	Yr	VG	VG+	NM
❑ CAS-1037	Fool's Mate	1972	3.75	7.50	15.00
❑ CH-1-2202	The Future Now	1978	3.00	6.00	12.00
❑ CH-1-2205	PH 7	1979	3.00	6.00	12.00

ENIGMA

Number	Title (A Side/B Side)	Yr	VG	VG+	NM
❑ ST-73206	Skin	1986	2.50	5.00	10.00
❑ ST-73246	And Close As This	1987	2.50	5.00	10.00

PVC

Number	Title (A Side/B Side)	Yr	VG	VG+	NM
❑ 8902	Sitting Targets	1981	3.00	6.00	12.00

HAMMOND, ALBERT
45s
COLUMBIA

Number	Title (A Side/B Side)	Yr	VG	VG+	NM
❑ 02470	Memories/I Want You Back with Me	1981	—	2.00	4.00
❑ 03412	Before You Change the World/ Somewhere in America	1982	—	2.00	4.00
❑ 60510	When I'm Gone/World of Love	1981	—	2.00	4.00

EPIC

Number	Title (A Side/B Side)	Yr	VG	VG+	NM
❑ 50277	Moonlight Lady/Cry Baby	1976	—	2.00	4.00

MUMS

Number	Title (A Side/B Side)	Yr	VG	VG+	NM
❑ 6009	Down by the River/The Last One to Know	1972	—	2.00	4.00
❑ 6011	It Never Rains in Southern California/Anyone Here in the Audience	1972	—	2.50	5.00

—Bizarrely, the stock copy is in rechanneled stereo

Number	Title (A Side/B Side)	Yr	VG	VG+	NM
❑ 6015	If You Gotta Break Another Heart/That Old American Dream	1973	—	2.00	4.00
❑ 6018	The Free Electric Band/ You Taught Me to Sing the Blues	1973	—	2.00	4.00
❑ 6021	The Peacemaker/Who's for Lunch Today	1973	—	2.00	4.00
❑ 6024	Half a Million Miles from Home/ I Think I'll Go That Way	1973	—	2.00	4.00
❑ 6026	I'm a Train/Brand New Day	1974	—	2.00	4.00
❑ 6030	Air Disaster/Candlelight, Sweet Candlelight	1974	—	2.00	4.00
❑ 6032	Fountain Avenue/ Names, Tags, Numbers, Labels	1974	—	2.00	4.00
❑ 6037	99 Miles from L.A./Rivers Are for Boats	1975	—	2.00	4.00

Albums
COLUMBIA

Number	Title (A Side/B Side)	Yr	VG	VG+	NM
❑ JC 36964	Your World and My World	1981	2.50	5.00	10.00
❑ FC 38181	Somewhere in America	1982	2.50	5.00	10.00

EPIC

Number	Title (A Side/B Side)	Yr	VG	VG+	NM
❑ JE 35049	When I Need You	1977	2.50	5.00	10.00

MUMS

Number	Title (A Side/B Side)	Yr	VG	VG+	NM
❑ KZ 31905	It Never Rains in Southern California	1972	2.50	5.00	10.00
❑ KZ 32267	The Free Electric Band	1973	2.50	5.00	10.00
❑ KZ 32834	Albert Hammond	1974	2.50	5.00	10.00

HAMMOND, JOHN
45s
ATLANTIC

Number	Title (A Side/B Side)	Yr	VG	VG+	NM
❑ 2696	I'm Tore Down/Shake for Me	1969	2.00	4.00	8.00

COLUMBIA

Number	Title (A Side/B Side)	Yr	VG	VG+	NM
❑ 45372	As the Years Go Passing By/Mellow Down Easy	1971	—	3.00	6.00

POINTBLANK/VIRGIN

Number	Title (A Side/B Side)	Yr	VG	VG+	NM
❑ 38775	Heartattack and Vine/2:19	2001	—	2.00	4.00

RED BIRD

Number	Title (A Side/B Side)	Yr	VG	VG+	NM
❑ 10-047	I Wish You Would/I Can Tell	1966	5.00	10.00	20.00

Albums
ATLANTIC

Number	Title (A Side/B Side)	Yr	VG	VG+	NM
❑ 8152 [M]	I Can Tell	1967	7.50	15.00	30.00
❑ SD 8152 [S]	I Can Tell	1967	7.50	15.00	30.00
❑ SD 8206	Sooner or Later	1968	3.75	7.50	15.00
❑ SD 8251	Southern Fried	1969	3.75	7.50	15.00

CAPRICORN

Number	Title (A Side/B Side)	Yr	VG	VG+	NM
❑ CP 0153	Can't Beat the Kid	1975	3.00	6.00	12.00

COLUMBIA

Number	Title (A Side/B Side)	Yr	VG	VG+	NM
❑ C 30458	Source Point	1971	3.00	6.00	12.00
❑ KC 31318	I'm Satisfied	1972	3.00	6.00	12.00

FLYING FISH

Number	Title (A Side/B Side)	Yr	VG	VG+	NM
❑ FF-502	Nobody But You	1988	2.50	5.00	10.00

ROUNDER

Number	Title (A Side/B Side)	Yr	VG	VG+	NM
❑ 3042	Mileage	1980	2.50	5.00	10.00
❑ 3060	Frogs for Snakes	1982	2.50	5.00	10.00
❑ 3074	John Hammond Live	1984	2.50	5.00	10.00

VANGUARD

Number	Title (A Side/B Side)	Yr	VG	VG+	NM
❑ VSD 11/12 [(2)]	The Best of John Hammond	1970	3.75	7.50	15.00
❑ VSD-2148 [S]	John Hammond	1964	10.00	20.00	40.00
❑ VRS-9132 [M]	John Hammond	1964	7.50	15.00	30.00
❑ VRS-9153 [M]	Big City Blues	1964	7.50	15.00	30.00
❑ VRS-9178 [M]	So Many Roads	1965	7.50	15.00	30.00
❑ VRS-9198 [M]	Country Blues	1966	7.50	15.00	30.00
❑ VRS-9245 [M]	Mirrors	1967	7.50	15.00	30.00
❑ VSD-79153 [S]	Big City Blues	1964	10.00	20.00	40.00
❑ VSD-79178 [S]	So Many Roads	1965	10.00	20.00	40.00
❑ VSD-79198 [S]	Country Blues	1966	10.00	20.00	40.00
❑ VSD-79245 [S]	Mirrors	1967	7.50	15.00	30.00
❑ VSD-79380	Solo	1976	2.50	5.00	10.00
❑ VSD-79400	Footwork	1978	2.50	5.00	10.00
❑ VSD-79424	Hot Tracks	1979	2.50	5.00	10.00

HAMMOND-HAZLEWOOD Also see ALBERT HAMMOND.
45s
CAPITOL

Number	Title (A Side/B Side)	Yr	VG	VG+	NM
❑ 2616	Wendy, Wendy/Broken Hearts Brigade	1969	2.50	5.00	10.00

HAMPTON, JOHN
45s
UNITED

Number	Title (A Side/B Side)	Yr	VG	VG+	NM
❑ 210	Honey Hush/Shadow Blues	1958	30.00	60.00	120.00

HANDS OF TIME, THE
45s
SIDEWALK

Number	Title (A Side/B Side)	Yr	VG	VG+	NM
❑ 903	Got to Get You Into My Life/Midnight Rider	1966	7.50	15.00	30.00

HANDY, WAYNE
45s
DIAL

Number	Title (A Side/B Side)	Yr	VG	VG+	NM
❑ 3002	Conscience Let Me Go/Pain Reliever	1961	3.00	6.00	12.00

RENOWN

Number	Title (A Side/B Side)	Yr	VG	VG+	NM
❑ 102	Say Yeah/Could It Be	195?	5.00	10.00	20.00
❑ 104	Betcha Didn't Know/Don't Be Unfair	195?	5.00	10.00	20.00
❑ 107	Problem Child/I'll Never Be the Same	195?	5.00	10.00	20.00

TREND

Number	Title (A Side/B Side)	Yr	VG	VG+	NM
❑ 30006	Betcha Didn't Know/Don't Be Unfair	195?	6.25	12.50	25.00
❑ 30015	Seminole Rock 'n' Roll/ I Think You Oughta Love Again	195?	6.25	12.50	25.00

HANEY, JACK, AND NIKITER ARMSTRONG
45s
MEL-O-DY

Number	Title (A Side/B Side)	Yr	VG	VG+	NM
❑ 107	The Interview/Peaceful	1963	5.00	10.00	20.00

HANGMEN, THE
45s
MONUMENT

Number	Title (A Side/B Side)	Yr	VG	VG+	NM
❑ 910	What a Girl Can't Do/The Girl Who Faded Away	1965	5.00	10.00	20.00
❑ 951	Faces/Bad Goodbye	1966	5.00	10.00	20.00

Albums
MONUMENT

Number	Title (A Side/B Side)	Yr	VG	VG+	NM
❑ MLP-8077 [M]	Bitter Sweet	1967	7.50	15.00	30.00
❑ SLP-18077 [S]	Bitter Sweet	1967	10.00	20.00	40.00

HANK AND CAROLEE
45s
MALA

Number	Title (A Side/B Side)	Yr	VG	VG+	NM
❑ 424	Go On and Go/I've Never Known	1960	10.00	20.00	40.00

HANK'S HOUNDS
45s
HIT

Number	Title (A Side/B Side)	Yr	VG	VG+	NM
❑ 223	Just a Little Bit Better/Catch Us If You Can	1965	3.00	6.00	12.00

—B-side by the Jalopy Five

HANNAN, JIMMY
45s
ATLANTIC

Number	Title (A Side/B Side)	Yr	VG	VG+	NM
❑ 2247	Beach Ball/You Gotta Have Love	1964	37.50	75.00	150.00

—Backing Hannan on this record are THE BEE GEES, three years before their first American release!

Number	Title (A Side/B Side)	Yr	VG	VG+	NM

HANS CHRISTIAN With Jon Anderson, pre-YES.
45s
TOWER
| ❑ 409 | Never My Love/All of the Time | 1968 | 25.00 | 50.00 | 100.00 |

HANSON
45s
MANTICORE
| ❑ 2001 | Love Knows Everything/(B-side unknown) | 1973 | — | 3.00 | 6.00 |
| ❑ 2004 | Boy Meets Girl/Modern Day Religion | 1973 | — | 3.00 | 6.00 |
Albums
MANTICORE
| ❑ MC 66670 | Now Hear This | 1973 | 3.00 | 6.00 | 12.00 |
| ❑ MC 66672 | Magic Dragon | 1974 | 2.50 | 5.00 | 10.00 |

HANSSON, BO
45s
CHARISMA
| ❑ 104 | The Black Riders/Flight to the Ford//(B-side unknown) | 1973 | 2.50 | 5.00 | 10.00 |
Albums
CHARISMA
| ❑ CAS-1059 | Lord of the Rings | 1973 | 3.00 | 6.00 | 12.00 |
| ❑ FC 6062 | Magician's Hat | 1974 | 3.00 | 6.00 | 12.00 |
SIRE
| ❑ SR 6044 | Music Inspired by Watership Down | 1977 | 2.50 | 5.00 | 10.00 |
| ❑ SASD-7525 | Attic Thoughts | 1976 | 2.50 | 5.00 | 10.00 |

HAPPENINGS, THE Also see BOB MIRANDA; THE TOKENS.
45s
B.T. PUPPY
❑ 181 [DJ]	Have Yourself a Merry Little Christmas (same on both sides)	1966	7.50	15.00	30.00
—Stock copies do not exist					
❑ 517	Girls on the Go/Go-Go	1966	2.50	5.00	10.00
❑ 520	See You in September/He Thinks He's a Hero	1966	2.50	5.00	10.00
❑ 522	Go Away Little Girl/Tea Time	1966	2.00	4.00	8.00
❑ 523	Goodnight My Love/Lillies By Money	1966	2.00	4.00	8.00
❑ 527	I Got Rhythm/You're in a Bad Way	1967	2.00	4.00	8.00
❑ 530	My Mammy/I Believe in Nothing	1967	2.00	4.00	8.00
❑ 530 [PS]	My Mammy/I Believe in Nothing	1967	3.75	7.50	15.00
❑ 532	Why Do Fools Fall in Love/ When the Summer Is Through	1967	2.00	4.00	8.00
❑ 532 [PS]	Why Do Fools Fall in Love/ When the Summer Is Through	1967	3.75	7.50	15.00
❑ 538	Music, Music, Music/When I Lock My Door	1968	2.00	4.00	8.00
❑ 538 [PS]	Music, Music, Music/When I Lock My Door	1968	3.75	7.50	15.00
❑ 540	Randy/Love Song of Mommy and Daddy	1968	2.00	4.00	8.00
❑ 542	Sealed with a Kiss/Anyway	1968	2.00	4.00	8.00
❑ 543	Breaking Up Is Hard to Do/Anyway	1968	2.00	4.00	8.00
❑ 545	Crazy Rhythm/Love Song of Mommy and Daddy	1968	2.00	4.00	8.00
❑ 549	That's All I Want from You/He Thinks He's a Hero	1968	2.00	4.00	8.00
BIG TREE
❑ 146	Strawberry Morning/ Workin' My Way Back to You	1972	—	2.00	4.00
❑ 153	Me Without You/God Bless Joanna	1972	—	2.00	4.00
JUBILEE
❑ 5666	Where Do I Go and Be In/New Day Comin'	1969	—	3.00	6.00
❑ 5677	El Paso County Jail/Won't Anybody Listen	1969	—	3.00	6.00
❑ 5686	Answer Me, My Love/I Need a Woman	1970	—	3.00	6.00
❑ 5698	Tomorrow, Today Will Be Yesterday/ Chain of Hands	1970	—	3.00	6.00
❑ 5702	Crazy Love/Chain of Hands	1970	—	3.00	6.00
❑ 5703	Condition Red/Sweet September	1970	2.50	5.00	10.00
—As "The Honor Society"					
❑ 5712	Lullaby in the Rain/I Wish You Could Know Me (Naomi)	1971	—	3.00	6.00
❑ 5721 [DJ]	Make Your Own Kind of Music (mono/stereo)	1971	—	3.00	6.00
—Stock copies may not exist					
MIDLAND INT'L.
❑ MB-10897	That's Why I Love You/Beyond the Hurt	1977	—	2.00	4.00
❑ MB-11127	Let Me Stay/Someone Special	1977	—	2.00	4.00
PHILCO-FORD
❑ HP-7	Go Away Little Girl/See You in September	1967	5.00	10.00	20.00
—4-inch plastic "Hip Pocket Record" with color sleeve					
Albums
B.T. PUPPY
❑ BTP-1001 [M]	The Happenings (Bye-Bye, So Long, Farewell…See You in September)	1966	6.25	12.50	25.00
❑ BTS-1001 [S]	The Happenings (Bye-Bye, So Long, Farewell…See You in September)	1966	7.50	15.00	30.00
❑ BT-1003 [M]	Psycle	1967	6.25	12.50	25.00
❑ BTS-1003 [S]	Psycle	1967	7.50	15.00	30.00
❑ BTS-1004	The Happenings Golden Hits!	1968	10.00	20.00	40.00
JUBILEE
❑ JGS-8028	Piece of Mind	1969	6.25	12.50	25.00
❑ JGS-8030	The Happenings' Greatest Hits	1969	6.25	12.50	25.00

HAPPY OTTO See CRAZY OTTO.

HAPSHASH AND THE COLOURED COAT
Albums
IMPERIAL
❑ LP-9377 [M]	Hapshash and the Coloured Coat	1968	12.50	25.00	50.00
❑ LP-12377 [S]	Hapshash and the Coloured Coat	1968	10.00	20.00	40.00
❑ LP-12430	Western Flyer	1969	10.00	20.00	40.00

HARBOR LIGHTS, THE Early JAY AND THE AMERICANS.
45s
JARO
| ❑ 77020 | Is That Too Much to Ask/ What Would I Do Without You | 1960 | 10.00 | 20.00 | 40.00 |
MALA
| ❑ 422 | Angel of Love/Tick-a-Tick-a-Tock | 1960 | 12.50 | 25.00 | 50.00 |

HARBOUR LITES, THE
45s
FONTANA
| ❑ 1544 | Run for Your Life/Lonely Journey | 1966 | 2.50 | 5.00 | 10.00 |

HARD, RANDY
45s
NRC
| ❑ 013 | Honey Doll/May It Be My Fortune | 1959 | 15.00 | 30.00 | 60.00 |
| ❑ 044 | Let Her Go/Make Me a Dreamer | 1959 | 12.50 | 25.00 | 50.00 |

HARD MEAT
Albums
WARNER BROS.
| ❑ WS 1852 | Hard Meat | 1969 | 3.75 | 7.50 | 15.00 |
| ❑ WS 1879 | Through a Window | 1970 | 3.75 | 7.50 | 15.00 |

HARD TIMES, THE
45s
WORLD PACIFIC
❑ 77816	There'll Be a Time/You're Bound to Cry	1966	2.50	5.00	10.00
❑ 77826	Come To Your Window/That's All I'll Do	1966	2.50	5.00	10.00
❑ 77851	Fortune Teller/Good-By	1966	2.50	5.00	10.00
❑ 77873	Blew Mind/Colours	1967	2.50	5.00	10.00
Albums
WORLD PACIFIC
| ❑ WP-1867 [M] | Blew Mind | 1968 | 6.25 | 12.50 | 25.00 |
| ❑ WPS-21867 [S] | Blew Mind | 1968 | 7.50 | 15.00 | 30.00 |

HARDEN TRIO, THE
45s
COLUMBIA
❑ 43229	Poor Boy/Let It Be Me	1965	2.00	4.00	8.00
❑ 43463	Tippy Toeing/Don't Remind Me	1965	2.00	4.00	8.00
❑ 43710	Little Boy Walk Like a Man/Dear Brother	1966	—	3.00	6.00
❑ 43844	Seven Days of Crying (Makes One Weak)/ Husbands and Wives	1966	—	3.00	6.00
❑ 44059	Sneaking 'Cross the Border/Childhood Place	1967	—	3.00	6.00
❑ 44249	Forbidden/Manana (Is Soon Enough for Me)	1967	—	3.00	6.00
❑ 44420	He Looks a Lot Like You/My Friend Mr. Echo	1968	—	2.50	5.00
❑ 44552	Everybody Wants to Be Somebody Else/Diddle Diddle Dumplin'	1968	—	2.50	5.00
Albums
COLUMBIA
| ❑ CL 2506 [M] | Tippy Toeing | 1966 | 5.00 | 10.00 | 20.00 |
| ❑ CS 9306 [S] | Tippy Toeing | 1966 | 6.25 | 12.50 | 25.00 |

HARDIN, ED
45s
HIT
❑ 02	Good Luck Charm/Slow Twistin'	1962	2.00	4.00	8.00
—B-side by Herbert Hunter					
❑ 03	Young World/Lover Please	1962	2.00	4.00	8.00
—B-side by Herbert Hunter					
❑ 13	Follow That Dream/Lovers Who Wander	1962	2.00	4.00	8.00
❑ 33	Only Love Can Break a Heart/Do You Love Me	1962	2.00	4.00	8.00
—B-side by Leroy Jones					
❑ 35	Return to Sender/Don't Go Near the Indians	1962	2.00	4.00	8.00
—B-side by Sandy Carmichael					
❑ 44	Love Came to Me/Everybody Loves a Lover	1962	2.00	4.00	8.00
—B-side by Alpha Zoe					
❑ 54	One Broken Heart for Sale/Let's Turkey Trot	1963	2.00	4.00	8.00
—B-side by Alpha Zoe					
❑ 87	Donna the Prima Donna/Washington Square	1963	2.00	4.00	8.00
—B-side by the Music City Five & Ten					
❑ 98	Drip Drop/Midnight Mary	1963	2.00	4.00	8.00
—B-side by Ricky Dickens					
❑ 103	For You/Um, Um, Um, Um, Um, Um	1964	2.00	4.00	8.00
—B-side by Thomas Henry					
❑ 112	Suspicion/Don't Let the Rain Come Down	1964	2.00	4.00	8.00
—B-side by the Music City Singers					
❑ 117	Little Children/My Guy	1964	2.00	4.00	8.00
—B-side by Clara Wilson					
❑ 130	Memphis/Bad to Me	1964	2.00	4.00	8.00
❑ 138	Such a Night/And I Love Her	1964	2.50	5.00	10.00
—B-side by the Jalopy Five					
❑ 142	Oh Pretty Woman/ Broken Hearted, Sad and Blue	1964	2.00	4.00	8.00
❑ 149	That's All That's Important Now/From a Window	1964	2.00	4.00	8.00
❑ 157	Ask Me/Pay It No Mind	1964	2.00	4.00	8.00
—B-side by Fred York					
❑ 175	My World's a Blue World/ Don't Forget I Still Love You	1965	2.00	4.00	8.00
—B-side by Shari Baker					
❑ 190	True Love You Can't Buy/You've Lost That Lovin' Feelin'	1965	2.00	4.00	8.00
—B-side by Wayne Harris					
❑ 199	Goodnight/Hearts Are Funny Things	1965	2.00	4.00	8.00
—B-side by Bobby Brooks					
❑ 211	Game of Love/One Fine Day	1965	2.00	4.00	8.00
❑ 219	Down in the Boondocks/What's New Pussycat?	1965	2.00	4.00	8.00
—B-side by Bobby Brooks					
❑ 245	It's Too Late/Nowhere Man	1966	3.00	6.00	12.00
—B-side by the Jalopy Five					
❑ 247	Sure Gonna Miss Her/The Cheater	1966	2.00	4.00	8.00
—B-side by the Chellows					
❑ 256	Green Grass/A Groovy Kind of Love	1966	2.00	4.00	8.00
—B-side by the Chords (2)					
❑ 261	Love Letters/Sweet Pea	1966	2.00	4.00	8.00
❑ 268	See See Rider/Psychotic Reaction	1966	2.00	4.00	8.00
—As "Ed Hardin and the Cadets"; B-side by the Jalopy Five					
❑ 279	Good Thing/Tell It Like It Is	1967	2.00	4.00	8.00
—As "Ed Hardin and the Cadets"; B-side by Leroy Jones					
❑ 280	Green, Green Grass of Home/ Mercy, Mercy, Mercy	1967	2.00	4.00	8.00
—B-side by the New Society Group					

Number	Title (A Side/B Side)	Yr	VG	VG+	NM
❑ 282	Baby I Need Your Lovin'/Pretty Ballerina	1967	2.00	4.00	8.00
—B-side by the Chords (2)					
❑ 285	Detroit City/A Little Bit Me, A Little Bit You	1967	2.00	4.00	8.00
—B-side by the Jalopy Five					
❑ 294	Release Me/Mirage	1967	2.00	4.00	8.00
—B-side by the Chords (2)					
❑ 315	By the Time I Get to Phoenix/Daydream Believer	1967	2.00	4.00	8.00
—B-side by the Jalopy Five					
❑ 320	The Ballad of Bonnie and Clyde/Honey	1968	2.00	4.00	8.00
—B-side by Bobby Sims					
❑ 329	I Wanna Live/Mony Mony	1968	2.00	4.00	8.00
—B-side by the Fantastics					
❑ 349	Hold Me Tight/Abraham, Martin and John	1968	2.00	4.00	8.00
—B-side by Joe Smith					

HARDIN, RETT
45s
HIT

Number	Title (A Side/B Side)	Yr	VG	VG+	NM
❑ 52	You're the Reason I'm Living/Ruby Baby	1963	2.00	4.00	8.00
—B-side by Larry Dexter					

HARDIN, TIM
45s
COLUMBIA

Number	Title (A Side/B Side)	Yr	VG	VG+	NM
❑ 44879	Once-Touched by Flame/A Question of Birth	1969	—	3.00	6.00
❑ 44920	Simple Song of Freedom/A Question of Birth	1969	—	3.00	6.00
❑ 45426	Bird on the Wire/Soft Summer Breeze	1971	—	2.50	5.00
❑ 45695	Do the Do/Sweet Lady	1972	—	2.50	5.00
VERVE FOLKWAYS					
❑ 5008	Hang On to a Dream/It'll Never Happen Again	1966	2.50	5.00	10.00
❑ 5017	Misty Roses/Don't Make Promises	1966	2.50	5.00	10.00
❑ 5031	If I Were a Carpenter/Hang On to a Dream	1966	2.50	5.00	10.00
❑ 5042	Green Rocky Road/Never Too Far	1967	2.00	4.00	8.00
❑ 5048	Black Sheep Boy/Misty Roses	1967	2.00	4.00	8.00
VERVE FORECAST					
❑ 5059	Tribute to Hank Williams/You Upset the Grace of Living When You Die	1967	—	3.00	6.00
❑ 5097	Reason to Believe/Smugglin' Man	1968	—	3.00	6.00
❑ 5116	Reason to Believe/Smugglin' Man	1971	—	2.50	5.00
Albums					
ANTILLES					
❑ 7023	Nine	1974	3.75	7.50	15.00
ATCO					
❑ 33-210 [M]	This Is Tim Hardin	1967	6.25	12.50	25.00
❑ SD 33-210 [R]	This Is Tim Hardin	1967	3.75	7.50	15.00
COLUMBIA					
❑ CS 9787	Suite for Susan Moore and Damion — We Are One, One, All in One	1969	6.25	12.50	25.00
—"360 Sound" label					
❑ C 30551	Bird on a Wire	1971	5.00	10.00	20.00
❑ KC 31764	Painted Head	1972	5.00	10.00	20.00
❑ PC 37164	The Shock of Grace	1981	3.00	6.00	12.00
MGM					
❑ GAS-104	Tim Hardin (Golden Archive Series)	1970	5.00	10.00	20.00
❑ M3G-4952	Archetypes	1974	3.75	7.50	15.00
POLYDOR					
❑ PD-1-6333	Memorial Album	1981	3.00	6.00	12.00
VERVE FOLKWAYS					
❑ FT-3004 [M]	Tim Hardin/1	1966	6.25	12.50	25.00
❑ FTS-3004 [S]	Tim Hardin/1	1966	7.50	15.00	30.00
VERVE FORECAST					
❑ FT-3004 [M]	Tim Hardin/1	1967	3.75	7.50	15.00
❑ FTS-3004 [S]	Tim Hardin/1	1967	5.00	10.00	20.00
❑ FTS-3022	Tim Hardin/2	1967	6.25	12.50	25.00
❑ FTS-3049	Tim Hardin/3 — Live in Concert	1968	6.25	12.50	25.00
❑ FTS-3064	Tim Hardin/4	1969	6.25	12.50	25.00
❑ FTS-3078	The Best of Tim Hardin	1970	5.00	10.00	20.00

HARDLY WORTHIT PLAYERS, THE See SENATOR BOBBY.

HARDWATER
45s
CAPITOL

Number	Title (A Side/B Side)	Yr	VG	VG+	NM
❑ 2230	Not So Hard/City Sidewalks	1968	3.00	6.00	12.00
Albums					
CAPITOL					
❑ ST-2954	Hardwater	1968	10.00	20.00	40.00

HARDY, FRANCOISE
45s
4 CORNERS OF THE WORLD

Number	Title (A Side/B Side)	Yr	VG	VG+	NM
❑ 103	Catch a Falling Star/Find Me a Boy	196?	2.50	5.00	10.00
❑ 123	How Ever Much/Only You Can Do It	196?	2.50	5.00	10.00
❑ 125	All Over the World/Another Place	196?	2.50	5.00	10.00
❑ 132	The Love of a Boy/Just Call and I'll Be There	196?	2.50	5.00	10.00
REPRISE					
❑ 0808	Loving You/Hang On to a Dream	1969	2.00	4.00	8.00
Albums					
4 CORNERS OF THE WORLD					
❑ FCL-4208 [M]	The "Yeh Yeh" Girl from Paris!	196?	5.00	10.00	20.00
❑ FCS-4208 [S]	The "Yeh Yeh" Girl from Paris!	196?	6.25	12.50	25.00
❑ FCL-4219 [M]	Maid in Paris	196?	5.00	10.00	20.00
❑ FCS-4219 [S]	Maid in Paris	196?	6.25	12.50	25.00
❑ FCL-4231 [M]	Francoise...	196?	5.00	10.00	20.00
❑ FCS-4231 [S]	Francoise...	196?	6.25	12.50	25.00
❑ FCL-4238 [M]	Je Vous Aime	196?	5.00	10.00	20.00
❑ FCS-4238 [S]	Je Vous Aime	196?	6.25	12.50	25.00
❑ FCS-4255 [S]	The Best of Francoise Hardy	196?	5.00	10.00	20.00
REPRISE					
❑ RS 6290	Francoise Hardy	1968	6.25	12.50	25.00
❑ RS 6318	Loving	1969	5.00	10.00	20.00
❑ RS 6345	Mon Amour, Adieu	1969	5.00	10.00	20.00

HARDY, HAGOOD
45s
CAPITOL

Number	Title (A Side/B Side)	Yr	VG	VG+	NM
❑ 4156	The Homecoming/The Queen	1975	—	2.00	4.00
❑ 4292	The Missouri Breaks/Afternoon in Venice	1976	—	2.00	4.00

HERITAGE

Number	Title (A Side/B Side)	Yr	VG	VG+	NM
❑ 833	I'll Take Love/Just a Little Lovin'	1971	—	2.50	5.00
Albums					
CAPITOL					
❑ ST-11488	The Homecoming	1975	2.50	5.00	10.00
❑ ST-11552	Maybe Tomorrow	1976	2.50	5.00	10.00
❑ SN-16300	The Homecoming	198?	2.00	4.00	8.00
—Budget-line reissue					

HARDY BOYS, THE
45s
RCA VICTOR

Number	Title (A Side/B Side)	Yr	VG	VG+	NM
❑ 47-9795	Wheels/Sha-La-La	1969	2.00	4.00	8.00
❑ 47-9831	Good, Good Lovin'/Love Train	1970	2.00	4.00	8.00
❑ 74-0228	Love and Let Love/Sink or Swim	1969	2.00	4.00	8.00
Albums					
RCA VICTOR					
❑ LSP-4217	Here Come the Hardy Boys	1969	5.00	10.00	20.00
❑ LSP-4315	Wheels	1970	5.00	10.00	20.00

HARGETT, JOHNNIE
45s
CHERRY

Number	Title (A Side/B Side)	Yr	VG	VG+	NM
❑ 1016	Rock This Town Tonight/God's Gift to Men	1960	25.00	50.00	100.00

HARGRAVE, RON
45s
CUB

Number	Title (A Side/B Side)	Yr	VG	VG+	NM
❑ 9025	Drive-In Movie/Buttercup	1959	3.00	6.00	12.00
MGM					
❑ 12344	A Fool Am I/Too Late	1956	5.00	10.00	20.00
❑ 12422	Latch On/Only a Daydream	1957	10.00	20.00	40.00
❑ 12475	Hold Me/Song of the Moonlight	1957	5.00	10.00	20.00
❑ 12571	If You Should Go/Heartbreaker	1957	5.00	10.00	20.00
❑ 12644	Young Romance/Should Have Been Home in Bed	1958	5.00	10.00	20.00

HARLAN, BILLY
45s
BRUNSWICK

Number	Title (A Side/B Side)	Yr	VG	VG+	NM
❑ 55066	I Wanna Bop/School House Rock	1958	50.00	100.00	200.00

HARMONAIRES, THE
45s
HOLIDAY

Number	Title (A Side/B Side)	Yr	VG	VG+	NM
❑ 2602	Come Back/Lorraine	1957	75.00	150.00	300.00
—Black label					
❑ 2602	Come Back/Lorraine	196?	6.25	12.50	25.00
—Red label, single horizontal line					
❑ 2602	Come Back/Lorraine	1960	15.00	30.00	60.00
—Red label, double horizontal lines					
LOST-NITE					
❑ 181	Come Back/Lorraine	196?	—	3.00	6.00
—Reissue					

HARMONICA FRANK
45s
SUN

Number	Title (A Side/B Side)	Yr	VG	VG+	NM
❑ 205	Rockin' Chair Daddy/The Great Musical Menagerist	1954	1500.	3000.	4500.

HARMONY GRITS, THE Members of the original DRIFTERS formed this group after their firing.
45s
END

Number	Title (A Side/B Side)	Yr	VG	VG+	NM
❑ 1051	Am I to Be the One/I Could Have Told You	1959	6.25	12.50	25.00
❑ 1063	Gee/I Could Have Told You	1959	6.25	12.50	25.00
❑ 1063	Gee/Santa Claus Is Coming to Town	1959	10.00	20.00	40.00

HARNELL, JOE
45s
COLUMBIA

Number	Title (A Side/B Side)	Yr	VG	VG+	NM
❑ 43549	Autumn Leaves/Near You	1966	—	2.50	5.00
❑ 43756	Our Concerto/Meeskeit	1966	—	2.50	5.00
❑ 43756 [DJ]	Our Concerto (same on both sides)	1966	3.75	7.50	15.00
—Promo only on red vinyl					
❑ 43902	Nature Boy/Bermuda Concerto	1966	—	2.50	5.00
❑ 44148	Un Poco Rio/Sunrise Serenade	1967	—	2.50	5.00
❑ 44244	Guantanamera/Seranata	1967	—	2.50	5.00
❑ 44365	Blame It on the Bossa Nova/So Soon	1967	—	2.50	5.00
❑ 44407	Theme to Candice/Spanish Eyes	1967	—	2.50	5.00
❑ 44571	The Mighty Quinn/Simon Says	1968	—	2.50	5.00
❑ 44670	Sky Hawk/Work Sunny Work	1968	—	2.50	5.00
EPIC					
❑ 9304	The Way of Love/You Are the Song	1959	2.50	5.00	10.00
❑ 9328	What Is This Thing Called Love/My Little Grass Shack in Kealakekua, Hawaii	1959	2.50	5.00	10.00
❑ 9406	Time on My Hands/Without a Song	1960	2.00	4.00	8.00
KAPP					
❑ 497	Fly Me to the Moon Bossa Nova/Harlem Nocturne	1962	2.00	4.00	8.00
❑ 521	Diane/Walking Song	1963	—	3.00	6.00
❑ 528	Our Day Will Come/My One and Only Love	1963	—	3.00	6.00
❑ 541	Hud/Come Away with Me	1963	—	3.00	6.00
❑ 562	Dawn of Love/Who Am I Kiddin'	1963	—	3.00	6.00
❑ 579	You're Nobody Till Somebody Loves You/When the World Was Young	1964	—	3.00	6.00
❑ 604	Sonata Portuguese/I'll Set My Love to Music	1964	—	3.00	6.00
❑ 633	St. Thomas/Ill Wind	1964	—	3.00	6.00
MCA					
❑ 40953	Theme from "The Incredible Hulk"/Love Theme from "The Incredible Hulk"	1978	—	2.50	5.00
MOTOWN					
❑ 1154	Midnight Cowboy/Green Grow the Lilacs	1969	—	3.00	6.00
❑ 1161	My Cherie Amour/Green Grow the Lilacs	1970	—	3.00	6.00
Albums					
CAPITOL					
❑ ST-11657	Harnell	1977	3.00	6.00	12.00

Number	Title (A Side/B Side)	Yr	VG	VG+	NM
COLUMBIA					
❑ CL 2466 [M]	Golden Piano Hits	1966	3.00	6.00	12.00
❑ CL 2699 [M]	Bossa Now	1967	3.75	7.50	15.00
❑ CS 9266 [S]	Golden Piano Hits	1966	3.75	7.50	15.00
❑ CS 9499 [S]	Bossa Now	1967	3.00	6.00	12.00
EPIC					
❑ LN (# unknown) [M]	I Want to Be Happy	1960	3.75	7.50	15.00
❑ BN 573 [S]	I Want to Be Happy	1960	5.00	10.00	20.00
JUBILEE					
❑ JLP-1015 [M]	Piano Inventions of Jo Harnell	1956	12.50	25.00	50.00
❑ JGM-5020 [M]	Joe Harnell and His Trio	1963	3.75	7.50	15.00
—Reissue of 1015					
KAPP					
❑ KL 1318 [M]	Fly Me to the Moon and the Bossa Nova Pops	1962	3.75	7.50	15.00
❑ KL 1325 [M]	More Joe Harnell, More Bossa Nova Pops	1963	3.75	7.50	15.00
❑ KL 1339 [M]	Joe Harnell	1963	3.75	7.50	15.00
❑ KL 1416 [M]	The Rhythm and the Fire	1965	3.00	6.00	12.00
❑ KL 1480 [M]	The Best of Joe Harnell	1966	3.00	6.00	12.00
❑ KS 3318 [S]	Fly Me to the Moon and the Bossa Nova Pops	1962	5.00	10.00	20.00
❑ KS 3325 [S]	More Joe Harnell, More Bossa Nova Pops	1963	5.00	10.00	20.00
❑ KS 3339 [S]	Joe Harnell	1963	5.00	10.00	20.00
❑ KS 3416 [S]	The Rhythm and the Fire	1965	3.75	7.50	15.00
❑ KS 3480 [S]	The Best of Joe Harnell	1966	3.75	7.50	15.00
MOTOWN					
❑ MS-698	Moving On!!	1969	10.00	20.00	40.00

HARNER, BILLY
45s

Number	Title (A Side/B Side)	Yr	VG	VG+	NM
ATLANTIC					
❑ 2351	A Message to My Babe/Everything's Hunky-Dory	1966	3.00	6.00	12.00
KAMA SUTRA					
❑ 226	Sally Sayin' Somethin'/Don't Want My Lovin'	1967	3.00	6.00	12.00
❑ 238	Homicide Dresser/Lavender Room	1967	3.00	6.00	12.00
❑ 242	What About the Music/Please Spare Me This Time	1968	3.00	6.00	12.00
KENT					
❑ 493	Irresistible You/Honky Dory	1968	3.00	6.00	12.00
LAWN					
❑ 239	Anymore/Whatcha Gonna Do	1964	10.00	20.00	40.00
❑ 244	Coney Island Wild Child/Feel Good	1964	17.50	35.00	70.00
MIDLAND INT'L.					
❑ MB-10783	Two Lonely People/Whenever I'm Away from You	1976	2.50	5.00	10.00
OPEN					
❑ 1253	She's Almost You/Fool Me	1969	3.75	7.50	15.00
OR					
❑ 1253	She's Almost You/Fool Me	1969	3.00	6.00	12.00
❑ 1255	I Struck It Rich/Watch Your Step	1969	6.25	12.50	25.00
PARKWAY					
❑ 950	Let's Get in Line/All Through the Night	1965	5.00	10.00	20.00
SOUND GEMS					
❑ (# unknown)	I Got It from Heaven/(B-side unknown)	197?	150.00	300.00	600.00
V-TONE					
❑ 1001	A Message to My Babe/Everything's Hunky-Dory	196?	10.00	20.00	40.00
❑ 1003	All in My Mind/Fool Me	196?	6.25	12.50	25.00

HAROLD AND THE CASUALS
45s

Number	Title (A Side/B Side)	Yr	VG	VG+	NM
SCOTTY					
❑ 628	Darling Do You Love Me/You Can Shake a Tail Feather	1959	75.00	150.00	300.00

HARPER, BEN
45s

Number	Title (A Side/B Side)	Yr	VG	VG+	NM
CENCO					
❑ 120	Red Dress Woman/Drop In to See Me	196?	3.00	6.00	12.00
TALENT					
❑ 106	Drive Away Blues/Here Comes My Girl	196?	2.50	5.00	10.00

HARPER, CHUCK As "Chuck Fassert," he recorded with THE REGENTS.
45s

Number	Title (A Side/B Side)	Yr	VG	VG+	NM
FELSTED					
❑ 8658	Summer Is Thru/Call on Me	1962	7.50	15.00	30.00

HARPER, ROY
45s

Number	Title (A Side/B Side)	Yr	VG	VG+	NM
EPIC					
❑ 10268	Midspring Dithering/Zengfm	1967	3.75	7.50	15.00
Albums					
CHRYSALIS					
❑ PRO-620 [DJ]	Introduction to Roy Harper	1976	7.50	15.00	30.00
❑ CHR 1105	When An Old Cricketer Leaves the Crease	1976	3.75	7.50	15.00
❑ CHR 1139	One of Those Days in England	1977	3.75	7.50	15.00
❑ CHR 1160	Flat Baroque and Berserk	1978	3.00	6.00	12.00
—Reissue of Harvest LP					
❑ CHR 1161	Stormcock	1978	3.00	6.00	12.00
—Released in the UK in 1971					
❑ CHR 1162	Lifemask	1978	3.00	6.00	12.00
—Released in the UK in 1973					
❑ CHR 1163	Valentine	1978	3.00	6.00	12.00
—Released in the UK in 1974					
❑ CH2 1164 [(2)]	Flashes from the Archives of Oblivion	1978	3.75	7.50	15.00
—Released in the UK in 1974					
HARVEST					
❑ SKAO-418	Flat Baroque and Berserk	1970	5.00	10.00	20.00
PVC					
❑ 8937	Whatever Happened to Jugula	198?	3.00	6.00	12.00
WORLD PACIFIC					
❑ WPS-21888	Folkjokeopus	1969	6.25	12.50	25.00

HARPERS BIZARRE
45s

Number	Title (A Side/B Side)	Yr	VG	VG+	NM
WARNER BROS.					
❑ 5890	The 59th Street Bridge Song (Feelin' Groovy)/Lost My Love Today	1967	2.50	5.00	10.00
❑ 7028	Come to the Sunshine/Debutante's Ball	1967	2.00	4.00	8.00
❑ 7063	Anything Goes/Malibu U.	1967	2.00	4.00	8.00
❑ 7090	Chattanooga Choo Choo/Hey, You in the Crowd	1967	2.00	4.00	8.00
❑ 7106	The 59th Street Bridge Song (Feelin' Groovy)/Come to the Sunshine	1968	—	3.00	6.00
—"Back to Back Hits" series -- originals have green labels with "W7" logo					
❑ 7123	Anything Goes/Chattanooga Choo Choo	1969	—	3.00	6.00
—"Back to Back Hits" series -- originals have green labels with "W7" logo					
❑ 7172	Virginia City/Cotton Candy Sandman	1968	—	3.00	6.00
❑ 7200	Both Sides Now/Small Talk	1968	—	3.00	6.00
❑ 7223	Battle of New Orleans/Green Apple Tree	1968	—	3.00	6.00
❑ 7238	I Love You, Alice B. Toklas/Look to the Rainbow	1968	—	3.00	6.00
❑ 7296	Knock on Wood/Witchi-Tai-Yo	1969	—	2.50	5.00
❑ 7377	Poly High/Soft Soundin' Music	1970	—	2.50	5.00
❑ 7388	Anything Goes/Virginia City	1970	—	2.50	5.00
❑ 7399	If We Ever Needed the Lord Before/Mad	1970	—	2.50	5.00
❑ 7647	Knock on Wood/Poly High	1972	—	2.00	4.00
7-Inch Extended Plays					
WARNER BROS.					
❑ S 1739	Battle of New Orleans/Las Mananitas/Sentimental Journey///I'll Build a Stairway to Paradise/Sit Down, You're Rocking the Boat/Green Apple Tree	1968	3.75	7.50	15.00
—Jukebox issue; small hole, plays at 33 1/3 rpm					
❑ S 1739 [PS]	The Secret Life of Harpers Bizarre	1968	3.75	7.50	15.00
Albums					
FOREST BAY					
❑ 7545	As Time Goes By	1976	3.75	7.50	15.00
WARNER BROS.					
❑ W 1693 [M]	Feelin' Groovy	1967	6.25	12.50	25.00
❑ WS 1693 [S]	Feelin' Groovy	1967	5.00	10.00	20.00
—Gold label					
❑ WS 1693 [S]	Feelin' Groovy	1968	3.75	7.50	15.00
—Green "W7" label					
❑ WS 1716	Anything Goes	1967	5.00	10.00	20.00
❑ WS 1739	The Secret Life of Harpers Bizarre	1968	5.00	10.00	20.00
❑ WS 1784	Harpers Bizarre Four	1969	5.00	10.00	20.00
❑ ST-91351	Anything Goes	1968	6.25	12.50	25.00
—Capitol Record Club edition					

HARPO, SLIM
45s

Number	Title (A Side/B Side)	Yr	VG	VG+	NM
EXCELLO					
❑ 2113	I'm a King Bee/I Got Love If You Want It	1957	15.00	30.00	60.00
❑ 2138	Wonderin' and Worryin'/Strange Love	1958	7.50	15.00	30.00
❑ 2162	One More Day/You'll Be Sorry One Day	1959	7.50	15.00	30.00
❑ 2171	Buzz Me Babe/Late Last Night	1960	7.50	15.00	30.00
❑ 2184	Blues Hangover/What a Dream	1960	7.50	15.00	30.00
❑ 2194	Rainin' in My Heart/Don't Start Cryin' Now	1961	5.00	10.00	20.00
❑ 2239	Buzzin'/I Love the Life I'm Livin'	1963	3.75	7.50	15.00
❑ 2246	Little Queen Bee (Got a Brand New King)/I Need Money (Keep Your Alibis)	1964	3.00	6.00	12.00
❑ 2253	Still Rainin' in My Heart/We're Two of a Kind	1964	3.00	6.00	12.00
❑ 2261	Sittin' Here Wondering/What's Goin' On Baby	1964	3.00	6.00	12.00
❑ 2265	Please Don't Turn Me Down/Harpo's Blues	1965	3.00	6.00	12.00
❑ 2273	Baby Scratch My Back/I'm Gonna Miss You (LIke the Devil)	1965	3.00	6.00	12.00
❑ 2276	Goin' Away Blues/Just a Lonely Stranger	1966	2.50	5.00	10.00
❑ 2278	Midnight Blues/Shake Your Hips	1966	2.50	5.00	10.00
❑ 2282	I'm Your Bread-Maker, Baby/Loving You (The Way I Do)	1966	2.50	5.00	10.00
❑ 2285	Tip On In (Part 1)/Tip On In (Part 2)	1967	2.50	5.00	10.00
❑ 2289	I'm Gonna Keep What I've Got/I've Got to Be with You Tonight	1967	2.50	5.00	10.00
❑ 2294	Te-Ni-Lee-Ni-Nu/Mailbox Bues	1968	2.50	5.00	10.00
❑ 2301	Mohair Sam/I Just Can't Leave You	1969	2.00	4.00	8.00
❑ 2305	Just for You/That's Why I Love You	1969	2.00	4.00	8.00
❑ 2306	Folsom Prison Blues/Mututal Friend	1969	2.00	4.00	8.00
❑ 2309	I've Got My Finger on Your Trigger/The Price Is Too High	1969	2.00	4.00	8.00
❑ 2316	Rainin' in My Heart/Jody Man	1970	2.00	4.00	8.00
Albums					
EXCELLO					
❑ LP-8003 [M]	Raining in My Heart	1961	62.50	125.00	250.00
—Orange and blue label					
❑ LPS-8003 [M]	Raining in My Heart	196?	25.00	50.00	100.00
—All-blue label					
❑ LP-8005 [M]	Baby Scratch My Back	1966	50.00	100.00	200.00
—Orange and blue label					
❑ LPS-8005 [M]	Baby Scratch My Back	196?	25.00	50.00	100.00
—All-blue label					
❑ LPS-8008 [M]	Tip On In	1968	12.50	25.00	50.00
❑ LPS-8010 [M]	The Best of Slim Harpo	1969	12.50	25.00	50.00
❑ LPS-8013 [M]	Slim Harpo Knew the Blues	1970	12.50	25.00	50.00
RHINO					
❑ RNLP-106	The Best of Slim Harpo	198?	3.75	7.50	15.00
❑ R1-70169	Scratch My Back: The Best of Slim Harpo	1989	3.00	6.00	12.00

HARPS, THE See THE CAMELOTS.

HARPTONES, THE
45s

Number	Title (A Side/B Side)	Yr	VG	VG+	NM
AMBIENT SOUND					
❑ 02807	Love Needs a Heart/It's You	1982	—	3.00	6.00
ANDREA					
❑ 100	What Is Your Decision/Gimme Some	1956	10.00	20.00	40.00
BRUCE					
❑ 101	A Sunday Kind of Love/I'll Never Tell	1953	20.00	40.00	80.00
—"Bruce" in block lettering					
❑ 101	A Sunday Kind of Love/I'll Never Tell	1953	1000.	2000.	3000.
—"Bruce" in script lettering					

Number	Title (A Side/B Side)	Yr	VG	VG+	NM
❏ 102	My Memories of You/The Laughs on You	1954	30.00	60.00	120.00
—Same B-side with different title (and missing the apostrophe)					
❏ 102	My Memories of You/It Was Just for Laughs	1954	50.00	100.00	200.00
❏ 104	I Depended on You/Mambo Boogie	1954	20.00	40.00	80.00
❏ 109	Forever Mine/Why Should I Love You	1954	20.00	40.00	80.00
❏ 113	Since I Fell for You/Oobidee-Oobidee-Oo	1954	20.00	40.00	80.00
❏ 123	High Flying Baby/Loving a Girl Like You	1955	15.00	30.00	60.00
❏ 128	I Almost Lost My Mind/Oh Wee Baby	1955	15.00	30.00	60.00
COED					
❏ 540	Answer Me My Love/Rain Down Kisses	1960	5.00	10.00	20.00
COMPANION					
❏ 102	All in Your Mind/The Last Dance	1961	7.50	15.00	30.00
❏ 103	What Will I Tell My Heart/Foolish Me	1961	20.00	40.00	80.00
CUB					
❏ 9097	Devil in Velvet/Your Love Is a Good Love	1961	5.00	10.00	20.00
GEE					
❏ 1045	Cry Like I Cried/So Good, So Fine, You're Mine	1957	15.00	30.00	60.00
—Red label					
KT					
❏ 201	Sunset/I Gotta Have Your Love	1963	12.50	25.00	50.00
LOST-NITE					
❏ 395	A Sunday Kind of Love/I'll Never Tell	197?	—	2.50	5.00
—Reissue					
❏ 397	My Memories of You/The Laughs on You	197?	—	2.50	5.00
—Reissue					
❏ 399	I Almost Lost My Mind/Oh Wee Baby	197?	—	2.50	5.00
—Reissue					
❏ 401	Forever Mine/Why Should I Love You	197?	—	2.50	5.00
—Reissue					
❏ 403	Since I Fell for You/Oobidee-Oobidee-Oo	197?	—	2.50	5.00
—Reissue					
❏ 405	I Depended on You/Mambo Boogie	197?	—	2.50	5.00
—Reissue					
❏ 407	What Is Your Decision/Gimme Some	197?	—	2.50	5.00
—Reissue					
❏ 409	High Flying Baby/Loving a Girl Like You	197?	—	2.50	5.00
PARADISE					
❏ 101	Life Is But a Dream/You Know You're Doing Me Wrong	1954	15.00	30.00	60.00
—Purple label					
❏ 101	Life Is But a Dream/You Know You're Doing Me Wrong	1954	37.50	75.00	150.00
—Maroon label					
❏ 103	My Success/I've Got a Notion	1955	75.00	150.00	300.00
❏ 105	It All Depends on You/Guitar Shuffle	1955	15.00	30.00	60.00
—Purple label					
❏ 105	It All Depends on You/Guitar Shuffle	1955	37.50	75.00	150.00
—Maroon label					
RAMA					
❏ 203	Three Wishes/That's the Way It Goes	1956	20.00	40.00	80.00
❏ 214	The Masquerade Is Over/On Sunday Afternoon	1956	20.00	40.00	80.00
❏ 221	The Shrine of St. Cecelia/Oo Wee Baby	1957	20.00	40.00	80.00
RAVEN					
❏ 8001	A Sunday Kind of Love/Mambo Boogie	1962	3.75	7.50	15.00
TIP TOP					
❏ 401	My Memories of You/High Flyin' Baby	1956	10.00	20.00	40.00
WARWICK					
❏ 500	I Remember/Laughing on the Outside	1959	6.25	12.50	25.00
❏ 512	Love Me Completely/Hep Teenager	1959	6.25	12.50	25.00
❏ 551	No Greater Miracle/What Kind of a Fool	1960	6.25	12.50	25.00
7-Inch Extended Plays					
BRUCE					
❏ BEP 201	A Sunday Kind of Love/Ou Wee Baby//Forever Mine/I Almost Lost My Mind	1954	2500.	3750.	5000.
❏ BEP 201 [PS]	The Sensational Harptones	1954	2500.	3750.	5000.
Albums					
AMBIENT SOUND					
❏ FZ 37718	Love Needs	1982	3.00	6.00	12.00
HARLEM HIT PARADE					
❏ 5006	The Harptones	197?	3.75	7.50	15.00
RELIC					
❏ LP-5001	The Greatest Hits of the Harptones, Vol. 1	197?	3.00	6.00	12.00
❏ LP-5003	The Greatest Hits of the Harptones, Vol. 2	197?	3.00	6.00	12.00

HARRIS, ANITA

45s

Number	Title (A Side/B Side)	Yr	VG	VG+	NM
BRUT					
❏ 1345	I Just Need a Lover/Music	197?	—	3.00	6.00
COLUMBIA					
❏ 44236	Just Loving You/Butterfly with Coloured Wings	1967	2.00	4.00	8.00
❏ 44438	Anniversary Waltz/Comes the Night	1968	2.00	4.00	8.00
LONDON					
❏ 9720	Lies/Don't Think About Love	1964	3.00	6.00	12.00
WARNER BROS.					
❏ 5638	Trains and Boats and Planes/Upside Down	1965	2.50	5.00	10.00

HARRIS, EMMYLOU

45s

Number	Title (A Side/B Side)	Yr	VG	VG+	NM
A&M					
❏ 2290	Wish We Were Back in Missouri/Riding with Jesse James	1980	—	2.00	4.00
—B-side by Charlie Daniels					
ASYLUM					
❏ 64570	Thanks to You/Lovin' You Again	1993	—	—	3.00
❏ 64610	High Powered Love/Ballad of a Runaway Horse	1992	—	—	3.00
JUBILEE					
❏ 5679	I'll Be Your Baby Tonight/I'll Never Fall in Love Again	1969	5.00	10.00	20.00
❏ 5697	Paddy/Fugue for the Ox	1970	5.00	10.00	20.00
MCA					
❏ 53236	I Still Dream of You/Back in Baby's Arms	1988	—	—	3.00
REPRISE					
❏ 1326	Too Far Gone/Boulder to Birmingham	1975	—	2.50	5.00

Number	Title (A Side/B Side)	Yr	VG	VG+	NM
❏ 1332	If I Could Only Win Your Love/Boulder to Birmingham	1975	—	2.50	5.00
❏ 1341	Light of the Stable/Bluebird Wine	1975	2.50	5.00	10.00
—A-side is a longer version than later releases					
❏ 1341 [PS]	Light of the Stable/Bluebird Wine	1975	3.00	6.00	12.00
❏ 1346	Together Again/Here, There and Everywhere	1976	—	2.50	5.00
❏ 1353	Till I Gain Control Again/One of These Days	1976	—	2.50	5.00
❏ 1371	Sweet Dreams/Amarillo	1976	—	2.50	5.00
❏ 1379	Light of the Stable/Boulder to Birmingham	1976	—	2.50	5.00
❏ 19281	Rollin' and Ramblin'/Sweet Dreams Of You	1991	—	—	3.00
❏ 19510	Wheels of Love/Better Off Without You	1991	—	—	3.00
❏ 19707	Never Be Anyone Else But You/Red, Red Rose	1990	—	—	3.00
❏ 19870	Gulf Coast Highway/Evangeline	1990	—	—	3.00
—A-side with Willie Nelson					
❏ 22850	I Still Miss Someone/No Regrets	1989	—	—	3.00
❏ 22999	Heaven Only Knows/A River for Him	1989	—	—	3.00
❏ 27635	Heartbreak Hill/Icy Blue Heart	1989	—	—	3.00
WARNER BROS.					
❏ PRO-S-2872 [DJ]	Light of the Stable/It Came Upon a Midnight Clear	1987	2.50	5.00	10.00
—B-side by Highway 101					
❏ 8329	C'est La Vie (You Never Can Tell)/You're Supposed to Be Feeling Good	1977	—	2.50	5.00
❏ 8388	Making Believe/I'll Be Your San Antone Rose	1977	—	2.50	5.00
❏ 8498	To Daddy/Tulsa Queen	1977	—	2.50	5.00
❏ 8553	Two More Bottles of Wine/I Ain't Living Long Like This	1978	—	2.50	5.00
❏ 8623	Easy from Now On/You're Supposed to Be Feeling Good	1978	—	2.50	5.00
❏ 8732	Too Far Gone/Tulsa Queen	1979	—	2.00	4.00
❏ 8815	Save the Last Dance for Me/Even Cowgirls Get the Blues	1979	—	2.50	5.00
❏ 28302	Someday My Ship Will Sail/When He Calls	1987	—	—	3.00
❏ 28714	Today I Started Loving You Again/When I Was Young	1986	—	—	3.00
❏ 28770	I Had My Heart Set on You/Your Long Journey	1986	—	—	3.00
❏ 28852	Timberline/Sweet Chariot	1985	—	2.00	4.00
❏ 28952	Rhythm Guitar/Diamond in My Crown	1985	—	—	3.00
❏ 29041	White Line/Long Tall Sally Rose	1985	—	2.00	4.00
❏ 29138	Someone Like You/Light of the Stable	1984	—	2.00	4.00
❏ 29218	Pledging My Love/Baby, Better Start Turnin' 'Em Down	1984	—	2.00	4.00
❏ 29329	In My Dreams/Like an Old Fashioned World	1984	—	2.00	4.00
❏ 29443	Drivin' Wheel/Good News	1983	—	2.00	4.00
❏ 29583	So Sad (To Watch Good Love Go Bad)/Amarillo	1983	—	2.00	4.00
❏ 29729	I'm Movin' On/Maybe Tonight	1983	—	2.00	4.00
❏ 29898	(Lost His Love) On Our Last Date/Another Pot O' Tea	1982	—	2.00	4.00
❏ 29993	Born to Run/Colors of My Heart	1982	—	2.00	4.00
❏ 49056	Blue Kentucky Girl/Leaving Louisiana in the Broad Daylight	1979	—	2.00	4.00
❏ 49164	Beneath Still Waters/Til I Gain Control Again	1980	—	2.00	4.00
❏ 49239	Wayfaring Stranger/Green Pastures	1980	—	2.00	4.00
❏ 49262	That Lovin' You Feeling Again/Lola	1980	—	2.50	5.00
—A-side with Roy Orbison; B-side by Craig Hundley					
❏ 49551	The Boxer/Precious Love	1980	—	2.00	4.00
❏ 49633	Beautiful Star of Bethlehem/The Little Drummer Boy	1980	—	2.00	4.00
❏ 49645	Little Drummer Boy/Light of the Stable	1980	—	2.00	4.00
❏ 49684	Mister Sandman/Fools' Thin Air	1981	—	2.00	4.00
❏ 49739	I Don't Have to Crawl/Colors of Your Heart	1981	—	2.00	4.00
❏ 49809	If I Needed You/Ashes By Now	1981	—	2.00	4.00
—A-side with Don Williams					
❏ 49892	Tennessee Rose/Mama Help	1982	—	2.00	4.00
Albums					
JUBILEE					
❏ JGS-8031	Gliding Bird	1969	30.00	60.00	120.00
—Originals have color covers; counterfeit covers are black and white					
MOBILE FIDELITY					
❏ 1-015	Quarter Moon in a Ten Cent Town	1979	10.00	20.00	40.00
—Audiophile vinyl					
REPRISE					
❏ MS 2213	Pieces of the Sky	1975	2.50	5.00	10.00
❏ MS 2236	Elite Hotel	1976	2.50	5.00	10.00
❏ MSK 2284	Pieces of the Sky	1977	2.00	4.00	8.00
—Reissue of 2213					
❏ MSK 2286	Elite Hotel	1977	2.00	4.00	8.00
—Reissue of 2236					
❏ 25776	Bluebird	1989	3.00	6.00	12.00
WARNER BROS.					
❏ BS 2998	Luxury Liner	1977	3.00	6.00	12.00
❏ BSK 3115	Luxury Liner	1977	2.50	5.00	10.00
—Reissue of 2998					
❏ BSK 3141	Quarter Moon in a Ten Cent Town	1978	2.50	5.00	10.00
❏ BSK 3258	Profile/Best of Emmylou Harris	1978	2.50	5.00	10.00
❏ BSK 3318	Blue Kentucky Girl	1979	2.50	5.00	10.00
❏ BSK 3422	Roses in the Snow	1980	2.50	5.00	10.00
❏ BSK 3484	Light of the Stable: The Christmas Album	1980	2.50	5.00	10.00
❏ BSK 3508	Evangeline	1981	2.50	5.00	10.00
❏ BSK 3603	Cimarron	1981	2.50	5.00	10.00
❏ 23740	Last Date	1982	2.50	5.00	10.00
❏ 23961	White Shoes	1983	2.50	5.00	10.00
❏ 25161	Profile II — The Best of Emmylou Harris	1984	2.50	5.00	10.00
❏ 25205	The Ballad of Sally Rose	1985	2.50	5.00	10.00
❏ 25352	Thirteen	1986	2.50	5.00	10.00
❏ 25585	Angel Band	1987	2.50	5.00	10.00

HARRIS, GENEE

45s

Number	Title (A Side/B Side)	Yr	VG	VG+	NM
ABC-PARAMOUNT					
❏ 9900	Bye Bye Elvis/You're Like a Jumping Jack	1958	12.50	25.00	50.00

HARRIS, GEORGIA, AND THE LYRICS

45s

Number	Title (A Side/B Side)	Yr	VG	VG+	NM
HY-TONE					
❏ 111	Let's Exchange Hearts for Christmas/It's Time to Rock	1958	125.00	250.00	500.00
❏ 117	Let's Exchange Hearts for Christmas/Kiss, Kiss, Kiss	1958	125.00	250.00	500.00

H

Number	Title (A Side/B Side)	Yr	VG	VG+	NM

HARRIS, JACKIE
45s
HIT
| ❑ 194 | Can't You Hear My Heartbeat/You Were Gone | 1965 | 2.00 | 4.00 | 8.00 |

—*B-side by John Preston*

HARRIS, JET, AND TONY MEECHAN Also see THE SHADOWS.
45s
LONDON
❑ 9589	Diamonds/Footstomp	1963	3.75	7.50	15.00
❑ 9608	Scarlet O'Hara/(Doin' the) Hully Gully	1963	3.75	7.50	15.00
❑ 9622	Applejack/Tall Texan	1963	3.75	7.50	15.00

HARRIS, KURT
45s
DIAMOND
| ❑ 158 | Go On/Emperor of My Baby's Heart | 1964 | 20.00 | 40.00 | 80.00 |

JOSIE
| ❑ 898 | Let Her Dance/I Can't Love Nobody Else | 1962 | 5.00 | 10.00 | 20.00 |
| ❑ 902 | Uh-Uh/You Better Shut Your Mouth | 1962 | 5.00 | 10.00 | 20.00 |

HARRIS, MAJOR Also see THE DELFONICS.
12-Inch Singles
POP ART
| ❑ 1401 | All My Life/(B-side unknown) | 1983 | — | 3.00 | 6.00 |

45s
ATLANTIC
❑ 3217	Each Morning I Wake Up/Just a Thing I Do	1974	—	2.50	5.00
❑ 3248	Love Won't Let Me Wait/After Loving You	1975	—	2.00	4.00
❑ 3299 [DJ]	Loving You Is Mellow (mono/stereo)	1975	—	2.50	5.00

—*May be promo-only*
❑ 3303	I Got Over Love/Loving You Is Mellow	1975	—	2.00	4.00
❑ 3321	Jealousy/Tynisa (What's Your Hurry)	1976	—	2.00	4.00
❑ 3336	It's Got to Be Magic/Just a Thing That I Do	1976	—	2.00	4.00

OKEH
| ❑ 7314 | Just Love Me/Loving You More | 1968 | 7.50 | 15.00 | 30.00 |
| ❑ 7327 | Like a Rolling Stone/Call Me Tomorrow | 1969 | 15.00 | 30.00 | 60.00 |

WMOT
| ❑ 02091 | Here We Are/Living's Easy Now | 1981 | — | 2.00 | 4.00 |
| ❑ 4002 | Laid Back Love/This Is What You Mean to Me | 1976 | — | 2.00 | 4.00 |

Albums
ATLANTIC
| ❑ SD 18119 | My Way | 1974 | 3.75 | 7.50 | 15.00 |
| ❑ SD 18160 | Jealousy | 1976 | 3.75 | 7.50 | 15.00 |

RCA VICTOR
| ❑ APL1-2803 | How Do You Take Your Love | 1978 | 3.00 | 6.00 | 12.00 |

WMOT
| ❑ 627 | Mellow Major | 1977 | 3.00 | 6.00 | 12.00 |
| ❑ PW 37067 | The Best of Major Harris, Now and Then | 1981 | 2.50 | 5.00 | 10.00 |

HARRIS, PEPPERMINT
45s
ALADDIN
| ❑ 3097 | I Got Loaded/It's You, Yes It's You | 1951 | 25.00 | 50.00 | 100.00 |

—*Black vinyl*
| ❑ 3097 | I Got Loaded/It's You, Yes It's You | 1951 | 62.50 | 125.00 | 250.00 |

—*Green vinyl*
❑ 3107	Have Another Drink and Talk to Me/ Middle of Winter	1951	20.00	40.00	80.00
❑ 3108	Let the Back Door Hit You/P.H. Blues	1951	20.00	40.00	80.00
❑ 3130	Right Back On It/Maggie's Boogie	1952	20.00	40.00	80.00
❑ 3141	I Cry for My Baby/There's a Dead Cat on the Line	1952	20.00	40.00	80.00
❑ 3154	I Sure Do Miss My Baby/Hey Little Schoolgirl	1952	20.00	40.00	80.00
❑ 3177	Wasted Love/Goodbye Blues	1953	20.00	40.00	80.00
❑ 3183	Don't Leave Me Alone/Wet Rat	1953	20.00	40.00	80.00
❑ 3206	I Never Get Enough of You/ Three Sheets in the Wind	1953	20.00	40.00	80.00

CASH
| ❑ 1003 | Cadillac Funeral/Treat Me Like I Treat You | 1954 | 37.50 | 75.00 | 150.00 |

COMBO
| ❑ 114 | Love at First Sight/I Don't Care | 1956 | 15.00 | 30.00 | 60.00 |

DART
| ❑ 103 | You Get Me Wondering/
Messing Around with the Blues | 1959 | 6.25 | 12.50 | 25.00 |

DUKE
| ❑ 319 | Ain't No Business/Angel Child | 1960 | 6.25 | 12.50 | 25.00 |

JEWEL
❑ 742	Marking Time/Bad, Mad Woman	1965	2.50	5.00	10.00
❑ 747	Ma Ma/Anything You Can Do	1965	2.50	5.00	10.00
❑ 762	Raining in My Heart/My Time After Awhile	1966	2.50	5.00	10.00
❑ 772	Anytime Is the Right Time/Wait Until It Happens to You	1966	2.50	5.00	10.00
❑ 789	Bad Bad Whiskey/Lonesome As Can Be	1967	2.50	5.00	10.00
❑ 795	24 Hours/Little Girl	1968	2.50	5.00	10.00

MODERN
| ❑ 936 | Bye Bye, Fare Thee Well/Black Cat Bone | 1951 | 25.00 | 50.00 | 100.00 |

SITTIN' IN WITH
| ❑ 543 | Raining in My Heart/My Blues Have Rolled Away | 1950 | 37.50 | 75.00 | 150.00 |

—*Other Peppermint Harris 45s on this label may exist.*
"X"
| ❑ 0142 | Need Your Lovin'/Just Me and You | 1955 | 25.00 | 50.00 | 100.00 |

Albums
TIME
| ❑ 5 [M] | Peppermint Harris | 1962 | 50.00 | 100.00 | 200.00 |

HARRIS, RAY
45s
SUN
| ❑ 254 | Come On Little Mama/
Where'd You Stay Last Night | 1956 | 37.50 | 75.00 | 150.00 |
| ❑ 272 | Greenback Dollar Watch and Chain/
Foolish Hearts | 1957 | 25.00 | 50.00 | 100.00 |

HARRIS, RICHARD
45s
ABC DUNHILL
| ❑ 4134 | MacArthur Park/Didn't We | 1968 | — | 3.00 | 6.00 |

—*With both ABC and Dunhill logos at top of label*
| ❑ 4134 [PS] | MacArthur Park/Didn't We | 1968 | 2.00 | 4.00 | 8.00 |

—*Regular stock sleeve*
❑ 4170	The Yard Went On Forever/Lucky Me	1968	—	2.50	5.00
❑ 4185	Watermark/One of the Nicer Things	1969	—	2.50	5.00
❑ 4194	Didn't We/Paper Chase	1969	—	2.50	5.00
❑ 4208	Fill the World with Love/What a Lot of Flowers	1969	—	2.50	5.00
❑ 4218	Fill the World with Love/What a Lot of Flowers	1969	—	2.50	5.00
❑ 4218 [PS]	Fill the World with Love/What a Lot of Flowers	1969	—	3.00	6.00
❑ 4241	Ballad of a Man Called Horse/Morning of the Mourning for Another	1970	—	2.50	5.00
❑ 4293	My Boy/Why Did You Leave Me	1971	—	2.50	5.00
❑ 4310	Half of Every Dream/Turning Back the Pages	1972	—	2.50	5.00
❑ 4322	There Are Too Many Saviours on My Cross/All the Broken Children	1972	—	2.50	5.00
❑ 4322 [PS]	There Are Too Many Saviours on My Cross/All the Broken Children	1972	—	3.00	6.00
❑ 4336	How I Spent My Summer/I Don't Have to Tell You	1973	—	2.50	5.00

ATLANTIC
| ❑ 3238 | On Crime and Punishment/
Theme from "The Prophet" | 1975 | — | 2.00 | 4.00 |
| ❑ 3238 [PS] | On Crime and Punishment/
Theme from "The Prophet" | 1975 | — | 2.50 | 5.00 |

DUNHILL
| ❑ 4134 | MacArthur Park/Didn't We | 1968 | 2.00 | 4.00 | 8.00 |

—*First pressings have Dunhill standing alone at top of label*
| ❑ 4134 [PS] | MacArthur Park/Didn't We | 1968 | 3.75 | 7.50 | 15.00 |

—*Special promotional issue, so marked on sleeve*
Albums
ABC DUNHILL
❑ DS-50032	A Tramp Shining	1968	3.75	7.50	15.00
❑ DS-50042	The Yard Went On Forever	1968	3.75	7.50	15.00
❑ DS-50074	The Love Album	1970	3.75	7.50	15.00
❑ DSX-50116	My Boy	1971	3.00	6.00	12.00
❑ DSX-50133	Slides	1972	3.00	6.00	12.00
❑ DSX-50139	The Great Performances	1973	3.00	6.00	12.00
❑ DSX-50159	I, In the Membership	1974	3.00	6.00	12.00
❑ DSX-50160	Jonathan Livingston Seagull	1973	3.00	6.00	12.00

—*Spoken-word recording*
ATLANTIC
| ❑ QD 18120 [Q] | The Prophet by Kahlil Gibran | 1974 | 5.00 | 10.00 | 20.00 |

—*Spoken-word recording*
| ❑ SD 18120 | The Prophet by Kahlil Gibran | 1974 | 3.00 | 6.00 | 12.00 |

—*Spoken-word recording*
MCA
| ❑ 27016 | A Tramp Shining | 198? | 2.00 | 4.00 | 8.00 |

—*Budget-line reissue*
PICKWICK
| ❑ SPC-3626 | A Tramp Shining | 1978 | 2.50 | 5.00 | 10.00 |

HARRIS, ROLF
45s
EPIC
❑ 9567	Sun Arise/Someone's Pinched My Winkles	1963	3.00	6.00	12.00
❑ 9596	Tie Me Kangaroo Down, Sport/The Big Black Hat	1963	3.75	7.50	15.00
❑ 9596 [PS]	Tie Me Kangaroo Down, Sport/The Big Black Hat	1963	5.00	10.00	20.00
❑ 9615	Nick Teen & Al K. Hall/I Know a Man	1963	3.00	6.00	12.00
❑ 9615 [PS]	Nick Teen & Al K. Hall/I Know a Man	1963	5.00	10.00	20.00
❑ 9641	Lost Little Boy/Six White Boomers	1963	2.50	5.00	10.00
❑ 9641 [PS]	Lost Little Boy/Six White Boomers	1963	5.00	10.00	20.00
❑ 9682	The Court of King Caractacus/Two Buffalos	1964	2.50	5.00	10.00
❑ 9721	Ringo for President/Click Go the Shears	1964	3.75	7.50	15.00
❑ 9756	The Thing/Wild Colonial Boy	1965	2.50	5.00	10.00
❑ 9780	Tie My Hunting Dog Down, Jed/ Five Young Apprentices	1965	2.50	5.00	10.00
❑ 10037	Jake the Peg/Big Dog	1966	2.50	5.00	10.00

MGM
| ❑ 14103 | Two Little Boys/I Love My Love | 1970 | 2.50 | 5.00 | 10.00 |

20TH FOX
| ❑ 207 | Tie Me Kangaroo Down, Sport/
Nick Teen & Al K. Hall | 1960 | 5.00 | 10.00 | 20.00 |

—*Different versions than the Epic recordings*
❑ 230	Lost Little Boy/The Big Black Hat	1960	3.75	7.50	15.00
❑ 295	Six White Boomers/Tame Eagle	1962	3.75	7.50	15.00
❑ 414	Lost Little Boy/The Big Black Hat	1963	3.00	6.00	12.00

Albums
EPIC
❑ LN 24053 [M]	Tie Me Kangaroo Down, Sport & Sun Arise	1963	5.00	10.00	20.00
❑ LN 24110 [M]	Join Rolf Harris Singing The Count of King Caractacus (And Other Fun Songs)	1964	5.00	10.00	20.00
❑ BN 26053 [S]	Tie Me Kangaroo Down, Sport & Sun Arise	1963	6.25	12.50	25.00
❑ BN 26110 [S]	Join Rolf Harris Singing The Count of King Caractacus (And Other Fun Songs)	1964	6.25	12.50	25.00

HARRIS, TED
45s
RCA VICTOR
| ❑ 47-7422 | Just Thought I'd Set You Straight/
Please Don't Say Take Me Home | 1958 | 7.50 | 15.00 | 30.00 |

HARRIS, THURSTON
45s
ALADDIN
❑ 3398	Little Bitty Pretty One/I Hope You Won't Hold It Against Me	1957	10.00	20.00	40.00
❑ 3399	Do What You Did/I'm Asking Forgiveness	1957	7.50	15.00	30.00
❑ 3415	Be Baby Leba/I'm Out to Getcha	1958	7.50	15.00	30.00
❑ 3428	Only One Love Is Blessed/Smokey Joe's	1958	7.50	15.00	30.00
❑ 3430	Over and Over/You're Gonna Miss Me	1958	5.00	10.00	20.00
❑ 3435	Over Someone Else's Shoulder/ Tears from My Heart	1958	5.00	10.00	20.00
❑ 3440	Purple Stew/I Heard a Rhapsody	1958	5.00	10.00	20.00

Number	Title (A Side/B Side)	Yr	VG	VG+	NM
❑ 3447	From the Bottom of My Heart/ You Don't Know How Much I Love You	1959	5.00	10.00	20.00
❑ 3448	Don't You Know/From the Bottom of My Heart	1959	5.00	10.00	20.00
❑ 3450	Hey Little Girl/My Love Will Last	1959	5.00	10.00	20.00
❑ 3452	Runk Bunk/Bless Your Heart	1959	5.00	10.00	20.00
❑ 3456	Slip Slop/Paradise Hill	1959	5.00	10.00	20.00
❑ 3462	Moonlight Cocktail/Recess in Heaven	1960	5.00	10.00	20.00
❑ 3468	One Scotch, One Bourbon, One Beer/ Send Me Some Loving	1960	5.00	10.00	20.00

CUB

❑ 9108	I'd Like to Start Over Again/Mr. Satan	1962	3.00	6.00	12.00

DOT

❑ 16415	Quiet As It's Kept/Goddess of Angels	1963	2.50	5.00	10.00
❑ 16427	Poop-A-Loop/She's the One	1963	2.50	5.00	10.00

IMPERIAL

❑ 5928	Got You on My Mind/Tears from My Heart	1963	2.50	5.00	10.00
❑ 5971	You're Gonna Need Me/I'm Asking Forgiveness	1963	2.50	5.00	10.00

REPRISE

❑ 0255	Dance On Little Girl/Dancing Silhouettes	1964	2.50	5.00	10.00

UNITED ARTISTS

❑ 0152	Little Bitty Pretty One/Over and Over	1973	—	2.00	4.00

—"Silver Spotlight Series" reissue

HARRIS, TONY
45s

DEE GEE

❑ 3014	Super Man/How Much Do I Love You	1966	4.00	8.00	16.00

EBB

❑ 104	Chicken Baby Chicken/I'll Forever Love You	1957	12.50	25.00	50.00
❑ 120	Try This Little Ol' Heart/When I Get You Back	1957	7.50	15.00	30.00
❑ 128	You Fascinate Me/Swing, Swing, Swing	1957	7.50	15.00	30.00

TRIUMPH

❑ 60	Go, Go, Little Scrambler/Poor Boy	1964	7.50	15.00	30.00

HARRIS, WAYNE
45s

HIT

❑ 75	(You're the) Devil in Disguise/Blowin' in the Wind	1963	2.00	4.00	8.00

—B-side by Jimmy, Wayne and Betty

❑ 86	Wonderful! Wonderful!/I Can't Stay Mad at You	1963	2.00	4.00	8.00

—B-side by Kathy Taylor

❑ 100	Forget Him/Drag City	1964	2.00	4.00	8.00

—B-side by the Jalopy Five

❑ 190	You've Lost That Lovin' Feelin'/True Love You Can't Buy	1965	2.00	4.00	8.00

—B-side by Ed Hardin

❑ 193	For Me/Tell Her No	1965	3.00	6.00	12.00

—B-side by the Mummies

HARRIS, WEE WILLIE
45s

CHARLIE PARKER

❑ 217	I Go Ape/Trouble in Mind	1963	2.50	5.00	10.00

HARRIS, WYNONIE
45s

ATCO

❑ 6081	Destination Love/Tell a Whale of a Tale	1956	7.50	15.00	30.00

KING

❑ 4210	Good Rockin' Tonight/Good Morning Mister Blues	1952	37.50	75.00	150.00

—78 originally released in 1948; the only known Wynonie Harris 45 on King before 4461

❑ 4461	Bloodshot Eyes/Confessin' the Blues	1951	30.00	60.00	120.00
❑ 4468	I'll Never Give Up/Man Have I Got Troubles	1951	30.00	60.00	120.00
❑ 4485	Lovin' Machine/Luscious Woman	1951	30.00	60.00	120.00

—Black vinyl

❑ 4485	Lovin' Machine/Luscious Woman	1951	100.00	200.00	400.00

—Blue vinyl

❑ 4507	My Playful Baby's Gone/Here Comes the Night	1952	25.00	50.00	100.00
❑ 4526	Keep On Churnin'/Married Women Stay Married	1952	25.00	50.00	100.00
❑ 4555	Do it Again Please/Night Train	1952	25.00	50.00	100.00
❑ 4565	Drinking Blues/Adam Come and Get Your Rib	1952	25.00	50.00	100.00
❑ 4592	Greyhound/Rot Gut	1953	25.00	50.00	100.00
❑ 4593	Bad News Baby (There'll Be Rockin' Tonight)/ Bring It Back	1953	25.00	50.00	100.00
❑ 4620	Mama Your Daughter Done Lied on Me/ Wasn't That Good	1953	25.00	50.00	100.00
❑ 4635	Song of the Bayou/The Deacon Doesn't Like It	1953	25.00	50.00	100.00
❑ 4662	Tremblin'/Rot Gut	1953	20.00	40.00	80.00
❑ 4668	Please Louise/Nearer My Love to Thee	1953	20.00	40.00	80.00
❑ 4685	Down Boy Down/Quiet Whiskey	1953	20.00	40.00	80.00
❑ 4716	Shake That Thing/Keep A-Talking	1954	20.00	40.00	80.00
❑ 4724	I Get a Thrill/ Don't Take My Whiskey Away from Me	1954	20.00	40.00	80.00
❑ 4763	All She Wants to Do Is Mambo/Christina	1955	15.00	30.00	60.00
❑ 4774	Good Mambo Tonight/Git to Gittin' Baby	1955	15.00	30.00	60.00
❑ 4789	Fishtail Blues/Mr. Dollar	1955	15.00	30.00	60.00
❑ 4814	Drinkin' Sherry Wine/Get With the Guts	1955	12.50	25.00	50.00
❑ 4826	Wine, Wine, Sweet Wine/Man's Best Friend	1955	12.50	25.00	50.00
❑ 4839	Shot Gun Wedding/I Don't Know Where to Go	1955	12.50	25.00	50.00
❑ 4852	Good Morning Judge/Bloodshot Eyes	1955	12.50	25.00	50.00
❑ 5050	Big Old Country Fool/That's Me Right Now	1957	7.50	15.00	30.00
❑ 5073	There's No Substitute for Love/A Tale of Woe	1957	7.50	15.00	30.00
❑ 5416	Good Rockin' Tonight/Bloodshot Eyes	1960	3.75	7.50	15.00
❑ 6011	Big Old Country Fool/Bloodshot Eyes	1965	2.50	5.00	10.00
❑ 6304	Good Rockin' Tonight/Good Morning Judge	1970	—	3.00	6.00

ROULETTE

❑ 4291	Bloodshot Eyes/Sweet Lucy Brown	1960	3.00	6.00	12.00

7-Inch Extended Plays

KING

❑ EP-260	*Good Rockin' Tonight/Bloodshot Eyes/All She Wants to Do Is Rock/Good Morning Judge	1954	125.00	250.00	500.00
❑ EP-260 [PS]	Wynonie Harris	1954	125.00	250.00	500.00

Albums

KING

❑ KS-1086	Good Rockin' Blues	1970	6.25	12.50	25.00

HARRIS BROTHERS, THE
45s

HIT

Number	Title (A Side/B Side)	Yr	VG	VG+	NM
❑ 258	The Sun Ain't Gonna Shine Anymore/Paint It Black	1966	3.00	6.00	12.00

—B-side by the Jalopy Five

HARRISON, GEORGE Also see THE BEATLES.
12-Inch Singles

COLUMBIA

❑ CAS 2085 [DJ]	I Don't Want to Do It (same on both sides)	1985	5.00	10.00	20.00

DARK HORSE

❑ PRO-A-949 [DJ]	All Those Years Ago (same on both sides)	1981	6.25	12.50	25.00
❑ PRO-A-1075 [DJ]	Wake Up My Love (same on both sides)	1982	6.25	12.50	25.00
❑ PRO-A-2845 [DJ]	Got My Mind Set on You (same on both sides)	1987	6.25	12.50	25.00
❑ PRO-A-2885 [DJ]	When We Was Fab (same on both sides)	1987	6.25	12.50	25.00
❑ PRO-A-2889 [DJ]	Devil's Radio (Gossip) (same on both sides)	1987	7.50	15.00	30.00

45s

APPLE

❑ 1828	What Is Life/Apple Scruffs	1971	2.00	4.00	8.00

—Without star on A-side label

❑ 1828	What Is Life/Apple Scruffs	1971	3.75	7.50	15.00

—With star on A-side label

❑ 1828 [PS]	What Is Life/Apple Scruffs	1971	10.00	20.00	40.00
❑ 1836	Bangla-Desh/Deep Blue	1971	2.00	4.00	8.00

—Without star on A-side label

❑ 1836	Bangla-Desh/Deep Blue	1971	6.25	12.50	25.00

—With star on A-side label

❑ 1836 [PS]	Bangla-Desh/Deep Blue	1971	5.00	10.00	20.00
❑ 1862	Give Me Love (Give Me Peace on Earth)/ Miss O'Dell (2:20)	1973	2.00	4.00	8.00

—B-side playing time corrected

❑ 1862	Give Me Love (Give Me Peace on Earth)/ Miss O'Dell (2:30)	1973	2.00	4.00	8.00

—With incorrect time for B-side listed

❑ P-1862 [DJ]	Give Me Love (Give Me Peace on Earth) (mono/stereo)	1973	12.50	25.00	50.00
❑ 1877	Dark Horse/I Don't Care Anymore	1974	2.00	4.00	8.00

—Light blue and white custom photo label

❑ 1877	Dark Horse/I Don't Care Anymore	1974	2.50	5.00	10.00

—White label; NOT a promo

❑ 1877 [PS]	Dark Horse/I Don't Care Anymore	1974	20.00	40.00	80.00
❑ P-1877 [DJ]	Dark Horse (full length mono/stereo).	1974	10.00	20.00	40.00
❑ P-1877 [DJ]	Dark Horse (edited mono/stereo).	1974	15.00	30.00	60.00
❑ 1879	Ding Dong, Ding Dong/Hari's on Tour (Express).	1974	5.00	10.00	20.00

—Black and white custom photo label

❑ 1879	Ding Dong, Ding Dong/Hari's on Tour (Express).	1974	62.50	125.00	250.00

—Blue and white custon photo label

❑ 1879 [PS]	Ding Dong, Ding Dong/Hari's on Tour (Express).	1974	5.00	10.00	20.00
❑ P-1879 [DJ]	Ding Dong, Ding Dong (remixed mono/edited stereo).	1974	10.00	20.00	40.00
❑ 1884	You/World of Stone.	1975	—	3.00	6.00
❑ 1884 [PS]	You/World of Stone.	1975	3.75	7.50	15.00
❑ P-1884 [DJ]	You (mono/stereo).	1975	10.00	20.00	40.00
❑ 1885	This Guitar (Can't Keep from Crying)/Maya Love.	1975	6.25	12.50	25.00

—The last Apple 45 until 1995

❑ P-1885 [DJ]	This Guitar (Can't Keep from Crying) (mono/stereo).	1975	12.50	25.00	50.00
❑ 2995	My Sweet Lord/Isn't It a Pity.	1970	2.00	4.00	8.00

—With "Mfd. by Apple" on label

❑ 2995	My Sweet Lord/Isn't It a Pity.	1970	10.00	20.00	40.00

—With black star on label

❑ 2995 [PS]	My Sweet Lord/Isn't It a Pity.	1970	10.00	20.00	40.00
❑ 2995	My Sweet Lord/Isn't It a Pity.	1975	6.25	12.50	25.00

—With "All Rights Reserved" disclaimer

CAPITOL

❑ 1828	What Is Life/Apple Scruffs	1976	7.50	15.00	30.00

—Orange label

❑ 1828	What Is Life/Apple Scruffs	1978	—	3.00	6.00

—Purple late-1970s label

❑ 1836	Bangla-Desh/Deep Blue	1976	7.50	15.00	30.00

—Orange label

❑ 1836	Bangla-Desh/Deep Blue	1978	—	3.00	6.00

—Purple late-1970s label

❑ 1836	Bangla-Desh/Deep Blue	1983	3.75	7.50	15.00

—Black colorband label

❑ 1862	Give Me Love (Give Me Peace on Earth)/ Miss O'Dell	1978	2.00	4.00	8.00

—Purple late-1970s label

❑ 1862	Give Me Love (Give Me Peace on Earth)/ Miss O'Dell	1978	3.75	7.50	15.00

—Black colorband label

❑ 1879	Ding Dong, Ding Dong/Hari's on Tour (Express)	1978	2.00	4.00	8.00

—Purple late-1970s label

❑ 2995	My Sweet Lord/Isn't It a Pity	1976	5.00	10.00	20.00

—Orange label with "Capitol" at bottom

❑ 2995	My Sweet Lord/Isn't It a Pity	1978	—	3.00	6.00

—Purple label; label has reeded edge

❑ 2995	My Sweet Lord/Isn't It a Pity	1983	—	3.00	6.00

—Black label with colorband

❑ 2995	My Sweet Lord/Isn't It a Pity	1988	—	2.50	5.00

—Purple label; label has smooth edge

❑ 15930 [DJ]	My Sweet Lord/My Sweet Lord 2000	2001	2.50	5.00	10.00

—White label, small hole

❑ 15930 [DJ]	My Sweet Lord/My Sweet Lord 2000	2001	3.75	7.50	15.00

—Promo item for the re-release of the All Things Must Pass CD

❑ 58983	My Sweet Lord (2000)/All Things Must Pass	2001	—	2.50	5.00

—Green vinyl

COLUMBIA

❑ 04887	I Don't Want to Do It/Queen of the Hop	1985	6.25	12.50	25.00

—B-side by Dave Edmunds

DARK HORSE

❑ 8294	This Song/Learning How to Love You	1976	2.00	4.00	8.00

—White label, NOT a promo

❑ 8294	This Song/Learning How to Love You	1976	2.50	5.00	10.00

—Tan label

Number	Title (A Side/B Side)	Yr	VG	VG+	NM
❏ 8294 [DJ]	This Song (mono/stereo)	1976	6.25	12.50	25.00
❏ 8294 [PS]	This Song/Learning How to Love You	1976	7.50	15.00	30.00
❏ 8294 [PS]	This Song (mono/stereo)	1976	10.00	20.00	40.00
—Flyer with "The Story Behind This Song"					
❏ 8294 [PS]	This Song (mono/stereo)	1976	10.00	20.00	40.00
—Promotional only sleeve, different from stock sleeve					
❏ 8313	Crackerbox Palace/Learning How to Love You	1977	—	2.50	5.00
❏ 8763	Blow Away/Soft-Hearted Hana	1979	—	2.50	5.00
—With "RE-1" on label					
❏ 8763	Blow Away/Soft-Hearted Hana	1979	5.00	10.00	20.00
—Without "RE-1" on label (no "Loka Productions S.A." on label)					
❏ 8763	Blow Away/Soft-Hearted Hana	1979	—	2.50	5.00
❏ 8844	Love Comes to Everyone/Soft Touch	1979	2.50	5.00	10.00
❏ 8844 [PS]	Love Comes to Everyone/Soft Touch	1979	250.00	500.00	750.00
❏ 21891	Got My Mind Set on You/When We Was Fab	198?	—	2.00	4.00
—"Back to Back Hits" series					
❏ 27913	This Is Love/Breath Away from Heaven	1988	—	2.50	5.00
❏ 27913 [PS]	This Is Love/Breath Away from Heaven	1988	—	2.50	5.00
❏ 28131	When We Was Fab/Zig Zag	1988	—	2.50	5.00
❏ 28131 [PS]	When We Was Fab/Zig Zag	1988	—	2.50	5.00
❏ 28178	Got My Mind Set on You/Lay His Head	1987	—	2.00	4.00
❏ 28178 [PS]	Got My Mind Set on You/Lay His Head	1987	—	2.00	4.00
❏ 29744	I Really Love You/Circles	1983	6.25	12.50	25.00
❏ 29864	Wake Up My Love/Greece	1982	2.50	5.00	10.00
❏ 49725	All Those Years Ago/Writing's on the Wall	1981	—	2.50	5.00
❏ 49725 [PS]	All Those Years Ago/Writing's on the Wall	1981	—	2.50	5.00
❏ 49785	Teardrops/Save the World	1981	2.50	5.00	10.00
WARNER BROS.					
❏ 22807	Cheer Down/That's What It Takes	1989	3.75	7.50	15.00
❏ 22807 [DJ]	Cheer Down (same on both sides)	1989	50.00	100.00	200.00
❏ 22807 [PS]	Cheer Down/That's What It Takes	1989	3.75	7.50	15.00
Albums					
APPLE					
❏ STCH-639 [(3)]	All Things Must Pass	1970	10.00	20.00	40.00
—Apple labels on first two records and "Apple Jam" labels on third; includes poster and lyric innersleeves					
❏ ST-3350	Wonderwall Music Bonus Photo	1968	—	2.50	5.00
❏ ST-3350	Wonderwall Music	1968	6.25	12.50	25.00
—With "Mfd. by Apple" on label					
❏ ST-3350	Wonderwall Music	1968	37.50	75.00	150.00
—With Capitol logo on Side 2 bottom					
❏ SMAS-3410	Living in the Material World	1973	3.75	7.50	15.00
❏ SMAS-3418	Dark Horse	1974	3.75	7.50	15.00
❏ SW-3420	Extra Texture (Read All About It)	1975	3.75	7.50	15.00
CAPITOL					
❏ STCH-639 [(3)]	All Things Must Pass	1976	7.50	15.00	30.00
—Orange labels with poster and lyric innersleeves					
❏ STCH-639 [(3)]	All Things Must Pass	1978	6.25	12.50	25.00
—Purple labels with poster and lyric innersleeves					
❏ STCH-639 [(3)]	All Things Must Pass	1983	25.00	50.00	100.00
—Black labels, print in colorband, with poster and lyric innersleeves					
❏ ST-11578	The Best of George Harrison	1976	3.75	7.50	15.00
—Custom label, no bar code on back					
❏ ST-11578	The Best of George Harrison	1976	45.00	90.00	180.00
—Orange label					
❏ ST-11578	The Best of George Harrison	1978	2.50	5.00	10.00
—Purple label, large Capitol logo					
❏ ST-11578	The Best of George Harrison	1983	6.25	12.50	25.00
—Black label, print in colorband					
❏ ST-11578	The Best of George Harrison	1988	6.25	12.50	25.00
—Odd reissue with custom label; large stand-alone "S" in trail-off area; bar code on cover					
❏ ST-11578	The Best of George Harrison	1989	20.00	40.00	80.00
—Purple label, small Capitol logo					
❏ SN-16055	Dark Horse	1980	3.75	7.50	15.00
—Budget-line reissue; reverses front and back covers					
❏ SN-16216	Living in the Material World	1980	5.00	10.00	20.00
—Budget-line reissue					
❏ SN-16217	Extra Texture (Read All About It)	1980	6.25	12.50	25.00
—Budget-line reissue					
CAPITOL/APPLE					
❏ STCH-639 [(3)]	All Things Must Pass	1988	20.00	40.00	80.00
—Odd pressing with Apple labels and Capitol cover (look for stand-alone "S" in trail-off wax); with large sticker on back cover					
DARK HORSE					
❏ (no #) [DJ]	Dark Horse Radio Special	1974	100.00	200.00	400.00
—Promo-only; George Harrison introduces his new record label and artists					
❏ PRO 649 [DJ]	A Personal Music Dialogue at Thirty Three and 1/3	1976	12.50	25.00	50.00
❏ DH 3005	Thirty Three and 1/3	1976	2.50	5.00	10.00
❏ DHK 3255	George Harrison	1979	2.50	5.00	10.00
—Deduct 30% for cut-outs					
❏ DHK 3255	George Harrison	1979	10.00	20.00	40.00
—Columbia House edition (back cover says "Manufactured by Columbia House Under License")					
❏ DHK 3492	Somewhere in England	1981	2.50	5.00	10.00
—Deduct 30% for cut-outs					
❏ 23724	Gone Troppo	1982	2.50	5.00	10.00
—Deduct 30% for cut-outs					
❏ 23724 [DJ]	Gone Troppo	1982	6.25	12.50	25.00
—Promo on Quiex II vinyl					
❏ 25643	Cloud Nine	1987	2.50	5.00	10.00
❏ W1-25643	Cloud Nine	1987	3.00	6.00	12.00
—Columbia House edition					
❏ 25726	Best of Dark Horse 1976-1989	1989	6.25	12.50	25.00
❏ W1-25726	Best of Dark Horse 1976-1989	1989	3.75	7.50	15.00
—Columbia House edition					
❏ R 174328	Cloud Nine	1987	3.75	7.50	15.00
—BMG Direct Marketing edition					
❏ R 180307	Best of Dark Horse 1976-1989	1989	3.75	7.50	15.00
—BMG Direct Marketing edition					
ZAPPLE					
❏ ST-3358	Electronic Sound	1969	10.00	20.00	40.00

Number	Title (A Side/B Side)	Yr	VG	VG+	NM
HARRISON, GEORGE, AND FRIENDS The "Friends" include BADFINGER; ERIC CLAPTON; BOB DYLAN; BILLY PRESTON; LEON RUSSELL; RAVI SHANKAR; RINGO STARR.					
Albums					
APPLE					
❏ STCX-3385 [(3)]	The Concert for Bangla Desh	1971	10.00	20.00	40.00
—With 64-page booklet and custom innersleeves					
❏ STCX-3385 [(3)]	The Concert for Bangla Desh	1975	12.50	25.00	50.00
—As above, but with "All Rights Reserved" on labels					
CAPITOL					
❏ SABB-12248 [(2)]	The Concert for Bangla Desh	1982	75.00	150.00	300.00
—Scheduled reissue that was never officially released, though a few copies got out by mistake					
HARRISON, GEORGE/JEFF BECK/DAVE EDMUNDS					
12-Inch Singles					
COLUMBIA					
❏ CAS 2034 [DJ]	I Don't Want to Do It/Sleepwalk/Queen of the Hop	1985	5.00	10.00	20.00
—Promo sampler from movie "Porky's Revenge"					
HARRISON, NOEL					
45s					
LONDON					
❏ 9755	One Too Many Mornings/Barbara Allen	1965	2.00	4.00	8.00
❏ 9795	A Young Girl/The Future Mrs. 'Awkins	1965	2.50	5.00	10.00
❏ 9815	It's All Over Now, Baby Blue/Much As I Love You	1966	2.00	4.00	8.00
❏ 20011	The Man Behind the Red Balloon/Marlene	1966	2.00	4.00	8.00
❏ 20017	Cheryl's Going Home/In a Dusty Old Room	1966	2.00	4.00	8.00
❏ 20017 [PS]	Cheryl's Going Home/In a Dusty Old Room	1966	3.00	6.00	12.00
❏ 20021	Out for the Day/Fly Sing Song	1967	2.00	4.00	8.00
REPRISE					
❏ 0599	Sign of the Queen/Mrs. Williams' Rose	1967	—	3.00	6.00
❏ 0615	Life Is a Dream/Suzanne	1967	—	3.00	6.00
❏ 0682	Santa Monica Pier/In Your Chidren	1968	—	3.00	6.00
❏ 0758	The Windmills of Your Mind/Leitch on the Beach	1968	2.00	4.00	8.00
❏ 0795	I'll Be Your Baby Tonight/The Greatest Experiment Is Over	1968	—	3.00	6.00
❏ 0914	Another Virgin Spring/Tin Wedding	1970	—	3.00	6.00
Albums					
LONDON					
❏ PS 459 [S]	Noel Harrison	1966	6.25	12.50	25.00
❏ LL 3459 [M]	Noel Harrison	1966	5.00	10.00	20.00
REPRISE					
❏ R-6263 [M]	Collage	1967	3.75	7.50	15.00
❏ RS-6263 [S]	Collage	1967	5.00	10.00	20.00
❏ RS-6295	Santa Monica Pier	1968	3.75	7.50	15.00
❏ RS-6321	The Great Electric Experiment Is Over	1969	3.75	7.50	15.00
HARRISON, WES					
45s					
LIN					
❏ 5002	There Y'Are/Uncle Winnie's Sound Stories	1956	7.50	15.00	30.00
PHILIPS					
❏ DJP-4 [DJ]	Wes' Car/Better Late Than Never	1963	3.00	6.00	12.00
—Promo only					
Albums					
PHILIPS					
❏ PHM 200103 [M]	You Won't Believe Your Ears	1963	5.00	10.00	20.00
❏ PHS 600103 [S]	You Won't Believe Your Ears	1963	6.25	12.50	25.00
HARRISON, WILBERT					
45s					
BELL					
❏ 869	C.C. Rider/Since I Fell for You	1970	—	3.00	6.00
BRUNSWICK					
❏ 55511	Lovin' Operator/Love You	1974	—	3.00	6.00
❏ 55519	I'm Going to the River/I Need Some (Honey Honey)	1975	—	3.00	6.00
CHART					
❏ 626	Cool Water/Calypso Man	1956	6.25	12.50	25.00
CONSTELLATION					
❏ 122	New York World's Fair/Mama, Mama, Mama	1964	2.50	5.00	10.00
DELUXE					
❏ 6002	This Woman of Mine/The Letter	1953	15.00	30.00	60.00
❏ 6031	Nobody Knows My Trouble/ Gin and Coconut Milk	1954	15.00	30.00	60.00
FURY					
❏ 1023	Kansas City/Listen, My Darling	1959	7.50	15.00	30.00
❏ 1027	Cheating Baby/Don't Wreck My Life	1959	3.75	7.50	15.00
❏ 1028	Goodbye Kansas City/1960	1960	3.75	7.50	15.00
❏ 1031	C.C. Rider/Why Did You Leave	1960	3.75	7.50	15.00
❏ 1037	Since I Fell for You/Little School Girl	1960	3.75	7.50	15.00
❏ 1041	The Horse/Da-De-Ya-Da (I'd Do Anything for You)	1961	3.75	7.50	15.00
❏ 1047	Happy in Love/Calypso Dance	1961	3.75	7.50	15.00
❏ 1055	Drafted/My Heart Is Yours	1961	3.75	7.50	15.00
❏ 1059	Let's Stick Together/Kansas City Twist	1962	3.75	7.50	15.00
❏ 1063	Let's Stick Together/My Heart Is Yours	1962	3.00	6.00	12.00
GLADES					
❏ 603	Gonna Tell You a Story/Letter Edged in Black	1959	3.00	6.00	12.00
LOST-NITE					
❏ 365	Kansas City/Listen, My Darling	197?	—	2.50	5.00
—Reissue					
PORT					
❏ 3003	Baby Move On/You're Still My Baby	1965	2.00	4.00	8.00
❏ 3009	Don't Take It So Hard/Sugar Lump	1965	2.00	4.00	8.00
ROCKIN'					
❏ 526	This Woman of Mine/The Letter	1952	25.00	50.00	100.00
ROULETTE					
❏ 4752	No One's Love But Yours/Mini-Parade	1967	2.00	4.00	8.00
SAVOY					
❏ 1138	Don't Drop It/The Ways of a Woman	1954	10.00	20.00	40.00
❏ 1149	Women and Whiskey/Da-De-Ya-Da (I'd Do Anything for You)	1955	7.50	15.00	30.00
❏ 1164	Florida Special/Darling, Listen to This Song	1955	7.50	15.00	30.00
❏ 1198	Confessin' My Dream/The Way I Feel	1956	7.50	15.00	30.00
❏ 1517	My Love Is True/I Know My Baby Loves Me	1957	6.25	12.50	25.00

Number	Title (A Side/B Side)	Yr	VG	VG+	NM
☐ 1531	Baby Don't You Know/				
	My Love for You Lingers On	1958	5.00	10.00	20.00
☐ 1571	Don't Drop It/Baby Don't You Know	1959	3.75	7.50	15.00
SEA HORN					
☐ 502	Say It Again/Near to You	1963	2.00	4.00	8.00
SSS INTERNATIONAL					
☐ 830	My Heart Is Yours/Pretty Little Woman	1971	—	3.00	6.00
☐ 830 [DJ]	My Heart Is Yours (mono/stereo)	1971	2.50	5.00	10.00
—Promo only on blue vinyl					
SUE					
☐ 11	Let's Work Together (Part 1)/				
	Let's Work Together (Part 2)	1969	—	3.00	6.00
WET SOUL					
☐ 4	My Heart Is Yours/Pretty Little Woman	1970	2.00	4.00	8.00
Albums					
BUDDAH					
☐ BDS-5002	Wilbert Harrison	1971	7.50	15.00	30.00
CHELSEA					
☐ CH 523	Wilbert Harrison	1977	5.00	10.00	20.00
JUGGERNAUT					
☐ ST-8803	Shoot You Full of Love	1971	12.50	25.00	50.00
SAVOY JAZZ					
☐ SJL-1182	Listen to My Song	1987	3.00	6.00	12.00
SPHERE SOUND					
☐ SSR-7000 [M]	Kansas City	1965	62.50	125.00	250.00
☐ SSSR-7000 [R]	Kansas City	1965	50.00	100.00	200.00
SUE					
☐ SSLP-8801	Let's Work Together	1970	12.50	25.00	50.00
WET SOUL					
☐ 1001	Anything You Want	197?	12.50	25.00	50.00

HARSHMAN, ROBERT LUKE See BOBBY HART.

HART, BILLY AND DON
45s
ROULETTE

Number	Title (A Side/B Side)	Yr	VG	VG+	NM
☐ 4133	Rock-a-Bop-a-Lena/More and More	1959	15.00	30.00	60.00
☐ 4172	Check-Mated and Bingoed/Blabbermouth	1959	7.50	15.00	30.00

HART, BOBBY
45s
ARIOLA AMERICA

Number	Title (A Side/B Side)	Yr	VG	VG+	NM
☐ 809	Lovers for the Night/				
	You Get Smoke in Your Eyes	1980	—	2.50	5.00
BAMBOO					
☐ 507	The Girl I Used to Know/The Spider and the Fly	1961	7.50	15.00	30.00
CHELSEA					
☐ BCBO-0026	Easy Evil/California	1973	—	2.50	5.00
DCP					
☐ 1113	That'll Be the Day/Turn On Your Lovelight	1964	5.00	10.00	20.00
☐ 1142	Baby Let Your Hair Down/Jealous Feeling	1965	6.25	12.50	25.00
☐ 1152	Around the Corner/Cry My Eyes Out	1966	5.00	10.00	20.00
ERA					
☐ 3039	Girl in the Window/Journey of Love	1961	5.00	10.00	20.00
GUYDEN					
☐ 2022	Is You Is Or Is You Ain't My Baby/Girl of My				
	Dreams	1959	7.50	15.00	30.00
—As "Robert Luke Harshman"					
INFINITY					
☐ 017	Too Many Teardrops/The People Next Door	1963	5.00	10.00	20.00
☐ 022	Lovesick Blues/I Think It's Called a Heartache	1963	5.00	10.00	20.00
RADIO					
☐ 122	Stop Talkin', Start Lovin'/Love Whatcha Doin' to				
	Me	1959	10.00	20.00	40.00
—As "Robert Luke Harshman"					
REEL					
☐ 100	Girl in the Window/Journey of Love	1961	10.00	20.00	40.00
WARNER BROS.					
☐ 8058	Hard Core Man/To Keep from Crying	1974	—	2.50	5.00
☐ 8058 [PS]	Hard Core Man/To Keep from Crying	1974	2.00	4.00	8.00
☐ 49079	The Loneliest Night/Sometimes Love	1979	—	2.50	5.00

HART, FREDDIE
45s
CAPITOL

Number	Title (A Side/B Side)	Yr	VG	VG+	NM
☐ F2524	Butterfly Love/My Heart Is a Playground	1953	6.25	12.50	25.00
☐ F2588	Secret Kisses/Whole Hog or None	1953	5.00	10.00	20.00
☐ 2692	The Whole World Holding Hands/Without You	1969	2.00	4.00	8.00
☐ F2726	Loose Talk/The Curtain Never Falls	1954	5.00	10.00	20.00
☐ 2768	One More Mountain to Climb/Just Another Girl	1970	2.00	4.00	8.00
☐ 2839	Fingerprints/I Can't Keep My Hands Off of You	1970	2.00	4.00	8.00
☐ F2873	Caught at Last/It Just Don't Seem Like Home	1954	5.00	10.00	20.00
☐ 2933	California Grapevine/				
	What's Wrong with Your Head, Fred	1970	2.00	4.00	8.00
☐ F2991	I'm Going Out on the Front Porch and Cry/				
	Please Don't Tell Her	1954	5.00	10.00	20.00
☐ F3090	Miss Lonely Heart/Oh Heart Let Her Go	1955	5.00	10.00	20.00
☐ 3115	Easy Living/Brother Bluebird	1971	—	3.00	6.00
☐ F3203	Canada to Tennessee/No Thanks to You	1955	5.00	10.00	20.00
☐ 3261	My Hang-Up Is You/Big Bad Wolf	1972	—	3.00	6.00
☐ F3299	Hiding in Darkness/That's What You Gave to Me	1955	5.00	10.00	20.00
☐ 3353	Bless Your Heart/Conscience Makes Cowards				
	(Of Us All)	1972		3.00	6.00
☐ 3453	Got the All Overs for You				
	(All Over Me)/Just Another Girl	1972		3.00	6.00
☐ 3524	Super Kind of Woman/				
	Mother Nature Made a Believer Out of Me	1973		3.00	6.00
☐ 3612	Trip to Heaven/Look-a Here	1973		3.00	6.00
☐ 3730	If You Can't Feel It (It Ain't There)/				
	Skid Row Street	1973		3.00	6.00
☐ 3789	Blue Christmas/I Believe in Santa Claus	1973		3.50	7.00
☐ 3827	Hang In There Girl/You Belong to Me	1974		3.00	6.00
☐ 3898	The Want-To's/Phenix City, Alabama	1974		3.00	6.00
☐ 3970	My Woman's Man/Let's Clean Up the Country	1974		3.00	6.00
☐ 4031	I'd Like to Sleep Til I Get Over You/Nothing's				
	Better Than That	1975		3.00	6.00

Number	Title (A Side/B Side)	Yr	VG	VG+	NM
☐ 4099	The First Time/Sexy	1975	—	3.00	6.00
☐ 4152	Warm Side of You/				
	I Love You, I Just Don't Like You	1975	—	3.00	6.00
☐ 4210	You Are the Song (Inside of Me)/I Can Almost				
	See Houston from Here	1976	—	3.00	6.00
☐ 4251	She'll Throw Stones at You/Love Makes It Alright	1976	—	3.00	6.00
☐ 4313	That Look in Her Eyes/Try My Love for Size	1976	—	3.00	6.00
☐ 4363	Why Lovers Turn to Strangers/Paper Sack Full				
	of Memories	1976	—	3.00	6.00
☐ 4409	Thank God She's Mine/Falling All Over Me	1977	—	2.00	4.00
☐ 4448	The Pleasure's Been All Mine/				
	It's Heaven Loving You	1977	—	2.00	4.00
☐ 4498	The Search/Honky Tonk Toys	1977	—	2.50	5.00
☐ 4530	So Good, So Rare, So Fine/				
	There's an Angel Living There	1978	—	2.50	5.00
☐ 4561	Only You/I Love You, I Just Don't Like You	1978	—	2.50	5.00
☐ 4609	Toe to Toe/And Then Some	1978	—	2.50	5.00
☐ 4684	My Lady/Guilty	1979	—	2.50	5.00
☐ 4720	Wasn't It Easy Baby/My Lady Loves	1979	—	2.50	5.00
COLUMBIA					
☐ 21512	Dig Boy Dig/Two of a Kind	1956	12.50	25.00	50.00
☐ 21550	Snatch It and Grab It/Human Thing to Do	1956	3.75	7.50	15.00
☐ 21558	Drink Up and Go Home/Blue	1956	3.75	7.50	15.00
☐ 40821	On the Prowl/Extra	1957	3.75	7.50	15.00
☐ 40896	Fraulein/Baby Don't Leave	1957	3.75	7.50	15.00
☐ 41005	Say No More/The Outside World	1957	3.75	7.50	15.00
☐ 41081	You Are My World/Heaven Only Knows	1957	3.75	7.50	15.00
☐ 41144	I Won't Be Home Tonight/Love, Come to Me	1958	3.75	7.50	15.00
☐ 41269	I'm No Angel/Midnight Date	1958	3.75	7.50	15.00
☐ 41345	The Wall/Davy Jones	1959	3.00	6.00	12.00
☐ 41439	Farther Than My Eyes Can See/My Kind of Love	1959	—	—	—
—Unreleased					
☐ 41456	Chain Gang/Rock Bottom	1959	3.00	6.00	12.00
☐ 41597	The Key's in the Mailbox/Starvation Days	1960	3.00	6.00	12.00
☐ 41805	Lying Again/Do My Heart a Favor	1960	3.00	6.00	12.00
☐ 42146	What a Laugh!/Heart Attack	1961	3.00	6.00	12.00
☐ 42285	Some Do, Some Don't, Some Will, Some Won't/				
	Like You Are	1962	3.00	6.00	12.00
☐ 42491	Stand Up/Ugly Duckling	1962	3.00	6.00	12.00
☐ 42679	I'll Hit It with a Stick/Stranger Drive Away	1963	3.00	6.00	12.00
☐ 42769	Angels Like You/Mary Ann	1963	3.00	6.00	12.00
EL DORADO					
☐ 101	I Don't Want to Lose You/				
	My Favorite Entertainer	1985	—	3.50	7.00
FIFTH ST.					
☐ 1091	Best Love I Never Had/I'm Not Going Hungry	1987	—	3.00	6.00
KAPP					
☐ 632	Love Can Make or Break a Heart/				
	Hurts Feel So Good	1964	2.50	5.00	10.00
☐ 661	Moon Gal/You've Got It Coming To Ya	1965	2.50	5.00	10.00
☐ 694	Hank Williams' Guitar/I Created a Monster	1965	2.50	5.00	10.00
☐ 743	Why Should I Cry Over You/Keys in the Mailbox	1966	2.50	5.00	10.00
☐ 765	Together Again/Waiting for a Train	1966	2.50	5.00	10.00
☐ 794	Misty Blue/Elm Street Pawn Shop	1966	2.50	5.00	10.00
☐ 820	I'll Hold You in My Heart/Too Much of You				
	(Left of Me)	1967	2.50	5.00	10.00
☐ 841	Anna Maria/Leon and the Rain	1967	2.50	5.00	10.00
☐ 879	Togetherness/Portrait of a Lonely Man	1967	2.50	5.00	10.00
☐ 879 [PS]	Togetherness/Portrait of a Lonely Man	1967	3.75	7.50	15.00
☐ 910	Born a Fool/Hands of a Man	1968	2.50	5.00	10.00
☐ 944	Don't Cry Baby/Here Lies a Heart	1968	2.50	5.00	10.00
☐ 976	Why Leave Something I Can't Use/				
	Hang On to Her	1969	2.50	5.00	10.00
☐ 993	I Lost All My Tomorrows/				
	That's How High a Man Can Go	1969	2.50	5.00	10.00
☐ 2183	Don't Cry Baby/Loving You Again	1972	—	3.50	7.00
MCA					
☐ 40011	Born a Fool/My Anna Maria	1973	—	3.00	6.00
MONUMENT					
☐ 826	For a Second There/The Almighty Dollar	1963	3.00	6.00	12.00
☐ 838	First You Go Through Me/Valentino	1964	3.00	6.00	12.00
SUNBIRD					
☐ 110	Sure Thing/Makin' Love to a Memory	1980	—	3.00	6.00
☐ 7550	Sure Thing/Makin' Love to a Memory	1980	—	2.50	5.00
☐ 7553	Roses Are Red/Battle of the Sexes	1980	—	2.50	5.00
☐ 7560	You're Crazy Man/Playboy's Centerfolk	1981	—	2.50	5.00
☐ 7565	You Were There/The Weaker Sex	1981	—	2.50	5.00
Albums					
CAPITOL					
☐ ST-469	New Sounds	1970	3.00	6.00	12.00
☐ ST-593	California Grapevine	1970	3.00	6.00	12.00
☐ ST-838	Easy Loving	1971	3.00	6.00	12.00
☐ ST-11014	My Hang-Up Is You	1972	3.00	6.00	12.00
☐ ST-11073	Bless Your Heart	1972	3.00	6.00	12.00
☐ ST-11107	Got the All-Overs	1972	3.00	6.00	12.00
☐ ST-11156	Super Kind of Woman	1973	3.00	6.00	12.00
☐ ST-11197	Trip to Heaven	1973	3.00	6.00	12.00
☐ ST-11252	If You Can't Feel It	1974	3.00	6.00	12.00
☐ ST-11296	Hang In There Girl	1974	3.00	6.00	12.00
☐ ST-11353	Country Heart 'N' Soul	1975	3.00	6.00	12.00
☐ ST-11374	Greatest Hits	1975	3.00	6.00	12.00
☐ ST-11449	The First Time	1975	2.50	5.00	10.00
☐ ST-11504	People Put to Music	1976	2.50	5.00	10.00
☐ ST-11568	That Look in Her Eyes	1976	2.50	5.00	10.00
☐ ST-11626	The Pleasure's Been All Mine	1977	2.50	5.00	10.00
☐ ST-11724	Only You	1978	2.50	5.00	10.00
COLUMBIA					
☐ CL 1792 [M]	The Spirited Freddie Hart	1962	10.00	20.00	40.00
☐ G 31550 [(2)]	The World of Freddie Hart	1972	3.75	7.50	15.00
HARMONY					
☐ HL 7412 [M]	The Best of Freddie Hart	1967	3.00	6.00	12.00
☐ HS 11212 [S]	The Best of Freddie Hart	1967	3.00	6.00	12.00
☐ KH 31165	Lonesome Love	1972	2.50	5.00	10.00
☐ KH 32467	You Are My World	1973	2.50	5.00	10.00
HILLTOP					
☐ 6117	From Canada to Tennessee	1972	2.50	5.00	10.00

Number	Title (A Side/B Side)	Yr	VG	VG+	NM
KAPP					
❏ KL-1456 [M]	The Hart of Country Music	1966	3.75	7.50	15.00
❏ KL-1492 [M]	Straight from the Heart	1966	3.75	7.50	15.00
❏ KL-1513 [M]	Hurtin' Man	1967	5.00	10.00	20.00
❏ KL-1539 [M]	The Neon and the Rain	1967	5.00	10.00	20.00
❏ KS-3456 [S]	The Hart of Country Music	1966	5.00	10.00	20.00
❏ KS-3492 [S]	Straight from the Heart	1966	5.00	10.00	20.00
❏ KS-3513 [S]	Hurtin' Man	1967	5.00	10.00	20.00
❏ KS-3539 [S]	The Neon and the Rain	1967	5.00	10.00	20.00
❏ KS-3546	Togetherness	1968	5.00	10.00	20.00
❏ KS-3568	Born a Fool	1968	5.00	10.00	20.00
❏ KS-3592	Greatest Hits	1969	3.75	7.50	15.00
MCA					
❏ 4088 [(2)]	The Best of Freddie Hart	1975	3.75	7.50	15.00
SUNBIRD					
❏ ST-50100	Sure Thing	1980	3.00	6.00	12.00

HART, MICKEY Also see THE GRATEFUL DEAD.
45s

Number	Title (A Side/B Side)	Yr	VG	VG+	NM
WARNER BROS.					
❏ 7644	Blind John/Pump Man	1972	2.50	5.00	10.00
Albums					
RELIX					
❏ 2026	Rolling Thunder	1987	3.00	6.00	12.00
WARNER BROS.					
❏ BS 2635	Rolling Thunder	1972	7.50	15.00	30.00

HART, MICKEY, AIRTO, FLORA PURIM, BATUCAJE
Albums

Number	Title (A Side/B Side)	Yr	VG	VG+	NM
REFERENCE RECORDINGS					
❏ RR-12	Dafos	1985	3.75	7.50	15.00

HART, ROCKY
45s

Number	Title (A Side/B Side)	Yr	VG	VG+	NM
BIG TOP					
❏ 3069	Crying/Baby You've Got It Made	1961	7.50	15.00	30.00
CUB					
❏ 9052	Every Day/Come with Me	1959	7.50	15.00	30.00
GLO					
❏ 216	I Play the Part of a Fool/Someone Stole My Baby While Doing the Twist	1961	50.00	100.00	200.00

HARTFORD, JOHN
45s

Number	Title (A Side/B Side)	Yr	VG	VG+	NM
AMPEX					
❏ 11019	One Too Many Mornings/(B-side unknown)	1971	—	2.50	5.00
FLYING FISH					
❏ 4013	Piece of My Heart/(B-side unknown)	1984	—	2.00	4.00
MCA DOT					
❏ 53104	Ohio River Rag/Love Wrote This Song	1987	—	2.00	4.00
RCA VICTOR					
❏ 47-8987	Tall Tall Grass/Jack's in the Sack	1966	2.00	4.00	8.00
❏ 47-9175	Gentle on My Mind/Electric Washing Machine	1967	2.00	4.00	8.00
❏ 47-9345	A Simple Thing As Love/Landscape Grown Cold	1967	2.00	4.00	8.00
❏ 47-9451	Big Blue Balloon/Six O'Clock Train and a Girl with Green Eyes	1968	2.00	4.00	8.00
❏ 47-9507	Shiny Rails of Steel/Natural to Be Gone	1968	2.00	4.00	8.00
❏ 47-9611	I Didn't Know the World Would Last This Long/The Category Stomp	1968	—	3.00	6.00
❏ 47-9668	California Earthquake/Mouth to Mouth Resuscitation	1968	—	3.00	6.00
❏ 47-9753	I Didn't Know the World Would Last This Long/Orphan of World War II	1969	—	3.00	6.00
❏ 47-9772	Like Unto a Mockingbird/Natural to Be Gone	1969	—	3.00	6.00
Albums					
FLYING FISH					
❏ FF-020	Mark Twang	1976	2.50	5.00	10.00
❏ FF-028	Nobody Knows What You Do	1977	2.50	5.00	10.00
❏ FF-044	All in the Name of Love	1983	2.50	5.00	10.00
❏ FF-063	Headin' Down Into the Mystery Below	1978	2.50	5.00	10.00
❏ FF-095	Slumberin' on the Cumberland	1979	2.50	5.00	10.00
—With Pat Burton and Benny Martin					
❏ FF-228	You and Me at Home	1980	2.50	5.00	10.00
❏ FF-259	Catalogue	1982	2.50	5.00	10.00
❏ FF-289	Gum Tree Canoe	1984	2.50	5.00	10.00
❏ FF-440	Me Oh My, How Time Flies	1987	2.50	5.00	10.00
MCA					
❏ 5861	Annual Waltz	1987	2.00	4.00	8.00
RCA VICTOR					
❏ LPM-3687 [M]	John Hartford Looks at Life	1966	5.00	10.00	20.00
❏ LSP-3687 [S]	John Hartford Looks at Life	1966	3.75	7.50	15.00
❏ LPM-3796 [M]	Earthwords and Music	1967	6.25	12.50	25.00
❏ LSP-3796 [S]	Earthwords and Music	1967	3.75	7.50	15.00
❏ LPM-3884 [M]	The Love Album	1967	6.25	12.50	25.00
❏ LSP-3884 [S]	The Love Album	1967	3.75	7.50	15.00
❏ LPM-3998 [M]	Housing Project	1968	12.50	25.00	50.00
❏ LSP-3998 [S]	Housing Project	1968	3.75	7.50	15.00
❏ LSP-4068	Gentle on My Mind and Other Originals	1968	3.75	7.50	15.00
❏ LSP-4156	John Hartford	1969	3.75	7.50	15.00
❏ LSP-4337	Iron Mountain Depot	1970	3.75	7.50	15.00
WARNER BROS.					
❏ WS 1916	Aereo-Plain	1971	3.00	6.00	12.00
❏ BS 2651	Morning Bugle	1972	3.00	6.00	12.00

HARTFORD, KEN
45s

Number	Title (A Side/B Side)	Yr	VG	VG+	NM
SOUTHERN SOUND					
❏ 119	Jay Walker/Little Joe, Go Lightly	1963	6.25	12.50	25.00
—With Frankie Valli					

HARTLEY, KEEF
45s

Number	Title (A Side/B Side)	Yr	VG	VG+	NM
DERAM					
❏ 85060	Don't Be Afraid/Don't Give Up	1970	—	3.00	6.00
❏ 85069	Roundabout (Part 1)/Roundabout (Part 2)	1971	—	3.00	6.00

Number	Title (A Side/B Side)	Yr	VG	VG+	NM
Albums					
DERAM					
❏ DES 18024	Halfbreed	1969	3.75	7.50	15.00
❏ DES 18035	The Battle of North West Six	1970	3.75	7.50	15.00
❏ DES 18047	The Time Is Near	1970	3.75	7.50	15.00
❏ DES 18057	Overdog	1971	3.75	7.50	15.00
❏ XDES 18065	The 72nd Brave	1972	3.75	7.50	15.00
❏ XDES 18070	Lancashire Hustler	1973	3.75	7.50	15.00

HARUMI
45s

Number	Title (A Side/B Side)	Yr	VG	VG+	NM
VERVE FORECAST					
❏ 5086	First Impressions/Talk About It	1968	3.00	6.00	12.00
Albums					
VERVE FORECAST					
❏ FTS-3030	Harumi	1968	6.25	12.50	25.00

HARVEY Also see ETTA AND HARVEY; THE MOONGLOWS.
45s

Number	Title (A Side/B Side)	Yr	VG	VG+	NM
CHESS					
❏ 1713	I Want Somebody/Da Da Goo Goo	1959	10.00	20.00	40.00
❏ 1725	Twelve Months of the Year/Don't Be Afraid of Love	1959	10.00	20.00	40.00
❏ 1749	Blue Skies/Ooh, Ouch, Stop!	1960	6.25	12.50	25.00
❏ 1760	If I Can't Have You/My Heart Cries	1960	6.25	12.50	25.00
—As "Etta and Harvey" (Etta is Etta James)					
❏ 1771	Spoonful/It's a Crying Shame	1960	6.25	12.50	25.00
—As "Etta and Harvey" (Etta is Etta James)					
❏ 1781	The First Time/Mama	1961	6.25	12.50	25.00
—As "Harvey Fuqua"					
HARVEY					
❏ 121	What Can You Do Now/Will I Do	1962	10.00	20.00	40.00
—As "Harvey and Ann"					
TRI-PHI					
❏ 1017	She Loves Me So/Any Way You Wanta	1962	10.00	20.00	40.00
❏ 1024	Memories of You/Come On and Answer Me	1963	15.00	30.00	60.00

HARVEY, ALEX (1) British; fronted the Sensational Alex Harvey Band.
45s

Number	Title (A Side/B Side)	Yr	VG	VG+	NM
ATLANTIC					
❏ 3293	Delilah/Soul in Chains	1975	—	2.50	5.00
DECCA					
❏ 31649	New Orleans/I Just Wanna Make Love to You	1964	5.00	10.00	20.00
VERTIGO					
❏ 113	Swamp Snake/Gang Bang	1974	—	2.50	5.00
❏ 200	Tomahawk Kid/Sergeant Fury	1974	—	2.50	5.00
Albums					
ATLANTIC					
❏ SD 18248	Live	1975	3.00	6.00	12.00
VERTIGO					
❏ VEL-1017	Next	1973	3.00	6.00	12.00
❏ VEL-2000	The Impossible Dream	1974	3.00	6.00	12.00
❏ VEL-2004	Tomorrow Belongs to Me	1975	3.00	6.00	12.00

HARVEY, ALEX (2) American country singer.
45s

Number	Title (A Side/B Side)	Yr	VG	VG+	NM
CAPITOL					
❏ 3172	To Make My Life Beautiful/Lady	1971	—	2.00	4.00
❏ 3336	Delta Dawn/Momma's Waiting	1972	—	2.00	4.00
❏ 3469	Angeline/Devil on My Shoulder	1972	—	2.00	4.00
❏ 3493	Good Time Christmas/Someone Who Cares	1972	—	2.00	4.00
—With Son Lex					
❏ 3649	Right On/Summer Days	1973	—	2.00	4.00
❏ 3703	You Don't Need a Reason/Goodbye Miss Carolina	1973	—	2.00	4.00
❏ 3847	Tangerine/Jody's Face	1974	—	2.00	4.00
METROMEDIA					
❏ 143	Louisiana River Bay/King of Oak Street	1969	—	3.00	6.00
❏ 173	Tell It All Brother/Mama Tried	1970	—	3.00	6.00
UNITED ARTISTS					
❏ 50494	It Takes a Lot of Tenderness/I'll Be Your Tomorrow	1969	2.00	4.00	8.00
Albums					
CAPITOL					
❏ ST-789	Alex Harvey	1972	3.00	6.00	12.00
❏ ST-11128	Souvenirs	1973	3.00	6.00	12.00

HARVEY, PHIL Actually PHIL SPECTOR.
45s

Number	Title (A Side/B Side)	Yr	VG	VG+	NM
IMPERIAL					
❏ 5583	Willy Boy/Bumbershoot	1959	37.50	75.00	150.00

HARVEY AND DOC WITH THE DWELLERS
45s

Number	Title (A Side/B Side)	Yr	VG	VG+	NM
ANNETTE					
❏ 1002	Oh, Baby/Uncle Kev	1964	62.50	125.00	250.00
—Phil Spector appeared on and produced this					

HARVEY AND THE MOONGLOWS See THE MOONGLOWS.

HASSAN, ALI Also see B. BUMBLE AND THE STINGERS.
45s

Number	Title (A Side/B Side)	Yr	VG	VG+	NM
PHILLES					
❏ 103	Malaguena/Chop Sticks	1962	7.50	15.00	30.00

HASSLES, THE BILLY JOEL was in this group.
45s

Number	Title (A Side/B Side)	Yr	VG	VG+	NM
UNITED ARTISTS					
❏ 50215	You've Got Me Hummin'/I'm Thinkin'	1967	3.00	6.00	12.00
❏ 50215 [PS]	You've Got Me Hummin'/I'm Thinkin'	1967	5.00	10.00	20.00
❏ 50258	I Hear Voices/Every Step I Take	1968	3.00	6.00	12.00
❏ 50450	4 O'Clock in the Morning/Let Me Bring You to the Sunshine	1968	3.00	6.00	12.00
❏ 50513	Night After Day/Country Boy	1969	3.00	6.00	12.00
❏ 50586	Traveling Band/Great Balls of Fire	1969	3.00	6.00	12.00

Number	Title (A Side/B Side)	Yr	VG	VG+	NM
Albums					
LIBERTY					
❑ LN-10138	The Hassles	1981	3.00	6.00	12.00
❑ LN-10139	Hour of the Wolf	1981	3.00	6.00	12.00
UNITED ARTISTS					
❑ UAS-6631	The Hassles	1968	6.25	12.50	25.00
❑ UAS-6699	Hour of the Wolf	1969	6.25	12.50	25.00
HATCH, TONY					
45s					
LONDON					
❑ 10505	Ghost Squad/What's All That About	1962	3.00	6.00	12.00
❑ 10523	Cyril's Tune/Out of This World	1963	3.00	6.00	12.00
❑ 10524	Theme from Dick Powell Theatre/Sharon	1963	3.00	6.00	12.00
REPRISE					
❑ 0356	Crossroads/The Marie Celeste	1965	2.50	5.00	10.00
WARNER BROS.					
❑ 5887	I Didn't Know What Time It Was/ Working in the Coal Mine	1967	2.00	4.00	8.00
❑ 7023	Beautiful Rain/While the City Sleeps	1967	2.00	4.00	8.00
HATCHER, WILLIE					
45s					
COLUMBIA					
❑ 44259	Good Things Come to Those Who Wait/ Searching	1968	12.50	25.00	50.00
KING					
❑ 6360	Head Over Heels/Who's Gotta Woman Like Mine	1971	7.50	15.00	30.00
HATFIELD, BOBBY Also see THE RIGHTEOUS BROTHERS.					
45s					
MOONGLOW					
❑ 220	I Need a Girl/Hot Tamale	1963	6.25	12.50	25.00
VERVE					
❑ 10598	Hang-Ups/Soul Cafe	1968	2.00	4.00	8.00
❑ 10621	Brothers/What's the Matter Baby	1968	2.00	4.00	8.00
❑ 10634	Only You/The Wonder of You	1969	2.00	4.00	8.00
❑ 10639	My Prayer/I Wish I Didn't Love You So	1969	2.00	4.00	8.00
❑ 10641	Answer Me My Love/I Only Have Eyes for You	1969	2.00	4.00	8.00
WARNER BROS.					
❑ 7566	Rock 'N Roll Woman/Oo Wee Baby, I Love You	1972	—	2.50	5.00
❑ 7649	Stay with Me/Rock 'N Roll Woman	1972	—	2.50	5.00
Albums					
MGM					
❑ SE-4727	Messin' in Muscle Shoals	1971	3.00	6.00	12.00
HATHAWAY, DONNY Also see ROBERTA FLACK.					
45s					
ATCO					
❑ 6719	The Ghetto (Part 1)/The Ghetto (Part 2)	1969	—	3.00	6.00
❑ 6759	Thank You Master/Je Vous Aime	1970	—	2.50	5.00
❑ 6768	Tryin' Times/Voices Inside	1970	—	2.50	5.00
❑ 6799	This Christmas/Be There	1970	2.00	4.00	8.00
❑ 6817	Take a Love Song/Magnificent Sanctuary Band	1971	—	2.50	5.00
❑ 6828	A Song for You/Put Your Hand in the Hand	1971	—	2.50	5.00
❑ 6880	Little Ghetto Boy/We're Still Friends	1972	—	2.50	5.00
❑ 6884	Giving Up/Jealous Love	1972	—	2.50	5.00
❑ 6899	Bossa Nova/Come Back Charleston Blue	1972	—	2.50	5.00
—With Margie Joseph					
❑ 6903	I Love You More Than You'll Ever Know/ Lord Help Me	1972	—	2.50	5.00
❑ 6928	Love, Love, Love/Someday We'll All Be Free	1973	—	2.50	5.00
❑ 6951	Come Little Children/The Slums	1973	—	2.50	5.00
❑ 7066	This Christmas/Be There	1975	—	2.50	5.00
❑ 7092	You Were Meant for Me/Valdez in the Country	1978	—	2.00	4.00
❑ 7320	This Christmas/Be There	1980	—	2.00	4.00
❑ 99956	This Christmas/Be There	1982	—	2.00	4.00
CURTOM					
❑ 1935	I Thank You Baby/What's This I See	1969	2.00	4.00	8.00
—By "June and Donnie"					
❑ 1971	I Thank You/Just Another Reason	1972	—	2.50	5.00
—By "June Conquest and Donnie Hathaway"; same A-side as 1935 but with revised title					
7-Inch Extended Plays					
ATCO					
❑ SD 7-7029	I Know It's You/Flying Easy//The Slums/Valdez in the Country	1973	2.00	4.00	8.00
—Jukebox issue; small hole, plays at 33 1/3 rpm					
❑ SD 7-7029 [PS]	Extension of a Man	1973	2.00	4.00	8.00
Albums					
ATCO					
❑ SD 38-107	The Best of Donny Hathaway	1978	2.50	5.00	10.00
❑ SD 33-332	Everything Is Everything	1970	3.00	6.00	12.00
❑ SD 33-360	Donny Hathaway	1971	3.00	6.00	12.00
❑ SD 33-386	Donny Hathaway Live	1972	3.00	6.00	12.00
❑ QD 7029 [Q]	Extension of a Man	1974	4.50	9.00	18.00
❑ SD 7029	Extension of a Man	1973	2.50	5.00	10.00
ATLANTIC					
❑ SD 19278	In Performance	1980	2.50	5.00	10.00
HAVEN, SHIRLEY					
45s					
FEDERAL					
❑ 12092	Troubles of My Own/Stop Foolin' Around	1952	75.00	150.00	300.00
—With the Four Jacks					
HAVENS, RICHIE					
45s					
A&M					
❑ 1869	We Can't Hide It Anymore/Dreaming as One	1976	—	2.00	4.00
❑ 1882	I'm Not in Love/Dreaming as One	1976	—	2.00	4.00
❑ 1901	You Can Close Your Eyes/ We Can't Hide It Anymore	1976	—	2.00	4.00
❑ 1984	We All Wanna Boogie/Nobody Left to Crown	1977	—	2.00	4.00
ELEKTRA					
❑ 46619	Every Night/Here's a Song	1980	—	2.00	4.00

Number	Title (A Side/B Side)	Yr	VG	VG+	NM
❑ 46657	The Girl, the Gold Watch and Everything/ Two Hearts in Perfect Time	1980	—	2.00	4.00
MGM					
❑ 14141	Sandy/Handsome Johnny	1970	—	2.50	5.00
ODE					
❑ 66032	Eyesight to the Blind/Underture	1973	2.00	4.00	8.00
STORMY FOREST					
❑ 650	Rocky Raccoon/Stop Pulling and Pushing Me	1970	—	3.00	6.00
❑ 651	Minstrel from Gault/There's a Hole in My Future	1970	—	2.50	5.00
❑ 653	Give All My Love Away/Nobody Knows	1970	—	2.50	5.00
❑ 656	Here Comes the Sun/Younger Men Get Older	1971	—	3.00	6.00
—Second (hit) pressing has full-length version of A-side and "REV" on label					
❑ 656	Here Comes the Sun/Younger Men Get Older	1971	2.00	4.00	8.00
—First pressing has an edited version of A-side					
❑ 658	Missing Train/I've Got to Get to Know Myself	1971	—	2.50	5.00
❑ 660	Fire and Rain/Think About the Children	1971	—	2.50	5.00
❑ 664	Where You Gonna Run To/ I've Got to Get to Know Myself	1972	—	2.50	5.00
❑ 666	Freedom/Handsome Johnny	1972	—	2.50	5.00
❑ 671	It Was a Very Good Year/ I Know I Won't Be There	1973	—	2.50	5.00
❑ 672	Tight Rope/Woman	1973	—	2.50	5.00
VERVE FOLKWAYS					
❑ 5022	I Can't Make It Anymore/Morning Morning	1966	2.00	4.00	8.00
❑ 5039	I've Gotta Go/Morning Morning	1967	2.00	4.00	8.00
VERVE FORECAST					
❑ 5068	Three Day Eternity/No Opportunity Necessary, No Experience Needed	1968	—	3.00	6.00
❑ 5092	Indian Rope Man/ Just Above My Hobby Horse's Head	1968	—	3.00	6.00
Albums					
A&M					
❑ SP-4598	The End of the Beginning	1976	2.50	5.00	10.00
❑ SP-4641	Mirage	1977	2.50	5.00	10.00
DOUGLAS					
❑ D-779 [M]	Richie Havens' Record	1966	3.75	7.50	15.00
❑ SD-779 [S]	Richie Havens' Record	1966	5.00	10.00	20.00
❑ D-780 [M]	Electric Havens	1966	6.25	12.50	25.00
❑ SD-780 [S]	Electric Havens	1966	5.00	10.00	20.00
ELEKTRA					
❑ 6E-242	Connections	1980	2.50	5.00	10.00
MGM					
❑ SE-4698	Mixed Bag	1970	3.75	7.50	15.00
—Reissue of Verve Forecast 3006					
❑ SE-4699	Something Else Again	1970	3.75	7.50	15.00
—Reissue of Verve Forecast 3034					
❑ SE-4700 [(2)]	Richard P. Havens, 1963	1970	5.00	10.00	20.00
—Reissue of Verve Forecast 3047					
RBI					
❑ 400	Simple Things	1987	2.50	5.00	10.00
STORMY FOREST					
❑ SFS-6001	Stonehenge	1969	3.75	7.50	15.00
❑ SFS-6005	Alarm Clock	1970	3.00	6.00	12.00
❑ SFS-6010	The Great Blind Degree	1971	3.00	6.00	12.00
❑ SFS-6012 [(2)]	Richie Havens On Stage	1972	3.75	7.50	15.00
❑ SFS-6013	Portfolio	1973	3.00	6.00	12.00
❑ SFS-6201	Mixed Bag II	1974	3.00	6.00	12.00
VERVE FOLKWAYS					
❑ FT-3006 [M]	Mixed Bag	1967	6.25	12.50	25.00
❑ FTS-3006 [S]	Mixed Bag	1967	5.00	10.00	20.00
VERVE FORECAST					
❑ FTS-3006	Mixed Bag	1968	3.75	7.50	15.00
❑ FT-3034 [M]	Something Else Again	1968	10.00	20.00	40.00
❑ FTS-3034 [S]	Something Else Again	1968	5.00	10.00	20.00
❑ FTS-3047 [(2)]	Richard P. Havens, 1983	1968	6.25	12.50	25.00
❑ FTS-3061	Richie Havens	1969			
—Canceled					
HAWK, THE See JERRY LEE LEWIS.					
HAWKETTS, THE					
45s					
CHESS					
❑ 1591	Mardi Gras Mambo/Your Time Is Up	1955	25.00	50.00	100.00
HAWKINS, DALE					
45s					
ABC-PARAMOUNT					
❑ 10668	I'll Fly High/La La Song	1965	2.50	5.00	10.00
ABNAK					
❑ 110	The Flag/And I Believed You	1965	3.00	6.00	12.00
ATLANTIC					
❑ 2126	Stay at Home, Lulu/I Can't Erase You	1961	5.00	10.00	20.00
❑ 2150	What a Feeling/Women, That's What's Happening	1962	5.00	10.00	20.00
BELL					
❑ 807	Back Street/Little Rain Cloud	1969	2.00	4.00	8.00
❑ 827	Heavy on My Mind/Joe	1969	2.00	4.00	8.00
CHECKER					
❑ 843	See You Soon, Baboon/Four Letter Word	1956	7.50	15.00	30.00
❑ 863	Susie-Q/Don't Treat Me This Way	1957	12.50	25.00	50.00
❑ 876	Baby, Baby/Mrs. Merguitory's Daughter	1957	7.50	15.00	30.00
❑ 892	Little Pig/Tornado	1958	6.25	12.50	25.00
❑ 900	La-Do-Dada/Cross Ties	1958	6.25	12.50	25.00
❑ 906	My Babe/A House, a Car, and a Wedding Ring	1958	6.25	12.50	25.00
❑ 913	Someday, One Day/Take My Heart	1959	6.25	12.50	25.00
❑ 916	Class Cutter (Yeah Yeah)/Lonely Nights	1959	6.25	12.50	25.00
❑ 923	Ain't That Lovin' You Baby/My Dream	1959	6.25	12.50	25.00
❑ 929	Our Turn/Lifeguard Man	1959	6.25	12.50	25.00
❑ 934	Liza Jane/Back to School Blues	1959	6.25	12.50	25.00
❑ 940	Hot Dog/Don't Break Your Promise to Me	1960	5.00	10.00	20.00
❑ 944	Poor Little Rhode Island/Every Little Girl	1960	5.00	10.00	20.00
❑ 944 [PS]	Poor Little Rhode Island/Every Little Girl	1960	75.00	150.00	300.00
❑ 962	Linda/Who	1960	5.00	10.00	20.00
❑ 970	Grandma's House/I Want to Love You	1961	5.00	10.00	20.00

H

Number	Title (A Side/B Side)	Yr	VG	VG+	NM
LINCOLN					
❑ 002	Johnny B. Goode/Baby We Had It	196?	2.00	4.00	8.00
NORTON					
❑ 45-055	Number Nine Train/On Account of You	1997	—	—	2.00
❑ 45-055 [PS]	Number Nine Train/On Account of You	1997	—	—	2.00
PAULA					
❑ 424	First Cut Is the Deepest/				
	Nothing Left to Do But Say Goodbye	1977	—	2.50	5.00
TILT					
❑ 781	Money Honey/The Same Old Way	1962	5.00	10.00	20.00
❑ 783	Forbidden Love/Wish I Hadn't Called Home	1962	5.00	10.00	20.00
❑ 785	Hawk Blows, Band Plays (Part 1)/Hawk Blows,				
	Band Plays (Part 2)	1962	5.00	10.00	20.00
ZONK					
❑ 1002	Gotta Dance/Peaches	1973	—	2.50	5.00
Albums					
BELL					
❑ 6036	L.A., Memphis and Tyler, Texas	1969	10.00	20.00	40.00
CHESS					
❑ ACRR-706	Dale Hawkins	1976	3.75	7.50	15.00
❑ LP-1429 [M]	Oh! Susie-Q	1958	500.00	1000.	1500.
ROULETTE					
❑ R 25175 [M]	Let's All Twist at the Miami Beach Peppermint				
	Lounge	1962	50.00	100.00	200.00
❑ SR 25175 [S]	Let's All Twist at the Miami Beach Peppermint				
	Lounge	1962	75.00	150.00	300.00

HAWKINS, EDWIN
45s

Number	Title (A Side/B Side)	Yr	VG	VG+	NM
BUDDAH					
❑ 145	Blowin' in the Wind/Pray for Peace	1970	—	2.50	5.00
❑ 155	I Believe/He's a Friend of Mine	1970	—	2.50	5.00
❑ 200	Try the Real Thing/Praise Him	1971	—	2.50	5.00
❑ 251	Children Get Together/There's a Place for Me	1971	—	2.50	5.00
❑ 271	Give Me a Star/Jesus	1971	—	2.50	5.00
❑ 324	Jesu, Joy of Man's Desiring/(B-side unknown)	1972	—	2.50	5.00
❑ 360	Jubilation/Do My Thing	1973	—	2.50	5.00
PAVILION					
❑ 20001	Oh Happy Day/Jesus, Lover of My Soul	1969	—	3.00	6.00
❑ 20002	Ain't It Like Him/Lord Don't Move That Mountain	1969	—	3.00	6.00
Albums					
ACCORD					
❑ SN-7120	The Genius of Edwin Hawkins	1981	2.50	5.00	10.00
BIRTHRIGHT					
❑ 4020	The Comforter	197?	3.00	6.00	12.00
❑ LS 5904	The Edwin Hawkins Christmas Album	1985	3.75	7.50	15.00
❑ WR-8119	Edwin Hawkins Live	198?	2.50	5.00	10.00
❑ ST-70200	The Edwin Hawkins Christmas Album	1987	2.00	4.00	8.00
—Reissue					
❑ ST-70201	Have Mercy	1987	2.00	4.00	8.00
❑ ST-70202	Angels Will Be Singing	1987	2.00	4.00	8.00
❑ D1-70208	Live with the Oakland Symphony, Vol. 1	1988	2.00	4.00	8.00
—Reissue of Myrrh 6691					
❑ D1-70210	Live with the Oakland Symphony, Vol. 2	1988	2.00	4.00	8.00
—Reissue of Myrrh 6700					
❑ ST-70300	Give Us Peace	1987	2.00	4.00	8.00
❑ D1-70315	The Name	1988	2.50	5.00	10.00
BUDDAH					
❑ BDS-5054	Peace Is Blowin' in the Wind	1969	3.75	7.50	15.00
❑ BDS-5064	More Happy Days	1970	3.75	7.50	15.00
❑ BDS-5070	Oh Happy Day	1970	3.00	6.00	12.00
—Reissue of Pavilion LP					
❑ BDS-5086	Children (Get Together)	1971	3.75	7.50	15.00
❑ BDS-5101	I'd Like to Teach the World to Sing	1972	3.75	7.50	15.00
❑ BDS-5606	The Edwin Hawkins Singers — Live	1974	3.75	7.50	15.00
LECTION					
❑ 501	Imagine Heaven	1982	2.50	5.00	10.00
❑ 810639-1	The Edwin Hawkins Mass Choir	198?	2.50	5.00	10.00
MYRRH					
❑ 6691	Live with the Oakland Symphony, Vol. 1	198?	2.50	5.00	10.00
❑ 6700	Live with the Oakland Symphony, Vol. 2	198?	2.50	5.00	10.00
PAVILION					
❑ BPS-10001	Let Us Go Into the House of the Lord	1969	3.75	7.50	15.00
❑ BPS-10002	He's a Friend of Mine	1969	3.75	7.50	15.00
SAVOY					
❑ 7077 [(2)]	The Best of the Edwin Hawkins Singers	198?	3.00	6.00	12.00

HAWKINS, HAWKSHAW
45s

Number	Title (A Side/B Side)	Yr	VG	VG+	NM
COLUMBIA					
❑ 4-41419	Soldier's Joy/Big Red Benson	1959	5.00	10.00	20.00
❑ 4-41574	Alaska Lil and Texas Bill/Patanio	1960	5.00	10.00	20.00
❑ 4-41714	Put a Nickel in the Jukebox/Your Conscience	1960	5.00	10.00	20.00
❑ 4-41811	You Know Me Too Well/My Story	1960	5.00	10.00	20.00
❑ 4-42002	No Love for Me/The Love I Have for You	1961	3.75	7.50	15.00
❑ 4-42223	Twenty Miles from Shore/Big Ole Heartache	1961	3.75	7.50	15.00
❑ 4-42441	I Can't Seem to Say Goodbye/				
	Darkness on the Face of the Earth	1962	3.75	7.50	15.00
KING					
❑ 969	I'm Waiting Just for You/A Heartache to Recall	1951	10.00	20.00	40.00
❑ 997	Sunny Side of the Mountain/				
	Blue Skies in Your Eyes	1951	10.00	20.00	40.00
❑ 998	Slow Poke/Two Roads	1951	10.00	20.00	40.00
❑ 1039	Be My Life's Companion/				
	Everybody's Got a Girl But Me	1952	7.50	15.00	30.00
❑ 1047	Over the Hill/I Am Slowly Dying of a Broken Heart	1952	7.50	15.00	30.00
❑ 1062	Unwanted/Got You on My Mind	1952	7.50	15.00	30.00
❑ 1081	Loaded with Love/I Love the Way You Say				
	Goodnight	1952	7.50	15.00	30.00
❑ 1133	Heavenly Road/An Empty Mansion	1952	7.50	15.00	30.00
❑ 1134	I'm a Lone Wolf/I Hope You're Cryin' Too	1952	7.50	15.00	30.00
❑ 1154	Tangled Heart/Betty Lorraine	1953	7.50	15.00	30.00
❑ 1174	The Life Story of Hank Williams/				
	Picking Sweethearts	1953	10.00	20.00	40.00
❑ 1175	Kaw-Liga/If I Ever Get Rich Mom	1953	7.50	15.00	30.00
❑ 1190	Barbara Allen/The Life Story of Hank Williams	1953	7.50	15.00	30.00

Number	Title (A Side/B Side)	Yr	VG	VG+	NM
❑ 5404	Nothing More to Say/Between the Lines	1960	3.75	7.50	15.00
❑ 5692	Silver Threads and Golden Needles/				
	Girl Without a Name	1962	3.75	7.50	15.00
❑ 5695	Bad News Travels Fast/Let Them Talk	1962	3.75	7.50	15.00
❑ 5712	Lonesome 7-7203/Everything Has Changed	1963	3.75	7.50	15.00
❑ 5765	Love Died Tonight/Sunny Side of the Mountain	1963	3.75	7.50	15.00
❑ 5810	Caught in the Middle of Two Hearts/				
	If I Ever Get Rich Mom	1963	3.75	7.50	15.00
❑ 5871	I'm Beginning to Forget/				
	Teardrops on Your Letter	1964	3.75	7.50	15.00
❑ 5909	This Particular Baby/The Shadows	1964	3.75	7.50	15.00
❑ 6047	The Last Letter/Never Mind the Tears	1967	3.00	6.00	12.00
❑ 6074	Jealous Fate/It's Easy to Remember	1967	3.00	6.00	12.00
RCA VICTOR					
❑ 47-5333	I'll Trade Yours for Mine/Long Way	1953	6.25	12.50	25.00
❑ 47-5444	A Heap of Lovin'/Mark Round My Finger	1953	6.25	12.50	25.00
❑ 47-5549	I'll Never Close My Heart to You/				
	When You Say Yes	1953	6.25	12.50	25.00
❑ 47-5623	Flashing Lights/Waitin' for My Baby	1954	6.25	12.50	25.00
❑ 47-5702	Rebound/Why Didn't I Hear It from You	1954	6.25	12.50	25.00
❑ 47-5808	One White Rose/I Wanna Be Hugged to Death	1954	6.25	12.50	25.00
❑ 47-5890	I'll Take a Chance with You/				
	Why Don't You Leave This Town	1954	6.25	12.50	25.00
❑ 47-6022	Ling Ting Tong/Ko Ko Mo, I Love You So	1955	6.25	12.50	25.00
—With Rita Robbins					
❑ 47-6103	How Can Anything So Pretty Be So Doggone				
	Mean/Pedro Gonzalez Tennessee Lopez	1955	6.25	12.50	25.00
❑ 47-6211	Car Hoppin' Mama/The Love You Steal	1955	6.25	12.50	25.00
❑ 47-6298	I Gotta Have You/				
	Standing at the End of My World	1955	6.25	12.50	25.00
❑ 47-6396	If It Ain't on the Menu/Borrowing	1956	6.25	12.50	25.00
❑ 47-6509	It Would Be a Doggone Lie/S				
	unny Side of the Mountain	1956	6.25	12.50	25.00
❑ 47-6716	I'll Be Gone/My Fate Is In Your Hands	1956	6.25	12.50	25.00
❑ 47-6794	Action/Oh How I Cried	1957	5.00	10.00	20.00
❑ 47-6910	Dark Moon/With This Pen	1957	5.00	10.00	20.00
❑ 47-7054	Is My Ring on Your Finger/Sensation	1957	5.00	10.00	20.00
❑ 47-7145	Guilty of Dreaming/It's Easier Said Than Done	1958	5.00	10.00	20.00
❑ 47-7222	I Don't Apologize/I'll Get Even with You	1958	5.00	10.00	20.00
❑ 47-7389	I've Got It Again/Freedom	1958	5.00	10.00	20.00
❑ 47-7486	Are You Happy/She Was Here	1959	5.00	10.00	20.00
Albums					
GLADWYNNE					
❑ G-2006 [M]	Country Western Cavalcade with				
	Hawkshaw Hawkins	195?	30.00	60.00	120.00
HARMONY					
❑ HL 7301 [M]	The Great Hawkshaw Hawkins	1963	5.00	10.00	20.00
❑ HS 11044 [R]	The Great Hawkshaw Hawkins	1963	3.75	7.50	15.00
KING					
❑ 587 [M]	Hawkshaw Hawkins	1958	25.00	50.00	100.00
❑ 592 [M]	Grand Ole Opry Favorites	1958	25.00	50.00	100.00
❑ 599 [M]	Hawkshaw Hawkins	1959	25.00	50.00	100.00
❑ 808 [M]	The All New Hawkshaw Hawkins	1963	20.00	40.00	80.00
❑ KS-808 [S]	The All New Hawkshaw Hawkins	1963	25.00	50.00	100.00
❑ 858 [M]	Taken From Our Vaults, Volume 1	1963	10.00	20.00	40.00
❑ 870 [M]	Taken From Our Vaults, Volume 2	1963	10.00	20.00	40.00
❑ 873 [M]	Taken From Our Vaults, Volume 3	1964	10.00	20.00	40.00
LABREA					
❑ 8020 [M]	Hawkshaw Hawkins	195?	25.00	50.00	100.00
RCA CAMDEN					
❑ CAL-808 [M]	Hawkshaw Hawkins Sings	1964	5.00	10.00	20.00
❑ CAS-808 [R]	Hawkshaw Hawkins Sings	1964	3.75	7.50	15.00
❑ CAL-931 [M]	The Country Gentleman	1966	5.00	10.00	20.00
❑ CAS-931 [R]	The Country Gentleman	1966	3.75	7.50	15.00

HAWKINS, JALACY See SCREAMIN' JAY HAWKINS.

HAWKINS, RONNIE His backing band, The Hawks, evolved into THE BAND.
45s

Number	Title (A Side/B Side)	Yr	VG	VG+	NM
COTILLION					
❑ 44060	Matchbox/Down in the Alley	1970	—	3.00	6.00
❑ 44067	Forty Days/Bitter Green	1970	—	3.00	6.00
❑ 44076	Little Bird/One More Night	1970	—	3.00	6.00
MONUMENT					
❑ 8548	Lawdy Miss Clawdy/Cora Mae	1972	—	2.50	5.00
❑ 8561	Lonesome Town/Kinky	1973	—	2.50	5.00
❑ 8573	Diddley Daddy/Cora Mae	1973	—	2.50	5.00
❑ 8583	Bo Diddley/Lonely Hours	1973	—	2.50	5.00
ROULETTE					
❑ 4154 [M]	Forty Days/One of These Days	1959	6.25	12.50	25.00
❑ SSR-4154 [S]	Forty Days/One of These Days	1959	12.50	25.00	50.00
❑ 4177 [M]	Mary Lou/Need Your Lovin'	1959	7.50	15.00	30.00
❑ SSR-4177 [S]	Mary Lou/Need Your Lovin'	1959	12.50	25.00	50.00
❑ 4209	Southern Love/Love Me Like You Can	1959	5.00	10.00	20.00
❑ 4228	Lonely Hours/Clara	1960	5.00	10.00	20.00
❑ 4231	The Ballad of Caryl Chessman/				
	The Tale of Floyd Collins	1960	5.00	10.00	20.00
❑ 4249	Ruby Baby/Hayride	1960	5.00	10.00	20.00
❑ 4267	Sumemrtime/Mister and Mississippi	1960	5.00	10.00	20.00
❑ 4311	Cold, Cold Heart/Nobody's Lonesome for Me	1960	5.00	10.00	20.00
❑ 4400	Come Love/I Feel Good	1961	5.00	10.00	20.00
❑ 4483	Bo Diddley/Who Do You Love	1963	5.00	10.00	20.00
❑ 4502	High Blood Pressure/There's a Screw Loose	1963	5.00	10.00	20.00
Albums					
ACCORD					
❑ SN-7213	Premonition	1983	2.50	5.00	10.00
COTILLION					
❑ SD 9019	Ronnie Hawkins	1970	3.75	7.50	15.00
❑ SD 9039	The Hawk	1971	3.75	7.50	15.00
MONUMENT					
❑ KZ 31330	Rock and Roll Resurrection	1972	3.00	6.00	12.00
❑ KZ 32940	The Giant of Rock 'n' Roll	1974	3.00	6.00	12.00
❑ ZG 33855 [(2)]	Rock and Roll Resurrection/				
	The Ghost of Rock and Roll	1976	3.75	7.50	15.00
ROULETTE					
❑ R 25078 [M]	Ronnie Hawkins	1959	37.50	75.00	150.00
—White label with spokes					

Number	Title (A Side/B Side)	Yr	VG	VG+	NM
❑ R 25078 [M]	Ronnie Hawkins	1964	12.50	25.00	50.00
—Orange/yellow label					
❑ SR 25078 [S]	Ronnie Hawkins	1959	50.00	100.00	200.00
—White label with spokes; black vinyl					
❑ SR 25078 [S]	Ronnie Hawkins	1959	150.00	300.00	600.00
—White label with spokes; red vinyl					
❑ SR 25078 [S]	Ronnie Hawkins	1964	15.00	30.00	60.00
—Orange/yellow label					
❑ R 25102 [M]	Mr. Dynamo	1960	37.50	75.00	150.00
❑ SR 25102 [S]	Mr. Dynamo	1960	50.00	100.00	200.00
—Black vinyl					
❑ SR 25102 [S]	Mr. Dynamo	1960	150.00	300.00	600.00
—Red vinyl					
❑ R 25120 [M]	The Folk Ballads of Ronnie Hawkins	1960	25.00	50.00	100.00
❑ SR 25120 [S]	The Folk Ballads of Ronnie Hawkins	1960	37.50	75.00	150.00
❑ R 25137 [M]	Ronnie Hawkins Sings the Songs of Hank Williams	1960	25.00	50.00	100.00
❑ SR 25137 [S]	Ronnie Hawkins Sings the Songs of Hank Williams	1960	37.50	75.00	150.00
❑ SR 42045	The Best of Ronnie Hawkins and His Band	1970	6.25	12.50	25.00
UNITED ARTISTS					
❑ UA-LA968-H	The Hawk	1979	2.50	5.00	10.00

HAWKINS, SCREAMIN' JAY
45s
APOLLO

Number	Title (A Side/B Side)	Yr	VG	VG+	NM
❑ 506	Please Try to Understand/Not Anymore	1957	6.25	12.50	25.00
❑ 528	Baptize Me in Wine/Not Anymore	1958	6.25	12.50	25.00
CHANCELLOR					
❑ 1117	Ashes/Nitty Gritty	1962	3.75	7.50	15.00
DECCA					
❑ 32019	All Night/I'm Not Made of Clay	1966	3.75	7.50	15.00
❑ 32100	I Put a Spell on You/ You're an Exception to the Rule	1967	10.00	20.00	40.00
ENRICA					
❑ 1010	I Hear Voices/I Just Don't Care	1962	6.25	12.50	25.00
GRAND					
❑ 135	Take Me Back/I Is	1957	6.25	12.50	25.00
MERCURY					
❑ 70549	This Is All/She Put the Whammee on Me	1955	20.00	40.00	80.00
OKEH					
❑ 7072	I Put a Spell on You/Little Demon	1956	12.50	25.00	50.00
❑ 7084	You Made Me Love You/ Darling, Please Forgive Me	1957	7.50	15.00	30.00
❑ 7087	Person to Person/Frenzy	1957	7.50	15.00	30.00
❑ 7101	Alligator Wine/ There's Something Wrong with You	1958	7.50	15.00	30.00
PHILIPS					
❑ 40606	Stone Crazy/I'm Lonely	1969	—	3.00	6.00
❑ 40636	Too Many Teardrops/Makaka Ways	1969	—	3.00	6.00
❑ 40645	Constipation Blues/Do You Really Love Me	1969	—	3.00	6.00
❑ 40668	Moanin'/Do You Really Love Me	1970	—	3.00	6.00
❑ 40674	Our Love Is Not for Three/Take Me Back	1970	—	3.00	6.00
PROVIDENCE					
❑ 411	My Kind of Love/Po' Folks	1965	3.00	6.00	12.00
QUEEN BEE					
❑ 1314	Monkberry Moon Delight/Sweet Ginny	1973	—	3.00	6.00
RCA VICTOR					
❑ PB-10127	You Put the Spell on Me/Voodoo	1974	—	2.50	5.00
ROULETTE					
❑ 4579	The Whammy/Strange	1964	3.00	6.00	12.00
TIMELY					
❑ 1004	Baptize Me in Wine/Not Anymore	1954	20.00	40.00	80.00
❑ 1005	I Found My Way to Wine/Please Try to Understand	1954	20.00	40.00	80.00
WING					
❑ 90005	Well, I Tried/You're All of Life to Me	1955	10.00	20.00	40.00
❑ 90055	Even Though/Talk About Me	1956	7.50	15.00	30.00

Albums
EPIC

Number	Title (A Side/B Side)	Yr	VG	VG+	NM
❑ LN 3448 [M]	At Home with Screamin' Jay Hawkins	1958	300.00	600.00	1200.
❑ LN 3457 [M]	I Put a Spell on You	1958	125.00	250.00	500.00
❑ BN 26457 [R]	I Put a Spell on You	1969	15.00	30.00	60.00
PHILIPS					
❑ PHS 600319	What That Is	1969	10.00	20.00	40.00
❑ PHS 600336	Screamin' Jay Hawkins	1970	10.00	20.00	40.00
SOUNDS OF HAWAII					
❑ 5015	A Night at Forbidden City	196?	12.50	25.00	50.00

HAWKS, THE (1)
45s
IMPERIAL

Number	Title (A Side/B Side)	Yr	VG	VG+	NM
❑ 5266	Joe the Grinder/Candy Girl	1954	62.50	125.00	250.00
❑ 5281	She's All Right/Good News	1954	50.00	100.00	200.00
❑ 5292	It Ain't That Way/I-Yi	1954	25.00	50.00	100.00
❑ 5306	Nobody But You/Give It Up	1954	25.00	50.00	100.00
❑ 5317	All Women Are the Same/That's What You Are	1954	25.00	50.00	100.00
❑ 5332	It's Too Late Now/I Can't See for Lookin'	1955	25.00	50.00	100.00
MODERN					
❑ 990	It's All Over/Ever Since You Been Gone	1956	62.50	125.00	250.00
POST					
❑ 2004	These Blues/Why Oh Why	1955	75.00	150.00	300.00

HAWKS, THE (U) None of these are group (1), but we don't know how many groups are represented below.
45s
ABC-PARAMOUNT

Number	Title (A Side/B Side)	Yr	VG	VG+	NM
❑ 10116	Grasshopper/The Grissle	1960	6.25	12.50	25.00
DEL-FI					
❑ 4108	A Little More Wine, My Dear?/Fussy	1958	10.00	20.00	40.00
MALA					
❑ 401	Cupcake/Lupp!!	1959	5.00	10.00	20.00

HAWKWIND
45s
ATCO

Number	Title (A Side/B Side)	Yr	VG	VG+	NM
❑ 7017	Kings of Speed/Motor Head	1975	—	2.50	5.00
UNITED ARTISTS					
❑ XW314	Urban Guerrilla/Brainbox Position	1973	—	2.50	5.00
❑ 50949	Seven by Seven/Silver Necklace	1972	—	2.50	5.00

Albums
ATCO

Number	Title (A Side/B Side)	Yr	VG	VG+	NM
❑ SD 36-115	Warrior on the Edge of Time	1975	3.75	7.50	15.00
GWR					
❑ 1237 [(2)]	Live Chronicles	1986	3.00	6.00	12.00
LIBERTY					
❑ LWB-120 [(2)]	Space Ritual/Alive in Liverpool and London	1981	3.00	6.00	12.00
—Reissue of United Artists 120					
❑ LW-5567	In Search of Space	1981	2.00	4.00	8.00
—Reissue of United Artists 5567					
SIRE					
❑ SRK 6047	Quark Strangeness and Charm	1978	3.00	6.00	12.00
UNITED ARTISTS					
❑ UA-LA001-F	Doremi Fasol Latido	1973	3.75	7.50	15.00
❑ UA-LA120-H [(2)]	Space Ritual/Alive in Liverpool and London	1973	5.00	10.00	20.00
❑ UA-LA328-G	Hall of the Mountain Grill	1974	3.75	7.50	15.00
❑ UAS-5519	Hawkwind	1971	3.75	7.50	15.00
❑ UAS-5567	In Search of Space	1972	3.75	7.50	15.00

HAWLEY, DEANE
45s
DORE

Number	Title (A Side/B Side)	Yr	VG	VG+	NM
❑ 524	New Fad/Pretty Little Mary	1959	3.75	7.50	15.00
❑ 536	Good Morning, Mr. Sun/Bossman	1959	3.75	7.50	15.00
❑ 543	Where Is My Angel/I'll Never Be a Fool Again	1960	3.75	7.50	15.00
❑ 554	Look for a Star/Bossman	1960	3.75	7.50	15.00
❑ 569	Like a Fool/Stay at Home Blues	1960	3.75	7.50	15.00
❑ 577	Hey There/Rainbow	1960	3.75	7.50	15.00
LIBERTY					
❑ 55359	Pocketful of Rainbows/ That Dream Could Never Be	1961	5.00	10.00	20.00
❑ 55446	Queen of the Angels/You Conquered Me	1962	6.25	12.50	25.00
SUNDOWN					
❑ 111	I Hate to See Me Go/ Love of the Common People	196?	2.50	5.00	10.00
❑ 113	That's the Name of the Game/ Canterbury Station	196?	2.50	5.00	10.00
VALOR					
❑ 2003	Mummy's Bracelet/Don't Keep Me Guessin'	1961	7.50	15.00	30.00
WARNER BROS.					
❑ 5484	I Know She'll Be There/ You'll Never Have to Cry Again	1964	3.00	6.00	12.00

HAWN, GOLDIE
45s
REPRISE

Number	Title (A Side/B Side)	Yr	VG	VG+	NM
❑ 1089	Butterfly/Uncle Pen	1972	2.00	4.00	8.00
❑ 1126	Pitta Patta/(Instrumental)	1972	2.00	4.00	8.00
❑ 1126 [PS]	Pitta Patta/(Instrumental)	1972	2.50	5.00	10.00

Albums
REPRISE

Number	Title (A Side/B Side)	Yr	VG	VG+	NM
❑ MS 2061	Goldie	1972	6.25	12.50	25.00

HAYES, BILL
45s
ABC-PARAMOUNT

Number	Title (A Side/B Side)	Yr	VG	VG+	NM
❑ 9785	Wringle, Wrangle/Westward Ho the Wagons	1957	3.00	6.00	12.00
❑ 9785 [PS]	Wringle, Wrangle/Westward Ho the Wagons	1957	5.00	10.00	20.00
❑ 9809	Ramshackle Daddy/On the Outside	1957	3.00	6.00	12.00
❑ 9895	Bop Boy/Uh Huh Oh Yeah	1958	15.00	30.00	60.00
CADENCE					
❑ 1245	I Knew an Old Lady//(B-side unknown)	1954	3.00	6.00	12.00
❑ 1256	The Ballad of Davy Crockett/Farewell	1955	3.75	7.50	15.00
❑ 1261	The Berry Tree/Blue Back Hair	1955	3.00	6.00	12.00
❑ 1274	That Do Make It Nice/Kwela Kwela	1955	3.00	6.00	12.00
❑ 1275	The Legend of Wyatt Earp/White Buffalo	1955	3.75	7.50	15.00
❑ 1294	I Knew an Old Lady/Das Ist Music	1956	3.00	6.00	12.00
❑ 1301	A Message from James Dean/The Trail's End	1956	3.75	7.50	15.00
KAPP					
❑ 258	Wimoweh/Goin' Down the Road Feelin' Bad	1959	2.50	5.00	10.00
❑ 298	Choppin' Mountains/Tall Teller of Tall Tales	1959	2.50	5.00	10.00
MERCURY					
❑ 5599	Too Young/Shenandoah Waltz	1951	5.00	10.00	20.00
MGM					
❑ 11006	Waltz of the Wind/Mine	1951	3.75	7.50	15.00
❑ 11042	The Love of a Gypsy/I've Got an Idea for a Song	1951	3.75	7.50	15.00
❑ 11064	I Love You/Never	1951	3.75	7.50	15.00
❑ 11112	Charmaine/For All We Know	1951	3.75	7.50	15.00
❑ 11142	We Won't Live in A.../Tulips and Heather	1952	3.75	7.50	15.00
❑ 11205	April Sings/Golden Haired Boy	1952	3.75	7.50	15.00
❑ 11210	When I Dream/Don't Send Me Home	1952	3.75	7.50	15.00
—With Judy Johnson					
❑ 11266	High Noon/Padam Padam	1952	3.75	7.50	15.00
❑ 11296	Say You'll Wait for Me/My Search for You	1952	3.75	7.50	15.00
❑ 11384	My Ever Lovin'/As Long As You Care	1952	3.75	7.50	15.00
❑ 11394	How Do You Speak to An Angel/The Donkey Song	1953	3.75	7.50	15.00
❑ 11492	I'm So Lonesome/There's Music in You	1953	3.75	7.50	15.00
❑ 11556	A Little Kiss Each Morning/Love You	1953	3.75	7.50	15.00
—With Judy Johnson					
❑ 12004	Wanderin'/You're Nearer	1955	3.00	6.00	12.00

7-Inch Extended Plays
ABC-PARAMOUNT

Number	Title (A Side/B Side)	Yr	VG	VG+	NM
❑ B-194	Lavender Blue/Zip-a-Dee Do-Dah/'Twas Brillig/ A Whale of a Tale	1957	3.75	7.50	15.00
❑ B-194 [PS]	Bill Hayes Sings the Best of Disney, Vol. 2	1957	3.75	7.50	15.00

H

Number	Title (A Side/B Side)	Yr	VG	VG+	NM

HAYES, ISAAC

Albums

ABC-PARAMOUNT

Number	Title (A Side/B Side)	Yr	VG	VG+	NM
□ 194 [M]	Bill Hayes Sings the Best of Disney	1957	10.00	20.00	40.00

DAYBREAK

□ DR-2020	The Look of Love	1972	6.25	12.50	25.00

KAPP

□ KL-1106 [M]	Jimmy Crack Corn	1958	6.25	12.50	25.00

HAYES, ISAAC

45s

ABC/HBS

Number	Title (A Side/B Side)	Yr	VG	VG+	NM
□ 12118	Chocolate Chip/(Instrumental)	1975	—	2.00	4.00
□ 12138	Come Live with Me/Body Language	1975	—	2.00	4.00
□ 12171	Disco Connection/St. Thomas Square	1976	—	2.00	4.00

—By the "Isaac Hayes Movement"

□ 12176	Rock Me Easy Baby (Pt. 1)/Rock Me Easy Baby (Pt. 2)	1976	—	2.00	4.00
□ 12206	Juicy Fruit (Disco Freak) (Pt. 1)/Juicy Fruit (Disco Freak) (Pt. 2)	1976	—	2.00	4.00

BRUNSWICK

□ 55258	Sweet Temptation/Laura	1964	2.50	5.00	10.00

CAPITOL

□ S7-18869	Walk On By/Tired of Being Alone	1995			3.00

—B-side by Al Green

COLUMBIA

Number	Title (A Side/B Side)	Yr	VG	VG+	NM
□ 06363	Ike's Rap/Hey Girl (Edited)	1986	—	—	3.00
□ 06363 [PS]	Ike's Rap/Hey Girl (Edited)	1986	—	2.00	4.00
□ 06655	Thing for You/Thank God for Love	1987	—	—	3.00
□ 07104	If You Want My Lovin' (Do Me Right)/(Instrumental)	1987	—	—	3.00
□ 07978	Showdown/(Instrumental)	1988	—	—	3.00
□ 08116	Let Me Be Your Everything/Curious	1988	—	—	3.00

ENTERPRISE

□ 002	Precious Precious/Going to Chicago Blues	1969	2.00	4.00	8.00
□ 9003	By the Time I Get to Phoenix/Walk On By	1969	—	3.00	6.00
□ 9006	The Mistletoe and Me/Winter Snow	1969	—	3.00	6.00
□ 9017	I Stand Accused/I Just Don't Know What to Do with Myself	1970	—	2.50	5.00
□ 9028	The Look of Love/Ike's Mood	1970	—	2.50	5.00
□ 9031	Never Can Say Goodbye/I Can't Help It If I'm Still in Love with You	1971	—	2.50	5.00
□ 9038	Theme from Shaft/Cafe Regio's	1971	—	2.50	5.00
□ 9042	Do Your Thing/Ellie's Love Theme	1972	—	2.50	5.00
□ 9045	Let's Stay Together/Soulville	1972	—	2.50	5.00
□ 9049	Ain't That Loving You (For More Reasons Than One)/Baby I'm-a Want You	1972	—	2.50	5.00

—With David Porter

□ 9058	Theme from The Men/Type Thang	1972	—	2.50	5.00
□ 9065	(If Loving You Is Wrong) I Don't Want to Be Right/Rolling Down a Mountainside	1973	—	2.50	5.00
□ 9085	Joy (Part 1)/Joy (Part 2)	1973	—	2.50	5.00
□ 9095	Wonderful/Someone Made You for Me	1974	—	2.50	5.00
□ 9104	Title Theme/Hung Up on My Baby	1974	—	2.50	5.00

POLYDOR

□ 2011	Don't Let Go/You Can't Hold Your Woman	1979	—	2.00	4.00
□ 2068	A Few More Kisses to Go/What Does It Take	1980	—	2.00	4.00
□ 2090	I Ain't Never/Love Has Been Good to Us	1980	—	2.00	4.00
□ 2102	It's All in the Game/Wherever You Are	1980	—	2.00	4.00
□ 2182	I'm So Proud/I'm Gonna Make Me Love You	1981	—	2.00	4.00
□ 2192	Fugitive/Lifetime Thing	1981	—	2.00	4.00
□ 14446	Out of the Ghetto/It's Heaven to Me	1977	—	2.00	4.00
□ 14464	Moonlight Lovin' (Menage a Trois)/It's Heaven to Me	1978	—	2.00	4.00
□ 14521	Zeke the Freak/If We Ever Needed Peace	1978	—	2.00	4.00
□ 14534	Just the Way You Are (Part 1)/Just the Way You Are (Part 2)	1979	—	2.00	4.00

STAX

□ 3209	Feel Like Makin' Love (Part 1)/Feel Like Makin' Love (Part 2)	1978	—	2.50	5.00

VIRGIN

□ S7-18950	Fragile/Thanks to the Fool	1995	—	2.00	4.00
□ 38759	Only If You Were Here/Oh Come All Ye Faithful	2000	—	2.00	4.00

—B-side by Ideal

Albums

ABC/HBS

Number	Title (A Side/B Side)	Yr	VG	VG+	NM
□ D-874	Chocolate Chip	1975	3.75	7.50	15.00
□ D-923	Disco Connection	1975	3.00	6.00	12.00
□ D-925	Groove-a-Thon	1976	3.00	6.00	12.00
□ D-953	Juicy Fruit (Disco Freak)	1976	3.00	6.00	12.00

ATLANTIC

□ SD 1599	In the Beginning	1972	3.75	7.50	15.00

—Reissue of Enterprise 100

COLUMBIA

□ FC 40316	U-Turn	1986	2.50	5.00	10.00
□ FC 40941	Love Attack	1988	2.50	5.00	10.00

ENTERPRISE

□ E-100 [M]	Presenting Isaac Hayes	1968	10.00	20.00	40.00
□ ES-100 [S]	Presenting Isaac Hayes	1968	7.50	15.00	30.00
□ ENS-1001	Hot Buttered Soul	1969	5.00	10.00	20.00
□ ENS-1010	The Isaac Hayes Movement	1970	5.00	10.00	20.00
□ ENS-1014	To Be Continued	1970	5.00	10.00	20.00
□ ENS-5002 [(2)]	Shaft	1971	5.00	10.00	20.00
□ EQS-2-5002 [(2)Q]	Shaft	1971	10.00	20.00	40.00
□ ENS-5003 [(2)]	Black Moses	1971	5.00	10.00	20.00
□ ENS-5005 [(2)]	Live at the Sahara Tahoe	1973	3.75	7.50	15.00
□ XQS-5005 [(2)Q]	Live at the Sahara Tahoe	1973	7.50	15.00	30.00
□ ENS-5007	Joy	1973	3.00	6.00	12.00
□ EQS-5007 [Q]	Joy	1973	5.00	10.00	20.00
□ ENS-7504	Tough Guys	1974	3.00	6.00	12.00
□ EQS-7504 [Q]	Tough Guys	1974	5.00	10.00	20.00
□ ENS-7507 [(2)]	Truck Turner	1974	3.75	7.50	15.00
□ ENS-7510	The Best of Isaac Hayes	1975	3.00	6.00	12.00

POINTBLANK

□ SPRO-12787 [DJ]	Funky Junky	1995	3.75	7.50	15.00

—Vinyl is promo only

POLYDOR

Number	Title (A Side/B Side)	Yr	VG	VG+	NM
□ PD-1-6120	New Horizon	1977	2.50	5.00	10.00
□ PD-1-6164	For the Sake of Love	1978	2.50	5.00	10.00
□ PD-1-6224	Don't Let Go	1979	2.50	5.00	10.00
□ PD-1-6269	And Once Again	1980	2.50	5.00	10.00

STAX

□ STX-4102	Hotbed	197?	2.50	5.00	10.00
□ STX-4114	Hot Buttered Soul	1978	2.50	5.00	10.00

—Reissue of Enterprise 1001

□ STX-4129	The Isaac Hayes Movement	197?	2.50	5.00	10.00

—Reissue of Enterprise 1010

□ STX-4133	To Be Continued	197?	2.50	5.00	10.00

—Reissue of Enterprise 1014

□ MPS-8509	Excerpts from Black Moses	1981	2.50	5.00	10.00
□ MPS-8515	His Greatest Hit Singles	1982	2.50	5.00	10.00
□ MPS-8530	Joy	1984	2.50	5.00	10.00

—Reissue of Enterprise 5007

□ STX-88002 [(2)]	Shaft	1979	3.00	6.00	12.00

—Reissue of Enterprise 5002

□ STX-88003 [(2)]	Enterprise: His Greatest Hits	1980	3.00	6.00	12.00
□ STX-88004 [(2)]	Live at the Sahara Tahoe	198?	3.00	6.00	12.00

—Reissue of Enterprise 5005

HAYES, ISAAC, AND DIONNE WARWICK Also see each artist's individual listings.

45s

ABC/HBS

Number	Title (A Side/B Side)	Yr	VG	VG+	NM
□ 12253	By the Time I Get to Phoenix—I Say a Little Prayer/That's the Way I Like It—Cry Down	1977	—	2.00	4.00

Albums

ABC/HBS

□ D-996 [(2)]	A Man and a Woman	1977	3.75	7.50	15.00

MCA

□ 10012 [(2)]	A Man and a Woman	198?	3.00	6.00	12.00

—Reissue of ABC/HBS 996

HAYES, JIMMY, AND THE SOUL SURFERS

45s

IMPERIAL

□ 5986	Summer Surfin'/Down on the Beach	1963	6.25	12.50	25.00

HAYES, LINDA

45s

ANTLER

□ 4000	I Had a Dream/You Ain't Movin' Me	1956	7.50	15.00	30.00

DECCA

□ 29644	Our Love's Forever Blessed/You're the Only One for Me	1955	7.50	15.00	30.00

HOLLYWOOD

□ 1003	Take Me Back/Yours for the Asking	1953	12.50	25.00	50.00
□ 1009	No Next Time/Don't Do Nothin' Baby	1954	10.00	20.00	40.00
□ 1016	Play It Right/Your Back's Out	1954	10.00	20.00	40.00
□ 1019	Non-Cooperation/Grrr! Mambo	1954	10.00	20.00	40.00
□ 1027	Change of Heart/Darling Angel	1954	10.00	20.00	40.00
□ 1031	Johnny Ace's Last Letter/Why Johnny Why	1955	12.50	25.00	50.00

—With Johnny Moore

□ 1032	Our Love's Forever Blessed/You're the Only One for Me	1955	15.00	30.00	60.00

KING

□ 4752	My Name Ain't Annie/Let's Babalu	1954	18.75	37.50	75.00
□ 4773	Please Have Mercy/Oochi Poochi	1955	12.50	25.00	50.00

RECORDED IN HOLLYWOOD

□ 244	Yes! I Know (What You're Putting Down)/Sister Ann	1953	12.50	25.00	50.00
□ 246	Big City (Part 1)/Big City (Part 2)	1953	12.50	25.00	50.00

HAYES, TOMMY

45s

PHILIPS

□ 40259	Trance/Glistening Lights	1965	7.50	15.00	30.00

—The Four Seasons sing backup

HAYMARKET SQUARE

Albums

CHAPARRAL

□ 201	Magic Lantern	1968	375.00	750.00	1500.

HAYWARD, JUSTIN Also see THE MOODY BLUES.

45s

COLUMBIA

Number	Title (A Side/B Side)	Yr	VG	VG+	NM
□ 10799	Forever Autumn/The Fighting Machine	1978	2.00	4.00	8.00

DERAM

□ 401	Night Flight/Suitcase	1980	—	2.00	4.00
□ 402	A Face in the Crowd/It's Not On	1980	—	2.00	4.00
□ 7541	Lay It On Me/Songwriter Part 2	1977	—	2.00	4.00
□ 7542	Country Girl/Songwriter Part 2	1977	—	2.00	4.00

RED BIRD

□ 10-049	London Is Behind Me/Day Must Come	1966	5.00	10.00	20.00

Albums

DERAM

□ DRL 4801	Night Flight	1980	3.00	5.00	12.00
□ DES 18073	Songwriter	1977	3.75	7.50	15.00

HAYWARD, JUSTIN, AND JOHN LODGE Also see JUSTIN HAYWARD; THE MOODY BLUES.

45s

THRESHOLD

□ 67019	I Dreamed Last Night/Remember Me, My Friend	1975	—	2.00	4.00
□ 67021	Blue Guitar/When You Wake Up	1975	—	2.00	4.00
□ 67021 [PS]	Blue Guitar/When You Wake Up	1975	—	2.50	5.00

Albums

THRESHOLD

□ THS 14	Blue Jays	1975	3.75	7.50	15.00
□ THSX 101 [DJ]	Blue Jays	1975	12.50	25.00	50.00

—Open-end interview with script; used to promote the LP of the same name

Number	Title (A Side/B Side)	Yr	VG	VG+	NM

HAYWOOD, LEON
12-Inch Singles
CASABLANCA

❏ 812164-1	I'm Out to Catch (LP version)/(Dub Version)	1983	—	3.00	6.00

MCA

❏ 13911	Disco Fever/Party	1978	3.00	6.00	12.00

45s
ATLANTIC

❏ 2799	You and Your Moody Ways/You Know What	1971	—	3.00	6.00
❏ 2858	Clean Up Your Own Back Yard/String Bean	1972	—	3.00	6.00

CAPITOL

❏ 2584	Just Your Fool/Consider the Source	1969	3.75	7.50	15.00
❏ 2752	I Wanna Thank You/I Was Sent to Love You	1970	3.75	7.50	15.00

CASABLANCA

❏ 812164-7	I'm Out to Catch/Keep It in the Family	1983	—	—	3.00
—With Karen Roberts					
❏ 814217-7	T.V. Mama/Steppin' Out	1983	—	—	3.00

COLUMBIA

❏ 10413	The Streets Will Love You to Death - Part 1/The Streets Will Love You to Death - Part 2	1976	—	2.00	4.00
❏ 10477	Dream Dream/Let Me Make It Good	1977	—	2.00	4.00

DECCA

❏ 32164	It's Got to Be Mellow/Cornbread & Buttermilk	1967	2.00	4.00	8.00
❏ 32230	Mellow Moonlight/Tennessee Waltz	1967	2.00	4.00	8.00
❏ 32310	Mercy, Mercy, Mercy/It's the Last Time	1968	2.00	4.00	8.00
❏ 32348	I Want to Talk About My Baby/You Don't Have to See Me Cry	1968	2.00	4.00	8.00
❏ 32414	Blues Get Off My Shoulder/Everyday Will Be Like a Holiday	1968	2.00	4.00	8.00

FANTASY

❏ 581	The Truth About Money/Would I	1964	6.25	12.50	25.00

FAT FISH

❏ 8005	Soul Cargo/Spice of the Blues	1966	7.50	15.00	30.00

IMPERIAL

❏ 66123	She's With Her Other Love/Pain in My Heart	1965	3.75	7.50	15.00
—As "Leon Hayward"					
❏ 66149	Soul-On/1-2-3	1965	3.00	6.00	12.00

MCA

❏ 40793	Super Sexy/Life Goes On	1977	—	2.00	4.00
❏ 40849	Double My Pleasure/It's Gonna Be Alright	1978	—	2.00	4.00
❏ 40889	Fine and Healthy Thing/She's Built, She's Stacked	1978	—	2.00	4.00
❏ 40941	Party/Life Goes On	1978	—	2.00	4.00
❏ 40989	Disco Fever/Self Respect	1979	—	2.00	4.00
❏ 41035	Energy/You Bring Out the Freak in Me	1979	—	2.00	4.00

MODERN

❏ 99708	Tenderoni/(Instrumental)	1984	—	—	3.00

20TH CENTURY

❏ 2003	One Way Ticket to Loveland/There Ain't Enough Love Around	1972	—	3.00	6.00
❏ 2022	La La Song/Sweet Loving Fair	1973	—	3.00	6.00
❏ 2065	Keep It in the Family/Long As There's You (I Got Love)	1974	—	2.50	5.00
❏ 2103	Sugar Lump/That Sweet Woman of Mine	1974	—	2.50	5.00
❏ 2146	Believe Half of What You See (And None of What You Hear)/The Day I Laid Eyes on You	1974	—	2.50	5.00
❏ 2191	Come an' Get Yourself Some/Who You Been Givin' It Up To	1975	—	2.50	5.00
❏ 2191	Come an' Get Yourself Some/B.M.F. Beautiful	1975	—	3.00	6.00
❏ 2228	I Want'a Do Something Freaky to You/I Know What Love Is	1975	—	2.50	5.00
❏ 2264	Just Your Fool/Consider the Source	1975	—	2.50	5.00
❏ 2285	Strokin' (Part 1)/Strokin' (Part 2)	1976	—	2.50	5.00
❏ 2443	Don't Push It Don't Force It/Who You Been Givin' It Up To	1980	—	2.00	4.00
❏ 2454	If You're Lookin' for a Night of Fun (Look Past Me, I'm Not the One)/That's What Time It Is	1980	—	2.00	4.00
❏ 2469	Daydream/Love Is What We Came Here For	1980	—	2.00	4.00

Albums
COLUMBIA

❏ PC 34363	Intimate	1976	2.50	5.00	10.00

DECCA

❏ DL 74949	It's Got to Be Mellow	1969	5.00	10.00	20.00

FAT FISH

❏ LP 2525	Soul Cargo	1966	15.00	30.00	60.00

GALAXY

❏ 8206	Mellow, Mellow	196?	5.00	10.00	20.00

MCA

❏ 2322	Double My Pleasure	1978	2.50	5.00	10.00
❏ 3090	Energy	1979	2.50	5.00	10.00

20TH CENTURY

❏ T-411	Back to Stay	1973	3.00	6.00	12.00
❏ T-440	Keep It in the Family	1974	3.00	6.00	12.00
❏ T-476	Come and Get Yourself Some	1975	2.50	5.00	10.00
❏ T-613	Naturally	1980	2.50	5.00	10.00

HEAD
Albums
BUDDAH

❏ BDS-5062	Head	1970	7.50	15.00	30.00

—With coloring book (deduct 1/3 if missing)

HEAD, JIM, AND HIS DEL RAYS
Albums
HP

❏ 22893 [M]	Jim Head and His Del Rays	1963	75.00	150.00	300.00

HEAD, MURRAY
45s
A&M

❏ 1796	Say It Ain't So, Joe/She's Such a Drag	1976	—	2.00	4.00
❏ 1836	Somebody's Rockin' My Dreamboat/She's Such a Drag	1976	—	2.00	4.00

DECCA

❏ 32603	Superstar/John Nineteen Forty-One	1969	—	3.00	6.00
—First pressings use this reference on the A-side: "Superstar (From JESUS CHRIST)"					
❏ 32603	Superstar/John Nineteen Forty-One	1970	—	2.50	5.00
—Reissues have the word "Superstar" without a subtitle, and small print mentions the LP "Jesus Christ Superstar"					
❏ 32603 [PS]	Superstar/John Nineteen Forty-One	1970	2.00	4.00	8.00
—Picture sleeve accompanies second pressings					
❏ 32709	Heaven on Their Minds/Strange Thing (Mystifying)	1970	—	2.50	5.00
❏ 32709 [PS]	Heaven on Their Minds/Strange Thing (Mystifying)	1970	2.00	4.00	8.00

RCA

❏ PB-13988	One Night in Bangkok/Merano	1985	—	2.00	4.00
❏ PB-13988 [PS]	One Night in Bangkok/Merano	1985	—	2.00	4.00
❏ PB-14152	Pity the Child/The Deal (No Deal)	1985	—	2.00	4.00
❏ GB-14339	One Night in Bangkok/Pity the Child	1986	—	—	3.00
—Gold Standard Series					

Albums
A&M

❏ SP-4558	Say It Ain't So	1976	3.00	6.00	12.00

HEAD, ROY

45s
ABC

❏ 12346	How You See 'Em, Now You Don't/Smooth Whiskey	1978	—	2.00	4.00
❏ 12383	Tonight's the Night/A Lady in My Room	1978	—	2.00	4.00
❏ 12418	Dixie/Love Survived	1978	—	2.00	4.00
❏ 12462	Kiss You and Make It Better/You Do It	1979	—	2.00	4.00

ABC DOT

❏ 17608	Lady Luck and Mother Nature/The Door I Used to Close	1976	—	2.00	4.00
❏ 17629	Ain't It Funny (How Times Haven't Changed)/A Bridge for Crawling Back	1976	—	2.00	4.00
❏ 17650	One Night/Deep Elem Blues	1976	—	2.00	4.00
❏ 17669	Just Because/Angel with a Broken Wing	1976	—	2.00	4.00
❏ 17706	Julianne/Velvet Strings	1977	—	2.00	4.00
❏ 17722	Come to Me/Georgia on My Mind	1977	—	2.00	4.00

ABC DUNHILL

❏ 4240	I'm Not a Fool Anymore/Mama Mama	1970	—	3.00	6.00

ATLANTIC AMERICA

❏ 99529	There's Something on Your Mind/Everything A Man Can Do (And I Love You)	1986	—	—	3.00

AVION

❏ 105	Where Did He Go Right/(B-side unknown)	1983	—	3.50	7.00

BACK BEAT

❏ 543	Teenage Letter/Pain	1965	3.00	6.00	12.00
❏ 546	Treat Her Right/So Long, My Love	1965	4.00	8.00	16.00
❏ 555	Apple of My Eye/I Pass the Day	1965	3.00	6.00	12.00
❏ 560	My Babe/Pain	1966	3.00	6.00	12.00
❏ 563	Driving Wheel/Wigglin' and Gigglin'	1966	3.00	6.00	12.00
❏ 571	Don't Cry No More/To Make a Big Man Cry	1966	3.00	6.00	12.00
❏ 576	You're (Almost) Tough/Tush Hog	1966	3.00	6.00	12.00
❏ 582	Nobody But Me/A Good Man Is Hard to Find	1967	2.50	5.00	10.00

CHURCHILL

❏ 7778	After Texas/California Day	1981	—	2.50	5.00

ELEKTRA

❏ 46549	In Our Room/Things I Never Could Have Left Behind	1979	—	2.00	4.00
❏ 46582	The Fire of Two Old Flames/Under Suspicion	1980	—	2.00	4.00
❏ 46653	Long Drop/Gonna Save It for My Baby	1980	—	2.00	4.00
❏ 47029	Drinking Them Long Necks/Baby's Found Another Way to Love Me	1980	—	2.00	4.00
❏ 47081	I've Never Gone to Bed With an Ugly Woman/All Night Long Is Gone	1981	—	2.00	4.00

MEGA

❏ 1219	Baby's Not Home/Do What You Can Do	1974	—	2.50	5.00

MERCURY

❏ 72750	Got Down on Saturday (Sunday in the Rain)/The Grass Was Green	1967	2.00	4.00	8.00
❏ 72799	Broadway Walk/Turn Out the Lights	1968	2.00	4.00	8.00
❏ 72848	Ain't Goin' Down Right!/Lovin' Man on Your Hands	1968	2.00	4.00	8.00
❏ 72922	I Miss You Baby/I Want Some Action	1969	2.00	4.00	8.00

NSD

❏ 129	Play Another Gettin' Drunk and Take Somebody Home Song/Your Next One and Only	1982	—	2.50	5.00
❏ 146	The Trouble with Hearts/Naughty Smile	1982	—	2.50	5.00
❏ 156	Your Mama Don't Dance/Party Time	1982	—	2.50	5.00

SCEPTER

❏ 12116	Just a Little Bit/Treat Me Right	1965	2.50	5.00	10.00
❏ 12117	Won't Be Blue/One More Time	1965	2.50	5.00	10.00
❏ 12124	Get Back — Part 1/Get Back — Part 2	1965	2.50	5.00	10.00
❏ 12138	Convicted/One More Time	1966	2.50	5.00	10.00

SHANNON

❏ 829	The Most Wanted Woman in Town/Gingerbread Man	1975	—	2.50	5.00
❏ 833	Help Yourself to Me/To Make a Big Man Cry	1975	—	2.50	5.00
❏ 838	I'll Take It/The One That Got Away	1975	—	2.50	5.00

TEXAS CRUDE

❏ 614	Break Out the Good Stuff/She Needs Time	1985	2.00	4.00	8.00

TMI

❏ 75-0103	Rock and Roll Mood/You Got the Power	1972	—	2.50	5.00
❏ 75-0106	Why Don't We Go Somewhere and Love/Smell-A-Woman	1972	—	2.50	5.00
❏ BTBO-0111	Small Town Girl/Chug All Night	1973	—	2.50	5.00
❏ 75-0113	Carol/Clyde O'Riley	1973	—	2.50	5.00
❏ 9000	Puff of Smoke/Lord Take a Bow	1971	—	3.00	6.00
❏ 9010	Bit By Bit/Wait Till I Arrive	1972	—	3.00	6.00

TNT

❏ 194	Don't Be Blue/One More Time	1965	3.75	7.50	15.00

Albums
ABC

❏ AB-1054	Tonight's the Night	1978	2.50	5.00	10.00

Number	Title (A Side/B Side)	Yr	VG	VG+	NM
ABC DOT					
❑ DO-2051	Head First	1976	3.00	6.00	12.00
❑ DO-2066	A Head of His Time	1977	3.00	6.00	12.00
ABC DUNHILL					
❑ DS-50080	Same People	1970	5.00	10.00	20.00
ELEKTRA					
❑ 6E-234	In Our Room	1979	2.50	5.00	10.00
❑ 6E-298	The Many Sides of Roy Head	1980	2.50	5.00	10.00
MCA					
❑ 796	Tonight's the Night	1980	2.00	4.00	8.00
—Reissue of ABC album					
SCEPTER					
❑ S-532 [M]	Treat Me Right	1965	7.50	15.00	30.00
❑ SS-532 [S]	Treat Me Right	1965	10.00	20.00	40.00
TMI					
❑ 1000	Dismal Prisoner	1972	3.75	7.50	15.00
TNT					
❑ 101 [M]	Roy Head and the Traits	1965	37.50	75.00	150.00
—Counterfeit alert: Authentics do NOT contain the hit "Treat Her Right."					

HEAD EAST
45s
A&M

Number	Title (A Side/B Side)	Yr	VG	VG+	NM
❑ 1718	Never Been Any Reason/One Against the Other	1975	—	2.00	4.00
❑ 1784	Love Me Tonight/Brother Jacob	1976	—	2.00	4.00
❑ 1930	Gettin' Lucky/Sands of Time	1977	—	2.00	4.00
❑ 2026	Since You Been Gone/Pictures	1978	—	2.00	4.00
❑ 2026 [PS]	Since You Been Gone/Pictures	1978	2.00	4.00	8.00
❑ 2122	Never Been Any Reason/I'm Feelin' Fine	1979	—	2.00	4.00
❑ 2208	Got to Be Real/Morning	1979	—	2.00	4.00
❑ 2222	Specialty/Morning	1980	—	2.00	4.00
❑ 2278	I Surrender/Out of the Blue	1980	—	2.00	4.00

Albums
A&M

Number	Title (A Side/B Side)	Yr	VG	VG+	NM
❑ SP-3162	Get Yourself Up	198?	2.00	4.00	8.00
—Budget-line reissue					
❑ SP-3196	Flat as a Pancake	198?	2.00	4.00	8.00
—Budget-line reissue					
❑ SP-4537	Flat as a Pancake	1975	2.50	5.00	10.00
❑ SP-4579	Get Yourself Up	1976	2.50	5.00	10.00
❑ SP-4624	Gettin' Lucky	1977	2.50	5.00	10.00
❑ SP-4680	Head East	1978	2.50	5.00	10.00
❑ SP-4795	A Different Kind of Crazy	1979	2.50	5.00	10.00
❑ SP-4826	U.S. 1	1980	2.50	5.00	10.00
❑ SP-6007 [(2)]	Head East Live!	1979	3.00	6.00	12.00
ALLEGIANCE					
❑ AV-432	Onward and Upward	1986	2.00	4.00	8.00
PYRAMID					
❑ (# unknown)	Flat as a Pancake	1974	50.00	100.00	200.00
—Original issue; 5,000 were pressed; has a different cover than the A&M version of the same album, plus the A and B sides are opposite the reissue					

HEAD OVER HEELS
Albums
CAPITOL

Number	Title (A Side/B Side)	Yr	VG	VG+	NM
❑ ST-797	Head Over Heels	1971	7.50	15.00	30.00

HEAD SHOP, THE
Albums
EPIC

Number	Title (A Side/B Side)	Yr	VG	VG+	NM
❑ BN 26476	The Head Shop	1969	15.00	30.00	60.00

HEADS, THE
45s
LIBERTY

Number	Title (A Side/B Side)	Yr	VG	VG+	NM
❑ 56025	Are You Lonely for Me, Baby/You	1968	2.50	5.00	10.00

Albums
LIBERTY

Number	Title (A Side/B Side)	Yr	VG	VG+	NM
❑ LST-7581	Heads Up	1968	6.25	12.50	25.00

HEADS, HANDS AND FEET
45s
ATCO

Number	Title (A Side/B Side)	Yr	VG	VG+	NM
❑ 6923	One Woman/Dirty, Heavy Weather Road	1973	—	3.00	6.00

Albums
ATCO

Number	Title (A Side/B Side)	Yr	VG	VG+	NM
❑ SD 7025	Old Soldiers Never Die	1973	5.00	10.00	20.00
CAPITOL					
❑ SVBB-680 [(2)]	Heads, Hands and Feet	1971	6.25	12.50	25.00
❑ ST-11051	Tracks	1972	5.00	10.00	20.00

HEADSTONE
Albums
STARR

Number	Title (A Side/B Side)	Yr	VG	VG+	NM
❑ (# unknown)	Still Looking	1974	37.50	75.00	150.00

HEART (2)
45s
EMI

Number	Title (A Side/B Side)	Yr	VG	VG+	NM
❑ 4008	Beautiful Woman/Lovemaker	1974	—	2.00	4.00

HEART (3)
45s
LOOK

Number	Title (A Side/B Side)	Yr	VG	VG+	NM
❑ 5023	Give Me a Happy Heart/Now	1969	—	3.00	6.00
❑ 5029	I Love You/Love	1970	—	3.00	6.00

Albums
LOOK

Number	Title (A Side/B Side)	Yr	VG	VG+	NM
❑ LLP-11000	Heart	1969	3.00	6.00	12.00

HEART (U) Some of these could be group (3), but others probably are not. None of these, by the way, are the Seattle-based group featuring Ann and Nancy Wilson. That group's first record did not come out in the U.S. until 1976, thus it is not in this book.
45s
REPRISE

Number	Title (A Side/B Side)	Yr	VG	VG+	NM
❑ 0772	Heartbeat/The Train	1968	—	3.00	6.00

Albums
KING

Number	Title (A Side/B Side)	Yr	VG	VG+	NM
❑ KS-1119	Have a Heart	1970	3.00	6.00	12.00
NATURAL RESOURCES					
❑ NR-102	Heart	1972	3.00	6.00	12.00

HEARTBEATS, THE Also see SHEP AND THE LIMELITES.
45s
GEE

Number	Title (A Side/B Side)	Yr	VG	VG+	NM
❑ 1043	When I Found You/Hands Off My Baby	1957	12.50	25.00	50.00
❑ 1047	500 Miles to Go/After New Year's Eve	1958	5.00	10.00	20.00
—Gray label					
❑ 1047	500 Miles to Go/After New Year's Eve	1958	10.00	20.00	40.00
—Red label					
❑ 1061	People Are Talking/Your Way	1960	5.00	10.00	20.00
❑ 1062	Darling How Long/Hurry Home Baby	1960	5.00	10.00	20.00
GUYDEN					
❑ 2011	One Million Years/Darling, I Want to Get Married	1959	7.50	15.00	30.00
—Purple label					
❑ 2011	One Million Years/Darling, I Want to Get Married	1959	10.00	20.00	40.00
—Yellow label					
HULL					
❑ 711	Crazy for You/Rockin-N-Rollin-N-Rhythm-N-Blues-N	1955	25.00	50.00	100.00
—Black label					
❑ 711	Crazy for You/Rockin-N-Rollin-N-Rhythm-N-Blues-N	1955	50.00	100.00	200.00
—Pink label, "Miller" as A-side composer					
❑ 711	Crazy for You/Rockin-N-Rollin-N-Rhythm-N-Blues-N	1955	75.00	150.00	300.00
—Pink label, "Sheppard-Miller" as A-side composers					
❑ 711 [DJ]	Crazy for You/Rockin-N-Rollin-N-Rhythm-N-Blues-N	1955	150.00	300.00	600.00
—White label					
❑ 713	Darling How Long/Hurry Home Baby	1956	50.00	100.00	200.00
❑ 716	People Are Talking/Your Way	1956	50.00	100.00	200.00
❑ 720	A Thousand Miles Away/Oh Baby Don't	1957	20.00	450.00	80.00
—Red label					
❑ 720	A Thousand Miles Away/Oh Baby Don't	1957	62.50	125.00	250.00
—Black label					
JUBILEE					
❑ 5202	Finally/Boil and Bubble	1955	7.50	15.00	30.00
NETWORK					
❑ 71200	Tormented/After Everybody's Gone	195?	6.25	12.50	25.00
—Red vinyl The Network release as "The Heart Beats Quintet"					
❑ 71200	Tormented/After Everybody's Gone	195?	30.00	60.00	120.00
—Yellow label, black vinyl					
❑ 71200	Tormented/After Everybody's Gone	1955	75.00	150.00	300.00
—Cream label, black vinyl					
RAMA					
❑ 216	A Thousand Miles Away/Oh Baby Don't	1956	20.00	40.00	80.00
❑ 222	Wedding Bells/I Won't Be the Fool Anymore	1957	25.00	50.00	100.00
❑ 231	I Want to Know/Everybody's Somebody's Fool	1957	25.00	50.00	100.00
ROULETTE					
❑ 4054	I Found a Job/Down on My Knees	1958	7.50	15.00	30.00
❑ 4091	One Day Next Year/Sometimes I Wonder	1958	7.50	15.00	30.00
❑ 4194	Crazy for You/Down on My Knees	1959	7.50	15.00	30.00

Albums
EMUS

Number	Title (A Side/B Side)	Yr	VG	VG+	NM
❑ ES-12033	A Thousand Miles Away	1979	6.25	12.50	25.00
ROULETTE					
❑ R 25107 [M]	A Thousand Miles Away	1960	100.00	200.00	400.00

HEARTBEATS, THE /SHEP AND THE LIMELITES Also see each artist's individual listings.
Albums
ROULETTE

Number	Title (A Side/B Side)	Yr	VG	VG+	NM
❑ RE-115 [(2)]	Echoes of a Rock Era: The Groups	1972	3.75	7.50	15.00

HEARTBREAKERS, THE Several different groups.
45s
ATCO

Number	Title (A Side/B Side)	Yr	VG	VG+	NM
❑ 6258	The Willow Wept/You Had Time	1963	5.00	10.00	20.00
BRENT					
❑ 7037	I'm Leaving It All Up to You/Corrido Mash	1962	7.50	15.00	30.00
DONNA					
❑ 1381	Everytime I See You/Cradle Rock	1963	30.00	60.00	120.00
—Frank Zappa plays guitar on this record					
LINDA					
❑ 114	Please Answer/She Is My Baby	1964	3.75	7.50	15.00
MARKAY					
❑ 106	Since You've Been Gone/John Law	1962	20.00	40.00	80.00
MGM					
❑ 13129	It's Hard Being a Girl/Special Occasions	1963	3.75	7.50	15.00
RCA VICTOR					
❑ 47-4327	Heartbreaker/Wanda	1951	150.00	300.00	600.00
❑ 47-4508	You're So Necessary to Me/I'm Only Following My Heart	1952	150.00	300.00	600.00
❑ 47-4662	Why Don't I/Rockin' Daddy-O	1952	125.00	250.00	500.00
❑ 47-4849	There Is Time/It's OK With Me	1952	125.00	250.00	500.00
SWAN					
❑ 4242	Baby Baby/I Told You So	1966	3.75	7.50	15.00
VIK					
❑ 0261	Without a Cause/One, Two, I Love You	1957	37.50	75.00	150.00
❑ 0299	My Love/Love You Till the Day I Die	1957	62.50	125.00	250.00

HEARTS, THE
45s
BATON

Number	Title (A Side/B Side)	Yr	VG	VG+	NM
❑ 208	Lonely Nights/Oo-Wee	1955	12.50	25.00	50.00
❑ 211	All My Love Belongs to You/Talk About Him Girlie	1955	12.50	25.00	50.00
❑ 215	Gone, Gone, Gone/Until the Real Thing Comes Along	1955	12.50	25.00	50.00
❑ 222	Disappointed Bride/Going Home to Stay	1956	7.50	15.00	30.00
❑ 228	He Drives Me Crazy/I Had a Guy	1956	6.25	12.50	25.00

Number	Title (A Side/B Side)	Yr	VG	VG+	NM
J&S					
❑ 425/6	My Love Has Gone/You or Me Have Got to Go	1959	12.50	25.00	50.00
❑ 995	A Thousand Years from Today/I Feel So Good	1960	10.00	20.00	40.00
❑ 1180/1	You Weren't Home/				
	I Couldn't Let You See Me Crying	1961	12.50	25.00	50.00
❑ 1626/7	I Want Your Love Tonight/Like Later Baby	1958	12.50	25.00	50.00
❑ 1657	Dancing in a Dream World/				
	You Needn't Tell, I Know	1957	15.00	30.00	60.00
❑ 1660	So Long, Baby/You Say You Love Me	1957	15.00	30.00	60.00
❑ 4571/2	Goodbye Baby/There Is No Love at All	1959	10.00	20.00	40.00
❑ 10002/3	If I Had Known/There Are So Many Ways	1958	12.50	25.00	50.00
TUFF					
❑ 370	Dear Abby/(Instrumental)	1963	3.75	7.50	15.00

HEARTS AND FLOWERS
45s

Number	Title (A Side/B Side)	Yr	VG	VG+	NM
CAPITOL					
❑ 2167	She Sang Hymns Out of Tune/Tin Angel (Will				
	You Ever Come Down)	1968	2.50	5.00	10.00
❑ 5897	View from Ward 3/Please	1967	2.50	5.00	10.00
Albums					
CAPITOL					
❑ ST 2762 [S]	Now Is the Time for Hearts and Flowers	1967	10.00	20.00	40.00
❑ T 2762 [M]	Now Is the Time for Hearts and Flowers	1967	10.00	20.00	40.00
❑ ST 2868	Of Horses, Kids and Forgotten Women	1968	12.50	25.00	50.00

HEARTS OF STONE
45s

Number	Title (A Side/B Side)	Yr	VG	VG+	NM
V.I.P.					
❑ 25058	It's a Lonesome Road/Yesterday's Love Is Over	1970	2.50	5.00	10.00
❑ 25064	If I Could Give You the World/You Gotta Sacrifice	1970	2.50	5.00	10.00
Albums					
V.I.P.					
❑ VIPS-404	Stop the World... We Wanna Get On	1970	10.00	20.00	40.00

HEARTSFIELD
45s

Number	Title (A Side/B Side)	Yr	VG	VG+	NM
MERCURY					
❑ 73449	Music Eyes/Gypsy Rider	1974	—	2.50	5.00
❑ 73600	Shine On/Eight Hours at a Time	1974	—	2.50	5.00
❑ 73628	Racin' the Sun/Pass Me By	1974	—	2.50	5.00
❑ 73706	Nashville/As I Look Into the Fire	1975	—	2.50	5.00
❑ 73742	Magic Mood/Rocking Chair	1975	—	2.50	5.00
Albums					
COLUMBIA					
❑ PC 34456	Collector's Item	1976	2.50	5.00	10.00
MERCURY					
❑ SRM-1-688	Heartsfield	1973	2.50	5.00	10.00
❑ SRM-1-1003	The Wonder of It All	1974	2.50	5.00	10.00
❑ SRM-1-1034	Foolish Pleasures	1975	2.50	5.00	10.00

HEAT BROTHERS '84 See CANNED HEAT.

HEATH, TED
45s

Number	Title (A Side/B Side)	Yr	VG	VG+	NM
LONDON					
❑ 1006	Sixty Seconds/The Girl in the Little Green Hat	1951	3.00	6.00	12.00
❑ 1014	Saxophone Mambo/Take a Letter Miss Smith	1951	3.00	6.00	12.00
❑ 1015	This Is the Time/In a Little Spanish Town	1951	3.00	6.00	12.00
❑ 1026	London Fog/Romanian Roundabout	1951	3.00	6.00	12.00
❑ 1056	The Nearness of You/Lyonia	1951	3.00	6.00	12.00
❑ 1057	Button Up Your Overcoat/You're Nearer	1951	3.00	6.00	12.00
❑ 1181	Turkey in the Straw/Entry of the Gladiators	1952	3.00	6.00	12.00
❑ 1182	L'Heure Bleu/A Kiss in the Dark	1952	3.00	6.00	12.00
❑ 1183	Live House Blues/The Black Bottom	1952	3.00	6.00	12.00
❑ 1184	Casey Jones/I Want to Be Happy	1952	3.00	6.00	12.00
❑ 1198	Obsession/Hawaiian Mambo	1952	3.00	6.00	12.00
❑ 1256	Vanessa/Early Autumn	1952	3.00	6.00	12.00
❑ 1259	Jungle Fantasy/The Piper's Patrol	1952	3.00	6.00	12.00
❑ 1290	Alpine Boogie/Floreintine	1952	3.00	6.00	12.00
❑ 1305	Beyond the Sea/On the Bridge	1953	3.00	6.00	12.00
❑ 1324	Phantom Regiment/Strike Up the Band	1953	3.00	6.00	12.00
❑ 1344	Alouette/Yours Is My Heart	1953	3.00	6.00	12.00
❑ 1379	Dragnet/Sloppy Joe	1953	3.00	6.00	12.00
❑ 1390	Lullaby of Birdland/Seven-Eleven	1953	3.00	6.00	12.00
❑ 1404	Slim Jim/The Original Creep	1954	3.00	6.00	12.00
❑ 1418	Jitterbug Waltz/Alligator Crawl	1954	3.00	6.00	12.00
❑ 1421	The Champ/Pick Yourself Up	1954	3.00	6.00	12.00
❑ 1495	Stomp and Whistle/Bernie's Tune	1954	3.00	6.00	12.00
❑ 1500	Skokiaan/Skokiaan	1954	3.00	6.00	12.00
—B-side by the Johnston Brothers					
❑ 1531	Asia Minor/Dig Deep	1955	2.50	5.00	10.00
❑ 1534	Peg o' My Heart Mambo/In the Mood	1955	2.50	5.00	10.00
❑ 1621	Malaguena/Barber Shop Jump	1955	2.50	5.00	10.00
❑ 1644	Main Title — The Man with the Golden Arm/				
	Siboney	1956	2.50	5.00	10.00
❑ 1647	Cloudburst/The Trouble with Harry	1956	2.50	5.00	10.00
❑ 1675	The Faithful Hussar/Have You Met Miss Jones	1956	2.50	5.00	10.00
❑ 1690	Autumn Concerto/Lost	1956	2.50	5.00	10.00
—B-side by Bobbie Britton					
❑ 1692	Canadian Sunset/Oriental Holiday	1956	2.50	5.00	10.00
❑ 1712	Madagascar/Jungle Drums	1957	2.50	5.00	10.00
❑ 1762	Witch Doctor/Headin' North	1957	2.50	5.00	10.00
❑ 1800	Little Serenade/I've Got the World on a String	1958	2.50	5.00	10.00
❑ 1809	Cha Cha Baby/Tom Hark	1958	2.50	5.00	10.00
❑ 1836	Bullfighters Patrol/Strolling Along with the Blues	1958	2.50	5.00	10.00
❑ 1867	Frogmarch/9:20 Special	1959	2.00	4.00	8.00
❑ 1887	Honky Tonk Train Blues/Bluest Kind of Blue	1959	2.00	4.00	8.00
❑ 1893	Swinging Ghosts/Indian Love Call	1959	2.00	4.00	8.00
❑ 1920	Slaughter on Tenth Avenue/Sleepy Lagoon	1960	2.00	4.00	8.00
❑ 1975	Man from Madrid/Theme from "Dangerman"	1961	2.00	4.00	8.00
❑ 2014	Peanut Vendor/Daddy	1961	2.00	4.00	8.00
❑ 9503	Charmaine Cha Cha/Sucu Sucu	1962	—	3.00	6.00
❑ 9602	Theme from Cleopatra/Mirage	1963	—	3.00	6.00
❑ 9629	Theme from "Lord of the Flies"/Paris Mist	1963	—	3.00	6.00
❑ 9680	Theme from "The Carpetbaggers"/Wigwam	1964	—	3.00	6.00

Number	Title (A Side/B Side)	Yr	VG	VG+	NM
7-Inch Extended Plays					
LONDON					
❑ BEP 6091	Twilight Boogie/Clair de Lune//Alouette/La Mer	195?	2.50	5.00	10.00
❑ BEP 6091 [PS]	Ted Heath and His Music	195?	2.50	5.00	10.00
❑ BEP.6270	The Man I Love/Love Walked In//Nice Work If				
	You Can Get It/Love Is Here to Stay	195?	2.50	5.00	10.00
❑ BEP.6270 [PS]	Love Is Here to Stay	195?	2.50	5.00	10.00
Albums					
EVEREST ARCHIVE OF FOLK & JAZZ					
❑ 215	Ted Heath's Big Band	1970	2.50	5.00	10.00
LONDON					
❑ PS 116 [S]	Hits I Missed	1958	6.25	12.50	25.00
❑ PS 117 [S]	All Time Top Twelve	1958	6.25	12.50	25.00
—Re-recorded version of LL 1716					
❑ PS 138 [S]	Swing Session	1958	6.25	12.50	25.00
—New stereo recordings of the same material as appears on LL 802					
❑ PS 140 [S]	Ted Heath Swings in High Stereo	1958	6.25	12.50	25.00
❑ PS 148 [S]	Shall We Dance	1959	6.25	12.50	25.00
❑ PS 159 [S]	Great Film Hits	1959	6.25	12.50	25.00
❑ PS 171 [S]	Pop Hits from the Classics	1959	6.25	12.50	25.00
❑ PS 172 [S]	Big Band Blues	1959	6.25	12.50	25.00
❑ PS 174 [S]	My Very Good Friends The Bandleaders	1959	6.25	12.50	25.00
❑ PS 175 [S]	The Hits of the Twenties	1960	5.00	10.00	20.00
❑ PS 184 [S]	The Big Band Dixie Sound	1960	5.00	10.00	20.00
❑ PS 187 [S]	Ted Heath in Concert	1960	5.00	10.00	20.00
❑ PS 190 [S]	Songs for the Young at Heart	1960	5.00	10.00	20.00
❑ PS 216 [S]	The Hits of the Thirties	1961	5.00	10.00	20.00
❑ PS 219 [S]	Latin Swingers	1961	5.00	10.00	20.00
❑ LPB-340 [10]	Tempo for Dancing	195?	10.00	20.00	40.00
❑ LPB-374 [10]	Ted Heath and His Orchestra	195?	10.00	20.00	40.00
❑ LB-511 [10]	Listen to My Music	195?	10.00	20.00	40.00
❑ PS 535	21st Anniversary Album	1968	3.00	6.00	12.00
❑ LB-732 [10]	Black and White Magic	195?	10.00	20.00	40.00
❑ LL 750 [M]	Ted Heath Strikes Up the Band	1953	5.00	10.00	20.00
❑ LL 802 [M]	Ted Heath at the London Palladium	1953	5.00	10.00	20.00
❑ LL 978 [M]	Ted Heath Plays the Music of Fats Waller	1954	5.00	10.00	20.00
❑ LL 1000 [M]	The 100th London Palladium Concert	1955	5.00	10.00	20.00
❑ LL 1211 [M]	Jazz Concert at the London Palladium, Vol. 3	1955	5.00	10.00	20.00
❑ LL 1217 [M]	Gershwin for Moderns	1956	5.00	10.00	20.00
❑ LL 1279 [M]	Kern for Moderns	1956	5.00	10.00	20.00
❑ LL 1379 [M]	Jazz Concert at the London Palladium, Vol. 4	1956	5.00	10.00	20.00
❑ LL 1475 [M]	Ted Heath Swings in Hi-Fi	1956	5.00	10.00	20.00
❑ LL 1500 [M]	Rodgers for Moderns	1956	5.00	10.00	20.00
❑ LL 1564 [M]	Ted Heath's First American Tour	1956	5.00	10.00	20.00
❑ LL 1566 [M]	Ted Heath at Carnegie Hall	1956	5.00	10.00	20.00
❑ LL 1676 [M]	A Yank in Europe	1956	5.00	10.00	20.00
❑ LL 1716 [M]	All Time Top Twelve	1957	5.00	10.00	20.00
❑ LL 1721 [M]	Spotlight on Sidemen	1957	5.00	10.00	20.00
❑ LL 1737 [M]	Showcase	1957	5.00	10.00	20.00
❑ LL 1743 [M]	Tribute to the Fabulous Dorseys	1957	5.00	10.00	20.00
❑ LL 1749 [M]	Rhapsody in Blue	1957	5.00	10.00	20.00
❑ LL 3047 [M]	Things to Come	1958	5.00	10.00	20.00
❑ LL 3057 [M]	Hits I Missed	1958	5.00	10.00	20.00
❑ LL 3058 [M]	Old English	1958	5.00	10.00	20.00
❑ LL 3062 [M]	Shall We Dance	1959	5.00	10.00	20.00
❑ LL 3106 [M]	Great Film Hits	1959	5.00	10.00	20.00
❑ LL 3124 [M]	Pop Hits from the Classics	1959	5.00	10.00	20.00
❑ LL 3125 [M]	Big Band Blues	1959	5.00	10.00	20.00
❑ LL 3127 [M]	My Very Good Friends The Bandleaders	1959	5.00	10.00	20.00
❑ LL 3128 [M]	The Hits of the Twenties	1960	3.75	7.50	15.00
❑ LL 3138 [M]	The Big Band Dixie Sound	1960	3.75	7.50	15.00
❑ LL 3143 [M]	Ted Heath in Concert	1960	3.75	7.50	15.00
❑ LL 3146 [M]	Songs for the Young at Heart	1960	3.75	7.50	15.00
❑ LL 3192 [M]	The Hits of the Thirties	1961	3.75	7.50	15.00
❑ LL 3195 [M]	Latin Swingers	1961	3.75	7.50	15.00
❑ LL 3325 [M]	Big Band Spirituals	1963	3.00	6.00	12.00
❑ LL 3367 [M]	New Palladium Performances	1964	3.00	6.00	12.00
LONDON PHASE 4					
❑ SP 44002 [S]	Big Band Percussion	1961	3.75	7.50	15.00
❑ SP 44017	Big Band Bash	1962	3.75	7.50	15.00
❑ SP 44023	Satin Strings and Bouncing Brass	1963	3.75	7.50	15.00
❑ SP 44036 [S]	Big Band Spirituals	1963	3.75	7.50	15.00
❑ SP 44038	Swing vs. Latin	1964	3.75	7.50	15.00
❑ SP 44046 [S]	New Palladium Performances	1964	3.00	6.00	12.00
❑ SP 44063	The Sound of Music	1965	3.00	6.00	12.00
❑ SP 44074	Chartbusters	1966	3.00	6.00	12.00
❑ SP 44079	Pow!	1966	3.00	6.00	12.00
❑ P 54002 [M]	Big Band Percussion	1961	3.00	6.00	12.00
RICHMOND					
❑ B 20034 [M]	Big Band Beat	196?	3.00	6.00	12.00
❑ B 20037 [M]	Ted Heath Plays Gershwin	196?	3.00	6.00	12.00
❑ B 20082 [M]	Ted Heath Plays the Music of Fats Waller	196?	3.00	6.00	12.00
❑ B 20096 [M]	Big Band Gershwin	196?	3.00	6.00	12.00
❑ B 20097 [M]	Big Band Kern	196?	3.00	6.00	12.00
❑ B 20098 [M]	Big Band Rodgers	196?	3.00	6.00	12.00

HEATHER BLACK
Albums

Number	Title (A Side/B Side)	Yr	VG	VG+	NM
AMERICAN PLAYBOY					
❑ 1001	Heather Black Live	197?	15.00	30.00	60.00
❑ 1001 [(2)]	Heather Black Live	197?	37.50	75.00	150.00
—Evidently, some copies of this were 2-record sets					
DOUBLE BAYOU					
❑ 2000	Heather Black	197?	7.50	15.00	30.00

HEATHERTON, JOEY
45s

Number	Title (A Side/B Side)	Yr	VG	VG+	NM
CORAL					
❑ 62422	That's How It Goes/I'll Be Seeing You	1964	7.50	15.00	30.00
❑ 62422 [PS]	That's How It Goes/I'll Be Seeing You	1964	10.00	20.00	40.00
❑ 62451	Hullabaloo/My Blood Runs Cold	1965	6.25	12.50	25.00
❑ 62459	Tomorrow Is Another Day/But He's Not Mine	1965	6.25	12.50	25.00
DECCA					
❑ 31962	Live and Learn/When You Call Me Baby	1966	15.00	30.00	60.00
❑ 31962 [PS]	Live and Learn/When You Call Me Baby	1966	20.00	40.00	80.00
MGM					
❑ 14387	Gone/The Road I Took to You	1972	—	2.50	5.00
❑ 14387 [PS]	Gone/The Road I Took to You	1972	2.50	5.00	10.00

H

Number	Title (A Side/B Side)	Yr	VG	VG+	NM
❏ 14434	I'm Sorry/Someone to Watch Over Me	1972	—	2.50	5.00
❏ 14434	I'm Sorry/Crazy	1972	—	3.00	6.00
❏ 14499	Crazy/God Only Knows	1973	—	2.50	5.00
Albums					
MGM					
❏ SE-4858	The Joey Heatherton Album	1972	3.75	7.50	15.00

HEAVY BALLOON, THE
Albums
ELEPHANT

Number	Title (A Side/B Side)	Yr	VG	VG+	NM
❏ EVS-104	32,000 Lbs.	1969	17.50	35.00	70.00

HEBB, BOBBY
45s
BOOM

Number	Title (A Side/B Side)	Yr	VG	VG+	NM
❏ 60017	Betty Jo from Ohio/Sam Hall Jr.	1966	2.00	4.00	8.00
CADET					
❏ 5690	I Was a Boy When You Needed a Man/Woman in the Window	1972	—	2.50	5.00
LAURIE					
❏ 3632	True, I Love You/Proud Soul Heritage	1975	—	2.50	5.00
❏ 3638	Sunny '76/Sunny Disco	1976	—	2.50	5.00
PHILIPS					
❏ 40365	Sunny/Bread	1966	2.50	5.00	10.00
❏ 40400	A Satisfied Mind/Love, Love, Love	1966	2.00	4.00	8.00
❏ 40400 [PS]	A Satisfied Mind/Love, Love, Love	1966	3.00	6.00	12.00
❏ 40421	Love Me/Crazy Baby	1966	2.00	4.00	8.00
❏ 40431	My Pretty Sunshine/Ooh La La	1967	2.00	4.00	8.00
❏ 40448	I Love Everything About You/Some Kind of Magic	1967	2.00	4.00	8.00
❏ 40482	Everything Is Coming Up Roses/Bound by Love	1967	2.00	4.00	8.00
❏ 40551	Dreamy/You Want to Change Me	1968	2.00	4.00	8.00
RICH					
❏ 1006	Cherry/Feel So Good	1960	3.75	7.50	15.00
❏ 1740	Just a Little Bit More/Walk Me On Alone	1962	3.75	7.50	15.00
SCEPTER					
❏ 12166	I Love Mary (Part 1)/I Love Mary (Part 2)	1966	2.00	4.00	8.00
Albums					
EPIC					
❏ BN 26523	Love Games	1970	3.00	6.00	12.00
PHILIPS					
❏ PHM 200212 [M]	Sunny	1966	6.25	12.50	25.00

—With "200-212" in trail-off; this record is mono

Number	Title (A Side/B Side)	Yr	VG	VG+	NM
❏ PHM 200212 [S]	Sunny	1966	6.25	12.50	25.00

—With "2/600-212" in trail-off; this record plays stereo, though labeled mono

Number	Title (A Side/B Side)	Yr	VG	VG+	NM
❏ PHS 600212 [S]	Sunny	1966	7.50	15.00	30.00

HEDGE & DONNA
45s
CAPITOL

Number	Title (A Side/B Side)	Yr	VG	VG+	NM
❏ 2695	Black Betty/Tomorrow Is the First Day of the Rest of Your Life	1969	2.00	4.00	8.00
❏ 2840	My God and I/Sunshine	1970	2.00	4.00	8.00
JANUS					
❏ 216	Guava Jelly/Well I Never	1973	—	3.50	7.00

—As "Capers & Carson"

Number	Title (A Side/B Side)	Yr	VG	VG+	NM
❏ 229	Mirror, Mirror/(B-side unknown)	1973	2.00	4.00	8.00

—As "Capers & Carson"
POLYDOR

Number	Title (A Side/B Side)	Yr	VG	VG+	NM
❏ 14090	Touch Caste on the Water/She Said She Said	1971	2.00	4.00	8.00
Albums					
CAPITOL					
❏ ST-107	2	1969	3.75	7.50	15.00

—Black label with rainbow ring

Number	Title (A Side/B Side)	Yr	VG	VG+	NM
❏ ST-279	All the Friendly Colours	1969	3.75	7.50	15.00

—Lime green label

Number	Title (A Side/B Side)	Yr	VG	VG+	NM
❏ ST-447	Special Circumstances	1970	3.75	7.50	15.00
❏ ST-2869	Hedge & Donna	1968	3.75	7.50	15.00

—The label calls this LP "Love"
JANUS

Number	Title (A Side/B Side)	Yr	VG	VG+	NM
❏ JLS-3045	Capers & Carson	1973	3.00	6.00	12.00
POLYDOR					
❏ 24-4063	Revolution	1971	3.00	6.00	12.00

HEDGEHOPPERS ANONYMOUS
45s
PARROT

Number	Title (A Side/B Side)	Yr	VG	VG+	NM
❏ 3002	Remember/Baby (You're My Everything)	1966	2.50	5.00	10.00
❏ 9800	It's Good News Week/Afraid of Love	1965	3.00	6.00	12.00
❏ 9817	Don't Push Me/Please Don't Hurt Your Heart for Me	1966	2.50	5.00	10.00

HEIGHT, RONNIE
45s
BAMBOO

Number	Title (A Side/B Side)	Yr	VG	VG+	NM
❏ 500	Dolores/I'm Confessin'	1961	3.00	6.00	12.00
DORE					
❏ 516	Come Softly to Me/So Young, So Wise	1959	5.00	10.00	20.00
ERA					
❏ 3000	Portrait of Linda/It's Not That Easy	1959	3.75	7.50	15.00
❏ 3005	Mr. Blue, I Presume/Juvenile	1959	3.75	7.50	15.00
❏ 3009	Maybe Tomorrow/A Kiss to Build a Dream On	1959	3.75	7.50	15.00
❏ 3017	Mem'ries and Habits/One Finger Symphony	1960	3.75	7.50	15.00
❏ 3031	No Date/Mr. Blue, I Presume	1960	3.75	7.50	15.00

HEINTJE
45s
MGM

Number	Title (A Side/B Side)	Yr	VG	VG+	NM
❏ 14183	Mama/Mother's Tears	1970	—	2.00	4.00
❏ 14272	When the Summer Comes/You Are the Best of All	1971	—	2.00	4.00
Albums					
MGM					
❏ SE-4739	Mama	1970	3.00	6.00	12.00
❏ SE-4772	Best of All	1971	3.00	6.00	12.00

HEINZ Also see FREDDIE AND THE DREAMERS.
45s
LONDON

Number	Title (A Side/B Side)	Yr	VG	VG+	NM
❏ 9619	Just Like Eddie/Don't You Knock on My Door	1963	3.75	7.50	15.00
TOWER					
❏ 110	Questions I Can't Answer/The Beating of My Heart	1964	5.00	10.00	20.00
❏ 172	Digging My Potatoes/Don't Think Twice, It's All Right	1965	5.00	10.00	20.00
❏ 195	Don't Worry Baby/Heart Full of Sorrow	1966	7.50	15.00	30.00
❏ 253	I'm Not a Bad Boy/Movin' In	1966	5.00	10.00	20.00

HELLERS, THE
Albums
COMMAND

Number	Title (A Side/B Side)	Yr	VG	VG+	NM
❏ RS 934 SD	Singers, Talkers, Players, Swingers and Doers	1968	10.00	20.00	40.00

HELLO PEOPLE, THE
45s
ABC

Number	Title (A Side/B Side)	Yr	VG	VG+	NM
❏ 12160	Book of Love/How High Is the Moon	1976	—	2.50	5.00
ABC DUNHILL					
❏ 15023	Future Shock/Destiny	1974	—	2.50	5.00
❏ 15031	Just One Victory/Take the Love in Your Body	1975	—	2.50	5.00
MEDIARTS					
❏ 109	Pass Me By/Maybe We Should Have Had Rain	1971	2.50	5.00	10.00
PHILIPS					
❏ 40481	Let's Go Hide in the Forest/Disparity Waterfront Blues	1967	2.00	4.00	8.00
❏ 40522	A Stranger at Her Door/Paisley Teddy Bear	1968	2.00	4.00	8.00
❏ 40531	(As I Went Down to) Jerusalem/It's a Monday Kind of Tuesday	1968	2.00	4.00	8.00
❏ 40572	If I Should Sing Too Softly/Pray for Rain	1968	2.00	4.00	8.00
❏ 40585	Anthem/Jelly Jam	1969	2.00	4.00	8.00
UNITED ARTISTS					
❏ 50797	Pass Me By/Maybe We Should Have Had Rain	1971	—	3.00	6.00
Albums					
ABC					
❏ D-882	Bricks	1975	2.50	5.00	10.00
ABC DUNHILL					
❏ DS-50184	The Handsome Devils	1974	2.50	5.00	10.00
MEDIARTS					
❏ 41-8	Have You Seen the Light	1970	3.00	6.00	12.00
PHILIPS					
❏ PHS 200265 [M]	The Hello People	1968	6.25	12.50	25.00

—Possibly white label promo only

Number	Title (A Side/B Side)	Yr	VG	VG+	NM
❏ PHS 600265 [S]	The Hello People	1968	3.75	7.50	15.00
❏ PHS 600276	Fusion	1969	3.75	7.50	15.00
UNITED ARTISTS					
❏ UAS 5524	Have You Seen the Light	1971	2.50	5.00	10.00

—Reissue of Mediarts LP

HELMS, BOBBY
45s
CERTRON

Number	Title (A Side/B Side)	Yr	VG	VG+	NM
❏ 10002	Mary Goes 'Round/Cold Winds Blow on Me	1970	2.00	4.00	8.00
❏ 10021	Jingle Bell Rock/The Old Year Is Gone	1970	2.00	4.00	8.00
❏ 10021 [PS]	Jingle Bell Rock/The Old Year Is Gone	1970	2.00	4.00	15.00
❏ 10023	I Wouldn't Take the World for You/Look What You've Done	1970	2.00	4.00	8.00
COLUMBIA					
❏ 4-42801	Fraulein/My Special Angel	1963	2.50	5.00	10.00
❏ 4-43031	It's a Girl/Put Your Arms Around Him	1964	2.50	5.00	10.00
DECCA					
❏ 9-29947	Tennessee Rock 'N' Roll/I Don't Owe You Nothing	1956	12.50	25.00	50.00
❏ 9-30194	Fraulein/(Got a) Heartsick Feeling	1957	5.00	10.00	20.00
❏ 9-30194 [PS]	Fraulein/(Got a) Heartsick Feeling	1957	12.50	25.00	50.00
❏ 9-30423	My Special Angel/Standing at the End of My World	1957	6.25	12.50	25.00
❏ 9-30513	Jingle Bell Rock/Captain Santa Claus	1957	6.25	12.50	25.00

—Black label, star under "Decca"

Number	Title (A Side/B Side)	Yr	VG	VG+	NM
❏ 9-30513	Jingle Bell Rock/Captain Santa Claus	1957	10.00	20.00	40.00

—Black label, lines on either side of "Decca"

Number	Title (A Side/B Side)	Yr	VG	VG+	NM
❏ 9-30513 [PS]	Jingle Bell Rock/Captain Santa Claus	1957	12.50	25.00	50.00
❏ 9-30513	Jingle Bell Rock/Captain Santa Claus	1960	3.00	6.00	12.00

—Black label with color bars

Number	Title (A Side/B Side)	Yr	VG	VG+	NM
❏ 9-30557	Just a Little Lonesome/Love My Baby	1958	5.00	10.00	20.00
❏ 9-30619	Jacqueline/Living in the Shadow of the Past	1958	5.00	10.00	20.00
❏ 9-30682	Schoolboy Crush/Borrowed Dreams	1958	5.00	10.00	20.00
❏ 9-30749	A Hundred Hearts/The Fool and the Angel	1958	5.00	10.00	20.00
❏ 9-30831	New River Train/Miss Memory	1959	3.75	7.50	15.00
❏ 9-30886	Soon It Can Be Told/I Guess I'll Miss the Prom	1959	3.75	7.50	15.00
❏ 9-30928	No Other Baby/You're No Longer Mine	1959	3.75	7.50	15.00
❏ 9-30976	My Lucky Day/Hurry Baby	1959	3.75	7.50	15.00
❏ 9-31041	To My Sorrow/Someone Was Already There	1960	3.75	7.50	15.00
❏ 31103	Let Me Be the One/I Wanna Be with You	1960	3.75	7.50	15.00
❏ 31148	Lonely River Rhine/Guess We Thought the World Would End	1960	3.75	7.50	15.00
❏ 31230	Sad-Eyed Baby/You're the One	1961	3.00	6.00	12.00
❏ 31287	How Can You Divide a Little Child/My Greatest Weakness	1961	3.00	6.00	12.00
❏ 31356	One Deep Love/Once in a Lifetime	1962	3.00	6.00	12.00
❏ 31403	Then Came You/Yesterday's Champagne	1962	3.00	6.00	12.00
GUSTO					
❏ 116	That Heart Belongs to Me/With Jenny on My Mind	1974	—	3.00	6.00
❏ 119	Work Things Out with Annie/With Jenny on My Mind	1974	—	3.00	6.00
KAPP					
❏ 708	I'm the Man/Have This Love on Me	1965	2.50	5.00	10.00
❏ 719	Jingle Bell Rock/The Bell That Couldn't Jingle	1965	3.00	6.00	12.00
❏ 732	Those Snowy Glowy Blowy Days of Winter/Sailor	1965	2.50	5.00	10.00
❏ 777	The Things I Remember Most/Sorry, My Name Isn't Fred	1966	2.50	5.00	10.00

Merle Haggard, *Okie from Muskogee,* Capitol ST-384, stereo LP, $10-$20.

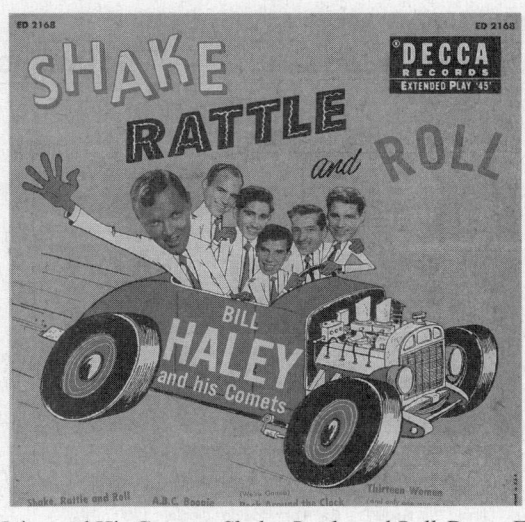

Bill Haley and His Comets, *Shake, Rattle and Roll*, Decca EP 2168, 7-inch EP, $60-$120 (cover and record together).

George Harrison, "Blow Away," Dark Horse DHS 8763, picture sleeve, $2.50-$5.

The Harptones, *The Sensational Harptones,* Bruce BEP-201, 7-inch EP, $7,500-$10,000 (cover and record together).

Head East, *Flat as a Pancake,* A&M SP-4537, stereo LP, $5-$10.

Bobby Hebb, *Sunny,* Philips PHS 600-212, stereo LP, $15-$30.

Number	Title (A Side/B Side)	Yr	VG	VG+	NM
❏ 876	I Miss My Fraulein/Where Does a Shadow Go	1967	2.00	4.00	8.00
LITTLE DARLIN'					
❏ 0030	He Thought He'd Die Laughing/				
	You'd Better Make Up Your Mind	1967	2.50	5.00	10.00
❏ 0034	The Day You Stop Loving Me/				
	You Can Tell the World	1967	2.50	5.00	10.00
❏ 0038	Jingle Bell Rock/I Wanta Go to Santa Claus Land	1967	3.00	6.00	12.00
❏ 0041	I Feel You, I Love You/				
	The Day You Stop Loving Me	1968	2.50	5.00	10.00
❏ 0049	Or Is It Love/Touch My Heart	1968	2.50	5.00	10.00
❏ 0054	My Special Angel/Expressing My Love	1968	2.50	5.00	10.00
❏ 0062	So Long/Just Do the Best You Can	1969	2.50	5.00	10.00
❏ 0073	Echoes and Shadows/Step Into My Soul	1969	2.50	5.00	10.00
❏ 7801	I'm Gonna Love the Devil Out of You/				
	I Can't Promise You	1978	—	3.00	6.00
❏ 7807	The Things I Remember Most/I'm Not Sorry	1978	—	3.00	6.00
❏ 7809	Jingle Bell Rock/I Wanta Go to Santa Claus Land	1978	—	3.00	6.00
❏ 7916	One More Dollar for the Band/Touch My Heart	1979	—	3.00	6.00
MCA					
❏ 65026	Jingle Bell Rock/Captain Santa Claus	1973	—	2.50	5.00
—Black label with rainbow					
❏ 65026	Jingle Bell Rock/Captain Santa Claus	1980	—	—	3.00
—Blue label with rainbow					
❏ 65029	Jingle Bell Rock/The Bell That Couldn't Jingle	1973	—	2.50	5.00
—Black label with rainbow; this contains the 1965 Kapp re-recording of the A-side					
❏ 65029	Jingle Bell Rock/The Bell That Couldn't Jingle	1980	—	—	3.00
—Blue label with rainbow					
MILLION					
❏ 5	It's the Little Things/Love's Sweet Mystery	1972	—	3.50	7.00
❏ 22	It's Starting to Rain Again/				
	Wouldn't Give Up on You	1972	—	3.50	7.00
MISTLETOE					
❏ 802	Jingle Bell Rock/Jingle Bells	197?	—	2.50	5.00
❏ 802 [PS]	Jingle Bell Rock/Jingle Bells	197?	2.00	4.00	8.00
PLAYBACK					
❏ 1305	Lay Me Down Look/Dance with Me	1988	—	3.00	6.00
❏ 1322	Somebody Wrong Is Looking Right/				
	This Song for You	1988	—	3.00	6.00
❏ 1328	Southern Belle/Troubles Wall to Wall	1989	—	3.00	6.00
❏ 75709	Southern Belle/Troubles Wall to Wall	1989	—	2.50	5.00
SPEED					
❏ 45-114	Yesterday's Lovin'/Hanging Around	1957	7.50	15.00	30.00
❏ 45-117	Freedom Lovin' Guy/I've Never Seen Anyone	1957	7.50	15.00	30.00
7-Inch Extended Plays					
DECCA					
❏ ED 2555	If Only I Knew/Far Away Heart//My Shoes Keep				
	Walking Back to You/Sugar Moon	1957	5.00	10.00	20.00
❏ ED 2555 [PS]	(title unknown)	1957	5.00	10.00	20.00
❏ ED 2586	Plaything/Magic Song//Tonight's the Night/Just				
	a Little Lonesome	1957	5.00	10.00	20.00
❏ ED 2586 [PS]	Tonight's the Night	1957	5.00	10.00	20.00
❏ ED 2629	Jacqueline/My Special Angel//Borrowed				
	Dreams/Schoolboy Crush	1957	5.00	10.00	20.00
❏ ED 2629 [PS]	Bobby Helms	1957	5.00	10.00	20.00
Albums					
COLUMBIA					
❏ CL 2060 [M]	The Best of Bobby Helms	1963	6.25	12.50	25.00
❏ CS 8860 [S]	The Best of Bobby Helms	1963	7.50	15.00	30.00
DECCA					
❏ DL 8638 [M]	Bobby Helms Sings to My Special Angel	1957	30.00	60.00	120.00
HARMONY					
❏ HL 7409 [M]	Fraulein	1967	3.00	6.00	12.00
❏ HS 11209 [S]	Fraulein	1967	3.00	6.00	12.00
KAPP					
❏ KL 1463 [M]	I'm the Man	1966	3.75	7.50	15.00
❏ KL 1505 [M]	Sorry My Name Isn't Fred	1966	3.75	7.50	15.00
❏ KS 3463 [S]	I'm the Man	1966	5.00	10.00	20.00
❏ KS 3505 [S]	Sorry My Name Isn't Fred	1966	5.00	10.00	20.00
LITTLE DARLIN'					
❏ 8088	All New Just for You	1968	6.25	12.50	25.00
MISTLETOE					
❏ MLP-1206	Jingle Bell Rock	197?	3.00	6.00	12.00
POWER PAK					
❏ 283	Greatest Hits	197?	2.50	5.00	10.00
VOCALION					
❏ VL 3743 [M]	Someone Already There	1965	3.75	7.50	15.00
❏ VL 73743 [R]	Someone Already There	1965	3.00	6.00	12.00
❏ VL 73874	My Special Angel	1969	3.00	6.00	12.00

HELMS, DON
45s
SMASH

Number	Title (A Side/B Side)	Yr	VG	VG+	NM
❏ 1781	Fire Ball Mail/I Can't Help It (If I'm Still in Love				
	with You)	1962	5.00	10.00	20.00
Albums					
SMASH					
❏ MGS-27001 [M]	The Steel Guitar Sounds of Hank Williams	1962	5.00	10.00	20.00
❏ MGS-27019 [M]	Don Helms' Steel Guitar	1962	5.00	10.00	20.00
❏ SRS-67001 [S]	The Steel Guitar Sounds of Hank Williams	1962	6.25	12.50	25.00
❏ SRS-67019 [S]	Don Helms' Steel Guitar	1962	6.25	12.50	25.00

HELMS, JIMMY
45s
CAPITOL

Number	Title (A Side/B Side)	Yr	VG	VG+	NM
❏ 3003	The Only Thing That Matters/Just Hold My Hand				
	and Sing	1970	2.00	4.00	8.00

HELP
45s
DECCA

Number	Title (A Side/B Side)	Yr	VG	VG+	NM
❏ 32879	Good Time Music/Hold On Child	1971	3.00	6.00	12.00
Albums					
DECCA					
❏ DL 75257	Help	1970	7.50	15.00	30.00
❏ DL 75304	Second Coming	1971	7.50	15.00	30.00

HEMLOCKS, THE
45s
FURY

Number	Title (A Side/B Side)	Yr	VG	VG+	NM
❏ 1004	Cora Lee/Joys of Love	1957	25.00	50.00	100.00
LOST-NITE					
❏ 361	Cora Lee/Joys of Love	197?	—	2.50	5.00
—Reissue					

HENDERSON, JOE
45s
FONTANA

Number	Title (A Side/B Side)	Yr	VG	VG+	NM
❏ 1638	Help Yourself/A Man Without Love	1969	—	3.00	6.00
❏ 1658	Don't Forget to Catch Me/Please Don't Go	1969	—	3.00	6.00
KAPP					
❏ 590	If We Could Start All Over/				
	You Take One Step, I'll Take Two	1964	2.50	5.00	10.00
RIC					
❏ 141	I Ain't Never/The River or the Railroad Track	1964	2.00	4.00	8.00
❏ 149	Honey on My Lips/Like a Child	1965	2.00	4.00	8.00
❏ 181	Sweet Lovin' Baby/Too Much to Lose	1966	2.00	4.00	8.00
TODD					
❏ 1066	Baby Don't Leave Me/Right Now	1961	3.75	7.50	15.00
❏ 1072	Snap Your Fingers/If You See Me Cry	1962	3.75	7.50	15.00
❏ 1077	Big Love/After Loving You	1962	3.00	6.00	12.00
❏ 1079	Three Steps/The Searching Is Over	1962	3.00	6.00	12.00
❏ 1082	Cause We're in Love/Sad Teardrops at Dawn	1963	3.00	6.00	12.00
❏ 1083	You Can't Lose/All Day Every Day	1963	3.00	6.00	12.00
❏ 1085	Love Me Sweet/My Hands Are Tied	1963	3.00	6.00	12.00
❏ 1091	Lovin' Part Time/Blues for a Four-String Guitar	1963	3.00	6.00	12.00
❏ 1096	If We Could Start All Over/				
	You Take One Step, I'll Take Two	1964	3.00	6.00	12.00
Albums					
FONTANA					
❏ SRF-67590	Hits, Hits, Hits!	1969	7.50	15.00	30.00
TODD					
❏ MT-2701 [M]	Snap Your Fingers	1962	12.50	25.00	50.00
❏ ST-2701 [S]	Snap Your Fingers	1962	17.50	35.00	70.00

HENDRICKS, BOBBY
45s
MERCURY

Number	Title (A Side/B Side)	Yr	VG	VG+	NM
❏ 71788	Happy Hearts/Pleasing You	1961	3.00	6.00	12.00
❏ 71810	Good Lovin'/Honey Crisp	1961	3.00	6.00	12.00
❏ 71881	I'm Comin' Home/Every Other Night	1961	3.00	6.00	12.00
MGM					
❏ 13179	Let's Get It Over/Love in My Heart	1963	5.00	10.00	20.00
SUE					
❏ 706	Itchy Twitchy Feeling/A Thousand Dreams	1958	7.50	15.00	30.00
❏ 708	Dreamy Eyes/Molly Be Good	1958	5.00	10.00	20.00
❏ 710	Cast Your Vote/It's Misery	1959	5.00	10.00	20.00
❏ 712	I'm a Big Boy Now/Good Things Will Come	1959	5.00	10.00	20.00
❏ 717	Little John Green/Sincerely, Your Lover	1959	5.00	10.00	20.00
❏ 727	City of Angels/If I Just Had Your Love	1960	5.00	10.00	20.00
❏ 732	Psycho/Too Good to Be True	1960	5.00	10.00	20.00
UNITED ARTISTS					
❏ 0142	Itchy Twitchy Feeling/Psycho	1973	—	2.00	4.00
—"Silver Spotlight Series" reissue					

HENDRIX, AL
45s
ABC-PARAMOUNT

Number	Title (A Side/B Side)	Yr	VG	VG+	NM
❏ 9901	Rhonda Lee/Go, Daddy. Rock	1958	6.25	12.50	25.00
LEGREE					
❏ 701	Young and Wild/I Need You	1960	30.00	60.00	120.00
TALLY					
❏ 119	Rhonda Lee/Go, Daddy Rock	1957	20.00	40.00	80.00

HENDRIX, JIMI
The albums list includes many posthumous "cash-in" records of early material.
12-Inch Singles
CAPITOL

Number	Title (A Side/B Side)	Yr	VG	VG+	NM
❏ SPRO 11284 [DJ]	Star Spangled Banner (same on both sides)	199?	25.00	50.00	100.00
—Promo only, blue vinyl with eight star-shaped holes in outer part of record					

45s
AUDIO FIDELITY

Number	Title (A Side/B Side)	Yr	VG	VG+	NM
❏ 167	No Such Animal (Part 1)/No Such Animal (Part 2)	1970	3.75	7.50	15.00
❏ 167 [PS]	No Such Animal (Part 1)/No Such Animal (Part 2)	1970	10.00	20.00	40.00
EXPERIENCE HENDRIX					
❏ RTH-1007	The Jimi Hendrix Classic Singles Collection	1998	15.00	30.00	60.00
—Boxed set of 10 45s, each with picture sleeves and white sleeve, with booklet					
❏ 5651-7	Little Drummer Boy-Auld Lang Syne/Three Little				
	Bears	1999	3.75	7.50	15.00
—Red vinyl, small hole					
❏ 5651-7 [PS]	Little Drummer Boy-Auld Lang Syne/Three Little				
	Bears	1999	—	2.50	5.00
—The same sleeve appears on both pressings of the single					
❏ 5651-7	Little Drummer Boy-Auld Lang Syne/Three Little				
	Bears	2001	—	2.50	5.00
—Green vinyl, small hole; reissue					
❏ 13487 [DJ]	Star Spangled Banner/Purple Haze	1999	3.75	7.50	15.00
—Promo-only picture disc					
MCA					
❏ 55336 [DJ]	Dolly Dagger/Night Bird Flying	1997	2.50	5.00	10.00
—Promo only on purple vinyl					
❏ 55336 [PS]	Dolly Dagger/Night Bird Flying	1997	2.50	5.00	10.00
❏ 55454 [DJ]	Can You Please Crawl Out Your Window?/				
	Burning of the Midnight Lamp	1998	—	2.00	5.00
—Promo only on orange vinyl					
❏ 55454 [PS]	Can You Please Crawl Out Your Window?/				
	Burning of the Midnight Lamp	1998	—	2.00	5.00
—Cardboard sleeve					
REPRISE					
❏ 0572	Hey Joe/51st Anniversary	1967	25.00	50.00	100.00
❏ 0572 [PS]	Hey Joe/51st Anniversary	1967	250.00	500.00	1000.
❏ PRO 595 [DJ]	Medley: The Little Drummer Boy-Silent Night/				
	Auld Lang Syne	1974	37.50	75.00	150.00
❏ PRO 595 [PS]	...And a Happy New Year	1974	20.00	40.00	80.00

Number	Title (A Side/B Side)	Yr	VG	VG+	NM
❑ 0597	Purple Haze/The Wind Cries Mary	1967	6.25	12.50	25.00
❑ 0641	Foxey Lady/Hey Joe	1967	6.25	12.50	25.00
❑ 0665	Up from the Skies/One Rainy Wish	1968	7.50	15.00	30.00
❑ 0728	Purple Haze/Foxey Lady	1968	3.75	7.50	15.00

—"Back to Back Hits" series -- originals have both "r:" and "W7" logos

Number	Title (A Side/B Side)	Yr	VG	VG+	NM
❑ 0742	All Along the Watchtower/Crosstown Traffic	1971	—	3.00	6.00

—"Back to Back Hits" series

Number	Title (A Side/B Side)	Yr	VG	VG+	NM
❑ 0767	All Along the Watchtower/Burning of the Midnight Lamp	1968	7.50	15.00	30.00
❑ 0792	Crosstown Traffic/Gypsy Eyes	1968	7.50	15.00	30.00
❑ 0853	If 6 Was 9/Stone Free	1969	10.00	20.00	40.00
❑ 0905	Stepping Stone/Izabella	1970	25.00	50.00	100.00

—As "Hendrix Band of Gypsys"

Number	Title (A Side/B Side)	Yr	VG	VG+	NM
❑ 1000	Freedom/Angel	1971	3.75	7.50	15.00
❑ 1044	Dolly Dagger/Star Spangled Banner	1971	3.75	7.50	15.00
❑ 1082	Johnny B. Goode/Lover Man	1972	3.75	7.50	15.00
❑ 1118	The Wind Cries Mary/Little Wing	1972	3.75	7.50	15.00
❑ EP 2239	Gloria (B-side blank)	1979	—	2.50	5.00
❑ EP 2239 [PS]	Gloria (B-side blank)	1979	—	2.50	5.00

—Above was a bonus record in "The Essential Jimi Hendrix, Volume 2"

Number	Title (A Side/B Side)	Yr	VG	VG+	NM
❑ 29845	Fire/Little Wing	1982	—	3.00	6.00

TRIP

Number	Title (A Side/B Side)	Yr	VG	VG+	NM
❑ 3002	Hot Trigger/Suspicious	1972	—	2.50	5.00

Albums

ACCORD

Number	Title (A Side/B Side)	Yr	VG	VG+	NM
❑ SN-7101	Kaleidoscope	1981	2.50	5.00	10.00
❑ SN-7112	Before London	1981	2.50	5.00	10.00
❑ SN-7139	Cosmic Feeling	1981	2.50	5.00	10.00

CAPITOL

Number	Title (A Side/B Side)	Yr	VG	VG+	NM
❑ STAO-472	Band of Gypsys	1970	5.00	10.00	20.00
❑ SWBB-659 [(2)]	Get That Feeling/Flashing	1971	6.25	12.50	25.00
❑ ST 2856 [S]	Get That Feeling	1967	10.00	20.00	40.00
❑ T 2856 [M]	Get That Feeling	1967	20.00	40.00	80.00
❑ ST 2894 [S]	Flashing	1968	10.00	20.00	40.00
❑ T 2894 [M]	Flashing	1968	25.00	50.00	100.00
❑ SJ-12416	Band of Gypsys 2	1986	2.50	5.00	10.00

—Side 2 lists, and plays, three songs

Number	Title (A Side/B Side)	Yr	VG	VG+	NM
❑ SJ-12416	Band of Gypsys 2	1986	37.50	75.00	150.00

—Side 2 lists three songs, but plays four completely different songs. Four bands are visible on the record.

Number	Title (A Side/B Side)	Yr	VG	VG+	NM
❑ MLP-15022 [EP]	Johnny B. Goode	1986	2.00	4.00	8.00
❑ SN-16319	Band of Gypsys	1985	2.50	5.00	10.00

—Budget-line reissue

Number	Title (A Side/B Side)	Yr	VG	VG+	NM
❑ C1-96414	Band of Gypsys	1995	3.75	7.50	15.00

—Numbered reissue

EXPERIENCE HENDRIX/CAPITOL

Number	Title (A Side/B Side)	Yr	VG	VG+	NM
❑ ST-472	Band of Gypsys	1997	6.25	12.50	25.00

—Limited edition on "heavy vinyl" with booklet; distributed by Classic Records

EXPERIENCE HENDRIX/CLASSIC

Number	Title (A Side/B Side)	Yr	VG	VG+	NM
❑ B0000698-01 [(2)]	Martin Scorsese Presents the Blues: Jimi Hendrix	2004	10.00	20.00	40.00

—Regular edition on black vinyl

Number	Title (A Side/B Side)	Yr	VG	VG+	NM
❑ B0000698-01 [(2)]	Martin Scorsese Presents the Blues: Jimi Hendrix	2004	12.50	25.00	50.00

—Limited edition of 1,000 on blue vinyl

Number	Title (A Side/B Side)	Yr	VG	VG+	NM
❑ RTH 2006 [(2)]	Blues	2002	15.00	30.00	60.00

—Limited edition on 200-gram blue vinyl

Number	Title (A Side/B Side)	Yr	VG	VG+	NM
❑ RTH 2006 [(2)]	Blues	2003	10.00	20.00	40.00

—Limited edition on 200-gram black vinyl

EXPERIENCE HENDRIX/MCA

Number	Title (A Side/B Side)	Yr	VG	VG+	NM
❑ 11599 [(2)]	First Rays of the New Rising Sun	1997	12.50	25.00	50.00

—Limited edition on "heavy vinyl" with booklet

Number	Title (A Side/B Side)	Yr	VG	VG+	NM
❑ 11600 [(2)]	Electric Ladyland	1997	10.00	20.00	40.00

—Limited edition on "heavy vinyl" with booklet

Number	Title (A Side/B Side)	Yr	VG	VG+	NM
❑ 11601	Axis: Bold As Love	1997	12.50	25.00	50.00

—Limited edition on "heavy vinyl" with booklet

Number	Title (A Side/B Side)	Yr	VG	VG+	NM
❑ 11602 [(2)]	Are You Experienced?	1997	12.50	25.00	50.00

—Limited edition on "heavy vinyl" with booklet

Number	Title (A Side/B Side)	Yr	VG	VG+	NM
❑ 11607	Band of Gypsys	1997	6.25	12.50	25.00

—Limited edition on "heavy vinyl" with booklet; pressed in U.S. for export to Europe

Number	Title (A Side/B Side)	Yr	VG	VG+	NM
❑ 11608	Are You Experienced?	1997	10.00	20.00	40.00

—Limited edition on "heavy vinyl" with booklet; pressed in U.S. for export to Europe; has different cover than US version

Number	Title (A Side/B Side)	Yr	VG	VG+	NM
❑ 11671 [(2)]	Experience Hendrix: The Best of Jimi Hendrix	1998	6.25	12.50	25.00

—Despite lower number, was released after South Saturn Delta

Number	Title (A Side/B Side)	Yr	VG	VG+	NM
❑ 11684 [(2)]	South Saturn Delta	1997	6.25	12.50	25.00

—Numbered, limited edition on "heavy vinyl"

Number	Title (A Side/B Side)	Yr	VG	VG+	NM
❑ 11742 [(3)]	BBC Sessions	1998	7.50	15.00	30.00
❑ 11931 [(3)]	Live at the Fillmore East	1999	7.50	15.00	30.00
❑ 11987 [(3)]	Live at Woodstock	1999	7.50	15.00	30.00
❑ 112316 [(8)]	The Jimi Hendrix Experience	2000	17.50	35.00	70.00

—Limited edition of 5,000 in purple felt box

Number	Title (A Side/B Side)	Yr	VG	VG+	NM
❑ 112984	Smash Hits	2002	3.75	7.50	15.00

—Limited edition on "heavy vinyl"

NUTMEG

Number	Title (A Side/B Side)	Yr	VG	VG+	NM
❑ 1001	High, Live 'N' Dirty	1978	6.25	12.50	25.00

—Black vinyl

Number	Title (A Side/B Side)	Yr	VG	VG+	NM
❑ 1001	High, Live 'N' Dirty	1978	6.25	12.50	25.00

—Red vinyl

Number	Title (A Side/B Side)	Yr	VG	VG+	NM
❑ 1002	Cosmic Turnaround	1981	3.00	6.00	12.00

PHOENIX 10

Number	Title (A Side/B Side)	Yr	VG	VG+	NM
❑ PHX 320	Rare Hendrix	1981	2.00	4.00	8.00
❑ PHX 324	Roots of Hendrix	1981	2.00	4.00	8.00

PICKWICK

Number	Title (A Side/B Side)	Yr	VG	VG+	NM
❑ SPC-3528	Jimi	197?	2.50	5.00	10.00

REPRISE

Number	Title (A Side/B Side)	Yr	VG	VG+	NM
❑ MS 2025	Smash Hits	1969	10.00	20.00	40.00

—With "W7" and "r:" logos on two-tone orange label

Number	Title (A Side/B Side)	Yr	VG	VG+	NM
❑ MS 2025	Smash Hits Bonus Poster	1969	10.00	20.00	40.00
❑ MS 2025	Smash Hits	1970	3.00	6.00	12.00

—With only "r:" logo on all-orange (tan) label

Number	Title (A Side/B Side)	Yr	VG	VG+	NM
❑ MS 2025	Smash Hits	198?	2.00	4.00	8.00

—Red and black label or gold and light blue label

Number	Title (A Side/B Side)	Yr	VG	VG+	NM
❑ MS 2029	Historic Performances As Recorded at the Monterey International Pop Festival	1970	5.00	10.00	20.00

—Side 1: Jimi Hendrix; Side 2: Otis Redding; with only "r:" logo on all-orange (tan) label

Number	Title (A Side/B Side)	Yr	VG	VG+	NM
❑ MS 2029	Historic Performances As Recorded at the Monterey International Pop Festival	1970	50.00	100.00	200.00

—Side 1: Jimi Hendrix; Side 2: Otis Redding; with "W7" and "r:" logos on two-tone orange label

Number	Title (A Side/B Side)	Yr	VG	VG+	NM
❑ MS 2034	The Cry of Love	1971	3.75	7.50	15.00

—With only "r:" logo on all-orange (tan) label

Number	Title (A Side/B Side)	Yr	VG	VG+	NM
❑ MS 2034	The Cry of Love	1971	125.00	250.00	500.00

—With "W7" and "r:" logos on two-tone orange label

Number	Title (A Side/B Side)	Yr	VG	VG+	NM
❑ MS 2040	Rainbow Bridge	1971	5.00	10.00	20.00
❑ MS 2049	Hendrix in the West	1972	5.00	10.00	20.00
❑ MS 2103	War Heroes	1972	5.00	10.00	20.00
❑ MS 2204	Crash Landing	1975	3.75	7.50	15.00
❑ MS 2229	Midnight Lightning	1975	3.75	7.50	15.00
❑ 2RS 2245 [(2)]	The Essential Jimi Hendrix	1978	5.00	10.00	20.00
❑ MSK 2276	Smash Hits	1977	2.50	5.00	10.00

—Reissue

Number	Title (A Side/B Side)	Yr	VG	VG+	NM
❑ HS 2293	The Essential Jimi Hendrix Volume Two	1979	3.75	7.50	15.00

—Add 100% if bonus single of "Gloria" with picture sleeve is enclosed

Number	Title (A Side/B Side)	Yr	VG	VG+	NM
❑ HS 2299	Nine to the Universe	1980	2.50	5.00	10.00
❑ R 6261 [M]	Are You Experienced?	1967	50.00	100.00	200.00
❑ RS 6261 [S]	Are You Experienced?	1967	12.50	25.00	50.00

—Pink, gold and green label

Number	Title (A Side/B Side)	Yr	VG	VG+	NM
❑ RS 6261 [S]	Are You Experienced?	1968	6.25	12.50	25.00

—With "W7" and "r:" logos on two-tone orange label

Number	Title (A Side/B Side)	Yr	VG	VG+	NM
❑ RS 6261 [S]	Are You Experienced?	1970	3.00	6.00	12.00

—With only "r:" logo on all-orange (tan) label

Number	Title (A Side/B Side)	Yr	VG	VG+	NM
❑ RS 6261 [S]	Are You Experienced?	198?	2.00	4.00	8.00

—Red and black label or gold and light blue label

Number	Title (A Side/B Side)	Yr	VG	VG+	NM
❑ R 6281 [M]	Axis: Bold As Love	1968	625.00	1250.	2500.
❑ RS 6281 [S]	Axis: Bold As Love	1968	6.25	12.50	25.00

—With "W7" and "r:" logos on two-tone orange label

Number	Title (A Side/B Side)	Yr	VG	VG+	NM
❑ RS 6281 [S]	Axis: Bold As Love	1968	20.00	40.00	80.00

—Pink, gold and green label

Number	Title (A Side/B Side)	Yr	VG	VG+	NM
❑ RS 6281 [S]	Axis: Bold As Love	1970	3.00	6.00	12.00

—With only "r:" logo on all-orange (tan) label

Number	Title (A Side/B Side)	Yr	VG	VG+	NM
❑ RS 6281 [S]	Axis: Bold As Love	198?	2.00	4.00	8.00

—Red and black label or gold and light blue label

Number	Title (A Side/B Side)	Yr	VG	VG+	NM
❑ 2R 6307 [(2)M]	Electric Ladyland	1968	2000.	3000.	4000.

—Mono is promo only

Number	Title (A Side/B Side)	Yr	VG	VG+	NM
❑ 2RS 6307 [(2)S]	Electric Ladyland	1968	25.00	50.00	100.00

—With "W7" and "r:" logos on two-tone orange label

Number	Title (A Side/B Side)	Yr	VG	VG+	NM
❑ 2RS 6307 [(2)S]	Electric Ladyland	1970	3.75	7.50	15.00

—With only "r:" logo on all-orange (tan) label

Number	Title (A Side/B Side)	Yr	VG	VG+	NM
❑ 2RS 6307 [(2)S]	Electric Ladyland	198?	3.00	6.00	12.00

—Red and black label or gold and light blue label

Number	Title (A Side/B Side)	Yr	VG	VG+	NM
❑ 2RS 6481 [(2)]	Soundtrack Recordings from the Film Jimi Hendrix	1973	6.25	12.50	25.00
❑ 22306 [(2)]	The Jimi Hendrix Concerts	1982	3.00	6.00	12.00
❑ 25119	Kiss the Sky	1984	2.50	5.00	10.00
❑ 25358	Jimi Plays Monterey	1986	2.50	5.00	10.00
❑ SKAO-91441	Axis: Bold As Love	1968	10.00	20.00	40.00

—Capitol Record Club edition; two-tone orange label with "W7" and "r:" at top

Number	Title (A Side/B Side)	Yr	VG	VG+	NM
❑ STBO-91568 [(2)]	Electric Ladyland	1968	37.50	75.00	150.00

—Capitol Record Club edition

Number	Title (A Side/B Side)	Yr	VG	VG+	NM
❑ SMAS-93467	The Cry of Love	1971	15.00	30.00	60.00

—Capitol Record Club edition

Number	Title (A Side/B Side)	Yr	VG	VG+	NM
❑ SMAS-93972	Rainbow Bridge	1971	12.50	25.00	50.00

—Capitol Record Club edition

RHINO

Number	Title (A Side/B Side)	Yr	VG	VG+	NM
❑ RNDF-254 [PD]	The Jimi Hendrix Interview	1982	6.25	12.50	25.00

RYKO ANALOGUE

Number	Title (A Side/B Side)	Yr	VG	VG+	NM
❑ RALP-0038 [(2)]	Live at Winterland	1988	3.75	7.50	15.00
❑ RALP-0078 [(2)]	Radio One	1988	3.75	7.50	15.00

—Clear vinyl

SPRINGBOARD

Number	Title (A Side/B Side)	Yr	VG	VG+	NM
❑ SPB-4010	Jimi Hendrix	197?	2.50	5.00	10.00

TRACK

Number	Title (A Side/B Side)	Yr	VG	VG+	NM
❑ 612003 [M]	Axis: Bold As Love	2000	6.25	12.50	25.00

—Classic Records issue of the original U.K. mono mix, on a reproduction of the original British label

TRIP

Number	Title (A Side/B Side)	Yr	VG	VG+	NM
❑ 3509 [(2)]	Superpak	197?	3.75	7.50	15.00
❑ TLP-9500	Rare Hendrix	1972	3.75	7.50	15.00
❑ TLP-9501	Roots of Hendrix	1972	3.00	6.00	12.00
❑ TLP-9512	Moods	1973	3.00	6.00	12.00
❑ TLP-9523	The Genius of Jimi Hendrix	1973	3.00	6.00	12.00

UNITED ARTISTS

Number	Title (A Side/B Side)	Yr	VG	VG+	NM
❑ UA-LA505-E	The Very Best of Jimi Hendrix	1975	3.00	6.00	12.00

WARNER BROS.

Number	Title (A Side/B Side)	Yr	VG	VG+	NM
❑ HS 2299	Nine to the Universe	1980	3.00	6.00	12.00

—Reprise cover, Warner Bros. tan "pinstripe" label; possibly Columbia House edition?

HENDRIX, JIMI, AND LITTLE RICHARD Also see each artist's individual listings.

45s

ALA

Number	Title (A Side/B Side)	Yr	VG	VG+	NM
❑ 1175	Goodnight Irene/Why Don't You Love Me	1972	2.00	4.00	8.00

Albums

EVEREST ARCHIVE OF FOLK & JAZZ

Number	Title (A Side/B Side)	Yr	VG	VG+	NM
❑ 296	Roots of Rock	1974	3.00	6.00	12.00

PICKWICK

Number	Title (A Side/B Side)	Yr	VG	VG+	NM
❑ SPC-3347	Jimi Hendrix and Little Richard Together	1973	3.00	6.00	12.00

HENDRIX, JIMI, AND LONNIE YOUNGBLOOD

Albums

MAPLE

Number	Title (A Side/B Side)	Yr	VG	VG+	NM
❑ 6004	Two Great Experiences Together	1971	12.50	25.00	50.00

HENHOUSE FIVE PLUS TOO See RAY STEVENS.

HENRY, CLARENCE

45s

ARGO

Number	Title (A Side/B Side)	Yr	VG	VG+	NM
❑ 5259	Ain't Got No Home/Troubles, Troubles	1956	5.00	10.00	20.00
❑ 5266	I'm a Country Boy/Lonely Tramp	1957	4.00	8.00	16.00
❑ 5273	I Found a Home/It Won't Be Long	1957	4.00	8.00	16.00
❑ 5305	I'm in Love/Baby Please	1958	4.00	8.00	16.00
❑ 5378	But I Do/Just My Baby and Me	1960	4.00	8.00	16.00

—A-side: Same song, new title

Number	Title (A Side/B Side)	Yr	VG	VG+	NM
❑ 5378	I Don't Know Why/Just My Baby and Me	1960	5.00	10.00	20.00

H

Number	Title (A Side/B Side)	Yr	VG	VG+	NM
❑ 5388	You Always Hurt the One You Love/Little Suzy	1961	4.00	8.00	16.00
❑ 5395	Lonely Street/Why Can't You	1961	3.75	7.50	15.00
❑ 5401	On Bended Knees/Standing in the Need of Love	1961	3.75	7.50	15.00
❑ 5408	A Little Too Much/I Wish I Could Stay the Same	1962	3.00	6.00	12.00
❑ 5414	Dream Myself a Sweetheart/Lost Without You	1962	3.00	6.00	12.00
❑ 5426	Jealous Kind/Come On and Dance	1962	3.00	6.00	12.00
❑ 5448	If I Didn't Care/It Takes Two to Tango	1963	3.00	6.00	12.00
❑ 5480	Looking Back/Long Lost and Worried	1964	2.50	5.00	10.00
CADET					
❑ 5259	Ain't Got No Home/Troubles, Troubles	1966	2.00	4.00	8.00
DIAL					
❑ 4057	This Time/Hummin' a Heartache	1967	—	3.00	6.00
❑ 4072	Shake Your Money Maker/				
	That's When I Guessed	1968	—	3.00	6.00
PARROT					
❑ 45004	Have You Ever Been Lonely/Little Green Frog	1964	2.50	5.00	10.00
❑ 45009	I Told My Pillow/Can't Hide My Tear	1964	2.50	5.00	10.00
❑ 45015	I Might As Well/Tore Up Over You	1965	2.50	5.00	10.00
Albums					
ARGO					
❑ LP-4009 [M]	You Always Hurt the One You Love	1961	75.00	125.00	250.00
CADET					
❑ LP-4009 [M]	You Always Hurt the One You Love	1966	12.50	25.00	50.00
—Includes copies of Cadet LP in Argo sleeves					
ROULETTE					
❑ SR 42039	Alive and Well and Living in New Orleans	1969	6.25	12.50	25.00

HENRY, EARL
45s
DOT

Number	Title (A Side/B Side)	Yr	VG	VG+	NM
❑ 15756	Whatcha Gonna Do?/I Am the Man	1958	12.50	25.00	50.00
❑ 15875	My Suzanne/Believe a Traveler	1958	7.50	15.00	30.00

HENRY, THOMAS
45s
HIT

Number	Title (A Side/B Side)	Yr	VG	VG+	NM
❑ 73	So Much in Love/No One	1963	2.00	4.00	8.00
—B-side by Leroy Jones					
❑ 103	Um, Um, Um, Um, Um, Um/For You	1964	2.00	4.00	8.00
—B-side by Ed Hardin					

HENRY TREE
45s
MAINSTREAM

Number	Title (A Side/B Side)	Yr	VG	VG+	NM
❑ 729	Penfield Town/(B-side unknown)	1970	3.00	6.00	12.00
Albums					
MAINSTREAM					
❑ S-6129	Electric Holy Man	1968	7.50	15.00	30.00

HENSLEE, GENE
45s
IMPERIAL

Number	Title (A Side/B Side)	Yr	VG	VG+	NM
❑ 8227	Diggin' and Datin'/A Girl Named Haertbreak	1954	17.50	35.00	70.00
❑ 8260	Naughty and Nice/Try As I May	1954	15.00	30.00	60.00
❑ 8277	Rockin' Baby/What Will I Do	1954	15.00	30.00	60.00
MEL-O-DY					
❑ 110	Beautiful Women/Shambles	1963	5.00	10.00	20.00
UNITED ARTISTS					
❑ 946	I Don't Wanna Go Home/Shambles	1964	3.75	7.50	15.00

HENSLEY, KEN
45s
MERCURY

Number	Title (A Side/B Side)	Yr	VG	VG+	NM
❑ 73410	When Evening Comes/Fortune	1973	—	2.50	5.00
Albums					
MERCURY					
❑ SRM-1-661	Proud Words on a Dusty Shelf	1973	3.00	6.00	12.00
WARNER BROS.					
❑ BS 2863	Eager to Please	1975	2.50	5.00	10.00

HENSON, JIM
45s
ATLANTIC

Number	Title (A Side/B Side)	Yr	VG	VG+	NM
❑ 3610	Rainbow Connection/I Hope That Somethin'				
	Better Comes Along	1979	—	3.00	6.00
—As "Kermit (Jim Henson)"; B-side by "Kermit and Fozzie"					
❑ 3642	Movin' Right Along/Never Before, Never Again	1980	—	3.00	6.00
—As "Kermit and Fozzie Bear (Jim Henson)"					
COLUMBIA					
❑ 4-45207	Rubber Duckie/Sesame Street	1970	2.00	4.00	8.00
—As "Ernie (Jim Henson)"; B-side by "The Kids"					
❑ 4-45247	Up and Down/I Love Trash	1970	2.00	4.00	8.00
—As "Two Monsters (Jim Henson, Frank Oz)"; B-side by Carroll Spinney as "Oscar"					
SIGNATURE					
❑ 12023	Tick-Tock Sick/The Countryside	1960	12.50	25.00	50.00

HEP STARS, THE With Benny Andersson, later of BJORN & BENNY and ABBA.
45s
CHARTMAKER

Number	Title (A Side/B Side)	Yr	VG	VG+	NM
❑ 414	It's Now Winter's Day/Musty Dusty	1969	5.00	10.00	20.00
DUNHILL					
❑ 4040	Sunny Girl/No Response	1966	6.25	12.50	25.00

HEPSTERS, THE
45s
RONEL

Number	Title (A Side/B Side)	Yr	VG	VG+	NM
❑ 107	Rockin' N' Rollin' with Santa Claus/				
	I Had To Let You Go	1955	100.00	200.00	400.00
❑ 110	I Gotta Sing the Blues/This-a-Way	1956	75.00	150.00	300.00
XMAS					
❑ 3711	Rockin' & Rollin' With Santa Claus/				
	Sleigh Bell Rock	19??	2.00	4.00	8.00
—B-side by Three Aces and a Joker; reissue of rare R&B sides					

HERALDS, THE
45s
HERALD

Number	Title (A Side/B Side)	Yr	VG	VG+	NM
❑ 435	Eternal Love/Gonna Love You	1954	62.50	125.00	250.00

HERD, THE PETER FRAMPTON was in this group.
45s
FONTANA

Number	Title (A Side/B Side)	Yr	VG	VG+	NM
❑ 1588	I Can Fly/Understand Me	1967	2.50	5.00	10.00
❑ 1602	Sweet William/From the Underworld	1967	2.50	5.00	10.00
❑ 1610	Paradise Lost/Come On, Believe Me	1968	2.50	5.00	10.00
❑ 1618	I Don't Want Our Loving to Die/Our Fairy Tale	1968	2.50	5.00	10.00
❑ 1646	The Game/Beauty Queen	1969	2.50	5.00	10.00
Albums					
FONTANA					
❑ SRF-67579	Lookin' Thru You	1968	6.25	12.50	25.00

HERMAN'S HERMITS Also see PETER NOONE.
45s
ABKCO

Number	Title (A Side/B Side)	Yr	VG	VG+	NM
❑ 4021	Mrs. Brown You've Got a Lovely Daughter/				
	I'm Henry VIII, I Am	1972	—	2.50	5.00
❑ 4022	I'm Into Something Good/				
	Can't You Hear My Heartbeat	1972	—	2.50	5.00
❑ 4023	There's a Kind of Hush (All Over the World)/				
	Wonderful World	1972	—	2.50	5.00
❑ 4024	Listen People/Dandy	1972	—	2.50	5.00
❑ 4042	Silhouettes/Just a Little Bit Better	1973	—	2.50	5.00
❑ 4043	A Must to Avoid/Leaning on the Lamp Post	1973	—	2.50	5.00
BUDDAH					
❑ 516	Lonely Situation (Love Is All I Need)/				
	Blond Haired Blue Eyed Boy	1976	2.00	4.00	8.00
MGM					
❑ (no #) [PS]	Hold On	1966	62.50	125.00	250.00
—Promo-only sleeve similar to the LP cover of the same name; rear of sleeve has "The Mod Shirts Are Here" advertisement; this may have come with some promos of MGM 13500					
❑ 13280	I'm Into Something Good/Your Hand in Mine	1964	2.50	5.00	10.00
❑ 13310	Can't You Hear My Heartbeat/I Know Why	1964	2.50	5.00	10.00
❑ 13310 [PS]	Can't You Hear My Heartbeat/I Know Why	1964	3.75	7.50	15.00
❑ 13332	Silhouettes/Walkin' With My Angel	1965	2.50	5.00	10.00
❑ 13341	Mrs. Brown You've Got a Lovely Daughter/I				
	Gotta Dream On	1965	2.50	5.00	10.00
❑ 13341 [PS]	Mrs. Brown You've Got a Lovely Daughter/I				
	Gotta Dream On	1965	3.75	7.50	15.00
❑ 13354	Wonderful World/Traveling Light	1965	2.50	5.00	10.00
❑ 13354 [PS]	Wonderful World/Traveling Light	1965	3.75	7.50	15.00
❑ 13367	I'm Henry VIII, I Am/The End of the World	1965	2.50	5.00	10.00
❑ 13367 [PS]	I'm Henry VIII, I Am/The End of the World	1965	5.00	10.00	20.00
❑ 13398	Just a Little Bit Better/Sea Cruise	1965	2.50	5.00	10.00
❑ 13398 [PS]	Just a Little Bit Better/Sea Cruise	1965	3.75	7.50	15.00
❑ 13437	A Must to Avoid/The Man with the Cigar	1966	2.00	4.00	8.00
❑ 13462	Listen People/Got a Feeling	1966	2.00	4.00	8.00
❑ 13500	Leaning on the Lamp Post/Hold On	1966	2.00	4.00	8.00
❑ 13548	This Door Swings Both Ways/For Love	1966	2.00	4.00	8.00
❑ 13603	Dandy/My Reservation's Been Confirmed	1966	2.00	4.00	8.00
❑ 13603 [PS]	Dandy/My Reservation's Been Confirmed	1966	3.75	7.50	15.00
❑ 13639	East West/What Is Wrong What Is Right	1966	2.00	4.00	8.00
❑ 13681	There's a Kind of Hush/No Milk Today	1967	2.00	4.00	8.00
❑ 13681	There's a Kind of Hush (All Over the World)/				
	No Milk Today	1967	2.50	5.00	10.00
❑ 13681 [PS]	There's a Kind of Hush/No Milk Today	1967	3.75	7.50	15.00
❑ 13761	Don't Go Out Into the Rain (You're Going to				
	Melt)/Moonshine Man	1967	2.00	4.00	8.00
❑ 13761 [PS]	Don't Go Out Into the Rain (You're Going to				
	Melt)/Moonshine Man	1967	3.75	7.50	15.00
❑ 13787	Museum/Last Bus Home	1967	2.00	4.00	8.00
❑ 13787 [PS]	Museum/Last Bus Home	1967	3.75	7.50	15.00
❑ 13885	I Can Take or Leave Your Loving/Marcel's	1967	2.00	4.00	8.00
❑ 13934	Sleepy Joe/Just One Girl	1968	2.00	4.00	8.00
—Blue and gold label					
❑ 13934	Sleepy Joe/Just One Girl	1968	2.50	5.00	10.00
—Black label					
❑ 13973	Sunshine Girl/Nobody Needs to Know	1968	2.50	5.00	10.00
❑ 13994	Ooh, She's Done It Again/The Most Beautiful				
	Thing in My Life	1968	2.50	5.00	10.00
❑ 14035	Something's Happening/Little Miss Sorrow,				
	Child of Tomorrow	1969	2.50	5.00	10.00
❑ 14060	My Lady/My Sentimental Friend	1969	2.50	5.00	10.00
❑ 14100	It's Alright Now/(Here Comes) The Star	1969	2.50	5.00	10.00
PRIVATE STOCK					
❑ 45,019	Ginny Go Softly/Blond Haired, Blue Eyed Boy	1975	2.00	4.00	8.00
ROULETTE					
❑ 7213	Truck Stop Mama/Heart Get Ready for Love	1977	3.75	7.50	15.00
Albums					
ABKCO					
❑ 4227-1	Their Greatest Hits	1988	2.00	4.00	8.00
—Abridged version of AB 4227					
❑ AB-4227 [(2)]	XX (Greatest Hits)	1973	3.00	6.00	12.00
MGM					
❑ E-4282 [M]	Introducing Herman's Hermits	1965	3.75	7.50	15.00
—Version 3: With "Including 'Mrs. Brown You've Got a Lovely Daughter' " on front cover					
❑ E-4282 [M]	Introducing Herman's Hermits	1965	5.00	10.00	20.00
—Version 2: Same as above, but with a sticker that says "Featuring "Mrs. Brown You Have a Lovely Daughter'."					
❑ E-4282 [M]	Introducing Herman's Hermits	1965	6.25	12.50	25.00
—Version 1: With "Including Their Hit Single 'I'm Into Something Good' " on front cover					
❑ SE-4282 [R]	Introducing Herman's Hermits	1965	2.50	5.00	10.00
—Version 3: With "Including 'Mrs. Brown You've Got a Lovely Daughter' " on front cover					
❑ SE-4282 [R]	Introducing Herman's Hermits	1965	3.75	7.50	15.00
—Version 2: Same as above, but with a sticker that says "Featuring "Mrs. Brown You Have a Lovely Daughter'."					
❑ SE-4282 [R]	Introducing Herman's Hermits	1965	5.00	10.00	20.00
—Version 1: With "Including Their Hit Single 'I'm Into Something Good' " on front cover					
❑ E-4295 [M]	Herman's Hermits On Tour	1965	3.00	6.00	12.00
❑ SE-4295 [R]	Herman's Hermits On Tour	1965	2.50	5.00	10.00
❑ E-4315 [M]	The Best of Herman's Hermits	1965	3.00	6.00	12.00

Number	Title (A Side/B Side)	Yr	VG	VG+	NM
❏ SE-4315 [R]	The Best of Herman's Hermits	1965	2.50	5.00	10.00
❏ E-4342 [M]	Hold On!	1966	2.50	5.00	10.00
❏ SE-4342 [P]	Hold On!	1966	3.00	6.00	12.00
❏ E-4386 [M]	Both Sides of Herman's Hermits	1966	2.50	5.00	10.00
❏ SE-4386 [R]	Both Sides of Herman's Hermits	1966	2.00	4.00	8.00
❏ E-4416 [M]	The Best of Herman's Hermits, Volume 2	1966	3.00	6.00	12.00

—Add 50% if bonus photo of Herman is included.

❏ SE-4416 [P]	The Best of Herman's Hermits, Volume 2	1966	2.50	5.00	10.00

—Add 50% if bonus photo of Herman is included. "Hold On" and "Leaning on the Lamp Post" are in true stereo.

❏ E-4438 [M]	There's a Kind of Hush All Over the World	1967	2.50	5.00	10.00
❏ SE-4438 [R]	There's a Kind of Hush All Over the World	1967	2.00	4.00	8.00
❏ E-4478 [M]	Blaze	1967	2.50	5.00	10.00
❏ SE-4478 [S]	Blaze	1967	2.50	5.00	10.00
❏ E-4505 [M]	The Best of Herman's Hermits, Volume 3	1967	2.50	5.00	10.00
❏ SE-4505 [P]	The Best of Herman's Hermits, Volume 3	1967	2.50	5.00	10.00

—"Don't Go Out Into the Rain," "Museum," "Last Bus Home" and "Mum and Dad" are in true stereo.

❏ SE-4548 [P]	Mrs. Brown You've Got a Lovely Daughter	1968	2.50	5.00	10.00

—"Mrs. Brown You've Got a Lovely Daughter" and "There's a Kind of Hush" are rechanneled

❏ ST-90416 [R]	Introducing Herman's Hermits	1965	5.00	10.00	20.00

—Capitol Record Club edition

❏ T-90416 [M]	Introducing Herman's Hermits	1965	6.25	12.50	25.00

—Capitol Record Club edition

❏ ST-90421 [R]	Herman's Hermits On Tour	1965	5.00	10.00	20.00

—Capitol Record Club edition

❏ T-90421 [M]	Herman's Hermits On Tour	1965	6.25	12.50	25.00

—Capitol Record Club edition

❏ KAO-90613 [M]	The Best of Herman's Hermits	1966	3.75	7.50	15.00

—Capitol Record Club edition

❏ ST-90646 [R]	Hold On!	1966	5.00	10.00	20.00

—Capitol Record Club edition

❏ T-90646 [M]	Hold On!	1966	6.25	12.50	25.00

—Capitol Record Club edition

❏ ST-91286 [S]	Blaze	1967	5.00	10.00	20.00

—Capitol Record Club edition

❏ T-91286 [M]	Blaze	1967	7.50	15.00	30.00

—Capitol Record Club edition

HERON, MIKE
45s
ELEKTRA

Number	Title (A Side/B Side)	Yr	VG	VG+	NM
❏ 45739	Call Me Diamond/Brindaban	1971	2.00	4.00	8.00

Albums
ELEKTRA

❏ EKS-74093	Smiling Men with Bad Reputations	1971	5.00	10.00	20.00

HERROLD, DENNIS
45s
IMPERIAL

❏ 5482	Hip Hip Baby/Make with the Lovin'	1957	20.00	40.00	80.00

HESITATIONS, THE
45s
GWP

❏ 504	Is This the Way to Treat a Girl/Yes I'm Ready	1969	2.00	4.00	8.00

KAPP

❏ 790	Soul Superman/I'm Not Built That Way	1966	2.50	5.00	10.00
❏ 810	Soul Kind of Love/Wait a Minute	1967	2.50	5.00	10.00
❏ 822	I'll Be Right There/She Won't Come Back	1967	2.50	5.00	10.00
❏ 848	You Can't Bypass Love/You'll Never Know	1967	2.50	5.00	10.00
❏ 878	Born Free/Love Is Everywhere	1967	2.50	5.00	10.00
❏ 899	The Impossible Dream/Nobody Knows You When You're Down and Out	1968	2.50	5.00	10.00
❏ 911	Climb Every Mountain/My World	1968	2.50	5.00	10.00
❏ 926	Who Will Answer/If You Ever Need a Hand	1968	2.50	5.00	10.00
❏ 948	A Whiter Shade of Pale/With Pen in Hand	1968	2.50	5.00	10.00

Albums
KAPP

❏ KL-1525 [M]	Soul Superman	1967	7.50	15.00	30.00
❏ KS-3525 [S]	Soul Superman	1967	6.25	12.50	25.00
❏ KS-3548	The New Born Free	1968	6.25	12.50	25.00
❏ KS-3561	Where We're At	1968	6.25	12.50	25.00
❏ KS-3574	Solid Gold	1969	6.25	12.50	25.00

HESS, FRED
45s
HIT

❏ 206	Something's Happened/Goldfinger	1965	2.00	4.00	8.00

—B-side by Sherry Young

❏ 213	Count Me In/You're Not the Same Now	1965	2.00	4.00	8.00

HESTER, CAROLYN
45s
CAPITOL

❏ 4101	Come On Home and Sing the Blues to Mama/Don't Touch Me	1975	—	3.00	6.00

DOT

❏ 16660	Stay Not Late/That's My Song	1964	2.50	5.00	10.00

METROMEDIA

❏ 120	Magic, Man/Big City Streets	1969	2.00	4.00	8.00

RCA VICTOR

❏ APBO-0008	You Made My Life a Song/Comin' On Back to You	1973	—	3.00	6.00

Albums
COLUMBIA

❏ CL 1796 [M]	Carolyn Hester	1962	15.00	30.00	60.00

—With Bob Dylan on harmonica on three tracks; black and red label with six "eye" logos

❏ CL 1796 [M]	Carolyn Hester	1963	5.00	10.00	20.00

—Red label with "Guaranteed High Fidelity"

❏ CL 2032 [M]	This Life I'm Living	1963	5.00	10.00	20.00
❏ CS 8596 [S]	Carolyn Hester	1962	20.00	40.00	80.00

—With Bob Dylan on harmonica on three tracks; black and red label with six "eye" logos

❏ CS 8596 [S]	Carolyn Hester	1963	6.25	12.50	25.00

—Red label, "360 Sound Stereo" in black

❏ CS 8832 [S]	This Life I'm Living	1963	6.25	12.50	25.00

CORAL

❏ CRL 57143 [M]	Scarlet Ribbons	1957	12.50	25.00	50.00

DOT

Number	Title (A Side/B Side)	Yr	VG	VG+	NM
❏ DLP-3604 [M]	That's My Song	1964	3.75	7.50	15.00
❏ DLP-3638 [M]	Carolyn Hester at Town Hall One	1965	3.75	7.50	15.00
❏ DLP-3649 [M]	Carolyn Hester at Town Hall Two	1965	3.75	7.50	15.00
❏ DLP-25604 [S]	That's My Song	1964	5.00	10.00	20.00
❏ DLP-25638 [S]	Carolyn Hester at Town Hall One	1965	5.00	10.00	20.00
❏ DLP-25649 [S]	Carolyn Hester at Town Hall Two	1965	5.00	10.00	20.00

FOLK ODYSSEY

❏ 32160264	Simply Carolyn Hester	196?	5.00	10.00	20.00

METROMEDIA

❏ MD-1001	The Carolyn Hester Coalition	1969	5.00	10.00	20.00
❏ MD-1022	Magazine	1970	15.00	30.00	60.00

RCA VICTOR

❏ APD1-0086 [Q]	Carolyn Hester	1973	5.00	10.00	20.00

—Only released in quadraphonic

TRADITION

❏ TLP-1043 [M]	Carolyn Hester	1961	10.00	20.00	40.00

HESTER, DOT
45s
HIT

❏ 80	My Boyfriend's Back/The Monkey Time	1963	2.00	4.00	8.00

—B-side by Sammy Fox

HEWITT, BEN
45s
MERCURY

❏ 71413	You Break Me Up/I Ain't Givin' Up Nothin'	1959	25.00	50.00	100.00
❏ 71472	Patricia June/For Quite a While	1959	12.50	25.00	50.00
❏ 71577	My Search/I Want a New Girl Now	1960	10.00	20.00	40.00
❏ 71612	The Queen in the Kingdom/Whirlwind Blues	1960	10.00	20.00	40.00

HEYWOOD, EDDIE Pianist on the Hugo Winterhalter hit single "Canadian Sunset."
45s
COLUMBIA

❏ 39316	Without a Song/A Pretty Girl Is Like a Melody	1951	2.50	5.00	10.00
❏ 39317	All the Things You Are/St. Louis Blues	1951	2.50	5.00	10.00
❏ 39318	Mighty Like a Rose/When Your Lover Has Gone	1951	2.50	5.00	10.00
❏ 39319	Try a Little Tenderness/The Birth of the Blues	1951	2.50	5.00	10.00

—The above four comprise a box set

DECCA

❏ 28549	Begin the Beguine/On the Sunny Side of the Street	1953	3.00	6.00	12.00
❏ 28893	The Moon Was Yellow/You Too, You Too	1953	3.00	6.00	12.00
❏ 30007	Jasmine/The Continental	1956	2.50	5.00	10.00

LIBERTY

❏ 55396	The Good Earth/Dream of Olwen	1961	2.00	4.00	8.00
❏ 55539	Harlem Blues/The Sidewalks of New York	1963	2.00	4.00	8.00
❏ 55575	Canadian Sunset Bossa Nova/The Good Life	1963	2.00	4.00	8.00

MERCURY

❏ 70645	Land of Dreams/Summer Holiday	1955	2.50	5.00	10.00
❏ 70677	Love for Love/Sunny Sunday	1955	2.50	5.00	10.00
❏ 70863	Soft Summer Breeze/Heywood's Bounce	1956	2.50	5.00	10.00
❏ 70950	Secret Love/Let's Fall in Love	1956	2.50	5.00	10.00
❏ 71014	Lover/If It's Sunny Sunday	1956	2.50	5.00	10.00
❏ 71462	Soft Summer Breeze/Castillian Rhapsody	1959	2.00	4.00	8.00
❏ 71504	High on a Windy Hill/Wings in Autumn	1959	2.00	4.00	8.00
❏ 71603	Out of Bounds/There You Are	1960	2.00	4.00	8.00
❏ 71650	(Love Theme) Rat Race/Everything in Manhattan	1960	2.00	4.00	8.00
❏ 71685	Jalousie/Cheek to Cheek	1960	2.00	4.00	8.00
❏ 71781	Velvet Rock/Mountains on the Moon	1961	2.00	4.00	8.00

RCA VICTOR

❏ 47-6674	Lost Love/Mozambique	1956	3.00	6.00	12.00
❏ 47-6816	Begin the Beguine/No Miracle Needed	1957	2.50	5.00	10.00
❏ 47-6956	Love Is All/Virgin Isle Vamp	1957	2.50	5.00	10.00
❏ 47-7058	Lies/All About You	1957	2.50	5.00	10.00
❏ 47-7262	Haiti Lady/It's Really Nothing	1957	2.50	5.00	10.00
❏ 47-7385	St. Louis Blues/Rendezvous	1958	2.50	5.00	10.00

20TH CENTURY FOX

❏ 453	Theme from "The Prize"/Li'l Darlin'	1963	2.00	4.00	8.00

7-Inch Extended Plays
DECCA

❏ ED 2032	Begin the Beguine/Laura//I Don't Know Why/Please Don't Talk About Me When I'm Gone	195?	3.00	6.00	12.00
❏ ED 2032 [PS]	Eddie Heywood, Vol. 1	195?	3.00	6.00	12.00

Albums
BRUNSWICK

❏ BL 58036 [10]	Eddie Heywood '45	1953	12.50	25.00	50.00

CAPITOL

❏ ST-163	Soft Summer Breeze	1969	3.00	6.00	12.00
❏ ST 2833	With Love and Strings	1968	3.00	6.00	12.00

COLUMBIA

❏ CL 6157 [10]	Piano Moods	1951	12.50	25.00	50.00

COMMODORE

❏ XFL-15876	The Biggest Little Band of the Forties	198?	3.00	6.00	12.00
❏ FL-20007 [10]	Eight Selections	1950	18.75	37.50	75.00

CORAL

❏ CRL 57095 [M]	Featuring Eddie Heywood	1957	10.00	20.00	40.00

DECCA

❏ DL 8202 [M]	Lightly and Politely	1956	7.50	15.00	30.00
❏ DL 8270 [M]	Swing Low Sweet Heywood	1956	7.50	15.00	30.00

EMARCY

❏ MG-36042 [M]	Eddie Heywood	1955	10.00	20.00	40.00

EPIC

❏ LN 3327 [M]	Eddie Heywood at Twilight	1956	7.50	15.00	30.00

LIBERTY

❏ LRP-3250 [M]	Eddie Heywood's Golden Encores	1962	3.00	6.00	12.00
❏ LRP-3279 [M]	Manhattan Beat	1963	3.00	6.00	12.00
❏ LRP-3313 [M]	Canadian Sunset Bossa Nova	1963	3.00	6.00	12.00
❏ LST-7250 [S]	Eddie Heywood's Golden Encores	1962	3.75	7.50	15.00
❏ LST-7279 [S]	Manhattan Beat	1963	3.75	7.50	15.00
❏ LST-7313 [S]	Canadian Sunset Bossa Nova	1963	3.75	7.50	15.00

MAINSTREAM

❏ S-6001 [S]	Begin the Beguine	1964	3.75	7.50	15.00
❏ 96001 [M]	Begin the Beguine	1964	3.00	6.00	12.00

Number	Title (A Side/B Side)	Yr	VG	VG+	NM
MERCURY					
❏ MG-20445 [M]	Breezin' Along with the Breeze	1959	5.00	10.00	20.00
❏ MG-20590 [M]	Eddie Heywood at the Piano	1960	5.00	10.00	20.00
❏ MG-20632 [M]	One for My Baby	1960	5.00	10.00	20.00
❏ SR-60115 [S]	Breezin' Along with the Breeze	1959	6.25	12.50	25.00
❏ SR-60248 [S]	Eddie Heywood at the Piano	1960	6.25	12.50	25.00
❏ SR-60632 [S]	One for My Baby	1960	6.25	12.50	25.00
MGM					
❏ E-135 [10]	It's Easy to Remember	1952	12.50	25.00	50.00
❏ E-3093 [M]	Pianorama	1955	10.00	20.00	40.00
❏ E-3260 [M]	Eddie Heywood	1956	10.00	20.00	40.00
RCA VICTOR					
❏ LPM-1466 [M]	The Touch of Eddie Heywood	1957	7.50	15.00	30.00
❏ LPM-1529 [M]	Canadian Sunset	1957	7.50	15.00	30.00
❏ LSP-1529 [S]	Canadian Sunset	1958	10.00	20.00	40.00
❏ LPM-1900 [M]	The Keys and I	1958	7.50	15.00	30.00
SUNSET					
❏ SUM-1121 [M]	An Affair to Remember	196?	3.00	6.00	12.00
❏ SUS-5121 [S]	An Affair to Remember	196?	3.00	6.00	12.00
VOCALION					
❏ VL 3748 [M]	The Piano Stylings of Eddie Heywood	1966	3.75	7.50	15.00
❏ VL 73748 [R]	The Piano Stylings of Eddie Heywood	1966	3.00	6.00	12.00
WING					
❏ MGW-12137 [M]	Eddie Heywood	196?	3.75	7.50	15.00
❏ MGW-12287 [M]	Breezin' Along	196?	3.75	7.50	15.00
❏ SRW-16137 [S]	Eddie Heywood	196?	3.00	6.00	12.00
❏ SRW-16287 [S]	Breezin' Along	196?	3.00	6.00	12.00

HI-FI'S, THE
45s
Number	Title (A Side/B Side)	Yr	VG	VG+	NM
CAMEO					
❏ 349	I Keep Forgettin'/Why Can't I Stop Loving You	1965	3.00	6.00	12.00
INTERPHON					
❏ 7701	Will Yer or Won't Yer/She's the One	1964	3.00	6.00	12.00
UNITED ARTISTS					
❏ 50160	I'm a Box/No Two Ways	1967	2.00	4.00	8.00

HI-FI-DELS, THE
45s
Number	Title (A Side/B Side)	Yr	VG	VG+	NM
ATLANTIC					
❏ 2121	Did I Cry/Tricky Tricky	1961	3.75	7.50	15.00

HI-FIVES, THE (1)
45s
Number	Title (A Side/B Side)	Yr	VG	VG+	NM
BELL					
❏ 634	Julie/Son of Raunchy	1965	10.00	20.00	40.00
JERDEN					
❏ 730	Goin' Away/Tort	1964	3.75	7.50	15.00

HI-FIVES, THE (2)
45s
Number	Title (A Side/B Side)	Yr	VG	VG+	NM
BINGO					
❏ 1006	Felicia/Windy City Special	1960	7.50	15.00	30.00
DECCA					
❏ 30576	My Friend/How Can I Win?	1958	10.00	20.00	40.00
❏ 30657	Dorothy/Just a Shoulder to Cry On	1958	12.50	25.00	50.00
❏ 30744	Lonely/What's New	1958	10.00	20.00	40.00

HI-LITERS, THE (1) With King Bassie and His Three Aces...Ben Vereen was a member.
45s
Number	Title (A Side/B Side)	Yr	VG	VG+	NM
HICO					
❏ 2432	Let Me Be True to You/In the Night	1958	25.00	50.00	100.00
❏ 2433	Over the Rainbow/(B-side unknown)	1958	37.50	75.00	150.00

HI-LITERS, THE (U) Probably not group (1), but we don't know if these are the same group or two different groups.
45s
Number	Title (A Side/B Side)	Yr	VG	VG+	NM
VEE JAY					
❏ 184	Bobby Sox Baby/Hello Dear	1956	250.00	500.00	1000.
WEN-DEE					
❏ 1927	Baby Don't Treat Me This Way/Route 66	1955	15.00	30.00	60.00

HI-LITES, THE (1) For records on Daran, see THE CHI-LITES.

HI-LITES, THE (2)
45s
Number	Title (A Side/B Side)	Yr	VG	VG+	NM
JULIA					
❏ 1105	Gloria/For Your Precious Love	1962	30.00	60.00	120.00
MONOGRAM					
❏ 119	Everybody's Somebody's Fool/Moonlight	1976	2.00	4.00	8.00
❏ 120	Zoom Zoom Zoom/To the Aisle	1976	2.00	4.00	8.00
❏ 121	Pretty Face/Maybe You'll Be There	1976	2.00	4.00	8.00
RECORD FAIR					
❏ 500	I'm Falling in Love/Walking My Baby Back Home	1961	12.50	25.00	50.00
❏ 501	For Sentimental Reasons/For Your Precious Love	1962	12.50	25.00	50.00
Albums					
DANDEE					
❏ DLP-206 [M]	For Your Precious Love	1961	500.00	1000.	2000.

HI-LITES, THE (U) None of these are group (1). Some could be group (2). The rest could be several more groups.
45s
Number	Title (A Side/B Side)	Yr	VG	VG+	NM
BRUNSWICK					
❏ 55102	Friday Night Go Go/Chicka-Rocka-Chee-Chi-Cho (Cha Cha)	1958	5.00	10.00	20.00
JET					
❏ 501	The Pony (Part 1)/The Pony (Part 2)	1961	5.00	10.00	20.00
❏ 502	4000 Miles Away/Woke Up This Morning	1961	7.50	15.00	30.00
KING					
❏ 5730	Death of an Angel/Our Winter Love	1963	5.00	10.00	20.00
MERCURY					
❏ 70987	The Next Four Years/The Girls with the Bells	1956	6.25	12.50	25.00
OKEH					
❏ 7046	I Found a Love/Zanzee	1954	125.00	250.00	500.00
RENO					
❏ 1030	Please Believe Me I Love You/Sweet and Lovely	1958	62.50	125.00	250.00

Number	Title (A Side/B Side)	Yr	VG	VG+	NM
TWIST TIME					
❏ 12	Twistin' Time/Twistin' Pony	1962	3.75	7.50	15.00
WASSEL					
❏ 701	Groovy/Hey Baby	1965	2.50	5.00	10.00

HI-LO'S, THE
45s
Number	Title (A Side/B Side)	Yr	VG	VG+	NM
COLUMBIA					
❏ 40915	A Face in the Crowd/Autumn Rain	1957	2.50	5.00	10.00
❏ 41050	A Very Special Love/My Sugar Is So Refined	1957	2.50	5.00	10.00
❏ 41197	Whistlin' Down the Lane/When I Remember	1958	2.50	5.00	10.00
❏ 41465	Goody Goody/Indiana	1959	2.50	5.00	10.00
❏ 41647	Cindy's Prayer/A Lot of Livin' to Do	1960	2.50	5.00	10.00
❏ 41867	The Trolley Song/Five Foot Two, Eyes of Blue	1960	2.50	5.00	10.00

7-Inch Extended Plays
Number	Title (A Side/B Side)	Yr	VG	VG+	NM
COLUMBIA					
❏ B-10231	Sunnyside Up/Laura//A Shine on Your Shoes/The Heather on the Hill	195?	3.00	6.00	12.00
❏ B-10231 [PS]	Sunnyside Up	195?	3.00	6.00	12.00
STARLITE					
❏ ST 455	Rockin' Chair/Jeepers Creepers//Nice Work If You Can Get It/Button Up Your Overcoat	195?	3.75	7.50	15.00
❏ ST 455 [PS]	The Hi-Lo's, I Presume	195?	3.75	7.50	15.00
❏ ST 456	Stars Fell on Alabama/Speak Low//I Thought About You/Put Your Dreams Away	195?	3.75	7.50	15.00
❏ ST 456 [PS]	The Hi-Lo's, I Presume	195?	3.75	7.50	15.00
❏ ST 457	Summertime/Through the Years//Skylark/Shadow Waltz	195?	3.75	7.50	15.00
❏ ST 457 [PS]	Under Glass, Part 1	195?	3.75	7.50	15.00

Albums
Number	Title (A Side/B Side)	Yr	VG	VG+	NM
COLUMBIA					
❏ CL 952 [M]	Suddenly It's the Hi-Lo's	1957	7.50	15.00	30.00
❏ CL 1023 [M]	Now Hear This	1957	7.50	15.00	30.00
❏ CL 1259 [M]	The Hi-Lo's and All That Jazz	1958	7.50	15.00	30.00
❏ CL 1416 [M]	Broadway Playbill	1959	7.50	15.00	30.00
❏ CL 1509 [M]	All Over the Place	1960	6.25	12.50	25.00
❏ CL 1723 [M]	This Time It's Love	1962	6.25	12.50	25.00
❏ CS 8057 [S]	Love Nest	1958	10.00	20.00	40.00
❏ CS 8077 [S]	The Hi-Lo's and All That Jazz	1958	10.00	20.00	40.00
❏ CS 8213 [S]	Broadway Playbill	1959	10.00	20.00	40.00
❏ CS 8300 [S]	All Over the Place	1960	7.50	15.00	30.00
❏ CS 8523 [S]	This Time It's Love	1962	7.50	15.00	30.00
COLUMBIA SPECIAL PRODUCTS					
❏ P 14387	Harmony in Jazz	1978	3.00	6.00	12.00
DRG					
❏ SL 5184	Clap Yo' Hands	198?	3.00	6.00	12.00
KAPP					
❏ KL 1027 [M]	The Hi-Lo's and the Jerry Fielding Band	1956	7.50	15.00	30.00
❏ KL 1184 [M]	Under Glass	1959	6.25	12.50	25.00
—Reissue of Starlite 7005					
❏ KL 1194 [M]	On Hand	1960	6.25	12.50	25.00
—Reissue of Starlite 7008					
MCA					
❏ 4171 [(2)]	The Hi-Lo's Collection	197?	3.75	7.50	15.00
OMEGA					
❏ OSL-11 [S]	The Hi-Lo's in Stereo	195?	7.50	15.00	30.00
PAUSA					
❏ 7040	Back Again	198?	3.00	6.00	12.00
❏ 7093	Now	198?	3.00	6.00	12.00
REPRISE					
❏ R-6066 [M]	The Hi-Lo's Happen to Bossa Nova	1963	5.00	10.00	20.00
❏ R9-6066 [S]	The Hi-Lo's Happen to Bossa Nova	1963	6.25	12.50	25.00
STARLITE					
❏ 6004 [10]	Listen!	1955	15.00	30.00	60.00
❏ 6005 [10]	The Hi-Lo's, I Presume	1955	15.00	30.00	60.00
❏ 7005 [M]	Under Glass	1956	10.00	20.00	40.00
❏ 7006 [M]	Listen!	1956	10.00	20.00	40.00
—Reissue of 6004					
❏ 7007 [M]	The Hi-Lo's. I Presume	1956	10.00	20.00	40.00
—Reissue of 6005					
❏ 7008 [M]	On Hand	1956	10.00	20.00	40.00

HIATT, JOHN
45s
Number	Title (A Side/B Side)	Yr	VG	VG+	NM
A&M					
❏ 1245	Slow Turning/Your Dad Did (Live)	1988	—	—	3.00
❏ 2950	Lipstick Sunset/Thank You Girl	1987	—	—	3.00
❏ 2970	Have a Little Faith in Me/Thank You Girl	1987	—	—	3.00
ATLANTIC					
❏ 89461	Snakecharmer/This Is Your Day	1985	—	2.00	4.00
CAPITOL					
❏ S7-19626	Little Head/Runaway	1997	—	—	3.00
EPIC					
❏ 10990	The Boulevard Ain't So Bad/We Make Spirit	1973	—	3.00	6.00
❏ 11095	Sure As I'm Sittin' Here/Ocean	1974	—	2.50	5.00
❏ 50022	Hangin' Around the Observatory/Full Moon	1974	—	2.50	5.00
❏ 50115	Down Home (Keep On Fallin')/Motorboat to Heaven	1975	—	2.50	5.00
GEFFEN					
❏ 29045	Living a Little, Laughing a Little/I'm a Real Man	1985	—	2.00	4.00
❏ 29945	I Look for Love/Take Time to Know Her	1982	—	2.00	4.00
MCA					
❏ 41019	Radio Girl/Sharon's Got a Drugstore	1979	—	2.00	4.00
❏ 41132	Madonna Road/Slug Line	1979	—	2.00	4.00
❏ 41300	I Spy (For the FBI)/It Hasn't Happened Yet	1980	—	2.00	4.00
THE RIGHT STUFF					
❏ S7-19856	Johnny 99/I Wish I Were Blind	1998	—	—	3.00
—B-side by the Yell Leaders					
Albums					
A&M					
❏ SP-5158	Bring the Family	1987	2.50	5.00	10.00
❏ SP-5206	Slow Turning	1988	2.50	5.00	10.00
❏ 75021 5310 1	Stolen Moments	1990	3.00	6.00	12.00
EPIC					
❏ KE 32688	Hangin' Around the Observatory	1974	3.75	7.50	15.00

Number	Title (A Side/B Side)	Yr	VG	VG+	NM
❑ KE 33190	Overcoats	1975	3.75	7.50	15.00
❑ PE 33190	Overcoats	198?	2.00	4.00	8.00
—Budget-line reissue					
GEFFEN					
❑ GHS 2009	All of a Sudden	1982	3.00	6.00	12.00
❑ GHS 4017	Riding with the King	1983	3.00	6.00	12.00
❑ GHS 24055	Warming Up to the Ice Age	1984	3.00	6.00	12.00
MCA					
❑ 741	Two-Bit Monster	198?	2.00	4.00	8.00
—Reissue					
❑ 747	Slug Line	198?	2.00	4.00	8.00
—Reissue					
❑ 3088	Slug Line	1979	3.00	6.00	12.00
❑ 5123	Two-Bit Monster	1980	3.00	6.00	12.00
MOBILE FIDEILTY					
❑ 1-210	Bring the Family	1994	12.50	25.00	50.00
—Audiophile vinyl					

HIBBLER, AL
45s
Number	Title (A Side/B Side)	Yr	VG	VG+	NM
ALADDIN					
❑ 3328	Don't Take Your Love from Me/I Got It So Bad and That Ain't Good	1956	3.75	7.50	15.00
ATLANTIC					
❑ 911	Danny Boy/Song of the Wanderer	1950	—	—	—
—Unconfimed on 45 rpm					
❑ 925	The Blues Come Falling Down/Old Folks	1951	12.50	25.00	50.00
❑ 932	Travelin' Light/If I Knew You Were There	1951	12.50	25.00	50.00
❑ 945	Now I Lay Me Down to Dream/This Is Always	1951	12.50	25.00	50.00
❑ 1071	Danny Boy/Now I Lay Me Down	1955	7.50	15.00	30.00
BRUNSWICK					
❑ 55027	Star Dust/Stormy Weather	1957	3.75	7.50	15.00
CLEF					
❑ 89095	I'm Getting Sentimental Over You/As Time Goes By	1954	3.75	7.50	15.00
DECCA					
❑ 29441	Unchained Melody/Daybreak	1955	5.00	10.00	20.00
❑ 29543	I Can't Put My Arms Around a Memory/They Say You're Laughing at Me	1955	3.75	7.50	15.00
❑ 29660	He/Breeze (Blow My Baby Back to Me)	1955	5.00	10.00	20.00
❑ 29789	11th Hour Melody/Let's Try Again	1956	3.75	7.50	15.00
❑ 29950	Away All Boats/Never Turn Back	1956	3.75	7.50	15.00
❑ 29982	After the Lights Go Down Low/I Was Telling Her About You	1956	3.75	7.50	15.00
❑ 30100	Nightfall/I'm Free	1956	3.75	7.50	15.00
❑ 30127	White Christmas/Silent Night	1956	3.75	7.50	15.00
❑ 30176	Trees/The Town Crier	1957	3.00	6.00	12.00
❑ 30268	Sweet Slumber/Because of You	1957	3.00	6.00	12.00
❑ 30337	Around the Corner from the Blues/I Complain	1957	3.00	6.00	12.00
❑ 30397	When Will I Forget You/Be Fair	1957	3.00	6.00	12.00
❑ 30483	The Crying Wind/A Wish	1957	3.00	6.00	12.00
❑ 30547	My Heart Tells Me/I'm Glad I'm Not Young Anymore	1958	3.00	6.00	12.00
❑ 30622	Honeysuckle Rose/Ain't Nothin' Wrong with That Baby	1958	3.00	6.00	12.00
❑ 30684	Softly, My Love/Your Hands	1958	3.00	6.00	12.00
❑ 30752	Love Land/Love Me Long, Hold Me Close	1958	3.00	6.00	12.00
❑ 30817	Warm Heart-Cold Feet/Mine All Mine	1959	3.00	6.00	12.00
❑ 30870	He Is Always There/What 'Tis, What 'Tis, 'Tis Spring	1959	3.00	6.00	12.00
❑ 30946	It Won't Be Easy/Lonesome and Cold	1959	3.00	6.00	12.00
MERCURY					
❑ 89011	Please/Believe It Love	1952	3.75	7.50	15.00
REPRISE					
❑ 20035	Look Away/Tall the Sky	1961	2.50	5.00	10.00
❑ 20077	Walk Away/I've Convinced Everyone But You	1962	2.50	5.00	10.00
TOP RANK					
❑ 2089	Strawberry Hill/Stranger	1960	2.50	5.00	10.00

7-Inch Extended Plays
Number	Title (A Side/B Side)	Yr	VG	VG+	NM
DECCA					
❑ ED 2410	*After the Lights Go Down Low/September in the Rain/You'll Never Know/Where Are You?	195?	5.00	10.00	20.00
❑ ED 2410 [PS]	Starring Al Hibbler, Part 1	195?	5.00	10.00	20.00
❑ ED 2447	I Hadn't Anyone Till You/I'll Get Along Somehow/It's Been a Long, Long Time/The Town Crier	195?	5.00	10.00	20.00
❑ ED 2447 [PS]	Here's Hibbler! Part 3	195?	5.00	10.00	20.00

Albums
Number	Title (A Side/B Side)	Yr	VG	VG+	NM
ARGO					
❑ LP-601 [M]	Melodies by Al Hibbler	1956	10.00	20.00	40.00
—Reissue of Marterry LP					
ATLANTIC					
❑ 1251 [M]	After the Lights Go Down Low	1957	12.50	25.00	50.00
—Black label					
❑ 1251 [M]	After the Lights Go Down Low	1961	6.25	12.50	25.00
—Mostly red label, white fan logo					
❑ 1251 [M]	After the Lights Go Down Low	1963	5.00	10.00	20.00
—Mostly red label, black fan logo					
BRUNSWICK					
❑ BL 54036 [M]	Al Hibbler with the Ellingtonians	1957	12.50	25.00	50.00
DECCA					
❑ DL 8328 [M]	Starring Al Hibbler	1956	7.50	15.00	30.00
❑ DL 8420 [M]	Here's Hibbler	1957	7.50	15.00	30.00
❑ DL 8697 [M]	Torchy and Blue	1958	7.50	15.00	30.00
❑ DL 8757 [M]	Hits by Hibbler	1958	7.50	15.00	30.00
❑ DL 8862 [M]	Al Hibbler Remembers the Big Songs of the Big Bands	1959	7.50	15.00	30.00
❑ DL 78862 [S]	Al Hibbler Remembers the Big Songs of the Big Bands	1959	10.00	20.00	40.00
DISCOVERY					
❑ 842	It's Monday Every Day	198?	3.00	6.00	12.00
—Reissue of Reprise LP					
LMI					
❑ 10001 [M]	Early One Morning	1964	7.50	15.00	30.00
MARTERRY					
❑ LP-601 [M]	Melodies by Al Hibbler	1956	20.00	40.00	80.00

Number	Title (A Side/B Side)	Yr	VG	VG+	NM
MCA					
❑ 4098 [(2)]	The Best of Al Hibbler	197?	3.75	7.50	15.00
NORGRAN					
❑ MGN-4 [10]	Al Hibbler Favorites	1954	37.50	75.00	150.00
❑ MGN-15 [10]	Al Hibbler Sings Duke Ellington	1954	37.50	75.00	150.00
OPEN SKY					
❑ OSR-3126	For Sentimental Reasons	1986	3.00	6.00	12.00
REPRISE					
❑ R-2005 [M]	It's Monday Every Day	1961	7.50	15.00	30.00
❑ R9-2005 [S]	It's Monday Every Day	1961	10.00	20.00	40.00
SCORE					
❑ SLP-4013 [M]	I Surrender, Dear	1957	25.00	50.00	100.00
VERVE					
❑ MGV-4000 [M]	Al Hibbler Sings Love Songs	1956	15.00	30.00	60.00
❑ V-4000 [M]	Al Hibbler Sings Love Songs	1961	5.00	10.00	20.00

HICKEY, ERSEL
45s
Number	Title (A Side/B Side)	Yr	VG	VG+	NM
APOLLO					
❑ 761	Upside Down Love/The Millionaire	1949	12.50	25.00	50.00
EPIC					
❑ 9263	Bluebirds Over the Mountain/Hangin' Around	1958	7.50	15.00	30.00
❑ 9278	Goin' Down That Road/Lovers' Land	1958	6.25	12.50	25.00
❑ 9298	You Never Can Tell/Wedding Day	1958	6.25	12.50	25.00
❑ 9309	Don't Be Afraid of Love/You Threw a Dart	1959	6.25	12.50	25.00
❑ 9320	I Can't Love Another/People Gotta Talk	1959	6.25	12.50	25.00
❑ 9357	Love in Bloom/What Do You Want	1960	6.25	12.50	25.00
❑ 9395	Another Wasted Day/Money Brought Me You	1960	6.25	12.50	25.00
JANUS					
❑ 151	Bluebirds Over the Mountain/Self Made Man	1971	—	2.50	5.00
KAPP					
❑ 372	Teardrops at Dawn/I Guess You Can Call It Love	1961	5.00	10.00	20.00
LAURIE					
❑ 3165	Some Enchanted Evening/Put Your Mind at Ease	1963	5.00	10.00	20.00
RAMESES II					
❑ 2003	Waitin' for Baby/In Spite of the Fool That I Am	1976	—	3.00	6.00
TOOT					
❑ 602	Tryin' to Get to You/Blue Skies	196?	2.50	5.00	10.00

7-Inch Extended Plays
Number	Title (A Side/B Side)	Yr	VG	VG+	NM
EPIC					
❑ EG-7206	(contents unknown)	1958	25.00	50.00	100.00
❑ EG-7206 [PS]	Ersel Hickey in Lover's Land	1958	25.00	50.00	100.00

Albums
Number	Title (A Side/B Side)	Yr	VG	VG+	NM
BACK-TRAC					
❑ P 18750	The Rockin' Bluebird	1985	15.00	30.00	60.00
—Allegedly, only 200 copies of this were pressed					

HICKMAN, DWAYNE Starred as Dobie Gillis on TV.
45s
Number	Title (A Side/B Side)	Yr	VG	VG+	NM
ABC-PARAMOUNT					
❑ 9908	School Dance/Pretty Baby	1958	6.25	12.50	25.00
❑ 9908 [PS]	School Dance/Pretty Baby	1958	10.00	20.00	40.00
CAPITOL					
❑ 4445	I'm a Lover, Not a Fighter/I Pass Your House	1960	5.00	10.00	20.00

Albums
Number	Title (A Side/B Side)	Yr	VG	VG+	NM
CAPITOL					
❑ ST 1441 [S]	Dobie!	1960	12.50	25.00	50.00
❑ T 1441 [M]	Dobie!	1960	10.00	20.00	40.00

HICKS, DAN, AND HIS HOT LICKS
45s
Number	Title (A Side/B Side)	Yr	VG	VG+	NM
BLUE THUMB					
❑ 211	Moody Richard/Walkin' One and Only	1972	—	2.50	5.00
❑ 213	I'm an Old Cowhand/Woe the Luck	1972	—	2.50	5.00
❑ 235	My Old Timey Baby/Cheaters Don't Win	1973	—	2.50	5.00
EPIC					
❑ 10511	How Can I Miss You When You Won't Go/Canned Music	1969	—	3.00	6.00

Albums
Number	Title (A Side/B Side)	Yr	VG	VG+	NM
BLUE THUMB					
❑ BTS-29	Where's the Money?	1971	3.00	6.00	12.00
❑ BTS-36	Striking It Rich!	1972	3.00	6.00	12.00
❑ BTS-51	Last Train to Hicksville…The Home of Happy Feet	1973	3.00	6.00	12.00
EPIC					
❑ BN 26464	Original Recordings	1969	3.75	7.50	15.00
—-Yellow label					
❑ BN 26464	Original Recordings	1973	2.50	5.00	10.00
—Orange label					
❑ PE 26464	Original Recordings	198?	2.00	4.00	8.00
—Reissue with new prefix					
MCA					
❑ 670	Striking It Rich!	198?	2.00	4.00	8.00
—Reissue					
❑ 671	Last Train to Hicksville…The Home of Happy Feet	198?	2.00	4.00	8.00
—Reissue					
WARNER BROS.					
❑ BSK 3158	It Happened One Bite	1978	2.50	5.00	10.00

HICKS, JEANETTE
45s
Number	Title (A Side/B Side)	Yr	VG	VG+	NM
COLUMBIA					
❑ 4-21374	Just Like in the Movies/Such a Wonderful Feeling	1955	6.25	12.50	25.00
OKEH					
❑ 18008	I Think of You/Still I Lost You	195?	6.25	12.50	25.00
❑ 18021	He Knows Why/All I Care About	195?	6.25	12.50	25.00
❑ 18055	Lipstick on a Glass/Kingless Hand	195?	6.25	12.50	25.00
STARDAY					
❑ 271	Extra Extra/Cry, Cry, It's Good for You	1956	5.00	10.00	20.00

Number	Title (A Side/B Side)	Yr	VG	VG+	NM

HICKS, JEANETTE, AND BILLY WALKER
45s
COLUMBIA

Number	Title (A Side/B Side)	Yr	VG	VG+	NM
❏ 4-21392	Which One of Us Is to Blame/Let's Make Memories Tonight	1955	5.00	10.00	20.00
❏ 4-21471	Blue Mountain Waltz/Why Does It Have to Be	1955	5.00	10.00	20.00

HIDE-A-WAYS, THE
45s
LOST-NITE

Number	Title (A Side/B Side)	Yr	VG	VG+	NM
❏ 119	Can't Help Loving That Girl of Mine/ I'm Coming Home	196?	2.00	4.00	8.00

—Reissue label
MGM

Number	Title (A Side/B Side)	Yr	VG	VG+	NM
❏ 55004	Cherie/Me Make Em Powwow	1955	125.00	250.00	500.00

RONNI

Number	Title (A Side/B Side)	Yr	VG	VG+	NM
❏ 1000	Can't Help Lovin' That Girl of Mine/ I'm Coming Home	1954	2000.	4000.	6000.

HIGH NUMBERS, THE See THE WHO.

HIGH TIDE
Albums
LIBERTY

Number	Title (A Side/B Side)	Yr	VG	VG+	NM
❏ LST-7638	Sea Shanties	1969	6.25	12.50	25.00

HIGH TREASON
Albums
ABBOTT

Number	Title (A Side/B Side)	Yr	VG	VG+	NM
❏ ABS-1209	High Treason	1968	15.00	30.00	60.00

HIGHLIGHTS, THE
45s
BALLY

Number	Title (A Side/B Side)	Yr	VG	VG+	NM
❏ 1016	City of Angels/Listen, My Love	1956	7.50	15.00	30.00
❏ 1027	To Be with You/Will I Ever Know	1957	7.50	15.00	30.00
❏ 1044	Indian Style/Turn Around Shoes	1957	6.25	12.50	25.00

HIGHWAYMEN, THE
45s
ABC

Number	Title (A Side/B Side)	Yr	VG	VG+	NM
❏ 10801	She's Not There/Little Bird, Little Bird	1966	2.00	4.00	8.00
❏ 10824	Fling/My Foolish Pride	1966	2.00	4.00	8.00

ABC-PARAMOUNT

Number	Title (A Side/B Side)	Yr	VG	VG+	NM
❏ 10688	Should I Go, Should I Stay/Permit to Be a Hermit	1965	2.00	4.00	8.00
❏ 10716	I'll Show You the Way/ Never a Thought for Tomorrow	1965	2.00	4.00	8.00

UNITED ARTISTS

Number	Title (A Side/B Side)	Yr	VG	VG+	NM
❏ 258	Michael/Santiano	1960	3.75	7.50	15.00
❏ 370	Cotton Fields/Gypsy Rover	1961	3.00	6.00	12.00
❏ 439	Whiskey in the Jar/I'm On My Way	1962	3.00	6.00	12.00
❏ 475	Cindy, Oh Cindy/The Birdman	1962	3.00	6.00	12.00
❏ 540	I Know Where I'm Going/Well, Well, Well	1963	3.00	6.00	12.00
❏ 568	I Never Will Marry/Pretoria	1963	3.00	6.00	12.00
❏ 602	All My Trials/Midnight Train	1963	3.00	6.00	12.00
❏ 647	Universal Soldier/I'll Fly Away	1963	3.00	6.00	12.00
❏ 679	Roll On Columbia, Roll On/ The Tale of Michael Flynn	1963	3.00	6.00	12.00
❏ 695	The Sinking of the Reuben James/Bon Soir	1964	2.50	5.00	10.00
❏ 752	Nellie/Sweet Mama Tree Top Tall	1964	2.50	5.00	10.00
❏ 788	Puttin' On the Style/Michael	1964	2.50	5.00	10.00
❏ 801	Michael '65/Puttin' On the Style	1964	2.50	5.00	10.00

Albums
ABC-PARAMOUNT

Number	Title (A Side/B Side)	Yr	VG	VG+	NM
❏ 522 [M]	On a New Road	1965	3.00	6.00	12.00
❏ S-522 [S]	On a New Road	1965	3.75	7.50	15.00

UNITED ARTISTS

Number	Title (A Side/B Side)	Yr	VG	VG+	NM
❏ UAL 3125 [M]	The Highwaymen	1961	3.75	7.50	15.00
❏ UAL 3168 [M]	Standing Room Only!	1962	3.75	7.50	15.00
❏ UAL 3225 [M]	Encore!	1962	3.75	7.50	15.00
❏ UAL 3245 [M]	March On, Brothers	1963	3.75	7.50	15.00
❏ UAL 3294 [M]	Hootenanny with the Highwaymen	1963	3.75	7.50	15.00
❏ UAL 3323 [M]	One More Time	1964	3.75	7.50	15.00
❏ UAL 3348 [M]	Homecoming	1964	3.75	7.50	15.00
❏ UAS 6125 [S]	The Highwaymen	1961	5.00	10.00	20.00
❏ UAS 6168 [S]	Standing Room Only!	1962	5.00	10.00	20.00
❏ UAS 6225 [S]	Encore!	1962	5.00	10.00	20.00
❏ UAS 6245 [S]	March On, Brothers	1963	5.00	10.00	20.00
❏ UAS 6294 [S]	Hootenanny with the Highwaymen	1963	5.00	10.00	20.00
❏ UAS 6323 [S]	One More Time	1964	5.00	10.00	20.00
❏ UAS 6348 [S]	Homecoming	1964	5.00	10.00	20.00

HIGHWAYMEN, THE (2) See JOHNNY CASH; WAYLON JENNINGS; KRIS KRISTOFFERSON; WILLIE NELSON.

HILDEBRAND, RAY See PAUL AND PAULA.
45s
PHILIPS

Number	Title (A Side/B Side)	Yr	VG	VG+	NM
❏ 40174	It's All Over, Paula/Snow Girl	1964	2.50	5.00	10.00

—As "Paul"

Number	Title (A Side/B Side)	Yr	VG	VG+	NM
❏ 40318	Hey Little Julie/The Way of the DJ	1965	2.00	4.00	8.00
❏ 40339	Hello Viet Nam (Goodbye My Love)/You, Wonderful You	1965	2.00	4.00	8.00

TOWER

Number	Title (A Side/B Side)	Yr	VG	VG+	NM
❏ 304	Paper Clown/Patsy	1966	2.00	4.00	8.00

—As "Paul (Paul and Paula)"
Albums
WORD

Number	Title (A Side/B Side)	Yr	VG	VG+	NM
❏ WST-8411	He's Everything to Me	196?	3.00	6.00	12.00
❏ WST-8465	I Need You Every Hour	1971	3.00	6.00	12.00

HILL, BUNKER
45s
MALA

Number	Title (A Side/B Side)	Yr	VG	VG+	NM
❏ 451	Hide and Go Seek (Part 1)/Hide and Go Seek (Part 2)	1962	5.00	10.00	20.00
❏ 457	Red Ridin' Hood and the Wolf/Nobody Knows	1962	5.00	10.00	20.00
❏ 464	The Girl Can't Dance/You Can't Make Me Doubt My Baby	1963	6.25	12.50	25.00

HILL, JESSIE
45s
BLUE THUMB

Number	Title (A Side/B Side)	Yr	VG	VG+	NM
❏ 204	Naturally/Livin' a Lie	1971	—	3.00	6.00

DOWNEY

Number	Title (A Side/B Side)	Yr	VG	VG+	NM
❏ 115	Chip Chop/Woodshed	1964	2.50	5.00	10.00
❏ 117	Understanding/Down the Street	1964	2.50	5.00	10.00
❏ 124	Never Thought/TV Guide	1964	2.50	5.00	10.00

MINIT

Number	Title (A Side/B Side)	Yr	VG	VG+	NM
❏ 607	Ooh Poo Pah Doo — Part 1/ Ooh Poo Pah Doo — Part 2	1960	3.75	7.50	15.00
❏ 611	Whip It On Me/I Need Your Love	1960	3.00	6.00	12.00
❏ 616	Scoop Scoobie Doobie/Highland Blues	1960	3.00	6.00	12.00
❏ 622	Oh My Oh My/I Got Mine	1961	3.00	6.00	12.00
❏ 628	Oogsey Moo/My Love	1961	3.00	6.00	12.00
❏ 638	Sweet Jelly Roll/It's My Fault	1961	3.00	6.00	12.00
❏ 646	Can't Get Enough of That Ooh Pah Doo/ Pot's on a Strike	1962	3.00	6.00	12.00

UNITED ARTISTS

Number	Title (A Side/B Side)	Yr	VG	VG+	NM
❏ 0081	Ooh Poo Pah Doo — Part 1/ Ooh Poo Pah Doo — Part 2	1973	—	2.00	4.00

—"Silver Spotlight Series" reissue

HILL, RAYMOND
45s
SUN

Number	Title (A Side/B Side)	Yr	VG	VG+	NM
❏ 204	Bourbon Street Jump/The Snuggle	1954	250.00	500.00	750.00

HILL, VERNELL
45s
TUFF

Number	Title (A Side/B Side)	Yr	VG	VG+	NM
❏ 381	Long Haired Daddy/Sometimes Love	1964	2.00	4.00	8.00

HILL, VINCE
45s
LONDON INT'L.

Number	Title (A Side/B Side)	Yr	VG	VG+	NM
❏ 10514	The River's Run Dry/Not Any More	1962	3.00	6.00	12.00

PARAMOUNT

Number	Title (A Side/B Side)	Yr	VG	VG+	NM
❏ 0132	(Love Story) Look Around/ In Every Corner of the World	1971	—	2.50	5.00

TOWER

Number	Title (A Side/B Side)	Yr	VG	VG+	NM
❏ 173	Yesterday's Hero/Unexpectedly	1965	2.00	4.00	8.00
❏ 207	Push Push/Take Me to Your Heart Again	1966	2.00	4.00	8.00
❏ 223	Looking at Me/Love Me True	1966	2.00	4.00	8.00
❏ 254	Heartaches/Merci Cherie	1966	2.00	4.00	8.00
❏ 323	Edelweiss/A Woman Needs Love	1967	2.00	4.00	8.00
❏ 358	When You Go/When the World Is Ready	1967	2.00	4.00	8.00
❏ 389	Why or When or Where/Why Can't I Remember	1968	—	3.00	6.00

HILL, Z.Z.
45s
ATLANTIC

Number	Title (A Side/B Side)	Yr	VG	VG+	NM
❏ 2659	It's a Hang-Up Baby/ (Home Just Ain't Home at) Suppertime	1969	2.00	4.00	8.00

COLUMBIA

Number	Title (A Side/B Side)	Yr	VG	VG+	NM
❏ 10552	Love Is So Good When You're Stealing It/ Need You By My Side	1977	—	2.50	5.00
❏ 10680	This Time They Told the Truth/ Near But Yet So Far	1978	—	2.50	5.00
❏ 10748	Universal Love/That's All That's Left	1978	—	2.50	5.00

HILL

Number	Title (A Side/B Side)	Yr	VG	VG+	NM
❏ 222	Don't Make Me Pay for His Mistakes/ (B-side unknown)	1971	—	3.00	6.00

KENT

Number	Title (A Side/B Side)	Yr	VG	VG+	NM
❏ 404	I Could Do It All Over/You Don't Love Me	1964	2.50	5.00	10.00
❏ 416	I Need Someone (To Love Me)/ Have Mercy Someone	1965	2.50	5.00	10.00
❏ 427	Hey Little Girl/Oh Darlin'	1965	2.50	5.00	10.00
❏ 432	That's It/What's More	1965	2.50	5.00	10.00
❏ 439	Everybody Has to Cry/Happiness Is All I Need	1965	2.50	5.00	10.00
❏ 444	No More Doggin'/The Kind of Love I Want	1966	2.50	5.00	10.00
❏ 449	I Found Love/Set Your Sights Higher	1966	2.50	5.00	10.00
❏ 453	You Can't Hide a Heartache/Gimme Gimme	1966	2.50	5.00	10.00
❏ 460	Oh Darling/Greatest Love	1967	2.50	5.00	10.00
❏ 464	Baby I'm Sorry/Where She At	1967	2.50	5.00	10.00
❏ 469	You Just Cheat and Lie/ Everybody Needs Somebody	1967	2.50	5.00	10.00
❏ 478	What Am I Living For/ You're Gonna Need My Lovin'	1967	2.50	5.00	10.00
❏ 481	Steal Away/ Nothing Can Change the Love I Have for You	1967	2.50	5.00	10.00
❏ 494	You Got What I Need/Have Mercy Someone	1968	2.50	5.00	10.00
❏ 502	Don't Make Promises (You Can't Keep)/ Set Your Sights Higher	1968	2.50	5.00	10.00
❏ 4547	I Need Someone (To Love Me)/Oh Darling	1971	2.00	4.00	8.00
❏ 4550	You Don't Love Me/Have Mercy Someone	1971	2.00	4.00	8.00
❏ 4560	If I Could Do It All Over/You Won't Hurt No More	1971	2.00	4.00	8.00
❏ 4577	Nothing Can Change This Love/ Everybody Has to Cry	1972	2.00	4.00	8.00

M.H.

Number	Title (A Side/B Side)	Yr	VG	VG+	NM
❏ 200	You Were Wrong/(B-side unknown)	1964	2.50	5.00	10.00

MALACO

Number	Title (A Side/B Side)	Yr	VG	VG+	NM
❏ 2069	Please Don't Make Me (Do Something Bad to You)/Blue Monday	1981	—	2.00	4.00
❏ 2074	Separate Ways/Chained to Your Love	1981	—	2.00	4.00
❏ 2076	Bump and Grind/Somethin' Goin' On	1981	—	2.00	4.00
❏ 2079	Cheating in the Next Room/ Right Arm for Your Love	1982	—	2.00	4.00
❏ 2082	When It Rains It Pours/ When Can We Do This Again	1982	—	2.00	4.00
❏ 2085	What Am I Gonna Tell Her/ Get You Some Business	1982	—	2.00	4.00
❏ 2090	Open House at My House/ Who You Been Givin' It To	1983	—	2.00	4.00
❏ 2094	Get a Little, Give a Little/Blind Side	1983	—	2.00	4.00
❏ 2097	Steal Away/Three Into Two Won't Go	1984	—	2.00	4.00

Number	Title (A Side/B Side)	Yr	VG	VG+	NM
❏ 2103	Someone Else Is Steppin' In/ Shade Tree Mechanic	1984	—	2.00	4.00
❏ 2109	I'm Gonna Stop You from Givin' Me the Blues/ Personally	1984	—	2.00	4.00
❏ 2141	Down Home Blues/ Please Don't Let Our Good Thing End	1988	—	2.00	4.00

MANKIND

Number	Title (A Side/B Side)	Yr	VG	VG+	NM
❏ 12003	Faithful and True/I Think I'd Do It	1971	2.00	4.00	8.00
❏ 12007	The Chokin' Kind/Hold Back	1971	2.00	4.00	8.00
❏ 12012	Second Chance/It Ain't No Use	1972	—	3.50	7.00
❏ 12015	It Ain't No Use/Ha Ha	1972	—	3.50	7.00
❏ 12017	The Chokin' Kind/A Man Needs a Woman	197?	—	3.50	7.00

UNITED ARTISTS

Number	Title (A Side/B Side)	Yr	VG	VG+	NM
❏ XW225	Ain't Nothing You Can Do/Love in the Street	1973	—	3.00	6.00
❏ XW307	I Don't Need Half a Love/Friendship Only Goes So Far	1973	—	3.00	6.00
❏ XW365	Let Them Talk/Red Rooster	1973	—	3.00	6.00
❏ XW412	Am I Groovin' You/Bad Mouth and Gossip	1974	—	3.00	6.00
❏ XW536	I Keep On Lovin' You/Whatever's Thrilling You Is Killing Me	1974	—	3.00	6.00
❏ XW631	I Created a Monster/Steppin' in the Shoes of a Fool	1975	—	3.00	6.00
❏ 50977	Your Love Makes Me Feel Good/I've Got to Get You Back	1972	—	3.50	7.00

Albums

COLUMBIA

Number	Title (A Side/B Side)	Yr	VG	VG+	NM
❏ JC 35030	Let's Make a Deal	1978	3.00	6.00	12.00
❏ JC 36125	The Mark of Z.Z.	1979	3.00	6.00	12.00

KENT

Number	Title (A Side/B Side)	Yr	VG	VG+	NM
❏ KST-528	A Whole Lot of Soul	1969	3.75	7.50	15.00
❏ KST-560	Dues Paid in Full	1971	3.75	7.50	15.00

MALACO

Number	Title (A Side/B Side)	Yr	VG	VG+	NM
❏ 7411	The Rhyhtm & The Blues	1983	2.50	5.00	10.00
❏ 7415	I'm a Blues Man	1984	2.50	5.00	10.00

MANKIND

Number	Title (A Side/B Side)	Yr	VG	VG+	NM
❏ 201	The Brand New Z.Z. Hill	1971	3.75	7.50	15.00

UNITED ARTISTS

Number	Title (A Side/B Side)	Yr	VG	VG+	NM
❏ UA-LA417-G	Keep On Lovin' You	1975	3.00	6.00	12.00
❏ UAS 5589	The Best Thing That's Ever Happened to Me	1972	3.00	6.00	12.00

HILL SISTERS, THE
45s

ANNA

Number	Title (A Side/B Side)	Yr	VG	VG+	NM
❏ 103	Hit and Run Away Love/Advertising for Love	1959	125.00	250.00	500.00
❏ 1103	Hit and Run Away Love/Advertising for Love	1959	12.50	25.00	50.00

HILLMEN, THE
Albums

TOGETHER

Number	Title (A Side/B Side)	Yr	VG	VG+	NM
❏ STT-1012	The Hillmen	1970	20.00	40.00	80.00

HILLOW HAMMET
Albums

HOUSE OF FOX

Number	Title (A Side/B Side)	Yr	VG	VG+	NM
❏ 2	Hammer	1968	37.50	75.00	150.00

HILLSIDE SINGERS, THE
45s

METROMEDIA

Number	Title (A Side/B Side)	Yr	VG	VG+	NM
❏ 231	I'd Like to Teach the World to Sing (In Perfect Harmony)/I Believe It All	1971	—	2.50	5.00
❏ 241	We're Together/Day by Day	1972	—	2.50	5.00
❏ 246	Kum Ba Yah/Tomorrow Belongs to Me	1972	—	2.50	5.00
❏ 255	The Last Happy Song/Ah Man, See What You've Done	1972	—	2.50	5.00

Albums

METROMEDIA

Number	Title (A Side/B Side)	Yr	VG	VG+	NM
❏ MD 1051	I'd Like to Teach the World to Sing	1971	3.00	6.00	12.00

HILLSIDERS, THE
45s

MEL-O-DY

Number	Title (A Side/B Side)	Yr	VG	VG+	NM
❏ 120	You Only Pass This Way One Time/Rain Is a Lonesome Thing	1964	7.50	15.00	30.00

HILLTOPPERS, THE
45s

DOT

Number	Title (A Side/B Side)	Yr	VG	VG+	NM
❏ 15018	Trying/You Made Up My Mind	1952	5.00	10.00	20.00

—As "The Hill Toppers"

Number	Title (A Side/B Side)	Yr	VG	VG+	NM
❏ 15034	Must I Cry Again/I Keep Telling Myself	1952	4.00	8.00	16.00
❏ 15055	If I Were King/I Can't Lie to Myself	1953	4.00	8.00	16.00
❏ 15085	P.S. I Love You/I'd Rather Die Young	1953	4.00	8.00	16.00
❏ 15105	Love Walked In/To Be Alone	1953	4.00	8.00	16.00
❏ 15127	From the Vine Came the Grape/Time Will Tell	1954	4.00	8.00	16.00
❏ 15132	Till Then/I Found Your Letter	1954	4.00	8.00	16.00
❏ 15156	Wrapped in a Dream/Poor Butterfly	1954	4.00	8.00	16.00
❏ 15201	Sweetheart/Old Cabaret	1954	4.00	8.00	16.00
❏ 15220	If I Didn't Care/Bertha	1954	4.00	8.00	16.00
❏ 15249	You Try Somebody Else/Time Waits for No One	1954	4.00	8.00	16.00
❏ 15318	D-A-R-L-I-N/Frivolette	1955	3.75	7.50	15.00
❏ 15351	The Door Is Still Open/Tears from My Eyes	1955	3.75	7.50	15.00
❏ 15375	The Kentuckian Song/I Must Be Dreaming	1955	3.75	7.50	15.00
❏ 15415	Searching/All I Need Is You	1955	3.75	7.50	15.00
❏ 15423	Only You (And You Alone)/Until the Real Thing Comes Along	1955	3.75	7.50	15.00
❏ 15437	My Treasure/The Last Word in Love	1955	3.75	7.50	15.00
❏ 15451	Do the Bop/When You're Alone	1956	3.75	7.50	15.00
❏ 15459	So Tired/Faded Rose	1956	3.75	7.50	15.00
❏ 15468	I'm Walking Thru Heaven/ Eyes of Fire, Lips of Wine	1956	3.75	7.50	15.00
❏ 15489	Ka-Ding-Dong/ Into Each Life Some Rain Must Fall	1956	3.00	6.00	12.00

—Second pressings have black labels

Number	Title (A Side/B Side)	Yr	VG	VG+	NM
❏ 15489	Ka-Ding-Dong/ Into Each Life Some Rain Must Fall	1956	3.75	7.50	15.00

—Originals have maroon labels

Number	Title (A Side/B Side)	Yr	VG	VG+	NM
❏ 15511	Until You're Mine/No Regrets	1956	3.00	6.00	12.00
❏ 15537	Marianne/You're Wasting Your Time	1957	3.00	6.00	12.00
❏ 15560	I Love My Girl/I'm Serious	1957	3.00	6.00	12.00
❏ 15594	A Fallen Star/Footsteps	1957	3.00	6.00	12.00
❏ 15626	My Cabin of Dreams/Dedicated to You	1957	3.00	6.00	12.00
❏ 15662	The Joker (That's What They Call Me)/ Chicken Chicken	1957	3.00	6.00	12.00
❏ 15712	Starry Eyes/You Sure Look Good to Me	1958	3.00	6.00	12.00
❏ 15814	Signorina/Peggy's Sister	1958	3.00	6.00	12.00
❏ 15857	You're Nobody Till Somebody Loves You/Trying	1958	3.00	6.00	12.00
❏ 15889	I'd Rather Die Young/Welcome to My Heart	1959	2.50	5.00	10.00
❏ 15958	Lots of Luck/Lizzie Darlin'	1959	2.50	5.00	10.00
❏ 16010	The Prisoner's Song/Phone	1959	2.50	5.00	10.00
❏ 16022	Trying/P.S. I Love You	1960	2.50	5.00	10.00
❏ 16024	From the Vine Came the Grape/Love Walked In	1960	2.50	5.00	10.00
❏ 16025	Only You (And You Alone)/Till Then	1960	2.50	5.00	10.00
❏ 16039	Marianne/To Be Alone	1960	2.50	5.00	10.00
❏ 16054	To Be Alone/P.S. I Love You	1960	2.50	5.00	10.00
❏ 16556	Only You/No Longer Lonely	1963	2.00	4.00	8.00

MGM

Number	Title (A Side/B Side)	Yr	VG	VG+	NM
❏ 14515	Jamaica Farewell/Sunshine and Love	1973	—	2.50	5.00

—As "Jimmy Sacca and the Hilltoppers"

Number	Title (A Side/B Side)	Yr	VG	VG+	NM
❏ 14603	Little Things You Do/Sunshine and Love	1973	—	2.50	5.00

—As "Jimmy Sacca and the Hilltoppers"

7-Inch Extended Plays

DOT

Number	Title (A Side/B Side)	Yr	VG	VG+	NM
❏ DEP-113	I Can't Lie to Myself/If I Were King//I'd Rather Die Young (Than Grow Old Without You)/P.S. I Love You	1953	3.75	7.50	15.00

—Maroon label

Number	Title (A Side/B Side)	Yr	VG	VG+	NM
❏ DEP-113 [PS]	(title unknown)	1953	3.75	7.50	15.00
❏ DEP-1-1006	*You Made Up My Mind/Trying//Must I Cry Again/ I Keep Telling Myself	1953	3.75	7.50	15.00
❏ DEP-1-1006 [PS]	The Hilltoppers	1953	3.75	7.50	15.00
❏ DEP-1007	(contents unknown)	195?	3.75	7.50	15.00
❏ DEP-1007 [PS]	The Hilltoppers Sing	195?	3.75	7.50	15.00
❏ DEP-1008	(contents unknown)	195?	3.75	7.50	15.00
❏ DEP-1008 [PS]	The Hilltoppers Sing	195?	3.75	7.50	15.00
❏ DEP-1009	(contents unknown)	195?	3.75	7.50	15.00
❏ DEP-1009 [PS]	The Hilltoppers Sing	195?	3.75	7.50	15.00
❏ DEP-1011	(contents unknown)	195?	3.75	7.50	15.00
❏ DEP-1011 [PS]	The Hilltoppers Sing	195?	3.75	7.50	15.00
❏ DEP-1012	(contents unknown)	195?	3.75	7.50	15.00
❏ DEP-1012 [PS]	The Hilltoppers Sing	195?	3.75	7.50	15.00

Albums

DOT

Number	Title (A Side/B Side)	Yr	VG	VG+	NM
❏ DLP-105 [10]	The Hilltoppers	1954	15.00	30.00	60.00
❏ DLP-106 [10]	The Hilltoppers	1954	15.00	30.00	60.00
❏ DLP-3003 [M]	The Hilltoppers Present Tops in Pops	1955	12.50	25.00	50.00

—Cartoon of female fan on cover

Number	Title (A Side/B Side)	Yr	VG	VG+	NM
❏ DLP-3003 [M]	The Hilltoppers Present Tops in Pops	1956	7.50	15.00	30.00

—Four caps with "W" on them on cover

Number	Title (A Side/B Side)	Yr	VG	VG+	NM
❏ DLP-3029 [M]	The Towering Hilltoppers	1957	7.50	15.00	30.00
❏ DLP-3073 [M]	Love in Bloom	1958	7.50	15.00	30.00

HIM See DOUG SAHM.

HINSON, DON, AND THE RIGAMORTICIANS
45s

CAPITOL

Number	Title (A Side/B Side)	Yr	VG	VG+	NM
❏ 5314	Riboflavin Flavored, Non-Carbonated, Polyunsaturated Blood/Monster Jerk	1964	3.00	6.00	12.00

Albums

CAPITOL

Number	Title (A Side/B Side)	Yr	VG	VG+	NM
❏ ST 2219 [S]	Monster Dance Party	1964	10.00	20.00	40.00
❏ T 2219 [M]	Monster Dance Party	1964	7.50	15.00	30.00

HINTON, JOE
45s

ARVEE

Number	Title (A Side/B Side)	Yr	VG	VG+	NM
❏ 5028	My Love Is Real/I Won't Be Your Fool	1961	3.00	6.00	12.00

—Arvee titles as "Little Joe Hinton"

Number	Title (A Side/B Side)	Yr	VG	VG+	NM
❏ 5029	Your Kind of Love/Let's Start a Romance	1961	3.00	6.00	12.00

BACK BEAT

Number	Title (A Side/B Side)	Yr	VG	VG+	NM
❏ 519	I Know/Ladder of Prayer	1958	3.75	7.50	15.00
❏ 526	Pretty Little Mama/Will You	1959	3.75	7.50	15.00
❏ 526 [PS]	Pretty Little Mama/Will You	1959	7.50	15.00	30.00
❏ 532	If You Love Me/A Thousand Cups of Happiness	1960	3.75	7.50	15.00
❏ 535	The Girls in My Life/Come On Baby	1961	3.75	7.50	15.00
❏ 537	You Know It Ain't Right/Lovre Sick Blues	1963	3.00	6.00	12.00
❏ 539	Better to Give Than Receive/There Is No In Between	1963	3.00	6.00	12.00
❏ 540	There Oughta Be a Law/You're My Girl	1964	3.00	6.00	12.00
❏ 541	Funny/You Gotta Have Love	1964	3.75	7.50	15.00
❏ 545	I Want a Little Girl/True Love	1965	3.00	6.00	12.00
❏ 547	Darling Come and Talk to Me/Everything	1965	3.00	6.00	12.00
❏ 550	Pledging My Love/Just a Kid Named Joe	1965	3.00	6.00	12.00
❏ 565	I'm Waiting/How Long Can I Last	1966	2.50	5.00	10.00
❏ 574	If I Had Only Known/Lots of Love	1966	2.50	5.00	10.00
❏ 581	Close to My Heart/You've Been Good to Me	1967	2.50	5.00	10.00
❏ 589	I'm Satisfied/Be Ever Wonderful	1968	2.50	5.00	10.00
❏ 594	Got You on My Mind/Please	1968	2.50	5.00	10.00

SOUL

Number	Title (A Side/B Side)	Yr	VG	VG+	NM
❏ 35080	Let's Save the Children/You Are Blue	1971	6.25	12.50	25.00

Albums

BACK BEAT

Number	Title (A Side/B Side)	Yr	VG	VG+	NM
❏ B-60 [M]	Funny (How Time Slips Away)	1965	12.50	25.00	50.00
❏ BS-60 [S]	Funny (How Time Slips Away)	1965	17.50	35.00	70.00

DUKE

Number	Title (A Side/B Side)	Yr	VG	VG+	NM
❏ DLPS-91	Duke-Peacock Remembers Joe Hinton	1969	5.00	10.00	20.00

HIPPIES, THE
45s

PARKWAY

Number	Title (A Side/B Side)	Yr	VG	VG+	NM
❏ 863	Memory Lane/A Lonely Piano	1963	5.00	10.00	20.00

—Originally released as "The Tams"; B-side by Reggie Harrison

Number	Title (A Side/B Side)	Yr	VG	VG+	NM
HIPPY DIPPYS, THE					
45s					
UNI					
❏ 55004	Thoroughly Modern Millie/Jimmy	1967	3.00	6.00	12.00
HIRT, AL Also see PETE FOUNTAIN.					
45s					
GWP					
❏ 516	I Still See Elisa/The Gospel of No-Name City	1969	—	3.00	6.00
❏ 519	Louisiana Man/Break My Mind	1969	—	3.00	6.00
❏ 522	Orange Blossom Special/				
	I Really Don't Want to Know	1970	—	3.00	6.00
❏ 529	Glory of Love/I Can Dream, Can't I	1970	—	3.00	6.00
MONUMENT					
❏ 8619	Melody for Michele/Sweet Sauce	1974	—	2.00	4.00
❏ 8652	Feudin' Pipers (Dueling Banjos)/				
	Southern Scramble	1975	—	2.00	4.00
❏ 8671	The Sound of Jazz and the Scent of Jasmine/				
	Monkey Farm	1975	—	2.00	4.00
RCA VICTOR					
❏ 47-7854	Janine/Elegie	1961	2.50	5.00	10.00
❏ 47-7854 [PS]	Janine/Elegie	1961	3.00	6.00	12.00
❏ 47-7903	Perky/I'm On My Way	1961	2.50	5.00	10.00
❏ 47-8016	Al Di La/Talkin' About That River	1962	2.50	5.00	10.00
❏ 47-8104	Theme from "The Eleventh Hour"/Song from				
	"Two for the See-Saw"	1962	2.50	5.00	10.00
❏ 47-8128	Pickin' Cotton/Roman Nocturne	1963	2.50	5.00	10.00
❏ 47-8128 [PS]	Pickin' Cotton/Roman Nocturne	1963	3.00	6.00	12.00
❏ 47-8280	Java/I Can't Get Started	1963	2.00	4.00	8.00
❏ 47-8346	Cotton Candy/Walkin'	1964	2.00	4.00	8.00
❏ 47-8391	Sugar Lips/Poupee Brisee	1964	2.00	4.00	8.00
❏ 47-8439	Up Above My Head (I Hear Music in the Air)/				
	September Song	1964	2.00	4.00	8.00
❏ 47-8478	Hooray for Santa Claus/White Christmas	1964	3.00	6.00	12.00
❏ 47-8478 [PS]	Hooray for Santa Claus/White Christmas	1964	3.75	7.50	15.00
❏ 47-8487	Fancy Pants/Star Dust	1964	2.00	4.00	8.00
❏ 47-8542	Al's Place/Mister Sandman	1965	2.00	4.00	8.00
❏ 47-8653	The Silence (Il Silenzio)/Love Theme from "The				
	Sandpiper"	1965	2.00	4.00	8.00
❏ 47-8684	Feelin' Fruggy/Louisiana Lullaby	1965	2.00	4.00	8.00
❏ 47-8706	Nutty Jingle Bells/Santa Claus Is Comin' to Town	1965	2.50	5.00	10.00
❏ 47-8706 [PS]	Nutty Jingle Bells/Santa Claus Is Comin' to Town	1965	3.00	6.00	12.00
❏ 47-8736	Yesterday/The Arena	1966	2.00	4.00	8.00
❏ 47-8774	Mame/Seven Days to Tahiti	1966	2.00	4.00	8.00
❏ 47-8774 [PS]	Mame/Seven Days to Tahiti	1966	2.50	5.00	10.00
❏ 47-8854	Skillet Lickin'/Trumpet Pickin'	1966	2.00	4.00	8.00
❏ 47-8925	Green Hornet Theme/Strawberry Jam	1966	3.00	6.00	12.00
❏ 47-9023	Theme from The Monkees/The Evil One	1966	2.50	5.00	10.00
❏ 47-9060	Music to Watch Girls By/His Girl	1967	2.00	4.00	8.00
❏ 47-9106	Boywatchers Theme/Yo Yo (Puppet Song)	1967	2.00	4.00	8.00
❏ 47-9198	Big Honey/Puppet on a String	1967	2.00	4.00	8.00
❏ 47-9285	Calypsoul/Honey Pot	1967	2.00	4.00	8.00
❏ 47-9381	Ludwig/Long Gone	1967	2.00	4.00	8.00
❏ 47-9417	Keep the Ball Rollin'/Manhattan Safari	1968	2.00	4.00	8.00
❏ 47-9500	We Can Fly-Up, Up and Away/The Glory of Love	1968	2.00	4.00	8.00
❏ 47-9539	The Odd Couple/				
	Do You Know the Way to San Jose	1968	2.50	5.00	10.00
❏ 47-9664	Those Were the Days/The Garbage	1968	2.00	4.00	8.00
❏ 47-9717	Penny Arcade/If	1969	2.00	4.00	8.00
Albums					
ACCORD					
❏ SN-7187	Java	1981	2.00	4.00	8.00
ALLEGIANCE					
❏ AV-5018	Showtime	1985	2.00	4.00	8.00
❏ AV-5032	Blues Line	1986	2.00	4.00	8.00
AUDIO FIDELITY					
❏ AFLP-1877 [M]	Swingin' Dixie (At Dan's Pier 600 in New				
	Orleans)	1959	3.75	7.50	15.00
❏ AFLP-1878 [M]	Swingin' Dixie	1959	3.75	7.50	15.00
❏ AFLP-1926 [M]	Swingin' Dixie (Vol. 3)	1961	3.75	7.50	15.00
❏ AFLP-1927 [M]	Swingin' Dixie (Vol. 4)	1961	3.75	7.50	15.00
❏ AFSD-5877 [S]	Swingin' Dixie (At Dan's Pier 600 in New				
	Orleans)	1959	5.00	10.00	20.00
❏ AFSD-5878 [S]	Swingin' Dixie	1959	5.00	10.00	20.00
❏ AFSD-5926 [S]	Swingin' Dixie (Vol. 3)	1961	5.00	10.00	20.00
❏ AFSD-5927 [S]	Swingin' Dixie (Vol. 4)	1961	5.00	10.00	20.00
❏ AF-6282	Hirt…So Good!	1978	2.50	5.00	10.00
❏ ST-90284 [S]	Swingin' Dixie (Vol. 3)	196?	5.00	10.00	20.00
—Capitol Record Club edition					
❏ T-90284 [M]	Swingin' Dixie (Vol. 3)	196?	5.00	10.00	20.00
—Capitol Record Club edition					
CORAL					
❏ CRL 57402 [M]	Al Hirt in New Orleans	1962	3.00	6.00	12.00
❏ CRL 757402 [S]	Al Hirt in New Orleans	1962	3.75	7.50	15.00
CROWN					
❏ CST-457 [S]	The Dawn Busters	196?	3.00	6.00	12.00
❏ CLP-5457 [M]	The Dawn Busters	196?	3.00	6.00	12.00
GHB					
❏ 107	Mardi Gras Parade Music	197?	2.50	5.00	10.00
GWP					
❏ 2002	Paint Your Wagon	1970	2.50	5.00	10.00
❏ 2004	Al Hirt Gold	1971	2.50	5.00	10.00
❏ 2005	Al Hirt Country	1971	2.50	5.00	10.00
LONGINES SYMPHONETTE					
❏ LWCP 1	The Best of Dixieland Jazz	196?	3.00	6.00	12.00
METRO					
❏ M-517 [M]	Al Hirt	1965	2.50	5.00	10.00
❏ MS-517 [S]	Al Hirt	1965	3.00	6.00	12.00
MONUMENT					
❏ 6642	Raw Sugar/Sweet Sauce/Banana Puddin'	1976	2.00	4.00	8.00
—Reissue of 32913					
❏ 7603	Jumbo's Gumbo	1977	2.00	4.00	8.00
—Reissue of 33885					
❏ KZ 32913	Raw Sugar/Sweet Sauce/Banana Puddin'	1974	2.50	5.00	10.00
❏ PZ 33885	Jumbo's Gumbo	1975	2.50	5.00	10.00

Number	Title (A Side/B Side)	Yr	VG	VG+	NM
PAIR					
❏ PDL2-1048 [(2)]	New Orleans By Night	1986	3.00	6.00	12.00
RCA CAMDEN					
❏ CAL-2138 [M]	Struttin' Down Royal Street	1967	3.00	6.00	12.00
❏ CAS-2138 [S]	Struttin' Down Royal Street	1967	2.50	5.00	10.00
❏ CAS-2316	Al's Place	1970	2.50	5.00	10.00
❏ CAS-2573	Have a Merry Little	1971	2.50	5.00	10.00
❏ CXS-9015 [(2)]	Al Hirt Blows His Own Horn	1972	3.00	6.00	12.00
RCA VICTOR					
❏ ANL1-1034	The Best of Al Hirt	1975	2.50	5.00	10.00
❏ LPM-2354 [M]	Al (He's the King) Hirt and His Band	1961	3.00	6.00	12.00
❏ LSP-2354 [S]	Al (He's the King) Hirt and His Band	1961	3.75	7.50	15.00
❏ LPM-2366 [M]	The Greatest Horn in the World	1961	3.00	6.00	12.00
❏ LSP-2366 [S]	The Greatest Horn in the World	1961	3.75	7.50	15.00
❏ LPM-2446 [M]	Horn A-Plenty	1962	3.00	6.00	12.00
❏ LSP-2446 [S]	Horn A-Plenty	1962	3.75	7.50	15.00
❏ LPM-2497 [M]	Al Hirt at the Mardi Gras	1962	3.00	6.00	12.00
❏ LSP-2497 [S]	Al Hirt at the Mardi Gras	1962	3.75	7.50	15.00
❏ LPM-2584 [M]	Trumpet and Strings	1962	3.00	6.00	12.00
❏ LSP-2584 [S]	Trumpet and Strings	1962	3.75	7.50	15.00
❏ LPM-2607 [M]	Our Man in New Orleans	1963	3.00	6.00	12.00
❏ LSP-2607 [S]	Our Man in New Orleans	1963	3.75	7.50	15.00
❏ LM-2729 [M]	"Pops" Goes the Trumpet	1964	3.75	7.50	15.00
❏ LSC-2729 [S]	"Pops" Goes the Trumpet	1964	5.00	10.00	20.00
—With the Boston Pops Orchestra conducted by Arthur Fiedler					
❏ LPM-2733 [M]	Honey in the Horn	1963	3.00	6.00	12.00
❏ LSP-2733 [S]	Honey in the Horn	1963	3.75	7.50	15.00
❏ LPM-2917 [M]	Cotton Candy	1964	3.00	6.00	12.00
❏ LSP-2917 [S]	Cotton Candy	1964	3.75	7.50	15.00
❏ LPM-2965 [M]	Sugar Lips	1964	3.00	6.00	12.00
❏ LSP-2965 [S]	Sugar Lips	1964	3.75	7.50	15.00
❏ LPM-3309 [M]	The Best of Al Hirt	1965	3.00	6.00	12.00
❏ LSP-3309 [S]	The Best of Al Hirt	1965	3.75	7.50	15.00
❏ LPM-3337 [M]	That Honey Horn Sound	1965	3.00	6.00	12.00
❏ LSP-3337 [S]	That Honey Horn Sound	1965	3.75	7.50	15.00
❏ LPM-3416 [M]	Live at Carnegie Hall	1965	3.00	6.00	12.00
❏ LSP-3416 [S]	Live at Carnegie Hall	1965	3.75	7.50	15.00
❏ LPM-3417 [M]	The Sound of Christmas	1965	2.50	5.00	10.00
❏ LSP-3417 [S]	The Sound of Christmas	1965	3.00	6.00	12.00
❏ LPM-3492 [M]	They're Playing Our Song	1966	3.00	6.00	12.00
❏ LSP-3492 [S]	They're Playing Our Song	1966	3.75	7.50	15.00
❏ LPM-3556 [M]	The Best of Al Hirt, Volume 2	1966	3.00	6.00	12.00
❏ LSP-3556 [S]	The Best of Al Hirt, Volume 2	1966	3.75	7.50	15.00
❏ LPM-3579 [M]	The Happy Trumpet	1966	3.00	6.00	12.00
❏ LSP-3579 [S]	The Happy Trumpet	1966	3.75	7.50	15.00
❏ LPM-3653 [M]	Latin in the Horn	1966	3.00	6.00	12.00
❏ LSP-3653 [S]	Latin in the Horn	1966	3.75	7.50	15.00
❏ LPM-3716 [M]	The Horn Meets the Hornet	1967	3.00	6.00	12.00
❏ LSP-3716 [S]	The Horn Meets the Hornet	1967	3.75	7.50	15.00
❏ LPM-3773 [M]	Music to Watch Girls By	1967	3.75	7.50	15.00
❏ LPM-3878 [M]	Soul in the Horn	1967	3.75	7.50	15.00
❏ LSP-3878 [S]	Soul in the Horn	1967	3.75	7.50	15.00
❏ LPM-3917 [M]	Al Hirt Plays Bert Kaempfert	1968	5.00	10.00	20.00
❏ LSP-3917 [S]	Al Hirt Plays Bert Kaempfert	1968	3.75	7.50	15.00
❏ LPM-3979 [M]	Unforgettable	1968	6.25	12.50	25.00
❏ LSP-3979 [S]	Unforgettable	1968	3.00	6.00	12.00
❏ LSP-4020	In Love with You	1968	3.00	6.00	12.00
❏ LSP-4101	Al Hirt Now	1969	3.00	6.00	12.00
❏ LSP-4161	Here in My Heart	1969	3.00	6.00	12.00
❏ LSP-4247	Al Hirt	1970	3.00	6.00	12.00
❏ VPS-6025 [(2)]	This Is Al Hirt	1970	3.75	7.50	15.00
❏ VPS-6057 [(2)]	This Is Al Hirt, Volume 2	1972	3.75	7.50	15.00
VERVE					
❏ MGV-1012 [M]	Swinging Dixie from Dan's Pier 600	1957	12.50	25.00	50.00
❏ MGV-1027 [M]	Blockbustin' Dixie!	195?	10.00	20.00	40.00
❏ V-1027 [M]	Blockbustin' Dixie!	1961	5.00	10.00	20.00
VOCALION					
❏ VL 73907	Floatin' Down to Cotton Town	1970	2.50	5.00	10.00
WYNCOTE					
❏ 9089	The Dawn Busters	196?	2.50	5.00	10.00
HIRT, AL, AND ANN-MARGRET Also see each artist's individual listings.					
Albums					
RCA VICTOR					
❏ LPM-2690 [M]	Beauty and the Beard	1964	6.25	12.50	25.00
❏ LSP-2690 [S]	Beauty and the Beard	1964	7.50	15.00	30.00
HIRT, AL, AND PETE FOUNTAIN See PETE FOUNTAIN AND AL HIRT.					
HIT COMBO, THE					
45s					
HIT					
❏ 08	Stranger on the Shore/Twist Twist Senora	1962	2.00	4.00	8.00
—B-side by Herbert Hunter					
❏ 09	Soul Twist/What'd I Say	1962	2.00	4.00	8.00
—B-side by Ray Fowler					
HIT PACK, THE					
45s					
SOUL					
❏ 35010	Never Say No to Your Baby/Let's Dance	1965	12.50	25.00	50.00
HO, DON					
45s					
HEL					
❏ 149	Christmas Is for Everyone/				
	Christmas Is You and Me	1977	—	2.00	4.00
❏ 149 [PS]	Christmas Is for Everyone/				
	Christmas Is You and Me	1977	—	2.00	4.00
MEGA					
❏ 1215	Watch Out Woman/A New Love Song	1974	—	2.00	4.00
❏ 1225	Today I Started Loving You Again/				
	Take a Walk in the Country	1975	—	2.00	4.00
REPRISE					
❏ 0388	I'll Remember You/E Lei Ka Lei Lei	1965	2.00	4.00	8.00
❏ 0441	Suck 'Em Up/La Haina Luna	1965	2.00	4.00	8.00
❏ 0451	Sweet Someone/La Haina Luna	1966	2.00	4.00	8.00

Number	Title (A Side/B Side)	Yr	VG	VG+	NM
❏ 0507	Tiny Bubbles/Born Free	1966	2.00	4.00	8.00
❏ 0573	I Love You/All That's Left Is the Lemon Tree	1967	2.00	4.00	8.00
❏ 0590	Tiny Bubbles/Macao	1967	2.50	5.00	10.00
❏ 0591	What Now My Love/One Paddle, Two Paddle	1967	2.00	4.00	8.00
❏ 0600	Tomorrow/This Sacred Hour	1967	2.00	4.00	8.00
❏ 0609	Forbidden Fruit/Sleepy Summer Days	1967	2.00	4.00	8.00
❏ 0643	The Windward Side (Of the Island)/Tu Tu Kane	1967	2.00	4.00	8.00
❏ 0669	Instant Happy/White Silver Sands	1968	—	3.00	6.00
❏ 0705	Tiny Bubbles/Do I Love You	1968	—	2.00	4.00

—"Back to Back Hits" series

Number	Title (A Side/B Side)	Yr	VG	VG+	NM
❏ 0754	Remembering/Sunny Days, Starry Nights	1968	—	3.00	6.00
❏ 0800	Galveston/Has Anybody Lost a Love	1968	—	3.00	6.00
❏ 0871	Honey Come Back/Sands of Waikiki	1969	—	3.00	6.00
❏ 0896	It Must Have Been the Wine/Questions	1970	—	2.50	5.00
❏ 0936	Melody Fair/Only Foolish People	1970	—	2.50	5.00
❏ 0950	Gotta Move Along/Home	1970	—	2.50	5.00
❏ 0960	This Is America/United We Stand	1970	—	2.50	5.00
❏ 1016	My God and I/What Do I Need to Be Free	1971	—	2.00	4.00
❏ 1059	Waikiki/Chotto Matte Kidasi	1971	—	2.00	4.00

Albums
REPRISE

Number	Title	Yr	VG	VG+	NM
❏ R-6161 [M]	The Don Ho Show	1965	3.00	6.00	12.00
❏ RS-6161 [S]	The Don Ho Show	1965	3.75	7.50	15.00
❏ R-6186 [M]	Don Ho…Again!	1966	2.50	5.00	10.00
❏ RS-6186 [S]	Don Ho…Again!	1966	3.00	6.00	12.00
❏ R-6219 [M]	You're Gonna Hear From Me	1966	2.50	5.00	10.00
❏ RS-6219 [S]	You're Gonna Hear From Me	1966	3.00	6.00	12.00
❏ R-6232 [M]	Tiny Bubbles	1966	2.50	5.00	10.00
❏ RS-6232 [S]	Tiny Bubbles	1966	3.00	6.00	12.00
❏ R-6244 [M]	East Coast/West Coast	1967	3.00	6.00	12.00
❏ RS-6244 [S]	East Coast/West Coast	1967	3.00	6.00	12.00
❏ RS-6283	Instant Happy	1968	3.00	6.00	12.00
❏ RS-6303	Hawaii-Ho!	1968	3.00	6.00	12.00
❏ RS-6331	Suck 'Em Up	1969	3.00	6.00	12.00
❏ RS-6357	Don Ho — Greatest Hits!	1969	3.00	6.00	12.00
❏ RS-6367	The Don Ho TV Show	1969	3.00	6.00	12.00
❏ RS-6418	Hawaii's Greatest Hits	1970	2.50	5.00	10.00
❏ RS-6461	Don Ho at the Polynesian Palace	1970	2.50	5.00	10.00

HO-DADS, THE
45s
IMPERIAL

Number	Title	Yr	VG	VG+	NM
❏ 66001	Legends/Honey	1963	7.50	15.00	30.00
❏ 66023	After Dark/Space Race	1964	7.50	15.00	30.00

HOBBITS, THE
45s
DECCA

Number	Title	Yr	VG	VG+	NM
❏ 32226	Sunny Day Girl/Daffodil Days	1967	3.00	6.00	12.00
❏ 32270	Pretty Young Thing/Strawberry Children	1968	3.00	6.00	12.00

ZAR

Number	Title	Yr	VG	VG+	NM
❏ 25	Frodo Lives/Jolly Good Fellow	1967	5.00	10.00	20.00

Albums
DECCA

Number	Title	Yr	VG	VG+	NM
❏ DL 4920 [M]	Down to Middle-Earth	1967	10.00	20.00	40.00
❏ DL 5009 [M]	Men and Doors	1968	20.00	40.00	80.00
❏ DL 74920 [S]	Down to Middle-Earth	1967	12.50	25.00	50.00
❏ DL 75009 [S]	Men and Doors	1968	7.50	15.00	30.00

HODGE, CHRIS
45s
APPLE

Number	Title	Yr	VG	VG+	NM
❏ 1850	We're On Our Way/Supersoul	1972	2.00	4.00	8.00
❏ 1850 [PS]	We're On Our Way/Supersoul	1972	2.50	5.00	10.00
❏ 1858	Goodnight Sweet Lorraine/Contact Love	1973	2.00	4.00	8.00

RCA VICTOR

Number	Title	Yr	VG	VG+	NM
❏ APBO-0289	Beautiful Love/Sweet Lady from the Sky	1974	—	2.50	5.00

HODGES, EDDIE
45s
AURORA

Number	Title	Yr	VG	VG+	NM
❏ 150	Across the Street (Is a Million Miles Away)/ She Doesn't Love Me	1965	2.50	5.00	10.00
❏ 153	New Orleans/Hard Times for Young Lovers	1965	2.50	5.00	10.00
❏ 156	Love Minus Zero (No Limit)/ The Water Is Over My Head	1965	2.50	5.00	10.00
❏ 161	Hitch Hike/Old Man Rag	1966	2.50	5.00	10.00

CADENCE

Number	Title	Yr	VG	VG+	NM
❏ 1397	I'm Gonna Knock on Your Door/ Ain't Gonna Wash for a Week	1961	3.75	7.50	15.00

—Red and black label with "Cadence Records" along edge three times

Number	Title	Yr	VG	VG+	NM
❏ 1397	I'm Gonna Knock on Your Door/Ain't Gonna Wash for a Week	1961	6.25	12.50	25.00

—Maroon and silver label with metronome at top

Number	Title	Yr	VG	VG+	NM
❏ 1397 [PS]	I'm Gonna Knock on Your Door/Ain't Gonna Wash for a Week	1961	6.25	12.50	25.00
❏ 1410	Bandit of My Dreams/Mugmates	1962	5.00	10.00	20.00
❏ 1421	(Girls, Girls, Girls) Made to Love/I Make Believe It's You	1962	3.75	7.50	15.00

COLUMBIA

Number	Title	Yr	VG	VG+	NM
❏ 42649	Seein' Is Believin'/Secret	1962	3.00	6.00	12.00
❏ 42649 [PS]	Seein' Is Believin'/Secret	1962	4.00	8.00	16.00
❏ 42697	Would You Come Back?/Too Soon to Know	1962	3.00	6.00	12.00
❏ 42811	Rainin' in My Heart/Halfway	1963	3.00	6.00	12.00

DECCA

Number	Title	Yr	VG	VG+	NM
❏ 30675	That Funny Little Dog/ What Would It Be Like in Heaven	1958	3.75	7.50	15.00
❏ 30903	High Hopes/Don't Dance on Momma's Rug	1959	3.75	7.50	15.00

MGM

Number	Title	Yr	VG	VG+	NM
❏ 13219	Avalanche/Just a Kid in Love	1964	2.50	5.00	10.00

HOFFMAN, ABBIE
Albums
BIG TOE

Number	Title	Yr	VG	VG+	NM
❏ 1	Wake Up, America!	196?	7.50	15.00	30.00

HOG HEAVEN   The Shondells after Tommy James went solo.
45s
ROULETTE

Number	Title (A Side/B Side)	Yr	VG	VG+	NM
❏ 7091	Theme from a Thought/(B-side unknown)	1970	2.00	4.00	8.00
❏ 7101	Happy/Prayer	1971	2.00	4.00	8.00
❏ 7106	If It Feels Good/(B-side unknown)	1971	2.00	4.00	8.00

Albums
ROULETTE

Number	Title	Yr	VG	VG+	NM
❏ SR 42057	Hog Heaven	1971	5.00	10.00	20.00

HOGG, SMOKEY
45s
COMBO

Number	Title	Yr	VG	VG+	NM
❏ 11	Where Have You Been/ Believe I'll Change My Towns	1952	50.00	100.00	200.00

—Also had releases on Combo 4 and 9, but these are unknown on 45

EBB

Number	Title	Yr	VG	VG+	NM
❏ 127	Good Morning Baby/Sure 'Nuff	1958	6.25	12.50	25.00

FEDERAL

Number	Title	Yr	VG	VG+	NM
❏ 12109	Keep a-Walkin'/Do It No More	1953	25.00	50.00	100.00
❏ 12117	Your Little Wagon/Penny Pinching Mama	1953	25.00	50.00	100.00
❏ 12127	Gone, Gone, Gone/I Ain't Got Over It Yet	1953	25.00	50.00	100.00

IMPERIAL

Number	Title	Yr	VG	VG+	NM
❏ 5269	When I've Been Drinkin'/Tear Me Down	1954	25.00	50.00	100.00
❏ 5290	My Baby's Gone/Train Whistle	1954	25.00	50.00	100.00

METEOR

Number	Title	Yr	VG	VG+	NM
❏ 5021	I Declare/Dark Clouds	1955	25.00	50.00	100.00

SPECIALTY

Number	Title	Yr	VG	VG+	NM
❏ 753	I Want My Baby for Christmas/I Want My Baby for Christmas	197?	2.50	5.00	10.00

—B-side by Jimmy Liggins

Albums
CROWN

Number	Title	Yr	VG	VG+	NM
❏ CLP-5226 [M]	Smokey Hogg Sings the Blues	1962	12.50	25.00	50.00

TIME

Number	Title	Yr	VG	VG+	NM
❏ 6 [M]	Smokey Hogg	1962	20.00	40.00	80.00

UNITED

Number	Title	Yr	VG	VG+	NM
❏ US-7745	Smokey Hogg	1970	3.00	6.00	12.00

HOGS, THE   Early version of THE CHOCOLATE WATCH BAND.
45s
HANNA-BARBERA

Number	Title	Yr	VG	VG+	NM
❏ 511	Loose Lip Sync Ships/Blues Theme	1967	37.50	75.00	150.00

—Contrary to previous reports, Frank Zappa was NOT involved with this record in any way

HOLDEN, RANDY
Albums
HOBBIT

Number	Title	Yr	VG	VG+	NM
❏ 5002	Population II	1968	50.00	100.00	200.00

HOLDEN, RON
45s
CHALLENGE

Number	Title	Yr	VG	VG+	NM
❏ 59360	I Tried/I'll Forgive and Forget	1967	10.00	20.00	40.00

DONNA

Number	Title	Yr	VG	VG+	NM
❏ 1315	Love You So/My Babe	1959	7.50	15.00	30.00
❏ 1324	Gee, But I'm Lonesome/Susie Jane	1960	6.25	12.50	25.00
❏ 1328	True Love Can Be/ Everything's Gonna Be Alright	1960	6.25	12.50	25.00
❏ 1331	Who Says There Ain't No Santa Claus/ Your Line Is Busy	1960	6.25	12.50	25.00
❏ 1335	The Big Shoe/Rock and Roll Call	1961	5.00	10.00	20.00

ELDO

Number	Title	Yr	VG	VG+	NM
❏ 117	I'll Be Happy/I'll Always Have You	1961	5.00	10.00	20.00

LANA

Number	Title	Yr	VG	VG+	NM
❏ 154	Love You So/My Babe	196?	2.00	4.00	8.00

—Oldies reissue

LOST-NITE

Number	Title	Yr	VG	VG+	NM
❏ 199	Love You So/My Babe	196?	—	2.50	5.00

—Reissue

Number	Title	Yr	VG	VG+	NM
❏ 207	Gee, But I'm Lonesome/Susie Jane	196?	—	2.50	5.00

—Reissue

NITE OWL

Number	Title	Yr	VG	VG+	NM
❏ 10	Love You So/My Babe	1959	200.00	400.00	800.00

NOW

Number	Title	Yr	VG	VG+	NM
❏ 6	Can You Talk?/I Need Ya	1974	—	3.00	6.00

RAMPART

Number	Title	Yr	VG	VG+	NM
❏ 645	Girl I Love You/Nothing I Wouldn't Do	1965	3.00	6.00	12.00

Albums
DONNA

Number	Title	Yr	VG	VG+	NM
❏ DLP-2111 [M]	I Love You So	1960	62.50	125.00	250.00
❏ DLPS-2111 [M]	I Love You So	1960	75.00	150.00	300.00

—Stereo records not known to exist; this is for a mono record in a stereo cover

HOLIDAY, BILLIE
45s
ATLANTIC

Number	Title	Yr	VG	VG+	NM
❏ 2923	Strange Fruit/I Love My Man	1973	—	3.00	6.00

CLEF

Number	Title	Yr	VG	VG+	NM
❏ 89089	My Man/He's Funny That Way	1954	3.75	7.50	15.00
❏ 89096	Remember/I Can't Face the Music	1954	3.75	7.50	15.00
❏ 89108	If the Moon Turns Green/Autumn in New York	1954	3.75	7.50	15.00
❏ 89132	How Deep Is the Ocean/ What a Little Moonlight Can Do	1955	3.75	7.50	15.00
❏ 89150	Love Me or Leave Me/I Thought About You	1955	3.75	7.50	15.00

COLUMBIA

Number	Title	Yr	VG	VG+	NM
❏ 1-613	Am I Blue/God Bless the Child	1950	12.50	25.00	50.00

—Microgroove 33 1/3 rpm 7-inch record, small hole

Number	Title	Yr	VG	VG+	NM
❏ S7 31706 [S]	(titles unknown)	1963	3.75	7.50	15.00
❏ S7 31707 [S]	(titles unknown)	1963	3.75	7.50	15.00
❏ S7 31708 [S]	(titles unknown)	1963	3.75	7.50	15.00
❏ S7 31709 [S]	You've Changed/It's Easy to Remember	1963	3.75	7.50	15.00
❏ S7 31710 [S]	But Beautiful/I'll Be Around	1963	3.75	7.50	15.00

—The above five are "Stereo Seven" 33 1/3 rpm jukebox singles from set "JS 7-71" entitled "Lady in Satin"

Number	Title (A Side/B Side)	Yr	VG	VG+	NM
DECCA					
❏ 27145	Them There Eyes/Keeps On Rainin'	1950	6.25	12.50	25.00
❏ 48259	Do Your Duty/The Blues Are Brewin'	1951	6.25	12.50	25.00
KENT GOSPEL					
❏ 3003	God Bless the Child/(Instrumental)	197?	2.00	4.00	8.00
MAINSTREAM					
❏ 614	Strange Fruit/Fine and Mellow	1964	2.00	4.00	8.00
MERCURY					
❏ 89002	These Foolish Things/I Only Have Eyes for You	1952	5.00	10.00	20.00
❏ 89003	You Turned the Tables on Me/Easy to Love	1952	5.00	10.00	20.00
❏ 89004	You Go to My Head/Blue Moon	1952	5.00	10.00	20.00
❏ 89005	East o' the Sun/Solitude	1952	5.00	10.00	20.00
❏ 89037	Lover Come Back to Me/Yesterdays	1953	5.00	10.00	20.00
❏ 89064	Stormy Weather/Tenderly	1953	5.00	10.00	20.00
MGM					
❏ 12813	Don't Worry 'Bout Me/Just One More Chance	1959	3.00	6.00	12.00
UNITED ARTISTS					
❏ 50999	My Man/Them There Eyes	1973	—	3.00	6.00
❏ 50999 [PS]	My Man/Them There Eyes	1973	2.50	5.00	10.00
VERVE					
❏ 10181	Strange Fruit/The Foolish Things	1959	3.00	6.00	12.00
7-Inch Extended Plays					
COLUMBIA					
❏ B-2534	*Gloomy Sunday/Am I Blue/Body and Soul/Long Gone Blues	195?	5.00	10.00	20.00
❏ B-2534 [PS]	Billie Holiday (Hall of Fame Series)	195?	5.00	10.00	20.00
DECCA					
❏ ED 2031	Easy Living/What Is This Thing Called Love// Them There Eyes/God Bless the Child	195?	5.00	10.00	20.00
❏ ED 2031 [PS]	Billie Holiday, Vol. 1	195?	5.00	10.00	20.00
Albums					
AMERICAN RECORDING SOCIETY					
❏ G-409 [M]	Billie Holiday Sings	1956	15.00	30.00	60.00
—Reissue of Clef 713					
❏ G-431 [M]	Lady Sings the Blues	1957	15.00	30.00	60.00
—Reissue of Clef 721					
ATLANTIC					
❏ 1614	Strange Fruit	1972	3.75	7.50	15.00
BLACKHAWK					
❏ BKH-50701	Billie Holiday at Monterey	1986	2.50	5.00	10.00
BULLDOG					
❏ 1007	Billie's Blues	198?	2.50	5.00	10.00
CLEF					
❏ MGC-118 [10]	Billie Holiday Sings	1953	45.00	90.00	180.00
❏ MGC-144 [10]	An Evening with Billie Holiday	1954	45.00	90.00	180.00
❏ MGC-161 [10]	Billie Holiday Favorites	1954	45.00	90.00	180.00
❏ MGC-169 [10]	Billie Holiday at Jazz at the Philharmonic	1955	45.00	90.00	180.00
❏ MGC-669 [M]	Music for Torching	1955	25.00	50.00	100.00
❏ MGC-686 [M]	A Recital by Billie Holiday	1956	30.00	60.00	120.00
—Reissue of 144 and 161 as one 12-inch LP					
❏ MGC-690 [M]	Solitude — Songs by Billie Holiday	1956	30.00	60.00	120.00
—Reissue of 118					
❏ MGC-713 [M]	Velvet Moods	1956	30.00	60.00	120.00
❏ MGC-721 [M]	Lady Sings the Blues	1956	30.00	60.00	120.00
COLLECTABLES					
❏ COL-5142	Fine and Mellow	198?	3.00	6.00	12.00
COLUMBIA					
❏ C3L 21 [(3)M]	The Golden Years	1962	12.50	25.00	50.00
—Red and black label with six "eye" logos					
❏ C3L 21 [(3)M]	The Golden Years	1963	6.25	12.50	25.00
—Red "Guaranteed High Fidelity" or "360 Sound" label					
❏ C3L 40 [(3)M]	The Golden Years, Volume 2	1966	7.50	15.00	30.00
—Red label, "Mono" at bottom					
❏ C3L 40 [(3)M]	The Golden Years, Volume 2	197?	5.00	10.00	20.00
—Orange labels					
❏ CL 637 [M]	Lady Day	1954	17.50	35.00	70.00
—Maroon label, gold print					
❏ CL 637 [M]	Lady Day	1956	10.00	20.00	40.00
—Red and black label with six "eye" logos					
❏ CL 637 [M]	Lady Day	1962	3.75	7.50	15.00
—Red "Guaranteed High Fidelity" or "360 Sound" label					
❏ CL 637 [M]	Lady Day	197?	3.00	6.00	12.00
—Orange label					
❏ CL 1157 [M]	Lady in Satin	1958	10.00	20.00	40.00
—Red and black label with six "eye" logos					
❏ CL 1157 [M]	Lady in Satin	1962	3.75	7.50	15.00
—Red "Guaranteed High Fidelity" or "360 Sound" label					
❏ CL 2666 [M]	Billie Holiday's Greatest Hits	1967	3.75	7.50	15.00
❏ CL 6129 [10]	Billie Holiday Sings	1950	50.00	100.00	200.00
❏ CL 6163 [10]	Billie Holiday Favorites	1951	50.00	100.00	200.00
❏ CS 8048 [S]	Lady in Satin	1958	10.00	20.00	40.00
—Red and black label with six "eye" logos					
❏ CS 8048 [S]	Lady in Satin	1962	3.75	7.50	15.00
—Red "Guaranteed High Fidelity" or "360 Sound" label					
❏ CS 8048 [S]	Lady in Satin	1999	6.25	12.50	25.00
—Classic Records reissue on audiophile vinyl					
❏ G 30782 [(2)]	God Bless the Child	1972	5.00	10.00	20.00
❏ C 32080	Billie's Blues/The Original Recordings by Billie Holiday	1973	3.75	7.50	15.00
❏ PC 32080	Billie's Blues/The Original Recordings by Billie Holiday	198?	2.00	4.00	8.00
—Reissue of Harmony LP					
❏ CG 32121 [(2)]	The Billie Holiday Story, Volume 1	1973	3.75	7.50	15.00
❏ CG 32124 [(2)]	The Billie Holiday Story, Volume 2	1973	3.75	7.50	15.00
❏ CG 32127 [(2)]	The Billie Holiday Story, Volume 3	1973	3.75	7.50	15.00
COLUMBIA JAZZ MASTERPIECES					
❏ CJ 40247	Lady in Satin	1987	2.50	5.00	10.00
❏ CJ 40646	The Quintessential Billie Holiday, Vol. 1	1987	2.50	5.00	10.00
❏ CJ 40790	The Quintessential Billie Holiday, Vol. 2	1987	2.50	5.00	10.00
❏ CJ 44048	The Quintessential Billie Holiday, Vol. 3	1988	2.50	5.00	10.00
❏ CJ 44252	The Quintessential Billie Holiday, Vol. 4	1988	2.50	5.00	10.00
❏ CJ 44423	The Quintessential Billie Holiday, Vol. 5	1989	2.50	5.00	10.00
❏ C 45449	The Quintessential Billie Holiday, Vol. 6	1990	2.50	5.00	10.00
❏ C 46180	The Quintessential Billie Holiday, Vol. 7	1990	2.50	5.00	10.00
COLUMBIA MUSICAL TREASURY					
❏ P3M 5869 [(3)]	The Golden Years	197?	5.00	10.00	20.00
COLUMBIA SPECIAL PRODUCTS					
❏ P 14338	Swing, Brother, Swing	198?	2.50	5.00	10.00
COMMODORE					
❏ FL-20005 [10]	Billie Holiday, Volume 1	1950	62.50	125.00	250.00
❏ FL-20006 [10]	Billie Holiday, Volume 2	1950	62.50	125.00	250.00
❏ DL-30008 [M]	Billie Holiday	1959	12.50	25.00	50.00
—Reissue of 20006					
❏ DL-30011 [M]	Billie Holiday with Eddie Heywood and His Orchestra	1959	12.50	25.00	50.00
—Reissue of 20005					
CROWN					
❏ CST-380 [R]	Billie Holiday & Vivian Fears	196?	3.00	6.00	12.00
❏ CLP-5380 [M]	Billie Holiday & Vivian Fears	196?	5.00	10.00	20.00
DECCA					
❏ DXB-161 [(2)M]	The Billie Holiday Story	1959	5.00	10.00	20.00
❏ DL 5345 [10]	Lover Man	1951	50.00	100.00	200.00
❏ DXSB-7161 [(2)R]	The Billie Holiday Story	1959	3.75	7.50	15.00
❏ DL 8215 [M]	The Lady Sings	1956	15.00	30.00	60.00
❏ DL 8701 [M]	The Blues Are Brewin'	1958	15.00	30.00	60.00
❏ DL 8702 [M]	Lover Man	1958	15.00	30.00	60.00
❏ DL 75040	Billie Holiday's Greatest Hits	1968	3.00	6.00	12.00
ESP-DISK'					
❏ 3002	The Lady Lives, Vol. 1	1973	3.00	6.00	12.00
❏ 3003	The Lady Lives, Vol. 2	1973	3.00	6.00	12.00
EVEREST ARCHIVE OF FOLK & JAZZ					
❏ 265	Billie Holiday	197?	3.00	6.00	12.00
❏ FS-310	Billie Holiday, Vol. 2	1976	3.00	6.00	12.00
HALL					
❏ 622	I've Gotta Right to Sing	197?	3.00	6.00	12.00
HARMONY					
❏ KH 32080	Billie's Blues	1973	2.50	5.00	10.00
INTERMEDIA					
❏ QS-5076	Billie Holiday Talks and Sings	198?	2.50	5.00	10.00
JAZZ MAN					
❏ 5005	Billie Holiday at Storyville	198?	2.50	5.00	10.00
JAZZTONE					
❏ J-1209 [M]	Billie Holiday Sings	1955	12.50	25.00	50.00
—Reissue of Commodore 20005					
JOLLY ROGER					
❏ 5020 [10]	Billie Holiday, Volume 1	1954	25.00	50.00	100.00
❏ 5021 [10]	Billie Holiday, Volume 2	1954	25.00	50.00	100.00
❏ 5022 [10]	Billie Holiday, Volume 3	1954	25.00	50.00	100.00
KENT GOSPEL					
❏ KST 600	Billie Holiday Sings	197?	3.75	7.50	15.00
MAINSTREAM					
❏ S-6000 [R]	The Commodore Recordings	1965	3.00	6.00	12.00
❏ S-6022 [R]	Once Upon a Time	1965	3.00	6.00	12.00
❏ 56000 [M]	The Commodore Recordings	1965	6.25	12.50	25.00
❏ 56022 [M]	Once Upon a Time	1965	6.25	12.50	25.00
MCA					
❏ 275	Billie Holiday's Greatest Hits	1973	2.50	5.00	10.00
—Reissue of Decca 75040					
❏ 4006 [(2)]	The Billie Holiday Story	1973	3.00	6.00	12.00
—Reissue of Decca 7161					
METRO					
❏ M-515 [M]	Billie Holiday	1965	3.75	7.50	15.00
❏ MS-515 [R]	Billie Holiday	1965	3.00	6.00	12.00
MGM					
❏ GAS-122	Billie Holiday (Golden Archive Series)	1970	3.00	6.00	12.00
❏ E-3764 [M]	Billie Holiday	1959	10.00	20.00	40.00
❏ SE-3764 [S]	Billie Holiday	1959	12.50	25.00	50.00
❏ M3G-4948	Archetypes	1974	3.00	6.00	12.00
MOBILE FIDELITY					
❏ 1-247	Body and Soul	1996	30.00	60.00	120.00
—Audiophile vinyl					
MONMOUTH/EVERGREEN					
❏ 7046	Gallant Lady	1973	3.00	6.00	12.00
PARAMOUNT					
❏ PA-6059	Songs and Conversations	1973	3.00	6.00	12.00
PHOENIX 10					
❏ PHX-312	Billie Holiday Live	1981	2.00	4.00	8.00
PICKWICK					
❏ PC-3335	Billie Holiday Sings the Blues	197?	2.50	5.00	10.00
RIC					
❏ M-2001 [M]	Rare Live Recording	1964	6.25	12.50	25.00
SCORE					
❏ SLP-4014 [M]	Billie Holiday Sings the Blues	1957	30.00	60.00	120.00
SOLID STATE					
❏ 18040	Lady Love	1969	3.00	6.00	12.00
SUNSET					
❏ SUM-1147 [M]	Shades of Blue	1967	3.00	6.00	12.00
❏ SUS-5147 [R]	Shades of Blue	1967	2.50	5.00	10.00
TIME-LIFE					
❏ STL-J-03 [(3)]	Giants of Jazz	1979	7.50	15.00	30.00
—Alternate number is Columbia Special Products P3 14786					
TOTEM					
❏ 1037	Billie Holiday On the Air	198?	2.50	5.00	10.00
TRIP					
❏ 5024	Billie Holiday Live	1974	2.50	5.00	10.00
UNITED ARTISTS					
❏ UAS-5625	Lady Love	1972	2.50	5.00	10.00
—Reissue of 15014					
❏ UAJ-14014 [M]	Lady Love	1962	10.00	20.00	40.00
❏ UASJ-15014 [S]	Lady Love	1962	12.50	25.00	50.00
VERVE					
❏ VSP-5 [M]	Lady	1966	3.75	7.50	15.00
❏ VSPS-5 [R]	Lady	1966	3.00	6.00	12.00
❏ VE-2-2503 [(2)]	The First Verve Sessions	1976	3.75	7.50	15.00
❏ VE-2-2515 [(2)]	Stormy Blues	1976	3.75	7.50	15.00
❏ VE-2-2529 [(2)]	All or Nothing at All	198?	3.75	7.50	15.00
❏ MGVS-6021 [S]	Songs for Distingue Lovers	1960	15.00	30.00	60.00

Number	Title (A Side/B Side)	Yr	VG	VG+	NM
❑ MGVS-6021 [S]Songs for Distingue Lovers		199?	6.25	12.50	25.00
—Classic Records reissue on audiophile vinyl					
❑ MGVS-6021-45 [(2)S]Songs for Distingue Lovers		1999	5.00	10.00	20.00
—Classic Records reissue on two 12-inch 45-rpm records					
❑ MGV-8026 [M] Music for Torching		1957	10.00	20.00	40.00
—Reissue of Clef 669					
❑ V-8026 [M]	Music for Torching	1961	5.00	10.00	20.00
❑ MGV-8027 [M] A Recital by Billie Holiday		1957	10.00	20.00	40.00
—Reissue of Clef 686					
❑ V-8027 [M]	A Recital by Billie Holiday	1961	5.00	10.00	20.00
❑ MGV-8074 [M] Solitude — Songs by Billie Holiday		1957	10.00	20.00	40.00
—Reissue of Clef 690					
❑ V-8074 [M]	Solitude — Songs by Billie Holiday	1961	5.00	10.00	20.00
❑ V6-8074 [R]	Solitude — Songs by Billie Holiday	196?	3.00	6.00	12.00
❑ MGV-8096 [M] Velvet Moods		1957	10.00	20.00	40.00
—Reissue of Clef 713					
❑ V-8096 [M]	Velvet Moods	1961	5.00	10.00	20.00
❑ MGV-8099 [M] Lady Sings the Blues		1957	10.00	20.00	40.00
—Reissue of Clef 721					
❑ V-8099 [M]	Lady Sings the Blues	1957	5.00	10.00	20.00
❑ MGV-8197 [M]	Body and Soul	1957	15.00	30.00	60.00
❑ V-8197 [M]	Body and Soul	1961	5.00	10.00	20.00
❑ MGV-8257 [M]	Songs for Distingue Lovers	1958	15.00	30.00	60.00
❑ V-8257 [M]	Songs for Distingue Lovers	1961	5.00	10.00	20.00
❑ V6-8257 [S]	Songs for Distingue Lovers	1961	6.25	12.50	25.00
❑ MGV-8302 [M]	Stay with Me	1959	12.50	25.00	50.00
❑ V-8302 [M]	Stay with Me	1961	5.00	10.00	20.00
❑ MGV-8329 [M]	All or Nothing at All	1959	12.50	25.00	50.00
❑ V-8329 [M]	All or Nothing at All	1959	5.00	10.00	20.00
❑ V6-8329 [R]	All or Nothing at All	196?	3.00	6.00	12.00
❑ MGV-8338-2 [(2)M]The Unforgettable Lady Day		1959	20.00	40.00	80.00
❑ V-8338-2 [(2)M]The Unforgettable Lady Day		1961	6.25	12.50	25.00
❑ V-8410 [M]	The Essential Billie Holiday	1961	5.00	10.00	20.00
❑ V6-8410 [R]	The Essential Billie Holiday	1961	3.00	6.00	12.00
❑ V-8505 [M]	The Essential Jazz Vocals	1963	5.00	10.00	20.00
❑ V6-8505 [R]	The Essential Jazz Vocals	1963	3.00	6.00	12.00
❑ V6-8808 [R]	The Best of Billie Holiday	1973	2.50	5.00	10.00
❑ 2V6S-8816 [(2)]History of the Real Billie Holiday		1973	3.75	7.50	15.00
❑ 817359-1 [(2)]	Embraceable You	198?	3.00	6.00	12.00
❑ 823230-1 [(2)]	Stormy Blues	198?	3.00	6.00	12.00
❑ 823233-1 [(2)]	History of the Real Billie Holiday	198?	3.00	6.00	12.00
❑ 823246-1	The Billie Holiday Songbook	198?	2.50	5.00	10.00
❑ 827160-1	All or Nothing at All	1987	2.50	5.00	10.00

HOLIDAY, BILLIE, AND STAN GETZ
Albums
DALE

Number	Title (A Side/B Side)	Yr	VG	VG+	NM
❑ 25 [10]	Billie and Stan	1951	100.00	200.00	400.00

HOLIDAY, BILLIE/AL HIBBLER
Albums
IMPERIAL

Number	Title (A Side/B Side)	Yr	VG	VG+	NM
❑ LP-9185 [M]	Billie Holiday, Al Hibbler and the Blues	1962	12.50	25.00	50.00
❑ LP-12185 [R]	Billie Holiday, Al Hibbler and the Blues	196?	7.50	15.00	30.00

HOLIDAY, GEORGIE
45s
DATE

Number	Title (A Side/B Side)	Yr	VG	VG+	NM
❑ 1541	Have a Gluey Christmas/ Clarence the Cross-Eyed Bear	1966	3.00	6.00	12.00
—As " 'Little' Georgie Holiday"					

MAP CITY

Number	Title (A Side/B Side)	Yr	VG	VG+	NM
❑ 302	Have a Gluey Christmas/ A Little Boy's Christmas Prayer	1969	2.50	5.00	10.00

HOLIDAY, JIMMY
45s
DIAL

Number	Title (A Side/B Side)	Yr	VG	VG+	NM
❑ 1004	Save Me/Sing a Song of Love	1971	2.00	4.00	8.00
DIPLOMACY					
❑ 20	The New Breed/Love Me One More Time	1965	3.00	6.00	12.00
❑ 23	I Can't Stand It/I've Been Done Wrong	1965	3.00	6.00	12.00
EVEREST					
❑ 2022	How Can I Forget/Janet	1963	3.75	7.50	15.00
❑ 2027	Don't Laugh/Poor Boy	1963	3.00	6.00	12.00
❑ 2034	Country Girl/I've Got a Woman	1963	3.00	6.00	12.00
❑ 2038	I Lied/Alison	1964	3.00	6.00	12.00
❑ 2049	I Believe in Love/One More Thing	1964	3.00	6.00	12.00
❑ 2056	Ol' Man River/Hollywood	1965	3.00	6.00	12.00
KENT					
❑ 482	I Can't Stand It/The New Breed	1968	2.50	5.00	10.00
MINIT					
❑ 32002	Baby I Love You/You Won't Get Away	1966	3.00	6.00	12.00
❑ 32011	Turning Point/I'm Gonna Move to the City	1966	2.50	5.00	10.00
❑ 32021	Ready, Willing and Able/ We Got a Good Thing Goin'	1967	2.50	5.00	10.00
—With Clydie King					
❑ 32023	We Forgot About Love/I'm Gonna Help Hurry My Brothers Home	1967	2.50	5.00	10.00
❑ 32028	The Beauty of a Girl in Love/Everything Is Love	1967	2.50	5.00	10.00
❑ 32040	Spread Your Love/We Got a Good Thing Goin'	1968	2.50	5.00	10.00
❑ 32053	I Don't Want to Hear It/I'm Gonna Use What I Got	1968	2.50	5.00	10.00
❑ 32058	If You've Got the Money, I've Got the Time/Baby Boy's in Love with You	1969	2.50	5.00	10.00
❑ 32079	Yesterday Died/Would You Like to Love Me	1969	2.50	5.00	10.00
❑ 32097	Man Ain't Nothin' Without a Woman/ I'm in Love with You	1970	2.50	5.00	10.00
OLDIES 45					
❑ 138	How Can I Forget/Janet	1964	2.50	5.00	10.00
—Reissue of Everest 2022					

Albums
MINIT

Number	Title (A Side/B Side)	Yr	VG	VG+	NM
❑ LP-24005 [M]	Turning Point	1966	7.50	15.00	30.00
❑ LP-40005 [S]	Turning Point	1966	10.00	20.00	40.00

HOLIDAY, JOHN E.
45s
ATLANTIC

Number	Title (A Side/B Side)	Yr	VG	VG+	NM
❑ 2091	Yes I Will Love You Tomorrow/ Till the End of Time	1961	5.00	10.00	20.00

HOLIDAY TRIO, THE
45s
SANTO

Number	Title (A Side/B Side)	Yr	VG	VG+	NM
❑ 500	Desperate/Dark Valley	196?	3.75	7.50	15.00

HOLIDAYS, THE (1) Detroit-based R&B group.
45s
GOLDEN WORLD

Number	Title (A Side/B Side)	Yr	VG	VG+	NM
❑ 36	Makin' Up Time/I'll Love You Forever	1966	6.25	12.50	25.00
❑ 47	No Greater Love/Watch Out Girl	1966	6.25	12.50	25.00
GROOVE CITY					
❑ 206	Easy Living/I've Lost You	196?	25.00	50.00	100.00
—As "The New Holidays"					
REVILOT					
❑ 205	Love's Creeping Up on Me/Never Alone	1967	7.50	15.00	30.00
❑ 210	I Know She Cares/I Keep Holding On	1967	7.50	15.00	30.00
❑ 226	I'll Keep Coming Back/ All That Is Required of You	1968	6.25	12.50	25.00

HOLIDAYS, THE (U) None of these are group (1), but exactly how many groups are represented here is not known.
45s
ANDIE

Number	Title (A Side/B Side)	Yr	VG	VG+	NM
❑ 5019	The Stars Will Remember/ Who Knows, Who Cares	1960	15.00	30.00	60.00
BRENT					
❑ 7018	Come Back to Me/No Other Love	1961	5.00	10.00	20.00
BRUNSWICK					
❑ 55084	Sands of Gold/French Riviera	1958	3.75	7.50	15.00
CORAL					
❑ 62430	Love and Learn/I Want You to Love Me	1964	5.00	10.00	20.00
DIXIE					
❑ 1156	Little Miss Hurt/I Got News for You	196?	7.50	15.00	30.00
GALAXY					
❑ 714	Send Back My Love/Deacon Brown	1962	5.00	10.00	20.00
❑ 714 [DJ]	Send Back My Love/Deacon Brown	1962	7.50	15.00	30.00
—Promo on colored vinyl					
KING					
❑ 1217	I'm a-Like a-You (Pizza Pie)/Rolling River	1953	7.50	15.00	30.00
❑ 1246	Just Out of Reach/Let the Dice Decide	1953	7.50	15.00	30.00
MELBA					
❑ 112	The Robin/Desperately	1957	75.00	150.00	300.00
MONUMENT					
❑ 431	Merry Christmas Song/A Very Merry Christmas	1960	3.75	7.50	15.00
NIX					
❑ 537	One Little Kiss/My Girl	1961	7.50	15.00	30.00
PAM					
❑ 111	Refreshing/Crazy Discharge	1959	50.00	100.00	200.00
ROBBEE					
❑ 103	Them There Eyes/The Kiss Cha Cha	1960	15.00	30.00	60.00
❑ 107	Lonely Summer/Then I'll Be Tired of You	1960	12.50	25.00	50.00
SPECIALTY					
❑ 533	Irene/Aw-Aw Baby	1954	10.00	20.00	40.00
TRACK					
❑ 101	Patty Ann/Big Brown Eyes	1962	3.75	7.50	15.00

HOLLAND, BRIAN
45s
INVICTUS

Number	Title (A Side/B Side)	Yr	VG	VG+	NM
❑ 1265	I'm So Glad (Part 1)/I'm So Glad (Part 2)	1974	—	2.50	5.00
❑ 1272	Super Woman/Let's Get Together	1974	—	2.50	5.00
KUDO					
❑ 667	(Where's the Joy?) In Nature Boy/Shock	1958	150.00	300.00	600.00
—First name as "Briant"					

HOLLAND, EDDIE Also see HOLLAND-DOZIER.
45s
MERCURY

Number	Title (A Side/B Side)	Yr	VG	VG+	NM
❑ 71290	You/Little Miss Ruby	1958	25.00	50.00	100.00
MOTOWN					
❑ 1021	Jamie/Take a Chance on Me	1961	6.25	12.50	25.00
❑ 1026	You Deserve What You Got/ Last Night I Had a Vision	1962	6.25	12.50	25.00
❑ 1030	If Cleopatra Took a Chance/What About Me	1962	6.25	12.50	25.00
❑ 1030 [PS]	If Cleopatra Took a Chance/What About Me	1962	25.00	50.00	100.00
❑ 1031	If It's Love (It's All Right)/It's Not Too Late	1962	6.25	12.50	25.00
❑ 1036	Darling I Hum Our Song/Just a Few Memories	1963	6.25	12.50	25.00
❑ 1043	Brenda/Baby Shake	1963	6.25	12.50	25.00
❑ 1049	I'm On the Outside Looking In /I Couldn't Cry If I Wanted To	1963	37.50	75.00	150.00
❑ 1052	Leaving Here/Brenda	1964	3.75	7.50	15.00
❑ 1058	Just Ain't Enough Love/Last Night I Had a Vision	1964	3.75	7.50	15.00
❑ 1063	Candy to Me/If You Don't Want My Love	1964	3.75	7.50	15.00
TAMLA					
❑ 102	Merry-Go-Round/It Moves Me	1959	62.50	125.00	250.00
UNITED ARTISTS					
❑ 172	Merry-Go-Round/It Moves Me	1959	7.50	15.00	30.00
❑ 191	Because I Love Her/Everybody's Going	1959	7.50	15.00	30.00
❑ 207	Magic Mirror/Will You Love Me	1960	7.50	15.00	30.00
❑ 280	The Last Laugh/Why Do You Want to Let Me Go	1960	7.50	15.00	30.00

Albums
MOTOWN

Number	Title (A Side/B Side)	Yr	VG	VG+	NM
❑ 604 [M]	Eddie Holland	1963	100.00	200.00	400.00

HOLLAND-DOZIER Also see LAMONT DOZIER; EDDIE HOLLAND.
45s
INVICTUS

Number	Title (A Side/B Side)	Yr	VG	VG+	NM
❑ 1253	Slipping Away/Can't Get Enough	1973	—	2.50	5.00
❑ 1254	If You Don't Wanta Be in My Life/New Breed Kinda Woman	1973	—	2.50	5.00

Number	Title (A Side/B Side)	Yr	VG	VG+	NM
❑ 1258	You Took Me from a World Outside/I'm Gonna Hijack Ya, Kidnap Ya, Take What I Want	1973	—	2.50	5.00
❑ 9110	Don't Leave Me (Part 1)/Don't Leave Me (Part 2)	1972	—	2.50	5.00
❑ 9125	Why Can't We Be Lovers/Don't Leave Me	1972	—	2.50	5.00
❑ 9133	Don't Leave Me Starvin' for Your Love (Part 1)/ Don't Leave Me Starvin' for Your Love (Part 2)	1972	—	2.50	5.00
MOTOWN					
❑ 1045	What Goes Up Must Come Down/ Come On Home	1963	6.25	12.50	25.00

HOLLIDAY, MICHAEL
45s
CAPITOL

Number	Title (A Side/B Side)	Yr	VG	VG+	NM
❑ F3720	Good Luck, Good Health, God Bless You/ John and Julie	1957	3.00	6.00	12.00
❑ F4018	Rooney/Keep Your Heart	1958	3.00	6.00	12.00

HOLLIES, THE Also see ALLAN CLARKE; GRAHAM NASH; TERRY SYLVESTER; THE TREMELOES/THE HOLLIES.
12-Inch Singles
ATLANTIC

Number	Title (A Side/B Side)	Yr	VG	VG+	NM
❑ PR 502 [DJ]	Stop in the Name of Love/If the Lights Go Out	1983	2.00	4.00	8.00
45s					
ATLANTIC					
❑ 89768 [DJ]	Casualty (same on both sides)	1983	—	2.50	5.00
—May be promo only					
❑ 89784	If the Lights Go Out/Someone Else's Eyes	1983	—	—	3.00
❑ 89819	Stop in the Name of Love/Musical Pictures	1983	—	—	3.00
❑ 89819 [PS]	Stop in the Name of Love/Musical Pictures	1983	—	2.50	5.00
EPIC					
❑ 10180	Carrie-Anne/Signs That Will Never Change	1967	2.00	4.00	8.00
❑ 10180 [PS]	Carrie-Anne/Signs That Will Never Change	1967	3.75	7.50	15.00
❑ 10234	King Midas in Reverse/Water on the Brain	1967	2.00	4.00	8.00
❑ 10234 [PS]	King Midas in Reverse/Water on the Brain	1967	3.75	7.50	15.00
❑ 10251	Dear Eloise/When Your Light's Turned On	1967	2.00	4.00	8.00
❑ 10251 [PS]	Dear Eloise/When Your Light's Turned On	1967	3.75	7.50	15.00
❑ 10298	Jennifer Eccles/Try It	1968	2.00	4.00	8.00
❑ 10361	Do the Best You Can/Elevated Observations	1968	2.00	4.00	8.00
❑ 10400	Listen to Me/Everything Is Sunshine	1968	2.00	4.00	8.00
❑ 10454	Sorry Suzanne/Not That Way at All	1969	2.00	4.00	8.00
❑ 10532	He Ain't Heavy, He's My Brother/Cos You Like to Love Me	1969	—	3.00	6.00
—A-side: Elton John on piano					
❑ 10613	I Can't Tell the Bottom from the Top/Mad Professor Blythe	1970	—	3.00	6.00
❑ 10677	Gasoline Alley Bred/Dandelion Wine	1970	2.50	5.00	10.00
❑ 10716	Survival of the Fittest/Man Without a Heart	1971	3.00	6.00	12.00
❑ 10754	Hey Willy/Row the Boat Together	1971	2.50	5.00	10.00
❑ 10842	The Baby/Oh Granny	1972	2.50	5.00	10.00
❑ 10842 [PS]	The Baby/Oh Granny	1972	25.00	50.00	100.00
❑ 10871	Long Cool Woman (In a Black Dress)/ Look What We've Got	1972	—	2.50	5.00
❑ 10920	Long Dark Road/Indian Girl	1972	—	2.50	5.00
❑ 10951	Magic Woman Touch/Blue in the Morning	1973	—	2.50	5.00
❑ 10989	Jesus Was a Crossmaker/I Had a Dream	1973	—	2.50	5.00
❑ 11025	Won't We Feel Good/Slow Down	1973	—	2.50	5.00
❑ 11051	The Day That Curley Billy Shot Down Crazy Sam McGee/Born a Man	1973	—	2.50	5.00
❑ 11100	The Air That I Breathe/No More Riders	1974	—	2.50	5.00
❑ 50029	Don't Let Me Down/Layin' to the Music	1974	—	2.50	5.00
❑ 50086	Sandy/Second Hand Hangups	1975	—	2.50	5.00
❑ 50110	Another Night/Time Machine Jive	1975	—	2.00	4.00
❑ 50144	Look Out Johnny/I'm Down	1975	—	2.00	4.00
❑ 50204	Crocodile Woman (She Bites)/Write On	1976	—	2.00	4.00
❑ 50359	Sandy/Second Hand Hangups	1977	—	2.00	4.00
❑ 50422	Draggin' My Heels/I Won't Move Over	1977	—	2.00	4.00
❑ 50522	Burn Out/Writing on the Wall	1978	—	2.00	4.00
IMPERIAL					
❑ 54050	Look Through My Window/I'm Alive	196?	3.75	7.50	15.00
—"The Golden Series" gold label reissue with incorrect A-side title					
❑ 66026	Just One Look/Keep Off That Friend of Mine	1964	5.00	10.00	20.00
❑ 66044	Here I Go Again/Lucille	1964	3.75	7.50	15.00
❑ 66070	Come On Back/We're Through	1964	3.75	7.50	15.00
❑ 66099	Yes I Will/Nobody	1965	10.00	20.00	40.00
❑ 66119	I'm Alive/You Know He Did	1965	3.75	7.50	15.00
❑ 66134	Look Through Any Window/So Lonely	1965	3.00	6.00	12.00
❑ 66158	I Can't Let Go/I've Got a Way of My Own	1966	3.75	7.50	15.00
❑ 66186	Bus Stop/Don't Run and Hide	1966	3.00	6.00	12.00
❑ 66214	Stop Stop Stop/It's You	1966	3.00	6.00	12.00
❑ 66231	On a Carousel/All the World Is Love	1967	3.00	6.00	12.00
❑ 66231 [PS]	On a Carousel/All the World Is Love	1967	7.50	15.00	30.00
❑ 66240	Pay You Back With Interest/Whatcha Gonna Do 'Bout It	1967	3.00	6.00	12.00
❑ 66258	Just One Look/Running Through the Night	1967	3.00	6.00	12.00
❑ 66271	If I Needed Someone/I'll Be True to You (Yes I Will)	1968	10.00	20.00	40.00
LIBERTY					
❑ 55674	Stay/Now's the Time	1964	15.00	30.00	60.00
UNITED ARTISTS					
❑ 50079	After the Fox/The Fox Trot	1966	5.00	10.00	20.00
—With Peter Sellers					
Albums					
ATLANTIC					
❑ 80076	What Goes Around	1983	2.50	5.00	10.00
CAPITOL					
❑ N-16056	Hollies' Greatest	1980	2.00	4.00	8.00
COLUMBIA LIMITED EDITION					
❑ LE 10178	He Ain't Heavy, He's My Brother	1976	3.00	6.00	12.00
EMI AMERICA					
❑ SN-16397	More Great Hits (1963-1968)	1986	2.00	4.00	8.00
EPIC					
❑ AS 138 [DJ]	Everything You Always Wanted to Hear by the Hollies but Were Afraid to Ask For	1976	5.00	10.00	20.00
—Promo-only sampler album					
❑ LN 24315 [M]	Evolution	1967	7.50	15.00	30.00
❑ LN 24344 [M]	Dear Eloise/King Midas in Reverse	1967	7.50	15.00	30.00

Number	Title (A Side/B Side)	Yr	VG	VG+	NM
❑ BN 26315 [S]	Evolution	1967	6.25	12.50	25.00
❑ BN 26344 [S]	Dear Eloise/King Midas in Reverse	1967	6.25	12.50	25.00
❑ BN 26447	Words and Music by Bob Dylan	1969	3.75	7.50	15.00
—Yellow label					
❑ BN 26447	Words and Music by Bob Dylan	1973	2.50	5.00	10.00
—Orange label					
❑ BN 26538	He Ain't Heavy, He's My Brother	1970	5.00	10.00	20.00
❑ E 30255	Moving Finger	1971	5.00	10.00	20.00
❑ KE 30958	Distant Light	1972	3.75	7.50	15.00
—Yellow label					
❑ KE 30958	Distant Light	1974	2.50	5.00	10.00
—Orange label					
❑ PE 30958	Distant Light	1986	2.00	4.00	8.00
—Blue label					
❑ KE 31992	Romany	1972	3.00	6.00	12.00
—Yellow label					
❑ KE 31992	Romany	1974	2.50	5.00	10.00
—Orange label					
❑ KE 32061	The Hollies' Greatest Hits	1973	3.00	6.00	12.00
—Yellow label					
❑ KE 32061	The Hollies' Greatest Hits	1974	2.50	5.00	10.00
—Orange label					
❑ PE 32061	The Hollies' Greatest Hits	1979	2.00	4.00	8.00
—Blue label					
❑ KE 32574	Hollies	1974	2.50	5.00	10.00
❑ PE 33387	Another Night	1975	2.50	5.00	10.00
❑ PE 34714	Clarke, Hicks, Sylvester, Calvert & Elliot	1977	2.50	5.00	10.00
❑ JE 35334	A Crazy Steal	1978	2.50	5.00	10.00
IMPERIAL					
❑ LP-9265 [M]	Here I Go Again	1964	12.50	25.00	50.00
—Black and pink label					
❑ LP-9265 [M]	Here I Go Again	1964	37.50	75.00	150.00
—Black label with stars					
❑ LP-9299 [M]	Hear! Here!	1965	12.50	25.00	50.00
❑ LP-9312 [M]	The Hollies — Beat Group	1966	7.50	15.00	30.00
❑ LP-9330 [M]	Bus Stop	1966	6.25	12.50	25.00
—Black and green label					
❑ LP-9330 [M]	Bus Stop	1966	7.50	15.00	30.00
—Black and pink label					
❑ LP-9339 [M]	Stop! Stop! Stop!	1966	6.25	12.50	25.00
❑ LP-9350 [M]	The Hollies' Greatest Hits	1967	5.00	10.00	20.00
❑ LP-12265 [R]	Here I Go Again	1964	7.50	15.00	30.00
—Black and pink label					
❑ LP-12265 [R]	Here I Go Again	1964	25.00	50.00	100.00
—Black label with silver print					
❑ LP-12299 [R]	Hear! Here!	1965	7.50	15.00	30.00
❑ LP-12312 [S]	The Hollies — Beat Group	1966	10.00	20.00	40.00
❑ LP-12330 [R]	Bus Stop	1966	5.00	10.00	20.00
—Black and green label					
❑ LP-12330 [R]	Bus Stop	1966	6.25	12.50	25.00
—Black and pink label					
❑ LP-12339 [S]	Stop! Stop! Stop!	1966	7.50	15.00	30.00
❑ LP-12350 [P]	The Hollies' Greatest Hits	1967	6.25	12.50	25.00
LIBERTY					
❑ LN-10216	Pay You Back with Interest	1982	2.00	4.00	8.00
PAIR					
❑ PDL2-1041 [(2)]	Hottest Hits	1986	3.75	7.50	15.00
REALM					
❑ 2V-8026 [(2)]	The Hollies, Volume 1	1976	3.75	7.50	15.00
—Two-record TV package					
❑ 1V-8027	The Hollies, Volume 2	1976	3.00	6.00	12.00
—TV package sold with Realm 8026					
UNITED ARTISTS					
❑ UA-LA329-E	The Very Best of the Hollies	1975	2.50	5.00	10.00

HOLLISTER, BOBBY
45s
PIKE

Number	Title (A Side/B Side)	Yr	VG	VG+	NM
❑ 5910	Ring Around Your Neck/Love's Gamble	1961	3.75	7.50	15.00
❑ 5910 [PS]	Ring Around Your Neck/Love's Gamble	1961	10.00	20.00	40.00

HOLLOWAY, BRENDA
45s
DONNA

Number	Title (A Side/B Side)	Yr	VG	VG+	NM
❑ 1358	Echo/Hey Fool	1962	10.00	20.00	40.00
❑ 1366	Game of Love/Echo-Echo-Echo	1962	12.50	25.00	50.00
❑ 1370	I'll Give My Life/More Echo	1962	12.50	25.00	50.00
TAMLA					
❑ 54094	Every Little Bit Hurts/Land of 1,000 Boys	1964	3.00	6.00	12.00
❑ 54099	I'll Always Love You/Sad Song	1964	3.75	7.50	15.00
❑ 54111	When I'm Gone/I've Been Good to You	1965	3.75	7.50	15.00
❑ 54111 [PS]	When I'm Gone/I've Been Good to You	1965	25.00	50.00	100.00
❑ 54115	Operator/I'll Be Available	1965	3.75	7.50	15.00
❑ 54121	You Can Cry on My Shoulder/How Many Times Did You Mean It	1965	5.00	10.00	20.00
❑ 54125	Sad Song/Together 'Til the End of Time	1965	5.00	10.00	20.00
❑ 54137	Hurt a Little Every Day/Where Were You	1966	7.50	15.00	30.00
❑ 54144	'Til Johnny Comes/Where Were You	1967	50.00	100.00	200.00
❑ 54148	Just Look What You've Done/Starting the Hurt All Over Again	1967	6.25	12.50	25.00
❑ 54155	You've Made Me So Very Happy/ I've Got to Find It	1967	5.00	10.00	20.00
❑ 206312 [DJ]	Play It Cool, Stay in School	1966	150.00	300.00	600.00
—Promo for Women's Ad Club of Detroit					
Albums					
MOTOWN					
❑ 5242 ML	Every Little Bit Hurts	1982	3.00	6.00	12.00
TAMLA					
❑ T 257 [M]	Every Little Bit Hurts	1964	50.00	100.00	200.00
❑ TS 257 [R]	Every Little Bit Hurts	1964	37.50	75.00	150.00

HOLLOWAY, LOLEATTA
12-Inch Singles
GOLD MIND

Number	Title (A Side/B Side)	Yr	VG	VG+	NM
❑ 402	Catch Me on the Rebound (10:51)/(7:22)	1978	3.75	7.50	15.00
❑ 4006	Hit and Run/It's Getting Stronger	1977	5.00	10.00	20.00

Number	Title (A Side/B Side)	Yr	VG	VG+	NM
SELECT					
❏ 5585	Strong Enough (5 versions)	1991	2.00	4.00	8.00
STREETWISE					
❏ 2230	Crash Goes Love/Sweet Thing	1984	2.50	5.00	10.00
45s					
AWARE					
❏ 033	Our Love/Mother of Shame	1973	—	3.00	6.00
❏ 039	H-E-L-P Me My Love/(B-side unknown)	1974	—	3.00	6.00
❏ 047	Cry to Me/So Can I	1974	—	3.00	6.00
❏ 050	The Show Must Go On/I Know Where You're Coming From	1975	—	3.00	6.00
❏ 054	Casanova/Only a Fool	1975	—	3.00	6.00
GALAXY					
❏ 780	Rainbow '71/Bring It On Up	1971	2.00	4.00	8.00
GOLD MIND					
❏ 4000	Dreamin'/Worn Out Broken Heart	1976	—	3.00	6.00
❏ 4001	Hit and Run/Is It Just a Man's Way	1977	—	3.00	6.00
❏ 4007	It's Getting Stronger/How Heartaches Are Made	1977	—	3.00	6.00
❏ 4012	Only You/Good Good Feeling	1978	—	3.00	6.00
—A-side with Bunny Sigler					
❏ 4016	Catch Me on the Rebound/Mama Don't, Papa Won't	1978	—	3.00	6.00
❏ 4021	That's What You Said/There'll Come a Time	1979	—	3.00	6.00
❏ 4024	Love Sensation/Short End of the Stick	1980	2.50	5.00	10.00
❏ 4025	I've Been Loving You Too Long/Two Became a Crowd	1980	—	3.00	6.00
SALSOUL					
❏ 2045	Run Away/Run Away (Part 2)	1977	—	3.00	6.00
—With the Salsoul Orchestra					
❏ 7034	Seconds/Columbia: The Space Shuttle	1981	—	3.00	6.00
—With the Salsoul Orchestra					
STREETWISE					
❏ 1130	Crash Goes Love/Sweet Thing	1984	—	3.00	6.00
Albums					
GOLD MIND					
❏ 7500	Loleatta	1977	5.00	10.00	20.00
❏ A-9501	Queen of the Night	1978	5.00	10.00	20.00
❏ GA-9506	Love Sensation	1979	5.00	10.00	20.00

HOLLOWAY, PATRICE Also see JOSIE AND THE PUSSYCATS.
45s

Number	Title (A Side/B Side)	Yr	VG	VG+	NM
CAPITOL					
❏ 5680	Stolen Hours/Lucky My Boy	1966	20.00	40.00	80.00
❏ 5778	Love and Desire/Ecstasy	1967	15.00	30.00	60.00
❏ 5985	Stay with Your Own Kind/That's All You Got to Do	1967	12.50	25.00	50.00
TASTE					
❏ 125	Do the Del Viking (Pt. 1)/Do the Del Viking (Pt. 2)	1963	7.50	15.00	30.00

HOLLY, BUDDY Also see THE CRICKETS (1).
45s

Number	Title (A Side/B Side)	Yr	VG	VG+	NM
CORAL					
❏ 61852	Words of Love/Mailman, Bring Me No More Blues	1957	150.00	250.00	400.00
—Promos for any Coral title valued at $50 or under Near Mint are worth 2-4 times the stock copy value.					
❏ 61885	Peggy Sue/Everyday	1957	12.50	25.00	50.00
—Orange label					
❏ 61885	Peggy Sue/Everyday	196?	6.25	12.50	25.00
—Black color bars label					
❏ 61947	I'm Gonna Love You Too/Listen to Me	1958	12.50	25.00	50.00
❏ 61985	Rave On/Take Your Time	1958	12.50	25.00	50.00
❏ 62006	Early in the Morning/Now We're One	1958	12.50	25.00	50.00
❏ 62051	Heartbeat/Well...All Right	1958	12.50	25.00	50.00
❏ 62074	It Doesn't Matter Anymore/Raining in My Heart	1959	10.00	20.00	40.00
❏ 62134	Peggy Sue Got Married/Crying, Waiting, Hoping	1959	15.00	30.00	60.00
❏ 62210	True Love Ways/That Makes It Tough	1960	12.50	25.00	50.00
❏ 62283	You're So Square (Baby I Don't Care)/Valley of Tears	1961	40.00	80.00	160.00
—Evidently only released in Canada					
❏ 62329	Reminiscing/Wait Till the Sun Shines, Nellie	1962	7.50	15.00	30.00
❏ 62352	True Love Ways/Bo Diddley	1963	15.00	30.00	60.00
❏ 62369	Brown Eyed Handsome Man/Wishing	1963	10.00	20.00	40.00
❏ 62390	Rock Around with Ollie Vee/I'm Gonna Love You Too	1963	10.00	20.00	40.00
❏ 62448	Slippin' and Slidin'/What to Do	1965	25.00	50.00	100.00
❏ 62554	Rave On/Early in the Morning	1968	7.50	15.00	30.00
❏ 62558	Love Is Strange/You're the One	1969	5.00	10.00	20.00
❏ 62558 [PS]	Love Is Strange/You're the One	1969	7.50	15.00	30.00
DECCA					
❏ 29854	Blue Days, Black Nights/Love Me	1956	75.00	150.00	300.00
—With star under "Decca"					
❏ 29854	Blue Days, Black Nights/Love Me	1956	150.00	300.00	600.00
—With lines on either side of "Decca"					
❏ 29854 [DJ]	Blue Days, Black Nights/Love Me	1956	100.00	200.00	400.00
—Promos have pink labels					
❏ 30166	Modern Don Juan/You Are My One Desire	1956	62.50	125.00	250.00
—With star under "Decca"					
❏ 30166	Modern Don Juan/You Are My One Desire	1956	125.00	250.00	500.00
—With lines on either side of "Decca"					
❏ 30166 [DJ]	Modern Don Juan/You Are My One Desire	1956	75.00	150.00	300.00
—Promos have pink labels					
❏ 30434	That'll Be the Day/Rock Around with Ollie Vee	1957	62.50	125.00	250.00
—With star under "Decca"					
❏ 30434	That'll Be the Day/Rock Around with Ollie Vee	1957	100.00	200.00	400.00
—With lines on either side of "Decca"					
❏ 30434 [DJ]	That'll Be the Day/Rock Around with Ollie Vee	1957	62.50	125.00	250.00
—Promos have pink labels					
❏ 30543	Love Me/You Are My One Desire	1958	75.00	150.00	300.00
❏ 30543 [DJ]	Love Me/You Are My One Desire	1958	50.00	100.00	200.00
—Pink label promos					
❏ 30543 [DJ]	Love Me/You Are My One Desire	1958	75.00	150.00	300.00
—Green label promos					
❏ 30650	Ting-a-Ling/Girl on My Mind	1958	75.00	150.00	300.00
❏ 30650 [DJ]	Ting-a-Ling/Girl on My Mind	1958	50.00	100.00	200.00
—Promos have pink labels					

Number	Title (A Side/B Side)	Yr	VG	VG+	NM
MCA					
❏ 40905	It Doesn't Matter Anymore/Peggy Sue	1978	—	2.50	5.00
❏ 40905 [PS]	It Doesn't Matter Anymore/Peggy Sue	1978	—	2.50	5.00
7-Inch Extended Plays					
CORAL					
❏ EC 81169	Listen to Me/Peggy Sue//I'm Gonna Love You Too/Everyday	1958	75.00	150.00	300.00
❏ EC 81169 [PS]	Listen to Me	1958	75.00	150.00	300.00
❏ EC 81182	It Doesn't Matter Anymore/Heartbeat//Raining in My Heart/Early in the Morning	1959	75.00	150.00	300.00
❏ EC 81182 [PS]	The Buddy Holly Story	1959	75.00	150.00	300.00
❏ EC 81191	Peggy Sue Got Married/Crying, Waiting, Hoping//Learning the Game/That Makes It Tough	1961	62.50	125.00	250.00
❏ EC 81191 [PS]	Buddy Holly	1961	62.50	125.00	250.00
❏ EC 81193	Brown Eyed Handsome Man/Wishing//Bo Diddley/True Love Ways	1961	62.50	125.00	250.00
❏ EC 81193 [PS]	Brown Eyed Handsome Man	1961	62.50	125.00	250.00
DECCA					
❏ ED 2575	*That'll Be the Day/Blue Days — Black Nights/Ting-a-Ling/You Are My One Desire	1958	150.00	300.00	600.00
❏ ED 2575 [PS]	That'll Be the Day	1958	150.00	300.00	600.00
—Sleeve has other EP ads on back					
❏ ED 2575 [PS]	That'll Be the Day	1958	500.00	1000.	2000.
—Sleeve has liner notes on back					
Albums					
CORAL					
❏ CXB 8 [(2)M]	The Best of Buddy Holly	1966	20.00	40.00	80.00
❏ CXSB 8 [(2)R]	The Best of Buddy Holly	1966	12.50	25.00	50.00
❏ CRL 57210 [M]	Buddy Holly	1958	100.00	200.00	400.00
—Maroon label					
❏ CRL 57210 [M]	Buddy Holly	1964	25.00	50.00	100.00
—Black label with color bars					
❏ CRL 57279 [M]	The Buddy Holly Story	1959	37.50	75.00	150.00
—Maroon label; back color print in all black					
❏ CRL 57279 [M]	The Buddy Holly Story	1959	75.00	150.00	300.00
—Maroon label; back color print in black and red					
❏ CRL 57279 [M]	The Buddy Holly Story	1963	20.00	40.00	80.00
—Black label with color bars					
❏ CRL 57326 [M]	The Buddy Holly Story, Vol. 2	1959	50.00	100.00	200.00
—Maroon label					
❏ CRL 57326 [M]	The Buddy Holly Story, Vol. 2	1963	20.00	40.00	80.00
—Black label with color bars					
❏ CRL 57405 [M]	Buddy Holly and the Crickets	1962	37.50	75.00	150.00
—Reissue of the Crickets LP on Brunswick 54038					
❏ CRL 57426 [M]	Reminiscing	1963	50.00	100.00	200.00
—Maroon label					
❏ CRL 57426 [M]	Reminiscing	1964	20.00	40.00	80.00
—Black label with color bars					
❏ CRL 57450 [M]	Buddy Holly Showcase	1964	25.00	50.00	100.00
❏ CRL 57463 [M]	Holly in the Hills	1965	30.00	60.00	120.00
❏ CRL 57492 [M]	Buddy Holly's Greatest Hits	1967	20.00	40.00	80.00
❏ CRL 757279 [R]	The Buddy Holly Story	1963	10.00	20.00	40.00
❏ CRL 757326 [R]	The Buddy Holly Story, Vol. 2	1963	10.00	20.00	40.00
❏ CRL 757405 [R]	Buddy Holly and the Crickets	1963	10.00	20.00	40.00
❏ CRL 757426 [R]	Reminiscing	1964	10.00	20.00	40.00
❏ CRL 757450 [R]	Buddy Holly Showcase	1964	20.00	40.00	80.00
❏ CRL 757463 [R]	Holly in the Hills	1965	25.00	50.00	100.00
❏ CRL 757492 [P]	Buddy Holly's Greatest Hits	1967	12.50	25.00	50.00
❏ CRL 757504 [S]	Giant	1969	12.50	25.00	50.00
CRICKET					
❏ C001000	Buddy Holly Live — Volume 1	197?	5.00	10.00	20.00
❏ C001001	Buddy Holly Live — Volume 1	197?	5.00	10.00	20.00
DECCA					
❏ DXSE 7207 [(2)]	A Rock 'n' Roll Collection	1972	10.00	20.00	40.00
❏ DL 8707 [M]	That'll Be the Day	1958	375.00	750.00	1500.
—Black label with silver print					
❏ DL 8707 [M]	That'll Be the Day	1961	75.00	150.00	300.00
—Black label with color bars					
GREAT NORTHWEST					
❏ GNW-4014	Visions of Buddy	197?	2.50	5.00	10.00
—Interview album					
MCA					
❏ 737	The Great Buddy Holly	197?	2.50	5.00	10.00
—Reissue of MCA Coral LP					
❏ 1484	Buddy Holly/The Crickets 20 Golden Greats	198?	2.00	4.00	8.00
—Reissue of 3040					
❏ 3040	Buddy Holly/The Crickets 20 Golden Greats	1978	3.75	7.50	15.00
❏ 4009 [(2)]	A Rock 'n' Roll Collection	1973	5.00	10.00	20.00
—Black labels with rainbow					
❏ 4009 [(2)]	A Rock 'n' Roll Collection	1978	3.00	6.00	12.00
—Later pressings on tan or blue/rainbow labels					
❏ 4184 [(2)]	Legend	1985	5.00	10.00	20.00
❏ 5540 [(2)]	From the Original Master Tapes	1986	6.25	12.50	25.00
❏ 11161	Buddy Holly	1995	10.00	20.00	40.00
—Audiophile "Heavy Vinyl" reissue with gatefold cover					
❏ 25239	Buddy Holly	1989	3.00	6.00	12.00
—Reissue of Coral 57210					
❏ 27059	For the First Time Anywhere	1983	2.50	5.00	10.00
❏ 80000 [(6)]	The Complete Buddy Holly	1981	12.50	25.00	50.00
—Box set with booklet and custom innersleeves					
MCA CORAL					
❏ CD-20101	The Great Buddy Holly	1973	3.00	6.00	12.00
VOCALION					
❏ VL 3811 [M]	The Great Buddy Holly	1967	20.00	40.00	80.00
❏ VL 73811 [R]	The Great Buddy Holly	1967	12.50	25.00	50.00
❏ VL 73923	Good Rockin'	1971	30.00	60.00	120.00

HOLLY TWINS, THE
45s

Number	Title (A Side/B Side)	Yr	VG	VG+	NM
LIBERTY					
❏ 55015	Take Me Back/It's Easy	1956	6.25	12.50	25.00
❏ 55048	I Want Elvis for Christmas/The Tender Age	1956	12.50	25.00	50.00
RENDEZVOUS					
❏ 180	Okee-Feenokee/Potato Chips	1962	3.00	6.00	12.00

Number	Title (A Side/B Side)	Yr	VG	VG+	NM

HOLLYHAWKS, THE With Niki Sullivan, ex-CRICKETS (1).
45s
JUBILEE

| ❑ 5441 | I Cry All the Time/When Came the Fall | 1962 | 20.00 | 40.00 | 80.00 |

HOLLYRIDGE STRINGS, THE
45s
CAPITOL

❑ 4557	Lucy's Theme/Hippodrome	1961	2.50	5.00	10.00
❑ 4600	The Thunder of Drums/The Guns of Navarone	1961	2.50	5.00	10.00
❑ 4631	Moon River/Something Big	1961	2.50	5.00	10.00
❑ 4664	The Comancheros/Theme from "The Devil at 4 O'Clock"	1961	2.50	5.00	10.00
❑ 4687	My Melancholy Baby/Light in the Piazza	1962	2.00	4.00	8.00
❑ 4720	It Happened in Athens/Song of Greece	1962	2.00	4.00	8.00
❑ 5165	The Seven Faces of Dr. Lao/The Fall of Love	1964	2.00	4.00	8.00
❑ 5207	Love Me Do/All My Loving	1964	3.00	6.00	12.00
❑ 5432	L-O-V-E/Those Lazy-Hazy-Crazy Days of Summer	1965	2.00	4.00	8.00
❑ 5533	Santa's Got a Brand New Bag/Have Yourself a Merry Little Christmas	1965	2.50	5.00	10.00
❑ 5551	Skyscraper/Gaiety	1965	2.00	4.00	8.00

7-Inch Extended Plays
CAPITOL

| ❑ SXA-2221 | Don't Be Cruel/Teddy Bear/Return to Sender//Bossa Nova, Baby/Good Luck Charm/Are You Lonesome Tonight? | 1964 | 5.00 | 10.00 | 20.00 |

—Jukebox issue; small hole, plays at 33 1/3 rpm

| ❑ SXA-2221 [PS] | The Hollyridge Strings Play Instrumental Versions of Hits Made Famous by Elvis Presley | 1964 | 5.00 | 10.00 | 20.00 |

—Title as listed on cover; title on label is "The Hollyridge Strings Play Hit Songs Made Famous by Elvis Presley"

Albums
CAPITOL

❑ ST-883	Hits of the 70's	1971	3.00	6.00	12.00
❑ SM-2116	The Beatles Song Book	197?	2.50	5.00	10.00
❑ ST 2116 [S]	The Beatles Song Book	1964	5.00	10.00	20.00
❑ T 2116 [M]	The Beatles Song Book	1964	3.75	7.50	15.00
❑ SM-2156	The Beach Boys Song Book	197?	2.50	5.00	10.00
❑ ST 2156 [S]	The Beach Boys Song Book	1964	5.00	10.00	20.00
❑ T 2156 [M]	The Beach Boys Song Book	1964	3.75	7.50	15.00
❑ ST 2199 [S]	Hits Made Famous by the Four Seasons	1965	5.00	10.00	20.00
❑ T 2199 [M]	Hits Made Famous by the Four Seasons	1965	3.75	7.50	15.00
❑ ST 2202 [S]	The Beatles Song Book, Vol. 2	1965	5.00	10.00	20.00
❑ T 2202 [M]	The Beatles Song Book, Vol. 2	1965	3.75	7.50	15.00
❑ ST 2221 [S]	Hits Made Famous by Elvis Presley	1965	5.00	10.00	20.00
❑ T 2221 [M]	Hits Made Famous by Elvis Presley	1965	3.75	7.50	15.00
❑ ST 2310 [S]	The Nat King Cole Song Book	1965	5.00	10.00	20.00
❑ T 2310 [M]	The Nat King Cole Song Book	1965	3.75	7.50	15.00
❑ ST 2404 [S]	Christmas Favorites by the Hollyridge Strings	1965	3.75	7.50	15.00
❑ T 2404 [M]	Christmas Favorites by the Hollyridge Strings	1965	3.00	6.00	12.00
❑ SM-2429	The New Beatles Song Book	197?	2.50	5.00	10.00
❑ ST 2429 [S]	The New Beatles Song Book	1966	5.00	10.00	20.00
❑ T 2429 [M]	The New Beatles Song Book	1966	3.75	7.50	15.00
❑ ST 2564 [S]	Oldies But Goldies	1966	5.00	10.00	20.00
❑ T 2564 [M]	Oldies But Goldies	1966	3.75	7.50	15.00
❑ ST 2611 [S]	Skyscraper	1966	5.00	10.00	20.00
❑ T 2611 [M]	Skyscraper	1966	3.75	7.50	15.00
❑ ST 2656 [S]	The Beatles Song Book, Vol. 4	1967	3.75	7.50	15.00
❑ T 2656 [M]	The Beatles Song Book, Vol. 4	1967	5.00	10.00	20.00
❑ ST 2749 [S]	The Beach Boys Song Book, Vol. 2	1967	3.75	7.50	15.00
❑ T 2749 [M]	The Beach Boys Song Book, Vol. 2	1967	5.00	10.00	20.00
❑ ST 2998	Hits Made Famous by Simon and Garfunkel	1968	3.75	7.50	15.00
❑ SM-11830	Christmas Favorites by the Hollyridge Strings	1978	2.50	5.00	10.00

—Abridged reissue of ST 2404

HOLLYWOOD ARGYLES, THE Also see FLESH GORDON AND THE NUDE HOLLYWOOD ARGYLES; GARY PAXTON.
45s
BRENT

| ❑ 7004 | Vacation Days Are Over/It Takes Time | 1959 | 7.50 | 15.00 | 30.00 |

—As "The Argyles"
CHATTAHOOCHIE

| ❑ 691 | Long Hair, Unsquare Dude Called Jack/Ole | 1965 | 3.75 | 7.50 | 15.00 |

FELSTED

| ❑ 8674 | Bossy Nover/Find Another Way | 1963 | 5.00 | 10.00 | 20.00 |

FINER ARTS

| ❑ 1002 | The Morning After/See You in the Morning | 1961 | 5.00 | 10.00 | 20.00 |

KAMMY

| ❑ 105 | Alley-Oop '65/Do the Funky Foot | 1965 | 5.00 | 10.00 | 20.00 |

—As "The New Hollywood Argyles"
LUTE

❑ 5905	Alley Oop/Sho' Know a Lot About Love	1960	6.25	12.50	25.00
❑ 5908	Gun Totin' Critter Called Jack/Bug-Eye	1960	5.00	10.00	20.00
❑ 6002	Hully Gully/So Fine	1960	5.00	10.00	20.00

PAXLEY

| ❑ 200 | Unemployment (same on both sides) | 196? | 2.50 | 5.00 | 10.00 |
| ❑ 752 | You've Been Torturing Me/The Grubble | 1960 | 5.00 | 10.00 | 20.00 |

TRILL

| ❑ 6311 | The Watermelon Song/Short Fat Outlaw | 196? | 6.25 | 12.50 | 25.00 |

Albums
LUTE

| ❑ L-9001 [M] | The Hollywood Argyles (Alley Oop) | 1960 | 175.00 | 350.00 | 700.00 |

HOLLYWOOD FLAMES, THE Also see BOBBY DAY.
45s
ATCO

❑ 6155	Every Day, Every Way/If I Thought I Needed You	1959	3.75	7.50	15.00
❑ 6164	Ball and Chain/I Found a Boy	1960	3.75	7.50	15.00
❑ 6171	Devil or Angel/Do You Ever Think of Me	1960	3.75	7.50	15.00
❑ 6180	Money Honey/My Heart's On Fire	1960	3.75	7.50	15.00

CHESS

| ❑ 1787 | Gee/Yes They Do | 1961 | 3.00 | 6.00 | 12.00 |

DECCA

| ❑ 29285 | Peggy/Ooh La La | 1954 | 18.75 | 37.50 | 75.00 |
| ❑ 48331 | Let's Talk It Over/I Know | 1955 | 18.75 | 37.50 | 75.00 |

EBB

❑ 119	Buzz-Buzz-Buzz/Crazy	1957	7.50	15.00	30.00
❑ 131	Give Me Back My Heart/A Little Bird	1958	6.25	12.50	25.00
❑ 144	Frankenstein's Den/Strollin' on the Beach	1958	6.25	12.50	25.00
❑ 146	Chains of Love/Let's Talk It Over	1958	6.25	12.50	25.00
❑ 149	A Star Fell/I'll Get By	1958	6.25	12.50	25.00
❑ 153	I'll Be Seeing You/Just for You	1959	7.50	15.00	30.00
❑ 158	So Good/There Is Something on Your Mind	1959	6.25	12.50	25.00
❑ 162	Now That You're Gone/Hawaiian Dream	1959	6.25	12.50	25.00
❑ 163	Much Too Much/In the Dark	1959	6.25	12.50	25.00

LUCKY

❑ 001	One Night with a Fool/Ride, Helen, Ride	1954	150.00	300.00	600.00
❑ 006	Peggy/Ooh-La-La	1954	150.00	300.00	600.00
❑ 009	Let's Talk It Over/I Know	1954	100.00	200.00	400.00

MONA-LEE

| ❑ 135 | Buzz-Buzz-Buzz/Crazy | 1958 | 6.25 | 12.50 | 25.00 |

MONEY

| ❑ 202 | Fare Thee Well/I'm Leaving | 1954 | 100.00 | 200.00 | 400.00 |

SWING TIME

| ❑ 345 | Let's Talk It Over/I Know | 1953 | 125.00 | 250.00 | 500.00 |
| ❑ 346 | Go and Get Some More/Another Soldier Gone | 1953 | 125.00 | 250.00 | 500.00 |

—B-side by the Question Marks
SYMBOL

| ❑ 211 | Dance Senorita/Annie Don't Love Me Anymore | 1965 | 3.00 | 6.00 | 12.00 |
| ❑ 215 | I'm Coming Home/I'm Gonna Stand By You | 1966 | 3.00 | 6.00 | 12.00 |

VEE JAY

| ❑ 515 | Drop Me a Line/Letter to My Love | 1963 | 3.75 | 7.50 | 15.00 |

HOLLYWOOD PERSUADERS, THE
45s
ORIGINAL SOUND

❑ 39	Tijuana Surf/Grunion Run	1964	12.50	25.00	50.00
❑ 39	Tijuana/Grunion Run	1964	12.50	25.00	50.00
❑ 44	Persuasion/Juarez	1964	6.25	12.50	25.00
❑ 50	Drums-A-Go-Go/Agua Caliente	1965	6.25	12.50	25.00
❑ 58	Hollywood A-Go-Go/Eve of Destruction	1965	6.25	12.50	25.00

Albums
ORIGINAL SOUND

| ❑ LPM-5013 [M] | Drums a-Go-Go | 1965 | 12.50 | 25.00 | 50.00 |
| ❑ LPS-8874 [S] | Drums a-Go-Go | 1965 | 15.00 | 30.00 | 60.00 |

HOLLYWOOD PLAYBOYS, THE With Nick Massi, later of THE FOUR SEASONS.
45s
SURE

| ❑ 105 | Ding Dong School Is Out/Talk to Audrey | 1960 | 7.50 | 15.00 | 30.00 |

HOLLYWOOD PRODUCERS, THE
45s
PARKWAY

| ❑ 993 | Whits Silk Glove/You're Not Welcome | 1966 | 7.50 | 15.00 | 30.00 |

HOLMAN, EDDIE
45s
ABC

❑ 11149	I Love You/I Surrender	1968	2.50	5.00	10.00
❑ 11240	Hey There Lonely Girl/It's All in the Game	1969	—	3.00	6.00
❑ 11261	Don't Stop Now/Since I Don't Have You	1970	—	3.00	6.00
❑ 11265	I'll Be There/Cause You're Mine Little Girl	1970	—	3.00	6.00
❑ 11276	Cathy Called/I Need Somebody	1970	—	3.00	6.00
❑ 11292	Love Story/Four Walls	1971	—	3.00	6.00

ASCOT

| ❑ 2142 | Go Get Your Own/Laughing at Me | 1963 | 3.75 | 7.50 | 15.00 |

BELL

| ❑ 712 | I'm Not Gonna Give Up/I'll Cry 1,000 Tears | 1968 | 5.00 | 10.00 | 20.00 |

GSF

| ❑ 6873 | My Mind Keeps Telling Me (That I Really Love You, Girl)/Stranded in a Dream | 1972 | — | 3.00 | 6.00 |
| ❑ 6885 | Young Girl/I'll Call You Joy | 1972 | — | 3.00 | 6.00 |

LEOPARD

| ❑ 45-5001 | What You Don't Know (Won't Hurt You)/I'm Counting Every Tear | 196? | 7.50 | 15.00 | 30.00 |

PARKWAY

❑ 106	Am I a Loser/You Know That I Will	1966	5.00	10.00	20.00
❑ 133	Somewhere Waits a Lonely Girl/Stay Mine for Heaven's Sake	1967	5.00	10.00	20.00
❑ 157	Why Do Fools Fall in Love/Never Let Me Go	1967	5.00	10.00	20.00
❑ 960	This Can't Be True/A Free Country	1965	5.00	10.00	20.00
❑ 981	Don't Stop Now/Eddie's My Name	1966	5.00	10.00	20.00
❑ 994	Return to Me/Stay Mine for Heaven's Sake	1966	5.00	10.00	20.00

SALSOUL

| ❑ 2026 | This Will Be a Night to Remember/Time Will Tell | 1977 | — | 2.50 | 5.00 |
| ❑ 2043 | You Make My Life Complete/Somehow You Make Me Feel | 1977 | — | 2.50 | 5.00 |

SILVER BLUE

| ❑ 807 | You're My Lady (Right Or Wrong)/(Instrumental) | 1974 | — | 2.50 | 5.00 |
| ❑ 815 | Just Say I Love Her/Darling Take Me Back | 1974 | — | 2.50 | 5.00 |

UNITED ARTISTS

| ❑ 609 | Go Get Your Own/Laughing at Me | 1963 | — | — | — |

—Unreleased
Albums
ABC

| ❑ S-701 | I Love You | 1970 | 7.50 | 15.00 | 30.00 |

SALSOUL

| ❑ 5511 | A Night to Remember | 1977 | 2.50 | 5.00 | 10.00 |

HOLMES, CARL, AND THE COMMANDERS
45s
ATLANTIC

| ❑ 2140 | Mashed Potatoes (Part 1)/(Part 2) | 1962 | 5.00 | 10.00 | 20.00 |

C.R.S.

| ❑ 000005 | The Pot's Hot/Your Game | 196? | 25.00 | 50.00 | 100.00 |

—As "Sherlock Holmes Investigation"
PARKWAY

| ❑ 900 | I Want My Ya Ya/I'm At My Best (When I'm Down) | 1964 | 5.00 | 10.00 | 20.00 |

Number	Title (A Side/B Side)	Yr	VG	VG+	NM
VERVE					
❑ 10510	Telegram/My Lonely Sad Eyes	1967	3.75	7.50	15.00
Albums					
ATLANTIC					
❑ 8060 [M]	Twist Party at the Roundtable	1962	10.00	20.00	40.00
❑ SD 8060 [S]	Twist Party at the Roundtable	1962	12.50	25.00	50.00

HOLMES, CECIL'S, SOULFUL SOUNDS
45s

Number	Title (A Side/B Side)	Yr	VG	VG+	NM
BUDDAH					
❑ 354	Superfly/Soulful Sounds	1973	—	2.50	5.00
❑ 391	Kung Fu/Soulful Love	1973	—	2.50	5.00
Albums					
BUDDAH					
❑ BDS-5129	The Black Motion Picture Experience	1973	3.00	6.00	12.00
❑ BDS-5139	Music for Soulful Lovers	1973	3.00	6.00	12.00

HOLMES, CLINT
45s

Number	Title (A Side/B Side)	Yr	VG	VG+	NM
ATCO					
❑ 6958	Playground in My Mind/Goodbye Maria	1974	—	2.50	5.00
❑ 7000	Let Me Hear It Out There/When You're No. 1	1974	—	2.50	5.00
❑ 7005	Bad Can Be Good/Hang In There Josie	1974	—	2.50	5.00
EPIC					
❑ 10891	Playground in My Mind/There's No Future in My Future	1972	—	2.50	5.00
—Originals have yellow labels					
❑ 10891	Playground in My Mind/There's No Future in My Future	1973	—	2.00	4.00
—Reissue have orange labels					
❑ 11033	Shiddle-Ee-Dee/Like the Fellow Once Said	1973	—	2.00	4.00
PRIVATE STOCK					
❑ 45,126	I Can Count on You	1976	—	2.00	4.00
❑ 45,186	It Wouldn't Have Made Any Difference/Got to Give In to Love	1978	—	2.00	4.00
❑ 45,201	No Walls, No Ceilings, No Floors	1979	—	2.00	4.00
Albums					
EPIC					
❑ KE 32269	Playground in My Mind	1973	2.50	5.00	10.00

HOLMES, JAKE
45s

Number	Title (A Side/B Side)	Yr	VG	VG+	NM
COLUMBIA					
❑ 45517	Trust Me/Just as Lost as Me	1971	—	2.50	5.00
❑ 45570	How Much Time/Silence	1972	—	2.50	5.00
POLYDOR					
❑ 14006	How Are You/(B-side unknown)	1969	—	2.50	5.00
❑ 14011	The Very First Time/Suitcase Room	1969	—	2.50	5.00
❑ 14023	A Little Later/Beautiful Girl Goodbye	1970	—	2.50	5.00
❑ 14041	So Close/Django and Friend	1970	—	2.50	5.00
TOWER					
❑ 392	Genuine Imitation Life/Hard to Keep My Mind on You	1968	—	3.00	6.00
❑ 393	Dazed and Confused/Penny's	1968	—	3.00	6.00
❑ 451	Saturday Night/Late Sleeping Day	1968	—	3.00	6.00
❑ 458	Sleeping Woman/Leaves Never Break	1969	—	3.00	6.00
❑ 459	High School Hero/The Diner Song	1969	—	3.00	6.00
Albums					
COLUMBIA					
❑ C 30996	Jake Holmes	1972	3.00	6.00	12.00
POLYDOR					
❑ 24-4007	Jake Holmes	1969	3.00	6.00	12.00
❑ 24-4034	So Close, So Very Far to Go	1970	3.00	6.00	12.00
TOWER					
❑ DT 5079 [R]	Above Ground	1967	3.75	7.50	15.00
❑ T 5079 [M]	Above Ground	1967	5.00	10.00	20.00
❑ ST 5127	Letter to Katherine December	1968	3.75	7.50	15.00

HOLMES, MARVIN
45s

Number	Title (A Side/B Side)	Yr	VG	VG+	NM
UNI					
❑ 55111	Ooh, Ooh, The Dragon (Part 1)/Ooh, Ooh, The Dragon (Part 2)	1969	6.25	12.50	25.00
❑ 55233	Sweet Talk/Thang	1970	6.25	12.50	25.00
Albums					
BROWN DOOR					
❑ MH-6573	Summer of '73	1973	6.25	12.50	25.00
❑ MH-6581	Honor Thy Father	1975	6.25	12.50	25.00
UNI					
❑ 73046	Ooh, Ooh, The Dragon And Other Monsters	1969	7.50	15.00	30.00

HOLMES, RUPERT
45s

Number	Title (A Side/B Side)	Yr	VG	VG+	NM
EPIC					
❑ 11014	Philly/Talk	1973	—	3.00	6.00
❑ 11117	Our National Pastime/Phantom of the Opera	1974	—	3.00	6.00
❑ 50013	Terminal/Bagdad	1974	—	3.00	6.00
❑ 50096	I Don't Wanna Hold Your Hand/The Man Behind the Woman	1975	—	3.00	6.00
❑ 50096 [PS]	I Don't Wanna Hold Your Hand	1975	2.50	5.00	10.00
—Promo-only sleeve					
❑ 50161	Terminal/Deco Lady	1975	—	3.00	6.00
❑ 50161 [PS]	Terminal/Deco Lady	1975	2.50	5.00	10.00
❑ 50223	Weekend Lover/Weekend Lover	1976	—	2.50	5.00
❑ 50295	You Make Me Real/Who, What, When, Where, How	1976	—	2.50	5.00
INFINITY					
❑ 50035	Escape (The Pina Colada Song)/Drop It	1979	—	2.50	5.00
❑ 50051	Him/Get Outta Yourself	1980	—	—	—
—Canceled					
MCA					
❑ 41173	Him/Get Outta Yourself	1980	—	2.00	4.00
❑ 41235	Answering Machine/Lunch Hour	1980	—	2.00	4.00
❑ 50035	Escape (The Pina Colada Song)/Drop It	1980	—	2.00	4.00
❑ 51019	Morning Man/The Mask	1980	—	2.00	4.00
❑ 51045	Blackjack/Crowd Pleaser	1981	—	2.00	4.00
❑ 51092	I Don't Need You/Cold	1981	—	2.00	4.00

Number	Title (A Side/B Side)	Yr	VG	VG+	NM
PRIVATE STOCK					
❑ 45,183	Bedside Companions/So Beautiful It Hurts	1978	—	2.50	5.00
❑ 45,199	Let's Get Crazy Tonight/Long Way Home	1978	—	2.50	5.00
Albums					
ELEKTRA					
❑ 5E-560	Full Circle	1982	2.50	5.00	10.00
EPIC					
❑ KE 32864	Widescreen	1974	3.00	6.00	12.00
❑ KE 33443	Rupert Holmes	1975	3.00	6.00	12.00
❑ PE 34288	Singles	1976	3.00	6.00	12.00
EXCELSIOR					
❑ XMP-6000	Rupert Holmes	1980	2.50	5.00	10.00
❑ XMP-6022	She Lets Her Hair Down	1981	2.50	5.00	10.00
INFINITY					
❑ 9020	Partners in Crime	1979	2.50	5.00	10.00
MCA					
❑ 5129	Adventure	1980	2.50	5.00	10.00
❑ 9020	Partners in Crime	1980	2.00	4.00	8.00
—Reissue of Infinity LP					
❑ 37166	Pursuit of Happiness	198?	2.00	4.00	8.00
—Reissue of Private Stock LP					
PRIVATE STOCK					
❑ PS-7006	Pursuit of Happiness	1978	3.00	6.00	12.00

HOLMES, SHERLOCK, INVESTIGATION See CARL HOLMES AND THE COMMANDERS.

HOLY MACKEREL, THE
Albums

Number	Title (A Side/B Side)	Yr	VG	VG+	NM
REPRISE					
❑ RS-6311	The Holy Mackerel	1968	6.25	12.50	25.00

HOLY MODAL ROUNDERS, THE
45s

Number	Title (A Side/B Side)	Yr	VG	VG+	NM
ELEKTRA					
❑ 45644	Bird Song/Dame Fortune	1968	3.75	7.50	15.00
METROMEDIA					
❑ 223	Boobs a Lot/Love Is the Closest Thing	1971	2.50	5.00	10.00
Albums					
ADELPHIA					
❑ 1030	Last Round	198?	2.50	5.00	10.00
ELEKTRA					
❑ EKS-74026	The Moray Eels Eat the Holy Modal Rounders	1968	7.50	15.00	30.00
ESP-DISK'					
❑ 1068 [M]	Indian War Whoop	1967	10.00	20.00	40.00
❑ 1068-S [S]	Indian War Whoop	1967	10.00	20.00	40.00
FANTASY					
❑ F-24711	Stampfel and Weber	1972	5.00	10.00	20.00
FOLKLORE					
❑ FRLP-14031 [M]	The Holy Modal Rounders	1964	20.00	40.00	80.00
METROMEDIA					
❑ MD-1039	Good Taste Is Timeless	1970	7.50	15.00	30.00
PRESTIGE					
❑ PRLP-7410 [M]	The Holy Modal Rounders 2	1965	10.00	20.00	40.00
❑ PRLP-7451 [M]	The Holy Modal Rounders	1966	10.00	20.00	40.00
—Reissue of Folklore LP					
❑ PR-7720	The Holy Modal Rounders	1969	6.25	12.50	25.00
ROUNDER					
❑ 3004	Alleged in Their Own Time	198?	2.50	5.00	10.00
SUNDAZED					
❑ LP 5126	The Moray Eels Eat the Holy Modal Rounders	2002	3.00	6.00	12.00
—Reissue on 180-gram vinyl					

HOMBRES, THE
45s

Number	Title (A Side/B Side)	Yr	VG	VG+	NM
SUN					
❑ 1104	If This Ain't Loving You Baby/You Made Me What I Am	1969	2.50	5.00	10.00
VERVE					
❑ 5058	Let It Out (Let It All Hang Out)/Go Girl, Go	196?	3.75	7.50	15.00
—Blue label; may be later than the Verve Forecast edition					
VERVE FORECAST					
❑ 5058	Let It Out (Let It All Hang Out)/Go Girl, Go	1967	3.00	6.00	12.00
❑ 5058	Let It All Hang Out/Go Girl, Go	1967	3.75	7.50	15.00
❑ 5076	It's a Gas/Am I High	1967	2.50	5.00	10.00
❑ 5083	The Prodigal/Mau, Mau, Mau	1968	2.50	5.00	10.00
❑ 5093	Take My Overwhelming Love (And Cram It Up Your Heart)/Pumpkin Man	1968	2.50	5.00	10.00
Albums					
VERVE FORECAST					
❑ FT-3036 [M]	Let It Out (Let It All Hang Out)	1967	7.50	15.00	30.00
❑ FTS-3036 [S]	Let It Out (Let It All Hang Out)	1967	6.25	12.50	25.00
❑ FTS-3068	The Hombres	1968	—	—	—
—Canceled					

HOMEMADE THEATER
45s

Number	Title (A Side/B Side)	Yr	VG	VG+	NM
A&M					
❑ 1776	Santa Jaws (Part 1)/Santa Jaws (Part 2)	1975	3.75	7.50	15.00
❑ 1887	C.B. Santa/Soup of the Day	1976	3.75	7.50	15.00

HOMER
45s

Number	Title (A Side/B Side)	Yr	VG	VG+	NM
UNITED					
❑ 123-6/7	I Never Cared for You/Dandilion Wine	1969	6.25	12.50	25.00
❑ 123-8	Texas Lights/(B-side unknown)	1970	5.00	10.00	20.00
❑ 123-10	Dandelion Wine/(B-side unknown)	1970	5.00	10.00	20.00
Albums					
UNITED					
❑ HS-101	Grown in U.S.A.	1970	62.50	125.00	250.00

HOMER AND JETHRO
45s

Number	Title (A Side/B Side)	Yr	VG	VG+	NM
KING					
❑ 1216	Don't Let Your Sweet Love Die/Long Handle Line	1953	7.50	15.00	30.00
❑ 5747	Five Minutes More/Tell a Woman	1963	3.00	6.00	12.00

RCA VICTOR

Number	Title (A Side/B Side)	Yr	VG	VG+	NM
❑ 47-4239	Sound Off #2/I Love You 1,000 Ways	1951	6.25	12.50	25.00
❑ 47-4290	Too Young/Too Old to Cut the Mustard	1951	7.50	15.00	30.00
❑ 47-4397	Cold, Cold Heart #2/Alabama Jubilee	1951	6.25	12.50	25.00
❑ 47-4557	Slow Poke #2/When It's Tooth Pickin' Time in False Teeth Valley	1952	6.25	12.50	25.00
❑ 47-4770	Li'l Ole Kiss of Fire/I'm Torn	1952	6.25	12.50	25.00
❑ 47-4936	The Billboard Song/Child Psychology	1952	6.25	12.50	25.00
❑ 47-5043	Jam Bowl Liar/You Belong to Me No. 2	1952	6.25	12.50	25.00
❑ 47-5099	A Screwball's Love Song/Settin' the Woods on Fire No. 2	1952	6.25	12.50	25.00
❑ 47-5214	Don't Let the Stars Get In Your Eyeballs/Unhappy Day	1953	6.25	12.50	25.00
❑ 47-5280	(How Much Is) That Hound Dog in the Window/Pore Ol' Koo-Liger	1953	7.50	15.00	30.00
❑ 47-5372	I'm Walking Behind You-All/Mexican Joe #6 7/8	1953	6.25	12.50	25.00
❑ 47-5429	Your Clobbered Heart/Gamblers Git Box	1953	6.25	12.50	25.00
❑ 47-5456	I Saw Mommy Smoochin' Santa Claus/(All I Want for Christmas Is) My Upper Plate	1953	5.00	10.00	20.00
❑ 47-5456 [PS]	I Saw Mommy Smoochin' Santa Claus/(All I Want for Christmas Is) My Upper Plate	1953	7.50	15.00	30.00
❑ 47-5555	You-Ewe-U/Hey Shmo!	1953	6.25	12.50	25.00
❑ 47-5633	Oh My Pappy/Swappin' Partners	1954	5.00	10.00	20.00
❑ 47-5708	Crazy Mixed Up Song/That Tired Run Down Feeling	1954	5.00	10.00	20.00
❑ 47-5788	Hernando's Hideaway/Wanted	1954	5.00	10.00	20.00
❑ 47-5903	The Night After Christmas/Santy Baby	1954	5.00	10.00	20.00
❑ 47-6029	Mister Sandman/The Nutty Lady of Shady Lane	1955	5.00	10.00	20.00
❑ 47-6053	Let Me Go, Blubber/Over the Rainbow	1955	5.00	10.00	20.00
❑ 47-6178	The Ballad of Davy Crew-Cut/Pickin' and Singin' (Medley)	1955	6.25	12.50	25.00
❑ 47-6241	The Yellow Rose of Texas, You All/Listen to the Gooney Bird	1955	5.00	10.00	20.00
❑ 47-6322	Nuttin' for Christmas/Santy's Movin' On	1955	5.00	10.00	20.00
❑ 47-6342	The Sifting, Whimpering Sands/They Laid Him in the Ground	1955	5.00	10.00	20.00
❑ 47-6374	Love and Marriage/This Is a Wife?	1955	5.00	10.00	20.00
❑ 47-6542	Two Tone Shoes/Hart Brake Motel	1956	6.25	12.50	25.00
❑ 47-6651	Where Is That Doggone Gal of Mine/Just Be Here	1956	5.00	10.00	20.00
❑ 47-6706	Houn' Dawg/Screen Door (Green Door)	1956	6.25	12.50	25.00
❑ 47-6765	I'm My Own Grand Paw/Mama from the Train	1956	5.00	10.00	20.00
❑ 47-6954	Gone/Ramblin' Rose	1957	3.75	7.50	15.00
❑ 47-7030	My Dog Likes Your Dog/Kentucky	1957	3.75	7.50	15.00
❑ 47-7162	At the Flop/My Special Angel	1958	3.75	7.50	15.00
❑ 47-7342	Lullaby of Bird Dog/I Guess Things Happen That Way	1958	3.75	7.50	15.00
❑ 47-7493	Don't Sing Along (On Top of Old Smoky)/Middle Aged Teenager	1959	3.75	7.50	15.00
❑ 47-7585	The Battle of Kookamonga/Waterloo	1959	3.75	7.50	15.00
❑ 47-7704	El Paso (Numero Dos)/That's Good, That's Bad	1960	3.75	7.50	15.00
❑ 47-7744	Sink the Bismarck/He'll Have to Go	1960	3.75	7.50	15.00
❑ 47-7790	Itsy Bitsy Teenie Weenie Yellow Polka Dot Bikini/Please Help Me, I'm Falling	1960	3.75	7.50	15.00
❑ 47-7852	Are You Lonesome Tonight/I Love Your Pizza	1961	3.75	7.50	15.00
❑ 47-8075	She Thinks I Don't Care/Are You Kissing More Now (But Enjoying It Less)	1962	3.00	6.00	12.00
❑ 47-8305	Joe Bean/Freda on the Freeway	1963	3.00	6.00	12.00
❑ 47-8345	I Want to Hold Your Hand/She Loves You	1964	3.75	7.50	15.00
❑ 47-8345 [PS]	I Want to Hold Your Hand/She Loves You	1964	7.50	15.00	30.00
❑ 47-8604	Misty/Tenderly	1965	3.00	6.00	12.00
❑ 47-8664	King of the Camp/Camp Runamuck	1965	3.00	6.00	12.00
❑ 47-8874	Act Naturally/Finished Musicians	1966	2.50	5.00	10.00
❑ 47-9130	Nashville Cats/Winchester Cathedral	1967	2.50	5.00	10.00
❑ 47-9299	Somethin' Stupid/The Ballad of Roger Miller	1967	2.50	5.00	10.00
❑ 47-9581	Hill Billy Boogie/I Crept Into the Crypt and Cried	1968	2.50	5.00	10.00
❑ 47-9674	The Gal from Possum Holler/There Ain't a Chicken Safe in Tennessee	1968	2.50	5.00	10.00
❑ 47-9866	Daddy Played First Base/You Smell Like Turtles	1970	2.00	4.00	8.00
❑ 47-9922	Hello Darlin' No. 2/Funny Farm	1970	2.00	4.00	8.00
❑ 48-0075	Baby, It's Cold Outside/Country Girl	1949	12.50	25.00	50.00
—With June Carter; originals on green vinyl						
❑ 48-0086	Waltz with Me/Roll Along Kentucky Moon	1949	10.00	20.00	40.00
—Originals on green vinyl						
❑ 48-0113	Tennessee Border — No. 2/I'm Gettin' Older Every Day	1949	10.00	20.00	40.00
—Originals on green vinyl						
❑ 48-0144	The Wedding of Hillbilly Lilli Marlene/The Hucklebuck	1950	10.00	20.00	40.00
—With June Carter; originals on green vinyl						
❑ 48-0170	She Made Toothpicks Out of the Timber of My Heart/I've Got Tears in My Ears	1950	10.00	20.00	40.00
—Originals on green vinyl						
❑ 48-0181	I Said My Nightshirt (And Put On My Prayers)/Music, Music, Music	1950	10.00	20.00	40.00
—Originals on green vinyl						
❑ 48-0308	You Tell Her I Stutter/Does the Spearmint Lose Its Flavor	1950	10.00	20.00	40.00
❑ 48-0349	Pistol Pete/Put That Knife Away Nellie	1950	10.00	20.00	40.00
—Originals on green vinyl						
❑ 48-0404	Oh Babe/Disc Jockey Nightmare	1951	7.50	15.00	30.00
❑ 48-0446	So Long — No. 2/I'm Movin' On — No. 2	1951	7.50	15.00	30.00
❑ 48-0468	King Sized Baby/That Texas Land	1951	7.50	15.00	30.00
❑ 48-0484	Knock-Kneed Susy/She Loves to Cry	1951	7.50	15.00	30.00
—With June Carter						
❑ 74-0566	We Didn't Make It Through the Night/Fer the Good Times	1971	2.00	4.00	8.00

7-Inch Extended Plays
RCA VICTOR

Number	Title (A Side/B Side)	Yr	VG	VG+	NM
❑ EPA 424	Jam-Bowl-Liar/Settin' the Woods on Fire No. 2//Li'l Ole Kiss of Fire/Hey, Good Lookin' No. 2	1952	5.00	10.00	20.00
❑ EPA 424 [PS]	Homer & Jethro Kid the Top Pops	1952	5.00	10.00	20.00
❑ EPA 534	Randolph the Flat-Nosed Reindeer/(All I Want for Christmas Is) My Upper Plate//I Saw Mommy Smoochin' Santa Claus/Frosty the De-Frosted Snow Man	195?	3.75	7.50	15.00
❑ EPA 534 [PS]	Seasoned Greetings	195?	3.75	7.50	15.00
❑ EPA 1-1412	Cigareetes, Whusky and Wild Wild Women/The West Virginny Hills//Keep Them Cold Icy Fingers Off of Me/Ground Hog	1956	5.00	10.00	20.00
❑ EPA 1-1412 [PS]	Barefoot Ballads, Vol. I	1956	5.00	10.00	20.00

Albums
AUDIO LAB

Number	Title (A Side/B Side)	Yr	VG	VG+	NM
❑ AL-1513 [M]	Musical Madness	1958	25.00	50.00	100.00
KING						
❑ 639 [M]	They Sure Are Corny	1959	25.00	50.00	100.00
❑ 848 [M]	Cornier Than Corn	1963	17.50	35.00	70.00
❑ KS-1005	24 Great Songs in the Homer & Jethro Style	1967	5.00	10.00	20.00
RCA CAMDEN						
❑ CAL-707 [M]	Homer and Jethro Strike Back	1961	3.75	7.50	15.00
RCA VICTOR						
❑ LPM-1412 [M]	Barefoot Ballads	1957	12.50	25.00	50.00
❑ LPM-1560 [M]	The Worst of Homer & Jethro	1958	12.50	25.00	50.00
❑ LPM-1880 [M]	Life Can Be Miserable	1958	7.50	15.00	30.00
❑ LSP-1880 [S]	Life Can Be Miserable	1958	12.50	25.00	50.00
❑ LPM-2181 [M]	Homer and Jethro at the Country Club	1960	6.25	12.50	25.00
❑ LSP-2181 [S]	Homer and Jethro at the Country Club	1960	10.00	20.00	40.00
❑ LPM-2286 [M]	Songs My Mother Never Sang	1961	6.25	12.50	25.00
❑ LSP-2286 [S]	Songs My Mother Never Sang	1961	7.50	15.00	30.00
❑ LPM-2455 [M]	Zany Songs of the '30s	1962	6.25	12.50	25.00
❑ LSP-2455 [S]	Zany Songs of the '30s	1962	7.50	15.00	30.00
❑ LPM-2459 [M]	Playing It Straight	1962	6.25	12.50	25.00
❑ LSP-2459 [S]	Playing It Straight	1962	7.50	15.00	30.00
❑ LPM-2492 [M]	Homer and Jethro at the Convention	1962	6.25	12.50	25.00
❑ LSP-2492 [S]	Homer and Jethro at the Convention	1962	7.50	15.00	30.00
❑ LPM-2674 [M]	Homer and Jethro Go West	1963	6.25	12.50	25.00
❑ LSP-2674 [S]	Homer and Jethro Go West	1963	7.50	15.00	30.00
❑ LPM-2743 [M]	Ooh, That's Corny	1963	6.25	12.50	25.00
❑ LSP-2743 [S]	Ooh, That's Corny	1963	7.50	15.00	30.00
❑ LPM-2928 [M]	Cornfucius Say	1964	6.25	12.50	25.00
❑ LSP-2928 [S]	Cornfucius Say	1964	7.50	15.00	30.00
❑ LPM-2954 [M]	Fractured Folk Songs	1964	6.25	12.50	25.00
❑ LSP-2954 [S]	Fractured Folk Songs	1964	7.50	15.00	30.00
❑ LPM-3112 [10]	Homer & Jethro Fracture Frank Loesser	1953	37.50	75.00	150.00
❑ LPM-3357 [M]	Homer and Jethro Sing Tenderly	1965	6.25	12.50	25.00
❑ LSP-3357 [S]	Homer and Jethro Sing Tenderly	1965	7.50	15.00	30.00
❑ LPM-3462 [M]	The Old Crusty Minstrels	1965	6.25	12.50	25.00
❑ LSP-3462 [S]	The Old Crusty Minstrels	1965	7.50	15.00	30.00
❑ LPM-3474 [M]	The Best of Homer and Jethro	1966	6.25	12.50	25.00
❑ LSP-3474 [S]	The Best of Homer and Jethro	1966	7.50	15.00	30.00
❑ LPM-3538 [M]	Any News from Nashville?	1966	6.25	12.50	25.00
❑ LSP-3538 [S]	Any News from Nashville?	1966	7.50	15.00	30.00
❑ LPM-3673 [M]	Wanted for Murder	1966	6.25	12.50	25.00
❑ LSP-3673 [S]	Wanted for Murder	1966	7.50	15.00	30.00
❑ LPM-3701 [M]	It Ain't Necessarily Square	1967	7.50	15.00	30.00
❑ LSP-3701 [S]	It Ain't Necessarily Square	1967	6.25	12.50	25.00
❑ LPM-3822 [M]	Nashville Cats	1967	10.00	20.00	40.00
❑ LSP-3822 [S]	Nashville Cats	1967	6.25	12.50	25.00
❑ LPM-3877 [M]	Somethin' Stupid	1967	12.50	25.00	50.00
❑ LSP-3877 [S]	Somethin' Stupid	1967	6.25	12.50	25.00
❑ LPM-3973 [M]	There's Nothing Like an Old Hippie	1968	25.00	50.00	100.00
❑ LSP-3973 [S]	There's Nothing Like an Old Hippie	1968	6.25	12.50	25.00
❑ LSP-4001	Cool, Crazy Christmas	1968	5.00	10.00	20.00
❑ LSP-4024	Homer and Jethro at Vanderbilt U.	1969	5.00	10.00	20.00
❑ LSP-4148	Homer and Jethro's Next Album	1969	5.00	10.00	20.00

HONDELLS, THE
45s
AMOS

Number	Title (A Side/B Side)	Yr	VG	VG+	NM
❑ 131	Follow the Bouncing Ball/The Legend of Frankie and Johnny	1969	3.00	6.00	12.00
❑ 150	Shine On Ruby Mountain/The Legend of Frankie and Johnny	1970	3.00	6.00	12.00
COLUMBIA						
❑ 44361	Just One More Chance/Yes to You	1967	5.00	10.00	20.00
❑ 44557	Another Woman/Atlanta Georgia Stray	1968	5.00	10.00	20.00
MERCURY						
❑ 72324	Little Honda/Hot Rod High	1964	5.00	10.00	20.00
❑ 72366	My Buddy Seat/You're Gonna Ride with Me	1964	5.00	10.00	20.00
❑ 72366 [PS]	My Buddy Seat/You're Gonna Ride with Me	1964	6.25	12.50	25.00
❑ 72405	Little Sidewalk Surfer Girl/Come On Baby (Pack It In)	1965	5.00	10.00	20.00
❑ 72443	Sea of Love/Do As I Say	1965	5.00	10.00	20.00
❑ 72479	You Meet the Nicest People on a Honda/Sea Cruise	1965	5.00	10.00	20.00
❑ 72479 [PS]	You Meet the Nicest People on a Honda/Sea Cruise	1965	7.50	15.00	30.00
❑ 72523	Endless Sleep/Follow Your Heart	1966	3.75	7.50	15.00
❑ 72563	Younger Girl/All American Girl	1966	3.75	7.50	15.00
❑ 72605	Country Love/Kissin' My Life Away	1966	3.75	7.50	15.00
❑ 72626	Cheryl's Goin' Home/Show Me	1966	3.75	7.50	15.00

Albums
MERCURY

Number	Title (A Side/B Side)	Yr	VG	VG+	NM
❑ MG-20940 [M]	Go Little Honda	1964	10.00	20.00	40.00
❑ MG-20982 [M]	The Hondells	1965	12.50	25.00	50.00
❑ SR-60940 [S]	Go Little Honda	1964	15.00	30.00	60.00
❑ SR-60982 [S]	The Hondells	1965	20.00	40.00	80.00

HONEY BEES, THE (1)
45s
FONTANA

Number	Title (A Side/B Side)	Yr	VG	VG+	NM
❑ 1505	You Turn Me On Boy/Some of Your Lovin'	1965	5.00	10.00	20.00
❑ 1939	One Wonderful Night/She Don't Deserve You	1964	5.00	10.00	20.00
GARRISON						
❑ 3005	Never in a Million Years/Let's Get Back Together	1966	62.50	125.00	250.00
VEE JAY						
❑ 611	One Girl, One Boy/No Guy	1964	6.25	12.50	25.00
WAND						
❑ 1141	Never in a Million Years/Let's Get Back Together	1966	3.00	6.00	12.00

Bobby Helms, *Bobby Helms Sings to My Special Angel,* Decca DL 8638, mono LP, all-black label with silver print, $60-$120.

Jimi Hendrix, *Are You Experienced,* Reprise RS-6261, stereo LP, pink, gold and green label, $25-$50.

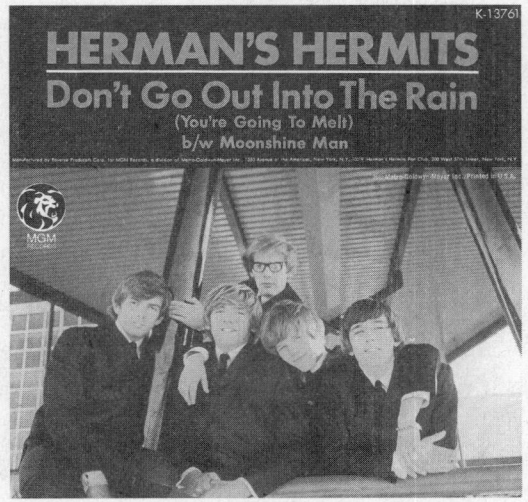

Herman's Hermits, "Don't Go Out Into the Rain (You're Going to Melt)," MGM K13761, picture sleeve, $7.50-$15.

The Hollies, *Hear! Here!,* Imperial LP-9299, mono LP, pink, white and black label, $25-$50.

Buddy Holly, *That'll Be the Day,* Decca ED 2575, 7-inch EP, cover has liner notes on back, $1,300-$2,600 (cover and record together).

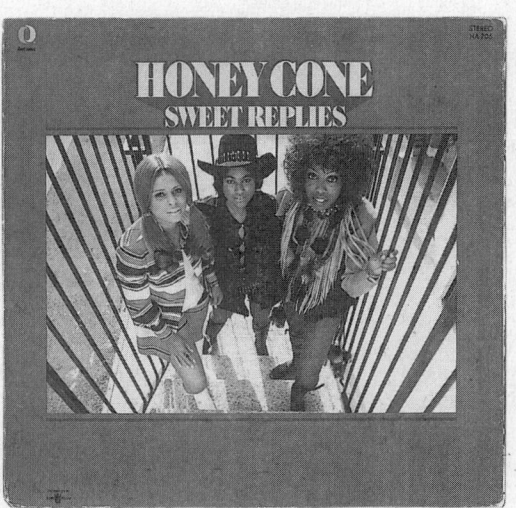

Honey Cone, *Sweet Replies,* Hot Wax HA-706, stereo LP, $6-$12.

Number	Title (A Side/B Side)	Yr	VG	VG+	NM

HONEY BEES, THE (2)
45s
IMPERIAL

Number	Title (A Side/B Side)	Yr	VG	VG+	NM
❏ 5400	Endless/Let's See What's Happening	1956	10.00	20.00	40.00
❏ 5436	Just to Live Again/What's to Become of Me	1957	10.00	20.00	40.00

HONEY CONE, THE
45s
HOT WAX

Number	Title (A Side/B Side)	Yr	VG	VG+	NM
❏ 6901	While You're Out Looking for Sugar?/The Feeling's Gone	1969	—	3.00	6.00
❏ 6903	Girls It Ain't Easy/The Feeling's Gone	1969	—	3.00	6.00
❏ 7001	Take Me With You/Take My Love	1970	—	3.00	6.00
❏ 7005	When Will It End/Take Me With You	1970	—	3.00	6.00
❏ 7011	Want Ads/We Belong Together	1970	—	2.50	5.00

—Mostly orange label

| ❏ 7011 | Want Ads/We Belong Together | 1970 | — | 3.00 | 6.00 |

—Mostly white label

❏ 7106	Stick-Up/V.I.P.	1971	—	3.00	6.00
❏ 7110	One Monkey Don't Stop No Show Part I/One Monkey Don't Stop No Show Part II	1971	—	3.00	6.00
❏ 7113	The Day I Found Myself/When Will It End	1971	—	3.00	6.00
❏ 7205	Sittin' on a Time Bomb (Waitin' for the Hurt to Come)/It's Better to Have Loved and Lost	1972	—	3.00	6.00
❏ 7208	Innocent Till Proven Guilty/Don't Send Me an Invitation	1972	—	3.00	6.00
❏ 7212	Ace in the Hole/Ooo Baby Baby	1972	—	3.00	6.00
❏ 7301	If I Can't Fly/Woman Can't Live by Bread Alone	1973	—	3.00	6.00
❏ 9255	The Truth Will Come Out/Somebody Is Always Messing Up a Good Thing	1974	—	3.00	6.00

Albums
HOT WAX

Number	Title (A Side/B Side)	Yr	VG	VG+	NM
❏ HA-701	Take Me With You	1970	3.00	6.00	12.00
❏ HA-706	Sweet Replies	1971	3.00	6.00	12.00
❏ HA-707	Soulful Tapestry	1971	3.00	6.00	12.00
❏ HA-713	Love, Peace & Soul	1972	3.00	6.00	12.00

HONEYCOMBS, THE
45s
INTERPHON

Number	Title (A Side/B Side)	Yr	VG	VG+	NM
❏ 7707	Have I the Right?/Please Don't Pretend Again	1964	3.00	6.00	12.00
❏ 7713	I Can't Stop/I'll Cry Tomorrow	1964	2.50	5.00	10.00
❏ 7713 [PS]	I Can't Stop/I'll Cry Tomorrow	1964	6.25	12.50	25.00
❏ 7716	Color Slide/That's the Way	1965	2.50	5.00	10.00
❏ 7716 [PS]	Colour Slide/That's the Way	1965	6.25	12.50	25.00

—Yes, the American sleeve spells the A-side the British way
WARNER BROS.

❏ 5634	I'll See You Tomorrow/Something Better Beginning	1965	2.50	5.00	10.00
❏ 5655	I Can't Get Through to You/That's the Way	1965	2.50	5.00	10.00
❏ 5803	How Will I Know/Who Is Sylvia	1966	2.50	5.00	10.00

Albums
INTERPHON

Number	Title (A Side/B Side)	Yr	VG	VG+	NM
❏ IN-88001 [M]	Here Are the Honeycombs	1964	10.00	20.00	40.00
❏ IN-88001 [R]	Here Are the Honeycombs	1964	7.50	15.00	30.00

VEE JAY

| ❏ IN-88001 [M] | Here Are the Honeycombs | 1964 | 12.50 | 25.00 | 50.00 |
| ❏ IN-88001 [R] | Here Are the Honeycombs | 1964 | 10.00 | 20.00 | 40.00 |

HONEYCONES, THE
45s
EMBER

Number	Title (A Side/B Side)	Yr	VG	VG+	NM
❏ 1033	Betty Moretti/Cool It Baby	1958	5.00	10.00	20.00
❏ 1036	Op/Vision of You	1958	6.25	12.50	25.00
❏ 1042	Gee Whiz/Rockin' in the Knees	1958	5.00	10.00	20.00
❏ 1049	Tell Me Baby/Your Face	1959	5.00	10.00	20.00

HONEYCUTT, GLENN
45s
FERNWOOD

Number	Title (A Side/B Side)	Yr	VG	VG+	NM
❏ 142	Campus Love/Tombigbee Queen	1964	25.00	50.00	100.00

SUN

| ❏ 264 | I'll Be Around/I'll Wait Forever | 1957 | 7.50 | 15.00 | 30.00 |

HONEYCUTT, JOHNNY
45s
TRIODE

Number	Title (A Side/B Side)	Yr	VG	VG+	NM
❏ 111	I'm Coming Over/(B-side unknown)	196?	300.00	600.00	1200.

HONEYS, THE
45s
CAPITOL

Number	Title (A Side/B Side)	Yr	VG	VG+	NM
❏ 2454	Goodnight My Love/Tonight You Belong to Me	1969	20.00	40.00	80.00
❏ 4952	Surfin' Down the Swanee River/Shoot the Curl	1963	37.50	75.00	150.00
❏ 4952 [PS]	Surfin' Down the Swanee River/Shoot the Curl	1963	200.00	400.00	800.00
❏ 5034	Hide Go Seek/Pray for Surf	1963	50.00	100.00	200.00
❏ 5093	The One You Can't Have/From Jimmy With Tears	1963	50.00	100.00	200.00

WARNER BROS.

| ❏ 5430 | He's a Doll/The Love of a Boy and Girl | 1964 | 150.00 | 300.00 | 600.00 |

—Stock copy; red label

| ❏ 5430 [DJ] | He's a Doll/The Love of a Boy and Girl | 1964 | 50.00 | 100.00 | 200.00 |

—Promotional copy; white label

HONEYTONES, THE
45s
BIG TOP

Number	Title (A Side/B Side)	Yr	VG	VG+	NM
❏ 3002	Don't Look Now, But/I Know, I Know	1958	5.00	10.00	20.00

MERCURY

| ❏ 70557 | Too Bad/Somewhere, Sometime, Someday | 1955 | 6.25 | 12.50 | 25.00 |

WING

| ❏ 90013 | False Alarm/Honeybun Cha Cha | 1955 | 7.50 | 15.00 | 30.00 |

HONK
45s
AMARET

Number	Title (A Side/B Side)	Yr	VG	VG+	NM
❏ 123	Don't Take Anything/Love Machine	1970	2.00	4.00	8.00

EPIC

Number	Title (A Side/B Side)	Yr	VG	VG+	NM
❏ 8-50056	Hesitation/Dog at Your Dog	1974	—	2.50	5.00

GRANITE

| ❏ 101 | Made My Statement/Pipeline Sequence | 1972 | 2.00 | 4.00 | 8.00 |

20TH CENTURY

| ❏ 2007 | Made My Statement/Pipeline Sequence | 1973 | — | 3.00 | 6.00 |
| ❏ 2029 | I Wanna Do for You/Another Light | 1973 | — | 3.00 | 6.00 |

Albums
EPIC

| ❏ KE 33094 | Honk | 1974 | 3.00 | 6.00 | 12.00 |

GRANITE

| ❏ GR 7720 | Five Summer Stories | 1972 | 3.75 | 7.50 | 15.00 |

20TH CENTURY

| ❏ T-406 | Honk | 1973 | 3.00 | 6.00 | 12.00 |

HONOR SOCIETY, THE See THE HAPPENINGS.

HOOK, THE
45s
UNI

Number	Title (A Side/B Side)	Yr	VG	VG+	NM
❏ 55057	Son of Fantasy/Plug Your Head In	1968	2.50	5.00	10.00
❏ 55077	Love Theme in E Major/Homes	1968	2.50	5.00	10.00
❏ 55149	In the Beginning/Show You the Way	1969	2.50	5.00	10.00

Albums
UNI

| ❏ 73023 | The Hook Will Grab You | 1968 | 6.25 | 12.50 | 25.00 |
| ❏ 73038 | Hooked | 1969 | 6.25 | 12.50 | 25.00 |

HOOKER, JOHN LEE
45s
ABC

Number	Title (A Side/B Side)	Yr	VG	VG+	NM
❏ 11298	Doin' the Shout/Kick Hit 4 Hit Kix U	1971	—	3.00	6.00
❏ 11320	Never Get Out of These Blues Alive/Boogie with the Hook	1972	—	3.00	6.00

BATTLE

| ❏ 45901 | No More Doggin'/I Need Some Money | 1962 | 2.50 | 5.00 | 10.00 |

BLUESWAY

❏ 61010	Motor City Is Burning/Want Ad Blues	1967	2.00	4.00	8.00
❏ 61014	Mr. Lucky/Cry Before I Go	1968	—	3.00	6.00
❏ 61017	Back Biters and Syndicators/Think Twice Before You Go	1968	—	3.00	6.00
❏ 61023	I Don't Wanna Go to Vietnam/Simply the Truth	1969	—	3.00	6.00

CHANCE

| ❏ 1108 | Miss Lorraine/Talkin' Boogie | 1951 | 750.00 | 1500. | 3000. |

—As "John Lee Booker"

| ❏ 1110 | Graveyard Blues/I Love to Boogie | 1952 | 750.00 | 1500. | 3000. |

—As "John Lee Booker"

| ❏ 1122 | 609 Boogie/Road Trouble | 1952 | 500.00 | 1000. | 2000. |

—As "John L. Booker"
CHART

| ❏ 609 | Going South/Wobbling Baby | 1955 | 12.50 | 25.00 | 50.00 |
| ❏ 614 | Blue Monday/My Baby Put Me Down | 1955 | 12.50 | 25.00 | 50.00 |

CHESS

❏ 1505	High Priced Woman/Union Station Blues	1952	300.00	600.00	1200.
❏ 1513	Sugar Mama/Walkin' the Boogie	1952	250.00	500.00	1000.
❏ 1562	It's My Own Fault/Women and Money	1954	62.50	125.00	250.00
❏ 1965	Let's Go Out Tonight/In the Mood	1966	2.50	5.00	10.00

DELUXE

| ❏ 6004 | Blue Monday/Lovin' Guitar Man | 1953 | 125.00 | 250.00 | 500.00 |

—As "John Lee Booker"

| ❏ 6009 | I Came to See You Baby/I'm a Boogie Man | 1953 | 200.00 | 400.00 | 800.00 |

—As "Johnny Lee"

| ❏ 6032 | Stuttering Blues/Pouring Down Rain | 1954 | 100.00 | 200.00 | 400.00 |

—As "John Lee Booker"

| ❏ 6046 | My Baby Don't Love Me/Real, Real Gone | 1954 | 100.00 | 200.00 | 400.00 |

—As "John Lee Booker"
ELMOR

| ❏ 303 | Blues for Christmas/Big Fine Woman | 1959 | 5.00 | 10.00 | 20.00 |

FEDERAL

| ❏ 12377 | Late Last Night/Don't You Remember Me | 1960 | 3.75 | 7.50 | 15.00 |

FORTUNE

❏ 846	609 Boogie/Curl My Baby's Hair	1959	5.00	10.00	20.00
❏ 853	Cry Baby/Love You Baby	1960	5.00	10.00	20.00
❏ 855	Crazy About That Walk/We're All God's Chillun	1960	5.00	10.00	20.00

GALAXY

| ❏ 716 | I Lost My Job/You Gotta Shake It Up and Go | 1963 | 2.50 | 5.00 | 10.00 |

HI-Q

| ❏ 5018 | Blues for Christmas/Big Fine Woman | 1960 | 5.00 | 10.00 | 20.00 |
| ❏ 5018X | 609 Blues/Blues for Christmas | 1961 | 5.00 | 10.00 | 20.00 |

IMPULSE

| ❏ 242 | Honey/Bottle Up and Go | 1966 | 2.50 | 5.00 | 10.00 |

JEWEL

| ❏ 824 | I Feel Good (Part 1)/I Feel Good (Part 2) | 1971 | — | 2.50 | 5.00 |
| ❏ 852 | Stand By (Part 1)/Stand By (Part 2) | 1977 | — | 2.00 | 4.00 |

JVB

| ❏ 30 | Boogie Rambler/No More Doggin' | 1953 | 375.00 | 750.00 | 1500. |

KENT

| ❏ 332 | Boogie Chillen/I'm in the Mood | 1960 | 5.00 | 10.00 | 20.00 |

KING

| ❏ 45-4504 | Moaning Blues/Stomp Boogie | 1952 | 250.00 | 500.00 | 1000. |

—As "John Lee Cooker"

| ❏ 6298 | Don't Go Baby/Moanin' and Stompin' Blues | 1970 | — | 3.00 | 6.00 |

LAUREN

| ❏ 361 | Ballad to Abraham Lincoln (He Got Assassinated)/Mojo Hand (Louisiana Voodoo) | 1961 | 5.00 | 10.00 | 20.00 |
| ❏ 362 | I Lost My Job/You Gotta Shake It Up and Go | 1961 | 5.00 | 10.00 | 20.00 |

MODERN

❏ 45x835	How Can You Do It/I'm in the Mood	1951	100.00	200.00	400.00
❏ 45x847	Anybody Seen My Baby? (Johnny Says Come Back)/Turn Over a New Leaf	1951	75.00	150.00	300.00
❏ 45x852	Ground Hog Blues/Louise	1951	30.00	60.00	120.00
❏ 45x862	Cold Chills All Over Me/Rock Me, Mama	1952	20.00	40.00	80.00
❏ 45x876	It Hurts Me So/I Got Eyes for You	1952	20.00	40.00	80.00

—With Little Eddie Kirkland

| ❏ 45x886 | Key to the Highway/Bluebird Blues | 1952 | 20.00 | 40.00 | 80.00 |

Number	Title (A Side/B Side)	Yr	VG	VG+	NM
❏ 45x893	New Boogie Chillen/I Tried	1952	20.00	40.00	80.00
❏ 45x897	It's Been a Long Time Baby/Rock House Boogie	1952	20.00	40.00	80.00
❏ 45x901	Ride Till I Die/It's Stormin' and Rainin'	1953	15.00	30.00	60.00
❏ 45x908	Please Take Me Back/Love Money Can't Buy	1953	15.00	30.00	60.00
❏ 45x916	Too Much Boogie/Need Somebody	1953	15.00	30.00	60.00
❏ 45x923	Gotta Boogie/Down Child	1953	15.00	30.00	60.00
❏ 45x931	Jump Me/I Wonder Little Darling	1954	15.00	30.00	60.00
❏ 45x935	I Tried Hard/Let's Talk it Over	1954	12.50	25.00	50.00
❏ 45x942	Cool Little Car/Bad Boy	1954	12.50	25.00	50.00
❏ 45x948	Half a Stranger/Shake, Holler and Run	1954	12.50	25.00	50.00
❏ 45x958	Taxi Driver/You Receive Me	1955	12.50	25.00	50.00
❏ 45x966	Hug and Squeeze/The Syndicator	1955	12.50	25.00	50.00
❏ 45x978	Looking for a Woman/I'm Ready	1955	15.00	30.00	60.00
POINTBLANK					
❏ S7-19518	Dimples/Don't Look Back	1997	—	2.00	4.00
❏ 38664	Burnin' Hell/Boogie at Russian Hill	1999	—	—	3.00
RIVERSIDE					
❏ 438	I Need Some Money/No More Diggin'	1960	6.25	12.50	25.00
ROCKIN'					
❏ 524	Blue Monday/Lovin' Guitar Man	1953	250.00	500.00	1000.
—As "John Lee Booker"					
❏ 525	Stuttering Blues/Pouring Down Rain	1953	250.00	500.00	1000.
—As "John Lee Booker"					
SPECIALTY					
❏ 528	Everybody's Blues/I'm Mad	1954	10.00	20.00	40.00
STAX					
❏ 0053	Slow and Easy/Grinder Man	1969	—	3.00	6.00
VEE JAY					
❏ 164	Mambo Chillen/Time Is Marching	1955	7.50	15.00	30.00
❏ 188	Every Night/Trouble Blues	1956	7.50	15.00	30.00
❏ 205	Dimples/Baby Lee	1956	7.50	15.00	30.00
❏ 233	The Road Is So Rough/I'm So Worried Baby	1957	6.25	12.50	25.00
❏ 245	I'm So Excited/I See You When You're Weak	1957	6.25	12.50	25.00
❏ 255	Little Wheel/Rosie Mae	1957	6.25	12.50	25.00
❏ 265	You Can Lead Me, Baby/Unfriendly Baby	1958	6.25	12.50	25.00
❏ 293	I Love You Honey/You've Taken My Woman	1958	6.25	12.50	25.00
❏ 308	Maudie/I'm In the Mood	1959	6.25	12.50	25.00
❏ 319	Tennessee Blues/Boogie Chillun	1959	6.25	12.50	25.00
❏ 331	Hobo Blues/Crawlin' King Snake	1959	6.25	12.50	25.00
❏ 349	No Shoes/Solid Sender	1960	6.25	12.50	25.00
❏ 366	Dusty Road/Tupelo	1960	6.25	12.50	25.00
❏ 379	I'm Mad Again/I'm Going Upstairs	1961	6.25	12.50	25.00
❏ 397	Want Ad Blues/Take Me As I Am	1961	6.25	12.50	25.00
❏ 438	Boom Boom/Drug Store Woman	1962	6.25	12.50	25.00
❏ 453	She's Mine/A New Leaf	1962	6.25	12.50	25.00
❏ 493	Take a Look at Yourself/Frisco Blues	1963	5.00	10.00	20.00
❏ 493	Take a Look at Yourself/I Love Her	1963	12.50	25.00	50.00
❏ 538	I'm Leaving/Birmingham Blues	1963	3.75	7.50	15.00
❏ 575	Send Me Your Pillow/Don't Look Back	1964	3.75	7.50	15.00
❏ 670	Big Legs, Tight Skirt/				
	Your Baby Ain't Sweet Like Mine	1965	3.00	6.00	12.00
❏ 708	It Serves Me Right/Flowers on the Hour	1966	2.50	5.00	10.00
Albums					
ABC					
❏ S-720 [(2)]	Endless Boogie	1971	5.00	10.00	20.00
❏ X-736	Never Get Out of These Blues Alive	1972	5.00	10.00	20.00
❏ XQ-736 [Q]	Never Get Out of These Blues Alive	1974	6.25	12.50	25.00
❏ X-761	Live at Soledad Prison	1972	5.00	10.00	20.00
❏ XQ-761 [Q]	Live at Soledad Prison	1974	6.25	12.50	25.00
❏ X-768	Born in Mississippi, Raised Up in Tennessee	1973	5.00	10.00	20.00
❏ XQ-768 [Q]	Born in Mississippi, Raised Up in Tennessee	1974	6.25	12.50	25.00
❏ X-838	Free Beer and Chicken	1974	3.75	7.50	15.00
❏ XQ-838 [Q]	Free Beer and Chicken	1974	6.25	12.50	25.00
ATCO					
❏ 33-151 [M]	Don't Turn Me From Your Door	1963	25.00	50.00	100.00
❏ SD 33-151 [R]	Don't Turn Me From Your Door	1967	12.50	25.00	50.00
ATLANTIC					
❏ SD 7228	Detroit Special	1972	5.00	10.00	20.00
BATTLE					
❏ BLP-6113 [M]	John Lee Hooker	196?	37.50	75.00	150.00
❏ BLP-6114 [M]	How Long Blues	196?	37.50	75.00	150.00
BLUESWAY					
❏ BL-6002 [M]	Live at Café A-Go-Go	1967	6.25	12.50	25.00
❏ BLS-6002 [S]	Live at Café A-Go-Go	1967	5.00	10.00	20.00
❏ BL-6012 [M]	Urban Blues	1967	6.25	12.50	25.00
❏ BLS-6012 [S]	Urban Blues	1967	5.00	10.00	20.00
❏ BLS-6023	Simply the Truth	1968	5.00	10.00	20.00
❏ BLS-6038	If You Miss 'Em	1969	5.00	10.00	20.00
❏ BLQ-6052 [Q]	Live at Kabuki-Wuki	1974	6.25	12.50	25.00
❏ BLS-6052	Live at Kabuki-Wuki	1973	3.75	7.50	15.00
BUDDAH					
❏ BDS-4002	The Very Best of John Lee Hooker	1970	3.75	7.50	15.00
❏ BDS-7506	Big Band Blues	1970	3.75	7.50	15.00
CHAMELEON					
❏ D1-74794	The Hook	1989	2.50	5.00	10.00
❏ D1-74808	The Healer	1989	2.50	5.00	10.00
CHESS					
❏ LP-1438 [M]	House of the Blues	1960	75.00	150.00	300.00
—Black label					
❏ LP-1438 [M]	House of the Blues	1966	12.50	25.00	50.00
—Blue and white label					
❏ LP-1454 [M]	John Lee Hooker Plays and Sings the Blues	1961	75.00	150.00	300.00
—Black label					
❏ LP-1454 [M]	John Lee Hooker Plays and Sings the Blues	1966	12.50	25.00	50.00
—Blue and white label					
❏ LP-1508 [M]	Real Folk Blues	1966	12.50	25.00	50.00
❏ LPS-1508 [R]	Real Folk Blues	1966	7.50	15.00	30.00
❏ CH-9199	John Lee Hooker Plays and Sings the Blues	1986	2.00	4.00	8.00
—Reissue					
❏ CH-9258	House of the Blues	1987	2.00	4.00	8.00
❏ CH-9271	The Real Folk Blues	1988	2.00	4.00	8.00
❏ 60011 [(2)]	Mad Man Blues	1973	5.00	10.00	20.00
❏ CH2-92507 [(2)]	Mad Man Blues	198?	3.00	6.00	12.00
COLLECTABLES					
❏ COL-5151	Golden Classics	198?	3.00	6.00	12.00

Number	Title (A Side/B Side)	Yr	VG	VG+	NM
CROWN					
❏ CLP-5157 [M]	The Blues	196?	3.00	6.00	12.00
—Black label with multi-color "Crown"					
❏ CLP-5157 [M]	The Blues	1960	25.00	50.00	100.00
—Black label with silver "Crown"					
❏ CLP-5157 [M]	The Blues	1962	7.50	15.00	30.00
—Gray label					
❏ CLP-5232 [M]	John Lee Hooker Sings the Blues	196?	3.00	6.00	12.00
—Black label with multi-color "Crown"					
❏ CLP-5232 [M]	John Lee Hooker Sings the Blues	1962	7.50	15.00	30.00
—Gray label					
❏ CLP-5232 [M]	John Lee Hooker Sings the Blues	1962	25.00	50.00	100.00
—Black label with silver "Crown"					
❏ CLP-5295 [M]	Folk Blues	1962	3.00	6.00	12.00
—Black label with multi-color "Crown"					
❏ CLP-5295 [M]	Folk Blues	1962	7.50	15.00	30.00
—Gray label					
❏ CLP-5353 [M]	The Great John Lee Hooker	1963	3.00	6.00	12.00
—Black label with multi-color "Crown"					
❏ CLP-5353 [M]	The Great John Lee Hooker	1963	7.50	15.00	30.00
—Gray label					
EVEREST ARCHIVE OF FOLK & JAZZ					
❏ 222	John Lee Hooker	1968	3.00	6.00	12.00
❏ 347	Hooked On Blues	1980	3.00	6.00	12.00
EXODUS					
❏ 325 [M]	Is He the World's Greatest Blues Singer?	1966	6.25	12.50	25.00
FANTASY					
❏ 24706 [(2)]	Boogie Chillun	1972	3.75	7.50	15.00
❏ 24722 [(2)]	Black Snake	197?	3.75	7.50	15.00
GALAXY					
❏ 8201 [M]	I'm John Lee Hooker	1962	62.50	125.00	250.00
❏ 8205 [M]	Live at Sugar Hill	196?	62.50	125.00	250.00
GNP CRESCENDO					
❏ GNPS-10007 [(2)]	The Best of John Lee Hooker	1974	3.75	7.50	15.00
GREENE BOTTLE					
❏ 3130 [(2)]	Johnny Lee	1972	3.75	7.50	15.00
IMPULSE!					
❏ A-9103 [M]	It Serves You Right to Suffer	1966	7.50	15.00	30.00
❏ AS-9103 [S]	It Serves You Right to Suffer	1966	10.00	20.00	40.00
JEWEL					
❏ 5005	I Feel Good	1971	3.75	7.50	15.00
KING					
❏ 727 [M]	John Lee Hooker Sings the Blues	1960	125.00	250.00	500.00
❏ KLP-727	John Lee Hooker Sings the Blues	1988	2.00	4.00	8.00
—Reissue of earlier 727					
❏ KS-1085	Moanin' and Stompin' Blues	1970	6.25	12.50	25.00
LABOR					
❏ 4	Alone	1982	2.50	5.00	10.00
MUSE					
❏ 5205	Sittin' Here Thinkin'	1980	3.00	6.00	12.00
PAUSA					
❏ PR-7197	Jealous	1986	2.50	5.00	10.00
RIVERSIDE					
❏ RLP 12-321 [M]	That's My Story	1960	25.00	50.00	100.00
❏ RLP 12-838 [M]	The Country Blues of John Lee Hooker	1959	25.00	50.00	100.00
SPECIALTY					
❏ SPS-2125	Alone	1970	7.50	15.00	30.00
❏ SPS-2127	Going Down Highway 51	1970	7.50	15.00	30.00
STAX					
❏ STS-2013	That's Where It's At	1970	3.75	7.50	15.00
❏ STX-4134	That's Where It's At	1979	2.50	5.00	10.00
—Reissue of 2013					
TOMATO					
❏ 7009 [(2)]	The Cream	1978	3.75	7.50	15.00
TRADITION					
❏ 2089	Real Blues	1970	3.75	7.50	15.00
UNITED ARTISTS					
❏ UA-LA127-J [(3)]	John Lee Hooker's Detroit	1974	6.25	12.50	25.00
❏ UAS-5512	Coast to Coast Blues Band	1971	3.75	7.50	15.00
VEE JAY					
❏ LP-1007 [M]	I'm John Lee Hooker	1959	75.00	150.00	300.00
—Maroon label					
❏ LP-1007 [M]	I'm John Lee Hooker	1960	20.00	40.00	80.00
—Black label with colorband					
❏ VJLP-1007 [(2)]	I'm John Lee Hooker	1986	2.00	4.00	8.00
—Reissue of original on flimsier vinyl					
❏ LP-1023 [M]	Travelin'	1960	20.00	40.00	80.00
❏ LP-1033 [M]	The Folk Lore of John Lee Hooker	1961	12.50	25.00	50.00
❏ SR-1033 [S]	The Folk Lore of John Lee Hooker	1961	20.00	40.00	80.00
❏ LP-1043 [M]	Burnin'	1962	12.50	25.00	50.00
❏ SR-1043 [S]	Burnin'	1962	37.50	75.00	150.00
❏ LP-1049 [M]	The Best of John Lee Hooker	1962	12.50	25.00	50.00
❏ SR-1049 [P]	The Best of John Lee Hooker	1962	20.00	40.00	80.00
❏ VJLP-1049	The Best of John Lee Hooker	1986	2.00	4.00	8.00
—Reissue of original on flimsier vinyl					
❏ LP-1058 [M]	The Big Soul of John Lee Hooker	1963	12.50	25.00	50.00
❏ SR-1058 [S]	The Big Soul of John Lee Hooker	1963	37.50	75.00	150.00
❏ VJLP-1058	The Big Soul of John Lee Hooker	1986	2.00	4.00	8.00
—Reissue of original on flimsier vinyl					
❏ LP-1066 [M]	John Lee Hooker On Campus	1963	12.50	25.00	50.00
❏ SR-1066 [S]	John Lee Hooker On Campus	1963	37.50	75.00	150.00
❏ LP-1078 [M]	John Lee Hooker at Newport	1964	12.50	25.00	50.00
❏ SR-1078 [S]	John Lee Hooker at Newport	1964	37.50	751.00	150.00
❏ VJLP-1078	John Lee Hooker at Newport	1986	2.00	4.00	8.00
—Reissue of original on flimsier vinyl					
❏ DY-7301	John Lee Hooker In Person	198?	2.00	4.00	8.00
❏ LP-8502 [M]	Is He the World's Greatest Blues Singer?	1966	10.00	20.00	40.00
—This is the title on the cover; the label calls it "Is He Really the World's Greatest Blues Singer?"					
❏ VJLP-8502	Is He the World's Greatest Blues Singer?	1986	2.00	4.00	8.00
—Reissue of original on flimsier vinyl; this is the title on the cover; the label calls it "Is He Really the World's Greatest Blues Singer?"					
VERVE FOLKWAYS					
❏ FT-3003 [M]	John Lee Hooker and Seven Nights	1965	6.25	12.50	25.00
❏ FTS-3003 [S]	John Lee Hooker and Seven Nights	1965	10.00	20.00	40.00
WAND					
❏ WDS-689	On the Waterfront	1972	3.75	7.50	15.00

Number	Title (A Side/B Side)	Yr	VG	VG+	NM
HOOKER, JOHN LEE, AND CANNED HEAT Also see each artist's individual listings.					
45s					
UNITED ARTISTS					
❑ 50779	Whiskey and Wimmen/Let's Make It	1971	—	2.50	5.00
Albums					
LIBERTY					
❑ 35002	Hooker 'n' Heat	1971	5.00	10.00	20.00
RHINO					
❑ RNLP-801	Recorded Live at the Fox Venice Theatre	1985	3.00	6.00	12.00
❑ RNDA-71105	Infinite Boogie	1987	3.00	6.00	12.00
HOOTCH					
Albums					
PROGRESS					
❑ PRS-4844	Hootch	1974	150.00	300.00	600.00
HOPE, BOB					
45s					
CAPITOL					
❑ F2109	Am I in Love/Wing Ding	1952	5.00	10.00	20.00
DECCA					
❑ 34117 [DJ]	Bob Hope Accepts 1962 Patriot's Award from University of Notre Dame/Bob Hope in Moscow	1962	3.75	7.50	15.00
RCA VICTOR					
❑ 47-6577	That Certain Feeling/ Zing! Went the Strings of My Heart	1956	3.75	7.50	15.00
❑ 47-7517	Ain't a-Hankerin'/Protection	1959	3.00	6.00	12.00
—With Rosemary Clooney					
UNITED ARTISTS					
❑ 603	Call Me Bwana/The Flip Side	1963	3.00	6.00	12.00
—B-side by Edie Adams					
❑ 603 [PS]	Call Me Bwana/The Flip Side	1963	7.50	15.00	30.00
Albums					
CADET					
❑ LP-4046	On the Road to Vietnam	1965	3.75	7.50	15.00
CAPITOL					
❑ ST-11538	America Is 200 Years Old ... And There's Still Hope!	1976	3.00	6.00	12.00
MCA					
❑ 906	Bob Hope in Hollywood	1984	3.00	6.00	12.00
RADIOLA					
❑ MR-1060	The Bob Hope Radio Show	197?	2.50	5.00	10.00
—Includes two radio shows: October 23, 1945 and December 18, 1945					
RCA VICTOR					
❑ LOC-1055 [M]	Not So Long Ago: NBC Project Twenty	1960	5.00	10.00	20.00
❑ LSO-1055 [S]	Not So Long Ago: NBC Project Twenty	1960	6.25	12.50	25.00
SPEAR					
❑ 4700	Holidays	1973	3.75	7.50	15.00
HOPE, EDDIE					
45s					
MARLIN					
❑ 804	A Fool No More/Lost Child	1956	50.00	100.00	200.00
HOPE, LYNN					
45s					
ALADDIN					
❑ 3095	Blue Moon/Blow, Lynn, Blow	1951	10.00	20.00	40.00
❑ 3103	Too Young/Free and Easy	1951	10.00	20.00	40.00
❑ 3109	She's Funny That Way/Eleven Till Two	1951	10.00	20.00	40.00
❑ 3134	Driftin'/Sentimental Journey	1952	7.50	15.00	30.00
❑ 3155	Move It/Don't Worry 'Bout Me	1952	7.50	15.00	30.00
❑ 3165	September Song/Blues for Anna Bocoa	1953	6.25	12.50	25.00
❑ 3178	Broken Heart/Morocco	1953	6.25	12.50	25.00
❑ 3185	Jet/Tenderly	1953	6.25	12.50	25.00
❑ 3208	Swing Train/Rose Room	1953	6.25	12.50	25.00
❑ 3229	Brazil/C. Jam Blues	1954	6.25	12.50	25.00
❑ 3297	All of Me/Summertime	1955	6.25	12.50	25.00
❑ 3322	Cherry/Blues in F	1956	6.25	12.50	25.00
KING					
❑ 5336	Tenderly/Full Moon	1960	3.00	6.00	12.00
❑ 5352	Body and Soul/Sands of Sahara	1960	3.00	6.00	12.00
❑ 5378	A Ghost of a Chance/Little Landslide	1960	3.00	6.00	12.00
❑ 5431	Shockin'/Blue and Sentimental	1960	3.00	6.00	12.00
HOPEFUL, THE					
45s					
MERCURY					
❑ 72637	7 O'Clock News (Silent Night)/6 O'Clock News (America The Beautiful)	1966	3.00	6.00	12.00
HOPKIN, MARY					
45s					
APPLE					
❑ 1801	Those Were the Days/Turn, Turn, Turn	1968	2.50	5.00	10.00
❑ 1806	Goodbye/Sparrow	1969	2.00	4.00	8.00
❑ 1806 [PS]	Goodbye/Sparrow	1969	3.00	6.00	12.00
❑ 1816	Temma Harbour/Lantano Dagli Occhi	1970	2.00	4.00	8.00
❑ 1816 [PS]	Temma Harbour/Lantano Dagli Occhi	1970	3.00	6.00	12.00
❑ 1823	Que Sera, Sera (Whatever Will Be, Will Be)/ Fields of St. Etienne	1970	2.00	4.00	8.00
❑ 1825	Think About Your Children/Heritage	1970	2.00	4.00	8.00
❑ 1825	Think About Your Children/Heritage	1970	3.00	6.00	12.00
—With star on A-side label					
❑ 1825 [PS]	Think About Your Children/Heritage	1970	3.00	6.00	12.00
❑ 1843	Water, Paper and Clay/Streets of London	1972	2.00	4.00	8.00
❑ 1843	Water, Paper and Clay/Streets of London	1972	3.00	6.00	12.00
—With star on A-side label					
❑ 1855	Knock Knock Who's There/International	1972	2.00	4.00	8.00
APPLE/AMERICOM					
❑ 1801P/M-238	Those Were the Days/Turn, Turn, Turn	1969	150.00	300.00	600.00
—Four-inch flexi-disc sold from vending machines					
RCA VICTOR					
❑ PB-10694	Tell Me Now/If You Love Me	1976	—	2.00	4.00

Number	Title (A Side/B Side)	Yr	VG	VG+	NM
Albums					
APPLE					
❑ ST-3351	Post Card	1969	6.25	12.50	25.00
❑ ST-5-3351	Post Card	1969	7.50	15.00	30.00
—Capitol Record Club edition					
❑ SMAS-3381	Earth Song/Ocean Song	1970	6.25	12.50	25.00
❑ SW-3395	Those Were the Days	1972	10.00	20.00	40.00
HOPKINS, LIGHTNIN'					
45s					
ACE					
❑ 516	Bad Boogie/Wonder What Is Wrong with Me	1956	10.00	20.00	40.00
ALADDIN					
❑ 3063	Shotgun Blues/Rolling Blues	1950	175.00	350.00	700.00
❑ 3077	Moonrise Blues/Honey, Honey Blues	1951	50.00	100.00	200.00
❑ 3096	Miss Me Blues/Abilene	1951	50.00	100.00	200.00
❑ 3117	You Are Not Going to Worry About My Life Anymore/Daddy Will Be Home Someday	1951	50.00	100.00	200.00
❑ 3262	So Long/My California	1954	25.00	50.00	100.00
ARHOOLIE					
❑ 508	My Woman/Lousiana Blues	1965	3.00	6.00	12.00
❑ 513	Come On Baby/Money Taker	1965	3.00	6.00	12.00
BLUESVILLE					
❑ 813	So Sorry to Leave You/Got to Move Your Baby	1960	5.00	10.00	20.00
❑ 814	Death Bells/Sail On	1961	5.00	10.00	20.00
❑ 817	Back to New Orleans/Hard to Love a Woman	1961	5.00	10.00	20.00
❑ 820	Happy Blues for John Glenn (Part 1)/Happy Blues for John Glenn (Part 2)	1962	5.00	10.00	20.00
❑ 821	Last Night Blues/Walkin' Blues	1962	5.00	10.00	20.00
❑ 822	Sinner's Prayer/Angel Child	1962	5.00	10.00	20.00
❑ 823	The Business You're Doing/Wake Up Old Lady	1963	5.00	10.00	20.00
❑ 824	Going Away/Better Stop Her	1963	5.00	10.00	20.00
❑ 825	Katie Mae/My Babe	1963	5.00	10.00	20.00
CHART					
❑ 636	Walkin' the Streets/Mussy Haired Woman	1957	7.50	15.00	30.00
DART					
❑ 123	Grievance Blues/Unsuccessful Blues	1959	5.00	10.00	20.00
❑ 152	Mary Lou/Wait to Go Home	1960	5.00	10.00	20.00
DECCA					
❑ 9-28841	The War Is Over/Policy Game	1953	20.00	40.00	80.00
❑ 9-48306	Merry Christmas/Happy New Year	1953	20.00	40.00	80.00
❑ 9-48312	Highway Blues/Cemetery Blues	1954	20.00	40.00	80.00
❑ 9-48321	I'm Wild About You Baby/Bad Things on My Mind	1954	25.00	50.00	100.00
FIRE					
❑ 1034	Mojo Hand/Glory Be	1961	5.00	10.00	20.00
HARLEM					
❑ 2321	Contrary Mary/I'm Begging You	1954	50.00	100.00	200.00
❑ 2324	Mad Man's Boogie/Nobody Cares for Me	1954	50.00	100.00	200.00
❑ 2331	Fast Life/The Jackstropper	1955	50.00	100.00	200.00
❑ 2336	Good Old Woman/Untrue	1955	50.00	100.00	200.00
HERALD					
❑ 425	Lightnin's Boogie/ Don't Think 'Cause You're Pretty	1954	7.50	15.00	30.00
❑ 428	Lightnin's Special/Life Is Used to Live	1954	7.50	15.00	30.00
❑ 436	Movin' On Out Boogie/Sick Feelin' Blues	1954	7.50	15.00	30.00
❑ 443	Nothin' But the Blues/Early Morning Boogie	1954	7.50	15.00	30.00
❑ 449	Evil Hearted Woman/They Wonder Who I Am	1955	7.50	15.00	30.00
❑ 456	My Baby's Gone/Don't Need No Job	1955	6.25	12.50	25.00
❑ 465	I Had a Gal Named Sal/Blues for My Cookie	1955	6.25	12.50	25.00
❑ 471	Hopkins Sky Hop/Lonesome in Your Home	1956	6.25	12.50	25.00
❑ 476	Grandma's Boogie/I Love You Baby	1956	6.25	12.50	25.00
❑ 483	Finally Met My Baby/That's Alright Baby	1956	6.25	12.50	25.00
❑ 490	Shine On Moon/Sitting and Thinking	1956	6.25	12.50	25.00
❑ 497	Remember Me/Please Don't Go Baby	1957	6.25	12.50	25.00
❑ 504	Boogie Woogie Dance/ The Blues Is a Mighty Bad Feeling	1957	5.00	10.00	20.00
❑ 520	Little Kewpie Doll/Lightnin' Don't Feel Well	1958	5.00	10.00	20.00
❑ 531	Hear Me Talkin'/Lightnin's Stomp	1958	5.00	10.00	20.00
❑ 542	Let's Move/I'm Achin'	1959	5.00	10.00	20.00
❑ 547	Flash Lightnin'/Gonna Change My Ways	1960	5.00	10.00	20.00
IMPERIAL					
❑ 5834	Feel So Bad/Shotgun	1962	3.75	7.50	15.00
❑ 5852	Picture on the Wall/Lightnin's Boogie	1962	3.75	7.50	15.00
IVORY					
❑ 91272	Got Me a Lousiana Woman/ War Is Starting Again	196?	3.75	7.50	15.00
JAX					
❑ 315	No Good Woman/Been a Bad Man	1953	75.00	150.00	300.00
—Red vinyl					
❑ 318	Automobile/Organ Blues	1953	75.00	150.00	300.00
—Red vinyl					
❑ 321	Contrary Mary/I'm Begging You	1953	75.00	150.00	300.00
—Red vinyl					
❑ 635	Coffee Blues/New Short Haired Woman	1954	62.50	125.00	250.00
—Reissue of Sittin' In With 635					
❑ 642	You Caused My Heart to Weep/ Tap Dance Boogie	1954	62.50	125.00	250.00
—Reissue of Sittin' In With 642					
❑ 649	New Worried Life Blues/One Kind of Favor	1954	62.50	125.00	250.00
—Reissue of Sittin' In With 649; this may be its first issue on 45 rpm					
❑ 660	Mad Blues/I've Been a Bad Man	1954	125.00	250.00	250.00
—Reissue of Sittin' In With 660					
❑ 661	Gone Again/Down to the River	1954	62.50	125.00	250.00
—Reissue of Sittin' In With 661					
JEWEL					
❑ 788	Back Door Friends/Fishing Clothes	1968	—	3.00	6.00
❑ 796	Wig Wearin' Woman/Move On Out, Part 2	1968	—	3.00	6.00
❑ 803	Lovin' Arms/Ride in Your New Auto	1969	—	3.00	6.00
❑ 807	Play with Your Poodle/Breakfast Time	1970	—	3.00	6.00
❑ 809	I'm Comin' Home/You're Too Fast	1970	—	3.00	6.00
❑ 816	My Charlie (Part 1)/My Charlie (Part 2)	1970	—	3.00	6.00
❑ 819	Rock Me Mama/Love Me This Morning	1971	—	3.00	6.00
❑ 825	Uncle Sam the Hip Hit Record Man/ Found My Baby Crying	1971	—	3.00	6.00
LIGHTNING					
❑ 104	Unsuccessful Blues/Grieving Blues	1955	125.00	250.00	500.00

Number	Title (A Side/B Side)	Yr	VG	VG+	NM
MERCURY					
❑ 8252x45	Everybody's Down on Me/You Do Too	1952	30.00	60.00	120.00
❑ 8274x45	Sad News from Korea/Let Me Fly Your Kite	1952	25.00	50.00	100.00
❑ 8293x45	Gone with the Wind/She's Almost Dead	1952	25.00	50.00	100.00
❑ 70081x45	Ain't It a Shame/Crazy About My Baby	1953	25.00	50.00	100.00
❑ 70191x45	My Mama Told Me/What's the Matter Now	1953	25.00	50.00	100.00
PRESTIGE					
❑ 326	I Like to Boogie/Let's Go Sit on the Lawn	1964	2.50	5.00	10.00
❑ 343	Mojo Hand/Automobile Blues	1964	2.50	5.00	10.00
❑ 374	T Model Blues/You Cook Alright	1965	2.50	5.00	10.00
❑ 391	Sinner's Prayer/Got to Move Your Baby	1965	2.50	5.00	10.00
❑ 405	I'm Gonna Build Me a Heaven (Part 1)/I'm Gonna Build Me a Heaven (Part 2)	1966	2.50	5.00	10.00
❑ 452	Mama Blues/Pneumonia Blues	1968	2.00	4.00	8.00
RPM					
❑ 45x337	Beggin' You to Stay/Bad Luck and Trouble	1951	150.00	300.00	600.00
❑ 45x346	Lonesome Dog Blues/Jake Head	1952	200.00	400.00	800.00
❑ 45x351	Don't Keep My Baby Long/Last Affair	1952	100.00	200.00	400.00
❑ 45x359	Needed Time/One Kind Favor	1952	100.00	200.00	400.00
❑ 45x378	Another Fool in Town/Candy Kitchen	1953	75.00	150.00	300.00
❑ 45x388	Black Cat/Mistreated Blues	1953	75.00	150.00	300.00
❑ 45x398	Santa Fe Blues/Some Day Baby	1954	50.00	100.00	200.00
SHAD					
❑ 5011	Hello Central/Mad As I Can Be	1959	3.75	7.50	15.00
SITTIN' IN WITH					
❑ 621	Give Me Central 209/New York Boogie	1951	125.00	250.00	500.00
❑ 621	Hello Central/New York Boogie	1952	100.00	200.00	400.00
❑ 635	Coffee Blues/New Short Haired Woman	1952	125.00	250.00	500.00
❑ 642	You Caused My Heart to Weep/Tap Dance Boogie	1952	125.00	250.00	500.00
❑ 644	Jail House Blues/"T" Model Blues	1952	125.00	250.00	500.00
❑ 647	Bald Headed Woman/Dirty House	1952	125.00	250.00	500.00
❑ 649	New Worried Life Blues/One Kind of Favor	1952	—	—	—
—Unreleased on 45 rpm?					
❑ 652	Papa Bones Boogie/Everything Happens to Me	1953	125.00	250.00	500.00
❑ 658	Freight Train Blues (When I Started Hoboing)/Broken Hearted Blues	1953	125.00	250.00	500.00
❑ 660	Mad Blues/I've Been a Bad Man	1953	125.00	250.00	500.00
❑ 661	Gone Again/Down to the River	1953	125.00	250.00	500.00
SPHERE SOUND					
❑ 710	Santa/Black Mare Trot	196?	2.50	5.00	10.00
TNT					
❑ 8002	Lightnin' Jump/Late in the Evening	1954	175.00	350.00	700.00
❑ 8003	Moanin' Blues/Leavin' Blues	1954	175.00	350.00	700.00
VAULT					
❑ 965	Easy on Your Heels/No Education	1970	—	3.00	6.00
Albums					
ANALOGUE PRODUCTIONS					
❑ AAPB-014	Goin' Away	199?	10.00	20.00	40.00
—Audiophile reissue					
ARHOOLIE					
❑ 1011	Lightnin' Hopkins and His Guitar	196?	5.00	10.00	20.00
❑ 1022	Lightnin' Hopkins, His Brother and Barbara Dane	196?	5.00	10.00	20.00
❑ 1030	Blues Festival	196?	3.75	7.50	15.00
❑ 1034	Texas Blues Man	1968	3.75	7.50	15.00
❑ 1063	Lightnin' Hopkins in Berkeley	1969	3.75	7.50	15.00
❑ 1087	Poor Lightnin'	1970	3.75	7.50	15.00
❑ 2007	Early Recordings	197?	3.75	7.50	15.00
❑ 2010	Early Recordings Volume 2	197?	3.75	7.50	15.00
BARNABY					
❑ Z 30247	Lightnin' Hopkins in New York	1970	3.75	7.50	15.00
BLUES CLASSICS					
❑ 30	Historic Recordings 1952-1953	1986	3.00	6.00	12.00
BLUESVILLE					
❑ BVLP-1019 [M] Lightnin'		1961	25.00	50.00	100.00
—Blue label, silver print					
❑ BVLP-1019 [M] Lightnin'		1964	7.50	15.00	30.00
—Blue label, trident logo on right					
❑ BVLP-1029 [M] Last Night Blues		1961	25.00	50.00	100.00
—Blue label, silver print					
❑ BVLP-1045 [M] Blues in My Bottle		1962	25.00	50.00	100.00
—Blue label, silver print					
❑ BVLP-1045 [M] Blues in My Bottle		1964	7.50	15.00	30.00
—Blue label, trident logo on right					
❑ BVLP-1057 [M] Walkin' This Street		1962	25.00	50.00	100.00
—Blue label, silver print					
❑ BVLP-1057 [M] Walkin' This Street		1964	7.50	15.00	30.00
—Blue label, trident logo on right					
❑ BVLP-1061 [M] Lightnin' & Co.		1963	25.00	50.00	100.00
—Blue label, silver print					
❑ BVLP-1061 [M] Lightnin' & Co.		1964	7.50	15.00	30.00
—Blue label, trident logo on right					
❑ BVLP-1070 [M] Smokes Like Lightnin'		1963	25.00	50.00	100.00
—Blue label, silver print					
❑ BVLP-1070 [M] Smokes Like Lightnin'		1964	7.50	15.00	30.00
—Blue label, trident logo on right					
❑ BVLP-1073 [M] Goin' Away		1963	25.00	50.00	100.00
—Blue label, silver print					
❑ BVLP-1073 [M] Goin' Away		1964	7.50	15.00	30.00
—Blue label, trident logo on right					
❑ BVLP-1081 [M] Gotta Move Your Baby		1964	7.50	15.00	30.00
—Blue label, trident logo on right					
❑ BVLP-1084 [M] Lightnin' Hopkins' Greatest Hits		1964	10.00	20.00	40.00
❑ BVLP-1086 [M] Down Home Blues		1964	6.25	12.50	25.00
BLUESWAY					
❑ S-6039	If You Miss 'Im	1969	5.00	10.00	20.00
BULLDOG					
❑ 1010	The Texas Bluesman	1965	3.75	7.50	15.00
CANDID					
❑ CM-8010 [M] Lightnin' in New York		1961	30.00	60.00	120.00
❑ CS-9010 [S] Lightnin' in New York		1961	37.50	75.00	150.00
COLLECTABLES					
❑ COL-5111	Golden Classics — Mojo Hand	198?	2.50	5.00	10.00
❑ COL-5121	The Herald Recordings/1954	198?	2.50	5.00	10.00
❑ COL-5143	Golden Classics, Part 1: Drinkin' the Blues	198?	2.50	5.00	10.00
❑ COL-5144	Golden Classics, Part 2: Prison Blues	198?	2.50	5.00	10.00

Number	Title (A Side/B Side)	Yr	VG	VG+	NM
❑ COL-5145	Golden Classics, Part 3: Mama and Papa Hopkins	198?	2.50	5.00	10.00
❑ COL-5146	Golden Classics, Part 4: Nothin' But the Blues	198?	2.50	5.00	10.00
❑ COL-5203	The Lost Texas Tapes, Vol. 1	198?	2.50	5.00	10.00
❑ COL-5204	The Lost Texas Tapes, Vol. 2	198?	2.50	5.00	10.00
❑ COL-5205	The Lost Texas Tapes, Vol. 3	198?	2.50	5.00	10.00
❑ COL-5206	The Lost Texas Tapes, Vol. 4	198?	2.50	5.00	10.00
❑ COL-5207	The Lost Texas Tapes, Vol. 5	198?	2.50	5.00	10.00
CROWN					
❑ CLP-5224 [M] Lightnin' Hopkins Sings the Blues		196?	6.25	12.50	25.00
—Black label, multi-color logo					
❑ CLP-5224 [M] Lightnin' Hopkins Sings the Blues		1962	12.50	25.00	50.00
—Gray label					
❑ CLP-5224 [M] Lightnin' Hopkins Sings the Blues		1962	25.00	50.00	100.00
—Black label, silver "Crown"					
DART					
❑ D-8000 [M]	Blues Underground	196?	50.00	100.00	200.00
—Retitled version of above					
❑ D-8000 [M]	Lightning Strikes Again	1960	100.00	200.00	400.00
DCC COMPACT CLASSICS					
❑ LPZ-2007	Blues Hoot	1996	7.50	15.00	30.00
—Audiophile vinyl					
EVEREST ARCHIVE OF FOLK & JAZZ					
❑ 241	Lightnin' Hopkins	1969	3.75	7.50	15.00
❑ 313	Lightnin' Hopkins, Vol. 2	197?	3.75	7.50	15.00
❑ 342	Autobiography in Blues	1979	3.00	6.00	12.00
FANTASY					
❑ OBC-506	Blues in My Bottle	198?	3.00	6.00	12.00
❑ OBC-522	Goin' Away	1988	3.00	6.00	12.00
❑ OBC-532	Lightnin'	1990	3.00	6.00	12.00
❑ 24702 [(2)]	Double Blues	1972	5.00	10.00	20.00
❑ 24725 [(2)]	How Many More Years	1981	3.75	7.50	15.00
FIRE					
❑ FLP 104 [M]	Mojo Hand	1960	375.00	750.00	1500.
FOLKLORE					
❑ FRLP-14021 [M] Hootin' the Blues		1964	15.00	30.00	60.00
❑ FRST-14021 [S] Hootin' the Blues		1964	17.50	35.00	70.00
FOLKWAYS					
❑ FS-3822 [M]	Lightnin' Hopkins	1962	10.00	20.00	40.00
❑ 31011	Roots	196?	3.75	7.50	15.00
GNP CRESCENDO					
❑ 10022	Legacy of the Blues, Volume 12	1978	3.00	6.00	12.00
GUEST STAR					
❑ G-1459 [M]	"Live" at the Bird Lounge, Houston, Texas	1964	7.50	15.00	30.00
❑ GS-1459 [R]	"Live" at the Bird Lounge, Houston, Texas	1964	5.00	10.00	20.00
HERALD					
❑ LP 1012 [M]	Lightnin' and the Blues	1959	200.00	400.00	800.00
—Yellow label					
❑ LP 1012 [M]	Lightnin' and the Blues	1959	750.00	1125.	1500.
—Black label					
❑ LP 1012 [M]	Lightnin' and the Blues	196?	125.00	250.00	500.00
—Multi-color label					
IMPERIAL					
❑ LP-9180 [M]	Lightnin' Hopkins On Stage	1962	75.00	150.00	300.00
❑ LP-9186 [M]	Lightnin' Hopkins Sings the Blues	1962	75.00	150.00	300.00
❑ LP-9211 [M]	Lightnin' Hopkins and the Blues	1963	50.00	100.00	200.00
❑ LP-12211 [R]	Lightnin' Hopkins and the Blues	1963	25.00	50.00	100.00
INTERNATIONAL ARTISTS					
❑ IA-6	Free Form Patterns	1968	12.50	25.00	50.00
—With psychedelic art on cover					
❑ IA-6	Free Form Patterns	1968	50.00	100.00	200.00
—With photo on cover					
JAZZ MAN					
❑ BLZ-5502	Lightnin' in New York	1982	2.50	5.00	10.00
JEWEL					
❑ 5000	Blue Lightnin'	1967	3.75	7.50	15.00
❑ 5001	Talkin' Some Sense	1968	3.75	7.50	15.00
❑ 5015	Great Electric Show and Dance	1970	3.75	7.50	15.00
KING					
❑ KS-1085	Moanin' Blues	1969	3.75	7.50	15.00
MAINSTREAM					
❑ 311	The Blues	1971	3.75	7.50	15.00
❑ 326	Dirty Blues	197?	3.75	7.50	15.00
❑ 405	Low Down Dirty Blues	1974	3.75	7.50	15.00
❑ S-6040 [S]	Blues	196?	7.50	15.00	30.00
❑ 56040 [M]	Blues	196?	6.25	12.50	25.00
MOUNT VERNON					
❑ 104 [M]	Nothin' But the Blues	196?	6.25	12.50	25.00
OLYMPIC GOLD MEDAL					
❑ 7110	Blues Giant	1974	3.00	6.00	12.00
POPPY					
❑ 60002 [(2)]	Lightnin'!	1969	6.25	12.50	25.00
PRESTIGE					
❑ PRLPT-7370 [(2)M] My Life with the Blues		1965	15.00	30.00	60.00
❑ PRST-7370 [(2)S] My Life with the Blues		1965	17.50	35.00	70.00
❑ PRLP-7377 [M] Soul Blues		1966	12.50	25.00	50.00
❑ PRST-7377 [S] Soul Blues		1966	15.00	30.00	60.00
❑ PRST-7592	Lightnin' Hopkins' Greatest Hits	1969	3.75	7.50	15.00
❑ PRST-7714	The Best of Lightnin' Hopkins & His Texas Blues Band	1969	3.75	7.50	15.00
❑ PRST-7806	Hootin' the Blues	1969	3.75	7.50	15.00
❑ PRST-7811	The Blues of Lightnin' Hopkins	1969	3.75	7.50	15.00
❑ PRST-7831	Gotta Move Your Baby	1970	3.75	7.50	15.00
RHINO					
❑ RNLP 103	Los Angeles Blues	1982	2.50	5.00	10.00
SCORE					
❑ SLP-4022 [M] Lightnin' Hopkins Strums the Blues		1958	300.00	600.00	1200.
SMITHSONIAN FOLKWAYS					
❑ SF-40019	Lightnin' Hopkins	1990	3.00	6.00	12.00
SPHERE SOUND					
❑ SSR-7001 [M] Lightnin' Hopkins		1964	100.00	200.00	400.00
❑ SSSR-7001 [R] Lightnin' Hopkins		1964	75.00	150.00	300.00
TIME					
❑ 1 [M]	Blues/Folk	1960	30.00	60.00	120.00
❑ 2 [M]	Blues/Folk Volume 2	1960	30.00	60.00	120.00

Number	Title (A Side/B Side)	Yr	VG	VG+	NM
❏ ST-70004 [S]	Last of the Great Blues Singers	1962	30.00	60.00	120.00
❏ T-70004 [M]	Last of the Great Blues Singers	1962	30.00	60.00	120.00
TOMATO					
❏ 7004 [(2)]	Lightnin'!	1977	3.75	7.50	15.00
TRADITION					
❏ TLP-1035 [M]	Country Blues	1960	7.50	15.00	30.00
❏ TLP-1040 [M]	Autobiography in Blues	1961	7.50	15.00	30.00
❏ TLP-2056 [M]	The Best of Lightnin' Hopkins	1967	5.00	10.00	20.00
❏ TLP-2103 [M]	Lightnin' Strikes	1972	3.75	7.50	15.00
TRIP					
❏ TLP-8015	Lightnin' Hopkins	1971	3.00	6.00	12.00
UNITED					
❏ US-7713	Lightnin' Hopkins Sings the Blues	196?	3.75	7.50	15.00
❏ US-7744	Original Folk Blues	196?	3.75	7.50	15.00
❏ US-7785	A Legend in His Time	196?	3.75	7.50	15.00
UNITED ARTISTS					
❏ UAS-5512	Coast to Coast Blues Band	197?	3.75	7.50	15.00
UP FRONT					
❏ 158	Lightnin' Blues	1973	3.00	6.00	12.00
VAULT					
❏ 129	California Mudslide	1969	6.25	12.50	25.00
VEE JAY					
❏ LP 1044 [M]	Lightnin' Strikes	1962	12.50	25.00	50.00
VERVE					
❏ V-8453 [M]	Fast Life Woman	1962	10.00	20.00	40.00
VERVE FOLKWAYS					
❏ FV-9000 [M]	The Roots of Lightnin' Hopkins	1965	6.25	12.50	25.00
❏ FVS-9000 [S]	The Roots of Lightnin' Hopkins	1965	7.50	15.00	30.00
❏ FV-9022 [M]	Lightnin' Strikes	1965	6.25	12.50	25.00
❏ FVS-9022 [S]	Lightnin' Strikes	1965	7.50	15.00	30.00
VERVE FORECAST					
❏ FT-3013 [M]	Something Blue	1967	5.00	10.00	20.00
❏ FTS-3013 [S]	Something Blue	1967	6.25	12.50	25.00
❏ FTS-3031	Lightnin' Strikes	1968	5.00	10.00	20.00
WORLD PACIFIC					
❏ ST-1817 [S]	First Meetin'	1963	10.00	20.00	40.00
—Black vinyl					
❏ ST-1817 [S]	First Meetin'	1963	20.00	40.00	80.00
—Red vinyl					
❏ WP-1817 [M]	First Meetin'	1963	7.50	15.00	30.00

HOPKINS, NICKY Prominent session keyboardist who played on BEATLES and ROLLING STONES sessions, among dozens of others.

45s

Number	Title (A Side/B Side)	Yr	VG	VG+	NM
COLUMBIA					
❏ 45869	Speed On/Sundown in Mexico	1973	—	2.50	5.00
DECCA					
❏ 32139	Mister Pleasant/Nothing As Yet	1967	3.00	6.00	12.00

Albums

Number	Title (A Side/B Side)	Yr	VG	VG+	NM
COLUMBIA					
❏ KC 32074	The Tin Man Was a Dreamer	1973	5.00	10.00	20.00

HORNE, LENA

45s

Number	Title (A Side/B Side)	Yr	VG	VG+	NM
BUDDAH					
❏ 215	Watch What Happens/Rocky Raccoon	1971	—	3.00	6.00
❏ 233	Feels So Good/Nature's Baby	1971	—	3.00	6.00
CAPITOL					
❏ S7-57888	Let It Snow! Let It Snow! Let It Snow!/Jingle Bells	1992		2.00	4.00
—B-side by Count Basie					
MCA					
❏ 40979	Believe in Yourself/Main Title Overture (Part 1)	1978	—	2.50	5.00
MGM					
❏ K30397	Is It Always Like This/Love of My Life	1951	3.00	6.00	12.00
—One record of box set K-72					
RCA VICTOR					
❏ 47-6073	Love Me or Leave Me/I Love to Love	1955	3.00	6.00	12.00
❏ 47-6175	It's All Right with Me/It's Love	1955	3.00	6.00	12.00
❏ 47-6431	If You Can Dream/What's Right for You	1956	3.00	6.00	12.00
❏ 47-7037	Push De Button/Coconut Street	1957	3.00	6.00	12.00
❏ 47-7332	When Johnny Comes Marching Home/You'd Better	1957	3.00	6.00	12.00
❏ 47-8092	Where Is Love/Come On Strong	1962	2.50	5.00	10.00
❏ 47-8092 [PS]	Where Is Love/Come On Strong	1962	3.75	7.50	15.00
SKYE					
❏ 4523	Watch What Happens/Rocky Raccoon	1970	2.00	4.00	8.00
THREE CHERRIES					
❏ 7301	I Wish I'd Met You/When I Fall in Love	1989	—	2.00	4.00
—A-side with Sammy Davis Jr.					
❏ 7301 [PS]	I Wish I'd Met You/When I Fall in Love	1989	—	2.00	4.00
20TH CENTURY FOX					
❏ 449	Now!/Silent Spring	1963	2.50	5.00	10.00
❏ 460	Blowin' in the Wind/The Eagle and Me	1964	2.50	5.00	10.00
UNITED ARTISTS					
❏ 851	Pleasures and Palaces/Feeling Good	1965	2.00	4.00	8.00
❏ 911	The Sand and the Sea/Softly, As I Leave You	1965	2.00	4.00	8.00
❏ 1661	Let It Snow! Let It Snow! Let It Snow!/What Are You Doing New Year's Eve	1966	2.50	5.00	10.00
—Silver Spotlight Series					
❏ 1661 [DJ]	Let It Snow! Let It Snow! Let It Snow! (same on both sides)	1966	2.00	4.00	8.00
—Silver Spotlight Series promo					
❏ 50051	Love Bug/Wonder What I'm Gonna Do	1966	2.00	4.00	8.00

7-Inch Extended Plays

Number	Title (A Side/B Side)	Yr	VG	VG+	NM
RCA CAMDEN					
❏ CAE 380	St. Louis Blues/Beale Street Blues//Aunt Hagar's Blues/Careless Love Blues	1956	3.00	6.00	12.00
❏ CAE 380 [PS]	Lena Horne Sings the Blues	1956	3.00	6.00	12.00
RCA VICTOR					
❏ 947-0164	Moanin' Low/I Gotta Right to Sing the Blues//The Man I Love/Where or When	1954	5.00	10.00	20.00
—Silver label, red print; part of 2-EP set EPBT-3061					
❏ 947-0165	Stormy Weather/Ill Wind//Mad About the Boy/What Is This Thing Called Love?	1954	5.00	10.00	20.00
—Silver label, red print; part of 2-EP set EPBT-3061					

Number	Title (A Side/B Side)	Yr	VG	VG+	NM
❏ VLP 2587	I've Grown Accustomed to His Face/I Concentrate on You/I Found a New Baby//I Surrender, Dear/I Let a Song Go Out of My Heart/I Want to Be Happy	1963	3.00	6.00	12.00
—Jukebox issue; small hole, plays at 33 1/3 rpm					
❏ VLP 2587 [PS]	Lena...Lovely and Alive	1963	3.00	6.00	12.00
❏ EPA-4038	Ain't It De Truth?/Take It Slow, Joe//Cocoanut Sweet/Push De Button	1957	3.75	7.50	15.00
❏ EPA-4038 [PS]	Jamaica	1957	3.75	7.50	15.00

Albums

Number	Title (A Side/B Side)	Yr	VG	VG+	NM
ACCORD					
❏ SN-7190	Standing Room Only	198?	2.50	5.00	10.00
BLUEBIRD					
❏ 9985-1-RB	Stormy Weather: The Legendary Lena	1990	3.00	6.00	12.00
BUDDAH					
❏ BDS-5084	Nature's Baby	1971	3.00	6.00	12.00
❏ BDS-5669 [(2)]	The Essential Lena Horne	197?	3.00	6.00	12.00
BULLDOG					
❏ BDL-2000	20 Golden Pieces of Lena Horne	198?	2.50	5.00	10.00
CHARTER					
❏ CLP-101 [M]	Lena Sings Your Requests	1963	3.75	7.50	15.00
❏ CLS-101 [S]	Lena Sings Your Requests	1963	5.00	10.00	20.00
❏ CLP-106 [M]	Like Latin	1964	3.75	7.50	15.00
❏ CLS-106 [S]	Like Latin	1964	5.00	10.00	20.00
DRG					
❏ MRS-501	Lena Horne With Lennie Hayton & the Marty Paich Orchestra	198?	2.50	5.00	10.00
❏ MRS-510	Lena Goes Latin	1986	2.50	5.00	10.00
JAZZTONE					
❏ J-1262 [M]	Lena and Ivie	1957	12.50	25.00	50.00
LIBERTY					
❏ LN-10194	Lena in Hollywood	198?	2.00	4.00	8.00
LION					
❏ L-70050 [M]	I Feel So Smoochie	1959	5.00	10.00	20.00
MGM					
❏ E-545 [10]	Lena Horne Sings	1952	12.50	25.00	50.00
❏ M3G-5409	The One and Only	197?	2.50	5.00	10.00
MOBILE FIDELITY					
❏ 2-094 [(2)]	Lena Horne: The Lady and Her Music	1982	10.00	20.00	40.00
—Audiophile vinyl					
MOVIETONE					
❏ MTM 71005 [M]	Once in a Lifetime	196?	3.75	7.50	15.00
❏ MTS 72005 [S]	Once in a Lifetime	196?	5.00	10.00	20.00
PAIR					
❏ PDL2-1055 [(2)]	Lena	1986	3.00	6.00	12.00
QWEST					
❏ 2QW 3597 [(2)]	Lena Horne: The Lady and Her Music	1981	3.00	6.00	12.00
RCA VICTOR					
❏ BGL1-1026	Lena and Michel	1975	3.00	6.00	12.00
—With Michel Legrand					
❏ LOC-1028 [M]	Lena Horne at the Waldorf Astoria	1957	7.50	15.00	30.00
❏ LSO-1028 [S]	Lena Horne at the Waldorf Astoria	1957	10.00	20.00	40.00
❏ LPM-1148 [M]	It's Love	1955	12.50	25.00	50.00
❏ LPM-1375 [M]	Stormy Weather	1956	12.50	25.00	50.00
❏ BGL1-1799	Lena	1976	3.00	6.00	12.00
❏ LPM-1879 [M]	Give the Lady What She Wants	1958	7.50	15.00	30.00
❏ LSP-1879 [S]	Give the Lady What She Wants	1958	10.00	20.00	40.00
❏ LPM-1895 [M]	Songs of Burke and Van Heusen	1959	7.50	15.00	30.00
❏ LSP-1895 [S]	Songs of Burke and Van Heusen	1959	10.00	20.00	40.00
❏ LPM-2364 [M]	Lena Horne at the Sands	1961	6.25	12.50	25.00
❏ LSP-2364 [S]	Lena Horne at the Sands	1961	7.50	15.00	30.00
❏ LPM-2465 [M]	Lena on the Blue Side	1962	6.25	12.50	25.00
❏ LSP-2465 [S]	Lena on the Blue Side	1962	7.50	15.00	30.00
❏ LPM-2587 [M]	Lena...Lovely and Alive	1963	6.25	12.50	25.00
❏ LSP-2587 [S]	Lena...Lovely and Alive	1963	7.50	15.00	30.00
❏ LPT-3061 [10]	This Is Lena Horne	1952	12.50	25.00	50.00
❏ AYL1-4389	Lena, A New Album	1983	2.00	4.00	8.00
—"Best Buy Series" reissue					
SKYE					
❏ 15	Lena & Gabor	1970	3.75	7.50	15.00
—With Gabor Szabo					
STANYAN					
❏ POW-3006	Stormy Weather	198?	2.50	5.00	10.00
—Reissue of 10126					
❏ 10126	Stormy Weather	197?	3.00	6.00	12.00
SUNBEAM					
❏ 212	A Date with Lena Horne	198?	2.50	5.00	10.00
—With Fletcher Henderson and His Orchestra					
THREE CHERRIES					
❏ TC-44411	The Men in My Life	1989	2.50	5.00	10.00
TIME-LIFE					
❏ SLGD-05 [(2)]	Legendary Singers: Lena Horne	1985	3.75	7.50	15.00
TOPS					
❏ L-910 [10]	Moanin' Low	195?	10.00	20.00	40.00
❏ L-931 [10]	Lena Horne Sings	195?	10.00	20.00	40.00
❏ L-1502 [M]	Lena Horne	1958	5.00	10.00	20.00
20TH CENTURY FOX					
❏ TF-4115 [M]	Here's Lena Now	1964	3.75	7.50	15.00
❏ TFS-4115 [S]	Here's Lena Now	1964	5.00	10.00	20.00
UNITED ARTISTS					
❏ UAL 3433 [M]	Feelin' Good	1965	3.75	7.50	15.00
❏ UAL 3470 [M]	Lena in Hollywood	1966	3.75	7.50	15.00
❏ UAL 3496 [M]	Soul	1966	3.75	7.50	15.00
❏ UAL 3546 [M]	Merry from Lena	1966	3.75	7.50	15.00
❏ UAS 6433 [S]	Feelin' Good	1965	5.00	10.00	20.00
❏ UAS 6470 [S]	Lena in Hollywood	1966	5.00	10.00	20.00
❏ UAS 6496 [S]	Soul	1966	5.00	10.00	20.00
❏ UAS 6546 [S]	Merry from Lena	1966	5.00	10.00	20.00
—Black label, "United Artists" in rounded box at top					
❏ UAS 6546 [S]	Merry from Lena	1972	3.00	6.00	12.00
—Tan label					

Number	Title (A Side/B Side)	Yr	VG	VG+	NM

HORNE, LENA, AND HARRY BELAFONTE Also see each artist's individual listings.
Albums
RCA VICTOR

Number	Title (A Side/B Side)	Yr	VG	VG+	NM
□ LOC-1507 [M]	Porgy and Bess	1959	6.25	12.50	25.00
□ LSO-1507 [S]	Porgy and Bess	1959	10.00	20.00	40.00

HORNETS, THE More than one group.
45s
COLUMBIA

Number	Title (A Side/B Side)	Yr	VG	VG+	NM
□ 42999	Fruit Cake/Seven Days to Tahiti	1964	15.00	30.00	60.00

EMERALD

□ 501	Runt/Breakfast in Bed	196?	7.50	15.00	30.00

FLASH

□ 125	Crying Over You/Tango Moon	1957	62.50	125.00	250.00

LIBERTY

□ 55688	Motorcycle U.S.A./On the Track	1964	7.50	15.00	30.00

REV

□ 3515	Slow Dance/Strollin'	1958	6.25	12.50	25.00

STATES

□ 127	I Can't Believe/Lonesome Baby	1953	4000.	6000.	8000.

—Black vinyl

□ 127	I Can't Believe/Lonesome Baby	1953	7500.	10000.	15000.

—Red vinyl

V.I.P.

□ 25004	She's My Baby/Give Me a Kiss	1964	15.00	30.00	60.00

Albums
LIBERTY

□ LRP-3348 [M]	Motorcycles U.S.A.	1963	10.00	20.00	40.00
□ LRP-3364 [M]	Big Drag Boats U.S.A.	1964	12.50	25.00	50.00
□ LST-7348 [S]	Motorcycles U.S.A.	1963	12.50	25.00	50.00
□ LST-7364 [S]	Big Drag Boats U.S.A.	1964	15.00	30.00	60.00

HORSES Don Johnson of "Miami Vice" and "Nash Bridges" fame was supposedly in this band.
45s
WHITE WHALE

□ 301	Class of '69/Country Boy	1969	2.00	4.00	8.00
□ 320	Freight Train/(B-side unknown)	1969	2.50	5.00	10.00

Albums
WHITE WHALE

□ WWS-7121	Horses	1970	10.00	20.00	40.00

HORSLIPS
45s
ATCO

□ 6935	High Reel/Furniture	1973	2.00	4.00	8.00

DJM

□ 1026	Warm Sweet Breath of Love/(B-side unknown)	1977	—	2.50	5.00
□ 1032	Trouble (With a Capital T)/(B-side unknown)	1978	—	2.50	5.00
□ 1036	Sure the Boy Was Green/Exiles	1978	2.50	5.00	10.00

—Green vinyl

□ 1105	Loneliness/Homesick	1979	—	2.50	5.00

MERCURY

□ 76030	Rescue Me/Soap Opera	1979	—	2.50	5.00
□ 76072 [DJ]	Shakin' All Over (mono/stereo)	1979	—	3.00	6.00

—May be promo only

RCA VICTOR

□ PB-10123	Nighttown Boys/We Bring the Summer With Me	1974	—	3.00	6.00

Albums
ATCO

□ SD 7030	Happy to Meet, Sorry to Part	1973	3.00	6.00	12.00
□ SD 7039	The Tain	1974	3.00	6.00	12.00

DJM

□ 10	Book of Invasions	1977	2.50	5.00	10.00
□ 16	Aliens	1978	2.50	5.00	10.00
□ 20	The Man Who Built America	1979	2.50	5.00	10.00

MERCURY

□ SRM-1-3809	Short Stories/Tall Tales	1979	2.50	5.00	10.00
□ SRM-1-3842	Belfast Gigs	1980	2.50	5.00	10.00

RCA VICTOR

□ CPL1-0709	Dancehall Sweethearts	1974	3.00	6.00	12.00

HORTON, JAY
45s
MUSTANG

□ 3010	I Trip on You Girl/(B-side unknown)	1965	7.50	15.00	30.00
□ 3021	It's Love/Come What May	1966	7.50	15.00	30.00

HORTON, JOHNNY
45s
ABBOTT

□ 100	Candy Jones/Devilish Lovelight	1951	10.00	20.00	40.00
□ 101	Happy Millionaire/Mean Mean Son of a Gun	1951	10.00	20.00	40.00
□ 102	Plaid and Calico/Done Roving	1951	10.00	20.00	40.00

—B-side by Bill Thompson's Westerners

□ 103	Birds and Butteflies/Coal Smoke, Valve Oil and Steam	1951	10.00	20.00	40.00
□ 104	Go and Wash (Those Dirty Feet)/In My Home in Shelby County	1951	10.00	20.00	40.00
□ 105	Shadows on the Old Bayou/Talk Gobbler Talk	1951	10.00	20.00	40.00
□ 106	Smokey Joe's Barbeque/Words	1951	10.00	20.00	40.00
□ 107	Long Rocky Road/On the Banks of the Beautiful Nile	1952	10.00	20.00	40.00
□ 108	Somebody Rocking in My Broken Chair/Betty Lorraine	1952	10.00	20.00	40.00

—With Hillbilly Barton

□ 109	Rhythm in My Baby's Walk/Bowlin' Baby	1952	10.00	20.00	40.00
□ 135	Plaid and Calico/Shadows on the Old Bayou	1953	7.50	15.00	30.00

COLUMBIA

□ 21504	Honky Tonk Man/I'm Ready If You're Willing	1956	7.50	15.00	30.00
□ 21538	I'm a One Woman Man/I Don't Like I Did	1956	6.25	12.50	25.00
□ 30568 [S]	Sink the Bismarck/The Same Old Tale the Crow Told Me	1960	6.25	12.50	25.00

—"Stereo Single 33"; small hole, plays at 33 1/3 rpm

□ S7 31104 [S]	North to Alaska/Whispering Pines	1961	5.00	10.00	20.00
□ S7 31105 [S]	Johnny Reb/The Mansion You Stole	1961	5.00	10.00	20.00
□ S7 31106 [S]	When It's Springtime in Alaska/The Battle of New Orleans	1961	5.00	10.00	20.00
□ S7 31107 [S]	All for the Love of a Girl/Sink the Bismarck	1961	5.00	10.00	20.00
□ S7 31108 [S]	Comanche (The Brave Horse)/Jim Bridger	1961	5.00	10.00	20.00

—The above five are "Stereo Seven" 33 1/3 rpm jukebox singles from "JS7-28" entitled "Johnny Horton's Greatest Hits"

□ 40813	I'm Coming Home/I Got a Hole in My Picture	1957	7.50	15.00	30.00
□ 40919	She Knows Why/The Woman I Need	1957	5.00	10.00	20.00
□ 40986	I'll Do It Every Time/Let's Take the Long Way Home	1957	5.00	10.00	20.00
□ 41043	You're My Baby/Lover's Rock	1957	7.50	15.00	30.00
□ 41110	Honky Tonk Hardwood Floor/The Wild One	1958	15.00	30.00	60.00
□ 41210	All Grown Up/Counterfeit Love	1958	5.00	10.00	20.00
□ 41308	When It's Springtime in Alaska (It's Forty Below)/Whispering Pines	1958	3.75	7.50	15.00
□ 41308 [PS]	When It's Springtime in Alaska (It's Forty Below)/Whispering Pines	1958	7.50	15.00	30.00

—Promo-only black and white sleeve

□ 41339	The Battle of New Orleans/All for the Love of a Girl	1959	3.75	7.50	15.00
□ 41339 [PS]	The Battle of New Orleans/All for the Love of a Girl	1959	5.00	10.00	20.00

—Red and black print sleeve with lyrics

□ 41339 [PS]	The Battle of New Orleans/All for the Love of a Girl	1959	15.00	30.00	60.00

—Promo-only four-page booklet sleeve

□ 41437	Johnny Reb/Sal's Got a Sugar Lip	1959	3.75	7.50	15.00
□ 41502	I'm Ready If You're Willing/Take Me Like I Am	1959	3.75	7.50	15.00
□ 41522	They Shined Up Rudolph's Nose/The Electrified Donkey	1959	3.75	7.50	15.00
□ 41522 [PS]	They Shined Up Rudolph's Nose/The Electrified Donkey	1959	25.00	50.00	100.00
□ 41568	Sink the Bismarck/The Same Old Tale the Crow Told Me	1960	3.00	6.00	12.00
□ 41568 [PS]	Sink the Bismarck/The Same Old Tale the Crow Told Me	1960	5.00	10.00	20.00
□ 41685	Johnny Freedom/Comanche	1960	3.00	6.00	12.00
□ 41685 [PS]	Johnny Freedom/Comanche	1960	5.00	10.00	20.00
□ 41782	North to Alaska/The Mansion You Stole	1960	3.00	6.00	12.00
□ 41782 [PS]	North to Alaska/The Mansion You Stole	1960	5.00	10.00	20.00
□ 41963	Sleepy Eyed John/They'll Never Take Her Love from Me	1961	3.00	6.00	12.00
□ 41963 [PS]	Sleepy Eyed John/They'll Never Take Her Love from Me	1961	5.00	10.00	20.00
□ 42063	Ole Slewfoot/Miss Marcy	1961	3.00	6.00	12.00
□ 42063 [PS]	Ole Slewfoot/Miss Marcy	1961	5.00	10.00	20.00
□ 42302	Honky Tonk Man/Words	1962	3.75	7.50	15.00
□ 42302 [PS]	Honky Tonk Man/Words	1962	5.00	10.00	20.00
□ 42653	All Grown Up/I'm a One Woman Man	1962	3.00	6.00	12.00
□ 42653 [PS]	All Grown Up/I'm a One Woman Man	1962	5.00	10.00	20.00
□ 42774	Sugar Coated Baby/When It's Springtime in Alaska (It's Forty Below)	1963	2.50	5.00	10.00
□ 42993	Hooray for That Little Difference/Tell My Baby I Love Her	1964	2.50	5.00	10.00
□ 42993 [PS]	Hooray for That Little Difference/Tell My Baby I Love Her	1964	5.00	10.00	20.00
□ 43143	Lost Highway/The Same Old Tale the Crow Told Me	1964	2.50	5.00	10.00
□ 43228	Rock Island Line/I Just Don't Like This Kind of Lovin'	1965	2.50	5.00	10.00
□ 43719	Sam Magee/All for the Love of a Girl	1966	2.00	4.00	8.00
□ 44156	The Battle of New Orleans/All for the Love of a Girl	1967	—	3.00	6.00

CORMAC

□ 1193	Plaid and Calico/Done Roving	1951	30.00	60.00	120.00
□ 1197	Birds and Butteflies/Coal Smoke, Valve Oil and Steam	1951	30.00	60.00	120.00

DOT

□ 15966	Plaid and Calico/Shadows on the Old Bayou	1959	3.00	6.00	12.00

MERCURY

□ 6412	The Devil Sent Me You/First Train Headin' South	1952	7.50	15.00	30.00
□ 6418	The Rest of Your Life/This Won't Be the First Time	1952	7.50	15.00	30.00
□ 70014	I Won't Forget/The Child's Side of Life	1952	7.50	15.00	30.00
□ 70100	Tennessee Jive/The Mansion You Stole	1953	7.50	15.00	30.00
□ 70156	S.S. Loveline/I Won't Get Dreamy-Eyed	1953	7.50	15.00	30.00
□ 70198	You, You, You/Red Lips and Warm Red Wine	1953	7.50	15.00	30.00
□ 70227	All for the Love of a Girl/Broken Hearted	1953	7.50	15.00	30.00
□ 70325	Move On Down the Line/Train with the Rhumba Beat	1954	7.50	15.00	30.00
□ 70399	The Door of Your Mansion/Ha Ha and Moonface	1954	7.50	15.00	30.00
□ 70462	No True Love/There'll Never Be Another Mary	1954	7.50	15.00	30.00
□ 70636	Journey with No End/Ridin' the Sunshine Special	1955	7.50	15.00	30.00
□ 70707	Big Wheels Rollin'/Hey Sweet, Sweet Thing	1955	7.50	15.00	30.00

7-Inch Extended Plays
COLUMBIA

□ B-13621	The Battle of New Orleans/Whispering Pines//The First Train Heading South/Lost Highway	1960	3.00	6.00	12.00
□ B-13621 [PS]	The Spectacular Johnny Horton, Vol. 1	1960	4.00	8.00	16.00
□ B-13622	Joe's Been a-Gettin' There/Sam Magee//When It's Springtime in Alaska/Cherokee Boogie	1960	3.00	6.00	12.00
□ B-13622 [PS]	The Spectacular Johnny Horton, Vol. 2	1960	4.00	8.00	16.00
□ B-13623	All for the Love of a Girl/The Golden Rocket/Mr. Moonlight/Got the Bull by the Horns	1960	3.00	6.00	12.00
□ B-13623 [PS]	The Spectacular Johnny Horton, Vol. 3	1960	4.00	8.00	16.00

Albums
BRIAR

□ 104 [M]	Done Rovin'	196?	37.50	75.00	150.00

COLUMBIA

□ CL 1362 [M]	The Spectacular Johnny Horton	1959	7.50	15.00	30.00
□ CL 1478 [M]	Johnny Horton Makes History	1960	7.50	15.00	30.00
□ 1596/8396	Johnny Horton's Greatest Hits Bonus Photo	1961	2.50	5.00	10.00
□ CL 1596 [M]	Johnny Horton's Greatest Hits	1961	6.25	12.50	25.00
□ CL 1721 [M]	Honky-Tonk Man	1962	7.50	15.00	30.00
□ CL 2299 [M]	I Can't Forget You	1965	6.25	12.50	25.00

Number	Title (A Side/B Side)	Yr	VG	VG+	NM
❑ CL 2566 [M]	Johnny Horton on Stage at the Louisiana Hayride	1966	5.00	10.00	20.00
❑ CS 8167 [S]	The Spectacular Johnny Horton	1959	10.00	20.00	40.00
❑ CS 8269 [S]	Johnny Horton Makes History	1960	10.00	20.00	40.00
❑ CS 8396 [S]	Johnny Horton's Greatest Hits	1961	7.50	15.00	30.00
❑ PC 8396	Johnny Horton's Greatest Hits	198?	2.00	4.00	8.00
—Budget-line reissue					
❑ CS 8779 [R]	Honky-Tonk Man	1962	3.75	7.50	15.00
❑ CS 9099 [R]	I Can't Forget You	1965	3.75	7.50	15.00
❑ CS 9366 [S]	Johnny Horton on Stage at the Louisiana Hayride	1966	6.25	12.50	25.00
❑ CS 9940	Johnny Horton On the Road	1969	3.75	7.50	15.00
❑ G 30884 [(2)]	The World of Johnny Horton	1971	3.75	7.50	15.00
DOT					
❑ DLP 3221 [M]	Johnny Horton	1962	7.50	15.00	30.00
❑ DLP 25221 [R]	Johnny Horton	1962	3.75	7.50	15.00
HARMONY					
❑ HS 11291 [R]	The Unforgettable Johnny Horton	196?	3.00	6.00	12.00
❑ HS 11384	The Legendary Johnny Horton	1970	3.00	6.00	12.00
❑ KH 30394	The Battle of New Orleans	1971	3.00	6.00	12.00
HILLTOP					
❑ 6012	The Voice of Johnny Horton	196?	3.00	6.00	12.00
❑ JS-6060	All for the Love of a Girl	196?	3.00	6.00	12.00
MERCURY					
❑ MG-20478 [M]	The Fantastic Johnny Horton	1959	12.50	25.00	50.00
SESAC					
❑ 1201 [M]	Free and Easy Songs	1959	37.50	75.00	150.00

HOSEA, DON
45s
SUN
Number	Title (A Side/B Side)	Yr	VG	VG+	NM
❑ 368	Since I Met You/Uh Huh Unh	1961	5.00	10.00	20.00

HOT BUTTER
45s
MUSICOR
Number	Title (A Side/B Side)	Yr	VG	VG+	NM
❑ 1458	Popcorn/At the Movies	1972	—	3.00	6.00
❑ 1466	Apache/Hot Butter	1972	—	2.50	5.00
❑ 1468	Tequila/Hot Butter	1972	—	2.50	5.00
❑ 1473	Percolator/Tristana	1973	—	2.50	5.00
❑ 1481	Slay Solution/Kappi Maki	1973	—	2.50	5.00
❑ 1491	Pipeline/Apache	1974	—	2.50	5.00
Albums					
MUSICOR					
❑ MS-3242	Popcorn	1972	3.00	6.00	12.00
—Regular cover					
❑ MS-3242	Popcorn	1972	5.00	10.00	20.00
—Die-cut cover					

HOT CHOCOLATE
45s
APPLE
Number	Title (A Side/B Side)	Yr	VG	VG+	NM
❑ 1812	Give Peace a Chance/Living Without Tomorrow	1969	2.50	5.00	10.00
—As "Hot Chocolate Band"					
BELL					
❑ 45390	Rumors/(B-side unknown)	1973	—	2.50	5.00
❑ 45466	Emma/(B-side unknown)	1974	—	3.50	7.00
BIG TREE					
❑ 16031	Emma/A Love Like Yours	1975	—	2.50	5.00
❑ 16038	Disco Queen/Makin' Music	1975	—	2.50	5.00
❑ 16047	You Sexy Thing/Amazing Skin Song	1975	—	2.50	5.00
❑ 16060	Don't Stop It Now/Beautiful Lady	1976	—	2.50	5.00
❑ 16078	Heaven Is in the Back Seat of My Cadillac//(B-side unknown)	1976	—	2.50	5.00
❑ 16096	So You Win Again/Part of Being with You	1977	—	2.50	5.00
❑ 16101	Man to Man/(B-side unknown)	1977	—	2.50	5.00
EMI AMERICA					
❑ 8143	Are You Getting Enough Happiness/One Night's Not Enough	1982	—	2.00	4.00
❑ 8157	Bed Games/It Started with a Kiss	1983	—	2.00	4.00
EMI-CAPITOL					
❑ S7-19894	You Sexy Thing/So You Win Again	1998	—	—	3.00
INFINITY					
❑ 50002	Every 1's a Winner/Power of Love	1978	—	2.00	4.00
❑ 50016	Going Through the Motions/Don't Turn It Off	1979	—	2.00	4.00
❑ 50033	I Just Love What You're Doing/Congas Man	1979	—	2.00	4.00
❑ 50048	Mindless Boogie/Dance (Get Down To It)	1979	—	2.00	4.00
RAK					
❑ 4503	You Could Have Been a Lady/Everybody's Laughing	1972	—	3.00	6.00
❑ 4506	I Believe in Love/Caveman Billy	1972	—	3.00	6.00
❑ 4508	Mary Anne/Ruth	1972	—	3.00	6.00
❑ 4513	Brother Louie/I Want to Be Free	1973	—	3.00	6.00
Albums					
BIG TREE					
❑ BT 76002	10 Greatest Hits	1977	2.50	5.00	10.00
❑ BT 89503	Cicero Park	1975	2.50	5.00	10.00
❑ BT 89512	Hot Chocolate	1975	2.50	5.00	10.00
❑ BT 89519	Man to Man	1976	2.50	5.00	10.00
EMI AMERICA					
❑ ST-17077	Mystery	1982	2.50	5.00	10.00
INFINITY					
❑ INF-9002	Every 1's a Winner	1978	2.50	5.00	10.00
❑ INF-9010	Going Through the Motions	1979	2.50	5.00	10.00

HOT DOGGERS, THE BRUCE JOHNSTON was in this group.
Albums
EPIC
Number	Title (A Side/B Side)	Yr	VG	VG+	NM
❑ LN 24054 [M]	Surfin' U.S.A.	1963	37.50	75.00	150.00
❑ BN 26054 [S]	Surfin' U.S.A.	1963	50.00	100.00	200.00

HOT POOP
Albums
HOT POOP
Number	Title (A Side/B Side)	Yr	VG	VG+	NM
❑ 3072	Hot Poop Does Their Own Thing	1971	75.00	150.00	300.00

HOT RODDERS, THE
Albums
CROWN
Number	Title (A Side/B Side)	Yr	VG	VG+	NM
❑ CST-378 [S]	Big Hot Rod	1963	6.25	12.50	25.00
❑ CLP-5378 [M]	Big Hot Rod	1963	5.00	10.00	20.00

HOT-TODDYS, THE See ROCKIN' REBELS.

HOT TUNA Offshoot of JEFFERSON AIRPLANE.
45s
GRUNT
Number	Title (A Side/B Side)	Yr	VG	VG+	NM
❑ 65-0502	Water Song/Keep On Truckin'	1972	—	3.00	6.00
❑ 65-0502 (PS)	Water Song/Keep On Truckin'	1972	3.00	6.00	12.00
❑ PB-10443	Hot Jellyroll Blues/Surphase Tension	1975	—	2.50	5.00
❑ PB-10776	It's So Easy/I Can't Be Satisfied	1976	—	2.50	5.00
RCA VICTOR					
❑ 74-0528	Candy Man/Been So Long	1971	—	3.00	6.00
❑ 74-0528 (PS)	Candy Man/Been So Long	1971	5.00	10.00	20.00
Albums					
GRUNT					
❑ BFL1-0348	The Phosphorescent Rat	1974	3.75	7.50	15.00
❑ BFD1-0820 [Q]	America's Choice	1975	6.25	12.50	25.00
❑ BFL1-0820	America's Choice	1975	3.75	7.50	15.00
❑ FTR-1004	Burgers	1972	3.75	7.50	15.00
❑ BFD1-1238 [Q]	Yellow Fever	1975	6.25	12.50	25.00
❑ BFL1-1238	Yellow Fever	1975	3.75	7.50	15.00
❑ BFL1-1920	Hoppkorv	1976	3.75	7.50	15.00
❑ CYL2-2545 [(2)]	Double Dose	1978	5.00	10.00	20.00
❑ BXL1-2591	Burgers	1978	3.00	6.00	12.00
—Reissue of 1004					
❑ DJL1-2852 [DJ]	The Last Interview? A Live Hot Tuna Radio Classic	1978	7.50	15.00	30.00
❑ BXL1-3357	Final Vinyl	1979	3.00	6.00	12.00
RCA VICTOR					
❑ AYL1-3864	Hot Tuna	1981	2.00	4.00	8.00
—"Best Buy Series" reissue					
❑ AYL1-3865	First Pull Up Then Pull Down	1981	2.00	4.00	8.00
—"Best Buy Series" reissue					
❑ AYL1-3951	Burgers	1981	2.00	4.00	8.00
—"Best Buy Series" reissue					
❑ LSP-4353	Hot Tuna	1970	3.75	7.50	15.00
❑ LSP-4550	First Pull Up Then Pull Down	1971	3.75	7.50	15.00

HOTLEGS Early incarnation of 10CC. Also see GRAHAM GOULDMAN.
45s
CAPITOL
Number	Title (A Side/B Side)	Yr	VG	VG+	NM
❑ 2886	Neanderthal Man/You Didn't Like It, Because You Didn't Think of It	1970	2.50	5.00	10.00
❑ 3043	Run Baby Run/How Many Times	1971	3.75	7.50	15.00
Albums					
CAPITOL					
❑ ST-587	Hotlegs Thinks: School Stinks	1970	6.25	12.50	25.00

HOUK, RALPH
Albums
CARLTON
Number	Title (A Side/B Side)	Yr	VG	VG+	NM
❑ HH-16 [M]	Hear How to Play Better Baseball	1961	10.00	20.00	40.00

HOUND DOG CLOWNS
45s
UNI
Number	Title (A Side/B Side)	Yr	VG	VG+	NM
❑ 55047	Superfox/Wicked Witch	1968	5.00	10.00	20.00

HOUR GLASS, THE Also see DUANE ALLMAN; DUANE AND GREGG ALLMAN; GREGG ALLMAN.
45s
LIBERTY
Number	Title (A Side/B Side)	Yr	VG	VG+	NM
❑ 56002	Heartbeat/Nothing But Tears	1967	3.00	6.00	12.00
❑ 56029	Power of Love/I Still Want Your Love	1968	3.00	6.00	12.00
❑ 56053	D-I-V-O-R-C-E/Changing of the Guard	1968	3.00	6.00	12.00
❑ 56065	She Is My Woman/Going Nowhere	1968	3.00	6.00	12.00
❑ 56072	Now Is the Time/She Is My Woman	1968	3.00	6.00	12.00
❑ 56091	I've Been Trying/Silently	1969	3.00	6.00	12.00
Albums					
LIBERTY					
❑ LRP-3536 [M]	The Hour Glass	1967	6.25	12.50	25.00
❑ LST-7536 [S]	The Hour Glass	1967	7.50	15.00	30.00
❑ LST-7555	The Power of Love	1968	7.50	15.00	30.00
SPRINGBOARD					
❑ SPB-4016	Duane and Gregg Allman with the Hour Glass	1976	2.50	5.00	10.00
UNITED ARTISTS					
❑ UA-LA013-G2 [(2)]	The Hour Glass	1973	3.75	7.50	15.00

HOUSTON, CISSY
12-Inch Singles
PRIVATE STOCK
Number	Title (A Side/B Side)	Yr	VG	VG+	NM
❑ PS 5108	Think It Over (6:00)/An Umbrella Song	1978	2.50	5.00	10.00
45s					
COLUMBIA					
❑ 11058	Warning-Danger (This Love Affair May Be Hazardous to You)/An Umbrella Song	1979	—	2.00	4.00
❑ 11208	Break It To Me Gently/Gonna Take the Easy Way Out	1980	—	2.00	4.00
COMMONWEALTH UNITED					
❑ 3010	I'll Be There/Me — I Believe	1970	—	3.00	6.00
CONGRESS					
❑ 268	Bring Him Back/World of Broken Hearts	1966	15.00	30.00	60.00
—As "Susie Houston"					
JANUS					
❑ 131	I Just Don't Know What to Do with Myself/Empty Place	1970	—	3.00	6.00
❑ 145	Be My Baby/I'll Be There	1971	—	3.00	6.00
❑ 159	Hang On to a Dream/Darling Take Me Back	1971	—	3.00	6.00
❑ 177	I Love You/Making Love	1971	—	3.00	6.00
❑ 190	Didn't We/It's Not Easy	1972	—	3.00	6.00

Number	Title (A Side/B Side)	Yr	VG	VG+	NM
❑ 206	Midnight Train to Georgia/				
	Will You Still Love Me Tomorrow	1972	—	3.00	6.00
❑ 230	I'm So Glad I Can Love Again/				
	One Time You Say You Love Me	1973	—	3.00	6.00
❑ 255	I Believe/Nothing Can Stop Me	1975	—	3.00	6.00
KAPP					
❑ 814	Don't Come Running to Me/				
	One Broken Heart for Sale	1967	7.50	15.00	30.00
—As "Sissie Houston"					
PRIVATE STOCK					
❑ 45,137	Love Is Something That Leads You/				
	If I Ever Lose This Heaven	1977	—	2.50	5.00
❑ 45,137	Love Is Something That Leads You/				
	It Never Really Ended	1977	—	2.50	5.00
❑ 45,153	Tomorrow/Love Is Holding On	1977	—	2.50	5.00
❑ 45,171	Things to Do/It Never Really Ended	1977	—	2.50	5.00
❑ 45,204	Think It Over/The Umbrella Song	1978	—	2.50	5.00
Albums					
COLUMBIA					
❑ JC 36112	Warning Danger	1979	2.50	5.00	10.00
❑ JC 36193	Step Aside for a Lady	1980	2.50	5.00	10.00
COMMONWEALTH UNITED					
❑ 6008	Cissy Houston	1970	—	—	—
—Canceled?					
JANUS					
❑ 3001	Cissy Houston	1970	3.75	7.50	15.00
PRIVATE STOCK					
❑ PS 2031	Cissy Houston	1977	3.00	6.00	12.00
❑ PS 7015	Think It Over	1978	3.00	6.00	12.00

HOUSTON, DAVID

45s

Number	Title (A Side/B Side)	Yr	VG	VG+	NM
COLONIAL					
❑ 101	Waltz of the Angels/(B-side unknown)	1978	2.00	4.00	8.00
COUNTRY INT'L.					
❑ 145	You're the Perfect Reason/❑ We Couldn't				
	Make It Love	1980	—	3.00	6.00
❑ 148	Sad Love Song Lady/				
	Thanks for Being You and Loving Me	1980	—	3.00	6.00
❑ 149	The Bottom Line/We Couldn't Make It Love	1980	—	3.00	6.00
❑ 155	Bandera Waltz/(B-side unknown)	1981	—	3.00	6.00
❑ 220	A Penny for Your Thoughts Tonight Virginia/				
	(B-side unknown)	1989	—	3.00	6.00
DERRICK					
❑ 126	Let Your Love Fall Back on Me/				
	Take Me to Your Heart	1979	—	3.00	6.00
❑ 127	Here's to All the Hard Working Husbands (In the				
	World)/Next Sunday I'm Gonna Be Saved	1979	—	3.00	6.00
ELEKTRA					
❑ 45513	Sunday I'm Gonna Be Saved/				
	Waltz of the Angels	1978	—	2.00	4.00
❑ 45552	Best Friends Make the Worst Enemies/				
	There Won't Be a Wedding	1978	—	2.00	4.00
❑ 46028	Faded Love and Winter Roses/				
	Beyond the Blue Horizon	1979	—	2.00	4.00
EPIC					
❑ 9625	Mountain of Love/Angeline	1963	2.00	4.00	8.00
❑ 9658	Chickashay/Passing Through	1964	2.00	4.00	8.00
❑ 9690	One If For Him, Two If For Me/Your Memories	1964	2.00	4.00	8.00
❑ 9720	Love Looks Good on You/My Little Lady	1964	2.00	4.00	8.00
❑ 9746	Sweet, Sweet Judy/Too Many Times				
	(Away from You)	1964	2.00	4.00	8.00
❑ 9782	Rose Colored Glasses/Ballad of the Fool Killer	1965	2.50	5.00	10.00
❑ 9831	Livin' in a House Full of Love/Cowpoke	1965	2.00	4.00	8.00
❑ 9884	Sammy/I'll Take You Home Again, Kathleen	1966	2.00	4.00	8.00
❑ 9884 [PS]	Sammy/I'll Take You Home Again, Kathleen	1966	2.50	5.00	10.00
❑ 10025	Almost Persuaded/We Got Love	1966	2.00	4.00	8.00
❑ 10102	A Loser's Cathedral/Where Could I Go? (But to				
	Her)	1966	—	3.00	6.00
❑ 10102 [PS]	A Loser's Cathedral/Where Could I Go? (But to				
	Her)	1966	2.50	5.00	10.00
❑ 10154	With One Exception/Sweet, Sweet Judy	1967	—	3.00	6.00
❑ 10154 [PS]	With One Exception/Sweet, Sweet Judy	1967	2.50	5.00	10.00
❑ 10224	You Mean the World to Me/Don't Mention				
	Tomorrow	1967	—	3.00	6.00
❑ 10224 [PS]	You Mean the World to Me/Don't Mention				
	Tomorrow	1967	2.50	5.00	10.00
❑ 10291	Have a Little Faith/Too Far Gone	1968	—	3.00	6.00
❑ 10291 [PS]	Have a Little Faith/Too Far Gone	1968	2.50	5.00	10.00
❑ 10338	Already It's Heaven/Lighter Shade of Pale	1968	—	3.00	6.00
❑ 10338 [PS]	Already It's Heaven/Lighter Shade of Pale	1968	2.50	5.00	10.00
❑ 10394	Where Love Used to Live/I Love a Rainbow	1968	—	3.00	6.00
❑ 10430	My Woman's Good to Me/Lullaby to a Little Girl	1968	—	3.00	6.00
❑ 10488	I'm Down to My Last "I Love You"/Watching My				
	World Walk Away	1969	—	3.00	6.00
❑ 10539	Baby, Baby (I Know You're a Lady)/				
	True Love's a Lasting Thing	1969	—	3.00	6.00
❑ 10596	I Do My Swinging at Home/				
	Then I'll Know You Care	1970	—	3.00	6.00
❑ 10643	Wonders of the Wine/If God Can Forgive Me	1970	—	3.00	6.00
❑ 10696	A Woman Always Knows/The Rest of My Life	1970	—	3.00	6.00
❑ 10748	Nashville/That's Why I Cry	1971	—	3.00	6.00
❑ 10778	Maiden's Prayer/Home Sweet Home	1971	—	3.00	6.00
❑ 10830	The Day That Love Walked In/Sweet Lovin'	1972	—	3.00	6.00
❑ 10870	Soft, Sweet and Warm/The Rest of My Life	1972	—	3.00	6.00
❑ 10911	I Wonder How John Felt (When He Baptized				
	Jesus)/Will the Circle Be Unbroken	1972	2.00	4.00	8.00
❑ 10939	Good Things/The Love She Gives	1973	—	3.00	6.00
❑ 10995	She's All Woman/Sweet Lovin'	1973	—	2.50	5.00
❑ 11048	The Lady of the Night/Thank You Teardrop	1973	—	2.50	5.00
❑ 11096	That Same Ol' Look of Love/Clinging Vine	1974	—	2.50	5.00
❑ 50009	Can't You Feel It/I Walk and I Walk and I Walk	1974	—	2.50	5.00
❑ 50066	A Man Needs Love/Flower of Love	1975	—	2.50	5.00
❑ 50113	I'll Be Your Steppin' Stone/				
	Then I'll Know You Care	1975	—	2.50	5.00

Number	Title (A Side/B Side)	Yr	VG	VG+	NM
❑ 50134	Sweet Molly/Old Blind Fiddler	1975	—	2.50	5.00
—With Calvin Crawford					
❑ 50156	The Woman on My Mind/I Can't Sit Still	1975	—	2.50	5.00
❑ 50186	What a Night/From the Bottom of My Heart	1976	—	2.50	5.00
❑ 50241	Lullaby Song/White Circle	1976	—	2.50	5.00
❑ 50275	Come On Down (To Our Favorite Forget-About-				
	Her Place)/Me and Susan Wright	1976	—	2.50	5.00
EXCELSIOR					
❑ 1007	My Lady/Something You've Never Heard	1981	—	2.50	5.00
❑ 1012	Texas Ida Red/(B-side unknown)	1981	—	3.00	6.00
❑ 1015	After All/(B-side unknown)	1981	—	2.00	4.00
GUSTO					
❑ 156	So Many Ways/Touch My World	1977	—	3.00	6.00
❑ 161	Amazing Grace/Return to Me	1977	—	—	—
—Canceled					
❑ 162	Ain't That Lovin' You Baby/Love Is a Mystery	1977	—	3.00	6.00
❑ 168	The Twelfth of Never/Barroom Champagne	1977	—	3.00	6.00
❑ 172	It Started All Over Again/Touch My World	1977	—	3.00	6.00
❑ 184	No Tell Motel/Hate to Tell Baby a Lie	1978	—	3.00	6.00
IMPERIAL					
❑ 8291	I'm Sorry I Made You Cry/Blue Prelude	1955	10.00	20.00	40.00
NRC					
❑ 005	Waited So Long/All I Do Is Dream of You	1958	5.00	10.00	20.00
❑ 012	The Key/So Young, So Unknowing	1958	5.00	10.00	20.00
❑ 047	It's Been So Long/Kalua	1959	5.00	10.00	20.00
PHILLIPS INTERNATIONAL					
❑ 3583	Sherry's Lips/Miss Brown	1961	7.50	15.00	30.00
RCA VICTOR					
❑ 47-6611	Sugar Sweet/Hasta Luego	1956	7.50	15.00	30.00
❑ 47-6696	Blue Prelude/I'll Always Have It on My Mind	1956	7.50	15.00	30.00
❑ 47-6837	Someone Else's Arms/				
	Ain't Going There No More	1957	7.50	15.00	30.00
❑ 47-6927	One and Only/Hackin' Around	1957	12.50	25.00	50.00
❑ 47-7001	The Teenage Frankie and Johnny/I'll Follow	1957	7.50	15.00	30.00
SOUNDWAVES					
❑ 4712	E.T. Still Means Ernest Tubb to Me/One Good				
	Cry Away from Happiness	1982	—	2.00	4.00
SUN					
❑ 403	Sherry's Lips/Miss Brown	1966	5.00	10.00	20.00
❑ 1127	Sherry's Lips/Miss Brown	1972	2.00	4.00	8.00
Albums					
EPIC					
❑ EGP 502 [(2)]	The World of David Houston	1970	5.00	10.00	20.00
❑ LN 24112 [M]	New Voice from Nashville	1964	3.75	7.50	15.00
❑ LN 24156 [M]	12 Great Country Hits	1965	3.75	7.50	15.00
❑ LN 24213 [M]	Almost Persuaded	1966	3.75	7.50	15.00
❑ LN 24303 [M]	A Loser's Cathedral	1967	5.00	10.00	20.00
❑ LN 24320 [M]	Golden Hymns	1967	5.00	10.00	20.00
❑ LN 24338 [M]	You Mean the World to Me	1967	5.00	10.00	20.00
❑ LN 24342 [M]	David Houston's Greatest Hits	1968	7.50	15.00	30.00
❑ BN 26112 [S]	New Voice from Nashville	1964	5.00	10.00	20.00
❑ BN 26156 [S]	12 Great Country Hits	1965	5.00	10.00	20.00
❑ BN 26213 [S]	Almost Persuaded	1966	5.00	10.00	20.00
❑ BN 26303 [S]	A Loser's Cathedral	1967	3.75	7.50	15.00
❑ BN 26320 [S]	Golden Hymns	1967	3.75	7.50	15.00
❑ BN 26338 [S]	You Mean the World to Me	1967	3.75	7.50	15.00
❑ BN 26342 [S]	David Houston's Greatest Hits	1968	3.75	7.50	15.00
❑ BN 26391	Already It's Heaven	1968	3.75	7.50	15.00
❑ BN 26432	Where Love Used to Live	1969	3.75	7.50	15.00
❑ BN 26482	David	1969	3.75	7.50	15.00
❑ BN 26539	Baby, Baby	1970	3.75	7.50	15.00
❑ E 30108	Wonders of the Wine	1970	3.75	7.50	15.00
❑ E 30437	Sweet Lovin'	1971	3.75	7.50	15.00
❑ E 30602	David Houston's Greatest Hits, Volume 2	1971	3.75	7.50	15.00
❑ E 30657	A Woman Always Knows	1971	3.75	7.50	15.00
❑ KE 31385	The Day Love Walked In	1972	3.00	6.00	12.00
❑ KE 32189	Good Things	1973	3.00	6.00	12.00
❑ KE 33350	A Man Needs Love	1975	3.00	6.00	12.00
❑ KE 33948	What a Night	1976	3.00	6.00	12.00
GUSTO					
❑ 0012	The Best of David Houston	1978	2.50	5.00	10.00
HARMONY					
❑ HS 11412	David Houston	1970	2.50	5.00	10.00
❑ KH 31778	The Many Sides of David Houston	1972	2.50	5.00	10.00
❑ KH 32287	Old Time Religion	1973	2.50	5.00	10.00
RCA CAMDEN					
❑ CAL-2126 [M]	David Houston Sings	1966	3.75	7.50	15.00
❑ CAS-2126 [R]	David Houston Sings	1966	2.50	5.00	10.00
STARDAY					
❑ 990	David Houston	1978	2.50	5.00	10.00

HOUSTON, DAVID, AND BARBARA MANDRELL
Also see each artist's individual listings.

45s

Number	Title (A Side/B Side)	Yr	VG	VG+	NM
EPIC					
❑ 10656	After Closing Time/My Song of Love	1970	2.00	4.00	8.00
❑ 10779	We've Got Everything But Love/Try a Little				
	Harder	1971	2.00	4.00	8.00
❑ 10908	A Perfect Match/Almost Persuaded	1972	2.00	4.00	8.00
❑ 11068	I Love You, I Love You/Let's Go Down Together	1973	—	3.00	6.00
❑ 11120	Lovin' You Is Worth It/How Can It Be Wrong	1974	—	3.00	6.00
❑ 20005	Ten Commandments of Love/Try a Little Harder	1974	—	3.00	6.00
Albums					
EPIC					
❑ KE 31705	A Perfect Match	1972	3.00	6.00	12.00
❑ KE 32915	The Best of David Houston and Barbara				
	Mandrell	1974	3.00	6.00	12.00

HOUSTON, DAVID, AND TAMMY WYNETTE
Also see each artist's individual listings.

45s

Number	Title (A Side/B Side)	Yr	VG	VG+	NM
EPIC					
❑ 10194	My Elusive Dreams/Marriage on the Rocks	1967	2.50	5.00	10.00
❑ 10274	It's All Over/Together We Stand	1967	2.50	5.00	10.00
Albums					
EPIC					
❑ LN 24325 [M]	My Elusive Dreams	1967	5.00	10.00	20.00
❑ BN 26325 [S]	My Elusive Dreams	1967	3.75	7.50	15.00

H

Number	Title (A Side/B Side)	Yr	VG	VG+	NM
HOUSTON, JOHNNY					
45s					
EVENT					
❏ 4277	Slick Chick/Playboy	1959	7.50	15.00	30.00
❏ 4280	Torrid Tessie Lee/Our Very First Kiss	1959	7.50	15.00	30.00
HOUSTON, SOLDIER BOY					
45s					
ATLANTIC					
❏ 971	Western Rider Blues/Hug Me Baby	1952	62.50	125.00	250.00
HOUSTON, THELMA					
12-Inch Singles					
CENTURY 2000					
❏ 1001	Hold On (4 versions)/Athens Grooves/ Olympus Thunder	1990	—	3.00	6.00
MCA					
❏ L33-1253 [DJ]	I'd Rather Spend the Bad Times with You (3 versions)	1984	2.00	4.00	8.00
❏ L33-1795 [DJ]	Working Girl (3:45)/(5:00)	1983	2.00	4.00	8.00
❏ 13963	Working Girl/Running in Circles	1983	—	3.00	
❏ 23520	You Used to Hold Me So Tight (12" Version)/ (Dub) (LP)	1984	—	3.00	6.00
❏ 23552	Fantasy and Heartbreak (Dance Version)/ (LP Version)	1985	—	3.00	6.00
MOTOWN					
❏ 00053	Ride to the Rainbow/Love Machine	1979	2.00	4.00	8.00
RCA VICTOR					
❏ PD-12293	96 Tears/There's No Runnin' Away from Love	1981	—	3.50	7.00
REPRISE					
❏ PRO-A-4475 [DJ]	High (4 versions)	1990	2.00	4.00	8.00
❏ PRO-A-4487 [DJ]	Out of My Hands (Remix) (same on both sides)	1990	2.00	4.00	8.00
❏ 21765	High (5 versions)	1990	—	3.00	6.00
❏ 21769	Our of My Hands (5 versions)	1990	—	3.00	6.00
❏ 40080	Throw You Down (4 version)/ What He Has (2 versions)	1990	—	3.00	6.00
45s					
ABC DUNHILL					
❏ 11 [DJ]	Everybody Gets to Go to the Moon (same on both sides)	1969	3.75	7.50	15.00
—Special Apollo 11 promotional item					
❏ 11 [PS]	Everybody Gets to Go to the Moon (same on both sides)	1969	5.00	10.00	20.00
—Special Apollo 11 promotional item					
❏ 4197	Sunshower/If This Was the Last Song	1969	2.50	5.00	10.00
❏ 4212	Jumpin' Jack Flash/This Is Your Life	1969	2.50	5.00	10.00
❏ 4222	Save the Country/I Just Can't Stay Away	1970	2.00	4.00	8.00
❏ 4260	The Good Earth/Ride, Louie, Ride	1970	2.00	4.00	8.00
CAPITOL					
❏ 5767	Baby Mine/Woman Behind Her Man	1966	12.50	25.00	50.00
❏ 5882	Don't Cry, My Soldier Boy/Let's Try to Make It	1967	12.50	25.00	50.00
MCA					
❏ 52196	Working Girl/Running in Circles	1983	—	—	3.00
❏ 52239	Make It Last/Just Like All the Rest	1983	—	—	3.00
❏ 52489	(I Guess) It Must Be Love/Running in Circles	1984	—	—	3.00
❏ 52491	Love Is a Dangerous Game/ You Used to Hold Me So Tight	1984	—	—	3.00
❏ 52574	Keep It Light/My Lucille	1985	—	—	3.00
—B-side by B.B. King					
❏ 52582	What a Woman Feels Inside/ Fantasy and Heartbreak	1985	—	—	3.00
MOTOWN					
❏ 1245	I'm Just a Part of Yesterday/Piano Man	1973	—	2.50	5.00
❏ 1260	Do You Know Where You're Going/Together	1973	—	2.50	5.00
❏ 1316	You've Been Doing Wrong for So Long/ Pick Up the Week	1974	—	2.50	5.00
❏ 1385	The Bingo Long Song/Razzle Dazzle	1976	—	2.50	5.00
—B-side by William Goldstein					
❏ 1385 [PS]	The Bingo Long Song/Razzle Dazzle	1976	3.00	6.00	12.00
—B-side by William Goldstein					
MOWEST					
❏ 5008	I Want to Go Back There Again/ Pick Up the Week	1972	—	3.00	6.00
❏ 5013	Me and Bobby McGee/No One's Gonna Be a Fool Forever	1972	—	3.00	6.00
❏ 5023	Piano Man/Me and Bobby McGee	1972	—	3.00	6.00
❏ 5027	What If/There Is a Fool	1972	—	3.00	6.00
❏ 5046	If It's the Last Thing I Do/And I Never Did	1973	—	—	—
—Unreleased					
❏ 5050	I'm Just a Part of Yesterday/Piano Man	1973	—	3.00	6.00
RCA					
❏ PB-11913	Suspicious Minds/Gone	1980	—	2.50	5.00
❏ PB-12215	If You Feel It/Hollywood	1981	—	2.00	4.00
❏ PB-12285	96 Tears/There's No Runnin' Away from Love	1981	—	2.00	4.00
TAMLA					
❏ 54275	One Out of Every Six (Censored)/ Pick of the Week	1976	2.50	5.00	10.00
❏ 54278	Don't Leave Me This Way (Short Version)/Today Will Soon Be Yesterday	1977	—	2.00	4.00
❏ 54278 [DJ]	Don't Leave Me This Way (Long Version)/Don't Leave Me This Way (Short Version)	1977	—	3.00	6.00
❏ 54283	If It's the Last Thing I Do/If You Won't Let Me Walk on the Water	1977	—	2.00	4.00
❏ 54287	I'm Here Again/Sharin' Something Perfect	1977	—	2.00	4.00
❏ 54292	I Can't Go On Living Without Your Love/ Any Way You Like It	1978	—	2.00	4.00
❏ 54295	I'm Not Strong Enough to Love You/Triplin'	1978	—	2.00	4.00
❏ 54297	Saturday Night, Sunday Morning/Come to Me	1979	—	2.00	4.00
Albums					
ABC DUNHILL					
❏ DS-50054	Sun Shower	1969	6.25	12.50	25.00
MCA					
❏ 5395	Thelma Houston	1983	2.50	5.00	10.00
❏ 5527	Qualifying Heat	1984	2.50	5.00	10.00
MOTOWN					
❏ M5-120V1	Superstar Series, Vol. 20	1981	2.50	5.00	10.00
❏ M5-127V1	Sunshower	1981	2.00	4.00	8.00

Number	Title (A Side/B Side)	Yr	VG	VG+	NM
❏ M5-226V1	Any Way You Like It	1982	2.50	5.00	10.00
MOWEST					
❏ MW-102	Thelma Houston	1972	5.00	10.00	20.00
RCA VICTOR					
❏ AFL1-3500	Breakwater Cat	1980	2.50	5.00	10.00
❏ AFL1-3842	Never Gonna Be Another One	1981	2.50	5.00	10.00
REPRISE					
❏ 26234	Throw You Down	1990	3.75	7.50	15.00
SHEFFIELD LABS					
❏ 2	I've Got the Music In Me	1975	10.00	20.00	40.00
SHEFFIELD TREASURY					
❏ ST-200	I've Got the Music In Me	1983	5.00	10.00	20.00
—Reissue of Sheffield Labs 2					
TAMLA					
❏ T6-345R1	Any Way You Like It	1976	3.00	6.00	12.00
❏ T7-358R1	The Devil in Me	1977	2.50	5.00	10.00
❏ T7-361R1	Ready to Roll	1978	2.50	5.00	10.00
HOUSTON, THELMA, AND JERRY BUTLER Also see each artist's individual listings.					
45s					
MOTOWN					
❏ 1422	It's a Lifetime Thing/Kiss Me Now	1977	—	2.50	5.00
Albums					
MOTOWN					
❏ M6-887	Thelma and Jerry	1977	2.50	5.00	10.00
❏ M7-903	Two to One	1978	2.50	5.00	10.00
HOUSTON FEARLESS					
45s					
IMPERIAL					
❏ 66354	Race with the Devil/Someone Else's Blues	1969	—	—	—
—Canceled					
Albums					
IMPERIAL					
❏ LP-12421	Houston Fearless	1969	5.00	10.00	20.00
HOUSTONS, THE					
45s					
HIT					
❏ 133	Where Did Our Love Go/Steal Away	1964	2.00	4.00	8.00
—B-side by Leroy Jones					
HOWARD, EDDY					
45s					
MERCURY					
❏ 5433	American Beauty Rose/Seems Like Only Yesterday	1950	3.75	7.50	15.00
—Note: Earlier Eddy Howard releases on Mercury may exist on 45.					
❏ 5439	Put Your Arms Around Me Honey/ Lassus Trombone	1950	3.75	7.50	15.00
❏ 5453	My Heart Isn't In It/I Do Better in the Mountains	1950	3.75	7.50	15.00
❏ 5475	Daddy's Little Boy/They Put the Lights Out	1950	3.75	7.50	15.00
❏ 5490	I'm Forever Blowing Bubbles/Red We Want	1950	3.75	7.50	15.00
❏ 5491	Patricia/So Long, Sally	1950	3.75	7.50	15.00
❏ 5516	I'll Be Home for Christmas/Dearest Santa	1950	3.75	7.50	15.00
❏ 5517	To Think You've Chosen Me/The One Rose	1950	3.75	7.50	15.00
❏ 5567	A Penny a kiss — A Penny a Hug/I Still Feel the Same About You	1951	3.75	7.50	15.00
❏ 5576	When You Return/Little Small Town Girl	1951	3.75	7.50	15.00
❏ 5578	Daddy's Little Girl/Daddy's Little Boy	1951	3.75	7.50	15.00
❏ 5590	Around the World/That's All That's Left	1951	3.75	7.50	15.00
❏ 5623	One Kind Word/How Thoughtful of You	1951	3.75	7.50	15.00
❏ 5630	What Will I Tell My Heart/The Strange Little Girl	1951	3.75	7.50	15.00
❏ 5663	(A Woman Is a) Deadly Weapon/ I'm in Love Again	1951	3.75	7.50	15.00
❏ 5678	Hello Young Lovers/We Kiss in a Shadow	1951	3.75	7.50	15.00
❏ 5697	I'm Cryin'/Put All Your Kisses in an Envelope	1951	3.75	7.50	15.00
❏ 5711	Sin/My Wife and I	1951	3.75	7.50	15.00
—Revised A-side title					
❏ 5711	It's No Sin/My Wife and I	1951	5.00	10.00	20.00
❏ 5722	Uncle Mistletoe/When Christmas Rolls Around	1951	3.75	7.50	15.00
❏ 5748	It's All Over But the Memories/Chances Are	1951	3.75	7.50	15.00
❏ 5752	There's a Christmas Tree/Auld Lang Syne	1951	3.75	7.50	15.00
❏ 5771	Stolen Love/I'll See You in My Dreams	1952	3.75	7.50	15.00
❏ 5791	My Adobe Hacienda/Wishin'	1952	3.75	7.50	15.00
❏ 5815	Be Anything (But Be Mine)/She Took	1952	3.75	7.50	15.00
❏ 5832	Singing in the Rain/All I Do Is Dream of You	1952	3.75	7.50	15.00
❏ 5837	The Family That Prays Together/ (B-side unknown)	1952	3.75	7.50	15.00
❏ 5871	Auf Wiederseh'n Sweetheart/I Don't Want to Take a Chance	1952	3.75	7.50	15.00
❏ 5898	Mademoiselle/I Don't Know Any Better	1952	3.75	7.50	15.00
❏ 70015	It's Worth Any Price You Pay/Kentucky Babe	1952	3.00	6.00	12.00
❏ 70071	Your Mother and Mine/You've Got Me Crying	1953	3.00	6.00	12.00
❏ 70107	Gomen Nasai (Forgive Me)/ Someone to Kiss Your Tears Away	1953	3.00	6.00	12.00
❏ 70134	Say You're Mine Again/Broken Wings	1953	3.00	6.00	12.00
❏ 70135	Am I Loving You/Almost Always	1953	3.00	6.00	12.00
❏ 70176	Love Every Moment That You Live/ The Right Way	1953	3.00	6.00	12.00
❏ 70225	That's the Price I Paid for You/Skirts	1953	3.00	6.00	12.00
❏ 70272	Ebenezer Scrooge/Bimbo	1953	3.75	7.50	15.00
❏ 70293	Little Miss One/Till We Two Are One	1954	3.00	6.00	12.00
❏ 70301	Bimbo/Call Me Darling	1954	3.00	6.00	12.00
❏ 70304	Melancholy Me/ I Wonder What's Become of Sally	1954	3.00	6.00	12.00
❏ 70388	Vieni Su/Don't Worry Baby	1954	3.00	6.00	12.00
❏ 70467	Love Me Tonight/You're Always Welcome Home	1954	3.00	6.00	12.00
❏ 70475	Happy Birthday/Anniversary Waltz	1954	3.75	7.50	15.00
❏ 70513	All of You/I'll Wrap You in My Arms	1954	3.00	6.00	12.00
❏ 70533	Old Memories/Finger of Suspicion	1955	3.00	6.00	12.00
❏ 70566	Words of Love/Forevermore	1955	3.00	6.00	12.00
❏ 70639	The Man from Laramie/The Three of Us	1955	3.00	6.00	12.00
❏ 70700	The Teen-Agers' Waltz/Choo Choo Cha Cha	1955	3.00	6.00	12.00
❏ 70763	Round, Round the Christmas Tree/Silver Bells	1955	3.00	6.00	12.00
❏ 70800	Why Is Your Dog Following Me/ Rustic Old Cathedral	1956	2.50	5.00	10.00

Number	Title (A Side/B Side)	Yr	VG	VG+	NM
❏ 70881	Whatever Will Be, Will Be/				
	You Can't Keep Running	1956	2.50	5.00	10.00
❏ 70946	Never, Never, Never/Thank You Lord	1956	2.50	5.00	10.00
❏ 70989	Confidential/Tiger Lily	1956	2.50	5.00	10.00
❏ 71002	Uncle Mistletoe/Silver Bells	1956	3.00	6.00	12.00
❏ 71008	Driftwood/The Hour of Love	1956	2.50	5.00	10.00
❏ 71072	Delia's Gone/Love Me a Little Bit	1957	2.50	5.00	10.00
❏ 71300	Just Foolin'/My Last Goodbye	1958	2.50	5.00	10.00
❏ 71773	I Want You to Want Me to Want You/				
	Just a Year Ago Tonight	1961	2.50	5.00	10.00

7-Inch Extended Plays
MERCURY

Number	Title (A Side/B Side)	Yr	VG	VG+	NM
❏ EP 1-3213	I Wonder What's Become of Sally/Little Miss				
	One//Call Me Darling/Yellow Roses	195?	3.75	7.50	15.00
❏ EP 1-3213 [PS]	Yellow Roses	195?	3.75	7.50	15.00

Albums
CIRCLE

Number	Title (A Side/B Side)	Yr	VG	VG+	NM
❏ 29	Eddy Howard 1949-1952	198?	2.50	5.00	10.00
❏ 79	Eddy Howard 1949-1953	1985	2.50	5.00	10.00
COLUMBIA					
❏ CL 6067 [10]	Eddy Howard	1949	15.00	30.00	60.00
HINDSIGHT					
❏ HSR-119	Eddy Howard 1946-1951	198?	2.50	5.00	10.00
❏ HSR-156	Eddy Howard 1945-1948	198?	2.50	5.00	10.00
❏ HSR-405 [(2)]	Eddy Howard and His Orchestra Play 22 Original				
	Big Band Favorites	198?	3.00	6.00	12.00
INSIGHT					
❏ 205	Eddy Howard and His Orchestra 1945-1951	198?	2.50	5.00	10.00
MERCURY					
❏ MG-20112 [M]	Singing in the Rain	195?	6.25	12.50	25.00
❏ MG-20312 [M]	Paradise Isle	195?	6.25	12.50	25.00
❏ MG-20432 [M]	Great for Dancing	1958	5.00	10.00	20.00
❏ MG-20562 [M]	Eddy Howard's Golden Hits	1961	3.75	7.50	15.00
❏ MG-20593 [M]	More Eddy Howard's Golden Hits	1962	3.75	7.50	15.00
❏ MG-20665 [M]	Eddy Howard Sings and Plays the				
	Great Old Waltzes	1962	3.75	7.50	15.00
❏ MG-20817 [M]	Eddy Howard Sings and Plays the				
	Great Band Hits	196?	3.75	7.50	15.00
❏ MG-20910 [M]	Intimately Yours	1965	3.75	7.50	15.00
❏ MG-21014 [M]	Softly and Sincerely	196?	3.75	7.50	15.00
❏ SR-60104 [S]	Great for Dancing	1959	6.25	12.50	25.00
❏ SR-60562 [S]	Eddy Howard's Golden Hits	1961	5.00	10.00	20.00
❏ SR-60593 [S]	More Eddy Howard's Golden Hits	1962	5.00	10.00	20.00
❏ SR-60665 [S]	Eddy Howard Sings and Plays the				
	Great Old Waltzes	1962	5.00	10.00	20.00
❏ SR-60817 [S]	Eddy Howard Sings and Plays the				
	Great Band Hits	196?	5.00	10.00	20.00
❏ SR-60910 [S]	Intimately Yours	1965	5.00	10.00	20.00
❏ SR-61014 [S]	Softly and Sincerely	196?	5.00	10.00	20.00
WING					
❏ MGW-12104 [M]	Saturday Night Dance Date	196?	3.00	6.00	12.00
❏ MGW-12171 [M]	Eddy Howard Sings Words of Love	196?	3.00	6.00	12.00
❏ MGW-12171 [M]	Words of Love	196?	3.00	6.00	12.00
❏ MGW-12194 [M]	Sleepy Serenade	196?	3.00	6.00	12.00
❏ MGW-12249 [M]	The Velvet Voice	196?	3.00	6.00	12.00
❏ SRW-16104 [S]	Saturday Night Dance Date	196?	3.00	6.00	12.00
❏ SRW-16171 [S]	Eddy Howard Sings Words of Love	196?	3.00	6.00	12.00
❏ SRW-16171 [S]	Words of Love	196?	3.00	6.00	12.00
❏ SRW-16194 [S]	Sleepy Serenade	196?	3.00	6.00	12.00
❏ SRW-16249 [S]	The Velvet Voice	196?	3.00	6.00	12.00

HOWARD, RONNIE
45s
BIG TOP

Number	Title (A Side/B Side)	Yr	VG	VG+	NM
❏ 3093	If Santa Fell/Give My Toy to the Boy Next Door	1961	3.75	7.50	15.00

HOWE, STEVE Also see YES.
Albums
ATLANTIC

Number	Title (A Side/B Side)	Yr	VG	VG+	NM
❏ SD 18154	Beginnings	1975	2.50	5.00	10.00
❏ SD 19243	The Steve Howe Album	1980	2.50	5.00	10.00

HOWELL, BILL
45s
PALLADIUM

Number	Title (A Side/B Side)	Yr	VG	VG+	NM
❏ 513	Rocket Rollin' Blues/Bayou City Blues	195?	12.50	25.00	50.00

HOWELL, REUBEN
45s
MOTOWN

Number	Title (A Side/B Side)	Yr	VG	VG+	NM
❏ 1274	When You Take Another Chance on Love/You				
	Can't Stop a Man in Love	1973	5.00	10.00	20.00
❏ 1274 [PS]	When You Take Another Chance on Love/You				
	Can't Stop a Man in Love	1973	7.50	15.00	30.00
❏ 1305	Rings/I'll Be Your Brother	1974	2.50	5.00	10.00
❏ 1325	Constant Disappointment/I Believe	1974	2.50	5.00	10.00

Albums
MOTOWN

Number	Title (A Side/B Side)	Yr	VG	VG+	NM
❏ M 771L	Reuben Howell	1973	5.00	10.00	20.00
❏ M6-799S1	Rings	1974	3.75	7.50	15.00

HOWL THE GOOD
45s
RARE EARTH

Number	Title (A Side/B Side)	Yr	VG	VG+	NM
❏ 5045	Long Way from Home/Why Do You Cry	1972	2.00	4.00	8.00

Albums
RARE EARTH

Number	Title (A Side/B Side)	Yr	VG	VG+	NM
❏ RS-537	Howl the Good	1972	5.00	10.00	20.00

HOWLIN' WOLF
45s
CADET CONCEPT

Number	Title (A Side/B Side)	Yr	VG	VG+	NM
❏ 7013	Evil/Tail Dragger	1969	2.00	4.00	8.00
CHESS					
❏ 1528	Oh! Red/My Last Affair	1952	175.00	350.00	700.00

—Note: Howlin' Wolf releases on Chess before 1528 are unknown on 45 rpm

Number	Title (A Side/B Side)	Yr	VG	VG+	NM
❏ 1557	All Night Boogie/I Love My Baby	1953	75.00	150.00	300.00

Number	Title (A Side/B Side)	Yr	VG	VG+	NM
❏ 1566	No Place to Go/Rockin' Daddy	1954	25.00	50.00	100.00
❏ 1575	How Long/Evil Is Going On	1954	25.00	50.00	100.00
❏ 1584	I'll Be Around/Forty Four	1955	12.50	25.00	50.00
❏ 1593	Who Will Be Next/I Have a Little Girl	1955	10.00	20.00	40.00
❏ 1607	Come to Me Baby/Don't Mess with My Baby	1955	10.00	20.00	40.00
❏ 1618	Smoke Stack Lightning/You Can't Be Beat	1956	10.00	20.00	40.00
❏ 1632	I Asked for Water/So Glad	1956	10.00	20.00	40.00
❏ 1648	Goin' Back Home/My Life	1957	10.00	20.00	40.00
❏ 1668	Somebody in My Home/Nature	1957	10.00	20.00	40.00
❏ 1679	Sittin' On Top of the World/Poor Boy	1958	10.00	20.00	40.00
❏ 1695	Moaning for My Baby/I Didn't Know	1958	10.00	20.00	40.00
❏ 1712	I'm Leaving You/Change My Way	1959	10.00	20.00	40.00
❏ 1726	Howlin' Blues/I Better Go Now	1959	10.00	20.00	40.00
❏ 1735	Mr. Airplane Man/I've Been Abused	1959	10.00	20.00	40.00
❏ 1744	The Natchez Burning/You Gonna Wreck My Life	1959	10.00	20.00	40.00
❏ 1762	Spoonful/Howlin' for My Baby	1960	7.50	15.00	30.00
❏ 1777	Wang Dang Doodle/Back Door Man	1961	7.50	15.00	30.00
❏ 1793	Little Baby/Down in the Bottom	1961	7.50	15.00	30.00
❏ 1804	The Red Rooster/Shake for Me	1961	6.25	12.50	25.00
❏ 1813	You'll Be Mine/Goin' Down Slow	1962	6.25	12.50	25.00
❏ 1823	Just Like I Treat You/I Ain't Superstitious	1962	6.25	12.50	25.00
❏ 1844	Do the Do/Mama's Baby	1962	6.25	12.50	25.00
❏ 1870	300 Pounds of Joy/Built for Comfort	1963	5.00	10.00	20.00
❏ 1890	Tail Dragger/Hidden Charms	1964	5.00	10.00	20.00
❏ 1911	Love Me Darlin'/My Country Sugar Mama	1964	5.00	10.00	20.00
❏ 1923	Killin' Floor/Louise	1965	5.00	10.00	20.00
❏ 1928	Tell Me What I've Done/Ooh Baby	1965	3.75	7.50	15.00
❏ 1945	I Walked from Dallas/Don't Laugh at Me	1965	3.75	7.50	15.00
❏ 1968	New Crawlin' King Snake/Wild Ramblin'	1966	3.75	7.50	15.00
❏ 2009	I Had a Dream/Pop It to Me	1967	3.75	7.50	15.00
❏ 2081	Mary Sue/Hard Luck	1970	2.00	4.00	8.00
❏ 2108	I Smell a Rat/Just As Long	1971	2.00	4.00	8.00
❏ 2118	Do the Do/Red Rooster	1971	2.00	4.00	8.00
❏ 2145	Back Door Wolf/Coon on the Moon	1973	2.00	4.00	8.00
RPM					
❏ 340	Passing By Blues/Crying at Daybreak	1952	1000.	2000.	3000.

—Note: Howlin' Wolf releases on RPM before 340 are unknown on 45 rpm

Number	Title (A Side/B Side)	Yr	VG	VG+	NM
❏ 347	My Baby Stole Off/I Want Your Picture	1952	800.00	1600.	2400.

Albums
CADET

Number	Title (A Side/B Side)	Yr	VG	VG+	NM
❏ LPS-319	This Is Howlin' Wolf's New Album	1969	6.25	12.50	25.00
CHESS					
❏ 201 [(2)]	Howlin' Wolf	1976	3.75	7.50	15.00
❏ LP-1434 [M]	Moanin' in the Moonlight	1958	150.00	300.00	600.00
❏ LP-1469 [M]	Howlin' Wolf	1962	150.00	300.00	600.00
❏ LP-1502 [M]	The Real Folk Blues	1966	12.50	25.00	50.00
❏ LP-1512 [M]	More Real Folk Blues	1966	12.50	25.00	50.00
❏ LP-1540	Evil	1969	6.25	12.50	25.00
❏ CH-9107	His Greatest Sides, Vol. 1	1985	2.50	5.00	10.00
❏ CH-9182	Chicago — 26 Golden Years	1985	2.50	5.00	10.00
❏ CH-9195	Moanin' in the Moonlight	1986	2.00	4.00	8.00
—Reissue of 1434					
❏ CH-9273	The Real Folk Blues	1988	2.50	5.00	10.00
—Reissue of 1502					
❏ CH-9279	More Real Folk Blues	1988	2.50	5.00	10.00
—Reissue of 1512					
❏ CH-9297	The London Howlin' Wolf Sessions	1989	2.50	5.00	10.00
—Reissue of 60008					
❏ CH5-9332 [(5)]	The Chess Box	1991	10.00	20.00	40.00
❏ CH-50002	Message to the Young	1971	5.00	10.00	20.00
❏ CH-50015	Live and Cookin'	1972	5.00	10.00	20.00
❏ CH-50045	Back Door Wolf	1974	5.00	10.00	20.00
❏ CH-60008	The London Howlin' Wolf Sessions	1971	5.00	10.00	20.00
❏ CH-60016 [(2)]	Howlin' Wolk, AKA Chester Burnett	1972	6.25	12.50	25.00
❏ CH-93001	Change My Way	198?	2.50	5.00	10.00
CROWN					
❏ CLP-5240 [M]	Howlin' Wolf Sings the Blues	1962	6.25	12.50	25.00
CUSTOM					
❏ CM-2055 [M]	Big City Blues	196?	10.00	20.00	40.00
❏ CS-2055 [R]	Big City Blues	196?	5.00	10.00	20.00
KENT					
❏ KLP-526 [M]	Original Folk Blues	1967	3.75	7.50	15.00
❏ KST-526 [R]	Original Folk Blues	1967	3.00	6.00	12.00
❏ KST-527	Howlin' Wolf's 20 Greatest R&B Hits	1968	3.00	6.00	12.00
❏ KST-535	Underground Blues	1968	3.00	6.00	12.00
ROUNDER					
❏ SS-28	Cadillac Daddy: Memphis Recordings, 1952	1989	3.00	6.00	12.00

HUBCAPS, THE ERNIE MARESCA is in this group.
45s
LAURIE

Number	Title (A Side/B Side)	Yr	VG	VG+	NM
❏ 3219	Hot Rod City (Vocal)/Hot Rod City (Instrumental)	1964	3.75	7.50	15.00

HUDDLE, JACK
45s
KAPP

Number	Title (A Side/B Side)	Yr	VG	VG+	NM
❏ 207	Starlight/Believe Me	1959	50.00	100.00	200.00

—Buddy Holly plays guitar on these tracks
PETSY

Number	Title (A Side/B Side)	Yr	VG	VG+	NM
❏ 1002	Starlight/Believe Me	1958	125.00	250.00	500.00

HUDSON, POOKIE Lead singer with THE SPANIELS.
45s
DOUBLE L

Number	Title (A Side/B Side)	Yr	VG	VG+	NM
❏ 711	Jealous Heart/I Know, I Know	1963	5.00	10.00	20.00
❏ 720	I Love You For Sentimental Reasons/Miracles	1963	5.00	10.00	20.00
JAMIE					
❏ 1319	This Gets To Me/All the Places I've Been	1966	15.00	30.00	60.00
PARKWAY					
❏ 839	John Brown/Turn Out the Lights	1962	5.00	10.00	20.00

HUDSON, ROCK
45s
DECCA

Number	Title (A Side/B Side)	Yr	VG	VG+	NM
❏ 30966	Pillow Talk/Roly Poly	1959	3.75	7.50	15.00
❏ 30966 [PS]	Pillow Talk/Roly Poly	1959	6.25	12.50	25.00

H

Number	Title (A Side/B Side)	Yr	VG	VG+	NM
Albums					
STANYAN					
❑ SR-10014	Rock Gently	1971	6.25	12.50	25.00
HUDSON AND LANDRY					
45s					
DORE					
❑ 852	The Hippie and the Redneck/Top 40 DJ's	1971	2.50	5.00	10.00
❑ 855	Ajax Liquor Store/The Hippie and the Redneck	1971	2.50	5.00	10.00
❑ 868	Ajax Airlines/Bruiser La Rue	1972	2.50	5.00	10.00
❑ 874	Obscene Phone Bust/The Prospectors	1972	2.50	5.00	10.00
❑ 879	Soul Bowl/Friar Shuck	1972	2.50	5.00	10.00
❑ 880	Frontier Christmas (Harlowe and The Mrs.)/The Soul Bowl	1972	2.50	5.00	10.00
❑ 881	Ajax Mortuary/Ajax Pet Store	1973	2.50	5.00	10.00
❑ 891	The Chocolate Freak/The Fate of the Mightiest Nation	1973	2.50	5.00	10.00
❑ 895	The Gas Man/Sir Basil	1974	2.50	5.00	10.00
❑ 898	The Weird Kingdom/Montague for President	1974	2.50	5.00	10.00
Albums					
DORE					
❑ 324	Hanging In There	1971	5.00	10.00	20.00
❑ 326	Losing Their Heads	1971	5.00	10.00	20.00
❑ 329	Right-Off!	1972	5.00	10.00	20.00
❑ 331	Weird Kingdom	1973	5.00	10.00	20.00
❑ 333	The Best of Hudson and Landry	1974	3.75	7.50	15.00
❑ 334	The Best of Hudson and Landry 2	1975	3.75	7.50	15.00
HUDSON BROTHERS, THE					
45s					
ARISTA					
❑ 0208	Help Wanted/Last Time I Looked	1976	—	2.50	5.00
❑ 0286	I Don't Wanna Be Lonely/Pauline	1977	—	2.50	5.00
❑ 0371	The Runaway/You Can't Make Me Cry	1978	—	2.50	5.00
CASABLANCA					
❑ 0108	So You Are a Star/Ma Ma Ma Baby	1974	—	3.00	6.00
—With long version of A-side					
❑ 801	So You Are a Star/Ma Ma Ma Baby	1974	—	2.50	5.00
—With short version of A-side					
❑ 816	Me and My Guitar/Coochie Coochie Coo	1975	—	2.50	5.00
COLUMBIA					
❑ 03976	Don't Try to Fight It/You Keep Me Up	1983	—	2.00	4.00
—As "The Hudsons"					
DECCA					
❑ 32634	Love Is a Word/Laugh, Funny, Funny	1970	—	3.00	6.00
—As "Everyday Hudson"					
ELEKTRA					
❑ 46648	Annie/Joni	1980	—	2.00	4.00
—As "Hudson"					
❑ 47049	Afraid to Love/Sidewalk	1980	—	2.00	4.00
—As "Hudson"					
LIONEL					
❑ 3211	Love Nobody/The World Would Be a Little Bit Better	1971	—	3.00	6.00
—As "Hudson"					
PLAYBOY					
❑ 50001	Someday/Leavin' It's Over	1972	—	3.00	6.00
ROCKET					
❑ 40141	America — Fight Back/If You Really Need Me	1973	—	3.00	6.00
—As "Hudson"					
❑ 40141 [PS]	America — Fight Back/If You Really Need Me	1973	2.50	5.00	10.00
❑ 40317	Sunday Driver/Be a Man	1974	—	3.00	6.00
❑ 40417	Rendezvous/Medley	1975	—	2.50	5.00
❑ 40464	Lonely School Year/If You Really Need Me	1975	—	2.50	5.00
❑ 40464 [PS]	Lonely School Year/If You Really Need Me	1975	2.00	4.00	8.00
❑ 40508	Spinning the Wheel (With the Girl You Love)/Bernie Was a Friend of Ours	1976	—	2.50	5.00
Albums					
ARISTA					
❑ AB 4199	The Truth About Us	1978	2.50	5.00	10.00
CASABLANCA					
❑ NBLP-7004	Hollywood Situation	1974	2.50	5.00	10.00
ELEKTRA					
❑ 6E-299	Damn Those Kids	1980	2.50	5.00	10.00
—As "Hudson"					
FIRST AMERICAN					
❑ 7708	The Hudson Brothers	1980	2.50	5.00	10.00
PLAYBOY					
❑ 102	Hudson	1972	3.75	7.50	15.00
ROCKET					
❑ PIG-460	Totally Out of Control	1974	2.50	5.00	10.00
❑ PIG-2169	Ba-Fa	1975	2.50	5.00	10.00
HUES CORPORATION, THE					
45s					
LIBERTY					
❑ 56204	Goodfootin'/We're Keepin' Our Business Together	1970	—	3.00	6.00
—As "The Hughes Corporation"					
RCA VICTOR					
❑ 74-0813	There He Is Again/Main Chance	1972	—	2.50	5.00
❑ 74-0900	Freedom for the Stallion/Off My Cloud	1973	—	2.50	5.00
❑ APBO-0139	Go to the Poet/Miracle Maker	1973	—	2.50	5.00
❑ APBO-0232	Rock the Boat/All Goin' Down Together	1974	—	2.50	5.00
❑ PB-10066	Rockin' Soul/Go to the Poet	1974	—	2.50	5.00
❑ PB-10200	Love Corporation/He's My Home	1975	—	2.50	5.00
❑ PB-10311	One Good Night Together/When You Look Down the Road	1975	—	2.50	5.00
❑ PB-10390	You Showed Me What Love Is/When You Look Down the Road	1975	—	2.50	5.00
❑ GB-10480	Rockin' Soul/Go to the Poet	1975	—	—	3.00
—Gold Standard Series					
❑ GB-10481	Rock the Boat/All Goin' Down Together	1975	—	—	3.00
—Gold Standard Series					
WARNER BROS.					
❑ 8400	I Caught Your Act/Natural Find	1977	—	2.00	4.00
❑ 8454	Telegram of Love/Dancing Together Again	1977	—	2.00	4.00
❑ 8454 [PS]	Telegram of Love/Dancing Together Again	1977	2.00	4.00	8.00
❑ 8559	Give Me Everything/Needed	1978	—	2.00	4.00
❑ 8638	Love Dance/With All My Love and Affection	1978	—	2.00	4.00
Albums					
RCA VICTOR					
❑ APL1-0323	Freedom for the Stallion	1973	2.50	5.00	10.00
❑ APD1-0755 [Q]	Rockin' Soul	1974	3.75	7.50	15.00
❑ APL1-0755	Rockin' Soul	1974	2.50	5.00	10.00
❑ APD1-0938 [Q]	Love Corporation	1975	3.75	7.50	15.00
❑ APL1-0938	Love Corporation	1975	2.50	5.00	10.00
❑ ANL1-2147	Rock the Boat	1976	2.00	4.00	8.00
❑ APL1-2408	The Best of the Hues Corporation	1977	2.50	5.00	10.00
WARNER BROS.					
❑ BS 3043	I Caught Your Act	1977	2.50	5.00	10.00
❑ BSK 3196	Your Place or Mine	1978	2.50	5.00	10.00
HUGHES, FRED					
45s					
BRUNSWICK					
❑ 55419	Baby Boy/Who You Really Are	1969	2.00	4.00	8.00
❑ 55439	Oo Wee Baby, I Love You/I Understand	1970	2.00	4.00	8.00
❑ 55446	Don't Let This Happen to Me/In My Time of Need	1971	2.00	4.00	8.00
CADET					
❑ 5616	Baby Don't Go/Love Is Ending	1968	2.50	5.00	10.00
VEE JAY					
❑ 684	Oo Wee Baby, I Love You/Love Me Baby	1965	3.75	7.50	15.00
❑ 703	You Can't Take It Away/My Heart Cries On	1965	3.75	7.50	15.00
❑ 718	Don't Let Me Down/My Heart Cries On	1965	3.75	7.50	15.00
Albums					
BRUNSWICK					
❑ BL 754147	Baby Boy	1970	3.75	7.50	15.00
HUGHES, FREDDY We're not sure if this is the same artist as the Fred Hughes above.					
45s					
WAND					
❑ 1182	Send My Baby Back/Where's My Baby	1968	2.50	5.00	10.00
❑ 1192	A Natural Man/I Gotta Keep My Bluff In	1968	2.50	5.00	10.00
❑ 1197	He's No Good/I Gotta Keep My Bluff In	1969	2.50	5.00	10.00
HUGHES, JIMMY					
45s					
ATLANTIC					
❑ 2454	Uncle Sam/It Ain't What You've Got	1967	2.00	4.00	8.00
FAME					
❑ 1000	Midnight Affair/When It Comes to Dancing	1965	2.50	5.00	10.00
❑ 1003	Neighbor, Neighbor/It's a Good Thing	1966	2.00	4.00	8.00
❑ 1006	I Worship the Ground You Walk On/A Shot of Rhythm and Blues	1966	2.00	4.00	8.00
❑ 1011	Why Not Tonight/I'm a Man of Action	1967	2.00	4.00	8.00
❑ 1014	Don't Lose Your Good Thing/You Can't Believe Everything That You Hear	1967	2.00	4.00	8.00
❑ 1015	Hi-Heel Sneakers/Time Will Bring You Back	1967	2.00	4.00	8.00
❑ 6401	Steal Away/Lollipops, Lace and Lipstick	1964	3.00	6.00	12.00
—Red label					
❑ 6401	Steal Away/Lollipops, Lace and Lipstick	1964	5.00	10.00	20.00
—Black label					
❑ 6403	Try Me/Lovely Ladies	1964	2.50	5.00	10.00
❑ 6404	I Want Justice/I'm Getting Better	1964	2.50	5.00	10.00
❑ 6407	Goodbye My Lover, Goodbye/It Was Nice	1965	2.50	5.00	10.00
❑ 6410	You Really Know How to Hurt a Guy/The Loving Physician	1965	2.50	5.00	10.00
GUYDEN					
❑ 2075	I'm Qualified/My Loving Time	1962	5.00	10.00	20.00
JAMIE					
❑ 1280	I'm Qualified/My Loving Time	1964	3.75	7.50	15.00
VOLT					
❑ 4002	I Like Everything About You/What Side of the Door	1968	2.00	4.00	8.00
❑ 4008	Let 'Em Down Baby/The Sweet Things You Do	1969	2.00	4.00	8.00
❑ 4017	Chains of Love/I'm Not Ashamed to Beg or Plead	1969	2.00	4.00	8.00
❑ 4024	I'm So Glad/Lay It on the Line	1969	2.00	4.00	8.00
Albums					
ATCO					
❑ 33-209 [M]	Why Not Tonight	1967	5.00	10.00	20.00
❑ SD 33-209 [S]	Why Not Tonight	1967	5.00	10.00	20.00
VEE JAY					
❑ VJ-1102 [M]	Steal Away	1965	6.25	12.50	25.00
❑ VJS-1102 [R]	Steal Away	1965	6.25	12.50	25.00
VOLT					
❑ VOS-6003	Something Special	1969	5.00	10.00	20.00
HUGO AND LUIGI					
45s					
MERCURY					
❑ 70563	Medley: Nobody's Sweetheart-Somebody Stole My Gal/The Crazy Otto Rag	1955	3.00	6.00	12.00
❑ 70676	A Satisfied Mind/The Goodbye Song	1955	3.00	6.00	12.00
❑ 70721	Young Abe Lincoln/Two-Thirds of the Tennessee Waltz	1955	3.00	6.00	12.00
❑ 70803	Our Melody/Anywhere Is Home with You	1956	3.00	6.00	12.00
RCA VICTOR					
❑ 47-7518	La Plume de Ma Tante/Honolulu Lu	1959	2.00	4.00	8.00
❑ 47-7569	Watusi Wedding/Yalaloo	1959	2.00	4.00	8.00
❑ 47-7639	Just Come Home/Lonesome Stranger	1959	2.00	4.00	8.00
❑ 47-7808	Smile/Tweedle Dee	1960	2.00	4.00	8.00
❑ 47-7868	La Pachange/Bimbombey	1961	2.00	4.00	8.00
❑ 47-7955	Brotherhood of Man/Love from a Heart of Gold	1961	2.00	4.00	8.00
❑ SP-45-101 [DJ]	RCA Victor Special DJ Spots	1959	2.50	5.00	10.00
ROULETTE					
❑ 4012	Rockabilly Party/Shenandoah Rose	1957	3.75	7.50	15.00
❑ 4050	76 Trombones/Twilight in Tennessee	1958	3.00	6.00	12.00
❑ 4074	Cha-Hua-Hua/Something's Always Happening on the River	1958	3.00	6.00	12.00
❑ 4074 [PS]	Cha-Hua-Hua/Something's Always Happening on the River	1958	3.00	6.00	12.00

Number	Title (A Side/B Side)	Yr	VG	VG+	NM
Albums					
RCA VICTOR					
❑ LPM-2254 [M]	The Sound of Children at Christmas	1960	3.75	7.50	15.00
❑ LSP-2254 [S]	The Sound of Children at Christmas	1960	5.00	10.00	20.00
❑ LPM-2641 [M]	The Cascading Voices of the Hugo & Luigi Chorus	1963	2.50	5.00	10.00
❑ LSP-2641 [S]	The Cascading Voices of the Hugo & Luigi Chorus	1963	3.00	6.00	12.00
❑ LPM-2717 [M]	Let's Fall in Love	1963	2.50	5.00	10.00
❑ LSP-2717 [S]	Let's Fall in Love	1963	3.00	6.00	12.00
❑ LPM-2789 [M]	The Cascading Voices of the Hugo & Luigi Chorus — With Brass	1964	2.50	5.00	10.00
❑ LSP-2789 [S]	The Cascading Voices of the Hugo & Luigi Chorus — With Brass	1964	3.00	6.00	12.00
❑ LPM-2863 [M]	The Cascading Voices of the Hugo & Luigi Chorus — With Strings	1964	2.50	5.00	10.00
❑ LSP-2863 [S]	The Cascading Voices of the Hugo & Luigi Chorus — With Strings	1964	3.00	6.00	12.00
❑ LSP-4083	Maggie Flynn	1968	2.50	5.00	10.00
ROULETTE					
❑ R-25044 [M]	When Good Fellows Get Together	1959	5.00	10.00	20.00
❑ R-25283 [M]	Cascading Voices	1965	3.00	6.00	12.00
❑ SR-25283 [S]	Cascading Voices	1965	3.75	7.50	15.00
WING					
❑ MGW 12207 [M]	Sing Along by the Fireside	195?	3.00	6.00	12.00

HULLABALLOOS, THE

Number	Title (A Side/B Side)	Yr	VG	VG+	NM
45s					
ROULETTE					
❑ 4587	I'm Gonna Love You Too/Party Doll	1964	5.00	10.00	20.00
❑ 4587 [PS]	I'm Gonna Love You Too/Party Doll	1964	10.00	20.00	40.00
❑ 4593	Beware/Did You Ever	1965	5.00	10.00	20.00
❑ 4593 [PS]	Beware/Did You Ever	1965	10.00	20.00	40.00
❑ 4612	Learning the Game/Don't Stop	1965	5.00	10.00	20.00
❑ 4612 [PS]	Learning the Game/Don't Stop	1965	10.00	20.00	40.00
❑ 4622	I Won't Turn Around Now/My Heart Keeps Telling Me	1965	5.00	10.00	20.00
❑ 4622 [PS]	I Won't Turn Around Now/My Heart Keeps Telling Me	1965	10.00	20.00	40.00
Albums					
ROULETTE					
❑ R-25297 [M]	England's Newest Singing Sensations	1965	12.50	25.00	50.00
❑ SR-25297 [P]	England's Newest Singing Sensations	1965	18.75	37.50	75.00
❑ R-25310 [M]	The Hullabaloos on Hullabaloo	1965	12.50	25.00	50.00
❑ SR-25310 [P]	The Hullabaloos on Hullabaloo	1965	18.75	37.50	75.00

HULLABALOO SINGERS AND ORCHESTRA, THE

Number	Title (A Side/B Side)	Yr	VG	VG+	NM
Albums					
COLUMBIA					
❑ CL 2410 [M]	The Hullabaloo Show	1965	5.00	10.00	20.00
❑ CS 9210 [S]	The Hullabaloo Show	1965	6.25	12.50	25.00

HUMAN BEINZ, THE

Number	Title (A Side/B Side)	Yr	VG	VG+	NM
45s					
CAPITOL					
❑ 2119	Turn On Your Love Light/It's Fun to Be Clean	1968	2.50	5.00	10.00
❑ 2119 [PS]	Turn On Your Love Light/It's Fun to Be Clean	1968	5.00	10.00	20.00
❑ 2198	Every Time Woman/The Face	1968	2.50	5.00	10.00
❑ 2431	I've Got to Keep On Pushin'/This Little Girl of Mine	1969	2.50	5.00	10.00
❑ 5990	Nobody But Me/Sueno	1967	3.75	7.50	15.00
GATEWAY					
❑ 828	Gloria/The Times They Are a-Changin'	1967	3.75	7.50	15.00
❑ 838	You Can't Make Me Cry/The Pied Piper	1967	3.75	7.50	15.00
Albums					
CAPITOL					
❑ ST 2906	Nobody But Me	1968	7.50	15.00	30.00
❑ ST 2926	Evolutions	1968	10.00	20.00	40.00
GATEWAY					
❑ GLP-3012	Nobody But Me	1968	10.00	20.00	40.00

—With added tracks by The Mammals

HUMAN EXPRESSION, THE

Number	Title (A Side/B Side)	Yr	VG	VG+	NM
45s					
ACCENT					
❑ 1214	Every Night/Love at Psychedelic Velocity	1967	50.00	100.00	200.00
❑ 1226	Calm Me Down/Optical Sound	1967	25.00	50.00	100.00
❑ 1252	I Don't Need Nobody/Sweet Child of Nothingness	1967	25.00	50.00	100.00

HUMBLE PIE

Number	Title (A Side/B Side)	Yr	VG	VG+	NM
45s					
A&M					
❑ 1282	I Don't Need No Doctor/Song for Jenny	1971	—	2.00	4.00
❑ 1282 [PS]	I Don't Need No Doctor/Song for Jenny	1971	—	3.00	6.00
❑ 1349	Hot and Nasty/You're So Good for Me	1972	—	2.00	4.00
❑ 1349 [PS]	Hot and Nasty/You're So Good for Me	1972	—	3.00	6.00
❑ 1366	Sweet Peace and Time/30 Days in the Hole	1972	—	2.00	4.00
❑ 1406	Black Coffee/Say No More	1973	—	2.00	4.00
❑ 1406 [PS]	Black Coffee/Say No More	1973	3.00	6.00	12.00
❑ 1440	Honky Tonk Woman/Get Down to It	1973	—	2.00	4.00
❑ 1484	Oh La De Da/The Out Crowd	1974	—	2.00	4.00
❑ 1530	Rally with Ali/Ninety-Nine Pounds	1974	—	2.00	4.00
❑ 1711	Road Hog/Rock and Roll Music	1975	—	2.00	4.00
ATCO					
❑ 7216	Fool for a Pretty Face/You Soppy Pratt	1980	—	2.50	5.00
IMMEDIATE					
❑ 001	Natural Born Woman/I'll Go Alone	1969	2.00	4.00	8.00
Albums					
A&M					
❑ SP-3127	Humble Pie	1981	2.00	4.00	8.00
—Budget-line reissue					
❑ SP-3132	Smokin'	1981	2.00	4.00	8.00
—Budget-line reissue					
❑ SP-3208	The Best of Humble Pie	1982	2.50	5.00	10.00
❑ SP-3506 [(2)]	Performance — Rockin' the Fillmore	1971	3.75	7.50	15.00
❑ SP-3513 [(2)]	Lost and Found	1972	3.75	7.50	15.00
❑ SP-3611	Thunderbox	1974	3.00	6.00	12.00
❑ SP-3701 [(2)]	Eat It	1973	3.75	7.50	15.00
❑ SP-4270	Humble Pie	1970	3.00	6.00	12.00
❑ SP-4301	Rock On	1971	3.00	6.00	12.00
❑ SP-4342	Smokin'	1972	3.00	6.00	12.00
❑ SP-4514	Street Rats	1975	3.00	6.00	12.00
❑ SP-6008 [(2)]	Performance — Rockin' the Fillmore	1981	2.50	5.00	10.00
—Budget-line reissue					
❑ SP-6009 [(2)]	Lost and Found	1981	2.50	5.00	10.00
—Budget-line reissue					
❑ SP-6503 [(2)]	Eat It	1981	2.50	5.00	10.00
—Budget-line reissue					
ACCORD					
❑ SN-7192	Recaptured	1981	2.50	5.00	10.00
ATCO					
❑ SD 38-122	On to Victory	1980	2.50	5.00	10.00
❑ SD 38-131	Go for the Throat	1981	2.50	5.00	10.00
COMPLEAT					
❑ 672009-1 [(2)]	A Slice of Humble Pie	1985	3.00	6.00	12.00
IMMEDIATE					
❑ IMOCS-101	As Safe As Yesterday Is	1969	6.25	12.50	25.00

HUMBLEBUMS, THE GERRY RAFFERTY was in this group.

Number	Title (A Side/B Side)	Yr	VG	VG+	NM
45s					
UNITED ARTISTS					
❑ 50771	All the Best People Do It/Cruisin'	1971	2.50	5.00	10.00
Albums					
LIBERTY					
❑ LST-7636	The Humblebums	1969	7.50	15.00	30.00
❑ LST-7656	Open Up the Door	1970	7.50	15.00	30.00

HUMES, ANITA

Number	Title (A Side/B Side)	Yr	VG	VG+	NM
45s					
ROULETTE					
❑ 4564	Don't Fight It Baby/When Somethin's Hard to Get	1964	3.75	7.50	15.00
❑ 4575	I'm Making It Over/Just for the Boy	1964	3.75	7.50	15.00
❑ 4750	Are You Going My Way/Everybody's Got You	1967	2.50	5.00	10.00

HUMPERDINCK, ENGELBERT

Number	Title (A Side/B Side)	Yr	VG	VG+	NM
45s					
EPIC					
❑ AE7 1170 [DJ]	Christmas Song/Silent Night	1978	—	2.00	4.00
❑ AE7 1170 [PS]	Christmas Song/Silent Night	1978	—	2.00	4.00
❑ 02060	Don't You Love Me Anymore/Till I Get It Right	1981	—	—	3.00
❑ 02245	Maybe This Time/When the Night Ends	1981	—	—	3.00
❑ 03817	Till You and Your Lover Are Lovers Again/What Will I Write	1983	—	—	3.00
❑ 50270	After the Lovin'/Let's Remember the Good Times	1976	—	2.50	5.00
❑ 50365	I Believe in Miracles/Goodbye My Friend	1977	—	2.00	4.00
❑ 50447	A Lover's Holiday/Look at Me	1977	—	2.00	4.00
❑ 50488	A Night to Remember/Silent Night	1977	—	2.00	4.00
❑ 50526	The Last of the Romantics/I Have Paid the Toll	1978	—	2.00	4.00
❑ 50566	Love Me Tender/This Time One Year Ago	1978	—	2.00	4.00
❑ 50579	Love's In Need of Love Today/Sweet Marjorene	1978	—	2.00	4.00
❑ 50632	This Moment in Time/And the Day Begins	1978	—	2.00	4.00
❑ 50692	Can't Help Falling in Love/You Know Me	1979	—	2.00	4.00
❑ 50732	Lovin' Too Well/Much, Much Greater Love	1979	—	2.00	4.00
❑ 50844	Love's Only Love/Burning Ember	1980	—	—	3.00
❑ 50899	A Chance to Be a Hero/Any Kind of Love at All	1980	—	—	3.00
❑ 50933	Don't Cry Out Loud/Don't Touch That Dial	1980	—	—	3.00
❑ 50958	It's Not Easy to Live Together/Royal Affair	1980	—	—	3.00
HICKORY					
❑ 1337	Baby Turn Around/If I Could Do the Things I Want to Do	1965	4.00	8.00	16.00
—As "Gerry Dorsey"					
PARROT					
❑ 40011 [M]	Release Me (And Let Me Love Again)/Ten Guitars	1967	2.00	4.00	8.00
❑ 40011 [S]	Release Me (And Let Me Love Again)/Ten Guitars	1967	5.00	10.00	20.00
—Both sides in true stereo. Letters "XDR" are stamped in run-off area before the matrix number					
❑ 40015	There Goes My Everything/You Love	1967	2.00	4.00	8.00
❑ 40019	The Last Waltz/That Promise	1967	2.00	4.00	8.00
❑ 40019 [PS]	The Last Waltz/That Promise	1967	3.00	6.00	12.00
❑ 40023	Am I That Easy to Forget/Pretty Ribbons	1967	2.00	4.00	8.00
❑ 40023 [PS]	Am I That Easy to Forget/Pretty Ribbons	1967	3.00	6.00	12.00
❑ 40027	A Man Without Love/Call on Me	1968	2.00	4.00	8.00
❑ 40032	Les Bicyclettes De Belsize/Three Little Words	1968	2.00	4.00	8.00
❑ 40032 [PS]	Les Bicyclettes De Belsize/Three Little Words	1968	3.00	6.00	12.00
❑ 40036	The Way It Used to Be/A Good Thing Going	1969	—	3.00	6.00
❑ 40036 [PS]	The Way It Used to Be/A Good Thing Going	1969	2.50	5.00	10.00
❑ 40040	I'm a Better Man/Cafe	1969	—	3.00	6.00
❑ 40044	Winter World of Love/Take My Heart	1969	—	3.00	6.00
❑ 40044 [PS]	Winter World of Love/Take My Heart	1969	2.50	5.00	10.00
❑ 40049	My Marie/Our Song (La Paloma)	1970	—	3.00	6.00
❑ 40049 [PS]	My Marie/Our Song (La Paloma)	1970	2.00	4.00	8.00
❑ 40054	Sweetheart/Born to Be Wanted	1970	—	3.00	6.00
❑ 40054 [PS]	Sweetheart/Born to Be Wanted	1970	2.00	4.00	8.00
❑ 40059	When There's No You/Stranger, Step In My World	1971	—	3.00	6.00
❑ 40059 [PS]	When There's No You/Stranger, Step In My World	1971	2.00	4.00	8.00
❑ 40065	Another Time, Another Place/You're the Window of My World	1971	—	3.00	6.00
❑ 40069	Too Beautiful to Last/A Hundred Times a Day	1972	—	2.50	5.00
❑ 40071	In Time/How Does It Feel	1972	—	2.50	5.00
❑ 40072	I Never Said Goodbye/Time After Time	1972	—	2.50	5.00
❑ 40073	I'm Leavin'/You My Summer Song	1973	—	2.00	4.00
❑ 40076	Love Is All/Lady of the Night	1973	—	2.00	4.00
❑ 40077	Free as the Wind/My Friend the Wind	1974	—	2.00	4.00
❑ 40079	Catch Me I'm Falling/Love, Oh Precious Love	1974	—	2.00	4.00
❑ 40082	Forever and Ever/Precious Love	1974	—	2.00	4.00
❑ 40085	This Is What You Mean to Me/A World Without Music	1975	—	2.00	4.00

Number	Title (A Side/B Side)	Yr	VG	VG+	NM
7-Inch Extended Plays					
PARROT					
❏ SBG 80	Raindrops Keep Fallin' on My Head/My Cherie Amour/Something//(B-side unknown)	1970	2.00	4.00	8.00
—Jukebox issue; small hole, plays at 33 1/3 rpm					
❏ SBG 80 [PS]	We Made It Happen	1970	2.00	4.00	8.00
Albums					
EPIC					
❏ (no #) [(PD)]	Last of the Romantics	1978	6.25	12.50	25.00
❏ PE 34381	After the Lovin'	1976	2.50	5.00	10.00
—Orange label					
❏ PE 34381	After the Lovin'	1979	2.00	4.00	8.00
—Dark blue label; back cover does not yet have bar code					
❏ PE 34381	After the Lovin'	198?	—	3.00	6.00
—Dark blue label; back cover has bar code					
❏ E 34436	The Ultimate	1977	2.50	5.00	10.00
—Orange label					
❏ PE 34436	The Ultimate	198?	2.00	4.00	8.00
—Reissue with bar code; dark blue label					
❏ E 34719	Golden Love Songs	1977	2.50	5.00	10.00
—Orange label					
❏ PE 34719	Golden Love Songs	198?	2.00	4.00	8.00
—Reissue with bar code; dark blue label					
❏ PE 34730	Miracles	1977	2.50	5.00	10.00
—Orange label					
❏ PE 34730	Miracles	198?	2.00	4.00	8.00
—Reissue with bar code; dark blue label					
❏ JE 35020	Last of the Romantics	1978	2.50	5.00	10.00
—Orange label					
❏ PE 35020	Last of the Romantics	198?	2.00	4.00	8.00
—Reissue with bar code; dark blue label					
❏ PE 35031	Christmas Tyme	1977	3.00	6.00	12.00
❏ JE 35791	This Moment in Time	1979	2.50	5.00	10.00
❏ PE 35791	This Moment in Time	198?	2.00	4.00	8.00
—Budget-line reissue					
❏ JE 36431	Love's Only Love	1980	2.50	5.00	10.00
❏ PE 36765	A Merry Christmas with Engelbert Humperdinck	1980	2.50	5.00	10.00
—Some copies of the record have a "JE" prefix					
❏ E2X 36782 [(2)]	All of Me/Live in Concert	1980	3.00	6.00	12.00
❏ FE 37128	Don't You Love Me Anymore	1981	2.50	5.00	10.00
❏ PE 37128	Don't You Love Me Anymore	1983	2.00	4.00	8.00
—Budget-line reissue					
❏ FE 38087	You and Your Lover	1983	2.50	5.00	10.00
❏ PE 39469	White Christmas	1984	2.50	5.00	10.00
LONDON					
❏ BP 688/9 [(2)]	Engelbert Humperdinck Sings for You	1977	3.75	7.50	15.00
❏ PS 709	Love Letters	1978	2.50	5.00	10.00
PARROT					
❏ PA 61012 [M]	Release Me	1967	5.00	10.00	20.00
❏ PA 61015 [M]	The Last Waltz	1967	5.00	10.00	20.00
❏ PAS 71012 [S]	Release Me	1967	3.75	7.50	15.00
❏ PAS 71015 [S]	The Last Waltz	1967	3.75	7.50	15.00
❏ PAS 71022	A Man Without Love	1968	3.75	7.50	15.00
❏ PAS 71026	Engelbert	1969	3.75	7.50	15.00
❏ XPAS 71030	Engelbert Humperdinck	1969	3.75	7.50	15.00
❏ XPAS 71038	We Made It Happen	1970	3.75	7.50	15.00
❏ XPAS 71043	Sweetheart	1971	3.75	7.50	15.00
❏ XPAS 71048	Another Time, Another Place	1971	3.75	7.50	15.00
❏ XPAS 71051	Live at the Riviera, Las Vegas	1971	3.75	7.50	15.00
❏ XPAS 71056	In Time	1972	3.75	7.50	15.00
❏ XPAS 71061	King of Hearts	1973	3.75	7.50	15.00
❏ APAS 71065	My Love	1974	3.75	7.50	15.00
❏ PAS 71067	His Greatest Hits	1974	3.75	7.50	15.00
❏ SW-93216	We Made It Happen	1970	5.00	10.00	20.00
—Capitol Record Club edition					
SILVER EAGLE					
❏ SE 1034 [(2)]	A Lovely Way to Spend an Evening	1985	3.75	7.50	15.00
—Mail-order offer					
HUMPHREY, BOBBI					
12-Inch Singles					
EPIC					
❏ 50537	Home-Made Jam/Sunset Burgundy	1978	2.50	5.00	10.00
❏ 50746	Love When I'm In Your Arms/Sweet and Low	1979	2.50	5.00	10.00
WARNER BROS.					
❏ 21716	Let's Get Started (2 versions)/Rainbows	1990	—	3.00	6.00
45s					
BLUE NOTE					
❏ XW395	Chicago, Damn/Just a Love Child	1974	—	2.50	5.00
❏ XW455	Harlem River Drive/Black and Blues	1974	—	2.50	5.00
❏ XW592	Fun House/San Francisco Lights	1975	—	2.50	5.00
❏ XW785	Uno Esta/Sweeter Than Sugar	1976	—	2.50	5.00
❏ 1971	Spanish Harlem/Sad Bag	1971	2.00	4.00	8.00
❏ 1974	Ain't No Sunshine/Sad Bag	1972	2.00	4.00	8.00
❏ 1980	Is This All/Lonely Town, Lonely Street	1972	2.00	4.00	8.00
EPIC					
❏ 50448	Dancin' to Keep From Cryin'/Theme I	1977	—	2.50	5.00
❏ 50529	Home-Made Jam/Sunset Burgundy	1978	—	2.50	5.00
❏ 50745	Love When I'm In Your Arms/Sweet and Low	1979	·	2.50	5.00
Albums					
BLUE NOTE					
❏ BN-LA142-G	Blacks and Blues	1974	2.50	5.00	10.00
❏ BN-LA344-G	Satin Doll	1974	2.50	5.00	10.00
❏ BN-LA550-G	Fancy Dancer	1975	2.50	5.00	10.00
❏ BN-LA699-G	The Best of Bobbi Humphrey	1976	2.50	5.00	10.00
❏ BST-84379	Flute-In	1971	3.00	6.00	12.00
❏ BST-84421	Dig This	1972	3.00	6.00	12.00
EPIC					
❏ PE 34704	Tailor Made	1977	2.50	5.00	10.00
❏ JE 35338	Freestyle	1978	2.50	5.00	10.00
❏ JE 35607	The Good Life	1979	2.50	5.00	10.00
❏ JE 36368	The Best of Bobbi Humphrey	1980	2.50	5.00	10.00

Number	Title (A Side/B Side)	Yr	VG	VG+	NM
HUMPHREY, PAUL					
45s					
LIZARD					
❏ 1009	Funky L.A./Baby Rice	1971	—	3.00	6.00
❏ 21006	Cool Aid/Detroit	1971	—	3.00	6.00
Albums					
BLUE THUMB					
❏ BTS 47	Supermellow	1973	3.00	6.00	12.00
❏ BTS 66	America, Wake Up!	1974	3.00	6.00	12.00
DISCOVERY					
❏ DS-850	Paul Humphrey Sextet	1981	2.50	5.00	10.00
LIZARD					
❏ 20106	Paul Humphrey & the Cool Aid Chemists	1971	3.75	7.50	15.00
HUNDLEY, CRAIG					
Albums					
WORLD PACIFIC					
❏ WPS-21880	Arrival of a Young Giant	1968	3.75	7.50	15.00
HUNGER					
45s					
PUBLIC					
❏ 101	Mind Machine/(B-side unknown)	1968	6.25	12.50	25.00
❏ 103	No Shame/(B-side unknown)	1968	6.25	12.50	25.00
❏ 1001	Colors/(B-side unknown)	1969	7.50	15.00	30.00
Albums					
PUBLIC					
❏ 1006	Strictly from Hunger	1969	150.00	300.00	600.00
HUNT, DANNY					
45s					
DYNAMITE					
❏ 8663	What's Happening to Our Love Affair/(B-side unknown)	1974	5.00	10.00	20.00
HUNT, GERALDINE					
45s					
ABC					
❏ 10859	Winner Take All/For Lovers Only	1966	7.50	15.00	30.00
BOMBAY					
❏ 4501	He's for Real/(B-side unknown)	1964	25.00	50.00	100.00
CHECKER					
❏ 1028	I Let Myself Go/I Wished I Had Listened	1962	7.50	15.00	30.00
PRISM					
❏ 315	Can't Fake the Feeling/(B-side unknown)	1980	—	2.00	4.00
❏ 323	Heart Heart/(B-side unknown)	1981	—	2.00	4.00
ROULETTE					
❏ 7068	Never, Never Leave Me/Push, Sweet	1970	—	3.00	6.00
❏ 7109	Now That There's You/Shades of Blue	1971	—	3.00	6.00
❏ 7129	Baby, I Need Your Loving/(B-side unknown)	1972	—	3.00	6.00
❏ 7132	Cold Blood/Just Believe in Me	1972	—	3.00	6.00
❏ 7149	You Brought Joy/Shades of Blue	1973	—	3.00	6.00
U.S.A.					
❏ 732	Sneak Around/It Never Happened Before	1962	7.50	15.00	30.00
❏ 737	Sneak Around/It Never Happened Before	1963	6.25	12.50	25.00
HUNTER, CHRISTINE					
45s					
ROULETTE					
❏ 4589	Santa Bring Me Ringo/Where Were You Daddy	1964	3.75	7.50	15.00
HUNTER, HERBERT					
45s					
HIT					
❏ 01	The Twist/Twistin' the Night Away	1962	2.00	4.00	8.00
❏ 02	Slow Twistin'/Good Luck Charm	1962	2.00	4.00	8.00
—B-side by Ed Hardin					
❏ 03	Lover Please/Young World	1962	2.00	4.00	8.00
—B-side by Ed Hardin					
❏ 08	Twist Twist Senora/Stranger on the Shore	1962	2.00	4.00	8.00
—B-side by the Hit Combo					
❏ 11	Hide 'Nor Hair/Shout! Shout! (Knock Yourself Out)	1962	2.00	4.00	8.00
—B-side by Bill Austin					
❏ 14	I Can't Stop Loving You/Second Hand Love	1962	2.00	4.00	8.00
—B-side by Connie Dee					
❏ 22	Dancin' Party/Ahab the Arab	1962	2.00	4.00	8.00
—B-side by John Dunn					
❏ 24	Bring It On Home to Me/The Loco-Motion	1962	2.00	4.00	8.00
—B-side by Peggy Gaines					
❏ 25	The Right String But the Wrong Yo-Yo/You Don't Know Me	1962	2.00	4.00	8.00
❏ 47	Loop-De-Loop/The Night Has a Thousand Eyes	1963	2.00	4.00	8.00
—B-side by Joe Cash					
❏ 61	Take These Chains from My Heart/I Will Follow Him	1963	2.00	4.00	8.00
—B-side by Connie and Clara					
❏ 78	Twist It Up/My Whole World Is Falling Down	1963	2.00	4.00	8.00
—B-side by Betty Scott					
HUNTER, IAN Also see MOTT THE HOOPLE.					
45s					
CHRYSALIS					
❏ 2324	When the Daylight Comes/Life After Death	1979	—	2.50	5.00
❏ 2352	Cleveland Rocks/Just Another Night	1979	—	2.50	5.00
❏ 2405	We Gotta Get Out of Here/Sons and Daughters	1980	—	2.00	4.00
❏ 2542	I Need Your Love/(B-side unknown)	1981	—	2.00	4.00
❏ 2569	Central Park 'N' West/(B-side unknown)	1981	—	2.00	4.00
COLUMBIA					
❏ 03929	All of the Good Ones Are Taken/Death 'N' Glory Boys	1983	—	2.00	4.00
❏ 04166	Seeing Double/That Girl Is Rock 'N' Roll	1983	—	2.00	4.00
❏ 10161	Once Bitten Twice Shy/3000 Miles from Here	1975	—	3.00	6.00
Albums					
CHRYSALIS					
❏ CHR 1214	You're Never Alone with a Schizophrenic	1979	2.50	5.00	10.00
❏ 2CHS 1269 [(2)]	Ian Hunter Live/Welcome to the Club	1980	3.00	6.00	12.00

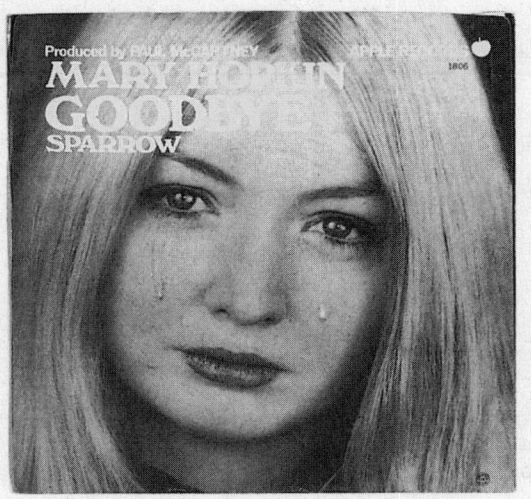

Mary Hopkin, "Goodbye," Apple 1806, picture sleeve, $6-$12.

The Honeycombs, "Colour Slide," Interphon 7716, picture sleeve, $12.50-$25.

H

Johnny Horton, *Johnny Horton's Greatest Hits*, Columbia CS 8396, stereo LP, red and black "6-eye" label, with bonus photo, $20-$40.

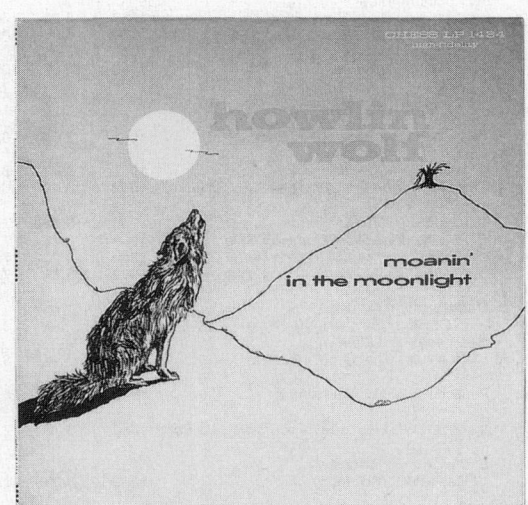

Howlin' Wolf, *Moanin' in the Moonlight*, Chess LP-1434, mono LP, $300-$600.

The Hullaballoos, *The Hullaballoos on Hullabaloo*, Roulette R 25310, mono LP, $25-$50.

Engelbert Humperdinck, *Release Me*, Parrot PAS 71012, stereo LP, $7.50-$15.

Number	Title (A Side/B Side)	Yr	VG	VG+	NM
❑ CHS 1326	Short Back N' Sides	1981	2.50	5.00	10.00
❑ PV 41214	You're Never Alone with a Schizophrenic	1982	2.00	4.00	8.00
—Budget-line reissue					
❑ PV 41326	Short Back N' Sides	1982	2.00	4.00	8.00
—Budget-line reissue					
COLUMBIA					
❑ PC 33480	Ian Hunter	1975	2.50	5.00	10.00
—No bar code on cover					
❑ PC 33480	Ian Hunter	198?	2.00	4.00	8.00
—Budget-line reissue with bar code					
❑ PC 34142	All American Alien Boy	1976	2.50	5.00	10.00
—No bar code on cover					
❑ PC 34142	All American Alien Boy	198?	2.00	4.00	8.00
—Budget-line reissue with bar code					
❑ PC 34721	Overnight Angels	1977	2.50	5.00	10.00
—No bar code on cover					
❑ C2 36251 [(2)]	Shades of Ian Hunter	1980	3.00	6.00	12.00
❑ FC 38628	All of the Good Ones Are Taken	1983	2.50	5.00	10.00

HUNTER, IVORY JOE
45s
ATLANTIC

Number	Title (A Side/B Side)	Yr	VG	VG+	NM
❑ 1049	It May Sound Silly/I Got to Learn to Do the Mambo	1954	6.25	12.50	25.00
❑ 1066	I Want Somebody/Heven Came Down to Earth	1955	6.25	12.50	25.00
❑ 1086	A Tear Fell/I Need You By My Side	1956	6.25	12.50	25.00
❑ 1095	You Mean Everything to Me/That's Why I Dream	1956	6.25	12.50	25.00
❑ 1111	Since I Met You Baby/You Can't Stop This Rocking and Rolling	1956	7.50	15.00	30.00
❑ 1128	Empty Arms/Love's a Hurting Game	1957	5.00	10.00	20.00
❑ 1151	She's Gone/Everytime I Hear That Song	1957	5.00	10.00	20.00
❑ 1164	All About the Blues/ If Only You Were Here with Me	1957	5.00	10.00	20.00
❑ 1173	You're On My Mind/Baby, Baby, Count on Me	1958	5.00	10.00	20.00
❑ 1183	I'm So Glad I Found You/Shooty Booty	1958	5.00	10.00	20.00
❑ 1191	You Flip Me Baby/Yes, I Want You	1958	5.00	10.00	20.00
❑ 2020	I Just Want to Love You/ Now I Don't Worry No More	1959	3.75	7.50	15.00
CAPITOL					
❑ 4587	I'm Hooked/Because I Love You	1961	3.00	6.00	12.00
❑ 4648	May the Best Man Win/ You Better Believe It Baby	1961	3.00	6.00	12.00
❑ 4688	The Life I Live/A Great Big Heart Full of Love	1962	3.00	6.00	12.00
DOT					
❑ 15880	City Lights/Stolen Moments	1958	3.75	7.50	15.00
❑ 15930	Old Fashioned Love/Cottage for Sale	1959	3.75	7.50	15.00
❑ 15957	I Love You So Much/Welcome Home Baby	1959	3.75	7.50	15.00
❑ 15986	My Search Was Ended/Did You Mean It	1959	3.75	7.50	15.00
EPIC					
❑ 10725	Heartbreak and Misery/ I'm Coming Down with the Blues	1971	—	3.00	6.00
❑ 10725	Heartbreak and Misery/ We All Like That Groovy Feeling	1971	—	3.00	6.00
4 STAR					
❑ 1634	Foolish Pride/Did You Mean It	1953	10.00	20.00	40.00
GOLDISC					
❑ 3010	It's Love, It's Love, It's Love/You Satisfy Me Baby	1960	3.75	7.50	15.00
GOLDWAX					
❑ 307	Every Little Bit Helped Me/ I Can Make You Happy	1966	5.00	10.00	20.00
KING					
❑ 4424	False Friend Blues/Send Me Pretty Mama	1951	10.00	20.00	40.00
—Ivory Joe Hunter records on King before 4422 are unconfirmed on 45 rpm					
❑ 4443	She's Gone Blues/Stop Rockin' That Train	1951	10.00	20.00	40.00
❑ 4455	Old Gal and New Gal Blues/Woo Wee Blues	1951	10.00	20.00	40.00
❑ 5166	Jealous Heart/I Like It	1958	3.75	7.50	15.00
❑ 5271	Guess Who/Don't Fall in Love with Me	1959	—	—	—
—Unreleased					
❑ 5280	Guess Who/Don't Fall in Love with Me	1959	3.75	7.50	15.00
MGM					
❑ 8011	I Almost Lost My Mind/If I Give You My Love	1949	12.50	25.00	50.00
—Original 45 issue of this record					
❑ K10578	I Almost Lost My Mind/If I Give You My Love	1949	10.00	20.00	40.00
❑ K10618	S.P. Blues/Why Fool Yourself	1950	7.50	15.00	30.00
❑ K10663	I Need You So/Leave Her Alone	1950	7.50	15.00	30.00
❑ K10733	Let Me Dream/Gimme a Pound of Round Ground	1950	7.50	15.00	30.00
❑ K10761	Old Man's Boogie/Living a Lie	1950	7.50	15.00	30.00
❑ K10818	It's A Sin/Don't You Believe Me	1950	7.50	15.00	30.00
❑ K10899	I Found My Baby/I Ain't Got No Gal	1951	7.50	15.00	30.00
❑ K10951	I Can't Get You Off My Mind/I Can't Resist You	1951	7.50	15.00	30.00
❑ K10995	You Lied/When I Lost You	1951	7.50	15.00	30.00
❑ K11052	I'm Yours/Wrong Woman Blues	1951	7.50	15.00	30.00
❑ K11132	Blue Moon/U Name It	1952	7.50	15.00	30.00
❑ K11165	Laugh/Where Shall I Go	1952	7.50	15.00	30.00
❑ K11195	I'm Sorry for You My Friend/I Will Be	1952	7.50	15.00	30.00
❑ K11263	I Get That Lonesome Feeling/ I Thought I Had Loved	1952	7.50	15.00	30.00
❑ K11325	Big Bounce/Tell Her for Me	1952	7.50	15.00	30.00
❑ K11378	Rockin' Chair Boogie/Music Before Dawn	1952	7.50	15.00	30.00
❑ K11459	I Had a Girl/If You See My Baby	1953	7.50	15.00	30.00
❑ K11549	I'm Afraid/Don't Make Me Cry	1953	7.50	15.00	30.00
❑ K11599	I Must Be Talking to Myself/My Best Wishes	1953	7.50	15.00	30.00
❑ K11702	I Have a Secret/I Feel So Good	1954	6.25	12.50	25.00
❑ K11818	Do You Miss Me/Whose Arms Are You Missing	1954	6.25	12.50	25.00
PARAMOUNT					
❑ 0253	He'll Never Love You/San Antonio Rose	1973	—	3.00	6.00
SMASH					
❑ 1825	My Arms Are Waiting/Congratulations	1963	3.00	6.00	12.00
❑ 1860	There's No Forgetting You/My Lover's Prayer	1963	3.00	6.00	12.00
SOUND STAGE 7					
❑ 2623	Ivory Tower/I'll Give You All Night to Stop	1968	2.00	4.00	8.00
❑ 2635	Until the Day I Die/I Built a Wall Around Me	1969	2.00	4.00	8.00
❑ 2643	Straighten Up Baby/Baby Me Baby	1969	2.00	4.00	8.00

Number	Title (A Side/B Side)	Yr	VG	VG+	NM
STAX					
❑ 155	This Kind of Woman/ Can't Explain Why It Happened	1964	3.00	6.00	12.00
TEARDROP					
❑ 3058	I've Asked You for the Last Time/Heart	196?	2.50	5.00	10.00
VEE JAY					
❑ 452	Somebody's Stealing My Love/ You Only Want Me When You Need Me	1962	3.00	6.00	12.00
VEEP					
❑ 1258	What's the Matter Baby/Don't You Believe Me	1967	2.00	4.00	8.00
❑ 1270	Did She Ask About Me/ From the First Time We Met	1967	2.00	4.00	8.00

7-Inch Extended Plays
ATLANTIC

Number	Title (A Side/B Side)	Yr	VG	VG+	NM
❑ EP 589	*Since I Met You Baby/I Got to Learn to Do the Mambo/It May Sound Silly/A Tear Fell	1958	12.50	25.00	50.00
❑ EP 589 [PS]	Ivory Joe Hunter (Since I Met You Baby)	1958	12.50	25.00	50.00
❑ EP 608	*Empty Arms/Love's a Hurting Game/She's Gone/Everytime I Hear That Song	1958	15.00	30.00	60.00
❑ EP 608 [PS]	Rock with Ivory Joe Hunter	1958	15.00	30.00	60.00
KING					
❑ 265	(contents unknown)	1954	20.00	40.00	80.00
❑ 265 [PS]	Ivory Joe Hunter	1954	20.00	40.00	80.00
MGM					
❑ X-1376	(contents unknown)	1957	12.50	25.00	50.00
❑ X-1376 [PS]	I Get That Lonesome Feeling, Volume 1	1957	12.50	25.00	50.00
❑ X-1377	I Get That Lonesome Feeling/I Found a New Baby//I Need You So/If You See My Baby	1957	12.50	25.00	50.00
❑ X-1377 [PS]	I Get That Lonesome Feeling, Volume 2	1957	12.50	25.00	50.00
❑ X-1378	(contents unknown)	1957	12.50	25.00	50.00
❑ X-1378 [PS]	I Get That Lonesome Feeling, Volume 3	1957	12.50	25.00	50.00

Albums
ATLANTIC

Number	Title (A Side/B Side)	Yr	VG	VG+	NM
❑ 8008 [M]	Ivory Joe Hunter	1957	50.00	100.00	200.00
—Black label					
❑ 8008 [M]	Ivory Joe Hunter	1960	25.00	50.00	100.00
—Purple and red label					
❑ 8015 [M]	The Old and the New	1958	50.00	100.00	200.00
—Black label					
❑ 8015 [M]	The Old and the New	1960	25.00	50.00	100.00
—Purple and red label					
DOT					
❑ DLP-3569 [M]	This Is Ivory Joe Hunter	1964	10.00	20.00	40.00
❑ DLP-25569 [S]	This Is Ivory Joe Hunter	1964	12.50	25.00	50.00
EPIC					
❑ E 30348	The Return of Ivory Joe Hunter	1971	5.00	10.00	20.00
EVEREST ARCHIVE OF FOLK & JAZZ					
❑ 289	Ivory Joe Hunter	1974	3.00	6.00	12.00
GOLDISC					
❑ 403 [M]	The Fabulous Ivory Joe Hunter	1961	15.00	30.00	60.00
HOME COOKING					
❑ 112	I'm Coming Down with the Blues	1989	3.00	6.00	12.00
KING					
❑ 605 [M]	16 of His Greatest Hits	1958	100.00	200.00	400.00
LION					
❑ L-70068 [M]	I Need You So	1959	15.00	30.00	60.00
MGM					
❑ E-3488 [M]	I Get That Lonesome Feeling	1957	75.00	150.00	300.00
PARAMOUNT					
❑ PAS-6080	I've Always Been Country	1974	3.00	6.00	12.00
POLYDOR					
❑ 830897-1	Since I Met You Baby	1987	3.00	6.00	12.00
SMASH					
❑ MGS-27037 [M]	Ivory Joe Hunter's Golden Hits	1963	10.00	20.00	40.00
❑ SRS-67037 [S]	Ivory Joe Hunter's Golden Hits	1963	12.50	25.00	50.00
SOUND					
❑ M-603 [M]	Ivory Joe Hunter	1959	37.50	75.00	150.00
STRAND					
❑ SL-1123 [M]	The Artistry of Ivory Joe Hunter	196?	10.00	20.00	40.00
❑ SLS-1123 [S]	The Artistry of Ivory Joe Hunter	196?	12.50	25.00	50.00

HUNTER, ROBERT
Albums
RELIX

Number	Title (A Side/B Side)	Yr	VG	VG+	NM
❑ 2002 [PD]	Promontory Rider	1982	5.00	10.00	20.00
—Limited edition of 1,000 picture discs					
ROUND					
❑ RX-101	Tales of the Great Rum Runners	1974	10.00	20.00	40.00
❑ RX-105	Tiger Rose	1975	10.00	20.00	40.00

HUNTER, TAB
45s
DOT

Number	Title (A Side/B Side)	Yr	VG	VG+	NM
❑ 15533	Young Love/Red Sails in the Sunset	1957	6.25	12.50	25.00
❑ 15548	Ninety-Nine Ways/Don't Get Around Much Anymore	1957	6.25	12.50	25.00
❑ 15657	Don't Let It Get Around/ I'm Alone Because I Love You	1957	5.00	10.00	20.00
❑ 15767	I'm a Runaway/It's All Over Town	1958	5.00	10.00	20.00
❑ 16036	Young Love/Ninety-Nine Ways	1960	5.00	10.00	20.00
❑ 16187	My Devotion/You Cheated	1961	3.75	7.50	15.00
❑ 16205	Wild Side of Life/My Devotion	1961	3.75	7.50	15.00
❑ 16264	The Way You Look Tonight/You Cheated	1961	3.75	7.50	15.00
❑ 16355	I Can't Stop Loving You/Born to Lose	1962	3.75	7.50	15.00
WARNER BROS.					
❑ 5008	Jealous Heart/Lonesome Road	1958	5.00	10.00	20.00
❑ 5021	Candy/My Baby Just Cares for Me	1958	5.00	10.00	20.00
❑ 5032 [M]	I'll Be With You in Apple Blossom Time/What Can I Give My Only Love	1959	5.00	10.00	20.00
❑ S-5032 [S]	I'll Be With You in Apple Blossom Time/What Can I Give My Only Love	1959	6.25	12.50	25.00
❑ 5051 [M]	There's No Fool Like a Young Fool/ I'll Never Smile Again	1959	5.00	10.00	20.00
❑ 5051 [PS]	There's No Fool Like a Young Fool/ I'll Never Smile Again	1959	5.00	10.00	20.00

Number	Title (A Side/B Side)	Yr	VG	VG+	NM
❏ S-5051 [S]	There's No Fool Like a Young Fool/				
	I'll Never Smile Again	1959	6.25	12.50	25.00
❏ 5093	Our Love/Waitin' for Fall	1959	5.00	10.00	20.00
❏ 5093 [PS]	Our Love/Waitin' for Fall	1959	6.25	12.50	25.00
❏ 5160	Again/Love Is Just Around the Corner	1960	5.00	10.00	20.00
❏ 5160 [PS]	Again/Love Is Just Around the Corner	1960	6.25	12.50	25.00

7-Inch Extended Plays
WARNER BROS.

Number	Title (A Side/B Side)	Yr	VG	VG+	NM
❏ EA 1221 [M]	(contents unknown)	1958	5.00	10.00	20.00
❏ EA 1221 [PS]	Tab Hunter	1958	5.00	10.00	20.00
❏ ESB 1221 [PS]	Tab Hunter	1959	6.25	12.50	25.00
❏ ESB 1221 [S]	(contents unknown)	1959	6.25	12.50	25.00

Albums
DOT

Number	Title (A Side/B Side)	Yr	VG	VG+	NM
❏ DLP-3370 [M]	Young Love	1961	7.50	15.00	30.00
❏ DLP-25370 [S]	Young Love	1961	7.50	15.00	30.00

WARNER BROS.

Number	Title (A Side/B Side)	Yr	VG	VG+	NM
❏ W 1221 [M]	Tab Hunter	1958	7.50	15.00	30.00
❏ WS 1221 [S]	Tab Hunter	1958	10.00	20.00	40.00
❏ W 1292 [M]	When I Fall in Love	1959	7.50	15.00	30.00
❏ WS 1292 [S]	When I Fall in Love	1959	10.00	20.00	40.00
❏ W 1367 [M]	R.F.D. Tab Hunter	1960	7.50	15.00	30.00
❏ WS 1367 [S]	R.F.D. Tab Hunter	1960	10.00	20.00	40.00

HUNTER, TY
45s
ANNA

Number	Title (A Side/B Side)	Yr	VG	VG+	NM
❏ 1114	Everything About You/Orphan Boy	1960	6.25	12.50	25.00
❏ 1123	Every Time/I'm Free	1960	7.50	15.00	30.00

CHECK MATE

Number	Title (A Side/B Side)	Yr	VG	VG+	NM
❏ 1002	Memories/The Envy of Every Man	1961	6.25	12.50	25.00
❏ 1015	Gladness to Sadness/Lonely Baby	1961	6.25	12.50	25.00

CHESS

Number	Title (A Side/B Side)	Yr	VG	VG+	NM
❏ 1857	Darling, My Babe/In Time	1963	5.00	10.00	20.00
❏ 1881	Am I Losing You/Love Walked Right Out on Me	1964	3.75	7.50	15.00
❏ 1893	Bad Loser/Something Like a Storm	1964	3.75	7.50	15.00

INVICTUS

Number	Title (A Side/B Side)	Yr	VG	VG+	NM
❏ 9120	Hey There Lonely Girl/I Don't See Me in Your				
	Eyes Anymore	1972	3.75	7.50	15.00

HUNTER MUSKETT
Albums
BRADLEY

Number	Title (A Side/B Side)	Yr	VG	VG+	NM
❏ 1003	Hunter Muskett	1973	20.00	40.00	80.00

HURRICANES, THE
45s
KING

Number	Title (A Side/B Side)	Yr	VG	VG+	NM
❏ 4817	Poor Little Dancin' Girl/Pistol Packin' Mama	1955	50.00	100.00	200.00
❏ 4867	Maybe It's All for the Best/Yours	1956	50.00	100.00	200.00
❏ 4898	Raining in My Heart/Tell Me Baby	1956	50.00	100.00	200.00
❏ 4926	Little Girl of Mine/Your Promise to Me	1956	37.50	75.00	150.00
❏ 4947	Dear Mother/You May Not Know	1956	30.00	60.00	120.00
❏ 5018	Fallen Angel/I'll Always Be in Love with You	1957	25.00	50.00	100.00
❏ 5042	Priceless/Now That I Need You	1957	25.00	50.00	100.00

HURT, MISSISSIPPI JOHN
Albums
BIOGRAPH

Number	Title (A Side/B Side)	Yr	VG	VG+	NM
❏ C-4 [M]	1928: His First Recordings	1972	6.25	12.50	25.00

PIEDMONT

Number	Title (A Side/B Side)	Yr	VG	VG+	NM
❏ PLP-13157 [M]	Folk Songs and Blues	1963	20.00	40.00	80.00
❏ PLP-13181 [M]	Worried Blues	1964	20.00	40.00	80.00

VANGUARD

Number	Title (A Side/B Side)	Yr	VG	VG+	NM
❏ VSD-19/20 [(2)]	The Best of Mississippi John Hurt	197?	6.25	12.50	25.00
❏ VRS-9145 [M]	Blues at Newport	1965	6.25	12.50	25.00
❏ VRS-9220 [M]	Mississippi John Hurt/Today	1966	6.25	12.50	25.00
❏ VRS-9248 [M]	The Immortal Mississippi John Hurt	1967	6.25	12.50	25.00
❏ VSD-79145 [S]	Blues at Newport	1965	7.50	15.00	30.00
❏ VSD-79220 [S]	Mississippi John Hurt/Today	1966	7.50	15.00	30.00
❏ VSD-79248 [S]	The Immortal Mississippi John Hurt	1967	7.50	15.00	30.00
❏ VSD-79327	The Last Session	1972	5.00	10.00	20.00

HURVITZ, SANDY
Albums
VERVE

Number	Title (A Side/B Side)	Yr	VG	VG+	NM
❏ V6-5064	Sandy's Album Is Here at Last	1968	7.50	15.00	30.00

—Produced by FRANK ZAPPA

HUSKY, FERLIN Also includes records as "Terry Preston" and "Simon Crum."
45s
ABC

Number	Title (A Side/B Side)	Yr	VG	VG+	NM
❏ 11345	True True Lovin'/A Legend in My Time	1973	—	3.00	6.00
❏ 11360	Between Me and Blue/My Special Angel	1973	—	3.00	6.00
❏ 11381	Baby's Blue/One	1973	—	3.00	6.00
❏ 11395	Rosie Cries a Lot/Shoes	1973	—	3.00	6.00
❏ 11432	Freckles and Polliwog Days/Everything Is				
	Nothing Without You	1974	—	3.00	6.00
❏ 12020	Drinkin' Man/Cuzz Yore So Sweet	1974	—	3.00	6.00

—As "Simon Crum"

Number	Title (A Side/B Side)	Yr	VG	VG+	NM
❏ 12021	A Room for a Boy...Never Used/A Ring of String	1974		2.50	5.00
❏ 12048	Champagne Ladies and Blue Ribbon Babies/I				
	Feel Better All Over	1974		2.50	5.00
❏ 12085	Burning/A Touch of Yesterday	1975		2.50	5.00

ABC DOT

Number	Title (A Side/B Side)	Yr	VG	VG+	NM
❏ 17574	An Old Memory (Got in My Eye)/She's Not Yours				
	Anymore	1975		2.50	5.00

CAPITOL

Number	Title (A Side/B Side)	Yr	VG	VG+	NM
❏ F1861	China Doll/Tennessee Central #9	1951	6.25	12.50	25.00
❏ F1947	I Want You So/Time	1952	5.00	10.00	20.00

—As "Terry Preston"

Number	Title (A Side/B Side)	Yr	VG	VG+	NM
❏ 2023	Christmas Dream/Christmas Is Holy	1967	2.00	4.00	8.00
❏ F2024	Words/I'm Missin' Lots of Lovin'	1952	5.00	10.00	20.00

—As "Terry Preston"

Number	Title (A Side/B Side)	Yr	VG	VG+	NM
❏ 2048	Just for You/Don't Hurt Me Anymore	1967	2.00	4.00	8.00
❏ 2048 [PS]	Just for You/Don't Hurt Me Anymore	1967	2.50	5.00	10.00
❏ F2105	Counting My Heartaches/I Love You	1952	5.00	10.00	20.00

—As "Terry Preston"

Number	Title (A Side/B Side)	Yr	VG	VG+	NM
❏ 2154	I Promised You the World/				
	You Should Live My Life	1968	2.00	4.00	8.00
❏ F2211	I'm Only Wishing/Are You Afraid	1952	5.00	10.00	20.00

—As "Terry Preston"

Number	Title (A Side/B Side)	Yr	VG	VG+	NM
❏ 2288	White Fences and Evergreen Trees/				
	Love's Been Good to Me	1968	2.00	4.00	8.00
❏ F2298	Gone/Out of Reach	1952	7.50	15.00	30.00

—As "Terry Preston"

Number	Title (A Side/B Side)	Yr	VG	VG+	NM
❏ F2391	My Foolish Heart/Undesired	1953	5.00	10.00	20.00

—As "Terry Preston"

Number	Title (A Side/B Side)	Yr	VG	VG+	NM
❏ F2397	Hank's Song/I'll Never Have You	1953	5.00	10.00	20.00
❏ 2411	Flat River, Mo./One Life to Live	1969	2.00	4.00	8.00
❏ F2467	I've Got a Woman's Love/				
	Watch the Company You Keep	1953	5.00	10.00	20.00

—As "Terry Preston"

Number	Title (A Side/B Side)	Yr	VG	VG+	NM
❏ F2495	Mini Ha Cha/I Lost My Love Today	1953	5.00	10.00	20.00
❏ 2512	That's Why I Love You So Much/Forever Yours	1969	2.00	4.00	8.00
❏ F2558	How Much Are You Mine/				
	You'll Die a Thousand Deaths	1953	5.00	10.00	20.00
❏ F2627	Walkin' and Hummin'/I Wouldn't Treat a Dog Like				
	You're Treating Me	1953	5.00	10.00	20.00
❏ 2666	Every Step of the Way/That's What I'd Do	1969	2.00	4.00	8.00
❏ F2746	Eli the Camel/Somebody Lied	1954	5.00	10.00	20.00
❏ 2793	Heavenly Sunshine/All My Little Loving Ways	1970	—	3.00	6.00
❏ F2814	Each Time You Leave/Deceived	1954	5.00	10.00	20.00

—As "Terry Preston"

Number	Title (A Side/B Side)	Yr	VG	VG+	NM
❏ F2835	The Drunken Driver/Homesick	1954	5.00	10.00	20.00
❏ 2882	Your Sweet Love Lifted Me/				
	You're the Happy Song I Sing	1970	—	3.00	6.00
❏ F2914	King of a Lonely Castle/				
	Very Seldom Frequently Ever	1954	5.00	10.00	20.00
❏ 2999	Sweet Misery/Because You're Mine	1970	—	3.00	6.00
❏ F3001	I Feel Better All Over				
	(More Than Anywhere's Else)/Little Tom	1954	3.75	7.50	15.00
❏ F3063	Cuzz Yore So Sweet/My Gallina	1955	5.00	10.00	20.00

—As "Simon Crum"

Number	Title (A Side/B Side)	Yr	VG	VG+	NM
❏ 3069	One More Time/				
	Don't Let the Good Life Pass You By	1971	—	3.00	6.00
❏ F3097	I'll Baby Sit with You/She's Always There	1955	3.75	7.50	15.00
❏ 3165	Open Up the Book (And Take a Look)/				
	Even If It's True	1971	—	3.00	6.00
❏ F3183	Don't Blame the Children/Saith the Lord	1955	3.75	7.50	15.00
❏ F3233	Dear Mr. Brown/I'll Be Here for a Lifetime	1955	3.75	7.50	15.00
❏ F3270	A Hillbilly Deck of Cards/Ooh I Want You	1955	5.00	10.00	20.00

—As "Simon Crum"

Number	Title (A Side/B Side)	Yr	VG	VG+	NM
❏ 3308	Just Plain Lonely/Always in All Ways	1972	—	3.00	6.00
❏ F3316	A Sinful Secret/Slow Down Brother	1956	3.75	7.50	15.00
❏ 3415	How Could You Be Anything But Love/I'd Walk				
	a Mile for a Smile	1972	—	3.00	6.00
❏ F3428	Aladdin's Lamp/That Big Old Moon	1956	3.75	7.50	15.00
❏ F3460	Bop Cat Bop/Muki Ruki	1956	5.00	10.00	20.00

—As "Simon Crum"

Number	Title (A Side/B Side)	Yr	VG	VG+	NM
❏ F3522	Nothing Looks As Good As You/Waiting	1956	3.75	7.50	15.00
❏ F3628	Gone/Missing Persons	1957	3.75	7.50	15.00
❏ F3742	A Fallen Star/Prize Possession	1957	3.00	6.00	12.00
❏ F3790	Make Me Live Again/This Moment of Love	1957	3.00	6.00	12.00
❏ F3862	What'cha Doin' After School/Wang Dang Doo	1957	3.00	6.00	12.00
❏ F3943	Kingdom of Love/Terrific Together	1958	3.00	6.00	12.00
❏ F4000	I Saw God/I Feel That Old Heartache Again	1958	3.00	6.00	12.00
❏ F4046	I Will/All of the Time	1958	3.00	6.00	12.00
❏ F4073	Country Music Is Here to Stay/Stand Up, Sit				
	Down, Shut Your Mouth	1958	5.00	10.00	20.00

—As "Simon Crum"

Number	Title (A Side/B Side)	Yr	VG	VG+	NM
❏ F4123	My Reason for Living/Wrong	1959	3.00	6.00	12.00
❏ F4186	Draggin' the River/Sea Sand	1959	3.00	6.00	12.00
❏ F4252	Morgan Poisoned the Water Hole/I Fell Out of				
	Love with You	1959	3.75	7.50	15.00

—As "Simon Crum"

Number	Title (A Side/B Side)	Yr	VG	VG+	NM
❏ F4278	Black Sheep/I'll Always Return	1959	3.00	6.00	12.00
❏ 4343	My Love for You/Asi Es La Vida	1960	3.00	6.00	12.00
❏ 4406	Wings of a Dove/Next to Jimmy	1960	3.00	6.00	12.00
❏ 4464	Country Music Fiddler/I Feel Better All Over	1960	3.75	7.50	15.00

—As "Simon Crum"

Number	Title (A Side/B Side)	Yr	VG	VG+	NM
❏ 4499	Enormity in Motion/Cuzz Yore So Sweet	1961	3.75	7.50	15.00

—As "Simon Crum"

Number	Title (A Side/B Side)	Yr	VG	VG+	NM
❏ 4548	Before I Lose My Mind/What Good Will I Ever Be	1961	3.00	6.00	12.00
❏ 4594	Willow Tree/Take a Look	1961	3.00	6.00	12.00
❏ 4650	The Waltz You Saved for Me/				
	Out of a Clear Blue Sky	1961	3.00	6.00	12.00
❏ 4650 [PS]	The Waltz You Saved for Me/				
	Out of a Clear Blue Sky	1961	6.25	12.50	25.00
❏ 4721	Somebody Save Me/Just Another Lonely Night	1962	2.50	5.00	10.00
❏ 4779	Stand Up/It Scares Me	1962	2.50	5.00	10.00
❏ 4853	It Was You/Near You	1962	2.50	5.00	10.00
❏ 4908	You Hurt Me/My Reason for Living	1963	2.50	5.00	10.00
❏ 4966	Don't Be Mad/Little Red Webb	1963	3.00	6.00	12.00

—As "Simon Crum"

Number	Title (A Side/B Side)	Yr	VG	VG+	NM
❏ 4977	Who's Next/As Close As We'll Ever Be	1963	2.50	5.00	10.00
❏ 5067	Face of a Clown/Love Looks Good on You	1963	2.50	5.00	10.00
❏ 5111	Timber I'm Falling/Don't Count the Diamonds	1964	2.50	5.00	10.00
❏ 5206	Up on the Mountain Top/Weaker Moments	1964	2.50	5.00	10.00
❏ 5355	True, True Lovin'/Love Built the House	1965	2.50	5.00	10.00
❏ 5438	Willie Was a Gamblin' Man/				
	Picking Up the Pieces	1965	2.50	5.00	10.00
❏ 5522	Money Greases the Wheels/Lasting Love	1965	2.50	5.00	10.00
❏ 5615	I Could Sing All Night/What Does Your				
	Conscience Say to You	1966	2.50	5.00	10.00
❏ 5679	I Hear Little Rock Calling/Stand Beside Me	1966	2.50	5.00	10.00
❏ 5775	Once/Why Do I Put Up with You	1966	2.50	5.00	10.00
❏ 5852	What Am I Gonna Do Now/General G	1967	2.00	4.00	8.00
❏ 5938	You Pushed Me Too Far/				
	A Bridge I Have Never Crossed	1967	2.00	4.00	8.00

4 STAR

Number	Title (A Side/B Side)	Yr	VG	VG+	NM
❏ 1516	Guilty Feeling/Road to Heaven	1950	12.50	25.00	50.00

—All 4 Star records as "Terry Preston"; it's possible that not all these exist on 45s

Number	Title (A Side/B Side)	Yr	VG	VG+	NM
❏ 1518	Let's Keep the Communists Out/The Sabbath	1950	12.50	25.00	50.00
❏ 1542	Irma/Put Me in Your Pocket	1950	12.50	25.00	50.00

H

Number	Title (A Side/B Side)	Yr	VG	VG+	NM
❑ 1566	Wise Guy/Cross Eyed Gal from the Ozarks	1951	10.00	20.00	40.00
❑ 1571	Jezebel/Tennessee Hillbilly Ghost	1951	10.00	20.00	40.00
❑ 1572	Crying Heart Blues/If You Don't Believe I'm Leaving (Just Count the Days I'm Gone)	1951	10.00	20.00	40.00
❑ 1573	Rotation Blues/Deadly Weapon	1951	10.00	20.00	40.00

KING

Number	Title (A Side/B Side)	Yr	VG	VG+	NM
❑ 5434	Irma/Cotton Pickin' Heart	1960	3.00	6.00	12.00
❑ 5476	Electrified Donkey/Guilty Feeling	1961	3.00	6.00	12.00

7-Inch Extended Plays

CAPITOL

Number	Title (A Side/B Side)	Yr	VG	VG+	NM
❑ EAP 1-609	(contents unknown)	1955	5.00	10.00	20.00
❑ EAP 1-609 [PS]	Ferlin Husky	1955	5.00	10.00	20.00
❑ EAP 1-718	Hang Your Head in Shame/That Silver Haired Daddy of Mine//Honky-Tonkin' Party Girl/Useless	1956	3.75	7.50	15.00
❑ EAP 1-718 [PS]	Songs of the Home and Heart, Part 1	1956	3.75	7.50	15.00
❑ EAP 2-718	I Can't Go On This Way/That Little Girl of Mine//You Make Me Feel Funny, Honey/Rockin' Alone in an Old Rockin' Chair	1956	3.75	7.50	15.00
❑ EAP 2-718 [PS]	Songs of the Home and Heart, Part 2	1956	3.75	7.50	15.00
❑ EAP 3-718	Farther and Farther Apart/Never Have, Never Will//I Dreamed of an Old Love Affair/Daddy's Little Girl	1956	3.75	7.50	15.00
❑ EAP 3-718 [PS]	Songs of the Home and Heart, Part 3	1956	3.75	7.50	15.00
❑ EAP 1-837	A Fallen Star/Prize Possession//I Feel Better All Over/Pick-a-Nickin'	1957	5.00	10.00	20.00
❑ EAP 1-837 [PS]	Husky Hits	1957	5.00	10.00	20.00
❑ EAP 1-880	Boulevard of Broken Dreams/I'll Walk Alone//But Where Are You/It All Comes Back to Me Now	1957	3.75	7.50	15.00
❑ EAP 1-880 [PS]	Boulevard of Broken Dreams, Part 1	1957	3.75	7.50	15.00
❑ EAP 2-880	Stormy Weather/It's the Talk of the Town//(Here Am I) Broken Hearted/Out in the Cold Again	1957	3.75	7.50	15.00
❑ EAP 2-880 [PS]	Boulevard of Broken Dreams, Part 2	1957	3.75	7.50	15.00
❑ EAP 3-880	(contents unknown)	1957	3.75	7.50	15.00
❑ EAP 3-880 [PS]	Boulevard of Broken Dreams, Part 3	1957	3.75	7.50	15.00
❑ EAP 1-921	Don't Walk Away/Somewhere There's Sunshine//My Home Town/This Whole Wide World	1958	3.00	6.00	12.00
❑ EAP 1-921 [PS]	Country Music Holiday	1958	3.00	6.00	12.00
❑ EAP 1-1280	(contents unknown)	1960	3.00	6.00	12.00
❑ EAP 1-1280 [PS]	Ferlin Favorites, Part 1	1960	3.00	6.00	12.00
❑ EAP 2-1280	(contents unknown)	1960	3.00	6.00	12.00
❑ EAP 2-1280 [PS]	Ferlin Favorites, Part 2	1960	3.00	6.00	12.00
❑ EAP 3-1280	(contents unknown)	1960	3.00	6.00	12.00
❑ EAP 3-1280 [PS]	Ferlin Favorites, Part 3	1960	3.00	6.00	12.00
❑ EAP 1-1516	Gone/Black Sheep//Wings of a Dove/My Love for You	1961	3.00	6.00	12.00
❑ EAP 1-1516 [PS]	Wings of a Dove	1961	3.00	6.00	12.00

Albums

ABC

Number	Title (A Side/B Side)	Yr	VG	VG+	NM
❑ X-776	True True Lovin'	1973	3.00	6.00	12.00
❑ X-803	Sweet Honky Tonk	1974	3.00	6.00	12.00
❑ X-818	Freckles and Polliwog Days	1974	3.00	6.00	12.00
❑ X-849	Champagne Ladies and Blue Ribbon Babies	1974	3.00	6.00	12.00
❑ X-884	The Foster-Rice Songbook	1975	3.00	6.00	12.00

CAPITOL

Number	Title (A Side/B Side)	Yr	VG	VG+	NM
❑ ST-115	White Fences and Evergreen Trees	1968	3.75	7.50	15.00
❑ SKAO-143	The Best of Ferlin Husky	1969	3.75	7.50	15.00
❑ SM-143	The Best of Ferlin Husky	197?	2.50	5.00	10.00
—Reissue with new prefix					
❑ ST-239	That's Why I Love You So Much	1969	3.75	7.50	15.00
❑ ST-433	Your Love Is Heavenly Sunshine	1970	3.75	7.50	15.00
❑ ST-591	Your Sweet Love Lifted Me	1970	3.75	7.50	15.00
❑ T 718 [M]	Songs of the Home and Heart	1956	15.00	30.00	60.00
—Turquoise label					
❑ T 718 [M]	Songs of the Home and Heart	1959	10.00	20.00	40.00
—Black colorband label, Capitol logo at left					
❑ T 718 [M]	Songs of the Home and Heart	1962	6.25	12.50	25.00
—Black colorband label, Capitol logo at top					
❑ ST-768	One More Time	1971	3.75	7.50	15.00
❑ T 880 [M]	Boulevard of Broken Dreams	1957	15.00	30.00	60.00
—Turquoise label					
❑ T 880 [M]	Boulevard of Broken Dreams	1958	10.00	20.00	40.00
—Black colorband label, Capitol logo at left					
❑ T 976 [M]	Sittin' On a Rainbow	1958	15.00	30.00	60.00
—Turquoise label					
❑ T 1204 [M]	Born to Lose	1959	10.00	20.00	40.00
—Black colorband label, Capitol logo at left					
❑ T 1204 [M]	Born to Lose	1962	6.25	12.50	25.00
—Black colorband label, Capitol logo at top					
❑ T 1280 [M]	Ferlin's Favorites	1960	10.00	20.00	40.00
—Black colorband label, Capitol logo at left					
❑ T 1280 [M]	Ferlin's Favorites	1962	6.25	12.50	25.00
—Black colorband label, Capitol logo at top					
❑ DT 1383 [R]	Gone	196?	3.00	6.00	12.00
❑ T 1383 [M]	Gone	196?	5.00	10.00	20.00
—Gold "The Star Line" label; "The Star Line" logo on cover					
❑ T 1383 [M]	Gone	1960	10.00	20.00	40.00
—Black colorband label, Capitol logo at left					
❑ T 1383 [M]	Gone	1962	6.25	12.50	25.00
—Black colorband label, Capitol logo at top					
❑ ST 1546 [S]	Walkin' and Hummin'	1961	7.50	15.00	30.00
—Black colorband label, Capitol logo at left					
❑ ST 1546 [S]	Walkin' and Hummin'	1962	5.00	10.00	20.00
—Black colorband label, Capitol logo at top					
❑ T 1546 [M]	Walkin' and Hummin'	1961	6.25	12.50	25.00
—Black colorband label, Capitol logo at left					
❑ T 1546 [M]	Walkin' and Hummin'	1962	3.75	7.50	15.00
—Black colorband label, Capitol logo at top					
❑ ST 1633 [S]	Memories of Home	1961	7.50	15.00	30.00
—Black colorband label, Capitol logo at left					
❑ ST 1633 [S]	Memories of Home	1962	5.00	10.00	20.00
—Black colorband label, Capitol logo at top					
❑ T 1633 [M]	Memories of Home	1961	6.25	12.50	25.00
—Black colorband label, Capitol logo at left					
❑ T 1633 [M]	Memories of Home	1962	3.75	7.50	15.00
—Black colorband label, Capitol logo at top					

Number	Title (A Side/B Side)	Yr	VG	VG+	NM
❑ ST 1720 [S]	Some of My Favorites	1962	5.00	10.00	20.00
❑ T 1720 [M]	Some of My Favorites	1962	3.75	7.50	15.00
❑ ST 1885 [S]	The Heart and Soul of Ferlin Husky	1963	5.00	10.00	20.00
❑ T 1885 [M]	The Heart and Soul of Ferlin Husky	1963	3.75	7.50	15.00
❑ DT 1991 [R]	The Hits of Ferlin Husky	1963	3.00	6.00	12.00
❑ T 1991 [M]	The Hits of Ferlin Husky	1963	3.75	7.50	15.00
❑ ST 2101 [S]	By Request	1964	5.00	10.00	20.00
❑ T 2101 [M]	By Request	1964	3.75	7.50	15.00
❑ ST 2305 [S]	True, True Lovin'	1965	5.00	10.00	20.00
❑ T 2305 [M]	True, True Lovin'	1965	3.75	7.50	15.00
❑ ST 2439 [S]	Ferlin Husky Sings the Songs of Music City, U.S.A.	1966	5.00	10.00	20.00
❑ T 2439 [M]	Ferlin Husky Sings the Songs of Music City, U.S.A.	1966	3.75	7.50	15.00
❑ ST 2548 [S]	I Could Sing All Night	1966	5.00	10.00	20.00
❑ T 2548 [M]	I Could Sing All Night	1966	3.75	7.50	15.00
❑ ST 2705 [S]	What Am I Gonna Do Now?	1967	3.75	7.50	15.00
❑ T 2705 [M]	What Am I Gonna Do Now?	1967	5.00	10.00	20.00
❑ ST 2793 [S]	Christmas All Year Long	1967	3.75	7.50	15.00
❑ T 2793 [M]	Christmas All Year Long	1967	3.75	7.50	15.00
❑ ST 2870 [S]	Just for You	1968	3.75	7.50	15.00
❑ T 2870 [M]	Just for You	1968	7.50	15.00	30.00
❑ ST 2913	Where No One Stands Alone	1968	3.75	7.50	15.00
❑ ST-11069	Just Plain Lonely	1972	3.75	7.50	15.00

HILLTOP

Number	Title (A Side/B Side)	Yr	VG	VG+	NM
❑ 6005	Ole Opry Favorites	196?	3.00	6.00	12.00
❑ 6086	Green, Green Grass of Home	1970	3.00	6.00	12.00
❑ 6099	Wings of a Dove	197?	3.00	6.00	12.00

KING

Number	Title (A Side/B Side)	Yr	VG	VG+	NM
❑ 647 [M]	Country Tunes Sung from the Heart	1959	17.50	35.00	70.00
❑ 728 [M]	Easy Livin'	1960	17.50	35.00	70.00

STARDAY

Number	Title (A Side/B Side)	Yr	VG	VG+	NM
❑ 3018	Greatest Hits	197?	3.00	6.00	12.00

HUTCH, WILLIE

45s

DUNHILL

Number	Title (A Side/B Side)	Yr	VG	VG+	NM
❑ 4012	The Duck/Love Runs Out	1965	15.00	30.00	60.00

MAVERICK

Number	Title (A Side/B Side)	Yr	VG	VG+	NM
❑ 1003	Use What You Got (Part 1)/Use What You Got (Part 2)	1968	3.75	7.50	15.00

MODERN

Number	Title (A Side/B Side)	Yr	VG	VG+	NM
❑ 1021	I Can't Get Enough/Your Love Has Made Me a Man	1966	10.00	20.00	40.00

MOTOWN

Number	Title (A Side/B Side)	Yr	VG	VG+	NM
❑ 1222	Brother's Gonna Work It Out/I Choose You	1973	—	2.50	5.00
❑ 1252	Slick/Mother's Theme	1973	—	2.50	5.00
❑ 1252 [PS]	Slick/Mother's Theme	1973	—	3.00	6.00
❑ 1282	Sunshine Lady/I Just Wanted to Make Her Happy	1973	—	2.50	5.00
❑ 1287	If You Ain't Got No Money (You Can't Get No Honey) Pt. 1/Pt. 2	1974	—	2.50	5.00
❑ 1292	Theme of Foxy Brown/Give Me Some of That Good Old Love	1974	—	2.50	5.00
❑ 1331	I'm Gonna Stay/Woman You Touched Me	1975	—	2.50	5.00
❑ 1339	Get Ready for the Get Down/Don't Let Nobody Tell You How to Do Your Thing	1975	—	2.50	5.00
❑ 1360	Love Power/Talk to Me	1975	—	2.00	4.00
❑ 1371	Party Down/Just Another Day	1976	—	2.00	4.00
❑ 1406	Let Me Be the One, Baby/She's Just Doing Her Thing	1976	—	2.00	4.00
❑ 1411	Shake It, Shake It/I Feel Like We Can Make It	1976	—	2.00	4.00
❑ 1416	We Gonna Have a House Party/Never Had It So Good	1977	—	2.00	4.00
❑ 1424	We Gonna Party Tonight/Precious Pearl	1977	—	2.00	4.00
❑ 1433	What You Gonna Do After the Party/I Feel Like We Can Make It	1977	—	2.00	4.00
❑ 1637	In and Out/Girl	1982	—	2.00	4.00
❑ 1797	Keep On Jammin'/The Glow	1985	—	2.00	4.00

RCA VICTOR

Number	Title (A Side/B Side)	Yr	VG	VG+	NM
❑ 74-0189	Ain't Gonna Stop/Do What You Wanna Do	1969	2.50	5.00	10.00
❑ 74-0294	When a Boy Falls in Love (Part 1)/When a Boy Falls in Love (Part 2)	1969	2.50	5.00	10.00
❑ 74-0327	Magic of Love/Walking on My Love	1970	2.50	5.00	10.00

WHITFIELD

Number	Title (A Side/B Side)	Yr	VG	VG+	NM
❑ 8615	All American Funkathon/And All Hell Broke Loose	1978	—	2.00	4.00
❑ 8689	Paradise/Hip Shakin' Sexy Lady	1978	—	2.00	4.00
❑ 49015	Deep in Your Love/Everybody Needs Money	1979	—	2.00	4.00
❑ 49102	Down Here on Disco Street/Kelly Green	1979	—	2.00	4.00

Albums

MOTOWN

Number	Title (A Side/B Side)	Yr	VG	VG+	NM
❑ M 766	The Mack	1973	3.00	6.00	12.00
❑ M 784	Fully Exposed	1973	3.00	6.00	12.00
❑ M6-811	Foxy Brown	1974	3.00	6.00	12.00
❑ M6-815	Mark of the Beast	1974	3.00	6.00	12.00
❑ M6-838	Ode to My Lady	1975	3.00	6.00	12.00
❑ M6-854	Concert in Blues	1976	3.00	6.00	12.00
❑ M6-871	Color Her...	1977	3.00	6.00	12.00
❑ M6-874	Havin' a House Party	1977	3.00	6.00	12.00
❑ 5281 ML	The Mack	1983	2.00	4.00	8.00
—Reissue of 766					

RCA VICTOR

Number	Title (A Side/B Side)	Yr	VG	VG+	NM
❑ LSP-4213	Soul Portrait: Willie Hutch	1969	3.75	7.50	15.00

WHITFIELD

Number	Title (A Side/B Side)	Yr	VG	VG+	NM
❑ BSK 3226	In Tune	1978	2.50	5.00	10.00
❑ BSK 3352	Midnight Dancer	1979	2.50	5.00	10.00

HUTTO, J.B.

45s

CHANCE

Number	Title (A Side/B Side)	Yr	VG	VG+	NM
❑ 1155	Now She's Gone/Combination Boogie	1954	250.00	500.00	1000.
❑ 1160	Lovin' You/Pet Cream Man	1954	1000.	2000.	4000.
—The above two may be listed on the label as "J.B. and the Hawks"					
❑ 1165	Dim Lights/Things Are So Slow	1955	750.00	1500.	3000.

Number	Title (A Side/B Side)	Yr	VG	VG+	NM

HUTTON, DANNY Also see THREE DOG NIGHT.
45s
ALMO

❏ 213	Why Don't You Love Me Anymore/Home in Pasadena	1964	5.00	10.00	20.00

—As "Daring Dan Hutton"
HANNA-BARBERA

❏ 447	Roses and Rainbows/Monster Shindig	1965	3.75	7.50	15.00
❏ 447 [PS]	Roses and Rainbows/Monster Shindig	1965	7.50	15.00	30.00
❏ 453	Big Bright Eyes/Monester Shindig (Part 2)	1965	3.75	7.50	15.00

MGM

❏ 13502	Funny How Love Can Be/Dreamin' Isn't Good for You	1966	2.50	5.00	10.00
❏ 13502 [PS]	Funny How Love Can Be/Dreamin' Isn't Good for You	1966	5.00	10.00	20.00
❏ 13613	Hang On to a Dream/Hit the Wall	1966	2.50	5.00	10.00

Albums
MGM

| ❏ SE-4664 | Pre-Dog Night | 1970 | 7.50 | 15.00 | 30.00 |

HYLAND, BRIAN
45s
ABC-PARAMOUNT

❏ 10236	Let Me Belong to You/Let It Die	1961	2.50	5.00	10.00
❏ 10262	I'll Never Stop Wanting You/The Night I Cried	1961	2.50	5.00	10.00
❏ 10262 [PS]	I'll Never Stop Wanting You/The Night I Cried	1961	5.00	10.00	20.00
❏ 10294	Ginny Come Lately/I Should Be Gettin' Better	1962	2.50	5.00	10.00
❏ 10294 [PS]	Ginny Come Lately/I Should Be Gettin' Better	1962	5.00	10.00	20.00
❏ 10336	Sealed with a Kiss/Summer Job	1962	3.00	6.00	12.00
❏ 10336 [PS]	Sealed with a Kiss/Summer Job	1962	5.00	10.00	20.00
❏ 10359	Warmed Over Kisses (Left Over Love)/Walk a Lonely Mile	1962	2.50	5.00	10.00
❏ 10359 [PS]	Warmed Over Kisses (Left Over Love)/Walk a Lonely Mile	1962	5.00	10.00	20.00
❏ 10374	I May Not Live to See Tomorrow/It Ain't That Way at All	1962	2.50	5.00	10.00
❏ 10374 [PS]	I May Not Live to See Tomorrow/It Ain't That Way at All	1962	5.00	10.00	20.00
❏ 10400	If Mary's There/Remember Me	1963	2.50	5.00	10.00
❏ 10400 [PS]	If Mary's There/Remember Me	1963	5.00	10.00	20.00
❏ 10427	Somewhere in the Night/I Wish Today Was Yesterday	1963	2.50	5.00	10.00
❏ 10452	I'm Afraid to Go Home/Save Your Heart for Me	1963	2.50	5.00	10.00
❏ 10494	Nothing Matters But You/Let Us Make Our Own Mistakes	1963	2.50	5.00	10.00
❏ 10549	Act Naturally/Out of Sight, Out of Mind	1964	2.50	5.00	10.00

DOT

❏ 17050	Apologize/Words on Paper	1967	—	3.00	6.00
❏ 17061	It's Christmas Time Once Again/Words on Paper	1967	3.00	6.00	12.00
❏ 17078	Come with Me/Delilah	1968	—	3.00	6.00
❏ 17109	The Lover/Springfield, Illinois	1968	—	3.00	6.00
❏ 17176	Tragedy/You'd Better Stop and Think It Over	1968	—	3.00	6.00
❏ 17222	A Million to One/It Could All Begin Again	1969	—	3.00	6.00
❏ 17258	Early April Morning/Stay and Love Me All Summer	1969		3.00	6.00
❏ 17291	Dreamy Eyes/Gonna Make a Woman Out of You	1970	—	3.00	6.00

KAPP

❏ 342	Itsy Bitsy Teeny Weeny Yellow Polka Dot Bikini/Don't Dilly Dally, Sally	1960	3.75	7.50	15.00
❏ 342 [PS]	Itsy Bitsy Teeny Weeny Yellow Polka Dot Bikini/Don't Dilly Dally, Sally	1960	7.50	15.00	30.00
❏ 352	Four Little Heels (The Clickety Clack Song)/That's How Much	1960	3.00	6.00	12.00
❏ 352 [PS]	Four Little Heels (The Clickety Clack Song)/That's How Much	1960	6.25	12.50	25.00
❏ 363	I Gotta Go/Lopsided, Over Loaded	1960	3.00	6.00	12.00
❏ 363 [PS]	I Gotta Go/Lopsided, Over Loaded	1960	6.25	12.50	25.00
❏ 401	Lipstick on Your Lips/When Will I Know	1961	3.00	6.00	12.00

LEADER

| ❏ 801 | Library Love Affair/Rosemary | 1960 | 5.00 | 10.00 | 20.00 |
| ❏ 805 | Itsy Bitsy Teeny Weeny Yellow Polka Dot Bikini/Don't Dilly Dally, Sally | 1960 | 7.50 | 15.00 | 30.00 |

PHILIPS

❏ 40179	Here's to Our Love/Two Kinds of Girls	1964	2.00	4.00	8.00
❏ 40179 [PS]	Here's to Our Love/Two Kinds of Girls	1964	3.00	6.00	12.00
❏ 40203	Devoted to You/Pledging My Love	1964	2.00	4.00	8.00
❏ 40203 [PS]	Devoted to You/Pledging My Love	1964	3.00	6.00	12.00
❏ 40221	Now I Belong to You/One Step Forward, Two Steps Back	1964	2.00	4.00	8.00
❏ 40263	He Don't Understand You/Love Will Find a Way	1965	2.00	4.00	8.00
❏ 40263 [PS]	He Don't Understand You/Love Will Find a Way	1965	3.00	6.00	12.00
❏ 40306	Stay Away from Her/I Can't Keep a Secret	1965	2.00	4.00	8.00
❏ 40354	3000 Miles/Sometimes They Do, Sometimes They Don't	1966	2.00	4.00	8.00
❏ 40377	The Joker Went Wild/I Can Hear the Rain	1966	2.50	5.00	10.00
❏ 40405	Why Did You Do It/Run, Look and See	1966	2.00	4.00	8.00
❏ 40424	Hung Up in Your Eyes/Why Mine	1967	2.00	4.00	8.00
❏ 40424 [PS]	Hung Up in Your Eyes/Why Mine	1967	3.00	6.00	12.00
❏ 40444	Holiday for Clowns/Yesterday I Had a Girl	1967	2.00	4.00	8.00
❏ 40472	Get the Message/Kinda Groovy	1967	—	3.00	6.00

UNI

❏ 55193	You and Me/Could You Dig It	1970	—	3.00	6.00
❏ 55240	Gypsy Woman/You and Me (#2)	1970	—	3.00	6.00
❏ 55272	Lonely Teardrops/Lorraine	1971	—	2.50	5.00
❏ 55287	So Long, Marianne/No Place to Run	1971	—	2.50	5.00
❏ 55306	Out of the Blue/If You Came Back	1971	—	2.50	5.00
❏ 55323	I Love Every Little Thing About You/With My Eyes Wide Open	1972		2.50	5.00
❏ 55334	Only Wanna Make You Happy/When You're Lovin' Me	1972	—	2.50	5.00

Albums
ABC-PARAMOUNT

❏ 400 [M]	Let Me Belong to You	1961	7.50	15.00	30.00
❏ S-400 [S]	Let Me Belong to You	1961	10.00	20.00	40.00
❏ 431 [M]	Sealed with a Kiss	1962	7.50	15.00	30.00
❏ S-431 [S]	Sealed with a Kiss	1962	10.00	20.00	40.00
❏ 463 [M]	Country Meets Folk	1964	7.50	15.00	30.00
❏ S-463 [S]	Country Meets Folk	1964	10.00	20.00	40.00

DOT

| ❏ DLP 25926 | Tragedy/A Million to One | 1969 | 3.75 | 7.50 | 15.00 |
| ❏ DLP 25954 | Stay and Love Me All Summer | 1969 | 3.75 | 7.50 | 15.00 |

KAPP

| ❏ KL 1202 [M] | The Bashful Blonde | 1960 | 12.50 | 25.00 | 50.00 |
| ❏ KS 3202 [S] | The Bashful Blonde | 1960 | 20.00 | 40.00 | 80.00 |

PHILIPS

❏ PHM 200136 [M]	Here's to Our Love	1964	5.00	10.00	20.00
❏ PHM 200158 [M]	Rockin' Folk	1965	5.00	10.00	20.00
❏ PHM 200217 [M]	Run, Run, Look and See/The Joker Went Wild	1966	5.00	10.00	20.00

—With "200-217" in trail-off; this record plays mono

| ❏ PHM 200217 [S] | Run, Run, Look and See/The Joker Went Wild | 1966 | 5.00 | 10.00 | 20.00 |

—With "2/600-217" in trail-off; this record plays stereo, though labeled mono

❏ PHS 600158 [S]	Here's to Our Love	1964	6.25	12.50	25.00
❏ PHS 600158 [S]	Rockin' Folk	1965	6.25	12.50	25.00
❏ PHS 600217 [S]	Run, Run, Look and See/The Joker Went Wild	1966	6.25	12.50	25.00

PICKWICK

| ❏ SPC-3261 | Young Years | 197? | 2.50 | 5.00 | 10.00 |

PRIVATE STOCK

| ❏ PS-7003 | In a State of Bayou | 1977 | 3.00 | 6.00 | 12.00 |

RHINO

| ❏ RNLP-70226 | Greatest Hits | 1987 | 2.50 | 5.00 | 10.00 |

UNI

| ❏ 73097 | Brian Hyland | 1970 | 3.75 | 7.50 | 15.00 |

—The album is listed as "stereo," but "Gypsy Woman" is rechanneled
WING

| ❏ MGW-12341 [M] | Here's to Our Love | 1967 | 3.00 | 6.00 | 12.00 |
| ❏ SRW-16341 [S] | Here's to Our Love | 1967 | 3.00 | 6.00 | 12.00 |

Number	Title (A Side/B Side)	Yr	VG	VG+	NM

I

I KADEZ
45s
HIT

Number	Title (A Side/B Side)	Yr	VG	VG+	NM
❏ 95	Louie Louie/Popsicles and Icicles	1963	2.00	4.00	8.00

—B-side by the Scotties

I.V. LEAGUERS, THE
45s
DOT

Number	Title (A Side/B Side)	Yr	VG	VG+	NM
❏ 15677	Ring Chimes/The Story	1957	5.00	10.00	20.00

NAU-VOO

Number	Title (A Side/B Side)	Yr	VG	VG+	NM
❏ 803	Told by the Stars/Jim Jam	1959	100.00	200.00	400.00

PORTER

Number	Title (A Side/B Side)	Yr	VG	VG+	NM
❏ 1004	Ring Chimes/The Story	1957	12.50	25.00	50.00

IAN, JANIS
45s
CAPITOL

Number	Title (A Side/B Side)	Yr	VG	VG+	NM
❏ 3107	He's a Rainbow/Here in Spain	1971	2.00	4.00	8.00

CASABLANCA

Number	Title (A Side/B Side)	Yr	VG	VG+	NM
❏ 2245	Night Rains/Fly Too High	1980	—	2.50	5.00

COLUMBIA

Number	Title (A Side/B Side)	Yr	VG	VG+	NM
❏ 02176	Sugar Mountain/Under the Covers	1981	—	2.00	4.00
❏ 02546	Restless Eyes/I Remember Yesterday	1981	—	2.00	4.00
❏ 10119	When the Party's Over/Bright Lights and Promises	1975	—	2.50	5.00
❏ 10154	At Seventeen/Stars	1975	—	2.50	5.00
❏ 10154 [PS]	At Seventeen/Stars	1975	2.00	4.00	8.00
❏ 10228	In the Winter/Thankyouse	1975	—	2.50	5.00
❏ 10297	Aftertones/Boy, I Really Tied One On	1976	—	2.50	5.00
❏ 10331	I Would Like to Dance/Goodbye to Morning	1976	—	2.50	5.00
❏ 10391	Roses/Love Is Blind	1976	—	2.50	5.00
❏ 10484	Miracle Row/Take It to the Sky	1977	—	2.50	5.00
❏ 10526	Candlelight/I Want to Make You Love Me	1977	—	2.50	5.00
❏ 10813	That Grand Illusion/Hopper Paining	1978	—	2.50	5.00
❏ 10864	The Bridge/Do You Wanna Dance	1978	—	2.50	5.00
❏ 10979	Here Comes the Night/Tonight Will Last Forever	1979	—	2.00	4.00
❏ 11111	Night Rains/Fly Too High	1979	—	2.00	4.00
❏ 11327	The Other Side of the Sun/Memories	1980	—	2.00	4.00
❏ 46034	Jesse/The Man You Are in Me	1974	—	2.50	5.00

POLYDOR

Number	Title (A Side/B Side)	Yr	VG	VG+	NM
❏ 14299	Society's Child (Baby I've Been Thinking)/I'll Give You a Stone If You Throw It	1975	—	3.00	6.00

VERVE

Number	Title (A Side/B Side)	Yr	VG	VG+	NM
❏ 5027	Society's Child (Baby I've Been Thinking)/Letter to Jon	1967	2.50	5.00	10.00

VERVE FOLKWAYS

Number	Title (A Side/B Side)	Yr	VG	VG+	NM
❏ 5027	Society's Child (Baby I've Been Thinking)/Letter to Jon	1966	3.00	6.00	12.00

VERVE FORECAST

Number	Title (A Side/B Side)	Yr	VG	VG+	NM
❏ 5027	Society's Child (Baby I've Been Thinking)/Letter to Jon	1967	2.00	4.00	8.00
❏ 5041	I'll Give You a Stone If You'll Throw It/Younger Generation Blues	1967	2.00	4.00	8.00
❏ 5072	Insanity Comes Quietly to the Structured Mind/Snowflakes Fall, Snowrays Call	1967	2.00	4.00	8.00
❏ 5079	Somg for All the Seasons of Your Mind/Lonely One	1968	2.00	4.00	8.00
❏ 5090	Lady of the Night/Friends Again	1968	2.00	4.00	8.00
❏ 5099	Everybody Knows/Janey's Blues	1968	2.00	4.00	8.00
❏ 5113	Month of May/Calling Your Name	1969	2.00	4.00	8.00

Albums
ANALOGUE PRODUCTIONS

Number	Title (A Side/B Side)	Yr	VG	VG+	NM
❏ AAP 027	Breaking Silence	1995	6.25	12.50	25.00

—Audiophile vinyl
CAPITOL

Number	Title (A Side/B Side)	Yr	VG	VG+	NM
❏ SKAO-683	Present Company	1971	3.75	7.50	15.00
❏ SN-683	Present Company	1975	2.50	5.00	10.00

COLUMBIA

Number	Title (A Side/B Side)	Yr	VG	VG+	NM
❏ KC 32857	Stars	1974	2.50	5.00	10.00
❏ PC 32857	Stars	197?	2.00	4.00	8.00
❏ PC 33394	Between the Lines	1975	2.50	5.00	10.00

—No bar code on cover

Number	Title (A Side/B Side)	Yr	VG	VG+	NM
❏ PC 33394	Between the Lines	1979	2.00	4.00	8.00

—With bar code on cover

Number	Title (A Side/B Side)	Yr	VG	VG+	NM
❏ PCQ 33394 [Q]	Between the Lines	1975	3.75	7.50	15.00
❏ PC 33919	Aftertones	1976	2.50	5.00	10.00

—No bar code on cover

Number	Title (A Side/B Side)	Yr	VG	VG+	NM
❏ PC 33919	Aftertones	1979	2.00	4.00	8.00

—With bar code on cover

Number	Title (A Side/B Side)	Yr	VG	VG+	NM
❏ PCQ 33919 [Q]	Aftertones	1976	3.75	7.50	15.00
❏ JC 34440	Miracle Row	1977	2.50	5.00	10.00
❏ JC 35325	Janis Ian	1978	2.50	5.00	10.00
❏ JC 36139	Night Rains	1979	2.50	5.00	10.00
❏ PC 36139	Night Rains	198?	2.00	4.00	8.00
❏ FC 37360	Restless Eyes	1981	2.50	5.00	10.00

MGM

Number	Title (A Side/B Side)	Yr	VG	VG+	NM
❏ GAS-121	Janis Ian (Golden Archive Series)	1970	6.25	12.50	25.00

POLYDOR

Number	Title (A Side/B Side)	Yr	VG	VG+	NM
❏ PD-6058	Janis Ian	1976	2.50	5.00	10.00

VERVE

Number	Title (A Side/B Side)	Yr	VG	VG+	NM
❏ V/VS-5027	Janis Ian	1967	—	—	—

—Scheduled, possibly not released; same LP is Verve Forecast 3017
VERVE FOLKWAYS

Number	Title (A Side/B Side)	Yr	VG	VG+	NM
❏ FT-3017 [M]	Janis Ian	1967	7.50	15.00	30.00
❏ FTS-3017 [S]	Janis Ian	1967	7.50	15.00	30.00

VERVE FORECAST

Number	Title (A Side/B Side)	Yr	VG	VG+	NM
❏ FT-3017 [M]	Janis Ian	1967	5.00	10.00	20.00
❏ FTS-3017 [S]	Janis Ian	1967	3.75	7.50	15.00
❏ FT-3024 [M]	For All the Seasons of Your Mind	1967	5.00	10.00	20.00
❏ FTS-3024 [S]	For All the Seasons of Your Mind	1967	3.75	7.50	15.00
❏ FTS-3048	The Secret Life of J. Eddy Fink	1968	3.75	7.50	15.00
❏ FTS-3063	Who Really Cares?	1969	3.75	7.50	15.00

IAN AND SYLVIA
45s
COLUMBIA

Number	Title (A Side/B Side)	Yr	VG	VG+	NM
❏ 45430	Creatures of Rain/Summer Wages	1971	—	3.00	6.00
❏ 45475	More Often Than Not/Some Kind of Fool	1971	—	3.00	6.00
❏ 45680	You Were On My Mind/Salmon in the Sea	1972	—	3.00	6.00

MGM

Number	Title (A Side/B Side)	Yr	VG	VG+	NM
❏ 13686	Lovin' Sound/Pilgrimage to Paradise	1967	2.00	4.00	8.00
❏ 14082	Give It to the World/Shinbone Alley	1969	2.00	4.00	8.00

VANGUARD

Number	Title (A Side/B Side)	Yr	VG	VG+	NM
❏ 35021	Four Strong Winds/C.C. Rider	1963	2.50	5.00	10.00
❏ 35025	You Were On My Mind/Someday Soon	1964	2.50	5.00	10.00
❏ 35035	Play One More/The French Girl	1964	2.50	5.00	10.00
❏ 35062	House of Cards/90" By 90"	1968	2.00	4.00	8.00

Albums
AMPEX

Number	Title (A Side/B Side)	Yr	VG	VG+	NM
❏ A-10103	Great Speckled Bird	1970	5.00	10.00	20.00

COLUMBIA

Number	Title (A Side/B Side)	Yr	VG	VG+	NM
❏ C 30736	Ian and Sylvia	1971	3.00	6.00	12.00
❏ KC 31337	You Were On My Mind	1972	3.00	6.00	12.00
❏ G 32516 [(2)]	The Best of Ian and Sylvia	1973	3.75	7.50	15.00

MGM

Number	Title (A Side/B Side)	Yr	VG	VG+	NM
❏ GAS-115	Ian and Sylvia (Golden Archive Series)	1970	3.75	7.50	15.00
❏ E-4388 [M]	Lovin' Sound	1967	5.00	10.00	20.00
❏ SE-4388 [S]	Lovin' Sound	1967	3.75	7.50	15.00
❏ SE-4550	Full Circle	1968	5.00	10.00	20.00

VANGUARD

Number	Title (A Side/B Side)	Yr	VG	VG+	NM
❏ VSD-5/6 [(2)]	Ian and Sylvia's Greatest Hits	1969	3.75	7.50	15.00
❏ VSD-23/24 [(2)]	Ian and Sylvia's Greatest Hits, Vol. 2	1970	3.75	7.50	15.00
❏ VSD-2113 [S]	Ian and Sylvia	1963	7.50	15.00	30.00
❏ VSD-2149 [S]	Four Strong Winds	1963	6.25	12.50	25.00
❏ VRS-9109 [M]	Ian and Sylvia	1963	6.25	12.50	25.00
❏ VRS-9133 [M]	Four Strong Winds	1963	5.00	10.00	20.00
❏ VRS-9154 [M]	Northern Journey	1964	5.00	10.00	20.00
❏ VRS-9175 [M]	Early Morning Rain	1965	5.00	10.00	20.00
❏ VRS-9215 [M]	Play One More	1966	5.00	10.00	20.00
❏ VRS-9241 [M]	So Much for Dreaming	1967	5.00	10.00	20.00
❏ VSD-73114	Greatest Hits	1985	2.50	5.00	10.00
❏ VSD-79154 [S]	Northern Journey	1964	6.25	12.50	25.00
❏ VSD-79175 [S]	Early Morning Rain	1965	6.25	12.50	25.00
❏ VSD-79215 [S]	Play One More	1966	6.25	12.50	25.00
❏ VSD-79241 [S]	So Much for Dreaming	1967	6.25	12.50	25.00
❏ VSD-79269	The Best of Ian & Sylvia	1968	3.75	7.50	15.00
❏ VSD-79284	Nashville	1968	3.75	7.50	15.00

IAN AND THE ZODIACS
45s
PHILIPS

Number	Title (A Side/B Side)	Yr	VG	VG+	NM
❏ 40244	The Cryin' Game/Livin' Lovin' Wreck	1964	2.50	5.00	10.00
❏ 40277	Good Morning Little Schoolgirl/Message to Martha	1965	2.50	5.00	10.00
❏ 40291	So Much in Love with You/This Empty Place	1965	2.50	5.00	10.00
❏ 40291 [PS]	So Much in Love with You/This Empty Place	1965	6.25	12.50	25.00
❏ 40343	Why Can't It Be Me/Leave It to Me	1965	2.50	5.00	10.00
❏ 40369	No Money, No Honey/Where Were You	1966	2.50	5.00	10.00

Albums
PHILIPS

Number	Title (A Side/B Side)	Yr	VG	VG+	NM
❏ PHM 200176 [M]	Ian and the Zodiacs	1965	10.00	20.00	40.00
❏ PHS 600176 [S]	Ian and the Zodiacs	1965	12.50	25.00	50.00

ID, THE
45s
RCA VICTOR

Number	Title (A Side/B Side)	Yr	VG	VG+	NM
❏ 47-9136	Short Circuit/Boil the Kettle, Mother	1967	3.00	6.00	12.00
❏ 47-9195	Wild Times/The Take	1967	3.00	6.00	12.00

Albums
AURA

Number	Title (A Side/B Side)	Yr	VG	VG+	NM
❏ 1000	Where Are We Going?	1976	12.50	25.00	50.00

RCA VICTOR

Number	Title (A Side/B Side)	Yr	VG	VG+	NM
❏ LPM-3805 [M]	The Inner Sounds of the Id	1967	10.00	20.00	40.00
❏ LSP-3805 [S]	The Inner Sounds of the Id	1967	10.00	20.00	40.00

IDEALS, THE (1)
Chicago-based group that, at one time, featured MAJOR LANCE. He is not on the Satellite singles, however.
45s
PASO

Number	Title (A Side/B Side)	Yr	VG	VG+	NM
❏ 6401	Together/What's the Matter with You Sam	1961	12.50	25.00	50.00
❏ 6402	Magic/Teens	1961	12.50	25.00	50.00

SATELLITE

Number	Title (A Side/B Side)	Yr	VG	VG+	NM
❏ 2007	You Lost and I Won/You Hurt Me	1965	6.25	12.50	25.00
❏ 2009	Kissing/I Had a Dream	1966	6.25	12.50	25.00
❏ 2011	Go Go Gorilla/Kissing Won't Go Out of Style	1966	6.25	12.50	25.00

IDEALS, THE (2)
45s
CHECKER

Number	Title (A Side/B Side)	Yr	VG	VG+	NM
❏ 920	Knee Socks/Mary's Lamb	1959	6.25	12.50	25.00
❏ 979	Knee Socks/Mary's Lamb	1961	3.75	7.50	15.00

—As "Johnny Brantley and the Ideals"

IDEALS, THE (U)
Some of these could be groups (1) or (2), but others are likely other groups.
45s
COOL

Number	Title (A Side/B Side)	Yr	VG	VG+	NM
❏ 108	Do I Have the Right/You Won't Like It	1958	75.00	150.00	300.00

CORTLAND

Number	Title (A Side/B Side)	Yr	VG	VG+	NM
❏ 110	Don Juan/Gorilla	1963	5.00	10.00	20.00
❏ 113	Mo Joe Hanna/Simple Simon	1964	3.75	7.50	15.00
❏ 115	Feeling of a Kiss/You Came a Long Way from St. Louis	1964	3.75	7.50	15.00
❏ 117	Local Boy/L.A.	1964	3.75	7.50	15.00

DECCA

Number	Title (A Side/B Side)	Yr	VG	VG+	NM
❏ 30720	Annie Has a Stroller/My Girl	1959	10.00	20.00	40.00
❏ 30800	Ivy League Lover/Don't Be a Baby, Baby	1959	6.25	12.50	25.00

FARGO

Number	Title (A Side/B Side)	Yr	VG	VG+	NM
❏ 1024	The Duchess/Trans Zizstor	1962	5.00	10.00	20.00

Number	Title (A Side/B Side)	Yr	VG	VG+	NM
ST. LAWRENCE					
❑ 1001	Cathy's Clown/Go Get a Wig	1965	3.00	6.00	12.00
❑ 1020	I Got Lucky (When I Found You)/				
	Tell Her I Apologize	1966	3.75	7.50	15.00
STARS OF HOLLYWOOD					
❑ 1001	Please, Jan/Always Yours	1959	10.00	20.00	40.00

IDES OF MARCH, THE

45s

Number	Title (A Side/B Side)	Yr	VG	VG+	NM
KAPP					
❑ 992	Nobody Loves Me/Strawberry Sunday	1969	2.50	5.00	10.00
PARROT					
❑ 304	I'll Keep Searching/You Wouldn't Listen	1966	2.50	5.00	10.00
❑ 310	Roller Coaster/				
	Things Aren't Always What They Seem	1966	2.50	5.00	10.00
❑ 312	You Need Love/Sha-La-La-La-Lee	1966	2.50	5.00	10.00
❑ 321	My Foolish Pride/Give Your Mind Wings	1967	2.50	5.00	10.00
❑ 326	Hole in My Soul/Girls Don't Grow on Trees	1967	2.50	5.00	10.00
RCA VICTOR					
❑ 74-0850	Mother America/Ladyland	1972	—	2.50	5.00
❑ APBO-0052	Hot Water/Heavy on the Country	1973	—	2.50	5.00
SUNDAZED					
❑ 142	I'm Gonna Say My Prayers/The Sun Ain't Gonna				
	Shine Anymore	1999	—	—	2.00
❑ 142 [PS]	I'm Gonna Say My Prayers/The Sun Ain't Gonna				
	Shine Anymore	1999	—	—	2.00
WARNER BROS.					
❑ 7140	Vehicle/L.A. Goodbye	1972	—	2.00	4.00
—"Back to Back Hits" series -- originals have green labels					
❑ 7334	High on a Hillside/One Woman Man	1969	—	3.00	6.00
❑ 7378	Vehicle/Lead Me Home, Gently	1970	2.00	4.00	8.00
❑ 7403	Superman/Home	1970	—	3.00	6.00
❑ 7426	Melody/The Sky Is Falling	1970	—	3.00	6.00
❑ 7466	L.A. Goodbye/Mrs. Grayson's Farm	1971	—	3.00	6.00
❑ 7507	Tie-Dye Princess/Friends of Feeling	1971	—	3.00	6.00
❑ 7526	Giddy-Up, Ride Me/Freedom Sweet	1971	—	3.00	6.00

Albums

Number	Title	Yr	VG	VG+	NM
RCA VICTOR					
❑ APL1-0143	Midnight Oil	1973	3.75	7.50	15.00
❑ LSP-4812	World Woven	1972	3.75	7.50	15.00
SUNDAZED					
❑ LP-5032	Ideology	199?	3.00	6.00	12.00
WARNER BROS.					
❑ WS 1863	Vehicle	1970	3.75	7.50	15.00
—Green "WB" label					
❑ WS 1863	Vehicle	1970	5.00	10.00	20.00
—Green "W7" label					
❑ WS 1896	Common Bond	1971	3.75	7.50	15.00

IDLE RACE, THE
Jeff Lynne, later of THE MOVE and ELECTRIC LIGHT ORCHESTRA, was in this group.

45s

Number	Title (A Side/B Side)	Yr	VG	VG+	NM
LIBERTY					
❑ 55997	Here We Go 'Round the Lemon Tree/				
	My Father's Son	1967	5.00	10.00	20.00
❑ 56064	The End of the Road/The Morning Sunshine	1968	6.25	12.50	25.00

Albums

Number	Title	Yr	VG	VG+	NM
LIBERTY					
❑ LST-7603	Birthday Party	1969	12.50	25.00	50.00

IDOLS, THE
Probably more than one group.

45s

Number	Title (A Side/B Side)	Yr	VG	VG+	NM
DOT					
❑ 16210	Just a Little Bit More/Why Must I Cry	1961	3.75	7.50	15.00
—B-side by the Swans					
E-Z					
❑ 1	Jeannine/Can't Tag Along	1961	10.00	20.00	40.00
RCA VICTOR					
❑ 47-7339	30 Days/The Prowler	1958	5.00	10.00	20.00
❑ 47-7417	Here in My Heart/The Counterfeiter	1958	5.00	10.00	20.00
REVEILLE					
❑ 1002	Just a Little Bit More/Why Must I Cry	1961	7.50	15.00	30.00
—B-side by the Swans					

IF

45s

Number	Title (A Side/B Side)	Yr	VG	VG+	NM
CAPITOL					
❑ 2909	The Promised Land/				
	I'm Reaching Out on All Sides	1970	2.00	4.00	8.00
❑ 2990	Raise the Level of Your Conscious Mind/What				
	Did I Say About the Box, Jack	1970	2.00	4.00	8.00
❑ 3068	Your City Is Falling/Woman Can't You See	1971	2.00	4.00	8.00
❑ 3932	I Believe in Rock and Roll/Still Alive	1974	—	3.00	6.00
METROMEDIA					
❑ 258	Waterfall/(B-side unknown)	1972	—	3.00	6.00

Albums

Number	Title	Yr	VG	VG+	NM
CAPITOL					
❑ ST-539	If	1970	5.00	10.00	20.00
❑ SW-676	If2	1971	5.00	10.00	20.00
❑ SMAS-820	If3	1971	5.00	10.00	20.00
❑ ST-11299	Not Just Another Bunch of Pretty Faces	1974	3.00	6.00	12.00
❑ ST-11344	Tea Break Over — Back On Your 'Eads!	1974	3.00	6.00	12.00
METROMEDIA					
❑ BML1-0174	Double Diamond	1973	3.00	6.00	12.00
❑ KMD-1057	Waterfall	1972	3.00	6.00	12.00

IFIELD, FRANK
Also see THE BEATLES.

45s

Number	Title (A Side/B Side)	Yr	VG	VG+	NM
CAPITOL					
❑ 5032	I'm Confessin' (That I Love You)/				
	Waltzing Matilda	1963	2.50	5.00	10.00
❑ 5089	Please/Mule Train	1963	2.50	5.00	10.00
❑ 5134	Don't Blame Me/Say It Isn't So	1964	2.50	5.00	10.00
❑ 5170	Sweet Lorraine/				
	You Came a Long Way from St. Louis	1964	2.50	5.00	10.00
❑ 5275	True Love Ways/I Should Care	1964	2.50	5.00	10.00
❑ 5349	Without You/Don't Make Me Laugh	1965	2.50	5.00	10.00

Number	Title (A Side/B Side)	Yr	VG	VG+	NM
HICKORY					
❑ 1397	No One Will Ever Know/I'm Saving All My Love				
	(For You)	1966	2.00	4.00	8.00
❑ 1411	Call Her Your Sweetheart/Give Myself a Party	1966	2.00	4.00	8.00
❑ 1435	I Remember You/Stranger to You	1967	2.00	4.00	8.00
❑ 1454	Kaw-Liga/Out of Nowhere	1967	2.00	4.00	8.00
❑ 1473	Just Let Me Make Believe/Fireball Mail	1967	2.00	4.00	8.00
❑ 1486	Oh, Such a Stranger/Then You Can Tell Me				
	Goodbye	1967	2.00	4.00	8.00
❑ 1499	Adios Matador/Movin' Lover	1968	2.00	4.00	8.00
❑ 1507	Don't Forget to Cry/Morning in Your Eyes	1968	2.00	4.00	8.00
❑ 1514	Good Morning Dear/Innocent Years	1968	2.00	4.00	8.00
❑ 1525	Maurie/I'm Learning Child	1968	2.00	4.00	8.00
❑ 1540	Let Me Into Your Life/Mary in the Morning	1969	—	3.00	6.00
❑ 1550	I Love You Because/It's My Time	1969	—	3.00	6.00
❑ 1556	Lights of Home/Love Hurts	1969	—	3.00	6.00
❑ 1574	Sweet Memories/You've Still Got a Place in My				
	Heart	1970	—	3.00	6.00
❑ 1595	Someone/One More Mile, One More Town (One				
	More Time)	1971	—	3.00	6.00
MAM					
❑ 3612	Lonesome Jubilee/Teach Me Little Children	1971	—	2.50	5.00
VEE JAY					
❑ 457	I Remember You/I Listen to My Heart	1962	3.75	7.50	15.00
—With Frank Ifield's name spelled correctly on label					
❑ 457	I Remember You/I Listen to My Heart	1962	5.00	10.00	20.00
—With both labels misspelled "Farnk Ifield"					
❑ 477	Lovesick Blues/Anytime	1962	3.00	6.00	12.00
❑ 499	The Wayward Wind/I'm Smiling Now	1963	3.00	6.00	12.00
❑ 525	Unchained Melody/Nobody's Darlin' But Mine	1963	3.00	6.00	12.00
❑ 553	I'm Confessin' (That I Love You)/Heart and Soul	1963	3.00	6.00	12.00
WARNER BROS.					
❑ 8730	Why Don't We Leave Together/Crawling Back	1979	—	2.00	4.00
❑ 8853	Crystal/Touch the Morning	1979	—	2.00	4.00
❑ 49095	Play Born to Lose Again/Yesterday Just Passed				
	My Way Again	1979	—	2.00	4.00

Albums

Number	Title	Yr	VG	VG+	NM
CAPITOL					
❑ ST 10356 [S]	I'm Confessin'	1963	6.25	12.50	25.00
❑ T 10356 [M]	I'm Confessin'	1963	5.00	10.00	20.00
HICKORY					
❑ LPM-132 [M]	The Best of Frank Ifield	1966	5.00	10.00	20.00
❑ LPS-132 [P]	The Best of Frank Ifield	1966	5.00	10.00	20.00
❑ LPM-136 [M]	Tale of Two Cities	1967	3.75	7.50	15.00
❑ LPS-136 [S]	Tale of Two Cities	1967	5.00	10.00	20.00
❑ ST-90753 [S]	The Best of Frank Ifield	1966	6.25	12.50	25.00
—Capitol Record Club edition					
❑ T-90753 [M]	The Best of Frank Ifield	1966	6.25	12.50	25.00
—Capitol Record Club edition					
VEE JAY					
❑ LP 1054 [M]	I Remember You	1962	7.50	15.00	30.00
❑ SR 1054 [S]	I Remember You	1962	12.50	25.00	50.00

IGGY AND THE STOOGES

12-Inch Singles

Number	Title (A Side/B Side)	Yr	VG	VG+	NM
BOMP!					
❑ 12139	I Got a Right/Gimme Some Skin	1991	—	2.50	5.00

45s

Number	Title (A Side/B Side)	Yr	VG	VG+	NM
BOMP!					
❑ 139	I Got a Right/Gimme Some Skin	1991	—	—	2.00
❑ 139 [PS]	I Got a Right/Gimme Some Skin	1991	—	—	2.00
COLUMBIA					
❑ 45877	Search and Destroy/Penetration	1973	2.50	5.00	10.00
ELEKTRA					
❑ 45664	I Wanna Be Your Dog (Part 1)/I Wanna Be Your				
	Dog (Part 2)	1970	7.50	15.00	30.00
—As "The Stooges"					
❑ 45695	Down on the Street/I Feel Alright	1970	7.50	15.00	30.00
—As "The Stooges"					
SIAMESE					
❑ 001	I Got a Right/Gimme Some Skin	1977	2.50	5.00	10.00
—Second pressing: "Siamese" in fake Asian lettering with iguana logo					
❑ 001	I Got a Right/Gimme Some Skin	1977	6.25	12.50	25.00
❑ 001 [PS]	I Got a Right/Gimme Some Skin	1977	—	3.00	6.00
—Only issued with Bomp!-distributed copies; has "Iggy && & The Stooges" on cover					

7-Inch Extended Plays

Number	Title (A Side/B Side)	Yr	VG	VG+	NM
BOMP!					
❑ 114	Jesus Loves the Stooges	1977	—	3.75	7.50
❑ 114 [PS]	Jesus Loves the Stooges	1977	—	3.75	7.50

Albums

Number	Title	Yr	VG	VG+	NM
BOMP!					
❑ 1018	Kill City	1978	2.00	4.00	8.00
—By "Iggy Pop and James Williamson"					
COLUMBIA					
❑ KC 32111	Raw Power	1973	12.50	25.00	50.00
ELEKTRA					
❑ EKS 74051	The Stooges	1969	12.50	25.00	50.00
—By "The Stooges"; red label with large stylized "E" (butterfly label, deduct 60%)					
❑ EKS 74101	Fun House	1970	12.50	25.00	50.00
—By "The Stooges"; red label with large stylized "E" (butterfly label, deduct 60%)					
IMPORT/BOMP!					
❑ 1015	Metallic K.O.	1977	4.50	9.00	18.00
❑ 1018	Kill City	1978	3.00	6.00	12.00
—By "Iggy Pop and James Williamson"; original issue on green vinyl					
SUNDAZED					
❑ LP 5149	The Stooges	2002	3.75	7.50	15.00
—By "The Stooges"; reissue on 180-gram vinyl					
❑ LP 5150	Fun House	2002	3.75	7.50	15.00
—By "The Stooges"; reissue on 180-gram vinyl					

IKETTES, THE
Also see THE MIRETTES.

45s

Number	Title (A Side/B Side)	Yr	VG	VG+	NM
ATCO					
❑ 6212	I'm Blue (The Gong-Gong Song)/Find My Baby	1961	5.00	10.00	20.00
❑ 6223	Troubles on My Mind/Come On and Truck	1962	3.75	7.50	15.00

I

Number	Title (A Side/B Side)	Yr	VG	VG+	NM
❑ 6232	Zizzy Zee Zum Zum/Heavenly Love	1962	3.75	7.50	15.00
❑ 6243	I Do Love You/I Had a Dream the Other Night	1962	3.75	7.50	15.00
MODERN					
❑ 1005	Peaches 'N' Cream/The Biggest Players	1965	2.50	5.00	10.00
❑ 1008	(He's Gonna Be) Fine, Fine, Fine/How Come	1965	2.50	5.00	10.00
❑ 1011	I'm So Thankful/Don't Feel Sorry for Me	1965	2.00	4.00	8.00
❑ 1015	Sally Go Round the Roses/Lonely for You	1965	2.00	4.00	8.00
❑ 1024	Da Doo Ron Ron/Not That I Recall	1966	2.00	4.00	8.00
PHI-DAN					
❑ 5009	Down Down/What'cha Gonna Do	1966	2.50	5.00	10.00
POMPEII					
❑ 66683	Beauty Is Just Skin Deep/Make Them Wait	1968	—	3.00	6.00
TEENA					
❑ 1702	Prisoner in Love/Those Words	1963	5.00	10.00	20.00
UNITED ARTISTS					
❑ 50866	If You Take a Close Look/Got What It Takes	1971	—	2.50	5.00
❑ 51103	I'm Just Not Ready for Love/				
	Two Timin' Double Dealin'	1973	—	2.50	5.00
Albums					
MODERN					
❑ M-102 [M]	Soul Hits	1965	7.50	15.00	30.00
❑ MST-102 [S]	Soul Hits	1965	10.00	20.00	40.00
UNITED ARTISTS					
❑ UA-LA190-F	(G)Old and New	1973	3.00	6.00	12.00

ILL WIND, THE
45s
ABC

Number	Title (A Side/B Side)	Yr	VG	VG+	NM
❑ 11107	In My Dark World/Walkin' and Singin'	1968	6.25	12.50	25.00
Albums					
ABC					
❑ S-641	Flashes	1968	25.00	50.00	100.00

ILL WINDS, THE Later incarnation of CHANTAY'S.
45s
REPRISE

Number	Title (A Side/B Side)	Yr	VG	VG+	NM
❑ 0423	So Be On Your Way (I Won't Cry)/Fear of the				
	Rain	1965	3.75	7.50	15.00
❑ 0492	I Idolize You/A Letter	1966	3.75	7.50	15.00

ILLINOIS SPEED PRESS, THE
45s
COLUMBIA

Number	Title (A Side/B Side)	Yr	VG	VG+	NM
❑ 44564	Get In the Wind (Part 1)/Get In the Wind (Part 2)	1968	2.50	5.00	10.00
❑ 45166	Country Dumplin'/Sadly Out of Place	1970	2.50	5.00	10.00
Albums					
COLUMBIA					
❑ CS 9792	The Illinois Speed Press	1969	3.75	7.50	15.00
❑ CS 9976	Duet	1970	3.75	7.50	15.00

ILLUSION, THE
45s
DYNO VOICE

Number	Title (A Side/B Side)	Yr	VG	VG+	NM
❑ 914	It's Groovy Time/My Party	1968	2.50	5.00	10.00
STEED					
❑ 712	Did You See Her Eyes/Falling in Love	1969	2.50	5.00	10.00
❑ 717	Run Run Run/I Love You Yes I Do	1969	2.00	4.00	8.00
❑ 718	Did You See Her Eyes/Falling in Love	1969	—	3.00	6.00
❑ 721	How Does It Feel/Once in a Lifetime	1969	—	3.00	6.00
❑ 722	Together/Don't Push It	1969	—	3.00	6.00
❑ 726	Let's Make Each Other Happy/Beside You	1970	—	3.00	6.00
❑ 732	Collection/Wait a Minute	1970	—	3.00	6.00
Albums					
STEED					
❑ ST-37003	The Illusion	1969	5.00	10.00	20.00
❑ ST-37005	Together (As a Way of Life)	1969	3.75	7.50	15.00
❑ ST-37006	If It's So	1970	3.75	7.50	15.00

ILLUSIONS, THE More than one group.
45s
COLUMBIA

Number	Title (A Side/B Side)	Yr	VG	VG+	NM
❑ 43700	I Know/Take My Heart	1966	2.50	5.00	10.00
CORAL					
❑ 62173	The Letter/Henry and Henrietta	1960	10.00	20.00	40.00
DIAL					
❑ 4004	I Don't Believe It/The World Outside	1965	2.50	5.00	10.00
DOT					
❑ 16752	Secrets of Love/Don't Put Me Down	1965	5.00	10.00	20.00
EMBER					
❑ 1071	How High Is the Mountain/Can't We Fall in Love	1961	7.50	15.00	30.00
KAPE					
❑ 1001	The Closer You Are/For Sentimental Reasons	196?	2.50	5.00	10.00
LAURIE					
❑ 3245	Maybe/In the Beginning	1964	5.00	10.00	20.00
LITTLE DEBBIE					
❑ 105	Story of My Life/Walking Boy	1964	37.50	75.00	150.00
MALI					
❑ 104	Hey Boy/Lonely Soldier	1962	12.50	25.00	50.00
NORTHEAST					
❑ 801	Hey Boy/Lonely Soldier	1962	3.75	7.50	15.00
RELIC					
❑ 512	Hey Boy/Lonely Soldier	1964	2.50	5.00	10.00
ROUND					
❑ 1018	Jezebel/Nightmare	1963	20.00	40.00	80.00
SHERATON					
❑ 104	Hey Boy/Lonely Soldier	1962	6.25	12.50	25.00

ILLUSTRATION
Albums
JANUS

Number	Title (A Side/B Side)	Yr	VG	VG+	NM
❑ JLP-3010	Illustration	1969	6.25	12.50	25.00

ILMO SMOKEHOUSE
Albums
BEAUTIFUL SOUND

Number	Title (A Side/B Side)	Yr	VG	VG+	NM
❑ 3002	Ilmo Smokehouse	1971	10.00	20.00	40.00
ROULETTE					
❑ RS-3002	Ilmo Smokehouse	1971	5.00	10.00	20.00

IMAGINATIONS, THE (1)
45s
BALLAD

Number	Title (A Side/B Side)	Yr	VG	VG+	NM
❑ 500	Wait a Little Longer Son/Mama's Little Baby	1962	5.00	10.00	20.00
BO MARC					
❑ 301	Guardian Angel/Hey You	1961	10.00	20.00	40.00
DUEL					
❑ 507	Guardian Angel/Hey You	1961	5.00	10.00	20.00
MUSIC MAKERS					
❑ 103	Goodnight Baby/The Search Is Over	1961	12.50	25.00	50.00
❑ 108	Guardian Angel/Hey You	1961	12.50	25.00	50.00
Albums					
RELIC					
❑ LP-5058	The Imaginations (1961-1962)	198?	2.50	5.00	10.00

IMAGINATIONS, THE (2) Another concoction of STEVE BARRI and P.F. SLOAN.
45s
DUNHILL

Number	Title (A Side/B Side)	Yr	VG	VG+	NM
❑ 4092	I Love You When You're Mad/				
	Summer in New York	1967	5.00	10.00	20.00

IMAGINATIONS, THE (3)
45s
FRATERNITY

Number	Title (A Side/B Side)	Yr	VG	VG+	NM
❑ 1001	I Just Can't Get Over Losing You/Strange				
	Neighborhood	1967	7.50	15.00	30.00
❑ 1006	No One Ever Lost More/Strange Voice	1968	6.25	12.50	25.00

IMPACS, THE
45s
KING

Number	Title (A Side/B Side)	Yr	VG	VG+	NM
❑ 5851	Jo-Ann/Two Strangers	1964	2.50	5.00	10.00
❑ 5863	Shimmy, Shimmy/Zot	1964	2.50	5.00	10.00
❑ 5891	She Didn't Even Say Hello/Kool It	1964	2.50	5.00	10.00
❑ 5910	Ain't That the Way Life Is/Don't Cry Baby	1964	2.50	5.00	10.00
❑ 5965	Your Mama Put the Hurt on Me/				
	Cape Kennedy, Florida	1964	2.50	5.00	10.00
PARKWAY					
❑ 865	I'm Gonna Make You Cry/Tears in My Heart	1963	3.00	6.00	12.00
Albums					
KING					
❑ 886 [M]	Impact!	1964	50.00	100.00	200.00
❑ KS-886 [S]	Impact!	1964	75.00	150.00	300.00
❑ 916 [M]	A Weekend with the Impacs	1964	50.00	100.00	200.00
❑ KS-916 [S]	A Weekend with the Impacs	1964	75.00	150.00	300.00

IMPACTS, THE Several different groups.
45s
ANDERSON

Number	Title (A Side/B Side)	Yr	VG	VG+	NM
❑ 104	Summer/Linda	1964	12.50	25.00	50.00
CARLTON					
❑ 548	Darling, Now You're Mine/Help Me Somebody	1961	7.50	15.00	30.00
❑ 548	Darling, No You're Mine/Help Me Somebody	1961	12.50	25.00	50.00
—With incorrect A-side title					
DCP					
❑ 1147	Wishing Well/Heartaches	1965	12.50	25.00	50.00
—As "Kenny and the Impacts"					
❑ 1150	Just Because/Pigtails	1965	10.00	20.00	40.00
KIP					
❑ 1890	Burnt Valves/Chrome Reverse	1963	12.50	25.00	50.00
RCA VICTOR					
❑ 47-7583	Bobby Sox Squaw/Croc-O-Doll	1959	5.00	10.00	20.00
❑ 47-7609	Canadian Sunset/They Say	1959	12.50	25.00	50.00
WATTS					
❑ 5599	Now Is the Time/Soup	1959	20.00	40.00	80.00
Albums					
DEL-FI					
❑ DFLP-1234 [M]	Wipe Out	1963	15.00	30.00	60.00
❑ DFS-1234 [S]	Wipe Out	1963	20.00	40.00	80.00
❑ DLF-1234	Wipe Out	199?	3.00	6.00	12.00
—Reissue with bar code					

IMPALA SYNDROME, THE
Albums
PARALLAX

Number	Title (A Side/B Side)	Yr	VG	VG+	NM
❑ 4002	The Impala Syndrome	1970	25.00	50.00	100.00

IMPALAS, THE
45s
BUNKY

Number	Title (A Side/B Side)	Yr	VG	VG+	NM
❑ 7760	Whay Should He Do/I Still Love You	1969	2.00	4.00	8.00
❑ 7762	Whip it On Me/I Still Love You	1969	2.00	4.00	8.00
CAPITOL					
❑ 2709	Speed Up/Soul	1969	2.00	4.00	8.00
CHECKER					
❑ 999	For the Love of Mike/I Need You So Much	1961	3.00	6.00	12.00
CUB					
❑ 9022	Sorry (I Ran All the Way Home)/Fool, Fool, Fool	1959	5.00	10.00	20.00
❑ 9022	I Ran All the Way Home/Fool, Fool, Fool	1959	15.00	30.00	60.00
—Original A-side title					
❑ 9033	Oh What a Fool/Sandy Went Away	1959	5.00	10.00	20.00
❑ 9053	Peggy Darling/Bye Everybody	1959	5.00	10.00	20.00
❑ 9066	All Alone/When My Heart Does All the Talking	1960	5.00	10.00	20.00
—As "Speedo and the Impalas"					
HAMILTON					
❑ 50026	I Was a Fool/First Date	1960	5.00	10.00	20.00
RED BOY					
❑ 113	When You Dance/I Can't See Me Without You	1966	6.25	12.50	25.00

Number	Title (A Side/B Side)	Yr	VG	VG+	NM
RITE-ON					
❏ 101	I Can't See Me Without You/Old Man Mose	196?	5.00	10.00	20.00
STEADY					
❏ 044	When You Dance/I Can't See Me Without You	1967	5.00	10.00	20.00
SUNDOWN					
❏ 115	The Lonely One/Lost Boogie	1959	3.75	7.50	15.00
20TH FOX					
❏ 428	Last Night I Saw a Girl/There Is Nothin' Like a Dame	1963	3.00	6.00	12.00
7-Inch Extended Plays					
CUB					
❏ 5000	(contents unknown)	1959	100.00	200.00	400.00
❏ 5000 [PS]	Sorry (I Ran All the Way Home)	1959	100.00	200.00	400.00
Albums					
CUB					
❏ 8003 [M]	Sorry (I Ran All the Way Home)	1959	100.00	200.00	400.00
❏ S-8003 [S]	Sorry (I Ran All the Way Home)	1959	150.00	300.00	600.00

IMPERIALITES, THE
45s

Number	Title (A Side/B Side)	Yr	VG	VG+	NM
IMPERIAL					
❏ 66015	Have Love, Will Travel/Let's Get One	1964	5.00	10.00	20.00

IMPERIALS, THE (1) See LITTLE ANTHONY AND THE IMPERIALS.

IMPERIALS, THE (2)
45s

Number	Title (A Side/B Side)	Yr	VG	VG+	NM
BUZZY					
❏ 1	My Darling/You Should Have Told Me	1962	5.00	10.00	20.00
—Red vinyl					
SAVOY					
❏ 1104	My Darling/You Should Have Told Me	1954	50.00	100.00	200.00

IMPERIALS, THE (3)
45s

Number	Title (A Side/B Side)	Yr	VG	VG+	NM
NEWTIME					
❏ 503	A Short Prayer/Where Will You Be	1962	3.75	7.50	15.00
❏ 505	The Letter/Go and Get Your Heart Broken	1962	3.75	7.50	15.00

IMPERIALS, THE (4)
45s

Number	Title (A Side/B Side)	Yr	VG	VG+	NM
OMNI					
❏ 5501	Who's Gonna Love Me/Better Take Time to Love	1978	—	2.50	5.00

IMPERIALS, THE (U) We're not sure which group these are.
45s

Number	Title (A Side/B Side)	Yr	VG	VG+	NM
CAPITOL					
❏ 4921	I'm Still Dancing/Bermuda Wonderful	1963	3.75	7.50	15.00
CARLTON					
❏ 566	Faithfully Yours/Vut Vut	1961	5.00	10.00	20.00

IMPERIALS MINUS TWO, THE
45s

Number	Title (A Side/B Side)	Yr	VG	VG+	NM
IMPERIAL					
❏ 5787	A Swingin' Dream/In Any Language	1961	5.00	10.00	20.00

IMPOSSIBLES, THE More than one group.
45s

Number	Title (A Side/B Side)	Yr	VG	VG+	NM
BLANCHE					
❏ 029	Chapel Bells/Little by Little	1960	100.00	200.00	400.00
REPRISE					
❏ 0305	Lonely Bluebird/Paint Me a Pretty Picture	1964	6.25	12.50	25.00
RMP					
❏ 501	Everywhere I Go/Well, It's Alright	1966	6.25	12.50	25.00
❏ 1030	Mr. Maestro/Well, It's Alright	1964	6.25	12.50	25.00
ROULETTE					
❏ 4745	I Wanna Know/It's All Right	1967	5.00	10.00	20.00

IMPRESSIONS, THE Also see JERRY BUTLER; CURTIS MAYFIELD.
45s

Number	Title (A Side/B Side)	Yr	VG	VG+	NM
ABC					
❏ 10831	Can't Satisfy/This Must End	1966	2.00	4.00	8.00
❏ 10869	Love's a-Comin'/Wade in the Water	1966	2.00	4.00	8.00
❏ 10900	You Always Hurt Me/Little Girl	1967	2.00	4.00	8.00
❏ 10932	It's Hard to Believe/You've Got Me Runnin'	1967	2.00	4.00	8.00
❏ 10964	I Can't Stay Away from You/You Ought to Be in Heaven	1967	2.00	4.00	8.00
❏ 11022	We're a Winner/It's All Over	1967	2.00	4.00	8.00
❏ 11071	We're Rolling On (Part 1)/We're Rolling On (Part 2)	1968	2.00	4.00	8.00
❏ 11103	I Loved and I Lost/Up, Up and Away	1968	2.00	4.00	8.00
❏ 11135	Don't Cry My Love/Sometimes I Wonder	1968	2.00	4.00	8.00
❏ 11188	East of Java/Just Before Sunrise	1969	2.00	4.00	8.00
ABC-PARAMOUNT					
❏ 10241	Gypsy Woman/As Long As You Love Me	1961	3.75	7.50	15.00
❏ 10289	Grow Closer Together/Can't You See	1962	3.75	7.50	15.00
❏ 10328	Little Young Lover/Never Let Me Go	1962	3.75	7.50	15.00
❏ 10357	You've Come Home/Minstrel and Queen	1962	3.75	7.50	15.00
❏ 10386	I'm the One Who Loves You/I Need Your Love	1962	3.75	7.50	15.00
❏ 10431	Sad, Sad Girl and Boy/Twist and Limbo	1963	3.75	7.50	15.00
❏ 10487	It's All Right/You'll Want Me Back	1963	3.75	7.50	15.00
❏ 10511	Talking About My Baby/Never Too Much Love	1963	3.75	7.50	15.00
❏ 10537	Girl You Don't Know Me/A Woman Who Loves Me	1964	3.75	7.50	15.00
❏ 10544	I'm So Proud/I Made a Mistake	1964	3.75	7.50	15.00
❏ 10554	Keep On Pushing/I Love You (Yeah)	1964	3.75	7.50	15.00
❏ 10581	You Must Believe Me/See the Real Me	1964	3.75	7.50	15.00
❏ 10602	Amen/Long, Long Winter	1964	3.75	7.50	15.00
❏ 10622	People Get Ready/I've Been Trying	1965	3.75	7.50	15.00
❏ 10647	Woman's Got Soul/Get Up and Move	1965	3.00	6.00	12.00
❏ 10670	Meeting Over Yonder/I've Found That I've Lost	1965	3.00	6.00	12.00
❏ 10710	I Need You/Never Could You Be	1965	3.00	6.00	12.00
❏ 10725	Just One Kiss from You/Twilight Time	1965	3.00	6.00	12.00
❏ 10750	You've Been Cheatin'/Man, Oh Man	1965	3.00	6.00	12.00
❏ 10761	Since I Lost the One I Love/Falling in Love with You	1966	2.50	5.00	10.00
❏ 10789	Too Slow/No One Else	1966	2.50	5.00	10.00

Number	Title (A Side/B Side)	Yr	VG	VG+	NM
ABNER					
❏ 1013	For Your Precious Love/Sweet Was the Wine	1958	10.00	20.00	40.00
—As "Jerry Butler and the Impressions"					
❏ 1017	Come Back My Love/Love Me	1958	7.50	15.00	30.00
❏ 1023	The Gift of Love/At the County Fair	1959	7.50	15.00	30.00
❏ 1025	Lonely One/Senorita I Love You	1959	7.50	15.00	30.00
❏ 1034	Say That You Love Me/A New Love	1960	7.50	15.00	30.00
BANDERA					
❏ 2504	Listen/Shorty's Got to Go	1959	12.50	25.00	50.00
CHI-SOUND					
❏ 2418	Sorry/All I Wanna Do Is Make Love to You	1979	—	2.50	5.00
❏ 2438	Maybe I'm Mistaken/All I Wanna Do Is Make Love to You	1980	—	2.50	5.00
❏ 2491	For Your Precious Love/You're Mine	1981	—	2.50	5.00
❏ 2499	Love, Love, Love/Fan the Fire	1981	—	2.50	5.00
COTILLION					
❏ 44210	This Time/I'm a Fool for Love	1976	—	2.50	5.00
❏ 44211	Silent Night/I Saw Mommy Kissing Santa Claus	1976	—	3.00	6.00
❏ 44214	You'll Never Find/Stardust	1977	—	2.50	5.00
❏ 44222	Can't Get Along/You're So Right for Me	1977	—	2.50	5.00
CURTOM					
❏ SP-3 [DJ]	Merry Christmas Happy New Year	197?	3.00	6.00	12.00
❏ 0103	Sooner or Later/Miracle Woman	1975	—	2.50	5.00
❏ 0106	Same Thing It Took/I'm So Glad	1975	—	2.50	5.00
❏ 0110	Loving Power/First Impressions	1975	—	2.50	5.00
❏ 0116	Sunshine/I Wish I'd Stayed in Bed	1976	—	2.50	5.00
❏ 1932	Fool for You/I'm Loving Nothing	1968	—	3.00	6.00
❏ 1932 [PS]	Fool for You/I'm Loving Nothing	1968	3.75	7.50	15.00
❏ 1934	This Is My Country/My Woman's Love	1968	—	3.00	6.00
❏ 1937	My Deceiving Heart/You Want Somebody Else	1969	—	3.00	6.00
❏ 1940	Seven Years/The Girl I Find	1969	—	3.00	6.00
❏ 1943	Choice of Colors/Mighty Mighty Spade and Whitey	1969	—	3.00	6.00
❏ 1946	Say You Love Me/You'll Be Always Mine	1969	—	3.00	6.00
❏ 1948	Wherever She Leadeth Me/Amen (1970)	1970	—	3.00	6.00
❏ 1951	Check Out Your Mind/Can't You See	1970	—	3.00	6.00
❏ 1954	(Baby) Turn On to Me/Soulful Love	1970	—	3.00	6.00
❏ 1957	Ain't Got Time/I'm So Proud	1971	—	3.00	6.00
❏ 1959	Love Me/Do You Wanna Win	1971	—	3.00	6.00
❏ 1966	Inner City Blues/We Must Be in Love	1971	—	3.00	6.00
❏ 1970	This Loves for Real/Times Have Changed	1972	—	3.00	6.00
❏ 1973	I Need to Belong to Someone/Love Me	1972	—	3.00	6.00
❏ 1982	Preacher Man/Times Have Changed	1973	—	3.00	6.00
❏ 1985	Thin Line/I'm Loving You	1973	—	3.00	6.00
❏ 1994	If It's In You to Do Wrong/Times Have Changed	1973	—	3.00	6.00
❏ 1997	Finally Got Myself Together (I'm a Changed Man)/I'll Always Be Here	1974	—	3.00	6.00
❏ 2003	Something's Mighty, Mighty Wrong/Three the Hard Way	1974	—	3.00	6.00
FALCON					
❏ 1013	For Your Precious Love/Sweet Was the Wine	1958	15.00	30.00	60.00
—As "Jerry Butler and the Impressions"					
LOST-NITE					
❏ 266	For Your Precious Love/Sweet Was the Wine	197?	—	2.50	5.00
—As "Jerry Butler and the Impressions"; reissue					
MCA					
❏ 52995	Can't Wait 'Til Tomorrow/Love Workin' On Me	1987	—	—	3.00
PORT					
❏ 70031	Listen/Shorty's Got to Go	1962	3.75	7.50	15.00
SWIRL					
❏ 107	I Need Your Love/Don't Leave Me	1962	5.00	10.00	20.00
20TH FOX					
❏ 172	All Through the Night/Meanwhile, Back in My Heart	1959	10.00	20.00	40.00
VEE JAY					
❏ 280	For Your Precious Love/Sweet Was the Wine	1958	4000.	6000.	8000.
—As "Jerry Butler and the Impressions"					
❏ 424	Say That You Love Me/Senorita I Love You	1962	5.00	10.00	20.00
❏ 574	The Gift of Love/At the County Fair	1963	3.75	7.50	15.00
❏ 621	Say That You Love Me/Senorita I Love You	1964	3.75	7.50	15.00
Albums					
ABC					
❏ 606 [M]	The Fabulous Impressions	1967	6.25	12.50	25.00
❏ S-606 [S]	The Fabulous Impressions	1967	5.00	10.00	20.00
❏ S-635	We're a Winner	1968	3.75	7.50	15.00
❏ S-654	The Best of the Impressions	1968	3.75	7.50	15.00
❏ S-668	The Versatile Impressions	1969	3.75	7.50	15.00
❏ S-727	16 Greatest Hits	1971	3.00	6.00	12.00
❏ D-780 [(2)]	Curtis Mayfield/His Early Years with the Impressions	1973	5.00	10.00	20.00
❏ ST-91540	The Best of the Impressions	1968	5.00	10.00	20.00
—Capitol Record Club edition					
ABC-PARAMOUNT					
❏ 450 [M]	The Impressions	1963	7.50	15.00	30.00
❏ S-450 [S]	The Impressions	1963	10.00	20.00	40.00
❏ 468 [M]	The Never Ending Impressions	1964	7.50	15.00	30.00
❏ S-468 [S]	The Never Ending Impressions	1964	10.00	20.00	40.00
❏ 493 [M]	Keep On Pushing	1964	7.50	15.00	30.00
❏ S-493 [S]	Keep On Pushing	1964	10.00	20.00	40.00
❏ 505 [M]	People Get Ready	1965	7.50	15.00	30.00
❏ S-505 [S]	People Get Ready	1965	10.00	20.00	40.00
❏ 515 [M]	The Impressions' Greatest Hits	1965	5.00	10.00	20.00
❏ S-515 [S]	The Impressions' Greatest Hits	1965	6.25	12.50	25.00
❏ 523 [M]	One By One	1965	5.00	10.00	20.00
❏ S-523 [S]	One By One	1965	6.25	12.50	25.00
❏ 545 [M]	Ridin' High	1966	5.00	10.00	20.00
❏ S-545 [S]	Ridin' High	1966	6.25	12.50	25.00
❏ ST-90097 [S]	People Get Ready	1965	12.50	25.00	50.00
—Capitol Record Club edition					
❏ ST-90106 [S]	Keep On Pushing	1965	12.50	25.00	50.00
—Capitol Record Club edition					
❏ T-90472 [M]	The Impressions	1965	10.00	20.00	40.00
—Capitol Record Club edition					
❏ ST-90492 [S]	The Never Ending Impressions	1965	12.50	25.00	50.00
—Capitol Record Club edition					

I

Number	Title (A Side/B Side)	Yr	VG	VG+	NM
❏ ST-90520 [S]	One By One	1965	7.50	15.00	30.00
—Capitol Record Club edition					
❏ T-90520 [M]	One By One	1965	6.25	12.50	25.00
—Capitol Record Club edition					
CHI-SOUND					
❏ T-596	Come to My Party	1979	2.50	5.00	10.00
❏ T-624	Fan the Fire	1981	2.50	5.00	10.00
COTILLION					
❏ SD 9912	It's About Time	1976	3.00	6.00	12.00
CURTOM					
❏ CUR-2006	Lasting Impressions	198?	2.50	5.00	10.00
❏ CU 5003	First Impressions	1975	3.00	6.00	12.00
❏ CU 5009	Loving Power	1976	3.00	6.00	12.00
❏ CRS-8001	This Is My Country	1968	3.75	7.50	15.00
❏ CRS-8003	The Young Mods' Forgotten Story	1969	3.75	7.50	15.00
❏ CRS-8004	Best Impressions — Curtis, Sam, Dave	1969	3.75	7.50	15.00
❏ CRS-8006	Check Out Your Mind	1970	3.75	7.50	15.00
❏ CRS-8012	Times Have Changed	1972	3.75	7.50	15.00
❏ CRS-8016	Preacher Man	1973	3.75	7.50	15.00
❏ CRS-8019	Finally Got Myself Together	1974	3.75	7.50	15.00
LOST-NITE					
❏ LLP-22 [10]	Jerry Butler and the Impressions	1981	3.75	7.50	15.00
—Red vinyl					
MCA					
❏ 1500	The Impressions Greatest Hits	1982	2.00	4.00	8.00
❏ 5373	In the Heat of the Night	1982	2.50	5.00	10.00
PICKWICK					
❏ SPC-3602	The Impressions	1978	2.00	4.00	8.00
SCEPTER CITATION					
❏ CTN-18018	The Best of Curtis Mayfield and the Impressions	1972	2.50	5.00	10.00
SIRE					
❏ SASH-3717 [(2)]	The Vintage Years	1977	3.75	7.50	15.00
—Includes solo hits by Jerry Butler and Curtis Mayfield					

IMUS, DON
45s
HAPPY TIGER

Number	Title (A Side/B Side)	Yr	VG	VG+	NM
❏ 576	From Adam's Rib to Women's Lib/The Ballad of Rick Nelson	1971	2.00	4.00	8.00
—As "Imus in the Morning"					
RCA VICTOR					
❏ 48-1031	Rev. Billy Sol Hargus/1200 Hamburgers to Go	1972	2.00	4.00	8.00
—As "Imus in the Morning"					
❏ 74-0789	Holy Land Record Package/ Rent-A-Car Phone Call	1972	2.00	4.00	8.00
—As "Imus in the Morning"					
❏ 74-0982	Son of Checkers (The Watergate Case)/ Oh, Billy Sol, Please Heal Us All	1973	2.00	4.00	8.00
❏ PB-10170	Everybody Needs Milk/Play That Country Juke Box	1975	2.00	4.00	8.00

Albums
BANG

Number	Title (A Side/B Side)	Yr	VG	VG+	NM
❏ 407	This Honky's Nuts	1974	6.25	12.50	25.00
RCA VICTOR					
❏ LSP-4699	1200 Hamburgers to Go	1972	6.25	12.50	25.00
—As "Imus in the Morning"					
❏ LSP-4819	One Sacred Chicken to Go	1973	6.25	12.50	25.00

IN CROWD, THE (1) Also see JON AND ROBIN & THE IN CROWD.
45s
ABNAK

Number	Title (A Side/B Side)	Yr	VG	VG+	NM
❏ 121	Inside Out/Big Cities	1967	2.00	4.00	8.00
❏ 121 [DJ]	Inside Out/Big Cities	1967	3.00	6.00	12.00
—Promo only on yellow vinyl					
❏ 129	Let's Take a Walk/ Hangin' From Your Lovin' Tree	1968	2.00	4.00	8.00
❏ 129 [DJ]	Let's Take a Walk/ Hangin' From Your Lovin' Tree	1968	3.00	6.00	12.00
—Promo only on yellow vinyl					

IN CROWD, THE (2) Includes two members of THE ELIGIBLES.
45s
VIVA

Number	Title (A Side/B Side)	Yr	VG	VG+	NM
❏ 604	Questions and Answers/Happiness in My Heart	1966	2.00	4.00	8.00
❏ 610	If I Knew a Magic Word/Never Ending Symphony	1967	2.00	4.00	8.00

IN CROWD, THE (3) British group.
45s
TOWER

Number	Title (A Side/B Side)	Yr	VG	VG+	NM
❏ 147	That's How Strong My Love Is/Things She Says	1965	6.25	12.50	25.00
❏ 196	Why Must They Criticize/I Don't Mind	1966	6.25	12.50	25.00

IN CROWD, THE (U) It's doubtful that any of these are group (1) or (3). Some may be group (2), though.
45s
BRENT

Number	Title (A Side/B Side)	Yr	VG	VG+	NM
❏ 7046	Grapevine/Cat Dance	1965	3.75	7.50	15.00
HICKORY					
❏ 1378	Speed Queen/Cry, Boy, Cry	1966	3.75	7.50	15.00
❏ 1413	In the Midnight Hour/Just Give Me Time	1966	3.00	6.00	12.00
MUSICOR					
❏ 1111	Do the Surfer Jerk/Girl in the Black Bikini	1965	5.00	10.00	20.00
RONN					
❏ 1	In the Midnight Hour/Nothing You Do	1967	2.50	5.00	10.00
SWAN					
❏ 4204	Let's Shindig/Klink	1965	3.75	7.50	15.00

IN GROUP, THE
Albums
IN

Number	Title (A Side/B Side)	Yr	VG	VG+	NM
❏ I-1002 [M]	Swinging 12 String	1964	5.00	10.00	20.00
❏ IS-1002 [S]	Swinging 12 String	1964	6.25	12.50	25.00

IN-SECT, THE
Albums
RCA CAMDEN

Number	Title (A Side/B Side)	Yr	VG	VG+	NM
❏ CAL-909 [M]	Introducing the In-Sect Direct from England	1964	10.00	20.00	40.00
❏ CAS-909 [S]	Introducing the In-Sect Direct from England	1964	12.50	25.00	50.00

IN-BETWEENS, THE Early incarnation of SLADE.
45s
HIGHLAND

Number	Title (A Side/B Side)	Yr	VG	VG+	NM
❏ 1173	Girl Child, I Am An Evil Witchman/Security	1966	75.00	150.00	300.00

INCREDIBLE BONGO BAND, THE
45s
MGM

Number	Title (A Side/B Side)	Yr	VG	VG+	NM
❏ 14588	Bongo Rock/Bongolia	1973	—	3.00	6.00
❏ 14635	Let There Be Drums/Dueling Bongos	1973	2.00	4.00	8.00
PRIDE					
❏ 1015	Bongo Rock/Bongolia	1972	3.00	6.00	12.00
❏ 7601	Kirburi/When the Bed Breaks Down, I'll Meet You in the Spring	1974	2.50	5.00	10.00

Albums
PRIDE

Number	Title (A Side/B Side)	Yr	VG	VG+	NM
❏ 0028	Bongo Rock	1973	20.00	40.00	80.00
—Note: This album has been reissued to look like the original					
❏ 6010	The Return of the Incredible Bongo Band	1974	5.00	10.00	20.00

INCREDIBLE STRING BAND, THE
45s
ELEKTRA

Number	Title (A Side/B Side)	Yr	VG	VG+	NM
❏ 45696	This Moment/Big Ted	1970	2.00	4.00	8.00

Albums
CARTHAGE

Number	Title (A Side/B Side)	Yr	VG	VG+	NM
❏ CGLP-4421	The Hangman's Beautiful Daughter	198?	3.00	6.00	12.00
ELEKTRA					
❏ EKM-322 [M]	The Incredible String Band	1967	7.50	15.00	30.00
❏ 7E-2002 [(2)]	'U'	1971	6.25	12.50	25.00
—Butterfly label					
❏ 7E-2004 [(2)]	Relics of the Incredible String Band	1971	5.00	10.00	20.00
—Butterfly label					
❏ EKM-4010 [M]	The 5,000 Spirits	1967	7.50	15.00	30.00
❏ EKS-7322 [S]	The Incredible String Band	1967	5.00	10.00	20.00
—Brown label					
❏ EKS-7322	The Incredible String Band	1969	3.75	7.50	15.00
—Red label, large stylized "E"					
❏ EKS-7322	The Incredible String Band	1971	3.00	6.00	12.00
—Butterfly label					
❏ EKS-74010 [S]	The 5,000 Spirits	1967	5.00	10.00	20.00
—Brown label					
❏ EKS-74010	The 5,000 Spirits	1969	3.75	7.50	15.00
—Red label, large stylized "E"					
❏ EKS-74010	The 5,000 Spirits	1971	3.00	6.00	12.00
—Butterfly label					
❏ EKS-74021	The Hangman's Beautiful Daughter	1968	5.00	10.00	20.00
—Brown label					
❏ EKS-74021	The Hangman's Beautiful Daughter	1969	3.75	7.50	15.00
—Red label, large stylized "E"					
❏ EKS-74021	The Hangman's Beautiful Daughter	1971	3.00	6.00	12.00
—Butterfly label					
❏ EKS-74036	Wee Tam	1969	3.75	7.50	15.00
—Red label, large stylized "E"					
❏ EKS-74036	Wee Tam	1969	5.00	10.00	20.00
—Brown label					
❏ EKS-74036	Wee Tam	1971	3.00	6.00	12.00
—Butterfly label					
❏ EKS-74037	The Big Huge	1969	3.75	7.50	15.00
—Red label, large stylized "E"					
❏ EKS-74037	The Big Huge	1969	5.00	10.00	20.00
—Brown label					
❏ EKS-74037	The Big Huge	1971	3.00	6.00	12.00
—Butterfly label					
❏ EKS-74057	Changing Horses	1969	3.75	7.50	15.00
—Red label, large stylized "E"					
❏ EKS-74057	Changing Horses	1971	3.00	6.00	12.00
—Butterfly label					
❏ EKS-74061	I Looked Up	1970	3.75	7.50	15.00
—Red label, large stylized "E"					
❏ EKS-74061	I Looked Up	1971	3.00	6.00	12.00
—Butterfly label					
❏ EKS-74112	Liquid Acrobat As Regards the Air	1972	3.75	7.50	15.00
—Butterfly label					
REPRISE					
❏ MS 2122	Earthspan	1973	3.00	6.00	12.00
❏ MS 2139	No Ruinous Feud	1973	3.00	6.00	12.00
❏ MS 2198	Hard Rope and Silver Twine	1974	3.00	6.00	12.00
SUNDAZED					
❏ LP 5127 [S]	The Incredible String Band	2003	3.00	6.00	12.00
—Reissue on 180-gram vinyl					
❏ LP 5128 [S]	The 5,000 Spirits	2003	3.00	6.00	12.00
—Reissue on 180-gram vinyl					
❏ LP 5129 [S]	The Hangman's Beautiful Daughter	2003	3.00	6.00	12.00
—Reissue on 180-gram vinyl					

INCREDIBLES, THE
45s
AUDIO ARTS

Number	Title (A Side/B Side)	Yr	VG	VG+	NM
❏ 60001	I'll Make It Easy (If You Come On Home)/ Crying Heart	1966	3.00	6.00	12.00
❏ 60006	There's Nothing Else to Say/Another Dirty Deal	1967	2.50	5.00	10.00
❏ 60007	Heart and Soul/I Found Another Love	1967	2.50	5.00	10.00
❏ 60009	Without a Word/Standing Here Crying	1967	2.50	5.00	10.00
❏ 60014	Fool, Fool, Fool/Lost Without You	1968	2.50	5.00	10.00
❏ 60016	Miss Treatment/All of a Sudden	1968	2.50	5.00	10.00
❏ 60017	Standing Here Crying/All of a Sudden	1968	2.50	5.00	10.00
❏ 60018	Stop the Raindrops/Fool, Fool, Fool	1968	2.50	5.00	10.00
TETRAGRAMMATON					
❏ 1515	All of a Sudden/Standing Here Crying	1969	2.00	4.00	8.00

Albums
AUDIO ARTS

Number	Title (A Side/B Side)	Yr	VG	VG+	NM
❏ AAS-7000	Heart and Soul	1970	5.00	10.00	20.00

Number	Title (A Side/B Side)	Yr	VG	VG+	NM

INDEPENDENTS, THE
45s
WAND
❏ 11245	Just As Long As You Need Me, Part 1/Part 2	1972	—	3.00	6.00
❏ 11249	I Just Want to Be There/Can't Understand It	1972	—	3.00	6.00
❏ 11252	Leaving Me/I Love You Yes I Do	1973	—	3.00	6.00
❏ 11258	Baby I've Been Missing You/Couldn't Hear Nobody Say	1973	—	3.00	6.00
❏ 11263	It's All Over/Sara Lee	1973	—	3.00	6.00
❏ 11267	The First Time We Met/Show Me How	1973	—	3.00	6.00
❏ 11273	Arise and Shine (Let's Get It On)/I Found Love	1974	—	3.00	6.00
❏ 11279	Let This Be a Lesson to You/No Wind, No Rain	1974	—	3.00	6.00
Albums
WAND
❏ WDS-694	The First Time We Met	1973	6.25	12.50	25.00
❏ WDS-696	The Independents	1973	6.25	12.50	25.00
❏ WDS-699	Discs of Gold	1974	6.25	12.50	25.00

INDEX
Albums
DC
| ❏ 71 | The Index | 1968 | 1500. | 2250. | 3000. |
—Black label; issued with black and white jacket; number is from deal wax
| ❏ 4736 | The Index | 1968 | 1000. | 1500. | 2000. |
—Red label; issued with generic white jacket, though sometimes found in first LP's jacket; number in dead wax

INDIAN SUMMER
Albums
RCA/NEON
| ❏ NE-3 | Indian Summer | 1971 | 5.00 | 10.00 | 20.00 |

INFLUENCE
Albums
ABC
| ❏ ABCS-630 | Influence | 1968 | 7.50 | 15.00 | 30.00 |

INGMANN, JORGEN
45s
ATCO
❏ 6184	Apache/Echo Boogie	1960	3.75	7.50	15.00
❏ 6195	Anna/Cherokee	1961	3.00	6.00	12.00
❏ 6205	Milord/Oceans of Love	1961	2.50	5.00	10.00
❏ 6216	Violetta/Pinetop's Boogie Woogie	1962	2.50	5.00	10.00
❏ 6235	Africa/Johnny's Tune	1962	2.50	5.00	10.00
❏ 6277	Fourth Man Theme/Drina	1963	2.00	4.00	8.00
❏ 6305	Tovarisch/Desert March	1964	2.00	4.00	8.00
❏ 6370	Theme from "Zorba the Greek"/Gorilla	1965	2.00	4.00	8.00
❏ 6403	Corfu/Seven Roses	1966	2.00	4.00	8.00
PARROT
❏ 45006	Sunrise Serenade/Tokyo Melody	1964	2.50	5.00	10.00
Albums
ATCO
| ❏ 33-130 [M] | Apache | 1961 | 10.00 | 20.00 | 40.00 |
| ❏ 33-139 [M] | The Many Guitars of Jorgen Ingmann | 1962 | 10.00 | 20.00 | 40.00 |
MERCURY
| ❏ MG-20200 [M] | Swinging Guitar | 1956 | 15.00 | 30.00 | 60.00 |
| ❏ MG-20292 [M] | Swing Softly | 1956 | 15.00 | 30.00 | 60.00 |
UNITED ARTISTS
| ❏ UAS-6785 | El Condor Pasa | 1970 | 5.00 | 10.00 | 20.00 |

INGRAM, LUTHER
45s
DECCA
| ❏ 31794 | Ain't That Nice/You Never Miss Your Water | 1965 | 3.00 | 6.00 | 12.00 |
HIB
| ❏ 698 | If It's All the Same To You Babe/Exus Trek | 1967 | 20.00 | 40.00 | 80.00 |
KOKO
❏ 101	I Can't Stop/You Got to Give Love to Get Love	1968	2.50	5.00	10.00
❏ 103	Missing You/Since You Don't Want Me	1968	2.50	5.00	10.00
❏ 721	Ain't Good for Nothing/These Are the Things	1976	—	3.00	6.00
❏ 724	Let's Steal Away to the Hideaway/I've Got Your Love in My Life	1977	—	3.00	6.00
❏ 725	I Like the Feeling/Gonna Be the Next Time	1977	—	3.00	6.00
❏ 728	Do You Love Somebody/How I Miss My Baby	1977	—	3.00	6.00
❏ 731	Get to Me/Trying to Find My Love	1978	—	3.00	6.00
❏ 2101	You Can Depend on Me/Looking for a New Love	1969	2.00	4.00	8.00
❏ 2102	Pity for the Lonely/Looking for a New Love	1969	2.00	4.00	8.00
❏ 2103	Puttin' Game Down/Since You Don't Want Me	1969	2.00	4.00	8.00
❏ 2104	My Honey and Me/I Can't Stop	1969	2.00	4.00	8.00
❏ 2105	Ain't That Loving You (For More Reasons Than One)/Home Don't Seem Like Home	1970	2.00	4.00	8.00
❏ 2106	To the Other Man/I'll Just Call You Honey	1970	2.00	4.00	8.00
❏ 2107	Be Good to Me Baby/Since You Don't Want Me	1971	2.00	4.00	8.00
❏ 2108	I'll Love You Until the End/Ghetto Train	1971	2.00	4.00	8.00
❏ 2110	You Were Made for Me/Missing You	1972	2.00	4.00	8.00
❏ 2111	(If Loving You Is Wrong) I Don't Want to Be Right/Puttin' Game Down	1972	2.00	4.00	8.00
❏ 2113	I'll Be Your Shelter (In Time of Storm)/I Can't Stop	1972	2.00	4.00	8.00
❏ 2115	Always/Help Me Love	1973	2.00	4.00	8.00
❏ 2116	Love Ain't Gonna Run Me Away/To the Other Man	1973	2.00	4.00	8.00
PROFILE
❏ 5125	Baby Don't Go Too Far/How Sweet It Would Be	1986	—	—	3.00
❏ 5132	Don't Turn Around/(B-side unknown)	1987	—	—	3.00
❏ 5143	Gotta Serve Somebody/All in the Name of Love	1987	—	—	3.00
SMASH
❏ 2019	(I Spy) For the F.B.I./Foxey Devil	1966	5.00	10.00	20.00
Albums
KOKO
| ❏ KOS-2201 | I've Been Here All the Time | 1971 | 3.75 | 7.50 | 15.00 |
| ❏ KOS-2202 | If Loving You Is Wrong I Don't Want to Be Right | 1972 | 3.75 | 7.50 | 15.00 |

INITIALS, THE (1)
45s
CONGRESS
❏ 207	School Day/The Song Is Number One	1964	3.00	6.00	12.00
❏ 219	Dancing on the Sand/Seventeen Guys on a Blanket at the Beach	1964	3.00	6.00	12.00
❏ 229	Someday She'll Love Me/I Should Have Listened	1964	3.00	6.00	12.00
—As "Angelo and the Initials"

INITIALS, THE (2)
45s
DEE
| ❏ 1001 | You/Bells of Joy | 1959 | 50.00 | 100.00 | 200.00 |
SHERRY
| ❏ 667 | You/Bells of Joy | 1959 | 12.50 | 25.00 | 50.00 |

INK SPOTS
45s
DECCA
| ❏ 9-5 [PS] | Ink Spots, Volume 2 | 1950 | 3.75 | 7.50 | 15.00 |
—Box for 25238, 25239 and 25240
| ❏ 23615 | To Each His Own/I Never Had a Dream Come True | 1960 | 2.00 | 4.00 | 8.00 |
—Black label, color bars at right
| ❏ 9-23615 | To Each His Own/I Never Had a Dream Come True | 1950 | 6.25 | 12.50 | 25.00 |
—Black label, lines on either side of "Decca"; reissue of 78 from 1946
| ❏ 9-23615 | To Each His Own/I Never Had a Dream Come True | 1955 | 3.00 | 6.00 | 12.00 |
—Black label, star under "Decca"
| ❏ 23632 | If I Didn't Care/Whispering Grass (Don't Tell the Trees) | 1961 | 2.50 | 5.00 | 10.00 |
—Black label, color bars at right
| ❏ 9-23632 | If I Didn't Care/Whispering Grass (Don't Tell the Trees) | 1950 | 6.25 | 12.50 | 25.00 |
—Black label, lines on either side of "Decca"
| ❏ 9-23632 | If I Didn't Care/Whispering Grass (Don't Tell the Trees) | 1955 | 3.00 | 6.00 | 12.00 |
—Black label, star under "Decca"
| ❏ 9-23633 | Java Jive/Do I Worry? | 1950 | 6.25 | 12.50 | 25.00 |
—Black label, lines on either side of "Decca"
| ❏ 9-25238 | I'll Get By (As Long As I Have You)/Just for a Thrill | 1950 | 5.00 | 10.00 | 20.00 |
—Side 1 and 6 of "Album No. 9-5"
| ❏ 9-25239 | I'd Climb the Highest Mountain/I'm Gettin' Sentimental Over You | 1950 | 5.00 | 10.00 | 20.00 |
—From "Album No. 9-5"
| ❏ 9-25240 | Coquette/When the Swallows Come Back to Capistrano | 1950 | 5.00 | 10.00 | 20.00 |
—From "Album No. 9-5"
❏ 25505	It's a Sin to Tell a Lie/That's When Your Heartaches Begin	1961	2.50	5.00	10.00
❏ 25533	All My Life/You Were Only Fooling	1961	3.00	6.00	12.00
❏ 9-27102	Sometime/I Was Dancing with Someone	1950	6.25	12.50	25.00
❏ 9-27214	The Way It Used to Be/Right About Now	1950	6.25	12.50	25.00
❏ 9-27256	Our Lady of Fatima/Stranger in the City	1950	6.25	12.50	25.00
❏ 9-27259	Dream Awhile/Time Out for Tears	1950	6.25	12.50	25.00
❏ 9-27391	If/A Friend of Johnny's	1951	5.00	10.00	20.00
❏ 9-27464	Tell Me You Love Me/Castles in the Sand	1951	5.00	10.00	20.00
❏ 9-27493	Do Something for Me/A Fool Grows Wise	1951	5.00	10.00	20.00
❏ 9-27632	More of the Same Sweet You/What Can You Do	1951	5.00	10.00	20.00
❏ 9-27742	I Don't Stand a Ghost of a Chance/I'm Lucky I Have You	1951	5.00	10.00	20.00
❏ 9-27996	Honest and Truly/All My Life	1952	5.00	10.00	20.00
❏ 9-29750	Memories of You/It's Funny to Everyone But Me	1955	5.00	10.00	20.00
❏ 9-29991	My Prayer/Bewildered	1956	5.00	10.00	20.00
❏ 9-30058	The Best Things in Life Are Free/I Don't Stand a Ghost of a Chance	1956	3.75	7.50	15.00
GRAND AWARD
❏ 1001	Rock and Roll Rag/Do I Worry	1956	5.00	10.00	20.00
KING
❏ 1297	Ebb Tide/If You Should Say Goodbye	1953	15.00	30.00	60.00
❏ 1304	Changing Partners/Stranger in Paradise	1954	17.50	35.00	70.00
❏ 1336	Melody of Love/Am I Too Late	1954	17.50	35.00	70.00
❏ 1378	Yesterdays/Planting Rice	1954	15.00	30.00	60.00
❏ 1425	When You Come to the End of the Day/Someone's Rocking My Dreamboat	1955	12.50	25.00	50.00
❏ 1429	Melody of Love/There Is Something Missing	1955	10.00	20.00	40.00
❏ 1512	Don't Laugh at Me/Keep It Movin'	1955	10.00	20.00	40.00
❏ 4670	Here in My Lonely Room/A Fool in Love	1953	37.50	75.00	150.00
❏ 4857	Command Me/I'll Walk a Country Mile	1955	10.00	20.00	40.00
SWIFT
❏ 1001	If I Didn't Care//Into Each Life Some Rain Must Fall/We Three	195?	3.75	7.50	15.00
VERVE
❏ 10198	Secret Love/A Little Bird Told Me	1960	3.00	6.00	12.00
7-Inch Extended Plays
DECCA
❏ ED 2008	The Gypsy/To Each His Own//Bless You/With My Eyes Wide Open, I'm Dreaming	195?	6.25	12.50	25.00
❏ ED 2008 [PS]	The Ink Spots, Vol. 1	195?	6.25	12.50	25.00
❏ ED 2047	*It's Funny to Everyone But Me/It's a Sin to Tell a Lie/Don't Get Around Much Anymore/My Prayer	195?	6.25	12.50	25.00
❏ ED 2047 [PS]	The Ink Spots, Volume 2	195?	6.25	12.50	25.00
KING
❏ EP-376	*Melody of Love/Ebb Tide/Stranger in Paradise/Yesterdays	195?	7.50	15.00	30.00
❏ EP-376 [PS]	Great Songs of Our Times	195?	7.50	15.00	30.00
Albums
COLORTONE
| ❏ 4901 [M] | The Ink Spots | 1958 | 15.00 | 30.00 | 60.00 |
| ❏ 4947 [M] | The Ink Spots, Vol. 2 | 1959 | 15.00 | 30.00 | 60.00 |

Number	Title (A Side/B Side)	Yr	VG	VG+	NM
CROWN					
☐ CST-144 [S]	The Ink Spots' Greatest Hits	1959	6.25	12.50	25.00
—Black vinyl					
☐ CST-144 [S]	The Ink Spots' Greatest Hits	1959	12.50	25.00	50.00
—Red vinyl					
☐ CST-175 [S]	The Ink Spots	1961	6.25	12.50	25.00
—Black vinyl					
☐ CST-175 [S]	The Ink Spots	1961	12.50	25.00	50.00
—Red vinyl					
☐ CST-217 [S]	The Sensational Ink Spots	1962	6.25	12.50	25.00
—Black vinyl					
☐ CST-217 [S]	The Sensational Ink Spots	1962	12.50	25.00	50.00
—Red vinyl					
☐ CLP-5112 [M]	The Ink Spots' Greatest Hits	1959	5.00	10.00	20.00
☐ CLP-5142 [M]	The Ink Spots	1961	5.00	10.00	20.00
☐ CLP-5187 [M]	The Sensational Ink Spots	1962	5.00	10.00	20.00
☐ CLP 5221 [M]	More Ink Spots	196?	3.75	7.50	15.00
DECCA					
☐ DXB 182 [(2)M]	The Best of the Ink Spots	1965	7.50	15.00	30.00
☐ DL 4297 [M]	Our Golden Favorites	1962	6.25	12.50	25.00
☐ DL 5056 [10]	The Ink Spots	1950	12.50	25.00	50.00
☐ DL 5071 [10]	The Ink Spots, Vol. 2	1950	12.50	25.00	50.00
☐ DL 5333 [10]	Precious Memories	1951	12.50	25.00	50.00
☐ DL 5541 [10]	Street of Dreams	1954	12.50	25.00	50.00
☐ DXSB 7182 [(2)P]	The Best of the Ink Spots	1965	5.00	10.00	20.00
☐ DL 8154 [M]	The Best of the Ink Spots	1955	10.00	20.00	40.00
—Black label, silver print					
☐ DL 8232 [M]	Time Our for Tears	1956	10.00	20.00	40.00
—Black label, silver print					
☐ DL 8768 [M]	Torch Time	1958	10.00	20.00	40.00
—Black label, silver print					
☐ DL 74297 [S]	Our Golden Favorites	1962	5.00	10.00	20.00
EVEREST ARCHIVE OF FOLK & JAZZ					
☐ 350	The Ink Spots in London	197?	2.50	5.00	10.00
GOLDEN TONE					
☐ C4024	The Fabulous Ink Spots	195?	3.00	6.00	12.00
☐ C4037	Ink Spots Vol. II	195?	3.00	6.00	12.00
GRAND AWARD					
☐ GA 232 SD [S]	The Ink Spots' Greatest, Volume 3	1959	10.00	20.00	40.00
☐ GA 33-328 [M]	The Ink Spots' Greatest, Volume 1	1958	6.25	12.50	25.00
☐ GA 33-354 [M]	The Ink Spots' Greatest, Volume 2	1958	6.25	12.50	25.00
☐ GA 33-396 [M]	The Ink Spots' Greatest, Volume 3	1959	6.25	12.50	25.00
KING					
☐ 535 [M]	Something Old, Something New	1956	100.00	200.00	400.00
☐ 642 [M]	Songs That Will Live Forever	1959	75.00	150.00	300.00
—Reissue of 535					
☐ 5001	18 Hits by the Ink Spots	197?	2.50	5.00	10.00
LONGINES SYMPHONETTE					
☐ SYS 5830	10 of the Best Ink Spots Hits	197?	2.50	5.00	10.00
—Label calls this "The Best of the Ink Spots"; also on label is "New Premiun for Mills Bros. V&R Offer"					
MCA					
☐ 4005 [(2)]	The Best of the Ink Spots	197?	3.00	6.00	12.00
☐ MSM2-35253 [(2)]	The Beautiful Music Company Presents the Ink Spots	1991	5.00	10.00	20.00
OPEN SKY					
☐ 3125	Just Like Old Times	198?	2.50	5.00	10.00
PAULA					
☐ 2212	The Ink Spots Sing Country	1972	2.50	5.00	10.00
TOPS					
☐ L-1561 [M]	The Ink Spots	1957	10.00	20.00	40.00
☐ L-1668 [M]	The Ink Spots, Vol. 2	1959	10.00	20.00	40.00
VERVE					
☐ MGV-2124 [M]	The Ink Spots' Favorites	1959	6.25	12.50	25.00
☐ MGVS-6096 [S]	The Ink Spots' Favorites	1959	10.00	20.00	40.00
VOCALION					
☐ VL 3606 [M]	Sincerely Yours	196?	3.00	6.00	12.00
☐ VL 3725 [M]	Lost in a Dream	1965	3.00	6.00	12.00
☐ VL 73606 [R]	Sincerely Yours	196?	2.50	5.00	10.00
☐ VL 73725 [R]	Lost in a Dream	1965	2.50	5.00	10.00
WALDORF MUSIC HALL					
☐ MH 33-144 [10]	Songs of the South Seas	195?	20.00	40.00	80.00
☐ MH 33-152 [10]	The Ink Spots Quartet	195?	20.00	40.00	80.00

INMAN, AUTRY
45s

Number	Title (A Side/B Side)	Yr	VG	VG+	NM
DECCA					
☐ 28290	Who Do You Love/Just Smile As You Go By	1952	5.00	10.00	20.00
☐ 28495	Does Your Sweetheart Seem Different Lately/ All of a Sudden	1952	5.00	10.00	20.00
☐ 28592	I'll Miss My Heart/Stop Stallin'	1953	5.00	10.00	20.00
☐ 28629	That's All Right/Uh Huh Honey	1953	6.25	12.50	25.00
☐ 28778	Pucker Up/That's When I Need You the Most	1953	5.00	10.00	20.00
☐ 28798	A Dear John Letter/Brown Eyed Baby	1953	5.00	10.00	20.00
☐ 28960	It Hurts Too Much to Cry/Happy Go Lucky	1953	5.00	10.00	20.00
☐ 29060	Just Reminiscing/Under the Moon	1954	5.00	10.00	20.00
☐ 29170	Little One/Once More	1954	5.00	10.00	20.00
☐ 29362	Finally I'm Free/Don't Put It Off	1954	5.00	10.00	20.00
☐ 29447	You Said Goodbye/It's a Shame	1955	5.00	10.00	20.00
☐ 29635	Tell Me Now/A Friend	1955	5.00	10.00	20.00
☐ 29690	Blue Monday/Look Over Your Shoulder	1955	6.25	12.50	25.00
☐ 29936	Be-Bop Baby/It Would Be a Doggone Lie	1956	25.00	50.00	100.00
☐ 46407	Let's Take the Long Way Home Tonight/I Hope Tomorrow Never Comes	1952	5.00	10.00	20.00
EPIC					
☐ 10232	Don't Call Me (I'll Call You)/Love Has to Die (All By Itself)	1967	2.00	4.00	8.00
☐ 10276	There Stands the Glass/ This Heart Was Made for Lovin'	1968	2.00	4.00	8.00
☐ 10327	I Can See an Angel/Wish in One Hand (Cry in the Other)	1968	2.00	4.00	8.00
☐ 10389	Ballad of Two Brothers/Don't Call Me (I'll Call You)	1968	2.00	4.00	8.00
☐ 10452	Home Is Heavy on My Mind/ You're the Only One in My Heart	1969	2.00	4.00	8.00
☐ 10494	I'll Be Waiting/Traveling Salesman	1969	2.00	4.00	8.00

Number	Title (A Side/B Side)	Yr	VG	VG+	NM
GLAD					
☐ 1002	I'm Still in Love with Mary/Please Cut Me Down	1960	3.75	7.50	15.00
JUBILEE					
☐ 9001	The Drinks Are On Me/You Don't Live There Anymore	1964	2.00	4.00	8.00
☐ 9010	Keep Her Out of Sight/Blue Is Next in Line	1965	2.00	4.00	8.00
☐ 9016	Hurtache/Mr. Love Passed Away	1965	2.00	4.00	8.00
☐ 9023	You Don't Live There Anymore/The Drinks Are on Me	1965	2.00	4.00	8.00
KOALA					
☐ 325	That's Why You're Being Paid/(B-side unknown)	1980	—	2.50	5.00
MERCURY					
☐ 71983	Living with One and Loving Two/I Guess I'm Crazy	1962	3.00	6.00	12.00
MILLION					
☐ 4	Please Let Me Love You/Maybe This Is the Day	1972	—	3.00	6.00
☐ 24	If You Were Mine/Please Let Me Love You	1972	—	3.00	6.00
RCA VICTOR					
☐ 47-7173	Dream Boat/Remember the Night	1958	7.50	15.00	30.00
☐ 47-7260	Mary Nell/The Hard Way	1958	7.50	15.00	30.00
SIMS					
☐ 131	The Volunteer/Unlucky Am I	1963	2.50	5.00	10.00
☐ 140	Big Sam/My Word	1963	2.50	5.00	10.00
☐ 170	The Ballad of John F. Kennedy/The World's Worst Lover	1964	2.50	5.00	10.00
☐ 188	My Past/You're Welcome Dear	1964	2.50	5.00	10.00
☐ 219	Give Me 40 Acres (To Turn This Rig Around)/ Six Rounds of Love and Hate	1964	2.50	5.00	10.00
UNITED ARTISTS					
☐ 278	That's All Right/Farther to Go Than I've Been	1960	3.75	7.50	15.00
☐ 303	Let's Take the Long Way Home/Too Blue to Cry	1961	3.75	7.50	15.00
Albums					
EPIC					
☐ BN 26428	Ballad of Two Brothers	1968	5.00	10.00	20.00
JUBILEE					
☐ JGM-2055 [M]	Riscoteque Saturday Night	1964	5.00	10.00	20.00
☐ JGS-2055 [S]	Riscoteque Saturday Night	1964	6.25	12.50	25.00
☐ JGM-2056 [M]	New Year's Eve with Autry Inman	1964	5.00	10.00	20.00
☐ JGS-2056 [S]	New Year's Eve with Autry Inman	1964	6.25	12.50	25.00
MOUNTAIN DEW					
☐ 7022 [M]	Autry Inman	1963	5.00	10.00	20.00
☐ S-7022 [S]	Autry Inman	1963	6.25	12.50	25.00
SIMS					
☐ 107 [M]	Autry Inman at the Frontier Club	1964	5.00	10.00	20.00
☐ S-107 [S]	Autry Inman at the Frontier Club	1964	6.25	12.50	25.00

INNER CIRCLE, THE Another STEVE BARRI and P.F. SLOAN creation.
45s

Number	Title (A Side/B Side)	Yr	VG	VG+	NM
DUNHILL					
☐ 4128	So Long Mary Ann/Goes to Show	1968	5.00	10.00	20.00
IMPACT					
☐ 1019	Sally Go Round the Roses/Sugar	1967	5.00	10.00	20.00

INNOCENCE, THE
45s

Number	Title (A Side/B Side)	Yr	VG	VG+	NM
KAMA SUTRA					
☐ 214	There's Got to Be a Word!/I t's Not Gonna Take Too Long	1966	2.00	4.00	8.00
☐ 222	Mairzy Doats/Lifetime Lovin' You	1967	2.50	5.00	10.00
☐ 228	All I Do Is Think About You/ Whence, I Make Thee Mine	1967	2.00	4.00	8.00
☐ 232	Someone Got Caught in My Eye/ Your Show Is Over	1967	2.00	4.00	8.00
☐ 237	Day Turns Me On (The Bufferin Song)/ It's Not Gonna Take Too Long	1967	2.00	4.00	8.00
Albums					
KAMA SUTRA					
☐ KLP-8059 [M]	The Innocence	1967	5.00	10.00	20.00
☐ KLPS-8059 [S]	The Innocence	1967	7.50	15.00	30.00

INNOCENTS, THE Also see KATHY YOUNG AND THE INNOCENTS.
45s

Number	Title (A Side/B Side)	Yr	VG	VG+	NM
DECCA					
☐ 31519	Don't Cry/Come On Lover	1963	5.00	10.00	20.00
INDIGO					
☐ 105	Honest I Do/My Baby Hully Gullys	1960	5.00	10.00	20.00
☐ 111	Gee Whiz/Please Mr. Sun	1960	5.00	10.00	20.00
☐ 116	Kathy/In the Beginning	1961	5.00	10.00	20.00
☐ 124	Beware/Because I Love You	1961	5.00	10.00	20.00
☐ 128	Donna/You Got Me Goin'	1961	5.00	10.00	20.00
☐ 132	Pains in My Heart/When I Become a Man	1961	5.00	10.00	20.00
PORT					
☐ 3026	Gee Whiz/Please Mr. Sun	196?	2.00	4.00	8.00
REPRISE					
☐ 20112	Be Mine/Oh How I Miss My Baby	1962	6.25	12.50	25.00
☐ 20122	Be Mine/Oh How I Miss My Baby	1962	—	—	—
—Unreleased					
☐ 20125	You're Never Satisfied/Oh How I Miss My Baby	1962	5.00	10.00	20.00
TRANS WORLD					
☐ 7001	Tick Tock/The Rut	196?	5.00	10.00	20.00
WARNER BROS.					
☐ 5450	My Heart Stood Still/ Don't Call Me Lonely Anymore	1964	7.50	15.00	30.00
Albums					
INDIGO					
☐ 503 [M]	Inocently Yours	1961	20.00	40.00	80.00
☐ 503 [M]	Inocently Yours	1961	125.00	250.00	500.00
—Plain white cover; promo only					

INSECT TRUST, THE
45s

Number	Title (A Side/B Side)	Yr	VG	VG+	NM
ATCO					
☐ 6764	Reciprocity/Reincarnations	1970	2.50	5.00	10.00
CAPITOL					
☐ 2386	Miss Fun City/Special Rider Blues	1969	3.75	7.50	15.00

Number	Title (A Side/B Side)	Yr	VG	VG+	NM

Albums
ATCO
- ❑ SD 33-313 — Hoboken Saturday Night — 1970 — 10.00 — 20.00 — 40.00

CAPITOL
- ❑ SKAO-109 — The Insect Trust — 1968 — 10.00 — 20.00 — 40.00

INSECTS, THE
45s
APPLAUSE
- ❑ 1002 — Let's Bug the Beatles/Dear Beatles — 1964 — 6.25 — 12.50 — 25.00
—*B-side by the Little Lady Beatles*

INSIDE OUT
Albums
FREDLO
- ❑ 6834 — Bringing It All Back — 1968 — 50.00 — 100.00 — 200.00

INSIDERS, THE
45s
RCA VICTOR
- ❑ 47-9225 — I'm Just a Man/I'm Better Off Without You — 1967 — 6.25 — 12.50 — 25.00
- ❑ 47-9325 — If You Had a Heart/Movin' On — 1967 — 3.75 — 7.50 — 15.00

RED BIRD
- ❑ 10-055 — Chapel Bells Are Calling/I'm Stuck on You — 1966 — 3.75 — 7.50 — 15.00

INSIGHT, THE
45s
CASCADE
- ❑ 364 — Please Come Home For Christmas/Out Of Sight — 1964 — 7.50 — 15.00 — 30.00

INSPIRATIONS, THE More than one group.
45s
AL-BRITE
- ❑ 1651 — Angel in Disguise/Stool Pigeon — 1960 — 20.00 — 40.00 — 80.00

BELTONE
- ❑ 2037 — The Girl By My Side/Neckin' — 1963 — 15.00 — 30.00 — 60.00

GONE
- ❑ 5097 — Angel in Disguise/Stool Pigeon — 1961 — 6.25 — 12.50 — 25.00

JAMIE
- ❑ 1034 — Dry Your Eyes/Good-Bye — 1956 — 18.75 — 37.50 — 75.00
- ❑ 1212 — Dry Your Eyes/Good-Bye — 1962 — 5.00 — 10.00 — 20.00

RONDAK
- ❑ 9787 — Ring Those Bells/The Cumberland and the Merrimac — 1961 — 200.00 — 400.00 — 800.00

SPARKLE
- ❑ 102 — Angel in Disguise/Stool Pigeon — 1960 — 37.50 — 75.00 — 150.00

SULTAN
- ❑ 1 — The Genie/The Feeling of Her Kiss — 1959 — 7.50 — 15.00 — 30.00
- ❑ 1 [PS] — The Genie/The Feeling of Her Kiss — 1959 — 12.50 — 25.00 — 50.00

INTENTIONS, THE Probably more than one group.
45s
JAMIE
- ❑ 1253 — Summertime Angel/Mr. Misery — 1963 — 375.00 — 750.00 — 1500.

MELRON
- ❑ 5014 — I'm in Love with a Go-Go Girl/Wonderful Girl — 1965 — 50.00 — 100.00 — 200.00

PHILIPS
- ❑ 40428 — Don't Forget That I Love You/Night Rider — 1967 — 6.25 — 12.50 — 25.00

INTERLUDES, THE Probably more than one group.
45s
ABC-PARAMOUNT
- ❑ 10213 — Number 1 in the Nation/Beautiful, Wonderful, Heavenly You — 1961 — 3.75 — 7.50 — 15.00

KING
- ❑ 5633 — Darling I'll Be True/Wilted Rose Bud — 1962 — 7.50 — 15.00 — 30.00

RCA VICTOR
- ❑ 47-7281 — I Shed a Million Tears/Oo-Wee — 1958 — 6.25 — 12.50 — 25.00

STAR-HI
- ❑ 103 — I Want You to Know/Split a Kiss — 1959 — 3.75 — 7.50 — 15.00

VALLEY
- ❑ 105 — Heartbreaker/Scandalous — 1959 — 3.75 — 7.50 — 15.00
- ❑ 106 — No One for Me/Fort Lauderdale — 1960 — 3.75 — 7.50 — 15.00
- ❑ 107 — White Sailor Hat/Evil — 1960 — 3.75 — 7.50 — 15.00

INTERNATIONAL SUBMARINE BAND, THE Also see GRAM PARSONS.
45s
ASCOT
- ❑ 2218 — The Russians Are Coming/Truck Driving Man — 1966 — 3.75 — 7.50 — 15.00
- ❑ 2218 [PS] — The Russians Are Coming/Truck Driving Man — 1966 — 12.50 — 25.00 — 50.00
—*Counterfeit identification: Fake copies are missing the Ascot logo and catalog number.*

COLUMBIA
- ❑ 43935 — Sum Up Broke/One Day Week — 1966 — 7.50 — 15.00 — 30.00

LHI
- ❑ 1205 — Luxury Liner/Blue Eyes — 1968 — 3.75 — 7.50 — 15.00
- ❑ 1217 — Miller's Cave/I Must Be Somebody Else — 1968 — 3.75 — 7.50 — 15.00

Albums
LHI
- ❑ 12001 — Safe at Home — 1968 — 25.00 — 50.00 — 100.00
—*Counterfeits have white labels, legitimate copies have multi-color labels.*

SUNDAZED
- ❑ LP 5112 — Safe at Home — 2001 — 3.00 — 6.00 — 12.00
—*Reissue on 180-gram vinyl*

INTERNS, THE
45s
CAPITOL
- ❑ 5747 — Is It Really What You Want/Just Like Me — 1966 — 3.00 — 6.00 — 12.00

UPTOWN
- ❑ 730 — Hard to Get/And I'm Glad — 1966 — 3.00 — 6.00 — 12.00

INTIMATES, THE
45s
EPIC
- ❑ 9743 — I've Got a Tiger in My Tank/Smart, Too Late — 1964 — 3.75 — 7.50 — 15.00

INTRIGUES, THE
45s
TOOT
- ❑ 609 — Soul Brother (Part 1)/Soul Brother (Part 2) — 1968 — 2.50 — 5.00 — 10.00

YEW
- ❑ 1001 — In a Moment/Scotchman Rock — 1969 — 3.00 — 6.00 — 12.00
- ❑ 1002 — I'm Gonna Love You/I Gotta Find Out for Myself — 1969 — 2.50 — 5.00 — 10.00
- ❑ 1007 — Just a Little Bit More/Let's Dance — 1970 — 2.50 — 5.00 — 10.00
- ❑ 1010 — Tuck a Little Love Away/Baseball Game/Friends No More — 1970 — 2.50 — 5.00 — 10.00
- ❑ 1012 — The Language of Love/I Got Love — 1971 — 2.50 — 5.00 — 10.00
- ❑ 1013 — Mojo Hannah/To Make a World — 1971 — 2.50 — 5.00 — 10.00

Albums
YEW
- ❑ YS-777 — In a Moment — 1970 — 7.50 — 15.00 — 30.00

INTRUDERS, THE (1) Early Philly Soul group.
45s
GAMBLE
- ❑ 201 — (We'll Be) United/Up and Down the Ladder — 1966 — 2.50 — 5.00 — 10.00
- ❑ 203 — Devil with an Angel's Smile/A Book for the Broken Hearted — 1966 — 2.50 — 5.00 — 10.00
- ❑ 203 [PS] — Devil with an Angel's Smile/A Book for the Broken Hearted — 1966 — 3.75 — 7.50 — 15.00
- ❑ 204 — It Must Be Love/Check Yourself — 1966 — 2.50 — 5.00 — 10.00
- ❑ 205 — Together/Up and Down the Ladder — 1967 — 2.50 — 5.00 — 10.00
- ❑ 209 — Baby I'm Lonely/A Love That's Real — 1967 — 2.50 — 5.00 — 10.00
- ❑ 214 — Cowboys to Girls/Turn the Hands of Time — 1968 — 2.50 — 5.00 — 10.00
- ❑ 217 — (Love Is Like a) Baseball Game/Friends No More — 1968 — 2.50 — 5.00 — 10.00
- ❑ 221 — Slow Drag/So Glad I'm Yours — 1968 — 2.50 — 5.00 — 10.00
- ❑ 223 — Give Her a Transplant/Girls, Girls, Girls — 1969 — 2.50 — 5.00 — 10.00
- ❑ 225 — Me Tarzan You Jane/Favorite Candidate — 1969 — 2.50 — 5.00 — 10.00
- ❑ 231 — Lollipop (I Like You)/Don't Give It Away — 1969 — 2.50 — 5.00 — 10.00
- ❑ 235 — Sad Girl/Let's Go Downtown — 1969 — 2.50 — 5.00 — 10.00
- ❑ 240 — Old Love/Every Day Is a Holiday — 1969 — 2.50 — 5.00 — 10.00
- ❑ 2501 — (Win, Place or Show) She's a Winner/Memories Are Here to Stay — 1972 — 2.00 — 4.00 — 8.00
- ❑ 2506 — I'll Always Love My Mama (Part 1)/I'll Always Love My Mama (Part 2) — 1973 — 2.00 — 4.00 — 8.00
- ❑ 2508 — I Wanna Know Your Name/Hang On In There — 1973 — 2.00 — 4.00 — 8.00
- ❑ 4001 — Tender (Was the Love We Knew)/By the Time I Get to Phoenix — 1970 — 2.00 — 4.00 — 8.00
- ❑ 4004 — When We Get Married/Doctor Doctor — 1970 — 2.00 — 4.00 — 8.00
- ❑ 4007 — This Is My Love Song/Let Me in Your Mind — 1970 — 2.00 — 4.00 — 8.00
- ❑ 4009 — I'm Girl Scoutin'/Wonder What Kind of Bag She's In — 1971 — 2.00 — 4.00 — 8.00
- ❑ 4014 — Pray for Me/Best Days of My Life — 1971 — 2.00 — 4.00 — 8.00
- ❑ 4016 — I Bet He Don't Love You (Like I Love You)/Do You Remember Yesterday — 1971 — 2.00 — 4.00 — 8.00
- ❑ 4019 — (Win, Place or Show) She's a Winner/Memories Are Here to Stay — 1972 — 2.50 — 5.00 — 10.00

GOWEN
- ❑ 1401 — I'm Sold on You/Come Home Soon — 1961 — 10.00 — 20.00 — 40.00

LOST-NITE
- ❑ 195 — I'm Sold on You/Come Home Soon — 196? — — — 3.00 — 6.00
—*Reissue*

PHILADELPHIA INT'L.
- ❑ 3624 — I'll Always Love My Mama (Part 1)/I'll Always Love My Mama (Part 2) — 1977 — — — 2.50 — 5.00
- ❑ 3689 — I'll Always Love My Mama/Save the Children — 1979 — — — 2.50 — 5.00

TSOP
- ❑ 4758 — A Nice Girl Like You/To Be Happy Is the Real Thing — 1974 — — — 3.00 — 6.00
- ❑ 4766 — Rainy Days and Mondays/Be on Time — 1975 — — — 3.00 — 6.00
- ❑ 4771 — Plain Old Fashioned Girl/Energy of Love — 1975 — — — 3.00 — 6.00

Albums
GAMBLE
- ❑ G-5001 [M] — The Intruders Are Together — 1967 — 10.00 — 20.00 — 40.00
- ❑ GS-5001 [S] — The Intruders Are Together — 1967 — 12.50 — 25.00 — 50.00
- ❑ GS-5004 — Cowboys to Girls — 1968 — 12.50 — 25.00 — 50.00
- ❑ GS-5005 — The Intruders Greatest Hits — 1969 — 10.00 — 20.00 — 40.00
- ❑ GS-5008 — When We Get Married — 1970 — 12.50 — 25.00 — 50.00
- ❑ KZ 31991 — Save the Children — 1973 — 5.00 — 10.00 — 20.00
- ❑ KZ 32131 — Super Hits — 1973 — 5.00 — 10.00 — 20.00

PHILADELPHIA INT'L.
- ❑ PZ 32131 — Super Hits — 198? — 2.00 — 4.00 — 8.00
—*Reissue of Gamble 32131*

TSOP
- ❑ KZ 33149 — Energy of Love — 1974 — 3.75 — 7.50 — 15.00

INTRUDERS, THE (2) Instrumental group from New Jersey.
45s
BELTONE
- ❑ 1009 — Camptown Rock/Morse Code — 1961 — 3.75 — 7.50 — 15.00

FAME
- ❑ 101 — Fried Eggs/Jeffrie's Rock — 1959 — 6.25 — 12.50 — 25.00
- ❑ 313 — Creepin'/Frankfurters and Sauerkraut — 1959 — 6.25 — 12.50 — 25.00
- ❑ 616 — Rock-A-Ma-Roll/Era-Rock-A — 1959 — 6.25 — 12.50 — 25.00

INVITATIONS, THE
45s
DIAMOND
- ❑ 253 — Got to Have It Now/Swingin' on the Love Vine — 1968 — 3.00 — 6.00 — 12.00

DYNO VOICE
- ❑ 206 — Written on the Wall/Hallelujah — 1965 — 7.50 — 15.00 — 30.00
- ❑ 210 — What's Wrong with Me Baby/Why Did My Baby Turn Bad — 1965 — 7.50 — 15.00 — 30.00
- ❑ 215 — Skiing in the Snow/Why Did My Baby Turn Bad — 1966 — 15.00 — 30.00 — 60.00

MGM
- ❑ 13574 — The Skate/Girl I'm Leavin' You — 1966 — 3.75 — 7.50 — 15.00
- ❑ 13666 — Watch Out Little Girl/You're Like a Mystery — 1967 — 3.75 — 7.50 — 15.00

SILVER BLUE
- ❑ 801 — They Say the Girl's Crazy/For Your Precious Love — 1973 — 2.00 — 4.00 — 8.00
- ❑ 804 — Let's Love/Love Has to Grow — 1973 — 2.00 — 4.00 — 8.00
- ❑ 809 — Living Together Is Keeping Us Apart/I Didn't Know — 1974 — 2.00 — 4.00 — 8.00
- ❑ 818 — Look on the Good Side/Look on the Good Side (Part 2) — 1974 — 2.00 — 4.00 — 8.00

Number	Title (A Side/B Side)	Yr	VG	VG+	NM
IRIDESCENTS, THE					
45s					
HUDSON					
❏ 8102	Three Coins in the Fountain/Strong Love	1963	6.25	12.50	25.00
❏ 8102	Three Coins in the Fountain/Strong Love	1963	25.00	50.00	100.00
—Blue vinyl					
ULTRASONIC					
❏ 109	I Know/The Angels Sang	1960	100.00	200.00	400.00
IRISH ROVERS, THE					
45s					
DECCA					
❏ 32254	The Unicorn/Black Velvet Band	1968	2.50	5.00	10.00
❏ 32333	(The Puppet Song) Whiskey on a Sunday/The Orange and the Green	1968	2.00	4.00	8.00
❏ 32371	Liverpool Lou/The Bi-Plane, Ever More	1968	2.00	4.00	8.00
❏ 32444	Lily the Pink/Mrs. Crandall's Boardinghouse	1969	2.00	4.00	8.00
❏ 32529	Peter Knight/Did She Mention My Name	1969	2.00	4.00	8.00
❏ 32575	Fifi O'Toole/Winkin', Blinkin', and Nod	1969	2.00	4.00	8.00
❏ 32616	Rhymes and Reasons/Penny Whistler Peddler	1970	—	3.00	6.00
❏ 32616 [PS]	Rhymes and Reasons/Penny Whistler Peddler	1970	2.50	5.00	10.00
❏ 32723	Two Little Boys/Years May Come, Years May Go	1970	—	3.00	6.00
❏ 32775	The Marvelous Toy/Marika's Lullaby	1970	—	3.00	6.00
Albums					
DECCA					
❏ DL 4835 [M]	First	1967	5.00	10.00	20.00
❏ DL 4951 [M]	The Unicorn	1968	6.25	12.50	25.00
❏ DL 74835 [S]	First	1967	3.75	7.50	15.00
❏ DL 74951 [S]	The Unicorn	1968	3.75	7.50	15.00
❏ DL 75037	All Hung Up	1968	3.75	7.50	15.00
❏ DL 75081	Tales to Warm Your Mind	1969	3.75	7.50	15.00
❏ DL 75157	Life of the Rover	1969	3.75	7.50	15.00
❏ DL 75302	On the Shores of Americay	1971	3.75	7.50	15.00
MCA					
❏ 15	The Unicorn	1973	2.50	5.00	10.00
—Reissue of Decca 74951					
❏ 175	On the Shores of Americay	1973	2.50	5.00	10.00
—Reissue of Decca 75302					
❏ 249	First	1973	2.50	5.00	10.00
—Reissue of Decca 74835					
❏ 284	Life of the Rover	1973	2.50	5.00	10.00
—Reissue of Decca 75157					
❏ 4066 [(2)]	Greatest Hits	1976	3.75	7.50	15.00
IRON BUTTERFLY					
45s					
ATCO					
❏ 6573	Possession/Unconscious Power	1968	2.00	4.00	8.00
❏ 6606	In-A-Gadda-Da-Vida/Iron Butterfly Theme	1968	2.50	5.00	10.00
❏ 6647	Soul Experience/In the Crowds	1969	2.00	4.00	8.00
❏ 6676	In the Times of Our Lives/It Must Be Love	1969	2.00	4.00	8.00
❏ 6712	Little Girl/I Can't Help But Deceive You	1969	2.00	4.00	8.00
❏ 6782	Easy Rider (Let the Wind Pay the Way)/Soldier in Town	1970	2.00	4.00	8.00
❏ 6818	Silly Sally/Stone Believer	1971	—	3.00	6.00
MCA					
❏ 40379	Pearly Gates/Searchin' Circles	1975	—	2.00	4.00
❏ 40493	Beyond the Milky Way/Get It Out	1975	—	2.00	4.00
Albums					
ATCO					
❏ 33-227 [M]	Heavy	1967	7.50	15.00	30.00
❏ SD 33-227 [S]	Heavy	1967	6.25	12.50	25.00
—Brown and purple label					
❏ SD 33-227 [S]	Heavy	1969	3.75	7.50	15.00
—Yellow label					
❏ 33-250 [M]	In-A-Gadda-Da-Vida	1968	12.50	25.00	50.00
❏ SD 33-250 [S]	In-A-Gadda-Da-Vida	1968	6.25	12.50	25.00
—Brown and purple label					
❏ SD 33-250 [S]	In-A-Gadda-Da-Vida	1969	3.75	7.50	15.00
—Yellow label					
❏ SD 33-250 [S]	In-A-Gadda-Da-Vida	197?	2.50	5.00	10.00
—Any later Atco label; LP was in print into the late 1980s					
❏ SD 33-280	Ball	1969	3.75	7.50	15.00
❏ SD 33-318	Iron Butterfly Live	197?	2.50	5.00	10.00
—Any later Atco label; LP was in print into the late 1980s					
❏ SD 33-318	Iron Butterfly Live	1970	3.75	7.50	15.00
—Yellow label					
❏ SD 33-339	Metamorphosis	1970	3.75	7.50	15.00
❏ SD 33-369	The Best of Iron Butterfly/Evolution	1971	3.75	7.50	15.00
MCA					
❏ 465	Scorching Beauty	1975	3.00	6.00	12.00
❏ 2164	Sun and Steel	1976	3.00	6.00	12.00
PAIR					
❏ PDL2-1065 [(2)]	Rare Flight	1986	3.75	7.50	15.00
IRRIDESCENTS, THE					
45s					
HAWK					
❏ 4001	Bali Ha'i/Swamp Surfer	1963	12.50	25.00	50.00
INFINITY					
❏ 037	Bali Ha'i/Swamp Surfer	1963	6.25	12.50	25.00
OLDIES 45					
❏ 183	Bali Ha'i/Swamp Surfer	1964	3.00	6.00	12.00
IRWIN, BIG DEE					
45s					
CUB					
❏ 9155	I Only Get This Feeling/Wrong Direction	1968	2.00	4.00	8.00
—As "Dee Erwin"					
DIMENSION					
❏ 1001	Everybody's Gotta Dance But Me/And Heaven Was There	1962	3.75	7.50	15.00
❏ 1010	Swinging on a Star/Another Night with the Boys	1963	5.00	10.00	20.00
❏ 1015	Soul Waltzin'/Happy Being Fat	1963	3.75	7.50	15.00
❏ 1018	You're My Inspiration/Skeeter	1963	3.75	7.50	15.00

Number	Title (A Side/B Side)	Yr	VG	VG+	NM
❏ 1021	The Christmas Song/I Wish You a Merry Christmas	1963	3.75	7.50	15.00
—With Little Eva					
❏ 1028	Heigh Ho/I Want So Much to Know You	1964	3.75	7.50	15.00
IMPERIAL					
❏ 66295	Wrong Direction/I Only Get This Feeling	1968	2.50	5.00	10.00
—As "Dee Irwin"					
❏ 66320	I Can't Stand the Pain/My Hope to Die Girl	1968	2.50	5.00	10.00
❏ 66334	All I Want for Christmas Is Your Love//By the Time I Get to Phoenix/I Say a Little Prayer	1968	3.00	6.00	12.00
—With Mamie Galore					
❏ 66359	Day Tripper/I Didn't Wanna Do It, But I Did	1969	2.00	4.00	8.00
—With Mamie Galore					
❏ 66420	Ain't No Way/Cherish	1969	2.00	4.00	8.00
PHIL-LA OF SOUL					
❏ 303	Better to Have Loved and Lost/Linda	1967	3.75	7.50	15.00
—As "Dee Erwin"					
ROULETTE					
❏ 4596	Discotheque/The Sun's Gonna Shine Tomorrow	1965	2.50	5.00	10.00
—As "Big Dee Erwin"					
ISLE, JIMMY					
45s					
BALLY					
❏ 1034	Baby-O/Hssle	1957	6.25	12.50	25.00
EVEREST					
❏ 19320	Oh Judy/Billy Boy	1959	6.25	12.50	25.00
MALA					
❏ 459	Our Town/Everybody Gotta Little Girl But Me	1963	5.00	10.00	20.00
ROULETTE					
❏ 4065	Goin' Wild/You and Johnny Smith	1959	7.50	15.00	30.00
SUN					
❏ 306	Diamond Ring/I've Been Waiting	1958	6.25	12.50	25.00
❏ 318	Time Will Tell/Without a Love	1959	6.25	12.50	25.00
❏ 332	What a Life/Together	1959	6.25	12.50	25.00
ISLEY BROTHERS, THE					
12-Inch Singles					
T-NECK					
❏ AS 947 [DJ]	Hurry Up and Wait (3:54) (4:09)	1981	2.00	4.00	8.00
❏ 2267	Livin' in the Life/Go for Your Guns	1977	3.75	7.50	15.00
❏ 2276	Tell Me When You Need It Again/Take Me to the Next Phase	1977	3.75	7.50	15.00
❏ 2283	I Wanna Be with You (6:20)/Rockin' with Fire (5:57)	1978	3.00	6.00	12.00
❏ 2289	It's a Disco Night (Rock Don't Stop)/Ain't Givin' Up on Love	1979	3.00	6.00	12.00
❏ 03282	It's Alright with Me (Vocal) (Instrumental)	1982	2.50	5.00	10.00
❏ 04148	I Need Your Body//(Instrumental)	1983	2.00	4.00	8.00
WARNER BROS.					
❏ PRO-A-2378 [DJ]	Colder Are My Night (Edit Version) (LP Version)	1985	2.00	4.00	8.00
❏ PRO-A-4511 [DJ]	Spend the Night (Edit)/Colder Are My Nights (Edit)/Smooth Sailin' Tonight (Edit)	1989	2.00	4.00	8.00
❏ PRO-A-5417 [DJ]	Sensitive Lover (4 versions)	1992	2.00	4.00	8.00
❏ 20827	I Wish (Vocal) (Instrumental)	1987	2.00	4.00	8.00
❏ 21415	You'll Never Walk Alone (4 versions)/One of a Kind	1989	2.00	4.00	8.00
45s					
ATLANTIC					
❏ 2092	Jeepers Creepers/Teach Me How to Shimmy	1961	3.75	7.50	15.00
❏ 2100	Shine On Harvest Moon/Standing on the Dance Floor	1961	3.75	7.50	15.00
❏ 2110	Your Old Lady/Write to Me	1961	3.75	7.50	15.00
❏ 2122	A Fool for You/Just One More Time	1961	3.75	7.50	15.00
❏ 2263	Looking for a Love/The Last Girl	1964	2.50	5.00	10.00
❏ 2277	Simon Says/Wild As a Tiger	1965	2.50	5.00	10.00
❏ 2303	Move Over and Let Me Dance/Have You Ever Been Disappointed	1965	3.75	7.50	15.00
CINDY					
❏ 3009	Don't Be Jealous/This Is the End	1958	18.75	37.50	75.00
—"Cindy" in regular print					
❏ 3009	Don't Be Jealous/This Is the End	1958	37.50	75.00	150.00
—"Cindy" in shadow print					
GONE					
❏ 5022	I Wanna Know/Everybody's Gonna Rock and Roll	1958	20.00	40.00	80.00
❏ 5048	My Love/The Drag	1958	20.00	40.00	80.00
MARK-X					
❏ 7003	The Drag/Rockin' MacDonald	1957	25.00	50.00	100.00
❏ 8000	The Drag/Rockin' MacDonald	1959	7.50	15.00	30.00
PHILCO-FORD					
❏ HP-41	Twist and Shout/Rubberleg Twist	1969	6.25	12.50	25.00
—4-inch plastic "Hip Pocket Record" with color sleeve					
RCA					
❏ 447-0589	Shout (Part 1)/Shout (Part 2)	1976	—	2.00	4.00
—Gold Standard Series; black label, dog near top					
RCA VICTOR					
❏ 47-7537	I'm Gonna Knock on Your Door/Turn to Me	1959	6.25	12.50	25.00
❏ 47-7588	Shout (Part 1)/Shout (Part 2)	1959	7.50	15.00	30.00
❏ 47-7657	Respectable/She's Got the Whole World in His Hands/How	1959	6.25	12.50	25.00
❏ 47-7718	He's Got the Whole World in His Hands/How Deep Is the Ocean	1960	6.25	12.50	25.00
❏ 47-7746	Gypsy Love Song/Open Up Your Heart	1960	6.25	12.50	25.00
❏ 47-7787	Say You Love Me Too/Tell Me Who	1960	6.25	12.50	25.00
❏ 61-7588 [S]	Shout (Part 1)/Shout (Part 2)	1959	15.00	30.00	60.00
—"Living Stereo" (large hole, plays at 45 rpm)					
❏ 447-0589	Shout (Part 1)/Shout (Part 2)	1962	3.00	6.00	12.00
—Gold Standard Series; black label, dog on top (this charted with this number in 1962)					
❏ 447-0589	Shout (Part 1)/Shout (Part 2)	1965	2.00	4.00	8.00
—Gold Standard Series; black label, dog on side					
❏ 447-0589	Shout (Part 1)/Shout (Part 2)	1969	—	2.50	5.00
—Gold Standard Series; red label					
T-NECK					
❏ 501	Testify (Part 1)/Testify (Part 2)	1964	3.75	7.50	15.00
❏ 901	It's Your Thing/Don't Give It Away	1969	—	3.00	6.00

Number	Title (A Side/B Side)	Yr	VG	VG+	NM
❏ 902	I Turned You On/				
	I Know Who You Been Socking It To	1969	—	3.00	6.00
❏ 906	Black Berries — Pt. 1/Black Berries — Pt. 2	1969	—	3.00	6.00
❏ 908	Was It Good to You/I Got to Get Myself Together	1969	—	3.00	6.00
❏ 912	Bless Your Heart/Give the Women What They				
	Want	1969	—	3.00	6.00
❏ 914	Keep On Doin'/Save Me	1970	—	3.00	6.00
❏ 919	If He Can, You Can/Holdin' On	1970	—	3.00	6.00
❏ 921	Girls Will Be Girls, Boys Will Be Boys/Get Down				
	Off of the Train	1970	—	3.00	6.00
❏ 924	Get Into Something/Get Into Something (Part 2)	1970	—	3.00	6.00
❏ 927	Freedom/I Need You So	1970	—	3.00	6.00
❏ 929	Warpath/I Got to Find Me One	1971	—	3.00	6.00
❏ 930	Love the One You're With/He's Got Your Love	1971	—	3.00	6.00
❏ 932	Spill the Wine/Take Inventory	1971	—	3.00	6.00
❏ 933	Lay Lady Lay/Vacuum Cleaner	1971	—	3.00	6.00
❏ 934	Lay-Away/Feel Like the World	1972	—	3.00	6.00
❏ 935	Pop That Thang/I Got to Find Me One	1972	—	3.00	6.00
❏ 936	Work to Do/Beautiful	1972	—	3.00	6.00
❏ 937	It's Too Late/Nothing to Do But Today	1973	—	3.00	6.00
❏ 02033	Hurry Up and Wait/(Instrumental)	1981	—	2.50	5.00
❏ 02151	Don't Say Goodnight (It's Time for Love)				
	(Parts 1 & 2)	1981	—	2.00	4.00
—Reissue					
❏ 02179	I Once Had Your Love (And I Can't Let Go)/				
	(Instrumental)	1981	—	2.50	5.00
❏ 2251	That Lady (Part 1)/That Lady (Part 2)	1973	—	2.50	5.00
❏ 2252	What It Comes Down To/Highways of My Life	1973	—	2.50	5.00
❏ 2253	Summer Breeze (Part 1)/				
	Summer Breeze (Part 2)	1974	—	2.50	5.00
❏ 2254	Live It Up (Part 1)/Live It Up (Part 2)	1974	—	2.50	5.00
❏ 2255	Midnight Sky (Part 1)/Midnight Sky (Part 2)	1974	—	2.50	5.00
❏ 2256	Fight the Power Part 1/Fight the Power Part 2	1975	—	2.50	5.00
❏ 2259	For the Love of You (Part 1&2)/				
	You Walk Your Way	1975	—	2.50	5.00
❏ 2260	Who Loves You Better-Part 1/				
	Who Loves You Better-Part 2	1976	—	2.50	5.00
❏ 2261	Harvest for the World/Harvest for the World				
	(Part 2)	1976	—	2.50	5.00
❏ 2262	The Pride (Part 1)/The Pride (Part 2)	1977	—	2.50	5.00
❏ 2264	Livin' in the Life/Go for Your Guns	1977	—	2.50	5.00
❏ 2270	Voyage to Atlantis/Do You Wanna Stay Down	1977	—	2.50	5.00
❏ 02270	Voyage to Atlantis/Do You Wanna Stay Down	1981	—	2.00	4.00
—Reissue					
❏ 2272	Take Me to the Next Phase (Part 1)/				
	Take Me to the Next Phase (Part 2)	1978	—	2.50	5.00
❏ 2277	Groove with You/Footsteps in the Dark	1978	—	2.50	5.00
❏ 2278	Showdown (Part 1)/Showdown (Part 2)	1978	—	2.50	5.00
❏ 2279	I Wanna Be with You (Part 1)/				
	I Wanna Be with You (Part 2)	1979	—	2.50	5.00
❏ 2284	Winner Takes All/Fun and Games	1979	—	2.50	5.00
❏ 2287	It's a Disco Night (Rock Don't Stop)/				
	Ain't Givin' Up on Love	1979	—	2.50	5.00
❏ 2290	Don't Say Goodnight (It's Time for Love) (Part				
	1)/Don't Say Goodnight				
	(It's Time for Love) (Part 2)	1980	—	2.50	5.00
❏ 2291	Here We Go Again (Part 1)/				
	Here We Go Again (Part 2)	1980	—	2.50	5.00
❏ 2292	Say You Will (Part 1)/Say You Will (Part 2)	1980	—	2.50	5.00
❏ 2293	Who Said?/(Can't You See)				
	What You've Done to Me	1980	—	2.50	5.00
❏ 02293	Who Said?/(Can't You See) What You Do to Me	1981	—	2.00	4.00
—Reissue					
❏ 02531	Inside You (Part 1)/Inside You (Part 2)	1981	—	2.50	5.00
❏ 02705	Party Night/Welcome Into My Night	1982	—	2.50	5.00
❏ 02985	The Real Deal/(Instrumental)	1982	—	2.50	5.00
❏ 03281	It's Alright with Me/(Instrumental)	1982	—	2.50	5.00
❏ 03797	Between the Sheets/(Instrumental)	1983	—	2.50	5.00
❏ 03994	Choosey Lover/(Instrumental)	1983	—	2.50	5.00
❏ 04320	Let's Make Love Tonight/(Instrumental)	1984	—	2.50	5.00
TAMLA					
❏ 54128	This Old Heart of Mine (Is Weak for You)/				
	There's No Love Left	1966	3.75	7.50	15.00
❏ 54133	Take Some Time Out for Love/Who Could Ever				
	Doubt My Love	1966	3.00	6.00	12.00
❏ 54135	I Guess I'll Always Love You/I Hear a Symphony	1966	3.00	6.00	12.00
❏ 54146	Got to Have You Back/Just Ain't Enough Love	1967	3.00	6.00	12.00
❏ 54154	One Too Many Heartaches/				
	That's the Way Love Is	1967	3.00	6.00	12.00
❏ 54164	Take Me in Your Arms (Rock Me a Little While)/				
	Why When Love Is Gone	1968	3.00	6.00	12.00
❏ 54175	Behind a Painted Smile/All Because I Love You	1968	3.00	6.00	12.00
❏ 54182	Take Some Time Out for Love/				
	Just Ain't Enough Love	1969	3.00	6.00	12.00
TEENAGE					
❏ 1004	Angels Cried/The Cow Jumped Over the Moon	1957	200.00	400.00	800.00
UNITED ARTISTS					
❏ 605	She's Gone/Tango	1963	5.00	10.00	20.00
❏ 638	Surf and Shout/Whatcha Gonna Do	1963	5.00	10.00	20.00
❏ 659	Please, Please, Please/You'll Never Leave Him	1963	5.00	10.00	20.00
❏ 714	Who's That Lady/My Little Girl	1964	5.00	10.00	20.00
❏ 798	Love Is a Wonderful Thing/Open Up Her Eyes	1964	—	—	—
—Unreleased					
❏ 923	Love Is a Wonderful Thing/Open Up Her Eyes	1965	—	—	—
—Unreleased					
V.I.P.					
❏ 25020	I Hear a Symphony/Who Could Ever Doubt My				
	Love	1965	200.00	400.00	800.00
VEEP					
❏ 1230	Love Is a Wonderful Thing/Open Up Her Eyes	1966	2.50	5.00	10.00
WAND					
❏ 118	Right Now/The Snake	1962	3.75	7.50	15.00
❏ 124	Twist and Shout/Spanish Twist	1962	5.00	10.00	20.00
❏ 127	Twistin' with Linda/You Better Come Home	1962	3.00	6.00	12.00
❏ 131	Nobody But Me/				
	I'm Laughing to Keep from Crying	1963	3.00	6.00	12.00
❏ 137	I Say Love/Hold On Baby	1963	3.00	6.00	12.00

Number	Title (A Side/B Side)	Yr	VG	VG+	NM
WARNER BROS.					
❏ 22748	One of a Kind/You'll Never Walk Alone	1989	—	—	3.00
❏ 22900	Spend the Night (Ce Soir)/(Instrumental)	1989	—	—	3.00
❏ 22900 [PS]	Spend the Night (Ce Soir)/(Instrumental)	1989	—	—	3.00
❏ 27954	It Takes a Good Woman/(Instrumental)	1988	—	2.00	4.00
❏ 28129	I Wish/(Instrumental)	1988	—	2.00	4.00
❏ 28129 [PS]	I Wish/(Instrumental)	1988	—	2.00	4.00
❏ 28241	Come My Way/(Instrumental)	1987	—	2.00	4.00
❏ 28385	Smooth Sailin' Tonight/(Instrumental)	1987	—	2.00	4.00
❏ 28385 [PS]	Smooth Sailin' Tonight/(Instrumental)	1987	—	2.00	4.00
❏ 28764	May I?/(Instrumental)	1986	—	2.00	4.00
❏ 28860	Colder Are My Nights/(Instrumental)	1985	—	2.00	4.00
Albums					
BUDDAH					
❏ BDS-5652 [(2)]	The Best of the Isley Brothers	1976	3.75	7.50	15.00
COLLECTABLES					
❏ COL-5103	Shout!	198?	2.50	5.00	10.00
ISLAND					
❏ 7243 [(2)DJ]	Mission to Please	1996	5.00	10.00	20.00
—Promo-only vinyl in generic cover					
MOTOWN					
❏ M5-106V1	Motown Superstar Series, Volume 6	1981	2.00	4.00	8.00
❏ M5-128V1	This Old Heart of Mine	1981	2.00	4.00	8.00
—Reissue of Tamla 269					
❏ M5-143V1	Doin' Their Thing (Best of the Isley Brothers)	1981	2.00	4.00	8.00
—Reissue of Tamla 287					
PICKWICK					
❏ SPC-3331	Soul Shout!	197?	2.50	5.00	10.00
RCA CAMDEN					
❏ ACL1-0126	Rock On Brother	1973	3.00	6.00	12.00
❏ ACL1-0861	Rock Around the Clock	1975	3.00	6.00	12.00
RCA VICTOR					
❏ LPM-2156 [M]	Shout!	1959	30.00	60.00	120.00
—"Long Play" label					
❏ LSP-2156 [S]	Shout!	1959	50.00	100.00	200.00
—"Living Stereo" label					
SCEPTER					
❏ SC-552 [M]	Take Some Time Out for the Isley Brothers	1966	7.50	15.00	30.00
❏ SCS-552 [S]	Take Some Time Out for the Isley Brothers	1966	10.00	20.00	40.00
SUNSET					
❏ SUS-5257	The Isley Brothers Do Their Thing	1969	3.75	7.50	15.00
T-NECK					
❏ ASZ 137 [DJ]	Everything You Always Wanted to Hear by the				
	Isley Brothers But Were Afraid to Ask For	1976	5.00	10.00	20.00
—Promo-only compilation					
❏ TNS-3001	It's Our Thing	1969	5.00	10.00	20.00
❏ TNS-3002	The Brothers: Isley	1969	5.00	10.00	20.00
❏ TNS-3006	Get Into Something	1970	3.75	7.50	15.00
❏ TNS-3007	In the Beginning (With Jimi Hendrix)	1970	5.00	10.00	20.00
❏ TNS-3008	Givin' It Back	1971	3.75	7.50	15.00
❏ TNS-3009	Brother, Brother, Brother	1972	3.75	7.50	15.00
❏ TNS-3010 [(2)]	The Isleys Live	1973	5.00	10.00	20.00
❏ TNS-3011	Isleys' Greatest Hits	1973	3.75	7.50	15.00
❏ KZ 32453	3 + 3	1973	3.00	6.00	12.00
❏ PZ 32453	3 + 3	197?	2.00	4.00	8.00
—Reissue with new prefix					
❏ ZQ 32453 [Q]	3 + 3	1974	5.00	10.00	20.00
❏ PZ 33070	Live It Up	1974	3.00	6.00	12.00
—No bar code on cover					
❏ PZQ 33070 [Q]	Live It Up	1974	5.00	10.00	20.00
❏ PZ 33536	The Heat Is On	1975	3.00	6.00	12.00
—No bar code on cover					
❏ PZ 33536	The Heat Is On	198?	2.00	4.00	8.00
—Budget-line reissue with bar code					
❏ PZ 33809	Harvest for the World	1976	3.00	6.00	12.00
—No bar code on cover					
❏ PZQ 33809 [Q]	Harvest for the World	1976	5.00	10.00	20.00
❏ PZ 34432	Go for Your Guns	1977	3.00	6.00	12.00
—No bar code on cover					
❏ PZ 34432	Go for Your Guns	198?	2.00	4.00	8.00
—Budget-line reissue with bar code					
❏ PZQ 34432 [Q]	Go for Your Guns	1977	5.00	10.00	20.00
❏ PZ 34452	Forever Gold	1977	2.50	5.00	10.00
❏ JZ 34930	Showdown	1978	2.50	5.00	10.00
❏ PZ 34930	Showdown	198?	2.00	4.00	8.00
—Budget-line reissue					
❏ KZ2 35650 [(2)]	Timeless	1978	3.00	6.00	12.00
❏ PZ2 36077 [(2)]	Winner Takes All	1979	3.00	6.00	12.00
❏ FZ 36305	Go All the Way	1980	2.50	5.00	10.00
❏ PZ 36305	Go All the Way	198?	2.00	4.00	8.00
—Budget-line reissue					
❏ FZ 37080	Grand Slam	1981	2.50	5.00	10.00
❏ PZ 37080	Grand Slam	198?	2.00	4.00	8.00
—Budget-line reissue					
❏ FZ 37533	Inside You	1981	2.50	5.00	10.00
❏ FZ 38047	The Real Deal	1982	2.50	5.00	10.00
❏ FZ 38674	Between the Sheets	1983	2.50	5.00	10.00
❏ PZ 38674	Between the Sheets	1985	2.00	4.00	8.00
—Budget-line reissue					
❏ FZ 39240	Greatest Hits, Vol. 1	1984	2.50	5.00	10.00
❏ PZ 39240	Greatest Hits, Vol. 1	1985	2.00	4.00	8.00
—Budget-line reissue					
TAMLA					
❏ T-269 [M]	This Old Heart of Mine	1966	6.25	12.50	25.00
❏ TS-269 [S]	This Old Heart of Mine	1966	7.50	15.00	30.00
❏ T-275 [M]	Soul on the Rocks	1967	6.25	12.50	25.00
❏ TS-275 [S]	Soul on the Rocks	1967	7.50	15.00	30.00
❏ TS-287	Doin' Their Thing (Best of the Isley Brothers)	1969	5.00	10.00	20.00
UNITED ARTISTS					
❏ UA-LA500-E	The Very Best of the Isley Brothers	1975	2.50	5.00	10.00
❏ UAL-3313 [M]	The Famous Isley Brothers	1963	12.50	25.00	50.00
❏ UAS-6313 [S]	The Famous Isley Brothers	1963	15.00	30.00	60.00
WAND					
❏ WD-653 [M]	Twist & Shout	1962	20.00	40.00	80.00
❏ WDS-653 [S]	Twist & Shout	1962	25.00	50.00	100.00

I

Number	Title (A Side/B Side)	Yr	VG	VG+	NM
WARNER BROS.					
❏ 25347	Masterpiece	1985	2.50	5.00	10.00
❏ 25586	Smooth Sailin'	1987	2.50	5.00	10.00
❏ 25940	Spend the Night	1989	2.50	5.00	10.00

IT'S A BEAUTIFUL DAY
45s

Number	Title (A Side/B Side)	Yr	VG	VG+	NM
COLUMBIA					
❏ 44928	White Bird/Wasted Union Blues	1969	2.00	4.00	8.00
❏ 45152	Good Lovin'/Soapstone Mountain	1970	—	3.00	6.00
❏ 45309	Do You Remember the Sun/Dolphin	1971	—	2.50	5.00
❏ 45536	Anytime/Apples and Oranges	1972	—	2.50	5.00
❏ 45788	White Bird/Wasted Union Blues	1973	—	2.50	5.00
❏ 45853	Ain't That Lovin' You Baby/Time	1973	—	3.00	6.00
SAN FRANCISCO SOUND					
❏ 11680	Aquarian Dream/Bulgaria	198?	2.50	5.00	10.00
Albums					
COLUMBIA					
❏ CS 1058	Marrying Maiden	1970	3.75	7.50	15.00
—Orange label					
❏ CS 1058	Marrying Maiden	1970	7.50	15.00	30.00
—Red "360 Sound" label					
❏ CS 9768	It's A Beautiful Day	1969	7.50	15.00	30.00
—Red "360 Sound" label					
❏ CS 9768	It's A Beautiful Day	1970	5.00	10.00	20.00
—Orange label					
❏ C 30734	Choice Quality Stuff/Anytime	1971	3.75	7.50	15.00
❏ KC 31338	It's a Beautiful Day at Carnegie Hall	1972	3.75	7.50	15.00
❏ KC 32181	It's a Beautiful Day...Today	1973	3.75	7.50	15.00
❏ KC 32660 [DJ]	A Thousand and One Nights	1973	12.50	25.00	50.00
—Canceled before commercial release?					
SAN FRANCISCO SOUND					
❏ 11790	It's A Beautiful Day	1985	6.25	12.50	25.00
—Limited reissue					

ITALIAN ASPHALT AND PAVEMENT COMPANY, THE See THE DUPREES.

IVAN
45s

Number	Title (A Side/B Side)	Yr	VG	VG+	NM
CORAL					
❏ 62017	Real Wild Child/Oh You Beautiful Doll	1958	50.00	100.00	200.00
—With Buddy Holly on guitar					
❏ 62081	That'll Be Alright/Frankie Frankenstein	1959	100.00	200.00	400.00
❏ 65607	Real Wild Child/That'll Be Alright	1967	12.50	25.00	50.00

IVERS, PETER
Albums

Number	Title (A Side/B Side)	Yr	VG	VG+	NM
EPIC					
❏ BN 26500	Knight of the Blue Communion	1970	10.00	20.00	40.00
WARNER BROS.					
❏ BS 2804	Terminal Love	1974	3.00	6.00	12.00
❏ BS 2930	Peter Ivers	1976	3.00	6.00	12.00

IVES, BURL
45s

Number	Title (A Side/B Side)	Yr	VG	VG+	NM
BELL					
❏ 930	Real Roses/Roll Up Some Inspiration	1970	—	2.50	5.00
❏ 943	Time/Galisteo	1970	—	2.50	5.00
BIG TREE					
❏ 130	Gingerbread House/Tumbleweed Snowman	1971	—	2.50	5.00
BUENA VISTA					
❏ 419	On the Front Porch/Ugly Bug Ball	1963	2.00	4.00	8.00
❏ 419 [PS]	On the Front Porch/Ugly Bug Ball	1963	3.00	6.00	12.00
COLUMBIA					
❏ 4-124	Grandfather Kringle/The 12 Days Of Christmas	1951	3.00	6.00	12.00
—Yellow-label "Chidren's Series" record; alternate number is 90138					
❏ 4-124 [PS]	Grandfather Kringle/The 12 Days Of Christmas	1951	3.75	7.50	15.00
❏ 1-173	Riders in the Sky (Cowboy Legend)/Wayfaring Stranger-Woolie Boogie Bee	1949	10.00	20.00	40.00
—Microgroove 33 1/3 rpm 7-inch single					
❏ 1-418	Mule Train/Greer County Bachelor	1950	7.50	15.00	30.00
—Microgroove 33 1/3 rpm 7-inch single					
❏ 1-550 (?)	John Henry/Mah Lindy Lou	1950	7.50	15.00	30.00
—Microgroove 33 1/3 rpm 7-inch single					
❏ 1-580 (?)	The Doughnut Song/I Got a Fever in My Bones	1950	7.50	15.00	30.00
—Microgroove 33 1/3 rpm 7-inch single					
❏ 1-630 (?)	Got the World by the Tail/My Momma Told Me	1950	7.50	15.00	30.00
—Microgroove 33 1/3 rpm 7-inch single					
❏ 1-780 (?)	Pig Pig/Last Night the Nightingale Woke Me	1950	7.50	15.00	30.00
—Microgroove 33 1/3 rpm 7-inch single					
❏ 6-780 (?)	Pig Pig/Last Night the Nightingale Woke Me	1950	6.25	12.50	25.00
❏ 1-910 (?)	There's a Little White House/Little White Duck	1950	7.50	15.00	30.00
—Microgroove 33 1/3 rpm 7-inch single					
❏ 6-910 (?)	There's a Little White House/Little White Duck	1950	6.25	12.50	25.00
❏ 39328	On Top of Old Smoky/The Syncopated Clock	1951	3.75	7.50	15.00
—With Percy Faith co-credited					
❏ 44508	I'll Be Your Baby Tonight/Maria	1968	—	3.00	6.00
❏ 44606	Little Green Apples/One Too Many Mornings	1968	—	3.00	6.00
❏ 44711	Santa Mouse/Oh What a Lucky Boy Am I	1968	—	3.00	6.00
❏ 44711 [PS]	Santa Mouse/Oh What a Lucky Boy Am I	1968	2.50	5.00	10.00
❏ 44974	Montego Bay/Tessie's Bar Mystery	1969	—	3.00	6.00
CYCLONE					
❏ 75014	One More Time Billy Brown/Tied Down Here at Home	1970	—	3.50	7.00
DECCA					
❏ 25524	Mockin' Bird Hill/Royal Telephone (Telephone to Glory)	196?	2.00	4.00	8.00
❏ 25585	Twelve Days of Christmas/The Indian Christmas Carol	1962	2.50	5.00	10.00
❏ 25691	You Know You Belong to Someone Else/Jealous	196?	2.00	4.00	8.00
❏ 25754	I Talk to the Trees/They Call the Wind Maria	1970	—	3.00	6.00
❏ 27079	This Time Tomorrow/One Hour Ahead of the Posse	1950	5.00	10.00	20.00
❏ 28055	Wild Side of Life/It's So Long and Goodbye to You	1952	3.75	7.50	15.00
❏ 28079	This Time Tomorrow/One Hour Ahead of the Posse	1952	3.75	7.50	15.00
❏ 28161	Diesel Smoke, Dangerous Curves/The Little Green Valley	1952	3.75	7.50	15.00
—With Grady Martin					
❏ 28299	There's a Mule Up in Tombstone, Arizona/Lonesome, So Lonesome	1952	3.75	7.50	15.00
❏ 28347	The Friendly Beasts/There Were Three Ships	1952	3.00	6.00	12.00
❏ 28348	Jesous Anatonia/What Child Is This	1952	3.00	6.00	12.00
❏ 28349	The Seven Joys of Mary (Part 1)/The Seven Joys of Mary (Part 2)	1952	3.00	6.00	12.00
❏ 28350	King Herod and the Clock/Down in Yon Forest	1952	3.00	6.00	12.00
—The above four comprise a box set					
❏ 28708	Close the Door Richard/Left My Gal in the Mountains	1953	3.75	7.50	15.00
❏ 28849	Great White Bird/Brighten the Corner Where You Are	1953	3.75	7.50	15.00
❏ 28935	The Crawdad Song/Hound Dog	1953	3.75	7.50	15.00
❏ 29039	There's Plenty of Fish in the Ocean/The Old Red Barn	1954	3.75	7.50	15.00
❏ 29088	True Love Goes On and On/Brave Man	1954	3.75	7.50	15.00
❏ 29129	Wait for Me Darling/Casey Jones	1954	3.00	6.00	12.00
❏ 29282	The Mission San Miguel/Tangled Web	1954	3.75	7.50	15.00
❏ 29423	The Ballad of Davy Crockett/Goober Peas	1955	3.75	7.50	15.00
❏ 29533	I Wonder What's Become of Sally/Wabash Cannonball	1955	3.00	6.00	12.00
❏ 29549	Be Sure You're Right (Then Go Ahead)/Ol' Betsy	1955	3.75	7.50	15.00
❏ 29910	Jack Was Every Inch a Sailor/Harlem Man	1956	3.00	6.00	12.00
❏ 30046	The Bus Stop Song/That's My Heart Strings	1956	3.00	6.00	12.00
❏ 30217	Marianne/Pretty Girl	1957	3.00	6.00	12.00
❏ 30855	We Love Ye, Jimmy/I Never See Maggie Alone	1959	3.00	6.00	12.00
❏ 31248	Long Black Veil/Forty Hour Week	1961	2.50	5.00	10.00
❏ 31330	A Little Bitty Tear/Shanghai	1961	2.50	5.00	10.00
❏ 31371	Funny Way of Laughin'/Mother Wouldn't Do That	1962	2.50	5.00	10.00
❏ 31405	Call Me Mr. In-Between/What You Gonna Do, Leroy	1962	2.50	5.00	10.00
❏ 31433	Mary Ann Regrets/How Do You Fall Out of Love	1962	2.50	5.00	10.00
❏ 31453	The Same Old Hurt/Curry Road	1963	2.50	5.00	10.00
❏ 31479	Roses and Orchids/Baby Come Home to Me	1963	2.50	5.00	10.00
❏ 31504	I'm the Boss/The Moon Is High	1963	2.50	5.00	10.00
❏ 31518	This Is All I Ask/There Goes Another Pal of Mine	1963	2.50	5.00	10.00
❏ 31543	It Comes and Goes/I Found My Best Friend in the Dog Pound	1963	2.50	5.00	10.00
❏ 31571	True Love Goes On and On/I Wonder What's Become of Sally	1963	2.50	5.00	10.00
❏ 31610	Four Initials on a Tree/This Is Your Day	1964	2.00	4.00	8.00
❏ 31659	Pearly Shells/What Little Tears Are Made Of	1964	2.00	4.00	8.00
❏ 31695	A Holly Jolly Christmas/Snow for Johnny	1964	2.50	5.00	10.00
❏ 31729	Call My Name/My Gal Sal	1965	2.00	4.00	8.00
❏ 31772	On the Beach at Waikiki/Some Hangin' Round You All the Time	1965	2.00	4.00	8.00
❏ 31811	Salt Water Guitar/The Story of Bobby Lee Trent	1965	2.00	4.00	8.00
❏ 31857	Frangipani/A Girl Sittin' Up in a Tree	1965	2.00	4.00	8.00
❏ 31918	The Sixties/Don't Forget Your Paddle	1966	2.00	4.00	8.00
❏ 31981	Here She Comes (There She Goes)/Atlantic Coastal Line	1966	2.00	4.00	8.00
❏ 31997	Evil Off My Mind/Taste of Heaven	1966	2.00	4.00	8.00
❏ 32078	Lonesome 7-7203/Hollow Words	1967	2.00	4.00	8.00
❏ 32165	Funny Little Show/Holding Hands for Joe	1967	2.00	4.00	8.00
❏ 32282	Bury the Bottle/That's Where My Baby Used to Be	1968	2.00	4.00	8.00
❏ 32990	Stayin' Song/The Best Is Yet to Come	1972	—	3.00	6.00
❏ 33049	Miss Johnson's Happiness Emporium/Anytime You Say	1972	—	3.00	6.00
DISNEYLAND					
❏ F-130	Chim Chim Chiree/Lavender Blue	1964	2.00	4.00	8.00
❏ F-130 [PS]	Chim Chim Chiree/Lavender Blue	1964	3.00	6.00	12.00
MCA					
❏ 31695	A Holly Jolly Christmas/Snow for Johnny	1989	—	2.50	5.00
—Double the NM value if insert is enclosed					
❏ 40082	Payin' My Dues Again/All Around	1973	—	2.50	5.00
❏ 40175	Tale of the Comet Kohoutek/A Very Fine Lady	1974	—	2.50	5.00
MONKEY JOE					
❏ MJ-1 [DJ]	The Christmas Legend of Monkey Joe/It's Gonna Be A Mixed Up Xmas	1978	2.50	5.00	10.00
UNITED ARTISTS					
❏ 293	Alexander's Ragtime Band/Say It Isn't So	1961	2.00	4.00	8.00
❏ 429	All Alone/Always	1962	2.00	4.00	8.00
❏ 1568	Go 'Way from My House/Two Maidens Went Milking	196?	2.00	4.00	8.00
❏ 1569	Willie Boy/Irish Rover	196?	2.00	4.00	8.00
❏ 1570	Alexander's Ragtime Band/What'll I Do	196?	2.00	4.00	8.00
❏ 1571	All Alone/Always	196?	2.00	4.00	8.00
—The above four all are "Silver Spotlight Series" releases					
7-Inch Extended Plays					
DECCA					
❏ ED 2103	*Dublin City/Cockle Shells/Old Dan Tucker/The Erie Canal/The Eddystone Light/Hullabaloo-Belay/Venezuela	195?	3.00	6.00	12.00
❏ ED 2103 [PS]	Burl Ives, Vol. 1	195?	3.00	6.00	12.00
❏ ED 2235	*The Locktender's Lament/Ox Driver's Song/The Bold Soldier/The Young Married Man (Cod Liver Oil)/Sad Man's Song (Fare Thee Well, O Honey)/The Harlem Man	195?	3.00	6.00	12.00
❏ ED 2235 [PS]	Songs For and About Men, Part 1	195?	3.00	6.00	12.00
❏ ED 2236	The Western Settler/Waltzing Matilda (The Jolly Swagman's Song)/The Wild Rover/Frankie and Johnny/The Deceiver	195?	3.00	6.00	12.00
❏ ED 2236 [PS]	Songs For and About Men, Part 2	195?	3.00	6.00	12.00
❏ ED 2714	(contents unknown)	1961	2.50	5.00	10.00
❏ ED 2714 [PS]	Burl Ives	1961	2.50	5.00	10.00
❏ ED 2720	Funny Way of Laughin'/Mother Wouldn't Do That/What You Gonna Do Leroy/I Ain't Comin' Home Tonight	1962	2.50	5.00	10.00
❏ ED 2720 [PS]	It's Just My Funny Way of Laughin'	1962	2.50	5.00	10.00
❏ ED 2726	Call Me Mr. In-Between/Poor Little Jimmie//In Foggy Old London/Thumbin' Johnny Brown	1962	2.50	5.00	10.00

Janis Ian, "At Seventeen," Columbia 3-10154, picture sleeve, $4-$8.

Ian and Sylvia, *Northern Journey,* Vanguard VSD-79154, stereo LP, $12.50-$25.

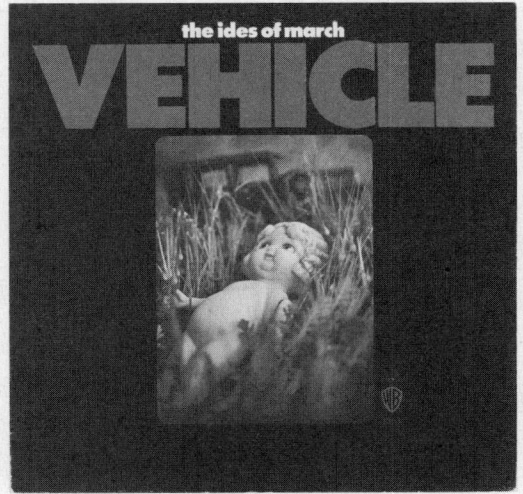

The Ides of March, *Vehicle,* Warner Bros. WS 1863, stereo LP, green label with "W7" logo in a box at top, $10-$20.

The Impressions, *Keep On Pushing,* ABC-Paramount ABC-493, mono LP, $15-$30.

The Isley Brothers, *Harvest for the World,* T-Neck PZ 33809, stereo LP, no bar code on cover, $6-$12.

Burl Ives, *The Wayfaring Stranger,* Columbia CL 628, mono LP, maroon label with silver print, $15-$30.

Number	Title (A Side/B Side)	Yr	VG	VG+	NM
❏ ED 2726 [PS]	Call Me Mr. In-Between	1962	2.50	5.00	10.00
❏ ED 2741	(contents unknown)	1962	2.50	5.00	10.00
❏ ED 2741 [PS]	Mary Ann Regrets	1962	2.50	5.00	10.00
❏ ED 2771	True Love Goes On and On/This Is All I Ask//It Comes and Goes/I'm the Boss	1963	2.50	5.00	10.00
❏ ED 2771 [PS]	True Love Goes On and On	1963	2.50	5.00	10.00

Albums
BELL

Number	Title (A Side/B Side)	Yr	VG	VG+	NM
❏ 6055	Time	1971	2.50	5.00	10.00

COLUMBIA

Number	Title (A Side/B Side)	Yr	VG	VG+	NM
❏ CL 628 [M]	The Wayfaring Stranger	1955	7.50	15.00	30.00
❏ CL 980 [M]	Burl Ives Sings Songs for All Ages	1956	7.50	15.00	30.00
❏ CL 1459 [M]	Return of the Wayfaring Stranger	1960	7.50	15.00	30.00
❏ CL 2570 [10]	Children's Favorites	1955	10.00	20.00	40.00
—"House Party Series" issue					
❏ CL 6058 [10]	The Return of the Wayfaring Stranger	1949	12.50	25.00	50.00
❏ CL 6109 [10]	The Wayfaring Stranger	1950	12.50	25.00	50.00
❏ CL 6144 [10]	More Folk Songs	1950	12.50	25.00	50.00
❏ CS 9041 [R]	The Wayfaring Stranger	1964	3.00	6.00	12.00
❏ CS 9675	The Times They Are a-Changin'	1969	3.00	6.00	12.00
❏ CS 9728	Burl Ives Christmas Album	1968	3.00	6.00	12.00
❏ CS 9925	Softly and Tenderly	1969	3.00	6.00	12.00

DECCA

Number	Title (A Side/B Side)	Yr	VG	VG+	NM
❏ DXB 167 [(2)M]	The Best of Burl Ives	1961	6.25	12.50	25.00
❏ DL 4152 [M]	The Versatile Burl Ives	1961	3.75	7.50	15.00
❏ DL 4179 [M]	Songs of the West	1961	3.75	7.50	15.00
❏ DL 4279 [M]	It's Just My Funny Way of Laughin'	1962	3.75	7.50	15.00
❏ DL 4304 [M]	Sing Out, Sweet Land	1962	3.75	7.50	15.00
❏ DL 4320 [M]	Sunshine in My Soul	1962	3.75	7.50	15.00
❏ DL 4361 [M]	Burl	1963	3.75	7.50	15.00
❏ DL 4390 [M]	The Best of Burl's for Boys and Girls	1963	3.75	7.50	15.00
❏ DL 4433 [M]	Singin' Easy	1964	3.75	7.50	15.00
❏ DL 4533 [M]	True Love	1964	3.75	7.50	15.00
❏ DL 4578 [M]	Pearly Shells	1964	3.75	7.50	15.00
❏ DL 4606 [M]	My Gal Sal	1965	3.00	6.00	12.00
❏ DL 4668 [M]	On the Beach at Waikiki	1965	3.00	6.00	12.00
❏ DL 4689 [M]	Have a Holly Jolly Christmas	1965	3.00	6.00	12.00
❏ DL 4734 [M]	Burl's Choice	1966	3.00	6.00	12.00
❏ DL 4789 [M]	Something Special	1966	3.00	6.00	12.00
❏ DL 4850 [M]	Burl Ives' Greatest Hits	1967	3.75	7.50	15.00
❏ DL 4876 [M]	Broadway	1967	3.75	7.50	15.00
❏ DL 4972 [M]	Big Country Hits	1968	3.75	7.50	15.00
❏ DL 5013 [10]	Ballads and Folk Songs, Volume II	1949	12.50	25.00	50.00
❏ DL 5080 [10]	A Collection of Ballads and Folk Songs, Volume One	1949	12.50	25.00	50.00
❏ DL 5093 [10]	Ballads, Folk and Country Songs	1949	12.50	25.00	50.00
❏ DL 5428 [10]	Christmas Day in the Morning	1952	12.50	25.00	50.00
❏ DL 5467 [10]	Folk Songs Dramatic and Dangerous	1953	12.50	25.00	50.00
❏ DL 5490 [10]	Women: Folk Songs About the Fair Sex	1954	12.50	25.00	50.00
❏ DXSB 7167 [(2)S]	The Best of Burl Ives	1961	7.50	15.00	30.00
❏ DL 8080 [M]	Coronation Concert	1953	10.00	20.00	40.00
❏ DL 8107 [M]	The Wild Side of Life	1955	6.25	12.50	25.00
❏ DL 8125 [M]	Men	1956	6.25	12.50	25.00
❏ DL 8245 [M]	Down to the Sea in Ships	1956	6.25	12.50	25.00
❏ DL 8246 [M]	Women	1956	6.25	12.50	25.00
❏ DL 8247 [M]	In the Quiet of Night	1956	6.25	12.50	25.00
❏ DL 8248 [M]	Burl Ives Sings for Fun	1956	6.25	12.50	25.00
❏ DL 8391 [M]	Christmas Eve	1957	6.25	12.50	25.00
❏ DL 8444 [M]	Songs of Ireland	1958	6.25	12.50	25.00
❏ DL 8587 [M]	Captain Burl Ives' Ark	1958	6.25	12.50	25.00
❏ DL 8637 [M]	Old Time Varieties	1958	6.25	12.50	25.00
❏ DL 8749 [M]	Australian Folk Songs	1959	6.25	12.50	25.00
❏ DL 8886 [M]	Cheers	1959	6.25	12.50	25.00
❏ DL 74152 [S]	The Versatile Burl Ives	1961	5.00	10.00	20.00
❏ DL 74179 [S]	Songs of the West	1961	5.00	10.00	20.00
❏ DL 74279 [S]	It's Just My Funny Way of Laughin'	1962	5.00	10.00	20.00
❏ DL 74304 [S]	Sing Out, Sweet Land	1962	5.00	10.00	20.00
❏ DL 74320 [S]	Sunshine in My Soul	1962	5.00	10.00	20.00
❏ DL 74361 [S]	Burl	1963	5.00	10.00	20.00
❏ DL 74390 [S]	The Best of Burl's for Boys and Girls	1963	5.00	10.00	20.00
❏ DL 74433 [S]	Singin' Easy	1964	5.00	10.00	20.00
❏ DL 74533 [S]	True Love	1964	5.00	10.00	20.00
❏ DL 74578 [S]	Pearly Shells	1964	5.00	10.00	20.00
❏ DL 74606 [S]	My Gal Sal	1965	3.75	7.50	15.00
❏ DL 74668 [S]	On the Beach at Waikiki	1965	3.75	7.50	15.00
❏ DL 74689 [S]	Have a Holly Jolly Christmas	1965	3.75	7.50	15.00
❏ DL 74734 [S]	Burl's Choice	1966	3.75	7.50	15.00
❏ DL 74789 [S]	Something Special	1966	3.75	7.50	15.00
❏ DL 74850 [S]	Burl Ives' Greatest Hits	1967	3.00	6.00	12.00
❏ DL 74876 [S]	Broadway	1967	3.00	6.00	12.00
❏ DL 74972 [S]	Big Country Hits	1968	3.00	6.00	12.00
❏ DL 78391 [R]	Christmas Eve	196?	2.50	5.00	10.00
❏ DL 78886 [S]	Cheers	1959	7.50	15.00	30.00

DISNEYLAND

Number	Title (A Side/B Side)	Yr	VG	VG+	NM
❏ ST-3927 [M]	Chim Chim Chiree and Other Children's Choices	1964	3.75	7.50	15.00
❏ STER-3927 [S]	Chim Chim Chiree and Other Children's Choices	1964	5.00	10.00	20.00

EVEREST ARCHIVE OF FOLK & JAZZ

Number	Title (A Side/B Side)	Yr	VG	VG+	NM
❏ 340	Burl Ives Live	1978	2.50	5.00	10.00

HARMONY

Number	Title (A Side/B Side)	Yr	VG	VG+	NM
❏ HL 9507 [M]	The Little White Duck	196?	3.75	7.50	15.00
❏ HL 9551 [M]	The Lollipop Tree	196?	3.75	7.50	15.00
❏ HS 11275	Got the World by the Tail	196?	2.50	5.00	10.00

MCA

Number	Title (A Side/B Side)	Yr	VG	VG+	NM
❏ 114	Burl Ives' Greatest Hits	1973	2.50	5.00	10.00
—Reissue of Decca 74850					
❏ 318	Paying My Dues Again	1973	2.50	5.00	10.00

Number	Title (A Side/B Side)	Yr	VG	VG+	NM
❏ 4034 [(2)]	The Best of Burl Ives	197?	3.00	6.00	12.00
❏ 4089 [(2)]	The Best of Burl Ives Volume 2	197?	3.00	6.00	12.00
❏ 15002	Have a Holly Jolly Christmas	1973	3.00	6.00	12.00
—Reissue of Decca 74689; black label with rainbow					
❏ 15002	Have a Holly Jolly Christmas	1980	2.00	4.00	8.00
—Blue label with rainbow					
❏ 15030	Santa Claus Is Coming to Town	198?	2.50	5.00	10.00

NATIONAL GEOGRAPHIC

Number	Title (A Side/B Side)	Yr	VG	VG+	NM
❏ 07806	We Americans	1978	3.00	6.00	12.00

PICKWICK

Number	Title (A Side/B Side)	Yr	VG	VG+	NM
❏ SPC-1018	Twelve Days of Christmas	197?	2.50	5.00	10.00

STINSON

Number	Title (A Side/B Side)	Yr	VG	VG+	NM
❏ SLP-1 [10]	The Wayfaring Stranger	1949	15.00	30.00	60.00

SUNSET

Number	Title (A Side/B Side)	Yr	VG	VG+	NM
❏ SUS-5280	Favorites	1970	2.50	5.00	10.00

UNITED ARTISTS

Number	Title (A Side/B Side)	Yr	VG	VG+	NM
❏ UAL 3060 [M]	Ballads	1959	3.75	7.50	15.00
❏ UAS 6060 [S]	Ballads	1959	5.00	10.00	20.00

WORD

Number	Title (A Side/B Side)	Yr	VG	VG+	NM
❏ 3259 [M]	Faith and Joy	196?	3.75	7.50	15.00
❏ 3339 [M]	Shall We Gather at the River	1966	3.00	6.00	12.00
❏ 3391 [M]	I Do Believe	1967	3.00	6.00	12.00
❏ 8140 [S]	Faith and Joy	196?	5.00	10.00	20.00
❏ 8339 [S]	Shall We Gather at the River	1966	3.75	7.50	15.00
❏ 8391 [S]	I Do Believe	1967	3.75	7.50	15.00
❏ 8537	How Great Thou Art	1971	3.00	6.00	12.00

IVEYS, THE See BADFINGER.

IVOLEERS, THE
45s
BUZZ

Number	Title (A Side/B Side)	Yr	VG	VG+	NM
❏ 101	Lover's Quarrel/Come with Me	1959	100.00	200.00	400.00

IVORY
Albums
PLAYBOY

Number	Title (A Side/B Side)	Yr	VG	VG+	NM
❏ 115	Ivory	1973	3.00	6.00	12.00

TETRAGRAMMATON

Number	Title (A Side/B Side)	Yr	VG	VG+	NM
❏ T-104	Ivory	1968	5.00	10.00	20.00

IVORY, JACKIE
45s
ATCO

Number	Title (A Side/B Side)	Yr	VG	VG+	NM
❏ 6398	Hi-Heel Sneakers/Three Tickets to Georgia	1966	2.50	5.00	10.00

Albums
ATCO

Number	Title (A Side/B Side)	Yr	VG	VG+	NM
❏ 33-178 [M]	Soul Discovery	1965	5.00	10.00	20.00
❏ SD 33-178 [S]	Soul Discovery	1965	6.25	12.50	25.00

IVORYS, THE
45s
DARLA

Number	Title (A Side/B Side)	Yr	VG	VG+	NM
❏ 1000	Wishing Well/Deep Freeze	1962	100.00	200.00	400.00

SPARTA

Number	Title (A Side/B Side)	Yr	VG	VG+	NM
❏ 001	Why Don't You Write Me/Deep Freeze	1962	20.00	40.00	80.00

IVY LEAGUE, THE
45s
CAMEO

Number	Title (A Side/B Side)	Yr	VG	VG+	NM
❏ 343	Wait a Minute/What More Do You Want	1965	3.75	7.50	15.00
❏ 356	Lonely Room/Funny How Love Can Be	1965	3.75	7.50	15.00
❏ 365	A Girl Like You/That's Why I'm Crying	1965	3.75	7.50	15.00
❏ 377	Tossing & Turning/Graduation Day	1965	3.75	7.50	15.00
❏ 388	Our Love Is Slipping Away/I Could Make You Fall in Love	1966	3.75	7.50	15.00
❏ 388 [PS]	Our Love Is Slipping Away/I Could Make You Fall in Love	1966	6.25	12.50	25.00
❏ 402	Rain Rain Go Away/Running Around in Circles	1966	3.75	7.50	15.00
❏ 449	When You're Young/My World Fell Down	1966	3.75	7.50	15.00

Albums
CAMEO

Number	Title (A Side/B Side)	Yr	VG	VG+	NM
❏ C 2000 [M]	Tossing and Turning	1965	7.50	15.00	30.00
❏ CS 2000 [R]	Tossing and Turning	1965	7.50	15.00	30.00

IVY THREE, THE
45s
SHELL

Number	Title (A Side/B Side)	Yr	VG	VG+	NM
❏ 302	Nine Out of Ten/I've Cried Enough for Two	1961	5.00	10.00	20.00
—Multicolored label					
❏ 302	Nine Out of Ten/I've Cried Enough for Two	1961	7.50	15.00	30.00
—Gold label					
❏ 306	Bagoo/Suicide	1961	3.75	7.50	15.00
❏ 720	Yogi/Was Judy There	1960	5.00	10.00	20.00
—Originals have blue labels					
❏ 720	Yogi/Was Judy There	1961	3.75	7.50	15.00
—Reissues have multicolored labels					
❏ 723	Alone in the Chapel/Hush Little Baby	1960	6.25	12.50	25.00

IVY-TONES, THE
45s
RED TOP

Number	Title (A Side/B Side)	Yr	VG	VG+	NM
❏ 105	Oo-Wee Baby/Each Time	1958	3.75	7.50	15.00
—Red label					
❏ 105	Oo-Wee Baby/Each Time	1958	5.00	10.00	20.00
—Blue label					

Number	Title (A Side/B Side)	Yr	VG	VG+	NM

J

J.B. AND THE HAWKS See J.B. HUTTO.

J.B.'S, THE See FRED WESLEY.

J.K. AND COMPANY
Albums
BEAT ROCKET
| ❏ BR-126 | Suddenly One Summer | 2000 | 3.00 | 6.00 | 12.00 |

—Reissue on 180-gram vinyl
WHITE WHALE
| ❏ WWS-7117 | Suddenly One Summer | 1969 | 6.25 | 12.50 | 25.00 |

JACKIE AND JILL
45s
U.S.A.
| ❏ 791 | I Want a Beatle for Christmas/Jingle Bells | 1964 | 5.00 | 10.00 | 20.00 |

JACKIE AND THE GIANTS
45s
HIT
❏ 185	I Go to Pieces/Ford G.T.	1965	2.50	5.00	10.00
❏ 209	I'm Telling You Now/Come On In	1965	2.50	5.00	10.00
❏ 230	Turn! Turn! Turn!/May the Bird of Paradise Fly Up Your Nose	1965	2.50	5.00	10.00

—B-side by Buddy Scott

JACKIE AND THE RAINDROPS
45s
COLPIX
| ❏ 738 | Down Our Street/My Heart Is Your Heart | 1964 | 2.50 | 5.00 | 10.00 |

JACKIE AND THE STARLITES
45s
EVERLAST
| ❏ 5027 | Valarie/Way Up in the Sky | 1964 | 3.75 | 7.50 | 15.00 |

—As "The Starlites"
FIRE & FURY
| ❏ 1000 | They Laughed at Me/You Put One Over on Me | 1959 | 500.00 | 1000. | 2000. |

FURY
| ❏ 1034 | Valarie/Way Up in the Sky | 1960 | 20.00 | 40.00 | 80.00 |

—As "The Starlites"
| ❏ 1045 | Silver Lining/Ain't Cha' Ever Coming Home | 1961 | 12.50 | 25.00 | 50.00 |

—As "The Starlites"
| ❏ 1057 | I Found Out Too Late/I'm Coming Home | 1962 | 7.50 | 15.00 | 30.00 |

HULL
| ❏ 760 | I Cried My Heart Out/I Still Remember | 1964 | 12.50 | 25.00 | 50.00 |

LANA
| ❏ 120 | Valarie/Lonesome Boy | 196? | 2.00 | 4.00 | 8.00 |

LOST-NITE
| ❏ 185 | Valarie/Way Up in the Sky | 196? | — | 3.00 | 6.00 |

—As "The Starlites"; reissue
| ❏ 444 | I Found Out Too Late/I'm Coming Home | 197? | — | 3.00 | 6.00 |

—Reissue
MASCOT
| ❏ 128 | For All We Know/I Heard You | 1962 | 10.00 | 20.00 | 40.00 |

—With horseshoe on label
| ❏ 128 | For All We Know/I Heard You | 1962 | 15.00 | 30.00 | 60.00 |

—No horseshoe on label
| ❏ 130 | You Keep Telling Me/Sha Pobo Baby | 1962 | 12.50 | 25.00 | 50.00 |
| ❏ 131 | I'll Burn Your Letter/Walking from School | 1963 | 12.50 | 25.00 | 50.00 |

SPHERE SOUND
| ❏ 705 | Seven Day Fool/Don't Be Afraid | 1966 | 20.00 | 40.00 | 80.00 |

—As "The Starlites"

JACKS, TERRY Also see THE POPPY FAMILY.
45s
BELL
❏ 45432	Seasons in the Sun/Put the Bone In	1974	—	2.50	5.00
❏ 45467	If You Go Away/Me and You	1974	—	2.00	4.00
❏ 45606	Love Game/Rock and Roll	1974	—	2.00	4.00

LONDON
| ❏ 181 | Concrete Sea/She Even Took the Cat | 1972 | — | 2.50 | 5.00 |
| ❏ 188 | I'm Gonna Love You, Too/Something Good Was Over Before It Ever Got to Start | 1972 | — | 2.50 | 5.00 |

PARROT
| ❏ 347 | A Good Thing Lost/I'm Gonna Capture You | 1970 | — | 3.00 | 6.00 |

PRIVATE STOCK
| ❏ 45,023 | Christina/The Feeling That We've Lost | 1975 | — | 2.00 | 4.00 |
| ❏ 45,094 | In My Father's Footsteps/Until You're Down | 1976 | — | 2.00 | 4.00 |

Albums
BELL
| ❏ 1307 | Seasons in the Sun | 1974 | 2.50 | 5.00 | 10.00 |

JACKS, THE Also see THE CADETS.
45s
KENT
| ❏ 344 | Why Don't You Write Me/This Empty Heart | 1960 | 3.75 | 7.50 | 15.00 |

RPM
❏ 428	Why Don't You Write Me/My Darling	1955	15.00	30.00	60.00
❏ 428	Why Don't You Write Me/Smack Dab in the Middle	1955	50.00	100.00	200.00
❏ 433	I'm Confessin'/Since My Baby's Been Gone	1955	15.00	30.00	60.00
❏ 444	This Empty Heart/My Clumsy Heart	1955	12.50	25.00	50.00
❏ 454	So Wrong/How Soon	1956	12.50	25.00	50.00
❏ 458	Sugar Baby/Why Did I Fall in Love	1956	15.00	30.00	60.00
❏ 467	Let's Make Up/Dream a Little Longer	1956	15.00	30.00	60.00

Albums
CROWN
❏ CST-372 [R]	Jumpin' with the Jacks	1962	12.50	25.00	50.00
❏ CLP-5021 [M]	Jumpin' with the Jacks	1960	50.00	100.00	200.00
❏ CLP-5372 [M]	Jumpin' with the Jacks	1962	25.00	50.00	100.00

RELIC
| ❏ 5023 | The Jacks' Greatest Hits | 198? | 2.50 | 5.00 | 10.00 |

RPM
| ❏ LRP-3006 [M] | Jumpin' with the Jacks | 1956 | 1000. | 1500. | 2000. |

UNITED
| ❏ US-7797 | Rock 'n' Roll Hits of the 50's | 197? | 3.75 | 7.50 | 15.00 |

JACKSON, BULL MOOSE
45s
BOGUS
| ❏ 12-042684 | Get Off the Table, Mable (The Two Dollars Is For the Beer)/I've Got a Gal Who Lives Up on a Hill | 1984 | — | 2.50 | 5.00 |
| ❏ 12-042684 [PS] | Get Off the Table, Mable (The Two Dollars Is For the Beer)/I've Got a Gal Who Lives Up on a Hill | 1984 | — | 2.50 | 5.00 |

ENCINO
| ❏ 1005 | Understanding/(B-side unknown) | 1957 | 15.00 | 30.00 | 60.00 |

KING
| ❏ 4181 | I Love You Yes I Do/Sneaky Pete | 1951 | 15.00 | 30.00 | 60.00 |

—78 originally released in 1947
| ❏ 4189 | I Want a Bowlegged Woman/All My Love Belongs to You | 1951 | 20.00 | 40.00 | 80.00 |

—78 originally released in 1948 -- 5191 and 5198 are the only legitimate 45s known before 4451
❏ 4451	Trust in Me/Wonder When My Baby's Coming Home	1951	15.00	30.00	60.00
❏ 4462	Unless/End This Misery	1951	15.00	30.00	60.00
❏ 4472	Cherokee Boogie/I'm Lucky I Have You	1951	15.00	30.00	60.00
❏ 4493	I'll Be Home for Christmas/I Never Loved Anyone But You	1951	15.00	30.00	60.00
❏ 4524	Nosey Joe/Sad	1952	20.00	40.00	80.00
❏ 4535	(Let Me Love You) All Night Long/Bootsie	1952	15.00	30.00	60.00
❏ 4551	Bearcat Blues/There Is No Greater Love	1952	15.00	30.00	60.00
❏ 4580	Big Ten Inch Record/I Needed You	1952	50.00	100.00	200.00
❏ 4634	Meet Me with Your Black Dress On/Try to Forget Him	1953	10.00	20.00	40.00
❏ 4655	If You'll Let Me/Hodge Podge	1953	10.00	20.00	40.00
❏ 4775	If You Ain't Lovin'/I Wanna Hug Ya, Kiss Ya	1955	6.25	12.50	25.00
❏ 4802	I'm Glad for Your Sake/Must You Keep On Pretending	1955	6.25	12.50	25.00

SEVEN ARTS
| ❏ 705 | I Love You Yes I Do/Aw Shucks Baby | 1961 | 5.00 | 10.00 | 20.00 |

WARWICK
| ❏ 575 | I Found My Love/More of the Same | 1960 | 5.00 | 10.00 | 20.00 |

7-Inch Extended Plays
KING
| ❏ EP-211 | *I Love You, Yes I Do/I Want a Bowlegged Woman/All My Love Belongs to You/Little Girl Don't Cry | 1953 | 37.50 | 75.00 | 150.00 |
| ❏ EP-211 [PS] | Bull Moose Jackson Sings His All Time Hits | 1953 | 37.50 | 75.00 | 150.00 |

Albums
AUDIO LAB
| ❏ AL-1524 [M] | Bull Moose Jackson | 1959 | 150.00 | 300.00 | 600.00 |

BOGUS
| ❏ 6-0214851 | Moosemania! | 1985 | 2.50 | 5.00 | 10.00 |

JACKSON, CHUCK
45s
ABC
❏ 11368	I Only Get This Feeling/Slowly But Surely	1973	—	3.00	6.00
❏ 11398	I Can't Break Away/Just a Little Tear	1973	—	3.00	6.00
❏ 11423	If Only You Believe/Maybe This Will Be the Morning	1974	—	3.00	6.00
❏ 12024	Take Off Your Make-Up/Talk a Little Less	1974	—	3.00	6.00

ALL PLATINUM
❏ 2357	Love Lights/(Instrumental)	1975	—	2.50	5.00
❏ 2360	I'm Needing You, Wanting You/We Can't Hide It Anymore	1975	—	2.50	5.00
❏ 2363	If You Were My Woman (Part 1)/If You Were My Woman (Part 2)	1976	—	2.50	5.00
❏ 2370	One of Those Yesterdays/Love Lights	1976	—	2.50	5.00
❏ 2373	I Fell Asleep/One of Those Yesterdays	1976	—	2.50	5.00

AMY
| ❏ 849 | Come On and Love Me/Ooh Baby | 1962 | 3.75 | 7.50 | 15.00 |
| ❏ 868 | I'm Yours/Hula Lula | 1962 | 3.75 | 7.50 | 15.00 |

ATCO
| ❏ 6197 | Never Let Me Go/Baby I Want to Marry You | 1961 | 3.00 | 6.00 | 12.00 |

BELTONE
| ❏ 1005 | Mr. Price/Hula Lula | 1961 | 5.00 | 10.00 | 20.00 |

CLOCK
| ❏ 1015 | Come On and Love Me/Ooh Baby | 1959 | 6.25 | 12.50 | 25.00 |

—Clock sides as "Charles Jackson"
| ❏ 1022 | Hula Lula/I'm Yours | 1960 | 6.25 | 12.50 | 25.00 |
| ❏ 1027 | This Is It/Mr. Pride | 1960 | 6.25 | 12.50 | 25.00 |

DAKAR
| ❏ 4512 | I Forgot to Tell You/The Man and the Woman | 1972 | — | 3.00 | 6.00 |

DOT
| ❏ 15673 | Woke Up This Morning/Wilette | 1957 | 7.50 | 15.00 | 30.00 |

—With Kripp Johnson
EMI AMERICA
| ❏ 8042 | I Wanna Give You Some Love/Waiting in Vain | 1980 | — | 2.00 | 4.00 |
| ❏ 8056 | After You/Let's Get Together | 1980 | — | 2.00 | 4.00 |

MOTOWN
❏ 1118	(Don't Let the Boy Overpower) The Man in You/Girls, Girls, Girls	1968	2.50	5.00	10.00
❏ 1144	Are You Lonely for Me Baby/Your Wonderful Love	1969	2.50	5.00	10.00
❏ 1152	Honey Come Back/What Am I Gonna Do Without You	1969	2.50	5.00	10.00
❏ 1160	The Day My World Stood Still/Baby, I'll Get It	1970	125.00	250.00	500.00

SUGARHILL
| ❏ 764 | Sometimes When We Touch/(B-side unknown) | 1981 | — | 2.00 | 4.00 |

V.I.P.
❏ 25052	The Day My World Stood Still/Baby, I'll Get It	1970	2.50	5.00	10.00
❏ 25056	Let Somebody Love Me/Two Feet from Happiness	1970	2.50	5.00	10.00
❏ 25059	Is There Anything Love Can't Do/Pet Names	1971	2.50	5.00	10.00
❏ 25067	Who You Gonna Run To/Forgive My Jealousy	1971	100.00	200.00	400.00

Number	Title (A Side/B Side)	Yr	VG	VG+	NM
VIBRATION					
❑ 569	We Can't Hide It Anymore/I'm Needing You, Wanting You	1977	—	2.50	5.00
—With Sylvia					
WAND					
❑ 106	I Don't Want to Cry/Just Once	1961	3.00	6.00	12.00
❑ 108	(It Never Happens) In Real Life/The Same Old Story	1961	3.00	6.00	12.00
❑ 110	I Wake Up Crying/Everybody Needs Love	1961	3.00	6.00	12.00
❑ 115	The Breaking Point/My Willow Tree	1961	3.00	6.00	12.00
❑ 119	What'cha Gonna Say Tomorrow/Angel of Angels	1962	3.00	6.00	12.00
❑ 122	Any Day Now (My Wild Beautiful Bird)/The Prophet	1962	3.75	7.50	15.00
❑ 126	I Keep Forgetting/Who's Gonna Pick Up the Pieces	1962	2.50	5.00	10.00
❑ 128	Gettin' Ready for the Heartbreak/In Between Tears	1962	2.50	5.00	10.00
❑ 132	Tell Him I'm Not Home/Lonely Am I	1963	2.50	5.00	10.00
❑ 132 [PS]	Tell Him I'm Not Home/Lonely Am I	1963	6.25	12.50	25.00
❑ 138	I Will Never Turn My Back on You/Tears of Joy	1963	2.50	5.00	10.00
❑ 141	Any Other Way/Big New York	1963	2.50	5.00	10.00
❑ 149	Hand It Over/Look Over Your Shoulder	1964	2.00	4.00	8.00
❑ 154	Beg Me/This Broken Heart	1964	2.00	4.00	8.00
❑ 161	Somebody New/Stand By Me	1964	2.00	4.00	8.00
❑ 169	Since I Don't Have You/Hand It Over	1964	2.00	4.00	8.00
❑ 179	I Need You/Soul Brother Twist	1965	2.00	4.00	8.00
❑ 188	If I Didn't Love You/Just a Little Bit of Your Soul	1965	2.00	4.00	8.00
❑ 1105	Good Things Come to Those Who Wait/Yah	1965	2.00	4.00	8.00
❑ 1119	All in My Mind/And That's Saying a Lot	1966	2.00	4.00	8.00
❑ 1129	These Chains of Love/Theme to the Blues	1966	2.00	4.00	8.00
❑ 1142	I've Got to Be Strong/Where Did She Stay	1967	2.00	4.00	8.00
❑ 1151	Every Man Needs a Down Home Girl/Need You There	1967	2.00	4.00	8.00
❑ 1159	Hound Dog/Love Me Tender	1967	2.00	4.00	8.00
❑ 1166	Shame on Me/Candy	1967	2.00	4.00	8.00
❑ 1178	My Child's Child/Theme to the Blues	1968	2.00	4.00	8.00
Albums					
ABC					
❑ X-798	Through All Times	1973	3.75	7.50	15.00
ALL PLATINUM					
❑ 3014	Needing You, Wanting You	1976	3.75	7.50	15.00
COLLECTABLES					
❑ COL-5115	Golden Classics	198?	2.50	5.00	10.00
EMI AMERICA					
❑ SW-17031	I Wanna Give You Some Love	1980	2.50	5.00	10.00
GUEST STAR					
❑ GS-1912 [M]	Chuck Jackson	196?	5.00	10.00	20.00
❑ GSS-1912 [R]	Chuck Jackson	196?	3.00	6.00	12.00
MOTOWN					
❑ M-667 [M]	Chuck Jackson Arrives!	1967	10.00	20.00	40.00
❑ MS-667 [S]	Chuck Jackson Arrives!	1967	6.25	12.50	25.00
❑ MS-687	Goin' Back to Chuck Jackson	1969	6.25	12.50	25.00
SCEPTER					
❑ 5100	A Tribute to Burt Bacharach	1972	3.75	7.50	15.00
SPIN-O-RAMA					
❑ 123 [M]	Starring Chuck Jackson	196?	5.00	10.00	20.00
❑ S-123 [R]	Starring Chuck Jackson	196?	3.00	6.00	12.00
STRAND					
❑ SL-1125 [M]	The Great Chuck Jackson	196?	6.25	12.50	25.00
❑ SLS-1125 [S]	The Great Chuck Jackson	196?	7.50	15.00	30.00
UNITED ARTISTS					
❑ UA-LA499-E	The Very Best of Chuck Jackson	1974	2.50	5.00	10.00
V.I.P.					
❑ 403	Teardrops Keep Fallin' on My Heart	1970	10.00	20.00	40.00
WAND					
❑ LP-650 [M]	I Don't Want to Cry	1961	10.00	20.00	40.00
❑ LP-654 [M]	Any Day Now	1962	10.00	20.00	40.00
❑ WD-655 [M]	Encore	1963	10.00	20.00	40.00
❑ WD-658 [M]	Chuck Jackson On Tour	1964	10.00	20.00	40.00
❑ WDM-667 [M]	Mr. Everything	1965	7.50	15.00	30.00
❑ WDS-667 [S]	Mr. Everything	1965	10.00	20.00	40.00
❑ WD-673 [M]	A Tribute to Rhythm and Blues	1966	7.50	15.00	30.00
❑ WDS-673 [S]	A Tribute to Rhythm and Blues	1966	10.00	20.00	40.00
❑ WD-676 [M]	A Tribute to Rhythm and Blues, Volume 2	1966	7.50	15.00	30.00
❑ WDS-676 [S]	A Tribute to Rhythm and Blues, Volume 2	1966	10.00	20.00	40.00
❑ WD-680 [M]	Dedicated to the King!!	1966	10.00	20.00	40.00
❑ WDS-680 [S]	Dedicated to the King!!	1966	12.50	25.00	50.00
❑ WD-683 [M]	Chuck Jackson's Greatest Hits	1967	5.00	10.00	20.00
❑ WDS-683 [S]	Chuck Jackson's Greatest Hits	1967	6.25	12.50	25.00

JACKSON, CHUCK, AND MAXINE BROWN Also see each artist's individual listings.

Number	Title (A Side/B Side)	Yr	VG	VG+	NM
45s					
WAND					
❑ 181	Something You Got/Baby Take Me	1965	2.00	4.00	8.00
❑ 191	Don't Go/Can't Let You Out of My Sight	1965	2.00	4.00	8.00
❑ 198	I Need You So/Cause We're in Love	1965	2.00	4.00	8.00
❑ 1109	Plerase Don't Hurt Me/I'm Satisfied	1966	2.00	4.00	8.00
❑ 1148	Hold On I'm Comin'/Never Had It So Good	1967	2.00	4.00	8.00
❑ 1155	Daddy's Home/Don't Go	1967	2.00	4.00	8.00
❑ 1162	See See Rider/Tennessee Waltz	1967	2.00	4.00	8.00
Albums					
WAND					
❑ WD-669 [M]	Say Something	1965	7.50	15.00	30.00
❑ WDS-669 [S]	Say Something	1965	10.00	20.00	40.00
❑ WD-678 [M]	Hold On, We're Coming	1966	7.50	15.00	30.00
❑ WDS-678 [S]	Hold On, We're Coming	1966	10.00	20.00	40.00

JACKSON, CHUCK, AND TAMMI TERRELL Also see each artist's individual listings.

Number	Title (A Side/B Side)	Yr	VG	VG+	NM
Albums					
WAND					
❑ WD-682 [M]	The Early Show	1967	7.50	15.00	30.00
❑ WDS-682 [S]	The Early Show	1967	7.50	15.00	30.00

JACKSON, DEON

Number	Title (A Side/B Side)	Yr	VG	VG+	NM
45s					
ATLANTIC					
❑ 2213	Hush Little Baby/You Said You Loved Me	1963	2.50	5.00	10.00
❑ 2252	Come Back Home/Nursery Rhymes	1964	2.50	5.00	10.00
CARLA					
❑ 1900	I Can't Go On/I Need a Love Like Yours	1968	2.00	4.00	8.00
❑ 1903	You'll Wake Up Wiser Baby/You Gotta Love	1968	2.00	4.00	8.00
❑ 2526	Love Makes the World Go Round/You Said You Loved Me	1966	2.50	5.00	10.00
❑ 2527	Love Takes a Long Time Growing/Hush Little Baby	1966	2.00	4.00	8.00
❑ 2530	I Can't Do Without You/That's What You Do to Me	1966	2.00	4.00	8.00
❑ 2533	When Your Love Has Gone/Hard to Get Thing Called Love	1967	2.00	4.00	8.00
❑ 2537	Ooh Baby/All on a Sunny Day	1967	2.00	4.00	8.00
SHOUT					
❑ 254	I'll Always Love You/Life Can Be That Way	1969	6.25	12.50	25.00
Albums					
ATCO					
❑ 33-188 [M]	Love Makes the World Go Round	1966	7.50	15.00	30.00
❑ SD 33-188 [S]	Love Makes the World Go Round	1966	10.00	20.00	40.00
COLLECTABLES					
❑ COL-5106	Golden Classics	198?	2.50	5.00	10.00

JACKSON, EARL

Number	Title (A Side/B Side)	Yr	VG	VG+	NM
45s					
ABC					
❑ 11142	Self Soul Satisfaction/Looking Through the Eyes of Love	1968	7.50	15.00	30.00

JACKSON, GEORGE

Number	Title (A Side/B Side)	Yr	VG	VG+	NM
45s					
ATLANTIC					
❑ 1024	Uh Huh/I'm Sorry	1954	12.50	25.00	50.00
CAMEO					
❑ 460	When I Stop Lovin' You/That Lonely Night	1967	3.00	6.00	12.00
CHESS					
❑ 2167	Things Are Gettin' Better/Mackin' on You	1975	—	3.00	6.00
DOT					
❑ 16724	Blinkety Blink/There Goes My Pride	1965	3.00	6.00	12.00
FAME					
❑ 1457	Find 'Em, Fool 'Em, and Forget 'Em/My Desires Are Getting the Best of Me	1969	2.00	4.00	8.00
❑ 1468	That's How Much You Mean to Me/I'm Gonna Hold On	1970	2.00	4.00	8.00
HI					
❑ 2130	I'm Gonna Wait/So Good to Me	1967	3.00	6.00	12.00
❑ 2212	Aretha, Sing One for Me/I'm Gonna Wait	1972	2.00	4.00	8.00
❑ 2236	Let Them Know You Care/Patricia	1973	2.00	4.00	8.00
MERCURY					
❑ 72736	Kiss Me/Tossin' and Turnin'	1967	2.50	5.00	10.00
❑ 72782	I Don't Have the Time to Love You/Don't Use Me	1968	2.50	5.00	10.00
MGM					
❑ 14680	We've Only Just Begun/You Can't Run Away from Love	1973	—	3.00	6.00
❑ 14732	Willie Lump Lump/How Can I Get Next to You	1974	—	3.00	6.00
❑ 14767	Soul Train/Smoking and Drinking	1974	—	3.00	6.00
RPM					
❑ 441	Hold Me Up/Heaven on Earth	1955	6.25	12.50	25.00
VERVE					
❑ 10658	Love Highjacker/I Found What I Wanted	1970	6.25	12.50	25.00

JACKSON, GEORGE, AND DAN GREER See GEORGE AND GREER.

JACKSON, J.J.

Number	Title (A Side/B Side)	Yr	VG	VG+	NM
45s					
CALLA					
❑ 119	But It's Alright/Boogaloo Baby	1966	3.00	6.00	12.00
❑ 125	I Dig Girls/That Ain't Right	1966	2.50	5.00	10.00
❑ 130	Til Love Goes Out of Style/Seems Like I've Been Here Before	1967	2.50	5.00	10.00
❑ 133	Four Walls (Three Windows and Two Doors)/Here We Go Again	1967	2.50	5.00	10.00
CONGRESS					
❑ 6008	Fat, Black and Together/That Woman Loving	1969	2.00	4.00	8.00
EVEREST					
❑ 2012	False Face/Ring Telephone	1963	3.00	6.00	12.00
LOMA					
❑ 2082	Try Me/Sho Nuff (Gotta Good Thing Goin')	1967	2.00	4.00	8.00
❑ 2090	Down But Not Out/Why Does It Take So Long	1968	2.00	4.00	8.00
❑ 2096	Come See Me (I'm Your Man)/I Don't Want to Live My Life Alone	1968	2.00	4.00	8.00
❑ 2102	Too Late/You Do It Cause You Wanna	1968	2.00	4.00	8.00
❑ 2104	That Ain't Right/Courage Ain't Strength	1968	2.00	4.00	8.00
MAGNA GLIDE					
❑ 5N-325	Let Me Try Again/(B-side unknown)	1975	—	3.00	6.00
PERCEPTION					
❑ 7	Nobody's Gonna Help You/Help Me Get to My Grits	1970	2.00	4.00	8.00
WARNER BROS.					
❑ 7130	But It's Alright/Four Walls (Three Windows and Two Doors)	1970	—	3.00	6.00
—"Back to Back Hits" series					
❑ 7278	But It's Alright/Ain't Too Proud to Beg	1969	2.00	4.00	8.00
❑ 7321	Four Walls (Three Windows and Two Doors)/That Ain't Right	1969	2.00	4.00	8.00
Albums					
CALLA					
❑ C-1101 [M]	But It's Alright/I Dig Girls	1967	5.00	10.00	20.00
❑ CS-1101 [S]	But It's Alright/I Dig Girls	1967	6.25	12.50	25.00
CONGRESS					
❑ CS-7000	The Greatest Little Soul Band in the World	1968	6.25	12.50	25.00

Number	Title (A Side/B Side)	Yr	VG	VG+	NM
PERCEPTION					
❏ 3	J.J. Jackson's Dilemma	1970	3.75	7.50	15.00
WARNER BROS.					
❏ WS 1797	The Great J.J. Jackson	1969	5.00	10.00	20.00

JACKSON, JACKIE
12-Inch Singles
POLYDOR

Number	Title (A Side/B Side)	Yr	VG	VG+	NM
❏ 871549-1	Stay (4 versions)/Who's Loving You Now	1989	2.00	4.00	8.00
❏ 889035-1	Cruzin' (12" Remix) (7" Remix) (7" Edit) (House Mix) (House Dub)	1989	2.00	4.00	8.00

45s
POLYDOR

Number	Title (A Side/B Side)	Yr	VG	VG+	NM
❏ 871548-7	Stay/Who's Loving You Now	1989	—	—	3.00
❏ 871548-7 [PS]	Stay/Who's Loving You Now	1989	—	—	3.00
❏ 889034-7	Cruzin'/(another mix)	1989	—	—	3.00
❏ 889034-7 [PS]	Cruzin'/(another mix)	1989	—	—	3.00

Albums
MOTOWN

Number	Title (A Side/B Side)	Yr	VG	VG+	NM
❏ M 785V1	Jackie Jackson	1973	3.75	7.50	15.00
POLYDOR					
❏ 837766-1	Be the One	1989	2.50	5.00	10.00

JACKSON, JERMAINE
12-Inch Singles
ARISTA

Number	Title (A Side/B Side)	Yr	VG	VG+	NM
❏ ADP 9189 [DJ]	Tell Me I'm Not Dreamin' (Too Good to Be True)/ Do What You Do/Escape from the Planet	1984	3.00	6.00	12.00
❏ AD1-9222	Dynamite/(Instrumental)/Tell Me I'm Not Dreaming (Instrumental)	1984	2.00	4.00	8.00
❏ AD1-9317	When the Rain Begins to Fall/Come to Me	1985	2.00	4.00	8.00
—A-side with Pia Zadora					
❏ AD1-9357	(Closest Thing to) Perfect/(Instrumental)	1985	2.00	4.00	8.00
❏ AD1-9445	I Think It's Love (4 versions)	1986	2.00	4.00	8.00
❏ AD1-9501	Do You Remember Me (6 versions)	1986	2.00	4.00	8.00
❏ ADP 9876 [DJ]	Don't Take It Personal (same on both sides)	1989	2.00	4.00	8.00
❏ AD1-9878	Don't Take It Personal (3 versions)	1989	2.00	4.00	8.00
❏ AD1-9934	Two Ships (In the Night) (4 versions)	1990	2.00	4.00	8.00
LAFACE					
❏ 24004	You Said, You Said (5 versions)	1991	2.00	4.00	8.00
❏ 24012	Word to the Badd!! (5 versions)	1991	3.00	6.00	12.00
❏ 24017	I Dream, I Dream (5 versions)	1992	2.50	5.00	10.00
MOTOWN					
❏ M 00001D1	Let's Be Young Tonight (5:07)/Down to Love Town (5:55)	1976	5.00	10.00	20.00
—B-side by the Originals on Soul					
❏ PR-66 [DJ]	Let's Get Serious (Short Version 3:33) (Long Version 7:55)	1980	5.00	10.00	20.00
❏ PR-73 [DJ]	Burnin' Hot (7:44)/Feelin' Free (6:32)	1980	6.25	12.50	25.00
—No label name on label					
❏ PR-101 [DJ]	Let Me Tickle Your Fancy (Vocal) (Instrumental)/ Hard to Get (Vocal) (Instrumental)	1982	3.75	7.50	15.00
—No label name on label; B-side by Rick James					
❏ PR-108 [DJ]	Very Special Part (6:32)/(Instrumental)	1982	3.00	6.00	12.00

45s
ARISTA

Number	Title (A Side/B Side)	Yr	VG	VG+	NM
❏ 2029	I'd Like to Get to Know You/ Spare the Rod, Love the Child	1990	—	—	3.00
❏ 9190	Dynamite/Tell Me I'm Not Dreaming (Too Good to Be True) (Instrumental)	1984	—	—	3.00
❏ 9190 [DJ]	Dynamite (same on both sides)	1984	2.00	4.00	8.00
—Promo only on red vinyl					
❏ 9190 [PS]	Dynamite/Tell Me I'm Not Dreaming (Too Good to Be True) (Instrumental)	1984	—	—	3.00
❏ 9275	Take Good Care of My Heart/Tell Me I'm Not Dreaming (Too Good to Be True) (Instrumental)	1984	—	2.50	5.00
—A-side with Whitney Houston					
❏ 9279	Do What You Do/Tell Me I'm Not Dreaming (Too Good to Be True)	1984	—	—	3.00
❏ 9356	(Closest Thing to) Perfect/(Instrumental)	1985	—	—	3.00
❏ 9356 [PS]	(Closest Thing to) Perfect/(Instrumental)	1985	—	—	3.00
❏ 9444	I Think It's Love/Voices in the Dark	1985	—	—	3.00
❏ 9444 [PS]	I Think It's Love/Voices in the Dark	1985	—	—	3.00
❏ 9495	Words Into Action/Our Love Story	1986	—	—	3.00
❏ 9495 [PS]	Words Into Action/Our Love Story	1986	—	—	3.00
❏ 9502	Do You Remember Me/Whatcha' Doin'	1986	—	—	3.00
❏ 9502 [PS]	Do You Remember Me/Whatcha' Doin'	1986	—	—	3.00
❏ 9788	Clean Up Your Act/I'm Gonna Git Ya Sucka	1988	—	—	3.00
—B-side by the Gap Band					
❏ 9788 [PS]	Clean Up Your Act/I'm Gonna Git Ya Sucka	1988	—	—	3.00
❏ 9875	Don't Take It Personal/Clean Up Your Act	1989	—	—	3.00
❏ 9875 [PS]	Don't Take It Personal/Clean Up Your Act	1989	—	—	3.00
❏ 9933	Two Ships (In the Night)/Next to You	1990	—	—	3.00
❏ 9933 [PS]	Two Ships (In the Night)/Next to You	1990	—	—	3.00
LAFACE					
❏ 24003	You Said, You Said/(Instrumental)	1991	—	2.00	4.00
MOTOWN					
❏ 1201	That's How Love Goes/ I Lost My Love in the Big City	1972	—	2.50	5.00
❏ 1216	Daddy's Home/Take Me in Your Arms (Rock Me for a Little While)	1972	—	2.50	5.00
❏ 1244	You're in Good Hands/ Does Your Mama Know About Me	1973	—	2.50	5.00
❏ 1386	She's the Ideal Girl/I'm So Glad You Chose Me	1976	—	—	—
—Unreleased					
❏ 1401	Let's Be Young Tonight/Boss Odyssey	1976	—	2.50	5.00
❏ 1409	You Need to Be Loved/My Touch of Madness	1977	—	2.50	5.00
❏ 1441	Castles of Sand/I Love Every Little Thing About You	1978	—	2.50	5.00
❏ 1469	Let's Get Serious/Je Vous Aime Beaucoups	1980	—	2.00	4.00
❏ 1490	You're Supposed to Keep Your Love for Me/Let It Ride	1980	—	2.00	4.00
❏ 1499	Little Girl Don't You Worry/We Can Put It Back Together	1980	—	2.00	4.00
❏ 1503	You Like Me Don't You/(Instrumental)	1981	—	2.00	4.00

Number	Title (A Side/B Side)	Yr	VG	VG+	NM
❏ 1525	I'm Just Too Shy/All Because of You	1981	—	2.00	4.00
❏ 1600	Paradise in Your Eyes/I'm My Brother's Keeper	1982	—	2.00	4.00
❏ 1628	Let Me Tickle Your Fancy/Maybe Next Time	1982	—	2.00	4.00
—Devo is the backing group					
❏ 1649	Very Special Part/You're Givin' Me the Runaround	1982	—	2.00	4.00

Albums
ARISTA

Number	Title (A Side/B Side)	Yr	VG	VG+	NM
❏ AL8-8203	Jermaine Jackson	1984	2.50	5.00	10.00
❏ AL8-8277	Precious Moments	1986	2.50	5.00	10.00
❏ AL-8421	Jermaine Jackson	1986	2.00	4.00	8.00
—Budget-line reissue					
❏ AL-8493	Don't Take It Personal	1989	2.50	5.00	10.00
MOTOWN					
❏ M5-117V1	Motown Superstar Series, Vol. 17	1981	2.50	5.00	10.00
❏ M-752L	Jermaine	1972	2.50	5.00	10.00
❏ M-775L	Come Into My Life	1973	2.50	5.00	10.00
❏ M6-842S1	My Name Is Jermaine	1976	2.50	5.00	10.00
❏ M6-888S1	Feel the Fire	1977	2.50	5.00	10.00
❏ M7-898R1	Frontiers	1978	2.50	5.00	10.00
❏ M7-928R1	Let's Get Serious	1980	2.50	5.00	10.00
❏ M8-948M1	Jermaine	1980	2.50	5.00	10.00
❏ M8-952M1	I Like Your Style	1981	2.50	5.00	10.00
❏ 6017 ML	Let Me Tickle Your Fancy	1982	2.50	5.00	10.00

JACKSON, JERRY
45s
CAPITOL

Number	Title (A Side/B Side)	Yr	VG	VG+	NM
❏ 2112	Miss You/Take Over Now	1968	2.50	5.00	10.00
COLUMBIA					
❏ 43056	Shrimp Boats/Always	1964	3.00	6.00	12.00
❏ 43158	Tell Her Johnny Said Goodbye/Are You Glad When We're Apart	1964	3.00	6.00	12.00
❏ 43231	You're Mine (And I Love You)/Hey, Sugarfoot	1965	3.00	6.00	12.00
KAPP					
❏ 387	Time/Se Habla Espanol	1961	5.00	10.00	20.00
❏ 420	I Don't Play Games/ You Might Be There With Him	1961	5.00	10.00	20.00
❏ 438	If I Only Had Known How to Keep Her (She Would Never Have Gone to You)/ Till the End of Time	1961	5.00	10.00	20.00
❏ 448	La-Dee-Dah (Ha-Ha-Ha)/ You Don't Wanna Hurt Me	1962	3.75	7.50	15.00
❏ 464	They Really Don't Know You/Blues in the Night	1962	3.75	7.50	15.00
❏ 496	She Lied/Wide Awake in a Dream	1962	3.75	7.50	15.00
❏ 511	Gypsy Eyes/Turn Back	1963	3.75	7.50	15.00
❏ 543	Blowin' in the Wind (Part 1)/ Blowin' in the Wind (Part 2)	1963	3.75	7.50	15.00
PARKWAY					
❏ 100	It's Rough Out There/I'm Gonna Paint a Picture	1966	5.00	10.00	20.00
TOP RANK					
❏ 2042	A Chance to Prove My Love/ For Every One There's Someone	1960	5.00	10.00	20.00
❏ 2072	Every Time You Kiss Me/Meaning of My Love	1960	5.00	10.00	20.00

JACKSON, JILL Also see PAUL AND PAULA.
45s
REPRISE

Number	Title (A Side/B Side)	Yr	VG	VG+	NM
❏ 0297	Hey Handsome Boy/All Over Again	1964	3.75	7.50	15.00
❏ 0323	Pixie Girl/ I Just Don't Know What to Do With Myself	1964	3.75	7.50	15.00
❏ 0362	Born Too Late/Here Comes the Night	1965	3.75	7.50	15.00
❏ 0411	Treasure of Love/I'll Love You for a While	1965	3.75	7.50	15.00

JACKSON, JUNE
45s
BELL

Number	Title (A Side/B Side)	Yr	VG	VG+	NM
❏ 45173	Little Dog Heaven/Tenderly with Feeling	1972	5.00	10.00	20.00
IMPERIAL					
❏ 66185	It's What's Up Front That Counts/ Fifty Per Cent Won't Do	1966	7.50	15.00	30.00
MUSETTE					
❏ 112	You're Welcome/(B-side unknown)	196?	250.00	500.00	1000.

JACKSON, LIL' SON
45s
IMPERIAL

Number	Title (A Side/B Side)	Yr	VG	VG+	NM
❏ 5204	Journey Back Home/Rockin' and Rollin' #2	1952	25.00	50.00	100.00
—Note: Lil' Son Jackson records on Imperial before 5204 are unconfirmed on 45 rpm					
❏ 5218	Black and Brown/Sad Letter Blues	1953	25.00	50.00	100.00
❏ 5229	Lonely Blues/Freight Train Blues	1953	25.00	50.00	100.00
❏ 5237	Spending Money Blues/All Alone	1953	25.00	50.00	100.00
❏ 5248	Movin' to the Country/Confession	1953	25.00	50.00	100.00
❏ 5259	Dirty Work/Little Girl	1953	25.00	50.00	100.00
❏ 5267	Thrill Me, Baby/Doctor, Doctor	1954	20.00	40.00	80.00
❏ 5276	Big Rat/Piggly Wiggly	1954	20.00	40.00	80.00
❏ 5286	Trouble Don't Last Always/Blues by the Hour	1954	20.00	40.00	80.00
❏ 5300	Get High Everybody/Let Me Down Easy	1954	20.00	40.00	80.00
❏ 5312	How Long/Good Ole Wagon	1954	20.00	40.00	80.00
❏ 5319	My Younger Days/I Wish to Go Home	1954	20.00	40.00	80.00
❏ 5339	Sugar Mama/Messin' Up	1955	20.00	40.00	80.00
❏ 5703	Rockin' and Rollin'/Peace Breaking People	1960	3.75	7.50	15.00
❏ 5851	Everybody's Blues/Travelin' Woman	1962	3.75	7.50	15.00
❏ 5963	Prison Bound/Rolling Mill	1963	3.00	6.00	12.00
POST					
❏ 2014	No Money/Lonely Blues	1955	10.00	20.00	40.00

Albums
ARHOOLIE

Number	Title (A Side/B Side)	Yr	VG	VG+	NM
❏ 1004 [M]	Lil' Son Jackson	1960	6.25	12.50	25.00
IMPERIAL					
❏ LP-9142 [M]	Rockin' and Rollin'	1961	100.00	200.00	400.00

J

Number	Title (A Side/B Side)	Yr	VG	VG+	NM

JACKSON, MAHALIA

45s

APOLLO

Number	Title (A Side/B Side)	Yr	VG	VG+	NM
❑ 235	Silent Night, Holy Night/Go Tell It On The Mountain	1951	5.00	10.00	20.00

—Note: Earlier Mahalia Jackson 45s on Apollo may exist

Number	Title (A Side/B Side)	Yr	VG	VG+	NM
❑ 240	Get Away Jordan/I Gave Up Everything	1951	5.00	10.00	20.00
❑ 245	Bless This House/The Lord's Prayer	1951	5.00	10.00	20.00
❑ 246	His Eyes Are On the Sparrow/It Is No Secret (What God Can Do)	1951	5.00	10.00	20.00
❑ 248	How I Got Over/Just As I Am	1951	5.00	10.00	20.00
❑ 258	He's the One/I'm Getting Nearer My Home	1952	5.00	10.00	20.00
❑ 262	In the Upper Room (Part 1)/ In the Upper Room (Part 2)	1952	5.00	10.00	20.00
❑ 269	He Said He Would/God Spoke to Me	1953	5.00	10.00	20.00
❑ 273	I'm Going Down the River/Do You Know Him	1953	5.00	10.00	20.00
❑ 278	I Wonder If I Will Ever Rest/Coming to Jesus	1953	5.00	10.00	20.00
❑ 282	Hands of God/It's Real	1954	5.00	10.00	20.00
❑ 286	I'm On My Way/My Story	1954	5.00	10.00	20.00
❑ 289	Walking to Jerusalem/What Then	1954	5.00	10.00	20.00
❑ 291	I Walked Into the Garden/I'm Going to Tell God	1955	5.00	10.00	20.00
❑ 298	Nobody Knows/Run All the Way	1955	5.00	10.00	20.00
❑ 304	He's My Light/If You Just Keep Still	1956	4.50	9.00	18.00
❑ 311	His Eyes Are On the Sparrow/ I Can Put My Trust in Jesus	1956	4.50	9.00	18.00
❑ 313	Didn't It Rain/Nobody Knows	1956	4.50	9.00	18.00
❑ 314	I'm On My Way/My Story	1956	4.50	9.00	18.00
❑ 539	Silent Night/The Lord's Prayer	1959	3.75	7.50	15.00
❑ 750	Silent Night/The Lord's Prayer	1962	3.00	6.00	12.00
❑ 750 [PS]	Silent Night/The Lord's Prayer	1962	5.00	10.00	20.00

COLUMBIA

Number	Title (A Side/B Side)	Yr	VG	VG+	NM
❑ 40411	A Rusty Old Halo/The Treasure of Love	1955	3.75	7.50	15.00
❑ 40412	Walk Over God's Heaven/Jesus Met the Woman	1955	3.75	7.50	15.00
❑ 40473	You'll Never Walk Alone/One God	1955	3.75	7.50	15.00
❑ 40529	His Hands/I See God	1955	3.75	7.50	15.00
❑ 40554	The Bible Tells Me So/Satisfied Mind	1955	3.75	7.50	15.00
❑ 40610	The Lord Is a Busy Man/You're Not Living in Vain	1955	3.75	7.50	15.00
❑ 40712	Round the Rainbow/An Evening Star	1956	3.75	7.50	15.00
❑ 40721	I Ask the Lord/I'm Going to Live	1956	3.75	7.50	15.00
❑ 40753	The Lord's Prayer/Precious Lord	1956	3.75	7.50	15.00
❑ 40777	Silent Night, Holy Night/Mary's Little Boy Chile	1956	3.75	7.50	15.00
❑ 40854	God Is So Good/I Complained	1957	3.75	7.50	15.00
❑ 41000	Trouble/He's a Light Unto My Pathway	1957	3.75	7.50	15.00
❑ 41055	Sweet Little Jesus Boy/A Star Stood Still	1957	3.00	6.00	12.00
❑ 41150	He's Got the Whole World In His Hands/ Didn't It Rain	1958	3.00	6.00	12.00
❑ 41258	For My Good Fortune/Have You Any Rivers	1958	3.00	6.00	12.00
❑ 41322	Elijah Rock/Hold Me	1959	3.00	6.00	12.00
❑ 41382	Tell the World About This/Trouble of the World	1959	3.00	6.00	12.00
❑ 41779	My Country 'Tis of Thee (America)/Onward, Christian Soldiers	1960	3.00	6.00	12.00
❑ 42633	Joy To The World!/Go Tell It On The Mountain	1962	2.50	5.00	10.00
❑ 42910	We Shall Overcome/Let's Pray Together	1963	2.50	5.00	10.00
❑ 42946	In the Summer of His Years/Song for My Brother	1964	2.50	5.00	10.00
❑ 43474	Sunrise, Sunset/Like the Breeze Blows	1965	2.50	5.00	10.00
❑ 44529	Take My Hand, Precious Lord/We Shall Overcome	1968	2.00	4.00	8.00
❑ 45068	Abraham, Martin and John/Day Is Done	1970	—	3.00	6.00
❑ JZSP 137705/6 [DJ]	Happy Birthday To You, Our Lord/Silver Bells	1968	—	2.50	5.00

GRAND AWARD

Number	Title (A Side/B Side)	Yr	VG	VG+	NM
❑ 1025	Dig a Little Deeper/I'm On My Way	1959	3.75	7.50	15.00

KENWOOD

Number	Title (A Side/B Side)	Yr	VG	VG+	NM
❑ 300	In the Upper Room (Part 1)/ In the Upper Room (Part 2)	1964	2.00	4.00	8.00
❑ 301	His Eyes Are On the Sparrow/Walking to Jerusalem	196?	2.00	4.00	8.00
❑ 302	How I Got Over/Didn't It Rain	196?	2.00	4.00	8.00
❑ 303	Go Tell It On the Mountain/Bless This House	196?	2.00	4.00	8.00
❑ 304	Move On Up a Little Higher (Part 1)/Move On Up a Little Higher (Part 2)	196?	2.00	4.00	8.00
❑ 305	These Are They/Get Away Jordan	196?	2.00	4.00	8.00
❑ 750	Silent Night/The Lord's Prayer	1964	2.50	5.00	10.00

NASHBORO

Number	Title (A Side/B Side)	Yr	VG	VG+	NM
❑ 750 [DJ]	Silent Night/The Lord's Prayer	197?	—	2.00	4.00

—Reissue of Kenwood 750

U.S.A.

Number	Title (A Side/B Side)	Yr	VG	VG+	NM
❑ 109	The Holy Bible (Part 1)/The Holy Bible (Part 2)	196?	2.50	5.00	10.00

7-Inch Extended Plays

COLUMBIA

Number	Title (A Side/B Side)	Yr	VG	VG+	NM
❑ B-2072	*Trouble in My Way/Down by the Riverside/ Joshua Fit the Battle of Jericho/You'll Never Walk Alone	195?	5.00	10.00	20.00
❑ B-2072 [PS]	You'll Never Walk Alone	195?	5.00	10.00	20.00

Albums

APOLLO

Number	Title (A Side/B Side)	Yr	VG	VG+	NM
❑ 201/202 [M]	Spirituals	1954	7.50	15.00	30.00
❑ 482 [M]	No Matter How You Pray	1959	6.25	12.50	25.00
❑ 499 [M]	Mahalia Jackson	1962	6.25	12.50	25.00
❑ 1001/2 [M]	Command Performance	1961	6.25	12.50	25.00

COLUMBIA

Number	Title (A Side/B Side)	Yr	VG	VG+	NM
❑ CL 644 [M]	Mahalia Jackson	1955	10.00	20.00	40.00
❑ CL 702 [M]	Sweet Little Jesus Boy	1955	10.00	20.00	40.00
❑ CL 899 [M]	Bless This House	1956	7.50	15.00	30.00
❑ CL 1244 [M]	Newport 1958	1959	5.00	10.00	20.00
❑ CL 1343 [M]	That Great Gettin' Up Morning	1959	5.00	10.00	20.00
❑ CL 1428 [M]	Come On Children, Let's Sing	1960	5.00	10.00	20.00
❑ CL 1473 [M]	The Power and the Glory	1960	5.00	10.00	20.00
❑ CL 1549 [M]	I Believe	1960	3.75	7.50	15.00
❑ CL 1643 [M]	Every Time I Feel the Spirit	1961	3.75	7.50	15.00
❑ CL 1726 [M]	Recorded in Europe During Her Latest Concert Tour	1962	3.75	7.50	15.00
❑ CL 1824 [M]	Great Songs of Love and Faith	1962	3.75	7.50	15.00
❑ CL 1903 [M]	Silent Night	1962	3.75	7.50	15.00
❑ CL 1936 [M]	Make a Joyful Noise Unto the Lord	1962	3.75	7.50	15.00
❑ CL 2004 [M]	Mahalia Jackson's Greatest Hits	1963	3.00	6.00	12.00
❑ CL 2130 [M]	Let's Pray Together	1964	3.00	6.00	12.00
❑ CL 2452 [M]	Mahalia Sings	1966	3.00	6.00	12.00
❑ CL 2546 [M]	Garden of Prayer	1967	3.75	7.50	15.00

Number	Title (A Side/B Side)	Yr	VG	VG+	NM
❑ CL 2552 [10]	You'll Never Walk Alone	1955	12.50	25.00	50.00
❑ CL 2605 [M]	My Faith	1967	3.75	7.50	15.00
❑ CL 2690 [M]	Mahalia Jackson In Concert, Easter Sunday 1967	1967	3.75	7.50	15.00
❑ CS 8071 [S]	Newport 1958	1959	7.50	15.00	30.00
❑ CS 8153 [S]	That Great Gettin' Up Morning	1959	6.25	12.50	25.00
❑ CS 8225 [S]	Come On Children, Let's Sing	1960	6.25	12.50	25.00
❑ CS 8264 [S]	The Power and the Glory	1960	6.25	12.50	25.00
❑ CS 8349 [S]	I Believe	1960	5.00	10.00	20.00
❑ CS 8443 [S]	Every Time I Feel the Spirit	1961	5.00	10.00	20.00
❑ CS 8526 [S]	Recorded in Europe During Her Latest Concert Tour	1962	5.00	10.00	20.00
❑ CS 8624 [S]	Great Songs of Love and Faith	1962	5.00	10.00	20.00
❑ CS 8703 [S]	Silent Night	1962	5.00	10.00	20.00
❑ CS 8736 [S]	Make a Joyful Noise Unto the Lord	1962	5.00	10.00	20.00
❑ CS 8759 [R]	Mahalia Jackson	1963	3.00	6.00	12.00
❑ CS 8761 [R]	Bless This House	1963	3.00	6.00	12.00
❑ PC 8761	Bless This House	198?	2.00	4.00	8.00

—Budget-line reissue

Number	Title (A Side/B Side)	Yr	VG	VG+	NM
❑ CS 8804 [S]	Mahalia Jackson's Greatest Hits	1963	3.75	7.50	15.00
❑ CS 8930 [S]	Let's Pray Together	1964	3.75	7.50	15.00
❑ CS 9252 [S]	Mahalia Sings	1966	3.75	7.50	15.00
❑ CS 9346 [S]	Garden of Prayer	1967	3.00	6.00	12.00
❑ CS 9405 [S]	My Faith	1967	3.00	6.00	12.00
❑ CS 9490 [S]	Mahalia Jackson In Concert, Easter Sunday 1967	1967	3.00	6.00	12.00
❑ CS 9659	A Mighty Fortress	1968	3.00	6.00	12.00
❑ CS 9686	The Best-Loved Hymns of Dr. Martin Luther King Jr.	1968	3.75	7.50	15.00
❑ PC 9686	The Best-Loved Hymns of Dr. Martin Luther King Jr.	198?	2.00	4.00	8.00

—Budget-line reissue

Number	Title (A Side/B Side)	Yr	VG	VG+	NM
❑ CS 9727	Christmas with Mahalia	1968	3.00	6.00	12.00
❑ CS 9813	Right Out of the Church	1969	3.00	6.00	12.00
❑ CS 9950	What the World Needs Now	1970	3.00	6.00	12.00
❑ CG 30744 [(2)]	America's Favorite Hymns	1971	3.75	7.50	15.00
❑ KG 31379 [(2)]	The Great Mahalia Jackson	1972	3.75	7.50	15.00
❑ KC 34073	How I Got Over	1976	2.50	5.00	10.00
❑ PC 37710	Mahalia Jackson's Greatest Hits	198?	2.00	4.00	8.00
❑ 3C 38304	Silent Night	1982	2.00	4.00	8.00

—Reissue

COLUMBIA SPECIAL PRODUCTS

Number	Title (A Side/B Side)	Yr	VG	VG+	NM
❑ P2 13200 [(2)]	(HRB Music Proudly Presents) The Best of Mahalia Jackson: Hymns, Spirituals & Songs of Inspiration	1976	3.75	7.50	15.00

FOLKWAYS

Number	Title (A Side/B Side)	Yr	VG	VG+	NM
❑ 31101	I Sing Because I'm Happy, Volume 1	198?	2.50	5.00	10.00
❑ 31102	I Sing Because I'm Happy, Volume 2	198?	2.50	5.00	10.00

GRAND AWARD

Number	Title (A Side/B Side)	Yr	VG	VG+	NM
❑ GA 265 SD	I Believe	1966	3.75	7.50	15.00

—Reissue of 326

Number	Title (A Side/B Side)	Yr	VG	VG+	NM
❑ GA 33-326 [M]	Mahalia Jackson	1955	7.50	15.00	30.00
❑ GA 33-390 [M]	Mahalia Jackson	195?	7.50	15.00	30.00

HARMONY

Number	Title (A Side/B Side)	Yr	VG	VG+	NM
❑ HS 11279	You'll Never Walk Alone	196?	2.50	5.00	10.00
❑ HS 11372	Abide with Me	1970	2.50	5.00	10.00
❑ H 30019	Sunrise, Sunset	1970	2.50	5.00	10.00
❑ KH 31111	Lord Don't Let Me Fall	1972	2.50	5.00	10.00

KENWOOD

Number	Title (A Side/B Side)	Yr	VG	VG+	NM
❑ 474	In the Upper Room	196?	3.75	7.50	15.00
❑ 479	Just As I Am	196?	3.75	7.50	15.00
❑ 482	No Matter How You Pray	196?	3.75	7.50	15.00
❑ 486	Mahalia	196?	3.75	7.50	15.00
❑ 489	Mahalia Jackson With the Greatest Spiritual Singers	196?	3.75	7.50	15.00
❑ 500	The Best of Mahalia Jackson	196?	3.75	7.50	15.00
❑ 501	I Lift My Voice	196?	3.75	7.50	15.00
❑ 502	Sing Out	196?	3.75	7.50	15.00
❑ 1001/2 [(2)]	Command Performance	196?	5.00	10.00	20.00

PICKWICK

Number	Title (A Side/B Side)	Yr	VG	VG+	NM
❑ SPC-3510	I Believe	197?	2.50	5.00	10.00

PRIORITY

Number	Title (A Side/B Side)	Yr	VG	VG+	NM
❑ PU 37710	Mahalia Jackson's Greatest Hits	1981	2.50	5.00	10.00

JACKSON, MICHAEL

12-Inch Singles

CBS INTERNATIONAL

Number	Title (A Side/B Side)	Yr	VG	VG+	NM
❑ EPSL-69007	Todo Mi Amor Eres Tu/I Just Can't Stop Loving You	1988	20.00	40.00	80.00

—Spanish version of "I Just Can't Stop Loving You," pressed in U.S. for Hispanic markets in the U.S. and elsewhere

EPIC

Number	Title (A Side/B Side)	Yr	VG	VG+	NM
❑ AS 654 [DJ]	Don't Stop 'Til You Get Enough (5:45) (same on both sides?)	1979	6.25	12.50	25.00
❑ AS 687 [DJ]	Rock with You (3:39) (same on both sides)	1979	6.25	12.50	25.00
❑ EAS 0781 [DJ]	Blood on the Dance Floor — The Dubs (T&G Pool of Blood Dub) (Refugee Camp Dub) (Fire Island Dub) (A Cappella)	1997	5.00	10.00	20.00
❑ AS 1624 [DJ]	Beat It (same on both sides)	1983	5.00	10.00	20.00
❑ 49-03557	Billie Jean (Extended Version 6:20) (Instrumental 6:20)	1983	6.25	12.50	25.00
❑ 49-03915	Wanna Be Startin' Somethin' (6:30)/ (Instrumental)	1983	3.00	6.00	12.00
❑ EAS 4363 [DJ]	Black or White (Club Mix) (Dub Mix) (Underground House Mix) (House Radio Mix with Guitars) (Tribal Beats)	1991	5.00	10.00	20.00
❑ EAS 4454 [DJ]	Remember the Time (unknown versions)	1992	5.00	10.00	20.00
❑ E2S 4467 [(2)DJ]	In the Closet (11 versions)	1991	7.50	15.00	30.00
❑ E2S 4533 [(2)DJ]	In the Closet (11 versions)	1991	7.50	15.00	30.00
❑ E2S 4580 [(2)DJ]	Jam (13 versions)	1991	7.50	15.00	30.00
❑ E2S 4582 [(2)DJ]	Jam (Atlanta Techno Dub 5:11) (Roger's Slam Jam Mix 4:51) (Silky Dub 4:22) (Acapella Mix 4:31) (More Than Enuff Dub 5:56) (Maurice's Jammin' Dub Mix 7:18) (Roger's Club Dub 6:14) (Roger's Club Mix 6:20) (More Than Enuff Mix 5:56) (E-Smoove's Jazzy Jam 6:44) (Atlanta Techno Mix 6:06) (Roger's Underground Mix 6:02) (Silky 12" 6:20)	1991	7.50	15.00	30.00

Number	Title (A Side/B Side)	Yr	VG	VG+	NM
❏ EAS 4656 [DJ]	Jam (Roger's Jeep Mix) (Teddy's 12" Mix) (Percapella) (Teddy's Jam) (Roger's Jeep Dub) (MJ's Raw Mix)	1992	5.00	10.00	20.00
❏ E2S 4686 [(2)DJ]	Who Is It (11 versions)	1993	7.50	15.00	30.00
❏ 49-04961	Thriller/(Instrumental)	1983	2.50	5.00	10.00
❏ 49-06911	Don't Stop 'Til You Get Enough/Wanna Be Startin' Somethin'	1987	3.00	6.00	12.00
—"Mixed Masters" series					
❏ E2S 7125 [(2)DJ]	Scream (12 versions)	1995	7.50	15.00	30.00
❏ E2S 7127 [(2)DJ]	Scream (unknown versions)	1995	7.50	15.00	30.00
❏ AED 7192 [DJ]	The Megamixes (10:33) (4:58) (MJ Urban Megamix)/Scream (Jam & Lewis Remix) (Jam & Lewis Instrumental)	1995	7.50	15.00	30.00
❏ AED 7298 [DJ]	You Are Not Alone (Franctified Club Mix) (Album Version) (Knuckluv Dub Version) (Classic Club Mix)	1995	5.00	10.00	20.00
❏ 49-07462	Bad (Dance Extended Mix) (7" Single Version) (Dance Remix Radio Edit) (Dub Version) (Acappella)	1987	2.50	5.00	10.00
❏ 49-07487	The Way You Make Me Feel (Dance Extended Mix) (Dance Remix Radio Edit) (Dub Version) (A Cappella)	1987	2.50	5.00	10.00
❏ 49-07510	Man in the Mirror (Single Mix) (Album Mix1)	1988	2.50	5.00	10.00
❏ 49-07583	Dirty Diana/(Instrumental)	1988	2.50	5.00	10.00
❏ E2S 7603 [DJ]	This Time Around (DM Mad Club) (DM Radio) (Maurice's Club) (Georgie's House 'n Around Mix) (Timeland Dub) (Neverland Dub) (Don's Control This Dub) (UBQ's Opera Vibe) (DM Bang Da Drums Mix)	1995	25.00	50.00	100.00
❏ EAS 7605 [DJ]	Earth Song (Hani's Around the World Experience) (Hani's Club Experience) (Hani's Extended Radio Experience)	1995	7.50	15.00	30.00
❏ EAS 7606 [DJ]	This Time Around (unknown versions)	1995	12.50	25.00	50.00
❏ EAS 7607 [DJ]	This Time Around (4 versions)	1995	12.50	25.00	50.00
❏ E2S 7770 [(2)DJ]	They Don't Care About Us (10 versions)	1996	7.50	15.00	30.00
❏ 49-07855	Another Part of Me (Extended Dance Mix) (Radio Edit) (Dub Mix) (Acappella)	1988	2.00	4.00	8.00
❏ EAS 8337 [DJ]	Stranger in Moscow (Tee's In-House Club Mix) (Basement Boys 12" Club Mix) (Hani's Num Club Mix) (Charlie Roane's Full R&B Mix)	1996	3.75	7.50	15.00
❏ EAS 8338 [DJ]	Stranger in Moscow (Tee's Freeze Mix) (Tee's Mission Mix) (Tee'sq Cappella) (Bonus Beats) (Hani's Extended Chili Hop Mix) (Basement Boys Danger Dub)	1996	3.75	7.50	15.00
❏ EAS 9961 [DJ]	Blood on the Dance Floor (TM's Switchblade Mix) (Refugee Camp Mix) (Fire Island Vocal Mix) (TM's O-Positive Dub)	1997	3.00	6.00	12.00
❏ 28-50658	You Can't Win (Part 1 7:14)/(Part 2 2:58)	1978	6.25	12.50	25.00
❏ EAS 54863 [DJ]	Butterflies (same on both sides)	2001	3.75	7.50	15.00
❏ EAS 54911 [DJ]	You Rock My World (Track Masters Remix with Jay-Z) (same on both sides)	2001	5.00	10.00	20.00
❏ EAS 56719 [DJ]	Butterflies (Master Mix Featuring Eve) (Michael A Cappella) (Eve A Cappella) (Instrumental)	2002	5.00	10.00	20.00
❏ 49-74099	Black or White (The Clivilles & Cole House/Club Mix) (The Clivilles and Core House/Dub Mix) (House with Guitar Radio Mix) (Single Version) (Instrumental) (Tribal Beats)	1991	2.50	5.00	10.00
❏ 49-74201	Remember the Time (4 versions)/Black or White (The Underground Club Mix)`	1991	2.50	5.00	10.00
❏ 49-74267	In the Closet (Club Mix) (The Underground Mix) (Touch Me Dub) (KI's 12" Mix)	1992	2.50	5.00	10.00
❏ 49-74304	In the Closet (The Mission 9:20) (Freestyle Mix 6:20)/(The Mix of Life 7:38) (The Underground Dub 6:24)	1992	3.00	6.00	12.00
❏ 49-74334	Jam (Roger's Club Mix) (Atlanta Techno Mix) (Teddy's Jam) (Roger's Jam) (E-Smoove's Jazzy Jam)/Don't Stop 'Til You Get Enough (Roger's Underground Solution Mix)	1992	2.50	5.00	10.00
❏ 49-74420	Who Is It (4 versions)/Beat It (Moby's Sub Mix)	1993	2.50	5.00	10.00
❏ 49-78001	Scream (5 versions)/Childhood	1995	2.50	5.00	10.00
❏ 49-78003	You Are Not Alone (Franctified Club Mix) (Album Version)/MJ Megaremix (10:33)/Scream Louder (Flyte Tyme Remix)	1995	2.50	5.00	10.00
❏ 49-78008	Blood on the Dance Floor (2 versions?)/Dangerous (Roger's Dangerous Mix)	1997	2.00	4.00	8.00
❏ 49-78013	Stranger in Moscow (Hani's Num Club Mix) (TNT Danger Dub) (Basement Boys 12" Club Mix)/Blood on the Dance Floor	1997	2.50	5.00	10.00
❏ 49X-78212 [(2)]	They Don't Care About Us (7 versions)/Earth Song/Rock with You (Club Mix)/This Time Around	1996	3.75	7.50	15.00
❏ 49-78581	Beat It/Working Day and Night	1997	3.00	6.00	12.00
—"Mixed Masters" series					
❏ 49-78582	Billie Jean/Off the Wall	1997	2.50	5.00	10.00
—"Mixed Masters" series					
MOTOWN					
❏ PR-153 [DJ]	Farewell My Summer Love (4:21)/Call on Me (3:38)//The Jackson 5 Motown Medley (6:49)	1984	3.00	6.00	12.00
45s					
EPIC					
❏ 15-02156	Rock with You/Off the Wall	1981	—	—	3.00
—"Memory Lane" reissue					
❏ 15-02157	She's Out of My Life/Lovely One	1981	—	—	3.00
—"Memory Lane" reissue; B-side by The Jacksons					
❏ 34-03509	Billie Jean/Can't Get Outta the Rain	1983	—	2.00	4.00
❏ ENR-03575	Billie Jean/(B-side blank)	1983	3.75	7.50	15.00
—One-sided budget release					
❏ 34-03759	Beat It/Get On the Floor	1983	—	2.00	4.00
❏ 34-03914	Wanna Be Startin' Somethin'/(Instrumental)	1983	—	2.00	4.00
❏ 34-03914 [PS]	Wanna Be Startin' Somethin'/(Instrumental)	1983	—	2.50	5.00
❏ 34-04026	Human Nature/Baby Be Mine	1983	—	2.00	4.00
❏ 34-04026 [PS]	Human Nature/Baby Be Mine	1983	—	2.50	5.00
❏ 34-04026 [PS]	Human Nature	1983	2.50	5.00	10.00
—"Demonstration -- Not for Sale" on sleeve					
❏ 34-04165	P.Y.T. (Pretty Young Thing)/Working Day and Night	1983	—	2.00	4.00

Number	Title (A Side/B Side)	Yr	VG	VG+	NM
❏ 34-04165 [PS]	P.Y.T. (Pretty Young Thing)/Working Day and Night	1983	—	2.50	5.00
❏ 34-04364	Thriller/Can't Get Outta the Rain	1984	—	2.00	4.00
❏ 34-07253	I Just Can't Stop Loving You/Baby Be Mine	1987	—	—	3.00
❏ 34-07253 [PS]	I Just Can't Stop Loving You/Baby Be Mine	1987	—	—	3.00
❏ 34-07418	Bad/I Can't Help It	1987	—	—	3.00
❏ 34-07418 [PS]	Bad/I Can't Help It	1987	—	—	3.00
❏ 34-07645	The Way You Make Me Feel/(Instrumental)	1987	—	—	3.00
❏ 34-07645 [PS]	The Way You Make Me Feel/(Instrumental)	1987	—	—	3.00
❏ 34-07668	Man in the Mirror/(Instrumental)	1988	—	—	3.00
❏ 34-07668 [PS]	Man in the Mirror/(Instrumental)	1988	—	—	3.00
❏ 34-07739	Dirty Diana/(Instrumental)	1988	—	—	3.00
❏ 34-07739 [PS]	Dirty Diana/(Instrumental)	1988	—	—	3.00
❏ 34-07962	Another Part of Me/(Instrumental)	1988	—	—	3.00
❏ 34-07962 [PS]	Another Part of Me/(Instrumental)	1988	—	—	3.00
❏ 34-08044	Smooth Criminal/(Instrumental)	1988	—	—	3.00
❏ 34-08044 [PS]	Smooth Criminal/(Instrumental)	1988	—	—	3.00
❏ 8-50654	You Can't Win (Part 1)/You Can't Win (Part 2)	1979	—	3.00	6.00
❏ 9-50742	Don't Stop 'Til You Get Enough/I Can't Help It	1979	—	2.00	4.00
❏ 9-50797	Rock with You/Working Day and Night	1979	—	2.00	4.00
❏ 9-50838	Off the Wall/Get On the Floor	1980	—	2.00	4.00
❏ 9-50871	She's Out of My Life/Get On the Floor	1980	—	2.00	4.00
❏ 34-74100	Black or White/(Instrumental)	1991	—	—	3.00
❏ 34-74200	Remember the Time/Black or White (The Underground Club Mix)	1992	—	—	3.00
❏ 34-74266	In the Closet (7" Edit)/(The Mission Radio Edit)	1992	—	—	3.00
❏ 34-74333	Jam/Rock with You (Masters At Work Remix)	1992	—	—	3.00
❏ 34-74406	Who Is It/Wanna Be Startin' Somethin'	1992	—	—	3.00
❏ 34-74708	Heal the World/She Drives Me Wild	1992	—	—	3.00
❏ 34-77060	Will You Be There/(Instrumental)	1993	—	—	3.00
❏ 34-77312	Gone Too Soon/(Instrumental)	1993	—	—	3.00
❏ 34-78000	Scream/Childhood	1995	—	—	3.00
—A-side: With Janet Jackson					
❏ 34-78002	You Are Not Alone/Scream Louder	1995	—	—	3.00
❏ 38-78007	Blood on the Dance Floor/Dangerous (Roger's Dangerous Edit)	1997	—	—	3.00
❏ 34-78012	Stranger in Moscow (Radio Edit)/(Tee's Radio Mix)	1997	—	—	3.00
❏ 34-78264	They Don't Care About Us/Rock with You (Frankie Knuckles Mix)	1996	—	—	3.00
❏ 34 79656	You Rock My World (same on both sides)	2001	—	—	2.00
❏ 34 79656 [PS]	You Rock My World (same on both sides)	2001	—	—	2.00
❏ 34 79660	Cry (same on both sides)	2001	—	—	3.00
MCA					
❏ S45-1786 [DJ]	Someone in the Dark (same on both sides)	1982	12.50	25.00	50.00
❏ S45-1786 [PS]	Someone in the Dark (same on both sides)	1982	12.50	25.00	50.00
❏ 40947	Ease On Down the Road/Poppy Girls	1978	—	2.50	5.00
—With Diana Ross					
❏ 40947 [PS]	Ease On Down the Road/Poppy Girls	1978	—	2.50	5.00
MOTOWN					
❏ 1191	Got to Be There/Maria (You Were the Only One)	1971	—	2.50	5.00
❏ 1197	Rockin' Robin/Love Is Here and Now You're Gone	1972	—	2.50	5.00
❏ 1202	I Wanna Be Where You Are/We Got a Good Thing Going	1972	—	2.50	5.00
❏ 1202 [PS]	I Wanna Be Where You Are/We Got a Good Thing Going	1972	2.50	5.00	10.00
❏ 1207	Ben/You Can Cry on My Shoulder	1972	—	2.50	5.00
❏ 1218	With a Child's Heart/Morning Glow	1973	—	2.50	5.00
❏ 1270	Doggin' Around/Up Again	1974	—	—	—
—Unreleased					
❏ 1341	We're Almost There/Take Me Back	1975	—	2.50	5.00
❏ 1349	Just a Little Bit of You/Dear Michael	1975	—	2.50	5.00
❏ 1512	One Day in Your Life/Take Me Back	1981	—	2.00	4.00
❏ 1739	Farewell My Summer Love/Call On Me	1984	—	2.00	4.00
❏ 1739 [PS]	Farewell My Summer Love/Call On Me	1984	—	2.50	5.00
❏ 1757	Girl You're So Together/Touch the One You Love	1984	—	2.00	4.00
❏ 1914	Twenty-Five Miles/Up on the House Top	1987	2.00	4.00	8.00
❏ 1914 [PS]	Twenty-Five Miles/Up on the House Top	1987	2.00	4.00	8.00
Albums					
EPIC					
❏ FE 35745	Off the Wall	1979	2.00	4.00	8.00
❏ QE 38112	Thriller	1982	2.00	4.00	8.00
❏ 8E8 38867 [PD]	Thriller	1983	5.00	10.00	20.00
❏ OE 40600	Bad	1987	2.00	4.00	8.00
❏ 9E9 44043 [PD]	Bad	1987	3.00	6.00	12.00
❏ E2 45400 [(2)]	Dangerous	1991	3.75	7.50	15.00
❏ HE 47545	Off the Wall	1982	10.00	20.00	40.00
—Half-speed mastered edition					
❏ HE 48112	Thriller	1982	10.00	20.00	40.00
—Half-speed mastered edition					
❏ E3 59000 [(3)]	HIStory: Past, Present and Future — Book I	1995	5.00	10.00	20.00
—Box set with 12x12 booklet					
❏ E2 68000 [(2)]	Blood on the Dance Floor: HIStory in the Mix	1997	3.75	7.50	15.00
❏ E2 69400 [(2)]	Invincible	2001	3.75	7.50	15.00
MOTOWN					
❏ M5-107V1	Motown Superstar Series, Vol. 7	1981	2.00	4.00	8.00
❏ M5-130V1	Got to Be There	1981	2.50	5.00	10.00
—Reissue of Motown 747					
❏ M5-153V1	Ben	1981	2.50	5.00	10.00
—Reissue of Motown 755					
❏ M5-194V1	The Best of Michael Jackson	1981	2.50	5.00	10.00
—Reissue of Motown 851					
❏ M 747	Got to Be There	1972	3.75	7.50	15.00
❏ M 755	Ben	1972	3.75	7.50	15.00
—With only Michael Jackson on front cover					
❏ M 755	Ben	1972	15.00	30.00	60.00
—With Michael Jackson on top half of cover, rats on the bottom half					
❏ M 767	Music and Me	1973	3.75	7.50	15.00
❏ M6-825S	Forever, Michael	1975	3.00	6.00	12.00
❏ M6-851S	The Best of Michael Jackson	1975	3.00	6.00	12.00
❏ M8-956M1	One Day in Your Life	1981	2.50	5.00	10.00
❏ 6099 ML	Michael Jackson and The Jackson 5 — 14 Greatest Hits	1984	2.50	5.00	10.00
—Picture disc packaged with one glove					
❏ 6101 ML	Farewell My Summer Love 1984	1984	2.50	5.00	10.00

J

Number	Title (A Side/B Side)	Yr	VG	VG+	NM

JACKSON, MICHAEL, AND PAUL MCCARTNEY Also see each artist's individual listings.
12-Inch Singles
COLUMBIA

Number	Title (A Side/B Side)	Yr	VG	VG+	NM
❑ AS 1758 [DJ]	Say Say Say (same on both sides)	1983	3.00	6.00	12.00
—As "Paul McCartney and Michael Jackson"					
❑ 44-04169	Say, Say, Say//(Instrumental)/				
	Ode to a Koala Bear	1983	2.50	5.00	10.00
—As "Paul McCartney and Michael Jackson"					

45s
COLUMBIA

Number	Title (A Side/B Side)	Yr	VG	VG+	NM
❑ 38-04168	Say, Say, Say/Ode to a Koala Bear	1983	—	2.00	4.00
—As "Paul McCartney and Michael Jackson"; B-side by Paul McCartney					
❑ 38-04168 [PS]	Say, Say, Say/Ode to a Koala Bear	1983	—	2.00	4.00
EPIC					
❑ 34-03288	The Girl Is Mine/Can't Get Outta the Rain	1982	—	2.50	5.00
—B-side by Michael Jackson					
❑ 34-03288 [PS]	The Girl Is Mine/Can't Get Outta the Rain	1982	—	2.50	5.00
❑ ENR-03372	The Girl Is Mine/(B-side blank)	1982	3.00	6.00	12.00
—One-sided budget release					

JACKSON, MILLIE
12-Inch Singles
JIVE

Number	Title (A Side/B Side)	Yr	VG	VG+	NM
❑ 1015	Hot! Wild! Unrestricted! Crazy Love (4 versions)	1986	—	3.00	6.00
❑ 1022	Love Is a Dangerous Game/(Instrumental)	1986	—	3.00	6.00
❑ 1057	It's a Thang (4 versions)	1987	—	3.00	6.00
❑ 1109	Something You Can Feel (3 versions)	1988	—	3.00	6.00
❑ 1194	You Knocked the Love (Right Out of My Heart)				
	(3 versions)/Let Me Show You	1989	—	3.00	6.00
❑ 1247	Will You Love Me Tomorrow				
	(same on both sides)	1989	—	3.00	6.00
SPRING					
❑ 028 [DJ]	All the Way Lover/You Created a Monster	1977	2.50	5.00	10.00
❑ 099	We Got to Hit It Off (same on both sides)	1979	2.50	5.00	10.00
❑ 195	Mess on Your Hands-Finger Rap				
	(censored & uncensored)	1982	3.00	6.00	12.00

45s
JIVE

Number	Title (A Side/B Side)	Yr	VG	VG+	NM
❑ 1007-7-J	Hot! Wild! Unrestricted! Crazy Love (long & short				
	version)	1986	—	—	3.00
❑ 1007-7-J [PS]	Hot! Wild! Unrestricted! Crazy Love (long & short				
	version)	1986	—	—	3.00
❑ 1009-7-J	Love Is a Dangerous Game/(Instrumental)	1986	—	—	3.00
❑ 1009-7-J [PS]	Love Is a Dangerous Game/(Instrumental)	1986	—	—	3.00
❑ 1040-7-J	An Imitation of Love/Mind Over Matter	1987	—	—	3.00
❑ 1040-7-J [PS]	An Imitation of Love/Mind Over Matter	1987	—	—	3.00
❑ 1056-7-J	It's a Thang/(Instrumental)	1987	—	—	3.00
❑ 1108-7-J	The Tide Is Turning/Cover Me (Wall to Wall)	1988	—	—	3.00
❑ 1111-7-J	Something You Can Feel/(Instrumental)	1988	—	—	3.00
❑ 1111-7-J [PS]	Something You Can Feel/(Instrumental)	1988	—	—	3.00
❑ 1246-7-J	Will You Love Me Tomorrow/Muffle That Fart	1989	—	2.00	4.00
MGM					
❑ 14050	Little Bit of Something/My Heart Took a Licking	1969	2.00	4.00	8.00
SPRING					
❑ 119	A Child of God (It's Hard to Believe)/				
	You're the Joy of My Life	1971	—	2.50	5.00
❑ 123	Ask Me What You Want/I Just Can't Stand It	1972	—	2.50	5.00
❑ 127	My Man, a Sweet Man/I Gotta Get Away	1972	—	2.50	5.00
❑ 131	I Miss You Baby/I Ain't Giving Up	1972	—	2.50	5.00
❑ 134	Breakaway/Strange Things	1973	—	2.50	5.00
❑ 139	Hurts So Good/Love Doctor	1973	—	2.50	5.00
❑ 144	I Got to Try It One Time/Get Your Love Right	1974	—	2.50	5.00
❑ 147	How Do You Feel the Morning After/In the Wash	1974	—	2.50	5.00
❑ 155	The Rap/If Loving You Is Wrong				
	I Don't Want to Be Right	1974	—	2.50	5.00
❑ 157	I'm Through Trying to Prove My Love to You/All				
	I Want Is a Fighting Chance	1975	—	2.50	5.00
❑ 161	Leftovers/Loving Arms	1975	—	2.50	5.00
❑ 164	Bad Risk/There You Are	1976	—	2.50	5.00
❑ 167	Feel Like Making Love/I'm in Love Again	1976	—	2.50	5.00
❑ 170	I Can't Say Goodbye/Help Me Finish My Song	1977	—	2.50	5.00
❑ 173	A Love of Your Own/Live My Love for You	1977	—	2.50	5.00
❑ 175	If You're Not Back in Love by Monday/A Taste				
	of Outside Love	1977	—	2.50	5.00
❑ 179	All the Way Lover/Cheatin' Is	1978	—	2.50	5.00
❑ 185	Sweet Music Man/Go Out and Get Some	1978	—	2.50	5.00
❑ 189	Keep the Home Fire Burnin'/Logs and Thangs	1978	—	2.50	5.00
❑ 192	Never Change Lovers in the Middle of the Night/				
	Seeing You Again	1979	—	2.50	5.00
❑ 197	A Moment's Pleasure/Once You've Had It	1979	—	2.50	5.00
❑ 3002	We Got to Hit It Off/What Went Wrong Last Night	1979	—	2.00	4.00
❑ 3007	Didn't I Blow Your Mind/Be a Sweetheart	1980	—	2.00	4.00
❑ 3011	Despair/Wish That I Could Have				
	Hurt That Way Again	1980	—	2.00	4.00
❑ 3013	This Is It (Part 1)/This Is It (Part 2)	1980	—	2.00	4.00
❑ 3017	I Had to Say It/It's Going to Take Some Time				
	This Time	1981	—	2.00	4.00
❑ 3019	I Can't Stop Loving You/Loving You	1981	—	2.00	4.00
❑ 3021	Anybody That Don't Like Millie Jackson/Rose				
	Colored Glasses	1981	—	2.50	5.00
❑ 3024	Passion/Lovers and Girlfriends	1982	—	2.00	4.00
❑ 3028	Special Occasion/Blues Don't Get Tired of Me	1982	—	2.00	4.00
❑ 3034	I Feel Like Walking in the Rain/(B-side unknown)	1983	—	2.00	4.00
❑ 3036	E.S.P./(B-side unknown)	1984	—	2.00	4.00
❑ 3040	Sister in the System/(B-side unknown)	1984	—	2.00	4.00

Albums
JIVE

Number	Title (A Side/B Side)	Yr	VG	VG+	NM
❑ 1016-1-J	An Imitation of Love	1986	2.00	4.00	8.00
❑ 1103-1-J	The Tide Is Turning	1988	2.00	4.00	8.00
❑ 1186-1-J	Back to the Shit	1989	2.50	5.00	10.00
❑ 1447-1-J	Young Man, Older Woman	1991	3.00	6.00	12.00
SPRING					
❑ SPR-5703	Millie Jackson	1972	3.00	6.00	12.00
❑ SPR-5706	It Hurts So Good	1973	3.00	6.00	12.00
❑ SPR-6701	Millie	1974	2.50	5.00	10.00
❑ SPR-6703	Caught Up	1974	2.50	5.00	10.00
❑ SPR-6708	Still Caught Up	1975	2.50	5.00	10.00
❑ SP-6712	Lovingly Yours	1976	2.50	5.00	10.00
❑ SP-6715	Feelin' Bitchy	1977	2.50	5.00	10.00
❑ SP-1-6719	Get It Out'cha System	1978	2.50	5.00	10.00
❑ SP-1-6722	A Moment's Pleasure	1979	2.50	5.00	10.00
❑ SP-2-6725 [(2)]	Live & Uncensored	1979	3.00	6.00	12.00
❑ SP-1-6727	For Men Only	1980	2.50	5.00	10.00
❑ SP-1-6730	I Had to Say It	1981	2.50	5.00	10.00
❑ SP-1-6735	Live and Outrageous (Rated XXX)	1982	2.50	5.00	10.00
❑ SP-1-6737	Hard Times	1983	2.50	5.00	10.00

JACKSON, MILLIE, AND ISAAC HAYES
45s
POLYDOR

Number	Title (A Side/B Side)	Yr	VG	VG+	NM
❑ 2036	Do You Wanna Make Love/I Changed My Mind	1979	—	2.00	4.00
❑ 2063	You Never Cross My Mind/				
	Feels Like the First Time	1980	—	2.00	4.00

Albums
POLYDOR

Number	Title (A Side/B Side)	Yr	VG	VG+	NM
❑ PD-1-6229	Royal Rappin's	1979	2.50	5.00	10.00

JACKSON, RUDY
45s
IMPERIAL

Number	Title (A Side/B Side)	Yr	VG	VG+	NM
❑ 5425	Teasing Me/Give Me Your Hand	1957	10.00	20.00	40.00
❑ 5945	Go On Lover, Go On/Who Do You Think You Are	1963	3.00	6.00	12.00
R & B					
❑ 1310	I'm Crying/Enfold Me	1955	20.00	40.00	80.00

JACKSON, SHIRLEY
45s
METRO

Number	Title (A Side/B Side)	Yr	VG	VG+	NM
❑ 20031	The Wedding/Wait for Me	1960	3.00	6.00	12.00

JACKSON, STONEWALL
45s
COLUMBIA

Number	Title (A Side/B Side)	Yr	VG	VG+	NM
❑ 4-40883	Don't Be Angry/Knock Off Your Naggin'	1957	6.25	12.50	25.00
❑ 4-40997	I Need You Real Bad/A Broken Heart, A				
	Wedding Band	1957	6.25	12.50	25.00
❑ 4-41114	Tears on Her Brodal Bouquet/Gettin' Older	1958	5.00	10.00	20.00
❑ 4-41199	Grieving in My Heart/				
	I Can't Go On Living This Way	1958	5.00	10.00	20.00
❑ 4-41257	Life to Go/Misery Known As Heartache	1958	5.00	10.00	20.00
❑ 4-41393	Waterloo/Smoke Along the Track	1959	3.75	7.50	15.00
❑ 4-41393 [PS]	Waterloo/Smoke Along the Track	1959	7.50	15.00	30.00
❑ 4-41488	Igmoo (The Pride of South Central High)/Uncle				
	Sam and Big John Bull	1959	3.75	7.50	15.00
❑ 4-41533	Mary Don't You Weep/Run	1959	3.75	7.50	15.00
❑ 4-41591	Why I'm Walkin'/Life of a Poor Boy	1960	3.75	7.50	15.00
❑ 4-41695	Thirty Links of Chain/Sixteen Fathoms	1960	3.75	7.50	15.00
❑ 4-41785	A Little Guy Called Joe/I'm Gonna Find You	1960	3.75	7.50	15.00
❑ 4-41932	Greener Pastures/				
	Wedding Bells for You and Me	1961	3.75	7.50	15.00
❑ 4-42028	Hungry for Love/For the Last Time	1961	3.75	7.50	15.00
❑ 4-42229	A Wound Time Can't Erase/Second Choice	1961	3.75	7.50	15.00
❑ 4-42426	Leona/One Look at Heaven	1962	3.00	6.00	12.00
❑ 4-42628	Can't Hang Up the Phone/Slowly	1962	3.00	6.00	12.00
❑ 4-42765	Old Showboat/A Toast to the Bride	1963	3.00	6.00	12.00
❑ 4-42846	Wild Wind Wind/The Water's So Cold	1963	3.00	6.00	12.00
❑ 4-42889	B.J. the D.J./Big House on the Corner	1963	3.00	6.00	12.00
❑ 4-43011	Not My Kind of People/Give It Back to the Indians	1964	3.00	6.00	12.00
❑ 4-43076	Don't Be Angry/It's Not Me	1964	3.00	6.00	12.00
❑ 4-43197	I Washed My Hands in Muddy Water/				
	I've Got to Change	1964	3.00	6.00	12.00
❑ 4-43304	Lost in the Shuffle/Trouble and Me	1965	2.50	5.00	10.00
❑ 4-43411	If This House Could Talk/Poor Red Georgia Dirt	1965	2.50	5.00	10.00
❑ 4-43552	The Minute Men (Are Turning in Their Graves)/				
	I Wish I Had a Girl	1966	2.50	5.00	10.00
❑ 4-43552 [PS]	The Minute Men (Are Turning in Their Graves)/				
	I Wish I Had a Girl	1966	5.00	10.00	20.00
❑ 4-43718	Blues Plus Booze (Means I Lose)/Still Awake	1966	2.50	5.00	10.00
❑ 4-43917	Mommy Look, Santa Is Crying/Blue Christmas	1966	3.00	6.00	12.00
❑ 4-43966	Stamp Out Loneliness/Road to Recovery	1967	2.50	5.00	10.00
❑ 4-44121	Promises and Hearts (Were Made to Break)/				
	While the Daisies Go Free	1967	2.50	5.00	10.00
❑ 4-44283	This World Means Nothing (Since You're Gone)/				
	Almost Hear the Blues	1967	2.50	5.00	10.00
❑ 4-44416	Nothing Takes the Place of Loving You/If				
	Heartaches Were Wine	1968	2.50	5.00	10.00
❑ 4-44501	I Believe in Love/Drinking and Driving	1968	2.50	5.00	10.00
❑ 4-44501 [PS]	I Believe in Love/Drinking and Driving	1968	3.75	7.50	15.00
❑ 4-44625	Angry Words/Red Roses Blooming Back Home	1968	2.50	5.00	10.00
❑ 4-44726	Somebody's Always Leaving/Recess Time	1969	2.50	5.00	10.00
❑ 4-44863	"Never More" Quoth the Raven/				
	How Many Lies Can I Tell	1969	2.50	5.00	10.00
❑ 4-44994	Ship in the Bottle/Thoughts of a Lonely Man	1969	2.50	5.00	10.00
❑ 4-45075	Better Days for Mama/The Harm You've Done	1970	2.00	4.00	8.00
❑ 4-45151	Born That Way/Blue Field	1970	2.00	4.00	8.00
❑ 4-45217	Oh, Lonesome Me/When He Was Nine	1970	2.00	4.00	8.00
❑ 4-45291	Save a Little Place for Me/Wings of a Dove	1970	2.00	4.00	8.00
❑ 4-45381	Me and You and a Dog Named Boo/				
	Here's to Hank	1971	2.00	4.00	8.00
❑ 4-45465	Push the Panic Button/				
	Waitin' for Dawn 'Til Dawn	1971	2.00	4.00	8.00
❑ 4-45546	That's All This Old World Needs/Big Busy World	1972	2.00	4.00	8.00
❑ 4-45632	Torn from the Pages of Life/Waterloo	1972	2.00	4.00	8.00
❑ 4-45738	I'm Not Strong Enough (To Build Another				
	Dream)/I've Run Out of Reasons	1972	2.00	4.00	8.00
❑ 4-45831	True Love Is the Thing/House of Bottles and Cans	1973	2.00	4.00	8.00
GRT					
❑ 013	Read Between the Lines/Don't Be Late	1975	—	3.00	6.00
❑ 023	Waterloo/I Washed My Hands in Muddy Water	1975	—	3.00	6.00
LITTLE DARLIN'					
❑ 7800	Spirits of St. Louis/Alcohol of Fame	1978	—	3.00	6.00
❑ 7802	Walk Out on Me Before I Walk Out on You/				
	Burned On Low	1978	—	3.00	6.00

Number	Title (A Side/B Side)	Yr	VG	VG+	NM
❏ 7806	I Can't Sing a Love Song/My Favorite Sin	1978	—	3.00	6.00
❏ 7915	Come On Home/Point of No Return	1979	—	3.00	6.00
❏ 7927	Listening to Johnny Paycheck/				
	Here's to the Ripoff	1979	—	3.00	6.00

MGM

Number	Title (A Side/B Side)	Yr	VG	VG+	NM
❏ 14569	Herman Schwartz/Lovin' the Fool Out of Me	1973	—	3.50	7.00

Albums

COLUMBIA

Number	Title (A Side/B Side)	Yr	VG	VG+	NM
❏ CL 1391 [M]	The Dynamic Stonewall Jackson	1959	6.25	12.50	25.00
❏ CL 1770 [M]	Sadness in a Song	1962	5.00	10.00	20.00
❏ CL 2059 [M]	I Love a Song	1963	5.00	10.00	20.00
❏ CL 2278 [M]	Trouble & Me	1964	3.75	7.50	15.00
❏ CL 2377 [M]	Stonewall Jackson's Greatest Hits	1965	3.75	7.50	15.00
❏ CL 2509 [M]	All's Fair in Love 'n' War	1966	3.75	7.50	15.00
❏ CL 2674 [M]	Help Stamp Out Loneliness	1967	6.25	12.50	25.00
❏ CL 2762 [M]	Stonewall Jackson Country	1967	6.25	12.50	25.00
❏ CS 8186 [S]	The Dynamic Stonewall Jackson	1959	7.50	15.00	30.00
❏ CS 8570 [S]	Sadness in a Song	1962	6.25	12.50	25.00
❏ CS 8859 [S]	I Love a Song	1963	6.25	12.50	25.00
❏ CS 9078 [S]	Trouble & Me	1964	5.00	10.00	20.00
❏ CS 9177 [S]	Stonewall Jackson's Greatest Hits	1965	5.00	10.00	20.00
❏ CS 9309 [S]	All's Fair in Love 'n' War	1966	5.00	10.00	20.00
❏ CS 9474 [S]	Help Stamp Out Loneliness	1967	5.00	10.00	20.00
❏ CS 9562 [S]	Stonewall Jackson Country	1967	5.00	10.00	20.00
❏ CS 9669	Nothing Takes the Place of Loving You	1968	5.00	10.00	20.00
❏ CS 9708	The Great Old Songs	1968	5.00	10.00	20.00
❏ CS 9754	The Old Country Church	1969	6.25	12.50	25.00
❏ CS 9880	Tribute to Hank Williams	1969	5.00	10.00	20.00
❏ C 30254	The Real Thing	1971	3.75	7.50	15.00

HARMONY

Number	Title (A Side/B Side)	Yr	VG	VG+	NM
❏ HS 11187	The Exciting Stonewall Jackson	196?	3.00	6.00	12.00

JACKSON, TONY, AND THE VIBRATIONS
45s

KAPP

Number	Title (A Side/B Side)	Yr	VG	VG+	NM
❏ 639	This Little Girl of Mine/You Beat Me to the Punch	1965	3.75	7.50	15.00

RED BIRD

Number	Title (A Side/B Side)	Yr	VG	VG+	NM
❏ 10-038	That's What I Want/Stage Door	1965	3.75	7.50	15.00

JACKSON, WALTER
45s

BRUNSWICK

Number	Title (A Side/B Side)	Yr	VG	VG+	NM
❏ 55502	It Doesn't Take Much/Let Me Come Back	1973	—	3.00	6.00

CHI-SOUND

Number	Title (A Side/B Side)	Yr	VG	VG+	NM
❏ XW908	Feelings/Words (Are Impossible)	1976	—	2.50	5.00
❏ XW964	Baby, I Love Your Way/What Would You Do	1977	—	2.50	5.00
❏ XW1044	It's All Over/Gonna Find Me an Angel	1977	—	2.50	5.00
❏ XW1140	If I Had My Way/We Could Fly	1978	—	2.50	5.00
❏ XW1216	Manhattan Skyline/I Won't Remember				
	Ever Loving You	1978	—	2.50	5.00
❏ 2426	Magic Man/Golden Rays	1979	—	2.00	4.00

COLUMBIA

Number	Title (A Side/B Side)	Yr	VG	VG+	NM
❏ 02037	Tell Me Where It Hurts/When I See You	1981	—	2.00	4.00
❏ 02294	What If I Walked Out on You/Come to Me	1981	—	2.00	4.00
❏ 42528	This World of Mine/I Don't Want to Suffer	1962	6.25	12.50	25.00
❏ 42659	Starting Tomorrow/Then, Only Then	1963	5.00	10.00	20.00
❏ 42823	Opportunity/It Will Be the Last Time	1963	5.00	10.00	20.00

COTILLION

Number	Title (A Side/B Side)	Yr	VG	VG+	NM
❏ 44053	Anyway That You Want Me/				
	Life Has Its Ups and Downs	1969	2.00	4.00	8.00

EPIC

Number	Title (A Side/B Side)	Yr	VG	VG+	NM
❏ 10408	Ad Lib/No Butterflies	1968	2.00	4.00	8.00

KELLI-ARTS

Number	Title (A Side/B Side)	Yr	VG	VG+	NM
❏ 1006	If I Had a Chance/(B-side unknown)	1982	—	2.50	5.00

OKEH

Number	Title (A Side/B Side)	Yr	VG	VG+	NM
❏ 7189	That's What Mama Say/What Would You Do	1964	3.00	6.00	12.00
❏ 7204	It's All Over/Lee Cross	1964	2.50	5.00	10.00
❏ 7215	Suddenly I'm All Alone/Special Love	1965	2.50	5.00	10.00
❏ 7219	Welcome Home/Blowin' in the Wind	1965	2.50	5.00	10.00
❏ 7229	I'll Keep On Trying/				
	Where Have All the Flowers Gone	1965	2.50	5.00	10.00
❏ 7236	Funny (Not Much)/One Heart Lonely	1965	2.50	5.00	10.00
❏ 7247	It's an Uphill Climb to the Bottom/Tear for Tear	1966	2.00	4.00	8.00
❏ 7247 [PS]	It's an Uphill Climb to the Bottom/Tear for Tear	1966	5.00	10.00	20.00
❏ 7256	After You There Can Be Nothing/				
	My Funny Valentine	1966	2.00	4.00	8.00
❏ 7260	A Corner in the Sun/Not You	1966	2.00	4.00	8.00
❏ 7272	Speak Her Name/They Don't Give Medals (To				
	Yesterday's Heroes)	1967	2.00	4.00	8.00
❏ 7272 [PS]	Speak Her Name/They Don't Give Medals (To				
	Yesterday's Heroes)	1967	5.00	10.00	20.00
❏ 7285	Deep in the Heart of Harlem/				
	My One Chance to Make It	1967	2.00	4.00	8.00
❏ 7285 [PS]	Deep in the Heart of Harlem/				
	My One Chance to Make It	1967	5.00	10.00	20.00
❏ 7295	Cold, Cold Winter/My Ship Is Comin' In	1967	2.00	4.00	8.00
❏ 7305	Everything/Road to Ruin	1968	2.00	4.00	8.00

U.S.A.

Number	Title (A Side/B Side)	Yr	VG	VG+	NM
❏ 104	Fool for You/Walls That Separate	196?	3.00	6.00	12.00

Albums

CHI-SOUND

Number	Title (A Side/B Side)	Yr	VG	VG+	NM
❏ CS-LA656-G	Feeling Good	1976	3.00	6.00	12.00
❏ CS-LA733-G	I Want to Come Back As A Song	1977	3.00	6.00	12.00
❏ CS-LA844-G	Good to See You	1978	3.00	6.00	12.00

COLUMBIA

Number	Title (A Side/B Side)	Yr	VG	VG+	NM
❏ FC 37132	Tell Me Where It Hurts	1981	2.50	5.00	10.00

EPIC

Number	Title (A Side/B Side)	Yr	VG	VG+	NM
❏ E 34657	Greatest Hits	1977	2.50	5.00	10.00
❏ PE 40434	Greatest Hits	1987	2.00	4.00	8.00

OKEH

Number	Title (A Side/B Side)	Yr	VG	VG+	NM
❏ OKM 12107 [M]	It's All Over	1965	6.25	12.50	25.00
❏ OKM 12108 [M]	Welcome Home	1966	6.25	12.50	25.00
❏ OKM 12120 [M]	Speak Her Name	1967	6.25	12.50	25.00
❏ OKS 14107 [S]	It's All Over	1965	7.50	15.00	30.00
❏ OKS 14108 [S]	Welcome Home	1966	7.50	15.00	30.00
❏ OKS 14120 [S]	Speak Her Name	1967	7.50	15.00	30.00
❏ OKS 14128	Walter Jackson's Greatest Hits	1969	3.75	7.50	15.00

JACKSON, WANDA
45s

ABC

Number	Title (A Side/B Side)	Yr	VG	VG+	NM
❏ 12116	Take a Look/I Can't Stand to Hear				
	You Say Goodbye	1975	—	2.50	5.00

CAPITOL

Number	Title (A Side/B Side)	Yr	VG	VG+	NM
❏ 2021	A Girl Don't Have to Drink to Have Fun/My Days				
	Are Darker Than Your Nights	1967	2.50	5.00	10.00
❏ 2085	By the Time You Get to Phoenix/Wishing Well	1968	2.00	4.00	8.00
❏ 2151	My Baby Walked Right Out on Me/				
	No Place to Go But Home	1968	2.00	4.00	8.00
❏ 2245	Little Boy Soldier/I Talk a Pretty Story	1968	2.00	4.00	8.00
❏ 2315	I Wish I Was Your Friend/Poor Old Me	1968	2.00	4.00	8.00
❏ 2379	If I Had a Hammer/The Pain of It All	1969	2.00	4.00	8.00
❏ 2472	Your Tender Love/As the Day Wears On	1969	2.00	4.00	8.00
❏ 2524	Everything's Leaving/You Cheated Me	1969	2.00	4.00	8.00
❏ 2614	My Big Iron Skillet/The Hunter	1969	2.00	4.00	8.00
❏ 2693	Two Separate Bar Stools/Two Wrongs Don't				
	Make a Right	1969	2.00	4.00	8.00
❏ 2761	A Woman Lives for Love/What Have We Done	1970	—	3.00	6.00
❏ 2872	Who Shot John/Stop the World	1970	—	3.00	6.00
❏ 2986	Fancy Satin Pillows/Why Don't We Love Like				
	That Anymore	1970	—	3.00	6.00
❏ 3070	People Gotta Be Loving/Glory Hallelujah	1971	—	3.00	6.00
❏ 3143	Back Then/I'm Gonna Walk Out of Your Life	1971	—	3.00	6.00
❏ 3218	I Already Know (What I'm Gettin' for My				
	Birthday)/The Man You Could Have Been	1971	—	3.00	6.00
❏ 3293	I'll Be Whatever You Say/				
	The More You See Me Less	1972	—	3.00	6.00
❏ 3385	I Wouldn't Want You Any Other Way/				
	Song of the Wind	1972	—	3.00	6.00
❏ F3485	I Gotta Know/Half As Good a Girl	1956	10.00	20.00	40.00
❏ 3498	Roll with the Tide/Tennessee Women's Prison	1972	—	3.00	6.00
❏ F3575	The Hot Dog That Made Him Mad/Silver Threads				
	and Golden Needles	1956	10.00	20.00	40.00
❏ 3599	I Don't Know How to Tell Him/Your Memory				
	Comes and Gets Me	1973	—	3.00	6.00
❏ F3637	Cryin' Through the Night/Baby Loves Him	1957	12.50	25.00	50.00
❏ F3683	Don'a Wan'a/Let Me Explain	1957	7.50	15.00	30.00
❏ F3764	Cool Love/Did You Miss Me	1957	7.50	15.00	30.00
❏ F3843	Fujiyama Mama/No Wedding Bells for Joe	1957	7.50	15.00	30.00
❏ F3941	Just a Queen for a Day/Honey Bop	1958	7.50	15.00	30.00
❏ F4026	(Every Time They Play) Our Song/				
	Mean, Mean Man	1958	7.50	15.00	30.00
❏ F4081	Sinful Heart/Rock Your Baby	1958	7.50	15.00	30.00
❏ F4142	Savin' My Love/I Wanna Waltz	1959	6.25	12.50	25.00
❏ F4207	A Date with Jerry/You're the One for Me	1959	6.25	12.50	25.00
❏ F4286	Reaching/I'd Rather Have You	1959	6.25	12.50	25.00
❏ 4354	My Destiny/Please Call Today	1960	6.25	12.50	25.00
❏ 4397	Let's Have a Party/Cool Love	1960	10.00	20.00	40.00
❏ 4469	Mean, Mean Man/Happy, Happy Birthday	1960	6.25	12.50	25.00
❏ 4520	Riot in Cell Block #9/Little Charm Bracelet	1961	6.25	12.50	25.00
❏ 4553	Right or Wrong/Funnel of Love	1961	6.25	12.50	25.00
❏ 4635	In the Middle of a Heartache/I'd Be Ashamed	1961	6.25	12.50	25.00
❏ 4681	A Little Bitty Tear/I Don't Wanta Go	1962	5.00	10.00	20.00
❏ 4723	If I Cried Every Time You Hurt Me/				
	Let My Love Walk In	1962	5.00	10.00	20.00
❏ 4723 [PS]	If I Cried Every Time You Hurt Me/				
	Let My Love Walk In	1962	7.50	15.00	30.00
❏ 4785	I Misunderstood/Between the Window				
	and the Phone	1962	3.75	7.50	15.00
❏ 4833	The Greatest Actor/You Bug Me Bad	1962	3.75	7.50	15.00
❏ 4884	Whirlpool/One Teardrop at a Time	1962	3.75	7.50	15.00
❏ 4917	But I Was Lying/Sympathy	1963	3.75	7.50	15.00
❏ 4973	This Should Go On Forever/We Haven't a				
	Moment to Lose	1963	3.75	7.50	15.00
❏ 5015	Memory Mountain/Let Me Talk to You	1963	3.75	7.50	15.00
❏ 5072	Slippin'/Just for You	1963	3.75	7.50	15.00
❏ 5142	The Violet and a Rose/To Tell You the Truth	1964	3.00	6.00	12.00
❏ 5228	Leave My Baby Alone/I'm Mad at Me	1964	3.00	6.00	12.00
❏ 5287	Candy Man/Weary Blues From Waitin'	1964	3.00	6.00	12.00
❏ 5364	My Baby's Gone/If I Were You	1965	3.00	6.00	12.00
❏ 5433	Have I Grown Used to Missing You/				
	Take Me Home	1965	3.00	6.00	12.00
❏ 5491	My First Day Without You/Send Me No Roses	1965	3.00	6.00	12.00
❏ 5559	The Box It Came In/Look Out Heart	1965	3.00	6.00	12.00
❏ 5645	Because It's You/Long As I Have You	1966	2.50	5.00	10.00
❏ 5712	This Gun Don't Care/I Wonder If She Knows	1966	2.50	5.00	10.00
❏ 5789	Tears Will Be the Chaser for Your Wine/				
	Reckless Love Affair	1967	2.50	5.00	10.00
❏ 5863	Both Sides of the Line/Famous Last Words	1967	2.50	5.00	10.00
❏ 5960	My Heart Gets All the Breaks/				
	You'll Always Have My Love	1967	2.50	5.00	10.00

DECCA

Number	Title (A Side/B Side)	Yr	VG	VG+	NM
❏ 29140	You Can't Have My Love/Lovin' Country Style	1954	15.00	30.00	60.00
—With Billy Gray					
❏ 29253	The Right to Love/If You Knew What I Know	1954	15.00	30.00	60.00
❏ 29267	If You Don't, Somebody Else Will/You'd Be the				
	First One to Know	1954	12.50	25.00	50.00
—With Billy Gray					
❏ 29514	Tears at the Grand Ole Opry/				
	Nobody's Darlin' But Mine	1955	12.50	25.00	50.00
❏ 29677	Don't Do the Things He'd Do/It's the Same World	1955	7.50	15.00	30.00
❏ 29803	Wasted/I Cried Again	1956	12.50	25.00	50.00
❏ 30153	You Won't Forget (About Me)/A Heart You Could				
	Have Had	1956	7.50	15.00	30.00

JIN

Number	Title (A Side/B Side)	Yr	VG	VG+	NM
❏ 300	Lonely Days, Lonely Nights/My Memories	197?	—	2.50	5.00

MYRRH

Number	Title (A Side/B Side)	Yr	VG	VG+	NM
❏ 122	When It's Time to Fall in Love Again/Say "I Do"	1973	—	2.50	5.00
❏ 126	Come On Home (To This Lonely Heart)/It's a				
	Long, Long Time to Cry	1973	—	2.50	5.00
❏ 143	Jesus Put a Yodel in My Soul/(B-side unknown)	1974	—	2.50	5.00
❏ 152	Where Do I Put His Memory/Take a Look	1975	—	2.50	5.00

J

Number	Title (A Side/B Side)	Yr	VG	VG+	NM

7-Inch Extended Plays
CAPITOL

Number	Title (A Side/B Side)	Yr	VG	VG+	NM
❑ SXA-1776	In the Middle of a Heartache/Is It Wrong/Don't Ask Me Why//If I Cried Every Time You Hurt Me/You Don't Know/A Little Bitty Tear	196?	7.50	15.00	30.00

—Stereo jukebox issue; small hole, plays at 33 1/3 rpm

| ❑ SXA-1776 [PS] | Wonderful Wanda | 196? | 7.50 | 15.00 | 30.00 |

Albums
CAPITOL

Number	Title	Yr	VG	VG+	NM
❑ ST-129	The Many Moods of Wanda Jackson	1969	3.75	7.50	15.00
❑ ST-238	The Happy Side of Wanda Jackson	1969	3.75	7.50	15.00
❑ ST 8-0345	Wanda Jackson In Person	1970	5.00	10.00	20.00

—Capitol Record Club edition

❑ ST-345	Wanda Jackson In Person	1970	3.75	7.50	15.00
❑ ST-434	Wanda Jackson Country!	1970	3.75	7.50	15.00
❑ ST-554	A Woman Lives for Love	1970	3.75	7.50	15.00
❑ ST-669	I've Gotta Sing!	1971	3.75	7.50	15.00
❑ T 1041 [M]	Wanda Jackson	1958	75.00	150.00	300.00

—Black colorband label, Capitol logo at left

| ❑ T 1041 [M] | Wanda Jackson | 1962 | 25.00 | 50.00 | 100.00 |

—Black colorband label, Capitol logo at top

| ❑ T 1384 [M] | Rockin' with Wanda | 1960 | 100.00 | 200.00 | 400.00 |

—Black colorband label, Capitol logo at left

| ❑ T 1384 [M] | Rockin' with Wanda | 1962 | 62.50 | 125.00 | 250.00 |

—Gold "Star Line" label

| ❑ T 1384 [M] | Rockin' with Wanda | 1963 | 37.50 | 75.00 | 150.00 |

—Black "Star Line" label

| ❑ ST 1511 [S] | There's a Party Goin' On | 1961 | 100.00 | 200.00 | 400.00 |

—Black colorband label, Capitol logo at left

| ❑ T 1511 [S] | There's a Party Goin' On | 1961 | 62.50 | 125.00 | 250.00 |

—Black colorband label, Capitol logo at left

| ❑ ST 1596 [S] | Right or Wrong | 1961 | 12.50 | 25.00 | 50.00 |

—Black colorband label, Capitol logo at left

| ❑ ST 1596 [S] | Right or Wrong | 1962 | 6.25 | 12.50 | 25.00 |

—Black colorband label, Capitol logo at top

| ❑ T 1596 [M] | Right or Wrong | 1961 | 10.00 | 20.00 | 40.00 |

—Black colorband label, Capitol logo at left

| ❑ T 1596 [M] | Right or Wrong | 1962 | 5.00 | 10.00 | 20.00 |

—Black colorband label, Capitol logo at top

❑ ST 1776 [S]	Wonderful Wanda	1962	7.50	15.00	30.00
❑ T 1776 [M]	Wonderful Wanda	1962	6.25	12.50	25.00
❑ ST 1911 [S]	Love Me Forever	1963	7.50	15.00	30.00
❑ T 1911 [M]	Love Me Forever	1963	6.25	12.50	25.00
❑ ST 2030 [S]	Two Sides of Wanda	1964	7.50	15.00	30.00
❑ T 2030 [M]	Two Sides of Wanda	1964	6.25	12.50	25.00
❑ ST 2306 [S]	Blues in My Heart	1965	7.50	15.00	30.00
❑ T 2306 [M]	Blues in My Heart	1965	6.25	12.50	25.00
❑ ST 2438 [S]	Wanda Jackson Sings Country Songs	1965	7.50	15.00	30.00
❑ T 2438 [M]	Wanda Jackson Sings Country Songs	1965	6.25	12.50	25.00
❑ ST 2606 [S]	Wanda Jackson Salutes the Country Music Hall of Fame	1966	5.00	10.00	20.00
❑ T 2606 [M]	Wanda Jackson Salutes the Country Music Hall of Fame	1966	3.75	7.50	15.00
❑ ST 2704 [S]	Reckless Love Affair	1967	3.75	7.50	15.00
❑ T 2704 [M]	Reckless Love Affair	1967	5.00	10.00	20.00
❑ ST 2812 [S]	You'll Always Have My Love	1967	3.75	7.50	15.00
❑ T 2812 [M]	You'll Always Have My Love	1967	5.00	10.00	20.00
❑ ST 2883 [S]	The Best of Wanda Jackson	1968	3.75	7.50	15.00
❑ T 2883 [M]	The Best of Wanda Jackson	1968	10.00	20.00	40.00

—Red and white "Starline" label

❑ ST 2976	Cream of the Crop	1968	3.75	7.50	15.00
❑ ST-11023	Praise the Lord	1972	3.75	7.50	15.00
❑ ST-11096	I Wouldn't Want You Any Other Way	1972	3.75	7.50	15.00
❑ ST-11161	Country Keepsakes	1973	3.75	7.50	15.00

DECCA

| ❑ DL 4224 [M] | Lovin' Country Style | 1962 | 12.50 | 25.00 | 50.00 |

GUSTO

| ❑ GT 0057 | Greatest Hits | 1980 | 2.50 | 5.00 | 10.00 |

HILLTOP

❑ 6058	Please Help Me I'm Falling	1968	2.50	5.00	10.00
❑ 6074	Leave My Baby Alone	1969	3.00	6.00	12.00
❑ 6116	We'll Sing in the Sunshine	1972	3.00	6.00	12.00
❑ 6123	By the Time I Get to Phoenix	1973	2.50	5.00	10.00
❑ 6182	Tears at the Grand Ole Opry	1974	2.50	5.00	10.00

MYRRH

❑ MSB-6513	When It's Time to Fall in Love Again	1974	3.00	6.00	12.00
❑ MSB-6533	Now I Have Everything	1975	3.00	6.00	12.00
❑ MSB-6556	Make Me Like a Child Again	1976	3.00	6.00	12.00

PICKWICK

| ❑ PTP-2053 [(2)] | Wanda Jackson | 1974 | 3.00 | 6.00 | 12.00 |

SYMPATHY FOR THE RECORD INDUSTRY

| ❑ SFTRI-724 | Heart Trouble | 2003 | 3.00 | 6.00 | 12.00 |

VARRICK

| ❑ VR-025 | Rock 'n' Roll Away Your Blues | 1987 | 3.00 | 6.00 | 12.00 |

VOCALION

| ❑ VL 73861 [R] | Nobody's Darlin' | 1968 | 3.00 | 6.00 | 12.00 |

WORD

| ❑ WST-8614 | Country Gospel | 1973 | 3.00 | 6.00 | 12.00 |
| ❑ WST-8781 | Closer to Jesus | 1977 | 3.00 | 6.00 | 12.00 |

JACKSON FIVE, THE See THE JACKSONS.

JACKSON HEIGHTS
45s
VERVE

| ❑ 10706 | Long Time Dying/Maureen | 1973 | 2.00 | 4.00 | 8.00 |

Albums
MERCURY

| ❑ SR-61331 | King Progress | 1970 | 6.25 | 12.00 | 25.00 |

VERVE

| ❑ V6-5089 | Jackson Heights | 1973 | 5.00 | 10.00 | 20.00 |

JACKSONS, THE Includes records as "The Jackson Five." Also see JACKIE JACKSON; JERMAINE JACKSON; MICHAEL JACKSON.
12-Inch Singles
EPIC

Number	Title (A Side/B Side)	Yr	VG	VG+	NM
❑ ASD 523 [DJ]	Blame It on the Boogie (Extended Disco Mix 7:00) (same on both sides)	1978	17.50	35.00	70.00
❑ AS 551 [DJ]	Shake Your Body (Down to the Ground) (7:58)/ Things I Do for You	1978	7.50	15.00	30.00
❑ AS 858 [DJ]	Lovely One (same on both sides?)	1980	3.75	7.50	15.00
❑ AS 894 [DJ]	Heartbreak Hotel (same on both sides)	1980	3.75	7.50	15.00
❑ AS 936 [DJ]	Can You Feel It (same on both sides)	1981	5.00	10.00	20.00
❑ AS 1244 [DJ]	Walk Right Now//(Instrumental)	1981	2.50	5.00	10.00
❑ AS 1351 [DJ]	Heartbreak Hotel/She's Out of My Life/ Jacksons Medley	1982	5.00	10.00	20.00
❑ AS 1387 [DJ]	Working Day and Night/Things I Do for You	1982	3.75	7.50	15.00
❑ EAS 1724 [DJ]	2300 Jackson Street (Short Version 4:12) (LP Version 5:06)	1989	3.00	6.00	12.00
❑ AS 1910 [DJ]	Torture/(Instrumental)	1984	3.00	6.00	12.00
❑ AS 1954 [DJ]	Body/(Instrumental)	1984	3.00	6.00	12.00
❑ 49-02403	Walk Right Now (Vocal 7:35) (Instrumental 6:55)	1981	3.75	7.50	15.00
❑ 49-05022	State of Shock (Dance Mix)/(Instrumental)	1984	2.50	5.00	10.00

—A-side vocal shared by Mick Jagger

| ❑ 49-05075 | Torture (Dance Mix)/(Instrumental) | 1984 | 2.50 | 5.00 | 10.00 |
| ❑ 49H-07548 | Lovely One/Can You Feel It | 198? | 2.50 | 5.00 | 10.00 |

—"Mixed Masters" reissue

| ❑ 49H-08142 | Blame It on the Boogie/Heartbreak Hotel | 1988 | 2.50 | 5.00 | 10.00 |

—"Mixed Masters" reissue

❑ 28-50721	Shake Your Body (Down to the Ground) (European Version 7:59)/That's What You Get (For Being Polite) (4:56)	1978	5.00	10.00	20.00
❑ 49-68233	Nothin' (That Compares 2 U) (5 versions)	1989	2.00	4.00	8.00
❑ 49-78583	Enjoy Yourself/Blame It on the Boogie/ Walk Right Now	1997	2.50	5.00	10.00

—"Mixed Masters" reissue

| ❑ 49-78584 | Shake Your Body (Down to the Ground)/Can You Feel It | 1997 | 2.50 | 5.00 | 10.00 |

—"Mixed Masters" reissue
MCA

| ❑ 23729 | Time Out for the Burglar (Extended Version 7:52) (Radio Edit 5:37) (Bonus Beats 7:44) (Instrumental 7:52) | 1987 | 2.50 | 5.00 | 10.00 |

MOTOWN

| ❑ 37463 1066 1 [DJ] | Who's Lovin' You (Live LP Version 5:40) (Live Radio Edit 4:02) (Original Version 3:42) | 1992 | 3.75 | 7.50 | 15.00 |
| ❑ 37463 3004 1 | I Want You Back '98 (6 versions) | 1998 | 5.00 | 10.00 | 20.00 |

45s
DYNAMO

| ❑ 146 | You Don't Have to Be Over Twenty-One to Fall in Love/Some Girls Want Me for Their Love | 1971 | 10.00 | 20.00 | 40.00 |

EPIC

❑ 19-01032	Can You Feel It/Everybody	1981	—	2.00	4.00
❑ 19-02132	Walk Right Now/Your Ways	1981	—	2.00	4.00
❑ 15-02157	Lovely One/She's Out of My Life	1981	—	—	3.00

—Reissue; B-side by Michael Jackson

| ❑ 14-02720 | The Things I Do for You/Working Day and Night | 1982 | — | 2.00 | 4.00 |
| ❑ 34-04503 | State of Shock/Your Ways | 1984 | — | 2.00 | 4.00 |

—A-side with Mick Jagger

❑ 34-04503 [PS]	State of Shock/Your Ways	1984	—	2.00	4.00
❑ 34-04575	Torture/(Instrumental)	1984	—	2.00	4.00
❑ 34-04575 [PS]	Torture/(Instrumental)	1984	—	2.00	4.00
❑ 34-04673	Body/(Instrumental)	1984	—	2.00	4.00
❑ 34-04673 [PS]	Body/(Instrumental)	1984	—	2.00	4.00
❑ 8-50595	Blame It on the Boogie/Do What You Wanna	1978	—	2.00	4.00
❑ 8-50656	Shake Your Body (Down to the Ground)/That's What You Get (For Being Polite)	1979	—	2.00	4.00

—Second issue has dark blue label

| ❑ 8-50656 | Shake Your Body (Down to the Ground)/That's What You Get (For Being Polite) | 1979 | — | 2.50 | 5.00 |

—Original issue has orange label

❑ 9-50938	Lovely One/Bless His Soul	1980	—	2.00	4.00
❑ 19-50959	Heartbreak Hotel/The Things I Do for You	1980	—	2.00	4.00
❑ 34-68688	Nothin' (That Compares 2 U)/Alright with Me	1989	—	—	3.00
❑ 34-69022	2300 Jackson Street/When I Look at You	1989	—	—	3.00

EPIC/PHILADELPHIA INT'L.

❑ 8-50289	Enjoy Yourself/Style of Life	1976	—	2.50	5.00
❑ 8-50350	Show You the Way to Go/Blues Away	1977	—	2.50	5.00
❑ 8-50454	Goin' Places/Do What You Wanna	1977	—	2.50	5.00
❑ 8-50496	Find Me a Girl/Different Kind of Lady	1977	—	2.50	5.00

MCA

| ❑ 53032 | Time Out for the Burglar/News at Eleven | 1987 | — | — | 3.00 |

—B-side by the Distants

| ❑ 53032 [PS] | Time Out for the Burglar/News at Eleven | 1987 | — | — | 3.00 |

MOTOWN

❑ 1157	I Want You Back/Who's Lovin' You	1969	2.00	4.00	8.00
❑ 1163	ABC/The Young Folks	1970	2.00	4.00	8.00
❑ 1166	The Love You Save/I Found That Girl	1970	2.00	4.00	8.00
❑ 1166 [DJ]	I Found That Girl (same on both sides)	1970	5.00	10.00	20.00

—Red vinyl

| ❑ 1166 [DJ] | The Love You Save | 1970 | 7.50 | 15.00 | 30.00 |

—Blank back promo

❑ 1171	I'll Be There/One More Chance	1970	2.00	4.00	8.00
❑ 1174	Santa Claus Is Coming to Town/Christmas Won't Be the Same This Year	1970	3.00	6.00	12.00
❑ 1177	Mama's Pearl/Darling Dear	1971	—	3.00	6.00
❑ 1177 [PS]	Mama's Pearl/Darling Dear	1971	3.75	7.50	15.00
❑ 1179	Never Can Say Goodbye/She's Good	1971	—	3.00	6.00
❑ 1186	Maybe Tomorrow/I Will Find a Way	1971	—	3.00	6.00
❑ 1194	Sugar Daddy/I'm So Happy	1971	—	3.00	6.00
❑ 1199	Little Bitty Pretty One/If I Had to Move a Mountain	1972	—	3.00	6.00
❑ 1205	Looking Through the Windows/Love Song	1972	—	3.00	6.00
❑ 1214	Corner of the Sky/To Know	1972	—	3.00	6.00
❑ 1224	Hallelujah Day/You Made Me What I Am	1973	—	3.00	6.00
❑ 1230	Boogie Man/Don't Let Your Baby Catch You	1973	—	—	—

—Unreleased

| ❑ 1277 | Get It Together/Touch | 1973 | — | 3.00 | 6.00 |

Number	Title (A Side/B Side)	Yr	VG	VG+	NM
❑ 1286	Dancing Machine/				
	It's Too Late to Change the Time	1974	—	3.00	6.00
❑ 1308	Whatever You Got, I Want/I Can't Quit Your Love	1974	—	3.00	6.00
❑ 1310	I Am Love (Parts 1 & 2)/I Am Love (Part 2)	1975	—	3.00	6.00
❑ 1310	I Am Love (Part 1)/I Am Love (Part 2)	1975	2.00	4.00	8.00
❑ 1356	Forever Came Today/All I Do Is Think of You	1975	—	3.00	6.00
❑ 1365	Body Language/Call of the Wild	1975	—	—	—
—Unreleased					
❑ 2193	Who's Lovin' You/In the Still of the Night				
	(I'll Remember)	1992	—	2.00	4.00
—B-side by Boyz II Men					
STEELTOWN					
❑ 681	Big Boy/You've Changed	1968	25.00	50.00	100.00
❑ 684	You Don't Have to Be Over Twenty-One to Fall in Love/Some Girls Want Me for Their Love	1968	25.00	50.00	100.00
❑ 689	Let Me Carry Your School Books/I Never Had a Girl	1969	20.00	40.00	80.00
—By "The Ripples and Waves plus Michael"					

7-Inch Extended Plays

Number	Title (A Side/B Side)	Yr	VG	VG+	NM
MOTOWN					
❑ M 60718	Ready or Not Here I Come/Goin' Back to Indiana/ Darling Dear//Oh How Happy/Reach In/Can I See You in the Morning	1970	3.75	7.50	15.00
—Jukebox issue; small hole, plays at 33 1/3 rpm					
❑ M 60718 [PS]	Third Album	1970	3.75	7.50	15.00
—Part of "Little LP" series (LLP #132)					

Albums

Number	Title (A Side/B Side)	Yr	VG	VG+	NM
EPIC					
❑ PE 34229	The Jacksons	1976	2.50	5.00	10.00
—Orange label					
❑ PE 34229	The Jacksons	198?	—	3.00	6.00
—Budget-line reissue with bar code and dark blue label					
❑ JE 34835	Goin' Places	1977	2.50	5.00	10.00
—Orange label					
❑ PE 34835	Goin' Places	198?	—	3.00	6.00
—Budget-line reissue					
❑ JE 35552	Destiny	1978	2.50	5.00	10.00
—Orange label					
❑ JE 35552	Destiny	1979	2.00	4.00	8.00
—Dark blue label					
❑ FE 36424	Triumph	1980	2.00	4.00	8.00
❑ KE2 37545 [(2)]	Jacksons Live	1981	3.00	6.00	12.00
❑ QE 38946	Victory	1984	2.00	4.00	8.00
❑ 8E8 39576 [PD]	Victory	1984	3.75	7.50	15.00
❑ OE 40911	2300 Jackson Street	1989	2.00	4.00	8.00
❑ HE 46424	Triumph	1982	15.00	30.00	60.00
—Half-speed mastered edition					
MOTOWN					
❑ M5-112V1	Motown Superstar Series, Vol. 12	1981	2.50	5.00	10.00
❑ M5-129V1	Diana Ross Presents the Jackson Five	1981	2.00	4.00	8.00
❑ M5-152V1	ABC	1981	2.00	4.00	8.00
❑ M5-157V1	Third Album	1981	2.00	4.00	8.00
❑ M5-201V1	Jackson 5 Greatest Hits	1981	2.00	4.00	8.00
❑ MS 700	Diana Ross Presents the Jackson 5	1969	6.25	12.50	25.00
❑ MS 709	ABC	1970	6.25	12.50	25.00
❑ MS 713	Christmas Album	1970	6.25	12.50	25.00
❑ MS 718	Third Album	1970	3.75	7.50	15.00
❑ M-735	Maybe Tomorrow	1971	3.75	7.50	15.00
❑ M-741	Jackson 5 Greatest Hits	1971	3.75	7.50	15.00
❑ M-742	Goin' Back to Indiana	1971	3.75	7.50	15.00
❑ M-750	Lookin' Through the Windows	1972	3.75	7.50	15.00
❑ M-761	Skywriter	1973	3.00	6.00	12.00
❑ M6-780	Dancing Machine	1974	3.00	6.00	12.00
❑ M6-783	Get It Together	1973	3.00	6.00	12.00
❑ M6-829	Moving Violation	1975	3.00	6.00	12.00
❑ M6-865	Joyful Jukebox Music	1976	3.00	6.00	12.00
❑ M7-868 [(3)]	Anthology	1976	5.00	10.00	20.00
❑ 37463 1294-1 [DJ]	Soulsation!	1995	5.00	10.00	20.00
—Vinyl is promo only; 4-song sampler from box set					
❑ 5228 ML	Maybe Tomorrow	1982	2.00	4.00	8.00
❑ 5250 ML	Christmas Album	1982	2.00	4.00	8.00
—Reissue of Motown 713					

JACOBI, LOU

Albums

Number	Title (A Side/B Side)	Yr	VG	VG+	NM
CAPITOL					
❑ ST 2596 [S]	Al Tijuana and His Jewish Brass	1966	5.00	10.00	20.00
❑ T 2596 [M]	Al Tijuana and His Jewish Brass	1966	3.75	7.50	15.00

JACOBS, HANK

45s

Number	Title (A Side/B Side)	Yr	VG	VG+	NM
IMPERIAL					
❑ 5894	Sting Ray/Sheryl Ann	1962	3.75	7.50	15.00
SUE					
❑ 102	Bacon Fat/Out of Sight	1964	2.50	5.00	10.00
❑ 113	Heide/Playboy's Penthouse	1964	2.50	5.00	10.00
❑ 795	So Far Away/Monkey Hips & Rice	1963	3.00	6.00	12.00

Albums

Number	Title (A Side/B Side)	Yr	VG	VG+	NM
SUE					
❑ LP-1023 [M]	So Far Away	1964	20.00	40.00	80.00

JADE, FAINE

45s

Number	Title (A Side/B Side)	Yr	VG	VG+	NM
RSVP					
❑ 1130	Introspection/(B-side unknown)	1968	6.25	12.50	25.00

Albums

Number	Title (A Side/B Side)	Yr	VG	VG+	NM
RSVP					
❑ 8002	Introspection: A Faine Jade Recital	1968	100.00	200.00	400.00

JADE WARRIOR

45s

Number	Title (A Side/B Side)	Yr	VG	VG+	NM
VERTIGO					
❑ 106	We Have Reason to Believe/Barazinbar	1972	2.00	4.00	8.00
❑ 108	A Winter's Tale/The Demon Trucker	1972	2.00	4.00	8.00

Albums

Number	Title (A Side/B Side)	Yr	VG	VG+	NM
ANTILLES					
❑ AN-7045	Floating World	198?	2.00	4.00	8.00
—Reissue of Island 9290					
❑ AN-7048	Waves	198?	2.00	4.00	8.00
—Reissue of Island 9318					
❑ AN-7056	Kites	198?	2.00	4.00	8.00
—Reissue of Island 9393					
❑ AN-7068	Way of the Sun	1978	2.50	5.00	10.00
ISLAND					
❑ ILPS 9290	Floating World	1974	2.50	5.00	10.00
❑ ILPS 9318	Waves	1975	2.50	5.00	10.00
❑ ILPS 9393	Kites	1976	2.50	5.00	10.00
VERTIGO					
❑ VEL-1007	Jade Warrior	1971	3.00	6.00	12.00
❑ VEL-1009	Released	1972	3.00	6.00	12.00
❑ VEL-1012	Last Autumn's Dream	1972	3.00	6.00	12.00

JADES, THE   Many different groups.

45s

Number	Title (A Side/B Side)	Yr	VG	VG+	NM
ADONA					
❑ 1445	Hey Senorita/(B-side unknown)	1962	7.50	15.00	30.00
CAPITOL					
❑ 2281	Ain't It Funny What Love Can Do/Baby I Need Your Love	1968	—	3.00	6.00
CHRISTY					
❑ 110	Oh Why/Big Beach Party	1959	125.00	250.00	500.00
❑ 111	Tell Me Pretty Baby/Applesauce	1959	62.50	125.00	250.00
❑ 113	Don't Be a Fool/Friday Night with My Baby	1959	125.00	250.00	500.00
❑ 114	Look for a Lie/Blue Memories	1959	375.00	750.00	1500.
DORE					
❑ 687	Hold Back the Dawn/When They Ask About You	1963	5.00	10.00	20.00
DOT					
❑ 15822	I'm Pretending/Beverly	1958	20.00	40.00	80.00
GAITY					
❑ 2-23-64	Surfin' Crow/Blue Black Hair	1964	45.00	90.00	180.00
IMPERIAL					
❑ 66383	Wheel of Fortune/Gotta Find Somebody to Love	1969	—	3.00	6.00
❑ 66425	L-O-V-E I Love You/ Don't Give What's Mine Away	1969	—	3.00	6.00
LIBERTY					
❑ 56192	All's Quiet on West 23rd/Love of a Woman	1970	—	2.50	5.00
MGM					
❑ 13399	There's a Kinder Way to Say Goodbye/ You're So Right for Me	1965	3.00	6.00	12.00
NAU VOO					
❑ 807	Walking All Alone/Hey Little Girl	1959	37.50	75.00	150.00
OXBORO					
❑ 2002	Surfin' Crow/Blue Black Hair	1964	30.00	60.00	120.00
❑ 2005	Little Marlene/Shake Baby Shake	1965	30.00	60.00	120.00
PORT					
❑ 70042	He's My Guy/There Will Come a Day	1964	6.25	12.50	25.00
TIME					
❑ 1002	Leave Her For Me/So Blue	1957	50.00	100.00	200.00
—Lou Reed is alleged to have been in this group, but he would have been 15 at the time.					
UNI					
❑ 55019	The Glide/Flower Power	1967	2.00	4.00	8.00
❑ 55032 [DJ]	Privilege (same on both sides)	1967	2.00	4.00	8.00
VERVE					
❑ 10385	For Just Another Day/I'm By Your Side (Baby)	1966	3.00	6.00	12.00

Albums

Number	Title (A Side/B Side)	Yr	VG	VG+	NM
JARRETT					
❑ 21517 [M]	Live at the Disco a-Go-Go	1965	30.00	60.00	120.00

JAGGED EDGE, THE

45s

Number	Title (A Side/B Side)	Yr	VG	VG+	NM
RCA VICTOR					
❑ 47-8880	Baby You Don't Know/Deep Inside	1966	2.50	5.00	10.00
TWIRL					
❑ 2024	How Many Times/Midnight to Six Man	1966	7.50	15.00	30.00

JAGGER, CHRIS

45s

Number	Title (A Side/B Side)	Yr	VG	VG+	NM
ASYLUM					
❑ 11028	Riddle Song/Handful of Dust	1973	—	3.00	6.00

Albums

Number	Title (A Side/B Side)	Yr	VG	VG+	NM
ASYLUM					
❑ 7E-1009	The Adventures of Valentine Vox the Ventriloquist	1974	3.00	6.00	12.00
❑ SD 5069	Chris Jagger	1973	3.00	6.00	12.00

JAGGERZ, THE

45s

Number	Title (A Side/B Side)	Yr	VG	VG+	NM
GAMBLE					
❑ 218	(That's Why) Baby I Love You/Bring It Back	1968	2.00	4.00	8.00
❑ 226	Gotta Find My Way Back Home/Forever Together, Together Forever	1968	2.00	4.00	8.00
❑ 238	Together/Let Me Be the One	1969	2.00	4.00	8.00
❑ 4008	Higher and Higher/Ain't No Sun	1970	2.00	4.00	8.00
❑ 4012	Need Your Love/Here's a Heart	1970	2.00	4.00	8.00
KAMA SUTRA					
❑ 502	The Rapper/Born Poor	1970	2.00	4.00	8.00
❑ 509	I Call My Baby Candy/Will She Believe Me	1970	—	3.00	6.00
❑ 513	What a Bummer/Memories of the Traveller	1970	—	3.00	6.00
❑ 517	Let's Talk About Love/I'll Never Forget You	1971	—	2.50	5.00
❑ 583	Let's Talk About Love/Ain't That Sad	1973	—	2.00	4.00
WOODEN NICKEL					
❑ PB-10194	Don't It Make You Want to Dance/2 Plus 2	1975	—	2.00	4.00

Albums

Number	Title (A Side/B Side)	Yr	VG	VG+	NM
GAMBLE					
❑ GS-5006	Introducing the Jaggerz	1969	5.00	10.00	20.00
KAMA SUTRA					
❑ KSBS-2017	We Went to Different Schools Together	1970	3.75	7.50	15.00
WOODEN NICKEL					
❑ BWL1-0772	Come Again	1975	3.00	6.00	12.00

J

Number	Title (A Side/B Side)	Yr	VG	VG+	NM
JAGUARS, THE (1)					
45s					
AARDELL					
❑ 0003	Rock It Davy, Rock It/I Wanted You	1955	12.50	25.00	50.00
❑ 0006	Be My Sweetie/Why Don't You Believe Me	1956	12.50	25.00	50.00
BARONET					
❑ 1	The Way You Look Tonight/Baby, Baby, Baby	1962	6.25	12.50	25.00
CLASSIC ARTISTS					
❑ 117	Happy Holiday/More Than Enough for Me	1989	—	3.00	6.00
—B-side by Johnny Staton and the Feathers					
❑ 136	Merry Christmas, Darling/Lost and Found	1990	—	3.00	6.00
ORIGINAL SOUND					
❑ 6	Thinking of You/Look Into My Eyes	1959	20.00	40.00	80.00
❑ 20	Thinking of You/Look Into My Eyes	1962	10.00	20.00	40.00
❑ 59	The Way You Look Tonight/Baby, Baby, Baby	1966	5.00	10.00	20.00
R-DELL					
❑ 11	The Way You Look Tonight/Baby, Baby, Baby	1956	12.50	25.00	50.00
❑ 11	The Way You Look Tonight/Moonlight and You	1956	62.50	125.00	250.00
—Black vinyl					
❑ 11	The Way You Look Tonight/Moonlight and You	1956	150.00	300.00	600.00
—Red vinyl					
❑ 16	I Love You Baby/Baby, Baby, Baby	1957	30.00	60.00	120.00
❑ 45	Rock It Davy, Rock It/I Wanted You	1958	10.00	20.00	40.00
❑ 107	Rock It Davy, Rock It/The Big Bear	1958	10.00	20.00	40.00
❑ 117	Girl of My Dreams/Don't Go Home	1960	15.00	30.00	60.00
JAGUARS, THE (2)					
45s					
DOT					
❑ 16723	Dead Sea/Supersonic	1965	2.50	5.00	10.00
❑ 16931	The Gorilla/He'll Turn Away	1966	2.50	5.00	10.00
JAGUARS, THE (3)					
45s					
EPIC					
❑ 9325	Drive-In/Exit 6	1959	5.00	10.00	20.00
JAGUARS, THE (4)					
45s					
FARO					
❑ 618	Where Lovers Go/Discover a Lover	1965	3.00	6.00	12.00
JAGUARS, THE (U) Some of these could be the above groups.					
45s					
EBB					
❑ 129	Hold Me Tight/Piccadilly	1958	25.00	50.00	100.00
RENDEZVOUS					
❑ 159	Fine, Fine, Fine/It Finally Happened	1961	5.00	10.00	20.00
❑ 216	Fine, Fine, Fine/It Finally Happened	1963	3.00	6.00	12.00
SKOOP					
❑ 1067	It's Gonna Be Alright/(B-side unknown)	1966	6.25	12.50	25.00
SPAY					
❑ 121	Rendezvous/(B-side unknown)	196?	15.00	30.00	60.00
JAIM					
Albums					
ETHEREAL					
❑ 1001	Prophecy Fulfilled	1970	12.50	25.00	50.00
JALOPY FIVE, THE					
45s					
HIT					
❑ 81	Surfer Girl/Then He Kissed Me	1963	2.00	4.00	8.00
—B-side by the Dacrons					
❑ 100	Drag City/Forget Him	1964	2.00	4.00	8.00
—B-side by Wayne Harris					
❑ 110	Fun, Fun, Fun/Glad All Over	1964	2.00	4.00	8.00
❑ 132	Can't You See That She's Mine/The Little Old Lady from Pasadena	1964	2.50	5.00	10.00
—B-side by the Roamers					
❑ 134	A Hard Day's Night/Rag Doll	1964	2.00	4.00	8.00
—B-side by the Chellows					
❑ 138	And I Love Her/Such a Night	1964	2.50	5.00	10.00
—B-side by Ed Hardin					
❑ 145	(I've Got a) Tiger in My Tank/Dancing in the Street	1964	2.50	5.00	10.00
—B-side by Mary Sue and the Trams					
❑ 147	Matchbox/When I Grow Up (To Be a Man)	1964	2.50	5.00	10.00
—B-side by the Roamers					
❑ 150	Little Honda/Making a Fool of Myself	1964	2.00	4.00	8.00
❑ 156	Be Yourself/Mountain of Love	1964	2.50	5.00	10.00
—B-side by Bobby Brooks					
❑ 161	Sidewalk Surfin'/Any Way You Want It	1964	3.00	6.00	12.00
—B-side by the Bugs					
❑ 171	I Feel Fine/She's a Woman	1965	3.00	6.00	12.00
❑ 183	Let's Lock the Door/California Street	1965	2.50	5.00	10.00
—As "Johnny and the Jalopy Five"					
❑ 192	Eight Days a Week/She's Come of Age	1965	3.00	6.00	12.00
—B-side by Bobby Brooks					
❑ 215	Wooly Bully/First Impressions	1965	2.50	5.00	10.00
❑ 217	(I Can't Get No) Satisfaction/I Want Candy	1965	3.00	6.00	12.00
—B-side by the Roamers					
❑ 218	I Like It Like That/I Want Candy	1965	3.00	6.00	12.00
—B-side by the Roamers					
❑ 220	Help!/California Girls	1965	3.00	6.00	12.00
—B-side by the Chellows					
❑ 223	Catch Us If You Can/Just a Little Bit Better	1965	3.00	6.00	12.00
—B-side by Hank's Hounds					
❑ 225	Yesterday/Kansas City Star	1965	3.00	6.00	12.00
—B-side by Richard Phillips					
❑ 228	Get Off of My Cloud/One, Two, Three	1965	3.00	6.00	12.00
—B-side by Henry Bary					
❑ 232	We Can Work It Out/Over and Over	1965	3.00	6.00	12.00
—B-side by the Chords (2)					
❑ 240	California Dreamin'/Uptight (Everything's Alright)	1966	2.50	5.00	10.00
—B-side by Ritchie Brown					

Number	Title (A Side/B Side)	Yr	VG	VG+	NM
❑ 245	Nowhere Man/It's Too Late	1966	3.00	6.00	12.00
—B-side by Ed Hardin					
❑ 252	Monday, Monday/Gloria	1966	3.00	6.00	12.00
—B-side by the Chellows					
❑ 253	Sloop John B/Rhapsody in the Rain	1966	3.00	6.00	12.00
—B-side by Fred York					
❑ 258	Paint It Black/The Sun Ain't Gonna Shine Anymore	1966	3.00	6.00	12.00
—B-side by the Harris Brothers					
❑ 259	Did You Ever Have to Make Up Your Mind/I Am a Rock	1966	2.00	4.00	8.00
—B-side by Sammy and Theodore					
❑ 262	Wild Thing/Little Red Riding Hood	1966	2.00	4.00	8.00
—B-side by the Chellows					
❑ 263	Mother's Little Helper/This Door Swings Both Ways	1966	2.50	5.00	10.00
—B-side by the Chords (2)					
❑ 266	Last Train to Clarksville/Yellow Submarine	1966	2.50	5.00	10.00
❑ 268	Psychotic Reaction/See See Rider	1966	2.00	4.00	8.00
—B-side by Ed Hardin and the Cadets					
❑ 271	The Hair on My Chinny Chin Chin/Have You Seen Your Mother, Baby	1966	2.50	5.00	10.00
—B-side by the Chords (2)					
❑ 273	I'm a Believer/Mellow Yellow	1966	2.00	4.00	8.00
—B-side by Joe King					
❑ 276	Music to Watch Girls By/Wild Thing	1967	2.00	4.00	8.00
—B-side by Bobby Sims					
❑ 277	98.6/Kind of a Drag	1967	2.00	4.00	8.00
—B-side by the Buchanans					
❑ 281	Sock It To Me Baby/The Beat Goes On	1967	2.00	4.00	8.00
—B-side by Bobby and Connie					
❑ 283	Then You Can Tell Me Goodbye/Ruby Tuesday	1967	2.00	4.00	8.00
—B-side by the Chellows					
❑ 285	A Little Bit Me, A Little Bit You/Detroit City	1967	2.00	4.00	8.00
—B-side by Ed Hardin					
❑ 287	Penny Lane/I Think We're Alone Now	1967	2.50	5.00	10.00
—B-side by Bobby Sims					
❑ 293	I Got Rhythm/Here Comes My Baby	1967	2.00	4.00	8.00
—B-side by the Fantastics					
❑ 295	Groovin'/Somebody to Love	1967	2.00	4.00	8.00
—B-side by the Chellows					
❑ 299	Windy/Up, Up and Away	1967	2.00	4.00	8.00
—B-side by the Chords (2)					
❑ 300	Pleasant Valley Sunday/Carrie-Anne	1967	2.00	4.00	8.00
—B-side by the Chords (2)					
❑ 307	Dandelion/The Letter	1967	2.50	5.00	10.00
—B-side by the Chords (2)					
❑ 311	Even the Bad Times Are Good/To Sir with Love	1967	2.00	4.00	8.00
—B-side by the Jalopy Five					
❑ 315	Daydream Believer/By the Time I Get to Phoenix	1967	2.00	4.00	8.00
—B-side by Ed Hardin					
❑ 317	We Can Fly/Judy in Disguise (With Glasses)	1967	2.00	4.00	8.00
—B-side by Jack Jones and the Jet Set Band					
❑ 325	Young Girl/The Unicorn	1968	2.00	4.00	8.00
—B-side by the Chords (2)					
❑ 327	Cry Like a Baby/Do You Know the Way to San Jose	1968	2.00	4.00	8.00
—B-side by Kathy Shannon					
❑ 332	D.W. Washburn/Reach Out of the Darkness	1968	2.00	4.00	8.00
—B-side by the Chords (2)					
❑ 334	Jumpin' Jack Flash/Angel of the Morning	1968	2.00	4.00	8.00
—B-side by Kathy Shannon					
❑ 336	Hurdy Gurdy Man/Stoned Soul Picnic	1968	2.00	4.00	8.00
—B-side by the Fantastics					
❑ 342	Revolution/Born to Be Wild	1968	2.50	5.00	10.00
—B-side by the Chords (2)					
❑ 343	Hey Jude/Harper Valley P.T.A.	1968	2.00	4.00	8.00
—B-side by Kathy Shannon					
❑ 345	Midnight Confessions/Suzie-Q	1968	2.00	4.00	8.00
—B-side by the Classmates					
❑ 347	Elenore/Little Green Apples	1968	2.00	4.00	8.00
—B-side by Leroy Jones					
❑ 352	Everyday People/Touch Me	1969	2.00	4.00	8.00
—B-side by the Fantastics					
JAMES, BOBBY					
45s					
INDIGO					
❑ 145	Memories Linger/5000 Years Ago	1962	3.75	7.50	15.00
KAROL					
❑ 3727	I Really Love You/(B-side unknown)	196?	300.00	600.00	1200.
LANOR					
❑ 530	Fortune Teller/Get Out of My Life Woman	1967	2.50	5.00	10.00
❑ 533	Going Back to Philly/That's What People Say	1967	2.50	5.00	10.00
JAMES, DICK					
45s					
LONDON					
❑ 1002	Eleanor/Mary Rose	1950	3.75	7.50	15.00
❑ 1013	Theater/My Life's Desire	1950	3.75	7.50	15.00
❑ 1027	Unless/Now That You've Left Me	1950	3.75	7.50	15.00
❑ 1044	We'll Keep a Welcome/The Minute Waltz	1951	3.75	7.50	15.00
❑ 1050	Happy Valley/My Truly Truly Fair	1951	3.75	7.50	15.00
❑ 1053	Tell Me Again/With All My Heart and Soul	1951	3.75	7.50	15.00
❑ 1139	Unforgettable/My Love for You	1951	3.75	7.50	15.00
❑ 1162	Pretending/It Would Break My Heart	1951	3.75	7.50	15.00
JAMES, ELMORE Some of the below were as "Elmo James."					
45s					
ACE					
❑ 508	I Believe My Time Ain't Long/I Wish I Was a Catfish	1955	62.50	125.00	250.00
CHECKER					
❑ 777	Country Boogie/She Just Won't Do Right	1953	250.00	500.00	1000.
CHESS					
❑ 1756	I Can't Hold Out/The Sun Is Shining	1960	3.75	7.50	15.00

Number	Title (A Side/B Side)	Yr	VG	VG+	NM
CHIEF					
❏ 7001	The Twelve Year Old Boy/Coming Home	1957	20.00	40.00	80.00
❏ 7004	It Hurts Me Too/Elmore's Contribution to Jazz	1957	20.00	40.00	80.00
❏ 7006	Cry for Me Baby/Take Me Where You Go	1957	15.00	30.00	60.00
❏ 7020	Knocking at Your Door/Calling All Blues	1960	10.00	20.00	40.00
ENJOY					
❏ 2015	It Hurts Me Too/Pickin' the Blues	1965	3.75	7.50	15.00
❏ 2015	It Hurts Me Too/Bleeding Heart	1965	5.00	10.00	20.00
❏ 2020	Mean Mistreatin' Mama/Bleeding	1965	3.75	7.50	15.00
❏ 2027	Dust My Broom/Everyday I Have the Blues	1965	3.75	7.50	15.00
FIRE					
❏ 504	Shake Your Moneymaker/Look on Yonder Wall	1962	10.00	20.00	40.00
❏ 1011	Make My Dreams Come True/Bobby's Rock	1960	7.50	15.00	30.00
❏ 1016	The Sky Is Crying/Held My Baby Last Night	1960	10.00	20.00	40.00
❏ 1024	I'm Worried/Rollin' and Tumblin'	1960	5.00	10.00	20.00
❏ 1031	Fine Little Mama/Done Somebody Wrong	1961	5.00	10.00	20.00
❏ 1503	Stranger Blues/Anna Lee	1963	3.75	7.50	15.00
❏ 2020	It Hurts Me Too/Pickin' the Blues	196?	3.75	7.50	15.00
—Red vinyl					
FLAIR					
❏ 1011	Early in the Morning/Hawaiian Boogie	1953	125.00	250.00	500.00
❏ 1014	Can't Stop Lovin'/Make a Little Love	1953	50.00	100.00	200.00
❏ 1022	Strange Kinda Feeling/Please Find My Baby	1953	50.00	100.00	200.00
❏ 1031	Make My Dreams Come True/Hand in Hand	1954	75.00	150.00	300.00
❏ 1039	Sho'nuff, I Do/1839 Blues	1954	75.00	150.00	300.00
❏ 1048	Dark and Dreary/Rock My Baby Right	1954	75.00	150.00	300.00
❏ 1057	Standing at the Cross Roads/Sunny Land	1955	62.50	125.00	250.00
❏ 1062	Late Hours at Midnight/The Way You Treat Me	1955	37.50	75.00	150.00
❏ 1069	Happy Home/No Love in My Heart	1955	37.50	75.00	150.00
❏ 1074	Dust My Blues/I Was a Fool	1955	62.50	125.00	250.00
❏ 1079	Blues Before Sunrise/Goodbye Baby	1955	50.00	100.00	200.00
JEWEL					
❏ 764	Dust My Broom/Gotta Find My Baby	1966	2.50	5.00	10.00
❏ 783	Catfish Blues/Make a Little Love	1967	2.50	5.00	10.00
KENT					
❏ 331	Dust My Blues/Happy Home	1960	3.00	6.00	12.00
❏ 394	Dust My Blues/Happy Home	1964	2.50	5.00	10.00
❏ 465	Sunnyland/Goodbye Baby	1967	2.00	4.00	8.00
❏ 508	I Believe/1839 Blues	1969	—	3.00	6.00
M-PAC					
❏ 7231	Cry for Me/Take Me Where You Go	1966	2.50	5.00	10.00
MEL					
❏ 7011	Cry for Me Baby/(B-side unknown)	197?	—	3.00	6.00
METEOR					
❏ 5000	I Believe/I Held My Baby Last Night	1953	200.00	400.00	800.00
❏ 5003	Baby What's Wrong/Sinful Woman	1953	125.00	250.00	500.00
❏ 5016	Saxony Boogie/Dumb Woman Blues	1954	75.00	150.00	300.00
❏ 5024	San Symphonic Boogie/Flaming Blues	1955	62.50	125.00	250.00
MODERN					
❏ 983	Wild About You/Long Tall Woman	1956	75.00	150.00	300.00
VEE JAY					
❏ 249	Coming Home/The 12-Year-Old Boy	1957	6.25	12.50	25.00
❏ 259	It Hurts Me Too/Elmore's Contribution to Jazz	1957	6.25	12.50	25.00
❏ 269	Cry for Me Baby/Take Me Where You Go	1958	6.25	12.50	25.00
Albums					
BELL					
❏ 6037	Elmore James	1969	6.25	12.50	25.00
CHESS					
❏ LP-1537	Whose Muddy Shoes	1969	6.25	12.50	25.00
COLLECTABLES					
❏ COL-5112	Golden Classics	198?	3.00	6.00	12.00
❏ COL-5184	The Complete Fire and Enjoy Sessions, Part 1	198?	2.50	5.00	10.00
❏ COL-5185	The Complete Fire and Enjoy Sessions, Part 2	198?	2.50	5.00	10.00
❏ COL-5186	The Complete Fire and Enjoy Sessions, Part 3	198?	2.50	5.00	10.00
❏ COL-5187	The Complete Fire and Enjoy Sessions, Part 4	198?	2.50	5.00	10.00
CROWN					
❏ CLP-5168 [M]	Blues After Hours	1961	62.50	125.00	250.00
—Black label, silver "Crown"					
❏ CLP-5168 [M]	Blues After Hours	1962	12.50	25.00	50.00
—Gray label					
INTERMEDIA					
❏ QS-5034	Red Hot Blues	198?	2.50	5.00	10.00
KENT					
❏ KST-522 [R]	Original Folk Blues	1964	6.25	12.50	25.00
❏ KLP-5022 [M]	Original Folk Blues	1964	10.00	20.00	40.00
❏ KLP-9001	Anthology of the Blues Legend	196?	6.25	12.50	25.00
❏ KLP-9010	The Resurrection of Elmore James	196?	6.25	12.50	25.00
SPHERE SOUND					
❏ SR-7002 [M]	The Sky Is Crying	1965	45.00	90.00	180.00
❏ SSR-7002 [R]	The Sky Is Crying	1965	30.00	60.00	120.00
❏ SR-7008 [M]	I Need You	1966	37.50	75.00	150.00
❏ SSR-7008 [R]	I Need You	1966	30.00	60.00	120.00
UP FRONT					
❏ UP-122	The Great Elmore James	1970	3.00	6.00	12.00

JAMES, ETTA
45s

Number	Title (A Side/B Side)	Yr	VG	VG+	NM
ARGO					
❏ 5359	All I Could Do Was Cry/Girl of My Dreams	1960	3.00	6.00	12.00
❏ 5368	My Dearest Darling/Tough Mary	1960	3.00	6.00	12.00
❏ 5380	At Last/I Just Want to Make Love to You	1961	3.75	7.50	15.00
❏ 5385	Trust in Me/Anything to Say You're Mine	1961	2.50	5.00	10.00
❏ 5390	Dream/Fool That I Am	1961	2.50	5.00	10.00
❏ 5393	Sunday Kind of Love/Don't Cry, Baby	1961	2.50	5.00	10.00
❏ 5402	It's Too Soon to Know/Seven Day Fool	1961	2.50	5.00	10.00
❏ 5409	Something's Got a Hold on Me/Waiting for Charlie to Come Home	1962	2.50	5.00	10.00
❏ 5418	Stop the Wedding/Street of Tears	1962	2.50	5.00	10.00
❏ 5424	Next Door to the Blues/Fools Rush In	1962	2.50	5.00	10.00
❏ 5430	How Do You Speak to An Angel/Would It Make Any Difference to You	1962	2.50	5.00	10.00
❏ 5437	Pushover/I Can't Hold It In Anymore	1963	2.50	5.00	10.00
❏ 5445	Be Honest with Me/Pay Back	1963	2.50	5.00	10.00
❏ 5452	Two Sides (To Every Story)/I Worry Bout You	1963	2.50	5.00	10.00
❏ 5459	Baby What You Want Me to Do/What I Say	1964	2.50	5.00	10.00
❏ 5465	Look Who's Blue/Loving You More Every Day	1964	2.50	5.00	10.00

Number	Title (A Side/B Side)	Yr	VG	VG+	NM
❏ 5477	Breaking Point/That Man Belongs Back Here with Me	1964	2.50	5.00	10.00
❏ 5485	Mellow Fellow/Bobby Is His Name	1964	2.50	5.00	10.00
CADET					
❏ 5519	Somewhere Down the Line/Do I Make Myself Clear	1966	2.00	4.00	8.00
—With Sugar Pie DeSanto					
❏ 5526	Only Time Will Tell/I'm Sorry for You	1966	2.00	4.00	8.00
❏ 5539	In the Basement — Part 1/In the Basement — Part 2	1966	2.00	4.00	8.00
—With Sugar Pie DeSanto					
❏ 5552	I Prefer You/I'm So Glad	1966	2.00	4.00	8.00
❏ 5564	Don't Take Me for Your Fool/It Must Be Your Love	1967	2.00	4.00	8.00
❏ 5568	Happiness/842-3089 (Call My Name)	1967	2.00	4.00	8.00
❏ 5578	Tell Mama/I'd Rather Go Blind	1967	2.00	4.00	8.00
❏ 5594	Security/I'm Gonna Take What He's Got	1968	2.00	4.00	8.00
❏ 5606	I Got You Babe/I Worship the Ground You Walk On	1968	2.00	4.00	8.00
❏ 5620	Fire/You Got It	1968	2.00	4.00	8.00
❏ 5630	Almost Persuaded/Steal Away	1968	2.00	4.00	8.00
❏ 5655	Miss Pitiful/Bobby Is His Name	1969	2.00	4.00	8.00
❏ 5664	Tighten Up Your Own Thing/What Fools We Mortals Be	1970	2.00	4.00	8.00
❏ 5671	The Sound of Love/When I Stop Dreaming	1970	2.00	4.00	8.00
❏ 5676	Losers Weepers — Part I/Weepers	1970	2.00	4.00	8.00
CAPITOL					
❏ B-44333	Avenue D/My Head Is a City	1989	—	2.00	4.00
—With David A. Stewart					
CHESS					
❏ 2100	The Love of My Man/Nothing from Nothing Leaves Nothing	1971	—	3.00	6.00
❏ 2112	I Think It's You/Take Out Some Insurance	1971	—	3.00	6.00
❏ 2125	I Found a Love/Nothing from Nothing Leaves Nothing	1972	—	3.00	6.00
❏ 2144	All the Way Down/Lay Back Daddy	1973	—	3.00	6.00
❏ 2148	Leave Your Hat On/Only a Fool	1974	—	3.00	6.00
❏ 2153	Out on the Street Again/Feeling Uneasy	1974	—	3.00	6.00
❏ 2171	Lovin' Arms/Take Out Some Insurance	1975	—	3.00	6.00
❏ 31001	Jump Into Love/(B-side unknown)	1976	—	2.50	5.00
EPIC					
❏ 68593	Baby What You Want Me to Do/Max's Theme (Instrumental)	1989	—	2.00	4.00
KENT					
❏ 304	Baby, Baby, Every Night/Sunshine of Love	1958	7.50	15.00	30.00
❏ 345	Roll with Me Henry/Good Rockin' Daddy	1960	6.25	12.50	25.00
❏ 352	How Big a Fool/Good Rockin' Daddy	1961	6.25	12.50	25.00
❏ 370	Do Something Crazy/Good Rockin' Daddy	1962	6.25	12.50	25.00
MODERN					
❏ 947	The Wallflower (Dance With Me Henry)/Hold Me, Squeeze Me	1955	6.25	12.50	25.00
❏ 947	The Wallflower (Roll With Me Henry)/Hold Me, Squeeze Me	1955	10.00	20.00	40.00
❏ 957	Hey Henry (Doin' Fine, Henry)/Be Mine	1955	6.25	12.50	25.00
❏ 962	Good Rockin' Daddy/Crazy Feeling	1955	7.50	15.00	30.00
❏ 972	That's All/W-O-M-A-N	1955	6.25	12.50	25.00
❏ 984	I'm a Fool/Number One (My One and Only)	1956	6.25	12.50	25.00
❏ 988	Shortnin' Bread Rock/Tears of Joy	1956	6.25	12.50	25.00
❏ 998	Fools We Mortals Be/Tough Lover	1956	7.50	15.00	30.00
❏ 1007	Good Lookin'/Then I'll Care	1957	6.25	12.50	25.00
❏ 1016	The Pick-Up/Market Place	1957	6.25	12.50	25.00
❏ 1022	By the Light of the Silvery Moon/Come What May	1957	6.25	12.50	25.00
PHILCO-FORD					
❏ HP-31	Tell Mama/Security	1968	5.00	10.00	20.00
—4-inch plastic "Hip Pocket Record" with color sleeve					
T-ELECTRIC					
❏ 41264	It Takes Love to Keep a Woman/Mean Mother	1980	—	2.50	5.00
WARNER BROS.					
❏ 8545	Piece of My Heart/Lovesick Blues	1978	—	2.50	5.00
❏ 8611	Sugar on the Floor/Lovesick Blues	1978	—	2.50	5.00
Albums					
ARGO					
❏ LP-4003 [M]	At Last!	1961	10.00	20.00	40.00
❏ LPS-4003 [S]	At Last!	1961	15.00	30.00	60.00
❏ LP-4011 [M]	The Second Time Around	1961	7.50	15.00	30.00
❏ LPS-4011 [S]	The Second Time Around	1961	10.00	20.00	40.00
❏ LP-4013 [M]	Etta James	1962	7.50	15.00	30.00
❏ LPS-4013 [P]	Etta James	1962	10.00	20.00	40.00
—Two duets with Harvey Fuqua are rechanneled					
❏ LP-4018 [M]	Etta James Sings for Lovers	1962	7.50	15.00	30.00
❏ LPS-4018 [S]	Etta James Sings for Lovers	1962	10.00	20.00	40.00
❏ LP-4025 [M]	Etta James Top Ten	1963	7.50	15.00	30.00
❏ LPS-4025 [S]	Etta James Top Ten	1963	10.00	20.00	40.00
❏ LP-4032 [M]	Etta James Rocks the House	1964	25.00	50.00	100.00
❏ LPS-4032 [S]	Etta James Rocks the House	1964	37.50	75.00	150.00
❏ LP-4040 [M]	The Queen of Soul	1965	7.50	15.00	30.00
❏ LPS-4040 [S]	The Queen of Soul	1965	10.00	20.00	40.00
CADET					
❏ LP-802 [M]	Tell Mama	1968	6.25	12.50	25.00
❏ LPS-802 [S]	Tell Mama	1968	5.00	10.00	20.00
❏ LPS-832	Etta James Sings Funk	1969	5.00	10.00	20.00
❏ LPS-847	Losers Weepers	1970	3.75	7.50	15.00
❏ LP-4003 [M]	At Last!	1966	3.00	6.00	12.00
❏ LPS-4003 [S]	At Last!	1966	3.75	7.50	15.00
❏ LP-4011 [M]	The Second Time Around	1966	3.00	6.00	12.00
❏ LPS-4011 [S]	The Second Time Around	1966	3.75	7.50	15.00
❏ LP-4013 [M]	Etta James	1966	3.00	6.00	12.00
❏ LPS-4013 [S]	Etta James	1966	3.75	7.50	15.00
❏ LP-4018 [M]	Etta James Sings for Lovers	1966	3.00	6.00	12.00
❏ LPS-4018 [S]	Etta James Sings for Lovers	1966	3.75	7.50	15.00
❏ LP-4025 [M]	Etta James Top Ten	1966	3.00	6.00	12.00
❏ LPS-4025 [S]	Etta James Top Ten	1966	3.75	7.50	15.00
❏ LP-4040 [M]	The Queen of Soul	1966	3.00	6.00	12.00
❏ LPS-4040 [S]	The Queen of Soul	1966	3.75	7.50	15.00
❏ LP-4055 [M]	Call My Name	1967	3.75	7.50	15.00
❏ LPS-4055 [S]	Call My Name	1967	5.00	10.00	20.00

J

CHESS

Number	Title (A Side/B Side)	Yr	VG	VG+	NM
CH2-6028 [(2)]	The Sweetest Peaches	1989	3.00	6.00	12.00
CH-9110	Her Greatest Sides, Vol. 1	1984	2.50	5.00	10.00
CH-9184	Etta James Rocks the House	1986	2.00	4.00	8.00
—Reissue					
CH-9266	At Last!	1987	2.00	4.00	8.00
—Reissue					
CH-9269	Tell Mama	1987	2.00	4.00	8.00
—Reissue					
CH-9287	The Second Time Around	1989	2.00	4.00	8.00
—Reissue					
ACH-19003	Etta Is Betta Than Evvah!	1976	3.75	7.50	15.00
CH-50042	Etta James	1973	3.75	7.50	15.00
2CH-60004 [(2)]	Peaches	1971	5.00	10.00	20.00
CH-60029	Come a Little Closer	1974	3.75	7.50	15.00
CH-91509	Come a Little Closer	198?	2.00	4.00	8.00
—Reissue					

CROWN

Number	Title (A Side/B Side)	Yr	VG	VG+	NM
CST-360 [R]	Etta James	1963	5.00	10.00	20.00
—With Etta smiling on cover					
CST-360 [R]	Etta James	1963	5.00	10.00	20.00
—With Etta somber on cover					
CLP-5209 [M]	Miss Etta James	1961	25.00	50.00	100.00
—First edition, with framed picture on cover					
CLP-5209 [M]	Miss Etta James	1962	15.00	30.00	60.00
—Second edition, all-white cover with "Miss Etta James"					
CLP-5234 [M]	The Best of Etta James	1962	15.00	30.00	60.00
—Black label					
CLP-5234 [M]	The Best of Etta James	1963	7.50	15.00	30.00
—Gray label					
CLP-5250 [M]	Twist with Etta James	1962	15.00	30.00	60.00
—Black label					
CLP-5250 [M]	Twist with Etta James	1963	7.50	15.00	30.00
—Gray label					
CLP-5360 [M]	Etta James	1963	7.50	15.00	30.00
—With Etta smiling on cover					
CLP-5360 [M]	Etta James	1963	7.50	15.00	30.00
—With Etta somber on cover					

INTERMEDIA

Number	Title (A Side/B Side)	Yr	VG	VG+	NM
QS-5014	Etta, Red Hot 'N' Live!	198?	2.50	5.00	10.00

ISLAND

Number	Title (A Side/B Side)	Yr	VG	VG+	NM
91018	Seven Year Itch	1988	2.50	5.00	10.00
842926-1	Sticking to My Guns	1990	3.00	6.00	12.00

KENT

Number	Title (A Side/B Side)	Yr	VG	VG+	NM
KST-500 [R]	Miss Etta James	1964	6.25	12.50	25.00
—Black vinyl					
KST-500 [R]	Miss Etta James	1964	20.00	40.00	80.00
—Red vinyl					
KLP-5000 [M]	Miss Etta James	1964	7.50	15.00	30.00

UNITED

Number	Title (A Side/B Side)	Yr	VG	VG+	NM
US 7712	Etta James Sings	197?	2.50	5.00	10.00

WARNER BROS.

Number	Title (A Side/B Side)	Yr	VG	VG+	NM
BSK 3156	Deep in the Night	1978	3.00	6.00	12.00

JAMES, JIMMY, AND THE VAGABONDS

12-Inch Singles

PYE

Number	Title (A Side/B Side)	Yr	VG	VG+	NM
121	I Am Somebody (same on both sides)	1976	3.75	7.50	15.00
125	Now Is the Time/I Go Where the Music Takes Me	1976	3.75	7.50	15.00

45s

ATCO

Number	Title (A Side/B Side)	Yr	VG	VG+	NM
6551	Come to Me Softly/Hi-Diddley Dee Dum Dum	1968	2.00	4.00	8.00
6608	Red Red Wine/No Good to Cry	1968	2.00	4.00	8.00

PYE

Number	Title (A Side/B Side)	Yr	VG	VG+	NM
71017	You Don't Stand a Chance If You Can't Dance (Part 1 & 2)	1975	—	3.00	6.00
71019	Lay Some Lovin' on Me/You Don't Stand a Chance If You Can't Dance	1975	—	2.50	5.00
71057	I Am Somebody/Chains of Love	1975	—	2.50	5.00
71068	I Go Where the Music Takes Me/Let's Love Together	1976	—	2.50	5.00
71075	Now Is the Time/Never Had This Dream Before	1976	—	2.50	5.00

Albums

ATCO

Number	Title (A Side/B Side)	Yr	VG	VG+	NM
33-222 [M]	The New Religion	1967	5.00	10.00	20.00
SD 33-222 [S]	The New Religion	1967	5.00	10.00	20.00

PYE

Number	Title (A Side/B Side)	Yr	VG	VG+	NM
12111	You Don't Stand a Chance If You Can't Dance	1975	2.50	5.00	10.00

JAMES, JONI

45s

MGM

Number	Title (A Side/B Side)	Yr	VG	VG+	NM
11223	Let There Be Love/My Baby Just Cares for Me	1952	6.25	12.50	25.00
11295	You Belong to Me/Yes, Yes, Yes	1952	6.25	12.50	25.00
11333	Why Don't You Believe Me/Purple Shades	1952	7.50	15.00	30.00
11390	Have You Heard/Wishing Ring	1953	5.00	10.00	20.00
11426	Your Cheatin' Heart/I'll Be Waiting for You	1953	5.00	10.00	20.00
11470	Is It Any Wonder/Almost Always	1953	5.00	10.00	20.00
11543	My Love, My Love/You're Fooling Someone	1953	5.00	10.00	20.00
11606	I'll Never Stand in Your Way/Why Can't I	1953	5.00	10.00	20.00
11637	Christmas and You/Nina-Non	1953	5.00	10.00	20.00
11696	Am I in Love/Maybe Next Time	1954	5.00	10.00	20.00
11753	In a Garden of Roses/Every Day	1954	5.00	10.00	20.00
11802	Mama, Don't Cry at My Wedding/Pa Pa Pa	1954	5.00	10.00	20.00
11865	Everytime You Tell Me You Love Me/When We Come of Age	1954	5.00	10.00	20.00
11919	How Important Can It Be?/This Is My Confession	1955	5.00	10.00	20.00
11960	When You Wish Upon a Star/Is This the End of the Line	1955	5.00	10.00	20.00
12020	The Moment I Saw You/Where Is That Someone for Me	1955	5.00	10.00	20.00
12066	You Are My Love/I Lay Me Down to Sleep	1955	5.00	10.00	20.00
12091	The Christmas Song/Have Yourself a Merry Little Christmas	1955	6.25	12.50	25.00
12126	My Believing Heart/You Never Fall in Love Again	1955	5.00	10.00	20.00
12175	Don't Tell Me Not to Love You/Somewhere Someone Is Lonely	1956	3.75	7.50	15.00
12213	I Woke Up Crying/The Maverick Queen	1956	3.75	7.50	15.00
12288	Give Us This Day/How Lucky You Are	1956	3.75	7.50	15.00
12353	Love Letters/Don't Take Your Love from Me	1956	3.75	7.50	15.00
12368	White Christmas/I'll Be Home for Christmas	1956	5.00	10.00	20.00
12369	Danny Boy/To You I Give My Heart	1956	3.75	7.50	15.00
12450	I Need You So/Only Trust Your Heart	1957	3.75	7.50	15.00
12480	Summer Love/I'm Sorry for You, My Friend	1957	3.75	7.50	15.00
12531	Crying in the Shadows/Day Dreaming	1957	3.75	7.50	15.00
12565	Never 'Til Now/I Give You My Heart	1957	3.75	7.50	15.00
12565 [PS]	Never 'Til Now/I Give You My Heart	1957	6.25	12.50	25.00
12607	Dansero/Love Works Miracles	1958	3.75	7.50	15.00
12627	Nothing Will Ever Change/Does It Show	1958	3.75	7.50	15.00
12639	Arrivederci Roma/Non Dimenticar	1958	3.75	7.50	15.00
12660	Coming from You/Junior Prom	1958	3.75	7.50	15.00
12706	There Goes My Heart/Funny	1958	3.75	7.50	15.00
12706 [PS]	There Goes My Heart/Funny	1958	12.50	25.00	50.00
SK-12706 [S]	There Goes My Heart/Funny	1958	10.00	20.00	40.00
—Note different prefix. Also, label will say "Stereo."					
12746	There Must Be a Way/Sorry for Myself	1959	3.75	7.50	15.00
12779	I Still Get a Thrill (Thinking of You)/Perhaps	1959	3.75	7.50	15.00
12779 [PS]	I Still Get a Thrill (Thinking of You)/Perhaps	1959	6.25	12.50	25.00
12807	I Still Get Jealous/My Prayer of Love	1959	3.75	7.50	15.00
12828	Are You Sorry/What I Don't Know Won't Hurt Me	1959	3.75	7.50	15.00
12849	Little Things Mean a Lot/I Laughed at Love	1959	3.75	7.50	15.00
12885	I Need You Now/You Belong to Me	1960	3.00	6.00	12.00
12895	They Really Don't Know You/We Know	1960	3.00	6.00	12.00
12933	My Last Date (With You)/I Can't Give You Anything But Love	1960	3.00	6.00	12.00
12933 [PS]	My Last Date (With You)/I Can't Give You Anything But Love	1960	5.00	10.00	20.00
12948	Be My Love/Tall As a Tree	1960	3.00	6.00	12.00
12948 [PS]	Be My Love/Tall As a Tree	1960	5.00	10.00	20.00
12990	Theme from "Carnival"/Can You Imagine That	1961	3.00	6.00	12.00
13016	Go Away (Bother Me No More)/I Gave My Love	1961	3.00	6.00	12.00
13037	Somebody Else Is Taking My Place/You Were Wrong	1961	3.00	6.00	12.00
13037 [PS]	Somebody Else Is Taking My Place/You Were Wrong	1961	5.00	10.00	20.00
13080	It's Magic/Tender and True	1962	3.00	6.00	12.00
13092	You Are My Sunshine/Lend Me Your Handkerchief	1962	3.75	7.50	15.00
13117	Anyone But Her/Forgive a Fool	1962	3.75	7.50	15.00
13159	Hey, Good Lookin'/He Says the Same Things to Me	1963	3.75	7.50	15.00
13180	Red Sails in the Sunset/Every Time I Meet You	1963	3.75	7.50	15.00
13206	Teach Me to Forget You/Un Cafe	1964	5.00	10.00	20.00
13243	Break, My Heart, Break/Don't Let the Neighbors Know	1964	5.00	10.00	20.00
13267	Pearly Shells/Hawaiian War Chant	1964	5.00	10.00	20.00
13288	Sentimental Me/You're Nearer	1964	20.00	40.00	80.00
13304	Dondi/Once I Loved	1964	5.00	10.00	20.00
13365	There Goes My Heart/I Still Get Jealous	1965	5.00	10.00	20.00
SK-50111 [S]	There Must Be a Way/Sorry for Myself	1959	7.50	15.00	30.00

SHARP

Number	Title (A Side/B Side)	Yr	VG	VG+	NM
46	Let There Be Love/My Baby Just Cares for Me	1952	75.00	150.00	300.00
50	You Belong to Me/Yes, Yes, Yes	1952	62.50	125.00	250.00

7-Inch Extended Plays

MGM

Number	Title (A Side/B Side)	Yr	VG	VG+	NM
X-222 [PS]	Let There Be Love	1953	12.50	25.00	50.00
—Cover for X-4047 and X-4048					
X-234 [PS]	Joni James	1954	12.50	25.00	50.00
—Cover with X-4090 and X-4091					
X272 [PS]	Little Girl Blue	195?	10.00	20.00	40.00
—Cover with X-4204 and X-4205					
X-326 [PS]	When I Fall in Love	1955	10.00	20.00	40.00
—Cover with X-4295 and X-4296					
X-1160	I'm in the Mood for Love/Where Can I Go Without You//People Will Say We're in Love/Love Letters	1955	15.00	30.00	60.00
X-1160 [PS]	Joni James	1955	15.00	30.00	60.00
X-1172	Have Yourself a Merry Little Christmas/Christmas and You//The Christmas Song (Merry Christmas to You)/Nina-Non	1955	15.00	30.00	60.00
X-1172 [PS]	Have Yourself a Merry Little Christmas	1955	15.00	30.00	60.00
X-1211	Star Dust/But Not for Me//Someone to Watch Over Me/My Heart Stood Still	1956	10.00	20.00	40.00
X-1211 [PS]	In the Still of the Night, Part 1	1956	10.00	20.00	40.00
X-1212	(contents unknown)	1956	10.00	20.00	40.00
X-1212 [PS]	In the Still of the Night, Part 2	1956	10.00	20.00	40.00
X-1213	In the Still of the Night/What's New//Deep Purple/You'd Be So Nice to Come Home To	1956	10.00	20.00	40.00
X-1213 [PS]	In the Still of the Night, Vol. 3	1956	10.00	20.00	40.00
X-1219	Have You Heard/Almost Always//Purple Shades/Your Cheatin' Heart	1956	10.00	20.00	40.00
X-1219 [PS]	Award Winning Album, Part 1	1956	10.00	20.00	40.00
X-1220	Why Don't You Believe Me/Is It Any Wonder//Wishing Ring/My Love, My Love	1956	10.00	20.00	40.00
X-1220 [PS]	Joni James, Volume 2	1956	10.00	20.00	40.00
X-1221	(contents unknown)	1956	10.00	20.00	40.00
X-1221 [PS]	Award Winning Album, Part 3	1956	10.00	20.00	40.00
X-1222	*Little Girl Blue/I'm Through with Love/These Foolish Things (Remind Me of You)/It's the Talk of the Town	1956	10.00	20.00	40.00
X-1222 [PS]	Little Girl Blue, Vol. 1	1956	10.00	20.00	40.00
X-1223	In Love in Vain/Too Late Now//Autumn Leaves/That Old Feeling	1956	10.00	20.00	40.00
X-1223 [PS]	Little Girl Blue, Vol. 2	1956	10.00	20.00	40.00
X-1227	I Need You Now/This Is My Confession//The Moment I Saw You/Am I in Love	1956	10.00	20.00	40.00
X-1227 [PS]	Let There Be Love	1956	10.00	20.00	40.00
X-1343	My Foolish Heart/I Don't Stand a Ghost of a Chance with You//Stella by Starlight/A Hundred Years from Today	1956	10.00	20.00	40.00
X-1343 [PS]	Joni Sings Songs by Victor Young (Vol. 1)	1956	10.00	20.00	40.00

Number	Title (A Side/B Side)	Yr	VG	VG+	NM
☐ X-1344	Song of Surrender/Everything I Do//If I Were a Bell.My Darling, My Darling	1956	10.00	20.00	40.00
☐ X-1344 [PS]	Joni Sings Songs by Victor Young/Songs by Frank Loesser (Vol. 2)	1956	10.00	20.00	40.00
☐ X-1345	On a Slow Boat to China/I'll Know//Spring Will Be a Little Late This Year/Anywhere I Wander	1956	10.00	20.00	40.00
☐ X-1345 [PS]	Joni Sings Songs by Frank Loesser (Vol. 3)	1956	10.00	20.00	40.00
☐ X-1389	(contents unknown)	1957	10.00	20.00	40.00
☐ X-1389 [PS]	Give Us This Day, Vol. 1	1957	10.00	20.00	40.00
☐ X-1390	Look for the Silver Lining/Panis Angelicus//I Believe/The Rosary	1957	10.00	20.00	40.00
☐ X-1390 [PS]	Give Us This Day, Vol. 2	1957	10.00	20.00	40.00
☐ X-1391	Count Your Blessings/Ave Maria (Gounod)// Abide with Me/May the Good Lord Bles and Keep You	1957	10.00	20.00	40.00
☐ X-1391 [PS]	Give Us This Day, Vol. 3	1957	10.00	20.00	40.00
☐ X-1399	(contents unknown)	1957	15.00	30.00	60.00
☐ X-1399 [PS]	Merry Christmas from Joni, Part 1	1957	15.00	30.00	60.00
☐ X-1400	The Christmas Song/It Came Upon the Midnight Clear//O Come All Ye Faithful/Nina-Non	1957	15.00	30.00	60.00
☐ X-1400 [PS]	Merry Christmas from Joni, Part 2	1957	15.00	30.00	60.00
☐ X-1401	(contents unknown)	1957	15.00	30.00	60.00
☐ X-1401 [PS]	Merry Christmas from Joni, Part 3	1957	15.00	30.00	60.00
☐ X-1545	Always/When You Were Sweet Sixteen//Let Me Call You Sweetheart/Alice Blue Gown	1957	10.00	20.00	40.00
☐ X-1545 [PS]	Among My Souvenirs, Vol. I	1957	10.00	20.00	40.00
☐ X-1546	(contents unknown)	1957	10.00	20.00	40.00
☐ X-1546 [PS]	Among My Souvenirs, Vol. II	1957	10.00	20.00	40.00
☐ X-1547	(contents unknown)	1957	10.00	20.00	40.00
☐ X-1547 [PS]	Among My Souvenirs, Vol. III	1957	10.00	20.00	40.00
☐ X1615	(contents unknown)	1958	10.00	20.00	40.00
☐ X1615 [PS]	Second Award Winning Album, Vol. 1	1958	10.00	20.00	40.00
☐ X1616	You're Fooling Someone/How Lucky You Are// You Belong to Me/Everyday	1958	10.00	20.00	40.00
☐ X1616 [PS]	Second Award Winning Album, Vol. 2	1958	10.00	20.00	40.00
☐ X1617	(contents unknown)	1958	10.00	20.00	40.00
☐ X1617 [PS]	Second Award Winning Album, Vol. 3	1958	10.00	20.00	40.00
☐ X-1652		1959	10.00	20.00	40.00
☐ X-1652 [PS]	Songs of Hank Williams, Part 1	1959	10.00	20.00	40.00
☐ X-1653	(contents unknown)	1959	10.00	20.00	40.00
☐ X-1653 [PS]	Songs of Hank Williams, Part 2	1959	10.00	20.00	40.00
☐ X-1654	(contents unknown)	1959	10.00	20.00	40.00
☐ X-1654 [PS]	Songs of Hank Williams, Part 3	1959	10.00	20.00	40.00
☐ X-1656	*All Through the Day/Too Young/My Heart Tells Me/Imagination	1959	10.00	20.00	40.00
☐ X-1656 [PS]	100 Strings and Joni, Part 1	1959	10.00	20.00	40.00
☐ X-1657	(contents unknown)	1959	10.00	20.00	40.00
☐ X-1657 [PS]	100 Strings and Joni, Part 2	1959	10.00	20.00	40.00
☐ X-1658	But Beautiful/Wait and See//It Could Happen to You/Maybe You'll Be There	1959	10.00	20.00	40.00
☐ X-1658 [PS]	100 Strings and Joni, Part 3	1959	10.00	20.00	40.00
☐ X-4047	Let There Be Love/My Romance//The Nearness of You/You're Mine You	1953	12.50	25.00	50.00
—One record of "X222"					
☐ X-4048	You're My Everything/You're Nearer//Love Is Here to Stay/I'll Be Seeing You	1953	12.50	25.00	50.00
—One record of "X222"					
☐ X-4090	Have You Heard/Almost Always//Purple Shades/Your Cheatin' Heart	1954	12.50	25.00	50.00
—One record of "X234"					
☐ X-4091	Why Don't You Believe Me/Is It Any Wonder// Wishing Ring/My Love, My Love	1954	12.50	25.00	50.00
—One record of "X234"					
☐ X4204	Little Girl Blue/I'm Through with Love//These Foolish Things/It's the Talk of the Town	195?	10.00	20.00	40.00
—One record of "X272"					
☐ X4205	In Love in Vain/Too Late Now//Autumn Leaves/ That Old Feeling	195?	10.00	20.00	40.00
—One record of "X272"					
☐ X-4295	When I Fall in Love/To Each His Own//I've Never Been in Love Before/Embraceable You	1955	10.00	20.00	40.00
—One record of "X326"					
☐ X-4296	I Could Write a Book/Don't Blame Me//My One and Only Love/As Time Goes By	1955	10.00	20.00	40.00
—One record of "X326"					

Albums

MGM

Number	Title (A Side/B Side)	Yr	VG	VG+	NM
☐ E-222 [10]	Let There Be Love	1953	50.00	100.00	200.00
☐ E-234 [10]	Award Winning Album	1954	50.00	100.00	200.00
☐ E-272 [10]	Little Girl Blue	1955	50.00	100.00	200.00
☐ E-3240 [M]	When I Fall in Love	1955	20.00	40.00	80.00
—Yellow label					
☐ E-3240 [M]	When I Fall in Love	1960	10.00	20.00	40.00
—Black label					
☐ E-3328 [M]	In the Still of the Night	1956	20.00	40.00	80.00
—Yellow label					
☐ E-3328 [M]	In the Still of the Night	1960	10.00	20.00	40.00
—Black label					
☐ E-3346 [M]	Award Winning Album	1956	20.00	40.00	80.00
—Yellow label					
☐ E-3346 [M]	Award Winning Album	1960	10.00	20.00	40.00
—Black label					
☐ E-3347 [M]	Little Girl Blue	1956	20.00	40.00	80.00
—Yellow label					
☐ E-3347 [M]	Little Girl Blue	1960	10.00	20.00	40.00
—Black label					
☐ E-3348 [M]	Let There Be Love	1956	20.00	40.00	80.00
—Yellow label					
☐ E-3348 [M]	Let There Be Love	1960	10.00	20.00	40.00
—Black label					
☐ E-3449 [M]	Songs by Victor Young and Frank Loesser	1956	20.00	40.00	80.00
—Yellow label					
☐ E-3449 [M]	Songs by Victor Young and Frank Loesser	1960	10.00	20.00	40.00
—Black label					
☐ E-3468 [M]	Merry Christmas from Joni	1956	30.00	60.00	120.00
—Yellow label original					

Number	Title (A Side/B Side)	Yr	VG	VG+	NM
☐ E-3468 [M]	Merry Christmas from Joni	1960	15.00	30.00	60.00
—Black label reissue					
☐ E-3528 [M]	Give Us This Day	1957	20.00	40.00	80.00
—Yellow label					
☐ E-3528 [M]	Give Us This Day	1960	10.00	20.00	40.00
—Black label					
☐ E-3533 [M]	Songs by Jerome Kern and Harry Warren	1957	20.00	40.00	80.00
—Yellow label					
☐ E-3533 [M]	Songs by Jerome Kern and Harry Warren	1960	10.00	20.00	40.00
—Black label					
☐ E-3602 [M]	Among My Souvenirs	1958	20.00	40.00	80.00
—Yellow label					
☐ E-3602 [M]	Among My Souvenirs	1960	10.00	20.00	40.00
—Black label					
☐ E-3623 [M]	Ti Voglio Bene	1958	20.00	40.00	80.00
—Yellow label					
☐ E-3623 [M]	Ti Voglio Bene	1960	10.00	20.00	40.00
—Black label					
☐ E-3706 [M]	Award Winning Album, Volume 2	1958	20.00	40.00	80.00
—Yellow label					
☐ E-3706 [M]	Award Winning Album, Volume 2	1960	10.00	20.00	40.00
—Black label					
☐ E-3718 [M]	Je T'aime (I Love You)	1958	20.00	40.00	80.00
—Yellow label					
☐ E-3718 [M]	Je T'aime (I Love You)	1960	10.00	20.00	40.00
—Black label					
☐ SE-3718 [S]	Je T'aime (I Love You)	1958	30.00	60.00	120.00
—Yellow label					
☐ SE-3718 [S]	Je T'aime (I Love You)	1960	12.50	25.00	50.00
—Black label					
☐ E-3739 [M]	Songs of Hank Williams	1959	20.00	40.00	80.00
—Yellow label					
☐ E-3739 [M]	Songs of Hank Williams	1960	10.00	20.00	40.00
—Black label					
☐ SE-3739 [S]	Songs of Hank Williams	1959	30.00	60.00	120.00
—Yellow label					
☐ SE-3739 [S]	Songs of Hank Williams	1960	12.50	25.00	50.00
—Black label					
☐ E-3749 [M]	Irish Favorites	1959	20.00	40.00	80.00
—Yellow label					
☐ E-3749 [M]	Irish Favorites	1960	10.00	20.00	40.00
—Black label					
☐ SE-3749 [S]	Irish Favorites	1959	30.00	60.00	120.00
—Yellow label					
☐ SE-3749 [S]	Irish Favorites	1960	12.50	25.00	50.00
—Black label					
☐ E-3755 [M]	100 Strings and Joni	1959	20.00	40.00	80.00
—Yellow label					
☐ E-3755 [M]	100 Strings and Joni	1960	10.00	20.00	40.00
—Black label					
☐ SE-3755 [S]	100 Strings and Joni	1959	30.00	60.00	120.00
—Yellow label					
☐ SE-3755 [S]	100 Strings and Joni	1960	12.50	25.00	50.00
—Black label					
☐ E-3772 [M]	Joni James Swings Sweet	1959	15.00	30.00	60.00
☐ SE-3772 [S]	Joni James Swings Sweet	1959	20.00	40.00	80.00
☐ E-3800 [M]	Joni James at Carnegie Hall	1959	15.00	30.00	60.00
☐ SE-3800 [S]	Joni James at Carnegie Hall	1959	20.00	40.00	80.00
☐ E-3837 [M]	I'm in the Mood for Love	1960	15.00	30.00	60.00
☐ SE-3837 [S]	I'm in the Mood for Love	1960	20.00	40.00	80.00
☐ E-3839 [M]	100 Strings and Joni On Broadway	1960	15.00	30.00	60.00
☐ SE-3839 [S]	100 Strings and Joni On Broadway	1960	17.50	35.00	70.00
☐ E-3840 [M]	100 Strings and Joni In Hollywood	1960	15.00	30.00	60.00
☐ SE-3840 [S]	100 Strings and Joni In Hollywood	1960	17.50	35.00	70.00
☐ E-3885 [M]	More Joni Hits	1960	12.50	25.00	50.00
☐ SE-3885 [S]	More Joni Hits	1960	15.00	30.00	60.00
☐ E-3892 [M]	100 Voices, 100 Strings	1960	12.50	25.00	50.00
☐ SE-3892 [S]	100 Voices, 100 Strings	1960	15.00	30.00	60.00
☐ E-3958 [M]	Folk Songs by Joni James	1961	12.50	25.00	50.00
☐ SE-3958 [S]	Folk Songs by Joni James	1961	15.00	30.00	60.00
☐ E-3987 [M]	The Mood Is Swinging	1961	12.50	25.00	50.00
☐ SE-3987 [S]	The Mood Is Swinging	1961	15.00	30.00	60.00
☐ E-3990 [M]	The Mood Is Romance	1961	12.50	25.00	50.00
☐ SE-3990 [S]	The Mood Is Romance	1961	15.00	30.00	60.00
☐ E-3991 [M]	The Mood Is Blue	1961	12.50	25.00	50.00
☐ SE-3991 [S]	The Mood Is Blue	1961	15.00	30.00	60.00
☐ E-4008 [M]	After Hours	1962	12.50	25.00	50.00
☐ SE-4008 [S]	After Hours	1962	15.00	30.00	60.00
☐ E-4053 [M]	I Feel a Song Comin' On	1962	12.50	25.00	50.00
☐ SE-4053 [S]	I Feel a Song Comin' On	1962	15.00	30.00	60.00
☐ E-4054 [M]	I'm Your Girl	1962	12.50	25.00	50.00
☐ SE-4054 [S]	I'm Your Girl	1962	15.00	30.00	60.00
☐ E-4101 [M]	Country Girl Style	1962	12.50	25.00	50.00
☐ SE-4101 [S]	Country Girl Style	1962	15.00	30.00	60.00
☐ E-4151 [M]	The Very Best of Joni James	1963	10.00	20.00	40.00
☐ SE-4151 [S]	The Very Best of Joni James	1963	12.50	25.00	50.00
☐ E-4158 [M]	Something for the Boys	1963	10.00	20.00	40.00
☐ SE-4158 [S]	Something for the Boys	1963	12.50	25.00	50.00
☐ E-4182 [M]	Three O'Clock in the Morning	1963	10.00	20.00	40.00
☐ SE-4182 [S]	Three O'Clock in the Morning	1963	12.50	25.00	50.00
☐ E-4200 [M]	My Favorite Things	1963	10.00	20.00	40.00
☐ SE-4200 [S]	My Favorite Things	1963	12.50	25.00	50.00
☐ E-4208 [M]	Italianissime!	1963	10.00	20.00	40.00
☐ SE-4208 [S]	Italianissime!	1963	12.50	25.00	50.00
☐ E-4248 [M]	Put On a Happy Face	1964	10.00	20.00	40.00
☐ SE-4248 [S]	Put On a Happy Face	1964	12.50	25.00	50.00
☐ E-4255 [M]	Joni James Sings the Gershwins	1964	10.00	20.00	40.00
☐ SE-4255 [S]	Joni James Sings the Gershwins	1964	12.50	25.00	50.00
☐ E-4263 [M]	Beyond the Reef	1964	10.00	20.00	40.00
☐ SE-4263 [S]	Beyond the Reef	1964	12.50	25.00	50.00
☐ E-4286 [M]	Bossa Nova Style	1965	10.00	20.00	40.00
☐ SE-4286 [S]	Bossa Nova Style	1965	12.50	25.00	50.00

JAMES, LEONARD

Albums

DECCA

Number	Title (A Side/B Side)	Yr	VG	VG+	NM
☐ DL 8772 [M]	Boppin' and a-Strollin'	1958	12.50	25.00	50.00

J

Number	Title (A Side/B Side)	Yr	VG	VG+	NM

JAMES, MARK
45s
BELL

Number	Title (A Side/B Side)	Yr	VG	VG+	NM
❏ 45323	Flyin' to Memphis//(B-side unknown)	1973	—	3.00	6.00
❏ 45355	Roller Coaster/I'd Get Enthused	1973	—	3.00	6.00

JAMIE

❏ 1261	Running Back/Free Me My Darling	1963	3.00	6.00	12.00

LIBERTY

❏ 55953	I Can't Let You Go/Bimbo Knows	1967	2.00	4.00	8.00

MERCURY

❏ 73718	Moody Blue/Wrong Kind of Love	1975	2.00	4.00	8.00

NEW DESIGN

❏ ZS7 1002	It's No Laughing Matter/Restless Mood	1971	—	3.50	7.00

PRIVATE STOCK

❏ 45,190	Who's Loving You//(B-side unknown)	1978	—	2.50	5.00

SCEPTER

❏ 12221	Suspicious Minds/Taste of Heaven	1968	2.50	5.00	10.00

JAMES, MILTON
45s
DORE

❏ 767	My Lonely Feeling//(B-side unknown)	1966	375.00	750.00	1500.

JAMES, RICK
12-Inch Singles
GORDY

❏ PR 72 [DJ]	Big Time (6:27)/Upside Down (4:05)	1980	12.50	25.00	50.00

—No label name on label; B-side by Diana Ross

❏ PR-101 [DJ]	Hard to Get (Vocal) (Instrumental)/Let Me Tickle Your Fancy (Vocal) (Instrumental)	1982	3.75	7.50	15.00

—No label name on label; B-side by Jermaine Jackson

MOTOWN

❏ 00012	High on Your Love Suite (7:20)/You and I (8:04)	1978	3.00	6.00	12.00
❏ PR-60 [DJ]	Love Gun (10:03) (3:45)	1979	3.00	6.00	12.00
❏ PR-81 [DJ]	Give It To Me Baby (3 versions)	1981	3.00	6.00	12.00
❏ 144	17 (6:40 vocal) (5:38 instrumental)	1984	—	3.00	6.00
❏ 981 [DJ]	You and I (8:04) (same on both sides)	1978	2.50	5.00	10.00
❏ 4511	Cold Blooded/(Instrumental)	1983	—	3.00	6.00
❏ 4528	Can't Stop/Oh What a Night	1985	—	3.00	6.00
❏ 4561	Sweet and Sexy Thing (3 versions)	1986	—	3.00	6.00
❏ 4565	Forever and a Day/(Instrumental)	1986	—	3.00	6.00

REPRISE

❏ PRO-A-3376 [DJ]	Sexual Love Affair (Club) (Remix Edit) (LP)	1988	2.00	4.00	8.00
❏ 20941	Loosey's Rap (5 versions)	1988	—	3.00	6.00
❏ 21035	This Magic Moment (3 versions)	1988	—	3.00	6.00
❏ 21036	Sexual Luv Affair (4 versions)/In the Girls Room	1988	—	3.00	6.00

45s
A&M

❏ 1615	Funkin' Around/My Mama	1974	6.25	12.50	25.00

GORDY

❏ 1619	Dance Wit' Me — Part 1/Dance Wit' Me — Part 2	1982	—	2.00	4.00
❏ 1619 [PS]	Dance Wit' Me — Part 1/Dance Wit' Me — Part 2	1982	—	2.50	5.00
❏ 1634	Hard to Get/My Love	1982	—	2.00	4.00
❏ 1646	She Blew My Mind (69 Times)//(B-side unknown)	1982	—	2.00	4.00
❏ 1658	Teardrops/Throwdown	1983	—	2.00	4.00
❏ 1687	Cold Blooded/(Instrumental)	1983	—	2.00	4.00
❏ 1703	U Bring the Freak Out/He Talks	1983	—	2.00	4.00
❏ 1714	Ebony Eyes/1,2,3	1983	—	2.00	4.00

—As "Rick James and Smokey Robinson"

❏ 1714	Ebony Eyes/1,2,3	1983	—	2.50	5.00

—As "Rick James and Friend"

❏ 1730	17/(Instrumental)	1984	—	2.00	4.00
❏ 1763	You Turn Me On/Fire and Desire	1984	—	2.00	4.00
❏ 1776	Can't Stop/Oh What a Night	1985	—	2.00	4.00
❏ 1776 [PS]	Can't Stop/Oh What a Night	1985	—	2.50	5.00
❏ 1796	Glow/(Instrumental)	1985	—	2.00	4.00
❏ 1806	Spend the Night with Me/(Instrumental)	1985	—	2.00	4.00
❏ 1844	Sweet and Sexy Thing/(Instrumental)	1986	—	—	3.00
❏ 1844 [PS]	Sweet and Sexy Thing/(Instrumental)	1986	2.00	4.00	8.00

—Sleeve may be promo only

❏ 1862	Forever and a Day/(Instrumental)	1986	—	—	3.00
❏ 7156	You & I/Hollywood	1978	—	2.50	5.00
❏ 7162	Mary Jane/Dream Maker	1978	—	2.50	5.00
❏ 7164	High on Your Love Suite/Stone City Band High	1979	—	2.50	5.00
❏ 7164 [PS]	High on Your Love Suite/Stone City Band High	1979	—	3.00	6.00
❏ 7167	Bustin' Out/Sexy Lady	1979	—	2.50	5.00
❏ 7171	Fool on the Street/Jefferson Hall	1979	—	2.50	5.00
❏ 7176	Love Gun/Stormy Love	1979	—	2.50	5.00
❏ 7177	Come Into My Life (Part 1)/Come Into My Life (Part 2)	1980	—	2.50	5.00
❏ 7185	Big Time/Island Lady	1980	—	2.50	5.00
❏ 7191	Gettin' it On (In the Summertime)/Summer Love	1980	—	2.50	5.00
❏ 7197	Give It to Me Baby/Don't Give Up on Love	1981	—	2.00	4.00
❏ 7205	Super Freak (Part 1)/Super Freak (Part 2)	1981	—	2.00	4.00
❏ 7215	Ghetto Life/Below the Funk (Pass the J)	1981	—	2.00	4.00

REPRISE

❏ 27764	Sexual Love Affair/In the Girls' Room	1988	—	—	3.00
❏ 27828	Wonderful/(Instrumental)	1988	—	—	3.00
❏ 27828 [PS]	Wonderful/(Instrumental)	1988	—	—	3.00
❏ 27885	Loosey's Rap/(Instrumental)	1988	—	—	3.00

—With Roxanne Shante

❏ 27885 [PS]	Loosey's Rap/(Instrumental)	1988	—	—	3.00

WARNER BROS.

❏ 27763	This Magic Moment-Dance with Me/(Instrumental)	1989	—	—	3.00
❏ 27763 [PS]	This Magic Moment-Dance with Me/(Instrumental)	1989	—	—	3.00

Albums
GORDY

❏ G7-981	Come Get It!	1978	2.50	5.00	10.00
❏ G7-984	Bustin' Out of L. Seven	1979	2.50	5.00	10.00
❏ G8-990	Fire It Up	1979	2.50	5.00	10.00
❏ G8-995	Garden of Love	1980	2.50	5.00	10.00
❏ G8-1002	Street Songs	1981	2.00	4.00	8.00
❏ 6005 GL	Throwin' Down	1982	2.00	4.00	8.00
❏ 6043 GL	Cold Blooded	1983	2.00	4.00	8.00
❏ 6095 GL	Reflections	1984	2.00	4.00	8.00
❏ 6135 GL	Glow	1985	2.00	4.00	8.00

MOTOWN

❏ 5263 ML	Come Get It!	198?	2.00	4.00	8.00
❏ 5382 ML	Greatest Hits	1986	2.00	4.00	8.00
❏ MOT-5405	Street Songs	1987	—	3.00	6.00

REPRISE

❏ 25659	Wonderful	1988	2.50	5.00	10.00

JAMES, SONNY
45s
CAPITOL

❏ 2067	A World of Our Own/An Old Sweetheart of Mine	1967	2.50	5.00	10.00
❏ 2067 [PS]	A World of Our Own/An Old Sweetheart of Mine	1967	3.75	7.50	15.00
❏ 2155	Heaven Says Hello/Fairy Tales	1968	2.50	5.00	10.00
❏ 2155 [PS]	Heaven Says Hello/Fairy Tales	1968	3.75	7.50	15.00
❏ F2164	Short Cut/It's So Nice to Make Up	1952	6.25	12.50	25.00
❏ F2259	That's Me Without You/Cool, Cold and Colder	1952	6.25	12.50	25.00
❏ 2271	Born to Be With You/In Waikiki	1968	2.50	5.00	10.00
❏ 2271 [PS]	Born to Be With You/In Waikiki	1968	3.00	6.00	12.00
❏ 2370	Only the Lonely/The Journey	1968	2.50	5.00	10.00
❏ 2370 [PS]	Only the Lonely/The Journey	1968	3.00	6.00	12.00
❏ F2399	The One I Can't Forget/Somebody's Heartache	1953	6.25	12.50	25.00
❏ 2486	Running Bear/Midnight Mood	1969	2.50	5.00	10.00
❏ 2486 [PS]	Running Bear/Midnight Mood	1969	3.00	6.00	12.00
❏ F2508	I Forgot More Than You'll Ever Know/ Poor Boy, Rich Lovin'	1953	6.25	12.50	25.00
❏ 2595	Since I Met You, Baby/Clinging to a Hope	1969	2.50	5.00	10.00
❏ 2595 [PS]	Since I Met You, Baby/Clinging to a Hope	1969	3.00	6.00	12.00
❏ F2641	Won't Somebody Tell Me/My Greatest Thrill	1953	6.25	12.50	25.00
❏ 2700	It's Just a Matter of Time/This World of Ours	1969	2.50	5.00	10.00
❏ 2700 [PS]	It's Just a Matter of Time/This World of Ours	1969	3.00	6.00	12.00
❏ F2734	I've Always Wanted You/That's How I Need You	1954	6.25	12.50	25.00
❏ 2782	My Love/Blue for You	1970	2.00	4.00	8.00
❏ 2782 [PS]	My Love/Blue for You	1970	2.50	5.00	10.00
❏ F2829	Table Next to Mine/Believe Another's Lips	1954	6.25	12.50	25.00
❏ 2834	Don't Keep Me Hangin' On/Woodbine Valley	1970	2.00	4.00	8.00
❏ 2834 [PS]	Don't Keep Me Hangin' On/Woodbine Valley	1970	2.50	5.00	10.00
❏ F2906	She Done Give Her Heart to Me/Oceans of Tears	1954	6.25	12.50	25.00
❏ 2914	Endlessly/Happy Memories	1970	2.00	4.00	8.00
❏ 2914 [PS]	Endlessly/Happy Memories	1970	2.50	5.00	10.00
❏ F2958	Christmas in My Home Town/I Forgot to Remember Santa Claus	1954	7.50	15.00	30.00
❏ 3015	Empty Arms/Everything Begins and Ends with You	1971	2.00	4.00	8.00
❏ 3015 [PS]	Empty Arms/Everything Begins and Ends with You	1971	2.50	5.00	10.00
❏ F3025	Lovin' Season/This Kiss Must Last Forever	1955	6.25	12.50	25.00
❏ F3112	Deceive Me Once Again/ Ain't Gonna Take No Chance	1955	6.25	12.50	25.00
❏ 3114	Bright Lights, Big City/True Love Lasts Forever	1971	2.00	4.00	8.00
❏ 3114 [PS]	Bright Lights, Big City/True Love Lasts Forever	1971	2.50	5.00	10.00
❏ F3163	Til the Last Leaf Shall Fall/ You Don't Have to Walk Alone	1955	6.25	12.50	25.00
❏ 3174	Here Comes Honey Again/ The Only Ones We Truly Hurt	1971	2.00	4.00	8.00
❏ 3174 [PS]	Here Comes Honey Again/ The Only Ones We Truly Hurt	1971	2.50	5.00	10.00
❏ F3198	Too Much/Let's Go Bunny Huggin'	1955	6.25	12.50	25.00
❏ 3232	Only Love Can Break a Heart/ He Has Walked This Way Before	1971	2.00	4.00	8.00
❏ 3232 [PS]	Only Love Can Break a Heart/ He Has Walked This Way Before	1971	2.50	5.00	10.00
❏ F3281	Careless with My Heart/Pigtails and Ribbons	1955	6.25	12.50	25.00
❏ 3322	That's Why I Love You Like I Do/ Still Water Runs Deep	1972	2.00	4.00	8.00
❏ F3357	For Rent (One Empty Heart)/My Stolen Love	1956	5.00	10.00	20.00
❏ 3398	Traces/I'm in Love with You	1972	—	3.50	7.00
❏ F3441	Twenty Feet of Muddy Water/All Mixed Up	1956	5.00	10.00	20.00
❏ 3475	Downfall of Me/I'll Follow You	1972	—	3.50	7.00
❏ F3542	The Cat Came Back/Hello, Old Broken Heart	1956	5.00	10.00	20.00
❏ 3564	Reach Out Your Hand and Touch Me/ Just Keep Thinking of Me	1973	—	3.50	7.00
❏ F3602	Young Love/You're the Reason I'm in Love	1956	5.50	11.00	22.00
❏ 3653	Heaven on Earth/She Believes in Me	1973	—	3.50	7.00
❏ F3674	First Date, First Kiss, First Love/Speak to Me	1957	5.00	10.00	20.00
❏ F3734	Lovesick Blues/Dear Love	1957	5.00	10.00	20.00
❏ 3779	Surprise, Surprise/What Am I Living For	1973	—	3.50	7.00
❏ F3792	Love Conquered/Mighty Loveable Man	1957	5.00	10.00	20.00
❏ F3840	Uh Huh-mm/Why Can't They Remember	1957	5.00	10.00	20.00
❏ F3888	Kathleen/Walk to the Dance	1958	5.00	10.00	20.00
❏ 3931	All the Way Together/Clinging Vine	1974	—	3.00	6.00
❏ F3962	Are You Mine/Let's Play Love	1958	5.00	10.00	20.00
❏ F4020	You Got That Touch/I Can See It in Your Eyes	1958	5.00	10.00	20.00
❏ F4066	Let Me Be the One to Love You/ I Can't Stay Away from You	1958	5.00	10.00	20.00
❏ F4127	Yo-Yo/Dream Big	1959	5.00	10.00	20.00
❏ F4178	Talk of the School/The Table	1959	5.00	10.00	20.00
❏ F4229	Pure Love/This Love of Mine	1959	5.00	10.00	20.00
❏ F4268	Who's Next in Line/Red Mud	1959	5.00	10.00	20.00
❏ F4268 [PS]	Who's Next in Line/Red Mud	1959	10.00	20.00	40.00
❏ 4307	Till Tomorrow/I Forgot More Than You'll Ever Know	1959	5.00	10.00	20.00
❏ 4969	The Minute You're Gone/Gold and Silver	1963	3.00	6.00	12.00
❏ 5057	Going Through the Motions (Of Living)/Bad Times a-Comin'	1963	3.00	6.00	12.00
❏ 5129	Baltimore/Least of All You	1964	3.00	6.00	12.00
❏ 5197	Ask Marie/Sugar Lump	1964	3.00	6.00	12.00
❏ 5280	You're the Only World I Know/ Tying Pieces Together	1964	3.00	6.00	12.00
❏ 5280 [PS]	You're the Only World I Know /Tying Pieces Together	1964	5.00	10.00	20.00
❏ 5375	I'll Keep Holding On (Just to Your Love) /I'm Getting Gray from Being Blue	1965	3.00	6.00	12.00
❏ 5375 [PS]	I'll Keep Holding On (Just to Your Love)/ I'm Getting Gray from Being Blue	1965	5.00	10.00	20.00
❏ 5454	Behind the Tear/Runnin'	1965	3.00	6.00	12.00

Number	Title (A Side/B Side)	Yr	VG	VG+	NM
❏ 5454 [PS]	Behind the Tear/Runnin'	1965	5.00	10.00	20.00
❏ 5536	True Love's a Blessing/Just Ask Your Heart	1965	3.00	6.00	12.00
❏ 5536 [PS]	True Love's a Blessing/Just Ask Your Heart	1965	5.00	10.00	20.00
❏ 5612	Take Good Care of Her/				
	On the Fingers of One Hand	1966	3.00	6.00	12.00
❏ 5612 [PS]	Take Good Care of Her/				
	On the Fingers of One Hand	1966	5.00	10.00	20.00
❏ 5690	Room in Your Heart				
	/How Many Times Can a Man Be a Fool	1966	3.00	6.00	12.00
❏ 5690 [PS]	Room in Your Heart/				
	How Many Times Can a Man Be a Fool	1966	5.00	10.00	20.00
❏ 5733	My Christmas Dream/Barefoot Santa Claus	1966	3.00	6.00	12.00
❏ 5733 [PS]	My Christmas Dream/Barefoot Santa Claus	1966	5.00	10.00	20.00
❏ 5833	Need You/On and On	1967	3.00	6.00	12.00
❏ 5833 [PS]	Need You/On and On	1967	5.00	10.00	20.00
❏ 5914	I'll Never Find Another You/				
	Goodbye, Maggie, Goodbye	1967	3.00	6.00	12.00
❏ 5914 [PS]	I'll Never Find Another You/				
	Goodbye, Maggie, Goodbye	1967	3.75	7.50	15.00
❏ 5987	It's the Little Things/				
	Don't Cut Timber on a Windy Day	1967	3.00	6.00	12.00
❏ 5987 [PS]	It's the Little Things/				
	Don't Cut Timber on a Windy Day	1967	3.75	7.50	15.00
COLUMBIA					
❏ 3-10001	A Mi Esposa Con Amor (To My Wife with Love)/				
	Just Don't Stop Lovin' Me	1974	—	2.50	5.00
❏ 3-10001 [PS]	A Mi Esposa Con Amor (To My Wife with Love)/				
	Just Don't Stop Lovin' Me	1974	2.00	4.00	8.00
❏ 3-10072	A Little Bit South of Saskatoon/				
	Home Style Lovin'	1974	—	2.50	5.00
❏ 3-10072 [PS]	A Little Bit South of Saskatoon/				
	Home Style Lovin'	1974	2.00	4.00	8.00
❏ 3-10121	Little Band of Gold/Pop and Me	1975	—	2.50	5.00
❏ 3-10121 [PS]	Little Band of Gold/Pop and Me	1975	2.00	4.00	8.00
❏ 3-10139	Indian Love Call/Maria Elena	1975	—	2.50	5.00
—As "The Guitars of Sonny James"					
❏ 3-10184	What in the World's Come Over You/Walking the				
	Railroad Trestle	1975	—	2.50	5.00
❏ 3-10184 [PS]	What in the World's Come Over You/Walking the				
	Railroad Trestle	1975	—	3.00	6.00
❏ 3-10249	Eres Tu (Touch the Wind)/Apache	1975	—	2.50	5.00
❏ 3-10276	The Prisoner's Song/Back in the Saddle Again	1975	—	2.50	5.00
❏ 3-10276 [PS]	The Prisoner's Song/Back in the Saddle Again	1975	—	3.00	6.00
❏ 3-10335	When Something Is Wrong with My Baby/				
	Big Silver Bird	1976	—	2.50	5.00
❏ 3-10392	Come On In/Baby's Eyes	1976	—	2.50	5.00
❏ 3-10466	You're Free to Go/Puttin' On the Dog Tonight	1976	—	2.50	5.00
❏ 3-10551	In the Jailhouse Now/Amazing Grace	1977	—	2.50	5.00
❏ 3-10551 [PS]	In the Jailhouse Now/Amazing Grace	1977	—	2.50	5.00
❏ 3-10628	Abilene/Pistol Packin' Mama	1977	—	2.50	5.00
❏ 3-10703	This Is the Love/It'll Still Be Worth It All	1978	—	2.50	5.00
❏ 3-10703 [PS]	This Is the Love/It'll Still Be Worth It All	1978	—	3.00	6.00
❏ 3-10764	Caribbean/Each Time I Look at You	1978	—	2.50	5.00
❏ 3-10852	Building Memories/Little Band of Gold	1978	—	2.50	5.00
❏ 4-45644	When the Snow Is On the Roses/				
	Love is a Rainbow	1972	—	3.50	7.00
❏ 4-45644 [PS]	When the Snow Is On the Roses				
	/Love is a Rainbow	1972	2.50	5.00	10.00
❏ 4-45706	White Silver Sands/Why Is It I'm the Last to Know	1972	—	3.50	7.00
❏ 4-45770	I Love You More and More Everyday/				
	I'll Think About That Tomorrow	1973	—	3.50	7.00
❏ 4-45770 [PS]	I Love You More and More Everyday/				
	I'll Think About That Tomorrow	1973	2.50	5.00	10.00
❏ 4-45871	If She Just Helps Me Get Over You/I Won't				
	Think About It Now	1973	—	3.00	6.00
❏ 4-46003	Is It Wrong (For Loving You)/				
	Suddenly There's a Valley	1974	—	3.00	6.00
DIMENSION					
❏ 1026	Innocent Lies/				
	Don't Let the Stars Get in Your Eyes	1981	—	2.50	5.00
❏ 1026 [PS]	Innocent Lies/				
	Don't Let the Stars Get in Your Eyes	1981	2.00	4.00	8.00
❏ 1033	A Place in the Sun/Lean On Me Girl	1982	—	2.50	5.00
❏ 1033 [PS]	A Place in the Sun/Lean On Me Girl	1982	2.00	4.00	8.00
❏ 1036	I'm Looking Over the Rainbow/Something's Got				
	a Hold on Me	1982	—	2.50	5.00
❏ 1036 [PS]	I'm Looking Over the Rainbow/Something's Got				
	a Hold on Me	1982	2.00	4.00	8.00
❏ 1040	The Fool in Me/Little Rainbow	1982	—	2.50	5.00
❏ 1045	A Free Roamin' Mind/Don't Let the Stars Get In				
	Your Eyes	1983	—	2.50	5.00
DOT					
❏ 16381	A Mile and a Quarter/Just One More Lie	1962	3.75	7.50	15.00
❏ 16419	On the Longest Day/The Only Cure	1963	3.75	7.50	15.00
GROOVE					
❏ 1	Young Love/Broken Wings	1961	5.00	10.00	20.00
MONUMENT					
❏ 45-280	Hold What You've Got/Hanging On to Yesterday	1979	—	2.50	5.00
❏ 45-280 [PS]	Hold What You've Got/Hanging On to Yesterday	1979	—	3.00	6.00
❏ 45-288	Lorelei/If I Ever Wanted You	1979	—	2.50	5.00
NRC					
❏ 050	Jenny Lou/Passin' Through	1960	6.25	12.50	25.00
❏ 050 [PS]	Jenny Lou/Passin' Through	1960	12.50	25.00	50.00
❏ 056	Cold in the Morning/Wondering	1960	6.25	12.50	25.00
❏ 061	Bimbo/I Wish This Night Would Never End	1960	5.00	10.00	20.00
RCA VICTOR					
❏ 47-7858	Apache/Magnetism	1961	3.75	7.50	15.00
❏ 47-7919	Innocent Angel/Hey Little Ducky	1961	3.75	7.50	15.00
❏ 47-7998	The Day's Not Over Yet/The Legend of Brown				
	Mountain Light	1962	3.75	7.50	15.00
7-Inch Extended Plays					
CAPITOL					
❏ SU-111	(contents unknown)	1969	3.75	7.50	15.00
—Jukebox issue; small hole, plays at 33 1/3 rpm					
❏ SU-111 [PS]	Born to Be with You	1969	3.75	7.50	15.00
—Above "For Coin Operated Phonographs Only"					

Number	Title (A Side/B Side)	Yr	VG	VG+	NM
❏ EAP 1-779	Can't Get Over Missin' You/Cold, Cold Heart//				
	Only One Heart to Give/I Got the Feeling	1957	5.00	10.00	20.00
❏ EAP 1-779 [PS]	Southern Gentleman, Part 1	1957	5.00	10.00	20.00
❏ EAP 2-779	I Wish I Knew/Forgive Me//I'll Always Wonder				
	(But I'll Never Know)/Lonesome	1957	5.00	10.00	20.00
❏ EAP 2-779 [PS]	Southern Gentleman, Part 2	1957	5.00	10.00	20.00
❏ EAP 3-779	'Til the Last Leaf Shall Fall/Only a Shadow				
	Between//May God Be With You/My God and I	1957	5.00	10.00	20.00
❏ EAP 3-779 [PS]	Southern Gentleman, Part 3	1957	5.00	10.00	20.00
❏ EAP 1-827	Young Love/Twenty Feet of Muddy Water//For				
	Rent/Hello Old Broken Heart	1957	6.25	12.50	25.00
❏ EAP 1-827 [PS]	Young Love	1957	6.25	12.50	25.00
❏ EAP 1-988	(contents unknown)	1958	5.00	10.00	20.00
❏ EAP 1-988 [PS]	Honey, Part 1	1958	5.00	10.00	20.00
❏ EAP 1-988 [PS]	Honey, Part 3	1958	5.00	10.00	20.00
❏ EAP 2-988	(contents unknown)	1958	5.00	10.00	20.00
❏ EAP 2-988 [PS]	Honey, Part 2	1958	5.00	10.00	20.00
❏ EAP 3-988	You're a Sweetheart/'Deed I Do//Goodnight				
	Sweetheart/I Love You So Much It Hurts	1958	5.00	10.00	20.00
❏ SXA-2209	Baltimore/I Guess It Doesn't Matter Anymore/				
	You're the Only World I Know//Least of All You/				
	Sugar Lump/Burning Bridges	196?	3.75	7.50	15.00
—Jukebox issue; small hole, plays at 33 1/3 rpm					
❏ SXA-2209 [PS]	You're the Only World I Know	196?	3.75	7.50	15.00
❏ SU-2415	I'll Never Be Anything But In Love with You/				
	Tonight I Found My True Love/On and On//I'll				
	Never Find Another You/Yes or No/I Truly Do	196?	3.75	7.50	15.00
—Jukebox issue; small hole, plays at 33 1/3 rpm					
❏ SU-2415 [PS]	Behind the Tear	196?	3.75	7.50	15.00
Albums					
ABC					
❏ AC-30027	The ABC Collection	1976	3.00	6.00	12.00
CAPITOL					
❏ ST-111	Born to Be with You	1968	3.75	7.50	15.00
❏ SKAO-144	The Best of Sonny James Vol. 2	1969	3.75	7.50	15.00
❏ ST 8-0193	Only the Lonely	1969	5.00	10.00	20.00
—Capitol Record Club edition					
❏ ST-193	Only the Lonely	1969	3.75	7.50	15.00
❏ SWBB-258 [(2)]	Close-Up	1969	5.00	10.00	20.00
—Combines ST 2500 and ST 2788 in one package					
❏ ST-320	The Astrodome Presents In Person Sonny				
	James	1969	3.75	7.50	15.00
❏ ST 8-0432	It's Just a Matter of Time	1970	5.00	10.00	20.00
—Capitol Record Club edition					
❏ ST-432	It's Just a Matter of Time	1970	3.75	7.50	15.00
❏ ST-478	My Love/Don't Keep Me Hangin' On	1970	3.75	7.50	15.00
❏ STBB-535 [(2)]	You're the Only World I Know/I'll Never Find				
	Another You	1970	5.00	10.00	20.00
—Combines the two listed albums in one package					
❏ ST-629	#1	1970	3.75	7.50	15.00
❏ ST-734	Empty Arms	1971	3.75	7.50	15.00
❏ T 779 [M]	The Southern Gentleman	1957	12.50	25.00	50.00
—Turquoise label					
❏ T 779 [M]	The Southern Gentleman	1964	5.00	10.00	20.00
—Black label with colorband, logo on top					
❏ ST-804	The Sensational Sonny James	1971	3.75	7.50	15.00
❏ ST-849	Here Comes Honey Again	1971	3.75	7.50	15.00
❏ T 867 [M]	Sonny	1957	12.50	25.00	50.00
—Turquoise label					
❏ T 867 [M]	Sonny	1964	5.00	10.00	20.00
—Black label with colorband, logo on top					
❏ T 988 [M]	Honey	1958	12.50	25.00	50.00
—Turquoise label					
❏ T 988 [M]	Honey	1964	5.00	10.00	20.00
—Black label with colorband, logo on top					
❏ T 1178 [M]	This Is Sonny James	1959	10.00	20.00	40.00
—Black label with colorband, logo at left					
❏ T 1178 [M]	This Is Sonny James	1964	5.00	10.00	20.00
—Black label with colorband, logo on top					
❏ ST 2017 [S]	The Minute You're Gone	1964	6.25	12.50	25.00
❏ T 2017 [M]	The Minute You're Gone	1964	5.00	10.00	20.00
❏ ST 2209 [S]	You're the Only World I Know	1965	6.25	12.50	25.00
❏ T 2209 [M]	You're the Only World I Know	1965	5.00	10.00	20.00
❏ ST 2317 [S]	I'll Keep Holding On	1965	6.25	12.50	25.00
❏ T 2317 [M]	I'll Keep Holding On	1965	5.00	10.00	20.00
❏ ST 2415 [S]	Behind the Tear	1965	6.25	12.50	25.00
❏ T 2415 [M]	Behind the Tear	1965	5.00	10.00	20.00
❏ ST 2500 [S]	True Love's a Blessing	1966	6.25	12.50	25.00
❏ T 2500 [M]	True Love's a Blessing	1966	5.00	10.00	20.00
❏ ST 2561 [S]	Till the Last Leaf Shall Fall	1966	6.25	12.50	25.00
❏ T 2561 [M]	Till the Last Leaf Shall Fall	1966	5.00	10.00	20.00
❏ ST 2589 [S]	My Christmas Dream	1966	6.25	12.50	25.00
❏ T 2589 [M]	My Christmas Dream	1966	5.00	10.00	20.00
❏ SM-2615	The Best of Sonny James	197?	2.50	5.00	10.00
❏ ST 2615 [S]	The Best of Sonny James	1966	5.00	10.00	20.00
—Black Starline label					
❏ T 2615 [M]	The Best of Sonny James	1966	3.75	7.50	15.00
❏ ST 2703 [S]	Need You	1967	3.75	7.50	15.00
❏ T 2703 [M]	Need You	1967	5.00	10.00	20.00
❏ ST 2788 [S]	I'll Never Find Another You	1967	3.75	7.50	15.00
❏ T 2788 [M]	I'll Never Find Another You	1967	5.00	10.00	20.00
❏ ST 2884 [S]	A World of Our Own	1968	3.75	7.50	15.00
❏ T 2884 [M]	A World of Our Own	1968	6.25	12.50	25.00
❏ ST 2937	Heaven Says Hello	1968	3.75	7.50	15.00
❏ SM-11013	The Biggest Hits of Sonny James	197?	2.50	5.00	10.00
❏ ST-11013	The Biggest Hits of Sonny James	1972	3.75	7.50	15.00
❏ ST-11067	That's Why I Love You Like I Do	1972	3.75	7.50	15.00
❏ ST-11108	Traces	1972	3.00	6.00	12.00
❏ ST-11144	The Gentleman from the South	1973	3.00	6.00	12.00
❏ ST-11196	Young Love	1973	3.00	6.00	12.00
❏ SQBO-91357 [(2)]	That Special Country Feeling	196?	7.50	15.00	30.00
—Capitol Record Club exclusive					
COLUMBIA					
❏ KC 31646	When the Snow Is On the Roses	1972	3.00	6.00	12.00
❏ KC 32028	Sonny James Sings the				
	Greatest Country Hits of '72	1973	3.00	6.00	12.00
❏ KC 32291	If She Just Helps Me Get Over You	1973	3.00	6.00	12.00

J

Number	Title (A Side/B Side)	Yr	VG	VG+	NM
❏ KC 32805	Is It Wrong	1974	3.00	6.00	12.00
❏ KC 33056	A Mi Esposa Con Amor (To My Wife with Love)	1974	3.00	6.00	12.00
❏ KC 33428	A Little Bit South of Saskatoon/				
	Little Band of Gold	1975	3.00	6.00	12.00
❏ KC 33477	The Guitars of Sonny James	1975	3.00	6.00	12.00
❏ CG 33627 [(2)]	When the Snow Is On the Roses/If She Just				
	Helps Me Get Over You	1975	3.75	7.50	15.00
❏ PC 33846	Country Male Artist of the Decade	1975	3.00	6.00	12.00
❏ PC 34035	200 Years of Country Music	1976	3.00	6.00	12.00
❏ PC 34309	When Something Is Wrong with My Baby	1976	3.00	6.00	12.00
❏ PC 34472	You're Free to Go	1977	3.00	6.00	12.00
❏ PC 34706	Sonny James In Prison, In Person	1977	3.00	6.00	12.00
❏ KC 35379	This Is the Love	1978	3.00	6.00	12.00
❏ KC 35626	Sonny James' Greatest Hits	1978	3.00	6.00	12.00
DOT					
❏ DLP 3462 [M]	Young Love	1962	10.00	20.00	40.00
❏ DLP 25462 [S]	Young Love	1962	12.50	25.00	50.00
DOT/MCA					
❏ 39087	Sonny James	198?	2.50	5.00	10.00
HILLTOP					
❏ 6067	Invisible Tears	1969	2.50	5.00	10.00
❏ 6079	Timberline	1969	2.50	5.00	10.00
PICKWICK					
❏ SPC-3594	Young Love	1977	2.00	4.00	8.00
RCA CAMDEN					
❏ CAL-2140 [M]	Young Love	1967	3.75	7.50	15.00
❏ CAS-2140 [S]	Young Love	1967	3.00	6.00	12.00

JAMES, TOMMY

45s

Number	Title (A Side/B Side)	Yr	VG	VG+	NM
FANTASY					
❏ 761	I Love You Love Me Love/Devil Gate Drive	1976	—	2.00	4.00
❏ 761 [PS]	I Love You Love Me Love/Devil Gate Drive	1976	—	2.50	5.00
❏ 776	Tighter, Tighter/Comin' Down	1976	—	2.50	5.00
❏ 811	Love Is Gonna Find a Way/				
	I Don't Love You Anymore	1977	—	2.50	5.00
❏ 886	Tighter, Tighter/Comin' Down	1980	—	2.00	4.00
MCA					
❏ 40289	Glory, Glory/Comin' Down	1974	—	2.50	5.00
MILLENNIUM					
❏ YB-11785	Three Times in Love/				
	I Just Wanna Play the Music	1980	—	2.00	4.00
❏ YB-11787	No Hay Dos Sin Tres (Three Times in Love)/I				
	Just Wanna Play the Music	1980	—	2.50	5.00
❏ YB-11787 [PS]	No Hay Dos Sin Tres (Three Times in Love)/I				
	Just Wanna Play the Music	1980	2.50	5.00	10.00
❏ YB-11788	It's Alright (For Now)/You Got Me	1980	—	2.00	4.00
❏ YB-11802	You're So Easy to Love/Halfway to Heaven	1981	—	2.00	4.00
❏ YB-11814	The Lady in White/Payin' for My Lover's Mistake	1981	—	2.00	4.00
ROULETTE					
❏ 7084	Ball and Chain/Candy Maker	1970	—	3.00	6.00
❏ 7093	Church Street Soul Revival/Draggin' the Line	1970	2.00	4.00	8.00
❏ 7100	Adrienne/Light of Day	1971	—	3.00	6.00
❏ 7103	Draggin' the Line/Bits & Pieces	1971	—	3.00	6.00
❏ 7110	I'm Coming Home/Sing, Sing, Sing	1971	—	2.50	5.00
❏ 7114	Nothing to Hide/Walk a Country Mile	1971	—	2.50	5.00
❏ 7119	Tell 'Em Willie Boy's A-Comin'/				
	Forty Days and Dorty Nights	1972	—	2.50	5.00
❏ 7126	Cat's Eye in the Window/Dark Is the Night	1972	—	2.50	5.00
❏ 7130	Love Song/Kingston Highway	1972	—	2.50	5.00
❏ 7135	Celebration/The Last One to Know	1972	—	2.50	5.00
❏ 7140	Boo, Boo, Don't Cha Be Blue/Rings and Things	1973	—	2.50	5.00
❏ 7147	Calico/Hey, My Lady	1973	—	2.50	5.00
21 RECORDS					
❏ 105	Two-Time Lover/Say Please	1983	—	—	3.00
❏ 105 [PS]	Two-Time Lover/Say Please	1983	—	2.00	4.00
Albums					
FANTASY					
❏ 9509	In Touch	1976	3.00	6.00	12.00
❏ 9532	Midnight Rider	1977	3.00	6.00	12.00
MILLENNIUM					
❏ BXL1-7748	Three Times in Love	1980	2.50	5.00	10.00
❏ BXL1-7758	Easy to Love	1981	2.50	5.00	10.00
ROULETTE					
❏ SR-3001	Christian of the World	1971	3.75	7.50	15.00
❏ SR-3007	My Head, My Bed, My Red Guitar	1972	3.75	7.50	15.00
❏ SR-42061	Tommy James	1970	3.75	7.50	15.00

JAMES, TOMMY, AND THE SHONDELLS Also see HOG HEAVEN; TOMMY JAMES.

45s

Number	Title (A Side/B Side)	Yr	VG	VG+	NM
PHILCO-FORD					
❏ HP-1	Mirage/I Think We're Alone Now	1967	3.75	7.50	15.00

—4-inch plastic "Hip Pocket Record" with color sleeve

| ❏ HP-2 | Hanky Panky/Gettin' Together | 1967 | 3.75 | 7.50 | 15.00 |

—4-inch plastic "Hip Pocket Record" with color sleeve

| **RED FOX** | | | | | |
| ❏ 110 | Hanky Panky/Thunderbolt | 1966 | 10.00 | 20.00 | 40.00 |

—As "The Shondells"

ROULETTE					
❏ 4686	Hanky Panky/Thunderbolt	1966	2.50	5.00	10.00
❏ 4695	Say I Am (What I Am)/Lots of Pretty Girls	1966	2.00	4.00	8.00
❏ 4695 [PS]	Say I Am (What I Am)/Lots of Pretty Girls	1966	3.75	7.50	15.00
❏ 4710	It's Only Love/Don't Let My Love Pass You By	1966	2.00	4.00	8.00
❏ 4710	It's Only Love/Ya Ya	1966	3.00	6.00	12.00
❏ 4720	I Think We're Alone Now/Gone, Gone, Gone	1967	2.50	5.00	10.00
❏ 4720 [PS]	I Think We're Alone Now/Gone, Gone, Gone	1967	3.75	7.50	15.00
❏ 4736	Mirage/Run, Run, Baby, Run	1967	2.00	4.00	8.00
❏ 4736 [PS]	Mirage/Run, Run, Baby, Run	1967	3.75	7.50	15.00
❏ 4756	I Like the Way/				
	(Baby) Baby I Can't Take No More	1967	2.00	4.00	8.00
❏ 4762	Gettin' Together/Real Girl	1967	2.00	4.00	8.00
❏ 4762 [PS]	Gettin' Together/Real Girl	1967	3.75	7.50	15.00
❏ 4775	Out of the Blue/Love's Closin' In on Me	1967	2.00	4.00	8.00
❏ 7000	Get Out Now/Wish It Were True	1968	2.00	4.00	8.00
❏ 7008	Mony Mony/One Two Three and I Fell	1968	2.50	5.00	10.00
❏ 7016	Somebody Cares/Do Unto Me	1968	2.00	4.00	8.00

Number	Title (A Side/B Side)	Yr	VG	VG+	NM
❏ 7024	Do Something to Me/Ginger Bread Man	1968	2.00	4.00	8.00
❏ 7028	Crimson and Clover/Some Kind of Love	1968	2.50	5.00	10.00
❏ 7028	Crimson and Clover/(I'm) Taken	1968	3.75	7.50	15.00
❏ 7039	Sweet Cherry Wine/Breakaway	1969	2.00	4.00	8.00
❏ 7050	Crystal Blue Persuasion/I'm Alive	1969	2.50	5.00	10.00
❏ 7060	Ball of Fire/Makin' Good Time	1969	2.00	4.00	8.00
❏ 7066	She/Loved One	1969	2.00	4.00	8.00
❏ 7071	Gotta Get Back to You/Red Rover	1970	2.00	4.00	8.00
❏ 7076	Come to Me/Talkin' and Signifyin'	1970	2.00	4.00	8.00
SNAP					
❏ 102	Hanky Panky/Thunderbolt	1963	20.00	40.00	80.00

—As "The Shondells"; no mention of Red Fox Records on label

| ❏ 102 | Hanky Panky/Thunderbolt | 1966 | 7.50 | 15.00 | 30.00 |

—As "The Shondells"; with "Dist. by Red Fox Records, Pgh, Pa." on label

Albums					
RHINO					
❏ R1-70920 [(2)]	Anthology	1989	3.75	7.50	15.00
ROULETTE					
❏ R 25336 [M]	Hanky Panky	1966	5.00	10.00	20.00
❏ SR 25336 [P]	Hanky Panky	1966	6.25	12.50	25.00

—"Hanky Panky" is rechanneled

❏ R 25344 [M]	It's Only Love	1967	7.50	15.00	30.00
❏ SR 25344 [S]	It's Only Love	1967	6.25	12.50	25.00
❏ R 25353 [M]	I Think We're Alone Now	1967	7.50	15.00	30.00
❏ SR 25353 [P]	I Think We're Alone Now	1967	3.75	7.50	15.00

—Photo cover

| ❏ SR 25353 [P] | I Think We're Alone Now | 1967 | 6.25 | 12.50 | 25.00 |

—Footprints cover; "I Think We're Alone Now" is rechanneled

❏ R 25355 [M]	Something Special! The Best of Tommy James				
	& The Shondells	1968	12.50	25.00	50.00
❏ SR 25355 [S]	Something Special! The Best of Tommy James				
	& The Shondells	1968	6.25	12.50	25.00
❏ R 25357 [M]	Gettin' Together	1968	10.00	20.00	40.00
❏ SR 25357 [S]	Gettin' Together	1968	6.25	12.50	25.00
❏ SR 42005	Something Special! The Best of Tommy James				
	& The Shondells	1968	3.75	7.50	15.00
❏ SR 42012	Mony Mony	1968	5.00	10.00	20.00
❏ SR 42023	Crimson and Clover	1969	5.00	10.00	20.00
❏ SR 42030	Cellophane Symphony	1969	5.00	10.00	20.00
❏ SR 42040	The Best of Tommy James & The Shondells	1969	5.00	10.00	20.00

—Original versions are in a Unipak (gatefold must be opened to remove record)

| ❏ SR 42040 | The Best of Tommy James & The Shondells | 197? | 3.75 | 7.50 | 15.00 |

—Later versions have gatefold covers, but record can be removed without opening it

| ❏ SR 42044 | Travelin' | 1970 | 3.75 | 7.50 | 15.00 |

JAMES GANG, THE (1) Also see TOMMY BOLIN; JOE WALSH.

45s

Number	Title (A Side/B Side)	Yr	VG	VG+	NM
ABC					
❏ 11272	Funk #49/Thanks	1970	—	3.00	6.00
❏ 11301	Walk Away/Yadig?	1971	—	3.00	6.00
❏ 11312	White Man—Black Man/Midnight	1971	—	3.00	6.00
❏ 11325	Looking for My Lady/Hairy Hypochondriac	1972	—	3.00	6.00
❏ 11336	Had Enough/Kick Back Man	1972	—	3.00	6.00
ATCO					
❏ 6953	Must Be Love/Got No Time for Trouble	1974	—	2.50	5.00
❏ 6966	Standing in the Rain/From Another Time	1974	—	2.50	5.00
❏ 7006	Cruisin' Down the Highway/Miami Two-Step	1974	—	2.50	5.00
❏ 7021	Merry Go Round/Red Satin Lover	1975	—	2.50	5.00
❏ 7067	I Need Love/Feelin' Alright	1975	—	2.50	5.00
BLUESWAY					
❏ 61027	I Don't Have the Time/Fred	1969	2.00	4.00	8.00
❏ 61030	Funk #48/Collage	1969	2.50	5.00	10.00
❏ 61033	Take a Look Around/Stop	1970	2.00	4.00	8.00
Albums					
ABC					
❏ S-688	Yer' Album	1970	3.00	6.00	12.00
❏ S-711	James Gang Rides Again	1970	3.00	6.00	12.00

—Standard pressing without "Bolero" as part of "The Bomber"; "RE-1" in trail-off wax

| ❏ S-711 | James Gang Rides Again | 1970 | 6.25 | 12.50 | 25.00 |

—First pressing with a short version of Ravel's "Bolero" as part of the song "The Bomber"; exists on both promos and early stock copies; no "RE-1" in trail-off wax

❏ X-721	Thirds	1971	3.00	6.00	12.00
❏ X-733	James Gang Live in Concert	1971	3.00	6.00	12.00
❏ X-741	Straight Shooter	1972	3.00	6.00	12.00
❏ X-760	Passin' Thru	1972	3.00	6.00	12.00
❏ ABCX-774	The Best of the James Gang				
	Featuring Joe Walsh	1973	3.00	6.00	12.00

—Most copies of this LP contain the edited version of "The Bomber". The full title of the LP is on the spine, and the record's trail-off wax has the number "ABCX-774-A-RE-1".

| ❏ ABCX-774 | The Best of the James Gang | | | | |
| | Featuring Joe Walsh | 1973 | 5.00 | 10.00 | 20.00 |

—A few copies of this LP contain the full version of "The Bomber" with the "Bolero" excerpt. The words "The Best Of" do NOT appear on the spine, and the record's trail-off wax has the number "ABCX-774-A".

❏ X-801 [(2)]	16 Greatest Hits	1973	3.75	7.50	15.00
ATCO					
❏ SD 36-102	Miami	1974	2.50	5.00	10.00
❏ SD 36-112	Newborn	1975	2.50	5.00	10.00
❏ SD 36-141	Jesse Come Home	1976	2.50	5.00	10.00
❏ SD 7037	Bang	1973	2.50	5.00	10.00
BLUESWAY					
❏ BLS-6034	Yer' Album	1969	3.75	7.50	15.00
MCA					
❏ 6012 [(2)]	16 Greatest Hits	1980	2.50	5.00	10.00

—Reissue

| ❏ 37111 | James Gang Rides Again | 1980 | 2.00 | 4.00 | 8.00 |

—Reissue

| ❏ 37112 | The Best of the James Gang | | | | |
| | Featuring Joe Walsh | 1980 | 2.00 | 4.00 | 8.00 |

—Reissue

JAMES GANG, THE (2)

45s

Number	Title (A Side/B Side)	Yr	VG	VG+	NM
ASCOT					
❏ 2168	Everybody Knows/Ladies' Man	1965	3.00	6.00	12.00
❏ 2196	Georgia Pines/Baby Take Me Back	1965	3.00	6.00	12.00
❏ 2205	Right String But the Wrong Yo-Yo/				
	Satin and Lace	1966	3.00	6.00	12.00

Number	Title (A Side/B Side)	Yr	VG	VG+	NM
JAMESON, BOBBY					
45s					
CURRENT					
❏ 103	All Alone/Your Sweet Lovin'	1964	3.00	6.00	12.00
LONDON					
❏ 9730	All I Want Is My Baby/Each and Everyday	1965	10.00	20.00	40.00
TALAMO					
❏ 1934	I'm So Lonely/I Wanna Love You	1964	2.50	5.00	10.00
JAMIE AND JANE "Jamie" is GENE PITNEY.					
45s					
DECCA					
❏ 30862	Snuggle Up Baby/Strollin' Thru the Park	1959	7.50	15.00	30.00
❏ 30934	Faithful Our Love/Classical Rock and Roll	1959	7.50	15.00	30.00
JAMIES, THE					
45s					
EPIC					
❏ 9281	Summertime, Summertime/Searching for You	1958	3.00	6.00	12.00
—Reissued in 1962 with the same catalog number and label design					
❏ 9281 [PS]	Summertime, Summertime/Searching for You	1958	5.00	10.00	20.00
❏ 9299	When the Sun Goes Down/Snow Train	1958	5.00	10.00	20.00
❏ 9565	When the Sun Goes Down/Snow Train	1963	3.00	6.00	12.00
❏ 11129	Summertime, Summertime/Searching for You	1974	—	2.50	5.00
UNITED ARTISTS					
❏ 193	The Evening Star/Don't Darken My Door	1959	5.00	10.00	20.00
JAMME					
45s					
ABC DUNHILL					
❏ 4231	Poor Widow/She Sits There	1970	2.00	4.00	8.00
Albums					
ABC DUNHILL					
❏ DS-50072	Jamme	1970	5.00	10.00	20.00
JAN AND ARNIE Also see JAN AND DEAN.					
45s					
ARWIN					
❏ 108	Jennie Lee/Gotta Getta Date	1958	10.00	20.00	40.00
❏ 111	Gas Money/Bonnie Lou	1958	10.00	20.00	40.00
❏ 113	I Love Linda/The Beat That Can't Be Beat	1958	15.00	30.00	60.00
DORE					
❏ 522	Baby Talk/Jeannette Get Your Hair Done	1959	150.00	300.00	600.00
—Actually by Jan and Dean, but incorrectly credited					
DOT					
❏ 16116	Gas Money/Gotta Getta Date	1960	12.50	25.00	50.00
7-Inch Extended Plays					
DOT					
❏ DEP-1097	Jennie Lee/Gas Money//Gotta Getta Date/The Beat That Can't Be Beat	1960	125.00	250.00	500.00
❏ DEP-1097 [PS]	Jan and Arnie	1960	125.00	250.00	500.00
JAN AND DEAN Also see JAN BERRY; THE LEGENDARY MASKED SURFERS; THE RALLY PACKS.					
45s					
CHALLENGE					
❏ 9111	Heart and Soul/A Midsummer Night's Dream	1961	5.00	10.00	20.00
❏ 9111	Heart and Soul/Those Words	1961	10.00	20.00	40.00
❏ 9120	Wanted: One Girl/Something a Little Bit Different	1961	7.50	15.00	30.00
COLUMBIA					
❏ 44036	Yellow Balloon/Taste of Rain	1967	7.50	15.00	30.00
DORE					
❏ 522	Baby Talk/Jeannette Get Your Hair Done	1959	7.50	15.00	30.00
❏ 531	There's a Girl/My Heart Sings	1959	6.25	12.50	25.00
❏ 539	Clementine/You're On My Mind	1960	6.25	12.50	25.00
❏ 548	Cindy/Whiter Tennis Sneakers	1960	6.25	12.50	25.00
❏ 555	We Go Together/Rosie Lane	1960	6.25	12.50	25.00
—B-side title was altered after the record no longer was issued with picture sleeve					
❏ 555	We Go Together/Rosilane	1960	6.25	12.50	25.00
❏ 555 [PS]	We Go Together/Rosilane	1960	30.00	60.00	120.00
❏ 576	Gee/Such a Good Night to Be Together	1960	6.25	12.50	25.00
❏ 576 [PS]	Gee/Such a Good Night to Be Together	1960	75.00	150.00	300.00
❏ 583	Baggy Pants/Judy's an Angel	1961	7.50	15.00	30.00
❏ 610	Julie/Don't Fly Away	1961	7.50	15.00	30.00
EVATONE					
❏ 7801X	Surf Bunkey	1980	2.00	4.00	8.00
—6-inch red flexi-disc; Dutch version of "Surf City"					
J&D					
❏ 001	California Lullabye/Summertime	1966	7.50	15.00	30.00
❏ 402	Like a Summer Rain/Louisiana Man	1966	7.50	15.00	30.00
❏ 1271 [DJ]	Ocean Park Angel/Wipe Out	1981	2.50	5.00	10.00
—B-side by the Surfaris					
JAN & DEAN					
❏ 10	Hawaii/Tijuana	1966	18.75	37.50	75.00
❏ 11	Fan Tan/Love and Hate	1966	30.00	60.00	120.00
LIBERTY					
❏ S7-19770	Frosty (The Snow Man)/Rudolph the Red-Nosed Reindeer	1997	—	—	3.00
—B-side by the Ventures on Dolton					
❏ 55397	A Sunday Kind of Love/Poor Little Puppet	1961	6.25	12.50	25.00
❏ 55454	Tennessee/Your Heart Has Changed Its Mind	1962	6.25	12.50	25.00
❏ 55496	Who Put the Bomp/My Favorite Dream	1962	12.50	25.00	50.00
❏ 55522	Frosty (The Snow Man)/(She's Still Talking) Baby Talk	1962	37.50	75.00	150.00
—Promos worth about half this value					
❏ 55531	Linda/When I Learn How to Cry	1963	6.25	12.50	25.00
❏ 55580	Surf City/She's My Summer Girl	1963	3.75	7.50	15.00
❏ 55580 [PS]	Surf City/She's My Summer Girl	1963	10.00	20.00	40.00
❏ 55613	Honolulu Lulu/Someday	1963	3.75	7.50	15.00
❏ 55613 [PS]	Honolulu Lulu/Someday	1963	10.00	20.00	40.00
❏ 55641	Drag City/Schlock Rod (Part 1)	1963	3.75	7.50	15.00
❏ 55641 [PS]	Drag City/Schlock Rod (Part 1)	1963	10.00	20.00	40.00
❏ 55672	Dead Man's Curve/The New Girl in School	1964	3.75	7.50	15.00
❏ 55672 [PS]	Dead Man's Curve/The New Girl in School	1964	10.00	20.00	40.00
❏ 55704	The Little Old Lady (From Pasadena)/My Mighty G.T.O.	1964	3.75	7.50	15.00
❏ 55704 [PS]	The Little Old Lady (From Pasadena)/My Mighty G.T.O.	1964	10.00	20.00	40.00
❏ 55724	Ride the Wild Surf/The Anaheim, Azusa and Cucamonga Sewing Circle, Book Review and Timing Association	1964	3.75	7.50	15.00
❏ 55724 [PS]	Ride the Wild Surf/The Anaheim, Azusa and Cucamonga Sewing Circle, Book Review and Timing Association	1964	10.00	20.00	40.00
❏ 55727	Sidewalk Surfin/When It's Over	1964	3.75	7.50	15.00
❏ 55727 [PS]	Sidewalk Surfin/When It's Over	1964	10.00	20.00	40.00
❏ 55766	(Here They Come) From All Over the World/Freeway Flyer	1965	3.00	6.00	12.00
❏ 55766 [PS]	(Here They Come) From All Over the World/Freeway Flyer	1965	50.00	100.00	200.00
❏ 55792	You Really Know How to Hurt a Guy/It's As Easy As 1-2-3	1965	3.00	6.00	12.00
❏ 55792 [PS]	You Really Know How to Hurt a Guy/It's As Easy As 1-2-3	1965	7.50	15.00	30.00
❏ 55816	It's a Shame to Say Goodbye/The Submarine Races	1965	—	—	—
—Unreleased					
❏ 55833	I Found a Girl/It's a Shame to Say Goodbye	1965	3.00	6.00	12.00
❏ 55849	Folk City/A Beginning from an End	1965	3.00	6.00	12.00
❏ 55849 [PS]	Folk City/A Beginning from an End	1965	7.50	15.00	30.00
❏ 55856	Norwegian Wood/I Can't Wait to Love You	1966	—	—	—
—Unreleased					
❏ 55860	Batman/Bucket "T"	1966	6.25	12.50	25.00
❏ 55886	Popsicle/Norwegian Wood	1966	3.00	6.00	12.00
❏ 55905	Fiddle Around/Surfer's Dream	1966	3.00	6.00	12.00
❏ 55923	The New Girl in School/School Days	1966	3.00	6.00	12.00
MAGIC LAMP					
❏ 401	California Lullabye/Summertime	1966	7.50	15.00	30.00
ODE					
❏ 66111	Fun City/Totally Wild	1975	6.25	12.50	25.00
UNITED ARTISTS					
❏ 0089	Jennie Lee/Baby Talk	1973	3.75	7.50	15.00
❏ 0090	Linda/The New Girl in School	1973	3.75	7.50	15.00
❏ 0091	Surf City/Ride the Wild Surf	1973	3.75	7.50	15.00
❏ 0092	Dead Man's Curve/Drag City	1973	3.75	7.50	15.00
❏ 0093	Honolulu Lulu/Sidewalk Surfin'	1973	3.75	7.50	15.00
❏ 0094	The Little Old Lady (From Pasadena)/Popsicle	1973	3.75	7.50	15.00
—0089 through 0094 are "Silver Spotlight Series" reissues					
❏ XW670	Sidewalk Surfin'/Gonna Hustle You	1975	3.75	7.50	15.00
❏ 50859	Jennie Lee/Vegetables	1971	3.75	7.50	15.00
❏ 50859 [PS]	Jennie Lee/Vegetables	1971	6.25	12.50	25.00
WARNER BROS.					
❏ 7151	Only a Boy/Love and Hate	1967	10.00	20.00	40.00
❏ 7219	Laurel and Hardy/I Know My Mind	1968	12.50	25.00	50.00
❏ 7240 [DJ]	In the Still of the Night/Girl, You're Blowing My Mind	1968	20.00	40.00	80.00
—Stock copy may not exist					
7-Inch Extended Plays					
SUNDAZED					
❏ SEP 125	Yellow Balloon/Raindrops//California Lullabye/Here Comes the Rain	1996	—	—	2.50
—Light blue marbled vinyl; instrumental versions of songs on the reissue of the "Save for a Rainy Day" LP					
❏ SEP 125 [PS]	Sounds for a Rainy Day	1996	—	—	2.50
Albums					
COLUMBIA					
❏ CL 2661 [M]	Save for a Rainy Day	1967	—	—	—
—Canceled					
❏ CS 9461 [S]	Save for a Rainy Day	1967	2000.	3000.	4000.
—LP not known to exist, but an acetate does, and possibly an import on this label and number					
DEADMAN'S CURVE					
❏ (no #)	Live at the Keystone Berkeley	1981	6.25	12.50	25.00
—With front and back covers pasted on					
❏ (no #)	Live at the Keystone Berkeley	1981	12.50	25.00	50.00
—Plain jacket with front and back cover inserts					
DORE					
❏ LP-101	Jan and Dean Bonus Photo	1960	30.00	60.00	120.00
❏ LP-101 [M]	Jan and Dean	1960	100.00	200.00	400.00
—Original with blue label					
❏ LP-101	Jan and Dean	197?	3.75	7.50	15.00
—Reissue with black label					
J&D					
❏ 101 [M]	Save for a Rainy Day	1967	75.00	150.00	300.00
—Private pressing by Dean Torrence of unreleased Columbia album					
LIBERTY					
❏ LRP-3248 [M]	Jan and Dean's Golden Hits	1962	7.50	15.00	30.00
❏ LRP-3294 [M]	Jan and Dean Take Linda Surfin'	1963	12.50	25.00	50.00
❏ LRP-3314 [M]	Surf City and Other Swingin' Cities	1963	10.00	20.00	40.00
❏ LRP-3339 [M]	Drag City	1963	10.00	20.00	40.00
❏ LRP-3361 [M]	The New Girl in School/Dead Man's Curve	1964	5.00	10.00	20.00
—Reissue with reversed title					
❏ LRP-3361 [M]	Dead Man's Curve/The New Girl in School	1964	7.50	15.00	30.00
—Full-color cover					
❏ LRP-3361 [M]	Dead Man's Curve/The New Girl in School	1964	10.00	20.00	40.00
—Black and white cover with pink tint					
❏ LRP-3368 [M]	Ride the Wild Surf	1964	7.50	15.00	30.00
❏ LRP-3377 [M]	The Little Old Lady from Pasadena	1964	7.50	15.00	30.00
❏ LRP-3403 [M]	Command Performance/Live in Person	1965	7.50	15.00	30.00
❏ LRP-3417 [M]	Jan and Dean's Golden Hits, Volume 2	1965	6.25	12.50	25.00
❏ LRP-3431 [M]	Folk 'N' Roll	1965	7.50	15.00	30.00
❏ LRP-3441 [M]	Filet of Soul	1966	7.50	15.00	30.00
❏ LRP-3444 [M]	Jan and Dean Meet Batman	1966	12.50	25.00	50.00
❏ LRP-3458 [M]	Popsicle	1966	7.50	15.00	30.00
❏ LRP-3460 [M]	Jan and Dean's Golden Hits, Volume 3	1966	6.25	12.50	25.00
❏ LST-7248 [S]	Jan and Dean's Golden Hits	1962	10.00	20.00	40.00
❏ LST-7294 [S]	Jan and Dean Take Linda Surfin'	1963	20.00	40.00	80.00
❏ LST-7314 [S]	Surf City and Other Swingin' Cities	1963	12.50	25.00	50.00
❏ LST-7339 [S]	Drag City	1963	12.50	25.00	50.00
❏ LST-7361 [S]	The New Girl in School/Dead Man's Curve	1964	7.50	15.00	30.00
—Reissue with reversed title					
❏ LST-7361 [S]	Dead Man's Curve/The New Girl in School	1964	10.00	2.00	40.00
—Full-color cover					

J

Number	Title (A Side/B Side)	Yr	VG	VG+	NM
❑ LST-7361 [S]	Dead Man's Curve/The New Girl in School	1964	12.50	25.00	50.00
—Black and white cover with pink tint					
❑ LST-7368 [S]	Ride the Wild Surf	1964	10.00	20.00	40.00
❑ LST-7377 [S]	The Little Old Lady from Pasadena	1964	10.00	20.00	40.00
❑ LST-7403 [S]	Command Performance/Live in Person	1965	10.00	20.00	40.00
❑ LST-7417 [S]	Jan and Dean's Golden Hits, Volume 2	1965	7.50	15.00	30.00
❑ LST-7431 [S]	Folk 'N' Roll	1965	10.00	20.00	40.00
❑ LST-7441 [S]	Filet of Soul	1966	10.00	20.00	40.00
❑ LST-7444 [S]	Jan and Dean Meet Batman	1966	17.50	35.00	70.00
❑ LST-7458 [S]	Popsicle	1966	10.00	20.00	40.00
❑ LST-7460 [S]	Jan and Dean's Golden Hits, Volume 3	1966	7.50	15.00	30.00
❑ LN-10011	Dead Man's Curve	1980	2.00	4.00	8.00
—Budget-line reissue					
❑ LN-10115	The Best of Jan and Dean	1981	2.00	4.00	8.00
❑ LN-10151	The Little Old Lady from Pasadena	1982	2.00	4.00	8.00
—Budget-line reissue					
PAIR					
❑ PDL2-1071 [(2)]	California Gold	1986	3.00	6.00	12.00
RHINO					
❑ RNDA 1498 [(2)]	One Summer Night — Live	1982	5.00	10.00	20.00
SUNDAZED					
❑ LP 5022 [(2)]	Save for a Rainy Day	1996	3.75	7.50	15.00
—First release to the general public; colored vinyl					
❑ LP 5040	Jan and Dean (The Dore Album)	1996	2.50	5.00	10.00
—Reissue of Dore LP on colored vinyl with extra tracks and poster					
SUNSET					
❑ SUM-1156 [M]	Jan and Dean	1967	3.75	7.50	15.00
❑ SUS-5156 [S]	Jan and Dean	1967	3.75	7.50	15.00
UNITED ARTISTS					
❑ UA-LA341-H2 [(2)]	Gotta Take That One Last Ride	1974	3.75	7.50	15.00
❑ UA-LA443-E	The Very Best of Jan and Dean	1975	2.50	5.00	10.00
❑ UA-LA515-E	The Very Best of Jan and Dean, Volume 2	1975	2.50	5.00	10.00
❑ UAS-9961 [(2)]	Anthology (Legendary Masters Series, Vol. 3)	1971	6.25	12.50	25.00

JAN AND LORRAINE
Albums
ABC
❑ S-691	Gypsy People	1969	6.25	12.50	25.00

JANIS, JOHNNY
45s
ABC-PARAMOUNT
❑ 45-9800	Pledge of Love/I Played the Field	1957	5.00	10.00	20.00
❑ 45-9840	All the Time/Later Baby	1957	5.00	10.00	20.00
BOMARC					
❑ 304	I Never Believed/Willing to Learn	1959	3.75	7.50	15.00
❑ 307	Living in a Candy Store/I Said You	1960	3.75	7.50	15.00
CARLTON					
❑ 463	The Better to Love You/Can This Be Love	1958	6.25	12.50	25.00
COLUMBIA					
❑ 4-41797	Gina/If the Lord's Willin'	1960	3.75	7.50	15.00
❑ 4-41933	Catch a Falling Star/As I Was Walkin'	1961	3.00	6.00	12.00
❑ 4-42040	I Get Ideas/Save a Thought for Me	1961	3.00	6.00	12.00
CORAL					
❑ 9-61552	Move It or Lose It/I'm Throwing Rice (At the Girl That I Love)	1956	6.25	12.50	25.00
MONUMENT					
❑ 977	You're Free to Go/Ninety Miles an Hour (Down a Dead End Street)	1966	2.50	5.00	10.00
❑ 1042	I Hear It Now/A Rose is a Rose	1967	2.50	5.00	10.00
❑ 1117	Anything's the Part of You/One of These Days	1968	2.50	5.00	10.00
❑ 1177	Walk Through This World with Me/All This World and the Seven Seas	1969	2.00	4.00	8.00
❑ 1205	Distant Dreams/Ride Me Donkey	1970	2.00	4.00	8.00
❑ ZS7 8532	I'll Need You Forever/No	1972	—	3.50	7.00

JANKOWSKI, HORST
45s
MERCURY
❑ 72425	A Walk in the Black Forest/Nola	1965	2.00	4.00	8.00
❑ 72465	Simple Gimple/Charming Vienna	1965	—	3.00	6.00
❑ 72465 [PS]	Simple Gimple/Charming Vienna	1965	2.00	4.00	8.00
❑ 72492	Heide/Happy Frankfurt	1965	—	3.00	6.00
❑ 72520	Cruisin' Down the River/Play a Simple Melody	1966	—	3.00	6.00
❑ 72567	Black Forest Holiday/Elmer's Tune	1966	—	3.00	6.00
❑ 72615	A Place in the Sun/So What's New	1966	—	3.00	6.00
❑ 72647	Spy with a Cold Nose/Big, Big River	1966	—	3.00	6.00
❑ 72740	A Man and a Woman/A Lover's Concerto	1967	—	3.00	6.00
❑ 72766	Glory of Love/Lazy	1968	—	2.50	5.00
❑ 72809	And We Got Love/Zabadak	1968	—	2.50	5.00
❑ 72851	Chitty Chitty Bang Bang/This Guy's in Love with You	1968	—	2.50	5.00
❑ 72948	Dream Flight/Pink Balloon	1969	—	2.50	5.00

Albums
MERCURY
❑ MG-20993 [M]	The Genius of Jankowski	1965	3.00	6.00	12.00
❑ MG-21054 [M]	More Genius of Jankowski	1965	3.00	6.00	12.00
❑ MG-21076 [M]	Still More Genius of Jankowski	1966	3.00	6.00	12.00
❑ MG-21093 [M]	So What's New?	1966	3.00	6.00	12.00
❑ MG-21106 [M]	Baby But Grand	1967	3.00	6.00	12.00
❑ MG-21125 [M]	With Love	1967	3.00	6.00	12.00
❑ SR-60993 [S]	The Genius of Jankowski	1965	3.75	7.50	15.00
❑ SR-61054 [S]	More Genius of Jankowski	1965	3.75	7.50	15.00
❑ SR-61076 [S]	Still More Genius of Jankowski	1966	3.75	7.50	15.00
❑ SR-61093 [S]	So What's New?	1966	3.75	7.50	15.00
❑ SR-61106 [S]	Baby But Grand	1967	3.75	7.50	15.00
❑ SR-61125 [S]	With Love	1967	3.75	7.50	15.00
❑ SR-61160	And We Got Love	1968	3.00	6.00	12.00
❑ SR-61195	Piano Affairs	1968	3.00	6.00	12.00
❑ SR-61219	Jankowski Plays Jankowski	1969	3.00	6.00	12.00
❑ SR-61232	A Walk in the Evergreens	1970	3.00	6.00	12.00

JANSSEN, DAVID
Albums
EPIC
❑ LN 24150 [M]	Hidden Island	1965	5.00	10.00	20.00
❑ BN 26150 [S]	Hidden Island	1965	6.25	12.50	25.00

JAPANESE BEATLES, THE
45s
GOLDEN CREST
❑ 584	The Beatle Song (Japanese Style) (Part 1)/The Beatle Song (Japanese Style) (Part 2)	1964	5.00	10.00	20.00

JARMELS, THE
45s
LAURIE
❑ 3085	Little Lonely One/She Loves to Dance	1961	3.75	7.50	15.00
❑ 3098	A Little Bit of Soap/The Way You Look Tonight	1961	5.00	10.00	20.00
❑ 3116	I'll Follow You/Gee Oh Gosh	1962	3.75	7.50	15.00
❑ 3124	Red Sails in the Sunset/Loneliness	1962	3.75	7.50	15.00
❑ 3142	Little Bug/One By One	1962	3.75	7.50	15.00
❑ 3174	Come On Girl/Keep Your Mind on Me	1963	3.75	7.50	15.00

Albums
COLLECTABLES
❑ COL-5044	Golden Classics	198?	2.50	5.00	10.00

JARRETT, CHARLIE
45s
HIT
❑ 12	Old Rivers/Everybody Loves Me But You	1962	2.00	4.00	8.00
—B-side by Connie Dee					

JARVIS, FELTON
45s
ABC-PARAMOUNT
❑ 10570	Be-I-Bye/Ski King	1964	3.75	7.50	15.00
❑ 10610	Honky Tonk Song/Everybody's Going to the Party	1964	3.75	7.50	15.00
❑ 10641	Too Many Tigers/Knuckie, Knuckie	1965	3.75	7.50	15.00
MGM					
❑ 12982	Indian Love Call/Goin' Downtown	1961	5.00	10.00	20.00
THUNDER INT'L.					
❑ 1023	Swingin' Cat/Honest John the Workin' Man's Friend	1960	25.00	50.00	100.00
VIVA					
❑ 1001	Don't Knock Elvis/Honest John	1959	10.00	20.00	40.00

JASPER WRATH
45s
SUNFLOWER
❑ 107	It's Up to You/Did You Know That	1971	2.50	5.00	10.00

Albums
SUNFLOWER
❑ SNF-5003	Jasper Wrath	1971	10.00	20.00	40.00

JAXON, BOB
45s
ABC-PARAMOUNT
❑ 10364	It's a Cruel, Cruel Thing/One Way to Love Me	1962	3.00	6.00	12.00
CADENCE					
❑ 1264	Ali Baba/Why Does a Woman Cry	1955	3.75	7.50	15.00
RCA VICTOR					
❑ 47-6945	Beach Party/I'm Hangin' Around	1957	3.75	7.50	15.00
❑ 47-7006	(Gotta Have Something in the) Bank Frank/Come On Down	1957	5.00	10.00	20.00
❑ 47-7106	Declaration of Love/I'm Hurtin' Inside	1957	3.75	7.50	15.00
❑ 47-7168	Me! Please! Me!/All About Me	1958	3.75	7.50	15.00
❑ 47-7232	For the Love of You/(Well It's) No Lie	1958	3.75	7.50	15.00
20TH CENTURY FOX					
❑ 441	Weep, Mary, Weep/Do the People	1963	2.50	5.00	10.00

JAY See JAY TRAYNOR.

JAY, IRA
45s
SUN
❑ 351	You Don't Love Me/More Than Anything	1960	5.00	10.00	20.00

JAY, JERRY California DJ, better known as Jerry Osborne.
45s
QUALITY
❑ 201	The King's Country/Merry Christmas To You	1966	50.00	100.00	200.00

JAY, PETER, AND THE JAYWALKERS
45s
WAND
❑ 180	What's Easy/Parchment Farm	1965	2.50	5.00	10.00

JAY AND THE AMERICANS Also see JAY BLACK; JAY TRAYNOR.
45s
EEOC
❑ 1140	Things Are Changing/Things Are Changing	1965	37.50	75.00	150.00
❑ 1140 [PS]	Things Are Changing/Things Are Changing	1965	37.50	75.00	150.00
—Promotional item for the Equal Employment Opportunity Commission					
UNITED ARTISTS					
❑ 0026	She Cried/Come a Little Bit Closer	1973	—	2.50	5.00
❑ 0027	Cara Mia/Let's Lock the Door (And Throw Away the Key)	1973	—	2.50	5.00
❑ 0028	This Magic Moment/Walking in the Rain	1973	—	2.50	5.00
—0026, 0027, 0028 are "Silver Spotlight Series" reissues					
❑ 353	Tonight/The Other Girls	1961	3.00	6.00	12.00
❑ 415	She Cried/Dawning	1962	3.75	7.50	15.00
❑ 479	It's My Turn to Cry/This Is It	1962	3.00	6.00	12.00
❑ 504	Tomorrow/Yes	1962	3.00	6.00	12.00
❑ 566	What's the Use/Strangers Tomorrow	1963	2.50	5.00	10.00
❑ 626	Only in America/My Clair De Lune	1963	2.50	5.00	10.00
❑ 669	Come Dance with Me/Look in My Eyes Maria	1963	2.50	5.00	10.00
❑ 693	To Wait for Love/Friday	1964	2.50	5.00	10.00
❑ 759	Come a Little Bit Closer/Goodbye Boys, Goodbye	1964	2.50	5.00	10.00
❑ 805	Let's Lock the Door (And Throw Away the Key)/I'll Remember You	1965	2.50	5.00	10.00
❑ 845	Think of the Good Times/If You Were Mine, Girl	1965	2.50	5.00	10.00
❑ 881	Cara Mia/When It's All Over	1965	2.50	5.00	10.00

Number	Title (A Side/B Side)	Yr	VG	VG+	NM
❏ 919	Some Enchanted Evening/Girl	1965	2.50	5.00	10.00
❏ 919 [PS]	Some Enchanted Evening/Girl	1965	3.75	7.50	15.00
❏ 948	Sunday and Me/Through This Doorway	1965	2.50	5.00	10.00
❏ 948 [PS]	Sunday and Me/Through This Doorway	1965	12.50	25.00	50.00
❏ 992	Why Can't You Bring Me Home/				
	Baby Stop Your Cryin'	1966	2.00	4.00	8.00
❏ 50016	Crying/I Don't Need a Friend	1966	2.00	4.00	8.00
❏ 50016 [PS]	Crying/I Don't Need a Friend	1966	3.00	6.00	12.00
❏ 50046	Livin' Above Your Head/				
	Look at Me, What Do You See	1966	2.00	4.00	8.00
❏ 50046 [PS]	Livin' Above Your Head/				
	Look at Me, What Do You See	1966	3.00	6.00	12.00
❏ 50086	Baby Come Home/Stop the Clock	1966	2.00	4.00	8.00
❏ 50094	(He's) Raining in My Sunshine/The Reason for				
	Living (For You My Darling)	1966	2.00	4.00	8.00
❏ 50139	Nature Boy/You Ain't As Hip As All That, Baby	1967	2.00	4.00	8.00
❏ 50196	(We'll Meet in) Yellow Forest/Got Hung Up				
	Along the Way	1967	2.00	4.00	8.00
❏ 50222	Shanghai Noodle Factory/French Provincial	1967	2.00	4.00	8.00
❏ 50282	No Other Love/No, I Don't Know Her	1968	2.00	4.00	8.00
❏ 50448	You Ain't Gonna Wake Up Cryin'/Gemini	1968	2.00	4.00	8.00
❏ 50475	This Magic Moment/Since I Don't Have You	1969	3.00	6.00	12.00
❏ 50510	When You Dance/No, I Don't Know Her	1969	—	3.00	6.00
❏ 50535	Hushabye/Gypsy Woman	1969	—	3.00	6.00
❏ 50567	(I'd Kill) For the Love of a Lady/				
	Learnin' How to Fly	1969	—	3.00	6.00
❏ 50605	Walkin' in the Rain/(I'd Kill) For the Love of a Lady	1969	2.00	4.00	8.00
❏ 50654	Do You Ever Think of Me/Capture the Moment	1970	—	3.00	6.00
❏ 50683	Do I Love You?/Tricia (Tell Your Daddy)	1970	—	3.00	6.00
❏ 50858	There Goes My Baby/Solitary Man	1971	—	3.00	6.00
Albums					
LIBERTY					
❏ LM-1010	Jay and the Americans Greatest Hits	1981	2.00	4.00	8.00
—Another reissue					
RHINO					
❏ RNLP 70224	All-Time Greatest Hits	1986	3.00	6.00	12.00
SUNSET					
❏ SUS-5252	Jay and the Americans!!	1968	3.00	6.00	12.00
❏ SUS-5278	Early American Hits	1969	3.75	7.50	15.00
UNART					
❏ M-20018 [M]	Jay and the Americans!!	196?	3.00	6.00	12.00
❏ MS-21018 [S]	Jay and the Americans!!	196?	3.00	6.00	12.00
UNITED ARTISTS					
❏ UA-LA357-E	The Very Best of Jay and the Americans	1975	3.00	6.00	12.00
❏ LM-1010	Jay and the Americans Greatest Hits	1980	2.50	5.00	10.00
—Reissue					
❏ UAL-3222 [M]	She Cried	1962	12.50	25.00	50.00
❏ UAL-3300 [M]	At the Café Wha?	1963	12.50	25.00	50.00
❏ UAL-3407 [M]	Come a Little Bit Closer	1964	6.25	12.50	25.00
❏ UAL-3417 [M]	Blockbusters	1965	6.25	12.50	25.00
❏ UAL-3453 [M]	Jay and the Americans Greatest Hits	1965	5.00	10.00	20.00
❏ UAL-3474 [M]	Sunday and Me	1966	5.00	10.00	20.00
❏ UAL-3534 [M]	Livin' Above Your Head	1966	5.00	10.00	20.00
❏ UAL-3555 [M]	Jay and the Americans Greatest Hits, Volume 2	1966	5.00	10.00	20.00
❏ UAL-3562 [M]	Try Some of This!	1967	5.00	10.00	20.00
❏ UAS-6222 [S]	She Cried	1962	25.00	50.00	100.00
❏ UAS-6300 [S]	At the Café Wha?	1963	25.00	50.00	100.00
❏ UAS-6407 [S]	Come a Little Bit Closer	1964	7.50	15.00	30.00
❏ UAS-6417 [S]	Blockbusters	1965	7.50	15.00	30.00
❏ UAS-6453 [S]	Jay and the Americans Greatest Hits	1965	6.25	12.50	25.00
❏ UAS-6474 [S]	Sunday and Me	1966	6.25	12.50	25.00
❏ UAS-6534 [S]	Livin' Above Your Head	1966	6.25	12.50	25.00
❏ UAS-6555 [S]	Jay and the Americans Greatest Hits, Volume 2	1966	5.00	10.00	20.00
❏ UAS-6562 [S]	Try Some of This!	1967	5.00	10.00	20.00
❏ UAS-6671	Sands of Time	1969	5.00	10.00	20.00
❏ UAS-6719	Wax Museum	1970	5.00	10.00	20.00
❏ UAS-6751	Wax Museum, Volume 2	1970	5.00	10.00	20.00
❏ UAS-6762	Capture the Moment	1970	5.00	10.00	20.00
❏ ST-90814 [S]	Jay and the Americans Greatest Hits	1966	7.50	15.00	30.00
—Capitol Record Club edition					
❏ ST-90815 [S]	Jay and the Americans Greatest Hits, Volume 2	1966	7.50	15.00	30.00
—Capitol Record Club edition					

JAY AND THE DELTAS
45s
WARNER BROS.

❏ 5404	Bells Are Ringing/Super Hawk	1964	12.50	25.00	50.00

JAY AND THE TECHNIQUES
45s
EVENT

❏ 222	I Feel Love Coming On/World of Mine	1975	—	2.50	5.00
❏ 228	Number Onederful/Don't Forget to Ask	1975	—	2.50	5.00
GORDY					
❏ 7123	I'll Be Here/Robot Man	1973	—	3.00	6.00
PHILCO-FORD					
❏ HP-22	Apples Peaches Pumpkin Pie/Loving for Money	1968	3.75	7.50	15.00
—4-inch plastic "Hip Pocket Record" with color sleeve					
SMASH					
❏ 2086	Apples, Peaches, Pumpkin Pie/Stronger Than				
	Dirt	1967	2.00	4.00	8.00
❏ 2124	Keep the Ball Rollin'/Here We Go Again	1967	2.00	4.00	8.00
❏ 2124 [PS]	Keep the Ball Rollin'/Here We Go Again	1967	3.00	6.00	12.00
❏ 2142	Strawberry Shortcake/Still (In Love with You)	1967	2.00	4.00	8.00
❏ 2142 [PS]	Strawberry Shortcake/Still (In Love with You)	1967	3.00	6.00	12.00
❏ 2154	Baby Make Your Own Sweet Music/Help				
	Yourself to All My Lovin'	1968	2.00	4.00	8.00
❏ 2154 [PS]	Baby Make Your Own Sweet Music/Help				
	Yourself to All My Lovin'	1968	3.00	6.00	12.00
❏ 2171	The Singles Game/				
	Baby How Easy Your Heart Forgets Me	1968	2.00	4.00	8.00
❏ 2171 [PS]	The Singles Game/				
	Baby How Easy Your Heart Forgets Me	1968	3.00	6.00	12.00
❏ 2185	Hey Diddle Diddle/If I Should Lose You	1968	2.00	4.00	8.00
❏ 2217	Change Your Mind/Are You Ready for This	1969	2.00	4.00	8.00
❏ 2237	Dancin' Mood/If I Should Lose You	1969	2.00	4.00	8.00

Number	Title (A Side/B Side)	Yr	VG	VG+	NM
Albums					
SMASH					
❏ MGS-27095 [M]	Apples, Peaches, Pumpkin Pie	1967	7.50	15.00	30.00
❏ MGS-27102 [M]	Love Lost and Found	1968	15.00	30.00	60.00
—Mono may be white-label promo only					
❏ SRS-67095 [S]	Apples, Peaches, Pumpkin Pie	1967	7.50	15.00	30.00
—First cover with "live" photo of the band					
❏ SRS-67095 [S]	Apples, Peaches, Pumpkin Pie	1968	5.00	10.00	20.00
—Second cover with "posed" photo of the band					
❏ SRS-67102 [S]	Love Lost and Found	1968	7.50	15.00	30.00

JAYBEES, THE
45s
RCA VICTOR

❏ 47-8904	Do You Think I'm in Love/I'm a Lover	1966	5.00	10.00	20.00

JAYE, JERRY
45s
COLUMBIA

❏ 10170	It's All in the Game/				
	Love Me 'Til the Morning Comes	1975	—	2.00	4.00
❏ 10269	Maybellene/Because It's Love	1975	—	2.00	4.00
HI					
❏ 2120	My Girl Josephine/Five Miles from Home	1967	2.00	4.00	8.00
❏ 2128	Let the Four Winds Blow/Singin' the Blues	1967	2.00	4.00	8.00
❏ 2139	Brown-Eyed Handsome Man/				
	In the Middle of Nowhere	1968	—	3.00	6.00
❏ 2150	Long Black Veil/(Today)				
	I Started Loving You Again	1968	—	3.00	6.00
❏ 2171	Never Going Back/You've Got to Go	1969	—	3.00	6.00
❏ 2310	Honky Tonk Women Love Redneck Men/				
	What's Left	1976	—	2.00	4.00
❏ 2318	Hot and Still Heatin'/Crazy	1976	—	2.00	4.00
❏ 2323	When Morning Comes to Memphis/				
	(B-side unknown)	1977	—	2.00	4.00
MEGA					
❏ 0033	I Didn't Hear a Thing/Love Is a Job	1971	—	2.50	5.00
❏ 0045	Don't Bring the Rain Back Again/				
	Tiny Praying Hands	1971	—	2.50	5.00
❏ 0066	Share Your Love with Me				
	/When My Ship Comes In	1972	—	2.50	5.00
❏ 0116	Honky Tonk Livin'/I'm Gonna Spend My Whole				
	Life Lovin' You	1973	—	2.50	5.00
❏ 209	Walkin' My Baby Back Home/				
	I Slipped But I Didn't Fall	1974	—	2.00	4.00
❏ 1218	Poor Side of Town/Lay Down	1974	—	2.00	4.00
STEPHENY					
❏ 1820	Sugar Dumplin'/				
	How Could You Lose Your Trust in Me	1958	10.00	20.00	40.00
Albums					
HI					
❏ HL-12038 [M]	My Girl Josephine	1967	5.00	10.00	20.00
❏ SHL-32038 [S]	My Girl Josephine	1967	5.00	10.00	20.00
❏ SHL-32102	Honky Tonk Women Love Redneck Men	1976	3.00	6.00	12.00

JAYHAWKS, THE Also see THE MARATHONS; THE VIBRATIONS.
45s
ALADDIN

❏ 3393	Everyone Should Know/The Creature	1957	20.00	40.00	80.00
ARGYLE					
❏ 1005	Lonely Highway/La Macerena	1961	6.25	12.50	25.00
EASTMAN					
❏ 792	Start the Fire/I Wish the World Owed Me a Living	1958	37.50	75.00	150.00
❏ 798	New Love/Betty Brown	1958	37.50	75.00	150.00
FLASH					
❏ 105	Counting Teardrops/The Devil's Cousin	1955	50.00	100.00	200.00
❏ 109	Starnded in the Jungle/My Only Darling	1956	12.50	25.00	50.00
❏ 111	Love Train/Don't Mind Dyin'	1956	7.50	15.00	30.00

JAYNELLS, THE
45s
CAMEO

❏ 286	I'll Stay Home New Year's Eve/Down Home	1963	5.00	10.00	20.00
DIAMOND					
❏ 153	I'll Stay Home (New Year's Eve)/Down Home	1963	10.00	20.00	40.00

JAYNETTS, THE
45s
J&S

❏ 1177	Out Behind the Daisies/Is It My Imagination	196?	2.00	4.00	8.00
❏ 1468/9	Chicken, Chicken, Crance or Crow/Winky Dinky	196?	2.00	4.00	8.00
❏ 1473	Peepin' In and Out the Window/				
	Extra, Extra, Read All About It	196?	2.00	4.00	8.00
❏ 1477	Who Stole the Cookie/That's My Boy	196?	2.50	5.00	10.00
❏ 1686	Looking for Wonderland, My Lover/				
	Make It an Extra	1965	2.00	4.00	8.00
❏ 1765/6	I Wanted to Be Free/Where Are You Tonight	196?	2.50	5.00	10.00
❏ 4418/9	Vangie Don't You Cry/				
	My Guy Is As Sweet As Can Be	196?	2.00	4.00	8.00
TUFF					
❏ 369	Sally, Go 'Round the Roses/(Instrumental)	1963	3.75	7.50	15.00
❏ 371	Keep an Eye on Her/(Instrumental)	1963	2.50	5.00	10.00
❏ 374	Snowman, Snowman, Sweet Potato Nose/				
	(Instrumental)	1963	3.75	7.50	15.00
❏ 377	No Love at All/Tonight You Belong to Me	1964	3.00	6.00	12.00
Albums					
TUFF					
❏ LP 13 [M]	Sally Go 'Round the Roses	1963	75.00	150.00	300.00

JAYTONES, THE
45s
BRUNSWICK

❏ 55087	The Clock/Gasoline	1958	30.00	60.00	120.00
CUB					
❏ 9057	My Only Love/Absolutely Right	1960	15.00	30.00	60.00
TIMELY					
❏ 1003/4	My Darling/The Bells	1958	375.00	750.00	1500.

J

Number	Title (A Side/B Side)	Yr	VG	VG+	NM

JAZZ CRUSADERS, THE See THE CRUSADERS.

JEFFERSON Also see ROCKIN' BERRIES.
45s
DECCA
| ☐ 32501 | The Colour of My Love/Look No Further | 1969 | 2.00 | 4.00 | 8.00 |

JANUS
☐ 106	Baby Take Me in Your Arms/				
	I Fell Flat on My Face	1969	2.00	4.00	8.00
☐ 117	You Know How It Is with a Woman/				
	Are You Growing Tired of My Love	1970	2.00	4.00	8.00

Albums
JANUS
| ☐ JLS-3006 | Jefferson | 1969 | 6.25 | 12.50 | 25.00 |

JEFFERSON, BLIND LEMON
Albums
MILESTONE
☐ MLP-2004 [M]	The Immortal Blind Lemon Jefferson	1968	6.25	12.50	25.00
☐ MLP-2007 [M]	The Immortal Blind Lemon Jefferson, Vol. 2	1969	6.25	12.50	25.00
☐ MLP-2013 [M]	Black Snake Moan	1970	6.25	12.50	25.00
RIVERSIDE
☐ RLP 12-125 [M]	Blind Lemon Jefferson — Classic Folk Blues	1957	30.00	60.00	120.00
☐ RLP 12-136 [M]	Blind Lemon Jefferson, Volume 2	1958	30.00	60.00	120.00
☐ 1014 [10]	The Folk Blues of Blind Lemon Jefferson	1953	62.50	125.00	250.00
☐ 1053 [10]	Penitentiary Blues	1955	62.50	125.00	250.00

JEFFERSON AIRPLANE Also see MARTY BALIN; PAPA JOHN CREACH; HOT TUNA; JEFFERSON STARSHIP; PAUL KANTNER; JORMA KAUKONEN; GRACE SLICK.
45s
EPIC
| ☐ 73044 | Summer of Love/Panda | 1989 | — | 2.50 | 5.00 |
GRUNT
☐ 65-0500	Pretty As You Feel/Wild Turkey	1971	—	2.50	5.00
☐ 65-0500 [PS]	Pretty As You Feel/Wild Turkey	1971	2.50	5.00	10.00
☐ 65-0506	Long John Silver/Milk Train	1972	—	2.50	5.00
☐ 65-0506 [PS]	Long John Silver/Milk Train	1972	3.75	7.50	15.00
☐ 65-0511	Trial by Fire/Twilight Double Leader	1972	—	2.50	5.00
☐ JB-10988 [DJ]	White Rabbit (mono/stereo)	1978	7.50	15.00	30.00
—White vinyl
RCA
| ☐ 5156-7-R | White Rabbit/Plastic Fantastic Lover | 1987 | — | 2.50 | 5.00 |
—White vinyl
| ☐ 5156-7-R [PS] | White Rabbit/Plastic Fantastic Lover | 1987 | — | 2.50 | 5.00 |
RCA VICTOR
☐ 47-8769	It's No Secret/Runnin' 'Round This World	1966	3.75	7.50	15.00
☐ 47-8848	Come Up the Years/Blues from an Airplane	1966	3.75	7.50	15.00
☐ 47-8967	Bringing Me Down/Let Me In	1966	3.75	7.50	15.00
☐ 47-9063	My Best Friend/How Do You Feel	1967	3.75	7.50	15.00
☐ 47-9140	Somebody to Love/She Has Funny Cars	1967	3.75	7.50	15.00
☐ 47-9248	White Rabbit/Plastic Fantastic Lover	1967	3.75	7.50	15.00
☐ 47-9297	Ballad of You & Me & Pooneil/Two Heads	1967	2.50	5.00	10.00
☐ 47-9389	Watch Her Ride/Martha	1967	2.50	5.00	10.00
☐ 47-9496	Greasy Heart/Share a Little Joke (With the World)	1968	2.00	4.00	8.00
☐ 47-9644	Crown of Creation/Lather	1968	2.00	4.00	8.00
☐ 47-9644 [PS]	Crown of Creation/Lather	1968	5.00	10.00	20.00
☐ 74-0150	Plastic Fantastic Lover/Other Side of This Life	1969	—	3.00	6.00
☐ 74-0150 [PS]	Plastic Fantastic Lover/Other Side of This Life	1969	5.00	10.00	20.00
☐ 74-0245	Volunteers/We Can Be Together	1969	—	3.00	6.00
☐ 74-0245 [PS]	Volunteers/We Can Be Together	1969	3.75	7.50	15.00
☐ 74-0343	Have You Seen the Saucers/Mexico	1970	—	3.00	6.00
☐ 74-0343 [PS]	Have You Seen the Saucers/Mexico	1970	3.75	7.50	15.00

Albums
DCC COMPACT CLASSICS
| ☐ LPZ-2033 | Surrealistic Pillow | 1997 | 6.25 | 12.50 | 25.00 |
—Audiophile vinyl
EPIC
| ☐ OE 45271 | Jefferson Airplane | 1989 | 3.75 | 7.50 | 15.00 |
GRUNT
☐ BFL1-0147	Thirty Seconds Over Winterland	1973	3.00	6.00	12.00
☐ APL1-0437	Early Flight	1974	3.00	6.00	12.00
☐ FTR-1001	Bark	1971	2.50	5.00	10.00
—Without brown paper bag
| ☐ FTR-1001 | Bark | 1971 | 3.75 | 7.50 | 15.00 |
—With brown paper bag
☐ FTR-1007	Long John Silver	1972	3.00	6.00	12.00
☐ CYL2-1255 [(2)]	Flight Log 1966-1976	1977	3.00	6.00	12.00
☐ AYL1-4386	Bark	1981	2.00	4.00	8.00
☐ AYL1-4391	Thirty Seconds Over Winterland	1981	2.00	4.00	8.00
MOBILE FIDELITY
☐ 1-148	Crown of Creation	1984	5.00	10.00	20.00
—Audiophile vinyl
PAIR
| ☐ PDL2-1090 [(2)] | Time Machine | 1986 | 3.00 | 6.00 | 12.00 |
RCA
| ☐ 5724-1-R [(2)] | 2400 Fulton Street: An Anthology | 1987 | 3.75 | 7.50 | 15.00 |
RCA VICTOR
| ☐ APD1-0320 [Q] | Volunteers | 1973 | 20.00 | 40.00 | 80.00 |
—Yellow/orange label
| ☐ APD1-0320 [Q] | Volunteers | 1975 | 12.50 | 25.00 | 50.00 |
—Tan label
| ☐ LOP-1511 [M] | After Bathing at Baxter's | 1967 | 12.50 | 25.00 | 50.00 |
| ☐ LSO-1511 [S] | After Bathing at Baxter's | 1967 | 5.00 | 10.00 | 20.00 |
—Black label, dog on top
| ☐ LSO-1511 [S] | After Bathing at Baxter's | 1969 | 3.00 | 6.00 | 12.00 |
—Orange label
| ☐ LSO-1511 [S] | After Bathing at Baxter's | 1975 | 2.50 | 5.00 | 10.00 |
—Tan label
| ☐ LPM-3584 [M] | Jefferson Airplane Takes Off! | 1966 | 6.25 | 12.50 | 25.00 |
—Version 3: No "Runnin' 'Round This World", altered lyrics to "Let Me In" ("Don't tell me it's so funny") and "Run Around ("That sway as you stay here by me"). All later versions confirm to Version 3.
| ☐ LPM-3584 [M] | Jefferson Airplane Takes Off! | 1966 | 250.00 | 500.00 | 1000. |
—Version 2: No "Runnin' 'Round This World", but "questionable" lyrics remain in "Let Me In" ("Don't tell me you want money") and "Run Around" ("That sway as you lay under me"). Until the exact matrix numbers are known, it must be heard to confirm.
| ☐ LPM-3584 [M] | Jefferson Airplane Takes Off! | 1966 | 1500. | 2250. | 3000. |
—Version 1: With "Runnin' 'Round This World" as last song on side 1. Count the number of bands on Side 1 of the record; don't rely on the cover listing, as some jackets list the title when it's not on the record
| ☐ LSP-3584 [S] | Jefferson Airplane Takes Off! | 1966 | 6.25 | 12.50 | 25.00 |
—Version 3: See Version 3 note under mono version
| ☐ LSP-3584 [S] | Jefferson Airplane Takes Off! | 1966 | 450.00 | 900.00 | 1800. |
—Version 2: See Version 2 note under mono version
| ☐ LSP-3584 [S] | Jefferson Airplane Takes Off! | 1966 | 2000. | 3500. | 5000. |
—Version 1: See Version 1 note under mono version
| ☐ LSP-3584 [S] | Jefferson Airplane Takes Off! | 1969 | 3.00 | 6.00 | 12.00 |
—Orange label
| ☐ LSP-3584 [S] | Jefferson Airplane Takes Off! | 1975 | 2.50 | 5.00 | 10.00 |
—Tan label
☐ AYL1-3661	The Worst of Jefferson Airplane	1980	2.00	4.00	8.00
☐ AYL1-3738	Surrealistic Pillow	1980	2.00	4.00	8.00
☐ AYL1-3739	Jefferson Airplane Takes Off!	1980	2.00	4.00	8.00
☐ LPM-3766 [M]	Surrealistic Pillow	1967	15.00	30.00	60.00
☐ LSP-3766 [S]	Surrealistic Pillow	1967	7.50	15.00	30.00
—Black label, dog on top
| ☐ LSP-3766 [S] | Surrealistic Pillow | 1969 | 3.00 | 6.00 | 12.00 |
—Orange label
| ☐ LSP-3766 [S] | Surrealistic Pillow | 1975 | 2.50 | 5.00 | 10.00 |
—Tan label
☐ AYL1-3797	Crown of Creation	1980	2.00	4.00	8.00
☐ AYL1-3798	Bless Its Pointed Little Head	1980	2.00	4.00	8.00
☐ AYL1-3867	Volunteers	1980	2.00	4.00	8.00
☐ LSP-4058	Crown of Creation	1968	7.50	15.00	30.00
—Black label, dog on top
| ☐ LSP-4058 | Crown of Creation | 1969 | 3.00 | 6.00 | 12.00 |
—Orange label
| ☐ LSP-4058 | Crown of Creation | 1975 | 2.50 | 5.00 | 10.00 |
—Tan label
| ☐ LSP-4133 | Bless Its Pointed Little Head | 1969 | 3.00 | 6.00 | 12.00 |
—Orange label
| ☐ LSP-4133 | Bless Its Pointed Little Head | 1975 | 2.50 | 5.00 | 10.00 |
—Tan label
| ☐ LSP-4238 | Volunteers | 1969 | 3.00 | 6.00 | 12.00 |
—Orange label
| ☐ LSP-4238 | Volunteers | 1975 | 2.50 | 5.00 | 10.00 |
—Tan label
☐ LSP-4459	The Worst of Jefferson Airplane	1970	3.00	6.00	12.00
☐ AFL1-4545	After Bathing at Baxter's	1981	2.00	4.00	8.00
☐ AYL1-4718	After Bathing at Baxter's	1983	2.00	4.00	8.00

JEFFERSON STARSHIP See cross-references under JEFFERSON AIRPLANE.
12-Inch Singles
GRUNT
☐ JD-11438 [DJ]	Light the Sky on Fire (LP Version 5:08) (3:56)	1978	3.75	7.50	15.00
☐ JD-11469 [DJ]	Light the Sky on Fire (same on both sides?)	1978	3.75	7.50	15.00
☐ JD-13409 [DJ]	Black Widow (stereo) (mono)	1982	2.50	5.00	10.00
45s
GRUNT
☐ FB-10080	Ride the Tiger/Devil's Den	1974	—	2.00	4.00
☐ FB-10206	Caroline/Be Young You	1975	—	2.00	4.00
☐ FB-10367	Miracles/Al Garimaso (There Is Love)	1975	—	2.50	5.00
☐ FB-10456	Play on Love/I Want to See Another World	1975	—	2.00	4.00
☐ FB-10746	With Your Love/Switchblade	1976	—	2.50	5.00
☐ FB-10791	St. Charles/Love Lovely Day	1976	—	2.00	4.00
☐ GB-10941	Miracles/With Your Love	1977	—	—	3.00
—Gold Standard Series
☐ FB-11196	Count on Me/Show Yourself	1978	—	2.00	4.00
☐ FB-11196 [PS]	Count on Me/Show Yourself	1978	—	2.50	5.00
☐ FB-11274	Runaway/Hot Water	1978	—	2.00	4.00
☐ FB-11274 [PS]	Runaway/Hot Water	1978	—	2.50	5.00
☐ JB-11274 [DJ]	Runaway (Long)/Runaway (Short)	1978	—	2.50	5.00
☐ JB-11274 [PS]	Runaway (Long)/Runaway (Short)	1978	—	3.00	6.00
—Promo-only sleeve (one song listed on jacket)
☐ FB-11374	Crazy Feelin'/Love Too Good	1978	—	2.00	4.00
☐ FB-11374 [PS]	Crazy Feelin'/Love Too Good	1978	—	2.50	5.00
☐ FB-11426	Light the Sky on Fire/Hyperdrive	1978	—	2.00	4.00
☐ FB-11426 [PS]	Light the Sky On Fire/Hyperdrive	1978	—	2.50	5.00
☐ GB-11506	Count on Me/Runaway	1979	—	—	3.00
—Gold Standard Series
☐ FB-11750	Jane/Freedom at Point Zero	1979	—	2.00	4.00
☐ FB-11750 [PS]	Jane/Freedom at Point Zero	1979	—	2.50	5.00
☐ FB-11921	Girl with the Hungry Eyes/Just the Same	1980	—	2.00	4.00
☐ FB-11921 [PS]	Girl with the Hungry Eyes/Just the Same	1980	—	2.50	5.00
☐ FB-11961	Rock Music/Lightning Rose	1980	—	2.00	4.00
☐ FB-12211	Find Your Way Back/Modern Times	1981	—	2.00	4.00
☐ FB-12212	Mary/Modern Times	1981	—	—	—
—Unreleased
☐ FB-12275	Stranger/Free	1981	—	2.00	4.00
☐ FB-12332	Save Your Love/Wild Eyes	1981	—	2.00	4.00
☐ FB-13350	Be My Lady/Out of Control	1982	—	2.00	4.00
☐ FB-13439	Winds of Change/Black Widow	1983	—	2.00	4.00
☐ FB-13531	Can't Find Love/I Will Stay	1983	—	2.00	4.00
☐ FB-13811	No Way Out/Rose Goes to Yale	1984	—	2.00	4.00
☐ FB-13872	Layin' It on the Line/Showdown	1984	—	2.00	4.00
☐ FB-13872 [PS]	Layin' It on the Line/Showdown	1984	—	2.00	4.00
Albums
DCC COMPACT CLASSICS
| ☐ LPZ-2036 | Red Octopus | 1997 | 6.25 | 12.50 | 25.00 |
—Audiophile vinyl
GRUNT
☐ BFD1-0717 [Q]	Dragon Fly	1974	3.75	7.50	15.00
☐ BFL1-0717	Dragon Fly	1974	2.50	5.00	10.00
☐ BFD1-0999 [Q]	Red Octopus	1975	3.75	7.50	15.00
☐ BFL1-0999	Red Octopus	1975	2.50	5.00	10.00
☐ BFD1-1557 [Q]	Spitfire	1976	3.75	7.50	15.00
☐ BFL1-1557	Spitfire	1976	2.50	5.00	10.00
☐ BXL1-2515	Earth	1978	2.50	5.00	10.00
☐ BZL1-3247	Gold	1978	2.50	5.00	10.00
☐ DJL1-3363 [PD]	Gold	1978	3.75	7.50	15.00
—Promo-only picture disc
| ☐ BZL1-3452 | Freedom at Point Zero | 1979 | 2.50 | 5.00 | 10.00 |
| ☐ AYL1-3660 | Red Octopus | 1980 | 2.00 | 4.00 | 8.00 |

The Jackson Five, *ABC,* Motown MS-709, stereo LP, $12.50-$25.

Joni James, *100 Strings and Joni,* MGM SE-3755, stereo LP, yellow label, $60-$120.

The James Gang, *Yer Album,* BluesWay BLS-6034, stereo LP, $7.50-$15.

Jan and Arnie, *Jan and Arnie,* Dot DEP-1097, 7-inch EP, $500-$1,000 (cover and record together).

Jan and Dean, *Drag City*, Liberty LRP-3339, mono LP, $20-$40.

Jefferson Airplane, *Crown of Creation*, RCA Victor LSP-4058, stereo LP, black label, white "RCA Victor" and dog at 12 o'clock, $15-$30.

Number	Title (A Side/B Side)	Yr	VG	VG+	NM
❏ AYL1-3796	Dragon Fly	1980	2.00	4.00	8.00
❏ BZL1-3848	Modern Times	1981	2.50	5.00	10.00
❏ AYL1-3953	Spitfire	1981	2.00	4.00	8.00
❏ AYL1-4172	Earth	1981	2.00	4.00	8.00
❏ BXL1-4372	Winds of Change	1982	2.50	5.00	10.00
❏ BXL1-4921	Nuclear Furniture	1984	2.50	5.00	10.00
❏ AYL1-5161	Freedom at Point Zero	1984	2.00	4.00	8.00

JEFFREY, JOE, GROUP
45s
WAND
❏ 11200	My Pledge of Love/Margie	1969	2.00	4.00	8.00
❏ 11207	The Train/Dreamin' Till Then	1969	—	3.00	6.00
❏ 11213	Chance of Loving You/Hey Hey Woman	1969	—	3.00	6.00
❏ 11219	My Baby Loves Lovin'/Chance of Loving You	1970	—	3.00	6.00
❏ 11235	A Hundred Pounds of Clay/Power of Love	1971	—	3.00	6.00
Albums
WAND
| ❏ WDS-686 | My Pledge of Love | 1969 | 7.50 | 15.00 | 30.00 |

JEFFREYS, GARLAND
12-Inch Singles
EPIC
| ❏ AS 962 [DJ] | Modern Lovers/R.O.C.K./Ghost of a Chance | 1981 | 2.50 | 5.00 | 10.00 |
RCA
| ❏ 62175 | Hail Hail Rock 'N' Roll (5 versions) | 1992 | 2.00 | 4.00 | 8.00 |
| ❏ 62295 | The Answer (6 versions) | 1992 | 2.50 | 5.00 | 10.00 |
45s
A&M
❏ 1934	Wild in the Streets/Ghost Writer	1977	—	2.00	4.00
❏ 1952	New York Skyline/Cool Down Boy	1977	—	2.00	4.00
❏ 2030	One-Eyed Jack/Reelin'	1978	—	2.00	4.00
❏ 2074	She Didn't Lie/Scream in the Night	1979	—	2.00	4.00
❏ 2178	American Boy and Girl/Livin' for Me	1979	—	2.00	4.00
❏ 2244	American Boy and Girl/Matador	1980	—	2.00	4.00
ARISTA
❏ 0119	The Disco Kid Part 1/The Disco Kid Part 2	1975	—	2.50	5.00
ATLANTIC
❏ 2948	She Didn't Lie/Lon Chaney	1973	—	2.50	5.00
❏ 2981	Wild in the Streets/Lon Chaney	1973	—	2.50	5.00
EPIC
❏ AE7 1225 [DJ]	Interview with Garland Jeffreys	1981	2.00	4.00	8.00
❏ AE7 1225 [PS]	Interview with Garland Jeffreys	1981	2.00	4.00	8.00
❏ 02073	Modern Lovers/Spanish Manners	1981	—	—	3.00
❏ 02173	R.O.C.K./Miami Beach	1981	—	—	3.00
❏ 03189	Surrender/Rebel Love	1982	—	—	3.00
❏ 03687	Rebel Love/What Does It Take (To Win Your Love)	1983	—	—	3.00
❏ 51008	96 Tears/Escape Goat Dab	1981	—	—	3.00
7-Inch Extended Plays
EPIC
| ❏ AE7 1223 [DJ] | (contents unknown) | 1981 | 2.00 | 4.00 | 8.00 |
| ❏ AE7 1223 [PS] | Escapades | 1981 | 2.00 | 4.00 | 8.00 |
Albums
A&M
❏ SP-4629	Ghost Writer	1977	3.00	6.00	12.00
❏ SP-4681	One-Eyed Jack	1978	2.50	5.00	10.00
❏ SP-4778	American Boy and Girl	1979	2.50	5.00	10.00
ATLANTIC
❏ SD 7253	Garland Jeffreys	1973	3.75	7.50	15.00
EPIC
❏ PE 36983	Escape Artist	1981	2.50	5.00	10.00
❏ FE 37436	Rock 'N' Roll Adult	1981	2.50	5.00	10.00
❏ ARE 38190	Guts for Love	1983	2.50	5.00	10.00

JELLY BEAN BANDITS, THE
45s
MAINSTREAM
| ❏ 674 | Country Woman/Generation | 1967 | 7.50 | 15.00 | 30.00 |
Albums
MAINSTREAM
| ❏ S-6103 [S] | The Jelly Bean Bandits | 1967 | 37.50 | 75.00 | 150.00 |
| ❏ 56103 [M] | The Jelly Bean Bandits | 1967 | 25.00 | 50.00 | 100.00 |

JELLY BEANS, THE
45s
ESKEE
| ❏ 001 | I'm Hip to You/You Don't Mean No Good to Me | 1965 | 3.75 | 7.50 | 15.00 |
RED BIRD
| ❏ 10-003 | I Wanna Love Him So Bad/So Long | 1964 | 5.00 | 10.00 | 20.00 |
| ❏ 10-011 | The Kind of Boy You Can't Forget/Baby Be Mine | 1964 | 5.00 | 10.00 | 20.00 |

JELLYBREAD
Albums
BLUE HORIZON
| ❏ BH-4801 | First Slice | 1970 | 7.50 | 15.00 | 30.00 |

JENKINS, FLORENCE FOSTER One of the worst singers ever to be recorded — and unlike MRS. MILLER, Jenkins sang arias!
Albums
RCA VICTOR
| ❏ LM-2597 [M] | The Glory (????) of the Human Voice | 1961 | 5.00 | 10.00 | 20.00 |
| ❏ LRT-7001 [10] | A Florence! Foster!! Jenkins!!! Recital!!!! | 195? | 12.50 | 25.00 | 50.00 |

JENKINS, NORMA See THE DOLLS.

JENNIFER See JENNIFER WARNES.

JENNINGS, WAYLON Also see JOHNNY CASH; WAYLON AND JESSI; WAYLON AND WILLIE.
12-Inch Singles
RCA
| ❏ WJ-01 [DJ] | Don't You Think This Outlaw Bit's Done Got Out of Hand/Medley of Buddy Holly Hits | 1979 | 3.75 | 7.50 | 15.00 |
| ❏ WJ-0283 [DJ] | Medley of Hits (7:14) (same on both sides) | 1983 | 3.75 | 7.50 | 15.00 |

Number	Title (A Side/B Side)	Yr	VG	VG+	NM
45s
A&M
❏ 722	Rave On/Love, Denise	1963	5.00	10.00	20.00
❏ 739	Four Strong Winds/Just to Satisfy You	1964	3.75	7.50	15.00
❏ 753	The Race Is On/Sing the Girls a Song	1964	3.75	7.50	15.00
ARK 21
❏ S7-58711	I Know About Me, Don't Know About You/Closing In on the Fire	1998	—	—	3.00
BAT
❏ 121636	White Lightning/(B-side unknown)	1962	12.50	25.00	50.00
❏ 121639	Dream Baby/Crying	1962	10.00	20.00	40.00
BRUNSWICK
❏ 55130	Jole Blon/When Sin Stops	1959	75.00	150.00	300.00
COLUMBIA
❏ 04881	Highwayman/The Human Condition	1985	—	—	3.00
—A-side: Willie Nelson/Waylon Jennings/Johnny Cash/Kris Kristofferson; B-side: Nelson, Cash
| ❏ 04881 [PS] | Highwayman/The Human Condition | 1985 | — | 2.00 | 4.00 |
—A-side: Willie Nelson/Waylon Jennings/Johnny Cash/Kris Kristofferson; B-side: Nelson, Cash
| ❏ 05594 | Desperadoes Waiting for a Train/The Twentieth Century Is Almost Over | 1985 | — | — | 3.00 |
—A-side: Willie Nelson/Waylon Jennings/Johnny Cash/Kris Kristofferson; B-side: Nelson, Cash
| ❏ 08406 | Highwayman/Desperadoes Waiting for a Train | 1988 | — | — | 3.00 |
—Waylon Jennings/Willie Nelson/Johnny Cash/Kris Kristofferson; reissue
| ❏ 73233 | Silver Stallion/America Remains | 1990 | — | — | 3.00 |
—Waylon Jennings/Willie Nelson/Johnny Cash/Kris Kristofferson
| ❏ 73381 | Born and Raised in Black and White/Texas | 1990 | — | — | 3.00 |
—The Highwaymen (Waylon Jennings/Willie Nelson/Johnny Cash/Kris Kristofferson)
| ❏ 73572 | American Remains/Texas | 1990 | — | — | 3.00 |
—The Highwaymen (Waylon Jennings/Willie Nelson/Johnny Cash/Kris Kristofferson)
EPIC
❏ 73352	Wrong/Waking Up with You	1990	—	—	3.00
❏ 73519	Where Corn Don't Grow/Waking Up with You	1990	—	—	3.00
❏ 73647	What Bothers Me Most/Wrong	1990	—	—	3.00
❏ 73718	The Eagle/What Bothers Me Most	1991	—	—	3.00
❏ 74403	Just Talkin'/I've Got My Faults	1992	—	—	3.00
❏ 74705	Too Dumb for New York City, Too Smart for L.A./I've Got My Faults	1992	—	—	3.00
LIBERTY
❏ S7-18486	It Is What It Is/The Devil's Right Hand	1995	—	—	3.00
—By The Highwaymen
MCA
❏ 52776	Working Without a Net/They Ain't Got 'Em All	1986	—	—	3.00
❏ 52830	Will the Wolf Survive/I've Got Me a Woman	1986	—	—	3.00
❏ 52915	What You'll Do When I'm Gone/That Dog Won't Hurt	1986	—	—	3.00
❏ 53009	Rose in Paradise/Crying Don't Even Come Close	1987	—	—	3.00
❏ 53088	Fallin' Out/Deep in the West	1987	—	—	3.00
❏ 53158	My Rough and Rowdy Days/Love Song (I Can't Sing Anymore)	1987	—	—	3.00
❏ 53243	If Ole Hank Could Only See Us Now (Chapter Five…Nashville)/You Went Out with Rock 'n' Roll	1988	—	—	3.00
❏ 53314	How Much Is It Worth to Live in L.A./G.I. Joe	1988	—	—	3.00
❏ 53476	Which Way Do I Go (Now That I'm Gone)/Hey Willie	1988	—	—	3.00
❏ 53634	Trouble Man/Yoyos, Bozos, Bimbos and Heroes	1989	—	—	3.00
❏ 53710	You Put the Soul in the Song/Woman I Hate It	1989	—	—	3.00
RAMCO
❏ 1997	My World/Another Blue Day	1968	3.00	6.00	12.00
RCA
❏ 5034-7-R	The Broken Promise Land/I Don't Have Any More Love Songs	1986	—	2.00	4.00
❏ PB-10842	Are You Ready for the Country/So Good Woman	1976	—	2.50	5.00
❏ PB-10924	Luckenbach, Texas (Back to the Basics of Love)/Belle of the Ball	1977	—	2.50	5.00
❏ GB-10927	Dreaming My Dreams with You/Can't You See	1977	—	—	3.00
—Gold Standard Series
❏ PB-11118	The Wurlitzer Prize (I Don't Want to Get Over You)/Lookin' for a Feeling	1977	—	2.50	5.00
❏ PB-11344	I've Always Been Crazy/I Never Said It Would Be Easy	1978	—	2.00	4.00
❏ PB-11390	Don't You Think This Outlaw Bit's Done Got Out of Hand/Girl I Can Tell (You're Trying to Work It Out)	1978	—	2.00	4.00
❏ GB-11500	Are You Ready for the Country/The Wurlitzer Prize (I Don't Want to Get Over You)	1978	—	—	3.00
—Gold Standard Series
❏ PB-11596	Amanda/Lonesome, On'ry and Mean	1979	—	2.00	4.00
❏ PB-11596 [PS]	Amanda/Lonesome, On'ry and Mean	1979	—	2.50	5.00
❏ PB-11723	Come with Me/Mes'kin	1979	—	2.00	4.00
❏ GB-11757	Luckenbach, Texas (Back to the Basics of Love)/Belle of the Ball	1979	—	—	3.00
—Gold Standard Series
| ❏ PB-11898 | I Ain't Living Long Like This/The World's Crazy | 1979 | — | 2.00 | 4.00 |
| ❏ GB-11991 | I've Always Been Crazy/Don't You Think This Outlaw Bit's Done Got Out of Hand | 1980 | — | — | 3.00 |
—Gold Standard Series
❏ PB-12007	Clyde/I Came Here to Party	1980	—	2.00	4.00
❏ PB-12067	Theme from "The Dukes of Hazzard" (Good Ol' Boys)/It's Alright	1980	—	2.00	4.00
❏ PB-12067 [PS]	Theme from "The Dukes of Hazzard" (Good Ol' Boys)/It's Alright	1980	—	2.50	5.00
❏ GB-12187	Theme from "The Dukes of Hazzard" (Good Ol' Boys)/Come with Me	1981	—	—	3.00
—Gold Standard Series
| ❏ GB-12313 | Amanda/I Ain't Living Long Like This | 1981 | — | — | 3.00 |
—"Gold Standard Series" reissue
❏ PB-12367	Shine/White Water	1981	—	2.00	4.00
❏ PB-13257	Women Do Know How to Carry On/Honky Tonk Blues	1982	—	2.00	4.00
❏ PB-13465	Lucille (You Won't Do Your Daddy's Will)/Medley of Hits	1983	—	2.00	4.00
❏ PB-13543	Breakin' Down/Livin' Legends (A Dyin' Breed)	1983	—	2.00	4.00
❏ PB-13631	The Conversation/Fancy Free	1983	—	2.00	4.00
—A-side with Hank Williams, Jr.

Number	Title (A Side/B Side)	Yr	VG	VG+	NM
PB-13729	I May Be Used (But Baby I Ain't Used Up)/So You Want to Be a Cowboy Singer	1984	—	2.00	4.00
PB-13827	Never Could Toe the Mark/Talk Good Boogie	1984	—	2.00	4.00
PB-13903	Silent Night, Holy Night/Precious Memories	1984	—	2.00	4.00

—A-side with Jessi Colter

Number	Title (A Side/B Side)	Yr	VG	VG+	NM
PB-13908	America/People Up in Texas	1984	—	2.00	4.00
PB-13984	Waltz Me to Heaven/Dream On	1984	—	2.00	4.00
PB-14094	Drinkin' and Dreamin'/Prophets Show Up in Strange Places	1985	—	2.00	4.00
PB-14215	The Devil's on the Loose/Good Morning John	1985	—	2.00	4.00
PB-14291	Sweet Mother Texas/Hanging On	1985	—	2.00	4.00

RCA VICTOR

Number	Title (A Side/B Side)	Yr	VG	VG+	NM
47-8572	That's the Chance I'll Have to Take/I Wonder Just Where I Went Wrong	1965	2.50	5.00	10.00
47-8652	Stop the World (And Let Me Off)/The Dark Side of Fame	1965	2.50	5.00	10.00
47-8729	Anita, You're Dreaming/Look Into My Teardrops	1965	2.50	5.00	10.00
47-8822	Time to Bum Again/Norwegian Wood	1966	2.50	5.00	10.00
47-8917	(That's What You Get) For Lovin' Me/Time Will Tell the Story	1966	2.50	5.00	10.00
47-9025	Green River/Silver Ribbons	1966	2.50	5.00	10.00
47-9146	Mental Revenge/Born to Love You	1967	2.50	5.00	10.00
47-9259	The Chokin' Kind/Love of the Common People	1967	2.50	5.00	10.00
47-9414	Walk On Out of My Mind/Julie	1967	2.50	5.00	10.00
47-9480	I Got You/No One's Gonna Miss Me	1968	2.50	5.00	10.00

—A-side with Anita Carter

Number	Title (A Side/B Side)	Yr	VG	VG+	NM
47-9561	Only Daddy That'll Walk the Line/Right Before My Eyes	1968	2.50	5.00	10.00
47-9642	Yours Love/Six Strings Away	1968	2.50	5.00	10.00
47-9819	Singer of Sad Songs/Lila	1970	2.00	4.00	8.00
47-9885	The Taker/Shadows of the Gallows	1970	2.00	4.00	8.00
47-9925	(Don't Let the Sun Set on You) Tulsa/You'll Look for Me	1970	2.00	4.00	8.00
47-9967	Mississippi Woman/Life Goes On	1971	2.00	4.00	8.00
48-1003	Cedartown, Georgia/I Think It's Time She Learned	1971	2.00	4.00	8.00
74-0105	Something's Wrong in California/Farewell Party	1969	2.00	4.00	8.00
74-0157	The Days of Sand and Shovels/Delia's Gone	1969	2.00	4.00	8.00
74-0210	MacArthur Park/But You Know I Love You	1969	2.00	4.00	8.00
74-0281	Brown Eyed Handsome Man/Sorrow (Breaks a Good Man Down)	1969	2.00	4.00	8.00
74-0615	Good Hearted Woman/It's All Over Now	1971	2.00	4.00	8.00
74-0716	Sweet Dream Woman/Sure Didn't Take Him Long	1972	2.00	4.00	8.00
74-0808	Pretend I Never Happened/Nothin' Worth Takin' or Leavin'	1972	2.00	4.00	8.00
74-0886	You Can Have Her/Gone to Denver	1973	2.00	4.00	8.00
74-0961	We Had It All/Do No Good Woman	1973	2.00	4.00	8.00
APBO-0086	You Asked Me To/Willy, the Wandering Gypsy and Me	1973	2.00	4.00	8.00
AMAO-0122	MacArthur Park/The Taker	1973	—	2.50	5.00
APBO-0251	This Time/Mona	1974	—	3.00	6.00
PB-10020	I'm a Ramblin' Man/Got a Lot Going for Me	1974	—	3.00	6.00
PB-10142	Rainy Day Woman/Let's All Help the Cowboys (Sing the Blues)	1974	—	3.00	6.00
GB-10169	This Time/You Asked Me To	1975	—	2.00	4.00

—Gold Standard Series

Number	Title (A Side/B Side)	Yr	VG	VG+	NM
PB-10270	Dreaming My Dreams with You/Waymore's Blues	1975	—	3.00	6.00
PB-10379	Are You Sure Hank Done It This Way/Bob Wills Is Still the King	1975	—	3.00	6.00
GB-10498	I'm a Ramblin' Man/Got a Lot Going for Me	1975	—	2.00	4.00

—Gold Standard Series

Number	Title (A Side/B Side)	Yr	VG	VG+	NM
GB-10499	Rainy Day Woman/Let's All Help the Cowboys (Sing the Blues)	1975	—	2.00	4.00

—Gold Standard Series

Number	Title (A Side/B Side)	Yr	VG	VG+	NM
GB-10673	Are You Sure Hank Done It This Way/Bob Wills Is Still the King	1976	—	2.00	4.00

—Gold Standard Series

Number	Title (A Side/B Side)	Yr	VG	VG+	NM
PB-10721	Can't You See/I'll Go Back to Her	1976	—	2.50	5.00

TREND

Number	Title (A Side/B Side)	Yr	VG	VG+	NM
102	Another Blue Day/Never Again	1962	7.50	15.00	30.00
106	The Stage/My Baby Walks All Over Me	1963	25.00	50.00	100.00

Albums

A&M

Number	Title	Yr	VG	VG+	NM
SP-4238	Don't Think Twice	1969	10.00	20.00	40.00

BAT

Number	Title	Yr	VG	VG+	NM
1001 [M]	Waylon Jennings at JD's	1964	175.00	350.00	700.00

—Approximately 500 copies pressed

COLUMBIA

Number	Title	Yr	VG	VG+	NM
FC 40056	Highwayman	1985	2.50	5.00	10.00

—Waylon Jennings/Willie Nelson/Johnny Cash/Kris Kristofferson

Number	Title	Yr	VG	VG+	NM
C 45240	Highwayman 2	1990	3.75	7.50	15.00

—Waylon Jennings/Willie Nelson/Johnny Cash/Kris Kristofferson

MCA

Number	Title	Yr	VG	VG+	NM
731	Waylon Jennings	198?	3.00	6.00	12.00

—Reissue of Vocalion LP

Number	Title	Yr	VG	VG+	NM
5688	Will the Wolf Survive	1986	2.50	5.00	10.00
5911	Hangin' Tough	1987	2.50	5.00	10.00
42038	A Man Called Hoss	1987	2.50	5.00	10.00
42038 [DJ]	A Man Called Hoss	1987	15.00	30.00	60.00

—Promo-only edition with letter and 48-page book

Number	Title	Yr	VG	VG+	NM
42222	Full Circle	1988	2.50	5.00	10.00
42287	New Classic Waylon	1989	2.50	5.00	10.00

PAIR

Number	Title	Yr	VG	VG+	NM
PDL1-1005 [(2)]	Waylon!	1986	3.00	6.00	12.00
PDL1-1033 [(2)]	A Couple More Years	1986	3.00	6.00	12.00
PDL1-1110 [(2)]	Honly Tonk Hero	1986	3.00	6.00	12.00

PICKWICK

Number	Title	Yr	VG	VG+	NM
ACL-0306	Only Daddy That'll Walk the Line	197?	2.00	4.00	8.00

—Reissue of RCA Camden LP

Number	Title	Yr	VG	VG+	NM
CAS-2556	Heartaches by the Number	197?	2.00	4.00	8.00

—Reissue of RCA Camden CAS-2556

Number	Title	Yr	VG	VG+	NM
ACL-7019 [S]	The Dark Side of Fame	1976	2.50	5.00	10.00

—Reissue of RCA Camden CAS-2183

RCA

Number	Title	Yr	VG	VG+	NM
5620-1-RB	The Best of Waylon	1987	2.50	5.00	10.00
9561-1-R	The Early Years (1965-1969)	1989	2.50	5.00	10.00

RCA CAMDEN

Number	Title	Yr	VG	VG+	NM
ACL-0306	Only Daddy That'll Walk the Line	1973	2.50	5.00	10.00
CAL-2183 [M]	The One and Only Waylon Jennings	1967	3.75	7.50	15.00
CAS-2183 [S]	The One and Only Waylon Jennings	1967	3.00	6.00	12.00
CAS-2556	Heartaches by the Number	1972	3.00	6.00	12.00
CAS-2608	Ruby, Don't Take Your Love to Town	1972	3.00	6.00	12.00

RCA VICTOR

Number	Title	Yr	VG	VG+	NM
APL1-0240	Honky Tonk Heroes	1973	3.75	7.50	15.00
APL1-0539	This Time	1974	3.00	6.00	12.00
APL1-0734	The Ramblin' Man	1974	3.00	6.00	12.00
APL1-1062	Dreaming My Dreams	1975	2.50	5.00	10.00
APL1-1108	Waylon Live	1976	2.50	5.00	10.00
AFL1-1816	Are You Ready for the Country	1977	2.00	4.00	8.00

—Black label, dog near side; new prefix

Number	Title	Yr	VG	VG+	NM
APL1-1816	Are You Ready for the Country	1976	2.50	5.00	10.00
AAL1-2317	Ol' Waylon	198?	2.00	4.00	8.00

—Reissue

Number	Title	Yr	VG	VG+	NM
APL1-2317	Ol' Waylon	1977	2.50	5.00	10.00
AFL1-2979	I've Always Been Crazy	1978	2.50	5.00	10.00
AHL1-3378	Greatest Hits	1979	2.50	5.00	10.00
AHL1-3493	What Goes Around Comes Around	1979	2.50	5.00	10.00
LPM-3523 [M]	Folk-Country	1966	7.50	15.00	30.00
LSP-3523 [S]	Folk-Country	1966	10.00	20.00	40.00
AHL1-3602	Music Man	1980	2.50	5.00	10.00
LPM-3620 [M]	Leavin' Town	1966	7.50	15.00	30.00
LSP-3620 [S]	Leavin' Town	1966	10.00	20.00	40.00
LPM-3660 [M]	Waylon Sings Ol' Harlan	1967	7.50	15.00	30.00
LSP-3660 [S]	Waylon Sings Ol' Harlan	1967	10.00	20.00	40.00
AYL1-3663	Are You Ready for the Country	1980	2.00	4.00	8.00

—Budget-line reissue

Number	Title	Yr	VG	VG+	NM
LPM-3736 [M]	Nashville Rebel	1967	10.00	20.00	40.00
LSP-3736 [S]	Nashville Rebel	1967	12.50	25.00	50.00
LPM-3825 [M]	Love of the Common People	1967	7.50	15.00	30.00
LSP-3825 [S]	Love of the Common People	1967	6.25	12.50	25.00
AYL1-3897	Honky Tonk Heroes	1980	2.00	4.00	8.00

—Budget-line reissue

Number	Title	Yr	VG	VG+	NM
LPM-3918 [M]	Hangin' On	1968	25.00	50.00	100.00
LSP-3918 [S]	Hangin' On	1968	6.25	12.50	25.00
LPM-4023 [M]	Only the Greatest	1968	—	—	—

—Canceled?

Number	Title	Yr	VG	VG+	NM
LSP-4023 [S]	Only the Greatest	1968	6.25	12.50	25.00
AYL1-4072	Dreaming My Dreams	1981	2.00	4.00	8.00

—Budget-line reissue

Number	Title	Yr	VG	VG+	NM
AYL1-4073	The Ramblin' Man	1981	2.00	4.00	8.00

—Budget-line reissue

Number	Title	Yr	VG	VG+	NM
LSP-4085	Jewels	1968	6.25	12.50	25.00
LSP-4137	Just to Satisfy You	1969	6.25	12.50	25.00
AYL1-4163	Waylon Live	1981	2.00	4.00	8.00

—Budget-line reissue

Number	Title	Yr	VG	VG+	NM
AYL1-4164	I've Always Been Crazy	1981	2.00	4.00	8.00

—Budget-line reissue

Number	Title	Yr	VG	VG+	NM
LSP-4180	Country-Folk	1969	6.25	12.50	25.00
AHL1-4247	Black On Black	1982	2.50	5.00	10.00
AYL1-4250	Music Man	1982	2.00	4.00	8.00

—Budget-line reissue

Number	Title	Yr	VG	VG+	NM
LSP-4260	Waylon	1970	5.00	10.00	20.00
LSP-4341	The Best of Waylon Jennings	1970	5.00	10.00	20.00
LSP-4418	Singer of Sad Songs	1970	5.00	10.00	20.00
LSP-4487	The Taker/Tulsa	1971	5.00	10.00	20.00
LSP-4567	Cedartown, Georgia	1971	5.00	10.00	20.00
LSP-4647	Good Hearted Woman	1972	5.00	10.00	20.00
AHL1-4673	It's Only Rock & Roll	1983	2.50	5.00	10.00
LSP-4751	Ladies Love Outlaws	1972	5.00	10.00	20.00
AHL1-4826	Waylon and Company	1983	2.50	5.00	10.00
AYL1-4828	The Best of Waylon Jennings	1983	2.00	4.00	8.00

—Budget-line reissue

Number	Title	Yr	VG	VG+	NM
LSP-4854	Lonesome, On'ry and Mean	1973	3.75	7.50	15.00
AHL1-5017	Never Could Toe the Mark	1984	2.50	5.00	10.00
AYL1-5126	Ol' Waylon	1984	2.00	4.00	8.00

—Budget-line reissue

Number	Title	Yr	VG	VG+	NM
AHL1-5325	Waylon's Greatest Hits, Vol. 2	1984	2.50	5.00	10.00
AHL1-5428	Turn the Page	1985	2.50	5.00	10.00
AYL1-5433	Waylon and Company	1985	2.00	4.00	8.00

—Budget-line reissue

Number	Title	Yr	VG	VG+	NM
AHL1-5473	Collector's Series	1985	2.50	5.00	10.00
AYL1-7046	Never Could Toe the Mark	1985	2.00	4.00	8.00

—Budget-line reissue

Number	Title	Yr	VG	VG+	NM
AHL1-7184	Sweet Mother Texas	1986	2.50	5.00	10.00

SOUNDS

Number	Title	Yr	VG	VG+	NM
1001 [M]	Waylon Jennings at JD's	1964	125.00	250.00	500.00

—Approximately 500 copies pressed; reissue of Bat 1001

TIME-LIFE

Number	Title	Yr	VG	VG+	NM
STW-102	Country Music	1981	2.50	5.00	10.00

VOCALION

Number	Title	Yr	VG	VG+	NM
VL 73873	Waylon Jennings	1969	6.25	12.50	25.00

JENNINGS, WAYLON; WILLIE NELSON; JESSI COLTER; TOMPALL GLASER
Also see JESSI COLTER; WAYLON JENNINGS; WILLIE NELSON; WAYLON AND JESSI; WAYLON AND WILLIE.
Albums
RCA VICTOR

Number	Title	Yr	VG	VG+	NM
AAL1-1321	Wanted! The Outlaws	198?	2.00	4.00	8.00

—Reissue

Number	Title	Yr	VG	VG+	NM
APL1-1321	Wanted! The Outlaws	1976	2.50	5.00	10.00

—Black label, dog near top

Number	Title	Yr	VG	VG+	NM
APL1-1321	Wanted! The Outlaws	1976	3.00	6.00	12.00

—Tan label

JENNINGS, WAYLON, AND JERRY REED Also see each artist's individual listings.
45s
RCA

Number	Title (A Side/B Side)	Yr	VG	VG+	NM
PB-13580	Hold On, I'm Comin'/Waiting On Down the Line	1983	—	2.00	4.00
GB-13789	Hold On, I'm Comin'/The Conversation	1984	—	—	3.00

—Gold Standard Series; B-side by Waylon and Hank Williams, Jr.

J

Number	Title (A Side/B Side)	Yr	VG	VG+	NM

JENNY AND THE JEWELS
45s
HIT

❏ 153	Baby Love/Baby Don't You Do It	1964	2.00	4.00	8.00
—B-side by Leroy Jones					
❏ 257	Love Is Like an Itching in My Heart/It's a Man's Man's Man's World	1966	2.00	4.00	8.00
—B-side by Leroy Jones					
❏ 313	In and Out of Love/Everlasting Love	1967	2.00	4.00	8.00
—B-side by Steve Miller					

JENSEN, KRIS
45s
A&M

❏ 1204	Dead End Street/Me and Bobby McGee	1970	—	2.50	5.00
COLPIX					
❏ 118	Bonnie Baby/Staying Up Late	1959	3.00	6.00	12.00
HICKORY					
❏ 1173	Torture/Let's Sit Down	1962	3.00	6.00	12.00
❏ 1195	Claudette/Don't Take Her from Me	1962	2.00	4.00	8.00
❏ 1203	Poor Unlucky Me/Cut Me Down (From Your Whipping Post)	1963	2.00	4.00	8.00
❏ 1224	Big As I Can Dream/Donna, Donna	1963	2.00	4.00	8.00
❏ 1224 [PS]	Big As I Can Dream/Donna, Donna	1963	5.00	10.00	20.00
❏ 1243	In Time/Lookin' for Love	1964	2.00	4.00	8.00
❏ 1256	Come Back to Me (My Love)/You've Only Got Me to Lose	1964	2.00	4.00	8.00
❏ 1285	Little Wind-Up Doll/Somebody's Smilin'	1964	2.00	4.00	8.00
❏ 1311	That's a Whole Lotta Love/What Should I Do	1965	2.00	4.00	8.00
KAPP					
❏ 393	The Jackie Look/Tender Hearted Baby	1961	2.50	5.00	10.00
❏ 410	Danny'd Dream/3 Vanilla, 2 Chocolate, 1 Pistachio Ice Cream Cones	1961	2.50	5.00	10.00
❏ 433	Busy Signal/Mary, Mary	1961	2.50	5.00	10.00
❏ 493	Busy Signal/Mary, Mary	1962	2.00	4.00	8.00
LEADER					
❏ 808	Perfect Love/School Bus	1960	3.00	6.00	12.00
❏ 813	Please Let Me Love You Tonight/Your Daddy Don't Like Me	1961	3.00	6.00	12.00
WHITE WHALE					
❏ 229	I Got You/I Can't Get Nowhere with You	1966	—	3.00	6.00
❏ 240	I Love to Call You Sweetheart/Good Pop Music	1966	—	3.00	6.00
Albums					
HICKORY					
❏ LP 110 [M]	Torture	1963	20.00	40.00	80.00

JEREMY AND THE SATYRS
45s
REPRISE

❏ 0664	Let's Go to the Movie Show/Lonely Child of Tears	1968	2.50	5.00	10.00
Albums					
REPRISE					
❏ R-6282 [M]	Jeremy and the Satyrs	1968	10.00	20.00	40.00
—Mono is white label promo only					
❏ RS-6282 [S]	Jeremy and the Satyrs	1968	5.00	10.00	20.00

JEREMY'S FRIENDS
Alan Arkin was a member of this group.
Albums
WARWICK

❏ W-2019 [M]	Jeremy's Friends	1960	12.50	25.00	50.00

JERICHO
45s
BEARSVILLE

❏ 31003	Cheater Man/Make It Better	1971	2.00	4.00	8.00
Albums					
AMPEX					
❏ A-10112	Jericho	1971	6.25	12.50	25.00

JERRY AND WAYNE
45s
ABC-PARAMOUNT

❏ 9806	Baby Baby Baby/I'm Sad, Blue and Lonesome	1957	5.00	10.00	20.00
❏ 9808	Baby Baby Baby, Be Mine/I'm Sad, Blue and Lonesome	1957	6.25	12.50	25.00

JESSE AND MARVIN
"Jesse" is JESSE BELVIN. "Marvin" later was with MARVIN AND JOHNNY.
45s
SPECIALTY

❏ 447	Dream Girl/Daddy Loves Baby	1952	18.75	37.50	75.00
—Black vinyl					
❏ 447	Dream Girl/Daddy Loves Baby	1952	50.00	100.00	200.00
—Red vinyl					

JESSIE MAE
45s
DRA

❏ 319	Don't Freeze on Me/It Might As Well Be Spring	1962	3.00	6.00	12.00

JESTERS, THE
Also see THE PARAGONS/THE JESTERS.
45s
AMY

❏ 859	Alexander Graham Bell/Buffalo	1962	2.00	4.00	8.00
CYCLONE					
❏ 5011	I Laughed/Now That You're Gone	1958	12.50	25.00	50.00
FEATURE					
❏ 101	Panther Pounce/Tiger Tail	1964	12.50	25.00	50.00
LOST-NITE					
❏ 117	The Wind/Sally Green	196?	2.00	4.00	8.00
—Reissue					
❏ 122	The Plea/Oh! Baby	196?	2.00	4.00	8.00
—Reissue					
❏ 124	Love No One But You/Oh! Baby	196?	2.00	4.00	8.00
❏ 126	So Strange/Oh! Baby	196?	2.00	4.00	8.00

Number	Title (A Side/B Side)	Yr	VG	VG+	NM
❏ 129	I Laughed/Now That You're Gone	196?	2.00	4.00	8.00
—Reissue					
❏ 131	I'm Falling in Love/Please Let Me Love You	196?	2.00	4.00	8.00
—Reissue					
SIDEWALK					
❏ 910	Leave Me Alone/Don't Try to Crawl Back	1967	2.50	5.00	10.00
❏ 916	Hands of Time/If You Love Her, Tell Her So	1967	2.50	5.00	10.00
SUN					
❏ 400	Cadillac Man/My Babe	1966	7.50	15.00	30.00
ULTIMA					
❏ 705	Drag Like Boogie/A-Rab	1964	7.50	15.00	30.00
WINLEY					
❏ 218	So Strange/Love No One But You	1957	12.50	25.00	50.00
❏ 221	I'm Falling in Love/Please Let Me Love You	1957	12.50	25.00	50.00
❏ 225	The Plea/Oh Baby	1958	10.00	20.00	40.00
❏ 242	The Wind/Sally Green	1959	10.00	20.00	40.00
❏ 248	That's How It Goes/Tutti Frutti	1961	7.50	15.00	30.00
—Black vinyl					
❏ 248	That's How It Goes/Tutti Frutti	1961	12.50	25.00	50.00
—Red vinyl					
❏ 252	Come Let Me Show You/Uncle Henry's Basement	1961	7.50	15.00	30.00
Albums					
COLLECTABLES					
❏ COL-5036	The Best of the Jesters	198?	2.50	5.00	10.00

JET SET, THE
45s
CAPITOL

❏ 5358	True to You/You Got Me Hooked	1965	6.25	12.50	25.00
❏ 5421	How Can I Know/Dancing Yet	1965	6.25	12.50	25.00
—As "Liza and the Jet Set"					

JETHRO TULL
12-Inch Singles
CHRYSALIS

❏ CHS 3 PDJ [DJ]	Ring Out, Solstice Bells/March, The Mad Scientist//Christmas Song/Pan Dance	1976	6.25	12.50	25.00

45s
CHRYSALIS

❏ 2006	Living in the Past/Christmas Song	1972	—	3.00	6.00
❏ 2012	A Passion Play (Edit #9)/A Passion Play (Edit #8)	1973	—	3.00	6.00
❏ 2017	A Passion Play (Edit #6)/A Passion Play (Edit #10)	1973	—	2.50	5.00
❏ 2101	Bungle in the Jungle/Back Door Angels	1974	—	2.50	5.00
❏ 2101 [PS]	Bungle in the Jungle/Back Door Angels	1974	2.50	5.00	10.00
❏ 2103	Skating Away (On the Thin Ice of a New Day)/Sealion	1975	—	2.50	5.00
❏ 2106	Minstrel in the Gallery/Sumer Day Sand	1975	—	2.50	5.00
❏ 2110	Locomotive Breath/Fat Man	1975	—	2.50	5.00
❏ 2114	Too Old to Rock and Roll, Too Young to Die/Bad Eyed and Loveless	1976	—	2.50	5.00
❏ 2135	The Whistler/Strip Cartoon	1977	—	2.50	5.00
❏ 2387	Home/Warm Sporran	1979	—	2.50	5.00
❏ 2613	Fallen on Hard Times/Pussy Willow	1982	—	2.00	4.00
❏ S7-18211	Christmas Song/Skating Away on the Thin Ice of a New Day	1994	—	2.50	5.00
—Green vinyl					
❏ 43172	Steel Monkey/Down at the End of Your Road	1987	—	2.00	4.00
REPRISE					
❏ 0815 [DJ]	Love Story/Song for Jeffrey	1969	3.75	7.50	15.00
—May be promo-only					
❏ 0845 [DJ]	Living in the Past/Driving Song	1969	5.00	10.00	20.00
—May be promo-only					
❏ 0886	Reasons for Waiting/Sweet Dream	1970	3.75	7.50	15.00
❏ 0899	Teacher/Witch's Promise	1970	3.75	7.50	15.00
❏ 0927	Inside/Time for Everything	1970	—	2.50	5.00
❏ 1024	Hymn 43/Mother Goose	1971	—	2.50	5.00
❏ 1054	Locomotive Breath/Wind-Up	1971	—	2.50	5.00
❏ 1153	Thick as a Brick (Edit)/Hymn 43	1972	—	2.50	5.00
—"Back to Back Hits" series					
Albums					
CHRYSALIS					
❏ PRO 623 [DJ]	The Jethro Tull Radio Show	1975	12.50	25.00	50.00
❏ CHR 1003	Thick as a Brick	1973	3.00	6.00	12.00
—Green label, "3300 Warner Blvd." address					
❏ CHR 1003	Thick as a Brick	1977	2.50	5.00	10.00
—Blue label, New York address					
❏ 2CH 1035 [(2)]	Living in the Past	1972	5.00	10.00	20.00
—Two-record set with booklet; green labels					
❏ CHR 1035 [(2)]	Living in the Past	1977	3.75	7.50	15.00
—Blue label, New York address					
❏ CHR 1040	A Passion Play	1973	3.00	6.00	12.00
—Green label, "3300 Warner Blvd." address					
❏ CHR 1040	A Passion Play	1977	2.50	5.00	10.00
—Blue label, New York address					
❏ CHR 1041	This Was	1973	3.00	6.00	12.00
—Green label, "3300 Warner Blvd." address					
❏ CHR 1041	This Was	1977	2.50	5.00	10.00
—Blue label, New York address					
❏ CHR 1042	Stand Up	1973	3.00	6.00	12.00
—Green label, "3300 Warner Blvd." address					
❏ CHR 1042	Stand Up	1977	2.50	5.00	10.00
—Blue label, New York address					
❏ CHR 1043	Benefit	1973	3.00	6.00	12.00
—Green label, "3300 Warner Blvd." address					
❏ CHR 1043	Benefit	1977	2.50	5.00	10.00
—Blue label, New York address					
❏ CH4 1044 [Q]	Aqualung	1974	10.00	20.00	40.00
❏ CHR 1044	Aqualung	1973	3.00	6.00	12.00
—Green label, "3300 Warner Blvd." address					
❏ CHR 1044	Aqualung	1977	2.50	5.00	10.00
—Blue label, New York address					
❏ CH4 1067 [Q]	War Child	1974	10.00	20.00	40.00
❏ CHR 1067	War Child	1974	2.50	5.00	10.00
—Blue label, New York address					

Number	Title (A Side/B Side)	Yr	VG	VG+	NM
CHR 1067	War Child	1974	3.00	6.00	12.00
—Green label, "3300 Warner Blvd." address					
CHR 1078	M.U. — The Best of Jethro Tull	1975	3.00	6.00	12.00
—Green label, "3300 Warner Blvd." address					
CHR 1078	M.U. — The Best of Jethro Tull	1977	2.50	5.00	10.00
—Blue label, New York address					
CHR 1082	Minstrel in the Gallery	1975	3.00	6.00	12.00
—Green label, "3300 Warner Blvd." address					
CHR 1082	Minstrel in the Gallery	1977	2.50	5.00	10.00
—Blue label, New York address					
CHR 1111	Too Old to Rock 'N' Roll; Too Young to Die!	1976	3.00	6.00	12.00
—Green label, "3300 Warner Blvd." address					
CHR 1111	Too Old to Rock 'N' Roll; Too Young to Die!	1977	2.50	5.00	10.00
—Blue label, New York address					
CHR 1132	Songs from the Wood	1977	2.50	5.00	10.00
CHR 1135	Repeat — The Best of Jethro Tull, Vol. II	1977	2.50	5.00	10.00
CHR 1175	Heavy Horses	1978	2.50	5.00	10.00
CHR2 1201 [(2)]	Jethro Tull Live — Bursting Out	1978	3.00	6.00	12.00
CHR 1238	Stormwatch	1979	2.50	5.00	10.00
CHR 1301	"A"	1980	2.50	5.00	10.00
CHR 1380	The Broadsword and the Beast	1982	2.50	5.00	10.00
F1-21708	Rock Island	1989	2.50	5.00	10.00
FV 41003	Thick as a Brick	1983	2.00	4.00	8.00
PV 41003	Thick as a Brick	1986	2.00	4.00	8.00
KV2 41035 [(2)]	Living in the Past	1983	3.00	6.00	12.00
PV 41040	A Passion Play	1983	2.00	4.00	8.00
PV 41041	This Was	1983	2.00	4.00	8.00
PV 41042	Stand Up	1983	2.00	4.00	8.00
PV 41043	Benefit	1983	2.00	4.00	8.00
FV 41044	Aqualung	1983	2.00	4.00	8.00
PV 41067	War Child	1983	2.00	4.00	8.00
FV 41078	M.U. — The Best of Jethro Tull	1983	2.00	4.00	8.00
PV 41082	Minstrel in the Gallery	1983	2.00	4.00	8.00
PV 41111	Too Old to Rock 'N' Roll; Too Young to Die!	1983	2.00	4.00	8.00
PV 41132	Songs from the Wood	1983	2.00	4.00	8.00
FV 41135	Repeat — The Best of Jethro Tull, Vol. II	1983	2.00	4.00	8.00
PV 41135	Repeat — The Best of Jethro Tull, Vol. II	1986	2.00	4.00	8.00
PV 41175	Heavy Horses	1983	2.00	4.00	8.00
V2X 41201 [(2)]	Jethro Tull Live — Bursting Out	1983	3.00	6.00	12.00
PV 41238	Stormwatch	1983	2.00	4.00	8.00
PV 41301	"A"	1983	2.00	4.00	8.00
FV 41380	The Broadsword and the Beast	1983	2.00	4.00	8.00
PV 41380	The Broadsword and the Beast	1986	2.00	4.00	8.00
FV 41461	Under Wraps	1984	2.50	5.00	10.00
PV 41461	Under Wraps	1986	2.00	4.00	8.00
FV 41515	Original Masters	1985	2.50	5.00	10.00
FV 41590	Crest of a Knave	1987	2.50	5.00	10.00
V5X 41653 [(5)]	20 Years of Jethro Tull	1988	20.00	40.00	80.00
VX2 41655 [(2)]	20 Years of Jethro Tull	1989	6.25	12.50	25.00
—Abridged version of Chrysalis 41653					

DCC COMPACT CLASSICS

Number	Title (A Side/B Side)	Yr	VG	VG+	NM
LPZ 2033	Aqualung	1997	25.00	50.00	100.00
—Audiophile vinyl					
LPZ-2059	Original Masters	1998	10.00	20.00	40.00
—Audiophile vinyl					

MOBILE FIDELITY

Number	Title (A Side/B Side)	Yr	VG	VG+	NM
1-061	Aqualung	1980	17.50	35.00	70.00
—Audiophile vinyl					
1-092	The Broadsword and the Beast	1982	10.00	20.00	40.00
—Audiophile vinyl					
1-187	Thick as a Brick	1985	7.50	15.00	30.00
—Audiophile vinyl					

REPRISE

Number	Title (A Side/B Side)	Yr	VG	VG+	NM
MS 2035	Aqualung	1971	3.75	7.50	15.00
MS 2072	Thick as a Brick	1972	3.75	7.50	15.00
2MS 2106 [(2)]	Living in the Past	1972	6.25	12.50	25.00
—Two-record set with booklet; original edition, rather than using cardboard outer sleeve for the records, has record sleeves attached to enclosed booklet, and thus is difficult to find intact					
RS 6336	This Was	1969	5.00	10.00	20.00
—Two-tone orange label with "r:" and "W7" logos on label					
RS 6336	This Was	1970	3.75	7.50	15.00
—All-one-color (orange/brown) label with no "W7" on label					
RS 6360	Stand Up	1969	5.00	10.00	20.00
—Two-tone orange label with "r:" and "W7" logos on label; band "stands up" when gatefold is opened					
RS 6360	Stand Up	1970	3.75	7.50	15.00
—All-one-color (orange/brown) label with no "W7" on label					
RS 6400	Benefit	1970	3.75	7.50	15.00
—All-one-color (orange/brown) label with no "W7" on label					
RS 6400	Benefit	1970	5.00	10.00	20.00
—Two-tone orange label with "r:" and "W7" logos on label					

JEWEL AND EDDIE
JEWEL AKENS and Eddie Daniels; EDDIE COCHRAN plays guitar.
45s

SILVER

Number	Title (A Side/B Side)	Yr	VG	VG+	NM
1004	Opportunity/Strollin' Guitar	1960	7.50	15.00	30.00
1004	Opportunity/Doin' the Hully Gully	1960	10.00	20.00	40.00
1008	My Eyes Are Cryin' for You/Sixteen Tons	1960	7.50	15.00	30.00

JEWELL, LEN
45s

TERI DE

Number	Title (A Side/B Side)	Yr	VG	VG+	NM
004	Bettin' on Love/(B-side unknown)	196?	200.00	400.00	800.00

JEWELL AND THE RUBIES
45s

ABC-PARAMOUNT

Number	Title (A Side/B Side)	Yr	VG	VG+	NM
10485	The Kidnapper/A Thrill	1963	3.00	6.00	12.00

LA LOUISIANNE

Number	Title (A Side/B Side)	Yr	VG	VG+	NM
8041	The Kidnapper/A Thrill	1963	7.50	15.00	30.00

JEWELS, THE (1) Female vocal group.
45s

DIMENSION

Number	Title (A Side/B Side)	Yr	VG	VG+	NM
1034	Opportunity/Gotta Find a Way	1964	5.00	10.00	20.00
1048	Smokey Joe/But I Do	1965	3.75	7.50	15.00

JEWELS, THE (2) Male vocal group, did the original version of the hit "Hearts of Stone."
45s

ANTLER

Number	Title (A Side/B Side)	Yr	VG	VG+	NM
1102	The Wind/Pearlie Mae	1959	10.00	20.00	40.00

IMPERIAL

Number	Title (A Side/B Side)	Yr	VG	VG+	NM
5351	Angel in My Life/Hearts Can Be Broken	1955	25.00	50.00	100.00
5362	Natural, Natural Ditty/Please Return	1955	25.00	50.00	100.00
5377	How/Rickety Rock	1956	25.00	50.00	100.00
5387	My Baby/Goin', Goin', Goin'	1956	25.00	50.00	100.00

ORIGINAL SOUND

Number	Title (A Side/B Side)	Yr	VG	VG+	NM
38	Hearts of Stone/Oh Yes I Know	1964	5.00	10.00	20.00

R&B

Number	Title (A Side/B Side)	Yr	VG	VG+	NM
1301	Hearts of Stone/Runnin'	1954	50.00	100.00	200.00
1303	Oh Yes I Know/A Fool in Paradise	1954	75.00	150.00	300.00

RPM

Number	Title (A Side/B Side)	Yr	VG	VG+	NM
474	She's a Flirt/Be-Bomp Baby	1956	17.50	35.00	70.00

JEWELS, THE (3)
45s

DYNAMITE

Number	Title (A Side/B Side)	Yr	VG	VG+	NM
2000	Papa Left Mama Holdin' the Bag/This Is My Story	1966	3.75	7.50	15.00

FEDERAL

Number	Title (A Side/B Side)	Yr	VG	VG+	NM
12541	My Song/This Is My Story	1966	5.00	10.00	20.00

KING

Number	Title (A Side/B Side)	Yr	VG	VG+	NM
6068	Smokie Joe's/Lookie Lookie	1967	3.00	6.00	12.00

JEWELS, THE (4) Probably an instrumental group.
45s

FERN

Number	Title (A Side/B Side)	Yr	VG	VG+	NM
806	Jewel Rock/Space Guitar	1961	5.00	10.00	20.00

JEWELS, THE (5) For recordings on Rama, see THE CROWS.

JEWELS, THE (U) We can't definitely put these with any of the above groups. This could be as many as three more groups!
45s

MGM

Number	Title (A Side/B Side)	Yr	VG	VG+	NM
13577	We Got Togetherness/I'm Forever Blowing Bubbles	1966	5.00	10.00	20.00

OLIMPIC

Number	Title (A Side/B Side)	Yr	VG	VG+	NM
244	Jimmy Lee/The Hash	1964	7.50	15.00	30.00

SHASTA

Number	Title (A Side/B Side)	Yr	VG	VG+	NM
115	I Worry 'Bout You/Are You Coming to the Party	1959	5.00	10.00	20.00

JIANTS, THE
45s

CLAUDRA

Number	Title (A Side/B Side)	Yr	VG	VG+	NM
112	Tornado/She's My Woman	1959	50.00	100.00	200.00

JILL AND RAY See PAUL AND PAULA.

JIMENEZ, JOSE Also includes records under his real name, Bill Dana.
45s

A&M

Number	Title (A Side/B Side)	Yr	VG	VG+	NM
773	Jose's Dream/Cry	1965	2.00	4.00	8.00
—As "Bill Dana"					
779	All I Need Is You/Make Nice	1965	2.00	4.00	8.00
—As "Bill Dana"					
811	Jose Jimenezchevitz/Childhood Scenes	1966	2.00	4.00	8.00
—As "Bill Dana"					

KAPP

Number	Title (A Side/B Side)	Yr	VG	VG+	NM
409	The Astronaut (Part 1)/The Astronaut (Part 2)	1961	2.00	4.00	8.00
409 [PS]	The Astronaut (Part 1)/The Astronaut (Part 2)	1961	3.00	6.00	12.00
434	Christmas Sing Along with Jose: Jingle Bells/Sing Along with Jose: Shine On Harvest Moon	1961	3.75	7.50	15.00
443	Jose Jimenez in Orbit/Press Conference with Jose Jimenez in Orbit	1962	2.50	5.00	10.00
540	Jose and Cleopatra (Part 1)/Jose and Cleopatra (Part 2)	1963	2.50	5.00	10.00
552	King of the Surf (Part 1)/King of the Surf (Part 2)	1963	3.75	7.50	15.00

SIGNATURE

Number	Title (A Side/B Side)	Yr	VG	VG+	NM
12041	My Name — Jose Jimenez/In the Wee Small Hours	1960	3.00	6.00	12.00
12046	Bob Sled Racer/U.S. Senator	1960	3.00	6.00	12.00
—As "Bill Dana"					

Albums

A&M

Number	Title (A Side/B Side)	Yr	VG	VG+	NM
SP-4144	Mashuganishi Yogi	1968	3.75	7.50	15.00

CAPITOL

Number	Title (A Side/B Side)	Yr	VG	VG+	NM
ST-464	Hoo Ha! Direct from Noshville	1970	3.75	7.50	15.00

KAPP

Number	Title (A Side/B Side)	Yr	VG	VG+	NM
KL 1215 [M]	More Jose Jimenez	1961	5.00	10.00	20.00
KL 1215 [M]	Jose Jimenez the Submarine Officer	1961	6.25	12.50	25.00
—Original title					
KL 1238 [M]	Jose Jimenez at the Hungry I	196?	3.75	7.50	15.00
—Reissue with new title					
KL 1238 [M]	Jose Jimenez — The Astronaut (The First Man in Space)	1961	5.00	10.00	20.00
KL-1257 [M]	Jose Jimenez in Orbit — Bill Dana on Earth	1961	5.00	10.00	20.00
KL 1304 [M]	Jose Jimenez Talks to Teenagers of All Ages	1962	5.00	10.00	20.00
KL-1320 [M]	Jose Jimenez — Our Secret Weapon	1963	5.00	10.00	20.00
KL-1332 [M]	Jose Jimenez in Jollywood	1963	5.00	10.00	20.00
KL-1402 [M]	Bill Dana in Las Vegas	1964	5.00	10.00	20.00
KS 3238 [S]	Jose Jimenez at the Hungry I	196?	3.75	7.50	15.00
—Reissue with new title					
KS 3238 [S]	Jose Jimenez — The Astronaut (The First Man in Space)	1961	6.25	12.50	25.00
KS-3257 [S]	Jose Jimenez in Orbit — Bill Dana on Earth	1961	6.25	12.50	25.00
KS 3304 [S]	Jose Jimenez Talks to Teenagers of All Ages	1962	6.25	12.50	25.00
KS-3332 [S]	Jose Jimenez in Jollywood	1963	6.25	12.50	25.00

ROULETTE

Number	Title (A Side/B Side)	Yr	VG	VG+	NM
R 25161 [M]	My Name...Jose Jimenez	1961	5.00	10.00	20.00
—Reissue of Signature LP					

SIGNATURE

Number	Title (A Side/B Side)	Yr	VG	VG+	NM
SM 1013 [M]	My Name...Jose Jimenez	1960	6.25	12.50	25.00

J

Number	Title (A Side/B Side)	Yr	VG	VG+	NM

JIMMIE DALE AND THE FLATLANDERS
45s
PLANTATION

Number	Title (A Side/B Side)	Yr	VG	VG+	NM
❏ 92	Dallas/Tonight I'm Gonna Go Downtown	1972	12.50	25.00	50.00
❏ 106	Jole Blon/You've Never Seen Me Cry	1972	12.50	25.00	50.00

Albums
PLANTATION

❏ 22	One Road More	1972	—	—	—

—May exist only as an 8-track tape. Should an LP exist, its value would be in the hundreds.
ROUNDER

❏ SS-34	More a Legend Than a Band	1990	3.00	6.00	12.00

—As "The Flatlanders"; reissue of Plantation material

JIMMY AND DUANE "Duane" is DUANE EDDY.
45s
EB X. PRESTON

❏ 213	Soda Fountain Girl/(B-side unknown)	1955	62.50	125.00	250.00

JIMMY AND JOE
45s
HIT

❏ 71	Surf City/Easier Said Than Done	1963	2.00	4.00	8.00

—B-side by Clara Wilson

JIMMY AND PAT
45s
HIT

❏ 224	Baby Don't Go/You Were On My Mind	1965	2.50	5.00	10.00

—B-side by the Roamers

JIMMY AND WALTER
45s
SUN

❏ 180	Easy/Before Long	1953	500.00	1000.	2000.

—The earliest known 45 on Sun

JIMMY, JOE AND BETTY
45s
HIT

❏ 59	Puff the Magic Dragon/Don't Be Afraid Little Darling	1963	2.00	4.00	8.00

—B-side by Fred York

JIMMY, WAYNE AND BETTY
45s
HIT

❏ 75	Blowin' in the Wind/(You're the) Devil in Diguise	1963	2.00	4.00	8.00
	—B-side by Wayne Harris				
❏ 88	Don't Think Twice, It's All Right/That Sunday, That Summer	1963	2.00	4.00	8.00

—B-side by Berry Bradley

JIVE BOMBERS, THE
45s
SAVOY

❏ 1508	Bad Boy/When Your Hair Has Turned to Silver	1957	6.25	12.50	25.00
❏ 1513	If I Had a Talking Picture of You/The Blues Don't Mean a Thing	1957	5.00	10.00	20.00
❏ 1515	You Took My Love/Cherry	1957	5.00	10.00	20.00
❏ 1535	Just Around the Corner/Is This the End	1958	5.00	10.00	20.00
❏ 1560	Star Dust/You Give Your Love to Me	1959	5.00	10.00	20.00

Albums
SAVOY JAZZ

❏ SJL-1150	Bad Boy	1986	2.50	5.00	10.00

JIVE FIVE, THE
45s
AMBIENT SOUND

❏ 02742	Magic Maker, Music Maker/Oh Baby	1982	—	2.50	5.00
❏ 03053	Hey Sam/Don't Believe Him Donna	1982	—	2.50	5.00

AVCO

❏ 4568	Come Down in Time/Love Is Pain	1971	—	3.00	6.00
❏ 4589	Follow the Lamb/Lay Lady Lay	1972	—	3.00	6.00
❏ 4589	Follow the Lamb/Let the Feeling Belong	1972	—	3.00	6.00

BELTONE

❏ 1006	My True Story/When I Was Single	1961	7.50	15.00	30.00
❏ 1014	Never, Never/People from Another World	1961	5.00	10.00	20.00
❏ 2019	Hully Gully Calling Time/No, Not Again	1962	5.00	10.00	20.00
❏ 2024	What Time Is It?/Beggin' You Please	1962	5.00	10.00	20.00
❏ 2029	These Golden Rings/Do You Hear Wedding Bells	1962	5.00	10.00	20.00
❏ 2030	Lily Marlene/Johnny Never Knew	1963	5.00	10.00	20.00
❏ 2034	She's My Girl/Rain	1963	5.00	10.00	20.00

BRUT

❏ 814	All I Ever Do Is Dream About You/Super Woman (Part 2)	1973	—	3.00	6.00

DECCA

❏ 32671	(If You Let Me Make Love to You) Why Can't I Touch You/You Showed Me the Light of Love	1970	2.00	4.00	8.00
❏ 32736	I Want You to Be My Baby/Give Me Just a Chance	1970	2.00	4.00	8.00

LANA

❏ 105	My True Story/When I Was Single	196?	2.00	4.00	8.00

—Oldies reissue
LOST-NITE

❏ 144	My True Story/When I Was Single	196?	—	3.00	6.00

—Reissue

❏ 147	What Time Is It?/Beggin' You Please	196?	—	3.00	6.00

—Reissue
MUSICOR

❏ 1250	Crying Like a Baby/You'll Fall in Love	1967	3.00	6.00	12.00
❏ 1270	No More Tears/You'll Fall in Love	1967	3.00	6.00	12.00
❏ 1305	Sugar (Don't Take Away My Candy)/Blues in the Ghetto	1968	3.00	6.00	12.00

SKETCH

❏ 219	United/Prove Every Word You Say	1964	3.75	7.50	15.00

UNITED ARTISTS

❏ 0100	I'm a Happy Man/It Will Stand	1973	—	2.50	5.00

—"Silver Spotlight Series" reissue; B-side by The Showmen

❏ 807	United/Prove Every Word You Say	1965	5.00	10.00	20.00
❏ 853	I'm a Happy Man/Kiss Kiss Kiss	1965	5.00	10.00	20.00
❏ 936	Please Baby Please/A Bench in the Park	1965	5.00	10.00	20.00
❏ 50004	Goin' Wild/Main Street	1966	3.75	7.50	15.00
❏ 50033	In My Neighborhood/Then Came Heartbreak	1966	3.75	7.50	15.00
❏ 50069	You're a Puzzle/Ha Ha	1966	3.75	7.50	15.00
❏ 50107	You/You Promised Me Great Things	1966	3.75	7.50	15.00

Albums
AMBIENT SOUND

❏ FZ 37717	Here We Are	1982	3.75	7.50	15.00

AMBIENT SOUND/ROUNDER

❏ ASR-801	Way Back	1985	3.00	6.00	12.00

COLLECTABLES

❏ COL-5022	Greatest Hits	198?	2.50	5.00	10.00

RELIC

❏ 5020	The Jive Five's Greatest Hits (1961-1963)	198?	2.50	5.00	10.00

UNITED ARTISTS

❏ UAL-3455 [M]	The Jive Five	1965	12.50	25.00	50.00
❏ UAS-6455 [S]	The Jive Five	1965	18.75	37.50	75.00

JIVERS, THE
45s
ALADDIN

❏ 3329	Cherie/Little Mama	1956	40.00	80.00	160.00
❏ 3347	Ray Pearl/Dear Little One	1956	30.00	60.00	120.00

JO JO GUNNE
45s
ASYLUM

❏ 11003	Run Run Run/Take It Easy	1972	—	2.50	5.00
❏ 11007	Shake That Fat/I Make Love	1972	—	2.50	5.00
❏ 11018	Ready Freddie/Wait a Lifetime	1973	—	2.50	5.00
❏ 11020	Take Me Down Easy/Rock Around the Symbol	1973	—	2.50	5.00
❏ 11031	I Wanna Love You/New City	1974	—	2.50	5.00
❏ 45225	Where Is the Show/Into My Life	1975	—	2.50	5.00

Albums
ASYLUM

❏ 7E-1022	So...Where's the Show?	1974	2.50	5.00	10.00
❏ SD 5053	Jo Jo Gunne	1972	3.75	7.50	15.00
❏ SD 5065	Bite Down Hard	1973	3.75	7.50	15.00
❏ SD 5071	Jumpin' the Gunne	1973	3.75	7.50	15.00

—Gatefold cover

❏ SD 5071	Jumpin' the Gunne	1974	2.50	5.00	10.00

—Regular cover

JODIMARS, THE Contains ex-members of BILL HALEY AND HIS COMETS.
45s
CAPITOL

❏ F3285	Well Now — Dig This/Let's All Rock Together	1955	6.25	12.50	25.00
❏ F3360	Dancin' the Bop/Boom Boom My Bayou Baby	1956	6.25	12.50	25.00
❏ F3436	Lotsa Love/Rattle My Bones	1956	6.25	12.50	25.00
❏ F3512	Rattle Shakin' Daddy/Eat Your Heart Out, Annie	1956	6.25	12.50	25.00
❏ F3588	Clarabella/Midnight	1956	6.25	12.50	25.00
❏ F3633	Cloud 99/Later	1957	6.25	12.50	25.00

PRESIDENT

❏ 1017	Shoo-Sue/Story-Telling Baby	1957	5.00	10.00	20.00

JOE & ANN
45s
ACE

❏ 577	Gee Baby/Wherever You May Be	1959	3.00	6.00	12.00

JOE & EDDIE
45s
CAPITOL

❏ F4149	The Fox/Lonesome Road	1959	2.50	5.00	10.00
❏ F4209	Green Grass/And I Believe	1959	2.50	5.00	10.00
❏ F4288	Take My Hand/Remember Me	1959	2.50	5.00	10.00

GNP CRESCENDO

❏ 185	I Got Shoes/Water Boy	1962	2.00	4.00	8.00
❏ 195	Lonesome Traveler/There's a Meetin' Here Tonight	1963	2.00	4.00	8.00
❏ 305	Children Go/I Laid Around	1963	2.00	4.00	8.00
❏ 306	What's That I Hear/Farewell My Cindy Jane	1963	2.00	4.00	8.00
❏ 316	Wild Is the Wind/Swing Down Chariot	1964	—	3.00	6.00
❏ 321	Frankie and Johnny Blues/Gonna Build a Mountain	1964	—	3.00	6.00
❏ 324	Goodnight Irene/Pearly Shells	1964	—	3.00	6.00
❏ 333	Lonesome Road/Tear Down the Walls	1964	—	3.00	6.00
❏ 338	He's Got the Whole World in His Hands/Gabrielle	1965	—	3.00	6.00
❏ 344	Depend On Yourself/With You in Mind	1965	—	3.00	6.00
❏ 353	It Ain't Me Babe/Walkin' Down the Line	1965	—	3.00	6.00
❏ 355	I Got You (I've Got Everything)/Petticoat White (Summer Blue Sky)	1965	—	3.00	6.00
❏ 366	Michael, Row the Boat Ashore/That Was the Last Thing on My Mind	1965	—	3.00	6.00

Albums
GNP CRESCENDO

❏ GNP-75 [M]	Joe & Eddie	1963	5.00	10.00	20.00
❏ GNP-86 [M]	There's a Meetin' Here Tonite	1963	5.00	10.00	20.00
❏ GNP-96 [M]	Coast to Coast	1964	5.00	10.00	20.00
❏ GNPS-96 [S]	Coast to Coast	1964	6.25	12.50	25.00
❏ GNP-99 [M]	Joe & Eddie, Volume 4	1964	5.00	10.00	20.00
❏ GNPS-99 [S]	Joe & Eddie, Volume 4	1964	6.25	12.50	25.00
❏ GNP-2005 [M]	Tear Down the Walls	1965	3.75	7.50	15.00
❏ GNPS-2005 [S]	Tear Down the Walls	1965	5.00	10.00	20.00
❏ GNP-2007 [M]	Joe & Eddie Live in Hollywood	1965	3.75	7.50	15.00
❏ GNPS-2007 [S]	Joe & Eddie Live in Hollywood	1965	5.00	10.00	20.00

Number	Title (A Side/B Side)	Yr	VG	VG+	NM
❑ GNP-2014 [M]	Walkin' Down the Line	1965	3.75	7.50	15.00
❑ GNPS-2014 [S]	Walkin' Down the Line	1965	5.00	10.00	20.00
❑ GNP-2021 [M]	The Magic of Their Singing	1966	3.75	7.50	15.00
❑ GNPS-2021 [S]	The Magic of Their Singing	1966	5.00	10.00	20.00
❑ GNP-2032 [M]	The Best of Joe & Eddie	1966	3.75	7.50	15.00
❑ GNPS-2032 [S]	The Best of Joe & Eddie	1966	5.00	10.00	20.00

JOEL, BILLY
12-Inch Singles
COLUMBIA

Number	Title (A Side/B Side)	Yr	VG	VG+	NM
❑ AS 1718 [DJ]	Tell Her About It/Easy Money/Keeping the Faith	1983	3.00	6.00	12.00
❑ AS 1738 [DJ]	Tell Her About It (12" Version) (same on both sides)	1983	2.50	5.00	10.00
❑ AS 1982 [DJ]	Keeping the Faith (Special Mix) (same on both sides)	1984	2.50	5.00	10.00
❑ CAS 2109 [DJ]	You're Only Human (Second Wind) (LP Version) (Short Version)	1985	2.00	4.00	8.00
❑ CAS 2321 [DJ]	Back in the U.S.S.R./ The Times They Are a-Changin'	1987	3.75	7.50	15.00
❑ CAS 2367 [DJ]	A Matter of Trust (same on both sides?)	1986	3.00	6.00	12.00
❑ 44-04138	Tell Her About It (Special 12" Version 5:35)// Easy Money/You Got Me Hummin' (Live)	1983	3.00	6.00	12.00

45s
COLUMBIA

Number	Title (A Side/B Side)	Yr	VG	VG+	NM
❑ AE7 1338 [DJ]	Nobody Knows But Me/Root Beer Rag	1981	3.75	7.50	15.00
—Promo-only release of song from the "In Harmony 2" album					
❑ 18-02518	Say Goodbye to Hollywood/Summer, Highland Falls	1981	—	2.00	4.00
❑ 18-02518 [PS]	Say Goodbye to Hollywood/Summer, Highland Falls	1981	—	2.00	4.00
❑ 18-02628	She's Got a Way/The Ballad of Billy the Kid	1981	—	2.00	4.00
❑ 18-02628 [PS]	She's Got a Way/The Ballad of Billy the Kid	1981	—	2.00	4.00
❑ 13-03238	It's Still Rock and Roll to Me/Don't Ask Me Why	1982	—	—	3.00
—Reissue					
❑ 13-03239	You May Be Right/She's Got a Way	1982	—	—	3.00
—Reissue					
❑ 13-03241	Honesty/Sometimes a Fantasy	1982	—	—	3.00
—Reissue					
❑ 38-03244	Pressure/Laura	1982	—	2.00	4.00
❑ 38-03244 [PS]	Pressure/Laura	1982	—	2.00	4.00
❑ CNR-03321	Pressure/(B-side blank)	1982	2.00	4.00	8.00
—One-sided budget release (large hole)					
❑ 38-03413	Allentown/Elvis Presley Blvd.	1982	—	2.00	4.00
❑ 38-03413 [PS]	Allentown/Elvis Presley Blvd.	1982	—	2.00	4.00
❑ CNR-03426	Allentown//(B-side blank)	1982	2.00	4.00	8.00
—One-sided budget release					
❑ 38-03780	Goodnight Saigon/A Room of Our Own	1983	—	2.00	4.00
❑ 38-03780 [PS]	Goodnight Saigon/A Room of Our Own	1983	—	2.00	4.00
❑ 38-04012	Tell Her About It/Easy Money	1983	—	—	3.00
❑ 38-04012 [PS]	Tell Her About It/Easy Money	1983	—	2.00	4.00
❑ 38-04012 [PS]	Tell Her About It	1983	2.00	4.00	8.00
—"Demonstration -- Not for Sale" on sleeve					
❑ 38-04149	Uptown Girl/Careless Talk	1983	—	—	3.00
❑ 38-04149 [PS]	Uptown Girl/Careless Talk	1983	—	2.00	4.00
❑ 38-04149 [PS]	Uptown Girl	1983	2.00	4.00	8.00
—"Demonstration -- Not for Sale" on sleeve					
❑ 53-04149	Uptown Girl/Careless Talk	1984	—	—	3.00
—Gold "Instant Classics" reissue label					
❑ 38-04259	An Innocent Man/I'll Cry Instead	1983	—	—	3.00
❑ 38-04259 [PS]	An Innocent Man/I'll Cry Instead	1983	—	2.00	4.00
❑ 38-04400	The Longest Time/Christie Lee	1984	—	—	3.00
❑ 38-04400 [PS]	The Longest Time/Christie Lee	1984	—	2.00	4.00
❑ 38-04514	Leave a Tender Moment Alone/This Night	1984	—	—	3.00
❑ 38-04514 [PS]	Leave a Tender Moment Alone/This Night	1984	—	2.00	4.00
❑ 38-04681	Keeping the Faith (Special Mix)/ She's Right On Time	1984	—	—	3.00
❑ 38-04681 [PS]	Keeping the Faith (Special Mix)/ She's Right On Time	1984	—	2.00	4.00
❑ 38-05417	You're Only Human (Second Wind)/Surprises	1985	—	—	3.00
❑ 38-05417 [PS]	You're Only Human (Second Wind)/Surprises	1985	—	—	3.00
❑ 38-05657	The Night Is Still Young/Summer, Highland Falls	1985	—	—	3.00
❑ 38-05657 [PS]	The Night Is Still Young/Summer, Highland Falls	1985	—	2.00	4.00
❑ 38-05657 [PS]	The Night Is Still Young	1985	2.50	5.00	10.00
—Promotional black & white sleeve, different from stock sleeve					
❑ 38-06108	A Matter of Trust/Getting Closer	1986	—	—	3.00
❑ 38-06526	This Is the Time/Code of Silence	1986	—	—	3.00
❑ 38-06526 [PS]	This Is the Time/Code of Silence	1986	—	—	3.00
❑ 38-06994	Baby Grand/Big Man on Mulberry Street	1987	—	—	3.00
—A-side with Ray Charles					
❑ 38-06994 [PS]	Baby Grand/Big Man on Mulberry Street	1987	—	—	3.00
❑ 38-07626	Back in the U.S.S.R./Big Shot	1987	—	—	3.00
❑ 38-07626 [DJ]	Back in the U.S.S.R.//Back in the U.S.S.R./The Times They Are a-Changin'	1987	2.50	5.00	10.00
—Promo-only coupling; white label					
❑ 38-07626 [PS]	Back in the U.S.S.R./Big Shot	1987	—	2.00	4.00
❑ 38-07626 [PS]	Back in the U.S.S.R.//Back in the U.S.S.R/The Times They Are a-Changin'	1987	3.75	7.50	15.00
—Promo-only picture sleeve for promo-only coupling; "Demonstration--Not for Sale" on upper right rear corner of sleeve					
❑ 38-07664	The Times They Are a-Changin'/Back in the U.S.S.R.	1987	—	2.00	4.00
❑ 13-08415	Tell Her About It/Easy Money	1988	—	—	3.00
—Reissue					
❑ 13-08416	An Innocent Man/I'll Cry Instead	1988	—	—	3.00
—Reissue					
❑ 13-08417	The Longest Time/Christie Lee	1988	—	—	3.00
—Reissue					
❑ 13-08418	Leave a Tender Moment Alone/This Night	1988	—	—	3.00
—Reissue					
❑ 13-08419	Keeping the Faith/She's Right on Time	1988	—	—	3.00
—Reissue					
❑ 13-08420	You're Only Human (Second Wind)/Surprises	1988	—	—	3.00
—Reissue					
❑ 3-10015	Travelin' Prayer/Ain't No Crime	1974	2.50	5.00	10.00
❑ 3-10064	The Entertainer/The Mexican Connection	1974	2.00	4.00	8.00
❑ 3-10412	James/Summer, Highland Falls	1976	2.50	5.00	10.00

Number	Title (A Side/B Side)	Yr	VG	VG+	NM
❑ 3-10562	Say Goodbye to Hollywood/ I've Loved These Days	1977	2.50	5.00	10.00
❑ 3-10624	Movin' Out (Anthony's Song)/ She's Always a Woman	1977	3.00	6.00	12.00
❑ 3-10646	Just the Way You Are/Get It Right the First Time	1977	—	2.50	5.00
❑ 3-10708	Movin' Out (Anthony's Song)/ Everybody Has a Dream	1978	—	2.50	5.00
❑ 3-10750	Only the Good Die Young/ Get It Right the First Time	1978	—	2.50	5.00
❑ 3-10788	She's Always a Woman/Vienna	1978	—	2.50	5.00
❑ 3-10853	My Life/52nd Street	1978	—	2.50	5.00
❑ 3-10913	Big Shot/Root Beer Rag	1979	—	2.50	5.00
❑ 3-10959	Honesty/The Mexican Connection	1979	—	2.50	5.00
❑ 1-11229	All for Leyna/Souvenir	1980	—	—	—
—Canceled					
❑ 1-11231	You May Be Right/Close to the Borderline	1980	—	2.00	4.00
❑ 1-11231 [PS]	You May Be Right/Close to the Borderline	1980	—	3.00	6.00
❑ 1-11276	It's Still Rock and Roll to Me/ Through the Long Night	1980	—	2.00	4.00
❑ 1-11276 [PS]	It's Still Rock and Roll to Me/ Through the Long Night	1980	—	3.00	6.00
❑ 1-11331	Don't Ask Me Why/C'etait Toi (You Were the One)	1980	—	2.00	4.00
❑ 1-11331 [PS]	Don't Ask Me Why/C'etait Toi (You Were the One)	1980	—	3.00	6.00
❑ 1-11379	Sometimes a Fantasy/All for Leyna	1980	—	2.50	5.00
❑ 1-11379 [PS]	Sometimes a Fantasy/All for Leyna	1980	2.00	4.00	8.00
❑ 4-45963	Piano Man/You're My Home	1973	2.00	4.00	8.00
❑ 4-46055	Worse Comes to Worst/ Somewhere Along the Line	1974	2.50	5.00	10.00
❑ 38-73021	We Didn't Start the Fire/House of Blue Light	1989	—	—	3.00
❑ 38-73091	I Go to Extremes/When in Rome	1989	—	—	3.00
❑ 38-73442	That's Not Her Style/And So It Goes	1990	—	—	3.00
❑ 38-77086	The River of Dreams/No Man's Land	1993	—	—	3.00
❑ 38-77254	All About Soul/Picked a Real Bad Time	1993	—	—	3.00
❑ 38-77363	Lullabye (Goodnight, My Angel)/ Two Thousand Years	1994	—	—	3.00
❑ 38-78641	To Make You Feel My Love//Intro/Summer, Highland Falls/Summer, Highland Falls	1997	—	—	3.00

EPIC

Number	Title (A Side/B Side)	Yr	VG	VG+	NM
❑ 34-06118	Modern Woman/Sleeping with the Television On	1986	—	—	3.00
❑ 34-06118 [PS]	Modern Woman/Sleeping with the Television On	1986	—	2.00	4.00
❑ 34-74422	All Shook Up/Wear My Ring Around Your Neck	1992	—	2.00	4.00
—B-side is instrumental track of Ricky Van Shelton's recording					

FAMILY PRODUCTIONS

Number	Title (A Side/B Side)	Yr	VG	VG+	NM
❑ 0900	She's Got a Way/Everybody Loves You Now	1971	7.50	15.00	30.00
❑ 0906	Tomorrow Is Today/Everybody Loves You Now	1971	7.50	15.00	30.00

Albums
COLUMBIA

Number	Title (A Side/B Side)	Yr	VG	VG+	NM
❑ AS 326 [DJ]	Souvenir	1976	7.50	15.00	30.00
—Promo-only LP with one side live, one side a compilation of studio tracks					
❑ AS 402 [DJ]	Inter Chords/Billy Joel Interview	1977	6.25	12.50	25.00
—Promo-only interview album					
❑ AS 1343 [DJ]	Billy Joel Interview	1982	6.25	12.50	25.00
❑ CQ 32544 [Q]	Piano Man	1974	5.00	10.00	20.00
❑ KC 32544	Piano Man	1973	3.00	6.00	12.00
—Some copies have the first song spelled "Travelin' Prayer," others have it "Travellin' Prayer." No difference in value.					
❑ PC 32544	Piano Man	1976	2.50	5.00	10.00
—No bar code on back cover					
❑ PC 32544	Piano Man	1979	2.00	4.00	8.00
—With bar code on back cover					
❑ PC 33146	Streetlife Serenade	1975	2.50	5.00	10.00
—No bar code on back cover					
❑ PC 33146	Streetlife Serenade	1979	2.00	4.00	8.00
—With bar code on back cover					
❑ PCQ 33146 [Q]	Streetlife Serenade	1975	5.00	10.00	20.00
❑ PC 33848	Turnstiles	1976	2.00	4.00	8.00
—With bar code on back cover					
❑ PC 33848	Turnstiles	1976	2.50	5.00	10.00
—No bar code on back cover					
❑ PCQ 33848 [Q]	Turnstiles	1976	5.00	10.00	20.00
❑ HC 34987	The Stranger	1981	7.50	15.00	30.00
—Original pressing of half-speed mastered edition					
❑ JC 34987	The Stranger	1977	2.50	5.00	10.00
❑ PC 34987	The Stranger	1979	2.00	4.00	8.00
❑ FC 35609	52nd Street	1978	2.50	5.00	10.00
❑ PC 35609	52nd Street	1985	2.00	4.00	8.00
❑ FC 36384	Glass Houses	1980	2.50	5.00	10.00
❑ PC 36384	Glass Houses	1986	2.00	4.00	8.00
❑ PC 37461	Songs in the Attic	1984	2.00	4.00	8.00
❑ TC 37461	Songs in the Attic	1981	2.50	5.00	10.00
❑ QC 38200	The Nylon Curtain	1982	2.50	5.00	10.00
❑ QC 38837	An Innocent Man	1983	2.50	5.00	10.00
❑ PC 38984	Cold Spring Harbor	1983	2.00	4.00	8.00
—Remixed, remastered version of Family Productions album					
❑ C2 40121 [(2)]	Greatest Hits, Volumes 1 and 2	1985	3.00	6.00	12.00
❑ OC 40402	The Bridge	1986	2.50	5.00	10.00
❑ C2 40996 [(2)]	KOHUEPT	1987	3.75	7.50	15.00
❑ OC 44366	Storm Front	1989	3.00	6.00	12.00
❑ HC 44987	The Stranger	1982	6.25	12.50	25.00
—Half-speed mastered edition (reissue)					
❑ HC 45609	52nd Street	1982	6.25	12.50	25.00
—Half-speed mastered edition					
❑ HC 47461	Songs in the Attic	1982	17.50	35.00	70.00
—Half-speed mastered edition					
❑ HC 48837	An Innocent Man	1983	7.50	15.00	30.00
—Half-speed mastered edition					

FAMILY PRODUCTIONS

Number	Title (A Side/B Side)	Yr	VG	VG+	NM
❑ FPS-2700	Cold Spring Harbor	1971	10.00	20.00	40.00
—Authentic copies have mostly dark blue labels; when reissued on Columbia, the entire LP was remixed and remastered, and "You Can Make Me Free" was shortened by three minutes					

JOEY AND DANNY
45s
SWAN

Number	Title (A Side/B Side)	Yr	VG	VG+	NM
❑ 4276	Santa's Got a Brand New Bag/Rats in My Room	1967	5.00	10.00	20.00

J

Number	Title (A Side/B Side)	Yr	VG	VG+	NM

JOEY AND THE CONTINENTALS
45s
CLARIDGE

Number	Title (A Side/B Side)	Yr	VG	VG+	NM
❑ 304	She Rides with Me/Rudy Vahoo	1966	6.25	12.50	25.00

—Reissued on Claridge 312 as "The G.T.O.'s"
KOMET

❑ 1001	Linda/Will Love Ever Come My Way	196?	3.75	7.50	15.00

LAURIE

❑ 3294	Sad Girl/Baby	1965	6.25	12.50	25.00

JOEY AND THE LEXINGTONS
45s
COMET

❑ 2154	Heaven/The Girl I Love	1962	37.50	75.00	150.00

DUNES

❑ 2029	Bobbie/Tears from My Eyes	1963	25.00	50.00	100.00

JOEY AND THE TEENAGERS
45s
COLUMBIA

❑ 42054	What's On Your Mind/The Draw	1961	20.00	40.00	80.00

JOHN, ELTON
12-Inch Singles
GEFFEN

Number	Title (A Side/B Side)	Yr	VG	VG+	NM
❑ PRO-A-948 [DJ]	Nobody Wins (5:20)/Nobody Wins (French Version) (5:09)	1981	3.75	7.50	15.00
❑ PRO-A-1018 [DJ]	Empty Garden (Hey Hey Johnny) (Long)/(Short)	1981	12.50	25.00	50.00
❑ PRO-A-2025 [DJ]	I'm Still Standing (same on both sides)	1983	3.00	6.00	12.00
❑ PRO-A-2066 [DJ]	Kiss the Bride (LP Version) (Edit)	1983	3.00	6.00	12.00
❑ PRO-A-2160 [DJ]	Sad Songs (Say So Much) (same on both sides)	1984	3.00	6.00	12.00
❑ PRO-A-2188 [DJ]	Who Wears These Shoes? (same on both sides)	1984	2.50	5.00	10.00
❑ PRO-A-2374 [DJ]	Wrap Her Up (same on both sides)	1985	2.50	5.00	10.00
❑ PRO-A-2440 [DJ]	Nikita (LP Version 5:42) (Edit 4:54)	1985	2.50	5.00	10.00
❑ PRO-A-2569 [DJ]	Heartache All Over the World (Edit) (Shorter Edit)	1986	3.00	6.00	12.00
❑ 20563	Heartache All Over the World (2 versions)/Highlander	1986	2.00	4.00	8.00

MCA

❑ L33-1172 [DJ]	Bite Your Lip (Get Up and Dance) (6:39) (same on both sides)	1977	6.25	12.50	25.00
❑ L33-1850 [DJ]	Victim of Love (same on both sides)	1979	2.50	5.00	10.00
❑ L33-1854 [DJ]	Johnny B. Goode (same on both sides)	1979	3.00	6.00	12.00
❑ L33-1979 [DJ]	Ego (same on both sides)	1978	12.50	25.00	50.00
❑ L33-17458 [DJ]	Candle in the Wind (Live) (same on both sides)	1987	2.50	5.00	10.00
❑ L33-17475 [DJ]	Take Me to the Pilot (Live) (same on both sides)	1987	2.50	5.00	10.00
❑ L33-17539 [DJ]	I Don't Wanna Go On with You Like That (4:34) (3:57)	1988	3.75	7.50	15.00
❑ 23870	I Don't Wanna Go On with You Like That (The Shep Pettibone Mix 7:29) (The Pub Dub 5:18) (Just for Radio Mix 4:00) (Just Elton and His Piano Mix 4:50)	1988	2.00	4.00	8.00
❑ 23917	Mona Lisas and Mad Hatters (Renaissance Mix) (Da Vinci Mix) (Slef Portrait Instrumental Mix)/A Word in Spanish	1988	3.00	6.00	12.00

ROCKET

❑ 852093-1	Made in England (Junior's Sound Factory Mix 10:59) (Junior's Sound Factory Dub 8:34) (Junior's Joyous Mix 4:21) /Believe (Hardkiss Mix 10:27)	1995	2.50	5.00	10.00

45s
CONGRESS

❑ 6017	Lady Samantha/It's Me That You Need	1970	12.50	25.00	50.00
❑ 6017 [DJ]	Lady Samantha/It's Me That You Need	1970	7.50	15.00	30.00
❑ 6022	Border Song/Bad Side of the Moon	1970	12.50	25.00	50.00
❑ 6022 [DJ]	Border Song/Bad Side of the Moon	1970	7.50	15.00	30.00

DJM

❑ 70008	Lady Samantha/All Across the Havens	1969	75.00	150.00	300.00
❑ 70008 [DJ]	Lady Samantha/All Across the Havens	1969	25.00	50.00	100.00

GEFFEN

❑ 28578	Heartache All Over the World/Highlander	1986	—	—	3.00
❑ 28578 [PS]	Heartache All Over the World/Highlander	1986	—	—	3.00
❑ 28800	Nikita/Restless	1985	—	—	3.00
❑ 28800 [PS]	Nikita/Restless	1985	—	—	3.00
❑ 28800DJ [DJ]	Nikita (U.S. Edit)/(U.K. Edit)	1985	—	3.00	6.00
❑ 28873	Wrap Her Up/The Man Who Never Died	1985	—	—	3.00
❑ 28873 [PS]	Wrap Her Up/The Man Who Never Died	1985	—	—	3.00
❑ 29111	In Neon/Tactics	1984	—	—	3.00
❑ 29189	Who Wears These Shoes?/Lonely Boy	1984	—	—	3.00
❑ 29189 [PS]	Who Wears These Shoes?/Lonely Boy	1984	—	—	3.00
❑ 29292	Sad Songs (Say So Much)/A Simple Man	1984	—	—	3.00
❑ 7-29292 [DJ]	Sad Songs (Say So Much) (Special Radio Mix) (same on both sides)	1984	2.50	5.00	10.00

—Contains a 4:05 mix unavailable elsewhere; label has "RE-1" on both sides

❑ 29402	Cold As Christmas (In the Middle of the Year)/(B-side unassigned)	1983			

—Unreleased

❑ 29460	I Guess That's Why They Call It the Blues/The Retreat	1983	—	—	3.00
❑ 29460 [PS]	I Guess That's Why They Call It the Blues/The Retreat	1983	—	—	3.00
❑ 29568	Kiss the Bride/Choc Ice Goes Mental	1983	—	—	3.00
❑ 29568 [PS]	Kiss the Bride/Choc Ice Goes Mental	1983	—	—	3.00
❑ 29639	I'm Still Standing/Love So Cold	1983	—	—	3.00
❑ 29639 [PS]	I'm Still Standing/Love So Cold	1983	—	—	3.00
❑ 29846	Ball & Chain/Where Have All the Good Times Gone?	1982	—	2.00	4.00
❑ 29954	Blue Eyes/Hey Papa Legba	1982	—	2.00	4.00
❑ 29954 [PS]	Blue Eyes/Hey Papa Legba	1982	—	2.50	5.00
❑ 49722	Nobody Wins/Fools in Fashion	1981	—	2.00	4.00
❑ 49722 [PS]	Nobody Wins/Fools in Fashion	1981	—	2.50	5.00
❑ 49788	Chloe/Tortured	1981	—	2.00	4.00
❑ 49788 [DJ]	Chloe//Fanfare/Chloe	1981	2.00	4.00	8.00

—B-side of this promo-only single is full-length version

❑ 50049	Empty Garden (Hey Hey Johnny)/Take Me Down to the Ocean	1982	—	2.00	4.00
❑ 50049 [DJ]	Empty Garden (LP version)/Empty Garden (Edit)	1982	2.00	4.00	8.00
❑ 50049 [PS]	Empty Garden (Hey Hey Johnny)/Take Me Down to the Ocean	1982	—	2.50	5.00

MCA

❑ S45-1938 [DJ]	Love Song (Long)/(Short)	1976	5.00	10.00	20.00

—Promo-only release from the Here And There live album

❑ 40000	Crocodile Rock/Elderberry Wine	1972	—	3.00	6.00

—Original pressings have a solid black label

❑ 40046	Daniel/Skyline Pigeon	1973	—	2.50	5.00
❑ 40105	Saturday Night's Alright for Fighting//Jack Rabbit/Whenever You're Ready	1973	—	2.50	5.00
❑ 40148	Goodbye Yellow Brick Road/Young Man's Blues	1973	—	2.50	5.00
❑ 40198	Bennie and the Jets/Harmony	1974	—	2.50	5.00
❑ 40259	Don't Let the Sun Go Down on Me/Sick City	1974	—	2.50	5.00
❑ 40297	The Bitch Is Back/Cold Highway	1974	—	2.50	5.00
❑ 40344	Lucy in the Sky with Diamonds/One Day at a Time	1974	—	2.50	5.00

—Both sides feature "Dr. Winston O'Boogie" (John Lennon)

❑ 40344 [PS]	Lucy in the Sky with Diamonds/One Day at a Time	1974	2.50	5.00	10.00
❑ 40364	Philadelphia Freedom/I Saw Her Standing There	1975	—	2.50	5.00

—B-side features John Lennon

❑ 40364 [PS]	Philadelphia Freedom/I Saw Her Standing There	1975	—	3.00	6.00
❑ 40364 [PS]	Philadelphia Freedom/I Saw Her Standing There	1975	10.00	20.00	40.00

—Promo-only sleeve from WFIL radio in Philadelphia

❑ 40421	Someone Saved My Life Tonight/House of Cards	1975	—	2.00	4.00

—With MCA black/rainbow label

❑ 40421	Someone Saved My Life Tonight/House of Cards	1975	—	2.50	5.00

—Original copies have "Captain Fantastic" label

❑ 40461	Island Girl/Sugar on the Floor	1975	—	2.00	4.00
❑ 40505	Grow Some Funk of Your Own/I Feel Like a Bullet (in the Gun of Robert Ford)	1976	—	2.00	4.00
❑ 40892	Ego/Flinstone Boy	1978	—	2.00	4.00
❑ 40892 [PS]	Ego/Flinstone Boy	1978	2.50	5.00	10.00
❑ 40973	Part-Time Love/I Cry at Night	1978	—	2.00	4.00
❑ 40973 [PS]	Part-Time Love/I Cry at Night	1978	—	2.00	4.00
❑ 40993	Song for Guy/Lovesick	1979	2.50	5.00	10.00

—The stock copy is much scarcer than the promo, the only Elton John MCA single where this is the case.

❑ 40993 [DJ]	Song for Guy/Lovesick	1979	—	2.50	5.00
❑ 40993 [PS]	Song for Guy/Lovesick	1979	—	2.50	5.00
❑ 41042	Mama Can't Buy You Love/Three Way Love Affair	1979	—	2.00	4.00
❑ 41042 [PS]	Mama Can't Buy You Love/Three Way Love Affair	1979	—	2.00	4.00
❑ 41126	Victim of Love/Strangers	1979	—	2.00	4.00

—Label correctly says "From the MCA LP...'Victim of Love'"

❑ 41126	Victim of Love/Strangers	1979	2.00	4.00	8.00

—Label incorrectly says "From the MCA LP...'Thunder in the Night'"

❑ 41159	Johnny B. Goode/Georgia	1980	—	2.50	5.00
❑ 41236	Little Jeannie/Conquer the Sun	1980	—	2.00	4.00

—Originals have a colorful custom label

❑ 41236 [PS]	Little Jeannie/Conquer the Sun	1980	—	2.50	5.00
❑ 41293	(Sartorial Eloquence) Don't Ya Wanna Play This Game No More?//Cartier/White Man Danger	1980	—	2.00	4.00
❑ 53196	Candle in the Wind/Sorry Seems to Be the Hardest Word	1987	—	—	3.00
❑ 53196 [PS]	Candle in the Wind/Sorry Seems to Be the Hardest Word	1987	—	—	3.00

—Yellow sleeve with album jackets pictured on back

❑ 53196 [PS]	Candle in the Wind/Sorry Seems to Be the Hardest Word	1987	—	2.00	4.00

—White sleeve

❑ 53260	Take Me to the Pilot/Tonight	1988	—	2.00	4.00
❑ 53260 [PS]	Take Me to the Pilot/Tonight	1988	—	2.00	4.00
❑ 53345	I Don't Wanna Go On with You Like That/Rope Around a Fool	1988	—	—	3.00
❑ 53345 [PS]	I Don't Wanna Go On with You Like That/Rope Around a Fool	1988	—	—	3.00
❑ 53408	A Word in Spanish/Heavy Traffic	1988	—	—	3.00
❑ 53408 [PS]	A Word in Spanish/Heavy Traffic	1988	—	—	3.00
❑ 53692	Healing Hands/Dancing in the End Zone	1989	—	—	3.00
❑ 53750	Sacrifice/Love Is a Cannibal	1989	—	—	3.00
❑ 54423	The One/Suit of Wolves	1992	—	—	3.00
❑ 54452	Runaway Train/Understanding Women	1992	—	—	3.00

—A-side with Eric Clapton

❑ 54581	Simple Life/The North	1993	—	—	3.00
❑ 54762	True Love/Runaway Train	1993	—	—	3.00

—A-side with Kiki Dee; B-side with Eric Clapton

❑ 65018	Step Into Christmas/Ho! Ho! Ho! (Who'd Be a Turkey at Christmas)	1973	—	2.50	5.00

—Originals have black labels with rainbow

❑ 65018	Step Into Christmas/Ho! Ho! Ho! (Who'd Be a Turkey at Christmas)	1978	—	2.00	4.00

—Second edition: Tan label

❑ 65018	Step Into Christmas/Ho! Ho! Ho! (Who'd Be a Turkey at Christmas)	1980	—	—	3.00

—Third edition: Blue label with rainbow

❑ 79026	Club at the End of the Street/Sacrifice	1990	—	—	3.00

POLYDOR

❑ PRO-002	Pinball Wizard/Acid Queen	1975	10.00	20.00	40.00

—Promo-only release; B-side by Tina Turner

ROCKET

❑ 31456 8108 7	Something About the Way You Look Tonight/Candle in the Wind 1997	1997	—	2.50	5.00
❑ 40645	Sorry Seems to Be the Hardest Word/Shoulder Holster	1976	—	2.00	4.00

Number	Title (A Side/B Side)	Yr	VG	VG+	NM
❏ 40677	Bite Your Lip (Get up and dance!)/Chameleon	1977	—	2.00	4.00
❏ 852172-7	Made in England/Lucy in the Sky with Diamonds	1995	—	2.00	4.00
—B-side recorded live at Madison Square Garden in 1974 with John Lennon					
❏ 852394-7	Blessed/Latitude	1995	—	2.00	4.00
❏ 856014-7	Believe/The One (Live)	1995	—	—	3.00
❏ 856014-7 [PS]	Believe/The One (Live)	1995	—	—	3.00
UNI					
❏ 55246	Border Song/Bad Side of the Moon	1970	—	3.00	6.00
❏ 55265	Your Song/Take Me to the Pilot	1970	—	3.00	6.00
❏ 55277	Friends/Honey Roll	1971	—	3.00	6.00
❏ 55314	Levon/Goodbye	1971	—	3.00	6.00
❏ 55318	Tiny Dancer/Razor Face	1971	—	3.00	6.00
—Stock copies have full-length version of A-side					
❏ 55318 [DJ]	Tiny Dancer/Razor Face	1971	2.50	5.00	10.00
—With a severely truncated version of the A-side					
❏ 55328	Rocket Man/Suzie (Dramas)	1972	—	3.00	6.00
❏ 55343	Honky Cat/Slave	1972	—	3.00	6.00
VIKING					
❏ 1010	From Denver to L.A./Warm Summer Rain	1970	15.00	30.00	60.00
—B-side by The Barbara Moore Singers					
❏ 1010 [DJ]	From Denver to L.A. (same on both sides)	1970	6.25	12.50	25.00
—The promo version of this has been counterfeited; some say all are counterfeits.					

7-Inch Extended Plays
MCA

Number	Title (A Side/B Side)	Yr	VG	VG+	NM
❏ 34961	Daniel/Teacher I Need You//High Flying Bird/Crocodile Rock	1973	3.75	7.50	15.00
—Jukebox issue; small hole, plays at 33 1/3 rpm					
❏ 34961 [PS]	Don't Shoot Me I'm Only the Piano Player	1973	3.75	7.50	15.00
—Part of "Little LP" series (LLP #207)					
UNI					
❏ 1903 [DJ]	Come Down in Time/Country Comfort//Amoreena/Love Song	1971	3.75	7.50	15.00
—Jukebox issue, small hole, plays at 33 1/3 rpm					
❏ 1903 [PS]	Tumbleweed Connection	1971	3.75	7.50	15.00
—Part of Little LP series (LLP 143)					

Albums
COLUMBIA SPECIAL PRODUCTS

Number	Title (A Side/B Side)	Yr	VG	VG+	NM
❏ P 16196	The Best of Elton John, Volume One	1981	3.00	6.00	12.00
❏ P 16197	The Best of Elton John, Volume Two	1981	3.00	6.00	12.00
—Both of the above "Distributed Exclusively by Scott Distributing Corp."					
DCC COMPACT CLASSICS					
❏ LPZ-2004	Madman Across the Water	1994	30.00	60.00	120.00
—Audiophile vinyl					
❏ LPZ-2013	Elton John's Greatest Hits	1995	25.00	50.00	100.00
—Audiophile vinyl					
❏ LPZ-2020	Elton John's Greatest Hits, Volume 2	1996	—	—	—
—Canceled					
DIRECT DISC					
❏ SD-16614 [(2)]	Goodbye Yellow Brick Road	1980	12.50	25.00	50.00
—Audiophile vinyl					
GEFFEN					
❏ GHS 2002	The Fox	1981	2.50	5.00	10.00
❏ GHS 2013	Jump Up!	1982	2.50	5.00	10.00
❏ PRO-A-2176 [DJ]	Sasson Presents Elton John	1983	7.50	15.00	30.00
—One-sided promo with four tracks on A-side and an etched facsimile autograph on B-side					
❏ GHS 4006	Too Low for Zero	1983	2.50	5.00	10.00
❏ GHS 24031	Breaking Hearts	1984	2.50	5.00	10.00
❏ GHS 24031 [DJ]	Breaking Hearts	1984	5.00	10.00	20.00
—Promo pressing on Quiex II vinyl					
❏ GHS 24077	Ice on Fire	1985	2.50	5.00	10.00
❏ GHS 24114	Leather Jackets	1986	2.50	5.00	10.00
❏ GHS 24153	Elton John's Greatest Hits, Vol. 3, 1979-1987	1987	2.50	5.00	10.00
MCA					
❏ 619	11-17-70	1979	2.00	4.00	8.00
❏ 620	Empty Sky	1979	2.00	4.00	8.00
❏ 621	Rock of the Westies	1979	2.00	4.00	8.00
❏ 622	Here and There	1979	2.00	4.00	8.00
❏ 771	Victim of Love	1981	2.00	4.00	8.00
❏ 772	21 at 33	1981	2.00	4.00	8.00
❏ L33-1173/4 [DJ]	Get Up and Dance	1977	25.00	50.00	100.00
—Promo-only sampler from "Blue Moves" LP; blue vinyl					
❏ 1689	Elton John's Greatest Hits	198?	2.00	4.00	8.00
❏ 4L33-1848 [(4)DJ]	Victim of Love	1979	25.00	50.00	100.00
—Promo-only collection of the entire album as four 12-inch singles					
❏ L33-1995 [PD]	A Single Man	1978	10.00	20.00	40.00
—Promo picture disc					
❏ 2012	Elton John	1973	2.50	5.00	10.00
❏ 2014	Tumbleweed Connection	1973	2.50	5.00	10.00
—With booklet					
❏ 2015	11-17-70	1973	2.50	5.00	10.00
❏ 2016	Madman Across the Water	1973	2.50	5.00	10.00
—With booklet					
❏ 2017	Honky Chateau	1973	2.50	5.00	10.00
❏ 2100	Don't Shoot Me, I'm Only the Piano Player	1973	2.50	5.00	10.00
—With black rainbow label and booklet					
❏ 2100	Don't Shoot Me, I'm Only the Piano Player	1973	5.00	10.00	20.00
—With all-black label (no rainbow) and booklet					
❏ 2116	Caribou	1974	2.50	5.00	10.00
❏ 2128	Elton John's Greatest Hits	1974	2.50	5.00	10.00
❏ 2130	Empty Sky	1975	2.50	5.00	10.00
—First American issue of his 1969 debut					
❏ 2142	Captain Fantastic and the Brown Dirt Cowboy	1975	3.00	6.00	12.00
—With custom label, two booklets and poster					
❏ 2142 [DJ]	Captain Fantastic and the Brown Dirt Cowboy	1975	75.00	150.00	300.00
—Brown vinyl promo, autographed by Elton John and Bernie Taupin					
❏ 2163	Rock of the Westies	1975	2.50	5.00	10.00
❏ 2197	Here and There	1976	2.50	5.00	10.00
❏ 3001	Tumbleweed Connection	1977	2.00	4.00	8.00
❏ 3003	Madman Across the Water	1977	2.00	4.00	8.00
❏ 3027	Elton John's Greatest Hits, Volume 2	1977	2.50	5.00	10.00
❏ 3065	A Single Man	1978	2.50	5.00	10.00
❏ 5104	Victim of Love	1979	2.50	5.00	10.00
❏ 5121	21 at 33	1980	2.50	5.00	10.00
—Originals have custom labels					
❏ 5224	Elton John's Greatest Hits	1981	2.00	4.00	8.00
❏ 5225	Elton John's Greatest Hits, Volume 2	1981	2.00	4.00	8.00

Number	Title (A Side/B Side)	Yr	VG	VG+	NM
❏ 6011 [(2)]	Blue Moves	1979	2.50	5.00	10.00
❏ 6240	Reg Strikes Back	1988	2.50	5.00	10.00
❏ 6321	Sleeping with the Past	1989	2.50	5.00	10.00
❏ 6894 [(2)]	Goodbye Yellow Brick Road	1980	2.50	5.00	10.00
❏ 8022 [(2)]	Live in Australia with the Melbourne Symphony Orchestra	1987	3.75	7.50	15.00
❏ 2-10003 [(2)]	Goodbye Yellow Brick Road	1973	3.75	7.50	15.00
❏ 13921 [EP]	The Thom Bell Sessions	1979	2.00	4.00	8.00
❏ 14951 [PD]	A Single Man	1978	5.00	10.00	20.00
—Stock picture disc					
❏ 37064	Honky Chateau	1979	2.00	4.00	8.00
❏ 37065	Caribou	1979	2.00	4.00	8.00
❏ 37066	Captain Fantastic and the Brown Dirt Cowboy	1979	2.00	4.00	8.00
❏ 37067	Elton John	1979	2.00	4.00	8.00
❏ 37068	A Single Man	1979	2.00	4.00	8.00
❏ 37113	Don't Shoot Me, I'm Only the Piano Player	1979	2.00	4.00	8.00
❏ 37199	Tumbleweed Connection	1982	2.00	4.00	8.00
❏ 37200	Madman Across the Water	1982	2.00	4.00	8.00
❏ 37215	Elton John's Greatest Hits	1983	2.00	4.00	8.00
❏ 37216	Elton John's Greatest Hits	1983	2.00	4.00	8.00
❏ 37266	Your Songs	1986	2.50	5.00	10.00
❏ 39115	The Complete Thom Bell Sessions	1989	3.75	7.50	15.00
MOBILE FIDELITY					
❏ 2-160 [(2)]	Goodbye Yellow Brick Road	1984	10.00	20.00	40.00
—Audiophile vinyl					
NAUTILUS					
❏ NR-42	Elton John's Greatest Hits	198?	25.00	50.00	100.00
—Audiophile vinyl					
PARAMOUNT					
❏ PAS 6004	Friends (Soundtrack)	1971	5.00	10.00	20.00
—Whitish gray label original					
❏ PAS 6004	Friends (Soundtrack)	1975	6.25	12.50	25.00
—Dark blue label with "Paramount" logo at top and ABC Records reference along edge; much rarer than the original					
ROCKET					
❏ 2-11004 [(2)]	Blue Moves	1976	3.75	7.50	15.00
—Originals have light blue labels with a train at the top of the label					
❏ 526915-1	Made in England	1995	5.00	10.00	20.00
—U.S. version is on 180-gram vinyl, distributed by Classic Records					
UNI					
❏ 73090	Elton John	1970	3.75	7.50	15.00
❏ 73096	Tumbleweed Connection	1971	3.75	7.50	15.00
—With booklet					
❏ 93090	Elton John	1971	3.00	6.00	12.00
❏ 93096	Tumbleweed Connection	1971	3.00	6.00	12.00
—With booklet					
❏ 93105	11-17-70	1971	3.75	7.50	15.00
❏ 93120	Madman Across the Water	1971	3.75	7.50	15.00
—With booklet					
❏ 93135	Honky Chateau	1972	3.75	7.50	15.00
—With "(P) 1972 This Record Co., Ltd." on label					
❏ 93135	Honky Chateau	1972	5.00	10.00	20.00
—With "(P) 1972 MCA Records, Inc." on label					

JOHN, ELTON, AND KIKI DEE Also see each artist's individual listings.
45s
ROCKET

Number	Title (A Side/B Side)	Yr	VG	VG+	NM
❏ 40585	Don't Go Breakin' My Heart/Snow Queen	1976	—	2.00	4.00
❏ 40585 [PS]	Don't Go Breakin' My Heart/Snow Queen	1976	—	2.50	5.00

JOHN, ELTON, AND MILLIE JACKSON Also see each artist's individual listings.
12-Inch Singles
GEFFEN

Number	Title (A Side/B Side)	Yr	VG	VG+	NM
❏ PRO-A-2324 [DJ]	Act of War (Edit)/(Instrumental)	1985	2.00	4.00	8.00
❏ 20347	Act of War (8:32)/(5:04)	1985	2.00	4.00	8.00

45s
GEFFEN

Number	Title (A Side/B Side)	Yr	VG	VG+	NM
❏ 28956	Act of War, Part 1/Act of War, Part 2	1985	—	2.00	4.00
❏ 28956 [PS]	Act of War, Part 1/Act of War, Part 2	1985	—	2.00	4.00

JOHN, LITTLE WILLIE
45s
ATLANTIC

Number	Title (A Side/B Side)	Yr	VG	VG+	NM
❏ 89189	Fever/Ruby Baby	1987	—	—	3.00
—B-side by the Drifters					
❏ 89189 [PS]	Fever/Ruby Baby	1987	—	—	3.00
—From the movie "Big Town"					
KING					
❏ 4818	All Around the World/Don't Leave Me Dear	1955	6.25	12.50	25.00
❏ 4841	Need Your Love So Bad/Home at Last	1955	6.25	12.50	25.00
❏ 4893	Are You Ever Coming Back?/I'm Stickin' with You Baby	1956	6.25	12.50	25.00
❏ 4935	Fever/Letter from My Darling	1956	7.50	15.00	30.00
❏ 4960	Do Something for Me/My Nerves	1956	6.25	12.50	25.00
❏ 4989	I've Been Around/Suffering with the Blues	1956	6.25	12.50	25.00
❏ 5003	Will the Sun Shine Tomorrow/A Little Bit of Loving	1956	6.25	12.50	25.00
❏ 5023	Love, Life and Money/You Got to Get Up Early in the Morning	1957	6.25	12.50	25.00
❏ 5045	I've Got to Go Cry/Look What You've Done to Me	1957	6.25	12.50	25.00
❏ 5066	Young Girl/If I Thought You Needed Me	1957	6.25	12.50	25.00
❏ 5083	Uh Uh Baby/Summer Date	1957	6.25	12.50	25.00
❏ 5091	Person to Person/Until You Do	1957	6.25	12.50	25.00
❏ 5108	Talk to Me, Talk to Me/Spasms	1958	6.25	12.50	25.00
❏ 5142	Let's Rock While the Rockin's Good/You're a Sweetheart	1958	6.25	12.50	25.00
❏ 5147	Tell It Like It Is/Don't Be Ashamed to Call My Name	1958	6.25	12.50	25.00
❏ 5154	All My Love Belongs to You/Why Don't You Haul Off and Love Me	1958	6.25	12.50	25.00
❏ 5170	No Regrets/I'll Carry Your Love Wherever I Go	1959	5.00	10.00	20.00
❏ 5179	Made for Me/Do More in Life	1959	5.00	10.00	20.00
❏ 5219	Leave My Kitten Alone/Let Nobody Love You	1959	5.00	10.00	20.00
❏ 5274	Let Them Talk/Right There	1959	5.00	10.00	20.00
❏ 5318	Loving Care/My Love Is	1960	5.00	10.00	20.00
❏ 5342	I'm Shakin'/Cottage for Sale	1960	5.00	10.00	20.00
❏ 5356	Heartbreak (It's Hurtin' Me)/Do You Love Me	1960	5.00	10.00	20.00
❏ 5394	Sleep/There's a Difference	1960	5.00	10.00	20.00

J

Number	Title (A Side/B Side)	Yr	VG	VG+	NM
❏ 5428	Walk Slow/You Hurt Me	1960	3.75	7.50	15.00
❏ 5428/30 [DJ]	Walk Slow/The Hoochi Coochi Coo	1960	6.25	12.50	25.00

—*White label; B-side by Hank Ballard and the Midnighters*

Number	Title (A Side/B Side)	Yr	VG	VG+	NM
❏ 5452	Leave My Kitten Alone/				
	I'll Never Go Back on My Word	1961	3.75	7.50	15.00
❏ 5458	I'm Sorry/The Very Thought of You	1961	3.75	7.50	15.00
❏ 5503	(I've Got) Spring Fever/Flamingo	1961	3.75	7.50	15.00
❏ 5516	Take My Love (I Want to Give It All to You)/				
	Now You Know	1961	3.75	7.50	15.00
❏ 5539	Need Your Love So Bad/Drive Me Home	1961	3.75	7.50	15.00
❏ 5577	There Is Someone in This World for Me/				
	Autumn Leaves	1961	3.75	7.50	15.00
❏ 5591	Fever/Bo-Da-Ley Dino-Ley	1962	3.75	7.50	15.00
❏ 5602	The Masquerade Is Over/Katanga	1962	3.75	7.50	15.00
❏ 5628	Until Again My Love/Mister Glenn	1962	3.75	7.50	15.00
❏ 5641	Every Beat of My Heart/I Wish I Could Cry	1962	3.75	7.50	15.00
❏ 5667	She Thinks I Still Care/Come Back to Me	1962	3.75	7.50	15.00
❏ 5681	Doll Face/Big Blue Diamonds	1962	3.75	7.50	15.00
❏ 5694	Without a Friend/Half a Love	1962	3.75	7.50	15.00
❏ 5717	Don't Play with Love/Heaven All Around Me	1963	3.00	6.00	12.00
❏ 5744	My Baby's in Love with Another Guy/				
	Come On Sugar	1963	3.00	6.00	12.00
❏ 5799	Let Them Talk/Talk to Me	1963	3.00	6.00	12.00
❏ 5818	So Lovely/Inside Information	1963	3.00	6.00	12.00
❏ 5823	Person to Person/I'm Shakin'	1963	3.00	6.00	12.00
❏ 5850	Bill Bailey/My Love Will Never Change	1964	3.00	6.00	12.00
❏ 5870	Rock Love/It Only Hurts for a Little While	1964	3.00	6.00	12.00
❏ 5886	All Around the World/All My Love Belongs to You	1964	3.00	6.00	12.00
❏ 5949	Do Something for Me/				
	Don't You Know I'm in Love	1964	3.00	6.00	12.00
❏ 6003	Talk to Me/Take My Love	1965	2.50	5.00	10.00
❏ 6170	Fever/Let Them Talk	1968	2.50	5.00	10.00
❏ 6302	All Around the World/Need Your Love So Bad	1970	2.00	4.00	8.00

7-Inch Extended Plays
KING

Number	Title (A Side/B Side)	Yr	VG	VG+	NM
❏ EP-423	*Talk to Me, Talk to Me/You're a Sweetheart/				
	Fever/Tell It Like It Is	1958	62.50	125.00	250.00
❏ EP-423 [PS]	Talk to Me	1958	62.50	125.00	250.00

Albums
BLUESWAY

Number	Title (A Side/B Side)	Yr	VG	VG+	NM
❏ BLS-6069	Free at Last	1973	6.25	12.50	25.00

KING

Number	Title (A Side/B Side)	Yr	VG	VG+	NM
❏ 564 [M]	Fever	1957	150.00	300.00	600.00

—*White cover with "Fever" in large colorful letters*

Number	Title (A Side/B Side)	Yr	VG	VG+	NM
❏ 395-564 [M]	Fever	1956	250.00	500.00	1000.

—*"Nurse with thermometer" cover*

Number	Title (A Side/B Side)	Yr	VG	VG+	NM
❏ 596 [M]	Talk to Me	1958	75.00	150.00	300.00
❏ 603 [M]	Mister Little Willie John	1958	62.50	125.00	250.00
❏ 691 [M]	Little Willie John In Action	1960	62.50	125.00	250.00
❏ 739 [M]	Sure Things	1961	37.50	75.00	150.00
❏ 767 [M]	The Sweet, the Hot, the Teenage Beat	1961	37.50	75.00	150.00
❏ 802 [M]	Come On and Join Little Willie John	1962	30.00	60.00	120.00
❏ 895 [M]	These Are My Favorite Songs	1964	25.00	50.00	100.00
❏ 949 [M]	Little Willie Sings All Originals	1966	25.00	50.00	100.00
❏ KS-949 [S]	Little Willie Sings All Originals	1966	37.50	75.00	150.00
❏ KS-1081	Free at Last	1970	10.00	20.00	40.00

JOHN, MABLE
45s
MOTOWN

Number	Title (A Side/B Side)	Yr	VG	VG+	NM
❏ 54031	Who Wouldn't Love a Man Like That/You Made				
	a Fool Out of Me	1960	125.00	250.00	500.00

—*Mispress with wrong label; may have been promo only*
STAX

Number	Title (A Side/B Side)	Yr	VG	VG+	NM
❏ 0016	Running Out/Shouldn't I Love Him	1968	5.00	10.00	20.00
❏ 192	Your Good Thing (Is About to End)/It's Catching	1966	5.00	10.00	20.00
❏ 205	If You Give Up What You Got/You're Taking Up				
	Another Man's Place	1967	5.00	10.00	20.00
❏ 215	Same Time, Same Place/Bigger and Better	1967	5.00	10.00	20.00
❏ 225	I'm a Big Girl Now/Wait You Dog	1967	5.00	10.00	20.00
❏ 234	Don't Hit Me No More/Left Over Love	1967	5.00	10.00	20.00
❏ 249	Don't Get Caught/Able Mable	1968	5.00	10.00	20.00

TAMLA

Number	Title (A Side/B Side)	Yr	VG	VG+	NM
❏ 54031	Who Wouldn't Love a Man Like That/				
	You Made a Fool Out of Me	1960	37.50	75.00	150.00
❏ 54040	No Love/Looking for a Love	1961	25.00	50.00	100.00

—*Version with no intro*

Number	Title (A Side/B Side)	Yr	VG	VG+	NM
❏ 54040	No Love/Looking for a Love	1961	30.00	60.00	120.00

—*Version with long intro*

Number	Title (A Side/B Side)	Yr	VG	VG+	NM
❏ 54050	Take Me/Action Speaks Louder Than Words	1962	20.00	40.00	80.00
❏ 54081	Who Wouldn't Love a Man Like That/Say You'll				
	Never Let Me Go	1963	30.00	60.00	120.00

JOHN, ROBERT
45s
A&M

Number	Title (A Side/B Side)	Yr	VG	VG+	NM
❏ 1210	When the Party Is Over/				
	Raindrops, Love and Sunshine	1970	—	2.50	5.00
❏ 1250	You Can't Hold On/				
	You're What's Been Missing from My Life	1971	—	2.50	5.00
❏ 1341	I'm Gonna Be Strong				
	/I Don't Want to Make You Love Me	1972	—	2.50	5.00

ARIOLA AMERICA

Number	Title (A Side/B Side)	Yr	VG	VG+	NM
❏ 7693	Poor Side of Town/Give a Little More	1978	—	2.00	4.00

ATLANTIC

Number	Title (A Side/B Side)	Yr	VG	VG+	NM
❏ 2846	The Lion Sleeps Tonight (Wimoweh)				
	(Mbube)/Janet	1971	—	3.00	6.00
❏ 2884	Hushabye/To Touch, To Feel	1972	—	2.50	5.00
❏ 2906	The Way You Do the Things You Do/To Touch,				
	To Feel	1972	—	2.50	5.00
❏ 2930	You and Me/You Don't Need a Gypsy	1973	—	2.50	5.00

BIG TOP

Number	Title (A Side/B Side)	Yr	VG	VG+	NM
❏ 3004	White Bucks and Saddle Shoes/Stranded	1958	12.50	25.00	50.00

—*As "Bobby Pedrick, Jr."*

Number	Title (A Side/B Side)	Yr	VG	VG+	NM
❏ 3008	Betty Blue Eyes/Pajama Party	1958	10.00	20.00	40.00

—*As "Bobby Pedrick, Jr."*

Number	Title (A Side/B Side)	Yr	VG	VG+	NM
❏ 3024	My Private Joy/Summer Nights	1959	10.00	20.00	40.00

—*As "Bobby Pedrick, Jr."*
COLUMBIA

Number	Title (A Side/B Side)	Yr	VG	VG+	NM
❏ 44435	If You Don't Want My Love/Don't Go	1968	2.00	4.00	8.00
❏ 44639	Don't Leave Me/Children	1968	2.00	4.00	8.00
❏ 44697	Can't Stop Loving You/Thirteen Times	1968	3.00	6.00	12.00
❏ 44706	Ooh Baby Baby/Children	1968	2.00	4.00	8.00
❏ 44950	Who Could Ever Believe It/				
	Children in the Making	1969	2.00	4.00	8.00

DUEL

Number	Title (A Side/B Side)	Yr	VG	VG+	NM
❏ 504	That Girl Is You/I'm Scared	1962	5.00	10.00	20.00

—*As "Bobby Pedrick, Jr."*

Number	Title (A Side/B Side)	Yr	VG	VG+	NM
❏ 516	Dining and Dancing/Two Ton Tessie	1962	5.00	10.00	20.00

—*As "Bobby Pedrick, Jr."*

Number	Title (A Side/B Side)	Yr	VG	VG+	NM
❏ 525	If I Had My Life to Live Over/If Mary Only Knew	1963	5.00	10.00	20.00

—*As "Bobby Pedrick, Jr."*
EMI AMERICA

Number	Title (A Side/B Side)	Yr	VG	VG+	NM
❏ 8013	Only Time/That's What Keeps Us Together	1979	—	2.00	4.00
❏ 8015	Sad Eyes/Am I Ever Gonna Hold You	1979	—	2.00	4.00
❏ 8023	Stay a Little Longer/Only Time	1979	—	2.00	4.00
❏ 8030	Lonely Eyes/Dance the Night Away	1979	—	2.00	4.00
❏ 8049	Hey There Lonely Girl/You Could Have Told Me	1980	—	2.00	4.00
❏ 8061	Sherry/On My Own	1980	—	2.00	4.00

MGM

Number	Title (A Side/B Side)	Yr	VG	VG+	NM
❏ 13384	Don't Try to Change My Ways/(I Have to) Teach				
	Myself How to Cry	1965	3.75	7.50	15.00

—*As "Bobby Pedrick"*
MOSAIC

Number	Title (A Side/B Side)	Yr	VG	VG+	NM
❏ 04445	Greased Lightning/(Instrumental)	1984	—	—	3.00

MOTOWN

Number	Title (A Side/B Side)	Yr	VG	VG+	NM
❏ 1664	Bread and Butter/If You Don't Want My Love	1983	—	—	3.00

SHELL

Number	Title (A Side/B Side)	Yr	VG	VG+	NM
❏ 722	School Crush/Come Out, Come Out	1960	5.00	10.00	20.00

—*As "Bobby Pedrick"*
VERVE

Number	Title (A Side/B Side)	Yr	VG	VG+	NM
❏ 10402	Maybe/Karine	1966	12.50	25.00	50.00

—*As "Bobby Pedrick"*
Albums
COLUMBIA

Number	Title (A Side/B Side)	Yr	VG	VG+	NM
❏ CS 9687	If You Don't Want My Love	1968	5.00	10.00	20.00

EMI AMERICA

Number	Title (A Side/B Side)	Yr	VG	VG+	NM
❏ SW-17007	Robert John	1979	2.50	5.00	10.00
❏ SW-17027	Back on the Street	1980	2.50	5.00	10.00

HARMONY

Number	Title (A Side/B Side)	Yr	VG	VG+	NM
❏ KH 31353	On the Way Up	1972	3.00	6.00	12.00

JOHN AND ERNEST Also see DICKIE GOODMAN.
45s
RAINY WEDNESDAY

Number	Title (A Side/B Side)	Yr	VG	VG+	NM
❏ 201	Super Fly Meets Shaft/Part Two	1973	—	2.50	5.00
❏ 201	Super Fly Meets Shaft/Problems	1973	—	2.50	5.00
❏ 203	Soul President Number One/Crossover	1973	—	2.50	5.00

JOHN'S CHILDREN
45s
WHITE WHALE

Number	Title (A Side/B Side)	Yr	VG	VG+	NM
❏ 239	Strange Affair/Smashed, Blocked	1966	5.00	10.00	20.00

Albums
WHITE WHALE

Number	Title (A Side/B Side)	Yr	VG	VG+	NM
❏ WWS 7128	Orgasm	1970	50.00	100.00	200.00

JOHNNIE AND JOE
45s
ABC-PARAMOUNT

Number	Title (A Side/B Side)	Yr	VG	VG+	NM
❏ 10079	I Adore You/I Want You Here Beside Me	1960	3.75	7.50	15.00
❏ 10117	Your Love/Why Do You Hurt Me So	1960	3.75	7.50	15.00

AMBIENT SOUND

Number	Title (A Side/B Side)	Yr	VG	VG+	NM
❏ 03410	Kingdom of Love/Tossin' Turnin' (Yearnin'				
	Burnin' For Your Love)	1982	—	2.50	5.00

CHESS

Number	Title (A Side/B Side)	Yr	VG	VG+	NM
❏ 1641	I'll Be Spinning/Feel Alright	1956	5.00	10.00	20.00
❏ 1654	Over the Mountain; Across the Sea/				
	My Baby's Gone, On, On	1957	6.25	12.50	25.00

—*Originals with blue and silver "chess pieces" label*

Number	Title (A Side/B Side)	Yr	VG	VG+	NM
❏ 1654	Over the Mountain; Across the Sea/				
	My Baby's Gone, On, On	1958	3.00	6.00	12.00

—*Reissues on blue labels with vertical "CHESS"*

Number	Title (A Side/B Side)	Yr	VG	VG+	NM
❏ 1654	Over the Mountain; Across the Sea/				
	My Baby's Gone, On, On	1963	2.50	5.00	10.00

—*Reissues on other labels (multicolor, black)*

Number	Title (A Side/B Side)	Yr	VG	VG+	NM
❏ 1677	I Was So Lonely/If You Tell Me You're Mine	1957	5.00	10.00	20.00
❏ 1693	Why Oh Why/Why Did She Go	1958	5.00	10.00	20.00
❏ 1706	My Baby's Gone/Darling	1958	5.00	10.00	20.00
❏ 1769	Across the Sea/You Said It, And Don't Forget It	1960	3.75	7.50	15.00

GONE

Number	Title (A Side/B Side)	Yr	VG	VG+	NM
❏ 5024	Who Do You Love/Trust in Me	1958	7.50	15.00	30.00

J&S

Number	Title (A Side/B Side)	Yr	VG	VG+	NM
❏ 1008	Over the Mountain (Part 2)/				
	Won't You Come Back to Me	1959	6.25	12.50	25.00
❏ 1603	I Was So Lonely/If You Tell Me You're Mine	1957	6.25	12.50	25.00
❏ 1605/6	Who Do You Love/Trust in Me	1958	6.25	12.50	25.00
❏ 1630/1	Warm, Soft and Lovely/				
	False Love Has Got to Go	1958	6.25	12.50	25.00
❏ 1654	Over the Mountain; Across the Sea/				
	My Baby's Gone, On, On	1957	37.50	75.00	150.00

—*With horizontal lines on label*

Number	Title (A Side/B Side)	Yr	VG	VG+	NM
❏ 1654	Over the Mountain; Across the Sea/				
	My Baby's Gone, On, On	1962	5.00	10.00	20.00

—*Without horizontal lines on label*

Number	Title (A Side/B Side)	Yr	VG	VG+	NM
❏ 1659	It Was There/There Goes My Heart	1957	6.25	12.50	25.00
❏ 1701	Where Did She Go/Red Sails in the Sunset	1959	6.25	12.50	25.00
❏ 4420	The Devil Said No, Gone With You Bad Self/You				
	Can Always Count on Me	196?	3.75	7.50	15.00
❏ 8719	Tell Me/Sincere Love	196?	3.75	7.50	15.00
❏ 42832	You're the Loveliest Song/				
	Let Your Mind Do the Walking	196?	3.75	7.50	15.00

Number	Title (A Side/B Side)	Yr	VG	VG+	NM
❏ 87187	False Love Has Got to Go/Jamaica — Our Thing	196?	3.75	7.50	15.00
LANA					
❏ 121	Over the Mountain; Across the Sea/				
	Shortening Bread	196?	2.50	5.00	10.00
TUFF					
❏ 379	Here We Go Baby/That's the Way You Go	1964	3.00	6.00	12.00
Albums					
AMBIENT SOUND					
❏ FZ 38345	Kingdom of Love	1982	3.00	6.00	12.00

JOHNNY AND JACKEY Also see JACKEY BEAVERS; JOHNNY BRISTOL.
45s

Number	Title (A Side/B Side)	Yr	VG	VG+	NM
ANNA					
❏ 1108	Let's Go to a Movie Baby/Lonely and Blue	1960	6.25	12.50	25.00
❏ 1120	Hoy Boy/No One Else But You	1960	6.25	12.50	25.00
TRI-PHI					
❏ 1002	Carry Your Own Load/So Disappointing	1961	6.25	12.50	25.00
❏ 1005	Someday We'll Be Together/She Don't Play	1961	7.50	15.00	30.00
❏ 1016	Do You See My Love for You Growing/				
	Carry Your Own Load	1962	6.25	12.50	25.00
❏ 1019	Baby Don'tcha Worry/Stop What You're Saying	1963	6.25	12.50	25.00

JOHNNY AND JON
45s

Number	Title (A Side/B Side)	Yr	VG	VG+	NM
JEWEL					
❏ 776	Christmas in Viet Nam/				
	Why Did You Leave Me Crawl	1966	7.50	15.00	30.00

JOHNNY AND THE BLUE BEATS
Albums

Number	Title (A Side/B Side)	Yr	VG	VG+	NM
WINSOR					
❏ 1001	Smile	196?	10.00	20.00	40.00

JOHNNY AND THE DREAMS
45s

Number	Title (A Side/B Side)	Yr	VG	VG+	NM
RICHIE					
❏ 457	You're Too Young/Are You for Me	1961	62.50	125.00	250.00
—Black vinyl					
❏ 457	You're Too Young/Are You for Me	1961	125.00	250.00	500.00
—Red vinyl					

JOHNNY AND THE HURRICANES
45s

Number	Title (A Side/B Side)	Yr	VG	VG+	NM
ATILA					
❏ 211	Saga of the Beatles/Rene	1967	2.50	5.00	10.00
❏ 214	Judy's Moody/I Love You	1967	2.50	5.00	10.00
❏ 215	Because I Love You/Wisdom's 5th Take	1967	2.50	5.00	10.00
❏ 216	Red River Rock '67/The Psychedlic Woman	1967	2.50	5.00	10.00
BIG TOP					
❏ 3036	Down Yonder/Sheba	1960	5.00	10.00	20.00
❏ 3036 [PS]	Down Yonder/Sheba	1960	10.00	20.00	40.00
❏ 3051	Revival/Rocking Goose	1960	5.00	10.00	20.00
❏ 3051 [PS]	Revival/Rocking Goose	1960	10.00	20.00	40.00
❏ 3056	You Are My Sunshine/Molly-O	1960	5.00	10.00	20.00
❏ 3056 [PS]	You Are My Sunshine/Molly-O	1960	10.00	20.00	40.00
❏ 3063	Ja-Da/Mr. Lonely	1961	5.00	10.00	20.00
❏ 3063 [PS]	Ja-Da/Mr. Lonely	1961	10.00	20.00	40.00
❏ 3076	Old Smokie/High Voltage	1961	5.00	10.00	20.00
❏ 3076 [PS]	Old Smokie/High Voltage	1961	10.00	20.00	40.00
❏ 3090	Traffic Jam/Farewell, Farewell	1961	5.00	10.00	20.00
❏ 3103	Misirlou/Salvation	1962	5.00	10.00	20.00
❏ 3113	San Antonio Rose/Come On Train	1962	5.00	10.00	20.00
❏ 3125	Shiek of Araby/Minnesota Fats	1962	5.00	10.00	20.00
❏ 3132	Whatever Happened to Baby Jane/				
	Greens and Beans	1963	5.00	10.00	20.00
❏ 3146	James Bond Theme/Hungry Eye	1963	5.00	10.00	20.00
❏ 3159	Rough Road/Kaw-Liga	1963	5.00	10.00	20.00
JEFF					
❏ 211	Saga of the Beatles/Rene	1964	3.75	7.50	15.00
LOST-NITE					
❏ 221	Reveille Rock/Sheba	196?	—	2.50	5.00
—Reissue					
MALA					
❏ 470	It's a Mad, Mad, Mad, Mad World/Shadows	1963	2.50	5.00	10.00
❏ 483	That's All/Honey, Honey	1964	2.50	5.00	10.00
TWIRL					
❏ 1001	Crossfire/Lazy	1958	12.50	25.00	50.00
WARWICK					
❏ 502	Crossfire/Lazy	1959	6.25	12.50	25.00
❏ 509 [M]	Red River Rock/Buckeye	1959	6.25	12.50	25.00
❏ 509 ST [S]	Red River Rock/Buckeye	1959	12.50	25.00	50.00
❏ 513 [M]	Reveille Rock/Time Bomb	1959	6.25	12.50	25.00
❏ 513 ST [S]	Reveille Rock/Time Bomb	1959	12.50	25.00	50.00
❏ 520	Beatnik Fly/Sand Storm	1960	5.00	10.00	20.00
❏ 520 [PS]	Beatnik Fly/Sand Storm	1960	15.00	30.00	60.00
7-Inch Extended Plays					
WARWICK					
❏ EX-700	Red River Rock/Storm Warning//Joy Ride/Bam				
	Boo	1959	20.00	40.00	80.00
❏ EX-700 [PS]	Johnny and the Hurricanes	1959	30.00	60.00	120.00
—Came with paper sleeve rather than cardboard sleeve					
Albums					
ATILA					
❏ 1030 [M]	Live at the Star-Club	1964	75.00	150.00	300.00
BIG TOP					
❏ 12-1302 [M]	The Big Sound of Johnny and the Hurricanes	1960	62.50	125.00	250.00
❏ ST 12-1302 [S]	The Big Sound of Johnny and the Hurricanes	1960	75.00	150.00	300.00
WARWICK					
❏ W-2007 [M]	Johnny and the Hurricanes	1959	37.50	75.00	150.00
❏ W-2007ST [S]	Johnny and the Hurricanes	1959	75.00	150.00	300.00
❏ W-2010 [M]	Stormsville	1960	37.50	75.00	150.00
❏ W-2010ST [S]	Stormsville	1960	62.50	125.00	250.00

JOHNNY AND THE JAMMERS "Johnny" is JOHNNY WINTER. His debut single.
45s

Number	Title (A Side/B Side)	Yr	VG	VG+	NM
DART					
❏ 131	School Day Blues/You Know I Love You	1959	75.00	150.00	300.00

JOHNNY AND THE TOKENS Also see THE TOKENS.
45s

Number	Title (A Side/B Side)	Yr	VG	VG+	NM
WARWICK					
❏ 658	The Taste of a Tear/Never Till Now	1961	5.00	10.00	20.00

JOHNS, LUCILLE
45s

Number	Title (A Side/B Side)	Yr	VG	VG+	NM
HIT					
❏ 39	Release Me/Desafinado	1962	2.00	4.00	8.00
—B-side by the Boots Purcell Combo					

JOHNS, SAMMY
45s

Number	Title (A Side/B Side)	Yr	VG	VG+	NM
ELEKTRA					
❏ 47189	Common Man/Easy to Be with You	1981	—	2.00	4.00
❏ 47248	Love Me Off the Road/This Time	1981	—	2.00	4.00
GRC					
❏ 1001	Shake a Hand/(B-side unknown)	1973	—	2.00	4.00
❏ 1007	America/(B-side unknown)	1973	—	2.00	4.00
❏ 2021	Early Morning Love/Holy Mother, Aging Father	1974	—	2.00	4.00
❏ 2046	Chevy Van/Hang My Head and Moan	1975	—	2.50	5.00
❏ 2062	Rag Doll/Friends of Mine	1975	—	2.00	4.00
MCA					
❏ 53398	Chevy Van/Love Me Off the Road	1988	—	—	3.00
REAL WORLD					
❏ 7307	Falling Over You/Six Feet Tall and Handsome	1980	—	2.00	4.00
SOUTHERN TRACKS					
❏ 1010	There! I've Said It Again/				
	All Wrapped Up in Your Love	1982	—	2.50	5.00
❏ 1031	I'd Rather Be Hurt by You/				
	All Wrapped Up in Your Love	1984	—	2.50	5.00
❏ 1036	Desperado Love/All Wrapped Up in Your Love	1985	—	2.50	5.00
❏ 1046	You Just Made Me Up in Your Mind/				
	Lifetime Thing	1985	—	2.50	5.00
❏ 1075	Rock You Like a Baby/Tennessee Valley Girl	1987	—	2.50	5.00
❏ 1086	Early Morning Love/(B-side unknown)	1988	—	2.50	5.00
❏ 1096	Sam's Song/Tennessee Valley Girl	1988	—	2.50	5.00
WARNER BROS.					
❏ 8224	Peas in a Pod/Friends of Mine	1976	—	2.00	4.00
❏ 8270	America/Bless Our Soul	1976	—	2.00	4.00
❏ 8335	Hey Mr. Dreamer/Female Chauvinist Sow	1977	—	2.00	4.00
❏ 8441	Chevy Van/Music of the Band	1977	—	2.00	4.00
Albums					
GRC					
❏ 5003	Sammy Johns	1975	3.00	6.00	12.00

JOHNSON, BETTY
45s

Number	Title (A Side/B Side)	Yr	VG	VG+	NM
ATLANTIC					
❏ 1169	The Little Blue Man/Winter in Miami	1958	3.75	7.50	15.00
❏ 1186	Dream/How Much	1958	3.00	6.00	12.00
❏ 2002	Hoopa Hoola/One More Time	1958	3.00	6.00	12.00
❏ 2009	You Can't Get to Heaven on Roller Skates/I Want				
	a Good Home for My Cat	1958	3.00	6.00	12.00
❏ 2019	Does Your Heart Beat for Me?/You and Only You	1959	3.00	6.00	12.00
❏ 2039	The Lonely Willow Tree/Waltz Me Around	1959	3.00	6.00	12.00
❏ 2056	Fantastic/You Don't Care a Rowboat	1960	3.00	6.00	12.00
BALLY					
❏ 1000	I'll Wait/Please Tell Me Why	1956	3.00	6.00	12.00
❏ 1005	Honky Tonk Rock/Say It Ain't So, Joe	1956	3.75	7.50	15.00
❏ 1013	Clay Idol/Why Do You Cry?	1956	3.00	6.00	12.00
❏ 1020	I Dreamed/If It's Wrong to Love You	1956	3.00	6.00	12.00
❏ 1033	Little White Lies/1492	1957	3.00	6.00	12.00
❏ 1041	The Song You Heard When You Fell in Love/I'm				
	Beginning to Wonder	1957	3.00	6.00	12.00
BELL					
❏ 1074	Make Yourself Comfortable/All of You	1955	3.75	7.50	15.00
—May or may not be the same Betty Johnson as the others					
COED					
❏ 532	There's a Star Spangled Banner Waving				
	Somewhere/Take a Little Look				
	(In the Good Book)	1960	2.50	5.00	10.00
DOT					
❏ 16127	Slipping Around/				
	One Has My Name, The Other Has My Heart	1960	2.50	5.00	10.00
NEW-DISC					
❏ 10013	I Want Eddie Fisher For Christmas/Show Me	1954	6.25	12.50	25.00
RCA VICTOR					
❏ 47-6034	Seven Pretty Dreams/Be a Lover	1955	3.00	6.00	12.00
❏ 47-6158	That's Happiness/				
	Give Me Something I Can Dream About	1955	3.00	6.00	12.00
❏ 47-6268	I'm a Sinner/Beginner's Luck	1955	3.00	6.00	12.00
❏ 47-8143	Betty's Bossa Nova/Ginny's Got a Phone	1963	2.00	4.00	8.00
REPUBLIC					
❏ 2011	Depend on Me/				
	I Don't Want to Go to Sleep Tonight	1961	2.50	5.00	10.00
❏ 2017	Let Me Be the One/Only When I Dream	1961	2.50	5.00	10.00
❏ 2021	My Kind of Guy/				
	A Gal's Best Friend Is Her Makeup	1961	2.50	5.00	10.00
❏ 2025	How Do You Tell Your Heart/Why, Why	1961	2.50	5.00	10.00
❏ 2026	I Dreamed/Luna Caprese	1962	2.50	5.00	10.00
WORLD ARTISTS					
❏ 1014	Wednesday's Child/What's the Matter	1963	2.00	4.00	8.00
Albums					
ATLANTIC					
❏ 8017 [M]	Betty Johnson	1958	12.50	25.00	50.00
❏ 8027 [M]	The Song You Heard When You Fell in Love	1959	12.50	25.00	50.00
—Black label					
❏ 8027 [M]	The Song You Heard When You Fell in Love	1960	5.00	10.00	20.00
—White "fan" logo on right					

J

Number	Title (A Side/B Side)	Yr	VG	VG+	NM
❏ SD 8027 [S]	The Song You Heard When You Fell in Love	1959	20.00	40.00	80.00
—Green label					
❏ SD 8027 [S]	The Song You Heard When You Fell in Love	1960	6.25	12.50	25.00
—White "fan" logo on right					

JOHNSON, BILL
45s
SUN

❏ 340	Bobaloo/Bad Times Ahead	1960	5.00	10.00	20.00

JOHNSON, BLIND WILLIE
Albums
FOLKWAYS

❏ FG-3585 [M]	Blind Willie Johnson: His Story	1957	25.00	50.00	100.00
RBF					
❏ 10 [M]	Blind Willie Johnson 1927-1930	1965	17.50	35.00	70.00

JOHNSON, BUBBER
45s
KING

❏ 4793	Drop Me a Line/Ding Dang Doo	1955	5.00	10.00	20.00
❏ 4822	Come Home/There'll Be No One	1955	5.00	10.00	20.00
❏ 4855	It's Christmas Time/Let's Make Everyday a Christmas Day	1955	5.00	10.00	20.00
❏ 4872	Wonderful Things Happen/Keep a Light in the Window	1956	5.00	10.00	20.00
❏ 4924	My One Desire/I Lost Track of Everything	1956	5.00	10.00	20.00
❏ 4939	My Lonely Heart/Have a Little Faith in Me	1956	5.00	10.00	20.00
❏ 4988	Confidential/Let's Take a Walk	1956	5.00	10.00	20.00
❏ 5014	Butterfly/Too Many Hearts	1957	5.00	10.00	20.00
❏ 5034	Little Girls Don't Cry/The Search	1957	5.00	10.00	20.00
❏ 5068	Crazy Afternoon/So Much Tonight	1957	5.00	10.00	20.00
❏ 5089	Muddy Water/The Whisperers	1957	5.00	10.00	20.00
❏ 5117	Dedicated to the One I Love/Prince of Players	1958	3.75	7.50	15.00
❏ 5132	Finger Tips/I'm Confessin'	1958	3.75	7.50	15.00
❏ 5143	I Surrender Dear/Everybody's With You When You're Winning	1958	3.75	7.50	15.00
❏ 5148	I Can't See Why/As Long As I Live	1958	3.75	7.50	15.00
❏ 5174	One Good Reason/Time Was	1959	3.75	7.50	15.00
❏ 5193	House of Love/Until Sunrise	1959	3.75	7.50	15.00
❏ 5232	I Do (Love You)/Come On	1959	3.75	7.50	15.00
❏ 5267	Tell Me Who/I Know My Way	1959	3.75	7.50	15.00
❏ 5298	Those Who Dream/Atlanta	1959	3.75	7.50	15.00
MERCURY					
❏ 8285	I've Got an Invitation/Forget It If You Can	1952	15.00	30.00	60.00
Albums					
KING					
❏ 569 [M]	Come Home	1957	50.00	100.00	200.00
❏ 624 [M]	Bubber Johnson Sings Sweet Love Songs	1959	37.50	75.00	150.00

JOHNSON, BUDDY
45s
ATLANTIC

❏ 1013	Don't Take Your Love from Me/Off Shore	1953	6.25	12.50	25.00
DECCA					
❏ 28907	Talkin' About Another Man's Wife/Jeannette	1953	6.25	12.50	25.00
❏ 29058	A Handful of Stars/Two Cigarettes in the Dark	1954	6.25	12.50	25.00
MERCURY					
❏ 70173	Jit Jit/That's What I Feel About You	1953	5.00	10.00	20.00
❏ 70488	I Never Had It So Good/There's No One Like You	1954	3.75	7.50	15.00
❏ 70656	Send Out for a Bottle of Beer/Bitter Sweet	1955	3.75	7.50	15.00
❏ 70695	It's Obdacious/Save Your Love for Me	1955	3.75	7.50	15.00
❏ 71017	Why Don't Cha Stop It/Kool Kitty	1956	3.00	6.00	12.00
❏ 71159	I've Surrendered/Slide's Mambo	1957	3.00	6.00	12.00
❏ 71262	Minglin/I Wonder Where Our Love Has Gone	1958	3.00	6.00	12.00
❏ 71799	The Last Laugh's on You (Ha, Ha, Baby)/Good Time Man	1961	2.50	5.00	10.00
WING					
❏ 90064	Doot Doot Dow/I Don't Want Nobody	1956	3.75	7.50	15.00
❏ 90074	Buddy's Boogie/I'll Dearly Love You	1956	3.75	7.50	15.00
❏ 90084	Goodbye Baby/I Still Love You	1956	3.75	7.50	15.00
Albums					
MCA					
❏ 1356	Fine Brown Frame	198?	2.50	5.00	10.00
MERCURY					
❏ MG-20209 [M]	Rock 'N' Roll	195?	20.00	40.00	80.00
❏ MG-20322 [M]	Walkin'	195?	20.00	40.00	80.00
❏ MG-20330 [M]	Buddy Johnson Wails	195?	20.00	40.00	80.00
❏ MG-20347 [M]	Swing Me	195?	20.00	40.00	80.00
❏ SR-60072 [S]	Buddy Johnson Wails	195?	25.00	50.00	100.00
WING					
❏ MGW-12005 [M]	Rock 'N' Roll	1956	37.50	75.00	150.00
❏ MGW-12111 [M]	Rock 'n' Roll Stage Show	1963	10.00	20.00	40.00
❏ MGW-12234 [M]	Buddy Johnson Wails	196?	7.50	15.00	30.00

JOHNSON, BUDDY & ELLA Also see BUDDY JOHNSON.
45s
MERCURY

❏ 70251	I'm Just Your Fool/A-12	1953	5.00	10.00	20.00
❏ 70321	One More Time/Mush Mouth	1954	5.00	10.00	20.00
❏ 70377	Ain't Cha Got Me/Let's Start All Over Again	1954	5.00	10.00	20.00
❏ 70421	Any Day Now/A Pretty Girl, a Cadillac and Money	1954	5.00	10.00	20.00
❏ 70459	We'll Do It/It Used to Hurt Me	1954	5.00	10.00	20.00
❏ 70523	Crazy 'Bout a Saxophone/Gotta Go Upside Your Head	1955	3.75	7.50	15.00
❏ 70775	Doot Doot Dow/I Don't Want Nobody	1956	3.00	6.00	12.00
❏ 70912	Bring It Home to Me/You Got It Made	1956	3.00	6.00	12.00
❏ 71723	I Don't Want Nobody (To Have My Love But You)/I'm Just Your Fool	1960	2.50	5.00	10.00
ROULETTE					
❏ 4134	Tune No. 1/Don't Fail Me Baby	1959	3.00	6.00	12.00
❏ 4188	Keep My Love for You/A Woman, a Lover, a Friend	1959	3.00	6.00	12.00

Albums
MERCURY

❏ MG-20347 [M]	Swing Me	195?	20.00	40.00	80.00
ROULETTE					
❏ R 25085 [M]	Go Ahead and Rock and Roll	1959	20.00	40.00	80.00
❏ SR 25085 [S]	Go Ahead and Rock and Roll	1959	30.00	60.00	120.00

JOHNSON, CLIFF
45s
COLUMBIA

❏ 40865	Go 'Way Hound Dog/Twenty Four Hours a Day	1957	20.00	40.00	80.00

JOHNSON, ERNIE Also see EDDIE AND ERNIE.
45s
ARTCO

❏ 45-104	I Can't Stand the Pain/These Very Tender Moments	1967	375.00	750.00	1500.
ASNES					
❏ 104	Tell Her For Me/You Need Love	1961	6.25	12.50	25.00
ROLO					
❏ 8800	You're Unforgettable (same on both sides)	198?	—	2.50	5.00
RONN					
❏ 102	Mouth to Mouth Resuscitation/You're Gonna Miss Me	1984	—	3.00	6.00
❏ 104	You're About to Succeed/Give Me a Little Bit of Your Lovin'	1984	2.50	5.00	10.00
❏ 109	Cold Woman/Party All Night	1984	2.50	5.00	10.00
❏ 113	Forever/Just in Time	198?	3.75	7.50	15.00
❏ 115	It's Party Time/Final Notice	198?	2.50	5.00	10.00
❏ 117	Dreams to Remember/Hard Times	198?	5.00	10.00	20.00
❏ 121	Honey I Love You/I'm Doing Alright	198?	—	3.00	6.00
❏ 124	I'm Doin' Alright/That Thang	198?	—	3.00	6.00
❏ 126	In My Dreams/Forever	198?	—	3.00	6.00
STEPH & LEE					
❏ 8667	Big Man Cry/Drowning in Misery	197?	15.00	30.00	60.00
WALDOXY					
❏ 109	Cold This Winter/I'm in the Mood for the Blues	1995	2.50	5.00	10.00
Albums					
RONN					
❏ LPS-8001	Just in Time	1985	3.75	7.50	15.00

JOHNSON, HOYT
45s
ERWIN

❏ 555	Eeny Meany Minie Mo/(B-side unknown)	1957	50.00	100.00	200.00
RCA VICTOR					
❏ 47-7522	Sylvia/Bella Renee	1959	10.00	20.00	40.00
❏ 47-7607	Little Boy Blue/My Special Girl	1959	37.50	75.00	150.00
❏ 47-7731	Too Shy/Eca-La	1960	10.00	20.00	40.00
SATELLITE					
❏ 110	Cindy/I Just Can't Learn	1961	6.25	12.50	25.00

JOHNSON, JIMMY
45s
ALLIGATOR

❏ 792	Serves Me Right to Suffer/Your Turn to Cry	1979	—	2.00	4.00
CLASS					
❏ 237	Cool, Cool School/Lone Ranger Gonna Get Married	1958	15.00	30.00	60.00
MID WEST					
❏ 1002	Mean Woman Blues/(B-side unknown)	195?	62.50	125.00	250.00
RENDEZVOUS					
❏ 145	Cool, Cool School/Lone Ranger Gonna Get Married	1961	6.25	12.50	25.00
VIV					
❏ 3001	How About Me? Pretty Baby/Cat Daddy	1956	50.00	100.00	200.00

JOHNSON, JOHNNY, AND THE BANDWAGON See THE BANDWAGON.

JOHNSON, LEN
45s
RAY-CO

❏ 503	Sweet Thing/One Day	1963	3.75	7.50	15.00

JOHNSON, LONNIE
45s
BLUESVILLE

❏ 806	Don't Ever Love/You Don't Move Me	196?	3.00	6.00	12.00
❏ 812	I'll Get Along Somehow/Memories of You	196?	3.00	6.00	12.00
FEDERAL					
❏ 12376	Friendless Blues/What a Real Woman	1960	3.75	7.50	15.00
KING					
❏ 4201	Tomorrow Night/What a Woman	1951	15.00	30.00	60.00
—78 released in 1948					
❏ 4459	Take Me I'm Yours/Why Should I Cry	1951	10.00	20.00	40.00
❏ 4473	It Was All in Vain/You Only Want Me When You're Lonely	1951	10.00	20.00	40.00
❏ 4492	Happy New Year, Darling/Christmas Blues	1951	12.50	25.00	50.00
—B-side by Gatemouth Moore					
❏ 4503	Seven Long Days/Darlin'	1951	10.00	20.00	40.00
❏ 4510	My Mother's Eyes/My Crazy Self	1951	10.00	20.00	40.00
❏ 4553	I'm Guilty/Can't Sleep Anymore	1952	10.00	20.00	40.00
❏ 4572	You Can't Buy Love/Just Another Day	1952	10.00	20.00	40.00
❏ 4758	Tomorrow Night/Pleasing You	1954	10.00	20.00	40.00
❏ 5293	Tomorrow Night/Pleasing You	1959	3.75	7.50	15.00
❏ 5907	Love Me Tonight/Brenda	1964	2.50	5.00	10.00
❏ 6303	Tomorrow Night/Blues Stay Away from Me	1970	—	3.00	6.00
PRESTIGE					
❏ 310	Mr. Jelly Roll Baker/I'll Get Along Somehow	1964	2.50	5.00	10.00
RAMA					
❏ 9	My Woman Is Gone/Don't Make Me Cry Baby	1953	15.00	30.00	60.00
—Black vinyl					
❏ 9	My Woman Is Gone/Don't Make Me Cry Baby	1953	37.50	75.00	150.00
—Red vinyl					
❏ 14	Stick With It Baby/Will You Remember	1953	15.00	30.00	60.00
❏ 19	It's Been So Long/Vaya Con Dios	1953	15.00	30.00	60.00
❏ 20	This Love of Mine/I Love a Dream	1953	15.00	30.00	60.00

Number	Title (A Side/B Side)	Yr	VG	VG+	NM

Albums

BLUESVILLE

Number	Title (A Side/B Side)	Yr	VG	VG+	NM
❏ BVLP-1007 [M] Blues by Lonnie		1960	50.00	100.00	200.00
—Blue label, silver print					
❏ BVLP-1007 [M] Blues by Lonnie		1964	15.00	30.00	60.00
—Blue label with trident logo at right					
❏ BVLP-1011 [M] Blues and Ballads		1960	50.00	100.00	200.00
—Blue label, silver print					
❏ BVLP-1011 [M] Blues and Ballads		1964	15.00	30.00	60.00
—Blue label with trident logo at right					
❏ BVLP-1024 [M] Losing Game		1961	50.00	100.00	200.00
—Blue label, silver print					
❏ BVLP-1024 [M] Losing Game		1964	15.00	30.00	60.00
—Blue label with trident logo at right					
❏ BVLP-1062 [M] Another Night to Cry		1963	50.00	100.00	200.
—Blue label, silver print					
❏ BVLP-1062 [M] Another Night to Cry		1964	15.00	30.00	60.00
—Blue label with trident logo at right					

COLUMBIA

Number	Title	Yr	VG	VG+	NM
❏ C 46221	Steppin' On the Blues	1990	5.00	10.00	20.00

FANTASY

| ❏ OBC-502 | Blues by Lonnie | 198? | 3.00 | 6.00 | 12.00 |
| ❏ OBC-531 | Blues and Ballads | 1990 | 3.00 | 6.00 | 12.00 |

KING

❏ 520 [M]	Lonesome Road	1958	750.00	1375.	2000.
❏ 958 [M]	Lonnie Johnson 24 Twelve-Bar Blues	1966	15.00	30.00	60.00
❏ KS-958 [R]	Lonnie Johnson 24 Twelve-Bar Blues	1966	15.00	30.00	60.00
❏ KS-1083	Tomorrow Night	1970	6.25	12.50	25.00

PRESTIGE

| ❏ PRST-7724 | The Blues of Lonnie Johnson | 1970 | 5.00 | 10.00 | 20.00 |

JOHNSON, LONNIE, AND VICTORIA SPIVEY

Albums

BLUESVILLE

❏ BVLP-1044 [M] Idle Hours		1962	37.50	75.00	150.00
—Blue label, silver print					
❏ BVLP-1044 [M] Idle Hours		1964	12.50	25.00	50.00
—Blue label with trident logo at right					
❏ BVLP-1054 [M] Woman Blues		1962	37.50	75.00	150.00
—Blue label, silver print					
❏ BVLP-1054 [M] Woman Blues		1964	12.50	25.00	50.00
—Blue label with trident logo at right					

FANTASY

| ❏ OBC-518 | Idle Hours | 198? | 3.00 | 6.00 | 12.00 |

JOHNSON, MARV

45s

GORDY

Number	Title (A Side/B Side)	Yr	VG	VG+	NM
❏ 7042	Why Do You Want to Let Me Go/I'm Not a Plaything	1965	3.75	7.50	15.00
❏ 7051	Just the Way You Are/Miss You Baby	1966	3.75	7.50	15.00
❏ 7077	I'll Pick a Rose for My Rose/You Got the Love I Love	1968	3.75	7.50	15.00

KUDO

| ❏ 663 | My Baby-O/Once Upon a Time | 1958 | 150.00 | 300.00 | 600.00 |

TAMLA

❏ 101	Come to Me/Whisper	1959	62.50	125.00	250.00
—With Gladstone St., Detroit, address on label					
❏ 101	Come to Me/Whisper	1959	75.00	150.00	300.00
—No address on label					

UNITED ARTISTS

❏ 0030	You've Got What It Takes/I Love the Way You Love	1973	—	2.50	5.00
—"Silver Spotlight Series" reissue					
❏ 0031	Move Two Mountains/Come to Me	1973	—	2.50	5.00
—"Silver Spotlight Series" reissue					
❏ 160	Come to Me/Whisper	1959	6.25	12.50	25.00
❏ 175	River of Tears/I'm Coming Home	1959	5.00	10.00	20.00
❏ 185	You Got What It Takes/Don't Leave Me	1959	5.00	10.00	20.00
❏ 208	I Love the Way You Love/Let Me Love You	1960	5.00	10.00	20.00
❏ 226	Ain't Gonna Be That Way/All the Love I've Got	1960	5.00	10.00	20.00
❏ 241	(You've Got to) Move Two Mountains/I Need You	1960	3.75	7.50	15.00
❏ 273	Happy Days/Baby, Baby	1960	3.75	7.50	15.00
❏ 294	Merry-Go-Round/Tell Me That You Love Me	1961	3.75	7.50	15.00
❏ 322	How Can We Tell Him/I've Got a Notion	1961	5.00	10.00	20.00
❏ 359	Show Me/Oh Mary	1961	5.00	10.00	20.00
❏ 386	Easier Said Than Done/Johnny One Stop	1961	5.00	10.00	20.00
❏ 423	Magic Mirror/With All That's In Me	1962	5.00	10.00	20.00
❏ 454	He Gave Me You/That's How Bad	1962	5.00	10.00	20.00
❏ 483	Let Yourself Go/That's Where I Lost My Baby	1962	5.00	10.00	20.00
❏ 556	Keep Tellin' Yourself/Everyone Who's Been in Love with You	1963	5.00	10.00	20.00
❏ 590	He's Got the Whole World In His Hands/Another Tear Falls	1963	5.00	10.00	20.00
❏ 617	Come On and Stop/Not Available	1963	5.00	10.00	20.00
❏ 643	Congratulations, You've Hurt Me Again/Crying on My Pillow	1963	5.00	10.00	20.00
❏ 691	Unbreakable Love/A Man Who Don't Believe in Love	1964	6.25	12.50	25.00

7-Inch Extended Plays

UNITED ARTISTS

❏ 10,007	I Love the Way You Love/Let Me Love You//You Got What It Takes/Don't Leave Me	1960	25.00	50.00	100.00
❏ 10,007 [PS]	Marv Johnson	1960	25.00	50.00	100.00
❏ 10,009	Ain't Gonna Be That Way/All the Love I've Got//Come to Me/Whisper	1960	25.00	50.00	100.00
❏ 10,009 [PS]	Marv Johnson	1960	25.00	50.00	100.00

Albums

UNITED ARTISTS

❏ UAL 3081 [M]	Marvelous Marv Johnson	1960	37.50	75.00	150.00
❏ UAL 3118 [M]	More Marv Johnson	1961	37.50	75.00	150.00
❏ UAL 3187 [M]	I Believe	1962	37.50	75.00	150.00
❏ UAS 6081 [S]	Marvelous Marv Johnson	1960	50.00	100.00	200.00
❏ UAS 6118 [S]	More Marv Johnson	1961	50.00	100.00	200.00
❏ UAS 6187 [S]	I Believe	1962	50.00	100.00	200.00

Number	Title (A Side/B Side)	Yr	VG	VG+	NM

JOHNSON, MIRRIAM See JESSI COLTER.

JOHNSON, ROBERT

Albums

COLUMBIA

❏ CL 1654 [M]	King of the Delta Blues Singers	1961	125.00	250.00	500.00
—Red and black label with six "eye" logos					
❏ CL 1654 [M]	King of the Delta Blues Singers	1963	12.50	25.00	50.00
—"Guaranteed High Fidelity" label					
❏ CL 1654 [M]	King of the Delta Blues Singers	1965	6.25	12.50	25.00
—"360 Sound Mono" label					
❏ CL 1654 [M]	King of the Delta Blues Singers	1970	3.00	6.00	12.00
—Orange label with "Columbia" circling the edge					
❏ CL 1654 [M]	King of the Delta Blues Singers	1998	2.50	5.00	10.00
—Red label, "Columbia" in white at top, "Sony Music" under side numbers					
❏ CL 1654 [M]	King of the Delta Blues Singers	2001	3.75	7.50	15.00
—Reissue on 180-gram vinyl (sealed copies have a sticker indicating this)					
❏ C 30034 [M]	King of the Delta Blues Singers, Volume 2	1970	5.00	10.00	20.00
❏ PC 30034 [M]	King of the Delta Blues Singers, Volume 2	1979	2.50	5.00	10.00
❏ C3 46222 [(3)]	Robert Johnson — The Complete Recordings	1990	12.50	25.00	50.00

JOHNSON, TERRY

45s

GORDY

| ❏ 7091 | My Springtime/Suzie | 1969 | 30.00 | 60.00 | 120.00 |
| ❏ 7095 | Whatcha Gonna Do/Suzie | 1970 | 6.25 | 12.50 | 25.00 |

JOHNSON BROTHERS, THE

45s

IMPERIAL

| ❏ 5550 | Love Ain't Got a Thing/Find Another Heart | 1958 | 5.00 | 10.00 | 20.00 |

VALOR

| ❏ 2006 | Zombie Lou/Castin' My Spell | 1958 | 25.00 | 50.00 | 100.00 |

JOHNSTON, BRUCE Also see THE BEACH BOYS; BRUCE AND TERRY; THE GAMBLERS; THE KUSTOM KINGS; PAPA DOO RUN RUN; THE REVERES (3); THE VETTES.

45s

COLUMBIA

| ❏ 10568 | Pipeline/Disney Girls | 1977 | 2.50 | 5.00 | 10.00 |
| —Promos (with "Pipeline" on both sides) worth 50% less | | | | | |

DEL-FI

❏ 4202	The Original Surfer Stomp/Pajama Party	1963	7.50	15.00	30.00
❏ 4202	The Original Surfer Stomp/Pajama Party	1963	15.00	30.00	60.00
—Originals credit "The Surf Stompers"					

DONNA

❏ 1354	Do the Surfer Stomp (Part 1)/Do the Surfer Stomp (Part 2)	1962	7.50	15.00	30.00
❏ 1354	Do the Surfer Stomp (Part 1)/Do the Surfer Stomp (Part 2)	1962	12.50	25.00	50.00
—Originals credit "The Surf Stompers"					
❏ 1354 [PS]	Do the Surfer Stomp (Part 1)/Do the Surfer Stomp (Part 2)	1962	25.00	50.00	100.00
❏ 1364	Soupy Shuffle Stomp (SSS)/Moon Shot	1962	7.50	15.00	30.00
❏ 1374	The Original Surfer Stomp (Part 1)/The Original Surfer Stomp (Part 2)	1962	7.50	15.00	30.00

RONDA

| ❏ 1003 | Do the Surfer Stomp (Part 1)/Do the Surfer Stomp (Part 2) | 1962 | 10.00 | 20.00 | 40.00 |

Albums

COLUMBIA

❏ CL 2057 [M]	Surfin' 'Round the World	1963	37.50	75.00	150.00
❏ CS 8857 [S]	Surfin' 'Round the World	1963	75.00	150.00	300.00
❏ PC 34459	Going Public	1976	3.75	7.50	15.00

DEL-FI

| ❏ DFLP-1228 [M] Surfers' Pajama Party | | 1963 | 25.00 | 50.00 | 100.00 |
| ❏ DFST-1228 [S] Surfers' Pajama Party | | 1963 | 50.00 | 100.00 | 200.00 |

JOHNSTON, COLONEL JUBILATION B., AND THE MYSTIC KNIGHTS BAND AND STREET SINGERS

Albums

COLUMBIA

| ❏ CL 2532 [M] | Moldy Goldies | 1966 | 6.25 | 12.50 | 25.00 |
| ❏ CS 9332 [S] | Moldy Goldies | 1966 | 7.50 | 15.00 | 30.00 |

JOINER, ARKANSAS, JUNIOR HIGH SCHOOL BAND

45s

LIBERTY

❏ 55244	National City/Big Ben	1959	2.50	5.00	10.00
❏ 55276	Arkansas Traveler/Hot Time in the Old Town	1960	2.50	5.00	10.00
❏ 55341	Highland Rock/Hop-Scotch	1960	2.50	5.00	10.00
—This one by the "Joiner, Arkansas, State College Band"					

JOLLY, PETE

45s

A&M

❏ 934	Dancing in the Streets/A Love So Fine	1968	—	3.00	6.00
❏ 963	Like a Lover/Serenta	1968	—	3.00	6.00
❏ 1032	Give a Damn/A Love So Fine	1969	—	3.00	6.00
❏ 1089	Little Green Apples/What the World Needs Now Is Love	1969	—	3.00	6.00

AVA

❏ 116	Falling in Love with Love/Little Bird	1963	2.00	4.00	8.00
❏ 149	Sweet September/Kiss Me Baby	1963	2.00	4.00	8.00
❏ 167	A Hard Day's Night/Three, Four, Five	1964	2.00	4.00	8.00
❏ 169	Moment of Truth/Sweet September	1964	2.00	4.00	8.00

MAINSTREAM

| ❏ 699 | Sweet September/Little Bird | 1969 | — | 3.00 | 6.00 |

Albums

A&M

❏ SP-3033	Seasons	1969	3.00	6.00	12.00
❏ SP-4145	Herb Alpert Presents Pete Jolly	1968	3.00	6.00	12.00
❏ SP-4184	Give a Damn	1970	3.00	6.00	12.00

AVA

❏ A-22 [M]	Little Bird	1963	5.00	10.00	20.00
❏ AS-22 [S]	Little Bird	1963	6.25	12.50	25.00
❏ A-39 [M]	Sweet September	1963	5.00	10.00	20.00
❏ AS-39 [S]	Sweet September	1963	6.25	12.50	25.00

J

Number	Title (A Side/B Side)	Yr	VG	VG+	NM
☐ A-51 [M]	Hello Jolly	1964	5.00	10.00	20.00
☐ AS-51 [S]	Hello Jolly	1964	6.25	12.50	25.00
CHARLIE PARKER					
☐ PLP-825 [M]	Pete Jolly Gasses Everybody	1962	5.00	10.00	20.00
☐ PLP-825S [S]	Pete Jolly Gasses Everybody	1962	6.25	12.50	25.00
COLUMBIA					
☐ CL 2397 [M]	Too Much, Baby	1965	5.00	10.00	20.00
☐ CS 9197 [S]	Too Much, Baby	1965	6.25	12.50	25.00
MAINSTREAM					
☐ S-6114	The Best of Pete Jolly	196?	3.75	7.50	15.00
METROJAZZ					
☐ E-1014 [M]	Impossible	1958	8.75	17.50	35.00
☐ SE-1014 [S]	Impossible	1958	8.75	17.50	35.00
MGM					
☐ E-4127 [M]	5 O'Clock Shadows	1963	5.00	10.00	20.00
☐ SE-4127 [S]	5 O'Clock Shadows	1963	6.25	12.50	25.00
RCA VICTOR					
☐ LPM-1105 [M]	Jolly Jumps In	1955	12.50	25.00	50.00
☐ LPM-1125 [M]	Duo, Trio, Quartet	1955	12.50	25.00	50.00
☐ LPM-1367 [M]	When Lights Are Low	1957	12.50	25.00	50.00
STEREO FIDELITY					
☐ SFS-11000 [S]	Continental Jazz	1960	6.25	12.50	25.00
TRIP					
☐ TLP-5817	A Touch of Jazz	197?	2.50	5.00	10.00

JOLSON, AL Almost his entire recording career predates the 45 and the LP. It's likely that other Decca 78s from the 23000 and 24000 series were reissued onto 45s, but we list only those for which we have confirmation.

45s
DECCA

Number	Title (A Side/B Side)	Yr	VG	VG+	NM
☐ 9-4 [PS]	Jolson Sings Again	1950	5.00	10.00	20.00
—Box for set of four 45s (24681, 24682, 24683, 24684)					
☐ 9-23612	Rock-a-Bye Your Baby with a Dixie Melody/ California Here I Come	1950	5.00	10.00	20.00
—Reissue of 78 from 1947					
☐ 9-23614	Sonny Boy/My Mammy	1950	5.00	10.00	20.00
☐ 9-23714	Avalon/Anniversary Song	1950	5.00	10.00	20.00
—Reissue of 78 from 1947					
☐ 9-24107	Golden Gate/I'm Sitting on Top of the World (Just Rolling Along — Just Rolling Along)	1950	5.00	10.00	20.00
—Side 3 and Side 4 of "Album No. 9-8"; reissue of 78 rpm material					
☐ 9-24108	Toot, Toot, Tootsie! (Goo'Bye)/Back in Your Own Back Yard	1950	5.00	10.00	20.00
—Side 5 and Side 6 of "Album No. 9-8"; reissue of 78 rpm material					
☐ 9-24681	Pretty Baby//I'm Looking Over a Four Leaf Clover/Baby Face	1950	5.00	10.00	20.00
—Side 1 and Side 2 of "Album No. 9-4"; reissue of 78 rpm material					
☐ 9-24682	Give My Regards to Broadway/I'm Just Wild About Harry	1950	5.00	10.00	20.00
—Side 3 and Side 4 of "Album No. 9-4"; reissue of 78 rpm material					
☐ 9-24683	After You've Gone/Chinatown, My Chinatown	1950	5.00	10.00	20.00
—Side 5 and Side 6 of "Album No. 9-4"; reissue of 78 rpm material					
☐ 9-24684	I Only Have Eyes for You/Is It True What They Say About Dixie?	1950	5.00	10.00	20.00
—Side 7 and Side 8 of "Album No. 9-4"; reissue of 78 rpm material					
☐ 9-27024	The Old Piano Roll Blues/Way Down Yonder in New Orleans	1950	5.00	10.00	20.00
☐ 9-27043	Are You Lonesome Tonight/No Sad Songs for Me	1950	5.00	10.00	20.00
☐ 9-27181	De Camptown Races/Oh Susannah	1950	5.00	10.00	20.00
☐ 9-27363	Beautiful Dreamer/Old Folks at Home	1951	3.75	7.50	15.00
☐ 9-27364	I Dream of Jeannie with the Light Brown Hair/ Old Black Joe	1951	3.75	7.50	15.00
☐ 9-27365	Massa's in De Cold, Cold Ground/My Old Kentucky Home	1951	3.75	7.50	15.00
—The above four comprise a box set					
☐ 9-27410	In Our House/I'm Crying Just for You	1951	3.75	7.50	15.00
MCA					
☐ 60037	Swanee/April Showers	1973	—	2.50	5.00
—Black label with rainbow					
☐ 60038	Avalon/Anniversary Song	1973	—	2.50	5.00
—Black label with rainbow					
☐ 60048	You Made Me Love You/Ma Blushin' Rosie	1973	—	2.50	5.00
—Black label with rainbow					
☐ 60096	My Mammy/Sonny Boy	197?	—	2.50	5.00
—Black label with rainbow					
☐ 60136	California Here I Come/Rock-a-Bye Your Baby with a Dixie Melody	197?	—	2.50	5.00
—Black label with rainbow					

7-Inch Extended Plays
DECCA

Number	Title (A Side/B Side)	Yr	VG	VG+	NM
☐ 7-34378	Way Down Yonder in New Orleans/California, Here I Come/I'm Sitting on Top of the World//I'm Looking Over a Four-Leaf Clover/Are You Lonesome Tonight/There's a Rainbow 'Round My Shoulder	196?	3.75	7.50	15.00
—Jukebox issue; small hole, plays at 33 1/3 rpm					
☐ 7-34378 [PS]	Rainbow 'Round My Shoulder	196?	3.75	7.50	15.00
☐ 7-34440	Margie/When the Red, Red Robin Comes Bob, Bob, Bobbin' Along/Baby Face//Dinah/My Melancholy Baby/I'm Always Chasing Rainbows	196?	3.75	7.50	15.00
—Jukebox issue; small hole, plays at 33 1/3 rpm					
☐ 7-34440 [PS]	The Best of Al Jolson, Volume 2	196?	3.75	7.50	15.00

Albums
DECCA

Number	Title (A Side/B Side)	Yr	VG	VG+	NM
☐ DXA 169 [(2)M]	The Best of Jolson	196?	6.25	12.50	25.00
☐ DLP 5006 [10]	Jolson Sings Again	1949	7.50	15.00	30.00
☐ DLP 5026 [10]	Al Jolson In Songs He Made Famous	1949	7.50	15.00	30.00
☐ DLP 5029 [10]	Souvenir Album, Vol. II	1949	7.50	15.00	30.00
☐ DLP 5030 [10]	Al Jolson, Vol. III	1949	7.50	15.00	30.00
☐ DLP 5031 [10]	Souvenir Album, Vol. IV	1949	7.50	15.00	30.00
☐ DL 5308 [10]	Stephen Foster Songs	1950	25.00	50.00	100.00
☐ DL 5314 [10]	Souvenir Album, Vol. V	1951	7.50	15.00	30.00
☐ DL 5315 [10]	Souvenir Album, Vol. VI	1951	7.50	15.00	30.00
☐ DXSA 7169 [(2)R]	The Best of Jolson	196?	3.75	7.50	15.00

Number	Title (A Side/B Side)	Yr	VG	VG+	NM
☐ DL 9034 [M]	You Made Me Love You	1957	6.25	12.50	25.00
—Black label, silver print					
☐ DL 9034 [M]	You Made Me Love You	196?	3.75	7.50	15.00
—Black label with color bars					
☐ DL 9035 [M]	Rock-a-Bye Your Baby	1957	6.25	12.50	25.00
—Black label, silver print					
☐ DL 9035 [M]	Rock-a-Bye Your Baby	196?	3.75	7.50	15.00
—Black label with color bars					
☐ DL 9036 [M]	Rainbow 'Round My Shoulder	1957	6.25	12.50	25.00
—Black label, silver print					
☐ DL 9036 [M]	Rainbow 'Round My Shoulder	196?	3.75	7.50	15.00
—Black label with color bars					
☐ DL 9037 [M]	You Ain't Heard Nothin' Yet!	1957	3.75	7.50	15.00
—Black label, silver print					
☐ DL 9037 [M]	You Ain't Heard Nothin' Yet!	1957	6.25	12.50	25.00
—Black label with color bars					
☐ DL 9038 [M]	Memories	1957	3.75	7.50	15.00
—Black label, silver print					
☐ DL 9038 [M]	Memories	1957	6.25	12.50	25.00
—Black label with color bars					
☐ DL 9050 [M]	Among My Souvenirs	1957	6.25	12.50	25.00
—Black label, silver print					
☐ DL 9050 [M]	Among My Souvenirs	196?	3.75	7.50	15.00
—Black label with color bars					
☐ DL 9063 [M]	The Immortal Al Jolson	1958	6.25	12.50	25.00
—Maroon label, silver print					
☐ DL 9063 [M]	The Immortal Al Jolson	196?	3.75	7.50	15.00
—Black label with color bars					
☐ DL 9070 [M]	Overseas	1959	7.50	15.00	30.00
—Black label, silver print					
☐ DL 9070 [M]	Overseas	196?	3.75	7.50	15.00
—Black label with color bars					
☐ DL 9074 [M]	The World's Greatest Entertainer	1959	6.25	12.50	25.00
—Black label, silver print					
☐ DL 9074 [M]	The World's Greatest Entertainer	196?	3.75	7.50	15.00
—Black label with color bars					
☐ DL 9095 [M]	Al Jolson with Oscar Levant at the Piano	1961	7.50	15.00	30.00
☐ DL 9099 [M]	Jolie	196?	6.25	12.50	25.00
—Black label, silver print					
☐ DL 79034 [R]	You Made Me Love You	196?	3.00	6.00	12.00
☐ DL 79035 [R]	Rock-a-Bye Your Baby	196?	3.00	6.00	12.00
☐ DL 79036 [R]	Rainbow 'Round My Shoulder	196?	3.00	6.00	12.00
☐ DL 79037 [R]	You Ain't Heard Nothin' Yet!	196?	3.00	6.00	12.00
☐ DL 79038 [R]	Memories	196?	3.00	6.00	12.00
☐ DL 79050 [R]	Among My Souvenirs	196?	3.00	6.00	12.00
☐ DL 79070 [R]	Overseas	196?	3.00	6.00	12.00
☐ DL 79074 [R]	The World's Greatest Entertainer	196?	3.00	6.00	12.00
☐ DL 79095 [R]	Al Jolson with Oscar Levant at the Piano	196?	3.00	6.00	12.00
MCA					
☐ 2057	You Made Me Love You	197?	2.50	5.00	10.00
☐ 2058	Rock-a-Bye Your Baby	197?	2.50	5.00	10.00
☐ 2059	Rainbow 'Round My Shoulder	197?	2.50	5.00	10.00
☐ 2060	You Ain't Heard Nothin' Yet!	197?	2.50	5.00	10.00
☐ 2061	Memories	197?	2.50	5.00	10.00
☐ 2064	Among My Souvenirs	197?	2.50	5.00	10.00
☐ 2066	The Immortal Al Jolson	197?	2.50	5.00	10.00
☐ 2067	The World's Greatest Entertainer	197?	2.50	5.00	10.00
☐ 10002 [(2)]	The Best of Jolson	1973	3.00	6.00	12.00
☐ 27051	You Made Me Love You	198?	2.00	4.00	8.00
☐ 27052	Rock-a-Bye Your Baby	198?	2.00	4.00	8.00
☐ 27053	Rainbow 'Round My Shoulder	198?	2.00	4.00	8.00
☐ 27054	You Ain't Heard Nothin' Yet!	198?	2.00	4.00	8.00
☐ 27055	Memories	198?	2.00	4.00	8.00
☐ 27057	The Immortal Al Jolson	198?	2.00	4.00	8.00
☐ 27058	The World's Greatest Entertainer	198?	2.00	4.00	8.00
SUNBEAM					
☐ 503	Steppin' Out	197?	2.50	5.00	10.00
☐ 505	California, Here I Come	197?	2.50	5.00	10.00
TOTEM					
☐ 1006	Al Jolson On the Air, Volume 1	197?	2.50	5.00	10.00
☐ 1012	Al Jolson On the Air, Volume 2	197?	2.50	5.00	10.00
☐ 1019	Al Jolson On the Air, Volume 3	197?	2.50	5.00	10.00
☐ 1030	Al Jolson On the Air, Volume 4	197?	2.50	5.00	10.00
☐ 1040	Al Jolson On the Air, Volume 5	197?	2.50	5.00	10.00

JON AND ROBIN AND THE IN CROWD Also see THE IN CROWD (1).

45s
ABNAK

Number	Title (A Side/B Side)	Yr	VG	VG+	NM
☐ 111	Lonely One/How Come	1965	2.50	5.00	10.00
☐ 111 [DJ]	Lonely One/How Come	1965	3.75	7.50	15.00
—Promo only on yellow vinyl					
☐ 113	Can't Make It With You/If I Need Someone	1966	2.50	5.00	10.00
☐ 113 [DJ]	Can't Make It With You/If I Need Someone	1966	3.75	7.50	15.00
—Promo only on yellow vinyl					
☐ 115	Hey Girl/If I Need Someone	1966	2.50	5.00	10.00
☐ 115 [DJ]	Hey Girl/If I Need Someone	1966	3.75	7.50	15.00
—Promo only on yellow vinyl					
☐ 119	Do It Again A Little Bit Slower/ If I Need Someone — It's You	1967	3.00	6.00	12.00
☐ 119 [DJ]	Do It Again A Little Bit Slower/ If I Need Someone — It's You	1967	4.00	8.00	16.00
—Promo only on yellow vinyl					
☐ 122	Drums/You Don't Care	1967	2.50	5.00	10.00
☐ 122 [DJ]	Drums/You Don't Care	1967	3.75	7.50	15.00
—Promo only on yellow vinyl					
☐ 124	I Want Some More/Love Me Baby	1967	2.50	5.00	10.00
☐ 124 [DJ]	I Want Some More/Love Me Baby	1967	3.75	7.50	15.00
—Promo only on yellow vinyl					
☐ 127	Dr. Jon (The Medicine Man)/Love Me Baby	1968	2.00	4.00	8.00
☐ 127 [DJ]	Dr. Jon (The Medicine Man)/Love Me Baby	1968	3.00	6.00	12.00
—Promo only on yellow vinyl					
☐ 130	You Got Style/Thursday Morning	1968	2.00	4.00	8.00
☐ 130 [DJ]	You Got Style/Thursday Morning	1968	3.00	6.00	12.00
—Promo only on yellow vinyl					
☐ 133	Save Me, Save Me/Thursday Morning	1968	2.00	4.00	8.00
—As "Jon and the In Crowd"					
☐ 133 [DJ]	Save Me, Save Me/Thursday Morning	1968	3.00	6.00	12.00
—Promo only on yellow vinyl					
☐ 135	Gift of Love/Gift of Love (Country Style)	1969	2.00	4.00	8.00

Number	Title (A Side/B Side)	Yr	VG	VG+	NM
□ 135 [DJ]	Gift of Love/Gift of Love (Country Style)	1969	3.00	6.00	12.00

—Promo only on yellow vinyl

Number	Title (A Side/B Side)	Yr	VG	VG+	NM
□ 138	Give Me Your Love/Lonely One	1969	2.00	4.00	8.00
□ 138 [DJ]	Give Me Your Love/Lonely One	1969	3.00	6.00	12.00

—Promo only on yellow vinyl

□ 140	There's An American Flag on the Moon (Part 1)/There's An American Flag on the Moon (Part 2)	1969	2.00	4.00	8.00
□ 140 [DJ]	There's An American Flag on the Moon (Part 1)/There's An American Flag on the Moon (Part 2)	1969	3.00	6.00	12.00

—Promo only on yellow vinyl

□ 141	If You Got It, Flaunt It/I'll Come Running to You	1969	2.00	4.00	8.00
□ 141 [DJ]	If You Got It, Flaunt It/I'll Come Running to You	1969	3.00	6.00	12.00

—Promo only on yellow vinyl

Albums
ABNAK

□ ABM-2068 [M]	Soul of a Boy and Girl	1967	5.00	10.00	20.00
□ ABST-2068 [S]	Soul of a Boy and Girl	1967	5.00	10.00	20.00
□ ABST-2070	Elastic Event	1968	5.00	10.00	20.00

JONES, BRIAN Also see THE ROLLING STONES.
Albums
ROLLING STONES

□ COC 49100	Brian Jones Presents the Pipes of Pan at Joujouka	1971	15.00	30.00	60.00

JONES, CORKY See BUCK OWENS.

JONES, DAVY Also see DOLENZ, JONES & TORK; DOLENZ, JONES, BOYCE & HART; THE MONKEES.
45s
BELL

□ 45111	Rainy Jane/Welcome to My Love	1971	2.50	5.00	10.00
□ 45136	I Really Love You/Sitting in the Apple Tree	1971	2.50	5.00	10.00
□ 45159	Girl/Take My Love	1971	12.50	25.00	50.00
□ 45178	I'll Believe in You/The Road to Love	1972	5.00	10.00	20.00

COLPIX

□ 764	Dream Girl/Take Me to Paradise	1965	5.00	10.00	20.00

—Colpix sides as "David Jones"

□ 764 [PS]	Dream Girl/Take Me to Paradise	1965	7.50	15.00	30.00
□ 784	What Are We Going to Do/This Bouquet	1965	5.00	10.00	20.00
□ 784 [PS]	What Are We Going to Do/This Bouquet	1965	7.50	15.00	30.00
□ 789	The Girl from Chelsea/Theme for a New Love	1965	5.00	10.00	20.00
□ 789 [PS]	The Girl from Chelsea/Theme for a New Love	1965	10.00	20.00	40.00

MGM

□ 14458	Who Was It/You're a Lady	1972	7.50	15.00	30.00
□ 14524	Rubberene/Who Was It	1973	7.50	15.00	30.00

Albums
BELL

□ 6067	Davy Jones	1971	5.00	10.00	20.00

COLPIX

□ CP 493 [M]	David Jones	1965	6.25	12.50	25.00
□ CPS 493 [S]	David Jones	1965	10.00	20.00	40.00

—This album charted in 1967 thanks to the singer's membership in The Monkees

JONES, DOROTHY
45s
COLUMBIA

□ 4-42062	Take That Long Walk Home/It's Unbelievable	1961	2.50	5.00	10.00

JONES, GEORGE Also see GENE PITNEY.
45s
D

□ 1226	New Baby for Christmas/Maybe Next Christmas	1961	3.00	6.00	12.00

EPIC

□ 02526	Still Doin' Time/Good Ones and Bad Ones	1981	—	—	3.00
□ 02696	Same Ol' Me/Together Alone	1982	—	—	3.00
□ 03489	Shine On (Shine All Your Sweet Love on Me)/Memories of Mama	1982	—	—	3.00
□ 03883	I Always Get Lucky with You/I'd Rather Have What We Had	1983	—	—	3.00
□ 04082	Tennessee Whiskey/Almost Persuaded	1983	—	—	3.00
□ 04413	You've Still Got a Place in My Heart/I'm Ragged But Right	1984	—	—	3.00
□ 04609	She's My Rock/(What Love Can Do) The Second Time Around	1984	—	—	3.00
□ 04876	Size Seven Round (Made of Gold)/All I Want to Do in Life	1985	—	—	3.00

—A-side with Lacy J. Dalton; B-side with Janie Frickie

□ 05439	Who's Gonna Fill Their Shoes/A Whole Lot of Trouble for You	1985	—	—	3.00
□ 05698	The One I Loved Back Then (The Corvette Song)/If Only You'd Love Me Again	1985	—	—	3.00
□ 05862	Somebody Wants Me Out of the Way/Call the Wrecker for My Heart	1986	—	—	3.00
□ 06296	Wine Colored Roses/These Old Eyes Have Seen It All	1986	—	—	3.00
□ 06593	The Right Left Hand/The Very Best on Me	1986	—	—	3.00
□ 07107	I Turn to You/Don't Leave Without Taking Your Silver	1987	—	—	3.00
□ 07655	The Bird/I'm Goin' Home Like I Never Did Before	1987	—	—	3.00
□ 07748	I'm a Survivor/The Real McCoy	1987	—	—	3.00
□ 07913	The Old Man No One Loves/One Hell of a Song	1988	—	—	3.00
□ 08011	If I Could Bottle This Up/I Always Get It Right with You	1988	—	—	3.00

—With Shelby Lynne

□ 08509	I'm a One Woman Man/Pretty Little Lady from Beaumont, Texas	1988	—	—	3.00
□ 10831	We Can Make It/One of These Days	1972	—	2.50	5.00
□ 10858	Loving You Could Never Be Better/Try It, You'll Like It	1972	—	2.50	5.00
□ 10917	A Picture of Me (Without You)/The Man Worth Loving You	1972	—	2.50	5.00
□ 10959	What My Woman Can't Do/My Loving Wife	1973	—	2.50	5.00
□ 11006	Nothing Ever Hurt Me (Half As Bad As Losing You)/Wine	1973	—	2.50	5.00
□ 11053	Once You've Had the Best/Mary Don't Go Round	1973	—	2.50	5.00
□ 11122	The Grand Tour/Our Private Life	1974	—	2.50	5.00

Number	Title (A Side/B Side)	Yr	VG	VG+	NM
□ 50038	The Door/Wean Me	1974	—	2.50	5.00
□ 50088	These Days (I Barely Get By)/Baby, There's Nothing Like You	1975	—	2.50	5.00
□ 50127	Memories of Us/I Just Don't Give a Damn	1975	—	2.50	5.00
□ 50187	The Battle/I'll Come Back	1976	—	2.50	5.00
□ 50227	You Always Look Your Best (Here in My Arms)/Have You Seen My Chicken	1976	—	2.50	5.00
□ 50271	Her Name Is…/Diary of My Mind	1976	—	2.50	5.00
□ 50385	Old King Kong/It's a 10-33 (Let's Get Jesus on the Line)	1977	—	2.00	4.00
□ 50423	If I Could Put Them All Together (I'd Have You)/You've Got the Best of Me Again	1977	—	2.00	4.00
□ 50495	Bartender's Blues/Rest in Peace	1977	—	2.00	4.00
□ 50564	I'll Just Take It Out in Love/Leaving Love All Over the Place	1978	—	2.00	4.00
□ 50684	Someday My Day Will Come/We Oughta Be Ashamed	1979	—	2.00	4.00
□ 50867	He Stopped Loving Her Today/A Hard Act to Follow	1980	—	3.00	6.00
□ 50922	I'm Not Ready Yet/Garage Sale Today	1980	—	2.00	4.00
□ 50968	If Drinkin' Don't Kill Me (Her Memory Will)/Brother to the Blues	1980	—	2.00	4.00
□ 68743	The King Is Gone (So Are You)/Don't You Ever Get Tired (Of Hurting Me)	1989	—	—	3.00

—Same song, different title (changed for legal reasons)

□ 68743	Ya Ba Da Ba Do (So Are You)/Don't You Ever Get Tired (Of Hurting Me)	1989	—	2.50	5.00
□ 68743 [PS]	Ya Ba Da Ba Do (So Are You)/Don't You Ever Get Tired (Of Hurting Me)	1989	—	2.50	5.00
□ 68991	Writing on the Wall/Burning Bridges	1989	—	—	3.00
□ 73070	Radio Lover/Burning Bridges	1989	—	—	3.00
□ 73424	Six Foot Deep, Six Foot Down/He Never Got the Picture at All	1990	—	2.00	4.00

MCA

□ 54187	You Couldn't Get the Picture/Heckle and Jeckle	1991	—	2.00	4.00
□ 54272	She Loved a Lot in Her Time/Come Home to Me	1991	—	2.00	4.00
□ 54370	Honky Tonk Myself to Death/Where the Tall Grass Grows	1992	—	2.00	4.00
□ 54470	I Don't Need Your Rockin' Chair/Finally Friday	1992	—	2.50	5.00
□ 54604	Wrong's What I Do Best/The Bottle Let Me Down	1993	—	2.00	4.00
□ 54687	Walls Can Fall/You Must Have Walked Across My Mind Again	1993	—	—	3.00
□ 54749	High-Tech Redneck/Forever's Here to Stay	1993	—	2.00	4.00
□ 54969	A Good Year for the Roses/I've Still Got Some Hurtin' Left to Do	1994	—	2.00	4.00

—A-side with Alan Jackson

□ 55228	Honky Tonk Song/The Lone Ranger	1996	—	2.00	4.00
□ 55287	Billy B. Bad/Back Down to Hung Up on You	1996	—	2.00	4.00
□ 72038	Wild Irish Rose/No Future for Me in Our Past	1998	—	—	3.00

MERCURY

□ 7045 [S]	White Lightning/Treasure of Love	196?	10.00	20.00	40.00
□ 7046 [S]	Why Baby Why/Hearts in My Dream	196?	10.00	20.00	40.00
□ 7047 [S]	The Window Up Above/Color of the Blues	196?	10.00	20.00	40.00
□ 7048 [S]	Tall, Tall Trees/Don't Stop the Music	196?	10.00	20.00	40.00
□ 7049 [S]	Who Shot Sam/Accidentally on Purpose	196?	10.00	20.00	40.00
□ 71049	Just One More/Gonna Come Get You	1957	6.25	12.50	25.00
□ 71096	Too Much Water/All I Want to Do	1957	6.25	12.50	25.00
□ 71139	Nothing Can Stop Me/I'm With the Wrong One	1957	6.25	12.50	25.00
□ 71176	Tall, Tall Trees/Hearts in My Dream	1957	5.00	10.00	20.00
□ 71224	Take the Devil Out of Me/A Cup of Loneliness	1957	5.00	10.00	20.00
□ 71225	New Baby for Christmas/Maybe Next Christmas	1957	5.00	10.00	20.00
□ 71257	Color of the Blues/Eskimo Pie	1958	5.00	10.00	20.00
□ 71340	Wandering Soul/Jesus Wants Me	1958	5.00	10.00	20.00
□ 71373	Treasure of Love/If I Don't Love You (Grits Ain't Groceries)	1958	5.00	10.00	20.00
□ 71406	White Lightning/Long Time to Forget	1959	3.75	7.50	15.00
□ 71464	Who Shot Sam/Into My Arms Again	1959	3.75	7.50	15.00
□ 71506	My Lord Has Called Me/If You Want to Wear a Crown	1959	5.00	10.00	20.00
□ 71514	Money to Burn/Big Harlan Taylor	1959	5.00	10.00	20.00
□ 71583	Accidently on Purpose/Sparkling Blue Eyes	1960	3.75	7.50	15.00
□ 71615	Have Mercy on Me/If You Believe	1960	5.00	10.00	20.00
□ 71636	Family Bible/Your Old Standby	1960	5.00	10.00	20.00
□ 71641	Out of Control/Just Little Boy Blue	1960	3.75	7.50	15.00
□ 71700	The Window Up Above/Candy Hearts	1960	3.75	7.50	15.00
□ 71721	Family Bible/Taggin' Along	1961	3.75	7.50	15.00
□ 71804	Tender Years/Battle of Love	1961	3.00	6.00	12.00
□ 71804 [PS]	Tender Years/Battle of Love	1961	3.75	7.50	15.00
□ 71910	Aching, Breaking Heart/When My Heart Hurts No More	1962	3.00	6.00	12.00
□ 71910 [PS]	Aching, Breaking Heart/When My Heart Hurts No More	1962	3.75	7.50	15.00
□ 72010	You're Still on My Mind/Cold, Cold Heart	1962	3.00	6.00	12.00
□ 72010 [PS]	You're Still on My Mind/Cold, Cold Heart	1962	3.75	7.50	15.00
□ 72087	I Love You Because/Revenoor Man	1963	3.00	6.00	12.00
□ 72087 [PS]	I Love You Because/Revenoor Man	1963	3.75	7.50	15.00
□ 72200	Mr. Fool/One Is a Lonely Number	1963	3.00	6.00	12.00
□ 72233	The Last Town I Painted/Tarnished Angel	1964	3.00	6.00	12.00
□ 72233 [PS]	The Last Town I Painted/Tarnished Angel	1964	3.75	7.50	15.00
□ 72293	Oh Lonesome Me/Life to Go	1964	3.00	6.00	12.00
□ 72293 [PS]	Oh Lonesome Me/Life to Go	1964	3.75	7.50	15.00
□ 72362	I Wouldn't Know About That/You Better Treat Your Man Right	1964	3.00	6.00	12.00

MUSICOR

□ 1067	Things Have Gone to Pieces/Wearing My Heart Away	1965	2.00	4.00	8.00
□ 1067 [PS]	Things Have Gone to Pieces/Wearing My Heart Away	1965	3.75	7.50	15.00
□ 1098	Love Bug/I Can't Get Used to Being Lonely	1965	2.00	4.00	8.00
□ 1117	Take Me/Ship of Love	1965	2.00	4.00	8.00
□ 1143	I'm a People/I Woke Up from Dreaming	1966	2.00	4.00	8.00
□ 1174	Old Brush Arbors/Flowers for Mama	1966	2.00	4.00	8.00
□ 1181	Four-O-Thirty Three/Don't Think I Don't	1966	2.00	4.00	8.00
□ 1226	Walk Through This World with Me/Developing My Pictures	1967	2.00	4.00	8.00
□ 1243	I Can't Get There from Here/A Poor Man's Riches	1967	2.00	4.00	8.00

J

Number	Title (A Side/B Side)	Yr	VG	VG+	NM
❏ 1244	A Cup of Loneliness/				
	That the World But Give Me Jesus	1967	3.00	6.00	12.00
❏ 1267	If My Heart Had Windows/Honky Tonk				
	Downstairs	1967	2.00	4.00	8.00
❏ 1289	Say It's Not You/Poor Chinee	1968	2.00	4.00	8.00
❏ 1297	Small Time Laboring Man/Well It's Alright	1968	2.00	4.00	8.00
❏ 1298	As Long As I Live/				
	Your Angel Steps Out of Heaven	1968	2.00	4.00	8.00
❏ 1333	When the Grass Grows Over Me/Heartaches				
	and Hangovers	1968	2.00	4.00	8.00
❏ 1339	Lonely Christmas Call/My Mom and Santa Claus	1968	2.00	4.00	8.00
❏ 1351	I'll Share My World with You/				
	I'll See You a While Ago	1969	2.00	4.00	8.00
❏ 1366	If Not for You/When the Wife Runs Off	1969	2.00	4.00	8.00
❏ 1381	She's Mine/No Blues Is Good News	1969	2.00	4.00	8.00
❏ 1392	Where Grass Won't Grow/Shoulder to Shoulder	1970	—	3.00	6.00
❏ 1404	Going Life's Way/Uncloudy Day	1970	—	3.00	6.00
❏ 1408	Tell Me My Lying Eyes Are Wrong/You've				
	Become My Everything	1970	—	3.00	6.00
❏ 1425	A Good Year for the Roses/				
	Let a Little Loving Come In	1970	2.00	4.00	8.00
❏ 1432	Sometimes You Just Can't Win/				
	Brothers of a Bottle	1971	—	3.00	6.00
❏ 1440	Right Won't Touch a Hand/				
	Someone Sweet to Love	1971	—	3.00	6.00
❏ 1446	I'll Follow You (Up to Our Cloud)/				
	Getting Over the Storm	1971	—	3.00	6.00
RCA VICTOR					
❏ 74-0625	A Day in the Life of a Fool/Old, Old House	1971	—	3.00	6.00
❏ 74-0700	I Made Leaving (Easy for You)/				
	How Proud I Would Have Been	1972	—	3.00	6.00
❏ 74-0792	Wrapped Around Her Finger/With Half a Heart	1972	—	3.00	6.00
❏ 74-0878	I Can Still See Him in Your Eyes/She's Mine	1973	—	3.00	6.00
❏ AMBO-0123	Tender Years/White Lightnin'	1973	—	2.50	5.00
❏ APBO-0218	My Favorite Lies/You Gotta Be My Baby	1974	—	2.50	5.00
❏ PB-10052	I Can Love You Enough/				
	Talk to Me Lonesome Heart	1974	—	2.50	5.00
STARDAY					
❏ 130	No Money in This Deal/You're in My Heart	1954	25.00	50.00	100.00
❏ 146	Play It Cool, Man/Wrong About You	1954	15.00	30.00	60.00
—B-side with Sonny Burns					
❏ 160	Let Him Know/Let Me Catch My Breath	1954	15.00	30.00	60.00
❏ 162	You All Goodnight/Let Him Know	1954	15.00	30.00	60.00
❏ 165	Tell Her/Heartbroken Me	1954	15.00	30.00	60.00
—B-side with Sonny Burns					
❏ 188	Hold Everything/What's Wrong with You	1955	12.50	25.00	50.00
❏ 202	Why Baby Why/Season of My Heart	1955	12.50	25.00	50.00
❏ 216	What Am I Worth/Still Hurtin'	1955	10.00	20.00	40.00
❏ 234	I'm Ragged But I'm Right/Your Heart	1956	10.00	20.00	40.00
❏ 240	Rock It/How Come It	1956	50.00	100.00	200.00
—As "Thumper Jones"					
❏ 247	You Gotta Be My Baby/It's OK	1956	10.00	20.00	40.00
❏ 256	Boat of Life/Taggin' Along	1956	10.00	20.00	40.00
❏ 264	Just One More/Gonna Come Get You	1956	10.00	20.00	40.00
❏ 7003	Seasons of My Heart/I'm Ragged But I'm Right	197?	—	2.50	5.00
❏ 7020	Wasted Words/Any Old Time	197?	—	2.50	5.00
❏ 7036	Why Baby Why/You Gotta Be My Baby	197?	—	2.50	5.00
❏ 8012	Why Baby Why/Seasons of My Heart	197?	—	2.50	5.00
UNITED ARTISTS					
❏ 424	She Thinks I Still Care/Sometimes You Just				
	Can't Win	1962	2.50	5.00	10.00
❏ 424 [PS]	She Thinks I Still Care/Sometimes You Just				
	Can't Win	1962	3.75	7.50	15.00
❏ 442	Beacon in the Night/He Made Me Free	1962	3.00	6.00	12.00
❏ 462	Open Pit Mine/Geronimo	1962	2.50	5.00	10.00
❏ 463	He Is So Good to Me/Magic Valley	1962	3.00	6.00	12.00
❏ 500	A Girl I Used to Know/Big Fool of the Year	1962	2.50	5.00	10.00
❏ 528	Not What I Had in Mind/I Saw Me	1962	2.50	5.00	10.00
❏ 530	Lonely Christmas Call/My Mom and Santa Claus	1962	3.75	7.50	15.00
❏ 578	You Comb Her Hair/				
	Ain't It Funny What a Fool Will Do	1963	2.50	5.00	10.00
❏ 578 [PS]	You Comb Her Hair/				
	Ain't It Funny What a Fool Will Do	1963	3.75	7.50	15.00
❏ 683	Your Heart Turned Left (And I Was On the Right)/				
	My Tears Are Overdue	1964	2.50	5.00	10.00
❏ 724	Where Does a Little Tear Come From/				
	Something I Dreamed	1964	2.50	5.00	10.00
❏ 751	The Race Is On/She's Lonesome Again	1964	2.50	5.00	10.00
❏ 804	Least of All/Brown to Blue	1965	2.50	5.00	10.00
❏ 858	Wrong Number/Old Old House	1965	2.50	5.00	10.00
❏ 901	What's Money/I Get Lonely in a Hurry	1965	2.50	5.00	10.00
❏ 965	World's Worse Loser/I Can't Change Overnight	1965	2.50	5.00	10.00
❏ 50014	Best Guitar Picker/A Good Old Fashioned Cry	1966	2.50	5.00	10.00
Albums					
ACCORD					
❏ SN-7201	Tender Years	1982	2.50	5.00	10.00
ALLEGIANCE					
❏ AV-5015	Cold Cold Heart	198?	2.50	5.00	10.00
BULLDOG					
❏ BDL-2009	20 Golden Pieces of George Jones	198?	2.50	5.00	10.00
EPIC					
❏ KE 31321	George Jones	1972	3.75	7.50	15.00
—Yellow label					
❏ KE 31321	George Jones	1973	3.00	6.00	12.00
—Orange label					
❏ KE 31718	A Picture of Me (Without You)	1972	3.75	7.50	15.00
—Yellow label					
❏ KE 31718	A Picture of Me (Without You)	1973	3.00	6.00	12.00
—Orange label					
❏ KE 32412	Nothing Ever Hurt Me				
	(Half As Bad As Losing You)	1973	3.75	7.50	15.00
❏ KE 32563	In a Gospel Way	1974	3.75	7.50	15.00
❏ KE 33083	The Grand Tour	1974	3.75	7.50	15.00
❏ KE 33352	The Best of George Jones	1975	3.75	7.50	15.00
❏ PE 33352	The Best of George Jones	198?	2.00	4.00	8.00
—Budget-line reissue					
❏ KE 33547	Memories of Us	1975	3.75	7.50	15.00

Number	Title (A Side/B Side)	Yr	VG	VG+	NM
❏ BG 33749 [(2)]	George Jones/A Picture of Me (Without You)	1976	3.75	7.50	15.00
❏ KE 34034	The Battle	1976	3.00	6.00	12.00
❏ KE 34290	Alone Again	1976	3.00	6.00	12.00
❏ PE 34692	All-Time Greatest Hits Volume 1	1977	3.00	6.00	12.00
—Orange label					
❏ PE 34692	All-Time Greatest Hits Volume 1	198?	2.00	4.00	8.00
—Dark blue label					
❏ PE 34717	I Wanta Sing	1977	3.00	6.00	12.00
—Orange label					
❏ PE 34717	I Wanta Sing	198?	2.00	4.00	8.00
—Dark blue label					
❏ KE 35414	Bartender's Blues	1978	3.00	6.00	12.00
❏ PE 35414	Bartender's Blues	198?	2.00	4.00	8.00
—Budget-line reissue					
❏ JE 35544	My Very Special Guests	1979	3.00	6.00	12.00
❏ PE 35544	My Very Special Guests	198?	2.00	4.00	8.00
—Budget-line reissue					
❏ JE 36586	I Am What I Am	1980	3.00	6.00	12.00
❏ FE 37106	Still the Same Old Me	1981	2.50	5.00	10.00
❏ PE 37106	Still the Same Ole Me	198?	2.00	4.00	8.00
—Budget-line reissue					
❏ FE 37346	Encore	1981	2.50	5.00	10.00
❏ KE2 38323 [(2)]	Anniversary — 10 Years of Hits	1982	3.00	6.00	12.00
❏ FE 38406	Shine On	1983	2.50	5.00	10.00
❏ PE 38406	Shine On	198?	2.00	4.00	8.00
—Budget-line reissue					
❏ FE 38978	Jones Country	1983	2.50	5.00	10.00
❏ PE 38978	Jones Country	1985	2.00	4.00	8.00
—Budget-line reissue					
❏ FE 39002	You've Still Got a Place in My Heart	1984	2.50	5.00	10.00
❏ FE 39272	Ladies' Choice	1984	2.50	5.00	10.00
❏ FE 39546	By Request	1984	2.50	5.00	10.00
❏ FE 39598	Who's Gonna Fill Their Shoes	1985	2.50	5.00	10.00
❏ FE 39899	First Time Live!	1985	2.50	5.00	10.00
❏ FE 40413	Wine Colored Roses	1986	2.50	5.00	10.00
❏ FE 40776	Super Hits	1987	2.50	5.00	10.00
❏ FE 40781	Too Wild Too Long	1988	2.50	5.00	10.00
❏ FE 44078	One Woman Man	1989	2.50	5.00	10.00
EVEREST ARCHIVE OF FOLK & JAZZ					
❏ 353	George Jones Sings Country Hits	198?	2.50	5.00	10.00
HILLTOP					
❏ 6048	You're In My Heart	1968	3.75	7.50	15.00
❏ 6092	Heartaches by the Number	1969	3.75	7.50	15.00
❏ 6133	Oh Lonesome Me	1970	3.75	7.50	15.00
INTERMEDIA					
❏ QS-5044	I Can't Change Overnight	198?	2.50	5.00	10.00
❏ QS-5061	How I Love These Old Songs	198?	2.50	5.00	10.00
LIBERTY					
❏ LN-10167	Trouble in Mind	1981	2.00	4.00	8.00
❏ LN-10168	I Get Lonely in a Hurry	1981	2.00	4.00	8.00
MCA					
❏ 10398	And Along Came Jones	1991	5.00	10.00	20.00
—Vinyl issued only through Columbia House					
MERCURY					
❏ ML-8014	Greatest Hits	1980	3.00	6.00	12.00
❏ MG-20282 [M]	Hillbilly Hit Parade, Volume 1	1957	37.50	75.00	150.00
—Five tracks by George Jones, one by George Jones with Benny Barnes, and four by other artists					
❏ MG-20306 [M]	14 Country Favorites	1957	37.50	75.00	150.00
❏ MG-20462 [M]	Country Church Time	1959	50.00	100.00	200.00
❏ MG-20477 [M]	George Jones Sings White Lightning and Other				
	Favorites	1959	37.50	75.00	150.00
❏ MG-20596 [M]	George Jones Salutes Hank Williams	1960	20.00	40.00	80.00
❏ MG-20621 [M]	George Jones' Greatest Hits	1961	10.00	20.00	40.00
❏ MG-20624 [M]	Country and Western Hits	1961	10.00	20.00	40.00
❏ MG-20694 [M]	George Jones Sings From the Heart	1962	10.00	20.00	40.00
❏ MG-20793 [M]	The Novelty Side of George Jones	1963	20.00	40.00	80.00
❏ MG-20836 [M]	The Ballad Side of George Jones	1963	10.00	20.00	40.00
❏ MG-20906 [M]	Blue and Lonesome	1964	6.25	12.50	25.00
❏ MG-20937 [M]	Country and Western No. 1 Male Singer	1964	6.25	12.50	25.00
❏ MG-20990 [M]	Heartaches and Tears	1965	6.25	12.50	25.00
❏ MG-21029 [M]	Singing the Blues	1965	6.25	12.50	25.00
❏ MG-21048 [M]	George Jones' Greatest Hits Volume 2	1965	6.25	12.50	25.00
❏ SR-60257 [S]	George Jones Salutes Hank Williams	1960	25.00	50.00	100.00
❏ SR-60621 [P]	George Jones' Greatest Hits	1961	12.50	25.00	50.00
❏ SR-60624 [P]	Country and Western Hits	1961	12.50	25.00	50.00
❏ SR-60694 [S]	George Jones Sings From the Heart	1962	12.50	25.00	50.00
❏ SR-60793 [S]	The Novelty Side of George Jones	1963	25.00	50.00	100.00
❏ SR-60836 [S]	The Ballad Side of George Jones	1963	12.50	25.00	50.00
❏ SR-60906 [S]	Blue and Lonesome	1964	7.50	15.00	30.00
❏ SR-60937 [S]	Country and Western No. 1 Male Singer	1964	7.50	15.00	30.00
❏ SR-60990 [S]	Heartaches and Tears	1965	7.50	15.00	30.00
❏ SR-61029 [S]	Singing the Blues	1965	7.50	15.00	30.00
❏ SR-61048 [S]	George Jones' Greatest Hits Volume 2	1965	7.50	15.00	30.00
❏ 822646-1	George Jones Salutes Hank Williams	1985	2.50	5.00	10.00
❏ 826095-1	Rockin' the Country	1985	2.50	5.00	10.00
❏ 826248-1	Greatest Hits	1986	2.50	5.00	10.00
MUSICOR					
❏ MM-2046 [M]	Mr. Country and Western Music	1965	7.50	15.00	30.00
❏ MM-2060 [M]	New Country Hits	1965	7.50	15.00	30.00
❏ MM-2061 [M]	Old Brush Arbors	1966	7.50	15.00	30.00
❏ MM-2088 [M]	Love Bug	1966	7.50	15.00	30.00
❏ MM-2099 [M]	I'm a People	1966	6.25	12.50	25.00
❏ MM-2106 [M]	We Found Heaven Right Here on Earth	1966	6.25	12.50	25.00
❏ MM-2116 [M]	George Jones' Greatest Hits	1967	6.25	12.50	25.00
❏ MM-2119 [M]	Walk Through This World with Me	1967	7.50	15.00	30.00
❏ MM-2124 [M]	Cup of Loneliness	1967	7.50	15.00	30.00
❏ MM-2128 [M]	Hits by George	1967	7.50	15.00	30.00
❏ MS-3046 [S]	Mr. Country and Western Music	1965	10.00	20.00	40.00
❏ MS-3060 [S]	New Country Hits	1965	10.00	20.00	40.00
❏ MS-3061 [S]	Old Brush Arbors	1966	10.00	20.00	40.00
❏ MS-3088 [S]	Love Bug	1966	10.00	20.00	40.00
❏ MS-3099 [S]	I'm a People	1966	7.50	15.00	30.00
❏ MS-3106 [S]	We Found Heaven Right Here on Earth	1966	7.50	15.00	30.00
❏ MS-3116 [S]	George Jones' Greatest Hits	1967	6.25	12.50	25.00
❏ MS-3119 [S]	Walk Through This World with Me	1967	5.00	10.00	20.00
❏ MS-3124 [S]	Cup of Loneliness	1967	5.00	10.00	20.00
❏ MS-3128 [S]	Hits by George	1967	5.00	10.00	20.00

Number	Title (A Side/B Side)	Yr	VG	VG+	NM
❑ MS-3149	The Songs of Dallas Frazier	1968	5.00	10.00	20.00
❑ MS-3158	If My Heart Had Windows	1968	5.00	10.00	20.00
❑ M2S-3159 [(2)]	The George Jones Story: The Musical Loves, Life and Sorrows of America's Great Country Star	1968	7.50	15.00	30.00
❑ M2S-3169 [(2)]	My Country	1969	7.50	15.00	30.00
❑ MS-3177	I'll Share My World with You	1969	5.00	10.00	20.00
❑ MS-3181	Where Grass Won't Grow	1969	5.00	10.00	20.00
❑ MS-3188	Will You Visit Me on Sunday?	1970	5.00	10.00	20.00
❑ MS-3191	The Best of George Jones	1970	5.00	10.00	20.00
❑ MS-3194	George Jones With Love	1971	5.00	10.00	20.00
❑ MS-3203	The Best of Sacred Music	1971	5.00	10.00	20.00
❑ MS-3204	The Great Songs of Leon Payne	1971	5.00	10.00	20.00
NASHVILLE					
❑ 2076	Seasons of My Heart	1970	3.75	7.50	15.00
PAIR					
❑ PDL2-1074 [(2)]	The Best of George Jones	1986	3.00	6.00	12.00
❑ PDL2-1080 [(2)]	Country, By George!	1986	3.00	6.00	12.00
POWER PAK					
❑ 271	The Crown Prince of Country Music	197?	2.50	5.00	10.00
QUICKSILVER					
❑ QS-1011	Frozen in Time	198?	2.50	5.00	10.00
❑ QS-1012	If My Heart Had Windows	198?	2.50	5.00	10.00
RCA CAMDEN					
❑ ACL1-0377	The Race Is On	1973	3.00	6.00	12.00
❑ CAS-2591	Flowers for Mama	1973	3.00	6.00	12.00
RCA VICTOR					
❑ APL1-0316	Best of George Jones Vol. II	1973	3.75	7.50	15.00
❑ APL1-0486	You Gotta Be My Baby	1974	3.75	7.50	15.00
❑ APL1-0612	His Songs	1974	3.75	7.50	15.00
❑ APL1-0815	I Can Love You Enough	1974	3.75	7.50	15.00
❑ APL1-1113	The Best of the Best	1975	3.75	7.50	15.00
❑ LSP-4672	First in the Hearts of Country Music Lovers	1972	3.75	7.50	15.00
❑ LSP-4716	Best of George Jones Vol. I	1972	3.75	7.50	15.00
❑ LSP-4725	Poor Man's Riches	1972	3.75	7.50	15.00
❑ LSP-4726	I Made Leaving (Easy for You)	1972	3.75	7.50	15.00
❑ LSP-4727	Country Singer	1972	3.75	7.50	15.00
❑ LSP-4733	George Jones And Friends	1972	3.75	7.50	15.00
❑ LSP-4785	Four-O Thirty-Three	1972	3.75	7.50	15.00
❑ LSP-4786	Tender Years	1972	3.75	7.50	15.00
❑ LSP-4787	Take Me	1972	3.75	7.50	15.00
❑ LSP-4801	Wrapped Around Her Finger	1973	3.75	7.50	15.00
❑ LSP-4847	I Can Still See Him	1973	3.75	7.50	15.00
ROUNDER					
❑ SS-15	Burn the Honky Tonk Down	198?	2.50	5.00	10.00
❑ SS-17	Heartaches & Hangovers	198?	2.50	5.00	10.00
SEARS					
❑ SPS-125	Maybe, Little Baby	196?	5.00	10.00	20.00
STARDAY					
❑ SLP 101 [M]	The Grand Ole Opry's New Star	1958	300.00	600.00	1200.
❑ SLP 125 [M]	The Crown Prince of Country Music	1960	40.00	80.00	160.00
❑ SLP 150 [M]	George Jones Sings His Greatest Hits	1962	12.50	25.00	50.00
❑ SLP 151 [M]	The Fabulous Country Music Sound of George Jones	1962	12.50	25.00	50.00
❑ SLP 335 [M]	George Jones	1965	10.00	20.00	40.00
❑ SLP 344 [M]	Long Live King George	1965	10.00	20.00	40.00
❑ SLP 366	The George Jones Story Bonus Photo	1966	5.00	10.00	20.00
❑ SLP 366 [(2)M]	The George Jones Story	1966	7.50	15.00	30.00
❑ SLP 401 [M]	The George Jones Song Book & Picture Album	1967	12.50	25.00	50.00
—With book					
❑ SLP 401 [M]	The George Jones Song Book & Picture Album	1967	7.50	15.00	30.00
—Without book					
❑ SLP 440 [M]	The Golden Country Hits of George Jones	1969	7.50	15.00	30.00
❑ 3021	16 Greatest Hits	197?	2.50	5.00	10.00
❑ DT-90080 [R]	George Jones Sings His Greatest Hits	1964	20.00	40.00	80.00
—Capitol Record Club edition					
TIME-LIFE					
❑ STW-103	Country Music	1981	2.50	5.00	10.00
UNITED ARTISTS					
❑ UXS-85 [(2)]	George Jones Superpak	1972	5.00	10.00	20.00
❑ UAL-3193 [M]	The New Favorites of George Jones	1962	7.50	15.00	30.00
❑ UAL-3218 [M]	George Jones Sings the Hits of His Country Cousins	1962	7.50	15.00	30.00
❑ UAL-3219 [M]	Homecoming in Heaven	1962	7.50	15.00	30.00
❑ UAL-3220 [M]	My Favorites of Hank Williams	1962	7.50	15.00	30.00
❑ UAL-3221 [M]	George Jones Sings Bob Wills	1962	10.00	20.00	40.00
❑ UAL-3270 [M]	I Wish the Night Would Never End	1963	6.25	12.50	25.00
❑ UAL-3291 [M]	The Best of George Jones	1963	6.25	12.50	25.00
❑ UAL-3338 [M]	More New Favorites	1964	6.25	12.50	25.00
❑ UAL-3364 [M]	George Jones Sings Like the Dickens	1964	10.00	20.00	40.00
❑ UAL-3388 [M]	I Get Lonely in a Hurry	1964	7.50	15.00	30.00
❑ UAL-3408 [M]	Trouble in Mind	1965	7.50	15.00	30.00
❑ UAL-3422 [M]	The Race Is On	1965	5.00	10.00	20.00
—With cartoon on front					
❑ UAL-3422 [M]	The Race Is On	1965	7.50	15.00	30.00
—With photo of George Jones on front					
❑ UAL-3442 [M]	King of Broken Hearts	1965	7.50	15.00	30.00
❑ UAL-3457 [M]	The Great George Jones	1966	7.50	15.00	30.00
❑ UAL-3532 [M]	George Jones' Golden Hits, Volume 1	1966	5.00	10.00	20.00
❑ UAL-3558 [M]	The Young George Jones	1967	7.50	15.00	30.00
❑ UAL-3566 [M]	George Jones' Golden Hits, Volume 2	1967	7.50	15.00	30.00
❑ UAS-6193 [S]	The New Favorites of George Jones	1962	10.00	20.00	40.00
❑ UAS-6218 [S]	George Jones Sings the Hits of His Country Cousins	1962	10.00	20.00	40.00
❑ UAS-6219 [S]	Homecoming in Heaven	1962	10.00	20.00	40.00
❑ UAS-6220 [S]	My Favorites of Hank Williams	1962	10.00	20.00	40.00
❑ UAS-6221 [S]	George Jones Sings Bob Wills	1962	12.50	25.00	50.00
❑ UAS-6270 [S]	I Wish the Night Would Never End	1963	7.50	15.00	30.00
❑ UAS-6291 [S]	The Best of George Jones	1963	7.50	15.00	30.00
❑ UAS-6328 [S]	More New Favorites	1964	7.50	15.00	30.00
❑ UAS-6364 [S]	George Jones Sings Like the Dickens	1964	12.50	25.00	50.00
❑ UAS-6388 [S]	I Get Lonely in a Hurry	1964	10.00	20.00	40.00
❑ UAS-6408 [S]	Trouble in Mind	1965	10.00	20.00	40.00
❑ UAS-6422 [S]	The Race Is On	1965	6.25	12.50	25.00
—With cartoon on front					

Number	Title (A Side/B Side)	Yr	VG	VG+	NM
❑ UAS-6422 [S]	The Race Is On	1965	10.00	20.00	40.00
—With photo of George Jones on front					
❑ UAS-6442 [S]	King of Broken Hearts	1965	10.00	20.00	40.00
❑ UAS-6457 [S]	The Great George Jones	1966	10.00	20.00	40.00
❑ UAS-6532 [S]	George Jones' Golden Hits, Volume 1	1966	6.25	12.50	25.00
❑ UAS-6558 [S]	The Young George Jones	1967	5.00	10.00	20.00
❑ UAS-6566 [S]	George Jones' Golden Hits, Volume 2	1967	5.00	10.00	20.00
❑ UAS-6696	George Jones' Golden Hits, Volume 3	1968	5.00	10.00	20.00
❑ ST-90829 [S]	The Race Is On	1965	10.00	20.00	40.00
—Capitol Record Club edition; photo on front					
❑ T-90829 [M]	The Race Is On	1965	7.50	15.00	30.00
—Capitol Record Club edition; photo on front					
WING					
❑ MGW-12266 [M]	The Great George Jones	196?	3.75	7.50	15.00
❑ SRW-16266 [S]	The Great George Jones	196?	3.75	7.50	15.00

JONES, GEORGE, AND BRENDA CARTER Also see each artist's individual listings.
45s

Number	Title (A Side/B Side)	Yr	VG	VG+	NM
MUSICOR					
❑ 1325	Milwaukee, Here I Come/Great Big Spirit of Love	1968	2.00	4.00	8.00
❑ 1375	Lonesome End of the Line/ Just Your Average Couple	1969	2.00	4.00	8.00

JONES, GEORGE, AND JEANETTE HICKS Also see each artist's individual listings.
45s

Number	Title (A Side/B Side)	Yr	VG	VG+	NM
MERCURY					
❑ 71029	Don't Stop the Music/Uh, Huh, No	1957	6.25	12.50	25.00
❑ 71061	Yearning/Cry, Cry	1957	6.25	12.50	25.00
❑ 71339	I'm with the Wrong One/Nothing Can Stop Me	1958	6.25	12.50	25.00
STARDAY					
❑ 279	Yearning/So Near Yet So Far Away	1956	7.50	15.00	30.00

JONES, GEORGE, AND BRENDA LEE Also see each artist's individual listings.
45s

Number	Title (A Side/B Side)	Yr	VG	VG+	NM
EPIC					
❑ 04723	Hallelujah I Love Her So/(What Love Can Do) The Second Time Around	1984	—	2.00	4.00

JONES, GEORGE, AND MELBA MONTGOMERY Also see each artist's individual listings.
45s

Number	Title (A Side/B Side)	Yr	VG	VG+	NM
MUSICOR					
❑ 1204	Close Together (As You and Me)/Long As We're Dreaming	1966	2.00	4.00	8.00
❑ 1238	Party Pickin'/Simply Divine	1967	2.00	4.00	8.00
UNITED ARTISTS					
❑ 575	We Must Have Been Out of Our Minds/ Until Then	1963	2.50	5.00	10.00
❑ 635	Let's Invite Them Over/What's In Our Hearts	1963	2.50	5.00	10.00
❑ 704	There's a Friend in the Way/Suppose Tonight Would Be Our Last	1964	2.50	5.00	10.00
❑ 732	Please Be My Love/Will There Ever Be Another	1964	2.50	5.00	10.00
❑ 784	Multiply the Heartaches/Once More	1964	2.50	5.00	10.00
❑ 828	House of Gold/I Dreamed My Baby Came Home	1965	2.50	5.00	10.00
❑ 899	Don't Go/I Let You Go	1965	2.50	5.00	10.00
❑ 941	Blue Moon of Kentucky/I Can't Get Over You	1965	2.50	5.00	10.00
❑ 50015	Afraid/Now Tell Me	1966	2.50	5.00	10.00
Albums					
GUEST STAR					
❑ GS 1465 [M]	George Jones and Melba Montgomery	196?	3.00	6.00	12.00
—Contains two solo records by each artist (no duets!) and assorted stuff by others					
LIBERTY					
❑ LN-10169	Singing What's In Our Hearts	1981	2.00	4.00	8.00
MUSICOR					
❑ MM-2109 [M]	Close Together (As You and Me)	1966	5.00	10.00	20.00
❑ MM-2127 [M]	Let's Get Together/Boy Meets Girl	1967	7.50	15.00	30.00
❑ MM-2127 [M]	Party Pickin'	1967	7.50	15.00	30.00
—Alternate title					
❑ MS-3109 [S]	Close Together (As You and Me)	1966	6.25	12.50	25.00
❑ MS-3127 [S]	Let's Get Together/Boy Meets Girl	1967	5.00	10.00	20.00
❑ MS-3127 [S]	Party Pickin'	1967	5.00	10.00	20.00
—Alternate title					
UNITED ARTISTS					
❑ UAL-3301 [M]	Singing What's In Our Hearts	1963	6.25	12.50	25.00
❑ UAL-3352 [M]	Bluegrass Hootenanny	1964	6.25	12.50	25.00
❑ UAL-3472 [M]	Blue Moon of Kentucky	1966	5.00	10.00	20.00
❑ UAS-6301 [S]	Singing What's In Our Hearts	1963	7.50	15.00	30.00
❑ UAS-6352 [S]	Bluegrass Hootenanny	1964	7.50	15.00	30.00
❑ UAS-6472 [S]	Blue Moon of Kentucky	1966	6.25	12.50	25.00
❑ T-90832 [M]	Blue Moon of Kentucky	1966	6.25	12.50	25.00
—Capitol Record Club edition					

JONES, GEORGE; MELBA MONTGOMERY; JUDY LYNN
Albums

Number	Title (A Side/B Side)	Yr	VG	VG+	NM
UNITED ARTISTS					
❑ UAL-3367 [M]	A King and Two Queens	1964	5.00	10.00	20.00
❑ UAS-6367 [S]	A King and Two Queens	1964	6.25	12.50	25.00

JONES, GEORGE; MELBA MONTGOMERY; GENE PITNEY
Albums

Number	Title (A Side/B Side)	Yr	VG	VG+	NM
MUSICOR					
❑ MM-2079 [M]	Famous Country Duets	1965	5.00	10.00	20.00

JONES, GEORGE, AND JOHNNY PAYCHECK Also see each artist's individual listings.
45s

Number	Title (A Side/B Side)	Yr	VG	VG+	NM
EPIC					
❑ 50647	Mabellene/Don't Want No Stranger Sleepin' in My Bed	1978	—	2.00	4.00
❑ 50708	You Can Have Her/Along Came Jones	1979	—	2.00	4.00
❑ 50891	When You're Ugly Like Us (You Just Naturally Got to Be Cool)/Kansas City	1980	—	2.00	4.00
❑ 50949	You Better Move On/Smack Dab in the Middle	1980	—	2.00	4.00
Albums					
EPIC					
❑ JE 35783	Double Trouble	1980	2.50	5.00	10.00

J

Number	Title (A Side/B Side)	Yr	VG	VG+	NM

JONES, GEORGE, AND MARGIE SINGLETON
45s
MERCURY

Number	Title (A Side/B Side)	Yr	VG	VG+	NM
❏ 71856	Did I Ever Tell You/Not Even Friends	1961	3.00	6.00	12.00
❏ 71955	Waltz of the Angels/Talk About Lovin'	1962	3.00	6.00	12.00
❏ 72159	Are You Mine/I Didn't Hear You	1963	3.00	6.00	12.00

Albums
MERCURY

Number	Title (A Side/B Side)	Yr	VG	VG+	NM
❏ MG-20747 [M]	Duets Country Style	1962	7.50	15.00	30.00
❏ SR-60747 [S]	Duets Country Style	1962	10.00	20.00	40.00

JONES, GEORGE, AND TAMMY WYNETTE Also see each artist's individual listings; TINA WITH DADDY AND MOMMY.
45s
EPIC

Number	Title (A Side/B Side)	Yr	VG	VG+	NM
❏ 10815	Take Me/We Go Together	1971	—	2.50	5.00
❏ 10881	The Ceremony/The Great Divide	1972	—	2.50	5.00
❏ 10923	Old Fashioned Singing/ We Love to Sing About Jesus	1972	—	2.50	5.00
❏ 10963	Let's Build a World Together/ Touching Shoulders	1973	—	2.50	5.00
❏ 11031	We're Gonna Hold On/My Elusive Dreams	1973	—	2.50	5.00
❏ 11077	Mr. and Mrs. Santa Claus/T he Greatest Christmas Gift	1973	—	2.50	5.00
❏ 11083	(We're Not) The Jet Set/The Crawdad Song	1974	—	2.50	5.00
❏ 11151	We Loved It Away/Ain't It Been Good	1974	—	2.50	5.00
❏ 50099	God's Gonna Getcha (For That)/ Those Were the Good Times	1975	—	2.50	5.00
❏ 50235	Golden Ring/We're Putting It Back Together	1976	—	2.50	5.00
❏ 50314	Near You/Tattletale Eyes	1976	—	2.50	5.00
❏ 50418	Southern California/Keep the Change	1977	—	2.00	4.00
❏ 50849	Two Story House/It Sure Was Good	1980	—	2.00	4.00
❏ 50930	A Pair of Old Sneakers/We'll Talk About It Later	1980	—	2.00	4.00

MCA

Number	Title (A Side/B Side)	Yr	VG	VG+	NM
❏ 55048	One/Golden Ring	1995	—	2.00	4.00

Albums
EPIC

Number	Title (A Side/B Side)	Yr	VG	VG+	NM
❏ EQ 30802 [Q]	We Go Together	1971	6.25	12.50	25.00
❏ KE 30802	We Go Together	1971	3.75	7.50	15.00
❏ KE 31554	Me and the First Lady	1972	3.75	7.50	15.00
—Yellow label					
❏ KE 31554	Me and the First Lady	1973	3.00	6.00	12.00
—Orange label					
❏ KE 31719	We Love to Sing About Jesus	1972	3.75	7.50	15.00
—Yellow label					
❏ KE 31719	We Love to Sing About Jesus	1973	3.00	6.00	12.00
—Orange label					
❏ KE 32113	Let's Build a World Together	1973	3.75	7.50	15.00
❏ KE 32757	We're Gonna Hold On	1973	3.75	7.50	15.00
❏ KE 33351	George & Tammy & Tina	1975	3.75	7.50	15.00
❏ BG 33752 [(2)]	We Go Together/Me and the First Lady	1976	3.75	7.50	15.00
❏ KE 34291	Golden Ring	1976	3.00	6.00	12.00
—Orange label					
❏ PE 34291	Golden Ring	198?	2.00	4.00	8.00
—Dark blue label					
❏ KE 34716	Greatest Hits	1977	3.00	6.00	12.00
❏ PE 34716	Greatest Hits	198?	2.00	4.00	8.00
—Budget-line reissue					
❏ JE 36764	Together Again	1980	2.50	5.00	10.00
❏ PE 36764	Together Again	198?	2.00	4.00	8.00
—Budget-line reissue					
❏ FE 37348	Encore	1981	2.50	5.00	10.00
❏ PE 37348	Encore	198?	2.00	4.00	8.00
—Budget-line reissue					

JONES, JACK
45s
CAPITOL

Number	Title (A Side/B Side)	Yr	VG	VG+	NM
❏ F3808	Good Luck Good Buddy/Baby Come Home	1957	3.00	6.00	12.00
❏ F3844	For Crying Out Loud/Born to Be Lucky	1957	3.00	6.00	12.00
❏ F3929	A Very Precious Love/What's the Use	1958	2.50	5.00	10.00
❏ F3991	Come On Baby Let's Go/You Laugh	1958	2.50	5.00	10.00
❏ F4089	Laffin' at Me/Deeply Devoted	1958	2.50	5.00	10.00
❏ F4161	Make Room for the Joy/ When I Love I'll Love Forever	1959	2.50	5.00	10.00
❏ F4161 [PS]	Make Room for the Joy/ When I Love I'll Love Forever	1959	3.75	7.50	15.00

KAPP

Number	Title (A Side/B Side)	Yr	VG	VG+	NM
❏ 341	It's a Lonesome Town/A Lot of Livin' to Do	1960	2.50	5.00	10.00
❏ 380	Big Time/She's My Darling, She's My Heart	1961	2.50	5.00	10.00
❏ 435	Lollipops and Roses/This Was My Love	1961	2.00	4.00	8.00
❏ 461	Gift of Love/Pick Up the Pieces	1962	2.00	4.00	8.00
❏ 477	Poetry/Dreamin' All the Time	1962	2.00	4.00	8.00
❏ 495	I've Got My Pride/That's Her Little Way	1962	2.00	4.00	8.00
❏ 507	La Paloma/The Lonely Bull	1963	2.00	4.00	8.00
❏ 516	Call Me Irresponsible/Mutiny on the Bounty	1963	2.00	4.00	8.00
❏ 534	Love Is a Ticklish Affair/That's the Way I Come to You	1963	2.00	4.00	8.00
❏ 551	Wives and Lovers/Toys in the Attic	1963	—	3.00	6.00
❏ 551 [PS]	Wives and Lovers/Toys in the Attic	1963	2.00	4.00	8.00
❏ 571	Love with the Proper Stranger/The Mood I'm In	1964	—	3.00	6.00
❏ 571 [PS]	Love with the Proper Stranger/The Mood I'm In	1964	2.00	4.00	8.00
❏ 589	The First Night of the Full Moon/Far Away	1964	—	3.00	6.00
❏ 589 [PS]	The First Night of the Full Moon/Far Away	1964	2.00	4.00	8.00
❏ 608	Where Love Has Gone/The Lorelei	1964	—	3.00	6.00
❏ 608 [PS]	Where Love Has Gone/The Lorelei	1964	2.00	4.00	8.00
❏ 629	Lullaby for Christmas Eve/The Village of St. Bernadette	1964	2.00	4.00	8.00
❏ 635	Dear Heart/Emily	1964	—	3.00	6.00
❏ 635 [PS]	Dear Heart/Emily	1964	2.00	4.00	8.00
❏ 651	The Race Is On/I Can't Believe I'm Losing You	1965	—	3.00	6.00
❏ 651 [PS]	The Race Is On/I Can't Believe I'm Losing You	1965	2.00	4.00	8.00
❏ 672	Seein' the Right Love Go Wrong/Travelin' On	1965	—	3.00	6.00
❏ 699	The True Picture/Just Yesterday	1965	—	3.00	6.00
❏ 722	Love Bug/And I Love Her	1965	—	3.00	6.00
❏ 722 [PS]	Love Bug/And I Love Her	1965	2.00	4.00	8.00
❏ 736	The Weekend/Wildflower	1966	—	3.00	6.00

(right column, continuation of KAPP)

Number	Title (A Side/B Side)	Yr	VG	VG+	NM
❏ 755	The Impossible Dream (The Quest)/ Strangers in the Night	1966	—	3.00	6.00
❏ 781	A Day in the Life of a Fool/Shining Sea	1966	—	3.00	6.00
❏ 781 [PS]	A Day in the Life of a Fool/Shining Sea	1966	—	—	—

—Rumored to exist, but without conclusive evidence, we will delete this from future editions

Number	Title (A Side/B Side)	Yr	VG	VG+	NM
❏ 800	Lady/Afraid to Love	1966	—	3.00	6.00
❏ 818	I'm Indestructible/Afterthoughts	1967	—	3.00	6.00
❏ 833	Now I Know/More and More	1967	—	3.00	6.00
❏ 847	Our Song/Michelle	1967	—	3.00	6.00
❏ 860	Open for Business As Usual/The Mood I'm In	1967	—	3.00	6.00
❏ 880	Don't Give Your Love Away/ Oh How Much I Love You	1967	—	3.00	6.00
❏ 900	Brother, Where Are You/ Gypsies, Jugglers and Clowns	1968	—	3.00	6.00
❏ 937	People/Don't Rain on My Parade	1968	—	3.00	6.00
❏ 964	Far Away/Meditation	1968	—	3.00	6.00
❏ 2022	Mathilda/Far Away	1969	—	2.50	5.00
❏ 2063	It Only Takes a Moment/Once Upon a Time	1969	—	2.50	5.00
❏ 2138	Mirrored Door/Feather Bed	1971	—	2.50	5.00
❏ 2143	Breathe Deep/Trippin' on a Country Road	1971	—	2.50	5.00
❏ 2154	I'll See You Through/No Concern	1971	—	2.50	5.00

MGM

Number	Title (A Side/B Side)	Yr	VG	VG+	NM
❏ 14851	The Love Boat Theme/ Ready to Take a Chance Again	197?	2.00	4.00	8.00
❏ 14852	Love Theme from "A Star Is Born" (Evergreen)/ I Could Have Been a Sailor	197?	—	2.00	4.00

POLYDOR

Number	Title (A Side/B Side)	Yr	VG	VG+	NM
❏ 815096-7	The Love Boat Theme/The Rockford Files	1983	—	2.00	4.00
—Reissue; B-side by Mike Post					

RCA VICTOR

Number	Title (A Side/B Side)	Yr	VG	VG+	NM
❏ 47-9365	Live for Life/That Tiny World	1967	—	2.50	5.00
❏ 47-9441	If You Ever Leave Me/Pretty	1968	—	2.50	5.00
❏ 47-9510	Without Her/Follow Me	1968	—	2.50	5.00
❏ 47-9564	I Really Want You to Know/This World Is Yours	1968	—	2.50	5.00
❏ 47-9639	The Way That I Live/Dirty Word	1968	—	2.50	5.00
❏ 47-9687	Love Story/L.A. Breakdown (And Take Me In)	1968	—	2.50	5.00
❏ 74-0185	Sweet Child/The Last Seven Days	1969	—	2.50	5.00
❏ 74-0278	Little Altar Boy/What's Out There for Me	1969	—	2.50	5.00
❏ 74-0350	Sweet Changes/I Wish We'd All Been Ready	1970	—	2.50	5.00
❏ 74-0425	Pieces of Dreams/Years of My Youth	1971	—	2.50	5.00
❏ 74-0475	Let Me Be the One/Talk It Over in the Morning	1971	—	2.50	5.00
❏ 74-0573	The Kind of Girl She Is/What Have They Done to the Moon	1971	—	2.50	5.00
❏ 74-0683	The Mountain/How Can We Run Away	1972	—	2.50	5.00
❏ 74-0734	Coming Apart/A Game of Magic	1972	—	2.50	5.00
❏ APBO-0220	Do Me Wrong, But Do Me/Fools in Love	1974	—	2.00	4.00
❏ PB-10025	She Doesn't Live Here Anymore/Write Me a Love Song Charlie	1974	—	2.00	4.00
❏ PB-10317	What I Did for Love/Don't Mention Love	1975	—	2.00	4.00
❏ PB-10845	Send In the Clowns/You Need a Man	1976	—	2.00	4.00
❏ PB-10955	Try It Again/With One More Look at You	1977	—	2.00	4.00
❏ PB-11076	Dixie Chicken/Perfect Strangers	1977	—	2.00	4.00

Albums
CAPITOL

Number	Title (A Side/B Side)	Yr	VG	VG+	NM
❏ ST 1274 [S]	This Love of Mine	1959	7.50	15.00	30.00
❏ T 1274 [M]	This Love of Mine	1959	6.25	12.50	25.00
❏ ST 2100 [S]	In Love	1964	5.00	10.00	20.00
—Reissue of 1274					
❏ T 2100 [M]	In Love	1964	3.75	7.50	15.00

KAPP

Number	Title (A Side/B Side)	Yr	VG	VG+	NM
❏ KL-1228 [M]	Shall We Dance	1961	3.00	6.00	12.00
❏ KL-1259 [M]	Lollipops and Roses	196?	3.00	6.00	12.00
—Revised title					
❏ KL-1259 [M]	This Was My Love	1962	5.00	10.00	20.00
—Original title					
❏ KL-1265 [M]	I've Got a Lot of Livin' to Do	1962	3.00	6.00	12.00
❏ KL-1328 [M]	Call Me Irresponsible	1963	3.00	6.00	12.00
❏ KL-1337 [M]	She Loves Me	1963	3.00	6.00	12.00
❏ KL-1352 [M]	Wives and Lovers	1963	3.00	6.00	12.00
❏ KL-1365 [M]	Bewitched	1964	3.00	6.00	12.00
❏ KL-1396 [M]	Where Love Has Gone	1964	3.00	6.00	12.00
❏ KL-1399 [M]	The Jack Jones Christmas Album	1964	3.00	6.00	12.00
❏ KL-1415 [M]	Dear Heart	1964	3.00	6.00	12.00
❏ KL-1433 [M]	My Kind of Town	1965	3.00	6.00	12.00
❏ KL-1435 [M]	There's Love & There's Love & There's Love	1965	3.00	6.00	12.00
❏ KL-1465 [M]	For the "In" Crowd	1966	3.00	6.00	12.00
❏ KL-1486 [M]	The Impossible Dream	1966	3.00	6.00	12.00
❏ KL-1500 [M]	Jack Jones Sings	1966	3.00	6.00	12.00
❏ KL-1511 [M]	Lady	1967	3.75	7.50	15.00
❏ KL-1531 [M]	Our Song	1967	3.75	7.50	15.00
❏ KL-1551 [M]	What the World Needs Now Is Love!	1968	5.00	10.00	20.00
—May only exist as a white label promo; covers are stereo with "Mono" sticker					
❏ KL-1559 [M]	Greatest Hits	1968	5.00	10.00	20.00
—May exist only as a white label promo; covers are stereo with a "Mono" sticker					
❏ KS-3228 [S]	Shall We Dance	1961	3.75	7.50	15.00
❏ KS-3259 [S]	Lollipops and Roses	196?	3.75	7.50	15.00
—Revised title					
❏ KS-3259 [S]	This Was My Love	1962	6.25	12.50	25.00
—Original title					
❏ KS-3265 [S]	I've Got a Lot of Livin' to Do	1962	3.75	7.50	15.00
❏ KS-3328 [S]	Call Me Irresponsible	1963	3.75	7.50	15.00
❏ KS-3337 [S]	She Loves Me	1963	3.75	7.50	15.00
❏ KS-3352 [S]	Wives and Lovers	1963	3.75	7.50	15.00
❏ KS-3365 [S]	Bewitched	1964	3.75	7.50	15.00
❏ KS-3396 [S]	Where Love Has Gone	1964	3.75	7.50	15.00
❏ KS 3399 [S]	The Jack Jones Christmas Album	1964	3.75	7.50	15.00
❏ KS-3415 [S]	Dear Heart	1964	3.75	7.50	15.00
❏ KS-3433 [S]	My Kind of Town	1965	3.75	7.50	15.00
❏ KS-3435 [S]	There's Love & There's Love & There's Love	1965	3.75	7.50	15.00
❏ KS-3465 [S]	For the "In" Crowd	1966	3.75	7.50	15.00
❏ KS-3486 [S]	The Impossible Dream	1966	3.75	7.50	15.00
❏ KS-3500 [S]	Jack Jones Sings	1966	3.75	7.50	15.00
❏ KS-3511 [S]	Lady	1967	3.00	6.00	12.00
❏ KS-3531 [S]	Our Song	1967	3.00	6.00	12.00
❏ KS-3551 [S]	What the World Needs Now Is Love!	1968	3.00	6.00	12.00
❏ KS-3559 [S]	Greatest Hits	1968	3.00	6.00	12.00
❏ KS-3566 [S]	Curtain Time	1968	3.00	6.00	12.00

Number	Title (A Side/B Side)	Yr	VG	VG+	NM
❏ KS-3590	Jack Jones in Hollywood	1969	3.00	6.00	12.00
❏ KS-3602	Greatest Hits Vol. 2	1970	3.00	6.00	12.00
❏ KXS-5009 [(2)]	The Best of Jack Jones	196?	3.75	7.50	15.00
MCA					
❏ 4115 [(2)]	The Best of Jack Jones	197?	3.00	6.00	12.00
—Reissue of Kapp KXS-5009					
❏ 15014	The Jack Jones Christmas Album	197?	2.50	5.00	10.00
—Reissue					
❏ 15036	White Christmas	198?	2.00	4.00	8.00
MGM					
❏ MG-1-5023	Nobody Does It Better	1979	2.50	5.00	10.00
❏ MG-1-5024	Don't Stop Now	1980	2.50	5.00	10.00
PICKWICK					
❏ PC-3001 [M]	This Love of Mine	196?	3.00	6.00	12.00
❏ SPC-3001 [S]	This Love of Mine	196?	3.00	6.00	12.00
❏ SPC-3041	A Very Precious Love	196?	2.50	5.00	10.00
RCA CAMDEN					
❏ ACL-1-0255	Christmas with Jack Jones	1973	3.00	6.00	12.00
—Reissue of RCA Victor LSP-4234					
RCA VICTOR					
❏ APL1-0139	Together	1973	2.50	5.00	10.00
❏ APL1-0408	Harbour	1974	2.50	5.00	10.00
❏ APL1-0773	Write Me a Love Song, Charlie	1975	2.50	5.00	10.00
❏ ANL1-1081	Jack Jones Sings Michel Legrand	1975	2.00	4.00	8.00
—Reissue					
❏ APL1-1111	What I Did for Love	1975	2.50	5.00	10.00
❏ APL1-2067	The Full Life	1976	2.50	5.00	10.00
❏ APL1-2361	With One More Look at You	1977	2.50	5.00	10.00
❏ LPM-3911 [M]	Without Her	1967	5.00	10.00	20.00
❏ LSP-3911 [S]	Without Her	1967	3.00	6.00	12.00
❏ LPM-3969 [M]	If You Ever Leave Me	1968	5.00	10.00	20.00
❏ LSP-3969 [S]	If You Ever Leave Me	1968	3.00	6.00	12.00
❏ LSP-4048	Where Is Love	1968	3.00	6.00	12.00
❏ LSP-4108	L.A. Break Down	1969	3.00	6.00	12.00
❏ LSP-4209	A Time for Us	1969	3.00	6.00	12.00
❏ LSP-4234	A Jack Jones Christmas	1969	3.75	7.50	15.00
❏ LSP-4413	In Person at the Sands, Las Vegas	1970	3.00	6.00	12.00
❏ LSP-4480	Jack Jones Sings Michel Legrand	1970	3.00	6.00	12.00
❏ LSP-4613	A Song for You	1971	3.00	6.00	12.00
❏ LSP-4692	Bread Winners	1972	2.50	5.00	10.00
VOCALION					
❏ VL 73913	Jack Jones Showcase	1970	2.50	5.00	10.00

JONES, JACK, AND THE JET SET BAND
45s
HIT

Number	Title (A Side/B Side)	Yr	VG	VG+	NM
❏ 317	Judy in Disguise (With Glasses)/We Can Fly	1967	2.00	4.00	8.00
—B-side by the Jalopy Five					

JONES, JIMMY Also see THE PRETENDERS (2).
45s
ABC-PARAMOUNT

Number	Title (A Side/B Side)	Yr	VG	VG+	NM
❏ 10094	Blue and Lonely/Daddy Needs Baby	1960	37.50	75.00	150.00
—As "Jimmy Jones and the Pretenders"					
ARROW					
❏ 717	Heaven in Your Eyes/The Whistlin' Man	1957	45.00	90.00	180.00
—As "Jimmy Jones and the Jones Boys"					
BELL					
❏ 682	Personal Property/39-21-40	1967	2.00	4.00	8.00
❏ 689	True Love Ways/Snap My Fingers	1967	2.00	4.00	8.00
CAPITOL					
❏ 3849	If I Knew Then (What I Know Now)/Everything's Gonna Be All Right	1974	—	2.50	5.00
CONCHILLO					
❏ 1	Ain't Nothing Wrong Makin' Love the First Night/Time and Changes	1976	—	3.00	6.00
CUB					
❏ 9049	Handy Man/The Search Is Over	1959	6.25	12.50	25.00
❏ 9067	Good Timin'/My Precious Angel	1960	6.25	12.50	25.00
❏ 9072	That's When I Cried/I Just Go for You	1960	5.00	10.00	20.00
❏ 9072 [PS]	That's When I Cried/I Just Go for You	1960	12.50	25.00	50.00
❏ 9076	Itchin'/Ee-I-Ee-I-Oh	1960	5.00	10.00	20.00
❏ 9082	Ready for Love/For You	1960	5.00	10.00	20.00
❏ 9085	I Told You So/You Got It	1961	3.75	7.50	15.00
❏ 9093	Dear One/I Say Love	1961	3.75	7.50	15.00
❏ 9102	Mr. Music Man/Holler Hey	1961	3.75	7.50	15.00
❏ 9110	You're Much Too Young/Nights of Mexico	1962	3.75	7.50	15.00
EPIC					
❏ 9339	Whenever You Need Me/You for Me to Love	1959	30.00	60.00	120.00
PARKWAY					
❏ 988	Don't You Just Know It/Dynamite	1966	2.50	5.00	10.00
RAMA					
❏ 210	Lover/Plain Old Love	1956	30.00	60.00	120.00
—As "Jimmy Jones and the Pretenders"					
ROULETTE					
❏ 4232	Lover/Plain Old Love	1960	7.50	15.00	30.00
—As "Jimmy 'Handyman' Jones"					
VEE JAY					
❏ 505	No Insurance (For a Broken Heart)/Mr. Fix-It	1963	3.75	7.50	15.00

Albums
JEN JILLUS

Number	Title (A Side/B Side)	Yr	VG	VG+	NM
❏ 1001	The Handy Man's Back in Town	1977	3.00	6.00	12.00
MGM					
❏ E-3847 [M]	Good Timin'	1960	30.00	60.00	120.00
❏ SE-3847 [S]	Good Timin'	1960	40.00	80.00	160.00

JONES, JOE
45s
CAPITOL

Number	Title (A Side/B Side)	Yr	VG	VG+	NM
❏ F2951	Adam Bit the Apple/Will Call	1954	10.00	20.00	40.00
HERALD					
❏ 488	You Done Me Wrong/When Your Hair Has Turned to Silver	1956	10.00	20.00	40.00
RIC					
❏ 972	You Talk Too Much/I Love You Still	1960	6.25	12.50	25.00

Number	Title (A Side/B Side)	Yr	VG	VG+	NM
ROULETTE					
❏ 4304	You Talk Too Much/I Love You Still	1960	3.75	7.50	15.00
❏ 4316	One Big Mouth/Here's What You Gotta Do	1960	3.00	6.00	12.00
❏ 4344	California Sun/Please Don't Talk About Me When I'm Gone	1961	3.00	6.00	12.00
❏ 4377	The Big Mule/I've Got a Uh Uh Wife	1961	3.00	6.00	12.00

Albums
ROULETTE

Number	Title (A Side/B Side)	Yr	VG	VG+	NM
❏ R 25143 [M]	You Talk Too Much	1961	37.50	75.00	150.00
❏ SR 25143 [R]	You Talk Too Much	1961	25.00	50.00	100.00

JONES, JOHN PAUL Also see LED ZEPPELIN.
45s
COTILLION

Number	Title (A Side/B Side)	Yr	VG	VG+	NM
❏ 44102	Got to Get Together Now/Man from Nazareth	1971	6.25	12.50	25.00
JERDEN					
❏ 761	Sound City/Broken Promises	1965	7.50	15.00	30.00
—B-side by Rosemary and Howard					
PARKWAY					
❏ 915	Baja/A Foggy Day in Vietnam	1964	10.00	20.00	40.00

Albums
COLUMBIA

Number	Title (A Side/B Side)	Yr	VG	VG+	NM
❏ KC 32047	John Paul Jones	1973	5.00	10.00	20.00

JONES, JONAH
45s
BETHLEHEM

Number	Title (A Side/B Side)	Yr	VG	VG+	NM
❏ 11014	You're the Cream in My Coffee/The Sheik of Araby	1959	3.00	6.00	12.00
CAPITOL					
❏ F3747	On the Street Where You Live/Rose Room	1957	2.50	5.00	10.00
❏ F3893	76 Trombones/Baubles, Bangles and Beads	1958	2.50	5.00	10.00
❏ F3999	Ballin' the Jack/Slowly But Surely	1958	2.50	5.00	10.00
❏ F4057	Night Train/Lots of Luck, Charlie	1958	2.50	5.00	10.00
❏ F4199	Cherry/I Dig Chicks	1959	2.50	5.00	10.00
❏ F4238	High Hopes/Hit Me Again	1959	2.50	5.00	10.00
❏ F4297	Where Did We Go? Out/Gentleman Jimmy	1959	2.50	5.00	10.00
❏ 4375	Blueberry Hill/Shanghai	1960	2.50	5.00	10.00
❏ 4497	I Ain't Down Yet/Blue Champagne	1961	2.00	4.00	8.00
❏ 4878	The Bells of St. Mary's/Brotherhood of Man	1962	2.00	4.00	8.00
❏ 4944	The Work Song/Jonah's Sermon	1963	2.00	4.00	8.00
❏ 4993	Doodles/Pink Shutters	1963	2.00	4.00	8.00
DECCA					
❏ 25672	People/Who Can I Turn To	196?	—	3.00	6.00
❏ 31765	Think Beautiful/Don't Forget 127th Street (127th Street March)	1965	—	3.00	6.00
GROOVE					
❏ 0140	Come Sit By Me/God Loves You Child	1956	3.75	7.50	15.00
MOTOWN					
❏ 1145	For Better or Worse/Don't Mess with Bill	1969	30.00	60.00	120.00

7-Inch Extended Plays
CAPITOL

Number	Title (A Side/B Side)	Yr	VG	VG+	NM
❏ EAP 1-839	*Rose Room/Mack the Knife/My Blue Heaven/Royal Garden Blues	1958	3.00	6.00	12.00
❏ EAP 1-839 [PS]	Muted Jazz, Part 1	1958	3.00	6.00	12.00
❏ EAP 1-963	*Baubles, Bangles and Beads/The Party's Over/Till There Was You/Seventy Six Trombones	1958	3.00	6.00	12.00
❏ EAP 1-963 [PS]	Swingin' on Broadway, Part 1	1958	3.00	6.00	12.00
❏ EAP 2-963	You're So Right for Me/Just My Luck/I Could Have Danced All Night/Whatever Lola Wants	195?	3.00	6.00	12.00
❏ EAP 2-963 [PS]	Swingin' on Broadway, Part 2	195?	3.00	6.00	12.00
❏ EAP 3-963	(contents unknown)	1958	3.00	6.00	12.00
❏ EAP 3-963 [PS]	Swingin' on Broadway, Part 3	1958	3.00	6.00	12.00
❏ EAP 1-1014	On the Street Where You Live/Rose Room//Baubles, Bangles and Beads/Seventy Six Trombones	195?	3.00	6.00	12.00
❏ EAP 1-1014 [PS]	On the Street Where You Live	195?	3.00	6.00	12.00
❏ EAP 1-1039	(contents unknown)	195?	3.00	6.00	12.00
❏ EAP 1-1039 [PS]	Jumpin' with Jonah, Part 1	195?	3.00	6.00	12.00
❏ EAP 2-1039	Bill Bailey, Won't You Please Come Home?/The Blues Don't Care (Who's Gort 'Em)//Dance Only with Me/Lots of Luck Charley	195?	3.00	6.00	12.00
❏ EAP 2-1039 [PS]	Jumpin' with Jonah, Part 2	195?	3.00	6.00	12.00
❏ EAP 3-1039	Night Train/Jumpin' with Jonah//Just a Gigolo/It's a Good Day	195?	3.00	6.00	12.00
❏ EAP 3-1039 [PS]	Jumpin' with Jonah, Part 3	195?	3.00	6.00	12.00

Albums
ANGEL

Number	Title (A Side/B Side)	Yr	VG	VG+	NM
❏ ANG.60005 [10]	Jonah Wails — 1st Blast	1954	18.75	37.50	75.00
❏ ANG.60006 [10]	Jonah Wails — 2nd Blast	1954	18.75	37.50	75.00
BETHLEHEM					
❏ BCP-1014 [10]	Jonah Jones Sextet	1954	20.00	40.00	80.00
CAPITOL					
❏ T 839 [M]	Muted Jazz	1957	10.00	20.00	40.00
❏ T 963 [M]	Swingin' On Broadway	1958	10.00	20.00	40.00
❏ ST 1039 [S]	Jumpin' with Jonah	1958	7.50	15.00	30.00
❏ T 1039 [M]	Jumpin' with Jonah	1958	6.25	12.50	25.00
❏ ST 1083 [S]	Swingin' at the Cinema	1958	7.50	15.00	30.00
❏ T 1083 [M]	Swingin' at the Cinema	1958	6.25	12.50	25.00
❏ ST 1115 [S]	Jonah Jumps Again	1959	7.50	15.00	30.00
❏ T 1115 [M]	Jonah Jumps Again	1959	6.25	12.50	25.00
❏ ST 1193 [S]	I Dig Chicks	1959	6.25	12.50	25.00
❏ T 1193 [M]	I Dig Chicks	1959	5.00	10.00	20.00
❏ ST 1237 [S]	Swingin' 'Round the World	1959	6.25	12.50	25.00
❏ T 1237 [M]	Swingin' 'Round the World	1959	5.00	10.00	20.00
❏ ST 1375 [S]	Hit Me Again!	1960	6.25	12.50	25.00
❏ T 1375 [M]	Hit Me Again!	1960	5.00	10.00	20.00
❏ ST 1404 [S]	Jumpin' with a Shuffle	1960	6.25	12.50	25.00
❏ T 1404 [M]	Jumpin' with a Shuffle	1960	5.00	10.00	20.00
❏ ST 1405 [S]	A Touch of Blue	1960	6.25	12.50	25.00
❏ T 1405 [M]	A Touch of Blue	1960	5.00	10.00	20.00
❏ ST 1532 [S]	The Unsinkable Molly Brown	1961	6.25	12.50	25.00
❏ T 1532 [M]	The Unsinkable Molly Brown	1961	5.00	10.00	20.00
❏ ST 1557 [S]	Great Instrumental Hits Styled by Jonah Jones	1961	6.25	12.50	25.00
❏ T 1557 [M]	Great Instrumental Hits Styled by Jonah Jones	1961	5.00	10.00	20.00
❏ ST 1641 [S]	Broadway Swings Again	1961	6.25	12.50	25.00

J

Number	Title (A Side/B Side)	Yr	VG	VG+	NM
❑ T 1641 [M]	Broadway Swings Again	1961	5.00	10.00	20.00
❑ SM-1660	Jonah Jones/Glenn Gray	197?	2.50	5.00	10.00
❑ ST 1660 [S]	Jonah Jones/Glenn Gray	1961	6.25	12.50	25.00
❑ T 1660 [M]	Jonah Jones/Glenn Gray	1961	5.00	10.00	20.00
❑ ST 1773 [S]	Jazz Bonus	1962	5.00	10.00	20.00
❑ T 1773 [M]	Jazz Bonus	1962	3.75	7.50	15.00
❑ ST 1948 [S]	And Now, In Person — Jonah Jones	1963	5.00	10.00	20.00
❑ T 1948 [M]	And Now, In Person — Jonah Jones	1963	3.75	7.50	15.00
❑ ST 2087 [S]	Blowin' Up a Storm	1964	5.00	10.00	20.00
❑ T 2087 [M]	Blowin' Up a Storm	1964	3.75	7.50	15.00
❑ ST 2594 [S]	The Best of Jonah Jones	1966	3.00	6.00	12.00
❑ T 2594 [M]	The Best of Jonah Jones	1966	3.75	7.50	15.00
CIRCLE					
❑ CLP-83	1944: Butterflies in the Rain	198?	2.50	5.00	10.00
DECCA					
❑ DL 4638 [M]	Hello Broadway	1965	3.00	6.00	12.00
❑ DL 4688 [M]	On the Sunny Side of the Street	1966	3.00	6.00	12.00
❑ DL 4765 [M]	Tijuana Taxi	1966	3.00	6.00	12.00
❑ DL 4800 [M]	Sweet with a Beat	1967	3.75	7.50	15.00
❑ DL 74638 [S]	Hello Broadway	1965	3.75	7.50	15.00
❑ DL 74688 [S]	On the Sunny Side of the Street	1966	3.75	7.50	15.00
❑ DL 74765 [S]	Tijuana Taxi	1966	3.75	7.50	15.00
❑ DL 74800 [S]	Sweet with a Beat	1967	3.00	6.00	12.00
❑ DL 74918	Jazz Tropical!	1968	3.00	6.00	12.00
GROOVE					
❑ LG-1001 [M]	Jonah Jones at the Embers	1956	12.50	25.00	50.00
HALL OF FAME					
❑ 613	After Hours Jazz	198?	2.50	5.00	10.00
JAZZ MAN					
❑ 5009	Confessin'	1981	2.50	5.00	10.00
MOTOWN					
❑ M-683	Along Came Jonah	1969	10.00	20.00	40.00
❑ M-690	Little Dis, Little Dat	1970	10.00	20.00	40.00
PICKWICK					
❑ SPC-3008	Swing Along	196?	3.00	6.00	12.00
RCA CAMDEN					
❑ CAS-2328	Jonah Jones Quartet	1969	3.00	6.00	12.00
RCA VICTOR					
❑ LPM-2004 [M]	Jonah Jones at the Embers	1959	10.00	20.00	40.00
—Reissue of Groove and Vik LP					
SWING					
❑ 8408	Paris 1954	198?	2.50	5.00	10.00
VIK					
❑ LXA-1135 [M]	Jonah Jones at the Embers	1958	10.00	20.00	40.00
—Reissue of Groove LP					

JONES, LEROY
45s
HIT

Number	Title (A Side/B Side)	Yr	VG	VG+	NM
❑ 33	Do You Love Me/Only Love Can Break a Heart	1962	2.00	4.00	8.00
—B-side by Ed Hardin					
❑ 51	Send Me Some Lovin'/Walk Like a Man	1963	2.00	4.00	8.00
—B-side by the Chellows					
❑ 53	Let's Limbo Some More/ Blame It on the Bossa Nova	1963	2.00	4.00	8.00
—B-side by Sylvia Richards					
❑ 60	Baby Workout/Can't Get Used to Losing You	1963	2.00	4.00	8.00
—B-side by Fred Brown					
❑ 68	Another Saturday Night/It's My Party	1963	2.00	4.00	8.00
—B-side by Connie Landers					
❑ 73	No One/So Much in Love	1963	2.00	4.00	8.00
—B-side by Thomas Henry					
❑ 79	Hey Girl/If I Had a Hammer	1963	2.00	4.00	8.00
—B-side by Ricky Dickens					
❑ 90	It's All Right/She's a Fool	1963	2.00	4.00	8.00
—B-side by Connie Dee					
❑ 97	Loddy Lo/Quicksand	1963	2.00	4.00	8.00
—B-side by Gerry and the Georgettes					
❑ 122	I Don't Want to Be Hurt Anymore/People	1964	2.00	4.00	8.00
—B-side by Morti Webb					
❑ 133	Steal Away/Where Did Our Love Go	1964	2.00	4.00	8.00
—B-side by the Houstons					
❑ 136	C'Mon and Swim/People Say	1964	2.00	4.00	8.00
—B-side by the Flower Sisters					
❑ 153	Baby Don't You Do It/Baby Love	1964	2.00	4.00	8.00
—B-side by Jenny and the Jewels					
❑ 176	Hold What You've Got/Wise Like Solomon	1965	2.00	4.00	8.00
—B-side by Bobby Brooks					
❑ 181	You Don't Want My Love/The Name Game	1965	2.00	4.00	8.00
—B-side by Lisa French					
❑ 184	Someday/Shake	1965	2.00	4.00	8.00
❑ 239	Crying Time/Lightnin' Strikes	1966	2.00	4.00	8.00
—B-side by Fred York					
❑ 249	I'm So Lonesome I Could Cry/ A Sign of the Times	1966	2.00	4.00	8.00
—B-side by Fred York					
❑ 255	When a Man Loves a Woman/Rainy Day Women #12 and 35	1966	2.00	4.00	8.00
—B-side by Bobby Brooks					
❑ 257	It's a Man's Man's Man's World/ Love Is Like an Itching in My Heart	1966	2.00	4.00	8.00
—B-side by Jenny and the Jewels					
❑ 267	Almost Persuaded/ My Uncle Used to Love Me But She Died	1966	2.00	4.00	8.00
—B-side by Roger Frolic					
❑ 270	Satisfied Mind/Reach Out I'll Be There	1966	2.00	4.00	8.00
—B-side by the Chellows					
❑ 279	Tell It Like It Is/Good Thing	1967	2.00	4.00	8.00
—B-side by Ed Hardin and the Cadets					
❑ 337	You Keep Me Hangin' On/Sunshine of Your Love	1968	2.00	4.00	8.00
—B-side by the Chords (2)					
❑ 347	Little Green Apples/Elenore	1968	2.00	4.00	8.00
—B-side by the Jalopy Five					

JONES, LEROY, AND LUCILLE JOHNS Also see each artist's individual listings.
45s
HIT

Number	Title (A Side/B Side)	Yr	VG	VG+	NM
❑ 41	You Are My Sunshine/Keep Your Hands Off My Baby	1962	2.00	4.00	8.00
—B-side by Alpha Zoe					

JONES, LITTLE ANTHONY Not the same Little Anthony who was with the Imperials.
45s
EMBER

Number	Title (A Side/B Side)	Yr	VG	VG+	NM
❑ 1090	Dear Gesu Bambino (Part 1)/Dear Gesu Bambino (Part 2)	1962	3.75	7.50	15.00

JONES, LITTLE JOHNNY
ATLANTIC

Number	Title (A Side/B Side)	Yr	VG	VG+	NM
❑ 1045	Hoy, Hoy/Doin' the Best I Can	1954	20.00	40.00	80.00
FLAIR					
❑ 1010	Sweet Little Woman/I May Be Wrong	1953	200.00	400.00	800.00

JONES, LITTLE SONNY
45s
IMPERIAL

Number	Title (A Side/B Side)	Yr	VG	VG+	NM
❑ 5275	I Got Booted/Tend to Your Business Blues	1954	25.00	50.00	100.00
❑ 5287	Winehead Baby/Going to the Country	1954	25.00	50.00	100.00
SPECIALTY					
❑ 443	Is Everything All Right/Do You Really Love Me	1952	20.00	40.00	80.00

JONES, MARY
45s
HIT

Number	Title (A Side/B Side)	Yr	VG	VG+	NM
❑ 121	Walk On By/Diane	1964	2.00	4.00	8.00
—B-side by the Concords					

JONES, PAUL Original lead singer for MANFRED MANN.
45s
BELL

Number	Title (A Side/B Side)	Yr	VG	VG+	NM
❑ 805	It's Getting Better/Not Before Time	1969	2.00	4.00	8.00
CAPITOL					
❑ 5745	I Can't Hold On Much Longer/Baby Tomorrow	1966	2.00	4.00	8.00
❑ 5800	High Time/It Is Coming Closer	1966	2.00	4.00	8.00
❑ 5857	Sonny Boy Williamson/I've Been a Bad, Bad Boy	1967	2.00	4.00	8.00
❑ 5970	Privilege/Free Me	1967	2.00	4.00	8.00
LONDON					
❑ 168	Mighty Ship/Who Are the Masters	1972	—	2.50	5.00
❑ 178	The Pod That Came Back/Construction Worker's Song	1972	—	2.50	5.00
PRIVATE STOCK					
❑ 45,004	Love Enough	1974	—	2.50	5.00
Albums					
CAPITOL					
❑ ST 2795 [S]	Paul Jones Sings Songs from the Film "Privilege" and Others	1967	7.50	15.00	30.00
❑ T 2795 [M]	Paul Jones Sings Songs from the Film "Privilege" and Others	1967	7.50	15.00	30.00
LONDON					
❑ XPS 605	Crucifix in a Horseshoe	1971	3.00	6.00	12.00

JONES, QUINCY
45s
A&M

Number	Title (A Side/B Side)	Yr	VG	VG+	NM
❑ 1115	Oh Happy Day/Love and Peace	1969	—	3.00	6.00
❑ 1139	Oh Happy Day/Love and Peace	1969	—	2.50	5.00
❑ 1163	Killer Joe/Maybe Tomorrow	1970	—	2.50	5.00
❑ 1184	Bridge Over Troubled Water (Part 1)/Bridge Over Troubled Water (Part 2)	1970	—	2.50	5.00
❑ 1316	What's Going On (Part 1)/What's Going On (Part 2)	1971	—	2.50	5.00
❑ 1323	Ironside/Cast Your Fate to the Wind	1972	—	2.50	5.00
❑ 1404	Love Theme from "The Getaway" (Part 1)/Love Theme from "The Getaway" (Part 2)	1973	—	2.00	4.00
❑ 1455	Sanford & Son Theme/Summer in the City	1973	—	2.00	4.00
❑ 1606	If I Ever Lose This Heaven/Along Came Betty	1974	—	2.00	4.00
❑ 1606 [PS]	If I Ever Lose This Heaven/Along Came Betty	1974	—	3.00	6.00
❑ 1638	Soul Saga/Boogie Joe, The Grinder	1974	—	2.00	4.00
❑ 1663	Body Heat/One Track Mind	1975	—	2.00	4.00
❑ 1743	Is It Love That We're Missing/Cry Baby	1975	—	2.00	4.00
❑ 1743 [PS]	Is It Love That We're Missing/Cry Baby	1975	—	3.00	6.00
❑ 1791	Mellow Madness/Paranoid	1976	—	2.00	4.00
❑ 1878	Midnight Soul Patrol/Brown Soft Shoe	1976	—	2.00	4.00
❑ 1909	"Roots" Medley/Many Rains Ago (Oluwu)	1977	—	2.00	4.00
❑ 1909 [PS]	"Roots" Medley/Many Rains Ago (Oluwu)	1977	—	3.00	6.00
❑ 1923	What Shall I Do (Hush, Hush, Somebody's Calling My Name)/Oh, Lord, Come By Here	1977	—	2.00	4.00
❑ 2043	Stuff Like That/There's a Train Leavin'	1978	—	2.00	4.00
❑ 2043 [PS]	Stuff Like That/There's a Train Leavin'	1978	—	3.00	6.00
❑ 2080	Love, I Never Had It So Good/I Heard That	1978	—	2.00	4.00
❑ 2309	Ai No Corrida/Lenta Letina	1981	—	2.00	4.00
❑ 2334	Razzamatazz/Velas	1981	—	2.00	4.00
—Featuring Patti Austin					
❑ 2357	Just Once/The Dude	1981	—	2.00	4.00
—Featuring James Ingram					
❑ 2387	One Hundred Ways/Velas	1981	—	2.00	4.00
—Featuring James Ingram					
❑ 2417	There's a Train Leavin'/Something Special	1981	—	2.00	4.00
—Featuring Patti Austin					
ABC					
❑ 11086	For Love of Ivy/The Pussyfoot	1968	2.00	4.00	8.00
BELL					
❑ 832	I'm a Believer/The Time for Love Is Anytime	1969	—	3.00	6.00
❑ 833	Cactus Flower Theme/ The Time for Love Is Anytime	1969	—	3.00	6.00
❑ 838	Bob & Carol & Ted & Alice/Giggle Grass	1969	—	3.00	6.00
COLGEMS					
❑ 66-1016	Hangin' Paper/Lonely Bottles	1968	2.00	4.00	8.00
IMPULSE					
❑ 206	Quintessence/For Lena and Lennie	1962	3.00	6.00	12.00

Number	Title (A Side/B Side)	Yr	VG	VG+	NM
MERCURY					
❏ 71425	The Syncopated Clock/Tuxedo Junction	1959	3.00	6.00	12.00
❏ 71460	Choo Choo Ch-Boogie/Marchin' the Blues	1959	3.00	6.00	12.00
❏ 71489	Moanin'/The Preacher	1959	3.00	6.00	12.00
❏ 71546	Birth of a Band/Change of Pace	1959	3.00	6.00	12.00
❏ 71665	Love Is Here to Stay/Moonglow	1960	3.00	6.00	12.00
❏ 71737	G-Man Train/Pleasingly Plump	1960	3.00	6.00	12.00
❏ 71825	Mack the Knife/Hot Saki	1961	3.00	6.00	12.00
❏ 71940	St. Louis Blues/Twistin' Chicken	1962	3.00	6.00	12.00
❏ 72012	A Taste of Honey/Shagnasty	1962	3.00	6.00	12.00
❏ 72105	Boogie Bossa Nova/Morning of the Carnival	1963	2.50	5.00	10.00
❏ 72160	Jive Samba/Comin' Home Baby	1963	2.50	5.00	10.00
❏ 72289	Baby Elephant Walk/Mr. Lucky	1964	2.50	5.00	10.00
❏ 72306	Theme from "Golden Boy"/Sea Weed	1964	2.50	5.00	10.00
❏ 72348	A Hard Day's Night/Soul Serenade	1964	2.50	5.00	10.00
❏ 72423	Non-Stop to Brazil/Gentle Rain	1965	2.50	5.00	10.00
❏ 72436	The Pawnbroker/Harlem Drive	1965	2.50	5.00	10.00
❏ 72460	Mirage/Pack It Up	1965	2.50	5.00	10.00
❏ 72496	(I Can't Get No) Satisfaction/What's New Pussycat	1965	2.50	5.00	10.00
❏ 72533	Baby Cakes/Mohair Sam	1966	2.50	5.00	10.00
QWEST					
❏ 17528	Stomp (Frankie Knuckles Mix)/Stomp (Mousse T.'s Radio Mix)	1996	—	—	3.00
❏ 17673	Slow Jams (New Edit)/Slow Jams (Remix)	1996	—	—	3.00
—Featuring Babyface and Tamia with Portrait and Barry White					
❏ 19881	Tomorrow (A Better You, A Better Me)/ (Instrumental)	1990	—	—	3.00
—Featuring Tevin Campbell					
❏ 19992	The Secret Garden (Sweet Seduction Suite)/ (Instrumental)	1990	—	—	3.00
—With Al B. Sure!, James Ingram, El DeBarge and Barry White					
❏ 19992 [PS]	The Secret Garden (Sweet Seduction Suite)/ (Instrumental)	1990	—	—	3.00
❏ 22697	I'll Be Good to You/(Instrumental)	1990	—	—	3.00
—With Ray Charles and Chaka Khan					
❏ 22697 [PS]	I'll Be Good to You/(Instrumental)	1990	—	—	3.00
RCA VICTOR					
❏ 74-0221	Ole Turkey Buzzard/Soul Full of Gold	1969	—	3.00	6.00
REPRISE					
❏ 1072	Passin' the Buck/Money Runner	1972	—	2.50	5.00
UNI					
❏ 55142	The Lost Man/Main Squeeze	1969	—	3.00	6.00
UNITED ARTISTS					
❏ 50706	Call Me Mister Tibbs/Soul Flower	1970	—	2.50	5.00
Albums					
A&M					
❏ SP-3023	Walking in Space	1969	3.00	6.00	12.00
❏ SP-3030	Gula Matari	1970	3.00	6.00	12.00
❏ SP-3037	Smackwater Jack	1971	3.00	6.00	12.00
❏ SP-3041	You've Got It Bad Girl	1973	3.00	6.00	12.00
❏ SP-3191	Body Heat	1982	2.00	4.00	8.00
—Budget-line reissue					
❏ SP-3200	The Best	1982	2.00	4.00	8.00
❏ SP-3248	The Dude	198?	2.00	4.00	8.00
—Budget-line reissue					
❏ SP-3249	Sounds…And Stuff Like That!	198?	2.00	4.00	8.00
—Budget-line reissue					
❏ SP-3278	The Best, Vol. 2	1985	2.00	4.00	8.00
❏ SP-3617	Body Heat	1974	2.50	5.00	10.00
❏ SP-3705 [(2)]	I Heard That!!	1976	3.00	6.00	12.00
❏ SP-3721	The Dude	1981	2.50	5.00	10.00
❏ SP-4526	Mellow Madness	1975	2.50	5.00	10.00
❏ SP-4626	Roots	1977	2.50	5.00	10.00
❏ SP-4685	Sounds…And Stuff Like That!	1978	2.50	5.00	10.00
❏ SP-6507 [(2)]	I Heard That!!	198?	2.50	5.00	10.00
—Budget-line reissue					
❏ QU-53041 [Q]	You've Got It Bad Girl	1974	5.00	10.00	20.00
❏ QU-53617 [Q]	Body Heat	1974	5.00	10.00	20.00
❏ QU-54526 [Q]	Mellow Madness	1975	5.00	10.00	20.00
ABC					
❏ D-782 [(2)]	Mode	1973	3.00	6.00	12.00
ABC IMPULSE!					
❏ AS-11 [S]	The Quintessence	1968	3.75	7.50	15.00
❏ IA-9342 [(2)]	Quintessential Charts	1978	3.00	6.00	12.00
ABC-PARAMOUNT					
❏ 149 [M]	This Is How I Feel About Jazz	1956	25.00	50.00	100.00
❏ 186 [M]	Go West, Man!	1957	25.00	50.00	100.00
CHESS					
❏ CH-91562	The Music of Quincy Jones	198?	2.50	5.00	10.00
COLGEMS					
❏ COM-107 [M]	In Cold Blood	1967	5.00	10.00	20.00
❏ COS-107 [S]	In Cold Blood	1967	6.25	12.50	25.00
EMARCY					
❏ MG-36083 [M]	Jazz Abroad	1956	25.00	50.00	100.00
❏ 818177-1 [(2)]	The Birth of a Band	1984	3.00	6.00	12.00
GRP/IMPULSE!					
❏ 222	The Quintessence	199?	3.75	7.50	15.00
—Reissue on audiophile vinyl					
IMPULSE!					
❏ A-11 [M]	The Quintessence	1962	7.50	15.00	30.00
❏ AS-11 [S]	The Quintessence	1962	10.00	20.00	40.00
LIBERTY					
❏ LOM-16004 [M]	Enter Laughing	1967	6.25	12.50	25.00
❏ LOS-17004 [S]	Enter Laughing	1967	7.50	15.00	30.00
MCA					
❏ 4145 [(2)]	Quintessential Charts	198?	2.50	5.00	10.00
—Reissue of ABC Impulse 9342					
❏ 5578	The Slugger's Wife	1985	3.00	6.00	12.00
MCA/IMPULSE!					
❏ 5728	The Quintessence	1986	2.00	4.00	8.00
MERCURY					
❏ SRM-2-623 [(2)]	Ndeda	1972	3.75	7.50	15.00
❏ PPS-2014 [M]	Around the World	1961	7.50	15.00	30.00
❏ PPS-6014 [S]	Around the World	1961	10.00	20.00	40.00

Number	Title (A Side/B Side)	Yr	VG	VG+	NM
❏ MG-20444 [M]	Birth of a Band	1959	12.50	25.00	50.00
❏ MG-20561 [M]	The Great, Wide World of Quincy Jones	1960	12.50	25.00	50.00
❏ MG-20612 [M]	I Dig Dancers	1960	10.00	20.00	40.00
❏ MG-20653 [M]	Quincy Jones at Newport '61	1961	7.50	15.00	30.00
❏ MG-20751 [M]	Big Band Bossa Nova	1962	7.50	15.00	30.00
❏ MG-20799 [M]	Quincy Jones Plays Hip Hits	1963	7.50	15.00	30.00
❏ MG-20863 [M]	Quincy Jones Explores the Music of Henry Mancini	1964	5.00	10.00	20.00
❏ MG-20938 [M]	Golden Boy	1964	5.00	10.00	20.00
❏ MG-21011 [M]	The Pawnbroker	1964	5.00	10.00	20.00
❏ MG-21025 [M]	Mirage	1965	5.00	10.00	20.00
❏ MG-21050 [M]	Quincy Jones Plays for Pussycats	1965	5.00	10.00	20.00
❏ MG-21063 [M]	Quincy's Got a Brand New Bag	1965	5.00	10.00	20.00
❏ MG-21070 [M]	Slender Thread	1966	5.00	10.00	20.00
❏ SR-60129 [S]	Birth of a Band	1959	15.00	30.00	60.00
❏ SR-60221 [S]	The Great, Wide World of Quincy Jones	1960	15.00	30.00	60.00
❏ SR-60612 [S]	I Dig Dancers	1960	12.50	25.00	50.00
❏ SR-60653 [S]	Quincy Jones at Newport '61	1961	10.00	20.00	40.00
❏ SR-60751 [S]	Big Band Bossa Nova	1962	10.00	20.00	40.00
❏ SR-60799 [S]	Quincy Jones Plays Hip Hits	1963	10.00	20.00	40.00
❏ SR-60863 [S]	Quincy Jones Explores the Music of Henry Mancini	1964	6.25	12.50	25.00
❏ SR-60938 [S]	Golden Boy	1964	6.25	12.50	25.00
❏ SR-61011 [S]	The Pawnbroker	1964	6.25	12.50	25.00
❏ SR-61025 [S]	Mirage	1965	6.25	12.50	25.00
❏ SR-61050 [S]	Quincy Jones Plays for Pussycats	1965	6.25	12.50	25.00
❏ SR-61063 [S]	Quincy's Got a Brand New Bag	1965	6.25	12.50	25.00
❏ SR-61070 [S]	Slender Thread	1966	6.25	12.50	25.00
MOBILE FIDELITY					
❏ 1-078	You've Got It Bad Girl	1981	6.25	12.50	25.00
—Audiophile vinyl					
NAUTILUS					
❏ NR-52	The Dude	198?	10.00	20.00	40.00
—Audiophile vinyl					
PRESTIGE					
❏ PRLP-172 [10]	Quincy Jones with the Swedish-American All Stars	1953	50.00	100.00	200.00
QWEST					
❏ 25356 [(2)]	The Color Purple	1985	5.00	10.00	20.00
—Boxed set on purple vinyl					
❏ 25389 [(2)]	The Color Purple	1985	3.75	7.50	15.00
—Gatefold package on purple vinyl					
❏ 26020	Back on the Block	1989	3.00	6.00	12.00
TRIP					
❏ 5514	The Great Wide World of Quincy Jones	1974	2.00	4.00	8.00
❏ 5554	Live at Newport '61	197?	2.00	4.00	8.00
UNITED ARTISTS					
❏ UAS-5214	They Call Me Mister Tibbs	1970	6.25	12.50	25.00
WING					
❏ SRW-16398	Around the World	1969	3.00	6.00	12.00

JONES, RONNIE, AND THE CLASSMATES

Number	Title (A Side/B Side)	Yr	VG	VG+	NM
45s					
END					
❏ 1002	Teenage Rock/Little Girl Next Door	1957	30.00	60.00	120.00
❏ 1014	Lonely Boy/Baby Cries	1958	30.00	60.00	120.00
❏ 1125	Teenage Rock/Little Girl Next Door	1963	6.25	12.50	25.00

JONES, SPIKE, AND THE CITY SLICKERS

Number	Title (A Side/B Side)	Yr	VG	VG+	NM
45s					
KAPP					
❏ 314	I Want the South to Win the War for Christmas/ Let's All Sing a Song for Christmas	1959	10.00	20.00	40.00
—B-side by the Happy Harts					
❏ 314 [PS]	I Want the South to Win the War for Christmas/ Let's All Sing a Song for Christmas	1959	15.00	30.00	60.00
LIBERTY					
❏ 55191	The Late Late Late Movies (Part 1)/The Late Late Late Movies (Part 2)	1959	3.00	6.00	12.00
❏ 55253	Ah-1, Ah-2, Ah-Sunset Strip (Part 1)/Ah-1, Ah-2, Ah-Sunset Strip (Part 2)	1960	3.00	6.00	12.00
❏ 55317	Keystone Kapers/Silence Please	1961	3.00	6.00	12.00
❏ 55649	The Ballad of Jed Clampett/Green, Green	1963	2.50	5.00	10.00
❏ 55684	Dominique/Sweet and Lovely	1964	2.50	5.00	10.00
❏ 55718	I'm in the Mood for Love/Paradise	1964	2.50	5.00	10.00
❏ 55788	Let's Kiss, Kiss, Kiss/Star Jenka	1965	2.50	5.00	10.00
RCA VICTOR					
❏ 27-0030	Cocktails for Two/Chloe	195?	5.00	10.00	20.00
❏ 47-2795	Nutcracker Suite — 1 (The Little Girl's Dream)/ Nutcracker Suite — 6 (End of the Little Girl's Dream)	1949	5.00	10.00	20.00
—Originals with aqua labels and gold print					
❏ 47-2795	Nutcracker Suite — 1 (The Little Girl's Dream)/ Nutcracker Suite — 6 (End of the Little Girl's Dream)	1951	3.75	7.50	15.00
—Reissue on black label with white print, outline of dog on right					
❏ 47-2796	Nutcracker Suite — 2 (Land of the Sugar Plum Fairy)/Nutcracker Suite — 5 (Back to the Fairy Ball)	1949	5.00	10.00	20.00
—Originals with aqua labels and gold print					
❏ 47-2796	Nutcracker Suite — 2 (Land of the Sugar Plum Fairy)/Nutcracker Suite — 5 (Back to the Fairy Ball)	1951	3.75	7.50	15.00
—Reissue on black label with white print, outline of dog on right					
❏ 47-2797	Nutcracker Suite — 3 (The Fairy Ball)/ Nutcracker Suite — 4 (The Mysterious Room)	1949	5.00	10.00	20.00
—Originals with aqua labels and gold print					
❏ 47-2797	Nutcracker Suite — 3 (The Fairy Ball)/ Nutcracker Suite — 4 (The Mysterious Room)	1951	3.75	7.50	15.00
—Reissue on black label with white print, outline of dog on right					
❏ 47-2894	Ya Wanna Buy a Bunny/Knock Knock	1949	5.00	10.00	20.00
❏ 47-2963	(All I Want for Christmas Is) My Two Front Teeth/ Happy New Year	1949	7.50	15.00	30.00
❏ 47-2992	Dance of the Hours/None But the Lonely Heart	1949	5.00	10.00	20.00
❏ 47-3126	Wild Bill Hiccup/Morpheus	1949	5.00	10.00	20.00
❏ 47-3198	The Charleston/Charlestone-Mio	1949	5.00	10.00	20.00
❏ 47-3199	Black Bottom/Doin' the New Raccoon	1949	5.00	10.00	20.00

J

Number	Title (A Side/B Side)	Yr	VG	VG+	NM
❏ 47-3200	I Wonder Where My Baby Is Tonight/❏ The Varsity Drag	1949	5.00	10.00	20.00
—The above three comprise a box set					
❏ 47-3287	That Old Black Magic/Liebestraum	1949	5.00	10.00	20.00
❏ 47-3288	Love in Bloom/My Old Flame	1949	5.00	10.00	20.00
❏ 47-3289	William Tell Overture/I Kiss Your Hand Madame	1949	5.00	10.00	20.00
—The above three comprise a box set					
❏ 47-3741	Chinese Mule Train/Riders in the Sky	1950	5.00	10.00	20.00
❏ 47-3827	I Know a Secret/Charlestone-Mio	1950	5.00	10.00	20.00
❏ 47-3912	Yaaha Hula Hickey Dula/Yes! We Have No Bananas	1950	5.00	10.00	20.00
❏ 47-3934	Rudolph the Red-Nosed Reindeer/Mommy, Won't You Buy a Baby Brother	1950	5.00	10.00	20.00
❏ 47-4011	Tennessee Waltz/I Haven't Been Home for Three Whole Nights	1950	5.00	10.00	20.00
❏ 47-4055	Peter Cottontail/Rhapsody from Hungary	1951	5.00	10.00	20.00
❏ 47-4125	My Daddy Is a General to Me/III Barkio	1951	5.00	10.00	20.00
❏ 47-4209	Too Young/So 'Elp Me	1951	5.00	10.00	20.00
❏ 47-4315	Rudolph the Red-Nosed Reindeer/(All I Want for Christmas Is) My Two Front Teeth	1951	5.00	10.00	20.00
❏ 47-4546	Deep Purple/It Never Rains in Sunny California	1952	5.00	10.00	20.00
❏ 47-4568	Down South/I've Turned a Gadabout	1952	5.00	10.00	20.00
❏ 47-4669	There's a Blue Sky Way Out Yonder/Stop Your Gamblin'	1952	5.00	10.00	20.00
❏ 47-4731	A Din Skal, A Min Skal (Swedish Polka)	1952	—	—	—
—Canceled?					
❏ 47-4831	(All of a Sudden) My Heart Sings/I'll Never Work There Anymore	1952	5.00	10.00	20.00
❏ 47-4875	Hotter Than a Pistol/Hot Lips	1952	5.00	10.00	20.00
❏ 47-5015	Barnyard Christmas/Socko the Smallest Snowball	1952	5.00	10.00	20.00
—With the Bell Sisters					
❏ 47-5067	I Saw Mommy Kissing Santa Claus/Winter	1952	5.00	10.00	20.00
❏ 47-5067 [PS]	I Saw Mommy Kissing Santa Claus/Winter	1952	10.00	20.00	40.00
❏ 47-5107	I Went to Your Wedding/I'll Never Work There Anymore	1952	5.00	10.00	20.00
❏ 47-5320	Three Little Fishes/A Din Skal, A Min Skal (Swedish Polka)	1953	5.00	10.00	20.00
❏ 47-5392	Captain of the Spaceship/Are My Ears On Straight	1953	—	—	—
—Canceled					
❏ 47-5472	Pal-Yat-Chee/Dragnet	1953	5.00	10.00	20.00
❏ 47-5497	Where Did My Snowman Go/Santa Brought Me Choo Choo Trains	1953	5.00	10.00	20.00
❏ 47-5602	Ricketshaw/My Heart Went Boom Boom	1954	—	—	—
—Canceled					
❏ 47-5742	Secret Love/I'm in the Mood for Love	1954	5.00	10.00	20.00
❏ 47-5917	Japanese Skokiaan/My Heart Went Boom Boom	1954	5.00	10.00	20.00
❏ 47-5920	I Want Eddie Fisher for Christmas/Japanese Skokiaan	1954	5.00	10.00	20.00
❏ 47-6064	This Song Is For the Birds/Hi Mister	1955	5.00	10.00	20.00
❏ 447-0172	(All I Want for Christmas Is) My Two Front Teeth/Rudolph the Red-Nosed Reindeer	195?	3.75	7.50	15.00
—Reissue (Gold Standard Series); black label, dog on top					
❏ WP 143 [(3)]	The Nutcracker Suite	1949	20.00	40.00	80.00
—Includes aqua label records 47-2795, 47-2796 and 47-2797 plus box					
❏ WP 143 [(3)]	The Nutcracker Suite	1951	15.00	30.00	60.00
—Includes black label records 47-2795, 47-2796 and 47-2797 plus box					
❏ WY-461	Barnyard Christmas/Socko the Smallest Snowball	1952	5.00	10.00	20.00
—With the Bell Sisters; "Little Nipper" children's series					
VERVE					
❏ 2026	My Birthday Comes on Christmas/Wouldn't It Be Fun	1956	3.75	7.50	15.00
❏ 10037	I'm Popeye the Sailor Man/My Heart Went Boom Boom	1957	3.75	7.50	15.00
WARNER BROS.					
❏ 5116	Monster Movie Babe/Teenage Brain Surgeon	1959	3.75	7.50	15.00
7-Inch Extended Plays					
RCA VICTOR					
❏ EPA 288	That Old Black Magic/Liebestraum//Love in Bloom/My Old Flame	1952	7.50	15.00	30.00
❏ EPA 288 [PS]	Spike Jones Favorites	1952	7.50	15.00	30.00
❏ EPA-5058	*Cocktails for Two/Chloe/William Tell Overture/Hawaiian War Chant	1958	7.50	15.00	30.00
❏ EPA-5058 [PS]	Spike Jones (Gold Standard Series)	1958	7.50	15.00	30.00
VERVE					
❏ 2003	Love and Marriage/Memories Are Made of This//16 Tacos/The Trouble with Pascual	1956	3.75	7.50	15.00
Albums					
CORNOGRAPHIC					
❏ 1001	King of Corn	197?	2.50	5.00	10.00
GOLDBERG & O'REILY					
❏ MF 205/4 [(3)]	The Craziest Show on Earth	1977	5.00	10.00	20.00
—Collection of radio show performances					
HINDSIGHT					
❏ HSR-185	The Uncollected Spike Jones 1946	198?	2.50	5.00	10.00
LIBERTY					
❏ LRP-3140 [M]	Omnibust	1959	12.50	25.00	50.00
❏ LRP-3154 [M]	60 Years of Music America Hates Best	1960	12.50	25.00	50.00
❏ LRP-3338 [M]	Washington Square	1963	5.00	10.00	20.00
❏ LRP-3349 [M]	Spike Jones' New Band	1964	7.50	15.00	30.00
❏ LRP-3370 [M]	My Man	1964	5.00	10.00	20.00
❏ LRP-3401 [M]	Spike Jones Plays Hank Williams Hits	1965	5.00	10.00	20.00
❏ LST-7140 [S]	Omnibust	1959	18.75	37.50	75.00
—Black vinyl					
❏ LST-7140 [S]	Omnibust	1959	37.50	75.00	150.00
—Red vinyl					
❏ LST-7154 [S]	60 Years of Music America Hates Best	1960	18.75	37.50	75.00
❏ LST-7338 [S]	Washington Square	1963	6.25	12.50	25.00
❏ LST-7349 [S]	Spike Jones' New Band	1964	10.00	20.00	40.00
❏ LST-7370 [S]	My Man	1964	6.25	12.50	25.00
❏ LST-7401 [S]	Spike Jones Plays Hank Williams Hits	1965	6.25	12.50	25.00
RCA GOLD SEAL					
❏ AGL1-4142	Spike Jones Is Murdering the Classics!	1982	2.00	4.00	8.00
—Reissue					

Number	Title (A Side/B Side)	Yr	VG	VG+	NM
RCA RED SEAL					
❏ LSC-3235 [R]	Spike Jones Is Murdering the Classics!	1971	5.00	10.00	20.00
RCA VICTOR					
❏ LPT-18 [10]	Spike Jones Plays the Charleston	1952	50.00	100.00	200.00
❏ ANL1-1035	The Best of Spike Jones	1975	2.50	5.00	10.00
—Reissue					
❏ LPM-2224 [M]	Thank You Music Lovers	1960	12.50	25.00	50.00
—"RCA Victor" in silver above dog, "Long 33 1/3 Play" at bottom of label					
❏ LPM-2224 [M]	Thank You Music Lovers	1965	6.25	12.50	25.00
—"RCA Victor" in white above dog, "Monaural" at bottom of label					
❏ ANL1-2312	The Best of Spike Jones, Volume 2	1977	2.50	5.00	10.00
—Reissue					
❏ LPM-3054 [10]	Bottoms Up	1952	50.00	100.00	200.00
❏ LPM-3128 [10]	Spike Jones Murders Carmen and Kids the Classics	1953	50.00	100.00	200.00
❏ AYL1-3748	The Best of Spike Jones, Volume 1	1980	2.00	4.00	8.00
—"Best Buy Series" reissue					
❏ LPM-3849 [M]	The Best of Spike Jones	1967	6.25	12.50	25.00
❏ LSP-3849 [R]	The Best of Spike Jones	1967	5.00	10.00	20.00
❏ AYL1-3870	The Best of Spike Jones, Volume 2	1981	2.00	4.00	8.00
—"Best Buy Series" reissue					
RHINO					
❏ R1 70196	It's a Spike Jones Christmas	1988	3.00	6.00	12.00
❏ R1 70261	Dinner Music…For People Who Aren't Very Hungry	1988	3.00	6.00	12.00
UNITED ARTISTS					
❏ UA-LA439-E	The Very Best of Spike Jones	1975	3.00	6.00	12.00
VERVE					
❏ MGV-2021 [M]	Let's Sing a Song for Christmas	1956	12.50	25.00	50.00
❏ V-2021 [M]	Let's Sing a Song for Christmas	1961	7.50	15.00	30.00
❏ MGV-4005 [M]	Dinner Music…For People Who Aren't Very Hungry	1957	12.50	25.00	50.00
❏ V-4005 [M]	Dinner Music…For People Who Aren't Very Hungry	1961	6.25	12.50	25.00
WARNER BROS.					
❏ W 1332 [M]	Spike Jones in Hi-Fi	1959	10.00	20.00	40.00
❏ WS 1332 [S]	Spike Jones in Stereo	1959	12.50	25.00	50.00

JONES, THUMPER See GEORGE JONES.

JONES, TOM
12-Inch Singles

Number	Title (A Side/B Side)	Yr	VG	VG+	NM
INTERSCOPE					
❏ 2172 [DJ]	If I Only Knew (4 versions)	1994	2.50	5.00	10.00
❏ 2194 [DJ]	Situation (5 versions)	1994	2.50	5.00	10.00
MCA					
❏ 55144	She's a Lady (3 versions)	1995	2.50	5.00	10.00
45s					
CHINA					
❏ 871038-7	Kiss/E.F.L.	1989	—	—	3.00
—A-side: The Art of Noise with Tom Jones; B-side by Art of Noise					
❏ 871038-7 [PS]	Kiss/E.F.L.	1989	—	—	3.00
EPIC					
❏ 50308	Say You'll Stay Until Tomorrow/Lady Lay	1976	—	2.00	4.00
❏ 50382	Take Me Tonight/I Hope You'll Understand	1977	—	2.00	4.00
❏ 50468	What a Night/That's Where I Belong	1977	—	2.00	4.00
❏ 50506	There's Nothing Stronger Than Our Love/No One Gave Me Love	1978	—	2.00	4.00
❏ 50636	Hey Love/Baby, As You Turn Away	1978	—	2.00	4.00
MCA					
❏ 41127	Dancing Endlessly/Never Had a Lady Before	1979	—	2.00	4.00
MERCURY					
❏ 76100	Darlin'/I Don't Want to Know You That Way	1981	—	2.00	4.00
❏ 76115	What in the World's Come Over You/The Things That Matter Most to Me	1981	—	2.00	4.00
❏ 76125	Lady Lay Down/A Daughter's Question	1981	—	2.00	4.00
❏ 76172	A Woman's Touch/I'll Never Get Over You	1982	—	2.00	4.00
❏ 810445-7	Touch Me (I'll Be Your Fool Once More)/We're Wasting Our Time	1983	—	—	3.00
❏ 812631-7	It'll Be Me/If I Ever Had to Say Goodbye to You	1983	—	—	3.00
❏ 814820-7	I've Been Rained On Too/That Old Piano	1983	—	—	3.00
❏ 818801-7	This Time/Memphis, Tennessee	1984	—	—	3.00
❏ 870233-7	Things That Matter Most to Me/Green, Green Grass of Home	1988	—	—	3.00
❏ 880173-7	All the Love Is On the Radio/(B-side unknown)	1984	—	—	3.00
❏ 880402-7	I'm an Old Rock and Roller (Dancin' to a Different Beat)/My Kind of Girl	1984	—	—	3.00
❏ 880569-7	Give Her All the Roses (Don't Wait Until Tomorrow)/A Picture of You	1985	—	—	3.00
❏ 884039-7	Not Another Heart Song/Only My Heart Knows	1985	—	—	3.00
❏ 884252-7	It's Four in the Morning/I'll Never Get Over You	1985	—	—	3.00
❏ 888911-7	Lover to Lover/A Daughter's Question	1987	—	—	3.00
PARROT					
❏ 9737	It's Not Unusual/To Wait for Love (Is to Waste Your Life Away)	1965	2.50	5.00	10.00
❏ 9765	What's New Pussycat/Once Upon a Time	1965	2.50	5.00	10.00
❏ 9765 [PS]	What's New Pussycat/Once Upon a Time	1965	3.75	7.50	15.00
❏ 9787	With These Hands/Some Other Guy	1965	2.00	4.00	8.00
❏ 9787 [PS]	With These Hands/Some Other Guy	1965	3.00	6.00	12.00
❏ 9801	Thunderball/Key to My Heart	1965	2.00	4.00	8.00
❏ 9801 [PS]	Thunderball/Key to My Heart	1965	3.00	6.00	12.00
—Version 2: without the above elements on sleeve					
❏ 9801 [PS]	Thunderball/Key to My Heart	1965	5.00	10.00	20.00
—Version 1: with a dead female and a spear gun					
❏ 9809	Promise Her Anything/Little You	1966	2.00	4.00	8.00
❏ 40006	Not Responsible/Once There Was a Time	1966	2.00	4.00	8.00
❏ 40008	City Girl/What a Party	1966	2.00	4.00	8.00
❏ 40009	Green, Green Grass of Home/If I Had You	1966	2.00	4.00	8.00
❏ 40012	Detroit City/Ten Guitars	1967	2.00	4.00	8.00
❏ 40014	Funny Familiar Forgotten Feelings/I'll Never Let You Go	1967	2.00	4.00	8.00
❏ 40016	Sixteen Tons/Things I Wanna Do	1967	2.00	4.00	8.00
❏ 40018	I'll Never Fall in Love Again/Once Upon a Time	1967	2.00	4.00	8.00
—Later pressings delete a verse from the A-side; time is listed at 2:55					
❏ 40018	I'll Never Fall in Love Again/Once Upon a Time	1967	3.00	6.00	12.00
—First pressings contain the full-length version of the A-side; time is listed at over four minutes					

Elton John, *Captain Fantastic and the Brown Dirt Cowboy,* MCA 2142, original with custom label, two booklets and a poster, $6-$12.

Johnny and the Hurricanes, "Rocking Goose," Big Top 3051, picture sleeve, $20-$40.

Robert Johnson, *King of the Delta Blues Singers,* Columbia CL 1654, mono LP, red and black label with six "eye" logos, $250-$500.

George Jones, *The Best of George Jones,* United Artists UAS 6291, stereo LP, $15-$30.

Jonah Jones, *Jumpin' with Jonah, Part 3,* Capitol EAP 3-1039, 7-inch EP, $12-$24 (cover and record together).

Tom Jones, *It's Not Unusual,* Parrot PA 61004, mono LP, $7.50-$15.

Number	Title (A Side/B Side)	Yr	VG	VG+	NM
❏ 40020	Land of a Thousand Dances/				
	I Can't Stop Loving You	1967	5.00	10.00	20.00
—May be promo only					
❏ 40024	I'm Coming Home/Lonely One	1967	2.00	4.00	8.00
❏ 40025	Delilah/Smile Away Your Blues	1968	2.00	4.00	8.00
❏ 40029	Help Yourself/Day by Day	1968	2.00	4.00	8.00
❏ 40035	A Minute of Your Time/Looking Out My Window	1968	2.00	4.00	8.00
❏ 40038	Love Me Tonight/Hide and Seek	1969	—	3.00	6.00
❏ 40038 [PS]	Love Me Tonight/Hide and Seek	1969	2.00	4.00	8.00
❏ 40045	Without Love (There Is Nothing)/				
	The Man Who Knows Too Much	1969	—	3.00	6.00
❏ 40045 [PS]	Without Love (There Is Nothing)/				
	The Man Who Knows Too Much	1969	2.00	4.00	8.00
❏ 40048	Daughter of Darkness/Tupelo Mississippi Flash	1970	—	3.00	6.00
❏ 40048 [PS]	Daughter of Darkness/Tupelo Mississippi Flash	1970	2.00	4.00	8.00
❏ 40051	I (Who Have Nothing)/Stop Breaking My Heart	1970	—	3.00	6.00
❏ 40051 [PS]	I (Who Have Nothing)/Stop Breaking My Heart	1970	2.00	4.00	8.00
❏ 40056	Can't Stop Loving You/Never Give Away Love	1970	—	3.00	6.00
❏ 40056 [PS]	Can't Stop Loving You/Never Give Away Love	1970	2.00	4.00	8.00
❏ 40058	She's a Lady/My Way	1971	—	3.00	6.00
❏ 40058 [PS]	She's a Lady/My Way	1971	2.00	4.00	8.00
❏ 40062	Puppet Man/Every Mile	1971	—	3.00	6.00
❏ 40062 [PS]	Puppet Man/Every Mile	1971	3.75	7.50	15.00
❏ 40064	Puppet Man/Resurrection Shuffle	1971	—	2.50	5.00
❏ 40067	Till/One Day Soon	1971	—	2.50	5.00
❏ 40070	The Young New Mexican Puppeteer/				
	All That I Need Is Time	1972	—	2.50	5.00
❏ 40074	Letter to Lucille/Thank the Lord	1973	—	2.50	5.00
❏ 40078	La, La, La (Just Having You Here)/				
	Love, Love, Love	1973	—	2.50	5.00
❏ 40080	Somethin' 'Bout You Baby I Like/				
	Keep a-Talkin' 'Bout Love	1973	—	2.50	5.00
❏ 40081	Pledging My Love/I'm Too Far Gone	1974	—	2.50	5.00
❏ 40083	Ain't No Love/When the Band Goes Home	1974	—	2.50	5.00
❏ 40084	I Got Your Number/The Pain of Love	1974	—	2.50	5.00
❏ 40086	Memories Don't Leave Like People Do/				
	Helping Hand	1975	—	2.50	5.00
TOWER					
❏ 126	Little Lonely One/That's What We'll All Do	1965	3.00	6.00	12.00
❏ 126 [PS]	Little Lonely One/That's What We'll All Do	1965	5.00	10.00	20.00
❏ 176	Lonely One/I Was a Fool	1965	3.00	6.00	12.00
❏ 176 [PS]	Lonely One/I Was a Fool	1965	5.00	10.00	20.00
❏ 190	Baby I'm in Love/Chills and Fever	1966	2.50	5.00	10.00
Albums					
EPIC					
❏ PE 34383	Classic Tom Jones	1976	3.00	6.00	12.00
❏ PE 34468	Say You'll Stay Until Tomorrow	1977	3.00	6.00	12.00
❏ PE 34720	Tom Is Love	1977	2.50	5.00	10.00
❏ JE 35023	What a Night	1978	2.50	5.00	10.00
JIVE					
❏ 1214-1-J	Move Closer	1989	3.00	6.00	12.00
LONDON					
❏ PS 717	The Country Side of Tom Jones	1978	2.50	5.00	10.00
❏ LC-50002	Tom Jones' Greatest Hits	1977	3.00	6.00	12.00
❏ 820234-1	This Is Tom Jones	1985	2.00	4.00	8.00
❏ 820319-1	Tom Jones' Greatest Hits	1985	2.50	5.00	10.00
MCA					
❏ 3182	Tom Jones	1979	2.50	5.00	10.00
❏ 37114	Rescue Me	1980	2.00	4.00	8.00
MERCURY					
❏ SRM-1-4010	Darlin'	1981	2.50	5.00	10.00
❏ SRM-1-4062	Tom Jones Country	1982	2.50	5.00	10.00
❏ 814448-1	Don't Let Our Dreams Die Young	1983	2.50	5.00	10.00
❏ 822701-1	Love Is on the Radio	1984	2.50	5.00	10.00
❏ 826140-1	Tender Loving Care	1985	2.50	5.00	10.00
❏ 830409-1	Things That Matter Most to Me	1987	2.50	5.00	10.00
PARROT					
❏ XPAS-1 [DJ]	Special Tom Jones Interview	1970	25.00	50.00	100.00
—Promo-only open-end interview with gatefold cover and script					
❏ PA 61004 [M]	It's Not Unusual	1965	3.75	7.50	15.00
❏ PA 61006 [M]	What's New Pussycat?	1965	3.75	7.50	15.00
❏ PA 61007 [M]	A-Tom-Ic Jones	1966	3.75	7.50	15.00
❏ PA 61009 [M]	Green, Green Grass of Home	1967	3.75	7.50	15.00
❏ PA 61011 [M]	Funny Familiar Forgotten Feelings	1967	3.75	7.50	15.00
❏ PA 61014 [M]	Tom Jones Live	1967	3.75	7.50	15.00
❏ PAS 71004 [S]	It's Not Unusual	1965	3.75	7.50	15.00
❏ PAS 71006 [S]	What's New Pussycat?	1965	3.75	7.50	15.00
❏ PAS 71007 [S]	A-Tom-Ic Jones	1966	3.75	7.50	15.00
❏ PAS 71009 [S]	Green, Green Grass of Home	1967	3.75	7.50	15.00
❏ PAS 71011 [S]	Funny Familiar Forgotten Feelings	1967	3.75	7.50	15.00
❏ PAS 71014 [S]	Tom Jones Live	1967	3.75	7.50	15.00
❏ PAS 71019	The Tom Jones Fever Zone	1968	3.00	6.00	12.00
❏ PAS 71025	Help Yourself	1969	3.00	6.00	12.00
❏ PAS 71028	This Is Tom Jones	1969	3.00	6.00	12.00
❏ PAS 71031	Live in Las Vegas	1969	3.00	6.00	12.00
❏ PAS 71037	Tom	1970	3.00	6.00	12.00
❏ PAS 71039	I (Who Have Nothing)	1970	3.00	6.00	12.00
❏ PAS 71046	She's a Lady	1971	3.00	6.00	12.00
❏ PAS 71049	Live at Caesar's Palace	1971	3.00	6.00	12.00
❏ XPAS 71055	Close Up	1972	3.00	6.00	12.00
❏ XPAS 71060	The Body and Soul of Tom Jones	197?	3.00	6.00	12.00
❏ XPAS 71062	Tom Jones' Greatest Hits	1973	3.00	6.00	12.00
❏ PAS 71066	Somethin' 'Bout You Baby I Like	1974	3.00	6.00	12.00
❏ PAS 71068	Memories Don't Leave Like People Do	197?	3.00	6.00	12.00
❏ ST-92025	This Is Tom Jones	1969	3.75	7.50	15.00
—Capitol Record Club edition					
❏ SW-93186	Tom	197?	3.75	7.50	15.00
—Capitol Record Club edition					

JONES, TOM (2)
45s
SYMBOL

Number	Title (A Side/B Side)	Yr	VG	VG+	NM
❏ 205	Nothing But Fine/Trying to Get to My Grits	1965	3.00	6.00	12.00

JONES, TONI
45s
SMASH

Number	Title (A Side/B Side)	Yr	VG	VG+	NM
❏ 1814	Love Is Strange/Dear (Here Comes My Baby)	1963	2.50	5.00	10.00

JONES BROTHERS, THE
45s
SUN

Number	Title (A Side/B Side)	Yr	VG	VG+	NM
❏ 213	Every Night/Look to Jesus	1954	200.00	400.00	800.00

JOPLIN, JANIS Also see BIG BROTHER AND THE HOLDING COMPANY.
45s
COLUMBIA

Number	Title (A Side/B Side)	Yr	VG	VG+	NM
❏ 45023	Kozmik Blues/Little Girl Blue	1969	—	3.00	6.00
❏ 45080	One Good Man/Try (Just a Little Bit Harder)	1970	—	3.00	6.00
❏ 45128	Wake Me, Lord/Maybe	1970	—	3.00	6.00
❏ 45314	Me and Bobby McGee/Half Moon	1971	—	2.50	5.00
❏ 45379	Mercedez Benz/Cry Baby	1971	—	2.50	5.00
❏ 45433	Get It While You Can/Move Over	1971	—	2.50	5.00
❏ 45630	Bye Bye Baby/Down on Me	1972	—	2.50	5.00
Albums					
COLUMBIA					
❏ AS 1377 [DJ]	A Collection	1982	5.00	10.00	20.00
❏ KCS 9913	I Got Dem Ol' Kozmik Blues Again Mama!	1969	5.00	10.00	20.00
—"360 Sound Stereo" on label					
❏ KCS 9913	I Got Dem Ol' Kozmik Blues Again Mama!	1970	3.00	6.00	12.00
—Orange label					
❏ PC 9913	I Got Dem Ol' Kozmik Blues Again Mama!	198?	2.00	4.00	8.00
—Budget-line reissue					
❏ CQ 30322 [Q]	Pearl	1974	5.00	10.00	20.00
❏ KC 30322	Pearl	1971	3.75	7.50	15.00
❏ PC 30322	Pearl	1975	3.00	6.00	12.00
—Reissue without bar code					
❏ PC 30322	Pearl	198?	2.00	4.00	8.00
—Reissue with bar code					
❏ C2X 31160 [(2)]	Joplin in Concert	1972	5.00	10.00	20.00
❏ CG 31160	Joplin in Concert	198?	3.00	6.00	12.00
❏ KC 32168	Janis Joplin's Greatest Hits	1973	3.75	7.50	15.00
❏ PC 32168	Janis Joplin's Greatest Hits	197?	2.00	4.00	8.00
❏ CG 33345 [(2)]	Janis	198?	3.00	6.00	12.00
❏ PG 33345 [(2)]	Janis	1975	3.75	7.50	15.00
❏ PC 37569	Farewell Song	1982	2.50	5.00	10.00
COLUMBIA SPECIAL PRODUCTS					
❏ 2P 13792 [(2)]	The Greatest Hits of Janis Joplin	1977	5.00	10.00	20.00

JORDAN, JERRY
45s
MCA

Number	Title (A Side/B Side)	Yr	VG	VG+	NM
❏ 40639	What It Was, Was Football/Phone Call from God	1976	—	2.00	4.00
Albums					
MCA					
❏ 473	Phone Call from God	1975	2.50	5.00	10.00
❏ 2174	Don't Call Me... I'll Call You	1976	2.50	5.00	10.00

JORDANAIRES, THE
45s
CAPITOL

Number	Title (A Side/B Side)	Yr	VG	VG+	NM
❏ F1254	Working on the Building/I Want to Rest	1950	7.50	15.00	30.00
❏ F1363	David and Goliath/Journey to the Sky	1951	6.25	12.50	25.00
❏ F1407	One Day/Something Within	1951	6.25	12.50	25.00
❏ F1499	He Bought My Soul/Read That Book	1951	6.25	12.50	25.00
❏ F2725	Tattler's Wagon/In My Saviour's Loving Arms	1954	5.00	10.00	20.00
❏ F2815	Bugle Call from Heaven/Oh Lord Stand By Me	1954	5.00	10.00	20.00
❏ F2915	This Ole House/Be Prepared	1954	5.00	10.00	20.00
❏ F3022	When the Saints Go Marching In/All the Way	1955	5.00	10.00	20.00
❏ F3158	Let's Make a Joyful Noise/Will You Be Ready	1955	5.00	10.00	20.00
❏ F3265	Shaking Bridges/What Will the Verdict Be	1955	5.00	10.00	20.00
❏ F3356	A House of Gold/Blow, Whistle, Blow	1956	5.00	10.00	20.00
❏ F3420	Rock 'n Roll Religion/Do Unto Others	1956	5.00	10.00	20.00
❏ F3492	Hands of God/Fighting for the Lord	1956	5.00	10.00	20.00
❏ F3684	Sugaree/Baby Won't You Please Come Home	1957	5.00	10.00	20.00
❏ F3684	Walk Away/Ridin' for a Fall	1957	5.00	10.00	20.00
❏ F3750	Summer Vacation/Each Day	1957	5.00	10.00	20.00
❏ F3807	Any Which-a-Way/Mood for the Blues	1957	5.00	10.00	20.00
❏ F3940	Little Miss Ruby/All I Need Is You	1958	3.75	7.50	15.00
❏ F4025	Wella Wella Honey/Where Many Go	1958	3.75	7.50	15.00
❏ 4431	Sit Down/Girl in the Valley	1960	3.00	6.00	12.00
COLUMBIA					
❏ 4-43283	Malibu Run/Who Does He Think He Is	1965	2.50	5.00	10.00
—Said to be a different group than the rest.					
DECCA					
❏ 9-46242	Dig a Little Deeper/I'm Free Again	1950	10.00	20.00	40.00
❏ 9-46366	Loafin' on a Lazy River/Sweet Roses of Morn	1951	6.25	12.50	25.00
DECCA FAITH SERIES					
❏ 9-14530	Peace in the Valley/(B-side unknown)	1950	7.50	15.00	30.00
RCA VICTOR					
❏ 47-4378	The Four Horsemen (Of the Apocalypse)/				
	Mansion Over the Hilltop	1951	6.25	12.50	25.00
❏ 47-4607	Who Can He Be/Gonna Walk Those Golden				
	Stairs	1952	6.25	12.50	25.00
❏ 47-4645	Goodbye Pharaoh/Roll, Jordan, Roll	1952	6.25	12.50	25.00
❏ 47-4943	Rag Mama/I Never Will Marry	1952	6.25	12.50	25.00
❏ 47-4948	My Rock/I'll Tell It Wherever I Go	1952	6.25	12.50	25.00
❏ 47-5021	He'll Understand and Say Well Done/I'm Moving				
	On to Glory	1952	6.25	12.50	25.00
❏ 47-5076	Beautiful City/Stand by Me	1952	5.00	10.00	20.00
❏ 47-5077	By the River of Life/Noah	1952	5.00	10.00	20.00
❏ 47-5078	You Better Run/Dry Bones	1952	5.00	10.00	20.00
❏ 47-5079	When Dey Ring Dem Golden Bells/Didn't They				
	Crucify My Lord	1952	5.00	10.00	20.00
❏ 47-5373	On the Jericho Road/The Lord Will Make a Way				
	Somehow	1953	6.25	12.50	25.00
❏ 47-5458	Is He Satisfied/I Am So Glad Jesus Lifted Me	1953	6.25	12.50	25.00
STOP					
❏ 259	You're Wasting Your Time Girl/				
	A Hundred Years of Real Estate	1969	2.00	4.00	8.00

Number	Title (A Side/B Side)	Yr	VG	VG+	NM

"X"

| ❏ 0034 | Say It Again/I Can't Smoke You Out of My Heart | 1954 | 5.00 | 10.00 | 20.00 |

7-Inch Extended Plays

RCA VICTOR

❏ 547-0246	The Beautiful City/Stand By Me//Noah/By the River of Life	195?	3.75	7.50	15.00
—Record 1 of 2-EP set EPB-3081					
❏ 547-0247	Dry Bones/You Better Run//When They Ring Dem Golden Bells/Didn't They Crucify My Lord	195?	3.75	7.50	15.00
—Record 2 of 2-EP set EPB-3081					
❏ EPB-3081 [PS]	Beautiful City	195?	3.75	7.50	15.00
—Two-pocket jacket for two-EP set (547-0246, 547-0247)					

SESAC

| ❏ AD 46 | Wanderin'/John Henry//Honey Baby Mine/ Twenty-One Froggies | 195? | 5.00 | 10.00 | 20.00 |
| ❏ AD 46 [PS] | Songs of the Plains | 195? | 5.00 | 10.00 | 20.00 |

Albums

CAPITOL

❏ T 1011 [M]	Heavenly Spirit	1958	10.00	20.00	40.00
❏ T 1167 [M]	Gloryland	1959	10.00	20.00	40.00
❏ ST 1311 [S]	Land of Jordan	1960	10.00	20.00	40.00
❏ T 1311 [M]	Land of Jordan	1960	7.50	15.00	30.00
❏ ST 1559 [S]	To God Be the Glory	1961	6.25	12.50	25.00
❏ T 1559 [M]	To God Be the Glory	1961	5.00	10.00	20.00
❏ ST 1742 [S]	Spotlight on the Jordanaires	1962	7.50	15.00	30.00
❏ T 1742 [M]	Spotlight on the Jordanaires	1962	6.25	12.50	25.00

CLASSIC

| ❏ CCR 1935 | Christmas to Elvis from the Jordanaires | 1978 | 3.00 | 6.00 | 12.00 |

COLUMBIA

❏ CL 2214 [M]	This Land	1964	5.00	10.00	20.00
❏ CL 2458 [M]	The Big Country Hits	1966	5.00	10.00	20.00
❏ CS 9014 [S]	This Land	1964	6.25	12.50	25.00
❏ CS 9258 [S]	The Big Country Hits	1966	6.25	12.50	25.00

DECCA

| ❏ DL 8681 [M] | Peace in the Valley | 1957 | 12.50 | 25.00 | 50.00 |

RCA VICTOR

| ❏ LPM-3081 [10] | Beautiful City | 1953 | 25.00 | 50.00 | 100.00 |

SESAC

| ❏ 1401/2 [M] | Of Rivers and Plains | 195? | 20.00 | 40.00 | 80.00 |

JORGENSON, CHRISTINE

Albums

J RECORDS

| ❏ J-1 [M] | Christine Jorgenson Reveals | 1958 | 12.50 | 25.00 | 50.00 |

JOSEFUS

45s

MAINSTREAM

| ❏ 725 | Jimmy Jimmy/Sephus Blues | 1970 | 3.75 | 7.50 | 15.00 |

Albums

HOOKAH

| ❏ 330 | Dead Man | 1969 | 75.00 | 150.00 | 300.00 |

MAINSTREAM

| ❏ S-6127 | Josefus | 1970 | 25.00 | 50.00 | 100.00 |

JOSEPH

Albums

SCEPTER

| ❏ SRS-674 | Stoned Age Man | 1970 | 20.00 | 40.00 | 80.00 |

JOSEPH, MARGIE

12-Inch Singles

H.C.R.C.

| ❏ 03338 | Knockout (Part 1)/Knockout (Part 2) | 1982 | 2.00 | 4.00 | 8.00 |

45s

ATLANTIC

❏ 2907	Born to Wander/Let's Go Somewhere and Love	1972	—	2.50	5.00
❏ 2933	Touch Your Woman/ I'm So Glad I'm Your Woman	1973	—	2.50	5.00
❏ 2954	Let's Stay Together/I'd Rather Go Blind	1973	—	2.50	5.00
❏ 2988	Come Lay Some Lovin' on Me/Ridin' High	1973	—	2.50	5.00
❏ 3032	My Love/Sweet Surrender	1974	—	2.50	5.00
❏ 3220	Words (Are Impossible)/I Still Love You	1974	—	2.50	5.00
❏ 3269	I Can't Move No Mountains/ Just As Soon As the Feeling's Over	1975	—	2.50	5.00
❏ 3290	Stay Still/Just As Soon As the Feeling's Over	1975	—	2.50	5.00
❏ 3445	Come On Back to Me Lover/ He Came Into My Life	1978	—	2.00	4.00
❏ 3509	I Feel His Love Getting Stronger/How Will I Know	1978	—	2.00	4.00
❏ 3525	I Don't Want to Get Over You/Love Takes Tears	1978	—	2.00	4.00

COTILLION

❏ 44201	Hear the Words, Feel the Feeling/ I Get Carried Away	1976	—	2.00	4.00
❏ 44207	Don't Turn the Lights Off/All Cried Out	1976	—	2.00	4.00
❏ 99737	Big Strong Man/(B-side unknown)	1984	—	2.00	4.00
❏ 99771	Ready for the Night/(B-side unknown)	1984	—	2.00	4.00

H.C.R.C.

| ❏ 03337 | Knockout (Part 1)/Knockout (Part 2) | 1982 | — | 2.00 | 4.00 |

VOLT

❏ 4012	One More Chance/Never Can You Be	1969	2.00	4.00	8.00
❏ 4023	What You Gonna Do/Nobody	1969	2.00	4.00	8.00
❏ 4037	Your Sweet Lovin'/What's Wrong Baby	1970	—	3.00	6.00
❏ 4046	Punish Me/A Sweeter Tomorrow	1970	—	3.00	6.00
❏ 4056	Stop! In the Name of Love/ Make Me Believe You'll Stay	1971	—	3.00	6.00
❏ 4061	The Other Woman Got My Man and Gone/ I'll Always Love You	1971	—	3.00	6.00

Albums

ATLANTIC

❏ SD 7248	Margie Joseph	1973	3.00	6.00	12.00
❏ SD 7277	Sweet Surrender	1974	3.00	6.00	12.00
❏ SD 18126	Margie	1975	3.00	6.00	12.00
❏ SD 19182	Feeling My Way	1978	2.50	5.00	10.00

COTILLION

| ❏ SD 9906 | Hear the Words, Feel the Feeling | 1976 | 3.00 | 6.00 | 12.00 |

H.C.R.C.

| ❏ 20009 | Knockout | 1983 | 2.50 | 5.00 | 10.00 |

VOLT

| ❏ VOS-6012 | Margie Joseph Makes a New Impression | 1971 | 7.50 | 15.00 | 30.00 |
| ❏ VOS-6016 | Phase II | 1971 | 7.50 | 15.00 | 30.00 |

JOSEPH, MARGIE, AND BLUE MAGIC Also see each artist's individual listings.

45s

ATCO/WMOT

| ❏ 7030 | What's Come Over Me/You and Me (Got a Good Thing Goin') | 1975 | — | 2.50 | 5.00 |

JOSHUA FOX

45s

TETRAGRAMMATON

| ❏ 1527 | Goin' Down for Big Numbers/Moontime Bore | 1969 | 3.00 | 6.00 | 12.00 |
| ❏ 1532 | Don't Tell Me a Story/It's Just Meant to Be | 1969 | 3.00 | 6.00 | 12.00 |

Albums

TETRAGRAMMATON

| ❏ T-125 | Joshua Fox | 1969 | 7.50 | 15.00 | 30.00 |

JOSIE AND THE PUSSYCATS Also see PATRICE HOLLOWAY; CHERYL LADD.

45s

CAPITOL

❏ CP 58-1	Letter to Mama/Inside, Outside, Upside Down	1970	5.00	10.00	20.00
❏ CP 58-1 [PS]	Letter to Mama/Inside, Outside, Upside Down	1970	7.50	15.00	30.00
❏ CP 59-2	With Every Beat of My Heart/Josie	1970	5.00	10.00	20.00
❏ CP 59-2 [PS]	With Every Beat of My Heart/Josie	1970	7.50	15.00	30.00
❏ CP 60-3	Voodoo/If That Isn't Love	1970	5.00	10.00	20.00
❏ CP 60-3 [PS]	Voodoo/If That Isn't Love	1970	7.50	15.00	30.00
❏ CP 61-4	I Wanna Make You Happy/It's Gotta Be Him	1970	5.00	10.00	20.00
❏ CP 61-4 [PS]	I Wanna Make You Happy/It's Gotta Be Him	1970	7.50	15.00	30.00
❏ 2967	Every Beat of My Heart/It's All Right with Me	1970	5.00	10.00	20.00
—Same song as CP 59, but a slightly different title and a mono mix					
❏ 3045	Stop, Look and Listen/ You've Come a Long Way, Baby	1971	5.00	10.00	20.00

Albums

CAPITOL

| ❏ ST-665 | Josie and the Pussycats | 1970 | 50.00 | 100.00 | 200.00 |

JOURNEY Original lead singer Gregg Rolie was also the original lead singer of SANTANA.

12-Inch Singles

COLUMBIA

| ❏ AS 568 [DJ] | Just the Same Way (3:14) (stereo/mono) | 1979 | 2.50 | 5.00 | 10.00 |
| ❏ AS 999 [DJ] | Who's Crying Now (5:01)/Stone in Love (4:25) | 1981 | 6.25 | 12.50 | 25.00 |

GEFFEN

| ❏ PRO-A-2240 [DJ] | Only the Young (same on both sides) | 1985 | — | 3.00 | 6.00 |

45s

COLUMBIA

❏ 02241	Who's Crying Now/Mother, Father	1981	—	—	3.00
❏ 02241 [PS]	Who's Crying Now/Mother, Father	1981	—	2.00	4.00
❏ 02567	Don't Stop Believin'/Natural Thing	1981	—	—	3.00
❏ 02567 [PS]	Don't Stop Believin'/Natural Thing	1981	—	2.00	4.00
❏ 02687	Open Arms/Little Girl	1982	—	—	3.00
❏ 02687 [PS]	Open Arms/Little Girl	1982	—	2.00	4.00
❏ 02883	Still They Ride/La Raza Del Sol	1982	—	—	3.00
❏ 02883 [PS]	Still They Ride/La Raza Del Sol	1982	—	2.00	4.00
❏ 03133	Open Arms/The Party's Over	1982	—	—	3.00
❏ 03134	Who's Crying Now/Don't Stop Believin'	1982	—	—	3.00
—Reissue					
❏ 38-03513	Separate Ways (Worlds Apart)/Frontiers	1983	—	—	3.00
❏ 38-03513 [PS]	Separate Ways (Worlds Apart)/Frontiers	1983	—	2.00	4.00
❏ CNR-03568	Separate Ways (Worlds Apart)	1983	—	2.50	5.00
—One-sided budget release					
❏ 03840	Faithfully/Frontiers	1983	—	—	3.00
❏ 04004	After the Fall/Only Solutions	1983	—	—	3.00
❏ 04151	Send Her My Love/Chain Reaction	1983	—	—	3.00
❏ 05869	Be Good to Yourself/Only the Young	1986	—	—	3.00
❏ 05869 [PS]	Be Good to Yourself/Only the Young	1986	—	—	3.00
❏ 06134	Suzanne/Ask the Lonely	1986	—	—	3.00
❏ 06134 [PS]	Suzanne/Ask the Lonely	1986	—	—	3.00
❏ 06301	I'll Be Alright Without You/The Eyes of a Woman	1986	—	—	3.00
❏ 06301 [PS]	I'll Be Alright Without You/The Eyes of a Woman	1986	—	—	3.00
❏ 06302	Girl Can't Help It/It Could Have Been You	1986	—	—	3.00
❏ 06302 [PS]	Girl Can't Help It/It Could Have Been You	1986	—	—	3.00
❏ 07043	Why Can't This Night Go On Forever/ Positive Touch	1987	—	—	3.00
❏ 07043 [PS]	Why Can't This Night Go On Forever/ Positive Touch	1987	—	—	3.00
❏ 10137	To Play Some Music/Topaz	1975	—	3.00	6.00
❏ 10324	On a Saturday Night/To Play Some Music	1976	—	3.00	6.00
❏ 10370	It's All Too Much/She Makes Me (Feel Alright)	1976	—	3.00	6.00
❏ 10522	Spaceman/Nickel and Dime	1977	—	3.00	6.00
❏ 10700	Wheel in the Sky/Can Do	1978	—	2.50	5.00
❏ 10757	Anytime/Can Do	1978	—	2.50	5.00
❏ 10800	Lights/Somethin' to Hide	1978	—	2.50	5.00
❏ 10928	Just the Same Way/Somethin' to Hide	1979	—	2.00	4.00
❏ 11036	Lovin', Touchin', Squeezin'/Daydream	1979	—	2.00	4.00
❏ 11143	Too Late/Do You Recall	1979	—	2.00	4.00
❏ 11213	Any Way You Want It/When You're Alone (It Ain't Easy)	1980	—	2.00	4.00
❏ 11275	Walks Like a Lady/People and Places	1980	—	2.00	4.00
❏ 11339	Good Morning Girl/Stay Awhile	1980	—	2.00	4.00
❏ 60505	The Party's Over (Hopelessly in Love)/Just the Same Way	1981	—	2.00	4.00
❏ 78428	When You Love a Woman/Message of Love	1996	—	—	3.00

GEFFEN

❏ 29090	Only the Young/I'll Only Fall in Love Again	1985	—	2.00	4.00
—B-side by Sammy Hagar					
❏ 29090 [PS]	Only the Young/I'll Only Fall in Love Again	1985	—	2.00	4.00

Albums

COLUMBIA

❏ AS 914 [DJ]	Journey	1975	3.75	7.50	15.00
—Promo-only sampler					
❏ AS 1606 [DJ]	A Candid Conversation with Journey	197?	3.75	7.50	15.00
—Promo-only interview and songs LP					

J

Number	Title (A Side/B Side)	Yr	VG	VG+	NM
❏ PC 33388	Journey	1975	2.50	5.00	10.00
—No bar code on cover					
❏ PC 33388	Journey	198?	—	3.00	6.00
—With bar code on cover					
❏ PC 33904	Look Into the Future	1976	2.50	5.00	10.00
—No bar code on cover					
❏ PC 33904	Look Into the Future	198?	—	3.00	6.00
—With bar code on cover					
❏ PCQ 33904 [Q]	Look Into the Future	1976	—	—	—
—Not released					
❏ PC 34311	Next	1977	2.50	5.00	10.00
—No bar code on cover					
❏ PC 34311	Next	198?	—	3.00	6.00
—With bar code on cover					
❏ JC 34912	Infinity	1978	2.50	5.00	10.00
—No bar code on cover					
❏ JC 34912	Infinity	1979	—	3.00	6.00
—With bar code on cover					
❏ FC 35797	Evolution	1979	2.00	4.00	8.00
❏ PC 35797	Evolution	1985	—	3.00	6.00
—Budget-line reissue					
❏ C2 36324 [(2)]	In the Beginning	1979	2.50	5.00	10.00
❏ FC 36339	Departure	1980	2.00	4.00	8.00
❏ KC2 37016 [(2)]	Captured	1981	2.50	5.00	10.00
❏ TC 37408	Escape	1981	2.00	4.00	8.00
❏ FC 37998	Dream After Dream	1982	3.00	6.00	12.00
❏ PC 37998	Dream After Dream	1986	2.00	4.00	8.00
—Budget-line reissue					
❏ QC 38504	Frontiers	1983	2.00	4.00	8.00
❏ OC 39936	Raised on Radio	1986	2.00	4.00	8.00
❏ OC 44493	Greatest Hits	1988	2.50	5.00	10.00
❏ HC 44912	Infinity	1982	7.50	15.00	30.00
—Half-speed mastered edition					
❏ HC 46339	Departure	1980	5.00	10.00	20.00
—Half-speed mastered edition					
❏ HC 47408	Escape	1982	5.00	10.00	20.00
—Half-speed mastered edition					
❏ HC 47998	Dream After Dream	1982	7.50	15.00	30.00
—Half-speed mastered edition					
❏ HC 48504	Frontiers	1983	7.50	15.00	30.00
—Half-speed mastered edition					
MOBILE FIDELITY					
❏ 1-144	Escape	1984	50.00	100.00	200.00
—Audiophile vinyl					

JOURNEYMEN, THE (1) Also see SCOTT McKENZIE; JOHN PHILLIPS.
45s
AMY

❏ 821	Cup-E-Co/Hush Storm	1961	3.00	6.00	12.00
CAPITOL					
❏ 4625	500 Miles/The River She Comes Down	1961	2.50	5.00	10.00
❏ 4678	Soft Blow the Summer Winds/Kumbaya	1962	2.50	5.00	10.00
❏ 4737	Don't Turn Around/Hush Now Sally	1962	2.50	5.00	10.00
❏ 4829	What'll I Do/Loadin' Coal	1962	2.50	5.00	10.00
❏ 4943	Rag Mama/I Never Will Marry	1963	2.50	5.00	10.00
❏ 4943 [PS]	Rag Mama/I Never Will Marry	1963	10.00	20.00	40.00
❏ 5031	Kumbaya/Ja Da	1963	2.50	5.00	10.00
Albums					
CAPITOL					
❏ ST 1629 [S]	The Journeymen	1961	7.50	15.00	30.00
❏ T 1629 [M]	The Journeymen	1961	6.25	12.50	25.00
❏ ST 1770 [S]	Coming Attraction — Live!	1962	7.50	51.00	30.00
❏ T 1770 [M]	Coming Attraction — Live!	1962	6.25	12.50	25.00
❏ ST 1951 [S]	New Directions in Folk Music	1963	7.50	15.00	30.00
❏ T 1951 [M]	New Directions in Folk Music	1963	6.25	12.50	25.00

JOURNEYMEN, THE (2)
45s
IONA

❏ 1111	Work Out/Bag's Groove	1961	12.50	25.00	50.00
❏ 1115	Surfer's Blues/Surfer's Rule	1963	10.00	20.00	40.00
—Rerelease as "The Baylanders"					
❏ 1115	Surfer's Blues/Surfer's Rule	1963	12.50	25.00	50.00

JOY, BENNY
45s
ANTLER

❏ 4011	Crash the Party/Little Red Book	1959	125.00	250.00	500.00
DECCA					
❏ 31199	New York, Hey Hey/Sincerely, Your Friend	1961	3.75	7.50	15.00
❏ 31280	Birds of a Feather Fly Together/ You Go Your Way (And I'll Go Mine)	1961	3.75	7.50	15.00
DIXIE					
❏ 2001	Steady with Betty/Spin the Bottle	1958	125.00	250.00	500.00
DOT					
❏ 16445	I'm of No More Use to You Old Earth/ Harry's Harem	1963	3.75	7.50	15.00
RAM					
❏ 1107	Ittie Bittie Everything/(B-side unknown)	1959	125.00	250.00	500.00
TRI-DEC					
❏ 8667	Steady with Betty/Spin the Bottle	1958	150.00	300.00	600.00

JOY, RODDIE
45s
PARKWAY

❏ 101	Something Strange Is Going On/Stop	1966	3.00	6.00	12.00
❏ 134	Every Breath I Take/Walkin' Back	1967	3.00	6.00	12.00
❏ 151	I Want You Back/Let's Start All Over	1967	3.00	6.00	12.00
❏ 991	A Boy Is Just a Toy/Stop	1966	3.75	7.50	15.00
RED BIRD					
❏ 10-021	Love Hit Me with a Wallop/Come Back Baby	1965	5.00	10.00	20.00
❏ 10-031	The La La Song/He's So Easy to Love	1965	6.25	12.50	25.00
❏ 10-037	If There's Anything Else You Want (Let Me Know)/Stop	1965	10.00	20.00	40.00

JOY OF COOKING
45s
CAPITOL

❏ 3075	Brownsville/Only Time Will Tell Me	1971	—	3.00	6.00
❏ 3224	Closer to the Ground/Pilot	1971	—	2.50	5.00
❏ 3330	Let Love Carry You Along/Home Town Man	1972	—	2.50	5.00
❏ 3396	Don't the Moon Look Fat and Round/ All Around the Sun and the Moon	1972	—	2.50	5.00
Albums					
CAPITOL					
❏ ST-661	Joy of Cooking	1971	3.75	7.50	15.00
❏ SMAS-828	Closer to the Ground	1971	3.75	7.50	15.00
❏ ST-11050	Castles	1972	3.00	6.00	12.00

JOY TONES, THE
45s
COED

❏ 600	This Love (That I'm Giving You)/I Wanna Party Some More	1965	3.00	6.00	12.00

JOYE, COL, AND THE JOY BOYS
45s
DECCA

❏ 30933	(Rockin' Rollin') Clementine/ Bye Bye Baby Goodbye	1959	7.50	15.00	30.00

JOYETTES, THE
45s
ONYX

❏ 502	Story of Love/The Boy Next Door	1956	25.00	50.00	100.00

JOYOUS NOISE
Albums
CAPITOL

❏ SMAS-844	Joyous Noise	1971	5.00	10.00	20.00

JOYTONES, THE
45s
RAMA

❏ 191	All My Love Belongs to You/ You Just Won't Treat Me Right	1956	37.50	75.00	150.00
❏ 202	Gee What a Boy/Is This Really the End	1956	75.00	150.00	300.00
❏ 215	My Foolish Heart/Jimbo Jango	1956	125.00	250.00	500.00

JULIAN, DON, AND THE MEADOWLARKS Also see THE LARKS.
45s
CLASSIC ARTISTS

❏ 101	Quickie Wedding/Our Love	1988	—	2.00	4.00
❏ 105	White Christmas/Marry Christmas, Baby	1988	—	3.00	6.00
DOOTO					
❏ 424	Blue Moon/Big Mama Wants to Rock	1957	12.50	25.00	50.00
DOOTONE					
❏ 359	Heaven and Paradise/Embarrassing Moments	1955	75.00	150.00	300.00
❏ 367	Always and Always/I Got Tore Up	1955	12.50	25.00	50.00
—Maroon label					
❏ 367	Always and Always/I Got Tore Up	1955	18.75	37.50	75.00
—Red label					
❏ 372	This Must Be Paradise/Mine All Mine	1955	15.00	30.00	60.00
❏ 394	Please Love a Fool/Oop Boopy Oop	1956	12.50	25.00	50.00
❏ 405	I Am a Believer/Boogie Woogie Teenager	1956	20.00	40.00	80.00
DYNAMITE					
❏ 1112	Heaven Only Knows/Popeye	1962	7.50	15.00	30.00
ORIGINAL SOUND					
❏ 3	Please Say You Want Me/ Doin' tha Cha Cha Cha	1959	10.00	20.00	40.00
❏ 12	There's a Girl/Blue Moon	1960	7.50	15.00	30.00
RPM					
❏ 399	Love Only You/Real Pretty Mama	1954	75.00	150.00	300.00
—As "The Meadow Larks"					
❏ 406	LSMFT Blues (Lord Find My Sweet Theresa)/ Pass the Gin	1954	750.00	1500.	3000.
—As "The Meadow Larks"					
7-Inch Extended Plays					
DOOTO					
❏ 203	(contents unknown)	1958	50.00	100.00	200.00
❏ 203 [PS]	Don Julian and the Meadowlarks	1958	50.00	100.00	200.00
—Reissue of Dootone 203					
DOOTONE					
❏ 203	(contents unknown)	1956	100.00	200.00	400.00
❏ 203 [PS]	Don Julian and the Meadowlarks	1956	100.00	200.00	400.00

JULIAN'S TREATMENT
Albums
DECCA

❏ DL 75224	A Time Before This	1970	5.00	10.00	20.00

JULIANA
45s
RCA VICTOR

❏ 47-7906	You Can Have Any Boy/ You're Saying Goodnight	1961	15.00	30.00	60.00

JULY
Albums
EPIC

❏ BN 26416	July	1969	50.00	100.00	200.00

JUMPIN' JACKS, THE
45s
DECCA

❏ 29973	You'll Wonder Where the Yellow Went/ A Frantic Antic	1956	7.50	15.00	30.00
❏ 29973 [PS]	You'll Wonder Where the Yellow Went/ A Frantic Antic	1956	10.00	20.00	40.00

Number	Title (A Side/B Side)	Yr	VG	VG+	NM
JUNIOR AND HIS FRIENDS					
45s					
ABC-PARAMOUNT					
❏ 10089	Who's Our Pet, Annette!/A.B.C. Love	1960	7.50	15.00	30.00
JUNIOR'S EYES					
Albums					
A&M					
❏ SP-4189	Junior's Eyes	1970	5.00	10.00	20.00
JURY, THE See BILL JUSTIS.					
JUST THREE					
45s					
HIT					
❏ 222	The "In" Crowd/Hang On Sloopy	1965	3.00	6.00	12.00
—B-side by the Roamers					
JUSTICE, BERGEN					
45s					
HIT					
❏ 305	Gimme Little Sign/Never My Love	1967	2.00	4.00	8.00
—B-side by the Chellows					
JUSTICE, JIMMY					
45s					
BLUE CAT					
❏ 101	Don't Let the Stars Get In Your Eyes/Guitar Player (Her and Him)	1964	2.50	5.00	10.00
KAPP					
❏ 469	Ain't That Funny/One	1962	3.00	6.00	12.00
❏ 482	When My Little Girl Is Smiling/If I Lost Your Love	1962	3.00	6.00	12.00
❏ 514	I Wake Up Crying/World of Lonely People	1963	3.00	6.00	12.00
Albums					
KAPP					
❏ KL-1308 [M]	Justice for All	1963	6.25	12.50	25.00
❏ KS-3308 [S]	Justice for All	1963	10.00	20.00	40.00
JUSTIS, BILL					
45s					
BELL					
❏ 921	Electric Dreams/Dark Continent Contribution	1970	—	2.50	5.00
MCA					
40810	Foxy Lady/Orange Blossom Special	1977	—	2.00	4.00
MONUMENT					
❏ 956	Yellow Summer/So Until I See You	1966	2.50	5.00	10.00
❏ 8699	Sea Dream/Touching, Feeling, Dreaming	1976	—	2.50	5.00
NRC					
❏ 1119	Boogie Woogie Rock/Blowing Rock	1959	5.00	10.00	20.00
PHILLIPS INTERNATIONAL					
❏ 3519	Raunchy/The Midnite Man	1957	5.00	10.00	20.00
❏ 3522	College Man/The Stranger	1958	5.00	10.00	20.00
❏ 3525	Wild Rice/Scroungie	1958	5.00	10.00	20.00
❏ 3529	Cattywampus/Summer Holiday	1958	5.00	10.00	20.00
❏ 3535	Bop Train/String of Pearls	1958	5.00	10.00	20.00
❏ 3544	Flea Circus/Cloud Nine	1959	5.00	10.00	20.00
PLAY ME					
❏ 1119	Boogie Woogie Rock/Blowing Rock	1959	7.50	15.00	30.00
—As "Bill Justis and the Jury"; second pressing					
❏ 1119	Boogie Woogie Rock/Blowing Rock	1959	10.00	20.00	40.00
—As "The Jury"; contains a different version of the A-side than those that give Bill Justis credit					
SMASH					
❏ 1812	I'm Gonna Learn to Dance/Tamoure	1963	2.50	5.00	10.00
❏ 1812 [PS]	I'm Gonna Learn to Dance/Tamoure	1963	4.00	8.00	16.00
❏ 1851	Sunday in Madrid/Satin and Velvet	1963	2.50	5.00	10.00
❏ 1902	Lavender Sax/Fia, Fia	1964	2.50	5.00	10.00
❏ 1955	How Soon/Ska-Ha	1964	2.50	5.00	10.00
❏ 1977	Late Game/Last Farewell	1965	2.50	5.00	10.00
Albums					
HARMONY					
❏ KH 31189	Enchanted Sea	1972	3.00	6.00	12.00
MONUMENT					
❏ MLP 8078 [M]	The Eternal Sea	1967	3.75	7.50	15.00
❏ SLP 18078 [S]	The Eternal Sea	1967	3.75	7.50	15.00
PHILLIPS INTERNATIONAL					
❏ PLP-1950 [M]	Cloud Nine	1959	100.00	200.00	400.00
SMASH					
❏ MGS-27021 [M]	Bill Justis Plays 12 Big Instrumental Hits (Alley Cat/Green Onions)	1962	3.75	7.50	15.00
❏ MGS-27030 [M]	Bill Justis Plays 12 More Big Instrumental Hits (Telstar/The Lonely Bull)	1963	3.75	7.50	15.00
❏ MGS-27031 [M]	Bill Justis Plays 12 Smash Instrumental Hits	1963	3.75	7.50	15.00
❏ MGS-27036 [M]	Bill Justis Plays 12 Top Tunes	1963	3.75	7.50	15.00
❏ MGS-27043 [M]	Bill Justis Plays 12 Other Instrumental Hits	1964	3.75	7.50	15.00
❏ MGS-27047 [M]	Dixieland Folk Style	1964	3.75	7.50	15.00
❏ MGS-27065 [M]	More Instrumental Hits	1965	3.75	7.50	15.00
❏ MGS-27077 [M]	Taste of Honey/The "In" Crowd	1966	3.75	7.50	15.00
❏ SRS-67021 [S]	Bill Justis Plays 12 Big Instrumental Hits (Alley Cat/Green Onions)	1962	5.00	10.00	20.00
❏ SRS-67030 [S]	Bill Justis Plays 12 More Big Instrumental Hits (Telstar/The Lonely Bull)	1963	5.00	10.00	20.00
❏ SRS-67031 [S]	Bill Justis Plays 12 Smash Instrumental Hits	1963	5.00	10.00	20.00
❏ SRS-67036 [S]	Bill Justis Plays 12 Top Tunes	1963	5.00	10.00	20.00
❏ SRS-67043 [S]	Bill Justis Plays 12 Other Instrumental Hits	1964	5.00	10.00	20.00
❏ SRS-67047 [S]	Dixieland Folk Style	1964	5.00	10.00	20.00
❏ SRS-67065 [S]	More Instrumental Hits	1965	5.00	10.00	20.00
❏ SRS-67077 [S]	Taste of Honey/The "In" Crowd	1966	5.00	10.00	20.00
❏ 830898-1	Raunchy	1987	2.50	5.00	10.00
SUN					
❏ LP-109	Raunchy	1969	3.00	6.00	12.00

Number	Title (A Side/B Side)	Yr	VG	VG+	NM
K					
K.C. AND THE SUNSHINE BAND Includes K.C. as a solo performer.					
12-Inch Singles					
EPIC					
❏ 49-03187	(You Said) You'd Gimme Some More (7:33) (Instrumental 5:37)	1982	2.00	4.00	8.00
MECA					
❏ D-5000	Give It Up (Vocal 5:18) (Instrumental 3:30)/ Are You Ready	1983	2.00	4.00	8.00
❏ D-5001	Don't Break My Heart (8:42)/ Are You Ready (6:20)	1984	2.00	4.00	8.00
—K.C. solo					
SISAPA/CURB					
❏ V-77201	Game of Love (Hot Radio Edit) (Radio Regular Edit) (Extended Edit) (D.I.Y. Beats)	1990	2.00	4.00	8.00
SUNSHINE SOUND					
❏ SSD-202	Do You Feel All Right/I Will Love You Tomorrow	1978	2.50	5.00	10.00
❏ SSD-207	Do You Wanna Go Party (7:27) (10:00)	1979	3.00	6.00	12.00
45s					
CASABLANCA					
❏ 2227	Yes I'm Ready/With Your Love	1979	—	2.00	4.00
—As "Teri DeSario with K.C."					
❏ 2278	Dancin' in the Streets/Moonlight Madness	1980	—	2.00	4.00
—As "Teri DeSario with K.C."					
❏ 812991-7	Yes I'm Ready/Dancin' in the Streets	1983	—	2.00	4.00
—As "Teri DeSario with K.C."; reissue					
EPIC					
❏ 14-02545	Love Me/Don't Say No	1981	—	2.00	4.00
❏ 14-02652	It Happens Every Night/Stand Up	1981	—	2.00	4.00
❏ 34-03286	(You Said) You'd Gimme Some More/When You Dance to the Music	1982	—	2.00	4.00
❏ 34-03556	Don't Run (Come Back to Me)/On the One	1983	—	2.00	4.00
MECA					
❏ 1001	Give It Up/Uptight	1983	—	2.00	4.00
—K.C. solo					
❏ 1003	On the Top/(B-side unknown)	1984	—	3.00	6.00
T.K.					
❏ 1001	Blow Your Whistle/I'm Going to Do Something Good to You	1973	—	2.50	5.00
—As "K.C. and the Sunshine Junkanoo Band"					
❏ 1003	Sound Your Funky Horn/Why Don't We Get Together	1974	—	2.50	5.00
❏ 1005	Queen of Clubs/Do It Good	1974	—	2.50	5.00
❏ 1008	I'm a Pushover/You Don't Know	1974	—	2.50	5.00
❏ 1009	Get Down Tonight/You Don't Know	1975	—	2.00	4.00
❏ 1010	Shotgun Shuffle/Hey J	1975	—	2.00	4.00
—As "The Sunshine Band"					
❏ 1015	That's the Way (I Like It)/What Makes You Happy	1975	—	2.00	4.00
❏ 1018	Rock Your Baby/S.O.S.	1976	—	2.00	4.00
—As "The Sunshine Band"					
❏ 1019	(Shake, Shake, Shake) Shake Your Booty/ Boogie Shoes	1976	—	2.00	4.00
❏ 1020	I Like to Do It/Come On In	1976	—	2.00	4.00
❏ 1022	I'm Your Boogie Man/ Wrap Your Arms Around Me	1977	—	2.00	4.00
❏ 1023	Keep It Comin' Love/Baby I Love You	1977	—	2.00	4.00
❏ 1023 [PS]	Keep It Comin' Love/Baby I Love You	1977	—	2.50	5.00
❏ 1025	Boogie Shoes/I Get Lifted	1978	—	2.00	4.00
❏ 1025 [PS]	Boogie Shoes/I Get Lifted	1978	2.00	4.00	8.00
❏ 1026	Black Water Gold (Part 1)/ Black Water Gold (Part 2)	1978	—	2.00	4.00
—As "The Sunshine Band"					
❏ 1028	It's the Same Old Song/Let's Go Party	1978	—	2.00	4.00
❏ 1028 [PS]	It's the Same Old Song/Let's Go Party	1978	—	2.00	4.00
❏ 1030	Do You Feel All Right/I Will Love You Tomorrow	1978	—	2.00	4.00
❏ 1030 [PS]	Do You Feel All Right/I Will Love You Tomorrow	1978	—	2.00	4.00
❏ 1031	Who Do Ya Love/Sho-Nuff	1978	—	2.00	4.00
❏ 1031 [PS]	Who Do Ya Love/Sho-Nuff	1978	—	2.00	4.00
❏ 1033	Do You Wanna Go Party/Come to My Island	1979	—	2.00	4.00
❏ 1035	Please Don't Go/I Betcha Didn't Know That	1979	—	2.00	4.00
❏ 1036	Let's Go Rock and Roll/I've Got the Feeling	1980	—	2.00	4.00
❏ 1037	Que Pasa?/Por Favor No Te Vayas	1980	—	2.00	4.00
❏ 1038	Make Me a Star/Do Me	1980	—	2.00	4.00
—K.C. solo					
❏ 1044	Space Cadet/Do Me	1981	—	2.00	4.00
—K.C. solo					
❏ 1048	Redlight/I Don't Wanna Make Love	1982	—	2.00	4.00
—K.C. solo					
Albums					
EPIC					
❏ FE 37490	The Painter	1981	2.50	5.00	10.00
❏ PE 37490	The Painter	1982	2.00	4.00	8.00
—Budget-line reissue					
❏ FE 38073	All in a Night's Work	1982	2.50	5.00	10.00
❏ PE 38073	All in a Night's Work	1984	2.00	4.00	8.00
—Budget-line reissue					
MECA					
❏ 8301	KC Ten	1984	2.50	5.00	10.00
SUNSHINE SOUND					
❏ 614	Space Cadet/Solo Flight	1981	2.50	5.00	10.00
T.K.					
❏ 500	Do It Good	1974	3.00	6.00	12.00
❏ 603	K.C. and the Sunshine Band	1975	2.50	5.00	10.00
❏ 604	The Sound of Sunshine	1975	2.50	5.00	10.00
—By "The Sunshine Band" (all instrumental)					
❏ 605	Part 3	1976	2.50	5.00	10.00
❏ 607	Who Do Ya (Love)	1978	2.50	5.00	10.00
❏ 611	Do You Wanna Go Party	1979	2.50	5.00	10.00
❏ 612	Greatest Hits	1980	2.50	5.00	10.00

Number	Title (A Side/B Side)	Yr	VG	VG+	NM

K.C. AND THE SUNSHINE BAND AND KOOL & THE GANG FEATURING JT TAYLOR
45s
EMI-CAPITOL

Number	Title (A Side/B Side)	Yr	VG	VG+	NM
❑ S7-19725	Casper, the Friendly Ghost/Delicious	1997	—	—	3.00

—B-side by Shampoo

K-DOE, ERNIE
45s
DUKE

Number	Title (A Side/B Side)	Yr	VG	VG+	NM
❑ 378	My Mother-in-Law (Is In My Hair Again)/Looking Into the Future	1964	2.00	4.00	8.00
❑ 387	Little Bit of Everything/Someone	1965	2.00	4.00	8.00
❑ 400	Please Don't Stop/Boomerang	1966	2.00	4.00	8.00
❑ 404	Little Marie/Somebody Told Me	1966	2.00	4.00	8.00
❑ 411	Later for Tomorrow/Dancin' Man	1966	2.00	4.00	8.00
❑ 420	Love Me Like I Wanna/Don't Kill My Groove	1967	2.00	4.00	8.00
❑ 423	(It Will Have to Do) Until the Real Thing Comes Along/Little Marie	1967	2.00	4.00	8.00
❑ 437	Gotta Pack My Bag/How Sweet You Are	1968	2.00	4.00	8.00
❑ 450	I'm Sorry/Trying to Make You Love Me	1969	2.00	4.00	8.00
❑ 456	I'll Make Everything Be Alright/Wishing in Vain	1969	2.00	4.00	8.00

EMBER

Number	Title (A Side/B Side)	Yr	VG	VG+	NM
❑ 1050	My Love for You/Tuff-Enuff	1959	6.25	12.50	25.00
❑ 1075	My Love for You/Shirley's Tuff	1961	3.75	7.50	15.00

INSTANT

Number	Title (A Side/B Side)	Yr	VG	VG+	NM
❑ 3260	Baby, SInce I Met You/Sufferin' So	1963	2.50	5.00	10.00
❑ 3264	Reaping What I Sow/Talking Out of My Head	1964	2.50	5.00	10.00

ISLAND

Number	Title (A Side/B Side)	Yr	VG	VG+	NM
❑ 031	Let Me Love You/So Good	1975	—	3.00	6.00

JANUS

Number	Title (A Side/B Side)	Yr	VG	VG+	NM
❑ 167	Here Come the Girls/Long Way Home	1971	—	3.00	6.00

MINIT

Number	Title (A Side/B Side)	Yr	VG	VG+	NM
❑ 604	Make You Love Me/There's a Will, There's a Way	1959	7.50	15.00	30.00
❑ 614	'Tain't It the Truth/Hello My Lover	1960	5.00	10.00	20.00
❑ 623	Mother-in-Law/Wanted, $10,000 Reward	1961	6.25	12.50	25.00

—Side 1 is at the correct speed. Trail-off number is "SO-738-2"

Number	Title (A Side/B Side)	Yr	VG	VG+	NM
❑ 623	Mother-in-Law/Wanted, $10,000 Reward	1961	50.00	100.00	200.00

—Side 1 was accidentally mis-mastered at 33 1/3 rpm. Trail-off number is "45-SO-738"

Number	Title (A Side/B Side)	Yr	VG	VG+	NM
❑ 627	Te-Ta-Te-Ta/Real Man	1961	3.75	7.50	15.00
❑ 634	A Certain Girl/I Cried My Last Tear	1961	3.75	7.50	15.00
❑ 641	Popeye Joe/Come On Home	1962	3.75	7.50	15.00
❑ 645	Hey Hey Hey/Love You the Best	1962	3.75	7.50	15.00
❑ 651	Beating Like a Tom-Tom/I Got to Find Somebody	1962	3.75	7.50	15.00
❑ 656	Loving You/Get Out of My House	1962	3.75	7.50	15.00
❑ 661	Easier Said Than Done/Be Sweet	1963	3.75	7.50	15.00
❑ 665	I'm the Boss/Pennies Worth o' Happiness	1963	3.75	7.50	15.00
❑ 32042	Real Man/Te Ta Te Ta Ta	1968	2.50	5.00	10.00

SANSU

Number	Title (A Side/B Side)	Yr	VG	VG+	NM
❑ 1006	Stoop Down/(B-side unknown)	197?	5.00	10.00	20.00
❑ 1016	Hotcha Mama/She Gave It All to Me	197?	5.00	10.00	20.00

SPECIALTY

Number	Title (A Side/B Side)	Yr	VG	VG+	NM
❑ 563	Eternity/Do Baby Do	1955	10.00	20.00	40.00

—As "Ernest Kador"
UNITED ARTISTS

Number	Title (A Side/B Side)	Yr	VG	VG+	NM
❑ 0110	Mother-in-Law/A Wonderful Dream	1973	—	2.50	5.00

—"Silver Spotlight Series" reissue; B-side by the Majors
Albums
JANUS

Number	Title (A Side/B Side)	Yr	VG	VG+	NM
❑ JLS-3030	Ernie K-Doe	1971	6.25	12.50	25.00

MINIT

Number	Title (A Side/B Side)	Yr	VG	VG+	NM
❑ LP-0002 [M]	Mother-in-Law	1961	50.00	100.00	200.00

—Orange label

Number	Title (A Side/B Side)	Yr	VG	VG+	NM
❑ LP-24002 [R]	Mother-in-Law	196?	37.50	75.00	150.00

—Black label, not issued until after Imperial bought Minit

KACT-TIES, THE
45s
ATCO

Number	Title (A Side/B Side)	Yr	VG	VG+	NM
❑ 6299	Oh What a Night/Let Me In Your Life	1964	3.75	7.50	15.00

—As "The Kac-Ties"
KAPE

Number	Title (A Side/B Side)	Yr	VG	VG+	NM
❑ 501	Happy Birthday/Girl in My Heart	1965	3.75	7.50	15.00

—As "The Kac-Ties"

Number	Title (A Side/B Side)	Yr	VG	VG+	NM
❑ 502	Walkin' in the Rain/Smile	1965	3.75	7.50	15.00

—As "The Kac-Ties"

Number	Title (A Side/B Side)	Yr	VG	VG+	NM
❑ 503	Let Your Love Light Shine/Were-Wolf	1965	3.75	7.50	15.00

—As "The Kac-Ties"
SHELLEY

Number	Title (A Side/B Side)	Yr	VG	VG+	NM
❑ 163	Let Your Love Light Shine/Were-Wolf	1963	6.25	12.50	25.00
❑ 165	Oh What a Night/Let Me In Your Life	1963	6.25	12.50	25.00

TRANS ATLAS

Number	Title (A Side/B Side)	Yr	VG	VG+	NM
❑ 695	Walkin' in the Rain/Smile	1962	37.50	75.00	150.00

—Without thunderstorm sound effects

Number	Title (A Side/B Side)	Yr	VG	VG+	NM
❑ 695	Walkin' in the Rain/Smile	1962	75.00	150.00	300.00

—With thunderstorm sound effects

KAEMPFERT, BERT
45s
DECCA

Number	Title (A Side/B Side)	Yr	VG	VG+	NM
❑ 30616	Midnight Blues/Ducky	1958	2.50	5.00	10.00
❑ 30866	Cerveza/Catalina	1959	2.00	4.00	8.00
❑ 31141	Wonderland by Night/Dreaming the Blues	1960	2.00	4.00	8.00
❑ 31236	Tenderly/Without Your Love	1961	2.00	4.00	8.00
❑ 31279	Now and Forever/Only Those in Love	1961	2.00	4.00	8.00
❑ 31350	Afrikaan Beat/Echo in the Night	1961	2.00	4.00	8.00
❑ 31388	That Happy Feeling/Take Me	1962	2.00	4.00	8.00
❑ 31420	Goden Wings in the Sun/Cinderella After Midnight	1962	2.00	4.00	8.00
❑ 31439	Happy Trumpeter/Tootsie Flutie	1962	2.00	4.00	8.00
❑ 31463	Gentleman Jim/Tipsy Gypsy	1963	—	3.00	6.00
❑ 31498	Danke Schoen/Give and Take	1963	—	3.00	6.00
❑ 31532	The Bass Walks/Don't Talk to Me	1963	—	3.00	6.00
❑ 31560	Jingo Jango/The Little Drummer Boy	1963	2.50	5.00	10.00

Number	Title (A Side/B Side)	Yr	VG	VG+	NM
❑ 31611	Dancing in a Dream/Big Build Up	1964	—	3.00	6.00
❑ 31638	Love/Blue Midnight	1964	—	3.00	6.00
❑ 31666	Almost There/Treat for Trumpet	1964	—	3.00	6.00
❑ 31722	Red Roses for a Blue Lady/Lonely Nightingale	1965	—	3.00	6.00
❑ 31778	Three O'Clock in the Morning/Nothing's New	1965	—	3.00	6.00
❑ 31812	Moon Over Naples/The Moon Is Making Eyes	1965	—	3.00	6.00
❑ 31873	Holiday for Bells/Jumpin' Jiminy Christmas	1965	2.00	4.00	8.00
❑ 31882	Bye Bye Blues/Remember When	1965	—	3.00	6.00
❑ 31882 [PS]	Bye Bye Blues/Remember When	1965	—	—	—

—Rumored to exist, but without conclusive evidence, we will delete this from future editions

Number	Title (A Side/B Side)	Yr	VG	VG+	NM
❑ 31945	Strangers in the Night/But Not Today	1966	—	3.00	6.00
❑ 32008	I Can't Give You Anything But Love/Milica	1966	—	3.00	6.00
❑ 32051	So What's New/Hold Back the Dawn	1966	—	3.00	6.00
❑ 32094	Pussy Footin'/Hold Me	1967	—	3.00	6.00
❑ 32159	Talk/Night Dreams	1967	—	3.00	6.00
❑ 32204	Love for Love/You Are My Sunshine	1967	—	3.00	6.00
❑ 32241	Caravan/Milina	1967	—	3.00	6.00
❑ 32283	The First Waltz/Somebody Loves You	1968	—	2.50	5.00
❑ 32329	Mister Sandman/Lonely Is the Name	1968	—	2.50	5.00
❑ 32379	My Way of Life/Malaysian Melody	1968	—	2.50	5.00
❑ 732471	One Lonely Night/The Maltese Melody	1969	—	2.50	5.00
❑ 32518	Games People Play/Here's My Life (Here's My Love)	1969	—	2.50	5.00
❑ 32647	Someday We'll Be Together/We Can Make It Girl	1970	—	2.50	5.00
❑ 32715	Theme from "You Can't Win Them All"/Flight to Mecca	1970	—	2.50	5.00
❑ 32772	Something/Sweet Caroline	1971	—	2.50	5.00
❑ 32809	(I'll Be With You) In Apple Blossom Time/My Life	1971	—	2.50	5.00
❑ 32875	Proud Mary/In Our Time	1971	—	2.50	5.00
❑ 32935	Lonely Is the Name/Only a Fool	1972	—	2.50	5.00

MCA

Number	Title (A Side/B Side)	Yr	VG	VG+	NM
❑ 40221	The Most Beautiful Girl/Moon Over Baja	1974	—	2.00	4.00

7-Inch Extended Plays
DECCA

Number	Title (A Side/B Side)	Yr	VG	VG+	NM
❑ ED 2697	Wonderland by Night/Dreaming the Blues//As I Love You/Tammy	1961	2.50	5.00	10.00
❑ ED 2697 [PS]	Wonderland by Night	1961	2.50	5.00	10.00
❑ ED 2721	That Happy Feeling/Take Me//Happy Trumpeter/Sunday in Madrid	196?	2.50	5.00	10.00
❑ ED 2721 [PS]	That Happy Feeling	196?	2.50	5.00	10.00
❑ ED 2766	Danke Schoen/Bass Walks//Gentleman Jim/Tipsy Wipsy	196?	2.50	5.00	10.00
❑ ED 2766 [PS]	Danke Schoen	196?	2.50	5.00	10.00
❑ ED 2796	(contents unknown)	196?	2.50	5.00	10.00
❑ ED 2796 [PS]	Red Roses for a Blue Lady	196?	2.50	5.00	10.00
❑ 7-34359	Bye Bye Blues/Remember When (We Made Those Memories)/Tahitian Sunset//It Makes No Difference/I'm Beginning to See the Light	196?	2.50	5.00	10.00

—Jukebox issue; small hole, plays at 33 1/3 rpm

Number	Title (A Side/B Side)	Yr	VG	VG+	NM
❑ 7-34359 [PS]	Bye Bye Blues	196?	2.50	5.00	10.00
❑ 7-34390	Wonderland by Night/Afrikaan Beat/Red Roses for a Blue Lady//Strangers in the Night/That Happy Feeling/Wiedershe'n	1966	2.50	5.00	10.00

—Jukebox issue; small hole, plays at 33 1/3 rpm; "Wiedershe'n" is the spelling on the label

Number	Title (A Side/B Side)	Yr	VG	VG+	NM
❑ 7-34390 [PS]	Bert Kaempfert's Greatest Hits	1966	2.50	5.00	10.00

Albums
DECCA

Number	Title (A Side/B Side)	Yr	VG	VG+	NM
❑ DL 4101 [M]	Wonderland by Night	1960	3.75	7.50	15.00
❑ DL 4117 [M]	The Wonderland of Bert Kaempfert	1961	3.75	7.50	15.00
❑ DL 4161 [M]	Dancing in Wonderland	1961	3.75	7.50	15.00
❑ DL 4228 [M]	With a "Sound" in My Heart	1962	3.00	6.00	12.00
❑ DL 4265 [M]	Lights Out, Sweet Dreams	1963	3.00	6.00	12.00
❑ DL 4273 [M]	Afrikaan Beat and Other Favorites	1962	3.00	6.00	12.00
❑ DL 4305 [M]	That Happy Feeling	1962	3.00	6.00	12.00
❑ DL 4374 [M]	Living It Up!	1963	3.00	6.00	12.00
❑ DL 4441 [M]	Christmas Wonderland	1963	3.75	7.50	15.00
❑ DL 4490 [M]	That Latin Feeling	1964	3.00	6.00	12.00
❑ DL 4569 [M]	Blue Midnight	1965	3.00	6.00	12.00
❑ DL 4616 [M]	The Magic Music of Far Away Places	1965	3.00	6.00	12.00
❑ DL 4670 [M]	Three O'Clock in the Morning	1965	3.00	6.00	12.00
❑ DL 4693 [M]	Bye Bye Blues	1966	3.00	6.00	12.00
❑ DL 4795 [M]	Strangers in the Night	1966	3.00	6.00	12.00
❑ DL 4810 [M]	Bert Kaempfert's Greatest Hits	1966	3.00	6.00	12.00
❑ DL 4860 [M]	Hold Me	1967	3.00	6.00	12.00
❑ DL 4925 [M]	The World We Knew	1967	5.00	10.00	20.00
❑ DL 4986 [M]	Love That	1968	5.00	10.00	20.00
❑ DXS 7200 [(2)]	The Best of Bert Kaempfert	197?	5.00	10.00	20.00
❑ DL 8881 [M]	April in Portugal	1959	3.75	7.50	15.00
❑ DL 34485 [M]	Bert Kaempfert's Best	1966	3.75	7.50	15.00

—Special Decca Custom Division edition

Number	Title (A Side/B Side)	Yr	VG	VG+	NM
❑ DL 74101 [S]	Wonderland by Night	1960	5.00	10.00	20.00
❑ DL 74117 [S]	The Wonderland of Bert Kaempfert	1961	5.00	10.00	20.00
❑ DL 74161 [S]	Dancing in Wonderland	1961	5.00	10.00	20.00
❑ DL 74228 [S]	With a "Sound" in My Heart	1962	3.75	7.50	15.00
❑ DL 74265 [S]	Lights Out, Sweet Dreams	1963	3.75	7.50	15.00
❑ DL 74273 [S]	Afrikaan Beat and Other Favorites	1962	3.75	7.50	15.00
❑ DL 74305 [S]	That Happy Feeling	1962	3.75	7.50	15.00
❑ DL 74374 [S]	Living It Up!	1963	3.75	7.50	15.00
❑ DL 74441 [S]	Christmas Wonderland	1963	4.00	8.00	16.00

—Same as above, but in stereo

Number	Title (A Side/B Side)	Yr	VG	VG+	NM
❑ DL 74490 [S]	That Latin Feeling	1964	3.75	7.50	15.00
❑ DL 74569 [S]	Blue Midnight	1965	3.75	7.50	15.00
❑ DL 74616 [S]	The Magic Music of Far Away Places	1965	3.75	7.50	15.00
❑ DL 74670 [S]	Three O'Clock in the Morning	1965	3.75	7.50	15.00
❑ DL 74693 [S]	Bye Bye Blues	1966	3.75	7.50	15.00
❑ DL 74795 [S]	Strangers in the Night	1966	3.75	7.50	15.00
❑ DL 74810 [S]	Bert Kaempfert's Greatest Hits	1966	3.75	7.50	15.00
❑ DL 74860 [S]	Hold Me	1967	3.75	7.50	15.00
❑ DL 74925 [S]	The World We Knew	1967	3.75	7.50	15.00
❑ DL 74986 [S]	Love That	1968	3.75	7.50	15.00
❑ DL 75059	My Way of Life	1968	3.75	7.50	15.00
❑ DL 75089	Warm and Wonderful	1969	3.75	7.50	15.00
❑ DL 75140	Traces of Love	1969	3.75	7.50	15.00
❑ DL 75175	The Kaempfert Touch	1970	3.75	7.50	15.00
❑ DL 75234	Free and Easy	1970	3.75	7.50	15.00
❑ DL 75256	Orange Colored Sky	1971	3.75	7.50	15.00
❑ DL 75305	Bert Kaempfert Now!	1971	3.75	7.50	15.00

Number	Title (A Side/B Side)	Yr	VG	VG+	NM
❏ DL 75322	Six Plus Six	1972	3.75	7.50	15.00
❏ DL 75367	Bert Kaempfert's Greatest Hits, Volume 2	1972	3.75	7.50	15.00
❏ DL 78881 [S]	April in Portugal	1959	5.00	10.00	20.00
❏ T-90995 [M]	Strangers in the Night	1966	3.75	7.50	15.00
—Capitol Record Club edition					
❏ ST-91165	Blue Midnight	196?	4.50	9.00	18.00
—Capitol Record Club edition					
❏ ST-91502	Love That	1968	4.50	9.00	18.00
—Capitol Record Club edition					
❏ ST-93495	Orange Colored Sky	1971	4.50	9.00	18.00
—Capitol Record Club edition					
❏ DL 734485 [S]	Bert Kaempfert's Best	1966	5.00	10.00	20.00
—Special Decca Custom Division edition					
LONGINES SYMPHONETTE					
❏ LWS 299/300/1/2/3 [(5)]	Strangers in the Night	196?	7.50	15.00	30.00
❏ LWS 304	Sweet and Gentle	196?	2.50	5.00	10.00
MCA					
❏ 11	Bert Kaempfert's Greatest Hits	1973	2.50	5.00	10.00
—Reissue of Decca 74810					
❏ 214	Christmas Wonderland	1973	3.00	6.00	12.00
—First MCA reissue of Decca 74441					
❏ 314	The Fabulous Fifties	1973	3.00	6.00	12.00
❏ 368	To the Good Life	1973	3.00	6.00	12.00
❏ 402	The Most Beautiful Girl	1974	3.00	6.00	12.00
❏ 447	Gallery	1974	3.00	6.00	12.00
❏ 466	Golden Memories	1974	3.00	6.00	12.00
❏ 489	Moon Over Miami	1975	3.00	6.00	12.00
❏ 4043 [(2)]	The Best of Bert Kaempfert	197?	3.75	7.50	15.00
—Reissue of Decca 7200; black label with rainbow					
❏ 4100 [(2)]	The Best of Bert Kaempfert, Volume 2	197?	3.75	7.50	15.00
—Black label with rainbow					
❏ 15020	Christmas Wonderland	197?	2.50	5.00	10.00
—Reissue; black label with rainbow					
❏ 15020	Christmas Wonderland	198?	2.00	4.00	8.00
—Reissue; blue label with rainbow					
POLYDOR					
❏ K2M 5051 [(2)M]	The Happy Wonderland of Bert Kaempfert	1966	3.75	7.50	15.00
—Columbia Record Club exclusive					
❏ K2S 5052 [(2)S]	The Happy Wonderland of Bert Kaempfert	1966	3.75	7.50	15.00
—Columbia Record Club exclusive					
❏ SPH 37553	Wonderland by Night	1967	3.00	6.00	12.00
—Columbia Record Club edition					
❏ SPH 37556	Afrikaan Beat and Other Favorites	1967	3.00	6.00	12.00
—Columbia Record Club edition					
❏ SPH 37580	With a "Sound" in My Heart	1967	3.00	6.00	12.00
—Columbia Record Club edition					
❏ SPH 37598	Lights Out, Sweet Dreams	1967	3.00	6.00	12.00
—Columbia Record Club edition					
❏ SPH 37599	Living It Up!	1967	3.00	6.00	12.00
—Columbia Record Club exclusive					

KAK Gary Yoder of BLUE CHEER was in this group.
45s
EPIC

Number	Title (A Side/B Side)	Yr	VG	VG+	NM
❏ 10383 [DJ]	Everything's Changing (Long Version)/ Everything's Changing (Edited Version)	1968	5.00	10.00	20.00
—May be promo only					
❏ 10446	I've Got Time/Disbelievin'	1969	5.00	10.00	20.00
Albums					
EPIC					
❏ BN 26429	Kak	1969	62.50	125.00	250.00
—Beware -- a reissue that looks almost identical to the original and sells for around $12 appeared in stores in 2000-2001					

KALABASH CORP., THE
Albums
UNCLE BILL

Number	Title (A Side/B Side)	Yr	VG	VG+	NM
❏ KB-3114	The Kalabash Corp.	1970	20.00	40.00	80.00

KALEIDOSCOPE, THE
45s
EPIC

Number	Title (A Side/B Side)	Yr	VG	VG+	NM
❏ 10117	Elevator Man/Please	1967	7.50	15.00	30.00
❏ 10219	Little Orphan Annie/Why Try	1967	7.50	15.00	30.00
❏ 10239	I Found Out/Rampe Rampe	1967	7.50	15.00	30.00
❏ 10332	Just a Taste/Hello Trouble	1968	7.50	15.00	30.00
❏ 10481	Lie to Me/Let the Good Love Flow	1969	7.50	15.00	30.00
❏ 10500	Killing Floor/Lie to Me	1969	7.50	15.00	30.00
FONTANA					
❏ 1633	Jimmy Artichoke/Just How Much You Are	1968	—	—	—
—Unreleased					
Albums					
EPIC					
❏ LN 24304 [M]	Side Trips	1967	7.50	15.00	30.00
❏ LN 24333 [M]	Beacon from Mars	1967	15.00	30.00	60.00
❏ BN 26304 [S]	Side Trips	1967	10.00	20.00	40.00
❏ BN 26333 [S]	Beacon from Mars	1967	25.00	50.00	100.00
❏ BN 26467	Incredible Kaleidoscope	1969	7.50	15.00	30.00
❏ BN 26508	Bernice	1970	7.50	15.00	30.00
PACIFIC ARTS					
❏ 102	When Scopes Collide	1978	3.00	6.00	12.00

KALIN TWINS, THE
45s
AMY

Number	Title (A Side/B Side)	Yr	VG	VG+	NM
❏ 969	Thinkin' About You Baby/Sometimes It Comes	1966	2.00	4.00	8.00
DECCA					
❏ 30552	Jumpin' Jack/Walkin' to School	1958	5.00	10.00	20.00
❏ 30642	When/Three O'Clock Thrill	1958	6.25	12.50	25.00
❏ 30745	Forget Me Not/Dream of Me	1958	6.25	12.50	25.00
❏ 30807	It's Only the Beginning/Oh My Goodness	1959	5.00	10.00	20.00
❏ 30868	Cool/When I Look in the Mirror	1959	5.00	10.00	20.00
❏ 30911	Sweet Sugar Lips/Moody	1959	5.00	10.00	20.00
❏ 30977	Why Don't You Believe Me/ The Meaning of the Blues	1959	5.00	10.00	20.00
❏ 30977 [PS]	Why Don't You Believe Me/ The Meaning of the Blues	1959	7.50	15.00	30.00

Number	Title (A Side/B Side)	Yr	VG	VG+	NM
❏ 31064	Loneliness/Chicken Thief	1960	3.75	7.50	15.00
❏ 31111	True to You/Blue, Blue Town	1960	3.75	7.50	15.00
❏ 31169	Zing! Went the Strings of My Heart/ No Money Can Buy	1960	3.75	7.50	15.00
❏ 31220	Momma-Poppa/You Mean the World to Me	1961	3.75	7.50	15.00
❏ 31286	Bubbles (I'm Forever Blowing Bubbles)/ One More Time	1961	3.75	7.50	15.00
❏ 31410	Trouble/A Picture of You	1962	3.75	7.50	15.00
7-Inch Extended Plays					
DECCA					
❏ ED 2623	When/Three O'Clock Thrill//Jumpin' Jack/ Walkin' to School	1958	15.00	30.00	60.00
❏ ED 2623 [PS]	When	1958	20.00	40.00	80.00
❏ ED 2641	(contents unknown)	1958	12.50	25.00	50.00
❏ ED 2641 [PS]	Forget Me Not	1958	15.00	30.00	60.00
Albums					
DECCA					
❏ DL 8812 [M]	The Kalin Twins	1959	25.00	50.00	100.00
VOCALION					
❏ VL 3771 [M]	When	1966	3.75	7.50	15.00
❏ VL 73771 [R]	When	1966	3.00	6.00	12.00

KALLEN, KITTY
45s
BELL

Number	Title (A Side/B Side)	Yr	VG	VG+	NM
❏ 673	Summer, Summer Wind/Oba, Oba	1967	2.00	4.00	8.00
COLUMBIA					
❏ 40298	The High and the Mighty/ Still You'd Break My Heart	1954	3.75	7.50	15.00
—With Harry James					
❏ 41236	When Will I Know/Love Is a Sacred Thing	1958	3.00	6.00	12.00
❏ 41473	If I Give My Heart to You/ The Door That Won't Open	1959	3.00	6.00	12.00
❏ 41546	That Old Feeling/Need Me	1959	3.00	6.00	12.00
❏ 41622	Always in My Heart/Got a Date with an Angel	1960	3.00	6.00	12.00
❏ 41671	Make Love to Me/Heaven Help Me	1960	3.00	6.00	12.00
❏ 41769	Come Live with Me/Be True to Me	1960	3.00	6.00	12.00
❏ 41857	I Believe in You/The Things You Left in My Heart	1960	3.00	6.00	12.00
❏ 41934	Hey Good Lookin'/Raining in My Heart	1961	3.00	6.00	12.00
❏ 42038	Summertime Lies/Yassu	1961	3.00	6.00	12.00
❏ 42247	It Wasn't God Who Made Honky Tonk Angels/ You Are My Sunshine	1961	3.00	6.00	12.00
DECCA					
❏ 28813	Lonely/Heartless Heart	1953	3.75	7.50	15.00
❏ 28904	A Little Lie/Are You Looking for a Sweetheart	1953	3.75	7.50	15.00
❏ 29037	Little Things Mean a Lot/ I Don't Think You Love Me Anymore	1954	3.75	7.50	15.00
❏ 29130	In the Chapel in the Moonlight/ Take Everything But You	1954	3.75	7.50	15.00
❏ 29268	I Want You All to Myself (Just You)/ Don't Let the Kitty Geddin	1954	3.75	7.50	15.00
❏ 29315	The Spirit of Christmas/Baby Brother (Santa Claus, Dear Santa Claus)	1954	3.00	6.00	12.00
❏ 29417	I'd Never Forgive Myself/Honestly	1955	3.00	6.00	12.00
❏ 29473	By Bayou Bay/Kitty Who?	1955	3.00	6.00	12.00
❏ 29548	If It's a Dream/Forgive Me	1955	3.00	6.00	12.00
❏ 29593	Let's Make the Most of Tonight/ Just Between Friends	1955	3.00	6.00	12.00
❏ 29663	Only Forever/Come Spring	1955	3.00	6.00	12.00
❏ 29708	Sweet Kentucky Rose/How Lonely Can I Get?	1955	3.00	6.00	12.00
❏ 29959	True Love/Will I Always Be Your Sweetheart	1956	3.00	6.00	12.00
❏ 30049	How About Me/The Lonely One	1956	3.00	6.00	12.00
❏ 30144	Saturday Blues/Ah, Ah, Ah (The Song That Haunts)	1956	3.00	6.00	12.00
❏ 30267	Star Bright/Gently, Johnny	1957	3.00	6.00	12.00
❏ 30346	Teen-Age Heart/Hideaway Heart	1957	3.00	6.00	12.00
❏ 30516	Crying Roses/I Never Was the One	1957	3.00	6.00	12.00
❏ 88181	The Spirit of Christmas/Baby Brother (Santa Claus, Dear Santa Claus)	1954	3.00	6.00	12.00
—Children's Series issue					
❏ 88181 [PS]	The Spirit of Christmas/Baby Brother (Santa Claus, Dear Santa Claus)	1954	5.00	10.00	20.00
—Children's Series issue					
MERCURY					
❏ 5417	Juke Box Annie/Choo'n Gum	1950	5.00	10.00	20.00
❏ 5587	If You Want Some Lovin'/Last Night	1951	3.75	7.50	15.00
❏ 5700	I Wish I Had a Daddy in the White House/ The Old Soft Shoe	1951	3.75	7.50	15.00
❏ 5727	Another Human Being of the Opposite Sex/ More, More, More	1951	3.75	7.50	15.00
PHILIPS					
❏ 40375	One Grain of Sand/ From Your Lips to the Arms of an Angel	1966	2.00	4.00	8.00
RCA VICTOR					
❏ 47-8124	My Coloring Book/Here's to Us	1962	2.50	5.00	10.00
❏ 47-8202	I'll Teach You How to Cry/ We'll Cross That Bridge	1963	2.50	5.00	10.00
20TH CENTURY FOX					
❏ 471	Make Somebody Love You/Lies and More Lies	1964	2.00	4.00	8.00
7-Inch Extended Plays					
DECCA					
❏ ED 2164	Little Things Mean a Lot/I Don't Think You Love Me Anymore//In the Chapel in the Moonlight/ Take Everything But You	1954	10.00	20.00	40.00
❏ ED 2164 [PS]	Kitty Kallen Sings	1954	10.00	20.00	40.00
❏ ED 2467	(contents unknown)	1956	6.25	12.50	25.00
❏ ED 2467 [PS]	It's a Lonesome Old Town, Part 1	1956	6.25	12.50	25.00
❏ ED 2468	(contents unknown)	1956	6.25	12.50	25.00
❏ ED 2468 [PS]	It's a Lonesome Old Town, Part 2	1956	6.25	12.50	25.00
❏ ED 2469	(contents unknown)	1956	6.25	12.50	25.00
❏ ED 2469 [PS]	It's a Lonesome Old Town, Part 3	1956	6.25	12.50	25.00
MERCURY					
❏ EP 1-3293	(contents unknown)	1955	10.00	20.00	40.00
❏ EP 1-3293 [PS]	Pretty Kitty Kallen Sings, Vol. 1	1955	10.00	20.00	40.00
❏ EP 1-3294	(contents unknown)	1955	10.00	20.00	40.00
❏ EP 1-3294 [PS]	Pretty Kitty Kallen Sings, Vol. 2	1955	10.00	20.00	40.00

Number	Title (A Side/B Side)	Yr	VG	VG+	NM

Albums
COLUMBIA

Number	Title (A Side/B Side)	Yr	VG	VG+	NM
❏ CL 1404 [M]	If I Give My Heart to You	1960	5.00	10.00	20.00
❏ CL 1662 [M]	Honky Tonk Angel	1961	5.00	10.00	20.00
❏ CS 8204 [S]	If I Give My Heart to You	1960	6.25	12.50	25.00
❏ CS 8462 [S]	Honky Tonk Angel	1961	6.25	12.50	25.00

DECCA

❏ DL 8397 [M]	It's a Lonesome Old Town	1958	10.00	20.00	40.00

MERCURY

❏ MG 25206 [10]	Pretty Kitty Kallen Sings	1955	12.50	25.00	50.00

MOVIETONE

❏ 71026 [M]	Delightfully	1967	3.75	7.50	15.00
❏ S-72026 [S]	Delightfully	1967	3.75	7.50	15.00

RCA VICTOR

❏ LPM-2640 [M]	My Coloring Book	1963	5.00	10.00	20.00
❏ LSP-2640 [S]	My Coloring Book	1963	6.25	12.50	25.00

VOCALION

❏ VL 3679 [M]	Little Things Mean a Lot	1959	6.25	12.50	25.00

WING

❏ MGW-12241 [M]	Kitty Kallen Sings	196?	3.75	7.50	15.00
❏ SRW-16241 [R]	Kitty Kallen Sings	196?	3.00	6.00	12.00

KALLEN, KITTY (WITH RICHARD HAYES)
45s
MERCURY

❏ 5466	Our Lady of Fatima/Honestly I Love You	1950	3.75	7.50	15.00
❏ 5499	Halls of Ivy/Dream	1950	3.75	7.50	15.00
❏ 5501	Silver Bells/A Bushel and a Peck	1950	3.75	7.50	15.00
❏ 5532	Silver Bells/Jing-a-Ling	1950	3.75	7.50	15.00
❏ 5564	It Is No Secret (What God Can Do) /Get Out the Old Records	1950	3.75	7.50	15.00
❏ 5586	The Aba Daba Honeymoon/I Don't Want to Love	1951	3.75	7.50	15.00
❏ 5661	Everyone Is Welcome (In the House of the Lord)/ Good Luck	1951	3.75	7.50	15.00

KALLEN, KITTY, AND GEORGIE SHAW
45s
DECCA

❏ 29776	Go On with the Wedding/ The Second Greatest Sex	1955	3.00	6.00	12.00

KALLMANN, GUNTER, CHORUS
45s
4 CORNERS OF THE WORLD

❏ 119	Music for Falling in Love/Serenade	1965	—	3.00	6.00
❏ 138	Wish Me a Rainbow/The Day the Rains Came	1966	—	3.00	6.00
❏ 139	Morning, Noon and Night/Chanson d'Amour	1967	—	3.00	6.00
❏ 144	Paint Yourself a Rainbow/This Is My Song	1967	—	3.00	6.00
❏ 146	Tammy/You Know What to Do	1967	—	3.00	6.00
❏ 148	Counting the Days/Our Day Will Come	1968	—	3.00	6.00
❏ 150	Talk to the Animals/In the Heat of the Night	1968	—	3.00	6.00

POLYDOR

❏ 15008	Where's the Playground Susie/Once in Each Life	1969	—	2.50	5.00

Albums
4 CORNERS OF THE WORLD

❏ FCL-4209 [M]	Serenade for Elisabeth	1965	3.00	6.00	12.00
❏ FCS-4209 [S]	Serenade for Elisabeth	1965	3.75	7.50	15.00
❏ FCL-4218 [M]	Serenade for a Lady in Love	1965	3.00	6.00	12.00
❏ FCS-4218 [S]	Serenade for a Lady in Love	1965	3.75	7.50	15.00
❏ FCL-4226 [M]	Songs for My Love	1966	3.00	6.00	12.00
❏ FCS-4226 [S]	Songs for My Love	1966	3.75	7.50	15.00
❏ FCL-4235 [M]	Wish Me a Rainbow	1966	3.00	6.00	12.00
❏ FCS-4235 [S]	Wish Me a Rainbow	1966	3.75	7.50	15.00
❏ FCL-4237 [M]	With All My Heart	1967	3.00	6.00	12.00
❏ FCS-4237 [S]	With All My Heart	1967	3.75	7.50	15.00
❏ FCS-4248 [S]	Live for Love	1968	3.00	6.00	12.00
❏ FCS-4256 [S]	Love Is Blue	1968	3.00	6.00	12.00

POLYDOR

❏ 24-4506	Early in the Morning	1970	2.50	5.00	10.00
❏ 24-6003	Once in Each Life	1969	2.50	5.00	10.00

KANE, EDEN
45s
FONTANA

❏ 1891	Boys Cry/Don't Come Crying to Me	1964	3.00	6.00	12.00
❏ 1961	Hangin' Around/Do Something About You	1964	3.00	6.00	12.00

LONDON

❏ 1993	Well, I Ask You/Before I Lose My Mind	1961	3.75	7.50	15.00
❏ 9508	Get Lost/I'm Telling You	1961	3.75	7.50	15.00
❏ 9516	Forget Me Not/New Kind of Lovin'	1962	3.75	7.50	15.00
❏ 9532	I Don't Know Why/Music for Strings	1962	3.75	7.50	15.00

T-A

❏ 193	Reason to Believe/(B-side unknown)	1970	—	3.00	6.00

KANE, PAUL See PAUL SIMON.

KANE'S COUSINS
Albums
SHOVE LOVE

❏ 9827	Undergum Bubbleground	1969	10.00	20.00	40.00

KANGAROO
45s
MGM

❏ 13960	I Never Tell Me Twice/Such a Long Long Time	1968	3.00	6.00	12.00
❏ 13961	Daydream Stallion/The Only Thing I Had	1968	3.00	6.00	12.00

—As "Barbara Keith and Kangaroo"

❏ 13962	Frogg Giggin'/Maybe Tomorrow	1968	3.00	6.00	12.00

—As "N.D. Smart and Kangaroo"

Albums
MGM

❏ SE-4586	Kangaroo	1968	6.25	12.50	25.00

KANNIBAL KOMIX
45s
COLOSSUS

❏ 118	Little Little/Neurotic Reaction	1970	2.00	4.00	8.00

Number	Title (A Side/B Side)	Yr	VG	VG+	NM

Albums
COLOSSUS

❏ 1004	Kannibal Komix	1970	5.00	10.00	20.00

KANSAS
12-Inch Singles
CBS ASSOCIATED

❏ AS 1747 [DJ]	Mainstream/Everybody's My Friend	1983	—	3.00	6.00

KIRSHNER

❏ AS 1451 [DJ]	Play the Game Tonight/Confessions Pre- Release Montage	1982	2.00	4.00	8.00
❏ AS 1534 [DJ]	Right Away/Diamonds and Pearls	1982	2.00	4.00	8.00

MCA

❏ L33-17209 [DJ]	All I Wanted (same on both sides?)	1986	2.00	4.00	8.00
❏ L33-17306 [DJ]	Can't Cry Anymore (same on both sides)	1987	—	3.00	6.00

45s
CBS ASSOCIATED

❏ ZS4-04057	Fight Fire with Fire/Incident on a Bridge	1983	—	—	3.00
❏ ZS4-04057 [PS]	Fight Fire with Fire/Incident on a Bridge	1983	—	2.00	4.00
❏ ZS4-04057 [PS]	Fight Fire with Fire/Incident on a Bridge	1983	2.00	4.00	8.00

—"Demonstration Only -- Not for Sale" on sleeve (sleeve lists both tracks, though the enclosed promo record only has the A-side on both sides)

❏ ZS4-04213	Everybody's My Friend/End of the Age	1983	—	—	3.00
❏ ZS4-04213 [PS]	Everybody's My Friend/End of the Age	1983	—	2.00	4.00
❏ ZS4-04213 [PS]	Everybody's My Friend	1983	2.00	4.00	8.00

—"Demonstration Only -- Not for Sale" on sleeve

KIRSHNER

❏ ZS5-02903	Play the Game Tonight/Play On	1982	—	2.00	4.00
❏ ZS5-03084	Right Away/Windows	1982	—	2.00	4.00
❏ ZS5-03084 [PS]	Right Away/Windows	1982	—	2.50	5.00
❏ ZS7 4253	Can I Tell You/The Pilgrimage	1974	—	3.00	6.00
❏ ZS8 4256	Lonely Wind/Bringing It Back	1974	—	3.00	6.00
❏ ZS8 4258	Song for America (Part 1)/(Part 2)	1975	—	3.00	6.00
❏ ZS8 4259	It's You/It Takes a Woman's Love to Make a Man	1975	—	3.00	6.00
❏ ZS8 4267	Carry On Wayward Son/Questions of My Childhood	1976	—	2.50	5.00
❏ ZS8 4270	What's On My Mind/Lonely Street	1977	—	2.00	4.00
❏ ZS8 4273	Point of Know Return/Closet Chronicles	1977	—	2.00	4.00
❏ ZS8 4274	Dust in the Wind/Paradox	1978	—	2.50	5.00
❏ ZS8 4276	Portrait (He Knew)/Lightning's Hand	1978	—	2.00	4.00
❏ ZS8 4280	Lonely Wind/Song for America	1979	—	2.00	4.00
❏ ZS8 4284	People of the South Wind/Stay Out of Trouble	1979	—	2.00	4.00
❏ ZS9 4285	Reason to Be/How My Soul Cries Out for You	1979	—	2.00	4.00
❏ ZS9 4291	Hold On/Don't Open Your Eyes	1980	—	2.00	4.00
❏ ZS6 4292	Got to Rock On/No Room for a Stranger	1980	—	2.00	4.00

MCA

❏ S45-17290 [DJ]	Power (same on both sides)	1987	—	2.00	4.00
❏ S45-17290 [PS]	Power (same on both sides)	1987	—	2.00	4.00
❏ 52958	All I Wanted/We're Not Alone Anymore	1986	—	—	3.00
❏ 52958 [PS]	All I Wanted/We're Not Alone Anymore	1986	—	—	3.00
❏ 53027	Power/Tomb 19	1987	—	—	3.00
❏ 53027 [PS]	Power/Tomb 19	1987	—	—	3.00
❏ 53070	Can't Cry Anymore/Three Pretenders	1987	—	—	3.00
❏ 53070 [PS]	Can't Cry Anymore/Three Pretenders	1987	—	—	3.00
❏ 53425	Stand Beside Me/House on Fire	1988	—	—	3.00
❏ 53425 [PS]	Stand Beside Me/House on Fire	1988	—	2.00	4.00

Albums
CBS ASSOCIATED

❏ QZ 38733	Drastic Measures	1983	2.00	4.00	8.00
❏ QZ 39283	The Best of Kansas	1984	2.00	4.00	8.00

KIRSHNER

❏ AS 555 [DJ]	Two for the Show (Sampler)	1978	5.00	10.00	20.00

—Promo-only single disc of selections from 35660

❏ KZ 32817	Kansas	1974	3.00	6.00	12.00
❏ PZ 32817	Kansas	197?	2.00	4.00	8.00

—Reissue

❏ PZ 33385	Song for America	1975	3.00	6.00	12.00

—Without bar code on cover

❏ PZ 33385	Song for America	198?	2.00	4.00	8.00

—With bar code on cover

❏ PZ 33806	Masque	1975	3.00	6.00	12.00

—Without bar code on cover

❏ PZ 33806	Masque	198?	2.00	4.00	8.00

—With bar code on cover

❏ JZ 34224	Leftoverture	1976	2.50	5.00	10.00
❏ PZ 34224	Leftoverture	198?	2.00	4.00	8.00

—Budget-line reissue

❏ JZ 34929	Point of Know Return	1977	2.50	5.00	10.00
❏ PZ2 35660 [(2)]	Two for the Show	1978	3.75	7.50	15.00
❏ FZ 36008	Monolith	1979	2.50	5.00	10.00
❏ PZ 36008	Monolith	198?	2.00	4.00	8.00

—Budget-line reissue

❏ FZ 36588	Audio-Visions	1980	2.50	5.00	10.00
❏ PZ 36588	Audio-Visions	198?	2.00	4.00	8.00

—Budget-line reissue

❏ FZ 38002	Vinyl Confessions	1982	2.50	5.00	10.00
❏ PZ 38002	Vinyl Confessions	198?	2.00	4.00	8.00

—Budget-line reissue

❏ HZ 44224	Leftoverture	1982	10.00	20.00	40.00

—Half-speed mastered edition

❏ HZ 44929	Point of Know Return	1982	10.00	20.00	40.00

—Half-speed mastered edition

❏ HZ 46008	Monolith	1982	12.50	25.00	50.00

—Half-speed mastered edition

❏ HZ 48002	Vinyl Confessions	1982	25.00	50.00	100.00

—Half-speed mastered edition

MCA

❏ 5838	Power	1986	2.00	4.00	8.00
❏ 6254	In the Spirit of Things	1988	2.00	4.00	8.00

KANTNER, PAUL/JEFFERSON STARSHIP Also see JEFFERSON STARSHIP.
45s
RCA VICTOR

❏ 74-0426	Let's Go Together/A Child Is Coming	1971	—	2.50	5.00
❏ 74-0426 [PS]	Let's Go Together/A Child Is Coming	1971	2.00	4.00	8.00

Number	Title (A Side/B Side)	Yr	VG	VG+	NM
Albums					
RCA VICTOR					
❑ AYL1-3868	Blows Against the Empire	1981	2.00	4.00	8.00
—Budget-line reissue					
❑ LSP-4448	Blows Against the Empire	1970	3.75	7.50	15.00
❑ LSP-4448 [DJ]	Blows Against the Empire	1970	37.50	75.00	150.00
—Clear vinyl promo					

KANTNER, PAUL, AND GRACE SLICK Also see JEFFERSON AIRPLANE; JEFFERSON STARSHIP; GRACE SLICK.

Number	Title (A Side/B Side)	Yr	VG	VG+	NM
45s					
GRUNT					
❑ BFBO-0094	Sketches of China/Ballad of Chrome Men	1973	—	2.50	5.00
—With David Freiberg					
❑ 65-0503	Sunfighter/China	1971	—	2.50	5.00
❑ 65-0503 [PS]	Sunfighter/China	1971	—	3.00	6.00
Albums					
GRUNT					
❑ BFL1-0148	Baron Von Tollbooth and the Chrome Nun	1977	2.50	5.00	10.00
—Reissue with new prefix					
❑ BXL1-0148	Baron Von Tollbooth and the Chrome Nun	1973	3.00	6.00	12.00
—Original prefix					
❑ FTR-1002	Sunfighter	1971	3.75	7.50	15.00
—With booklet (deduct 33% if missing)					
❑ AYL1-3799	Baron Von Tollbooth and the Chrome Nun	1980	2.00	4.00	8.00
—Budget-line reissue					

KAPLAN, GABRIEL

Number	Title (A Side/B Side)	Yr	VG	VG+	NM
45s					
ABC					
❑ 12027	De Amerikans/Ed Sullivan, Ed Sullivan	1974	2.00	4.00	8.00
ELEKTRA					
❑ 45369	Up Your Nose/Bye Centennial Minutes	1976	—	3.00	6.00
❑ 45369 [PS]	Up Your Nose/Bye Centennial Minutes	1976	2.00	4.00	8.00
Albums					
ABC					
❑ ABC-102 [10]	Holes and Mellow Rolls	1974	3.75	7.50	15.00
—Promo-only 10-inch sampler					
❑ ABCD-815	Holes and Mellow Rolls	1974	3.75	7.50	15.00
—Original release with painting of ice-cream bars on cover					
❑ ABCD-905	Holes and Mello-Rolls	1976	3.00	6.00	12.00
—Reissue with photo of the "Welcome Back, Kotter" cast on cover					

KAPTIONS, THE

Number	Title (A Side/B Side)	Yr	VG	VG+	NM
45s					
HAM-MIL					
❑ 1520	Dreaming of You/I Know Somewhere	196?	5.00	10.00	20.00

KAREN, KENNY

Number	Title (A Side/B Side)	Yr	VG	VG+	NM
45s					
BIG TREE					
❑ 16007	That's Why You Remember/A Nice Place to Live	1973	3.00	6.00	12.00
COLUMBIA					
❑ 4-42264	Oh Susie Forgive Me/The Light in Your Window	1962	7.50	15.00	30.00
❑ 4-42452	To Sandy with Love/A Face in the Crowd	1962	7.50	15.00	30.00
❑ 4-42638	Sixteen Years Ago Tonight/Take Me Back	1962	7.50	15.00	30.00
STRAND					
❑ 25008	Little Boy/Nature Boy	1959	5.00	10.00	20.00
❑ 25017	Broken Dreams/You're the Only One I Love	1960	5.00	10.00	20.00

KARL, FRANKIE

Number	Title (A Side/B Side)	Yr	VG	VG+	NM
45s					
CONGRESS					
❑ 255	You Should 'O Held On/The Boy Next Door	1965	30.00	60.00	120.00
—Reissue; as "The 7th Avenue Aviators"					
DC					
❑ 180	Don't Be Afraid (Do As I Say)/I'm So Glad	1968	5.00	10.00	20.00
LIBERTY					
❑ 56164	Don't Sleep Too Long/Put a Little Love in Your Heart	1970	7.50	15.00	30.00
PHILTOWN					
❑ 105	You Should 'O Held On/The Boy Next Door	1965	125.00	250.00	500.00
—Original issue; as "Frankie Karl and the Chevrons"					

KARTUNES, THE

Number	Title (A Side/B Side)	Yr	VG	VG+	NM
45s					
MGM					
❑ 12598	Raindrops/Will You Marry Me	1957	7.50	15.00	30.00
❑ 12680	Dedicated to Love/Willie the Weeper	1958	6.25	12.50	25.00

KASANDRA Also recorded as "John KaSandra," though his only hits were under the abbreviated name.

Number	Title (A Side/B Side)	Yr	VG	VG+	NM
45s					
CAPITOL					
❑ 2342	Don't Pat Me On the Back and Call Me Brother/Just Look in My Face	1968	2.00	4.00	8.00
RESPECT					
❑ 2501	(What's Under) The Natural Do/Tired Old Subject	1972	—	3.50	7.00
❑ 2502	Ain't I Good/Down Home Ups-Good Whiskey and Bad Women	1972	—	3.50	7.00
❑ 2504	Mose Part III/Tired Old Subject	1972	—	3.50	7.00
Albums					
CAPITOL					
❑ ST-157	A Higher Plateau	1969	3.75	7.50	15.00
❑ ST-2957	John W. Anderson Presents KaSandra	1968	3.75	7.50	15.00
RESPECT					
❑ TAS-2602	Color Me Human	1972	3.75	7.50	15.00
❑ TAS-2603	Beautiful New World	1972	3.75	7.50	15.00
❑ TAS-2604	True Genius	1972	3.75	7.50	15.00
❑ TAS-2605	The Mod Messiah	1974	3.75	7.50	15.00

KASENETZ-KATZ SINGING ORCHESTRAL CIRCUS

Number	Title (A Side/B Side)	Yr	VG	VG+	NM
45s					
BELL					
❑ 966	When He Come/Ah-La	1970	2.50	5.00	10.00
—As "Kasenetz-Katz Fighter Squadron"					
BUDDAH					
❑ 52	Down in Tennessee/Mrs. Green	1968	2.00	4.00	8.00
❑ 64	Quick Joey Small (Run Joey Run)/Mr. Jensen	1968	2.00	4.00	8.00
❑ 82	I'm in Love with You/To You, With Love	1969	2.00	4.00	8.00
❑ 90	Embrasez-Moi/Mrs. Green	1969	2.00	4.00	8.00
EPIC					
❑ 50443	Heart Get Ready for Love/Jungle Junk	1977	—	2.50	5.00
—As "K&K Super Cirkus"					
SUPER K					
❑ 109	Bubblegum March/Dong-Dong-Diki-Di-Ki-Dong	1970	2.00	4.00	8.00
Albums					
BUDDAH					
❑ BDM-1020 [M]	Kasenetz-Katz Singing Orchestral Circus	1968	10.00	20.00	40.00
—Mono is promo only; in stereo cover with "Mono" sticker					
❑ BDS-5020 [S]	Kasenetz-Katz Singing Orchestral Circus	1968	3.75	7.50	15.00
❑ BDS-5028	Kasenetz-Katz Super Circus	1969	3.75	7.50	15.00

KATFISH

Number	Title (A Side/B Side)	Yr	VG	VG+	NM
45s					
BIG TREE					
❑ 16045	Dear Prudence/Street Walkin'	1975	2.00	4.00	8.00

KATMANDU

Number	Title (A Side/B Side)	Yr	VG	VG+	NM
Albums					
MAINSTREAM					
❑ S-6131	Katmandu	1971	10.00	20.00	40.00

KAUKONEN, JORMA Also see HOT TUNA; JEFFERSON AIRPLANE.

Number	Title (A Side/B Side)	Yr	VG	VG+	NM
Albums					
GRUNT					
❑ BFL1-0209	Quah	1973	3.00	6.00	12.00
❑ BXL1-0209	Quah	197?	2.50	5.00	10.00
—Reissue with new prefix					
❑ AYL1-3747	Quah	1981	2.00	4.00	8.00
—"Best Buy Series" reissue					
RCA VICTOR					
❑ AFL1-3446	Jorma	1979	2.50	5.00	10.00
❑ AFL1-3725	Barbecue King	1981	2.50	5.00	10.00

KAY, JOANNE

Number	Title (A Side/B Side)	Yr	VG	VG+	NM
45s					
HIT					
❑ 94	Wonderful Summer/Be True to Your School	1963	2.00	4.00	8.00
—B-side by the Roamers					
❑ 148	Lonesome Fool/Chug-a-Lug	1964	2.00	4.00	8.00
—B-side by Harvey Frolic					
❑ 250	Wonderful Summer/Be True to Your School	1966	2.00	4.00	8.00
—B-side by the Roamers					

KAY, JOHN Also see SPARROW; STEPPENWOLF.

Number	Title (A Side/B Side)	Yr	VG	VG+	NM
45s					
ABC DUNHILL					
❑ 4309	I'm Movin' On/Walk Beside Me	1972	—	2.00	4.00
❑ 4319	You Win Again/Somebody	1972	—	2.00	4.00
❑ 4351	Moonshine/Nobody Lives Here Anymore	1973	—	2.00	4.00
❑ 4360	Dance to My Song/Easy Evil	1973	—	2.00	4.00
COLUMBIA					
❑ 4-44769	Twistin'/Square-Headed People	1969	2.00	4.00	8.00
MERCURY					
❑ 74004	Say You Will/Give Me Some News I Can Use	1978	—	2.00	4.00
Albums					
ABC DUNHILL					
❑ DSX-50120	Forgotten Songs & Unsung Heroes	1972	2.50	5.00	10.00
❑ DSX-50147	My Sportin' Life	1973	2.50	5.00	10.00
MERCURY					
❑ SRM-1-3715	All in Good Time	1978	2.50	5.00	10.00

KAY, JOHN, AND SPARROW See SPARROW.

KAY, JOHN, AND STEPPENWOLF See STEPPENWOLF.

KAY-GEES, THE

Number	Title (A Side/B Side)	Yr	VG	VG+	NM
45s					
DELITE					
❑ 903	Kilowatt/Kilowatt Invasion	1978	—	2.00	4.00
❑ 906	Cheek to Cheek/Tango Hustle	1978	—	2.00	4.00
❑ 913	Heavenly Love/Burn Me Up	1979	—	2.00	4.00
GANG					
❑ 321	You've Got to Keep On Bumpin' (Pt 1)/You've Got to Keep On Bumpin' (Pt 2)	1974	—	2.50	5.00
❑ 1322	Master Plan/(B-side unknown)	1974	—	2.50	5.00
❑ 1323	Get Down/My Favorite Song	1975	—	2.50	5.00
❑ 1325	Hustle Wit Every Muscle (Theme from "Party" TV Show)/(Instrumental)	1975	—	2.50	5.00
❑ 1326	Waiting at the Bus Stop (Part 1)/Waiting at the Bus Stop (Part 2)	1976	—	2.50	5.00
Albums					
DE-LITE					
❑ 9505	Kilowatt	1978	2.50	5.00	10.00
❑ 9510	Burn Me Up	1979	2.50	5.00	10.00
GANG					
❑ 101	Keep On Bumpin' & Masterplan	1975	2.50	5.00	10.00
❑ 102	Find a Friend	1975	2.50	5.00	10.00

KAYAK

Number	Title (A Side/B Side)	Yr	VG	VG+	NM
45s					
JANUS					
❑ 274	I Want You to Be Mine/Irene	1978	—	2.50	5.00
❑ 278	Keep the Change/Ivory Dance	1979	—	2.50	5.00
MERCURY					
❑ 76059	Periscope Life/Stop That Song	1980	—	2.00	4.00

K

Number	Title (A Side/B Side)	Yr	VG	VG+	NM

Albums
HARVEST
| ☐ ST-11305 | See See the Sun | 1973 | 3.75 | 7.50 | 15.00 |

JANUS
| ☐ (no #) [PD] | Phantom of the Night | 1979 | 6.25 | 12.50 | 25.00 |

—Numbered limited edition of 3,000
☐ NXS-7023	Royal Bed Bouncer	1975	2.50	5.00	10.00
☐ NXS-7034	Starlight Dancer	1978	2.50	5.00	10.00
☐ NXS-7039	Phantom of the Night	1979	2.50	5.00	10.00

MERCURY
| ☐ SRM-1-3824 | Periscope Life | 1980 | 2.50 | 5.00 | 10.00 |

KAYE, MARY, TRIO
45s
CAMELOT
| ☐ 132 | Can't Get You Off My Mind/Writing on the Wall | 1967 | 2.00 | 4.00 | 8.00 |

COLUMBIA
| ☐ 1-230 (?) | I'm in the Mood for Love/The Monkey Song | 1949 | 10.00 | 20.00 | 40.00 |

—Microgroove 33 1/3 rpm 7-inch single, small hole

DECCA
☐ 9-29622	Mad About the Boy/My Funny Valentine	1955	3.00	6.00	12.00
☐ 9-29761	Lonesome Road/Get Out of Town	1955	3.00	6.00	12.00
☐ 9-30145	Fools Rush In/Add Another Leaf	1956	3.00	6.00	12.00
☐ 9-30241	Almost Like Being in Love/Spring Reunion	1957	3.00	6.00	12.00
☐ 9-30344	Calypso Rock/Boy on a Dolphin	1957	3.75	7.50	15.00
☐ 9-30596	Another Time, Another Place/With a Love That's True	1958	3.00	6.00	12.00

RCA VICTOR
☐ 47-5586	Do You Believe in Dreams?/Toreador	1954	3.75	7.50	15.00
☐ 47-5751	Almost/Don't Laugh at Me	1954	3.75	7.50	15.00
☐ 47-5784	Anyone Can Dream/The Cuddlin' Song	1954	3.75	7.50	15.00

20TH CENTURY FOX
| ☐ 457 | Man's Favourite Sport/What's Yours? | 1964 | 2.00 | 4.00 | 8.00 |

VERVE
| ☐ 10228 | Kiss Me Again/When My Sugar Walks Down the Street | 1960 | 2.50 | 5.00 | 10.00 |

WARNER BROS.
☐ 5020	Home Before Dark/Belong to Me	1958	2.50	5.00	10.00
☐ 5041	Believe in Me/Wonder Why	1959	2.50	5.00	10.00
☐ 5050	You Can't Be True Dear/Because of You	1959	2.50	5.00	10.00
☐ 5095	My Isle of Golden Dreams/That Wasn't Me	1959	2.50	5.00	10.00

Albums
COLUMBIA
| ☐ CL 1910 [M] | Our Hawaii | 1962 | 3.75 | 7.50 | 15.00 |
| ☐ CS 8710 [S] | Our Hawaii | 1962 | 5.00 | 10.00 | 20.00 |

DECCA
☐ DL 8238 [M]	The Mary Kaye Trio	1956	7.50	15.00	30.00
☐ DL 8434 [M]	Music on a Silver Platter	1957	7.50	15.00	30.00
☐ DL 8650 [M]	You Don't Know What Love Is	1958	7.50	15.00	30.00

MOVIETONE
| ☐ 71027 [M] | Just Us | 1967 | 3.00 | 6.00 | 12.00 |
| ☐ S 72027 [S] | Just Us | 1967 | 3.00 | 6.00 | 12.00 |

20TH CENTURY FOX
| ☐ TFM-3117 [M] | Night Life | 1964 | 3.00 | 6.00 | 12.00 |
| ☐ TFS-4117 [S] | Night Life | 1964 | 3.75 | 7.50 | 15.00 |

VERVE
☐ MGV-2142 [M]	Up Front!	1960	10.00	20.00	40.00
☐ V-8446 [M]	For the Record	1962	5.00	10.00	20.00
☐ V6-8446 [S]	For the Record	1962	6.25	12.50	25.00

WARNER BROS.
☐ B 1222 [M]	Too Much!	1958	5.00	10.00	20.00
☐ W 1263 [M]	Jackpot	1959	5.00	10.00	20.00
☐ WS 1263 [S]	Jackpot	1959	6.25	12.50	25.00
☐ W 1342 [M]	The Mary Kaye Trio on the Sunset Strip	1959	5.00	10.00	20.00
☐ WS 1342 [S]	The Mary Kaye Trio on the Sunset Strip	1959	6.25	12.50	25.00

KAYE, SAMMY
45s
COLUMBIA
| ☐ 1-740 (?) | Guilty/Checky-Checky Hoopla | 1950 | 7.50 | 15.00 | 30.00 |

—Microgroove 33 1/3 rpm 7-inch single
☐ 6-740 (?)	Guilty/Checky-Checky Hoopla	1950	5.00	10.00	20.00
☐ 38963	Harbor Lights/Sugar Sweet	1950	3.75	7.50	15.00
☐ 39030	Patricia/Petite Waltz	1950	3.75	7.50	15.00
☐ 39036	To Think You've Chosen Me/You Oughta Be in Pictures	1950	3.75	7.50	15.00
☐ 39113	Tennessee Waltz/Get Out Those Old Records	1950	3.75	7.50	15.00
☐ 39140	Tell Me You Love Me/Dear Little Girl of Theta Chi	1950	3.75	7.50	15.00
☐ 39156	You and Beautiful You/Tonda Wonda Hoy	1951	3.75	7.50	15.00
☐ 39186	Peter Cottontail/Easter Parade	1951	3.75	7.50	15.00
☐ 39270	I Love You Because/Pretty Little Bells	1951	3.75	7.50	15.00
☐ 3-39270	I Love You Because/Pretty Little Bells	1951	5.00	10.00	20.00

—Microgroove 33 1/3 rpm 7-inch single (note prefix)
☐ 39325	I'm Yours to Command/Shenandoah Waltz	1951	3.75	7.50	15.00
☐ 39360	My Prayer/Down the Trail of Aching Hearts	1951	3.75	7.50	15.00
☐ 39376	Come Back to Angeuleme/Please Don't Talk About Me	1951	3.75	7.50	15.00
☐ 39421	Del Rio/Would Mind	1951	3.75	7.50	15.00
☐ 39492	Dixie/Tennessee Tears	1951	3.75	7.50	15.00
☐ 39499	Longing for You/Mary Rose	1951	3.75	7.50	15.00
☐ 39531	It's All in the Game/Be Mine Tonight	1951	3.75	7.50	15.00
☐ 39567	(It's No) Sin/Jealous Eyes	1951	3.75	7.50	15.00
☐ 39572	Silent Night-O Little Town Of Bethlehem/Joy To The World-Hark the Herald Angels Sing-O Come All Ye Faithful	1951	3.00	6.00	12.00
☐ 39573	White Christmas/Jingle Bells	1951	3.00	6.00	12.00
☐ 39574	Winter Wonderland/Rudolph the Red-Nosed Reindeer	1951	3.00	6.00	12.00
☐ 39575	Frosty the Snow Man/Santa Claus Is Coming to Town	1951	3.00	6.00	12.00

—The above four comprise a box set
☐ 39583	Daddy/Bouquet of Roses	1951	3.75	7.50	15.00
☐ 39602	The Three Bells/I Only Have One Life	1951	3.75	7.50	15.00
☐ 39633	You Know You Belong to Someone Else/My Lei-Ee-Yana	1952	3.75	7.50	15.00
☐ 39667	Wheel of Fortune/Goodbye Sweetheart	1952	3.75	7.50	15.00
☐ 39688	Winnipesaukee/I Ain't Lazy	1952	3.75	7.50	15.00
☐ 39724	You/Oh How I Miss You	1952	3.75	7.50	15.00
☐ 39731	You/Pittsburgh, Pennsylvania	1952	3.00	6.00	12.00

—B-side by Guy Mitchell; part of a 4-record box set
☐ 39769	Walkin' to Missouri/One for the Wonder	1952	3.75	7.50	15.00
☐ 39771	Girl of My Dreams/My Extraordinary Girl	1952	3.00	6.00	12.00
☐ 39772	All the Things You Are/Who	1952	3.00	6.00	12.00
☐ 39773	Josephine/Would You Like to Take a Walk	1952	3.00	6.00	12.00
☐ 39774	Little Girl/We'll Meet Again	1952	3.00	6.00	12.00

—The above four comprise a box set
☐ 39816	I Don't Know Any Better/God's Little Candles	1952	3.75	7.50	15.00
☐ 39856	It Wasn't God Who Made Honky Tonk Angels/I Went to Your Wedding	1952	3.75	7.50	15.00
☐ 39883	Forget Me Not/Sailin' Along the Ohio	1952	3.75	7.50	15.00
☐ 39894	All Around the Christmas Tree/Santa, Santa, Santa Claus	1952	3.75	7.50	15.00
☐ 39917	Hurry, Hurry, Hurry/Dance of Mexico	1953	3.00	6.00	12.00
☐ 39936	Lighthouse in the Harbor/Angel Made of Ice	1953	3.00	6.00	12.00
☐ 39957	Gomen-Sasai (Forgive Me)/Until Tomorrow	1953	3.00	6.00	12.00
☐ 39977	Sweet Sue-Just You/I Couldn't Keep from Crying	1953	3.00	6.00	12.00
☐ 39999	Orange Blossom Serenade/The Tattle-Tale Duck	1953	3.00	6.00	12.00
☐ 40025	The Midnight Ride/The One in Your Heart	1953	3.00	6.00	12.00
☐ 40061	In the Mission of St. Augustine/No Stone Unturned	1953	3.00	6.00	12.00
☐ 40151	Bella Bella Donna Mis/Y (That's Why)	1954	3.00	6.00	12.00
☐ 40205	Godspeed to You/Till You Kiss Me at the Altar	1954	3.00	6.00	12.00
☐ 40248	Dream for Sale/Sittin' 'n' Waitin'	1954	3.00	6.00	12.00
☐ 40269	Friends and Neighbors/Through	1954	3.00	6.00	12.00
☐ 40299	Sentimental/If We Should Ever Meet Again	1954	3.00	6.00	12.00
☐ 40417	Melody of Love/You Are the One	1955	3.00	6.00	12.00
☐ 40431	Hindustan/She Went That-a-Way	1955	3.00	6.00	12.00
☐ 40485	Impossible/Jim, Johnny and Jonas	1955	3.00	6.00	12.00
☐ 40517	The Banjo's Back in Town/Joe, Joe, Joe	1955	3.00	6.00	12.00
☐ 40518	Sweet and Lovely/Yearning	1955	3.00	6.00	12.00
☐ 40556	Queen of My Lonesome Heart/I'll Never Learn Cha-Cha-Cha	1955	3.00	6.00	12.00
☐ 40574	The Lucky Little Bell/Don't Cry Baby	1955	3.00	6.00	12.00
☐ 40621	Hey Pretty Girl/In the Valley of the Moon	1955	3.00	6.00	12.00
☐ 40645	We All Need Love/Try Another Cherry Tree	1956	3.00	6.00	12.00
☐ 40698	Once Again/Every Sunday Morning	1956	3.00	6.00	12.00
☐ 40707	I Could Have Danced All Night/I've Grown Accustomed to Your Face	1956	3.00	6.00	12.00
☐ 40752	The Rich People of Brooklyn/Dreamy River	1956	3.00	6.00	12.00
☐ 40795	Faded Roses/I'm Through with Love	1956	3.00	6.00	12.00
☐ 40839	I Met a Girl/Mountain of Kisses	1957	2.50	5.00	10.00
☐ 40869	Money/The Ship That Never Sailed	1957	2.50	5.00	10.00
☐ 40909	What a Saturday Night/A Young Lover's Dream	1957	2.50	5.00	10.00
☐ 40936	Past My Prime/Charm Bracelet	1957	2.50	5.00	10.00
☐ 40966	Charleston/Posin'	1957	2.50	5.00	10.00
☐ 40988	Mary Lou/Moonlight Swim	1957	2.50	5.00	10.00
☐ 41028	Ha, Ha, Ha/You'd Be Surprised	1957	2.50	5.00	10.00
☐ 41084	Garden of Allah/Well, Anyway	1957	2.50	5.00	10.00
☐ 41140	That Girl Next Door/Our First Formal Dance	1958	2.50	5.00	10.00
☐ 41178	That Daffodil Feelin'/Spain	1958	2.50	5.00	10.00
☐ 41206	Why Can't This Night Go On Forever/Yearning	1958	2.50	5.00	10.00
☐ 41255	Roses Remind Me of You/At the High School Prom	1958	2.50	5.00	10.00
☐ 41293	Sweet Leilani/How Good Can a Good Girl Be	1958	2.50	5.00	10.00
☐ 41348	Leave the Door Wide Open/Dah Dee (Daddy)	1959	2.50	5.00	10.00
☐ 41398	Until Tomorrow/Sammy Kaye's Theme Song	1959	2.50	5.00	10.00
☐ 41508	Deep Purple/Till Tomorrow	1959	2.50	5.00	10.00
☐ 41552	My Happiness/Melody of Love	1960	2.50	5.00	10.00
☐ 41656	Chopsticks Boogie/Harvey's Melody	1960	2.50	5.00	10.00

DECCA
☐ 25511	Oh Johnny, Oh Johnny, Oh!/Got a Date with an Angel	1962	2.00	4.00	8.00
☐ 25555	After You've Gone/Who's Sorry Now	1962	2.00	4.00	8.00
☐ 25604	Roses Are Red/Ramblin' Rose	1963	2.00	4.00	8.00
☐ 25722	The Whiffenpoof Song/There Is a Tavern in the Town	1967	—	3.00	6.00
☐ 25752	Charley, My Boy/Hot Lips	1969	—	2.50	5.00
☐ 31174	Merry Merry Christmas (To You)/Silver Bells	1960	2.50	5.00	10.00
☐ 31175	Christmas Child (Loo, Loo, Loo)/Let It Snow, Let It Snow, Let It Snow	1960	2.50	5.00	10.00
☐ 31204	Welcome Home/What's New at the Zoo	1961	2.00	4.00	8.00
☐ 31264	I'm a Big Girl Now/Strange Interlude	1961	2.00	4.00	8.00
☐ 31294	Lydia, the Tattooed Lady/I'm Married to a Strip Tease Dancer	1961	2.00	4.00	8.00
☐ 31336	Swing and Sway Twist/Mama and Papa Twist	1961	3.00	6.00	12.00
☐ 31448	Big Deal/Shoot the Piano Player	1962	2.00	4.00	8.00
☐ 31589	Charade/Maria Elena	1964	—	3.00	6.00
☐ 31642	Night Train/Bedtime Story	1964	—	3.00	6.00
☐ 31700	House of the Rising Sun/Theme from Golden Boy	1964	—	3.00	6.00
☐ 31738	Night Walker/Sophia	1965	—	3.00	6.00
☐ 31773	Goldfinger/Blue Prelude	1965	—	3.00	6.00
☐ 31854	Hush…Hush, Sweet Charlotte/The Hucklebuck	1965	—	3.00	6.00
☐ 31935	Lara's Theme (from Dr. Zhivago)/Swedish Rhapsody (Madame X Love Theme)	1966	—	3.00	6.00
☐ 32034	Smile/In the Arms of Love	1966	—	3.00	6.00
☐ 32071	Oh, How I Miss You Tonight/Gambit	1966	—	3.00	6.00
☐ 32258	Talk to the Animals/Glory of Love	1968	—	2.50	5.00
☐ 32442	I Love to Cry at Weddings/I'm a Brass Band	1969	—	2.50	5.00
☐ 32624	Something/Juanita (Love Theme from "Topaz")	1970	—	2.50	5.00

PROJECT 3
| ☐ 1421 | For the Good Times/If You've Got the Time | 1972 | — | 2.00 | 4.00 |

RCA VICTOR
☐ 47-2810	Cuddle Up a Little Closer, Lovey Mine/I Want a Girl (Just Like the Girl That Married Dear Old Dad)	1949	3.75	7.50	15.00
☐ 47-2811	Down Among the Sheltering Palms/The World Is Waiting for the Sunrise	1949	3.75	7.50	15.00
☐ 47-2812	There But For You Go I/My Son	1949	3.75	7.50	15.00
☐ 47-2813	I Still Love You/We Just Couldn't Say Goodbye	1949	3.75	7.50	15.00
☐ 47-2862	April Showers/June Is Bustin' Out All Over	1949	3.75	7.50	15.00
☐ 47-2863	Indian Summer/September Song	1949	3.75	7.50	15.00

Number	Title (A Side/B Side)	Yr	VG	VG+	NM
❏ 47-2864	White Christmas/Winter Wonderland	1949	3.75	7.50	15.00
❏ 47-2901	Careless Hands/				
	Powder Your Face with Sunshine	1949	3.75	7.50	15.00
❏ 47-2908	Room Full of Roses/It's Springtime Again	1949	3.75	7.50	15.00
❏ 47-2923	The Four Winds and the Seven Seas/Out of Love	1949	3.75	7.50	15.00
❏ 47-2936	Belmont Boogie/Hollywood Square Dance	1949	3.75	7.50	15.00
❏ 47-2942	Fiddle Dee Dee/It's a Great Feeling	1949	3.75	7.50	15.00
❏ 47-3010	Dime a Dozen/Everything They Said Came True	1949	3.75	7.50	15.00
❏ 47-3038	The Last Mile Home/Hawaiian Sunset	1949	3.75	7.50	15.00
❏ 47-3048	Let's Harmonize/Makin' Love Ukulele Style	1949	3.75	7.50	15.00
❏ 47-3067	Funny Face/Toot Toot Tootsie	1949	3.75	7.50	15.00
❏ 47-3071	Here Comes Santa Claus/				
	I Want to Wish You a Merry Christmas	1949	3.75	7.50	15.00
❏ 47-3075	My Little Grass Shack in Kaelakekua, Hawaii/				
	My Tan	1949	3.75	7.50	15.00
❏ 47-3076	My Isle of Golden Dreams/Sweet Leilani	1949	3.75	7.50	15.00
❏ 47-3077	Hawaiian War Chant/Hawaiian Sunset	1949	3.75	7.50	15.00
❏ 47-3101	Careless Kisses/Echoes	1949	3.75	7.50	15.00
❏ 47-3115	It Isn't Fair/My Lily and My Rose	1950	3.75	7.50	15.00
❏ 47-3168	Always/Blue Skies	1950	3.75	7.50	15.00
❏ 47-3169	How Deep Is the Ocean/Say It Isn't So	1950	3.75	7.50	15.00
❏ 47-3170	Alexander's Ragtime Band/				
	A Pretty Girl Is Like a Melody	1950	3.75	7.50	15.00
❏ 47-3203	Wanderin'/The Bicycle Song	1950	3.75	7.50	15.00
❏ 47-3754	Roses/Tiddley Winkle Woe	1950	3.75	7.50	15.00
❏ 47-3828	The Object of My Affection/				
	I Thought She Was a Local	1950	3.75	7.50	15.00
❏ 47-3891	Miss You/There's No Use	1950	3.75	7.50	15.00

7-Inch Extended Plays
COLUMBIA

Number	Title (A Side/B Side)	Yr	VG	VG+	NM
❏ B-2546	Daddy/Harbor Lights//Walkin' to Missouri/In the Mission of St. Augustine	195?	3.75	7.50	15.00
❏ B-2546 [PS]	Sammy Kaye (Hall of Fame Series)	195?	3.75	7.50	15.00

RCA CAMDEN

Number	Title (A Side/B Side)	Yr	VG	VG+	NM
❏ CAE-264	You Always Hurt the One You Love/Taking a Chance on Love//Amapola/Taboo	195?	2.50	5.00	10.00
❏ CAE-264 [PS]	Sammy Kaye and His Orchestra Play	195?	2.50	5.00	10.00
❏ CAE-271	Easter Parade/Baby Face//Begin the Beguine/Pretty Baby	195?	2.50	5.00	10.00
❏ CAE-271	Sammy Kaye and His Orchestra	195?	2.50	5.00	10.00

RCA VICTOR

Number	Title (A Side/B Side)	Yr	VG	VG+	NM
❏ EPA 258	Sweet Leilani/My Isle of Golden Dreams//Hawaiian War Chant/Hawaiian Sunset	1952	3.00	6.00	12.00
❏ EPA 258 [PS]	The Heart of the Islands in Song	1952	3.00	6.00	12.00

Albums
COLUMBIA

Number	Title (A Side/B Side)	Yr	VG	VG+	NM
❏ CL 561 [M]	Swing and Sway with Sammy Kaye	195?	7.50	15.00	30.00
❏ CL 668 [M]	Music, Maestro, Please!	195?	7.50	15.00	30.00
❏ CL 885 [M]	My Fair Lady (For Dancing)	1956	5.00	10.00	20.00
❏ CL 891 [M]	What Makes Sammy Swing and Sway	1956	5.00	10.00	20.00
❏ CL 964 [M]	Sunday Serenade	1957	5.00	10.00	20.00
❏ CL 1018 [M]	Popular American Waltzes	1957	5.00	10.00	20.00
❏ CL 1236 [M]	Strauss Waltzes for Dancing	1959	3.75	7.50	15.00
❏ CL 2541 [10]	Christmas Serenade	1955	10.00	20.00	40.00
—"House Party Series" issue					
❏ CL 6155 [10]	Sunday Serenade	1953	10.00	20.00	40.00

DECCA

Number	Title (A Side/B Side)	Yr	VG	VG+	NM
❏ DL 4070 [M]	Christmas Day with Sammy Kaye	1960	3.00	6.00	12.00
❏ DL 4071 [M]	Sing and Sway with Sammy Kaye	1960	3.00	6.00	12.00
❏ DL 4121 [M]	Dance to My Golden Favorites	1961	3.00	6.00	12.00
❏ DL 4154 [M]	Songs I Wish I Had Played… The First Time Around	1961	3.00	6.00	12.00
❏ DL 4215 [M]	Sexy Strings and Subtle Saxes	1962	3.00	6.00	12.00
❏ DL 4247 [M]	New Twists on Old Favorites	1962	3.00	6.00	12.00
❏ DL 4306 [M]	For Your Dancing Pleasure	1962	3.00	6.00	12.00
❏ DL 4357 [M]	Come Dance with Me	1963	3.00	6.00	12.00
❏ DL 4424 [M]	Dreamy Serenades	1963	3.00	6.00	12.00
❏ DL 4502 [M]	Come Dance to the Hits	1964	3.00	6.00	12.00
❏ DL 4590 [M]	Come Dance with Me (Vol. 2)	1965	3.00	6.00	12.00
❏ DL 4655 [M]	Dancetime	1965	3.00	6.00	12.00
❏ DL 4687 [M]	Swing and Sway Au-Go-Go	1965	3.00	6.00	12.00
❏ DL 4754 [M]	Shall We Dance	1966	3.00	6.00	12.00
❏ DL 4823 [M]	Let's Face the Music	1967	3.00	6.00	12.00
❏ DL 4862 [M]	Swing & Sway in Hawaii	1967	3.75	7.50	15.00
❏ DL 4924 [M]	Dance and Be Happy	1967	3.75	7.50	15.00
❏ DL 4970 [M]	Glory of Love	1967	3.75	7.50	15.00
❏ DL 74070 [S]	Christmas Day with Sammy Kaye	1960	3.75	7.50	15.00
❏ DL 74071 [S]	Sing and Sway with Sammy Kaye	1960	3.75	7.50	15.00
❏ DL 74121 [S]	Dance to My Golden Favorites	1961	3.75	7.50	15.00
❏ DL 74154 [S]	Songs I Wish I Had Played… The First Time Around	1961	3.75	7.50	15.00
❏ DL 74215 [S]	Sexy Strings and Subtle Saxes	1962	3.75	7.50	15.00
❏ DL 74247 [S]	New Twists on Old Favorites	1962	3.75	7.50	15.00
❏ DL 74306 [S]	For Your Dancing Pleasure	1962	3.75	7.50	15.00
❏ DL 74357 [S]	Come Dance with Me	1963	3.75	7.50	15.00
❏ DL 74424 [S]	Dreamy Serenades	1963	3.75	7.50	15.00
❏ DL 74502 [S]	Come Dance to the Hits	1964	3.75	7.50	15.00
❏ DL 74590 [S]	Come Dance with Me (Vol. 2)	1965	3.75	7.50	15.00
❏ DL 74655 [S]	Dancetime	1965	3.75	7.50	15.00
❏ DL 74687 [S]	Swing and Sway Au-Go-Go	1965	3.75	7.50	15.00
❏ DL 74754 [S]	Shall We Dance	1966	3.75	7.50	15.00
❏ DL 74823 [S]	Let's Face the Music	1967	3.75	7.50	15.00
❏ DL 74862 [S]	Swing & Sway in Hawaii	1967	3.00	6.00	12.00
❏ DL 74924 [S]	Dance and Be Happy	1967	3.00	6.00	12.00
❏ DL 74970 [S]	Glory of Love	1967	3.00	6.00	12.00
❏ DL 75106	The 30's Are Here to Stay	1968	3.00	6.00	12.00

HARMONY

Number	Title (A Side/B Side)	Yr	VG	VG+	NM
❏ HL 7187 [M]	Dancing with Sammy Kaye in Hi-Fi	196?	3.75	7.50	15.00
❏ HL 7230 [M]	In a Dancing Mood	196?	3.75	7.50	15.00
❏ HL 7321 [M]	My Fair Lady	1964	3.75	7.50	15.00
❏ HL 7357 [M]	Beautiful Waltzes for Dancing	196?	3.75	7.50	15.00
❏ HS 11087 [R]	Dancing with Sammy Kaye in Hi-Fi	196?	3.00	6.00	12.00
❏ HS 11121 [R]	My Fair Lady	1964	3.00	6.00	12.00
❏ HS 11157 [R]	Beautiful Waltzes for Dancing	196?	3.00	6.00	12.00
❏ HS 11261	All-Time Waltz Favorites	1968	3.00	6.00	12.00
❏ HS 11377	Harbor Lights	1970	2.50	5.00	10.00
❏ KH 32013	Best of the Big Bands	1971	2.50	5.00	10.00

HINDSIGHT

Number	Title (A Side/B Side)	Yr	VG	VG+	NM
❏ HSR-158	1940-41	198?	2.50	5.00	10.00
❏ HSR-163	1942-43	198?	2.50	5.00	10.00
❏ HSR-207	1944-46	198?	2.50	5.00	10.00
❏ HSR-402 [(2)]	22 Original Big Band Recordings	198?	3.00	6.00	12.00

MCA

Number	Title (A Side/B Side)	Yr	VG	VG+	NM
❏ 191	Dance to My Golden Favorites	1973	2.50	5.00	10.00
—Reissue of Decca 74121					
❏ 205	Plays Swing & Sway	1973	2.50	5.00	10.00
—Reissue of Decca 74306					
❏ 278	The 30's Are Here to Stay	197?	2.50	5.00	10.00
—Reissue of Decca material					
❏ 4027 [(2)]	The Best of Sammy Kaye	197?	3.00	6.00	12.00

PROJECT 3

Number	Title (A Side/B Side)	Yr	VG	VG+	NM
❏ PR-5065 QD [Q]	If You've Got the Time	1972	3.75	7.50	15.00
❏ PR-5065 SD	If You've Got the Time	1972	2.50	5.00	10.00

RCA CAMDEN

Number	Title (A Side/B Side)	Yr	VG	VG+	NM
❏ CAL-355 [M]	Swing and Sway with Sammy Kaye	1957	5.00	10.00	20.00

RCA VICTOR

Number	Title (A Side/B Side)	Yr	VG	VG+	NM
❏ LPM 15 [10]	Sammy Kaye Plays Irving Berlin for Dancing	1950	12.50	25.00	50.00
❏ LPM-3966 [M]	The Best of Sammy Kaye	1967	5.00	10.00	20.00
❏ LSP-3966 [R]	The Best of Sammy Kaye	1967	3.00	6.00	12.00
❏ VPM-6070 [(2)]	This Is Sammy Kaye	1972	3.00	6.00	12.00

VOCALION

Number	Title (A Side/B Side)	Yr	VG	VG+	NM
❏ VL 73919	Theme from "Love Story"	1971	2.50	5.00	10.00

KAYLI, BOB
45s
ANNA

Number	Title (A Side/B Side)	Yr	VG	VG+	NM
❏ 1104	Never More/Peppermint (You Know What to Do)	1959	10.00	20.00	40.00

CARLTON

Number	Title (A Side/B Side)	Yr	VG	VG+	NM
❏ 482	Everyone Was There/I Took a Dare	1958	7.50	15.00	30.00

GORDY

Number	Title (A Side/B Side)	Yr	VG	VG+	NM
❏ 7004	Toodle Loo/Everyone Was There	1962	20.00	40.00	80.00
❏ 7008	Toodle Loo/Hold On Pearl	1962	7.50	15.00	30.00

TAMLA

Number	Title (A Side/B Side)	Yr	VG	VG+	NM
❏ 54051	Small Sad Sam/Tie Me Tight	1962	7.50	15.00	30.00

KAZAN, LAINIE
45s
COLPIX

Number	Title (A Side/B Side)	Yr	VG	VG+	NM
❏ 768	Color of Love/Ouzo	1965	2.50	5.00	10.00

MGM

Number	Title (A Side/B Side)	Yr	VG	VG+	NM
❏ 13479	I'm Shooting High/No More Songs for Me	1966	2.00	4.00	8.00
❏ 13526	Can I Trust You/I Can't Remember (Ever Loving You)	1966	2.00	4.00	8.00
❏ 13657	Kiss Tomorrow Goodbye/Sweet Talk	1967	2.00	4.00	8.00
❏ 13777	Road to Ruin/What Did I Lose by Loving You	1967	2.00	4.00	8.00
❏ 13877	Sunny/When I Look in Your Eyes	1967	2.00	4.00	8.00
❏ 13943	Night Song/They Don't Give Medals	1968	2.00	4.00	8.00

POMPEII

Number	Title (A Side/B Side)	Yr	VG	VG+	NM
❏ 7001	Window on My Mind/It's You	1971	—	3.00	6.00

Albums
MGM

Number	Title (A Side/B Side)	Yr	VG	VG+	NM
❏ E-4340 [M]	Right Now	1966	5.00	10.00	20.00
❏ SE-4340 [S]	Right Now	1966	6.25	12.50	25.00
❏ E-4385 [M]	Lainie Kazan	1966	5.00	10.00	20.00
❏ SE-4385 [S]	Lainie Kazan	1966	6.25	12.50	25.00
❏ E-4451 [M]	The Love Album	1967	6.25	12.50	25.00
❏ SE-4451 [S]	The Love Album	1967	5.00	10.00	20.00
❏ SE-4496	Love Is	1968	5.00	10.00	20.00
❏ SE-4631	The Best of Lainie Kazan	1969	5.00	10.00	20.00

KEATON, JOHNNY
45s
HIT

Number	Title (A Side/B Side)	Yr	VG	VG+	NM
❏ 10	PT 109/Funny Way of Laughin'	1962	2.00	4.00	8.00
—B-side by Tom Walls					

KEGGS, THE
45s
ORBIT

Number	Title (A Side/B Side)	Yr	VG	VG+	NM
❏ 20959	To Find Out/(B-side unknown)	1967	1000.	2000.	4000.
—Counterfeit identification: The producer's first name, "Yolanda," is misspelled "Yalanda" on fakes.					

KEITH
45s
COLUMBIA

Number	Title (A Side/B Side)	Yr	VG	VG+	NM
❏ 43268	Dream/Caravan of Lonely Men	1965	3.75	7.50	15.00
—As "Keith and the Admirations"					

DISCREET

Number	Title (A Side/B Side)	Yr	VG	VG+	NM
❏ 1193	What Did You Do in the Revolution, Dad/In and Out of Love	1974	—	2.50	5.00

MERCURY

Number	Title (A Side/B Side)	Yr	VG	VG+	NM
❏ 72596	Ain't Gonna Lie/Our Love Started All Over Again	1966	2.00	4.00	8.00
❏ 72639	98.6/The Teenie Bopper Song	1966	2.50	5.00	10.00
❏ 72639 [PS]	98.6/The Teenie Bopper Song	1966	3.75	7.50	15.00
❏ 72652	Tell Me To My Face/Pretty Little Shy One	1967	2.00	4.00	8.00
❏ 72652 [PS]	Tell Me To My Face/Pretty Little Shy One	1967	3.75	7.50	15.00
❏ 72695	Daylight Savin' Time/Happy Walking Around	1967	2.00	4.00	8.00
❏ 72695 [PS]	Daylight Savin' Time/Happy Walking Around	1967	3.00	6.00	12.00
❏ 72715	Easy-As-Pie/Sugar Man	1967	2.00	4.00	8.00
❏ 72715 [PS]	Easy-As-Pie/Sugar Man	1967	3.00	6.00	12.00
❏ 72746	I'm So Proud/Candy Candy	1967	2.00	4.00	8.00
❏ 72746 [PS]	I'm So Proud/Candy Candy	1967	5.00	10.00	20.00
❏ 72794	Hurry/Pleasure of Your Company	1968	2.00	4.00	8.00
❏ 72824	Always Tomorrow/I Can't Go Wrong	1968	2.00	4.00	8.00

PHILCO-FORD

Number	Title (A Side/B Side)	Yr	VG	VG+	NM
❏ HP-20	98.6/Ain't Gonna Lie	1968	3.75	7.50	15.00
—4-inch plastic "Hip Pocket Record" with color sleeve					

RCA VICTOR

Number	Title (A Side/B Side)	Yr	VG	VG+	NM
❏ 74-0140	Marstrand/The Problem	1969	—	3.00	6.00
❏ 74-0222	Trixin's Election/A Fairy Tale or Two	1969	—	3.00	6.00

Albums
MERCURY

Number	Title (A Side/B Side)	Yr	VG	VG+	NM
❏ MG-21102 [M]	98.6/Ain't Gonna Lie	1967	3.75	7.50	15.00
❏ MG-21129 [M]	Out of Crank	1967	3.75	7.50	15.00

Number	Title (A Side/B Side)	Yr	VG	VG+	NM
☐ SR-61102 [S]	98.6/Ain't Gonna Lie	1967	5.00	10.00	20.00
☐ SR-61129 [S]	Out of Crank	1967	5.00	10.00	20.00
RCA VICTOR					
☐ LSP-4143	The Adventures of Keith	1969	5.00	10.00	20.00

KEITH AND DONNA Also see THE GRATEFUL DEAD.
Albums
ROUND

Number	Title (A Side/B Side)	Yr	VG	VG+	NM
☐ RX-104	Keith and Donna	1975	7.50	15.00	30.00

KELLEM, MANNY
45s
EPIC

Number	Title (A Side/B Side)	Yr	VG	VG+	NM
☐ 10282	Love Is Blue/Claudine	1968	—	3.00	6.00
☐ 10308	Trains and Boats and Planes/Free Again	1968	—	3.00	6.00
METROMEDIA					
☐ 104	Red White and Maddox/Jubilee Joe	1969	—	3.00	6.00
Albums					
EPIC					
☐ BN 26367	Love Is Blue	1968	2.50	5.00	10.00

KELLER, JERRY
45s
CAPITOL

Number	Title (A Side/B Side)	Yr	VG	VG+	NM
☐ 4630	Never Wake Up/Be Careful How You Drive, Young Joey	1961	3.00	6.00	12.00
☐ 4668	I'll Get By/My Year of Love	1961	3.00	6.00	12.00
CORAL					
☐ 62348	It's Too Late/What Will I Tell My Darling	1963	2.50	5.00	10.00
☐ 62361	Sume Summer/Goodnight Pretty Girl	1963	2.50	5.00	10.00
☐ 62378	Sea Shell Sherry/What Happens When He Comes Home	1963	2.50	5.00	10.00
☐ 62409	Small Wonder/The Tears Keep Falling Down	1964	2.50	5.00	10.00
KAPP					
☐ 277 [M]	Here Comes Summer/Time Has a Way	1959	3.75	7.50	15.00
☐ 277 [PS]	Here Comes Summer/Time Has a Way	1959	6.25	12.50	25.00
☐ KS-277 [S]	Here Comes Summer/Time Has a Way	1959	7.50	15.00	30.00
☐ 295	If I Had a Girl/Lovable	1959	3.00	6.00	12.00
☐ 295 [PS]	If I Had a Girl/Lovable	1959	6.25	12.50	25.00
☐ 310	Now, Now, Now/There Are Such Things	1959	3.00	6.00	12.00
☐ 322	American Beauty Rose/Lonesome Lullaby	1960	3.00	6.00	12.00
☐ 337	My Name Ain't Joe/White for You and Bless for Me	1960	3.00	6.00	12.00
☐ 353	What More Can I Say/Whole-Heartedly	1960	3.00	6.00	12.00
RCA VICTOR					
☐ 47-9221	You're Leanin' On My Mind/My Heart Loves the Samba (Best of All)	1967	2.00	4.00	8.00
REPRISE					
☐ 0351	Fickle Finger of Fate/Glory of Love	1965	2.00	4.00	8.00
☐ 0397	Ma (She's Such a Quiet Girl)/The Mack	1965	2.00	4.00	8.00
Albums					
KAPP					
☐ KL-1178 [M]	Here Comes Jerry Keller	1959	10.00	20.00	40.00
☐ KS-3178 [S]	Here Comes Jerry Keller	1959	12.50	25.00	50.00

KELLERMAN, SALLY
45s
DECCA

Number	Title (A Side/B Side)	Yr	VG	VG+	NM
☐ 33024	Roll with the Feelin'/Child of Mine	1972	—	3.00	6.00
Albums					
DECCA					
☐ DL 75359	Roll with the Feelin'	1972	5.00	10.00	20.00

KELLIN, MIKE
Albums
VERVE FORECAST

Number	Title (A Side/B Side)	Yr	VG	VG+	NM
☐ FT-3028 [M]	Mike Kellin	1967	6.25	12.50	25.00
☐ FTS-3028 [S]	Mike Kellin	1967	6.25	12.50	25.00

KELLUM, MURRY
45s
CINNAMON

Number	Title (A Side/B Side)	Yr	VG	VG+	NM
☐ 765	Walking Tall/Huckleberry's Ferry Boat Building Blues	1973	—	2.50	5.00
☐ 777	Lovely Lady/Alive and Doing Well	1973	—	2.50	5.00
☐ 794	Girl of My Life/Since You've Been Gone	1974	—	2.50	5.00
EPIC					
☐ 10741	Joy to the World/In a Phone Booth on My Knees	1971	—	2.50	5.00
☐ 10784	Train Train (Carry Me Away)/What's Made Milwaukee Famous	1971	—	2.50	5.00
☐ 10832	Love You to Sleep Tonight/You Do the Callin' (I'll Do the Crawlin')	1972	—	2.50	5.00
M.O.C.					
☐ 653	Long, Tall Texan/I Gotta Leave This Town	1963	3.00	6.00	12.00
—B-side by Glenn Sutton					
☐ 657	Red Ryder/Texas Lil	1964	3.00	6.00	12.00
☐ 658	I Dreamed I Was a Beatle/Oh How Sweet It Could Be	1964	5.00	10.00	20.00
PLANTATION					
☐ 176 [DJ]	Memphis Sun (mono/stereo)	1978	—	2.50	5.00
—Released only as a promo					
RANWOOD					
☐ 1047	Shoot Low Sheriff/How Long Has It Been (Since They Played Something You Could Dance To)	1976	—	2.50	5.00

KELLY, CASEY
45s
ELEKTRA

Number	Title (A Side/B Side)	Yr	VG	VG+	NM
☐ 45804	Poor Boy/You'll Never Leave My Mind	1972	2.00	4.00	8.00
☐ 45826	Can't Get There from Here/Making Believe	1972	2.00	4.00	8.00
☐ 45885	Reach Out for Me/Sometimes	1974	2.00	4.00	8.00
PRIVATE STOCK					
☐ 45,145	Where You Been/Out of Sight, Out of Mind	1977	2.00	4.00	8.00
Albums					
ELEKTRA					
☐ EKS-75040	Casey Kelly	1972	3.75	7.50	15.00
☐ EKS-75072	For Sale	1974	3.75	7.50	15.00

KELLY, EMMETT
Albums
ROULETTE

Number	Title (A Side/B Side)	Yr	VG	VG+	NM
☐ R-25130 [M]	Sing Along with Emmett Kelly	1962	6.25	12.50	25.00
☐ SR-25130 [S]	Sing Along with Emmett Kelly	1962	7.50	15.00	30.00

KELLY, MONTY
45s
CARLTON

Number	Title (A Side/B Side)	Yr	VG	VG+	NM
☐ 495	Willingly/The Blue Cha Cha	1959	2.50	5.00	10.00
☐ 517	I Loves You Porgy/Tango Bongo	1959	2.50	5.00	10.00
☐ 527	Summer Set/Amalia	1960	2.50	5.00	10.00
ESSEX					
☐ 325 [S]	Tropicana/Life in New York	1953	3.00	6.00	12.00
☐ 328	Three O'Clock in the Morning/Doreen	1953	3.00	6.00	12.00
☐ 341	Granada/Snow, Snow	1953	3.00	6.00	12.00
☐ 351	Cubamba/Cross Winds	1954	3.00	6.00	12.00
☐ 373	Shangri-La/Monte Carlo	1954	3.00	6.00	12.00
☐ 375	Neapolitan Nights/Majorca	1954	3.00	6.00	12.00
☐ 386	Blue Mirage/That Sweetheart of Mine	1955	3.00	6.00	12.00
☐ 404	Bali Ha'i/To You with Love	1955	3.00	6.00	12.00
OLYMPIA					
☐ 815	Ski Song/The Clicking of the Skis	196?	2.00	4.00	8.00
Albums					
ALSHIRE					
☐ SAS 610	Passport to Romance	196?	2.50	5.00	10.00
ESSEX					
☐ ESLP-106 [10]	I Love	1954	7.50	15.00	30.00
☐ ESLP-108 [10]	Monty Kelly Takes Me to Far Away Places	1954	7.50	15.00	30.00
☐ ESLP-203 [M]	Tropicana	1955	6.25	12.50	25.00
SOMERSET					
☐ P 7300 [M]	Tropicana	196?	2.50	5.00	10.00
—Reissue of Trans World 203					
TRANS WORLD					
☐ TWLP-203 [M]	Tropicana	1956	5.00	10.00	20.00
—Reissue of Essex 203					

KELLY, PAT
45s
CHIC

Number	Title (A Side/B Side)	Yr	VG	VG+	NM
☐ 1009	She's a Devil/The Stranger Dressed in Black	1957	7.50	15.00	30.00
JUBILEE					
☐ 5315	Hey Doll Baby/Cloud 13	1958	15.00	30.00	60.00
☐ 5333	Patsy/That Is Where My Money Goes	1958	6.25	12.50	25.00

KELLY, PAUL
45s
DIAL

Number	Title (A Side/B Side)	Yr	VG	VG+	NM
☐ 4021	Chills and Fever/Only Your Love	1965	2.50	5.00	10.00
☐ 4025	Since I Found You/Can't Help It	1966	2.50	5.00	10.00
☐ 4088	Call Another Doctor/We're Gonna Make It	1968	2.50	5.00	10.00
HAPPY TIGER					
☐ 541	Stealing in the Name of the Lord/Day After Forever	1970	—	3.00	6.00
☐ 555	Sailing/509	1970	—	3.00	6.00
☐ 568	Poor But Proud/Hot Runnin' Soul	1971	—	3.00	6.00
☐ 573	Hangin' On In There/Soul Flow	1971	—	3.00	6.00
PHILIPS					
☐ 40409	I Need Your Love So Bad/Nine Times Out of Ten	1966	3.75	7.50	15.00
☐ 40457	Cryin' for My Baby/Sweet Sweet Lovin'	1967	3.75	7.50	15.00
☐ 40480	If This Old House Could Talk/You Don't Know, You Just Don't Know	1967	3.75	7.50	15.00
☐ 40513	Glad to Be Sad/My Love Is Growing Stronger	1968	3.75	7.50	15.00
WARNER BROS.					
☐ 7614	Travelin' Man/Here Comes Old Jezebel	1972	—	2.50	5.00
☐ 7657	Don't Burn Me/Love Me Now	1972	—	2.50	5.00
☐ 7707	Come Lay Some Lovin' on Me/Come By Here	1973	—	2.50	5.00
☐ 7765	I'm Into Something I Can't Shake Loose/Joy	1974	—	2.50	5.00
☐ 7823	Hooked, Hogtied & Collared/I Wanna Be Close to You	1974	—	2.50	5.00
☐ 8040	Let Your Love Come Down (Let It Fall on Me)/I Wanna Be Close to You	1974	—	2.50	5.00
☐ 8067	Take It Away from Him (Put It On Me)/Try My Love	1975	—	2.50	5.00
☐ 8120	Get Sexy/I Believe I Can	1975	—	2.50	5.00
☐ 8187	Play Me a Love Song/Stealin' Love on the Side	1976	—	2.50	5.00
Albums					
HAPPY TIGER					
☐ 1015	Stealing in the Name of the Lord	1970	3.75	7.50	15.00
WARNER BROS.					
☐ BS 2605	Dirt	1972	3.00	6.00	12.00
☐ BS 2689	Don't Burn Me	1973	3.00	6.00	12.00
☐ BS 2812	Hooked, Hogtied & Collared	1974	3.00	6.00	12.00
☐ BS 3026	Stand on the Positive Side	1976	3.00	6.00	12.00

KELLY FOUR, THE
45s
CANDIX

Number	Title (A Side/B Side)	Yr	VG	VG+	NM
☐ 325	Annie Had a Party/Sweet Angelina	1961	6.25	12.50	25.00
—A-side is an alternate take of Silver 1006					
☐ 325	Annie Had a Party/Sweet Angelina	1961	6.25	12.50	25.00
—As "Big Daddy Greenfield"; same recordings as above					
SILVER					
☐ 1001	Strollin' Guitar/Guybo	1959	10.00	20.00	40.00
—A-side was reissued on Silver 1004 by "Jewel and Eddie"					
☐ 1006	Annie Had a Party/So Fine, Be Mine	1960	10.00	20.00	40.00
—A-side was reissued on Crest 1088 by "The Gee Cees"					

KEMPER, JIMMY, AND THE TIERS
45s
LE MANS

Number	Title (A Side/B Side)	Yr	VG	VG+	NM
☐ 002	Lonely for Kathy/I'm Free to Choose	1964	37.50	75.00	150.00

Number	Title (A Side/B Side)	Yr	VG	VG+	NM

KENDALL SISTERS, THE
45s
ARGO
❏ 5278	I'm Available/Don't Bother Me	1957	3.75	7.50	15.00
❏ 5291	Yea, Yea/Won't You Be My Baby	1958	3.75	7.50	15.00
❏ 5310	Billy, Billy, Billy/Let's Wait	1958	3.75	7.50	15.00
CHECKER
❏ 884	Make It Soon/Three Wishes	1958	3.75	7.50	15.00
❏ 889	Yea, Yea/Won't You Be My Baby	1958	6.25	12.50	25.00

KENDRICK, NAT, AND THE SWANS James Brown's backing band, later known as the J.B.'s. Also see FRED WESLEY.
45s
DADE
❏ 1804	(Do the) Mashed Potatoes (Part 1)/(Do the) Mashed Potatoes (Part 2)	1959	3.75	7.50	15.00
❏ 1808	Dish Rag (Part 1)/Dish Rag (Part 2)	1960	3.75	7.50	15.00
❏ 1812	Hot Chili/Slow Down	1960	3.75	7.50	15.00
❏ 5003	Wobble Wobble (Part 1)/Wobble Wobble (Part 2)	1961	3.75	7.50	15.00
❏ 5004	(Do the) Mashed Potatoes (Part 1)/(Do the) Mashed Potatoes (Part 2)	1961	3.00	6.00	12.00

KENDRICKS, EDDIE Also see DARYL HALL AND JOHN OATES; THE TEMPTATIONS.
12-Inch Singles
ARISTA
| ❏ SP-15 [DJ] | Ain't No Smoke Without Fire (5:58)/Whip (5:05) | 1978 | 3.00 | 6.00 | 12.00 |
CORNER STONE
| ❏ 3001 | Surprise Attack (3 versions) | 1984 | 2.00 | 4.00 | 8.00 |
45s
ARISTA
❏ 0325	Ain't No Smoke Without Fire/Love, Love, Love	1978	—	2.00	4.00
❏ 0346	The Best of Strangers Now/Don't Underestimate the Power of Love	1978	—	2.00	4.00
❏ 0466	I Just Want to Be the One in Your Life/I Can't Let You Walk Away	1979	—	2.00	4.00
❏ 0500	Your Love Has Been So Good/I Never Used to Dance	1980	—	2.00	4.00
ATLANTIC
❏ 3796	Looking for Love/Need Your Lovin'	1981	—	2.00	4.00
❏ 3874 [DJ]	I Don't Need Nobody Else (same on both sides)	1981	—	2.50	5.00
—May be promo only
CORNER STONE
| ❏ 1001 | Surprise Attack/(B-side unknown) | 1984 | — | 2.00 | 4.00 |
TAMLA
❏ 54203	It's So Hard for Me to Say Good-Bye/This Used to Be the Home of Johnnie Mae	1971	—	2.50	5.00
❏ 54210	Can I/I Did It All for You	1971	—	2.50	5.00
❏ 54218	Eddie's Love/Let Me Run Into Your Lonely Heart	1972	—	2.50	5.00
❏ 54222	If You Let Me/Just Memories	1972	—	2.50	5.00
❏ 54230	Girl You Need a Change of Mind (Part 1)/Girl You Need a Change of Mind (Part 2)	1973	—	2.50	5.00
❏ 54236	Darling Come Back Home/Loving You the Second Time Around	1973	—	2.50	5.00
❏ 54238	Keep On Truckin' (Part 1)/Keep On Truckin' (Part 2)	1973	—	2.50	5.00
❏ 54243	Boogie Down/Can't Help What I Am	1974	—	2.50	5.00
❏ 54247	Son of Sagittarius/Trust Your Heart	1974	—	2.50	5.00
❏ 54249	Tell Her Love Has Felt the Need/Loving You the Second Time Around	1974	—	2.50	5.00
❏ 54255	One Tear/The Thin Man	1974	—	2.50	5.00
❏ 54257	Shoeshine Boy/Hooked on Your Love	1975	—	2.50	5.00
❏ 54260	Get the Cream Off the Top/Honey Brown	1975	—	2.50	5.00
❏ 54263	Happy/Deep and Quiet Love	1975	—	2.50	5.00
❏ 54266	He's a Friend/All of My Life	1976	—	2.50	5.00
❏ 54266 [DJ]	He's a Friend (stereo/mono)	1976	3.75	7.50	15.00
—Promo only on red vinyl
❏ 54270	Get It While It's Hot/Never Gonna Leave You	1976	—	2.50	5.00
❏ 54277	Goin' Up in Smoke/Thanks for the Memories	1976	—	2.50	5.00
❏ 54285	Date with the Rain/Born Again	1977	—	2.50	5.00
❏ 54289	Baby/I Want to Live (My Life with You)	1977	—	—	—
—Unreleased
| ❏ 54290 | Baby/Intimate Friends | 1977 | — | 2.50 | 5.00 |
Albums
ARISTA
| ❏ AB 4170 | Vintage '78 | 1978 | 2.50 | 5.00 | 10.00 |
| ❏ AB 4250 | Something More | 1979 | 2.50 | 5.00 | 10.00 |
ATLANTIC
| ❏ SD 19294 | Love Keys | 1981 | 2.50 | 5.00 | 10.00 |
MOTOWN
| ❏ M5-151V1 | Eddie Kendricks | 1981 | 2.00 | 4.00 | 8.00 |
—Reissue of Tamla 327
| ❏ M5-196V1 | He's a Friend | 1981 | 2.00 | 4.00 | 8.00 |
—Reissue of Tamla 343
TAMLA
❏ T-309	All By Myself	1971	2.50	5.00	10.00
❏ T 315L	People...Hold On	1972	2.50	5.00	10.00
❏ T 327L	Eddie Kendricks	1973	2.50	5.00	10.00
❏ T 330V1	Boogie Down!	1974	2.50	5.00	10.00
❏ T6-335	For You	1974	2.50	5.00	10.00
❏ T6-338	The Hit Man	1975	2.50	5.00	10.00
❏ T6-343	He's a Friend	1976	2.50	5.00	10.00
❏ T6-346	Goin' Up in Smoke	1976	2.50	5.00	10.00
❏ T7-354	Eddie Kendricks at His Best	1977	2.50	5.00	10.00
❏ T8-356	Slick	1978	2.50	5.00	10.00

KENNEDY, JOHN FITZGERALD Various tribute records, most of which were released in the immediate aftermath of his assassination in 1963.
Albums
CAEDMON
| ❏ TC-2021 [(2)] | Self-Portrait | 196? | 5.00 | 10.00 | 20.00 |
CAPITOL
| ❏ ST 2486 [S] | Years of Lightning, Day of Drums | 1966 | 7.50 | 15.00 | 30.00 |
| ❏ T 2486 [M] | Years of Lightning, Day of Drums | 1966 | 5.00 | 10.00 | 20.00 |
—Narrated by Gregory Peck; U.S. Information Agency movie soundtrack

COLPIX
| ❏ CP 2500 [M] | Four Days That Shocked the World | 1964 | 12.50 | 25.00 | 50.00 |
—Narrated by Reid Collins; covers Nov. 22-25, 1963
DECCA
| ❏ DL 9116 [M] | That Was The Week That Was | 1963 | 5.00 | 10.00 | 20.00 |
—BBC show's tribute to JFK, broadcast Nov. 23, 1963
DIPLOMAT
| ❏ 10000 [M] | John F. Kennedy — A Memorial Album | 1963 | 3.75 | 7.50 | 15.00 |
DOCUMENTARIES UNLIMITED
| ❏ (no #) [M] | JFK The Man, The President | 1963 | 5.00 | 10.00 | 20.00 |
—Narrated by Barry Gray
HARMONICA
| ❏ HLP-3005 [M] | Kennedy Speaks | 1963 | 5.00 | 10.00 | 20.00 |
LEGACY
| ❏ L2L 1017 [(2)M] | John Fitzgerald Kennedy...As We Remember Him | 1965 | 6.25 | 12.50 | 25.00 |
—Narrated by Charles Kuralt; with 240-page book
PICKWICK
| ❏ 169 [M] | The Presidential Years (1960-1963) | 1963 | 3.75 | 7.50 | 15.00 |
PREMIER
| ❏ 2099 [M] | A Memorial Album | 1963 | 5.00 | 10.00 | 20.00 |
—From WMCA Radio, New York, Nov. 22, 1963
RCA VICTOR
| ❏ VDM-101 [M] | The Kennedy Wit | 1964 | 3.75 | 7.50 | 15.00 |
—Narrated by David Brinkley with introduction by Adlai E. Stevenson
SOMERSET
| ❏ 16100 [M] | Actual Speeches of Franklin D. Roosevelt and John F. Kennedy | 1963 | 3.75 | 7.50 | 15.00 |
—One side has FDR speeches, the other, JFK speeches
20TH CENTURY
| ❏ TCF 3127 [M] | The Presidential Years 1960-1963 | 1963 | 5.00 | 10.00 | 20.00 |
—Narrated by David Teig

KENNEDY, JOYCE
12-Inch Singles
A&M
❏ SP-12117	Tailor Made (Specially Remixed Version 6:27) (Instrumental 5:30)/Stronger Than Before (4:04)	1984	2.00	4.00	8.00
❏ SP-12127	Didn't I Tell You (Album Version) (Single Version)	1985	2.00	4.00	8.00
❏ SP-12158	Hold On (For Love's Sake) (Specially Remixed Version 5:20) (Instrumental 5:44)	1985	2.00	4.00	8.00
❏ SP-17319 [DJ]	Didn't I Tell You/Fire in the Twilight	1985	2.50	5.00	10.00
—B-side by Wang Chung
45s
A&M
| ❏ 2656 | The Last Time I Made Love/Different Now | 1984 | — | 2.00 | 4.00 |
—A-side with Jeffrey Osborne
| ❏ 2665 [DJ] | Tailor Made (same on both sides?) | 1984 | 2.00 | 4.00 | 8.00 |
—45 is promo only
❏ 2685	Stronger Than Before/Chain Reaction	1984	—	2.00	4.00
❏ 2685 [PS]	Stronger Than Before/Chain Reaction	1984	—	2.00	4.00
❏ 2710	Tailor Made/Watch My Body	1985	2.00	4.00	8.00
❏ 2727	Didn't I Tell You/Different Now	1985	—	2.00	4.00
❏ 2790	Hold On (For Love's Sake)/Oh	1985	—	2.00	4.00
❏ 2809	Do Me Right/Too Much Smoke (Not Enough Fire)	1986	—	2.00	4.00
BLUE ROCK
❏ 4016	I'm a Good Girl/Does Anybody Love Me	1965	25.00	50.00	100.00
❏ 4023	Does Anybody Love Me/Hi Fi Albums and I	1965	7.50	15.00	30.00
FONTANA
❏ 1924	Paddle My Own Canoe/Could This Be Love	1964	5.00	10.00	20.00
RAN-DEE
❏ 110	I Still Love You (Darling)/Misunderstood	1963	7.50	15.00	30.00
Albums
A&M
| ❏ SP-4996 | Lookin' for Trouble | 1984 | 2.50 | 5.00 | 10.00 |
| ❏ SP-5073 | Wanna Play Your Game! | 1985 | 2.50 | 5.00 | 10.00 |

KENNEDY, MIKE Also see LOS BRAVOS.
45s
ABC
❏ 11309	Louisianna/The Lover (Of the Lost Face of the Moon)	1972	—	3.00	6.00
❏ 11326	Livin' I'm Doin'/Forgive and Forget	1972	2.50	5.00	10.00
❏ 11333	Mother America/Naked in the Cradle	1972	3.00	6.00	12.00
Albums
ABC
| ❏ ABCX-754 | Louisianna | 1972 | 5.00 | 10.00 | 20.00 |

KENNEDY, RAY (1) Pop-rock singer; not to be confused with the country singer-songwriter of the same name, who is outside the scope of this book.
45s
ARC
| ❏ 1-11298 | Starlight/Let Me Sing You a Love Letter | 1980 | — | 2.00 | 4.00 |
CREAM
| ❏ 1001 | She's a Lady/Try Acting Like a Woman, Woman | 1972 | — | 3.00 | 6.00 |
Albums
ARC
| ❏ NJC 36395 | Ray Kennedy | 1980 | 3.00 | 6.00 | 12.00 |
CREAM
| ❏ CR 9001 | Raymond Louis Kennedy | 1972 | 3.75 | 7.50 | 15.00 |

KENNEDY, ROBERT FRANCIS Tribute album released shortly after his death.
Albums
COLUMBIA
| ❏ C2S 792 [(2)] | A Memorial | 1968 | 5.00 | 10.00 | 20.00 |

KENNER, CHRIS
45s
BATON
| ❏ 220 | Grandma's House/Don't Let Her Pin That Charge | 1956 | 10.00 | 20.00 | 40.00 |

Number	Title (A Side/B Side)	Yr	VG	VG+	NM
IMPERIAL					
❑ 5448	Sick and Tired/Nothing Will Keep Me from You	1957	6.25	12.50	25.00
❑ 5488	Will You Be Mine/I Have News for You	1958	6.25	12.50	25.00
❑ 5767	Sick and Tired/Nothing Will Keep Me from You	1961	3.00	6.00	12.00
INSTANT					
❑ 3229	I Like It Like That, Part 1/I Like It Like That, Part 2	1961	3.75	7.50	15.00
❑ 3234	A Very True Story/Packin' Up	1961	3.00	6.00	12.00
❑ 3237	Something You Got/Come See About Me	1961	3.00	6.00	12.00
❑ 3244	How Far/Time	1962	3.00	6.00	12.00
❑ 3247	Let Me Show You How (To Twist)/Johnny Little	1962	3.00	6.00	12.00
❑ 3252	Land of 1000 Dances/That's My Girl	1962	3.00	6.00	12.00
❑ 3257	Come Back and See/Go Thru Life	1963	3.00	6.00	12.00
❑ 3263	What's Wrong with Life/Never Reach Perfection	1963	3.00	6.00	12.00
❑ 3265	She Can Dance/Anybody Here See My Baby	1964	3.00	6.00	12.00
❑ 3277	I'm Lonely, Take Me/Cinderella	1966	2.50	5.00	10.00
❑ 3280	All Night Rambler, Part 1/All Night Rambler, Part 2	1966	2.50	5.00	10.00
❑ 3283	Shoo Rah/Stretch My Hands to You	1967	2.50	5.00	10.00
❑ 3286	Fumigate Funky Broadway/Wind the Clock	1967	2.50	5.00	10.00
❑ 3290	Memories of a King (Let Freedom Ring), Part 1/Memories of a King (Let Freedom Ring), Part 2	1968	3.00	6.00	12.00
❑ 3293	Mini-Skirts and Soul/Sad Mistake	1968	2.50	5.00	10.00
PRIGAN					
❑ 2002	Don't Make No Noise/Right Kind of Girl	196?	5.00	10.00	20.00
RON					
❑ 335	Rocket to the Moon/Life's Just a Struggle	1961	3.00	6.00	12.00
UPTOWN					
❑ 708	Life of My Baby/They Took My Money	1965	2.50	5.00	10.00
❑ 716	I'm the Greatest/Get On This Train	1965	2.50	5.00	10.00
VALIANT					
❑ 3229	I Like It Like That, Part 1/I Like It Like That, Part 2	1960	10.00	20.00	40.00
Albums					
ATLANTIC					
❑ 8117 [M]	Land of 1,000 Dances	1965	20.00	40.00	80.00
COLLECTABLES					
❑ COL-5116	Golden Classics: I Like It Like That	198?	3.00	6.00	12.00

KENNY AND CORKY
45s

Number	Title (A Side/B Side)	Yr	VG	VG+	NM
BIG TOP					
❑ 3031	Nuttin' for Christmas/Suzy Snowflake	1959	5.00	10.00	20.00
❑ 3031 [PS]	Nuttin' for Christmas/Suzy Snowflake	1959	10.00	20.00	40.00

KENNY AND THE CADETS Also see THE BEACH BOYS.
45s

Number	Title (A Side/B Side)	Yr	VG	VG+	NM
RANDY					
❑ 422	Barbie/What Is a Young Man Made Of	1962	100.00	200.00	400.00
—Pink label original (white labels are counterfeits)					
❑ 422	Barbie/What Is a Young Man Made Of	1962	250.00	500.00	1000.
—Red and gold vinyl					

KENNY AND THE FIENDS
45s

Number	Title (A Side/B Side)	Yr	VG	VG+	NM
DOT					
❑ 16568	House on Haunted Hill (Part 1)/House on Haunted Hill (Part 2)	1963	5.00	10.00	20.00
❑ 16596	Moon Shot/One-Two-Three-Four	1964	5.00	10.00	20.00
POSEA					
❑ 80	The Raven (Part 1)/The Raven (Part 2)	1963	7.50	15.00	30.00
❑ 87	House on Haunted Hill/Green Door	1963	10.00	20.00	40.00
—As "Kenny and the Beach Fiends"					
PRINCESS					
❑ 51	House on Haunted Hill (Part 1)/House on Haunted Hill (Part 2)	1963	7.50	15.00	30.00

KENNY AND THE KASUALS
45s

Number	Title (A Side/B Side)	Yr	VG	VG+	NM
MARK IV					
❑ 911	Nothin' Better to Do/Floatin'	1965	7.50	15.00	30.00
❑ 1002	Don't Let Your Baby Go/(B-side unknown)	1966	7.50	15.00	30.00
❑ 1003	It's All Right/You Make Me Feel So Good	1966	7.50	15.00	30.00
❑ 1004	Strings of Time/(B-side unknown)	1966	7.50	15.00	30.00
❑ 1006	I'm Gonna Make It/Journey to Tyme	1966	10.00	20.00	40.00
❑ 1008	See-Saw Ride/As I Knew	1967	7.50	15.00	30.00
UNITED ARTISTS					
❑ 50085	I'm Gonna Make It/Journey to Tyme	1966	5.00	10.00	20.00
Albums					
MARK					
❑ 5000 [M]	The Impact Sound of Kenny and the Kasuals Live at the Studio Club	1966	250.00	500.00	1000.
❑ 5000 [M]	The Impact Sound of Kenny and the Kasuals Live at the Studio Club	1977	6.25	12.50	25.00
—"Reissue, 1977" appears on cover					
❑ 6000 [M]	Teen Dreams	1978	62.50	125.00	250.00
—Red vinyl; numbered, signed limited edition					
❑ 7000 [S]	Garage Kings	1979	6.25	12.50	25.00

KENNY AND THE SOCIALITES
45s

Number	Title (A Side/B Side)	Yr	VG	VG+	NM
CROSSTOWN					
❑ 001	I'll Have to Decide/King Tut Rock	1958	37.50	75.00	150.00

KENSINGTON MARKET
45s

Number	Title (A Side/B Side)	Yr	VG	VG+	NM
WARNER BROS.					
❑ 7221	I Would Be the One/Speaking of Dreams	1968	2.00	4.00	8.00
Albums					
WARNER BROS.					
❑ WS 1754	Avenue Road	1968	5.00	10.00	20.00
❑ WS 1780	Aardvark	1969	5.00	10.00	20.00

KENT, AL
45s

Number	Title (A Side/B Side)	Yr	VG	VG+	NM
BARITONE					
❑ 942	Hold Me/Tell Me Why	1960	37.50	75.00	150.00
CHECKER					
❑ 881	Dat's Why (I Love You So)/Am I the Man	1958	15.00	30.00	60.00

Number	Title (A Side/B Side)	Yr	VG	VG+	NM
RIC-TIC					
❑ 123	The Way You Been Acting Lately/(Instrumental)	1967	5.00	10.00	20.00
❑ 127	You've Got to Pay the Price/Where Do I Go from Here	1967	5.00	10.00	20.00
❑ 133	Finders Keepers/Ooh! Pretty Lady	1967	5.00	10.00	20.00
❑ 140	Bless You (My Love)/(Instrumental)	1968	3.75	7.50	15.00
WINGATE					
❑ 004	You Know I Love You/Country Boy	1965	6.25	12.50	25.00
WIZARD					
❑ 100	Hold Me/You Know Me	1959	25.00	50.00	100.00

KENT, BILLY, AND THE ANDANTES
45s

Number	Title (A Side/B Side)	Yr	VG	VG+	NM
MAH'S					
❑ 000.2	Your Love/Take All of Me	1960	15.00	30.00	60.00
—Second pressing, without address and with Roulette distribution mentioned on label					
❑ 000.2	Your Love/Take All of Me	1960	30.00	60.00	120.00
—First pressing, with Detroit address on label					

KENTON, STAN
45s

Number	Title (A Side/B Side)	Yr	VG	VG+	NM
CAPITOL					
❑ F899	Intermission Riff/Minor Riff	1950	5.00	10.00	20.00
—Note: Earlier Stan Kenton 45s on Capitol may exist					
❑ F900	Artistry in Boogie/Machito	1950	5.00	10.00	20.00
❑ F901	Concerto to End All Concertos, Part 1/Part 2	1950	5.00	10.00	20.00
❑ F902	Painted Rhythm/Southern Scandal	1950	5.00	10.00	20.00
❑ F903	Eager Beaver/Harlem Folk Dance	1950	5.00	10.00	20.00
❑ F904	The Peanut Vendor/Lover	1950	5.00	10.00	20.00
❑ F905	Theme to the West/Collaboration	1950	5.00	10.00	20.00
❑ F906	Harlem Holiday/Ricka Jicka Jack	1950	5.00	10.00	20.00
❑ F907	Unison Riff/Bongo Riff	1950	5.00	10.00	20.00
❑ F908	Interlude/Thermopolae	1950	5.00	10.00	20.00
❑ F909	Peg o' My Heart/How Am I to Know	1950	5.00	10.00	20.00
❑ F910	Tampico/And Her Tears Flowed Like Wine	1950	5.00	10.00	20.00
❑ F911	Willow Weep for Me/How High the Moon	1950	5.00	10.00	20.00
❑ F912	Just a-Sittin' a-Rockin'/Soothe Me	1950	5.00	10.00	20.00
❑ F913	His Feets Too Big for De Bed/Down in Chihuahua	1950	5.00	10.00	20.00
❑ F1043	Evening in Pakistan/Jolly Rogers	1950	5.00	10.00	20.00
❑ F1191	Easy Go/But Then You Kissed Me	1950	5.00	10.00	20.00
❑ F1236	Love for Sale, Be Easy, Be Tender	1950	5.00	10.00	20.00
❑ F1279	Viva Prado/I'm So in the Mood	1950	5.00	10.00	20.00
❑ F1306	Pagliacci/Santa Lucia	1950	3.75	7.50	15.00
❑ F1480	September Song/Artistry in Tango1	1951	3.75	7.50	15.00
❑ F1535	Tortillas and Beans/Dynaflow	1951	3.75	7.50	15.00
❑ F1616	The Spider and the Fly/Are You Livin' Old Man	1951	3.00	6.00	12.00
—Reissue of 78 rpm material					
❑ F1625	Love for Sale/Opus in Pastels	1951	3.00	6.00	12.00
❑ F1636	Artistry in Rhythm/Artistry Jumps	1951	3.00	6.00	12.00
—Reissue of 78 rpm material					
❑ F1661	Across the Alley from the Alamo/After You	1951	3.00	6.00	12.00
—Reissue of 78 rpm material					
❑ F1680	September Song/Laura	195?	3.00	6.00	12.00
—Reissue					
❑ F1704	Laura/Jump for Joe	1951	3.75	7.50	15.00
❑ F1774	Francesca/Night Watch	1951	3.75	7.50	15.00
❑ F1823	Daddy/Street of Dreams	1951	3.75	7.50	15.00
—A-side with June Christy, vocals					
❑ F1874	Blues in Burlesque (Part 1)/Blues in Burlesque (Part 2)	1951	3.75	7.50	15.00
❑ F2020	Yes/Mambo Rhapsody	1952	3.75	7.50	15.00
❑ F2040	Delicado/Bag and Baggage	1952	3.75	7.50	15.00
❑ F2064	Cool Eyes/She's a Comely Wench	1952	3.75	7.50	15.00
❑ F2214	Stardust/Beehive	1952	3.75	7.50	15.00
❑ F2250	Taboo/Lonesome Train	1952	3.75	7.50	15.00
❑ 2278	The Odd Couple/MacArthur Park	1968	2.50	5.00	10.00
❑ F2373	Hushabye/Harlem Nocturne	1953	3.75	7.50	15.00
❑ F2388	Jeepers Creepers/And the Bull Walked Around Olay	1953	3.75	7.50	15.00
❑ F2409	Do Nothing Till You Hear from Me/How Many Hearts Have You Broken	1953	3.00	6.00	12.00
❑ F2410	Sweet Dreams Sweetheart/Gotta Be Gettin'	1953	3.00	6.00	12.00
❑ F2411	Don't Let Me Dream/It's Been a Long, Long Time	1953	3.00	6.00	12.00
❑ F2412	Every Time We Say Goodbye/Four Months, Three Weeks, Two Days	1953	3.00	6.00	12.00
❑ F2413	Shoo Fly Pie and Apple Pie Down/I Been Down in Texas	1953	3.00	6.00	12.00
❑ F2414	It's a Pity to Say Goodnight/There Is No Greater Love	1953	3.00	6.00	12.00
❑ F2415	Curiosity/Theme to the West	1953	3.00	6.00	12.00
❑ F2416	Unison Riff/I Told Ya I Love Ya Now Get Out	1953	3.00	6.00	12.00
❑ F2418	Harlem Holiday/Don't Want That Man Around	1953	3.00	6.00	12.00
❑ F2419	How Am I to Know/He Was a Good Man	1953	3.00	6.00	12.00
❑ F2446	Sophisticated Lady/Begin the Beguine	1953	3.00	6.00	12.00
❑ F2447	There's a Small Hotel/Shadow Waltz	1953	3.00	6.00	12.00
❑ F2449	Fascinating Rhythm/Over the Rainbow	1953	3.00	6.00	12.00
❑ F2511	Baja/All About Ronnie	1953	3.00	6.00	12.00
❑ F2685	Tenderly/The Creep	1953	3.00	6.00	12.00
❑ F2789	Alone Too Long/Don't Take Your Love from Me	1954	3.00	6.00	12.00
❑ F2822	The Lady in Red/Under a Blanket of Blue	1954	3.00	6.00	12.00
❑ F2871	More Love Than Your Love/Skoot	1954	3.00	6.00	12.00
❑ F2879	Sambo Mambo/Mambo Riff	1954	3.00	6.00	12.00
❑ F3046	A-Ting-a-Ling/Malaguena	1955	3.00	6.00	12.00
❑ F3110	Casanova/Dark Eyes	1955	3.00	6.00	12.00
❑ F3134	23 Degrees N — 82 Degrees W/Falling	1955	3.00	6.00	12.00
❑ F3151	Freddy/Handwriting on the Wall	1955	3.00	6.00	12.00
❑ F3243	Sunset Tower/Opus in Chartreuse	1955	3.00	6.00	12.00
❑ F3345	Baa Too Kee/Winter in Madrid	1955	3.00	6.00	12.00
❑ F3836	Lemon Twist/Baby You're Through	1957	2.50	5.00	10.00
❑ F3928	Tequila/Cuban Mumble	1958	2.50	5.00	10.00
❑ F4196	Whistle Walk/Tamer Lane	1959	2.50	5.00	10.00
❑ 4370	Opus in Chartreuse Cha Cha Cha/Chocolate Caliente	1960	2.50	5.00	10.00
❑ 4500	Carnival/Malibu Moonlight	1961	2.00	4.00	8.00
❑ 4629	Theme from "Splendor in the Grass"/Officer Krupke	1961	2.00	4.00	8.00

Number	Title (A Side/B Side)	Yr	VG	VG+	NM
❏ 4666	Maria/Tonight	1961	2.00	4.00	8.00
❏ 4707	Magic Moment/Waltz of the Prophet	1962	2.00	4.00	8.00
❏ 4764	Come On Back/Warm Blue Stream	1962	2.00	4.00	8.00
❏ 4847	Mama Sang a Song/Whispering Hope	1962	2.00	4.00	8.00
❏ 5085	O Tannenbaum/What Is a Santa Claus	1963	2.50	5.00	10.00
❏ 5480	Peyton Place Theme/007	1965	2.00	4.00	8.00
❏ 5572	Patch of Blue/Make Me Love You	1966	2.00	4.00	8.00
❏ 5828	Dragnet/Spanish Eyes	1967	2.50	5.00	10.00
❏ F15530	Artistry in Bolero/Come Back to Sorrento	1950	3.75	7.50	15.00
❏ F15531	Willow Weep for Me/Fantasy	1950	3.75	7.50	15.00
❏ F15532	Safranski (Artistry in Bass)/Opus in Pastels	1950	3.75	7.50	15.00
❏ F15533	Artistry in Percussion/Ain't No Misery in Me	1950	3.75	7.50	15.00

—The above four comprise a box set

CREATIVE WORLD

Number	Title (A Side/B Side)	Yr	VG	VG+	NM
❏ 1001 [DJ]	The Twelve Days of Christmas//O Tannenbaum/				
	We Three Kings Of Orient Are	197?	—	2.00	4.00

7-Inch Extended Plays

CAPITOL

Number	Title (A Side/B Side)	Yr	VG	VG+	NM
❏ EAP 1-358	Tampico/Artistry in Boogie//Across the Valley				
	from the Alamo/Unison Riff	1954	3.75	7.50	15.00
❏ EAP 1-358 [PS]	A Collection of Stan Kenton Classics, Part 1	1954	3.75	7.50	15.00
❏ EAP 2-358	Southern Scandal/Machito//And Her Tears				
	Flowed Like Wine/Minor Riff	1954	3.75	7.50	15.00
❏ EAP 2-358 [PS]	A Collection of Stan Kenton Classics, Part 2	1954	3.75	7.50	15.00
❏ EBF 358 [PS]	A Collection of Stan Kenton Classics	1954	5.00	10.00	20.00

—Gatefold sleeve for some editions of 1-358 and 2-358

Number	Title (A Side/B Side)	Yr	VG	VG+	NM
❏ 1-383	23 degrees N — 82 degrees W/Portrait of a				
	Count//Young Blood/Frank Speaking	195?	3.00	6.00	12.00
❏ 2-383	Improvisation//Invention for Guitar and Trumpet/				
	My Lady	195?	3.00	6.00	12.00
❏ EBF 383 [PS]	New Concepts of Artistry in Rhythm	195?	3.00	6.00	12.00

—Cover for 2-EP set

Number	Title (A Side/B Side)	Yr	VG	VG+	NM
❏ EAP 1-421	September Song/Delicado//Laura/Stardust	195?	3.75	7.50	15.00
❏ EAP 1-421 [PS]	Popular Favorites by Stan Kenton	195?	3.75	7.50	15.00
❏ EAP 1-426	Sophisticated Lady/Begin the Beguine//There's				
	a Small Hotel/Shadow Waltz	195?	3.75	7.50	15.00
❏ EAP 1-426 [PS]	Sketches on Standards, Part 1	195?	3.75	7.50	15.00
❏ EAP 2-426	Lover Man, Oh Where Can You Be?/Pennies				
	from Heaven//Over the Rainbow/Fascinating				
	Rhythm	195?	3.75	7.50	15.00
❏ EAP 2-426 [PS]	Sketches on Standards, Part 2	195?	3.75	7.50	15.00
❏ EAP 1-462	You and the Night and the Music/Reverie//Crazy				
	Rhythm/I Got It Bad and That Ain't Good	195?	3.75	7.50	15.00
❏ EAP 1-462 [PS]	Portraits on Standards, Part 1	195?	3.75	7.50	15.00
❏ EAP 2-462	I've Got You Under My Skin/Autumn in New				
	York//April in Paris/How High the Moon	195?	3.75	7.50	15.00
❏ EAP 2-462 [PS]	Portraits on Standards, Part 2	195?	3.75	7.50	15.00
❏ EBF 462 [PS]	Portraits on Standards	195?	6.25	12.50	25.00

—Both of above EPs in gatefold sleeve

Number	Title (A Side/B Side)	Yr	VG	VG+	NM
❏ EAP 1-508	(contents unknown)	195?	3.75	7.50	15.00
❏ EAP 1-508 [PS]	Stan Kenton Plays the Compositions of Pete				
	Rugolo	195?	3.75	7.50	15.00
❏ EAP 1-610	(contents unknown)	195?	3.00	6.00	12.00
❏ EAP 1-610 [PS]	Kenton with Voices, Part 1	195?	3.00	6.00	12.00
❏ EAP 2-610	(contents unknown)	195?	3.00	6.00	12.00
❏ EAP 2-610 [PS]	Kenton with Voices, Part 2	195?	3.00	6.00	12.00
❏ EAP 3-610	Temptation/Opus in Chartreuse//All About				
	Ronnie/Interlude	195?	3.00	6.00	12.00
❏ EAP 3-610 [PS]	Kenton with Voices, Part 3	195?	3.00	6.00	12.00
❏ EAP 1-666	What's New/Stella by Starlight	195?	3.00	6.00	12.00
❏ EAP 1-666 [PS]	Contemporary Concepts, Part 1	195?	3.00	6.00	12.00
❏ EAP 1-666 [PS]	Contemporary Concepts, Part 3	195?	3.00	6.00	12.00
❏ EAP 2-666	Cherokee/Limelight//Yesterdays	195?	3.00	6.00	12.00
❏ EAP 2-666 [PS]	Contemporary Concepts, Part 2	195?	3.00	6.00	12.00
❏ EAP 3-666	I've Got You Under My Skin/Stompin' at the				
	Savoy	195?	3.00	6.00	12.00
❏ EAP 1-731	(contents unknown)	195?	3.00	6.00	12.00
❏ EAP 1-731 [PS]	Cuban Fire, Part 1	195?	3.00	6.00	12.00
❏ EAP 2-731	El Congo Valiente/La Guera Baila	195?	3.00	6.00	12.00
❏ EAP 2-731 [PS]	Cuban Fire, Part 2	195?	3.00	6.00	12.00
❏ EAP 3-731	Recuerdos/Quien Sabe	195?	3.00	6.00	12.00
❏ EAP 3-731 [PS]	Cuban Fire, Part 3	195?	3.00	6.00	12.00
❏ SXA-1796	Lime House Blues/Misty//Waltz of the Prophets	196?	2.50	5.00	10.00

—Jukebox issue; small hole, plays at 33 1/3 rpm

Number	Title (A Side/B Side)	Yr	VG	VG+	NM
❏ SXA-1796 [PS]	Adventures in Jazz	196?	2.50	5.00	10.00

Albums

CAPITOL

Number	Title (A Side/B Side)	Yr	VG	VG+	NM
❏ H 155 [10]	Encores	1950	15.00	30.00	60.00
❏ T 155 [M]	Encores	195?	10.00	20.00	40.00

—Turquoise label

Number	Title (A Side/B Side)	Yr	VG	VG+	NM
❏ DT 167 [R]	Artistry in Rhythm	1969	2.50	5.00	10.00
❏ H 167 [10]	Artistry in Rhythm	1950	15.00	30.00	60.00
❏ SM-167 [R]	Artistry in Rhythm	1975	2.00	4.00	8.00

—Reissue with new prefix

Number	Title (A Side/B Side)	Yr	VG	VG+	NM
❏ T 167 [M]	Artistry in Rhythm	195?	10.00	20.00	40.00

—Turquoise label

Number	Title (A Side/B Side)	Yr	VG	VG+	NM
❏ T 167 [M]	Artistry in Rhythm	1959	3.75	7.50	15.00

—Black label with colorband, Capitol logo at left

Number	Title (A Side/B Side)	Yr	VG	VG+	NM
❏ T 167 [M]	Artistry in Rhythm	1962	3.00	6.00	12.00

—Black label with colorband, Capitol logo at top

Number	Title (A Side/B Side)	Yr	VG	VG+	NM
❏ H 172 [10]	A Presentation of Progressive Jazz	1950	15.00	30.00	60.00
❏ T 172 [M]	A Presentation of Progressive Jazz	195?	10.00	20.00	40.00
❏ P 189 [10]	Innovations in Modern Music	1950	15.00	30.00	60.00
❏ H 190 [10]	Milestones	1950	15.00	30.00	60.00
❏ T 190 [M]	Milestones	195?	10.00	20.00	40.00

—Turquoise label

Number	Title (A Side/B Side)	Yr	VG	VG+	NM
❏ T 190 [M]	Milestones	196?	6.25	12.50	25.00

—Black colorband label, logo at left

Number	Title (A Side/B Side)	Yr	VG	VG+	NM
❏ PRO-206/7 [DJ]	The Kenton Era (Excerpts)	1955	10.00	20.00	40.00
❏ L 248 [10]	Stan Kenton Presents	1951	15.00	30.00	60.00
❏ T 248 [M]	Stan Kenton Presents	195?	10.00	20.00	40.00

—Turquoise label

Number	Title (A Side/B Side)	Yr	VG	VG+	NM
❏ T 248 [M]	Stan Kenton Presents	196?	3.75	7.50	15.00

—Black colorband label, logo at top

Number	Title (A Side/B Side)	Yr	VG	VG+	NM
❏ T 248 [M]	Stan Kenton Presents	196?	6.25	12.50	25.00

—Black colorband label, logo at left

Number	Title (A Side/B Side)	Yr	VG	VG+	NM
❏ ST-305	Music from "Hair"	1969	3.75	7.50	15.00

Number	Title (A Side/B Side)	Yr	VG	VG+	NM
❏ H 353 [10]	City of Glass	1952	15.00	30.00	60.00
❏ H 358 [10]	Classics	1952	15.00	30.00	60.00
❏ T 358 [M]	Classics	195?	10.00	20.00	40.00

—Turquoise label

Number	Title (A Side/B Side)	Yr	VG	VG+	NM
❏ H 383 [10]	New Concepts of Artistry in Rhythm	1953	15.00	30.00	60.00
❏ T 383 [M]	New Concepts of Artistry in Rhythm	195?	10.00	20.00	40.00

—Turquoise label

Number	Title (A Side/B Side)	Yr	VG	VG+	NM
❏ H 386 [10]	Prologue: This Is an Orchestra	1953	15.00	30.00	60.00
❏ H 421 [10]	Popular Favorites	1953	15.00	30.00	60.00
❏ T 421 [M]	Popular Favorites	195?	10.00	20.00	40.00

—Turquoise label

Number	Title (A Side/B Side)	Yr	VG	VG+	NM
❏ H 426 [10]	Sketches on Standards	1953	15.00	30.00	60.00
❏ T 426 [M]	Sketches on Standards	195?	10.00	20.00	40.00

—Turquoise label

Number	Title (A Side/B Side)	Yr	VG	VG+	NM
❏ H 460 [10]	This Modern World	1953	15.00	30.00	60.00
❏ H 462 [10]	Portraits on Standards	1953	15.00	30.00	60.00
❏ T 462 [M]	Portraits on Standards	195?	10.00	20.00	40.00

—Turquoise label

Number	Title (A Side/B Side)	Yr	VG	VG+	NM
❏ T 462 [M]	Portraits on Standards	196?	6.25	12.50	25.00

—Black colorband label, logo at left

Number	Title (A Side/B Side)	Yr	VG	VG+	NM
❏ W 524 [M]	Kenton Showcase	1954	10.00	20.00	40.00
❏ H 525 [10]	Kenton Showcase — The Music of Bill Russo	1954	15.00	30.00	60.00
❏ H 526 [10]	Kenton Showcase — The Music of Bill Holman	1954	15.00	30.00	60.00
❏ TDB 569 [(4)M]	The Kenton Era	1955	25.00	50.00	100.00

—Box set with 44-page book

Number	Title (A Side/B Side)	Yr	VG	VG+	NM
❏ WDX 569 [(4)M]	The Kenton Era	196?	17.50	35.00	70.00

—Box set with 44-page book; limited edition reissue with black label, Capitol logo at left

Number	Title (A Side/B Side)	Yr	VG	VG+	NM
❏ STCL-575 [(3)]	Stan Kenton	1970	5.00	10.00	20.00
❏ T 656 [M]	Duet	1955	10.00	20.00	40.00

—With June Christy; turquoise label

Number	Title (A Side/B Side)	Yr	VG	VG+	NM
❏ T 666 [M]	Contemporary Concepts	1955	10.00	20.00	40.00

—Turquoise label

Number	Title (A Side/B Side)	Yr	VG	VG+	NM
❏ SW 724 [S]	Kenton in Hi-Fi	1959	12.50	25.00	50.00

—Black label with colorband, logo at left; one fewer track than mono version

Number	Title (A Side/B Side)	Yr	VG	VG+	NM
❏ SW 724 [S]	Kenton in Hi-Fi	1962	7.50	15.00	30.00

—Black label with colorband, logo at top; one fewer track than mono version

Number	Title (A Side/B Side)	Yr	VG	VG+	NM
❏ W 724 [M]	Kenton in Hi-Fi	1956	10.00	20.00	40.00

—Gray label

Number	Title (A Side/B Side)	Yr	VG	VG+	NM
❏ W 724 [M]	Kenton in Hi-Fi	1959	5.00	10.00	20.00

—Black label with colorband, logo at left

Number	Title (A Side/B Side)	Yr	VG	VG+	NM
❏ T 731 [M]	Cuban Fire!	1956	10.00	20.00	40.00

—Turquoise label

Number	Title (A Side/B Side)	Yr	VG	VG+	NM
❏ T 731 [M]	Cuban Fire!	1959	5.00	10.00	20.00

—Black label with colorband, Capitol logo at left

Number	Title (A Side/B Side)	Yr	VG	VG+	NM
❏ T 731 [M]	Cuban Fire!	1962	3.75	7.50	15.00

—Black label with colorband, Capitol logo at top

Number	Title (A Side/B Side)	Yr	VG	VG+	NM
❏ T 736 [M]	City of Glass/This Modern World	1956	10.00	20.00	40.00

—Combination of 353 and 460 onto one 12-inch LP, turquoise label

Number	Title (A Side/B Side)	Yr	VG	VG+	NM
❏ T 810 [M]	Kenton with Voices	1957	10.00	20.00	40.00

—Turquoise label

Number	Title (A Side/B Side)	Yr	VG	VG+	NM
❏ T 932 [M]	Rendezvous with Kenton	1957	10.00	20.00	40.00

—Turquoise label

Number	Title (A Side/B Side)	Yr	VG	VG+	NM
❏ T 995 [M]	Back to Balboa	1958	10.00	20.00	40.00

—Turquoise label

Number	Title (A Side/B Side)	Yr	VG	VG+	NM
❏ ST 1068 [S]	The Ballad Style of Stan Kenton	1959	5.00	10.00	20.00

—Black label with colorband, Capitol logo at left

Number	Title (A Side/B Side)	Yr	VG	VG+	NM
❏ ST 1068 [S]	The Ballad Style of Stan Kenton	1962	3.00	6.00	12.00

—Black label with colorband, Capitol logo at top

Number	Title (A Side/B Side)	Yr	VG	VG+	NM
❏ T 1068 [M]	The Ballad Style of Stan Kenton	1959	6.25	12.50	25.00

—Black label with colorband, Capitol logo at left

Number	Title (A Side/B Side)	Yr	VG	VG+	NM
❏ T 1068 [M]	The Ballad Style of Stan Kenton	1962	3.75	7.50	15.00

—Black label with colorband, Capitol logo at top

Number	Title (A Side/B Side)	Yr	VG	VG+	NM
❏ ST 1130 [S]	Lush Interlude	1959	5.00	10.00	20.00

—Black label with colorband, Capitol logo at left

Number	Title (A Side/B Side)	Yr	VG	VG+	NM
❏ T 1130 [M]	Lush Interlude	1959	6.25	12.50	25.00

—Black label with colorband, Capitol logo at left

Number	Title (A Side/B Side)	Yr	VG	VG+	NM
❏ ST 1166 [S]	The Stage Door Swings	1959	5.00	10.00	20.00

—Black label with colorband, Capitol logo at left

Number	Title (A Side/B Side)	Yr	VG	VG+	NM
❏ T 1166 [M]	The Stage Door Swings	1959	6.25	12.50	25.00

—Black label with colorband, Capitol logo at left

Number	Title (A Side/B Side)	Yr	VG	VG+	NM
❏ ST 1276 [S]	The Kenton Touch	1960	5.00	10.00	20.00

—Black label with colorband, Capitol logo at left

Number	Title (A Side/B Side)	Yr	VG	VG+	NM
❏ T 1276 [M]	The Kenton Touch	1960	6.25	12.50	25.00

—Black label with colorband, Capitol logo at left

Number	Title (A Side/B Side)	Yr	VG	VG+	NM
❏ SW 1305 [S]	Viva Kenton!	1960	5.00	10.00	20.00

—Black label with colorband, Capitol logo at left

Number	Title (A Side/B Side)	Yr	VG	VG+	NM
❏ W 1305 [M]	Viva Kenton!	1960	6.25	12.50	25.00

—Black label with colorband, Capitol logo at left

Number	Title (A Side/B Side)	Yr	VG	VG+	NM
❏ STBO 1327 [(2)S]	Road Show	1960	7.50	15.00	30.00

—Black label with colorband, Capitol logo at left

Number	Title (A Side/B Side)	Yr	VG	VG+	NM
❏ STBO 1327 [(2)S]	Road Show	1962	3.75	7.50	15.00

—Black label with colorband, Capitol logo at top

Number	Title (A Side/B Side)	Yr	VG	VG+	NM
❏ TBO 1327 [(2)M]	Road Show	1960	10.00	20.00	40.00

—Black label with colorband, Capitol logo at left

Number	Title (A Side/B Side)	Yr	VG	VG+	NM
❏ TBO 1327 [(2)M]	Road Show	1962	5.00	10.00	20.00

—Black label with colorband, Capitol logo at top

Number	Title (A Side/B Side)	Yr	VG	VG+	NM
❏ ST 1394 [S]	Standards in Silhouette	1960	5.00	10.00	20.00

—Black label with colorband, Capitol logo at left

Number	Title (A Side/B Side)	Yr	VG	VG+	NM
❏ ST 1394 [S]	Standards in Silhouette	1962	3.00	6.00	12.00

—Black label with colorband, Capitol logo at top

Number	Title (A Side/B Side)	Yr	VG	VG+	NM
❏ T 1394 [M]	Standards in Silhouette	1960	6.25	12.50	25.00

—Black label with colorband, Capitol logo at top

Number	Title (A Side/B Side)	Yr	VG	VG+	NM
❏ T 1394 [M]	Standards in Silhouette	1962	3.75	7.50	15.00

—Black label with colorband, Capitol logo at top

Number	Title (A Side/B Side)	Yr	VG	VG+	NM
❏ ST 1460 [S]	Kenton at the Las Vegas Tropicana	1961	5.00	10.00	20.00

—Black label with colorband, Capitol logo at left

Number	Title (A Side/B Side)	Yr	VG	VG+	NM
❏ T 1460 [M]	Kenton at the Las Vegas Tropicana	1961	6.25	12.50	25.00

—Black label with colorband, Capitol logo at left

Number	Title (A Side/B Side)	Yr	VG	VG+	NM
❏ ST 1533 [S]	The Romantic Approach	1961	3.00	6.00	12.00

—Black label with colorband, Capitol logo at top

Number	Title (A Side/B Side)	Yr	VG	VG+	NM
❏ ST 1533 [S]	The Romantic Approach	1961	5.00	10.00	20.00

—Black label with colorband, Capitol logo at left

Number	Title (A Side/B Side)	Yr	VG	VG+	NM
❏ T 1533 [M]	The Romantic Approach	1961	3.75	7.50	15.00

—Black label with colorband, Capitol logo at top

Number	Title (A Side/B Side)	Yr	VG	VG+	NM
❏ T 1533 [M]	The Romantic Approach	1961	6.25	12.50	25.00

—Black label with colorband, Capitol logo at left

K

Number	Title (A Side/B Side)	Yr	VG	VG+	NM
❑ ST 1609 [S]	Kenton's West Side Story	1961	3.00	6.00	12.00
—Black label with colorband, Capitol logo at top					
❑ ST 1609 [S]	Kenton's West Side Story	1961	5.00	10.00	20.00
—Black label with colorband, Capitol logo at left					
❑ T 1609 [M]	Kenton's West Side Story	1961	3.75	7.50	15.00
—Black label with colorband, Capitol logo at top					
❑ T 1609 [M]	Kenton's West Side Story	1961	6.25	12.50	25.00
—Black label with colorband, Capitol logo at left					
❑ ST 1621 [S]	A Merry Christmas	1961	5.00	10.00	20.00
❑ T 1621 [M]	A Merry Christmas	1961	3.75	7.50	15.00
❑ ST 1674 [S]	The Sophisticated Approach	1962	3.75	7.50	15.00
—Black label with colorband, Capitol logo at top					
❑ T 1674 [M]	The Sophisticated Approach	1962	3.00	6.00	12.00
—Black label with colorband, Capitol logo at top					
❑ ST 1796 [S]	Adventures in Jazz	1962	3.75	7.50	15.00
—Black label with colorband, Capitol logo at top					
❑ T 1796 [M]	Adventures in Jazz	1962	3.00	6.00	12.00
—Black label with colorband, Capitol logo at top					
❑ ST 1844 [S]	Adventures in Time	1963	3.75	7.50	15.00
—Black label with colorband, Capitol logo at top					
❑ T 1844 [M]	Adventures in Time	1963	3.00	6.00	12.00
—Black label with colorband, Capitol logo at top					
❑ ST 1931 [S]	Artistry in Bossa Nova	1963	3.75	7.50	15.00
❑ T 1931 [M]	Artistry in Bossa Nova	1963	3.00	6.00	12.00
❑ ST 1985 [S]	Adventures in Blues	1963	3.75	7.50	15.00
—Black label with colorband, Capitol logo at top					
❑ T 1985 [M]	Adventures in Blues	1963	3.00	6.00	12.00
—Black label with colorband, Capitol logo at top					
❑ ST 2132 [S]	Artistry in Voices and Brass	1964	3.75	7.50	15.00
—Black label with colorband, Capitol logo at top					
❑ T 2132 [M]	Artistry in Voices and Brass	1964	3.00	6.00	12.00
—Black label with colorband, Capitol logo at top					
❑ STAO 2217 [S]	Kenton Plays Wagner	1964	3.75	7.50	15.00
—Black label with colorband, Capitol logo at top					
❑ TAO 2217 [M]	Kenton Plays Wagner	1964	3.00	6.00	12.00
—Black label with colorband, Capitol logo at top					
❑ DT 2327 [R]	Stan Kenton's Greatest Hits	1965	2.50	5.00	10.00
—Black label with colorband, Capitol logo at top					
❑ SM-2327	Stan Kenton's Greatest Hits	197?	2.00	4.00	8.00
—Reissue with new prefix					
❑ T 2327 [M]	Stan Kenton's Greatest Hits	1965	3.00	6.00	12.00
—Black label with colorband, Capitol logo at top					
❑ MAS 2424 [M]	Stan Kenton Conducts the Los Angeles Neophonic Orchestra	1966	3.00	6.00	12.00
—Black label with colorband, Capitol logo at top					
❑ SMAS 2424 [S]	Stan Kenton Conducts the Los Angeles Neophonic Orchestra	1966	3.75	7.50	15.00
—Black label with colorband, Capitol logo at top					
❑ ST 2655 [S]	Kenton Plays for Today	1966	3.75	7.50	15.00
—Black label with colorband, Capitol logo at top					
❑ T 2655 [M]	Kenton Plays for Today	1966	3.00	6.00	12.00
—Black label with colorband, Capitol logo at top					
❑ ST 2810	The World We Know	1968	3.00	6.00	12.00
❑ ST 2932	Jazz Compositions of Dee Barton	1968	3.00	6.00	12.00
❑ ST 2974	Finian's Rainbow	1968	3.00	6.00	12.00
❑ STCL 2989 [(3)]	The Stan Kenton Deluxe Set	1968	5.00	10.00	20.00
❑ M-11027	Artistry in Jazz	1972	2.50	5.00	10.00
❑ SM-11794 [M]	Cuban Fire!	1978	2.50	5.00	10.00
—Reissue of Capitol T 731					
❑ STB-12016 [(2)]	The Comprehensive Kenton	1979	3.75	7.50	15.00
❑ SM-12037	Kenton's West Side Story	1979	2.50	5.00	10.00
—Reissue of Capitol ST 1609					
❑ N-16182	Stan Kenton's Greatest Hits	1984	2.00	4.00	8.00
—Budget-line reissue					
CREATIVE WORLD					
❑ ST 1001	Kenton's Christmas	1970	3.00	6.00	12.00
❑ ST 1002 [R]	New Concepts of Artistry in Rhythm	197?	2.50	5.00	10.00
—Reissue of Capitol T 383					
❑ ST 1003 [R]	Contemporary Concepts	197?	2.00	4.00	8.00
—Reissue of Capitol T 666					
❑ ST 1004 [R]	Kenton in Stereo	197?	2.50	5.00	10.00
—Reissue of Capitol W 724					
❑ ST 1005	Lush Interlude	197?	2.50	5.00	10.00
—Reissue of Capitol ST 1130					
❑ ST 1006 [R]	City of Glass/This Modern World	197?	2.00	4.00	8.00
—Reissue of Capitol T 736					
❑ ST 1007	Kenton's West Side Story	197?	2.50	5.00	10.00
—Reissue of Capitol ST 1609					
❑ ST 1008 [R]	Cuban Fire!	197?	2.00	4.00	8.00
—Reissue of Capitol T 731					
❑ ST 1009 [R]	Innovations in Modern Music	197?	2.00	4.00	8.00
—Reissue of Capitol P 189					
❑ ST 1010	Adventures in Jazz	197?	2.50	5.00	10.00
—Reissue of Capitol ST 1796					
❑ ST 1011	Adventures in Time	197?	2.50	5.00	10.00
—Reissue of Capitol ST 1844					
❑ ST 1012	Adventures in Blues	197?	2.50	5.00	10.00
—Reissue of Capitol ST 1985					
❑ ST 1013	Stan Kenton Conducts the Los Angeles Neophonic Orchestra	197?	2.50	5.00	10.00
—Reissue of Capitol SMAS 2424					
❑ ST 1015 [(2)]	Live at Redlands University	1971	2.50	5.00	10.00
❑ ST 1017	The Romantic Approach	197?	2.00	4.00	8.00
—Reissue of Capitol ST 1533					
❑ ST 1018	The Sophisticated Approach	197?	2.50	5.00	10.00
—Reissue of Capitol ST 1674					
❑ ST 1019	Road Show, Volume 1	197?	2.50	5.00	10.00
—Partial reissue of Capitol STBO 1327					
❑ ST 1020	Road Show, Volume 2	197?	2.50	5.00	10.00
—Partial reissue of Capitol STBO 1327					
❑ ST 1022	Jazz Compositions of Dee Barton	197?	2.50	5.00	10.00
—Reissue of Capitol ST 2932					
❑ ST 1023 [R]	Stan Kenton Presents	197?	2.00	4.00	8.00
—Reissue of Capitol T 248					
❑ ST 1024	Kenton Plays Wagner	197?	2.50	5.00	10.00
—Reissue of Capitol STAO 2217					
❑ ST 1025	Adventures in Standards	197?	2.50	5.00	10.00
❑ ST 1026 [R]	Kenton Showcase	197?	2.00	4.00	8.00
—Reissue of Capitol W 524					
❑ ST 1027 [R]	Collector's Choice	197?	2.00	4.00	8.00
❑ ST 1028 [R]	The Fabulous Alumni of Stan Kenton	197?	2.00	4.00	8.00
❑ ST 1029 [R]	Some Women I've Known	197?	2.00	4.00	8.00
❑ ST 1030 [(4)R]	The Kenton Era	197?	5.00	10.00	20.00
—Reissue of Capitol TDB 569					
❑ ST 1031	Back to Balboa	197?	2.50	5.00	10.00
—Reissue of Capitol T 995					
❑ ST 1032	Kenton at the Las Vegas Tropicana	197?	2.50	5.00	10.00
—Reissue of Capitol ST 1460					
❑ ST 1033	The Kenton Touch	197?	2.50	5.00	10.00
—Reissue of Capitol ST 1276					
❑ ST 1034 [R]	Encores	197?	2.00	4.00	8.00
—Reissue of Capitol T 155					
❑ ST 1035 [R]	The Christy Years	197?	2.00	4.00	8.00
❑ ST 1036 [R]	Kenton By Request, Vol. I	197?	2.00	4.00	8.00
❑ ST 1037 [R]	A Concert in Progessive Jazz	197?	2.00	4.00	8.00
—Reissue of Capitol T 172					
❑ ST 1038	Artistry in Voices and Brass	197?	2.50	5.00	10.00
—Reissue of Capitol ST 2132					
❑ ST 1039 [Q]	Live at Brigham Young	1971	3.75	7.50	15.00
❑ ST 1040 [R]	Kenton By Request, Vol. II	197?	2.00	4.00	8.00
❑ ST 1041 [R]	Sketches on Standards	197?	2.00	4.00	8.00
—Reissue of Capitol T 426					
❑ ST 1042 [R]	Portraits on Standards	197?	2.00	4.00	8.00
—Reissue of Capitol T 462					
❑ ST 1043 [R]	Artistry in Rhythm	197?	2.00	4.00	8.00
—Reissue of Capitol DT 167					
❑ ST 1044	The Stage Door Swings	197?	2.50	5.00	10.00
—Reissue of Capitol ST 1166					
❑ ST 1045	Artistry in Bossa Nova	197?	2.50	5.00	10.00
❑ ST 1046	Stan Kenton with Jean Turner	197?	2.50	5.00	10.00
❑ ST 1047 [R]	Milestones	197?	2.00	4.00	8.00
—Reissue of Capitol T 190					
❑ ST 1048 [R]	Duet	197?	2.00	4.00	8.00
—Reissue of Capitol T 656					
❑ ST 1049	Standards in Silhouette	197?	2.50	5.00	10.00
—Reissue of Capitol ST 1394					
❑ ST 1050 [R]	The Lighter Side of Stan Kenton	197?	2.00	4.00	8.00
❑ ST 1057	Rendezvous with Kenton	197?	2.50	5.00	10.00
—Reissue of Capitol T 932					
❑ ST 1058 [(2)Q]	Live at Butler University	1972	5.00	10.00	20.00
❑ ST 1059 [(2)Q]	Stan Kenton with the Four Freshmen at Butler University	1972	5.00	10.00	20.00
❑ ST 1060 [(2)Q]	National Anthems of the World	1972	5.00	10.00	20.00
❑ ST 1061 [R]	Stan Kenton — Formative Years	197?	2.00	4.00	8.00
—Reissue of Decca DL 8259					
❑ ST 1062 [R]	Kenton By Request, Vol. III	197?	2.00	4.00	8.00
❑ ST 1063	Viva Kenton!	197?	2.50	5.00	10.00
—Reissue of Capitol SW 1305					
❑ ST 1064 [R]	Kenton By Request, Vol. IV	197?	2.00	4.00	8.00
❑ ST 1065	Birthday in Britain	1973	2.50	5.00	10.00
❑ ST 1066 [R]	Kenton By Request, Vol. V	197?	2.00	4.00	8.00
❑ ST 1067	Too Much	197?	2.50	5.00	10.00
❑ STCL 1068	The Ballad Style of Stan Kenton	197?	2.00	4.00	8.00
—Reissue of Capitol ST 1068					
❑ ST 1069	Kenton By Request, Vol. VI	197?	2.50	5.00	10.00
❑ ST 1070	7.5 on the Richter Scale	1973	2.50	5.00	10.00
❑ ST 1071	Solo	1973	2.50	5.00	10.00
❑ ST 1072	Kenton Plays Chicago	1974	2.50	5.00	10.00
❑ ST 1073	Fire, Fury and Fun	1974	2.50	5.00	10.00
❑ ST 1074	Hits in Concert	197?	2.50	5.00	10.00
❑ ST 1076	Kenton '76	1976	2.50	5.00	10.00
❑ ST 1077	Journey Into Capricorn	1977	2.50	5.00	10.00
❑ ST 1078 [R]	The Jazz Compositions of Stan Kenton	197?	2.00	4.00	8.00
❑ ST 1079	Street of Dreams	197?	2.50	5.00	10.00
❑ ST 1080	The Exciting Stan Kenton	197?	2.50	5.00	10.00
❑ CW-3005	Stan Kenton Presents Gabe Baltazar	1979	2.50	5.00	10.00
DECCA					
❑ DL 8259 [M]	Stan Kenton — Formative Years	195?	6.25	12.50	25.00
—All-black label with silver print					
❑ DL 8259 [M]	Stan Kenton — Formative Years	1960	3.75	7.50	15.00
—Black label with color bars					
HINDSIGHT					
❑ HSR-118	Stan Kenton 1941	1984	2.00	4.00	8.00
❑ HSR-124	Stan Kenton 1941, Volume 2	1984	2.00	4.00	8.00
❑ HSR-136	Stan Kenton 1943-44	1984	2.00	4.00	8.00
❑ HSR-147	Stan Kenton 1944-45	1984	2.00	4.00	8.00
❑ HSR-157	Stan Kenton 1945-47	1984	2.00	4.00	8.00
❑ HSR-195	Stan Kenton 1962	1984	2.00	4.00	8.00
INSIGHT					
❑ 206	Stan Kenton and His Orchestra, Volume 1	197?	2.50	5.00	10.00
❑ 217	Stan Kenton and His Orchestra, Volume 2	197?	2.50	5.00	10.00
LONDON PHASE 4					
❑ BP 44179/80 [(2)]	Stan Kenton Today	1972	10.00	20.00	40.00
❑ ST-44276	Live in Europe	1976	2.50	5.00	10.00
MOBILE FIDELITY					
❑ 1-091	Kenton Plays Wagner	1982	6.25	12.50	25.00
—Audiophile vinyl					
MOSAIC					
❑ MR6-136 [(6)]	The Complete Capitol Recordings of the Holman and Russo Charts	199?	30.00	60.00	120.00
❑ MQ10-163 [(10)]	The Complete Capitol Studio Recordings of Stan Kenton 1943-47	199?	50.00	100.00	200.00
SUNBEAM					
❑ 213	Artistry in Rhythm, 1944-45	197?	2.50	5.00	10.00
TIME-LIFE					
❑ STBB-13 [(2)]	Big Bands: Stan Kenton	1984	3.75	7.50	15.00

KENTON, STAN/JUNE CHRISTY/THE FOUR FRESHMEN
Albums
CAPITOL

Number	Title (A Side/B Side)	Yr	VG	VG+	NM
❑ STCL-575 [(3)]	Stan Kenton/June Christy/The Four Freshmen	1970	6.25	12.50	25.00

—Reissue of an album by each artist in a 3-LP box -- ST 1796 (Kenton), ST 516 (Christy), ST 1008 (Four Freshmen)

Number	Title (A Side/B Side)	Yr	VG	VG+	NM

KENTON, STAN, AND TEX RITTER Also see each artist's individual listings.
Albums
CAPITOL

Number	Title (A Side/B Side)	Yr	VG	VG+	NM
❑ ST 1757 [S]	Stan Kenton/Tex Ritter	1962	20.00	40.00	80.00
❑ T 1757 [M]	Stan Kenton/Tex Ritter	1962	15.00	30.00	60.00

KENTS, THE
45s
ARGO

❑ 5299	I Found My Girl/With All My Heart and Soul	1958	7.50	15.00	30.00

DOME

❑ 501	I Love You So/Happy Beat	1958	125.00	250.00	500.00

KERMIT; KERMIT AND FOZZIE BEAR; TWO MONSTERS See JIM HENSON.

KEROUAC, JACK
Albums
DOT

❑ DLP-3154 [M]	Poetry for the Beat Generation	1959	5000.	7500.	10000.

—Acknowledged to be extremely rare; approximately 130 copies were distributed and only a small handful are known to exist today; the same performance is on Hanover 5000

HANOVER

❑ HML-5000 [M]	Poetry for the Beat Generation	1959	100.00	200.00	400.00

—Reissue of Dot LP with new cover; STEVE ALLEN plays piano on this record

❑ HML-5006 [M]	Blues and Haikus	1959	62.50	125.00	250.00

—AL COHN and ZOOT SIMS play saxophones behind Kerouac on this album

RHINO

❑ R1-70939 [(4)]	The Jack Kerouac Collection	1990	15.00	30.00	60.00

—Box set compiling the Hanover and Verve LPs plus an LP of unreleased material

VERVE

❑ MGV-15005 [M]	Readings on the Beat Generation	1960	62.50	125.00	250.00

KERR, ANITA, SINGERS Includes records by "Anita and th' So-and-So's" and "The Little Dippers."
45s
AMPEX

Number	Title (A Side/B Side)	Yr	VG	VG+	NM
❑ 11042	Eli's Comin'/Something in the Way She Moves	1971	—	2.50	5.00
❑ 11050	Shine, Shine//Medley: O Come All Ye Faithful-Noel	1970	—	3.00	6.00
❑ 11051	Oh Holy Night/Medley: Angels We Have Heard on High-What Child Is This?-Joy to the World	1970	—	3.00	6.00

DECCA

❑ 27767	Borrowed Angel/My Evening	1951	3.00	6.00	12.00
❑ 27872	Have Faith/Pray	1951	3.00	6.00	12.00
❑ 28053	The Road Up Ahead/God Has Been Good to Me	1952	2.50	5.00	10.00
❑ 28260	A Promise and a Prayer/Mt Grandmother's Place	1952	2.50	5.00	10.00
❑ 28962	A Vision of the Blessed Mother/God Is Everywhere	1953	2.50	5.00	10.00
❑ 28996	After You/Not Mine	1954	2.50	5.00	10.00
❑ 30756	Give In, Give In/Keep Your Belt Buttoned Up, Baby	1958	2.00	4.00	8.00
❑ 9-31002	My Love Is a Kitten/Strange Little Melody	1959	2.00	4.00	8.00

—As "Anita Kerr Quartet"

❑ 33032	Mary Kaye's Theme/Where Do I Go from Here	1972	—	3.00	6.00

DOT

❑ 16602	Sails/For Just a Little While Tonight	1964	2.00	4.00	8.00

—As "The Little Dippers"

❑ 17210	Alfie/A House Is Not a Home	1969	—	2.50	5.00
❑ 17270	Lalena/Suppose	1969	—	2.50	5.00
❑ 17315	Ob-La-Di, Ob-La-Da/You and I	1969	—	2.50	5.00
❑ 17334	Coco/Money Rings Out Like Freedom	1969	—	2.50	5.00

RCA VICTOR

❑ 47-8246	Guitar Country/Waitin' for the Evening Train	1963	3.00	6.00	12.00

—With Chet Atkins

| ❑ 47-8332 | Copper Kettle/Summer Green and Winter White | 1964 | — | 3.00 | 6.00 |
| ❑ 47-7974 | Joey Baby/Rinky Tinky Rhythm | 1961 | 3.75 | 7.50 | 15.00 |

—As "Anita and th' So-and-So's"

❑ 47-8050	To Each His Own/Tell Tale	1962	3.00	6.00	12.00

—As "Anita and th' So-and-So's"

❑ PB-10388	The Masterpiece/At Seventeen	1975	—	2.00	4.00

UNIVERSITY

❑ 210	Forever/Two by Four	1959	2.50	5.00	10.00

—As "The Little Dippers"

❑ 603	Tonight/Be Sincere	1960	2.50	5.00	10.00

—As "The Little Dippers"

❑ 608	Lonely/I Wonder, I Wonder, I Wonder	1960	2.50	5.00	10.00

—As "The Little Dippers"

WARNER BROS.

❑ 5866	A Man and a Woman/Just Say Goodbye	1966	—	3.00	6.00
❑ 7010	One in a Row/The Ever Constant Sea	1967	—	3.00	6.00
❑ 7065	For Bert/I Can't Help Remembering You	1967	—	3.00	6.00
❑ 7085	In the Morning/The Smile You Save for Strangers	1967	—	3.00	6.00
❑ 7161	All This (She Does to Me)/No Salt on Her Tail	1967	—	3.00	6.00
❑ 7185	One Day/One Up on Me	1968	—	2.50	5.00
❑ 7211	Happiness/Wine in the Wind	1968	—	2.50	5.00

7-Inch Extended Plays
SESAC

❑ AD-49 [DJ]	On This Holy Night/Bring a Torch, Jeanette, Isabella//Sleep, Sweet Jesus, Sleep/The 12 Days Of Christmas	197?	—	3.00	6.00
❑ AD-56 [DJ]	Deck the Halls/All Through The Night//Rise Up Shepherd and Foller/Christmas Is the Day	197?	—	3.00	6.00
❑ AD-56 [PS]	Deck the Halls/All Through The Night//Rise Up Shepherd and Foller/Christmas Is the Day	197?	—	3.00	6.00

Albums
AMPEX

| ❑ A-10136 | Grow to Know Me | 1971 | 2.50 | 5.00 | 10.00 |
| ❑ A-10142 | A Christmas Story | 1971 | 3.00 | 6.00 | 12.00 |

—With the Royal Philharmonic Orchestra

BAINBRIDGE

❑ 6224	Slightly Baroque	1981	2.50	5.00	10.00
❑ 6226	I Sang with Jim Reeves	1981	2.50	5.00	10.00
❑ 6227	The Simon and Garfunkel Songbook	1981	2.50	5.00	10.00
❑ 6228	'Round Midnight	1981	2.50	5.00	10.00

CENTURY

Number	Title (A Side/B Side)	Yr	VG	VG+	NM
❑ 1160	Anita Kerr Performs Wonder's	1979	2.50	5.00	10.00

DECCA

❑ DL 4061 [M]	For You, For Me, Forevermore	1960	3.75	7.50	15.00
❑ DL 8647 [M]	Quartet Voices in Hi-Fi	1958	3.75	7.50	15.00
❑ DL 74061 [S]	For You, For Me, Forevermore	1960	5.00	10.00	20.00
❑ DL 75159	Till the End of Time	1970	2.50	5.00	10.00

DOT

❑ DLP 25906	The Anita Kerr Singers Reflect on the Hits of Burt Bacharach & Hal David	1969	2.50	5.00	10.00
❑ DLP 25944	Precious Teresa	1969	2.50	5.00	10.00
❑ DLP 25961	Velvet Voices and Bold Brass	1969	2.50	5.00	10.00
❑ DLP 25970	Touchlove	1970	2.50	5.00	10.00

RCA CAMDEN

❑ CAS-2209	Georgia on My Mind	1968	2.50	5.00	10.00

RCA VICTOR

❑ APL1-1166	The Anita Kerr Singers	1975	2.50	5.00	10.00
❑ APL1-2298	Anite Kerr and the French Connection	1977	2.50	5.00	10.00
❑ LPM-2480 [M]	From Nashville…The Hit Sound	1962	3.00	6.00	12.00
❑ LSP-2480 [S]	From Nashville…The Hit Sound	1962	3.75	7.50	15.00
❑ LPM-2581 [M]	"The Genius" In Harmony	1962	3.00	6.00	12.00
❑ LSP-2581 [S]	"The Genius" In Harmony	1962	3.75	7.50	15.00
❑ LPM-2679 [M]	Tender Words	1963	3.00	6.00	12.00
❑ LSP-2679 [S]	Tender Words	1963	3.75	7.50	15.00
❑ LPM-3322 [M]	Mellow Moods of Love	1965	3.00	6.00	12.00
❑ LSP-3322 [S]	Mellow Moods of Love	1965	3.75	7.50	15.00
❑ LPM-3428 [M]	We Dig Mancini	1965	3.00	6.00	12.00
❑ LSP-3428 [S]	We Dig Mancini	1965	3.75	7.50	15.00
❑ LPM-3485 [M]	Sunday Serenade	1966	3.00	6.00	12.00
❑ LSP-3485 [S]	Sunday Serenade	1966	3.75	7.50	15.00

VOCALION

❑ VL 73899	For You	1969	2.50	5.00	10.00

WARNER BROS.

❑ W 1665 [M]	Slightly Baroque	1966	3.00	6.00	12.00
❑ WS 1665 [S]	Slightly Baroque	1966	3.75	7.50	15.00
❑ W 1707 [M]	Bert Kaempfert Turns Us On!	1967	3.75	7.50	15.00
❑ WS 1707 [S]	Bert Kaempfert Turns Us On!	1967	3.00	6.00	12.00
❑ W 1724 [M]	All You Need Is Love	1967	3.75	7.50	15.00
❑ WS 1724 [S]	All You Need Is Love	1967	3.00	6.00	12.00

WORD

| ❑ 8647 | Hallelujah Brass | 197? | 2.50 | 5.00 | 10.00 |
| ❑ 8692 | Hymns | 197? | 2.50 | 5.00 | 10.00 |

—With Kurt Kaiser

❑ 8696	Walk a Little Slower	197?	2.50	5.00	10.00
❑ 8706	Precious Memories	197?	2.50	5.00	10.00
❑ 8707	Hallelujah Guitars	197?	2.50	5.00	10.00
❑ 8741	Hallelujah Woodwinds	197?	2.50	5.00	10.00
❑ 8808	Hallelujah Voices	197?	2.50	5.00	10.00

KERSHAW, RUSTY AND DOUG
45s
FEATURE

❑ 2003	It's Better to Be a Has Been (Than Be a Never Was)/No, No, It's Not So	1954	25.00	50.00	100.00

HICKORY

❑ 1027	So Lovely, Baby/Why Cry for You	1955	7.50	15.00	30.00
❑ 1036	Can I Be Dreaming/Look Around	1955	7.50	15.00	30.00
❑ 1042	Honey Honey/Let's Stay Together	1956	7.50	15.00	30.00
❑ 1048	Hey You There/Your Crazy, Crazy Heart	1956	7.50	15.00	30.00
❑ 1055	I'll Understand/Mister Love	1956	7.50	15.00	30.00
❑ 1061	If I Win, I Win/Money	1957	7.50	15.00	30.00

—B-side by Al Terry

❑ 1063	Going Down the Road/You'll See	1957	10.00	20.00	40.00
❑ 1068	Love Me to Pieces/I Never Had the Blues	1957	10.00	20.00	40.00
❑ 1072	Dream Queen/Take My Love	1957	7.50	15.00	30.00
❑ 1077	Hey Mae/Why Don't You Love Me	1958	7.50	15.00	30.00
❑ 1083	Hey Sheriff/Sweet Thing	1958	7.50	15.00	30.00
❑ 1091	It's Too Late/We'll Do It Anyway	1958	7.50	15.00	30.00
❑ 1095	Kaw-Liga/Never Love Again	1959	15.00	30.00	60.00
❑ 1101	Dancing Shoes/I Love You Like This	1959	15.00	30.00	60.00
❑ 1110	The Love I Want/Oh Love	1959	7.50	15.00	30.00
❑ 1137	Louisiana Man/Make Me Realize	1960	12.50	25.00	50.00
❑ 1151	Diggy Liggy Lo/Hey Mae	1961	15.00	30.00	60.00
❑ 1163	Cheated Too/So Lovely Baby	1961	7.50	15.00	30.00
❑ 1177	Cajun Joe (Bully of the Bayou)/Sweet Sweet to Me	1962	7.50	15.00	30.00
❑ 1575	Louisiana Man/(Our Own) Jole Blon	1970	2.50	5.00	10.00

RCA VICTOR

❑ 47-8266	Cajun Stripper/Half the Time	1963	3.75	7.50	15.00
❑ 47-8362	Cleopatra/Malinda	1964	3.75	7.50	15.00
❑ 47-8415	St. Louis Blues/I Can't See Myself	1964	3.75	7.50	15.00

Albums
HICKORY

❑ LPM-103 [M]	Rusty and Doug Sing Louisiana Man	1960	30.00	60.00	120.00

HICKORY/MGM

❑ H3G-4506	Louisiana Man	1974	5.00	10.00	20.00

KESEY, KEN
Albums
SOUND CITY

❑ 27690 [M]	The Acid Test	1967	75.00	150.00	300.00

—THE GRATEFUL DEAD appear on this LP

KESNER, DICK
Albums
BRUNSWICK

❑ BL 54044 [M]	Lawrence Welk Presents Dick Kesner	1958	5.00	10.00	20.00
❑ BL 54051 [M]	Dick Kesner and His Magic Stradivarius	1959	3.75	7.50	15.00
❑ BL 54054 [M]	Intermezzo	1960	3.75	7.50	15.00
❑ BL 754044 [S]	Lawrence Welk Presents Dick Kesner	1959	6.25	12.50	25.00
❑ BL 754051 [S]	Dick Kesner and His Magic Stradivarius	1959	5.00	10.00	20.00
❑ BL 754054 [S]	Intermezzo	1960	5.00	10.00	20.00

CORAL

❑ CRL 57352 [M]	Music of Hawaii	1960	3.00	6.00	12.00
❑ CRL 57360 [M]	A "New" Old Refrain	1961	3.00	6.00	12.00
❑ CRL 57376 [M]	The Sound of Gypsy Music	1961	3.00	6.00	12.00

K

Number	Title (A Side/B Side)	Yr	VG	VG+	NM
❏ CRL 57393 [M] Amor Latino		1962	3.00	6.00	12.00
❏ CRL 57435 [M] Golden Favorites		1964	3.00	6.00	12.00
❏ CRL 757352 [S] Music of Hawaii		1960	3.75	7.50	15.00
❏ CRL 757360 [S] A "New" Old Refrain		1961	3.75	7.50	15.00
❏ CRL 757376 [S] The Sound of Gypsy Music		1961	3.75	7.50	15.00
❏ CRL 757393 [S] Amor Latino		1962	3.75	7.50	15.00
❏ CRL 757435 [S] Golden Favorites		1964	3.75	7.50	15.00

VOCALION

Number	Title	Yr	VG	VG+	NM
❏ VL 3777 [M]	Latin Favorites	196?	3.00	6.00	12.00
❏ VL 73777 [S]	Latin Favorites	196?	3.75	7.50	15.00

KESTRELS, THE
45s
LAURIE

Number	Title	Yr	VG	VG+	NM
❏ 3053	There Comes a Time/In the Chapel in the Moonlight	1960	6.25	12.50	25.00

KEY, JOANIE
45s
HIT

❏ 179	Anything/My Love, Forgive Me	1965	2.00	4.00	8.00

—B-side by Fred York

KEYES, TROY
45s
ABC

❏ 11027	Love Explosion/I'm Crying (Inside)	1967	2.50	5.00	10.00
❏ 11060	No Sad Songs/You Told Your Story (Now Let Me Tell Mine)	1968	3.75	7.50	15.00
❏ 11116	A Good Love Gone Bad/I Can Wait My Turn	1968	5.00	10.00	20.00

—With Norma Jenkins

KEYMEN, THE
45s
ABC-PARAMOUNT

❏ 9976	Sentimental Journey/Like Help, Man	1958	3.75	7.50	15.00
❏ 9977 [M]	Miss You/Isle of Capri	1958	3.75	7.50	15.00
❏ S-9977 [S]	Miss You/Isle of Capri	1958	6.25	12.50	25.00
❏ 9991 [M]	Gazachstahagen/Miss You	1959	3.75	7.50	15.00
❏ S-9991 [S]	Gazachstahagen/Miss You	1959	6.25	12.50	25.00
❏ 10016	Dream/Nancy Lee	1959	3.00	6.00	12.00
❏ 10039	Camilia/Cha Cha Marcha Congo	1959	3.00	6.00	12.00

Albums
ABC-PARAMOUNT

❏ 258 [M]	Dance with Dick Clark	1958	7.50	15.00	30.00
❏ S-258 [S]	Dance with Dick Clark	1958	12.50	25.00	50.00
❏ 288 [M]	Dance with Dick Clark, Volume 2	1959	7.50	15.00	30.00
❏ S-288 [S]	Dance with Dick Clark, Volume 2	1959	12.50	25.00	50.00

CORAL

❏ CRL 57112 [M]	Vocal Sounds of the Keymen	1957	7.50	15.00	30.00

GOLDUST

❏ LPS-153 [M]	The Keymen Live	196?	12.50	25.00	50.00

KEYNOTES, THE Possibly all the same group.
45s
APOLLO

❏ 478	Suddenly/Zenda	1955	37.50	75.00	150.00
❏ 484	I Don't Know/A Star	1955	20.00	40.00	80.00
❏ 493	Really Wish You Were Here/Bye Bye Baby	1956	30.00	60.00	120.00
❏ 498	Now I Know/Zup Zup	1956	25.00	50.00	100.00
❏ 503	In the Evening/O Yeah Hm-m-m	1956	20.00	40.00	80.00
❏ 513	One Little Kiss/Now I Know	1957	20.00	40.00	80.00

DOT

❏ 15225	Who/They Say	1954	7.50	15.00	30.00

INDEX

❏ 101	Open the Door (To Your Heart)/Dum-De, Dum-Dum	1958	25.00	50.00	100.00

POP

❏ 111	Carelessly/Congratulations Baby	1957	20.00	40.00	80.00

TOP RANK

❏ 2005	With These Rings/We're Not Getting Along	1959	3.75	7.50	15.00

KEYSTONERS, THE
45s
EPIC

❏ 9187	The Magic Kiss/After I Propose	1956	15.00	30.00	60.00

G&M

❏ 102	The Magic Kiss/I'd Write About the Blues	1956	75.00	150.00	300.00

OKEH

❏ 7210	The Magic Kiss/After I Propose	1964	5.00	10.00	20.00

RIFF

❏ 202	Sleep and Dream/T.V. Gal	1961	50.00	100.00	200.00

KEYTONES, THE
45s
CHELSEA

❏ 101	I Don't Care/La-Do-Da Da	1962	7.50	15.00	30.00
❏ 1013	Sweet Chariot/One, Two, Three	1963	3.75	7.50	15.00

OLD TOWN

❏ 1041	Seven Wonders of the World/A Fool in Love	1957	25.00	50.00	100.00
❏ 1041	Wonders of the World/A Fool in Love	1957	75.00	150.00	300.00

KHAZAD DOOM
Albums
LPL

❏ 892	Level 6 1/2	1970	250.00	500.00	1000.

KICKSTANDS, THE
Albums
CAPITOL

❏ ST 2078 [S]	Black Boots and Bikes	1964	37.50	75.00	150.00
❏ T 2078 [M]	Black Boots and Bikes	1964	30.00	60.00	120.00
❏ T/ST 2078	Black Boots and Bikes Bonus Fold-Out	1964	12.50	25.00	50.00

KID, THE
45s
RUMBLE

❏ 1347	Sleep Tight/True Love	1959	45.00	90.00	180.00

KIDD, JOHNNY, AND THE PIRATES
45s
APT

❏ 25040	Shakin' All Over/Yes Sir, That's My Baby	1960	6.25	12.50	25.00

CAPITOL

❏ 5065	I'll Never Get Over You/Then I Got Everything	1963	3.75	7.50	15.00

KIDDS, THE
45s
IMPERIAL

❏ 5335	Are You Forgetting Me/Drunk, Drunk, Drunk	1955	125.00	250.00	500.00

POST

❏ 2003	You Broke My Heart/I Won't Be Back	1955	75.00	150.00	300.00

KIDS NEXT DOOR, THE
45s
DECCA

❏ 32157	The Devil Rides in Jericho/Hold Me, Now and Forever	1967	2.00	4.00	8.00

4 CORNERS OF THE WORLD

❏ 129	Inky Dinky Spider (The Spider Song)/Goodbye, Don't Cry (Fare Thee Well)	1965	2.00	4.00	8.00
❏ 129 [PS]	Inky Dinky Spider (The Spider Song)/Goodbye, Don't Cry (Fare Thee Well)	1965	3.00	6.00	12.00

KILGORE, MERLE
45s
ASHLEY

❏ 6000	Packing and Unpacking/Beyond My Conscience and the Door	1968	2.50	5.00	10.00
❏ 35007	That's Alright/God Bless the Working Man	197?	—	3.50	7.00

COLUMBIA

❏ 4-44279	Fast Talking Louisiana Man/Avenue of Tears	1967	2.50	5.00	10.00
❏ 4-44463	Patches (Made the Change)/Wild Rose	1968	2.50	5.00	10.00

D

❏ 1042	It'll Be My First Time/I Take a Trip to the Moon	1959	5.00	10.00	20.00

ELEKTRA

❏ 47252	Mister Garfield/I'm a One Woman Man	1981	—	2.50	5.00
❏ 69895	The Night They Drove Old Dixie Down/She Went a Little Bit Farther	1982	—	2.50	5.00

EPIC

❏ 5-9762	Every Day's a Holiday/It's All Over Now	1965	3.00	6.00	12.00
❏ 5-9816	Dig, Dig, Dig (There's No More)/Help Me Up Darling (All Fools Fall Down)	1965	3.00	6.00	12.00
❏ 5-9873	Baby, I Got It/Mama's Killing Daddy	1965	3.00	6.00	12.00
❏ 5-10049	Nevada Smith/Too Many Mountains	1966	3.00	6.00	12.00
❏ 5-10146	I Just Don't Care Anymore/I'd Cry Like a Baby	1967	3.00	6.00	12.00

IMPERIAL

❏ 5379	Please, Please, Please/Teen-Ager's Holiday	1956	7.50	15.00	30.00
❏ 5409	Ernie/Trying to Find (Someone Like You)	1956	15.00	30.00	60.00
❏ 5555	Tom Dooley, Jr./Hang Doll	1958	5.00	10.00	20.00
❏ 5584	Start All Over Again/Static	1959	5.00	10.00	20.00
❏ 8256	More and More/What Makes Me Love You	1954	10.00	20.00	40.00
❏ 8266	Seeing Double, Feeling Single/It Can't Rain	1954	10.00	20.00	40.00
❏ 8300	Everybody Needs a Little Lovin'/Funny Feelin'	1955	12.50	25.00	50.00

MERCURY

❏ 71839	Wicked City/I'll Take Ginger and Run Away	1961	5.00	10.00	20.00
❏ 71918	42 in Chicago/Lover's Hell	1962	5.00	10.00	20.00
❏ 71978	A Girl Named Liz/Trouble at the Towers	1962	5.00	10.00	20.00
❏ 72048	Ain't Nothin' but a Man/Somethin' Goin' On	1962	5.00	10.00	20.00

MGM

❏ 13168	Five Miles Down the Road/Whiskey Road	1963	3.75	7.50	15.00
❏ 13277	The Bell Witch/Slow Hard Way	1964	3.75	7.50	15.00

PARKWAY

❏ 864	I Am/When It Rains the Blues on You	1963	3.75	7.50	15.00

STARDAY

❏ 469	Dear Mama/Jimmie Brings Sunshine	1959	5.00	10.00	20.00
❏ 497	Love Has Made You Beautiful/Gettin' Old Before My Time	1960	5.00	10.00	20.00
❏ 533	Daddy's Place/Just Another Song Now	1961	5.00	10.00	20.00
❏ 644	Pinball Machine/Old Smokey	1963	3.75	7.50	15.00
❏ 964	Different Kind of Pretty/My Side of Life	1973	2.00	4.00	8.00

WARNER BROS.

❏ 7831	Montgomery Mable/Old Home Filler-Up An' Keep On-a Truckin' Cafe	1974	—	2.50	5.00
❏ 8039	Love o' Love/Baby's Comin' Home to Stay	1974	—	2.50	5.00
❏ 8081	I'm Not Responsible/Tied	1975	—	2.50	5.00
❏ 29062	Guilty/When You Leave That Way You Can Never Go Back	1985	—	2.00	4.00
❏ 29267	Just Out of Reach/Road Women	1984	—	2.00	4.00

Albums
STARDAY

❏ SLP-251 [M]	There's Gold in Them Thar Hills	1963	7.50	15.00	30.00

WING

❏ MGW-12316 [M]	Tall Texan	196?	3.75	7.50	15.00
❏ SRW-16316 [S]	Tall Texan	196?	3.00	6.00	12.00

KILGORE, THEOLA
45s
CANDIX

❏ 311	The Sound of My Man/Later I'll Cry	1960	6.25	12.50	25.00

KT

❏ 501	I'll Keep Trying/He's Coming Back to Me	1964	3.75	7.50	15.00

MERCURY

❏ 72564	I Can't Stand It/It's Gonna Be Alright	1966	3.00	6.00	12.00

SCEPTER

❏ 12170	The Love of My Man/As Long As You Need Me	1966	3.00	6.00	12.00

SEROCK

❏ 2004	The Love of My Man/I Know That He Loves Me	1963	3.75	7.50	15.00
❏ 2006	This Is My Prayer/As Long As You Need Me (Want Me, Love Me)	1963	3.75	7.50	15.00

Number	Title (A Side/B Side)	Yr	VG	VG+	NM

KILLEBREW, GEORGE
45s
HIT

Number	Title (A Side/B Side)	Yr	VG	VG+	NM
❏ 27	She's Not You/Sheila	1962	2.00	4.00	8.00

—B-side by Sandy Gold

| ❏ 46 | Half Heaven Half Heartache/I'm Gonna Be Warm This Winter | 1962 | 2.00 | 4.00 | 8.00 |

—B-side by Connie Landers

KILLING FLOOR
Albums
SIRE

| ❏ SES-97019 | Killing Floor | 1970 | 12.50 | 25.00 | 50.00 |

KIM, ANDY
45s
CAPITOL

❏ 3895	Rock Me Gently/Rock Me Gently (Part 2)	1974	—	2.50	5.00
❏ 3962	Fire, Baby, I'm on Fire/Here Comes the Mornin'	1974	—	2.00	4.00
❏ 3962 [PS]	Fire, Baby, I'm on Fire/Here Comes the Mornin'	1974	—	3.00	6.00
❏ 4032	Hang Up Those Rock 'N' Roll Shoes/Essence of Joan	1975	—	2.00	4.00
❏ 4086	Mary Ann/You Are My Everything	1975	—	2.00	4.00
❏ 4130	(She Got Me) Dancin'/Baby, You're All I Got	1975	—	2.00	4.00
❏ 4234	Oh, Pretty Woman/Baby You're All I Got	1976	—	2.00	4.00

RED BIRD

| ❏ 10-040 | I Hear You Say (I Love You Baby)/Falling in Love | 1965 | 3.75 | 7.50 | 15.00 |

STEED

❏ 707	How'd We Ever Get This Way?/Are You Ever Coming Home	1968	2.00	4.00	8.00
❏ 710	Shoot 'Em Up Baby/Ordinary Kind of Girl	1968	2.00	4.00	8.00
❏ 711	Rainbow Ride/Resurrection	1968	2.00	4.00	8.00
❏ 715	Foundation of My Soul/Tricia Tell Your Daddy	1969	2.00	4.00	8.00
❏ 716	Baby I Love You/Gee Girl	1969	2.00	4.00	8.00
❏ 720	So Good Together/I Got to Know	1969	—	3.00	6.00
❏ 720 [PS]	So Good Together/I Got to Know	1969	3.00	6.00	12.00
❏ 723	A Friend in the City/You	1970	—	3.00	6.00
❏ 723 [PS]	A Friend in the City/You	1970	3.00	6.00	12.00
❏ 727	It's Your Life/To Be Continued	1970	—	3.00	6.00
❏ 729	Be My Baby/Love That Little Woman	1970	—	3.00	6.00
❏ 731	I Wish I Were/Walking My La De La	1971	—	3.00	6.00
❏ 734	I Been Moved/If I Had You Here	1971	—	3.00	6.00
❏ 734 [PS]	I Been Moved/If I Had You Here	1971	3.00	6.00	12.00

TCF

| ❏ 5 | Give Me Your Love/Li'l Liz (I Love You) | 1964 | 3.75 | 7.50 | 15.00 |

20TH CENTURY FOX

| ❏ 6709 | Give Me Your Love/That Girl | 1968 | 2.00 | 4.00 | 8.00 |

UNI

❏ 55332	Who Has the Answers?/Shady Hollow Dreamers	1972	—	2.50	5.00
❏ 55353	Love Song/Love the Poor Boy	1972	—	2.50	5.00
❏ 55356	Oh What a Day/Sunshine	1972	—	2.50	5.00

UNITED ARTISTS

| ❏ 591 | Love Me, Love Me/I Loved You Once | 1963 | 3.75 | 7.50 | 15.00 |

Albums
ABC DUNHILL

| ❏ DSDP-50193 | Andy Kim's Greatest Hits | 1974 | 3.00 | 6.00 | 12.00 |

—Reissue of Steed 37008
CAPITOL

| ❏ ST-11318 | Andy Kim | 1974 | 3.00 | 6.00 | 12.00 |
| ❏ ST-11368 | The Pilot | 1975 | 3.00 | 6.00 | 12.00 |

STEED

| ❏ ST-7001 [M] | How Did We Ever Get This Way? | 1968 | 10.00 | 20.00 | 40.00 |

—In stereo cover with "Monaural" sticker

❏ STS-37001 [S]	How Did We Ever Get This Way?	1968	3.75	7.50	15.00
❏ STS-37002	Rainbow Ride	1969	3.75	7.50	15.00
❏ ST 37004	Baby I Love You	1969	3.75	7.50	15.00
❏ ST 37008	Andy Kim's Greatest Hits	1970	3.75	7.50	15.00

UNI

| ❏ 73137 | Andy Kim | 1972 | 3.00 | 6.00 | 12.00 |

KIMBERLY, ADRIAN Actually DON EVERLY.
45s
CALLIOPE

❏ 6501	The Graduation Song...Pomp and Circumstance/Black Mountain Stomp	1961	10.00	20.00	40.00
❏ 6503	Greensleeves/God Bless America	1961	10.00	20.00	40.00
❏ 6504	When You Wish Upon a Star/Draggin' Dragon	1961	10.00	20.00	40.00

KIMBERLYS, THE
45s
CANADIAN AMERICAN

❏ 138	Kimberly/Once	1962	2.50	5.00	10.00
❏ 147	Save Me a Kiss at Your Wedding/You Just Smiled	1962	2.50	5.00	10.00
❏ 154	Since the Word Got Around/One Room Flat	1963	2.50	5.00	10.00
❏ 160	Forever/I Won't Be Back This Year	1963	2.50	5.00	10.00

COLUMBIA

❏ 4-43287	You Can't Roller Skate in a Buffalo Herd/Four Long Seasons	1965	2.50	5.00	10.00
❏ 4-43399	Denver/Pretty Little Children	1965	2.50	5.00	10.00
❏ 4-43601	Soldiers and Lilies/Don't Send Me Away	1965	2.50	5.00	10.00
❏ 4-44403	I Never Will Marry/Early Morning Sun	1967	2.00	4.00	8.00

HAPPY TIGER

❏ 535	Elusive Butterfly/Take Me with You	1970	—	3.50	7.00
❏ 547	Family/Leavin' California	1970	—	3.50	7.00
❏ 548	Let It Be/Hello and Happy Birthday	1970	—	3.50	7.00

—As "Verna and the Kimberlys"

❏ 561	And I Love Her/Sal's Got a Sugar Lip	1970	—	3.50	7.00
❏ 572	I Don't Know How to Love Him-Everything's Alright/Hello and Happy Birthday	1971	—	3.50	7.00
❏ 577	Any Way That You Want Me/Sunny Day Blues	1971	—	3.50	7.00

RCA VICTOR

| ❏ 47-9782 | Drivin' Nails in the Wall/These New Changing Times | 1969 | 2.00 | 4.00 | 8.00 |

HAPPY TIGER

| ❏ HT-1006 | The Kimberlys | 1970 | 3.75 | 7.50 | 15.00 |
| ❏ HT-1014 | New Horizon | 1970 | 3.75 | 7.50 | 15.00 |

KIME, WARREN, AND HIS BRASS IMPACT ORCHESTRA
45s
COMMAND

❏ 4093	The Breeze and I/Mas Que Nada	1967	—	2.50	5.00
❏ 4106	Feeling Good/No Moon at All	1967	—	2.50	5.00
❏ 4118	Let's Get Away From It All/On My Mind	1968	—	2.50	5.00

Albums
COMMAND

❏ 33-910 [M]	Brass Impact	1967	2.50	5.00	10.00
❏ SD-910 [S]	Brass Impact	1967	3.00	6.00	12.00
❏ 33-919 [M]	Explosive Brass Impact	1967	2.50	5.00	10.00
❏ SD-919 [S]	Explosive Brass Impact	1967	3.00	6.00	12.00

KING, ALBERT
45s
ATLANTIC

| ❏ 2604 | The Hunter/As the Years Go Passing By | 1969 | 2.00 | 4.00 | 8.00 |

BOBBIN

❏ 114	Why Are You So Mean to Me?/Ooh-Ee Baby	1959	6.25	12.50	25.00
❏ 119	Need You By My Side/The Time Has Come	1960	6.25	12.50	25.00
❏ 126	Blues at Sunrise/Let's Have a Natural Ball	1960	6.25	12.50	25.00
❏ 129	I Walked All Night Long/I've Made Nights By Myself	1961	6.25	12.50	25.00
❏ 130	Travelin' to California/Dyna-Flow	1961	6.25	12.50	25.00
❏ 131	Don't Thow Your Love on Me So Strong/This Morning	1961	6.25	12.50	25.00
❏ 135	I Get Evil/What Can I Do to Change Your Mind	1962	6.25	12.50	25.00
❏ 141	I'll Do Anything for You/Got to Be Some Changes Made	1963	6.25	12.50	25.00
❏ 143	Old Blue Ribbon/I've Made Nights By Myself	1963	6.25	12.50	25.00

KING

❏ 5575	Don't Throw Your Love on Me So Strong/This Morning	1961	3.00	6.00	12.00
❏ 5588	Travelin' to California/Dyna-Flow	1961	3.00	6.00	12.00
❏ 5751	This Funny Feeling/Had You Told It Like It Was	1963	3.00	6.00	12.00
❏ 6265	Travelin' to California/Don't Throw Your Love on Me So Strong	1969	2.00	4.00	8.00

PARROT

| ❏ 798 | Bad Luck Blues/Be On Your Merry Way | 1954 | 400.00 | 800.00 | 1200. |

STAX

❏ 0020	Night Stomp/Blues Power	1968	2.00	4.00	8.00
❏ 0034	Drowning on Dry Land (Vocal)/(Instrumental)	1969	2.00	4.00	8.00
❏ 0058	Wrapped Up in Love Again/Cockroach	1969	2.00	4.00	8.00
❏ 0069	Can't You See What You're Doing to Me/Cold Sweat	1970	2.00	4.00	8.00
❏ 0101	Everybody Wants to Go to Heaven/Lovejoy, Ill.	1971	—	3.50	7.00
❏ 0121	Angel of Mercy/Funky London	1972	—	3.50	7.00
❏ 0135	I'll Play the Blues for You (Part 1)/I'll Play the Blues for You (Part 2)	1972	—	3.50	7.00
❏ 0147	Breaking Up Somebody's Home/Little Brother	1972	—	3.50	7.00
❏ 0166	The High Cost of Loving/Playing on Me	1973	—	3.50	7.00
❏ 0189	That's What the Blues Is All About/I Wanna Get Funky	1973	—	3.50	7.00
❏ 190	Laundromat Blues/Overall Junction	1966	2.50	5.00	10.00
❏ 197	Funk-Shun/Pretty Woman (Can't Make You Love Me)	1966	2.50	5.00	10.00
❏ 201	Crosscut Saw/Down Don't Bother Me	1966	2.50	5.00	10.00
❏ 217	Born Under a Bad Sign/Personal Manager	1967	2.50	5.00	10.00
❏ 0217	I Can Hear Nothing But the Blues/Flat Tire	1974	—	3.50	7.00
❏ 0228	Crosscut Saw/Don't Burn Down the Bridge	1974	—	3.50	7.00
❏ 0234	Santa Claus Wants Some Lovin'/Don't Burn Down the Bridges	1974	—	3.50	7.00
❏ 241	Cold Feet/Drive a Hard Bargain	1967	2.50	5.00	10.00
❏ 252	(I Love) Lucy/You're Gonna Need Me	1968	2.50	5.00	10.00
❏ 1056	Santa Claus Wants Some Lovin'/What Do The Lonely Do At Christmas?	197?	—	3.00	6.00

—B-side by Emotions; reissue

| ❏ 1073 | Christmas Comes Once A Year/I'll Be Your Santa Claus | 197? | — | 2.50 | 5.00 |

—B-side by Rufus Thomas; reissue

| ❏ 3203 | The Pinch Paid Off (Part 1)/The Pinch Paid Off (Part 2) | 1978 | — | 2.50 | 5.00 |
| ❏ 3225 | Santa Claus Wants Some Lovin'/Don't Burn Down the Bridges | 1979 | — | 3.00 | 6.00 |

TOMATO

❏ 10001	Call My Job/Love Shack	1978	—	2.50	5.00
❏ 10002	Chump Change/Good Time Charlie	1978	—	2.50	5.00
❏ 10009	The Very Thought of You/I Get Evil	1979	—	2.50	5.00
❏ 10012	Born Under a Bad Sign/I've Got the Blues	1979	—	2.50	5.00

UTOPIA

❏ PB-10544	Cadillac Assembly Line/Nobody Wants a Loser	1976	—	2.50	5.00
❏ PB-10682	Sensation, Communication Together/Gonna Make It Somehow	1976	—	2.50	5.00
❏ PB-10770	Guitar Man/Rub My Back	1976	—	2.50	5.00
❏ PB-10879	Ain't Nothing You Can Do/I Don't Care What My Baby Do	1977	—	2.50	5.00

Albums
ATLANTIC

| ❏ SD 8213 | King of the Blues Guitar | 1969 | 6.25 | 12.50 | 25.00 |

FANTASY

| ❏ 9627 | San Francisco '83 | 1983 | 2.50 | 5.00 | 10.00 |
| ❏ 9633 | I'm in a Phone Booth, Baby | 1984 | 2.50 | 5.00 | 10.00 |

KING

| ❏ 852 [M] | Big Blues | 1963 | 125.00 | 250.00 | 500.00 |
| ❏ KS-1060 | Travelin' to California | 1969 | 6.25 | 12.50 | 25.00 |

MODERN BLUES

| ❏ MBLP-723 | Let's Have a Natural Ball | 198? | 2.50 | 5.00 | 10.00 |

STAX

❏ ST-723 [M]	Born Under a Bad Sign	1967	20.00	40.00	80.00
❏ STS-723 [S]	Born Under a Bad Sign	1967	30.00	60.00	120.00
❏ STS-2003	Live Wire/Blues Power	1968	12.50	25.00	50.00

K

Number	Title (A Side/B Side)	Yr	VG	VG+	NM
❏ STS-2010	Years Gone By	1969	6.25	12.50	25.00
❏ STS-2015	King Does the King's Thing	1969	6.25	12.50	25.00
❏ STS-2040	Lovejoy	1971	5.00	10.00	20.00
❏ STS-3009	I'll Play the Blues for You	1972	5.00	10.00	20.00
❏ STX-4101	The Pinch	1977	3.00	6.00	12.00
❏ STX-4128	Live Wire/Blues Power	1979	2.50	5.00	10.00
—Reissue of 2003					
❏ STX-4132	Montreux Festival	1980	2.50	5.00	10.00
—Retitled reissue of 5520					
❏ STS-5505	I Wanna Get Funky	1974	3.75	7.50	15.00
❏ STS-5520	Montreux Festival	1975	3.75	7.50	15.00
❏ MPS-8504	Blues for Elvis	1981	2.50	5.00	10.00
—Retitled reissue of 2015					
❏ MPS-8513	I'll Play the Blues for You	1981	2.50	5.00	10.00
—Reissue of 3309					
❏ MPS-8517	Lovejoy	1981	2.50	5.00	10.00
—Reissue of 2040					
❏ MPS-8522	Years Gone By	1982	2.50	5.00	10.00
—Reissue of 2010					
❏ MPS-8534	The Lost Session	1986	2.50	5.00	10.00
❏ MPS-8536	I Wanna Get Funky	1987	2.50	5.00	10.00
—Reissue of 5505					
❏ MPS-8546	Blues at Sunrise	1988	2.50	5.00	10.00
❏ MPS-8556	Wednesday Night in San Francisco	1990	2.50	5.00	10.00
❏ MPS-8557	Tuesday Night in San Francisco	1990	2.50	5.00	10.00
SUNDAZED					
❏ LP 5031	Born Under a Bad Sign	1999	3.75	7.50	15.00
—Reissue on 180-gram vinyl					
TOMATO					
❏ TOM-6002	King Albert	1978	3.00	6.00	12.00
❏ TOM-7022	New Orleans Heat	1979	3.00	6.00	12.00
UTOPIA					
❏ BUL1-1387	Truckload of Lovin'	1976	3.00	6.00	12.00
❏ BUL1-1731	Albert	1976	3.00	6.00	12.00
❏ CUL2-2205 [(2)]	Albert Live	1977	3.75	7.50	15.00

KING, ALBERT/STEVE CROPPER/POP STAPLES

45s
STAX

Number	Title (A Side/B Side)	Yr	VG	VG+	NM
❏ 0047	Tupelo (Part 1)/Tupelo (Part 2)	1969	2.00	4.00	8.00
❏ 0048	Water/Opus de Soul	1969	2.00	4.00	8.00
Albums					
STAX					
❏ STS-2020	Jammed Together	1969	6.25	12.50	25.00
❏ MPS-8544	Jammed Together	1988	2.50	5.00	10.00
—Reissue					

KING, ALBERT/LITTLE MILTON

Albums
STAX

Number	Title (A Side/B Side)	Yr	VG	VG+	NM
❏ STX-4123	Chronicle	1979	3.00	6.00	12.00
—One side devoted to each artist					

KING, ALBERT/OTIS RUSH

Albums
CHESS

Number	Title (A Side/B Side)	Yr	VG	VG+	NM
❏ LPS 1538	Door to Door	1969	6.25	12.50	25.00
❏ CH-9322	Door to Door	1990	2.50	5.00	10.00
—Reissue					

KING, ANNA

45s
END

Number	Title (A Side/B Side)	Yr	VG	VG+	NM
❏ 1126	Mama's Got a Bag of Her Own/Sally	1963	7.50	15.00	30.00
LUDIX					
❏ 103	You Don't Love Me Anymore/Big Change	1963	10.00	20.00	40.00
SMASH					
❏ 1858	If Somebody Told You/				
	Come and Get These Memories	1963	5.00	10.00	20.00
❏ 1884	Baby, Baby, Baby/(Instrumental)	1964	5.00	10.00	20.00
—With Bobby Byrd					
❏ 1904	If You Don't Think/Make Up Your Mind	1964	5.00	10.00	20.00
❏ 1942	Come On Home/Sittin' in the Dark	1964	5.00	10.00	20.00
❏ 1970	That's When I Cry/Tennessee Waltz	1965	3.75	7.50	15.00
Albums					
SMASH					
❏ MGS-27059 [M]	Back to Soul	1964	25.00	50.00	100.00
❏ SRS-67059 [S]	Back to Soul	1964	30.00	60.00	120.00

KING, B.B. Also see BOBBY BLAND AND B.B. KING.

12-Inch Singles
MCA

Number	Title (A Side/B Side)	Yr	VG	VG+	NM
❏ L33-1284 [DJ]	My Lucille (Extended)/Into the Night	1985	2.00	4.00	8.00
❏ 2118 [DJ]	The Blues Come Over Me (6 versions)	1991	—	3.00	6.00
❏ L33-17810 [DJ]	Lay Another Log on the Fire/Go On	1989	—	3.00	6.00
❏ 23831	Habit to Me (LP Version) (TV Mix)	1988	—	3.00	6.00
45s					
ABC					
❏ 10856	Don't Answer the Door (Part 1)/				
	Don't Answer the Door (Part 2)	1966	3.75	7.50	15.00
❏ 10889	Waitin' on You/Night Life	1966	3.75	7.50	15.00
❏ 11268	Hummingbird/Ask Me No Questions	1970	2.00	4.00	8.00
❏ 11280	Chains and Things/King's Special	1970	2.00	4.00	8.00
❏ 11290	Ask Me No Questions/				
	Nobody Loves Me But My Mother	1971	2.00	4.00	8.00
❏ 11302	Help the Poor/Lucille's Granny	1971	2.00	4.00	8.00
❏ 11310	Ghetto Woman/Seven Minutes	1971	2.00	4.00	8.00
❏ 11316	Ain't Nobody Home/Alexi's Boogie	1971	2.00	4.00	8.00
❏ 11319	Sweet Sixteen/I've Been Blue Too Long	1972	—	3.00	6.00
❏ 11321	I Got Some Help I Don't Need/Lucille's Granny	1972	—	3.00	6.00
❏ 11330	Guess Who/Better Lovin' Man	1972	—	3.00	6.00
❏ 11339	Summer in the City/Five Long Years	1972	—	3.00	6.00
❏ 11373	To Know You Is to Love You/I Can't Leave	1973	—	3.00	6.00
❏ 11406	I Like to Live the Love/Love	1973	—	3.00	6.00
❏ 11433	Who Are You/On to Me	1974	—	3.00	6.00
❏ 12029	Philadelphia/Up at 5 A.M.	1974	—	3.00	6.00
❏ 12053	Friends/My Song	1974	—	3.00	6.00
❏ 12158	When I'm Wrong/Have Faith	1976	—	3.00	6.00
❏ 12247	Slow and Easy/I Wonder Why	1977	—	3.00	6.00
❏ 12380	Never Make a Move Too Soon/				
	Let Me Make You Cry a Little Longer	1978	—	3.00	6.00
❏ 12412	I Just Can't Leave Your Love Alone/				
	Midnight Believer	1978	—	3.00	6.00
ABC-PARAMOUNT					
❏ 10316	I'm Gonna Sit In Till You Give In/You Ask Me	1962	3.75	7.50	15.00
❏ 10334	Blues at Midnight/My Baby's Coming Home	1962	3.75	7.50	15.00
❏ 10361	Chains of Love/Sneakin' Around	1962	3.75	7.50	15.00
❏ 10367	Tomorrow Night/Mother's Love	1962	3.75	7.50	15.00
❏ 10390	Guess Who/By Myself	1962	3.75	7.50	15.00
❏ 10455	On My Word of Honor/Young Dreamers	1963	3.75	7.50	15.00
❏ 10486	How Do I Love You/Slowly Losing My Mind	1963	3.75	7.50	15.00
❏ 10527	How Blue Can You Get/Please Accept My Love	1964	3.75	7.50	15.00
❏ 10552	Help the Poor/I Wouldn't Have It Any Other Way	1964	3.75	7.50	15.00
❏ 10576	Whole Lotta Lovin'/The Hurt	1964	3.75	7.50	15.00
❏ 10597	Never Trust a Woman/Worryin' Blues	1964	3.75	7.50	15.00
❏ 10616	Please Send Me Someone to Love/				
	The Worst Thing in My Life	1965	3.75	7.50	15.00
❏ 10634	Everyday I Have the Blues/It's My Own Fault	1965	3.75	7.50	15.00
❏ 10675	Tired of Your Jive/Night Owl	1965	3.75	7.50	15.00
❏ 10724	All Over Again/The Things You Put Me Through	1965	3.75	7.50	15.00
❏ 10754	Goin' to Chicago Blues/				
	I'd Rather Drink Muddy Water	1965	3.75	7.50	15.00
❏ 10766	Tormented/You're Still a Square	1966	3.75	7.50	15.00
BLUESWAY					
❏ 61004	Think It Over/				
	I Don't Want You Cutting Off Your Hair	1967	2.50	5.00	10.00
❏ 61007	Worried Dream/That's Wrong, Little Mama	1967	2.50	5.00	10.00
❏ 61011	Raining in My Heart/Heartbreaker	1967	2.50	5.00	10.00
❏ 61012	Sweet Sixteen (Part 1)/Sweet Sixteen (Part 2)	1968	2.50	5.00	10.00
❏ 61015	Paying the Cost to Be the Boss/Having My Say	1968	2.50	5.00	10.00
❏ 61018	I'm Gonna Do What They Do to Me/				
	Losing Faith in You	1968	2.50	5.00	10.00
❏ 61019	You Put It On Me/B.B. Jones	1968	2.50	5.00	10.00
❏ 61021	Dance with Me/				
	Please Send Me Someone to Love	1968	2.50	5.00	10.00
❏ 61022	Don't Waste My Time/Get Myself Somebody	1969	2.50	5.00	10.00
❏ 61024	Why I Sing the Blues/Friends	1969	2.50	5.00	10.00
❏ 61026	Get Off My Back Woman/I Want You So Bad	1969	2.50	5.00	10.00
❏ 61029	Just a Little Love/My Mood	1969	2.50	5.00	10.00
❏ 61032	The Thrill Is Gone/You're Mean	1969	3.00	6.00	12.00
❏ 61032 [PS]	The Thrill Is Gone/You're Mean	1969	5.00	10.00	20.00
❏ 61035	So Excited/Confessin' the Blues	1970	2.00	4.00	8.00
KENT					
❏ 301	You Know I Go for You/				
	Why Do Everything Happen to Me	1958	5.00	10.00	20.00
❏ 307	Days of Old/				
	Don't Look Now, But You Got the Blues	1958	5.00	10.00	20.00
❏ 315	Please Accept My Love/You've Been an Angel	1958	6.25	12.50	25.00
—With the Vocal Chords					
❏ 317	Worry Worry/I Am	1959	5.00	10.00	20.00
❏ 319	The Fool/Come By Here	1959	5.00	10.00	20.00
❏ 325	A Lonely Lover's Plea/Woman in Love	1959	5.00	10.00	20.00
❏ 327	Everyday I Have the Blues/Time to Say Goodbye	1959	5.00	10.00	20.00
❏ 329	Sugar Mama/Mean Old Friend	1959	5.00	10.00	20.00
❏ 330	Sweet Sixteen, Pt. 1/Sweet Sixteen, Pt. 2	1960	5.00	10.00	20.00
❏ 333	Got a Right to Love My Baby/My Own Fault	1960	3.75	7.50	15.00
❏ 336	Please Love Me/Crying Won't Help You	1960	3.75	7.50	15.00
❏ 337	Blind Love/You Upset Me Baby	1960	3.75	7.50	15.00
❏ 338	Ten Long Years/Everyday I Have the Blues	1960	3.75	7.50	15.00
❏ 339	Did You Ever Love a Woman/				
	Three O'Clock Blues	1960	3.75	7.50	15.00
❏ 340	Sweet Little Angel/				
	You Done Lost Your Good Thing Now	1960	3.75	7.50	15.00
❏ 346	Partin' Time/Good Man Gone Bad	1960	3.75	7.50	15.00
❏ 350	Waking Dr. Bill/				
	You Done Lost Your Good Thing Now	1960	3.75	7.50	15.00
❏ 351	Things Are Not the Same/Fishin' After Me	1961	3.75	7.50	15.00
❏ 353	Bad Luck Soul/Get Out of Here	1961	3.75	7.50	15.00
❏ 358	Hold That Train/Understand	1961	3.75	7.50	15.00
❏ 360	Peace of Mind/Someday	1961	3.75	7.50	15.00
❏ 362	You're Breaking My Heart/Bad Case of Love	1961	3.75	7.50	15.00
❏ 365	My Sometime Baby/Lonely	1962	3.00	6.00	12.00
❏ 372	Gonna Miss You Around Here/Hully Gully Twist	1962	3.00	6.00	12.00
❏ 373	3 O'Clock Stomp/Mashed Potato Twist	1962	3.00	6.00	12.00
❏ 381	Tell Me Baby/Mashing the Popeye	1962	3.00	6.00	12.00
❏ 383	Going Down Slow/				
	When My Heart Beats Like a Hammer	1962	3.00	6.00	12.00
❏ 386	Your Letter/Blues for Me	1962	3.00	6.00	12.00
❏ 387	Christmas Celebration/Easy Listening	1962	3.00	6.00	12.00
❏ 388	Whole Lot of Loving/Down Now	1963	3.00	5.00	10.00
❏ 389	Trouble in Mind/Long Nights	1963	3.00	5.00	10.00
❏ 390	My Reward/The Road I Travel	1963	3.00	5.00	10.00
❏ 391	The Letter/You Never Know	1963	3.00	5.00	10.00
❏ 392	Army of the Lord/Precious Lord	1964	3.00	7.50	15.00
❏ 393	Rock Me Baby/I Can't Lose	1964	3.00	5.00	10.00
❏ 396	Let Me Love You/You're Gonna Miss Me	1964	3.00	5.00	10.00
❏ 403	Beautician Blues/I Can Hear My Name	1964	3.00	5.00	10.00
❏ 412	Christmas Celebration/Easy Listening	1964	3.00	6.00	12.00
❏ 415	Got 'Em Bad/The Worst Thing in My Life	1965	3.00	6.00	12.00
❏ 421	Please Love Me/Baby Look at You	1965	3.00	6.00	12.00
❏ 426	Blue Shadows/And Like That	1965	3.00	6.00	12.00
❏ 429	Just a Dream/Why Do Everything Happen to Me	1965	3.00	6.00	12.00
❏ 435	Mercy, Mercy/Broken Promise	1965	3.00	6.00	12.00
❏ 441	Eyesight to the Blind/Just Like a Woman	1966	3.00	6.00	12.00
❏ 445	Five Long Years/Love, Honor and Obey	1966	3.00	6.00	12.00
❏ 447	Ain't Nobody's Business/I Wonder Why	1966	3.00	6.00	12.00
❏ 450	I Stay in the Mood/Early Every Morning	1966	3.00	6.00	12.00
❏ 458	It's a Mean World/Blues Stay Away	1966	2.00	4.00	8.00
❏ 462	The Jungle/Long Gone Baby	1967	2.00	4.00	8.00
❏ 467	Treat Me Right/Who Can Your Good Man Be	1967	2.00	4.00	8.00
❏ 470	Bad Breaks/Growing Old	1967	2.00	4.00	8.00
❏ 475	Sweet Thing/Soul Beat	1967	2.00	4.00	8.00
❏ 484	Worry, Worry, Worry/				
	Why Do Everything Happen to Me	1968	—	3.00	6.00

Number	Title (A Side/B Side)	Yr	VG	VG+	NM
❏ 492	The Woman I Love/Blues for Me	1968	—	3.00	6.00
❏ 499	Slow Burn/3 O'Clock Blues	1968	—	3.00	6.00
❏ 510	Your Fool/Shoutin' the Blues	1969	—	3.00	6.00
❏ 4513	I'm Cracking Up Over You/Powerhouse	1969	2.50	5.00	10.00
❏ 4515	Dreams/House Rocker	1970	2.50	5.00	10.00
❏ 4526	Worried Life/Walkin' Dr. Bill	1970	2.50	5.00	10.00
❏ 4542	That Evil Child/Tell Me Baby	1971	2.00	4.00	8.00
❏ 4549	I'll Survive/Long Nights	1971	2.00	4.00	8.00
❏ 4562	Precious Lord/Swing Low, Sweet Chariot	1972	2.00	4.00	8.00
❏ 4566	Don't Get Around Much Anymore/Poontanging	1972	2.00	4.00	8.00
❏ 4572	Recession Blues/Walkin' Dr. Bill	1972	2.00	4.00	8.00
MCA					
❏ 41062	Happy Birthday Blues/Better Not Look Down	1979	—	2.00	4.00
❏ 51101	There Must Be a Better World Somewhere/ You're Going with Me	1981	—	2.00	4.00
❏ 52057	Since I Met You Baby/One of Those Nights	1982	—	—	3.00
❏ 52098	Street Life/Overture	1982	—	—	3.00
—With the Crusaders and the London Symphony Orchestra					
❏ 52125	Love Me Tender/The World I Never Made	1982	—	—	3.00
❏ 52218	Sell My Monkey/Inflation Blues	1983	—	—	3.00
❏ 52530	Into the Night/Century City Chase of J.B. in Teheran	1985	—	—	3.00
❏ 52530 [PS]	Into the Night/Century City Chase of J.B. in Teheran	1985	—	—	3.00
❏ 52574	My Lucille/Keep It Light	1985	—	—	3.00
—B-side by Thelma Houston					
❏ 52675	Big Boss Man/My Guitar Sings the Blues	1985	—	—	3.00
❏ 52751	Memory Lane/Six Silver Strings	1985	—	—	3.00
❏ 53269	(You've Become a) Habit to Me/(You've Become a) Habit to Me (Long)	1988	—	—	3.00
❏ 53644	Lay Another Log on the Fire/Go On	1989	—	—	3.00
❏ 54339	The Blues Come Over Me (Wild & Bluesy Club Mix Edit)/The Blues Come Over Me (Integrity Mix)	1992	—	2.00	4.00
POINTBLANK					
❏ 58820	Christmas Celebration/White Christmas	1999	—	—	3.00
—B-side by Hadda Brooks					
RPM					
❏ 339	3 O'Clock Blues/That Ain't the Way to Do It	1951	225.00	450.00	900.00
—B.B. King singles on RPM before 339 are unconfirmed on 45 rpm					
❏ 348	Fine Lookin' Woman/She Don't Move Me No More	1952	75.00	150.00	300.00
❏ 355	Shake It Up and Go/My Own Fault, Darling	1952	37.50	75.00	150.00
❏ 360	Gotta Find My Baby/Someday Somewhere	1952	25.00	50.00	100.00
❏ 363	You Know I Love You/You Didn't Want Me	1952	20.00	40.00	80.00
❏ 374	Story from My Heart and Soul/Boogie Woogie Woman	1952	37.50	75.00	150.00
❏ 380	Woke Up This Morning (My Baby She Was Gone)/Don't Have to Cry	1953	25.00	50.00	100.00
❏ 386	Please Love Me/Highway Bound	1953	37.50	75.00	150.00
❏ 391	Please Hurry Home/Neighborhood Affair	1953	20.00	40.00	80.00
❏ 395	Why Did You Leave Me/Blind Love	1953	20.00	40.00	80.00
❏ 403	Praying to the Lord/Please Help Me	1954	7.50	15.00	30.00
❏ 408	Love Me Baby/The Woman I Love	1954	7.50	15.00	30.00
❏ 411	Everything I Do Is Wrong/ Don't You Want a Man Like Me	1954	7.50	15.00	30.00
❏ 412	When My Heart Beats Like a Hammer/ Bye Bye Baby	1954	7.50	15.00	30.00
❏ 416	You Upset Me Baby/Whole Lotta' Love	1954	7.50	15.00	30.00
❏ 421	Every Day I Have the Blues/Sneakin' Around	1955	7.50	15.00	30.00
❏ 425	Lonely and Blue/Jump with You Baby	1955	7.50	15.00	30.00
❏ 430	I'm in Love/Shut Your Mouth	1955	7.50	15.00	30.00
❏ 435	Talkin' the Blues/Boogie Rock	1955	7.50	15.00	30.00
❏ 437	Ten Long Years/What Can I Do	1955	7.50	15.00	30.00
❏ 450	I'm Cracking Up Over You/Ruby Lee	1956	6.25	12.50	25.00
❏ 451	Crying Won't Help You/Can't We Talk It Over	1956	6.25	12.50	25.00
❏ 451	Crying Won't Help You/Sixteen Tons	1956	6.25	12.50	25.00
❏ 457	Did You Ever Love a Woman/Let's Do the Boogie	1956	6.25	12.50	25.00
❏ 459	Dark Is the Night (Part 1)/ Dark Is the Night (Part 2)	1956	6.25	12.50	25.00
❏ 468	Bad Luck/Sweet Little Angel	1956	6.25	12.50	25.00
❏ 479	On My Word of Honor/Bim Bam	1956	6.25	12.50	25.00
❏ 486	You Don't Know/Early in the Morning	1957	6.25	12.50	25.00
❏ 490	How Do I Love You/You Can't Fool My Heart	1957	6.25	12.50	25.00
❏ 492	Troubles, Troubles, Troubles/ I Want to Get Married	1957	6.25	12.50	25.00
❏ 494	Quit My Baby/Be Careful with a Fool	1957	6.25	12.50	25.00
❏ 498	I Wonder/I Need You So Bad	1957	6.25	12.50	25.00
❏ 501	The Key to My Kingdom/ My Heart Belongs to Only You	1957	6.25	12.50	25.00
Albums					
ABC					
❏ D-704	Blues Is King	1970	3.00	6.00	12.00
—Reissue of BluesWay 6001					
❏ D-709	Blues on Top of Blues	1970	3.00	6.00	12.00
—Reissue of BluesWay 6011					
❏ D-712	Lucille	1970	3.00	6.00	12.00
—Reissue of BluesWay 6016					
❏ D-713	Indianola Mississippi Seeds	1970	3.00	6.00	12.00
❏ D-723	Live in Cook County Jail	1971	3.00	6.00	12.00
❏ D-724	Live at the Regal	1971	3.00	6.00	12.00
—Reissue of ABC-Paramount 509					
❏ D-730	B.B. King in London	1971	3.00	6.00	12.00
❏ D-743	L.A. Midnight	1972	3.00	6.00	12.00
❏ X-759	Guess Who	1972	3.00	6.00	12.00
❏ X-767	The Best of B.B. King	1973	3.00	6.00	12.00
❏ X-794	To Know You Is to Love You	1973	3.00	6.00	12.00
❏ D-813	His Best/The Electric B.B. King	1974	3.00	6.00	12.00
—Reissue of BluesWay 6022					
❏ D-819	Live and Well	1974	3.00	6.00	12.00
—Reissue of BluesWay 6031					
❏ D-825	Friends	1974	3.00	6.00	12.00
❏ D-868	Completely Well	1975	3.00	6.00	12.00
—Reissue of BluesWay 6037					
❏ D-878	Back in the Alley	1975	3.00	6.00	12.00
—Reissue of BluesWay 6050					
❏ D-898	Lucille Talks Back	1975	3.00	6.00	12.00

Number	Title (A Side/B Side)	Yr	VG	VG+	NM
❏ AB-977	King Size	1977	3.00	6.00	12.00
❏ AA-1061	Midnight Believer	1978	3.00	6.00	12.00
ABC-PARAMOUNT					
❏ 456 [M]	Mr. Blues	1963	7.50	15.00	30.00
❏ S-456 [S]	Mr. Blues	1963	10.00	20.00	40.00
❏ 509 [M]	Live at the Regal	1965	10.00	20.00	40.00
❏ S-509 [S]	Live at the Regal	1965	12.50	25.00	50.00
❏ 528 [M]	Confessin' the Blues	1965	7.50	15.00	30.00
❏ S-528 [S]	Confessin' the Blues	1965	10.00	20.00	40.00
BLUESWAY					
❏ BL-6001 [M]	Blues Is King	1967	10.00	20.00	40.00
❏ BLS-6001 [S]	Blues Is King	1967	6.25	12.50	25.00
❏ BLS-6011	Blues on Top of Blues	1968	6.25	12.50	25.00
❏ BLS-6016	Lucille	1968	6.25	12.50	25.00
❏ BLS-6022	His Best/The Electric B.B. King	1969	5.00	10.00	20.00
❏ BLS-6031	Live and Well	1969	5.00	10.00	20.00
❏ BLS-6037	Completely Well	1969	5.00	10.00	20.00
❏ BLS-6050	Back in the Alley	1970	5.00	10.00	20.00
COMMAND					
❏ CQD-40022 [Q]	Friends	1974	5.00	10.00	20.00
CROWN					
❏ CST-147 [R]	B.B. King Wails	1960	3.00	6.00	12.00
—Black vinyl					
❏ CST-147 [R]	B.B. King Wails	1960	25.00	50.00	100.00
—Red vinyl					
❏ CST-152 [R]	B.B. King Sings Spirituals	1960	3.00	6.00	12.00
—Black vinyl					
❏ CST-152 [R]	B.B. King Sings Spirituals	1960	25.00	50.00	100.00
—Red vinyl					
❏ CST-195 [S]	King of the Blues	1961	5.00	10.00	20.00
—Black vinyl; this album is in true stereo, contrary to prior reports					
❏ CST-195 [S]	King of the Blues	1961	30.00	60.00	120.00
—Red vinyl; this album is in true stereo, contrary to prior reports					
❏ CST-309 [R]	Blues in My Heart	1963	3.00	6.00	12.00
❏ CST-359 [P]	B.B. King	1963	3.00	6.00	12.00
—Half of the album is in stereo, half is rechanneled					
❏ CLP-5020 [M]	Singin' the Blues	1957	25.00	50.00	100.00
—Black label, silver "Crown"					
❏ CLP-5020 [M]	Singin' the Blues	196?	3.00	6.00	12.00
—Black label, multi-color "Crown"					
❏ CLP-5020 [M]	Singin' the Blues	1963	5.00	10.00	20.00
—Gray label, black "Crown"					
❏ CLP-5063 [M]	The Blues	1958	20.00	40.00	80.00
—Black label, silver "Crown"					
❏ CLP-5063 [M]	The Blues	196?	3.00	6.00	12.00
—Black label, multi-color "Crown"					
❏ CLP-5063 [M]	The Blues	1963	5.00	10.00	20.00
—Gray label, black "Crown"					
❏ CLP-5115 [M]	B.B. King Wails	1959	20.00	40.00	80.00
—Black label, silver "Crown"					
❏ CLP-5115 [M]	B.B. King Wails	196?	3.00	6.00	12.00
—Black label, multi-color "Crown"					
❏ CLP-5115 [M]	B.B. King Wails	1963	5.00	10.00	20.00
—Gray label, black "Crown"					
❏ CLP-5119 [M]	B.B. King Sings Spirituals	196?	3.00	6.00	12.00
—Black label, multi-color "Crown"					
❏ CLP-5119 [M]	B.B. King Sings Spirituals	1960	15.00	30.00	60.00
—Gray label, black "Crown"					
❏ CLP-5143 [M]	The Great B.B. King	196?	3.00	6.00	12.00
—Black label, multi-color "Crown"					
❏ CLP-5143 [M]	The Great B.B. King	1961	15.00	30.00	60.00
—Gray label, black "Crown"					
❏ CLP-5167 [M]	King of the Blues	196?	3.00	6.00	12.00
—Black label, multi-color "Crown"					
❏ CLP-5167 [M]	King of the Blues	1961	15.00	30.00	60.00
—Gray label, black "Crown"					
❏ CLP-5188 [M]	My Kind of Blues	196?	3.00	6.00	12.00
—Black label, multi-color "Crown"					
❏ CLP-5188 [M]	My Kind of Blues	1961	15.00	30.00	60.00
—Gray label, black "Crown"					
❏ CLP-5230 [M]	More B.B. King	196?	3.00	6.00	12.00
—Black label, multi-color "Crown"					
❏ CLP-5230 [M]	More B.B. King	1962	15.00	30.00	60.00
—Gray label, black "Crown"					
❏ CLP-5248 [M]	Twist with B.B. King	196?	3.00	6.00	12.00
—Black label, multi-color "Crown"					
❏ CLP-5248 [M]	Twist with B.B. King	1962	15.00	30.00	60.00
—Gray label, black "Crown"					
❏ CLP-5286 [M]	Easy Listening Blues	196?	3.00	6.00	12.00
—Black label, multi-color "Crown"					
❏ CLP-5286 [M]	Easy Listening Blues	1962	15.00	30.00	60.00
—Gray label, black "Crown"					
❏ CLP-5309 [M]	Blues in My Heart	196?	3.00	6.00	12.00
—Black label, multi-color "Crown"					
❏ CLP-5309 [M]	Blues in My Heart	1963	10.00	20.00	40.00
—Gray label, black "Crown"					
❏ CLP-5359 [M]	B.B. King	196?	3.00	6.00	12.00
—Black label, multi-color "Crown"					
❏ CLP-5359 [M]	B.B. King	1963	10.00	20.00	40.00
—Gray label, black "Crown"					
CRUSADERS					
❏ 16013	Live in London	1982	6.25	12.50	25.00
—Part of MCA's "Audiophile Series"					
CUSTOM					
❏ CM-2046 [M]	Blues for Me	196?	3.00	6.00	12.00
❏ CM-2049 [M]	I Love You So	196?	3.00	6.00	12.00
❏ CM-2052 [M]	The Soul of B.B. King	196?	3.00	6.00	12.00
DIRECT DISK					
❏ SD-16616	Midnight Believer	1980	12.50	25.00	50.00
—Audiophile vinyl					
GALAXY					
❏ 202 [M]	16 Greatest Hits	1963	15.00	30.00	60.00
❏ 8202 [S]	16 Greatest Hits	1963	20.00	40.00	80.00
GRP					
❏ GR-9637	Live at the Apollo	1991	3.75	7.50	15.00

Number	Title (A Side/B Side)	Yr	VG	VG+	NM
KENT					
❏ KST-512 [R]	Rock Me Baby	1964	3.75	7.50	15.00
❏ KST-513 [R]	Let Me Love You	1965	3.75	7.50	15.00
❏ KST-515 [R]	B.B. King Live on Stage	1965	3.75	7.50	15.00
❏ KST-516 [R]	The Soul of B.B. King	1966	3.75	7.50	15.00
❏ KST-517 [R]	Pure Soul	1966	3.75	7.50	15.00
❏ KST-521 [R]	The Jungle	1967	3.75	7.50	15.00
❏ KST-529 [R]	Boss of the Blues	1968	3.75	7.50	15.00
❏ KST-533 [(2)]	From the Beginning	1969	5.00	10.00	20.00
❏ KST-535	Underground Blues	1969	3.75	7.50	15.00
❏ KST-539	The Incredible Soul of B.B. King	1970	3.75	7.50	15.00
❏ KST-548	Turn On to B.B. King	1970	3.75	7.50	15.00
❏ KST-552	Greatest Hits, Volume 1	1971	3.75	7.50	15.00
❏ KST-561	Better Than Ever	1971	3.75	7.50	15.00
❏ KST-563	Doing My Thing, Lord	1971	3.75	7.50	15.00
❏ KST-565	B.B. King Live	1972	3.75	7.50	15.00
❏ KST-568	The Original Sweet Sixteen	1972	3.75	7.50	15.00
❏ KLP-2008	Incredible Soul of B.B. King	1987	3.00	6.00	12.00
❏ KLP-5012 [M]	Rock Me Baby	1964	5.00	10.00	20.00
❏ KLP-5013 [M]	Let Me Love You	1965	5.00	10.00	20.00
❏ KLP-5015 [M]	B.B. King Live on Stage	1965	5.00	10.00	20.00
❏ KLP-5016 [M]	The Soul of B.B. King	1966	5.00	10.00	20.00
❏ KLP-5017 [M]	Pure Soul	1966	5.00	10.00	20.00
❏ KLP-5021 [M]	The Jungle	1967	5.00	10.00	20.00
❏ KLP-5029 [M]	Boss of the Blues	1968	5.00	10.00	20.00
MCA					
❏ 3151	Take It Home	1979	2.50	5.00	10.00
❏ 5162	There Must Be a Better World Somewhere	1981	2.50	5.00	10.00
❏ 5307	Love Me Tender	1982	2.50	5.00	10.00
❏ 5413	Blues 'N' Jazz	1983	2.50	5.00	10.00
❏ 5616	Six Silver Strings	1985	2.50	5.00	10.00
❏ 6455	Live at San Quentin	1990	3.00	6.00	12.00
❏ 2-8016 [(2)]	"Now Appearing" at Ole Miss	1980	3.00	6.00	12.00
❏ 27005	Live in Cook County Jail	1980	2.00	4.00	8.00
—Reissue of ABC 723					
❏ 27006	Live at the Regal	1980	2.00	4.00	8.00
—Reissue of ABC 724					
❏ 27007	His Best/The Electric B.B. King	1980	2.00	4.00	8.00
—Reissue of ABC 813					
❏ 27008	Live and Well	1980	2.00	4.00	8.00
—Reissue of ABC 819					
❏ 27009	Completely Well	1980	2.00	4.00	8.00
—Reissue of ABC 868					
❏ 27010	Back in the Alley	1980	2.00	4.00	8.00
—Reissue of ABC 878					
❏ 27011	Midnight Believer	1980	2.00	4.00	8.00
—Reissue of ABC 1061					
❏ 27028	Take It Home	1981	2.00	4.00	8.00
—Reissue of MCA 3151					
❏ 27034	There Must Be a Better World Somewhere	1983	2.00	4.00	8.00
—Reissue of MCA 5162					
❏ 27074	The Best of B.B. King	1984	2.00	4.00	8.00
—Reissue of ABC 767					
❏ 42183	The King of the Blues: 1989	1989	2.50	5.00	10.00
MCA IMPULSE!					
❏ MCA2-4124 [(2)]	Great Moments with B.B. King	1981	3.00	6.00	12.00
MOBILE FIDELITY					
❏ 1-235	Lucille	1995	6.25	12.50	25.00
—Audiophile vinyl					
PICKWICK					
❏ SPC-3593	Live at the Regal	197?	2.00	4.00	8.00
❏ SPC-3654	Live in Cook County Jail	197?	2.00	4.00	8.00
STAX					
❏ ORS-4508	16 Original Big Hits	198?	2.00	4.00	8.00
UNITED					
❏ US-7703	Heart Full of Blues	197?	2.00	4.00	8.00
❏ US-7705	Easy Listening Blues	197?	2.00	4.00	8.00
—Reissue of Crown 5286					
❏ US-7708	Blues for Me	197?	2.00	4.00	8.00
—Reissue of Custom 2046					
❏ US-7711	I Love You So	197?	2.00	4.00	8.00
—Reissue of Custom 2049					
❏ US-7714	The Soul of B.B. King	197?	2.00	4.00	8.00
—Reissue of Custom 2052					
❏ US-7721	Swing Low	197?	2.00	4.00	8.00
❏ US-7724	My Kind of Blues	197?	2.00	4.00	8.00
—Reissue of Crown 5188					
❏ US-7726	Singin' the Blues	197?	2.00	4.00	8.00
—Reissue of Crown 5020					
❏ US-7728	The Great B.B. King	197?	2.00	4.00	8.00
—Reissue of Crown 5143					
❏ US-7732	The Blues	197?	2.00	4.00	8.00
—Reissue of Crown 5063					
❏ US-7733	Rock Me, Baby	197?	2.00	4.00	8.00
—Reissue of Kent 5012					
❏ US-7734	Let Me Love You	197?	2.00	4.00	8.00
—Reissue of Kent 513					
❏ US-7736	B.B. King Live on Stage	197?	2.00	4.00	8.00
—Reissue of Kent 515					
❏ US-7742	The Jungle	197?	2.00	4.00	8.00
—Reissue of Kent 521					
❏ US-7750	Boss of the Blues	197?	2.00	4.00	8.00
—Reissue of Kent 529					
❏ US-7756	The Incredible Soul of B.B. King	197?	2.00	4.00	8.00
—Reissue of Kent 539					
❏ US-7763	Turn On with B.B. King	197?	2.00	4.00	8.00
—Reissue of Kent 548					
❏ US-7766	Greatest Hits, Volume 1	197?	2.00	4.00	8.00
—Reissue of Kent 552					
❏ US-7773	The Original Sweet Sixteen	197?	2.00	4.00	8.00
—Reissue of Kent 568					
❏ US-7788	9 x 9	197?	2.00	4.00	8.00

KING, B.B./ERIC CLAPTON Also see each artist's individual listings.
45s
REPRISE

Number	Title (A Side/B Side)	Yr	VG	VG+	NM
❏ 7-16831	Riding with the King/Key to the Highway	2000	—	—	3.00

Number	Title (A Side/B Side)	Yr	VG	VG+	NM
❏ 7-16832	Worried Life Blues/Days of Old	2000	—	—	3.00
❏ 7-16833	Marry You/Three O'Clock Blues (Edit)	2000	—	—	3.00
❏ 7-16834	When My Heart Beats Like a Hammer (Edit)/I Wanna Be	2000	—	—	3.00
❏ 7-16835	Help the Poor/Hold On I'm Coming	2000	—	—	3.00
❏ 7-16836	Come Rain or Come Shine/Ten Long Years	2000	—	—	3.00

KING, BEN E. Also see AVERAGE WHITE BAND; THE DRIFTERS.
45s
ATCO

Number	Title (A Side/B Side)	Yr	VG	VG+	NM
❏ 6166	Show Me the Way/Brace Yourself	1960	4.00	8.00	16.00
❏ 6185	Spanish Harlem/First Taste of Love	1960	5.00	10.00	20.00
❏ 6194	Stand By Me/On the Horizon	1961	5.00	10.00	20.00
❏ 6203	Amor/Souvenir of Mexico	1961	4.00	8.00	16.00
❏ 6207	Young Boy Blues/Here Comes the Night	1961	4.00	8.00	16.00
❏ 6215	Ecstasy/Yes	1962	4.00	8.00	16.00
❏ 6222	Don't Play That Song (You Lied)/Hermit of Misty Mountain	1962	4.00	8.00	16.00
❏ 6231	Too Bad/My Heart Cries for You	1962	3.00	6.00	12.00
❏ 6237	I'm Standing By/Walking in the Footsteps of a Fool	1962	3.00	6.00	12.00
❏ 6246	Tell Daddy/Auf Wiedersehn, My Dear	1962	3.00	6.00	12.00
❏ 6256	How Can I Forget/Gloria Gloria	1963	3.00	6.00	12.00
❏ 6267	I (Who Have Nothing)/The Beginning of Time	1963	3.00	6.00	12.00
❏ 6275	I Could Have Danced All Night/Gypsy	1963	3.00	6.00	12.00
❏ 6284	What Now My Love/Groovin'	1964	2.50	5.00	10.00
❏ 6288	That's When It Hurts/Around the Corner	1964	2.50	5.00	10.00
❏ 6303	What Can a Man Do/Si, Senor	1964	2.50	5.00	10.00
❏ 6315	It's All Over/Let the Water Run Down	1964	2.50	5.00	10.00
❏ 6328	Seven Letters/River of Tears	1964	2.50	5.00	10.00
❏ 6343	The Record (Baby I Love You)/The Way You Shake It	1965	2.50	5.00	10.00
❏ 6357	She's Gone Again/Not Now (I'll Tell You When)	1965	2.50	5.00	10.00
❏ 6371	Cry No More/There's No Place to Hide	1965	2.50	5.00	10.00
❏ 6390	Goodnight My Love/I Can't Break the News to Myself	1965	2.50	5.00	10.00
❏ 6413	So Much Love/Don't Drive Me Away	1966	2.00	4.00	8.00
❏ 6431	Get in a Hurry/I Swear by Stars Above	1966	2.00	4.00	8.00
❏ 6454	They Don't Give Medals to Yesterday's Heroes/What Is Soul	1966	2.00	4.00	8.00
❏ 6472	A Man Without a Dream/Tears, Tears, Tears	1967	2.00	4.00	8.00
❏ 6493	Katherine/Teeny Weeny Little Bit	1967	2.00	4.00	8.00
❏ 6527	Don't Take Your Sweet Love Away/She Knows What to Do for Me	1967	2.50	5.00	10.00
❏ 6557	We Got a Thing Goin' On/What 'Cha Gonna Do About It	1968	2.00	4.00	8.00
—With Dee Dee Sharp					
❏ 6571	Don't Take Your Love from Me/Forgive This Soul	1968	2.00	4.00	8.00
❏ 6596	Where's the Girl/It's Amazing	1968	2.00	4.00	8.00
❏ 6637	It Ain't Fair/Till I Can't Take It Anymore	1968	2.00	4.00	8.00
❏ 6666	Hey Little One/When You Love Someone	1969	2.50	5.00	10.00
ATLANTIC					
❏ 3241	Supernatural Thing — Part 1/Supernatural Thing — Part 2	1975	—	2.50	5.00
❏ 3274	Do It in the Name of Love/Imagination	1975	—	2.50	5.00
❏ 3308	We Got Love/I Had a Love	1975	—	2.50	5.00
❏ 3337	I Betch'a You Didn't Know/Smooth Sailing	1976	—	2.50	5.00
❏ 3359	One More Time/Somebody's Knocking	1976	—	2.50	5.00
❏ 3402	Get It Up/Keepin' It To Myself	1977	—	2.50	5.00
—With the Average White Band					
❏ 3427	A Star in the Ghetto/What Is Soul?	1977	—	2.50	5.00
—With the Average White Band					
❏ 3444	Fool for You Anyway/The Message	1977	—	2.50	5.00
—With the Average White Band					
❏ 3494	I See the Light/Tippin'	1978	—	2.50	5.00
❏ 3535	Fly Away to My Wonderland/Spoiled	1978	—	2.50	5.00
❏ 3635	Music Trance/And This Is Love	1979	—	2.00	4.00
❏ 3808	Street Tough/Why Is the Question	1981	—	2.00	4.00
❏ 3839	You Made the Difference in My Life/Souvenirs of Love	1981	—	2.00	4.00
❏ 89234	Spanish Harlem/First Taste of Love	1987	—	—	3.00
❏ 89361	Stand By Me/Yakety Yak	1986	—	—	3.00
—B-side by the Coasters					
❏ 89361 [DJ]	Stand By Me Medley (same on both sides)	1986	2.00	4.00	8.00
—Contains excerpts from all 10 songs on the "Stand By Me" soundtrack album. It is listed here because it uses the same number as the stock release of "Stand By Me."					
❏ 89361 [PS]	Stand By Me/Yakety Yak	1986	—	—	3.00
❏ 89361 [PS]	Stand By Me Medley	1986	2.00	4.00	8.00
—Promo-only sleeve accompanying above medley. Stock and promo sleeves are identical in front but different on back.					
ICHIBAN					
❏ 254	You've Got All of Me/It's All Right	1992	—	—	3.00
❏ 257	You Still Move Me/I'm Gonna Be Somebody	1992	—	—	3.00
MANDALA					
❏ 2512	Take Me to the Pilot/I Guess It's Goodbye	1972	—	2.50	5.00
❏ 2513	Into the Mystic/White Moon	1972	—	2.50	5.00
❏ 2518	Spread Myself Around/Travellin' Woman	1973	—	2.50	5.00
MANHATTAN					
❏ 50078	Save the Last Dance for Me/Wheel of Love	1987	—	—	3.00
❏ 50078 [PS]	Save the Last Dance for Me/Wheel of Love	1987	—	—	3.00
MAXWELL					
❏ 800	I Can't Take It Like a Man/(B-side unknown)	1969	2.00	4.00	8.00
THE RIGHT STUFF					
❏ S7-19728	4th of July, Asbury Park (Sandy)/Janey, Don't You Lose Heart	1997	—	—	3.00
—B-side by Mrs. Fun/Tina & The B-Side Movement					
Albums					
ATCO					
❏ 33-133 [M]	Spanish Harlem	1961	25.00	50.00	100.00
—Yellow label with harp					
❏ 33-133 [M]	Spanish Harlem	1962	10.00	20.00	40.00
—Gold and gray label					
❏ SD 33-133 [S]	Spanish Harlem	1961	37.50	75.00	150.00
—Yellow label with harp					
❏ SD 33-133 [S]	Spanish Harlem	1962	12.50	25.00	50.00
—Purple and brown label					
❏ 33-137 [M]	Ben E. King Sings for Soulful Lovers	1962	10.00	20.00	40.00
❏ SD 33-137 [S]	Ben E. King Sings for Soulful Lovers	1962	15.00	30.00	60.00

Number	Title (A Side/B Side)	Yr	VG	VG+	NM
❑ 33-142 [M]	Don't Play That Song	1962	10.00	20.00	40.00
❑ SD 33-142 [S]	Don't Play That Song	1962	15.00	30.00	60.00
❑ 33-165 [M]	Ben E. King's Greatest Hits	1964	7.50	15.00	30.00
❑ SD 33-165 [S]	Ben E. King's Greatest Hits	1964	10.00	20.00	40.00
—Purple and brown label					
❑ SD 33-165 [S]	Ben E. King's Greatest Hits	1969	3.00	6.00	12.00
—Yellow label					
❑ SD 33-165 [S]	Ben E. King's Greatest Hits	197?	2.00	4.00	8.00
—Any other color label					
❑ 33-174 [M]	Seven Letters	1965	10.00	20.00	40.00
❑ SD 33-174 [S]	Seven Letters	1965	12.50	25.00	50.00
ATLANTIC					
❑ SD 18132	Supernatural	1975	3.00	6.00	12.00
❑ SD 18169	I Have a Love	1976	3.00	6.00	12.00
❑ SD 18191	Rhapsody	1976	3.00	6.00	12.00
❑ SD 19200	Let Me Live in Your Life	1978	3.00	6.00	12.00
❑ SD 19269	Music Trance	1980	2.50	5.00	10.00
❑ SD 19300	Street Tough	1981	2.50	5.00	10.00
❑ 81716	Stand By Me: The Best of Ben E. King	1987	2.00	4.00	8.00
—Includes seven Ben E. King tracks and three by the Drifters					
CLARION					
❑ 606 [M]	Young Boy Blues	1966	6.25	12.50	25.00
❑ SD 606 [S]	Young Boy Blues	1966	7.50	15.00	30.00
MANDALA					
❑ MLP 3007	The Beginning of It All for Ben E. King	1972	5.00	10.00	20.00
❑ MLP-3008 [DJ]	Audio Biography	1972	7.50	15.00	30.00
—Promo-only interview by Richard Robinson					
MAXWELL					
❑ ML-88001	Rough Edges	1969	5.00	10.00	20.00

KING, CAROLE   Also see THE CITY; BERTELL DACHE.

12-Inch Singles

Number	Title (A Side/B Side)	Yr	VG	VG+	NM
ATLANTIC					
❑ PR 427 [DJ]	One to One (same on both sides)	1982	2.00	4.00	8.00
CAPITOL					
❑ SPRO-8863/4 [DJ]	Main Street Saturday Night/Disco Tech	1978	3.00	6.00	12.00

45s

Number	Title (A Side/B Side)	Yr	VG	VG+	NM
ABC-PARAMOUNT					
❑ 9921	Goin' Wild/The Right Girl	1958	37.50	75.00	150.00
❑ 9986	Baby Sittin'/Under the Stars	1958	37.50	75.00	150.00
ALPINE					
❑ 57	Oh, Neil/A Very Special Boy	1959	175.00	350.00	700.00
ATLANTIC					
❑ 4026	One to One/Goat Annie	1982	—	2.00	4.00
❑ 4026 [PS]	One to One/Goat Annie	1982	—	2.50	5.00
❑ 4062	Read Between the Lines/Life Without Love	1982	—	2.00	4.00
❑ 89694 [DJ]	Speeding Time (same on both sides)	1984	—	2.00	4.00
—May be promo only					
❑ 89756	Crying in the Rain/Sacred Heart of Stone	1983	—	2.00	4.00
CAPITOL					
❑ 4455	Hard Rock Cafe/To Know That I Love You	1977	—	2.00	4.00
❑ 4455 [PS]	Hard Rock Cafe/To Know That I Love You	1977	—	2.50	5.00
❑ 4497	Simple Things/Hold On	1977	—	2.00	4.00
❑ 4593	Main Street Saturday Night/Changes	1978	—	2.00	4.00
❑ 4649	Sunbird/Morning Sun	1978	—	2.00	4.00
❑ 4718	Move Lightly/Whiskey	1979	—	2.00	4.00
❑ 4718 [PS]	Move Lightly/Whiskey	1979	—	2.50	5.00
❑ 4766	Time Gone By/Dreamlike I Wander	1979	—	2.00	4.00
❑ 4864	One Fine Day/Rulers of This World	1980	—	2.00	4.00
❑ 4864 [PS]	One Fine Day/Rulers of This World	1980	—	2.00	4.00
—Second pressing sleeves don't list a B-side at all					
❑ 4864 [PS]	One Fine Day/Recipients of History	1980	2.00	4.00	8.00
—First pressing sleeves list the wrong title for the B-side (no records are known to exist with this title)					
❑ 4911	The Locomotion/Oh No Not My Baby	1980	—	2.00	4.00
❑ 4941	Chains/Bad Girl	1980	—	2.00	4.00
❑ B-44336	City Streets/Time Heals All Wounds	1989	—	—	3.00
❑ B-44336 [PS]	City Streets/Time Heals All Wounds	1989	—	—	3.00
❑ 7PRO-79520 [DJ]	City Streets (same on both sides)	1989	—	2.00	4.00
❑ 7PRO-79520 [PS]	City Streets (same on both sides)	1989	—	2.00	4.00
❑ 7PRO-79873 [DJ]	Lovelight (same on both sides)	1989	—	2.50	5.00
—Vinyl is promo only					
COMPANION					
❑ 2000	It Might As Well Rain Until September/Nobody's Perfect	1962	75.00	150.00	300.00
DIMENSION					
❑ 1004	School Bells Are Ringing/I Didn't Have Any Summer Romance	1962	5.00	10.00	20.00
❑ 1009	He's a Bad Boy/We Grew Up Together	1963	5.00	10.00	20.00
❑ 2000	It Might As Well Rain Until September/Nobody's Perfect	1962	3.00	6.00	12.00
—Blue label					
❑ 2000	It Might As Well Rain Until September/Nobody's Perfect	1962	3.75	7.50	15.00
—Purple label					
ODE					
❑ 66006	Eventually/Up On the Roof	1970	2.00	4.00	8.00
❑ 66015	It's Too Late/I Feel the Earth Move	1971	—	2.00	4.00
❑ 66015 [PS]	It's Too Late/I Feel the Earth Move	1971	—	2.50	5.00
❑ 66019	So Far Away/Smackwater Jack	1971	—	2.00	4.00
❑ 66019 [PS]	So Far Away/Smackwater Jack	1971	—	2.50	5.00
❑ 66022	Sweet Seasons/Pocket Money	1971	—	2.00	4.00
❑ 66022 [PS]	Sweet Seasons/Pocket Money	1971	—	2.50	5.00
❑ 66026	It's Going to Take Some Time/Brother Brother	1972	—	3.00	6.00
❑ 66031	Been to Canaan/Bitter with the Sweet	1972	—	2.00	4.00
❑ 66031 [PS]	Been to Canaan/Bitter with the Sweet	1972	—	2.50	5.00
❑ 66035	Believe in Humanity/You Light Up My Life	1973	—	2.00	4.00
❑ 66035 [PS]	Believe in Humanity/You Light Up My Life	1973	—	2.50	5.00
❑ 66039	Corazon/That's How Things Go Down	1973	—	2.00	4.00
❑ 66047	Jazzman/You Go Your Way, I'll Go Mine	1974	—	2.50	5.00
❑ 66047 [PS]	Jazzman/You Go Your Way, I'll Go Mine	1974	—	3.00	6.00
❑ 66101	Jazzman/You Go Your Way, I'll Go Mine	1974	—	2.00	4.00
❑ 66101 [PS]	Jazzman/You Go Your Way, I'll Go Mine	1974	—	2.50	5.00
❑ 66106	Nightingale/You're Something New	1975	—	2.00	4.00
❑ 66112 SP	Chicken Soup with Rice/Pierre	1975	2.00	4.00	8.00
—33 1/3 rpm 7-inch record					
❑ 66112 SP [PS]	Chicken Soup with Rice/Pierre	1975	2.50	5.00	10.00

Number	Title (A Side/B Side)	Yr	VG	VG+	NM
❑ 66119	Only Love Is Real/Still Here Thinking of You	1976	—	2.00	4.00
❑ 66123	High Out of Time/I'd Like to Know You Better	1976	—	2.00	4.00
RCA VICTOR					
❑ 47-7560	Short Mort/Queen of the Beach	1959	25.00	50.00	100.00
TOMORROW					
❑ 7502	A Road to Nowhere/Some of Your Lovin'	1966	10.00	20.00	40.00

7-Inch Extended Plays

Number	Title (A Side/B Side)	Yr	VG	VG+	NM
ODE					
❑ LLP 77013	Brother, Brother/Song of Long Ago/Brighter// Some Kind of Wonderful/Sweet Seasons	1971	2.00	4.00	8.00
—Jukebox issue; small hole, plays at 33 1/3 rpm					
❑ LLP 77013 [PS]	Music	1971	2.00	4.00	8.00
—Part of "Little LP" series (LLP #180)					

Albums

Number	Title (A Side/B Side)	Yr	VG	VG+	NM
ATLANTIC					
❑ SD 19344	One to One	1982	2.50	5.00	10.00
❑ 80118	Speeding Time	1983	2.50	5.00	10.00
CAPITOL					
❑ SPRO-9103/4 [EP]	Touch the Sky Sampler	1979	3.75	7.50	15.00
—Promo-only four-song excerpt from "Touch the Sky"					
❑ SMAS-11667	Simple Things	1977	2.50	5.00	10.00
❑ SW-11785	Welcome Home	1978	2.50	5.00	10.00
❑ SW-11785	Welcome Home	1978	2.50	5.00	10.00
❑ ST-11953	Touch the Sky	1979	2.50	5.00	10.00
❑ SWAK-11963	Touch the Sky	1979	2.50	5.00	10.00
❑ SOO-12073	Pearls — Songs of Goffin and King	1980	2.50	5.00	10.00
❑ SN-16057	Simple Things	1980	2.00	4.00	8.00
—Budget-line reissue					
❑ SN-16058	Welcome Home	1980	2.00	4.00	8.00
—Budget-line reissue					
❑ SN-16059	Touch the Sky	1980	2.00	4.00	8.00
—Budget-line reissue					
❑ C1-90885	City Streets	1989	3.00	6.00	12.00
ODE					
❑ PE 34944	Carole King: Writer	1977	2.50	5.00	10.00
—Reissue of 77006					
❑ FE 34946	Tapestry	1979	2.50	5.00	10.00
—Reissue with new prefix					
❑ PE 34946	Tapestry	1977	2.50	5.00	10.00
—Reissue of 77009					
❑ PE 34949	Music	1977	2.50	5.00	10.00
—Reissue of 77013					
❑ PE 34950	Rhymes and Reasons	1977	2.50	5.00	10.00
—Reissue of 77016					
❑ PE 34953	Wrap Around Joy	1977	2.50	5.00	10.00
—Reissue of 77024					
❑ PE 34955	Really Rosie	1977	2.50	5.00	10.00
—Reissue of 77027					
❑ PE 34962	Fantasy	1977	2.50	5.00	10.00
—Reissue of 77018					
❑ PE 34963	Thoroughbred	1977	2.50	5.00	10.00
—Reissue of 77034					
❑ JE 34967	Her Greatest Hits	1978	2.50	5.00	10.00
❑ HE 44946	Tapestry	1980	12.50	25.00	50.00
—Half-speed mastered edition					
❑ SP-77006	Writer: Carole King	1970	3.00	6.00	12.00
❑ SP-77009	Tapestry	1971	3.00	6.00	12.00
❑ SP-77013	Music	1971	3.00	6.00	12.00
❑ SP-77016	Rhymes and Reasons	1972	3.00	6.00	12.00
❑ SP-77018	Fantasy	1973	3.00	6.00	12.00
❑ SP-77024	Wrap Around Joy	1974	3.00	6.00	12.00
❑ SP-77027	Really Rosie	1975	3.00	6.00	12.00
❑ SP-77034	Thoroughbred	1976	3.00	6.00	12.00
❑ QU-88013 [Q]	Music	1974	5.00	10.00	20.00

KING, CLAUDE

45s

Number	Title (A Side/B Side)	Yr	VG	VG+	NM
CINNAMON					
❑ 808	Don't Do Me Mad/It's Such a Perfect Day for Making Love	1974	—	2.50	5.00
COLUMBIA					
❑ 42043	Big River, Big Man/Sweet Lovin'	1961	2.50	5.00	10.00
❑ 42196	The Comancheros/I Can't Get Over the Way You Got Over Me	1961	2.50	5.00	10.00
❑ 42196 [PS]	The Comancheros/I Can't Get Over the Way You Got Over Me	1961	3.75	7.50	15.00
❑ 42352	Wolverton Mountain/Little Bitty Heart	1962	3.00	6.00	12.00
❑ 42352 [PS]	Wolverton Mountain/Little Bitty Heart	1962	3.75	7.50	15.00
❑ 42581	The Burning of Atlanta/Don't That Moon Look Lonesome	1962	2.50	5.00	10.00
❑ 42581 [PS]	The Burning of Atlanta/Don't That Moon Look Lonesome	1962	3.75	7.50	15.00
❑ 42630	I've Got the World by the Tail/Shopping Center	1962	2.50	5.00	10.00
❑ 42630 [PS]	I've Got the World by the Tail/Shopping Center	1962	3.75	7.50	15.00
❑ 42688	Sheepskin Valley/I Backed Out	1963	2.50	5.00	10.00
❑ 42688 [PS]	Sheepskin Valley/I Backed Out	1963	3.75	7.50	15.00
❑ 42782	Building a Bridge/What Will I Do	1963	2.50	5.00	10.00
❑ 42782 [PS]	Building a Bridge/What Will I Do	1963	3.75	7.50	15.00
❑ 42833	Hey Lucille!/Scarlet O'Hara	1963	2.50	5.00	10.00
❑ 42833 [PS]	Hey Lucille!/Scarlet O'Hara	1963	3.75	7.50	15.00
❑ 42959	That's What Makes the World Go Around/A Lace Mantilla and a Rose of Red	1964	2.00	4.00	8.00
❑ 43083	Sam Hill/Big Ole Shoulder	1964	2.00	4.00	8.00
❑ 43157	Whirlpool (Of Your Love)/This Land of Yours and Mine	1964	2.00	4.00	8.00
❑ 43298	Tiger Woman/When You Gotta Go	1965	2.00	4.00	8.00
❑ 43416	Little Buddy/Come On Home	1965	2.00	4.00	8.00
❑ 43510	Catch a Little Raindrop/Hold That Tiger	1966	2.00	4.00	8.00
❑ 43714	The Juggler/I Won't Be Long in Your Town	1966	2.50	5.00	10.00
❑ 43867	Little Things That Every Girl Should Know/The Right Place	1966	2.00	4.00	8.00
❑ 44035	The Watchman/That's the Way the Wind Blows	1967	2.00	4.00	8.00
❑ 44237	Laura (What's He Got That I Ain't Got)/Good-By My Love	1967	2.00	4.00	8.00
❑ 44340	Yellow Haired Woman/Ninety-Nine Years	1967	2.00	4.00	8.00
❑ 44504	Parchman Farm Blues/Birmingham Bus Station	1968	2.00	4.00	8.00

K

Number	Title (A Side/B Side)	Yr	VG	VG+	NM
□ 44642	The Power of Your Sweet Love/Beertops and Teardrops	1968	2.00	4.00	8.00
□ 44749	Sweet Love on My Mind/Four Roses	1969	2.00	4.00	8.00
□ 44833	All for the Love of a Girl/I Remember Johnny	1969	2.00	4.00	8.00
□ 44833 [PS]	All for the Love of a Girl/I Remember Johnny	1969	3.00	6.00	12.00
□ 45015	Friend, Lover, Woman, Wife/The House of the Rising Sun	1969	2.00	4.00	8.00
□ 45142	I'll Be Your Baby Tonight/It's Good to Have My Baby Home	1970	—	3.00	6.00
□ 45248	Mary's Vineyard/Johnny Valentine	1970	—	3.00	6.00
□ 45340	Chip 'n' Dale's Place/Highway Lonely	1971	—	3.00	6.00
□ 45441	When You're Twenty-One/Heart	1971	—	3.00	6.00
□ 45515	Darlin' Raise the Shade (Let the Sun Shine In)/Sweet Mary Ann	1971	—	3.00	6.00
□ 45614	The Lady of Our Town/Just As Soon As I Get Over Loving You	1972	—	3.00	6.00
□ 45704	He Ain't Country/This Time I'm Through	1972	—	3.00	6.00

TRUE

Number	Title (A Side/B Side)	Yr	VG	VG+	NM
□ 103	Cotton Dan/I'll Spend My Lifetime Loving You	1977	—	3.00	6.00
□ 106	Sugar Baby, Candy Girl/(B-side unknown)	1977	—	3.00	6.00
□ 124	Wobble Water/(B-side unknown)	197?	—	3.00	6.00

Albums
COLUMBIA

Number	Title (A Side/B Side)	Yr	VG	VG+	NM
□ CS 1024	Friend, Lover, Woman, Wife	1970	3.75	7.50	15.00
□ CL 1810 [M]	Meet Claude King	1962	6.25	12.50	25.00
—Six "eye" logos on label					
□ CL 1810 [M]	Meet Claude King	1963	3.75	7.50	15.00
—"Guaranteed High Fidelity" or "Mono" on red label					
□ CL 2415 [M]	Tiger Woman	1965	5.00	10.00	20.00
□ CS 8610 [S]	Meet Claude King	1962	10.00	20.00	40.00
—Six "eye" logos on label					
□ CS 8610 [S]	Meet Claude King	1963	5.00	10.00	20.00
—"360 Sound Stereo" on red label					
□ CS 9215 [S]	Tiger Woman	1965	6.25	12.50	25.00
—"360 Sound Stereo" on red label					
□ CS 9789	I Remember Johnny Horton	1968	3.75	7.50	15.00
—"360 Sound Stereo" on red label					
□ C 30804	Chip 'n' Dale's Place	1971	3.75	7.50	15.00

HARMONY

Number	Title (A Side/B Side)	Yr	VG	VG+	NM
□ HS 11300	The Best of Claude King	1969	3.00	6.00	12.00

KING, CLYDIE
45s
IMPERIAL

Number	Title (A Side/B Side)	Yr	VG	VG+	NM
□ 66109	The Thrill Is Gone/If You Were a Man	1965	5.00	10.00	20.00
□ 66139	My Love Grows Deeper/Missin' My Baby	1965	5.00	10.00	20.00
□ 66172	He Always Comes Back to Me/Soft and Gentle Ways	1966	5.00	10.00	20.00

LIZARD

Number	Title (A Side/B Side)	Yr	VG	VG+	NM
□ 21007	'Bout Love/(B-side unknown)	1971	—	3.00	6.00

MINIT

Number	Title (A Side/B Side)	Yr	VG	VG+	NM
□ 32025	Good for Cryin' Over You Days/Mistakes of Yesterday	1967	3.00	6.00	12.00
□ 32054	Love Now, Pay Later/One Part, Two Part	1969	2.00	4.00	8.00

PHILIPS

Number	Title (A Side/B Side)	Yr	VG	VG+	NM
□ 40001	Boys in My Life/Promises	1962	5.00	10.00	20.00
□ 40051	Turn Around/Don't Hang Up the Phone	1962	5.00	10.00	20.00
□ 40107	Only the Guilty Cry/By Noro	1963	5.00	10.00	20.00

SPECIALTY

Number	Title (A Side/B Side)	Yr	VG	VG+	NM
□ 605	Our Romance/Written on the Wall	1957	7.50	15.00	30.00

Albums
LIZARD

Number	Title (A Side/B Side)	Yr	VG	VG+	NM
□ A-20104	Direct Me	1971	3.00	6.00	12.00

KING, CURTIS No, not King Curtis.
45s
COLUMBIA

Number	Title (A Side/B Side)	Yr	VG	VG+	NM
□ 44096	Bad Habits/So Nice While It Lasted	1967	5.00	10.00	20.00

KING, EARL
45s
ACE

Number	Title (A Side/B Side)	Yr	VG	VG+	NM
□ 509	Those Lonely, Lonely Nights/Baby You Can Get Your Gun	1955	15.00	30.00	60.00
□ 514	My Love Is Strong/Little Girl	1956	12.50	25.00	50.00
□ 517	It Must Have Been Love/I'll Take You Back Home	1956	12.50	25.00	50.00
□ 520	Is Everything Alright/Mother Told Me Not to Go	1956	12.50	25.00	50.00
□ 529	Those Lonely, Lonely Feelings/You Can Fly High	1957	12.50	25.00	50.00
□ 543	I'll Never Get Tired/Well'o, Well'o, Well'o Baby	1958	12.50	25.00	50.00
□ 564	Weary Silent Night/Everybody's Carried Away	1959	10.00	20.00	40.00
□ 598	Don't You Know You're Wrong/Buddy It's Time to Go	1960	10.00	20.00	40.00

IMPERIAL

Number	Title (A Side/B Side)	Yr	VG	VG+	NM
□ 5713	Come On — Part 1/Come On — Part 2	1960	6.25	12.50	25.00
□ 5730	Love Me Now/The Things That I Used to Do	1961	6.25	12.50	25.00
□ 5750	Come Along with Me/You're More to Me Than Gold	1961	6.25	12.50	25.00
□ 5774	You Better Know/Mama and Papa	1961	6.25	12.50	25.00
□ 5811	Trick Bag/Always a First Time	1962	6.25	12.50	25.00
□ 5858	We Are Just Friends/You're More to Me That Gold	1962	6.25	12.50	25.00
□ 5891	Come Along with Me/Case of Love	1962	6.25	12.50	25.00

REX

Number	Title (A Side/B Side)	Yr	VG	VG+	NM
□ 1015	I Can't Help Myself/Darling Honey, Angel Child	1961	5.00	10.00	20.00

SPECIALTY

Number	Title (A Side/B Side)	Yr	VG	VG+	NM
□ 495	A Mother's Love/I'm Your Best Bet Baby	1954	15.00	30.00	60.00
□ 531	No One But Me/Eating and Sleeping	1954	15.00	30.00	60.00
□ 558	Funny Face/Sittin' and Wonderin'	1955	15.00	30.00	60.00

KING, FREDDIE
45s
COTILLION

Number	Title (A Side/B Side)	Yr	VG	VG+	NM
□ 44015	Funky/Play It Cool	1968	2.00	4.00	8.00
□ 44058	I Wonder Why/Yonder Wall	1970	2.00	4.00	8.00

EL-BEE

Number	Title (A Side/B Side)	Yr	VG	VG+	NM
□ 157	Country Boy/That's What You Think	1956	100.00	200.00	400.00

FEDERAL

Number	Title (A Side/B Side)	Yr	VG	VG+	NM
□ 12384	Have You Ever Loved a Woman/You've Got to Love Her with a Feeling	1960	10.00	20.00	40.00
□ 12401	Hideaway/I Love the Woman	1961	7.50	15.00	30.00
□ 12415	Lonesome Whistle Blues/It's Too Bad Things Are Going So Tough	1961	7.50	15.00	30.00
□ 12428	San-Ho-Zay/See See Baby	1961	7.50	15.00	30.00
□ 12432	I'm Tore Down/Sen-Say-Shun	1961	7.50	15.00	30.00
□ 12439	Christmas Tears/I Hear Jingle Bells	1961	7.50	15.00	30.00
□ 12443	If You Believe in What You Do/Heads Up	1961	5.00	10.00	20.00
□ 12450	Takin' Care of Business/The Stumble	1962	5.00	10.00	20.00
□ 12456	Side Tracked/Sittin' on the Boat Dock	1962	5.00	10.00	20.00
□ 12462	What About Love/Texas Oil	1962	5.00	10.00	20.00
□ 12470	Come On/Just Pickin'	1962	5.00	10.00	20.00
□ 12475	In the Open/I'm On My Way to Atlanta	1962	5.00	10.00	20.00
□ 12482	The Bossa Nova Watusi Twist/Look Ma, I'm Crying	1963	3.75	7.50	15.00
□ 12491	(I'd Love To) Make Love to You/One Hundred Years	1963	3.75	7.50	15.00
□ 12499	(The Welfare) Turns Its Back on You/You're Barkin' Up the Wrong Tree	1963	3.75	7.50	15.00
□ 12509	Surf Monkey/Monkey Donkey	1963	5.00	10.00	20.00
□ 12515	Meet Me at the Station/Ting-a-Ling	1964	3.75	7.50	15.00
□ 12518	Driving Sideways/Someday After Awhile (You'll Be Gone)	1964	3.00	6.00	12.00
□ 12521	She Put the Whammy on Me/High Rise	1964	3.00	6.00	12.00
□ 12529	Now I've Got a Woman/Onion Rings	1964	3.00	6.00	12.00
□ 12532	Some Other Day, Some Other Time/Manhole	1965	3.00	6.00	12.00
□ 12535	If You Have It/I Love You More Every Day	1965	3.00	6.00	12.00
□ 12537	Full Time Love/She's the One	1965	3.00	6.00	12.00

KING

Number	Title (A Side/B Side)	Yr	VG	VG+	NM
□ 6057	Use What You've Got/Double Eyed Whammy	1966	3.00	6.00	12.00
□ 6080	You've Got Me Licked/The Girl from Kookamunga	1967	3.00	6.00	12.00
□ 6264	Have You Ever Loved a Woman/Hideaway	1969	2.00	4.00	8.00

RSO

Number	Title (A Side/B Side)	Yr	VG	VG+	NM
□ 505	My Credit Didn't Go Through/Texas Flyer	1975	—	2.50	5.00
□ 516	Boogie Bump/It's Your Love	1975	—	2.50	5.00

SHELTER

Number	Title (A Side/B Side)	Yr	VG	VG+	NM
□ 7303	Going Down/Toke Down	1971	—	3.00	6.00
□ 7320	Me and My Guitar/Downtown in Lodi	1972	—	3.00	6.00
□ 7333	Woman Across the River/Help Me Through the Day	1973	—	3.00	6.00
□ 40410	Going Down/Me and My Guitar	1975	—	2.50	5.00

Albums
COTILLION

Number	Title (A Side/B Side)	Yr	VG	VG+	NM
□ SD 9004	Freddie King Is a Blues Master	1969	6.25	12.50	25.00
□ SD 9016	My Feeling for the Blues	1970	6.25	12.50	25.00

KING

Number	Title (A Side/B Side)	Yr	VG	VG+	NM
□ 762 [M]	Freddie King Sings the Blues	1961	62.50	125.00	250.00
□ 773 [M]	Let's Hide Away and Dance Away	1961	62.50	125.00	250.00
□ 821 [M]	Bossa Nova and Blues	1962	37.50	75.00	150.00
□ 856 [M]	Freddie King Goes Surfin'	1963	20.00	40.00	80.00
□ KS-856 [S]	Freddie King Goes Surfin'	1963	30.00	60.00	120.00
□ 928 [M]	A Bonanza of Instrumentals	1965	12.50	25.00	50.00
□ KS-928 [S]	A Bonanza of Instrumentals	1965	15.00	30.00	60.00
□ 964 [M]	24 Vocals and Instrumentals	1966	6.25	12.50	25.00
□ KS-1059	Hide Away	1969	3.75	7.50	15.00

MCA

Number	Title (A Side/B Side)	Yr	VG	VG+	NM
□ 690	The Best of Freddie King	1979	2.00	4.00	8.00
—Reissue of Shelter 52021					

MODERN BLUES

Number	Title (A Side/B Side)	Yr	VG	VG+	NM
□ MB2LP-721 [(2)]	Just Pickin'	198?	3.75	7.50	15.00
□ MBLP-722	Freddie King Sings	198?	2.50	5.00	10.00

RSO

Number	Title (A Side/B Side)	Yr	VG	VG+	NM
□ RS-1-3025	Freddie King 1934-1976	1977	3.00	6.00	12.00
□ SD 4803	Burglar	1974	3.00	6.00	12.00
□ SD 4811	Larger Than Life	1975	3.00	6.00	12.00

SHELTER

Number	Title (A Side/B Side)	Yr	VG	VG+	NM
□ 2140	The Best of Freddie King	1975	3.75	7.50	15.00
—Original with MCA distribution					
□ SW-8905	Getting Ready	1971	3.75	7.50	15.00
□ SW-8913	Texas Cannonball	1972	3.75	7.50	15.00
□ SW-8919	Woman Across the River	1973	3.75	7.50	15.00
□ SRL 52021	The Best of Freddie King	1977	3.00	6.00	12.00
—Second edition with ABC distribution					

STARDAY/GUSTO

Number	Title (A Side/B Side)	Yr	VG	VG+	NM
□ 5012	17 Original Hits	1977	2.50	5.00	10.00
□ 5033	Hide Away	1978	2.50	5.00	10.00

KING, FREDDIE/LULA REED/BOBBY THOMPSON
Albums
KING

Number	Title (A Side/B Side)	Yr	VG	VG+	NM
□ 777 [M]	Boy-Girl-Boy	1962	62.50	125.00	250.00

KING, JEAN
45s
HANNA-BARBERA

Number	Title (A Side/B Side)	Yr	VG	VG+	NM
□ 497	Don't Say Goodbye/It's Good Enough for Me	1966	2.50	5.00	10.00

Albums
HANNA-BARBERA

Number	Title (A Side/B Side)	Yr	VG	VG+	NM
□ HLP-8505 [M]	Jean King Sings for the In Crowd	1966	5.00	10.00	20.00

KING, JOE
45s
HIT

Number	Title (A Side/B Side)	Yr	VG	VG+	NM
□ 265	Sunshine Superman/Dandy	1966	2.00	4.00	8.00
—B-side by the Chords (2)					
□ 273	Mellow Yellow/I'm a Believer	1966	2.00	4.00	8.00
—B-side by the Jalopy Five					

Number	Title (A Side/B Side)	Yr	VG	VG+	NM

KING, JONATHAN Also see HEDGEHOPPERS ANONYMOUS.
45s
PARROT

Number	Title (A Side/B Side)	Yr	VG	VG+	NM
❑ 3005	Just Like a Woman/Land of the Golden Tree	1966	2.00	4.00	8.00
❑ 3008	Icicles (Fell from the Heart of a Bluebird)/In a Hundred Years from Now	1966	2.00	4.00	8.00
❑ 3011	Round, Round/Time and Motion	1967	2.00	4.00	8.00
❑ 3021	1968 (Message to the Presidential Candidates)/Colloquial Sex	1968	2.00	4.00	8.00
❑ 3027	Lazy Bones/Just Want to Say Thank You	1968	2.00	4.00	8.00
❑ 3029	Hooked on a Feeling/I Don't Want to Be Gay	1969	—	3.00	6.00
❑ 3030	Flirt/Hey Jim	1969	—	3.00	6.00
❑ 9774	Everyone's Gone to the Moon/Summer's Coming	1965	2.50	5.00	10.00
❑ 9804	Green Is the Grass/Where the Sun Has Never Shown	1965	2.00	4.00	8.00
❑ 40047	Let It All Hang Out/Colloquial Sex	1970	—	3.00	6.00
❑ 40055	Cherry Cherry/Gay Girl	1970	—	3.00	6.00

UK

Number	Title (A Side/B Side)	Yr	VG	VG+	NM
❑ 49002	It's a Tall Order for a Short Guy/Learned Tax Counsel	1972	—	2.50	5.00
❑ 49014	Mary, My Love/A Little Bit Left of Right	1973	—	2.50	5.00
❑ 49018	The Kung Fu Anthem/A Little Bit Left of Right	1973	—	2.50	5.00
❑ 49034	The Way You Look Tonight/The True Story of Molly Malone	1974	—	2.50	5.00

Albums
PARROT

Number	Title (A Side/B Side)	Yr	VG	VG+	NM
❑ PA 61013 [M]	Jonathan King Or Then Again....	1967	10.00	20.00	40.00
❑ PAS 71013 [P]	Jonathan King Or Then Again....	1967	12.50	25.00	50.00

—Only "Where the Sun Has Never Shown" is rechanneled.
U.K.

Number	Title (A Side/B Side)	Yr	VG	VG+	NM
❑ 53101	Bubble Rock Is Here to Stay	1972	6.25	12.50	25.00
❑ 53104	Pandora's Box	1973	6.25	12.50	25.00

KING, MORGANA
45s
MAINSTREAM

Number	Title (A Side/B Side)	Yr	VG	VG+	NM
❑ 600	A Taste of Honey/Corcavado	1964	2.50	5.00	10.00
❑ 602	When the World Was Young/Lazy Afternoon	1964	2.50	5.00	10.00
❑ 623	Try to Remember/Cuore di Mama	1964	2.50	5.00	10.00

MERCURY

Number	Title (A Side/B Side)	Yr	VG	VG+	NM
❑ 70927	Homesick in Paris/For You and Me	1956	3.75	7.50	15.00
❑ 70967	Four Walls, Two Windows, One Broken Heart/Mine for the Taking	1956	3.75	7.50	15.00

PARAMOUNT

Number	Title (A Side/B Side)	Yr	VG	VG+	NM
❑ 0245	A Song for You/You Are the Sunshine of My Life	1973	—	2.50	5.00
❑ 0275	Jennifer Had/Like a Seed	1974	—	2.50	5.00

REPRISE

Number	Title (A Side/B Side)	Yr	VG	VG+	NM
❑ 0481	If You Should Leave Me (E Se Domani)/Mountain High, Valley Low	1966	2.00	4.00	8.00
❑ 0604	The Look of Love/I Have Loved Me a Man	1967	2.00	4.00	8.00

20TH FOX

Number	Title (A Side/B Side)	Yr	VG	VG+	NM
❑ 142	Give Me Love/Lost, Lonely and Looking for Love	1959	3.00	6.00	12.00

VERVE

Number	Title (A Side/B Side)	Yr	VG	VG+	NM
❑ 10615	I Know How It Feels to Be Lonely/I Only Know I Loved You	1968	—	3.00	6.00
❑ 10630	Didn't We/Eleanor Rigby	1968	—	3.00	6.00

WING

Number	Title (A Side/B Side)	Yr	VG	VG+	NM
❑ 90073	In the Wee Small Hours of the Morning/It's De-Lovely	1956	3.75	7.50	15.00

Albums
ASCOT

Number	Title (A Side/B Side)	Yr	VG	VG+	NM
❑ AM 13014 [M]	The Winter of My Discontent	1964	6.25	12.50	25.00
❑ AM 13019 [M]	The End of a Love Affair	1965	6.25	12.50	25.00

—Reissue of United Artists 30020

Number	Title (A Side/B Side)	Yr	VG	VG+	NM
❑ AM 13020 [M]	Everybody Loves Saturday Night	1965	6.25	12.50	25.00
❑ AM 13025 [M]	More Morgana	1965	6.25	12.50	25.00
❑ AS 16014 [S]	The Winter of My Discontent	1964	7.50	15.00	30.00
❑ AS 16019 [S]	The End of a Love Affair	1965	7.50	15.00	30.00

—Reissue of United Artists 40020

Number	Title (A Side/B Side)	Yr	VG	VG+	NM
❑ AS 16020 [S]	Everybody Loves Saturday Night	1965	7.50	15.00	30.00
❑ AS 16025 [S]	More Morgana	1965	7.50	15.00	30.00

EMARCY

Number	Title (A Side/B Side)	Yr	VG	VG+	NM
❑ MG-36079 [M]	For You, For Me, Forever More	1956	20.00	40.00	80.00

MAINSTREAM

Number	Title (A Side/B Side)	Yr	VG	VG+	NM
❑ MRL-321	Taste of Honey	1972	3.75	7.50	15.00
❑ MRL-355	Cuore di Mama	1974	3.75	7.50	15.00
❑ S-6015 [S]	With a Taste of Honey	1964	6.25	12.50	25.00
❑ S-6052 [S]	Miss Morgana King	1965	6.25	12.50	25.00
❑ 56015 [M]	With a Taste of Honey	1964	5.00	10.00	20.00
❑ 56052 [M]	Miss Morgana King	1965	5.00	10.00	20.00

MERCURY

Number	Title (A Side/B Side)	Yr	VG	VG+	NM
❑ MG-20231 [M]	Morgana King Sings the Blues	1958	20.00	40.00	80.00

MUSE

Number	Title (A Side/B Side)	Yr	VG	VG+	NM
❑ MR-5166	Stretchin' Out	1977	2.50	5.00	10.00
❑ MR-5190	Everything Must Change	1978	2.50	5.00	10.00
❑ MR-5224	Higher Ground	1979	2.50	5.00	10.00
❑ MR-5257	Looking Through the Eyes of Love	1981	2.50	5.00	10.00
❑ MR-5301	Portraits	1983	2.50	5.00	10.00
❑ MR-5326	Simply Eloquent	1986	2.50	5.00	10.00
❑ MR-5339	Another Time, Another Space	1988	2.50	5.00	10.00

PARAMOUNT

Number	Title (A Side/B Side)	Yr	VG	VG+	NM
❑ PAS-6067	New Beginnings	1973	3.00	6.00	12.00

RCA CAMDEN

Number	Title (A Side/B Side)	Yr	VG	VG+	NM
❑ CAL-543 [M]	The Greatest Songs Ever Swung	1959	5.00	10.00	20.00
❑ CAS-543 [S]	The Greatest Songs Ever Swung	1959	7.50	15.00	30.00

REPRISE

Number	Title (A Side/B Side)	Yr	VG	VG+	NM
❑ R 6192 [M]	It's a Quiet Thing	1966	5.00	10.00	20.00
❑ RS 6192 [S]	It's a Quiet Thing	1966	6.25	12.50	25.00
❑ R 6205 [M]	Wild Is Love	1966	5.00	10.00	20.00
❑ RS 6205 [S]	Wild Is Love	1966	6.25	12.50	25.00
❑ R 6257 [M]	Gemini Changes	1967	5.00	10.00	20.00
❑ RS 6257 [S]	Gemini Changes	1967	6.25	12.50	25.00

TRIP

Number	Title (A Side/B Side)	Yr	VG	VG+	NM
❑ 5533	Morgana King Sings	197?	2.50	5.00	10.00

UNITED ARTISTS

Number	Title (A Side/B Side)	Yr	VG	VG+	NM
❑ UAL 3028 [M]	Folk Songs A La King	1960	10.00	20.00	40.00
❑ UAS 6028 [S]	Folk Songs A La King	1960	12.50	25.00	50.00
❑ UAL 30020 [M]	Let Me Love You	1960	12.50	25.00	50.00
❑ UAS 40020 [S]	Let Me Love You	1960	15.00	30.00	60.00

VERVE

Number	Title (A Side/B Side)	Yr	VG	VG+	NM
❑ V-5061 [M]	I Know How It Feels	1968	6.25	12.50	25.00
❑ V6-5061 [S]	I Know How It Feels	1968	6.25	12.50	25.00

WING

Number	Title (A Side/B Side)	Yr	VG	VG+	NM
❑ MGW-12307 [M]	More Morgana King	1965	3.75	7.50	15.00
❑ SRW-16307 [S]	More Morgana King	1965	5.00	10.00	20.00

KING, PEGGY
45s
BUENA VISTA

Number	Title (A Side/B Side)	Yr	VG	VG+	NM
❑ 397	Bon Voyage/I Get a Kick Out of Kissin'	1962	2.50	5.00	10.00

BULLET

Number	Title (A Side/B Side)	Yr	VG	VG+	NM
❑ 77	I Can't Make It on My Own/I Can't Get Over Gettin'	1971	—	3.00	6.00

COLUMBIA

Number	Title (A Side/B Side)	Yr	VG	VG+	NM
❑ 4-40273	Burn 'Em Up/The Hottentot	1954	3.75	7.50	15.00
❑ 4-40362	I'm Gonna Put Some Glue 'Round The Christmas Tree/Counting Sheep	1954	3.75	7.50	15.00
❑ 4-40363	Make Yourself Comfortable/The Gentleman in the Next Apartment	1954	3.00	6.00	12.00
❑ 4-40437	Any Questions/You Never Gave It a Try	1955	3.00	6.00	12.00
❑ 4-40524	Please Wait for Me/You Did, You Did	1955	3.00	6.00	12.00
❑ 4-40562	Learning to Love/Song of Seventeen	1955	3.00	6.00	12.00
❑ 4-40614	You Better Go Now/Learning to Love	1955	3.00	6.00	12.00
❑ 4-40638	Kiss and Run/Angel Pie (Postillon!)	1956	3.00	6.00	12.00
❑ 4-40744	Tall Boy/The Test of Time	1956	3.00	6.00	12.00
❑ 4-40773	Love Sick/He Never Looks My Way	1956	3.00	6.00	12.00
❑ 4-40863	Mircle Man/In My Own Little Corner	1957	3.00	6.00	12.00
❑ 4-40996	If You Don't Love Me/C'mon Over	1957	3.00	6.00	12.00
❑ 4-41054	Zero Hour/No Sleep Till Dawn	1957	3.00	6.00	12.00

MGM

Number	Title (A Side/B Side)	Yr	VG	VG+	NM
❑ K11260	There's Doubt in My Mind/I Cried for You	1952	3.75	7.50	15.00

ROULETTE

Number	Title (A Side/B Side)	Yr	VG	VG+	NM
❑ 4327	I'll Be Around/Up, Up, Up (Flying High)	1961	2.50	5.00	10.00

Albums
COLUMBIA

Number	Title (A Side/B Side)	Yr	VG	VG+	NM
❑ CL 2549 [10]	Wish Upon a Star	1955	12.50	25.00	50.00

IMPERIAL

Number	Title (A Side/B Side)	Yr	VG	VG+	NM
❑ LP-9078 [M]	Lazy Afternoon	1959	5.00	10.00	20.00
❑ LP-12026 [S]	Lazy Afternoon	1959	7.50	15.00	30.00

STASH

Number	Title (A Side/B Side)	Yr	VG	VG+	NM
❑ 246	Peggy King Sings Jerome Kern: Till the Clouds Roll By	198?	2.00	4.00	8.00

KING, REV. MARTIN LUTHER The 1968 releases are posthumous tributes.
45s
GORDY

Number	Title (A Side/B Side)	Yr	VG	VG+	NM
❑ 7023	I Have a Dream/We Shall Overcome	1963	7.50	15.00	30.00
❑ 7023	I Have a Dream/We Shall Overcome	1968	2.00	4.00	8.00

—B-side by Liz Lands; "Gordy" on side of label
MERCURY

Number	Title (A Side/B Side)	Yr	VG	VG+	NM
❑ 72814	I Have a Dream/I've Been to the Mountain Top-Eulogy	1968	2.00	4.00	8.00

Albums
BUDDAH

Number	Title (A Side/B Side)	Yr	VG	VG+	NM
❑ BDS-2002	Man of Love	1968	5.00	10.00	20.00

CREED

Number	Title (A Side/B Side)	Yr	VG	VG+	NM
❑ 3201 [M]	I Have a Dream	1968	5.00	10.00	20.00

DOOTO

Number	Title (A Side/B Side)	Yr	VG	VG+	NM
❑ DTL-831 [M]	Martin Luther King at Zion Hill	1962	7.50	15.00	30.00
❑ DTL-841	The American Dream	1968	5.00	10.00	20.00

GORDY

Number	Title (A Side/B Side)	Yr	VG	VG+	NM
❑ G-906 [M]	The Great March to Freedom	1963	10.00	20.00	40.00

—"Gordy" in script at top of label

Number	Title (A Side/B Side)	Yr	VG	VG+	NM
❑ G-906 [M]	The Great March to Freedom	1968	3.75	7.50	15.00

—Later pressings

Number	Title (A Side/B Side)	Yr	VG	VG+	NM
❑ G-908 [M]	The Great March on Washington	1963	10.00	20.00	40.00

—"Gordy" in script at top of label

Number	Title (A Side/B Side)	Yr	VG	VG+	NM
❑ G-908 [M]	The Great March on Washington	1968	3.75	7.50	15.00

—Later pressings

Number	Title (A Side/B Side)	Yr	VG	VG+	NM
❑ G-929	...Free at Last	1968	7.50	15.00	30.00

—Original with gatefold cover
MERCURY

Number	Title (A Side/B Side)	Yr	VG	VG+	NM
❑ SR-61170	In Search of Freedom	1968	5.00	10.00	20.00

MR. MAESTRO

Number	Title (A Side/B Side)	Yr	VG	VG+	NM
❑ 1000 [M]	The March on Washington	1963	7.50	15.00	30.00

SUNSET

Number	Title (A Side/B Side)	Yr	VG	VG+	NM
❑ 21033	The Struggle for Freedom	1968	3.75	7.50	15.00

20TH CENTURY

Number	Title (A Side/B Side)	Yr	VG	VG+	NM
❑ TCF-3110 [M]	Freedom March on Washington	1963	7.50	15.00	30.00
❑ S-3201	The Rev. Dr. Martin Luther King, Jr.	1968	5.00	10.00	20.00

UNART

Number	Title (A Side/B Side)	Yr	VG	VG+	NM
❑ S 21033	In the Struggle for Freedom and Human Dignity	1968	5.00	10.00	20.00

KING, SLEEPY
45s
AWAKE

Number	Title (A Side/B Side)	Yr	VG	VG+	NM
❑ 852	Rock Rock/Still in My Heart	196?	12.50	25.00	50.00
❑ 909	Lost Man/The Pillow	196?	15.00	30.00	60.00

JOY

Number	Title (A Side/B Side)	Yr	VG	VG+	NM
❑ 257	Pushin' Your Luck/The King Steps Out	1961	3.75	7.50	15.00
❑ 261	It's Written All Over Your Face/Happy Music	1962	3.75	7.50	15.00
❑ 263	Lovin' Time/Slowly But Surely	1962	3.75	7.50	15.00

SYMBOL

Number	Title (A Side/B Side)	Yr	VG	VG+	NM
❑ 904	Begging/My Time Ain't Long	1959	7.50	15.00	30.00

VEEP

Number	Title (A Side/B Side)	Yr	VG	VG+	NM
❑ 1236	Hello Martha/Please Let a Fool In Out of the Rain	1966	3.00	6.00	12.00

K

Number	Title (A Side/B Side)	Yr	VG	VG+	NM
KING, TEDDI					
45s					
CORAL					
❏ 9-62094	BLue Tango/River of Regret	1959	2.50	5.00	10.00
RCA VICTOR					
❏ 47-6392	Mr. Wonderful/Are You Slipping Through My Fingers	1956	3.00	6.00	12.00
❏ 47-6392 [PS]	Mr. Wonderful/Are You Slipping Through My Fingers	1956	6.25	12.50	25.00
—Promo-only "This Is Her Life" cartoon sleeve					
❏ 47-6575	Impossible/I Can Honestly Say It's a Lie	1956	3.00	6.00	12.00
❏ 47-6660	Married I Can Always Get/Traveling Down a Lonely Road	1956	3.00	6.00	12.00
❏ 47-6866	Say It Isn't So/There's So Much More	1956	3.00	6.00	12.00
❏ 47-7026	I Was a Child Till Tonight/Then It Starts Again	1956	3.00	6.00	12.00
❏ 47-7074	Every Woman/A Lot in Common	1957	3.00	6.00	12.00
❏ 47-7297	Say a Prayer/Baisez-Moi (Kiss Me)	1958	3.00	6.00	12.00
Albums					
AUDIOPHILE					
❏ AP-117	Lovers and Losers	1976	3.75	7.50	15.00
❏ AP-150	Someone to Light Up Your Life	1979	3.00	6.00	12.00
CORAL					
❏ CRL 57278 [M]	All the King's Songs	1959	15.00	30.00	60.00
❏ CRL 757278 [S]	All the King's Songs	1959	20.00	40.00	80.00
RCA VICTOR					
❏ LPM-1147 [M]	Bidin' My Time	1956	20.00	40.00	80.00
❏ LPM-1313 [M]	To You from Teddi King	1957	20.00	40.00	80.00
❏ LPM-1454 [M]	A Girl and Her Songs	1957	20.00	40.00	80.00
STORYVILLE					
❏ STLP-302 [10]	'Round Midnight	1954	50.00	100.00	200.00
❏ STLP-314 [10]	Storyville Presents Teddi King	1954	50.00	100.00	200.00
❏ STLP-903 [M]	Now In Vogue	1956	30.00	60.00	120.00
KING, TEDDI, AND DAVE MCKENNA					
Albums					
INNER CITY					
❏ IC-1044	This Is New	1977	3.75	7.50	15.00
KING BEES, THE More than one group.					
45s					
CHECKER					
❏ 909	Buzzin'/Good Rockin' Tonight	1958	20.00	40.00	80.00
FLIP					
❏ 323	Puppy Love/Give Me Your Number	1957	10.00	20.00	40.00
KRC					
❏ 302	Lovely Love/Can't You Understand?	1957	10.00	20.00	40.00
NOBLE					
❏ 715	Tender Love/What Could Have Been Can't Be	1959	62.50	125.00	250.00
RCA VICTOR					
❏ 47-8688	What She Does to Me/That Ain't Love	1965	3.00	6.00	12.00
❏ 47-8787	On Your Way Down the Drain/Rhythm and Blues	1966	3.00	6.00	12.00
❏ 47-8979	Lost in the Shuffle/Hardly (Part 3)	1966	3.00	6.00	12.00
KING BISCUIT BOY					
45s					
EPIC					
❏ 50129	New Orleans/I'm Writing You a Letter	1975	—	2.50	5.00
PARAMOUNT					
❏ 0052	Corrina, Corrina/Cookin' Little Baby	1970	—	2.50	5.00
❏ 0076	King Biscuit's Boogie/Badly Bent	1971	—	2.50	5.00
Albums					
EPIC					
❏ KE 32891	King Biscuit Boy	1974	3.00	6.00	12.00
PARAMOUNT					
❏ PAS-5030	Official Music	1970	3.75	7.50	15.00
—As "King Biscuit Boy with Crowbar"					
❏ PAS-6023	Gooduns	1972	3.75	7.50	15.00
KING CRIMSON					
12-Inch Singles					
WARNER BROS.					
❏ PRO-A-2131 [DJ]	Sleepless (Long Version)/Sleepless (Short Version)	1984	2.00	4.00	8.00
❏ PRO-A-2148 [DJ]	3 of a Perfect Pair/Man with an Open Heart	1984	2.00	4.00	8.00
❏ 20193	Sleepless (Dance Mix)/(Instrumental)	1984	—	3.00	6.00
45s					
ATLANTIC					
❏ 2702	The Court of the Crimson King - Part 1/Part 2	1970	3.00	6.00	12.00
❏ 3016	Night Watch/The Great Deceiver	1974	—	3.00	6.00
WARNER BROS.					
❏ 29309	Sleepless/Nuages (That Which Passes, Passes Like Clouds)	1984	—	2.50	5.00
❏ 29964	Heartbeat/Requiem	1982	—	2.50	5.00
Albums					
ATLANTIC					
❏ SD 7212	Islands	1972	5.00	10.00	20.00
❏ SD 7263	Larks' Tongues in Aspic	1973	5.00	10.00	20.00
❏ SD 7298	Starless and Bible Black	1974	5.00	10.00	20.00
❏ 8245 [M]	In the Court of the Crimson King — An Observation by King Crimson	1969	12.50	25.00	50.00
—Mono is white label promo only; comes in stereo cover with "DJ Copy Monaural" sticker on front					
❏ SD 8245	In the Court of the Crimson King — An Observation by King Crimson	1969	5.00	10.00	20.00
❏ SD 8266	In the Wake of Poseidon	1970	5.00	10.00	20.00
❏ SD 8278	Lizard	1971	5.00	10.00	20.00
❏ SD 18110	Red	1974	3.75	7.50	15.00
❏ SD 18136	USA	1975	3.75	7.50	15.00
❏ SD 19155	In the Court of the Crimson King — An Observation by King Crimson	1978	3.00	6.00	12.00
—Reissue of Atlantic 8245					
EDITIONS EG					
❏ EGKC-1	In the Court of the Crimson King — An Observation by King Crimson	1985	2.50	5.00	10.00
—Reissue of Atlantic 19155					

Number	Title (A Side/B Side)	Yr	VG	VG+	NM
❏ EGKC-2	In the Wake of Poseidon	1985	2.50	5.00	10.00
—Reissue of Atlantic 8266					
❏ EGKC-3	Lizard	1985	2.50	5.00	10.00
—Reissue of Atlantic 8278					
❏ EGKC-4	Islands	1985	2.50	5.00	10.00
—Reissue of Atlantic 7212					
❏ EGKC-6	Lark's Tongue in Aspic	1985	2.50	5.00	10.00
—Reissue of Atlantic 7263					
❏ EGKC-7	Starless and Bible Black	1985	2.50	5.00	10.00
—Reissue of Atlantic 7298					
❏ EGKC-8	Red	1985	2.50	5.00	10.00
—Reissue of Atlantic 18110					
❏ EGKC-9	USA	1985	2.50	5.00	10.00
—Reissue of Atlantic 18135					
❏ EGKC-10 [(2)]	The Young Person's Guide to King Crimson	1985	3.75	7.50	15.00
MOBILE FIDELITY					
❏ 1-075	In the Court of the Crimson King — An Observation by King Crimson	1981	20.00	40.00	80.00
—Audiophile vinyl					
WARNER BROS.					
❏ WBMS-119 [DJ]	The Return of King Crimson	1981	15.00	30.00	60.00
—Promo-only interview and music show					
❏ BSK 3629	Discipline	1981	2.50	5.00	10.00
❏ 23692	Beat	1982	2.50	5.00	10.00
❏ 25071	Three of a Perfect Pair	1984	2.50	5.00	10.00
KING CROONERS, THE					
45s					
EXCELLO					
❏ 2168	Won't You Let Me Know/Now That She's Gone	1959	10.00	20.00	40.00
❏ 2187	Memoirs/School Daze	1960	15.00	30.00	60.00
HART					
❏ 1002	She's Mine All Mine/Lonely Nights	1959	100.00	200.00	400.00
KING CURTIS					
45s					
ABC-PARAMOUNT					
❏ 10133	Beatnick Hoedown/King Neptune's Guitar	1960	3.75	7.50	15.00
ALCOR					
❏ 1016	Jay Walk/The Lone Prairie	1961	5.00	10.00	20.00
APOLLO					
❏ 507	King's Rock/Dynamite at Midnight	1957	7.50	15.00	30.00
ATCO					
❏ 6114	The Birth of the Blues/Just Smoochin'	1958	5.00	10.00	20.00
❏ 6124	You Made Me Love You/Ific	1958	5.00	10.00	20.00
❏ 6135	Castle Rock/Chili	1959	5.00	10.00	20.00
❏ 6143	Honey Dripper (Part 1)/Honey Dripper (Part 2)	1959	5.00	10.00	20.00
❏ 6152	Heavenly Blues/Restless Guitar	1959	5.00	10.00	20.00
❏ 6387	Spanish Harlem/The Boss	1965	2.50	5.00	10.00
❏ 6406	On Broadway/Quicksand	1966	2.00	4.00	8.00
❏ 6419	Make the World Go Away/You've Lost That Lovin' Feeling	1966	2.00	4.00	8.00
❏ 6429	Dancing in the Streets/He'll Have to Go	1966	2.00	4.00	8.00
❏ 6447	Pots and Pans (Part 1)/Pots and Pans (Part 2)	1966	2.00	4.00	8.00
❏ 6457	Something on Your Mind/Soul Theme	1966	2.00	4.00	8.00
❏ 6476	Jump Back/When Something Is Wrong with My Baby	1967	2.00	4.00	8.00
❏ 6496	You Don't Miss Your Water/Green Onions	1967	2.00	4.00	8.00
❏ 6511	Memphis Soul Stew/Blue Nocturne	1967	2.00	4.00	8.00
❏ 6516	Ode to Billie Joe/In the Pocket	1967	2.00	4.00	8.00
—As "The Kingpins"					
❏ 6534	For What It's Worth/Cook Out	1968	2.00	4.00	8.00
❏ 6547	I Never Loved a Man (The Way I Love You)/I Was Made to Love Her	1968	2.00	4.00	8.00
❏ 6562	(Sittin' On) The Dock of the Bay/This Is Soul	1968	2.00	4.00	8.00
❏ 6582	(Theme from) Valley of the Dolls/Eighth Wonder	1968	2.00	4.00	8.00
❏ 6598	I Heard It Through the Grapevine/Whiter Shade of Pale	1968	2.00	4.00	8.00
❏ 6613	Harper Valley P.T.A./Makin' Hey	1968	2.00	4.00	8.00
❏ 6630	The Christmas Song/What Are You Doing New Year's Eve?	1968	3.00	6.00	12.00
❏ 6664	Games People Play/Foot Pattin' (Part 2)	1969	2.00	4.00	8.00
❏ 6680	Instant Groove/Sweet Inspiration	1969	2.00	4.00	8.00
❏ 6695	Little Green Apples/La Jeanne	1969	2.00	4.00	8.00
❏ 6711	C.C. Rider/Rocky Roll	1969	2.00	4.00	8.00
❏ 6720	Pop Corn Willie/Patty Cake	1969	2.00	4.00	8.00
❏ 6738	Soulin'/Teasin'	1970	—	3.00	6.00
❏ 6762	Get Ready/Bridge Over Troubled Water	1970	—	3.00	6.00
❏ 6779	Whole Lotta Love/Floatin'	1970	—	3.00	6.00
❏ 6785	Changes (Part 1)/Changes (Part 2)	1970	—	3.00	6.00
❏ 6834	Changes (Part 1)/Changes (Part 2)	1971	—	3.00	6.00
❏ 6908	Ridin' Thumb (Part 1)/Ridin' Thumb (Part 2)	1972	—	3.00	6.00
CAPITOL					
❏ 4788	Beach Party/Turn 'Em On	1962	2.50	5.00	10.00
❏ 4841	Beautiful Brown Eyes/Your Cheatin' Heart	1962	2.50	5.00	10.00
❏ 4891	Strollin' Home/Mess Around	1962	2.50	5.00	10.00
❏ 4998	Do the Monkey/Feel All Right	1963	2.50	5.00	10.00
❏ 5061	Theme from "Lilies of the Field" (Part 1)/Theme from "Lilies of the Field" (Part 2)	1963	2.50	5.00	10.00
❏ 5109	Soul Serenade/More Soul	1964	2.50	5.00	10.00
❏ 5212	Summer Dream/Melancholy Serenade	1964	2.50	5.00	10.00
❏ 5270	Stranger on the Shore/Hide Away	1964	2.50	5.00	10.00
❏ 5324	Sister Sadie/Tanya	1964	2.50	5.00	10.00
❏ 5377	Bill Bailey/Soul Twine	1965	2.50	5.00	10.00
❏ 5490	The Prance/Slow Drag	1965	2.50	5.00	10.00
DELUXE					
❏ 6142	The Stranger/Steel Guitar Rag	1957	6.25	12.50	25.00
❏ 6157	Wicky Wacky (Part 1)/Wicky Wacky (Part 2)	1958	6.25	12.50	25.00
ENJOY					
❏ 1000	Soul Twist/Twisting Time	1962	3.75	7.50	15.00
❏ 1001	Twisting with the King/Wobble Twist	1962	3.75	7.50	15.00
EVEREST					
❏ 19406	Jay Walk/The Lone Prairie	1961	3.75	7.50	15.00
EVERLAST					
❏ 5030	Soul Twist/Twisting Time	1965	2.50	5.00	10.00
GEM					
❏ 208	Tenor in the Sky/No More Crying on My Pillow	1954	10.00	20.00	40.00

Number	Title (A Side/B Side)	Yr	VG	VG+	NM
GROOVE					
❏ 1060	Movin' On/Rockabye Baby	1956	6.25	12.50	25.00
KING					
❏ 5647	King Curtis Stomp/Steel Guitar Rag	1962	3.00	6.00	12.00
MONARCH					
❏ 702	Wine Head/I've Got News for You Baby	1953	15.00	30.00	60.00
NEW JAZZ					
❏ 45-510	Soul Meeting/All the Way	1961	3.75	7.50	15.00
SEG-WAY					
❏ 1006	Hot Rod/Bonaparte's Retreat	1962	3.75	7.50	15.00
SKY ROCKET					
❏ 106	Madisonville (Part 1)/Madisonville (Part 2)	1960	5.00	10.00	20.00
TRU SOUND					
❏ 401	Trouble in Mind/But That's Alright	1961	3.75	7.50	15.00
❏ 406	Twistin' and Jivin'/I Have to Worry	1961	3.75	7.50	15.00
❏ 412	So Rare/Hucklebuck Twist	1961	3.75	7.50	15.00
❏ 415	Free for All/When the Saints Go Marching In	1962	3.75	7.50	15.00
❏ 422	Low Down/I'll Wait for You	1962	3.75	7.50	15.00
Albums					
ATCO					
❏ 33-113 [M]	Have Tenor Sax, Will Blow	1959	10.00	20.00	40.00
❏ SD 33-113 [S]	Have Tenor Sax, Will Blow	1959	15.00	30.00	60.00
❏ 33-189 [M]	That Lovin' Feeling	1966	5.00	10.00	20.00
❏ SD 33-189 [S]	That Lovin' Feeling	1966	6.25	12.50	25.00
❏ 33-198 [M]	Live at Small's Paradise	1966	5.00	10.00	20.00
❏ SD 33-198 [S]	Live at Small's Paradise	1966	6.25	12.50	25.00
❏ 33-211 [M]	The Great Memphis Hits	1967	5.00	10.00	20.00
❏ SD 33-211 [S]	The Great Memphis Hits	1967	6.25	12.50	25.00
❏ 33-231 [M]	King Size Soul	1967	6.25	12.50	25.00
❏ SD 33-231 [S]	King Size Soul	1967	5.00	10.00	20.00
❏ 33-247 [M]	Sweet Soul	1968	7.50	15.00	30.00
❏ SD 33-247 [S]	Sweet Soul	1968	5.00	10.00	20.00
❏ SD 33-266	The Best of King Curtis	1968	5.00	10.00	20.00
❏ SD 33-293	Instant Groove	1969	5.00	10.00	20.00
❏ SD 33-338	Get Ready	1970	5.00	10.00	20.00
❏ SD 33-359	Live at Fillmore West	1971	5.00	10.00	20.00
❏ SD 33-385	Everybody's Talkin'	1972	5.00	10.00	20.00
ATLANTIC					
❏ SD 1637	Blues Montreux	1973	3.00	6.00	12.00
CAPITOL					
❏ ST 1756 [S]	Country Soul	1963	10.00	20.00	40.00
❏ T 1756 [M]	Country Soul	1963	7.50	15.00	30.00
❏ ST 2095 [S]	Soul Serenade	1964	7.50	15.00	30.00
❏ T 2095 [M]	Soul Serenade	1964	6.25	12.50	25.00
❏ ST 2341 [S]	King Curtis Plays the Hits Made Famous by Sam Cooke	1965	7.50	15.00	30.00
❏ T 2341 [M]	King Curtis Plays the Hits Made Famous by Sam Cooke	1965	6.25	12.50	25.00
❏ ST 2858 [S]	The Best of King Curtis	1968	6.25	12.50	25.00
❏ T 2858 [M]	The Best of King Curtis	1968	12.50	25.00	50.00
—Red and white "Starline" label; may be promo only					
❏ SM-11798	Soul Serenade	1978	2.50	5.00	10.00
—Reissue					
❏ SM-11963	The Best of King Curtis	1979	2.50	5.00	10.00
—Reissue					
CLARION					
❏ 615 [M]	The Great "K" Curtis	1966	5.00	10.00	20.00
❏ SD 615 [S]	The Great "K" Curtis	1966	6.25	12.50	25.00
COLLECTABLES					
❏ COL-5119	Soul Twist	198?	2.50	5.00	10.00
❏ COL-5156	Golden Classics: Enjoy…The Best of King Curtis	198?	2.50	5.00	10.00
ENJOY					
❏ ENLP-2001 [M]	Soul Twist	1962	12.50	25.00	50.00
EVEREST					
❏ SDBR-1121 [S]	Azure	1961	18.75	37.50	75.00
❏ LPBR-5121 [M]	Azure	1961	12.50	25.00	50.00
FANTASY					
❏ OJC-198	The New Scene of King Curtis	1985	2.50	5.00	10.00
—Reissue of New Jazz 8237					
❏ OBC-512	Trouble in Mind	1988	2.50	5.00	10.00
—Reissue of Tru-Sound 15001					
NEW JAZZ					
❏ NJLP-8237 [M]	The New Scene of King Curtis	1960	15.00	30.00	60.00
—Purple label					
❏ NJLP-8237 [M]	The New Scene of King Curtis	1965	7.50	15.00	30.00
—Blue label with trident logo on right					
PRESTIGE					
❏ PRLP-7222 [M]	Soul Meeting	1962	12.50	25.00	50.00
❏ PRST-7222 [S]	Soul Meeting	1962	18.75	37.50	75.00
❏ PRST-7709	The Best of King Curtis	1969	3.75	7.50	15.00
❏ PRST-7775	The Best of King Curtis — One More Time	1970	3.75	7.50	15.00
❏ PRST-7789	King Soul	1970	3.75	7.50	15.00
❏ PRST-7833	Soul Meeting	1971	3.75	7.50	15.00
—Reissue of 7222					
❏ 24033 [(2)]	Jazz Groove	198?	3.75	7.50	15.00
RCA CAMDEN					
❏ CAS-2242	Sax in Motion	1968	3.75	7.50	15.00
RCA VICTOR					
❏ LPM-2494 [M]	Arthur Murray's Music for Dancing: The Twist!	1962	6.25	12.50	25.00
❏ LSP-2494 [S]	Arthur Murray's Music for Dancing: The Twist!	1962	7.50	15.00	30.00
TRU-SOUND					
❏ TS-15001 [M]	Trouble in Mind	1961	12.50	25.00	50.00
❏ TS-15008 [M]	It's Party Time	1962	12.50	25.00	50.00
❏ TS-15009 [M]	Doin' the Dixie Twist	1962	12.50	25.00	50.00

KING FAMILY, THE
45s
WARNER BROS.

Number	Title (A Side/B Side)	Yr	VG	VG+	NM
❏ PRO 216 [DJ]	Go Tell It on the Mountain/Here the Sledges with the Bells	1965	2.50	5.00	10.00
❏ 5647	The Sweetheart Tree/Amen	1965	—	3.00	6.00
❏ 5678	Just One Smile/Today I'm in Love	1965	—	3.00	6.00
❏ 5869	The Men in My Little Girl's Life/Bill Bailey (Won't You Please Come Home)	1966	—	3.00	6.00

Number	Title (A Side/B Side)	Yr	VG	VG+	NM
Albums					
CAPITOL					
❏ DT 2352 [R]	Love at Home	1965	3.00	6.00	12.00
❏ T 2352 [M]	Love at Home	1965	3.75	7.50	15.00
FANNY FARMER/FLEETWOOD					
❏ FCLP 3039	Fanny Farmer Presents The King Family Christmas Album	196?	3.00	6.00	12.00
HARMONY					
❏ HS 11293	The Wonderful King Family	196?	2.50	5.00	10.00
WARNER BROS.					
❏ W 1601 [M]	The King Family Show!	1965	3.00	6.00	12.00
❏ WS 1601 [S]	The King Family Show!	1965	3.75	7.50	15.00
❏ W 1613 [M]	The King Family Album	1965	3.00	6.00	12.00
❏ WS 1613 [S]	The King Family Album	1965	3.75	7.50	15.00
❏ W 1627 [M]	Christmas with the King Family	1965	3.00	6.00	12.00
❏ WS 1627 [S]	Christmas with the King Family	1965	3.75	7.50	15.00
❏ W 1633 [M]	Sunday with the King Family	1966	3.00	6.00	12.00
❏ WS 1633 [S]	Sunday with the King Family	1966	3.75	7.50	15.00

KING FLOYD Because this is a male singer whose first name is "King" and last name is "Floyd," he can be found in the letter F under "Floyd."

KING HARVEST
45s
A&M

Number	Title (A Side/B Side)	Yr	VG	VG+	NM
❏ 1726	Little Bit Like Magic/Vaea	1975	—	2.00	4.00
❏ 1761	Lovestruck/Hickory	1975	—	2.00	4.00
PERCEPTION					
❏ 515	Dancing in the Moonlight/Marty and the Captain	1972	—	2.50	5.00
❏ 527	A Little Bit Like Magic/Elmore Bacon	1973	—	2.00	4.00
❏ 534	Take It Slow/Idaho	1973	—	2.00	4.00
❏ 556	Celestial Navigator/Angels of Mercy	1974	—	2.00	4.00
Albums					
A&M					
❏ SP-4540	King Harvest	1975	2.50	5.00	10.00
PERCEPTION					
❏ 36	Dancing in the Moonlight	1973	3.00	6.00	12.00

KING PINS, THE (1)
45s
FEDERAL

Number	Title (A Side/B Side)	Yr	VG	VG+	NM
❏ 12480	Believe in Me/Don't Wait Pretty Baby	1963	5.00	10.00	20.00
❏ 12484	It Won't Be This Way (Always)/How Long Will It Last	1963	5.00	10.00	20.00
❏ 12505	The Monkey One More Time/With the Other Guy	1963	3.75	7.50	15.00
❏ 12512	Hop Scotch/Wonderful One	1964	3.75	7.50	15.00
❏ 12517	Two Hearts/I Won't Have It	1964	3.75	7.50	15.00
❏ 12519	I Got the Monkey Off My Back/You're Using Me	1964	3.75	7.50	15.00
Albums					
KING					
❏ 865 [M]	It Won't Be This Way Always	1963	75.00	150.00	300.00

KING PINS, THE (2)
45s
LARSE

Number	Title (A Side/B Side)	Yr	VG	VG+	NM
❏ 101	94 Second Turf/Rod Hot Rod	1966	10.00	20.00	40.00
MGM					
❏ 13535	Rod Hot Rod/Door Banger	1966	7.50	15.00	30.00

KING RICHARD'S FLUEGEL KNIGHTS
45s
MTA

Number	Title (A Side/B Side)	Yr	VG	VG+	NM
❏ 101	Milord/Happiness Is	1966	—	3.00	6.00
❏ 107	A Sign of the Times/England Swings	1966	—	3.00	6.00
❏ 110	The Crusades/Castle Holiday	1966	—	3.00	6.00
❏ 115	Cabaret/Sing, Sing, Sing	1966	—	3.00	6.00
❏ 120	Two Different Worlds/Everybody Loves My Baby	1967	—	3.00	6.00
❏ 131	Miniskirt Waltz/Horn Duey	1967	—	3.00	6.00
❏ 138	Camelot/Bye Bye Blues	1967	—	3.00	6.00
❏ 151	Feelin' Good/To Life	1968	—	2.50	5.00
❏ 154	Mrs. Robinson/Dessert	1968	—	2.50	5.00
❏ 161	Gentle on My Mind/Something Classic	1968	—	2.50	5.00
❏ 166	Memories Are Made of This/One of Those Songs	1969	—	2.50	5.00
❏ 187	Everybody Loves My Baby/Horn Duey	1970	—	2.50	5.00
Albums					
MTA					
❏ 5001	A Sign of the Times	1966	3.00	6.00	12.00
❏ 5005	Something Super	1967	3.00	6.00	12.00
❏ 5005	Something Super!	1968	3.00	6.00	12.00
❏ 5014	One of Those Songs	1969	3.00	6.00	12.00

KINGDOM
45s
SPECIALTY

Number	Title (A Side/B Side)	Yr	VG	VG+	NM
❏ 722	Seven Fathoms Deep/If I Never Was to See Her Again	1970	3.00	6.00	12.00
Albums					
SPECIALTY					
❏ SPS-2135	Kingdom	1970	15.00	30.00	60.00

KINGS, THE   Several different groups.
45s
BATON

Number	Title (A Side/B Side)	Yr	VG	VG+	NM
❏ 245	Long Lonely Nights/Let Me Know	1957	10.00	20.00	40.00
EPIC					
❏ 9370	I Want to Know/Bomp-I-Ty Bump	1960	7.50	15.00	30.00
GONE					
❏ 5013	Don't Go/Love Is Something from Within	1957	25.00	50.00	100.00
GOTHAM					
❏ 316	God Made You Mine/The Good Book	1956	25.00	50.00	100.00
HARLEM					
❏ 2322	Fire in My Heart/You Never Know	1954	37.50	75.00	150.00
JALO					
❏ 203	Angel/Come On Little Baby	1958	10.00	20.00	40.00
JAY-WING					
❏ 5805	Surrender/Hold Me	1959	37.50	75.00	150.00

K

Number	Title (A Side/B Side)	Yr	VG	VG+	NM
JOX					
❑ 052	I've Got a License/Just a Little Bit of You	1965	10.00	20.00	40.00
LOOKIE					
❑ 18	I Want to Know/Bomp-I-Ty Bump	1960	10.00	20.00	40.00
RCA VICTOR					
❑ 47-7419	Till You/Elephant Walk	1958	6.25	12.50	25.00
❑ 47-7544	Troubles Don't Last/Your Sweet Love	1959	6.25	12.50	25.00
SPECIALTY					
❑ 497	What Can I Do/Till I Say Well Done	1954	30.00	60.00	120.00

KINGSMEN, THE (1) Northwest garage band. Also see JACK EELY.
45s

Number	Title (A Side/B Side)	Yr	VG	VG+	NM
FOREVER OLDIES					
❑ 21011	Louie Louie/Haunted Castle	197?	—	2.00	4.00
—Later issue of Scepter-Wand Forever 21011, "a product of Springboard International" at bottom					
JERDEN					
❑ 712	Louie Louie/Haunted Castle	1963	15.00	30.00	60.00
SCEPTER-WAND FOREVER					
❑ 21011	Louie Louie/Haunted Castle	197?	—	2.50	5.00
—Reissue					
WAND					
❑ 143	Louie Louie/Little Green Thing	196?	3.75	7.50	15.00
❑ 143	Louie, Louie/Haunted Castle	1963	5.00	10.00	20.00
❑ 143	Louie Louie 64-65-66.../Haunted Castle	1966	3.75	7.50	15.00
❑ 150	Money/Bent Scepter	1964	3.00	6.00	12.00
❑ 157	Little Latin Lupe Lu/David's Mood	1964	2.50	5.00	10.00
❑ 164	Death of an Angel/Searching for Love	1964	2.50	5.00	10.00
❑ 172	The Jolly Green Giant/Long Green	1965	3.00	6.00	12.00
❑ 183	The Climb/I'm Waiting	1965	2.50	5.00	10.00
❑ 189	Annie Fanny/Give Her Lovin'	1965	2.50	5.00	10.00
❑ 1107	(You Got) Gamma Goochie/It's Only the Dog	1965	3.75	7.50	15.00
❑ 1115	Killer Joe/Little Green Thing	1966	3.75	7.50	15.00
❑ 1118	The Krunch/The Climb	1966	3.75	7.50	15.00
❑ 1118 [PS]	The Krunch/The Climb	1966	6.25	12.50	25.00
❑ 1127	My Wife Can't Dance/Little Sally Tease	1966	2.50	5.00	10.00
❑ 1137	If I Need Someone/The Grass Is Green	1966	2.50	5.00	10.00
❑ 1147	Trouble/Daytime Shadows	1967	2.00	4.00	8.00
❑ 1154	The Wolf of Manhattan/Children's Caretaker	1967	2.00	4.00	8.00
❑ 1157	(I Have Found) Another Girl/Don't Say No	1967	2.00	4.00	8.00
❑ 1164	Bo Diddley Bach/Just Before the Break of Day	1968	2.00	4.00	8.00
❑ 1174	Get Out of My Life Woman/ Since You've Been Gone	1968	2.00	4.00	8.00
❑ 1180	I Guess I Was Dreamin'/Oh Love	1968	2.00	4.00	8.00
Albums					
RHINO					
❑ RNLP-126	The Best of the Kingsmen	1985	2.50	5.00	10.00
SCEPTER					
❑ CTN-18002	The Best of the Kingsmen	1972	2.50	5.00	10.00
WAND					
❑ WDM-657 [M]	The Kingsmen In Person	1964	7.50	15.00	30.00
❑ WDS-657 [P]	The Kingsmen In Person	1964	10.00	20.00	40.00
❑ WDM-659 [M]	The Kingsmen, Volume II	1964	7.50	15.00	30.00
—With "Death of an Angel"					
❑ WDM-659 [M]	The Kingsmen, Volume II	1964	10.00	20.00	40.00
—Without "Death of an Angel" (replaced by untitled instrumental)					
❑ WDS-659 [S]	The Kingsmen, Volume II	1964	10.00	20.00	40.00
—With "Death of an Angel"					
❑ WDS-659 [S]	The Kingsmen, Volume II	1964	12.50	25.00	50.00
—Without "Death of an Angel" (replaced by untitled instrumental)					
❑ WDM-662 [M]	The Kingsmen, Volume 3	1965	6.25	12.50	25.00
❑ WDS-662 [S]	The Kingsmen, Volume 3	1965	7.50	15.00	30.00
❑ WDM-670 [M]	The Kingsmen On Campus	1965	6.25	12.50	25.00
❑ WDS-670 [S]	The Kingsmen On Campus	1965	7.50	15.00	30.00
❑ WDM-674 [M]	15 Great Hits	1966	5.00	10.00	20.00
❑ WDS-674 [P]	15 Great Hits	1966	6.25	12.50	25.00
❑ WDM-675 [M]	Up and Away	1966	5.00	10.00	20.00
❑ WDS-675 [S]	Up and Away	1966	6.25	12.50	25.00
❑ WDM-681 [M]	The Kingsmen's Greatest Hits	1967	3.75	7.50	15.00
❑ WDS-681 [S]	The Kingsmen's Greatest Hits	1967	5.00	10.00	20.00
❑ ST-91011 [S]	Up and Away	1966	7.50	15.00	30.00
—Capitol Record Club edition					

KINGSMEN, THE (2) Instrumental group composed of former members of BILL HALEY AND HIS COMETS.
45s

Number	Title (A Side/B Side)	Yr	VG	VG+	NM
EASTWEST					
❑ 115	Week End/Better Believe It	1958	10.00	20.00	40.00
❑ 120	Conga Rock/The Cat Walk	1958	10.00	20.00	40.00

KINGSMEN, THE (3)
45s

Number	Title (A Side/B Side)	Yr	VG	VG+	NM
ALL STAR					
❑ 500	Guardian Angel/I'm Your Lover Man	1957	20.00	40.00	80.00

KINGSMEN, THE (U) Some of these could have been by groups (1), (2) or (3).
45s

Number	Title (A Side/B Side)	Yr	VG	VG+	NM
ARNOLD					
❑ 2106	Goodnight Sweetheart/Humpty Dumpty	196?	30.00	60.00	120.00
CAPITOL					
❑ 3576	You Better Do Right/Today	1973	—	2.50	5.00
JALYNNE					
❑ 108	Ladies Choice/Dig This	1960	5.00	10.00	20.00
NEIL					
❑ 102	One Foolish Mistake/Stranded Love	1956	15.00	30.00	60.00

KINGSTON TRIO, THE Also see DAVE GUARD AND THE WHISKEYHILL SINGERS; BOB SHANE; JOHN STEWART.
45s

Number	Title (A Side/B Side)	Yr	VG	VG+	NM
CAPITOL					
❑ PRO 856 [DJ]	The Merry Minuet/Tick, Tick, Tick	1959	10.00	20.00	40.00
❑ X1-1407 [S]	When I Was Young/Leave My Woman Alone	1960	5.00	10.00	20.00
—33 1/3 rpm, small hole jukebox pressing					
❑ X2-1407 [S]	This Mornin', This Evenin', So Soon/Everglades	1960	5.00	10.00	20.00
—33 1/3 rpm, small hole jukebox pressing					
❑ X3-1407 [S]	Buddy Better Get On Down the Line/South Wind	1960	5.00	10.00	20.00
—33 1/3 rpm, small hole jukebox pressing					

Number	Title (A Side/B Side)	Yr	VG	VG+	NM
❑ X4-1407 [S]	Who's Gonna Hold Her Hand/To Morrow	1960	5.00	10.00	20.00
—33 1/3 rpm, small hole jukebox pressing					
❑ X5-1407 [S]	Colorado Trail/The Tattooed Lady	1960	5.00	10.00	20.00
—33 1/3 rpm, small hole jukebox pressing					
❑ XE1-1446 [S]	We Wish You a Merry Christmas/The Last Month of the Year	1960	3.75	7.50	15.00
—33 1/3 rpm, small hole jukebox pressing					
❑ XE2-1446 [S]	Sing We Noel/Go Where I Send Thee	1960	3.75	7.50	15.00
—33 1/3 rpm, small hole jukebox pressing					
❑ XE3-1446 [S]	The White Snows of Winter/All Through the Night	1960	3.75	7.50	15.00
—33 1/3 rpm, small hole jukebox pressing					
❑ XE4-1446 [S]	Follow Now, Oh Shepherd/Somerset Gloucestershire Wassail	1960	3.75	7.50	15.00
—33 1/3 rpm, small hole jukebox pressing					
❑ XE5-1446 [S]	Bye Bye Thou Little Tiny Child/Mary Mild	1960	3.75	7.50	15.00
—33 1/3 rpm, small hole jukebox pressing					
❑ SM-1705 [S]	Billy Goat Hill/Take Her Out of Pity	1962	3.75	7.50	15.00
—Small hole, plays at 33 1/3 rpm					
❑ SXE1-1809 [S]	Some Fool Made a Soldier Out of Me/To Be Redeemed	1963	3.75	7.50	15.00
—33 1/3 rpm, small hole jukebox pressing					
❑ SXE2-1809 [S]	Honey, Are You Mad at Your Man/Adios Farewell	1963	3.75	7.50	15.00
—33 1/3 rpm, small hole jukebox pressing					
❑ SXE3-1809 [S]	Poor Ellie Smith/My Lord What a Mornin'	1963	3.75	7.50	15.00
—33 1/3 rpm, small hole jukebox pressing					
❑ SXE4-1809 [S]	Long Black Veil/Genny Glen	1963	3.75	7.50	15.00
—33 1/3 rpm, small hole jukebox pressing					
❑ SXE5-1809 [S]	The First Time/Dogie's Lament	1963	3.75	7.50	15.00
—33 1/3 rpm, small hole jukebox pressing					
❑ 2006/7 [DJ]	Farewell Adelita/Corey, Corey	1960	3.75	7.50	15.00
❑ 2006/7 [PS]	Farewell Adelita/Corey, Corey	1960	6.25	12.50	25.00
—Promo item for Welgrume Sportswear					
❑ 2782/3 [DJ]	Molly Dee/Haul Away	1959	3.75	7.50	15.00
❑ 2782/3 [PS]	Molly Dee/Haul Away	1959	6.25	12.50	25.00
—Promo item for "The New March of Dimes"					
❑ 3149	Tell the Riverboat Captain/Windy Wakefield	1971	2.50	5.00	10.00
—As "The New Kingston Trio"					
❑ F3970	Scarlet Ribbons (For Her Hair)/Three Jolly Coachmen	1958	5.00	10.00	20.00
❑ F4049	Tom Dooley/Ruby Red	1958	6.25	12.50	25.00
❑ F4114	Raspberries, Strawberries/Sally	1959	5.00	10.00	20.00
❑ F4167 [M]	The Tijuana Jail/Oh Cindy	1959	5.00	10.00	20.00
❑ SF4167 [S]	The Tijuana Jail/Oh Cindy	1959	12.50	25.00	50.00
❑ F4221	M.T.A./All My Sorrows	1959	5.00	10.00	20.00
❑ F4271	A Worried Man/San Miguel	1959	5.00	10.00	20.00
❑ 4303	Coo Coo-U/Green Grasses	1959	3.75	7.50	15.00
❑ 4338	El Matador/Home from the Hill	1960	3.75	7.50	15.00
❑ 4338 [PS]	El Matador/Home from the Hill	1960	10.00	20.00	40.00
—This sleeve's existence has been confirmed					
❑ 4379	Bad Man Blunder/Escape of Old John Webb	1960	3.75	7.50	15.00
❑ 4441	Everglades/This Mornin', This Evenin', So Soon	1960	3.75	7.50	15.00
❑ 4475	Somerset Gloucestershire Wassail/ Goodnight My Baby	1960	3.75	7.50	15.00
❑ 4475 [PS]	Somerset Gloucestershire Wassail/ Goodnight My Baby	1960	15.00	30.00	60.00
❑ 4536	You're Gonna Miss Me/En El Aqua	1961	3.75	7.50	15.00
❑ 4642	Coming from the Mountains/ Nothing More to Look Forward To	1961	3.75	7.50	15.00
❑ 4671	Where Have All the Flowers Gone/ O Ken Karanga	1961	3.75	7.50	15.00
❑ 4740	Scotch and Soda/Jane, Jane, Jane	1962	2.50	5.00	10.00
❑ 4740 [PS]	Scotch and Soda/Jane, Jane, Jane	1962	7.50	15.00	30.00
❑ 4808	Old Joe Clark/C'mon Betty Home	1962	2.50	5.00	10.00
❑ 4842	One More Town/She Was Too Good to Me	1962	2.50	5.00	10.00
❑ 4842 [PS]	One More Town/She Was Too Good to Me	1962	7.50	15.00	30.00
❑ 4898	Greenback Dollar/New Frontier	1963	2.50	5.00	10.00
❑ 4898 [PS]	Greenback Dollar/New Frontier	1963	—	—	—
—Rumored to exist as a U.S. edition (an import exists), but without conclusive evidence, we will delete this from future editions					
❑ 4951	Reverend Mr. Black/One More Round	1963	2.50	5.00	10.00
❑ 5005	Desert Pete/Ballad of the Thresher	1963	2.50	5.00	10.00
❑ 5078	Ally Ally Oxen Free/Marcelle Vanine	1963	2.50	5.00	10.00
❑ 5132	Last Night I Had the Strangest Dream/ Patriot Game	1964	2.50	5.00	10.00
❑ 5166	Seasons in the Sun/If You Don't Look Around	1964	2.50	5.00	10.00
❑ S7-19762	Somerset Gloucestershire Wassail/ Goodnight My Baby	1997	—	2.00	4.00
CAPITOL CUSTOM					
❑ NKB-2670/1	Tom Dooley/A Worried Man//The Hunter/ With You My Johnny	1960	7.50	15.00	30.00
❑ NKB-2670/1 [PS]	Cool Cargo	1960	7.50	15.00	30.00
—Promotional item for 7-Up					
CAPITOL STARLINE					
❑ 6002	Tom Dooley/M.T.A.	1962	2.00	4.00	8.00
—Originals have two-tone green swirl labels					
❑ 6046	A Worried Man/Scotch and Soda	1964	2.00	4.00	8.00
—Originals have two-tone green swirl labels					
❑ 6071	Greenback Dollar/Reverend Mr. Black	1965	2.00	4.00	8.00
—Originals have two-tone green swirl labels; "Greenback Dollar" does NOT have the word "damn" obliterated by a guitar chord, as the original 45 does					
DECCA					
❑ 31702	My Ramblin' Boy/Hope You Understand	1964	3.75	7.50	15.00
❑ 31702 [PS]	My Ramblin' Boy/Hope You Understand	1964	6.25	12.50	25.00
❑ 31730	Little Play Soldiers/I'm Going Home	1965	2.50	5.00	10.00
❑ 31790	Stay Awhile/Yes I Can Feel It	1965	2.50	5.00	10.00
❑ 31790 [PS]	Stay Awhile/Yes I Can Feel It	1965	6.25	12.50	25.00
❑ 31860	The Runaway Song/Parchment Farm (Blues)	1965	2.50	5.00	10.00
❑ 31860 [PS]	The Runaway Song/Parchment Farm (Blues)	1965	6.25	12.50	25.00
❑ 31922	Norwegian Wood/Put Your Money Away	1966	2.50	5.00	10.00
❑ 31961	The Spinnin' of the World/A Little Soul Is Born	1966	2.50	5.00	10.00
❑ 32010	Lock All the Windows/Hit and Run	1966	2.50	5.00	10.00
❑ 32040	Babe, You've Been On My Mind/ Texas Across the River	1966	2.50	5.00	10.00
MOUNTAIN CREEK					
❑ 301/2	Big Ship Glory/Johnson Party of Four	1977	6.25	12.50	25.00
NAUTILUS					
❑ NR2-45	Aspen Gold/Longest Beer of the Night	1979	—	2.50	5.00

Number	Title (A Side/B Side)	Yr	VG	VG+	NM
TETRAGRAMMATON					
❏ 1526	One Too Many Mornings/Scotch and Soda	1969	2.50	5.00	10.00
XERES					
❏ 10004	Looking for the Sunshine/Reverend Mr. Black	1982	—	2.00	4.00
❏ 10004 [PS]	Looking for the Sunshine/Reverend Mr. Black	1982	—	2.00	4.00
7-Inch Extended Plays					
CAPITOL					
❏ EAP 1-996	Three Jolly Coachmen/Sloop John B//Bay of Mexico/Saro Jane	1958	7.50	15.00	30.00
❏ EAP 1-996 [PS]	The Kingston Trio	1958	7.50	15.00	30.00
❏ EAP 1-1119	M.T.A./Como Se Viene, Se Va//All My Sorrows/Sail Away Ladies	1959	7.50	15.00	30.00
❏ EAP 1-1119 [PS]	M.T.A.	1959	7.50	15.00	30.00
❏ EAP 1-1129	The Tijuana Jail/Oh Cindy//Coplas/Tom Dooley	1959	7.50	15.00	30.00
❏ EAP 1-1129 [PS]	Tijuana Jail	1959	7.50	15.00	30.00
❏ EAP 1-1136	Tom Dooley/Coplas//Banua/Santy Anno	1959	7.50	15.00	30.00
❏ EAP 1-1136 [PS]	Tom Dooley	1959	7.50	15.00	30.00
❏ EAP 1-1182	Raspberries, Strawberries/Ruby Red//Sally/Scarlet Ribbons	1959	7.50	15.00	30.00
❏ EAP 1-1182 [PS]	Raspberries, Strawberries	1959	7.50	15.00	30.00
❏ EAP 1-1199	M.T.A./All My Sorrows//Scarlet Ribbons/Remember the Alamo	1959	6.25	12.50	25.00
❏ EAP 1-1199 [PS]	The Kingston Trio at Large, Part 1	1959	6.25	12.50	25.00
❏ EAP 2-1199	Blow Ye Winds/Corey Corey//The Long Black Rifle/Early in the Mornin'	1959	6.25	12.50	25.00
❏ EAP 2-1199 [PS]	The Kingston Trio at Large, Part 2	1959	6.25	12.50	25.00
❏ EAP 3-1199	The Seine/I Bawled//Good News/Getaway John	1959	6.25	12.50	25.00
❏ EAP 3-1199 [PS]	The Kingston Trio at Large, Part 3	1959	6.25	12.50	25.00
❏ EAP 1-1258	Molly Dee/Across the Wide Missouri//Goober Peas/A Worried Man	1959	6.25	12.50	25.00
❏ EAP 1-1258 [PS]	Here We Go Again! Part 1	1959	6.25	12.50	25.00
❏ EAP 2-1258	Haul Away/The Wanderer//E Inu Tatou E/A Rollin' Stone	1959	6.25	12.50	25.00
❏ EAP 2-1258 [PS]	Here We Go Again! Part 2	1959	6.25	12.50	25.00
❏ EAP 3-1258	Round About a Mountain/Oleanna//The Unfortunate Miss Bailey/San Miguel	1959	6.25	12.50	25.00
❏ EAP 3-1258 [PS]	Here We Go Again! Part 3	1959	6.25	12.50	25.00
❏ EAP 1-1322	A Worried Man/Molly Dee//San Miguel/Oleanna	1959	6.25	12.50	25.00
❏ EAP 1-1322 [PS]	A Worried Man	1959	6.25	12.50	25.00
❏ EAP 1-1352	El Matador/The Mountains o' Mourne//The Hunter/Farewell Adelita	1960	6.25	12.50	25.00
❏ EAP 1-1352 [PS]	Sold Out, Part 1	1960	6.25	12.50	25.00
❏ EAP 2-1352	Don't Cry Katie/Medley: Tanga Tiki-Toerau//Mangwani Mpulele/With You My Johnny	1960	6.25	12.50	25.00
❏ EAP 2-1352 [PS]	Sold Out, Part 2	1960	6.25	12.50	25.00
❏ EAP 3-1352	With Her Head Tucked Underneath Her Arm/Carrier Pigeon//Bimini/Raspberries, Strawberries	1960	6.25	12.50	25.00
❏ EAP 3-1352 [PS]	Sold Out, Part 3	1960	6.25	12.50	25.00
❏ EAP 1-1407	Bad Man Blunder/The Escape of Old John Webb//Colorado Trail/The Tattooed Lady	1960	6.25	12.50	25.00
❏ EAP 1-1407 [PS]	String Along, Part 1	1960	6.25	12.50	25.00
❏ EAP 2-1407	When I Was Young/Leave My Woman Alone//Who's Gonna Hold Her Hand/To Morrow	1960	6.25	12.50	25.00
❏ EAP 2-1407 [PS]	String Along, Part 2	1960	6.25	12.50	25.00
❏ EAP 3-1407	This Mornin', This Evenin', So Soon/Everglades//Buddy Better Get On Down the Line/South Wind	1960	6.25	12.50	25.00
❏ EAP 3-1407 [PS]	String Along, Part 3	1960	6.25	12.50	25.00
❏ EAP 1-1446	Bye Bye Thou Little Tiny Child/The Snows of Winter//Sing We Noel/The Last Month of the Year	1960	6.25	12.50	25.00
❏ EAP 1-1446 [PS]	The Last Month of the Year, Part 1	1960	6.25	12.50	25.00
❏ EAP 2-1446	We Wish You a Merry Christmas/All Through the Night//Mary Mild/A Round About Christmas	1960	6.25	12.50	25.00
❏ EAP 2-1446 [PS]	The Last Month of the Year, Part 2	1960	6.25	12.50	25.00
❏ EAP 3-1446	Goodnight My Baby Goodnight/Go Where I Send Thee//Follow Now, Oh Shepherds/Somerset Gloucestershire Wassail	1960	6.25	12.50	25.00
❏ EAP 3-1446 [PS]	The Last Month of the Year, Part 3	1960	6.25	12.50	25.00
❏ EAP 1-1474	En El Agua/Come All You Fair and Tender Ladies//Blow the Candle Out/Blue Eyed Gal	1961	6.25	12.50	25.00
❏ EAP 1-1474 [PS]	Make Way, Part 1	1961	6.25	12.50	25.00
❏ EAP 2-1474	The Jug of Punch/Bonny Heilan' Laddie//The River Is Wide/Oh Yes, Oh	1961	6.25	12.50	25.00
❏ EAP 2-1474 [PS]	Make Way, Part 2	1961	6.25	12.50	25.00
❏ EAP 3-1474	Utawena/Hear Travelin'//Hangman/Speckled Roan	1961	6.25	12.50	25.00
❏ EAP 3-1474 [PS]	Make Way, Part 3	1961	6.25	12.50	25.00
❏ EAP 1-1642	Coming from the Mountains/Oh Sail Away//Weeping Willow/Reuben James	1961	6.25	12.50	25.00
❏ EAP 1-1642 [PS]	Close Up, Part 1	1961	6.25	12.50	25.00
❏ EAP 2-1642	Take Her Out of Pity/Don't You Weep, Mary//When My Love Was Here/Karu	1961	6.25	12.50	25.00
❏ EAP 2-1642 [PS]	Close Up, Part 2	1961	6.25	12.50	25.00
❏ EAP 3-1642	The Whistling Gypsy/O Ken Karanga//Jessie James/Glorious Kingdom	1961	6.25	12.50	25.00
❏ EAP 3-1642 [PS]	Close Up, Part 3	1961	6.25	12.50	25.00
Albums					
CAPITOL					
❏ STBB-513 [(2)]	Tom Dooley/Scarlet Ribbons	1970	5.00	10.00	20.00
❏ DT 996 [R]	The Kingston Trio	196?	3.00	6.00	12.00
❏ T 996 [M]	The Kingston Trio	1958	10.00	20.00	40.00
—*Black label with colorband, Capitol logo at left*					
❏ T 996 [M]	The Kingston Trio	1958	12.50	25.00	50.00
—*Turquoise label*					
❏ T 996 [M]	The Kingston Trio	1962	5.00	10.00	20.00
—*Black label with colorband, Capitol logo at top*					
❏ T 1107 [M]	From the Hungry I	1959	10.00	20.00	40.00
—*Black label with colorband, Capitol logo at left*					
❏ T 1107 [M]	From the Hungry I	1962	5.00	10.00	20.00
—*Black label with colorband, Capitol logo at top*					
❏ ST 1183 [S]	Stereo Concert	1959	12.50	25.00	50.00
—*Black label with colorband, Capitol logo at left*					
❏ ST 1183 [S]	Stereo Concert	1962	6.25	12.50	25.00
—*Black label with colorband, Capitol logo at top*					

Number	Title (A Side/B Side)	Yr	VG	VG+	NM
❏ ST 1199 [S]	The Kingston Trio at Large	1959	10.00	20.00	40.00
—*Black label with colorband, Capitol logo at left*					
❏ ST 1199 [S]	The Kingston Trio at Large	1962	5.00	10.00	20.00
—*Black label with colorband, Capitol logo at top*					
❏ T 1199 [M]	The Kingston Trio at Large	1959	7.50	15.00	30.00
—*Black label with colorband, Capitol logo at left, "Long Playing High-Fidelity"*					
❏ T 1199 [M]	The Kingston Trio at Large	1960	6.25	12.50	25.00
—*Black label with colorband, Capitol logo at left, white line replaces "Long Playing High-Fidelity"*					
❏ T 1199 [M]	The Kingston Trio at Large	1962	3.75	7.50	15.00
—*Black label with colorband, Capitol logo at top*					
❏ ST 1258 [S]	Here We Go Again!	1959	10.00	20.00	40.00
—*Black label with colorband, Capitol logo at left*					
❏ ST 1258 [S]	Here We Go Again!	1962	5.00	10.00	20.00
—*Black label with colorband, Capitol logo at top*					
❏ T 1258 [M]	Here We Go Again!	1959	7.50	15.00	30.00
—*Black label with colorband, Capitol logo at left*					
❏ T 1258 [M]	Here We Go Again!	1962	3.75	7.50	15.00
—*Black label with colorband, Capitol logo at top*					
❏ ST 1352 [S]	Sold Out	1960	10.00	20.00	40.00
—*Black label with colorband, Capitol logo at left*					
❏ ST 1352 [S]	Sold Out	1962	5.00	10.00	20.00
—*Black label with colorband, Capitol logo at top*					
❏ T 1352 [M]	Sold Out	1960	7.50	15.00	30.00
—*Black label with colorband, Capitol logo at left*					
❏ T 1352 [M]	Sold Out	1962	3.75	7.50	15.00
—*Black label with colorband, Capitol logo at top*					
❏ ST 1407 [S]	String Along	1960	10.00	20.00	40.00
—*Black label with colorband, Capitol logo at left*					
❏ ST 1407 [S]	String Along	1962	5.00	10.00	20.00
—*Black label with colorband, Capitol logo at top*					
❏ T 1407 [M]	String Along	1960	7.50	15.00	30.00
—*Black label with colorband, Capitol logo at left*					
❏ T 1407 [M]	String Along	1962	3.75	7.50	15.00
—*Black label with colorband, Capitol logo at top*					
❏ ST 1446 [S]	The Last Month of the Year	1960	10.00	20.00	40.00
—*Same as above, but in stereo*					
❏ T 1446 [M]	The Last Month of the Year	1960	7.50	15.00	30.00
❏ ST 1474 [S]	Make Way!	1961	10.00	20.00	40.00
—*Black label with colorband, Capitol logo at left*					
❏ ST 1474 [S]	Make Way!	1962	5.00	10.00	20.00
—*Black label with colorband, Capitol logo at top*					
❏ T 1474 [M]	Make Way!	1961	7.50	15.00	30.00
—*Black label with colorband, Capitol logo at left*					
❏ T 1474 [M]	Make Way!	1962	3.75	7.50	15.00
—*Black label with colorband, Capitol logo at top*					
❏ ST 1564 [S]	Goin' Places	1961	10.00	20.00	40.00
—*Black label with colorband, Capitol logo at left*					
❏ ST 1564 [S]	Goin' Places	1962	5.00	10.00	20.00
—*Black label with colorband, Capitol logo at top*					
❏ T 1564 [M]	Goin' Places	1961	7.50	15.00	30.00
—*Black label with colorband, Capitol logo at left*					
❏ T 1564 [M]	Goin' Places	1962	3.75	7.50	15.00
—*Black label with colorband, Capitol logo at top*					
❏ DT 1612 [R]	Encores	1961	5.00	10.00	20.00
❏ DT 1612 [R]	Encores	1962	2.50	5.00	10.00
❏ T 1612 [M]	Encores	1961	7.50	15.00	30.00
—*Black label with colorband, Capitol logo at left*					
❏ T 1612 [M]	Encores	1962	3.75	7.50	15.00
—*Black label with colorband, Capitol logo at top*					
❏ ST 1642 [S]	Close-Up	1961	10.00	20.00	40.00
—*Black label with colorband, Capitol logo at left*					
❏ ST 1642 [S]	Close-Up	1962	5.00	10.00	20.00
—*Black label with colorband, Capitol logo at top*					
❏ T 1642 [M]	Close-Up	1961	7.50	15.00	30.00
—*Black label with colorband, Capitol logo at left*					
❏ T 1642 [M]	Close-Up	1962	3.75	7.50	15.00
—*Black label with colorband, Capitol logo at top*					
❏ ST 1658 [S]	College Concert	1962	6.25	12.50	25.00
❏ T 1658 [M]	College Concert	1962	5.00	10.00	20.00
❏ SM-1705	The Best of the Kingston Trio	197?	2.50	5.00	10.00
❏ ST 1705 [P]	The Best of the Kingston Trio	1962	5.00	10.00	20.00
❏ T 1705 [M]	The Best of the Kingston Trio	1962	5.00	10.00	20.00
❏ ST 1747 [S]	Something Special	1962	6.25	12.50	25.00
❏ T 1747 [M]	Something Special	1962	5.00	10.00	20.00
❏ ST 1809 [S]	New Frontier	1962	6.25	12.50	25.00
❏ T 1809 [M]	New Frontier	1962	5.00	10.00	20.00
❏ ST 1871 [S]	The Kingston Trio #16	1963	6.25	12.50	25.00
❏ T 1871 [M]	The Kingston Trio #16	1963	5.00	10.00	20.00
❏ ST 1935 [S]	Sunny Side!	1963	6.25	12.50	25.00
❏ T 1935 [M]	Sunny Side!	1963	5.00	10.00	20.00
❏ KAO 2005 [M]	Sing a Song with the Kingston Trio	1963	6.25	12.50	25.00
❏ SKAO 2005 [S]	Sing a Song with the Kingston Trio	1963	7.50	15.00	30.00
❏ ST 2011 [S]	Time to Think	1964	5.00	10.00	20.00
❏ T 2011 [M]	Time to Think	1964	3.75	7.50	15.00
❏ ST 2081 [S]	Back in Town	1964	5.00	10.00	20.00
❏ T 2081 [M]	Back in Town	1964	3.75	7.50	15.00
❏ STCL 2180 [(3)S]	The Folk Era	1964	12.50	25.00	50.00
—*Box set with booklet*					
❏ TCL 2180 [(3)M]	The Folk Era	1964	10.00	20.00	40.00
—*Box set with booklet*					
❏ SM-2280	The Best of the Kingston Trio, Volume 2	197?	2.50	5.00	10.00
❏ ST 2280 [S]	The Best of the Kingston Trio, Volume 2	1965	5.00	10.00	20.00
❏ T 2280 [M]	The Best of the Kingston Trio, Volume 2	1965	3.75	7.50	15.00
❏ SM-2614	The Best of the Kingston Trio, Volume 3	197?	2.50	5.00	10.00
❏ ST 2614 [S]	The Best of the Kingston Trio, Volume 3	1966	5.00	10.00	20.00
❏ T 2614 [M]	The Best of the Kingston Trio, Volume 3	1966	3.75	7.50	15.00
❏ M-11577	The Kingston Trio	1976	2.50	5.00	10.00
❏ M-11968	From the Hungry I	1979	2.50	5.00	10.00
❏ SN-16183	The Kingston Trio	1981	2.00	4.00	8.00
—*Budget-line reissue*					
❏ SN-16184	The Best of the Kingston Trio, Volume 2	1981	2.00	4.00	8.00
—*Budget-line reissue*					
❏ N-16185	Tom Dooley	1981	2.00	4.00	8.00
❏ SN-16186	Scarlet Ribbons	1981	2.00	4.00	8.00

Number	Title (A Side/B Side)	Yr	VG	VG+	NM

DECCA

Number	Title (A Side/B Side)	Yr	VG	VG+	NM
❑ DL 4613 [M]	The Kingston Trio (Nick-Bob-John)	1965	6.25	12.50	25.00
❑ DL 4656 [M]	Stay Awhile	1965	6.25	12.50	25.00
❑ DL 4694 [M]	Somethin' Else	1965	6.25	12.50	25.00
❑ DL 4758 [M]	Children of the Morning	1966	6.25	12.50	25.00
❑ DL 74613 [S]	The Kingston Trio (Nick-Bob-John)	1965	7.50	15.00	30.00
❑ DL 74656 [S]	Stay Awhile	1965	7.50	15.00	30.00
❑ DL 74694 [S]	Somethin' Else	1965	7.50	15.00	30.00
❑ DL 74758 [S]	Children of the Morning	1966	7.50	15.00	30.00

FOLK ERA

Number	Title (A Side/B Side)	Yr	VG	VG+	NM
❑ FE-2001	Rediscover the Kingston Trio	198?	2.50	5.00	10.00
❑ FE-2036	Hidden Treasures	198?	2.50	5.00	10.00

NAUTILUS

Number	Title (A Side/B Side)	Yr	VG	VG+	NM
❑ NR-2	Aspen Gold	1979	10.00	20.00	40.00

—*Audiophile vinyl*

PAIR

Number	Title (A Side/B Side)	Yr	VG	VG+	NM
❑ PDL2-1067 [(2)]	Early American Heroes	1986	3.00	6.00	12.00

PICKWICK

Number	Title (A Side/B Side)	Yr	VG	VG+	NM
❑ SPC-3260	Tom Dooley	196?	3.00	6.00	12.00

TETRAGRAMMATON

Number	Title (A Side/B Side)	Yr	VG	VG+	NM
❑ T-5101 [(2)]	Once Upon a Time	1969	6.25	12.50	25.00

XERES

Number	Title (A Side/B Side)	Yr	VG	VG+	NM
❑ 1-10001	25 Years Non-Stop	1982	3.00	6.00	12.00

KINKS, THE Also see DAVE DAVIES.

12-Inch Singles

ARISTA

Number	Title (A Side/B Side)	Yr	VG	VG+	NM
❑ SP-34 [DJ]	Father Christmas/A Rock 'n' Roll Fantasy	1978	6.25	12.50	25.00
❑ SP-45 [DJ]	(Wish I Could Fly Like) Superman (3:45) (5:58)	1979	3.75	7.50	15.00
❑ SP-152 [DJ]	Come Dancing (same on both sides)	1983	3.75	7.50	15.00
❑ CP 700	(Wish I Could Fly Like) Superman/Low Budget	1979	2.00	4.00	8.00
❑ ADP 9095 [DJ]	Don't Forget to Dance (same on both sides)	1983	—	3.00	6.00
❑ ADP 9297 [DJ]	Do It Again (same on both sides)	1984	—	3.00	6.00
❑ ADP 9337 [DJ]	Summer's Gone (same on both sides)	1983	—	3.00	6.00

MCA

Number	Title (A Side/B Side)	Yr	VG	VG+	NM
❑ L33-17207 [DJ]	Rock 'n' Roll Cities (same on both sides)	1987	—	3.00	6.00
❑ L33-17260 [DJ]	Lost and Found (same on both sides)	1987	—	3.00	6.00
❑ L33-17345 [DJ]	How Are You (same on both sides)	1987	—	3.00	6.00
❑ L33-17460 [DJ]	The Road (same on both sides)	1988	2.00	4.00	8.00
❑ L33-17498 [DJ]	The Road (Edit) (same on both sides)	1988	—	3.00	6.00
❑ L33-17531 [DJ]	Art Lover (Live)/Destroyer (Live)	1988	—	3.00	6.00

45s

ARISTA

Number	Title (A Side/B Side)	Yr	VG	VG+	NM
❑ SP-5 [DJ]	Sleepwalker/All the Kids on the Street	1977	2.50	5.00	10.00

—*Gold vinyl; B-side by the Hollywood Stars*

Number	Title (A Side/B Side)	Yr	VG	VG+	NM
❑ SP-5 [PS]	Sleepwalker/All the Kids on the Street	1977	2.50	5.00	10.00
❑ 0240	Sleepwalker/Full Moon	1977	—	2.00	4.00
❑ 0247	Life Goes On/Juke Box Music	1977	—	2.00	4.00
❑ 0296	Father Christmas/Prince of the Punks	1977	—	2.50	5.00
❑ 0296 [PS]	Father Christmas/Prince of the Punks	1977	—	2.50	5.00
❑ 0342	A Rock and Roll Fantasy/Live Life	1978	—	2.00	4.00
❑ 0372	Black Messiah/Live Life	1978	—	2.00	4.00
❑ 0409	(Wish I Could Fly Like) Superman/Party Line	1979	—	2.00	4.00
❑ 0409	Superman/Low Budget	1979	—	2.50	5.00
❑ 0448	Low Budget/A Gallon of Gas	1979	—	2.00	4.00
❑ 0458	Catch Me Now I'm Falling/Low Budget	1979	—	2.00	4.00
❑ 0541	Lola/Celluloid Heroes	1980	—	2.00	4.00
❑ 0541 [PS]	Lola/Celluloid Heroes	1980	—	2.50	5.00
❑ 0577	You Really Got Me/Attitude	1980	—	2.00	4.00
❑ 0619	Destroyer/Back to Back	1981	—	2.00	4.00
❑ 0649	Better Things/Yo-Yo	1981	—	2.00	4.00
❑ 1054	Come Dancing/Noise	1983	—	2.00	4.00
❑ 1054 [PS]	Come Dancing/Noise	1983	—	2.00	4.00
❑ 9016	Come Dancing/Noise	1983	—	—	3.00
❑ 9016 [PS]	Come Dancing/Noise	1983	—	—	3.00
❑ 9075	Don't Forget to Dance/Young Conservatives	1983	—	—	3.00
❑ 9309	Do It Again/Guilty	1984	—	—	3.00
❑ 9309 [PS]	Do It Again/Guilty	1984	—	—	3.00
❑ 9334	Summer's Gone/Going Solo	1985	—	—	3.00

CAMEO

Number	Title (A Side/B Side)	Yr	VG	VG+	NM
❑ 308	Long Tall Sally/I Took My Baby Home	1964	150.00	300.00	600.00
❑ 345	Long Tall Sally/I Took My Baby Home	1965	75.00	150.00	300.00
❑ 348	You Still Want Me/You Do Something to Me	1965	—	—	—

—*Canceled. NOTE: An EP on Cameo, which contains the four songs assigned to Cameo in the U.S., is a bootleg with little collector value.*

MCA

Number	Title (A Side/B Side)	Yr	VG	VG+	NM
❑ 52960	Rock 'N' Roll Cities/Sleazy Town	1986	—	—	3.00
❑ 52960 [PS]	Rock 'N' Roll Cities/Sleazy Town	1986	—	—	3.00
❑ 53015	Lost and Found/Killing Time	1987	—	—	3.00
❑ 53015 [PS]	Lost and Found/Killing Time	1987	—	—	3.00
❑ 53093	Working at the Factory/How Are You	1987	2.50	5.00	10.00
❑ 53699	How Do I Get Close/War Is Over	1989	2.50	5.00	10.00

RCA VICTOR

Number	Title (A Side/B Side)	Yr	VG	VG+	NM
❑ 74-0620	20th Century Man/Skin and Bones	1971	2.00	4.00	8.00
❑ 74-0807	Supersonic Rocket Ship/You Don't Know My Name	1972	2.00	4.00	8.00
❑ 74-0852	Celluloid Heroes/Hot Potatoes	1972	2.00	4.00	8.00
❑ 74-0940	One of the Survivors/Scrap Heap City	1973	50.00	100.00	200.00

—*Released with acoustic versions of the two songs rather than the LP versions and quickly deleted*

Number	Title (A Side/B Side)	Yr	VG	VG+	NM
❑ APBO-0275	Money Talks/Here Comes Flash	1974	2.50	5.00	10.00
❑ DJBO-0275 [DJ]	Money Talks (short/long versions)	1974	2.00	4.00	8.00
❑ LPBO-5001	Sitting in the Midday Sun/Sweet Lady Genevieve	1973	2.50	5.00	10.00
❑ PB-10019	Mirror of Love/It's Evil	1974	—	3.00	6.00
❑ PB-10121	Preservation/Salvation Road	1974	—	3.00	6.00
❑ PB-10251	Everybody's a Star (Starmaker)/Ordinary People	1975	—	3.00	6.00
❑ PB-10551	I'm in Disgrace/The Hard Way	1976	—	3.00	6.00

REPRISE

Number	Title (A Side/B Side)	Yr	VG	VG+	NM
❑ 0306	You Really Got Me/It's All Right	1964	3.75	7.50	15.00

—*Second pressings have orange and brown labels*

Number	Title (A Side/B Side)	Yr	VG	VG+	NM
❑ 0306	You Really Got Me/It's All Right	1964	6.25	12.50	25.00

—*Originals have peach labels*

Number	Title (A Side/B Side)	Yr	VG	VG+	NM
❑ 0334	All Day and All of the Night/I Gotta Move	1964	5.00	10.00	20.00
❑ 0347	Tired of Waiting for You/Come On Now	1965	5.00	10.00	20.00

Number	Title (A Side/B Side)	Yr	VG	VG+	NM
❑ 0366	Who'll Be the Next in Line/Everybody's Gonna Be Happy	1965	5.00	10.00	20.00
❑ 0379	Set Me Free/I Need You	1965	5.00	10.00	20.00
❑ 0409	See My Friends/Never Met a Girl Like You Before	1965	3.75	7.50	15.00
❑ 0420	A Well Respected Man/Such a Shame	1965	3.75	7.50	15.00
❑ 0454	Till the End of the Day/Where Have All the Good Times Gone	1966	3.75	7.50	15.00
❑ 0471	Dedicated Follower of Fashion/Sittin' on My Sofa	1966	3.75	7.50	15.00
❑ 0497	Sunny Afternoon/I'm Not Like Everybody Else	1966	3.75	7.50	15.00
❑ 0540	Dead End Street/Big Black Smoke	1966	10.00	20.00	40.00
❑ 0587	Mr. Pleasant/Harry Rag	1967	10.00	20.00	40.00
❑ 0612	Waterloo Sunset/Two Sisters	1967	10.00	20.00	40.00
❑ 0647	Autumn Almanac/David Watts	1967	10.00	20.00	40.00
❑ 0691	Wonderboy/Polly	1968	10.00	20.00	40.00
❑ 0708	Sunny Afternoon/Dead End Street	1968	2.50	5.00	10.00
❑ 0712	Dedicated Follower of Fashion/Who'll Be the Next in Line	1968	2.50	5.00	10.00
❑ 0715	A Well Respected Man/Set Me Free	1968	2.50	5.00	10.00
❑ 0719	Tired of Waiting for You/All Day and All of the Night	1968	2.50	5.00	10.00
❑ 0722	You Really Got Me/It's All Right	1968	2.50	5.00	10.00

—*0708 through 0722 are "Back to Back Hits" series -- originals have both "r:" and "W7" on label*

Number	Title (A Side/B Side)	Yr	VG	VG+	NM
❑ 0743	Lola/Apeman	1972	—	2.50	5.00

—*"Back to Back Hits" series*

Number	Title (A Side/B Side)	Yr	VG	VG+	NM
❑ 0762	Days/She's Got Everything	1968	10.00	20.00	40.00
❑ 0806	Starstruck/Picture Book	1969	10.00	20.00	40.00
❑ 0847	The Village Green Preservation Society/Do You Remember Walter	1969	10.00	20.00	40.00
❑ 0863	Victoria/Brainwashed	1969	3.75	7.50	15.00
❑ 0930	Lola/Mindless Child of Motherhood	1970	2.50	5.00	10.00
❑ 0979	Apeman/Rats	1970	2.50	5.00	10.00
❑ 1017	God's Children/The Way Love Used to Be	1971	5.00	10.00	20.00
❑ 1094	King Kong/Waterloo Sunset	1972	3.75	7.50	15.00

7-Inch Extended Plays

CAMEO

Number	Title (A Side/B Side)	Yr	VG	VG+	NM
❑ 315	Long Tall Sally/I Took My Baby Home//You Still Want Me/You Do Something To Me	196?	—	—	—

—*This is a fake with little collector value; also comes with title sleeve; no such item was ever issued by Cameo*

Albums

ARISTA

Number	Title (A Side/B Side)	Yr	VG	VG+	NM
❑ SP-69 [DJ]	Low Budget Radio Interview	1979	10.00	20.00	40.00

—*Promo-only radio show featuring Ray Davies*

Number	Title (A Side/B Side)	Yr	VG	VG+	NM
❑ SP-85 [EP]	A Fistful of Kinks	1980	6.25	12.50	25.00

—*Promo-only four-song sampler from "One for the Road"*

Number	Title (A Side/B Side)	Yr	VG	VG+	NM
❑ AL 4106	Sleepwalker	1977	2.50	5.00	10.00
❑ AL 4106 [DJ]	Sleepwalker	1977	7.50	15.00	30.00

—*White label promo*

Number	Title (A Side/B Side)	Yr	VG	VG+	NM
❑ AL 4167	Misfits	1978	2.50	5.00	10.00
❑ AL 4167 [DJ]	Misfits	1978	7.50	15.00	30.00

—*White label promo*

Number	Title (A Side/B Side)	Yr	VG	VG+	NM
❑ AB 4240	Low Budget	1979	2.50	5.00	10.00
❑ AL 8-8018	State of Confusion	1983	2.50	5.00	10.00
❑ AL13 8041 [(2)]	One for the Road	1983	2.50	5.00	10.00

—*Reissue of 8609*

Number	Title (A Side/B Side)	Yr	VG	VG+	NM
❑ AL 8264	Word of Mouth	1984	2.50	5.00	10.00
❑ ALB6 8300	Low Budget	1985	2.00	4.00	8.00

—*Budget-line reissue*

Number	Title (A Side/B Side)	Yr	VG	VG+	NM
❑ ALB6 8328	Give the People What They Want	1985	2.00	4.00	8.00

—*Budget-line reissue*

Number	Title (A Side/B Side)	Yr	VG	VG+	NM
❑ ALB6 8375	Sleepwalker	1985	2.00	4.00	8.00

—*Budget-line reissue*

Number	Title (A Side/B Side)	Yr	VG	VG+	NM
❑ ALB6 8377	Misfits	1985	2.00	4.00	8.00

—*Budget-line reissue*

Number	Title (A Side/B Side)	Yr	VG	VG+	NM
❑ A2L 8401 [(2)]	One for the Road	1980	3.75	7.50	15.00

—*Original edition has this number*

Number	Title (A Side/B Side)	Yr	VG	VG+	NM
❑ AL11 8428 [(2)]	Come Dancing with the Kinks	1986	3.00	6.00	12.00
❑ A2L 8609 [(2)]	One for the Road	198?	3.00	6.00	12.00

—*Second edition of 8401*

Number	Title (A Side/B Side)	Yr	VG	VG+	NM
❑ AL 9567	Give the People What They Want	1981	2.50	5.00	10.00

COMPLEAT

Number	Title (A Side/B Side)	Yr	VG	VG+	NM
❑ CPL2-2001 [(2)]	A Compleat Collection	1984	3.00	6.00	12.00
❑ CPL2-2003 [(2)]	20th Anniversary Edition	1984	3.00	6.00	12.00

MCA

Number	Title (A Side/B Side)	Yr	VG	VG+	NM
❑ 5822	Think Visual	1987	2.50	5.00	10.00
❑ 6337	UK Jive	1989	3.00	6.00	12.00
❑ L33-17281 [DJ]	A Look at "Think Visual"	1987	12.50	25.00	50.00

—*Promo only in white jacket*

Number	Title (A Side/B Side)	Yr	VG	VG+	NM
❑ 42107	Live: The Road	1988	2.50	5.00	10.00

MOBILE FIDELITY

Number	Title (A Side/B Side)	Yr	VG	VG+	NM
❑ 1-070	Misfits	1981	5.00	10.00	20.00

—*Audiophile vinyl*

PICKWICK

Number	Title (A Side/B Side)	Yr	VG	VG+	NM
❑ ACL-7072	Preservation Act 1	197?	3.00	6.00	12.00

—*Reissue of RCA Victor LPL1-5002*

PYE

Number	Title (A Side/B Side)	Yr	VG	VG+	NM
❑ 505	The Kinks	1975	3.00	6.00	12.00
❑ 509	The Kinks, Vol. 2	1976	3.00	6.00	12.00

RCA VICTOR

Number	Title (A Side/B Side)	Yr	VG	VG+	NM
❑ APL1-1743	Celluloid Heroes (The Kinks' Greatest)	1976	2.50	5.00	10.00
❑ APL1-3520	Second Time Around	1980	2.50	5.00	10.00
❑ AYL1-3749	Schoolboys in Disgrace	1980	2.00	4.00	8.00

—*Budget-line reissue*

Number	Title (A Side/B Side)	Yr	VG	VG+	NM
❑ AYL1-3750	Soap Opera	1980	2.00	4.00	8.00

—*Budget-line reissue*

Number	Title (A Side/B Side)	Yr	VG	VG+	NM
❑ AYL1-3869	Celluloid Heroes (The Kinks' Greatest)	1981	2.00	4.00	8.00

—*Budget-line reissue*

Number	Title (A Side/B Side)	Yr	VG	VG+	NM
❑ AYL1-4558	Muswell Hillbillies	1982	2.00	4.00	8.00

—*Budget-line reissue*

Number	Title (A Side/B Side)	Yr	VG	VG+	NM
❑ LSP-4644	Muswell Hillbillies	1971	7.50	15.00	30.00
❑ AYL1-4719	Second Time Around	1983	2.00	4.00	8.00

—*Budget-line reissue*

Number	Title (A Side/B Side)	Yr	VG	VG+	NM
❑ LPL1-5002	Preservation Act 1	1973	3.75	7.50	15.00
❑ CPL2-5040 [(2)]	Preservation Act 2	1974	5.00	10.00	20.00
❑ LPL1-5081	Soap Opera	1975	2.50	5.00	10.00

—*Brown label*

Number	Title (A Side/B Side)	Yr	VG	VG+	NM
❏ LPL1-5081	Soap Opera	1975	3.75	7.50	15.00
—Orange label					
❏ LPL1-5102	Schoolboys in Disgrace	1975	2.50	5.00	10.00
❏ VPS-6065 [(2)]	Everybody's in Showbiz	1972	5.00	10.00	20.00
—Orange label					
❏ VPS-6065 [(2)]	Everybody's in Showbiz	1975	3.00	6.00	12.00
—Brown label					
REPRISE					
❏ PRO 328 [P]	Then Now and In Between	1969	12.50	25.00	50.00
—Album that came with above box is sometimes found by itself without all the other goodies.					
❏ PRO 328 [P]	God Save the Kinks	1969	125.00	250.00	500.00
—Mail-order box with decal, postcard, bag of grass, two pins, letter, Kinks consumer guide and "Then Now and In Between" LP. Price is for complete package.					
❏ MS-2127	The Great Lost Kinks Album	1973	12.50	25.00	50.00
❏ R-6143 [M]	You Really Got Me	1965	15.00	30.00	60.00
❏ R-6143 [M]	You Really Got Me	1965	100.00	200.00	400.00
—White label promo					
❏ RS-6143 [P]	You Really Got Me	1965	20.00	40.00	80.00
—Pink, gold and green label					
❏ RS-6143 [P]	You Really Got Me	1971	2.50	5.00	10.00
—Orange label with "r:" and steamboat at top					
❏ R-6158 [M]	Kinks-Size	1965	12.50	25.00	50.00
❏ R-6158 [M]	Kinks-Size	1965	50.00	100.00	200.00
—White label promo					
❏ RS-6158 [R]	Kinks-Size	1965	7.50	15.00	30.00
❏ R-6173 [M]	Kinda Kinks	1965	12.50	25.00	50.00
❏ R-6173 [M]	Kinda Kinks	1965	50.00	100.00	200.00
—White label promo					
❏ RS-6173 [R]	Kinda Kinks	1965	7.50	15.00	30.00
❏ R-6184 [M]	Kinks Kinkdom	1965	12.50	25.00	50.00
❏ R-6184 [M]	Kinks Kinkdom	1965	50.00	100.00	200.00
—White label promo					
❏ RS-6184 [R]	Kinks Kinkdom	1965	7.50	15.00	30.00
❏ R-6197 [M]	The Kink Kontroversy	1966	12.50	25.00	50.00
❏ R-6197 [M]	The Kink Kontroversy	1966	50.00	100.00	200.00
—White label promo					
❏ RS-6197 [R]	The Kink Kontroversy	1966	7.50	15.00	30.00
❏ R-6217 [M]	The Kinks Greatest Hits!	1966	10.00	20.00	40.00
❏ RS-6217 [R]	The Kinks Greatest Hits!	1966	6.25	12.50	25.00
—Pink, gold and green label					
❏ RS-6217 [R]	The Kinks Greatest Hits!	1971	2.50	5.00	10.00
—Orange label with "r:" and steamboat at top					
❏ R-6228 [M]	Face to Face	1967	10.00	20.00	40.00
❏ RS-6228 [P]	Face to Face	1967	7.50	15.00	30.00
—Pink, gold and green label					
❏ RS-6228 [P]	Face to Face	1971	2.50	5.00	10.00
—Orange label with "r:" and steamboat at top					
❏ R-6260 [M]	The Live Kinks	1967	8.75	17.50	35.00
❏ RS-6260 [S]	The Live Kinks	1967	6.25	12.50	25.00
—Pink, gold and green label					
❏ RS-6260 [S]	The Live Kinks	1971	2.50	5.00	10.00
—Orange label with "r:" and steamboat at top					
❏ R-6279 [M]	Something Else by the Kinks	1968	75.00	150.00	300.00
—White label promo; no stock copies were issued in mono					
❏ RS-6279 [S]	Something Else by the Kinks	1968	5.00	10.00	20.00
—Two-tone orange label with "r: and "W7" logos with steamboat					
❏ RS-6279 [S]	Something Else by the Kinks	1968	7.50	15.00	30.00
—Pink, gold and green label					
❏ RS-6279 [S]	Something Else by the Kinks	1971	2.50	5.00	10.00
—Orange label with "r:" and steamboat at top					
❏ RS-6327	The Kinks Are the Village Green Preservation Society	1969	7.50	15.00	30.00
—Two-tone orange label with "r: and "W7" logos with steamboat					
❏ RS-6327	The Kinks Are the Village Green Preservation Society	1971	2.50	5.00	10.00
—Orange label with "r:" and steamboat at top					
❏ RS-6366	Arthur (Or The Decline and Fall of the British Empire)	1969	6.25	12.50	25.00
—Two-tone orange label with "r: and "W7" logos with steamboat					
❏ RS-6366	Arthur (Or The Decline and Fall of the British Empire)	1971	2.50	5.00	10.00
—Orange label with "r:" and steamboat at top					
❏ RS-6423	Lola Versus Powerman and the Moneyground, Part One	1970	3.75	7.50	15.00
—Original pressings have blue printing on a white cover					
❏ RS-6423	Lola Versus Powerman and the Moneyground, Part One	1971	2.50	5.00	10.00
—Later pressings have black printing on a white cover					
❏ 2XS-6454 [(2)]	The Kink Kronicles	1972	3.75	7.50	15.00
❏ SMAS-93034	Arthur (Or The Decline and Fall of the British Empire)	1970	10.00	20.00	40.00
—Capitol Record Club edition					
RHINO					
❏ R1 70086	The Kinks Greatest Hits! Vol. 1	1989	3.00	6.00	12.00
❏ R1 70315	You Really Got Me	1988	3.00	6.00	12.00
❏ R1 70316	Kinda Kinks	1988	3.00	6.00	12.00
❏ R1 70317	Kinks-Size	1988	3.00	6.00	12.00
❏ R1 70318	Kinks Kinkdom	1988	3.00	6.00	12.00

KIPPINGTON LODGE　With Nick Lowe.
45s

Number	Title (A Side/B Side)	Yr	VG	VG+	NM
CAPITOL					
❏ 2236	And She Cried/Rumors	1968	7.50	15.00	30.00

KIRBY, BUZZ
45s

Number	Title (A Side/B Side)	Yr	VG	VG+	NM
PARKWAY					
❏ 906	Speedo/She's My Girl	1964	3.00	6.00	12.00

KIRBY, DAVE
45s

Number	Title (A Side/B Side)	Yr	VG	VG+	NM
BOONE					
❏ 1078	Marie St. John/My Faults Will Fade Away	1969	2.00	4.00	8.00
❏ 1083	A Walk on the Outside/Mary and Jane	1969	2.00	4.00	8.00
CAPITOL					
❏ 4119	Colorado/Good to Be Back on the Road	1975	—	3.00	6.00

Number	Title (A Side/B Side)	Yr	VG	VG+	NM
DIMENSION					
❏ 1013	Great All American Good Timin' Honky Tonk Man/Ain't Nothing Older Than That	1980	—	2.50	5.00
❏ 1019	North Alabama/How Can I Tell You Goodbye	1981	—	2.50	5.00
❏ 1022	Moccasin Man/When Will Forgetting Begin	1981	—	2.50	5.00
❏ 1030	Something New to Love/Cowboy Connection	1982	—	2.50	5.00
DOT					
❏ 17437	Lila Is My Kind of Woman/So Long Train Whistle	1972	—	3.00	6.00
MONUMENT					
❏ 1168	Her and the Car and the Mobile Home/Don't It Make You Want to Go Home	1969	—	3.00	6.00
❏ 1215	I Came Out Smelling Like a Rose/The Hobo	1970	—	3.00	6.00
RED FEATHER					
❏ 18174	The Old Old House/Cantaloupe Jones	196?	5.00	10.00	20.00
—Red vinyl					
SOMA					
❏ 1416	The Old, Old House/Cantalope Jones	1964	3.00	6.00	12.00
ZODIAC					
❏ 1007	What Kind of Bird Is That/Gonna Ride the Santa Fe to Santa Fe	1976	—	3.00	6.00
Albums					
DOT					
❏ DLP-26014	Singer, Picker, Writer	1973	3.00	6.00	12.00

KIRBY, KATHY
45s

Number	Title (A Side/B Side)	Yr	VG	VG+	NM
ASCOT					
❏ 2232	In All the World/Time	1967	2.00	4.00	8.00
LONDON					
❏ 9572	(He's a) Big Man/Slowly	1963	3.75	7.50	15.00
❏ 9621	Dance On/Playboy	1963	3.75	7.50	15.00
❏ 9628	Secret Love/Too Bad for Johnny	1964	3.75	7.50	15.00
❏ 9645	Let Me Go Lover/Sweetest Sounds	1964	3.75	7.50	15.00
❏ 9677	Love Me Baby/You're the One	1964	3.75	7.50	15.00
❏ 9750	I Belong/I'll Try Not to Cry	1965	3.75	7.50	15.00
PARROT					
❏ 9767	Secret Love/Soon I'll Wed My Love	1965	3.00	6.00	12.00
❏ 9775	The Way of Love/Oh Darling How I Miss You	1965	3.00	6.00	12.00
❏ 9805	Where in the World/Wonderful Feeling of Love	1965	3.00	6.00	12.00
❏ 9827	Till the End of Time/Spanish Flea	1966	2.50	5.00	10.00

KIRK, DAVE
45s

Number	Title (A Side/B Side)	Yr	VG	VG+	NM
HI-Q					
❏ 5024	Oh! Baby/Those Lonely Blue Nights	1962	12.50	25.00	50.00

KISS
12-Inch Singles

Number	Title (A Side/B Side)	Yr	VG	VG+	NM
CASABLANCA					
❏ 20169	I Was Made for Lovin' You/Charisma	1979	6.25	12.50	25.00
MERCURY					
❏ PRO 229-1 [DJ]	Lick It Up (same on both sides)	1983	3.75	7.50	15.00
❏ PRO 244-1 [DJ]	All Hell's Breaking Loose (same on both sides)	1983	3.75	7.50	15.00
❏ PRO 311-1 [DJ]	Heaven's on Fire (same on both sides)	1984	3.75	7.50	15.00
❏ PRO 326-1 [DJ]	Thrills in the Night (same on both sides)	1984	3.75	7.50	15.00
❏ PRO 377-1 [DJ]	Tears Are Falling (3:55) (same on both sides)	1985	3.75	7.50	15.00
❏ PRO 395-1 [DJ]	Uh! All Night (3:43) (same on both sides)	1985	3.75	7.50	15.00
❏ PRO 531-1 [DJ]	Crazy Crazy Nights (same on both sides)	1987	3.00	6.00	12.00
❏ PRO 559-1 [DJ]	Reason to Live (same on both sides)	1987	3.00	6.00	12.00
❏ PRO 572-1 [DJ]	Turn On the Night (same on both sides)	1987	3.00	6.00	12.00
❏ PRO 693-1 [DJ]	Let's Put the X in Sex (X-Cessive Mix 7:33)//(Hot Urban Mix 3:58) (Sex-A-Pella Mix 4:37)/Calling Dr. Love	1989	10.00	20.00	40.00
45s					
CASABLANCA					
❏ 0004	Love Theme from Kiss/Nothin' to Lose	1974	3.75	7.50	15.00
❏ 0011	Kissin' Time/Nothin' to Lose	1974	3.75	7.50	15.00
❏ 0015	Strutter/100,000 Years	1974	3.75	7.50	15.00
❏ 823	Let Me Go, Rock and Roll/Hotter Than Hell	1975	5.00	10.00	20.00
—Blue label					
❏ 823	Let Me Go, Rock and Roll/Hotter Than Hell	1977	3.00	6.00	12.00
—"Casablanca Record and FilmWorks" label					
❏ 829	Rock and Roll All Nite/Getaway	1975	5.00	10.00	20.00
❏ 841	C'mon and Love Me/Getaway	1975	5.00	10.00	20.00
—Blue label					
❏ 841	C'mon and Love Me/Getaway	1977	3.00	6.00	12.00
—"Casablanca Record and FilmWorks" label					
❏ 850	Rock and Roll All Nite (Live)/Rock and Roll All Nite (Studio)	1975	2.50	5.00	10.00
—Blue label					
❏ 850	Rock and Roll All Nite (Live)/Rock and Roll All Nite (Studio)	1977	3.00	6.00	12.00
—"Casablanca Record and FilmWorks" label					
❏ 854	Shout It Out Loud/Sweet Pain	1976	2.50	5.00	10.00
—Blue label					
❏ 854	Shout It Out Loud/Sweet Pain	1977	2.00	4.00	8.00
—"Casablanca Record and FilmWorks" label					
❏ 858	Flaming Youth/God of Thunder	1976	2.50	5.00	10.00
❏ 858 [PS]	Flaming Youth/God of Thunder	1976	15.00	30.00	60.00
❏ 863	Beth/Detroit Rock City	1976	—	3.00	6.00
—With "Beth" listed as "Side A"; brown label with camel					
❏ 863	Detroit Rock City/Beth	1976	2.50	5.00	10.00
—With "Detroit Rock City" listed as "Side A"					
❏ 863	Beth/Detroit Rock City	1977	—	2.50	5.00
—With "Beth" listed as "Side A"; "Casablanca Record and FilmWorks" label					
❏ 873	Hard Luck Woman/Mr. Speed	1976	—	3.00	6.00
❏ 880	Calling Dr. Love/Take Me	1977	—	2.50	5.00
—"Casablanca Record and FilmWorks" label					
❏ 880	Calling Dr. Love/Take Me	1977	—	3.00	6.00
—Brown label with camel					
❏ 889	Christine Sixteen/Shock Me	1977	—	2.50	5.00
—A-side time listed as 2:52, B-side time listed as 4:17; "Casablanca Record and FilmWorks" label					
❏ 889	Christine Sixteen/Shock Me	1977	—	2.50	5.00
—A-side time listed as 3:10, B-side time listed as 3:45; "Casablanca Record and FilmWorks" label					
❏ 889	Christine Sixteen/Shock Me	1977	—	3.00	6.00
—A-side time listed as 2:52, B-side time listed as 4:17; brown label with camel					

K

Number	Title (A Side/B Side)	Yr	VG	VG+	NM
❏ 889	Christine Sixteen/Shock Me	1977	—	3.00	6.00
—A-side time listed as 3:10, B-side time listed as 3:45; brown label with camel					
❏ 895	Love Gun/Hooligan	1977	—	3.00	6.00
❏ 906	Shout It Out Loud (Live)/Nothin' to Lose	1977	—	3.00	6.00
❏ 915	Rocket Ride/Tomorrow and Tonight	1978	—	3.00	6.00
❏ 928	Strutter '78/Shock Me	1978	—	3.00	6.00
❏ 983	I Was Made for Lovin' You/Hard Times	1979	—	2.50	5.00
❏ 2205	Sure Know Something/Dirty Livin'	1979	—	2.50	5.00
❏ 2282	Shandi/She's So European	1980	—	2.50	5.00
❏ 2299	Tomorrow/Naked City	1980	—	2.50	5.00
❏ 2343	A World Without Heroes/Dark Light	1981	—	2.50	5.00
❏ 2365	I Love It Loud/Danger	1982	—	2.50	5.00
❏ 2365 [PS]	I Love It Loud/Danger	1982	5.00	10.00	20.00
LOOKOUT!					
❏ 238	Detroit Rock City/Strutter	1999	—	—	3.00
—B-side by The Donnas; small hole, clear vinyl					
❏ 238 [PS]	Detroit Rock City/Strutter	1999	—	—	3.00
MERCURY					
❏ PRO 694-7 [DJ]	Let's Put the X in Sex (Hot Urban Mix)/(Hot Rock Mix)	1989	6.25	12.50	25.00
❏ PRO 1086-7 [DJ]	Rock and Roll All Nite	1993	7.50	15.00	30.00
—White label; small hole; B-side blank; comes in white sleeve that says "It's the Music Stupid" (included in above value)					
❏ 814671-7	Lick It Up/Dance All Over Your Face	1983	—	2.00	4.00
❏ 818216-7	All Hell's Breaking Loose/Young and Wasted	1984	—	2.00	4.00
❏ 858894-7	Detroit Rock City/Detroit Rock City	1994	—	2.00	4.00
—B-side by Mighty Mighty Bosstones; small center hole; green vinyl					
❏ 858894-7 [PS]	Detroit Rock City/Detroit Rock City	1994	—	2.00	4.00
❏ 870022-7	Reason to Live/Thief in the Night	1987	—	2.00	4.00
❏ 870022-7 [PS]	Reason to Live/Thief in the Night	1987	—	2.50	5.00
❏ 870215-7	Turn On the Night/Hell or High Water	1988	—	2.00	4.00
❏ 870215-7 [PS]	Turn On the Night/Hell or High Water	1988	—	2.50	5.00
❏ 872244-7	Let's Put the X in Sex/Calling Dr. Love	1989	—	2.50	5.00
❏ 872244-7 [PS]	Let's Put the X in Sex/Calling Dr. Love	1989	—	3.00	6.00
❏ 876146-7	Hide Your Heart/Betrayed	1989	—	2.50	5.00
❏ 876716-7	Forever/The Street Giveth and the Street Taketh Away	1990	—	2.50	5.00
❏ 880205-7	Heaven's on Fire/Lonely Is the Hunter	1984	—	2.00	4.00
❏ 880535-7	Thrills in the Night/Burn Bitch Burn	1985	—	2.00	4.00
❏ 884141-7	Tears Are Falling/Any Way You Slice It	1985	—	2.00	4.00
❏ 884141-7 [PS]	Tears Are Falling/Any Way You Slice It	1985	—	2.50	5.00
❏ 888796-7	Crazy Crazy Nights/No, No, No	1987	—	2.00	4.00
❏ 888796-7 [PS]	Crazy Crazy Nights/No, No, No	1987	—	2.50	5.00
Albums					
CASABLANCA					
❏ Kiss '76 [DJ]	Special Kiss Tour Album	1976	20.00	40.00	80.00
—Special four-track sampler					
❏ NBLP 737 [DJ]	Rock and Roll Over Special Edition	1977	30.00	60.00	120.00
—Five-track sampler from the LP					
❏ NBLP 7001	Kiss	1974	7.50	15.00	30.00
—All renumbered versions have "Kissin' Time"; dark blue label					
❏ NBLP 7001	Kiss	1976	3.75	7.50	15.00
—Tan label with desert scene, "Casablanca" label					
❏ NBLP 7001	Kiss	1977	3.00	6.00	12.00
—Tan label with desert scene, "Casablanca Record and FilmWorks" label					
❏ NBLP 7006	Hotter Than Hell	1974	7.50	15.00	30.00
—Dark blue label					
❏ NBLP 7006	Hotter Than Hell	1976	3.75	7.50	15.00
—Tan label with desert scene, "Casablanca" label					
❏ NBLP 7006	Hotter Than Hell	1977	3.00	6.00	12.00
—Tan label with desert scene, "Casablanca Record and FilmWorks" label					
❏ NBLP 7016	Dressed to Kill	1975	7.50	15.00	30.00
—Dark blue label					
❏ NBLP 7016	Dressed to Kill	1976	3.75	7.50	15.00
—Tan label with desert scene, "Casablanca" label					
❏ NBLP 7016	Dressed to Kill	1977	3.00	6.00	12.00
—Tan label with desert scene, "Casablanca Record and FilmWorks" label					
❏ NBLP 7020 [(2)]	Alive!	1975	10.00	20.00	40.00
—Dark blue labels; with booklet					
❏ NBLP 7020 [(2)]	Alive!	1976	5.00	10.00	20.00
—Tan labels with desert scene, "Casablanca" label					
❏ NBLP 7020 [(2)]	Alive!	1977	3.75	7.50	15.00
—Tan labels with desert scene, "Casablanca Record and FilmWorks" label					
❏ NBLP 7025	Destroyer	1976	3.75	7.50	15.00
—Tan label with desert scene, "Casablanca" label					
❏ NBLP 7025	Destroyer	1976	7.50	15.00	30.00
—Dark blue label					
❏ NBLP 7025	Destroyer	1977	3.00	6.00	12.00
—Tan label with desert scene, "Casablanca Record and FilmWorks" label					
❏ NBLP 7032 [(3)]	The Originals	1976	25.00	50.00	100.00
—Tan label with desert scene, "Casablanca" label; without extras					
❏ NBLP 7032 [(3)]	The Originals	1976	37.50	75.00	150.00
—Tan label with desert scene, "Casablanca" label; with booklet, six Kiss cards, a Kiss Army sticker					
❏ NBLP 7032 [(3)]	The Originals	1977	12.50	25.00	50.00
—Tan label with desert scene, "Casablanca Record and FilmWorks" label; "Second Printing" on cover; without extras					
❏ NBLP 7032 [(3)]	The Originals	1977	25.00	50.00	100.00
—Tan label with desert scene, "Casablanca Record and FilmWorks" label; "Second Printing" on cover; with extras listed above					
❏ NBLP 7037	Rock and Roll Over	1976	5.00	10.00	20.00
—Tan label with desert scene, "Casablanca" label; comes with sticker and Kiss Army paraphenalia order form					
❏ NBLP 7037	Rock and Roll Over	1977	3.00	6.00	12.00
—Tan label with desert scene, "Casablanca Record and FilmWorks" label, with inserts					
❏ NBLP 7057	Love Gun	1977	3.00	6.00	12.00
—Without inserts					
❏ NBLP 7057	Love Gun	1977	10.00	20.00	40.00
—with "Hot Goods from the Supply Depot" order form, unpunched-out cardboard gun and "Bang!" sticker. All items must be intact to get top dollar for this.					
❏ NBLP 7076 [(2)]	Alive II	1977	3.75	7.50	15.00
—Without inserts					
❏ NBLP 7076 [(2)]	Alive II	1977	10.00	20.00	40.00
—With 8-page booklet, tattoo insert and "Combat Gear" order form; back cover contents are correct					
❏ NBLP 7076 [(2)]	Alive II	1977	100.00	200.00	400.00
—With 8-page booklet, tattoo insert and "Combat Gear" order form; back cover lists three tracks -- "Take Me," "Hooligan" and "Do You Love Me" -- that were not included on the record; no records with these tracks were made; perhaps as few as 50 copies of this cover were made					

Number	Title (A Side/B Side)	Yr	VG	VG+	NM
❏ NBLP 7100 [(2)]	Double Platinum	1978	3.75	7.50	15.00
—Without inserts					
❏ NBLP 7100 [(2)]	Double Platinum	1978	10.00	20.00	40.00
—With "platinum award" cardboard insert and "Double Platinum Kiss Gear" order form					
❏ NBLP 7152	Dynasty	1979	2.50	5.00	10.00
—With neither poster nor order form					
❏ NBLP 7152	Dynasty	1979	3.75	7.50	15.00
—With poster and merchandise order form					
❏ NBLP 7225	Kiss Unmasked	1980	2.50	5.00	10.00
—With neither poster nor order form					
❏ NBLP 7225	Kiss Unmasked	1980	3.75	7.50	15.00
—With poster and "Kiss Essential Gear" order form					
❏ NBLP 7261	Music from The Elder	1981	7.50	15.00	30.00
—Various editions have paper or plastic innersleeves, lyric sheets, even incorrect track listings on the back cover; no difference in value is noted between variations					
❏ NBLP 7270	Creatures of the Night	1982	10.00	20.00	40.00
—Original version has band with makeup					
❏ NB 9001	Kiss	1974	12.50	25.00	50.00
—Second Warner Bros.-distributed version DOES have "Kissin' Time" on Side 2 (RE-1 on label)					
❏ NB 9001	Kiss	1974	20.00	40.00	80.00
—First Warner Bros.-distributed version does NOT have "Kissin' Time"					
❏ NB 20128 [DJ]	A Taste of Platinum	1978	12.50	25.00	50.00
—Promo-only sampler from Double Platinum					
❏ NB 20137 [DJ]	Peter Criss, Ace Frehley, Gene Simmons, Paul Stanley	1978	10.00	20.00	40.00
—Promo-only sampler from the band's solo albums					
❏ 812770-1	Dynasty	1983	2.00	4.00	8.00
—Reissue					
❏ 822780-1 [(2)]	Alive!	1984	2.50	5.00	10.00
—Reissue					
❏ 822781-1 [(2)]	Alive II	1984	2.50	5.00	10.00
—Reissue					
❏ 824146-1	Kiss	1984	2.00	4.00	8.00
—Reissue					
❏ 824147-1	Hotter Than Hell	1984	2.00	4.00	8.00
—Reissue					
❏ 824148-1	Dressed to Kill	1984	2.00	4.00	8.00
—Reissue					
❏ 824149-1	Destroyer	1984	2.00	4.00	8.00
—Reissue					
❏ 824150-1	Rock and Roll Over	1984	2.00	4.00	8.00
—Reissue					
❏ 824151-1	Love Gun	1984	2.00	4.00	8.00
—Reissue					
❏ 824153-1	Music from The Elder	1984	2.00	4.00	8.00
—Reissue					
❏ 824154-1	Creatures of the Night	1984	2.00	4.00	8.00
—Reissue; features band without its makeup on cover					
❏ 824154-1	Creatures of the Night	1994	6.25	12.50	25.00
—Reissue; glow-in-the-dark vinyl; gatefold edition; makeup cover restored					
❏ 824155-1 [(2)]	Double Platinum	1984	2.50	5.00	10.00
—Reissue					
❏ 826242-1	Unmasked	1985	2.00	4.00	8.00
—Reissue					
MERCURY					
❏ 792-1 [DJ]	First Kiss, Last Licks	1990	25.00	50.00	100.00
—Promo-only sampler					
❏ 522647-1 [(2)]	Alive III	1994	6.25	12.50	25.00
—Limited edition black vinyl					
❏ 522647-1 [(2)]	Alive III	1994	6.25	12.50	25.00
—Limited edition blue vinyl					
❏ 522647-1 [(2)]	Alive III	1994	6.25	12.50	25.00
—Limited edition red vinyl					
❏ 522647-1 [(2)]	Alive III	1994	6.25	12.50	25.00
—Limited edition white vinyl					
❏ 528674-1 [PD]	Creatures of the Night	1995	6.25	12.50	25.00
—Reissue; picture disc of makeup cover					
❏ 528950-1 [(2)]	MTV Unplugged	1996	5.00	10.00	20.00
—First editions are on black vinyl					
❏ 528950-1 [(2)]	MTV Unplugged	1996	5.00	10.00	20.00
—Second editions are on yellow marbled vinyl					
❏ 532741-1 [(2)]	You Wanted the Best, You Got the Best!!	1996	5.00	10.00	20.00
❏ 814297-1	Lick It Up	1983	3.00	6.00	12.00
❏ 822495-1	Animalize	1984	3.00	6.00	12.00
❏ 826099-1	Asylum	1985	2.50	5.00	10.00
❏ 832632-1	Crazy Nights	1987	2.50	5.00	10.00
❏ 832903-1 [PD]	Crazy Nights	1987	6.25	12.50	25.00
❏ 836427-1	Smashes, Thrashes and Hits	1988	2.50	5.00	10.00
❏ 836887-1 [PD]	Smashes, Thrashes and Hits	1988	6.25	12.50	25.00
❏ 838913-1	Hot in the Shade	1989	2.50	5.00	10.00

KISSOON, MAC AND KATIE
45s
ABC

Number	Title (A Side/B Side)	Yr	VG	VG+	NM
❏ 11306	Chirpy Chirpy Cheep Cheep/Walking Around	1971	—	3.00	6.00
BELL					
❏ 45198	I Found My Freedom/Love Game Today	1972	—	2.50	5.00
❏ 45436	Love Will Keep Us Together/I'm Up in Heaven	1974	—	2.50	5.00
MCA					
❏ 40409	Black Rose/Sugar Candy Kisses	1975	—	2.00	4.00
❏ 40482	Like a Butterfly/Beautiful Day	1975	—	2.00	4.00
❏ 40550	Two of Us/Dream of Me	1976	—	2.00	4.00
❏ 40609	Fly Away/Where Would Our Love Be	1976	—	2.00	4.00
Albums					
STATE/MCA					
❏ 2192	The Two of Us	1976	3.00	6.00	12.00

KIT AND THE OUTLAWS
45s
PHILIPS

Number	Title (A Side/B Side)	Yr	VG	VG+	NM
❏ 40420	Midnight Hour/Don't Tread on Me	1966	3.00	6.00	12.00

KIT KATS, THE
45s
JAMIE

Number	Title (A Side/B Side)	Yr	VG	VG+	NM
❏ 1321	That's the Way/Won't Find Better Than Me	1966	3.00	6.00	12.00
❏ 1326	Let's Get Lost on a Country Road/Find Someone (Who'll Make You Happy)	1966	3.00	6.00	12.00
❏ 1331	You've Got to Know/Cold Walls	1967	3.00	6.00	12.00

Number	Title (A Side/B Side)	Yr	VG	VG+	NM
❏ 1337	Breezy/Won't Find Better Than Me	1967	3.00	6.00	12.00
❏ 1343	Sea of Love/Cold Walls	1967	3.00	6.00	12.00
❏ 1345	Distance/Find Someone	1968	2.50	5.00	10.00
❏ 1346	I Got the Feeling/That's the Way	1968	2.50	5.00	10.00
❏ 1353	I Want to Be/Need You	1968	2.50	5.00	10.00
❏ 1354	You're So Good to Me/Need You	1968	2.50	5.00	10.00
❏ 1362	Hey Saturday Noon/That's the Way	1968	2.50	5.00	10.00
❏ 1381	Won't Find Better (Than Me)/(They Call It) Love	1969	2.00	4.00	8.00

—As "New Hope"

Number	Title (A Side/B Side)	Yr	VG	VG+	NM
❏ 1385	Rain/Let's Get Lost on a Country Road	1970	2.00	4.00	8.00

—As "New Hope"

Number	Title (A Side/B Side)	Yr	VG	VG+	NM
❏ 1388	Look Away/The Money Game	1970	2.00	4.00	8.00

—As "New Hope"

Number	Title (A Side/B Side)	Yr	VG	VG+	NM
❏ 1422	Find Someone/Breezy	1974	—	3.00	6.00

—As "New Hope"

LAURIE

Number	Title (A Side/B Side)	Yr	VG	VG+	NM
❏ 3186	Good Luck Charlie/Aba Daba Honeymoon	1963	5.00	10.00	20.00

LAWN

Number	Title (A Side/B Side)	Yr	VG	VG+	NM
❏ 249	You're No Angel/Cold Walls	1964	3.75	7.50	15.00

PARAMOUNT

Number	Title (A Side/B Side)	Yr	VG	VG+	NM
❏ 0110	That You Love/Taking My Time	1971	2.00	4.00	8.00

Albums

JAMIE

Number	Title (A Side/B Side)	Yr	VG	VG+	NM
❏ LPM-3029 [M]	It's Just a Matter of Time	1966	6.25	12.50	25.00
❏ LPS-3029 [S]	It's Just a Matter of Time	1966	7.50	15.00	30.00
❏ LPM-3032 [M]	The Kit Kats Do Their Thing — Live!	1967	7.50	15.00	30.00
❏ LPS-3032 [S]	The Kit Kats Do Their Thing — Live!	1967	10.00	20.00	40.00
❏ JLPS-3034	To Understand Is to Love	1970	7.50	15.00	30.00

—As "New Hope"

KITCHEN CINQ, THE
45s

DECCA

Number	Title (A Side/B Side)	Yr	VG	VG+	NM
❏ 32262	Good Lovin'/For Never We Met	1968	2.50	5.00	10.00
❏ 32374	She's So Fine/The Minstrel	1968	2.50	5.00	10.00

LHI

Number	Title (A Side/B Side)	Yr	VG	VG+	NM
❏ 17000	You'll Be Sorry Someday/Determination	1966	3.00	6.00	12.00
❏ 17005	If You Think/Ride the Wind	1967	3.00	6.00	12.00
❏ 17010	Still in Love with You Baby/Ride the Wind	1967	3.00	6.00	12.00
❏ 17015	Street Song/When the Rain Disappears	1967	3.00	6.00	12.00

Albums

LHI

Number	Title (A Side/B Side)	Yr	VG	VG+	NM
❏ E-12000 [M]	Everything But the Kitchen Cinq	1967	7.50	15.00	30.00
❏ E7-12000 [S]	Everything But the Kitchen Cinq	1967	10.00	20.00	40.00

KITTENS, THE Probably more than one group.
45s

ABC

Number	Title (A Side/B Side)	Yr	VG	VG+	NM
❏ 10835	The Masquerade Is Over/It's Gotta Be Love	1966	2.50	5.00	10.00

ABC-PARAMOUNT

Number	Title (A Side/B Side)	Yr	VG	VG+	NM
❏ 10619	Shindig/I Got to Know Him	1965	3.00	6.00	12.00
❏ 10730	Lookie Lookie/We Find Him Guilty	1965	3.00	6.00	12.00
❏ 10783	Is It Our Baby/Undecided You	1966	3.00	6.00	12.00

ALPINE

Number	Title (A Side/B Side)	Yr	VG	VG+	NM
❏ 64	Dark, Dark Sunglasses/Itsy Bitsy Teeny Weeny Yellow Polka Dot Bikini	1960	7.50	15.00	30.00
❏ 67	A Letter on His Sweater/Broken Dreams	1960	7.50	15.00	30.00

CHESS

Number	Title (A Side/B Side)	Yr	VG	VG+	NM
❏ 2027	Hey Operator/Ain't No More Room	1967	2.00	4.00	8.00
❏ 2055	How Long Can I Go On/I've Got to Get Over You	1968	2.00	4.00	8.00

CHESTNUT

Number	Title (A Side/B Side)	Yr	VG	VG+	NM
❏ 203	Count Every Star/I'm Worried	1963	12.50	25.00	50.00

DON-EL

Number	Title (A Side/B Side)	Yr	VG	VG+	NM
❏ 122	Walter/Lite Bulb	1963	3.75	7.50	15.00
❏ 205	I Need Your Love Tonight/Johnny's Place	1963	3.75	7.50	15.00

MURBO

Number	Title (A Side/B Side)	Yr	VG	VG+	NM
❏ 1015	Joey Has a New Love/Lonely Summer	1967	2.50	5.00	10.00

UNART

Number	Title (A Side/B Side)	Yr	VG	VG+	NM
❏ 2010	It's All Over Now/Letter to Donna	1959	12.50	25.00	50.00

KLAATU
45s

CAPITOL

Number	Title (A Side/B Side)	Yr	VG	VG+	NM
❏ 4377	Calling Occupants/Doctor Marvello	1976	2.00	4.00	8.00
❏ 4412	Calling Occupants/Sub-Rosa Subway	1977	—	2.50	5.00
❏ 4516	Around the Universe in 80 Days/We're Off You Know	1977	—	2.50	5.00
❏ 4627	Dear Christine/Older	1978	—	2.50	5.00
❏ 4866	Knee Deep in Love/Dog Star	1980	—	2.50	5.00

ISLAND

Number	Title (A Side/B Side)	Yr	VG	VG+	NM
❏ 011	California Jam/Doctor Marvello	1975	2.50	5.00	10.00

Albums

CAPITOL

Number	Title (A Side/B Side)	Yr	VG	VG+	NM
❏ ST-11542	Klaatu	1976	3.75	7.50	15.00
❏ ST-11633	Hope	1977	3.00	6.00	12.00
❏ SW-11836	Sir Army Suit	1978	3.00	6.00	12.00
❏ ST-12080	Endangered Species	1980	3.00	6.00	12.00
❏ SN-16060	Klaatu	1980	2.00	4.00	8.00

—Budget-line reissue

Number	Title (A Side/B Side)	Yr	VG	VG+	NM
❏ SN-16061	Hope	1980	2.00	4.00	8.00

—Budget-line reissue

Number	Title (A Side/B Side)	Yr	VG	VG+	NM
❏ SN-16062	Sir Army Suit	1980	2.00	4.00	8.00

—Budget-line reissue

KLEIN, GEORGE
45s

SUN

Number	Title (A Side/B Side)	Yr	VG	VG+	NM
❏ 358	U.T. Party (Part 1)/U.T. Party (Part 2)	1961	5.00	10.00	20.00

KLEIN, ROBERT
45s

BRUT

Number	Title (A Side/B Side)	Yr	VG	VG+	NM
❏ 802	The Fabulous Fifties/(B-side unknown)	1973	—	3.00	6.00

CASABLANCA

Number	Title (A Side/B Side)	Yr	VG	VG+	NM
❏ 972	Fallin'/Fill In the Words	1979	—	2.00	4.00

Albums

BRUT

Number	Title (A Side/B Side)	Yr	VG	VG+	NM
❏ 6001	Child of the 50's	1973	3.00	6.00	12.00
❏ 6600	Mind Over Matter	1974	3.00	6.00	12.00

CAEDMON

Number	Title (A Side/B Side)	Yr	VG	VG+	NM
❏ TC 9100	The Unauthorized Biography of Howard Who	1969	3.00	6.00	12.00

EPIC

Number	Title (A Side/B Side)	Yr	VG	VG+	NM
❏ PE 33535	New Teeth	1975	2.50	5.00	10.00

KLINT, PETE, QUINTET
45s

ATLANTIC

Number	Title (A Side/B Side)	Yr	VG	VG+	NM
❏ 2533	Just Holding On/Hey Diddle Diddle	1968	3.00	6.00	12.00

MERCURY

Number	Title (A Side/B Side)	Yr	VG	VG+	NM
❏ 72709	Walkin' Proud/Shake	1967	2.50	5.00	10.00

KLOWNS, THE
45s

RCA VICTOR

Number	Title (A Side/B Side)	Yr	VG	VG+	NM
❏ 74-0393	Lady Love/If You Can't Be a Clown	1970	—	2.50	5.00
❏ 74-0393 [PS]	Lady Love/If You Can't Be a Clown	1970	2.00	4.00	8.00
❏ 74-0485	Flower in My Garden/I Don't Believe in Magic	1971	—	2.50	5.00

Albums

RCA VICTOR

Number	Title (A Side/B Side)	Yr	VG	VG+	NM
❏ LSP-4438	The Klowns	1970	2.50	5.00	10.00

KNACK, THE No relation to the late-1970s pop group.
45s

CAPITOL

Number	Title (A Side/B Side)	Yr	VG	VG+	NM
❏ 2075	Freedom Now/Lady in the Window	1968	2.50	5.00	10.00
❏ 5774	Time Waits for No One/I'm Aware	1966	2.50	5.00	10.00
❏ 5889	The Spell/Softly, Softly	1967	2.50	5.00	10.00
❏ 5940	Banana Man/Pretty Daisy	1967	2.50	5.00	10.00

KNICKERBOCKERS, THE
45s

CHALLENGE

Number	Title (A Side/B Side)	Yr	VG	VG+	NM
❏ 59268	All I Need Is You/Bite, Bite Barracuda	1965	10.00	20.00	40.00
❏ 59293	Jerktown/Room for One More	1965	3.75	7.50	15.00
❏ 59321	Lies/The Coming Generation	1965	4.00	8.00	16.00
❏ 59326	One Track Mind/I Must Be Doing Something Right	1966	3.75	7.50	15.00
❏ 59332	High on Love/Stick with Me	1966	3.75	7.50	15.00
❏ 59335	Just One Girl/Chapel in the Fields	1966	3.75	7.50	15.00
❏ 59341	Love Is a Bird/Rumors, Gossip, Words Untrue	1966	3.75	7.50	15.00
❏ 59348	Can You Help Me/Please Don't Love Him	1966	3.75	7.50	15.00
❏ 59359	What Does That Make You/Sweet Green Fields	1967	3.75	7.50	15.00
❏ 59366	Come and Get It/Wishful Thinking	1967	3.75	7.50	15.00
❏ 59380	You'll Never Walk Alone/I Can Do It Better	1967	3.75	7.50	15.00
❏ 59384	As a Matter of Fact/They Ran for Their Lives	1968	3.75	7.50	15.00

LANA

Number	Title (A Side/B Side)	Yr	VG	VG+	NM
❏ 156	Lies/The Coming Generation	196?	2.00	4.00	8.00

—Oldies reissue

Albums

CHALLENGE

Number	Title (A Side/B Side)	Yr	VG	VG+	NM
❏ CH-621 [M]	Jerk and Twine Time	1965	100.00	200.00	400.00
❏ CH-622 [M]	Lies	1966	25.00	50.00	100.00
❏ CHS-622 [S]	Lies	1966	50.00	100.00	200.00
❏ LP-12664 [M]	Llyod Thaxton Presents the Knickerbockers	1965	50.00	100.00	200.00

SUNDAZED

Number	Title (A Side/B Side)	Yr	VG	VG+	NM
❏ LP-5000	The Great Lost Knickerbockers Album	1990	3.00	6.00	12.00

—Blue vinyl

Number	Title (A Side/B Side)	Yr	VG	VG+	NM
❏ LP-5154	Rockin' with the Knickerbockers	2003	3.00	6.00	12.00

KNIGHT, CHRIS "Peter Brady" of THE BRADY BUNCH.
45s

PARAMOUNT

Number	Title (A Side/B Side)	Yr	VG	VG+	NM
❏ 0177	Good for Each Other/Over and Over	1972	3.75	7.50	15.00
❏ 0177 [PS]	Good for Each Other/Over and Over	1972	3.75	7.50	15.00

KNIGHT, CHRIS, AND MAUREEN MCCORMICK Also see each artist's individual listings; THE BRADY BUNCH.
45s

PARAMOUNT

Number	Title (A Side/B Side)	Yr	VG	VG+	NM
❏ 0246	Little Bird/Just a-Singin' Along	1973	3.75	7.50	15.00

Albums

PARAMOUNT

Number	Title (A Side/B Side)	Yr	VG	VG+	NM
❏ PAS-6062	Chris Knight and Maureen McCormick	1973	30.00	60.00	120.00

KNIGHT, FREDERICK
45s

JUANA

Number	Title (A Side/B Side)	Yr	VG	VG+	NM
❏ 1948	Let Me Ring Your Bell Again/When It Ain't Right	1980	—	2.50	5.00
❏ 3402	I'm Falling in Love Again/Done Got Over Lover	1976	—	2.50	5.00
❏ 3404	Sugar/I'm Falling in Love	1976	—	2.50	5.00
❏ 3408	High Society/(Instrumental)	1976	—	2.50	5.00
❏ 3411	Staying Power/Wrapped in Your Love	1977	—	2.50	5.00
❏ 3415	Sit Down on Your Love/Staying Power	1977	—	2.50	5.00
❏ 3418	You and Me/When It Ain't Right with My Baby	1978	—	2.50	5.00
❏ 3420	My Music Makes Me Feel Good/When It Ain't Right with My Baby	1978	—	2.50	5.00
❏ 3423	You Can't Deny Me/If You Love Your Baby	1979	—	2.50	5.00
❏ 3700	The Old Songs/Bundle of Love	1981	—	2.50	5.00
❏ 3702	You're the Best Thing in My Life/(B-side unknown)	1981	—	2.50	5.00

1-2-3

Number	Title (A Side/B Side)	Yr	VG	VG+	NM
❏ 1724	Have a Little Mercy/Sauerkraut	1970	3.75	7.50	15.00

STAX

Number	Title (A Side/B Side)	Yr	VG	VG+	NM
❏ 0117	I've Been Lonely for So Long/Lean on Me	1972	2.00	4.00	8.00
❏ 0139	Trouble/A Friend	1972	—	3.50	7.00
❏ 0167	Take Me On Home Witcha/This Is My Song of Love to You	1973	—	3.50	7.00
❏ 0201	I Let My Chance Go By/Suzy	1974	—	3.50	7.00

TRUTH

Number	Title (A Side/B Side)	Yr	VG	VG+	NM
❏ 3202	Passing Through/Sometimes Storm	1974	—	3.00	6.00
❏ 3216	I Betcha Didn't Know That/Let's Make a Deal	1974	—	3.00	6.00
❏ 3228	I Wanna Play with You/I Miss You	1975	—	3.00	6.00

K

Number	Title (A Side/B Side)	Yr	VG	VG+	NM
Albums					
STAX					
❏ STS-3011	I've Been Lonely So Long	1973	5.00	10.00	20.00

KNIGHT, GLADYS, AND THE PIPS Includes Gladys Knight solo and the Pips without Gladys.

Number	Title (A Side/B Side)	Yr	VG	VG+	NM
12-Inch Singles					
BUDDAH					
❏ DSC 115	Love Is Always On Your Mind/(Instrumental)	1977	3.00	6.00	12.00
❏ DSC 126	It's a Better Than Good Time/(Instrumental)	1978	3.00	6.00	12.00
COLUMBIA					
❏ AS 803 [DJ]	Taste of Bitter Love/Bourgie, Bourgie	1980	3.00	6.00	12.00
❏ AS 1307 [DJ]	I Will Fight (4:10)/God Is (3:48)	1981	2.50	5.00	10.00
❏ AS 1643 [DJ]	Save the Overtime (For Me) (5:07) (same on both sides)	1983	3.00	6.00	12.00
❏ CAS 2052 [DJ]	Keep Givin' Me Love (same on both sides)	1985	2.00	4.00	8.00
❏ 44-03969	Save the Overtime (For Me)/(Instrumental)	1983	2.00	4.00	8.00
❏ 44-04965	When You're Far Away/(Instrumental)	1983	—	3.00	6.00
❏ 44-05161	My Time (2 versions)	1984	2.50	5.00	10.00
❏ 23-10996	You Bring Out the Best in Me (8:20)/You Loved Away the Pain	1979	3.75	7.50	15.00
MCA					
❏ L33-1456 [DJ]	Men (5 versions)	1990	2.00	4.00	8.00
❏ L33-1621 [DJ]	Where Would I Be (Vocal) (Instrumental) (Suite)	1991	2.00	4.00	8.00
❏ L33-1653 [DJ]	Meet Me in the Middle (LP Version) (Instrumental) (7" Version) (Suite)	1991	3.75	7.50	15.00
❏ L33-1694 [DJ]	Superwoman (LP Mix 6:19) (Radio Edit 5:37) (Instrumental Mix 6:15) (Single Version 4:29)	1991	2.00	4.00	8.00
❏ L33-2080 [DJ]	Meet Me in the Middle (6 versions)	1991	2.00	4.00	8.00
❏ MCA8P-3311 [DJ]	This Time (Spike Club Mix 8:48) (Spike Beats Mix) (Radio Mix) (Spike Next Dub 9:35)	1994	2.00	4.00	8.00
❏ L33-17429 [DJ]	Lovin' On Next to Nothin' (Extended) (Radio Edit) (Instrumental) (Percussapella)	1987	2.00	4.00	8.00
❏ L33-17431 [DJ]	Love Overboard (4 versions)	1987	2.00	4.00	8.00
❏ L33-17444 [DJ]	Love Overboard (6:10) (5:44)	1987	2.00	4.00	8.00
❏ L33-17546 [DJ]	Lovin' on Next to Nothin' (5 versions)	1988	2.50	5.00	10.00
❏ L33-17561 [DJ]	It's Gonna Take All Our Love (same on both sides)	1988	2.00	4.00	8.00
❏ 23713	Send It To Me (Extended Version 7:34)/When You Love Somebody (It's Christmas Everyday) (6:12)	1986	3.00	6.00	12.00
❏ 23803	Love Overboard (Extended Version 6:00)/(Instrumental)	1987	—	3.00	6.00
❏ 23804	Lovin' On Next to Nothin' (Extended Version) (Instrumental)	1987	—	3.00	6.00
❏ 23871	It's Gonna Take All Our Love/(Instrumental)	1988	2.00	4.00	8.00
❏ 25371 [DJ]	If I Were Your Woman II (LP Version) (Instrumental) (Acappella)/(same on both sides)	2001	3.00	6.00	12.00
❏ 54130	Men (Extended Club Version 7:13) (Instrumental)	1990	—	3.00	6.00
45s					
BRUNSWICK					
❏ 55048	Whistle My Love/Ching Ching	1958	30.00	60.00	120.00
BUDDAH					
❏ 363	Where Peaceful Waters Flow/Perfect Love	1973	—	2.50	5.00
❏ 363 [PS]	Where Peaceful Waters Flow/Perfect Love	1973	2.00	4.00	8.00
❏ 383	Midnight Train to Georgia/Window Raising Granny	1973	—	2.50	5.00
❏ 383	Midnight Train to Georgia/(Instrumental)	1973	—	3.00	6.00
❏ 393	I've Got to Use My Imagination/I Can See Clearly Now	1973	—	2.50	5.00
❏ 403	Best Thing That Ever Happened to Me/Once in a Lifetime	1974	—	2.50	5.00
❏ 423	On and On/The Makings of You	1974	—	2.50	5.00
❏ 423 [PS]	On and On/The Makings of You	1974	2.00	4.00	8.00
❏ 433	I Feel a Song (In My Heart)/Don't Burn Down the Bridge	1974	—	2.50	5.00
❏ 453	Love Finds It's Own Way/Better You Go Your Way	1975	—	2.50	5.00
❏ 463	The Way We Were-Try to Remember/The Need to Be	1975	—	2.50	5.00
❏ 487	Money/Street Brothers	1975	—	2.50	5.00
❏ 513	Part Time Love/Where Did I Put His Memory	1975	—	2.50	5.00
❏ 523	Make Yours a Happy Home/The Going Up and the Coming Down	1976	—	2.50	5.00
❏ 544	So Sad the Song/(Instrumental)	1976	—	2.50	5.00
❏ 569	Baby Don't Change Your Mind/I Love to Feel That Feelin'	1977	—	2.50	5.00
❏ 584	Sorry Doesn't Always Make It Right/You Put a New Life in My Body	1977	—	2.50	5.00
❏ 592	The One and Only/Pipe Dreams	1978	—	2.50	5.00
❏ 598	It's a Better Than Good Time/Everybody's Got to Find a Way	1978	—	2.50	5.00
❏ 601	I'm Coming Home Again/Love Gives You the Power	1978	—	2.50	5.00
❏ 605	Sail Away/I'm Still Caught Up with You	1979	—	2.50	5.00
❏ 1974 [DJ]	Do You Hear What I Hear/Silent Night	1974	—	3.00	6.00
❏ 1974 [PS]	Do You Hear What I Hear/Silent Night	1974	—	3.00	6.00
CASABLANCA					
❏ 912	If I Could Bring Back Yesterday/Since I Found Love	1978	—	2.00	4.00
—As "The Pips"					
❏ 949	Baby I'm Your Fool/Lights of the City	1978	—	2.00	4.00
—As "The Pips"					
COLUMBIA					
❏ 11-02113	Forever Yesterday (For the Children)/(Instrumental)	1981	—	2.00	4.00
❏ 11-02113 [PS]	Forever Yesterday (For the Children)/(Instrumental)	1981	—	2.50	5.00
❏ 18-02413	If That'll Make You Happy/Love Was Made for Two	1981	—	2.00	4.00
❏ 18-02549	I Will Fight/God Is	1981	—	2.00	4.00
❏ 18-02706	Friend of Mine/Reach High	1982	—	2.00	4.00
❏ 38-03418	That Special Time of Year/Santa Claus Is Comin' to Town	1982	—	2.50	5.00
❏ 38-03761	Save the Overtime (For Me)/Ain't No Greater Love	1983	—	2.00	4.00

Number	Title (A Side/B Side)	Yr	VG	VG+	NM
❏ 38-04033	You're Number 1 in My Book/Oh La De Dah	1983	—	2.00	4.00
❏ 38-04219	Hero (The Wind Beneath My Wings)/Seconds	1983	—	2.50	5.00
❏ 38-04333	Here's That Sunny Day/Oh La De Da	1984	—	2.00	4.00
❏ 38-04369	When You're Far Away/Seconds	1984	—	2.00	4.00
❏ 38-04761	My Time/(Instrumental)	1985	—	2.00	4.00
❏ 38-04761 [PS]	My Time/(Instrumental)	1985	—	2.50	5.00
❏ 38-04873	Keep Givin' Me Love/Do You Wanna Have Some Fun	1985	—	2.00	4.00
❏ 38-05679	Till I See You Again/Strivin'	1985	—	2.00	4.00
❏ 3-10922	Am I Too Late/It's the Same Old Song	1979	—	2.00	4.00
❏ 3-10997	You Bring Out the Best in Me/You Loved Away the Pain	1979	—	2.00	4.00
❏ 3-11088	The Best Thing We Can Do Is Say Goodbye/You Don't Have to Say I Love You	1979	—	2.00	4.00
❏ 1-11239	Landlord/We Need Hearts	1980	—	2.00	4.00
❏ 1-11330	Taste of Bitter Love/Add It Up	1980	—	2.00	4.00
❏ 1-11375	Bourgie', Bourgie'/Get the Love	1980	—	2.00	4.00
❏ 11-11409	When a Child Is Born/The Lord's Prayer	1980	—	2.50	5.00
—With Johnny Mathis					
ENJOY					
❏ 2012	What Shall I Do/Love Call	1964	3.75	7.50	15.00
EVERLAST					
❏ 5025	Happiness/I Had a Dream Last Night	1963	6.25	12.50	25.00
—As "The Pips"					
FURY					
❏ 1050	Every Beat of My Heart/Room in Your Heart	1961	6.25	12.50	25.00
—Re-recordings of the same songs on Huntom and Vee Jay					
❏ 1052	Guess Who/Stop Running Around	1961	3.75	7.50	15.00
❏ 1054	Letter Full of Tears/You Broke Your Promise	1961	3.75	7.50	15.00
❏ 1064	Operator/I'll Trust in You	1962	3.75	7.50	15.00
❏ 1067	Darling/Linda	1962	5.00	10.00	20.00
—As "The Pips"					
❏ 1073	Come See About Me/I Want That Kind of Love	1963	7.50	15.00	30.00
HUNTOM					
❏ 2510	Every Beat of My Heart/Room in Your Heart	1961	125.00	250.00	500.00
—As "The Pips"					
LOST-NITE					
❏ 261	Giving Up/Lovers Always Forgive	196?	—	2.50	5.00
—Reissue					
❏ 382	Every Beat of My Heart/Room in Your Heart	197?	—	3.00	6.00
—Reissue of Fury versions					
❏ 386	Letter Full of Tears/You Broke Your Promise	197?	—	2.50	5.00
—Reissue					
❏ 389	Darling/Linda	197?	—	2.50	5.00
—As "The Pips"; reissue					
MAXX					
❏ 326	Giving Up/Maybe, Maybe Baby	1964	3.75	7.50	15.00
❏ 329	Lovers Always Forget/Another Love	1964	3.75	7.50	15.00
❏ 331	Either Way I Lose/Go Away, Stay Away	1964	3.75	7.50	15.00
❏ 334	Who Knows/Stop and Get a Hold of Myself	1965	3.75	7.50	15.00
❏ 335	Tell Her You're Mine/If I Should Ever Be in Love	1965	3.75	7.50	15.00
MCA					
❏ 53002	Send It to Me/When You Love Somebody (It's Christmas Every Day)	1987	—	—	3.00
❏ 53002 [PS]	Send It to Me/When You Love Somebody (It's Christmas Every Day)	1987	—	—	3.00
❏ 53210	Love Overboard/(Instrumental)	1987	—	—	3.00
❏ 53210 [PS]	Love Overboard/(Instrumental)	1987	—	—	3.00
❏ 53211	Lovin' on Next to Nothin'/(Instrumental)	1988	—	—	3.00
❏ 53211 [PS]	Lovin' on Next to Nothin'/(Instrumental)	1988	—	—	3.00
❏ 53351	It's Gonna Take All Our Love/(Instrumental)	1988	—	—	3.00
❏ 53657	Licence to Kill/You	1989	—	—	3.00
❏ 53676	Licence to Kill/Pam	1989	—	—	3.00
—B-side by National Philharmonic Orchestra					
❏ 54117	Men/(Instrumental)	1991	—	—	3.00
SCOTTI BROS.					
❏ ZS4-06267	Loving on Borrowed Time (Love Theme from Cobra)/Angel of the City	1986	—	—	3.00
—A-side: Gladys Knight and Bill Medley; B-side: Robert Tepper					
SOUL					
❏ 35023	Just Walk in My Shoes/Stepping Closer to Your Heart	1966	2.00	4.00	8.00
❏ 35033	Take Me in Your Arms and Love Me/Do You Love Me Just a Little More?	1967	2.00	4.00	8.00
❏ 35034	Everybody Needs Love/Since I've Lost You	1967	2.00	4.00	8.00
❏ 35039	I Heard It Through the Grapevine/It's Time to Go Now	1967	2.50	5.00	10.00
❏ 35042	The End of Our Road/Don't Let Her Take Your Love from Me	1968	2.00	4.00	8.00
❏ 35045	It Should Have Been Me/You Don't Love Me No More	1968	2.00	4.00	8.00
❏ 35047	I Wish It Would Rain/It's Summer	1968	2.00	4.00	8.00
❏ 35057	Didn't You Know (You'd Have to Cry Sometime)/Keep an Eye	1969	2.00	4.00	8.00
❏ 35063	The Nitty Gritty/Got Myself a Good Man	1969	2.00	4.00	8.00
❏ 35068	Friendship Train/Cloud Nine	1969	2.00	4.00	8.00
❏ 35071	You Need Love Like I Do (Don't You)/You're My Everything	1970	2.00	4.00	8.00
❏ 35078	If I Were Your Woman/The Tracks of My Tears	1970	—	3.50	7.00
❏ 35083	I Don't Want to Do Wrong/Is There a Place In His Heart for Me	1971	—	3.00	6.00
❏ 35091	Make Me the Woman You Come Home To/If You're Gonna Leave (Just Leave)	1972	—	3.00	6.00
❏ 35094	Help Me Make It Through the Night/If You're Gonna Leave (Just Leave)	1972	—	3.00	6.00
❏ 35098	Neither One of Us (Wants to Be the First to Say Goodbye)/Can't Give It Up No More	1972	—	3.00	6.00
❏ 35105	Daddy Could Swear I Declare/For Once in My Life	1973	—	3.00	6.00
❏ 35107	All I Need Is Time/The Only Time You Love Me (Is When You're Losing Me)	1973	—	3.00	6.00
❏ 35111	Between Her Goodbye and My Hello/This Child Needs Its Father	1974	—	3.00	6.00
TRIP					
❏ 3004	It Hurt Me So Bad/What Will Become of Me	1973	—	3.00	6.00
❏ 3004 [PS]	It Hurt Me So Bad/What Will Become of Me	1973	3.00	6.00	12.00

K.C. and the Sunshine Band, "Boogie Shoes," T.K. 1025, picture sleeve, $4-$8.

Carole King, "It Might As Well Rain Until September," Companion 2000, 45 rpm single, $150-$300.

The Kingsmen, *The Kingsmen In Person Featuring Louie, Louie*, Wand WDS-657, stereo LP, $20-$40.

The Kinks, *You Really Got Me*, Reprise R-6143, mono LP, $30-$60.

Kiss, *Alive!*, Casablanca NBLP-7020, stereo 2-LP set, blue labels, with booklet, $20-$40.

Gladys Knight & the Pips, *If I Were Your Woman*, Soul SS-731, stereo LP, $7.50-$15.

Number	Title (A Side/B Side)	Yr	VG	VG+	NM
VEE JAY					
❏ 386	Every Beat of My Heart/Ain'tcha Got Some Room (In Your Heart for Me)	1961	5.00	10.00	20.00
—By "The Pips"; same B-side, different title					
❏ 386	Every Beat of My Heart/Room in Your Heart	1961	5.00	10.00	20.00
—By "The Pips"					
❏ 545	A Love Like Mine/Queen of Tears	1963	5.00	10.00	20.00
Albums					
ACCORD					
❏ SN-7103	Every Beat of My Heart	1981	2.50	5.00	10.00
❏ SN-7105	Letter Full of Tears	1981	2.50	5.00	10.00
❏ SN-7131	I Feel a Song	1981	2.50	5.00	10.00
❏ SN-7188	It's Showtime	1982	2.50	5.00	10.00
ALLEGIANCE					
❏ AV-5002	Glad to Be...	198?	2.50	5.00	10.00
BELL					
❏ 1323	In the Beginning	1975	3.00	6.00	12.00
❏ 6013	Tastiest Hits	1968	5.00	10.00	20.00
BUDDAH					
❏ BDS-5141	Imagination	1973	3.00	6.00	12.00
❏ BDS-5602	Claudine	1974	7.50	15.00	30.00
❏ BDS-5612	I Feel a Song	1974	3.00	6.00	12.00
❏ BDS-5639	2nd Anniversary	1975	3.00	6.00	12.00
❏ BDS-5653	The Best of Gladys Knight & The Pips	1976	3.00	6.00	12.00
❏ BDS-5676	Pipe Dreams	1976	3.00	6.00	12.00
❏ BDS-5689	Still Together	1977	3.00	6.00	12.00
❏ BDS-5701	The One and Only	1978	3.00	6.00	12.00
❏ BDS-5714	Miss Gladys Knight	1978	3.00	6.00	12.00
CASABLANCA					
❏ NBLP 7081	At Last…The Pips	1977	2.50	5.00	10.00
—As "The Pips"					
❏ NBLP 7113	Callin'	1978	2.50	5.00	10.00
—As "The Pips"					
COLLECTABLES					
❏ COL-5154	Golden Classics: Letter Full of Tears	198?	2.50	5.00	10.00
COLUMBIA					
❏ JC 35704	Gladys Knight	1979	2.50	5.00	10.00
❏ PC 35704	Gladys Knight	198?	2.00	4.00	8.00
—Budget-line reissue					
❏ JC 36387	About Love	1980	2.50	5.00	10.00
❏ PC 36387	About Love	198?	2.00	4.00	8.00
—Budget-line reissue					
❏ FC 37086	Touch	1981	2.50	5.00	10.00
❏ PC 37086	Touch	198?	2.00	4.00	8.00
—Budget-line reissue					
❏ FC 38114	That Special Time of Year	1982	2.50	5.00	10.00
❏ PC 38114	That Special Time of Year	1983	2.00	4.00	8.00
—Same as above with new prefix					
❏ FC 38205	Visions	1983	2.50	5.00	10.00
❏ PC 38205	Visions	198?	2.00	4.00	8.00
—Budget-line reissue					
❏ FC 39423	Life	1985	2.50	5.00	10.00
❏ PC 39423	Life	198?	2.00	4.00	8.00
—Budget-line reissue					
❏ FC 40376	Greatest Hits	1986	2.50	5.00	10.00
❏ FC 40878	The Best of Gladys Knight and the Pips/The Columbia Years	1988	2.50	5.00	10.00
FURY					
❏ 1003 [M]	Letter Full of Tears	1962	125.00	250.00	500.00
LOST-NITE					
❏ LLP-17 [10]	The Best of Gladys Knight and the Pips	1981	3.00	6.00	12.00
—Red vinyl					
MAXX					
❏ 3000 [M]	Gladys Knight and the Pips	1964	37.50	75.00	150.00
MCA					
❏ 10329	Good Woman	1991	3.75	7.50	15.00
❏ 42004	All Our Love	1987	2.50	5.00	10.00
MOTOWN					
❏ M5-113V	Motown Superstar Series, Vol. 13	1981	2.50	5.00	10.00
❏ M5-126V1	Everybody Needs Love	1981	3.00	6.00	12.00
—Reissue of Soul 706					
❏ M5-148V1	Nitty Gritty	1981	3.00	6.00	12.00
—Reissue of Soul 713					
❏ M5-193V1	Neither One of Us	1981	3.00	6.00	12.00
—Reissue of Soul 737					
❏ M 792S2 [(2)]	Anthology	1974	3.75	7.50	15.00
❏ MOT 5303	All the Great Hits of Gladys Knight and the Pips	198?	2.00	4.00	8.00
NATURAL RESOURCES					
❏ NR 4004T1	Silk N' Soul	1978	2.50	5.00	10.00
—Reissue of Soul 711					
PAIR					
❏ PDL2-1198	The Best of Gladys Knight and the Pips	1987	3.00	6.00	12.00
PICKWICK					
❏ SPC-3349	Every Beat of My Heart	197?	2.50	5.00	10.00
SOUL					
❏ S 706 [M]	Everybody Needs Love	1967	5.00	10.00	20.00
❏ SS 706 [S]	Everybody Needs Love	1967	6.25	12.50	25.00
❏ S 707 [M]	Feelin' Bluesy	1968	10.00	20.00	40.00
—Mono copies are white label promo only; cover has "Monaural Record DJ Copy" sticker					
❏ SS 707 [S]	Feelin' Bluesy	1968	6.25	12.50	25.00
❏ SS 711	Silk N' Soul	1968	6.25	12.50	25.00
❏ SS 713	Nitty Gritty	1969	6.25	12.50	25.00
❏ SS 723	Gladys Knight and the Pips Greatest Hits	1970	3.75	7.50	15.00
❏ SS 730	All in a Knight's Work	1970	3.75	7.50	15.00
❏ SS 731	If I Were Your Woman	1971	3.75	7.50	15.00
❏ S 736L	Standing Ovation	1971	3.75	7.50	15.00
❏ S 737L	Neither One of Us	1973	3.75	7.50	15.00
❏ S 739L	All I Need Is Time	1973	3.75	7.50	15.00
❏ S 741	Knight Time	1974	3.00	6.00	12.00
❏ S 744	A Little Knight Music	1975	3.00	6.00	12.00
SPHERE SOUND					
❏ SR-7006 [M]	Gladys Knight and the Pips	196?	50.00	100.00	200.00
❏ SSR-7006 [R]	Gladys Knight and the Pips	196?	30.00	60.00	120.00
SPRINGBOARD					
❏ SPB-4035	Early Hits	1972	2.50	5.00	10.00
❏ SPB-4050	How Do You Say Goodbye	1973	2.50	5.00	10.00
TRIP					
❏ TLP-9509	It Hurt Me So Bad	1973	2.50	5.00	10.00
UNITED ARTISTS					
❏ UA-LA503-E	The Very Best of Gladys Knight and the Pips	1975	3.00	6.00	12.00
UPFRONT					
❏ UPF 130	Gladys Knight and the Pips	197?	2.50	5.00	10.00
❏ UPF 185	Gladys Knight and the Pips	197?	2.50	5.00	10.00
VEE JAY					
❏ D1-74796	Every Beat of My Heart: The Greatest Hits of the Early Years	1989	3.75	7.50	15.00

KNIGHT, JEAN

45s

Number	Title (A Side/B Side)	Yr	VG	VG+	NM
CHELSEA					
❏ 3020	Don't Ask for 24 Hours/Hold Back the Night	1975	—	2.50	5.00
❏ 3035	Jesse James Is an Outlaw/Hold Back the Night	1975	—	2.50	5.00
COTILLION					
❏ 46020	You Got the Papers (But I Got the Man)/Anything You Can Do (I Can Do As Well)	1981	—	2.00	4.00
❏ 46027	Keep It Comin'/One on One	1981	—	2.00	4.00
❏ 47002	You Show Me Yours, I'll Show You Mine/(B-side unknown)	1982	—	2.00	4.00
—All of the above with Premium					
DIAL					
❏ 1026	Dirt/Jesse Joe	1974	—	2.50	5.00
ICHIBAN					
❏ 97-422	Bill/Bus Stop	1997	—	—	3.00
JETSTREAM					
❏ 706	Doggin' Around/The Man That Left Me	1965	2.50	5.00	10.00
MIRAGE					
❏ 99606	Let the Good Times Roll/Magic	1985	—	—	3.00
❏ 99643	My Toot Toot/My Heart Is Willing (And My Body Is Too)	1985	—	—	3.00
❏ 99643 [PS]	My Toot Toot/My Heart Is Willing (And My Body Is Too)	1985	—	—	3.00
STAX					
❏ 0088	Mr. Big Stuff/Why I Keep Living These Memories	1971	—	3.00	6.00
❏ 0105	You Think You're Hot Stuff/Don't Talk About Jody	1971	—	2.50	5.00
❏ 0116	Carry On/Call Me Your Fool	1972	—	2.50	5.00
❏ 0136	Helping Man/Pick Up the Pieces	1972	—	2.50	5.00
❏ 0150	Do Me/Save the Last Kiss for Me	1972	—	2.50	5.00
TRIBE					
❏ 8304	Lonesome Tonight/Love	1964	3.00	6.00	12.00
❏ 8306	T'Ain't It the Truth/I'm So Glad for Your Sake	1965	3.00	6.00	12.00
❏ 8313	Anyone Can Love Him/A Tear	1966	3.00	6.00	12.00
Albums					
COTILLION					
❏ SD 5230	Jean Knight and Premium	1981	3.75	7.50	15.00
MIRAGE					
❏ 90282	My Toot Toot	1985	2.50	5.00	10.00
STAX					
❏ STS-2045	Mr. Big Stuff	1971	10.00	20.00	40.00
❏ MPS-8554	Mr. Big Stuff	198?	2.50	5.00	10.00

KNIGHT, ROBERT Also see THE PARAMOUNTS (3).

45s

Number	Title (A Side/B Side)	Yr	VG	VG+	NM
DOT					
❏ 16256	Because/Dance Only with Me	1961	3.00	6.00	12.00
❏ 16303	Free Me/The Other Half of Man	1962	3.00	6.00	12.00
ELF					
❏ 90019	Isn't It Lonely Together/We'd Better Stop	1968	—	3.00	6.00
❏ 90030	Smokey/If I Had My Way	1969	—	3.00	6.00
❏ 90037	I Only Have Eyes for You/I'm Sticking with You	1969	—	3.00	6.00
MONUMENT					
❏ 8612	Better Get Ready for Love/Somebody's Baby	1974	—	2.50	5.00
❏ 8629	Dynamite/The Outsider	1974	—	2.50	5.00
PRIVATE STOCK					
❏ 45,038	I'm Coming Home to You/(B-side unknown)	1975	—	2.50	5.00
❏ 45,069	Second Chance/Glitter Lady	1976	—	2.50	5.00
❏ 45,118	I've Got News for You/(B-side unknown)	1976	—	2.50	5.00
RISING SONS					
❏ 705	Everlasting Love/Somebody's Baby	1967	2.00	4.00	8.00
❏ 707	Blessed Are the Lonely/It's Been Worth It All	1967	—	3.00	6.00
❏ 708	Power of Love/Love on a Mountain Top	1968	—	3.00	6.00
Albums					
RISING SONS					
❏ RSM-7000 [M]	Everlasting Love	1967	7.50	15.00	30.00
❏ RSS-17000 [S]	Everlasting Love	1967	10.00	20.00	40.00

KNIGHT, SONNY

45s

Number	Title (A Side/B Side)	Yr	VG	VG+	NM
A&M					
❏ 718	Evil Minded Woman/Georgia Town	1963	2.50	5.00	10.00
❏ 728	Be True to Your Dog/State Street	1964	2.50	5.00	10.00
ALADDIN					
❏ 3357	But Officer/Dear Wonderful God	1957	7.50	15.00	30.00
AURA					
❏ 403	If You Want This Love/I Just Called to Say Hello	1964	2.00	4.00	8.00
❏ 4505	Love Me As Though There Were No Tomorrow/Fool Like Me	1964	2.00	4.00	8.00
❏ 4505 [PS]	Love Me As Though There Were No Tomorrow/Fool Like Me	1964	5.00	10.00	20.00
❏ 4508	Rose Mary/(B-side unknown)	1965	2.00	4.00	8.00
DOT					
❏ 15507	Confidential/Jailbird	1956	3.75	7.50	15.00
—Second pressings have black labels					
❏ 15507	Confidential/Jailbird	1956	5.00	10.00	20.00
—Originals have maroon labels					
❏ 15542	End of a Dream/Worthless and Lowdown	1957	3.75	7.50	15.00
❏ 15597	Lovesick Blues/Insha Allot	1957	3.75	7.50	15.00
❏ 15635	Dedicated to You/Short Walk	1957	3.75	7.50	15.00
EASTMAN					
❏ 787	Lipstick Kisses/East Your Mush and Hush	1959	12.50	25.00	50.00

Number	Title (A Side/B Side)	Yr	VG	VG+	NM
FIFO					
❑ 102	Cold, Cold Night/Saving My Love	1961	3.75	7.50	15.00
❑ 105	A Swingin' Door/(B-side unknown)	1961	3.75	7.50	15.00
MERCURY					
❑ 72033	Just One More Chance/Lost Child	1962	2.50	5.00	10.00
ORIGINAL SOUND					
❑ 2	Once in Awhile/School's Out	1959	5.00	10.00	20.00
❑ 18	Those Oldies But Goodies Are Dedicated to You/ She Had Me Reelin'	1961	3.75	7.50	15.00
SPECIALTY					
❑ 594	Keep a-Walkin'/My Baby Don't Want Me	1957	3.75	7.50	15.00
STARLA					
❑ 1	Dedicated to You/Short Walk	1957	7.50	15.00	30.00
❑ 10	Once in a While/School's Out	1958	3.75	7.50	15.00
VITA					
❑ 137	Confidential/Jailbird	1956	10.00	20.00	40.00
WORLD PACIFIC					
❑ 403	If You Want This Love/I Just Called to Say Hello	1964	3.00	6.00	12.00
❑ 77811	If I May/Need Your Love So Bad	1966	2.00	4.00	8.00
❑ 77832	Angel Love/If I Ruled the World	1966	2.00	4.00	8.00
❑ 77858	A Quiet Man/I Can't Let You Go	1966	6.25	12.50	25.00
—This record exists as a promo at least (we have listed it as "Unreleased" in the past)					
Albums					
AURA					
❑ AR-3001 [M]	If You Want This Love	1964	6.25	12.50	25.00
❑ AS-3001 [S]	If You Want This Love	1964	7.50	15.00	30.00

KNIGHT, TERRY, AND THE PACK Group evolved into GRAND FUNK RAILROAD.
45s

Number	Title (A Side/B Side)	Yr	VG	VG+	NM
A&M					
❑ 769	Kids Will Be the Same/You Lie	1965	3.75	7.50	15.00
CAMEO					
❑ 482	Forever and a Day/Lizbeth Peach	1967	2.50	5.00	10.00
❑ 495	Come Home Baby/Dirty Lady	1967	2.50	5.00	10.00
CAPITOL					
❑ 2174	Without a Woman/Let Me Stand Next to Your Fire	1968	3.00	6.00	12.00
—As "The Pack"					
❑ 2409	Such a Lonely Life/Lullaby	1969	2.50	5.00	10.00
❑ 2506	St. Paul/(Legend of) William and Mary	1969	2.50	5.00	10.00
❑ 2737	I'll Keep Waiting Patiently/Lullaby	1970	2.50	5.00	10.00
LUCKY ELEVEN					
❑ 003	Harlem Shuffle/I've Got News for You	1965	4.00	8.00	16.00
—As "The Pack"					
❑ 007	Does It Matter to You Girl/Wide Trackin'	1965	4.00	8.00	16.00
—As "The Fabulous Pack"					
❑ 007 [PS]	Does It Matter to You Girl/Wide Trackin'	1965	6.25	12.50	25.00
—As "The Fabulous Pack"					
❑ 225	How Much More/I've Been Told	1966	3.75	7.50	15.00
❑ 226	I Got Love/Better Man Than I	1966	3.75	7.50	15.00
❑ 228	Lady Jane/Lovin' Kind	1966	3.75	7.50	15.00
❑ 229	What's On Your Mind/A Change on the Way	1966	3.75	7.50	15.00
❑ 230	I (Who Have Nothing)/Numbers	1966	3.75	7.50	15.00
❑ 235	This Precious Time/ Love, Love, Love, Love, Love	1967	3.75	7.50	15.00
❑ 236	One Monkey Don't Stop No Show/The Train	1967	3.75	7.50	15.00
WINGATE					
❑ 007	The Tears Come Rollin'/The Colour of My Love	1965	6.25	12.50	25.00
—As "The Pack"					
Albums					
ABKCO					
❑ AB-4217 [(2)]	Mark, Don and Terry 1966-67	1972	5.00	10.00	20.00
CAMEO					
❑ C 2007 [M]	Reflections	1967	5.00	10.00	20.00
—Reissue of Lucky Eleven LE-8001					
❑ CS 2007 [S]	Reflections	1967	6.25	12.50	25.00
—Reissue of Lucky Eleven LES-8001					
LUCKY ELEVEN					
❑ LE-8000 [M]	Terry Knight and the Pack	1966	10.00	20.00	40.00
❑ LES-8000 [R]	Terry Knight and the Pack	1966	6.25	12.50	25.00
❑ LE-8001 [M]	Reflections	1967	6.25	12.50	25.00
❑ LES-8001 [S]	Reflections	1967	10.00	20.00	40.00

KNIGHT BROS., THE
45s

Number	Title (A Side/B Side)	Yr	VG	VG+	NM
CHECKER					
❑ 1064	I Really Love You/Second Hand Lover	1963	6.25	12.50	25.00
❑ 1076	Come On Girl/City Life	1964	6.25	12.50	25.00
❑ 1107	Temptation 'Bout to Get Me/Sinking Low	1965	6.25	12.50	25.00
❑ 1124	I Owe Her My Life/I'm Never Gonna Live It Down	1965	6.25	12.50	25.00
❑ 1146	All I Have to Do Is Dream/Hand of Faith	1966	5.00	10.00	20.00
❑ 1153	That'll Get It/She's A-1	1966	5.00	10.00	20.00
MERCURY					
❑ 72718	Nobody's Fault/You're My Love	1967	5.00	10.00	20.00
❑ 72829	Ghetto Joe/Tried So Hard to Please Her	1968	5.00	10.00	20.00

KNIGHT RIDERS, THE Featuring BILLY VERA.
45s

Number	Title (A Side/B Side)	Yr	VG	VG+	NM
UNITED ARTISTS					
❑ 366	Annie's Place/Unchained Melody	1961	6.25	12.50	25.00

KNIGHTS, THE At least three, and perhaps four, different groups.
45s

Number	Title (A Side/B Side)	Yr	VG	VG+	NM
CAPITOL					
❑ 5302	Hot Rod High/Theme for Teen Love	1964	12.50	25.00	50.00
FELSTED					
❑ 8640	White Fang/Night Train	1962	3.00	6.00	12.00
Albums					
ACE					
❑ 4763	Cold Days, Hot Knights	196?	100.00	200.00	400.00
❑ 200854	Across the Board	1966	100.00	200.00	400.00
❑ 201302	The Knights 1967	1967	100.00	200.00	400.00
CAPITOL					
❑ DT 2189 [R]	Hot Rod High	1964	100.00	200.00	400.00
❑ T 2189 [M]	Hot Rod High	1964	100.00	200.00	400.00
JUSTICE					
❑ JLP-156	On the Move	196?	75.00	150.00	300.00

KNIGHTSBRIDGE STRINGS, THE
45s

Number	Title (A Side/B Side)	Yr	VG	VG+	NM
TOP RANK					
❑ 2006	Cry/My Prayer	1959	2.50	5.00	10.00
❑ 2014	Wheel of Fortune/Cow Cow Boogie	1959	2.50	5.00	10.00
❑ 2031	Blues from "An American in Paris"/ Fiddler's Boogie	1959	2.50	5.00	10.00
❑ 2082	If I Didn't Care/I Hear a Rhapsody	1960	2.50	5.00	10.00
❑ 3000	The Singer Not the Song/Anacleto's Theme	1961	2.50	5.00	10.00
Albums					
MONUMENT					
❑ MAM-3000 [M]	Espana	1966	2.50	5.00	10.00
❑ MAM-3001 [M]	3/4 Time	1966	2.50	5.00	10.00
❑ MAM-3002 [M]	Cinema	1966	2.50	5.00	10.00
❑ MAM-3003 [M]	The Knightsbridge Strings Go Pop	1966	2.50	5.00	10.00
❑ MAM-3004 [M]	Reverie	1966	2.50	5.00	10.00
❑ MAM-3005 [M]	Hawaii	1967	3.00	6.00	12.00
❑ MAM-3006 [M]	Gilbert and Sullivan	1967	3.00	6.00	12.00
❑ MAS-13000 [S]	Espana	1966	3.00	6.00	12.00
❑ MAS-13001 [S]	3/4 Time	1966	3.00	6.00	12.00
❑ MAS-13002 [S]	Cinema	1966	3.00	6.00	12.00
❑ MAS-13003 [S]	The Knightsbridge Strings Go Pop	1966	3.00	6.00	12.00
❑ MAS-13004 [S]	Reverie	1966	3.00	6.00	12.00
❑ MAS-13005 [S]	Hawaii	1967	3.00	6.00	12.00
❑ MAS-13006 [S]	Gilbert and Sullivan	1967	3.00	6.00	12.00
❑ MAS-13007	Marching Strings	1969	2.50	5.00	10.00
❑ MAS-13008	Nashville	1969	2.50	5.00	10.00
PURIST					
❑ SR-3	Spanish Mood	196?	3.00	6.00	12.00
❑ SR-9	Nostalgic Swing Mood	196?	3.00	6.00	12.00
RIVERSIDE					
❑ RM-7518 [M]	Strings on the March	196?	2.50	5.00	10.00
❑ RM-7532 [M]	Waltzing Strings	196?	2.50	5.00	10.00
❑ RM-7533 [M]	Big Beat	196?	2.50	5.00	10.00
❑ RS-97518 [S]	Strings on the March	196?	3.00	6.00	12.00
❑ RS-97532 [S]	Waltzing Strings	196?	3.00	6.00	12.00
❑ RS-97533 [S]	Big Beat	196?	3.00	6.00	12.00
SESAC					
❑ C-1701/2 [M]	Songs of America Vol. 1	195?	3.75	7.50	15.00
❑ C-1703/4 [M]	Songs of America Vol. 2	195?	3.75	7.50	15.00
TOP RANK					
❑ RM-303 [M]	The Strings Sing	1959	3.00	6.00	12.00
❑ RM-308 [M]	The Strings Swing	1959	3.00	6.00	12.00
❑ RM-315 [M]	Latin Cameos	1960	3.00	6.00	12.00
❑ RM-325 [M]	More Swinging Strings	1960	3.00	6.00	12.00
❑ RM-341 [M]	Soft Swaying Strings	1960	3.00	6.00	12.00
—Title on label is "More Swaying Strings"					
❑ RS-603 [S]	The Strings Sing	1959	3.75	7.50	15.00
❑ RS-608 [S]	The Strings Swing	1959	3.75	7.50	15.00
❑ RS-615 [S]	Latin Cameos	1960	3.75	7.50	15.00
❑ RS-625 [S]	More Swinging Strings	1960	3.75	7.50	15.00
❑ RS-641 [S]	Soft Swaying Strings	1960	3.75	7.50	15.00
—Title on label is "More Swaying Strings"					

KNOCKOUTS, THE (1)
45s

Number	Title (A Side/B Side)	Yr	VG	VG+	NM
SCEPTER					
❑ 1269	Got My Mojo Workin'/Every Day of the Week	1964	3.00	6.00	12.00
SHAD					
❑ 5013	Darling Lorraine/Riot in Room 3C	1959	6.25	12.50	25.00
—With short ending on A-side					
❑ 5013	Darling Lorraine/Riot in Room 3C	1959	12.50	25.00	50.00
—With long ending on A-side					
❑ 5018	Please Be Mine/Rich Boy, Poor Boy	1960	6.25	12.50	25.00
TRIBUTE					
❑ 199	Got My Mojo Working (Part 1)/Got My Mojo Working (Part 2)	1964	3.75	7.50	15.00
❑ 201	Tweet-Tweet/What's On Your Mind	1964	4.00	8.00	16.00
Albums					
TRIBUTE					
❑ 1202 [M]	Go Ape with the Knockouts	1964	50.00	100.00	200.00

KNOCKOUTS, THE (U) May be different or the same group as above, but we're not sure.
45s

Number	Title (A Side/B Side)	Yr	VG	VG+	NM
MGM					
❑ 13010	Fever/You Can Take My Girl	1961	5.00	10.00	20.00

KNOTT SISTERS, THE
45s

Number	Title (A Side/B Side)	Yr	VG	VG+	NM
BIG TOP					
❑ 3003	Undivided Attention/Sun Glasses	1958	25.00	50.00	100.00

KNOX, BUDDY
45s

Number	Title (A Side/B Side)	Yr	VG	VG+	NM
LIBERTY					
❑ 55290	Lovey Dovey/I Got You	1960	3.00	6.00	12.00
❑ 55305	Ling, Ting, Tong/The Kisses	1961	3.00	6.00	12.00
❑ 55305 [PS]	Ling, Ting, Tong/The Kisses	1961	7.50	15.00	30.00
❑ 55366	All By Myself/Three Eyed Man	1961	3.00	6.00	12.00
❑ 55411	Cha-Hua-Hua/Open	1962	3.00	6.00	12.00
❑ 55473	She's Gone/There's Only Me	1962	3.00	6.00	12.00
❑ 55503	Dear Abby/Three Way Love Affair	1962	3.00	6.00	12.00
❑ 55592	Shadaroom/Tomorrow Is a-Comin'	1963	2.50	5.00	10.00
❑ 55650	Thanks a Lot/Hitchhike Back to Georgia	1963	2.50	5.00	10.00
❑ 55694	Good Lovin'/All Time Loser	1964	2.50	5.00	10.00
REPRISE					
❑ 0395	Livin' in a House Full of Love/Good Time Girl	1965	2.50	5.00	10.00
❑ 0431	A Lover's Question/You Said Goodbye	1965	2.50	5.00	10.00
❑ 0463	A White Sport Coat/That Don't Do Me No Good	1966	2.50	5.00	10.00
❑ 0501	Love Has Many Ways/Sixteen Feet of Patio	1966	2.50	5.00	10.00
ROULETTE					
❑ 4002	Party Doll/My Baby's Gone	1957	6.25	12.50	25.00
—Red label, no roulette wheel					
❑ 4002	Party Doll/My Baby's Gone	1957	7.50	15.00	30.00
—Red label, roulette wheel on top half of label					

K

Number	Title (A Side/B Side)	Yr	VG	VG+	NM
❏ 4002	Party Doll/My Baby's Gone	1957	10.00	20.00	40.00
—Red label, black print, with roulette wheel around outside					
❏ 4002	Party Doll/My Baby's Gone	1957	12.50	25.00	50.00
—Maroon label, silver print, with roulette wheel around outside					
❏ 4002	Party Doll/My Baby's Gone	1958	3.75	7.50	15.00
—White label with color spokes					
❏ 4009	Rock Your Little Baby to Sleep/ Don't Make Me Cry	1957	5.00	10.00	20.00
—Red label, no roulette wheel					
❏ 4009	Rock Your Little Baby to Sleep/ Don't Make Me Cry	1957	6.25	12.50	25.00
—Red label, roulette wheel on top half of label					
❏ 4009	Rock Your Little Baby to Sleep/ Don't Make Me Cry	1957	10.00	20.00	40.00
—Red label with roulette wheel around outside					
❏ 4018	Hula Love/Devil Woman	1957	6.25	12.50	25.00
❏ 4042	Swingin' Daddy/Whenever I'm Lonely	1958	6.25	12.50	25.00
❏ 4082	Somebody Touched Me/C'mon Baby	1958	6.25	12.50	25.00
❏ 4120	That's Why I Cry/Teaseable, Pleaseable You	1958	6.25	12.50	25.00
❏ 4140	I Think I'm Gonna Kill Myself/To Be with You	1959	6.25	12.50	25.00
❏ 4179	Taste of the Blues/I Ain't Sharin' Sharon	1959	6.25	12.50	25.00
❏ 4262	Long Lonely Nights/Storm Clouds	1960	6.25	12.50	25.00
RUFF					
❏ 1001	Jo-Ann/Don't Make a Ripple	1965	2.50	5.00	10.00
TRIPLE D					
❏ 798	Party Doll/I'm Stickin' With You	1956	250.00	500.00	1000.
—B-side by Jimmy Bowen					
UNITED ARTISTS					
❏ 50301	This Time Tomorrow/Gypsy Man	1968	2.00	4.00	8.00
❏ 50463	Today My Sleepless Nights Came Back to Town/ A Million Years or So	1968	2.00	4.00	8.00
❏ 50526	God Knows I Love You/Night Runners	1969	2.00	4.00	8.00
❏ 50596	Salt Lake City/I'm Only Rockin'	1969	2.00	4.00	8.00
❏ 50644	Yesterday Is Gone/Back to New Orleans	1970	—	3.00	6.00
❏ 50722	White Dove/Glory Train	1970	—	3.00	6.00
❏ 50789	Come Softly to Me/Travelin' Light	1971	—	3.00	6.00
7-Inch Extended Plays					
ROULETTE					
❏ EPR-1-301	Party Doll/Rock Your Little Baby to Sleep//Hula Love/Rock Around the Clock	1957	20.00	40.00	80.00
❏ EPR-1-301 [PS]	Buddy Knox	1957	20.00	40.00	80.00
Albums					
ACCORD					
❏ SN-7218	Party Doll and Other Hits	1981	2.50	5.00	10.00
LIBERTY					
❏ LRP-3251 [M]	Buddy Knox's Golden Hits	1962	7.50	15.00	30.00
❏ LST-7251 [S]	Buddy Knox's Golden Hits	1962	10.00	20.00	40.00
ROULETTE					
❏ R 25003 [M]	Buddy Knox	1957	37.50	75.00	150.00
—Black label, red and silver print					
❏ R 25003 [M]	Buddy Knox	1957	50.00	100.00	200.00
—Black label, all silver print (original)					
❏ R 25003 [M]	Buddy Knox	1959	25.00	50.00	100.00
—White label with colored spokes					
❏ R 25048 [M]	Buddy Knox and Jimmy Bowen	1959	25.00	50.00	100.00
—White label with colored spokes					
❏ R 25048 [M]	Buddy Knox and Jimmy Bowen	1959	50.00	100.00	200.00
—Black label, red and silver print					
UNITED ARTISTS					
❏ UAS 6689	Gypsy Man	1969	6.25	12.50	25.00

KOALA, THE
45s
CAPITOL

Number	Title (A Side/B Side)	Yr	VG	VG+	NM
❏ 2365	Don't You Know What I Mean/Scattered Children's Toys	1968	3.75	7.50	15.00
Albums					
CAPITOL					
❏ SKAO-176	The Koala	1969	15.00	30.00	60.00

KODAKS, THE
45s
LOST-NITE

Number	Title (A Side/B Side)	Yr	VG	VG+	NM
❏ 355	Oh Gee Oh Gosh/Make Believe World	197?	—	2.50	5.00
—Reissue					
❏ 358	Runaround Baby/Guardian Angel	197?	—	2.50	5.00
—Reissue					
❏ 362	Teenager's Dream/Little Boy and Girl	197?	—	2.50	5.00
—Reissue					

KOFFMAN, MOE
45s
ASCOT

Number	Title (A Side/B Side)	Yr	VG	VG+	NM
❏ 2100	Swingin' Shepherd Blues Twist/Train Whistle Twist	1962	2.00	4.00	8.00
❏ 2111	Bumpin'/The Pretzel	1962	2.00	4.00	8.00
❏ 2118	Growing Up/Jazz Merengue	1963	2.00	4.00	8.00
ATCO					
❏ 6382	Bulldog Walk/Big Bad Irving	1965	2.00	4.00	8.00
GOLD EAGLE					
❏ 1804	Wishbone/Keep Walkin', Little Flock	196?	2.00	4.00	8.00
❏ 1811	Theme from Rocco and His Brothers/Hi-Fiver	196?	2.00	4.00	8.00
JUBILEE					
❏ 5311	The Swingin' Shepherd Blues/Hamburg Bound	1958	2.50	5.00	10.00
❏ 5324	Little Pixie/Koko-Mamey	1958	2.50	5.00	10.00
❏ 5352	Shepherd's Cha Cha/The Great Healer	1958	2.50	5.00	10.00
❏ 5367	Shepherd's Hoedown/Stroll Along with the Blues	1959	2.50	5.00	10.00
❏ 5471	Coffee House/Flootenanny	1964	2.00	4.00	8.00
❏ 5485	I Want to Hold Your Hand/Soul Brothers	1964	2.50	5.00	10.00
❏ 5615	Norwegian Wood/Trains and Boats and Planes	1968	—	3.50	7.00
❏ 5632	Do You Know the Way to San Jose/ Funky Monkey	1968	—	3.50	7.00
PALETTE					
❏ 5045	Black Eyed Peas/Sapphire	1959	2.50	5.00	10.00
❏ 5106	Cool Ghoul/Sapphire	1963	2.00	4.00	8.00
Albums					
ASCOT					
❏ AM 13001 [M]	Moe Koffman Plays for the Teens	1962	5.00	10.00	20.00
❏ AS 16001 [S]	Moe Koffman Plays for the Teens	1962	6.25	12.50	25.00

Number	Title (A Side/B Side)	Yr	VG	VG+	NM
JANUS					
❏ 7037	Museum Pieces	1978	3.75	7.50	15.00
JUBILEE					
❏ JLP-1037 [M]	Cool and Hot Sax	1957	10.00	20.00	40.00
❏ JLP-1074 [M]	The Shepherd Swings Again	1958	10.00	20.00	40.00
❏ JGS-8009	Moe Koffman Goes Electric	1968	7.50	15.00	30.00
❏ JGS-8016	Turned On	1968	6.25	12.50	25.00
KAMA SUTRA					
❏ KSBS-2018	Moe's Curried Soul	1970	5.00	10.00	20.00
SOUNDWINGS/DUKE STREET					
❏ SW 2108	Oop-Pop-A-Da	1988	3.00	6.00	12.00
—With Dizzy Gillespie					
UNITED ARTISTS					
❏ UAJ-14029 [M]	Tales of Koffman	1963	6.25	12.50	25.00
❏ UAJS-15029 [S]	Tales of Koffman	1963	7.50	15.00	30.00

KOKOMO (1) Pseudonym for producer Jimmy "Wiz" Wisner.
45s
FELSTED

Number	Title (A Side/B Side)	Yr	VG	VG+	NM
❏ 8612	Asia Minor/Roy's Tune	1961	2.50	5.00	10.00
❏ 8612 [PS]	Asia Minor/Roy's Tune	1961	3.75	7.50	15.00
❏ 8622	Humorous/Theme from a Silent Movie	1961	2.00	4.00	8.00
❏ 8628	Piano Rhapsody/Sweet Memories	1961	2.00	4.00	8.00
❏ 8635	Journey Home/Like Teen	1961	2.00	4.00	8.00
❏ 8641	Poinciana/The Good Earth	1962	2.00	4.00	8.00
Albums					
FELSTED					
❏ FL 7513 [M]	Asia Minor	1961	10.00	20.00	40.00
❏ FS 17513 [S]	Asia Minor	1961	12.50	25.00	50.00

KOKOMO (2)
45s
COLUMBIA

Number	Title (A Side/B Side)	Yr	VG	VG+	NM
❏ 3-10207	Kitty Sittin' Pretty/It Ain't Cool (To Be Cool No More)	1975	—	2.50	5.00
❏ 3-10213	Kitty Sittin' Pretty/Anytime	1975	—	2.50	5.00
❏ 3-10283	Rise and Shine/Do It Right	1976	—	2.50	5.00
❏ 3-10380	Use Your Imagination/That's Enough	1976	—	2.50	5.00
Albums					
COLUMBIA					
❏ PC 33442	Kokomo	1975	2.50	5.00	10.00
❏ PC 34031	Rise and Shine!	1976	2.50	5.00	10.00

KOKOMOS, THE
45s
GONE

Number	Title (A Side/B Side)	Yr	VG	VG+	NM
❏ 5134	Mama's Boy/Yours Truly	1962	3.75	7.50	15.00
JOSIE					
❏ 906	Open House Party/No Lies	1963	3.00	6.00	12.00

KOLBY, DIANE
45s
COLUMBIA

Number	Title (A Side/B Side)	Yr	VG	VG+	NM
❏ 4-45169	Holy Man/Hallelujah Baby	1970	—	3.00	6.00
❏ 4-45290	Juju Woman/Nivey Klaine	1970	—	3.00	6.00
❏ 4-45712	Death of the Sun/Reincarnation	1972	2.00	4.00	8.00
❏ 4-45844	Once Around the Park/Bessie Kimble	1973	2.00	4.00	8.00
Albums					
COLUMBIA					
❏ KC 31386	Diane Kolby	1972	3.75	7.50	15.00

KOLE, JERRY, AND THE STRINGERS
Albums
CROWN

Number	Title (A Side/B Side)	Yr	VG	VG+	NM
❏ CST-385 [S]	Hot Rod Alley	1963	10.00	20.00	40.00
❏ CLP-5385 [M]	Hot Rod Alley	1963	7.50	15.00	30.00

KONGOS, JOHN
45s
ELEKTRA

Number	Title (A Side/B Side)	Yr	VG	VG+	NM
❏ 45729	He's Gonna Step on You Again/ Sometimes It's Not Enough	1971	—	3.00	6.00
❏ 45760	Tokoloshe Man/Can Someone Please Direct Me Back to Earth	1972	—	2.50	5.00
❏ 45779	Jubilee Cloud/I Would Have Had a Good Time	1972	—	2.50	5.00
❏ 45809	He's Gonna Step on You Again/Tokoloshe Man	1972	—	2.50	5.00
GROOVE					
❏ 58-0009	Johnny and the Mermaid/Raunchy Twist	1963	3.00	6.00	12.00
KAPP					
❏ 799	I Love Mary/Good Time Party Companion	1966	2.50	5.00	10.00
RCA VICTOR					
❏ 47-8226	The Enchanted Sea/Tulips for 'Toinette	1963	3.00	6.00	12.00
Albums					
ELEKTRA					
❏ EKS-75019	Kongos	1971	3.00	6.00	12.00
JANUS					
❏ JLS 3032	Confusions About a Goldfish	1970	3.75	7.50	15.00

KONRADS, THE
45s
DECCA

Number	Title (A Side/B Side)	Yr	VG	VG+	NM
❏ 32060	I Didn't Know How Much/ I Thought of You Last Night	1966	2.00	4.00	8.00

KOOBAS, THE
45s
CAPITOL

Number	Title (A Side/B Side)	Yr	VG	VG+	NM
❏ 2416	First Cut is the Deepest/Walking Out	1969	2.00	4.00	8.00
KAPP					
❏ 737	Take Me for a Little While/Give a Little Bit	1965	3.75	7.50	15.00
❏ 737 [PS]	Take Me for a Little While/Give a Little Bit	1965	5.00	10.00	20.00

KOOL AND THE GANG Also see K.C. AND THE SUNSHINE BAND.
12-Inch Singles
DE-LITE

Number	Title (A Side/B Side)	Yr	VG	VG+	NM
❏ MK 179-1 [DJ]	Take My Heart (same on both sides)	1983	—	3.00	6.00
❏ MK 208-1 [DJ]	Big Fun (same on both sides)	1982	3.75	7.50	15.00

Number	Title (A Side/B Side)	Yr	VG	VG+	NM
❏ PRO 245-1 [DJ]	Home Is Where the Heart Is (same on both sides)	1983	2.00	4.00	8.00
❏ PRO 261-1 [DJ]	Tonight (Dance Mix) (same on both sides)	1983	2.00	4.00	8.00
❏ PRO 274-1 [DJ]	Tonight (AOR Mix) (same on both sides)	1984	2.50	5.00	10.00
❏ PRO 278-1 [DJ]	Straight Ahead (same on both sides)	1983	—	3.00	6.00
❏ DDS 503 [DJ]	Celebremos (5:25)/Morning Star	1981	7.50	15.00	30.00
❏ DDS 507	Tonight/Celebration	1984	3.00	6.00	12.00
❏ 880623-1	Fresh (Remix) (Dance Mix)	1985	2.00	4.00	8.00
❏ 880947-1	Cherish (Remix 5:40)/Fresh-Misled (Remix 6:10)	1985	2.00	4.00	8.00
❏ 884199-1	Emergency (Remix) (Dub Mix) (Special Mix)/ You Are the One	1985	3.00	6.00	12.00
MERCURY					
❏ PRO 478-1 [DJ]	Stone Love (Club Mix) (House Mix)/Dance Champion	1986	2.00	4.00	8.00
❏ PRO 739-1 [DJ]	Raindrops (3 versions)	1989	2.00	4.00	8.00
❏ 870513-1	Rags to Riches (5 versions)	1988	2.00	4.00	8.00
❏ 870572-1	Rags to Riches (4 versions)	1988	2.00	4.00	8.00
❏ 874403-1	Raindrops (3 versions)/Amor, Amore	1989	2.00	4.00	8.00
❏ 888074-1	Victory (12" Version) (7" Version)/Bad Woman	1986	2.00	4.00	8.00
❏ 888292-1	Stone Love (Club Version) (House Mix)/ Dance Champion	1986	2.00	4.00	8.00
❏ 888712-1	Holiday (12" Club Remix 5:48) (Dub Version 5:45) (7" Version 3:35) (Jam Mix 5:20)	1988	2.00	4.00	8.00
45s					
DE-LITE					
❏ 519	Kool and the Gang/Raw Hamburger	1969	—	3.00	6.00
❏ 523	The Gangs Back Again/Kools Back Again	1969	—	3.00	6.00
❏ 525	Kool It (Here Comes the Fuzz)/Can't Stop	1970	—	3.00	6.00
❏ 529	Let the Music Take Your Mind/ Chocolate Buttermilk	1970	—	3.00	6.00
❏ 534	Funky Man/1,2,3,4,5,6,7,8	1970	—	3.00	6.00
❏ 538	Who's Gonna Take the Weight (Part One)/Who's Gonna Take the Weight (Part Two)	1970	—	3.00	6.00
❏ 540	I Want to Take You Higher/Pneumonia	1971	—	3.00	6.00
❏ 543	The Penguin/Lucky for Me	1971	—	3.00	6.00
❏ 544	N.T. (Part One)/N.T. (Part Two)	1971	—	3.00	6.00
❏ 546	Love the Life You Live, Part I/Love the Life You Live, Part II	1972	—	3.00	6.00
❏ 547	You've Lost That Lovin' Feeling/Ike's Mood	1972	—	3.00	6.00
❏ 550	Music Is the Messenger, Part I/Music Is the Messenger, Part II	1972	—	3.00	6.00
❏ 552	Good Times/The Frog	1972	—	3.00	6.00
❏ 553	Funky Granny/Blowing with the Wind	1973	—	3.00	6.00
❏ 555	Country Junkie/I Remember John W. Coltrane	1973	—	3.00	6.00
❏ 557	Funky Stuff/More Funky Stuff	1973	—	3.00	6.00
❏ 559	Jungle Boogie/North, East, South, West	1973	—	2.50	5.00
❏ 561	Hollywood Swinging/Dujii	1974	—	2.50	5.00
❏ 801	Ladies Night/If You Feel Like Dancin'	1979	—	2.00	4.00
❏ 802	Too Hot/Tonight's the Night	1979	—	2.00	4.00
❏ 804	Hangin' Out/Got You Into My Life	1980	—	2.00	4.00
❏ 807	Celebration/Morning Star	1980	—	2.00	4.00
❏ 810	Take It to the Top/Love Affair	1981	—	2.00	4.00
❏ 813	Jones Vs. Jones/Night People	1981	—	2.00	4.00
❏ 815	Take My Heart (You Can Have It If You Want It)/ Just Friends	1981	—	2.00	4.00
❏ 815	Take My Heart/Just Friends	1981	—	2.50	5.00
—First pressings have no subtitle					
❏ 816	Steppin' Out/Love Festival	1982	—	2.00	4.00
❏ 818	Get Down On It/Steppin' Out	1982	—	2.00	4.00
❏ 822	Big Fun/No Show	1982	—	2.00	4.00
❏ 824	Let's Go Dancin' (Ooh, La, La, La)/Be My Lady	1982	—	2.00	4.00
❏ 825	Street Kids/As One	1983	—	2.00	4.00
❏ 829	Joanna/A Place for Us	1983	—	—	3.00
❏ 830	Tonight/Home Is Where the Heart Is	1984	—	—	3.00
❏ 831	Straight Ahead/September Love	1984	—	—	3.00
❏ 901	Slick Superchick/Life's a Song	1978	—	2.50	5.00
❏ 905	A Place in Space/The Force	1978	—	2.50	5.00
❏ 909	I Like Music/It's All You Need	1978	—	2.50	5.00
❏ 910	Everybody's Dancin'/Stay Awhile	1978	—	2.50	5.00
❏ 1562	Higher Plane/Wild Is Love	1974	—	2.50	5.00
❏ 1563	Rhyme Tyme People/Father, Father	1974	—	2.50	5.00
❏ 1567	Spirit of the Boogie/Summer Madness	1975	—	2.50	5.00
❏ 1573	Caribbean Festival/Caribbean Festival (Disco Version)	1975	—	2.50	5.00
❏ 1577	Winter Sadness/Father, Father	1975	—	2.50	5.00
❏ 1579	Love and Understanding (Come Together)/ Sunshine and Love	1976	—	2.50	5.00
❏ 1583	Universal Sound/Ancestral Ceremony	1976	—	2.50	5.00
❏ 1586	Open Sesame — Part 1/Open Sesame — Part 2	1976	—	2.50	5.00
❏ 1590	Super Band/Sunshine	1977	—	2.50	5.00
❏ 880431-7	Misled/Rollin'	1984	—	—	3.00
❏ 880623-7	Fresh/In the Heart	1985	—	—	3.00
❏ 880623-7 [PS]	Fresh/In the Heart	1985	—	2.00	4.00
❏ 880869-7	Cherish/(Instrumental)	1985	—	—	3.00
❏ 880869-7 [PS]	Cherish/(Instrumental)	1985	—	2.00	4.00
❏ 884199-7	Emergency/You Are the One	1985	—	—	3.00
MERCURY					
❏ PRO 621-7 [DJ]	Rags to Riches (Lightnin' Licks Remix) (same on both sides)	1988	—	3.00	6.00
❏ PRO 621-7 [PS]	Rags to Riches (Lightnin' Licks Remix) (same on both sides)	1988	—	3.00	6.00
❏ 870513-7	Rags to Riches/Rags to Riches (Remix)	1988	—	—	3.00
❏ 870513-7 [PS]	Rags to Riches/Rags to Riches (Remix)	1988	—	—	3.00
❏ 872038-7	Strong/Funky Stuff	1988	—	—	3.00
❏ 874402-7	Raindrops/Amor Amore	1989	—	—	3.00
❏ 876072-7	Never Give Up/Amor Amore	1989	—	—	3.00
❏ 888074-7	Victory/Bad Woman	1986	—	—	3.00
❏ 888074-7 [PS]	Victory/Bad Woman	1986	—	—	3.00
❏ 888292-7	Stone Love/Dance Champion	1987	—	—	3.00
❏ 888292-7 [PS]	Stone Love/Dance Champion	1987	—	—	3.00
❏ 888712-7	Holiday/(Jam Mix)	1987	—	—	3.00
❏ 888712-7 [PS]	Holiday/(Jam Mix)	1987	—	—	3.00
❏ 888867-7	In a Special Way/God's Country	1987	—	—	3.00
❏ 888867-7 [PS]	In a Special Way/God's Country	1987	—	—	3.00
Albums					
DE-LITE					
❏ MK-48 [DJ]	History of Kool and the Gang	1979	3.75	7.50	15.00
❏ 2003	Kool and the Gang	1969	6.25	12.50	25.00
❏ 2008	Live at the Sex Machine	1971	3.00	6.00	12.00
❏ 2009	The Best of Kool and the Gang	1971	3.00	6.00	12.00

Number	Title (A Side/B Side)	Yr	VG	VG+	NM
❏ 2010	Live at PJ's	1971	3.00	6.00	12.00
❏ 2011	Music Is the Message	1972	3.00	6.00	12.00
❏ 2012	Good Times	1973	3.00	6.00	12.00
❏ 2013	Wild and Peaceful	1973	2.50	5.00	10.00
❏ 2014	Light of Worlds	1974	2.50	5.00	10.00
❏ 2015	Kool & the Gang Greatest Hits!	1975	2.50	5.00	10.00
❏ 2016	Spirit of the Boogie	1975	2.50	5.00	10.00
❏ 2018	Love and Understanding	1976	2.50	5.00	10.00
❏ 2023	Open Sesame	1976	2.50	5.00	10.00
❏ 4001	Kool Jazz	1973	2.50	5.00	10.00
❏ 8502	Something Special	1981	2.50	5.00	10.00
❏ 8505	As One	1982	2.50	5.00	10.00
❏ 8508	In the Heart	1983	2.50	5.00	10.00
❏ 9501	The Force	1978	2.50	5.00	10.00
❏ 9507	Kool & the Gang Spin Their Top Ten Hits	1978	2.50	5.00	10.00
❏ 9509	Everybody's Dancin'	1979	2.50	5.00	10.00
❏ 9513	Ladies Night	1979	2.50	5.00	10.00
❏ 9518	Celebrate!	1980	2.50	5.00	10.00
❏ 814351-1	In the Heart	1984	2.00	4.00	8.00
—Reissue					
❏ 822534-1	Something Special	1984	2.00	4.00	8.00
—Reissue					
❏ 822535-1	As One	1984	2.00	4.00	8.00
—Reissue					
❏ 822536-1	Kool & The Gang Spin Their Top Ten Hits	1984	2.00	4.00	8.00
—Reissue					
❏ 822537-1	Ladies Night	1984	2.00	4.00	8.00
—Reissue					
❏ 822538-1	Celebrate!	1984	2.00	4.00	8.00
—Reissue					
❏ 822943-1	Emergency	1984	2.00	4.00	8.00
MERCURY					
❏ 830398-1	Forever	1986	2.00	4.00	8.00
❏ 834780-1	Everything's Kool & the Gang: Greatest Hits & More	1988	2.00	4.00	8.00
❏ 838233-1	Sweat	1989	2.00	4.00	8.00

KOOL GENTS DEE CLARK was a member of this group.
45s
VEE JAY

Number	Title (A Side/B Side)	Yr	VG	VG+	NM
❏ 173	This Is the Night/Do Ya Do	1956	50.00	100.00	200.00
❏ 207	You Know/I Can't Help Myself	1956	50.00	100.00	200.00

KOOPER, AL Also see BLOOD, SWEAT AND TEARS; MIKE BLOOMFIELD; THE BLUES PROJECT.
45s
AURORA

Number	Title (A Side/B Side)	Yr	VG	VG+	NM
❏ 164	New York's My Town/My Voice, My Piano	1967	3.00	6.00	12.00
COLUMBIA					
❏ 03312	Two Sides (To Every Situation)/Snowblind	1982	—	2.00	4.00
❏ 44748	You Never Know Who Your Friends Are/ Soft Landing on the Moon	1969	—	2.50	5.00
❏ 44811	I Stand Alone/Hey, Western Union Man	1969	—	2.50	5.00
❏ 45093	One Room Country Shack/Bury My Body	1970	—	2.50	5.00
❏ 45148	She Gets Me Where I Live/ God Sheds His Grace on Thee	1970	—	2.50	5.00
❏ 45179	Love Theme from "The Landlord"/ Brand New Day	1970	—	2.50	5.00
❏ 4-45243	I Got a Woman/Easy Does It	1970	—	2.50	5.00
❏ 45412	John the Baptist/Back on My Feet	1971	—	2.50	5.00
❏ 45566	The Monkey Time/Bended Knees (Please Don't Let Me Down)	1972	—	2.50	5.00
❏ 45691	Sam Stone/Be Real	1972	—	2.50	5.00
❏ 45735	Jolie/Be Real	1972	—	2.50	5.00
UNITED ARTISTS					
❏ XW879	This Diamond Ring/Hollywood Vampire	1976	—	2.00	4.00
VERVE FOLKWAYS					
❏ 5026	Changes/Pack Up Your Sorrows	1966	3.00	6.00	12.00
Albums					
COLUMBIA					
❏ CS 9718	I Stand Alone	1969	3.75	7.50	15.00
—"360 Sound" label					
❏ CS 9718	I Stand Alone	1970	2.50	5.00	10.00
—Orange label					
❏ CS 9855	You Never Know Who Your Friends Are	1969	3.75	7.50	15.00
—"360 Sound" label					
❏ CS 9855	You Never Know Who Your Friends Are	1970	2.50	5.00	10.00
—Orange label					
❏ CS 9951	Kooper Session	1970	2.50	5.00	10.00
—With Shuggie Otis; orange label					
❏ CS 9951	Kooper Session	1970	3.75	7.50	15.00
—With Shuggie Otis; "360 Sound" label					
❏ G 30031 [(2)]	Easy Does It	1970	5.00	10.00	20.00
❏ KC 30309	New York City (You're a Woman)	1971	3.75	7.50	15.00
❏ KC 31159	A Possible Projection of the Future/ Childhood's End	1972	3.75	7.50	15.00
❏ KC 31723	Naked Songs	1973	3.75	7.50	15.00
❏ PG 33169 [(2)]	Unclaimed Freight (Al's Big Deal)	1975	3.75	7.50	15.00
❏ FC 38137	Championship Wrestling	1982	2.50	5.00	10.00
UNITED ARTISTS					
❏ UA-LA702-G	Act Like Nothing's Wrong	1976	3.00	6.00	12.00

KORNER, ALEXIS
45s
COLUMBIA

Number	Title (A Side/B Side)	Yr	VG	VG+	NM
❏ 10166	Get Off My Cloud/Strange N' Deranged	1975	2.00	4.00	8.00
Albums					
COLUMBIA					
❏ PC 33427	Get Off of My Cloud	1975	3.75	7.50	15.00
JUST SUNSHINE					
❏ 13	All Star Blues Incorporated	1974	3.00	6.00	12.00
MOBILE FIDELITY					
❏ 1-265	Blues at the Marquee	1996	5.00	10.00	20.00
—Audiophile vinyl					
WARNER BROS.					
❏ 2XS 1966 [(2)]	Bootleg Him	1972	6.25	12.50	25.00
❏ BS 2647	Accidentally Borne in New Orleans	1972	3.75	7.50	15.00

K

Number	Title (A Side/B Side)	Yr	VG	VG+	NM

KOSSOFF, PAUL Also see FREE.

Albums
DJM
| ☐ 2300 [(2)] | Koss | 1977 | 3.75 | 7.50 | 15.00 |

ISLAND
| ☐ ILPS 9264 | Back Street Crawler | 1975 | 2.50 | 5.00 | 10.00 |

KOSTELANETZ, ANDRE

45s
COLUMBIA
☐ 40044	Playing Around/Time on My Hands	1953	2.50	5.00	10.00
☐ 40350	Sweet Surrender/April in Paradise	1954	2.50	5.00	10.00
☐ 41534	Sabre Dance/Gypsy Fiddler	1959	2.00	4.00	8.00
☐ 42604	Washington Twist/Secret Service	1962	2.00	4.00	8.00
☐ 43034	Bluesette/Fall in Love	1964	—	3.00	6.00
☐ 44147	The Impossible Dream/Born Free	1967	—	3.00	6.00
☐ 44255	You Are There/One of These Songs	1967	—	3.00	6.00
☐ 45061	Come Saturday Morning/Leaving on a Jet Plane	1970	—	2.50	5.00
☐ 45244	Things of Life/Valse de Rothschild	1970	—	2.50	5.00
☐ 45357	Theme from "Love Story"/Mr. Bojangles	1971	—	2.00	4.00
☐ JZSP 76389/90 [DJ]	Medley: Santa Claus Is Coming To Town & Have Yourself A Merry Little Christmas/ Christmas Chopsticks	1963	2.50	5.00	10.00
☐ JZSP 111905/6 [DJ]	O Come All Ye Faithful/Oh Tannenbaum	1965	2.00	4.00	8.00
—Black vinyl					
☐ JZSP 111905/6 [DJ]	O Come All Ye Faithful/Oh Tannenbaum	1965	3.00	6.00	12.00
—Green vinyl					
☐ JZSP 116040/1 [DJ]	Galop from "Moscow, Cheremushki"/Galop from "Ballet Suite No. 2"	1966	2.00	4.00	8.00
—White label promo only					
☐ JZSP 116040/1 [PS]	Galop from "Moscow, Cheremushki"/Galop from "Ballet Suite No. 2"	1966	3.00	6.00	12.00
—Title on sleeve: "Kosty Plays Shosty"					

COLUMBIA MASTERWORKS
☐ A-753 [(4)]	Carnival Tropicana	195?	2.50	5.00	10.00
—Box for 4-record set					
☐ A-925 [(5)]	Swan Lake	195?	2.50	5.00	10.00
—Box for five-record set					
☐ 4-7603-M	Malaguena/No Taboleiro De Bahiana	195?	2.00	4.00	8.00
☐ 4-7604-M	La Cumparasita/Adios	195?	2.00	4.00	8.00
☐ 4-7605-M	Mexicana/Caminito	195?	2.00	4.00	8.00
☐ 4-7606-M	Yours/Siboney	195?	2.00	4.00	8.00
—The above four comprise box set A-753					
☐ 4-7648-M	Swan Lake (Part 1)/Swan Lake (Part 10)	195?	2.00	4.00	8.00
☐ 4-7649-M	Swan Lake (Part 2)/Swan Lake (Part 9)	195?	2.00	4.00	8.00
☐ 4-7650-M	Swan Lake (Part 3)/Swan Lake (Part 8)	195?	2.00	4.00	8.00
☐ 4-7651-M	Swan Lake (Part 4)/Swan Lake (Part 7)	195?	2.00	4.00	8.00
☐ 4-7652-M	Swan Lake (Part 5)/Swan Lake (Part 6)	195?	2.00	4.00	8.00
—The above five comprise box set A-925					

7-Inch Extended Plays
COLUMBIA
| ☐ KZP-1 | Where or When/Celeste Aida//Tales from the Vienna Woods/The Love for Three Oranges - March | 195? | 2.50 | 5.00 | 10.00 |
| ☐ KZP-1 [PS] | Meet Andre Kostelanetz, Music's Leading Man | 195? | 2.50 | 5.00 | 10.00 |

COLUMBIA MASTERWORKS
☐ A-502 [PS]	Musical Comedy Favorites, Vol. II	195?	2.50	5.00	10.00
—Cover for 2-EP set (1429 and 1430)					
☐ 7-1155	Begin the Beguine/Blow, Gabriel, Blow//Night and Day/Just One of Those Things	195?	2.50	5.00	10.00
—Alternate number is "A 1506"					
☐ 7-1266	Schumann: Traumerei, Op. 15, No. 7/Brahms: Lullaby, Op. 49, No. 4//Francois Schubert: The Bee (L'abeille)/Londonderry Air	195?	2.50	5.00	10.00
—Alternate number is "A 1571"					
☐ 7-1429	Night and Day/Time on My Hands//I'll See You Again/Dancing in the Dark	195?	2.50	5.00	10.00
—Alternate numbers are "A 502-1" and "A 502-4"					
☐ 7-1430	The Touch of Your Hand/Somebody Loves Me/ /With a Song in My Heart/Easter Parade	195?	2.50	5.00	10.00
—Alternate numbers are "A 502-2" and "A 502-3"					
☐ A 1506 [PS]	(title unknown)	195?	2.50	5.00	10.00
☐ A 1571 [PS]	(title unknown)	195?	2.50	5.00	10.00

Albums
COLUMBIA
☐ AK 1 [M]	Musical Tour of the World	195?	5.00	10.00	20.00
☐ KZ 1 [M]	Meet Andre Kostelanetz	1955	5.00	10.00	20.00
—Red and black label with six "eye" logos					
☐ GP 10 [(2)]	Sounds of Love	1969	3.00	6.00	12.00
☐ C2L 11 [M]	The Romantic Music of Tchaikovsky	195?	6.25	12.50	25.00
—Red and black label with six "eye" logos					
☐ CL 704 [M]	Mood for Love	1956	5.00	10.00	20.00
—Red and black label with six "eye" logos					
☐ CL 720 [M]	Peter and the Wolf; Carnival of the Animals	1956	5.00	10.00	20.00
—Red and black label with six "eye" logos					
☐ CL 734 [M]	The Music of Victor Youmans	1956	5.00	10.00	20.00
—Red and black label with six "eye" logos					
☐ CL 765 [M]	The Music of Victor Herbert	1956	5.00	10.00	20.00
—Red and black label with six "eye" logos					
☐ CL 768 [M]	Music of Irving Berlin	1956	5.00	10.00	20.00
—Red and black label with six "eye" logos					
☐ CL 780 [M]	Lure of the Tropics	1956	5.00	10.00	20.00
—Red and black label with six "eye" logos					
☐ CL 781 [M]	Stardust	1956	5.00	10.00	20.00
—Red and black label with six "eye" logos					
☐ CL 797 [M]	La Boheme for Orchestra	1956	5.00	10.00	20.00
—Red and black label with six "eye" logos					
☐ CL 806 [M]	Show Boat/South Pacific/Slaughter on 10th Avenue	1956	5.00	10.00	20.00
—Red and black label with six "eye" logos					
☐ CL 811 [M]	Calendar Girl	1956	5.00	10.00	20.00
—Red and black label with six "eye" logos					
☐ CL 843 [M]	The Very Thought of You	1956	5.00	10.00	20.00
—Red and black label with six "eye" logos					
☐ CL 863 [M]	Café Continental	1956	5.00	10.00	20.00
—Red and black label with six "eye" logos					
☐ CL 864 [M]	Beautiful Dreamer	1956	5.00	10.00	20.00
—Red and black label with six "eye" logos					
☐ CL 1220 [M]	Romantic Music of...	1958	3.75	7.50	15.00
☐ CL 1335 [M]	The Lure of Paradise	1959	3.00	6.00	12.00
☐ CL 1354 [M]	Strauss Waltzes	1959	3.00	6.00	12.00
☐ CL 1431 [M]	Gypsy Passion	1960	3.00	6.00	12.00
☐ CL 1495 [M]	Gershwin: Rhapsody in Blue; Previn: Concerto in F	1960	3.00	6.00	12.00
☐ CL 1528 [M]	Joy to the World: Music for Christmas	1959	3.75	7.50	15.00
☐ CL 1657 [M]	Wonderland of Sound	1961	3.00	6.00	12.00
☐ CL 1718 [M]	Star-Spangled Marches	1962	3.00	6.00	12.00
☐ CL 1827 [M]	Wonderland of Sound (Broadway's Greatest Hits)	1962	3.00	6.00	12.00
☐ CL 1898 [M]	Wonderland of Sound (Fire and Jealousy)	1962	3.00	6.00	12.00
☐ CL 1938 [M]	Wonderland of Sound (The World's Greatest Waltzes)	1963	2.50	5.00	10.00
☐ CL 1995 [M]	Wonderland of Opera	1963	2.50	5.00	10.00
☐ CL 2039 [M]	Wonderland of Golden Hits	1963	2.50	5.00	10.00
☐ CL 2068 [M]	Wonderland of Christmas	1963	3.00	6.00	12.00
☐ CL 2078 [M]	Kostelanetz in Wonderland	1964	2.50	5.00	10.00
☐ CL 2133 [M]	Gershwin Wonderland	1964	2.50	5.00	10.00
☐ CL 2138 [M]	New York Wonderland	1964	2.50	5.00	10.00
☐ CL 2185 [M]	I Wish You Love	1964	2.50	5.00	10.00
☐ CL 2250 [M]	New Orleans Wonderland	1965	2.50	5.00	10.00
☐ CL 2359 [M]	Thunder (The Spectacular Sound of John Philip Sousa)	1965	2.50	5.00	10.00
☐ CL 2467 [M]	The Shadow of Your Smile and Other Great Movie Themes	1966	2.50	5.00	10.00
☐ CL 2534 [M]	Today's Golden Hits	1966	2.50	5.00	10.00
☐ CL 2581 [M]	Exotic Nights	1966	2.50	5.00	10.00
☐ CL 2609 [M]	The Kostelanetz Sound of Today	1967	2.50	5.00	10.00
☐ CL 2688 [M]	Concert in the Park	1967	2.50	5.00	10.00
☐ CL 2756 [M]	Today's Greatest Movie Hits	1967	3.00	6.00	12.00
☐ CL 2823 [M]	Scarborough Fair	1968	3.75	7.50	15.00
☐ CL 2891 [M]	For the Young at Heart	1968	3.75	7.50	15.00
☐ CS 8144 [S]	The Lure of Paradise	1959	3.75	7.50	15.00
☐ CS 8162 [S]	Strauss Waltzes	1959	3.75	7.50	15.00
☐ CS 8228 [S]	Gypsy Passion	1960	3.75	7.50	15.00
☐ CS 8286 [S]	Gershwin: Rhapsody in Blue; Previn: Concerto in F	1960	3.75	7.50	15.00
☐ CS 8328 [S]	Joy to the World: Music for Christmas	1959	5.00	10.00	20.00
—Red and black label with six "eye" logos					
☐ CS 8457 [S]	Wonderland of Sound	1961	3.75	7.50	15.00
☐ CS 8518 [S]	Star-Spangled Marches	1962	3.75	7.50	15.00
☐ CS 8627 [S]	Wonderland of Sound (Broadway's Greatest Hits)	1962	3.75	7.50	15.00
☐ CS 8698 [S]	Wonderland of Sound (Fire and Jealousy)	1962	3.75	7.50	15.00
☐ CS 8738 [S]	Wonderland of Sound (The World's Greatest Waltzes)	1963	3.00	6.00	12.00
☐ CS 8795 [S]	Wonderland of Opera	1963	3.00	6.00	12.00
☐ CS 8839 [S]	Wonderland of Golden Hits	1963	3.00	6.00	12.00
☐ CS 8868 [S]	Wonderland of Christmas	1963	3.75	7.50	15.00
☐ CS 8878 [S]	Kostelanetz in Wonderland	1964	3.00	6.00	12.00
☐ CS 8933 [S]	Gershwin Wonderland	1964	3.00	6.00	12.00
☐ CS 8938 [S]	New York Wonderland	1964	3.00	6.00	12.00
☐ CS 8985 [S]	I Wish You Love	1964	3.00	6.00	12.00
☐ CS 9050 [S]	New Orleans Wonderland	1965	3.00	6.00	12.00
☐ CS 9159 [S]	Thunder (The Spectacular Sound of John Philip Sousa)	1965	3.00	6.00	12.00
☐ CS 9267 [S]	The Shadow of Your Smile and Other Great Movie Themes	1966	2.50	5.00	10.00
☐ CS 9334 [S]	Today's Golden Hits	1966	3.00	6.00	12.00
☐ CS 9381 [S]	Exotic Nights	1966	2.50	5.00	10.00
☐ CS 9409 [S]	The Kostelanetz Sound of Today	1967	2.50	5.00	10.00
☐ CS 9488 [S]	Concert in the Park	1967	2.50	5.00	10.00
☐ CS 9556 [S]	Today's Greatest Movie Hits	1967	2.50	5.00	10.00
☐ CS 9623 [S]	Scarborough Fair	1968	2.50	5.00	10.00
☐ CS 9691 [S]	For the Young at Heart	1968	2.50	5.00	10.00
☐ CS 9724	Hits from Funny Girl, Finian's Rainbow, and Star!	1968	2.50	5.00	10.00
☐ CS 9740	Andre Kostelanetz' Greatest Hits	1969	2.50	5.00	10.00
☐ CS 9823	Traces	1969	2.50	5.00	10.00
☐ CS 9973	Greatest Hits of the 60's	1970	2.50	5.00	10.00
☐ CS 9998	I'll Never Fall in Love Again	1970	2.50	5.00	10.00
☐ C 30037	Everything Is Beautiful	1970	2.50	5.00	10.00
☐ C 30501	Love Story	1971	2.50	5.00	10.00
☐ C 30672	For All We Know	1971	2.50	5.00	10.00
☐ C 31002	Kostelanetz Plays Chicago	1971	2.50	5.00	10.00
☐ KG 31491 [(2)]	Andre Kostelanetz Plays Cole Porter	1972	3.75	7.50	15.00
☐ KG 32002 [(2)]	The World's Greatest Love Songs	1973	3.00	6.00	12.00
☐ CQ 32147 [Q]	A Quadraphonic Concert	1972	3.75	7.50	15.00
☐ KC 32187	Last Tango in Paris	1973	2.50	5.00	10.00
☐ KC 32451	Kostelanetz Plays Great Hits of Today	1973	2.50	5.00	10.00
☐ KC 32580	Andre Kostelanetz Plays Legrand's Greatest Hits	1974	2.50	5.00	10.00
☐ KG 32825 [(2)]	Andre Kostelanetz Plays Gershwin	1974	3.00	6.00	12.00
☐ CQ 32856 [Q]	Quadraphonic Pop Concert	1973	3.75	7.50	15.00
☐ KC 33061	Musical Reflections of Broadway and Hollywood	1974	2.50	5.00	10.00
☐ KG 33065 [(2)]	Strike Up the Band	1974	3.00	6.00	12.00
☐ KC 33437	Orient Express	1975	2.50	5.00	10.00
☐ C 33550	Never Can Say Goodbye	1975	2.00	4.00	8.00
☐ KC 33550	Never Can Say Goodbye	1975	2.50	5.00	10.00
☐ KC 33954	Music from A Chorus Line and Treemonisha	1975	2.50	5.00	10.00
☐ KC 34157	I'm Easy and Other Themes	1976	2.50	5.00	10.00
☐ PC 34352	Dance with Me	1977	2.50	5.00	10.00
☐ PC 34660	Music of Charlie Chaplin and Duke Ellington	1977	2.50	5.00	10.00
☐ JC 35328	You Light Up My Life	1978	2.50	5.00	10.00
☐ JC 35788	Superman	1979	2.00	4.00	8.00
☐ JC 36382	Various Themes	1980	2.00	4.00	8.00

COLUMBIA LIMITED EDITION
☐ LE 10083	Joy to the World: Music for Christmas	197?	2.50	5.00	10.00
—Reissue of CS 8328					
☐ LE 10086	Wonderland of Christmas	197?	2.50	5.00	10.00
—Reissue of CS 8868					

COLUMBIA MASTERWORKS
☐ ML 2007 [10]	Music of Stephen Foster	195?	6.25	12.50	25.00
☐ ML 2011 [10]	Waltzes of Johann Strauss	195?	6.25	12.50	25.00
☐ ML 2014 [10]	Songs of Cole Porter	195?	7.50	15.00	30.00
☐ ML 2022 [10]	Motion Picture Favorites	195?	6.25	12.50	25.00
☐ ML 2056 [10]	Chopin-Kostelanetz	195?	6.25	12.50	25.00
☐ ML 4065 [M]	Favorites	195?	5.00	10.00	20.00
☐ ML 4066 [M]	Clair de Lune	195?	5.00	10.00	20.00
☐ ML 4082 [M]	Carnival Tropicana	195?	5.00	10.00	20.00
☐ ML 4253 [M]	Music of Fritz Kreisler and Sigmund Romberg	195?	5.00	10.00	20.00
☐ ML 4308 [M]	Swan Lake (Highlights)	195?	5.00	10.00	20.00

Number	Title (A Side/B Side)	Yr	VG	VG+	NM
❏ ML 4409 [M]	Bizet: L'arlesienne Suites 1 & 2	195?	5.00	10.00	20.00
❏ ML 4455 [M]	An American in Paris	195?	5.00	10.00	20.00
❏ ML 4822 [M]	Lure of the Tropics	1956	5.00	10.00	20.00
❏ MS 6106 [S]	Offenbach: Gaite Parisienne; Bizet: Carmen (Highlights)	195?	5.00	10.00	20.00
❏ ML 6111 [M]	Romantic Strings	1960	3.00	6.00	12.00
❏ ML 6129 [M]	Showstoppers	1960	3.00	6.00	12.00
❏ ML 6179 [M]	Wishing You a Merry Christmas	1960	3.00	6.00	12.00
❏ ML 6206 [M]	Promenade Favorites	1966	3.00	6.00	12.00
❏ ML 6224 [M]	Romantic Waltzes of Tchaikovsky	1961	3.00	6.00	12.00
❏ ML 6226 [M]	Favorite Romantic Concertos	1961	3.00	6.00	12.00
❏ MS 6711 [S]	Romantic Strings	1960	3.75	7.50	15.00
❏ MS 6729 [S]	Showstoppers	1960	3.75	7.50	15.00
❏ MS 6779 [S]	Wishing You a Merry Christmas	1960	3.75	7.50	15.00
❏ MS 6806 [S]	Promenade Favorites	1966	3.75	7.50	15.00
❏ MS 6824 [S]	Romantic Waltzes of Tchaikovsky	1961	3.75	7.50	15.00
❏ MS 6826 [S]	Favorite Romantic Concertos	1961	3.75	7.50	15.00
❏ MS 7087	Vienna, City of Dreams	1968	3.00	6.00	12.00
❏ MS 7108 [S]	Andre Kostelanetz Conducts Great Romantic Ballads	196?	2.50	5.00	10.00
❏ MS 7319	Musical Evenings	1969	2.50	5.00	10.00
❏ MS 7427	Extravaganza	1970	2.50	5.00	10.00
❏ M 30075	Music for Strings	1970	2.50	5.00	10.00
❏ M 35114	Festive Overtures	1978	2.00	4.00	8.00

COLUMBIA SPECIAL PRODUCTS

Number	Title (A Side/B Side)	Yr	VG	VG+	NM
❏ C 10975	Wishing You a Merry Christmas	1972	2.50	5.00	10.00

—Reissue of Columbia Masterworks MS 6779

| ❏ P 13286 | Scarborough Fair | 197? | 2.00 | 4.00 | 8.00 |

HARMONY

Number	Title (A Side/B Side)	Yr	VG	VG+	NM
❏ HL 7368 [M]	You and the Night and the Music	196?	2.50	5.00	10.00
❏ HL 7371 [M]	Broadway Theatre Party	196?	2.50	5.00	10.00
❏ HL 7395 [M]	Grand Canyon Suite	196?	2.50	5.00	10.00
❏ HL 7432 [M]	Joy to the World: Music for Christmas	1967	3.00	6.00	12.00

—Reissue of Columbia 1528

❏ HS 11168 [S]	You and the Night and the Music	196?	2.50	5.00	10.00
❏ HS 11171 [S]	Broadway Theatre Party	196?	2.50	5.00	10.00
❏ HS 11195 [S]	Grand Canyon Suite	196?	2.50	5.00	10.00
❏ HS 11232 [S]	Joy to the World: Music for Christmas	1967	3.00	6.00	12.00

—Reissue of Columbia 8328

❏ HS 11281	The Magic of Music	1968	2.50	5.00	10.00
❏ H 30014	Be My Love	1970	2.50	5.00	10.00
❏ KH 31414	Greatest Hits of Broadway and Hollywood	1972	2.50	5.00	10.00
❏ KH 31500	Love Theme from "The Godfather"	1972	2.50	5.00	10.00
❏ KH 31571	Andre Kostelanetz Plays Richard Rogers	1973	2.50	5.00	10.00
❏ KH 32170	Strike Up the Band	1973	2.50	5.00	10.00

READER'S DIGEST

Number	Title (A Side/B Side)	Yr	VG	VG+	NM
❏ RD-120-A [(8)]	The Best of Andre Kostelanetz	197?	7.50	15.00	30.00

KOTTKE, LEO
45s
CAPITOL

Number	Title (A Side/B Side)	Yr	VG	VG+	NM
❏ 3854	Pamela Brown/A Child Should Be a Fish	1974	—	3.00	6.00
❏ 4177	Can't Quite Put It Into Words/Power Failure	1975	—	2.50	5.00

Albums
CAPITOL

Number	Title (A Side/B Side)	Yr	VG	VG+	NM
❏ ST-682	Mudlark	1971	3.00	6.00	12.00
❏ ST-11000	Greenhouse	1972	2.50	5.00	10.00
❏ ST-11164	My Feet Are Smiling	1973	2.50	5.00	10.00
❏ ST-11262	Ice Water	1974	2.50	5.00	10.00
❏ ST-11335	Dreams and All That Stuff	1974	2.50	5.00	10.00
❏ ST-11446	Chewing Pine	1975	2.50	5.00	10.00
❏ ST-11576	Leo Kottke 1971-1976 — Did You Hear Me?	1976	2.50	5.00	10.00
❏ SWBC-11867 [(2)]	The Best of Leo Kottke	1979	3.00	6.00	12.00
❏ SN-16063	Mudlark	1979	2.00	4.00	8.00

—Budget-line reissue

| ❏ SN-16064 | Ice Water | 1979 | 2.00 | 4.00 | 8.00 |

—Budget-line reissue

| ❏ SN-16065 | Greenhouse | 1979 | 2.00 | 4.00 | 8.00 |

—Budget-line reissue

| ❏ SN-16187 | Dreams and All That Stuff | 1980 | 2.00 | 4.00 | 8.00 |

—Budget-line reissue

| ❏ SN-16188 | Chewing Pine | 1980 | 2.00 | 4.00 | 8.00 |

—Budget-line reissue

| ❏ SN-16189 | Leo Kottke 1971-1976 — Did You Hear Me? | 1980 | 2.00 | 4.00 | 8.00 |

—Budget-line reissue

CHRYSALIS

Number	Title (A Side/B Side)	Yr	VG	VG+	NM
❏ CHR 1106	Leo Kottke	1977	2.50	5.00	10.00
❏ CHR 1191	Burnt Lips	1978	2.50	5.00	10.00
❏ CHR 1234	Balance	1979	2.50	5.00	10.00
❏ CHR 1328	Guitar Music	1981	2.50	5.00	10.00
❏ PV 41106	Leo Kottke	1985	2.00	4.00	8.00

—Budget-line reissue

| ❏ PV 41191 | Burnt Lips | 1985 | 2.00 | 4.00 | 8.00 |

—Budget-line reissue

| ❏ PV 41234 | Balance | 1985 | 2.00 | 4.00 | 8.00 |

—Budget-line reissue

| ❏ PV 41328 | Guitar Music | 1983 | 2.00 | 4.00 | 8.00 |

—Budget-line reissue

| ❏ FV 41411 | Time Step | 1983 | 2.50 | 5.00 | 10.00 |
| ❏ PV 41411 | Time Step | 1986 | 2.00 | 4.00 | 8.00 |

—Budget-line reissue

OBLIVION

Number	Title (A Side/B Side)	Yr	VG	VG+	NM
❏ S-1	12-String Blues/Live at the Scholar Coffee House	1969	6.25	12.50	25.00

PRIVATE MUSIC

Number	Title (A Side/B Side)	Yr	VG	VG+	NM
❏ 2007-1-P	A Shout Toward Noon	1986	2.50	5.00	10.00
❏ 2025-1-P	Regards from Chuck Pink	1988	2.50	5.00	10.00
❏ 2050-1-P	My Father's Face	1989	2.50	5.00	10.00

SYMPOSIUM

Number	Title (A Side/B Side)	Yr	VG	VG+	NM
❏ 2001	Circle Round the Sun	1970	3.00	6.00	12.00

TAKOMA

Number	Title (A Side/B Side)	Yr	VG	VG+	NM
❏ 1024	6 and 12 String Guitar	1969	3.00	6.00	12.00

KOTTKE, LEO/PETER LANG/JOHN FAHEY Also see JOHN FAHEY; LEO KOTTKE.
Albums
TAKOMA

Number	Title (A Side/B Side)	Yr	VG	VG+	NM
❏ 1040	Leo Kottke/Peter Lang/John Fahey	1974	3.00	6.00	12.00

KRAFTWERK
12-Inch Singles
CAPITOL

Number	Title (A Side/B Side)	Yr	VG	VG+	NM
❏ 8502	Showroom Dummies (6:00)/Les Mannequins (6:02)	1977	5.00	10.00	20.00
❏ 8526	Neon Lights (9:03)/The Model	1978	6.25	12.50	25.00

ELEKTRA

| ❏ ED 5551 [DJ] | Robotnik/The Robots/Robotronik | 1991 | 3.00 | 6.00 | 12.00 |

WARNER BROS.

| ❏ PRO-A-951 [DJ] | Pocket Calculator/Dentaku | 1981 | 3.00 | 6.00 | 12.00 |
| ❏ 20549 | Musique Nonstop (LP Version)/Musique Nonstop (7" Version) | 1986 | 2.00 | 4.00 | 8.00 |

45s
CAPITOL

Number	Title (A Side/B Side)	Yr	VG	VG+	NM
❏ 4211	Radioactivity/Antenna	1976	—	2.50	5.00
❏ 4211 [PS]	Radioactivity/Antenna	1976	2.00	4.00	8.00
❏ 4460	Trans-Europe Express/Franz Schubert	1977	—	2.50	5.00
❏ 4620	Neon Lights/The Robots	1978	—	2.50	5.00

VERTIGO

| ❏ 203 | Autobahn/Morgan Spaziergang | 1975 | 2.00 | 4.00 | 8.00 |
| ❏ 204 | Mitternacht (Midnight)/Kometen Melodie (Comet Melody 2) | 1975 | 2.00 | 4.00 | 8.00 |

WARNER BROS.

❏ 28441	The Telephone Call/Der Telefon Anruf	1987	—	—	3.00
❏ 28441 [PS]	The Telephone Call/Der Telefon Anruf	1987	—	—	3.00
❏ 28532	Musique Non-Stop (Long)/Musique Non-Stop (Short)	1986	—	—	2.00
❏ 28532 [PS]	Musique Non-Stop (Long)/Musique Non-Stop (Short)	1986	—	—	2.00
❏ 29342	Tour de France (Remix)/Tour de France (French)	1984	—	—	3.00
❏ 49723	Pocket Calculator/Dentaku	1981	—	—	3.00
❏ 49723	Pocket Calculator/Dentaku	1981	—	2.50	5.00

—Yellow vinyl

| ❏ 49723 [PS] | Pocket Calculator/Dentaku | 1981 | — | 2.50 | 5.00 |

—Plastic sleeve that goes with yellow vinyl pressing

| ❏ 49795 | Numbers/Computer Love | 1981 | — | — | 3.00 |

Albums
CAPITOL

Number	Title (A Side/B Side)	Yr	VG	VG+	NM
❏ ST-11457	Radio-Activity	1975	4.00	8.00	16.00
❏ SW 11603	Trans-Europe Express	1977	4.00	8.00	16.00
❏ SW-11728	The Man-Machine	1978	4.00	8.00	16.00
❏ SN-16301	Trans-Europe Express	198?	2.50	5.00	10.00

—Reissue

| ❏ SN-16302 | The Man-Machine | 198? | 2.50 | 5.00 | 10.00 |

—Reissue

| ❏ SN-16380 | Radio-Activity | 1986 | 2.50 | 5.00 | 10.00 |

—Reissue

ELEKTRA

| ❏ 60789 | Computer World | 1988 | 2.00 | 4.00 | 8.00 |

—Reissue

| ❏ 60797 | Autobahn | 1988 | 2.00 | 4.00 | 8.00 |

—Still another reissue of this album

| ❏ 60798 | Electric Cafe | 1988 | 2.00 | 4.00 | 8.00 |

—Reissue

| ❏ 60869 [(2)] | The Mix | 1991 | 3.00 | 6.00 | 12.00 |

MERCURY

| ❏ SRM-1-3704 | Autobahn | 1977 | 3.75 | 7.50 | 15.00 |

—Reissue of Vertigo VEL-2003

VERTIGO

| ❏ VEL-2003 | Autobahn | 1974 | 5.00 | 10.00 | 20.00 |
| ❏ VEL-2006 | Ralf & Florian | 1976 | 4.00 | 8.00 | 16.00 |

—Recorded in 1973

WARNER BROS.

| ❏ HS 3549 | Computer World | 1981 | 2.50 | 5.00 | 10.00 |
| ❏ 25326 | Autobahn | 1985 | 3.00 | 6.00 | 12.00 |

—Another reissue of Vertigo VEL-2003

| ❏ 25525 | Electric Cafe | 1986 | 3.00 | 6.00 | 12.00 |

KRAMER, BILLY J., AND THE DAKOTAS
45s
EPIC

Number	Title (A Side/B Side)	Yr	VG	VG+	NM
❏ 10331	1941/His Love Is Just a Lie	1968	2.50	5.00	10.00

IMPERIAL

❏ 66027	Little Children/Bad to Me	1964	3.00	6.00	12.00
❏ 66048	I'll Keep You Satisfied/I Know	1964	3.00	6.00	12.00
❏ 66051	From a Window/I'll Be On My Way	1964	3.00	6.00	12.00
❏ 66051 [PS]	From a Window/I'll Be On My Way	1964	6.25	12.50	25.00
❏ 66085	It's Gotta Last Forever/They Remind Me of You	1965	3.00	6.00	12.00
❏ 66115	Trains and Boats and Planes/That's the Way I Feel	1965	2.50	5.00	10.00
❏ 66115	Trains and Boats and Planes/I'll Be On My Way	1965	3.00	6.00	12.00
❏ 66135	Irresistible You/Twilight Time	1965	2.50	5.00	10.00
❏ 66143	I'll Be Doggone/Neon City	1965	2.50	5.00	10.00
❏ 66210	You Make Me Feel Like Someone/Take My Hand	1966	2.50	5.00	10.00

LIBERTY

❏ 55586	Do You Want to Know a Secret/I'll Be On My Way	1963	7.50	15.00	30.00
❏ 55618	The Cruel Surf/The Millionaire	1963	10.00	20.00	40.00
❏ 55626	Bad to Me/I Call Your Name	1963	7.50	15.00	30.00
❏ 55643	I'll Keep You Satisfied/I Know	1963	7.50	15.00	30.00
❏ 55667	Bad to Me/Do You Want to Know a Secret	1964	6.25	12.50	25.00
❏ 55687	Little Children/They Remind Me of You	1964	—	—	—

—Unreleased

Albums
CAPITOL

Number	Title (A Side/B Side)	Yr	VG	VG+	NM
❏ SM-11897 [P]	The Best of Billy J. Kramer and the Dakotas	1979	2.50	5.00	10.00

IMPERIAL

| ❏ LP 9267 [M] | Little Children | 1964 | 7.50 | 15.00 | 30.00 |

—Black and pink label

| ❏ LP 9267 [M] | Little Children | 1964 | 12.50 | 25.00 | 50.00 |

—Black label with stars

❏ LP 9273 [M]	I'll Keep You Satisfied/From a Window	1964	7.50	15.00	30.00
❏ LP 9291 [M]	Trains and Boats and Planes	1965	7.50	15.00	30.00
❏ LP 12267 [P]	Little Children	1964	10.00	20.00	40.00

—Black and pink label

K

Number	Title (A Side/B Side)	Yr	VG	VG+	NM
❏ LP 12267 [P]	Little Children	1964	20.00	40.00	80.00
—Black label with silver print					
❏ LP 12273 [P]	I'll Keep You Satisfied/From a Window	1964	10.00	20.00	40.00
❏ LP 12921 [R]	Trains and Boats and Planes	1965	6.25	12.50	25.00

KREED
Albums
VISION OF SOUND

Number	Title (A Side/B Side)	Yr	VG	VG+	NM
❏ 71-56	Kreed	1971	300.00	600.00	1200.

KRISTOFFERSON, KRIS *Also see WILLIE NELSON.*
45s
COLUMBIA

Number	Title (A Side/B Side)	Yr	VG	VG+	NM
❏ 04881	Highwayman/The Human Condition	1985	—	—	3.00
—A-side: Willie Nelson/Waylon Jennings/Johnny Cash/Kris Kristofferson; B-side: Nelson, Cash					
❏ 04881 [PS]	Highwayman/The Human Condition	1985	—	2.00	4.00
—A-side: Willie Nelson/Waylon Jennings/Johnny Cash/Kris Kristofferson; B-side: Nelson, Cash					
❏ 05594	Desperadoes Waiting for a Train/The Twentieth Century Is Almost Over	1985	—	—	3.00
—A-side: Willie Nelson/Waylon Jennings/Johnny Cash/Kris Kristofferson; B-side: Nelson, Cash					
❏ 08406	Highwayman/Desperadoes Waiting for a Train	1988	—	—	3.00
—Waylon Jennings/Willie Nelson/Johnny Cash/Kris Kristofferson; reissue					
❏ 10525	Watch Closely Now/Crippled Crow	1977	—	2.00	4.00
❏ 10731	The Fighter/Forever in Your Love	1978	—	2.00	4.00
❏ 11160	Prove It to You One More Time Again/Fallen Angel	1979	—	2.00	4.00
❏ 11383	I'll Take Any Chance I Can with You/Maybe You Heard	1980	—	2.00	4.00
❏ 60507	Nobody Loves Anybody Anymore/Maybe You Heard	1981	—	2.00	4.00
❏ 73381	Born and Raised in Black and White/Texas	1990	—	—	3.00
—The Highwaymen (Waylon Jennings/Willie Nelson/Johnny Cash/Kris Kristofferson)					
❏ 73572	American Remains/Texas	1990	—	—	3.00
—The Highwaymen (Waylon Jennings/Willie Nelson/Johnny Cash/Kris Kristofferson)					

EPIC

Number	Title (A Side/B Side)	Yr	VG	VG+	NM
❏ 10225	Golden Idol/Killing Time	1967	3.75	7.50	15.00

LIBERTY

Number	Title (A Side/B Side)	Yr	VG	VG+	NM
❏ S7-18486	It Is What It Is/The Devil's Right Hand	1995	—	—	3.00
—By The Highwaymen					

MERCURY

Number	Title (A Side/B Side)	Yr	VG	VG+	NM
❏ 888345-7	They Killed Him/Anthem '84	1987	—	—	3.00
❏ 888554-7	Love Is the Way/This Old Road	1987	—	—	3.00
❏ 888723-7	El Coyote/They Killed Him	1987	—	—	3.00

MONUMENT

Number	Title (A Side/B Side)	Yr	VG	VG+	NM
❏ 1210	Sunday Morning Comin' Down/To Beat the Devil	1970	2.00	4.00	8.00
❏ 8525	Loving Her Was Easier (Than Anything I'll Ever Do Again)/Epitaph	1971	—	3.00	6.00
❏ 8531	The Taker/Pilgrim: Chapter 33	1971	—	3.00	6.00
❏ 8536	Josie/Border Lord	1972	—	3.00	6.00
❏ 8558	Jesus Was a Capricorn/Enough for You	1972	—	3.00	6.00
❏ 8564	Jesse Younger/Give It Time to Be Tender	1973	—	3.00	6.00
❏ 8571	Why Me/Help Me	1973	—	2.50	5.00
❏ 8618	I May Smoke Too Much/Lights of Magdala	1974	—	2.50	5.00
❏ 8658	Easy, Come On/Rocket to Star	1975	—	2.00	4.00
❏ 8679	If It's All the Same to You/The Year 2000 Minus 25	1975	—	2.00	4.00
❏ 8707	The Prisoner/It's Never Gonna Be the Same Again	1976	—	2.00	4.00
❏ 21000	Here Comes That Rainbow Again/(B-side unknown)	1981	—	2.00	4.00

7-Inch Extended Plays
MONUMENT

Number	Title (A Side/B Side)	Yr	VG	VG+	NM
❏ Z7-31909	Jesus Was a Capricorn/Out of Mind, Out of Sight/Give It Time to Be Tender// It Sure Was (Love)/Nobody Wins/Enough for You	1973	2.00	4.00	8.00
—Jukebox issue; small hole, plays at 33 1/3 rpm					
❏ Z7-31909 [PS]	Jesus Was a Capricorn	1973	2.00	4.00	8.00

Albums
COLUMBIA

Number	Title (A Side/B Side)	Yr	VG	VG+	NM
❏ PZ 30679	The Silver Tongued Devil and I	1976	2.00	4.00	8.00
—Reissue					
❏ PZ 30817	Me and Bobby McGee	1976	2.00	4.00	8.00
—Reissue					
❏ PZ 31302	Border Lord	1976	2.00	4.00	8.00
—Reissue					
❏ PZ 31909	Jesus Was a Capricorn	1976	2.00	4.00	8.00
—Reissue					
❏ PZ 32914	Spooky Lady's Sideshow	1976	2.00	4.00	8.00
—Reissue					
❏ PZ 33379	Who's to Bless…And Who's to Blame	1976	2.00	4.00	8.00
—Reissue					
❏ PZ 34687	Songs of Kristofferson	1977	3.00	6.00	12.00
❏ JZ 35310	Easter Island	1978	3.00	6.00	12.00
❏ JZ 36135	Shake Hands with the Devil	1979	3.00	6.00	12.00
❏ JZ 36885	To the Bone	1980	3.00	6.00	12.00
❏ FC 40056	Highwayman	1985	2.50	5.00	10.00
—Waylon Jennings/Willie Nelson/Johnny Cash/Kris Kristofferson					
❏ C 45240	Highwayman 2	1990	3.75	7.50	15.00
—Waylon Jennings/Willie Nelson/Johnny Cash/Kris Kristofferson					

MERCURY

Number	Title (A Side/B Side)	Yr	VG	VG+	NM
❏ 830406-1	Repossessed	1987	2.50	5.00	10.00

MONUMENT

Number	Title (A Side/B Side)	Yr	VG	VG+	NM
❏ SLP-18139	Kristofferson	1970	6.25	12.50	25.00
—Original label is light green with a yellow ring					
❏ Z 30679	The Silver Tongued Devil and I	1971	3.00	6.00	12.00
❏ ZQ 30679 [Q]	The Silver Tongued Devil and I	1972	5.00	10.00	20.00
❏ Z 30817	Me and Bobby McGee	1971	3.00	6.00	12.00
—Reissue of 18139 with new title					
❏ KZ 31302	Border Lord	1972	3.00	6.00	12.00
❏ ZQ 31302 [Q]	Border Lord	1972	5.00	10.00	20.00
❏ KZ 31909	Jesus Was a Capricorn	1972	3.00	6.00	12.00
❏ ZQ 31909 [Q]	Jesus Was a Capricorn	1973	5.00	10.00	20.00
❏ PZ 32914	Spooky Lady's Sideshow	1974	3.00	6.00	12.00
❏ PZQ 32914 [Q]	Spooky Lady's Sideshow	1974	5.00	10.00	20.00
❏ PZ 33379	Who's to Bless…And Who's to Blame	1975	3.00	6.00	12.00
❏ PZ 34254	Surreal Thing	1976	3.00	6.00	12.00
❏ PW 38392	Songs of Kristofferson	1982	2.00	4.00	8.00
—Reissue of 34687					

PAIR

Number	Title (A Side/B Side)	Yr	VG	VG+	NM
❏ PDL2-1078 [(2)]	My Songs	1986	3.00	6.00	12.00

KRISTOFFERSON, KRIS, AND RITA COOLIDGE *Also see each artist's individual listings.*
45s
A&M

Number	Title (A Side/B Side)	Yr	VG	VG+	NM
❏ 1475	A Song I'd Like to Sing/From the Bottle to the Bottom	1973	—	2.00	4.00
❏ 1475 [PS]	A Song I'd Like to Sing/From the Bottle to the Bottom	1973	—	3.00	6.00
❏ 1498	Loving Arms/I'm Down	1974	—	2.00	4.00
❏ 2121	Not Everyone Knows/Blue As I Do	1979	—	2.00	4.00

MONUMENT

Number	Title (A Side/B Side)	Yr	VG	VG+	NM
❏ 8630	Rain/What'cha Gonna Do	1974	—	2.00	4.00
❏ 8636	Lover Please/Slow Down	1975	—	2.00	4.00
❏ 8646	We Must Have Been Out of Our Minds/Sweet Susannah	1975	—	2.00	4.00

Albums
A&M

Number	Title (A Side/B Side)	Yr	VG	VG+	NM
❏ SP-4403	Full Moon	1973	3.00	6.00	12.00
❏ SP-4690	Natural Act	1979	2.50	5.00	10.00

MONUMENT

Number	Title (A Side/B Side)	Yr	VG	VG+	NM
❏ PZ 33278	Breakaway	1974	3.00	6.00	12.00

KRISTYL
Albums
(NO LABEL)

Number	Title (A Side/B Side)	Yr	VG	VG+	NM
❏ (no #)	Kristyl	1975	50.00	100.00	200.00

KUBAN, BOB, AND THE IN-MEN
45s
MUSICLAND U.S.A.

Number	Title (A Side/B Side)	Yr	VG	VG+	NM
❏ 20001	The Cheater/Try Me Baby	1966	2.50	5.00	10.00
—With no mention of "Vocal by Walter Scott"					
❏ 20001	The Cheater/Try Me Baby	1966	3.00	6.00	12.00
—With "Vocal by Walter Scott" on only B-side label					
❏ 20001	The Cheater/Try Me Baby	1966	5.00	10.00	20.00
—With "Vocal by Walter Scott" on both sides' labels					
❏ 20006	The Teaser/All I Want	1966	2.50	5.00	10.00
❏ 20007	Drive My Car/The Pretzel	1966	2.50	5.00	10.00
❏ 20013	Harlem Shuffle/Theme from "Virginia Wolff"	1967	2.00	4.00	8.00
❏ 20017	Batman Theme/You Better Run, You Better Hide	1967	2.00	4.00	8.00

NORMAN

Number	Title (A Side/B Side)	Yr	VG	VG+	NM
❏ 558	Jerkin' Time/Turn On Your Lovelight	1965	3.00	6.00	12.00
❏ 567	Little Girl/I Don't Want to Know	1965	3.00	6.00	12.00

REPRISE

Number	Title (A Side/B Side)	Yr	VG	VG+	NM
❏ 0937	Soul Man/Hard to Handle	1970	2.00	4.00	8.00

Albums
MUSICLAND U.S.A.

Number	Title (A Side/B Side)	Yr	VG	VG+	NM
❏ LP-3500 [M]	Look Out for the Cheater	1966	7.50	15.00	30.00
❏ SLP-3500 [S]	Look Out for the Cheater	1966	10.00	20.00	40.00

KUF-LINX, THE
45s
CHALLENGE

Number	Title (A Side/B Side)	Yr	VG	VG+	NM
❏ 1013	So Tough/What'cha Gonna Do	1957	10.00	20.00	40.00
❏ 1013	So Tough/What'cha Gonna Do	1958	6.25	12.50	25.00
❏ 59004	Eyeballin'/Service with a Smile	1958	3.75	7.50	15.00
❏ 59015	Climb Love Mountain/All That's Good	1958	3.75	7.50	15.00
❏ 59102	So Tough/What'cha Gonna Do	1961	3.00	6.00	12.00

KULIS, CHARLIE
45s
PLAYBOY

Number	Title (A Side/B Side)	Yr	VG	VG+	NM
❏ 6023	Runaway/When I See Her	1975	—	2.50	5.00
❏ 6044	Save a Rose for Me/Somebody Help Me Now	1975	—	2.50	5.00

KUSTOM KINGS, THE *BRUCE JOHNSTON appears on the below.*
45s
SMASH

Number	Title (A Side/B Side)	Yr	VG	VG+	NM
❏ 1883	In My '40 Ford/Clutch Rider	1964	12.50	25.00	50.00

Albums
SMASH

Number	Title (A Side/B Side)	Yr	VG	VG+	NM
❏ MGS-27051 [M]	Kustom City, U.S.A.	1964	30.00	60.00	120.00
❏ SRS-67051 [S]	Kustom City, U.S.A.	1964	50.00	100.00	200.00

KWESKIN, JIM
45s
REPRISE

Number	Title (A Side/B Side)	Yr	VG	VG+	NM
❏ 0624	The Sheik of Araby/Minglewood	1967	2.00	4.00	8.00

VANGUARD

Number	Title (A Side/B Side)	Yr	VG	VG+	NM
❏ 35027	Rag Momma/Don't You Leave Me Here	1964	2.50	5.00	10.00

Albums
MOUNTAIN RAILROAD

Number	Title (A Side/B Side)	Yr	VG	VG+	NM
❏ MR-52672	Jug Band Blues	198?	2.50	5.00	10.00
❏ MR-52782	Jim Kweskin Lives Again	198?	2.50	5.00	10.00
❏ MR-52790	Side by Side	198?	2.50	5.00	10.00
❏ MR-52793	Swing on a Star	198?	2.50	5.00	10.00

REPRISE

Number	Title (A Side/B Side)	Yr	VG	VG+	NM
❏ R 6266 [M]	Garden of Joy	1967	5.00	10.00	20.00
❏ RS 6266 [S]	Garden of Joy	1967	3.75	7.50	15.00
❏ RS 6464	America	1971	3.75	7.50	15.00

VANGUARD

Number	Title (A Side/B Side)	Yr	VG	VG+	NM
❏ VSD 13/14 [(2)]	Greatest Hits	1970	3.75	7.50	15.00
❏ VSD-2158 [S]	Jim Kweskin and the Jug Band	1963	6.25	12.50	25.00
❏ VRS-9139 [M]	Jim Kweskin and the Jug Band	1963	5.00	10.00	20.00
❏ VRS-9163 [M]	Jug Band Music	1965	5.00	10.00	20.00
❏ VRS-9188 [M]	Relax Your Mind	1966	5.00	10.00	20.00
❏ VRS-9234 [M]	See Reverse Side for Title	1967	5.00	10.00	20.00
❏ VRS-9243 [M]	Jump for Joy	1967	5.00	10.00	20.00
❏ VRS-9270 [M]	The Best of Jim Kweskin and the Jug Band	1968	10.00	20.00	40.00
❏ VSD-79163 [S]	Jug Band Music	1965	6.25	12.50	25.00
❏ VSD-79188 [S]	Relax Your Mind	1966	6.25	12.50	25.00
❏ VSD-79234 [S]	See Reverse Side for Title	1967	6.25	12.50	25.00
❏ VSD-79243 [S]	Jump for Joy	1967	5.00	10.00	20.00
❏ VSD-79270 [S]	The Best of Jim Kweskin and the Jug Band	1968	3.75	7.50	15.00

Number	Title (A Side/B Side)	Yr	VG	VG+	NM

L

L.T.D.
45s
A&M

Number	Title (A Side/B Side)	Yr	VG	VG+	NM
❑ 1514	Elegant Love/Success	1974	—	2.50	5.00
❑ 1537	What Goes Around/To the Bone	1974	—	2.50	5.00
❑ 1665	Don't Lose Your Cool/Thank You Mother	1975	—	2.50	5.00
❑ 1681	Trying to Find a Way/I Told You I'd Be Back	1975	—	2.50	5.00
❑ 1731	Rated X/Ain't No Way	1975	—	2.50	5.00
❑ 1847	Love Ballad/Let the Music Keep Playing	1976	—	2.50	5.00
❑ 1847 [PS]	Love Ballad/Let the Music Keep Playing	1976	—	3.00	6.00
❑ 1897	Love to the World/Get Your It Together	1976	—	2.50	5.00
❑ 1974	(Every Time I Turn Around) Back in Love Again/ Material Things	1977	—	2.50	5.00
❑ 1974 [PS]	(Every Time I Turn Around) Back in Love Again/ Material Things	1977	2.00	4.00	8.00
❑ 2005	Never Get Enough of Your Love/Make Someone Smile Today	1978	—	2.50	5.00
❑ 2005 [PS]	Never Get Enough of Your Love/Make Someone Smile Today	1978	—	3.00	6.00
❑ 2057	Holding On (When Love Is Gone)/Together Forever	1978	—	2.50	5.00
❑ 2095	We Both Deserve Each Other's Love/It's Time to Be Real	1978	—	2.50	5.00
❑ 2142	Dance "N" Sing "N"/Give It All	1979	—	2.50	5.00
❑ 2142 [PS]	Dance "N" Sing "N"/Give It All	1979	—	3.00	6.00
❑ 2176	Share My Love/Sometimes	1979	—	2.50	5.00
❑ 2192	Stranger/Sometimes	1979	—	2.50	5.00
❑ 2250	Where Did We Go Wrong/Stand Up L.T.D.	1980	—	2.50	5.00
❑ 2283	Shine On/Love Is What You Need	1980	—	2.50	5.00
❑ 2346	Shine On (Spanish Version)/Where Did We Go Wrong	1981	—	2.50	5.00
❑ 2382	Kickin' Back/Now	1981	—	2.50	5.00
❑ 2395	April Love/Stay on the One	1982	—	2.50	5.00
❑ 2414	Cuttin' It Up/Love Magic	1982	—	2.00	4.00

MONTAGE

Number	Title (A Side/B Side)	Yr	VG	VG+	NM
❑ 908	For You/Party with You (All Night)	1983	—	2.00	4.00

Albums
A&M

Number	Title (A Side/B Side)	Yr	VG	VG+	NM
❑ SP-3119	L.T.D.	198?	2.00	4.00	8.00
—Budget-line reissue					
❑ SP-3146	Love to the World	198?	2.00	4.00	8.00
—Budget-line reissue					
❑ SP-3148	Something to Love	198?	2.00	4.00	8.00
—Budget-line reissue					
❑ SP-3602	L.T.D.	1974	3.00	6.00	12.00
❑ SP-3660	Gittin' Down	1975	3.00	6.00	12.00
❑ SP-4589	Love to the World	1976	2.50	5.00	10.00
❑ SP-4646	Something to Love	1977	2.50	5.00	10.00
❑ SP-4705	Togetherness	1978	2.50	5.00	10.00
❑ SP-4771	Devotion	1979	2.50	5.00	10.00
❑ SP-4819	Shine On	1980	2.50	5.00	10.00
❑ SP-4881	Love Magic	1981	2.50	5.00	10.00

LA LUPE
45s
ROULETTE

Number	Title (A Side/B Side)	Yr	VG	VG+	NM
❑ 7043	Down on Me/Touch Me	1969	2.00	4.00	8.00
❑ 7054	Don't Ever Leave Me/(B-side unknown)	1969	2.00	4.00	8.00
❑ 7141	Unchained Melody/Carlos Dominguez	1973	—	3.00	6.00

Albums
ROULETTE

Number	Title (A Side/B Side)	Yr	VG	VG+	NM
❑ SR-42024	The Queen Does Her Thing	1969	7.50	15.00	30.00

LABEEF, SLEEPY
45s
COLUMBIA

Number	Title (A Side/B Side)	Yr	VG	VG+	NM
❑ 43452	Everybody's Got to Have Somebody (To Love)/ You Can't Catch Me	1965	3.00	6.00	12.00
❑ 43875	I Feel a Lot More Like I Do Now/I'm Too Broke	1966	3.00	6.00	12.00
❑ 44068	Sure Beats the Heck Out of Settlin' Down/ Schneider	1967	2.50	5.00	10.00
❑ 44261	Completely Destroyed/Go Ahead On Baby	1967	2.50	5.00	10.00
❑ 44455	Every Day/If I'm Right I'm Wrong	1968	2.50	5.00	10.00

CRESCENT

Number	Title (A Side/B Side)	Yr	VG	VG+	NM
❑ 102	Turn Me Loose/(B-side unknown)	195?	50.00	100.00	200.00

MERCURY

Number	Title (A Side/B Side)	Yr	VG	VG+	NM
❑ 71112	I'm Through/All Alone	1957	25.00	50.00	100.00
❑ 71179	All the Time/Lonely	1957	25.00	50.00	100.00

PICTURE

Number	Title (A Side/B Side)	Yr	VG	VG+	NM
❑ 1937	Ride On Josephine/(B-side unknown)	1959	37.50	75.00	150.00

PLANTATION

Number	Title (A Side/B Side)	Yr	VG	VG+	NM
❑ 55	Too Much Monkey Business/Got You on My Mind	1970	6.25	12.50	25.00
❑ 66	Asphalt Cowboy/Got You on My Mind	1971	2.50	5.00	10.00
❑ 74	Blackland Farmer/Got You on My Mind	1971	2.50	5.00	10.00
❑ 74 [DJ]	Blackland Farmer (mono/stereo)	1971	3.00	6.00	12.00
—Promo only on green vinyl					

STARDAY

Number	Title (A Side/B Side)	Yr	VG	VG+	NM
❑ 292	I'm Through/All Alone	1957	37.50	75.00	150.00

SUN

Number	Title (A Side/B Side)	Yr	VG	VG+	NM
❑ 1132	Thunder Road/A Hundred Pounds of Lovin'	1974	—	2.00	4.00
❑ 1133 [DJ]	Ghost Riders in the Sky (same on both sides)	1975	—	2.00	4.00
—Promo only					
❑ 1134	There Ain't Much After Taxes/ A Hundred Pounds of Lovin'	1976	—	2.00	4.00
❑ 1137	Good Rockin' Boogie (Part 1)/ Good rockin' Boogie (Part 2)	1978	—	2.00	4.00
❑ 1145	Flying Saucers Rock and Roll/ Boogie Woogie Country Girl	1979	—	2.00	4.00

WAYSIDE

Number	Title (A Side/B Side)	Yr	VG	VG+	NM
❑ 1651	Ride On Josephine/(B-side unknown)	1959	50.00	100.00	200.00
—Wayside titles as "Tommy LaBeef"					
❑ 1652	Walkin' Slowly/(B-side unknown)	1959	62.50	125.00	250.00
❑ 1654	Tore Up/Lonely	1959	75.00	150.00	300.00

Albums
ROUNDER

Number	Title (A Side/B Side)	Yr	VG	VG+	NM
❑ 3052	It Ain't What You Eat...	198?	2.50	5.00	10.00
❑ 3070	Electricity	198?	2.50	5.00	10.00
❑ 3072	Nothin' But the Truth	198?	2.50	5.00	10.00

SUN

Number	Title (A Side/B Side)	Yr	VG	VG+	NM
❑ 130	Bull's Night Out	1974	3.00	6.00	12.00
❑ 138	Western Gold	197?	3.00	6.00	12.00
❑ 1004	Rockabilly 1977	1977	3.00	6.00	12.00
❑ 1018	Downtown Rockabilly	1978	3.00	6.00	12.00

LABELLE   Also see PATTI LaBELLE; PATTI LaBELLE AND THE BLUE BELLES.
45s
EPIC

Number	Title (A Side/B Side)	Yr	VG	VG+	NM
❑ 50048	Lady Marmalade/Space Children	1974	—	3.00	6.00
❑ 50097	Night Bird/What Can I Do for You	1975	—	3.00	6.00
❑ 50140	Messin' My Mind/Take the Night Off	1975	—	3.00	6.00
❑ 50168	Slow Burn/Far As We Felt Like Going	1975	—	3.00	6.00
❑ 50262	Get You Somebody New/Who's Watching the Watcher	1976	—	3.00	6.00
❑ 50315	Isn't It a Shame/Gypsy Moths	1976	—	3.00	6.00

RCA VICTOR

Number	Title (A Side/B Side)	Yr	VG	VG+	NM
❑ 74-0965	Open Up Your Heart/Going Up a Holiday	1973	2.00	4.00	8.00
❑ APBO-0157	Mr. Sunshine Man/Sunshine	1973	2.00	4.00	8.00

WARNER BROS.

Number	Title (A Side/B Side)	Yr	VG	VG+	NM
❑ 7512	Morning Much Better/Shades of Difference	1971	2.00	4.00	8.00
❑ 7579	Moonshadow/If I Can't Have You	1972	2.00	4.00	8.00
❑ 7624	Touch Me All Over/Ain't It Sad It's All Over	1972	2.00	4.00	8.00

Albums
EPIC

Number	Title (A Side/B Side)	Yr	VG	VG+	NM
❑ KE 33075	Nightbirds	1974	3.00	6.00	12.00
❑ PE 33075	Nightbirds	197?	2.00	4.00	8.00
—Reissue with new prefix					
❑ PEQ 33075 [Q]	Nightbirds	1975	5.00	10.00	20.00
❑ PE 33579	Phoenix	1975	2.50	5.00	10.00
❑ PEQ 33579 [Q]	Phoenix	1975	3.75	7.50	15.00
❑ PE 34189	Chameleon	1976	2.50	5.00	10.00
—Original with no bar code and orange label					
❑ PE 34189	Chameleon	198?	2.00	4.00	8.00
—Reissue with bar code and dark blue label					

RCA VICTOR

Number	Title (A Side/B Side)	Yr	VG	VG+	NM
❑ APL1-0205	Pressure Cookin'	1973	3.00	6.00	12.00
❑ AYL1-4176	Pressure Cookin'	1982	2.00	4.00	8.00
—"Best Buy Series" reissue					

WARNER BROS.

Number	Title (A Side/B Side)	Yr	VG	VG+	NM
❑ WS 1943	LaBelle	1971	3.75	7.50	15.00
❑ BS 2618	Moonshadow	1972	3.75	7.50	15.00

LABELLE, PATTI   Also see LaBELLE; PATTI LaBELLE AND THE BLUE BELLES.
12-Inch Singles
EPIC

Number	Title (A Side/B Side)	Yr	VG	VG+	NM
❑ 50664	Music Is My Way of Life (2 versions)	1979	3.00	6.00	12.00

MCA

Number	Title (A Side/B Side)	Yr	VG	VG+	NM
❑ 1131 [DJ]	'Twas Love/Reason for the Season	1990	2.00	4.00	8.00
❑ 2074 [DJ]	Somebody Loves You Baby (4 versions)	1991	2.00	4.00	8.00
❑ 2433 [DJ]	All Right Now (6 versions)	1992	2.00	4.00	8.00
❑ 3140 [DJ]	All This Love (3 versions)	1994	2.00	4.00	8.00
❑ 3160 [DJ]	All This Love (4 versions)	1994	2.00	4.00	8.00
❑ L33-17339 [DJ]	Just the Facts (same on both sides)	1987	2.00	4.00	8.00
❑ L33-18014 [DJ]	Yo Mister (same on both sides)	1989	2.00	4.00	8.00
❑ L33-18108 [DJ]	I Can't Complain/(Instrumental)	1989	2.00	4.00	8.00
❑ 23534	New Attitude (Extended Mix)/Axel F (Extended Mix)	1985	2.50	5.00	10.00
—B-side by Harold Faltermeyer					
❑ 23567	Stir It Up (3 versions)	1985	2.50	5.00	10.00
❑ 23607	On My Own/Stir It Up	1986	—	3.00	6.00
—A-side with Michael McDonald					
❑ 23649	Something Special (5 versions)	1986	2.00	4.00	8.00
❑ 23651	Oh, People (Extended)/(Instrumental)	1986	2.00	4.00	8.00
❑ 23773	Just the Facts (4 versions)	1987	2.50	5.00	10.00
❑ 23984	Yo Mister (3 versions)	1989	2.00	4.00	8.00
❑ 54541	All Right Now (Extended) (Remix) (Dub)	1992	2.00	4.00	8.00
❑ 54851	The Right Kinda Lover (Fusion Extended Remix) (Def Jam Remix) (Club Remix)	1994	2.50	5.00	10.00
❑ 54933	All This Love (Hip Hop Mix) (Patti's Buttah Mix)/ Our World	1994	2.00	4.00	8.00
❑ 55113	Turn It Out (4 mixes)	1995	2.00	4.00	8.00

PHILADELPHIA INT'L.

Number	Title (A Side/B Side)	Yr	VG	VG+	NM
❑ 04176	If Only You Knew/I'll Never, Never Give Up	1983	2.50	5.00	10.00
❑ 05296	Shy (Remix)/Shy (Dub Mix)	1985	2.00	4.00	8.00

45s
ARISTA

Number	Title (A Side/B Side)	Yr	VG	VG+	NM
❑ 12929	My Love, Sweet Love/Sittin' Up in My Room	1996	—	—	3.00
—B-side by Brandy					

BEVERLY GLEN

Number	Title (A Side/B Side)	Yr	VG	VG+	NM
❑ 2012	Love Has Finally Come at Last/American Dream	1984	—	2.00	4.00
—With Bobby Womack					
❑ 2018	It Takes a Lot of Strength to Say Goodbye/ Who's Foolin' Who	1984	—	2.00	4.00
—With Bobby Womack					

ELEKTRA

Number	Title (A Side/B Side)	Yr	VG	VG+	NM
❑ 69887	The Best Is Yet to Come/Bye Bye Love	1982	—	2.00	4.00
—With Grover Washington Jr.					

EPIC

Number	Title (A Side/B Side)	Yr	VG	VG+	NM
❑ 50445	Joy to Have Your Love/Do I Stand a Chance	1977	—	3.00	6.00
❑ 50487	You Are My Friend/I Think About You	1977	—	3.00	6.00
❑ 50510	Since I Don't Have You/Dan Swit Me	1978	—	3.00	6.00
❑ 50550	Teach Me Tonight/Quiet Time	1978	—	3.00	6.00
❑ 50583	Little Girls/You Make It So Hard	1978	—	3.00	6.00
❑ 50659	It's Alright with Me/Music Is My Way of Life	1979	—	2.50	5.00
❑ 50718	Music Is My Way of Life/ My Best Was Good Enough	1979	—	2.50	5.00
❑ 50763	Love Is Just a Touch Away/Love and Learn	1979	—	2.50	5.00
❑ 50852	Come and Dance with Me/Release	1980	—	2.50	5.00

Number	Title (A Side/B Side)	Yr	VG	VG+	NM
❏ 50872	I Don't Go Shopping/Come and Dance with Me	1980	—	2.50	5.00
❏ 50910	Ain't That Enough/Don't Make Your Angel Cry	1980	—	2.50	5.00
MCA					
❏ 52517	New Attitude/Shoot Out	1984	—	2.00	4.00
—B-side by Harold Faltermeyer					
❏ 52517 [PS]	New Attitude/Shoot Out	1984	—	2.00	4.00
❏ 52610	Stir It Up/The Discovery	1985	—	2.00	4.00
—B-side by Harold Faltermeyer					
❏ 52610 [PS]	Stir It Up/The Discovery	1985	—	2.00	4.00
❏ 52770	On My Own/Stir It Up	1986	—	—	3.00
—A-side with Michael McDonald					
❏ 52770 [PS]	On My Own/Stir It Up	1986	—	2.00	4.00
❏ 52876	Something Special (Is Gonna Happen Tonight)/(Instrumental)	1986	—	—	3.00
❏ 52877	Oh, People/Love Attack	1986	—	—	3.00
❏ 52877 [PS]	Oh, People/Love Attack	1986	—	2.00	4.00
❏ 52945	Kiss Away the Pain/(Instrumental)	1986	—	—	3.00
❏ 53064	The Last Unbroken Heart/Miami Vice: New York Theme	1987	—	—	3.00
—A-side with Bill Champlin; B-side by Harold Faltermeyer					
❏ 53064 [PS]	The Last Unbroken Heart/Miami Vice: New York Theme	1987	—	—	3.00
❏ 53100	Just the Facts/(Instrumental)	1987	—	—	3.00
❏ 53358	If You Asked Me To/(Instrumental)	1988	—	—	3.00
❏ 53728	Yo Mister/I Can Fly	1989	—	—	3.00
❏ 53774	I Can't Complain/I Can Fly	1989	—	—	3.00
❏ 54481	When You Love Somebody (I'm Saving My Love for You)/Temptation	1992	—	—	3.00
❏ 54513	All Right Now/All Right Now (Remix Dub)	1992	—	—	3.00
❏ 54673	The Right Kinda Lover/(Instrumental)	1993	—	—	3.00
PHILADELPHIA INT'L.					
❏ 02309	Rocking Pneumonia and the Boogie Woogie Flu/Over the Rainbow	1981	—	2.00	4.00
❏ 02655	The Spirit's In It/The Family	1981	—	2.00	4.00
❏ 04248	If Only You Knew/I'll Never, Never Give Up	1983	—	2.00	4.00
❏ 04399	I'm in Love Again/Love, Need and Want It	1984	—	2.00	4.00
❏ 05436	I Can't Forget You/Living Doubt	1985	—	2.00	4.00
❏ 05755	If You Don't Know Me By Now/(Instrumental)	1986	—	2.00	4.00
❏ 05877	Look to the Rainbow/What Can I Do for You	1986	—	2.00	4.00
Albums					
EPIC					
❏ PE 34847	Patti LaBelle	1977	2.50	5.00	10.00
—Original with no bar code and orange label					
❏ PE 34847	Patti LaBelle	1986	2.00	4.00	8.00
—Reissue with bar code and dark blue label					
❏ JE 35335	Tasty	1978	2.50	5.00	10.00
❏ JE 35772	It's Alright with Me	1979	2.50	5.00	10.00
❏ JE 36381	Released	1980	2.50	5.00	10.00
❏ FE 36997	Best of Patti LaBelle	1981	2.50	5.00	10.00
❏ PE 36997	Best of Patti LaBelle	198?	2.00	4.00	8.00
—Budget-line reissue					
MCA					
❏ 5737	Winner in You	1986	2.50	5.00	10.00
❏ 6292	Be Yourself	1989	2.50	5.00	10.00
❏ 10439	Burnin'	1991	3.00	6.00	12.00
PHILADELPHIA INT'L.					
❏ FZ 37380	The Spirit's In It	1981	2.50	5.00	10.00
❏ PZ 37380	The Spirit's In It	198?	2.00	4.00	8.00
—Budget-line reissue					
❏ FZ 38539	I'm in Love Again	1983	2.50	5.00	10.00
❏ FZ 40020	Patti	1985	2.50	5.00	10.00

LABELLE, PATTI, AND THE BLUE BELLES Also see THE BLUE BELLES; LaBELLE.
45s

Number	Title (A Side/B Side)	Yr	VG	VG+	NM
ATLANTIC					
❏ 2311	All or Nothing/You Forgot How to Love	1965	3.00	6.00	12.00
❏ 2318	A Groovy Kind of Love/Over the Rainbow	1966	2.50	5.00	10.00
❏ 2333	Ebb Tide/Patti's Prayer	1966	2.50	5.00	10.00
❏ 2347	I'm Still Waiting/Family Man	1966	2.50	5.00	10.00
❏ 2373	Take Me for a Little While/I Don't Want to Go On Without You	1967	2.50	5.00	10.00
❏ 2390	(There's) Always Something There to Remind Me/Tender Words	1967	2.50	5.00	10.00
❏ 2408	Unchained Melody/Dreamer	1967	2.50	5.00	10.00
❏ 2446	Oh My Love/I Need Your Love	1967	2.50	5.00	10.00
❏ 2548	He's My Man/Wonderful	1968	2.50	5.00	10.00
❏ 2610	Dance to the Rhythm of Love/He's Alone	1969	2.50	5.00	10.00
❏ 2629	Loving Blues/Pride's No Match for Love	1969	2.50	5.00	10.00
❏ 2712	Suffer/Trustin' in You	1970	2.50	5.00	10.00
KING					
❏ 5777	Down the Aisle (Wedding Song)/C'est La Vie	1963	3.75	7.50	15.00
LOST-NITE					
❏ 250	You'll Never Walk Alone/Decatur Street	196?	—	2.50	5.00
—Reissue					
❏ 251	Down the Aisle (Wedding Song)/C'est La Vie	196?	—	2.50	5.00
—Reissue					
❏ 252	I Sold My Heart to the Junkman/Itty Bitty Twist	196?	—	2.50	5.00
—Reissue					
NEWTIME					
❏ 510	Love Me Just a Little/The Joke's On You	1962	5.00	10.00	20.00
NEWTOWN					
❏ 5000	I Sold My Heart to the Junkman/Itty Bitty Twist	1962	5.00	10.00	20.00
—Credited to "The Blue-Belles" but actually recorded by The Starlets					
❏ 5006	I Found a New Love/Pitter Patter	1962	5.00	10.00	20.00
—Most of the Newtown sides credit "The Blue-Belles"					
❏ 5007	Tear After Tear/Go On, This Is Goodbye	1962	5.00	10.00	20.00
❏ 5009	Cool Water/When Johnny Comes Marching Home	1962	5.00	10.00	20.00
❏ 5019	Academy Award/Decatur Street	1963	5.00	10.00	20.00
❏ 5777	Down the Aisle (Wedding Song)/C'est La Vie	1963	3.75	7.50	15.00
NICETOWN					
❏ 5020	You'll Never Walk Alone/Where Are You	1963	3.75	7.50	15.00
PARKWAY					
❏ 896	You'll Never Walk Alone/Decatur Street	1964	3.00	6.00	12.00
❏ 896 [PS]	You'll Never Walk Alone/Decatur Street	1964	20.00	40.00	80.00
❏ 913	One Phone Call/You Will Fill My Eyes No More	1964	3.00	6.00	12.00

Number	Title (A Side/B Side)	Yr	VG	VG+	NM
❏ 935	Danny Boy/I Believe	1964	3.00	6.00	12.00
PEAK					
❏ 7042	I've Got to Let Him Know/I Sold My Heart to the Junkman	1962	6.25	12.50	25.00
—Credited to "The Blue-Belles" but actually recorded by The Starlets					
❏ 7042 [PS]	I've Got to Let Him Know/I Sold My Heart to the Junkman	1962	20.00	40.00	80.00
Albums					
ATLANTIC					
❏ 8119 [M]	Over the Rainbow	1966	7.50	15.00	30.00
❏ SD 8119 [S]	Over the Rainbow	1966	10.00	20.00	40.00
❏ 8147 [M]	Dreamer	1967	7.50	15.00	30.00
❏ SD 8147 [S]	Dreamer	1967	10.00	20.00	40.00
MISTLETOE					
❏ MLP-1204	Merry Christmas from LaBelle	1976	5.00	10.00	20.00
NEWTOWN					
❏ 631 [M]	Sweethearts of the Apollo	1963	100.00	200.00	400.00
❏ 632 [M]	Sleigh Bells, Jingle Bells and Blue Bells	1963	75.00	150.00	300.00
PARKWAY					
❏ P-7043 [M]	The Bluebelles On Stage	1965	30.00	60.00	120.00
—Without bonus single					
❏ P-7043 [M]	The Bluebelles On Stage	1965	37.50	75.00	150.00
—With bonus single					
TRIP					
❏ 3508	Patti LaBelle and the Bluebelles	197?	2.50	5.00	10.00
❏ 8000	Patti LaBelle and the Bluebelles' Greatest Hits	1971	2.50	5.00	10.00
❏ 9525	Early Hits	197?	2.50	5.00	10.00
UNITED ARTISTS					
❏ UA-LA504-E	The Very Best of Patti LaBelle and the Bluebelles	1975	2.50	5.00	10.00

LACEWING
45s

Number	Title (A Side/B Side)	Yr	VG	VG+	NM
MAINSTREAM					
❏ 731	Paradox/(B-side unknown)	1971	3.00	6.00	12.00
Albums					
MAINSTREAM					
❏ S-6132	Lacewing	1971	12.50	25.00	50.00

LADD, CHERYL Also see JOSIE AND THE PUSSYCATS.
45s

Number	Title (A Side/B Side)	Yr	VG	VG+	NM
CAPITOL					
❏ 4215	Country Love/He's Lookin' More Everyday Like the Man Who Broke My Heart	1976	—	2.50	5.00
❏ 4599	Think It Over/Here Is a Song	1978	—	2.00	4.00
❏ 4599 [PS]	Think It Over/Here Is a Song	1978	—	3.00	6.00
❏ 4650	Good Good Lovin'/Skinnydippin'	1978	—	2.00	4.00
❏ 4650 [PS]	Good Good Lovin'/Skinnydippin'	1978	—	3.00	6.00
❏ 4698	Missing You/Thunder in the Distance	1979	—	2.00	4.00
❏ B-5115	Can't Say No to You/You Make It Beautiful	1982	—	2.00	4.00
—With Frankie Valli					
❏ B-5115 [PS]	Can't Say No to You/You Make It Beautiful	1982	—	2.00	4.00
WARNER BROS.					
❏ 7821	Mama Don't Be Blue/The Family	1974	—	3.00	6.00
❏ 7821 [PS]	Mama Don't Be Blue/The Family	1974	2.50	5.00	10.00
Albums					
CAPITOL					
❏ SW-11808	Cheryl Ladd	1978	3.00	6.00	12.00
❏ ST-11927	Dance Forever	1979	3.00	6.00	12.00

LADDERS, THE
45s

Number	Title (A Side/B Side)	Yr	VG	VG+	NM
HOLIDAY					
❏ 2611	Counting the Stars/I Want to Know	1957	75.00	150.00	300.00
—Red label, double lines					
❏ 2611	Counting the Stars/I Want to Know	196?	20.00	40.00	80.00
—Red label, single line					
LOST-NITE					
❏ 178	My Love Is Gone/Hey, Pretty Baby	196?	—	3.00	6.00
—Reissue					
❏ 191	Counting the Stars/I Want to Know	196?	—	3.00	6.00
—Reissue					
VEST					
❏ 826	My Love Is Gone/Hey, Pretty Baby	1959	37.50	75.00	150.00
—No stars around "Vest" logo					
❏ 826	My Love Is Gone/Hey, Pretty Baby	1960	12.50	25.00	50.00
—With stars around "Vest" logo					

LADY BUGS, THE May be three different groups, two different groups, or all the same group.
45s

Number	Title (A Side/B Side)	Yr	VG	VG+	NM
CHATTAHOOCHIE					
❏ 637	How Do You Do It/Liverpool	1964	3.75	7.50	15.00
DEL-FI					
❏ 4233	Sooner or Later/It's the Last Time	1964	5.00	10.00	20.00
LEGRAND					
❏ 1033	Who Sends the Love Note/Fraternity U.S.A.	1964	5.00	10.00	20.00

LADYBIRDS, THE
45s

Number	Title (A Side/B Side)	Yr	VG	VG+	NM
ATCO					
❏ 6329	Memories/Lady Bird	1964	3.00	6.00	12.00
LAWN					
❏ 231	Handsome Boy/Yes I Know	1964	2.50	5.00	10.00

LAFLORE, JOHNNY
45s

Number	Title (A Side/B Side)	Yr	VG	VG+	NM
HIT					
❏ 195	Ferry Cross the Mersey/Berlin Melody	1965	2.00	4.00	8.00
—B-side by the Music City Orchestra					

LAINE, DENNY Also see THE MOODY BLUES; WINGS.
45s

Number	Title (A Side/B Side)	Yr	VG	VG+	NM
ARISTA					
❏ 0511	Japanese Tears/Guess I'm Only Fooling	1980	—	2.00	4.00
CAPITOL					
❏ 4340	It's So Easy-Listen to Me/I'm Lookin' for Someone to Love	1976	—	3.00	6.00

Number	Title (A Side/B Side)	Yr	VG	VG+	NM
❑ 4425	Heartbeat/Moondreams	1977	—	3.00	6.00
DERAM					
❑ 7509	Ask the People/Say You Don't Mind	1967	3.75	7.50	15.00
Albums					
CAPITOL					
❑ ST-11588	Holly Days	1977	3.75	7.50	15.00
REPRISE					
❑ MS 2190	Ah, Laine!	1972	3.00	6.00	12.00
TAKOMA					
❑ 7034	Japanese Tears	1983	2.50	5.00	10.00

LAINE, FRANKIE
45s
ABC

Number	Title (A Side/B Side)	Yr	VG	VG+	NM
❑ 10891	I'll Take Care of Your Cares/Every Street's a Boulevard	1966	—	3.00	6.00
❑ 10924	Making Memories/Moment of Truth	1967	—	3.00	6.00
❑ 10946	You Wanted Someone to Play With (I Wanted Someone to Love)/The Real Meaning of Love	1967	—	3.00	6.00
❑ 10967	Laura, What's He Got That I Ain't Got/Sometimes (I Just Can't Stand You)	1967	—	3.00	6.00
❑ 10983	You, No One But You/Somewhere There's Someone	1967	—	3.00	6.00
❑ 11032	To Each His Own/I'm Happy to Hear You're Sorry	1967	—	3.00	6.00
❑ 11057	I Don't Want to Set the World On Fire/I Found You	1968	—	3.00	6.00
❑ 11097	Forsaking All Others/Take Me Back	1968	—	3.00	6.00
❑ 11129	Please Forgive Me/Pretty Little Princess	1968	—	3.00	6.00
❑ 11174	You Gave Me a Mountain/The Secret of Happiness	1969	—	3.00	6.00
❑ 11224	Dammit Isn't God's Last Name/Fresh Out of Tears	1969	—	3.00	6.00
❑ 11231	If I Didn't Believe in You/Allegra	1969	—	3.00	6.00
AMOS					
❑ 138	I Believe/On the Sunny Side of the Street	1970	—	2.50	5.00
❑ 153	Put Your Hand in the Hand/Going to Newport	1971	—	2.50	5.00
❑ 161	Don't Blame the Child/My God and I	1971	—	2.50	5.00
CAPITOL					
❑ 5299	Go On With Your Dancing/Halfway	1964	2.00	4.00	8.00
❑ 5472	House of Laughter/A Girl	1965	2.00	4.00	8.00
❑ 5525	Seven Days of Love/Heartaches Can Be Fun	1965	2.00	4.00	8.00
❑ 5569	The Meaning of It All/Pray and He Will Answer You	1966	2.00	4.00	8.00
❑ 5658	Johnny Willow/What Do You Know	1966	2.00	4.00	8.00
COLUMBIA					
❑ J-4-275	Robin Hood/Champion, the Wonder Horse	1955	5.00	10.00	20.00
❑ 39367	Jezebel/Rose, Rose, I Love You	1951	3.75	7.50	15.00
❑ 39489	Wonderful, Wasn't It?/The Girl in the Wood	1951	3.75	7.50	15.00
❑ 39585	Jealousy (Jalousie)/Flamenco	1951	3.75	7.50	15.00
❑ 39597	One for My Baby/Tomorrow Mountain	1951	3.00	6.00	12.00
❑ 39598	Song of the Islands/Necessary Evil	1951	3.00	6.00	12.00
❑ 39599	She Reminds Me of You/Love Is Such a Cheat	1951	3.00	6.00	12.00
❑ 39600	Sleepy Time Down South/To Be Worthy	1951	3.00	6.00	12.00
—The above four comprise a box set					
❑ 39662	Jealousy (Jalousie)/Charmaine	1952	3.00	6.00	12.00
—B-side by Paul Weston; part of a box set					
❑ 39665	The Gandy Dancers' Ball/When You're in Love	1952	3.75	7.50	15.00
❑ 39716	That's How It Goes/Snow in Lover's Lane	1952	3.75	7.50	15.00
❑ 39770	High Noon (Do Not Forsake Me)/Rock of Gibraltar	1952	3.75	7.50	15.00
❑ 39798	There's a Rainbow 'Round My Shoulder/She's Funny That Way	1952	3.00	6.00	12.00
❑ 39799	Wonderful, Wasn't It?/The Girl in the Wood	1952	3.00	6.00	12.00
❑ 39862	The Mermaid/The Ruby and the Pearl	1952	3.75	7.50	15.00
❑ 39903	I'm Just a Poor Bachelor/Tonight You Belong to Me	1952	3.75	7.50	15.00
❑ 39938	I Believe/Your Cheatin' Heart	1953	3.75	7.50	15.00
❑ 39979	Ramblin' Man/I Let Her Go	1953	3.75	7.50	15.00
❑ 40022	When the Wind Blows/Te Amo	1953	3.75	7.50	15.00
❑ 40036	Hey Joe!/Sittin' in the Sun	1953	3.75	7.50	15.00
❑ 40079	Another Me/Blowing Wild	1953	3.75	7.50	15.00
❑ 40136	Granada/I'd Give My Life	1953	3.75	7.50	15.00
❑ 40178	The Kid's Last Fight/Long Distance Love	1954	3.75	7.50	15.00
❑ 40235	Some Day/There Must Be a Reason	1954	3.75	7.50	15.00
❑ 40295	Rain, Rain, Rain/Your Heart, My Heart	1954	3.75	7.50	15.00
—With the Four Lads					
❑ 40378	In the Beginning/Old Shoes	1954	3.75	7.50	15.00
❑ 40433	The Tarrier Song/Bubbles	1955	3.00	6.00	12.00
❑ 40457	Cool Water/Strange Lady in Town	1955	3.00	6.00	12.00
❑ 40526	Humming Bird/My Little One	1955	3.00	6.00	12.00
❑ 40558	Hawk-Eye/Your Love	1955	3.00	6.00	12.00
❑ 40583	A Woman in Love/Walking the Night Away	1955	3.00	6.00	12.00
❑ 40600	I Heard the Angels Singing/Ain't It a Pity and a Shame	1955	3.00	6.00	12.00
—With the Four Lads					
❑ 40663	Hell Hath No Fury/The Most Happy Fella	1956	3.00	6.00	12.00
❑ 40669	Moby Dick/A Capitol Ship	1956	3.00	6.00	12.00
❑ 40693	Don't Cry/Ticky Ticky Tick (I'm Gonna Tell on You)	1956	3.00	6.00	12.00
—With Paul Weston					
❑ 40720	Make Me a Child Again/The Thief	1956	3.00	6.00	12.00
❑ 40741	On the Road to Mandalay/Only If We Love	1956	3.00	6.00	12.00
❑ 40780	Moonlight Gambler/Lotus Land	1956	3.00	6.00	12.00
❑ 40780 [PS]	Moonlight Gambler/Lotus Land	1956	6.25	12.50	25.00
❑ 40856	Love Is a Golden Ring/There's Not a Moment to Spare	1957	3.00	6.00	12.00
❑ 40916	Gunfight at the O.K. Corral/Without Him	1957	3.00	6.00	12.00
❑ 40962	The 3:10 to Yuma/You Know How It Is	1957	3.00	6.00	12.00
❑ 41036	East Is East/The Greater Sin	1957	3.00	6.00	12.00
❑ 41106	Annabelle Lee/All of These…And More	1958	3.00	6.00	12.00
❑ 41139	My Gal and a Prayer/Lonesome Road	1958	3.00	6.00	12.00
❑ 41163	Lovin' Up a Storm/A Kiss Can Change the World	1958	3.00	6.00	12.00
❑ 41187	I Have to Cry/Choombala Bay	1958	3.00	6.00	12.00
❑ 41230	Rawhide/Magnificent Obsession	1958	6.25	12.50	25.00
❑ 41283	A Cottage for Sale/When I Speak Your Name	1958	3.00	6.00	12.00

Number	Title (A Side/B Side)	Yr	VG	VG+	NM
❑ 41299	When I Speak Your Name/Midnight on a Rainy Monday	1958	3.00	6.00	12.00
❑ 41331	That's My Desire/In My Wildest Dreams	1959	2.50	5.00	10.00
❑ 41376	My Little Love/Journey's End	1959	2.50	5.00	10.00
❑ 41430	El Diablo/The Valley of a Hundred Hills	1959	2.50	5.00	10.00
❑ 41486	Rockin' Mother/Rocks and Gravel	1959	2.50	5.00	10.00
❑ 41613	St. James Infirmary/Et Voila	1960	2.50	5.00	10.00
❑ 41700	Seven Women/And Doesn't She Roll	1960	2.50	5.00	10.00
❑ 41787	Kisses That Shake the World/Here She Comes Now	1960	2.50	5.00	10.00
❑ 41974	Gunslinger/Wanted Man	1961	2.50	5.00	10.00
❑ 42233	Miss Satan/Ride Through the Night	1961	2.50	5.00	10.00
❑ 42383	A Wedded Man/We'll Be Together Again	1962	2.50	5.00	10.00
❑ 42767	Don't Make My Baby Blue/The Moment of Truth	1963	2.50	5.00	10.00
❑ 42767 [DJ]	Don't Make My Baby Blue (same on both sides)	1963	5.00	10.00	20.00
—Promo only on red vinyl					
❑ 42767 [PS]	Don't Make My Baby Blue	1963	7.50	15.00	30.00
—Promo-only custom "This Sleeve Contains One Broken Record"					
❑ 42843	I'm Gonna Be Strong/And Doesn't She Roll	1963	2.50	5.00	10.00
❑ 42884	Take Her/I'm Gonna Be Strong	1963	2.50	5.00	10.00
❑ 42966	Lonely Days of Winter/Up Among the Stars	1964	2.50	5.00	10.00
❑ 50006	Jezebel/Jalousie	1954	2.50	5.00	10.00
—Early "Hall of Fame Series" issue					
MAINSTREAM					
❑ 5579	Tell Me 'Bout the Hard Times/(B-side unknown)	1975	—	2.00	4.00
MERCURY					
❑ A-81 [PS]	Frankie Laine	195?	5.00	10.00	20.00
—Box for records 525, 526 and 527					
❑ 525	Cherie I Love You/I'm in the Mood for Love	195?	5.00	10.00	20.00
❑ 526	Exactly Like You/You're Wonderful	195?	5.00	10.00	20.00
❑ 527	Till We Meet Again/Rockin' Chair	195?	5.00	10.00	20.00
—The above three comprise box set A-81					
❑ 1026	Black and Blue/Wrap Your Troubles in Dreams	195?	6.25	12.50	25.00
❑ 1027	On the Sunny Side of the Street/Blue Turning Grey Over You	1950	6.25	12.50	25.00
❑ 1275	The Cry of the Wild Goose/Don't Cry Little Children	195?	5.00	10.00	20.00
—Part of box set A-113					
❑ 1277	Mule Train/God Bless the Child	195?	5.00	10.00	20.00
—Part of box set A-113					
❑ 5028-X45	Stay As Sweet As You Are/I May Be Wrong	1950	6.25	12.50	25.00
—Reissue of 78 rpm					
❑ 5177-X45	You're All I Want for Christmas/Tara Talara Tara	1950	7.50	15.00	30.00
—Reissue of 78 rpm; secondary number is "A-1027-X45"					
❑ 5316-X45	That Lucky Old Sun/I Get Sentimental Over Nothing	1950	6.25	12.50	25.00
—Reissue of 78 rpm; black vinyl					
❑ 5316-X45	That Lucky Old Sun/I Get Sentimental Over Nothing	1950	10.00	20.00	40.00
—Reissue of 78 rpm; red vinyl					
❑ 5345-X45	Mule Train/Carry Me Back to Old Virginny	1950	7.50	15.00	30.00
—Turquoise label					
❑ 5358-X45	Satan Wears a Satin Gown/Baby Just for Me	1950	6.25	12.50	25.00
❑ 5363-X45	The Cry of the Wild Goose/Black Lace	1950	6.25	12.50	25.00
—Maroon label					
❑ 5363-X45	The Cry of the Wild Goose/Black Lace	1950	7.50	15.00	30.00
—Turquoise label					
❑ 5390-X45	Swamp Girl/A Kiss for Tomorrow	1950	6.25	12.50	25.00
❑ 5421-X45	Stars and Stripes Forever/Thanks for the Kisses	1950	6.25	12.50	25.00
❑ 5458-X45	Music, Maestro, Please/Dream a Little Dream of Me	1950	5.00	10.00	20.00
❑ 5495-X45	Nevertheless/I Was Dancing with Someone	1950	5.00	10.00	20.00
❑ 5500-X45	If I Were a Bell/Sleepy Ol' River	1950	5.00	10.00	20.00
❑ 5544-X45	I'm Gonna Live 'Til I Die/A Man Gets Awfully Lonesome	1950	5.00	10.00	20.00
❑ 5553-X45	Merry Christmas Everywhere/What Am I Gonna Do This Christmas	1950	5.00	10.00	20.00
❑ 5580-X45	Dear, Dear, Dear/May the Good Lord Bless and Keep You	1951	5.00	10.00	20.00
❑ 5581-X45	Metro Polka/The Jalopy Song	1951	5.00	10.00	20.00
❑ 5656-X45	The Gang That Sang Heart of My Heart/Out in the Rain	1951	5.00	10.00	20.00
❑ 5685-X45	Isle of Capri/The Day Isn't Long Enough	1951	5.00	10.00	20.00
❑ 5733-X45	Get Happy/I Would Do Most Anything for You	1951	5.00	10.00	20.00
❑ 5768-X45	Baby I Need You/Yes My Darling Daughter	1951	5.00	10.00	20.00
❑ 5892-X45	All of Me/South of the Border	1952	5.00	10.00	20.00
❑ C-30056X45	September in the Rain/Georgia on My Mind	1958	2.50	5.00	10.00
—Pink label; early "Celebrity Series" reissue					
❑ 70099	Ain't Misbehavin'/How Rhythm Was Born	1953	3.75	7.50	15.00
❑ 70262	(The Gang That Sang) Heart of My Heart/South of the Border	1953	3.75	7.50	15.00
❑ 70275	West End Blues/I Can't Believe That You're in Love with Me	1953	3.75	7.50	15.00
SUNFLOWER					
❑ 125	My Own True Love/Time to Ride	1972	—	2.50	5.00
WARNER BROS.					
❑ 7774	Blazing Saddles/I'm Tired	1974	—	3.00	6.00
—B-side by Madeline Kahn					
7-Inch Extended Plays					
COLUMBIA					
❑ B-367 [PS]	Mr. Rhythm	195?	3.00	6.00	12.00
—Cover for 2-EP set (5-1810, 5-1811)					
❑ 5-1169	There's a Rainbow 'Round My Shoulder/She's Funny That Way//Wonderful Wasn't It?/The Girl in the Wood	195?	5.00	10.00	20.00
—Alternate number is B-1512					
❑ 5-1325	Jezebel/Jealousy (Jalousie)//The Gandy Dancers' Ball/When You're in Love	195?	5.00	10.00	20.00
—Alternate number is B-1582					
❑ B-1512 [PS]	Rainbow 'Round My Shoulder	195?	5.00	10.00	20.00
❑ 5-1569	Your Cheatin' Heart/I Believe//Love Is Such a Cheat/High Noon (Do Not Forsake Me)	195?	5.00	10.00	20.00
—Alternate number is B-1685					
❑ B-1582 [PS]	Frankie Laine Spotlite	195?	5.00	10.00	20.00
❑ B-1685 [PS]	Frankie Laine Favorites	195?	5.00	10.00	20.00

L

Number	Title (A Side/B Side)	Yr	VG	VG+	NM
❑ 5-1810	Some Day, Sweetheart/A Hundred Years from Today//Judy/After You've Gone	195?	3.00	6.00	12.00

—Alternate numbers are B-367-1 and B-367-4

Number	Title (A Side/B Side)	Yr	VG	VG+	NM
❑ 5-1811	Laughing at Life/Lullaby in Rhythm//Willow Weep for Me/My Ohio Home	195?	3.00	6.00	12.00

—Alternate numbers are B-367-2 and B-367-3

Number	Title (A Side/B Side)	Yr	VG	VG+	NM
❑ B-1897	(contents unknown)	195?	5.00	10.00	20.00
❑ B-1897 [PS]	Popular Favorites	195?	5.00	10.00	20.00
❑ B-2086	(contents unknown)	1956	5.00	10.00	20.00
❑ B-2086 [PS]	Bring Your Smile Along	1956	5.00	10.00	20.00
❑ B-2121	(contents unknown)	1957	5.00	10.00	20.00
❑ B-2121 [PS]	Moonlight Gambler	1957	5.00	10.00	20.00
❑ B-2132	Love Is a Golden Ring/There's Not a Moment to Spare//After You've Gone/Lullaby in Rhythm	1957	5.00	10.00	20.00
❑ B-2132 [PS]	Love Is a Golden Ring and Other Hits	1957	5.00	10.00	20.00
❑ B-2590	*Shine/That's My Desire/That Lucky Old Sun/ Moonlight Gambler	1960	3.75	7.50	15.00
❑ B-2590 [PS]	Frankie Laine (Hall of Fame Series)	1960	3.75	7.50	15.00
❑ B-11161	Mona Lisa/Quiereme Mucho (Yours)//Besame Mucho (Kiss Me Much)/Laura	195?	5.00	10.00	20.00
❑ B-11161 [PS]	Foreign Affair, Vol. 1	195?	5.00	10.00	20.00
❑ B-11162	(contents unknown)	195?	5.00	10.00	20.00
❑ B-11162 [PS]	Foreign Affair, Vol. 2	195?	5.00	10.00	20.00

MERCURY

Number	Title (A Side/B Side)	Yr	VG	VG+	NM
❑ EP 1-3001	(contents unknown)	195?	6.25	12.50	25.00
❑ EP 1-3001 [PS]	Music, Maestro, Please	195?	6.25	12.50	25.00
❑ EP 1-3010	Two Loves Have I/I May Be Wrong//All of Me/ Old Fashioned Love	195?	6.25	12.50	25.00
❑ EP 1-3010 [PS]	Frankie Laine	195?	6.25	12.50	25.00
❑ EP-1-3016	Don't Cry Little Children/Lucky Old Sun//By the Light of the Stars/Mule Train	195?	6.25	12.50	25.00
❑ EP-1-3016 [PS]	Frankie Laine	195?	6.25	12.50	25.00
❑ EP 1-3021	But Beautiful/That's My Desire//We Will Be Together Again/Shine	195?	6.25	12.50	25.00
❑ EP 1-3021 [PS]	Frankie Laine Favorites	195?	6.25	12.50	25.00
❑ EP 1-3028	(contents unknown)	195?	6.25	12.50	25.00
❑ EP 1-3028 [PS]	Christmas Favorites	195?	6.25	12.50	25.00
❑ EP-1-3057	(title unknown)	195?	5.00	10.00	20.00
❑ EP-1-3057	I May Be Wrong/On the Sunny Side of the Street//Too Marvelous for Words/I Get a Kick Out of You	195?	5.00	10.00	20.00

—B-side by Billy Daniels

Number	Title (A Side/B Side)	Yr	VG	VG+	NM
❑ EP 1-3071	(contents unknown)	195?	6.25	12.50	25.00
❑ EP 1-3071 [PS]	Georgia on My Mind	195?	6.25	12.50	25.00
❑ EP 1-3165	(contents unknown)	195?	6.25	12.50	25.00
❑ EP 1-3165 [PS]	Get Happy	195?	6.25	12.50	25.00
❑ EP 1-3175	(contents unknown)	195?	6.25	12.50	25.00
❑ EP 1-3175 [PS]	With All My Heart	195?	6.25	12.50	25.00

Albums

ABC

Number	Title (A Side/B Side)	Yr	VG	VG+	NM
❑ 604 [M]	I'll Take Care of Your Cares	1967	3.00	6.00	12.00
❑ S-604 [S]	I'll Take Care of Your Cares	1967	3.75	7.50	15.00
❑ 608 [M]	I Wanted Someone to Love	1967	3.00	6.00	12.00
❑ S-608 [S]	I Wanted Someone to Love	1967	3.75	7.50	15.00
❑ 628 [M]	To Each His Own	1968	5.00	10.00	20.00
❑ S-628 [S]	To Each His Own	1968	3.75	7.50	15.00
❑ S-657	Take Me Back to Laine Country	1968	3.75	7.50	15.00
❑ S-682	You Gave Me a Mountain	1969	3.75	7.50	15.00

AMOS

Number	Title (A Side/B Side)	Yr	VG	VG+	NM
❑ 7009	Frankie Laine's Greatest Hits	1970	3.00	6.00	12.00
❑ 7013	Brand New Day	1971	3.00	6.00	12.00

BULLDOG

Number	Title (A Side/B Side)	Yr	VG	VG+	NM
❑ BDL-1035	All of Me	198?	2.50	5.00	10.00

CAPITOL

Number	Title (A Side/B Side)	Yr	VG	VG+	NM
❑ ST 2277 [S]	I Believe	1965	3.75	7.50	15.00
❑ T 2277 [M]	I Believe	1965	3.00	6.00	12.00

COLUMBIA

Number	Title (A Side/B Side)	Yr	VG	VG+	NM
❑ CL 625 [M]	Command Performance	1954	10.00	20.00	40.00
❑ CL 808 [M]	Jazz Spectacular	1956	7.50	15.00	30.00
❑ CL 975 [M]	Rockin'	1957	7.50	15.00	30.00
❑ CL 1116 [M]	Foreign Affair	1958	7.50	15.00	30.00
❑ CL 1176 [M]	Torchin'	1959	5.00	10.00	20.00
❑ CL 1231 [M]	Frankie Laine's Greatest Hits	1958	6.25	12.50	25.00

—Red and black label with six "eye" logos

Number	Title (A Side/B Side)	Yr	VG	VG+	NM
❑ CL 1231 [M]	Frankie Laine's Greatest Hits	1962	3.75	7.50	15.00

—"Guaranteed High Fidelity" or "360 Sound Mono" label

Number	Title (A Side/B Side)	Yr	VG	VG+	NM
❑ CL 1277 [M]	Reunion in Rhythm	1959	5.00	10.00	20.00
❑ CL 1317 [M]	You Are My Love	1960	5.00	10.00	20.00
❑ CL 1393 [M]	Frankie Laine, Balladeer	1960	5.00	10.00	20.00
❑ CL 1615 [M]	Hell Bent for Leather!	1961	5.00	10.00	20.00

—Red and black label with six "eye" logos

Number	Title (A Side/B Side)	Yr	VG	VG+	NM
❑ CL 1615 [M]	Hell Bent for Leather!	1962	3.75	7.50	15.00

—"Guaranteed High Fidelity" or "360 Sound Mono" label

Number	Title (A Side/B Side)	Yr	VG	VG+	NM
❑ CL 1696 [M]	Deuces Wild	1962	3.75	7.50	15.00

—"Guaranteed High Fidelity" or "360 Sound Mono" label

Number	Title (A Side/B Side)	Yr	VG	VG+	NM
❑ CL 1696 [M]	Deuces Wild	1962	5.00	10.00	20.00

—Red and black label with six "eye" logos

Number	Title (A Side/B Side)	Yr	VG	VG+	NM
❑ CL 1829 [M]	Call of the Wild	1962	3.75	7.50	15.00
❑ CL 1962 [M]	Wanderlust	1963	3.75	7.50	15.00
❑ CL 2504 [10]	Lover's Laine	1955	10.00	20.00	40.00
❑ CL 2548 [10]	One for My Baby	1955	10.00	20.00	40.00
❑ CL 6200 [10]	One for My Baby	1952	12.50	25.00	50.00
❑ CL 6278 [10]	Mr. Rhythm	1954	12.50	25.00	50.00
❑ CS 8024 [S]	Torchin'	1959	7.50	15.00	30.00
❑ CS 8087 [S]	Reunion in Rhythm	1959	7.50	15.00	30.00
❑ CS 8119 [S]	You Are My Love	1960	6.25	12.50	25.00
❑ CS 8188 [S]	Frankie Laine, Balladeer	1960	6.25	12.50	25.00
❑ CS 8415 [S]	Hell Bent for Leather!	1961	7.50	15.00	30.00

—Red and black label with six "eye" logos

Number	Title (A Side/B Side)	Yr	VG	VG+	NM
❑ CS 8415 [S]	Hell Bent for Leather!	1962	5.00	10.00	20.00

—"360 Sound Stereo" label

Number	Title (A Side/B Side)	Yr	VG	VG+	NM
❑ CS 8496 [S]	Deuces Wild	1962	5.00	10.00	20.00

—"360 Sound Stereo" label

Number	Title (A Side/B Side)	Yr	VG	VG+	NM
❑ CS 8496 [S]	Deuces Wild	1962	6.25	12.50	25.00

—Red and black label with six "eye" logos

Number	Title (A Side/B Side)	Yr	VG	VG+	NM
❑ CS 8629 [S]	Call of the Wild	1962	5.00	10.00	20.00
❑ CS 8636 [R]	Frankie Laine's Greatest Hits	1963	3.00	6.00	12.00

Number	Title (A Side/B Side)	Yr	VG	VG+	NM
❑ PC 8636	Frankie Laine's Greatest Hits	198?	2.00	4.00	8.00

—Reissue with new prefix

Number	Title (A Side/B Side)	Yr	VG	VG+	NM
❑ CS 8762 [S]	Wanderlust	1963	5.00	10.00	20.00

GALAXY SERIES

Number	Title (A Side/B Side)	Yr	VG	VG+	NM
❑ 4821 [M]	Frankie Laine Sings	195?	3.00	6.00	12.00

HARMONY

Number	Title (A Side/B Side)	Yr	VG	VG+	NM
❑ HL 7329 [M]	Roving Gambler	196?	3.00	6.00	12.00
❑ HL 7382 [M]	That's My Desire	196?	3.00	6.00	12.00
❑ HL 7425 [M]	Memories	196?	3.00	6.00	12.00
❑ HS 11129 [S]	Roving Gambler	196?	3.00	6.00	12.00
❑ HS 11182 [S]	That's My Desire	196?	3.00	6.00	12.00
❑ HS 11225 [S]	Memories	196?	3.00	6.00	12.00
❑ HS 11345	I'm Gonna Live 'Til I Die	1969	3.00	6.00	12.00
❑ H 30406	High Noon	1971	3.00	6.00	12.00

HINDSIGHT

Number	Title (A Side/B Side)	Yr	VG	VG+	NM
❑ HSR-216	Frankie Laine with Carl Fischer and His Orchestra, 1947	1985	2.50	5.00	10.00

MERCURY

Number	Title (A Side/B Side)	Yr	VG	VG+	NM
❑ PKW-2-111 [(2)]	The Great Years	1969	3.75	7.50	15.00
❑ MG-20069 [M]	Songs by Frankie Laine	1956	10.00	20.00	40.00
❑ MG-20080 [M]	That's My Desire	1957	10.00	20.00	40.00
❑ MG-20083 [M]	Frankie Laine Sings For Us	1957	10.00	20.00	40.00
❑ MG-20085 [M]	Concert Date	1957	10.00	20.00	40.00
❑ MG-20105 [M]	With All My Heart	1957	10.00	20.00	40.00
❑ MG-20587 [M]	Frankie Laine's Golden Hits	1960	6.25	12.50	25.00
❑ MG-25007 [10]	Favorites	1949	12.50	25.00	50.00
❑ MG-25024 [10]	Songs from the Heart	1950	12.50	25.00	50.00
❑ MG-25025 [10]	Frankie Laine	1950	12.50	25.00	50.00
❑ MG-25026 [10]	Frankie Laine	1950	12.50	25.00	50.00
❑ MG-25027 [10]	Frankie Laine	1950	12.50	25.00	50.00
❑ MG-25082 [10]	Christmas Favorites	1951	12.50	25.00	50.00
❑ MG-25097 [10]	Mr. Rhythm Sings	1951	12.50	25.00	50.00
❑ MG-25124 [10]	Listen to Laine	1952	12.50	25.00	50.00
❑ SR-60587 [R]	Frankie Laine's Golden Hits	196?	3.00	6.00	12.00

PICKWICK

Number	Title (A Side/B Side)	Yr	VG	VG+	NM
❑ SPC-3526	That Lucky Old Sun	197?	2.50	5.00	10.00
❑ SPC-3601	You Gave Me a Mountain	197?	2.50	5.00	10.00

TOWER

Number	Title (A Side/B Side)	Yr	VG	VG+	NM
❑ ST 5092 [S]	Memory Laine	1967	3.75	7.50	15.00
❑ T 5092 [M]	Memory Laine	1967	3.00	6.00	12.00

WING

Number	Title (A Side/B Side)	Yr	VG	VG+	NM
❑ MGW 12110 [M]	All-Time Favorites	196?	3.75	7.50	15.00
❑ MGW 12158 [M]	Singing the Blues	196?	3.75	7.50	15.00
❑ MGW 12202 [M]	That's My Desire	196?	3.75	7.50	15.00
❑ SRW 16110 [R]	All-Time Favorites	196?	3.00	6.00	12.00
❑ SRW 16158 [R]	Singing the Blues	196?	3.00	6.00	12.00
❑ SRW 16202 [R]	That's My Desire	196?	3.00	6.00	12.00

LAINE, FRANKIE, AND JIMMY BOYD
Also see each artist's individual listings.

45s

COLUMBIA

Number	Title (A Side/B Side)	Yr	VG	VG+	NM
❑ 39945	Tell Me a Story/The Little Boy and the Old Man	1953	3.75	7.50	15.00
❑ 40069	Let's Go Fishin'/Poor Little Piggy Bank	1953	3.75	7.50	15.00
❑ 40650	Little Child/Let's Go Fishin'	1956	3.00	6.00	12.00

LAINE, FRANKIE, AND PATTI PAGE
Also see each artist's individual listings.

45s

MERCURY

Number	Title (A Side/B Side)	Yr	VG	VG+	NM
❑ 5442	I Love You for That/ If I Were You Baby, I'd Love Me	1950	5.00	10.00	20.00

LAINE, FRANKIE, AND JOHNNIE RAY
Also see each artist's individual listings.

45s

COLUMBIA

Number	Title (A Side/B Side)	Yr	VG	VG+	NM
❑ 4-40976	Up Above My Head/Good Evening Friends	1957	3.00	6.00	12.00

LAINE, FRANKIE, AND JO STAFFORD
Also see each artist's individual listings.

45s

COLUMBIA

Number	Title (A Side/B Side)	Yr	VG	VG+	NM
❑ 39388	Pretty Eyed Baby/That's One for Me	1951	3.75	7.50	15.00
❑ 39466	In the Cool of the Evening/That's Good, That's Bad	1951	3.75	7.50	15.00
❑ 39570	Hey, Good Lookin'/Gambella (The Gamblin' Lady)	1951	3.75	7.50	15.00
❑ 39672	Hambone/Let's Have a Party	1952	3.75	7.50	15.00
❑ 39867	Settin' the Woods on Fire/Piece a-Puddin'	1952	3.75	7.50	15.00
❑ 39893	Christmas Roses/Chow Willy	1952	3.75	7.50	15.00
❑ 40116	Way Down Yonder in New Orleans/Floatin' Down to Cotton Town	1953	3.75	7.50	15.00
❑ 40198	Rollin' Down the Line/Goin' Like Wildfire	1954	3.75	7.50	15.00
❑ 40401	High Society/Back Where I Belong	1954	3.75	7.50	15.00

LAINE, LINDA, AND THE SINNERS
Also see FREDDIE AND THE DREAMERS.

45s

TOWER

Number	Title (A Side/B Side)	Yr	VG	VG+	NM
❑ 108	Low Grades and High Fever/After Today	1964	3.00	6.00	12.00

LAKE, GREG

45s

ATLANTIC

Number	Title (A Side/B Side)	Yr	VG	VG+	NM
❑ 3305	I Believe in Father Christmas/Humbug	1975	—	3.00	6.00
❑ 3305 [PS]	I Believe in Father Christmas/Humbug	1975	2.50	5.00	10.00
❑ 3405	C'est La Vie/Jeremy Bender	1977	—	2.50	5.00

CHRYSALIS

Number	Title (A Side/B Side)	Yr	VG	VG+	NM
❑ 2517	Let Me Love You Once/(B-side unknown)	1981	—	2.00	4.00
❑ 2571	Retribution Drive/Let Me Love You Once	1981	—	2.00	4.00

Albums

CHRYSALIS

Number	Title (A Side/B Side)	Yr	VG	VG+	NM
❑ CHR 1357	Greg Lake	1981	2.50	5.00	10.00

LAKE, KAREN

45s

ABC-PARAMOUNT

Number	Title (A Side/B Side)	Yr	VG	VG+	NM
❑ 10050	Nine O'Clock/Will I Know	1959	5.00	10.00	20.00
❑ 10087	Kiss Me Quick and Go/ When I'm Not Teen Age Anymore	1960	5.00	10.00	20.00

Number	Title (A Side/B Side)	Yr	VG	VG+	NM

BIG TOP
| □ 3077 | Air Mail Special Delivery/
I'd Like to Miss My Graduation | 1961 | 7.50 | 15.00 | 30.00 |

—Produced by Phil Spector

LALA AND THE LALARETTES
45s
ELPECO
| □ 2922 | This Day of Ours/Getting Ready for Freddy | 1963 | 15.00 | 30.00 | 60.00 |

LAMARR, GENE
45s
SPRY
□ 113	Crazy Little House on the Hill/ You Don't Love Me Anymore	1959	37.50	75.00	150.00
□ 114	You Can Count on Me/Just a Little Bit Longer	1959	37.50	75.00	150.00
□ 115	Close to Me/Moon Eyes	1959	25.00	50.00	100.00

LAMAS, FERNANDO
Albums
ROULETTE
| □ R-25041 [M] | With Love, Fernando Lamas | 1958 | 10.00 | 20.00 | 40.00 |

LAMB
Albums
FILLMORE
| □ F 30003 | Sign of Change | 1970 | 5.00 | 10.00 | 20.00 |
WARNER BROS.
| □ WS 1920 | Cross Between | 1971 | 5.00 | 10.00 | 20.00 |
| □ WS 1952 | Bring Out the Sun | 1972 | 5.00 | 10.00 | 20.00 |

LAMB, BECKY
45s
WARNER BROS.
| □ 7154 | Little Becky's Christmas Wish/Go to Sleep, Little
Lambs | 1967 | 3.00 | 6.00 | 12.00 |

—B-side by Bill Lamb

LAMBERT, RUDY See THE MONDELLOS.

LAMM, ROBERT Of CHICAGO.
45s
COLUMBIA
| □ 10068 | Skinny Boy/Temporary Jones | 1974 | — | 2.50 | 5.00 |
Albums
COLUMBIA
| □ PC 33095 | Skinny Boy | 1974 | 3.00 | 6.00 | 12.00 |

LAMONT, BILLY
45s
KING
| □ 5403 | Come On Right Now/Hear Me Now | 1960 | 3.00 | 6.00 | 12.00 |
OKEH
| □ 7125 | Country Boy/Can't Make It By Myself | 1959 | 6.25 | 12.50 | 25.00 |
| □ 7131 | I'm Gonna Try/Now Darling | 1960 | 6.25 | 12.50 | 25.00 |
SAVOY
| □ 1522 | I'm So Lonely/I Got a Rock 'n' Roll Gal | 1957 | 3.75 | 7.50 | 15.00 |
THREE-D
| □ 850 | Country Boy/Can't Make It By Myself | 1959 | 37.50 | 75.00 | 150.00 |

LAMP, BUDDY
45s
ABC-PARAMOUNT
| □ 10398 | I'm Comin' Home/Promised Land | 1963 | 3.75 | 7.50 | 15.00 |
D-TOWN
| □ 1064 | Next Best Thing/Just a Little Bit of Lovin' | 1966 | 7.50 | 15.00 | 30.00 |
DOUBLE L
| □ 716 | Thank You Love/My Tears | 1963 | 7.50 | 15.00 | 30.00 |
DUKE
□ 438	I'm Coming Home/Where Have You Been	1968	2.50	5.00	10.00
□ 461	Devil's Gonna Get You/Wall Around Your Heart	1970	2.00	4.00	8.00
□ 468	Hen Pecked/If You See Kate	1971	2.00	4.00	8.00
GONE
□ 5104	Good News/What Here Can I Do	1961	3.75	7.50	15.00
WHEELSVILLE
□ 113	You've Got the Lovin' Touch/I Wanna Go Home	196?	10.00	20.00	40.00
□ 120	Confusion/I Wanna Go Home	196?	10.00	20.00	40.00
□ 122	Save Your Love/I Wanna Go Home	196?	17.50	35.00	70.00

LAMP OF CHILDHOOD, THE
45s
DUNHILL
□ 4051	Season of the Witch/You Can't Blame Me	1966	2.00	4.00	8.00
□ 4063	First Time Last Time/2 O'Clock Morning	1967	2.00	4.00	8.00
□ 4063 [PS]	First Time Last Time/2 O'Clock Morning	1967	3.00	6.00	12.00
□ 4089	No More Running Around/2 O'Clock Morning	1967	2.00	4.00	8.00

LAMPLIGHTERS, THE
45s
FEDERAL
□ 12149	Part of Me/Turn Me Loose	1953	75.00	150.00	300.00
□ 12152	Give Me/Be-Bop Wino	1953	37.50	75.00	150.00
□ 12166	Smootchie/I Can't Stand It	1954	37.50	75.00	150.00
□ 12176	Tell Me You Came/I Used to Cry Mercy, Mercy	1954	37.50	75.00	150.00
□ 12182	Salty Dog/Ride, Jockey, Ride	1954	37.50	75.00	150.00
□ 12192	Five Minutes Longer/You Hear	1954	37.50	75.00	150.00
□ 12197	Yum! Yum!/Goody Good Times	1954	37.50	75.00	150.00
□ 12206	I Wanna Know/Believe in Me	1955	37.50	75.00	150.00
□ 12212	Roll On/Love, Rock and Thrill	1955	37.50	75.00	150.00
□ 12242	Don't Make It So Good/Hug a Little, Kiss a Little	1955	37.50	75.00	150.00
□ 12255	You Were Sent Down from Heaven/Bo-Peep	1956	25.00	50.00	100.00
□ 12261	It Ain't Right/Everything's All Right	1956	25.00	50.00	100.00
KING
□ 5890	Be-Bop Wino/Thunderbird	1964	3.75	7.50	15.00

—B-side by Dossie Terry

LANCASTRIANS, THE
45s
CAPITOL
| □ 5501 | Never Gonna Come On Home/
There'll Be No More Goodbyes | 1965 | 2.50 | 5.00 | 10.00 |
JERDEN
| □ 798 | The World Keeps Going Round/
Not the Same Anymore | 1966 | 2.50 | 5.00 | 10.00 |

LANCE, HERB
45s
DELUXE
| □ 6150 | You Can't Be Sure of Anything/By the
Candleglow | 1957 | 12.50 | 25.00 | 50.00 |
MALA
□ 404	Like a Baby/My Good Mind	1959	5.00	10.00	20.00
□ 405	Some Love/Until the Real Thing	1959	5.00	10.00	20.00
□ 426	Deep in My Heart/Prayer in My Heart	1961	5.00	10.00	20.00
Albums
CHESS
| □ LP-1506 [M] | The Comeback | 1966 | 6.25 | 12.50 | 25.00 |
| □ LPS-1506 [S] | The Comeback | 1966 | 7.50 | 15.00 | 30.00 |

LANCE, MAJOR
45s
COLUMBIA
| □ 10488 | Come On, Have Yourself a Good Time/
Come What May | 1977 | — | 2.50 | 5.00 |
CURTOM
| □ 1953 | Stay Away from Me (I Love You Too Much)/
Gypsy Woman | 1970 | — | 3.00 | 6.00 |
| □ 1956 | Must Be Love Coming Down/Little Young Lover | 1970 | — | 3.00 | 6.00 |
DAKAR
| □ 608 | Follow the Leader/Since You've Been Gone | 1969 | 2.00 | 4.00 | 8.00 |
| □ 612 | Shadows of a Memory/
Sweeter As the Days Go By | 1969 | 2.00 | 4.00 | 8.00 |
KAT FAMILY
| □ 03024 | I Wanna Go Home/(Instrumental) | 1982 | — | 2.00 | 4.00 |
| □ 04185 | Are You Leaving Me/I Wanna Go Home | 1983 | — | 2.00 | 4.00 |
MERCURY
| □ 71582 | I've Got a Girl/Phyllis | 1960 | 7.50 | 15.00 | 30.00 |
OKEH
□ 7175	The Monkey Time/Mama Didn't Know	1963	3.75	7.50	15.00
□ 7181	Hey Little Girl/Crying in the Rain	1963	3.00	6.00	12.00
□ 7187	Um, Um, Um, Um, Um, Um/Sweet Music	1964	3.75	7.50	15.00
□ 7187 [PS]	Um, Um, Um, Um, Um, Um/Sweet Music	1964	7.50	15.00	30.00
□ 7191	The Matador/Gonna Get Married	1964	2.50	5.00	10.00
□ 7197	It Ain't No Use/Girls	1964	2.50	5.00	10.00
□ 7200	Think Nothing About It/It's Alright	1964	12.50	25.00	50.00
□ 7203	Rhythm/Please Don't Say No More	1964	2.50	5.00	10.00
□ 7203 [PS]	Rhythm/Please Don't Say No More	1964	3.75	7.50	15.00
□ 7209	Sometimes I Wonder/I'm So Lost	1965	2.50	5.00	10.00
□ 7216	Come See/You Belong to Me My Love	1965	2.50	5.00	10.00
□ 7216 [PS]	Come See/You Belong to Me My Love	1965	3.75	7.50	15.00
□ 7223	Ain't It a Shame/Gotta Get Away	1965	2.50	5.00	10.00
□ 7226	Too Hot to Hold/Dark and Lovely	1965	2.50	5.00	10.00
□ 7233	Everybody Loves a Good Time/ I Just Can't Help It	1965	3.75	7.50	15.00
□ 7250	Little Young Lover/Investigate	1966	3.75	7.50	15.00
□ 7250 [PS]	Little Young Lover/Investigate	1966	5.00	10.00	20.00
□ 7255	It's the Beat/You'll Want Me Back	1966	2.50	5.00	10.00
□ 7266	Ain't No Soul (In These Shoes)/I	1966	3.75	7.50	15.00
□ 7284	You Don't Want Me No More/ Wait Till I Get You in Your Arms	1967	12.50	25.00	50.00
□ 7298	Without a Doubt/Forever	1967	2.50	5.00	10.00
OSIRIS
□ 001	You're Everything I Need/(Instrumental)	1975	—	2.50	5.00
PLAYBOY
□ 6017	Um, Um, Um, Um, Um, Um/ Last of the Red Hot Lovers	1974	—	2.50	5.00
□ 6020	Sweeter/Wild and Free	1975	—	2.50	5.00
SOUL
□ 35123	I Never Thought I'd Be Losing You/ Chicago Disco	1977	—	2.50	5.00
VOLT
□ 4079	I Wanna Make Up/That's the Story of My Life	1972	—	3.00	6.00
□ 4085	Ain't No Sweat/Since I Lost My Baby's Love	1972	—	3.00	6.00
Albums
KAT FAMILY
| □ FZ 38898 | The Major's Back | 1983 | 3.00 | 6.00 | 12.00 |
OKEH
□ OKM-12105 [M]	The Monkey Time	1963	10.00	20.00	40.00
□ OKM-12106 [M]	Um, Um, Um, Um, Um, Um	1964	10.00	20.00	40.00
□ OKM-12110 [M]	Major's Greatest Hits	1965	7.50	15.00	30.00
□ OKS-14105 [S]	The Monkey Time	1963	12.50	25.00	50.00
□ OKS-14106 [S]	Um, Um, Um, Um, Um, Um	1964	12.50	25.00	50.00
□ OKS-14110 [S]	Major's Greatest Hits	1965	10.00	20.00	40.00
SOUL
□ S7-751	Now Arriving	1978	3.00	6.00	12.00

LANCELOT LINK AND THE EVOLUTION REVOLUTION
45s
ABC
| □ 11278 | Sha La Love You/Blind Date | 1970 | 2.50 | 5.00 | 10.00 |
| □ 11285 | Daydreams/Magic Feelings | 1970 | 2.50 | 5.00 | 10.00 |
Albums
ABC
| □ S-715 | Lancelot Link and the Evolution Revolution | 1970 | 10.00 | 20.00 | 40.00 |

LANCERS, THE
45s
CLOUD
| □ 500 | Baja/When Johnny Comes Draggin' Home | 1965 | 6.25 | 12.50 | 25.00 |
CORAL
| □ 61288 | Mr. Sandman/Little White Light | 1954 | 3.00 | 6.00 | 12.00 |

Number	Title (A Side/B Side)	Yr	VG	VG+	NM
❏ 61314	'Twas the Night Before Christmas/I Wanna Do				
	More Than Whistle (Under the Mistletoe)	1954	3.00	6.00	12.00
❏ 61332	Tweedlee Dee/Open Up Your Heart				
	(And Let the Sun Shine In)	1955	3.00	6.00	12.00
❏ 61343	Timberjack/Crazy Music	1955	3.00	6.00	12.00
—With Lawrence Welk and His Orchestra					
❏ 61374	Somebody Else Is Taking My Place/Cherry	1955	3.00	6.00	12.00
❏ 61382	Two Hearts, Two Kisses/Afraid	1955	3.00	6.00	12.00
❏ 61416	Leave the Door Partly Open/				
	The Lucky Black Cat	1955	3.00	6.00	12.00
❏ 61468	It Shouldn't Hurt to Love You				
	/It Takes a Heap of Livin'	1955	3.00	6.00	12.00
❏ 61527	Alphabet Rock/How Lonely Can I Get	1955	3.00	6.00	12.00
❏ 61550	Rock Around the Island/The Walking Doll	1956	3.00	6.00	12.00
❏ 61611	Sorry/A Man Is As Good As His Word	1956	3.00	6.00	12.00
❏ 61614	Joey, Joey, Joey/When You're in Love	1956	3.00	6.00	12.00
❏ 61616	Little Fool/A Man Is As Good As His Word	1956	3.00	6.00	12.00
❏ 61665	The First Traveling Saleslady/Free	1956	3.00	6.00	12.00
❏ 61686	The Bonnie Banks of Loch Lomon'/Maybe Now	1956	3.00	6.00	12.00
❏ 61712	I Came Back to Say I'm Sorry/Never Leave Me	1956	3.00	6.00	12.00
❏ 61769	Freckle Face Sara Jane/				
	It Happened in Monterey	1957	3.00	6.00	12.00
❏ 61831	Charm Bracelets/And I Don't Feel Bad	1957	3.00	6.00	12.00
❏ 61866	Lover's Rendezvous/Follow the River	1957	3.00	6.00	12.00
❏ 61887	I'm Awfully Strong for You/				
	I'd Move Heaven and Earth	1957	3.00	6.00	12.00
❏ 61899	Don't Go Near the Water/A Hundred Heartbeats	1957	3.00	6.00	12.00
❏ 61930	The Stroll/Jo-Ann	1958	3.00	6.00	12.00
❏ 61966	Sorry/The Sound	1958	3.00	6.00	12.00
❏ 61998	It Was Great While It Lasted/				
	The Lord Is a Generous Man	1958	3.00	6.00	12.00
OLD TIMER					
❏ 604	Baja/When Johnny Comes Draggin' Home	1965	2.50	5.00	10.00
—Red vinyl (reissue)					
❏ 604	Baja/When Johnny Comes Draggin' Home	1965	10.00	20.00	40.00
—Black vinyl					
VEE JAY					
❏ 654	The Warmth of the Sun/Hush-A-Bye	1965	2.50	5.00	10.00
Albums					
CORAL					
❏ CRL 57100 [M]	Dixieland Ball	1957	6.25	12.50	25.00
IMPERIAL					
❏ LP-9075 [M]	Concert in Contrasts	1959	7.50	15.00	30.00
❏ LP-12023 [S]	Concert in Contrasts	1959	10.00	20.00	40.00
TREND					
❏ TL-1009 [10]	The Lancers	1954	10.00	20.00	40.00

LANDERS, CONNIE
45s
HIT

Number	Title (A Side/B Side)	Yr	VG	VG+	NM
❏ 23	Heart in Hand/Things	1962	2.00	4.00	8.00
—B-side by Harvey Frolic					
❏ 26	Vacation/Rinky Dink	1962	2.00	4.00	8.00
—B-side by the Boots Purcell Combo					
❏ 34	He Thinks I Still Care/All Alone Am I	1962	2.00	4.00	8.00
—B-side by Katy Richards					
❏ 40	Bobby's Girl/Ride!	1962	2.00	4.00	8.00
—B-side by Peggy Gaines					
❏ 43	My Coloring Book/Go Away Little Girl	1962	2.00	4.00	8.00
—B-side by Fred York					
❏ 46	I'm Gonna Be Warm This Winter/				
	Half Heaven Half Heartache	1962	2.00	4.00	8.00
—B-side by George Killebrew					
❏ 48	Shake Me I Rattle/My Dad	1962	2.00	4.00	8.00
—B-side by Woody Martin					
❏ 57	Follow the Boys/He's So Fine	1963	2.00	4.00	8.00
—B-side by the Dacrons					
❏ 68	It's My Party/Another Saturday Night	1963	2.00	4.00	8.00
—B-side by Leroy Jones					

LANDIS, JERRY See PAUL SIMON.

LANDS, HOAGY
45s
ABC-PARAMOUNT

Number	Title (A Side/B Side)	Yr	VG	VG+	NM
❏ 10171	(I'm Gonna) Cry Some Tears/Lighted Windows	1960	6.25	12.50	25.00
❏ 10392	Tender Years/I'm Yours	1963	3.75	7.50	15.00
ATLANTIC					
❏ 2217	Baby Come On Home/				
	Baby Let Me Hold Your Hand	1964	3.75	7.50	15.00
JUDI					
❏ 054	(I'm Gonna) Cry Some Tears/Lighted Windows	1960	20.00	40.00	80.00
LAURIE					
❏ 3349	Theme from The Other Side/Friends and Lovers				
	Don't Go Together	1966	5.00	10.00	20.00
❏ 3372	Yesterday/Forever	1967	5.00	10.00	20.00
❏ 3381	The Next in Line/Please Don't Talk About Me				
	When I'm Gone	1967	6.25	12.50	25.00
—Backing group: THE CHIFFONS.					
MGM					
❏ K-13041	My Tears Are Dry/It's Gonna Be Morning	1961	5.00	10.00	20.00
❏ K-13062	Goodnight Irene/It Ain't As Easy As That	1962	5.00	10.00	20.00

LANDS, LIZ
45s
GORDY

Number	Title (A Side/B Side)	Yr	VG	VG+	NM
❏ 7023	We Shall Overcome/I Have a Dream	1963	6.25	12.50	25.00
—B-side by Rev. Martin Luther King					
❏ 7026	May What He Lived For Live/He's Got the Whole				
	World in His Hands	1963	7.50	15.00	30.00
❏ 7030	Midnight Journey/Keep Me	1964	12.50	25.00	50.00
—The Temptations sing backup					
ONE-DERFUL					
❏ 4847	One Man's Poison/Don't Shut Me Out	1967	3.75	7.50	15.00
T&L					
❏ 201	Silent Night (Part 1)/Silent Night (Part 2)	19??	2.00	4.00	8.00

LANDSLIDE
Albums
CAPITOL

Number	Title (A Side/B Side)	Yr	VG	VG+	NM
❏ ST-11006	Two-Sided Fantasy	1972	10.00	20.00	40.00

LANE, BILLY
45s
TABA

Number	Title (A Side/B Side)	Yr	VG	VG+	NM
❏ 201	Beginner in Love/Space Ship Blues	196?	40.00	80.00	160.00

LANE, MICKEY
45s
BRUNSWICK

Number	Title (A Side/B Side)	Yr	VG	VG+	NM
❏ 55098	Daddy's Little Baby/Toasted Love	1958	5.00	10.00	20.00
LAURIE					
❏ 3071	Dum Dee Dee Dum/Night Cap	1960	6.25	12.50	25.00

LANE, MICKEY LEE
45s
MALA

Number	Title (A Side/B Side)	Yr	VG	VG+	NM
❏ 12032	Tutti Frutti/With Your Love	1968	2.00	4.00	8.00
SWAN					
❏ 4183	Shaggy Dog/Oo-Oo	1964	3.00	6.00	12.00
❏ 4199	The Zoo/(They're All in the) Senior Class	1965	2.50	5.00	10.00
❏ 4210	Little Girl (I Was Wrong)/When You're in Love	1965	2.50	5.00	10.00
❏ 4222	Hey Sah-Lo-Ney/Of Yesterday	1965	2.50	5.00	10.00
❏ 4252	The Only Thing to Do/She Don't Want To	1966	2.50	5.00	10.00

LANE, ROCKI, AND THE GROSS GROUP
45s
EPIC

Number	Title (A Side/B Side)	Yr	VG	VG+	NM
❏ 10556	Happy Hairy Hippy Harry Claus/Santa Soul	1969	6.25	12.50	25.00

LANI & BONI See DELANEY AND BONNIE.

LANIN, LESTER
45s
AUDIO FIDELITY

Number	Title (A Side/B Side)	Yr	VG	VG+	NM
❏ 134	All You Need Is Love/The Windows of the World	1968	—	2.50	5.00
❏ 135	Mame/Cabaret	1968	—	2.50	5.00
❏ 148	Up-Up and Away/The Windows of the World	1968	—	2.50	5.00
EPIC					
❏ 9279	Lester Lanin Cha-Cha-Cha (And Medley)/				
	Toreador Song	1958	2.50	5.00	10.00
❏ 9296	Over the Rainbow Cha-Cha-Cha/				
	I Want My Mama	1958	2.50	5.00	10.00
❏ 9349	Winter Wonderland/				
	Dance of the Sugar-Plum Fairies	1959	3.00	6.00	12.00
❏ 9350	Sleigh Ride/Christmas Carol Medley	1959	3.00	6.00	12.00
❏ 9396	Glow-Worm Cha Cha/				
	Yellow Rose of Texas Meringue	1960	2.00	4.00	8.00
❏ 9426	Blue Tango Rock/This Could Be the Start of				
	Something Big	1960	2.00	4.00	8.00
❏ 9444	The Bells/Bow and Arrow	1961	2.00	4.00	8.00
❏ 9482	Organ Twist/Sweet Georgia Brown	1961	2.00	4.00	8.00
❏ 9501	Russian Roulette/Twelfth Street Rag	1962	2.00	4.00	8.00
❏ 9514	Give Me a Song/You Can't Be True, Dear	1962	2.00	4.00	8.00
❏ 9571	Ballad of the Red River Valley/Tumbling				
	Tumbleweeds	1963	2.00	4.00	8.00
❏ 9618	Theme from "The Seven Capital Sins"/Hora				
	(Happiness)	1963	2.00	4.00	8.00
❏ 9624	Tamoure Shake/Theme from "The Seven				
	Capital Sins"	1963	2.00	4.00	8.00
❏ JZSP 123255/6 [DJ]	Winter Wonderland/Sleigh Ride	1967	2.00	4.00	8.00
❏ JZSP 123257/8 [DJ]	Dance of the Sugar-Plum Fairies/Ring In the				
	New	1967	2.00	4.00	8.00
❏ JZSP 123259/60 [DJ]	Christmas Medley/Jingle Bells	1967	2.00	4.00	8.00
METROMEDIA					
❏ 118	Love Theme from Romeo and Juliet/Aquarius	1969	—	2.00	4.00
❏ 135	Ob-La-Di, Ob-La-Da/Dizzy	1969	—	2.00	4.00
PHILIPS					
❏ 40217	Down by the Riverside/West Indies Ska	1964	—	3.00	6.00
❏ 40344	Theme from "The Yearling"/Dancing				
	Tambourines	1965	—	3.00	6.00

7-Inch Extended Plays
EPIC

Number	Title (A Side/B Side)	Yr	VG	VG+	NM
❏ EG 7184	*September Song/Marianne/Ballin' the Jack/				
	Waltz from "Eugen Onegin"/Anything Goes/				
	Love for Sale/Sunny/Greensleeves/At the				
	Darktown Strutters' Ball	195?	2.50	5.00	10.00
❏ EG 7184 [PS]	Dance to the Music of Lester Lanin, Volume 1	195?	2.50	5.00	10.00
❏ EG 7203	*Laura/Deep Purple/Tin Roof Blues/After You've				
	Gone/Do I Love You Because You're Beautiful/				
	Hawaiian War Chant/It's Delovely/You're				
	Sensational/Everything I've Got/Love Walked				
	In/Charleston/Alexander's Ragtime Band	195?	2.50	5.00	10.00
❏ EG 7203 [PS]	Lester Lanin Goes to College	195?	2.50	5.00	10.00

Albums
AUDIO FIDELITY

Number	Title (A Side/B Side)	Yr	VG	VG+	NM
❏ AFLP-2180 [M]	Thoroughly Modern	1968	3.75	7.50	15.00
❏ AFSD-6180 [S]	Thoroughly Modern	1968	3.00	6.00	12.00
EPIC					
❏ BSN 146 [(2)S]	The Dance Album	1964	5.00	10.00	20.00
❏ BN 501 [S]	Lester Lanin Goes to College	1959	5.00	10.00	20.00
❏ BN 505 [S]	Lester Lanin at the Tiffany Ball	1959	5.00	10.00	20.00
❏ BN 516 [S]	Cocktail Dancing	1959	5.00	10.00	20.00
❏ BN 517 [S]	Have Band, Will Travel	1959	5.00	10.00	20.00
❏ BN 547 [S]	Christmas Dance Party (Volume 9)	1959	5.00	10.00	20.00
❏ BN 556 [S]	Dance to the Lester Lanin Beat	1960	5.00	10.00	20.00
❏ BN 570 [S]	High Society	1961	3.75	7.50	15.00
❏ BN 620 [S]	Twistin' in High Society!	1961	3.75	7.50	15.00
❏ BN 628 [R]	Lester Lanin and His Orchestra	1962	3.00	6.00	12.00
❏ BN 633 [R]	Dance to the Music of Lester Lanin	1962	3.00	6.00	12.00
❏ LN 3242 [M]	Lester Lanin and His Orchestra	1956	3.75	7.50	15.00
❏ LN 3340 [M]	Dance to the Music of Lester Lanin	1957	3.75	7.50	15.00
❏ LN 3410 [M]	Lester Lanin at the Tiffany Ball	1957	3.75	7.50	15.00
❏ LN 3474 [M]	Lester Lanin Goes to College	1958	3.75	7.50	15.00

Number	Title (A Side/B Side)	Yr	VG	VG+	NM
❑ LN 3525 [M]	Have Band, Will Travel	1958	3.75	7.50	15.00
❑ LN 3531 [M]	Cocktail Dancing	1959	3.75	7.50	15.00
❑ LN 3617 [M]	Christmas Dance Party (Volume 9)	1959	3.75	7.50	15.00
❑ LN 3656 [M]	Dance to the Lester Lanin Beat	1960	3.75	7.50	15.00
❑ LN 3699 [M]	High Society	1961	3.00	6.00	12.00
❑ LN 3825 [M]	Twistin' in High Society!	1961	3.00	6.00	12.00
❑ SN 6046 [(2)M]	The Dance Album	1964	3.75	7.50	15.00
❑ LN 24016 [M]	Dancing Theatre Party	1962	3.00	6.00	12.00
❑ LN 24105 [M]	Richard Rogers Hits	1964	3.00	6.00	12.00
❑ LN 24317 [M]	Cole Porter's Greatest Hits	1967	3.00	6.00	12.00
❑ BN 26016 [S]	Dancing Theatre Party	1962	3.75	7.50	15.00
❑ BN 26105 [S]	Richard Rogers Hits	1964	3.75	7.50	15.00
❑ BN 26317 [S]	Cole Porter's Greatest Hits	1967	3.00	6.00	12.00
HARMONY					
❑ HS 11262	Everybody Dance	1968	2.50	5.00	10.00
HINDSIGHT					
❑ HSR-210	Dance Instrumentals: 1960-1962	198?	2.00	4.00	8.00
METROMEDIA					
❑ MD-1006	Narrowing the Generation Gap	1969	3.00	6.00	12.00
PHILIPS					
❑ PHM 200132 [M]	Lester Lanin Plays for Dancing	1964	2.50	5.00	10.00
❑ PHM 200145 [M]	Dancing at the Discotheque	1964	2.50	5.00	10.00
❑ PHM 200165 [M]	I Had a Ball	1965	2.50	5.00	10.00
❑ PHM 200181 [M]	Hits for Dancing	1965	2.50	5.00	10.00
❑ PHM 200192 [M]	Lester Lanin at the Country Club	1966	2.50	5.00	10.00
❑ PHM 200211 [M]	Forty Beatles Hits	1966	3.00	6.00	12.00
❑ PHS 600132 [S]	Lester Lanin Plays for Dancing	1964	3.00	6.00	12.00
❑ PHS 600145 [S]	Dancing at the Discotheque	1964	3.00	6.00	12.00
❑ PHS 600165 [S]	I Had a Ball	1965	3.00	6.00	12.00
❑ PHS 600192 [S]	Hits for Dancing	1965	3.00	6.00	12.00
❑ PHS 600192 [S]	Lester Lanin at the Country Club	1966	3.00	6.00	12.00
❑ PHS 600211 [S]	Forty Beatles Hits	1966	3.75	7.50	15.00

LANZA, MARIO

45s
RCA VICTOR

Number	Title (A Side/B Side)	Yr	VG	VG+	NM
❑ 47-6334	Ave Maria/I'll Walk with God	1955	3.75	7.50	15.00
❑ 47-6644	Earthbound/This Land	1956	3.00	6.00	12.00
❑ 47-6915	A Night to Remember/Behold	1957	3.00	6.00	12.00
❑ 47-7119	Come Dance with Me/Never Till Now	1957	3.00	6.00	12.00
❑ 47-7164	Arrividerci Roma/Younger Than Springtime	1958	3.00	6.00	12.00
❑ 47-7439	For the First Time/O Sole Mio	1959	3.00	6.00	12.00
❑ 47-7622	I'll Walk with God/Guardian Angels	1959	3.00	6.00	12.00
❑ 447-0774	Ave Maria/The Lord's Prayer	196?	2.00	4.00	8.00

—Reissue; black label, dog on top

❑ 447-0777	Oh, Holy Night/I'll Walk With God	196?	2.00	4.00	8.00

—Reissue; black label, dog on top
RCA VICTOR RED SEAL

❑ 49-0902	O Sole Mio/Mattinata	1950	5.00	10.00	20.00

—Red vinyl

❑ 49-1169	Granada/Lolita	1950	5.00	10.00	20.00

—Red vinyl

❑ 49-1353	Be My Love/I'll Never Love You	1950	6.25	12.50	25.00

—Red vinyl

❑ 49-1353	Be My Love/I'll Never Love You	1951	5.00	10.00	20.00

—Black vinyl

❑ 49-3155	Serenade (Toselli)/Serenade (Drigo)	1951	5.00	10.00	20.00

—Red vinyl

❑ 49-3207	Because/For You Alone	1951	5.00	10.00	20.00

—Red vinyl

❑ 49-3208	My Song, My Love/I Love Thee	1951	5.00	10.00	20.00

—Red vinyl

❑ 49-3209	O Tu Che in Seno Agli Angeli/Addio Alla Madre	1951	5.00	10.00	20.00

—Red vinyl

❑ 49-3228	Vesti La Giubba (On with the Play)/Ave Maria (Bach-Gounod)	1951	5.00	10.00	20.00

—Red vinyl

❑ 49-3300	The Loveliest Night of the Year/La Donna E Mobile	1951	5.00	10.00	20.00

—Red vinyl

❑ 49-3435	Marechiare/'A Vucchella	195?	5.00	10.00	20.00

—Red vinyl

❑ 49-3639	The Lord's Prayer/Guardian Angels	195?	2.00	4.00	8.00

—Side 1 and Side 8 of WDM-1649; black vinyl

❑ 49-3639	The Lord's Prayer/Guardian Angels	195?	3.00	6.00	12.00

—Side 1 and Side 8 of WDM-1649; red vinyl

❑ 49-3640	The First Noel/Silent Night	195?	2.00	4.00	8.00

—Side 2 and Side 7 of WDM-1649; black vinyl

❑ 49-3640	The First Noel/Silent Night	195?	3.00	6.00	12.00

—Side 2 and Side 7 of WDM-1649; red vinyl

❑ 49-3641	O Come, All Ye Faithful/Oh Little Town of Bethlehem	195?	2.00	4.00	8.00

—Side 3 and Side 6 of WDM-1649; black vinyl

❑ 49-3641	O Come, All Ye Faithful/Oh Little Town of Bethlehem	195?	3.00	6.00	12.00

—Side 3 and Side 6 of WDM-1649; red vinyl

❑ 49-3642	Away In A Manger/We Three Kings Of Orient Are	195?	2.00	4.00	8.00

—Side 4 and Side 5 of WDM-1649; black vinyl

❑ 49-3642	Away In A Manger/We Three Kings Of Orient Are	195?	3.00	6.00	12.00

—Side 4 and Side 5 of WDM-1649; red vinyl

❑ 49-3914	Because You're Mine/The Song Angels Sing	1952	3.75	7.50	15.00

—Red vinyl

❑ 49-4209	Song of India/If You Were Mine	1953	3.75	7.50	15.00
❑ 49-4216	I'll Walk with God/Beloved	1954	3.75	7.50	15.00
❑ 49-4218	Deep in My Heart, Dear/Serenade	1954	3.75	7.50	15.00
❑ 49-4220	Drink, Drink, Drink/(B-side unknown)	1954	3.75	7.50	15.00
❑ WDM-1649 [PS]	Mario Lanza Sings Christmas Songs	195?	2.50	5.00	10.00

—Box for 4-record set (49-3639, 49-3640, 49-3641, 49-3642); may contain either red vinyl or black vinyl 45s

7-Inch Extended Plays
RCA VICTOR

❑ LPC-117	Deep in My Heart, Dear/Gaudeamus Igitur//Serenade/Drink, Drink, Drink	1961	3.75	7.50	15.00

—33 1/3 rpm, small hole

❑ LPC-117 [PS]	The Student Prince	1961	3.75	7.50	15.00
❑ EPA-4222	*Seven Hills of Rome/Arrividerci Roman/Come Dance with Me/Lolita	1958	3.00	6.00	12.00

Number	Title (A Side/B Side)	Yr	VG	VG+	NM
❑ EPA-4222 [PS]	Seven Hills of Rome	1958	3.00	6.00	12.00
❑ EPA-4344	*Come Prima/Pineapple Pickers/O, Mon Amour/O Sole Mio/Hofbrauhaus Song	1959	3.00	6.00	12.00
❑ EPA-4344 [PS]	For the First Time	1959	3.00	6.00	12.00

RCA VICTOR RED SEAL

❑ ERA 51	Addio Alla Madre (Turiddu's Farewell)/Granada//Mama Mia Che Vo Sape?/The Lord's Prayer	1952	3.00	6.00	12.00

—Red vinyl

❑ ERA 51 [PS]	Selections from "Because You're Mine"	1952	3.00	6.00	12.00
❑ ERA 110	Un Diall-Azzurro Spazio/Questa O Quella//Come Un Bel Di Di Maggio/La Donna E Mobile	195?	3.00	6.00	12.00
❑ ERA 110 [PS]	Rigoletto	195?	3.00	6.00	12.00
❑ ERA 115	O Come All Ye Faithful/Silent Night//We Three Kings Of Orient Are/The First Noel	195?	3.00	6.00	12.00
❑ ERA 115 [PS]	Four Favorite Christmas Carols	195?	3.00	6.00	12.00

—Ornament-shaped sleeve

❑ ERA 130	I Know, I Know, I Know/Be My Love//The Loveliest Night of the Year/Because You're Mine	1953	3.00	6.00	12.00
❑ ERA 130 [PS]	Mario Lanza In Movie Hits	1953	3.00	6.00	12.00
❑ ERA 222	Because/Vesta La Giubba//Core 'Ingrato/Toselli's Serenade	1954	3.00	6.00	12.00
❑ ERA 222 [PS]	Mario Lanza Sings Because	1954	3.00	6.00	12.00
❑ ERA-288	Away in a Manger/Deck the Halls/Joy to the World//O Little Town of Bethlehem/It Came Upon a Midnight Clear	1956	3.00	6.00	12.00
❑ ERA-288 [PS]	Mario Lanza Sings Christmas Carols	1956	3.00	6.00	12.00
❑ ERB 1837 [PS]	The Student Prince	195?	3.75	7.50	15.00

—Gatefold cover for 2-EP set (549-5078, 549-5079)

❑ ERB 1860 [PS]	A Kiss and Other Love Songs	1955	3.00	6.00	12.00
❑ 549-5078	Orchestral Introduction/Serenade//Deep in My Heart, Dear/I'll Walk with God	195?	3.00	6.00	12.00

—Record 1 of 2-EP set ERB 1837

❑ 549-5079	Golden Days/Drink, Drink, Drink//Summertime in Heidelburg/Beloved/Gaudeamus Igitur	195?	3.75	7.50	15.00

—Record 2 of 2-EP set ERB 1837

❑ 549-5127	A Kiss/Begin the Beguine//My Romance/Night and Day	195?	3.00	6.00	12.00

—Record 1 of 2-EP set ERB 1860

❑ 549-5128	Long Ago/The Night Is Young and You're So Beautiful//My Heart Stood Still/The Moon Was Yellow	195?	3.00	6.00	12.00

—Record 1 of 2-EP set ERB 1860

Albums
PAIR

❑ PDL2-1059 [(2)]	The Voice of the Century	1986	3.00	6.00	12.00

PICKWICK

❑ CAS-777(e) [R]	Christmas Hymns and Carols	1977	2.00	4.00	8.00

—Same contents as RCA Camden CAS-777(e)
RCA CAMDEN

❑ CAL-450 [M]	You Do Something to Me	195?	3.75	7.50	15.00
❑ CAS-450(e) [R]	You Do Something to Me	195?	3.00	6.00	12.00
❑ CAL-777 [M]	Christmas Hymns and Carols	196?	3.75	7.50	15.00
❑ CAS-777(e) [R]	Christmas Hymns and Carols	196?	3.00	6.00	12.00

RCA RED SEAL

❑ ARL1-0134	Lanza Sings Caruso	1973	2.50	5.00	10.00
❑ CRL1-1750	A Legendary Performer	1976	2.50	5.00	10.00
❑ ANL1-2874	Pure Gold	1978	2.50	5.00	10.00
❑ CRM5-4158 [(5)]	The Mario Lanza Collection	1981	15.00	30.00	60.00
❑ ARL1-4405	The Great Caruso	198?	2.00	4.00	8.00
❑ VCS-6192 [(3)]	Mario Lanza's Greatest Hits	1970	6.25	12.50	25.00
❑ VCS-7073 [(2)]	Opera's Greatest Hits	1971	4.50	9.00	18.00

RCA VICTOR RED SEAL

❑ LM-155 [10]	Mario Lanza Sings Christmas Songs	1951	12.50	25.00	50.00
❑ LM-1127 [M]	The Great Caruso	195?	10.00	20.00	40.00
❑ LSC-1127(e) [R]	The Great Caruso	196?	3.00	6.00	12.00
❑ LM-1188 [M]	Love Songs and a Neapolitan Serenade	195?	10.00	20.00	40.00
❑ LSC-1188(e) [R]	Love Songs and a Neapolitan Serenade	196?	3.00	6.00	12.00
❑ LM 1837 [M]	Mario Lanza Sings the Hit Songs from "The Student Prince" and Other Great Musical Comedies	1955	10.00	20.00	40.00
❑ LSC 1837(e) [R]	Mario Lanza Sings the Hit Songs from "The Student Prince" and Other Great Musical Comedies	196?	3.00	6.00	12.00
❑ LM-1860 [M]	"A Kiss" and Other Love Songs	1955	10.00	20.00	40.00
❑ LSC-1860(e) [R]	"A Kiss" and Other Love Songs	196?	3.00	6.00	12.00
❑ LM-1927 [M]	The Touch of Your Hand	1955	10.00	20.00	40.00
❑ LSC-1927(e) [R]	The Touch of Your Hand	196?	3.00	6.00	12.00
❑ LM-1943 [M]	Magic Mario	1955	10.00	20.00	40.00
❑ LM-1996 [M]	Serenade	1956	10.00	20.00	40.00
❑ LM-2070 [M]	Lanza on Broadway	1956	7.50	15.00	30.00
❑ LSC-2070(e) [R]	Lanza on Broadway	196?	3.00	6.00	12.00
❑ LM-2090 [M]	Cavalcade of Show Tunes	1957	7.50	15.00	30.00
❑ LSC-2090(e) [R]	Cavalcade of Show Tunes	196?	3.00	6.00	12.00
❑ LM-2211 [M]	Seven Hills of Rome	1958	7.50	15.00	30.00
❑ LM-2331 [M]	Mario	1959	5.00	10.00	20.00
❑ LSC-2331 [S]	Mario!	1959	7.50	15.00	30.00
❑ LM-2333 [M]	Lanza Sings Christmas Carols	1959	3.75	7.50	15.00
❑ LSC-2333 [S]	Lanza Sings Christmas Carols	1959	5.00	10.00	20.00

—Original copies have "shaded dog" on labels

❑ LM-2338 [M]	For the First Time	1959	3.75	7.50	15.00
❑ LSC-2338 [S]	For the First Time	1959	5.00	10.00	20.00
❑ LM-2339 [M]	The Student Prince	1959	3.75	7.50	15.00
❑ LSC-2339 [S]	The Student Prince	1959	5.00	10.00	20.00
❑ LM-2393 [M]	Mario Lanza Sings Caruso Favorites	1960	3.75	7.50	15.00
❑ LSC-2393 [S]	Mario Lanza Sings Caruso Favorites	1960	5.00	10.00	20.00
❑ LM-2422 [M]	Double Feature — Mario Lanza	1960	5.00	10.00	20.00
❑ LM-2440 [M]	The Desert Song	1960	3.75	7.50	15.00
❑ LSC-2440 [S]	The Desert Song	1960	5.00	10.00	20.00
❑ LM-2454 [M]	A Mario Lanza Program	1960	3.75	7.50	15.00
❑ LSC-2454 [S]	A Mario Lanza Program	1960	5.00	10.00	20.00
❑ LM-2509 [M]	The Vagabond King	1961	3.75	7.50	15.00
❑ LSC-2509 [S]	The Vagabond King	1961	5.00	10.00	20.00
❑ LM-2607 [M]	I'll Walk with God	1962	5.00	10.00	20.00
❑ LSC-2607(e) [R]	I'll Walk with God	1962	3.00	6.00	12.00
❑ LM-2720 [M]	I'll See You in My Dreams	1964	3.00	6.00	12.00
❑ LSC-2720 [S]	I'll See You in My Dreams	1964	3.75	7.50	15.00

Number	Title (A Side/B Side)	Yr	VG	VG+	NM
❑ LM-2748 [M]	The Best of Mario Lanza	1964	3.00	6.00	12.00
❑ LSC-2748 [S]	The Best of Mario Lanza	1964	3.75	7.50	15.00
❑ LM-2790 [M]	If You Are But a Dream	196?	3.00	6.00	12.00
❑ LSC-2790 [S]	If You Are But a Dream	196?	3.75	7.50	15.00
❑ LM-2932 [M]	His Favorite Arias	196?	3.00	6.00	12.00
❑ LSC-2932 [S]	His Favorite Arias	196?	3.75	7.50	15.00
❑ LM-2998 [M]	The Best of Mario Lanza, Volume 2	1968	5.00	10.00	20.00
❑ LSC-2998 [S]	The Best of Mario Lanza, Volume 2	1968	3.75	7.50	15.00
❑ LSC-3049	Younger Than Springtime	1968	3.00	6.00	12.00
❑ LSC-3101	Mario Lanza in Opera	1969	3.75	7.50	15.00
❑ LSC-3102	Mario Lanza Memories	1969	3.75	7.50	15.00
❑ LSC-3103	Mario Lanza…Speak to Me of Love	1969	3.75	7.50	15.00
❑ LSC-3216	The Student Prince	1971	3.00	6.00	12.00
❑ LSC-3289	Be My Love	1972	3.00	6.00	12.00

LAPELS, THE
45s
DOT
❑ 16129	Sneakin' Around/Sneakin' Blues	1960	3.00	6.00	12.00
MELKER
| ❑ 103 | Sneakin' Around/Sneakin' Blues | 1960 | 10.00 | 20.00 | 40.00 |

LARADOS, THE Members of this group were later in THE REFLECTIONS.
45s
FOX
❑ 962/3	Now the Parting Begins/Bad Guitar Man	1958	50.00	100.00	200.00
MADOG
| ❑ 801 | Will You Love Me Tomorrow/You Didn't Care | 1980 | 3.75 | 7.50 | 15.00 |

LARKIN, BILLY Includes The Delegates; Billy Larkin and the Delegates.
45s
AURA
❑ 4504	Pigmy (Part 1)/Pigmy (Part 2)	1965	3.75	7.50	15.00
—As "The Delegates"					
❑ 4508	The Peeper/Hainty	1965	3.75	7.50	15.00
—As "The Delegates"					
CASINO
| ❑ 097 | Here's to the Next Time/Lonely Woman | 1976 | — | 2.50 | 5.00 |
SUNBIRD
❑ 107	I Can't Stop Now/Lovin' a Lie	1980	—	2.00	4.00
❑ 7557	20-20 Hindsight/Lonely Woman	1981	—	2.00	4.00
❑ 7562	Longing for the High/Is There Nothing Left to Say	1981	—	2.00	4.00
WORLD PACIFIC
❑ 4504	Pigmy (Part 1)/Pigmy (Part 2)	1965	3.00	6.00	12.00
—As "The Delegates"					
❑ 77844	Hold On! I'm a-Comin'/Dirty Water	1966	2.00	4.00	8.00
❑ 88120	Pigmy (Part 1)/The Peeper	1966	2.50	5.00	10.00
—As "The Delegates"					
Albums
AURA
❑ 23002 [S]	Pigmy	1964	6.25	12.50	25.00
—As "The Delegates"					
❑ ARS 23003 [S]	Blue Lights	196?	6.25	12.50	25.00
❑ 83002 [M]	Pigmy	1964	5.00	10.00	20.00
—As "The Delegates"					
❑ AR 83003 [M]	Blue Lights	196?	5.00	10.00	20.00
WORLD PACIFIC
❑ WP-1837 [M]	Hole in the Wall	1966	5.00	10.00	20.00
❑ WP-1843 [M]	Ain't That a Groove	1966	5.00	10.00	20.00
❑ WP-1850 [M]	Hold On	1967	5.00	10.00	20.00
❑ WPS-21837 [S]	Hole in the Wall	1966	6.25	12.50	25.00
❑ WPS-21843 [S]	Ain't That a Groove	1966	6.25	12.50	25.00
❑ WPS-21850 [S]	Hold On	1967	6.25	12.50	25.00

LARKS, THE (1) Also see DON JULIAN AND THE MEADOWLARKS.
45s
MONEY
❑ 106	The Jerk/Forget Me	1964	5.00	10.00	20.00
❑ 109	Mickey's East Coast Jerk/Soul Jerk	1965	3.00	6.00	12.00
❑ 110	The Slauson Shuffle/Soul Jerk	1965	3.00	6.00	12.00
❑ 112	The Roman/Heavenly Father	1965	3.00	6.00	12.00
❑ 115	Can You Do the Duck/Sad Sad Boy	1965	3.00	6.00	12.00
❑ 119	Lost My Love Yesterday/ The Answer Came Too Late	1966	3.00	6.00	12.00
❑ 122	Philly Dog/Heaven Only Knows	1966	3.00	6.00	12.00
❑ 127	The Skate/Come Back Baby	1967	3.00	6.00	12.00
❑ 601	I Love You/I Want You Back	1973	—	3.00	6.00
❑ 604	My Favorite Beer Joint/(Instrumental)	1973	—	3.00	6.00
❑ 607	Shorty the Pimp (Part 1)/Shorty the Pimp (Part 2)	1974	—	3.00	6.00
—Money 604 and 607 as "Don Julian and the Larks"					
Albums
COLLECTABLES
| ❑ COL-5176 | Golden Classics: The Jerk | 198? | 2.50 | 5.00 | 10.00 |
MONEY
❑ LP-1102 [M]	The Jerk	1965	10.00	20.00	40.00
❑ ST-1102 [S]	The Jerk	1965	12.50	25.00	50.00
❑ LP-1107 [M]	Soul Kaleidoscope	1966	10.00	20.00	40.00
❑ ST-1107 [S]	Soul Kaleidoscope	1966	12.50	25.00	50.00
❑ LP-1110 [M]	Superslick	1967	10.00	20.00	40.00
❑ ST-1110 [S]	Superslick	1967	12.50	25.00	50.00

LARKS, THE (2)
45s
SHERYL
❑ 334	It's Unbelievable/I Can't Believe It	1961	7.50	15.00	30.00
❑ 338	There Is a Girl/Let's Drink a Toast	1961	6.25	12.50	25.00

LARKS, THE (3)
45s
APOLLO
❑ 429	Little Side Car/Hey Little Girl	1951	1000.	2000.	4000.
❑ 430	Ooh, It Feels So Good/ I Don't Believe in Tomorrow	1951	1000.	2000.	4000.
❑ 435	My Lost Love/How Long Must I Wait for You	1952	250.00	500.00	1000.
❑ 437	Darlin'/Lucy Brown	1952	250.00	500.00	1000.
❑ 475	No Mama No/Honey from the Bee	1955	100.00	200.00	400.00

Number	Title (A Side/B Side)	Yr	VG	VG+	NM
❑ 1180	Hopefully Yours/ When I Leave These Prison Walls	1951	1000.	2000.	4000.
❑ 1184	My Reverie/Let's Say a Prayer	1951	500.00	1000.	2000.
—Black vinyl					
❑ 1184	My Reverie/Let's Say a Prayer	1951	4000.	6000.	8000.
—Red vinyl					
❑ 1189	Shadrack/Honey in the Rock	1952	500.00	1000.	2000.
❑ 1190	Stolen Love/In My Lonely Room	1952	625.00	1250.	2500.
—Black vinyl					
❑ 1190	Stolen Love/In My Lonely Room	1952	2500.	3750.	5000.
—Red vinyl					
❑ 1194	I Live True to You/Hold Me	1952	250.00	500.00	1000.

LLOYDS
❑ 108	Margie/Rockin' in the Rockin' Room	1954	200.00	400.00	800.00
❑ 110	Tippin' In/If It's a Crime	1954	200.00	400.00	800.00
❑ 112	No Other Girl/The World Is Waiting for the Sunrise	1954	200.00	400.00	800.00
❑ 114	Forget It/I Live True to You	1954	150.00	300.00	600.00

LARKS, THE (U) It's doubtful that any of these are groups (1) or (3). Some could be by group (2).
45s
CROSS FIRE
❑ 74-49/50	Fabulous Cars and Diamond Rings/ Life Is Sweeter Now	1961	5.00	10.00	20.00
GUYDEN
| ❑ 2098 | I Want Her to Love Me/(Instrumental) | 1963 | 3.00 | 6.00 | 12.00 |
| ❑ 2103 | Fabulous Cars and Diamond Rings/Life Is Sweeter Now | 1964 | 3.00 | 6.00 | 12.00 |
JETT
| ❑ 3001 | Love You So/Love Me True | 1965 | 15.00 | 30.00 | 60.00 |
NASCO
| ❑ 028 | I Love You/I Want You Back | 1972 | 2.00 | 4.00 | 8.00 |
STACY
| ❑ 969 | Food Sticks/Scavenger | 1963 | 3.00 | 6.00 | 12.00 |
VIOLET
| ❑ 1051 | I Want Her to Love Me/(Instrumental) | 1962 | 5.00 | 10.00 | 20.00 |

LARKTONES, THE
45s
ABC-PARAMOUNT
❑ 9909	The Letter/Rockin' Swingin' Man	1958	7.50	15.00	30.00
RIKI
| ❑ 140 | Why Are You Tearing Us Apart/Nosy Neighbor | 1960 | 15.00 | 30.00 | 60.00 |

LAROSA, JULIUS
45s
ABC
❑ 10959	For Once in My Life/Summer Love	1967	—	3.00	6.00
CADENCE
❑ 1230	Anywhere I Wander/This Is Heaven	1953	3.75	7.50	15.00
❑ 1231	My Lady Loves to Dance/ Let's Make Up Before We Say Goodnight	1953	3.75	7.50	15.00
❑ 1232	Eh, Cumpari/Till They've All Gone Home	1953	3.75	7.50	15.00
❑ 1235	The Big Bell and the Little Bell/ I Couldn't Believe My Eyes	1954	3.00	6.00	12.00
❑ 1236	My Funny Valentine/Roseanne	1954	3.00	6.00	12.00
❑ 1237	When You're in Love/Have a Heart	1954	3.00	6.00	12.00
❑ 1240	Three Coins in the Fountain/Me Gotta Have You	1954	3.00	6.00	12.00
❑ 1244	My Heart's on a Fast Express/ In My Own Quiet Way	1954	3.00	6.00	12.00
❑ 1251	Mobile/I Hate to Say Hello	1954	3.00	6.00	12.00
❑ 1252	Campanelle (Jingle Bells)/I Hope You'll Be Very Happy	1954	3.00	6.00	12.00
❑ 1253	Jingle Dingle/Campanelle (Jingle Bells)	1954	3.00	6.00	12.00
❑ 1258	Let's Stay Home Tonight/Pass It On	1955	3.00	6.00	12.00
❑ 1265	Domani (Tomorrow)/Mama Rosa	1955	3.00	6.00	12.00
❑ 1270	Suddenly There's a Valley/ Everytime That I Kiss Carrie	1955	3.00	6.00	12.00
❑ 1440	David and Lisa's Love Song/ Suddenly There's a Valley	1963	2.00	4.00	8.00
❑ 1444	Gonna Build a Mountain/JE	1964	2.00	4.00	8.00
CREWE
| ❑ 335 | Where Do I Go/This Is All I Had | 1969 | — | 3.00 | 6.00 |
| —With the Bob Crewe Generation | | | | | |
GP
| ❑ 592 | A Christmas Gift/To Find Our Children | 1981 | — | 3.00 | 6.00 |
KAPP
❑ 323	Green Fields/Your Hand in Mine	1960	2.00	4.00	8.00
❑ 348	Bewitched/It's Alright with Me	1960	2.00	4.00	8.00
❑ 371	Let Your Lips Tell Me/Seventeen	1961	2.00	4.00	8.00
❑ 417	There's No Other Love/Caress Me	1961	2.00	4.00	8.00
❑ 444	You Can't Keep Me from Loving You/If I Had My Way	1962	2.00	4.00	8.00
METROMEDIA
| ❑ 186 | Brooklyn Roads/Being Alive | 1970 | — | 2.50 | 5.00 |
MGM
❑ CS5-5	Celebrity Scene: Julius LaRosa	1967	12.50	25.00	50.00
—Box set of five singles (13671-13675). Price includes box, all 5 singles, jukebox title strips, bio. Records are sometimes found by themselves, so they are also listed separately.					
❑ 13454	Small, Small World/Unless	1966	—	3.00	6.00
❑ 13497	Lonely As I Leave You/ You're Gonna Hear from Me	1966	—	3.00	6.00
❑ 13575	I Think It's Going to Rain Today/ You Only See Her	1966	—	3.00	6.00
❑ 13651	We Need A Little Christmas/Our Venetian Affair	1966	2.00	4.00	8.00
❑ 13671	(titles unknown)	1967	2.00	4.00	8.00
❑ 13672	Somethin' Special/You're Gonna Hear from Me	1967	2.00	4.00	8.00
❑ 13673	(titles unknown)	1967	2.00	4.00	8.00
❑ 13674	What Did I Have That I Don't Have/Spring	1967	2.00	4.00	8.00
❑ 13675	Who Am I/What'll I Do	1967	2.00	4.00	8.00
RCA VICTOR
❑ 47-6416	Lipstick and Candy and Rubber Sole Shoes/ Winter in New England	1956	2.50	5.00	10.00
❑ 47-6499	I've Got Love/Augustine	1956	2.50	5.00	10.00
❑ 47-6567	Get Me to the Church On Time/ I've Grown Accustomed to Her Face	1956	2.50	5.00	10.00

Number	Title (A Side/B Side)	Yr	VG	VG+	NM
47-6648	The Opposite Sex/Namely You	1956	2.50	5.00	10.00
47-6700	All I Want/Priscilla	1956	2.50	5.00	10.00
47-6802	Jeanette/Stashu Pandowski	1957	2.50	5.00	10.00
47-6878	Mama Guitar/Man to Man	1957	2.50	5.00	10.00
47-6923	Crying My Heart Out for You/When You're With the One You Love	1957	2.50	5.00	10.00
47-6998	Worlds Apart/Famous Last Words	1957	2.50	5.00	10.00
47-7059	Just Forever/Since When (Is It a Sin)	1957	2.50	5.00	10.00
47-7186	Lover, Lover/A Heart for a Heart	1958	2.50	5.00	10.00
47-7227	Torero/Milano	1958	2.50	5.00	10.00
74-0938	The Good Life/Sing Me a Song	1973	—	2.50	5.00

ROULETTE

Number	Title (A Side/B Side)	Yr	VG	VG+	NM
4135	Where's the Girl/Protect Me	1959	2.50	5.00	10.00
4162	Honey Bunch/Port of Love	1959	2.50	5.00	10.00

7-Inch Extended Plays

CADENCE

Number	Title (A Side/B Side)	Yr	VG	VG+	NM
EP 1233	No Other Love/I Believe//My Funny Valentine/Roseanne	1953	3.75	7.50	15.00
EP 1233 [PS]	Requestfully Yours	1953	3.75	7.50	15.00
EP 1234	Ave Maria/Adeste Fideles//Silent Night/Oh Holy Night	1953	3.75	7.50	15.00
EP 1234 [PS]	Julius LaRosa Sings…	1953	3.75	7.50	15.00

RCA VICTOR

Number	Title (A Side/B Side)	Yr	VG	VG+	NM
SPA-7-38	No Love, No Nothin'/Intermission Time/1001 Nighters//Sweet Substitute/I Can't Believe That You're in Love with Me/The Little Boy Blew	1956	3.00	6.00	12.00

—Continuously banded; narrated by LaRosa; artists, in order, are Julius LaRosa/The Three Suns/Ralph Flanagan//Bob Scobey/Teddi King/Dennis Farnon

Number	Title (A Side/B Side)	Yr	VG	VG+	NM
SPA-7-38 [PS]	Pajama Party	1956	3.00	6.00	12.00
EPA 841	(contents unknown)	1956	3.75	7.50	15.00
EPA 841 [PS]	Julius LaRosa	1956	3.75	7.50	15.00
547-1025	Candy/Don't You Know I Care//No Love, No Nothin'/Wait 'Till You See Her	1956	2.50	5.00	10.00

—One record of EPB 1299

Number	Title (A Side/B Side)	Yr	VG	VG+	NM
547-1026	But Not for Me/I Love My Bed//Our Love Is Here to Stay/Ev'ry Time	1956	2.50	5.00	10.00

—One record of EPB 1299

Number	Title (A Side/B Side)	Yr	VG	VG+	NM
EPB-1299 [PS] Julius LaRosa		1956	2.50	5.00	10.00

—Cover for 2-EP set (547-1025, 547-1026)

Albums

AUDIOPHILE

Number	Title (A Side/B Side)	Yr	VG	VG+	NM
AP-190	It's a Wrap!	1985	3.00	6.00	12.00

CADENCE

Number	Title (A Side/B Side)	Yr	VG	VG+	NM
CLP 1007 [M]	Julius LaRosa (Julie's Best)	1955	10.00	20.00	40.00

FORUM

Number	Title (A Side/B Side)	Yr	VG	VG+	NM
F-16012 [M]	Just Say I Love Her	1960	3.75	7.50	15.00
FS-16012 [S]	Just Say I Love Her	1960	5.00	10.00	20.00

KAPP

Number	Title (A Side/B Side)	Yr	VG	VG+	NM
KL-1245 [M]	The New Julie LaRosa	1961	3.75	7.50	15.00
KS-3245 [S]	The New Julie LaRosa	1961	5.00	10.00	20.00

METROMEDIA

Number	Title (A Side/B Side)	Yr	VG	VG+	NM
MD-1036	Words	1971	3.00	6.00	12.00

MGM

Number	Title (A Side/B Side)	Yr	VG	VG+	NM
E-4398 [M]	You're Gonna Hear From Me	1966	3.00	6.00	12.00
SE-4398 [S]	You're Gonna Hear From Me	1966	3.75	7.50	15.00
E-4437 [M]	Hey Look Me Over	1967	3.00	6.00	12.00
SE-4437 [S]	Hey Look Me Over	1967	3.75	7.50	15.00

RCA VICTOR

Number	Title (A Side/B Side)	Yr	VG	VG+	NM
LPM-1299 [M]	Julius LaRosa	1956	10.00	20.00	40.00

ROULETTE

Number	Title (A Side/B Side)	Yr	VG	VG+	NM
R 25054 [M]	Love Songs A LaRosa	1959	5.00	10.00	20.00
SR 25054 [S]	Love Songs A LaRosa	1959	6.25	12.50	25.00
R 25083 [M]	On the Sunny Side	1960	5.00	10.00	20.00
SR 25083 [S]	On the Sunny Side	1960	6.25	12.50	25.00

LARRY AND THE CROSSFIRES
45s

SEARCY

Number	Title (A Side/B Side)	Yr	VG	VG+	NM
711	Torquay '65/Wee Wee Hours	1965	12.50	25.00	50.00

LARRY AND THE LEGENDS
45s

ATLANTIC

Number	Title (A Side/B Side)	Yr	VG	VG+	NM
2220	Don't Pick On My Baby/The Creep	1964	6.25	12.50	25.00

—With the Four Seasons

LASALLE, DENISE
45s

ABC

Number	Title (A Side/B Side)	Yr	VG	VG+	NM
12225	Hellfire Loving/I Get What I Want	1976	—	2.50	5.00
12238	Freedom to Express Yourself/Second Breath	1977	—	2.00	4.00
12312	Love Me Right/Fool Me Good	1977	—	2.00	4.00
12353	One Life to Live/Before You Take It to the Streets	1978	—	2.00	4.00
12419	Workin' Overtime/No Matter What They Say	1978	—	2.00	4.00
12443	P.A.R.T.Y. (Where It Is)/Under the Influence	1979	—	2.00	4.00

CHESS

Number	Title (A Side/B Side)	Yr	VG	VG+	NM
2005	A Love Reputation/One Little Thing	1967	2.50	5.00	10.00
2044	Private Property/I've Been Waiting	1968	2.50	5.00	10.00
2058	Count Down (And Fly Me to the Moon)/A Promise Is a Promise	1968	2.50	5.00	10.00

MALACO

Number	Title (A Side/B Side)	Yr	VG	VG+	NM
2089	Lady in the Street/I Was Not the Best Woman	198?	—	2.00	4.00
2092	Lay Me Down/I Was Telling Him About You	198?	—	2.00	4.00
2095	Down Home Blues/Down Home Blues (X-Rated)	198?	—	2.00	4.00
2098	Right Place, Right Time/He's Not Available	1984	—	2.00	4.00

—With Latimore

Number	Title (A Side/B Side)	Yr	VG	VG+	NM
2105	Treat Your Man Like a Baby/Come to Bed	1985	—	2.00	4.00
2112	My Tu-Tu/Give Me Yo' Strongest Whiskey	1985	—	2.00	4.00
2124	Santa Claus Got the Blues/Love Is a Five Letter Word	1985	—	2.50	5.00
2131	What's Going On in My House/He's That Way Sometime	1986	—	2.00	4.00
2138	Hold What You Got/Footsteps of a Fool	1986	—	2.00	4.00
2152	Bring It On Home to Me/Write This One Off (As Actors)	1987	—	2.00	4.00
2156	Caught in Your Mess/I Forgot to Remember	1987	—	2.00	4.00
2167	Drop That Zero/Chain Letter	1988	—	2.00	4.00

MCA

Number	Title (A Side/B Side)	Yr	VG	VG+	NM
41222	I'm So Hot/Miracle, You and Me	1980	—	2.00	4.00
51046	I'm Trippin' on You/I'll Get You Some Help	1981	—	2.00	4.00
51098	Sharing Your Love/I'll Get You Some Help	1981	—	2.00	4.00

TARPEN

Number	Title (A Side/B Side)	Yr	VG	VG+	NM
6603	A Love Reputation/One Little Thing	1967	6.25	12.50	25.00

WESTBOUND

Number	Title (A Side/B Side)	Yr	VG	VG+	NM
162	Heartbreaker of the Year/Hung Up, Strung Out	1971	2.00	4.00	8.00
182	Trapped by a Thing Called Love/Keep It Coming	1971	—	3.00	6.00
201	Now Run and Tell That/The Deeper I Go	1972	—	3.00	6.00
206	Man Sized Job/I'm Over You	1972	—	3.00	6.00
215	What It Takes to Get a Good Woman (That's What It's Gonna Take to Keep Her)/Making a Good Thing Better	1973	—	3.00	6.00
219	Your Man and Your Best Friend/What Am I Doing Wrong	1973	—	3.00	6.00
221	Don't Nobody Live Here (By the Name of Fool)/Goody Goody Getter	1973	—	3.00	6.00
223	Get Up Off My Mind/The Best Thing I Ever Had	1974	—	3.00	6.00
229	Trying to Forget/We've Got Love	1974	—	3.00	6.00
5004	My Brand on You/Anytime Is the Right Time	1975	—	2.50	5.00
5008	Here I Am Again/Hung Up, Strung Out	1975	—	2.50	5.00
5019	Married, But Not to Each Other/Who's the Fool	1976	—	2.50	5.00

Albums

ABC

Number	Title (A Side/B Side)	Yr	VG	VG+	NM
D-966	Second Breath	1976	3.00	6.00	12.00
D-1027	The Bitch Is Bad	1977	3.00	6.00	12.00
AA-1087	Under the Influence	1978	3.00	6.00	12.00

MALACO

Number	Title (A Side/B Side)	Yr	VG	VG+	NM
7412	A Lady in the Street	198?	2.50	5.00	10.00
7417	Right Place, Right Time	1984	2.50	5.00	10.00
7422	Love Talkin'	198?	2.50	5.00	10.00
7434	Rain and Fire	198?	2.50	5.00	10.00
7441	It's Lying Time Again	198?	2.50	5.00	10.00
7447	Hittin' Where It Hurts	198?	2.50	5.00	10.00
7454	Still Trapped	198?	2.50	5.00	10.00
7464	Love Me Right	198?	2.50	5.00	10.00

MCA

Number	Title (A Side/B Side)	Yr	VG	VG+	NM
759	Unwrapped	198?	2.00	4.00	8.00

—Reissue of 3089

Number	Title (A Side/B Side)	Yr	VG	VG+	NM
760	I'm So Hot	198?	2.00	4.00	8.00

—Reissue of 3239

Number	Title (A Side/B Side)	Yr	VG	VG+	NM
3089	Unwrapped	1979	2.50	5.00	10.00
3239	I'm So Hot	1980	2.50	5.00	10.00

WESTBOUND

Number	Title (A Side/B Side)	Yr	VG	VG+	NM
209	Here I Am Again	1975	3.00	6.00	12.00
2012	Trapped by a Thing Called Love	1972	3.75	7.50	15.00
2016	On the Loose	1973	3.75	7.50	15.00

LAST, JAMES
45s

MGM

Number	Title (A Side/B Side)	Yr	VG	VG+	NM
13599	Lara's Theme/Games That Lovers Play	1966	2.50	5.00	10.00

POLYDOR

Number	Title (A Side/B Side)	Yr	VG	VG+	NM
2071	The Seduction (Love Theme)/Night Drive	1980	—	—	3.00
2108	Fantasy/Last Glow	1980	—	—	3.00
2119	So Excited/Last Glow	1980	—	—	3.00
15004	Happy Heart/A Man and a Woman	1969	—	2.00	4.00
15017	Proud Mary/Washington Square	1970	—	2.00	4.00
15024	Girl of the North Country/The Party Is Over	1971	—	2.00	4.00
15028	Music from Across the Way/Endless Journey	1971	—	2.00	4.00
15045	Wedding Song (There Is Love)/Love Must Be the Reason	1972	—	2.00	4.00
15050	Heart of Gold/It's Going to Take Some Time	1972	—	2.00	4.00
15082	Jenny Jenny/But I Can Sleep in a Park	1973	—	2.00	4.00
15108	Summertime/Love for Sale	1975	—	2.00	4.00
15115	Theme from Prisoner of Second Avenue/Jubilation	197?	—	2.00	4.00

Albums

POLYDOR

Number	Title (A Side/B Side)	Yr	VG	VG+	NM
24-4505	Classics Up to Date	1970	3.00	6.00	12.00
24-4507	Soft Rock	1970	3.00	6.00	12.00
24-4509	El Condor Pasa	1971	3.00	6.00	12.00
24-4512	Good Times	1971	3.00	6.00	12.00
PD-5505	Music from Across the Way	1972	2.50	5.00	10.00
PD-5506	The Love Album	197?	2.50	5.00	10.00
PD-5512	Love Must Be the Reason	1972	2.50	5.00	10.00
PD-5534	Non Stop Dancing	1973	2.50	5.00	10.00
PD-5538	M.O.R.	1973	2.50	5.00	10.00
24-6004	Hair	1969	3.00	6.00	12.00
PD-6040	Well Kept Secret	1975	2.50	5.00	10.00
PD-1-6283	Seduction	1980	2.50	5.00	10.00

LAST CALL OF SHILOH, THE
Albums

LAST CALL

Number	Title (A Side/B Side)	Yr	VG	VG+	NM
5136	The Last Call	196?	50.00	100.00	200.00

LAST POETS, THE
45s

BLUE THUMB

Number	Title (A Side/B Side)	Yr	VG	VG+	NM
216	Tribute to Orabi/Bird's Word	1972	3.00	6.00	12.00

DOUGLAS

Number	Title (A Side/B Side)	Yr	VG	VG+	NM
ADS 8	O.D./Black Thighs	1971	3.75	7.50	15.00
ADS 8 [PS]	O.D./Black Thighs	1971	7.50	15.00	30.00
ZS7 6500	True Blues/Black Is	1971	3.00	6.00	12.00

Albums

BLUE THUMB

Number	Title (A Side/B Side)	Yr	VG	VG+	NM
BT-39	Chastisement	1972	7.50	15.00	30.00
BT-52	At Last	1973	7.50	15.00	30.00

CASABLANCA

Number	Title (A Side/B Side)	Yr	VG	VG+	NM
NBLP 7051	Delights of the Garden	1977	6.25	12.50	25.00

CELLULOID

Number	Title (A Side/B Side)	Yr	VG	VG+	NM
6101	The Last Poets	198?	2.50	5.00	10.00

L

Number	Title (A Side/B Side)	Yr	VG	VG+	NM
❑ 6105	This Is Madness	198?	2.50	5.00	10.00
❑ 6108	Oh My People	198?	2.50	5.00	10.00
❑ 6136	Delights of the Garden	198?	2.50	5.00	10.00
COLLECTABLES					
❑ COL-6500	Right On!	198?	2.50	5.00	10.00
DOUGLAS					
❑ 3	The Last Poets	1970	12.50	25.00	50.00
❑ Z 30583	This Is Madness	1971	12.50	25.00	50.00
❑ Z 30811	The Last Poets	1971	10.00	20.00	40.00
JUGGERNAUT					
❑ 8802	Right On!	1971	12.50	25.00	50.00
—As "The Original Last Poets"					

LATIMORE
12-Inch Singles
T.K. DISCO

Number	Title (A Side/B Side)	Yr	VG	VG+	NM
❑ 400	Goodbye Heartache/We Got to Hit It Off	1979	3.75	7.50	15.00
45s					
ATLANTIC					
❑ 2639	I Pity the Fool/I'm Just an Ordinary Man	1969	2.00	4.00	8.00
DADE					
❑ 2013	Girl, I Got News for You/Ain't Gonna Cry No More	1967	2.50	5.00	10.00
❑ 2014	There She Is/It Was So Nice While It Lasted	1967	2.50	5.00	10.00
❑ 2015	It's Just a Matter of Time/ Let's Move and Groove Together	1967	2.50	5.00	10.00
❑ 2017	The Power and the Glory/Love Don't Love Me	1968	2.50	5.00	10.00
❑ 2020	Have a Little Faith/I'm a Believer	1968	2.50	5.00	10.00
❑ 2022	I Pity the Fool/I'm Just an Ordinary Man	1968	2.50	5.00	10.00
❑ 2026	I'll Be Good to You/Life's Little Ups and Downs	1969	2.50	5.00	10.00
GLADES					
❑ 1714	Jolie/There's No End	1973	2.00	4.00	8.00
❑ 1716	Stormy Monday/There's No End	1973	—	3.00	6.00
❑ 1720	If You Were My Woman/Put Pride Aside	1974	—	3.00	6.00
❑ 1722	Let's Straighten It Out/Ain't Nobody Gonna Make Me Change My Mind	1974	—	3.00	6.00
❑ 1726	Keep the Home Fires Burnin'/That's How It Is	1975	—	3.00	6.00
❑ 1729	There's a Red-Neck in the Soul Band/ Just One Step	1975	—	3.00	6.00
❑ 1733	Qualified Man/She Don't Ever Lose Her Groove	1976	—	3.00	6.00
❑ 1739	Somethin' 'Bout 'Cha/Sweet Vibrations	1976	—	3.00	6.00
❑ 1742	I Get Lifted/All the Way Lover	1977	—	3.00	6.00
❑ 1744	Let Me Live the Life I Love/ It Ain't Where You Been	1977	—	3.00	6.00
❑ 1750	Dig a Little Deeper/Let Me Go	1978	—	3.00	6.00
❑ 1752	Long Distance Love/Out to Get 'Cha	1979	—	3.00	6.00
❑ 1755	Goodbye Heartache/We Got to Hit It Off	1979	—	3.00	6.00
❑ 1756	Discoed to Death/Just One Step	1979	—	3.00	6.00
❑ 1761	Take Me to the Mountaintop/Joy	1980	—	3.00	6.00
MALACO					
❑ 2083	Let the Doorknob Hit'cha/ Do That To Me One More Time	1982	—	2.00	4.00
❑ 2084	Ain't Nothing You Can Do/Bad Risk	198?	—	2.00	4.00
❑ 2093	I'll Do Anything for You/Hell Fire Lovin'	198?	—	2.00	4.00
❑ 2098	Right Place, Right Time/He's Not Available	1984	—	2.00	4.00
—With Denise LaSalle					
❑ 2099	One Shirt, Soulless Shoes/You	1984	—	2.00	4.00
❑ 2119	Good Time Man/You Crowed in My Bed	198?	—	2.00	4.00
❑ 2130	Sunshine Lady/There's No Limit to My Love	1986	—	2.00	4.00
Albums					
GLADES					
❑ 6502	Latimore	1973	3.00	6.00	12.00
❑ 6503	More, More, More	1974	3.00	6.00	12.00
❑ 7505	Latimore 3	1975	3.00	6.00	12.00
❑ 7509	It Ain't Where You Been	1976	2.50	5.00	10.00
❑ 7515	Dig a Little Deeper	1978	2.50	5.00	10.00
MALACO					
❑ 7409	Singing in the Key of Love	198?	2.50	5.00	10.00
❑ 7414	I'll Do Anything for You	198?	2.50	5.00	10.00
❑ 7423	Good Time Man	198?	2.50	5.00	10.00
❑ 7436	Every Way But Wrong	198?	2.50	5.00	10.00
❑ 7443	Slow Down	198?	2.50	5.00	10.00
❑ 7456	The Only Way Is Up	198?	2.50	5.00	10.00
❑ 7468	Catchin' Up	1993	3.00	6.00	12.00

LATIN SOULS, THE
45s
KAPP

Number	Title (A Side/B Side)	Yr	VG	VG+	NM
❑ 844	La Bamba/The Party Is Over	1967	2.00	4.00	8.00
❑ 898	I've Got You/Look But Don't Touch	1968	2.00	4.00	8.00
Albums					
KAPP					
❑ KL-1524 [M]	Boo-Ga-Loo and Shing-a-Ling	1967	6.25	12.50	25.00
❑ KS-3524 [S]	Boo-Ga-Loo and Shing-a-Ling	1967	5.00	10.00	20.00
❑ KS-3553	Tigar Boo-Ga-Loo	1968	5.00	10.00	20.00

LATTIMORE, BENNY
45s
HIT

Number	Title (A Side/B Side)	Yr	VG	VG+	NM
❑ 15	Snap Your Fingers/I Sold My Heart to the Junkman	1962	2.00	4.00	8.00
—B-side by Peggy Thompson					

LAUGHING GRAVY
45s
WHITE WHALE

Number	Title (A Side/B Side)	Yr	VG	VG+	NM
❑ 261	Vegetables/Snow Flakes on Laughing Gravy's Whiskers	1968	50.00	100.00	200.00

LAURELS, THE (1)
45s
ABC-PARAMOUNT

Number	Title (A Side/B Side)	Yr	VG	VG+	NM
❑ 10048	Hand in Hand/Picture of Love	1959	12.50	25.00	50.00

LAURELS, THE (2)
45s
"X"

Number	Title (A Side/B Side)	Yr	VG	VG+	NM
❑ 0143	Truly, Truly/'Tis Night	1955	62.50	125.00	250.00

LAURELS, THE (U) May also be by group (2), but we're not sure.
45s
SPRING

Number	Title (A Side/B Side)	Yr	VG	VG+	NM
❑ 1112	Baby Talk/You Left Me	1959	15.00	30.00	60.00

LAUREN, ROD
45s
CHANCELLOR

Number	Title (A Side/B Side)	Yr	VG	VG+	NM
❑ 1126	I Ain't Got You/Mexicali Rose	1962	3.00	6.00	12.00
❑ 1132	Oh How I Miss You Tonight/Blame Your Friends	1963	3.00	6.00	12.00
❑ 1136	Yesterday's Lovers/I Know	1963	3.00	6.00	12.00
❑ 1141	I Wanna Know/Searcher for Love	1963	3.00	6.00	12.00
❑ 1146	Let Me Tell You 'Bout My Baby/I can't Get You Out of My Heart	1963	3.00	6.00	12.00
RCA VICTOR					
❑ 47-7645	If I Had a Girl/No Wonder	1959	3.75	7.50	15.00
❑ 47-7645 [PS]	If I Had a Girl/No Wonder	1959	5.00	10.00	20.00
❑ 47-7720	Listen My Love/This I Know	1960	3.75	7.50	15.00
❑ 47-7786	A Wild Imagination/The One Finger Symphony	1960	3.75	7.50	15.00
❑ 47-8020	I Dreamed/A Wondrous Place	1962	3.00	6.00	12.00
Albums					
RCA VICTOR					
❑ LPM-2176 [M]	I'm Rod Lauren	1961	10.00	20.00	40.00
❑ LSP-2176 [S]	I'm Rod Lauren	1961	12.50	25.00	50.00

LAURIE, ANNIE
45s
DELUXE

Number	Title (A Side/B Side)	Yr	VG	VG+	NM
❑ 6107	It Hurts to Be in Love/Hand in Hand	1957	5.00	10.00	20.00
❑ 6135	It Must Be You/Please Honey Don't Go	1957	3.75	7.50	15.00
❑ 6140	You're the Only One for Me/Out of My Mind	1957	3.75	7.50	15.00
❑ 6151	Love Is a Funny Thing/ Nobody's Gonna Hurt You Baby	1957	3.75	7.50	15.00
❑ 6173	Someday Someway/Hold On to What You Got	1958	3.75	7.50	15.00
❑ 6182	Since I Fell for You/Lost Love	1959	3.75	7.50	15.00
❑ 6189	If You're Lonely/It's Gonna Come Out in the Wash Someday	1960	3.75	7.50	15.00
OKEH					
❑ 6915	You Belong to Me/I Feel So Right Tonight	1952	6.25	12.50	25.00
❑ 6933	Stop Talkin' and Start Walkin'/ Give Me Half a Chance	1953	6.25	12.50	25.00
❑ 6973	It's Been a Long, Long Time/ I Ain't Got It Bad No More	1953	6.25	12.50	25.00
❑ 7025	I'm in the Mood for You/Feeling the Need	1954	5.00	10.00	20.00
SAVOY					
❑ 1197	You Promised Love/Rockin' and Rollin' Again	1956	5.00	10.00	20.00
Albums					
AUDIO LAB					
❑ AL-1510 [M]	It Hurts to Be in Love	1959	75.00	150.00	300.00

LAURIE, LINDA
45s
ANDIE

Number	Title (A Side/B Side)	Yr	VG	VG+	NM
❑ 5015	All Winter Long/Stay with Me	1960	3.00	6.00	12.00
GLORY					
❑ 290	Ambrose (Part Five)/Ooh! What a Lover	1958	3.75	7.50	15.00
❑ 294	Forever Ambrose/Wherever He Goes, I Go	1959	3.00	6.00	12.00
KEETCH					
❑ 6001	Jose He Say/Chico	197?	—	2.50	5.00
MCA					
❑ 40119	Leave Me Alone (Ruby Red Dress)/Sweet Deceiver	1973	—	3.00	6.00
RUST					
❑ 5022	Prince Charming/Soupin' Up Your Motor	1960	2.50	5.00	10.00
❑ 5042	Stay at Home Sue/Lazy Love	1961	2.50	5.00	10.00
❑ 5061	The Return of Ambrose/Chicken Little	1963	2.50	5.00	10.00

LAVELLE, RONNIE
45s
PARKWAY

Number	Title (A Side/B Side)	Yr	VG	VG+	NM
❑ 831	Cartoons/The Crazy Way of Love	1961	3.00	6.00	12.00
❑ 837	Let Her Go/A Dog's Life	1962	3.00	6.00	12.00

LAVETTE, BETTY
45s
ATCO

Number	Title (A Side/B Side)	Yr	VG	VG+	NM
❑ 6891	Heart of Gold/You'll Wake Up Wisely	1972	—	3.00	6.00
❑ 6913	Your Turn to Cry/Soul Tambourine	1973	—	3.00	6.00
ATLANTIC					
❑ 2160	My Man — He's a Lovin' Man/Shut Your Mouth	1962	3.00	6.00	12.00
—As "Betty LaVett"					
❑ 2198	You'll Never Change/Here I Am	1963	3.00	6.00	12.00
—As "Betty LaVett"					
CALLA					
❑ 102	Let Me Down Easy/What I Don't Know (Won't Hurt Me)	1965	2.50	5.00	10.00
❑ 104	I Feel Good (All Over)/Only Your Love Can Save Me	1965	2.50	5.00	10.00
❑ 106	Stand Up Like a Man/I'm Just a Fool for You	1965	2.50	5.00	10.00
KAREN					
❑ 1540	Love Makes the World Go Round/Almost	1968	2.00	4.00	8.00
❑ 1544	Get Away/What Condition My Condition Is In	1968	2.00	4.00	8.00
❑ 1545	With a Little Help from My Friends/Hey Love	1969	2.00	4.00	8.00
❑ 1548	Ticket to the Moon/Let Me Down Easy	1969	2.00	4.00	8.00
LUPINE					
❑ 123	Witch Craft in the Air/You Killed the Love	1964	10.00	20.00	40.00
—As "Betty LaVett"					
❑ 1021	Witch Craft in the Air/You Killed the Love	1964	6.25	12.50	25.00
—As "Betty LaVett"					

Number	Title (A Side/B Side)	Yr	VG	VG+	NM

MOTOWN

| ☐ 1532 | Right in the Middle (Of Falling in Love)/You Seen One, You Seen 'Em All | 1981 | — | 2.50 | 5.00 |

—As "Bettye LaVette"

| ☐ 1614 | Either Way, We Lose/I Can't Stop | 1982 | — | 2.50 | 5.00 |

—As "Bettye LaVette"

SILVER FOX

☐ 17	He Made a Woman Out of Me/Nearer to You	1969	—	3.00	6.00
☐ 21	Do Your Duty/Love's Made a Fool Out of Me	1970	—	3.00	6.00
☐ 24	Games People Play/My Train's Comin' In	1970	—	3.00	6.00

SSS INTERNATIONAL

| ☐ 839 | Take Another Piece of My Heart/ At the Mercy of a Man | 1971 | — | 3.00 | 6.00 |

WEST END

| ☐ 1213 | Doin' the Best That I Can/(Instrumental) | 1983 | — | 2.50 | 5.00 |

—As "Bettye LaVette"

Albums

MOTOWN

| ☐ 6000 ML | Tell Me a Lie | 1982 | 3.00 | 6.00 | 12.00 |

—As "Bettye LaVette"

LAVOIE, KENT See LOBO.

LAWRENCE, BILL
45s

BERTRAM INT'L.

| ☐ 207 | Hey Baby!/Caribbean | 1959 | 25.00 | 50.00 | 100.00 |
| ☐ 227 | Please Don't Leave Me/Billy Boy | 1960 | 15.00 | 30.00 | 60.00 |

FREEDOM

| ☐ 44004 | Hey Baby!/Caribbean | 1958 | 37.50 | 75.00 | 150.00 |

MOOD

| ☐ 1013 | Little Girl/(B-side unknown) | 195? | 17.50 | 35.00 | 70.00 |

Albums

TOPS

| ☐ L-1576 [M] | Bill Lawrence Sings I'm in the Mood for Love | 1957 | 5.00 | 10.00 | 20.00 |

LAWRENCE, EDDIE
45s

CORAL

☐ 61168	Old, Old Vienna (Part 1)/Old, Old Vienna (Part 2)	1954	3.00	6.00	12.00
☐ 61671	The Old Philosopher/King Arthur's Mine	1956	3.75	7.50	15.00
☐ 61713	The New Philosopher/Loco Baseball	1956	3.00	6.00	12.00
☐ 61799	German Baseball/Golden Baskos	1957	3.00	6.00	12.00
☐ 61821	Abner the Baseball (Part 1)/ Abner the Baseball (Part 2)	1957	3.00	6.00	12.00
☐ 61863	The Old Philosopher on the Range/ Memories of Louise	1957	3.00	6.00	12.00
☐ 61915	The Merry Old Philosopher/That Holiday Spirit	1957	5.00	10.00	20.00
☐ 61940	The Visitor/Fix Your Watch	1958	3.00	6.00	12.00
☐ 61978	The Philosopher Strikes Back/ Frankensteiner Polka	1958	3.00	6.00	12.00
☐ 62005	The Good Old Days/Hi-Fi Blues	1958	3.00	6.00	12.00
☐ 62049	The Space Philosopher/Outta This World	1958	3.00	6.00	12.00
☐ 62070	The Mother Philosopher/The Salesman's Philosopher	1959	2.50	5.00	10.00
☐ 62267	The Suburban Philosopher/We Sure Had Fun	1961	2.50	5.00	10.00
☐ 62298	The Philosopher Twist/The D.J. Philosopher Returns	1961	2.50	5.00	10.00
☐ 62367	The Mets' Philosopher/We Love the Mets	1963	3.75	7.50	15.00

EPIC

| ☐ 9804 | The World's Fair Philosopher/The Old Philosopher and the Single Girl | 1965 | 3.00 | 6.00 | 12.00 |

SHASTA

| ☐ 139 | Stardust/Harlem Nocturne | 196? | 2.00 | 4.00 | 8.00 |
| ☐ 144 | Cattle Call/Cielito Lindo | 196? | 2.00 | 4.00 | 8.00 |

SIGNATURE

| ☐ 12010 | The Doctor's Philosopher/Blackouts of 1984 | 1960 | 2.50 | 5.00 | 10.00 |
| ☐ 12031 | Anyone for President/Unequal | 1960 | 2.50 | 5.00 | 10.00 |

Albums

CORAL

☐ CRL 57103 [M]	The Old Philosopher	1956	7.50	15.00	30.00
☐ CRL 57155 [M]	Eddie "The Old Philosopher" Lawrence	1957	7.50	15.00	30.00
☐ CRL 57203 [M]	The Kingdom of Eddie Lawrence	1958	7.50	15.00	30.00
☐ CRL 57371 [M]	The Side Splitting Personality of Eddie Lawrence	1961	7.50	15.00	30.00
☐ CRL 57411 [M]	Seven Characters In Search of Eddie Lawrence	1962	7.50	15.00	30.00
☐ CRL 757411 [S]	Seven Characters In Search of Eddie Lawrence	1962	10.00	20.00	40.00

EPIC

| ☐ LN 24149 [M] | Is That What's Bothering You Bunkie? | 1965 | 7.50 | 15.00 | 30.00 |
| ☐ BN 26149 [S] | Is That What's Bothering You Bunkie? | 1965 | 10.00 | 20.00 | 40.00 |

SIGNATURE

| ☐ SM-1003 [M] | The Garden of Eddie Lawrence | 1960 | 10.00 | 20.00 | 40.00 |

LAWRENCE, MARK
45s

GNP CRESCENDO

| ☐ 419 | Is There A Santa Claus?/The Heavenly Forest | 1968 | — | 3.00 | 6.00 |

JERDEN

| ☐ 110 | Is There A Santa Claus/ Santa Claus Square Dance | 196? | 2.00 | 4.00 | 8.00 |

LAWRENCE, STEVE
45s

ABC-PARAMOUNT

☐ 10005	(I Don't Care) Only Love Me/ Loving Is a Way of Living	1959	2.50	5.00	10.00
☐ 10031	There'll Be Some Changes Made/You're Everything Wonderful	1959	2.50	5.00	10.00
☐ 10058	Pretty Blue Eyes/You're Nearer	1959	2.50	5.00	10.00
☐ 10085	Footsteps/You Don't Know	1960	2.50	5.00	10.00
☐ 10113	You're Everything Wonderful/Why Why Why	1960	2.50	5.00	10.00
☐ 10146	Come Back Silly Girl/Going Steady	1960	2.50	5.00	10.00

CALENDAR

| ☐ 63-1001 | I've Gotta Be Me/Love's a Game | 1968 | — | 3.00 | 6.00 |
| ☐ 63-1005 | Runaround/I'm Falling Down | 1968 | — | 3.00 | 6.00 |

COLUMBIA

☐ S7 31545 [S]	Remember/Come Waltz with Me	1962	3.00	6.00	12.00
☐ S7 31546 [S]	(titles unknown)	1962	3.00	6.00	12.00
☐ S7 31547 [S]	It's a Sin to Tell a Lie/ I'll Always Be in Love with You	1962	3.00	6.00	12.00
☐ S7 31548 [S]	(titles unknown)	1962	3.00	6.00	12.00
☐ S7 31549 [S]	(titles unknown)	1962	3.00	6.00	12.00

—The above five are "Stereo Seven" 33 1/3 rpm jukebox singles from "JS 7-62"

☐ 42396	The Lady Wants to Twist/Tell Her I Said Hello	1962	2.50	5.00	10.00
☐ 42455	A House Without Windows/The Endless Night	1962	2.50	5.00	10.00
☐ 42601	Go Away Little Girl/If You Love Her Tell Her So	1962	2.00	4.00	8.00
☐ 42601 [PS]	Go Away Little Girl/If You Love Her Tell Her So	1962	3.00	6.00	12.00
☐ 42699	Don't Be Afraid, Little Darlin'/ Don't Come Runnin' Back	1963	2.00	4.00	8.00
☐ 42699 [PS]	Don't Be Afraid, Little Darlin'/ Don't Come Runnin' Back	1963	3.00	6.00	12.00
☐ 42795	Poor Little Rich Girl/More (Theme from Mondo Cane)	1963	2.00	4.00	8.00
☐ 42837	One Love Too Late/Walking Proud	1963	—	—	—

—Canceled?

☐ 42865	Walking Proud/All the Way Home	1963	2.00	4.00	8.00
☐ 42865 [PS]	Walking Proud/All the Way Home	1963	3.00	6.00	12.00
☐ 42952	My Home Town/A Room Without Windows	1964	2.00	4.00	8.00
☐ 43047	Everybody Knows/One Love Too Late	1964	2.00	4.00	8.00
☐ 43095	Yet…I Know/Put Away Your Teardrops	1964	2.00	4.00	8.00
☐ 43192	I Will Wait for You/Bewitched	1964	2.00	4.00	8.00
☐ 43303	Where Can I Go/Last Night I Made a Girl Cry	1965	—	3.50	7.00
☐ 43362	The Sounds of Summer/Millions of Roses	1965	—	3.50	7.00
☐ 43487	Only the Young/The Week-End	1965	—	3.50	7.00
☐ 43610	Today Will Be Yesterday Tomorrow/I'm Making the Same Mistakes	1966	—	3.50	7.00
☐ 43681	The Warm Hours/Good Times	1966	—	3.50	7.00
☐ 43758	I'm a Fool to Want You/ The Ballad of the Sad Young Men	1966	—	3.50	7.00
☐ 44022	Did I Ever Really Live/Girl in the White Glove	1967	—	3.00	6.00
☐ 44084	The Impossible Dream/Sweet Maria	1967	—	3.00	6.00
☐ 44384	Remember When/You've Got to Learn	1967	—	3.00	6.00
☐ 44514	I Want to Be with You/Dulcinea	1968	—	3.00	6.00

CORAL

☐ 61279	Tell Me What to Do (To Make You Mine)/Willow	1954	3.00	6.00	12.00
☐ 61327	Kiss Me Now/How Do I Break Away	1954	3.00	6.00	12.00
☐ 61486	Open Up the Gates of Mercy/ My Impression of Jamie	1955	3.00	6.00	12.00
☐ 61537	Adelaide/The Lord Is a Busy Man	1955	3.00	6.00	12.00
☐ 61563	Speedoo/The Chicken and the Hawk	1956	3.00	6.00	12.00
☐ 61667	Ethel Baby/Never My Love	1956	3.00	6.00	12.00
☐ 61708	Never Mind/If You Would Say You're Mine	1956	3.00	6.00	12.00
☐ 61761	The Banana Boat Song/Long Before I Knew You	1956	3.00	6.00	12.00
☐ 61792	Party Doll/(The Bad Donkey) Pum-Pa-Lum	1957	3.75	7.50	15.00
☐ 61834	Can't Wait for Summer/Fabulous	1957	3.00	6.00	12.00
☐ 61876	Fraulein/Blue Rememberin' You	1957	3.00	6.00	12.00
☐ 61904	A Long Last Look/At a Time Like This	1957	3.00	6.00	12.00
☐ 61925	Geisha Girl/I Don't Know	1958	3.00	6.00	12.00
☐ 61950	Uh-Huh, Oh Yeah/Lover in the House	1958	2.50	5.00	10.00
☐ 61992	Stranger in Mexico/ Those Nights at the Round Table	1958	2.50	5.00	10.00
☐ 62025	Many a Time/All About Love	1958	2.50	5.00	10.00
☐ 62052	I Only Have Eyes for You/These Things Are Free	1958	2.50	5.00	10.00
☐ 62080	Blah, Blah, Blah/Lover in the House	1959	2.50	5.00	10.00

KING

☐ 1223	To the Birds/With Every Breath I Take	1953	5.00	10.00	20.00
☐ 1252	King for a Day/ You Can't Hold a Memory in Your Arms	1953	5.00	10.00	20.00
☐ 1315	Remember Me/Too Little Time	1954	5.00	10.00	20.00
☐ 5360	Poinciana/Mine and Mine Alone	1960	2.50	5.00	10.00
☐ 5913	King for a Day/Liebscher	1964	2.00	4.00	8.00
☐ 15185	Never Leave Me/(B-side unknown)	1952	6.25	12.50	25.00
☐ 15190	Poinciana/All My Love Belongs to You	1952	5.00	10.00	20.00
☐ 15199	Sudden Fear/Always Love Me	1952	5.00	10.00	20.00
☐ 15208	How Many Stars Have to Shine/Tango	1952	5.00	10.00	20.00
☐ 15218	Tomorrow/If Not for You	1953	5.00	10.00	20.00

MGM

☐ 14257	Lookin' Good/Frosty Morning	1971	—	2.00	4.00
☐ 14288	The Last Run/Frosty Morning	1971	—	2.00	4.00
☐ 14368	Ain't No Sunshine-You Are My Sunshine/ In My Own Lifetime	1972	—	2.00	4.00
☐ 14531	The Best Thing That Ever Happened (To Me)/ Hello, Los Angeles	1973	—	2.00	4.00
☐ 14631	The End/You Light Up My Life	1973	—	2.00	4.00

RCA VICTOR

☐ 74-0169	Pickin' Up the Pieces/I've Got My Eyes on You	1969	—	2.50	5.00
☐ 74-0237	The Drifter/To Say Goodbye	1969	—	2.50	5.00
☐ 74-0303	Cry for Us All/Mama, a Rainbow	1969	—	2.50	5.00
☐ 74-0357	Groovin'/Being Alone	1970	—	2.50	5.00

20TH CENTURY

| ☐ 2246 | Now That We're in Love/ I Just Needed Your Lovin' | 1975 | — | 2.00 | 4.00 |

UNITED ARTISTS

☐ 233	Girls, Girls, Girls/Little Boy Blue	1960	2.50	5.00	10.00
☐ 233 [PS]	Girls, Girls, Girls/Little Boy Blue	1960	5.00	10.00	20.00
☐ 240	Tears from Heaven/Hold Back the Dike	1960	2.50	5.00	10.00
☐ 291	Portrait of My Love/Oh How You Lied	1961	2.00	4.00	8.00
☐ 335	My Clair de Lune/In Time	1961	2.00	4.00	8.00
☐ 364	Somewhere Along the Way/While There's Still Time	1961	2.00	4.00	8.00
☐ 403	Our Concerto/Send Someone to Love Me	1962	2.00	4.00	8.00
☐ XW927	You Take My Heart Away/ (Everybody Has To) Begin Again	1976	—	2.00	4.00
☐ XW1050	Everytime I Sing a Love Song/ I Wasn't Man Enough	1977	—	2.00	4.00

WARNER BROS.

| ☐ 8584 | Take My Hand/Don't Wish Too Hard | 1978 | — | 2.00 | 4.00 |

Number	Title (A Side/B Side)	Yr	VG	VG+	NM

7-Inch Extended Plays

COLUMBIA

Number	Title (A Side/B Side)	Yr	VG	VG+	NM
❏ 7-9565 [DJ]	Go Away Little Girl/More/Millions of Roses//The Impossible Dream (The Quest)/Sweet Maria/ Love Me with All Your Heart	1967	2.50	5.00	10.00

—"Stereo Seven" jukebox issue, small hole

| ❏ 7-9565 [PS] | Steve Lawrence's Greatest Hits | 1967 | 2.50 | 5.00 | 10.00 |

Albums

ABC-PARAMOUNT

❏ 290 [M]	Swing Softly with Me	1959	6.25	12.50	25.00
❏ S-290 [S]	Swing Softly with Me	1959	7.50	15.00	30.00
❏ 392 [M]	The Best of Steve Lawrence	1960	5.00	10.00	20.00
❏ S-392 [S]	The Best of Steve Lawrence	1960	6.25	12.50	25.00

APPLAUSE

| ❏ 1001 | Take It On Home | 1981 | 2.50 | 5.00 | 10.00 |

COLUMBIA

❏ CL 1953 [M]	Winners!	1963	3.00	6.00	12.00
❏ CL 2121 [M]	Academy Award Losers	1964	3.00	6.00	12.00
❏ CL 2227 [M]	Everybody Knows	1964	3.00	6.00	12.00
❏ CL 2419 [M]	The Steve Lawrence Show	1965	3.00	6.00	12.00
❏ CL 2540 [M]	Of Love and… Sad Young Men	1966	3.00	6.00	12.00
❏ CS 8753 [S]	Winners!	1963	3.75	7.50	15.00
❏ CS 8921 [S]	Academy Award Losers	1964	3.75	7.50	15.00
❏ CS 9027 [S]	Everybody Knows	1964	3.75	7.50	15.00
❏ CS 9219 [S]	The Steve Lawrence Show	1965	3.75	7.50	15.00
❏ CS 9340 [S]	Of Love and… Sad Young Men	1966	3.75	7.50	15.00
❏ CS 9565	Greatest Hits	1968	3.00	6.00	12.00
❏ PC 9565	Greatest Hits	198?	2.00	4.00	8.00

—Reissue with new prefix

CORAL

❏ CRL 57050 [M]	About That Girl	1956	10.00	20.00	40.00
❏ CRL 57182 [M]	Songs by Steve Lawrence	1957	10.00	20.00	40.00
❏ CRL 57204 [M]	Here's Steve Lawrence	1958	10.00	20.00	40.00
❏ CRL 57268 [M]	All About Love	1959	7.50	15.00	30.00
❏ CRL 57434 [M]	Songs Everybody Knows	1963	6.25	12.50	25.00
❏ CRL 757268 [S]	All About Love	1959	10.00	20.00	40.00
❏ CRL 757434 [S]	Songs Everybody Knows	1963	7.50	15.00	30.00

HARMONY

❏ HS 11257	Moon River	196?	2.50	5.00	10.00
❏ HS 11327	Ramblin' Rose	1969	2.50	5.00	10.00
❏ HS 11397	Love Me	1970	2.50	5.00	10.00

KING

| ❏ 593 [M] | Steve Lawrence | 1959 | 20.00 | 40.00 | 80.00 |

MGM

| ❏ SE-4824 | Portrait | 1973 | 2.50 | 5.00 | 10.00 |

RCA VICTOR

| ❏ LSP-4167 | I've Gotta Be Me | 1969 | 3.00 | 6.00 | 12.00 |
| ❏ LSP-4347 | On a Clear Day | 1970 | 3.00 | 6.00 | 12.00 |

UNITED ARTISTS

❏ UAL-3098 [M]	The Steve Lawrence Sound	1960	5.00	10.00	20.00
❏ UAL-3114 [M]	Steve Lawrence Goes Latin	1960	5.00	10.00	20.00
❏ UAL-3150 [M]	Portrait of My Love	1961	5.00	10.00	20.00
❏ UAL-3190 [M]	The Very Best of Steve Lawrence	1962	5.00	10.00	20.00
❏ UAL-3265 [M]	People Will Say We're in Love	1963	5.00	10.00	20.00
❏ UAL-3368 [M]	Steve Lawrence Conquers Broadway	1964	3.75	7.50	15.00
❏ UAS-6098 [S]	The Steve Lawrence Sound	1960	6.25	12.50	25.00
❏ UAS-6114 [S]	Steve Lawrence Goes Latin	1960	6.25	12.50	25.00
❏ UAS-6150 [S]	Portrait of My Love	1961	6.25	12.50	25.00
❏ UAS-6190 [S]	The Very Best of Steve Lawrence	1962	6.25	12.50	25.00
❏ UAS-6265 [S]	People Will Say We're in Love	1963	6.25	12.50	25.00
❏ UAS-6368 [S]	Steve Lawrence Conquers Broadway	1964	5.00	10.00	20.00

VOCALION

❏ VL 3775 [M]	Here's Steve Lawrence	196?	3.00	6.00	12.00
❏ VL 73775 [R]	Here's Steve Lawrence	196?	2.50	5.00	10.00
❏ VL 73886	The More I See You	1970	2.50	5.00	10.00

LAWRENCE, STEVE, AND EYDIE GORME Also see each artist's individual listings.

45s

ABC-PARAMOUNT

| ❏ 10104 | This Could Be the Start of Something Big/Darn It, Baby, That's Love | 1960 | 2.50 | 5.00 | 10.00 |

CALENDAR

| ❏ 63-1003 | Two of Us/Mr. Spoons | 1968 | — | 3.00 | 6.00 |

COLUMBIA

| ❏ 42815 | I Want to Stay Here/Ain't Love | 1963 | 2.00 | 4.00 | 8.00 |
| ❏ 4-42815 [DJ] | I Want to Stay Here (same on both sides) | 1963 | 5.00 | 10.00 | 20.00 |

—Promo only on red vinyl

❏ 42932	I Can't Stop Talking About You/ To the Movies We Go	1963	2.00	4.00	8.00
❏ 43179	Happy Holiday/That Holiday Feeling	1964	2.50	5.00	10.00
❏ 43930	The Honeymoon Is Over/Together Forever	1966	—	3.50	7.00
❏ 44123	Cabaret/Mame	1967	—	3.00	6.00
❏ 44228	Summer Wind/Be Still	1967	—	3.00	6.00

CORAL

❏ 61313	Make Yourself Comfortable/I've Gotta Crow	1954	3.00	6.00	12.00
❏ 61411	Besame Mucho/ Close Your Eyes, Take a Deep Breath	1955	3.00	6.00	12.00
❏ 61440	Knickerbocker Mambo/Give a Fool a Chance	1955	3.00	6.00	12.00

MGM

| ❏ 14340 | Lead Me On/Tea for Two | 1971 | — | 2.00 | 4.00 |
| ❏ 14383 | We Can Make It Together/E Fini | 1972 | — | 2.00 | 4.00 |

—With the Osmonds

| ❏ 14493 | Feelin'/Lead Me On | 1973 | — | 2.00 | 4.00 |

RCA VICTOR

❏ 47-9656	Dear World/A Break at Love	1968	—	2.50	5.00
❏ 47-9694	Hurry Home for Christmas/Dedicated to Love	1968	2.00	4.00	8.00
❏ 74-0123	Chapter One/Real True Lovin'	1969	—	2.50	5.00
❏ 74-0334	(You're My) Soul and Inspiration/ Now I Love the World Again	1970	—	2.50	5.00
❏ 74-0386	For All We Know/ Did You Give the World My Love Today, Babe	1970	—	2.50	5.00
❏ 74-0420	Love Is Blue-Autumn Leaves/Hi Sweetie	1971	—	2.50	5.00

UNITED ARTISTS

| ❏ 282 | The Facts of Life/I'm a Girl, You're a Boy | 1960 | 2.50 | 5.00 | 10.00 |
| ❏ XW1163 | You Take My Heart Away/What I Did for Love | 1978 | — | 2.00 | 4.00 |

—Steve Lawrence is on A-side, Eydie Gorme on B-side

Albums

ABC

| ❏ X-764 [(2)] | 20 Golden Performances | 1974 | 3.00 | 6.00 | 12.00 |

ABC-PARAMOUNT

❏ 300 [M]	We Got Us	1960	5.00	10.00	20.00
❏ S-300 [S]	We Got Us	1960	6.25	12.50	25.00
❏ 311 [M]	Steve and Eydie Sing the Golden Hits	1960	5.00	10.00	20.00
❏ S-311 [S]	Steve and Eydie Sing the Golden Hits	1960	6.25	12.50	25.00
❏ 469 [M]	Our Best to You	1964	3.75	7.50	15.00
❏ S-469 [S]	Our Best to You	1964	5.00	10.00	20.00

CALENDAR

| ❏ KOM-1001 [M] | Golden Rainbow | 1968 | 7.50 | 15.00 | 30.00 |
| ❏ KOS-1001 [S] | Golden Rainbow | 1968 | 10.00 | 20.00 | 40.00 |

COLUMBIA

❏ CL 2021 [M]	Steve and Eydie at the Movies	1964	3.00	6.00	12.00
❏ CL 2262 [M]	That Holiday Feeling	1964	3.00	6.00	12.00
❏ CL 2636 [M]	Steve and Eydie Together On Broadway	1967	3.00	6.00	12.00
❏ CL 2730 [M]	Bonfa and Brazil	1968	3.75	7.50	15.00
❏ CS 8821 [S]	Steve and Eydie at the Movies	1964	3.75	7.50	15.00
❏ CS 9062 [S]	That Holiday Feeling	1964	3.75	7.50	15.00
❏ CS 9436 [S]	Steve and Eydie Together On Broadway	1967	3.75	7.50	15.00
❏ CS 9530 [S]	Bonfa and Brazil	1968	3.00	6.00	12.00

CORAL

| ❏ CRL 57336 [M] | Steve and Eydie | 1962 | 5.00 | 10.00 | 20.00 |

HARMONY

| ❏ H 30292 | Something's Gotta Give | 1971 | 2.50 | 5.00 | 10.00 |

MATI-MOR

| ❏ 8003 | It's Us Again | 196? | 5.00 | 10.00 | 20.00 |

—Promotional item for Silvirkin shampoo

MGM

| ❏ SE-4803 | The World of Steve Lawrence and Eydie Gorme | 1972 | 2.50 | 5.00 | 10.00 |
| ❏ SE-4881 | Feelin' | 1973 | 2.50 | 5.00 | 10.00 |

RCA VICTOR

❏ LSP-4107	Real True Lovin'	1969	3.00	6.00	12.00
❏ LSP-4115	What It Was, Was Love	1969	3.00	6.00	12.00
❏ LSP-4393	A Man and a Woman	1971	3.00	6.00	12.00
❏ VPS-6035 [(2)]	This Is Steve Lawrence and Eydie Gorme	1971	3.75	7.50	15.00
❏ VPS-6050 [(2)]	This Is Steve Lawrence and Eydie Gorme, Vol. 2	1972	3.75	7.50	15.00

STAGE 2

| ❏ 712 | Hallelujah | 198? | 2.50 | 5.00 | 10.00 |

UNITED ARTISTS

❏ UAL-3191 [M]	The Very Best of Eydie and Steve	1962	5.00	10.00	20.00
❏ UAL-3268 [M]	Two on the Aisle	1963	5.00	10.00	20.00
❏ WWL-4509 [M]	Cozy	1961	5.00	10.00	20.00
❏ UAS-6191 [S]	The Very Best of Eydie and Steve	1962	6.25	12.50	25.00
❏ UAS-6268 [S]	Two on the Aisle	1963	6.25	12.50	25.00
❏ WWS-8509 [S]	Cozy	1961	6.25	12.50	25.00

VOCALION

| ❏ VL 3825 [M] | Presenting Steve and Eydie | 1968 | 3.00 | 6.00 | 12.00 |
| ❏ VL 73825 [R] | Presenting Steve and Eydie | 1968 | 2.50 | 5.00 | 10.00 |

LAWRENCE, SYD

45s

COSMIC

| ❏ 1001 | The Answer to the Flying Saucer/Haunted Guitar | 1956 | 10.00 | 20.00 | 40.00 |

—B-side by Billy Mure

LAWRENCE, VICKI

45s

BELL

❏ 45303	The Night the Lights Went Out in Georgia/ Dime a Dance	1973	—	2.50	5.00
❏ 45362	He Did with Me/Mr. Allison	1973	—	2.00	4.00
❏ 45409	Sensual Man/Ships in the Night	1973	—	2.00	4.00
❏ 45437	Mama's Gonna Make It Better/Cameo	1974	—	2.00	4.00

ELF

| ❏ 90035 | And I'll Go/The Whole State of Alabama | 1970 | — | 3.00 | 6.00 |

PRIVATE STOCK

❏ 45,036	The Other Woman/Cameo	1975	—	2.00	4.00
❏ 45,067	There's a Gun Still Smokin' in Nashville	1976	—	2.00	4.00
❏ 45,121	Love in the Hot Afternoon/(B-side unknown)	1976	—	2.00	4.00

SOMA

| ❏ 5248 | The Night the Lights Went Out in Georgia/ He Did with Me | 197? | — | 2.50 | 5.00 |

—Original, reissue or bootleg? Please advise.

UNITED ARTISTS

| ❏ 50748 | No, No/Lincoln Street Chapel | 1971 | — | 3.00 | 6.00 |

Albums

BELL

| ❏ 1120 | The Night the Lights Went Out in Georgia | 1973 | 3.00 | 6.00 | 12.00 |

LAWRENCE, WALT

45s

HOLLYWOOD INT'L.

| ❏ 2 | Cascade/Twilight Adrift | 195? | 10.00 | 20.00 | 40.00 |

LAWSON, LINDA

Albums

CHANCELLOR

| ❏ CHL-5010 [M] | Introducing Linda Lawson | 1960 | 5.00 | 10.00 | 20.00 |

LAWSON, ROBBY

45s

KYSER

| ❏ 2122 | Burning Sensation/(B-side unknown) | 196? | 300.00 | 600.00 | 1200. |

LAY, SAM

Albums

BLUE THUMB

| ❏ BTS 14 | Sam Lay in Bluesland | 1970 | 6.25 | 12.50 | 25.00 |

LEADBELLY

7-Inch Extended Plays

CAPITOL

| ❏ EAP 1-369 | Back Water Blues/Take This Hammer// On a Christmas Day/Irene | 1954 | 25.00 | 50.00 | 100.00 |

Number	Title (A Side/B Side)	Yr	VG	VG+	NM
❏ EAP 1-369 [PS]Classics in Jazz, Part 1		1954	25.00	50.00	100.00
❏ EAP 2-369	Sweet Mary Blues/Ella Speed//Tell Me Baby/ Western Plain	1954	25.00	50.00	100.00
❏ EAP 2-369 [PS]Classics in Jazz, Part 2		1954	25.00	50.00	100.00

Albums
ALLEGRO

Number	Title (A Side/B Side)	Yr	VG	VG+	NM
❏ L-4027 [10]	Sinful Songs	195?	62.50	125.00	250.00

CAPITOL

Number	Title (A Side/B Side)	Yr	VG	VG+	NM
❏ H 369 [10]	Classics in Jazz	1953	62.50	125.00	250.00
❏ T 1821 [M]	Leadbelly: Huddie Ledbetter's Best	1962	10.00	20.00	40.00

ELEKTRA

Number	Title (A Side/B Side)	Yr	VG	VG+	NM
❏ EKL-301/2 [(2)]	The Library of Congress Recordings	1966	6.25	12.50	25.00

FOLKWAYS

Number	Title (A Side/B Side)	Yr	VG	VG+	NM
❏ FP-4 [10]	Lead Belly's Legacy, Vol. 1: Take This Hammer	1950	30.00	60.00	120.00
❏ FP-14 [10]	Lead Belly's Legacy, Vol. 2: Rock Island Line	1951	30.00	60.00	120.00
❏ FP-24 [10]	Lead Belly's Legacy, Vol. 3: Early Recordings	1951	30.00	60.00	120.00
❏ FP-34 [10]	Lead Belly's Legacy, Vol. 4: Easy Rider	1951	30.00	60.00	120.00
❏ FP-241 [(2)M]	Leadbelly's Last Sessions, Vol. 1	196?	10.00	20.00	40.00
❏ FP-242 [(2)M]	Leadbelly's Last Sessions, Vol. 2	196?	10.00	20.00	40.00
❏ FA-2004 [10]	Lead Belly's Legacy, Vol. 1: Take This Hammer	195?	12.50	25.00	50.00
—Reissue of FP-4					
❏ FA-2014 [10]	Lead Belly's Legacy, Vol. 2: Rock Island Line	195?	12.50	25.00	50.00
—Reissue of FP-14					
❏ FA-2024 [10]	Lead Belly's Legacy, Vol. 3: Early Recordings	195?	12.50	25.00	50.00
—Reissue of FP-24					
❏ FA-2034 [10]	Lead Belly's Legacy, Vol. 4: Easy Rider	195?	12.50	25.00	50.00
—Reissue of FP-34					
❏ FA-2941 [M]	Leadbelly's Last Sessions, Vol. 3	196?	6.25	12.50	25.00
❏ FA-2942 [M]	Leadbelly's Last Sessions, Vol. 4	196?	6.25	12.50	25.00
❏ FA-3106 [M]	Leadbelly Sings Folk Songs	196?	6.25	12.50	25.00

RCA VICTOR

Number	Title (A Side/B Side)	Yr	VG	VG+	NM
❏ LPV-505 [M]	Midnight Special	1964	10.00	20.00	40.00

ROYALE

Number	Title (A Side/B Side)	Yr	VG	VG+	NM
❏ 18131 [10]	Blues Songs	1954	30.00	60.00	120.00
—As "The Lonesome Blues Singer"					

VERVE FOLKWAYS

Number	Title (A Side/B Side)	Yr	VG	VG+	NM
❏ FT-3019 [M]	From the Last Sessions	1967	6.25	12.50	25.00
❏ FTS-3019 [R]	From the Last Sessions	1967	3.75	7.50	15.00
❏ FV-9001 [M]	Take This Hammer	1965	6.25	12.50	25.00
❏ FVS-9001 [R]	Take This Hammer	1965	3.75	7.50	15.00
❏ FV-9021 [M]	Keep Your Hands Off Her	1965	6.25	12.50	25.00
❏ FVS-9021 [R]	Keep Your Hands Off Her	1965	3.75	7.50	15.00

LEADERS, THE
45s
GLORY

Number	Title (A Side/B Side)	Yr	VG	VG+	NM
❏ 239	Nobody Loves Me/Dearest Beloved Darling	1956	20.00	40.00	80.00
❏ 243	Can't Help Lovin' That Girl of Mine/Lovers	1956	20.00	40.00	80.00

LEAPER, BOB
45s
REPRISE

Number	Title (A Side/B Side)	Yr	VG	VG+	NM
❏ 0274	Sunday Morning/Come and Join Us	1964	2.50	5.00	10.00

Albums
LONDON

Number	Title (A Side/B Side)	Yr	VG	VG+	NM
❏ LL 3391 [M]	Big Band Beatle Songs	1964	3.75	7.50	15.00
❏ SP 4056 [S]	Big Band Beatle Songs	1964	5.00	10.00	20.00

LEAPING FERNS, THE   Also recorded as CHANTAY'S.
45s
X-PANDED SOUND

Number	Title (A Side/B Side)	Yr	VG	VG+	NM
❏ 103	It Never Works Out for Me/Maybe Baby	1964	7.50	15.00	30.00

LEAPY LEE
45s
CADET

Number	Title (A Side/B Side)	Yr	VG	VG+	NM
❏ 5635	It's All Happening/It's Great	1969	—	3.50	7.00

DECCA

Number	Title (A Side/B Side)	Yr	VG	VG+	NM
❏ 32380	Little Arrows/Time Will Tell	1968	2.00	4.00	8.00
❏ 32436	Here Comes the Rain/I'm Gonna Spend My Love	1969	—	3.50	7.00
❏ 32492	Little Yellow Aeroplane/Boom Boom (That's How My Heart Beats)	1969	—	3.50	7.00
❏ 32584	Someone's in Love/Best to Forget	1969	—	3.50	7.00
❏ 32625	Good Morning/Teresa	1970	—	3.50	7.00
❏ 32692	Tupelo Mississippi Flash/Green Green Trees	1970	—	3.00	6.00
❏ 32808	Best to Forget/I'll Be Your Baby Tonight	1971	—	3.00	6.00

MAM

Number	Title (A Side/B Side)	Yr	VG	VG+	NM
❏ 3618	Just Another Night/My Advice to You	1972	—	3.00	6.00
❏ 3622	Summer Rain/No Full Moon	1972	—	3.00	6.00

MCA

Number	Title (A Side/B Side)	Yr	VG	VG+	NM
❏ 40470	Every Road Leads Back to You/ Honey Go Drift Away	1975	—	2.50	5.00

Albums
DECCA

Number	Title (A Side/B Side)	Yr	VG	VG+	NM
❏ DL 75076	Little Arrows	1968	5.00	10.00	20.00
❏ DL 75237	Leapy Lee	1970	3.75	7.50	15.00

LEARY, DR. TIMOTHY
45s
MERCURY

Number	Title (A Side/B Side)	Yr	VG	VG+	NM
❏ 72713	Turn On, Tune In, Drop Out (Part 1)/Turn On, Tune In, Drop Out (Part 2)	1967	7.50	15.00	30.00

Albums
DOUGLAS

Number	Title (A Side/B Side)	Yr	VG	VG+	NM
❏ 1	You Can Be Anyone This Time Around	1969	25.00	50.00	100.00

ESP-DISK'

Number	Title (A Side/B Side)	Yr	VG	VG+	NM
❏ 1027 [M]	Turn On, Tune In, Drop Out	1966	37.50	75.00	150.00

MERCURY

Number	Title (A Side/B Side)	Yr	VG	VG+	NM
❏ MG-21131 [M]	Turn On, Tune In, Drop Out	1967	10.00	20.00	40.00
❏ SR-61131 [S]	Turn On, Tune In, Drop Out	1967	12.50	25.00	50.00

PIXIE

Number	Title (A Side/B Side)	Yr	VG	VG+	NM
❏ CA-1069 [M]	L.S.D.	1966	20.00	40.00	80.00

LEATHER BOY
45s
FLOWER

Number	Title (A Side/B Side)	Yr	VG	VG+	NM
❏ 100	My Prayer/You Gotta Have Soul	1968	7.50	15.00	30.00

MGM

Number	Title (A Side/B Side)	Yr	VG	VG+	NM
❏ 13724	I'm a Leather Boy/Shadows	1967	7.50	15.00	30.00
❏ 13724 [PS]	I'm a Leather Boy/Shadows	1967	15.00	30.00	60.00
❏ 13790	On the Go/Soulin'	1967	7.50	15.00	30.00

PARKWAY

Number	Title (A Side/B Side)	Yr	VG	VG+	NM
❏ 125	Jersey Thursday/Black Friday	1966	7.50	15.00	30.00

LEATHERCOATED MINDS, THE
Albums
VIVA

Number	Title (A Side/B Side)	Yr	VG	VG+	NM
❏ V-6003 [M]	Trip Down Sunset Strip	1967	15.00	30.00	60.00
❏ V-36003 [S]	Trip Down Sunset Strip	1967	20.00	40.00	80.00

LEAVES, THE
45s
CAPITOL

Number	Title (A Side/B Side)	Yr	VG	VG+	NM
❏ 5799	Lemon Princess/Twilight Sanctuary	1966	3.00	6.00	12.00

LOST-NITE

Number	Title (A Side/B Side)	Yr	VG	VG+	NM
❏ 314	Hey Joe/Girl from the East	197?	—	3.00	6.00
—Reissue					

MIRA

Number	Title (A Side/B Side)	Yr	VG	VG+	NM
❏ 202	Love Minus Zero-No Limit/Too Many People	1965	12.50	25.00	50.00
❏ 207	Hey Joe, Where You Gonna Go/Be with You	1965	25.00	50.00	100.00
❏ 213	You Better Move On/A Different Story	1966	12.50	25.00	50.00
❏ 220	Be with You/Funny Little World	1966	12.50	25.00	50.00
❏ 222	Hey Joe/Girl from the East	1966	10.00	20.00	40.00
❏ 222	Hey Joe/Funny Little World	1966	12.50	25.00	50.00
❏ 227	Too Many People/Girl from the East	1966	10.00	20.00	40.00
❏ 231	Get Out of My Life Woman/Girl from the East	1966	10.00	20.00	40.00
❏ 234	Be with You/You Better Move On	1966	10.00	20.00	40.00

Albums
CAPITOL

Number	Title (A Side/B Side)	Yr	VG	VG+	NM
❏ ST 2638 [S]	All the Good That's Happening	1967	7.50	15.00	30.00
❏ T 2638 [M]	All the Good That's Happening	1967	6.25	12.50	25.00

MIRA

Number	Title (A Side/B Side)	Yr	VG	VG+	NM
❏ LP-3005 [M]	Hey Joe	1966	10.00	20.00	40.00
❏ LPS-3005 [S]	Hey Joe	1966	12.50	25.00	50.00

SURREY

Number	Title (A Side/B Side)	Yr	VG	VG+	NM
❏ LPS-3005	Hey Joe	196?	37.50	75.00	150.00
—Issued in Mira jackets					

LED ZEPPELIN
45s
ATLANTIC

Number	Title (A Side/B Side)	Yr	VG	VG+	NM
❏ PR 157 [DJ]	Gallows Pole (mono/stereo)	1971	50.00	100.00	200.00
❏ PR 175 [DJ]	Stairway to Heaven (mono/stereo)	1972	25.00	50.00	100.00
❏ PR 175 [PS]	Stairway to Heaven (mono/stereo)	1972	62.50	125.00	250.00
❏ PR 269 [DJ]	Stairway to Heaven (stereo/stereo)	1973	12.50	25.00	50.00
❏ 2613	Communication Breakdown/ Good Times Bad Times	1969	6.25	12.50	25.00
❏ 2613	Communication Breakdown/ Good Times Bad Times	198?	2.00	4.00	8.00

—Later edition with Warner Communcations logo in perimeter print and a reference to "From Atlantic LP 19126 -- 'Led Zeppelin'" at bottom, plus a "(P) 1969 Atlantic Recording Corp." underneath

Number	Title (A Side/B Side)	Yr	VG	VG+	NM
❏ 2690	Whole Lotta Love/Living Loving Maid (She's Just a Woman)	1969	3.75	7.50	15.00

—With A-side time of 3:12

Number	Title (A Side/B Side)	Yr	VG	VG+	NM
❏ 2690	Whole Lotta Love/Living Loving Maid (She's Just a Woman)	1969	5.00	10.00	20.00

—With A-side time of 5:33; no Warner Communications logo in perimeter print

Number	Title (A Side/B Side)	Yr	VG	VG+	NM
❏ 2690	Whole Lotta Love/Living Loving Maid (She's Just a Woman)	198?	2.00	4.00	8.00

—Later edition with Warner Communcations logo in perimeter print, "(P) 1969 Atlantic Recording Corp." at right and a reference to "From Atlantic LP 19127 -- 'Led Zeppelin II'" at bottom

Number	Title (A Side/B Side)	Yr	VG	VG+	NM
❏ 2777 [DJ]	Immigrant Song	1970	30.00	60.00	120.00
—One-sided promo					
❏ 2777	Immigrant Song/Hey, Hey, What Can I Do	1970	6.25	12.50	25.00
—First pressings with "Do What Thou Wilt Shalt Be the Whole of the Law" in trail-off					
❏ 2777	Immigrant Song/Hey, Hey, What Can I Do	1970	3.75	7.50	15.00

—Second pressings without "Do What Thou Wilt Shalt Be the Whole of the Law" in trail-off; no Warner Commuications logo in perimeter print

Number	Title (A Side/B Side)	Yr	VG	VG+	NM
❏ 2777	Immigrant Song/Hey, Hey, What Can I Do	1977	—	2.50	5.00

—Third pressings with smaller, bolder type and Warner Communications logo in perimeter print; available well into the late 1980s

Number	Title (A Side/B Side)	Yr	VG	VG+	NM
❏ 2849	Black Dog/Misty Mountain Hop	1971	2.50	5.00	10.00
❏ 2865	Rock and Roll/Four Sticks	1972	2.50	5.00	10.00
❏ 2865	Rock and Roll/Four Sticks	198?	2.00	4.00	8.00

—Label has smaller, bolder type, "From Atlantic LP 19129 -- 'Led Zeppelin'," and Warner Commuications logo in perimeter print

Number	Title (A Side/B Side)	Yr	VG	VG+	NM
❏ 2970	Over the Hills & Far Away/Dancing Days	1973	2.50	5.00	10.00
❏ 2986	D'yer Mak'er/The Crunge	1973	—	3.00	6.00

—Defective pressing -- the left channel starts to fade out midway through the A-side, making it sound like rechanneled stereo. The number "3" follows the matrix number in the trail-off wax of those copies we've encountered.

Number	Title (A Side/B Side)	Yr	VG	VG+	NM
❏ 2986	D'yer Mak'er/The Crunge	1973	2.50	5.00	10.00

—Normal pressing in true stereo throughout

ATLANTIC OLDIES SERIES

Number	Title (A Side/B Side)	Yr	VG	VG+	NM
❏ 13116	Whole Lotta Love/Living Loving Maid (She's Just a Woman)	197?	—	2.00	4.00
❏ 13129	Black Dog/Misty Mountain Hop	197?	—	2.00	4.00
❏ 13130	Rock and Roll/Four Sticks	197?	—	2.00	4.00
❏ 13131	Immigrant Song/Hey, Hey, What Can I Do	197?	—	2.00	4.00

SWAN SONG

Number	Title (A Side/B Side)	Yr	VG	VG+	NM
❏ 70102	Trampled Under Foot/Black Country Woman	1975	—	3.00	6.00
❏ 70110	Candy Store Rock/Royal Orleans	1976	—	3.00	6.00
❏ 71003	Fool in the Rain/Hot Dog	1979	—	3.00	6.00
❏ 71003 [DJ]	Fool in the Rain (Short 3:20)/(Long 6:08)	1979	3.75	7.50	15.00

7-Inch Extended Plays
ATLANTIC

Number	Title (A Side/B Side)	Yr	VG	VG+	NM
❏ SD 7-7208	Black Dog/Rock and Roll//Stairway to Heaven	1972	25.00	50.00	100.00
—Jukebox issue; small hole, plays at 33 1/3 rpm					

L

Number	Title (A Side/B Side)	Yr	VG	VG+	NM
❏ SD 7-7208 [PS]	Led Zeppelin (IV)	1972	37.50	75.00	150.00
❏ SD 7-7255	Dancing Days/D'yer Mak'er//The Song Remains the Same/The Crunge	1973	20.00	40.00	80.00

—Jukebox issue; small hole, plays at 33 1/3 rpm

Number	Title (A Side/B Side)	Yr	VG	VG+	NM
❏ SD 7-7255 [PS]	Houses of the Holy	1973	25.00	50.00	100.00

Albums
ATLANTIC

Number	Title (A Side/B Side)	Yr	VG	VG+	NM
❏ 7201 [M]	Led Zeppelin III	1970	50.00	100.00	200.00

—White label promo only

Number	Title (A Side/B Side)	Yr	VG	VG+	NM
❏ SD 7201 [DJ]	Led Zeppelin III	1970	50.00	100.00	200.00

—Stereo white label promo

Number	Title (A Side/B Side)	Yr	VG	VG+	NM
❏ SD 7201 [S]	Led Zeppelin III	1970	3.75	7.50	15.00

—Die-cut cover with movable wheel; "1841 Broadway" address on label

Number	Title (A Side/B Side)	Yr	VG	VG+	NM
❏ SD 7201 [S]	Led Zeppelin III	1974	2.50	5.00	10.00

—"75 Rockefeller Plaza" address on label

Number	Title (A Side/B Side)	Yr	VG	VG+	NM
❏ SD 7201 [S]	Led Zeppelin III	2001	6.25	12.50	25.00

—Classic Records reissue on audiophile vinyl

Number	Title (A Side/B Side)	Yr	VG	VG+	NM
❏ 7208 [M]	Led Zeppelin (IV) (Runes)	1971	75.00	150.00	300.00

—White label promo only

Number	Title (A Side/B Side)	Yr	VG	VG+	NM
❏ SD 7208 [DJ]	Led Zeppelin (IV) (Runes)	1971	37.50	75.00	150.00

—Stereo white label promo

Number	Title (A Side/B Side)	Yr	VG	VG+	NM
❏ SD 7208 [S]	Led Zeppelin (IV) (Runes)	1971	3.00	6.00	12.00

—"1841 Broadway" address on label

Number	Title (A Side/B Side)	Yr	VG	VG+	NM
❏ SD 7208 [S]	Led Zeppelin (IV) (Runes)	1974	2.50	5.00	10.00

—"75 Rockefeller Plaza" address on label

Number	Title (A Side/B Side)	Yr	VG	VG+	NM
❏ SD 7208 [S]	Led Zeppelin (IV) (Runes)	2001	6.25	12.50	25.00

—Classic Records reissue on audiophile vinyl

Number	Title (A Side/B Side)	Yr	VG	VG+	NM
❏ 7255 [M]	Houses of the Holy	1973	250.00	500.00	1000.

—White label promo only

Number	Title (A Side/B Side)	Yr	VG	VG+	NM
❏ SD 7255 [S]	Houses of the Holy	1973	3.00	6.00	12.00

—"1841 Broadway" address on label

Number	Title (A Side/B Side)	Yr	VG	VG+	NM
❏ SD 7255 [S]	Houses of the Holy	1974	2.50	5.00	10.00

—"75 Rockefeller Plaza" address on label

Number	Title (A Side/B Side)	Yr	VG	VG+	NM
❏ SD 7255 [S]	Houses of the Holy	2001	6.25	12.50	25.00

—Classic Records reissue on audiophile vinyl

Number	Title (A Side/B Side)	Yr	VG	VG+	NM
❏ 8216 [M]	Led Zeppelin	1969	100.00	200.00	400.00

—White label promo only

Number	Title (A Side/B Side)	Yr	VG	VG+	NM
❏ SD 8216 [DJ]	Led Zeppelin	1969	50.00	100.00	200.00

—Stereo white label promo

Number	Title (A Side/B Side)	Yr	VG	VG+	NM
❏ SD 8216 [S]	Led Zeppelin	1969	5.00	10.00	20.00

—"1841 Broadway" address on label

Number	Title (A Side/B Side)	Yr	VG	VG+	NM
❏ SD 8216 [S]	Led Zeppelin	1969	62.50	125.00	250.00

—Possible mispress with purple and brown labels

Number	Title (A Side/B Side)	Yr	VG	VG+	NM
❏ SD 8216 [S]	Led Zeppelin	1974	2.50	5.00	10.00

—"75 Rockefeller Plaza" address on label

Number	Title (A Side/B Side)	Yr	VG	VG+	NM
❏ SD 8216 [S]	Led Zeppelin	2000	6.25	12.50	25.00

—Classic Records reissue on audiophile vinyl

Number	Title (A Side/B Side)	Yr	VG	VG+	NM
❏ 8236 [M]	Led Zeppelin II	1969	50.00	100.00	200.00

—White label promo only

Number	Title (A Side/B Side)	Yr	VG	VG+	NM
❏ SD 8236 [DJ]	Led Zeppelin II	1969	75.00	150.00	300.00

—Stereo white label promo

Number	Title (A Side/B Side)	Yr	VG	VG+	NM
❏ SD 8236 [S]	Led Zeppelin II	1969	5.00	10.00	20.00

—"1841 Broadway" address on label

Number	Title (A Side/B Side)	Yr	VG	VG+	NM
❏ SD 8236 [S]	Led Zeppelin II	1974	2.50	5.00	10.00

—"75 Rockefeller Plaza" address on label

Number	Title (A Side/B Side)	Yr	VG	VG+	NM
❏ SD 8236 [S]	Led Zeppelin II	2000	6.25	12.50	25.00

—Classic Records reissue on audiophile vinyl

Number	Title (A Side/B Side)	Yr	VG	VG+	NM
❏ SD 19126	Led Zeppelin	1977	2.00	4.00	8.00
❏ SD 19127	Led Zeppelin II	1977	2.00	4.00	8.00
❏ SD 19128	Led Zeppelin III	1977	2.00	4.00	8.00
❏ SD 19129	Led Zeppelin (IV) (Runes)	1977	2.00	4.00	8.00
❏ SD 19130	Houses of the Holy	1977	2.00	4.00	8.00
❏ 82144 [(6)]	Led Zeppelin (Box Set)	1990	25.00	50.00	100.00
❏ 83061 [(4)]	BBC Sessions	2000	15.00	30.00	60.00

—Classic Records limited edition; each LP is in its own cardboard sleeve inside a box with a sheet of liner notes

Number	Title (A Side/B Side)	Yr	VG	VG+	NM
❏ 83268 [(2)]	Early Days: The Best of Led Zeppelin Vol. 1	1999	3.75	7.50	15.00
❏ 83278 [(2)]	Latter Days: The Best of Led Zeppelin Vol. 2	2000	3.75	7.50	15.00
❏ SMAS-94019	Led Zeppelin (IV) (Runes)	1972	10.00	20.00	40.00

—Capitol Record Club edition
MOBILE FIDELITY

Number	Title (A Side/B Side)	Yr	VG	VG+	NM
❏ 1-065	Led Zeppelin II	1981	20.00	40.00	80.00

—Audiophile vinyl
SWAN SONG

Number	Title (A Side/B Side)	Yr	VG	VG+	NM
❏ SS 2-200 [(2)]	Physical Graffiti	1975	3.75	7.50	15.00
❏ SS 2-200 [(2)]	Physical Graffiti	2002	10.00	20.00	40.00

—Classic Records reissue on audiophile vinyl

Number	Title (A Side/B Side)	Yr	VG	VG+	NM
❏ SS 2-201 [(2)]	The Song Remains the Same	1976	3.75	7.50	15.00
❏ SS 2-201 [(2)]	The Song Remains the Same	2003	10.00	20.00	40.00

—Classic Records edition on 200-gram vinyl

Number	Title (A Side/B Side)	Yr	VG	VG+	NM
❏ SS 8416	Presence	1976	2.50	5.00	10.00
❏ SS 8416	Presence	2002	6.25	12.50	25.00

—Classic Records reissue on audiophile vinyl

Number	Title (A Side/B Side)	Yr	VG	VG+	NM
❏ SS 16002	In Through the Out Door	1979	2.50	5.00	10.00

—Letter "B" on spine; add 50% if brown paper bag is still with jacket

Number	Title (A Side/B Side)	Yr	VG	VG+	NM
❏ SS 16002	In Through the Out Door	1979	2.50	5.00	10.00

—Letter "C" on spine; add 50% if brown paper bag is still with jacket

Number	Title (A Side/B Side)	Yr	VG	VG+	NM
❏ SS 16002	In Through the Out Door	1979	2.50	5.00	10.00

—Letter "D" on spine; add 50% if brown paper bag is still with jacket

Number	Title (A Side/B Side)	Yr	VG	VG+	NM
❏ SS 16002	In Through the Out Door	1979	2.50	5.00	10.00

—Letter "E" on spine; add 50% if brown paper bag is still with jacket

Number	Title (A Side/B Side)	Yr	VG	VG+	NM
❏ SS 16002	In Through the Out Door	1979	2.50	5.00	10.00

—Letter "F" on spine; add 50% if brown paper bag is still with jacket

Number	Title (A Side/B Side)	Yr	VG	VG+	NM
❏ SS 16002	In Through the Out Door	1979	2.50	5.00	10.00

—Letter "A" on spine; add 50% if brown paper bag is still with jacket

Number	Title (A Side/B Side)	Yr	VG	VG+	NM
❏ SS 16002	In Through the Out Door	2003	7.50	15.00	30.00

—Classic Records reissue on 200-gram vinyl; contains a 12-page insert with all six covers; we don't know if the label actually pressed these with six different covers

Number	Title (A Side/B Side)	Yr	VG	VG+	NM
❏ 90051	Coda	1982	2.50	5.00	10.00

LEE See LEE MARENO.

LEE, ALVIN Also see TEN YEARS AFTER.
12-Inch Singles
21 RECORDS

Number	Title (A Side/B Side)	Yr	VG	VG+	NM
❏ PR 918 [DJ]	Detroit Diesel (same on both sides)	1986	—	3.00	6.00
❏ PR 956 [DJ]	Shot in the Dark (same on both sides)	1986	—	3.00	6.00

45s
ATLANTIC

Number	Title (A Side/B Side)	Yr	VG	VG+	NM
❏ 3792 [DJ]	Ridin' Truckin' (same on both sides)	1981	—	2.00	4.00

—May be promo only

Number	Title (A Side/B Side)	Yr	VG	VG+	NM
❏ 4004 [DJ]	Can't Stop (same on both sides)	1982	—	2.00	4.00

—May be promo only
COLUMBIA

Number	Title (A Side/B Side)	Yr	VG	VG+	NM
❏ 45987	So Sad/Riffin'	1974	—	2.00	4.00

—With Mylon LeFevre
RSO

Number	Title (A Side/B Side)	Yr	VG	VG+	NM
❏ 936	Ride On Cowboy/Can't Sleep at Night	1979	—	2.00	4.00

—With "Ten Years Later"
21 RECORDS

Number	Title (A Side/B Side)	Yr	VG	VG+	NM
❏ 99501	Heart of Stone/She's So Cute	1986	—	—	3.00
❏ 99527	Detroit Diesel/Let's Go	1986	—	—	3.00

Albums
ATLANTIC

Number	Title (A Side/B Side)	Yr	VG	VG+	NM
❏ SD 19287	Free Fall	1980	2.50	5.00	10.00
❏ SD 19306	RX5	1981	2.50	5.00	10.00

COLUMBIA

Number	Title (A Side/B Side)	Yr	VG	VG+	NM
❏ KC 32729	On the Road to Freedom	1973	3.00	6.00	12.00

—With Mylon LeFevre

Number	Title (A Side/B Side)	Yr	VG	VG+	NM
❏ PC 32729	On the Road to Freedom	197?	2.00	4.00	8.00

—With Mylon LeFevre; reissue with new prefix

Number	Title (A Side/B Side)	Yr	VG	VG+	NM
❏ PG 33187 [(2)]	In Flight	1974	3.75	7.50	15.00
❏ PC 33796	Pump Iron!	1975	3.00	6.00	12.00

RSO

Number	Title (A Side/B Side)	Yr	VG	VG+	NM
❏ RS-1-3033	Rocket Fuel	1978	3.00	6.00	12.00

—With "Ten Years Later"

Number	Title (A Side/B Side)	Yr	VG	VG+	NM
❏ RS-1-3049	Ride On	1979	3.00	6.00	12.00

—With "Ten Years Later"
21 RECORDS

Number	Title (A Side/B Side)	Yr	VG	VG+	NM
❏ 90517	Detroit Diesel	1986	2.50	5.00	10.00

LEE, ARTHUR Also see LOVE.
45s
A&M

Number	Title (A Side/B Side)	Yr	VG	VG+	NM
❏ 1361	Everybody's Gotta Live/Love Jumped Through My Window	1972	—	2.00	4.00
❏ 1381	Sad Song/You Want Change for Your Re-Run	1972	—	2.00	4.00

CAPITOL

Number	Title (A Side/B Side)	Yr	VG	VG+	NM
❏ 4980	Ninth Wave/Rumble Still Skins	1963	7.50	15.00	30.00

Albums
A&M

Number	Title (A Side/B Side)	Yr	VG	VG+	NM
❏ SP-4356	Vindicator	1972	7.50	15.00	30.00

RHINO

Number	Title (A Side/B Side)	Yr	VG	VG+	NM
❏ RNLP 020	Arthur Lee	1981	2.50	5.00	10.00

LEE, BILLY, AND THE RIVIERAS Early version of MITCH RYDER AND THE DETROIT WHEELS.
45s
HYLAND

Number	Title (A Side/B Side)	Yr	VG	VG+	NM
❏ 3016	Won't You Dance with Me/You Know	1964	6.25	12.50	25.00

LEE, BRENDA
45s
DECCA

Number	Title (A Side/B Side)	Yr	VG	VG+	NM
❏ 30050	Jambalaya (On the Bayou)/Bigelow 6-2000	1956	7.50	15.00	30.00
❏ 30107	Christy Christmas/I'm Gonna Lasso Santa Claus	1956	6.25	12.50	25.00
❏ 30198	One Step at a Time/Fairyland	1957	6.25	12.50	25.00
❏ 30333	Dynamite/Love You 'Til I Die	1957	6.25	12.50	25.00
❏ 30411	Ain't That Love/One Teenager to Another	1957	6.25	12.50	25.00
❏ 30535	Rock-a-Bye Baby Blues/Rock the Bop	1958	6.25	12.50	25.00
❏ 30673	Ring-a My Phone/Little Jonah	1958	7.50	15.00	30.00
❏ 30776	Rockin' Around the Christmas Tree/Papa Noel	1958	6.25	12.50	25.00

—Originals have black labels with star under "Decca"

Number	Title (A Side/B Side)	Yr	VG	VG+	NM
❏ 30776	Rockin' Around the Christmas Tree/Papa Noel	1960	3.75	7.50	15.00

—Reissues have black labels with color bars

Number	Title (A Side/B Side)	Yr	VG	VG+	NM
❏ 30776 [PS]	Rockin' Around the Christmas Tree/Papa Noel	1960	12.50	25.00	50.00
❏ 30806	Bill Bailey Won't You Please Come Home/Hummin' the Blues	1959	6.25	12.50	25.00
❏ 30885	Let's Jump the Broomstick/One of These Days	1959	7.50	15.00	30.00
❏ 30967	Sweet Nothin's/Weep No More My Baby	1959	5.00	10.00	20.00
❏ 30967 [PS]	Sweet Nothin's/Weep No More My Baby	1959	30.00	60.00	120.00
❏ 31093	I'm Sorry/That's All You Gotta Do	1960	5.00	10.00	20.00
❏ 31093 [PS]	I'm Sorry/That's All You Gotta Do	1960	12.50	25.00	50.00
❏ 31149	I Want to Be Wanted/Just a Little	1960	3.75	7.50	15.00
❏ 31149 [PS]	I Want to Be Wanted/Just a Little	1960	10.00	20.00	40.00
❏ 31195	Emotions/I'm Learning About Love	1961	3.75	7.50	15.00
❏ 31195 [PS]	Emotions/I'm Learning About Love	1961	7.50	15.00	30.00
❏ 31231	You Can Depend on Me/It's Never Too Late	1961	3.75	7.50	15.00
❏ 31231 [PS]	You Can Depend on Me/It's Never Too Late	1961	7.50	15.00	30.00
❏ 31272	Dum Dum/Eventually	1961	3.75	7.50	15.00
❏ 31309	Fool #1/Anybody But Me	1961	3.75	7.50	15.00
❏ 31309 [PS]	Fool #1/Anybody But Me	1961	7.50	15.00	30.00
❏ 31348	Break It To Me Gently/So Deep	1962	3.75	7.50	15.00
❏ 31348 [PS]	Break It To Me Gently/So Deep	1962	6.25	12.50	25.00
❏ 31379	Everybody Loves Me But You/Here Comes That Feelin'	1962	3.75	7.50	15.00
❏ 31407	Heart in Hand/It Started All Over Again	1962	3.75	7.50	15.00
❏ 31424	All Alone Am I/Save All Your Lovin' for Me	1962	3.75	7.50	15.00
❏ 31424 [PS]	All Alone Am I/Save All Your Lovin' for Me	1962	6.25	12.50	25.00
❏ 31454	Your Used to Be/She'll Never Know	1963	3.75	7.50	15.00
❏ 31454 [PS]	Your Used to Be/She'll Never Know	1963	6.25	12.50	25.00
❏ 31478	Losing You/He's So Heavenly	1963	3.75	7.50	15.00
❏ 31478 [PS]	Losing You/He's So Heavenly	1963	6.25	12.50	25.00
❏ 31510	My Whole World Is Falling Down/I Wonder	1963	3.75	7.50	15.00
❏ 31510 [PS]	My Whole World Is Falling Down/I Wonder	1963	6.25	12.50	25.00
❏ 31539	The Grass Is Greener/Sweet Impossible You	1963	3.75	7.50	15.00
❏ 31539 [PS]	The Grass Is Greener/Sweet Impossible You	1963	6.25	12.50	25.00
❏ 31570	As Usual/Lonely Lonely Lonely Me	1963	3.75	7.50	15.00
❏ 31599	Think/The Waiting Game	1964	2.50	5.00	10.00
❏ 31599 [PS]	Think/The Waiting Game	1964	3.75	7.50	15.00
❏ 31628	Alone with You/My Dreams	1964	2.50	5.00	10.00
❏ 31628 [PS]	Alone with You/My Dreams	1964	3.75	7.50	15.00

Number	Title (A Side/B Side)	Yr	VG	VG+	NM
31654	When You Loved Me/He's Sure to Remember Me	1964	2.50	5.00	10.00
31654 [PS]	When You Loved Me/He's Sure to Remember Me	1964	3.75	7.50	15.00
31687	Jingle Bell Rock/Winter Wonderland	1964	3.00	6.00	12.00
31687 [PS]	Jingle Bell Rock/Winter Wonderland	1964	4.00	8.00	16.00
31688	This Time of the Year/Christmas Will Be Just Another Lonely Day	1964	3.00	6.00	12.00
31688 [PS]	This Time of the Year/Christmas Will Be Just Another Lonely Day	1964	4.00	8.00	16.00
31690	Is It True/Just Behind the Rainbow	1964	2.50	5.00	10.00
31690 [PS]	Is It True/Just Behind the Rainbow	1964	3.75	7.50	15.00
31728	Thanks a Lot/The Crying Game	1965	2.50	5.00	10.00
31762	Truly, Truly, True/I Still Miss Someone	1965	2.50	5.00	10.00
31762 [PS]	Truly, Truly, True/I Still Miss Someone	1965	3.75	7.50	15.00
31792	Too Many Rivers/No One	1965	2.50	5.00	10.00
31849	Rusty Bells/If You Don't (Not Like You)	1965	2.50	5.00	10.00
31917	Too Little Time/Time and Time Again	1966	2.00	4.00	8.00
31970	Ain't Gonna Cry No More/It Takes One to Know One	1966	2.00	4.00	8.00
32018	Coming On Strong/You Keep Coming Back to Me	1966	2.00	4.00	8.00
32079	Ride, Ride, Ride/Lonely People Do Foolish Things	1967	2.00	4.00	8.00
32119	Born to Be By Your Side/Take Me	1967	2.00	4.00	8.00
32161	My Heart Keeps Hangin' On/Where Love Is	1967	2.00	4.00	8.00
32213	Where's the Melody/Save Me for a Rainy Day	1967	2.00	4.00	8.00
32248	That's All Right/Fantasy	1967	2.00	4.00	8.00
32299	Cabaret/Mood Indigo	1968	2.00	4.00	8.00

—With Pete Fountain

Number	Title (A Side/B Side)	Yr	VG	VG+	NM
32330	Kansas City/Each Day Is a Rainbow	1968	2.00	4.00	8.00
32428	Johnny One Time/I Must Have Been Out of My Mind	1968	2.00	4.00	8.00
32428 [PS]	Johnny One Time/I Must Have Been Out of My Mind	1968	3.75	7.50	15.00
32491	You Don't Need Me for Anything Anymore/Bring Me Sunshine	1969	—	3.00	6.00
32560	Let It Be Me/You Better Move On	1969	—	3.00	6.00
32675	I Think I Love You Again/Hello Love	1970	—	3.00	6.00
32734	Do Right Woman, Do Right Man/Sisters in Sorrow	1970	—	3.00	6.00
32848	If This Is Our Last Time/Everybody's Reaching Out for Someone	1971	—	3.00	6.00
32918	I'm a Memory/Misty Memories	1972	—	3.00	6.00
32975	Always on My Mind/That Ain't Right	1972	—	3.00	6.00
7-34060 [S]	Lazy River/You Always Hurt the One You Love	1962	5.00	10.00	20.00
7-34061 [S]	It's the Talk of the Town/You've Got Me Crying Again	1962	5.00	10.00	20.00
7-34062 [S]	How Deep Is the Ocean (How High Is the Sky)/Send Me Some Lovin'	1962	5.00	10.00	20.00
7-34063 [S]	Fools Rush In (Where Angels Fear to Tread)/I'll Always Be in Love with You	1962	5.00	10.00	20.00
7-34064 [S]	I'll Be Seeing You/Hold Me	1962	5.00	10.00	20.00

—The above five are 7-inch 33 1/3 rpm singles with small holes

Number	Title (A Side/B Side)	Yr	VG	VG+	NM
34494 [DJ]	Where's the Melody? (same on both sides)	1967	3.75	7.50	15.00

—Promo-only number, pink label

Number	Title (A Side/B Side)	Yr	VG	VG+	NM
38236 [DJ]	Voice Tracks by Brenda Lee: For Brenda Lee Day, March 29, 1961/Introduction and Station Breaks for General Use	1961	10.00	20.00	40.00

—Pink label promo

Number	Title (A Side/B Side)	Yr	VG	VG+	NM
38275 [S]	If You Love Me (Really Love Me)/Just Another Lie	1961	5.00	10.00	20.00
38276 [S]	When I Fall in Love/Crazy Talk	1961	5.00	10.00	20.00
38277 [S]	Swanee River Rock/Around the World	1961	5.00	10.00	20.00
38278 [S]	Will You Love Me Tomorrow/Georgia on My Mind	1961	5.00	10.00	20.00
38279 [S]	I'm in the Mood for Love/Cry	1961	5.00	10.00	20.00

—The above five are 7-inch 33 1/3 rpm singles with small holes

Number	Title (A Side/B Side)	Yr	VG	VG+	NM
88215	Christy Christmas/I'm Gonna Lasso Santa Claus	1956	12.50	25.00	50.00

—As "Little Brenda Lee" on Decca's Children's Series

Number	Title (A Side/B Side)	Yr	VG	VG+	NM
88215 [PS]	Christy Christmas/I'm Gonna Lasso Santa Claus	1956	20.00	40.00	80.00

ELEKTRA

Number	Title (A Side/B Side)	Yr	VG	VG+	NM
45492	Left-Over Love/Could It Be I Found Love Tonight	1978	—	2.50	5.00

MCA

Number	Title (A Side/B Side)	Yr	VG	VG+	NM
40003	Nobody Wins/We Had a Good Thing Goin'	1973	—	2.50	5.00
40107	Sunday Sunrise/Must I Believe	1973	—	2.50	5.00
40171	Wrong Ideas/Something For A Rainy Day	1973	—	2.50	5.00
40262	Big Four Poster Bed/Castles In The Sand	1974	—	2.50	5.00
40318	Rock On Baby/More Than A Memory	1974	—	2.50	5.00
40385	He's My Rock/Feel Free	1975	—	2.50	5.00
40442	Bringing It Back/Papa's Knee	1975	—	2.50	5.00
40511	Find Yourself Another Puppet/What I Had With You	1976	—	2.50	5.00
40584	Brother Shelton/Now He's Coming Home	1976	—	2.50	5.00
40640	Takin' What I Can Get/Your Favorite Wornout Nightmare's Coming Home	1976	—	2.50	5.00
40683	Ruby's Lounge/Oklahoma Superstar	1977	—	2.50	5.00
41130	Tell Me What It's Like/Let Your Love Fall Back On Me	1979	—	2.50	5.00
41187	The Cowgirl And The Dandy/Do You Wanna Spend The Night	1980	—	2.50	5.00
41262	Keeping Me Warm For You/At The Moonlight	1980	—	2.50	5.00
41270	Don't Promise Me Anything (Do It)/You Only Broke My Heart	1980	—	2.50	5.00
41322	Broken Trust/Right Behind The Rain	1980	—	2.50	5.00

—With the Oak Ridge Boys

Number	Title (A Side/B Side)	Yr	VG	VG+	NM
51047	Every Now and Then/He'll Play The Music	1981	—	2.00	4.00
51113	Fool, Fool/Right Behind The Rain	1981	—	2.00	4.00
51154	Enough For You/What Am I Gonna Do	1981	—	2.00	4.00
51195	Only When I Laugh/Too Many Nights Alone	1981	—	2.00	4.00
51230	From Levis To Calvin Klein Jeans/I Know A Lot About Love	1982	—	2.00	4.00
52060	Keeping Me Warm For You/There's More To Me Than You Can See	1982	—	2.00	4.00
52124	Just For The Moment/Love Letters	1982	—	2.00	4.00

—With the Oak Ridge Boys

Number	Title (A Side/B Side)	Yr	VG	VG+	NM
52268	Didn't We Do It Good/We're So Close	1983	—	2.00	4.00
52394	A Sweeter Love (I'll Never Know)/A Woman's Mind	1984	—	2.00	4.00
52654	I'm Takin' My Time/That's The Way It Was Then	1985	—	2.00	4.00
52720	Why You Been Gone So Long/He Can't Make Your Kind of Love	1985	—	2.00	4.00
52720 [PS]	Why You Been Gone So Long/He Can't Make Your Kind of Love	1985	—	2.00	4.00
52804	Two Hearts/Loving Arms	1986	—	2.00	4.00
52804 [DJ]	Two Hearts (same on both sides)	1986	2.50	5.00	10.00

—Promo only on red vinyl

Number	Title (A Side/B Side)	Yr	VG	VG+	NM
60069	Sweet Nothin's/I Want to Be Wanted	197?	—	2.00	4.00

—Reissue; originals have black rainbow label

Number	Title (A Side/B Side)	Yr	VG	VG+	NM
60070	I'm Sorry/All Alone Am I	197?	—	2.00	4.00

—Reissue; originals have black rainbow label

Number	Title (A Side/B Side)	Yr	VG	VG+	NM
65027	Rockin' Around the Christmas Tree/Papa Noel	1973	—	2.00	4.00

—Black label with rainbow

Number	Title (A Side/B Side)	Yr	VG	VG+	NM
65027	Rockin' Around the Christmas Tree/Papa Noel	1980	—	—	3.00

—Blue label with rainbow

Number	Title (A Side/B Side)	Yr	VG	VG+	NM
65028	Jingle Bell Rock/Winter Wonderland	1973	—	2.00	4.00

—Black label with rainbow

Number	Title (A Side/B Side)	Yr	VG	VG+	NM
65028	Jingle Bell Rock/Winter Wonderland	1980	—	—	3.00

—Blue label with rainbow

MONUMENT

Number	Title (A Side/B Side)	Yr	VG	VG+	NM
03781	You're Gonna Love Yourself (In the Morning)/What Do You Think About Lovin'	1983	—	2.00	4.00

—A-side: With Willie Nelson; B-side: With Dolly Parton

WARNER BROS.

Number	Title (A Side/B Side)	Yr	VG	VG+	NM
19303	A Little Unfair/Some of These Days	1991	—	—	3.00
19397	Your One and Only/You Better Do Better	1991	—	—	3.00

7-Inch Extended Plays

DECCA

Number	Title (A Side/B Side)	Yr	VG	VG+	NM
ED 2678	(contents unknown)	1960	5.00	10.00	20.00
ED 2678 [PS]	Sweet Nothin's	1960	5.00	10.00	20.00
ED 2682	Be My Love Again/Just Let Me Dream//Jambalaya/Wee Wee Willie	1960	5.00	10.00	20.00
ED 2682 [PS]	(title unknown)	1960	5.00	10.00	20.00
ED 2683	Dynamite/Heading Home//I'm Sorry/That's All You Gotta Do	1960	5.00	10.00	20.00
ED 2683 [PS]	I'm Sorry	1960	5.00	10.00	20.00
ED 2695	I Want to Be Wanted/Just a Little//Teach Me Tonite/Walkin' to New Orleans	1961	5.00	10.00	20.00
ED 2695 [PS]	(title unknown)	1961	5.00	10.00	20.00
ED 2702	Dum Dum/Eventually//When I Fall in Love/Build a Big Fence	1961	5.00	10.00	20.00
ED 2702 [PS]	(title unknown)	1961	5.00	10.00	20.00
ED 2704	Lover Come Back to Me/All the Way//Kansas City/On the Sunny Side of the Street	1961	5.00	10.00	20.00
ED 2704 [PS]	Lover Come Back to Me	1961	5.00	10.00	20.00
ED 2712	Fool #1/Anybody But Me//You Can Depend on Me/It's Never Too Late	1961	5.00	10.00	20.00
ED 2712 [PS]	(title unknown)	1961	5.00	10.00	20.00
ED 2716	Break It to Me Gently/Will You Love Me Tomorrow//Tragedy/So Deep	1962	5.00	10.00	20.00
ED 2716 [PS]	Break It to Me Gently	1962	5.00	10.00	20.00
ED 2725	Here Comes That Feeling/Everybody Loves Me But You//You've Got Me Crying Again/Lazy River	1962	5.00	10.00	20.00
ED 2725 [PS]	Everybody Loves Me But You	1962	5.00	10.00	20.00
ED 2730	It Started All Over Again/Heart in Hand//You Always Hurt the One You Love/Cry	1962	5.00	10.00	20.00
ED 2730 [PS]	(title unknown)	1962	5.00	10.00	20.00
ED 2738	All Alone Am I/Why Me//It's a Lonely Old Town/Save All Your Loving for Me	1962	5.00	10.00	20.00
ED 2738 [PS]	All Alone Am I	1962	5.00	10.00	20.00
ED 2745	My Coloring Book/I Left My Heart in San Francisco//What Kind of Fool Am I/Fly Me to the Moon	1962	5.00	10.00	20.00
ED 2745 [PS]	Fly Me to the Moon	1962	5.00	10.00	20.00
ED 2764	The Grass Is Greener/I Wonder//My Whole World Is Falling Down/Losing You	1963	5.00	10.00	20.00
ED 2764 [PS]	The Grass Is Greener	1963	5.00	10.00	20.00
ED 2775	As Usual/The End of the World//There Goes My Heart/Out in the Cold Again	1963	5.00	10.00	20.00
ED 2775 [PS]	As Usual	1963	5.00	10.00	20.00
ED 2801	Thanks a Lot/Think//Is It True/When You Love Me	1965	5.00	10.00	20.00
ED 2801 [PS]	(title unknown)	1965	5.00	10.00	20.00
7-4216 [DJ]	You Always Hurt the One You Love/Lazy River//You've Got Me Crying//I Miss You So/Fools Rush In/I'll Be Seeing You	1962	5.00	10.00	20.00

—Jukebox EP, stereo, small hole, plays at 33 1/3 rpm

Number	Title (A Side/B Side)	Yr	VG	VG+	NM
7-4216 [PS]	Sincerely	1962	5.00	10.00	20.00
7-4439 [DJ]	I Wanna Be Around/Our Day Will Come/You're the Reason I'm in Love//End of the World/Losing You/Break It to Me Gently	1963	5.00	10.00	20.00

—Jukebox EP, stereo, small hole, plays at 33 1/3 rpm

Number	Title (A Side/B Side)	Yr	VG	VG+	NM
7-4439 [PS]	Let Me Sing	1963	5.00	10.00	20.00
7-4825 [DJ]	What Now My Love/You Don't Have to Say You Love Me/You've Got Your Troubles//Up Tight/Strangers in the Night/Call Me	1966	5.00	10.00	20.00

—Jukebox EP, stereo, small hole, plays at 33 1/3 rpm

Number	Title (A Side/B Side)	Yr	VG	VG+	NM
7-4825 [PS]	Coming On Strong	1966	5.00	10.00	20.00
7-34243	Days of Wine and Roses/Blue Velvet/As Usual//I Love You Becuase/I'm Confessin' (That I Love You)/My Whole World Is Falling Down	1964	6.25	12.50	25.00

—Jukebox issue; small hole, plays at 33 1/3 rpm

Number	Title (A Side/B Side)	Yr	VG	VG+	NM
7-34243 [PS]	By Request	1964	6.25	12.50	25.00
7-34254	This Time of the Year/Blue Christmas/Jingle Bell Rock//Rockin' Around the Christmas Tree/Marshmallow World/Winter Wonderland	1964	6.25	12.50	25.00

—Jukebox EP, stereo, small hole, plays at 33 1/3 rpm

Number	Title (A Side/B Side)	Yr	VG	VG+	NM
7-34254 [PS]	Merry Christmas	1964	6.25	12.50	25.00

—Sleeve says this is "DL 74583"; price includes title strips

Number	Title (A Side/B Side)	Yr	VG	VG+	NM
7-34363	Bye Bye Blues/September in the Rain/What a Difference a Day Makes//The Good Life/Shadow of Your Smile/Softly As I Leave You	1966	5.00	10.00	20.00

—Jukebox EP, stereo, small hole, plays at 33 1/3 rpm

Number	Title (A Side/B Side)	Yr	VG	VG+	NM
7-34363 [PS]	Bye Bye Blues	1966	5.00	10.00	20.00

L

Number	Title (A Side/B Side)	Yr	VG	VG+	NM
Albums					
DECCA					
☐ DL 4039 [M]	Brenda Lee	1960	6.25	12.50	25.00
☐ DL 4082 [M]	This Is...Brenda	1960	6.25	12.50	25.00
☐ DL 4104 [M]	Emotions	1961	6.25	12.50	25.00
☐ DL 4176 [M]	All the Way	1961	6.25	12.50	25.00
☐ DL 4216 [M]	Sincerely	1962	6.25	12.50	25.00
☐ DL 4326 [M]	Brenda, That's All	1962	6.25	12.50	25.00
☐ DL 4370 [M]	All Alone Am I	1963	6.25	12.50	25.00
☐ DL 4439 [M]	Let Me Sing	1963	6.25	12.50	25.00
☐ DL 4509 [M]	By Request	1964	5.00	10.00	20.00
☐ DL 4583 [M]	Merry Christmas from Brenda Lee	1964	5.00	10.00	20.00
☐ DL 4626 [M]	Top Teen Hits	1965	5.00	10.00	20.00
☐ DL 4661 [M]	The Versatile Brenda Lee	1965	5.00	10.00	20.00
☐ DL 4684 [M]	Too Many Rivers	1965	5.00	10.00	20.00
☐ DL 4755 [M]	Bye Bye Blues	1966	5.00	10.00	20.00
☐ DL 4757 [M]	10 Golden Years	196?	3.75	7.50	15.00
—With regular cover					
☐ DL 4757 [M]	10 Golden Years	1966	6.25	12.50	25.00
—With gatefold cover					
☐ DL 4825 [M]	Coming On Strong	1966	3.75	7.50	15.00
☐ DL 4941 [M]	Reflections in Blue	1967	5.00	10.00	20.00
☐ DL 8873 [M]	Grandma, What Great Songs You Sang	1960	10.00	20.00	40.00
☐ DL 74039 [S]	Brenda Lee	1960	7.50	15.00	30.00
☐ DL 74082 [S]	This Is...Brenda	1960	7.50	15.00	30.00
☐ DL 74104 [S]	Emotions	1961	7.50	15.00	30.00
☐ DL 74176 [S]	All the Way	1961	7.50	15.00	30.00
☐ DL 74216 [S]	Sincerely	1962	7.50	15.00	30.00
☐ DL 74326 [S]	Brenda, That's All	1962	7.50	15.00	30.00
☐ DL 74370 [S]	All Alone Am I	1963	7.50	15.00	30.00
☐ DL 74439 [S]	Let Me Sing	1963	7.50	15.00	30.00
☐ DL 74509 [S]	By Request	1964	6.25	12.50	25.00
☐ DL 74583 [S]	Merry Christmas from Brenda Lee	1964	6.25	12.50	25.00
☐ DL 74626 [S]	Top Teen Hits	1965	6.25	12.50	25.00
☐ DL 74661 [S]	The Versatile Brenda Lee	1965	6.25	12.50	25.00
☐ DL 74684 [S]	Too Many Rivers	1965	6.25	12.50	25.00
☐ DL 74755 [S]	Bye Bye Blues	1966	6.25	12.50	25.00
☐ DL 74757 [S]	10 Golden Years	196?	5.00	10.00	20.00
—With regular cover					
☐ DL 74757 [S]	10 Golden Years	1966	7.50	15.00	30.00
—With gatefold cover					
☐ DL 74825 [S]	Coming On Strong	1966	5.00	10.00	20.00
☐ DL 74941 [S]	Reflections in Blue	1967	3.75	7.50	15.00
☐ DL 74955 [S]	For the First Time	1968	3.75	7.50	15.00
—With Pete Fountain					
☐ DL 75111	Johnny One Time	1969	3.75	7.50	15.00
☐ DL 75232	Memphis Portrait	1970	3.75	7.50	15.00
☐ DL 78873 [S]	Grandma, What Great Songs You Sang	1960	12.50	25.00	50.00
☐ ST-90997 [S]	10 Golden Years	1966	6.25	12.50	25.00
—Capitol Record Club edition					
☐ ST-92062	Johnny One Time	1969	5.00	10.00	20.00
—Capitol Record Club edition					
☐ R 103619 [S]	Merry Christmas from Brenda Lee	1971	5.00	10.00	20.00
—RCA Music Service edition					
MCA					
☐ 232 [S]	Merry Christmas from Brenda Lee	1973	3.00	6.00	12.00
☐ 305	Brenda	1973	3.75	7.50	15.00
☐ 373	New Sunrise	1973	3.00	6.00	12.00
☐ 433	Brenda Lee Now	1974	3.00	6.00	12.00
☐ 477	Sincerely, Brenda Lee	1975	2.50	5.00	10.00
☐ 758	Even Better	198?	2.00	4.00	8.00
—Reissue of 3211					
☐ 824	Only When I Laugh	1982	2.00	4.00	8.00
—Reissue of 5278					
☐ 2233	L.A. Sessions	1976	2.50	5.00	10.00
☐ 3211	Even Better	1979	2.50	5.00	10.00
☐ 2-4012 [(2)]	The Brenda Lee Story — Her Greatest Hits	1973	5.00	10.00	20.00
☐ 5143	Take Me Back	1980	2.50	5.00	10.00
☐ 5278	Only When I Laugh	1981	2.50	5.00	10.00
☐ 5342	Greatest Country Hits	1982	2.50	5.00	10.00
☐ 5626	Feels So Right	1985	2.50	5.00	10.00
☐ 15021 [S]	Merry Christmas from Brenda Lee	197?	2.50	5.00	10.00
☐ 15038	Rockin' Around the Christmas Tree	198?	2.50	5.00	10.00
MCA CORAL					
☐ CB-20044	Let It Be Me	197?	2.50	5.00	10.00
VOCALION					
☐ VL 3795 [M]	Here's Brenda Lee	1967	3.00	6.00	12.00
☐ VL 73795 [S]	Here's Brenda Lee	1967	3.00	6.00	12.00
☐ VL 73890	Let It Be Me	1970	3.00	6.00	12.00

LEE, BRENDA (2) Not the same Brenda Lee as the others; this one's real name is Brenda Lee Jones.
45s

Number	Title (A Side/B Side)	Yr	VG	VG+	NM
APOLLO					
☐ 490	I Ain't Gonna Give Nobody None/I'll Never Get Rich Again	1956	7.50	15.00	30.00

LEE, CURTIS Also see C.L. AND THE PICTURES.
45s

Number	Title (A Side/B Side)	Yr	VG	VG+	NM
DUNES					
☐ 801	California GH-903/Then I'll Know	1960	5.00	10.00	20.00
☐ 2001	Special Love/"D" in Love	1960	5.00	10.00	20.00
☐ 2003	Pledge of Love/Then I'll Know	1961	5.00	10.00	20.00
☐ 2003 [PS]	Pledge of Love/Then I'll Know	1961	6.25	12.50	25.00
☐ 2007	Pretty Little Angel Eyes/Gee, How I Wish You Were Here	1961	6.25	12.50	25.00
☐ 2008	Under the Moon of Love/Beverly Jean	1961	6.25	12.50	25.00
—2007 and 2008 were Phil Spector productions					
☐ 2012	Just Another Fool/A Night at Daddy Gee's	1962	5.00	10.00	20.00
☐ 2015	Does He Mean That Much to You/The Wobble	1962	5.00	10.00	20.00
☐ 2020	Lonely Weekends/Better Him Than Me	1963	5.00	10.00	20.00
☐ 2021	Pickin' Up the Pieces of My Heart/Mr. Mistaker	1963	5.00	10.00	20.00
HOT					
☐ 7	I Never Knew What Love Could Do/Gotta Have You	1960	18.75	37.50	75.00
LOST-NITE					
☐ 217	Pretty Little Angel Eyes/Gee, How I Wish You Were Here	196?	—	2.50	5.00
—Reissue					

Number	Title (A Side/B Side)	Yr	VG	VG+	NM
MIRA					
☐ 240	Sweet Baby/Is She In Your Town	1967	5.00	10.00	20.00
ROJAC					
☐ 114	Get In My Bag/Everybody's Going Wild	1967	3.00	6.00	12.00
SABRA					
☐ 517	Let's Take a Ride/I'm Asking Forgiveness	1960	6.25	12.50	25.00
WARRIOR					
☐ 1555	With All My Heart/Pure Love	1959	7.50	15.00	30.00

LEE, DICKEY
45s

Number	Title (A Side/B Side)	Yr	VG	VG+	NM
ATCO					
☐ 6546	Run Right Back/Red, Green, Yellow, Blue	1968	2.00	4.00	8.00
☐ 6580	All My Life/Hang-Ups	1968	2.00	4.00	8.00
☐ 6609	You're Young and You'll Forget/Waitin' for Love to Come My Way	1968	2.00	4.00	8.00
DIAMOND					
☐ 266	Ruby Baby/I Remember Barbara	1969	2.00	4.00	8.00
DOT					
☐ 16087	Life in a Teenage World/Why Don't You Write On	1960	3.75	7.50	15.00
HALLWAY					
☐ 1924	Big Brother/She's Walking Away	1964	2.50	5.00	10.00
MERCURY					
☐ 55068	I'm Just a Heartache Away/Midnight Flyer	1979	—	2.00	4.00
☐ 57005	He's an Old Rock 'N' Roller/It Hurts to Be in Love	1979	—	2.00	4.00
☐ 57017	Don't Look Back/I'm Trustin' a Feelin'	1980	—	2.00	4.00
☐ 57027	Workin' My Way to Your Heart/If You Want Me	1980	—	2.00	4.00
☐ 57036	Lost in Love/Again	1980	—	2.00	4.00
—A-side with Kathy Burdick					
☐ 57052	Honky Tonk Hearts/Best I Hit the Road	1981	—	2.00	4.00
☐ 57056	I Wonder If I Care As Much/Further Than a Country Mile	1981	—	2.00	4.00
☐ 76129	Everybody Loves a Winner/You Won't Be Here Tonight	1982	—	2.00	4.00
RCA					
☐ PB-10764	9,999,999 Tears/I Never Will Get Over You	1976	—	2.00	4.00
☐ PB-10914	If You Gotta Make a Fool of Somebody/My Love Shows Thru	1977	—	2.00	4.00
☐ GB-10929	Rocky/9,999,999 Tears	1977	—	—	3.00
—Gold Standard Series					
☐ PB-11009	Virginia, How Far Will You Go/My Love Shows Thru	1977	—	2.00	4.00
☐ PB-11125	Peanut Butter/Breezy Was Her Name	1977	—	2.00	4.00
☐ PB-11191	Love Is a Word/I'll Be Leaving Alone	1978	—	2.00	4.00
☐ PB-11294	My Heart Won't Cry Anymore/Danna	1978	—	2.00	4.00
☐ PB-11389	It's Not Easy/I've Been Honky-Tonkin' Too Long	1978	—	2.00	4.00
RCA VICTOR					
☐ 47-9862	All Too Soon/Charlie	1970	—	3.00	6.00
☐ 47-9941	Home To/Special	1971	—	3.00	6.00
☐ 47-9988	The Mahogany Pulpit/Everybody's Reaching Out for Someone	1971	—	3.00	6.00
☐ 48-1013	Never Ending Song of Love/On the Southbound	1971	—	3.00	6.00
☐ 74-0623	I Saw My Lady/What We Used to Hang On To	1971	—	3.00	6.00
☐ 74-0710	Ashes of Love/The Kingdom I Call Home	1972	—	2.50	5.00
☐ 74-0798	Baby, Bye Bye/She Thinks I Still Care	1972	—	2.50	5.00
☐ 74-0892	Crying Over You/My World Around You	1973	—	2.50	5.00
☐ 74-0980	Put Me Down Softly/If She Turns Up in Atlanta	1973	—	2.50	5.00
☐ APBO-0082	Sparklin' Brown Eyes/Country Song	1973	—	2.50	5.00
☐ APBO-0227	I Use the Soap/Strawberry Women	1974	—	2.50	5.00
☐ PB-10014	Give Me One Good Reason/Sweet Fever	1974	—	2.50	5.00
☐ PB-10091	The Busiest Memory in Town/Way to Go On	1974	—	2.50	5.00
☐ PB-10289	You Make It Look So Easy/The Door's Always Open	1975	—	2.00	4.00
☐ PB-10361	Rocky/The Closest Thing to You	1975	—	2.00	4.00
☐ PB-10543	Angels, Roses and Rain/Danna	1976	—	2.00	4.00
☐ PB-10684	Makin' Love Don't Always Make Love Grow/I Never Will Get Over You	1976	—	2.00	4.00
RENDEZVOUS					
☐ 188	Dream Boy/Stay True Baby	1962	6.25	12.50	25.00
SMASH					
☐ 1758	Patches/More or Less	1962	3.75	7.50	15.00
☐ 1791	I Saw Linda Yesterday/The Girl I Can't Forget	1962	3.00	6.00	12.00
☐ 1808	Don't Wanna Talk About Paula/Just a Friend	1963	3.00	6.00	12.00
☐ 1822	I Go Lonely/Ten Million Faces	1963	3.00	6.00	12.00
☐ 1844	She Wants to Be Bobby's Girl/The Day the Sawmill Closed Down	1963	3.00	6.00	12.00
☐ 1871	To the Aisle/Mother Nature	1964	3.00	6.00	12.00
☐ 1913	Me and My Teardrops/Only Trust in Me	1964	3.00	6.00	12.00
SUN					
☐ 280	Good Lovin'/Memories Never Grow Old	1957	7.50	15.00	30.00
☐ 297	Dreamy Nights/Fool, Fool, Fool	1958	20.00	40.00	80.00
TAMPA					
☐ 131	Dream Boy/Stay True Baby	1957	7.50	15.00	30.00
TCF HALL					
☐ 102	Laurie (Strange Things Happen)/Party Doll	1965	2.50	5.00	10.00
☐ 111	The Girl from Peyton Place/The Girl I Used to Know	1965	2.50	5.00	10.00
☐ 118	Good Girl Goin' Bad/Pretty White Dress	1965	2.50	5.00	10.00
☐ 128	Good Guy/Annie	1966	2.50	5.00	10.00
Albums					
MERCURY					
☐ SRM-1-5020	Dickey Lee	1979	2.50	5.00	10.00
☐ SRM-1-5026	Dickey Lee Again	1980	2.50	5.00	10.00
RCA VICTOR					
☐ APL1-0311	Sparklin' Brown Eyes	1974	3.00	6.00	12.00
☐ APL1-1243	Rocky	1975	3.00	6.00	12.00
☐ APL1-1725	Angels, Roses and Rain	1976	3.00	6.00	12.00
☐ LSP-4637	Never Ending Song of Love	1971	3.00	6.00	12.00
☐ LSP-4715	Ashes of Love	1972	3.00	6.00	12.00
☐ LSP-4791	Baby, Bye Bye	1972	3.00	6.00	12.00
☐ LSP-4857	Crying Over You	1973	3.00	6.00	12.00
SMASH					
☐ MGS-27020 [M]	The Tale of Patches	1962	7.50	15.00	30.00
☐ SRS-67020 [S]	The Tale of Patches	1962	10.00	20.00	40.00

Number	Title (A Side/B Side)	Yr	VG	VG+	NM
TCF HALL					
❏ TCF-8001 [M]	Dickey Lee Sings "Laurie" and "The Girl from Peyton Place"	1965	5.00	10.00	20.00
❏ TCF-9001 [S]	Dickey Lee Sings "Laurie" and "The Girl from Peyton Place"	1965	6.25	12.50	25.00

LEE, JACKIE (1) Male R&B singer whose biggest hit was "The Duck."
45s

Number	Title (A Side/B Side)	Yr	VG	VG+	NM
ABC					
❏ 11146	One for the Road/Darkest Days	1968	5.00	10.00	20.00
CAPITOL					
❏ 3145	25 Miles to Louisiana/Pershing Square	1971	—	3.00	6.00
KEYMEN					
❏ 109	Glory of Love/Bring It Home	1968	2.50	5.00	10.00
❏ 114	African Boo-Ga-Loo/Bring It Home	1968	2.50	5.00	10.00
MIRWOOD					
❏ 5502	The Duck/Let Your Conscience Be Your Guide	1965	3.00	6.00	12.00
❏ 5509	Your P-E-R-S-O-N-A-L-I-T-Y/Try My Method	1966	2.50	5.00	10.00
❏ 5510	The Shotgun and the Duck/Do the Temptation Walk	1966	2.50	5.00	10.00
❏ 5519	You're Everything/Would You Believe	1966	2.50	5.00	10.00
❏ 5527	Don't Be Ashamed/Oh, My Darlin'	1966	2.50	5.00	10.00
❏ 5528	Baby I'm Satisfied/Whether It's Right or Wrong	1966	2.50	5.00	10.00
—With Dolores Hall					
UNI					
❏ 55206	The Chicken/I Love You	1970	—	4.00	8.00
❏ 55259	Your Sweetness Is My Weakness/You Were Searching for a Love	1970	2.00	4.00	8.00
Albums					
MIRWOOD					
❏ MW-7000 [M]	The Duck	1966	5.00	10.00	20.00
❏ SW-7000 [S]	The Duck	1966	6.25	12.50	25.00

LEE, JACKIE (2) Phialdelphia-based keyboard player.
45s

Number	Title (A Side/B Side)	Yr	VG	VG+	NM
ABC-PARAMOUNT					
❏ 9892	The Storm/Bye Bye Blues	1958	2.50	5.00	10.00
CORAL					
❏ 61214	The Donkey Serenade/Mr. Hot Piano	1954	3.00	6.00	12.00
❏ 61259	Bei Mir Bist Du Schoen/Missouri Waltz	1954	3.00	6.00	12.00
❏ 61304	I Can't Give You Anything But Love/Blue Boogie	1954	3.00	6.00	12.00
❏ 61400	Chop Sticks/Luigi's Wedding	1955	3.00	6.00	12.00
❏ 61461	Cannibal King/The Spoon Song	1955	3.00	6.00	12.00
❏ 61534	Aloha Oe/More, More, More	1955	3.00	6.00	12.00
❏ 61579	A String of Pearls/Always Love Me	1956	2.50	5.00	10.00
❏ 61638	Crazy Polka/Elmer's Tune	1956	2.50	5.00	10.00
❏ 61734	Chatterbox/Dardanella	1956	2.50	5.00	10.00
❏ 61827	Baby Buggy Boogie/Sippin' Soda	1957	2.50	5.00	10.00
SURE					
❏ 1005	Bongo Shuffle Boogie/Isle of Capri Boogie	196?	3.00	6.00	12.00
❏ 1738	Do the New Hully Gully/Patricia	1962	2.50	5.00	10.00
❏ 1767	Hungarian Rhapsody Boogie/Bumpy	1962	2.50	5.00	10.00
SWAN					
❏ 4034	Happy Vacation/The Huckelbuck	1959	3.00	6.00	12.00
❏ 4039	Like Sunset/Rancho	1959	3.00	6.00	12.00

LEE, JACKIE (3) Female singer.
45s

Number	Title (A Side/B Side)	Yr	VG	VG+	NM
EPIC					
❏ 9807	I Cry Alone/'Cause I Love Him	1965	2.50	5.00	10.00
❏ 10183	Love Is Gone/The Lonely Clown	1967	2.00	4.00	8.00

LEE, JACKIE, AND THE RAINDROPS
45s

Number	Title (A Side/B Side)	Yr	VG	VG+	NM
LONDON INT'L.					
❏ 10602	The Last One to Know/There's No One in the Whole Wide World	1962	3.00	6.00	12.00

LEE, JENNY, AND THE STARLETS
45s

Number	Title (A Side/B Side)	Yr	VG	VG+	NM
CONGRESS					
❏ 107	What I Gotta Do/Show Me a Man	1962	3.75	7.50	15.00

LEE, JOHNNY For records on DeLuxe, see JOHN LEE HOOKER.

LEE, JULIA
45s

Number	Title (A Side/B Side)	Yr	VG	VG+	NM
CAPITOL					
❏ F838	Ain't It a Crime/Don't Save It Too Long	1950	10.00	20.00	40.00
—Note: Julia Lee singles before 838 are unknown on 45 rpm					
❏ F956	Do You Want It/Decent Woman Blues	1950	10.00	20.00	40.00
❏ F1009	There Goes My Heart/Nobody Knows You When You're Down and Out	1950	10.00	20.00	40.00
❏ F1111	My Man Stands Out/Don't Come Too Soon	1950	12.50	25.00	50.00
❏ F1149	Pagan Love Song/I'm Forever Blowing Bubbles	1950	12.50	25.00	50.00
❏ F1252	It Won't Be Long/Bleeding Hearted Blues	1950	10.00	20.00	40.00
❏ F1376	Lotus Blossom/Pipe Dreams	1951	7.50	15.00	30.00
❏ F1432	Ugly Papa/I Know It's Wrong	1951	7.50	15.00	30.00
❏ F1589	Mama Don't Allow It/The Breeze	1951	7.50	15.00	30.00
❏ F1798	Scream in the Night/If You Hadn't Gone Away	1951	7.50	15.00	30.00
❏ F1896	Charmaine/Out in the Cold Again	1951	7.50	15.00	30.00
Albums					
CAPITOL					
❏ H 228 [10]	Party Time	1950	30.00	60.00	120.00
❏ T 228 [M]	Party Time	195?	20.00	40.00	80.00

LEE, LAURA
12-Inch Singles

Number	Title (A Side/B Side)	Yr	VG	VG+	NM
FANTASY					
❏ D-133	Sat-Is-Fac-Tion (6:20)/Your Song	1979	3.00	6.00	12.00
45s					
ARIOLA AMERICA					
❏ 7652	Love's Got Me Tired (But I Ain't Tired of Love)/You're Barking Up the Wrong Tree	1976	—	2.50	5.00
CHESS					
❏ 1989	Stop Giving Your Man Away/You Need Me	1967	3.00	6.00	12.00
❏ 2013	Dirty Man/It's Mighty Hard	1967	2.50	5.00	10.00
❏ 2030	Wanted: Lover, No Experience Necessary/Up Tight, Good Man	1967	2.50	5.00	10.00
❏ 2041	As Long As I Got You/A Man with Some Backbone	1968	2.50	5.00	10.00
❏ 2052	Need to Belong/He Will Break Your Heart	1968	2.50	5.00	10.00
❏ 2062	Hang It Up/It's How You Make It Good	1968	2.50	5.00	10.00
❏ 2068	Mama's Got a Good Thing/Love More Than Pride	1969	2.50	5.00	10.00
COTILLION					
❏ 44054	What a Man/Separation Line	1970	2.00	4.00	8.00
❏ 44073	Together/But You Know I Love You	1970	2.00	4.00	8.00
FANTASY					
❏ 865	Sat-Is-Fac-Tion/Your Song	1979	—	2.50	5.00
HOT WAX					
❏ 7007	Wedlock Is a Padlock/Her Picture Matches Mine	1970	2.00	4.00	8.00
❏ 7105	Women's Love Rights/Her Picture Matches Mine	1971	2.00	4.00	8.00
❏ 7111	Love and Liberty/I Don't Want Nothing Old But Money	1971	2.00	4.00	8.00
❏ 7201	Since I Fell for You/I Don't Want Nothing Old But Money	1972	—	3.50	7.00
❏ 7204	Rip Off/Two Lovely Pillows	1972	—	3.50	7.00
❏ 7207	If You Can Beat Me Rockin' (You Can Have My Chair)/If I'm Good Enough to Love	1972	—	3.50	7.00
❏ 7210	Crumbs Off the Table/You've Got to Save Me	1972	—	3.50	7.00
❏ 7302	(If You Want to Try Love Again) Remember Me/If I'm Good Enough to Love	1973	—	3.50	7.00
❏ 7305	I'll Catch You When You Fall/I Can't Hold On Much Longer	1973	—	3.50	7.00
INVICTUS					
❏ 1264	I Need It Just As Bad As You/If I'm Good Enough to Love	1974	—	3.00	6.00
❏ 1273	Don't Leave Me Starving for Your Love/Remember Me	1974	—	3.00	6.00
RIC-TIC					
❏ 111	To Win Your Heart/So Will I	1966	3.75	7.50	15.00
Albums					
CHESS					
❏ CH-50031	Love More Than Pride	1972	5.00	10.00	20.00
HOT WAX					
❏ HA-708	Women's Love Rights	1971	3.75	7.50	15.00
❏ HA-714	Laura Lee	1972	3.75	7.50	15.00
❏ HA-715	The Best of Laura Lee	1973	3.75	7.50	15.00
INVICTUS					
❏ KZ 33133	Laura Lee	1974	2.50	5.00	10.00

LEE, MICHELE
45s

Number	Title (A Side/B Side)	Yr	VG	VG+	NM
ABC-PARAMOUNT					
❏ 10365	I'm Sorry Missus Murray (But I Cannot Baby-Sit for You Tonight)/Havin' a Party for One	1962	3.75	7.50	15.00
❏ 10365 [PS]	I'm Sorry Missus Murray (But I Cannot Baby-Sit for You Tonight)/Havin' a Party for One	1962	7.50	15.00	30.00
❏ 10411	He's Not Good Enough for You/I See It All Now	1963	3.75	7.50	15.00
COLUMBIA					
❏ 4-43288	Pretty Lies, Pretty Make Believe/Somewhere in the World	1965	2.00	4.00	8.00
❏ 4-43376	Call Me/You Were There	1965	2.00	4.00	8.00
❏ 4-43476	Feeling Good/Steady, Steady	1965	2.00	4.00	8.00
❏ 4-43575	Laugh, Clown, Laugh/I'll Never Go There Anymore	1966	2.00	4.00	8.00
❏ 4-43923	If You Go Away/Wednesday's Child	1966	2.00	4.00	8.00
❏ 4-44165	Being Good Isn't Good Enough/I Believe in You	1967	2.00	4.00	8.00
❏ 4-44413	L. David Sloane/Everybody Loves My Baby (But My Baby Don't Love Nobody But Me)	1967	2.00	4.00	8.00
❏ 4-44554	I Can't Believe I'm Losing You/I Didn't Come to New York to Meet a Guy from My Home Town	1968	2.00	4.00	8.00
❏ 4-44698	Knowing When to Leave/The Look of Love	1968	2.00	4.00	8.00
❏ 4-44835	It's a Long Way to Fall/You'll Remember Me	1969	—	3.00	6.00
Albums					
COLUMBIA					
❏ CL 2486 [M]	A Taste of the Fantastic	1966	3.75	7.50	15.00
❏ CS 9286 [S]	A Taste of the Fantastic	1966	5.00	10.00	20.00
❏ CS 9682	L. David Sloane and Other Hits of Today	1968	5.00	10.00	20.00

LEE, PEGGY
45s

Number	Title (A Side/B Side)	Yr	VG	VG+	NM
A&M					
❏ 1771	I Remember/Some Cats Know	1975	—	2.00	4.00
ATLANTIC					
❏ 3215	Let's Love/Always	1974	—	2.00	4.00
CAPITOL					
❏ 54-547	Bali Ha'i/There Is Nothing Like a Dame	1949	10.00	20.00	40.00
❏ F791	The Old Master Painter/Bless You	1949	6.25	12.50	25.00
—With Mel Torme					
❏ F801	My Small Senor/When You Speak with Your Eyes	1950	5.00	10.00	20.00
❏ F810	Save Your Sorrow for Tomorrow/Sugar	1950	5.00	10.00	20.00
❏ F849	Sunshine Cake/Goodbye John	1950	5.00	10.00	20.00
❏ F898	Crazy He Calls Me/Them There Eyes	1950	5.00	10.00	20.00
❏ F961	Cry, Cry, Cry/Once Around the Moon	1950	5.00	10.00	20.00
❏ F1105	Show Me the Way to Get Out of This World ('Cause That's Where Everything Is)/Happy Music	1950	5.00	10.00	20.00
❏ F1161	Lover Come Back to Me/Helpless	1950	5.00	10.00	20.00
❏ F1244	Once in a Lifetime/Love Is So Peculiar	1950	5.00	10.00	20.00
❏ F1298	Where Are You/Ay-Ay-Chug-a-Lug	1950	5.00	10.00	20.00
❏ F1366	Climb Up the Mountain/The Mill on the Floss	1951	3.75	7.50	15.00
❏ F1428	Yeah, Yeah, Yeah/Rock Me to Sleep	1951	3.75	7.50	15.00
❏ F1450	That Ol' Devil/Cannonball Express	1951	3.75	7.50	15.00
❏ F1513	He's Only Wonderful/It Never Happens to Me	1951	3.75	7.50	15.00
❏ F1544	Boulevard Café/If You Turn Me Down	1951	3.75	7.50	15.00
❏ F1573	(When I Dance with You) I Get Ideas/Tonight You Belong to Me	1951	3.75	7.50	15.00
❏ F1586	My Magic Heart/So Far So Good	1951	3.75	7.50	15.00

Number	Title (A Side/B Side)	Yr	VG	VG+	NM
❑ F1601	It's a Good Day/Them There Eyes	1951	3.75	7.50	15.00
—Reissue of 78 rpm recordings from the 1940s					
❑ F1602	Manana (Is Soon Enough for Me)/				
	Why Don't You Do It Right	1951	3.75	7.50	15.00
—Reissue of 78 rpm recordings from the 1940s					
❑ F1609	That Old Feeling/Solitude	1951	3.75	7.50	15.00
—B-side by the Capitol Jazzmen; reissue of 1940s material					
❑ F1667	I Can't Give You Anything But Love/I Don't Know				
	Enough About You	1951	3.75	7.50	15.00
—Reissue of 78 rpm recordings from the 1940s					
❑ F1683	While We're Young/Golden Earrings	195?	3.00	6.00	12.00
—Reissue					
❑ F1749	I Love You But I Don't Like You/Wandering				
	Swallow	1951	3.75	7.50	15.00
❑ F1776	While We're Young/Birmingham Jail	1951	3.75	7.50	15.00
❑ SM-1857 [S]	Mack the Knife/(B-side unknown)	1963	3.75	7.50	15.00
—Small hole, plays at 33 1/3 rpm					
❑ F1926	Shame on You/Would You Dance	1952	3.75	7.50	15.00
❑ F2025	Everytime/Goin' On a Hayride	1952	3.75	7.50	15.00
❑ 2171	Reason to Believe/Didn't Want to Have to Do It	1968	—	3.00	6.00
❑ 2308	Misty Roses/It'll Never Happen Again	1968	—	3.00	6.00
❑ 2477	Spinning Wheel/Lean On Me	1969	—	3.00	6.00
❑ 2602	Is That All There Is/Me and My Shadow	1969	—	3.00	6.00
❑ 2696	Something/Whistle for Happiness	1969	—	3.00	6.00
❑ 2721	My Old Flame/Love Story	1970	—	2.50	5.00
❑ 2817	Have You Seen My Baby/You'll Remember Me	1970	—	2.50	5.00
❑ 2910	One More Ride on the Merry-Go-Round/				
	Pieces of Dreams	1970	—	2.50	5.00
❑ 3113	Where Did They Go/All I Want	1971	—	2.50	5.00
❑ 3439	Someone Who Cares/Love Song	1972	—	2.50	5.00
❑ F3722	Every Night/Baby, Baby, Wait for Me	1957	3.00	6.00	12.00
❑ F3811	Listen to the Rockin' Bird/Uninvited Dream	1957	3.00	6.00	12.00
❑ F3998	Fever/You Don't Know	1958	3.00	6.00	12.00
❑ F4071	Light of Love/Sweetheart	1958	3.00	6.00	12.00
❑ F4115	Alright, OK, You Win/My Man	1959	3.00	6.00	12.00
❑ F4189	Hallelujah I Love Him So/				
	I'm Looking Out the Window	1959	3.00	6.00	12.00
❑ F4243	You Came a Long Way from St. Louis/				
	I Lost My Sugar in Salt Lake City	1959	3.00	6.00	12.00
❑ 4298	You Deserve/Where Do I Go from Here	1959	3.00	6.00	12.00
❑ 4311	The Tree/The Christmas List	1959	3.75	7.50	15.00
❑ 4311 [PS]	The Tree/The Christmas List	1959	5.00	10.00	20.00
❑ 4349	Heart/C'est Magnifique	1960	2.50	5.00	10.00
❑ 4449	I'm Gonna Go Fishin'/My Gentle Young Johnny	1960	2.50	5.00	10.00
❑ 4474	I Like a Sleighride (Jingle Bells)/				
	Christmas Carousel	1960	3.00	6.00	12.00
❑ 4474 [PS]	I Like a Sleighride (Jingle Bells)/				
	Christmas Carousel	1960	10.00	20.00	40.00
❑ 4498	Bucket of Tears/I Love Being Here with You	1961	2.50	5.00	10.00
❑ 4576	Boston Beans/Yes Indeed	1961	2.50	5.00	10.00
❑ 4610	Hey, Look Me Over/When He Makes Music	1961	2.50	5.00	10.00
❑ 4750	The Sweetest Sounds/Loads of Love	1962	2.50	5.00	10.00
❑ 4812	Tell All the World About You/Amazing	1962	2.50	5.00	10.00
❑ 4888	I'm a Woman/Big Bad Bill	1962	2.50	5.00	10.00
❑ 4942	Alley Cat Song/O Barquinho (Little Boat)	1963	2.50	5.00	10.00
❑ 5001	The Doodlin' Song/Got That Magic	1963	2.50	5.00	10.00
❑ 5121	I Can't Stop Loving You/A Lot of Livin' to Do	1964	2.50	5.00	10.00
❑ 5241	In the Name of Love/My Sin	1964	2.50	5.00	10.00
❑ 5289	Talk to Me Baby/After You've Gone	1964	2.50	5.00	10.00
❑ 5346	That's What It Takes/Pass Me By	1965	2.00	4.00	8.00
❑ 5404	Bewitched/Sneakin' Up on You	1965	2.00	4.00	8.00
❑ 5469	The Sandpiper Love Theme (The Shadow of				
	Your Smile)/Maybe This Summer	1965	2.00	4.00	8.00
❑ 5488	I Go to Sleep/Stop Living in the Past	1965	2.00	4.00	8.00
❑ 5521	Everybody Has the Right to Be Wrong/				
	Free Spirits	1965	2.00	4.00	8.00
❑ 5557	Big Spender/Trapped	1965	2.00	4.00	8.00
❑ 5605	That Man/You Don't Know	1966	2.00	4.00	8.00
❑ 5653	Come Back to Me/You've Got Possibilities	1966	2.00	4.00	8.00
❑ 5678	Stay with Me/Happy Feet	1966	2.00	4.00	8.00
❑ 5758	So What's New/Walking Happy	1966	2.00	4.00	8.00
❑ 5988	I Feel It/Lonesome Road	1967	—	3.00	6.00
❑ S7-19343	Happy Holiday/Auld Lang Syne	1996	—	—	3.00
—B-side by Guy Lombardo					
DECCA					
❑ 27238	Watermelon Weather/The Moon Came Up	1950	3.75	7.50	15.00
—With Bing Crosby					
❑ 27813	Just One of Those Things/I'm Glad There Is You	1951	3.75	7.50	15.00
❑ 28142	Be Anything/Forgive Me	1952	3.75	7.50	15.00
❑ 28215	Lover/You Go to My Head	1952	3.75	7.50	15.00
❑ 28313	Just One of Those Things/I'm Glad There Is You	1952	3.75	7.50	15.00
❑ 28395	San Souci/River, River	1952	3.75	7.50	15.00
❑ 28565	This Is a Very Special Day/I Hear the Music Now	1953	3.75	7.50	15.00
❑ 28631	Who's Gonna Pay the Check/Sorry, Baby, You				
	Let My Love Get Cold	1953	3.75	7.50	15.00
❑ 28737	I've Got You Under My Skin/				
	My Heart Belongs to Daddy	1953	3.75	7.50	15.00
❑ 28889	Apples, Peaches and Cherries/				
	Night Holds No Fear	1953	3.75	7.50	15.00
❑ 28890	Baubles, Bangles and Beads/Love You So	1953	3.75	7.50	15.00
❑ 28939	Ring Those Christmas Bells/				
	It's Christmas Time Again	1953	3.75	7.50	15.00
❑ 29003	Go You Where You Go/				
	Where Can I Go Without You	1954	3.75	7.50	15.00
❑ 29076	Johnny Guitar/Autumn in Rome	1954	3.75	7.50	15.00
❑ 29164	Summer Vacation/That's What a Woman Is For	1954	3.75	7.50	15.00
❑ 29250	Love, You Didn't Do Right by Me/Sisters	1954	3.75	7.50	15.00
❑ 29342	God Rest Ye Merry Gentlemen/White Christmas	1954	3.75	7.50	15.00
—A-side with Trudi Stevens; B-side by Bing Crosby and Danny Kaye					
❑ 29359	It Must Be So/Straight Ahead	1954	3.00	6.00	12.00
—With the Mills Brothers					
❑ 29373	Let Me Go Lover/Bouquet of Roses	1954	3.00	6.00	12.00
❑ 29427	He's a Tramp/The Siamese Cat Song	1955	3.00	6.00	12.00
❑ 29429	I Belong to You/How Bitter, My Sweet	1955	3.00	6.00	12.00
❑ 29460	Bella Notte/La La Lu	1955	3.00	6.00	12.00
❑ 29534	Ooh, That Kiss/Oh! No!	1955	3.00	6.00	12.00
❑ 29605	Sing a Rainbow/He Needs Me	1955	3.00	6.00	12.00
❑ 29608	What Can I Say After I Say I'm Sorry/Sugar	1955	3.00	6.00	12.00
❑ 29681	Me/Pablo Pasablo	1955	3.00	6.00	12.00
❑ 29834	Mr. Wonderful/Crazy in the Heart	1956	3.00	6.00	12.00
❑ 29837	The Comeback/				
	You've Got to See Mamma Every Night	1956	3.00	6.00	12.00
❑ 29877	Joey, Joey, Joey/				
	They Can't Take That Away from Me	1956	3.00	6.00	12.00
❑ 29994	That's Alright Honey/We Laughed at Love	1956	3.00	6.00	12.00
❑ 30059	You Oughta Be Mine/				
	I Don't Know Enough About You	1956	3.00	6.00	12.00
❑ 30117	Where Flamingos Fly/				
	Gypsy with Fire in Her Shoes	1956	3.00	6.00	12.00
❑ 30494	Never Mind/Wrong, Wrong, Wrong	1956	2.50	5.00	10.00
❑ 30879	It Ain't Necessarily So/Swing Low Sweet Chariot	1959	2.50	5.00	10.00
7-Inch Extended Plays					
CAPITOL					
❑ EAP 1-864	(contents unknown)	1957	3.00	6.00	12.00
❑ EAP 1-864 [PS]	The Man I Love, Part 1	1957	3.00	6.00	12.00
❑ EAP 2-864	Please Be Kind/If I Should Lose You//He's My				
	Guy/Then I'll Be Tired of You	1957	3.00	6.00	12.00
❑ EAP 2-864 [PS]	The Man I Love, Part 2	1957	3.00	6.00	12.00
❑ EAP 3-864	(contents unknown)	1957	3.00	6.00	12.00
❑ EAP 3-864 [PS]	The Man I Love, Part 3	1957	3.00	6.00	12.00
❑ MA 1-1591	Manana/Golden Earrings//Fever/Alright, Okay,				
	You Win	196?	3.00	6.00	12.00
—Small hole, plays at 33 1/3 rpm					
Albums					
A&M					
❑ SP-4547	Mirrors	1975	3.00	6.00	12.00
ATLANTIC					
❑ SD 18108	Let's Love	1974	3.00	6.00	12.00
CAPITOL					
❑ ST-105	Two Shows Nightly	1969	50.00	100.00	200.00
—Withdrawn immediately after release					
❑ H 151 [10]	Rendezvous with Peggy Lee	1952	25.00	50.00	100.00
❑ T 151 [M]	Rendezvous with Peggy Lee	1954	12.50	25.00	50.00
—Turquoise or gray label					
❑ T 151 [M]	Rendezvous with Peggy Lee	1959	6.25	12.50	25.00
—Black label with colorband, Capitol logo at left					
❑ ST-183	A Natural Woman	1969	3.75	7.50	15.00
❑ H 204 [10]	My Best to You	1952	25.00	50.00	100.00
❑ T 204 [M]	My Best to You	1954	12.50	25.00	50.00
—Turquoise or gray label					
❑ T 204 [M]	My Best to You	1959	6.25	12.50	25.00
—Black label with colorband, Capitol logo at left					
❑ DKAO-377	Peggy Lee's Greatest	1969	3.00	6.00	12.00
❑ SM-386	Is That All There Is?	197?	2.50	5.00	10.00
—Reissue with new prefix					
❑ ST-386	Is That All There Is?	1969	3.00	6.00	12.00
❑ ST-463	Bridge Over Troubled Water	1970	3.00	6.00	12.00
❑ STBB-517 [(2)]	Folks Who Live on the Hill/Broadway Ala Lee	1970	3.75	7.50	15.00
❑ STCL-576 [(3)]	Peggy Lee	1970	6.25	12.50	25.00
❑ ST-622	Make It with You	1970	3.00	6.00	12.00
❑ ST-810	Where Did They Go	1971	3.00	6.00	12.00
❑ ST 864 [S]	The Man I Love	1959	7.50	15.00	30.00
❑ T 864 [M]	The Man I Love	1957	12.50	25.00	50.00
—Turquoise label					
❑ T 864 [M]	The Man I Love	1959	6.25	12.50	25.00
—Black label with colorband, Capitol logo at left					
❑ ST 979 [S]	Jump for Joy	1959	7.50	15.00	30.00
❑ T 979 [M]	Jump for Joy	1958	10.00	20.00	40.00
—Turquoise or gray label					
❑ T 979 [M]	Jump for Joy	1959	6.25	12.50	25.00
—Black label with colorband, Capitol logo at left					
❑ ST 1049 [S]	Things Are Swingin'	1959	7.50	15.00	30.00
❑ T 1049 [M]	Things Are Swingin'	1958	6.25	12.50	25.00
❑ ST 1131 [S]	I Like Men	1959	7.50	15.00	30.00
❑ T 1131 [M]	I Like Men	1959	6.25	12.50	25.00
❑ ST 1213 [S]	Alright, Okay, You Win	1959	7.50	15.00	30.00
❑ T 1213 [M]	Alright, Okay, You Win	1959	6.25	12.50	25.00
❑ ST 1219 [S]	Beauty and the Beat	1959	7.50	15.00	30.00
—With George Shearing; black label with colorband, Capitol logo at left					
❑ ST 1219 [S]	Beauty and the Beat	1962	5.00	10.00	20.00
—With George Shearing; black label with colorband, Capitol logo at top					
❑ T 1219 [M]	Beauty and the Beat	1959	6.25	12.50	25.00
—With George Shearing; black label with colorband, Capitol logo at left					
❑ T 1219 [M]	Beauty and the Beat	1962	3.75	7.50	15.00
—With George Shearing; black label with colorband, Capitol logo at top					
❑ SM-1290	Latin Ala Lee!	1977	2.50	5.00	10.00
—Reissue with new prefix					
❑ ST 1290 [S]	Latin Ala Lee!	1960	6.25	12.50	25.00
—Black label with colorband, Capitol logo at left					
❑ ST 1290 [S]	Latin Ala Lee!	1962	3.75	7.50	15.00
—Black label with colorband, Capitol logo at top					
❑ T 1290 [M]	Latin Ala Lee!	1960	5.00	10.00	20.00
—Black label with colorband, Capitol logo at left					
❑ T 1290 [M]	Latin Ala Lee!	1962	3.00	6.00	12.00
—Black label with colorband, Capitol logo at top					
❑ ST 1366 [S]	All Aglow Again	1960	6.25	12.50	25.00
—Black label with colorband, Capitol logo at left					
❑ ST 1366 [S]	All Aglow Again	1962	3.75	7.50	15.00
—Black label with colorband, Capitol logo at top					
❑ T 1366 [M]	All Aglow Again	1960	5.00	10.00	20.00
—Black label with colorband, Capitol logo at left					
❑ T 1366 [M]	All Aglow Again	1962	3.00	6.00	12.00
—Black label with colorband, Capitol logo at top					
❑ ST 1401 [S]	Pretty Eyes	1960	6.25	12.50	25.00
—Black label with colorband, Capitol logo at left					
❑ ST 1401 [S]	Pretty Eyes	1962	3.75	7.50	15.00
—Black label with colorband, Capitol logo at top					
❑ T 1401 [M]	Pretty Eyes	1960	5.00	10.00	20.00
—Black label with colorband, Capitol logo at left					
❑ T 1401 [M]	Pretty Eyes	1962	3.00	6.00	12.00
—Black label with colorband, Capitol logo at top					
❑ ST 1423 [S]	Christmas Carousel	1960	6.25	12.50	25.00
❑ T 1423 [M]	Christmas Carousel	1960	5.00	10.00	20.00

Number	Title (A Side/B Side)	Yr	VG	VG+	NM
ST 1475 [S]	Ole Ala Lee!	1961	6.25	12.50	25.00
T 1475 [M]	Ole Ala Lee!	1961	5.00	10.00	20.00
SM-1520	Basin Street East	1977	2.50	5.00	10.00
—Reissue with new prefix					
ST 1520 [S]	Basin Street East	1961	6.25	12.50	25.00
—Black label with colorband, Capitol logo at left					
ST 1520 [S]	Basin Street East	1962	3.75	7.50	15.00
—Black label with colorband, Capitol logo at top					
T 1520 [M]	Basin Street East	1961	5.00	10.00	20.00
—Black label with colorband, Capitol logo at left					
T 1520 [M]	Basin Street East	1962	3.00	6.00	12.00
—Black label with colorband, Capitol logo at top					
ST 1630 [S]	If You Go	1962	6.25	12.50	25.00
T 1630 [M]	If You Go	1962	5.00	10.00	20.00
ST 1671 [S]	Blue Cross Country	1962	6.25	12.50	25.00
T 1671 [M]	Blue Cross Country	1962	5.00	10.00	20.00
DT 1743 [R]	Bewitching-Lee!	1962	3.75	7.50	15.00
T 1743 [M]	Bewitching-Lee!	1962	6.25	12.50	25.00
—Black "The Star Line" label					
ST 1772 [S]	Sugar 'n' Spice	1962	6.25	12.50	25.00
T 1772 [M]	Sugar 'n' Spice	1962	5.00	10.00	20.00
ST 1850 [S]	Mink Jazz	1963	6.25	12.50	25.00
T 1850 [M]	Mink Jazz	1963	5.00	10.00	20.00
SM-1857	I'm a Woman	1977	2.50	5.00	10.00
—Reissue with new prefix					
ST 1857 [S]	I'm a Woman	1963	6.25	12.50	25.00
T 1857 [M]	I'm a Woman	1963	5.00	10.00	20.00
ST 1969 [S]	In Love Again	1963	6.25	12.50	25.00
T 1969 [M]	In Love Again	1963	5.00	10.00	20.00
ST 2096 [S]	In the Name of Love	1964	5.00	10.00	20.00
T 2096 [M]	In the Name of Love	1964	3.75	7.50	15.00
ST 2320 [S]	Pass Me By	1965	5.00	10.00	20.00
T 2320 [M]	Pass Me By	1965	3.75	7.50	15.00
ST 2388 [S]	That Was Then, Now Is Now	1965	5.00	10.00	20.00
T 2388 [M]	That Was Then, Now Is Now	1965	3.75	7.50	15.00
ST 2390 [S]	Happy Holiday	1965	3.75	7.50	15.00
T 2390 [M]	Happy Holiday	1965	3.00	6.00	12.00
ST 2469 [S]	Guitars Ala Lee	1966	5.00	10.00	20.00
T 2469 [M]	Guitars Ala Lee	1966	3.75	7.50	15.00
ST 2475 [S]	Big $pender	1966	5.00	10.00	20.00
T 2475 [M]	Big $pender	1966	3.75	7.50	15.00
ST 2732 [S]	Extra Special	1967	3.75	7.50	15.00
T 2732 [M]	Extra Special	1967	5.00	10.00	20.00
ST 2781	Somethin' Groovy	1968	3.75	7.50	15.00
ST 2887	The Hits of Peggy Lee	1968	3.75	7.50	15.00
ST-11077	Norma Deloris Egstrom from Jamestown, North Dakota	1972	3.00	6.00	12.00
SN-16140	Peggy Lee Sings Songs of Cy Coleman	198?	2.00	4.00	8.00
COLUMBIA					
CL 6033 [10]	Benny Goodman and Peggy Lee	1949	15.00	30.00	60.00
DECCA					
DXB 164 [(2)M]	The Best of Peggy Lee	1964	7.50	15.00	30.00
DL 4458 [M]	Lover	1964	6.25	12.50	25.00
DL 4461 [M]	The Fabulous Peggy Lee	1964	6.25	12.50	25.00
DL 5482 [10]	Black Coffee	1953	25.00	50.00	100.00
DL 5539 [10]	Songs in an Intimate Style	1953	20.00	40.00	80.00
DXSB 7164 [(2)R]	The Best of Peggy Lee	1964	5.00	10.00	20.00
DL 8358 [M]	Black Coffee	1956	15.00	30.00	60.00
DL 8411 [M]	Dream Street	1957	15.00	30.00	60.00
DL 8591 [M]	Sea Shells	1958	15.00	30.00	60.00
DL 8816 [M]	Miss Wonderful	1959	15.00	30.00	60.00
DL 74458 [R]	Lover	1964	3.75	7.50	15.00
DL 74461 [R]	The Fabulous Peggy Lee	1964	3.75	7.50	15.00
DRG					
SL-5190	Close Enough for Love	1979	3.00	6.00	12.00
EVEREST ARCHIVE OF FOLK & JAZZ					
294	Peggy Lee	197?	2.50	5.00	10.00
GLENDALE					
6023	You Can Depend on Me	1982	2.50	5.00	10.00
HARMONY					
HL 7005 [M]	Peggy Lee Sings with Benny Goodman	195?	6.25	12.50	25.00
H 30024	Miss Peggy Lee	1970	2.50	5.00	10.00
HINDSIGHT					
HSR-220	Peggy Lee with the David Barbour and Billy May Bands, 1948	1985	2.50	5.00	10.00
MCA					
4049 [(2)]	The Best of Peggy Lee	197?	3.00	6.00	12.00
MERCURY					
SRM-1-1172	Live in London	1977	3.00	6.00	12.00
MUSICMASTERS					
5005	Peggy Sings the Blues	1988	3.00	6.00	12.00
PAUSA					
PR-9043	Sugar 'n' Spice	1985	2.50	5.00	10.00
PICKWICK					
SPC-3090	Once More with Feeling	196?	2.50	5.00	10.00
SPC-3192	I've Got the World	1971	2.50	5.00	10.00
TIME-LIFE					
SLGD-07 [(2)]	Legendary Singers: Peggy Lee	1985	3.75	7.50	15.00
VOCALION					
VL 3776 [M]	So Blue	1966	3.75	7.50	15.00
VL 73776 [R]	So Blue	1966	2.50	5.00	10.00
VL 73903	Crazy in the Heart	1969	2.50	5.00	10.00

LEE AND THE LEOPARDS
45s

Number	Title (A Side/B Side)	Yr	VG	VG+	NM
FORTUNE					
867	What About Me/Don't Press Your Luck	1964	12.50	25.00	50.00
GORDY					
7002	Come Into My Palace/Trying to Make It	1962	15.00	30.00	60.00
LAURIE					
3197	Come Into My Palace/Trying to Make It	1963	6.25	12.50	25.00

LEFEVRE, RAYMOND
45s

Number	Title (A Side/B Side)	Yr	VG	VG+	NM
ATLANTIC					
2093	Come Softly to Me/Havah Nagilah	1961	2.50	5.00	10.00
BUDDAH					
269	Mammy Blue/What Have They Done to My Song, Ma	1971	—	2.50	5.00
4 CORNERS OF THE WORLD					
142	When a Man Loves a Woman/Black Is Black	1967	—	2.50	5.00
145	Groovin'/A Whiter Shade of Pale	1967	—	2.50	5.00
147	Ame Caline (Soul Coaxing)/If I Were a Carpenter	1968	—	2.50	5.00
149	La, La, La (He Gives Me Love)/C'est La Rose	1968	—	2.50	5.00
151	Delilah/If I Only Had Time	1968	—	2.50	5.00
JAMIE					
1161	Never on Sunday/Sleepy Time	1960	2.50	5.00	10.00
1171	Rendezvous/The Right Girl on the Left Bank	1960	2.50	5.00	10.00
KAPP					
231	The Day the Rains Came/Butterfingers	1958	2.50	5.00	10.00
279	You Are My Destiny/Le Belle Helene	1959	2.50	5.00	10.00
766	You Don't Have to Say You Love Me/La Boheme	1966	—	3.00	6.00
809	Spanish Eyes/Stars of the Way	1967	—	3.00	6.00
AS-949 [DJ]	Silver Bells (mono/stereo)	196?	2.00	4.00	8.00
MERCURY					
71599	What Good Does It Do Me/(Instrumental)	1960	2.50	5.00	10.00
VERVE					
10263	Come Une Symphonie/Un Voms Vivo	1962	2.00	4.00	8.00
Albums					
ATLANTIC					
8044 [M]	Romantica	1961	5.00	10.00	20.00
SD 8044 [S]	Romantica	1961	6.25	12.50	25.00
BUDDAH					
BDS-5095	Raymond Lefevre	1971	2.50	5.00	10.00
BDS-5109	Oh Happy Day	1972	2.50	5.00	10.00
4 CORNERS OF THE WORLD					
FCL-4239 [M]	Love Me, Please Love Me	1967	3.00	6.00	12.00
FCS-4239 [S]	Love Me, Please Love Me	1967	3.00	6.00	12.00
FCS-4244	Soal Coaxing (Ame Caline)	1968	3.00	6.00	12.00
FCS-4250	La La La (He Gives Me Love)	1968	3.00	6.00	12.00
FCS-4257	Merry Christmas	1968	3.00	6.00	12.00
KAPP					
KL-1510 [M]	You Don't Have to Stay	1967	3.75	7.50	15.00
KS-3510 [S]	You Don't Have to Stay	1967	3.00	6.00	12.00
MONUMENT					
MLP-8067 [M]	Paris Cancan	1967	3.75	7.50	15.00
SLP-18067 [S]	Paris Cancan	1967	3.00	6.00	12.00

LEFT BANKE, THE
45s

Number	Title (A Side/B Side)	Yr	VG	VG+	NM
CAMERICA					
005	Queen of Paradise/And One Day	1978	—	2.50	5.00
SMASH					
2041	Walk Away Renee/I Haven't Got the Nerve	1966	3.75	7.50	15.00
2074	Pretty Ballerina/Lazy Day	1966	3.75	7.50	15.00
2089	Ivy, Ivy/And Suddenly	1967	3.00	6.00	12.00
2097	She May Call You Up Tonight/Barterers and Their Wives	1967	3.00	6.00	12.00
2119	Desiree/I've Got Something on My Mind	1967	3.00	6.00	12.00
2119 [PS]	Desiree/I've Got Something on My Mind	1967	6.25	12.50	25.00
2165	Dark Is the Bark/My Friend Today	1968	3.00	6.00	12.00
2198	Goodbye Holly/Sing, Little Bird, Sing	1968	3.00	6.00	12.00
2209	Bryant Hotel/Give the Man a Hand	1969	3.00	6.00	12.00
2243	Myrah/Pedestal	1969	10.00	20.00	40.00
—Picture sleeves are bootlegs					
Albums					
RHINO					
RNLP-123	History of the Left Banke	1985	2.50	5.00	10.00
SMASH					
MGS-27088 [M]	Walk Away Renee/Pretty Ballerina	1967	10.00	20.00	40.00
SRS-67088 [S]	Walk Away Renee/Pretty Ballerina	1967	10.00	20.00	40.00
SRS-67088	Walk Away Renee/Pretty Ballerina	198?	2.50	5.00	10.00
—Reissue with thinner vinyl					
SRS-67113	The Left Banke, Too	1968	12.50	25.00	50.00

LEGENDARY MASKED SURFERS, THE
45s

Number	Title (A Side/B Side)	Yr	VG	VG+	NM
UNITED ARTISTS					
XW270	Summer Means Fun/Gonna Hustle You	1973	5.00	10.00	20.00
—Original pressings have a Jan & Dean recording on them by mistake					
XW270	Summer Means Fun/Gonna Hustle You	1973	30.00	60.00	120.00
—With the intended recording, a newly-recorded vocal track					
XW270 [PS]	Summer Means Fun/Gonna Hustle You	1973	7.50	15.00	30.00
50958	Summertime, Summertime/Gonna Hustle You	1972	7.50	15.00	30.00

LEGENDARY STARDUST COWBOY, THE
45s

Number	Title (A Side/B Side)	Yr	VG	VG+	NM
MERCURY					
72862	Paralyzed/Who's Knocking on My Door	1968	5.00	10.00	20.00
72891	Down in the Wrecking Yard/I Took a Trip on a Gemini Spaceship	1969	5.00	10.00	20.00
72912	Everything's Getting Bigger But Our Love/Kiss and Run	1969	5.00	10.00	20.00
NORTON					
012	I Hate CDs's/Linda	199?	—	—	2.00
012 [PS]	I Hate CD's/Linda	199?	—	—	2.00
PSYCHO-SUAVE					
1033	Paralyzed/Who's Knocking on My Door	1968	7.50	15.00	30.00

LEGENDS, THE   Several different groups.
45s

Number	Title (A Side/B Side)	Yr	VG	VG+	NM
BRIDGE SOCIETY					
2204	Keep On Running/Cheating	1968	10.00	20.00	40.00
CALDWELL					
410	Go Away with Me/Jungle Lullaby	1962	6.25	12.50	25.00
CAPITOL					
5014	Summertime Blues/Run to the Movies	1963	5.00	10.00	20.00
COLUMBIA					
41949	Theme from "Exodus"/Later	1961	3.00	6.00	12.00
DOC HOLLIDAY					
107	Surf's Up/Dance with the Drummer Man	1963	10.00	20.00	40.00
107 [PS]	Surf's Up/Dance with the Drummer Man	1963	12.50	25.00	50.00

L

Number	Title (A Side/B Side)	Yr	VG	VG+	NM
EPIC					
❏ 10937	Rock and Roll Woman/Problems	1973	2.00	4.00	8.00
ERMINE					
❏ 39	My Love for You/Say Mama	1962	12.50	25.00	50.00
❏ 41	Lariat/Late Train	1962	10.00	20.00	40.00
❏ 43	Bop-A-Lena/I Wish I Knew	1962	12.50	25.00	50.00
❏ 45	Temptation/Marionette	1962	10.00	20.00	40.00
HART-VAN					
❏ 18003	Traction/As Long As I Live	1962	7.50	15.00	30.00
HEART					
❏ 7672	Rock and Roll Woman/Problems	1972	5.00	10.00	20.00
HULL					
❏ 727	The Legend of Love/Now I'm Telling You	1958	25.00	50.00	100.00
—Red label					
❏ 727	The Legend of Love/Now I'm Telling You	1962	7.50	15.00	30.00
—Multicolor label					
JAMIE					
❏ 1228	Tell the Truth/You'll Never See the Forest	1962	5.00	10.00	20.00
KEY					
❏ 1002	Lariat/Gail	1961	10.00	20.00	40.00
❏ 1002	Lariat/Late Train	1961	10.00	20.00	40.00
MELBA					
❏ 109	I'll Never Fall in Love Again/Eyes of an Angel	1957	37.50	75.00	150.00
—Label with double horizontal lines					
❏ 109	I'll Never Fall in Love Again/Eyes of an Angel	1961	10.00	20.00	40.00
—Label with no horizontal lines					
PARROT					
❏ 45010	Just in Case/If I Only Had Her Back	1965	3.00	6.00	12.00
❏ 45011	Alright/How Can I Find Her	1965	3.00	6.00	12.00
RAILROAD HOUSE					
❏ 12003	High Towers/Fever Games	1969	5.00	10.00	20.00
❏ 12003 [PS]	High Towers/Fever Games	1969	7.50	15.00	30.00
THAMES					
❏ 104	Raining in My Heart/(B-side unknown)	1964	7.50	15.00	30.00
UP					
❏ 2202	Baby, Get Your Head Screwed On/Why	1968	12.50	25.00	50.00
WARNER BROS.					
❏ 5457	Here Comes the Rain/Don't Be Ashamed	1964	3.75	7.50	15.00
Albums					
CAPITOL					
❏ ST 1925 [S]	The Legends Let Loose	1963	20.00	40.00	80.00
❏ T 1925 [M]	The Legends Let Loose	1963	15.00	30.00	60.00
COLUMBIA					
❏ CL 1707 [M]	Hit Sounds of Today's Smash Hit Combos	1961	7.50	15.00	30.00
❏ CS 8507 [S]	Hit Sounds of Today's Smash Hit Combos	1961	10.00	20.00	40.00
ERMINE					
❏ LP-101 [M]	The Legends Let Loose	1963	50.00	100.00	200.00

LEGRAND, MICHEL
45s

Number	Title (A Side/B Side)	Yr	VG	VG+	NM
BELL					
❏ 45118	The Summer Knows/I Will Say Goodbye	1971	—	2.50	5.00
❏ 45171	Brian's Song/Theme from "The Go-Between"	1972	—	2.50	5.00
❏ 45215	Jesus Christ Superstar-Day by Day/Amy's Theme	1972	—	2.50	5.00
COLUMBIA					
❏ 40661	Under Paris Skies/Merry-Go-Round	1956	3.00	6.00	12.00
❏ 40692	Smile/Bon Jour, Paris	1956	3.00	6.00	12.00
❏ 40732	Love Theme from "La Strada"/Paris Canaille	1956	3.00	6.00	12.00
❏ 40751	Friendly Persuasion/Lovers and Lollipops	1956	3.00	6.00	12.00
❏ 41312	Cheek to Cheek/Only You	1958	2.50	5.00	10.00
DECCA					
❏ 32287	Pretty Polly/The Race Is to the Swift	1968	—	3.00	6.00
MCA					
❏ 40160	Walking on the Beach/Breezy's Song	1973	—	2.00	4.00
❏ 40523	Gable and Lombard Love Theme/I Can't Give You Anything But Love, Baby	1976	—	2.00	4.00
MGM					
❏ 13816	Tara's Theme (Part 1)/Tara's Theme (Part 2)	1967	—	3.00	6.00
❏ 13816	Tara's Theme (Part 1)/Theme from Orfell Negro	1967	—	3.00	6.00
❏ 13894	Love Theme from "Elvira Madigan"/Melange	1968	—	3.00	6.00
PHILIPS					
❏ 40098	Love Is a Ball/Millie's Theme	1963	2.00	4.00	8.00
❏ 40188	Monkey Business/Come Ray or Come Charles	1964	2.00	4.00	8.00
❏ 40257	Love Theme from Parapailies de Cherbourg/Garage Scene	1965	2.00	4.00	8.00
❏ 40357	I Will Wait for You/Melody from the Stars	1966	2.00	4.00	8.00
RCA VICTOR					
❏ PB-10234	Blue, Green, Gray and Gone/Brian's Song	1975	—	2.00	4.00
20TH CENTURY					
❏ 2346	The Other Side of Midnight (Noelle's Theme)/Drive to Demeris	1977	—	2.00	4.00
UNITED ARTISTS					
❏ 50618	What Are You Doing the Rest of Your Life/Floating Time	1969	—	3.50	7.00
❏ 50662	What Are You Doing the Rest of Your Life (English)/What Are You Doing the Rest of Your Life (French)	1970	—	3.00	6.00
WARNER BROS.					
❏ 7486	Theme from "Summer of '42"/Summer Song	1971	—	2.50	5.00
7-Inch Extended Plays					
COLUMBIA					
❏ B-441 [PS]	I Love Paris, Vol. I	195?	3.00	6.00	12.00
—Cover for 2-EP set (5-1944, 5-1945)					
❏ 5-1944	I Love Paris/Mademoiselle de Paris//Paris in the Spring/Paris Canaille	195?	2.50	5.00	10.00
—Alternate numbers are "B-441-1" and "B-441-4"					
❏ 5-1945	Paris/Autumn Leaves//Under the Bridges of Paris (Sous les ponts de Paris)/La Seine	195?	2.50	5.00	10.00
—Alternate numbers are "B-441-2" and "B-441-3"					
❏ B-2554	*I Love Paris/April in Paris/La Vie En Rose/The Last Time I Saw Paris	195?	2.50	5.00	10.00
❏ B-2554 [PS]	Michel Legrand (Hall of Fame Series)	195?	2.50	5.00	10.00

Number	Title (A Side/B Side)	Yr	VG	VG+	NM
Albums					
BELL					
❏ 4200 [(2)]	Twenty Songs of the Century	1974	3.00	6.00	12.00
❏ 6071	Brian's Song Themes & Variations	1972	2.50	5.00	10.00
COLUMBIA					
❏ CL 555 [M]	I Love Paris	1954	10.00	20.00	40.00
❏ CL 647 [M]	Holiday in Rome	1955	6.25	12.50	25.00
❏ CL 706 [M]	Vienna Holiday	1955	6.25	12.50	25.00
❏ CL 888 [M]	Castles in Spain	1956	6.25	12.50	25.00
❏ CL 1115 [M]	Michel Legrand Plays Cole Porter	1957	6.25	12.50	25.00
❏ CL 1139 [M]	Legrand in Rio	1957	6.25	12.50	25.00
❏ CL 1250 [M]	Legrand Jazz	1958	10.00	20.00	40.00
—Miles Davis appears on this record					
❏ CL 1437 [M]	I Love Paris	1960	6.25	12.50	25.00
❏ CS 8079 [S]	Legrand Jazz	1959	10.00	20.00	40.00
—Miles Davis appears on this record					
❏ CS 8237 [S]	I Love Paris	1960	5.00	10.00	20.00
❏ PC 9237	I Love Paris	1987	2.00	4.00	8.00
—Reissue with new prefix					
GRYPHON					
❏ 786	Jazz Grand	1978	2.50	5.00	10.00
HARMONY					
❏ HL 7331 [M]	I Love Paris	196?	3.00	6.00	12.00
❏ HS 11131 [S]	I Love Paris	196?	3.00	6.00	12.00
❏ KH 31540	Cole Porter, Volume II	1972	2.50	5.00	10.00
❏ KH 31549	Cole Porter, Volume I	1972	2.50	5.00	10.00
MERCURY					
❏ MG 20342 [M]	C'est Magnifique	1958	5.00	10.00	20.00
MGM					
❏ SE-4491	Cinema La Grand	1967	3.75	7.50	15.00
MOBILE FIDELITY					
❏ 1-504	Jazz Grand	198?	12.50	25.00	50.00
—Audiophile vinyl					
PABLO TODAY					
❏ 2312139	After the Rain	198?	2.50	5.00	10.00
PHILIPS					
❏ PHM 200074 [M]	The Michel Legrand Big Band Plays Richard Rogers	1963	5.00	10.00	20.00
❏ PHM 200143 [M]	Michel Legrand Sings	1964	6.25	12.50	25.00
❏ PHS 600074 [S]	The Michel Legrand Big Band Plays Richard Rogers	1963	6.25	12.50	25.00
❏ PHS 600143 [S]	Michel Legrand Sings	1964	7.50	15.00	30.00
RCA VICTOR					
❏ BGL1-0850	Jimmy's	1975	2.50	5.00	10.00
❏ BXL1-0850	Jimmy's	1978	2.00	4.00	8.00
—Reissue with new prefix					
❏ BGL1-1028	Concert	1976	2.50	5.00	10.00
❏ BXL1-1028	Concert	1978	2.00	4.00	8.00
—Reissue with new prefix					
❏ BGL1-1392	Michel Legrand and Friends	1976	2.50	5.00	10.00
❏ BXL1-1392	Michel Legrand and Friends	1978	2.00	4.00	8.00
—Reissue with new prefix					
VERVE					
❏ V6-8760	Michel Legrand at Shelly's Mann-Hole	1969	3.00	6.00	12.00

LEHRER, TOM
45s

Number	Title (A Side/B Side)	Yr	VG	VG+	NM
REPRISE					
❏ 0862	Pollution/Who's Next	1969	2.00	4.00	8.00
7-Inch Extended Plays					
LEHRER					
❏ TLEP-1 [PS]	Songs by Tom Lehrer	1955	12.50	25.00	50.00
—Cover for F8-OH-0421/0422 and F8-OH-0423/0424					
❏ F8-OH-0421/2	Fight Fiercely, Harvard/The Old Dope Peddler/Be Prepared//The Wild West/I Wanna Go Home to Dixie/Lobachevsky	1955	10.00	20.00	40.00
—Side 1 and Side 2 of 2-EP set					
❏ F8-OH-0423/4	The Irish Ballad/The Hunting Song/My Home Town//When You Are Old and Grey/I Hold Your Hand in Mine/The Wiener Schnitzel Waltz	1955	10.00	20.00	40.00
—Side 3 and Side 4 of 2-EP set					
Albums					
LEHRER					
❏ TLP-1 [10]	Songs by Tom Lehrer	1953	25.00	50.00	100.00
❏ TL-101 [M]	Songs by Tom Lehrer	1959	10.00	20.00	40.00
❏ TL-102 [M]	More of Tom Lehrer	1958	10.00	20.00	40.00
❏ TL-102S [S]	More of Tom Lehrer	1959	10.00	20.00	40.00
❏ TL-101 [M]	Tom Lehrer Revisited	1959	6.25	12.50	25.00
❏ TL-202 [M]	An Evening Wasted with Tom Lehrer	1959	6.25	12.50	25.00
❏ TL-202S [S]	An Evening Wasted with Tom Lehrer	1959	10.00	20.00	40.00
REPRISE					
❏ R-6179 [M]	That Was the Year That Was	1965	5.00	10.00	20.00
❏ RS-6179 [S]	That Was the Year That Was	1965	6.25	12.50	25.00
—Pink, yellow and green label					
❏ RS-6179 [S]	That Was the Year That Was	1968	3.75	7.50	15.00
—Two-tone orange label with "W7" and "r:" logos					
❏ RS-6179 [S]	That Was the Year That Was	1970	2.50	5.00	10.00
—Orange/tan label with "r:" logo					
❏ R 6199 [M]	An Evening Wasted with Tom Lehrer	1966	5.00	10.00	20.00
—Reissue of Lehrer 202					
❏ RS 6199 [S]	An Evening Wasted with Tom Lehrer	1966	6.25	12.50	25.00
—Reissue of Lehrer 202					
❏ R-6216 [M]	Songs by Tom Lehrer	1966	5.00	10.00	20.00
❏ RS-6216 [S]	Songs by Tom Lehrer	1966	6.25	12.50	25.00

LEIBER, JERRY
Albums

Number	Title (A Side/B Side)	Yr	VG	VG+	NM
KAPP					
❏ KL-1127 [M]	Scooby-Doo	1959	12.50	25.00	50.00

LEIBER AND STOLLER BIG BAND, THE
45s

Number	Title (A Side/B Side)	Yr	VG	VG+	NM
UNITED ARTISTS					
❏ 441	Blue Baion/Café Espresso	1962	3.00	6.00	12.00

Number	Title (A Side/B Side)	Yr	VG	VG+	NM

Albums
ATLANTIC

☐ 8047 [M] Yakety Yak — 1960 — 10.00 — 20.00 — 40.00
—*White "fan" logo on right side of label*
☐ 8047 [M] Yakety Yak — 1962 — 5.00 — 10.00 — 20.00
—*Black "fan" logo on right side of label*
☐ SD 8047 [S] Yakety Yak — 1960 — 12.50 — 25.00 — 50.00
—*White "fan" logo on right side of label*
☐ SD 8047 [S] Yakety Yak — 1962 — 6.25 — 12.50 — 25.00
—*Black "fan" logo on right side of label*

LEIGH, LINDA
45s
AMERICAN INT'L.
☐ 540 — I Promise You/My Guy — 1959 — 6.25 — 12.50 — 25.00
☐ 543 — Beri-Beri/The Plan — 1959 — 12.50 — 25.00 — 50.00
☐ 546 — Foolish Dreams/The Scent — 1960 — 5.00 — 10.00 — 20.00
KASH
☐ 1028 — Heart/Here I Go Out of Your Life — 1965 — 3.00 — 6.00 — 12.00
RENDEZVOUS
☐ 103 — Move Out/It's Real — 1958 — 5.00 — 10.00 — 20.00
☐ 106 — Please Please (Let Me Go Steady)/Teardrops — 1959 — 5.00 — 10.00 — 20.00
REPRISE
☐ 20060 — Someone Special/Please — 1962 — 3.00 — 6.00 — 12.00
☐ 20078 — Lover's Beach/A Thousand Violins — 1962 — 3.00 — 6.00 — 12.00

LEMMON, JACK
45s
EPIC
☐ 9318 — Daphne/Sleepy Lagoon — 1959 — 2.50 — 5.00 — 10.00
☐ 9364 — I Cover the Waterfront/ I'm Forever Blowing Bubbles — 1960 — 2.50 — 5.00 — 10.00
☐ 9399 — Theme from The Apartment/ Lemmon Flavored Blues — 1960 — 2.50 — 5.00 — 10.00
☐ 9399 [PS] — Theme from The Apartment/ Lemmon Flavored Blues — 1960 — 5.00 — 10.00 — 20.00
Albums
CAPITOL
☐ ST 1943 [S] — Jack Lemmon Plays Piano Selections from Irma La Douce — 1963 — 15.00 — 30.00 — 60.00
☐ T 1943 [M] — Jack Lemmon Plays Piano Selections from Irma La Douce — 1963 — 12.50 — 25.00 — 50.00
EPIC
☐ BN 523 [S] — A Twist of Lemmon — 1959 — 12.50 — 25.00 — 50.00
☐ BN 528 [S] — Jack Lemmon Sings and Plays Music from Some Like It Hot — 1959 — 12.50 — 25.00 — 50.00
☐ LN 3491 [M] — A Twist of Lemmon — 1959 — 10.00 — 20.00 — 40.00
☐ LN 3559 [M] — Jack Lemmon Sings and Plays Music from Some Like It Hot — 1959 — 10.00 — 20.00 — 40.00

LEMON PIPERS, THE
45s
BUDDAH
☐ 11 — Turn Around and Take a Look/Danger — 1967 — 2.50 — 5.00 — 10.00
☐ 23 — Green Tambourine/No Help from Me — 1967 — 3.00 — 6.00 — 12.00
☐ 31 — Rice Is Nice/Blueberry Blue — 1968 — 2.50 — 5.00 — 10.00
☐ 31 [PS] — Rice Is Nice/Blueberry Blue — 1968 — 3.75 — 7.50 — 15.00
☐ 41 — Jelly Jungle (Of Orange Marmalade)/ Shoe Shine Boy — 1968 — 2.50 — 5.00 — 10.00
☐ 63 — Wine and Violet/Lonely Atmosphere — 1968 — 2.50 — 5.00 — 10.00
☐ 136 — I Was Not Born to Follow/Rainbow Tree — 1969 — 2.00 — 4.00 — 8.00
CAROL
☐ 107 — Quiet Please/Monaural 78 — 1966 — 3.75 — 7.50 — 15.00
Albums
BUDDAH
☐ BD-5009 [M] — Green Tambourine — 1968 — 6.25 — 12.50 — 25.00
☐ BDS-5009 [S] — Green Tambourine — 1968 — 6.25 — 12.50 — 25.00
☐ BDS-5016 — Jungle Marmalade — 1968 — 6.25 — 12.50 — 25.00

LENNON, FREDDIE
45s
JERDEN
☐ 792 — That's My Life (My Love and My Home)/Next Time You Feel Important — 1966 — 20.00 — 40.00 — 80.00

LENNON, JOHN Includes records as "Plastic Ono Band," "John Ono Lennon," "John Lennon/ Plastic Ono Band" and other records he made with Yoko Ono. Also see THE BEATLES.
12-Inch Singles
CAPITOL
☐ SPRO-9585/6 [DJ] Imagine/Come Together — 1986 — 10.00 — 20.00 — 40.00
☐ SPRO-9894 [DJ] Happy Xmas (War Is Over) (same on both sides) — 1986 — 50.00 — 100.00 — 200.00
—*Limited edition for the Central Virginia Food Bank*
☐ SPRO-9917 [DJ] Rock and Roll People (same on both sides) — 1986 — 15.00 — 30.00 — 60.00
☐ SPRO-9929 [DJ] Happy Xmas (War Is Over)/Listen, the Snow Is Falling — 1986 — 12.50 — 25.00 — 50.00
—*Custom silver label, plastic sleeve with sticker*
☐ SPRO-79463 [DJ] Stand By Me (same on both sides) — 1988 — 10.00 — 20.00 — 40.00
GEFFEN
☐ PRO-A-919 [DJ] (Just Like) Starting Over/Kiss Kiss Kiss — 1980 — 20.00 — 40.00 — 80.00
—*A-side is slightly longer (4:17) than any other release of this song*
☐ PRO-A-1079 [DJ] Happy Xmas (War Is Over)/ Beautiful Boy (Darling Boy) — 1982 — 7.50 — 15.00 — 30.00
POLYDOR
☐ PRO 250-1 [DJ] Nobody Told Me/O' Sanity — 1983 — 7.50 — 15.00 — 30.00
45s
APPLE
☐ 1809 — Give Peace a Chance/Remember Love — 1969 — — — 2.50 — 5.00
—*As "Plastic Ono Band"*
☐ 1809 [PS] — Give Peace a Chance/Remember Love — 1969 — 3.75 — 7.50 — 15.00
—*As "Plastic Ono Band"*
☐ 1813 — Cold Turkey/Don't Worry Kyoko (Mummy's Only Looking for a Hand in the Snow) — 1969 — — — 2.50 — 5.00
—*As "Plastic Ono Band"; most copies skip on A-side on the third chorus because of a pressing defect*

☐ 1813 — Cold Turkey/Don't Worry Kyoko (Mummy's Only Looking for a Hand in the Snow) — 1969 — 2.50 — 5.00 — 10.00
—*As "Plastic Ono Band"; some copies don't skip on A-side. They tend to have wider, bolder print than those that do.*
☐ 1813 [PS] — Cold Turkey/Don't Worry Kyoko (Mummy's Only Looking for a Hand in the Snow) — 1969 — 10.00 — 20.00 — 40.00
—*As "Plastic Ono Band"*
☐ 1818 — Instant Karma! (We All Shine On)/Who Has Seen the Wind? — 1970 — — — 2.00 — 4.00
—*As "John Ono Lennon"; B-side by "Yoko Ono Lennon"*
☐ 1818 [DJ] — Instant Karma! (We All Shine On) — 1970 — 50.00 — 100.00 — 200.00
—*As "John Ono Lennon"; one-sided promo*
☐ 1818 [PS] — Instant Karma! (We All Shine On)/Who Has Seen the Wind? — 1970 — 3.75 — 7.50 — 15.00
—*As "John Ono Lennon"; B-side by "Yoko Ono Lennon"*
☐ 1827 — Mother/Why — 1970 — 2.00 — 4.00 — 8.00
—*As "John Lennon/Plastic Ono Band"; B-side by "Yoko Ono/Plastic Ono Band"*
☐ 1827 — Mother/Why — 1970 — 3.00 — 6.00 — 12.00
—*As "John Lennon/Plastic Ono Band"; star on A-side label*
☐ 1827 — Mother/Why — 1970 — 10.00 — 20.00 — 40.00
—*As "John Lennon/Plastic Ono Band"; "MONO" on A-side label*
☐ 1827 [PS] — Mother/Why — 1970 — 30.00 — 60.00 — 120.00
—*As "John Lennon/Plastic Ono Band"; B-side by "Yoko Ono/Plastic Ono Band"*
☐ 1830 — Power to the People/Touch Me — 1971 — 2.00 — 4.00 — 8.00
—*As "John Lennon/Plastic Ono Band"; with star on A-side label*
☐ 1830 — Power to the People/Touch Me — 1971 — 2.00 — 4.00 — 8.00
—*As "John Lennon/Plastic Ono Band"; B-side by "Yoko Ono/Plastic Ono Band"*
☐ 1830 [PS] — Power to the People/Touch Me — 1971 — 7.50 — 15.00 — 30.00
—*As "John Lennon/Plastic Ono Band"; B-side by "Yoko Ono/Plastic Ono Band"*
☐ 1840 — Imagine/It's So Hard — 1971 — 2.00 — 4.00 — 8.00
—*As "John Lennon Plastic Ono Band"; tan label*
☐ 1840 — Imagine/It's So Hard — 1975 — 3.00 — 6.00 — 12.00
—*As "John Lennon Plastic Ono Band"; green label with "All Rights Reserved"*
☐ 1842 — Happy Xmas (War Is Over)/Listen, the Snow Is Falling — 1971 — 2.50 — 5.00 — 10.00
—*As "John & Yoko/Plastic Ono Band with the Harlem Community Choir"; green vinyl, Apple label*
☐ 1842 — Happy Xmas (War Is Over)/Listen, the Snow Is Falling — 1971 — 3.75 — 7.50 — 15.00
—*As "John & Yoko/Plastic Ono Band with the Harlem Community Choir"; green vinyl, faces label*
☐ 1842 [PS] — Happy Xmas (War Is Over)/Listen, the Snow Is Falling — 1971 — 5.00 — 10.00 — 20.00
—*As "John & Yoko/Plastic Ono Band with the Harlem Community Choir"*
☐ 1848 — Woman Is the Nigger of the World/Sisters O Sisters — 1972 — 2.00 — 4.00 — 8.00
—*As "John Lennon/Plastic Ono Band..."; B-side by "Yoko Ono/Plastic Ono Band..."*
☐ 1848 [PS] — Woman Is the Nigger of the World/Sisters O Sisters — 1972 — 6.25 — 12.50 — 25.00
—*As "John Lennon/Plastic Ono Band..."; B-side by "Yoko Ono/Plastic Ono Band..."*
☐ 1868 — Mind Games/Meat City — 1973 — — — 3.00 — 6.00
☐ 1868 [PS] — Mind Games/Meat City — 1973 — 3.75 — 7.50 — 15.00
☐ P-1868 [DJ] — Mind Games (mono/stereo) — 1973 — 12.50 — 25.00 — 50.00
☐ 1874 — Whatever Gets You Thru the Night/Beef Jerky — 1974 — — — 3.00 — 6.00
—*As "John Lennon and the Plastic Ono Nuclear Band"*
☐ P-1874 [DJ] — Whatever Gets You Thru the Night (mono/ stereo) — 1974 — 12.50 — 25.00 — 50.00
—*As "John Lennon and the Plastic Ono Nuclear Band"*
☐ 1878 — #9 Dream/What You Got — 1974 — 2.00 — 4.00 — 8.00
☐ P-1878 [DJ] — #9 Dream (edited mono/stereo) — 1974 — 12.50 — 25.00 — 50.00
☐ P-1878 [DJ] — What You Got (mono/stereo) — 1974 — 25.00 — 50.00 — 100.00
☐ 1881 — Stand By Me/Move Over Ms. L — 1975 — 2.00 — 4.00 — 8.00
☐ P-1881 [DJ] — Stand By Me (mono/stereo) — 1975 — 12.50 — 25.00 — 50.00
☐ P-1883 [DJ] — Ain't That a Shame (mono/stereo) — 1975 — 50.00 — 100.00 — 200.00
—*No stock copies issued*
☐ P-1883 [DJ] — Slippin' and Slidin' (mono/stereo) — 1975 — 50.00 — 100.00 — 200.00
—*No stock copies issued*
☐ S45X-47663/4 [DJ] Happy Xmas (War Is Over)/Listen, the Snow Is Falling — 1971 — 200.00 — 400.00 — 800.00
—*As "John & Yoko/Plastic Ono Band with the Harlem Community Choir"; white label on styrene*
APPLE/AMERICOM
☐ 1809P/M-435 Give Peace a Chance/Remember Love — 1969 — 187.50 — 375.00 — 750.00
—*As "Plastic Ono Band"; four-inch flexi-disc sold in vending machines*
ATLANTIC
☐ PR-104/5 [DJ] — John Lennon on Ronnie Hawkins: The Short Rap/The Long Rap — 1970 — 25.00 — 50.00 — 100.00
CAPITOL
☐ 1840 — Imagine/It's So Hard — 1978 — — — 3.00 — 6.00
—*As "John Lennon Plastic Ono Band"; purple late 1970s label*
☐ 1840 — Imagine/It's So Hard — 1983 — — — 3.00 — 6.00
—*As "John Lennon Plastic Ono Band"; black colorband label*
☐ 1840 — Imagine/It's So Hard — 1988 — — — 2.50 — 5.00
—*As "John Lennon Plastic Ono Band"; purple late-1980s label (wider)*
☐ 1842 — Happy Xmas (War Is Over)/Listen, the Snow Is Falling — 1976 — 12.50 — 25.00 — 50.00
—*As "John & Yoko/Plastic Ono Band with the Harlem Community Choir"; orange label*
☐ 1842 — Happy Xmas (War Is Over)/Listen, the Snow Is Falling — 1978 — — — 3.00 — 6.00
—*As "John & Yoko/Plastic Ono Band with the Harlem Community Choir"; purple late-1970s label*
☐ 1842 — Happy Xmas (War Is Over)/Listen, the Snow Is Falling — 1983 — — — 3.00 — 6.00
—*As "John & Yoko/Plastic Ono Band with the Harlem Community Choir"; black colorband label*
☐ 1842 — Happy Xmas (War Is Over)/Listen, the Snow Is Falling — 1988 — 5.00 — 10.00 — 20.00
—*As "John & Yoko/Plastic Ono Band with the Harlem Community Choir"; purple late-1980s label (wider)*
☐ 1868 — Mind Games/Meat City — 1978 — — — 3.00 — 6.00
—*Purple late-1970s label*
☐ 1868 — Mind Games/Meat City — 1983 — 3.00 — 6.00 — 12.00
—*Black colorband label*
☐ 1874 — Whatever Gets You Thru the Night/Beef Jerky — 1978 — — — 3.00 — 6.00
—*Purple late-1970s label*
☐ 1874 — Whatever Gets You Thru the Night/Beef Jerky — 1983 — — — 3.00 — 6.00
—*Black colorband label*
☐ 1874 — Whatever Gets You Thru the Night/Beef Jerky — 1988 — — — 3.00 — 6.00
—*Purple late-1980s label*
☐ 1878 — #9 Dream/What You Got — 1976 — 10.00 — 20.00 — 40.00
—*Orange label*

Number	Title (A Side/B Side)	Yr	VG	VG+	NM
❑ 1878	#9 Dream/What You Got	1978	—	3.00	6.00

—*Purple late-1970s label*

❑ 1878	#9 Dream/What You Got	1983	2.50	5.00	10.00

—*Black colorband label*

❑ 7PRO 6 15998 7 [DJ]	Every Man Has a Woman Who Loves Him (Lennon Version)/(Ono Version)	2001	3.75	7.50	15.00

—*White label promo, small hole; B-side has Yoko Ono's version of the song with Lennon backing her*

❑ 7PRO 6 15998 7 [PS]	Every Man Has a Woman Who Loves Him (Lennon Version)/(Ono Version)	2001	3.75	7.50	15.00
❑ S7-17644	Happy Xmas (War Is Over)/ Listen, the Snow Is Falling	1993	—	2.00	4.00

—*John & Yoko/The Plastic Ono Band; green vinyl*

❑ S7-17783	Give Peace a Chance/Remember Love	1994	25.00	50.00	100.00

—*CEMA Special Markets issue; meant for gold-plating in a special plaque. About 100 were not.*

❑ B-44230	Jealous Guy/Give Peace a Chance	1988	—	2.50	5.00
❑ B-44230 [PS]	Jealous Guy/Give Peace a Chance	1988	—	2.50	5.00
❑ S7-57849	Imagine/It's So Hard	1992	12.50	25.00	50.00

—*CEMA Special Markets issue; meant for gold-plating in a special plaque. About 1,000 were not.*

❑ 58894	(Just Like) Starting Over/Watching the Wheels	2000	—	2.50	4.00

—*Blue vinyl*

❑ 58895	Woman/Walking on Thin Ice	2000	—	2.50	5.00

—*Clear vinyl; B-side as "John Lennon and Yoko Ono" though originally issued as a Yoko Ono solo single*

COTILLION

❑ PR-104/5 [DJ]	John Lennon on Ronnie Hawkins: The Short Rap/The Long Rap	1970	20.00	40.00	80.00

—*White label with promo markings*

❑ PR-104/5 [DJ]	John Lennon on Ronnie Hawkins: The Short Rap/The Long Rap	1970	22.50	45.00	90.00

—*No promo markings on white label*

GEFFEN

❑ 29855	Happy Xmas (War Is Over)/ Beautiful Boy (Darling Boy)	1982	—	2.50	5.00
❑ 29855 [PS]	Happy Xmas (War Is Over)/ Beautiful Boy (Darling Boy)	1982	—	2.50	5.00
❑ 49604	(Just Like) Starting Over/Kiss Kiss Kiss	1980	—	2.00	4.00

—*B-side by Yoko Ono*

❑ 49604 [PS]	(Just Like) Starting Over/Kiss Kiss Kiss	1980	—	2.00	4.00

—*B-side by Yoko Ono*

❑ 49644	Woman/Beautiful Boys	1980	—	2.00	4.00

—*B-side by Yoko Ono*

❑ 49644 [PS]	Woman/Beautiful Boys	1980	—	2.00	4.00

—*B-side by Yoko Ono*

❑ 49695	Watching the Wheels/Yes, I'm Your Angel	1981	—	2.00	4.00

—*B-side by Yoko Ono*

❑ 49695 [PS]	Watching the Wheels/Yes, I'm Your Angel	1981	—	2.00	4.00

—*B-side by Yoko Ono*

KYA

❑ 1260 [DJ]	The KYA 1969 Peace Talk	1969	50.00	100.00	200.00

—*Blue vinyl copies are counterfeits*

NOISEVILLE

❑ 43	John Lennon Talks About David Peel	199?	2.50	5.00	10.00

—*Black vinyl*

❑ 43	John Lennon Talks About David Peel	199?	10.00	20.00	40.00

—*Red vinyl, signed by David Peel*

❑ 43 [PS]	John Lennon Talks About David Peel	199?	2.50	5.00	10.00

POLYDOR

❑ 817254-7	Nobody Told Me/O' Sanity	1983	—	2.50	5.00

—*With "Manufactured and Marketed by Polygram..." on label; B-side by Yoko Ono*

❑ 817254-7	Nobody Told Me/O' Sanity	1983	2.50	5.00	10.00

—*With "Manufactured by Polydor Incorporated..." on label; B-side by Yoko Ono*

❑ 817254-7 [PS]	Nobody Told Me/O' Sanity	1983	—	2.50	5.00
❑ 821107-7	I'm Stepping Out/Sleepless Night	1984	—	2.00	4.00

—*B-side by Yoko Ono*

❑ 821107-7 [PS]	I'm Stepping Out/Sleepless Night	1984	—	2.00	4.00
❑ 821204-7	Borrowed Time/Your Hands	1984	—	2.50	5.00

—*B-side by Yoko Ono*

❑ 821204-7 [PS]	Borrowed Time/Your Hands	1984	—	2.50	5.00
❑ 881378-7	Every Man Has a Woman Who Loves Him/It's Alright	1984	2.00	4.00	8.00

—*B-side by Sean Ono Lennon*

❑ 881378-7 [PS]	Every Man Has a Woman Who Loves Him/It's Alright	1984	2.00	4.00	8.00

QUAKER GRANOLA DIPPS

❑ (no #)	A Tribute to John Lennon	1986	3.75	7.50	15.00

—*Cardboard record included in specially marked boxes of Quaker Granola Dipps*

QUAYE/TRIDENT

❑ SK 3419 [DJ]	Rock 'N' Roll	1975	125.00	250.00	500.00

—*Radio spot to promote the album Rock 'N' Roll*

Albums

ADAM VIII

❑ A-8018	John Lennon Sings the Great Rock & Roll Hits (Roots)	1975	250.00	500.00	1000.

—*Counterfeits abound. On authentic copies, cover is posterboard (not slicks); labels are normal size (not overly large); printing on cover is sharp, not blurry; the word "Greatest" does NOT appear on the spine. Authentic copies usually have ad sleeve also.*

APPLE

❑ SMAX-3361	Wedding Album	1969	37.50	75.00	150.00

—*With photo strip, postcard, poster of wedding photos, poster of lithographs, "Bagism" bag, booklet, photo of slice of wedding cake. Missing inserts reduce the value.*

❑ SW-3362	Live Peace in Toronto 1969	1970	3.75	7.50	15.00

—*By "The Plastic Ono Band" -- without calendar*

❑ SW-3362	Live Peace in Toronto 1969	1970	5.00	10.00	20.00

—*By "The Plastic Ono Band"; with calendar*

❑ SW-3372	John Lennon Plastic Ono Band	1970	5.00	10.00	20.00
❑ SW-3379	Imagine	1971	5.00	10.00	20.00

—*With either of two postcard inserts, lyric sleeve, poster*

❑ SW-3379	Imagine	1975	5.00	10.00	20.00

—*"All Rights Reserved" label*

❑ SVBB-3392 [(2)]	Some Time in New York City	1972	7.50	15.00	30.00

—*By John and Yoko; with photo card and petition*

❑ SVBB-3392 [(2)DJ]	Some Time in New York City	1972	250.00	500.00	1000.

—*White label promo*

❑ SW-3414	Mind Games	1973	5.00	10.00	20.00
❑ SW-3416	Walls and Bridges	1974	5.00	10.00	20.00

—*With fold-open segmented front cover*

❑ SK-3419	Rock 'N' Roll	1975	5.00	10.00	20.00
❑ SW-3421	Shaved Fish	1975	5.00	10.00	20.00
❑ T-5001	Two Virgins — Unfinished Music No. 1	1968	12.50	25.00	50.00

—*With Yoko Ono; without brown bag*

❑ T-5001	Two Virgins — Unfinished Music No. 1	1968	37.50	75.00	150.00

—*With Yoko Ono; with die-cut bag*

❑ T-5001	Two Virgins — Unfinished Music No. 1	1968	37.50	75.00	150.00

—*With Yoko Ono; price with brown bag*

❑ T-5001	Two Virgins — Unfinished Music No. 1	1985	3.75	7.50	15.00

—*With Yoko Ono; reissue, flat label*

CAPITOL

❑ SW-3372	John Lennon Plastic Ono Band	1978	3.00	6.00	12.00

—*Purple label, large Capitol logo*

❑ SW-3372	John Lennon Plastic Ono Band	1982	5.00	10.00	20.00

—*Black label, print in colorband*

❑ SW-3372	John Lennon Plastic Ono Band	1988	7.50	15.00	30.00

—*Purple label, small Capitol logo*

❑ SW-3379	Imagine	1978	2.50	5.00	10.00

—*Purple label, large Capitol logo*

❑ SW-3379	Imagine	1986	7.50	15.00	30.00

—*Black label, print in colorband*

❑ SW-3379	Imagine	1987	6.25	12.50	25.00

—*Black label, print in colorband; "Digitally Re-Mastered" at top of front cover*

❑ SW-3379	Imagine	1988	7.50	15.00	30.00

—*Purple label, small Capitol logo*

❑ SVBB-3392 [(2)]	Some Time in New York City	197?	6.25	12.50	25.00

—*By John and Yoko; purple label, large Capitol logo*

❑ SVBB-3392 [(2)]	Some Time in New York City	197?	25.00	50.00	100.00

—*Both discs in single-pocket gatefold (the other pocket is glued shut)*

❑ SW-3414	Mind Games	1978	10.00	20.00	40.00

—*Purple label, large Capitol logo*

❑ SW-3416	Walls and Bridges	1978	3.75	7.50	15.00

—*Purple label, large Capitol logo; standard front cover*

❑ SW-3416	Walls and Bridges	1982	7.50	15.00	30.00

—*Black label, print in colorband*

❑ SW-3416	Walls and Bridges	1989	7.50	15.00	30.00

—*Purple label, small Capitol logo*

❑ SK-3419	Rock 'N' Roll	1978	10.00	20.00	40.00

—*Purple label, large Capitol logo*

❑ SW-3421	Shaved Fish	1978	3.00	6.00	12.00

—*Purple Capitol label with Apple logo on cover*

❑ SW-3421	Shaved Fish	1978	10.00	20.00	40.00

—*Purple Capitol label with Capitol logo on cover*

❑ SW-3421	Shaved Fish	1983	5.00	10.00	20.00

—*Black Capitol label with Apple logo on cover*

❑ SW-3421	Shaved Fish	1983	10.00	20.00	40.00

—*Black Capitol label with Capitol logo on cover*

❑ SW-3421	Shaved Fish	1989	10.00	20.00	40.00

—*Purple Capitol label (small logo) with Capitol logo on cover*

❑ ST-12239	Live Peace in Toronto 1969	1982	2.50	5.00	10.00

—*By "The Plastic Ono Band"; reissue, purple Capitol label*

❑ ST-12239	Live Peace in Toronto 1969	1983	12.50	25.00	50.00

—*By "The Plastic Ono Band"; reissue, black Capitol label*

❑ SV-12451	Live in New York City	1986	3.00	6.00	12.00
❑ SJ-12533	Menlove Ave.	1986	3.75	7.50	15.00
❑ SN-16068	Mind Games	1980	3.00	6.00	12.00

—*Budget-line reissue*

❑ SN-16069	Rock 'N' Roll	1980	3.00	6.00	12.00

—*Budget-line reissue*

❑ C1-90803 [(2)]	Imagine: Music from the Motion Picture	1988	5.00	10.00	20.00
❑ C1-91425	Double Fantasy	1989	5.00	10.00	20.00

—*Very briefly available reissue*

❑ R 144136	Menlove Ave.	198?	12.50	25.00	50.00

—*BMG Direct Marketing edition*

❑ R 144136	Menlove Ave.	1986	12.50	25.00	50.00

—*RCA Music Service edition*

❑ R 144497	Live in New York City	1986	3.75	7.50	15.00

—*RCA Music Service edition*

❑ SV-512451	Live in New York City	1986	3.75	7.50	15.00

—*Columbia House edition*

❑ C1-591425	Double Fantasy	1989	15.00	30.00	60.00

—*Columbia House edition of reissue*

GEFFEN

❑ GHS 2001	Double Fantasy	1980	2.50	5.00	10.00

—*Seven tracks by John, seven by Yoko; off-white label; titles on back cover out of order*

❑ GHS 2001	Double Fantasy	1981	3.00	6.00	12.00

—*Columbia House edition (all have corrected back cover) without "CH" on label*

❑ GHS 2001	Double Fantasy	1981	3.00	6.00	12.00

—*Off-white label, titles in order on the back cover*

❑ GHS 2001	Double Fantasy	1981	18.75	37.50	75.00

—*Columbia House edition (all have corrected back cover) with "CH" on label*

❑ GHS 2001	Double Fantasy	1986	12.50	25.00	50.00

—*Same as above, but with black Geffen label*

❑ GHSP 2023	The John Lennon Collection	1982	5.00	10.00	20.00
❑ GHSP 2023 [DJ]	The John Lennon Collection	1982	12.50	25.00	50.00

—*Promo only on Quiex II audiophile vinyl*

❑ R 104689	Double Fantasy	1981	10.00	20.00	40.00

—*RCA Music Service edition*

MOBILE FIDELITY

❑ 1-153	Imagine	1984	12.50	25.00	50.00

—*Audiophile vinyl*

NAUTILUS

❑ NR-47	Double Fantasy	1982	20.00	40.00	80.00

—*Half-speed master*

❑ NR-47	Double Fantasy	1982	500.00	1000.	2000.

—*Half-speed master; alternate experimental cover with yellow and red added to black and white front*

PARLOPHONE

❑ 21954 [(2)]	Lennon Legend	1998	5.00	10.00	20.00

—*"Made in U.S.A." on back cover*

POLYDOR

❑ 817160-1	Milk and Honey	1983	2.50	5.00	10.00

—*Six tracks by John, six by Yoko*

❑ 817160-1	Milk and Honey	1984	37.50	75.00	150.00

—*Yellow or green vinyl; unauthorized "inside jobs"*

❑ 817238-1	Heart Play (Unfinished Dialogue)	1983	3.00	6.00	12.00

—*Interviews with John Lennon and Yoko Ono*

SILHOUETTE

❑ SM-10012 [(2)]	Reflections and Poetry	1984	6.25	12.50	25.00

Number	Title (A Side/B Side)	Yr	VG	VG+	NM
ZAPPLE					
❏ ST-3357	Life with the Lions — Unfinished Music No. 2	1969	5.00	10.00	20.00
—With Yoko Ono					

LENNON SISTERS, THE Also see LAWRENCE WELK.
45s

Number	Title (A Side/B Side)	Yr	VG	VG+	NM
BRUNSWICK					
❏ 55000	Young and In Love/Teenage Waltz	1957	2.50	5.00	10.00
❏ 55013	White Silver Sands/One Day a Little Girl	1957	2.50	5.00	10.00
❏ 55028	Shake Me I Rattle/Pocahontas	1957	2.50	5.00	10.00
❏ 55044	Let's Light the Christmas Tree/ Merry, Merry Christmas	1957	3.00	6.00	12.00
❏ 55051	To Know You Is to Love You/Hide Your Troubles Behind a Smile	1958	2.50	5.00	10.00
❏ 55058	Dear One/Mr. Clarinet Man	1958	2.50	5.00	10.00
❏ 55063	How Will I Know My Love/Graduation Dance	1958	2.50	5.00	10.00
❏ 55075	Bubble Gum/Have You Ever Been Lonely	1958	2.50	5.00	10.00
—With Larry Dean					
❏ 55082	Walk with Me/Goodnight God	1958	2.50	5.00	10.00
❏ 55113	The Children's Marching Song/Slumber Party	1959	2.50	5.00	10.00
DOT					
❏ 15965	A Hundred and One in the Sun/Vacation Waltz	1959	2.00	4.00	8.00
❏ 16131	Freckles/I Wakled with the Wind	1960	2.00	4.00	8.00
❏ 16184	Did'Ja Know/What a Sky	1961	2.00	4.00	8.00
❏ 16215	Darlin' Meggie/On the Double	1961	2.00	4.00	8.00
❏ 16255	Sad Movies (Make Me Cry)/I Don't Know Why	1961	2.00	4.00	8.00
❏ 16277	Kaw-Liga/We Live in Two Different Worlds	1961	2.00	4.00	8.00
❏ 16423	Bei Mir Bist Du Schoen/Lida Rose	1963	2.00	4.00	8.00
❏ 16489	The Heartstrings/Speak, Sugar, Speak	1963	2.00	4.00	8.00
❏ 16681	Little Stranger/Little Lady Make Believe	1964	—	3.00	6.00
❏ 16748	Chim Chim Cheree/A Step in Time	1965	—	3.00	6.00
❏ 17010	He's Got a Lotta Lovin'/I'm Coming Back to You	1967	—	3.00	6.00
❏ 17046	I Love/Gypsy, What Can I Do	1967	—	3.00	6.00
MERCURY					
❏ 72830	As Long As There's an Apple Tree/I'm So Glad That You've Found Me	1968	—	3.00	6.00
❏ 72883	The Christmas Waltz/Lullaby for Christmas	1968	—	3.00	6.00
Albums					
BRUNSWICK					
❏ BL 54031 [M]	Let's Get Acquainted	1957	6.25	12.50	25.00
❏ BL 54039 [M]	Lawrence Welk Presents the Lennon Sisters	1958	6.25	12.50	25.00
DOT					
❏ DLP-3250 [M]	Best-Loved Catholic Hymns	1959	3.75	7.50	15.00
❏ DLP-3292 [M]	The Lennon Sisters Sing 12 Great Hits	1960	3.75	7.50	15.00
❏ DLP 3343 [M]	Christmas with the Lennon Sisters	1961	3.75	7.50	15.00
❏ DLP-3398 [M]	Sad Movies (Make Me Cry)	1961	3.75	7.50	15.00
❏ DLP-3417 [M]	Can't Help Falling in Love	1962	3.00	6.00	12.00
❏ DLP-3481 [M]	The Lennon Sisters' Favorites	1963	3.00	6.00	12.00
❏ DLP-3557 [M]	Dominique and Other Great Folk Songs	1964	3.00	6.00	12.00
❏ DLP-3619 [M]	No. 1 Hits of the 1960s	1964	3.00	6.00	12.00
❏ DLP-3622 [M]	Twelve Great Hits, Volume 2	1965	3.00	6.00	12.00
❏ DLP-3659 [M]	Solos	1965	3.00	6.00	12.00
❏ DLP-3797 [M]	Somethin' Stupid	1967	3.75	7.50	15.00
❏ DLP-25250 [S]	Best-Loved Catholic Hymns	1959	5.00	10.00	20.00
❏ DLP-25292 [S]	The Lennon Sisters Sing 12 Great Hits	1960	5.00	10.00	20.00
❏ DLP 25343 [S]	Christmas with the Lennon Sisters	1961	5.00	10.00	20.00
❏ DLP-25398 [S]	Sad Movies (Make Me Cry)	1961	5.00	10.00	20.00
❏ DLP-25417 [S]	Can't Help Falling in Love	1962	3.75	7.50	15.00
❏ DLP-25481 [S]	The Lennon Sisters' Favorites	1963	3.75	7.50	15.00
❏ DLP-25557 [S]	Dominique and Other Great Folk Songs	1964	3.75	7.50	15.00
❏ DLP-25589 [S]	No. 1 Hits of the 1960s	1964	3.75	7.50	15.00
❏ DLP-25622 [S]	Twelve Great Hits, Volume 2	1965	3.75	7.50	15.00
❏ DLP-25659 [S]	Solos	1965	3.75	7.50	15.00
❏ DLP-25797 [S]	Somethin' Stupid	1967	3.00	6.00	12.00
HAMILTON					
❏ HLP-119 [M]	Melody of Love	196?	3.00	6.00	12.00
❏ HLP-12119 [S]	Melody of Love	196?	3.00	6.00	12.00
MERCURY					
❏ SR-61164	The Lennon Sisters Today!!	1968	3.00	6.00	12.00
❏ SR-61201	Pop Country	1969	3.00	6.00	12.00
PICKWICK					
❏ PTP-2014 [(2)]	America's Sweethearts	1973	3.00	6.00	12.00
❏ SPC-3084	Our Favorite Songs	196?	2.50	5.00	10.00
❏ SPC-3110	Goodnight Sweetheart	197?	2.50	5.00	10.00
RANWOOD					
❏ 7027 [(2)]	22 Songs of Faith and Inspiration	198?	2.50	5.00	10.00
❏ 8205	Best of the Lennon Sisters	198?	2.00	4.00	8.00
❏ 8212	How Great Thou Art	198?	2.00	4.00	8.00
VOCALION					
❏ VL 73864	Too Marvelous for Words	1969	2.50	5.00	10.00
❏ VL 73887	The Lennon Sisters with Lawrence Welk	1970	2.50	5.00	10.00

LENNY AND THE CHIMES
45s

Number	Title (A Side/B Side)	Yr	VG	VG+	NM
VEE JAY					
❏ 605	Only Forever/Two Times Two	1964	3.00	6.00	12.00

LENNY AND THE THUNDERTONES
45s

Number	Title (A Side/B Side)	Yr	VG	VG+	NM
DOT					
❏ 16177	The Street Beat/Happy Little Jug	1961	6.25	12.50	25.00

LENOIR, J.B.
45s

Number	Title (A Side/B Side)	Yr	VG	VG+	NM
CHECKER					
❏ 844	Let Me Die with the One I Love/ If I Give My Love to You	1956	10.00	20.00	40.00
❏ 856	Don't Touch My Head/I've Been Down So Long	1957	10.00	20.00	40.00
❏ 874	What About Your Daughter/Five Years	1957	7.50	15.00	30.00
❏ 901	Daddy Talk to Your Son/She Don't Know	1958	7.50	15.00	30.00
J.O.B.					
❏ 1012	The Mojo/How Can I Leave	1952	50.00	100.00	200.00
❏ 1102	Play a Little While/Louise	1952	30.00	60.00	120.00
PARROT					
❏ 802	Eisenhower Blues/I'm in Korea	1954	100.00	200.00	400.00
❏ 802	Tax Paying Blues/I'm in Korea	1954	250.00	500.00	1000.
—A-side is similar, though not identical, to "Eisenhower Blues"					

Number	Title (A Side/B Side)	Yr	VG	VG+	NM
❏ 802	Tax Paying Blues/I'm in Korea	1954	500.00	1000.	2000.
—Red vinyl					
❏ 809	Mama Talk to Your Daughter/ Man, Watch Your Woman	1955	20.00	40.00	80.00
❏ 814	Mama Your Daughter Is Going to Miss Me/ What Have I Done	1955	25.00	50.00	100.00
❏ 821	Fine Girls/I Lost My Baby	1955	37.50	75.00	150.00
SHAD					
❏ 5012	Back Door/Louella	1959	5.00	10.00	20.00
U.S.A.					
❏ 744	I Feel So Good/Sing Um the Way I Feel	1963	5.00	10.00	20.00
VEE JAY					
❏ 352	Do What I Say/Oh Baby	1960	3.00	6.00	12.00
—As "J.B. Lenore"					
Albums					
CHESS					
❏ LP-410	Natural Man	1970	10.00	20.00	40.00
❏ CH-9323	Natural Man	1990	3.00	6.00	12.00
POLYDOR					
❏ 24-4011	J.B. Lenoir	1970	3.75	7.50	15.00

LEON AND THE DREAMERS
45s

Number	Title (A Side/B Side)	Yr	VG	VG+	NM
PARKWAY					
❏ 843	Haircut/If It Hadn't Been for You	1962	3.75	7.50	15.00

LEONARD, JACK E.
Albums

Number	Title (A Side/B Side)	Yr	VG	VG+	NM
VIK					
❏ LX-1080 [M]	Rock 'n Roll for People Over Sixteen	1957	10.00	20.00	40.00

LES CHANSONETTES
45s

Number	Title (A Side/B Side)	Yr	VG	VG+	NM
SHRINE					
❏ 114	Don't Let Him Hurt You/Deeper	1966	200.00	400.00	800.00

LESTER, BOBBY, AND THE MOONLIGHTERS The Moonlighters are THE MOONGLOWS.
45s

Number	Title (A Side/B Side)	Yr	VG	VG+	NM
CHECKER					
❏ 806	So All Alone/Shoo Doo-Be Do (My Loving Baby)	1954	25.00	50.00	100.00
—Maroon label with checkerboard top					
❏ 806	So All Alone/Shoo Doo-Be Do (My Loving Baby)	1958	10.00	20.00	40.00
—Maroon label, vertical logo					
❏ 813	New Gal/The Hug and a Kiss	1955	20.00	40.00	80.00

LESTER, KETTY
45s

Number	Title (A Side/B Side)	Yr	VG	VG+	NM
ERA					
❏ 3068	Love Letters/I'm a Fool to Want You	1962	3.00	6.00	12.00
❏ 3080	But Not for Me/Once Upon a Time	1962	2.50	5.00	10.00
❏ 3088	You Can't Lie to a Liar/River of Salt	1962	2.50	5.00	10.00
❏ 3094	This Land Is Your Land/Love Is for Everyone	1962	2.50	5.00	10.00
❏ 3103	Fallen Angel/Lullaby for Lovers	1963	2.50	5.00	10.00
EVEREST					
❏ 20007	Queen for a Day/I Said Goodbye to My Love	1962	2.50	5.00	10.00
PETE					
❏ 706	I Wil Lead You/Now That I Need Him	1968	—	3.00	6.00
❏ 710	Measure of a Man/Cracker Box Living	1968	—	3.00	6.00
❏ 714	Show Me/Since I Fell for You	1969	—	3.00	6.00
RCA VICTOR					
❏ 47-8331	The House Is Haunted/ Some Things Are Better Left Unsaid	1964	2.00	4.00	8.00
❏ 47-8371	Please Don't Cry Anymore/ Roses Grow With Thorns	1964	2.00	4.00	8.00
❏ 47-8424	I Trust You Baby/ Theme from The Luck of Ginger Coffey	1964	2.00	4.00	8.00
❏ 47-8471	You Go Your Way/ Variations on a Theme by Byrd	1964	2.00	4.00	8.00
❏ 47-8573	(Looking for a) Better World/Pretty Lies, Pretty Make Believes	1965	2.00	4.00	8.00
TOWER					
❏ 166	I'll Be Looking Back/West Coast	1965	2.00	4.00	8.00
❏ 208	Secret Love/Love Me Just a Little Bit	1966	2.00	4.00	8.00
❏ 236	When a Woman Loves a Man/We'll Be Together Again	1966	2.00	4.00	8.00
Albums					
AVI					
❏ 6116	A Collection of Her Best	1982	3.75	7.50	15.00
ERA					
❏ EL-108 [M]	Love Letters	1962	10.00	20.00	40.00
❏ ES-108 [S]	Love Letters	1962	15.00	30.00	60.00
PETE					
❏ 1109	Ketty Lester	1969	3.75	7.50	15.00
RCA VICTOR					
❏ LPM-2945 [M]	The Soul of Me	1964	6.25	12.50	25.00
❏ LSP-2945 [S]	The Soul of Me	1964	7.50	15.00	30.00
❏ LPM-3326 [M]	Where Is Love	1965	6.25	12.50	25.00
❏ LSP-3326 [S]	Where Is Love	1965	7.50	15.00	30.00
SHEFFIELD					
❏ 15	Ketty Lester In Concert	1977	3.75	7.50	15.00
TOWER					
❏ ST 5029 [S]	When a Woman Loves a Man	1966	6.25	12.50	25.00
❏ T 5029 [M]	When a Woman Loves a Man	1966	6.25	12.50	25.00

LETTERMEN, THE
45s

Number	Title (A Side/B Side)	Yr	VG	VG+	NM
ALPHA OMEGA					
❏ 078501	It Feels Like Christmas/I Believe	1985	—	2.00	4.00
❏ 078501 [PS]	It Feels Like Christmas/I Believe	1985	—	2.00	4.00
APPLAUSE					
❏ 104	What I Did for Love/Cherish-Precious and Few	1983	—	2.00	4.00
CAPITOL					
❏ 2054	Goin' Out of My Head-Can't Take My Eyes Off You/I Believe	1967	2.00	4.00	8.00
❏ 2132	Sherry Don't Go/Never My Love	1968	—	3.00	6.00

Number	Title (A Side/B Side)	Yr	VG	VG+	NM
❑ 2196	Anyone Who Had a Heart/				
	All the Gray-Haired Men	1968	—	3.00	6.00
❑ 2218	Love Is Blue-Greensleeves/Where Were You				
	When the Lights Went Out	1968	—	3.00	6.00
❑ 2254	Playing the Piano/Sally Le Roy	1968	—	3.00	6.00
❑ 2324	Put Your Head on My Shoulder/Mary's Rainbow	1968	—	3.00	6.00
❑ 2414	I Have Dreamed/				
	The Pendulum Swings Both Ways	1969	—	3.00	6.00
❑ 2482	Hurt So Bad/Catch the Wind	1969	—	3.00	6.00
❑ 2643	Shangri-La/When Summer Ends	1969	—	3.00	6.00
❑ 2697	Traces-Memories Medley/For Once in a Lifetime	1969	—	3.00	6.00
❑ 2774	Hang On Sloopy/For Love	1970	—	2.50	5.00
❑ 2820	She Cried/For Love	1970	—	2.50	5.00
❑ 2938	Hey Girl/Worlds	1970	—	2.50	5.00
❑ 3020	Everything Is Good About You/It's Over	1971	—	2.50	5.00
❑ 3098	Love Is a Hurtin' Thing/Feelings	1971	—	2.50	5.00
❑ 3192	Love/Maybe Tomorrow	1971	—	2.50	5.00
❑ 3285	Oh My Love/An Old Fashioned Love Song	1972	—	2.00	4.00
❑ 3285 [PS]	Oh My Love/An Old Fashioned Love Song	1972	—	3.00	6.00
❑ 3449	Maybe We Should/Spin Away	1972	—	2.00	4.00
❑ 3512	Sandman/Love Song	1973	—	2.00	4.00
❑ 3619	A Summer Song/Mac Arthur Park	1973	—	2.00	4.00
❑ 3810	Goodbye/The You Part of Me	1973	—	2.00	4.00
❑ 3912	The Way We Were-Isn't It a Shame/Touch Me				
	in the Morning	1974	—	2.00	4.00
❑ 4005	Song from Some Came Running (To Love and				
	Be Loved)/Eastward	1974	—	2.00	4.00
❑ 4096	You Are My Sunshine Girl/Make a Time for Lovin'	1975	—	2.00	4.00
❑ 4161	If You Feel the Way I Do/Love Me Like a Stranger	1975	—	2.00	4.00
❑ 4226	Storms of Troubled Times/				
	The Way You Look Tonight	1976	—	2.00	4.00
❑ 4586	The Way You Look Tonight/That's My Desire	1961	3.00	6.00	12.00
❑ 4586 [PS]	The Way You Look Tonight/That's My Desire	1961	5.00	10.00	20.00
❑ 4658	When I Fall in Love/Smile	1961	3.00	6.00	12.00
❑ 4658 [PS]	When I Fall in Love/Smile	1961	5.00	10.00	20.00
❑ 4699	Come Back Silly Girl/A Song for Young Love	1962	3.00	6.00	12.00
❑ 4699 [PS]	Come Back Silly Girl/A Song for Young Love	1962	5.00	10.00	20.00
❑ 4746	How Is Julie?/Turn Around, Look at Me	1962	3.00	6.00	12.00
❑ 4746 [PS]	How Is Julie?/Turn Around, Look at Me	1962	5.00	10.00	20.00
❑ 4810	Silly Boy (She Doesn't Love You)/I Told the Stars	1962	3.00	6.00	12.00
❑ 4810 [PS]	Silly Boy (She Doesn't Love You)/I Told the Stars	1962	5.00	10.00	20.00
❑ 4851	Again/A Tree in the Meadow	1962	3.00	6.00	12.00
❑ 4851 [PS]	Again/A Tree in the Meadow	1962	5.00	10.00	20.00
❑ 4914	No Other Love/Heartache Oh Heartache	1963	2.50	5.00	10.00
❑ 4976	Two Brothers/The Allentown Jail	1963	2.50	5.00	10.00
❑ 5091	Where or When/Be My Girl	1963	2.50	5.00	10.00
❑ 5218	Put Away Your Teardrops/				
	Seventh Dawn Theme	1964	2.50	5.00	10.00
❑ 5273	When Summer Ends/				
	You Don't Know Just How Lucky You Are	1964	2.50	5.00	10.00
❑ 5370	The Girl with a Little Tin Heart/It's Over	1965	2.00	4.00	8.00
❑ 5437	Theme from "A Summer Place"/				
	Sealed with a Kiss	1965	2.00	4.00	8.00
❑ 5499	Secretly/The Things We Did Last Summer	1965	2.00	4.00	8.00
❑ 5499 [PS]	Secretly/The Things We Did Last Summer	1965	3.00	6.00	12.00
❑ 5544	I Believe/Sweet September	1965	2.00	4.00	8.00
❑ 5583	You'll Be Needin' Me/Run to My Loving Arms	1966	2.00	4.00	8.00
❑ 5649	I Only Have Eyes for You/Love Letters	1966	2.00	4.00	8.00
❑ 5649 [PS]	I Only Have Eyes for You/Love Letters	1966	3.00	6.00	12.00
❑ 5749	Chanson D'Amour/She Don't Want Me Now	1966	2.00	4.00	8.00
❑ 5813	Our Winter Love/Warm	1966	2.00	4.00	8.00
❑ 5913	Volare/Mr. Sun	1967	2.00	4.00	8.00

WARNER BROS.

Number	Title (A Side/B Side)	Yr	VG	VG+	NM
❑ 5152	Their Hearts Were Full of Spring/When	1960	3.75	7.50	15.00
❑ 5178	Two Hearts/Magic Sound	1960	3.75	7.50	15.00

Albums

APPLAUSE

Number	Title	Yr	VG	VG+	NM
❑ 1006	Love Is...	198?	2.50	5.00	10.00

CAPITOL

❑ SKAO-138	The Best of the Lettermen, Vol. 2	1969	3.00	6.00	12.00
❑ SM-147	Put Your Head on My Shoulder	1977	2.00	4.00	8.00
—Reissue with new prefix					
❑ ST-147	Put Your Head on My Shoulder	1968	3.75	7.50	15.00
❑ ST-202	I Have Dreamed	1969	3.00	6.00	12.00
❑ SWBB-251 [(2)]	Close-Up	1969	3.75	7.50	15.00
—Reissue of ST 2013 and ST 2083 in one package					
❑ ST 8-0269	Hurt So Bad	1969	3.75	7.50	15.00
—Capitol Record Club edition					
❑ ST-269	Hurt So Bad	1969	3.00	6.00	12.00
❑ ST-390	Traces/Memories	1970	3.00	6.00	12.00
❑ ST 8-0496	Reflections	1970	3.75	7.50	15.00
—Capitol Record Club edition					
❑ ST-496	Reflections	1970	3.00	6.00	12.00
❑ STCL-577 [(3)]	The Lettermen	1970	6.25	12.50	25.00
❑ ST-634	Everything's Good About You	1971	3.00	6.00	12.00
❑ STBB-710 [(2)]	Let It Be Me/And I Love Her	1971	3.75	7.50	15.00
❑ SW-781	Feelings	1971	3.00	6.00	12.00
❑ ST-836	Love Book	1971	3.00	6.00	12.00
❑ ST 1669 [S]	A Song for Young Love	1962	5.00	10.00	20.00
❑ T 1669 [M]	A Song for Young Love	1962	3.75	7.50	15.00
❑ ST 1711 [S]	Once Upon a Time	1962	5.00	10.00	20.00
❑ T 1711 [M]	Once Upon a Time	1962	3.75	7.50	15.00
❑ ST 1761 [S]	Jim, Tony and Bob	1962	5.00	10.00	20.00
❑ T 1761 [M]	Jim, Tony and Bob	1962	3.75	7.50	15.00
❑ ST 1829 [S]	College Standards	1963	5.00	10.00	20.00
❑ T 1829 [M]	College Standards	1963	3.75	7.50	15.00
❑ ST 1936 [S]	The Lettermen In Concert	1963	5.00	10.00	20.00
❑ T 1936 [M]	The Lettermen In Concert	1963	3.75	7.50	15.00
❑ ST 2013 [S]	A Lettermen Kind of Love	1964	3.75	7.50	15.00
❑ T 2013 [M]	A Lettermen Kind of Love	1964	3.00	6.00	12.00
❑ ST 2083 [S]	The Lettermen Look at Love	1964	3.75	7.50	15.00
❑ T 2083 [M]	The Lettermen Look at Love	1964	3.00	6.00	12.00
❑ ST 2142 [S]	She Cried	1964	3.75	7.50	15.00
❑ T 2142 [M]	She Cried	1964	3.00	6.00	12.00
❑ ST 2213 [S]	You'll Never Walk Alone	1965	3.75	7.50	15.00
❑ T 2213 [M]	You'll Never Walk Alone	1965	3.00	6.00	12.00
❑ ST 2270 [S]	Portrait of My Love	1965	3.75	7.50	15.00

Number	Title (A Side/B Side)	Yr	VG	VG+	NM
❑ T 2270 [M]	Portrait of My Love	1965	3.00	6.00	12.00
❑ ST 2359 [S]	The Hit Sounds of the Lettermen	1965	3.75	7.50	15.00
❑ T 2359 [M]	The Hit Sounds of the Lettermen	1965	3.00	6.00	12.00
❑ ST 2428 [S]	More Hit Sounds of the Lettermen!	1966	3.75	7.50	15.00
❑ T 2428 [M]	More Hit Sounds of the Lettermen!	1966	3.00	6.00	12.00
❑ ST 2496 [S]	A New Song for Young Love	1966	3.75	7.50	15.00
❑ T 2496 [M]	A New Song for Young Love	1966	3.00	6.00	12.00
❑ ST 2554 [S]	The Best of the Lettermen	1966	3.75	7.50	15.00
❑ T 2554 [M]	The Best of the Lettermen	1966	3.00	6.00	12.00
❑ ST 2587 [S]	For Christmas This Year	1966	3.75	7.50	15.00
❑ ST-8-2587 [S]	For Christmas This Year	1966	5.00	10.00	20.00
—Capitol Record Club edition					
❑ T 2587 [M]	For Christmas This Year	1966	3.00	6.00	12.00
❑ ST 2633 [S]	Warm	1967	3.75	7.50	15.00
❑ T 2633 [M]	Warm	1967	3.75	7.50	15.00
❑ SM-2711	Spring!	1977	2.00	4.00	8.00
—Reissue with new prefix					
❑ ST 2711 [S]	Spring!	1967	3.75	7.50	15.00
❑ T 2711 [M]	Spring!	1967	3.75	7.50	15.00
❑ ST 2758 [S]	The Lettermen!!!... And "Live!"	1967	3.75	7.50	15.00
❑ T 2758 [M]	The Lettermen!!!... And "Live!"	1967	5.00	10.00	20.00
❑ ST 2865	Goin' Out of My Head	1968	3.75	7.50	15.00
❑ ST 2934	Special Request	1968	3.75	7.50	15.00
❑ SPRO-4798/9 [DJ]	A Collection of Their Finest Songs	1969	6.25	12.50	25.00
—Promo-only collection of excerpts of 20 songs					
❑ SW-11010	Lettermen 1	1972	2.50	5.00	10.00
❑ SW-11124	Spin Away	1972	2.50	5.00	10.00
❑ SW-11183	"Alive" Again ... Naturally	1973	2.50	5.00	10.00
❑ SW-11249	All-Time Greatest Hits	1973	2.50	5.00	10.00
❑ SW-11319	Now and Forever	1974	2.50	5.00	10.00
❑ SW-11364	There Is No Greater Love	1974	2.50	5.00	10.00
❑ SW-11424	Make Time	1975	2.50	5.00	10.00
❑ SW-11470	The Time Is Right	1975	2.50	5.00	10.00
❑ SW-11508	Kind of Country	1976	2.50	5.00	10.00
❑ SM-11678	Hurt So Bad	1977	2.00	4.00	8.00
—Reissue of 269					
❑ SM-11814	The Lettermen!!! ... And "Live!"	1978	2.00	4.00	8.00
—Reissue of 2758					
❑ SM-11970	Goin' Out of My Head	1979	2.00	4.00	8.00
—Reissue of 2865					
❑ SN-16071	The Best of the Lettermen	1980	2.00	4.00	8.00
—Budget-line reissue					
❑ SN-16190	Let It Be Me	1981	2.00	4.00	8.00
—Budget-line reissue					
❑ SN-16191	And I Love Her	1981	2.00	4.00	8.00
—Budget-line reissue					
❑ SN-16222	The Best of the Lettermen, Vol. 2	198?	2.00	4.00	8.00
—Budget-line reissue					
❑ SN-16312	All-Time Greatest Hits	198?	2.00	4.00	8.00
—Budget-line reissue					

LONGINES SYMPHONETTE

❑ 220 [(5)]	A Time for Us	1972	7.50	15.00	30.00

PICKWICK

❑ SPC-3294	Soft Hits	1972	2.50	5.00	10.00
❑ SPC-3565	With Love	1978	2.00	4.00	8.00

LETTERMEN, THE (2) Different group from above.

45s

LIBERTY

❑ 55141	Hey, Big Brain/Guiro	1958	2.50	5.00	10.00

LEVIATHAN

Albums

MACH

❑ XMA-12501	Leviathan	1974	10.00	20.00	40.00

LEVON AND THE HAWKS Early version of THE BAND.

45s

ATCO

❑ 6383	He Don't Love You (And He'll Break Your Heart)/				
	Stones I Throw	1965	7.50	15.00	30.00
❑ 6625	He Don't Love You (And He'll Break Your Heart)/				
	Go Go Lisa Jane	1968	7.50	15.00	30.00

LEWIS, BARBARA

45s

ATLANTIC

❑ 2141	My Heart Went Do Dat Da/				
	The Longest Night of the Year	1962	3.00	6.00	12.00
❑ 2159	My Mama Told Me/				
	Gonna Love You Till the Day I Die	1962	3.00	6.00	12.00
❑ 2184	Hello Stranger/Think a Little Sugar	1963	5.00	10.00	20.00
❑ 2200	Straighten Up Your Heart/If You Love Her	1963	3.00	6.00	12.00
❑ 2214	Puppy Love/Snap Your Fingers	1963	3.00	6.00	12.00
❑ 2227	Someday We're Gonna Love Again/Spend a				
	Little Time	1964	2.50	5.00	10.00
❑ 2255	Come Home/Pushin' a Good Thing Too Far	1964	2.50	5.00	10.00
❑ 2283	Baby, I'm Yours/I Say Love	1965	3.75	7.50	15.00
❑ 2300	Make Me Your Baby/Love to Be Loved	1965	3.75	7.50	15.00
❑ 2316	Don't Forget About Me/It's Magic	1965	2.50	5.00	10.00
❑ 2346	Make Me Belong to You/Girls Need Loving Care	1966	2.00	4.00	8.00
❑ 2361	I Remember the Feeling/Baby What You Want				
	Me to Do	1966	2.00	4.00	8.00
❑ 2400	Love Makes the World Go Round/I'll Make Him				
	Love Me	1967	2.00	4.00	8.00
❑ 2413	Fool, Fool, Fool/Only All the Time	1967	2.00	4.00	8.00
❑ 2482	Thankful for What I Got/Sho Nuff	1968	2.00	4.00	8.00
❑ 2514	On Bended Knees/I'll Keep Believing	1968	2.00	4.00	8.00
❑ 2550	I'm All You've Got/You're a Dream Maker	1968	2.00	4.00	8.00

ENTERPRISE

❑ 9012	You Made Me a Woman/				
	Just the Way You Are Today	1970	—	3.00	6.00
❑ 9027	Ask the Lonely/Why Did It Take You So Long	1970	—	3.00	6.00
❑ 9029	Anyway/That's the Way I Like It	1970	—	3.00	6.00

KAREN

❑ 313	My Heart Went Do Dat Da/				
	The Longest Night of the Year	1961	7.50	15.00	30.00

Number	Title (A Side/B Side)	Yr	VG	VG+	NM
REPRISE					
❏ 1146	Rock and Roll Lullaby/I'm So Thankful	1972	—	2.50	5.00
7-Inch Extended Plays					
ATLANTIC					
❏ LSD 8110 [DJ]	Baby I'm Yours/Hy Heart Went Do Da Dat/Puppy Love//Hello Stranger/Someday We're Gonna Love Again/Snap Your Fingers	196?	3.75	7.50	15.00
—Jukebox mini-LP, small hole, plays at 33 1/3 rpm					
❏ LSD 8110 [PS]	Baby I'm Yours	196?	3.75	7.50	15.00
Albums					
ATLANTIC					
❏ 8086 [M]	Hello Stranger	1963	10.00	20.00	40.00
❏ SD 8086 [S]	Hello Stranger	1963	12.50	25.00	50.00
❏ 8090 [M]	Snap Your Fingers	1964	10.00	20.00	40.00
❏ SD 8090 [S]	Snap Your Fingers	1964	12.50	25.00	50.00
❏ 8110 [M]	Baby, I'm Yours	1965	10.00	20.00	40.00
❏ SD 8110 [S]	Baby, I'm Yours	1965	12.50	25.00	50.00
❏ 8118 [M]	It's Magic	1966	7.50	15.00	30.00
❏ SD 8118 [S]	It's Magic	1966	10.00	20.00	40.00
❏ SD 8173	Workin' on a Groovy Thing	1968	6.25	12.50	25.00
❏ SD 8286	The Best of Barbara Lewis	1971	5.00	10.00	20.00
COLLECTABLES					
❏ COL-5104	Golden Classics	198?	2.50	5.00	10.00
ENTERPRISE					
❏ ENS-1006	The Many Grooves of Barbara Lewis	1970	6.25	12.50	25.00

LEWIS, BOBBY (1) R&B singer.
45s

Number	Title (A Side/B Side)	Yr	VG	VG+	NM
ABC-PARAMOUNT					
❏ 10565	That's Right/Fannie Lewis	1964	3.00	6.00	12.00
❏ 10592	Jealous Love/Stark Raving Wild	1964	3.00	6.00	12.00
BELTONE					
❏ 1002	Tossin' and Turnin'/Oh Yes I Love You	1961	6.25	12.50	25.00
❏ 1012	One Track Mind/Are You Ready	1961	6.25	12.50	25.00
❏ 1015	What a Walk/Cry No More	1961	3.75	7.50	15.00
❏ 1016	Yes, Oh Yes, It Did/Mamie in the Afternoon	1962	3.75	7.50	15.00
❏ 2018	A Man's Gotta Be a Man/ Day by Day I Need Your Love	1962	3.75	7.50	15.00
❏ 2023	I'm Tossin' and Turnin' Again/ Nothin' But the Blues	1962	3.75	7.50	15.00
❏ 2026	Lonely Teardrops/Boom-a-Chick-Chick	1962	3.75	7.50	15.00
❏ 2035	Nothin' But the Blues/Intermission	1963	3.75	7.50	15.00
LANA					
❏ 104	Tossin' and Turnin'/Oh Yes I Love You	196?	2.00	4.00	8.00
—Oldies reissue					
LOST-NITE					
❏ 146	Tossin' An' Turnin'/Oh Yes I Love You	196?	—	3.00	6.00
—Reissue; note slightly different spelling of A-side					
MERCURY					
❏ 71245	Mumbles Blues/Oh Baby	1957	6.25	12.50	25.00
PHILIPS					
❏ 40519	Soul Seekin'/Give Me Your Yesterdays	1968	5.00	10.00	20.00
ROULETTE					
❏ 4182	You Better Stop/Fire of Love	1959	3.75	7.50	15.00
❏ 4382	Solid as a Rock/Oh Mr. Somebody	1961	3.75	7.50	15.00
SPOTLIGHT					
❏ 394	Mumbles Blues/Oh Baby	1957	7.50	15.00	30.00
❏ 397	Solid as a Rock/You Even Forgot My Name	1957	7.50	15.00	30.00
Albums					
BELTONE					
❏ 4000 [M]	Tossin' and Turnin'	1961	50.00	100.00	200.00

LEWIS, BOBBY (2) Country singer.
45s

Number	Title (A Side/B Side)	Yr	VG	VG+	NM
ACE OF HEARTS					
❏ 0463	Already Gone to My Heart/Mr. President	1973	—	3.00	6.00
❏ 0466	Here with You/Where Happiness Is	1973	—	3.00	6.00
❏ 0472	Too Many Memories/With Meaning	1973	—	3.00	6.00
❏ 0480	I Never Get Through Missing You/Lady Lover	1974	—	3.00	6.00
❏ 0502	Let Me Take Care of You/Where Happiness Is	1975	—	3.00	6.00
❏ 7503	It's So Nice to Be with You/(B-side unknown)	1975	—	3.00	6.00
CAPRICORN					
❏ 0318	She's Been Keeping Me Up Nights/I Keep Falling in Love with You	1979	—	2.50	5.00
❏ 0331	Love Won't Be Love Without You/This Is a Man and Woman Kind of Night	1979	—	2.50	5.00
GRT					
❏ 007	Lady Lover/I Never Get Through Missing You	1974	—	3.00	6.00
❏ 008	I See Love/Your Love	1974	—	3.00	6.00
HME					
❏ 04853	Love Is An Overload/Treat Her Like a Stranger	1985	—	2.00	4.00
RPA					
❏ 7603	For Your Love/(B-side unknown)	1976	—	3.00	6.00
❏ 7613	I'm Getting High Remembering/With Meaning	1976	—	3.00	6.00
❏ 7622	What a Diff'rence a Day Made/I Can Feel It	1977	—	3.00	6.00
UNITED ARTISTS					
❏ 842	Everybody's Baby/Perfect Example of a Fool	1965	2.50	5.00	10.00
❏ 920	Why Me/Six Days a Week, Twice on Sunday	1965	2.50	5.00	10.00
❏ 50009	You Remind Me Of Myself/I Hope You Find in Him What You Were Looking for in Me	1966	2.00	4.00	8.00
❏ 50067	How Long Has It Been/Easy to Say, Hard to Do	1966	2.00	4.00	8.00
❏ 50133	Two of the Usual/ Your B.A.B.Y. Baby Don't Love You	1967	2.00	4.00	8.00
❏ 50161	Love Me and Make It All Better/My Tears Don't Care (They Fall Anywhere)	1967	2.00	4.00	8.00
❏ 50208	I Doubt It/Laughing Girl, She's Not Happy	1967	2.00	4.00	8.00
❏ 50263	Ordinary Miracle/These Are Things I Miss	1968	2.00	4.00	8.00
❏ 50327	From Heaven to Heartache/Only for Me	1968	2.00	4.00	8.00
❏ 50476	Each and Every Part of Me/ My (Is Such a Lonely Word)	1969	2.00	4.00	8.00
❏ 50528	Til Something Better Comes Along/ I'm Only a Man	1969	2.00	4.00	8.00
❏ 50573	Things for You and I/Somebody Lied to Me	1969	2.00	4.00	8.00
❏ 50620	I'm Going Home/I May Never Be Free	1969	2.00	4.00	8.00
❏ 50668	Hello Mary Lou/Love, Wonderful Love	1970	—	3.50	7.00
❏ 50719	Simple Days and Simple Ways/Love's Garden	1970	—	3.50	7.00

Number	Title (A Side/B Side)	Yr	VG	VG+	NM
❏ 50754	Come Sundown/He Gives Us All His Love	1971	—	3.50	7.00
❏ 50791	If I Had You/Doggone This Heartache	1971	—	3.50	7.00
❏ 50850	Today's Teardrops/Love's Satisfaction	1971	—	3.50	7.00
❏ 50885	Only Love Can Break a Heart/ We Ran Out of Time	1972	—	3.50	7.00
Albums					
ACE OF HEARTS					
❏ 1002	Too Many Memories	1974	3.75	7.50	15.00
RPA					
❏ 1002	Portrait in Love	1976	2.50	5.00	10.00
❏ 1013	Soul Full of Music	1977	2.50	5.00	10.00
UNITED ARTISTS					
❏ UAL-3582 [M]	How Long Has It Been	1967	6.25	12.50	25.00
❏ UAS-6582 [S]	How Long Has It Been	1967	6.25	12.50	25.00
❏ UAS-6616	A World of Love from Bobby Lewis	1967	5.00	10.00	20.00
❏ UAS-6629	An Ordinary Miracle	1968	5.00	10.00	20.00
❏ UAS-6673	From Heaven to Heartache	1968	5.00	10.00	20.00
❏ UAS-6717	Thanks for You and I	1969	5.00	10.00	20.00
❏ UAS-6760	The Best of Bobby Lewis, Vol. 1	1970	3.75	7.50	15.00

LEWIS, CLARENCE
45s

Number	Title (A Side/B Side)	Yr	VG	VG+	NM
FURY					
❏ 1032	Cupid's Little Helper/Half a Heart	1960	3.75	7.50	15.00
RED ROBIN					
❏ 136	Lost Everything/ Your Heart Must Be Made of Stone	1955	20.00	40.00	80.00

LEWIS, EARL, AND THE CHANNELS See THE CHANNELS.

LEWIS, GARY, AND THE PLAYBOYS
45s

Number	Title (A Side/B Side)	Yr	VG	VG+	NM
EPIC					
❏ 50068	One Good Woman/Ooh Baby	1975	2.00	4.00	8.00
—Gary Lewis solo					
LIBERTY					
❏ (no #) [DJ]	Way Way Out (same on both sides)	1967	125.00	250.00	500.00
❏ 65-227	Doin' the Flake//This Diamond Ring/Little Miss Go-Go	1965	6.25	12.50	25.00
—Record available from mail order from Kellogg's Corn Flakes; all copies have black labels with silver print					
❏ 65-227 [PS]	Doin' the Flake//This Diamond Ring/ Little Miss Go-Go	1965	12.50	25.00	50.00
—Kellogg's Corn Flakes giveaway					
❏ 55756	This Diamond Ring/Tijuana Wedding	1964	2.50	5.00	10.00
❏ 55756	This Diamond Ring/Hard to Find	1964	3.00	6.00	12.00
❏ 55778	Count Me In/Little Miss Go-Go	1965	2.50	5.00	10.00
❏ 55809	Save Your Heart for Me/ Without a Word of Warning	1965	2.50	5.00	10.00
❏ 55818	Everybody Loves a Clown/Time Stands Still	1965	2.50	5.00	10.00
❏ 55818 [PS]	Everybody Loves a Clown/Time Stands Still	1965	3.75	7.50	15.00
❏ 55846	She's Just My Style/ I Won't Make That Mistake Again	1965	2.50	5.00	10.00
❏ 55846 [PS]	She's Just My Style/ I Won't Make That Mistake Again	1965	3.75	7.50	15.00
❏ 55865	Sure Gonna Miss Her/ I Don't Wanna Say Goodnight	1966	2.50	5.00	10.00
❏ 55865 [PS]	Sure Gonna Miss Her/ I Don't Wanna Say Goodnight	1966	3.75	7.50	15.00
❏ 55880	Green Grass/I Can Read Between the Lines	1966	2.50	5.00	10.00
❏ 55880 [PS]	Green Grass/I Can Read Between the Lines	1966	3.75	7.50	15.00
❏ 55898	My Heart's Symphony/Tina	1966	2.50	5.00	10.00
❏ 55898 [PS]	My Heart's Symphony/Tina	1966	3.75	7.50	15.00
❏ 55914	(You Don't Have to) Paint Me a Picture/ Looking for the Stars	1966	2.50	5.00	10.00
❏ 55914 [PS]	(You Don't Have to) Paint Me a Picture/ Looking for the Stars	1966	3.75	7.50	15.00
❏ 55932	Down on the Sloop John B/Ice Melts in the Sun	1966	—	—	—
—Unreleased					
❏ 55933	Where Will the Words Come From/ May the Best Man Win	1966	2.50	5.00	10.00
❏ 55949	The Loser (With a Broken Heart)/ Ice Melts in the Sun	1967	2.50	5.00	10.00
❏ 55949 [PS]	The Loser (With a Broken Heart)/ Ice Melts in the Sun	1967	3.75	7.50	15.00
❏ 55971	Girls in Love/Let's Be More Than Friends	1967	2.00	4.00	8.00
❏ 55985	Jill/New in Town	1967	2.00	4.00	8.00
❏ 56011	Has She Got the Nicest Eyes/Happiness	1967	2.00	4.00	8.00
❏ 56037	Sealed with a Kiss/Sara Jane	1968	2.00	4.00	8.00
❏ 56075	C.C. Rider/Main Street	1968	—	3.00	6.00
❏ 56093	Every Day I Have to Cry Some/Mister Memory	1969	—	3.00	6.00
❏ 56093	Rhythm of the Rain/Mister Memory	1969	—	3.00	6.00
❏ 56121	Hayride/Gary's Groove	1969	—	3.00	6.00
❏ 56144	I Saw Elvis Presley Last Night/ Something Is Wrong	1969	3.00	6.00	12.00
❏ 56158	Great Balls of Fire/I'm On the Road Right Now	1970	—	3.00	6.00
SCEPTER					
❏ 12359	Peace of Mind/Then Again Maybe	1972	2.00	4.00	8.00
—Gary Lewis solo					
UNITED ARTISTS					
❏ 0064	This Diamond Ring/My Heart's Symphony	1973	—	2.00	4.00
❏ 0065	Count Me In/Save Your Heart for Me	1973	—	2.00	4.00
❏ 0066	Everybody Loves a Clown/Sure Gonna Miss Her	1973	—	2.00	4.00
❏ 0067	She's Just My Style/Green Grass	1973	—	2.00	4.00
—0064 through 0067 are "Silver Spotlight Series" reissues					
Albums					
LIBERTY					
❏ LM-1003	This Diamond Ring	1981	2.00	4.00	8.00
—Reissue of United Artists 1008					
❏ LRP-3408 [M]	This Diamond Ring	1965	5.00	10.00	20.00
❏ LRP-3419 [M]	A Session with Gary Lewis and the Playboys	1965	5.00	10.00	20.00
❏ LRP-3428 [M]	Everybody Loves a Clown	1965	5.00	10.00	20.00
❏ LRP-3435 [M]	She's Just My Style	1966	3.75	7.50	15.00
❏ LRP-3452 [M]	Hits Again!	1966	3.75	7.50	15.00
❏ LRP-3468 [M]	Golden Greats	1966	3.75	7.50	15.00
❏ LRP-3487 [M]	(You Don't Have to) Paint Me a Picture	1967	3.75	7.50	15.00
—Side 1 plays as listed					

L

Number	Title (A Side/B Side)	Yr	VG	VG+	NM
❑ LRP-3487 [M]	(You Don't Have to) Paint Me a Picture	1967	5.00	10.00	20.00
—Side 1, Song 4 claims to be "Tina" but plays "Ice Melts in the Sun"					
❑ LRP-3519 [M]	New Directions	1967	3.75	7.50	15.00
❑ LRP-3524 [M]	Listen	1967	3.75	7.50	15.00
❑ LST-7408 [S]	This Diamond Ring	1965	6.25	12.50	25.00
❑ LST-7419 [S]	A Session with Gary Lewis and the Playboys	1965	6.25	12.50	25.00
❑ LST-7428 [S]	Everybody Loves a Clown	1965	6.25	12.50	25.00
❑ LST-7435 [S]	She's Just My Style	1966	5.00	10.00	20.00
❑ LST-7452 [S]	Hits Again!	1966	5.00	10.00	20.00
❑ LST-7468 [S]	Golden Greats	1966	5.00	10.00	20.00
—Side 2 plays as listed					
❑ LST-7468 [S]	Golden Greats	1966	7.50	15.00	30.00
—Side 2, Song 2 claims to be "I Won't Make That Mistake Again" but it plays "You've Got to Hide Your Love Away"					
❑ LST-7487 [S]	(You Don't Have to) Paint Me a Picture	1967	5.00	10.00	20.00
—Side 1 plays as listed					
❑ LST-7487 [S]	(You Don't Have to) Paint Me a Picture	1967	6.25	12.50	25.00
—Side 1, Song 4 claims to be "Tina" but plays "Ice Melts in the Sun"					
❑ LST-7519 [S]	New Directions	1967	3.75	7.50	15.00
❑ LST-7524 [S]	Listen	1967	3.75	7.50	15.00
❑ LST-7568	Gary Lewis Now!	1968	3.75	7.50	15.00
❑ LST-7589	More Golden Greats	1968	3.75	7.50	15.00
❑ LST-7606	Close Cover Before Playing	1969	3.75	7.50	15.00
❑ LST-7623	Rhythm of the Rain	1969	3.75	7.50	15.00
❑ LST-7633	I'm On the Right Road Now	1970	3.75	7.50	15.00
❑ LN-10241	Golden Greats	198?	2.00	4.00	8.00
—Budget-line reissue					
RHINO					
❑ RNLP-163	Greatest Hits (1965-1968)	1985	2.50	5.00	10.00
SUNSET					
❑ SUM-1168 [M]	Gary Lewis and the Playboys	1967	3.00	6.00	12.00
❑ SUS-5168 [S]	Gary Lewis and the Playboys	1967	3.00	6.00	12.00
❑ SUS-5262	Rhythm!	1969	3.00	6.00	12.00
UNITED ARTISTS					
❑ UA-LA430-E	The Very Best of Gary Lewis and the Playboys	1975	2.50	5.00	10.00
❑ LM-1003	This Diamond Ring	1980	2.50	5.00	10.00
—Edited reissue of Liberty 7408					

LEWIS, HERMAN
45s
STONE BLUE

Number	Title (A Side/B Side)	Yr	VG	VG+	NM
❑ 101	Who's Kissing You Tonite/(B-side unknown)	196?	1000.	1750.	2500.

LEWIS, JERRY Also see DEAN MARTIN.
45s
CAPITOL

Number	Title (A Side/B Side)	Yr	VG	VG+	NM
❑ F1045	I'm a Little Busybody/Sunday Driving	1950	5.00	10.00	20.00
❑ F1385	The Navy Gets the Gravy/Pa-Pa-Pa Polka	1951	3.75	7.50	15.00
❑ F1482	A-Hunting We Will Go/Never Been Kissed	1951	3.75	7.50	15.00
❑ F1740	I Like It, I Like It/I'll Tell a Policeman on You	1951	3.75	7.50	15.00
❑ F1868	I Love Girls/Lay Something on the Bar	1951	3.75	7.50	15.00
❑ F1969	The Book Was So Much Better Than the Picture/ North Dakota, South Dakota	1952	3.75	7.50	15.00
❑ F2141	Crazy Words/I Can't Carry a Tune	1952	3.75	7.50	15.00
❑ F2202	They Go Wild, Simply Wild Over Me/ I Keep Her Picture Hanging	1952	3.75	7.50	15.00
❑ F2317	I've Had a Very Merry Christmas/ Strictly for the Birds	1952	5.00	10.00	20.00
❑ F2481	If You Love Me Truly/ Little Man You've Had a Busy Day	1953	3.75	7.50	15.00
—With Patti Lewis					
❑ F2576	Give Me a Little Kiss, Will Ya Huh/Yyyup	1953	3.75	7.50	15.00
DECCA					
❑ 30124	Rock-a-Bye Your Baby with a Dixie Melody/ Come Rain or Come Shine	1956	3.00	6.00	12.00
❑ 30263	Let Me Sing and I'm Happy/It All Depends on You	1957	2.50	5.00	10.00
❑ 30345	My Mammy/With These Hands	1957	2.50	5.00	10.00
❑ 30370	By Myself/No One	1957	2.50	5.00	10.00
❑ 30503	Sad Sack/The Lord Loves a Laughing Man	1957	2.50	5.00	10.00
❑ 30607	Long Black Nylons/Back to Kenya	1958	2.50	5.00	10.00
❑ 30664	Dormi-Dormi-Dormi/Love Is a Lonely Thing	1958	2.50	5.00	10.00
❑ 30808	Song from "The Geisha Boy"/The More I See	1959	2.50	5.00	10.00
❑ 31019	Makin' Whoopee/Have a Girl, Have a Boy	1959	2.50	5.00	10.00
❑ 31115	Smile/Everything's Coming Up Roses	1960	2.00	4.00	8.00
❑ 31400	My Mammy/Let Me Sing and I'm Happy	1962	2.00	4.00	8.00
DOT					
❑ 16164	Somebody/Turn It On	1960	2.00	4.00	8.00
❑ 16772	Green, Green/I'll See Your Light	1965	—	3.00	6.00
—As "The Jerry Lewis Singers"					
LIBERTY					
❑ 55633	Kids/Witchcraft	1963	2.00	4.00	8.00

7-Inch Extended Plays
DECCA

Number	Title (A Side/B Side)	Yr	VG	VG+	NM
❑ ED 2455	Jerry Lewis Just Sings, Vol. 1	1957	3.75	7.50	15.00
❑ ED 2455 [PS]	Come Rain or Come Shine/Shine On Your Shoes//How Long Has This Been Going On/ Get Happy	1957	3.75	7.50	15.00
❑ ED 2456	(contents unknown)	1957	3.75	7.50	15.00
❑ ED 2456 [PS]	Jerry Lewis Just Sings, Vol. 2	1957	3.75	7.50	15.00
❑ ED 2457	Birth of the Blues/Bye Bye Baby//Back in Your Own Backyard/Sometimes I'm Happy	1957	3.75	7.50	15.00
❑ ED 2457 [PS]	Jerry Lewis Just Sings, Vol. 3	1957	3.75	7.50	15.00

Albums
DECCA

Number	Title (A Side/B Side)	Yr	VG	VG+	NM
❑ DL 8410 [M]	Jerry Lewis Just Sings	1956	15.00	30.00	60.00
❑ DL 8595 [M]	More Jerry Lewis	1957	15.00	30.00	60.00
❑ DL 8936 [M]	Big Songs for Little People	1959	12.50	25.00	50.00
❑ DL 78936 [S]	Big Songs for Little People	1959	15.00	30.00	60.00
DOT					
❑ DLP 3664 [M]	The Jerry Lewis Singers	1964	3.75	7.50	15.00
❑ DLP 25664 [S]	The Jerry Lewis Singers	1964	5.00	10.00	20.00

LEWIS, JERRY LEE
45s
ELEKTRA

Number	Title (A Side/B Side)	Yr	VG	VG+	NM
❑ 46030	Rockin' My Life Away/ I Wish I Was Eighteen Again	1979	—	2.00	4.00

Number	Title (A Side/B Side)	Yr	VG	VG+	NM
❑ 46067	Who Will the Next Fool Be/Rita May	1979	—	2.00	4.00
❑ 46591	When Two Worlds Collide/ Good News Travels Fast	1980	—	2.00	4.00
❑ 46642	Honky Tonk Stuff/Rockin' Jerry Lee	1980	—	2.00	4.00
❑ 47026	Over the Rainbow/Folsom Prison Blues	1980	—	2.00	4.00
❑ 47095	Thirty-Nine and Holding/Change Places with Me	1980	—	2.00	4.00
❑ 69962	I'd Do It All Again/Who Will Buy the Wine	1982	—	2.00	4.00
MCA					
❑ 52151	My Fingers Do the Talkin'/Forever Forgiving	1983	—	—	3.00
❑ 52188	Come As You Were/Circumstantial Evidence	1983	—	—	3.00
❑ 52233	She Sings Amazing Grace/ Why You Been Gone So Long	1983	—	—	3.00
❑ 52369	I Am What I Am/That Was the Way It Was Then	1984	—	—	3.00
MERCURY					
❑ 55011	Middle Age Crazy/Georgia on My Mind	1977	—	3.00	6.00
❑ 55021	Come On In/Who's Sorry Now	1977	—	3.00	6.00
❑ 55028	I'll Find It Where I Can/ Don't Let the Stars Get In Your Eyes	1977	—	3.00	6.00
❑ 73099	There Must Be More to Love Than This/ Home Away from Home	1970	2.00	4.00	8.00
❑ 73155	I Can't Have a Merry Christmas, Mary (Without You)/In Loving Memories	1970	2.50	5.00	10.00
❑ 73192	Touching Home/Woman, Woman	1971	2.00	4.00	8.00
❑ 73227	When He Walks on You (Like You Have Walked on Me)/Foolish Kind of Man	1971	2.00	4.00	8.00
❑ 73248	Would You Take Another Chance on Me/ Me and Bobby McGee	1971	2.00	4.00	8.00
❑ 73273	Chantilly Lace/Think About It Darlin'	1972	2.00	4.00	8.00
❑ 73296	Lonely Weekends/Turn On Your Love Light	1972	2.00	4.00	8.00
❑ 73328	Who's Gonna Play This Old Piano/ No Honky Tonks in Heaven	1972	2.00	4.00	8.00
❑ 73361	No More Hanging On/Mercy of a Letter	1973	2.00	4.00	8.00
❑ 73374	Drinking Wine Spo-Dee O'Dee/ Rock and Roll Medley	1973	2.00	4.00	8.00
❑ 73402	No Headstone on My Grave/Jack Daniels	1973	2.00	4.00	8.00
❑ 73423	Sometimes a Memory Ain't Enough/ I Think I Need to Pray	1973	2.00	4.00	8.00
❑ 73452	I'm Left, You're Right, She's Gone/ I've Fallen to the Bottom	1974	2.00	4.00	8.00
❑ 73462	Meat Man/Just a Little Bit	1974	2.00	4.00	8.00
❑ 73491	Tell Tale Signs/Cold, Cold Morning Light	1974	2.00	4.00	8.00
❑ 73618	He Can't Fill My Shoes/ Tomorrow's Taking Baby Away	1974	—	3.00	6.00
❑ 73661	I Can Still Hear the Music in the Restroom/ Remember Me	1975	—	3.00	6.00
❑ 73685	Boogie Woogie Country Man/ I'm Still Jealous of You	1975	—	3.00	6.00
❑ 73729	A Damn Good Country Song/ When I Take My Vacation in Heaven	1975	—	3.00	6.00
❑ 73763	Don't Boogie Woogie/That Kind of Fool	1976	—	3.00	6.00
❑ 73822	Let's Put It Back Together Again/Jerry Lee's Rock and Roll Revival Show	1976	—	3.00	6.00
❑ 73872	The Closest Thing to You/You Belong to Me	1976	—	3.00	6.00
❑ 76148	I'm So Lonesome I Could Cry/ Pick Me Up on Your Way Down	1982	—	2.50	5.00
PHILLIPS INT'L.					
❑ 3559	In the Mood/I Get the Blues When It Rains	1960	12.50	25.00	50.00
—As "The Hawk"					
POLYDOR					
❑ 889312-7	Breathless/Great Balls of Fire	1989	—	2.00	4.00
❑ 889312-7 [PS]	Breathless/Great Balls of Fire	1989	—	2.00	4.00
❑ 889798-7	Crazy Arms/Great Balls of Fire	1989	—	2.00	4.00
SCR					
❑ 386	Get Out Your Big Roll, Daddy/Honky Tonkin' Rock 'N' Roll Piano Man	1985	—	2.50	5.00
SIRE					
❑ 19809	It Was the Whiskey Talkin' (Not Me)/same (Rock and Roll Version)	1990	—	—	3.00
❑ 64423	Goose Bumps/Crown Victoria 51	1995	—	2.50	5.00
SMASH					
❑ 1857	Pen and Paper/Hit the Road Jack	1963	3.75	7.50	15.00
❑ 1886	I'm on Fire/Bread and Butter Man	1964	10.00	20.00	40.00
❑ 1906	She Was My Baby (He Was My Friend)/The Hole He Said He'd Dig for Me	1964	3.75	7.50	15.00
❑ 1930	High Heel Sneakers/ You Went Back on Your Word	1964	3.75	7.50	15.00
❑ 1969	Baby Hold Me Close/I Believe in You	1965	3.75	7.50	15.00
❑ 1992	This Must Be the Place/Rocking Pneumonia and the Boogie Woogie Flu	1965	3.75	7.50	15.00
❑ 2006	Green, Green Grass of Home/ You've Got What It Takes	1965	3.75	7.50	15.00
❑ 2027	Sticks and Stones/What a Heck of a Mess	1966	3.00	6.00	12.00
❑ 2053	If I Had It All to Do Over/Memphis Beat	1966	3.00	6.00	12.00
❑ 2103	Holding On/It's a Hang-Up, Baby	1967	3.00	6.00	12.00
❑ 2122	Turn On Your Love Light/Shotgun Man	1967	3.00	6.00	12.00
❑ 2146	Another Place, Another Time/Walking the Floor Over You	1968	2.50	5.00	10.00
❑ 2164	What's Made Milwaukee Famous (Has Made a Loser Out of Me)/All the Good Is Gone	1968	2.50	5.00	10.00
❑ 2186	She Still Comes Around (To Love What's Left of Me)/Slipping Around	1968	2.50	5.00	10.00
❑ 2202	To Make Love Sweeter for You/ Let's Talk About Us	1968	2.50	5.00	10.00
❑ 2224	One Has My Name (The Other Has My Heart)/I Can't Stop Loving You	1969	2.50	5.00	10.00
❑ 2244	She Even Woke Me Up to Say Goodbye/Echoes	1969	2.50	5.00	10.00
❑ 2257	Once More with Feeling/You Went Out of Your Way (To Walk on Me)	1970	2.50	5.00	10.00
❑ 884934-7	Sixteen Candles/Rock and Roll (Fais-Do-Do)	1986	—	2.00	4.00
—B-side with Roy Orbison, Carl Perkins and Johnny Cash					
❑ 888142-7	We Remember the King/Class of '55	1987	—	2.00	4.00
—With Johnny Cash, Roy Orbison and Carl Perkins; B-side by Carl Perkins solo					
SUN					
❑ 259	Crazy Arms/End of the Road	1957	12.50	25.00	50.00
—As "Jerry Lee Lewis and His Pumping Piano"					
❑ 259	Crazy Arms/End of the Road	1957	25.00	50.00	100.00
—As "Jerry Lee Lewis"					

Frankie Laine, *Frankie Laine Favorites,* Columbia B-1685, 7-inch
EP, $20-$40 (cover and record together).

Led Zeppelin, *Houses of the Holy,* Atlantic SD 7255, stereo LP,
with "1841 Broadway" address on label, $6-$12.

Brenda Lee, "Fool #1," Decca 31309, picture sleeve,
$15-$30.

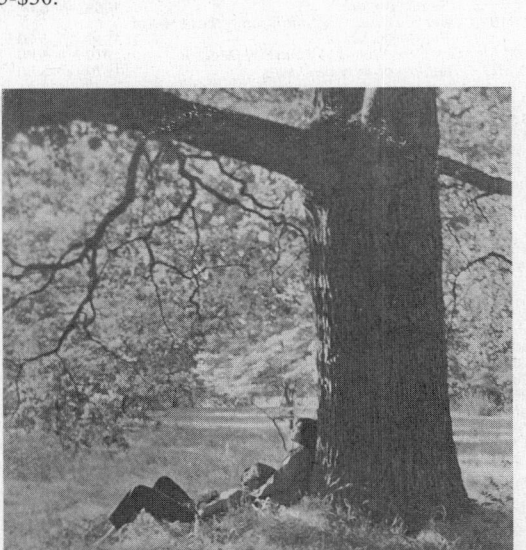

Tom Lehrer, *Songs by Tom Lehrer,* Lehrer TLEP-1, 7-inch
EP set, $65-$130 (cover and both records together).

John Lennon, *John Lennon Plastic Ono Band,* Apple SW-
3372, stereo LP, $10-$20.

Jerry Lee Lewis, "High School Confidential," Sun 296,
picture sleeve, $40-$80.

L

Number	Title (A Side/B Side)	Yr	VG	VG+	NM
❏ 267	Whole Lot of Shakin' Going On/It'll Be Me	1957	10.00	20.00	40.00
❏ 281	Great Balls of Fire/You Win Again	1957	10.00	20.00	40.00
❏ 281 [PS]	Great Balls of Fire/You Win Again	1957	20.00	40.00	80.00
❏ 288	Breathless/Down the Line	1958	10.00	20.00	40.00
❏ 296	High School Confidential/Fools Like Me	1958	7.50	15.00	30.00
❏ 296 [PS]	High School Confidential/Fools Like Me	1958	20.00	40.00	80.00
❏ 301	Lewis Boogie/The Return of Jerry Lee	1958	7.50	15.00	30.00
—B-side by George and Louis					
❏ 303	I'll Make It All Up to You/Break-Up	1958	6.25	12.50	30.00
❏ 312	I'll Sail My Ship Alone/It Hurt Me So	1958	6.25	12.50	25.00
❏ 317	Lovin' Up a Storm/Big Blon' Baby	1959	6.25	12.50	25.00
❏ 324	Let's Talk About Us/Ballad of Billy Joe	1959	6.25	12.50	25.00
❏ 330	Little Queenie/I Could Never Be Ashamed of You	1959	6.25	12.50	25.00
❏ 337	Old Black Joe/Baby Baby, Bye Bye	1960	5.00	10.00	20.00
❏ 344	Hang Up My Rock and Roll Shoes/John Henry	1960	5.00	10.00	20.00
❏ 352	Love Made a Fool of Me/When I Get Paid	1960	5.00	10.00	20.00
❏ 356	What'd I Say/Livin' Lovin' Wreck	1961	5.00	10.00	20.00
❏ 364	Cold, Cold Heart/It Won't Happen with Me	1961	5.00	10.00	20.00
❏ 367	Save the Last Dance for Me/As Long As I Live	1961	5.00	10.00	20.00
❏ 371	Money/Bonnie B	1961	5.00	10.00	20.00
❏ 374	I've Been Twistin'/Ramblin' Rose	1962	5.00	10.00	20.00
❏ 379	Sweet Little Sixteen/How's My Ex Treating You	1962	5.00	10.00	20.00
❏ 382	Good Golly Miss Molly/I Can't Trust You	1962	5.00	10.00	20.00
❏ 384	Teenage Letter/Seasons of My Heart	1963	5.00	10.00	20.00
❏ 396	Carry Me Back to Old Virginny/				
	I Know What It Means	1965	5.00	10.00	20.00
❏ 1101	Invitation to Your Party/				
	I Could Never Be Ashamed of You	1969	—	3.00	6.00
❏ 1107	One Minute Past Eternity/Frankie and Johnny	1969	—	3.00	6.00
❏ 1115	I Can't Seem to Say Goodbye/Goodnight Irene	1970	—	2.50	5.00
❏ 1119	Waiting for the Train (All Around the Watertank)/				
	Big Legged Woman	1970	—	2.50	5.00
❏ 1125	Love on Broadway/Matchbox	1971	—	2.50	5.00
❏ 1128	Your Loving Ways/				
	I Can't Trust Me in Your Arms Anymore	1972	—	2.50	5.00
❏ 1130	Good Rockin' Tonight/I Can't Trust Me in Your				
	Arms Anymore	1973	—	2.50	5.00
❏ 1138	Matchbox/Am I to Be the One	1978	—	2.00	4.00
❏ 1139	Save the Last Dance for Me/Am I to Be the One	1978	—	2.00	4.00
—With uncredited "duet" partner, actually Orion (Jimmy Ellis); a shameless attempt to concoct a "lost Elvis Presley duet"					
❏ 1141	Cold, Cold Heart/Hello Josephine	1979	—	2.00	4.00
❏ 1151	Be-Bop-a-Lula/The Breakup	1980	—	2.00	4.00
—B-side by Charlie Rich; both sides are duets with Orion					

7-Inch Extended Plays

SUN

Number	Title (A Side/B Side)	Yr	VG	VG+	NM
❏ EPA-107	Mean Woman Blues/I'm Feelin' Sorry//Whole				
	Lot of Shakin' Goin' On/Turn Around	1958	20.00	30.00	80.00
❏ EPA-107 [PS]	The Great Ball of Fire	1958	20.00	30.00	80.00
❏ EP-108	One Minute Past Eternity/Cold, Cold Heart/				
	Invitation to Your Party// I Can't Trust Me in				
	Your Arms Anymore//How's My Ex Treating				
	You//Ramblin' Rose	197?	5.00	10.00	20.00
—Jukebox issue; small hole, plays at 33 1/3 rpm					
❏ EP-108 [PS]	The Golden Cream of the Country	197?	5.00	10.00	20.00
—Part of "Little LP" series (LLP #155)					
❏ EPA-108	Don't Be Cruel/Goodnight Irene//Put Me Down/				
	It All Depends	1958	12.50	25.00	50.00
❏ EPA-108 [PS]	Jerry Lee Lewis	1958	12.50	25.00	50.00
❏ EPA-109	Ubangi Stomp/Crazy Arms//Jambalaya/Fools				
	Like Me	1958	12.50	25.00	50.00
❏ EPA-109 [PS]	Jerry Lee Lewis	1958	12.50	25.00	50.00
❏ EPA-110	High School Confidential/When the Saints Go				
	Marching In//Matchbox/It'll Be Me	1958	12.50	25.00	50.00
❏ EPA-110 [PS]	Jerry Lee Lewis	1958	12.50	25.00	50.00
❏ EP-114	You Win Again/I Can't Seem to Say Goodbye/				
	Am I to Be the One//As Long As I Live/I Love				
	You So Much It Hurts/Night Train to Memphis	197?			
—Jukebox issue; small hole, plays at 33 1/3 rpm					
❏ EP-114 [PS]	A Taste of Country	197?	5.00	10.00	20.00

Albums

ACCORD

Number	Title (A Side/B Side)	Yr	VG	VG+	NM
❏ SN-7133	I Walk the Line	1981	2.50	5.00	10.00

DESIGN

| ❏ DLP-165 [M] | Rockin' with Jerry Lee Lewis | 1963 | 6.25 | 12.50 | 25.00 |
| ❏ DST-165 [R] | Rockin' with Jerry Lee Lewis | 1963 | 5.00 | 10.00 | 20.00 |

ELEKTRA

❏ 6E-184	Jerry Lee Lewis	1979	3.00	6.00	12.00
❏ 6E-254	When Two Worlds Collide	1980	3.00	6.00	12.00
❏ 6E-291	Killer Country	1980	3.00	6.00	12.00
❏ 60191	The Best of Jerry Lee Lewis				
	Featuring 39 and Holding	1982	2.50	5.00	10.00

HILLTOP

❏ 6102	Sunday After Church	1971	2.50	5.00	10.00
❏ 6110	Roll Over Beethoven	1972	2.50	5.00	10.00
❏ 6120	Rural Route #1	1972	2.50	5.00	10.00

MCA

| ❏ 5387 | My Fingers Do the Talkin' | 1983 | 2.50 | 5.00 | 10.00 |
| ❏ 5478 | I Am What I Am | 1984 | 2.50 | 5.00 | 10.00 |

MERCURY

❏ SRM-1-637	The "Killer" Rocks On	1972	3.75	7.50	15.00
❏ SRM-1-677	Sometimes a Memory Ain't Enough	1973	3.75	7.50	15.00
❏ 690 [DJ]	A Jerry Lee Lewis Radio Special	1973	12.50	25.00	50.00
❏ SRM-1-690	Southern Roots — Back Home to Memphis	1973	3.75	7.50	15.00
❏ SRM-1-710	I-40 Country	1974	3.75	7.50	15.00
❏ SRM-2-803 [(2)]	The Session	1973	5.00	10.00	20.00
❏ SRM-1-1030	Boogie Woogie Country Man	1975	3.75	7.50	15.00
❏ SRM-1-1064	Odd Man In	1975	3.75	7.50	15.00
❏ SRM-1-1109	Country Class	1976	3.75	7.50	15.00
❏ SRM-1-5004	Country Memories	1977	3.75	7.50	15.00
❏ SRM-1-5006	The Best of Jerry Lee Lewis Volume II	1978	3.75	7.50	15.00
❏ SRM-1-5010	Jerry Lee Lewis Keeps Rockin'	1978	3.75	7.50	15.00
❏ SR-61278	Live at the International, Las Vegas	1970	3.75	7.50	15.00
❏ SR-61318	In Loving Memories	1970	7.50	15.00	30.00
❏ SR-61323	There Must Be More to Love Than This	1971	3.75	7.50	15.00

Number	Title (A Side/B Side)	Yr	VG	VG+	NM
❏ SR-61343	Touching Home	1971	3.75	7.50	15.00
—With photo of Jerry Lee in front of a brick wall					
❏ SR-61343	Touching Home	1971	5.00	10.00	20.00
—With drawing on cover and small photo of Jerry Lee					
❏ SR-61364	Would You Take Another Chance on Me?	1971	3.75	7.50	15.00
❏ SR-61366	Who's Gonna Play This Old Piano…				
	(Think About It Darlin')	1972	3.75	7.50	15.00
❏ 822789-1	The Best of Jerry Lee Lewis Volume II	198?	2.50	5.00	10.00
❏ 826251-1	Greatest Hits	198?	2.50	5.00	10.00
❏ 830399-1	Would You Take Another Chance on Me	1987	2.50	5.00	10.00
—Reissue of 61346					
❏ 836935-1	Killer: The Mercury Years Volume One,				
	1963-1968	1989	3.00	6.00	12.00
❏ 836938-1	Killer: The Mercury Years Volume Two,				
	1969-1972	1989	3.00	6.00	12.00
❏ 836941-1	Killer: The Mercury Years Volume Three,				
	1973-1977	1989	3.00	6.00	12.00

PAIR

| ❏ PDL2-1132 [(2)] | Solid Gold | 1986 | 3.00 | 6.00 | 12.00 |

PICKWICK

❏ PTP-2055 [(2)]	Jerry Lee Lewis	1973	3.00	6.00	12.00
❏ SPC-3224	High Heel Sneakers	1970	2.50	5.00	10.00
❏ SPC-3344	Drinking Wine Spo-Dee-O-Dee	1973	2.50	5.00	10.00

POLYDOR

| ❏ 826139-1 | I'm on Fire | 1985 | 2.50 | 5.00 | 10.00 |
| ❏ 839516-1 | Great Balls of Fire! | 1989 | 3.00 | 6.00 | 12.00 |

POWER PAK

| ❏ 247 | From the Vaults of Sun | 1974 | 2.50 | 5.00 | 10.00 |

RHINO

❏ RNDF-255 [PD]	Original Sun Greatest Hits	1983	3.75	7.50	15.00
❏ RNDA-1499 [(2)]	Milestones	1985	3.75	7.50	15.00
❏ R1-70255	Original Sun Greatest Hits	1989	2.50	5.00	10.00
—Reissue of 255 on black vinyl					
❏ R1-70656	Jerry Lee Lewis	1989	3.00	6.00	12.00
—Reissue of Sun 1230					
❏ R1-70657	Jerry Lee's Greatest	1989	3.00	6.00	12.00
—Reissue of Sun 1265					
❏ R1-70899	Wild One: Rare Tracks from Jerry Lee Lewis	1989	3.00	6.00	12.00
❏ R1-71499 [(2)]	Milestones	1989	3.00	6.00	12.00
—Reissue of 1499					

SEARS

| ❏ SPS-610 | Hound Dog | 1970 | 6.25 | 12.50 | 25.00 |

SMASH

❏ SL-17001	Golden Hits	1980	3.00	6.00	12.00
❏ MGS-27040 [M]	The Golden Hits of Jerry Lee Lewis	1964	6.25	12.50	25.00
❏ MGS-27056 [M]	The Greatest Live Show on Earth	1964	25.00	50.00	100.00
❏ MGS-27063 [M]	The Return of Rock	1965	7.50	15.00	30.00
❏ MGS-27071 [M]	Country Songs for City Folks	1965	6.25	12.50	25.00
❏ MGS-27079 [M]	Memphis Beat	1966	6.25	12.50	25.00
❏ MGS-27086 [M]	By Request — More of the Greatest Live				
	Show on Earth	1966	7.50	15.00	30.00
❏ MGS-27097 [M]	Soul My Way	1967	7.50	15.00	30.00
❏ SRS-67040 [S]	The Golden Hits of Jerry Lee Lewis	1964	7.50	15.00	30.00
❏ SRS-67040 [S]	The Golden Rock Hits of Jerry Lee Lewis	1969	3.75	7.50	15.00
—Retitled reissue					
❏ SRS-67056 [S]	The Greatest Live Show on Earth	1964	37.50	75.00	150.00
❏ SRS-67063 [S]	The Return of Rock	1965	10.00	20.00	40.00
❏ SRS-67071 [S]	Country Songs for City Folks	1965	7.50	15.00	30.00
❏ SRS-67071 [S]	All Country	1969	3.75	7.50	15.00
—Retitled reissue					
❏ SRS-67079 [S]	Memphis Beat	1966	7.50	15.00	30.00
❏ SRS-67086 [S]	By Request — More of the Greatest				
	Live Show on Earth	1966	10.00	20.00	40.00
❏ SRS-67097 [S]	Soul My Way	1967	10.00	20.00	40.00
❏ SRS-67104	Another Place Another Time	1968	5.00	10.00	20.00
❏ SRS-67112	She Still Comes Around (To Love What's Left of Me)	1969	5.00	10.00	20.00
❏ SRS-67117	Jerry Lee Lewis Sings the Country Music Hall of				
	Fame Hits, Vol. 1	1969	5.00	10.00	20.00
❏ SRS-67118	Jerry Lee Lewis Sings the Country Music Hall of				
	Fame Hits, Vol. 2	1969	5.00	10.00	20.00
❏ SRS-67128	She Even Woke Me Up to Say Goodbye	1970	5.00	10.00	20.00
❏ SRS-67131	The Best of Jerry Lee Lewis	1970	5.00	10.00	20.00

SUN

❏ LP-102	Original Golden Hits — Volume 1	1969	3.75	7.50	15.00
❏ LP-103	Original Golden Hits — Volume 2	1969	3.75	7.50	15.00
❏ LP-107	Rockin' Rhythm and Blues	1969	3.75	7.50	15.00
❏ SUN-108	The Golden Cream of the Country	1969	3.75	7.50	15.00
❏ SUN-108 [M]	The Golden Cream of the Country	1969	10.00	20.00	40.00
—Mono version is white label promo only; the word "MONO" appears at 9 o'clock on the label					
❏ LP-114	A Taste of Country	1970	3.75	7.50	15.00
❏ LP-121	Ole Tyme Country Music	1971	3.75	7.50	15.00
❏ LP-124	Monsters	1971	3.75	7.50	15.00
❏ LP-128	Original Golden Hits — Volume 3	1972	3.75	7.50	15.00
❏ SUN-145	Roots	1982	3.00	6.00	12.00
❏ 1005	The Original	1978	3.00	6.00	12.00
❏ SUN-1011	Duets	1978	3.75	7.50	15.00
—As "Jerry Lee Lewis and Friends"; gold vinyl					
❏ 1018	Trio +	1979	3.00	6.00	12.00
—With Carl Perkins, Charlie Rich and (uncredited) Orion					
❏ SLP-1230 [M]	Jerry Lee Lewis	1958	50.00	100.00	200.00
❏ SLP-1265 [M]	Jerry Lee's Greatest	1961	62.50	125.00	250.00
❏ SLP-1265 [M]	Jerry Lee's Greatest	1961	200.00	400.00	800.00
—White label promo					

SUNNYVALE

| ❏ 905 | The Sun Story, Vol. 5 | 1977 | 2.50 | 5.00 | 10.00 |

WING

❏ PKW2-125 [(2)]	The Legend of Jerry Lee Lewis	1969	6.25	12.50	25.00
❏ MGW-12340 [M]	The Return of Rock	1967	3.00	6.00	12.00
❏ SRW-16340 [S]	The Return of Rock	1967	3.00	6.00	12.00
❏ SRW-16340	In Demand	1968	2.50	5.00	10.00
❏ SRW-16406	Unlimited	1968	3.00	6.00	12.00

LEWIS, JERRY LEE, AND LINDA GAIL LEWIS

45s

MERCURY

Number	Title (A Side/B Side)	Yr	VG	VG+	NM
❏ 73303	Writing on the Wall/Me and Jesus	1972	—	3.50	7.00

SMASH

| ❏ 2220 | Don't Let Me Cross Over/ | | | | |
| | We Live in Two Different Worlds | 1969 | 2.50 | 5.00 | 10.00 |

Number	Title (A Side/B Side)	Yr	VG	VG+	NM
❏ 2220 [PS]	Don't Let Me Cross Over/				
	We Live in Two Different Worlds	1969	5.00	10.00	20.00
❏ 2254	Roll Over Beethoven/Secret Places	1969	2.50	5.00	10.00

Albums
SMASH

Number	Title (A Side/B Side)	Yr	VG	VG+	NM
❏ SRS-67126	Together	1969	5.00	10.00	20.00

LEWIS, JIMMY, AND THE ELFS
45s
HIT

Number	Title (A Side/B Side)	Yr	VG	VG+	NM
❏ 306	Come Back When You Grow Up/				
	How Can I Be Sure	1967	2.00	4.00	8.00

—B-side by the Olives

Number	Title (A Side/B Side)	Yr	VG	VG+	NM
❏ 312	Keep the Ball Rollin'/An Open Letter to My				
	Teenage Son	1967	2.00	4.00	8.00

—B-side by Bobby Sims

LEWIS, RAMSEY Includes releases by "Ramsey Lewis Trio."
12-Inch Singles
COLUMBIA

Number	Title (A Side/B Side)	Yr	VG	VG+	NM
❏ 05311	This Ain't No Fantasy (Extended with Male)/				
	(Extended with Female)	1985	—	3.00	6.00
❏ 06850	7-11 (Club Mix) (Booster Mix)	1987	—	3.00	6.00
❏ 10937	Aquarius-Let the Sunshine In/				
	Just Can't Give You Up	1979	3.00	6.00	12.00

45s
ARGO

Number	Title (A Side/B Side)	Yr	VG	VG+	NM
❏ 108-S [S]	Scarlet Ribbons/Here 'Tis	1960	5.00	10.00	20.00
❏ 110-S [S]	Solo Para Ti/These Foolish Things	1960	5.00	10.00	20.00
❏ 5303	Black Eyed Peas/Carmen	1958	3.00	6.00	12.00
❏ 5322	Tracy Blues/Delilah	1958	3.00	6.00	12.00
❏ 5344	C.C. Rider/Consider the Source	1959	3.00	6.00	12.00
❏ 5351	Ol' Devil Moon/				
	Please Send Me Someone to Love	1959	3.00	6.00	12.00
❏ 5352	The Chant/Here 'Tis	1959	3.00	6.00	12.00
❏ 5362	Little Liza Jane/Put Your Little Foot Right Out	1960	3.00	6.00	12.00
❏ 5377	Santa Claus Is Coming to Town/				
	Winter Wonderland	1960	3.00	6.00	12.00
❏ 5387	Blues for the Night Owl/Hello, Cello	1961	2.50	5.00	10.00
❏ 5398	Never on Sunday/The Ripper	1961	2.50	5.00	10.00
❏ 5407	Sound of Christmas/Merry Christmas Baby	1961	3.00	6.00	12.00
❏ 5411	I Got Plenty of Nothin'/Thanks for the Memory	1962	2.50	5.00	10.00
❏ 5413	Blue Spring/Spring Fever	1962	2.50	5.00	10.00
❏ 5423	Blueberry Hill/Memphis in June	1962	2.50	5.00	10.00
❏ 5431	Maha de Carnaval/				
	Tangleweed 'Round My Heart	1963	2.00	4.00	8.00
❏ 5438	Look-a Here/Andaluza	1963	2.00	4.00	8.00
❏ 5454	Lonely Avenue/Come On Baby	1963	2.00	4.00	8.00
❏ 5467	Dance Mystique/For the Love of a Princess	1964	2.00	4.00	8.00
❏ 5474	Why Don't You Do It Right/Travel On	1964	2.00	4.00	8.00
❏ 5481	Something You Got/My Babe	1964	2.00	4.00	8.00
❏ 5488	Jingle Bells/Egg Nog	1964	2.50	5.00	10.00
❏ 5496	Let It Be Me/It Had Better Be Tonight	1965	2.00	4.00	8.00
❏ 5506	The "In" Crowd/Since I Fell for You	1965	2.50	5.00	10.00

CADET

Number	Title (A Side/B Side)	Yr	VG	VG+	NM
❏ 5377	Santa Claus Is Coming to Town/				
	Winter Wonderland	1966	2.00	4.00	8.00

—Reissue of Argo 5377

Number	Title (A Side/B Side)	Yr	VG	VG+	NM
❏ 5423	Blueberry Hill/Memphis in June	1966	—	3.00	6.00
❏ 5431	Maha de Carnaval/				
	Tangleweed 'Round My Heart	1966	—	3.00	6.00
❏ 5481	Something You Got/My Babe	1966	—	3.00	6.00
❏ 5496	Let It Be Me/It Had Better Be Tonight	1966	—	3.00	6.00
❏ 5506	The "In" Crowd/Since I Fell for You	1966	—	3.00	6.00
❏ 5522	Hang On Sloopy/Movin' Easy	1965	2.00	4.00	8.00
❏ 5525	A Hard Day's Night/All My Love Belongs to You	1966	2.00	4.00	8.00
❏ 5531	Hi Heel Sneakers — Pt. 1/				
	Hi Heel Sneakers — Pt. 2	1966	2.00	4.00	8.00
❏ 5541	Wade in the Water/Ain't That Peculiar	1966	2.00	4.00	8.00
❏ 5547	Up Tight/Money in the Pocket	1966	2.00	4.00	8.00
❏ 5553	Rudolph the Red-Nosed Reindeer/Day Tripper	1966	2.00	4.00	8.00
❏ 5556	One, Two, Three/Down by the Riverside	1967	2.00	4.00	8.00
❏ 5562	Function at the Junction/Hey, Mrs. Jones	1967	2.00	4.00	8.00
❏ 5565	Saturday Night After the Movies/China Gate	1967	2.00	4.00	8.00
❏ 5573	Dancing in the Street/Girls Talk	1967	2.00	4.00	8.00
❏ 5583	Soul Man/Struttin' Lightly	1967	2.00	4.00	8.00
❏ 5593	The Look of Love/Bear Mash	1968	—	3.00	6.00
❏ 5596	Jade Easy/Party Time	1968	—	3.00	6.00
❏ 5609	Since You've Been Gone/Les Fleurs	1968	—	3.00	6.00
❏ 5629	Mary's Boy Child/Have Yourself a Merry Little				
	Christmas	1968	—	3.00	6.00
❏ 5640	Julia/Do What You Wanna	1969	—	3.00	6.00
❏ 5645	If You've Got It, Flaunt It/Wanderin' Rose	1969	—	3.00	6.00
❏ 5662	Mary's Boy Child/My Cherie Amour	1969	—	3.00	6.00
❏ 5668	Everybody's Talkin'/Love I Feel for You	1970	—	3.00	6.00
❏ 5674	Them Changes/Unsilent Minority	1970	—	3.00	6.00
❏ 5678	Do Whatever Sets You Free/Close Your Eyes				
	and Remember	1970	—	3.00	6.00
❏ 5681	Candida/Love Me Now	1971	—	3.00	6.00
❏ 5684	He Ain't Heavy, He's My Brother/Up in Yonder	1971	—	3.00	6.00
❏ 5695	Summertime/Look-a There	1973	—	3.00	6.00

COLUMBIA

Number	Title (A Side/B Side)	Yr	VG	VG+	NM
❏ 02043	So Much More/Romance Me	1981	—	2.00	4.00
❏ 02572	Lakeshore Cowboy/Michelle	1981	—	2.00	4.00
❏ 02704	You Never Know/Lynn	1982	—	2.00	4.00
❏ 03274	Up Where We Belong/Chance Encounter	1982	—	2.00	4.00
❏ 04524	The Two of Us/Song Without Words				
	(Remembering)	1984	—	2.00	4.00
❏ 04655	Quiet Storm/Ram	1984	—	2.00	4.00
❏ 05640	This Ain't No Fantasy/The Quest	1985	—	—	3.00
❏ 05819	Ram Jam/Slow Dancin'	1986	—	—	3.00
❏ 07220	7-11/My Love Will Lead You Home	1987	—	—	3.00
❏ 10056	Hot Dawgit/R.L. Tambura			—	2.50	5.00

—A-side with Earth, Wind and Fire

Number	Title (A Side/B Side)	Yr	VG	VG+	NM
❏ 10103	Sun Goddess/Jungle Strut	1975	—	2.50	5.00

—A-side with Earth, Wind and Fire

Number	Title (A Side/B Side)	Yr	VG	VG+	NM
❏ 10235	What's the Name of This Funk				
	(Spider Man)/Juacklyn	1975	—	2.50	5.00
❏ 10293	Don't It Feel Good/Fish Bite	1976	—	2.50	5.00
❏ 10382	Brazilica/Salongo	1976	—	2.50	5.00
❏ 10571	Spring High/The Messenger	1977	—	2.50	5.00
❏ 10643	Skippin'/Camino El Bueno	1977	—	2.50	5.00
❏ 10698	Tequila Mockingbird/My Angel's Smile	1978	—	2.50	5.00
❏ 10827	All the Way Live/Toccata	1978	—	2.50	5.00
❏ 10932	Aquarius-Let the Sunshine In/				
	Just Can't Give You Up	1979	—	2.50	5.00
❏ 11042	Wearin' It Out/Spanoletta	1979	—	2.50	5.00
❏ 45634	Slipping Into Darkness/Collage	1972	—	2.50	5.00
❏ 45707	Upendo Mi Pamoja/Eternal Peace	1972	—	2.50	5.00
❏ 45766	Kufanya Mapenzi (Making Love)/What It Is	1973	—	2.50	5.00
❏ 45847	Dreams/Hang On Sloopy	1973	—	2.50	5.00
❏ 45973	Hi-Heel Sneakers/Wade in the Water	1973	—	2.50	5.00
❏ 46037	Summer Breeze/Everywhere Calypso	1974	—	2.50	5.00

7-Inch Extended Plays
ARGO

Number	Title (A Side/B Side)	Yr	VG	VG+	NM
❏ EP-1084	Sleigh Ride/Christmas Blues//Sound of				
	Christmas/The Christmas Song	1961	2.50	5.00	10.00
❏ EP-1084 [PS]	Sound of Christmas	1961	3.00	6.00	12.00

Albums
ARGO

Number	Title (A Side/B Side)	Yr	VG	VG+	NM
❏ LP-611 [M]	Gentleman of Swing	1958	12.50	25.00	50.00
❏ LPS-611 [S]	Gentleman of Swing	1959	15.00	30.00	60.00
❏ LP-627 [M]	Gentleman of Jazz	1958	12.50	25.00	50.00
❏ LPS-627 [S]	Gentleman of Jazz	1959	15.00	30.00	60.00
❏ LP-642 [M]	The Ramsey Lewis Trio with Lee Winchester	1959	10.00	20.00	40.00
❏ LPS-642 [S]	The Ramsey Lewis Trio with Lee Winchester	1959	12.50	25.00	50.00
❏ LP-645 [M]	An Hour with the Ramsey Lewis Trio	1959	10.00	20.00	40.00
❏ LPS-645 [S]	An Hour with the Ramsey Lewis Trio	1959	12.50	25.00	50.00
❏ LP-665 [M]	Stretching Out	1960	10.00	20.00	40.00
❏ LPS-665 [S]	Stretching Out	1960	12.50	25.00	50.00
❏ LP-671 [M]	The Ramsey Lewis Trio in Chicago	1961	10.00	20.00	40.00
❏ LPS-671 [S]	The Ramsey Lewis Trio in Chicago	1961	12.50	25.00	50.00
❏ LP-680 [M]	More Music from the Soil	1961	10.00	20.00	40.00
❏ LPS-680 [S]	More Music from the Soil	1961	12.50	25.00	50.00
❏ LP-687 [M]	Sound of Christmas	1961	10.00	20.00	40.00
❏ LPS-687 [S]	Sound of Christmas	1961	12.50	25.00	50.00
❏ LP-693 [M]	The Sound of Spring	1962	6.25	12.50	25.00
❏ LPS-693 [S]	The Sound of Spring	1962	7.50	15.00	30.00
❏ LP-701 [M]	Country Meets the Blues	1962	6.25	12.50	25.00
❏ LPS-701 [S]	Country Meets the Blues	1962	7.50	15.00	30.00
❏ LP-705 [M]	Bossa Nova	1962	6.25	12.50	25.00
❏ LPS-705 [S]	Bossa Nova	1962	7.50	15.00	30.00
❏ LP-715 [M]	Pot Luck	1963	6.25	12.50	25.00
❏ LPS-715 [S]	Pot Luck	1963	7.50	15.00	30.00
❏ LP-723 [M]	Barefoot Sunday Blues	1963	6.25	12.50	25.00
❏ LPS-723 [S]	Barefoot Sunday Blues	1963	7.50	15.00	30.00
❏ LP-732 [M]	Bach to the Blues	1964	6.25	12.50	25.00
❏ LPS-732 [S]	Bach to the Blues	1964	7.50	15.00	30.00
❏ LP-741 [M]	The Ramsey Lewis Trio				
	at the Bohemian Caverns	1964	6.25	12.50	25.00
❏ LPS-741 [S]	The Ramsey Lewis Trio				
	at the Bohemian Caverns	1964	7.50	15.00	30.00
❏ LP-745 [M]	More Sounds of Christmas	1964	6.25	12.50	25.00
❏ LPS-745 [S]	More Sounds of Christmas	1964	7.50	15.00	30.00
❏ LP-755 [M]	Choice! The Best of the Ramsey Lewis Trio	1965	7.50	15.00	30.00
❏ LPS-755 [S]	Choice! The Best of the Ramsey Lewis Trio	1965	10.00	20.00	40.00
❏ LP-757 [M]	The In Crowd	1965	6.25	12.50	25.00
❏ LPS-757 [S]	The In Crowd	1965	7.50	15.00	30.00

CADET

Number	Title (A Side/B Side)	Yr	VG	VG+	NM
❏ LP-611 [M]	Gentleman of Swing	1966	3.00	6.00	12.00
❏ LPS-611 [S]	Gentleman of Swing	1966	3.75	7.50	15.00
❏ LP-627 [M]	Gentleman of Jazz	1966	3.00	6.00	12.00
❏ LPS-627 [S]	Gentleman of Jazz	1966	3.75	7.50	15.00
❏ LP-645 [M]	An Hour with the Ramsey Lewis Trio	1966	3.00	6.00	12.00
❏ LPS-645 [S]	An Hour with the Ramsey Lewis Trio	1966	3.75	7.50	15.00
❏ LP-665 [M]	Stretching Out	1966	3.00	6.00	12.00
❏ LPS-665 [S]	Stretching Out	1966	3.75	7.50	15.00
❏ LP-671 [M]	The Ramsey Lewis Trio in Chicago	1966	3.00	6.00	12.00
❏ LPS-671 [S]	The Ramsey Lewis Trio in Chicago	1966	3.75	7.50	15.00
❏ LP-680 [M]	More Music from the Soil	1966	3.00	6.00	12.00
❏ LPS-680 [S]	More Music from the Soil	1966	3.75	7.50	15.00
❏ LPS-680 [S]	More Music from the Soil	197?	3.00	6.00	12.00

—Reissue with "A Division of All Platinum Record Group" on label

Number	Title (A Side/B Side)	Yr	VG	VG+	NM
❏ LP-687X [M]	Sound of Christmas	1966	5.00	10.00	20.00

—Reissue of Argo 687

Number	Title (A Side/B Side)	Yr	VG	VG+	NM
❏ LPS-687X [S]	Sound of Christmas	1966	5.00	10.00	20.00

—Reissue of Argo 687-S

Number	Title (A Side/B Side)	Yr	VG	VG+	NM
❏ LP-693 [M]	The Sound of Spring	1966	3.00	6.00	12.00
❏ LPS-693 [S]	The Sound of Spring	1966	3.75	7.50	15.00
❏ LP-701 [M]	Country Meets the Blues	1966	3.00	6.00	12.00
❏ LPS-701 [S]	Country Meets the Blues	1966	3.75	7.50	15.00
❏ LP-705 [M]	Bossa Nova	1966	3.00	6.00	12.00
❏ LPS-705 [S]	Bossa Nova	1966	3.75	7.50	15.00
❏ LP-715 [M]	Pot Luck	1966	3.00	6.00	12.00
❏ LPS-715 [S]	Pot Luck	1966	3.75	7.50	15.00
❏ LP-723 [M]	Barefoot Sunday Blues	1966	3.00	6.00	12.00
❏ LPS-723 [S]	Barefoot Sunday Blues	1966	3.75	7.50	15.00
❏ LP-732 [M]	Bach to the Blues	1966	3.00	6.00	12.00
❏ LPS-732 [S]	Bach to the Blues	1966	3.75	7.50	15.00
❏ LP-741 [M]	The Ramsey Lewis Trio				
	at the Bohemian Caverns	1966	3.00	6.00	12.00
❏ LPS-741 [S]	The Ramsey Lewis Trio				
	at the Bohemian Caverns	1966	3.75	7.50	15.00
❏ LP-745 [M]	More Sounds of Christmas	1966	3.75	7.50	15.00
❏ LPS-745 [S]	More Sounds of Christmas	1966	5.00	10.00	20.00
❏ LP-750 [M]	You Better Believe It	1966	3.00	6.00	12.00
❏ LPS-750 [S]	You Better Believe It	1966	3.75	7.50	15.00
❏ LP-755 [M]	Choice! The Best of the Ramsey Lewis Trio	1965	3.75	7.50	15.00
❏ LPS-755 [S]	Choice! The Best of the Ramsey Lewis Trio	1965	5.00	10.00	20.00
❏ LP-757 [M]	The In Crowd	1965	3.00	6.00	12.00
❏ LPS-757 [S]	The In Crowd	1965	3.75	7.50	15.00
❏ LP-761 [M]	Hang On Ramsey!	1966	3.75	7.50	15.00
❏ LPS-761 [S]	Hang On Ramsey!	1966	5.00	10.00	20.00

L

Number	Title (A Side/B Side)	Yr	VG	VG+	NM
❑ LP-771 [M]	Swingin'	1966	3.75	7.50	15.00
❑ LPS-771 [S]	Swingin'	1966	5.00	10.00	20.00
❑ LP-774 [M]	Wade in the Water	1966	3.75	7.50	15.00
❑ LPS-774 [S]	Wade in the Water	1966	5.00	10.00	20.00
❑ LP-782 [M]	The Movie Album	1967	5.00	10.00	20.00
❑ LPS-782 [S]	The Movie Album	1967	3.75	7.50	15.00
❑ LP-790 [M]	Goin' Latin	1967	5.00	10.00	20.00
❑ LPS-790 [S]	Goin' Latin	1967	3.75	7.50	15.00
❑ LP-794 [M]	Dancing in the Street	1967	5.00	10.00	20.00
❑ LPS-794 [S]	Dancing in the Street	1967	3.75	7.50	15.00
❑ LPS-799	Up Pops Ramsey Lewis	1968	3.75	7.50	15.00
❑ LPS-811	Maiden Voyage	1968	3.75	7.50	15.00
❑ LPS-821	Mother Nature's Son	1969	3.75	7.50	15.00
❑ LPS-827	Another Voyage	1969	3.75	7.50	15.00
❑ LPS-836	Ramsey Lewis, The Piano Player	1970	3.75	7.50	15.00
❑ LPS-839	The Best of Ramsey Lewis	1970	3.75	7.50	15.00
❑ LPS-844	Them Changes	1970	3.75	7.50	15.00
❑ 50020	Groover	1973	3.00	6.00	12.00
❑ 50058 [(2)]	Solid Ivory	1974	3.75	7.50	15.00
❑ 60001	Back to the Roots	1971	3.00	6.00	12.00
❑ 60018 [(2)]	Inside Ramsey Lewis	1972	3.75	7.50	15.00
CBS					
❑ FM 42661	A Classic Encounter	1988	2.50	5.00	10.00
CHESS					
❑ 9001 [(2)]	Solid Ivory	197?	3.00	6.00	12.00
—Reissue of Cadet 50058					
❑ CH 9716	Sound of Christmas	1984	2.50	5.00	10.00
—Reissue of Argo 687-S					
COLUMBIA					
❑ CQ 31096 [Q]	Upendo Ni Pamoja	1972	4.50	9.00	18.00
❑ KC 31096	Upendo Ni Pamoja	1972	3.00	6.00	12.00
❑ KC 32030	Funky Serenity	1973	3.00	6.00	12.00
❑ KC 32490	Ramsey Lewis' Newly Recorded All-Time, Non-Stop Golden Hits	1973	3.00	6.00	12.00
❑ PC 32490	Ramsey Lewis' Newly Recorded All-Time, Non-Stop Golden Hits	197?	2.00	4.00	8.00
—Reissue with new prefix					
❑ KC 32897	Solar Wind	1974	3.00	6.00	12.00
❑ KC 33194	Sun Goddess	1974	2.50	5.00	10.00
❑ PC 33194	Sun Goddess	197?	2.00	4.00	8.00
—Reissue with new prefix					
❑ CG 33663 [(2)]	Upendo Ni Pamoja/Funky Serenity	1975	3.00	6.00	12.00
❑ PC 33800	Don't It Feel Good	1975	2.50	5.00	10.00
—Originals have no bar code					
❑ PC 33800	Don't It Feel Good	198?	2.00	4.00	8.00
—Budget-line reissue with bar code					
❑ PC 34173	Salongo	1976	2.50	5.00	10.00
—Originals have no bar code					
❑ PC 34173	Salongo	198?	2.00	4.00	8.00
—Budget-line reissue with bar code					
❑ PC 34696	Love Notes	1977	2.50	5.00	10.00
❑ JC 35018	Tequila Mockingbird	1977	2.50	5.00	10.00
❑ JC 35483	Legacy	1978	2.50	5.00	10.00
❑ PC 35483	Legacy	198?	2.00	4.00	8.00
—Budget-line reissue					
❑ JC 35815	Ramsey	1979	2.50	5.00	10.00
❑ FC 36364	The Best of Ramsey Lewis	1980	2.50	5.00	10.00
❑ JC 36423	Routes	1980	2.50	5.00	10.00
❑ PC 36423	Routes	198?	2.00	4.00	8.00
—Budget-line reissue					
❑ FC 37153	Three Piece Suite	1981	2.50	5.00	10.00
❑ FC 37687	Live at the Savoy	1982	2.50	5.00	10.00
❑ PC 37687	Live at the Savoy	198?	2.00	4.00	8.00
—Budget-line reissue					
❑ FC 38294	Chance Encounter	1983	2.50	5.00	10.00
❑ FC 38787	Les Fleurs	1983	2.50	5.00	10.00
❑ FC 39158	Reunion	1983	2.50	5.00	10.00
❑ FC 40108	Fantasy	1985	2.50	5.00	10.00
❑ FC 40677	Keys to the City	1987	2.50	5.00	10.00
❑ HC 43194	Sun Goddess	1982	12.50	25.00	50.00
—Half-speed mastered edition					
❑ FC 44190	Urban Renewal	1989	3.75	7.50	15.00
❑ HC 47687	Live at the Savoy	1982	20.00	40.00	80.00
—Half-speed mastered edition					
COLUMBIA JAZZ ODYSSEY					
❑ PC 37019	Blues for the Night Owl	1981	2.50	5.00	10.00
EMARCY					
❑ MG-36150 [M]	Down to Earth	1958	10.00	20.00	40.00
❑ SR-80029 [S]	Down to Earth	1958	12.50	25.00	50.00
MERCURY					
❑ MG-20536 [M]	Down to Earth	1965	5.00	10.00	20.00
❑ SR-60536 [S]	Down to Earth	1965	6.25	12.50	25.00

LEWIS, RAMSEY, AND JEAN DUSHON
Albums

Number	Title (A Side/B Side)	Yr	VG	VG+	NM
ARGO					
❑ 750 [M]	You Better Believe Me	1965	6.25	12.50	25.00
❑ 750S [S]	You Better Believe Me	1965	7.50	15.00	30.00

LEWIS, RAMSEY, AND NANCY WILSON Also see each artist's individual listings.
Albums

Number	Title (A Side/B Side)	Yr	VG	VG+	NM
COLUMBIA					
❑ FC 39326	The Two of Us	1984	2.50	5.00	10.00

LEWIS, RUDY Also see THE DRIFTERS.
45s

Number	Title (A Side/B Side)	Yr	VG	VG+	NM
ATLANTIC					
❑ 2193	I've Loved You So Long/Baby I Dig Love	1963	3.00	6.00	12.00
RCA VICTOR					
❑ 47-7792	Moonbeam/Beer, Beer and More Beer	1960	5.00	10.00	20.00
—With the Sputniks					

LEWIS, SABBY
45s

Number	Title (A Side/B Side)	Yr	VG	VG+	NM
ABC-PARAMOUNT					
❑ 9685	Ding-a-Ling/Kenny's Blues	1956	10.00	20.00	40.00
❑ 9687	Forgive Me, My Love/Regretting	1956	10.00	20.00	40.00

Number	Title (A Side/B Side)	Yr	VG	VG+	NM
GONE					
❑ 5074	Swana/Sabby	1959	6.25	12.50	25.00
—With the Uniques					

LEWIS, SAMMIE
45s

Number	Title (A Side/B Side)	Yr	VG	VG+	NM
SUN					
❑ 218	So Long Baby Goodbye/I Feel So Worried	1955	20.00	40.00	80.00

LEWIS, SMILEY
45s

Number	Title (A Side/B Side)	Yr	VG	VG+	NM
DOT					
❑ 16674	I Wonder/Lookin' for My Woman	1964	2.50	5.00	10.00
IMPERIAL					
❑ 5194	The Bells Are Ringing/Lillie Mae	1952	30.00	60.00	120.00
—Note: Smiley Lewis records on Imperial before 5194 are unconfirmed on 45 rpm					
❑ 5208	Gumbo Blues/It's So Peaceful	1952	25.00	50.00	100.00
❑ 5224	Gypsy Blues/You're Not the One	1953	25.00	50.00	100.00
❑ 5234	Play Girl/Big Mamou	1953	20.00	40.00	80.00
❑ 5234	Play Girl/Big Mamou	1953	62.50	125.00	250.00
—Red vinyl					
❑ 5241	Caldonia's Party/Oh Baby	1953	20.00	40.00	80.00
❑ 5252	Little Fernandez/It's Music	1953	20.00	40.00	80.00
❑ 5268	Down the Road/Blue Monday	1954	20.00	40.00	80.00
❑ 5279	I Love You for Sentimental Reasons/The Rocks	1954	20.00	40.00	80.00
❑ 5296	Can't Stop Loving You/That Certain Door	1954	20.00	40.00	80.00
❑ 5316	Too Many Drivers/Ooh La La	1954	20.00	40.00	80.00
❑ 5325	Jailbird/Farewell	1955	20.00	40.00	80.00
❑ 5349	Real Gone Lover/Nobody Knows	1955	20.00	40.00	80.00
❑ 5356	I Hear You Knocking/Bumpity Bump	1955	20.00	40.00	80.00
❑ 5372	Queen of Hearts/Come On	1956	20.00	40.00	80.00
❑ 5380	One Night/Ain't Gonna Do It	1956	20.00	40.00	80.00
❑ 5389	She's Got Me (Hook, Line and Sinker)/ Please Listen to Me	1956	20.00	40.00	80.00
❑ 5404	Down Yonder We Go Ballin'/ Someday You'll Want Me	1956	20.00	40.00	80.00
❑ 5418	Shame, Shame, Shame/No No	1957	15.00	30.00	60.00
❑ 5431	You Are My Sunshine/Sweeter Words Have Never Been Spoken	1957	10.00	20.00	40.00
❑ 5450	Go On Fool/Goin' to Jump and Shout	1957	7.50	15.00	30.00
❑ 5470	Rootin' and Tootin'/I Can't Believe	1957	7.50	15.00	30.00
❑ 5478	Bad Luck Blues/School Days Are Back Again	1957	7.50	15.00	30.00
❑ 5531	Lil' Liza Jane/My Love Is Gone	1958	6.25	12.50	25.00
❑ 5662	Oh Red!/I Want to Be with Her	1960	3.75	7.50	15.00
❑ 5676	Last Night/Ain't Goin' There No More	1960	3.75	7.50	15.00
❑ 5719	Stormy Monday Blues/Tell Me Who	1961	3.75	7.50	15.00
❑ 5820	Gumbo Blues/Tee Nah Nah	1962	3.75	7.50	15.00
KNIGHT					
❑ 2007	Baby Please/I Shall Not Be Moved	1959	3.75	7.50	15.00
❑ 2011	Lost Weekend/By the Water	1959	3.75	7.50	15.00
LOMA					
❑ 2024	Bells Are Ringing/Walkin' the Girl	1965	2.50	5.00	10.00
OKEH					
❑ 7146	I'm Coming Down with the Blues/Tune-Up	1962	3.00	6.00	12.00
Albums					
IMPERIAL					
❑ LP-9141 [M]	I Hear You Knocking	1961	150.00	300.00	600.00
—Black vinyl					
❑ LP-9141 [M]	I Hear You Knocking	1961	1500.00	3000.	6000.
—Green vinyl (one copy known)					

LEWIS AND CLARKE EXPEDITION, THE
45s

Number	Title (A Side/B Side)	Yr	VG	VG+	NM
CHARTMAKER					
❑ 402	Expedition West/For Your Freedom Tonight	1966	2.00	4.00	8.00
COLGEMS					
❑ 66-1006	I Feel Good (I Feel Bad)/Blue Revelations	1967	2.00	4.00	8.00
❑ 66-1006 [PS]	I Feel Good (I Feel Bad)/Blue Revelations	1967	3.75	7.50	15.00
❑ 66-1011	Destination Unknown/Freedom Bird	1967	2.00	4.00	8.00
❑ 66-1011 [PS]	Destination Unknown/Freedom Bird	1967	3.75	7.50	15.00
❑ 66-1022	Chain Around the Flowers/ Why Need They Pretend	1968	2.00	4.00	8.00
❑ 66-1028	Daddy's Plastic Child/Gypsy Song Man	1968	2.00	4.00	8.00
Albums					
COLGEMS					
❑ COM-105 [M]	The Lewis and Clarke Expedition	1967	6.25	12.50	25.00
❑ COS-105 [S]	The Lewis and Clarke Expedition	1967	7.50	15.00	30.00

LEYTON, JOHN
45s

Number	Title (A Side/B Side)	Yr	VG	VG+	NM
ABC-PARAMOUNT					
❑ 10292	Son, This Is She/Six White Horses	1962	3.00	6.00	12.00
ATCO					
❑ 6319	Make Love to Me/I'll Cut Your Tail Off	1964	3.00	6.00	12.00
LIVERPOOL SOUND					
❑ 901	Beautiful Dreamer/ I Guess You Are Always On My Mind	1964	3.00	6.00	12.00

LIBERACE
45s

Number	Title (A Side/B Side)	Yr	VG	VG+	NM
AVI					
❑ 101	The Way We Were/The Entertainer	1976	—	2.00	4.00
❑ 112	My Melody of Love/El Bimbo	1976	—	2.00	4.00
COLUMBIA					
❑ 39709	September Song/I Want My Mama	1952	3.75	7.50	15.00
❑ 39777	Star Dust/Malaguena	1952	3.00	6.00	12.00
❑ 39778	As Time Goes By/Liebestraum	1952	3.00	6.00	12.00
❑ 39779	Carioca/Warsaw Concerto	1952	3.00	6.00	12.00
❑ 39780	Polish National Dance/Moonlight Sonata	1952	3.00	6.00	12.00
—The above four comprise a box set					
❑ 39895	I Miss You So/I Don't Care	1952	3.75	7.50	15.00
❑ 39919	Yakety Yak Polka/Begin the Beguine	1953	3.00	6.00	12.00
❑ 39920	Chopsticks/The Old Piano Roll Blues	1953	3.00	6.00	12.00
❑ 39921	Cement Mixer/Slaughter on Tenth Avenue	1953	3.00	6.00	12.00
❑ 39922	Cumana/Lover	1953	3.00	6.00	12.00
—The above four comprise a box set					

Number	Title (A Side/B Side)	Yr	VG	VG+	NM
❑ 39984	Tchakovsky's Piano Concerto #1/September Song	1953	3.00	6.00	12.00
❑ 39985	I Don't Care/Jalousie	1953	3.00	6.00	12.00
❑ 39986	Autumn Nocturne/Concerto #2 in A Major for Piano and Orchestra	1953	3.00	6.00	12.00
❑ 39987	Tales from the Vienna Woods/I'll Be Seeing You	1953	3.00	6.00	12.00

—*The above four comprise a box set*

Number	Title (A Side/B Side)	Yr	VG	VG+	NM
❑ 39995	I'm Loved/I'd Never Forgive Myself	1953	3.75	7.50	15.00
❑ 40065	Warsaw Concerto (Beginning)/Cornish Rhapsody (Conclusion)	1953	3.00	6.00	12.00
❑ 40066	Warsaw Concerto (Conclusion)/Cornish Rhapsody (Beginning)	1953	3.00	6.00	12.00
❑ 40067	Grieg's Piano Concerto (Beginning)/Chopin's Fantasia (Conclusion)	1953	3.00	6.00	12.00
❑ 40068	Grieg's Piano Concerto (Conclusion)/Chopin's Fantasia (Beginning)	1953	3.00	6.00	12.00

—*The above four comprise a box set*

Number	Title (A Side/B Side)	Yr	VG	VG+	NM
❑ 40099	A Story of Three Loves/Maiden's Wish Samba	1953	3.75	7.50	15.00
❑ 40145	Spellbound Concerto (Beginning)/Rachmaninoff Fantasia (Conclusion)	1953	3.00	6.00	12.00
❑ 40146	Spellbound Concerto (Conclusion)/Rachmaninoff Fantasia (Beginning)	1953	3.00	6.00	12.00
❑ 40147	Dream of Olwen/Laura (Conclusion)	1953	3.00	6.00	12.00
❑ 40148	Stella by Starlight/Laura (Beginning)	1953	3.00	6.00	12.00

—*The above four comprise a box set*

Number	Title (A Side/B Side)	Yr	VG	VG+	NM
❑ 40217	Twelfth Street Rag/Beer Barrel Polka	1954	3.00	6.00	12.00
❑ 40285	Polonaise/Liebestraum (Love's Dream)	1954	3.00	6.00	12.00
❑ 40314	Rhapsody by Candlelight/Star of India	1954	3.00	6.00	12.00
❑ 40331	Waltz in C-Sharp Minor/Polonaise in A Major	1954	2.50	5.00	10.00
❑ 40332	Nocturne No. 5 in E-Flat Major/Etude in A-Flat Major	1954	2.50	5.00	10.00
❑ 40333	Fantasie-Impromptu (Beginning)/Nocturne No. 2 in E Flat Major (Conclusion)	1954	2.50	5.00	10.00
❑ 40334	Fantasie-Impromptu (Conclusion)/Nocturne No. 2 in E Flat Major (Beginning)	1954	2.50	5.00	10.00

—*The above four comprise a box set*

Number	Title (A Side/B Side)	Yr	VG	VG+	NM
❑ 40335	Polonaise in A-Flat Major (Beginning)/Grande Valse	1954	2.50	5.00	10.00
❑ 40336	Polonaise in A-Flat Major (Conclusion)/Prelude No. 4 in E Minor	1954	2.50	5.00	10.00
❑ 40337	Etude No. 3 in E Major (Beginning)/Etude in F Minor	1954	2.50	5.00	10.00
❑ 40338	Etude No. 3 in E Major (Conclusion)/Waltz No. 6 in D-Flat Major	1954	2.50	5.00	10.00

—*The above four comprise a box set*

Number	Title (A Side/B Side)	Yr	VG	VG+	NM
❑ 40379	The Spirit of Christmas/O Holy Night	1954	3.00	6.00	12.00
❑ 40380	The Christmas Song/The Toy Piano//The Beauty of Holiness/Santa Claus Medley	1954	3.00	6.00	12.00
❑ 40381	Gesu Bambino/Sleigh Ride//Star Bright/Ave Maria	1954	3.00	6.00	12.00
❑ 40382	Twas the Night Before Christmas/Christmas Medley	1954	3.00	6.00	12.00
❑ 40394	Cornish Rhapsody/Rhapsody by Candlelight	1954	2.50	5.00	10.00
❑ 40395	Alexander's Ragtime Band/El Cumbanchero	1954	2.50	5.00	10.00
❑ 40396	My TV Sponsors/Clair de Lune	1954	2.50	5.00	10.00
❑ 40397	Cement Mixer/Beer Barrel Polka	1954	2.50	5.00	10.00

—*The above four comprise a box set*

Number	Title (A Side/B Side)	Yr	VG	VG+	NM
❑ 40454	I'll Get By/Finger of Suspicion	1955	3.00	6.00	12.00
❑ 40455	Unchained Melody/The Bridges at Toko-Ri	1955	3.00	6.00	12.00
❑ 40570	Sincerely Yours/Under Paris Skies	1955	3.00	6.00	12.00
❑ 40647	We All Need Love/Dancing Skeletons	1956	3.00	6.00	12.00
❑ 40686	Faith Unlocks the Door/Nocturne No. 2	1956	3.00	6.00	12.00
❑ 40768	The Magic of Believing/Cuba	1956	3.00	6.00	12.00
❑ 48001	Ave Maria/Christmas Medley (White Christmas/Jingle Bells/ O Come All Ye Faithful/Silent Night)	1954	3.75	7.50	15.00
❑ 48001 [PS]	Ave Maria/Christmas Medley (White Christmas/Jingle Bells/O Come All Ye Faithful/Silent Night)	1954	5.00	10.00	20.00
❑ 48008	I Love You Truly/Oh Promise Me	1954	3.00	6.00	12.00
❑ 48008 [PS]	I Love You Truly/Oh Promise Me	1954	3.75	7.50	15.00

CORAL

Number	Title (A Side/B Side)	Yr	VG	VG+	NM
❑ 62112	Gigi/This Earth Is Mine	1959	2.50	5.00	10.00
❑ 65539	I Believe/Gigi	1961	2.00	4.00	8.00
❑ 65556	I'll Be Seeing You/Laura	1961	2.00	4.00	8.00

DECCA

Number	Title (A Side/B Side)	Yr	VG	VG+	NM
❑ 28279	Velvet Moon/It's Shadow Time	1952	3.75	7.50	15.00

DOT

Number	Title (A Side/B Side)	Yr	VG	VG+	NM
❑ 16594	Alley Cat/Theme from "Outer Space"	1964	—	3.00	6.00
❑ 17033	Happy Barefoot Boy/Two for the Road	1967	—	3.00	6.00

LIBERACE

Number	Title (A Side/B Side)	Yr	VG	VG+	NM
❑ R 4069/70	Ciao/When Irish Eyes Are Smiling	197?	2.50	5.00	10.00
❑ R 4069/70 [PS]	Ciao/When Irish Eyes Are Smiling	197?	3.75	7.50	15.00

—*No number on sleeve; sleeve calls this "Never Say Goodbye, Say Ciao"; promotional item for Ciao Liqueur*

MGM

Number	Title (A Side/B Side)	Yr	VG	VG+	NM
❑ 14518	The Morning After/Theme from "Above San Francisco"	1973	—	2.50	5.00

WARNER BROS.

Number	Title (A Side/B Side)	Yr	VG	VG+	NM
❑ 7465	Ciao/Theme from Love Story	1971	—	2.50	5.00

7-Inch Extended Plays

COLUMBIA

Number	Title (A Side/B Side)	Yr	VG	VG+	NM
❑ B-308 [PS]	Liberace	195?	3.75	7.50	15.00

—*Cover for 2-EP set (5-1101 and 5-1102)*

Number	Title (A Side/B Side)	Yr	VG	VG+	NM
❑ B-329 [PS]	An Evening with Liberace	195?	2.50	5.00	10.00

—*Cover for 2-EP set (5-1371 and 5-1372)*

Number	Title (A Side/B Side)	Yr	VG	VG+	NM
❑ B-378 [PS]	Concertos for You, Vol. II	195?	2.50	5.00	10.00

—*Cover for 2-EP set (5-1832 and 5-1833)*

Number	Title (A Side/B Side)	Yr	VG	VG+	NM
❑ B-454 [PS]	(title unknown)	1954	3.75	7.50	15.00
❑ 5-1101	Star Dust/Liebestraum (Love's Dream)//As Time Goes By/Malaguena	195?	3.00	6.00	12.00

—*Alternate numbers are "B 308-1" and "B 308-4"*

Number	Title (A Side/B Side)	Yr	VG	VG+	NM
❑ 5-1102	Carioca/Polish National Dance in E-flat Minor, Op. 47//Moonlight Sonata/Warsaw Concerto	195?	3.00	6.00	12.00

—*Alternate numbers are "B 308-2" and "B 308-3"*

Number	Title (A Side/B Side)	Yr	VG	VG+	NM
❑ 5-1270	Tchaikovsky's Piano Concerto No. 1/I Don't Care (As Long As You Care for Me)//Jalousie (Jealousy)/September Song	195?	2.50	5.00	10.00

—*Alternate number is B-1562*

Number	Title (A Side/B Side)	Yr	VG	VG+	NM
❑ 5-1371	"Yakety Yak" Polka/Begin the Beguine//Chopsticks/The Old Piano Roll Blues	195?	2.50	5.00	10.00

—*Alternate numbers are "B 329-1" and "B 329-4"*

Number	Title (A Side/B Side)	Yr	VG	VG+	NM
❑ 5-1372	Cement Mixer (Put-Ti, Put-Ti)/Slaughter on Tenth Avenue//Cumana/Lover	195?	2.50	5.00	10.00

—*Alternate numbers are "B 329-2" and "B 329-3"*

Number	Title (A Side/B Side)	Yr	VG	VG+	NM
❑ B-1562 [PS]	Liberace by Candlelight	195?	2.50	5.00	10.00

—*Contains record 5-1270*

Number	Title (A Side/B Side)	Yr	VG	VG+	NM
❑ 5-1832	Spellbound Concerto/Rachmaninoff Fantasia	195?	2.50	5.00	10.00

—*Alternate numbers are "B 378-1" and "B 378-4"*

Number	Title (A Side/B Side)	Yr	VG	VG+	NM
❑ 5-1833	The Dream of Olwen/Stella by Starlight/Laura	195?	2.50	5.00	10.00

—*Alternate numbers are "B 378-2" and "B 378-3"*

Number	Title (A Side/B Side)	Yr	VG	VG+	NM
❑ 5-2049	Santa Claus Medley/'Twas the Night Before Christmas//Ave Maria/Gesu Bambino (The Infant Jesus)	195?	3.00	6.00	12.00
❑ 5-2050	The Spirit of Christmas/Christmas Medley//Star Bright/The Beauty of Holiness	1954	3.00	6.00	12.00

—*Alternate numbers are "B-454-2" and "B-454-5"*

Number	Title (A Side/B Side)	Yr	VG	VG+	NM
❑ 5-2051	O Holy Night/The Toy Piano//Sleigh Ride/The Christmas Song	1954	3.00	6.00	12.00

—*Alternate numbers are "B-454-3" and "B-454-4"*

DECCA

ABC

Number	Title (A Side/B Side)	Yr	VG	VG+	NM
❑ ED 2197	(contents unknown)	195?	5.00	10.00	20.00
❑ ED 2197 [PS]	Piano Solos	195?	5.00	10.00	20.00

Albums

ABC

Number	Title (A Side/B Side)	Yr	VG	VG+	NM
❑ 4002	16 Great Performances	1974	3.00	6.00	12.00

AVI

Number	Title (A Side/B Side)	Yr	VG	VG+	NM
❑ 1023	Candlelight Classics	1973	3.00	6.00	12.00
❑ 1029	The World of Liberace	1974	3.00	6.00	12.00

CBS

Number	Title (A Side/B Side)	Yr	VG	VG+	NM
❑ FM 42244	Concert Favorites	1986	2.50	5.00	10.00

COLUMBIA

Number	Title (A Side/B Side)	Yr	VG	VG+	NM
❑ CL 575 [M]	Liberace at the Piano	1954	10.00	20.00	40.00

—*Maroon label, gold print*

Number	Title (A Side/B Side)	Yr	VG	VG+	NM
❑ CL 589 [M]	Christmas at Liberace's	1954	12.50	25.00	50.00

—*Maroon label, gold print*

Number	Title (A Side/B Side)	Yr	VG	VG+	NM
❑ CL 600 [M]	Liberace at the Hollywood Bowl	1955	10.00	20.00	40.00
❑ CL 645 [M]	Hollywood Bowl Encore	1955	10.00	20.00	40.00
❑ CL 661 [M]	Liberace by Candlelight	1955	10.00	20.00	40.00
❑ CL 800 [M]	Sincerely Yours	1956	12.50	25.00	50.00
❑ CL 896 [M]	Liberace at Home	1956	12.50	25.00	50.00
❑ CL 2516 [10]	Piano Reverie	1955	15.00	30.00	60.00
❑ CL 2592 [10]	Kiddin' on the Keys	1955	15.00	30.00	60.00
❑ CL 6217 [10]	Liberace at the Piano	1952	20.00	40.00	80.00
❑ CL 6239 [10]	An Evening with Liberace	1953	20.00	40.00	80.00
❑ CL 6251 [10]	Liberace by Candlelight	1953	20.00	40.00	80.00
❑ CL 6269 [10]	Concertos for You	1953	20.00	40.00	80.00
❑ CL 6283 [10]	Concertos for You, Volume 2	1953	20.00	40.00	80.00
❑ CL 6327 [10]	Liberace Plays Chopin	1954	20.00	40.00	80.00
❑ CL 6328 [10]	Liberace Plays Chopin, Volume 2	1954	20.00	40.00	80.00
❑ CS 9845	Liberace's Greatest Hits	1969	3.00	6.00	12.00

—*Red "360 Sound" label*

Number	Title (A Side/B Side)	Yr	VG	VG+	NM
❑ CS 9845	Liberace's Greatest Hits	1970	2.50	5.00	10.00

—*Orange label*

CORAL

Number	Title (A Side/B Side)	Yr	VG	VG+	NM
❑ 7CXB 9 [(2)S]	The Best of Liberace	1965	5.00	10.00	20.00
❑ CXB 9 [(2)M]	The Best of Liberace	1965	3.75	7.50	15.00
❑ CRL 57292 [M]	Piano Song Book — Movie Themes	1959	3.75	7.50	15.00
❑ CRL 57305 [M]	The Magic Pianos of Liberace	1960	3.00	6.00	12.00
❑ CRL 57305 [M]	The Magic Pianos of Liberace	1960	3.75	7.50	15.00
❑ CRL 57344 [M]	My Inspiration	1961	3.00	6.00	12.00
❑ CRL 57346 [M]	Liberace at the Palladium	1961	3.00	6.00	12.00
❑ CRL 57377 [M]	My Parade of Golden Favorites	1961	3.00	6.00	12.00
❑ CRL 57392 [M]	As Time Goes By	1962	3.00	6.00	12.00
❑ CRL 57395 [M]	Rhapsody by Candlelight	1962	3.00	6.00	12.00
❑ CRL 57452 [M]	Golden Themes from Hollywood	1964	3.00	6.00	12.00
❑ CRL 757292 [S]	Piano Song Book — Movie Themes	1959	5.00	10.00	20.00
❑ CRL 757305 [S]	The Magic Pianos of Liberace	1960	3.75	7.50	15.00
❑ CRL 757305 [S]	The Magic Pianos of Liberace	1960	5.00	10.00	20.00
❑ CRL 757344 [S]	My Inspiration	1961	3.75	7.50	15.00
❑ CRL 757346 [S]	Liberace at the Palladium	1961	3.75	7.50	15.00
❑ CRL 757377 [S]	My Parade of Golden Favorites	1961	3.75	7.50	15.00
❑ CRL 757392 [S]	As Time Goes By	1962	3.75	7.50	15.00
❑ CRL 757395 [S]	Rhapsody by Candlelight	1962	3.75	7.50	15.00
❑ CRL 757452 [S]	Golden Themes from Hollywood	1964	3.75	7.50	15.00

DOT

Number	Title (A Side/B Side)	Yr	VG	VG+	NM
❑ DLP-3547 [M]	Mr. Showmanship	1964	3.00	6.00	12.00
❑ DLP-3550 [M]	A Liberace Christmas	1964	3.00	6.00	12.00
❑ DLP-3563 [M]	My Most Requested	1965	3.00	6.00	12.00
❑ DLP-3595 [M]	Liberace at the Americana, Volume 1	1965	3.00	6.00	12.00
❑ DLP-3596 [M]	Liberace at the Americana, Volume 2	1965	3.00	6.00	12.00
❑ DLP-3755 [M]	New Sounds	1966	3.00	6.00	12.00
❑ DLP-3816 [M]	Liberace Now!	1967	3.75	7.50	15.00
❑ DLP-9502 [M]	Silver Anniversary	1965	3.00	6.00	12.00
❑ DLP-25547 [S]	Mr. Showmanship	1964	3.75	7.50	15.00
❑ DLP-25550 [S]	A Liberace Christmas	1964	3.75	7.50	15.00
❑ DLP-25563 [S]	My Most Requested	1965	3.75	7.50	15.00
❑ DLP-25595 [S]	Liberace at the Americana, Volume 1	1965	3.75	7.50	15.00
❑ DLP-25596 [S]	Liberace at the Americana, Volume 2	1965	3.75	7.50	15.00
❑ DLP-25755 [S]	New Sounds	1966	3.75	7.50	15.00
❑ DLP-25816 [S]	Liberace Now!	1967	3.75	7.50	15.00
❑ DLP-25858	The Love Album	1968	3.00	6.00	12.00
❑ DLP-25901	Sound of Love	1969	3.00	6.00	12.00
❑ DLP-29502 [S]	Silver Anniversary	1965	3.75	7.50	15.00

HARMONY

Number	Title (A Side/B Side)	Yr	VG	VG+	NM
❑ HL 7154 [M]	The Liberace Show	1959	3.75	7.50	15.00
❑ HL 7237 [M]	Rhapsody in Blue	196?	3.00	6.00	12.00
❑ HL 7361 [M]	Concerto by Candlelight	196?	3.00	6.00	12.00
❑ HS 11054 [R]	The Liberace Show	196?	2.50	5.00	10.00
❑ HS 11161 [R]	Concerto by Candlelight	196?	3.00	6.00	12.00

L

Number	Title (A Side/B Side)	Yr	VG	VG+	NM
❏ HL 11175 [R]	Rhapsody in Blue	196?	2.50	5.00	10.00
❏ HS 11325	Tenderly	1969	2.50	5.00	10.00
❏ HS 11391	The Very Thought of You	1970	2.50	5.00	10.00

MCA

Number	Title (A Side/B Side)	Yr	VG	VG+	NM
❏ 740	Here's Liberace	198?	2.00	4.00	8.00

—Reissue of Vocalion 73821

Number	Title (A Side/B Side)	Yr	VG	VG+	NM
❏ 4060 [(2)]	The Best of Liberace	197?	3.00	6.00	12.00
❏ 4167 [(2)]	The Artistry of Liberace	198?	3.00	6.00	12.00

MISTLETOE

Number	Title (A Side/B Side)	Yr	VG	VG+	NM
❏ MLP-1208	Twas the Night Before Christmas	1974	2.50	5.00	10.00

PARAMOUNT

Number	Title (A Side/B Side)	Yr	VG	VG+	NM
❏ PAS-1009	The Best of Liberace	1973	3.00	6.00	12.00
❏ PAS-1032 [(2)]	Liberace In Concert	1974	3.75	7.50	15.00

PICKWICK

Number	Title (A Side/B Side)	Yr	VG	VG+	NM
❏ SPC-3085	You Made Me Love You	196?	2.50	5.00	10.00
❏ SPC-3124	Strangers in the Night	196?	2.50	5.00	10.00
❏ SPC-3159	What Now My Love	1969	2.50	5.00	10.00
❏ SPC-3208	By the Time I Get to Phoenix	197?	2.50	5.00	10.00

VOCALION

Number	Title (A Side/B Side)	Yr	VG	VG+	NM
❏ VL 3821 [M]	Here's Liberace	196?	3.00	6.00	12.00
❏ VL 73821 [R]	Here's Liberace	196?	3.00	6.00	12.00

WARNER BROS.

Number	Title (A Side/B Side)	Yr	VG	VG+	NM
❏ WS 1847	A Brand New Me	1969	3.00	6.00	12.00
❏ WS 1889	Love and Music Festival "Live"	1970	3.00	6.00	12.00

LIEBERMAN, LORI

45s

CAPITOL

Number	Title (A Side/B Side)	Yr	VG	VG+	NM
❏ 3370	L.A. Texas Boy/Louisiana Cock Fight	1972	—	2.50	5.00
❏ 3379	Killing Me Softly with His Song/Back to Before	1972	—	3.00	6.00
❏ 3577	And the Feeling's Good/My Lover Do You Know	1973	—	2.50	5.00
❏ 3709	Becoming/House Full of Women	1973	—	2.50	5.00
❏ 3889	Make No Mistake/The World Is Turning	1974	—	2.50	5.00
❏ 4020	Raise Up Off of Me/Legacy	1974	—	2.50	5.00

MILLENNIUM

Number	Title (A Side/B Side)	Yr	VG	VG+	NM
❏ 622	Let Me Down Easy/Boston	1978	—	2.00	4.00

Albums

CAPITOL

Number	Title (A Side/B Side)	Yr	VG	VG+	NM
❏ ST-11081	Lori Lieberman	1972	3.00	6.00	12.00
❏ ST-11203	Becoming	1973	3.00	6.00	12.00
❏ ST-11297	A Piece of Time	1974	3.00	6.00	12.00

LIFEGUARDS, THE (1)

45s

ABC-PARAMOUNT

Number	Title (A Side/B Side)	Yr	VG	VG+	NM
❏ 10021	Everybody Out'a the Pool/Teenage Tango	1959	10.00	20.00	40.00

CASA BLANCA

Number	Title (A Side/B Side)	Yr	VG	VG+	NM
❏ 5535	Everybody Out'a the Pool/Teenage Tango	1959	12.50	25.00	50.00

DR

Number	Title (A Side/B Side)	Yr	VG	VG+	NM
❏ 69	Everybody Out'a the Pool/Teenage Tango	1965	3.75	7.50	15.00

LIFEGUARDS, THE (2) Yet another production of STEVE BARRI and P.F. SLOAN.

45s

CATCH

Number	Title (A Side/B Side)	Yr	VG	VG+	NM
❏ 104	State Beach/Big Swim	1964	7.50	15.00	30.00

REPRISE

Number	Title (A Side/B Side)	Yr	VG	VG+	NM
❏ 0277	Swim Party/Swimtime U.S.A.	1964	6.25	12.50	25.00

LIFEGUARDS, THE (U) May be group (1); may be group (2); may be neither.

Albums

WYNCOTE

Number	Title (A Side/B Side)	Yr	VG	VG+	NM
❏ SW-9043 [S]	C'mon and Swim	1964	3.75	7.50	15.00
❏ W-9043 [M]	C'mon and Swim	1964	3.00	6.00	12.00

LIGHT, ENOCH Includes records made by the same musicians under other names; examples include "Terry Snyder and the All-Stars" and "The Command All-Stars."

45s

COMMAND

Number	Title (A Side/B Side)	Yr	VG	VG+	NM
❏ 4008	The Private Life of a Private Eye/ Gum Shoe Lullaby	1960	2.50	5.00	10.00
❏ 4009	Young at Heart Cha Cha/Travel Now, Pay Next Year, Pleasure Cruise	1960	2.50	5.00	10.00
❏ 4010	Mack the Knife Cha Cha/(B-side unknown)	1960	2.50	5.00	10.00
❏ 4011	Rock-a-Bongo Boogie/Blue Is the Night	1960	2.50	5.00	10.00

—By "Terry Snyder and the All-Stars"

Number	Title (A Side/B Side)	Yr	VG	VG+	NM
❏ 4013	No Rest for the Drummer Man/American Patrol	196?	2.50	5.00	10.00
❏ 4014	Waltzing Matilda/Sunrise Over Sumatra	196?	2.50	5.00	10.00
❏ 4019	Satan Never Sleeps/The Four Horsemen of the Apocalypse	1961	2.00	4.00	8.00
❏ 4028	Perdido/Rio Junction	1962	2.00	4.00	8.00
❏ 4029	Meditation (Meditacao)/Big Ben Bossa	1962	2.00	4.00	8.00
❏ 4031	Ching Ching Chow Chow/Istanbul	196?	2.00	4.00	8.00
❏ 4033	Nola/Big Ben Bossa	196?	2.00	4.00	8.00
❏ 4035	Hud/Speak Not a Word	196?	2.00	4.00	8.00
❏ 4050	A Hard Day's Night/Carribe	1964	2.00	4.00	8.00
❏ 4062	Begin the Beguine/(B-side unknown)	196?	2.00	4.00	8.00
❏ 4067	Downtown/Easy Baby, Go Easy Baby	1965	2.00	4.00	8.00
❏ 4068	Forget Domani/Love Me Now	1965	2.00	4.00	8.00
❏ 4069	Theme from "Zorba the Greek"/ Von Ryan's Express	1965	2.00	4.00	8.00
❏ 4072	Love Theme from "The Sandpiper"/ Forget Domani	1966	2.00	4.00	8.00

GRAND AWARD

Number	Title (A Side/B Side)	Yr	VG	VG+	NM
❏ 1020	I Want to Be Happy Cha Cha/Cara Mia Cha Cha	1958	3.00	6.00	12.00
❏ 1026	Baby, It's Cold Outside Cha Cha/ Chiquita Cha Cha	1958	3.00	6.00	12.00
❏ 1032	With My Eyes Wide Open I'm Dreaming/ I Cried for You	1959	3.00	6.00	12.00
❏ 1035	Scarlet Ribbons/Greensleeves	1959	3.00	6.00	12.00

PROJECT 3

Number	Title (A Side/B Side)	Yr	VG	VG+	NM
❏ 1305	Is Paris Burning/And We Were Lovers	1967	—	3.00	6.00
❏ 1310	Come On, Come On, Come On, Don't Be Timid/ I Love, I Live, I Love	1967	—	3.00	6.00
❏ 1322	In the Heat of the Night/Live for Life	1967	—	3.00	6.00
❏ 1330	Green Tambourine/ I Wonder What She's Doing Tonight	1968	—	3.00	6.00
❏ 1339	Lullaby from "Rosemary's Baby"/ The Windmills of Your Mind	1968	—	3.00	6.00
❏ 1341	Hang 'Em High/The Windmills of Your Mind	1968	—	3.00	6.00
❏ 1344	A Man Without Love/ Whoever You Are, I Love You	1969	—	3.00	6.00
❏ 1346	Interlude/Now	1969	—	3.00	6.00
❏ 1348	Funny Girl/Ol' Devil Moon	1969	—	3.00	6.00
❏ 1354	Blowin' in the Wind/Happy Ever After	1969	—	3.00	6.00
❏ 1359	Hair/(B-side unknown)	1969	—	3.00	6.00
❏ 1367	Alice's Restaurant/ Raindrops Keep Fallin' on My Head	1970	—	2.50	5.00
❏ 1368	My Silent Song/Little Fugue for You and Me	1970	—	2.50	5.00
❏ 1369	Day of Anger/Song from "The Wild Bunch"	1970	—	2.50	5.00
❏ 1379	A Lover's Concerto/Bond Street	197?	—	2.50	5.00
❏ 1385	The Out-of-Towners/Patton Theme	197?	—	2.50	5.00
❏ 1389	In the Mood/Let's Dance	197?	—	2.50	5.00
❏ 1394	One O'Clock Jump/Take the "A" Train	197?	—	2.50	5.00
❏ 1395	South Rampart Street Parade/ Woodchopper's Ball	197?	—	2.50	5.00
❏ 1396	Marie/I'll Never Smile Again	197?	—	2.50	5.00
❏ 1397	Jersey Bounce/Tuxedo Junction	197?	—	2.50	5.00
❏ 1398	I'm Getting Sentimental Over You/ A String of Pearls	197?	—	2.50	5.00
❏ 1399	Cherokee/Flying Home	197?	—	2.50	5.00
❏ 1401	Moonlight Serenade/Snowfall	197?	—	2.50	5.00
❏ 1405	Chicago/Happy Days Are Here Again	197?	—	2.50	5.00
❏ 1406	Bye Bye Blackbird/Charleston	197?	—	2.50	5.00
❏ 1407	If You Knew Susie/ I'm Looking Over a Four-Leaf Clover	197?	—	2.50	5.00
❏ 1408	Ain't She Sweet/Yes Sir, That's My Baby	197?	—	2.50	5.00
❏ 1409	Tea for Two/Toot, Toot, Tootsie	197?	—	2.50	5.00
❏ 1411	The Theme from "Shaft"/ The Night They Drove Old Dixie Down	197?	—	2.50	5.00
❏ 1412	Diamonds Are Forever/Fiddler on the Roof	197?	—	2.50	5.00
❏ 1416	The Godfather Waltz/The French Connection	197?	—	2.50	5.00
❏ 1420	Cecelia/Eglantine	197?	—	2.50	5.00
❏ 1427	Give Joy to the World/(B-side unknown)	197?	—	2.50	5.00

Albums

ABC WESTMINSTER/GRAND AWARD

Number	Title (A Side/B Side)	Yr	VG	VG+	NM
❏ 68008	Sing Along with the Original Roaring 20's	1974	2.50	5.00	10.00
❏ 68009	The Flirty 30's	1974	2.50	5.00	10.00
❏ 68012	The Torchy Thirties	1974	2.50	5.00	10.00

COMMAND

Number	Title (A Side/B Side)	Yr	VG	VG+	NM
❏ 800 SD [S]	Persuasive Percussion	1960	3.75	7.50	15.00

—By "Terry Snyder and the All-Stars"

Number	Title (A Side/B Side)	Yr	VG	VG+	NM
❏ 33-800 [M]	Persuasive Percussion	1960	3.00	6.00	12.00

—By "Terry Snyder and the All-Stars"

Number	Title (A Side/B Side)	Yr	VG	VG+	NM
❏ 804 SD [S]	The Sound of Strings	1960	3.75	7.50	15.00
❏ 5 33-804 [M]	The Sound of Strings	1960	3.00	6.00	12.00
❏ 805 SD [S]	Paperback Ballet	1960	3.75	7.50	15.00
❏ 33-805 [M]	Paperback Ballet	1960	3.00	6.00	12.00
❏ 806 SD [S]	Provocative Percussion	1960	3.75	7.50	15.00

—By "The Command All-Stars"

Number	Title (A Side/B Side)	Yr	VG	VG+	NM
❏ 33-806 [M]	Provocative Percussion	1960	3.00	6.00	12.00

—By "The Command All-Stars"

Number	Title (A Side/B Side)	Yr	VG	VG+	NM
❏ 808 SD [S]	Persuasive Percussion, Volume 2	1960	3.75	7.50	15.00

—By "Terry Snyder and the All-Stars"

Number	Title (A Side/B Side)	Yr	VG	VG+	NM
❏ 33-808 [M]	Persuasive Percussion, Volume 2	1960	3.00	6.00	12.00

—By "Terry Snyder and the All-Stars"

Number	Title (A Side/B Side)	Yr	VG	VG+	NM
❏ 810 SD [S]	Provocative Percussion, Volume 2	1960	3.75	7.50	15.00
❏ 33-810 [M]	Provocative Percussion, Volume 2	1960	3.00	6.00	12.00
❏ 814 SD [S]	Pertinent Percussion Cha-Cha's	1960	3.75	7.50	15.00
❏ 33-814 [M]	Pertinent Percussion Cha-Cha's	1960	3.00	6.00	12.00
❏ 817 SD [S]	Persuasive Percussion, Volume 3	1961	3.75	7.50	15.00

—By "The Command All-Stars"

Number	Title (A Side/B Side)	Yr	VG	VG+	NM
❏ 33-817 [M]	Persuasive Percussion, Volume 3	1961	3.00	6.00	12.00

—By "The Command All-Stars"

Number	Title (A Side/B Side)	Yr	VG	VG+	NM
❏ 818 SD [S]	Big Bold and Brassy	1961	3.75	7.50	15.00
❏ 33-818 [M]	Big Bold and Brassy	1961	3.00	6.00	12.00
❏ 821 SD [S]	Provocative Percussion, Volume 3	1961	3.75	7.50	15.00
❏ 33-821 [M]	Provocative Percussion, Volume 3	1961	3.00	6.00	12.00
❏ 822 SD [S]	Far Away Places	1961	3.75	7.50	15.00
❏ 33-822 [M]	Far Away Places	1961	3.00	6.00	12.00
❏ 826 SD [S]	Stereo 35/MM	1961	3.75	7.50	15.00
❏ 830 SD [S]	Persuasive Percussion, Volume 4	1962	3.75	7.50	15.00
❏ 33-830 [M]	Persuasive Percussion, Volume 4	1962	3.00	6.00	12.00
❏ 831 SD [S]	Stereo 35/MM, Volume Two	1962	3.75	7.50	15.00
❏ 833 SD [S]	Vibrations	1962	3.75	7.50	15.00
❏ 33-833 [M]	Vibrations	1962	3.00	6.00	12.00
❏ 834 SD [S]	Provocative Percussion, Volume 4	1962	3.75	7.50	15.00
❏ 33-834 [M]	Provocative Percussion, Volume 4	1962	3.00	6.00	12.00
❏ 835 SD [S]	Great Themes from Hit Films	1962	3.75	7.50	15.00
❏ 33-835 [M]	Great Themes from Hit Films	1962	3.00	6.00	12.00
❏ 840 SD [S]	Enoch Light and His Orchestra At Carnegie Hall Play Irving Berlin	1962	3.75	7.50	15.00
❏ 33-840 [M]	Enoch Light and His Orchestra At Carnegie Hall Play Irving Berlin	1962	3.00	6.00	12.00
❏ 844 SD [S]	Big Band Bossa Nova	1962	3.75	7.50	15.00
❏ 33-844 [M]	Big Band Bossa Nova	1962	3.00	6.00	12.00
❏ 850 SD [S]	Far Away Places, Volume 2	1963	3.75	7.50	15.00
❏ 33-850 [M]	Far Away Places, Volume 2	1963	3.00	6.00	12.00
❏ 851 SD [S]	Let's Dance the Bossa Nova	1963	3.75	7.50	15.00
❏ 33-851 [M]	Let's Dance the Bossa Nova	1963	3.00	6.00	12.00
❏ 854 SD [S]	1963 — The Year's Most Popular Themes	1963	3.75	7.50	15.00
❏ 33-854 [M]	1963 — The Year's Most Popular Themes	1963	3.00	6.00	12.00
❏ 863 SD [S]	Rome 35/MM	1964	3.75	7.50	15.00
❏ 33-863 [M]	Rome 35/MM	1964	3.00	6.00	12.00
❏ 867 SD [S]	Dimension "3"	1964	3.75	7.50	15.00
❏ 33-867 [M]	Dimension "3"	1964	3.00	6.00	12.00
❏ 868 SD [S]	Command Performances	1964	3.75	7.50	15.00
❏ 33-868 [M]	Command Performances	1964	3.00	6.00	12.00
❏ 871 SD [S]	Great Themes from Hit Films	1964	3.75	7.50	15.00
❏ 33-871 [M]	Great Themes from Hit Films	1964	3.00	6.00	12.00
❏ 873 SD [S]	Discotheque Dance...Dance...Dance	1964	3.75	7.50	15.00
❏ 33-873 [M]	Discotheque Dance...Dance...Dance	1964	3.00	6.00	12.00
❏ 879 SD [S]	Great Cole Porter Songs	1965	3.75	7.50	15.00
❏ 33-879 [M]	Great Cole Porter Songs	1965	3.00	6.00	12.00

Number	Title (A Side/B Side)	Yr	VG	VG+	NM
❑ 882 SD [S]	Discotheque Dance…Dance…Dance, Volume 2	1965	3.75	7.50	15.00
❑ 33-882 [M]	Discotheque Dance…Dance…Dance, Volume 2	1965	3.00	6.00	12.00
❑ 887 SD [S]	Magnificent Movie Themes	1965	3.75	7.50	15.00
❑ 33-887 [M]	Magnificent Movie Themes	1965	3.00	6.00	12.00
❑ 895 SD [S]	Persuasive Percussion 1966	1966	3.75	7.50	15.00
❑ 33-895 [M]	Persuasive Percussion 1966	1966	3.00	6.00	12.00
❑ 915 SD	Command Performances, Volume 2	1969	3.75	7.50	15.00
❑ QD-40002 [Q]	A New Concept	1972	3.75	7.50	15.00
GRAND AWARD					
❑ GA-201 SD [S]	The Roaring Twenties	1958	6.25	12.50	25.00
❑ GA-202 SD [S]	The Flirty Thirties	1958	6.25	12.50	25.00
❑ GA-203 SD [S]	Waltzes for Dancing	1958	6.25	12.50	25.00
❑ GA-206 SD [S]	Tommy Dorsey's Song Hits	1958	6.25	12.50	25.00
❑ GA-207 SD [S]	Glenn Miller's Song Hits	1958	6.25	12.50	25.00
❑ GA-211 SD [S]	The Roaring Twenties, Volume 2	1958	6.25	12.50	25.00
❑ GA-214 SD [S]	Around the World in 80 Days	1958	6.25	12.50	25.00
❑ GA-215 SD [S]	Gigi	1958	6.25	12.50	25.00
❑ GA-216 SD [S]	My Fair Lady	1958	6.25	12.50	25.00
❑ GA-217 SD [S]	Oklahoma/South Pacific	1958	6.25	12.50	25.00
❑ GA-220 SD [S]	The Torchy Thirties	1958	6.25	12.50	25.00
❑ GA-222 SD [S]	I Want to Be Happy Cha Cha's	1959	6.25	12.50	25.00
❑ GA-224 SD [S]	New World Symphony	1958	6.25	12.50	25.00
❑ GA-225 SD [S]	The Great Themes of America's Great Bands	1958	6.25	12.50	25.00
❑ GA-227 SD [S]	Happy Cha Cha's, Vol. 2	1959	6.25	12.50	25.00
❑ GA-228 SD [S]	Show Spectacular	1959	6.25	12.50	25.00
❑ GA-229 SD [S]	The Roaring Twenties, Volume 3	1959	6.25	12.50	25.00
❑ GA-236 SD [S]	All the Things You Are	1959	6.25	12.50	25.00
❑ GA-237 SD [S]	Come to Hawaii	1959	6.25	12.50	25.00
❑ GA-238 SD [S]	With My Eyes Wide Open I'm Dreaming	1959	6.25	12.50	25.00
❑ GA-242 SD [S]	Something to Remember You By	1959	6.25	12.50	25.00
❑ GA-246 SD [S]	Just for Kicks	1959	6.25	12.50	25.00
❑ GA-251 SD [S]	Sing Along with the Original Roaring 20's	1959	6.25	12.50	25.00
❑ GA 33-327 [M]	The Roaring Twenties	1958	5.00	10.00	20.00
❑ GA 33-353 [M]	The Roaring Twenties, Volume 3	1959	5.00	10.00	20.00
❑ GA 33-371 [M]	The Flirty Thirties	1958	5.00	10.00	20.00
❑ GA 33-372 [M]	Waltzes for Dancing	1958	5.00	10.00	20.00
❑ GA 33-380 [M]	Paris Spectacular	1959	5.00	10.00	20.00
❑ GA 33-381 [M]	Glenn Miller's Song Hits	1958	5.00	10.00	20.00
❑ GA 33-382 [M]	Tommy Dorsey's Song Hits	1958	5.00	10.00	20.00
❑ GA 33-388 [M]	I Want to Be Happy Cha Cha's	1959	5.00	10.00	20.00
❑ GA 33-391 [M]	Happy Cha Cha's, Vol. 2	1959	5.00	10.00	20.00
❑ GA 33-392 [M]	The Great Themes of America's Great Bands	1958	5.00	10.00	20.00
❑ GA 33-399 [M]	All the Things You Are	1959	5.00	10.00	20.00
❑ GA 33-405 [M]	Come to Hawaii	1959	5.00	10.00	20.00
❑ GA 33-406 [M]	With My Eyes Wide Open I'm Dreaming	1959	5.00	10.00	20.00
❑ GA 33-410 [M]	Something to Remember You By	1959	5.00	10.00	20.00
❑ GA 33-419 [M]	Sing Along with the Original Roaring 20's	1959	5.00	10.00	20.00
PROJECT 3					
❑ PR-5000 SD	Spanish Strings	1967	3.00	6.00	12.00
❑ PR4C-5000 [Q]	Spanish Strings	1973	3.75	7.50	15.00
❑ PR-5004 SD	It's Happening	1967	3.00	6.00	12.00
❑ PR-5005 SD	Film on Film — Great Movie Themes	1967	3.00	6.00	12.00
❑ PR-5013 SD	Film Fame	1968	3.00	6.00	12.00
❑ PR-5021 SD	Twelve Smash Hits	1968	3.00	6.00	12.00
❑ PR-5027 SD	The Best of Hollywood '68–'69	1968	3.00	6.00	12.00
❑ PR-5030 SD	Whoever You Are, I Love You	1968	3.00	6.00	12.00
❑ PR-5036 SD	Enoch Light and the Brass Menagerie	1969	3.00	6.00	12.00
❑ PR4C-5036 [Q]	Enoch Light and the Brass Menagerie	1973	3.75	7.50	15.00
❑ PR-5038 SD	Glittering Guitars	1969	3.00	6.00	12.00
❑ PR-5042 SD	Enoch Light and the Brass Menagerie, Volume 2	1969	3.00	6.00	12.00
❑ PR4C-5042 [Q]	Enoch Light and the Brass Menagerie, Volume 2	1973	3.75	7.50	15.00
❑ PR-5043 SD	Spaced Out	1970	3.00	6.00	12.00
❑ PR4C-5043 [Q]	Spaced Out	1973	3.75	7.50	15.00
❑ PR-5046 SD	Best of the Movie Themes 1970	1970	3.00	6.00	12.00
❑ PR4C-5046 [Q]	Best of the Movie Themes 1970	1973	3.75	7.50	15.00
❑ PR-5048 SD	Permissive Polyphonics	1970	3.00	6.00	12.00
❑ PR4C-5048 [Q]	Permissive Polyphonics	1973	3.75	7.50	15.00
❑ PR-5049 SD	Big Band Hits of the 30's	1971	3.00	6.00	12.00
❑ PR4C-5049 [Q]	Big Band Hits of the 30's	1973	3.75	7.50	15.00
❑ PR-5051 SD	Hit Movie Themes	1971	3.00	6.00	12.00
❑ PR4C-5051 [Q]	Hit Movie Themes	1973	3.75	7.50	15.00
❑ PR-5056 SD	Big Band Hits of the 30's & 40's!	1971	3.00	6.00	12.00
❑ PR4C-5056 [Q]	Big Band Hits of the 30's & 40's!	1973	3.75	7.50	15.00
❑ PR-5059 SD	Big Hits of the 20's	1971	3.00	6.00	12.00
❑ PR4C-5059 [Q]	Big Hits of the 20's	1973	3.75	7.50	15.00
❑ PR-5060 SD	Enoch Light and the Brass Menagerie 1973	1972	3.00	6.00	12.00
❑ PR4C-5060 [Q]	Enoch Light and the Brass Menagerie 1973	1973	3.75	7.50	15.00
❑ PR-5063 SD	Movie Hits!	1972	3.00	6.00	12.00
❑ PR4C-5063 [Q]	Movie Hits!	1973	3.75	7.50	15.00
❑ PR4C-5068 [Q]	4 Channel Dynamite!	1973	3.75	7.50	15.00
❑ PR4C-5073 [Q]	Charge!	1973	3.75	7.50	15.00
❑ PR4C-5076 [Q]	Big Band Hits of the 40's & 50's	1973	3.75	7.50	15.00
❑ PR4C-5073 [Q]	Future Sound Shock	1973	3.75	7.50	15.00
❑ PR-5084 SD	Beatles Classics	1974	3.00	6.00	12.00
❑ PR4C-5084 [Q]	Beatles Classics	1974	3.75	7.50	15.00
❑ PR-5086 SD	Great Hits from the Gatsby Era	1974	3.00	6.00	12.00
❑ PR4C-5086 [Q]	Great Hits from the Gatsby Era	1974	3.75	7.50	15.00
❑ PR-5089 SD	Big Band Hits of the 30's, Volume 2	1975	3.00	6.00	12.00
❑ PR4C-5089 [Q]	Big Band Hits of the 30's, Volume 2	1975	3.75	7.50	15.00
❑ PR-5092 SD	Disco Disque	197?	3.00	6.00	12.00
❑ PR4C-5092 [Q]	Disco Disque	197?	3.75	7.50	15.00
❑ PR-5100	Let It Be	197?	3.00	6.00	12.00
❑ PR-5109	The Most Beautiful Music in the World	1981	3.00	6.00	12.00
❑ PR-6003/4 [(2)]	Big Hits of the Seventies	1974	3.75	7.50	15.00
❑ PR4C-6003/4 [(2)Q]	Big Hits of the Seventies	1974	5.00	10.00	20.00
❑ PR-6005/6 [(2)]	Big Band Hits of the 30's, 40's & 50's	1974	3.75	7.50	15.00
❑ PR4C-6005/6 [(2)Q]	Big Band Hits of the 30's, 40's & 50's	1974	5.00	10.00	20.00
❑ PR-6011/12 [(2)]	Music Maestro, Please	197?	3.75	7.50	15.00
❑ PR-6013/14 [(2)]	Big Band Hits of the 30's and 40's	197?	3.75	7.50	15.00
❑ PR4C-6013/14 [(2)Q]	Big Band Hits of the 30's and 40's	197?	5.00	10.00	20.00
❑ PR-6034 [(2)]	20 Great Movie Themes	1980	3.75	7.50	15.00
SEAGULL					
❑ LG-8204	Blowin' in the Wind	198?	2.50	5.00	10.00
❑ LG-8207	Music from the Movies	198?	2.50	5.00	10.00

LIGHTFOOT, GORDON

Number	Title (A Side/B Side)	Yr	VG	VG+	NM
45s					
ABC-PARAMOUNT					
❑ 10352	Daisy-Doo/I'm the One (Remember Me)	1962	6.25	12.50	25.00
—As "Gord Lightfoot"					
❑ 10373	It's Too Late, He Wins/Negotiations	1962	6.25	12.50	25.00
CHATEAU					
❑ 142	Daisy-Doo/I'm the One (Remember Me)	1962	12.50	25.00	50.00
❑ 148	It's Too Late, He Wins/Negotiations	1962	12.50	25.00	50.00
❑ 152	I'll Meet You in Michigan/ Is My Baby Blue Tonight	1962	10.00	20.00	40.00
REPRISE					
❑ 0744	If You Could Read My Mind/ Me and Bobby McGee	1972	—	2.00	4.00
—"Back to Back Hits" series					
❑ 0745	Talking in Your Sleep/Summer Side of Life	1972	—	2.00	4.00
—"Back to Back Hits" series					
❑ 0926	Me and Bobby McGee/Pony Man	1970	—	2.50	5.00
❑ 0974	If You Could Read My Mind/Poor Little Allison	1970	—	3.00	6.00
❑ 1020	Talking in Your Sleep/Nous Vivons Ensemble	1971	—	2.50	5.00
❑ 1035	Summer Side of Life/Love and Maple Syrup	1971	—	2.50	5.00
❑ 1088	Beautiful/Don Quixote	1972	—	2.50	5.00
❑ 1128	You Are What I Am/The Same Old Obsession	1972	—	2.50	5.00
❑ 1145	Can't Depend on You/It's Worth Believin'	1972	—	2.50	5.00
❑ 1194	Sundown/Too Late for Prayin'	1974	—	2.00	4.00
❑ 1309	Carefree Highway/Seven Island Suite	1974	—	2.00	4.00
❑ 1328	Rainy Day People/Cherokee Bend	1975	—	2.00	4.00
❑ 1369	The Wreck of the Edmund Fitzgerald/The House You Live In	1976	—	2.00	4.00
❑ 1380	Race Among the Ruins/Protocol	1976	—	2.00	4.00
UNITED ARTISTS					
❑ 929	Just Like Tom Thumb's Blues/Ribbon of Darkness	1965	2.50	5.00	10.00
❑ 50055	For Lovin' Me/Spin, Spin	1966	2.00	4.00	8.00
❑ 50114	I'll Be Alright/Go Go Round	1967	2.00	4.00	8.00
❑ 50152	The Way I Feel/Peaceful Waters	1967	2.00	4.00	8.00
❑ 50281	Pussywillows, Cat-Tails/Black Day in July	1968	2.00	4.00	8.00
❑ 50447	Does Your Mother Know/Bitter Green	1968	2.00	4.00	8.00
❑ 50765	If I Could/Softly	1971	—	2.50	5.00
WARNER BROS.					
❑ 5621	For Lovin' Me/I'm Not Sayin'	1965	3.75	7.50	15.00
❑ 8518	The Circle Is Small (I Can See It In Your Eyes)/ Sweet Guinevere	1978	—	2.00	4.00
—Subtitle added to later pressings					
❑ 8518	The Circle Is Small/Sweet Guinevere	1978	—	2.50	5.00
—Without A-side subtitle					
❑ 8579	Daylight Katy/Hangdog Hotel Room	1978	—	2.00	4.00
❑ 8644	Dreamland/Songs the Minstrel Sang	1978	—	2.00	4.00
❑ 28222	Ecstasy Made Easy/Morning Glory	1987	—	—	3.00
❑ 28422	East of Midnight/I'll Tag Along	1987	—	—	3.00
❑ 28553	Stay Loose/Morning Glory	1986	—	—	3.00
❑ 28655	Anything for Love/Let It Ride	1986	—	—	3.00
❑ 28655 [PS]	Anything for Love/Let It Ride	1986	—	2.00	4.00
❑ 29466	Someone to Believe In/Without You	1983	—	2.00	4.00
❑ 29511	Knotty Pine/Salute	1983	—	2.00	4.00
❑ 29859	Shadows/In My Fashion	1982	—	2.00	4.00
❑ 29963	Blackberry Wine/(B-side unknown)	1982	—	2.00	4.00
❑ 49230	Dream Street Rose/Make Way for the Lady	1980	—	2.00	4.00
❑ 49516	If You Need Me/Mister Rock of Ages	1980	—	2.00	4.00
❑ 50012	Baby Step Back/Thank You for the Promises	1982	—	2.00	4.00
Albums					
LIBERTY					
❑ LN-10038	The Best of Lightfoot	198?	2.00	4.00	8.00
—Budget-line reissue					
❑ LN-10039	Sunday Concert	198?	2.00	4.00	8.00
—Budget-line reissue					
❑ LN-10040	Back Here on Earth	198?	2.00	4.00	8.00
—Budget-line reissue					
❑ LN-10041	Did She Mention My Name	198?	2.00	4.00	8.00
—Budget-line reissue					
❑ LN-10043	The Way I Feel	198?	2.00	4.00	8.00
—Budget-line reissue					
❑ LN-10044	Lightfoot	198?	2.00	4.00	8.00
—Budget-line reissue					
MOBILE FIDELITY					
❑ 1-018	Sundown	1979	10.00	20.00	40.00
—Audiophile vinyl					
PAIR					
❑ PDL2-1081 [(2)]	Songbook	1986	3.00	6.00	12.00
REPRISE					
❑ MS 2037	Summer Side of Life	1971	3.00	6.00	12.00
❑ MS 2056	Don Quixote	1972	3.00	6.00	12.00
❑ MS 2116	Old Dan's Records	1972	3.00	6.00	12.00
❑ MS 2177	Sundown	1974	3.00	6.00	12.00
❑ MS4-2177 [Q]	Sundown	1974	5.00	10.00	20.00
❑ MS 2206	Cold on the Shoulder	1975	3.00	6.00	12.00
❑ MS4-2206 [Q]	Cold on the Shoulder	1975	5.00	10.00	20.00
❑ 2RS 2237 [(2)]	Gord's Gold	1975	3.75	7.50	15.00
❑ MS 2246	Summertime Dream	1976	3.00	6.00	12.00
❑ RS 6392	Sit Down Young Stranger	1970	3.75	7.50	15.00
❑ RS 6392	If You Could Read My Mind	1971	2.50	5.00	10.00
—Retitled version					
❑ ST-93228	Sit Down Young Stranger	1970	5.00	10.00	20.00
—Capitol Record Club edition					
UNITED ARTISTS					
❑ UA-LA243-G	The Very Best of Gordon Lightfoot	1974	3.00	6.00	12.00
❑ UAL-3487 [M]	Lightfoot	1966	5.00	10.00	20.00
❑ UAL-3587 [M]	The Way I Feel	1967	5.00	10.00	20.00
❑ UAS-5510	Classic Lightfoot (The Best of Lightfoot/Volume 2)	1971	3.75	7.50	15.00
❑ UAS-6487 [S]	Lightfoot	1966	6.25	12.50	25.00
❑ UAS-6587 [S]	The Way I Feel	1967	6.25	12.50	25.00
❑ UAS-6649	Did She Mention My Name	1968	5.00	10.00	20.00
❑ UAS-6672	Back Here on Earth	1969	5.00	10.00	20.00
❑ UAS-6714	Sunday Concert	1969	3.75	7.50	15.00
❑ UAS-6754	The Best of Gordon Lightfoot	1970	3.75	7.50	15.00

L

Number	Title (A Side/B Side)	Yr	VG	VG+	NM
WARNER BROS.					
❏ BSK 3149	Endless Wire	1978	2.50	5.00	10.00
❏ HS 3426	Dream Street Rose	1980	2.50	5.00	10.00
❏ BSK 3633	Shadows	1982	2.50	5.00	10.00
❏ 23901	Salute	1983	2.50	5.00	10.00
❏ 25482	East of Midnight	1986	2.50	5.00	10.00
❏ 25784	Gord's Gold, Volume II	1989	3.00	6.00	12.00

LIGHTFOOT, PAPA
45s
Number	Title (A Side/B Side)	Yr	VG	VG+	NM
ALADDIN					
❏ 3171	After a While (Blue Lights)/P.L.'s Blues	1953	50.00	100.00	200.00
❏ 3304	Blue Lights/Jumpin' with Jarvis	1955	37.50	75.00	150.00
IMPERIAL					
❏ 5289	Wine, Women, Whiskey/Mean Old Train	1954	37.50	75.00	150.00
SAVOY					
❏ 1161	Mean Old Train/Wild Fire	1955	7.50	15.00	30.00
Albums					
VAULT					
❏ 130	Natchez Trace	1969	3.75	7.50	15.00
—As "Papa George Lightfoot"					

LIGHTHOUSE
45s
Number	Title (A Side/B Side)	Yr	VG	VG+	NM
EVOLUTION					
❏ 1041	Hats Off/Sing, Sing, Sing	1971	—	2.50	5.00
❏ 1048	One Fine Morning/Little Kind Words	1971	—	3.00	6.00
❏ 1052	Take It Slow (Out in the Country)/Sweet Lullaby	1971	—	2.50	5.00
❏ 1058	I Just Wanna Be Your Friend/1849	1972	—	2.50	5.00
❏ 1061	I'd Be So Happy/Old Man	1972	—	2.50	5.00
❏ 1069	Sunny Days/Lonely Places	1972	—	2.50	5.00
❏ 1072	You Girl/Merlin	1972	—	2.50	5.00
❏ 1076	Broken Guitar Blues/Merlin	1973	—	2.50	5.00
POLYDOR					
❏ 14197	Can You Feel It/Bright Side	1973	—	2.00	4.00
❏ 14198	Pretty Lady/Bright Side	1973	—	2.00	4.00
❏ 14220	Magic's in the Dancing/Disagreeable man	1974	—	2.00	4.00
❏ 14246	Good Day/Going Downtown	1974	—	2.00	4.00
RCA VICTOR					
❏ 47-9808	The Chant (Nam-Myo-Ho Renge Kyo)/Could You Be Concerned	1969	—	3.00	6.00
❏ 74-0224	Eight Miles High/If There Ever Was a Time	1969	—	3.00	6.00
❏ 74-0285	Feel So Good/ Places on Faces Four Blue Carpet Traces	1969	—	3.00	6.00
Albums					
EVOLUTION					
❏ 3007	One Fine Morning	1971	3.75	7.50	15.00
❏ 3010	Thoughts of Movin' On	1972	3.75	7.50	15.00
❏ 3014 [(2)]	Lighthouse Live!	1972	5.00	10.00	20.00
❏ 3016	Sunny Days	1973	3.75	7.50	15.00
JANUS					
❏ JSX-7025	The Best of Lighthouse	1976	3.00	6.00	12.00
POLYDOR					
❏ PD-5056	Can You Feel It	1973	3.00	6.00	12.00
❏ PD-1-6028	Good Day	1974	3.00	6.00	12.00
RCA VICTOR					
❏ LSP-4173	Lighthouse	1969	3.75	7.50	15.00
❏ LSP-4241	Suite Feeling	1969	3.75	7.50	15.00
❏ LSP-4325	Peacing It All Together	1970	3.75	7.50	15.00

LIGHTNIN' SLIM
45s
Number	Title (A Side/B Side)	Yr	VG	VG+	NM
ACE					
❏ 505	Bad Feeling Blues/Lightning Slim Boogie	1955	37.50	75.00	150.00
EXCELLO					
❏ 2066	I Can't Be Successful/Lightnin' Blues	1955	10.00	20.00	40.00
❏ 2075	Sugar Plum/Just Made Twenty One	1956	7.50	15.00	30.00
❏ 2080	Goin' Home/Wonderin' and Goin'	1956	7.50	15.00	30.00
❏ 2096	Have Your Way/Bad Luck and Trouble	1956	7.50	15.00	30.00
❏ 2106	Mean Old Lonesome Train/I'm Grown	1957	7.50	15.00	30.00
❏ 2116	I'm a Rollin' Stone/Love Me Mama	1957	7.50	15.00	30.00
❏ 2131	Hoo-Doo Blues/It's Mighty Crazy	1958	7.50	15.00	30.00
❏ 2142	My Starter Won't Work/Long Leanie Mama	1958	7.50	15.00	30.00
❏ 2150	Feelin' Awful Blues/I'm Leavin' You Baby	1959	7.50	15.00	30.00
❏ 2160	Sweet Little Woman/Lightnin's Troubles	1959	7.50	15.00	30.00
❏ 2169	Rooster Blues/G.I. Slim	1959	7.50	15.00	30.00
❏ 2179	My Little Angel Child/Too Close Blues	1960	6.25	12.50	25.00
❏ 2186	Cool Down Baby/Nothin' But the Devil	1960	6.25	12.50	25.00
❏ 2195	Somebody Knockin'/I Just Don't Know	1961	6.25	12.50	25.00
❏ 2203	Hello Mary Lee/I'm Tired Waitin' Baby	1961	6.25	12.50	25.00
❏ 2215	Mind Your Own Business/ You're Old Enough to Understand	1962	6.25	12.50	25.00
❏ 2224	Winter Time Blues/I'm Warnin' You Baby	1962	6.25	12.50	25.00
❏ 2228	If You Ever Need Me/I'm Evil	1963	6.25	12.50	25.00
❏ 2234	Loving Around the Clock/ You Know You're So Fine	1963	6.25	12.50	25.00
❏ 2240	Blues at Night/Don't Mistreat Me Baby	1963	6.25	12.50	25.00
❏ 2245	You Give Me the Blues/Strangest Feelin'	1964	6.25	12.50	25.00
❏ 2252	Greyhound Blues/She's My Crazy Little Baby	1964	6.25	12.50	25.00
❏ 2258	Baby Please Come Back/You Move Me Baby	1964	6.25	12.50	25.00
❏ 2262	Have Mercy on Me Baby/ I've Been a Fool for You Darlin'	1965	6.25	12.50	25.00
❏ 2267	Bad Luck Blues/Can't Live This Life No More	1965	6.25	12.50	25.00
❏ 2269	Don't Start Me Talkin'/Darlin' You're the One	1965	5.00	10.00	20.00
❏ 2272	I Hate to See You Leave/Love Is Just a Gamble	1965	5.00	10.00	20.00
❏ 2320	My Babe/Good Morning Heartaches	1971	2.50	5.00	10.00
FEATURE					
❏ 3006	Rock Me, Mama/Bad Luck	1954	75.00	150.00	300.00
❏ 3008	I Can't Live Happy/New Orleans Bound	1954	15.00	30.00	60.00
❏ 3012	Bugger Bugger Boy/Ethel Mae	1954	15.00	30.00	60.00
Albums					
EXCELLO					
❏ LP 8000 [M]	Rooster Blues	1960	200.00	400.00	800.00
❏ LPS 8000 [M]	Rooster Blues	196?	12.50	25.00	50.00
—Thogh labeled "Electronic Stereo," this record is mono					
❏ LP 8004 [M]	Lightnin' Slim's Bell Ringer	1965	75.00	150.00	300.00

Number	Title (A Side/B Side)	Yr	VG	VG+	NM
❏ LPS 8004 [M]	Lightnin' Slim's Bell Ringer	196?	12.50	25.00	50.00
—Thogh labeled "Electronic Stereo," this record is mono					
❏ LPS 8018	High and Low Down	1971	3.75	7.50	15.00
❏ LPS 8023	London Gumbo	1972	3.75	7.50	15.00
INTERMEDIA					
❏ QS-5062	That's All Right	198?	2.50	5.00	10.00

LIGHTNING
45s
Number	Title (A Side/B Side)	Yr	VG	VG+	NM
P.I.P.					
❏ 8921	Hideaway/Freedom	1970	5.00	10.00	20.00
Albums					
P.I.P.					
❏ 6807	Lightning	1971	7.50	15.00	30.00

LIMELIGHTERS, THE
45s
Number	Title (A Side/B Side)	Yr	VG	VG+	NM
JOSIE					
❏ 795	Cabin Hideaway/My Sweet Norma Lee	1956	37.50	75.00	150.00

LIMELITERS, THE　Also see GLENN YARBROUGH.
45s
Number	Title (A Side/B Side)	Yr	VG	VG+	NM
RCA VICTOR					
❏ 47-7859	A Dollar Down/ When Twice the Moon Has Come and Gone	1961	2.00	4.00	8.00
❏ 47-7859 [PS]	A Dollar Down/When Twice the Moon Has Come and Gone	1961	3.00	6.00	12.00
❏ 47-7913	Paco Peco/A Hundred Years Ago	1961	2.00	4.00	8.00
❏ 47-7942	Milk and Honey/Red Roses and White Wine	1961	2.00	4.00	8.00
❏ 47-7966	Jonah/Just an Honest Mistake	1961	2.00	4.00	8.00
❏ 47-8069	The Riddle Song/I Had a Mule	1962	2.00	4.00	8.00
❏ 47-8094	Who Will Buy/Funk	1962	2.00	4.00	8.00
❏ 47-8094 [PS]	Who Will Buy/Funk	1962	3.00	6.00	12.00
❏ 47-8255	Midnight Special/McClintock's Theme	1963	2.00	4.00	8.00
❏ 47-8361	No Man Is an Island/A Casinda Pequenina	1964	2.00	4.00	8.00
WARNER BROS.					
❏ 7254	Time to Gather Seed/ The Importance of the Rose	1968	—	3.00	6.00
7-Inch Extended Plays					
RCA VICTOR					
❏ VLP 2445	A Wayfaring Stranger/Charmin' Betsy/Gotta Travel On//(B-side unknown)	196?	5.00	10.00	20.00
—Jukebox issue; small hole, plays at 33 1/3 rpm					
❏ VLP 2445 [PS]	(title unknown)	196?	5.00	10.00	20.00
Albums					
ELEKTRA					
❏ EKM-180 [M]	The Limeliters	1960	5.00	10.00	20.00
❏ EKS-7180 [S]	The Limeliters	1960	6.25	12.50	25.00
GNP CRESCENDO					
❏ GNPS-2188	Alive! In Concert, Vol. 1	1986	2.50	5.00	10.00
❏ GNPS-2190	Alive! In Concert, Vol. 2	1987	2.50	5.00	10.00
LEGACY					
❏ 113	Their First Historic Album	1970	3.00	6.00	12.00
RCA CAMDEN					
❏ ACL1-0602	This Train	1974	2.50	5.00	10.00
RCA VICTOR					
❏ LPM-2272 [M]	Tonight: In Person	1961	5.00	10.00	20.00
❏ LSP-2272 [S]	Tonight: In Person	1961	6.25	12.50	25.00
❏ ANL1-2336	Pure Gold	1977	2.00	4.00	8.00
❏ LPM-2393 [M]	The Slightly Fabulous Limeliters	1961	5.00	10.00	20.00
❏ LSP-2393 [S]	The Slightly Fabulous Limeliters	1961	6.25	12.50	25.00
❏ LPM-2445 [M]	Sing Out!	1962	5.00	10.00	20.00
❏ LSP-2445 [S]	Sing Out!	1962	6.25	12.50	25.00
❏ LPM-2512 [M]	Through Children's Eyes	1962	5.00	10.00	20.00
❏ LSP-2512 [S]	Through Children's Eyes	1962	6.25	12.50	25.00
❏ LPM-2547 [M]	Folk Matinee	1962	5.00	10.00	20.00
❏ LSP-2547 [S]	Folk Matinee	1962	6.25	12.50	25.00
❏ LPM-2588 [M]	Makin' a Joyful Noise	1963	5.00	10.00	20.00
❏ LSP-2588 [S]	Makin' a Joyful Noise	1963	6.25	12.50	25.00
❏ LPM-2609 [M]	Our Men in San Francisco	1963	5.00	10.00	20.00
❏ LSP-2609 [S]	Our Men in San Francisco	1963	6.25	12.50	25.00
❏ LPM-2671 [M]	Fourteen 14K Folk Songs	1963	5.00	10.00	20.00
❏ LSP-2671 [S]	Fourteen 14K Folk Songs	1963	6.25	12.50	25.00
❏ LPM-2844 [M]	More of Everything!	1964	3.75	7.50	15.00
❏ LSP-2844 [S]	More of Everything!	1964	5.00	10.00	20.00
❏ LPM-2889 [M]	The Best of the Limeliters	1964	3.75	7.50	15.00
❏ LSP-2889 [S]	The Best of the Limeliters	1964	5.00	10.00	20.00
❏ LPM-2906 [M]	Leave It to the Limeliters	1964	3.75	7.50	15.00
❏ LSP-2906 [S]	Leave It to the Limeliters	1964	5.00	10.00	20.00
❏ LPM-2907 [M]	London Concert	1964	3.75	7.50	15.00
❏ LSP-2907 [S]	London Concert	1964	5.00	10.00	20.00
❏ LPM-3385 [M]	The Limeliters Look at Love… In Depth	1965	3.75	7.50	15.00
❏ LSP-3385 [S]	The Limeliters Look at Love… In Depth	1965	5.00	10.00	20.00
❏ LSP-4100	The Original "Those Were the Days"	1969	3.75	7.50	15.00
WEST KNOLL					
❏ WK-1001	Alive! In Concert, Vol. 1	198?	2.50	5.00	10.00
❏ WK-1002	Alive! In Concert, Vol. 2	198?	2.50	5.00	10.00

LIMEYS, THE
45s
Number	Title (A Side/B Side)	Yr	VG	VG+	NM
DOT					
❏ 16725	Don't Cry/I Can't Find My Way Through	1965	3.75	7.50	15.00
SCEPTER					
❏ 12156	Come Back/Scraped: Green and Blue	1966	3.75	7.50	15.00

LIMOUSINE
Albums
Number	Title (A Side/B Side)	Yr	VG	VG+	NM
GSF					
❏ 1002	Limousine	1972	5.00	10.00	20.00

LIND, BOB
45s
Number	Title (A Side/B Side)	Yr	VG	VG+	NM
CAPITOL					
❏ 3169	Theme from the Music Box/She Can Get Along	1971	—	2.50	5.00
UNITED ARTISTS					
❏ 0032	Elusive Butterfly/Truly Julie's Blues	1973	—	2.00	4.00
—"Silver Spotlight Series" reissue					

Number	Title (A Side/B Side)	Yr	VG	VG+	NM
VERVE FOLKWAYS					
❑ 5018	Wandering/Hey Nellie Hellie	1966	2.00	4.00	8.00
❑ 5029	Black Night/White Snow	1966	2.00	4.00	8.00
WORLD PACIFIC					
❑ 77808	Elusive Butterfly/Cheryl's Goin' Home	1965	2.50	5.00	10.00
❑ 77822	Remember the Rain/Truly Julie's Blues					
	(I'll Be There)	1966	2.00	4.00	8.00
❑ 77830	We've Never Spoken/I Just Let It Take Me	1966	2.00	4.00	8.00
❑ 77839	San Francisco Woman/Baby Take Me Home	1966	2.00	4.00	8.00
❑ 77865	Good Time Special/Just My Love	1967	2.00	4.00	8.00
❑ 77879	Goodbye Neon Lies/We May Have Touched	1967	2.00	4.00	8.00
Albums					
CAPITOL					
❑ ST-780	Since There Were Circles	1971	3.75	7.50	15.00
VERVE FOLKWAYS					
❑ FT-3005 [M]	The Elusive Bob Lind	1966	6.25	12.50	25.00
❑ FTS-3005 [S]	The Elusive Bob Lind	1966	7.50	15.00	30.00
WORLD PACIFIC					
❑ WP-1841 [M]	Don't Be Concerned	1966	5.00	10.00	20.00
❑ WP-1851 [M]	Photographs of Feeling	1966	5.00	10.00	20.00
❑ ST-21841 [S]	Don't Be Concerned	1966	6.25	12.50	25.00
❑ ST-21851 [S]	Photographs of Feeling	1966	6.25	12.50	25.00
LINDA AND THE VISTAS					
45s					
SHRINE					
❑ 0100	Bad Apple/She Went Away	1965	62.50	125.00	250.00
LINDE, JOHN					
45s					
CADET					
❑ 5611	Accordingly/I Learned Some Things Today	1968	2.00	4.00	8.00
PARKWAY					
❑ 856	Bossa Nova Bill/Round Sound	1962	3.00	6.00	12.00
LINDEN, KATHY					
45s					
CAPITOL					
❑ 4700	Remember Me (To Jimmy)/					
	Beautiful Brown Eyes	1962	2.00	4.00	8.00
❑ 4770	Words/There'll Always Be Sadness	1962	2.00	4.00	8.00
❑ 4811	If You Really Love Me/Jimmy	1962	2.00	4.00	8.00
❑ 5018	People Say/There'll Always Be Sadness	1963	2.00	4.00	8.00
FELSTED					
❑ 8510	Billy/If I Could Hold You in My Arms	1958	3.75	7.50	15.00
❑ 8521	You'd Be Surprised/Why Oh Why	1958	3.75	7.50	15.00
❑ 8533	Oh Johnny Oh/Georgie	1958	3.75	7.50	15.00
❑ 8544	Kissin' Conversation/Just a Sandy Haired Boy					
	Called Sandy	1958	3.75	7.50	15.00
❑ 8554	Somebody Loves You/You Walked Into My Life	1959	3.75	7.50	15.00
❑ 8571	Goodbye, Jimmy, Goodbye/Heartaches at					
	Sweet Sixteen	1959	3.75	7.50	15.00
❑ 8587	You Don't Know Girls/So Close to My Heart	1959	3.00	6.00	12.00
❑ 8596	Think Love/Mary Lou Wilson and Johnny Brown	1959	3.00	6.00	12.00
MONUMENT					
❑ 420	Allentown Jail/That's What Love Is	1960	2.50	5.00	10.00
❑ 423	Midnight/The Willow Weeps	1960	2.50	5.00	10.00
❑ 428	Take Me Home (To My Lover)/We Had Words	1960	2.50	5.00	10.00
❑ 436	So in Love (With You)/Take Me Home, Jimmy	1961	2.50	5.00	10.00
Albums					
FELSTED					
❑ 7501 [M]	That Certain Boy	1959	15.00	30.00	60.00
LINDISFARNE					
45s					
ATCO					
❑ 7093	Run for Home/Stick Together	1978	—	2.00	4.00
❑ 7095	Warm Feeling/Woman	1979	—	2.00	4.00
ELEKTRA					
❑ 45733	We Can Swing Together/					
	Float Me Down the River	1971	—	—	—
—Canceled					
❑ 45778	Fog on the Tyne/Meet Me on the Corner	1972	—	3.50	7.00
❑ 45799	Lady Eleanor/Down	1972	—	3.00	6.00
❑ 45819	Don't Ask Him/All Fall Down	1972	—	2.50	5.00
❑ 45835	Court in the Act/Poor Old Ireland	1973	—	2.50	5.00
Albums					
ATCO					
❑ SD 38-108	Back and Fourth	1978	3.00	6.00	12.00
ELEKTRA					
❑ 7E-1018	Happy Daze	1975	3.00	6.00	12.00
❑ EKS-74099	Nicely Out of Tune	1971	3.75	7.50	15.00
❑ EKS-75021	Fog on the Tyne	1972	3.75	7.50	15.00
❑ EKS-75043	Dingly Dell	1972	3.75	7.50	15.00
❑ EKS-75077	Roll On, Ruby	1974	3.75	7.50	15.00
LINDSAY, MARK Also see PAUL REVERE AND THE RAIDERS; THE UNKNOWNS.					
45s					
COLUMBIA					
❑ 10081	Mamacita/Song for a Friend	1974	—	2.50	5.00
❑ 10114	Photograph/Song for a Friend	1975	—	2.50	5.00
❑ 44875	First Hymn from Grand Terrace/					
	The Old Man at the Fair	1969	—	3.00	6.00
❑ 45037	Arizona/Man from Houston	1969	—	3.00	6.00
❑ 45125	Miss America/Small Town Woman	1970	—	3.00	6.00
❑ 45180	Silver Bird/So Hard to Leave You	1970	—	3.00	6.00
❑ 45229	And the Grass Won't Pay No Mind/					
	Funny How Little Men Care	1970	—	3.00	6.00
❑ 45286	Problem Child/Bookends	1970	—	3.00	6.00
❑ 45385	Been Too Long on the Road/					
	All I Really See Is You	1971	—	2.50	5.00
❑ 45462	Are You Old Enough/Don't You Know	1971	—	2.50	5.00
❑ 45506	Pretty Pretty/Something Big	1971	—	2.50	5.00
❑ 45895	California/Someone's Been Hiding	1973	—	2.50	5.00

Number	Title (A Side/B Side)	Yr	VG	VG+	NM
ELKA					
❑ 310	Sing Your Own Song/Sing Your Own Song					
	(Theme)	1976	2.50	5.00	10.00
GREEDY					
❑ 106	Sing Your Own Song/Sing Your Own Song					
	(Theme)	1976	—	3.00	6.00
WARNER BROS.					
❑ 8359	Sing Me High, Sing Me Low/Flips-Eyed	1977	—	2.00	4.00
❑ 8479	Little Ladies of the Night/Flips-Eyed	1977	—	2.00	4.00
Albums					
COLUMBIA					
❑ CS 9986	Arizona	1970	3.00	6.00	12.00
—Orange label					
❑ CS 9986	Arizona	1970	3.75	7.50	15.00
—Red "360 Sound" label					
❑ C 30111	Silver Bird	1970	3.00	6.00	12.00
❑ C 30735	You've Got a Friend	1971	3.00	6.00	12.00
LINK-EDDY COMBO					
45s					
REPRISE					
❑ 20002	Big Mr. C./The Man with the Golden Arm	1961	3.75	7.50	15.00
❑ 20008	Katrina/The Cat's Pajamas	1961	3.75	7.50	15.00
LINKLETTER, BOB					
45s					
CHATTAHOOCHIE					
❑ 702	The Out Crowd/Final Season	1965	5.00	10.00	20.00
LINKS, THE					
45s					
TEENAGE					
❑ 1009	Ba-Bee/She's the One	1958	250.00	500.00	1000.
LINN COUNTY					
45s					
MERCURY					
❑ 72852	Cave Song/Think	1968	2.00	4.00	8.00
❑ 72882	Fast Days/Lower Lemons	1969	2.00	4.00	8.00
❑ 72907	The Girl Can't Help It/Fever Shot	1969	2.00	4.00	8.00
PHILIPS					
❑ 40644	Let the Music Begin/Wine Take Me Away	1969	2.00	4.00	8.00
Albums					
MERCURY					
❑ SR-61181	Proud Flesh Soothseer	1968	5.00	10.00	20.00
❑ SR-61218	Fever Shot	1969	5.00	10.00	20.00
PHILIPS					
❑ PHS 600326	Till the Break of Dawn	1970	3.75	7.50	15.00
LINNEAS, THE					
45s					
DIAMOND					
❑ 241	It's a Good Kind of Hurt/Forever Baby	1968	3.00	6.00	12.00
❑ 248	My Baby Comes Home Today/					
	Born to Be Your Baby	1968	3.00	6.00	12.00
LIONS, THE					
45s					
EVEREST					
❑ 19388	No One But You/Giggles	1961	3.75	7.50	15.00
IMPERIAL					
❑ 5678	Hickory Dickory/The Yodel	1960	3.75	7.50	15.00
RENDEZVOUS					
❑ 116	The Feast of the Beasts/Two-Timing Lovers	1960	3.75	7.50	15.00
LIPTON, PEGGY					
45s					
ODE					
❑ 111	Let Me Pass By/Stoney End	1968	2.00	4.00	8.00
❑ 114	San Francisco Glide/Stoney End	1968	2.00	4.00	8.00
❑ 114 [PS]	San Francisco Glide/Stoney End	1968	3.00	6.00	12.00
❑ 118	Just a Little Lovin' (Early in the Morning)/					
	Red Clay County Line	1969	2.00	4.00	8.00
❑ 124	Lu/Let Me Pass By	1969	2.00	4.00	8.00
❑ 124 [PS]	Lu/Let Me Pass By	1969	3.00	6.00	12.00
❑ 66001	Wear Your Love Like Heaven/					
	Honey Won't Let Me	1970	—	3.00	6.00
❑ 66001 [PS]	Wear Your Love Like Heaven/					
	Honey Won't Let Me	1970	3.00	6.00	12.00
Albums					
ODE					
❑ Z12 44006	Peggy Lipton	1968	6.25	12.50	25.00
LIQUID SMOKE					
45s					
AVCO EMBASSY					
❑ 4522	I Who Have Nothing/Warm Touch	1970	2.00	4.00	8.00
❑ 4532	The Shelter of Your Arms/Let Me Down Easy	1970	2.00	4.00	8.00
❑ 4546	Hard to Handle/(B-side unknown)	1970	2.00	4.00	8.00
ROULETTE					
❑ 7166	Dance, Dance, Dance/Where's Our Love	1975	—	3.00	6.00
Albums					
AVCO EMBASSY					
❑ AVE-33005	Liquid Smoke	1970	6.25	12.50	25.00
LISTEN (1) With Robert Plant, later of LED ZEPPELIN.					
45s					
COLUMBIA					
❑ 43967	You Better Run/Everybody's Gonna Say	1967	75.00	150.00	300.00
—Promotional copies go for about half these values					
LISTENING					
45s					
VANGUARD					
❑ 35077	I Can Teach You/Cuando	1968	5.00	10.00	20.00
❑ 35094	Life Stories/Hello You	1968	5.00	10.00	20.00

L

Number	Title (A Side/B Side)	Yr	VG	VG+	NM
Albums					
VANGUARD					
❏ VSD-6504	Listening	1968	15.00	30.00	60.00

LITTER
45s
PROBE

Number	Title (A Side/B Side)	Yr	VG	VG+	NM
❏ 461	Silly People/Feeling	1968	6.25	12.50	25.00
❏ 467	Blue Ice/On Our Minds	1969	6.25	12.50	25.00
SCOTTY					
❏ 6710	Action Woman/A Legal Matter	1967	25.00	50.00	100.00
WARICK					
❏ 6711	Somebody Help Me/I'm a Man	1967	50.00	100.00	200.00
❏ 6712	Action Woman/Whatcha Gonna Do About It	1967	37.50	75.00	150.00
Albums					
EVA					
❏ 12013	Rare Tracks	1983	3.75	7.50	15.00
HEXAGON					
❏ 681	$100 Fine	1968	100.00	200.00	400.00
PROBE					
❏ 4504	Emerge	1969	12.50	25.00	50.00
WARICK					
❏ 671	Distortions	1967	125.00	250.00	500.00

LITTLE ANTHONY AND THE IMPERIALS
45s
APOLLO

Number	Title (A Side/B Side)	Yr	VG	VG+	NM
❏ 521	The Fires Burn No More/Lift Up Your Hands	1957	15.00	30.00	60.00
—As "The Chesters"					
AVCO					
❏ 4635	I'm Falling in Love with You/What Good Am I Without You	1974	—	2.50	5.00
❏ 4645	I Don't Have to Worry/Loneliest House on the Block	1974	—	2.50	5.00
❏ 4651	Hold On (Just a Little Bit Longer)/I've Got to Let You Go (Part 1)	1975	—	2.50	5.00
❏ 4655	I'll Be Loving You Sooner or Later/Young Girl	1975	—	2.50	5.00
DCP					
❏ 1104	I'm On the Outside (Looking In)/Please Go	1964	2.50	5.00	10.00
❏ 1119	Goin' Out of My Head/Make It Easy on Yourself	1964	2.50	5.00	10.00
❏ 1128	Hurt So Bad/Reputation	1965	2.50	5.00	10.00
❏ 1128 [PS]	Hurt So Bad/Reputation	1965	10.00	20.00	40.00
❏ 1136	Take Me Back/Our Song	1965	2.00	4.00	8.00
❏ 1149	I Miss You So/Get Out of My Life	1965	2.00	4.00	8.00
❏ 1154	Hurt/Never Again	1966	2.00	4.00	8.00
END					
❏ 1027	Tears on My Pillow/Two People in the World	1958	6.25	12.50	25.00
—As "Little Anthony and the Imperials"					
❏ 1027	Tears on My Pillow/Two People in the World	1958	10.00	20.00	40.00
—As "The Imperials"					
❏ 1036	So Much/Oh Yeah	1958	6.25	12.50	25.00
❏ 1038	The Diary/Cha Cha Henry	1959	6.25	12.50	25.00
❏ 1039	When You Wish Upon a Star/Wishful Thinking	1959	6.25	12.50	25.00
❏ 1047	A Prayer and a Juke Box/River Path	1959	6.25	12.50	25.00
❏ 1053	So Near and Yet So Far/I'm Alright	1959	6.25	12.50	25.00
❏ 1060	Shimmy, Shimmy, Ko-Ko Bop/I'm Still in Love with You	1959	7.50	15.00	30.00
❏ 1067	My Empty Room/Bayou, Bayou, Baby	1960	3.75	7.50	15.00
❏ 1074	I'm Taking a Vacation from Love/Only Sympathy	1960	3.75	7.50	15.00
❏ 1080	Limbo (Part 1)/Limbo (Part 2)	1960	3.75	7.50	15.00
❏ 1083	Formula of Love/Dream	1961	3.75	7.50	15.00
❏ 1086	Please Say You Want Me/So Near Yet So Far	1961	3.75	7.50	15.00
❏ 1091	Traveling Stranger/Say Yea	1961	3.75	7.50	15.00
❏ 1104	Dream/A Lovely Way to Spend an Evening	1961	3.75	7.50	15.00
JANUS					
❏ 160	Father, Father/Each One, Teach One	1971	—	3.00	6.00
❏ 166	Madeline/Universe	1971	—	3.00	6.00
❏ 178	(Where Do I Begin) Love Story/There's an Island	1972	—	3.00	6.00
LIBERTY					
❏ 55119	The Glory of Love/C'mon Tiger (Gimme a Growl)	1958	7.50	15.00	30.00
—As "The Imperials"					
MCA					
❏ 41258	Daylight/Your Love	1980	—	2.00	4.00
—Little Anthony solo					
NEWTIME					
❏ 503	A Short Prayer/Where Will You Be	196?	3.00	6.00	12.00
—As "Anthony and the Imperials"					
PCM					
❏ 202	This Time We're Winning/Your Love	1983	—	2.00	4.00
PURE GOLD					
❏ 101	Nothing from Nothing/Running with the Wrong Crowd	1976	—	2.50	5.00
ROULETTE					
❏ 4379	That Lil' Ole Lovemaker Me/It Just Ain't Fair	1961	3.00	6.00	12.00
—Little Anthony solo					
❏ 4477	Lonesome Romeo/I've Got a Lot to Offer Darling	1963	3.00	6.00	12.00
—Little Anthony solo					
UNITED ARTISTS					
❏ 0117	Goin' Out of My Head/I'm On the Outside (Looking In)	1973	—	2.00	4.00
—"Silver Spotlight Series" reissue					
❏ 0118	Hurt So Bad/Take Me Back	1973	—	2.00	4.00
—"Silver Spotlight Series" reissue					
❏ 50552	Out of Sight, Out of Mind/Summer's Comin'	1969	—	3.00	6.00
❏ 50598	The Ten Commandments of Love/Let the Sunshine In	1969	—	3.00	6.00
❏ 50625	It'll Never Be the Same Again/Don't Get Close	1970	—	3.00	6.00
❏ 50677	World of Darkness/The Change	1970	—	3.00	6.00
❏ 50720	Help Me Find a Way (To Say I Love You)/If I Love You	1970	—	3.00	6.00
VEEP					
❏ 1228	Better Use Your Head/The Wonder of It All	1966	2.00	4.00	8.00
❏ 1228 [PS]	Better Use Your Head/The Wonder of It All	1966	10.00	20.00	40.00
❏ 1233	You Better Take It Easy Baby/Gonna Fix You Good (Every Time You're Bad)	1966	2.00	4.00	8.00
❏ 1239	Tears on My Pillow/Who's Sorry Now	1966	—	3.00	6.00
❏ 1240	I'm On the Outside (Looking In)/Please Go	1966	—	3.00	6.00
❏ 1241	Goin' Out of My Head/Shing-a-Ling	1966	—	3.00	6.00
❏ 1242	Hurt So Bad/Reputation	1966	—	3.00	6.00
❏ 1243	Take Me Back/Our Song	1966	—	3.00	6.00
❏ 1244	I Miss You So/Get Out of My Life	1966	—	3.00	6.00
❏ 1245	Hurt/Never Again	1966	—	3.00	6.00
❏ 1248	It's Not the Same/Down on Love	1966	2.00	4.00	8.00
❏ 1255	Don't Tie Me Down/Where There's a Will There's a Way	1967	2.00	4.00	8.00
❏ 1262	Hold On to Someone/Lost in Love	1967	2.00	4.00	8.00
❏ 1269	You Only Live Twice/Hungry Heart	1967	2.00	4.00	8.00
❏ 1275	Beautiful People/If I Remember to Forget	1967	2.00	4.00	8.00
❏ 1278	I'm Hypnotized/Hungry Heart	1968	2.00	4.00	8.00
❏ 1283	What Greater Love/In the Back of My Heart	1968	2.00	4.00	8.00
❏ 1285	Yesterday Has Gone/My Love Is a Rainbow	1968	2.00	4.00	8.00
❏ 1293	The Flesh Failures (Let the Sunshine In)/Gentle Rain	1969	2.00	4.00	8.00
❏ 1303	Anthem (Revelation)/Goodbye Good Times	1969	2.00	4.00	8.00
7-Inch Extended Plays					
END					
❏ 203	*The Diary/Tears on My Pillow/Traveling Stranger/So Much	1959	50.00	100.00	200.00
❏ 203 [PS]	Little Anthony and the Imperials	1959	75.00	150.00	300.00
❏ 204	(contents unknown)	1959	50.00	100.00	200.00
❏ 204 [PS]	We Are Little Anthony and the Imperials	1959	75.00	150.00	300.00
Albums					
ACCORD					
❏ SN-7216	Tears on My Pillow	1983	2.50	5.00	10.00
AVCO					
❏ AV-11012	On a New Street	1973	5.00	10.00	20.00
DCP					
❏ DCL-3801 [M]	I'm On the Outside Looking In	1964	6.25	12.50	25.00
❏ DCL-3808 [M]	Goin' Out of My Head	1965	6.25	12.50	25.00
❏ DCL-3809 [M]	The Best of Little Anthony and the Imperials	1965	5.00	10.00	20.00
❏ DCS-6801 [S]	I'm On the Outside Looking In	1964	7.50	15.00	30.00
❏ DCS-6808 [S]	Goin' Out of My Head	1965	7.50	15.00	30.00
❏ DCS-6809 [S]	The Best of Little Anthony and the Imperials	1965	6.25	12.50	25.00
END					
❏ LP 303 [M]	We Are The Imperials Featuring Little Anthony	1959	62.50	125.00	250.00
❏ LP 311 [M]	Shades of the 40's	1960	50.00	100.00	200.00
FORUM					
❏ F-9107 [M]	Little Anthony and the Imperials' Greatest Hits	196?	3.75	7.50	15.00
❏ FS-9107 [R]	Little Anthony and the Imperials' Greatest Hits	196?	3.00	6.00	12.00
LIBERTY					
❏ LM-1017	Out of Sight, Out of Mind	1981	2.00	4.00	8.00
—Reissue of United Artists 1017					
❏ LN-10133	The Best of Little Anthony and the Imperials	1981	2.00	4.00	8.00
—Budget-line reissue					
PICKWICK					
❏ SPC-3029	The Hits of Little Anthony and the Imperials	196?	3.00	6.00	12.00
RHINO					
❏ R1-70919	The Best of Little Anthony and the Imperials	1989	3.00	6.00	12.00
ROULETTE					
❏ R-25294 [M]	Little Anthony and the Imperials' Greatest Hits	1965	6.25	12.50	25.00
❏ SR-25294 [R]	Little Anthony and the Imperials' Greatest Hits	1965	5.00	10.00	20.00
❏ SR-42007	Forever Yours	1968	3.75	7.50	15.00
SONGBIRD					
❏ 3245	Daylight	1980	2.50	5.00	10.00
SUNSET					
❏ SUS-5287	Little Anthony and the Imperials	1970	3.75	7.50	15.00
UNITED ARTISTS					
❏ UA-LA026-G [(2)]	Legendary Masters Series	1972	6.25	12.50	25.00
❏ UA-LA255-G	The Very Best of Little Anthony and the Imperials	1974	2.50	5.00	10.00
❏ LM-1017	Out of Sight, Out of Mind	1980	2.50	5.00	10.00
—Reissue of United Artists 6720					
❏ UAS 6720	Out of Sight, Out of Mind	1969	5.00	10.00	20.00
VEEP					
❏ VP 13510 [M]	I'm On the Outside Looking In	1966	3.75	7.50	15.00
❏ VP 13511 [M]	Goin' Out of My Head	1966	3.75	7.50	15.00
❏ VP 13512 [M]	The Best of Little Anthony and the Imperials	1966	3.75	7.50	15.00
❏ VP 13513 [M]	Payin' Our Dues	1966	3.75	7.50	15.00
❏ VP 13514 [M]	Reflections	1967	3.75	7.50	15.00
❏ VP 13516 [M]	Movie Grabbers	1967	3.75	7.50	15.00
❏ VPS 16510 [S]	I'm On the Outside Looking In	1966	5.00	10.00	20.00
❏ VPS 16511 [S]	Goin' Out of My Head	1966	5.00	10.00	20.00
❏ VPS 16512 [S]	The Best of Little Anthony and the Imperials	1966	5.00	10.00	20.00
❏ VPS 16513 [S]	Payin' Our Dues	1966	5.00	10.00	20.00
❏ VPS 16514 [S]	Reflections	1967	5.00	10.00	20.00
❏ VPS 16516 [S]	Movie Grabbers	1967	5.00	10.00	20.00
❏ VPS 16519	The Best of Little Anthony, Volume 2	1968	3.75	7.50	15.00

LITTLE BILL AND THE BLUENOTES
45s
DOLTON

Number	Title (A Side/B Side)	Yr	VG	VG+	NM
❏ 4	I Love an Angel/Bye Bye Baby	1959	7.50	15.00	30.00
Albums					
CAMELOT					
❏ 102 [M]	The Fiesta Club Presents Little Bill and the Bluenotes	1960	100.00	200.00	400.00

LITTLE BILLY
45s
ABC-PARAMOUNT

Number	Title (A Side/B Side)	Yr	VG	VG+	NM
❏ 9896	I Found Me a Girl/Say It Like You Mean It	1958	3.75	7.50	15.00

LITTLE BOOKER
45s
ACE

Number	Title (A Side/B Side)	Yr	VG	VG+	NM
❏ 547	Open the Door/Teen-Age Rock	1958	6.25	12.50	25.00
IMPERIAL					
❏ 5293	Thinkin' 'Bout My Baby/Doing the Ham Bone	1954	25.00	50.00	100.00

Number	Title (A Side/B Side)	Yr	VG	VG+	NM

LITTLE BOY BLUES
45s
FONTANA
| ❏ 1623 | It's Only You/Is Love? | 1968 | 3.75 | 7.50 | 15.00 |

IRC
❏ 6928	Look at the Sun/Love for a Day	1966	5.00	10.00	20.00
❏ 6936	I'm Ready/Little Boy Blues' Blues	1966	7.50	15.00	30.00
❏ 6939	I Can Only Give You Everything/				
	You Don't Love Me	1966	7.50	15.00	30.00

Albums
FONTANA
| ❏ SRF-67578 | In the Woodland of Weir | 1968 | 75.00 | 15.00 | 30.00 |

LITTLE BUBBER
45s
IMPERIAL
| ❏ 5225 | High Class Woman/Come Back Baby | 1953 | 20.00 | 40.00 | 80.00 |
| ❏ 5238 | Runnin' Around/Never Trust a Woman | 1953 | 20.00 | 40.00 | 80.00 |

LITTLE CAESAR
45s
BIG TOWN
| ❏ 106 | Can't Stand It All Alone/Big Eyes | 195? | 15.00 | 30.00 | 60.00 |
| ❏ 110 | What Kind of Fool Is He/Wonder Why I'm Leaving (Rat Song) | 195? | 15.00 | 30.00 | 60.00 |

RCA VICTOR
| ❏ 47-7270 | Who Slammed the Door/I'm Reachin' | 1958 | 6.25 | 12.50 | 25.00 |

RECORDED IN HOLLYWOOD
❏ 234	Long Time Baby/(Going Down to) The River	1952	15.00	30.00	60.00
❏ 235	Goodbye Baby/If I Could See My Baby	1952	15.00	30.00	60.00
❏ 236	Move Me/Lying Woman	1953	15.00	30.00	60.00
❏ 237	You're Part of Me/Here Is a Letter	1953	15.00	30.00	60.00
❏ 238	Do Right/Money Ain't Long Enough	1953	15.00	30.00	60.00
❏ 239	Atomic Love/You Can't Bring Me Down	1953	15.00	30.00	60.00

RPM
| ❏ 393 | Chains of Love Have Disappeared/Tried to Reason with You Baby | 1953 | 15.00 | 30.00 | 60.00 |

LITTLE CAESAR AND THE CONSULS
45s
MALA
❏ 512	(My Girl) Sloopy/Poison Ivy	1965	3.75	7.50	15.00
❏ 518	You've Really Got a Hold on Me/It's So Easy	1965	3.00	6.00	12.00
❏ 523	Hey Girl/You Laugh Too Much	1966	3.00	6.00	12.00

LITTLE CAESAR AND THE EMPIRE
45s
PARKWAY
| ❏ 152 | Everybody Dance Now/(Instrumental) | 1967 | 6.25 | 12.50 | 25.00 |

LITTLE CAESAR AND THE ROMANS
45s
DEL-FI
❏ 4158	Those Oldies But Goodies (Remind Me of You)/She Don't Wanna Dance	1961	7.50	15.00	30.00
❏ 4164	Hully Gully Again/Frankie and Johnny	1961	6.25	12.50	25.00
❏ 4166	Memories of Those Oldies But Goodies/Fever	1961	15.00	30.00	60.00
❏ 4170	Ten Commandments of Love/C.C. Rider	1961	12.50	25.00	50.00
❏ 4176	Popeye One More Time/Yoyo Yo Yoyo	1962	6.25	12.50	25.00

LANA
| ❏ 152 | Those Oldies But Goodies (Remind Me of You)/She Don't Wanna Dance | 196? | 2.00 | 4.00 | 8.00 |
—Oldies reissue

LOST-NITE
| ❏ 204 | Those Oldies But Goodies (Remind Me of You)/She Don't Wanna Dance | 196? | — | 2.50 | 5.00 |
—Reissue

SCEPTER
| ❏ 12237 | Baby Love/When Will I Get Over You | 1969 | 2.00 | 4.00 | 8.00 |
—As "Caesar and the Romans"
| ❏ 12264 | Jailhouse Rock/Leavin' My Past Behind | 1969 | 2.00 | 4.00 | 8.00 |
—As "Caesar and the Romans"

Albums
DEL-FI
| ❏ DFLP-1218 [M] | Memories of Those Oldies But Goodies | 1961 | 75.00 | 150.00 | 300.00 |

LITTLE CHARLES AND THE SIDEWINDERS
45s
DECCA
❏ 31980	I'm Available/It's a Heartache	1966	10.00	20.00	40.00
❏ 32095	Talkin' About You, Babe/A Taste of the Good Life	1967	7.50	15.00	30.00
❏ 32233	The Loner (Part 1)/The Loner (Part 2)	1967	5.00	10.00	20.00
❏ 32321	Sweet Lorene/Twice as Much for My Baby	1968	5.00	10.00	20.00

JEWEL
| ❏ 752 | Give Me a Chance/Guess I'll Have to Take What's Left | 1965 | 5.00 | 10.00 | 20.00 |

LITTLE CHERYL
45s
CAMEO
❏ 270	Heaven Only Knows/Can't We Just Be Friends	1963	10.00	20.00	40.00
❏ 276	Mama Let the Phone Bell Ring/Can't We Just Be Friends	1963	3.00	6.00	12.00
❏ 292	Come On Home/I Love You Conrad	1964	3.00	6.00	12.00
❏ 307	Yeh Yeh We Love 'Em All/Nick and Joe Callin'	1964	4.00	8.00	16.00

REPRISE
| ❏ 20109 | Jim/Pocketful of Money | 1962 | 3.75 | 7.50 | 15.00 |

LITTLE COOLBREEZERS, THE See THE COOLBREEZERS.

LITTLE DIPPERS, THE See ANITA KERR SINGERS.

LITTLE DOUG See DOUG SAHM.

LITTLE ESTHER See LITTLE ESTHER PHILLIPS.

LITTLE EVA
45s
AMY
| ❏ 943 | Stand By Me/That's My Man | 1965 | 2.00 | 4.00 | 8.00 |

BELL
| ❏ 45264 | The Loco-Motion/Will You Love Me Tomorrow | 1972 | — | 2.50 | 5.00 |

DIMENSION
| ❏ 1000 | The Loco-Motion/He Is the Boy | 1962 | 5.00 | 10.00 | 20.00 |
| ❏ 1003 | Keep Your Hands Off My Baby/Where Do I Go | 1962 | 3.00 | 6.00 | 12.00 |
—Most copies have longer, and correct, title
| ❏ 1003 | Keep Your Hands Off/Where Do I Go | 1962 | 3.75 | 7.50 | 15.00 |
—Some copies have this shortened title
❏ 1006	Let's Turkey Trot/Down Home	1963	3.00	6.00	12.00
❏ 1011	Old Smokey Locomotion/Just a Little Girl	1963	3.00	6.00	12.00
❏ 1013	The Trouble with Boys/What I Gotta Do	1963	3.00	6.00	12.00
❏ 1019	Let's Start the Party Again/Please Hurt Me	1963	3.00	6.00	12.00
❏ 1021	The Christmas Song/I Wish You a Merry Christmas	1963	3.75	7.50	15.00
—With Big Dee Irwin
| ❏ 1021 [PS] | The Christmas Song/I Wish You a Merry Christmas | 1963 | 10.00 | 20.00 | 40.00 |
—With Big Dee Irwin
❏ 1035	Makin' with the Magilla/Conga	1964	2.50	5.00	10.00
❏ 1035	Makin' with the Magilla/Run to Her	1964	2.50	5.00	10.00
❏ 1035 [PS]	Makin' with the Magilla/Run to Her	1964	10.00	20.00	40.00
❏ 1042	Wake Up John/Takin' Back What I Said	1964	2.50	5.00	10.00

SPRING
| ❏ 101 | Mama Said/Something About You Boy | 1970 | — | 3.00 | 6.00 |
| ❏ 107 | Night After Night/Something About You Boy | 1970 | — | 3.00 | 6.00 |

VERVE
| ❏ 10459 | Bend It/Just One Word Isn't Enough | 1966 | 2.00 | 4.00 | 8.00 |
| ❏ 10529 | Everything Is Beautiful About You Boy/Take a Step in My Direction | 1967 | 2.00 | 4.00 | 8.00 |

Albums
DIMENSION
| ❏ DLP-6000 [M] | LLLLLoco-Motion | 1962 | 37.50 | 75.00 | 150.00 |
—Without "Keep Your Hands Off My Baby"
| ❏ DLP-6000 [M] | LLLLLoco-Motion | 1962 | 50.00 | 100.00 | 200.00 |
—With "Keep Your Hands Off My Baby"
| ❏ DLPS-6000 [R] | LLLLLoco-Motion | 1962 | 37.50 | 75.00 | 150.00 |
—Without "Keep Your Hands Off My Baby"
| ❏ DLPS-6000 [R] | LLLLLoco-Motion | 1962 | 50.00 | 100.00 | 200.00 |
—With "Keep Your Hands Off My Baby"

LITTLE FEAT
45s
WARNER BROS.
❏ 7431	Strawberry Flats/Hamburger Midnight	1970	2.00	4.00	8.00
❏ 7553	Easy to Slip/Cat Fever	1972	2.00	4.00	8.00
❏ 7689	Dixie Chicken/Lafayette Railroad	1973	—	3.00	6.00
❏ 8054	Oh Atlanta/Down the Road	1974	—	2.50	5.00
❏ 8174	Long Distance Love/Romance Dance	1975	—	2.50	5.00
❏ 8219	All That You Dream/One Love Stand	1976	—	2.50	5.00
❏ 8420	Time Loves a Hero/Sailin' Shoes	1977	—	2.50	5.00
❏ 8566	Oh Atlanta/Willin'	1978	—	2.50	5.00
❏ 27684	One Clear Moment/Changin' Luck	1988	—	—	3.00
❏ 27684 [PS]	One Clear Moment/Changin' Luck	1988	—	—	3.00
❏ 27728	Hate to Lose Your Lovin'/Cajun Girl	1988	—	—	3.00
❏ 27728 [PS]	Hate to Lose Your Lovin'/Cajun Girl	1988	—	—	3.00
❏ 49169	Wake Up Dreaming/Front Page News	1980	—	2.50	5.00
❏ 49801	Front Page News/Easy to Sleep	1981	—	2.50	5.00
❏ 49841	Strawberry Flats/Gringo	1981	—	2.50	5.00

Albums
MOBILE FIDELITY
| ❏ 1-013 [(2)] | Waiting for Columbus | 1979 | 20.00 | 40.00 | 80.00 |
—Audiophile vinyl

NAUTILUS
| ❏ NR-24 | Time Loves a Hero | 198? | 12.50 | 25.00 | 50.00 |
—Audiophile vinyl

WARNER BROS.
| ❏ PRO-A-984 [DJ] | Hoy-Hoy! | 1981 | 5.00 | 10.00 | 20.00 |
—Single-album sampler of 2-LP set
| ❏ WS 1890 | Little Feat | 1971 | 3.75 | 7.50 | 15.00 |
—Green "WB" label; without photo on back cover
| ❏ WS 1890 | Little Feat | 1971 | 5.00 | 10.00 | 20.00 |
—Green "WB" label; with photo on back cover
| ❏ WS 1890 | Little Feat | 1973 | 2.50 | 5.00 | 10.00 |
—"Burbank" palm trees label
| ❏ WS 1890 | Little Feat | 1979 | 2.00 | 4.00 | 8.00 |
—Tan or white label
| ❏ BS 2600 | Sailin' Shoes | 1972 | 3.75 | 7.50 | 15.00 |
—Green "WB" label
| ❏ BS 2600 | Sailin' Shoes | 1973 | 2.50 | 5.00 | 10.00 |
—"Burbank" palm trees label
| ❏ BS 2600 | Sailin' Shoes | 1979 | 2.00 | 4.00 | 8.00 |
—Tan or white label
| ❏ BS 2686 | Dixie Chicken | 1973 | 3.75 | 7.50 | 15.00 |
—"Burbank" palm trees label
| ❏ BS 2686 | Dixie Chicken | 1979 | 2.00 | 4.00 | 8.00 |
—Tan or white label
| ❏ BS 2748 | Feats Don't Fail Me Now | 1974 | 3.75 | 7.50 | 15.00 |
—"Burbank" palm trees label
| ❏ BS 2748 | Feats Don't Fail Me Now | 1979 | 2.00 | 4.00 | 8.00 |
—Tan or white label
| ❏ BS 2884 | The Last Record Album | 1975 | 3.75 | 7.50 | 15.00 |
—"Burbank" palm trees label
| ❏ BS 2884 | The Last Record Album | 1979 | 2.00 | 4.00 | 8.00 |
—Tan or white label

L

Number	Title (A Side/B Side)	Yr	VG	VG+	NM
❏ BS 3015	Time Loves a Hero	1977	3.00	6.00	12.00
—"Burbank" palm trees label					
❏ BS 3015	Time Loves a Hero	1979	2.00	4.00	8.00
—Tan or white label					
❏ 2WS 3140 [(2)]	Waiting for Columbus	1978	3.75	7.50	15.00
—"Burbank" palm trees label					
❏ 2WS 3140 [(2)]	Waiting for Columbus	1979	2.50	5.00	10.00
—Tan or white label					
❏ HS 3345	Down on the Farm	1979	2.50	5.00	10.00
❏ 2BSK 3538 [(2)]	Hoy-Hoy!	1981	3.00	6.00	12.00
❏ 25750	Let It Roll	1988	2.50	5.00	10.00
❏ 26263	Representing the Mambo	1990	3.75	7.50	15.00
ZOO/CLASSIC					
❏ 11097 [(2)]	Ain't Had Enough Fun	1995	4.50	9.00	18.00
—150-gram vinyl					
❏ 11097 [(2)]	Ain't Had Enough Fun	1995	5.00	10.00	20.00
—180-gram vinyl					

LITTLE GUY AND THE GIANTS
45s
LAWN
| ❏ 103 | It's You/So Young | 1960 | 50.00 | 100.00 | 200.00 |

LITTLE IKE
45s
CHAMPION
| ❏ 1011 | She Can Rock/Am I Losin' You | 1959 | 25.00 | 50.00 | 100.00 |

LITTLE IVA AND HER BAND
45s
MIRACLE
| ❏ 2 | When I Needed You/Continental Strut | 1960 | 500.00 | 1000. | 1500. |

LITTLE JOE
45s
BRUNSWICK
| ❏ 55369 | Holiday/Fool on the Hill | 1968 | 2.00 | 4.00 | 8.00 |
Albums
BRUNSWICK
| ❏ BL 754135 | Little Joe (Sure Can Sing) | 1968 | 5.00 | 10.00 | 20.00 |

LITTLE JOE AND THE THRILLERS
45s
ENJOY
| ❏ 2011 | Peanuts and Popcorn/Chicken Little Boo Boo | 1964 | 2.50 | 5.00 | 10.00 |
EPIC
| ❏ 9293 | Mine/It's Too Bad We Had to Say Goodbye | 1958 | 3.75 | 7.50 | 15.00 |
| ❏ 9431 | Run Little Girl/Public Opinion | 1961 | 3.00 | 6.00 | 12.00 |
MGM
❏ 14129	Somehow, Someway/Days 'Til Morning	1970	—	2.50	5.00
❏ 14230	People Show/ Baby I Could Be So Good at Lovin' You	1971	—	2.50	5.00
❏ 14290	Don't Take the Rain Away/The Children	1971	—	2.50	5.00
❏ 14361	Shelly Made Me Smile/Words and Music	1972	—	2.50	5.00
❏ 14466	Baby I Could Be So Good at Lovin' You/Cherry Pink and Apple Blossom White	1972	—	2.50	5.00
❏ 14662	Folks Who Live on the Hill/ Baby I Could Be So Good at Lovin' You	1973	—	2.50	5.00
OKEH
❏ 7075	Let's Do the Slop/This I Know	1956	3.75	7.50	15.00
❏ 7088	Peanuts/Lilly Lou	1957	5.00	10.00	20.00
❏ 7094	Lonesome/The Echoes Keep Calling Me	1957	3.75	7.50	15.00
❏ 7099	Don't Leave Me Alone/What's Happened to Your Halo	1958	3.75	7.50	15.00
❏ 7107	Mine/It's Too Bad We Had to Say Goodbye	1958	3.75	7.50	15.00
❏ 7116	Cherry (Part 1)/Cherry (Part 2)	1959	3.00	6.00	12.00
❏ 7121	I'm Tryin'/Strange Dreams	1959	3.00	6.00	12.00
❏ 7127	Give Me All Your Love/I'll Never Let You Go	1959	3.00	6.00	12.00
❏ 7134	Ev'ry Now and Then/Goodnight, Little Girl	1960	3.00	6.00	12.00
❏ 7136	Stay/Please Don't Go	1960	3.00	6.00	12.00
❏ 7140	Run Little Girl/Public Opinion	1961	3.00	6.00	12.00
REPRISE
❏ 20142	Peanuts/No, No, I Can't Stop	1963	2.50	5.00	10.00
7-Inch Extended Plays
EPIC
| ❏ EG-7198 | (contents unknown) | 1958 | 25.00 | 50.00 | 100.00 |
| ❏ EG-7198 [PS] | Little Joe and the Thrillers | 1958 | 25.00 | 50.00 | 100.00 |

LITTLE JOEY AND THE FLIPS
45s
JOY
| ❏ 262 | Bongo Stomp/Lost Love | 1962 | 3.75 | 7.50 | 15.00 |
| ❏ 268 | Bongo Gully/It Was Like Heaven | 1962 | 3.00 | 6.00 | 12.00 |

LITTLE JUNIOR'S BLUE FLAMES See JUNIOR PARKER.

LITTLE LADY BEATLES, THE See THE INSECTS.

LITTLE MILTON
45s
BOBBIN
❏ 101	I'm a Lonely Man/That Will Never Do	1958	6.25	12.50	25.00
❏ 103	Long Distance Operator/I Found Me a New Love	1959	6.25	12.50	25.00
❏ 112	Strange Dreams/I'm Tryin'	1959	6.25	12.50	25.00
❏ 117	Hold Me Tight/Same Old Blues	1959	6.25	12.50	25.00
❏ 120	Dead Love/My Baby Pleases Me	1960	6.25	12.50	25.00
❏ 125	Let It Be Known/Hey Girl	1960	6.25	12.50	25.00
❏ 128	I'm in Love/Cross My Heart	1961	6.25	12.50	25.00
CHECKER
❏ 977	Saving My Love for You/Lonely No More	1961	3.75	7.50	15.00
❏ 994	So Mean to Me/I Need Somebody	1961	3.75	7.50	15.00
❏ 1012	Satisfied/Someone to Love	1962	3.75	7.50	15.00
❏ 1020	I Wonder Why/Losing Hand	1962	3.75	7.50	15.00
❏ 1048	She Put a Spell on Me/Never Too Old	1963	3.75	7.50	15.00
❏ 1063	Meddlin'/One of These Old Days	1963	3.75	7.50	15.00
❏ 1078	Sacrifice/What Kind of Love Is This	1964	3.75	7.50	15.00
❏ 1096	Blind Man/Blues in the Night	1964	3.75	7.50	15.00
❏ 1105	We're Gonna Make It/Can't Hold Back the Tears	1965	3.75	7.50	15.00

Number	Title (A Side/B Side)	Yr	VG	VG+	NM
❏ 1113	Who's Cheating Who?/Ain't No Big Deal on You	1965	3.75	7.50	15.00
❏ 1118	Help Me Help You/Without My Sweet Baby	1965	3.75	7.50	15.00
❏ 1128	My Baby's Something Else/Your People	1965	3.75	7.50	15.00
❏ 1132	Sometimes/We Got the Winning Hand	1965	3.75	7.50	15.00
❏ 1138	I'm Mightry Grateful/When Does Heartache End	1966	3.75	7.50	15.00
❏ 1149	Man Loves Two/Believe in Me	1966	3.75	7.50	15.00
❏ 1162	Feel So Bad/You Colored My Blues Right	1966	5.00	10.00	20.00
❏ 1172	I'll Never Turn My Back on You/Don't Leave Her	1967	3.00	6.00	12.00
❏ 1178	I'm Shorty/Sitting Home Alone	1967	3.00	6.00	12.00
❏ 1186	A Whole Lot of Fun Before the Weekend Is Done/ Real True Love	1967	3.00	6.00	12.00
❏ 1189	More and More/Cost of Living	1967	3.00	6.00	12.00
❏ 1194	I Know What I Want/You Mean Everything to Me	1968	3.00	6.00	12.00
❏ 1203	At the Dark End of the Street/ I (Who Have Nothing)	1968	3.00	6.00	12.00
❏ 1208	Let Me Down Easy/Lonely Drifter	1968	3.00	6.00	12.00
❏ 1212	Grits Ain't Groceries (All Around the World)/I Can't Quit You Baby	1969	3.00	6.00	12.00
❏ 1217	Just a Little Bit/Spring	1969	3.00	6.00	12.00
❏ 1221	Poor Man/So Blue	1969	3.00	6.00	12.00
❏ 1225	Let's Get Together/I'll Always Love You	1969	3.00	6.00	12.00
❏ 1226	If Walls Could Talk/Loving You	1969	3.00	6.00	12.00
❏ 1227	Baby I Love You/Don't Talk Back	1970	3.00	6.00	12.00
❏ 1231	Somebody's Changin' My Sweet Baby's Mind/ I'm Tired	1970	3.00	6.00	12.00
—As "Little Milton Campbell"					
❏ 1236	Many Rivers to Cross/Mother's Love	1970	3.00	6.00	12.00
❏ 1239	I Play Dirty/Nothing Beats a Failure	1971	2.00	4.00	8.00
GLADES					
❏ 1734	Friend of Mine/(Instrumental)	1976	—	2.50	5.00
❏ 1738	Baby It Ain't No Way/Bring It On Back	1976	—	2.50	5.00
❏ 1741	Just One Step/(Instrumental)	1977	—	2.50	5.00
❏ 1743	Loving You (Is the Best Thing to Happen to Me)/ 9:59 A.M.	1977	—	2.50	5.00
❏ 1747	Me for You, You for Me/My Thing Is You	1977	—	2.50	5.00
MALACO					
❏ 2104	The Blues Is All Right/Come Back Kind of Loving	1985	—	2.00	4.00
❏ 2108	Misty Blue/Catch You on the Way Down	1985	—	2.00	4.00
❏ 2123	Lonesome Christmas/Come To Me	1985	—	2.00	4.00
❏ 2127	I Will Survive/4:59 A.M.	1986	—	2.00	4.00
❏ 2134	Real Good Woman/Annie Mae's Café	198?	—	2.00	4.00
❏ 2147	His Old Lady and My Old Lady/(B-side unknown)	198?	—	2.00	4.00
❏ 2162	Bad Dream/The Woman I Love	198?	—	2.00	4.00
MCA					
❏ 52184	Age Ain't Nothin' But a Number/(Instrumental)	1983	—	2.00	4.00
❏ 52254	Living on the Dark Side of Love/Why Are You So Hard to Please	1983	—	2.00	4.00
METEOR					
❏ 5040	Love at First Sight/Let's Boogie Baby	1957	50.00	100.00	200.00
❏ 5045	Let My Baby Be/Oh My Little Baby	1957	200.00	400.00	800.00
STAX					
❏ 0100	If That Ain't a Reason (For Your Woman to Leave You)/Mr. Mailman	1971	—	3.00	6.00
❏ 0111	That's What Love Will Make You Do/ I'm Livin' Off the Love You Give	1972	—	3.00	6.00
❏ 0124	Walking the Back Streets and Crying/ Before the Honeymoon	1972	—	3.00	6.00
❏ 0141	I'm Gonna Cry a River/What It Is	1972	—	3.00	6.00
❏ 0148	Lovin' Stick/Rainy Day	1972	—	3.00	6.00
❏ 0174	What It Is/Who Can Handle Me Is You	1973	—	3.00	6.00
❏ 0191	Tin Pan Alley/Sweet Woman of Mine	1974	—	3.00	6.00
❏ 0210	Behind Closed Doors/Bet You I Win	1974	—	3.00	6.00
❏ 0229	Let Me Back In/Let Your Loss Be Your Lesson	1974	—	3.00	6.00
❏ 0238	If You Talk in Your Sleep/Sweet Woman of Mine	1975	—	3.00	6.00
❏ 0252	How Could You Do It to Me/ Packed Up and Took My Mind	1975	—	3.00	6.00
SUN					
❏ 194	Beggin' My Baby/Somebody Told Me	1954	75.00	150.00	300.00
❏ 200	If You Love Me/Alone and Blue	1954	150.00	300.00	600.00
❏ 220	Lookin' for My Baby/Homesick for My Baby	1955	200.00	400.00	800.00
Albums					
CHECKER					
❏ LP-2995 [M]	We're Gonna Make It	196?	6.25	12.50	25.00
—Blue, fading to white, label					
❏ LP-2995 [M]	We're Gonna Make It	1965	25.00	50.00	100.00
—Black label					
❏ LP-2995 [M]	We're Gonna Make It	1966	17.50	35.00	70.00
—Blue label with red and black checkers					
❏ LP-3002 [M]	Little Milton Sings Big Blues	1966	12.50	25.00	50.00
❏ LP-3011	Grits Ain't Groceries	1969	6.25	12.50	25.00
❏ LP-3012	If Walls Could Talk	1970	6.25	12.50	25.00
CHESS					
❏ 204 [(2)]	Little Milton	1976	3.75	7.50	15.00
❏ CH-9252	We're Gonna Make It	1986	2.50	5.00	10.00
—Reissue of Checker 2995					
❏ CH-9265	Little Milton Sings Big Blues	1987	2.50	5.00	10.00
—Reissue of Checker 3002					
❏ CH-9289	If Walls Could Talk	1989	2.50	5.00	10.00
—Reissue of Checker 3012					
❏ CH-50013	Little Milton's Greatest Hits	1972	3.75	7.50	15.00
GLADES					
❏ 7508	Friend of Mine	1976	3.00	6.00	12.00
❏ 7511	Me for You, You for Me	1977	3.00	6.00	12.00
MALACO					
❏ 7419	Playin' for Keeps	198?	3.00	6.00	12.00
❏ 7427	I Will Survive	198?	3.00	6.00	12.00
❏ 7435	Annie Mae's Café	198?	3.00	6.00	12.00
❏ 7445	Movin' to the Country	198?	3.00	6.00	12.00
❏ 7448	Back to Back	198?	3.00	6.00	12.00
❏ 7453	Too Much Pain	198?	3.00	6.00	12.00
MCA					
❏ 5414	Age Ain't Nothin' But a Number	1983	2.50	5.00	10.00
ROUNDER					
❏ SS-35	The Sun Masters	198?	3.00	6.00	12.00
STAX					
❏ STS-3012	Waiting for Little Milton	1973	5.00	10.00	20.00

Number	Title (A Side/B Side)	Yr	VG	VG+	NM
❏ 4117	Waiting for Little Milton	1978	3.00	6.00	12.00
—Reissue of 3012					
❏ 5514	Blues 'n' Soul	1974	5.00	10.00	20.00
❏ MPS-8514	Walking the Back Streets	1981	2.50	5.00	10.00
❏ MPS-8518	Blues 'n' Soul	1981	2.50	5.00	10.00
—Reissue of 5514					
❏ MPS-8529	Grits Ain't Groceries	198?	2.50	5.00	10.00
—Despite the title, this is NOT a reissue of Checker 3011, but a later live recording					
❏ MPS-8550	What It Is	198?	2.50	5.00	10.00

LITTLE MISS CORNSHUCKS
45s
CHESS
| ❏ 1785 | No Teasing Around/It Do Me No Good | 1961 | 3.75 | 7.50 | 15.00 |
Albums
CHESS
| ❏ LP-1453 [M] | The Loneliest Gal in Town | 1961 | 50.00 | 100.00 | 200.00 |

LITTLE OTIS
45s
TAMLA
| ❏ 54058 | I Out-Duked the Duke/Baby I Need You | 1962 | 7.50 | 15.00 | 30.00 |

LITTLE PEOPLE
45s
ENTRANCE
| ❏ ZS7 7504 | I Don't Want to Go On Without You/You've Really Got a Hold on Me | 1972 | — | 3.50 | 7.00 |

LITTLE RICHARD Also see THE DEUCES OF RHYTHM AND THE TEMPO TOPPERS; JIMI HENDRIX.
12-Inch Singles
MCA
| ❏ L33-17101 [DJ] | Great Gosh A' Mighty! (same on both sides) | 1986 | 2.00 | 4.00 | 8.00 |
SPECIALTY
| ❏ SPS 4000 | Lucille/Heebie-Jeebies Love | 198? | 2.00 | 4.00 | 8.00 |
WTG
| ❏ 08169 | Twins (5 versions) | 1988 | — | 3.00 | 6.00 |
| —With Philip Bailey | | | | | |
45s
ATLANTIC
| ❏ 2181 | Crying in the Chapel/Hole in the Wall | 1963 | 3.00 | 6.00 | 12.00 |
| ❏ 2192 | It Is No Secret (What God Can Do)/Travelin' Shoes | 1963 | 3.00 | 6.00 | 12.00 |
BELL
| ❏ 45385 | Good Golly Miss Molly/Good Golly Miss Molly (Part 2) | 1973 | — | 2.50 | 5.00 |
BRUNSWICK
❏ 55362	She's Together/Try Some of Mine	1968	2.00	4.00	8.00
❏ 55377	Stingy Jenny/Baby Don't You Tear My Clothes	1968	2.00	4.00	8.00
❏ 55386	Soul Train/Can I Count on You	1968	2.00	4.00	8.00
CORAL
| ❏ 62366 | Milky White Way/Need Him | 1963 | 2.50 | 5.00 | 10.00 |
CRITIQUE
| ❏ 99392 | Happy Endings/California Girls | 1987 | — | 2.00 | 4.00 |
| —A-side with the Beach Boys; B-side is The Beach Boys without Little Richard | | | | | |
ELEKTRA
❏ 69370	Tutti Frutti/Rave On	1988	—	—	3.00
—B-side by John Cougar Mellencamp					
❏ 69384	Tutti Frutti/Powerful Stuff	1988	—	—	3.00
—B-side by the Fabulous Thunderbirds					
❏ 69385	Tutti Frutti/Kokomo	1988	—	—	3.00
—B-side by the Beach Boys					
END
| ❏ 1057 | Troubles of the World/Save Me Lord | 1959 | 3.75 | 7.50 | 15.00 |
| ❏ 1058 | Milky White Way/I've Just Come From the Fountain | 1959 | 3.75 | 7.50 | 15.00 |
GREEN MOUNTAIN
| ❏ 413 | In the Middle of the Night/Where Will I Find a Place to Sleep This Evening | 1973 | — | 2.50 | 5.00 |
KENT
❏ 4567	Mississippi/In the Name	1972	—	—	—
—Unreleased					
❏ 4568	Don't You Know I/In the Name	1972	—	2.50	5.00
LOST-NITE
❏ 296	Keep a-Knockin'/She's Got It	197?	—	3.00	6.00
—Reissue from Vee-Jay masters (not the original versions)					
❏ 302	Lucille/Good Golly Miss Molly	197?	—	3.00	6.00
—Reissue from Vee-Jay masters (not the original versions)					
❏ 309	Tutti Frutti/Long Tall Sally	197?	—	3.00	6.00
—Reissue from Vee-Jay masters (not the original versions)					
❏ 315	The Girl Can't Help It/Rip It Up	197?	—	3.00	6.00
—Reissue from Vee-Jay masters (not the original versions)					
MAINSTREAM
| ❏ 5572 | Try to Help Your Brother/Funk Proof | 1975 | — | 2.50 | 5.00 |
MANTICORE
| ❏ 7007 | Call My Name/Steal Miss Liza (Miss Liza Jane) | 1975 | — | 2.00 | 4.00 |
MCA
❏ 52780	Great Gosh A-Mighty! (It's a Matter of Time)/The Ride	1986	—	—	3.00
—B-side by Charlie Midnight					
❏ 52780 [PS]	Great Gosh A-Mighty! (It's a Matter of Time)/The Ride	1986	—	—	3.00
MERCURY
❏ 71884	He's Not Just a Soldier/Joy, Joy, Joy	1962	3.75	7.50	15.00
❏ 71911	Do You Care/Ride On King Jesus	1962	3.75	7.50	15.00
❏ 71965	Why Don't You Change Your Ways/He Got What He Wanted	1962	3.75	7.50	15.00
MODERN
❏ 1018	Holy Mackerel/Baby, Don't You Want a Man Like Me	1966	3.00	6.00	12.00
❏ 1018 [PS]	Holy Mackerel/Baby, Don't You Want a Man Like Me	1966	5.00	10.00	20.00
❏ 1019	Do You Feel It (Part 1)/Do You Feel It (Part 2)	1966	3.00	6.00	12.00
❏ 1022	Directly from My Heart to You/I'm Back	1966	3.00	6.00	12.00
❏ 1030	Slippin' and Slidin'/Bring It Back Home to Me	1967	3.00	6.00	12.00

Number	Title (A Side/B Side)	Yr	VG	VG+	NM
❏ 1043	Baby What You Want Me to Do (Part 1)/Baby What You Want Me to Do (Part 2)	1967	3.00	6.00	12.00
OKEH
❏ 7251	Poor Dog (Who Can't Wag His Own Tail)/Well	1966	3.75	7.50	15.00
❏ 7251 [PS]	Poor Dog (Who Can't Wag His Own Tail)/Well	1966	6.25	12.50	25.00
❏ 7262	I Need Love/Commandments of Love	1966	3.00	6.00	12.00
❏ 7271	Hurry Sundown/I Don't Want to Discuss It	1967	3.00	6.00	12.00
❏ 7278	Don't Deceive Me (Please Don't Go)/Never Gonna Let You Go	1967	3.00	6.00	12.00
❏ 7286	Money/Little Bit of Something	1967	3.00	6.00	12.00
❏ 7325	Lucille/Whole Lotta Shakin' Goin' On	1969	2.50	5.00	10.00
PEACOCK
| ❏ 1658 | Little Richard's Boogie/Directly from My Heart to You | 1956 | 37.50 | 75.00 | 150.00 |
| ❏ 1673 | Maybe I'm Right/I Love My Baby | 1957 | 20.00 | 40.00 | 80.00 |
RCA VICTOR
❏ 47-4392	Taxi Blues/Every Hour	1951	225.00	450.00	900.00
❏ 47-4582	Get Rich Quick/Thinkin' 'Bout My Mother	1952	200.00	400.00	800.00
❏ 47-4772	Why Did You Leave Me?/Ain't Nothin' Happenin'	1952	200.00	400.00	800.00
❏ 47-5025	Please Have Mercy on Me/I Brought It All on Myself	1952	150.00	300.00	600.00
REPRISE
❏ 0907	Freedom Blues/Dew Drop Inn	1970	2.50	5.00	10.00
❏ 0942	Greenwood Mississippi/I Saw Her Standing There	1970	2.50	5.00	10.00
❏ 1005	Shake a Hand (If You Can)/Somebody Saw You	1971	2.00	4.00	8.00
❏ 1043	Green Power/Dancing in the Street	1971	2.00	4.00	8.00
❏ 1062	Money Is/Money Runner	1972	2.00	4.00	8.00
—B-side by Quincy Jones					
❏ 1130	Mockingbird Sally/Nuki Suki	1972	2.00	4.00	8.00
SPECIALTY
❏ 561	Tutti-Frutti/I'm Just a Lonely Guy	1955	12.50	25.00	50.00
❏ 572	Long Tall Sally/Slippin' and Slidin' (Peepin' and Hidin')	1956	10.00	20.00	40.00
❏ 579	Rip It Up/Ready Teddy	1956	10.00	20.00	40.00
❏ 584	Heebie-Jeebies/She's Got it	1956	10.00	20.00	40.00
❏ 591	The Girl Can't Help It/All Around the World	1956	10.00	20.00	40.00
❏ 598	Lucille/Send Me Some Lovin'	1957	10.00	20.00	40.00
❏ 606	Jenny, Jenny/Miss Ann	1957	10.00	20.00	40.00
❏ 606 [PS]	Jenny, Jenny/Miss Ann	1957	15.00	30.00	60.00
❏ 611	Keep a Knockin'/Can't Believe You Wanna Leave	1957	7.50	15.00	30.00
❏ 611 [PS]	Keep a Knockin'/Can't Believe You Wanna Leave	1957	15.00	30.00	60.00
❏ 624	Good Golly, Miss Molly/Hey-Hey-Hey-Hey!	1958	7.50	15.00	30.00
❏ 624 [PS]	Good Golly, Miss Molly/Hey-Hey-Hey-Hey!	1958	12.50	25.00	50.00
❏ 633	Ooh! My Soul/True, Fine Mama	1958	6.25	12.50	25.00
❏ 633 [PS]	Ooh! My Soul/True, Fine Mama	1958	12.50	25.00	50.00
❏ 633/624	Ooh! My Soul/True, Fine Mama	1958	20.00	40.00	80.00
—Some copies have the B-side misnumbered; all other information is correct, including the master number					
❏ 645	Baby Face/I'll Never Let You Go	1958	6.25	12.50	25.00
❏ 652	She Knows How to Rock/Early One Morning	1958	6.25	12.50	25.00
❏ 660	By the Light of the Silvery Moon/Wonderin'	1959	6.25	12.50	25.00
❏ 664	Kansas City/Lonesome and Blue	1959	6.25	12.50	25.00
❏ 670	Shake a Hand/All Night Long	1959	6.25	12.50	25.00
❏ 680	Whole Lotta Shakin' Goin' On/Maybe I'm Right	1959	6.25	12.50	25.00
❏ 681	I Got It/Baby	1960	6.25	12.50	25.00
❏ 686	The Most I Can Offer/Directly from My Heart	1964	3.75	7.50	15.00
❏ 692	Bama Lama Bama Loo/Annie Is Back	1964	3.75	7.50	15.00
❏ 697	Keep a Knockin'/Bama Lama Bama Loo	1964	3.75	7.50	15.00
❏ 699	Poor Boy Paul/Wonderin'	1964	3.75	7.50	15.00
❏ 734	Chicken Little Baby/Oh Why	1974	—	3.00	6.00
VEE JAY
❏ 612	Whole Lotta Shakin' Goin' On/Goodnight Irene	1964	2.50	5.00	10.00
❏ 625	Blueberry Hill/Cherry Red	1964	2.50	5.00	10.00
❏ 652	It Ain't Whatcha Do/Cross Over	1965	2.50	5.00	10.00
❏ 665	Without Love/Dance What You Wanna	1965	2.50	5.00	10.00
❏ 698	I Don't Know What You've Got But It's Got Me — Part I/I Don't Know What You've Got But It's Got Me — Part II	1965	2.50	5.00	10.00
WARNER BROS.
| ❏ 28491 | Big House Reunion/Somebody's Comin' | 1987 | — | 2.00 | 4.00 |
WTG
| ❏ 08492 | Twins (Long)/Twins (Short) | 1988 | — | 2.00 | 4.00 |
| —With Philip Bailey | | | | | |
7-Inch Extended Plays
RCA CAMDEN
❏ CAE-416	Ain't Nothin' Happenin'/Why Did You Leave Me/Every Hour/I Brought It All on Myself	1955	37.50	75.00	150.00
❏ CAE-416 [PS]	Little Richard	1955	37.50	75.00	150.00
❏ CAE-446	Taxi Blues/Please Have Mercy on Me/Get Rich Quick/Thinkin' 'Bout My Mother	1956	25.00	50.00	100.00
❏ CAE-446 [PS]	Little Richard Rocks	1956	25.00	50.00	100.00
SPECIALTY
❏ SEP-400	Long Tall Sally/Miss Ann//She's Got It/Can't Believe You Wanna Leave	1957	25.00	50.00	100.00
❏ SEP-400 [PS]	Here's Little Richard	1957	25.00	50.00	100.00
❏ SEP-401	Slippin' and Slidin'/Oh Why//Ready Teddy/Baby	1957	25.00	50.00	100.00
❏ SEP-401 [PS]	Here's Little Richard	1957	25.00	50.00	100.00
❏ SEP-402	Tutti-Frutti/True, Fine Mama//Rip It Up/Jenny, Jenny	1957	25.00	50.00	100.00
❏ SEP-402 [PS]	Here's Little Richard	1957	25.00	50.00	100.00
❏ SEP-403	Keep a Knockin'/By the Light of the Silvery Moon//Lucille/Hey-Hey-Hey-Hey	1958	20.00	40.00	80.00
❏ SEP-403 [PS]	Little Richard	1958	20.00	40.00	80.00
❏ SEP-404	Ooh! My Soul/All Around the World//Good Golly, Miss Molly/Babyface	1958	20.00	40.00	80.00
❏ SEP-404 [PS]	Little Richard	1958	20.00	40.00	80.00
❏ SEP-405	Boo Hoo Hoo Hoo/The Girl Can't Help It//Send Me Some Lovin'/Heeby-Jeebies	1958	20.00	40.00	80.00
❏ SEP-405 [PS]	Little Richard	1958	20.00	40.00	80.00
Albums
ACCORD
| ❏ SN-7123 | Tutti Frutti | 1981 | 2.50 | 5.00 | 10.00 |
AUDIO ENCORES
| ❏ 1002 | Little Richard | 1980 | 6.25 | 12.50 | 25.00 |

L

Number	Title (A Side/B Side)	Yr	VG	VG+	NM
BUDDAH					
❏ BDS-7501	Little Richard	1969	7.50	15.00	30.00
CORAL					
❏ CRL 57446 [M]	Coming Home	1963	10.00	20.00	40.00
❏ CRL 757446 [S]	Coming Home	1963	12.50	25.00	50.00
CROWN					
❏ CLP-5362 [M]	Little Richard Sings Freedom Songs	1963	5.00	10.00	20.00
CUSTOM					
❏ 2061 [M]	Little Richard Sings Spirituals	196?	3.00	6.00	12.00
EPIC					
❏ EG 30428 [(2)]	Cast a Long Shadow	1971	5.00	10.00	20.00
❏ PE 40389	Little Richard's Greatest Hits	1986	2.50	5.00	10.00
❏ PE 40390	The Explosive Little Richard	1986	2.50	5.00	10.00
EXACT					
❏ 206	The Best of Little Richard	1980	2.50	5.00	10.00
GNP CRESCENDO					
❏ GNP-9033	The Big Hits	1974	3.00	6.00	12.00
GRT					
❏ 2103	The Original Little Richard	1977	2.50	5.00	10.00
GUEST STAR					
❏ GS-1429 [M]	Little Richard with Sister Rosetta Tharpe	196?	3.00	6.00	12.00
❏ GSS-1429 [R]	Little Richard with Sister Rosetta Tharpe	196?	3.00	6.00	12.00
KAMA SUTRA					
❏ KSBS-2023	Little Richard	1970	6.25	12.50	25.00
MERCURY					
❏ MG-20656 [M]	It's Real	1961	12.50	25.00	50.00
❏ SR-60656 [S]	It's Real	1961	15.00	30.00	60.00
MODERN					
❏ 100 [M]	His Greatest Hits/Recorded Live	1966	5.00	10.00	20.00
❏ 103 [M]	The Explosive Little Richard	1966	5.00	10.00	20.00
❏ 1000 [S]	His Greatest Hits/Recorded Live	1966	6.25	12.50	25.00
❏ 1003 [S]	The Explosive Little Richard	1966	6.25	12.50	25.00
OKEH					
❏ OKM 12117 [M]	The Explosive Little Richard	1967	6.25	12.50	25.00
❏ OKM 12121 [M]	Little Richard's Greatest Hits	1967	6.25	12.50	25.00
❏ OKS 14117 [S]	The Explosive Little Richard	1967	5.00	10.00	20.00
❏ OKS 14121 [S]	Little Richard's Greatest Hits	1967	5.00	10.00	20.00
PICKWICK					
❏ SPC-3258	King of the Gospel Singers	197?	2.50	5.00	10.00
RCA CAMDEN					
❏ CAL-420 [M]	Little Richard	1956	50.00	100.00	200.00
❏ CAS-2430(e)	Every Hour with Little Richard	1970	3.00	6.00	12.00
REPRISE					
❏ MS 2107	The Second Coming	1973	5.00	10.00	20.00
❏ RS 6406	The Rill Thing	1971	5.00	10.00	20.00
❏ RS 6462	King of Rock and Roll	1972	5.00	10.00	20.00
RHINO					
❏ R1-70236	Shut Up! A Collection of Rare Tracks, 1951-1964	1988	3.00	6.00	12.00
SCEPTER					
❏ CTN-18020	The Best of Little Richard	1972	3.00	6.00	12.00
SPECIALTY					
❏ 100 [M]	Here's Little Richard	1957	175.00	350.00	700.00
❏ SP-2100 [M]	Here's Little Richard	1957	50.00	100.00	200.00
—Thick vinyl					
❏ SP-2103 [M]	Little Richard	1958	37.50	75.00	150.00
—Front cover photo occupies the entire cover					
❏ SP-2103 [M]	Little Richard	196?	25.00	50.00	100.00
—Front cover photo partially obscured by a black triangle at uper right; thick vinyl					
❏ SP-2103 [M]	Little Richard	197?	5.00	10.00	20.00
—Reissue with thinner vinyl					
❏ SP-2104 [M]	The Fabulous Little Richard	1958	37.50	75.00	150.00
—Thick vinyl					
❏ SP-2104 [M]	The Fabulous Little Richard	197?	5.00	10.00	20.00
—Reissue with thinner vinyl					
❏ SP-2111 [M]	Little Richard — His Biggest Hits	1963	12.50	25.00	50.00
—Thick vinyl					
❏ SP-2111 [M]	Little Richard — His Biggest Hits	197?	5.00	10.00	20.00
—Reissue with thinner vinyl					
❏ SP-2113	Little Richard's Grooviest 17 Original Hits	1968	6.25	12.50	25.00
—Thick vinyl					
❏ SP-2136	Well Alright!	1970	5.00	10.00	20.00
❏ SP-8508 [(5)]	The Specialty Sessions	1989	10.00	20.00	40.00
SPIN-O-RAMA					
❏ 119 [M]	Clap Your Hands	196?	3.00	6.00	12.00
TRIP					
❏ 8013 [(2)]	Greatest Hits	1972	3.00	6.00	12.00
20TH FOX					
❏ FXG-5010 [M]	Little Richard Sings Gospel	1959	25.00	50.00	100.00
❏ SGM-5010 [S]	Little Richard Sings Gospel	1959	37.50	75.00	150.00
UNITED					
❏ US-7775	His Greatest Hits/Recorded Live	197?	2.50	5.00	10.00
❏ US-7777	The Wild and Frantic Little Richard	197?	2.50	5.00	10.00
UNITED ARTISTS					
❏ UA-LA497-E	The Very Best of Little Richard	1975	2.50	5.00	10.00
UPFRONT					
❏ UPF-123	The Best of Little Richard	197?	2.50	5.00	10.00
❏ UPF-197	Little Richard Sings Gospel	197?	2.50	5.00	10.00
VEE JAY					
❏ LP-1107 [M]	Little Richard Is Back!	1964	12.50	25.00	50.00
❏ LPS-1107 [S]	Little Richard Is Back!	1964	17.50	35.00	70.00
❏ VJLP-1107	Little Richard's Back	198?	2.50	5.00	10.00
—Reissue with thin vinyl					
❏ LP-1124 [M]	Little Richard's Greatest Hits	1965	6.25	12.50	25.00
❏ LPS-1124 [S]	Little Richard's Greatest Hits	1965	10.00	20.00	40.00
❏ VJLP-1124	Little Richard's Greatest Hits	198?	2.50	5.00	10.00
—Reissue with thin vinyl					
❏ DY-7304	Talkin' 'Bout Soul	198?	3.00	6.00	12.00
VEE JAY/CHAMELEON					
❏ D1-74797	Rip It Up	1989	3.00	6.00	12.00
WARNER BROS.					
❏ 25529	Lifetime Friend	1986	3.00	6.00	12.00
WING					
❏ MGW-12288 [M]	King of the Gospel Singers	1964	3.75	7.50	15.00
❏ SRW-16288 [S]	King of the Gospel Singers	1964	5.00	10.00	20.00

Number	Title (A Side/B Side)	Yr	VG	VG+	NM
LITTLE SAMMY AND THE TONES					
45s					
JACLYN					
❏ 1761	Christine/Over the Rainbow	1962	12.50	25.00	50.00
LITTLE STANLEY					
45s					
VANCE					
❏ 00111	Out of Sight Loving/(B-side unknown)	196?	250.00	500.00	1000.
LITTLE SYLVIA See SYLVIA (1).					
LITTLE TOMMY AND THE ELGINS					
45s					
ABC-PARAMOUNT					
❏ 10358	Never Love Again/I Walk On	1962	6.25	12.50	25.00
ELMAR					
❏ 1084	Never Love Again/I Walk On	1962	15.00	30.00	60.00
LITTLE WALTER					
45s					
CHANCE					
❏ 1116	That's All Right/Just Keep Loving Her	1952	1000.	2000.	3000.
—As "Little Walter J."					
CHECKER					
❏ 758	Juke/Can't Hold On Much Longer	1952	50.00	100.00	200.00
❏ 764	Mean Old World/Sad Hours	1952	30.00	60.00	120.00
❏ 767	Don't Have to Hunt No More/Tonight with a Fool	1953	20.00	40.00	80.00
❏ 770	Off the Wall/Tell Me Mama	1953	20.00	40.00	80.00
—Black vinyl					
❏ 770	Off the Wall/Tell Me Mama	1953	750.00	1500.	3000.
—Red vinyl					
❏ 780	Blues with a Feeling/Quarter to Twelve	1953	25.00	50.00	100.00
❏ 786	Lights Out/You're So Fine	1953	12.50	25.00	50.00
❏ 793	Oh Baby/Rocker	1954	10.00	20.00	40.00
❏ 799	You'd Better Watch Yourself/Blue Light	1954	10.00	20.00	40.00
—Black vinyl					
❏ 799	You'd Better Watch Yourself/Blue Light	1954	25.00	50.00	100.00
—Red vinyl					
❏ 805	Last Night/Mellow Down Easy	1954	15.00	30.00	60.00
❏ 811	My Babe/Thunder Bird	1955	10.00	20.00	40.00
❏ 817	Roller Coaster/I Got to Go	1955	10.00	20.00	40.00
❏ 825	Too Late/I Hate to See You Go	1955	10.00	20.00	40.00
❏ 833	Who/It Ain't Right	1956	10.00	20.00	40.00
❏ 838	Flying Saucer/One More Chance with You	1956	10.00	20.00	40.00
❏ 845	Teenage Beat/What a Feeling	1956	10.00	20.00	40.00
❏ 852	It's Too Late Brother/Take Me Back	1957	10.00	20.00	40.00
❏ 859	Everybody Needs Somebody/Nobody But You	1957	10.00	20.00	40.00
❏ 867	Boom, Boom — Out Goes the Light/Temperature	1957	10.00	20.00	40.00
❏ 890	The Toddle/Confessin' the Blues	1958	7.50	15.00	30.00
❏ 904	Key to the Highway/Rock Bottom	1958	7.50	15.00	30.00
❏ 919	My Baby's Sweeter/Crazy Mixed-Up World	1959	6.25	12.50	25.00
❏ 930	Everything's Gonna Be All Right/Back Track	1959	6.25	12.50	25.00
❏ 938	Break It Up/Me and Piney Brown	1960	5.00	10.00	20.00
❏ 945	Ah'w Baby/I Had My Fun	1960	5.00	10.00	20.00
❏ 955	My Babe/Blue Midnight	1960	5.00	10.00	20.00
❏ 968	I Don't Play/As Long As I Have You	1961	5.00	10.00	20.00
❏ 986	Crazy Legs/Crazy for My Baby	1961	5.00	10.00	20.00
❏ 1013	Just You Fool/I Got to Find My Baby	1962	3.75	7.50	15.00
❏ 1043	Up the Line/Southern Feeling	1963	3.75	7.50	15.00
❏ 1071	Diggin' My Potatoes/Snake Dancer	1964	3.75	7.50	15.00
❏ 1081	Dead Presidents/I'm a Business Man	1964	3.75	7.50	15.00
❏ 1117	Mean Ole Frisco/Blue and Lonesome	1965	3.75	7.50	15.00
Albums					
CHECKER					
❏ LP-1428 [M]	The Best of Little Walter	1957	125.00	250.00	500.00
—Black or maroon label					
❏ LP-3004 [M]	The Best of Little Walter	1967	12.50	25.00	50.00
—Reissue of 1428					
CHESS					
❏ 2ACMB-202 [(2)]	Little Walter	1976	5.00	10.00	20.00
—Reissue of 60014					
❏ CHV-416 [M]	Confessin' the Blues	1974	3.00	6.00	12.00
❏ LP-1535 [M]	Hate to See You Go	1969	6.25	12.50	25.00
❏ 2CH-60014 [(2)]	Boss Blues Harmonica	1972	5.00	10.00	20.00
LITTLE WHEELS, THE With RAY HILDEBRAND and JILL JACKSON, better known as PAUL AND PAULA.					
45s					
DOT					
❏ 16676	Four Wheeles, Ball Bearing Surfing Board/The Bumper	1964	7.50	15.00	30.00
LITTLEFIELD, LITTLE WILLIE					
45s					
BULLSEYE					
❏ 1005	Ruby-Ruby/Easy Go	1958	7.50	15.00	30.00
FEDERAL					
❏ 12101	Sticking on You Baby/Blood Is Redder Than Wine	1952	25.00	50.00	100.00
❏ 12110	K.C. Loving/Pleading at Midnight	1953	25.00	50.00	100.00
❏ 12137	The Midnight Hour Was Shining/My Best Wishes and Regards	1953	25.00	50.00	100.00
❏ 12148	Miss K.C.'s Fine/Rock-a-Bye Baby	1953	25.00	50.00	100.00
❏ 12163	Please Don't Go-o-o-o-oh/Don't Take My Heart Little Girl	1954	20.00	40.00	80.00
❏ 12174	Goofy Dust Blues/Falling Tears	1954	20.00	40.00	80.00
❏ 12221	Jim Wilson's Boogie/Sitting on the Curbstone	1955	15.00	30.00	60.00
❏ 12351	Kansas City/Midnight Hour Was Shining	1959	7.50	15.00	30.00
RHYTHM					
❏ 107	Baby Shame/Mistreated	1956	37.50	75.00	150.00
❏ 108	Ruby-Ruby/Easy Go	1956	37.50	75.00	150.00
❏ 115	I Need a Pay Day/I Want a Little Girl	195?	25.00	50.00	100.00
❏ 124	Theresa/The Day the Rains Came	195?	20.00	40.00	80.00
❏ 130	I Wanna Love You/Goodbye Baby	195?	20.00	40.00	80.00

Number	Title (A Side/B Side)	Yr	VG	VG+	NM
LITTLES, HATTIE					
45s					
GORDY					
❑ 7004	Back in My Arms Again/(B-side unknown)	1962	200.00	400.00	800.00
❑ 7007	Here You Come/Your Love Is Wonderful	1962	20.00	40.00	80.00
LITTLETON, JOHN, AND THE CAPISTRANOS					
45s					
DUKE					
❑ 179	Po Mary/Now Darling	1959	20.00	40.00	80.00
LIVELY ONES, THE					
45s					
DEL-FI					
❑ 4184	Guitarget/Crying Guitar	1962	7.50	15.00	30.00
❑ 4189	Misirlou/Blue Tears	1962	7.50	15.00	30.00
❑ 4189	Misirlou/Livin'	1962	7.50	15.00	30.00
❑ 4196	Surf Rider/Surfer's Lament	1963	7.50	15.00	30.00
❑ 4205	Surfer Boogie/Ric-a-Tic	1963	6.25	12.50	25.00
❑ 4210	High Tide/Goofy Foot	1963	6.25	12.50	25.00
❑ 4217	Surf City/Telstar Surf	1963	6.25	12.50	25.00
MGM					
❑ 13691	Bugalu Movement/Take It While You Can	1967	3.75	7.50	15.00
SMASH					
❑ 1880	Night and Day/Hey Scrounge	1964	6.25	12.50	25.00
Albums					
DEL-FI					
❑ DFLP-1226 [M]	Surf Rider	1963	25.00	50.00	100.00
❑ DFST-1226 [S]	Surf Rider	1963	37.50	75.00	150.00
❑ DFLP-1231 [M]	Surf Drums	1963	12.50	25.00	50.00
❑ DFST-1231 [S]	Surf Drums	1963	17.50	35.00	70.00
❑ DLF 1231	Surf Drums	1997	3.00	6.00	12.00
❑ DFLP-1237 [M]	Surf City	1963	10.00	20.00	40.00
❑ DFST-1237 [S]	Surf City	1963	12.50	25.00	50.00
❑ DLF 1237	Surf City	1997	3.00	6.00	12.00
❑ DFLP-1240 [M]	Surfin' South of the Border	1964	10.00	20.00	40.00
❑ DFST-1240 [S]	Surfin' South of the Border	1964	12.50	25.00	50.00
MGM					
❑ E-4449 [M]	Bugalu Party	1967	5.00	10.00	20.00
❑ SE-4449 [S]	Bugalu Party	1967	6.25	12.50	25.00
LIVERBIRDS, THE					
45s					
PHILIPS					
❑ 40276	Shop Around/It's Got to Be You	1965	2.50	5.00	10.00
❑ 40288	Why Do You Hang Around Me/Diddley Daddy	1965	2.50	5.00	10.00
LIVERPOOL BEATS, THE					
Albums					
RONDO					
❑ 2026 [M]	The New Merseyside Sound	1964	7.50	15.00	30.00
LIVERPOOL SPINNERS, THE British group known as "The Spinners" in their homeland; because of its existence, the R&B group The Spinners was called the "Motown Spinners" or the "Detroit Spinners" in the U.K.					
45s					
FONTANA					
❑ 1574	Seth Davey/All For Me Grog	1967	2.50	5.00	10.00
LIVERPOOLS, THE					
Albums					
WYNCOTE					
❑ SW-9001 [S]	Beatle Mania! In the U.S.A.	1964	6.25	12.50	25.00
❑ W-9001 [M]	Beatle Mania! In the U.S.A.	1964	5.00	10.00	20.00
❑ SW-9061 [S]	The Hit Sounds from England	1964	5.00	10.00	20.00
❑ W-9061 [M]	The Hit Sounds from England	1964	3.75	7.50	15.00
LIVERS, THE					
45s					
CONSTELLATION					
❑ 118	Beatle Time/This Is the Night	1964	3.75	7.50	15.00
LIVIGNI, JOHN See JOHN VALENTI.					
LIVIN' BLUES					
Albums					
DWARF					
❑ 2003	Dutch Treat	1971	7.50	15.00	30.00
LLOYD, DAVID					
Albums					
EPIC					
❑ LN 24151 [M]	Confidential (Sounds for a Secret Agent)	1965	5.00	10.00	20.00
❑ BN 26151 [S]	Confidential (Sounds for a Secret Agent)	1965	6.25	12.50	25.00
LLOYD, JIMMY					
45s					
ROULETTE					
❑ 4062	I Got a Rocket in My Pocket/You're Gone Baby	1958	25.00	50.00	100.00
❑ 7001	Where the Rio De Rosa Flows/The Beginning of the End	1957	15.00	30.00	60.00
LOAD OF MISCHIEF					
45s					
HOLIDAY INN					
❑ 2205	I'm a Lover/Back in My Arms Again	1967	5.00	10.00	20.00
SUN					
❑ 407	I'm a Lover/Back in My Arms Again	1967	20.00	40.00	80.00
—The last of the Sam Phillips Sun 45s					
LOBO					
45s					
ATLANTIC					
❑ 3851 [DJ]	Caribbean Carnival (same on both sides)	1981	—	2.50	5.00
—May be promo only					
BIG TREE					
❑ 112	Me and You and a Dog Named Boo/ Walk Away from It All	1971	—	3.00	6.00

Number	Title (A Side/B Side)	Yr	VG	VG+	NM
❑ 116	She Didn't Do Magic/I'm the Only One	1971	—	2.50	5.00
❑ 119	California Kid and Reemo/A Little Different	1971	—	2.50	5.00
❑ 134	The Albatross/We'll Make It, I Know We Will	1972	—	2.50	5.00
❑ 141	A Simple Man/ Don't Expect Me to Be Your Friend	1972	—	2.50	5.00
❑ 147	I'd Love You to Want Me/Am I True to Myself	1972	—	2.50	5.00
❑ 158	Don't Expect Me to Be Your Friend/ A Big Red Kite	1973	—	2.00	4.00
❑ 15001	Standing at the End of the Line/Stoney	1974	—	2.00	4.00
❑ 15008	Rings/I'm Only Sleeping	1974	—	2.00	4.00
❑ 16001	It Sure Took a Long, Long Time/Running Deer	1973	—	2.00	4.00
❑ 16004	How Can I Tell Her/Hope You're Proud of Me Girl	1973	—	2.00	4.00
❑ 16012	There Ain't No Way/Love Me for What I Am	1973	—	2.00	4.00
❑ 16033	Don't Tell Me Goodnight/My Mama Had Soul	1975	—	2.00	4.00
❑ 16040	Would I Still Have You/Morning Sun	1975	—	2.00	4.00
ELEKTRA					
❑ 47099	I Can't Believe You Anymore/Fight Fire with Fire	1980	—	2.00	4.00
EVERGREEN					
❑ 1028	Am I Going Crazy (Or Just Out of My Mind)/I Don't Want to Want You	1985	—	2.50	5.00
—Stock copies have corrected title					
❑ 1028 [DJ]	Am I Going Crazy (Or Just Out of Her Mind) (same on both sides)	1985	—	3.00	6.00
—Promo copies have incorrect title					
LAURIE					
❑ 3526	Happy Days in New York City/My Friend Is Here	1969	3.75	7.50	15.00
—As "Kent LaVoie"					
LOBO					
❑ I	I Don't Want to Want You/No One Will Ever Know	1981	—	2.50	5.00
❑ IV	Come Looking for Me/I Don't Want to Want You	1982	—	2.50	5.00
❑ X	Living My Life Without You/A Simple Man	1982	—	2.50	5.00
MCA					
❑ 41065	Where Were You When I Was Falling in Love/I Don't Wanna Make Love Anymore	1979	—	2.00	4.00
❑ 41152	Holdin' On for Dear Love/Gus, the Dancing Dog	1979	—	2.00	4.00
WARNER BROS.					
❑ 8493	Afterglow/Our Best Time	1977	—	2.00	4.00
❑ 8537	You Are All I'll Ever Need/Our Best Time	1978	—	2.00	4.00
Albums					
BIG TREE					
❑ 2003	Introducing Lobo	1971	3.75	7.50	15.00
❑ 2013	Of a Simple Man	1972	3.75	7.50	15.00
❑ 2100	Introducing Lobo	1973	3.00	6.00	12.00
—Reissue of 2003 with new cover					
❑ 2101	Calumet	1973	3.75	7.50	15.00
❑ BT 89501	Just a Singer	1974	3.00	6.00	12.00
❑ BT 89505	A Cowboy Afraid of Horses	1975	3.00	6.00	12.00
❑ BT 89513	The Best of Lobo	1976	3.00	6.00	12.00
MCA					
❑ 3194	Lobo	1979	2.50	5.00	10.00
LOCKETS, THE					
45s					
ARGO					
❑ 5455	Little Boy/Don'tcha Know	1963	3.00	6.00	12.00
LOCKLIN, HANK					
45s					
DECCA					
❑ 9-28526	I Like to Play with Your Kisses/Picking Sweethearts	1953	6.25	12.50	25.00
❑ 9-28740	I Can't Run Away/Red Rose	1953	6.25	12.50	25.00
❑ 9-28826	Lessons in Love/Shadows	1953	6.25	12.50	25.00
❑ 9-29030	Queen of Hearts/Mysteries of Life	1954	6.25	12.50	25.00
❑ 9-29270	Baby You Can Count on Me/ Whispering Scandal	1954	6.25	12.50	25.00
❑ 9-29564	Let Me Confess/I'll Always Be Standing By	1955	6.25	12.50	25.00
4 STAR					
❑ 1556	I Could Love You Darling/ The Song of the Whispering Leaves	1951	10.00	20.00	40.00
❑ 1564	Your House of Love Won't Stand/ Who Do You Think You're Fooling	1951	10.00	20.00	40.00
❑ 1574	Send Me the Pillow You Dream On, No. 2/I Always Lose	1951	10.00	20.00	40.00
❑ 1582	Stumpy Joe/I'm Going to Copyright Your Kisses	1951	10.00	20.00	40.00
❑ 1594	Tell Me You Love Me!/ Tomorrow's Just Another Day to Cry	1952	10.00	20.00	40.00
❑ 1605	Could You/Down Texas Way	1952	7.50	15.00	30.00
❑ 1608	Who's Knocking at My Heart/The Harvest Is Ripe	1952	7.50	15.00	30.00
❑ 1624	Alone at a Table for Two/Golden Wristwatch	1953	7.50	15.00	30.00
❑ 1632	Won't You Change Your Mind/Crazy Over You	1953	7.50	15.00	30.00
❑ 1641	Let Me Be the One/I'm Tired of Runnin' Around	1953	7.50	15.00	30.00
❑ 1688	Who Will It Be/Empty Bottle, Empty Heart	1954	7.50	15.00	30.00
❑ 1747	The Same Sweet Girl/ You Burned a Hole in My Heart	1960	3.75	7.50	15.00
KING					
❑ 5283	Send Me the Pillow You Dream On/ Let Me Be the One	1959	3.75	7.50	15.00
MGM					
❑ 14753	Send Me Your Coffee Cup/ True Love Is Always Hard to Find	1974	—	2.50	5.00
❑ 14777	The Sweetest Mistake/ Hang My Picture in Your Heart	1975	—	2.50	5.00
❑ 14802	Irish Eyes/Please Let Me Have You	1975	—	2.50	5.00
PLANTATION					
❑ 135	These Arms You Push Away/Baby I Need You	1976	—	2.50	5.00
❑ 142	Daytime Love Affair/You Never Miss the Water	1976	—	2.50	5.00
❑ 151	You Love Me Don't Cha/(B-side unknown)	1977	—	2.50	5.00
❑ 160	There Never Was a Time/(B-side unknown)	1977	—	2.50	5.00
RCA VICTOR					
❑ 47-6170	Your Heart Is an Island/You're Out of Step	1955	5.00	10.00	20.00
❑ 47-6242	Who Am I to Cast the First Stone/ These Ruins Belong to You	1955	5.00	10.00	20.00
❑ 47-6347	Why Baby Why/Love or Spite	1955	5.00	10.00	20.00
❑ 47-6434	I'm a Fool/A Good Woman's Love	1956	5.00	10.00	20.00
❑ 47-6571	Seven or Eleven/You Can't Never Tell	1956	5.00	10.00	20.00

L

Number	Title (A Side/B Side)	Yr	VG	VG+	NM
❏ 47-6672	How Much/She's Better Than Most	1956	5.00	10.00	20.00
❏ 47-6778	14 Karat Gold/By the Sweat of My Brow	1956	5.00	10.00	20.00
❏ 47-6867	Goin' Home All By Myself/The Rich and the Poor	1957	5.00	10.00	20.00
❏ 47-6967	Geisha Girl/Livin' Alone	1957	5.00	10.00	20.00
❏ 47-7127	Send Me the Pillow You Dream On/Why Don't You Haul Off and Love Me	1957	5.00	10.00	20.00
❏ 47-7203	It's a Little More Like Heaven/Blue Grass Skirt	1958	3.75	7.50	15.00
❏ 47-7317	That Inner Glow/The Upper Room	1958	3.75	7.50	15.00
❏ 47-7393	I Gotta Talk to Your Heart/The Other Side of the Door	1958	3.75	7.50	15.00
❏ 47-7472	Foreign Car/When the Band Plays the Blues	1959	3.75	7.50	15.00
❏ 47-7561	Hiding in My Heart/The Border of the Blues	1959	3.75	7.50	15.00
❏ 47-7612	Seven Days (The Humming Song)/Blues in Advance	1959	3.75	7.50	15.00
❏ 47-7692	Please Help Me, I'm Falling/My Old Home Town	1960	3.75	7.50	15.00
❏ 47-7813	One Step Ahead of My Past/Toujours Moi	1960	3.00	6.00	12.00
❏ 47-7871	From Here to There to You/This Song Is Just for You	1961	3.00	6.00	12.00
❏ 47-7921	You're the Reason/Happy Birthday to Me	1961	3.00	6.00	12.00
❏ 47-7965	Happy Journey/I Need You Now	1961	3.00	6.00	12.00
❏ 47-8034	We're Gonna Go Fishin'/Welcome Home, Mister Blues	1962	3.00	6.00	12.00
❏ 47-8106	Wabash Cannonball/Once More	1962	3.00	6.00	12.00
❏ 47-8156	Flyin' South/Behind the Footlights	1963	3.00	6.00	12.00
❏ 47-8248	Wooden Soldier/Kiss on the Door	1963	3.00	6.00	12.00
❏ 47-8318	Followed Closely by My Teardrops/You Never Want to Love Me	1964	3.00	6.00	12.00
❏ 47-8399	Hello Heartache/I Was Coming Home to You	1964	3.00	6.00	12.00
❏ 47-8497	I'm Blue/Give Your Wife a Kiss for Me	1965	2.50	5.00	10.00
❏ 47-8560	Forty Nine, Fifty One/Faith and Trust	1965	2.50	5.00	10.00
❏ 47-8695	The Girls Get Prettier (Every Day)/To Him	1965	2.50	5.00	10.00
❏ 47-8783	Insurance/I Feel a Cry Coming On	1966	2.50	5.00	10.00
❏ 47-8891	There's More Pretty Girls Than One/A Good Woman's Love	1966	2.50	5.00	10.00
❏ 47-8928	The Best Part of Loving You/The Last Thing on My Mind	1966	2.50	5.00	10.00
❏ 47-9092	Hasta Luego (See You Later)/Wishing on a Star	1967	2.50	5.00	10.00
❏ 47-9218	Nashville Women/Behind My Back	1967	2.50	5.00	10.00
❏ 47-9323	The Country Hall of Fame/Evergreen	1967	2.50	5.00	10.00
❏ 47-9476	Love Song for You/Little Geisha Girl	1968	2.50	5.00	10.00
❏ 47-9582	Everlasting Love/I'm Slowly Going Out of Your Mind	1968	2.50	5.00	10.00
❏ 47-9646	Lovin' You (The Way I Do)/Hot Pepper Doll	1968	2.50	5.00	10.00
❏ 47-9710	Where the Blue of the Night Meets the Gold of the Day/The Girls Who Wait	1969	2.00	4.00	8.00
❏ 47-9849	Flying South/Rosalita	1970	2.00	4.00	8.00
❏ 47-9894	Bless Her Heart...I Love Her/Morning	1970	2.00	4.00	8.00
❏ 47-9955	She's As Close As I Can Get to Loving You/I Like a Woman	1971	2.00	4.00	8.00
❏ 47-9986	My Heart Needs a Friend/Only a Fool	1971	2.00	4.00	8.00
❏ 48-1014	The Devil Out of Me/Softly	1971	2.00	4.00	8.00
❏ 74-0196	Jeannie/Cuban Girl	1969	2.00	4.00	8.00
❏ 74-0287	Please Help Me, I'm Falling/Anna	1969	2.00	4.00	8.00
❏ 74-0634	Imagination Running Wild/Love Has a Mind of Its Own	1972	—	3.00	6.00
❏ 74-0772	Eventually/I Forgot to Live Today	1972	—	3.00	6.00
❏ 74-0848	Goodbye Dear Ole Ryman/Just Call Me Darling	1972	—	3.00	6.00
❏ 74-0941	Before My Time/If Loving You Means Anything	1973	—	3.00	6.00
❏ APBO-0031	Jonas P. Jones/Send Me the Pillow You Dream On	1973	—	3.00	6.00
❏ SP-45-177 [DJ]	Hurt Me Again (same on both sides)	1968	5.00	10.00	20.00
❏ APBO-0226	Wildwood Flower/Sweet Inspiration	1974	—	3.00	6.00

Albums
DESIGN

Number	Title	Yr	VG	VG+	NM
❏ DLP-603 [M]	Hank Locklin	196?	3.75	7.50	15.00

HILLTOP

❏ JM-6003	Born to Ramble	196?	3.75	7.50	15.00
❏ JM-6041 [M]	Hank Locklin Sings Hank Locklin	196?	3.75	7.50	15.00
❏ JS-6041 [R]	Hank Locklin Sings Hank Locklin	196?	3.00	6.00	12.00
❏ JM-6083	Queen of Hearts	196?	3.75	7.50	15.00

KING

| ❏ 672 [M] | The Best of Hank Locklin | 1961 | 15.00 | 30.00 | 60.00 |
| ❏ 738 [M] | Encores | 1961 | 15.00 | 30.00 | 60.00 |

METRO

| ❏ M 541 [M] | Down Texas Way | 196? | 3.75 | 7.50 | 15.00 |
| ❏ MS 541 [R] | Down Texas Way | 196? | 3.00 | 6.00 | 12.00 |

RCA CAMDEN

❏ CAL-705 [M]	Hank Locklin	1962	3.75	7.50	15.00
❏ CAL-912 [M]	My Kind of Country Music	196?	3.75	7.50	15.00
❏ CAS-912 [R]	My Kind of Country Music	196?	3.00	6.00	12.00

RCA VICTOR

❏ LPM-1673 [M]	Foreign Love	1958	15.00	30.00	60.00
❏ LPM-2291 [M]	Please Help Me, I'm Falling	1960	7.50	15.00	30.00
❏ LSP-2291 [S]	Please Help Me, I'm Falling	1960	10.00	20.00	40.00
❏ LPM-2464 [M]	Happy Journey	1962	6.25	12.50	25.00
❏ LSP-2464 [S]	Happy Journey	1962	7.50	15.00	30.00
❏ LPM-2597 [M]	A Tribute to Roy Acuff, the King of Country Music	1962	6.25	12.50	25.00
❏ LSP-2597 [S]	A Tribute to Roy Acuff, the King of Country Music	1962	7.50	15.00	30.00
❏ LPM-2680 [M]	The Ways of Life	1963	6.25	12.50	25.00
❏ LSP-2680 [S]	The Ways of Life	1963	7.50	15.00	30.00
❏ LPM-2801 [M]	Irish Songs, Country Style	1964	5.00	10.00	20.00
❏ LSP-2801 [S]	Irish Songs, Country Style	1964	6.25	12.50	25.00
❏ LPM-2997 [M]	Hank Locklin Sings Hank Williams	1964	5.00	10.00	20.00
❏ LSP-2997 [S]	Hank Locklin Sings Hank Williams	1964	6.25	12.50	25.00
❏ LPM-3391 [M]	Hank Locklin Sings Eddy Arnold	1965	5.00	10.00	20.00
❏ LSP-3391 [S]	Hank Locklin Sings Eddy Arnold	1965	6.25	12.50	25.00
❏ LPM-3465 [M]	Once Over Lightly	1965	5.00	10.00	20.00
❏ LSP-3465 [S]	Once Over Lightly	1965	6.25	12.50	25.00
❏ LPM-3559 [M]	The Best of Hank Locklin	1966	5.00	10.00	20.00
❏ LSP-3559 [S]	The Best of Hank Locklin	1966	6.25	12.50	25.00
❏ LPM-3588 [M]	The Girls Get Prettier	1966	5.00	10.00	20.00
❏ LSP-3588 [S]	The Girls Get Prettier	1966	6.25	12.50	25.00
❏ LPM-3656 [M]	The Gloryland Way	1966	5.00	10.00	20.00
❏ LSP-3656 [S]	The Gloryland Way	1966	6.25	12.50	25.00
❏ LPM-3770 [M]	Send Me the Pillow You Dream On	1967	6.25	12.50	25.00
❏ LSP-3770 [S]	Send Me the Pillow You Dream On	1967	5.00	10.00	20.00
❏ LPM-3841 [M]	Nashville Women	1967	6.25	12.50	25.00

Number	Title (A Side/B Side)	Yr	VG	VG+	NM
❏ LSP-3841 [S]	Nashville Women	1967	5.00	10.00	20.00
❏ LPM-3946 [M]	Country Hall of Fame	1968	25.00	50.00	100.00
❏ LSP-3946 [S]	Country Hall of Fame	1968	5.00	10.00	20.00
❏ LSP-4030	My Love Song for You	1968	5.00	10.00	20.00
❏ LSP-4113	Softly	1969	5.00	10.00	20.00
❏ LSP-4191	Lookin' Back	1969	3.75	7.50	15.00

SEARS

| ❏ SPS-104 | Send Me the Pillow You Dream On | 196? | 6.25 | 12.50 | 25.00 |

STEREO SPECTRUM

| ❏ SDLP-603 [R] | Hank Locklin | 196? | 3.00 | 6.00 | 12.00 |

—"Stereo" version of Design DLP-603

WRANGLER

| ❏ 1004 [M] | Hank Locklin | 1962 | 6.25 | 12.50 | 25.00 |

LOCOMOTIONS, THE
45s
GONE

Number	Title (A Side/B Side)	Yr	VG	VG+	NM
❏ 5142	Little Eva/Adios My Love	1962	5.00	10.00	20.00

SWAN

| ❏ 4237 | Weekend Workout/Make It Saturday Night | 1965 | 2.50 | 5.00 | 10.00 |

LODI
45s
MOWEST

| ❏ 5003 | Happiness/I Hope I See It in My Lifetime | 1971 | 2.00 | 4.00 | 8.00 |

Albums
MOWEST

| ❏ MW 101L | Happiness | 1972 | 6.25 | 12.50 | 25.00 |

LOE AND JOE
45s
HARVEY

| ❏ 112 | Little Ole Boy, Little Ole Girl/That's How I Am Without You | 1962 | 7.50 | 15.00 | 30.00 |

LOFGREN, NILS
Also see GRIN. Also was a member of BRUCE SPRINGSTEEN's E Street Band in the 1980s.
12-Inch Singles
BACKSTREET

Number	Title (A Side/B Side)	Yr	VG	VG+	NM
❏ L33-1127 [DJ]	Across the Tracks/Daddy Dream	1983	2.00	4.00	8.00

COLUMBIA

| ❏ CAS 2100 [DJ] | Secrets in the Street (same on both sides) | 1985 | — | 3.00 | 6.00 |
| ❏ CAS 2173 [DJ] | Delivery Night (same on both sides) | 1985 | — | 3.00 | 6.00 |

45s
A&M

❏ 1692	Back It Up/If I Say It, It's So	1975	—	2.50	5.00
❏ 1812	Cry Tough/Share a Little	1976	—	2.50	5.00
❏ 1839	It's Not a Crime/Share a Little	1976	—	2.50	5.00
❏ 1927	I Came to Dance/Code of the Road	1977	—	2.00	4.00
❏ 2173	Kool Skool/No Mercy	1979	—	2.00	4.00

BACKSTREET

| ❏ 51191 | Night Fades Away/Ancient History | 1981 | — | 2.00 | 4.00 |

COLUMBIA

| ❏ 05406 | Secrets in the Street/From the Heart | 1985 | — | — | 3.00 |
| ❏ 05598 | Delivery Night/Flip Ya Flip | 1985 | — | — | 3.00 |

Albums
A&M

| ❏ SP-3145 | Cry Tough | 198? | 2.00 | 4.00 | 8.00 |

—Reissue of 4573

❏ SP-3201	The Best	1982	2.50	5.00	10.00
❏ SP-3707 [(2)]	Night After Night	1977	3.00	6.00	12.00
❏ SP-4509	Nils Lofgren	1975	2.50	5.00	10.00
❏ SP-4573	Cry Tough	1976	2.50	5.00	10.00
❏ SP-4628	I Came to Dance	1977	2.50	5.00	10.00
❏ SP-4756	Nils	1979	2.50	5.00	10.00
❏ SP-6509 [(2)]	Night After Night	198?	2.50	5.00	10.00

—Reissue of 3707

| ❏ SP-8362 [DJ] | Authorized Bootleg | 1976 | 6.25 | 12.50 | 25.00 |

BACKSTREET

| ❏ 5251 | Night Fades Away | 1981 | 2.50 | 5.00 | 100.00 |
| ❏ 5421 | Wonderland | 1983 | 2.50 | 5.00 | 10.00 |

COLUMBIA

| ❏ BFC 39982 | Flip | 1985 | 2.50 | 5.00 | 10.00 |

LOGGINS, DAVE
45s
EPIC

| ❏ 02152 | Please Come to Boston/Someday | 1981 | — | — | 3.00 |

—Reissue

❏ 11115	Please Come to Boston/Let Me Go Now	1974	—	2.50	5.00
❏ 50035	Someday/Girl from Knoxville	1974	—	2.00	4.00
❏ 50069	Second Hand Lady/So You Couldn't Get to Me	1975	—	2.00	4.00
❏ 50221	Saviour of My Natural Life/You've Got Me to Hold On To	1976	—	2.00	4.00
❏ 50246	Movin' to the Country/Wild Millie the Country Girl	1976	—	2.00	4.00
❏ 50326	Three Little Words (I Love You)/Don't Treat Me Like a Stranger	1976	—	2.00	4.00
❏ 50491	Ship in a Bottle/The Ballad of Cowboy 20	1977	—	2.00	4.00
❏ 50509	One-Way Ticket to Paradise/Crowd of Lonely People	1978	—	—	4.00
❏ 50578	So Much for Dreams/You Found It Now	1978	—	2.00	4.00
❏ 50711	Pieces of April/Color of My Mood	1979	—	2.00	4.00
❏ 50783	One Way Ticket to Paradise/The Fool in Me	1979	—	2.00	4.00

VANGUARD

❏ 35147	Claudia/Think'n of You	1972	—	2.50	5.00
❏ 35167	Pieces of April/Think'n of You	1972	—	2.50	5.00
❏ 35177	Building Condemned/Lady in an Orange Silk Blouse	1973	—	2.50	5.00

Albums
EPIC

❏ KE 32833	Apprentice (In a Musical Workshop)	1974	2.50	5.00	10.00
❏ PE 33946	Country Suite	1975	2.50	5.00	10.00
❏ PE 34713	One Way	1977	2.50	5.00	10.00
❏ JE 35792	David Loggins	1979	2.50	5.00	10.00

VANGUARD

| ❏ VSD-6580 | Personal Belongings | 1972 | 3.75 | 7.50 | 15.00 |

Number	Title (A Side/B Side)	Yr	VG	VG+	NM
LOGGINS AND MESSINA Also see JIM MESSINA.					
45s					
COLUMBIA					
❏ JBQ 507 [Q]	Your Mama Don't Dance/Thinking of You	1973	2.50	5.00	10.00
—"Special Coin Operator Release" in quadraphonic					
❏ 10077	Changes/Get a Hold	1974	—	2.50	5.00
❏ 10118	Growin'/Keep Me in Mind	1975	—	2.50	5.00
❏ 10188	I Like It Like That/Angry Eyes	1975	—	2.50	5.00
❏ 10222	A Lover's Question/Oh, Lonesome Me	1975	—	2.50	5.00
❏ 10311	When I Was a Child/Peacemaker	1976	—	2.50	5.00
❏ 10376	Native Son/Pretty Princess	1976	—	2.50	5.00
❏ 10444	Angry Eyes/Watching the River Run	1976	—	2.50	5.00
❏ 45550	Same Old Wine/Vahevelia	1972	—	3.00	6.00
—As "Kenny Loggins and Jim Messina"					
❏ 45617	Nobody But You/Danny's Song	1972	—	3.00	6.00
—As "Kenny Loggins and Jim Messina"					
❏ 45664	Peace of Mind/House at Pooh Corner	1972	—	3.00	6.00
—As "Kenny Loggins and Jim Messina"					
❏ 45719	Your Mama Don't Dance/Golden Ribbons	1972	—	2.50	5.00
—As "Kenny Loggins and Jim Messina"; orange label					
❏ 45719	Your Mama Don't Dance/Golden Ribbons	1972	—	3.00	6.00
—As "Kenny Loggins and Jim Messina"; gray label					
❏ 45815	Thinking of You/'Till the Ends Meet	1973	—	2.50	5.00
—A-side is a different version than on most LPs					
❏ 45952	My Music/A Love Song	1973	—	2.50	5.00
❏ 46010	Watching the River Run/Travelin' Blues	1974	—	2.50	5.00
Albums					
COLUMBIA					
❏ C 31044	Kenny Loggins with Jim Messina Sittin' In	1972	2.50	5.00	10.00
❏ PC 31044	Kenny Loggins with Jim Messina Sittin' In	197?	2.00	4.00	8.00
—Reissue with new prefix					
❏ CQ 31748 [Q]	Loggins and Messina	1973	3.75	7.50	15.00
❏ KC 31748	Loggins and Messina	1972	2.50	5.00	10.00
❏ PC 31748	Loggins and Messina	197?	2.00	4.00	8.00
—Reissue with new prefix					
❏ CQ 32540 [Q]	Full Sail	1973	3.75	7.50	15.00
❏ KC 32540	Full Sail	1973	2.50	5.00	10.00
❏ PC 32540	Full Sail	197?	2.00	4.00	8.00
—Reissue with new prefix					
❏ PG 32848 [(2)]	On Stage	1974	3.00	6.00	12.00
—Original with no bar code					
❏ PG 32848 [(2)]	On Stage	198?	2.50	5.00	10.00
—With bar code					
❏ PC 33175	Mother Lode	1974	2.50	5.00	10.00
—Original with no bar code					
❏ PC 33175	Mother Lode	198?	2.00	4.00	8.00
—With bar code					
❏ PC 33578	Native Sons	1976	2.50	5.00	10.00
—Original with no bar code					
❏ PC 33578	Native Sons	198?	2.00	4.00	8.00
—With bar code					
❏ PCQ 33578 [Q]	Native Sons	1976	3.75	7.50	15.00
❏ PC 33810	So Fine	1975	2.50	5.00	10.00
—Original with no bar code					
❏ PC 33810	So Fine	198?	2.00	4.00	8.00
—With bar code					
❏ JG 34167 [(2)]	Finale	1977	3.00	6.00	12.00
❏ PC 34388	The Best of Friends	1976	2.50	5.00	10.00
—Original with no bar code					
❏ PC 34388	The Best of Friends	198?	2.00	4.00	8.00
—With bar code					
❏ HC 44388	The Best of Friends	1982	12.50	25.00	50.00
—Half-speed mastered edition					
DIRECT DISC					
❏ SD 16606	Full Sail	198?	7.50	15.00	30.00
—Audiophile vinyl					
EPIC					
❏ PC 34388	The Best of Friends	1976	5.00	10.00	20.00
—Mispressing with wrong label					
LOLITA					
45s					
4 CORNERS OF THE WORLD					
❏ 131	Come Back/When Our Father Is Happy	1965	—	3.50	7.00
KAPP					
❏ 349	Sailor (Your Home Is the Sea)/La Luna (Quando La Luna)	1960	2.00	4.00	8.00
—Black label					
❏ 349	Sailor (Your Home Is the Sea)/La Luna (Quando La Luna)	1960	3.00	6.00	12.00
—Maroon and silver label					
❏ 349 [PS]	Sailor (Your Home Is the Sea)/La Luna (Quando La Luna)	1960	5.00	10.00	20.00
❏ 370	Cowboy Jimmy Joe (Die Sterne Der Prarie)/Theme from "A Summer Place"	1961	2.00	4.00	8.00
❏ 370 [PS]	Cowboy Jimmy Joe (Die Sterne Der Prarie)/Theme from "A Summer Place"	1961	5.00	10.00	20.00
❏ 402	For the First Time (I've Fallen in Love)/Souvenir d'Amour	1961	2.00	4.00	8.00
Albums					
KAPP					
❏ KL-1219 [M]	Sailor	1961	6.25	12.50	25.00
❏ KL-1229 [M]	Songs You Will Never Forget	1961	6.25	12.50	25.00
❏ KS-3219 [S]	Sailor	1961	7.50	15.00	30.00
❏ KS-3229 [S]	Songs You Will Never Forget	1961	7.50	15.00	30.00
LOLLIPOP SHOPPE, THE					
45s					
SHAMLEY					
❏ 44005	Someone I Know/Through My Window	1969	3.00	6.00	12.00
UNI					
❏ 55050	You Must Be a Witch/Don't Close the Door	1968	3.75	7.50	15.00
❏ 55050 [PS]	You Must Be a Witch/Don't Close the Door	1968	6.25	12.50	25.00
Albums					
UNI					
❏ 73019	The Lollipop Shoppe	1968	20.00	40.00	80.00

Number	Title (A Side/B Side)	Yr	VG	VG+	NM
LOLLIPOPS, THE (1)					
45s					
ATCO					
❏ 6787	Nothing's Gonna Stop Our Love/I Believe in Love	1970	—	3.00	6.00
GORDY					
❏ 7089	Cheating Is Telling On You/Need Your Love	1969	200.00	400.00	800.00
IMPACT					
❏ 1021	Lovin' Good Feelin'/Step Aside Baby	1967	7.50	15.00	30.00
V.I.P.					
❏ 25051	Cheating Is Telling On You/Need Your Love	1968	6.25	12.50	25.00
LOLLIPOPS, THE (2)					
45s					
SSS INTERNATIONAL					
❏ 777	You Don't Know/Feel So Comfortable	1969	3.75	7.50	15.00
LOLLIPOPS, THE (3)					
45s					
WARNER BROS.					
❏ 5122	Mister Santa/Little Donkey (Carry Mary Safely on Her Way)	1959	3.00	6.00	12.00
LOLLIPOPS, THE (U) Some of these could be group (1).					
45s					
RCA VICTOR					
❏ 47-8344	Peggy Got Engaged/I'll Set My Love to Music	1964	5.00	10.00	20.00
❏ 47-8390	Don't Monkey With Me/Love Is the Only Answer	1964	5.00	10.00	20.00
❏ 47-8430	Billy, Billy Baby/Big Brother	1964	5.00	10.00	20.00
❏ 47-8494	Busy Signal/I Want You Back Again	1965	3.75	7.50	15.00
SMASH					
❏ 2057	He's the Boy/Gee Whiz Baby	1966	3.00	6.00	12.00
LOMAX, JACKIE					
45s					
APPLE					
❏ 1802	Sour Milk Sea/The Eagle Laughs at You	1968	5.00	10.00	20.00
—With B-side author listed as "(George Harrison)"					
❏ 1802	Sour Milk Sea/The Eagle Laughs at You	1968	5.00	10.00	20.00
—With B-side author listed as "(Jackie Lomax)"					
❏ 1807	New Day/Thumbin' a Ride	1969	15.00	30.00	60.00
—Without star on A-side label					
❏ 1807	New Day/Thumbin' a Ride	1969	18.75	37.50	75.00
—With star on A-side label					
❏ 1819	How the Web Was Woven/I Fall Inside Your Eyes	1970	2.00	4.00	8.00
❏ 1819 [PS]	How the Web Was Woven/I Fall Inside Your Eyes	1970	2.50	5.00	10.00
❏ 1834	Sour Milk Sea/(I) Fall Inside Your Eyes	1971	2.00	4.00	8.00
❏ PRO-6240/1 [DJ]	Sour Milk Sea/(I) Fall Inside Your Eyes	1971	7.50	15.00	30.00
CAPITOL					
❏ 4384	More (Livin' for Lovin')/I Remember (Memorabilia)	1976	—	2.50	5.00
EPIC					
❏ 10270	One Minute Woman/Genuine Imitation of Life	1967	3.00	6.00	12.00
WARNER BROS.					
❏ 7503	Helluva Woman/Higher Ground	1971	—	3.00	6.00
❏ 7564	Lavender Dream/Lost	1972	—	3.00	6.00
❏ 7589	Roll On/Hellfire, Night Crier	1972	—	3.00	6.00
Albums					
APPLE					
❏ ST-3354	Is This What You Want?	1969	6.25	12.50	25.00
CAPITOL					
❏ ST-11558	Livin' for Lovin'	1976	2.50	5.00	10.00
❏ ST-11668	Did You Ever	1977	2.50	5.00	10.00
WARNER BROS.					
❏ PRO 520 [DJ]	An Interview with Jackie Lomax	1972	10.00	20.00	40.00
❏ WS 1914	Home Is In My Head	1971	3.00	6.00	12.00
❏ BS 2591	Three	1972	3.00	6.00	12.00
LONDON, JULIE					
45s					
BETHLEHEM					
❏ 11003	Sometimes I Feel Like a Motherless Child/A Foggy Day	1958	5.00	10.00	20.00
❏ 11015	Don't Worry 'Bout Me/You're Blase	1959	3.00	6.00	12.00
LIBERTY					
❏ 33006 [S]	Lonesome Road/Goodbye	1960	5.00	10.00	20.00
❏ 33007 [S]	When I Fall in Love/The More I See You	1960	5.00	10.00	20.00
❏ 33008 [S]	Blue Moon/I Guess I'll Have to Change My Plan	1960	5.00	10.00	20.00
❏ 33009 [S]	Bye Bye Blues/Basin Street Blues	1960	5.00	10.00	20.00
❏ 33010 [S]	Daddy/Bye Bye Blackbird	1960	5.00	10.00	20.00
—The above four are 33 1/3 rpm jukebox singles					
❏ 55006	Cry Me a River/S'Wonderful	1955	3.00	6.00	12.00
❏ 55009	Baby, Baby, All the Time/Shadow Woman	1955	2.50	5.00	10.00
❏ 55025	September in the Rain/Lonely Girl	1956	2.50	5.00	10.00
❏ 55032	Tall Boy/Now, Baby, Now	1956	2.50	5.00	10.00
❏ 55052	The Meaning of the Blues/Boy on a Dolphin	1957	2.50	5.00	10.00
❏ 55076	It Had to Be You/Dark	1957	2.50	5.00	10.00
❏ 55108	I'd Like You for Christmas/Saddle the Wind	1957	3.00	6.00	12.00
❏ 55131	Tell Me You're Home/The Freshman	1958	2.50	5.00	10.00
❏ 55139	It's Easy/Voice in the Mirror	1958	2.50	5.00	10.00
❏ 55157	Blue Moon/Man of the West	1958	2.50	5.00	10.00
❏ 55175	Come On-a My House/My Strange Affair	1959	2.50	5.00	10.00
❏ 55182	Must Be Catchin'/Something I Dreamed Last Night	1959	2.50	5.00	10.00
❏ 55216	Comin' Through the Rye/Makin' Whoopee	1959	2.50	5.00	10.00
❏ 55227	Cry Me a River/It's a Blue World	1959	2.50	5.00	10.00
❏ 55269	In the Wee Small Hours of the Morning/Time for Lovers	1960	2.50	5.00	10.00
❏ 55300	Send for Me/Evenin'	1961	2.00	4.00	8.00
❏ 55309	Sanctuary/Every Chance I Get	1961	2.00	4.00	8.00
❏ 55337	My Darling, My Darling/My Love, My Love	1961	2.00	4.00	8.00
❏ 55512	Desafinado/Where Did the Gentleman Go	1962	2.00	4.00	8.00
❏ 55605	I'm Coming Back to You/When Snowflakes Fall in the Summer	1963	2.00	4.00	8.00

Number	Title (A Side/B Side)	Yr	VG	VG+	NM
❏ 55666	Guilty Heart/I Want to Find Out for Myself	1964	—	3.00	6.00
❏ 55702	Girl (Boy) from Ipanema/My Lover Is a Stranger	1964	—	3.00	6.00
❏ 55759	We Proved Them Wrong/You're Free to Go	1964	—	3.00	6.00
❏ 55830	Girl Talk/Won't Somebody Please Belong to Me	1965	—	3.00	6.00
❏ 55911	Nice Girls Don't Stay for Breakfast/Bill Bailey (Won't You Please Come Home)	1966	—	3.00	6.00
❏ 55966	Mickey Mouse March/Baby Won't You Please	1967	—	3.00	6.00
❏ 56074	Yummy, Yummy, Yummy/Come to Me Slowly	1968	—	2.50	5.00
❏ 56085	Louie Louie/Hushabye Mountain	1969	—	2.50	5.00
❏ 56112	Too Much of a Man/Sittin' Pretty	1969	—	—	—
—Unreleased					

UNITED ARTISTS

Number	Title (A Side/B Side)	Yr	VG	VG+	NM
❏ 0013	Cry Me a River/Come On-a My House	1973	·	2.00	4.00
—"Silver Spotlight Series" reissue					

7-Inch Extended Plays
LIBERTY

Number	Title (A Side/B Side)	Yr	VG	VG+	NM
❏ LEP-1-3006	Laura/S' Wonderful//I'm in the Mood for Love/ Can't Help Lovin' That Man	1956	3.00	6.00	12.00
❏ LEP-1-3006 [PS]	Julie Is Her Name, Part One	1956	3.00	6.00	12.00
❏ LEP-2-3006	(contents unknown)	1956	3.00	6.00	12.00
❏ LEP-2-3006 [PS]	Julie Is Her Name, Part Two	1956	3.00	6.00	12.00
❏ LEP-3-3006 [PS]	Julie Is Her Name, Part Three	1956	3.00	6.00	12.00
❏ LEP-1-3012	*Lonely Girl/Fools Rush In/How Deep Is the Ocean/Mean to Me	195?	3.00	6.00	12.00
❏ LEP-1-3012 [PS]	Lonely Girl, Part One	195?	3.00	6.00	12.00
❏ LEP-2-3012	(contents unknown)	195?	3.00	6.00	12.00
❏ LEP-2-3012 [PS]	Lonely Girl, Part Two	195?	3.00	6.00	12.00
❏ LEP-3-3012	Don't Take Your Love from Me/Where or When/ /It's the Talk of the Town/What'll I Do	195?	3.00	6.00	12.00
❏ LEP-3-3012 [PS]	Lonely Girl, Part Three	195?	3.00	6.00	12.00
❏ LEP-1-3043	Basin Street Blues/Get Set for the Blues// Invitation to the Blues/Meaning of the Blues	195?	3.00	6.00	12.00
❏ LEP-1-3043 [PS]	About the Blues, Part One	195?	3.00	6.00	12.00
❏ LST-7342	Since I Fell for You/Fools Rush In/You Don't Have to Be a Baby to Cry/I Wish You Love/ Charade/Wives and Lovers	1964	3.75	7.50	15.00
—Jukebox issue; small hole, plays at 33 1/3 rpm					
❏ LST-7342 [PS]	Julie London	1964	3.75	7.50	15.00
❏ LEP-1-9002	*June in January/February Brings the Rain/ Melancholy March/I'll Remember April	1956	3.00	6.00	12.00
❏ LEP-1-9002 [PS]	Calendar Girl, Part One	1956	3.00	6.00	12.00
❏ LEP-2-9002	*People Who Are Born in May/Memphis in June/ Sleigh Ride in July/Time for August	1956	3.00	6.00	12.00
❏ LEP-2-9002 [PS]	Calendar Girl, Part Two	1956	3.00	6.00	12.00
❏ LEP-3-9002	*September in the Rain/This October/November Twilight/Warm December	1956	3.00	6.00	12.00
❏ LEP-3-9002 [PS]	Calendar Girl, Part Three	1956	3.00	6.00	12.00

Albums
LIBERTY

Number	Title (A Side/B Side)	Yr	VG	VG+	NM
❏ MCR-1 [M]	By Myself	196?	6.25	12.50	25.00
—Columbia Record Club exclusive					
❏ SCR-1 [S]	By Myself	196?	7.50	15.00	30.00
—Columbia Record Club exclusive					
❏ LRP-3006 [M]	Julie Is Her Name	1956	12.50	25.00	50.00
—Green label					
❏ LRP-3006 [M]	Julie Is Her Name	1960	5.00	10.00	20.00
—Black label, colorband and logo at left					
❏ LRP-3012 [M]	Lonely Girl	1956	12.50	25.00	50.00
—Green label					
❏ LRP-3012 [M]	Lonely Girl	1960	5.00	10.00	20.00
—Black label, colorband and logo at left					
❏ LRP-3043 [M]	About the Blues	1957	10.00	20.00	40.00
—Green label					
❏ LRP-3043 [M]	About the Blues	1960	5.00	10.00	20.00
—Black label, colorband and logo at left					
❏ LRP-3060 [M]	Make Love to Me	1957	10.00	20.00	40.00
—Green label					
❏ LRP-3060 [M]	Make Love to Me	1960	5.00	10.00	20.00
—Black label, colorband and logo at left					
❏ LRP-3096 [M]	Julie	1957	10.00	20.00	40.00
—Green label					
❏ LRP-3100 [M]	Julie Is Her Name, Volume 2	1958	10.00	20.00	40.00
—Green label					
❏ LRP-3100 [M]	Julie Is Her Name, Volume 2	1960	5.00	10.00	20.00
—Black label, colorband and logo at left					
❏ LRP-3105 [M]	London By Night	1958	7.50	15.00	30.00
—Green label					
❏ LRP-3119 [M]	Swing Me an Old Song	1959	7.50	15.00	30.00
—Green label					
❏ LRP-3130 [M]	Your Number Please	1959	7.50	15.00	30.00
—Green label					
❏ LRP-3130 [M]	Your Number Please	1960	5.00	10.00	20.00
—Black label, colorband and logo at left					
❏ LRP-3152 [M]	Julie…At Home	1960	7.50	15.00	30.00
❏ LRP-3164 [M]	Around Midnight	1960	7.50	15.00	30.00
❏ LRP-3171 [M]	Send for Me	1961	7.50	15.00	30.00
❏ LRP-3192 [M]	Whatever Julie Wants	1961	7.50	15.00	30.00
❏ LRP-3203 [M]	Sophisticated Lady	1962	6.25	12.50	25.00
❏ LRP-3231 [M]	Love Letters	1962	6.25	12.50	25.00
❏ LRP-3249 [M]	Love on the Rocks	1963	6.25	12.50	25.00
❏ LRP-3278 [M]	Latin in a Satin Mood	1963	6.25	12.50	25.00
❏ LRP-3291 [M]	Julie's Golden Hits	1963	6.25	12.50	25.00
—Black cover					
❏ LRP-3291 [M]	Julie's Golden Hits	1963	6.25	12.50	25.00
—White cover					
❏ LRP-3300 [M]	The End of the World	1963	6.25	12.50	25.00
❏ LRP-3324 [M]	The Wonderful World of Julie London	1963	6.25	12.50	25.00
❏ LRP-3342 [M]	Julie London	1964	6.25	12.50	25.00
❏ LRP-3375 [M]	Julie London In Person at the Americana	1964	6.25	12.50	25.00
❏ LRP-3392 [M]	Our Fair Lady	1965	6.25	12.50	25.00
❏ LRP-3416 [M]	Feeling Good	1965	6.25	12.50	25.00
❏ LRP-3434 [M]	All Through the Night	1965	6.25	12.50	25.00
❏ LRP-3478 [M]	For the Night People	1966	6.25	12.50	25.00
❏ LRP-3493 [M]	Nice Girls Don't Stay for Breakfast	1967	6.25	12.50	25.00
❏ LRP-3514 [M]	With Body and Soul	1967	7.50	15.00	30.00
❏ L-5501 [M]	The Best of Julie London	1962	7.50	15.00	30.00

Number	Title (A Side/B Side)	Yr	VG	VG+	NM
❏ S-6601 [S]	The Best of Julie London	1962	10.00	20.00	40.00
❏ LST-7004 [S]	Julie	1958	17.50	35.00	70.00
—Black label, silver print					
❏ LST-7012 [S]	About the Blues	1958	17.50	35.00	70.00
—Black label, silver print					
❏ LST-7012 [S]	About the Blues	1960	6.25	12.50	25.00
—Black label, colorband and logo at left					
❏ LST-7027 [S]	Julie Is Her Name	1958	10.00	20.00	40.00
—Black label, silver print					
❏ LST-7027 [S]	Julie Is Her Name	1958	25.00	50.00	100.00
—Blue vinyl					
❏ LST-7027 [S]	Julie Is Her Name	1958	25.00	50.00	100.00
—Red vinyl					
❏ LST-7027 [S]	Julie Is Her Name	1960	6.25	12.50	25.00
—Black label, colorband and logo at left					
❏ LST-7029 [S]	Lonely Girl	1958	10.00	20.00	40.00
—Black label, silver print					
❏ LST-7029 [S]	Lonely Girl	1960	6.25	12.50	25.00
—Black label, colorband and logo at left					
❏ LST-7060 [S]	Make Love to Me	1958	10.00	20.00	40.00
—Black label, silver print					
❏ LST-7060 [S]	Make Love to Me	1960	6.25	12.50	25.00
—Black label, colorband and logo at left					
❏ LST-7100 [S]	Julie Is Her Name, Volume 2	1958	10.00	20.00	40.00
—Black label, silver print					
❏ LST-7100 [S]	Julie Is Her Name, Volume 2	1960	6.25	12.50	25.00
—Black label, colorband and logo at left					
❏ LST-7105 [S]	London By Night	1958	10.00	20.00	40.00
—Black label, silver print					
❏ LST-7119 [S]	Swing Me an Old Song	1959	10.00	20.00	40.00
—Black label, silver print					
❏ LST-7130 [S]	Your Number Please	1959	10.00	20.00	40.00
—Black label, silver print					
❏ LST-7130 [S]	Your Number Please	1960	6.25	12.50	25.00
—Black label, colorband and logo at left					
❏ LST-7152 [S]	Julie…At Home	1960	10.00	20.00	40.00
—Black vinyl					
❏ LST-7152 [S]	Julie…At Home	1960	25.00	50.00	100.00
—Blue vinyl					
❏ LST-7164 [S]	Around Midnight	1960	10.00	20.00	40.00
❏ LST-7171 [S]	Send for Me	1961	10.00	20.00	40.00
❏ LST-7192 [S]	Whatever Julie Wants	1961	10.00	20.00	40.00
❏ LST-7203 [S]	Sophisticated Lady	1962	7.50	15.00	30.00
❏ LST-7231 [S]	Love Letters	1962	7.50	15.00	30.00
❏ LST-7249 [S]	Love on the Rocks	1963	7.50	15.00	30.00
❏ LST-7278 [S]	Latin in a Satin Mood	1963	7.50	15.00	30.00
❏ LST-7291 [S]	Julie's Golden Hits	1963	7.50	15.00	30.00
—Black cover					
❏ LST-7291 [S]	Julie's Golden Hits	1963	7.50	15.00	30.00
—White cover					
❏ LST-7300 [S]	The End of the World	1963	7.50	15.00	30.00
❏ LST-7324 [S]	The Wonderful World of Julie London	1963	7.50	15.00	30.00
❏ LST-7342 [S]	Julie London	1964	7.50	15.00	30.00
❏ LST-7375 [S]	Julie London In Person at the Americana	1964	7.50	15.00	30.00
❏ LST-7392 [S]	Our Fair Lady	1965	7.50	15.00	30.00
❏ LST-7416 [S]	Feeling Good	1965	7.50	15.00	30.00
❏ LST-7434 [S]	All Through the Night	1965	7.50	15.00	30.00
❏ LST-7478 [S]	For the Night People	1966	7.50	15.00	30.00
❏ LST-7493 [S]	Nice Girls Don't Stay for Breakfast	1967	6.25	12.50	25.00
❏ LST-7514 [S]	With Body and Soul	1967	6.25	12.50	25.00
❏ LST-7546	Easy Does It	1968	5.00	10.00	20.00
❏ LST-7609	Yummy, Yummy, Yummy	1969	5.00	10.00	20.00
❏ SL-9002 [M]	Calendar Girl	1956	25.00	50.00	100.00

SUNSET

Number	Title (A Side/B Side)	Yr	VG	VG+	NM
❏ SUM-1104 [M]	Julie London	196?	3.00	6.00	12.00
❏ SUM-1161 [M]	Soft and Sweet	196?	3.00	6.00	12.00
❏ SUS-5104 [S]	Julie London	196?	3.75	7.50	15.00
❏ SUS-5161 [S]	Soft and Sweet	196?	3.75	7.50	15.00
❏ SUS-5207	Gone with the Wind	196?	3.00	6.00	12.00

UNITED ARTISTS

Number	Title (A Side/B Side)	Yr	VG	VG+	NM
❏ UA-LA437-E	The Very Best of Julie London	1975	3.00	6.00	12.00

LONDON, LAURIE
45s
CAPITOL

Number	Title (A Side/B Side)	Yr	VG	VG+	NM
❏ F3891	He's Got the Whole World (In His Hands)/ Handed Down	1958	3.75	7.50	15.00
❏ F3973	Joshua/I Gotta Robe	1958	3.00	6.00	12.00
❏ F4133	My Mother/Three O'Clock	1959	3.00	6.00	12.00

ROULETTE

Number	Title (A Side/B Side)	Yr	VG	VG+	NM
❏ 4176	Pretty Eyed Baby/Boom Ladda Boom Boom	1959	2.50	5.00	10.00

7-Inch Extended Plays
CAPITOL

Number	Title (A Side/B Side)	Yr	VG	VG+	NM
❏ EAP 1-10182	He's Got the Whole World in His Hands/Handed Down//The Gospel Train/Boomerang	1958	5.00	10.00	20.00
❏ EAP 1-10182 [PS]	Laurie London!	1958	5.00	10.00	20.00

Albums
CAPITOL

Number	Title (A Side/B Side)	Yr	VG	VG+	NM
❏ T 10169 [M]	England's 14 Year Old Singing Sensation — Laurie London	1958	12.50	25.00	50.00

LONDON SOUND 70 ORCHESTRA AND CHORUS
Albums
DECCA

Number	Title (A Side/B Side)	Yr	VG	VG+	NM
❏ DEB 7-7 [(3)]	The Sounds of Christmas	1970	6.25	12.50	25.00

LONE TWISTER, THE
45s
ATLANTIC

Number	Title (A Side/B Side)	Yr	VG	VG+	NM
❏ 2130	The Lone Twister/Twistin' Up a Storm	1961	3.75	7.50	15.00

Number	Title (A Side/B Side)	Yr	VG	VG+	NM
LONELY HEARTS CLUB BAND See BEE GEES.					
LONESOME BLUES SINGER, THE See LEADBELLY.					
LONESOME DRIFTER, THE					
45s					
K					
❏ 5812	Eager Boy/Teardrop Valley	1958	500.00	1000.	2000.
LONESOME RHODES					
45s					
RCA VICTOR					
❏ 47-9305	The Delight of My Day//(B-side unknown)	1967	5.00	10.00	20.00
Albums					
RCA VICTOR					
❏ LPM-3759 [M]	Lonesome Rhodes	1967	7.50	15.00	30.00
❏ LSP-3759 [S]	Lonesome Rhodes	1967	5.00	10.00	20.00
LONG, HUEY					
45s					
FIDELITY					
❏ 4054	How to Tell My Heart/Waiting for a Letter	1962	5.00	10.00	20.00
❏ 4055	Elvis Stole My Gal/Ballad of John Glenn	1962	12.50	25.00	50.00
LONG, SHORTY (1) R&B singer.					
45s					
SOUL					
❏ 35001	Devil with the Blue Dress/Wind It Up	1964	6.25	12.50	25.00
❏ 35005	It's a Crying Shame/Out to Get You	1964	6.25	12.50	25.00
❏ 35021	Function at the Junction/Call On Me	1966	3.75	7.50	15.00
❏ 35031	Chantilly Lace/Your Love Is Amazing	1966	3.75	7.50	15.00
❏ 35040	Night Fo' Last/(Instrumental)	1968	2.50	5.00	10.00
❏ 35044	Here Comes the Judge/Sing What You Wanna	1968	2.50	5.00	10.00
❏ 35054	I Had a Dream/Ain't No Justice	1969	2.50	5.00	10.00
❏ 35064	A Whiter Shade of Pale/When You Are Available	1969	2.50	5.00	10.00
TRI-PHI					
❏ 1006	I'll Be There/Bad Willie	1962	12.50	25.00	50.00
❏ 1015	Too Smart/I'll Be There	1962	17.50	35.00	70.00
❏ 1021	What's the Matter/Going Away	1963	15.00	30.00	60.00
Albums					
SOUL					
❏ SM-709 [M]	Here Comes the Judge	1968	12.50	25.00	50.00
—Mono is white label promo only; mono sticker on stereo cover					
❏ SS-709 [S]	Here Comes the Judge	1968	5.00	10.00	20.00
❏ SS-719	The Prime of Shorty Long	1969	3.75	7.50	15.00
LONG, SHORTY (2) C&W singer.					
45s					
DOT					
❏ 1154	Pretend/Crying Street Guitar Waltz	1953	6.25	12.50	25.00
KING					
❏ 5605	Take Me to the Happy Land/Mary, Oh Mary	1962	6.25	12.50	25.00
RCA VICTOR					
❏ 47-6472	Hey, Doll Baby/Luscious	1956	25.00	50.00	100.00
❏ 47-6572	Vacation Rock/Burnt Toast and Black Coffee	1956	25.00	50.00	100.00
❏ 47-6804	Another Love Has Ended/Little White Horse	1957	25.00	50.00	100.00
❏ 47-6873	You Don't Have to Be a Baby to Cry/I'd Crawl Back	1957	25.00	50.00	100.00
❏ 48-0057	The Morning After/Please Daddy Forgive	1949	10.00	20.00	40.00
—Originals on green vinyl; second pressing on black vinyl is unconfirmed					
❏ 48-0098	The Warm Red Wine/I Got Mine	1949	10.00	20.00	40.00
—Originals on green vinyl; second pressing on black vinyl is unconfirmed					
❏ 48-0347	A Bottle and a Blonde/Waltz of Colorado	1950	10.00	20.00	40.00
—Originals on green vinyl; second pressing on black vinyl is unconfirmed					
"X"					
❏ 0024	Standing in the Station/Make with Me De Love	1954	5.00	10.00	20.00
Albums					
FORD					
❏ FXM-712 [M]	Country Jamboree	1963	5.00	10.00	20.00
LONGBRANCH PENNYWHISTLE GLENN FREY, J.D. SOUTHER and RY COODER all were members of this group.					
45s					
AMOS					
❏ 121	Don't Talk Now/Jubilee Anne	1969	3.75	7.50	15.00
❏ 129	Lucky Love/Rebecca	1969	3.75	7.50	15.00
❏ 148	Star Spangled Bus/Bring Back Founky Women	1970	3.75	7.50	15.00
Albums					
AMOS					
❏ AAS-7007	Longbranch Pennywhistle	1969	12.50	25.00	50.00
LONGET, CLAUDINE					
45s					
A&M					
❏ 817	Meditation (Meditacao)/Sunrise, Sunset	1966	—	3.00	6.00
❏ 832	A Man and a Woman/Here, There and Everywhere	1967	—	3.00	6.00
❏ 846	Hello, Hello/Wonderlove	1967	—	3.00	6.00
❏ 864	Good Day Sunshine/The Look of Love	1967	—	3.00	6.00
❏ 877	Small Talk/A Man in a Raincoat	1967	—	3.00	6.00
❏ 895	Snow/I Don't Intend to Spend My Christmas Without You	1967	2.00	4.00	8.00
❏ 897	When I'm Sixty-Four/I Love How You Love Me	1968	—	2.50	5.00
❏ 909	Love Is Blue (L'amour Est Bleu)/Think of Rain	1968	—	2.50	5.00
❏ 936	Nothing to Lose/White Horses	1968	—	2.50	5.00
❏ 954	Lullaby from "Rosemary's Baby" (Sleep Safe and Warm)/It's Hard to Say Goodbye	1968	—	2.50	5.00
❏ 967	A Walk in the Park/Who Needs You	1968	—	2.50	5.00
❏ 1002	Am I Blue/Flea in Her Ear	1968	—	2.50	5.00
❏ 1024	I Think It's Gonna Rain Today/Hurry On Down	1969	—	2.50	5.00
❏ 1059	Colours/Love Can Never Die	1969	—	2.50	5.00
❏ 1098	Quentin's Theme/Lazy Summer Night	1969	—	2.50	5.00
❏ 1181	A Bushel and a Peck/Run Wild, Run Free	1970	—	2.50	5.00
BARNABY					
❏ 603	Goodbye Jimmy Goodbye//(B-side unknown)	1974	—	2.00	4.00
❏ 2022	Broomstick Cowboy/Long Long Time	1970	—	2.00	4.00
❏ 2028	Ain't No Mountain High Enough/Electric Moon	1971	—	2.00	4.00
❏ 2033	Anytime of the Year/Guess Who I Saw in Paris	1971	—	2.00	4.00
❏ 2060	Let's Spend the Night Together/Wake Up to Me Gentle	1972	—	2.00	4.00
❏ 5001	Remember the Good/While You're Sleeping	1972	—	2.00	4.00
❏ 5021	Every Beat of My Heart/Sugar Me	1973	—	2.00	4.00
Albums					
A&M					
❏ LP-121 [M]	Claudine	1967	3.75	7.50	15.00
❏ LP-128 [M]	The Look of Love	1967	3.75	7.50	15.00
❏ SP-4121 [S]	Claudine	1967	3.00	6.00	12.00
❏ SP-4128 [S]	The Look of Love	1967	3.00	6.00	12.00
❏ SP-4142	Love Is Blue	1968	3.00	6.00	12.00
❏ SP-4163	Colours	1969	3.00	6.00	12.00
❏ SP-4232	Run Wild, Run Free	1970	3.00	6.00	12.00
BARNABY					
❏ Z 30377	We've Only Just Begun	1971	3.00	6.00	12.00
❏ KZ 31383	Let's Spend the Night Together	1972	3.00	6.00	12.00
LONNIE AND THE CAROLLONS					
45s					
MOHAWK					
❏ 108	Chapel of Tears/My Heart	1958	37.50	75.00	150.00
—Green label					
❏ 108	Chapel of Tears/My Heart	1961	7.50	15.00	30.00
—Red label					
❏ 108	Chapel of Tears/My Heart	1965	5.00	10.00	20.00
—White label					
❏ 111	Hold Me Close/Trudy	1958	12.50	25.00	50.00
❏ 112	Back Yard Rock/You Say	1958	12.50	25.00	50.00
❏ 113	The Gang All Knows/Ike Hammer	1959	15.00	30.00	60.00
❏ 122	Need Your Lovin'/Beeline	1960	6.25	12.50	25.00
—As "Lonnie"					
LONNIE AND THE CRISIS					
45s					
RELIC					
❏ 532	Bells in the Chapel/Santa Town USA	196?	—	3.00	6.00
—Reissue of Universal 103					
TIMES SQUARE					
❏ 25	Bells in the Chapel/Santa Town USA	196?	2.00	4.00	8.00
—Reissue of Universal 103					
UNIVERSAL					
❏ 103	Bells in the Chapel/Santa Town USA	1961	50.00	100.00	200.00
LOOKING GLASS Also see ELLIOTT LURIE.					
45s					
EPIC					
❏ 10834	Don't It Make You Feel Good/Catherine Street	1972	—	2.50	5.00
❏ 10874	Brandy (You're a Fine Girl)/One by One	1972	—	3.00	6.00
❏ 10900	Jenn-Lyne/Golden Rainbow	1972	—	2.50	5.00
❏ 10953	Sweet Somethin'/Rainbow Man	1973	—	2.50	5.00
❏ 11001	Jimmy Loves Mary-Anne/Wooly Eyes	1973	—	2.50	5.00
❏ 11061	City Lady/Who's Gonna Sing My Rock 'N' Roll Song	1973	—	2.50	5.00
❏ 11085	Sweet Somethin'/Who's Gonna Sing My Rock 'N' Roll Song	1974	—	2.50	5.00
❏ 20001	Rock This Town/Highway to Hollywood	1974	—	2.50	5.00
Albums					
EPIC					
❏ KE 31320	Looking Glass	1972	3.75	7.50	15.00
❏ KE 32167	Subway Serenade	1973	3.75	7.50	15.00
LOOKING GLASS, THE This group pre-dates the one on Epic, which did not use the word "The" in its name.					
45s					
UNI					
❏ 55034	Virginia Day's Ragtime/Cry//Memories/What Am I Doin'	1967	2.50	5.00	10.00
VALIANT					
❏ 750	Silver and Sunshine (How Wonderful My Love)/If I Never Love Again	1966	2.50	5.00	10.00
WARNER BROS.					
❏ 7050	Lonely Stranger/Love Is Not Everything	1967	2.50	5.00	10.00
LOOKINLAND, MIKE "Bobby Brady" of THE BRADY BUNCH.					
45s					
CAPITOL					
❏ 3914	Gum Drop/Love Doesn't Care Who's In It	1974	2.50	5.00	10.00
❏ 3914 [PS]	Gum Drop/Love Doesn't Care Who's In It	1974	3.75	7.50	15.00
LOOSE					
45s					
NOCTURNE					
❏ 1909	Freaky Billy the Wheelie King/It's Happenin'	1969	2.50	5.00	10.00
Albums					
NOCTURNE					
❏ 906	Freaky Billie, The Wheelie King	1970	7.50	15.00	30.00
LOPEZ, TRINI					
45s					
CAPITOL					
❏ 3195	Some Kind of a Summer/Poor Old Billy	1971	—	2.50	5.00
❏ 3312	Ruby Mountain/Y Voluere	1972	—	2.50	5.00
❏ 3402	Mammy Blue/Viva	1972	—	2.50	5.00
D.R.A.					
❏ 7008	Rosita/Only in My Dreams	1962	3.75	7.50	15.00
GRIFFIN					
❏ 504	Butterfly/Don't Burn Your Bridges Behind You	1973	—	2.50	5.00
❏ 508	Bring Back the Sunshine/We Gotta Make It Together	1974	—	2.50	5.00
KING					
❏ 5173	Rosalia/Nola	1959	5.00	10.00	20.00
❏ 5187	Since I Don't Have You/Rock On	1959	6.25	12.50	25.00
❏ 5198	Love Me Tonight/Here Comes Sally	1959	5.00	10.00	20.00
❏ 5234	Don't Let Your Sweet Love Die/I'm Grateful	1959	5.00	10.00	20.00
❏ 5284	Nobody Loves Me/Nobody Listens to Our Teenage Problems	1959	5.00	10.00	20.00

L

Number	Title (A Side/B Side)	Yr	VG	VG+	NM
❏ 5304	Chain of Love/Sweet Thing	1960	5.00	10.00	20.00
❏ 5324	Schemes/Jeannie Marie	1960	5.00	10.00	20.00
❏ 5344	It Hurts to Be in Love/The Search Goes On	1960	5.00	10.00	20.00
❏ 5418	Don't Treat Me That Way/Then You Know	1960	5.00	10.00	20.00
❏ 5487	One Heart, One Life, One Love/				
	You Broke the Only Heart	1961	5.00	10.00	20.00
❏ 5801	Jeannie Marie/Love Me Tonight	1963	3.00	6.00	12.00
❏ 5820	Don't Go/It Seems	1963	3.00	6.00	12.00
❏ 5824	Nobody Loves Me/The Club for Broken Hearts	1963	3.00	6.00	12.00
❏ 5849	Yes You Do/Won't You Be	1963	3.00	6.00	12.00
❏ 6000	Jeannie Marie/Nobody Listens, Nobody Cares	1965	2.00	4.00	8.00
❏ 6021	The Search Goes On/Chain of Love	1966	2.00	4.00	8.00
PRIVATE STOCK					
❏ 45,024	Somethin' 'Bout You Baby I Like/Sweet Life	1975	—	2.50	5.00
❏ 45,035	Seco Sulto Y Tonton	1975	—	2.50	5.00
❏ 45,044	Heavy Makes You Happy (Sha-La-Boom-				
	Boom-Yeah)/Satisfaction	1975	—	2.50	5.00
REPRISE					
❏ S 195 [S]	Bye Bye Blackbird/A-Mer-I-Ca	196?	3.75	7.50	15.00
❏ S 196 [S]	If I Had a Hammer/Unchain My Heart	196?	3.75	7.50	15.00
❏ S 197 [S]	This Land Is Your Land/Granada	196?	3.75	7.50	15.00
❏ S 198 [S]	Cielito Lindo/La Bamba	196?	3.75	7.50	15.00
❏ S 199 [S]	What'd I Say/Medley	196?	3.75	7.50	15.00
—The above five are small hole, 33 1/3 rpm jukebox singles					
❏ 0260	Jailer, Bring Me Water/You Can't Say Goodbye	1964	2.00	4.00	8.00
❏ 0276	Ya Ya/What Have I Got of My Own	1964	2.00	4.00	8.00
❏ 0300	Michael/San Fransico De Assisi	1964	2.00	4.00	8.00
❏ 0328	Sad Tomorrows/I've Lost My Love for You	1964	2.00	4.00	8.00
❏ 0328 [PS]	Sad Tomorrows/I've Lost My Love for You	1964	3.75	7.50	15.00
❏ 0336	Lemon Tree/Pretty Eyes	1965	2.50	5.00	10.00
❏ 0336 [PS]	Lemon Tree/Pretty Eyes	1965	3.75	7.50	15.00
❏ 0376	Are You Sincere/You'll Be Sorry	1965	2.00	4.00	8.00
❏ 0405	Sinner Man/Double Trouble	1965	2.00	4.00	8.00
❏ 0405 [PS]	Sinner Man/Double Trouble	1965	3.75	7.50	15.00
❏ 0421	Regressa A Mi/Mi Felicidad	1965	2.00	4.00	8.00
❏ 0435	Made in Paris/Pretty Little Girl	1965	2.00	4.00	8.00
❏ 0435 [PS]	Made in Paris/Pretty Little Girl	1965	3.75	7.50	15.00
❏ 0455	The 32nd of May/I'm Coming Home, Cindy	1966	2.00	4.00	8.00
❏ 0480	La Bamba — Part 1/Trini's Tune	1966	2.00	4.00	8.00
❏ 0508	Hall of Fame/Pancho Lopez	1966	2.00	4.00	8.00
❏ 0536	Your Ever Changin' Mind/Takin' the Back Roads	1966	2.00	4.00	8.00
❏ 0547	Gonna Get Along Without Ya' Now/Love Letters	1967	—	3.00	6.00
❏ 0574	In the Land of Plenty/Up To Now	1967	—	3.00	6.00
❏ 0596	Ballad of the Dirty Dozen/The Bramble Bush	1967	—	3.00	6.00
❏ 0618	I Wanna Be Free/Together	1967	—	3.00	6.00
❏ 0648	It's a Great Life/Let's Take a Walk	1967	—	3.00	6.00
❏ 0659	Sally Was a Good Old Girl/It's a Great Life	1968	—	3.00	6.00
❏ 0687	Good Old Mountain Dew/Mental Journey	1968	—	3.00	6.00
❏ 0700	If I Had a Hammer/Lemon Tree	1968	—	2.50	5.00
—"Back to Back Hits" series					
❏ 0725	La Bamba/Kansas City	1968		2.50	5.00
—"Back to Back Hits" series					
❏ 0770	Something Tells Me/Malaguena Salerosa	1968	—	3.00	6.00
❏ 0801 [DJ]	El Nino Del Tambor/Nocho De Paz				
	(Let There Be Peace)	1968	2.00	4.00	8.00
—Stock copy may not exist					
❏ 0814	Come a Little Bit Closer/				
	My Baby Loves Sad Songs	1969	—	3.00	6.00
❏ 0825	Don't Let the Sun Catch You Cryyin'/				
	My Baby Loves Sad Songs	1969	—	3.00	6.00
❏ 0879	Games People Play/Love Story	1969	—	3.00	6.00
❏ 0912	5 O'Clock World/You Make My Day	1970	—	2.50	5.00
❏ 0933	Mexican Medicine Man/Time to Get It Together	1970	—	2.50	5.00
❏ 0947	Su-Kal-De-Don/Mexican Medicine Man	1970	—	2.50	5.00
❏ 0975	Let's Think About Living/				
	There Was a Crooked Man	1970	—	2.50	5.00
❏ 20168	A-M-E-R-I-C-A/Let It Be Known	1963	2.50	5.00	10.00
❏ 20190	La Bamba (Part 1)/La Bamba (Part 2)	1963	2.50	5.00	10.00
❏ 20198	If I Had a Hammer/Unchain My Heart	1963	3.00	6.00	12.00
❏ 20236	Kansas City/Lonesome Traveler	1963	2.00	4.00	8.00
ROULETTE					
❏ 7214	Beautiful People/Helplessly	1977	—	2.50	5.00
VOLK					
❏ 101	The Right to Rock/Just Once More	1958	7.50	15.00	30.00
7-Inch Extended Plays					
FRESCA					
❏ ZTEP-124178	A-Mer-I-Ca/Kansas City//If I Had a Hammer/The				
	Blizzard Song	1967	2.50	5.00	10.00
❏ ZTEP-124178 [PS]	Trini Lopez Sings His Greatest Hits	1967	3.75	7.50	15.00
—Available on specially marked packages of Fresca soda					
KING					
❏ EP-483	Jeanie Marie/It Seems//Don't Go/Love Me				
	Tonight	1963	10.00	20.00	40.00
—Possibly promo only; not known if issued with sleeve					
Albums					
CAPITOL					
❏ SK 11009	Viva	1972	2.50	5.00	10.00
GUEST STAR					
❏ GS-1499 [M]	Trini Lopez and Scott Gregory	1964	12.50	25.00	50.00
—"Scott Gregory" is said to be a pseudonym for BILL HALEY.					
HARMONY					
❏ H 30012	Bye Bye Love	1970	2.50	5.00	10.00
KING					
❏ 863 [M]	Teenage Love Songs	1963	15.00	30.00	60.00
❏ 877 [M]	More of Trini Lopez	1964	15.00	30.00	60.00
❏ 962 [M]	24 Songs by the Great Trini Lopez	1966	7.50	15.00	30.00
REPRISE					
❏ R-6093 [M]	Trini Lopez at PJ's	1963	3.00	6.00	12.00
❏ R9-6093 [S]	Trini Lopez at PJ's	1963	3.75	7.50	15.00
❏ R-6103 [M]	More Trini Lopez at PJ's	1963	3.00	6.00	12.00
❏ RS-6103 [S]	More Trini Lopez at PJ's	1963	3.75	7.50	15.00
❏ R-6112 [M]	On the Move	1964	3.00	6.00	12.00
❏ RS-6112 [S]	On the Move	1964	3.75	7.50	15.00
❏ R-6125 [M]	The Latin Album	1964	3.00	6.00	12.00
❏ RS-6125 [S]	The Latin Album	1964	3.75	7.50	15.00
❏ R-6134 [M]	Live at Basin St. East	1964	3.00	6.00	12.00
❏ RS-6134 [S]	Live at Basin St. East	1964	3.75	7.50	15.00
❏ R-6147 [M]	The Folk Album	1965	3.00	6.00	12.00
❏ RS-6147 [S]	The Folk Album	1965	3.75	7.50	15.00
❏ R-6165 [M]	The Love Album	1965	3.00	6.00	12.00
❏ RS-6165 [S]	The Love Album	1965	3.75	7.50	15.00
❏ R-6171 [M]	The Rhythm & Blues Album	1965	3.00	6.00	12.00
❏ RS-6171 [S]	The Rhythm & Blues Album	1965	3.75	7.50	15.00
❏ R-6183 [M]	The Sing-Along World of Trini Lopez	1965	3.00	6.00	12.00
❏ RS-6183 [S]	The Sing-Along World of Trini Lopez	1965	3.75	7.50	15.00
❏ R-6196 [M]	Trini	1966	3.00	6.00	12.00
❏ RS-6196 [S]	Trini	1966	3.75	7.50	15.00
❏ R-6215 [M]	The Second Latin Album	1966	3.00	6.00	12.00
❏ RS-6215 [S]	The Second Latin Album	1966	3.75	7.50	15.00
❏ R-6226 [M]	Greatest Hits!	1966	3.00	6.00	12.00
❏ RS-6226 [S]	Greatest Hits!	1966	3.75	7.50	15.00
❏ R-6238 [M]	Trini Lopez in London	1967	3.75	7.50	15.00
❏ RS-6238 [S]	Trini Lopez in London	1967	3.00	6.00	12.00
❏ R-6255 [M]	Trini Lopez — Now!	1967	3.75	7.50	15.00
❏ RS-6255 [S]	Trini Lopez — Now!	1967	3.00	6.00	12.00
❏ RS-6285	It's a Great Life	1968	3.00	6.00	12.00
❏ RS-6300	Welcome to Trini Country	1968	3.00	6.00	12.00
❏ RS-6337	The Whole Enchilada	1969	3.00	6.00	12.00
❏ RS-6361	The Trini Lopez Show	1970	3.75	7.50	15.00
ROULETTE					
❏ 3020	Transformed by Time	1978	2.50	5.00	10.00

LORD, BOBBY

45s

COLUMBIA

Number	Title (A Side/B Side)	Yr	VG	VG+	NM
❏ 21339	No More/Why Were You Only Fooling Me	1955	6.25	12.50	25.00
❏ 21339	No More No More/				
	Why Were You Only Fooling Me	1955	12.50	25.00	50.00
—With longer A-side title					
❏ 21367	I'm the Devil Who Made Her That Way/				
	Ain'tcha Ever Gonna	1955	6.25	12.50	25.00
❏ 21397	Something's Missing/				
	Sittin' Home Prayin' for Rain	1955	5.00	10.00	20.00
❏ 21437	Hawk-Eye/I Can't Make My Dreams Understand	1955	7.50	15.00	30.00
❏ 21459	I Can't Do Without You Anymore/				
	Don't Make Me Laugh	1955	5.00	10.00	20.00
❏ 21498	So Doggone Lonesome/Pie Peachie Pie Pie	1956	5.00	10.00	20.00
❏ 21539	Everybody's Rockin' But Me/Without Your Love	1956	20.00	40.00	80.00
—"Without Your Love" was the hit, but "Everybody's Rockin' But Me" is the collectible side					
❏ 40666	Fire of Love/Beautiful Baby	1956	7.50	15.00	30.00
❏ 40819	Your Sweet Love/				
	My Baby's Not My Baby Anymore	1957	5.00	10.00	20.00
❏ 40927	High Voltage/Just Wonderful	1957	10.00	20.00	40.00
❏ 41030	Am I a Fool/I Know It Was You	1957	5.00	10.00	20.00
❏ 41155	Sack/Fire of Love	1958	6.25	12.50	25.00
❏ 41288	When I've Learned/Walking Alone	1958	5.00	10.00	20.00
❏ 41352	Party Pooper/What a Thrill	1959	6.25	12.50	25.00
❏ 41505	Too Many Miles/Swamp Fox	1959	6.25	12.50	25.00
❏ 41596	Give Me a Woman/Where Did My Woman Go	1960	5.00	10.00	20.00
❏ 41824	Before I Lose My Mind/When the Snow Falls	1960	5.00	10.00	20.00
❏ 42012	A Rose and a Thorn/Fascination	1961	5.00	10.00	20.00
DECCA					
❏ 32115	Look What You're Doing/				
	On and On Goes the Hurt	1967	2.00	4.00	8.00
❏ 32174	Shadows on the Wall/One Day Down	1967	2.00	4.00	8.00
❏ 32277	Live Your Life Out Loud/				
	Charlotte, North Carolina	1968	—	3.00	6.00
❏ 32373	The True and Lasting Kind/It's My Life	1968	—	3.00	6.00
❏ 32431	Yesterday's Letters/Don't Forget to Smell the				
	Flowers (Along the Way)	1969	—	3.00	6.00
❏ 32578	Rainbow Girl/Do You Ever Think of Me	1969	—	3.00	6.00
❏ 32657	You and Me Against the World/Something Real	1970	—	3.00	6.00
❏ 32718	Wake Me Up Early in the Morning/				
	Violets Are Red	1970	—	3.00	6.00
❏ 32797	Do It to Someone You Love/So in Love with You	1970	2.00	4.00	8.00
❏ 32797	Goodbye Jukebox/Do It to Someone You Love	1971	—	3.00	6.00
❏ 32841	They've Got Something in the Country/				
	Peace of Mind	1971	—	3.00	6.00
❏ 32932	Everybody's Here/Sweet Inspiration	1972	—	3.00	6.00
HICKORY					
❏ 1158	I'll Go On Alone/My Heart Tells Me So	1961	3.00	6.00	12.00
❏ 1169	Precious Jewel/Trail of Tears	1962	3.00	6.00	12.00
❏ 1190	Don't Shed Any Tears for Me/Out Behind the				
	Barn	1962	3.00	6.00	12.00
❏ 1210	Cry, Cry Darling/Shopping Center	1963	2.50	5.00	10.00
❏ 1232	Life Can Have Meaning/Pickin' White Gold	1963	2.50	5.00	10.00
❏ 1259	A Man Needs a Woman/Take a Bucket to the				
	Wall	1964	2.50	5.00	10.00
❏ 1310	I'm Going Home Next Summer/That Room in the				
	Corner of the House	1965	2.50	5.00	10.00
❏ 1361	Cash on the Barrelhead/That's Love	1965	2.50	5.00	10.00
❏ 1389	It Only Hurts When I'm Laughing/Losers Like Me	1966	2.00	4.00	8.00
RICE					
❏ 5056	I've Had You/Got Yourself Something	1973	2.00	4.00	8.00
❏ 5062	Hello Wine/(B-side unknown)	1973	2.00	4.00	8.00
❏ 5063	Looking for a Cold, Lonely Winter/Hello Wine	1973	2.00	4.00	8.00
❏ 5068	The Look of Love/Your Song	1974	2.00	4.00	8.00
Albums					
DECCA					
❏ DL 75246	Bobby Lord	1970	3.00	6.00	12.00
HARMONY					
❏ HL 7322 [M]	Bobby Lord's Best	1964	6.25	12.50	25.00
HICKORY					
❏ LP-126 [M]	The Bobby Lord Show	1965	5.00	10.00	20.00

LORD, BRIAN, AND THE MIDNIGHTERS FRANK ZAPPA was a member of this group.

45s

CAPITOL

Number	Title (A Side/B Side)	Yr	VG	VG+	NM
❏ 4981	Big Surfer/Not Another One	1963	37.50	75.00	150.00
VIGAH					
❏ 001	Big Surfer/Not Another One	1963	75.00	150.00	300.00

Number	Title (A Side/B Side)	Yr	VG	VG+	NM
LORD ROCKINGHAM'S XI					
45s					
LONDON					
❏ 1810	Fried Onions/The Squelch	1958	3.00	6.00	12.00
❏ 1839	Hoots Mon/Blue Train	1958	3.00	6.00	12.00
LORD SITAR Sometimes rumored to be GEORGE HARRISON, but it's not.					
45s					
CAPITOL					
❏ 5972	Black Is Black/Have You Seen Your Mother, Baby, Standing in the Shadow	1967	5.00	10.00	20.00
Albums					
CAPITOL					
❏ ST 2916	Lord Sitar	1968	7.50	15.00	30.00
LORDAN, JERRY					
45s					
CAPITOL					
❏ 4389	Who Could Be Bluer/Do I Worry	1960	3.75	7.50	15.00
LORDS OF LONDON, THE					
45s					
DECCA					
❏ 32196	Time Waits for No One/Cornflakes and Ice Cream	1967	5.00	10.00	20.00
MGM					
❏ 13919	Candy Rainbow/Within Your Mind	1968	5.00	10.00	20.00
LORELEIS, THE					
45s					
BRUNSWICK					
❏ 55271	Strange Way/Why Do I Put Up with You	1964	2.00	4.00	8.00
LORRAINE AND THE SOCIALITES					
45s					
MERCURY					
❏ 72163	Any Old Way/The Conqueror	1963	3.00	6.00	12.00
LORY, DICK					
45s					
COLUMBIA					
❏ 41224	Wild Blooded Woman/No One But You Knows When	1958	12.50	25.00	50.00
❏ 41276	Crazy Little Daisy/Don't Be a Fool for Love	1958	10.00	20.00	40.00
DOT					
❏ 15496	Cool It Baby/Ball Room Baby	1956	15.00	30.00	60.00
LIBERTY					
❏ 55306	The Pain Is Here/You	1961	3.75	7.50	15.00
❏ 55319	Hello Walls/City of Love	1961	3.75	7.50	15.00
❏ 55529	I Got Over You/Welcome Home Again	1963	3.75	7.50	15.00
❏ 55600	Crazy Arms/There's Going to Be a Fight	1963	3.75	7.50	15.00
❏ 55707	I Will/I Catch Myself Crying	1964	3.00	6.00	12.00
LOS ADMIRADORES					
Albums					
COMMAND					
❏ 809 SD [S]	Bongos Bongos Bongos	1960	3.75	7.50	15.00
❏ 812 SD [S]	Bongos/Flutes/Guitars	1960	3.75	7.50	15.00
LOS BRAVOS Also see MIKE KENNEDY.					
45s					
PARROT					
❏ 3020	Bring a Little Lovin'/Make It Last	1968	3.00	6.00	12.00
❏ 3023	Dirty Street/Two People in Me	1968	2.50	5.00	10.00
PRESS					
❏ 60002	Black Is Black/I Want a Name	1966	3.75	7.50	15.00
❏ 60003	Going Nowhere/Brand New Baby	1966	2.50	5.00	10.00
❏ 60004	You'll Never Get the Chance Again/I'm All Ears	1967	2.50	5.00	10.00
Albums					
PARROT					
❏ PAS 71021	Bring a Little Lovin'	1968	20.00	40.00	80.00
—Among the other tracks, "Black Is Black" in in true stereo.					
PRESS					
❏ PR 73003 [M]	Black Is Black	1966	12.50	25.00	50.00
❏ PRS 83003 [R]	Black Is Black	1966	7.50	15.00	30.00
LOS INDIOS TABAJARAS					
45s					
RCA VICTOR					
❏ 47-8216	Maria Elena/Jungle Dream	1963	2.00	4.00	8.00
❏ 47-8313	Always in My Heart/Moonlight and Shadows	1964	—	3.00	6.00
❏ 47-8401	Marta/St. Louis Blues	1964	—	3.00	6.00
❏ 47-8510	Darktown Strutters' Ball/The Third Man Theme	1965	—	3.00	6.00
❏ 47-9094	The Petite Waltz/Sentimental Journey	1967	—	2.50	5.00
❏ 47-9388	Rio Antigo/Os Quindins De Ya Ya	1967	—	2.50	5.00
Albums					
RCA CAMDEN					
❏ CXS-9031 [(2)] Los Indios Tabajaras		1973	3.75	7.50	15.00
RCA INTERNATIONAL					
❏ IL5-7367	Los Grandes Exitos	198?	3.00	6.00	12.00
RCA VICTOR					
❏ AFL1-0210	Favorite Movie Themes	1977	2.50	5.00	10.00
—Reissue with new prefix					
❏ APL1-0210	Favorite Movie Themes	1973	3.00	6.00	12.00
❏ FSP-296	Maria Elena	1971	3.00	6.00	12.00
❏ FSP-300	Siempre En Mi Corazon	1972	3.00	6.00	12.00
❏ FSP-310	Softly	1972	3.00	6.00	12.00
❏ AFL1-0668	Classical Guitars	1977	2.50	5.00	10.00
—Reissue with new prefix					
❏ CPL1-0668	Classical Guitars	1974	3.00	6.00	12.00
❏ AFL1-1033	Secret Love	1977	2.50	5.00	10.00
—Reissue with new prefix					
❏ APL1-1033	Secret Love	1975	3.00	6.00	12.00
❏ ANL1-1179	Maria Elena	1976	2.50	5.00	10.00
—Reissue					
❏ LPM-1788 [M]	Sweet and Savage	1958	10.00	20.00	40.00
❏ LSP-1788 [S]	Sweet and Savage	1958	12.50	25.00	50.00

Number	Title (A Side/B Side)	Yr	VG	VG+	NM
❏ APL1-2082	Mellow Nostalgia	1977	3.00	6.00	12.00
❏ ANL1-2321	In a Sentimental Mood	1977	2.50	5.00	10.00
❏ AFL1-2526	Masterpieces	1978	3.00	6.00	12.00
❏ LPM-2822 [M]	Maria Elena	1963	5.00	10.00	20.00
—Reissue of LPM-1788					
❏ LSP-2822 [S]	Maria Elena	1963	6.25	12.50	25.00
—Reissue of LSP-1788					
❏ AFL1-2912	Always in My Heart	1977	2.50	5.00	10.00
—Reissue with new prefix					
❏ LPM-2912 [M]	Always in My Heart	1964	3.75	7.50	15.00
❏ LSP-2912 [S]	Always in My Heart	1964	5.00	10.00	20.00
❏ LPM-2959 [M]	Twin Guitar Moods	1964	3.75	7.50	15.00
❏ LSP-2959 [S]	Twin Guitar Moods	1964	5.00	10.00	20.00
❏ AFL1-3241	Two Guitars	1979	2.50	5.00	10.00
❏ LPM-3413 [M]	Many-Splendored Guitars	1965	3.75	7.50	15.00
❏ LSP-3413 [S]	Many-Splendored Guitars	1965	5.00	10.00	20.00
❏ AFL1-3505	Casually Classical	1977	2.50	5.00	10.00
—Reissue with new prefix					
❏ LPM-3505 [M]	Casually Classical	1966	3.75	7.50	15.00
❏ LSP-3505 [S]	Casually Classical	1966	5.00	10.00	20.00
❏ AFL1-3535	Rainbows	1980	2.50	5.00	10.00
❏ LPM-3611 [M]	Twin Guitars — In a Mood for Lovers	1966	3.75	7.50	15.00
❏ LSP-3611 [S]	Twin Guitars — In a Mood for Lovers	1966	5.00	10.00	20.00
❏ LPM-3723 [M]	Their Very Special Touch	1967	3.75	7.50	15.00
❏ LSP-3723 [S]	Their Very Special Touch	1967	5.00	10.00	20.00
❏ LPM-3909 [M]	Fascinating Rhythms of Their Brazil	1968	5.00	10.00	20.00
❏ LSP-3909 [S]	Fascinating Rhythms of Their Brazil	1968	3.75	7.50	15.00
❏ AFL1-3990	Beautiful Sounds	1981	2.50	5.00	10.00
❏ AFL1-4007	The Best of Los Indios Tabajaras	1977	2.50	5.00	10.00
—Reissue with new prefix					
❏ LSP-4007	The Best of Los Indios Tabajaras	1968	3.75	7.50	15.00
❏ LSP-4013	In a Sentimental Mood	1968	3.75	7.50	15.00
❏ LSP-4129	Song of the Islands	1969	3.75	7.50	15.00
❏ AFL1-4273	Music for Romance	1982	2.50	5.00	10.00
❏ LSP-4365	Dreams of Love	1970	3.75	7.50	15.00
❏ LSP-4496	The Very Thought of You	1971	3.75	7.50	15.00
❏ LSP-4615	What the World Needs Now	1971	3.00	6.00	12.00
❏ AFL1-4649	Guitars on the Go	1983	2.50	5.00	10.00
LOS LOCOS DEL RITMO					
Albums					
DIMSA					
❏ 8178	Rock!	196?	25.00	50.00	100.00
LOS SEVEN DAYS					
Albums					
ECO					
❏ 314	Sha-La-La	196?	12.50	25.00	50.00
LOST, THE					
45s					
CAPITOL					
❏ 5519	Back Door Blues/Maybe More Than You Do	1965	3.75	7.50	15.00
❏ 5708	Mean Motorcycle/Violet Gown	1966	3.75	7.50	15.00
❏ 5725	No Reason Why/Violet Gown	1966	3.75	7.50	15.00
JANUS					
❏ 109	I Shall Be Released/Shame	1969	2.50	5.00	10.00
LOST & FOUND					
45s					
INTERNATIONAL ARTISTS					
❏ 120	Everybody's Here/ Forever Lasting Plastic Words	1968	6.25	12.50	25.00
❏ 125	When Will You Come Through/Professor Black	1968	6.25	12.50	25.00
Albums					
INTERNATIONAL ARTISTS					
❏ IA-3	Everybody's Here	1968	25.00	50.00	100.00
—Original pressing, no "Masterfonics" in dead wax					
❏ IA-3	Everybody's Here	1979	3.75	7.50	15.00
—Reissue with "Masterfonics" in trail-off wax					
LOST NATION, THE					
Albums					
RARE EARTH					
❏ RS-518	Paradise Lost	1970	5.00	10.00	20.00
LOTHAR AND THE HAND PEOPLE					
45s					
CAPITOL					
❏ 2008	Have Mercy (Mercy, Mercy, Mercy)/ Let the Boy Pretend	1967	2.50	5.00	10.00
❏ 2376	Machines/Milkweed Love	1969	2.00	4.00	8.00
❏ 2556	Midnight Ranger/Yes, I Love You	1969	2.00	4.00	8.00
❏ 5874	L-O-V-E/Rose Colored Glasses	1967	2.50	5.00	10.00
❏ 5945	Comic Strip/Every Single Word	1967	2.50	5.00	10.00
Albums					
CAPITOL					
❏ ST-247	Space Hymn	1969	10.00	20.00	40.00
❏ SM-2997	Presenting Lothar and the Hand People	1977	2.00	4.00	8.00
—Reissue with new prefix					
❏ ST 2997	Presenting Lothar and the Hand People	1968	10.00	20.00	40.00
LOU, HERB B., AND THE LEGAL EAGLES Break-in record with HERB ALPERT involvement.					
45s					
ARCH					
❏ 1607	The Trial/Kiss Me	1958	10.00	20.00	40.00
LOUDERMILK, JOHN D.					
45s					
COLONIAL					
❏ 430	Sittin' in the Balcony/A-Plus in Love	1957	7.50	15.00	30.00
—As "Johnny Dee"					
❏ 430 [PS]	Sittin' in the Balcony/A-Plus in Love	1957	100.00	200.00	400.00
—As "Johnny Dee"					
❏ 433	Teenage Queen/It's Gotta Be You	1957	7.50	15.00	30.00
—As "Johnny Dee"					

L

Number	Title (A Side/B Side)	Yr	VG	VG+	NM

COLUMBIA

Number	Title (A Side/B Side)	Yr	VG	VG+	NM
❏ 4-41165	Yearbook/Susie's House	1958	3.75	7.50	15.00
❏ 4-41165 [PS]	Yearbook/Susie's House	1958	6.25	12.50	25.00
❏ 4-41209	Lover's Lane/Yo Yo	1958	3.75	7.50	15.00
❏ 4-41247	Goin' Away to School/This Cold War with You	1958	3.75	7.50	15.00
❏ 4-41507	The Happy Wanderer/Red Headed Stranger	1959	3.75	7.50	15.00
❏ 4-41562	Tobacco Road/Midnight Bus	1960	5.00	10.00	20.00

DOT

Number	Title (A Side/B Side)	Yr	VG	VG+	NM
❏ 15699	Somebody Sweet/They Were Right	1958	7.50	15.00	30.00

—As "Johnny Dee"

RCA VICTOR

Number	Title (A Side/B Side)	Yr	VG	VG+	NM
❏ 47-7938	Language of Love/Darling Jane	1961	3.00	6.00	12.00
❏ 47-7993	Thou Shalt Not Steal/Mister Jones	1962	3.00	6.00	12.00
❏ 47-8054	Callin' Doctor Casey/Oh How Sad	1962	3.00	6.00	12.00
❏ 47-8101	Road Hog/Angela Jones	1962	3.00	6.00	12.00
❏ 47-8101 [PS]	Road Hog/Angela Jones	1962	5.00	10.00	20.00
❏ 47-8154	Bad News/The Guitar Player	1963	3.00	6.00	12.00
❏ 47-8308	Blue Train (Of the Heartbreak Line)/Rhythm and Blues	1962	3.00	6.00	12.00
❏ 47-8389	Th' Wife/Nothing to Gain	1964	3.00	6.00	12.00
❏ 47-8826	Run On Home Baby Brother/Silver Cloud Talking Blues	1966	2.50	5.00	10.00
❏ 47-8973	I Hear It Now/You're the Guilty One	1966	2.50	5.00	10.00
❏ 47-9189	It's My Time/Bahama Mama	1967	2.50	5.00	10.00
❏ 47-9592	Sidewalks/The Odd Folks of Okracoke	1968	2.00	4.00	8.00
❏ 74-0121	Brown Girl/The Jones'	1969	2.00	4.00	8.00

WARNER BROS.

Number	Title (A Side/B Side)	Yr	VG	VG+	NM
❏ 7489	When I Was Nine/Lord Have Mercy	1971	—	3.50	7.00

Albums

RCA VICTOR

Number	Title (A Side/B Side)	Yr	VG	VG+	NM
❏ LPM-2434 [M]	Language of Love	1961	6.25	12.50	25.00
❏ LSP-2434 [S]	Language of Love	1961	7.50	15.00	30.00
❏ LPM-2539 [M]	Twelve Sides of Loudermilk	1962	5.00	10.00	20.00
❏ LSP-2539 [S]	Twelve Sides of Loudermilk	1962	6.25	12.50	25.00
❏ LPM-3497 [M]	A Bizarre Collection of the Most Unusual Songs	1965	5.00	10.00	20.00
❏ LSP-3497 [S]	A Bizarre Collection of the Most Unusual Songs	1965	6.25	12.50	25.00
❏ LPM-3807 [M]	Suburban Attitudes in Country Music	1967	6.25	12.50	25.00
❏ LSP-3807 [S]	Suburban Attitudes in Country Music	1967	5.00	10.00	20.00
❏ LSP-4040	Country Love Songs	1968	5.00	10.00	20.00
❏ LSP-4097	The Open Mind of John D. Loudermilk	1968	5.00	10.00	20.00

WARNER BROS.

Number	Title (A Side/B Side)	Yr	VG	VG+	NM
❏ WS 1922	Volume 1, Elloree	1971	3.75	7.50	15.00

LOUIE AND THE LOVERS

45s

EPIC

Number	Title (A Side/B Side)	Yr	VG	VG+	NM
❏ 5-10616	Driver Go Slow/I Know You Know	1970	2.00	4.00	8.00
❏ 5-10678	Rise/I Don't Want to Be Seen with You	1970	2.00	4.00	8.00
❏ 5-10825	Little Georgie Baker/Tomorrows Just Might Change	1972	2.00	4.00	8.00

Albums

EPIC

Number	Title (A Side/B Side)	Yr	VG	VG+	NM
❏ E 30026	Rise	1970	5.00	10.00	20.00

LOUIS, BOBBY

45s

CAPITOL

Number	Title (A Side/B Side)	Yr	VG	VG+	NM
❏ F4224	Adult Western/Love at First Sight	1959	7.50	15.00	30.00
❏ F4272	I'm a Coward/Cell of Love	1959	7.50	15.00	30.00

LOUISE, TINA

Albums

CONCERT HALL

Number	Title (A Side/B Side)	Yr	VG	VG+	NM
❏ H-1503 [M]	Her Portrait in Hi-Fi	1958	12.50	25.00	50.00
❏ H-1521 [M]	It's Time for Tina	1958	50.00	100.00	200.00

URANIA

Number	Title (A Side/B Side)	Yr	VG	VG+	NM
❏ ULM-2005 [M]	It's Time for Tina	1959	50.00	100.00	200.00
❏ USD-2005 [S]	It's Time for Tina	1959	75.00	150.00	300.00

LOUVIN, CHARLIE

45s

CAPITOL

Number	Title (A Side/B Side)	Yr	VG	VG+	NM
❏ 2007	The Only Way Out (Is to Walk Over Me)/Too Little and Too Late	1967	2.50	5.00	10.00
❏ 2106	Will You Visit Me on Sundays?/Tears, Wine and Flowers	1968	2.00	4.00	8.00
❏ 2231	Hey Daddy/She Will Get Lonesome	1968	2.00	4.00	8.00
❏ 2350	What Are Those Things (With Big Black Wings)/What Then	1968	2.00	4.00	8.00
❏ 2448	Let's Put Our World Back Together/Heart of Clay	1969	2.00	4.00	8.00
❏ 2612	Little Reasons/After Awhile	1969	2.00	4.00	8.00
❏ 2703	Here's a Toast to Mama/Show Me the Way Back to Your Heart	1969	2.00	4.00	8.00
❏ 2770	Tiny Wings/I Ain't Gonna Work Tomorrow	1970	2.00	4.00	8.00
❏ 2824	Come and Get It Mama/Is Home Sweet Home	1970	2.00	4.00	8.00
❏ 2972	Sittin' Bull/It Ain't No Big Thing	1970	2.00	4.00	8.00
❏ 3048	Love Has to Die All By Itself/I Wish It Had Been a Dream	1971	2.00	4.00	8.00
❏ 3243	I Placed a Call/I'm Going Home	1971	2.00	4.00	8.00
❏ 3319	Just in Time (To Watch Love Die)/She Just Wants to Be Needed	1972	2.00	4.00	8.00
❏ 3528	Bottom of the Fifth/The Roses and the Rain	1973	2.00	4.00	8.00
❏ 3607	Funny Man/Harvest Time	1973	2.00	4.00	8.00
❏ 5173	I Don't Love You Anymore/My Book of Memories	1964	2.50	5.00	10.00
❏ 5296	Less and Less/I Don't Want It	1964	2.50	5.00	10.00
❏ 5369	See the Big Man Cry/I Just Don't Understand	1965	2.50	5.00	10.00
❏ 5475	Think I'll Go Somewhere and Cry Myself to Sleep/Life Begins at Love	1965	2.50	5.00	10.00
❏ 5550	You Finally Said Something Good (When You Said Goodbye)/Something to Think About	1965	2.50	5.00	10.00
❏ 5606	To Tell the Truth (I Told a Lie)/That's What Your Leaving's Done to Me	1966	2.50	5.00	10.00
❏ 5665	Something's Wrong/I Want a Happy Life	1966	2.50	5.00	10.00
❏ 5729	The Proof Is in the Kissing/Scared of the Blues	1966	2.50	5.00	10.00
❏ 5791	Off and On/Still Loving You	1967	2.50	5.00	10.00
❏ 5872	On the Other Hand/Someone's Heartache	1967	2.50	5.00	10.00
❏ 5948	I Forgot to Cry/Drive Me Out of My Mind	1967	2.50	5.00	10.00

LITTLE DARLIN'

Number	Title (A Side/B Side)	Yr	VG	VG+	NM
❏ 7922	Love Don't Care/Who's Gonna Love Me Now	1979	—	2.50	5.00

—A-side with Emmylou Harris

UNITED ARTISTS

Number	Title (A Side/B Side)	Yr	VG	VG+	NM
❏ XW368	You're My Wife, She's My Woman/If I Had to Build a Bridge	1973	—	3.00	6.00
❏ XW430	It Almost Felt Like Love/Until I'm Out of Sight	1974	—	3.00	6.00
❏ XW540	When Love Is Gone/I Want to See You One More Time	1974	—	3.00	6.00
❏ XW616	When You Have to Fly Alone/I Just Want a Happy Life	1975	—	3.00	6.00
❏ XW689	I Just Went Out, That's All/Is I Love You That Easy to Say	1975	—	3.00	6.00
❏ XW919	Sweet Texas/(B-side unknown)	1976	—	3.00	6.00

Albums

CAPITOL

Number	Title (A Side/B Side)	Yr	VG	VG+	NM
❏ ST-142	Hey Daddy	1969	5.00	10.00	20.00
❏ ST-8-0142	Hey Daddy	1969	6.25	12.50	25.00

—Capitol Record Club edition

Number	Title (A Side/B Side)	Yr	VG	VG+	NM
❏ ST-248	The Kind of Man I Am	1969	5.00	10.00	20.00
❏ ST-416	Here's a Toast to Mama	1970	5.00	10.00	20.00
❏ ST-555	Ten Times	1970	5.00	10.00	20.00
❏ ST 2208 [S]	Less and Less and I Don't Love You Anymore	1965	6.25	12.50	25.00
❏ T 2208 [M]	Less and Less and I Don't Love You Anymore	1965	5.00	10.00	20.00
❏ ST 2437 [S]	The Many Moods of Charlie Louvin	1966	6.25	12.50	25.00
❏ T 2437 [M]	The Many Moods of Charlie Louvin	1966	5.00	10.00	20.00
❏ ST 2482 [S]	Lonesome Is Me	1966	6.25	12.50	25.00
❏ T 2482 [M]	Lonesome Is Me	1966	5.00	10.00	20.00
❏ ST 2689 [S]	I'll Remember Always	1967	6.25	12.50	25.00
❏ T 2689 [M]	I'll Remember Always	1967	6.25	12.50	25.00
❏ ST 2787 [S]	I Forgot to Cry	1967	5.00	10.00	20.00
❏ T 2787 [M]	I Forgot to Cry	1967	6.25	12.50	25.00
❏ ST 2958	Will You Visit Me on Sundays	1968	5.00	10.00	20.00

LOUVIN, CHARLIE, AND ROY ACUFF Also see each artist's individual listings.

45s

HAL KAT

Number	Title (A Side/B Side)	Yr	VG	VG+	NM
❏ 63058	The Precious Jewel/Buried Alive	1989	2.00	4.00	8.00

LOUVIN, CHARLIE, AND MELBA MONTGOMERY Also see each artist's individual listings.

45s

CAPITOL

Number	Title (A Side/B Side)	Yr	VG	VG+	NM
❏ 2915	Something to Brag About/Let's Help Each Other to Forget	1970	2.00	4.00	8.00
❏ 3029	Did You Ever/Don't Believe Me	1971	2.00	4.00	8.00
❏ 3111	Baby, You've Got What It Takes/If We Don't Make It	1971	2.00	4.00	8.00
❏ 3208	I'm Gonna Leave You/When I Stop Dreaming	1971	2.00	4.00	8.00
❏ 3388	Baby, What's Wrong with Us/Unmatched Wedding Bands	1972	2.00	4.00	8.00
❏ 3508	A Man Likes Things Like That/That Don't Mean I Don't Love You	1973	2.00	4.00	8.00

Albums

CAPITOL

Number	Title (A Side/B Side)	Yr	VG	VG+	NM
❏ ST-686	Somethin' to Brag About	1971	5.00	10.00	20.00
❏ ST-808	Baby, You've Got What It Takes	1971	5.00	10.00	20.00

LOUVIN, IRA Also see THE LOUVIN BROTHERS.

45s

CAPITOL

Number	Title (A Side/B Side)	Yr	VG	VG+	NM
❏ 5190	Make Believe It's Me/Who Threw Dat Rock	1964	2.50	5.00	10.00
❏ 5428	Yodel, Sweet Molly/You're Looking for an Angel	1965	2.50	5.00	10.00

Albums

CAPITOL

Number	Title (A Side/B Side)	Yr	VG	VG+	NM
❏ ST 2413 [S]	The Unforgettable Ira Louvin	1965	7.50	15.00	30.00
❏ T 2413 [M]	The Unforgettable Ira Louvin	1965	6.25	12.50	25.00

LOUVIN BROTHERS, THE Also see CHARLIE LOUVIN; IRA LOUVIN.

45s

CAPITOL

Number	Title (A Side/B Side)	Yr	VG	VG+	NM
❏ F2296	The Family Who Prays Together/Let Us Travel On	1952	6.25	12.50	25.00
❏ F2381	Broadminded/I Know What You're Talking About	1953	6.25	12.50	25.00
❏ F2510	Born Again/From Mother's Arms to Korea	1952	6.25	12.50	25.00
❏ F2612	Preach the Gospel/I Love God's Way of Living	1953	6.25	12.50	25.00
❏ F2753	God Bless Her/No One to Sing for Me	1954	6.25	12.50	25.00
❏ F2852	If We Forget God/Satan Lied to Me	1954	6.25	12.50	25.00
❏ F2965	Satan and the Saint/Swing Low Sweet Chariot	1954	6.25	12.50	25.00
❏ F3083	Love Thy Neighbor As Thyself/Make Him a Soldier	1955	6.25	12.50	25.00
❏ F3177	When I Stop Dreaming/Pitfall	1955	5.00	10.00	20.00
❏ F3241	Just Rehearsing/Pray for Me	1955	5.00	10.00	20.00
❏ F3300	I Don't Believe You've Met My Baby/In the Middle of Nowhere	1955	5.00	10.00	20.00
❏ F3413	Hoping That You're Hoping/Childish Love	1956	5.00	10.00	20.00
❏ F3467	Where Will You Build/That's All He's Asking of Me	1956	5.00	10.00	20.00
❏ F3523	You're Running Wild/Cash on the Barrel Head	1956	5.00	10.00	20.00
❏ F3630	Don't Laugh/New Partner Waltz	1957	5.00	10.00	20.00
❏ F3715	Plenty of Everything But You/The First One to Love You	1957	5.00	10.00	20.00
❏ F3770	Praying/There's No Excuse	1957	5.00	10.00	20.00
❏ F3804	Call Me/I Wish You Knew	1957	5.00	10.00	20.00
❏ F3871	Dog Sled/When I Loved You	1958	3.75	7.50	15.00
❏ F3974	My Baby Came Back/She Didn't Even Know I Was Gone	1958	3.75	7.50	15.00
❏ F4055	My Baby's Gone/Lorene	1958	3.75	7.50	15.00
❏ F4112	The River of Jordan/He Can Be Found	1959	3.75	7.50	15.00
❏ F4117	Knoxville Girl/I Wish It Had Been a Dream	1959	3.75	7.50	15.00
❏ F4200	Blue from Now On/While You're Cheating on Me	1959	3.75	7.50	15.00
❏ F4255	You're Learning/My Curly Headed Baby	1959	3.75	7.50	15.00
❏ 4331	Nellie Moved to Town/Stagger	1960	3.75	7.50	15.00
❏ 4359	Just Suppose/I See a Bridge	1960	3.75	7.50	15.00
❏ 4395	Ruby's Song/If You Love Me, Stay Away	1960	3.75	7.50	15.00
❏ 4430	Love Is a Lonely Street/What a Change	1960	3.75	7.50	15.00
❏ 4473	Santa Claus Parade/It's Christmas Time	1960	3.75	7.50	15.00

Number	Title (A Side/B Side)	Yr	VG	VG+	NM
❑ 4473 [PS]	Santa Claus Parade/It's Christmas Time	1960	7.50	15.00	30.00
❑ 4506	I Love You Best of All/Scared of the Blues	1961	3.75	7.50	15.00
❑ 4559	I Ain't Gonna Work Tomorrow/				
	I Can't Keep You in Love with Me	1961	3.75	7.50	15.00
❑ 4628	How's the World Treating You/It Hurts Me More	1961	3.75	7.50	15.00
❑ 4686	Weapon of Prayer/Great Atomic Power	1962	3.75	7.50	15.00
❑ 4757	Broken Engagement/Time Goes So Slow	1962	3.75	7.50	15.00
❑ 4822	Must You Throw Dirt in My Face/				
	The First Time in Life	1962	3.75	7.50	15.00
❑ 4886	Keep Your Eyes on Jesus/				
	Don't Let Them Take the Bible	1962	3.75	7.50	15.00
❑ 4941	Love Turns to Hate/I Cried After You Left	1963	3.00	6.00	12.00
❑ 4999	I'm Glad That I'm Not Him/				
	Message to Your Heart	1963	3.00	6.00	12.00
❑ 5075	Every Time You Leave/There Is No Easy Way	1963	3.00	6.00	12.00

MGM

Number	Title (A Side/B Side)	Yr	VG	VG+	NM
❑ K10988	Weapon of Prayer/They've Got the Church				
	Outnumbered	1951	7.50	15.00	30.00
❑ K11065	You'll Be Rewarded Over There/Robe of White	1951	7.50	15.00	30.00
❑ K11221	Get Acquainted/My Love Song	1952	7.50	15.00	30.00
❑ K11277	Insured Before the Grave/Great Atomic Power	1952	7.50	15.00	30.00
❑ K11392	Do You Live What You Preach/I'll Live with God	1953	7.50	15.00	30.00

7-Inch Extended Plays
MGM

Number	Title (A Side/B Side)	Yr	VG	VG+	NM
❑ X1324	(contents unknown)	1956	3.75	7.50	15.00
❑ X1324 [PS]	The Louvin Brothers (Ira and Charles), Vol. 1	1956	3.75	7.50	15.00
❑ X1325	(contents unknown)	1956	3.75	7.50	15.00
❑ X1325 [PS]	The Louvin Brothers (Ira and Charles), Vol. 2	1956	3.75	7.50	15.00
❑ X1326	(contents unknown)	1956	3.75	7.50	15.00
❑ X1326 [PS]	The Louvin Brothers (Ira and Charles), Vol. 3	1956	3.75	7.50	15.00

Albums
CAPITOL

Number	Title (A Side/B Side)	Yr	VG	VG+	NM
❑ DT 769 [R]	Tragic Songs of Life	196?	5.00	10.00	20.00
❑ T 769 [M]	Tragic Songs of Life	1956	25.00	50.00	100.00
—Turquoise label					
❑ T 769 [M]	Tragic Songs of Life	1959	10.00	20.00	40.00
—Black colorband label, logo at left					
❑ T 769 [M]	Tragic Songs of Life	1962	6.25	12.50	25.00
—Black colorband label, logo at top					
❑ T 825 [M]	Nearer My God to Thee	1957	25.00	50.00	100.00
—Turquoise label					
❑ T 825 [M]	Nearer My God to Thee	1959	10.00	20.00	40.00
—Black colorband label, logo at left					
❑ T 825 [M]	Nearer My God to Thee	1962	6.25	12.50	25.00
—Black colorband label, logo at top					
❑ T 910 [M]	Ira and Charlie	1958	25.00	50.00	100.00
—Turquoise label					
❑ T 910 [M]	Ira and Charlie	1959	10.00	20.00	40.00
—Black colorband label, logo at left					
❑ T 910 [M]	Ira and Charlie	1962	6.25	12.50	25.00
—Black colorband label, logo at top					
❑ DT 1061 [R]	The Family Who Prays	196?	5.00	10.00	20.00
❑ T 1061 [M]	The Family Who Prays	1958	20.00	40.00	80.00
—Black colorband label, logo at left					
❑ T 1061 [M]	The Family Who Prays	1962	6.25	12.50	25.00
—Black colorband label, logo at top					
❑ T 1106 [M]	Country Love Ballads	1959	20.00	40.00	80.00
—Black colorband label, logo at left					
❑ T 1106 [M]	Country Love Ballads	1962	6.25	12.50	25.00
—Black colorband label, logo at top					
❑ T 1277 [M]	Satan Is Real	1960	20.00	40.00	80.00
—Black colorband label, logo at left					
❑ T 1277 [M]	Satan Is Real	1962	6.25	12.50	25.00
—Black colorband label, logo at top					
❑ T 1385 [M]	My Baby's Gone	1960	20.00	40.00	80.00
—Black colorband label, logo at left					
❑ T 1385 [M]	My Baby's Gone	1962	6.25	12.50	25.00
—Black colorband label, logo at top					
❑ T 1449 [M]	A Tribute to the Delmore Brothers	1960	20.00	40.00	80.00
—Black colorband label, logo at left					
❑ T 1449 [M]	A Tribute to the Delmore Brothers	1962	6.25	12.50	25.00
—Black colorband label, logo at top					
❑ T 1547 [M]	Encore	1961	20.00	40.00	80.00
—Black colorband label, logo at left					
❑ T 1547 [M]	Encore	1962	6.25	12.50	25.00
—Black colorband label, logo at top					
❑ ST 1616 [S]	Country Christmas	1961	20.00	40.00	80.00
—Black rainbow label with "Capitol" at left					
❑ ST 1616 [S]	Country Christmas	1962	6.25	12.50	25.00
—Black rainbow label with "Capitol" at top					
❑ T 1616 [M]	Country Christmas	1961	12.50	25.00	50.00
—Black rainbow label with "Capitol" at left					
❑ T 1616 [M]	Country Christmas	1962	5.00	10.00	20.00
—Black rainbow label with "Capitol" at top					
❑ ST 1721 [S]	Weapon of Prayer	1962	12.50	25.00	50.00
❑ T 1721 [M]	Weapon of Prayer	1962	10.00	20.00	40.00
❑ ST 1834 [S]	Keep Your Eyes on Jesus	1963	12.50	25.00	50.00
❑ T 1834 [M]	Keep Your Eyes on Jesus	1963	10.00	20.00	40.00
❑ ST 2091 [S]	The Louvin Brothers Sing and Play				
	Their Current Hits	1964	7.50	15.00	30.00
❑ T 2091 [M]	The Louvin Brothers Sing and Play				
	Their Current Hits	1964	6.25	12.50	25.00
❑ ST 2331 [S]	Thank God for My Christian Home	1965	7.50	15.00	30.00
❑ T 2331 [M]	Thank God for My Christian Home	1965	6.25	12.50	25.00
❑ ST 2827 [S]	The Great Roy Acuff Songs	1967	7.50	15.00	30.00
❑ T 2827 [M]	The Great Roy Acuff Songs	1967	10.00	20.00	40.00

METRO

Number	Title (A Side/B Side)	Yr	VG	VG+	NM
❑ M-598 [M]	The Louvin Brothers	1966	6.25	12.50	25.00
❑ MS-598 [R]	The Louvin Brothers	1966	5.00	10.00	20.00

MGM

Number	Title (A Side/B Side)	Yr	VG	VG+	NM
❑ E-3426 [M]	The Louvin Brothers	1957	50.00	100.00	200.00

SEARS

Number	Title (A Side/B Side)	Yr	VG	VG+	NM
❑ SP-119 [M]	Ira & Charles Louvin	196?	5.00	10.00	20.00
❑ SPS-119 [R]	Ira & Charles Louvin	196?	3.75	7.50	15.00

TOWER

Number	Title (A Side/B Side)	Yr	VG	VG+	NM
❑ DT 5038 [R]	Two Different Worlds	1966	5.00	10.00	20.00
❑ T 5038 [M]	Two Different Worlds	1966	7.50	15.00	30.00
❑ DT 5122	Country Heart and Soul	1968	5.00	10.00	20.00

LOVE
45s
BLUE THUMB

Number	Title (A Side/B Side)	Yr	VG	VG+	NM
❑ 106	Stand Out/I'll Pray for You	1970	—	3.00	6.00
❑ 7116	Keep On Shining/Everlasting First	1970	—	3.00	6.00

ELEKTRA

Number	Title (A Side/B Side)	Yr	VG	VG+	NM
❑ 45603	My Little Red Book/Message to Pretty	1966	2.50	5.00	10.00
❑ 45605	7 and 7 Is/No. Fourteen	1966	2.50	5.00	10.00
❑ 45608	She Comes in Colors/Orange Sky	1966	2.50	5.00	10.00
❑ 45608	Stephanie Knows Who/Orange Sky	1966	7.50	15.00	30.00
❑ 45613	Que Vida/Hey Joe	1967	12.50	25.00	50.00
❑ 45629	Alone Again Or/A House Is Not a Motel	1968	2.50	5.00	10.00
❑ 45633	Laughing Stock/				
	You're Mine and We Belong Together	1968	3.75	7.50	15.00
❑ 45700	Alone Again Or/Good Times	1970	2.00	4.00	8.00

RSO

Number	Title (A Side/B Side)	Yr	VG	VG+	NM
❑ 502	Time Is Like a River/With a Little Energy	1974	—	2.50	5.00
❑ 506	Good Old Fashioned Dream/				
	You Said You Would	1975	—	2.50	5.00

Albums
BLUE THUMB

Number	Title (A Side/B Side)	Yr	VG	VG+	NM
❑ BTS-8822	False Start	1970	5.00	10.00	20.00
❑ BTS-9000 [(2)]	Out Here	1969	6.25	12.50	25.00

ELEKTRA

Number	Title (A Side/B Side)	Yr	VG	VG+	NM
❑ EKL-4001 [M]	Love	1966	25.00	50.00	100.00
❑ EKL-4001 [M]	Love	1966	75.00	150.00	300.00
—White label promo					
❑ EKL-4005 [M]	Da Capo	1967	25.00	50.00	100.00
❑ EKL-4013 [M]	Forever Changes	1967	12.50	25.00	50.00
❑ EKL-4013 [M]	Forever Changes	1967	37.50	75.00	150.00
—White label promo					
❑ EKS-74001 [S]	Love	1966	12.50	25.00	50.00
—Brown label					
❑ EKS-74001 [S]	Love	1969	3.75	7.50	15.00
—Red label with large stylized "E"					
❑ EKS-74001 [S]	Love	1971	3.00	6.00	12.00
—Butterfly label					
❑ EKS-74005 [S]	Da Capo	1967	10.00	20.00	40.00
—Brown label					
❑ EKS-74005 [S]	Da Capo	1969	3.75	7.50	15.00
—Red label with large stylized "E"					
❑ EKS-74005 [S]	Da Capo	1971	3.00	6.00	12.00
—Butterfly label					
❑ EKS-74013 [S]	Forever Changes	1967	7.50	15.00	30.00
—Brown label					
❑ EKS-74013 [S]	Forever Changes	1969	3.75	7.50	15.00
—Red label with large stylized "E"					
❑ EKS-74013 [S]	Forever Changes	1971	3.00	6.00	12.00
—Butterfly label					
❑ EKS-74013 [S]	Forever Changes	1980	2.50	5.00	10.00
—Red label, small "E," Warner Communications logo on label					
❑ EKS-74013 [S]	Forever Changes	1984	2.00	4.00	8.00
—Red and black label					
❑ EKS-74049	Four Sail	1969	6.25	12.50	25.00
—Red label with large stylized "E"					
❑ EKS-74049 [DJ]	Four Sail	1969	20.00	40.00	80.00
—White label promo					
❑ EKS-74049	Four Sail	1971	3.00	6.00	12.00
—Butterfly label					
❑ EKS-74058	Revisited	1970	6.25	12.50	25.00
—Red label with large stylized "E"					
❑ EKS-74058	Revisited	1971	3.00	6.00	12.00
—Butterfly label					
❑ EKS-74058	Revisited	198?	2.50	5.00	10.00
—Red label, small "E," Warner Communications logo on label					
❑ EKS-74058	Revisited	1984	2.00	4.00	8.00
—Red and black label					

MCA

Number	Title (A Side/B Side)	Yr	VG	VG+	NM
❑ 27025	Studio/Live	1982	2.50	5.00	10.00

RHINO

Number	Title (A Side/B Side)	Yr	VG	VG+	NM
❑ RNDF-251 [PD]	Love Live	1981	3.75	7.50	15.00
❑ RNLP-800	Best of Love	1980	2.50	5.00	10.00
❑ RNLP-70175	The Best of Love (1966-1969) (Golden Archive				
	Series)	1987	2.50	5.00	10.00

RSO

Number	Title (A Side/B Side)	Yr	VG	VG+	NM
❑ SO 4804	Reel to Real	1974	3.75	7.50	15.00

SUNDAZED

Number	Title (A Side/B Side)	Yr	VG	VG+	NM
❑ LP 5100	Love	2001	3.00	6.00	12.00
—Reissue on 180-gram vinyl					
❑ LP 5101	Da Capo	2001	3.00	6.00	12.00
—Reissue on 180-gram vinyl					
❑ LP 5102	Forever Changes	2001	3.00	6.00	12.00
—Reissue on 180-gram vinyl					
❑ LP 5103	Four Sail	2004	3.00	6.00	12.00
❑ LP 5104	Revisited	2001	3.00	6.00	12.00
—Reissue on 180-gram vinyl					

LOVE, DARLENE Also see THE BLOSSOMS; THE CRYSTALS.
45s
COLUMBIA

Number	Title (A Side/B Side)	Yr	VG	VG+	NM
❑ 07984	He's Sure the Man I Love/Everybody Needs	1988	—	2.50	5.00

ELEKTRA

Number	Title (A Side/B Side)	Yr	VG	VG+	NM
❑ 69647	River Deep, Mountain High/Leader of the Pack	1985	—	2.00	4.00
—B-side by Leader of the Pack					
❑ 69647 [PS]	River Deep, Mountain High/Leader of the Pack	1985	—	2.00	4.00

PASSPORT

Number	Title (A Side/B Side)	Yr	VG	VG+	NM
❑ 7926	Christmas (Baby Please Come Home)/				
	Playing for Keeps	1983	3.00	6.00	12.00

PHILLES

Number	Title (A Side/B Side)	Yr	VG	VG+	NM
❑ 111	(Today I Met) The Boy I'm Gonna Marry/Playing				
	for Keeps	1963	5.00	10.00	20.00
❑ 111	(Today I Met) The Boy I'm Gonna Marry/				
	My Heart Beat a Little Bit Faster	1963	7.50	15.00	30.00

L

Number	Title (A Side/B Side)	Yr	VG	VG+	NM
❏ 114	Wait 'Til My Bobby Gets Home/Take It From Me	1963	5.00	10.00	20.00
❏ 117	A Fine Fine Boy/Nino & Sonny (Big Trouble)	1963	5.00	10.00	20.00
❏ 119	Christmas (Baby Please Come Home)/Harry and Milt Meet Hal B.	1963	10.00	20.00	40.00
❏ 123	Stumble and Fall/(He's a) Quiet Guy	1964	75.00	150.00	300.00
—Yellow and red label, "D.J. Copy Not for Sale" on label					
❏ 123	Stumble and Fall/(He's a) Quiet Guy	1964	200.00	400.00	800.00
—Yellow and red label stock copy; has been verified to exist					
❏ 123 [DJ]	Stumble and Fall/(He's a) Quiet Guy	1964	37.50	75.00	150.00
—White label promo					
❏ 125	Christmas (Baby Please Come Home)/X-Mas Blues	1964	100.00	200.00	400.00
❏ 125X	Christmas (Baby Please Come Home)/Winter Wonderland	1965	6.25	12.50	25.00
REPRISE					
❏ 0534	Too Late to Say You're Sorry/If	1966	2.50	5.00	10.00
WARNER/SPECTOR					
❏ 0401	Christmas (Baby Please Come Home)/Winter Wonderland	1974	2.50	5.00	10.00
❏ 0410	Lord, If You're a Woman/Stumble and Fall	1975	2.50	5.00	10.00
Albums					
COLUMBIA					
❏ FC 40605	Paint Another Picture	1988	3.00	6.00	12.00

LOVE, HONEY, AND THE LOVE NOTES
45s
CAMEO

Number	Title (A Side/B Side)	Yr	VG	VG+	NM
❏ 380	We Belong Together/Mary Ann	1965	3.00	6.00	12.00
❏ 409	Baby Baby You/Beg Me	1966	3.00	6.00	12.00
—As "The Lovenotes"					

LOVE, HOT SHOT
45s
SUN

Number	Title (A Side/B Side)	Yr	VG	VG+	NM
❏ 196	Wolf Call Boogie/Harmonica Jam	1954	1000.	2000.	4000.

LOVE, JOHNNY See RONNIE LOVE.

LOVE, MICHAEL Not the Beach Boy.
45s
COLUMBIA

Number	Title (A Side/B Side)	Yr	VG	VG+	NM
❏ 44253	Mrs. MacAbee/I Love Those Trees	1967	2.00	4.00	8.00

LOVE, RONNIE
45s
D-TOWN

Number	Title (A Side/B Side)	Yr	VG	VG+	NM
❏ 1021	Judy/Show Me What You Got	1963	30.00	60.00	120.00
❏ 1027	'Deed I Do/Always Be Good	1964	7.50	15.00	30.00
❏ 1040	Come Dance with Me/She's Got Love	196?	12.50	25.00	50.00
❏ 1047	Judy/Detroit, Michigan	1965	12.50	25.00	50.00
DOT					
❏ 16144	Chills and Fever/No Use Pledging My Love	1960	5.00	10.00	20.00
❏ 16186	Just to Be Loved/North to St. Louis	1961	5.00	10.00	20.00
MERCURY					
❏ 71492	Bless Your Heart/Lead Me	1959	6.25	12.50	25.00
—As "Johnny Love"					
❏ 71575	Because You Love Me/While Our Hearts Are Young	1960	6.25	12.50	25.00
—As "Johnny Love"					
❏ 71667	There Goes My Heart/I Love You, Yes I Do	1960	6.25	12.50	25.00
—As "Johnny Love"					
STARTIME					
❏ 5001	Chills and Fever/No Use Pledging My Love	1960	12.50	25.00	50.00
—As "Johnny Love"					
❏ 5003	Shakin' and a Breakin'/(B-side unknown)	1961	7.50	15.00	30.00

LOVE AFFAIR, THE
45s
DATE

Number	Title (A Side/B Side)	Yr	VG	VG+	NM
❏ 2-1591	Everlasting Love/Gone Are the Songs of Yesterday	1968	2.50	5.00	10.00
❏ 2-1608	Rainbow Valley/Someone Like Me	1968	2.50	5.00	10.00
❏ 2-1627	A Day Without Love/I'm Happy	1968	2.50	5.00	10.00
❏ 2-1646	Let Me Know/One Road	1968	2.50	5.00	10.00
❏ 2-1652	Bringing On Back the Good Times/Another Day	1969	2.50	5.00	10.00

LOVE CHILDS AFRO CUBAN BLUES BAND
12-Inch Singles
MIDSONG INT'L.

Number	Title (A Side/B Side)	Yr	VG	VG+	NM
❏ MD-10983	Oye Como Va (9:56)/Medley: Spanish Harlem-Dancin' to Spandisco	1977	3.00	6.00	12.00
45s					
ROULETTE					
❏ 7172	Life and Death in G & A/Bang Bang	1975	—	2.50	5.00
❏ 7180	Black Skin Blue Eyed Boys/Ask Me	1975	—	2.50	5.00
Albums					
MIDSONG INT'L.					
❏ BKL1-2292	Spandisco	1977	2.50	5.00	10.00
ROULETTE					
❏ 3016	Out Among 'Em	1975	2.50	5.00	10.00

LOVE EXCHANGE, THE
45s
UPTOWN

Number	Title (A Side/B Side)	Yr	VG	VG+	NM
❏ 755	Swallow the Sun/Mellow Memory	1968	6.25	12.50	25.00
Albums					
TOWER					
❏ ST 5115	The Love Exchange	1968	6.25	12.50	25.00

LOVE GENERATION, THE
45s
IMPERIAL

Number	Title (A Side/B Side)	Yr	VG	VG+	NM
❏ 66243	Groovy Summertime/Playin' on the Strings of the Wind	1967	2.00	4.00	8.00
❏ 66254	Meet Me at the Love-In/She Touched Me	1967	2.00	4.00	8.00
❏ 66275	Maman (Mama)/W.C. Fields	1968	2.00	4.00	8.00
❏ 66289	Love and Sunshine/Magic Land	1968	2.00	4.00	8.00
❏ 66310	Montage from "How Sweet It Is" (I Know That You Know)/Consciousness Expansion	1968	2.00	4.00	8.00
❏ 66336	Let the Good Time In/Catching Up on Fun	1968	2.00	4.00	8.00
Albums					
IMPERIAL					
❏ LP-9351 [M]	The Love Generation	1967	5.00	10.00	20.00
❏ LP-12351 [S]	The Love Generation	1967	5.00	10.00	20.00
❏ LP-12364	A Generation of Love	1968	5.00	10.00	20.00
❏ LP-12408	Montage	1968	5.00	10.00	20.00

LOVE NOTES, THE (1)
45s
HOLIDAY

Number	Title (A Side/B Side)	Yr	VG	VG+	NM
❏ 2605	United/Tonight	1957	5.00	10.00	20.00
—Flat (matte) label					
❏ 2605	United/Tonight	1957	15.00	30.00	60.00
—Glossy label					
❏ 2607	If I Could Make You Mine/Don't Go	1957	10.00	20.00	40.00
LOST-NITE					
❏ 179	United/Tonight	196?	—	3.00	6.00
—Reissue					

LOVE NOTES, THE (2)
45s
IMPERIAL

Number	Title (A Side/B Side)	Yr	VG	VG+	NM
❏ 5254	Surrender Your Heart/Get On My Train	1953	300.00	600.00	1200.
RAINBOW					
❏ 266	I'm Sorry/Sweet Lulu	1954	75.00	150.00	300.00
RIVIERA					
❏ 970	I'm Sorry/Sweet Lulu	1954	200.00	400.00	800.00
❏ 975	Since I Fell for You/Don't Be No Fool	1954	250.00	500.00	1000.
—Authentic copies have a lavender (light purple) label, counterfeits have a pink label					

LOVE NOTES, THE (3)
45s
WILSHIRE

Number	Title (A Side/B Side)	Yr	VG	VG+	NM
❏ 200	Nancy/Our Songs of Love	1963	10.00	20.00	40.00
❏ 203	Gloria/The Mathematics of Love	1963	25.00	50.00	100.00

LOVE, PEACE AND HAPPINESS Also see THE NEW BIRTH; THE NITE-LITERS.
45s
RCA VICTOR

Number	Title (A Side/B Side)	Yr	VG	VG+	NM
❏ 74-0402	Don't Blame the Young Folks for the Drug Society/You've Got to Be the One for Me	1970	—	3.00	6.00
❏ 74-0468	Message to the Establishment/Love Is Far Stronger Than We	1971	—	2.50	5.00
❏ 74-0584	Strip Me Naked/Unborn Child	1971	—	2.50	5.00
❏ 74-0740	I Don't Want to Do Wrong/Lonely Room	1972	—	2.50	5.00
Albums					
RCA VICTOR					
❏ LSP-4535	Love Is Stronger	1971	3.00	6.00	12.00
❏ LSP-4721	Here 'Tis	1972	3.00	6.00	12.00

LOVE POTION, THE
45s
KAPP

Number	Title (A Side/B Side)	Yr	VG	VG+	NM
❏ 979	This Love/Moby Binks	1969	2.00	4.00	8.00
TCB					
❏ 1601	This Love/Mr. Farouk	1968	3.75	7.50	15.00

LOVE SCULPTURE DAVE EDMUNDS was in this group.
45s
PARROT

Number	Title (A Side/B Side)	Yr	VG	VG+	NM
❏ 335	Sabre Dance/Think of Love	1969	3.75	7.50	15.00
❏ 362	In the Land of the Few/Farandole	1970	3.75	7.50	15.00
Albums					
EMI AMERICA					
❏ SQ-17208	Blues Helping	1986	3.00	6.00	12.00
—Reissue of Rare Earth LP					
PARROT					
❏ PAS 71035	Forms and Feelings	1970	6.25	12.50	25.00
RARE EARTH					
❏ RS-505	Blues Helping	1969	10.00	20.00	40.00

LOVE SOCIETY, THE
45s
MERCURY

Number	Title (A Side/B Side)	Yr	VG	VG+	NM
❏ 73130	America/Wanda	1970	3.75	7.50	15.00
RCA VICTOR					
❏ 74-0257	Don't Worry Baby/You Know How I Feel (And Why)	1969	2.50	5.00	10.00
SCEPTER					
❏ 12223	Without You/Do You Wanna Dance	1968	3.00	6.00	12.00
❏ 12236	Tobacco Road/Drops of Rain	1969	3.00	6.00	12.00

LOVE UNLIMITED
12-Inch Singles
UNLIMITED GOLD

Number	Title (A Side/B Side)	Yr	VG	VG+	NM
❏ 1410	High Steppin', Hip Dressin' Fella (You Got It Together)/(Instrumental)	1979	3.00	6.00	12.00
45s					
MCA					
❏ 40009	Fragile/I'll Be Yours Forever	1973	—	3.00	6.00
20TH CENTURY					
❏ 2025	Oh Love, Well We Finally Made It/Yes, We Finally Made It	1973	—	2.50	5.00
❏ 2062	It May Be Winter Outside (But In My Heart It's Spring)/It's Winter Again	1973	—	2.50	5.00
❏ 2082	Under the Influence of Love/(Instrumental)	1974	—	2.50	5.00
❏ 2110	People of Tomorrow Are the Children of Today/So Nice to Hear	1974	—	2.50	5.00
❏ 2141	I Belong to You/And Only You	1974	—	2.50	5.00
❏ 2183	Share a Little Love in Your Heart/I Love You So, Never Gonna Let You Go	1975	—	2.50	5.00

Number	Title (A Side/B Side)	Yr	VG	VG+	NM
UNI					
❑ 55319	Walkin' in the Rain with the One I Love/				
	I Should Have Known	1972	—	3.00	6.00
❑ 55342	Is It Really True Boy — Is It Really Me?/				
	Another Chance	1972	—	3.00	6.00
❑ 55349	Are You Really Sure/Another Chance	1972	—	3.00	6.00
UNLIMITED GOLD					
❑ 1409	High Steppin', Hip Dressin' Fella				
	(You Got It Together)/(Instrumental)	1979	—	2.50	5.00
❑ 1412	I'm So Glad That I'm a Woman/				
	Gotta Be Where You Are	1980	—	2.50	5.00
❑ 1417	If You Want Me, Say It/				
	When I'm In Your Arms, Everything's Okay	1980	—	2.50	5.00
❑ 7001	I Did It for Love/(Instrumental)	1977	—	2.50	5.00
Albums					
MCA					
❑ 181	Love Unlimited	1973	3.00	6.00	12.00
—Reissue of Uni 73131					
❑ 316	Under the Influence of…	1973	—	—	—
—Canceled; issued on 20th Century 414					
20TH CENTURY					
❑ T-414	Under the Influence of…	1973	2.50	5.00	10.00
❑ T-443	In Heat	1974	2.50	5.00	10.00
UNI					
❑ 73131	Love Unlimited	1972	3.75	7.50	15.00
UNLIMITED GOLD					
❑ 101	He's All I Got	1977	2.50	5.00	10.00
❑ JZ 36130	Love Is Back	1979	2.50	5.00	10.00

LOVE UNLIMITED ORCHESTRA

12-Inch Singles

Number	Title (A Side/B Side)	Yr	VG	VG+	NM
20TH CENTURY					
❑ TCD-61	Theme from King Kong/Blues Concerto	1976	3.75	7.50	15.00
❑ TCD-66	Don't You Know How Much I Love You/Hey Look				
	at Me, I'm in Love	1978	3.75	7.50	15.00
UNLIMITED GOLD					
❑ 1406	Jamaican Girl/I'm in the Mood	1979	3.00	6.00	12.00
❑ 1414	Young America/Freeway Flyer	1980	3.00	6.00	12.00
❑ 02135	Lift Your Voice and Say (United We Can Live in				
	Peace Today)/My Fantasies	1981	2.50	5.00	10.00
❑ 02479	Welcome Aboard/Strange	1981	2.50	5.00	10.00
❑ 02636	Night Life in the City/Wind	1981	2.50	5.00	10.00
❑ 03882	My Laboratory Is Ready for You/				
	Goodbye Concerto	1983	2.50	5.00	10.00

45s

Number	Title (A Side/B Side)	Yr	VG	VG+	NM
20TH CENTURY					
❑ 2069	Love's Theme/Sweet Moments	1973	—	2.50	5.00
❑ 2090	Rhapsody in White/Barry's Theme	1974	—	2.50	5.00
❑ 2107	Theme from "Together Brothers"/Find the Man				
	Brothers	1974	—	2.50	5.00
❑ 2145	Baby Blues/What a Groove	1974	—	2.50	5.00
❑ 2162	Satin Soul/Just Living It Up	1975	—	2.50	5.00
❑ 2197	Forever in Love/Only You Can Make Me Blue	1975	—	2.50	5.00
❑ 2281	Midnight Groove/It's Only What I Feel	1976	—	2.50	5.00
❑ 2301	My Sweet Summer Suite/Just Living It Up	1976	—	2.50	5.00
❑ 2325	Theme from King Kong (Pt. 1)/Theme from King				
	Kong (Pt. 2)	1977	—	2.50	5.00
❑ 2348	Brazilian Love Song/My Sweet Summer Suite	1977	—	2.50	5.00
❑ 2364	Whisper Softly/Hey Look at Me, I'm in Love	1978	—	2.50	5.00
❑ 2367	Don't You Know How Much I Love You/Hey Look				
	at Me, I'm in Love	1978	—	2.50	5.00
❑ 2399	Theme from "Superman"/Theme from "Shaft"	1978	—	2.50	5.00
UNLIMITED GOLD					
❑ 1405	Jamaican Girl/I'm in the Mood	1979	—	2.50	5.00
❑ 1413	Young America/Freeway Flyer	1980	—	2.50	5.00
❑ 1421	I Wanna Boogie and Woogie with You/I'm in the				
	Mood	1980	—	2.50	5.00
❑ 1423	Vieni Qua Bella Mi/Bayou	1980	—	2.50	5.00
❑ 02134	Lift Your Voice and Say (United We Can Live in				
	Peace Today)/My Fantasies	1981	—	2.00	4.00
❑ 02478	Welcome Aboard/Strange	1981	—	2.00	4.00
❑ 02635	Night Life in the City/Wind	1981	—	2.00	4.00
❑ 03881	My Laboratory Is Ready for You/Goodbye				
	Concerto	1983	—	2.00	4.00

Albums

Number	Title (A Side/B Side)	Yr	VG	VG+	NM
20TH CENTURY					
❑ T-101	Together Brothers	1974	3.00	6.00	12.00
❑ T-433	Rhapsody in White	1974	2.50	5.00	10.00
❑ T-458	White Gold	1974	2.50	5.00	10.00
❑ T-480	Music Maestro Please	1975	2.50	5.00	10.00
❑ T-517	My Sweet Summer Suite	1976	2.50	5.00	10.00
❑ T-554	My Musical Bouquet	1978	2.50	5.00	10.00
❑ T-582	Movie Themes	1978	2.50	5.00	10.00
UNLIMITED GOLD					
❑ FZ 37425	Welcome Aboard	1981	2.50	5.00	10.00
❑ FZ 38366	Rise	1983	2.50	5.00	10.00

LOVECRAFT See H.P. LOVECRAFT.

LOVEJOYS, THE

45s

Number	Title (A Side/B Side)	Yr	VG	VG+	NM
RED BIRD					
❑ 10-004	Payin'/It's Mighty Nice	1964	7.50	15.00	30.00

LOVELITES, THE

45s

Number	Title (A Side/B Side)	Yr	VG	VG+	NM
BANDERA					
❑ 2515	I Found Me a Lover/You Better Stop It	1967	3.75	7.50	15.00

LOVENOTES, THE See HONEY LOVE AND THE LOVE NOTES.

LOVERS, THE (1) Husband-and-wife R&B duo.

45s

Number	Title (A Side/B Side)	Yr	VG	VG+	NM
ALADDIN					
❑ 3419	Tell Me/Love Bug Bit Me	1958	10.00	20.00	40.00
IMPERIAL					
❑ 5845	Darling It's Wonderful/I Want to Be Loved	1962	5.00	10.00	20.00

Number	Title (A Side/B Side)	Yr	VG	VG+	NM
❑ 5960	Tell Me/Let's Elope	1963	5.00	10.00	20.00
❑ 66055	Darling It's Wonderful/I Want to Be Loved	1964	3.75	7.50	15.00
LAMP					
❑ 2005	Darling It's Wonderful/				
	Gotta Whole Lot of Livin' to Do	1957	12.50	25.00	50.00
❑ 2013	I Wanna Be Loved/Let's Elope	1957	12.50	25.00	50.00
❑ 2018	Tell Me/Love Bug Bit Me	1958	12.50	25.00	50.00
POST					
❑ 10007	Darling It's Wonderful/				
	Gotta Whole Lot of Livin' to Do	1963	3.75	7.50	15.00

LOVERS, THE (2)

45s

Number	Title (A Side/B Side)	Yr	VG	VG+	NM
AGON					
❑ 1011	Caravan of Lonely Men/In My Tenement	1965	6.25	12.50	25.00
GATE					
❑ 501	Someone/Do This for Me	1965	25.00	50.00	100.00
PHILIPS					
❑ 40353	Someone/Do This for Me	1966	5.00	10.00	20.00

LOVERS, THE (3)

45s

Number	Title (A Side/B Side)	Yr	VG	VG+	NM
CASINO					
❑ 103	Let's/Big Axe	1958	5.00	10.00	20.00

LOVERS, THE (4)

45s

Number	Title (A Side/B Side)	Yr	VG	VG+	NM
MARLIN					
❑ 3313	Discomania (Part 1)/Discomania (Part 2)	1977	—	2.50	5.00

LOVERS, THE (U) These could be groups (1) or (2).

45s

Number	Title (A Side/B Side)	Yr	VG	VG+	NM
CHECKER					
❑ 1100	It's Too Late/Security	1965	2.50	5.00	10.00
DECCA					
❑ 29862	Don't Touch Me/Let Me Be the First to Know	1956	10.00	20.00	40.00
KELLER					
❑ 101	Party Line/Strange As It Seems	1961	10.00	20.00	40.00

LOVETONES, THE

45s

Number	Title (A Side/B Side)	Yr	VG	VG+	NM
LOVE-TONE					
❑ 101	You Can Tell Me That This Is Christmas/				
	When I Asked My Love	1961	5.00	10.00	20.00
PLUS					
❑ 108	Talk to an Angel/Take It Easy, Baby	1956	125.00	250.00	500.00

LOVIN' SPOONFUL, THE Also see JOE BUTLER; JOHN SEBASTIAN; ZALMAN YANOVSKY.

L

45s

Number	Title (A Side/B Side)	Yr	VG	VG+	NM
KAMA SUTRA					
❑ 201	Do You Believe in Magic/On the Road Again	1965	2.00	4.00	8.00
—Mostly yellow label with "Kama Sutra" in black					
❑ 201	Do You Believe in Magic/On the Road Again	1965	2.50	5.00	10.00
—Mostly yellow label with "Kama Sutra" in red					
❑ 201	Do You Believe in Magic/On the Road Again	1965	3.75	7.50	15.00
—Mostly red-orange label					
❑ 205	You Didn't Have to Be So Nice/My Gal	1965	2.00	4.00	8.00
—Mostly yellow label with "Kama Sutra" in black					
❑ 205	You Didn't Have to Be So Nice/My Gal	1965	2.50	5.00	10.00
—Mostly yellow label with "Kama Sutra" in red					
❑ 205	You Didn't Have to Be So Nice/My Gal	1965	3.00	6.00	12.00
—Mostly red-orange label					
❑ 205 [PS]	You Didn't Have to Be So Nice/My Gal	1965	3.75	7.50	15.00
❑ 208	Daydream/Night Owl Blues	1966	2.50	5.00	10.00
—Mostly yellow label with "Kama Sutra" in black					
❑ 208	Daydream/Night Owl Blues	1966	3.00	6.00	12.00
—Mostly yellow label with "Kama Sutra" in red					
❑ 208	Daydream/Night Owl Blues	1966	3.75	7.50	15.00
—Mostly red-orange label					
❑ 208 [PS]	Daydream/Night Owl Blues	1966	3.75	7.50	15.00
❑ 209	Did You Ever Have to Make Up Your Mind/Didn't				
	Want to Have to Do It	1966	2.50	5.00	10.00
❑ 209 [PS]	Did You Ever Have to Make Up Your Mind/Didn't				
	Want to Have to Do It	1966	3.75	7.50	15.00
❑ 211	Summer in the City/Butchie's Tune	1966	2.50	5.00	10.00
❑ 211 [PS]	Summer in the City/Butchie's Tune	1966	3.75	7.50	15.00
❑ 216	Rain on the Roof/Pow	1966	2.50	5.00	10.00
❑ 216 [PS]	Rain on the Roof/Pow	1966	3.75	7.50	15.00
❑ 219	Nashville Cats/Full Measure	1966	2.50	5.00	10.00
❑ 219 [PS]	Nashville Cats/Full Measure	1966	3.75	7.50	15.00
❑ 220	Darling Be Home Soon/Darlin' Companion	1967	2.50	5.00	10.00
❑ 220 [PS]	Darling Be Home Soon/Darlin' Companion	1967	3.75	7.50	15.00
❑ 225	Six O'Clock/The Finale	1967	2.50	5.00	10.00
❑ 225 [PS]	Six O'Clock/The Finale	1967	3.75	7.50	15.00
❑ 231	Lonely (Amy's Theme)/You're a Big Boy Now	1967	3.75	7.50	15.00
❑ 239	She Is Still a Mystery/Only Pretty, What a Pity	1967	2.50	5.00	10.00
❑ 239 [PS]	She Is Still a Mystery/Only Pretty, What a Pity	1967	3.75	7.50	15.00
❑ 241	Money/Close Your Eyes	1967	2.00	4.00	8.00
❑ 250	Never Going Back/Forever	1968	2.00	4.00	8.00
❑ 251	Revelation Revolution '69/Run with You	1968	2.00	4.00	8.00
❑ 255	Me About You/Amazing Air	1968	2.00	4.00	8.00
❑ 551	Summer in the City/				
	You and Me and Rain on the Roof	1972	—	3.00	6.00
❑ 551 [PS]	Summer in the City/				
	You and Me and Rain on the Roof	1972	3.75	7.50	15.00
—Sleeve evidently is promo only					
❑ 608 [DJ]	Daydream (mono/stereo)	1976	—	3.00	6.00
—Stock copy not known to exist					

7-Inch Extended Plays

Number	Title (A Side/B Side)	Yr	VG	VG+	NM
KAMA SUTRA					
❑ EK-1 [DJ]	It's Not Time Now/Nashville Cats//Henry				
	Thomas/Darlin' Companion	1967	5.00	10.00	20.00
❑ EK-1 [PS]	The Lovin' Spoonful	1967	12.50	25.00	50.00

Albums

Number	Title (A Side/B Side)	Yr	VG	VG+	NM
ACCORD					
❑ SN-7196	Distant Echoes	1981	2.50	5.00	10.00

Number	Title (A Side/B Side)	Yr	VG	VG+	NM
BUDDAH					
❑ BDM-5706	The Best of the Lovin' Spoonful	197?	3.00	6.00	12.00
❑ BLB6-8339	The Best of the Lovin' Spoonful	198?	2.50	5.00	10.00
—Reissue of 5706					
51 WEST					
❑ Q 16023	... So Nice	1979	2.50	5.00	10.00
KAMA SUTRA					
❑ KLPS-750-2 [(2)]	24 Karat Hits	1968	5.00	10.00	20.00
❑ KSBS-2011	The John Sebastian Song Book	1970	3.75	7.50	15.00
❑ KSBS-2013	The Very Best of the Lovin' Spoonful	1970	3.75	7.50	15.00
❑ KSBS-2029	Once Upon a Time	1971	3.75	7.50	15.00
❑ KSBS-2608 [(2)]	The Best…Lovin' Spoonful	1976	5.00	10.00	20.00
❑ KLP-8050 [M]	Do You Believe in Magic	1965	5.00	10.00	20.00
❑ KLPS-8050 [S]	Do You Believe in Magic	1965	7.50	15.00	30.00
❑ KLP-8051 [M]	Daydream	1966	5.00	10.00	20.00
❑ KLPS-8051 [S]	Daydream	1966	7.50	15.00	30.00
❑ KLP-8053 [M]	What's Up, Tiger Lily?	1966	5.00	10.00	20.00
❑ KLPS-8053 [S]	What's Up, Tiger Lily?	1966	7.50	15.00	30.00
❑ KLP-8054 [M]	Hums of the Lovin' Spoonful	1966	5.00	10.00	20.00
❑ KLPS-8054 [S]	Hums of the Lovin' Spoonful	1966	7.50	15.00	30.00
❑ KLP-8056 [M]	The Best of the Lovin' Spoonful	1967	3.75	7.50	15.00
—Came with four bonus photos of the band, which are priced separately					
❑ KLP/S-8056	The Best of the Lovin' Spoonful Bonus Photos (4)	1967	2.50	5.00	10.00
❑ KLPS-8056 [S]	The Best of the Lovin' Spoonful	1967	3.75	7.50	15.00
—Came with four bonus photos of the band, which are priced separately					
❑ KLP-8058 [M]	You're a Big Boy Now	1967	5.00	10.00	20.00
❑ KLPS-8058 [S]	You're a Big Boy Now	1967	5.00	10.00	20.00
❑ KLP-8061 [M]	Everything Playing	1968	7.50	15.00	30.00
❑ KLPS-8061 [S]	Everything Playing	1968	5.00	10.00	20.00
❑ KLP-8064 [M]	The Best of the Lovin' Spoonful, Volume 2	1968	12.50	25.00	50.00
❑ KLPS-8064 [S]	The Best of the Lovin' Spoonful, Volume 2	1968	5.00	10.00	20.00
❑ KLPS-8073	Revelation: Revolution '69	1969	6.25	12.50	25.00
❑ ST-90597 [S]	Do You Believe in Magic	1965	10.00	20.00	40.00
—Capitol Record Club edition					
❑ T-90597 [M]	Do You Believe in Magic	1965	7.50	15.00	30.00
—Capitol Record Club edition					
❑ ST-90675 [S]	Daydream	1966	10.00	20.00	40.00
—Capitol Record Club edition					
❑ T-90675 [M]	Daydream	1966	6.25	12.50	25.00
—Capitol Record Club edition					
❑ ST-90988 [S]	Hums of the Lovin' Spoonful	1966	10.00	20.00	40.00
—Capitol Record Club edition					
❑ KAO-91102 [M]	The Best of the Lovin' Spoonful	1967	6.25	12.50	25.00
—Capitol Record Club edition					
❑ SKAO-91102 [S]	The Best of the Lovin' Spoonful	1967	5.00	10.00	20.00
—Capitol Record Club edition					
❑ ST-91198 [S]	You're a Big Boy Now	1967	6.25	12.50	25.00
—Capitol Record Club edition					
KOALA					
❑ KO 14221	Day Dream	1979	2.50	5.00	10.00
PAIR					
❑ PDL2-1200 [(2)]	The Best of the Lovin' Spoonful	1986	3.00	6.00	12.00
RHINO					
❑ RNLP-114	The Best of the Lovin' Spoonful, Vol. 2	1985	2.50	5.00	10.00
SUNDAZED					
❑ LP 5159	Do You Believe in Magic	2002	3.75	7.50	15.00
—Reissue on 180-gram vinyl					
❑ LP 5160	Daydream	2002	3.75	7.50	15.00
—Reissue on 180-gram vinyl					
❑ LP 5166	Hums of the Lovin' Spoonful	2003	3.75	7.50	15.00
—Reissue on 180-gram vinyl					

LOWE, JIM
45s

Number	Title (A Side/B Side)	Yr	VG	VG+	NM
BUDDAH					
❑ 44	Michael J. Polaird for President/				
	The Ol' Racetrack	1968	—	3.00	6.00
DECCA					
❑ 31153	Someone Else's Arms/Man of the Cloth	1960	2.50	5.00	10.00
❑ 31198	That Do Make It Nice/Two Sides to Every Story	1961	2.50	5.00	10.00
DOT					
❑ 15381	Close the Door/Nuevo Laredo	1955	3.00	6.00	12.00
❑ 15407	Maybellene/Rene La Rue	1955	3.00	6.00	12.00
❑ 15429	John Jacob Jingleheimer Smith/				
	St. James Avenue	1955	3.00	6.00	12.00
❑ 15456	The Sixty-Four Thousand Dollar Question/				
	Blue Suede Shoes	1956	3.00	6.00	12.00
❑ 15486	The Green Door/(				
	The Story of) The Little Man in Chinatown	1956	3.00	6.00	12.00
—Second pressings have black labels					
❑ 15486	The Green Door/				
	(The Story of) The Little Man in Chinatown	1956	3.75	7.50	15.00
—Originals have maroon labels					
❑ 15525	By You, By You, By You/I Feel the Beat	1957	2.50	5.00	10.00
❑ 15569	Four Walls/Talkin' to the Blues	1957	3.00	6.00	12.00
❑ 15611	From a Jack to a King/Slow Train	1957	2.50	5.00	10.00
❑ 15665	Rick-a-Chickie/The Bright Light	1957	2.50	5.00	10.00
❑ 15693	Kewpie Doll/The Lady from Johannesburg	1958	2.50	5.00	10.00
❑ 15753	Take Us To Your President/Later On Tonight	1958	2.50	5.00	10.00
❑ 15832	Chapel Bells on Chapel Hill/Ja, Ja, Ja	1958	2.50	5.00	10.00
❑ 15869	Play Number Eleven/Come Away from Her Arms	1958	2.50	5.00	10.00
❑ 15954	I'm Movin' On/Without You	1959	2.50	5.00	10.00
❑ 16046	He'll Have to Go/Dress Rehearsal	1960	2.50	5.00	10.00
❑ 16074	The Midnight Ride of Paul Revere/A Tomorrow				
	That Never Comes	1960	2.50	5.00	10.00
❑ 16636	Addis Ababa/Have You Ever Been Lonely	1964	—	3.00	6.00
MERCURY					
❑ 70163	Gambler's Guitar/The Martins and the Coys	1953	5.00	10.00	20.00
❑ 70265	Santa Claus Rides a Strawberry Roan/Love in				
	Both Directions	1953	5.00	10.00	20.00
❑ 70319	Goodbye Little Sweetheart/River Boat	1954	5.00	10.00	20.00
❑ 71016	Prince of Peace/				
	Santa Claus Rides a Strawberry Roan	1956	3.75	7.50	15.00
SIGNATURE					
❑ 75001	Green Door/San Francisco Bay	197?	—	2.50	5.00

Number	Title (A Side/B Side)	Yr	VG	VG+	NM
20TH CENTURY FOX					
❑ 426	Hootenanny Granny/				
	These Bones Gonna Rise Again	1963	2.00	4.00	8.00
UNITED ARTISTS					
❑ 874	Mr. Moses/Make Your Back Strong	1965	—	3.00	6.00
❑ 50124	Gambler's Guitar/Blotson Bottom	1967	—	3.00	6.00
7-Inch Extended Plays					
DOT					
❑ DEP 1061	Rainbow/Love Ya//The Crossing/				
	Honky Tonk Rock	1957	3.75	7.50	15.00
❑ DEP 1061 [PS]	Rainbow	1957	3.75	7.50	15.00
Albums					
DOT					
❑ DLP-3051 [M]	The Green Door	1956	37.50	75.00	150.00
❑ DLP-3114 [M]	Wicked Women	1958	25.00	50.00	100.00
❑ DLP-3681 [M]	Songs They Sing Behind the Green Door	1965	6.25	12.50	25.00
❑ DLP-25881 [S]	Songs They Sing Behind the Green Door	1965	7.50	15.00	30.00
MERCURY					
❑ MG-20246 [M]	The Door of Fame	1957	37.50	75.00	150.00

LOWE, VIRGINIA
45s

Number	Title (A Side/B Side)	Yr	VG	VG+	NM
MELBA					
❑ 107	I'm in Love with Elvis Presley/Empty Feeling	1956	12.50	25.00	50.00

LRY
Albums

Number	Title (A Side/B Side)	Yr	VG	VG+	NM
CONGRESS OF THE CROW					
❑ 8031002	The LRY Record	1968	50.00	100.00	200.00

LUCAS, AL
45s

Number	Title (A Side/B Side)	Yr	VG	VG+	NM
CHALLENGE					
❑ 59042	She's My Baby/Got the Ring	1959	15.00	30.00	60.00
❑ 59050	Sweet Tooth for My Baby Ruth/Always	1959	10.00	20.00	40.00

LUCAS, JIMMY
45s

Number	Title (A Side/B Side)	Yr	VG	VG+	NM
HIT					
❑ 19	Roses Are Red (My Love)/Gravy				
	(For My Mashed Potatoes)	1962	2.00	4.00	8.00
—B-side by Peggy Gaines					

LUCAS, MITCH
45s

Number	Title (A Side/B Side)	Yr	VG	VG+	NM
HIT					
❑ 31	Patches/You Beat Me to the Punch	1962	2.00	4.00	8.00
—B-side by Alpha Zoe					

LUDDEN, ALLEN
Albums

Number	Title (A Side/B Side)	Yr	VG	VG+	NM
RCA VICTOR					
❑ LPM-2934 [M]	Allen Ludden Sings His Favorite Songs	1964	5.00	10.00	20.00
❑ LSP-2934 [S]	Allen Ludden Sings His Favorite Songs	1964	6.25	12.50	25.00

LUKE, ROBIN
45s

Number	Title (A Side/B Side)	Yr	VG	VG+	NM
BERTRAM INTERNATIONAL					
❑ 206	Susie Darlin'/Living's Loving You	1958	15.00	30.00	60.00
❑ 206 [PS]	Susie Darlin'/Living's Loving You	1958	25.00	50.00	100.00
❑ 208	My Girl/Chicka Chicka Honey	1958	7.50	15.00	30.00
❑ 210	Strollin' Blues/You Can't Stop Me from Dreaming	1959	7.50	15.00	30.00
❑ 212	Five Minutes More/				
	Who's Gonna Hold Your Hand	1959	7.50	15.00	30.00
DOT					
❑ 15781	Susie Darlin'/Living's Loving You	1958	6.25	12.50	25.00
❑ 15839	My Girl/Chicka Chicka Honey	1958	5.00	10.00	20.00
❑ 15899	Strollin' Blues/You Can't Stop Me from Dreaming	1959	5.00	10.00	20.00
❑ 15959	Five Minutes More/Who's Gonna Hold Your				
	Hand	1959	5.00	10.00	20.00
❑ 16001	Make Me a Dreamer/Walkin' in the Moonlight	1959	5.00	10.00	20.00
❑ 16040	Bad Boy/School Bus Love Affair	1960	5.00	10.00	20.00
❑ 16096	Everlovin'/Well Oh Well Oh	1960	5.00	10.00	20.00
❑ 16096 [PS]	Everlovin'/Well Oh Well Oh	1960	15.00	30.00	60.00
❑ 16170	So Alone/All Because of You	1960	5.00	10.00	20.00
❑ 16229	Part of a Fool/Poor Little Rich Boy	1961	3.75	7.50	15.00
❑ 16366	Foggin' Up the Windows/Time	1962	3.75	7.50	15.00
—With Roberta Shore					
INTERNATIONAL					
❑ 206	Susie Darlin'/Living's Loving You	1958	250.00	500.00	1000.
—Light blue label					
7-Inch Extended Plays					
DOT					
❑ DEP-1092	Susie Darlin'/Bad Boy//Won't You Please Be				
	Mine/Chicka Chicka Honey	1958	100.00	200.00	400.00
❑ DEP-1092 [PS]	Susie Darlin'	1958	100.00	200.00	400.00

LUKE THE DRIFTER See HANK WILLIAMS.

LUKE THE DRIFTER, JR. See HANK WILLIAMS, JR.

LULU
12-Inch Singles

Number	Title (A Side/B Side)	Yr	VG	VG+	NM
SBK					
❑ 19777	Independence (5 versions)	1993	2.00	4.00	8.00

45s

Number	Title (A Side/B Side)	Yr	VG	VG+	NM
ALFA					
❑ 7006	I Could Never Miss You (More Than I Do)/				
	Dance to the Feeling	1981	—	2.00	4.00
❑ 7006 [PS]	I Could Never Miss You (More Than I Do)/				
	Dance to the Feeling	1981	—	2.50	5.00
—With Lulu wearing a spotted headband					
❑ 7006 [PS]	I Could Never Miss You (More Than I Do)/				
	Dance to the Feeling	1981	—	3.00	6.00
—With Lulu not wearing a headband (original)					
❑ 7011	If I Were You/You Win, I Lose	1981	—	2.00	4.00
❑ 7011 [PS]	If I Were You/You Win, I Lose	1981	—	2.50	5.00

Number	Title (A Side/B Side)	Yr	VG	VG+	NM
❏ 7021	Who's Foolin' Who/You Win, I Lose	1982	—	2.00	4.00
ATCO					
❏ 6722	Oh Me Oh My (I'm a Fool for You Baby)/Sweep Around Your Own Back Door	1969	2.00	4.00	8.00
❏ 6749	Hum a Song (From Your Heart)/Where's Eddie	1970	—	3.00	6.00
❏ 6761	Good Day Sunshine/After the Feeling Is Gone	1970	—	3.00	6.00
❏ 6774	Melody Fair/To the Other Woman	1970	—	3.00	6.00
❏ 6819	Goodbye My Love, Goodbye/Everybody's Got to Clap	1971	—	3.00	6.00
❏ 6885	It Takes a Real Man/You Ain't Wrong, You Just Ain't Right	1972	—	3.00	6.00
CHELSEA					
❏ 78-0121	Make Believe World/Help Me Help You	1973	2.00	4.00	8.00
❏ 3001	The Man Who Sold the World/Watch That Man	1974	7.50	15.00	30.00
—A David Bowie song on the A-side...and produced by Bowie, too					
❏ 3009	The Man with a Golden Gun/Baby I Don't Care	1974	5.00	10.00	20.00
❏ 3011	Take Your Mama for a Ride (Long)/Take Your Mama for a Ride (Short)	1975	2.50	5.00	10.00
❏ 3019	Boy Meets Girl/(B-side unknown)	1975	2.50	5.00	10.00
❏ 3038	Heaven and Earth and the Stars/(B-side unknown)	1976	5.00	10.00	20.00
EPIC					
❏ 10187	To Sir with Love/The Boat That I Row	1967	2.50	5.00	10.00
❏ 10210	Dreamy Nights and Days/Let's Pretend	1967	2.00	4.00	8.00
❏ 10260	Best of Both Worlds/Love Loves to Love Love	1967	2.00	4.00	8.00
❏ 10260 [PS]	Best of Both Worlds/Love Loves to Love Love	1967	5.00	10.00	20.00
❏ 10260/65 [DJ]	Best of Both Worlds/Everybody Knows	1968	6.25	12.50	25.00
—B-side by the Dave Clark Five; odd promo					
❏ 10302	Me, the Peaceful Heart/Look Out	1968	2.00	4.00	8.00
❏ 10302 [PS]	Me, the Peaceful Heart/Look Out	1968	5.00	10.00	20.00
❏ 10346	Sad Memories/Boy	1968	2.00	4.00	8.00
❏ 10367	Morning Dew/You and I	1968	2.00	4.00	8.00
❏ 10403	Without Him/This Time	1968	2.00	4.00	8.00
❏ 10420	Rattler/I'm a Tiger	1968	2.00	4.00	8.00
PARROT					
❏ 9678	Shout/Forget Me Baby	1964	5.00	10.00	20.00
❏ 9714	Here Comes the Night/I'll Come Running	1964	5.00	10.00	20.00
❏ 9778	Leave a Little Love/He Don't Want Your Love Anymore	1965	5.00	10.00	20.00
❏ 9791	Try to Understand/Not in This Whole World	1965	5.00	10.00	20.00
❏ 40021	Shout/When He Touches Me	1967	2.50	5.00	10.00
ROCKET					
❏ YB-11355	Don't Take Love for Granted/Love Is the Sweetest Mistake	1978	—	2.50	5.00

7-Inch Extended Plays

EPIC

Number	Title (A Side/B Side)	Yr	VG	VG+	NM
❏ 5-26339 [DJ]	To Sir With Love/Morning Dew/Love Loves to Love Love//Best of Both Worlds/Day Tripper/Take Me in Your Arms (And Love Me)	1967	3.75	7.50	15.00
—Jukebox mini-LP, small hole, plays at 33 1/3 rpm					
❏ 5-26339 [PS]	To Sir with Love	1967	3.75	7.50	15.00

Albums

ALFA

Number	Title	Yr	VG	VG+	NM
❏ 10006	Lulu	1981	3.00	6.00	12.00
ATCO					
❏ 33-310 [M]	New Routes	1970	7.50	15.00	30.00
—White label promo; no stock copies were issued in mono					
❏ SD 33-310 [S]	New Routes	1970	3.00	6.00	12.00
❏ 33-330 [M]	Melody Fair	1970	7.50	15.00	30.00
—White label promo, "DJ Copy Monaural" on cover; no stock copies were issued in mono					
❏ SD 33-330 [S]	Melody Fair	1970	3.00	6.00	12.00
CHELSEA					
❏ BCL1-0144	Lulu	1973	3.00	6.00	12.00
❏ CHL-518	Heaven and Earth and the Stars	1976	5.00	10.00	20.00
EPIC					
❏ LN 24339 [M]	To Sir with Love	1967	6.25	12.50	25.00
❏ BN 26339 [P]	To Sir with Love	1967	7.50	15.00	30.00
❏ BN 26536	It's Lulu	1970	3.00	6.00	12.00
HARMONY					
❏ H 30249	To Love Somebody	1970	5.00	10.00	20.00
PARROT					
❏ PA 61016 [M]	From Lulu with Love	1967	15.00	30.00	60.00
❏ PAS 71016 [S]	From Lulu with Love	1967	20.00	40.00	80.00
PICKWICK					
❏ SPC-3237	Lulu	1973	2.00	4.00	8.00
ROCKET					
❏ BXL1-3073	Don't Take Love for Granted	1978	3.00	6.00	12.00

LUMAN, BOB

45s

CAPITOL

Number	Title (A Side/B Side)	Yr	VG	VG+	NM
❏ F3972	Try Me/I Know My Baby Cares	1958	7.50	15.00	30.00
❏ F4059	Precious/Svengali	1958	7.50	15.00	30.00
EPIC					
❏ 10312	Ain't Got Time to Be Unhappy/I Can't Remember to Forget	1968	—	3.00	6.00
❏ 10381	I Like Trains/A World of Unhappiness	1968	—	3.00	6.00
❏ 10416	I'm In This Town for Good/A Woman Without Love	1968	—	3.00	6.00
❏ 10439	Come On Home and Sing the Blues to Daddy/Big, Big World	1969	—	3.00	6.00
❏ 10480	Every Day I Have to Cry Some/Livin' in a House Full of Love	1969	—	3.00	6.00
❏ 10535	The Gun/Cleanin' Up the Streets of Memphis	1969	—	3.00	6.00
❏ 10581	Gettin' Back to Norma/Maybelline	1970	—	3.00	6.00
❏ 10631	Honky Tonk Man/I Ain't Built That Way	1970	—	3.00	6.00
❏ 10667	What About the Hurt/The Time to Remember	1970	—	3.00	6.00
❏ 10699	Is It Any Wonder That I Love You?/Give Us One More Chance	1971	—	2.50	5.00
❏ 10755	I Got a Woman/One Hundred Songs on the Jukebox	1971	—	2.50	5.00
❏ 10786	A Chain Don't Take to Me/Don't Let Love Pass You By	1971	—	2.50	5.00
❏ 10823	When You Say Love/Have a Little Faith	1972	—	2.50	5.00
❏ 10869	It Takes You/Let's Think About Livin'	1972	—	2.50	5.00

Number	Title (A Side/B Side)	Yr	VG	VG+	NM
❏ 10905	Lonely Women Make Good Lovers/Love Ought to Be a Happy Thing	1972	—	2.50	5.00
❏ 10943	Neither One of Us/Anything But Lonesome	1973	—	2.00	4.00
❏ 10994	A Good Love Is Like a Good Song/Have I Ever Said "I Love You" to a Lady	1973	—	2.00	4.00
❏ 11039	Still Loving You/I'm Gonna Write a Song	1973	—	2.00	4.00
❏ 11087	Just Enough to Make Me Stay/Baby Make It Good	1974	—	2.00	4.00
❏ 11138	Let Me Make the Bright Lights Shine for You/The Closest Thing to Heaven That I Love	1974	—	2.00	4.00
❏ 50065	Proud of You Baby/Tonight Your Baby's Coming Home	1975	—	2.00	4.00
❏ 50136	Shame on Me/How Do You Start Over	1975	—	2.00	4.00
❏ 50183	A Satisfied Mind/Cleanin' Up the Streets of Memphis	1975	—	2.00	4.00
❏ 50216	The Man from Bowling Green/It's Only Make Believe	1976	—	2.00	4.00
❏ 50247	How Do You Start Over/Red Cadillac and Black Mustache	1976	—	2.00	4.00
❏ 50297	Labor of Love/Blond Haired Woman	1976	—	2.00	4.00
❏ 50323	He's Got a Way with Women/Here We Are Making Love Again	1976	—	2.00	4.00
HICKORY					
❏ 1201	You're Welcome/Interstate 40	1963	3.00	6.00	12.00
❏ 1219	Can't Take the Country from the Boy/I'm Gonna Write a Song of Love	1963	3.00	6.00	12.00
❏ 1221	Too Hot to Dance/I Like Your Kind of Love	1963	3.00	6.00	12.00
—With Sue Thompson					
❏ 1238	The File/Bigger Men Than I (Have Cried)	1964	3.00	6.00	12.00
❏ 1266	Lonely Room (Empty Walls)/Run On Home Baby Brother	1964	3.00	6.00	12.00
❏ 1277	Fire Engine Red/Old George Dickel	1964	3.00	6.00	12.00
❏ 1289	Bad, Bad Day/Tears from Out of Nowhere	1965	2.50	5.00	10.00
❏ 1307	Jealous Heart/Go On Home Boy	1965	2.50	5.00	10.00
❏ 1333	I Love You Because/Love Worked a Miracle	1965	2.50	5.00	10.00
❏ 1355	Five Miles from Home (Soon I'll See Mary)/(I Get So) Sentimental	1965	2.50	5.00	10.00
❏ 1382	Poor Boy Blues/(Can't Get You) Off My Mind	1966	2.50	5.00	10.00
❏ 1410	Come On and Sing/It's a Sin	1966	2.50	5.00	10.00
❏ 1430	Hardly Anymore/Freedom of Living	1967	2.00	4.00	8.00
❏ 1460	If You Don't Love Me (Then Why Don't You Leave Me Alone)/Throwin' Kisses	1967	2.00	4.00	8.00
❏ 1481	Running Scared/The Best Years of My Wife	1967	2.00	4.00	8.00
❏ 1536	It's All Over (But the Shouting)/Still Loving You	1969	—	3.00	6.00
❏ 1564	Still Loving You/Meet Mr. Mud	1970	—	3.00	6.00
IMPERIAL					
❏ 5705	A Red Cadillac and a Black Moustache/All Night Long	1960	6.25	12.50	25.00
❏ 8311	A Red Cadillac and a Black Moustache/All Night Long	1957	20.00	40.00	80.00
❏ 8313	Red Hot/Whenever You're Ready	1957	20.00	40.00	80.00
❏ 8315	Make Up Your Mind, Baby/Your Love	1958	15.00	30.00	60.00
—The same coupling was slated for Imperial 8314 but not released.					
POLYDOR					
❏ 14408	I'm a Honky-Tonk Woman's Man/Lonely Women Make Good Lovers	1977	—	2.00	4.00
❏ 14431	The Pay Phone/He'll Be the One	1977	—	2.00	4.00
❏ 14444	A Christmas Tribute/Give Someone You Love (A Little Bit of Love This Year)	1977	—	2.00	4.00
❏ 14454	Proud Lady/Let Me Love Him Out of You	1978	—	2.00	4.00
ROLLIN' ROCK					
❏ 028	Stranger Than Fiction/You're the Cause of It All	1978	—	2.00	4.00
WARNER BROS.					
❏ 5081	My Baby Walks All Over Me/Class of '59	1959	6.25	12.50	25.00
❏ 5105	Dreamy Doll/Buttercup	1959	6.25	12.50	25.00
❏ 5105 [PS]	Dreamy Doll/Buttercup	1959	15.00	30.00	60.00
❏ 5172	Let's Think About Living/You've Got Everything	1960	5.00	10.00	20.00
❏ 5172 [PS]	Let's Think About Living/You've Got Everything	1960	10.00	20.00	40.00
❏ 5184	Why, Why, Bye, Bye/Oh Lonesome Me	1960	5.00	10.00	20.00
❏ 5184 [PS]	Why, Why, Bye, Bye/Oh Lonesome Me	1960	10.00	20.00	40.00
❏ 5204	The Great Snow Man/The Pig Latin Song	1961	5.00	10.00	20.00
❏ 5204 [PS]	The Great Snow Man/The Pig Latin Song	1961	10.00	20.00	40.00
❏ 5233	Private Eyes/You've Turned Down the Lights	1961	5.00	10.00	20.00
❏ 5233 [PS]	Private Eyes/You've Turned Down the Lights	1961	10.00	20.00	40.00
❏ 5255	Louisiana Man/Rocks of Reno	1962	5.00	10.00	20.00
❏ 5272	Big River Rose/Belonging to You	1962	5.00	10.00	20.00
❏ 5299	Hey Joe/The Fool	1962	5.00	10.00	20.00
❏ 5321	You're Everything/Envy	1962	5.00	10.00	20.00
❏ 5506	Boston Rocker/Old Friends//Bad Bad Day/Let's Think About Living	1960	25.00	50.00	100.00
—Part of Warner Bros. "+2" series, with two new songs and excerpts of two prior hits					
❏ 5506 [PS]	Boston Rocker/Old Friends//Bad Bad Day/Let's Think About Living	1960	25.00	50.00	100.00

Albums

EPIC

Number	Title	Yr	VG	VG+	NM
❏ BN 26393	Ain't Got Time to Be Unhappy	1968	5.00	10.00	20.00
❏ BN 26463	Come On Home and Sing the Blues	1969	5.00	10.00	20.00
❏ BN 26541	Gettin' Back	1970	5.00	10.00	20.00
❏ E 30617	Is It Any Wonder	1971	5.00	10.00	20.00
❏ E 30923	Chain Don't Take to Me	1972	5.00	10.00	20.00
❏ KE 31375	When You Say Love	1972	5.00	10.00	20.00
❏ KE 31746	Lonely Women Make Good Lovers	1972	5.00	10.00	20.00
❏ KE 32192	Neither One of Us	1973	3.75	7.50	15.00
❏ KE 32759	Bob Luman's Greatest Hits	1974	3.75	7.50	15.00
❏ KE 33942	Satisfied Mind	1975	3.00	6.00	12.00
❏ KE 34445	Alive and Well!	1976	3.00	6.00	12.00
HARMONY					
❏ KH 32006	Bob Luman	1973	3.00	6.00	12.00
HICKORY					
❏ LPM-124 [M]	Livin' Lovin' Sounds	1965	6.25	12.50	25.00
❏ LPS-124 [S]	Livin' Lovin' Sounds	1965	7.50	15.00	30.00
HICKORY/MGM					
❏ H3G-4508	Still Loving You	1974	3.75	7.50	15.00
POLYDOR					
❏ PD-1-6135	Bob Luman	1978	3.00	6.00	12.00

L

Number	Title (A Side/B Side)	Yr	VG	VG+	NM
WARNER BROS.					
❑ W 1396 [M]	Let's Think About Livin'	1960	12.50	25.00	50.00
❑ WS 1396 [S]	Let's Think About Livin'	1960	17.50	35.00	70.00
LUMPKIN, HENRY					
45s					
MOTOWN					
❑ 1005	I've Got a Notion/We Really Love Each Other	1961	20.00	40.00	80.00
❑ 1013	What Is a Man/Don't Leave Me	1961	10.00	20.00	40.00
❑ 1029	Mo Jo Hanna/Break Down and Sing	1962	10.00	20.00	40.00
LUND, GARRETT					
Albums					
(NO LABEL)					
❑ (no #)	Almost Grown	1975	75.00	150.00	300.00
LUREX, LARRY See FREDDIE MERCURY.					
LURIE, ELLIOTT Also see LOOKING GLASS.					
45s					
ARISTA					
❑ 0219	Rich Girl/Night Ride Part 2	1976	—	2.00	4.00
EPIC					
❑ 11153	Your Love Song/(B-side unknown)	1974	—	2.00	4.00
❑ 50083	Disco/I Don't Wanna Lose You	1975	—	2.00	4.00
❑ 50101	I Think I'm Fallin'/Rainbow Girl	1975	—	2.00	4.00
Albums					
EPIC					
❑ PE 33337	Elliott Lurie	1975	2.50	5.00	10.00
LUVWORTH, RITCHIE					
45s					
DATE					
❑ 2-1597	Girl of Mine/Hey Baby, Where You Gonna Go	1968	2.50	5.00	10.00
❑ 2-1624	Can You Dig It/Let's Dance	1968	2.50	5.00	10.00
LY-DELLS, THE					
45s					
LOST-NITE					
❑ 116	There Goes the Boy/Talking to Myself	196?	2.00	4.00	8.00
—Reissue					
MASTER					
❑ 111	Genie of the Lamp/Teenage Tears	1961	62.50	125.00	250.00
❑ 251	Wizard of Love/Let This Night Last	1961	15.00	30.00	60.00
PAM					
❑ 103	There Goes the Boy/Talking to Myself	1959	50.00	100.00	200.00
PARKWAY					
❑ 897	There Goes the Boy/Talking to Myself	1964	5.00	10.00	20.00
ROULETTE					
❑ 4493	Karen/Doing the Wiggle Wobble	1963	6.25	12.50	25.00
SCA					
❑ 18001	Book of Songs/Hear That Train	1962	10.00	20.00	40.00
SOUTHERN SOUND					
❑ 122	Three Little Monkeys/Playing Hide and Seek	1965	15.00	30.00	60.00
LYMAN, ARTHUR					
45s					
GNP CRESCENDO					
❑ 315	Shangri-La/Pearly Shells	1964	—	3.00	6.00
❑ 349	Cast Your Fate to the Wind/Night Train	1965	—	3.00	6.00
❑ 497	Skybird/Puka Shells	1975	—	2.00	4.00
HIFI					
❑ 533	76 Trombones/House on a Haunted Hill	1959	2.50	5.00	10.00
❑ 550	Taboo/Dahil Sayo	1959	2.50	5.00	10.00
❑ 564	Bahia/Jungle Jalopy	1959	2.50	5.00	10.00
❑ 591	Legend of the Rain/Vera Cruz	1960	2.50	5.00	10.00
❑ 599	Jungle Fantasy/Koni Au I Ka Wai	1960	2.50	5.00	10.00
❑ 5002	Taboo Tu/Ebb Tide	1960	2.50	5.00	10.00
❑ 5024	Yellow Bird/Havah Nagilah	1961	2.50	5.00	10.00
❑ 5040	(The Sloop) John B/Honolulu Nites	1961	2.50	5.00	10.00
❑ 5047	Never on Sunday/I Talk to the Trees	1961	2.50	5.00	10.00
❑ 5049	Moanin'/Aloha No Honolulu	1962	2.50	5.00	10.00
❑ 5055	Anna/(B-side unknown)	1962	2.50	5.00	10.00
❑ 5057	America (West Side Story)/Planning Rice	1962	2.50	5.00	10.00
❑ 5058	We Three Kings/Little Drummer Boy	1962	3.00	6.00	12.00
❑ 5065	Mutiny on the Bounty/Pagan Love Song	1963	2.00	4.00	8.00
❑ 5066	Love for Sale/Dahil Sayo	1963	2.00	4.00	8.00
❑ 5071	Cottonfields/Limbo Rock	1963	2.00	4.00	8.00
❑ 5076	Sentimental Journey/Jungle Drums	1963	2.00	4.00	8.00
❑ 5078	Blowin' in the Wind/I've Been Workin' on the Railroad	1963	2.00	4.00	8.00
❑ 5079	He's Gone Away/Suzy's Waltz	1963	2.00	4.00	8.00
❑ 5080	Charade/Arthur's Line	1963	2.00	4.00	8.00
❑ 5081	Winter Wonderland/Rudolph, the Red-Nosed Reindeer	1963	3.00	6.00	12.00
❑ 5082	Petticoat Junction/Gently, Gently	1963	3.00	6.00	12.00
❑ 5083	We Three Kings/Little Drummer Boy	1963	3.00	6.00	12.00
❑ 5088	Swingin' Shephard Blues/(B-side unknown)	1964	2.00	4.00	8.00
❑ 5089	Wheel of Fortune/La Montana	1964	2.00	4.00	8.00
❑ 5091	Hello, Dolly/Get Me to the Church On Time	1964	2.00	4.00	8.00
❑ 5092	Taboo/Black Orchid	1965	2.00	4.00	8.00
❑ 5096	Afro Blues/Waltzing Matilda	1965	2.00	4.00	8.00
❑ 5100	Lemon Tree/The Car	1966	2.00	4.00	8.00
❑ 5101	The Shadow of Your Smile/Imua Kamehameha	1966	2.00	4.00	8.00
❑ 5105	The Windmills of Your Mind/Lonely Winds	1969	2.00	4.00	8.00
Albums					
GNP CRESCENDO					
❑ GNP-605 [M]	Exotic Sounds	1963	3.75	7.50	15.00
❑ GNPS-605 [S]	Exotic Sounds	1963	5.00	10.00	20.00
❑ GNP-606 [M]	Paradise	1964	3.75	7.50	15.00
❑ GNPS-606 [S]	Paradise	1964	5.00	10.00	20.00
❑ GNP-607 [M]	Cast Your Fate to the Wind	1965	3.75	7.50	15.00
❑ GNPS-607 [S]	Cast Your Fate to the Wind	1965	5.00	10.00	20.00
❑ GNPS-2091	Puka Shells	1975	2.50	5.00	10.00
HIFI					
❑ R-607 [M]	Leis of Jazz	1958	5.00	10.00	20.00
❑ SR-607 [S]	Leis of Jazz	1958	7.50	15.00	30.00

Number	Title (A Side/B Side)	Yr	VG	VG+	NM
❑ R-806 [M]	Taboo	1958	5.00	10.00	20.00
❑ SR-806 [S]	Taboo	1958	7.50	15.00	30.00
❑ R-807 [M]	Hawaiian Sunset	1959	5.00	10.00	20.00
❑ SR-807 [S]	Hawaiian Sunset	1959	7.50	15.00	30.00
❑ R-808 [M]	Bwan-A	1959	5.00	10.00	20.00
❑ SR-808 [S]	Bwan-A	1959	7.50	15.00	30.00
❑ R-813 [M]	The Legend of Pele	1959	5.00	10.00	20.00
❑ SR-813 [S]	The Legend of Pele	1959	7.50	15.00	30.00
❑ R-815 [M]	Bahia	1959	5.00	10.00	20.00
❑ SR-815 [S]	Bahia	1959	7.50	15.00	30.00
❑ R-818 [M]	Arthur Lyman On Broadway	1960	5.00	10.00	20.00
❑ SR-818 [S]	Arthur Lyman On Broadway	1960	7.50	15.00	30.00
❑ R-822 [M]	Taboo (Volume 2)	1960	5.00	10.00	20.00
❑ SR-822 [S]	Taboo (Volume 2)	1960	7.50	15.00	30.00
LIFE					
❑ L 1004 [M]	Yellow Bird	1961	5.00	10.00	20.00
—Reissue with new title reflecting the hit single					
❑ L 1004 [M]	Percussion Spectacular	1961	7.50	15.00	30.00
❑ SL 1004 [S]	Yellow Bird	1961	6.25	12.50	25.00
—Reissue with new title reflecting the hit single					
❑ SL 1004 [S]	Percussion Spectacular	1961	10.00	20.00	40.00
❑ L 1005 [M]	The Colorful Percussions of Arthur Lyman	1962	5.00	10.00	20.00
❑ SL 1005 [S]	The Colorful Percussions of Arthur Lyman	1962	6.25	12.50	25.00
❑ L 1007 [M]	The Many Moods of Arthur Lyman	1962	5.00	10.00	20.00
❑ SL 1007 [S]	The Many Moods of Arthur Lyman	1962	6.25	12.50	25.00
❑ L 1009 [M]	I Wish You Love	1963	5.00	10.00	20.00
❑ L 1009 [M]	Love for Sale!	1963	6.25	12.50	25.00
—Alternate title					
❑ SL 1009 [S]	I Wish You Love	1963	6.25	12.50	25.00
❑ SL 1009 [S]	Love for Sale!	1963	7.50	15.00	30.00
—Alternate title					
❑ L 1010 [M]	Cotton Fields	1963	5.00	10.00	20.00
❑ SL 1010 [S]	Cotton Fields	1963	6.25	12.50	25.00
❑ L 1014 [M]	Blowin' in the Wind	1963	5.00	10.00	20.00
❑ SL 1014 [S]	Blowin' in the Wind	1963	6.25	12.50	25.00
❑ L 1018 [M]	Mele Kalikimaka (Merry Christmas)	1963	5.00	10.00	20.00
❑ SL 1018 [S]	Mele Kalikimaka (Merry Christmas)	1963	6.25	12.50	25.00
❑ L 1023 [M]	Isle of Enchantment	1964	5.00	10.00	20.00
❑ SL 1023 [S]	Isle of Enchantment	1964	6.25	12.50	25.00
❑ L 1024 [M]	Call of the Midnight Sun	1964	5.00	10.00	20.00
❑ SL 1024 [S]	Call of the Midnight Sun	1964	6.25	12.50	25.00
❑ L 1025 [M]	Hawaiian Sunset, Volume 2	1965	3.75	7.50	15.00
❑ SL 1025 [S]	Hawaiian Sunset, Volume 2	1965	5.00	10.00	20.00
❑ L 1027 [M]	Polynesia	1965	3.75	7.50	15.00
❑ SL 1027 [S]	Polynesia	1965	5.00	10.00	20.00
❑ L 1030 [M]	Greatest Hits	1965	3.00	6.00	12.00
❑ SL 1030 [S]	Greatest Hits	1965	3.75	7.50	15.00
❑ L 1031 [M]	Lyman '66	1965	3.75	7.50	15.00
❑ SL 1031 [S]	Lyman '66	1965	5.00	10.00	20.00
❑ L 1033 [M]	The Shadow of Your Smile	1966	3.75	7.50	15.00
❑ SL 1033 [S]	The Shadow of Your Smile	1966	5.00	10.00	20.00
❑ L 1034 [M]	Aloha, Amigo	1966	3.75	7.50	15.00
❑ SL 1034 [S]	Aloha, Amigo	1966	5.00	10.00	20.00
❑ L 1035 [M]	Ilikai	1967	3.75	7.50	15.00
❑ SL 1035 [S]	Ilikai	1967	5.00	10.00	20.00
❑ L 1036 [M]	Arthur Lyman at the Port of L.A.	1967	3.75	7.50	15.00
❑ SL 1036 [S]	Arthur Lyman at the Port of L.A.	1967	5.00	10.00	20.00
❑ SL 1037	Latitude 20	1968	3.75	7.50	15.00
❑ SL 1038	Aphrodisia	1968	3.75	7.50	15.00
❑ SL 1039	Winner's Circle	1969	3.75	7.50	15.00
❑ SL 1040	Today's Greatest Hits	1970	3.75	7.50	15.00
LYMAN, JONI					
45s					
REPRISE					
❑ 0378	Happy Birthday Blue/I Just Don't Know What to Do with Myself	1965	10.00	20.00	40.00
LYMON, FRANKIE Also see FRANKIE LYMON AND THE TEENAGERS.					
45s					
BIG KAT					
❑ 7008	I Want You to Be My Girl/Portable on My Shoulder	1968	2.50	5.00	10.00
❑ 7008 [PS]	I Want You to Be My Girl/Portable on My Shoulder	1968	3.00	6.00	12.00
COLUMBIA					
❑ 43094	Somewhere/Sweet and Lovely	1964	12.50	25.00	50.00
GEE					
❑ 1039	Goody Goody/Creation of Love	1957	6.25	12.50	25.00
❑ 1052	I'm Not Too Young to Dream/Goody Good Girl	1959	6.25	12.50	25.00
ROULETTE					
❑ 4026	So Goes My Love/My Girl	1957	6.25	12.50	25.00
❑ 4035	It's Christmas Once Again/Little Girl	1957	6.25	12.50	25.00
❑ 4044	Footsteps/Thumb Thumb	1958	5.00	10.00	20.00
❑ 4068	Mama Don't Allow It/Portable on My Shoulder	1958	5.00	10.00	20.00
❑ 4093	Melinda/The Only Way to Love	1958	5.00	10.00	20.00
❑ 4128	No Matter What You've Done/Up Jumped a Rabbit	1959	5.00	10.00	20.00
❑ 4150	Before I Fall Asleep/What a Little Moonlight Can Do	1959	5.00	10.00	20.00
❑ 4257	Little Bitty Pretty One/Creation of Love	1960	5.00	10.00	20.00
❑ 4283	Buzz, Buzz, Buzz/Waitin' in School	1960	5.00	10.00	20.00
❑ 4310	Jailhouse Rock/Silhouettes	1961	5.00	10.00	20.00
❑ 4348	Change Partners/So Young	1961	5.00	10.00	20.00
❑ 4391	I Put the Bomp/So Young	1962	5.00	10.00	20.00
TCF					
❑ 11	Teacher Teacher/To Each His Own	1964	3.75	7.50	15.00
7-Inch Extended Plays					
ROULETTE					
❑ EPR-1-304	Let's Fall in Love/My Baby Just Cares for Me//Goody Goody/Somebody Loves Me	1958	50.00	100.00	200.00
❑ EPR-1-304 [PS]	Frankie Lymon at the London Palladium	1958	50.00	100.00	200.00
Albums					
GUEST STAR					
❑ GS-1406 [M]	Teen Time Tunes Starring Frankie Lymon	1959	10.00	20.00	40.00
—Various-artists compilation; color cover					

Number	Title (A Side/B Side)	Yr	VG	VG+	NM
GS-1406 [M]	Rock & Roll Party Starring Frankie Lymon	196?	6.25	12.50	25.00

—Various-artists compilation; retitled, black and white cover

ROULETTE

Number	Title (A Side/B Side)	Yr	VG	VG+	NM
R-25013 [M]	Frankie Lymon at the London Palladium	1958	75.00	150.00	300.00
R-25036 [M]	Rock 'N' Roll	1958	75.00	150.00	300.00
R-25250 [M]	Frankie Lymon's Greatest	1964	7.50	15.00	30.00
SR-25250 [R]	Frankie Lymon's Greatest	1964	6.25	12.50	25.00

LYMON, FRANKIE, AND THE TEENAGERS Also see FRANKIE LYMON; THE TEENAGERS.

45s

GEE

Number	Title (A Side/B Side)	Yr	VG	VG+	NM
1002	Why Do Fools Fall in Love/Please Be Mine	1956	7.50	15.00	30.00

—Red and black label; vocal solo on B-side. All of the above credit "The Teenagers featuring Frankie Lymon"

1002	Why Do Fools Fall in Love/Please Be Mine	1956	12.50	25.00	50.00

—Red and black label; vocal duet on B-side

1002	Why Do Fools Fall in Love/Please Be Mine	1956	20.00	40.00	80.00

—Red and gold label

1002	Why Do Fools Fall in Love/My Girl	1958	6.25	12.50	25.00

—White label, "Gee Records" at top; note different B-side

1002	Why Do Fools Fall in Love/Please Be Mine	1959	3.75	7.50	15.00

—Gray label, "Gee Records" at bottom; label credit is "The Teenagers featuring Frankie Lymon"

1012	I Want You to Be My Girl/I'm Not a Know-It-All	1956	7.50	15.00	30.00

—As "Frankie Lymon and the Teenagers"

1012	I Want You to Be My Girl/I'm Not a Know-It-All	1956	12.50	25.00	50.00

—As "The Teenagers featuring Frankie Lymon"

1018	I Promise to Remember/Who Can Explain	1956	7.50	15.00	30.00
1022	The ABC's of Love/Share	1956	7.50	15.00	30.00
1026	I'm Not a Juvenile Delinquent/Baby Baby	1957	7.50	15.00	30.00
1032	Teenage Love/Paper Castles	1957	7.50	15.00	30.00
1035	Am I Fooling Myself Again/Love Is a Clown	197?	—	—	—

—Evidently a 1970s bootleg to fill in a gap in the Gee Records discography

1036	Miracle of Love/Out in the Cold Again	1957	7.50	15.00	30.00
1039	Goody Goody/Creation of Love	1957	10.00	20.00	40.00

—Actually a Frankie Lymon solo recording; the first pressing credited the entire group

7-Inch Extended Plays

GEE

Number	Title (A Side/B Side)	Yr	VG	VG+	NM
GEP-601	Teenage Love/Why Do Fools Fall in Love//I Want You to Be My Girl/Love Is a Clown	1956	37.50	75.00	150.00
GEP-601 [PS]	The Teenagers Go Rock'n	1956	50.00	100.00	200.00
GEP-602	Paper Castles/Share//Am I Fooling Myself Again/I'm Not a Know-It-All	1957	50.00	100.00	200.00
GEP-602 [PS]	The Teenagers Go Romantic	1957	50.00	100.00	200.00

Albums

ACCORD

Number	Title (A Side/B Side)	Yr	VG	VG+	NM
SN-7203	Why Do Fools Fall in Love	1982	2.50	5.00	10.00

GEE

GLP-701 [M]	The Teenagers Featuring Frankie Lymon	1956	125.00	250.00	500.00

—Red label

GLP-701 [M]	The Teenagers Featuring Frankie Lymon	1961	37.50	75.00	150.00

—Gray label

GLP-701 [M]	The Teenagers Featuring Frankie Lymon	197?	3.00	6.00	12.00

—White label on thinner vinyl

MURRAY HILL

148 [(5)]	Frankie Lymon and the Teenagers	198?	17.50	35.00	70.00

RHINO

R1-70918	The Best of Frankie Lymon and the Teenagers	1989	3.00	6.00	12.00

LYMON, LEWIS, AND THE TEENCHORDS

45s

END

Number	Title (A Side/B Side)	Yr	VG	VG+	NM
1003	Too Young/Your Last Chance	1957	25.00	50.00	100.00
1007	I Found Out Why/Tell Me Love	1958	20.00	40.00	80.00
1113	Too Young/Your Last Chance	1962	5.00	10.00	20.00

FURY

1000	I'm So Happy (Tra-La-La-La-La-La)/Lydia	1957	50.00	100.00	200.00

—Maroon label

1000	I'm So Happy (Tra-La-La-La-La-La)/Lydia	1958	10.00	20.00	40.00

—Yellow label

1003	Honey, Honey (You Don't Know)/Please Tell the Angels	1957	20.00	40.00	80.00
1006	I'm Not Too Young to Fall in Love/Falling in Love	1957	20.00	40.00	80.00

JUANITA

101	Dance Girl/Them There Eyes	1958	12.50	25.00	50.00

LOST-NITE

357	I'm So Happy (Tra-La-La-La-La-La)/Lydia	197?	—	2.50	5.00

—Reissue

360	Honey, Honey (You Don't Know)/Please Tell the Angels	197?	—	2.50	5.00

—Reissue

364	I'm Not Too Young to Fall in Love/Falling in Love	197?	—	2.50	5.00

—Reissue

Albums

COLLECTABLES

COL-5049	Lewis Lymon and the Teenchords Meet the Kodaks	198?	2.50	5.00	10.00

LOST-NITE

LLP-13 [10]	Lewis Lymon and the Teenchords	1981	2.50	5.00	10.00

—Red vinyl

LYNCH, KENNY

45s

ARLEN

Number	Title (A Side/B Side)	Yr	VG	VG+	NM
750	Make It Easy on Yourself/Monument	1964	3.00	6.00	12.00

BIG TOP

3140	Poof (Up in Smoke)/Happy That's Me	1963	3.00	6.00	12.00

IMPERIAL

66088	So Much to Love You For/My Own Two Feet	1964	3.00	6.00	12.00

LIBERTY

55740	That's What Girls Are Made For/What Am I to You	1964	3.00	6.00	12.00
55811	For Lovin' You Baby/I'll Stay By You	1965	2.50	5.00	10.00

WHITE WHALE

307	Along Comes Love/Sweet Situation	1969	—	3.00	6.00

LYNN, BARBARA

45s

ATLANTIC

Number	Title (A Side/B Side)	Yr	VG	VG+	NM
2450	This Is the Thanks I Get/Ring, Telephone, Ring	1967	2.00	4.00	8.00
2513	Why Can't You Love Me/You're Losing Me	1968	2.00	4.00	8.00
2553	Love Ain't Never Hurt Nobody/You're Gonna See a Lot More	1968	2.00	4.00	8.00
2585	People Like Me/He Ain't Gonna Do Right	1968	2.00	4.00	8.00
2812	(Until Then) I'll Suffer/Take Your Love and Run	1971	—	3.00	6.00
2853	Nice and Easy/I'm a One Woman Man	1972	—	3.00	6.00
2880	(Daddy Hotstuff) You're Too Hot to Hold/You Better Quit It	1972	—	3.00	6.00
2931	You Make Me So Hot/It Ain't No Good to Be Too Good	1973	—	3.00	6.00

JAMIE

1220	You'll Lose a Good Thing/Lonely Heartache	1962	5.00	10.00	20.00
1233	Second Fiddle Girl/Letter to Mommy and Daddy	1962	3.00	6.00	12.00
1240	You're Gonna Need Me/I'm Sorry I Met You	1962	3.00	6.00	12.00
1244	Don't Be Cruel/You Can't Be Satisfied	1963	3.00	6.00	12.00
1251	To Love or Not to Love/Promises	1963	3.00	6.00	12.00
1260	(I Cried at) Laura's Wedding/You Better Stop	1963	3.00	6.00	12.00
1265	Everybody Loves Somebody/Dedicate the Blues to Me	1963	3.00	6.00	12.00
1269	Money/Jealous Love	1964	3.00	6.00	12.00
1277	Oh! Baby (We Got a Good Thing Goin')/Unfair	1964	3.00	6.00	12.00
1286	Don't Spread It Around/Let Her Knock Herself Out	1964	3.00	6.00	12.00
1292	It's Better to Have It/People Gonna Talk	1964	3.00	6.00	12.00
1295	(Don't Pretend) Just Lay It on the Line/Careless Hands	1965	2.00	4.00	8.00

—With Lee Maye

1297	Keep On Pushing Your Luck/I've Taken All I'm Gonna Take	1965	2.00	4.00	8.00
1301	Can't Buy Me Love/That's What Friends Are For	1965	2.00	4.00	8.00
1304	All I Need Is Your Love/You're Gonna Be Sorry	1965	2.00	4.00	8.00

TRIBE

8316	Running Back/I'm a Good Woman	1966	2.00	4.00	8.00
8319	You Left the Water Running/Until I'm Free	1966	2.00	4.00	8.00
8322	Watch the One That Brings Bad News/AUB A-Go-Go	1967	2.00	4.00	8.00
8324	I Don't Want a Playboy/New Kind of Love	1967	2.00	4.00	8.00

Albums

ATLANTIC

8171 [M]	Here Is Barbara Lynn	1968	12.50	25.00	50.00
SD 8171 [S]	Here Is Barbara Lynn	1968	10.00	20.00	40.00

JAMIE

JLP-3023 [M]	You'll Lose a Good Thing	1962	12.50	25.00	50.00
JLPS-3023 [R]	You'll Lose a Good Thing	1962	12.50	25.00	50.00
JLP-3026 [M]	Sister of Soul	1964	—	—	—

—Canceled

JLPS-3026 [S]	Sister of Soul	1964	—	—	—

—Canceled

LYNN, DONNA

45s

CAPITOL

Number	Title (A Side/B Side)	Yr	VG	VG+	NM
5087	Ronnie/That's Me, I'm the Brother	1963	3.75	7.50	15.00
5127	My Boyfriend Got a Beatle Haircut/That Winter Weekend	1964	5.00	10.00	20.00
5156	Java Jones/Things That I Feel	1964	3.75	7.50	15.00
5213	Silly Girl/There Goes the Boy I Love with Mary	1964	3.75	7.50	15.00
5378	I'd Much Rather Be with the Girls/I'm Sorry More Than You Know	1965	3.00	6.00	12.00
5456	True Blue/When Your Heart Rings, Answer	1965	3.00	6.00	12.00

EPIC

9580	Donna Loves Jerry/Oh, I'm in Love (With George Maharis)	1963	2.00	4.00	8.00

—The B-side is the full title of the song -- George Maharis does NOT appear on this record!

PALMER

5016	Don't You Dare/I Was Raining	1967	6.25	12.50	25.00

Albums

CAPITOL

ST 2085 [S]	Java Jones/My Boyfriend Got a Beatle Haircut	1964	7.50	15.00	30.00
T 2085 [M]	Java Jones/My Boyfriend Got a Beatle Haircut	1964	5.00	10.00	20.00

LYNN, LORETTA Also see DOLLY PARTON; ERNEST TUBB AND LORETTA LYNN; CONWAY TWITTY AND LORETTA LYNN.

45s

DECCA

Number	Title (A Side/B Side)	Yr	VG	VG+	NM
31323	The Girl That I Am Now/I Walked Away from the Wreck	1961	3.75	7.50	15.00
31384	Success/Hundred Proof Heartache	1962	3.00	6.00	12.00
31435	World of Forgotten People/Get Set for a Heartache	1962	3.75	7.50	15.00
31471	The Other Woman/Who'll Help Me Get Over You	1963	2.50	5.00	10.00
31541	Before I'm Over You/Where Were You	1963	2.50	5.00	10.00
31608	Wine, Women and Song/This Haunted House	1964	2.50	5.00	10.00
31707	Happy Birthday/When Lonely Hits Your Heart	1964	2.50	5.00	10.00
31769	Blue Kentucky Girl/Two Steps Forward	1965	2.50	5.00	10.00
31836	The Home You're Tearin' Down/The Farther You Go	1965	2.50	5.00	10.00
31879	When I Hear My Children Play/Everybody Wants to Go to Heaven	1965	3.00	6.00	12.00
31893	Dear Uncle Sam/Hurtin' for Certain	1966	2.50	5.00	10.00
31966	You Ain't Woman Enough/God Gave Me a Heart to Forgive	1966	2.50	5.00	10.00
32043	It Won't Seem Like Christmas/To Heck with Santa Claus	1966	2.50	5.00	10.00
32043 [PS]	It Won't Seem Like Christmas/To Heck with Santa Claus	1966	3.75	7.50	15.00
32045	Don't Come Home a-Drinkin' (With Lovin' on Your Mind)/A Saint to a Sinner	1966	2.50	5.00	10.00
32127	If You're Not Gone Too Long/A Man I Hardly Know	1967	2.50	5.00	10.00
32184	What Kind of a Girl (Do You Think I Am?)/Bargain Basement Dress	1967	2.50	5.00	10.00

L

Number	Title (A Side/B Side)	Yr	VG	VG+	NM
❏ 32264	Fist City/Slowly Killing Me	1968	2.00	4.00	8.00
❏ 32332	You've Just Stepped In (From Stepping Out on Me)/Taking the Place of My Man	1968	2.00	4.00	8.00
❏ 32392	Your Squaw Is On the Warpath/Let Me Go, You're Hurtin' Me	1968	2.00	4.00	8.00
❏ 32439	Woman of the World (Leave My World Alone)/Sneakin' In	1969	2.00	4.00	8.00
❏ 32513	To Make a Man (Feel Like a Man)/One Little Reason	1969	2.00	4.00	8.00
❏ 32586	Wings Upon Your Horns/Let's Get Back Down to Earth	1969	2.00	4.00	8.00
❏ 32637	I Know How/The End of My World	1970	2.00	4.00	8.00
❏ 32693	You Wanna Give Me a Lift/What's the Bottle Done Today Baby	1970	2.00	4.00	8.00
❏ 32749	Coal Miner's Daughter/Man of the House	1970	2.50	5.00	10.00
❏ 32749 [PS]	Coal Miner's Daughter/Man of the House	1970	3.00	6.00	12.00
❏ 32796	I Wanna Be Free/If I Never Love Again	1971	—	3.50	7.00
❏ 32851	You're Lookin' at Country/When You're Poor	1971	—	3.50	7.00
❏ 32900	One's On the Way/Kinfolks Holler	1971	—	3.50	7.00
—Retitled version of A-side					
❏ 32900	Here in Topeka/Kinfolks Holler	1971	5.00	10.00	20.00
❏ 32974	Here I Am Again/My Kind of Man	1972	—	3.50	7.00
❏ 33039	Rated "X"/'Til the Pain Outwears the Shame	1972	—	3.50	7.00
MCA					
❏ 40058	Love Is the Foundation/What Sundown Does to You	1973	—	2.50	5.00
❏ 40150	Hey Loretta/Turn Me Any Way But Loose	1973	—	2.50	5.00
❏ 40223	They Don't Make 'Em Like My Daddy/Nothin'	1974	—	2.50	5.00
❏ 40283	Trouble in Paradise/We've Already Tasted Love	1974	—	2.50	5.00
❏ 40358	The Pill/Will You Be There	1975	—	2.50	5.00
❏ 40438	Home/You Take Me to Heaven Every Night	1975	—	2.50	5.00
❏ 40484	When the Tingle Becomes a Chill/All I Want from You (Is Away)	1975	—	2.50	5.00
❏ 40541	Red, White and Blue/Sounds of a New Love (Being Born)	1976	—	2.50	5.00
❏ 40607	Somebody Somewhere (Don't Know What He's Missin' Tonight)/Sundown Tavern	1976	—	2.50	5.00
❏ 40679	She's Got You/The Lady That Lived Here Before	1977	—	2.50	5.00
❏ 40747	Why Can't He Be You/I Keep On Putting On	1977	—	2.50	5.00
❏ 40832	Out of My Head and Back in My Bed/Old Rooster	1977	—	2.50	5.00
❏ 40910	Spring Fever/God Bless the Children	1978	—	2.00	4.00
❏ 40954	We've Come a Long Way, Baby/I Can't Feel You Anymore	1978	—	2.00	4.00
❏ 40954 [PS]	We've Come a Long Way, Baby/I Can't Feel You Anymore	1978	—	3.00	6.00
❏ 41021	I Can't Feel You Anymore/True Love Needs to Keep in Touch	1979	—	2.00	4.00
❏ 41129	I've Got a Picture of Us on My Mind/I Don't Feel Like a Movie Tonight	1979	—	2.00	4.00
❏ 41185	Pregnant Again/You're a Cross I Can't Bear	1980	—	2.00	4.00
❏ 41250	Naked in the Rain/I Should Be Over You by Now	1980	—	2.00	4.00
❏ 51015	Cheatin' On a Cheater/Until I Met You	1980	—	2.00	4.00
❏ 51058	Somebody Led Me Away/Everybody's Lookin' for Somebody New	1981	—	2.00	4.00
❏ 51226	I Lie/If I Ain't Got It	1982	—	2.50	5.00
❏ 52005	I Lie/If I Ain't Got It	1982	—	2.00	4.00
❏ 52092	Making Love from Memory/Don't It Feel Good	1982	—	2.00	4.00
❏ 52158	Breakin' It/There's All Kinds of Smoke (In the Barroom)	1983	—	2.00	4.00
❏ 52219	Lyin', Cheatin', Woman Chasin', Honky Tonkin', Whiskey Drinkin' You/Star Light, Star Bright	1983	—	2.00	4.00
❏ 52289	Walking with My Memories/It's Gone	1983	—	2.00	4.00
❏ 52621	Heart Don't Do This to Me/Adam's Rib	1985	—	—	3.00
❏ 52621 [PS]	Heart Don't Do This to Me/Adam's Rib	1985	—	2.00	4.00
❏ 52706	Wouldn't It Be Great/One Man Band	1985	—	—	3.00
❏ 52766	Just a Woman/Take Me in Your Arms (And Hold Me)	1986	—	—	3.00
❏ 53320	Who Was That Stranger/Elsie Banks	1988	—	—	3.00
❏ 53397	Fly Away/Your Used to Be	1988	—	—	3.00
❏ 65034	Shadrack, the Black Reindeer/Let's Put Christ Back in Christmas	1974	—	2.00	4.00
—Black label with rainbow					
❏ 65034	Shadrack, the Black Reindeer/Let's Put Christ Back in Christmas	1980	—	—	3.00
—Blue label with rainbow					
ZERO					
❏ 107	I'm a Honky Tonk Girl/Whispering Sea	1960	125.00	250.00	500.00
❏ 110	New Rainbow/Heartaches Meet Mr. Blues	1960	100.00	200.00	400.00
❏ 112	The Darkest Day/Gonna Pack My Troubles	1961	100.00	200.00	400.00
7-Inch Extended Plays					
DECCA					
❏ ED 2762	The Other Woman/Where Were You//Success/Before I'm Over You	1964	5.00	10.00	20.00
❏ ED 2762 [PS]	The Other Woman	1964	5.00	10.00	20.00
❏ ED 2784	(contents unknown)	1965	5.00	10.00	20.00
❏ ED 2784 [PS]	Wine, Women and Song	1965	5.00	10.00	20.00
❏ ED 2793	(contents unknown)	1965	5.00	10.00	20.00
❏ ED 2793 [PS]	The End of the World	1965	5.00	10.00	20.00
❏ ED 2800	(contents unknown)	1965	5.00	10.00	20.00
❏ ED 2800 [PS]	Songs from the Heart	1965	5.00	10.00	20.00
❏ 7-34333	Blue Kentucky Girl/Night Girl/Farther to Go//The Race Is On/The Beginning of the End/Send Me the Pillow You Dream On	1965	6.25	12.50	25.00
—Jukebox issue; small hole, plays at 33 1/3 rpm					
❏ 7-34333 [PS]	Blue Kentucky Girl	1965	6.25	12.50	25.00
❏ DL 734731	Big Ole Hurt/I'm Dynamite/When I Reach the Bottom//Wings Upon Your Horns/I'll Still Be Missing You/Let's Get Back to Earth	1970	3.00	6.00	12.00
—Jukebox issue; small hole, plays at 33 1/3 rpm					
❏ DL 734731 [PS]	Wings Upon Your Horns	1970	3.00	6.00	12.00
Albums					
DECCA					
❏ DL 4457 [M]	Loretta Lynn Sings	1963	15.00	30.00	60.00
❏ DL 4541 [M]	Before I'm Over You	1964	7.50	15.00	30.00
❏ DL 4620 [M]	Songs from My Heart	1965	7.50	15.00	30.00
❏ DL 4665 [M]	Blue Kentucky Girl	1965	7.50	15.00	30.00
❏ DL 4695 [M]	Hymns	1965	7.50	15.00	30.00

Number	Title (A Side/B Side)	Yr	VG	VG+	NM
❏ DL 4744 [M]	I Like 'Em Country	1966	6.25	12.50	25.00
❏ DL 4783 [M]	You Ain't Woman Enough	1966	6.25	12.50	25.00
❏ DL 4817 [M]	Country Christmas	1966	6.25	12.50	25.00
❏ DL 4842 [M]	Don't Come Home a-Drinkin' (With Lovin' on Your Mind)	1967	7.50	15.00	30.00
❏ DL 4928 [M]	Who Says God Is Dead!	1967	10.00	20.00	40.00
❏ DL 4930 [M]	Singin' with Feelin'	1967	7.50	15.00	30.00
❏ DL 4997 [M]	Fist City	1968	12.50	25.00	50.00
—Mono version appears to exist only as a white label promo					
❏ DL 74457 [S]	Loretta Lynn Sings	1963	20.00	40.00	80.00
❏ DL 74541 [S]	Before I'm Over You	1964	10.00	20.00	40.00
❏ DL 74620 [S]	Songs from My Heart	1965	10.00	20.00	40.00
❏ DL 74665 [S]	Blue Kentucky Girl	1965	10.00	20.00	40.00
❏ DL 74695 [S]	Hymns	1965	10.00	20.00	40.00
❏ DL 74744 [S]	I Like 'Em Country	1966	7.50	15.00	30.00
❏ DL 74783 [S]	You Ain't Woman Enough	1966	7.50	15.00	30.00
❏ DL 74817 [S]	Country Christmas	1966	7.50	15.00	30.00
❏ DL 74842 [S]	Don't Come Home a-Drinkin' (With Lovin' on Your Mind)	1967	6.25	12.50	25.00
❏ DL 74928 [S]	Who Says God Is Dead!	1967	6.25	12.50	25.00
❏ DL 74930 [S]	Singin' with Feelin'	1967	6.25	12.50	25.00
❏ DL 74997 [S]	Fist City	1968	6.25	12.50	25.00
❏ DL 75000	Loretta Lynn's Greatest Hits	1968	6.25	12.50	25.00
❏ DL 75084	Your Squaw Is On the Warpath	1969	6.25	12.50	25.00
—Later editions delete the track "Barney"					
❏ DL 75084	Your Squaw Is On the Warpath	1969	10.00	20.00	40.00
—First editions had a track called "Barney"					
❏ DL 75113	Woman of the World/To Make a Man	1969	6.25	12.50	25.00
❏ DL 75163	Wings Upon Your Horns	1970	6.25	12.50	25.00
❏ DL 75198	Loretta Lynn Writes 'Em and Sings 'Em	1970	6.25	12.50	25.00
❏ DL 75253	Coal Miner's Daughter	1971	5.00	10.00	20.00
❏ DL 75282	I Wanna Be Free	1971	5.00	10.00	20.00
❏ DL 75310	You're Lookin' at Country	1971	5.00	10.00	20.00
❏ DL 75334	One's On the Way	1972	5.00	10.00	20.00
❏ DL 75351	God Bless America Again	1972	5.00	10.00	20.00
❏ DL 75381	Here I Am Again	1972	5.00	10.00	20.00
❏ ST-91604	Loretta Lynn's Greatest Hits	1968	7.50	15.00	30.00
—Capitol Record Club edition					
MCA					
❏ 1	Loretta Lynn's Greatest Hits	1973	3.75	7.50	15.00
—Reissue of Decca 75000					
❏ 5	Hymns	1973	3.75	7.50	15.00
—Reissue of Decca 74695					
❏ 6	You Ain't Woman Enough	1973	3.75	7.50	15.00
—Reissue of Decca 74783					
❏ 7	Who Says God Is Dead!	1973	3.75	7.50	15.00
—Reissue of Decca 74928					
❏ 58	Here I Am Again	1973	3.75	7.50	15.00
—Reissue of Decca 75381					
❏ 113	Don't Come Home a-Drinkin' (With Lovin' on Your Mind)	1973	3.75	7.50	15.00
—Reissue of Decca 74842					
❏ 248	Country Christmas	1973	3.75	7.50	15.00
—First reissue of Decca LP					
❏ 300	Entertainer of the Year — Loretta	1973	3.75	7.50	15.00
❏ 355	Love Is the Foundation	1973	3.75	7.50	15.00
❏ 420	Loretta Lynn's Greatest Hits Vol. II	1974	3.75	7.50	15.00
❏ 444	They Don't Make 'Em Like My Daddy	1974	3.75	7.50	15.00
❏ 471	Back to the Country	1975	3.00	6.00	12.00
❏ 628	When the Tingle Becomes a Chill	198?	2.00	4.00	8.00
—Budget-line reissue					
❏ 630	Somebody Somewhere	198?	2.00	4.00	8.00
—Budget-line reissue					
❏ 721	We've Come a Long Way, Baby	198?	2.00	4.00	8.00
—Budget-line reissue					
❏ 735	Alone with You	198?	2.50	5.00	10.00
❏ L33-1934 [DJ]	Loretta Lynn	1974	10.00	20.00	40.00
—Promo-only compilation					
❏ 2146	Home	1975	3.00	6.00	12.00
❏ 2179	When the Tingle Becomes a Chill	1976	3.00	6.00	12.00
❏ 2228	Somebody Somewhere	1976	3.00	6.00	12.00
❏ 2265	I Remember Patsy	1977	3.00	6.00	12.00
❏ 2330	Out of My Head and Back in My Bed	1978	3.00	6.00	12.00
❏ 2341	Loretta Lynn's Greatest Hits	1978	3.00	6.00	12.00
—Reissue of MCA 1					
❏ 2342	Coal Miner's Daughter	1978	3.00	6.00	12.00
—Reissue					
❏ 2353	Loretta Lynn's Greatest Hits Vol. II	1978	3.00	6.00	12.00
—Reissue of MCA 420					
❏ 3073	We've Come a Long Way, Baby	1979	3.00	6.00	12.00
❏ 3217	Loretta	1980	2.50	5.00	10.00
❏ 5148	Lookin' Good	1980	2.50	5.00	10.00
❏ 5293	I Lie	1982	2.50	5.00	10.00
❏ 5426	Lyin', Cheatin', Woman Chasin', Honky Tonkin', Whiskey Drinkin' You	1983	2.50	5.00	10.00
❏ 5613	Just a Woman	1985	2.50	5.00	10.00
❏ 15022	Country Christmas	1974	3.00	6.00	12.00
—Second reissue of Decca LP; black rainbow label					
❏ 15022	Country Christmas	1980	2.50	5.00	10.00
—Blue rainbow label					
❏ 15032	Christmas Without Daddy	198?	3.00	6.00	12.00
❏ 35013	Allis-Chalmers Presents Loretta Lynn	1978	10.00	20.00	40.00
—Special products compilation					
❏ 35018	Crisco Presents Loretta Lynn's Country Classics	1979	10.00	20.00	40.00
—Special products compilation					
❏ 37080	I Remember Patsy Cline	198?	2.00	4.00	8.00
—Budget-line reissue					
❏ 37165	Loretta	198?	2.00	4.00	8.00
—Budget-line reissue					
❏ 37205	Loretta Lynn's Greatest Hits Vol. II	198?	2.00	4.00	8.00
—Budget-line reissue					
❏ 37235	Loretta Lynn's Greatest Hits	198?	2.00	4.00	8.00
—Budget-line reissue					
❏ 37236	Coal Miner's Daughter	198?	2.00	4.00	8.00
—Budget-line reissue					
❏ 42174	Who Was That Stranger	1988	2.50	5.00	10.00

Little Richard, *The Specialty Sessions*, Specialty SP-8508, 5-LP boxed set, $20-$40.

The Lovin' Spoonful, "Six O'Clock," Kama Sutra 225, picture sleeve, $7.50-$15.

Robin Luke, "Susie Darlin'," International 206, picture sleeve, $50-$100.

Lulu, *Melody Fair*, Atco 33-330, mono LP, white label promo only with "dj copy monaural" sticker on cover, $15-$30.

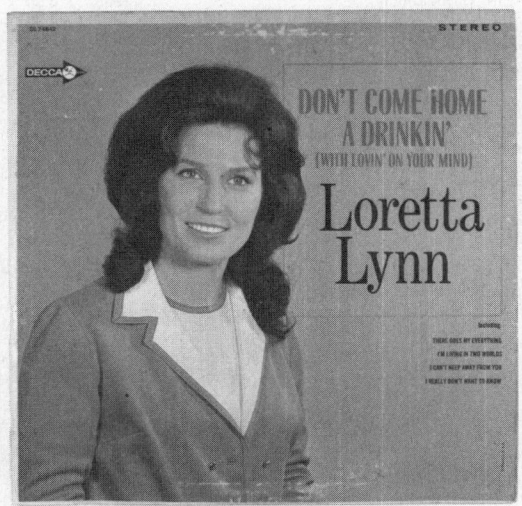

Loretta Lynn, *Don't Come Home a Drinkin' (With Lovin' on Your Mind)*, Decca DL 74842, stereo LP, $12.50-$25.

Lynyrd Skynyrd, *Street Survivors*, MCA 3029, stereo LP, with band's photo in flames, $12.50-$25.

Number	Title (A Side/B Side)	Yr	VG	VG+	NM

VOCALION
❏ VL 73853　Here's Loretta Lynn　1968　3.75　7.50　15.00

LYNN, LORETTA, AND ERNEST TUBB See ERNEST TUBB AND LORETTA LYNN.

LYNN, LORETTA, AND CONWAY TWITTY See CONWAY TWITTY AND LORETTA LYNN.

LYNN, SANDRA
45s
CONSTELLATION
❏ 140　Where Would I Be/Sometime　1964　3.00　6.00　12.00

LYNNE, GLORIA
45s
ABC IMPULSE!
❏ 31003　Out of This World/Thank You Early Bird　1976　—　2.00　4.00
CANYON
❏ 36　Love's Finally Found Me/If You Don't Get It Yourself　1970　—　2.50　5.00
EVEREST
❏ 2023　I'll Buy You a Star/Record Company Blues　1963　2.00　4.00　8.00
❏ 2030　Stormy Monday Blues/Humming Blues　1963　2.00　4.00　8.00
❏ 2036　I Wish You Love/Through a Long and Sleepless Night　1963　2.00　4.00　8.00
❏ 2042　I Should Care/Indian Love Call　1964　2.00　4.00　8.00
❏ 2044　Don't Take Your Love from Me/You Don't Know What Love Is　1964　2.00　4.00　8.00
❏ 2047　Serenade in Blue/Without a Song　1964　2.00　4.00　8.00
❏ 2051　On Christmas Day/Wouldn't It Be Loverly　1964　2.00　4.00　8.00
❏ 2055　Fly Me to the Moon/The Night Has a Thousand Eyes　1965　2.00　4.00　8.00
❏ 2058　Out of This World/Squeeze Me　1965　2.00　4.00　8.00
❏ 2059　Lonely Street/Try a Little Tenderness　1965　2.00　4.00　8.00
❏ 2061　Folks Who Live on the Hill/That's a Joy　1965　2.00　4.00　8.00
❏ 2062　My Devotion/I'm Glad There Is You　1965　2.00　4.00　8.00
❏ 19303　June Night/Perdido　1959　3.00　6.00　12.00
❏ 19308　But Not for Me/Just in Time　1959　3.00　6.00　12.00
❏ 19326　Be My Love/My Prayer for You　1960　2.50　5.00　10.00
❏ 19337　Happiness Is Just a Thing Called Joe/My Reverie　1960　2.50　5.00　10.00
❏ 19367　Gypsy Boy/Recommend to Love　1960　2.50　5.00　10.00
❏ 19373　Condemned Without Trial/Dreamy　1960　2.50　5.00　10.00
❏ 19390　Jazz in You/Love, I've Found You　1961　2.00　4.00　8.00
❏ 19409　He Needs Me/The Lamp Is Low　1961　2.00　4.00　8.00
❏ 19418　Impossible/This Little Boy of Mine　1961　2.00　4.00　8.00
❏ 19428　You Don't Have to Be a Tower of Strength/I Will Follow You　1961　3.00　6.00　12.00
❏ 19431　I'm Glad There Is You/And This Is My Beloved　1962　2.00　4.00　8.00
❏ 20008　I Know Love/It Just Happened to Me　1962　2.00　4.00　8.00
❏ 29343 [S]　Perdido/June Night　1960　3.00　6.00　12.00
—Jukebox issue, small hole, plays at 33 1/3 rpm
❏ 29344 [S]　Bye Bye Blackbird/April in Paris　1960　3.00　6.00　12.00
—Jukebox issue, small hole, plays at 33 1/3 rpm
❏ 29345 [S]　For All We Know/'Tis Autumn　1960　3.00　6.00　12.00
—Jukebox issue, small hole, plays at 33 1/3 rpm
❏ 29346 [S]　Little Girl Blue/Am I Blue　1960　3.00　6.00　12.00
—Jukebox issue, small hole, plays at 33 1/3 rpm
❏ 29347 [S]　Without a Song/They Didn't Believe Me　1960　3.00　6.00　12.00
—Jukebox issue, small hole, plays at 33 1/3 rpm
FONTANA
❏ 1507　The Touch of Your Lips/Intimate Moments　1965　—　3.00　6.00
❏ 1511　Watermelon Man/All Alone　1965　—　3.00　6.00
❏ 1523　The Whisperers/I Understand　1965　—　3.00　6.00
❏ 1538　Speaking of Happiness/Somtimes It Be's That Way　1966　—　3.00　6.00
❏ 1554　Strangers in the Night/Hey, Candy Man　1966　—　3.00　6.00
❏ 1560　Honey Machine/I Got What You Want　1966　—　3.00　6.00
❏ 1567　Love Is/It's Not the Truth　1967　—　3.00　6.00
❏ 1594　Foolish Dreamer/I Can't Stand It　1967　—　3.00　6.00
❏ 1617　I've Never Ever Loved Before/Down Here on the Ground　1968　—　2.50　5.00
❏ 1627　The Guy Who Lived Up There/Hold Back the Dawn　1968　—　2.50　5.00
❏ 1639　I've Got to Be Someone/Problem Child　1969　—　2.50　5.00
❏ 1660　No Easy Way Down/Darlin'　1969　—　2.50　5.00
❏ 1674　Hold It/Untouched by Human Love　1969　—　2.50　5.00
❏ 1890　Be Anything (But Be Mine)/Soul Serenade　1964　2.00　4.00　8.00
❏ 1890 [PS]　Be Anything (But Be Mine)/Soul Serenade　1964　3.00　6.00　12.00
❏ 1966　Soul Serenade/Do Anything　1965　—　3.00　6.00
HIFI
❏ 5103　I Wish You Love/Long Long Story　1966　—　3.00　6.00
MERCURY
❏ 73267　Never My Love/The Summer Knows　1972　—　2.50　5.00
❏ 73294　Just Let Me Be Me/Kickin' Life　1972　—　2.50　5.00
SEECO
❏ 6037　Little Boy Blues/Way Beyond the Hills　1959　3.00　6.00　12.00
❏ 6077　Is There Someone for Me/I'm Not Afraid Anymore　1961　2.50　5.00　10.00

7-Inch Extended Plays
EVEREST
❏ SDBR-196137　And This Is My Beloved/Drinking Again/I Got Rhythm//It Just Happened to Me/Wouldn't It Be Loverly/I Get a Kick Out of You　196?　3.75　7.50　15.00
—Jukebox issue; small hole, plays at 33 1/3 rpm
❏ SDBR-196137 [PS]　Gloria Lynne at Basin Street East　196?　3.75　7.50　15.00
FONTANA
❏ SRF-751-C　It's Just a Matter of Time/Til There Was You/I Understand//A Sunday Kind of Love/The Whisperers/It May Sound Silly　196?　3.00　6.00　12.00
—Stereo jukebox issue; small hole, plays at 33 1/3 rpm
❏ SRF-751-C [PS]　Love and a Woman　196?　3.00　6.00　12.00
Albums
ABC IMPULSE!
❏ ASD-9311　I Don't Know How to Love Him　1976　3.00　6.00　12.00
CANYON
❏ 7709　Happy and In Love　1970　3.75　7.50　15.00

COLLECTABLES
❏ COL-5138　Golden Classics　198?　2.50　5.00　10.00
DESIGN
❏ D-177 [M]　My Funny Valentine　196?　2.50　5.00　10.00
❏ DS-177 [S]　My Funny Valentine　196?　3.00　6.00　12.00
EVEREST
❏ ES-1001 [S]　Gloria Lynne Live! Take 1　1959　10.00　20.00　40.00
❏ SDBR-1022 [S]　Miss Gloria Lynne　1959　7.50　15.00　30.00
❏ SDBR-1063 [S]　Lonely and Sentimental　1960　7.50　15.00　30.00
❏ SDBR-1090 [S]　Try a Little Tenderness　1960　7.50　15.00　30.00
❏ SDBR-1101 [S]　Day In, Day Out　1961　7.50　15.00　30.00
❏ SDBR-1126 [S]　I'm Glad There Is You　1961　7.50　15.00　30.00
❏ SDBR-1128 [S]　He Needs Me　1961　7.50　15.00　30.00
❏ SDBR-1131 [S]　This Little Boy of Mine　1961　7.50　15.00　30.00
❏ SDBR-1132 [S]　Gloria Lynne at Basin Street East　1962　7.50　15.00　30.00
❏ SDBR-1203 [S]　Gloria Blue　1962　7.50　15.00　30.00
❏ SDBR-1208 [S]　Gloria Lynne at the Las Vegas Thunderbird　1963　7.50　15.00　30.00
❏ EV-1220 [S]　Gloria, Marty & Strings　1963　7.50　15.00　30.00
❏ EV-1226 [S]　I Wish You Love　1964　6.25　12.50　25.00
❏ EV-1228 [S]　Glorious Gloria Lynne　1964　6.25　12.50　25.00
❏ EV-1230 [S]　After Hours　1965　6.25　12.50　25.00
❏ EV-1231 [S]　The Best of Gloria Lynne　1965　5.00　10.00　20.00
❏ EV-1237 [S]　Go! Go! Go!　1965　5.00　10.00　20.00
❏ EV-1238 [S]　Gloria Lynne '66　1966　5.00　10.00　20.00
❏ E-5001 [M]　Gloria Lynne Live! Take 1　1959　7.50　15.00　30.00
❏ LPBR-5022 [M]　Miss Gloria Lynne　1959　5.00　10.00　20.00
❏ LPBR-5063 [M]　Lonely and Sentimental　1960　5.00　10.00　20.00
❏ LPBR-5090 [M]　Try a Little Tenderness　1960　5.00　10.00　20.00
❏ LPBR-5101 [M]　Day In, Day Out　1961　5.00　10.00　20.00
❏ LPBR-5126 [M]　I'm Glad There Is You　1961　5.00　10.00　20.00
❏ LPBR-5128 [M]　He Needs Me　1961　5.00　10.00　20.00
❏ LPBR-5131 [M]　This Little Boy of Mine　1961　5.00　10.00　20.00
❏ LPBR-5132 [M]　Gloria Lynne at Basin Street East　1962　5.00　10.00　20.00
❏ LPBR-5203 [M]　Gloria Blue　1962　5.00　10.00　20.00
❏ LPBR-5208 [M]　Gloria Lynne at the Las Vegas Thunderbird　1963　5.00　10.00　20.00
❏ EV-5220 [M]　Gloria, Marty & Strings　1963　5.00　10.00　20.00
❏ EV-5226 [M]　I Wish You Love　1964　5.00　10.00　20.00
❏ EV-5228 [M]　Glorious Gloria Lynne　1964　5.00　10.00　20.00
❏ EV-5230 [M]　After Hours　1965　5.00　10.00　20.00
❏ EV-5231 [M]　The Best of Gloria Lynne　1965　3.75　7.50　15.00
❏ EV-5237 [M]　Go! Go! Go!　1965　3.75　7.50　15.00
❏ EV-5238 [M]　Gloria Lynne '66　1966　3.75　7.50　15.00
❏ ST-90057 [M]　I Wish You Love　196?　6.25　12.50　25.00
—Capitol Record Club edition
FONTANA
❏ MGF-27528 [M]　Intimate Moments　1964　3.75　7.50　15.00
❏ MGF-27541 [M]　Soul Serenade　1965　3.75　7.50　15.00
❏ MGF-27546 [M]　Love and a Woman　1965　3.75　7.50　15.00
❏ MGF-27555 [M]　Where It's At　1966　3.75　7.50　15.00
❏ MGF-27561 [M]　Gloria　1966　3.75　7.50　15.00
❏ MGF-27571 [M]　The Other Side of Gloria Lynne　1967　5.00　10.00　20.00
❏ SRF-67528 [S]　Intimate Moments　1964　5.00　10.00　20.00
❏ SRF-67541 [S]　Soul Serenade　1965　5.00　10.00　20.00
❏ SRF-67546 [S]　Love and a Woman　1965　5.00　10.00　20.00
❏ SRF-67555 [S]　Where It's At　1966　5.00　10.00　20.00
❏ SRF-67561 [S]　Gloria　1966　5.00　10.00　20.00
❏ SRF-67571 [S]　The Other Side of Gloria Lynne　1967　3.75　7.50　15.00
❏ SRF-67577　Here, There and Everywhere　1968　3.75　7.50　15.00
HIFI
❏ L-440 [M]　The Gloria Lynne Calendar　1966　3.75　7.50　15.00
❏ SL-440 [S]　The Gloria Lynne Calendar　1966　5.00　10.00　20.00
❏ SR-441　Greatest Hits　1969　3.75　7.50　15.00
INTERMEDIA
❏ QS-5069　Classics　198?　2.50　5.00　10.00
MERCURY
❏ SRM-1-633　A Very Gentle Sound　1972　3.75　7.50　15.00
MUSE
❏ MR-5381　A Time for Love　198?　2.50　5.00　10.00
SUNSET
❏ SUM-1145 [M]　Gloria Lynne　1966　3.00　6.00　12.00
❏ SUM-1171 [M]　I Wish You Love　1967　3.00　6.00　12.00
❏ SUS-5145 [S]　Gloria Lynne　1966　3.00　6.00　12.00
❏ SUS-5171 [S]　I Wish You Love　1967　3.00　6.00　12.00
❏ SUS-5221　Golden Greats　1968　3.00　6.00　12.00
UPFRONT
❏ 146　Gloria Lynne　197?　3.00　6.00　12.00

LYNYRD SKYNYRD
12-Inch Singles
MCA
❏ L33-17385 [DJ]　Truck Drivin' Man/Simple Man　1987　2.00　4.00　8.00
❏ L33-17444 [DJ]　Georgia Peaches (same on both sides)　1987　2.00　4.00　8.00
❏ L33-17488 [DJ]　Swamp Music (same on both sides)　1987　2.00　4.00　8.00
❏ L33-17569 [DJ]　Gimme Back My Bullets/Comin' Home　198?　2.00　4.00　8.00
45s
ATINA
❏ 129　Need All My Friends/Michelle　1978　3.75　7.50　15.00
COLUMBIA
❏ 78284　White Knuckle Ride/Tearin' It Up　1996　—　2.00　4.00
—B-side by Joe Diffie
MCA
❏ L45-1966 [DJ]　Gimme Back My Bullets (same on both sides)　1976　6.25　12.50　25.00
❏ 40258　Sweet Home Alabama/Take Your Time　1974　—　2.50　5.00
❏ 40328　Free Bird/Down South Jukin'　1974　—　2.50　5.00
❏ 40416　Saturday Night Special/Made in the Shade　1975　—　2.50　5.00
❏ 40532　Double Trouble/Roll Gypsy Roll　1975　—　2.50　5.00
❏ 40565　Gimme Back My Bullets/All I Can Do Is Write About It　1976　—　2.50　5.00
❏ 40647　Gimme Three Steps/Travelin' Man　1976　—　2.50　5.00
❏ 40665　Free Bird/Searching　1976　—　2.50　5.00
❏ 40819　What's Your Name/I Know a Little　1977　—　2.50　5.00
—"What's Your Name" is a different mix than that on the Street Survivors LP.
❏ 40888　You Got That Right/Ain't No Good Life　1978　—　2.50　5.00
❏ 40957　Down South Jukin'/Wino　1978　—　2.50　5.00
❏ 53206　When You Got Good Friends/Truck Drivin' Man　1987　—　2.00　4.00

Number	Title (A Side/B Side)	Yr	VG	VG+	NM
❏ 60191	Sweet Home Alabama/Saturday Night Special	1976	—	2.00	4.00

—*Reissue*

SHADE TREE

Number	Title (A Side/B Side)	Yr	VG	VG+	NM
❏ 101	Need All My Friends/Michelle	1971	375.00	750.00	1500.

—*As "Lynard Skynard"; approximately 300 copies pressed*

SOUNDS OF THE SOUTH

Number	Title (A Side/B Side)	Yr	VG	VG+	NM
❏ 40158	Gimme Three Steps/Mr. Banker	1973	2.00	4.00	8.00
❏ 40231	Don't Ask Me No Questions/Take Your Time	1974	2.00	4.00	8.00
❏ 40258	Sweet Home Alabama/Take Your Time	1974	2.00	4.00	8.00

Albums

ATLANTIC

Number	Title (A Side/B Side)	Yr	VG	VG+	NM
❏ A1-82258	Lynyrd Skynyrd 1991	1991	5.00	10.00	20.00

—*The only U.S. vinyl version was released through Columbia House*

MCA

Number	Title (A Side/B Side)	Yr	VG	VG+	NM
❏ 363	(pronounced leh-nerd skin-nerd)	1975	3.00	6.00	12.00
—*Reissue on black rainbow label*					
❏ 413	Second Helping	1975	3.00	6.00	12.00
—*Reissue on black rainbow label*					
❏ 1448	Best of the Rest	1985	2.00	4.00	8.00
❏ L33-1946 [(2)DJ]	One More From the Road	1976	6.25	12.50	25.00
—*Promo only on black vinyl*					
❏ L33-1946 [(2)DJ]	One More From the Road	1976	12.50	25.00	50.00
—*Promo on blue, gold, purple or red vinyl (each has the same value)*					
❏ L33-1988 [DJ]	Skynyrd's First and…Last	1978	6.25	12.50	25.00
—*Promo sampler*					
❏ 2137	Nuthin' Fancy	1975	3.00	6.00	12.00
❏ 2170	Gimme Back My Bullets	1976	3.00	6.00	12.00
❏ 3019	(pronounced leh-nerd skin-nerd)	1976	2.50	5.00	10.00
—*Second reissue with new number on black rainbow label*					
❏ 3020	Second Helping	1976	2.50	5.00	10.00
—*Second reissue with new number on black rainbow label*					
❏ 3021	Nuthin' Fancy	1976	2.50	5.00	10.00
—*Reissue with new number on black rainbow label*					
❏ 3022	Gimme Back My Bullets	1977	2.50	5.00	10.00
—*Reissue with new number on black rainbow label*					
❏ 3029	Street Survivors	1977	2.50	5.00	10.00
—*After the band's plane crash, the "flames" photo was replaced with the back cover photo; the back cover is black with only the song titles*					
❏ 3029	Street Survivors	1977	6.25	12.50	25.00
—*Originals with the band in flames on the front cover and a smaller band photo on the back cover*					
❏ 3047	Skynyrd's First and…Last	1978	3.00	6.00	12.00
—*Originals with tan labels and gatefold cover*					
❏ 5221	(pronounced leh-nerd skin-nerd)	1980	2.00	4.00	8.00
❏ 5222	Second Helping	1980	2.00	4.00	8.00
❏ 5223	Street Survivors	1980	2.00	4.00	8.00
❏ 5370	Best of the Rest	1982	2.50	5.00	10.00
—*Original version*					
❏ 6001 [(2)]	One More From the Road	1976	3.75	7.50	15.00
—*Originals with black rainbow label and gatefold cover*					
❏ 6897 [(2)]	One More From the Road	1985	2.50	5.00	10.00
—*Most, if not all, of these pressings have no gatefold*					
❏ 6898 [(2)]	Gold & Platinum	1985	2.50	5.00	10.00
—*Most, if not all, of these pressings have no gatefold*					
❏ 8011 [(2)]	One More From the Road	1977	3.00	6.00	12.00
—*First reissue with new number*					
❏ 8027 [(2)]	Southern by the Grace of God	1988	3.00	6.00	12.00
❏ 10014 [(2)]	One More From the Road	1980	2.50	5.00	10.00
—*Second reissue*					
❏ 11008 [(2)]	Gold & Platinum	1979	3.00	6.00	12.00
—*Originals with embossed gatefold cover*					
❏ 37069	Gimme Back My Bullets	1980	2.00	4.00	8.00
❏ 37070	Nuthin' Fancy	1980	2.00	4.00	8.00
❏ 37071	Skynyrd's First and…Last	1980	2.00	4.00	8.00
❏ 37211	(pronounced leh-nerd skin-nerd)	1985	2.00	4.00	8.00
❏ 37212	Second Helping	1985	2.00	4.00	8.00
❏ 37213	Street Survivors	1985	2.00	4.00	8.00
❏ 42084	Legend	1987	2.50	5.00	10.00
❏ 42293	Skynyrd's Innyrds	1989	3.00	6.00	12.00

SOUNDS OF THE SOUTH

Number	Title (A Side/B Side)	Yr	VG	VG+	NM
❏ 363	(pronounced leh-nerd skin-nerd)	1973	5.00	10.00	20.00
❏ 413	Second Helping	1974	5.00	10.00	20.00

—*Both of the above are original pressings with yellow labels*

LYONS, MARIE
45s

DELUXE

Number	Title (A Side/B Side)	Yr	VG	VG+	NM
❏ 101	Drown in My Own Tears/Try Me	1968	3.00	6.00	12.00
—*As "Queenie Lyons"*					
❏ 103	Fever/Your Key Don't Fit No More	1969	2.50	5.00	10.00
—*As "Marie 'Queenie' Lyons"*					
❏ 123	Daddy's House/See and Don't See	1970	2.50	5.00	10.00

Albums

DELUXE

Number	Title (A Side/B Side)	Yr	VG	VG+	NM
❏ 12001	Soul Fever	1970	6.25	12.50	25.00

LYZER, TONY
45s

LAURIE

Number	Title (A Side/B Side)	Yr	VG	VG+	NM
❏ 3019	Six Little Men/Loco	1958	37.50	75.00	150.00

M

M.H. ROYALS, THE
45s

ABC

Number	Title (A Side/B Side)	Yr	VG	VG+	NM
❏ 10907	Tomorrow's Dead/She's Gone Forever	1967	6.25	12.50	25.00
❏ 10957	Old Town/Now She's Crying	1967	6.25	12.50	25.00

M.P.D. LIMITED
45s

LTD

Number	Title (A Side/B Side)	Yr	VG	VG+	NM
❏ 400	Little Boy Sad/Wendy Don't Go	1965	10.00	20.00	40.00

M-3'S, THE
45s

ABC-PARAMOUNT

Number	Title (A Side/B Side)	Yr	VG	VG+	NM
❏ 10772	Funny Cafe/So Give Me Love	1966	6.25	12.50	25.00

UNITED ARTISTS

Number	Title (A Side/B Side)	Yr	VG	VG+	NM
❏ 737	When the Party's Over/Magic Kiss	1964	3.00	6.00	12.00
❏ 889	Three Lonely Nights/I See a Rainbow	1965	3.00	6.00	12.00

MABLEY, MOMS
45s

MERCURY

Number	Title (A Side/B Side)	Yr	VG	VG+	NM
❏ 72935	Abraham, Martin and John/Sunny	1969	—	3.00	6.00
❏ 72958	His Way/Yes Indeed	1969	—	3.00	6.00
❏ 72974	It's Your Thing/He's Got the Whole World in His Hands	1969	—	3.00	6.00
❏ 73240	I Surrender Dear/That's Pops	1971	—	2.50	5.00

Albums

CHESS

Number	Title (A Side/B Side)	Yr	VG	VG+	NM
❏ LP-1447 [M]	Moms Mabley, Funniest Woman in the World, Onstage	1961	6.25	12.50	25.00
❏ LP-1452 [M]	Moms Mabley at the "UN"	1961	6.25	12.50	25.00
❏ LP-1460 [M]	Moms Mabley at the Playboy Club	1961	6.25	12.50	25.00
❏ LP-1463 [M]	Moms Mabley at Geneva Conference	1962	6.25	12.50	25.00
❏ LP-1472 [M]	Moms Mabley Breaks It Up	1962	6.25	12.50	25.00
❏ LP-1477 [M]	Young Men, Si — Old Men, No	1962	6.25	12.50	25.00
❏ LP-1479 [M]	I Got Somethin' to Tell You!	1963	6.25	12.50	25.00
❏ LP-1482 [M]	The Funny Sides of Moms Mabley	1963	6.25	12.50	25.00
❏ LP-1486 [M]	Moms Wows	1964	6.25	12.50	25.00
❏ LP-1487 [M]	The Best of Moms	1964	6.25	12.50	25.00
❏ LP-1497 [M]	The Man in My Life	1965	5.00	10.00	20.00
❏ LPS-1525	Moms Mabley Breaks Up the Network	1968	5.00	10.00	20.00
❏ LPS-1530	Moms Mabley Sings	1969	5.00	10.00	20.00

MERCURY

Number	Title (A Side/B Side)	Yr	VG	VG+	NM
❏ MG-20889 [M]	Out on a Limb	1964	3.75	7.50	15.00
❏ MG-20907 [M]	Moms the Word	1964	3.75	7.50	15.00
❏ MG-21012 [M]	Now Hear This	1965	3.75	7.50	15.00
❏ MG-21090 [M]	Moms Mabley at the White House	1966	3.75	7.50	15.00
❏ MG-21139 [M]	The Best of Moms Mabley	1967	6.25	12.50	25.00
❏ SR-60889 [S]	Out on a Limb	1964	5.00	10.00	20.00
❏ SR-60907 [S]	Moms the Word	1964	5.00	10.00	20.00
❏ SR-61012 [S]	Now Hear This	1965	5.00	10.00	20.00
❏ SR-61090 [S]	Moms Mabley at the White House	1966	5.00	10.00	20.00
❏ SR-61139 [S]	The Best of Moms Mabley	1967	3.75	7.50	15.00
❏ SR-61205	Her Young Thing	1969	3.75	7.50	15.00
❏ SR-61229	The Youngest Teenager	1969	3.75	7.50	15.00
❏ SR-61235	Abraham, Martin and John	1969	3.75	7.50	15.00
❏ SR-61263	Live at Sing Sing	1970	3.75	7.50	15.00

MACH, LEON
45s

LAVENDER

Number	Title (A Side/B Side)	Yr	VG	VG+	NM
❏ 1554	You Hurt Me So/It's You I Love	1960	25.00	50.00	100.00

MACK, LONNIE
45s

BUCCANEER

Number	Title (A Side/B Side)	Yr	VG	VG+	NM
❏ 3001	Memphis/Lonnie on the Move	196?	2.00	4.00	8.00

—*Reissue of Fraternity material*

CAPITOL

Number	Title (A Side/B Side)	Yr	VG	VG+	NM
❏ 4441	Running Wild/Funky Country Living	1977	—	2.50	5.00

ELEKTRA

Number	Title (A Side/B Side)	Yr	VG	VG+	NM
❏ 45638	Memphis/Why	1968	2.50	5.00	10.00
❏ 45652	Save Your Money/In the Band	1969	2.50	5.00	10.00
❏ 45715	Lay It Down/ She Even Woke Me Up to Say Goodbye	1971	2.00	4.00	8.00
❏ 45715 [PS]	Lay It Down/ She Even Woke Me Up to Say Goodbye	1971	3.75	7.50	15.00
❏ 45761	Rings/Florida	1972	2.00	4.00	8.00

EPIC

Number	Title (A Side/B Side)	Yr	VG	VG+	NM
❏ 07973	Too Rock for Country, Too Country for Rock and Roll/Lucille	1988	—	2.00	4.00
❏ 08117	Hard Life/50's-60's Man	1988	—	2.00	4.00

FRATERNITY

Number	Title (A Side/B Side)	Yr	VG	VG+	NM
❏ 906	Memphis/Down in the Dumps	1963	3.75	7.50	15.00
❏ 912	Wham!/Susie-Q	1963	3.75	7.50	15.00
❏ 918	Baby, What's Wrong/Where There's a Will	1963	3.00	6.00	12.00
❏ 920	Say Something Nice to Me/Lonnie on the Move	1964	3.00	6.00	12.00
❏ 925	I've Had It/Nashville	1964	3.00	6.00	12.00
❏ 932	Chicken Pickin'/Sa-Ba-Hoola	1964	3.00	6.00	12.00
❏ 938	Don't Make My Baby Blue/Oh Boy	1964	3.00	6.00	12.00
❏ 942	Crying Over You/Coastin'	1965	3.00	6.00	12.00
❏ 946	Tonky Go Go/When I'm Alone	1965	3.00	6.00	12.00
❏ 951	Honky Tonk '65/Chicken Pickin'	1965	3.00	6.00	12.00
❏ 957	Crying Over You/Are You Guilty	1966	3.00	6.00	12.00
❏ 959	The Circus/Bucaroo	1966	3.00	6.00	12.00
❏ 967	Tension (Part 1)/Tension (Part 2)	1966	3.00	6.00	12.00
❏ 969	Wildwood Flower/Snow on the Mountain	1966	3.00	6.00	12.00
❏ 981	I Left My Heart in San Francisco/Omaha	1967	2.50	5.00	10.00
❏ 986	Save Your Money/Snow on the Mountain	1967	2.50	5.00	10.00
❏ 1004	Soul Express/Down and Out	1968	2.50	5.00	10.00
❏ 1278	Soul Express/I Found a Love	197?	—	3.00	6.00

L

Number	Title (A Side/B Side)	Yr	VG	VG+	NM
ROULETTE					
❏ 7175	All We Need Is Love, You and Me/Highway 56	1975	—	3.00	6.00
Albums					
ALLIGATOR					
❏ AL-3903	The Wham of That Memphis Man	1987	2.50	5.00	10.00
—Reissue of Fraternity LP					
❏ AL-4739	Strike Like Lightning	1985	2.50	5.00	10.00
❏ AL-4750	Second Sight	1987	2.50	5.00	10.00
❏ AL-4786	Live!: Attack of the Killer V	1990	3.00	6.00	12.00
CAPITOL					
❏ ST-11619	Home at Last	1976	3.00	6.00	12.00
❏ ST-11703	Lonnie Mack and Pismo	1977	3.00	6.00	12.00
ELEKTRA					
❏ EKS-74040	Glad I'm in the Band	1969	6.25	12.50	25.00
❏ EKS-74050	Whatever's Right	1969	6.25	12.50	25.00
❏ EKS-74077	For Collectors Only	1970	6.25	12.50	25.00
❏ EKS-74102	The Hills of Indiana	1971	6.25	12.50	25.00
EPIC					
❏ FE 44075	Roadhouses and Dance Halls	1989	3.00	6.00	12.00
FRATERNITY					
❏ SF-1014 [M]	The Wham of That Memphis Man	1963	30.00	60.00	120.00
❏ SSF-1014 [S]	The Wham of That Memphis Man	1963	75.00	150.00	300.00
TRIP					
❏ TLX-9522 [(2)]	The Memphis Sounds of Lonnie Mack	1975	3.00	6.00	12.00

MACKENZIE, GISELE

45s

Number	Title (A Side/B Side)	Yr	VG	VG+	NM
CAPITOL					
❏ F1722	Jolie Jacqueline/Fairyland	1951	3.75	7.50	15.00
❏ F1768	J'Attendrai/My Greatest Love	1951	3.75	7.50	15.00
❏ F1807	On Rosary Hill/Lovers' Waltz	1951	3.75	7.50	15.00
—With Gordon MacRae					
❏ F1826	Sans Souci/I Never Was Loved by Anyone Else	1951	3.75	7.50	15.00
❏ F1865	Sweetheart/It's All Over But the Memories	1951	3.75	7.50	15.00
❏ F1878	Please/Love Makes the World Go Round	1951	3.75	7.50	15.00
❏ F1907	La Fiacre/Thu Pocket Thu Pocket	1951	3.75	7.50	15.00
❏ F1959	My Buick, My Lover and I/Lovers' Waltz	1952	3.00	6.00	12.00
—With Gordon MacRae					
❏ F1983	Wishin'/Goodbye Sweetheart	1952	3.00	6.00	12.00
❏ F1997	Eggbert the Easter Egg/Benny the Bob-Tailed Bunny	1952	3.75	7.50	15.00
❏ F2059	What'll I Do/I'm So Easy to Satisfy	1952	3.00	6.00	12.00
❏ F2110	Johnny/Whistle My Love	1952	3.00	6.00	12.00
❏ F2156	Adios/Darling You Can't Love Two	1952	3.00	6.00	12.00
❏ F2256	Don't Let the Stars Get In Your Eyes/My Favorite Song	1952	3.00	6.00	12.00
❏ F2266	Crazy Waltz/Water Can't Quench the Fire of Love	1952	3.00	6.00	12.00
—With Helen O'Connell					
❏ F2307	Gone/The New Wears Off Too Fast	1952	3.00	6.00	12.00
❏ F2354	Let Me Know/Friend of the Family	1953	3.00	6.00	12.00
❏ F2404	Lipstick and Powder and Paint/Get It While You're Young	1953	3.00	6.00	12.00
—With Helen O'Connell					
❏ F2501	I'd Rather Die Young/I Didn't Want to Love You	1953	3.00	6.00	12.00
❏ F2521	Give Me a Name/When the Hands of the Clock Pray at Midnight	1953	3.00	6.00	12.00
—With Helen O'Connell					
❏ F2556	Half Hearted/Till They've All Come Home	1953	3.00	6.00	12.00
❏ F2600	Walkin' Tune/Embrasse	1953	3.00	6.00	12.00
❏ F2695	A Letter and a Ring/Le Gros Bill	1954	3.00	6.00	12.00
❏ F2743	Doggone It Baby, I'm in Love/Ridin' to Tennessee	1954	3.00	6.00	12.00
❏ F2827	El Recicario/The One Who Broke My Heart Is Back in Town	1954	3.00	6.00	12.00
EVEREST					
❏ 19352	In Milano/You Dream of Me (And I'll Dream of You)	1960	2.00	4.00	8.00
MERCURY					
❏ 72113	Loser's Lullaby/By Myself	1963	—	3.50	7.00
RCA VICTOR					
❏ 47-7086	Never Go Away/This I Know	1957	2.50	5.00	10.00
❏ 47-7183	They're Playing Our Song/Come to Me My True Love	1958	2.00	4.00	8.00
VIK					
❏ 0233	The Star You Wished Upon Last Night/It's Delightful to Be Married	1956	2.50	5.00	10.00
❏ 0249	He Knows/Hello There	1957	2.50	5.00	10.00
❏ 0274	The Waltz That Broke My Heart/Oh Pain, Oh Agony	1957	2.50	5.00	10.00
❏ 0300	Too Fat for the Chimney/Jingle Bells	1957	3.00	6.00	12.00
❏ 0300 [PS]	Too Fat for the Chimney/Jingle Bells	1957	5.00	10.00	20.00
"X"					
❏ 0137	Hard to Get/Boston Fancy	1955	3.00	6.00	12.00
❏ 0137 [PS]	Hard to Get/Boston Fancy	1955	5.00	10.00	20.00
❏ 0172	Pepper Hot Baby/That's the Chance I've Got to Take	1955	2.50	5.00	10.00
❏ 0189	Reserved/The Little Child	1956	2.50	5.00	10.00
—With Billy Quinn					
❏ 0202	Mr. Telephone/Dance If You Want to Dance	1956	2.50	5.00	10.00

7-Inch Extended Plays

Number	Title (A Side/B Side)	Yr	VG	VG+	NM
CAPITOL					
❏ EAP 1-430	(contents unknown)	195?	3.75	7.50	15.00
❏ EAP 1-430 [PS]	J'Attendrai	195?	3.75	7.50	15.00
Albums					
EVEREST					
❏ SDBR-1069 [S]	In Person at the Empire Room	1959	7.50	15.00	30.00
❏ LPBR-5069 [M]	In Person at the Empire Room	1959	6.25	12.50	25.00
GLENDALE					
❏ 6017	Gisele MacKenzie Sings	1978	3.00	6.00	12.00
RCA VICTOR					
❏ LPM-1790 [M]	Gisele	1958	7.50	15.00	30.00
❏ LSP-1790 [S]	Gisele	1958	10.00	20.00	40.00
❏ LPM-2006 [M]	Christmas with Gisele	1959	7.50	15.00	30.00
❏ LSP-2006 [S]	Christmas with Gisele	1959	10.00	20.00	40.00

Number	Title (A Side/B Side)	Yr	VG	VG+	NM
SUNSET					
❏ SUM-1155 [M]	In Person at the Empire Room	196?	3.00	6.00	12.00
❏ SUS-5155 [S]	In Person at the Empire Room	196?	3.75	7.50	15.00
VIK					
❏ LX-1055 [M]	Gisele MacKenzie	1956	10.00	20.00	40.00
❏ LX-1075 [M]	Mam'selle MacKenzie	1956	10.00	20.00	40.00
❏ LX-1099 [M]	Christmas with Gisele	1957	10.00	20.00	40.00

MACRAE, GORDON   Also see JO STAFFORD AND GORDON MacRAE.

45s

Number	Title (A Side/B Side)	Yr	VG	VG+	NM
CAPITOL					
❏ 54-777	Mule Train/Dear Hearts and Gentle People	1949	6.25	12.50	25.00
—Earlier Gordon MacRae 45s on Capitol may exist; this is the earliest we can confirm					
❏ F812	I'm Yours/Just One More Chance	1950	5.00	10.00	20.00
❏ F842	Half a Heart Is All You Left Me/Poison Ivy	1950	5.00	10.00	20.00
❏ F924	Oh, Oh, Ophelia/Two-Faced Heart	1950	5.00	10.00	20.00
❏ F935	Kisses and Tears/As We Are Today	1950	5.00	10.00	20.00
❏ F959	River of Smoke/This Is Heaven to Me	1950	5.00	10.00	20.00
❏ F1021	The Stars and Stripes Forever/Hongi-Tongi-Goki-Poki	1950	5.00	10.00	20.00
❏ F1168	Love 'Em All/Pigskin Polka	1950	5.00	10.00	20.00
❏ F1193	Honestly, I Love You/Just the Way You Are	1950	5.00	10.00	20.00
❏ F1214	You Love Me/You're Gonna Lose Your Gal	1950	5.00	10.00	20.00
❏ F1289	Use Your Imagination/I Am Loved	1950	5.00	10.00	20.00
❏ F1317	You Did Your Hair Chartreuse/Honky Tonk 10 Cent Dance	1950	5.00	10.00	20.00
❏ F1374	O Kive Neabs Kive (Love Means Love)/Wait for Me	1951	3.75	7.50	15.00
❏ F1471	I'm Yours to Command/I'll Buy You a Star	1951	3.75	7.50	15.00
❏ F1545	Cuban Love Song/Last Night When We Were Young	1951	3.75	7.50	15.00
❏ F1684	So in Love/Ramona	1951	3.00	6.00	12.00
—Reissue					
❏ F1705	Ol' Man River/On Sunday at Coney Island	1951	3.75	7.50	15.00
❏ F1750	Cuddle Up a Little Closer/Down Old Ox Road	1951	3.75	7.50	15.00
❏ F1836	Be My Guest/Laughing at Love	1951	3.75	7.50	15.00
❏ F1846	My Love/How Close	1951	3.75	7.50	15.00
❏ F1941	Baby Doll/Green Acres, Purple Mountains	1952	3.00	6.00	12.00
❏ F1959	My Buick, My Lover and I/Lovers' Waltz	1952	3.00	6.00	12.00
—With Gisele MacKenzie					
❏ F1990	Call Her Sweetheart/900 Miles	1952	3.00	6.00	12.00
❏ F2010	Gentle Hands/These Things Shall Pass	1952	3.00	6.00	12.00
❏ F2047	No Other Girl/If Someone Had Told Me	1952	3.00	6.00	12.00
❏ F2115	Peace in the Valley/Mansion Over the Hilltop	1952	3.00	6.00	12.00
❏ F2196	Blame it on My Youth/There's a Lull in My Life	1952	3.00	6.00	12.00
❏ F2311	Starlight and Narrow/Brotherly Love	1952	3.00	6.00	12.00
❏ 2329	Only Love/Knowing When to Leave	1968	—	3.50	7.00
❏ F2352	Congratulations to Someone/How Do You Speak to an Angel	1953	3.00	6.00	12.00
❏ F2465	C'est Magnifique/Homin' Time	1953	3.00	6.00	12.00
❏ F2603	I Still Dream of You/I Don't Want to Walk Without You	1953	3.00	6.00	12.00
❏ F2652	Stranger in Paradise/Never in a Million Years	1953	3.00	6.00	12.00
❏ F2672	Soothe My Lonely Heart/High on a Windy Hill	1953	3.00	6.00	12.00
❏ F2760	Face to Face/Backward Turn Backward	1954	3.00	6.00	12.00
❏ F2784	Coney Island Boat/Open Your Arms	1954	3.00	6.00	12.00
—With June Hutton					
❏ F2927	Count Your Blessings Instead of Sheep/Cara Mia	1954	3.00	6.00	12.00
❏ F2988	Here's What I'm Here For/Love Can Change the Stars	1954	3.00	6.00	12.00
❏ F3085	You Forgot to Tell Me/Tikatee Tikatay	1955	2.50	5.00	10.00
❏ F3122	Bella Notte/Follow Your Heart	1955	2.50	5.00	10.00
❏ F3191	Jim Bowie/Why Break the Heart That Loves You	1955	2.50	5.00	10.00
❏ F3214	People Will Say We're in Love/Surrey with the Fringe on Top	1955	2.50	5.00	10.00
❏ F3284	(Here's to) A Wonderful Christmas/A Woman in Love	1955	3.00	6.00	12.00
❏ F3315	Fate/Never Before and Never Again	1956	2.50	5.00	10.00
❏ F3384	I've Grown Accustomed to Your Face/Who Are We	1956	2.50	5.00	10.00
❏ F3438	I Asked the Lord/One Misty Morning	1956	2.50	5.00	10.00
❏ F3519	Without Love/Obey	1956	2.50	5.00	10.00
❏ F3641	Till We Meet Again/Lonely	1957	2.50	5.00	10.00
❏ F3724	When You Kiss Me/Endless Love	1957	2.50	5.00	10.00
❏ F3816	Sayonara/Never Till Now	1957	2.50	5.00	10.00
❏ F3864	If I Forget You/Now	1957	2.50	5.00	10.00
❏ F4033	The Secret/A Man Once Said	1958	2.50	5.00	10.00
❏ F4116	Fly Little Bluebird/Little Do You Know	1959	2.00	4.00	8.00
❏ F4179	Stranger/Palace of Love	1959	2.00	4.00	8.00
❏ 4323	The Sound of Music/When Did I Fall in Love	1959	2.00	4.00	8.00
❏ 4357	Our Love Story/You Were There	1960	2.00	4.00	8.00
—With Sheila MacRae					
❏ 4483	Dolce Par Niente/If Ever I Would Leave You	1960	2.00	4.00	8.00
❏ 4613	Face to Face/Sail Away	1961	2.00	4.00	8.00
❏ 4626	Impossible/Ordinary People	1961	2.00	4.00	8.00
❏ 4736	Nobody Told Me/The Sweetest Sounds	1962	2.00	4.00	8.00
❏ 4773	Lovely/Warmer Than a Whisper	1962	2.00	4.00	8.00
❏ 5693	If She Walked Into My Life/I Want to Be with You	1966	—	3.50	7.00
❏ F15597	I Surrender Dear/I'm Yours	195?	3.75	7.50	15.00
❏ F15598	You Were Meant for Me/A Kiss in the Dark	195?	3.75	7.50	15.00
❏ F15599	Body and Soul/The Sunshine of Your Smile	195?	3.75	7.50	15.00
—The above three comprise a box set					
❏ 54-90034	Merry Christmas Waltz/Adeste Fideles	1949	10.00	20.00	40.00
MGM					
❏ K10734	They Say It's Wonderful/Prisoner of Love	1950	7.50	15.00	30.00

7-Inch Extended Plays

Number	Title (A Side/B Side)	Yr	VG	VG+	NM
CAPITOL					
❏ EAP 1-765	(contents unknown)	1956	2.50	5.00	10.00
❏ EAP 1-765 [PS]	The Best Things in Life Are Free, Part 1	1956	2.50	5.00	10.00
❏ EAP 2-765	(contents unknown)	1956	2.50	5.00	10.00
❏ EAP 2-765 [PS]	The Best Things in Life Are Free, Part 2	1956	2.50	5.00	10.00
❏ EAP 3-765	(contents unknown)	1956	2.50	5.00	10.00
❏ EAP 3-765 [PS]	The Best Things in Life Are Free, Part 3	1956	2.50	5.00	10.00
❏ EAP 3-834	*The Last Round-Up/Green Grow the Lilacs/Wagon Wheels/I Went to the City	1957	2.50	5.00	10.00
❏ EAP 3-834 [PS]	Cowboy's Lament, Part 3	1957	2.50	5.00	10.00
Albums					
ALLEGRO ROYALE					
❏ 1606 [M]	Gordon MacRae	1952	5.00	10.00	20.00

Number	Title (A Side/B Side)	Yr	VG	VG+	NM

ANGEL

| □ S 37318 | The Student Prince | 1973 | 2.50 | 5.00 | 10.00 |

—Operetta with Dorothy Kirsten; reissue of Capitol SW 1841

| □ S 37319 | The Desert Song | 1973 | 2.50 | 5.00 | 10.00 |

—Operetta with Dorothy Kirsten; reissue of Capitol SW 1842

| □ S 37320 | The New Moon | 1973 | 2.50 | 5.00 | 10.00 |

—Operetta with Dorothy Kirsten; reissue of Capitol SW 1966

CAPITOL

| □ ST-125 | Only Love | 1969 | 3.00 | 6.00 | 12.00 |
| □ H 218 [10] | The Vagabond King | 1951 | 12.50 | 25.00 | 50.00 |

—Operetta with Lucille Norman

| □ P 219 [M] | New Moon and The Vagabond King | 1951 | 7.50 | 15.00 | 30.00 |

—Operettas with Lucille Norman; original

| □ T 219 [M] | New Moon and The Vagabond King | 195? | 7.50 | 15.00 | 30.00 |

—Operettas with Lucille Norman; turquoise label

| □ H 231 [10] | Gordon MacRae Sings | 1951 | 10.00 | 20.00 | 40.00 |
| □ L 334 [10] | Roberta | 1952 | 10.00 | 20.00 | 40.00 |

—Operetta with Lucille Norman and Anne Triola

| □ L 335 [10] | The Merry Widow | 1952 | 10.00 | 20.00 | 40.00 |

—With Lucille Norman

| □ L 351 [10] | The Desert Song | 1953 | 10.00 | 20.00 | 40.00 |

—Operetta with Lucille Norman and Bob Sands

| □ T 394 [M] | The Desert Song and Roberta | 195? | 7.50 | 15.00 | 30.00 |

—Turquoise label original

| □ L 407 [10] | The Student Prince | 1953 | 10.00 | 20.00 | 40.00 |

—Operetta with Dorothy Warenskjold and Harry Stanton

| □ H 422 [10] | By the Light of the Silvery Moon | 1953 | 10.00 | 20.00 | 40.00 |

—With June Hutton; not the soundtrack from the movie because MacRae and movie co-star Doris Day were on different labels

| □ P 437 [M] | The Student Prince and The Merry Widow | 1953 | 10.00 | 20.00 | 40.00 |

—Original

| □ T 437 [M] | The Student Prince and The Merry Widow | 195? | 7.50 | 15.00 | 30.00 |

—Turqiouse label original

| □ L 468 [10] | Naughty Marietta | 1954 | 10.00 | 20.00 | 40.00 |

—Operetta with Marguerite Piazza

| □ L 485 [10] | 3 Sailors and a Girl | 1953 | 15.00 | 30.00 | 60.00 |

—With Jane Powell and Gene Nelson

| □ L 530 [10] | The Red Mill | 1954 | 10.00 | 20.00 | 40.00 |

—Operetta with Lucille Norman

| □ T 537 [M] | Romantic Ballads | 1955 | 7.50 | 15.00 | 30.00 |

—Turquoise or gray label

| □ T 551 [M] | Naughty Marietta and The Red Mill | 1955 | 7.50 | 15.00 | 30.00 |

—Turquoise label original

| □ T 681 [M] | Operetta Favorites | 1956 | 7.50 | 15.00 | 30.00 |

—Turquoise or gray label

| □ T 765 [M] | The Best Things in Life Are Free | 1956 | 7.50 | 15.00 | 30.00 |

—Turquoise or gray label

| □ T 834 [M] | Cowboy's Lament | 1957 | 7.50 | 15.00 | 30.00 |

—Turquoise or gray label

| □ T 875 [M] | Motion Picture Soundstage | 1957 | 7.50 | 15.00 | 30.00 |

—Turquoise or gray label

| □ ST 980 [S] | Gordon MacRae in Concert | 1959 | 10.00 | 20.00 | 40.00 |

—Black colorband label, logo at left

| □ T 980 [M] | Gordon MacRae in Concert | 1957 | 7.50 | 15.00 | 30.00 |

—Turquoise or gray label

| □ T 1050 [M] | This Is Gordon MacRae | 1958 | 7.50 | 15.00 | 30.00 |

—Turquoise label

| □ ST 1146 [S] | The Seasons of Love | 1959 | 5.00 | 10.00 | 20.00 |

—Black colorband label, Capitol logo at left

| □ T 1146 [M] | The Seasons of Love | 1959 | 3.75 | 7.50 | 15.00 |

—Black colorband label, Capitol logo at left

| □ ST 1251 [S] | Songs for an Evening at Home | 1959 | 5.00 | 10.00 | 20.00 |

—Black colorband label, Capitol logo at left

| □ T 1251 [M] | Songs for an Evening at Home | 1959 | 3.75 | 7.50 | 15.00 |

—Black colorband label, Capitol logo at left

| □ ST 1353 [S] | Our Love Story | 1960 | 5.00 | 10.00 | 20.00 |

—With Sheila MacRae; black colorband label, Capitol logo at left

| □ T 1353 [M] | Our Love Story | 1960 | 3.75 | 7.50 | 15.00 |

—With Sheila MacRae; black colorband label, Capitol logo at left

| □ ST 1466 [S] | Hallowed Be Thy Name | 1960 | 5.00 | 10.00 | 20.00 |

—Black colorband label, Capitol logo at left

| □ T 1466 [M] | Hallowed Be Thy Name | 1960 | 3.75 | 7.50 | 15.00 |

—Black colorband label, Capitol logo at left

| □ SW 1841 [S] | The Student Prince | 1963 | 3.75 | 7.50 | 15.00 |

—Operetta with Dorothy Kirsten

| □ W 1841 [M] | The Student Prince | 1963 | 3.00 | 6.00 | 12.00 |

—Opertta with Dorothy Kirsten

| □ SW 1842 [S] | The Desert Song | 1963 | 3.75 | 7.50 | 15.00 |

—Operetta with Dorothy Kirsten

| □ W 1842 [M] | The Desert Song | 1963 | 3.00 | 6.00 | 12.00 |

—Operetta with Dorothy Kirsten

| □ SW 1966 [S] | The New Moon | 1963 | 3.75 | 7.50 | 15.00 |

—Operetta with Dorothy Kirsten

| □ W 1966 [M] | The New Moon | 1963 | 3.00 | 6.00 | 12.00 |

—Operetta with Dorothy Kirsten

| □ SW 2022 [S] | Kismet | 1964 | 3.75 | 7.50 | 15.00 |

—Operetta with Dorothy Kirsten

| □ W 2022 [M] | Kismet | 1964 | 3.00 | 6.00 | 12.00 |

—Operetta with Dorothy Kirsten

| □ ST 2578 [S] | If She Walked Into My Life | 1966 | 3.75 | 7.50 | 15.00 |
| □ T 2578 [M] | If She Walked Into My Life | 1966 | 3.00 | 6.00 | 12.00 |

COLORTONE

| □ 4939 [M] | Gordon MacRae Sings | 1958 | 3.75 | 7.50 | 15.00 |

EVON

| □ 320 [M] | Gordon MacRae Sings | 1958 | 3.75 | 7.50 | 15.00 |

—Reissue of Allegro Royale LP

GALAXY

| □ 4805 [M] | Gordon MacRae | 1958 | 3.75 | 7.50 | 15.00 |

—Reissue of Allegro Royale LP

RONDO-LETTE

| □ A5 [M] | Gordon MacRae | 1958 | 3.75 | 7.50 | 15.00 |

—Reissue of Allegro Royale LP

ROYALE

| □ 18106 [10] | Gordon MacRae and Walter Gross Orchestra | 195? | 7.50 | 15.00 | 30.00 |
| □ 18155 [10] | Gordon MacRae and Orchestra | 195? | 7.50 | 15.00 | 30.00 |

SUTTON

| □ SSU 292 [R] | Gordon MacRae Sings Broadway's Best! | 196? | 2.50 | 5.00 | 10.00 |
| □ SU 292 [M] | Gordon MacRae Sings Broadway's Best! | 196? | 2.50 | 5.00 | 10.00 |

MACRAE, GORDON, AND JO STAFFORD See JO STAFFORD AND GORDON MacRAE.

MACRAE, SHEILA

Albums

ABC

| □ ABCS-611 | How Sweet She Is | 1968 | 6.25 | 12.50 | 25.00 |

MAD HATTERS, THE

45s

ASCOT

| □ 2197 | I Need Love/Blowin' in the Wind | 1965 | 6.25 | 12.50 | 25.00 |

FONTANA

| □ 1582 | I'll Come Running/Hello Girl | 1967 | 5.00 | 10.00 | 20.00 |

IGL

| □ 117 | Her Love/Route 66 | 196? | 3.75 | 7.50 | 15.00 |

MAD LADS, THE

45s

CAPITOL

| □ 5284 | Don't Cry at the Party/I'll Survive | 1964 | 3.75 | 7.50 | 15.00 |

STAX

| □ 160 | Surf Jerk/Sidewalk Surf | 1964 | 3.75 | 7.50 | 15.00 |

VOLT

□ 127	Don't Have to Shop Around/Tear-Maker	1965	2.50	5.00	10.00
□ 131	I Want Someone/Nothing Can Break Through	1965	2.50	5.00	10.00
□ 135	Come Closer to Me/Sugar Sugar	1966	2.50	5.00	10.00
□ 137	I Want a Girl/What Will Love Tend to Make You Do	1966	2.50	5.00	10.00
□ 139	Patch My Heart/You Mean So Much to Me	1966	2.50	5.00	10.00
□ 143	These Simple Reasons/I Don't Want to Lose Your Love	1967	2.50	5.00	10.00
□ 150	My Inspiration/Mr. Fix-It	1967	2.50	5.00	10.00
□ 162	Whatever Hurts You/No Time Is Better Than Right Now	1968	2.50	5.00	10.00
□ 4003	So Nice/Make Room	1968	2.00	4.00	8.00
□ 4009	Love Is Here Today and Gone Tomorrow/Make This Young Lady Mine	1969	2.00	4.00	8.00
□ 4016	By the Time I Get to Phoenix/No Strings Attached	1969	2.00	4.00	8.00
□ 4041	Seeing Is Believing/These Old Memories	1970	2.00	4.00	8.00
□ 4068	Gone! The Promises of Yesterday/I'm So Glad I Fell in Love with You	1971	2.00	4.00	8.00
□ 4080	Let Me Repair Your Heart/Did My Baby Call	1972	2.00	4.00	8.00
□ 4098	I Forgot to Be Your Lover/I'm So Glad I Fell in Love with You	1973	2.00	4.00	8.00

WAND

| □ 11221 | Let's Have Some Fun (Part 1)/Let's Have Some Fun (Part 2) | 1970 | 2.50 | 5.00 | 10.00 |

Albums

STAX

| □ MPS-8525 | The Best of the Mad Lads | 198? | 2.50 | 5.00 | 10.00 |

VOLT

□ 414 [M]	The Mad Lads In Action	1966	7.50	15.00	30.00
□ S-414 [S]	The Mad Lads In Action	1966	10.00	20.00	40.00
□ VOS-6005	The Mad, Mad, Mad, Mad, Mad Lads	1969	7.50	15.00	30.00
□ VOS-6020	A New Beginning	1973	5.00	10.00	20.00

MAD MILO

45s

COMBO

| □ 131 | Elvis on Trial/A Date with Elvis | 1957 | 12.50 | 25.00 | 50.00 |

MILLION

| □ 20018 | Elvis for Christmas/New Year | 1957 | 12.50 | 25.00 | 50.00 |

—B-side by Ron Tan and Combo

MAD RIVER

45s

CAPITOL

| □ 2310 | A Gazelle/High All the Time | 1968 | 3.00 | 6.00 | 12.00 |
| □ 2559 | Copper Plates/Harfy Magnum | 1969 | 3.00 | 6.00 | 12.00 |

Albums

CAPITOL

| □ ST-185 | Paradise Bar and Grill | 1969 | 10.00 | 20.00 | 40.00 |
| □ ST 2985 | Mad River | 1968 | 12.50 | 25.00 | 50.00 |

MADHATTANS, THE

45s

ATLANTIC

| □ 1142 | Wowie/A Basketful of Blueberries | 1957 | 5.00 | 10.00 | 20.00 |

MADISONS, THE

45s

LAWN

| □ 240 | Can You Imagine It/The Wind and the Rain | 1964 | 10.00 | 20.00 | 40.00 |

LIMELIGHT

| □ 3018 | Bad Baboon/Because I Got You | 1964 | 5.00 | 10.00 | 20.00 |

MGM

| □ 13312 | Cheryl Anne/Looking for True Love | 1965 | 10.00 | 20.00 | 40.00 |

MADRIGAL

45s

SSS INTERNATIONAL

| □ 824 | I Believe in Sunshine/Lady | 1971 | 2.00 | 4.00 | 8.00 |

Albums

SSS INTERNATIONAL

| □ 18 | Madrigal | 1971 | 7.50 | 15.00 | 30.00 |

MADURA

45s

COLUMBIA

| □ 45483 | Johnny B. Goode/(B-side unknown) | 1971 | 2.00 | 4.00 | 8.00 |
| □ 46022 | Save the Miracle/Windy One | 1974 | 2.00 | 4.00 | 8.00 |

Number	Title (A Side/B Side)	Yr	VG	VG+	NM

Albums

COLUMBIA

| ❏ G 30794 [(2)] | Madura | 1971 | 5.00 | 10.00 | 20.00 |
| ❏ KC 32545 | Madura II | 1973 | 3.75 | 7.50 | 15.00 |

MAESTRO, JOHNNY Also see THE BROOKLYN BRIDGE; THE CRESTS.

45s

APT

| ❏ 25075 | Phone Booth on the Highway/
She's All Mine Alone | 1965 | 12.50 | 25.00 | 50.00 |

BUDDAH

❏ 201	The Rains Came/Never Knew THis Kind of Hurt Before	1971	2.50	5.00	10.00
❏ 236	Yours Until Tomorrow/Man in a Band	1971	2.50	5.00	10.00
❏ 289 [DJ]	Snow (mono/stereo)	1971	2.50	5.00	10.00

—May be promo only

CAMEO

| ❏ 256 | Over the Weekend/I'll Be There | 1963 | 7.50 | 15.00 | 30.00 |
| ❏ 305 | Lean on Me/(It's Harder to) Make Up My Mind | 1964 | 5.00 | 10.00 | 20.00 |

COED

| ❏ 527 | Say It Isn't So/The Great Physician | 1960 | 6.25 | 12.50 | 25.00 |

—As "Johnny Masters"

| ❏ 545 | Model Girl/We've Got to Tell Them | 1961 | 6.25 | 12.50 | 25.00 |

—As "Johnny Mastro"

❏ 549	What a Surprise/Warning Voice	1961	6.25	12.50	25.00
❏ 552	Mr. Happiness/Test of Love	1961	6.25	12.50	25.00
❏ 557	I.O.U./The Way You Look Tonight	1961	7.50	15.00	30.00
❏ 562	Besame Baby/It Must Be Love	1962	25.00	50.00	100.00

PARKWAY

❏ 118	My Times/Is It You	1966	5.00	10.00	20.00
❏ 987	Heartburn/Try Me	1966	3.75	7.50	15.00
❏ 987 [DJ]	Heartburn	1966	15.00	30.00	60.00

—One-sided white label promo

| ❏ 999 | I Care About You/Come See Me (I'm Your Man) | 1966 | 3.75 | 7.50 | 15.00 |

UNITED ARTISTS

| ❏ 474 | Before I Loved Her/Fifty Million Heartbeats | 1962 | 10.00 | 20.00 | 40.00 |

Albums

BUDDAH

| ❏ BDS-5091 | The Johnny Maestro Story | 1971 | 10.00 | 20.00 | 40.00 |

—With inserts; deduct 40% if missing

MAGI, THE

Albums

UNCLE DIRTY

| ❏ 6102-N13 | Win or Lose | 1975 | 75.00 | 150.00 | 300.00 |

MAGIC CHRISTIANS, THE Trevor Burton of THE MOVE was in this studio group.

45s

COMMONWEALTH UNITED

| ❏ 3006 | Come and Get It/Nats | 1970 | 3.00 | 6.00 | 12.00 |

MAGIC FERN, THE

45s

JERDEN

| ❏ 813 | Maggie/I Wonder Why | 1966 | 5.00 | 10.00 | 20.00 |

PICCADILLY

| ❏ 240 | Nellie/Candy Day | 1967 | 3.75 | 7.50 | 15.00 |

Albums

PANORAMA

| ❏ 108 | The Magic Fern | 1980 | 37.50 | 75.00 | 150.00 |

MAGIC LANTERNS Contrary to some opinions, Ozzy Osbourne was never in this group. (The bass player was Michael "Oz" Osborne; notice the difference in last name spelling.) But ALBERT HAMMOND was.

45s

ATLANTIC

❏ 2560	Shame, Shame/Baby, I Gotta Go Now	1968	2.50	5.00	10.00
❏ 2600	Give Me Love/Biding My Time	1969	2.00	4.00	8.00
❏ 2626	Melt All Your Troubles Away/Bossa Nova 1940- Hello You Lovers	1969	2.00	4.00	8.00
❏ 2715	One Night Stand/Frisco Annie	1970	2.00	4.00	8.00

BIG TREE

| ❏ 109 | One Night Stand/Frisco Annie | 1970 | — | 3.00 | 6.00 |
| ❏ 113 | Let the Sunshine In/Old Pa Bradley | 1971 | — | 3.00 | 6.00 |

CHARISMA

| ❏ 100 | Country Woman/Pa Bradley | 1972 | — | 2.50 | 5.00 |

EPIC

❏ 10062	Excuse Me Baby/Greedy Girl	1966	2.00	4.00	8.00
❏ 10062 [PS]	Excuse Me Baby/Greedy Girl	1966	5.00	10.00	20.00
❏ 10111	Knight in Rusty Armour/Simple Things	1966	2.00	4.00	8.00

Albums

ATLANTIC

| ❏ SD 8217 | Shame, Shame | 1969 | 5.00 | 10.00 | 20.00 |

MAGIC MUSHROOM, THE

45s

WARNER BROS.

| ❏ 5846 | I'm Gone/Cry Baby | 1966 | 6.25 | 12.50 | 25.00 |

MAGIC MUSHROOMS, THE

45s

A&M

| ❏ 815 | It's a-Happening/Never More | 1966 | 3.75 | 7.50 | 15.00 |

PHILIPS

| ❏ 40483 | Look in My Face/Never Let Go | 1968 | 3.75 | 7.50 | 15.00 |

MAGIC SAND

Albums

UNI

| ❏ 73094 | Magic Sand | 1971 | 6.25 | 12.50 | 25.00 |

MAGIC TOUCH, THE (1) Female group.

45s

BLACK FALCON

| ❏ 19102 | Step Into My World/Step Into My World (Part 2) | 1971 | 2.00 | 4.00 | 8.00 |

MAGIC TOUCH, THE (2) Male group.

45s

ROULETTE

| ❏ 7143 | Baby You Belong to Me/Lost and Lonely Boy | 1973 | 3.00 | 6.00 | 12.00 |

MAGISTRATES, THE

45s

MGM

| ❏ 13946 | Here Comes the Judge/Girl | 1968 | 3.00 | 6.00 | 12.00 |
| ❏ 13980 | After the Fox/Tear Down the Walls | 1968 | 3.00 | 6.00 | 12.00 |

MAGNETICS, THE

45s

BONNIE

| ❏ (# unknown) | Lady in Green/(B-side unknown) | 196? | 500.00 | 1000. | 2000. |

MAGNETS, THE (1)

45s

GROOVE

| ❏ 58-0058 | Surprise/You Just Say the Word | 1965 | 10.00 | 20.00 | 40.00 |

MAGNETS, THE (2)

45s

LONDON INT'L.

| ❏ 10036 | Drag Race/Joker | 1963 | 6.25 | 12.50 | 25.00 |

MAGNETS, THE (3)

45s

RCA VICTOR

| ❏ 47-7391 | When the School Bells Ring/
Don't Tarry, Little Mary | 1958 | 6.25 | 12.50 | 25.00 |

MAGNIFICENT FOUR, THE

45s

BLAST

| ❏ 210 | The Closer You Are/Uncle Sam | 1963 | 10.00 | 20.00 | 40.00 |

WHALE

| ❏ 506 | The Closer You Are/Uncle Sam | 1961 | 20.00 | 40.00 | 80.00 |

MAGNIFICENT MEN, THE

45s

CAPITOL

❏ 2062	Baby, I'm Crazy About You/Forever Together	1967	2.00	4.00	8.00
❏ 2134	By the Time I Get to Phoenix/Tired of Pushing	1968	2.00	4.00	8.00
❏ 2202	Almost Persuaded/I Found What I Wanted in You	1968	2.00	4.00	8.00
❏ 2319	Save the Country/So Much Love Waiting	1968	2.00	4.00	8.00
❏ 5608	Peace of Mind/All Your Lovin's Gone To My Head	1966	2.00	4.00	8.00
❏ 5732	I've Got News/Maybe, Maybe, Baby	1966	2.00	4.00	8.00
❏ 5812	Stormy Weather/Much, Much More of Your Love	1966	2.00	4.00	8.00
❏ 5905	I Could Be So Happy/You Changed My Life	1967	2.00	4.00	8.00
❏ 5976	Swet Soul Medley — Part 1/ Sweet Soul Medley — Part 2	1967	2.00	4.00	8.00

MERCURY

| ❏ 72988 | Holly Go Softly/Open Up and Get Richer | 1969 | — | 3.00 | 6.00 |
| ❏ 73028 | Lay Lady Lay/Whatever It Takes | 1970 | — | 3.00 | 6.00 |

Albums

CAPITOL

❏ ST 2678 [S]	The Magnificent Men	1967	3.75	7.50	15.00
❏ T 2678 [M]	The Magnificent Men	1967	5.00	10.00	20.00
❏ ST 2775 [S]	The Magnificent Men "Live!"	1967	3.75	7.50	15.00
❏ T 2775 [M]	The Magnificent Men "Live!"	1967	5.00	10.00	20.00
❏ ST 2846 [S]	World of Soul	1968	3.75	7.50	15.00
❏ T 2846 [M]	World of Soul	1968	5.00	10.00	20.00

MERCURY

| ❏ SR-61252 | Better Than a Ten Cent Movie | 1970 | 3.75 | 7.50 | 15.00 |

MAGNIFICENT 7, THE

45s

DIAL

| ❏ 4074 | Ooh, Baby Baby/
Never Will I (Make My Baby Cry) | 1968 | 6.25 | 12.50 | 25.00 |

DIMENSION

| ❏ 1050 | Show Me/Boogidy | 1965 | 5.00 | 10.00 | 20.00 |

—As "Magnificent VII"

EASTERN

| ❏ 611 | She's Called a Woman/
Since You've Been Gone So Long | 1966 | 10.00 | 20.00 | 40.00 |

MAGNIFICENTS, THE

45s

CHECKER

| ❏ 1016 | The Dribble Twist/Do You Mind | 1962 | 3.75 | 7.50 | 15.00 |

KANSOMA

| ❏ 03 | The Dribble Twist/Do You Mind | 1962 | 7.50 | 15.00 | 30.00 |

LOST-NITE

| ❏ 267 | Up On the Mountain/Why Did She Go | 197? | — | 2.50 | 5.00 |

—Reissue

| ❏ 282 | Don't Leave Me/Ozeta | 197? | — | 2.50 | 5.00 |

—Reissue

VEE JAY

❏ 183	Up On the Mountain/Why Did She Go	1956	18.75	37.50	75.00
❏ 208	Hiccup/Caddy Bo	1956	25.00	50.00	100.00
❏ 235	Off the Mountain/Lost Lovers	1957	18.75	37.50	75.00
❏ 281	Don't Leave Me/Ozeta	1958	25.00	50.00	100.00
❏ 367	Up On the Mountain/Let's Do the Cha Cha	1960	5.00	10.00	20.00

MAHAL, TAJ

45s

COLUMBIA

❏ 10055	Why Did You Have to Desert Me/Cajun Waltz	1974	—	2.00	4.00
❏ 10109	Salve Drive/Cajun Waltz	1975	—	2.00	4.00
❏ 10260	Why, And We Repeat Why, And We Repeat.../ (B-side unknown)	1975	—	2.00	4.00
❏ 10368	Ain't Nobody's Business/Easy to Love	1976	—	2.00	4.00

Number	Title (A Side/B Side)	Yr	VG	VG+	NM
❏ 44051	Let the Good Times Roll/				
	Shimmy Like My Sister Kate	1967	2.00	4.00	8.00
❏ 44405	E-Z Rider/Leaving Trunk	1967	2.00	4.00	8.00
❏ 44476	Statesboro Blues/Everybody's Got to Change				
	Sometime	1968	2.00	4.00	8.00
❏ 44696	You Don't Miss Your Water/Going Down to the				
	Country-Paint My Mailbox Blue	1968	2.00	4.00	8.00
❏ 44767	Corinna/A Lot of Love	1969	2.00	4.00	8.00
❏ 44991	Six Days on the Road/Light Rain Blues	1969	2.00	4.00	8.00
❏ 45419	Fishin' Blues/Diving Duck Blues	1971	—	2.50	5.00
❏ 45455	Ain't Gwine to Whistle Dixie Anymore				
	(Part 1/Part 2)	1971	—	2.50	5.00
❏ 45539	Chevrolet/Oh Susanna	1972	—	2.50	5.00
❏ 45990	Buck Dancer's Choice/Little Red Hen	1974	—	2.50	5.00
❏ 46031	Built for Comfort/Teacup's Jazzy Blues Tune	1974	—	2.50	5.00
WARNER BROS.					
❏ 8528	Sing a Happy Song/				
	Southbound with the Hammer Down	1978	—	2.00	4.00
Albums					
COLUMBIA					
❏ CG 18 [(2)]	Giant Step/De Ole Folks at Home	198?	2.50	5.00	10.00
—Reissue with new prefix					
❏ GP 18 [(2)]	Giant Step/De Ole Folks at Home	1969	5.00	10.00	20.00
—Red "360 Sound" label					
❏ GP 18 [(2)]	Giant Step/De Ole Folks at Home	1971	3.75	7.50	15.00
—Orange label					
❏ CL 2779 [M]	Taj Mahal	1967	7.50	15.00	30.00
❏ CS 9579 [S]	Taj Mahal	1967	3.75	7.50	15.00
—Red "360 Sound" label					
❏ CS 9579 [S]	Taj Mahal	1971	3.00	6.00	12.00
—Orange label					
❏ PC 9579 [S]	Taj Mahal	198?	2.00	4.00	8.00
—Reissue with new prefix					
❏ CS 9698	The Natch'l Blues	1968	3.75	7.50	15.00
—Red "360 Sound" label					
❏ CS 9698	The Natch'l Blues	1971	3.00	6.00	12.00
—Orange label					
❏ PC 9698	The Natch'l Blues	198?	2.00	4.00	8.00
—Reissue with new prefix					
❏ CG 30619 [(2)]	The Real Thing	198?	2.50	5.00	10.00
—Reissue with new prefix					
❏ G 30619 [(2)]	The Real Thing	1971	5.00	10.00	20.00
❏ C 30767	Happy to Be Like I Am	1971	3.00	6.00	12.00
❏ PC 30767	Happy to Be Like I Am	198?	2.00	4.00	8.00
—Budget-line reissue					
❏ KC 31605	Recycling the Blues & Other Related Stuff	1972	3.00	6.00	12.00
❏ PC 31605	Recycling the Blues & Other Related Stuff	198?	2.00	4.00	8.00
—Budget-line reissue					
❏ KC 32600	Oooh So Good 'N Blues	1973	3.00	6.00	12.00
❏ PC 32600	Oooh So Good 'N Blues	198?	2.00	4.00	8.00
—Budget-line reissue					
❏ KC 33051	Mo' Roots	1974	3.00	6.00	12.00
❏ PC 33051	Mo' Roots	198?	2.00	4.00	8.00
—Budget-line reissue					
❏ PC 33801	Music Keeps Me Together	1975	3.00	6.00	12.00
❏ PC 34103	Satisfied & Tickled Too	1976	3.00	6.00	12.00
❏ PC 34466	Anthology Volume 1	1977	3.00	6.00	12.00
❏ FC 36528	The Best of Taj Mahal	1981	2.50	5.00	10.00
❏ PC 36528	The Best of Taj Mahal	198?	2.00	4.00	8.00
—Budget-line reissue					
CRYSTAL CLEAR					
❏ 5011	Live and Direct	1980	6.25	12.50	25.00
—Direct-to-disc recording					
WARNER BROS.					
❏ BS 2994	Music Fuh Ya' (Musica Para Tu)	1977	2.50	5.00	10.00
❏ BS 3024	Brothers	1977	2.50	5.00	10.00
❏ BS 3094	Evolution (Recent)	1978	2.50	5.00	10.00

MAHARIS, GEORGE
45s
EPIC

Number	Title (A Side/B Side)	Yr	VG	VG+	NM
❏ 9504	Teach Me Tonight/After the Lights Go Down Low	1962	2.00	4.00	8.00
❏ 9504 [PS]	Teach Me Tonight/After the Lights Go Down Low	1962	2.50	5.00	10.00
❏ 9522	Love Me as I Love You/They Knew About You	1962	2.00	4.00	8.00
❏ 9522 [PS]	Love Me as I Love You/They Knew About You	1962	2.50	5.00	10.00
❏ 9555	Baby Has Gone Bye Bye/After One Kiss	1962	2.00	4.00	8.00
❏ 9555 [PS]	Baby Has Gone Bye Bye/After One Kiss	1962	2.50	5.00	10.00
❏ 9569	Don't Fence Me In/Alright, Okay, You Win	1963	2.00	4.00	8.00
❏ 9569 [PS]	Don't Fence Me In/Alright, Okay, You Win	1963	2.50	5.00	10.00
❏ 9600	Where Can You Go				
	(For a Broken Heart)/Kiss Me	1963	2.00	4.00	8.00
❏ 9600 [PS]	Where Can You Go				
	(For a Broken Heart)/Kiss Me	1963	2.50	5.00	10.00
❏ 9613	That's How It Goes/It Isn't There	1963	2.00	4.00	8.00
❏ 9613 [PS]	That's How It Goes/It Isn't There	1963	2.50	5.00	10.00
❏ 9653	It's a Sin to Tell a Lie/Sara Darling	1964	—	3.00	6.00
❏ 9696	The Object of My Affection/				
	Tonight You Belong to Me	1964	—	3.00	6.00
❏ 9696 [PS]	The Object of My Affection/				
	Tonight You Belong to Me	1964	3.00	6.00	12.00
❏ 9753	I'm Coming Back for You/				
	Lonely People Do Foolish Things	1965	—	3.00	6.00
❏ 9772	More I Cannot Do/Where Does Happiness Go	1965	—	3.00	6.00
❏ 9844	Quien Sabe (Who Knows, Who Knows)/You				
	Always Hurt the One You Love	1965	—	3.00	6.00
❏ 9858	Ivy/A World Without Sunshine	1965	—	3.00	6.00
❏ 10039	Never Is a Long, Long Time/Goodbye, Good				
	Luck and God Bless You	1966	—	3.00	6.00
Albums					
EPIC					
❏ LN 24001 [M]	George Maharis Sings!	1962	3.00	6.00	12.00
❏ LN 24021 [M]	Portrait in Music	1962	3.00	6.00	12.00
❏ LN 24037 [M]	Just Turn Me Loose!	1963	3.00	6.00	12.00
❏ LN 24064 [M]	Where Can You Go for a Broken Heart?	1963	3.00	6.00	12.00
❏ LN 24079 [M]	Make Love to Me	1964	3.00	6.00	12.00
❏ LN 24111 [M]	Tonight You Belong to Me	1964	3.00	6.00	12.00
❏ LN 24191 [M]	A New Route: George Maharis	1966	3.00	6.00	12.00

Number	Title (A Side/B Side)	Yr	VG	VG+	NM
❏ BN 26001 [S]	George Maharis Sings!	1962	3.75	7.50	15.00
❏ BN 26021 [S]	Portrait in Music	1962	3.75	7.50	15.00
❏ BN 26037 [S]	Just Turn Me Loose!	1963	3.75	7.50	15.00
❏ BN 26064 [S]	Where Can You Go for a Broken Heart?	1963	3.75	7.50	15.00
❏ BN 26079 [S]	Make Love to Me	1964	3.75	7.50	15.00
❏ BN 26111 [S]	Tonight You Belong to Me	1964	3.75	7.50	15.00
❏ BN 26191 [S]	A New Route: George Maharis	1966	3.75	7.50	15.00

MAHOGANY RUSH
45s
NINE

Number	Title (A Side/B Side)	Yr	VG	VG+	NM
❏ 369	Buddy/All in Your Mind	1973	2.00	4.00	8.00
20TH CENTURY					
❏ 2111	New Rock and Roll/Child of the Novelty	1974	—	2.50	5.00
❏ 2166	Buddy/Satisfy Your Soul	1975	—	2.50	5.00
Albums					
COLUMBIA					
❏ PC 34190	Mahogany Rush IV	1976	3.75	7.50	15.00
—Original with no bar code					
❏ PC 34190	Mahogany Rush IV	198?	2.00	4.00	8.00
—Reissue with bar code					
❏ PC 34677	World Anthem	1977	3.75	7.50	15.00
—Original with no bar code					
❏ PC 34677	World Anthem	198?	2.00	4.00	8.00
—Reissue with bar code					
❏ JC 35257	Frank Marino & Mahogany Rush Live	1978	3.75	7.50	15.00
❏ PC 35257	Frank Marino & Mahogany Rush Live	198?	2.00	4.00	8.00
—Budget-line reissue					
❏ JC 35753	Tales of the Unexpected	1979	3.75	7.50	15.00
❏ PC 35753	Tales of the Unexpected	198?	2.00	4.00	8.00
—Budget-line reissue					
❏ JC 36204	What's Next	1980	3.75	7.50	15.00
❏ PC 36204	What's Next	198?	2.00	4.00	8.00
—Budget-line reissue					
NINE					
❏ 936	Maxoom	1973	12.50	25.00	50.00
20TH CENTURY					
❏ T-451	Child of the Novelty	1974	6.25	12.50	25.00
❏ T-463	Maxoom	1975	6.25	12.50	25.00
—Reissue of Nine 936					
❏ T-482	Strange Universe	1975	5.00	10.00	20.00

MAIN ATTRACTION, THE
45s
TOWER

Number	Title (A Side/B Side)	Yr	VG	VG+	NM
❏ 420	I Remember Yesterday/If I'm Wrong	1968	2.50	5.00	10.00
❏ 435	Everyday/One Must Cry	1968	2.50	5.00	10.00
❏ 464	Friends/Jonathan	1969	2.50	5.00	10.00
Albums					
TOWER					
❏ ST-5117 [S]	And Now...The Main Attraction	1968	6.25	12.50	25.00
❏ T-5117 [M]	And Now...The Main Attraction	1968	12.50	25.00	50.00

MAIN INGREDIENT, THE
12-Inch Singles
RCA

Number	Title (A Side/B Side)	Yr	VG	VG+	NM
❏ PD-13046	Party People/Save Me	1981	3.00	6.00	12.00
45s					
MERCURY					
❏ 73831	Magic Touch/Very White	1976	—	2.50	5.00
—As "Tony Sylvester and the New Ingredient"					
❏ 73871	Puzuzu/Soca	1977	—	2.50	5.00
—As "Tony Sylvester and the New Ingredient"					
POLYDOR					
❏ 889910-7	I Just Wanna Love You/When We Need It Bad	1989	—	—	3.00
RCA					
❏ PB-12060	Think Positive/Spoiled	1980	—	2.00	4.00
—RCA 1980s titles as "Cuba Gooding and the Main Ingredient"					
❏ PB-12107	What Can a Miracle Do/				
	Makes No Diff'rence to Me	1980	—	2.00	4.00
❏ PB-12320	Evening of Love/(Instrumental)	1981	—	—	—
—Unreleased					
❏ PB-12340	I Only Have Eyes for You/Only	1981	—	2.00	4.00
❏ PB-12340 [PS]	I Only Have Eyes for You/Only	1981	2.50	5.00	10.00
—Sleeve is not seam sealed, but folds open to promote the album from which the songs came					
❏ PB-13045	Party People/Save Me	1982	—	2.00	4.00
RCA VICTOR					
❏ 47-9748	I Was Born to Lose You/Psychedelic Ride	1969	—	3.00	6.00
❏ 74-0252	Get Back/Brotherly Love	1969	—	3.00	6.00
❏ 74-0313	The Girl I Left Behind/Can't Stand Your Love	1970	—	2.50	5.00
❏ 74-0340	You've Been My Inspiration/Life Won't Be the				
	Same (Without You)	1970	—	2.50	5.00
❏ 74-0385	Need Your Love/I'm Better Off Without You	1970	—	2.50	5.00
❏ 74-0401	I'm So Proud/Brother Love	1970	—	2.50	5.00
❏ 74-0456	Spinning Around (I Must Be Falling in Love)/				
	Magic Shoes	1971	—	2.50	5.00
❏ 74-0517	Black Seeds Keep On Growing/				
	Baby Change Your Mind	1971	—	2.50	5.00
❏ 74-0603	I'm Leaving This Time/Another Day Has Come	1971	—	2.50	5.00
❏ 74-0731	Everybody Plays the Fool/Who Can I Turn To	1972	—	3.00	6.00
❏ 74-0856	You've Got to Take It (If You Want It)/Travelling	1973	—	2.50	5.00
❏ 74-0939	You Can Call Me Rover/				
	I'm Better Off Without You	1973	—	2.50	5.00
❏ APBO-0046	Girl Blue/Movin' On	1973	—	2.50	5.00
❏ AMBO-0124	Everybody Plays the Fool/I'm So Proud	1973	—	2.00	4.00
—Gold Standard Series					
❏ APBO-0205	Just Don't Want to Be Lonely/Goodbye My Love	1974	—	2.50	5.00
❏ APBO-0305	Happiness Is Just Around the Bend/Why Can't				
	We All Unite	1974	—	2.50	5.00
❏ PB-10095	California My Way/Looks Like Rain	1974	—	2.50	5.00
❏ PB-10224	Rolling Down a Mountainside/Family Man	1975	—	2.50	5.00
❏ PB-10334	The Good Old Days/I Want to Make You Glad	1975	—	2.50	5.00
❏ PB-10431	Shame on the World/Lillian	1975	—	2.50	5.00
❏ GB-10482	Why Can't We All Unite/Happiness Is Just				
	Around the Corner	1975	—	2.00	4.00
—Gold Standard Series					

M

Number	Title (A Side/B Side)	Yr	VG	VG+	NM
❏ GB-10483	Just Don't Want to Be Lonely/Goodbye My Love	1975	—	2.00	4.00

—Gold Standard Series

ZAKIA

Number	Title (A Side/B Side)	Yr	VG	VG+	NM
❏ 015	Do Me Right/(B-side unknown)	1986	—	2.00	4.00

Albums
COLLECTABLES

| ❏ COL-5101 | Golden Classics | 198? | 2.50 | 5.00 | 10.00 |

POLYDOR

| ❏ 841249-1 | I Just Wanna Love You | 1989 | 3.00 | 6.00 | 12.00 |

RCA VICTOR

❏ APL1-0314	Greatest Hits	1974	3.00	6.00	12.00
❏ APD1-0335 [Q]	Euphrates River	1974	5.00	10.00	20.00
❏ APL1-0335	Euphrates River	1974	3.00	6.00	12.00
❏ APL1-0644	Rolling Down a Mountainside	1975	3.00	6.00	12.00
❏ APL1-1003	Shame On the World	1975	3.00	6.00	12.00
❏ APL1-1558	Music Maximus	1977	3.00	6.00	12.00
❏ APL1-1858	Super Hits	1977	3.00	6.00	12.00
❏ ANL1-2667	Rolling Down a Mountainside	1978	2.50	5.00	10.00

—Reissue of APL1-0644

❏ AFL1-3641	Ready for Love	1980	2.50	5.00	10.00
❏ AFL1-3963	I Only Have Eyes for You	1981	2.50	5.00	10.00
❏ LSP-4253	The Main Ingredient L.T.D.	1970	3.00	6.00	12.00
❏ LSP-4412	Tasteful Soul	1971	3.00	6.00	12.00
❏ LSP-4483	Black Seeds	1971	3.00	6.00	12.00
❏ LSP-4677	Bitter Sweet	1972	3.00	6.00	12.00
❏ LSP-4834	Afrodisiac	1973	3.00	6.00	12.00

MAJESTICS, THE (1)
45s
CHESS

| ❏ 1802 | Oasis (Part 1)/Oasis (Part 2) | 1961 | 5.00 | 10.00 | 20.00 |

V.I.P.

| ❏ 25028 [DJ] | Say You/All for Someone | 1965 | 250.00 | 500.00 | 1000. |

—Promo only; stock copies credited "The Monitors"

MAJESTICS, THE (2)
45s
CHEX

❏ 1000	Give Me a Cigarette/So I Can Forget	1962	10.00	20.00	40.00
❏ 1000	Give Me a Cigarette/Shoppin' and Hoppin'	1962	25.00	50.00	100.00
❏ 1004	Unhappy and Blue/Treat Me Like You Want	1962	12.50	25.00	50.00
❏ 1006	Lonely Heart/Gwendolyn	1962	7.50	15.00	30.00
❏ 1009	Baby/Teach Me How to Limbo	1963	6.25	12.50	25.00

MAJESTICS, THE (3)
45s
CONTOUR

| ❏ 501 | Teen Age Gossip/Hard Times | 1960 | 20.00 | 40.00 | 80.00 |

FARO

| ❏ 592 | TV Cowboys/So You Want to Rock | 1959 | 6.25 | 12.50 | 25.00 |

FOXIE

| ❏ 7004 | The Lone Stranger/Sweet One | 1960 | 5.00 | 10.00 | 20.00 |

NRC

| ❏ 502 | Please Don't Say No/Divided Heart | 1958 | 62.50 | 125.00 | 250.00 |

SIOUX

| ❏ 91459 | The Lone Stranger/Sweet One | 1959 | 12.50 | 25.00 | 50.00 |

20TH FOX

| ❏ 171 | The Lone Stranger/Sweet One | 1959 | 6.25 | 12.50 | 25.00 |

MAJESTICS, THE (4)
45s
DUNES

| ❏ 2014 | The Boss Walk (Part 1)/The Boss Walk (Part 2) | 1962 | 10.00 | 20.00 | 40.00 |

SAM

❏ 112	Jaguar/Blue Feeling	1962	12.50	25.00	50.00
❏ 117	Riptide/Big Noise from Makaba	1962	12.50	25.00	50.00
❏ 123	XL-3/My Little Baby	1963	12.50	25.00	50.00

MAJESTICS, THE (5)
45s
JORDAN

| ❏ 1057 | Angel of Love/Searching for a New Love | 1961 | 12.50 | 25.00 | 50.00 |

—Black vinyl

| ❏ 1057 | Angel of Love/Searching for a New Love | 1961 | 75.00 | 150.00 | 300.00 |

—Yellow vinyl

LINDA

| ❏ 111 | Strange World/Everything Is Gonna Be All Right | 1963 | 15.00 | 30.00 | 60.00 |
| ❏ 121 | Girl of My Dreams/It Hurts Me | 1963 | 25.00 | 50.00 | 100.00 |

NU-TONE

| ❏ 123 | Angel of Love/Searching for a New Love | 1961 | 17.50 | 35.00 | 70.00 |

PIXIE

| ❏ 6901 | Angel of Love/Searching for a New Love | 1961 | 7.50 | 15.00 | 30.00 |

MAJESTICS, THE (6) Sam Moore of SAM AND DAVE was in this group.
45s
MARLIN

| ❏ 802 | Nitey Nite/Cave Man Rock | 1956 | 250.00 | 500.00 | 1000. |

MAJESTICS, THE (7)
45s
MGM

| ❏ 13488 | Love Has Forgotten Me/Smile Through My Tears | 1966 | 3.00 | 6.00 | 12.00 |

MAJOR LANCE See listing under LANCE, MAJOR.

MAJORETTES, THE
45s
TROY

| ❏ 1000 | White Levi's/Please Come Back | 1963 | 5.00 | 10.00 | 20.00 |
| ❏ 1000 [PS] | White Levi's/Please Come Back | 1963 | 10.00 | 20.00 | 40.00 |

MAJORS, THE (1)
45s
IMPERIAL

| ❏ 5855 | A Wonderful Dream/Time Will Tell | 1962 | 5.00 | 10.00 | 20.00 |
| ❏ 5879 | She's a Troublemaker/ A Little Bit Now, A Little Bit Later | 1962 | 3.75 | 7.50 | 15.00 |

Number	Title (A Side/B Side)	Yr	VG	VG+	NM
❏ 5914	What in the World/Anything You Can Do	1963	3.00	6.00	12.00
❏ 5936	Tra La La/What Have You Been Doin'	1963	3.00	6.00	12.00
❏ 5968	One Happy Ending/Get Up Now	1963	3.00	6.00	12.00
❏ 5991	Which Way Did She Go/ Your Life Begins (Sweet 16)	1963	3.00	6.00	12.00
❏ 66009	I'll Be There/Ooh Wee Baby	1963	3.00	6.00	12.00

UNITED ARTISTS

| ❏ 0110 | A Wonderful Dream/Mother-in-Law | 1973 | — | 2.50 | 5.00 |

—"Silver Spotlight Series" reissue; B-side by Ernie K-Doe

Albums
IMPERIAL

| ❏ LP-9222 [M] | Meet the Majors | 1963 | 37.50 | 75.00 | 150.00 |
| ❏ LP-12222 [S] | Meet the Majors | 1963 | 75.00 | 150.00 | 300.00 |

MAJORS, THE (2)
45s
DERBY

| ❏ 763 | At Last/You Ran Away from My Heart | 1951 | 200.00 | 400.00 | 800.00 |
| ❏ 779 | Laughing on the Outside/ Come On Up to My Room | 1951 | 150.00 | 300.00 | 600.00 |

MAJORS, THE (3)
45s
FELSTED

❏ 8501	Blue Sunset/Rockin' the Boogie	1958	7.50	15.00	30.00
❏ 8576	Come Go with Me/Les Qua	1959	6.25	12.50	25.00
❏ 8707	Come Go with Me/Les Qua	1964	3.75	7.50	15.00

MAJORS, THE (4)
45s
ORIGINAL

| ❏ 1003 | Big Eyes/Go 'Way | 1954 | 100.00 | 200.00 | 400.00 |

MAKEBA, MIRIAM Also see HARRY BELAFONTE.
45s
KAPP

| ❏ 452 | Carnival/Can't Cross Over | 1962 | 3.00 | 6.00 | 12.00 |

LONDON

| ❏ 1610 | Lovely Lies/Kilimanjaro | 1956 | 3.75 | 7.50 | 15.00 |

—With the Manhattan Brothers

MERCURY

| ❏ 72642 | Ballad of the Sad Young Men/Mommy, Mommy, What Is Heaven Like | 1966 | 2.00 | 4.00 | 8.00 |

RCA VICTOR

| ❏ 47-8326 | Dubula/Forbidden Games | 1964 | 2.50 | 5.00 | 10.00 |

REPRISE

❏ 0578	Reza/When I've Passed On	1967	—	3.00	6.00
❏ 0606	Pata Pata/Ballad of the Sad Young Men	1967	2.00	4.00	8.00
❏ 0654	Malaysha/Ring Bell, Ring Bell	1967	—	3.00	6.00
❏ 0671	What Is Love/Ho Po Zamani	1968	—	3.00	6.00
❏ 0732	Pata Pata/Malaysha	1969	—	2.00	4.00

—"Back to Back Hits" series

❏ 0755	Ibabalazie/Emavungivini (Down in the Dumps)	1968	—	3.00	6.00
❏ 0804	I Shall Be Released/Iphi Ndilela	1969	—	3.00	6.00
❏ 0921	I Shall Sing/In My Life	1970	—	3.00	6.00

Albums
KAPP

| ❏ KL-1274 [M] | The Many Voices of Miriam Makeba | 1962 | 5.00 | 10.00 | 20.00 |
| ❏ KS-3274 [S] | The Many Voices of Miriam Makeba | 1962 | 6.25 | 12.50 | 25.00 |

MERCURY

❏ MG-21082 [M]	The Magnificent Miriam Makeba	1966	3.00	6.00	12.00
❏ MG-21095 [M]	All About Miriam	1967	3.00	6.00	12.00
❏ SR-61082 [S]	The Magnificent Miriam Makeba	1966	3.75	7.50	15.00
❏ SR-61095 [S]	All About Miriam	1967	3.75	7.50	15.00

MERCURY/URBAN AFRICA

| ❏ 838208-1 | Welela | 1989 | 3.00 | 6.00 | 12.00 |

RCA VICTOR

❏ LPM-2267 [M]	Miriam Makeba	1960	5.00	10.00	20.00
❏ LSP-2267 [S]	Miriam Makeba	1960	6.25	12.50	25.00
❏ LPM-2750 [M]	The World of Miriam Makeba	1963	3.75	7.50	15.00
❏ LSP-2750 [S]	The World of Miriam Makeba	1963	5.00	10.00	20.00
❏ LPM-2845 [M]	The Voice of Africa	1964	3.75	7.50	15.00
❏ LSP-2845 [S]	The Voice of Africa	1964	5.00	10.00	20.00
❏ LPM-3321 [M]	Makeba Sings	1965	3.75	7.50	15.00
❏ LSP-3321 [S]	Makeba Sings	1965	5.00	10.00	20.00
❏ LPM-3512 [M]	The Magic of Makeba	1966	3.75	7.50	15.00
❏ LSP-3512 [S]	The Magic of Makeba	1966	5.00	10.00	20.00
❏ LPM-3982 [M]	The Best of Miriam Makeba	1968	6.25	12.50	25.00
❏ LSP-3982 [S]	The Best of Miriam Makeba	1968	3.00	6.00	12.00

REPRISE

❏ R-6253 [M]	Miriam Makeba In Concert!	1967	3.75	7.50	15.00
❏ RS-6253 [S]	Miriam Makeba In Concert!	1967	3.00	6.00	12.00
❏ R-6274 [M]	Pata Pata	1967	3.75	7.50	15.00
❏ RS-6274 [S]	Pata Pata	1967	3.00	6.00	12.00
❏ RS-6310	Makeba!	1968	3.00	6.00	12.00
❏ RS-6381	Keep Me in Mind	1970	3.00	6.00	12.00

WARNER BROS.

| ❏ 25673 | Sangoma | 1988 | 2.50 | 5.00 | 10.00 |

MALACHI
Albums
VERVE

| ❏ V-5024 [M] | Holy Music | 1967 | 7.50 | 15.00 | 30.00 |
| ❏ V6-5024 [S] | Holy Music | 1967 | 10.00 | 20.00 | 40.00 |

MALCOLM X
Albums
DOUGLAS

❏ SD 795 [M]	Malcolm X Talks to Young People	1968	7.50	15.00	30.00
❏ SD 797	His Wit and Wisdom	196?	7.50	15.00	30.00
❏ Z 30743 [M]	By Any Means Necessary	1971	7.50	15.00	30.00

PAUL WINLEY

| ❏ 135 | The Ballot or the Bullet | 197? | 5.00 | 10.00 | 20.00 |

RCA

| ❏ 66132 | Words from the Frontlines: Excerpts from the Great Speeches of Malcolm X | 1992 | 5.00 | 10.00 | 20.00 |

Number	Title (A Side/B Side)	Yr	VG	VG+	NM
UPFRONT					
❏ UPF-152	Malcolm X Speaks to the People in Harlem	197?	3.75	7.50	15.00
WARNER BROS.					
❏ BS 2619	Malcolm X	1972	6.25	12.50	25.00
❏ PRO-A-5943 [DJ]	Malcolm X Speaks	1992	5.00	10.00	20.00
❏ PRO-A-5957 [DJ]	Music and Dialog from the Historic 1992 Documentary Film Malcolm X	1992	5.00	10.00	20.00

MALLETT, SAUNDRA, AND THE VANDELLAS
45s

Number	Title (A Side/B Side)	Yr	VG	VG+	NM
TAMLA					
❏ 54067	Camel Walk/It's Gonna Be Hard Times	1962	250.00	500.00	1000.

MALO
12-Inch Singles

Number	Title (A Side/B Side)	Yr	VG	VG+	NM
TRAQ					
❏ TR-109	Lady I Love (Dance Version 8:00) (Radio Version 3:40)	1981	2.00	4.00	8.00

45s

Number	Title (A Side/B Side)	Yr	VG	VG+	NM
TRAQ					
❏ 106	Fernando/Lady I Love	1981	—	3.00	6.00
WARNER BROS.					
❏ 7559	Suavecito/Nena	1972	—	2.50	5.00
❏ 7605	Café/Peace	1972	—	2.50	5.00
❏ 7651	Suavecito/Café	1973	—	2.00	4.00
—"Back to Back Hits" reissue					
❏ 7668	Oye Mama/I'm For Real	1972	—	2.50	5.00
❏ 7677	Latin Bugaloo/Midnight Thoughts	1973	—	2.50	5.00
❏ 7692	I Don't Know/Merengue	1973	—	2.50	5.00

Albums

Number	Title (A Side/B Side)	Yr	VG	VG+	NM
WARNER BROS.					
❏ BS 2584	Malo	1972	3.00	6.00	12.00
❏ BS 2652	Dos	1972	3.00	6.00	12.00
❏ BS 2702	Evolution	1973	3.00	6.00	12.00
❏ BS 2769	Ascencion	1974	3.00	6.00	12.00

MALTAIS, GENE
45s

Number	Title (A Side/B Side)	Yr	VG	VG+	NM
DECCA					
❏ 30387	Crazy Baby/Deep River Blues	1957	50.00	100.00	200.00
LILAC					
❏ 3159	The Raging Sea/(B-side unknown)	1957	100.00	200.00	400.00
REGAL					
❏ 7502	Lovemakin'/The Bug	1958	37.50	75.00	150.00

MAMA CASS See CASS ELLIOT.

MAMA LION
45s

Number	Title (A Side/B Side)	Yr	VG	VG+	NM
FAMILY PRODUCTIONS					
❏ 0903	Ain't Too Proud to Beg/Cry	1971	2.00	4.00	8.00
❏ 0921	Sister Sister/Give It Everything I've Got	1972	2.00	4.00	8.00

Albums

Number	Title (A Side/B Side)	Yr	VG	VG+	NM
FAMILY PRODUCTIONS					
❏ FPS-2702	Mama Lion	1972	5.00	10.00	20.00
❏ FPS-2713	Give It Everything I've Got	1973	5.00	10.00	20.00

MAMAS AND THE PAPAS, THE Also see DENNY DOHERTY; CASS ELLIOT; JILL GIBSON; JOHN PHILLIPS; MICHELLE PHILLIPS.
45s

Number	Title (A Side/B Side)	Yr	VG	VG+	NM
ABC DUNHILL					
❏ 4125	Safe in My Garden/Too Late	1968	2.00	4.00	8.00
❏ 4150	For the Love of Ivy/Strange Young Girls	1968	2.00	4.00	8.00
❏ 4171	Do You Wanna Dance/My Girl	1968	2.00	4.00	8.00
❏ 4301	Step Out/Shooting Star	1972	—	3.00	6.00
DUNHILL					
❏ 4018 [DJ]	Go Where You Wanna Go/Somebody Groovy	1966	5.00	10.00	20.00
—Withdrawn before stock copies were released					
❏ 4018 [PS]	Go Where You Wanna Go/Somebody Groovy	1966	100.00	200.00	400.00
—Yes, a picture sleeve has been confirmed!					
❏ 4020	California Dreamin'/Somebody Groovy	1966	2.50	5.00	10.00
—Most of the 1966 Dunhill singles credited "The Mama's and the Papa's"					
❏ 4020 [PS]	California Dreamin'/Somebody Groovy	1966	75.00	150.00	300.00
—Sleeve is promo only					
❏ 4026	Monday, Monday/Got a Feeling	1966	2.50	5.00	10.00
❏ 4026 [PS]	Monday, Monday/I Call Your Name	1966	150.00	300.00	600.00
—The sleeve was printed, but after Dunhill changed the flip side of the 45 before release, most of them were destroyed					
❏ 4031	I Saw Her Again/Even If I Could	1966	2.50	5.00	10.00
❏ 4050	Look Through My Window/ Once Was a Time I Thought	1966	2.50	5.00	10.00
❏ 4057	Words of Love/Dancing in the Street	1966	2.50	5.00	10.00
❏ 4077	Dedicated to the One I Love/Free Advice	1967	2.50	5.00	10.00
❏ 4083	Creeque Alley/Did You Ever Want to Cry	1967	2.50	5.00	10.00
❏ 4083 [PS]	Creeque Alley/Did You Ever Want to Cry	1967	10.00	20.00	40.00
—Sleeve is promo only					
❏ 4099	Twelve Thirty (Young Girls Are Coming to the Canyon)/Straight Shooter	1967	2.50	5.00	10.00
❏ 4107	Glad to Be Unhappy/Hey Girl	1967	2.50	5.00	10.00
❏ 4113	Dancing Bear/John's Music Box	1967	2.50	5.00	10.00
❏ 4113 [PS]	Dancing Bear/John's Music Box	1967	3.00	6.00	12.00
❏ 4125	Safe in My Garden/Too Late	1968	6.25	12.50	25.00
—Without the "ABC" logo at top of label					

7-Inch Extended Plays

Number	Title (A Side/B Side)	Yr	VG	VG+	NM
ABC DUNHILL					
❏ LP-DS-50031	Safe in My Garden/For the Love of Ivy// Mansions/Dream a Little Dream of Me	1968	3.75	7.50	15.00
—Jukebox issue; small hole, plays at 33 1/3 rpm					
❏ LP-DS-50031 [PS]	The Papas and the Mamas	1968	3.75	7.50	15.00
❏ PRO-50106	People Like Us/I Wanna Be a Star/Pearl// Pacific Coast Highway/ Snowqueen of Texas/Step Out	1972	5.00	10.00	20.00
—Jukebox issue; small hole, plays at 33 1/3 rpm					
❏ PRO-50106 [PS]	People Like Us	1972	7.50	15.00	30.00

Number	Title (A Side/B Side)	Yr	VG	VG+	NM
Albums					
ABC					
❏ AC-30005	The ABC Collection	1976	3.75	7.50	15.00
ABC DUNHILL					
❏ DS-50006	If You Can Believe Your Eyes and Ears	1968	3.00	6.00	12.00
❏ DS-50010	The Mamas and the Papas	1968	3.00	6.00	12.00
❏ DS-50014	The Mamas and the Papas Deliver	1968	3.00	6.00	12.00
❏ DS-50025	Farewell to the First Golden Era	1968	3.00	6.00	12.00
❏ DS-50031	The Papas and the Mamas	1968	3.75	7.50	15.00
—The five LPs above are reissues of records originally without the ABC logo					
❏ DS-50038	Golden Era, Volume 2	1968	5.00	10.00	20.00
❏ DS-50064	16 of Their Greatest Hits	1969	3.75	7.50	15.00
❏ DS-50073 [(2)]	A Gathering of Flowers	1970	6.25	12.50	25.00
❏ DSX-50100	Monterey International Pop Festival	1970	3.75	7.50	15.00
❏ DSX-50106	People Like Us	1971	3.00	6.00	12.00
❏ DSX-50145 [(2)]	20 Golden Hits	1973	5.00	10.00	20.00
DUNHILL					
❏ D-50006 [M]	If You Can Believe Your Eyes and Ears	1966	5.00	10.00	20.00
—With scroll over toilet					
❏ D-50006 [M]	If You Can Believe Your Eyes and Ears	1966	10.00	20.00	40.00
—Black cover with photo cropped to render toilet invisible					
❏ D-50006 [M]	If You Can Believe Your Eyes and Ears	1966	20.00	40.00	80.00
—With toilet completely visible in lower right					
❏ DS-50006 [S]	If You Can Believe Your Eyes and Ears	1966	6.25	12.50	25.00
—With scroll over toilet proclaiming "Includes California Dreamin' "					
❏ DS-50006 [S]	If You Can Believe Your Eyes and Ears	1966	6.25	12.50	25.00
—With scroll over toilet proclaiming "Includes California Dreamin'... Monday Monday... I Call Your Name"					
❏ DS-50006 [S]	If You Can Believe Your Eyes and Ears	1966	12.50	25.00	50.00
—Black cover with photo cropped to render toilet invisible					
❏ DS-50006 [S]	If You Can Believe Your Eyes and Ears	1966	25.00	50.00	100.00
—With toilet completely visible in lower right					
❏ D-50010 [M]	The Mamas and the Papas	1966	5.00	10.00	20.00
❏ DS-50010 [S]	The Mamas and the Papas	1966	6.25	12.50	25.00
❏ D-50014 [M]	The Mamas and the Papas Deliver	1967	5.00	10.00	20.00
❏ DS-50014 [S]	The Mamas and the Papas Deliver	1967	6.25	12.50	25.00
❏ D-50025 [M]	Farewell to the First Golden Era	1967	5.00	10.00	20.00
❏ DS-50025 [S]	Farewell to the First Golden Era	1967	5.00	10.00	20.00
❏ DS-50031	The Papas and the Mamas	1968	6.25	12.50	25.00
❏ ST-90797 [S]	If You Can Believe Your Eyes and Ears	1966	12.50	25.00	50.00
—Capitol Record Club edition; known copies have scroll proclaiming "Includes California Dreamin'."					
❏ T-90797 [M]	If You Can Believe Your Eyes and Ears	1966	12.50	25.00	50.00
—Capitol Record Club edition; known copies have scroll proclaiming "Includes California Dreamin'."					
❏ ST-90924 [S]	The Mamas and the Papas	1966	10.00	20.00	40.00
—Capitol Record Club edition					
❏ T-90924 [M]	The Mamas and the Papas	1966	7.50	15.00	30.00
—Capitol Record Club edition					
MCA					
❏ 709	Farewell to the First Golden Era	1980	2.00	4.00	8.00
❏ 710	The Papas and the Mamas	1980	2.00	4.00	8.00
❏ 6019 [(2)]	The Best of the Mamas and the Papas	1986	3.00	6.00	12.00
❏ 37145	16 of Their Greatest Hits	1980	2.00	4.00	8.00
PICKWICK					
❏ SPC-3352	California Dreaming	1972	3.00	6.00	12.00

MANCHA, STEVE
45s

Number	Title (A Side/B Side)	Yr	VG	VG+	NM
GROOVESVILLE					
❏ 1001	You're Still in My Heart/She's So Good	1965	6.25	12.50	25.00
❏ 1002	I Don't Want to Lose You/Need to Be Needed	1966	5.00	10.00	20.00
❏ 1004	Friday Night/Monday Through Thursday	1966	25.00	50.00	100.00
❏ 1005	Don't Make Me a Storyteller/ I Won't Love and Leave You	1967	5.00	10.00	20.00
❏ 1007	Just Keep On Loving Me/ Sweet Baby Don't Ever Be Untrue	1967	6.25	12.50	25.00
WHEELSVILLE					
❏ 102	Did My Baby Call/Whirlpool	1965	37.50	75.00	150.00

MANCHESTER, MELISSA Also see NATIONAL LAMPOON.
12-Inch Singles

Number	Title (A Side/B Side)	Yr	VG	VG+	NM
MCA					
❏ 23563	Energy (Vocal)/Energy (Dub)	1985	—	3.00	6.00

45s

Number	Title (A Side/B Side)	Yr	VG	VG+	NM
ANGEL					
❏ S7-19771	Have Yourself a Merry Little Christmas/I've Got My Love to Keep Me Warm	1997	—	—	3.00
ARISTA					
❏ 0116	Midnight Blue/I Got Eyes	1975	—	2.00	4.00
❏ 0146	Just Too Many People/This Lady's Not Home	1975	—	2.00	4.00
❏ 0168	Just You and I/My Sweet Thing	1976	—	2.00	4.00
❏ 0183	Better Days/Sing, Sing, Sing	1976	—	2.00	4.00
❏ 0196	Happy Endings/Rescue Me	1976	—	2.00	4.00
❏ 0218	Monkey See, Monkey Do/So's My Old Man	1976	—	2.00	4.00
❏ 0237	Dirty Work/Be Somebody	1977	—	2.00	4.00
❏ 0267	I Wanna Be Where You Are/No One's Ever Seen This Side of Me	1977	—	2.00	4.00
❏ 0373	Don't Cry Out Loud/We Had This Time	1978	—	2.00	4.00
—Originals have black labels					
❏ 0373	Don't Cry Out Loud/We Had This Time	1979	—	—	3.00
—Second pressings have whitish labels					
❏ 0405	Theme from "Ice Castles"/Such a Night	1979	—	2.00	4.00
❏ 0456	Pretty Girls/It's All in the Sky Above	1979	—	2.00	4.00
❏ 0485	Fire in the Morning/Lights of Dawn	1980	—	2.00	4.00
❏ 0551	If This Is Love/Talk	1980	—	2.00	4.00
❏ 0579	Without You/Boys in the Back Room	1980	—	2.00	4.00
❏ 0587	Lovers After All/Happier Than I've Ever Been	1981	—	2.00	4.00
—With Peabo Bryson					
❏ 0657	Race to the End/Long Goodbyes	1982	—	2.00	4.00
❏ 0676	You Should Hear How She Talks About You/ Long Goodbyes	1982	—	2.00	4.00
❏ 1028	Come In from the Rain/ Hey Ricky (You're a Low Down Heel)	1982	—	2.00	4.00
❏ 1045	Nice Girls/Hey Ricky (You're a Low Down Heel)	1983	—	2.00	4.00
❏ 1057	My Boyfriend's Back/Looking for the Perfect Aah	1983	—	2.00	4.00
❏ 9014	My Boyfriend's Back/Looking for the Perfect Aah	1983	—	—	3.00

Number	Title (A Side/B Side)	Yr	VG	VG+	NM
9087	No One Can Love You More Than Me/White Rose	1983	—	—	3.00
9162	I Don't Care What the People Say/Emergency	1984	—	—	3.00
BELL					
45399	Never Never Land/Be Happy Now	1973	—	2.50	5.00
45465	Heaven/Inclined	1974	—	2.50	5.00
CASABLANCA					
880308-7	Thief of Hearts/(B-side unknown)	1984	—	—	3.00
MB					
1005	Beautiful People/A Song for You	1967	3.75	7.50	15.00
MCA					
52575	Mathematics/So Full of Yourself	1985	—	—	3.00
52575 [PS]	Mathematics/So Full of Yourself	1985	—	—	3.00
52616	Energy/So Full of Yourself	1985	—	—	3.00
52616 [PS]	Energy/So Full of Yourself	1985	—	—	3.00
52688	Just One Lifetime/So Full of Yourself	1985	—	—	3.00
52784	Music of Goodbye (Love Theme from Out of Africa)/Have You Got a Story for Me	1986	—	—	3.00
—With Al Jarreau					
52784 [PS]	Music of Goodbye (Love Theme from Out of Africa)/Have You Got a Story for Me	1986	—	—	3.00
—With Al Jarreau					
RCA VICTOR					
74-0366	Tellin' the World/(B-side unknown)	1970	3.00	6.00	12.00
—With Grover Kimball					
Albums					
ARISTA					
AL 4006	Home to Myself	1975	2.50	5.00	10.00
—Reissue of Bell 1123					
AL 4011	Bright Eyes	1975	2.50	5.00	10.00
—Reissue of Bell 1303					
AL 4031	Melissa	1975	2.50	5.00	10.00
AQ 4031 [Q]	Melissa	1975	3.75	7.50	15.00
AL 4067	Better Days & Happy Endings	1976	2.50	5.00	10.00
AQ 4067 [Q]	Better Days & Happy Endings	1976	3.75	7.50	15.00
AL 4095	Help Is On the Way	1976	2.50	5.00	10.00
AL 4136	Singin'	1977	2.50	5.00	10.00
AB 4186	Don't Cry Out Loud	1978	2.50	5.00	10.00
AL 8055	Melissa	1983	2.00	4.00	8.00
—Budget-line reissue of 4031					
AL 8094	Emergency	1983	2.00	5.00	10.00
AL 8293	Greatest Hits	198?	2.00	4.00	8.00
—Budget-line reissue of 9611					
AL 8350	Hey Ricky	198?	2.00	4.00	8.00
—Budget-line reissue of 9574					
AL 8373	Don't Cry Out Loud	198?	2.00	4.00	8.00
—Budget-line reissue of 4186					
AL 9506	Melissa Manchester	1979	2.50	5.00	10.00
AL 9533	For the Working Girl	1980	2.50	5.00	10.00
AL 9574	Hey Ricky	1982	2.50	5.00	10.00
AL 9611	Greatest Hits	1983	2.50	5.00	10.00
BELL					
1123	Home to Myself	1973	3.00	6.00	12.00
1303	Bright Eyes	1974	3.00	6.00	12.00
MCA					
5587	Mathematics	1985	2.50	5.00	10.00
MIKA					
841273-1	Tribute	1989	3.00	6.00	12.00
MOBILE FIDELITY					
1-028	Melissa	1980	5.00	10.00	20.00
—Audiophile vinyl					
NAUTILUS					
NR-33	Don't Cry Out Loud	198?	10.00	20.00	40.00
—Audiophile vinyl					
PAIR					
PDL2-1086 [(2)]	The Many Moods of Melissa Manchester	1986	3.00	6.00	12.00

MANCHESTERS, THE (1)
Albums

Number	Title (A Side/B Side)	Yr	VG	VG+	NM
DIPLOMAT					
D-2307 [M]	Beatlerama	1964	3.75	7.50	15.00
—No artist credited on label or cover					
D-2307 [M]	Beatlerama	1964	3.75	7.50	15.00
—With artist credited					
DS-2307 [S]	Beatlerama	1964	5.00	10.00	20.00
—No artist credited on label or cover					
DS-2307 [S]	Beatlerama	1964	5.00	10.00	20.00
—With artist credited					
GUEST STAR					
G-2307 [M]	Beatlerama	1964	3.75	7.50	15.00
GS-2307 [S]	Beatlerama	1964	5.00	10.00	20.00

MANCHESTERS, THE (2) Featuring DAVID GATES.
45s

Number	Title (A Side/B Side)	Yr	VG	VG+	NM
VEE JAY					
700	I Don't Come from England/Dragonfly	1965	6.25	12.50	25.00

MANCINI, HENRY
45s

Number	Title (A Side/B Side)	Yr	VG	VG+	NM
AVCO EMBASSY					
4531	Love Theme from Sunflower/Giovanna	1970	—	2.50	5.00
CORAL					
61974	The Long Hot Summer/Paris Holiday	1958	3.00	6.00	12.00
61990	Love Theme from "The Brothers Karamazov"/Tana's Theme	1958	3.00	6.00	12.00
LIBERTY					
1489	Trail of the Pink Panther (Soundtrack)/The Inspector Clouseau Theme (Soundtrack)	1983	—	2.00	4.00
55045	(Main Theme from) Four Girls in Town/Cha Cha Cha for Gia	1956	3.00	6.00	12.00
55060	Hot Rod/Big Band Rock and Roll	1957	3.00	6.00	12.00
55184	Pow/Cha Cha Cha for Gia	1959	2.50	5.00	10.00
RCA					
PB-10888	Theme from "Charlie's Angels"/Bumper's Theme	1977	—	2.50	5.00
PB-11054	What's Happening Theme/Silver Streak	1977	—	2.50	5.00
PB-11142	The Money Changers/Just You and Me Together, Love	1977	—	2.50	5.00
PB-11423	Theme from Battlestar Galactica/NBC Nightly News Theme	1978	—	2.50	5.00
RCA VICTOR					
47-7442	Fallout/Dreamsville	1959	3.00	6.00	12.00
47-7460	Peter Gunn/The Brothers Go to Mother's	1959	3.00	6.00	12.00
47-7512	Spook!/Timothy	1959	3.00	6.00	12.00
47-7682	Bijou/Let's Walk	1960	3.00	6.00	12.00
47-7705	Mr. Lucky/Floating Pad	1960	3.00	6.00	12.00
47-7785	Big Noise from Winnetka/The Blues	1960	3.00	6.00	12.00
47-7791	High Time/The Second Time Around	1960	3.00	6.00	12.00
47-7830	Theme from The Great Impostor/Love Music	1961	2.50	5.00	10.00
47-7830 [PS]	Theme from The Great Impostor/Love Music	1961	3.75	7.50	15.00
47-7902	Fanny/My Cousin from Naples	1961	2.50	5.00	10.00
47-7916	Moon River/Breakfast at Tiffany's	1961	2.00	4.00	8.00
47-7916 [PS]	Moon River/Breakfast at Tiffany's	1961	3.75	7.50	15.00
47-8008	Experiment in Terror/Tooty Tooty	1962	2.00	4.00	8.00
47-8037	Theme from "Hatari!"/Your Father's Feathers	1962	2.00	4.00	8.00
47-8037 [PS]	Theme from "Hatari!"/Your Father's Feathers	1962	3.75	7.50	15.00
47-8099	Love Theme from Phaedra/Dreamsville	1962	2.00	4.00	8.00
47-8120	Days of Wine and Roses/Seventy Six Trombones	1962	2.00	4.00	8.00
47-8120 [PS]	Days of Wine and Roses/Seventy Six Trombones	1962	3.75	7.50	15.00
47-8184	Banzai Pipeline/Rhapsody in Blue	1963	5.00	10.00	20.00
47-8184 [PS]	Banzai Pipeline/Rhapsody in Blue	1963	6.25	12.50	25.00
47-8256	Charade/Orange Tamoure	1963	2.00	4.00	8.00
47-8256 [PS]	Charade/Orange Tamoure	1963	3.75	7.50	15.00
47-8286	The Pink Panther Theme/It Had Better Be Tonight	1963	2.00	4.00	8.00
47-8286 [PS]	The Pink Panther Theme/It Had Better Be Tonight	1963	3.75	7.50	15.00
47-8381	A Shot in the Dark/The Shadows of Paris	1964	2.00	4.00	8.00
47-8381 [PS]	A Shot in the Dark/The Shadows of Paris	1964	3.00	6.00	12.00
47-8458	Dear Heart/How Soon	1964	2.00	4.00	8.00
47-8458 [PS]	Dear Heart/How Soon	1964	3.00	6.00	12.00
47-8574	Senor Peter Gunn/La Raspa	1965	2.00	4.00	8.00
47-8624	Pie in the Face Polka/Sweetheart Tree	1965	2.00	4.00	8.00
47-8691	He Shouldn't-A, Hadn't-A, Oughtn't-A Swang on Me/Push the Button, Man	1965	2.00	4.00	8.00
47-8718	Moment to Moment/Soldier in the Rain	1965	2.00	4.00	8.00
47-8798	House of the Rising Sun/Turtles	1966	—	3.00	6.00
47-8856	Arabesque/We've Loved Before	1966	—	3.00	6.00
47-8951	Hawaii/Driftwood and Dreams	1966	—	3.00	6.00
47-9200	Two for the Road/Happy Barefoot Boy	1967	—	3.00	6.00
47-9340	Wait Until Dark/Theme for Three	1967	—	3.00	6.00
47-9483	The Party/Party Poop	1968	—	3.00	6.00
47-9483 [PS]	The Party/Party Poop	1968	2.50	5.00	10.00
47-9521	Nothing to Lose/Norma De La Guadalajara	1968	—	3.00	6.00
47-9585	The Magnificent Seven/Springtime for Hitler	1968	2.00	4.00	8.00
47-9654	A Man, a Horse, and a Gun/Las Cruces	1968	—	3.00	6.00
47-9857	Love Theme from Sunflower/Darling Lili	1970	—	2.50	5.00
47-9927	Theme from Love Story/Phone Call to the Past	1970	—	2.50	5.00
74-0131	Love Theme from Romeo and Juliet/The Windmills of Your Mind	1969	2.50	5.00	10.00
74-0212	Moonlight Sonata/Natalie	1969	—	3.00	6.00
74-0297	Midnight Cowboy/There's Enough to Go Around	1969	—	3.00	6.00
74-0315	Theme from "The Molly Maguires"/Theme from "Z"	1970	—	2.50	5.00
74-0454	Theme from "The Night Visitor"/Whistling Away the Dark	1971	—	2.50	5.00
74-0575	Mystery Movie Theme/Theme from "Cade's Country"	1971	—	2.50	5.00
74-0618	Nicholas and Alexandra's Theme/Two for the Road	1971	—	2.50	5.00
74-0685	Brass in Ivory/Poor Butterfly	1972	—	2.50	5.00
—With Doc Severinson					
74-0756	Theme from The Mancini Generation/Bluish Bag	1972	—	2.50	5.00
74-0890	Theme from "The Thief Who Came to Dinner"/Charade	1973	—	2.50	5.00
74-0974	Oklahoma Crude/Amazing Grace	1973	—	2.50	5.00
47-7785 [PS]	Big Noise from Winnetka/The Blues	1960	3.75	7.50	15.00
47-8008 [PS]	Experiment in Terror/Tooty Tooty	1962	3.75	7.50	15.00
47-8099 [PS]	Love Theme from Phaedra/Dreamsville	1962	3.75	7.50	15.00
47-8624 [PS]	Pie in the Face Polka/Sweetheart Tree	1965	3.00	6.00	12.00
47-8857	The Swing March/In the Arms of Love	1966	—	3.00	6.00
47-8857 [PS]	The Swing March/In the Arms of Love	1966	3.00	6.00	12.00
47-8951 [PS]	Hawaii/Driftwood and Dreams	1966	3.00	6.00	12.00
47-9200 [PS]	Two for the Road/Happy Barefoot Boy	1967	2.50	5.00	10.00
47-9340 [PS]	Wait Until Dark/Theme for Three	1967	2.50	5.00	10.00
74-0890 [PS]	Theme from "The Thief Who Came to Dinner"/Charade	1973	2.00	4.00	8.00
APBO-0117	Ludmilla's Theme/Pretty Girls	1973	—	2.50	5.00
APBO-0249	Olympic Village/Dolce	1974	—	2.50	5.00
APBO-0323	Hangin' Out/Send a Little Love My Way	1974	—	2.50	5.00
PB-10060	Sex Symbol/Theme from "White Dawn"	1974	—	2.50	5.00
PB-10288	The Greatest Gift/The Pink Panther Theme	1975	—	2.50	5.00
PB-10355	Once Is Not Enough/The Greatest Gift	1975	—	2.50	5.00
PB-10463	Satin Soul/African Symphony	1975	—	2.50	5.00
PB-10731	Slow Hot Wind/Symphonic Soul	1976	—	2.50	5.00
UNITED ARTISTS					
XW1237	Pink Panther Theme '78/Touch of Red	1978	—	2.00	4.00
WARNER BROS.					
5019	The Star Spangled Banner/The Stars and Stripes Forever	1959	2.50	5.00	10.00
29697	The Thorn Birds Theme/Luke and Meggie	1983	—	2.00	4.00
29697 [PS]	The Thorn Birds Theme/Luke and Meggie	1983	—	3.00	6.00
49139	Ravel's Bolero/It's Easy to Say	1979	—	2.00	4.00
—B-side by Julie Andrews and Dudley Moore					
49139 [PS]	Ravel's Bolero/It's Easy to Say	1979	3.00	6.00	12.00
—Fold-out poster sleeve of Bo Derek and scenes from the movie "10"					

7-Inch Extended Plays

Number	Title (A Side/B Side)	Yr	VG	VG+	NM
RCA VICTOR					
LPC-104	(contents unknown)	1961	2.50	5.00	10.00
—"Compact 33 Double"; small hole, plays at 33 1/3 rpm					
LPC-104 [PS]	Henry Mancini Showcase	1961	2.50	5.00	10.00

Number	Title (A Side/B Side)	Yr	VG	VG+	NM
❑ LPC-130	Mr. Lucky (Goes Latin)/Lu Jon//No-Cal Sugar Loaf/Siesta	1961	2.50	5.00	10.00
—"Compact 33 Double"; small hole, plays at 33 1/3 rpm					
❑ LPC-130 [PS]	Mr. Lucky Goes Latin	1961	2.50	5.00	10.00
❑ EPA-4333 [M]	Peter Gunn/A Profound Gass// Fallout!/Sorta Blue	1959	3.00	6.00	12.00
❑ EPA-4333 [PS]	The Music from Peter Gunn	1959	3.00	6.00	12.00
❑ ESP-4333 [S]	The Music from Peter Gunn	1959	5.00	10.00	20.00
❑ ESP-4333 [S]	Peter Gunn/A Profound Gass// Fallout!/Sorta Blue	1959	5.00	10.00	20.00
❑ EPA-4339 [M]	*Walkin' Bass/Spook!/The Little Man Theme/ Goofin' at the Coffee House	1959	3.00	6.00	12.00
❑ EPA-4339 [PS]	More Music from Peter Gunn	1959	3.00	6.00	12.00
❑ ESP-4339 [PS]	More Music from Peter Gunn	1959	3.75	7.50	15.00
❑ ESP-4339 [S]	*Walkin' Bass/Spook!/The Little Man Theme/ Goofin' at the Coffee House	1959	3.75	7.50	15.00
❑ EPA-4363	Mr. Lucky/My Friend Andamo// Lightly Latin/Tipsy	1960	3.00	6.00	12.00
❑ EPA-4363 [PS]	Music from Mr. Lucky	1960	3.00	6.00	12.00
Albums					
AVCO EMBASSY					
❑ AVE 0110	Sunflower	1970	3.75	7.50	15.00
DECCA					
❑ DL 79185	Sometimes a Great Notion	1971	3.75	7.50	15.00
LIBERTY					
❑ LRP-3121 [M]	The Versatile Henry Mancini	1959	5.00	10.00	20.00
❑ LST-7121 [S]	The Versatile Henry Mancini	1959	7.50	15.00	30.00
❑ LT-51135	Trail of the Pink Panther	1982	2.50	5.00	10.00
MCA					
❑ 2085	The Great Waldo Pepper	1975	3.00	6.00	12.00
❑ 6222	The Glass Menagerie	1987	2.50	5.00	10.00
PAIR					
❑ PDL2-1092 [(2)]	The Mancini Collection (Film Music)	1986	3.00	6.00	12.00
PARAMOUNT					
❑ PAS-6000	The Molly Maguires	1970	5.00	10.00	20.00
RCA CAMDEN					
❑ ACL2-0293 [(2)]	Film Music	1973	3.00	6.00	12.00
❑ CAL-928 [M]	The Second Time Around and Others	1966	3.00	6.00	12.00
❑ CAS-928 [S]	The Second Time Around and Others	1966	3.00	6.00	12.00
❑ CAL-2158 [M]	Mancini Plays Mancini and Other Composers	1968	3.00	6.00	12.00
❑ CAS-2158 [S]	Mancini Plays Mancini and Other Composers	1968	2.50	5.00	10.00
❑ CAS-2510	Dream of You	1971	2.50	5.00	10.00
❑ CXS-9005 [(2)]	Mancini Magic	1971	3.00	6.00	12.00
❑ CXS-9034	Everybody's Favorite	1972	2.50	5.00	10.00
RCA SPECIAL PRODUCTS					
❑ DPL1-0678	Taking It Easy	1984	3.75	7.50	15.00
—Manufactured for Abbott Laboratories					
RCA VICTOR					
❑ APD1-0013 [Q]	Mancini Salutes Sousa	1973	4.50	9.00	18.00
❑ APL1-0013	Mancini Salutes Sousa	1972	3.00	6.00	12.00
❑ APD1-0098 [Q]	Brass, Ivory and Strings	1973	4.50	9.00	18.00
❑ APL1-0098	Brass, Ivory and Strings	1973	3.00	6.00	12.00
❑ PRM-175 [M]	Academy Award Songs, Volume Two	1965	3.75	7.50	15.00
—Made for the B.F. Goodrich tire company					
❑ PRS-175 [S]	Academy Award Songs, Volume Two	1965	5.00	10.00	20.00
—Made for the B.F. Goodrich tire company					
❑ ABL1-0231	Visions of Eight	1973	3.00	6.00	12.00
❑ AFL1-0270	Country Gentlemen	1977	2.50	5.00	10.00
—Reissue with new prefix					
❑ APD1-0270 [Q]	Country Gentlemen	1973	4.50	9.00	18.00
❑ APL1-0270	Country Gentlemen	1973	3.00	6.00	12.00
❑ APL1-0271	Oklahoma Crude	1973	3.00	6.00	12.00
❑ AFL1-0672	Hangin' Out	1977	2.50	5.00	10.00
—Reissue with new prefix					
❑ APD1-0672 [Q]	Hangin' Out	1974	4.50	9.00	18.00
❑ CPL1-0672	Hangin' Out	1974	3.00	6.00	12.00
❑ ABD1-0968 [Q]	Return of the Pink Panther	1975	4.50	9.00	18.00
❑ ABL1-0968	Return of the Pink Panther	1975	3.00	6.00	12.00
❑ ANL1-0980	Pure Gold	1975	2.50	5.00	10.00
❑ AFL1-1025	Symphonic Soul	1977	2.00	4.00	8.00
—Reissue with new prefix					
❑ APD1-1025 [Q]	Symphonic Soul	1975	4.50	9.00	18.00
❑ APL1-1025	Symphonic Soul	1975	2.50	5.00	10.00
❑ APL1-1379	Concert of Film Music	1975	2.50	5.00	10.00
❑ CPL1-1843	A Legendary Performer	1976	2.50	5.00	10.00
❑ APL1-1896	Cop Show Themes	1976	2.50	5.00	10.00
❑ ANL1-1928 [S]	A Merry Mancini Christmas	1976	2.00	4.00	8.00
—Reissue with new number and new front cover					
❑ LPM-1956 [M]	The Music from Peter Gunn	1959	3.00	6.00	12.00
—Second reissue cover is green/blue on front with huge "Peter Gunn" in center; back cover has a figure with a gun and a large photo of Henry Mancini at the upper left; catalog number on back is followed by "RE 2"					
❑ LPM-1956 [M]	The Music from Peter Gunn	1959	5.00	10.00	20.00
—First reissue cover is green/blue on front with huge "Peter Gunn" in center; back cover has a figure with a gun and a small photo of Henry Mancini at the lower left positioned so that it appears the gun is aimed at his head; catalog number on back cover is followed by "RE"					
❑ LPM-1956 [M]	The Music from Peter Gunn	1959	10.00	20.00	40.00
—Original cover is a "block" design with "Peter Gunn" at top					
❑ LSP-1956 [S]	The Music from Peter Gunn	1959	3.75	7.50	15.00
—Second reissue cover is green/blue on front with huge "Peter Gunn" in center; back cover has a figure with a gun and a large photo of Henry Mancini at the upper left; catalog number on back is followed by "RE 2"					
❑ LSP-1956 [S]	The Music from Peter Gunn	1959	6.25	12.50	25.00
—First reissue cover is green/blue on front with huge "Peter Gunn" in center; back cover has a figure with a gun and a small photo of Henry Mancini at the lower left positioned so that it appears the gun is aimed at his head; catalog number on back cover is followed by "RE"					
❑ LSP-1956 [S]	The Music from Peter Gunn	1959	12.50	25.00	50.00
—Original cover is a "block" design with "Peter Gunn" at top					
❑ LPM-2040 [M]	More Music from Peter Gunn	1959	5.00	10.00	20.00
❑ LSP-2040 [S]	More Music from Peter Gunn	1959	6.25	12.50	25.00
❑ LPM-2101 [M]	The Mancini Touch	1959	5.00	10.00	20.00
❑ LSP-2101 [S]	The Mancini Touch	1959	6.25	12.50	25.00
❑ LPM-2147 [M]	The Blues and the Beat	1960	6.25	12.50	25.00
❑ LSP-2147 [S]	The Blues and the Beat	1960	7.50	15.00	30.00
❑ LPM-2198 [M]	Music from Mr. Lucky	1960	5.00	10.00	20.00
❑ LSP-2198 [S]	Music from Mr. Lucky	1960	6.25	12.50	25.00

Number	Title (A Side/B Side)	Yr	VG	VG+	NM
❑ LPM-2258 [M]	Combo!	1960	5.00	10.00	20.00
❑ LSP-2258 [S]	Combo!	1960	6.25	12.50	25.00
❑ APL1-2290	Mancini's Angels	1977	2.50	5.00	10.00
❑ LPM-2360 [M]	Mr. Lucky Goes Latin	1961	5.00	10.00	20.00
❑ LSP-2360 [S]	Mr. Lucky Goes Latin	1961	6.25	12.50	25.00
❑ LPM-2362 [M]	Breakfast at Tiffany's	1961	5.00	10.00	20.00
❑ LSP-2362 [S]	Breakfast at Tiffany's	1961	6.25	12.50	25.00
❑ LPM-2442 [M]	Experiment in Terror	1962	5.00	10.00	20.00
—Reissue cover has two mannequins					
❑ LPM-2442 [M]	Experiment in Terror	1962	6.25	12.50	25.00
—Original cover has Lee Remick under attack					
❑ LSP-2442 [S]	Experiment in Terror	1962	6.25	12.50	25.00
—Reissue cover has two mannequins					
❑ LSP-2442 [S]	Experiment in Terror	1962	10.00	20.00	40.00
—Original cover has Lee Remick under attack					
❑ ANL1-2484	Mancini Plays the Theme from Love Story	1977	2.50	5.00	10.00
—Reissue of LSP-4466					
❑ LPM-2559 [M]	Hatari!	1962	5.00	10.00	20.00
❑ LSP-2559 [S]	Hatari!	1962	6.25	12.50	25.00
❑ LPM-2604 [M]	Our Man in Hollywood	1963	3.75	7.50	15.00
❑ LSP-2604 [S]	Our Man in Hollywood	1963	5.00	10.00	20.00
❑ LPM-2692 [M]	Uniquely Mancini	1963	3.75	7.50	15.00
❑ LSP-2692 [S]	Uniquely Mancini	1963	5.00	10.00	20.00
❑ AFL1-2693	The Best of Mancini	1977	2.50	5.00	10.00
—Reissue with new prefix					
❑ LPM-2693 [M]	The Best of Mancini	1964	3.00	6.00	12.00
❑ LSP-2693 [S]	The Best of Mancini	1964	3.75	7.50	15.00
❑ LPM-2755 [M]	Charade	1963	3.75	7.50	15.00
❑ LSP-2755 [S]	Charade	1963	5.00	10.00	20.00
❑ LPM-2795 [M]	The Pink Panther	1964	3.75	7.50	15.00
❑ LSP-2795 [S]	The Pink Panther	1964	5.00	10.00	20.00
❑ LPM-2897 [M]	The Concert Sound of Henry Mancini	1964	3.00	6.00	12.00
❑ LSP-2897 [S]	The Concert Sound of Henry Mancini	1964	3.75	7.50	15.00
❑ LPM-2990 [M]	Dear Heart and Other Songs About Love	1965	3.00	6.00	12.00
❑ LSP-2990 [S]	Dear Heart and Other Songs About Love	1965	3.75	7.50	15.00
❑ AQL1-3052	The Theme Scene	1978	2.50	5.00	10.00
❑ AQL1-3347	The Best of Mancini, Volume 3	1979	2.50	5.00	10.00
❑ LPM-3356 [M]	The Latin Sound of Henry Mancini	1965	3.00	6.00	12.00
❑ LSP-3356 [S]	The Latin Sound of Henry Mancini	1965	3.75	7.50	15.00
❑ LPM-3402 [M]	The Great Race	1965	3.00	6.00	12.00
❑ LSP-3402 [S]	The Great Race	1965	3.75	7.50	15.00
❑ AFL1-3557	The Best of Mancini, Volume 2	1977	2.50	5.00	10.00
—Reissue with new prefix					
❑ LPM-3557 [M]	The Best of Mancini, Volume 2	1966	3.00	6.00	12.00
❑ LSP-3557 [S]	The Best of Mancini, Volume 2	1966	3.75	7.50	15.00
❑ LPM-3612 [M]	A Merry Mancini Christmas	1966	2.50	5.00	10.00
—Original front cover has a photo of Henry Mancini and family					
❑ LSP-3612 [S]	A Merry Mancini Christmas	1966	3.00	6.00	12.00
—Same as above, but in stereo					
❑ LPM-3623 [M]	Arabesque	1966	3.00	6.00	12.00
❑ LSP-3623 [S]	Arabesque	1966	3.75	7.50	15.00
❑ LPM-3648 [M]	What Did You Do in the War, Daddy?	1966	3.00	6.00	12.00
❑ LSP-3648 [S]	What Did You Do in the War, Daddy?	1966	3.75	7.50	15.00
❑ AYL1-3667	Pure Gold	1980	2.00	4.00	8.00
—"Best Buy Series" reissue					
❑ AYL1-3668	Mancini Country	1980	2.00	4.00	8.00
—"Best Buy Series" reissue					
❑ LPM-3694 [M]	Mancini '67	1967	3.75	7.50	15.00
❑ LSP-3694 [S]	Mancini '67	1967	3.75	7.50	15.00
❑ AFL1-3713	Music of Hawaii	1977	2.50	5.00	10.00
—Reissue with new prefix					
❑ LPM-3713 [M]	Music of Hawaii	1966	3.00	6.00	12.00
❑ LSP-3713 [S]	Music of Hawaii	1966	3.75	7.50	15.00
❑ AYL1-3756	Brass on Ivory	1980	2.00	4.00	8.00
—"Best Buy Series" reissue					
❑ AYL1-3757	A Warm Shade of Ivory	1980	2.00	4.00	8.00
—"Best Buy Series" reissue					
❑ LPM-3802 [M]	Two for the Road	1967	5.00	10.00	20.00
❑ LSP-3802 [S]	Two for the Road	1967	3.75	7.50	15.00
❑ AYL1-3822	The Best of Mancini	1981	2.00	4.00	8.00
—"Best Buy Series" reissue					
❑ LPM-3840 [M]	Gunn	1967	5.00	10.00	20.00
❑ LSP-3840 [S]	Gunn	1967	7.50	15.00	30.00
❑ AYL1-3877	Music of Hawaii	1981	2.00	4.00	8.00
—"Best Buy Series" reissue					
❑ LPM-3887 [M]	Encore! More of the Concert Sound of Henry Mancini	1967	5.00	10.00	20.00
❑ LSP-3887 [S]	Encore! More of the Concert Sound of Henry Mancini	1967	3.75	7.50	15.00
❑ LPM-3943 [M]	The Mancini Sound	1968	5.00	10.00	20.00
❑ LSP-3943 [S]	The Mancini Sound	1968	3.75	7.50	15.00
❑ AYL1-3954	Country Gentlemen	1981	2.00	4.00	8.00
—"Best Buy Series" reissue					
❑ LPM-3997 [M]	Party	1968	6.25	12.50	25.00
❑ LSP-3997 [S]	Party	1968	3.75	7.50	15.00
❑ LSP-4049	The Big Latin Band of Henry Mancini	1968	3.75	7.50	15.00
❑ AFL1-4140	A Warm Shade of Ivory	1977	2.00	4.00	8.00
—Reissue with new prefix					
❑ LSP-4140	A Warm Shade of Ivory	1969	3.75	7.50	15.00
❑ LSP-4239	Six Hours Past Sunset	1969	3.75	7.50	15.00
❑ AFL1-4307	Mancini Country	1977	2.50	5.00	10.00
—Reissue with new prefix					
❑ LSP-4307	Mancini Country	1970	3.75	7.50	15.00
❑ LSP-4350	Theme from "Z" and Other Film Music	1970	3.75	7.50	15.00
❑ LSP-4466	Mancini Plays the Theme from Love Story	1971	3.75	7.50	15.00
❑ AFL1-4542	Mancini Concert	1977	2.50	5.00	10.00
—Reissue with new prefix					
❑ LSP-4542	Mancini Concert	1971	3.75	7.50	15.00
❑ AFL1-4629	Brass on Ivory	1977	2.00	4.00	8.00
—Reissue with new prefix					
❑ LSP-4629	Brass on Ivory	1972	3.00	6.00	12.00
❑ LSP-4630	Big Screen — Little Screen	1972	3.75	7.50	15.00
❑ LSP-4689	The Mancini Generation	1972	3.00	6.00	12.00
❑ LPM-6013 [(2)M]	The Academy Award Songs	1966	3.75	7.50	15.00
❑ LSP-6013 [(2)S]	The Academy Award Songs	1966	5.00	10.00	20.00
❑ VPS-6029 [(2)]	This Is Henry Mancini	1970	5.00	10.00	20.00
❑ VPS-6053 [(2)]	This Is Henry Mancini, Volume 2	1972	5.00	10.00	20.00

Number	Title (A Side/B Side)	Yr	VG	VG+	NM
SUNSET					
❏ SUM-1105 [M]	Sounds and Voices	1966	3.00	6.00	12.00
❏ SUS-5105 [S]	Sounds and Voices	1966	3.00	6.00	12.00
UNITED ARTISTS					
❏ UA-LA694-G	The Pink Panther Strikes Again	1976	3.75	7.50	15.00
❏ UAS-5210	The Hawaiians	1970	3.00	6.00	12.00
❏ SW-93297	The Hawaiians	1970	5.00	10.00	20.00
—Capitol Record Club edition					
WARNER BROS.					
❏ W 1312 [M]	March Step in Hi-Fi	1959	5.00	10.00	20.00
❏ WS 1312 [S]	March Step in Stereo	1959	7.50	15.00	30.00
❏ W 1465 [M]	Sousa's Greatest Marches	1962	3.75	7.50	15.00
❏ WS 1465 [S]	Sousa's Greatest Marches	1962	5.00	10.00	20.00
❏ W 1491 [M]	Marches	1963	3.75	7.50	15.00
❏ WS 1491 [S]	Marches	1963	5.00	10.00	20.00
❏ BS 2700	The Thief Who Came to Dinner	1973	3.75	7.50	15.00
❏ BSK 3399	10	1979	3.75	7.50	15.00

MANDEL, HARVEY
45s

Number	Title (A Side/B Side)	Yr	VG	VG+	NM
JANUS					
❏ 144	Midnight Sun/Baby Batter	1970	—	3.00	6.00
❏ 198	Pegasus/Uni Ino	1972	—	3.00	6.00
PHILIPS					
❏ 40566	Cristo Redentor/Bradley's Barn	1968	2.00	4.00	8.00
❏ 40579	Wade in the Water (Part 1)/Wade in the Water (Part 2)	1968	2.00	4.00	8.00
❏ 40607	Campus Blues/Righteous	1969	2.00	4.00	8.00
❏ 40627	Moontan/Summer Sequence	1969	2.00	4.00	8.00
❏ 40643	Dry Your Eyes/Ridin' High	1969	2.00	4.00	8.00
Albums					
EDITIONS EG					
❏ CAROL-1535-1	Cristo Redentor	198?	2.50	5.00	10.00
—Reissue of Philips 600-281					
JANUS					
❏ JLS-3017	Baby Batter	1970	3.00	6.00	12.00
❏ JLS-3037	The Snake	1972	3.00	6.00	12.00
❏ JLS-3047	Shangrenade	1973	3.00	6.00	12.00
❏ JSX-3067	Feel the Sound of Harvey Mandel	1974	3.00	6.00	12.00
❏ JXS-7014	The Best of Harvey Mandel	1975	3.00	6.00	12.00
OVATION					
❏ OV-1415	Get Off in Chicago	1971	3.75	7.50	15.00
PHILIPS					
❏ PHS 600281	Cristo Redentor	1969	6.25	12.50	25.00
❏ PHS 600306	Righteous	1969	6.25	12.50	25.00
❏ PHS 600325	Games Guitars Play	1970	6.25	12.50	25.00

MANDEL, MIKE
Albums

Number	Title (A Side/B Side)	Yr	VG	VG+	NM
VANGUARD					
❏ VSD-79409	Sky Music	1978	3.00	6.00	12.00
❏ VSD-79437	Utopia Parkway	1979	3.00	6.00	12.00

MANDO AND THE CHILI PEPPERS
Albums

Number	Title (A Side/B Side)	Yr	VG	VG+	NM
GOLDEN CREST					
❏ CR-3023 [M]	On the Road with Rock and Roll	1957	125.00	250.00	500.00

MANDRAKE MEMORIAL
45s

Number	Title (A Side/B Side)	Yr	VG	VG+	NM
POPPY					
❏ 90103	Something in the Air/Musical Man	1969	2.50	5.00	10.00
❏ 90103 [PS]	Something in the Air/Musical Man	1969	6.25	12.50	25.00
Albums					
POPPY					
❏ PYS 40002	Mandrake Memorial	1968	10.00	20.00	40.00
❏ PYS 40003	Medium	1969	10.00	20.00	40.00
❏ PYS 40006	Puzzle	1970	10.00	20.00	40.00

MANDRELL, BARBARA
45s

Number	Title (A Side/B Side)	Yr	VG	VG+	NM
ABC					
❏ 12362	Tonight/If I Were a River	1978	—	2.00	4.00
❏ 12403	Sleeping Single in a Double Bed/Just One More of Your Goodbyes	1978	—	2.00	4.00
❏ 12451	(If Loving You Is Wrong) I Don't Want to Be Right/I Feel the Hurt Coming On	1979	—	2.50	5.00
ABC DOT					
❏ 17601	Standing Room Only/Can't Help But Wonder	1975	—	2.00	4.00
❏ 17623	Beginning of the End/That's What Friends Are For	1976	—	2.00	4.00
❏ 17644	Love Is Thin Ice/Will We Ever Make Love In Love Again	1976	—	2.00	4.00
❏ 17668	Midnight Angel/I Count on You	1976	—	2.00	4.00
❏ 17688	Married But Not to Each Other/Fools Gold	1977	—	2.00	4.00
❏ 17716	Hold Me/This Is Not Another Cheatin' Song	1977	—	2.00	4.00
❏ 17736	Woman to Woman/Let the Rain Out	1977	—	2.00	4.00
CAPITOL					
❏ B-44220	I Wish That I Could Fall in Love Today/I'll Be Your Jukebox Tonight	1988	—	—	3.00
❏ B-44276	My Train of Thought/Blanket of Love	1989	—	—	3.00
❏ B-44383	Mirror Mirror/Blanket of Love	1989	—	—	3.00
❏ B-44494	You Wouldn't Know Love/Why Do Bad Things Happen to Good People	1990	—	2.00	4.00
CAPITOL NASHVILLE					
❏ 7PRO-79029	You've Become the Dream (same on both sides)	1990	—	2.50	5.00
—Vinyl is promo only					
❏ 7PRO-79334	Men and Trains (same on both sides)	1991	—	2.50	5.00
—Vinyl is promo only					
COLUMBIA					
❏ 10082	Wonder When My Baby's Comin' Home/Kiss the Hurt Away	1974	—	2.50	5.00
❏ 44955	I've Been Loving You Too Long (To Stop Now)/Baby Come Home	1969	—	3.00	6.00
❏ 45143	Playin' Around with Love/I Almost Lost My Mind	1970	—	2.50	5.00
❏ 45307	Do Right Woman — Do Right Man/The Letter	1971	—	2.50	5.00

Number	Title (A Side/B Side)	Yr	VG	VG+	NM
❏ 45391	Treat Him Right/Break My Mind	1971	—	2.50	5.00
❏ 45505	Tonight My Baby's Coming Home/He'll Never Take the Place of You	1971	—	2.50	5.00
❏ 45580	Show Me/Satisfied	1972	—	2.50	5.00
❏ 45702	Holdin' On (To the Love I Got)/Smile, Somebody Loves You	1972	—	2.50	5.00
❏ 45819	Give a Little, Take a Little/Ain't It Good	1973	—	2.50	5.00
❏ 45904	The Midnight Oil/In the Name of Love	1973	—	2.50	5.00
❏ 46054	This Time I Almost Made It/Son-of-a-Gun	1974	—	2.50	5.00
EMI AMERICA					
❏ 43032	Child Support/I'm Glad I Married You	1987	—	—	3.00
❏ 43032 [PS]	Child Support/I'm Glad I Married You	1987	—	2.00	4.00
❏ 43042	Angels Love Bad Men/Sunshine Street	1988	—	—	3.00
EMI MANHATTAN					
❏ 50102	Sure Feels Good/Sunshine Street	1987	—	—	3.00
MCA					
❏ S45-1241 [DJ]	Santa, Bring My Baby Back Home//It Must Have Been the Mistletoe (Our First Christmas)/From Our House to Yours	1984	2.50	5.00	10.00
❏ 12451	(If Loving You Is Wrong) I Don't Want to Be Right/I Feel the Hurt Coming On	1979	—	2.00	4.00
—Reissue of ABC 12451					
❏ 41077	Fooled by a Feeling/Love Takes a Long Time to Die	1979	—	—	3.00
❏ 41162	Years/Darlin'	1979	—	—	3.00
❏ 41162 [PS]	Years/Darlin'	1979	—	2.00	4.00
❏ 41263	Crackers/Using Him to Get to You	1980	—	—	3.00
❏ 51001	The Best of Strangers/Sometime, Somewhere, Somehow	1980	—	—	3.00
❏ 51062	Love Is Fair/Sometime, Somewhere, Somehow	1981	—	—	3.00
❏ 51107	I Was Country When Country Wasn't Cool/Woman's Got a Right	1981	—	2.00	4.00
❏ 51171	Wish You Were Here/She's Out There Dancin' Alone	1981	—	—	3.00
❏ 52038	'Till You're Gone/You're Not Supposed to Be Here	1982	—	—	3.00
❏ 52111	Operator, Long Distance Please/Black and White	1982	—	—	3.00
❏ 52206	In Times Like These/Loveless	1983	—	—	3.00
❏ 52258	One of a Kind Pair of Fools/As Well As Can Be Expected	1983	—	—	3.00
❏ 52340	Happy Birthday Dear Heartache/A Man's Not a Man ('Til He's Loved by a Woman)	1984	—	—	3.00
❏ 52397	Only a Lonely Heart Knows/I Wonder What the Rich Folk Are Doin' Tonight	1984	—	—	3.00
❏ 52465	Crossword Puzzle/If It's Not One Thing It's Another	1984	—	—	3.00
❏ 52537	There's No Love in Tennessee/Sincerely I'm Yours	1985	—	—	3.00
❏ 52537 [PS]	There's No Love in Tennessee/Sincerely I'm Yours	1985	—	—	3.00
❏ 52645	Angel in Your Arms/Don't Look in My Eyes	1985	—	—	3.00
❏ 52737	Fast Lanes and Country Roads/You Only You	1985	—	—	3.00
❏ 52737 [DJ]	Fast Lanes and Country Roads (same on both sides)	1985	2.50	5.00	10.00
—Promo only on yellow vinyl					
❏ 52737 [PS]	Fast Lanes and Country Roads/You Only You	1985	—	—	3.00
❏ 52802	When You Get to the Heart/Survivors	1986	—	—	3.00
—With the Oak Ridge Boys					
❏ 52802 [DJ]	When You Get to the Heart (same on both sides)	1986	2.50	5.00	10.00
—Promo only on red vinyl					
❏ 52900	No One Mends a Broken Heart Like You/Love Is Adventure in the Great Unknown	1986	—	—	3.00
MOSRITE					
❏ 190	Queen for a Day/Alone in the Crowd	196?	6.25	12.50	25.00
Albums					
ABC					
❏ AB-1088	Moods	1978	3.00	6.00	12.00
❏ AB-1119	The Best of Barbara Mandrell	1979	3.00	6.00	12.00
ABC DOT					
❏ DOSD-2045	This Is Barbara Mandrell	1976	3.00	6.00	12.00
❏ DOSD-2067	Midnight Angel	1976	3.00	6.00	12.00
❏ DO-2076	Lovers, Friends and Strangers	1977	3.00	6.00	12.00
❏ DO-2098	Love's Ups and Downs	1977	3.00	6.00	12.00
CAPITOL					
❏ C1-90416	I'll Be Your Jukebox Tonight	1988	2.50	5.00	10.00
❏ C1-91977	Morning Sun	1990	3.00	6.00	12.00
COLUMBIA					
❏ C 30967	Treat Him Right	1971	5.00	10.00	20.00
❏ KC 32743	The Midnight Oil	1973	3.75	7.50	15.00
❏ PC 32743	The Midnight Oil	198?	2.00	4.00	8.00
—Budget-line reissue					
❏ KC 32959	This Time I Almost Made It	1974	3.75	7.50	15.00
❏ PC 34876	The Best of Barbara Mandrell	1977	3.00	6.00	12.00
—No bar code on cover					
❏ PC 34876	The Best of Barbara Mandrell	198?	2.00	4.00	8.00
—Reissue with bar code on cover					
❏ FC 37437	Looking Back	1982	2.50	5.00	10.00
❏ PC 37437	Looking Back	198?	2.00	4.00	8.00
—Budget-line reissue					
COLUMBIA LIMITED EDITION					
❏ LE 10550	Treat Him Right	197?	2.50	5.00	10.00
EMI AMERICA					
❏ ET-46956	Sure Feels Good	1987	2.50	5.00	10.00
MCA					
❏ 641	Midnight Angel	198?	2.00	4.00	8.00
—Reissue of ABC Dot 2067					
❏ 672	This Is Barbara Mandrell	198?	2.00	4.00	8.00
—Reissue of ABC Dot 2045					
❏ 673	Lovers, Friends and Strangers	198?	2.00	4.00	8.00
—Reissue of ABC Dot 2076					
❏ 674	Love's Ups and Downs	198?	2.00	4.00	8.00
—Reissue of ABC Dot 2098					
❏ 3165	Just for the Record	1979	2.50	5.00	10.00
❏ 3280	Moods	1980	2.00	4.00	8.00
—Reissue of ABC 1088					

Number	Title (A Side/B Side)	Yr	VG	VG+	NM
❏ 5136	Love Is Fair	1980	2.50	5.00	10.00
❏ 5243	Barbara Mandrell Live	1981	2.50	5.00	10.00
❏ 5295	...In Black and White	1982	2.50	5.00	10.00
❏ 5330	He Set My Life to Music	1982	2.50	5.00	10.00
❏ 5377	Spun Gold	1983	2.50	5.00	10.00
❏ 5474	Clean Cut	1984	2.50	5.00	10.00
❏ 5519	Christmas at Our House	1984	3.00	6.00	12.00
❏ 5566	Greatest Hits	1985	2.50	5.00	10.00
❏ 5619	Get to the Heart	1985	2.50	5.00	10.00
❏ 37173	Just for the Record	198?	2.00	4.00	8.00
—Budget-line reissue					
❏ 37202	Moods	198?	—	3.00	6.00
—Budget-line reissue					
❏ 37224	Barbara Mandrell Live	198?	2.00	4.00	8.00
—Budget-line reissue					
PAIR					
❏ PDL1-1079 [(2)]	The Best of Barbara Mandrell	1986	3.00	6.00	12.00
TIME-LIFE					
❏ STW-104	Country Music	1981	2.50	5.00	10.00

MANDRELL, BARBARA, AND LEE GREENWOOD
45s
MCA

Number	Title (A Side/B Side)	Yr	VG	VG+	NM
❏ 52415	To Me/We Were Meant for Each Other	1984	—	—	3.00
❏ 52415 [PS]	To Me/We Were Meant for Each Other	1984	—	—	3.00
❏ 52525	It Should Have Been Love By Now/Can't Get Too Much of a Good Thing	1985	—	2.00	4.00

MANDRILL
45s
ARISTA

Number	Title (A Side/B Side)	Yr	VG	VG+	NM
❏ 0274	Funky Monkey/Gilley Hines	1977	—	2.00	4.00
❏ 0304	Can You Get It/Holiday	1978	—	2.00	4.00
❏ 0326	Happy Beat/Holiday	1978	—	2.00	4.00
❏ 0375	Too Late/Holiday	1978	—	2.00	4.00
❏ 0490	My Kind of Girl/Lo Siento Mucho	1980	—	2.00	4.00
❏ 0507	Getting in the Mood/(B-side unknown)	1980	—	2.00	4.00
❏ 0529	Dance of Love/When You Shake	1980	—	2.00	4.00
MONTAGE					
❏ 1222	Put Your Money Where the Funk Is/(B-side unknown)	1982	—	2.00	4.00
❏ 1224	Soar Like an Eagle/Starry-Eyed	1982	—	2.00	4.00
POLYDOR					
❏ 14070	Mandrill/Warning Blues	1971	—	2.50	5.00
❏ 14085	Rollin' On/Symphonic Revolution	1971	—	2.50	5.00
❏ 14127	Kofijahm/I Refuse to Smile	1972	—	2.50	5.00
❏ 14142	Cohelo/Git It All	1972	—	2.50	5.00
❏ 14156	Children of the Sun/Ace Is High	1972	—	2.50	5.00
❏ 14163	Fencewalk/Hagalo	1973	—	2.50	5.00
❏ 14187	Hang Loose/Polk Street Carnival	1973	—	2.50	5.00
❏ 14200	Mango Meat/Afrikus Retrospectus	1973	—	2.50	5.00
❏ 14214	Love Song/Two Sisters of Mystery	1974	—	2.50	5.00
❏ 14235	Positive Thing/Positive Thing Plus	1974	—	2.50	5.00
❏ 14257	Road to Love/Armadillo	1974	—	2.50	5.00
UNITED ARTISTS					
❏ XW673	Tee Vee/Silk	1975	—	2.00	4.00
❏ XW778	Disco-Lypso/Solid	1976	—	2.00	4.00
Albums					
ARISTA					
❏ AL 4144	We Are One	1977	2.50	5.00	10.00
❏ AL 4195	New Worlds	1978	2.50	5.00	10.00
❏ AL 9527	Getting In the Mood	1980	2.50	5.00	10.00
LIBERTY					
❏ LN-10196	Rebirth	1983	2.00	4.00	8.00
MONTAGE					
❏ ST-72008	Energize	1982	3.00	6.00	12.00
POLYDOR					
❏ 24-4060	Mandrill	1971	3.00	6.00	12.00
❏ PD-5025	Mandrill Is	1972	3.00	6.00	12.00
❏ PD-5043	Composite Truth	1973	3.00	6.00	12.00
❏ PD-5059	Just Outside of Town	1973	3.00	6.00	12.00
❏ PD-1-6047	The Best of Mandrill	1975	3.00	6.00	12.00
❏ PD-2-9002 [(2)]	Mandrilland	1976	3.75	7.50	15.00
UNITED ARTISTS					
❏ UA-LA408-G	Solid	1975	3.00	6.00	12.00
❏ UA-LA577-G	Beast from the East	1976	3.00	6.00	12.00

MANGIONE, CHUCK
12-Inch Singles
A&M

Number	Title (A Side/B Side)	Yr	VG	VG+	NM
❏ 8448 [DJ]	Feels So Good (4:40) (same on both sides)	1978	3.00	6.00	12.00
COLUMBIA					
❏ AS 1903 [DJ]	Love Wears No Disguise/Diana "D"	1984	2.00	4.00	8.00
❏ 07827	Long Hair Soulful (Extended) (Edit)	1988	2.00	4.00	8.00

45s
A&M

Number	Title (A Side/B Side)	Yr	VG	VG+	NM
❏ 1707	Chase the Clouds Away/Soft	1975	—	2.00	4.00
❏ 1773	Bellavia/Listen to the Wind	1975	—	2.00	4.00
❏ 1827	Soft/Can't We Do This All Night	1976	—	2.00	4.00
❏ 1886	Main Squeeze/Come Take a Ride with Me	1976	—	2.00	4.00
❏ 1886 [PS]	Main Squeeze/Come Take a Ride with Me	1976	—	3.00	6.00
❏ 1919	Bellavia/Doin' Everything With You	1977	—	2.00	4.00
❏ 2001	Feels So Good/Maui-Waui	1977	—	2.00	4.00
❏ 2001 [PS]	Feels So Good/Maui-Waui	1977	—	2.50	5.00
❏ 2088	Children of Sanchez/Doin' Everything with You	1978	—	2.00	4.00
❏ 2088 [PS]	Children of Sanchez/Doin' Everything with You	1978	—	2.50	5.00
❏ 2118	Bellavia/Lullabye	1979	—	2.00	4.00
❏ 2167	Land of Make Believe/Children of Sanchez	1979	—	2.00	4.00
❏ 2211	Give It All You Got/B'Bye	1980	—	2.00	4.00
❏ 2211 [PS]	Give It All You Got/B'Bye	1980	—	2.00	4.00
❏ 2236	Fun and Games/Children of Sanchez (Finale)	1980	—	2.00	4.00
❏ 2236 [PS]	Fun and Games/Children of Sanchez (Finale)	1980	—	2.00	4.00
❏ 2341	Give It All You Got, But Slowly/Neapolitan Tarantella	1981	—	—	3.00
❏ 2354	Cannonball Run Theme/Can't We Do This All Night	1981	—	—	3.00

COLUMBIA

Number	Title (A Side/B Side)	Yr	VG	VG+	NM
❏ 03008	Steppin' Out/Memories of Scirocco	1982	—	—	3.00
❏ 03329	No Problem/Memories of Scirocco	1982	—	—	3.00
❏ 03986	Journey to a Rainbow/Please Stay the Night	1983	—	—	3.00
❏ 04649	Diana "D"/Josephine	1984	—	—	3.00
❏ 05866	Save Tonight for Me/T.J.'s Gingerbread House	1986	—	—	3.00
❏ 07917	Long Hair Soulful/Do You Ever Think About Me	1988	—	—	3.00
MERCURY					
❏ 73208	Hill Where the Lord Hides/Friends and Lovers	1971	2.00	4.00	8.00
❏ 73238	And In the Beginning/Feel a Vision	1972	—	3.00	6.00
❏ 73262	Freddie's Walkin'/Look to the Children	1972	—	3.00	6.00
❏ 73371	Last Tango in Paris/Legend of the One-Eyed Sailor	1973	—	3.00	6.00
❏ 73453	As Long As We're Together/Legend of the One-Eyed Sailor	1974	—	3.00	6.00
❏ 73635	Land of Make Believe/As Long As We're Together	1975	—	3.00	6.00
❏ 73920	Land of Make Believe/As Long As We're Together	1977	—	2.50	5.00
❏ 74016	Hill Where the Lord Hides/Land of Make Believe	1978	—	2.50	5.00

Albums
A&M

Number	Title (A Side/B Side)	Yr	VG	VG+	NM
❏ SP-3115	Chase the Clouds Away	198?	—	3.00	6.00
—Budget-line reissue					
❏ SP-3172	Bellavia	198?	—	3.00	6.00
—Budget-line reissue					
❏ SP-3193	Fun and Games	1983	—	3.00	6.00
—Budget-line reissue					
❏ SP-3219	Feels So Good	198?	—	3.00	6.00
—Budget-line reissue					
❏ SP-3220	Main Squeeze	198?	—	3.00	6.00
—Budget-line reissue					
❏ SP-3237	70 Miles Young	198?	—	3.00	6.00
—Budget-line reissue					
❏ SP-3282	The Best of Chuck Mangione	1985	2.50	5.00	10.00
❏ SP-3715	Fun and Games	1980	2.50	5.00	10.00
❏ SP-4518	Chase the Clouds Away	1975	2.50	5.00	10.00
❏ SP-4557	Bellavia	1975	2.50	5.00	10.00
❏ SP-4612	Main Squeeze	1976	2.50	5.00	10.00
❏ SP-4658	Feels So Good	1977	2.50	5.00	10.00
❏ SP-4911	70 Miles Young	1982	2.50	5.00	10.00
❏ SP-6513 [(2)]	Tarantella	1981	3.00	6.00	12.00
❏ SP-6700 [(2)]	Children of Sanchez	1978	3.00	6.00	12.00
❏ SP-6701 [(2)]	An Evening of Magic — Chuck Mangione Live at the Hollywood Bowl	1979	3.00	6.00	12.00
❏ QU-54518 [Q]	Chase the Clouds Away	1975	4.50	9.00	18.00
❏ QU-54557 [Q]	Bellavia	1975	4.50	9.00	18.00
COLUMBIA					
❏ FC 38101	Love Notes	1982	2.50	5.00	10.00
❏ PC 38101	Love Notes	198?	—	3.00	6.00
—Budget-line reissue					
❏ FC 38686	Journey to a Rainbow	1983	2.50	5.00	10.00
❏ PC 38686	Journey to a Rainbow	1986	—	3.00	6.00
—Budget-line reissue					
❏ FC 39479	Disguise	1984	2.50	5.00	10.00
❏ FC 40254	Save Tonight for Me	1986	2.50	5.00	10.00
❏ FC 40984	Eyes of the Veiled Temptress	1988	2.50	5.00	10.00
FANTASY					
❏ OJC-495	Recuerdo	1991	3.00	6.00	12.00
—Reissue of Jazzland 984					
JAZZLAND					
❏ JLP-84 [M]	Recuerdo	1962	10.00	20.00	40.00
❏ JLP-984 [S]	Recuerdo	1962	12.50	25.00	50.00
MERCURY					
❏ SRM-1-631	The Chuck Mangione Quartet	1972	3.00	6.00	12.00
❏ SRM-1-650	Alive!	1973	3.00	6.00	12.00
❏ SRM-1-681	Friends & Love/Highlights	1973	3.00	6.00	12.00
❏ SRM-1-684	Land of Make Believe	1973	3.00	6.00	12.00
❏ SRM-2-800 [(2)]	Friends & Love — A Chuck Mangione Concert	1971	3.75	7.50	15.00
❏ SRM-1-1050	Encore: The Chuck Mangione Concerts	1975	2.50	5.00	10.00
❏ SRM-2-7501 [(2)]	Together: A New Chuck Mangione Concert	1971	3.75	7.50	15.00
❏ SRM-2-8601 [(2)]	The Best of Chuck Mangione	1978	3.00	6.00	12.00
❏ 824301-1	Alive!	198?	2.00	4.00	8.00
—Reissue of 650					
MILESTONE					
❏ 47042 [(2)]	Jazz Brother	1977	3.00	6.00	12.00
—Reissue of material issued by "The Jazz Brothers"					
MOBILE FIDELITY					
❏ 1-068	Feels So Good	1981	6.25	12.50	25.00
—Audiophile vinyl					

MANHATTAN TRANSFER
12-Inch Singles
ATLANTIC

Number	Title (A Side/B Side)	Yr	VG	VG+	NM
❏ PR 525 [DJ]	Spice of Life/The Night That Monk Returned to Heaven	1983	—	3.00	6.00
❏ PR 560 [DJ]	American Pop/Why Not	1983	—	3.00	6.00
❏ PR 2272 [DJ]	So You Say (same on both sides)	1987	—	3.00	6.00

45s
(NO LABEL)

Number	Title (A Side/B Side)	Yr	VG	VG+	NM
❏ 1984 [DJ]	The Christmas Song (same on both sides)	1984	10.00	20.00	40.00
❏ 1984 [PS]	The Christmas Song (same on both sides)	1984	10.00	20.00	40.00
—Above sleeve and record are a private pressing for friends and associates of the group					
ATLANTIC					
❏ 3277	Sweet Talking Guy/Clap Your Hands	1975	2.00	4.00	8.00
❏ 3292	Operator/Tuxedo Junction	1975	—	2.50	5.00
❏ 3349	Helpless/My Cat Fell in the Well	1976	—	2.50	5.00
❏ 3374	Chanson d'Amour/Popsicle Toes	1976	—	2.50	5.00
❏ 3472	Where Did Our Love Go/Inside and Out	1978	—	2.50	5.00
❏ 3491	Four Brothers/It's Not the Spotlight	1978	—	2.50	5.00
❏ 3636	Birdland/Shaker Song	1979	—	2.50	5.00
❏ 3649	Twilight Zone-Twilight Tone/Body and Soul	1980	—	2.50	5.00
❏ 3756 [DJ]	Nothin' You Can Do About It (same on both sides)	1980	—	2.50	5.00
—May be promo only					
❏ 3772	Trickle, Trickle/Foreign Affair	1980	2.50	5.00	10.00

Number	Title (A Side/B Side)	Yr	VG	VG+	NM
❑ 3816	Boy from New York City/				
	(The World of) Confirmation	1981	—	2.00	4.00
❑ 3855	Smile Again/Until I Met You	1981	—	2.00	4.00
❑ 3877	Spies in the Night/Kafka	1981	—	2.00	4.00
❑ 4034	Route 66/On the Boulevard	1982	—	2.00	4.00
❑ 89094	So You Say/Notes from the Underground	1988	—	2.00	4.00
❑ 89094 [PS]	So You Say/Notes from the Underground	1988	—	2.00	4.00
❑ 89156	Soul Food to Go/Hear the Voices	1988	—	2.00	4.00
❑ 89156 [PS]	Soul Food to Go/Hear the Voices	1988	—	2.00	4.00
❑ 89467	That's Killer Joe/Airegin II	1985	—	2.50	5.00
❑ 89533	Ray's Rockhouse/Another Life in Tunisia	1985	—	2.00	4.00
❑ 89533 [PS]	Ray's Rockhouse/Another Life in Tunisia	1985	—	2.00	4.00
❑ 89594	Baby Come Back to Me (Morse Code of Love)/				
	That's the Way It Goes	1984	2.50	5.00	10.00
❑ 89647	This Independence/Code of Ethics	1984	—	2.50	5.00
❑ 89695	Mystery/Goodbye Love	1984	—	2.00	4.00
❑ 89720	American Pop/Why Not!	1983	—	2.00	4.00
—Featuring Frankie Valli					
❑ 89720 [PS]	American Pop/Why Not!	1983	—		4.00
❑ 89786	Spice of Life/The Night That Monk Returned to				
	Heaven	1983	—	2.00	4.00
❑ 89786 [PS]	Spice of Life/The Night That Monk Returned to				
	Heaven	1983	—	2.50	5.00
CAPITOL					
❑ 2968	Care for Me/Rosianna	1970	2.50	5.00	10.00
—With Gene Pistilli					
❑ 3036	Maybe Mexico/Winterlude	1971	2.50	5.00	10.00
—With Gene Pistilli					
❑ 3108	Java Jive/Chicken Bone Bone	1971	2.50	5.00	10.00
—With Gene Pistilli					
Albums					
ATLANTIC					
❑ SD 16036	Mecca for Moderns	1981	2.50	5.00	10.00
❑ SD 18133	The Manhattan Transfer	1975	2.50	5.00	10.00
❑ SD 18183	Coming Out	1976	2.50	5.00	10.00
❑ SD 19163	Pastiche	1978	2.50	5.00	10.00
❑ SD 19258	Extensions	1979	2.50	5.00	10.00
❑ SD 19319	The Best of the Manhattan Transfer	1981	2.50	5.00	10.00
❑ 80104	Bodies and Souls	1983	2.50	5.00	10.00
❑ 81233	Bop Doo-Wopp	1984	3.00	6.00	12.00
❑ 81266	Vocalese	1985	2.50	5.00	10.00
❑ 81723	Live	1987	2.50	5.00	10.00
❑ 81803	Brasil	1987	2.50	5.00	10.00
CAPITOL					
❑ ST-778	Jukin'	1971	3.75	7.50	15.00
—With Gene Pistilli					
❑ ST-11405	Jukin'	1975	2.50	5.00	10.00
—With Gene Pistilli; reissue of 778					
❑ SN-16223	Jukin'	198?	2.00	4.00	8.00
—With Gene Pistilli; budget-line reissue					
COLUMBIA					
❑ C 47079	The Offbeat of Avenues	1991	3.75	7.50	15.00
MOBILE FIDELITY					
❑ 1-022	Manhattan Transfer Live	1979	5.00	10.00	20.00
—Audiophile vinyl					
❑ 1-199	Extensions	1994	6.25	12.50	25.00
—Audiophile vinyl					

MANHATTANS, THE (1) Well-known male R&B vocal group.

12-Inch Singles

COLUMBIA

Number	Title (A Side/B Side)	Yr	VG	VG+	NM
❑ AS 1316 [DJ]	Let Your Love Come Down (same on both sides)	1981	2.50	5.00	10.00
❑ 03940	Crazy (5:00) (Instrumental)	1983	2.00	4.00	8.00
❑ 05973	Maybe Tomorrow/Where Did We Go Wrong	1986	2.00	4.00	8.00

45s

CARNIVAL

Number	Title (A Side/B Side)	Yr	VG	VG+	NM
❑ 504	I've Got Everything But You/				
	For the Very First Time	1964	5.00	10.00	20.00
❑ 506	There Goes a Fool/Call Somebody Please	1964	10.00	20.00	40.00
❑ 507	I Wanna Be (Your Everything)/				
	What's It Gonna Be	1965	3.75	7.50	15.00
❑ 509	Searchin' for My Baby/				
	I'm the One That Love Forgot	1965	3.75	7.50	15.00
❑ 512	Follow Your Heart/The Boston Money	1965	3.75	7.50	15.00
❑ 514	Baby I Need You/Teach Me the Philly Dog	1966	3.75	7.50	15.00
❑ 517	Can I/That New Girl	1966	3.75	7.50	15.00
❑ 522	I Betcha (Couldn't Love Me)/Sweet Little Girl	1966	3.75	7.50	15.00
❑ 524	It's That Time of the Year/				
	Alone on New Year's Eve	1966	5.00	10.00	20.00
❑ 526	All I Need Is Your Love/Our Love Will Never Die	1967	3.75	7.50	15.00
❑ 529	When We're Made As One/Baby I'm Sorry	1967	3.75	7.50	15.00
❑ 533	I Call It Love/Manhattan Stomp	1967	3.75	7.50	15.00
❑ 542	I Don't Wanna Go/Love Is Breaking Out	1968	3.75	7.50	15.00
❑ 545	Til You Come Back to Me/Call Somebody Please	1968	3.75	7.50	15.00
COLUMBIA					
❑ 02164	Shining Star/Summertime in the City	1981	—	—	3.00
—Reissue					
❑ 02191	Just One Moment Away/When I Leave				
	Tomorrow	1981	—	2.00	4.00
❑ 02548	Let Your Love Come Down/I Gotta Thank You	1981	—	2.00	4.00
❑ 02666	Money, Money/I Wanta Thank You	1982	—	2.00	4.00
❑ 03939	Crazy/Gonna Find You	1983	—	2.00	4.00
❑ 04110	Forever By Your Side/Locked Up in Your Love	1983	—	2.00	4.00
❑ 04754	You Send Me/				
	You're Gonna Love Being Loved By Me	1985	—	2.00	4.00
❑ 04754 [PS]	You Send Me/				
	You're Gonna Love Being Loved By Me	1985	—	2.00	4.00
❑ 04930	Don't Say No/Dreamin'	1985	—	2.00	4.00
❑ 06376	Where Did We Go Wrong/Maybe Tomorrow	1986	—	2.00	4.00
—With Regina Belle					
❑ 07010	Mr. D.J./All I Need	1987	—	2.00	4.00
❑ 10045	Don't Take Your Love/The Day the Robins Sang				
	to Me	1974	—	2.50	5.00
❑ 10140	Hurt/Nursery Rhymes	1975	—	2.50	5.00
❑ 10310	Kiss and Say Goodbye/Wonderful World of Love	1976	—	2.50	5.00
❑ 10430	I Kinda Miss You/Gypsy Man	1976	—	2.50	5.00

Number	Title (A Side/B Side)	Yr	VG	VG+	NM
❑ 10495	It Feels So Good to Be Loved By You/				
	On the Street (Where I Live)	1977	—	2.50	5.00
❑ 10586	We Never Danced to a Love Song/Let's Start It				
	All Over Again	1977	—	2.50	5.00
❑ 10674	Am I Losing You/Movin'	1978	—	2.50	5.00
❑ 10766	Everybody Has a Dream/Happiness	1978	—	2.50	5.00
❑ 10921	Here Comes the Hurt Again/Don't Say Goodbye	1979	—	2.50	5.00
❑ 11024	The Way We Were-Memories/New York City	1979	—	2.50	5.00
❑ 11222	Shining Star/				
	I'll Never Run Away from Love Again	1980	—	2.00	4.00
❑ 11321	Girl of My Dreams/The Closer You Are	1980	—	2.00	4.00
❑ 11398	I'll Never Find Another (Another Just Like You)/				
	Rendezvous	1980	—	2.00	4.00
❑ 45838	There's No Me Without You/I'm Not a Run-				
	Around	1973	—	3.00	6.00
❑ 45927	You'd Better Believe It/Soul Train	1973	—	3.00	6.00
❑ 45971	Wish That You Were Mine/				
	It's So Hard Loving You	1973	—	3.00	6.00
❑ 46081	Summertime in the City/The Other Side of Me	1974	—	3.00	6.00
❑ 60511	Do You Really Mean Goodbye/Rendezvous	1981	—	2.00	4.00
DELUXE					
❑ 109	The Picture Became Quite Clear/Oh Lord, How				
	I Wish I Could Sleep	1969	2.50	5.00	10.00
❑ 115	It's Gonna Take a Lot to Bring Me Back/				
	Give Him Up	1970	2.50	5.00	10.00
❑ 122	If My Heart Could Speak/Loneliness	1970	2.50	5.00	10.00
❑ 129	From Atlanta to Goodbye/Fantastic Journey	1970	2.50	5.00	10.00
❑ 132	Let Them Talk/Straight to My Heart	1970	2.50	5.00	10.00
❑ 136	Do You Ever/I Can't Stand for You to Leave Me	1971	2.50	5.00	10.00
❑ 137	A Million to One/Cry If You Wanna Cry	1971	2.50	5.00	10.00
❑ 139	One Life to Live/It's the Only One	1972	2.50	5.00	10.00
❑ 144	Back Up/Fever	1972	2.50	5.00	10.00
❑ 146	Rainbow Week/Loneliness	1973	2.50	5.00	10.00
❑ 152	Do You Ever/If My Heart Could Speak	1973	2.50	5.00	10.00
STARFIRE					
❑ 121	Alone on New Year's Eve/It's That Time of the				
	Year	1979	—	2.50	5.00
VALLEY VUE					
❑ 75723	Sweet Talk/(B-side unknown)	1989	—	3.00	6.00
❑ 75749	Why You Wanna Love Me Like That/(B-side				
	unknown)	1989	—	3.00	6.00
Albums					
CARNIVAL					
❑ CMLP-201 [M]	Dedicated to You	1966	62.50	125.00	250.00
❑ CSLP-201 [S]	Dedicated to You	1966	125.00	250.00	500.00
❑ CMLP-202 [M]	For You and Yours	1967	37.50	75.00	150.00
❑ CSLP-202 [S]	For You and Yours	1967	75.00	150.00	300.00
COLLECTABLES					
❑ COL-5135	Dedicated to You: Golden Carnival Classics,				
	Part One	198?	2.50	5.00	10.00
❑ COL-5136	For You and Yours: Golden Carnival Classics,				
	Part Two	198?	2.50	5.00	10.00
COLUMBIA					
❑ KC 32444	There's No Me Without You	1973	3.75	7.50	15.00
❑ PC 32444	There's No Me Without You	198?	2.00	4.00	8.00
—Budget-line reissue					
❑ KC 33064	That's How Much I Love You	1975	3.75	7.50	15.00
❑ PC 33820	The Manhattans	1976	3.00	6.00	12.00
—No bar code on back cover					
❑ PC 33820	The Manhattans	198?	2.00	4.00	8.00
—With bar code on back cover					
❑ PC 34450	It Feels So Good	1977	3.00	6.00	12.00
—No bar code on back cover					
❑ PC 34450	It Feels So Good	198?	2.00	4.00	8.00
—With bar code on back cover					
❑ PCQ 34450 [Q]	It Feels So Good	1977	5.00	10.00	20.00
❑ JC 35252	There's No Good in Goodbye	1978	3.00	6.00	12.00
❑ JC 35693	Love Talk	1979	3.00	6.00	12.00
❑ PC 35693	After Midnight	198?	2.00	4.00	8.00
—Budget-line reissue					
❑ JC 36411	After Midnight	1980	3.00	6.00	12.00
❑ JC 36861	Manhattans Greatest Hits	1980	3.00	6.00	12.00
❑ FC 37156	Black Tie	1981	2.50	5.00	10.00
❑ PC 37156	Black Tie	198?	2.00	4.00	8.00
—Budget-line reissue					
❑ FC 38600	Forever By Your Side	1983	2.50	5.00	10.00
❑ FC 39277	Too Hot to Stop It	1985	2.50	5.00	10.00
DELUXE					
❑ 12000	With These Hands	1971	6.25	12.50	25.00
❑ 12004	A Million to One	1972	6.25	12.50	25.00
SOLID SMOKE					
❑ 8007	Follow Your Heart	1981	2.50	5.00	10.00
VALLEY VUE					
❑ D1-72946	Sweet Talk	1989	3.00	6.00	12.00

MANHATTANS, THE (2)

45s

COLPIX

Number	Title (A Side/B Side)	Yr	VG	VG+	NM
❑ 115	Big Wheel Express/Powder Blue	1959	7.50	15.00	30.00

MANHATTANS, THE (U) Some of these are likely group (1); others could be group (2); others are probably neither.

45s

AVANTI

Number	Title (A Side/B Side)	Yr	VG	VG+	NM
❑ 1401	What Should I Do/Later for You	1963	6.25	12.50	25.00
BIG MACK					
❑ 3911	Why Should I Cry/The Feeling Is Mutual	196?	50.00	100.00	200.00
CAPITOL					
❑ 4591	Molly Brown Medley/I Ain't Down Yet	1961	5.00	10.00	20.00
❑ 4730	La La La/Sing All the Day	1962	5.00	10.00	20.00
ENJOY					
❑ 2008	Come On Back/Long Time No See	1964	5.00	10.00	20.00
—As "Ronnie and the Manhattans"					
GOLDEN WORLD					
❑ 14	Just a Little Loving/Beautiful Brown Eyes	1964	7.50	15.00	30.00

Number	Title (A Side/B Side)	Yr	VG	VG+	NM
KING					
❑ 5228	Ebb Tide (Part 1)/Ebb Tide (Part 2)	1959	3.75	7.50	15.00
❑ 5259	Sugar Tooth/Like Saying Something	1959	3.75	7.50	15.00
PINEY					
❑ 107	Live It Up/Go Baby Go	1962	15.00	30.00	60.00
❑ 108	Crazy Love/The Hawk and the Crow	1962	12.50	25.00	50.00
WARNER					
❑ 1015	How Do I Say I'm Sorry/				
	Love Is Where You Find It	1958	30.00	60.00	120.00

MANILOW, BARRY Also see FEATHERBED.
12-Inch Singles

Number	Title (A Side/B Side)	Yr	VG	VG+	NM
ARISTA					
❑ (# unknown)	En El Copa (Long) (Short)	1978	7.50	15.00	30.00
❑ SP-18 [DJ]	Copacabana (At the Copa)/(B-side blank)	1978	7.50	15.00	30.00
—The B-side is banded to appear as if it has three tracks, but the groove is blank!					
❑ SP-21 [DJ]	En El Copa (same on both sides)	1978	6.25	12.50	25.00
—Spanish version of "Copacabana"					
❑ ADP 3291 [DJ]	I'd Really Love to See You Tonight (3 versions)	1997	2.50	5.00	10.00
❑ ADP 9295 [DJ]	When October Goes (same on both sides)	1984	2.50	5.00	10.00
❑ ADP 9648 [DJ]	Brooklyn Blues (same on both sides)	1987	5.00	10.00	20.00
—With Tom Scott; blue vinyl					
❑ AD1-9665	Hey Mambo (2 versions)	1988	3.00	6.00	12.00
❑ 13379	I'd Really Love to See You Tonight (2 versions)/				
	Could It Be Magic (1993 remix)	1997	3.00	6.00	12.00
RCA					
❑ PD-14330	I'm Your Man (Club Mix)/I'm Your Man (Dub)	1986	2.50	5.00	10.00

45s

Number	Title (A Side/B Side)	Yr	VG	VG+	NM
ARISTA					
❑ SP-11 [DJ]	It's Just Another New Year's Eve				
	(same on both sides)	1977	2.00	4.00	8.00
❑ SP-11 [PS]	It's Just Another New Year's Eve				
	(same on both sides)	1977	3.00	6.00	12.00
❑ SP-25 [DJ]	Ready to Take a Chance Again				
	(same on both sides)	1978	2.00	4.00	8.00
❑ SP-25 [PS]	Ready to Take a Chance Again				
	(same on both sides)	1978	3.00	6.00	12.00
❑ 0108	It's a Miracle/One of These Days	1975	—	2.00	4.00
❑ 0126	Could It Be Magic/I Am Your Child	1975	—	2.00	4.00
❑ 0157	I Write the Songs/A Nice Boy Like Me	1975	—	2.00	4.00
❑ 0172	Tryin' to Get the Feeling Again/Beautiful Music	1976	—	2.00	4.00
❑ 0206	This One's for You/Riders to the Stars	1976	—	2.00	4.00
❑ 0212	Weekend in New England/Say the Words	1976	—	2.00	4.00
❑ 0244	Looks Like We Made It/New York City Rhythm	1977	—	2.00	4.00
❑ 0273	Daybreak/Jump Shout Boogie	1977	—	2.00	4.00
❑ 0305	Can't Smile Without You/Sunrise	1978	—	2.00	4.00
❑ 0330	Even Now/I Was a Fool (To Let You Go)	1978	—	2.00	4.00
❑ 0330 [PS]	Even Now/I Was a Fool (To Let You Go)	1978	—	2.00	4.00
❑ 0339	Copacabana (Short Version)/Copacabana				
	(Long Version)	1978	—	2.00	4.00
❑ 0357	Ready to Take a Chance Again/Sweet Life	1978	—	2.00	4.00
❑ 0382	Somewhere in the Night/Leavin' in the Morning	1978	—	2.00	4.00
❑ 0464	Ships/They Gave In to the Blues	1979	—	2.00	4.00
❑ 0481	When I Wanted You/Bobbie Lee (What's the				
	Difference I Gotta Live)	1979	—	2.00	4.00
❑ 0501	I Don't Want to Walk Without You/One Voice	1980	—	2.00	4.00
❑ 0566	I Made It Through the Rain/Only in Chicago	1980	—	2.00	4.00
❑ 0596	Lonely Together/The Last Duet	1981	—	2.00	4.00
—B-side with Lily Tomlin					
❑ 0633	The Old Songs/Don't Fall in Love with Me	1981	—	2.00	4.00
❑ 0658	Somewhere Down the Road/Let's Take All Night				
	to Say Goodbye	1982	—	2.00	4.00
❑ 0675	Let's Hang On/No Other Love	1982	—	2.00	4.00
❑ 0698	Oh Julie/Break Down the Door	1982	—	2.00	4.00
❑ 1025	Memory/Heart of Steel	1982	—	2.00	4.00
❑ 1046	Some Kind of Friend/Heaven	1983	—	2.00	4.00
❑ 2094	Jingle Bells/Because It's Christmas (For All the				
	Children)	1990	—	—	3.00
—A-side with Expose					
❑ 9003	Some Kind of Friend/Heaven	1983	—	—	3.00
❑ 9101	Read 'Em and Weep/One Voice	1983	—	—	3.00
❑ 9185	You're Lookin' Hot Tonight/Put a Quarter in the				
	Jukebox	1984	—	—	3.00
—B-side with Ronnie Milsap					
❑ 9666	Hey Mambo/When October Goes	1988	—	—	3.00
—With Kid Creole and the Coconuts					
❑ 9666 [PS]	Hey Mambo/When October Goes	1988	—	—	3.00
❑ 9811	Please Don't Be Scared/				
	A Little Traveling Music, Please	1989	—	—	3.00
❑ 9838	Keep Each Other Warm/				
	A Little Traveling Music, Please	1989	—	2.50	5.00
❑ 9838 [PS]	Keep Each Other Warm/				
	A Little Traveling Music, Please	1989	—	2.50	5.00
❑ 9873 [DJ]	When the Good Times Come Again				
	(same on both sides)	1989	2.50	5.00	10.00
—Record appears to be promo only					
BELL					
❑ 45357	Sweetwater Jones/One of These Days	1973	—	3.00	6.00
❑ 45422	Cloudburst/Could It Be Magic	1973	—	3.00	6.00
❑ 45443	Let's Take Some Time to Say Goodbye/Seven				
	More Years	1974	—	3.00	6.00
❑ 45613	Mandy/Something's Comin' Up	1974	—	2.50	5.00
RCA					
❑ PB-14223	In Search of Love/At the Dance	1985	—	—	3.00
❑ PB-14223 [PS]	In Search of Love/At the Dance	1985	—	2.00	4.00
❑ PB-14302	He Doesn't Care (But I Do)/It's All Behind Us Now	1986	—	—	3.00
❑ PB-14302 [PS]	He Doesn't Care (But I Do)/It's All Behind Us Now	1986	—	2.00	4.00
❑ PB-14397	I'm Your Man/I'm Your Man (Dub)	1986	—	—	3.00
❑ PB-14397 [PS]	I'm Your Man/I'm Your Man (Dub)	1986	—	—	3.00
SBK					
❑ S7-17906	Let Me Be Your Wings/Follow Your Heart	1994	—	2.00	4.00
—A-side with Debra Byrd; B-side by Gino Conforti					

Albums

Number	Title (A Side/B Side)	Yr	VG	VG+	NM
ARISTA					
❑ AB 2500 [EP]	Oh, Julie!	1982	5.00	10.00	20.00

Number	Title (A Side/B Side)	Yr	VG	VG+	NM
❑ AB 4007	Barry Manilow I	1977	2.00	4.00	8.00
—Reissue of AL 4007 with new prefix					
❑ AL 4007	Barry Manilow I	1975	2.50	5.00	10.00
—Revised version of Bell 1129 with new cover; "Could It Be Magic" especially is noticeably different between the Bell and Arista versions					
❑ AB 4016	Barry Manilow II	1977	2.00	4.00	8.00
—Reissue of AL 4016 with new prefix					
❑ AL 4016	Barry Manilow II	1975	2.50	5.00	10.00
—Reissue of Bell 1314					
❑ AQ 4016 [Q]	Barry Manilow II	1975	3.75	7.50	15.00
❑ AB 4060	Tryin' to Get the Feeling	1977	2.00	4.00	8.00
—Reissue of AL 4060 with new prefix					
❑ AL 4060	Tryin' to Get the Feeling	1975	2.50	5.00	10.00
❑ AQ 4060 [Q]	Tryin' to Get the Feeling	1975	3.75	7.50	15.00
❑ AB 4090	This One's for You	1977	2.00	4.00	8.00
—Reissue of AL 4090 with new prefix					
❑ AL 4090	This One's for You	1976	2.50	5.00	10.00
❑ AQ 4090 [Q]	This One's for You	1976	5.00	10.00	20.00
❑ AB 4164	Even Now	1978	2.00	4.00	8.00
❑ AL8-8003	Here Comes the Night	198?	—	3.00	6.00
—Reissue of 9610					
❑ AL13-8039 [(2)]	Greatest Hits	1983	2.50	5.00	10.00
❑ AL5-8046	One Voice	198?	—	3.00	6.00
—Reissue of 9505					
❑ AL13-8049 [(2)]	Barry Manilow/Live	1983	2.50	5.00	10.00
❑ AL5-8052	Even Now	198?	—	3.00	6.00
—Reissue of 8322					
❑ AL5-8070	Tryin' to Get the Feeling	198?	—	3.00	6.00
—Reissue of 8336					
❑ AL5-8085	Barry Manilow II	198?	—	3.00	6.00
—Reissue of 8370					
❑ AL8-8102	Barry Manilow/Greatest Hits, Vol. II	1983	2.00	4.00	8.00
❑ AL8-8117	Barry	198?	—	3.00	6.00
—Reissue of 9537					
❑ AL8-8123	If I Should Love Again	198?	—	3.00	6.00
—Reissue of 9573					
❑ AL5-8153	Barry Manilow I	198?	—	3.00	6.00
—Reissue of 8372					
❑ AL5-8160	This One's for You	198?	—	3.00	6.00
—Reissue of 8331					
❑ AL8-8254	2:00 A.M. Paradise Café	1984	2.00	4.00	8.00
❑ AL9-8274	The Manilow Collection — 20 Classic Hits	1985	2.00	4.00	8.00
❑ AL8-8291	Barry Manilow/Greatest Hits, Vol. II	1985	—	3.00	6.00
❑ AL8-8322	Even Now	1985	—	3.00	6.00
❑ AL8-8331	This One's for You	1985	—	3.00	6.00
❑ AL8-8336	Tryin' to Get the Feeling	1985	—	3.00	6.00
❑ AL8-8370	Barry Manilow II	1985	—	3.00	6.00
❑ AL8-8372	Barry Manilow I	1985	—	3.00	6.00
❑ AL 8500 [(2)]	Barry Manilow/Live	1977	3.00	6.00	12.00
❑ AL-8527	Swing Street	1987	2.00	4.00	8.00
❑ AL-8570	Barry Manilow	1989	2.00	4.00	8.00
❑ AL-8598	Greatest Hits, Vol. 1	1989	2.50	5.00	10.00
❑ AL-8599	Greatest Hits, Vol. 2	1989	2.50	5.00	10.00
❑ AL-8600	Greatest Hits, Vol. 3	1989	2.50	5.00	10.00
❑ A2L 8601 [(2)]	Greatest Hits	1978	3.00	6.00	12.00
❑ A2L 8601 [(2)PD]	Greatest Hits	1979	10.00	20.00	40.00
—Entire contents on two picture discs (yes, it has the same number as the regular issue)					
❑ AL-8638 [(2)]	Live on Broadway	1990	5.00	10.00	20.00
❑ AL-8644	Because It's Christmas	1990	3.75	7.50	15.00
❑ AL 9505	One Voice	1979	—	4.00	8.00
❑ AL 9537	Barry	1980	2.00	4.00	8.00
❑ AL 9573	If I Should Love Again	1981	—	4.00	8.00
❑ AL-9610	Here Comes the Night	1982	2.00	4.00	8.00
❑ NU 9740	Manilow Magic	1982	3.00	6.00	12.00
—Manufactured by K-Tel					
BELL					
❑ 1129	Barry Manilow	1973	6.25	12.50	25.00
❑ 1314	Barry Manilow II	1974	3.75	7.50	15.00
MOBILE FIDELITY					
❑ 1-097	Barry Manilow I	1981	5.00	10.00	20.00
—Audiophile vinyl					
RCA VICTOR					
❑ AFL1-7044	Manilow	1985	2.00	4.00	8.00

MANN, BARRY
45s

Number	Title (A Side/B Side)	Yr	VG	VG+	NM
ABC-PARAMOUNT					
❑ 10143	War Paint/Counting Teardrops	1960	5.00	10.00	20.00
❑ 10180	Happy Birthday, Broken Heart/Millionaire	1961	5.00	10.00	20.00
❑ 10237	Who Put the Bomp				
	(In the Bomp, Bomp, Bomp)/Love, True Love	1961	6.25	12.50	25.00
❑ 10263	Little Miss U.S.A./Find Another Fool	1961	5.00	10.00	20.00
❑ 10356	Hey Baby I'm Dancin'/Like I Don't Love You	1962	5.00	10.00	20.00
❑ 10380	Teenage Has-Been/Bless You	1962	5.00	10.00	20.00
ARISTA					
❑ 0194	The Princess and the Punk/Jennifer	1976	—	2.00	4.00
CAPITOL					
❑ 2082	Young Electric Psychedelic Hippy Flippy Folk &				
	Funky Philosophic Turned On Groovy Twelve-				
	String Band/Take Your Love	1968	3.75	7.50	15.00
❑ 2217	I Just Can't Help Believin'/				
	Where Do I Go from Here	1968	2.50	5.00	10.00
❑ 5695	Looking at Tomorrow/Angelica	1966	2.50	5.00	10.00
❑ 5894	Where Do I Go from Here/She Is Today	1967	2.50	5.00	10.00
CASABLANCA					
❑ 2287	Brown-Eyed Woman/In My Own Way	1980	—	2.00	4.00
COLLECTABLES					
❑ 90000	Who Put the Bomp/For You	199?	—	—	3.00
—B-side by Rick Nelson					
COLPIX					
❑ 691	Graduation Time/Johnny Surfboard	1963	5.00	10.00	20.00
JDS					
❑ 5002	I Love to Last a Lifetime/All the Things You Are	1959	7.50	15.00	30.00
NEW DESIGN					
❑ 1000	Carry Me Home/Sundown	1971	—	2.50	5.00
❑ 1005	When You Get Right Down to It/				
	Don't Give Up on Me	1972	—	2.50	5.00

M

Number	Title (A Side/B Side)	Yr	VG	VG+	NM
❑ 1006	Too Many Mornings/Lay It All Out	1972	—	2.50	5.00
❑ 1006	Too Many Mornings/On Broadway	1972	—	2.50	5.00

RCA VICTOR

Number	Title (A Side/B Side)	Yr	VG	VG+	NM
❑ PB-10104	Nobody But You/Woman, Woman, Woman	1974	—	2.50	5.00
❑ PB-10230	Nothing Good Comes Easy/Woman, Woman, Woman	1975	—	2.50	5.00
❑ PB-10319	Don't Seem Right/I'm a Survivor	1975	—	2.50	5.00

RED BIRD

Number	Title (A Side/B Side)	Yr	VG	VG+	NM
❑ 10-015	Talk to Me Baby/Amy	1964	3.75	7.50	15.00

SCEPTER

Number	Title (A Side/B Side)	Yr	VG	VG+	NM
❑ 12281	Feelings/Let Me Stay with You	1970	—	3.00	6.00

UNITED ARTISTS

Number	Title (A Side/B Side)	Yr	VG	VG+	NM
❑ XW1021	Best That I Know How/Lettin' Good Times Get Away	1977	—	2.00	4.00

WARNER BROS.

Number	Title (A Side/B Side)	Yr	VG	VG+	NM
❑ 8752	For No Reason at All/Almost Gone	1979	—	2.00	4.00
❑ 8752 [PS]	For No Reason at All/Almost Gone	1979	—	2.50	5.00

Albums

ABC-PARAMOUNT

Number	Title (A Side/B Side)	Yr	VG	VG+	NM
❑ 399 [M]	Who Put the Bomp	1963	30.00	60.00	120.00
❑ S-399 [S]	Who Put the Bomp	1963	75.00	150.00	300.00

CASABLANCA

Number	Title (A Side/B Side)	Yr	VG	VG+	NM
❑ NBLP 7226	Barry Mann	1980	2.50	5.00	10.00

NEW DESIGN

Number	Title (A Side/B Side)	Yr	VG	VG+	NM
❑ Z 30876	Lay It All Out	1971	3.00	6.00	12.00

RCA VICTOR

Number	Title (A Side/B Side)	Yr	VG	VG+	NM
❑ APL1-0860	Survivor	1975	3.00	6.00	12.00
❑ DJL1-1162 [DJ]	Flo and Eddie Interview Barry Mann	1975	12.50	25.00	50.00

MANN, BOBBY See BOBBY BLOOM.

MANN, CARL
45s

ABC

Number	Title (A Side/B Side)	Yr	VG	VG+	NM
❑ 12035	Burnin' Holes in the Eyes of Abraham Lincoln/Ballad of Johnny Clyde	1974	—	2.50	5.00
❑ 12071	Neon Lights/Just About Out	1975	—	2.50	5.00
❑ 12092	It's Not the Coffee/Cheatin' Time	1975	—	2.50	5.00

ABC/DOT

Number	Title (A Side/B Side)	Yr	VG	VG+	NM
❑ 17596	Back Loving/Annie Over Time	1975	—	2.50	5.00
❑ 17621	Twilight Time/Belly-Rubbin' Country Soul	1976	—	2.50	5.00

JAXON

Number	Title (A Side/B Side)	Yr	VG	VG+	NM
❑ 502	Gonna Rock and Roll Tonight/Rockin' Love	1957	750.00	1500.	3000.

MONUMENT

Number	Title (A Side/B Side)	Yr	VG	VG+	NM
❑ 974	Down to My Last I Forgive You/Serenade of the Bells	1966	3.75	7.50	15.00

PHILLIPS INT'L.

Number	Title (A Side/B Side)	Yr	VG	VG+	NM
❑ 3539	Mona Lisa/Foolish One	1959	6.25	12.50	25.00
❑ 3546	Pretend/Rockin' Love	1959	6.25	12.50	25.00
❑ 3550	Some Enchanted Evening/I Can't Forget	1960	6.25	12.50	25.00
❑ 3555	South of the Border/I'm Comin' Home	1960	6.25	12.50	25.00
❑ 3564	The Wayward Wind/Born to Be Bad	1961	6.25	12.50	25.00
❑ 3569	I Ain't Got No Home/If I Could Change You	1961	6.25	12.50	25.00
❑ 3579	When I Grow Too Old to Dream/Mountain Dew	1962	6.25	12.50	25.00

Albums

PHILLIPS INT'L.

Number	Title (A Side/B Side)	Yr	VG	VG+	NM
❑ PLP-1960 [M]	Like Mann	1960	150.00	300.00	600.00

MANN, JOHNNY, SINGERS
45s

EPIC

Number	Title (A Side/B Side)	Yr	VG	VG+	NM
❑ 10895	Stand Up and Cheer/America, There's So Much to Say	1972	—	2.50	5.00

LIBERTY

Number	Title (A Side/B Side)	Yr	VG	VG+	NM
❑ 55249	Varsity Drag/Sweet Georgia Brown	1959	2.50	5.00	10.00
❑ 55327	East of the Sun/(B-side unknown)	1961	2.00	4.00	8.00
❑ 55355	Don't/Love Me	1961	2.00	4.00	8.00
❑ 55466	Summersong/Mr. and Mrs. Millionaire	1962	2.00	4.00	8.00
❑ 55525	Cotton Fields/Shenandoah	1962	2.00	4.00	8.00
❑ 55653	African Noel/Children, Board That Train	1963	2.00	4.00	8.00

—By "The Johnny Mann Children's Choir"

Number	Title (A Side/B Side)	Yr	VG	VG+	NM
❑ 55799	The Voice of Freedom/Try to Remember	1965	—	3.00	6.00
❑ 55871	Cinnamint Shuffle/Rovin' Gambler	1966	—	3.00	6.00
❑ 55938	Whither Thou Goest/A Joyful Noise	1966	—	3.00	6.00
❑ 55972	Up-Up and Away/Joey Is the Name	1967	—	3.00	6.00
❑ 56010	Don't Look Back/Instant Happy	1967	—	3.00	6.00
❑ 56083	Snow/If I Only Had Time	1968	2.00	4.00	8.00
❑ 56107	Carolina on My Mind/Little Sister	1969	—	3.00	6.00

Albums

EPIC

Number	Title (A Side/B Side)	Yr	VG	VG+	NM
❑ KE 31954	Stand Up and Cheer!	1973	3.00	6.00	12.00

LIBERTY

Number	Title (A Side/B Side)	Yr	VG	VG+	NM
❑ LRP-3134 [M]	Alma Mater	1959	3.75	7.50	15.00
❑ LRP-3149 [M]	Roar Along with the Singing Twenties	1960	3.75	7.50	15.00
❑ LRP-3156 [M]	Swing Along with the Singing Thirties	1960	3.75	7.50	15.00
❑ LRP-3198 [M]	Ballads of the King	1961	3.75	7.50	15.00
❑ LRP-3217 [M]	Ballads of the King, Volume 2	1961	3.75	7.50	15.00
❑ LRP-3253 [M]	Golden Folk Song Hits	1963	3.00	6.00	12.00
❑ LRP-3296 [M]	Golden Folk Song Hits, Volume 2	1963	3.00	6.00	12.00
❑ LRP-3355 [M]	Golden Folk Song Hits, Volume 3	1964	3.00	6.00	12.00
❑ LRP-3387 [M]	Invisible Tears	1964	3.00	6.00	12.00
❑ LRP-3391 [M]	The Ballad Sound (Beatle Songs)	1964	3.75	7.50	15.00
❑ LRP-3414 [M]	If I Loved You	1965	3.00	6.00	12.00
❑ LRP-3436 [M]	I'll Remember You	1965	3.00	6.00	12.00
❑ LRP-3447 [M]	Daydream	1966	3.00	6.00	12.00
❑ LRP-3522 [M]	We Wish You a Merry Christmas	1967	3.75	7.50	15.00
❑ LRP-3523 [M]	We Can Fly! Up-Up and Away	1967	3.00	6.00	12.00
❑ LST-7134 [S]	Alma Mater	1959	5.00	10.00	20.00
❑ LST-7149 [S]	Roar Along with the Singing Twenties	1960	5.00	10.00	20.00
❑ LST-7156 [S]	Swing Along with the Singing Thirties	1960	5.00	10.00	20.00
❑ LST-7198 [S]	Ballads of the King	1961	5.00	10.00	20.00
❑ LST-7217 [S]	Ballads of the King, Volume 2	1961	5.00	10.00	20.00
❑ LST-7253 [S]	Golden Folk Song Hits	1963	3.75	7.50	15.00
❑ LST-7296 [S]	Golden Folk Song Hits, Volume 2	1963	3.75	7.50	15.00
❑ LST-7355 [S]	Golden Folk Song Hits, Volume 3	1964	3.75	7.50	15.00
❑ LST-7387 [S]	Invisible Tears	1964	3.75	7.50	15.00
❑ LST-7391 [S]	The Ballad Sound (Beatle Songs)	1964	5.00	10.00	20.00
❑ LST-7411 [S]	If I Loved You	1965	3.75	7.50	15.00
❑ LST-7426 [S]	I'll Remember You	1965	3.75	7.50	15.00
❑ LST-7447 [S]	Daydream	1966	3.75	7.50	15.00
❑ LST-7522 [S]	We Wish You a Merry Christmas	1967	3.75	7.50	15.00
❑ LST-7523 [S]	We Can Fly! Up-Up and Away	1967	3.75	7.50	15.00
❑ LST-7629	Golden	1969	3.00	6.00	12.00
❑ LMM-13017 [M]	The Great Bands with Great Voices Swing the Great Voices of the Great Bands	1962	3.75	7.50	15.00
❑ LSS-14017 [S]	The Great Bands with Great Voices Swing the Great Voices of the Great Bands	1962	5.00	10.00	20.00

SUNSET

Number	Title (A Side/B Side)	Yr	VG	VG+	NM
❑ SUM-1115 [M]	The Flowing Voices of the Johnny Mann Singers	196?	2.50	5.00	10.00
❑ SUS-5115 [S]	The Flowing Voices of the Johnny Mann Singers	196?	3.00	6.00	12.00
❑ SUS-5196	Heart Full of Song	1968	3.00	6.00	12.00
❑ SUS-5231	Country Style	1969	3.00	6.00	12.00
❑ SUS-5288	At Our Best	1970	3.00	6.00	12.00

UNITED ARTISTS

Number	Title (A Side/B Side)	Yr	VG	VG+	NM
❑ UXS-87 [(2)]	The Johnny Mann Singers Superpak	1972	3.75	7.50	15.00

MANN, MANFRED Also see MIKE D'ABO; PAUL JONES; MANFRED MANN'S EARTH BAND.
45s

ASCOT

Number	Title (A Side/B Side)	Yr	VG	VG+	NM
❑ 2151	Hubble Bubble (Toil and Trouble)/I'm Your Kingpin	1964	50.00	100.00	200.00
❑ 2157	Do Wah Diddy Diddy/What You Gonna Do?	1964	3.75	7.50	15.00
❑ 2165	Sha La La/John Hardy	1964	2.50	5.00	10.00
❑ 2165 [PS]	Sha La La/John Hardy	1964	6.25	12.50	25.00
❑ 2170	Come Tomorrow/What Did I Do Wrong	1965	2.50	5.00	10.00
❑ 2170 [PS]	Come Tomorrow/What Did I Do Wrong	1965	6.25	12.50	25.00
❑ 2181	Poison Ivy/I Can't Believe What You Say	1965	—	—	—

—Unreleased?

Number	Title (A Side/B Side)	Yr	VG	VG+	NM
❑ 2184	My Little Red Book/What Am I Doing Wrong	1965	2.50	5.00	10.00
❑ 2194	If You Gotta Go, Go Now/The One in the Middle	1965	2.50	5.00	10.00
❑ 2210	She Needs Company/Hi Lili, Hi Lo	1966	2.50	5.00	10.00
❑ 2241	My Little Red Book/I Can't Believe What You Say	1967	2.50	5.00	10.00

MERCURY

Number	Title (A Side/B Side)	Yr	VG	VG+	NM
❑ 72607	Just Like a Woman/I Wanna Be Rich	1966	2.50	5.00	10.00
❑ 72607 [PS]	Just Like a Woman/I Wanna Be Rich	1966	6.25	12.50	25.00
❑ 72629	Semi-Detached Suburban Mr. Jones/Each and Every Day	1966	2.50	5.00	10.00
❑ 72675	Ha, Ha, Said the Clown/Feeling So Good	1967	2.50	5.00	10.00
❑ 72770	The Mighty Quinn (Quinn the Eskimo)/By Request — Edwin Garvey	1968	2.00	4.00	8.00

—Red label with white "Mercury" in a circle

Number	Title (A Side/B Side)	Yr	VG	VG+	NM
❑ 72770	Quinn the Eskimo/By Request — Edwin Garvey	1968	2.50	5.00	10.00

—Red label with white "Mercury" in a circle

Number	Title (A Side/B Side)	Yr	VG	VG+	NM
❑ 72770	The Mighty Quinn (Quinn the Eskimo)/By Request — Edwin Garvey	1968	2.50	5.00	10.00

—Orange and red swirl label

Number	Title (A Side/B Side)	Yr	VG	VG+	NM
❑ 72770	Quinn the Eskimo/By Request — Edwin Garvey	1968	3.00	6.00	12.00

—Orange and red swirl label

Number	Title (A Side/B Side)	Yr	VG	VG+	NM
❑ 72770	The Mighty Quinn (Quinn the Eskimo)/By Request — Edwin Garvey	1968	3.00	6.00	12.00

—Red label with "Mercury" in all capital letters

Number	Title (A Side/B Side)	Yr	VG	VG+	NM
❑ 72770	The Mighty Quinn (Quinn the Eskimo)/By Request — Edwin Garvey	1968	3.75	7.50	15.00

—Black label, silver print, "Mercury Records" in double oval at top; as this label was last used in 1964, this shouldn't exist, but it does

Number	Title (A Side/B Side)	Yr	VG	VG+	NM
❑ 72822	My Name Is Jack/There Is a Man	1968	2.00	4.00	8.00
❑ 72822 [PS]	My Name Is Jack/There Is a Man	1968	3.75	7.50	15.00
❑ 72879	Fox on the Run/Too Many People	1968	2.00	4.00	8.00
❑ 72921	Ragamuffin Man/A B-Side	1969	2.00	4.00	8.00

POLYDOR

Number	Title (A Side/B Side)	Yr	VG	VG+	NM
❑ 14026	Sometimes/Snakeskin Garter	1970	—	3.00	6.00
❑ 14074	California Coastline/Part Time	1971	—	—	—

—Unreleased

Number	Title (A Side/B Side)	Yr	VG	VG+	NM
❑ 14097	Please Mrs. Henry/Prayers	1971	—	2.50	5.00

PRESTIGE

Number	Title (A Side/B Side)	Yr	VG	VG+	NM
❑ 312	5-4-3-2-1/Without You	1964	10.00	20.00	40.00
❑ 314	Blue Brave/Brother Jack	1964	25.00	50.00	100.00

UNITED ARTISTS

Number	Title (A Side/B Side)	Yr	VG	VG+	NM
❑ 0048	Do Wah Diddy Diddy/Sha La La	1973	—	2.50	5.00

—"Silver Spotlight Series" reissue

Number	Title (A Side/B Side)	Yr	VG	VG+	NM
❑ 0049	Pretty Flamingo/Come Tomorrow	1973	—	2.50	5.00

—"Silver Spotlight Series" reissue

Number	Title (A Side/B Side)	Yr	VG	VG+	NM
❑ 50040	Pretty Flamingo/You're Standing By	1966	2.50	5.00	10.00
❑ 50066	When Will I Be Loved/Do You Have to Do That	1966	2.50	5.00	10.00

Albums

ASCOT

Number	Title (A Side/B Side)	Yr	VG	VG+	NM
❑ AM-13015 [M]	The Manfred Mann Album	1964	10.00	20.00	40.00
❑ AM-13018 [M]	The Five Faces of Manfred Mann	1965	10.00	20.00	40.00
❑ AM-13021 [M]	My Little Red Book of Winners	1965	10.00	20.00	40.00
❑ AM-13024 [M]	Mann Made	1966	10.00	20.00	40.00
❑ AS-16015 [P]	The Manfred Mann Album	1964	12.50	25.00	50.00
❑ AS-16018 [P]	The Five Faces of Manfred Mann	1965	12.50	25.00	50.00
❑ AS-16021 [S]	My Little Red Book of Winners	1965	12.50	25.00	50.00
❑ AS-16024 [S]	Mann Made	1966	12.50	25.00	50.00

CAPITOL

Number	Title (A Side/B Side)	Yr	VG	VG+	NM
❑ SM-11688	The Best of Manfred Mann	1977	2.50	5.00	10.00
❑ SN-16073	The Best of Manfred Mann	1980	2.00	4.00	8.00

JANUS

Number	Title (A Side/B Side)	Yr	VG	VG+	NM
❑ JXS-3064	The Best of Manfred Mann	1974	3.00	6.00	12.00

MERCURY

Number	Title (A Side/B Side)	Yr	VG	VG+	NM
❑ SR-61168	The Mighty Quinn	1968	6.25	12.50	25.00

POLYDOR

Number	Title (A Side/B Side)	Yr	VG	VG+	NM
❑ 24-4013	Chapter Three	1970	3.75	7.50	15.00

UNITED ARTISTS

Number	Title (A Side/B Side)	Yr	VG	VG+	NM
❑ 94 [DJ]	Manfred Mann Interview	1966	50.00	100.00	200.00

—Promotional album in plain white jacket

Number	Title (A Side/B Side)	Yr	VG	VG+	NM
❑ UAL 3549 [M]	Pretty Flamingo	1966	7.50	15.00	30.00
❑ UAL 3551 [M]	Manfred Mann's Greatest Hits	1966	7.50	15.00	30.00
❑ UAS 6549 [S]	Pretty Flamingo	1966	10.00	20.00	40.00
❑ UAS 6551 [P]	Manfred Mann's Greatest Hits	1966	10.00	20.00	40.00

—"Do Wah Diddy Diddy," "Sha La La," "I Got You Babe" and "Satisfaction" are rechanneled.

Number	Title (A Side/B Side)	Yr	VG	VG+	NM

MANN, MANFRED'S, EARTH BAND Also see MANFRED MANN.
12-Inch Singles
ARISTA
- ADP 9110 [DJ] Demolition Man (same on both sides) 1983 2.00 4.00 8.00
- ADP 9147 [DJ] Runner (same on both sides) 1983 2.00 4.00 8.00

45s
ARISTA
- 9143 Runner/Where Do They Send Them 1984 — — 3.00
—Second pressing has black label
- 9143 Runner/Where Do They Send Them 1984 — 2.00 4.00
—First pressing has whitish label
- 9203 Rebel/Figures on a Rock 1984 — — 3.00
POLYDOR
- 14113 Living Without You/Tribute 1972 — 2.50 5.00
- 14130 I'm Up and Leaving/Part Time Man 1972 — 2.50 5.00
- 14130 [PS] I'm Up and Leaving/Part Time Man 1972 2.50 5.00 10.00
- 14160 It's All Over Now, Baby Blue/Ashes 1973 — 2.50 5.00
- 14173 Mardi Gras Day/Sad Joy 1973 — 2.50 5.00
- 14191 Get Your Rocks Off/Wind 1973 — 2.50 5.00
- 14205 Joybringer/Cloudy Eyes 1973 — 2.50 5.00
- 14225 Father of Night/Solar Fire Two 1974 — 2.50 5.00
WARNER BROS.
- 8152 Spirit in the Night/As Above So Below 1975 2.00 4.00 8.00
- 8176 Spirit in the Night/As Above So Below 1976 — 3.00 6.00
- 8176 [DJ] Spirit in the Night (Long)/Spirit in the Night (Short) 1976 — 3.00 6.00
- 8252 Blinded by the Light/Starbird No. 2 1976 — 2.50 5.00
- 8252 [PS] Blinded by the Light/Starbird No. 2 1976 2.00 4.00 8.00
- 8355 Spirit in the Night/Questions 1977 — 2.50 5.00
—This has newly-recorded vocal tracks by Chris Thompson
- 8355 [DJ] Spirit (same on both sides) 1977 2.50 5.00 10.00
—Newly-recorded vocal tracks by Chris Thompson; some early promos use this title in error and include a card that says "The correct title should be 'Spirit in the Night.' WBS 8355"
- 8574 California/Bouillabaise 1978 — 2.50 5.00
- 8620 Davy's on the Road Again/Bouillabaise 1978 — 2.50 5.00
- 8850 You Angel You/"Belle" of the Earth 1979 — 2.00 4.00
- 49678 For You/Fool I Am 1981 — 2.50 5.00
- 49762 Adolescent Dream/Lies (Through the 80's) 1981 — 2.00 4.00
Albums
ARISTA
- AL 8194 Somewhere in Afrika 1983 2.50 5.00 10.00
POLYDOR
- PD-5015 Manfred Mann's Earth Band 1971 3.75 7.50 15.00
- PD-5031 Glorified, Magnified 1972 3.75 7.50 15.00
- PD-5050 Get Your Rocks Off 1973 3.75 7.50 15.00
- PD-1-6019 Solar Fire 1974 3.75 7.50 15.00
WARNER BROS.
- BS 2826 The Good Earth 1974 3.00 6.00 12.00
- BS 2877 Nightingales and Bombers 1975 3.00 6.00 12.00
- BS 2965 The Roaring Silence 1976 3.00 6.00 12.00
—Orange cover
- BSK 3055 The Roaring Silence 1977 2.50 5.00 10.00
—Blue cover; re-recording of "Spirit in the Night" is added
- BSK 3157 Watch 1978 2.50 5.00 10.00
- BSK 3302 Angel Station 1979 2.50 5.00 10.00
- BSK 3498 Chance 1980 2.50 5.00 10.00

MANN, REV. COLUMBUS
45s
CYE
- 1001 Soon Very Soon (He's Coming Back)/(B-side unknown) 196? 10.00 20.00 40.00
TAMLA
- 54047 Jesus Loves/They Shall Be Mine 1961 12.50 25.00 50.00
Albums
TAMLA
- T-227 [M] They Shall Be Mine 1962 2000. 3000. 4000.
WINGATE
- 701 [M] He Satisfies Me 196? 300.00 600.00 900.00

MANN, SHADOW
Albums
TOMORROW
- TPS-69001 Come Live with Me 1974 15.00 30.00 60.00

MANNA, CHARLIE
45s
DECCA
- 31320 I Want Me Crayons (Part 1)/I Want Me Crayons (Part 2) 1961 2.50 5.00 10.00
- 31320 [PS] I Want Me Crayons (Part 1)/I Want Me Crayons (Part 2) 1961 3.00 6.00 12.00
- 38238 The Astronaut/War at Sea 1961 2.50 5.00 10.00
- 38238 [PS] The Astronaut/War at Sea 1961 5.00 10.00 20.00
JUBILEE
- 5498 Dear Sally, Mary, Lou/Give Me a Chance to Explain 1965 2.00 4.00 8.00
Albums
DECCA
- DL 4159 [M] Manna Overboard!! 1961 6.25 12.50 25.00
- DL 4213 [M] Manna Live!! 1962 6.25 12.50 25.00
- DL 74159 [R] Manna Overboard!! 1961 3.75 7.50 15.00
- DL 74213 [R] Manna Live!! 1962 3.75 7.50 15.00
VERVE
- V-15051 [M] The Rise and Fall of the Great Society 1966 3.00 6.00 12.00
- V6-15051 [S] The Rise and Fall of the Great Society 1966 3.75 7.50 15.00

MANNING, TERRY
Albums
ENTERPRISE
- ENS-1008 Home Sweet Home 1969 10.00 20.00 40.00

MANNO, TOMMY
45s
ATLANTIC
- 2149 Too Good to Be True/That's for Me to Know 1962 3.00 6.00 12.00

MANSON, CHARLES
Albums
AWARENESS
- 08903-1056 Lie: The Love and Terror Cult 1987 5.00 10.00 20.00
- LP-2144 Lie: The Love and Terror Cult 197? 10.00 20.00 40.00
ESP-DISK'
- 2003 Lie: The Love and Terror Cult 1970 50.00 100.00 200.00

MANTLE, MICKEY Also see TERESA BREWER.
Albums
RCA VICTOR
- LPM-1704 [M] My Favorite Hits 1958 100.00 200.00 400.00

MANTOVANI
45s
LONDON
- 1000 Tell Me You Love Me/Le Chaland Qui Passe 1951 3.00 6.00 12.00
- 1017 Wyoming/Under the Roofs of Paris 1951 3.00 6.00 12.00
- 1018 For You/Kisses in the Dark 1951 3.00 6.00 12.00
- 1019 Diane/Babette 1951 3.00 6.00 12.00
- 1020 Charmaine/Just for a Little While 1951 3.00 6.00 12.00
- 1170 At Dawning/I Love You Truly 1952 3.00 6.00 12.00
- 1171 Greensleeves/Love Makes the World Go Round 1952 3.00 6.00 12.00
- 1173 Love Here in My Heart/Poeme 1952 3.00 6.00 12.00
- 1174 Lovely Lady/Mexicali Rose 1952 3.00 6.00 12.00
- 1175 Dancing with Tears in My Eyes/Dear Love, My Love 1952 3.00 6.00 12.00
- 1205 Was It a Dream/It Happened in Monterey 1952 3.00 6.00 12.00
- 1223 Symphony/Faith 1952 3.00 6.00 12.00
- 1236 Agnes Waltz/Die Schonbrunner Waltz 1952 3.00 6.00 12.00
- 1237 Some Enchanted Evening/Gypsy Love Waltz 1952 3.00 6.00 12.00
- 1245 La Comparsita/Tango Della Luna 1952 3.00 6.00 12.00
- 1253 Teddy Bear's Christmas/The Whistling Boy 1952 3.00 6.00 12.00
- 1268 Roses from the South/Blue Danube 1952 3.00 6.00 12.00
- 1269 Wine, Women and Song Waltz/Village Swallows 1952 3.00 6.00 12.00
- 1271 Acceleration/Emperor Waltz 1952 3.00 6.00 12.00
- 1272 Vienna Blood Waltz/You and You 1952 3.00 6.00 12.00
- 1273 Voices of Spring Waltz/An Artist's Life 1952 3.00 6.00 12.00
- 1274 Treasure Waltz/1001 Nights 1952 3.00 6.00 12.00
- 1280 White Christmas/Adeste Fideles 1952 3.00 6.00 12.00
- 1287 Gypsy Legend/Czardas 1953 2.50 5.00 10.00
- 1300 Love's Dream After the Ball/Red Petticoats 1953 2.50 5.00 10.00
- 1307 Ah! Sweet Mystery of Life/Kiss in the Dark 1953 2.50 5.00 10.00
- 1308 Kiss Me Again/Italian Street Song 1953 2.50 5.00 10.00
- 1309 Sweethearts/Falling in Love with Someone 1953 2.50 5.00 10.00
- 1310 Indian Summer/Land of Romance 1953 2.50 5.00 10.00
- 1328 The Moulin Rouge Theme (Where Is Your Heart)/Vola Columba 1953 2.50 5.00 10.00
- 1332 Adios Muchachos/Speakeasy 1953 2.50 5.00 10.00
- 1333 Ave Maria/Ombra Mai Fa (Largo) 1953 2.50 5.00 10.00
- 1354 Queen Elizabeth Waltz/Royal Blue Waltz 1953 2.50 5.00 10.00
- 1355 Suddenly/Beautiful Dreamer 1953 2.50 5.00 10.00
- 1361 Chiquita Mia/Ramona 1953 2.50 5.00 10.00
- 1369 Jamaican Rumba/Swedish Rhapsody 1953 2.50 5.00 10.00
- 1380 The Melba Waltz/We'll Gather Lilacs 1953 2.50 5.00 10.00
- 1394 The Skaters' Waltz/The Midnight Waltz 1953 2.50 5.00 10.00
- 1443 I Live for You/Luxembourg Polka 1954 2.50 5.00 10.00
- 1466 Wanting You/I Bring a Love Song 1954 2.50 5.00 10.00
- 1467 Desert Song/When I Grow Too Old to Dream 1954 2.50 5.00 10.00
- 1468 Lover, Come Back to Me/You Will Remember Vienna 1954 2.50 5.00 10.00
- 1469 Will You Remember/Softly As In Morning Sunrise 1954 2.50 5.00 10.00
- 1471 Dream, Dream, Dream/Bewitched 1954 2.50 5.00 10.00
- 1483 June Night/Little Swiss Waltz 1954 2.50 5.00 10.00
- 1507 Lonely Ballerina/You Stepped Out of a Dream 1954 2.50 5.00 10.00
- 1510 Lazy Gondolier/Longing 1954 2.50 5.00 10.00
- 1543 Begin the Beguine/Our Dream Waltz 1955 2.50 5.00 10.00
- 1547 Me Chere Amie/Amoreuse 1955 2.50 5.00 10.00
- 1604 Brass Buttons/Edelma 1955 2.50 5.00 10.00
- 1617 When You Lose the One You Love/Angelus 1956 2.00 4.00 8.00
- 1646 Candlelight/Spring in Montmartre 1956 2.00 4.00 8.00
- 1669 Hearts of Paris/Merry-Go-Round Waltz 1956 2.00 4.00 8.00
- 1698 Song of Sorrento/Valse Campestre 1957 2.00 4.00 8.00
- 1708 Toyshop Ballet/Habanero 1957 2.00 4.00 8.00
- 1746 Around the World/The Road to Ballingarry 1957 2.00 4.00 8.00
- 1746 [PS] Around the World/The Road to Ballingarry 1957 3.00 6.00 12.00
- 1761 Let Me Be Loved/Call of the West 1957 3.75 7.50 15.00
- 1761 [PS] Let Me Be Loved/Call of the West 1957 15.00 30.00 60.00
—Sought-after sleeve has a photo of James Dean
- 1790 To My Love/The Story of Three Loves 1958 2.00 4.00 8.00
- 1823 Only Yesterday/Tulips from Amsterdam 1958 2.00 4.00 8.00
- 1840 Come Prima/The Canary 1958 2.00 4.00 8.00
- 1859 Summertime/This Nearly Was Mine 1959 2.00 4.00 8.00
- 1919 Tenderly/Jamaica Farewell 1960 2.00 4.00 8.00
- 1927 In the Spring/Song Without End 1960 2.00 4.00 8.00
- 1946 Theme from "The Sundowners"/Mine Alone 1960 2.00 4.00 8.00
- 1947 Irma La Douce/Count of Luxembourg Waltz 1960 2.00 4.00 8.00
- 1953 Main Theme from Exodus (Ari's Theme)/Karen 1960 2.00 4.00 8.00
- 1953 [PS] Main Theme from Exodus (Ari's Theme)/Karen 1960 2.50 5.00 10.00
- 1983 Theme from "The Valiant Years"/Non Dimenticar 1961 2.00 4.00 8.00
- 1999 Theme from "Carnival"/Do Re Mi 1961 2.00 4.00 8.00
- 2000 Theme from "Greengage Summer"/Theme from "Rocco and His Brothers" 1961 2.00 4.00 8.00
- 2021 Moon River/Sail Away 1961 2.00 4.00 8.00
- 2021 [PS] Moon River/Sail Away 1961 3.00 6.00 12.00
- 9520 The Waltz You Saved for Me/Whistle Down the Wind 1962 — 3.00 6.00
- 9543 Advise and Consent/Let Me Call You Sweetheart 1962 — 3.00 6.00
- 9552 What Kind of Fool Am I/Someone Nice Like You 1962 — 3.00 6.00
- 9567 Mutiny on the Bounty Theme/Love Song from Mutiny on the Bounty 1962 — 3.00 6.00
- 9595 Elizabethan Serenade/A Girl Named Tamiko 1963 — 3.00 6.00
- 9604 My Moonlight Madonna/Home in the Meadow 1963 — 3.00 6.00
- 9624 Take the "A" Train/Manhattan Lullaby 1963 — 3.00 6.00

Number	Title (A Side/B Side)	Yr	VG	VG+	NM
❑ 9626	The Bowery/Take the "A" Train	1963	—	3.00	6.00
❑ 9653	Two Guitars/Hava Nagila	1964	—	3.00	6.00
❑ 9655	Charade/The Fall of Love	1964	—	3.00	6.00
❑ 9674	The Churchill March/ Love Theme from The Carpetbaggers	1964	—	3.00	6.00
❑ 9711	Return to Peyton Place/ I Left My Heart in San Francisco	1964	—	3.00	6.00
❑ 9734	Fiddler on the Roof/Kanshi I (Sad Am I)	1965	—	3.00	6.00
❑ 20013	Ebb Tide/Games That Lovers Play	1966	—	3.00	6.00
❑ 20040	The Willow Tree/Villa Rides	1967	—	3.00	6.00
❑ 20045	Delilah/Both Sides Now	1968	—	2.50	5.00
❑ 20056	Aquarius/Where Did Our Summers Go	1969	—	2.50	5.00
❑ 20064	Theme from "Love Story"/Loss of Love	1970	—	2.00	4.00
❑ 20070	All of a Sudden/Winter World of Love	1971	—	2.00	4.00

7-Inch Extended Plays

LONDON

Number	Title (A Side/B Side)	Yr	VG	VG+	NM
❑ BEP 6001	*Blue Danube/Roses from the South/Wine, Women and Song/Village Swallows	195?	2.50	5.00	10.00
❑ BEP 6001 [PS]	Strauss Waltzes	195?	2.50	5.00	10.00
❑ BEP 6002	*Tales from the Vienna Woods/Morning Papers/ You and You/Vienna Blood	195?	2.50	5.00	10.00
❑ BEP 6002 [PS]	Strauss Waltzes	195?	2.50	5.00	10.00
❑ BEP.6003	Emperor Waltz/Accelerations//Voices of Spring/ Artist's Life	195?	2.50	5.00	10.00
❑ BEP.6003 [PS]	Mantovani Plays Strauss Waltzes	195?	2.50	5.00	10.00
❑ BEP 6004	*Greensleeves/Love Makes the World Go Round/A Dawning/I Love You Truly	195?	2.50	5.00	10.00
❑ BEP 6004 [PS]	Favorite Waltzes	195?	2.50	5.00	10.00
❑ BEP 6005	*Mexicali Rose/Lovely Lady Love/Here Is My Heart/My Moonlight Madonna	195?	2.50	5.00	10.00
❑ BEP 6005 [PS]	Favorite Waltzes	195?	2.50	5.00	10.00
❑ BEP 6006	*Dancing with Tears in My Eyes/Dear Love, My Love/Was It a Dream?/It Happened in Monterey	195?	2.50	5.00	10.00
❑ BEP 6006 [PS]	Favorite Waltzes	195?	2.50	5.00	10.00
❑ BEP 6007	*El Gracio/Tango D'Amore/The Agnes Waltz/ Die Schonbrunner Waltz	195?	2.50	5.00	10.00
❑ BEP 6007 [PS]	Dance Time	195?	2.50	5.00	10.00
❑ BEP 6008	Tell Me You Love Me/Love's Last Word Is Spoken//Symphony/Faith	195?	2.50	5.00	10.00
❑ BEP 6008 [PS]	Dancetime	195?	2.50	5.00	10.00
—Cover calls the second song "Le Chaland Qui Passe"					
❑ BEP 6009	*Carriage and Pair/Bees in the Bonnet/Oh Mama Mama/Gypsy Trumpeter	195?	2.50	5.00	10.00
❑ BEP 6009 [PS]	Highlights	195?	2.50	5.00	10.00
❑ BEP 6010	*La Cumpasita/Tango de la Luna/Mexican Starlight/Tango Bolero	195?	2.50	5.00	10.00
❑ BEP 6010 [PS]	Dance Time	195?	2.50	5.00	10.00
❑ BEP 6011	*Some Enchanted Evening/Gypsy Love/Hejra Kati/Love Is a Song	195?	2.50	5.00	10.00
❑ BEP 6011 [PS]	Highlights	195?	2.50	5.00	10.00
❑ BEP 6012	*Under the Roofs of Paris/Wyoming/Kisses in the Dark/For You	195?	2.50	5.00	10.00
❑ BEP 6012 [PS]	Waltzing with Mantovani	195?	2.50	5.00	10.00
❑ BEP 6013	*Diane/Babette/Charmaine/Just for Awhile	195?	2.50	5.00	10.00
❑ BEP 6013 [PS]	Waltzing with Mantovani	195?	2.50	5.00	10.00
❑ BEP 6014	The Sea (La Mer)/Night and Day//The Green Cockatoo/El Toreador	195?	2.50	5.00	10.00
❑ BEP 6014 [PS]	Mantovani Concert	195?	2.50	5.00	10.00
❑ BEP 6015	Clair de Lune//Lullaby of the Bells	195?	2.50	5.00	10.00
❑ BEP 6015 [PS]	Music from the Films	195?	2.50	5.00	10.00
❑ BEP 6016	*Prelude to the Stars/The Way to the Stars/ Nature Boy/Ritual Fire Dance	195?	2.50	5.00	10.00
❑ BEP 6016 [PS]	Mantovani Concert	195?	2.50	5.00	10.00
❑ BEP 6017	Warsaw Concerto//Cornish Rhapsody	195?	2.50	5.00	10.00
❑ BEP 6017 [PS]	Music from the Films	195?	2.50	5.00	10.00
❑ BEP.6074	Indian Summer/Kiss in the Dark//Sweethearts/ I'm Falling in Love with Someone	195?	2.00	4.00	8.00
❑ BEP.6074 [PS]	The Music of Victor Herbert	195?	2.00	4.00	8.00
❑ BEP.6075	Ah! Sweet Mystery of Life/To the Land of My Own Romance//Kiss Me Again/ Indian Street Song	195?	2.00	4.00	8.00
❑ BEP.6075 [PS]	The Music of Victor Herbert	195?	2.00	4.00	8.00
❑ BEP 6178	Romona/Amoureuse//Midnight Bells/ Beautiful Dreamer	195?	2.00	4.00	8.00
❑ BEP 6178 [PS]	Beautiful Dreamer	195?	2.00	4.00	8.00
❑ BEP 6320	*September Song/Intermezzo/Over the Rainbow/Laura	195?	2.00	4.00	8.00
❑ BEP 6320 [PS]	Mantovani Film Encores, Vol. 1	195?	2.00	4.00	8.00
❑ BEP 6324	The Dream of Olwen/The Legend of the Glass Mountain//Story of Three Loves/ Serenata D'Amour	195?	2.00	4.00	8.00
❑ BEP 6324 [PS]	Music from the Films, Vol. 2	195?	2.00	4.00	8.00

Albums

BAINBRIDGE

Number	Title (A Side/B Side)	Yr	VG	VG+	NM
❑ BT-6277	Mantovani's Italia	1988	2.00	4.00	8.00
❑ 8001 [(2)]	The Magic of Mantovani: Live at the Royal Festival Hall	1982	3.00	6.00	12.00

FLEETWOOD

Number	Title (A Side/B Side)	Yr	VG	VG+	NM
❑ FMS 1019	90 Minutes with Mantovani	1978	3.00	6.00	12.00

—Side 1: Great Songs of Christmas (reissue of London recordings); Side 2: Great Songs for All Seasons

HOLIDAY

Number	Title (A Side/B Side)	Yr	VG	VG+	NM
❑ HDY 1928	Holy Night	1981	2.50	5.00	10.00

LONDON

Number	Title (A Side/B Side)	Yr	VG	VG+	NM
❑ SS 1 [S]	Mantovani Stereo Showcase	1959	5.00	10.00	20.00
❑ PS 106 [S]	Gems Forever	1959	5.00	10.00	20.00
❑ PS 112 [S]	Music from the Films	1959	3.75	7.50	15.00
❑ PS 118 [S]	Strauss Waltzes	1959	5.00	10.00	20.00
❑ PS 119 [S]	Waltz Encores	1959	5.00	10.00	20.00
❑ PS 124 [S]	Film Encores	1959	3.75	7.50	15.00
❑ PS 125 [S]	Song Hits from Theatreland	1959	3.75	7.50	15.00
❑ PS 133 [S]	Concert Encores	1959	5.00	10.00	20.00
❑ PS 142 [S]	Christmas Carols	1959	5.00	10.00	20.00

—Originals have blue back cover, "Stereophonic" on upper left front cover and dark blue "FFSS" labels

Number	Title (A Side/B Side)	Yr	VG	VG+	NM
❑ PS 142 [S]	Christmas Carols	196?	3.75	7.50	15.00
—Reissue with white back cover					
❑ PS 147 [S]	Continental Encores	1959	5.00	10.00	20.00
❑ PS 164 [S]	Film Encores, Vol. 2	1959	5.00	10.00	20.00
❑ PS 165 [S]	The Music of Victor Herbert and Sigmund Romberg	1959	5.00	10.00	20.00
❑ PS 165/6 [(2)S]	All-American Showcase	1959	6.25	12.50	25.00
❑ PS 166 [S]	The Music of Irving Berlin and Rudolf Friml	1959	5.00	10.00	20.00
❑ PS 182 [S]	The American Scene	1960	3.75	7.50	15.00
❑ PS 193 [S]	Songs to Remember	1960	3.75	7.50	15.00
❑ PS 202 [S]	Operetta Memories	1960	3.75	7.50	15.00
❑ PS 224 [S]	Mantovani Plays Music from Exodus and Other Great Themes	1960	3.75	7.50	15.00
❑ PS 232 [S]	Italia Mia	1961	3.75	7.50	15.00
❑ PS 242 [S]	Themes from Broadway (Carnival)	1961	3.75	7.50	15.00
❑ PS 245 [S]	Songs of Praise	1961	3.00	6.00	12.00
❑ PS 248 [S]	American Waltzes	1962	3.00	6.00	12.00
❑ PS 249 [S]	Moon River and Other Great Film Themes	1962	3.00	6.00	12.00
❑ PS 269 [S]	Classical Encores	1963	3.00	6.00	12.00
❑ PS 270 [S]	Stop the World—I Want to Get Off/Oliver	1962	3.00	6.00	12.00
❑ PS 280 [S]	The World's Great Love Songs	1963	3.00	6.00	12.00
❑ PS 295 [S]	Latin Rendezvous	1963	3.00	6.00	12.00
❑ PS 328 [S]	Mantovani/Manhattan	1963	3.00	6.00	12.00
❑ PS 338 [S]	Christmas Greetings from Mantovani	1963	3.75	7.50	15.00
❑ PS 360 [S]	Folk Songs Around the World	1964	3.00	6.00	12.00
❑ PS 392 [S]	The Incomparable Mantovani	1964	3.00	6.00	12.00
❑ PS 419 [S]	The Mantovani Sound — Big Hits from Broadway and Hollywood	1965	3.00	6.00	12.00
❑ PS 422 [S]	Mantovani Ole	1965	3.00	6.00	12.00
❑ PS 448 [S]	Mantovani Magic	1966	3.00	6.00	12.00
❑ PS 474 [S]	Mr. Music…Mantovani	1966	3.00	6.00	12.00
❑ PS 483 [S]	Mantovani's Golden Hits	1967	3.00	6.00	12.00
❑ PS 516 [S]	Mantovani/Hollywood	1967	3.00	6.00	12.00
❑ PS 526 [S]	The Mantovani Touch	1968	3.00	6.00	12.00
❑ PS 532 [S]	Mantovani/Tango	1968	3.00	6.00	12.00
❑ PS 542 [S]	Mantovani…Memories	1968	3.00	6.00	12.00
❑ PS 548 [S]	The Mantovani Scene	1969	3.00	6.00	12.00
❑ PS 565 [S]	The World of Mantovani	1969	3.00	6.00	12.00
❑ LL 570 [M]	Greensleeves (A Selection of Favorite Waltzes)	1952	5.00	10.00	20.00
❑ PS 570	Greensleeves	1970	3.00	6.00	12.00
❑ PS 572 [S]	Mantovani Today	1970	3.00	6.00	12.00
❑ PS 578 [S]	Mantovani In Concert	1970	3.00	6.00	12.00
❑ XPS 585/6 [(2)S]	From Monty with Love	1971	3.75	7.50	15.00
❑ XPS 598 [S]	To Lovers Everywhere U.S.A.	1971	3.00	6.00	12.00
❑ XPS 610 [S]	Annunzio Paolo Mantovani (25th Anniversary)	1972	3.00	6.00	12.00
❑ LL 685 [M]	Strauss Waltzes	1953	5.00	10.00	20.00
❑ BP 720/1 [(2)]	Christmas Favorites	19??	3.75	7.50	15.00
❑ LL 766 [M]	An Enchanted Evening with Mantovani	1953	5.00	10.00	20.00
❑ LL 768 [M]	Mantovani Plays Tangos	1953	5.00	10.00	20.00
❑ XPS 900	Gypsy Soul	1972	2.50	5.00	10.00
❑ XPS 902	An Evening with Mantovani	1973	2.50	5.00	10.00
❑ XPS 906	All-Time Greatest Hits, Volume 1	1973	2.50	5.00	10.00
❑ APS 907	Musical Moments	1974	2.50	5.00	10.00
❑ BP 910/1 [(2)]	Romantic Hits	197?	3.00	6.00	12.00
❑ LL 913 [M]	Christmas Carols	1953	3.75	7.50	15.00
—Original recordings in mono					
❑ LL 913 [M]	Christmas Carols	1959	3.00	6.00	12.00
—Mono versions of stereo re-recordings					
❑ XPS 913	The Greatest Gift Is Love	197?	2.50	5.00	10.00
❑ XPS 914	More Golden Hits	197?	2.50	5.00	10.00
❑ XPS 915	American Encores	1976	2.50	5.00	10.00
❑ XPS 917	Strictly Mantovani	1977	2.50	5.00	10.00
❑ PS 921	Favorite Melodies from Opera	1978	2.50	5.00	10.00
❑ LL 979 [M]	Romantic Melodies	1954	5.00	10.00	20.00
❑ LL 1094 [M]	Waltz Time	1954	5.00	10.00	20.00
❑ LL 1150 [M]	The Music of Rudolf Frimi	1955	5.00	10.00	20.00
❑ LL 1219 [M]	Song Hits from Theatreland	1955	5.00	10.00	20.00
❑ LL 1259 [M]	Lonely Ballerina (Musical Modes)	1955	5.00	10.00	20.00
❑ LL 1262 [M]	Gershwin: Concerto	1955	5.00	10.00	20.00
❑ LL 1262 [M]	Gershwin: Rhapsody in Blue	1955	5.00	10.00	20.00
❑ LL 1331 [M]	Operatic Arias	1955	5.00	10.00	20.00
❑ LL 1452 [M]	Waltzes of Irving Berlin	1956	5.00	10.00	20.00
❑ LL 1502 [M]	Candlelight	195?	3.75	7.50	15.00
❑ LL 1513 [M]	Music from the Films	1956	5.00	10.00	20.00
❑ LL 1525 [M]	Music from the Ballet	1956	5.00	10.00	20.00
❑ LL 1700 [M]	Film Encores	1957	5.00	10.00	20.00
❑ LL 1748 [M]	The World's Favorite Love Songs	1957	5.00	10.00	20.00
❑ LL 3004 [M]	Concert Encores	1958	3.75	7.50	15.00
❑ LL 3032 [M]	Gems Forever	1958	3.75	7.50	15.00
❑ LL 3095 [M]	Continental Encores	1959	3.75	7.50	15.00
❑ LL 3117 [M]	Film Encores, Vol. 2	1959	3.75	7.50	15.00
❑ LL 3122 [M]	The Music of Victor Herbert and Sigmund Romberg	1959	3.75	7.50	15.00
❑ LL 3122/3 [(2)M]	All-American Showcase	1959	5.00	10.00	20.00
❑ LL 3123 [M]	The Music of Irving Berlin and Rudolf Friml	1959	3.75	7.50	15.00
❑ LL 3136 [M]	The American Scene	1960	3.00	6.00	12.00
❑ LL 3149 [M]	Songs to Remember	1960	3.00	6.00	12.00
❑ LL 3181 [M]	Operetta Memories	1960	3.00	6.00	12.00
❑ LL 3231 [M]	Mantovani Plays Music from Exodus and Other Great Themes	1960	3.00	6.00	12.00
❑ LL 3239 [M]	Italia Mia	1961	3.00	6.00	12.00
❑ LL 3250 [M]	Themes from Broadway (Carnival)	1961	3.00	6.00	12.00
❑ LL 3251 [M]	Songs of Praise	1961	2.50	5.00	10.00
❑ LL 3260 [M]	American Waltzes	1962	2.50	5.00	10.00
❑ LL 3261 [M]	Moon River and Other Great Film Themes	1962	2.50	5.00	10.00
❑ LL 3269 [M]	Classical Encores	1963	2.50	5.00	10.00
❑ LL 3270 [M]	Stop the World—I Want to Get Off/Oliver	1962	2.50	5.00	10.00
❑ LL 3280 [M]	The World's Great Love Songs	1963	2.50	5.00	10.00
❑ LL 3295 [M]	Latin Rendezvous	1963	2.50	5.00	10.00
❑ LL 3328 [M]	Mantovani/Manhattan	1963	2.50	5.00	10.00
❑ LL 3338 [M]	Christmas Greetings from Mantovani	1963	3.00	6.00	12.00
❑ LL 3360 [M]	Folk Songs Around the World	1964	2.50	5.00	10.00
❑ LL 3392 [M]	The Incomparable Mantovani	1964	2.50	5.00	10.00
❑ LL 3419 [M]	The Mantovani Sound — Big Hits from Broadway and Hollywood	1965	2.50	5.00	10.00
❑ LL 3422 [M]	Mantovani Ole	1965	2.50	5.00	10.00
❑ LL 3448 [M]	Mantovani Magic	1966	2.50	5.00	10.00
❑ LL 3474 [M]	Mr. Music…Mantovani	1966	2.50	5.00	10.00

Number	Title (A Side/B Side)	Yr	VG	VG+	NM
❏ LL 3483 [M]	Mantovani's Golden Hits	1967	3.00	6.00	12.00
❏ LL 3516 [M]	Mantovani/Hollywood	1967	3.00	6.00	12.00
❏ LL 3526 [M]	The Mantovani Touch	1968	3.75	7.50	15.00
❏ PM 55001 [M]	Kismet	1964	3.00	6.00	12.00
❏ 820085-1	Mantovani's Golden Hits	198?	2.00	4.00	8.00
—Reissue of 483					
❏ 820333-1	Mantovani/Tango	198?	2.00	4.00	8.00
—Reissue of 532					
❏ 820334-1	The Incomparable Mantovani	198?	2.00	4.00	8.00
—Reissue of 392					
LONDON PHASE 4					
❏ SP-44043 [S]	Kismet	1964	3.75	7.50	15.00
❏ BP 44302/3 [(2)]	Million Sellers	1978	3.00	6.00	12.00

MANZAREK, RAY Also see THE DOORS; RICK AND THE RAVENS.
45s
MERCURY

❏ 73477	Solar Boat/Moorish Idol	1974	—	2.50	5.00
❏ 73601	Downbound Train/Choose Up and Choose Off	1974	—	2.50	5.00
❏ 73644	The Whole Thing Started with Rock and Roll				
	(And Now It's Out of Control)/Art Deco				
	Fandango	1974	—	2.50	5.00

Albums
A&M

❏ SP-4945	Carmina Burana	1984	2.50	5.00	10.00
MERCURY					
❏ SRM-1-703	The Golden Scarab	1974	3.00	6.00	12.00
❏ SRM-1-1014	The Whole Thing Started with Rock & Roll Now				
	It's Out of Control	1975	3.00	6.00	12.00

MAR-KEYS
45s
SATELLITE

❏ 107	Last Night/Night Before	1960	7.50	15.00	30.00
STAX					
❏ 112	Morning After/Diana	1961	3.00	6.00	12.00
❏ 114	About Noon/Sack-O-Woe	1961	3.00	6.00	12.00
❏ 115	Foxy/One Degree North	1961	3.00	6.00	12.00
❏ 121	Pop-Eye Stroll/Po-Dunk	1962	3.00	6.00	12.00
❏ 124	What's Happening/You Got It	1962	3.00	6.00	12.00
❏ 129	Sailor Man Waltz/Sack-O-Woe	1963	3.00	6.00	12.00
❏ 133	The Dribble/Bo Time	1963	3.00	6.00	12.00
❏ 156	Beach Bash/Bush Bash	1964	2.50	5.00	10.00
❏ 166	The Shovel/Banana Juice	1965	2.50	5.00	10.00
❏ 181	Grab This Thing (Part 1)/Grab This Thing (Part 2)	1965	2.50	5.00	10.00
❏ 185	Philly Dog/Honey Pot	1966	2.50	5.00	10.00

Albums
ATLANTIC

❏ 8055 [M]	Last Night	1961	25.00	50.00	100.00
—White "fan" logo on right					
❏ 8055 [M]	Last Night	1962	12.50	25.00	50.00
—Black "fan" logo on right					
❏ SD 8055 [R]	Last Night	1966	10.00	20.00	40.00
❏ 8062 [M]	Do the Pop-Eye with the Mar-Keys	1962	12.50	25.00	50.00
❏ SD 8062 [R]	Do the Pop-Eye with the Mar-Keys	1966	10.00	20.00	40.00
STAX					
❏ ST-707 [M]	The Great Memphis Sound	1966	12.50	25.00	50.00
❏ STS-707 [R]	The Great Memphis Sound	1966	10.00	20.00	40.00
❏ STS-2025	Damifiknew	1969	5.00	10.00	20.00
❏ STS-2036	Memphis Experience	1971	5.00	10.00	20.00

MAR-KEYS/BOOKER T. AND THE MG'S Also see each artist's individual listings.
Albums
STAX

| ❏ ST-720 [M] | Back to Back | 1967 | 5.00 | 10.00 | 20.00 |
| ❏ STS-720 [S] | Back to Back | 1967 | 6.25 | 12.50 | 25.00 |

MAR-VELS, THE
45s
ANGIE

❏ 1005	Go On and Have Yourself a Ball/				
	How Do I Keep the Girls Away	1963	5.00	10.00	20.00
BUTANE					
❏ 778	Go On and Have Yourself a Ball/				
	How Do I Keep the Girls Away	1963	3.75	7.50	15.00
IN					
❏ 102	Surfing at Makeha/Endless Nights	1964	12.50	25.00	50.00
LOVE					
❏ 5011/2	Cherry Lips/Could Be You	1958	7.50	15.00	30.00
TAMMY					
❏ 1016	Somewhere in Life/Voo Doo Hurt	1961	75.00	150.00	300.00
❏ 1019	My Guardian Angel/Marble Stomp	1961	75.00	150.00	300.00

MARAINEY, BIG MEMPHIS
45s
SUN

| ❏ 184 | Call Me Anything, But Call Me/Baby No, No | 1953 | 2000. | 3000. | 4000. |

MARATHONS, THE (1) Two different groups posing as one. After the success of "Peanut Butter" on Arvee, the label hired another group to be The Marathons after losing a legal battle to keep the "real" group, which was really THE VIBRATIONS in disguise. And the Vibrations had formerly been THE JAYHAWKS. Confused yet?
45s
ARGO

❏ 5389	Peanut Butter/Down in New Orleans	1961	3.75	7.50	15.00
—As "Vibrations Named By Others As MARATHONS"					
ARVEE					
❏ 5027	Peanut Butter/Talkin' Trash	1961	5.00	10.00	20.00
❏ 5038	Tight Sweater/C. Percy Mercy of Scotland	1961	3.00	6.00	12.00
❏ 5048	Chicken Spaceman/You Bug Me Baby	1962	3.00	6.00	12.00
CHESS					
❏ 1790	Peanut Butter/Down in New Orleans	1961	4.00	8.00	16.00
PLAZA					
❏ 507	Mashed Potatoes One More Time/Little Pancho	1962	3.00	6.00	12.00

Number	Title (A Side/B Side)	Yr	VG	VG+	NM
Albums					
ARVEE					
❏ A-428 [M]	Peanut Butter	1961	45.00	90.00	180.00

MARATHONS, THE (2) Completely unrelated to groups (1).
45s
SABRINA

| ❏ 334 | Don't Know Why/The Stranger | 1959 | 30.00 | 60.00 | 120.00 |

MARAUDERS, THE More than one group.
45s
ALMO

❏ 221	Like You/Slippin' and Slidin'	1965	3.75	7.50	15.00
HAWK					
❏ 4002	Sand Flea/Stomp Watch	1962	12.50	25.00	50.00
LAURIE					
❏ 3356	Out of Sight, Out of Mind/Jug Band Music	1966	5.00	10.00	20.00
LEE					
❏ 9449	Nightmare/Lovin'	1965	7.50	15.00	30.00
SKYVIEW					
❏ 001	Since I Met You/I Don't Know How	1966	5.00	10.00	20.00
❏ 001 [PS]	Since I Met You/I Don't Know How	1966	12.50	25.00	50.00

MARBLE PHROGG, THE
45s
DERRICK

❏ 8568	Fire/(B-side unknown)	1968	20.00	40.00	80.00
Albums					
DERRICK					
❏ 8868	The Marble Phrogg	1968	250.00	500.00	1000.

MARCEAU, MARCEL
Albums
GONE

❏ LP 1F	The Best of Marcel Marceau	196?	12.50	25.00	50.00
MGM					
❏ SE-4	The Best of Marcel Marceau	196?	10.00	20.00	40.00
—The above records are identical: 38 minutes of silence and 2 minutes of applause!					

MARCELLO Known as "Marcello Minerbi" outside the United States.
45s
PARKWAY

| ❏ 962 | Zorba's Dance/L'Isola Del Dole | 1965 | 2.00 | 4.00 | 8.00 |

MARCELS, THE
45s
ALL EARS

❏ 810085	Blue Moon/Clap Your Hands				
	(When I Clap My Hands)	1981	—	3.00	6.00
BARON					
❏ 109	Betty Lou/Take Me Back	197?	2.00	4.00	8.00
CHARTBOUND					
❏ 009	Letter Full of Tears/Tell Me	197?	2.00	4.00	8.00
COLPIX					
❏ TL-147	Blue Moon/Friendly Loans	196?	3.75	7.50	15.00
—"Torchlite Series" reissue on red label					
❏ 186	Blue Moon/Goodbye to Love	1961	7.50	15.00	30.00
❏ 186 [PS]	Blue Moon/Goodbye to Love	1961	15.00	30.00	60.00
❏ 196	Summertime/Teeter-Totter Love	1961	6.25	12.50	25.00
❏ 606	You Are My Sunshine/Find Another Fool	1961	6.25	12.50	25.00
❏ 612	Heartaches/My Love for You	1961	6.25	12.50	25.00
❏ 612 [PS]	Heartaches/My Love for You	1961	25.00	50.00	100.00
❏ 617	Merry Twist-Mas/				
	Don't Cry for Me This Christmas	1961	6.25	12.50	25.00
❏ 617 [PS]	Merry Twist-Mas/				
	Don't Cry for Me This Christmas	1961	30.00	60.00	120.00
❏ 624	My Melancholy Baby/Really Need Your Love	1962	5.00	10.00	20.00
❏ 629	Footprints in the Sand/Twistin' Fever	1962	12.50	25.00	50.00
❏ 640	Flowerpot/Hold On	1962	7.50	15.00	30.00
❏ 651	Loved Her the Whole Week Through/				
	Friendly Loans	1962	6.25	12.50	25.00
❏ 665	Alright, Okay, You Win/Lollipop Baby	1962	6.25	12.50	25.00
❏ 683	That Old Black Magic/				
	Don't Turn Your Back on Me	1963	6.25	12.50	25.00
❏ 687	Give Me Back Your Love/I Wanna Be the Leader	1963	7.50	15.00	30.00
❏ 694	One Last Kiss/Teeter-Totter Love	1963	25.00	50.00	100.00
❏ 694	One Last Kiss/You Got to Be Sincere	1963	50.00	100.00	200.00
888					
❏ 101	How Deep Is the Ocean/Lonely Boy	1964	3.75	7.50	15.00
KYRA					
❏ 100	Comes Love/Your Red Wagon	1964	12.50	25.00	50.00
❏ 100	Comes Love/Your Red Wagon	1964	25.00	50.00	100.00
—Red vinyl					
MONOGRAM					
❏ 112	I'll Be Forever Loving You/A Fallen Tear	1974	3.00	6.00	12.00
❏ 113	Sweet Was the Wine/Over the Rainbow	1974	3.00	6.00	12.00
❏ 115	Two People in the World/Most of All	1974	3.00	6.00	12.00
OWL					
❏ 324	(You Gave Me) Peace of Mind/Crazy Bells	197?	2.00	4.00	8.00
QUEEN BEE					
❏ 47001	In the Still of the Night/High on a Hill	1973	3.75	7.50	15.00
ROCKY					
❏ 13711	(You Gave Me) Peace of Mind/				
	That Lucky Old Sun	1975	2.00	4.00	8.00
—As "The Fabulous Marcels"					
ST. CLAIR					
❏ 13711	(You Gave Me) Peace of Mind/				
	That Lucky Old Sun	1975	2.50	5.00	10.00
—As "The Fabulous Marcels"					
Albums					
COLPIX					
❏ CP-416 [M]	Blue Moon	1961	87.50	175.00	350.00
—Gold label					
❏ CP-416 [M]	Blue Moon	1963	30.00	60.00	120.00
—Blue label					

M

Number	Title (A Side/B Side)	Yr	VG	VG+	NM

MARCH, LITTLE PEGGY
45s
OLDE WORLD

Number	Title (A Side/B Side)	Yr	VG	VG+	NM
❑ 1105	Average People/Isn't This the Way We Are	1975	2.00	4.00	8.00

RCA VICTOR

Number	Title (A Side/B Side)	Yr	VG	VG+	NM
❑ 47-8107	Little Me/Pagan Love Song	1962	3.75	7.50	15.00
❑ 47-8139	I Will Follow Him/Wind-Up Doll	1963	5.00	10.00	20.00
❑ 47-8189	I Wish I Were a Princess/My Teenage Castle	1963	3.75	7.50	15.00
❑ 47-8189 [PS]	I Wish I Were a Princess/My Teenage Castle	1963	7.50	15.00	30.00
❑ 47-8221	Hello Heartache, Goodbye Love/Boy Crazy	1963	3.75	7.50	15.00
❑ 47-8221 [PS]	Hello Heartache, Goodbye Love/Boy Crazy	1963	7.50	15.00	30.00
❑ 47-8267	The Impossible Happened/Waterfall	1963	3.00	6.00	12.00
❑ 47-8291	My Heart Keeps Telling Me/His	1963	—	—	—

—Unreleased

Number	Title (A Side/B Side)	Yr	VG	VG+	NM
❑ 47-8302	(I'm Watching) Every Little Move You Make/After You	1963	3.00	6.00	12.00
❑ 47-8357	Takin' the Long Way Home/Leave Me Alone	1964	2.50	5.00	10.00

—All records from 1964 on are as "Peggy March"

Number	Title (A Side/B Side)	Yr	VG	VG+	NM
❑ 47-8418	Oh My, What a Guy/Only You Could Do That to My Heart	1964	2.50	5.00	10.00
❑ 47-8460	Watch What You Do With My Baby/Can't Stop Thinking About Him	1964	2.50	5.00	10.00
❑ 47-8534	Why Can't He Be You/Losin' My Touch	1965	2.50	5.00	10.00
❑ 47-8605	Let Her Go/Your Girl	1965	2.50	5.00	10.00
❑ 47-8710	He Couldn't Care Less/Heaven for Lovers	1965	2.50	5.00	10.00
❑ 47-8840	Ein Boy Wie Du (A Boy Like You)/Sechs Tage Lang (Six Long Days)	1966	5.00	10.00	20.00
❑ 47-8877	Play a Simple Melody/Old Fashioned Wedding	1966	2.50	5.00	10.00

—With Gary Marshall

Number	Title (A Side/B Side)	Yr	VG	VG+	NM
❑ 47-8903	He's Back Again/Running Scared	1966	2.50	5.00	10.00
❑ 47-9033	Fool, Fool, Fool (Look in the Mirror)/Try to See It My Way	1966	2.50	5.00	10.00
❑ 47-9143	January First/How Can I Tell Him	1967	2.50	5.00	10.00
❑ 47-9223	Mama Dear, Papa Dear/Your Good Girl's Gonna Go Bad	1967	2.50	5.00	10.00
❑ 47-9283	This Heart Wasn't Made to Kick Around/Foolin' Around	1967	2.50	5.00	10.00
❑ 47-9359	Have a Good Time/Let Me Down Hard	1967	2.50	5.00	10.00
❑ 47-9494	If You Would Love Me/Thinking Through My Tears	1968	2.50	5.00	10.00
❑ 47-9566	Roses on the Sea/Time and Time Again	1968	2.50	5.00	10.00
❑ 47-9627	I've Been Here Before/Aren't You Glad	1968	2.50	5.00	10.00
❑ 47-9718	Purple Hat/Try to See It My Way	1969	2.50	5.00	10.00
❑ 74-0136	Boom Bang-a Bang/Lilac Skies	1969	2.50	5.00	10.00

Albums
RCA VICTOR

Number	Title (A Side/B Side)	Yr	VG	VG+	NM
❑ LPM-2732 [M]	I Will Follow Him	1963	15.00	30.00	60.00
❑ LSP-2732 [S]	I Will Follow Him	1963	20.00	40.00	80.00
❑ LPM-3883 [M]	No Foolin'	1968	10.00	20.00	40.00
❑ LSP-3883 [S]	No Foolin'	1968	6.25	12.50	25.00

MARCH, LITTLE PEGGY/BENNIE THOMAS
Albums
RCA VICTOR

Number	Title (A Side/B Side)	Yr	VG	VG+	NM
❑ LPM-3408 [M]	In Our Fashion	1965	10.00	20.00	40.00
❑ LSP-3408 [S]	In Our Fashion	1965	12.50	25.00	50.00

MARCHAN, BOBBY
45s
ACE

Number	Title (A Side/B Side)	Yr	VG	VG+	NM
❑ 523	Chickee Wah-Wah/Don't Take Your Love from Me	1956	10.00	20.00	40.00
❑ 532	I'll Never Let You Go/I Can't Stop Loving You	1957	7.50	15.00	30.00
❑ 557	Rockin' Behind the Iron Curtain/You Can't Stop Her	1959	7.50	15.00	30.00
❑ 3004	Push the Button/My Day Is Coming	1974	—	2.50	5.00
❑ 3008	God Bless Our Love/My Day Is Coming	1975	—	2.50	5.00
❑ 3016	Baby Get Your Yo-Yo/What Can I Do	1975	—	2.50	5.00

ALADDIN

Number	Title (A Side/B Side)	Yr	VG	VG+	NM
❑ 3189	Just a Little Walk/Have Mercy	1953	15.00	30.00	60.00

BOBBY ROBINSON

Number	Title (A Side/B Side)	Yr	VG	VG+	NM
❑ (# unknown)	There's Something on Your Mind/(B-side unknown)	1973	—	3.00	6.00

CAMEO

Number	Title (A Side/B Side)	Yr	VG	VG+	NM
❑ 405	There's Something About My Baby/Everything a Poor Man Needs	1966	2.50	5.00	10.00
❑ 429	Shake Your Tambourine/Just Be Yourself	1966	2.50	5.00	10.00
❑ 453	Meet Me in Church/Hooked	1967	2.00	4.00	8.00
❑ 469	You Better Hold On/Help Yourself	1967	2.00	4.00	8.00
❑ 489	Rockin' Pneumonia/Someone to Take Your Place	1967	2.00	4.00	8.00

DIAL

Number	Title (A Side/B Side)	Yr	VG	VG+	NM
❑ 1152	Bump Your Bootie/Ain't Nothing Wrong with Whitey	1975	—	2.50	5.00
❑ 3022	I Gotta Sit Down and Cry/I Got a Thing Going	1964	2.50	5.00	10.00
❑ 4002	Get Down to It/Half a Mind	1964	2.50	5.00	10.00
❑ 4007	Hello Happiness/Funny Style	1965	2.50	5.00	10.00
❑ 4020	I Feel It Coming/Gimme Your Love	1965	2.50	5.00	10.00
❑ 4065	I Just Want What Belongs to Me/Sad Sack	1967	2.00	4.00	8.00

FIRE

Number	Title (A Side/B Side)	Yr	VG	VG+	NM
❑ 510	Yes It's Written All Over Your Face/Look at My Heart	1962	3.75	7.50	15.00
❑ 1014	Snoopin' and Accusin'/This Is the Life	1959	3.75	7.50	15.00
❑ 1022	There's Something On Your Mind (Part 1)/There's Something On Your Mind (Part 2)	1960	6.25	12.50	25.00
❑ 1027	Booty Green/It Hurts Me to My Heart	1960	3.75	7.50	15.00
❑ 1028	You're Still My Baby (Part 1)/You're Still My Baby (Part 2)	1960	3.75	7.50	15.00
❑ 1035	All in My Mind/I Miss You So	1961	3.75	7.50	15.00
❑ 1037	What You Don't Know Don't Hurt You/I Need Someone (I Need You)	1961	3.75	7.50	15.00

GALE

Number	Title (A Side/B Side)	Yr	VG	VG+	NM
❑ 4M-101	Chickee Wah Wah/Give a Helping Hand	1957	6.25	12.50	25.00

GAMBLE

Number	Title (A Side/B Side)	Yr	VG	VG+	NM
❑ 216	(Ain't No Reason) For Girls to Be Lonely Part 1/Part 2	1968	2.00	4.00	8.00

LOST-NITE

Number	Title (A Side/B Side)	Yr	VG	VG+	NM
❑ 390	There's Something On Your Mind (Part 1)/(Part 2)	197?	—	2.50	5.00

—Reissue
MERCURY

Number	Title (A Side/B Side)	Yr	VG	VG+	NM
❑ 73908	I Wanna Bump with the Big Fat Woman/Disco Rabbit	1977	—	2.50	5.00

VOLT

Number	Title (A Side/B Side)	Yr	VG	VG+	NM
❑ 108	What Can I Do (Part 1)/What Can I Do (Part 2)	1963	3.00	6.00	12.00

Albums
COLLECTABLES

Number	Title (A Side/B Side)	Yr	VG	VG+	NM
❑ COL-5113	Golden Classics	198?	2.50	5.00	10.00

SPHERE SOUND

Number	Title (A Side/B Side)	Yr	VG	VG+	NM
❑ SSR-7004 [M]	There's Something on Your Mind	1964	75.00	150.00	300.00

MARCHING OTTO   See CRAZY OTTO.

MARENO, LEE
45s
NEW ART

Number	Title (A Side/B Side)	Yr	VG	VG+	NM
❑ 103	Goddess of Love/He's Gone	1961	30.00	60.00	120.00

SCEPTER

Number	Title (A Side/B Side)	Yr	VG	VG+	NM
❑ 1222	Goddess of Love/He's Gone	1961	7.50	15.00	30.00
❑ 12222	Goddess of Love/Lonely Summer	1968	3.00	6.00	12.00

—As "Lee"

MARESCA, ERNIE
45s
LAURIE

Number	Title (A Side/B Side)	Yr	VG	VG+	NM
❑ 3345	The Good Life/A Bum Can't Cry	1966	2.50	5.00	10.00
❑ 3371	My Son/My Shadow and Me	1967	2.50	5.00	10.00
❑ 3447	What Is a Marine/The Night My Papa Died	1968	2.00	4.00	8.00
❑ 3496	Blind Date/People Get Jealous	1969	2.00	4.00	8.00
❑ 3519	The Spirit of Woodstock/Web of Love	1969	2.00	4.00	8.00
❑ 3671	The Night My Poppa Died/Please Don't Play Me a Seven	1978	—	3.00	6.00
❑ 3698	You're the Only Girl for Me/Medley	1980	—	3.00	6.00

—B-side by the Belmonts
PROVIDENCE

Number	Title (A Side/B Side)	Yr	VG	VG+	NM
❑ 417	Rockin' Blvd. St./Am I Better Off Than Them	1965	12.50	25.00	50.00

RUST

Number	Title (A Side/B Side)	Yr	VG	VG+	NM
❑ 5076	The Beetle Dance/Theme from Lilly, Lilly	1964	3.75	7.50	15.00

SEVILLE

Number	Title (A Side/B Side)	Yr	VG	VG+	NM
❑ 107	Lonesome Blues/I Don't Know Why	1960	3.75	7.50	15.00
❑ 45-117	Shout! Shout! (Knock Yourself Out)/Crying Like a Baby	1962	6.25	12.50	25.00
❑ 5N-117	Shout! Shout! (Knock Yourself Out)/Crying Like a Baby	197?	—	3.00	6.00

—Reissue on all-black label; note different prefix

Number	Title (A Side/B Side)	Yr	VG	VG+	NM
❑ 119	Down on the Beach/Mary Jane	1962	3.75	7.50	15.00
❑ 119 [PS]	Down on the Beach/Mary Jane	1962	5.00	10.00	20.00
❑ 122	Something to Shout About/How Many Times	1962	3.75	7.50	15.00
❑ 125	Love Express/Lorelei	1963	12.50	25.00	50.00
❑ 129	The Rovin' Kind/Please Be Fair	1963	3.75	7.50	15.00
❑ 138	I Can't Dance/It's Their World	1965	3.75	7.50	15.00

Albums
SEVILLE

Number	Title (A Side/B Side)	Yr	VG	VG+	NM
❑ SV 77001 [M]	Shout! Shout! Knock Yourself Out	1962	30.00	60.00	120.00
❑ SV 87001 [S]	Shout! Shout! Knock Yourself Out	1962	50.00	100.00	200.00

MARGO AND THE MARVETTES
45s
AMERICAN ARTS

Number	Title (A Side/B Side)	Yr	VG	VG+	NM
❑ 8	Cherry Pie/Say You Will	1965	3.75	7.50	15.00

MARGO, MARGO, MEDRESS AND SIEGEL   See THE TOKENS.

MARGULIS, CHARLIE
45s
CARLTON

Number	Title (A Side/B Side)	Yr	VG	VG+	NM
❑ 456	Heartache for Sale/Gigi	1958	3.00	6.00	12.00
❑ 494	Malaguena/Theme from El Salon Mexico	1959	3.00	6.00	12.00

Albums
CARLTON

Number	Title (A Side/B Side)	Yr	VG	VG+	NM
❑ LP 12-103 [M]	Marvelous Margulis	1958	6.25	12.50	25.00
❑ STLP 12-103 [S]	Marvelous Margulis	1959	7.50	15.00	30.00

MARIACHI BRASS, THE
45s
WORLD PACIFIC

Number	Title (A Side/B Side)	Yr	VG	VG+	NM
❑ 77815	Tequila/Flowers on the Wall	1966	2.00	4.00	8.00
❑ 77823	Bang Bang/Happiness Is	1966	2.00	4.00	8.00
❑ 77848	Dancing in the Street/When You're Smiling	1966	2.00	4.00	8.00
❑ 77853	La Bamba/Colonel Bogey March	1966	2.00	4.00	8.00
❑ 77857	A Man and a Woman/All	1966	2.00	4.00	8.00
❑ 77863	The Dating Game/In the Mood	1967	5.00	10.00	20.00

—Contrary to popular belief, the A-side was never done by Herb Alpert and the Tijuana Brass

Albums
WORLD PACIFIC

Number	Title (A Side/B Side)	Yr	VG	VG+	NM
❑ WP-1839 [M]	A Taste of Tequila	1966	3.00	6.00	12.00
❑ WP-1842 [M]	Hats Off!!!	1966	3.00	6.00	12.00
❑ WP-1852 [M]	Double Shot	1966	3.00	6.00	12.00
❑ WP-1859 [M]	In the Mood	1967	3.00	6.00	12.00
❑ WPS-21839 [S]	A Taste of Tequila	1966	3.75	7.50	15.00
❑ WPS-21842 [S]	Hats Off!!!	1966	3.75	7.50	15.00
❑ WPS-21852 [S]	Double Shot	1966	3.75	7.50	15.00
❑ WPS-21859 [S]	In the Mood	1967	3.75	7.50	15.00

MARIE AND THE DECCORS
45s
CUB

Number	Title (A Side/B Side)	Yr	VG	VG+	NM
❑ 9115	I'm the One/Queen of Fools	1962	6.25	12.50	25.00

Number	Title (A Side/B Side)	Yr	VG	VG+	NM
MARINO, FRANK, AND MAHOGANY RUSH See MAHOGANY RUSH.					
MARIONETTES, THE					
45s					
LONDON					
❏ 9738	Whirlpool of Love/Nobody But You	1965	3.00	6.00	12.00
MARK-ALMOND					
45s					
ABC					
❏ 12221	New York State of Mind/Return to the City	1976	—	2.00	4.00
BLUE THUMB					
❏ 201	The City/The Ghetto	1971	—	3.00	6.00
❏ 206	One Way Sunday/The Bay	1971	—	3.00	6.00
COLUMBIA					
❏ 45745	Organ Grinder/What Am I Living For	1972	—	2.50	5.00
❏ 45951	Get Yourself Together/Lonely Girl	1973	—	2.50	5.00
HORIZON					
❏ 118	You Look Just Like a Girl Again/The City	1978	—	2.00	4.00
Albums					
ABC					
❏ D-945	To the Heart	1976	2.50	5.00	10.00
BLUE THUMB					
❏ BTS 27	Mark-Almond	1971	3.00	6.00	12.00
—Reissue of 8827					
❏ BTS 32	Mark-Almond II	1971	3.00	6.00	12.00
❏ BTS 50	The Best of Mark-Almond	1973	3.00	6.00	12.00
❏ BTS-8827	Mark-Almond	1971	3.75	7.50	15.00
COLUMBIA					
❏ KC 31917	Rising	1972	3.00	6.00	12.00
❏ PC 31917	Rising	198?	2.00	4.00	8.00
—Budget-line reissue					
❏ KC 32486	Mark-Almond 73	1973	3.00	6.00	12.00
❏ CG 33648 [(2)]	Rising/Mark-Almond 73	1976	3.75	7.50	15.00
HORIZON					
❏ SP-730	Other People's Rooms	1978	2.50	5.00	10.00
MCA					
❏ 711	Mark-Almond II	198?	2.00	4.00	8.00
—Reissue of Blue Thumb 32					
❏ 792	The Best of Mark-Almond	198?	2.00	4.00	8.00
—Reissue of Blue Thumb 50					
❏ 793	To the Heart	198?	2.00	4.00	8.00
—Reissue of ABC 945					
PACIFIC ARTS					
❏ 7-142	The Best of the Mark-Almond Band…Live	1980	2.50	5.00	10.00
MARKETTS, THE					
45s					
ARVEE					
❏ 5063	Beach Bum/Sweet Potatoes	1962	5.00	10.00	20.00
CALLIOPE					
❏ 8003	Mary Hartman, Mary Hartman/(B-side unknown)	1977	—	2.50	5.00
—As "The New Marketts"					
❏ 8009	City Nights/Soul Coaxing	1977	—	2.50	5.00
—As "The New Marketts"					
FARR					
❏ 007	Song from M.A.S.H./Song from M.A.S.H. (Disco Version)	1976	—	2.50	5.00
—As "The New Marketts"					
❏ 019	The Hustle/Song from M.A.S.H.	1977	—	2.50	5.00
—As "The New Marketts"					
❏ 021	Looking for Mr. Goodbar (Terry's Theme)/Black	1977	—	2.50	5.00
—As "Danny Welton and the New Marketts"					
LIBERTY					
❏ 55401	Surfer's Stomp/Start	1962	5.00	10.00	20.00
—As "The Mar-Kets"					
❏ 55443	Balboa Blue/Stompede	1962	5.00	10.00	20.00
—As "The Mar-Kets"					
❏ 55506	Stomping Room Only/Canadian Sunset	1962	5.00	10.00	20.00
—As "The Mar-Kets"					
MERCURY					
❏ 73433	Mystery Movie Theme/Sister Candy	1973	2.00	4.00	8.00
SEMINOLE					
❏ 501	Song from M.A.S.H./Song from M.A.S.H. (Disco Version)	1976	2.00	4.00	8.00
—As "The New Marketts"					
UNI					
❏ 55173	The Undefeated/They Call the Wind Maria	1969	2.00	4.00	8.00
UNION					
❏ 501	Surfer's Stomp/Start	1961	7.50	15.00	30.00
❏ 504	Balboa Blue/Stompede	1962	7.50	15.00	30.00
❏ 507	Stomping Room Only/Canadian Sunset	1962	7.50	15.00	30.00
UNITED ARTISTS					
❏ 0043	Surfer's Stomp/Balboa Blue	1973	—	2.50	5.00
—"Silver Spotlight Series" reissue					
WARNER BROS.					
❏ 5365	Woody Wagon/Cobra	1963	3.75	7.50	15.00
❏ 5391	Out of Limits/Bella Dalena	1963	5.00	10.00	20.00
❏ 5391	Outer Limits/Bella Dalena	1963	7.50	15.00	30.00
—Original title of A-side					
❏ 5423	Vanishing Point/Borealis	1964	3.00	6.00	12.00
❏ 5468	Come See, Come Ska/Look for a Star	1964	3.00	6.00	12.00
❏ 5641	Miami's Blue/Napoleon's Solo	1965	2.50	5.00	10.00
❏ 5670	Ready Steady Go/Lady in the Cage	1965	2.50	5.00	10.00
❏ 5696	Batman Theme/Richie's Theme	1966	3.00	6.00	12.00
❏ 5814	Theme from "The Avengers"/A Touch of Velvet, a Sting of Brass	1966	5.00	10.00	20.00
❏ 5847	Tarzan/Stirrin' Up Some Soul	1966	2.50	5.00	10.00
❏ 7116	Out of Limits/Batman Theme	1968	—	3.00	6.00
—"Back to Back Hits" series -- originals have green labels with "W7" logo					
WORLD PACIFIC					
❏ 77874	Sunshine Girl/Sun Power	1967	2.50	5.00	10.00
❏ 77899	California Summer (People Moving West)/Groovin' Time	1968	2.50	5.00	10.00

Number	Title (A Side/B Side)	Yr	VG	VG+	NM
Albums					
LIBERTY					
❏ LRP-3226 [M]	The Surfing Scene	196?	7.50	15.00	30.00
—Retitled version of above					
❏ LRP-3226 [M]	Surfer's Stomp	1962	10.00	20.00	40.00
—Add 20% if "Surfer's Stomp" instruction sheet is enclosed					
❏ LST-7226 [S]	The Surfing Scene	196?	10.00	20.00	40.00
—Retitled version of above					
❏ LST-7226 [S]	Surfer's Stomp	1962	12.50	25.00	50.00
—Add 20% if "Surfer's Stomp" instruction sheet is enclosed					
MERCURY					
❏ SRM-1-679	AM, FM, Etc.	1973	3.75	7.50	15.00
WARNER BROS.					
❏ W 1509 [M]	The Marketts Take to Wheels	1963	10.00	20.00	40.00
❏ WS 1509 [S]	The Marketts Take to Wheels	1963	12.50	25.00	50.00
❏ W 1537 [M]	Out of Limits!	1964	7.50	15.00	30.00
❏ WS 1537 [S]	Out of Limits!	1964	10.00	20.00	40.00
❏ W 1642 [M]	The Batman Theme	1966	10.00	20.00	40.00
❏ WS 1642 [S]	The Batman Theme	1966	12.50	25.00	50.00
WORLD PACIFIC					
❏ WP-1870 [M]	Sun Power	1967	6.25	12.50	25.00
❏ WPS-21870 [S]	Sun Power	1967	5.00	10.00	20.00
MARKEYS, THE No relation to THE MAR-KEYS.					
45s					
GONE					
❏ 5028	Special Delivery/Along Came Love	1958	7.50	15.00	30.00
RCA VICTOR					
❏ 47-7256	Hot Rod/Yakkaty Yal	1958	6.25	12.50	25.00
❏ 47-7412	Time to Love/Make a Record Man	1958	6.25	12.50	25.00
20TH CENTURY					
❏ 1210	Eternal Love/You've Got Me on a String	1956	12.50	25.00	50.00
MARKHAM, PIGMEAT					
45s					
CHESS					
❏ 1828	Hold That Ladder (Part 1)/Hold That Ladder (Part 2)	1962	2.50	5.00	10.00
❏ 1891	Open the Door, Richard (Part 1)/Open the Door, Richard (Part 2)	1964	2.00	4.00	8.00
❏ 2049	Here Comes the Judge/The Trial	1968	—	3.50	7.00
❏ 2059	Sock It To 'Em Judge/The Hip Judge	1968	—	3.00	6.00
❏ 2087	Pig's Popcorn/Who's Got the Number	1969	—	3.00	6.00
Albums					
CHESS					
❏ LP-1451 [M]	The Trial	1961	6.25	12.50	25.00
❏ LP-1462 [M]	Pigmeat Markham At the Party	1962	6.25	12.50	25.00
❏ LP-1467 [M]	Anything Goes	1962	6.25	12.50	25.00
❏ LP-1475 [M]	The World's Greatest Clown	1963	6.25	12.50	25.00
❏ LP-1484 [M]	Open the Door, Richard	1964	6.25	12.50	25.00
❏ LP-1493 [M]	Mr. Funny Man	1965	6.25	12.50	25.00
❏ LP-1500 [M]	This'll Kill Ya	1965	6.25	12.50	25.00
❏ LP-1505 [M]	If You Can't Be Good, Be Careful	1966	3.75	7.50	15.00
❏ LPS-1505 [S]	If You Can't Be Good, Be Careful	1966	5.00	10.00	20.00
❏ LP-1515 [M]	Mr. Vaudeville	1967	3.75	7.50	15.00
❏ LPS-1515 [S]	Mr. Vaudeville	1967	5.00	10.00	20.00
❏ LP-1517 [M]	Save Your Soul, Baby	1967	5.00	10.00	20.00
❏ LPS-1517 [S]	Save Your Soul, Baby	1967	5.00	10.00	20.00
❏ LP-1521 [M]	Backstage	1968	5.00	10.00	20.00
❏ LPS-1521 [S]	Backstage	1968	5.00	10.00	20.00
❏ LPS-1525	Here Comes the Judge	1968	5.00	10.00	20.00
❏ LPS-1526	Tune Me In	1968	3.75	7.50	15.00
❏ LPS-1529	Hustlers	1969	3.75	7.50	15.00
❏ LPS-1534	Bag	1970	3.75	7.50	15.00
❏ CH-9166	Here Comes the Judge	1985	2.50	5.00	10.00
—Reissue of 1525					
JEWEL					
❏ 5007	Crap-Shootin' Rev	1972	3.00	6.00	12.00
❏ 5012	Will the Real Pigmeat Markham Please Sit Down	1973	3.00	6.00	12.00
MARKLEY					
Albums					
FORWARD					
❏ 1007	A Group	1969	7.50	15.00	30.00
MARKS, GUY					
45s					
ABC					
❏ 11055	Loving You Has Made Me Bananas/Forgive Me, My Love	1968	2.00	4.00	8.00
❏ 11099	Meet Me Tonight by the Postage Machine/This Is Forever	1968	—	3.00	6.00
❏ 11148	How the West Was Really Won/This Is Forever	1968	—	3.00	6.00
ARIOLA AMERICA					
❏ 7646	The Bridge/Man in the Glass	1976	—	2.00	4.00
Albums					
ABC					
❏ 549 [M]	Hollywood Sings	1966	3.75	7.50	15.00
❏ S-549 [S]	Hollywood Sings	1966	3.75	7.50	15.00
❏ S-648	Loving You Has Made Me Bananas	1968	5.00	10.00	20.00
MARKSMEN, THE (1) With Don Wilson of THE VENTURES.					
45s					
BLUE HORIZON					
❏ 6052	Night Run/Scratch	1960	37.50	75.00	150.00
MARKSMEN, THE (2)					
45s					
JUBILEE					
❏ 5531	Coming In on a Wing and a Prayer/Just One More Mile	1966	3.00	6.00	12.00
MARLEY, BOB, AND THE WAILERS					
12-Inch Singles					
COTILLION					
❏ PR 291 [DJ]	Reggae on Broadway (6:00) (3:15)	1981	3.00	6.00	12.00
❏ PR 414 [DJ]	Chances Are (same on both sides)	1981	3.75	7.50	15.00

M

Number	Title (A Side/B Side)	Yr	VG	VG+	NM
ISLAND					
❑ DMD 628 [DJ]	Buffalo Soldier/Buffalo Dub	1983	2.50	5.00	10.00
❑ DMD 668 [DJ]	Mix Up, Mix Up (LP Version) (Edit Version)	1983	2.50	5.00	10.00
TUFF GONG					
❑ 864693-1	Iron Zion Lion (4 versions)/Could You Be Loved	1992	3.00	6.00	12.00
45s					
BLACK HEART					
❑ 8042	African Herbsman/Stand Alone	1974	3.00	6.00	12.00
CLOCK TOWER					
❑ 505	Duppy Conqueror/Duppy Version	1971	6.25	12.50	25.00
COTILLION					
❑ 46023	Reggae on Broadway/Gonna Get You	1981	—	2.50	5.00
❑ 46029	Chances Are/(B-side unknown)	1981	—	2.50	5.00
G&C					
❑ C&G-5000	Trench Town Rock/Version	197?	5.00	10.00	20.00
ISLAND					
❑ 005	I Shot the Sheriff/Put It On	1974	—	3.00	6.00
❑ 027	Lively Up Yourself/So Jah Seh	1975	—	3.00	6.00
❑ 037	No Woman, No Cry/Kinky Reggae	1975	—	3.00	6.00
❑ 060	Roots, Rock, Reggae/Cry to Me	1976	—	3.00	6.00
❑ 072	Who the Cap Fit/(B-side unknown)	1976	—	3.00	6.00
❑ 089	Exodus/(Instrumental)	1977	—	3.00	6.00
❑ 092	Waiting in Vain/Roots	1977	—	3.00	6.00
❑ 099	Is This Love/Crisis	1978	—	3.00	6.00
❑ PR 670 [DJ]	Stir It Up (same on both sides)	1984	2.50	5.00	10.00
❑ 1211	Rock It Baby/Stop That Train	1972	2.00	4.00	8.00
❑ 1215	Concrete Jungle/No More Trouble	1973	2.00	4.00	8.00
❑ 1218	Get Up, Stand Up/Slave Driver	1973	2.00	4.00	8.00
❑ 49080	Wake Up and Live/Wake Up and Live (Dub)	1979	—	3.00	6.00
❑ 49156	Kaya/One Drop	1980	—	3.00	6.00
❑ 49547	Ride Natty Ride/Could You Be Loved	1980	—	3.00	6.00
❑ 49636	Redemption Song/Coming In from the Cold	1980	—	3.00	6.00
❑ 49755	Jamming/No Woman, No Cry	1981	—	3.00	6.00
❑ 99740	Blackman Redemption/Is This Love	1984	—	2.00	4.00
❑ 99837	Mix Up, Mix Up/French Town	1983	—	2.00	4.00
❑ 99882	Buffalo Soldier/Buffalo Dub	1983	—	2.00	4.00
❑ 99882 [PS]	Buffalo Soldier/Buffalo Dub	1983	—	3.00	6.00
❑ 562356-7	Kinky Reggae (Raga Mix)/Kinky Reggae (Kinky Mix)	1999	—	2.00	4.00
JAD					
❑ 211	Bend Down Low/Mellow Mood	1968	25.00	50.00	100.00
—As "Bob, Rita and Peter"					
SHELTER					
❑ 7309	Doppy Conquer/Justice	1971	3.00	6.00	12.00
—B-side by the Upsetters					
TRANQUILITY					
❑ T0024	It Hurts to Be Alone/(B-side unknown)	1965	50.00	100.00	200.00
—As "The Wailers"					
TUFF GONG					
❑ TG-5002	Ammunition/Kingston 12 Shuffle	197?	5.00	10.00	20.00
—B-side by U-Roy					
❑ TG-5004	Lick Samba/Version	197?	5.00	10.00	20.00
❑ TG-5005	Lively Up Yourself/Guava Jelly	197?	5.00	10.00	20.00
❑ TG-5007	Craven Choke Puppy/Version	197?	5.00	10.00	20.00
❑ TG-5009	Steppin' (Walking) Razor/The Letter	197?	5.00	10.00	20.00
❑ TG-5014	Midnight Ravers/Version	197?	5.00	10.00	20.00
UPSETTER					
❑ (# unknown)	More Axe/The Axe Man	1971	6.25	12.50	25.00
❑ 007	Cross the Nation/All in One (Medley)	1970	5.00	10.00	20.00
❑ 007	Cross the Nation/Version	1970	5.00	10.00	20.00
—B-side by the Upsetters					
❑ 009	Small Axe/Version	1970	5.00	10.00	20.00
—B-side by the Upsetters					
❑ 9001	Secondhand/Secondhand Part 2	1971	5.00	10.00	20.00
Albums					
ACCORD					
❑ SN-7211	Jamaican Storm	1982	2.50	5.00	10.00
CALLA					
❑ CAS-1240 [(2)]	The Birth of a Legend	1976	3.75	7.50	15.00
❑ ZX 34759	The Birth of a Legend	1977	2.50	5.00	10.00
—Reissue of Record 1 of Calla 1240					
❑ ZX 34760	Early Music	1977	2.50	5.00	10.00
—Reissue of Record 2 of Calla 1240					
COLUMBIA					
❑ PZ 34759	The Birth of a Legend	198?	2.00	4.00	8.00
—Budget-line reissue of Calla 34759					
❑ PZ 34760	Early Music	198?	2.00	4.00	8.00
—Budget-line reissue of Calla 34760					
COTILLION					
❑ SD 5228	Chances Are	1981	2.50	5.00	10.00
ISLAND					
❑ ISLD 11 [(2)]	Babylon by Bus	1978	3.75	7.50	15.00
—Island distribution					
❑ ISLD 11 [(2)]	Babylon by Bus	1979	3.00	6.00	12.00
—Warner Bros. distribution					
❑ ILPS 9241	Catch a Fire	1975	3.75	7.50	15.00
—Reissue with standard cover; Island distribution					
❑ ILPS 9241	Catch a Fire	1978	3.00	6.00	12.00
—Reissue; Warner Bros. distribution					
❑ ILPS 9256	Burnin'	1974	3.75	7.50	15.00
—Island distribution					
❑ ILPS 9256	Burnin'	1978	3.00	6.00	12.00
—Warner Bros. distribution					
❑ ILPS 9281	Natty Dread	1974	3.75	7.50	15.00
—Island distribution					
❑ ILPS 9281	Natty Dread	1978	3.00	6.00	12.00
—Warner Bros. distribution					
❑ SW-9329	Catch a Fire	1973	12.50	25.00	50.00
—"Cigarette lighter" cover with flip-open top; Capitol distribution					
❑ SMAS-9338	Burnin'	1973	5.00	10.00	20.00
—Capitol distribution					
❑ ILPS 9376	Live!	1975	3.00	6.00	12.00
—Island distribution					
❑ ILPS 9376	Live!	1978	2.50	5.00	10.00
—Warner Bros. distribution					

Number	Title (A Side/B Side)	Yr	VG	VG+	NM
❑ ILPS 9383	Rastaman Vibration	1976	3.00	6.00	12.00
—Island distribution					
❑ ILPS 9383 [DJ]	Rastaman Vibration	1976	25.00	50.00	100.00
—Promotional package with burlap box and press kit					
❑ ILPS 9383	Rastaman Vibration	1978	2.50	5.00	10.00
—Warner Bros. distribution					
❑ ILPS 9498	Exodus	1977	3.00	6.00	12.00
—Island distribution (all have multicolor labels)					
❑ ILPS 9498	Exodus	1978	2.50	5.00	10.00
—Warner Bros. distribution					
❑ ILPS 9517	Kaya	1978	3.00	6.00	12.00
—Island distribution					
❑ ILPS 9517	Kaya	1979	2.50	5.00	10.00
—Warner Bros. distribution					
❑ ILPS 9542	Survival	1979	3.00	6.00	12.00
❑ ILPS 9596	Uprising	1980	3.00	6.00	12.00
❑ 90029 [(2)]	Babylon by Bus	1983	3.00	6.00	12.00
❑ 90030	Catch a Fire	1983	2.00	4.00	8.00
❑ 90031	Burnin'	1983	2.00	4.00	8.00
❑ 90032	Live!	1983	2.00	4.00	8.00
❑ 90033	Rastaman Vibration	1983	2.00	4.00	8.00
❑ 90034	Exodus	1983	2.00	4.00	8.00
❑ 90035	Kaya	1983	2.00	4.00	8.00
❑ 90036	Uprising	1983	2.00	4.00	8.00
❑ 90037	Natty Dread	1983	2.00	4.00	8.00
—90029-90037 are reissues with Atco distribution					
❑ 90085	Confrontation	1983	2.50	5.00	10.00
❑ 90169	Legend	1984	2.50	5.00	10.00
❑ 90520	Rebel Music	1986	2.50	5.00	10.00
❑ 524419-1	Dreams of Freedom	1997	3.00	6.00	12.00
❑ 546404-1	Chant Down Babylon	1999	3.00	6.00	12.00
MOBILE FIDELITY					
❑ 1-221	Exodus	1995	6.25	12.50	25.00
—Audiophile vinyl					
❑ 1-236	Catch a Fire	1995	6.25	12.50	25.00
—Audiophile vinyl					
TUFF GONG					
❑ 524103-1	Natural Mystic	1995	3.75	7.50	15.00
❑ 846197-1 [(2)]	Babylon by Bus	1990	3.75	7.50	15.00
❑ 846200-1	Burnin'	1990	3.00	6.00	12.00
❑ 846201-1	Catch a Fire	1990	3.00	6.00	12.00
❑ 846202-1	Survival	1990	3.00	6.00	12.00
❑ 846203-1	Live!	1990	3.00	6.00	12.00
❑ 846204-1	Natty Dread	1990	3.00	6.00	12.00
❑ 846205-1	Rastaman Vibration	1990	3.00	6.00	12.00
❑ 846206-1	Rebel Music	1990	3.00	6.00	12.00
❑ 846207-1	Confrontation	1990	3.00	6.00	12.00
❑ 846208-1	Exodus	1990	3.00	6.00	12.00
❑ 846209-1	Kaya	1990	3.00	6.00	12.00
❑ 846210-1	Legend	1990	3.00	6.00	12.00
❑ 846211-1	Uprising	1990	3.00	6.00	12.00
❑ 848243-1	Talkin' Blues	1991	3.00	6.00	12.00

MARLO, MICKI
45s

Number	Title (A Side/B Side)	Yr	VG	VG+	NM
ABC-PARAMOUNT					
❑ 9762	Little By Little/It All Started With Your Kiss	1956	6.25	12.50	25.00
❑ 9807	Ain't That Love/The Beginning of Love	1957	3.75	7.50	15.00
❑ 9841	What You've Done to Me/That's Right	1957	3.75	7.50	15.00
—New mix, without "Vocal assist by Paul Anka"					
❑ 9841	What You've Done to Me/That's Right	1957	7.50	15.00	30.00
—With "Vocal assist by Paul Anka"					
CAPITOL					
❑ F2736	I'm Gonna Rock, Rock, Rock/Love's Like That	1954	5.00	10.00	20.00
❑ F2801	I'm Going to Sit Right Down and Cry Over You/Forever Is Now	1954	5.00	10.00	20.00
❑ F2874	I'm Flying/Why Should I Cry	1954	3.75	7.50	15.00
❑ F2932	Show Me/Every Road Must Have a Turning	1954	3.75	7.50	15.00
❑ F3016	Don't Go, Don't Go, Don't Go/Can You	1955	3.75	7.50	15.00
❑ F3062	Prize of Gold/Foolish Notion	1955	3.75	7.50	15.00
❑ F3148	I've Got Rhythm in My Nursery Rhymes/Dream Boy	1955	3.75	7.50	15.00
❑ F3266	Pet Me, Poppa/Like I Love Nobody Before	1955	3.75	7.50	15.00
❑ F3346	How Come You Love Me Like You Do/Way Down by the Cherry Tree	1956	3.75	7.50	15.00
Albums					
ABC-PARAMOUNT					
❑ 295 [M]	Married I Can Always Get	1959	5.00	10.00	20.00
❑ S-295 [S]	Married I Can Always Get	1959	6.25	12.50	25.00

MARMALADE, THE
45s

Number	Title (A Side/B Side)	Yr	VG	VG+	NM
ARIOLA AMERICA					
❑ 7619	Falling Apart at the Seams/Fly, Fly, Fly	1976	—	2.00	4.00
❑ 7631	My Everything/Walking a Tightrope	1976	—	2.00	4.00
EMI					
❑ 3676	Engine Driver/Wishing Well	1973	—	2.00	4.00
EPIC					
❑ 10162	Can't Stop Now/There Ain't No Use in Hanging On	1967	2.50	5.00	10.00
❑ 10236	Otherwise It's Been a Perfect Day/I See the Rain	1967	2.50	5.00	10.00
❑ 10284	Cry/Man in a Shop	1968	2.00	4.00	8.00
❑ 10340	Hey Joe/Lovin' Things	1968	2.00	4.00	8.00
❑ 10404	Wait for Me Mary-Ann/Mess Around	1968	2.00	4.00	8.00
❑ 10428	Ob-La-Di, Ob-La-Da/Chains	1969	2.50	5.00	10.00
❑ 10493	Time Is On My Side/Baby Make It Soon	1969	2.00	4.00	8.00
LONDON					
❑ 20058	Reflections of My Life/Rollin' My Thing	1970	—	3.00	6.00
❑ 20059	Rainbow/The Ballad of Cherry Flavar	1970	—	2.50	5.00
❑ 20066	My Little One/Is Your Life Your Own	1971	—	2.50	5.00
❑ 20068	Lonely Man/Cousin Norman	1971	—	2.50	5.00
❑ 20072	Just One Woman/Radancer	1971	—	2.50	5.00
Albums					
EPIC					
❑ BN 26553	The Best of the Marmalade	1970	5.00	10.00	20.00

Number	Title (A Side/B Side)	Yr	VG	VG+	NM
LONDON					
❑ PS 575	Reflections of My Life	1970	5.00	10.00	20.00
MARQUEES, THE (1)					
45s					
DAY-SEL					
❑ 1001	Ecstasy/Close to Me	1959	150.00	300.00	600.00
MARQUEES, THE (2)					
45s					
GRAND					
❑ 141	The Bells/The Rain	195?	12.50	25.00	50.00
—With address on label					
❑ 141	The Bells/The Rain	1956	75.00	150.00	300.00
—With no address on label					
LOST-NITE					
❑ 330	The Bells/The Rain	197?	—	2.50	5.00
—Reissue					
MARQUEES, THE (3)					
45s					
JO-ANN					
❑ 128	Stay with Me/That's the Way I Feel	1960	37.50	75.00	150.00
❑ 130	I Need a Helping Hand/				
	Don't You Do Me Like That	1961	25.00	50.00	100.00
MARQUEES, THE (4)					
45s					
LEN					
❑ 100	Say Hey/I'm in Misery	1958	25.00	50.00	100.00
MARQUEES, THE (5) MARVIN GAYE was in this group.					
45s					
OKEH					
❑ 7096	Hey Little School Girl/Wyatt Earp	1957	30.00	60.00	120.00
MARQUEES, THE (6)					
45s					
WARNER BROS.					
❑ 5072	Who Will Be the First One/Love Machine	1959	10.00	20.00	40.00
❑ 5127	Christmas in the Crowd/Sunset to Sunrise	1959	10.00	20.00	40.00
❑ 5139	Until the Day I Die/Don't Be Mean, Geraldine	1960	20.00	40.00	80.00
MARS, SYLVIA					
Albums					
LYRIC					
❑ 124	Blues Walk Right In	196?	15.00	30.00	60.00
MARSDEN, BERYL					
45s					
CAPITOL					
❑ 5552	Who You Gonna Hurt/				
	Gonna Make Him My Baby	1965	2.50	5.00	10.00
MARSDEN, GERRY Also see GERRY AND THE PACEMAKERS.					
45s					
COLUMBIA					
❑ 44309	Gilbert Green/Please Let Them Be	1967	2.50	5.00	10.00
MARSH, RICHIE Also known as Dick Marsh, he later recorded as "Sky Saxon" in THE SEEDS.					
45s					
ACAMA					
❑ 125	Baby, Baby, Baby/Half Angel	1960	7.50	15.00	30.00
AVA					
❑ 122	Goodbye/Crying Inside My Heart	1963	5.00	10.00	20.00
ROSCO					
❑ 412	There's Only One Girl/What Chance Have I	1960	5.00	10.00	20.00
SHEPHERD					
❑ 2203	They Say Darling/I Swear That It's True	1962	6.25	12.50	25.00
MARSHALL, CHUCK					
Albums					
DECCA					
❑ DL 4267 [M]	Twist to Songs Everybody Knows	1962	3.75	7.50	15.00
❑ DL 74267 [S]	Twist to Songs Everybody Knows	1962	5.00	10.00	20.00
MARSHALL, PETER					
Albums					
DOT					
❑ DLP-25930	For the Love of Pete	1969	6.25	12.50	25.00
MARSHALL BROTHERS, THE					
45s					
SAVOY					
❑ 825	Mr. Santa's Boogie/				
	Who'll Be the Fool from Now On	1951	125.00	250.00	500.00
❑ 833	Why Make a Fool Out of Me/				
	Just a Poor Boy in Love	1952	100.00	200.00	400.00
MARSHALL TUCKER BAND, THE					
12-Inch Singles					
WARNER BROS.					
❑ PRO-A-816 [DJ]	Running Like the Wind (Edit)/Last of the Singing Cowboys	1979	2.50	5.00	10.00
❑ PRO-A-863 [DJ]	It Takes Time (Single Version)//Sing My Blues/ Cattle Drive	1980	3.00	6.00	12.00
45s					
CAPRICORN					
❑ 0021	Can't You See/See You Later, I'm Gone	1973	—	3.00	6.00
❑ 0030	Take the Highway/Jesus Told Me So	1973	—	3.00	6.00
❑ 0049	Another Cruel Love/Blue Ridge Mountain Sky	1974	—	2.50	5.00
❑ 0228	This Ol' Cowboy/Try One More Time	1975	—	2.50	5.00
❑ 0244	Fire on the Mountain/Bop Away My Blues	1975	—	2.50	5.00
❑ 0251	Searchin' for a Rainbow/Walkin' and Talkin'	1976	—	2.50	5.00
❑ 0258	Long Hard Ride/Windy City Blues	1976	—	2.50	5.00
❑ 0270	Heard It in a Love Song/Life in a Song	1977	—	2.50	5.00
❑ 0278	Can't You See/Fly Like an Eagle	1977	—	2.50	5.00
❑ 0300	Dream Lover/A Change Is Gonna Come	1978	—	2.50	5.00

Number	Title (A Side/B Side)	Yr	VG	VG+	NM
❑ 0307	I'll Be Seeing You/Everybody Needs Somebody	1978	—	2.50	5.00
MERCURY					
❑ 870050-7	Once You Get the Feel of It/Slow Down	1987	—	—	3.00
❑ 870505-7	Dancin' Shoes/I'm Glad It's Gone	1988	—	—	3.00
❑ 872096-7	Still Holdin' On/Same Old Moon	1989	—	—	3.00
❑ 888774-7	Hangin' Out in Smokey Places/He Don't Know	1987	—	—	3.00
WARNER BROS.					
❑ 8841	Last of the Singing Cowboys/Pass It On	1979	—	2.50	5.00
❑ 8841 [PS]	Last of the Singing Cowboys/Pass It On	1979	—	3.00	6.00
❑ 29355	I May Be Easy But You Make It Hard/Shot Down Where You Stand	1984	—	2.00	4.00
❑ 29619	A Place I've Never Been/8:05	1983	—	2.00	4.00
❑ 29939	Reachin' for a Little Bit More/Sweet Elaine	1982	—	2.00	4.00
❑ 29995	Mr. President/The Sea, Dreams and Fairy Tales	1982	—	2.00	4.00
❑ 49068	Running Like the Wind/(B-side unknown)	1979	—	2.50	5.00
❑ 49215	It Takes Time/Jimi	1980	—	2.50	5.00
❑ 49259	Disillusioned/Without You	1980	—	2.00	4.00
❑ 49724	This Time I Believe/ Tell the Blues to Take Off the Night	1981	—	2.00	4.00
❑ 49764	Time Has Come/Love Some	1981	—	2.00	4.00
7-Inch Extended Plays					
CAPRICORN					
❑ SCP 0124	24 Hours at a Time/Blue Ridge Mountain Sky// A New Life	1973	2.50	5.00	10.00
—Jukebox issue; small hole, plays at 33 1/3 rpm					
❑ SCP 0124 [PS]	A New Life	1973	2.50	5.00	10.00
—Part of "Little LP" series (LLP #249)					
Albums					
CAPRICORN					
❑ CP 0112	The Marshall Tucker Band	1973	3.00	6.00	12.00
❑ CP 0124	A New Life	1974	3.00	6.00	12.00
❑ 2CP 0145 [(2)]	Where We All Belong	1974	3.75	7.50	15.00
❑ CP 0161	Searchin' for a Rainbow	1975	3.00	6.00	12.00
❑ CP 0170	Long Hard Ride	1976	3.00	6.00	12.00
❑ CPK 0180	Carolina Dreams	1977	3.00	6.00	12.00
❑ CP 0205	Together Forever	1978	3.00	6.00	12.00
❑ CPN-0214	Greatest Hits	1978	3.00	6.00	12.00
MERCURY					
❑ 832794-1	Still Holdin' On	1988	2.50	5.00	10.00
WARNER BROS.					
❑ BSK 3317	Running Like the Wind	1979	2.50	5.00	10.00
❑ HS 3410	Tenth	1980	2.50	5.00	10.00
❑ HS 3525	Dedicated	1981	2.50	5.00	10.00
❑ BSK 3606	The Marshall Tucker Band	1982	2.50	5.00	10.00
—Reissue of Capricorn 0112					
❑ 2WS 3608 [(2)]	Where We All Belong	1982	3.00	6.00	12.00
—Reissue of Capricorn 0145					
❑ BSK 3609	Searchin' for a Rainbow	1982	2.50	5.00	10.00
—Reissue of Capricorn 0161					
❑ BSK 3610	Carolina Dreams	1982	2.50	5.00	10.00
—Reissue of Capricorn 0180					
❑ BSK 3611	Greatest Hits	1982	2.50	5.00	10.00
—Reissue of Capricorn 0214					
❑ BSK 3662	A New Life	1982	2.50	5.00	10.00
—Reissue of Capricorn 0124					
❑ BSK 3663	Long Hard Ride	1982	2.50	5.00	10.00
—Reissue of Capricorn 0170					
❑ BSK 3664	Together Forever	1982	2.50	5.00	10.00
—Reissue of Capricorn 0205					
❑ BSK 3684	Tuckerized	1982	2.50	5.00	10.00
❑ 23803	Just Us	1983	2.50	5.00	10.00
MARSHANS, THE					
45s					
ETIQUETTE					
❑ 8	I Remember/It's Almost Tomorrow	1964	5.00	10.00	20.00
JOHNSON					
❑ 736	My Letter To Santa/Main Man	1966	5.00	10.00	20.00
MARSHMALLOW WAY					
45s					
UNITED ARTISTS					
❑ 50611	Good Day/Music, Music	1969	2.00	4.00	8.00
Albums					
UNITED ARTISTS					
❑ UAS-6708	Marshmallow Way	1969	5.00	10.00	20.00
MARTELLS, THE					
45s					
BELLA					
❑ 20	Rockin' Santa Claus/Carol Lee	1959	10.00	20.00	40.00
—B-side by Eulis Mason					
❑ 45	Forgotten Spring/Va Va Voom	1961	12.50	25.00	50.00
CESSNA					
❑ 477	Forgotten Spring/Va Va Voom	1961	20.00	40.00	80.00
RELIC					
❑ 517	Forgotten Spring/Va Va Voom	1964	2.50	5.00	10.00
MARTHA AND THE VANDELLAS Also see SAUNDRA MALLETT AND THE VANDELLAS; MARTHA REEVES; THE VELLS.					
45s					
A&M					
❑ 3022	Nowhere to Run/I Got You (I Feel Good)	1988	—	2.00	4.00
—B-side by James Brown					
❑ 3022 [PS]	Nowhere to Run/I Got You (I Feel Good)	1988		2.00	4.00
—"Good Morning Vietnam" sleeve					
GORDY					
❑ 7011	I'll Have to Let Him Go/ My Baby Won't Come Back	1962	6.25	12.50	25.00
❑ 7014	Come and Get These Memories/Jealous Love	1963	7.50	15.00	30.00
❑ 7022	Heat Wave/A Love Like Yours	1963	5.00	10.00	20.00
❑ 7025	Quicksand/Darling, I Hum Our Song	1963	3.75	7.50	15.00
❑ 7027	Live Wire/Old Love	1964	3.75	7.50	15.00
❑ 7031	In My Lonely Room/A Tear for the Girl	1964	3.75	7.50	15.00
❑ 7033	Dancing in the Street/There He Is (At My Door)	1964	3.75	7.50	15.00
❑ 7033 [PS]	Dancing in the Street/There He Is (At My Door)	1964	30.00	60.00	120.00

M

Number	Title (A Side/B Side)	Yr	VG	VG+	NM
❑ 7036	Wild One/Dancing Slow	1964	3.00	6.00	12.00
❑ 7039	Nowhere to Run/Motoring	1965	3.00	6.00	12.00
❑ 7045	You've Been in Love Too Long/Love (Makes You Do Foolish Things)	1965	3.00	6.00	12.00
❑ 7048	My Baby Loves Me/ Never Leave Your Baby's Side	1965	3.00	6.00	12.00
❑ 7053	What Am I Gonna Do Without Your Love/ Go Ahead and Laugh	1966	3.00	6.00	12.00
❑ 7056	I'm Ready for Love/He Doesn't Love Her Anymore	1966	3.00	6.00	12.00
—"Gordy" logo at left					
❑ 7056	I'm Ready for Love/He Doesn't Love Her Anymore	1966	3.75	7.50	15.00
—"Gordy" logo at top					
❑ 7058	Jimmy Mack/Third Finger, Left Hand	1967	2.50	5.00	10.00
❑ 7062	Love Bug Leave My Heart Alone/One Way Out	1967	2.50	5.00	10.00
❑ 7067	Honey Chile/Show Me the Way	1967	2.50	5.00	10.00
—Starting here, as "Martha Reeves and the Vandellas"					
❑ 7070	I Promise to Wait My Love/Forget Me Not	1968	2.50	5.00	10.00
❑ 7075	I Can't Dance to That Music You're Playin'/I Tried	1968	2.50	5.00	10.00
❑ 7080	Sweet Darlin'/Without You	1968	2.50	5.00	10.00
❑ 7085	(We've Got) Honey Love/I'm In Love (And I Know It)	1969	2.00	4.00	8.00
❑ 7094	Taking My Love (And Leaving Me)/Heartless	1969	2.00	4.00	8.00
❑ 7098	I Should Be Pround/Love, Guess Who	1970	2.00	4.00	8.00
❑ 7103	I Gotta Let You Go/You're the Loser Now	1970	2.00	4.00	8.00
❑ 7110	Bless You/Hope I Don't Get My Heart Broke	1971	2.00	4.00	8.00
❑ 7113	In and Out of My Life/ Your Love Makes It All Worthwhile	1972	2.00	4.00	8.00
❑ 7118	Tear It On Down/I Want You Back	1972	2.00	4.00	8.00
❑ 7127	Baby Don't Leave Me /I Won't Be the Fool I've Been Again	1973	2.00	4.00	8.00
TOPPS/MOTOWN					
❑ 7	Dancing in the Street	1967	18.75	37.50	75.00
—Cardboard record					
❑ 14	Love Is Like a Heat Wave	1967	18.75	37.50	75.00
—Cardboard record					
Albums					
GORDY					
❑ G-902 [M]	Come and Get These Memories	1963	100.00	200.00	400.00
❑ GS-902 [S]	Come and Get These Memories	1963	200.00	400.00	800.00
❑ G-907 [M]	Heat Wave	1963	37.50	75.00	150.00
❑ GS-907 [R]	Heat Wave	1963	37.50	75.00	150.00
—"Stereo" banner pre-printed on cover					
❑ GS-907 [S]	Heat Wave	1963	100.00	200.00	400.00
—Mono cover with "Stereo" sticker					
❑ G-915 [M]	Dance Party	1965	10.00	20.00	40.00
❑ GS-915 [S]	Dance Party	1965	15.00	30.00	60.00
❑ G-917 [M]	Greatest Hits	1966	6.25	12.50	25.00
❑ GS-917 [S]	Greatest Hits	1966	7.50	15.00	30.00
❑ G-920 [M]	Watchout!	1966	6.25	12.50	25.00
❑ GS-920 [S]	Watchout!	1966	7.50	15.00	30.00
❑ G-925 [M]	Martha and the Vandellas Live!	1967	7.50	15.00	30.00
❑ GS-925 [S]	Martha and the Vandellas Live!	1967	6.25	12.50	25.00
❑ G-926 [M]	Ridin' High	1968	10.00	20.00	40.00
—Mono is promo only					
❑ GS-926 [S]	Ridin' High	1968	5.00	10.00	20.00
❑ GS-944	Sugar 'N Spice	1969	5.00	10.00	20.00
❑ GS-952	Natural Resources	1970	5.00	10.00	20.00
❑ GS-958	Black Magic	1972	5.00	10.00	20.00
MOTOWN					
❑ M5-111V1	Motown Superstar Series, Vol. 11	1981	2.50	5.00	10.00
❑ M5-145V1	Heat Wave	1981	2.50	5.00	10.00
—Reissue of Gordy 907					
❑ M5-204V1	Greatest Hits	1981	2.50	5.00	10.00
—Reissue of Gordy 917					
❑ M7-778 [(2)]	Anthology	1974	3.75	7.50	15.00

MARTIN, BARRY
45s

Number	Title (A Side/B Side)	Yr	VG	VG+	NM
FREEDOM					
❑ 44019	Minnie the Moocher/The Willies	1959	3.00	6.00	12.00
RCA VICTOR					
❑ 47-7834	Got a Whole Lot of Lovin' to Do/ Why'd I Have to Fall	1961	5.00	10.00	20.00

MARTIN, BOBBI
45s

Number	Title (A Side/B Side)	Yr	VG	VG+	NM
BUDDAH					
❑ 217	No Love at All/A Place for Me	1971	—	2.00	4.00
❑ 227	Devotion/A Place for Me	1971	—	2.00	4.00
❑ 253	Tomorrow/Sentimental Journey	1971	—	2.00	4.00
❑ 286	Something Tells Me (Something's Gonna Happen Tonight)/Give Me a Star to Live On	1972	—	2.00	4.00
CORAL					
❑ 62263	I Need Your Love/Cry, Cry, Cry (I Never Thought I'd Make You Cry)	1961	2.00	4.00	8.00
❑ 62285	Wooden Heart/How Should I Cry	1961	2.00	4.00	8.00
❑ 62321	Forgive Me/Tired and Blue	1962	2.00	4.00	8.00
❑ 62340	Afraid/Brenda, Brenda	1962	2.00	4.00	8.00
❑ 62351	I'll Never Stop Loving You/Why, Tell Me Why	1963	2.00	4.00	8.00
❑ 62384	"A" You're Adorable/A Girl's Prayer	1963	2.00	4.00	8.00
❑ 62410	I'm a Fool (To Go On Loving You)/ Does Your Heart Hurt a Little	1964	—	3.00	6.00
❑ 62426	Don't Forget I Still Love You/ On the Outside (Looking In)	1964	—	3.00	6.00
❑ 62447	I Can't Stop Thinking of You/ A Million Thanks to You	1965	—	3.00	6.00
❑ 62452	I Love You So/When Will the Torch Go Out	1965	—	3.00	6.00
❑ 62452 [PS]	I Love You So/When Will the Torch Go Out	1965	2.50	5.00	10.00
❑ 62457	Holding Back the Tears/I Don't Want to Love	1965	—	3.00	6.00
❑ 62466	Auf Wiedersehn Good Bye/There Are No Rules	1965	—	3.00	6.00
❑ 62472	Just One Time/Trying to Get You Off My Mind	1965	—	3.00	6.00
❑ 62475	Don't Take It Out on Me/Something on My Mind	1965	—	3.00	6.00
❑ 62485	I Can Give You Love/Sometimes	1966	—	3.00	6.00
❑ 62488	Oh, Lonesome Me/It's a Sin to Tell a Lie	1966	—	3.00	6.00
❑ 62503	Just As Much As Ever/You Have No Idea	1966	—	3.00	6.00

Number	Title (A Side/B Side)	Yr	VG	VG+	NM
❑ 62512	Anytime/How Long	1967	—	3.00	6.00
MGM					
❑ 14587	Smile for Me/Now Lonely Is Only a Word	1973	—	2.00	4.00
UNITED ARTISTS					
❑ 0148	For the Love of Him/I Think of You	1973	—	2.00	4.00
—"Silver Spotlight Series" reissue					
❑ 50253	Only You (And You Alone)/Would You Believe	1968	—	2.50	5.00
❑ 50297	A Man and a Woman/Before You	1968	—	2.50	5.00
❑ 50443	Harper Valley P.T.A./He Called Me Baby	1968	—	2.50	5.00
❑ 50456	I Love Him/I Think of You	1968	—	2.50	5.00
❑ 50523	Your Cheatin' Heart/Tennessee Waltz	1969	—	2.50	5.00
❑ 50602	For the Love of Him/I Fall to Pieces	1969	—	2.50	5.00
❑ 50602	For the Love of Him/I Think of You	1969	—	2.50	5.00
❑ 50687	Goin' South/Give a Woman Love	1970	—	2.50	5.00
❑ 50728	No Love at All/What Greater Love	1970	—	2.50	5.00
7-Inch Extended Plays					
UNITED ARTISTS					
❑ UALP 9-6668	Harper Valley P.T.A./I Love Him/Little Green Apples//She'll Have to Go/He Called Me Baby/I Think of You	1968	2.50	5.00	10.00
—Jukebox issue; small hole, plays at 33 1/3 rpm					
❑ UALP 9-6668 [PS]	Harper Valley P.T.A.	1968	2.50	5.00	10.00
Albums					
BUDDAH					
❑ BDS-5090	Tomorrow	1971	3.00	6.00	12.00
CORAL					
❑ CRL 57472 [M]	Don't Forget I Still Love You	1965	3.75	7.50	15.00
❑ CRL 57478 [M]	I Love You So	1965	3.75	7.50	15.00
❑ CRL 757472 [S]	Don't Forget I Still Love You	1965	5.00	10.00	20.00
❑ CRL 757478 [S]	I Love You So	1965	5.00	10.00	20.00
SUNSET					
❑ SUS-5319	Thinking of You	197?	2.50	5.00	10.00
UNITED ARTISTS					
❑ UAS-6668	Harper Valley P.T.A.	1968	3.00	6.00	12.00
❑ UAS-6700	For the Love of Him	1969	3.00	6.00	12.00
❑ UAS-6755	With Love	1970	3.00	6.00	12.00
VOCALION					
❑ VL 73906	Have You Ever Been Lonely	196?	2.50	5.00	10.00

MARTIN, DEAN
45s

Number	Title (A Side/B Side)	Yr	VG	VG+	NM
CAPITOL					
❑ 54-691	Just for Fun/My One, My Only, My All	1949	5.00	10.00	20.00
—Note: Dean Martin singles on Capitol before 691 are unconfirmed on 45 rpm					
❑ 54-726	That Lucky Old Sun/Vieni Su	1949	5.00	10.00	20.00
❑ F937	Rain/Zing-a, Zing-a, Boom	1950	3.75	7.50	15.00
❑ F948	Muskrat Ramble/I'm Gonna Paper All My Walls with Love Letters	1950	3.75	7.50	15.00
❑ F981	Choo'n Gum/I Don't Care If the Sun Don't Shine	1950	3.75	7.50	15.00
❑ F1002	I Still Get a Thrill/Be Honest with Me	1950	3.75	7.50	15.00
❑ F1028	I'll Always Love You/Baby Obey Me	1950	3.75	7.50	15.00
❑ F1052	Bye Bye Blackbird/Happy Feet	1950	3.75	7.50	15.00
❑ F1139	Peddler's Serenade/Wham, Bam, Thank You, Ma'am	1950	3.75	7.50	15.00
❑ F1160	Don't Rock the Boat/I'm in Love with You	1950	3.75	7.50	15.00
—With Margaret Whiting					
❑ F1342	If/I Love the Way	1950	3.75	7.50	15.00
❑ F1358	You and Your Beautiful Eyes/Tonda Wanda Hoy	1951	3.75	7.50	15.00
❑ F1458	Beside You/Who's Sorry Now	1951	3.75	7.50	15.00
❑ F1682	Oh Marie/I'll Always Love You	1951	3.00	6.00	12.00
❑ F1703	In the Cool, Cool, Cool of the Evening/Bonne Nuit	1951	3.75	7.50	15.00
❑ F1724	Go Go Go Go/Luna Mezzo Mare	1951	3.75	7.50	15.00
❑ F1797	Hanging Around with You/Aw C'mon	1951	3.75	7.50	15.00
❑ F1811	Meanderin'/Bella Bimba	1951	3.75	7.50	15.00
❑ F1817	Solitaire/I Ran All the Way Home	1951	3.75	7.50	15.00
❑ F1885	Night Train to Memphis/Blue Smoke	1951	3.75	7.50	15.00
❑ F1901	Never Before/Sailors Polka	1951	3.75	7.50	15.00
❑ F1921	As You Are/Oh Boy	1952	3.75	7.50	15.00
❑ F1938	Until/My Heart Found Home	1952	3.75	7.50	15.00
❑ F1975	All I Have to Give/When You're Smiling	1952	3.75	7.50	15.00
❑ F2001	Pretty as a Picture/Won't You Surrender	1952	3.75	7.50	15.00
❑ F2071	Bet-i-Cha/I Passed Your House Tonight	1952	3.75	7.50	15.00
❑ F2140	Oh Marie/Come Back to Sorrento	1952	3.75	7.50	15.00
❑ F2165	You Belong to Me/Hominy Grits	1952	3.75	7.50	15.00
❑ F2240	I Know a Dream When I See One/Second Chance	1952	3.75	7.50	15.00
❑ F2319	What Could Be More Beautiful/The Kiss	1953	3.00	6.00	12.00
❑ F2378	Little Did We Know/There's My Lover	1953	3.00	6.00	12.00
❑ F2485	Love Me, Love Me/Till I Find You	1953	3.00	6.00	12.00
❑ F2555	If I Could Sing Like Bing/Don't You Remember	1953	3.00	6.00	12.00
❑ F2589	That's Amore/You're the Right One	1953	3.75	7.50	15.00
❑ F2640	The Christmas Blues/If I Should Love Again	1953	3.00	6.00	12.00
❑ F2749	Hey Brother Pour the Wine/I'd Cry Like a Baby	1954	3.00	6.00	12.00
❑ F2818	Money Burns a Hole in My Pocket/Sway	1954	3.00	6.00	12.00
❑ F2870	That's What I Like/Peddler Man	1954	3.00	6.00	12.00
❑ F2911	Try Again/One More Time	1954	3.00	6.00	12.00
❑ F2985	Open Up the Doghouse/Long, Long Ago	1954	3.75	7.50	15.00
—With Nat King Cole					
❑ F3011	Confused/Belle from Barcelona	1955	2.50	5.00	10.00
❑ F3036	Young and Foolish/Under the Bridges of Paris	1955	2.50	5.00	10.00
❑ F3133	Chee Chee Oo-Chee/Ridin' Into Love	1955	2.50	5.00	10.00
❑ F3153	Simpatico/Love Is All That Matters	1955	2.50	5.00	10.00
❑ F3196	Two Sleepy People/Relax Ay Voo	1955	2.50	5.00	10.00
—With Line Renaud					
❑ F3238	I Like Them All/In Napoli	1955	2.50	5.00	10.00
❑ F3295	Memories Are Made of This/Change of Heart	1955	3.00	6.00	12.00
❑ F3352	Innamorata/Lady with a Big Umbrella	1956	2.50	5.00	10.00
❑ F3414	Standing on the Corner/ Watching the World Go By	1956	2.50	5.00	10.00
❑ F3468	Street of Love/I'm Gonna Steal You Away	1956	2.50	5.00	10.00
❑ F3521	Mississippi Dreamboat/Test of Time	1956	2.50	5.00	10.00
❑ F3577	The Look/Give Me a Sign	1956	2.50	5.00	10.00
❑ F3604	Just Kiss Me/I Know I Can't Forget	1956	2.50	5.00	10.00
❑ F3648	Captured/The Man Who Plays the Mandolino	1957	2.50	5.00	10.00
❑ F3680	Bamboozled/Only Trust Your Heart	1957	2.50	5.00	10.00

Number	Title (A Side/B Side)	Yr	VG	VG+	NM
❏ F3718	I Can't Give You Anything But Love/				
	I Never Had a Chance	1957	2.50	5.00	10.00
❏ F3752	Write to Me from Naples/Beau James	1957	2.50	5.00	10.00
❏ F3787	Promise Her Anything/Triche Trache	1957	2.50	5.00	10.00
❏ F3842	Makin' Love Ukulele Style/Good Morning Life	1957	2.50	5.00	10.00
❏ F3894	Return to Me/Forgetting You	1958	2.00	4.00	8.00
❏ F3988	Angel Baby/				
	I'll Gladly Make the Same Mistake Again	1958	2.00	4.00	8.00
❏ F4028	Volare (Nel Blu Dipinto Di Blu)/Outa My Mind	1958	2.00	4.00	8.00
❏ F4028 [PS]	Volare (Nel Blu Dipinto Di Blu)/Outa My Mind	1958	6.25	12.50	25.00
❏ F4065	Once Upon a Time/The Magician	1958	2.00	4.00	8.00
❏ F4124	It Takes So Long/You Were Made for Love	1959	2.00	4.00	8.00
❏ F4174	Rio Bravo/My Rifle, My Pony and Me	1959	2.00	4.00	8.00
❏ F4222	On an Evening in Roma/You Can't Love 'Em All	1959	2.00	4.00	8.00
❏ F4222 [PS]	On an Evening in Roma/You Can't Love 'Em All	1959	6.25	12.50	25.00
❏ F4287	I Ain't Gonna Lead This Life No More/Career	1959	2.00	4.00	8.00
❏ 4328	Love Me, My Love/Who Was That Lady	1960	2.00	4.00	8.00
❏ 4361	Napoli/Professor, Professor	1960	2.00	4.00	8.00
❏ 4391	Just in Time/Buttercup a Golden Hair	1960	2.00	4.00	8.00
❏ 4420	Ain't That a Kick in the Head/Humdinger	1960	2.00	4.00	8.00
❏ 4472	How Sweet It Is/Sogni D'Oro	1960	2.00	4.00	8.00
❏ 4518	Sparklin' Eyes/Tu Sei Bella Signorina	1961	2.00	4.00	8.00
❏ 4551	Bella, Bella Bambina/All in a Night's Work	1961	2.00	4.00	8.00
❏ 4570	The Story of Life/Giuggiola	1961	2.00	4.00	8.00
❏ B-44153	That's Amore/It Must Be Him	1988	—	2.00	4.00
—B-side by Vikki Carr					
❏ B-44153 [PS]	That's Amore/It Must Be Him	1988	—	2.50	5.00
❏ S7-57889	Rudolph, the Red-Nosed Reindeer/				
	White Christmas	1992	—	2.50	5.00
❏ 58742	The Christmas Blues/				
	Let It Snow! Let It Snow! Let It Snow!	1998	—	—	3.00
❏ 77683	When You're Smiling/Witchcraft	2001	—	—	3.00
—B-side by Frank Sinatra					
MCA					
❏ 52662	L.A. Is My Home/Drinking Champagne	1985	—	2.00	4.00
REPRISE					
❏ PRO 248 [DJ]	White Christmas (same on both sides)	1966	2.50	5.00	10.00
❏ 0252	La Giostra (Merry-Go-Round)/				
	Grazie, Prego, Scusi	1964	2.00	4.00	8.00
❏ 0281	Everybody Loves Somebody/A Little Voice	1964	2.50	5.00	10.00
❏ 0307	The Door Is Still Open to My Heart/Every Minute,				
	Every Hour	1964	2.00	4.00	8.00
❏ 0333	You're Nobody Till Somebody Loves You/You'll				
	Always Be the One I Love	1964	2.00	4.00	8.00
❏ 0344	Send Me the Pillow You Dream On/				
	I'll Be Seeing You	1965	2.00	4.00	8.00
❏ 0369	(Remember Me) I'm the One Who Loves You/				
	Born to Lose	1965	2.00	4.00	8.00
❏ 0393	Houston/Bumming Around	1965	2.00	4.00	8.00
❏ 0415	I Will/You're the Reason I'm in Love	1965	2.00	4.00	8.00
❏ 0443	Somewhere There's a Someone/				
	That Old Clock on the Wall	1965	2.00	4.00	8.00
❏ 0466	Come Running Back/Bouquet of Roses	1966	—	3.00	6.00
❏ 0500	A Million and One/Shades	1966	—	3.00	6.00
❏ 0516	Nobody's Baby Again/				
	It Just Happened That Way	1966	—	3.00	6.00
❏ 0538	(Open Up the Door) Let the Good Times In/I'm				
	Not the Marrying Kind	1966	—	3.00	6.00
❏ 0542	Blue Christmas/A Marshmallow World	1966	—	3.00	6.00
❏ 0571	Lay Some Happiness on Me/Think About Me	1967	—	3.00	6.00
❏ 0601	In the Chapel in the Moonlight/				
	Welcome to My World	1967	—	3.00	6.00
❏ 0608	Little Ole Wine Drinker, Me/I Can't Help				
	Remembering You	1967	—	3.00	6.00
❏ 0640	In the Misty Moonlight/The Glory of Love	1967	—	3.00	6.00
❏ 0640	In the Misty Moonlight/Wallpaper Roses	1967	—	3.00	6.00
❏ 0672	You've Still Got a Place in My Heart/				
	Old Yellow Line	1968	—	2.50	5.00
❏ 0703	Lay Some Happiness on Me/(Open Up the Door)				
	Let the Good Times In	1968	—	2.50	5.00
❏ 0709	Everybody Loves Somebody/A Million and One	1968	—	2.50	5.00
❏ 0711	Somewhere There's a Someone/				
	Come Running Back	1968	—	2.50	5.00
❏ 0714	Houston/I Will	1968	—	2.50	5.00
❏ 0717	You're Nobody Till Somebody Loves You/				
	(Remember Me) I'm the One Who Loves You	1968	—	2.50	5.00
❏ 0718	Send Me the Pillow You Dream On/The Door Is				
	Still Open to My Heart	1968	—	2.50	5.00
❏ 0730	In the Chapel in the Moonlight/				
	Little Ole Wine Drinker, Me	1968	—	2.50	5.00
❏ 0735	In the Misty Moonlight/Not Enough Indians	1970	—	2.00	4.00
—0703 through 0735 are "Back to Back Hits" reissues					
❏ 0761	April Again/That Old Time Feelin'	1968	—	2.50	5.00
❏ 0765	Five Card Stud/One Lonely Boy	1968	—	2.50	5.00
❏ 0780	Not Enough Indians/Rainbows Are Back in Style	1968	—	2.50	5.00
❏ 0812	Gentle on My Mind/That's When I See the Blues	1969	—	2.50	5.00
❏ 0841	I Take a Lot of Pride in What I Am/				
	Drowning in My Tears	1969	—	2.50	5.00
❏ 0857	Crying Time/One Cup of Happiness	1969	—	2.50	5.00
❏ 0893	Down Home/Come On Down	1970	—	2.50	5.00
❏ 0915	For the Love of a Woman/				
	The Tracks of My Tears	1970	—	2.50	5.00
❏ 0934	My Woman, My Woman, My Wife/				
	Here We Go Again	1970	—	2.50	5.00
❏ 0955	Detroit City/Turn the World Around	1970	—	2.50	5.00
❏ 0973	For the Good Times/Georgia Sunshine	1970	—	2.50	5.00
❏ 1004	She's a Little Bit Country/Raining in My Heart	1971	—	2.50	5.00
❏ 1060	What's Yesterday/The Right Kind of Woman	1971	—	2.50	5.00
❏ 1085	I Can Give You What You Want Now/Guess Who	1972	—	2.50	5.00
❏ 1141	Amor Mio/You Made Me Love You	1972	—	2.50	5.00
❏ 1166	Smile/Get On With Your Livin'	1973	—	2.50	5.00
❏ 1178	You're the Best Thing That Ever Happened to				
	Me/Free to Carry On	1973	—	2.50	5.00
❏ 20058	Just Close Your Eyes/Tik-A-Tee Tik-A-Tay	1962	3.00	6.00	12.00
❏ 20082	Baby-O/Dame Su Amor	1962	2.50	5.00	10.00
❏ 20116	From the Bottom of My Heart (Dammi, Dammi,				
	Dammi)/Who's Got the Action	1962	2.50	5.00	10.00

Number	Title (A Side/B Side)	Yr	VG	VG+	NM
❏ 20116 [PS]	From the Bottom of My Heart (Dammi, Dammi,				
	Dammi)/Who's Got the Action	1962	5.00	10.00	20.00
❏ 20128	Sam's Song/Me and My Shadow	1962	3.75	7.50	15.00
—A-side with Sammy Davis, Jr.; B-side: Sammy Davis Jr. and Frank Sinatra					
❏ 20128 [PS]	Sam's Song/Me and My Shadow	1962	10.00	20.00	40.00
❏ 20140	Who's Got the Action/Send a Fine	1963	2.50	5.00	10.00
❏ 20150	Ain't Gonna Try Anymore/A Face in the Crowd	1963	2.50	5.00	10.00
❏ 20194	Corrine, Corrina/My Sugar's Gone	1963	2.50	5.00	10.00
❏ 20215	Via Veneto/Mama Roma	1963	2.50	5.00	10.00
❏ 20217	Fugue for Tinhorns/The Oldest Established				
	(Permanent Floating Crap Game in New York)	1963	3.75	7.50	15.00
—By Frank Sinatra/Bing Crosby/Dean Martin					
❏ 20217 [PS]	Fugue for Tinhorns/The Oldest Established				
	(Permanent Floating Crap Game in New York)	1963	20.00	40.00	80.00
—By Frank Sinatra/Bing Crosby/Dean Martin					
WARNER BROS.					
❏ 29480	Drinking Champagne/Since I Met You Baby	1983	—	2.00	4.00
❏ 29584	My First Country Song/Hangin' Around	1983	—	2.00	4.00
7-Inch Extended Plays					
CAPITOL					
❏ EAP 1-401	(contents unknown)	195?	5.00	10.00	20.00
❏ EAP 1-401 [PS]	Dean Martin Sings	195?	5.00	10.00	20.00
❏ EAP 1-481	That's Amore/Oh Marie//Come Back to				
	Sorrento/Luna Mezzo Mare	1954	5.00	10.00	20.00
❏ EAP 1-481 [PS]	Sunny Italy	1954	5.00	10.00	20.00
❏ EAP 1-576	(contents unknown)	195?	3.75	7.50	15.00
❏ EAP 1-576 [PS]	Swingin' Down Yonder, Part 1	195?	3.75	7.50	15.00
❏ EAP 2-576 [PS]	Swingin' Down Yonder, Part 2	195?	3.75	7.50	15.00
❏ EAP 3-576	Alabamy Bound/Dinah//Carolina in the Morning/				
	Way Down Yonder in New Orleans	195?	3.75	7.50	15.00
❏ EAP 3-576 [PS]	Swingin' Down Yonder, Part 3	195?	3.75	7.50	15.00
❏ EAP 1-701	Memories Are Made of This/I Like Them All//				
	Change of Heart/Ridin' Into Love	1956	3.75	7.50	15.00
❏ EAP 1-701 [PS]	Memories Are Made of This	1956	3.75	7.50	15.00
❏ EAP 1-702	(contents unknown)	1956	3.75	7.50	15.00
❏ EAP 1-702 [PS]	Artists and Models	1956	3.75	7.50	15.00
❏ EAP 1-806	(contents unknown)	1957	3.75	7.50	15.00
❏ EAP 1-806 [PS]	Hollywood or Bust	1957	3.75	7.50	15.00
❏ EAP 1-840	(contents unknown)	1957	3.75	7.50	15.00
❏ EAP 1-840 [PS]	Ten Thousand Bedrooms	1957	3.75	7.50	15.00
❏ EAP 1-849	(contents unknown)	1957	3.00	6.00	12.00
❏ EAP 1-849 [PS]	Pretty Baby, Part 1	1957	3.00	6.00	12.00
❏ EAP 2-849	(contents unknown)	1957	3.00	6.00	12.00
❏ EAP 2-849 [PS]	Pretty Baby, Part 2	1957	3.00	6.00	12.00
❏ EAP 3-849	(contents unknown)	1957	3.00	6.00	12.00
❏ EAP 3-849 [PS]	Pretty Baby, Part 3	1957	3.00	6.00	12.00
❏ EAP 1-939	*Return to Me/Don't You Remember/Forgetting				
	You/Buona Sera	1958	3.75	7.50	15.00
❏ EAP 1-939 [PS]	Return to Me	1958	3.75	7.50	15.00
❏ EAP 1-1285	(contents unknown)	1959	3.00	6.00	12.00
❏ EAP 1-1285 [PS]	A Winter Romance, Part 1	1959	3.00	6.00	12.00
❏ EAP 2-1285	(contents unknown)	1959	3.00	6.00	12.00
❏ EAP 2-1285 [PS]	A Winter Romance, Part 2	1959	3.00	6.00	12.00
❏ EAP 3-1285	(contents unknown)	1959	3.00	6.00	12.00
❏ EAP 3-1285 [PS]	A Winter Romance, Part 3	1959	3.00	6.00	12.00
❏ SU 1659	Just Say I Love Her/Arrivideci, Roma/Non				
	Dimenticar//Vieni Su/Take Me in Your Arms/I				
	Have But One Love	196?	3.75	7.50	15.00
❏ SU 1659 [PS]	Italian Love Songs	196?	3.75	7.50	15.00
❏ DU 2601	That's Amore/Return to Me/Volare//Memories				
	Are Made of This/Just in Time/				
	Come Back to Sorrento	196?	2.50	5.00	10.00
—Jukebox issue; small hole, plays at 33 1/3 rpm; red and white "Starline" label					
❏ DU 2601 [PS]	The Best of Dean Martin	196?	2.50	5.00	10.00
REPRISE					
❏ 6130	Everybody Loves Somebody/Corrine Corrina/				
	Face in the Crowd//Just Close Your Eyes/				
	Things/My Heart Cries for You	196?	2.50	5.00	10.00
—Jukebox issue; small hole, plays at 33 1/3 rpm; brown and orange label with white spot in middle					
❏ 6130	Everybody Loves Somebody/Corrine Corrina/				
	Face in the Crowd//Just Close Your Eyes/				
	Things/My Heart Cries for You	1964	3.75	7.50	15.00
—Jukebox issue; small hole, plays at 33 1/3 rpm; white label with "Promotion" at bottom					
❏ 6130 [PS]	Everybody Loves Somebody	1964	2.50	5.00	10.00
—Both versions have virtually identical sleeves					
❏ SR 6170	Walk On By/King of the Road/(Remember Me)				
	I'm the One Who Loves You//Here Comes My				
	Baby/My Shoes Keep Walking Back to You/				
	The Birds and the Bees	1965	2.50	5.00	10.00
—Jukebox issue; small hole, plays at 33 1/3 rpm					
❏ SR 6170 [PS]	(Remember Me) I'm the One Who Loves You	1965	2.50	5.00	10.00
❏ SR 6181	Houston/Snap Your Fingers/Little Lovely One//I				
	Will/The First Thing Ev'ry Morning (And the				
	Last Thing Ev'ry Night)/Down Home	1965	2.50	5.00	10.00
—Jukebox issue; small hole, plays at 33 1/3 rpm					
❏ SR 6181 [PS]	Houston	1965	2.50	5.00	10.00
❏ SR 6201	Second Hand Rose/Bouquet of Roses/Just a				
	Little Lovin'//Somewhere There's a Someone/				
	I Can't Help It/Anytime	1966	2.50	5.00	10.00
—Jukebox issue; small hole, plays at 33 1/3 rpm					
❏ SR 6201 [PS]	Somewhere There's a Someone	1966	2.50	5.00	10.00
❏ SR 6211	The Glory of Love/Empty Saddles in the Old				
	Corral/Side by Side//On the Sunny Side of the				
	Street/The Last Round-up/Red Sails in the				
	Sunset	1966	2.50	5.00	10.00
—Jukebox issue; small hole, plays at 33 1/3 rpm					
❏ SR 6211 [PS]	The Silencers	1966	2.50	5.00	10.00
❏ 40045	Tangerine/South of the Border/In a Little				
	Spanish Town//What a Diff'rence a Day Made/				
	Magic Is the Moonlight/Besame Mucho	196?	5.00	10.00	20.00
—Jukebox issue; small hole, plays at 33 1/3 rpm					
❏ 40045 [PS]	Dino Latino	196?	5.00	10.00	20.00
Albums					
CAPITOL					
❏ SKAO-140	The Best of Dean Martin, Vol. 2	1968	3.75	7.50	15.00
❏ H 401 [10]	Dean Martin Sings	1953	25.00	50.00	100.00

M

Number	Title (A Side/B Side)	Yr	VG	VG+	NM
❏ T 401 [M]	Dean Martin Sings	1953	12.50	25.00	50.00
❏ STBB-523 [(2)]	You're Nobody 'Til Somebody Loves You/ Return to Me	1970	5.00	10.00	20.00
❏ T 576 [M]	Swingin' Down Yonder	1955	7.50	15.00	30.00
❏ T 849 [M]	Pretty Baby	1957	7.50	15.00	30.00
❏ DT 1047 [R]	This Is Dean Martin	196?	3.00	6.00	12.00
❏ T 1047 [M]	This Is Dean Martin	1958	7.50	15.00	30.00
❏ ST 1150 [S]	Sleep Warm	1959	7.50	15.00	30.00
❏ T 1150 [M]	Sleep Warm	1959	6.25	12.50	25.00
❏ ST 1285 [S]	A Winter Romance	1959	7.50	15.00	30.00
❏ T 1285 [M]	A Winter Romance	1959	5.00	10.00	20.00
❏ ST 1442 [S]	This Time I'm Swingin'	1961	7.50	15.00	30.00
❏ T 1442 [M]	This Time I'm Swingin'	1961	5.00	10.00	20.00
❏ SW 1580 [S]	Dean Martin	1961	7.50	15.00	30.00
❏ W 1580 [M]	Dean Martin	1961	5.00	10.00	20.00
❏ SM-1659	Dino — Italian Love Songs	197?	2.50	5.00	10.00
—Reissue with new prefix					
❏ ST 1659 [S]	Dino — Italian Love Songs	1962	7.50	15.00	30.00
❏ T 1659 [M]	Dino — Italian Love Songs	1962	5.00	10.00	20.00
❏ ST 1702 [S]	Cha Cha De Amor	1962	7.50	15.00	30.00
❏ T 1702 [M]	Cha Cha De Amor	1962	5.00	10.00	20.00
❏ DT 2212 [R]	Hey Brother Pour the Wine	1964	3.00	6.00	12.00
❏ T 2212 [M]	Hey Brother Pour the Wine	1964	5.00	10.00	20.00
❏ ST 2297 [S]	Dean Martin Sings — Sinatra Conducts	1965	5.00	10.00	20.00
❏ T 2297 [M]	Dean Martin Sings — Sinatra Conducts	1965	3.75	7.50	15.00
❏ DT 2333 [R]	Dean Martin — Southern Style	1965	3.00	6.00	12.00
❏ T 2333 [M]	Dean Martin — Southern Style	1965	3.75	7.50	15.00
❏ STT 2343 [S]	Holiday Cheer	1965	5.00	10.00	20.00
—Some copies of this LP have labels that state the title as "Baby, It's Cold Outside."					
❏ TT 2343 [M]	Holiday Cheer	1965	3.75	7.50	15.00
—Reissue of 1285 with one fewer track					
❏ DT 2601 [R]	The Best of Dean Martin	1966	3.00	6.00	12.00
❏ SM-2601	The Best of Dean Martin	197?	2.50	5.00	10.00
—Reissue with new prefix					
❏ T 2601 [M]	The Best of Dean Martin	1966	3.75	7.50	15.00
❏ DTCL 2815 [(3)R]	The Dean Martin Deluxe Set	1967	5.00	10.00	20.00
❏ TCL 2815 [(3)M]	The Dean Martin Deluxe Set	1967	7.50	15.00	30.00
PAIR					
❏ PDL2-1029 [(2)]	Dreams and Memories	1986	3.00	6.00	12.00
PICKWICK					
❏ PTP-2051 [(2)]	Dean Martin	197?	3.00	6.00	12.00
❏ SPC-3057	You Can't Love 'Em All	196?	2.50	5.00	10.00
❏ SPC-3089	I Can't Give You Anything But Love	196?	2.50	5.00	10.00
❏ SPC-3136	Young and Foolish	196?	2.50	5.00	10.00
❏ SPC-3175	You Were Made for Love	197?	2.50	5.00	10.00
❏ SPC-3283	Deluxe	197?	2.50	5.00	10.00
REPRISE					
❏ MS 2053	Dino	1972	3.75	7.50	15.00
❏ MS 2113	Sittin' on Top of the World	1973	3.75	7.50	15.00
❏ MS 2174	You're the Best Thing That Ever Happened to Me	1973	3.75	7.50	15.00
❏ MS 2267	Once in a Lifetime	1978	3.00	6.00	12.00
❏ R-6021 [M]	French Style	1962	3.75	7.50	15.00
❏ R9-6021 [S]	French Style	1962	5.00	10.00	20.00
❏ R-6054 [M]	Dino Latino	1962	3.75	7.50	15.00
❏ R9-6054 [S]	Dino Latino	1962	5.00	10.00	20.00
❏ R-6061 [M]	Country Style	1963	3.75	7.50	15.00
❏ R9-6061 [S]	Country Style	1963	5.00	10.00	20.00
❏ R-6085 [M]	Dean "Tex" Martin Rides Again	1963	3.75	7.50	15.00
❏ R9-6085 [S]	Dean "Tex" Martin Rides Again	1963	5.00	10.00	20.00
❏ R-6123 [M]	Dream with Dean	1964	3.00	6.00	12.00
❏ RS-6123 [S]	Dream with Dean	1964	3.75	7.50	15.00
❏ R-6130 [M]	Everybody Loves Somebody	1964	3.00	6.00	12.00
❏ RS-6130 [S]	Everybody Loves Somebody	1964	3.75	7.50	15.00
❏ R-6140 [M]	The Door Is Still Open to My Heart	1964	3.00	6.00	12.00
❏ RS-6140 [S]	The Door Is Still Open to My Heart	1964	3.75	7.50	15.00
❏ R-6146 [M]	Dean Martin Hits Again	1965	3.00	6.00	12.00
❏ RS-6146 [S]	Dean Martin Hits Again	1965	3.75	7.50	15.00
❏ R-6170 [M]	(Remember Me) I'm the One Who Loves You	1965	3.00	6.00	12.00
❏ RS-6170 [S]	(Remember Me) I'm the One Who Loves You	1965	3.75	7.50	15.00
❏ R-6181 [M]	Houston	1965	3.00	6.00	12.00
❏ RS-6181 [S]	Houston	1965	3.75	7.50	15.00
❏ R-6201 [M]	Somewhere There's a Someone	1966	3.00	6.00	12.00
❏ RS-6201 [S]	Somewhere There's a Someone	1966	3.75	7.50	15.00
❏ R-6211 [M]	The Silencers	1966	5.00	10.00	20.00
❏ RS-6211 [S]	The Silencers	1966	6.25	12.50	25.00
❏ R-6213 [M]	The Hit Sound of Dean Martin	1966	3.00	6.00	12.00
❏ RS-6213 [S]	The Hit Sound of Dean Martin	1966	3.75	7.50	15.00
❏ R 6222 [M]	The Dean Martin Christmas Album	1966	3.75	7.50	15.00
❏ RS 6222 [S]	The Dean Martin Christmas Album	1966	5.00	10.00	20.00
❏ R-6233 [M]	The Dean Martin TV Show	1966	3.00	6.00	12.00
❏ RS-6233 [S]	The Dean Martin TV Show	1966	3.75	7.50	15.00
❏ R-6242 [M]	Happiness Is Dean Martin	1967	3.75	7.50	15.00
❏ RS-6242 [S]	Happiness Is Dean Martin	1967	3.75	7.50	15.00
❏ R-6250 [M]	Welcome to My World	1967	3.75	7.50	15.00
❏ RS-6250 [S]	Welcome to My World	1967	3.75	7.50	15.00
❏ RS-6301	Dean Martin's Greatest Hits! Vol. 1	1968	3.75	7.50	15.00
❏ RS-6320	Dean Martin's Greatest Hits! Vol. 2	1968	3.75	7.50	15.00
❏ RS-6330	Gentle on My Mind	1968	3.75	7.50	15.00
❏ RS-6338	I Take a Lot of Pride in What I Am	1969	3.75	7.50	15.00
❏ RS-6403	My Woman, My Woman, My Wife	1970	3.75	7.50	15.00
❏ RS-6428	For the Good Times	1971	3.75	7.50	15.00
❏ SW-94345	Dino	1972	5.00	10.00	20.00
—Capitol Record Club edition					
TOWER					
❏ DT 5006 [R]	The Lush Years	1965	3.75	7.50	15.00
❏ T 5006 [M]	The Lush Years	1965	5.00	10.00	20.00
❏ DT 5018 [R]	Relaxin'	1966	3.75	7.50	15.00
❏ T 5018 [M]	Relaxin'	1966	5.00	10.00	20.00
❏ ST 5036 [S]	Happy in Love	1966	5.00	10.00	20.00
❏ T 5036 [M]	Happy in Love	1966	3.75	7.50	15.00
WARNER BROS.					
❏ 23870	The Nashville Sessions	1983	3.00	6.00	12.00

MARTIN, DEAN, AND JERRY LEWIS
7-Inch Extended Plays
CAPITOL

Number	Title (A Side/B Side)	Yr	VG	VG+	NM
❏ EAP 1-533	(contents unknown)	1954	20.00	40.00	80.00
❏ EAP 1-533 [PS]	Living It Up	1954	20.00	40.00	80.00
❏ EAP 1-733	(contents unknown)	1956	15.00	30.00	60.00
❏ EAP 1-733 [PS]	Pardners	1956	15.00	30.00	60.00

MARTIN, DEWEY, AND MEDICINE BALL
Dewey is a former member of BUFFALO SPRINGFIELD.
45s
RCA VICTOR

Number	Title (A Side/B Side)	Yr	VG	VG+	NM
❏ 74-0489	There Must Be a Reason/Caress Me Pretty Music	1971	2.00	4.00	8.00
UNI					
❏ 55178	Jambalaya (On the Bayou)/Ala-Bam	1969	2.00	4.00	8.00
❏ 55245	Indian Child/I Do Believe	1970	2.00	4.00	8.00
Albums					
UNI					
❏ 73088	Dewey Martin and Medicine Ball	1970	6.25	12.50	25.00

MARTIN, DICK
45s
HIT

Number	Title (A Side/B Side)	Yr	VG	VG+	NM
❏ 77	Hello Muddah, Hello Faddah/Candy Girl	1963	2.00	4.00	8.00
—B-side by the Chellows					

MARTIN, GEORGE
45s
UNITED ARTISTS

Number	Title (A Side/B Side)	Yr	VG	VG+	NM
❏ 745	Ringo's Theme (This Boy)/And I Love Her	1964	6.25	12.50	25.00
❏ 745 [PS]	Ringo's Theme (This Boy)/And I Love Her	1964	75.00	150.00	300.00
❏ 750	A Hard Day's Night/I Should Have Known Better	1964	25.00	50.00	100.00
❏ 750 [PS]	A Hard Day's Night/I Should Have Known Better	1964	500.00	1000.	2000.
❏ 831	All Quiet on the Mersey Front/ Cast Your Fate to the Wind	1965	3.75	7.50	15.00
❏ 873	I Feel Fine/Downtown	1965	3.75	7.50	15.00
❏ 50148	Love in the Open Air/Bahama Sound	1967	7.50	15.00	30.00
Albums					
UNITED ARTISTS					
❏ UAL 3377 [M]	Off the Beatle Track	1964	20.00	40.00	80.00
❏ UAL 3383 [M]	A Hard Day's Night	1964	10.00	20.00	40.00
❏ UAL 3420 [M]	George Martin	1965	10.00	20.00	40.00
❏ UAL 3448 [M]	George Martin Plays "Help"	1965	12.50	25.00	50.00
❏ UAL 3539 [M]	George Martin Salutes the Beatle Girls	1966	12.50	25.00	50.00
❏ UAL 3647 [M]	London by George	1967	7.50	15.00	30.00
❏ UAS 6377 [S]	Off the Beatle Track	1964	25.00	50.00	100.00
❏ UAS 6383 [S]	A Hard Day's Night	1964	12.50	25.00	50.00
❏ UAS 6420 [S]	George Martin	1965	12.50	25.00	50.00
❏ UAS 6448 [S]	George Martin Plays "Help"	1965	20.00	40.00	80.00
❏ UAS 6539 [S]	George Martin Salutes the Beatle Girls	1966	20.00	40.00	80.00
❏ UAS 6647 [S]	London by George	1967	10.00	20.00	40.00

MARTIN, JANIS
45s
PALETTE

Number	Title (A Side/B Side)	Yr	VG	VG+	NM
❏ 5058	Hard Times Ahead/ Here Today and Gone Tomorrow	1960	6.25	12.50	25.00
❏ 5071	Teen Street/Cry Guitar	1961	6.25	12.50	25.00
RCA VICTOR					
❏ 47-6491	Drugstore Rock and Roll/Will You, Willyum	1956	10.00	20.00	40.00
❏ 47-6560	Ooby-Dooby/One More Year to Go	1956	10.00	20.00	40.00
❏ 47-6652	My Boy Elvis/Little Bit	1956	17.50	35.00	70.00
❏ 47-6744	Let's Elope, Baby/Barefoot Baby	1956	7.50	15.00	30.00
❏ 47-6832	Love Me to Pieces/Two Long Years	1957	7.50	15.00	30.00
❏ 47-6983	Love and Kisses/I'll Never Be Free	1957	7.50	15.00	30.00
❏ 47-7104	All Right Baby/Billy Boy, Billy Boy	1957	7.50	15.00	30.00
❏ 47-7184	Cracker Jack/Good Love	1958	7.50	15.00	30.00
7-Inch Extended Plays					
RCA VICTOR					
❏ EPA-4093	Just Squeeze Me (But Don't Tease Me)/My Confession/I Don't Hurt Anymore/Half Loved	1957	37.50	75.00	150.00
❏ EPA-4093 [PS]	Just Squeeze Me	1957	50.00	100.00	200.00

MARTIN, MARTY
45s
ANVIL

Number	Title (A Side/B Side)	Yr	VG	VG+	NM
❏ 1001	All I Got for Christmas Was a Broken Heart/ Hootenanny Santa	1963	2.50	5.00	10.00

MARTIN, RAY
45s
CAPITOL

Number	Title (A Side/B Side)	Yr	VG	VG+	NM
❏ F3393	Tickled Pink/If Hearts Could Talk	1956	3.00	6.00	12.00
❏ F3516	Street Symphony/Tambourine	1956	3.00	6.00	12.00
❏ F3670	Whistling Sergeant/Tango in the Rain	1957	3.00	6.00	12.00
❏ F3767	Heladero/Manhattan Tango	1957	3.00	6.00	12.00
ESSEX					
❏ 335	Begorrah/Hi-Lilli, Hi-Lo	1953	3.75	7.50	15.00
❏ 346	Tango Waltz/Carnivalito	1954	3.75	7.50	15.00
❏ 357	Veradero/Strings on Parade	1954	3.75	7.50	15.00
RCA VICTOR					
❏ 47-7344	Wild Gypsy/Big Dipper	1958	2.50	5.00	10.00
❏ 47-7769	Never on Sunday/Never on Sunday	1960	2.00	4.00	8.00
—B-side by Marty Gold					
❏ 47-7920	The Boulevard of Broken Dreams/ The Mime's Theme	1961	2.00	4.00	8.00
UNITED ARTISTS					
❏ 103	Song from "The Quiet American"/ The Grape Stompers	1958	2.50	5.00	10.00
❏ 116	Argentina Ballerina/Spring in Spain	1958	2.50	5.00	10.00
7-Inch Extended Plays					
CAPITOL					
❏ EAP-1-10017	A Fine Romance/You Stepped Out of a Dream/ /Isn't It Romantic/Love Walked In	195?	3.75	7.50	15.00
❏ EAP-1-10017 [PS]	Rainy Night in London, Part 1	195?	3.75	7.50	15.00
ESSEX					
❏ EXP-110	14th Variation/Ecstasy//Veradero/Begorrah	195?	3.75	7.50	15.00
❏ EXP-110 [PS]	(title unknown)	195?	3.75	7.50	15.00
Albums					
CAPITOL					
❏ T 10017 [M]	Rainy Night in London	195?	3.75	7.50	15.00
❏ T 10056 [M]	My London	195?	3.75	7.50	15.00
❏ T 10066 [M]	International Vibrations	195?	3.75	7.50	15.00

Number	Title (A Side/B Side)	Yr	VG	VG+	NM
❑ T 10067 [M]	High Barbaree	195?	3.75	7.50	15.00
❑ T 10101 [M]	Global Hop	195?	3.75	7.50	15.00
COLUMBIA					
❑ CL 529 [M]	Pop Concert	1953	6.25	12.50	25.00
ESSEX					
❑ ESLP-105 [10]	I Love	1954	7.50	15.00	30.00
IMPERIAL					
❑ LP-9083 [M]	Love of My Life	1959	3.00	6.00	12.00
❑ LP-9085 [M]	Boots and Saddle	1959	3.00	6.00	12.00
❑ LP-9087 [M]	Martin Goes Latin	1959	3.00	6.00	12.00
❑ LP-12018 [S]	Love of My Life	1959	3.75	7.50	15.00
❑ LP-12020 [S]	Boots and Saddle	1959	3.75	7.50	15.00
❑ LP-12022 [S]	Martin Goes Latin	1959	3.75	7.50	15.00
JUBILEE					
❑ JLP-1055 [M]	Witchcraft	1958	3.75	7.50	15.00
LONDON PHASE 4					
❑ SP-44040 [S]	The Sound of Sight: Music for an Experiment in Imagination	1964	5.00	10.00	20.00
MONUMENT					
❑ LP8068 [M]	Romance in Vienna	1966	2.50	5.00	10.00
❑ LP18068 [S]	Romance in Vienna	1966	3.00	6.00	12.00
RCA CAMDEN					
❑ CAL-913 [M]	Goldfinger and Other Music from James Bond Thrillers	1965	2.50	5.00	10.00
❑ CAS-913 [S]	Goldfinger and Other Music from James Bond Thrillers	1965	3.00	6.00	12.00
❑ CAL-927 [M]	Thunderball and Other Thriller Music	1965	2.50	5.00	10.00
❑ CAS-927 [S]	Thunderball and Other Thriller Music	1965	3.00	6.00	12.00
❑ CAL-976 [M]	Michelle Going for Baroque	1966	2.50	5.00	10.00
❑ CAS-976 [S]	Michelle Going for Baroque	1966	3.00	6.00	12.00
❑ CAL-2102 [M]	Comic Strip Favorites	1967	3.00	6.00	12.00
❑ CAS-2102 [S]	Comic Strip Favorites	1967	2.50	5.00	10.00
❑ CAL-2181 [M]	Up-Up and Away	1967	3.00	6.00	12.00
❑ CAS-2181 [S]	Up-Up and Away	1967	2.50	5.00	10.00
RCA VICTOR					
❑ LPM-1771 [M]	Pop Goes the Swingin' Marchin' Band	1958	3.00	6.00	12.00
❑ LSP-1771 [S]	Pop Goes the Swingin' Marchin' Band	1958	5.00	10.00	20.00
❑ LPM-2130 [M]	The Rockin' Strings of Ray Martin	1959	3.00	6.00	12.00
❑ LSP-2130 [S]	The Rockin' Strings of Ray Martin	1959	3.75	7.50	15.00
❑ LPM-2287 [M]	Dynamica	1961	3.00	6.00	12.00
❑ LSA-2287 [S]	Dynamica	1961	3.75	7.50	15.00
❑ LPM-2422 [M]	Excitement, Incorporated	1961	3.00	6.00	12.00
❑ LSA-2422 [S]	Excitement, Incorporated	1961	3.75	7.50	15.00
STRAND					
❑ SL-1037 [M]	Dancing After Dark	1962	3.00	6.00	12.00

MARTIN, VINCE
45s

Number	Title (A Side/B Side)	Yr	VG	VG+	NM
ABC-PARAMOUNT					
❑ 9992	Goodnight Irene/The Old Grey Goose	1959	3.00	6.00	12.00
❑ 10029	Strawberry Fair/Homing Pigeon	1959	3.00	6.00	12.00
CAPITOL					
❑ 2565	Summer Wind/I Can't Escape from You	1969	—	3.00	6.00
GLORY					
❑ 247	Cindy, Oh Cindy/Only If You Praise the Lord	1956	5.00	10.00	20.00
—With the Tarriers					
❑ 252	Katie-O/1-2-3-4 Anyplace Road	1957	3.75	7.50	15.00
❑ 259	Big Dreams/Wait for Me	1957	3.75	7.50	15.00
❑ 262	The Midnight Special/Ginny My Joy	1957	3.75	7.50	15.00
❑ 266	Goodbye My Love/Oh My Darling, Oh	1957	3.75	7.50	15.00
❑ 283	Keep a-Movin'/Sail Me Back	1958	3.75	7.50	15.00
20TH FOX					
❑ 214	The Sea Is Green/Is There Somebody Somewhere	1960	3.00	6.00	12.00

MARTIN, VINCE, AND FRED NEIL
45s

Number	Title (A Side/B Side)	Yr	VG	VG+	NM
ELEKTRA					
❑ 45009	Tear Down the Walls/I Know You Rider	1964	2.50	5.00	10.00

Albums

Number	Title (A Side/B Side)	Yr	VG	VG+	NM
ELEKTRA					
❑ EKL-248 [M]	Tear Down the Walls	1964	12.50	25.00	50.00
❑ EKS-7248 [S]	Tear Down the Walls	1964	15.00	30.00	60.00

MARTIN, WOODY
45s

Number	Title (A Side/B Side)	Yr	VG	VG+	NM
HIT					
❑ 48	My Dad/Shake Me I Rattle	1962	2.00	4.00	8.00
—B-side by Connie Landers					

MARTINEZ, TONY
Albums

Number	Title (A Side/B Side)	Yr	VG	VG+	NM
DEL-FI					
❑ DFLP-1205 [M]	The Many Sides of Pepino	1959	7.50	15.00	30.00
❑ DFLP-1205S [S]	The Many Sides of Pepino	1959	10.00	20.00	40.00

MARTINI, LUIGI, AND THE BAY CITY 5
45s

Number	Title (A Side/B Side)	Yr	VG	VG+	NM
JAGUAR					
❑ 3001	Basin Street Blues/Please Don't Talk About Me	1954	75.00	150.00	300.00
❑ 3002	Oh Marie/I'm Sorry I Made You Cry	1954	75.00	150.00	300.00

MARTINO, AL
45s

Number	Title (A Side/B Side)	Yr	VG	VG+	NM
BBS					
❑ 101	Here in My Heart/I Cried Myself to Sleep	1952	7.50	15.00	30.00
—With "BBS Records" at top of label					
❑ 101	Here in My Heart/I Cried Myself to Sleep	1952	10.00	20.00	40.00
—With "BBS Record Co., Phila. 7, Pa." at top of label					
❑ 101	Here in My Heart/I Cried Myself to Sleep	1952	15.00	30.00	60.00
—Red vinyl					
CAPITOL					
❑ 2053	A Voice in the Choir/The Glory of Love	1967	—	3.00	6.00
❑ 2102	Love Is Blue/I'm Carrying the World on My Shoulders	1968	—	3.00	6.00
❑ F2122	Take My Heart/I Never Cared	1952	5.00	10.00	20.00
❑ 2158	Lili Marlene/Georgia	1968	—	3.00	6.00

Number	Title (A Side/B Side)	Yr	VG	VG+	NM
❑ F2185	Say You'll Wait for Me/I've Never Seen	1952	5.00	10.00	20.00
❑ F2260	Now/In All This World	1952	5.00	10.00	20.00
❑ 2285	Wake Up to Me Gentle/If You Must Leave My Life	1968	—	3.00	6.00
❑ F2353	One Lonely Night/Rachel	1953	5.00	10.00	20.00
❑ 2355	I Can't Help It (If I'm Still in Love with You)/I Can Only See You	1968	—	3.00	6.00
❑ F2431	Here Are My Arms/There's Music in You	1953	5.00	10.00	20.00
❑ 2468	Sausalito/Take My Hand for Awhile	1969	—	3.00	6.00
❑ F2480	This Night I'll Remember/When You're Mine	1953	5.00	10.00	20.00
❑ F2535	All I Want Is a Chance/You Can't Go On Forever Breaking My Heart	1953	5.00	10.00	20.00
❑ F2649	Before/Sweetheart of Mine	1953	5.00	10.00	20.00
❑ 2674	I Started Loving You Again/Let Me Stay Awhile (With You)	1969	—	3.00	6.00
❑ F2737	Melancholy Serenade/Way Paesano	1954	5.00	10.00	20.00
❑ 2746	Can't Help Falling in Love/You're All the Woman That I Need	1970	—	2.50	5.00
❑ F2826	On and On/Give Me Something to Go with the Wine	1954	5.00	10.00	20.00
❑ 2830	Walking in the Sand/One More Mile (And Darlin' I'll Be Home)	1970	—	2.50	5.00
❑ F2899	Don't Go to Strangers/When	1954	5.00	10.00	20.00
❑ 2956	True Love Is Greater Than Friendship/The Call	1970	—	2.50	5.00
❑ F2982	Say It Again/The Story of Tina	1954	5.00	10.00	20.00
❑ 3056	Come Into My Life/One Pair of Hands	1971	—	2.50	5.00
❑ F3080	Love Is Eternal/Snowy, Snowy Mountains	1955	3.75	7.50	15.00
❑ 3120	Too Many Mornings/Losing My Mind	1971	—	2.50	5.00
❑ F3171	To Please My Lady/The Man from Laramie	1955	3.75	7.50	15.00
❑ 3256	More Than Ever Now/The Summer Knows	1972	—	2.50	5.00
❑ F3307	Close to Me/The Journey's End	1955	3.75	7.50	15.00
❑ 3313	Speak Softly Love/I Have But One Heart	1972	—	2.00	4.00
❑ 3444	Take Me Back/Canta Libre	1972	—	2.00	4.00
❑ F3501	The Girl I Left in Rome/Love to Call My Own	1956	3.75	7.50	15.00
❑ 3604	If I Give My Heart to You/Hey Mama	1973	—	2.00	4.00
❑ F3605	I'm Sorry/I'm a Funny Guy	1956	3.75	7.50	15.00
❑ 3748	Roses in the Sky/Daddy Let's Play	1973	—	2.00	4.00
❑ 3763	She/Mary Go Lightly (Como Un Nino)	1973	—	2.00	4.00
❑ 3771	Mary Go Lightly (Como Un Nino)/Daddy Let's Play	1973	—	2.00	4.00
❑ 3918	Daddy Loves You Honey/More Than Ever Now	1974	—	2.00	4.00
❑ 3987	To the Door of the Sun (Alle Porte Del Sol)/Mary Go Lightly	1974	—	2.00	4.00
❑ 4071	Charmer/Wake Up	1975	—	2.00	4.00
❑ 4134	Volare/You Belong to Me	1975	—	2.00	4.00
❑ 4241	The More I See You/My Thrill	1976	—	2.00	4.00
❑ 4322	May I Have the Next Dream with You/Sing My Love Song	1976	—	2.00	4.00
❑ 4362	Dream of Me/There's Nothing Greater Than Our Love	1976	—	2.00	4.00
❑ 4444	Kentucky Mornin'/Sweet Marjorene	1977	—	2.00	4.00
❑ 4508	The Next Hundred Years/After the Lovin'	1977	—	2.00	4.00
❑ 4551	One Last Time/Here I Go Again	1978	—	2.00	4.00
❑ 4593	Here in My Heart/Granada	1961	2.50	5.00	10.00
❑ 4643	Pardon/Another Time, Another Place	1961	2.50	5.00	10.00
❑ 4681	Torero/Now That I Found You	1979	—	2.00	4.00
❑ 4710	Exodus/Love, Where Are You Now	1962	2.50	5.00	10.00
❑ 4797	Make Me Believe/Because You're Mine	1962	2.50	5.00	10.00
❑ 4798	I Think About You/Only a Dream Away	1979	—	2.00	4.00
—With Kathy Keates					
❑ 4897	Almost Gone/Doors	1980	—	2.00	4.00
❑ 4930	I Love You Because/Merry-Go-Round	1963	2.00	4.00	8.00
❑ 4957	Look Around (You'll Find Me There)/More Than Ever Now	1980	—	2.00	4.00
❑ 5000	Painted, Tainted Rose/That's the Way It's Got to Be	1963	2.00	4.00	8.00
❑ 5060	Living a Lie/I Love You Truly	1963	2.00	4.00	8.00
❑ A-5094	You and I/Warm Is When You Touch Me	1982	—	—	3.00
❑ 5108	I Love You More and More Every Day/I'm Living My Heaven with You	1964	2.00	4.00	8.00
❑ 5183	Tears and Roses/A Year Ago Tonight	1964	2.00	4.00	8.00
❑ B-5191	What Your Love Did for Me/Warm Is When You Touch Me	1982	—	—	3.00
❑ 5239	Always Together/Thank You for Loving Me	1964	2.00	4.00	8.00
❑ 5293	We Could/Sunrise to Sunrise	1964	2.00	4.00	8.00
❑ 5311	Silver Bells/You're All I Want for Christmas	1964	2.00	4.00	8.00
❑ 5341	My Heart Would Know/Hush, Hush, Sweet Charlotte	1965	2.00	4.00	8.00
❑ 5341 [PS]	My Heart Would Know/Hush, Hush, Sweet Charlotte	1965	3.00	6.00	12.00
❑ 5384	Somebody Else Is Taking My Place/With All My Heart	1965	2.00	4.00	8.00
❑ 5434	My Cherie/Romana	1965	2.00	4.00	8.00
❑ 5506	Forgive Me/What Now My Love	1965	2.00	4.00	8.00
❑ 5542	Spanish Eyes/Melody of Love	1965	2.00	4.00	8.00
❑ 5598	Think I'll Go Somewhere and Cry Myself to Sleep/Hello Memory	1966	—	3.00	6.00
❑ 5652	Wiederseh'n/The Minute You're Gone	1966	—	3.00	6.00
❑ 5652 [PS]	Wiederseh'n/The Minute You're Gone	1966	2.50	5.00	10.00
❑ 5702	Just Yesterday/By the River of Roses	1966	—	3.00	6.00
❑ 5741	The Wheel of Hurt/Somewhere in This World	1966	—	3.00	6.00
❑ 5825	Daddy's Little Girl/Devotion	1967	—	3.00	6.00
❑ 5904	Mary in the Morning/I Love You and You Love Me	1967	—	3.00	6.00
❑ 5989	More Than the Eye Can See/Red Is Red	1967	—	3.00	6.00
20TH CENTURY FOX					
❑ 508	My Side of the Story/It's All Over But the Shouting	1964	2.00	4.00	8.00
❑ 530	I Can't Get You Out of My Heart/Come Back to Me	1964	2.00	4.00	8.00
❑ 575	Mama/My Bella Amore	1965	2.00	4.00	8.00
20TH FOX					
❑ 132	I Can't Get You Out of My Heart/Two Hearts Are Better Than One	1959	3.00	6.00	12.00
❑ 153	Darling, I Love You/Memory of You	1959	3.00	6.00	12.00
❑ 173	I Sold My Heart/Summertime	1960	3.00	6.00	12.00
❑ 180	Mama/And I Have You My Love	1960	3.00	6.00	12.00
❑ 184	Dearest (Cara)/Hello My Love	1960	3.00	6.00	12.00
❑ 200	Journey to Love/Only the Broken Hearted	1960	3.00	6.00	12.00

Number	Title (A Side/B Side)	Yr	VG	VG+	NM
❏ 213	Heart of Hearts/Our Concerto	1960	3.00	6.00	12.00
❏ 232	Come Back to Me/It's All Over But the Shouting	1960	3.00	6.00	12.00
❏ 237	Little Boy, Little Girl/My Side of the Story	1961	3.00	6.00	12.00

7-Inch Extended Plays
CAPITOL

Number	Title (A Side/B Side)	Yr	VG	VG+	NM
❏ EAP 1-405	*Take My Heart/I've Never Seen/Say You'll Wait for Me/Now	195?	3.75	7.50	15.00
❏ EAP 1-405 [PS]	Al Martino Sings	195?	3.75	7.50	15.00

Albums
CAPITOL

Number	Title (A Side/B Side)	Yr	VG	VG+	NM
❏ ST-180	Sausalito	1969	3.00	6.00	12.00
❏ ST-379	Jean	1969	3.00	6.00	12.00
❏ ST-405	Can't Help Falling in Love	1970	3.00	6.00	12.00
❏ ST-497	My Heart Sings	1970	3.00	6.00	12.00
❏ STBB-526 [(2)]	Here in My Heart/Yesterday	1970	3.75	7.50	15.00
❏ STCL-572 [(3)]	Al Martino	1971	6.25	12.50	25.00
❏ STBB-713 [(2)]	I Wish You Love/Losing You	1971	3.75	7.50	15.00
❏ ST-793	Summer of '42	1971	3.00	6.00	12.00
❏ ST 1774 [S]	The Exciting Voice of Al Martino	1962	5.00	10.00	20.00
❏ T 1774 [M]	The Exciting Voice of Al Martino	1962	3.75	7.50	15.00
❏ ST 1907 [S]	The Italian Voice of Al Martino	1963	5.00	10.00	20.00
❏ T 1907 [M]	The Italian Voice of Al Martino	1963	3.75	7.50	15.00
❏ ST 1914 [S]	I Love You Because	1963	3.75	7.50	15.00
❏ T 1914 [M]	I Love You Because	1963	3.00	6.00	12.00
❏ ST 1975 [S]	Painted, Tainted Rose	1963	3.75	7.50	15.00
❏ T 1975 [M]	Painted, Tainted Rose	1963	3.00	6.00	12.00
❏ ST 2040 [S]	Living a Lie	1964	3.75	7.50	15.00
❏ T 2040 [M]	Living a Lie	1964	3.00	6.00	12.00
❏ ST 2107 [S]	I Love You More and More Every Day/Tears and Roses	1964	3.75	7.50	15.00
❏ T 2107 [M]	I Love You More and More Every Day/Tears and Roses	1964	3.00	6.00	12.00
❏ ST 2165 [S]	A Merry Christmas from Al Martino	1964	3.75	7.50	15.00
❏ T 2165 [M]	A Merry Christmas from Al Martino	1964	3.00	6.00	12.00
❏ ST 2200 [S]	We Could	1964	3.75	7.50	15.00
❏ T 2200 [M]	We Could	1964	3.00	6.00	12.00
❏ ST 2312 [S]	Somebody Else Is Taking My Place	1965	3.75	7.50	15.00
❏ T 2312 [M]	Somebody Else Is Taking My Place	1965	3.00	6.00	12.00
❏ ST 2362 [S]	My Cherie	1965	3.75	7.50	15.00
❏ T 2362 [M]	My Cherie	1965	3.00	6.00	12.00
❏ ST 2435 [S]	Spanish Eyes	1966	3.75	7.50	15.00
❏ T 2435 [M]	Spanish Eyes	1966	3.00	6.00	12.00
❏ ST 2528 [S]	Think I'll Go Somewhere and Cry Myself to Sleep	1966	3.75	7.50	15.00
❏ T 2528 [M]	Think I'll Go Somewhere and Cry Myself to Sleep	1966	3.00	6.00	12.00
❏ ST 2592 [S]	This Is Love	1966	3.75	7.50	15.00
❏ T 2592 [M]	This Is Love	1966	3.00	6.00	12.00
❏ ST 2654 [S]	This Love for You	1967	3.75	7.50	15.00
❏ T 2654 [M]	This Love for You	1967	3.75	7.50	15.00
❏ ST 2733 [S]	Daddy's Little Girl	1967	3.75	7.50	15.00
❏ T 2733 [M]	Daddy's Little Girl	1967	3.75	7.50	15.00
❏ ST 2780 [S]	Mary in the Morning	1967	3.75	7.50	15.00
❏ T 2780 [M]	Mary in the Morning	1967	3.75	7.50	15.00
❏ ST 2843	This Is Al Martino	1968	3.75	7.50	15.00
❏ ST 2908	Love Is Blue	1968	3.75	7.50	15.00
❏ SKAO 2946	The Best of Al Martino	1968	3.75	7.50	15.00
❏ SM-2946	The Best of Al Martino	197?	2.50	5.00	10.00

—Reissue with new prefix

Number	Title (A Side/B Side)	Yr	VG	VG+	NM
❏ ST 2983	Wake Up to Me Gentle	1968	3.75	7.50	15.00
❏ SM-11071	Love Theme from "The Godfather"	1977	2.00	4.00	8.00

—Reissue with new prefix

Number	Title (A Side/B Side)	Yr	VG	VG+	NM
❏ ST-11071	Love Theme from "The Godfather"	1972	2.50	5.00	10.00
❏ ST-11302	I Won't Last a Day Without You	1974	2.50	5.00	10.00
❏ ST-11366	To the Door of the Sun	1975	2.50	5.00	10.00
❏ ST-11572	Sing My Love Songs	1976	2.50	5.00	10.00
❏ SM-11679	To the Door of the Sun	1977	2.00	4.00	8.00

—Reissue of 11366

Number	Title (A Side/B Side)	Yr	VG	VG+	NM
❏ ST-11741	The Next Hundred Years	1978	2.50	5.00	10.00
❏ SN-16074	The Best of Al Martino	1981	2.00	4.00	8.00

—Budget-line reissue

Number	Title (A Side/B Side)	Yr	VG	VG+	NM
❏ SQBO-91280 [(2)]	The Romantic World of Al Martino	196?	5.00	10.00	20.00

—Capitol Record Club exclusive
MOVIETONE

Number	Title (A Side/B Side)	Yr	VG	VG+	NM
❏ MTM 2002 [M]	That Old Feeling	196?	3.75	7.50	15.00
❏ MTM 2015 [M]	All of Me	1967	5.00	10.00	20.00
❏ MTS 72002 [S]	That Old Feeling	196?	5.00	10.00	20.00
❏ MTS 72015 [S]	All of Me	1967	3.75	7.50	15.00

PICKWICK

Number	Title (A Side/B Side)	Yr	VG	VG+	NM
❏ SPC-3049	Don't Go to Strangers	196?	3.00	6.00	12.00
❏ SPC-3276	Mary in the Morning	197?	2.50	5.00	10.00

SPRINGBOARD

Number	Title (A Side/B Side)	Yr	VG	VG+	NM
❏ 4074	Time After Time	1978	2.00	4.00	8.00

20TH CENTURY FOX

Number	Title (A Side/B Side)	Yr	VG	VG+	NM
❏ SF-3025 [M]	Al Martino	1959	6.25	12.50	25.00
❏ SFX-3025 [S]	Al Martino	1959	7.50	15.00	30.00
❏ SF-3032 [M]	Sing Along with Al Martino	1959	6.25	12.50	25.00
❏ SFX-3032 [S]	Sing Along with Al Martino	1959	7.50	15.00	30.00
❏ TF-4168 [M]	Al Martino Sings	196?	5.00	10.00	20.00
❏ TFS-4168 [S]	Al Martino Sings	196?	6.25	12.50	25.00
❏ SXG-5009 [S]	When Your Lover Has Gone	1963	6.25	12.50	25.00
❏ XG-5009 [M]	When Your Lover Has Gone	1963	5.00	10.00	20.00

MARTY
45s
NOVELTY

Number	Title (A Side/B Side)	Yr	VG	VG+	NM
❏ 101	Marty on Planet Mars (Part 1)/Marty on Planet Mars (Part 2)	1956	10.00	20.00	40.00

MARTY AND THE SYMBOLS
45s
GRAPHIC ARTS

Number	Title (A Side/B Side)	Yr	VG	VG+	NM
❏ 1000	You're the One/Rip Van Winkle	1963	20.00	40.00	80.00

MARVELETTES, THE
45s
A&M

Number	Title (A Side/B Side)	Yr	VG	VG+	NM
❏ 1201	Danger Heartbreak Dead Ahead/Baby Please Don't Go	1988	—	2.00	4.00

—B-side by Them

Number	Title (A Side/B Side)	Yr	VG	VG+	NM
❏ 1201 [PS]	Danger Heartbreak Dead Ahead/Baby Please Don't Go	1988	—	2.00	4.00

—"Good Morning Vietnam" sleeve
GORDY

Number	Title (A Side/B Side)	Yr	VG	VG+	NM
❏ 7024	Too Hurt to Cry, Too Much in Love to Say Goodbye/Come On Home	1963	20.00	40.00	80.00

—As "The Darnells"
TAMLA

Number	Title (A Side/B Side)	Yr	VG	VG+	NM
❏ 54046	Please Mr. Postman/So Long Baby	1961	6.25	12.50	25.00
❏ 54046 [PS]	Please Mr. Postman/So Long Baby	1961	30.00	60.00	120.00
❏ 54054	Twistin' Postman/I Want a Guy	1962	5.00	10.00	20.00
❏ 54054 [PS]	Twistin' Postman/I Want a Guy	1962	25.00	50.00	100.00
❏ 54060	Playboy/All the Love I've Got	1962	5.00	10.00	20.00
❏ 54065	Beechwood 4-5789/Someday, Someway	1962	5.00	10.00	20.00
❏ 54072	Strange I Know/Too Strong to Be Strung Along	1962	3.75	7.50	15.00
❏ 54077	Forever/Locking Up My Heart	1963	3.75	7.50	15.00
❏ 54082	Tie a String Around My Finger/My Daddy Knows Best	1963	5.00	10.00	20.00
❏ 54088	As Long As I Know He's Mine/Little Girl Blue	1963	3.00	6.00	12.00
❏ 54091	He's a Good Guy (Yes He Is)/Goddess of Love	1964	3.00	6.00	12.00
❏ 54091 [DJ]	Yes He Is	1964	18.75	37.50	75.00

—One-sided promo with different title than stock copy

Number	Title (A Side/B Side)	Yr	VG	VG+	NM
❏ 54097	You're My Remedy/A Little Bit of Sympathy, A Little Bit of Love	1964	2.50	5.00	10.00
❏ 54097 [PS]	You're My Remedy/A Little Bit of Sympathy, A Little Bit of Love	1964	15.00	30.00	60.00
❏ 54105	Too Many Fish in the Sea/A Need for Love	1964	2.50	5.00	10.00
❏ 54105	Two Many Fish in the Sea/A Need for Love	1964	10.00	20.00	40.00

—Some copies feature the above incorrect A-side title

Number	Title (A Side/B Side)	Yr	VG	VG+	NM
❏ 54116	I'll Keep Holding On/No Time for Tears	1965	2.50	5.00	10.00
❏ 54120	Danger, Heartbreak Dead Ahead/Your Cheating Ways	1965	2.50	5.00	10.00
❏ 54126	Don't Mess with Bill/Anything You Wanna Do	1965	2.50	5.00	10.00
❏ 54131	You're the One/Paper Boy	1966	2.50	5.00	10.00
❏ 54143	The Hunter Gets Captured by the Game/I Think I Can Change You	1967	2.50	5.00	10.00
❏ 54150	When You're Young and In Love/The Day You Take One, You Have to Take the Other	1967	2.50	5.00	10.00
❏ 54158	My Baby Must Be a Magician/I Need Someone	1967	2.50	5.00	10.00
❏ 54166	Here I Am Baby/Keep Off, No Trespassing	1968	2.50	5.00	10.00
❏ 54171	Destination: Anywhere/What's So Easy for Two Is So Hard for One	1968	2.50	5.00	10.00
❏ 54177	I'm Gonna Hold On Long As I Can/Don't Make Hurting Me a Habit	1968	2.50	5.00	10.00
❏ 54186	That's How Heartaches Are Made/Rainy Mourning	1969	2.50	5.00	10.00
❏ 54198	Marionette/After All	1970	2.00	4.00	8.00
❏ 54213	A Breath Taking Guy/You're the One for Me Baby	1972	2.00	4.00	8.00

TOPPS/MOTOWN

Number	Title (A Side/B Side)	Yr	VG	VG+	NM
❏ 12	Please Mr. Postman	1967	18.75	37.50	75.00

—Cardboard record

7-Inch Extended Plays
TAMLA

Number	Title (A Side/B Side)	Yr	VG	VG+	NM
❏ 60274	The Hunter Gets Captured by the Game/When You're Young and In Love/I Know Better//I Was Really Sayin' Somethin'/The Day You Take One/Keep Off, No Trespassing	196?	10.00	20.00	40.00

—Jukebox issue; small hole, plays at 33 1/3 rpm

Number	Title (A Side/B Side)	Yr	VG	VG+	NM
❏ 60274 [PS]	The Marvelettes	196?	10.00	20.00	40.00

Albums
MOTOWN

Number	Title (A Side/B Side)	Yr	VG	VG+	NM
❏ M5-180V1	Greatest Hits	1981	2.50	5.00	10.00

—Reissue of Tamla 253

Number	Title (A Side/B Side)	Yr	VG	VG+	NM
❏ M7-827 [(2)]	Anthology	1975	3.75	7.50	15.00
❏ 5266 ML	Please Mr. Postman	1982	2.50	5.00	10.00

—Reissue of Tamla 228
TAMLA

Number	Title (A Side/B Side)	Yr	VG	VG+	NM
❏ T-228 [M]	Please Mr. Postman	1961	150.00	300.00	600.00

—White label

Number	Title (A Side/B Side)	Yr	VG	VG+	NM
❏ T-228 [M]	Please Mr. Postman	1963	75.00	150.00	300.00

—Yellow label with globes logo

Number	Title (A Side/B Side)	Yr	VG	VG+	NM
❏ T-229 [M]	The Marveletts Sing	1962	125.00	250.00	500.00

—Title as listed on front cover (misspelled); all-black cover with white circles

Number	Title (A Side/B Side)	Yr	VG	VG+	NM
❏ T-229 [M]	Smash Hits of 62'	1962	600.00	900.00	1200.

—Title as listed on front cover; large black "M" with song titles in circles

Number	Title (A Side/B Side)	Yr	VG	VG+	NM
❏ T-229 [M]	The Marveletts Sing	1963	62.50	125.00	250.00

—Yellow label with side-by-side globes logo

Number	Title (A Side/B Side)	Yr	VG	VG+	NM
❏ T-231 [M]	Playboy	1962	125.00	250.00	500.00

—Yellow label with overlapping record and globe logo

Number	Title (A Side/B Side)	Yr	VG	VG+	NM
❏ T-231 [M]	Playboy	1962	150.00	300.00	600.00

—White label

Number	Title (A Side/B Side)	Yr	VG	VG+	NM
❏ T-231 [M]	Playboy	1963	62.50	125.00	250.00

—Yellow label with side-by-side globes logo

Number	Title (A Side/B Side)	Yr	VG	VG+	NM
❏ T-237 [M]	The Marvelous Marvelettes	1963	37.50	75.00	150.00
❏ T-243 [M]	Recorded Live on Stage	1963	20.00	40.00	80.00
❏ T-253 [M]	Greatest Hits	1966	7.50	15.00	30.00

—Yellow cover

Number	Title (A Side/B Side)	Yr	VG	VG+	NM
❏ T-253 [M]	Greatest Hits	1967	6.25	12.50	25.00

—Green cover

Number	Title (A Side/B Side)	Yr	VG	VG+	NM
❏ TS-253 [S]	Greatest Hits	1966	10.00	20.00	40.00

—Yellow cover

Number	Title (A Side/B Side)	Yr	VG	VG+	NM
❏ TS-253 [S]	Greatest Hits	1967	5.00	10.00	20.00

—Green cover

Number	Title (A Side/B Side)	Yr	VG	VG+	NM
❏ T-274 [M]	The Marvelettes	1967	7.50	15.00	30.00
❏ TS-274 [S]	The Marvelettes	1967	5.00	10.00	20.00
❏ T-286 [M]	Sophisticated Soul	1968	10.00	20.00	40.00
❏ TS-286 [S]	Sophisticated Soul	1968	5.00	10.00	20.00
❏ TS-288	In Full Bloom	1969	3.75	7.50	15.00
❏ TS-305	Return of the Marvelettes	1970	3.75	7.50	15.00

Number	Title (A Side/B Side)	Yr	VG	VG+	NM

MARVELLOS, THE (1)
45s
CHA CHA
□ 756 — Come Back My Love/Boyee Yoing — 1963 — 7.50 — 15.00 — 30.00
STEPHENY
□ 1818 — Come Back My Love/Boyee Yoing — 1958 — 50.00 — 100.00 — 200.00

MARVELLOS, THE (2)
45s
EXODUS
□ 6214 — Salty Sam/She Told Me Lies — 1962 — 50.00 — 100.00 — 200.00
□ 6216 — I Ask of You/Hip Enough — 1962 — 30.00 — 60.00 — 120.00
REPRISE
□ 20088 — Salty Sam/She Told Me Lies — 1962 — 7.50 — 15.00 — 30.00

MARVELLOS, THE (3)
45s
LOMA
□ 2045 — Something's Burning/We Go Together — 1966 — 3.00 — 6.00 — 12.00
□ 2061 — You're Such a Sweet Thing/Why Do You Want to Hurt the One You Love — 1966 — 3.00 — 6.00 — 12.00
MODERN
□ 1054 — Down in the City/In the Sunshine — 1967 — 2.50 — 5.00 — 10.00
WARNER BROS.
□ 7011 — Don't Play with My Heart/Let Me Keep You Satisfied — 1967 — 2.50 — 5.00 — 10.00
□ 7054 — Piece of Silk/Yes I Do — 1967 — 2.50 — 5.00 — 10.00

MARVELLOS, THE (U) Could be group (1); it's doubtful that these could be either of the other two.
45s
MARVELLO
□ 5005 — Red Hot Momma/I Need a Girl — 1955 — 75.00 — 150.00 — 300.00
THERON
□ 117 — You're the Dream/Calypso Mama — 1957 — 100.00 — 200.00 — 400.00

MARVELOWS, THE
45s
ABC
□ 10820 — Fade Away/You've Been Going to Sally — 1966 — 2.50 — 5.00 — 10.00
□ 11011 — In the Morning/Talkin' 'Bout Ya, Baby — 1967 — 2.00 — 4.00 — 8.00
—As "The Mighty Marvelows"
□ 11073 — I'm So Confused/I'm Without a Girl — 1968 — 2.00 — 4.00 — 8.00
—As "The Mighty Marvelows"
□ 11139 — Hey, Hey Girl/Wait, Be Cool — 1968 — 2.00 — 4.00 — 8.00
—As "The Mighty Marvelows"
□ 11189 — You're Breaking My Heart/This Town's Too Much — 1969 — 2.00 — 4.00 — 8.00
—As "The Mighty Marvelows"
ABC-PARAMOUNT
□ 10613 — A Friend/Hey, Hey Baby — 1965 — 2.50 — 5.00 — 10.00
□ 10629 — I Do/My Heart — 1965 — 3.75 — 7.50 — 15.00
□ 10708 — Shim Sham/Your Little Sister — 1965 — 2.50 — 5.00 — 10.00
□ 10756 — Do It/I've Got My Eyes on You — 1965 — 2.50 — 5.00 — 10.00
Albums
ABC
□ S-643 — The Mighty Marvelows — 1968 — 7.50 — 15.00 — 30.00

MARVELS, THE (1) Early version of THE DUBS.
45s
ABC-PARAMOUNT
□ 9771 — I Won't Have You Breaking My Heart/Jump Rock and Roll — 1956 — 150.00 — 300.00 — 600.00

MARVELS, THE (2)
45s
LAURIE
□ 3106 — I Shed So Many Tears/So Young, So Sweet — 1958 — 17.50 — 35.00 — 70.00
—Also released as "The Marvells"

MARVELS, THE (3)
45s
MUN-RAB
□ 1008 — Just Another Fool/You Crack Me Up — 1959 — 375.00 — 750.00 — 1500.

MARVELS, THE (U) May be group (2).
45s
WINN
□ 1916 — For Sentimental Reasons/Come Back — 1961 — 50.00 — 100.00 — 200.00

MARVIN AND JOHNNY
45s
ALADDIN
□ 3371 — Yak Yak/Pretty Eyes — 1957 — 7.50 — 15.00 — 30.00
□ 3408 — You're in My Heart/Smack Smack — 1958 — 7.50 — 15.00 — 30.00
□ 3439 — It's Christmas/The Valley of Love — 1958 — 7.50 — 15.00 — 30.00
FELSTED
□ 8681 — Hot Biscuits and Gravy/Tired of Being Alone — 1963 — 3.00 — 6.00 — 12.00
JAMIE
□ 1188 — Once Upon a Time/Tick Tock — 1961 — 3.00 — 6.00 — 12.00
LANA
□ 127 — Cherry Pie/Ain't That Right — 196? — 2.50 — 5.00 — 10.00
—Oldies reissue
LIBERTY
□ 1394 — It's Christmas/It's Christmas Time — 1980 — — — 2.50 — 5.00
—B-side by the Five Keys
MODERN
□ 933 — Tick Tock/Cherry Pie — 1954 — 18.75 — 37.50 — 75.00
□ 941 — Sugar/Kiss Me — 1954 — 12.50 — 25.00 — 50.00
□ 946 — Little Honey/Honey Girl — 1955 — 12.50 — 25.00 — 50.00
□ 949 — Ko Ko Mo/Sometimes I Wonder — 1955 — 10.00 — 20.00 — 40.00
□ 952 — I Love You, Yes I Do/Baby Won't You Marry Me — 1955 — 10.00 — 20.00 — 40.00
□ 959 — Butler Ball/Sugar Mama — 1955 — 10.00 — 20.00 — 40.00
□ 968 — Will You Love Me/Sweet Dreams — 1956 — 7.50 — 15.00 — 30.00
□ 974 — Ain't That Right/Let Me Know — 1956 — 7.50 — 15.00 — 30.00
SPECIALTY
□ 479 — Baby Doll/I'm Not a Fool — 1953 — 15.00 — 30.00 — 60.00

□ 479 — Baby Doll/I'm Not a Fool — 1953 — 25.00 — 50.00 — 100.00
—Red vinyl
□ 488 — Jo Jo/How Long Has She Been Gone — 1954 — 15.00 — 30.00 — 60.00
□ 498 — School of Love/Boy Loves Girl — 1954 — 15.00 — 30.00 — 60.00
□ 530 — Day In — Day Out/Flip — 1954 — 15.00 — 30.00 — 60.00
□ 554 — Ding Dong Baby/Mamo Mamo — 1955 — 12.50 — 25.00 — 50.00
SWINGIN'
□ 641 — I'm Tired of Being Alone/Baby You Don't Know — 1962 — 3.00 — 6.00 — 12.00
□ 645 — Pretty One/Second Helping of Cherry Pie — 1963 — 3.00 — 6.00 — 12.00
Albums
CROWN
□ CST-381 [R] — Marvin and Johnny — 1963 — 3.00 — 6.00 — 12.00
□ CLP-5381 [M] — Marvin and Johnny — 1963 — 12.50 — 25.00 — 50.00

MARVIN AND THE CHIRPS
45s
TIP TOP
□ 202 — I'll Miss You This Christmas/Sixteen Tons — 1958 — 50.00 — 100.00 — 200.00

MARX, THE
45s
CHANTE
□ 1002 — One Minute More/You Are My Love — 19?? — 50.00 — 100.00 — 200.00
DAHLIA
□ 1002 — One Minute More/You Are My Love — 19?? — 25.00 — 50.00 — 100.00

MARY BUTTERWORTH
Albums
CUSTOM FIDELITY
□ 2092 — Mary Butterworth — 1969 — 75.00 — 150.00 — 300.00

MARY SUE AND THE TRAMS
45s
HIT
□ 145 — Dancing in the Street/(I've Got a) Tiger in My Tank — 1964 — 2.50 — 5.00 — 10.00
—B-side by the Jalopy Five

MARYLANDERS, THE
45s
JUBILEE
□ 5079 — I'm a Sentimental Fool/Sittin' By the River — 1952 — 100.00 — 200.00 — 400.00
□ 5091 — Make Me Thrill Again/Please Love Me — 1952 — 100.00 — 200.00 — 400.00
□ 5114 — Fried Chicken/Good Old 99 — 1953 — 75.00 — 150.00 — 300.00
□ 5114 — Fried Chicken/Good Old 99 — 1953 — 100.00 — 200.00 — 400.00
—Red vinyl

MASCOTS, THE (1)
ABC
□ 11152 — Baby, You're So Wrong/Moreen — 1968 — 2.00 — 4.00 — 8.00

MASCOTS, THE (2)
45s
BLAST
□ 206 — Once Upon a Love/Hey Little Angel — 1963 — 5.00 — 10.00 — 20.00
—White label
□ 206 — Once Upon a Love/Hey Little Angel — 1963 — 10.00 — 20.00 — 40.00
—Red label
MERMAID
□ 107 — Bluebirds Over the Mountain/Timberlands — 1962 — 20.00 — 40.00 — 80.00

MASCOTS, THE (3) Later recorded as THE O'JAYS.
45s
KING
□ 5377 — The Story of My Heart/Do the Wiggle — 1960 — 25.00 — 50.00 — 100.00
□ 5435 — Lonely Rain/That's the Way I Feel — 1960 — 15.00 — 30.00 — 60.00

MASCOTS, THE (4)
45s
MGM
□ 12027 — Relax-Ay-Voo/The Others I Like — 1955 — 5.00 — 10.00 — 20.00
□ 12107 — Nobody's Arms/Little Mustard Seed — 1955 — 5.00 — 10.00 — 20.00
□ 12236 — Who Put the Devil in Evelyn's Eyes/Java Jive — 1956 — 5.00 — 10.00 — 20.00

MASCOTS, THE (U) If this is any of the above groups, it's most likely group (1).
45s
RUMBLE
□ 4197 — I Want Love/Waited So Long — 196? — 5.00 — 10.00 — 20.00

MASEKELA, HUGH
12-Inch Singles
JIVE
□ 9194 — Don't Go Lose It Baby (3 versions) — 1984 — 2.00 — 4.00 — 8.00
□ 9361 — Lady (Remix)/Lady (LP Version)//Coal Train (Live 17:16) — 1985 — 2.50 — 5.00 — 10.00
WARNER BROS.
□ 20634 — Bring Him Back Home (Extended) (Instrumental)/Serengeti — 1987 — 2.00 — 4.00 — 8.00
□ 20684 — Bring Him Back Home (Extended) (Live)/Stimela (Live) — 1987 — 2.00 — 4.00 — 8.00
45s
A&M
□ 2107 — Foreign Natives/Mama Way — 1979 — — — 2.00 — 4.00
—With Herb Alpert
BLUE THUMB
□ 244 — Languta/Rekpete — 1973 — — — 2.50 — 5.00
□ 255 — Been Such a Long Time Gone/Jungle Jim — 1974 — — — 2.00 — 4.00
□ 260 — African Secret Society/Jungle Jim — 1974 — — — 2.00 — 4.00
CASABLANCA
□ 848 — Excuse Me Please/The Boy's Doin' It — 1975 — — — 2.00 — 4.00
□ 857 — For the Love of You/Witch Doctor — 1976 — — — 2.00 — 4.00
□ 861 — A Person Is a Sometime Thing/Mama — 1976 — — — 2.00 — 4.00
□ 862 — Dance/(B-side unknown) — 1976 — — — 2.00 — 4.00
□ 879 — Hi-Life/Toejam — 1977 — — — 2.00 — 4.00
CHISA
□ 003 — Chisa/What Is Wrong with Groovin' — 1970 — — — 3.00 — 6.00

M

Number	Title (A Side/B Side)	Yr	VG	VG+	NM
❏ 8009	You Keep Me Hangin' On/Make Me a Potion	1971	—	3.00	6.00
❏ 8014	Dyambo/Shebeen	1971	—	3.00	6.00
HORIZON					
❏ 115	Skokiaan/African Summer	1978	—	2.00	4.00
—With Herb Alpert					
❏ 116	Lobo/African Summer	1978	—	2.00	4.00
—With Herb Alpert					
JIVE					
❏ 9198	Don't Go Lose It Baby/(Instrumental)	1984	—	—	3.00
❏ 9360	Lady/Cool Train	1985	—	—	3.00
MERCURY					
❏ 72853	Emavungwani (Green Home)/U-Dwi (Smallpox)	1968	—	3.00	6.00
MGM					
❏ CS3-5 [DJ]	Celebrity Scene: Hugh Masekela	1966	12.50	25.00	50.00
—Box set of five singles (13643-13647). Price includes box, all 5 singles, jukebox title strips, bio. Records are sometimes found by themselves, so they are also listed separately.					
❏ 13601	Along Comes Mary/Little Star	1966	—	3.00	6.00
❏ 13643 [DJ]	California Dreamin'/U-Dwi	1966	2.00	4.00	8.00
❏ 13644 [DJ]	Norwegian Wood/Cantaloupe Island	1966	2.00	4.00	8.00
❏ 13645 [DJ]	She's Comin' My Way/Unhlanhla	1966	2.00	4.00	8.00
❏ 13646 [DJ]	Along Comes Mary/Little Star	1966	2.00	4.00	8.00
❏ 13647 [DJ]	If I Needed Someone/From Me to You	1966	2.00	4.00	8.00
❏ 13901	Norwegian Wood/Sound of Silence	1968	—	3.00	6.00
UNI					
❏ 55024	Baby, Baby, Baby/Lily the Fox	1967	—	3.00	6.00
❏ 55037	Up-Up and Away/Son of the Ice Bag	1967	—	3.00	6.00
❏ 55049	There Are Seeds to Sow/Ha Lese Le Di Khana	1968	—	3.00	6.00
❏ 55066	Grazing in the Grass/Bajabula Bounce	1968	—	3.00	6.00
❏ 55085	Puffin' On Down the Track/Do Me So Lo, So So	1968	—	3.00	6.00
❏ 55102	Riot/Mace and Grenades	1968	—	3.00	6.00
❏ 55116	A Long Ways from Home/Home Boy	1969	—	3.00	6.00
❏ 55130	10,000 Miles to Memphis/Gettin' It On	1969	—	3.00	6.00
❏ 55165	Where Has All the Grass Grown/I Haven't Slept	1969	—	3.00	6.00
WARNER BROS.					
❏ 28419	Bring Him Back Home/Serengeti	1987	—	—	3.00
Albums					
ABC IMPULSE!					
❏ IA-9343 [(2)]	African Connection	1978	3.00	6.00	12.00
BLUE THUMB					
❏ BT-62	Introducing Hedzoleh Sounds	1972	2.50	5.00	10.00
❏ BT-6003	Home Is Where the Music Is	1973	2.50	5.00	10.00
❏ BT-6015	I Am Not Afraid	1974	2.50	5.00	10.00
CASABLANCA					
❏ NBLP 7017	The Boy's Doin' It	1975	2.50	5.00	10.00
❏ NBLP 7023	Colonial Man	1976	2.50	5.00	10.00
❏ NBLP 7036	Melody Maker	1977	2.50	5.00	10.00
❏ NBLP 7079	You Told Your Mama	1978	2.50	5.00	10.00
CHISA					
❏ CS-803	Reconstruction	1970	3.00	6.00	12.00
❏ CS-808	Union of South Africa	1971	3.00	6.00	12.00
JIVE					
❏ JL-8210	Techno Bush	1984	2.50	5.00	10.00
❏ JL-8382	Waiting for the Rain	1985	2.50	5.00	10.00
MERCURY					
❏ MG-20797 [M]	The Trumpet of Hugh Masekela	1963	3.75	7.50	15.00
❏ SR-60797 [S]	The Trumpet of Hugh Masekela	1963	5.00	10.00	20.00
❏ SR-61109	Grr	1969	3.00	6.00	12.00
MGM					
❏ GAS-116	Hugh Masekela (Golden Archive Series)	1970	3.00	6.00	12.00
❏ E-4372 [M]	The Americanization of Ooga Booga	1966	3.00	6.00	12.00
❏ SE-4372 [S]	The Americanization of Ooga Booga	1966	3.75	7.50	15.00
❏ E-4415 [M]	Hugh Masekela's Next Album	1966	3.00	6.00	12.00
❏ SE-4415 [S]	Hugh Masekela's Next Album	1966	3.75	7.50	15.00
❏ E-4468 [M]	The Lasting Impression of Hugh Masekela	1967	3.75	7.50	15.00
❏ SE-4468 [S]	The Lasting Impression of Hugh Masekela	1967	3.00	6.00	12.00
NOVUS					
❏ 3070-1-R	Uptownship	1990	3.00	6.00	12.00
UNI					
❏ 3010 [M]	Hugh Masekela's Latest	1967	3.75	7.50	15.00
❏ 3015 [M]	Hugh Masekela Is Alive and Well at the Whisky	1967	5.00	10.00	20.00
❏ 73010 [S]	Hugh Masekela's Latest	1967	3.00	6.00	12.00
❏ 73015 [S]	Hugh Masekela Is Alive and Well at the Whisky	1967	3.00	6.00	12.00
❏ 73028	The Promise of a Future	1968	3.00	6.00	12.00
❏ 73041	Masekela	1969	3.00	6.00	12.00
❏ 73051	Masekela — Vol. 2	1970	3.00	6.00	12.00
VERVE					
❏ V6-8651 [(2)]	24 Karat Hits	1968	3.75	7.50	15.00
WARNER BROS.					
❏ 25566	Tomorrow	1987	2.50	5.00	10.00

MASH, THE
45s
COLUMBIA

Number	Title (A Side/B Side)	Yr	VG	VG+	NM
❏ 45130	Song from M*A*S*H/M*A*S*H March	1970	2.00	4.00	8.00
—Alternate A-side title					
❏ 45130	Suicide Is Painless/M*A*S*H March	1970	3.00	6.00	12.00

MASHMAKHAN Early version of APRIL WINE.
45s
EPIC

Number	Title (A Side/B Side)	Yr	VG	VG+	NM
❏ 10634	As the Years Go By/The Days When We Are Free	1970	—	3.00	6.00
JAMIE					
❏ 1418	One Night Stand/Dance a Little Step	1969	2.00	4.00	8.00
Albums					
EPIC					
❏ E 30235	Mashmakhan	1970	3.00	6.00	12.00
❏ E 30813	The Family	1971	3.00	6.00	12.00

MASKED MARAUDERS, THE
Fictional supergroup from a Rolling Stone magazine album review, which noted the presence of Bob Dylan, Mick Jagger, John Lennon and Paul McCartney. The below, recorded using the bogus review as a guide, was actually THE CLEANLINESS AND GODLINESS SKIFFLE BAND.
45s
DEITY

Number	Title (A Side/B Side)	Yr	VG	VG+	NM
❏ 0870	I Can't Get No Nookie/Cow Pie	1969	3.75	7.50	15.00
Albums					
DEITY					
❏ RS 6378	The Masked Marauders	1969	5.00	10.00	20.00

MASON, BARBARA
12-Inch Singles
WEST END

Number	Title (A Side/B Side)	Yr	VG	VG+	NM
❏ 22164	Another Man (4 versions)	1983	—	3.00	6.00
WMOT					
❏ 02237	Let Me Give You Love/(Instrumental)	1981	2.00	4.00	8.00
45s					
ARCTIC					
❏ 102	Girls Have Feelings Too/Come to Me	1964	3.00	6.00	12.00
❏ 105	Yes I'm Ready/Keep Him	1965	5.00	10.00	20.00
❏ 108	Sad, Sad Girl/Come to Me	1965	3.00	6.00	12.00
❏ 112	You Got What It Takes/If You Don't (Love Me, Tell Me So)	1965	3.00	6.00	12.00
❏ 116	Don't Ever Want to Lose Your Love/Is It Me	1965	3.00	6.00	12.00
❏ 120	I Need Love/Bobby Is My Baby	1966	2.50	5.00	10.00
❏ 126	Hello Baby/Poor Girl I'm in Trouble	1966	2.50	5.00	10.00
❏ 134	You Can Depend on Me/Game of Love	1967	2.00	4.00	8.00
❏ 137	Oh, How It Hurts/Ain't Got Nobody	1967	2.00	4.00	8.00
❏ 140	Dedicated to the One I Love/Half a Love	1968	2.00	4.00	8.00
❏ 142	Half a Love/(I Can Feel Your Love) Slipping Away	1968	2.00	4.00	8.00
❏ 146	Don't Ever Go Away/I'm No Good for You	1968	2.00	4.00	8.00
❏ 148	Take It Easy/You Never Loved Me	1969	2.00	4.00	8.00
❏ 154	You Better Stop It/Happy Girl	1969	2.00	4.00	8.00
BUDDAH					
❏ 249	The Pow Pow Song (Sorry Sorry Baby)/Your Old Flame	1971	—	3.00	6.00
❏ 296	Bed and Board/Yes It's You	1972	—	2.50	5.00
❏ 319	Woman and Man/Who Will You Hurt Next	1972	—	2.50	5.00
❏ 331	Give Me Your Love/You Can Be with the One You Don't Love	1972	—	2.50	5.00
❏ 355	Yes I'm Ready/Who Will You Hurt Next	1973	—	2.50	5.00
❏ 375	Child of Tomorrow/Out of This World	1973	—	2.50	5.00
❏ 395	Caught in the Middle/Give Him Up	1973	—	2.50	5.00
❏ 405	World War III/I Miss You Gordon	1974	—	2.50	5.00
❏ 424	Our Day Will Come/Half Sister, Half Brother	1974	—	2.50	5.00
❏ 441	From His Woman to You/When You Wake Up in Georgia	1974	—	2.50	5.00
❏ 459	Shackin' Up/One Man Between Us	1975	—	2.50	5.00
❏ 481	Make It Last/We Got Each Other	1975	—	2.50	5.00
—With the Futures					
❏ 481 [PS]	Make It Last/We Got Each Other	1975	2.00	4.00	8.00
CRUSADER					
❏ 111	Dedicated to You/Trouble Child	1965	2.50	5.00	10.00
NATIONAL GENERAL					
❏ 005	Raindrops Keep Fallin' on My Head/If You Knew Him Like I Do	1970	—	3.00	6.00
PRELUDE					
❏ 71103	I Am Your Woman, She Is Your Wife/Take Me Tonight	1978	—	2.50	5.00
❏ 71111	Darling Come Back Home Soon/It Was You Boy	1978	—	2.50	5.00
WEST END					
❏ 1264	Another Man (Vocal) (Short)/Another Man (Instrumental)	1984	—	—	4.00
WMOT					
❏ 02506	She's Got the Papers (But I've Got the Man)/(Instrumental)	1981	—	2.00	4.00
❏ 5352	I'll Never Love the Same Way Twice/(B-side unknown)	1980	—	2.00	4.00
❏ 70077	On and Off/You're All Inside of Me	1981	—	2.00	4.00
Albums					
ARCTIC					
❏ ALP-1000 [M]	Yes, I'm Ready	1965	7.50	15.00	30.00
❏ ALPS-1000 [P]	Yes, I'm Ready	1965	12.50	25.00	50.00
❏ ALPS-1004	Oh, How It Hurts	1968	7.50	15.00	30.00
BUDDAH					
❏ BDS-5117	Give Me Your Love	1972	3.00	6.00	12.00
❏ BDS-5140	Lady Love	1973	3.00	6.00	12.00
❏ BDS-5610	Transition	1974	3.00	6.00	12.00
❏ BDS-5628	Love's the Thing	1975	3.00	6.00	12.00
NATIONAL GENERAL					
❏ 2001	If You Knew Him Like I Do	1970	7.50	15.00	30.00

MASON, BARBARA, AND BUNNY SIGLER Also see each artist's individual listings.
12-Inch Singles
CURTOM

Number	Title (A Side/B Side)	Yr	VG	VG+	NM
❏ PRO-A-689 [DJ]	Locked in This Position (10:05)/Love Song (6:14)	1977	3.75	7.50	15.00
Albums					
CURTOM					
❏ CU 5014	Locked in This Position	1977	2.50	5.00	10.00

MASON, BONNIE JO See CHER.

MASON, DAVE Also see FLEETWOOD MAC; DAVE MASON AND CASS ELLIOT; TRAFFIC.
12-Inch Singles
COLUMBIA

Number	Title (A Side/B Side)	Yr	VG	VG+	NM
❏ ASF 308 [DJ]	So High (same on both sides)	1977	3.00	6.00	12.00
MCA					
❏ L33-17468 [DJ]	Dreams I Dream (same on both sides)	1987	—	3.00	6.00
—With Phoebe Snow					
❏ L33-17541 [DJ]	Two Hearts (same on both sides)	1988	—	3.00	6.00
45s					
BLUE THUMB					
❏ 112	World and Changes/Can't Stop Worrying	1970	—	3.00	6.00

Number	Title (A Side/B Side)	Yr	VG	VG+	NM
❏ 114	Only You Know and I Know/				
	Sad and Deep As You	1970	—	3.00	6.00
❏ 205	A Heartache, a Shadow, a Lifetime/				
	Can't Stop Worrying	1972	—	3.00	6.00
❏ 209	To Be Free/Pearly Queen	1972	—	3.00	6.00
❏ 276	Only You Know and I Know/				
	Sad and Deep As You	1975	—	2.50	5.00
❏ 7117	Satin and Red Velvet Woman/Shouldn't Have				
	Took More Than You Gave	1971	—	3.00	6.00
❏ 7122	Just a Song/Waitin' on You	1971	—	3.00	6.00
CHUMLEY					
❏ 45-01	I Love the Music/In Love with You	1987	2.00	4.00	8.00
COLUMBIA					
❏ 10074	Bring it On Home to Me/Harmony and Melody	1974	—	2.50	5.00
❏ 10104	Every Woman/Relationships	1975	—	2.50	5.00
❏ 10162	Show Me Some Affection/Get a Hold on Love	1975	—	2.50	5.00
❏ 10246	Long Lost Friend/Split Coconut	1975	—	2.50	5.00
❏ 10469	All Along the Watchtower/Sad and Deep As You	1976	—	2.50	5.00
❏ 10509	So High (Rock Me Baby and Roll Me Away)/You				
	Just Have to Wait Now	1977		2.50	5.00
❏ 10575	We Just Disagree/Mystic Traveler	1977	—	2.50	5.00
❏ 10662	Let It Go, Let It Flow/Takin' the Time to Find	1978	—	2.50	5.00
❏ 10749	Will You Still Love Me Tomorrow/Mystic Traveler	1978	—	2.50	5.00
❏ 10819	Warm Desire/Don't It Make You Wonder	1978	—	2.50	5.00
❏ 11289	Save Me/Tryin' to Get Back to You	1980	—	2.00	4.00
❏ 45947	Baby... Please/Side-Tracked	1973	—	2.50	5.00
MCA					
❏ 53205	Dreams I Dream/Fighting for Love	1987	—	2.00	4.00
—A-side with Phoebe Snow					
❏ 53205 [PS]	Dreams I Dream/Fighting for Love	1987	—	2.00	4.00
Albums					
BLUE THUMB					
❏ BTS-19	Alone Together	1970	5.00	10.00	20.00
—Originals on multicolored vinyl					
❏ BTS-19	All Together	1970	50.00	100.00	200.00
—Erroneous pressing of "Alone Together"					
❏ BTS-19	Alone Together	1975	3.00	6.00	12.00
—Multicolor label with "ABC" logo					
❏ BTS-34	Headkeeper	1972	3.75	7.50	15.00
❏ BTS-54	Dave Mason Is Alive!	1973	3.75	7.50	15.00
❏ ABCD-880	Dave Mason At His Best	1975	2.50	5.00	10.00
❏ BT-6013	The Best of Dave Mason	1974	2.50	5.00	10.00
❏ BT-6032	Very Best of Dave Mason	1978	2.50	5.00	10.00
❏ BTS-8819	Alone Together	1971	12.50	25.00	50.00
—Capitol-distributed black vinyl reissue					
CHUMLEY					
❏ 00101	Some Assembly Required	1987	2.50	5.00	10.00
COLUMBIA					
❏ CQ 31721 [Q]	It's Like You Never Left	1973	4.50	9.00	18.00
❏ KC 31721	It's Like You Never Left	1973	2.50	5.00	10.00
❏ PC 31721	It's Like You Never Left	197?	2.00	4.00	8.00
—Reissue with new prefix					
❏ PC 33096	Dave Mason	1974	2.50	5.00	10.00
—No bar code on cover					
❏ PC 33096	Dave Mason	198?	2.00	4.00	8.00
—Budget-line reissue with bar code					
❏ PCQ 33096 [Q]	Dave Mason	1974	4.50	9.00	18.00
❏ PC 33698	Split Coconut	1975	2.50	5.00	10.00
❏ PCQ 33698 [Q]	Split Coconut	1975	4.50	9.00	18.00
❏ PG 34174 [(2)]	Certified Live	1976	3.00	6.00	12.00
❏ PC 34680	Let It Flow	1977	2.50	5.00	10.00
—No bar code on cover					
❏ PC 34680	Let It Flow	198?	2.00	4.00	8.00
—Budget-line reissue with bar code					
❏ JC 35285	Mariposa de Oro	1978	2.50	5.00	10.00
❏ JC 36144	Old Crest on a New Wave	1980	2.50	5.00	10.00
❏ FC 37089	The Best of Dave Mason	1981	2.50	5.00	10.00
❏ PC 37089	The Best of Dave Mason	1983	2.00	4.00	8.00
—Budget-line reissue					
MCA					
❏ 712	Headkeeper	198?	2.00	4.00	8.00
—Reissue of Blue Thumb 34					
❏ 713	Dave Mason Is Alive	198?	2.00	4.00	8.00
—Reissue of Blue Thumb 54					
❏ 714	Dave Mason At His Best	198?	2.00	4.00	8.00
—Reissue of Blue Thumb 880					
❏ 715	Very Best of Dave Mason	198?	2.00	4.00	8.00
—Reissue of Blue Thumb 6032					
❏ 800	The Best of Dave Mason	1981	2.00	4.00	8.00
—Reissue of Blue Thumb 6013					
❏ 11319	Alone Together	1995	5.00	10.00	20.00
—"Heavy Vinyl" gatefold reissue					
❏ 27035	Alone Together	198?	2.00	4.00	8.00
—Reissue of Blue Thumb 19					
❏ 42086	Two Hearts	1988	2.50	5.00	10.00

MASON, DAVE, AND CASS ELLIOT Also see each artist's individual listings.
45s
ABC DUNHILL

Number	Title (A Side/B Side)	Yr	VG	VG+	NM
❏ 4266	Something to Make You Happy/Next to You	1971	—	3.00	6.00
❏ 4271	Walking to the Point/				
	Too Much Truth, Too Much Love	1971	—	3.00	6.00
Albums					
BLUE THUMB					
❏ BTS-8825	Dave Mason and Cass Elliot	1971	5.00	10.00	20.00

MASON, EULIS
45s
BELLA

Number	Title (A Side/B Side)	Yr	VG	VG+	NM
❏ 20	Carol Lee/Rockin' Santa Claus	1959	10.00	20.00	40.00
—B-side by the Martels					

MASON, JACKIE
45s
VERVE

Number	Title (A Side/B Side)	Yr	VG	VG+	NM
❏ 10289	Don't Blame the Bossa Nova/I Gave My Love	1963	3.00	6.00	12.00

Albums
VERVE

Number	Title (A Side/B Side)	Yr	VG	VG+	NM
❏ V-15033 [M]	I'm the Greatest Comedian in the World Only				
	Nobody Knows It Yet	1962	5.00	10.00	20.00
❏ V-15034 [M]	I Want to Leave You with the				
	Words of a Great Comedian	1963	5.00	10.00	20.00
❏ V-15045 [M]	Great Moments in Comedy	1964	5.00	10.00	20.00
WARNER BROS.					
❏ 25603	The World According to Me!	1987	2.50	5.00	10.00

MASON PROFFIT
45s
AMPEX

Number	Title (A Side/B Side)	Yr	VG	VG+	NM
❏ 11048	Hope/Jewel	1971	—	3.00	6.00
HAPPY TIGER					
❏ 545	Voice of Change/A Rectangle Picture	1970	—	3.00	6.00
❏ 552	Two Hangmen/Sweet Lady of Love	1970	—	3.00	6.00
❏ 570	Hard Luck Woman/Good Friend of Mary's	1971	—	3.00	6.00
WARNER BROS.					
❏ 7709	I Saw the Light/Lilly	1973	—	2.50	5.00
Albums					
AMPEX					
❏ A-10138	Last Night I Had the Strangest Dream	1971	3.00	6.00	12.00
HAPPY TIGER					
❏ HT-1009	Wanted! Mason Proffit	1970	3.75	7.50	15.00
❏ HT-1019	Movin' Toward Happiness	1971	3.75	7.50	15.00
WARNER BROS.					
❏ BS 2657	Rockfish Crossing	1972	2.50	5.00	10.00
❏ BS 2704	Bareback Rider	1973	2.50	5.00	10.00
❏ 2WS 2746 [(2)]	Come and Gone	1974	3.00	6.00	12.00

MASONICS, THE
45s
INTERPHON

Number	Title (A Side/B Side)	Yr	VG	VG+	NM
❏ 7714	Mariner II/Call It a Day	1965	2.50	5.00	10.00

MASQUERADERS, THE
45s
SOULTOWN

Number	Title (A Side/B Side)	Yr	VG	VG+	NM
❏ 201	That's the Same Thing/(B-side unknown)	196?	—	—	1500.

MASTER-TONES, THE
45s
BRUCE

Number	Title (A Side/B Side)	Yr	VG	VG+	NM
❏ 111	What'll You Do/Tell Me	1954	75.00	150.00	300.00
—Blue vinyl					
❏ 111	What'll You Do/Tell Me	1954	125.00	250.00	500.00
—Black vinyl, "New York 19, N.Y." address					
❏ 111	What'll You Do/Tell Me	1962	12.50	25.00	50.00
—Black vinyl, "New York, N.Y." address					
LOST-NITE					
❏ 396	What'll You Do/Tell Me	197?	—	3.00	6.00
—Reissue					

MASTERETTES, THE
45s
LE SAGE

Number	Title (A Side/B Side)	Yr	VG	VG+	NM
❏ 716	Never Ever/Follow the Leader	1961	37.50	75.00	150.00

MASTERS, JOHNNY; MASTRO, JOHNNY See JOHNNY MAESTRO.

MASTERS, KEN
45s
DECCA

Number	Title (A Side/B Side)	Yr	VG	VG+	NM
❏ 31084	Too Late/Parting Hour	1960	5.00	10.00	20.00

MATADORS, THE (1)
45s
CHART MAKER

Number	Title (A Side/B Side)	Yr	VG	VG+	NM
❏ 404	Let Me Dream/Wiggle Wobble	1966	37.50	75.00	150.00
FORBES					
❏ 230	Let Me Dream/Wiggle Wobble	1966	6.25	12.50	25.00

MATADORS, THE (2)
45s
COLPIX

Number	Title (A Side/B Side)	Yr	VG	VG+	NM
❏ 698	Ace of Hearts/Perfidia	1963	6.25	12.50	25.00
❏ 718	I've Gotta Drive/La Corrida	1963	12.50	25.00	50.00
—A-side is a Jan and Dean track with a new spoken introduction					
❏ 741	C'mon, Let Yourself Go (Part 1)/C'mon, Let				
	Yourself Go (Part 2)	1964	6.25	12.50	25.00

MATADORS, THE (3)
45s
KEITH

Number	Title (A Side/B Side)	Yr	VG	VG+	NM
❏ 6502	If You Left Me Today/It Ain't Nothin' But Rock 'N'				
	Roll	1962	10.00	20.00	40.00
❏ 6504	You'd Be Crying, Too/My Foolish Heart	1963	20.00	40.00	80.00

MATADORS, THE (4)
45s
SUE

Number	Title (A Side/B Side)	Yr	VG	VG+	NM
❏ 700	Pennies from Heaven/Vengeance	1957	30.00	60.00	120.00
❏ 701	Be Good to Me/Have Mercy Baby	1957	20.00	40.00	80.00

MATADORS, THE (U) Could be group (2) or (3).
45s
JAMIE

Number	Title (A Side/B Side)	Yr	VG	VG+	NM
❏ 1226	Listen/So Near	1962	5.00	10.00	20.00

MATHERS, JERRY Better known as "The Beaver."
45s
ATLANTIC

Number	Title (A Side/B Side)	Yr	VG	VG+	NM
❏ 2156	Don'tcha Cry/Wind-Up Toy	1962	5.00	10.00	20.00
❏ 2156 [PS]	Don'tcha Cry/Wind-Up Toy	1962	10.00	20.00	40.00

M

Number	Title (A Side/B Side)	Yr	VG	VG+	NM

MATHIS, BOBBY, AND THE SEVILLES
45s
SIOUX

Number	Title (A Side/B Side)	Yr	VG	VG+	NM
☐ 51860	Girl in the Drugstore/Going to the City	1960	37.50	75.00	150.00

MATHIS, JOHNNY
12-Inch Singles
COLUMBIA

Number	Title (A Side/B Side)	Yr	VG	VG+	NM
☐ CAS 1400 [DJ]	Daydreamin' (same on both sides)	1988	2.50	5.00	10.00
☐ CAS 1805 [DJ]	In the Still of the Night (same on both sides)	1989	2.50	5.00	10.00
—With Take 6					
☐ AS 1867 [DJ]	Simple (Vocal Version 5:55)/(Instrumental)	1984	2.50	5.00	10.00
☐ 38-05034	Simple/(Instrumental)	1984	—	3.00	6.00
☐ 38-07837	Begin the Beguine/Simple	198?	—	3.00	6.00
—"Mixed Masters" reissue					
☐ CAS 8322 [DJ]	Let Your Heart Remember/(Dub Mix)	199?	2.50	5.00	10.00
☐ 23-11002	Begin the Beguine (Thompson Disco Remix 8:28)/Gone, Gone, Gone (Luongo Disco Remix 6:30)	1979	3.75	7.50	15.00

45s
COLUMBIA

Number	Title (A Side/B Side)	Yr	VG	VG+	NM
☐ (no #) [DJ]	Columbia Records Presents Johnny Mathis — Take 2	1957	7.50	15.00	30.00
—Promo-only gatefold sleeve containing white-label promos of 40784 and 40851					
☐ SS-7 [S]	The Best of Everything/The Theme from "A Summer Place"	1960	3.75	7.50	15.00
—B-side by Percy Faith; "Stereo Seven" single, small hole, plays at 33 1/3 rpm					
☐ AS 93 [DJ]	The Heart of a Woman (same on both sides)	1974	2.50	5.00	10.00
—Promo release for the Helena Rubenstein cosmetics firm					
☐ AS 93 [PS]	Helena Rubenstein Presents Johnny Mathis for Courant	1974	3.75	7.50	15.00
—Promo sleeve with above single					
☐ AE7 1148 [DJ]	Christmas Is/Sleigh Ride	1977	2.00	4.00	8.00
☐ AE7 1148 [PS]	Christmas Is/Sleigh Ride	1977	3.00	6.00	12.00
—Above single and sleeve were the 1977 Christmas Seals record					
☐ 18-02194	Nothing Between Us But Love/Deep Purple	1981	—	—	3.00
☐ 38-03222	When the Lovin' Goes Out of the Lovin'/Warm	1982	—	—	3.00
☐ 38-04468	Simple/Lead Me to Your Love	1984	—	—	3.00
☐ 38-04856	Right From the Heart/Hold On	1985	—	—	3.00
☐ 38-05588	Just One Touch/I Need You (The Journey)	1985	—	—	3.00
☐ 38-06561	Where Can I Find Christmas?/It's Beginning to Look a Lot Like Christmas	1986	—	2.00	4.00
☐ 38-07797	I'm on the Outside Looking In/Just Like You	1988	—	—	3.00
☐ 38-08524	Daydreamin'/Love Brought Us Here Tonight	1988	—	—	3.00
☐ 10080	Sail On White Moon/The Heart of a Woman	1974	—	2.50	5.00
☐ 10112	I'm Stone in Love with You/Foolish	1975	—	2.50	5.00
☐ 10175	The Greatest Gift/You're As Right As Rain	1975	—	2.50	5.00
☐ 10250	Stardust/What I Did for Love	1975	—	2.50	5.00
☐ 3-10291	One Day in Your Life/Midnight Blue	1976	—	2.50	5.00
☐ 3-10350	Yellow Roses on Her Gown/Every Time You Touch Me (I Get High)	1976	—	2.50	5.00
☐ 3-10404	Do Me Wrong, But Do Me/Send In the Clowns	1976	—	2.50	5.00
☐ 3-10447	When a Child Is Born/Turn the Lights Down	1976	—	2.50	5.00
☐ 3-10496	Loving You, Losing You/World of Laughter	1977	—	2.50	5.00
☐ 3-10574	Arianne/99 Miles from L.A.	1977	—	2.50	5.00
☐ 3-10611	Hold Me, Thrill Me, Kiss Me/The Most Beautiful Girl	1977	—	2.50	5.00
☐ 3-10640	When a Child Is Born/Every Time You Touch Me (I Get High)	1977	—	2.50	5.00
☐ 3-10902	The Last Time I Felt Like This/As Time Goes By	1979	—	2.00	4.00
—A-side with Jane Olivor					
☐ 3-11001	Begin the Beguine/Gone, Gone, Gone	1979	—	2.00	4.00
☐ 1-11091	No One Else But the One You Love/To the Ends of the Earth	1979	—	2.00	4.00
—A-side with Stephanie Lawrence					
☐ 1-11158	Christmas in the City of the Angels/The Very First Christmas Day	1979	—	2.50	5.00
☐ 1-11313	Different Kinda Different/The Lights of Rio	1980	—	2.00	4.00
—A-side with Paulette					
☐ 11-11409	When a Child Is Born/The Lord's Prayer	1980	—	2.00	4.00
—With Gladys Knight and the Pips					
☐ 30355 [S]	Someone/Very Much in Love	1959	5.00	10.00	20.00
—"Stereo Seven" single, small hole, plays at 33 1/3 rpm					
☐ 30410 [S]	Small World/You Are Everything to Me	1959	5.00	10.00	20.00
—"Stereo Seven" single, small hole, plays at 33 1/3 rpm					
☐ 30483 [S]	Misty/The Story of Our Love	1959	5.00	10.00	20.00
—"Stereo Seven" single, small hole, plays at 33 1/3 rpm					
☐ 30583 [S]	The Best of Everything/Cherie	1959	5.00	10.00	20.00
—"Stereo Seven" single, small hole, plays at 33 1/3 rpm					
☐ 30598 [S]	Heavenly/Hello, Young Lovers	1959	3.75	7.50	15.00
—"Stereo Seven" single, small hole, plays at 33 1/3 rpm					
☐ 30599 [S]	Misty/Stranger in Paradise	1959	3.75	7.50	15.00
—"Stereo Seven" single, small hole, plays at 33 1/3 rpm					
☐ 30600 [S]	Tonight/Maria	1959	3.75	7.50	15.00
—"Stereo Seven" single, small hole, plays at 33 1/3 rpm					
☐ 30601 [S]	Secret Love/And This Is My Beloved	1959	3.75	7.50	15.00
—"Stereo Seven" single, small hole, plays at 33 1/3 rpm					
☐ 30684 [S]	Maria/Hey Love	1960	3.75	7.50	15.00
—"Stereo Seven" single, small hole, plays at 33 1/3 rpm					
☐ 30764 [S]	My Love for You/Oh That Feeling	1960	3.75	7.50	15.00
—"Stereo Seven" single, small hole, plays at 33 1/3 rpm					
☐ S7 30828 [S]	Everything's Coming Up Roses/I Wish I Were in Love Again	1960	3.00	6.00	12.00
☐ S7 30829 [S]	You Do Something To Me/Let's Misbehave	1960	3.00	6.00	12.00
☐ S7 30830 [S]	I Could Have Danced All Night/A Cock-Eyed Optimist	1960	3.00	6.00	12.00
☐ S7 30831 [S]	I Just Found Out About Love/Let's Do It	1960	3.00	6.00	12.00
☐ S7 30832 [S]	I Am in Love/Love Eyes	1960	3.00	6.00	12.00
—The above five are "Stereo Seven" 33 1/3 rpm jukebox singles from set "JS7-9" entitled "The Rhythms and Ballads of Broadway"					
☐ 30866 [S]	How to Handle a Woman/While You're Young	1960	3.75	7.50	15.00
—"Stereo Seven" single, small hole, plays at 33 1/3 rpm					
☐ 30980 [S]	You Set My Heart to Music/Jenny	1961	3.75	7.50	15.00
—"Stereo Seven" single, small hole, plays at 33 1/3 rpm					
☐ 31048 [S]	Laurie, My Love/Should I Wait	1961	3.75	7.50	15.00
—"Stereo Seven" single, small hole, plays at 33 1/3 rpm					
☐ 31238 [S]	Christmas Eve/My Kind of Christmas	1961	6.25	12.50	25.00
—"Stereo Seven" single, small hole, plays at 33 1/3 rpm					
☐ 31261 [S]	Sweet Thursday/One Look	1962	5.00	10.00	20.00
—"Stereo Seven" single, small hole, plays at 33 1/3 rpm					
☐ S7 31344 [S]	Live It Up/Just Friends	1962	3.00	6.00	12.00
☐ S7 31345 [S]	Why Not/On a Cold and Rainy Day	1962	3.00	6.00	12.00
☐ S7 31346 [S]	I Won't Dance/Johnny One Note	1962	3.00	6.00	12.00
☐ S7 31347 [S]	Crazy in the Heart/Too Much Too Soon	1962	3.00	6.00	12.00
☐ S7 31348 [S]	Hey Look Me Over/Love	1962	3.00	6.00	12.00
—The above five are "Stereo Seven" 33 1/3 rpm jukebox singles from set "JS7-47" entitled "Live It Up!"					
☐ 31420 [S]	Marianna/Unaccustomed As I Am	1962	5.00	10.00	20.00
—"Stereo Seven" single, small hole, plays at 33 1/3 rpm					
☐ 31509 [S]	That's the Way It Is/I'll Never Be Lonely Again	1962	5.00	10.00	20.00
—"Stereo Seven" single, small hole, plays at 33 1/3 rpm					
☐ 31582 [S]	Gina/I Love Her That's Why	1962	5.00	10.00	20.00
—"Stereo Seven" single, small hole, plays at 33 1/3 rpm					
☐ 31666 [S]	What Will Mary Say/Quiet Girl	1963	6.25	12.50	25.00
—"Stereo Seven" single, small hole, plays at 33 1/3 rpm					
☐ 31666 [S]	What Will My Mary Say/Quiet Girl	1963	6.25	12.50	25.00
—"Stereo Seven" single, small hole, plays at 33 1/3 rpm; revised A-side title					
☐ S7 31731 [S]	Rapture/Love Me As Though There Were No Tomorrow	1963	3.00	6.00	12.00
☐ S7 31732 [S]	Moments Like This/You've Come Home	1963	3.00	6.00	12.00
☐ S7 31733 [S]	Here I'll Stay/My Darling, My Darling	1963	3.00	6.00	12.00
☐ S7 31734 [S]	Stars Fell on Alabama/I Was Telling Her About You	1963	3.00	6.00	12.00
☐ S7 31735 [S]	Lost in Loveliness/Stella by Starlight	1963	3.00	6.00	12.00
—The above five are "Stereo Seven" 33 1/3 rpm jukebox singles from "JS7-76" entitled "Rapture"					
☐ 31799 [S]	Every Step of the Way/No Man Can Stand Alone	1963	3.75	7.50	15.00
—"Stereo Seven" single, small hole, plays at 33 1/3 rpm					
☐ 31836 [S]	Sooner or Later/In Wisconsin	1963	3.75	7.50	15.00
—"Stereo Seven" single, small hole, plays at 33 1/3 rpm					
☐ 31916 [S]	I'll Search My Heart/All the Sad Young Men	1963	3.75	7.50	15.00
—"Stereo Seven" single, small hole, plays at 33 1/3 rpm					
☐ 33001	It's Not for Me to Say/Chances Are	196?	—	3.00	6.00
—Red label					
☐ 33001	It's Not for Me to Say/Chances Are	198?	—	—	3.00
—Gray label					
☐ 3-33001	It's Not for Me to Say/Chances Are	196?	3.75	7.50	15.00
—"Hall of Fame Series"; "Columbia Single 33"; small hole					
☐ 33042	Maria/Misty	196?	—	3.00	6.00
—Red label					
☐ 33042	Maria/Misty	198?	—	—	3.00
—Gray label					
☐ 33048	Wonderful, Wonderful/The Twelfth of Never	196?	—	3.00	6.00
—Red label					
☐ 33048	Wonderful, Wonderful/The Twelfth of Never	198?	—	—	3.00
—Gray label					
☐ 33056	Small World/A Certain Smile	196?	—	3.00	6.00
—Red label					
☐ 33056	Small World/A Certain Smile	198?	—	—	3.00
—Gray label					
☐ 33142	Venus/Gina	196?	—	3.00	6.00
—Red label					
☐ 33142	Venus/Gina	198?	—	—	3.00
—Gray label					
☐ 33174	I'll Never Fall in Love Again/A Time for Us	197?	—	2.00	4.00
—Red label					
☐ 33174	I'll Never Fall in Love Again/A Time for Us	198?	—	—	3.00
—Gray label					
☐ 33226	What Will My Mary Say/Call Me	197?	—	2.00	4.00
—Red label					
☐ 33226	What Will My Mary Say/Call Me	198?	—	—	3.00
—Gray label					
☐ 33253	Show and Tell/Soul and Inspiration-Just Once in My Life	197?	—	2.00	4.00
—Red label					
☐ 33253	Show and Tell/Soul and Inspiration-Just Once in My Life	198?	—	—	3.00
—Gray label					
☐ 33264	I'm Coming Home/I'm Stone in Love with You	197?	—	2.00	4.00
—Red label					
☐ 33264	I'm Coming Home/I'm Stone in Love with You	198?	—	—	3.00
—Gray label					
☐ JZSP 39330 [DJ]	In Other Words (Complete Version)/In Other Words (Short Version)	1956	6.25	12.50	25.00
—Promo only, possibly his first single. Came with a "Columbia Records Introduces" sleeve, the presence of which doubles the value					
☐ 40784	Wonderful! Wonderful!/When Sunny Gets Blue	1956	3.00	6.00	12.00
☐ 40851	It's Not for Me to Say/Warm and Tender	1957	3.00	6.00	12.00
☐ 40993	Chances Are/The Twelfth of Never	1957	2.50	5.00	10.00
☐ 40993 [PS]	Chances Are/The Twelfth of Never	1957	5.00	10.00	20.00
☐ 41060	No Love (But Your Love)/Wild Is the Wind	1957	2.50	5.00	10.00
☐ 41060 [PS]	No Love (But Your Love)/Wild Is the Wind	1957	3.75	7.50	15.00
☐ 41082	Come to Me/When I Am With You	1957	2.50	5.00	10.00
☐ 41152	All the Time/Teacher, Teacher	1958	2.50	5.00	10.00
☐ 41193	A Certain Smile/Let It Rain	1958	2.50	5.00	10.00
☐ 41193 [PS]	A Certain Smile/Let It Rain	1958	3.75	7.50	15.00
☐ 41253	Call Me/Stairway to the Sea	1958	2.50	5.00	10.00
☐ 41253 [PS]	Call Me/Stairway to the Sea	1958	3.75	7.50	15.00
☐ 41304	Let's Love/You Are Beautiful	1958	2.50	5.00	10.00
☐ 41355	Someone/Very Much in Love	1959	2.50	5.00	10.00
☐ 41410	Small World/You Are Everything to Me	1959	2.50	5.00	10.00
☐ 41483	Misty/The Story of Our Love	1959	2.50	5.00	10.00
☐ 41483 [PS]	Misty/The Story of Our Love	1959	3.75	7.50	15.00
☐ 41491	The Best of Everything/Cherie	1959	2.50	5.00	10.00
☐ 41491 [PS]	The Best of Everything/Cherie	1959	3.75	7.50	15.00
☐ 41583	Starbright/All Is Well	1960	2.00	4.00	8.00
☐ 41583 [PS]	Starbright/All Is Well	1960	3.00	6.00	12.00
☐ 41684	Maria/Hey Love	1960	2.00	4.00	8.00
—Reissued in 1961 with the same catalog number					
☐ 41764	My Love for You/Oh That Feeling	1960	2.00	4.00	8.00
☐ 3-41764	My Love for You/Oh That Feeling	1960	3.75	7.50	15.00
—"Columbia Single 33"; small hole					
☐ 41866 [PS]	How to Handle a Woman/While You're Young	1960	3.00	6.00	12.00
☐ 41866	How to Handle a Woman/While You're Young	1960	2.00	4.00	8.00

Number	Title (A Side/B Side)	Yr	VG	VG+	NM
❏ 3-41866	How to Handle a Woman/While You're Young	1960	3.75	7.50	15.00
—"Columbia Single 33"; small hole					
❏ 41980 [PS]	You Set My Heart to Music/Jenny	1961	3.00	6.00	12.00
❏ 41980	You Set My Heart to Music/Jenny	1961	2.00	4.00	8.00
❏ 3-41980	You Set My Heart to Music/Jenny	1961	3.75	7.50	15.00
—"Columbia Single 33"; small hole					
❏ 42005	Should I Wait/Oh How I Try	1961	—	—	—
—Unreleased?					
❏ 3-42005	Should I Wait/Oh How I Try	1961	—	—	—
—Unreleased?					
❏ 42048 [PS]	Laurie My Love/Should I Wait (Or Should I Run to Her)	1961	3.00	6.00	12.00
❏ 42048	Laurie My Love/Should I Wait (Or Should I Run to Her)	1961	2.00	4.00	8.00
❏ 3-42048	Laurie My Love/Should I Wait (Or Should I Run to Her)	1961	3.75	7.50	15.00
—"Columbia Single 33"; small hole					
❏ 42156 [PS]	Wasn't the Summer Short/There You Are	1961	3.00	6.00	12.00
❏ 42156	Wasn't the Summer Short/There You Are	1961	2.00	4.00	8.00
❏ 3-42156	Wasn't the Summer Short/There You Are	1961	3.75	7.50	15.00
—"Columbia Single 33"; small hole					
❏ 42238 [PS]	My Kind of Christmas/Christmas Eve	1961	5.00	10.00	20.00
❏ 42238	My Kind of Christmas/Christmas Eve	1961	3.00	6.00	12.00
❏ 3-42238	My Kind of Christmas/Christmas Eve	1961	5.00	10.00	20.00
—"Columbia Single 33"; small hole					
❏ 42261 [PS]	Sweet Thursday/One Look	1962	3.00	6.00	12.00
❏ 42261	Sweet Thursday/One Look	1962	2.00	4.00	8.00
❏ 3-42261	Sweet Thursday/One Look	1962	3.75	7.50	15.00
—"Columbia Single 33"; small hole					
❏ 42420 [PS]	Marianna/Unaccustomed As I Am	1962	3.00	6.00	12.00
❏ 42420	Marianna/Unaccustomed As I Am	1962	2.00	4.00	8.00
❏ 3-42420	Marianna/Unaccustomed As I Am	1962	3.75	7.50	15.00
—"Columbia Single 33"; small hole					
❏ 42509 [PS]	That's the Way It Is/I'll Never Be Lonely Again	1962	2.50	5.00	10.00
❏ 42509	That's the Way It Is/I'll Never Be Lonely Again	1962	2.00	4.00	8.00
❏ 3-42509	That's the Way It Is/I'll Never Be Lonely Again	1962	3.75	7.50	15.00
—"Columbia Single 33"; small hole					
❏ 42582 [DJ]	Gina (same on both sides)	1962	5.00	10.00	20.00
—Promo only on red vinyl					
❏ 42582 [PS]	Gina/I Love Her That's Why	1962	2.50	5.00	10.00
❏ 42582	Gina/I Love Her That's Why	1962	2.00	4.00	8.00
❏ 3-42582	Gina/I Love Her That's Why	1962	3.75	7.50	15.00
—"Columbia Single 33"; small hole					
❏ 42666 [DJ]	What Will My Mary Say (same on both sides)	1963	5.00	10.00	20.00
—Promo only on red vinyl					
❏ 42666 [PS]	What Will Mary Say/Quiet Girl	1963	3.00	6.00	12.00
❏ 42666	What Will Mary Say/Quiet Girl	1963	2.00	4.00	8.00
—Revised A-side title					
❏ 42666	What Will My Mary Say/Quiet Girl	1963	2.50	5.00	10.00
❏ 3-42666	What Will My Mary Say/Quiet Girl	1963	3.75	7.50	15.00
—"Columbia Single 33"; small hole; revised A-side title					
❏ 3-42666	What Will Mary Say/Quiet Girl	1963	5.00	10.00	20.00
—"Columbia Single 33"; small hole					
❏ 42799 [PS]	Every Step of the Way/No Man Can Stand Alone	1963	2.50	5.00	10.00
❏ 42799	Every Step of the Way/No Man Can Stand Alone	1963	2.00	4.00	8.00
❏ 3-42799	Every Step of the Way/No Man Can Stand Alone	1963	5.00	10.00	20.00
—"Columbia Single 33"; small hole					
❏ 42836	Sooner or Later/In Wisconsin	1963	2.00	4.00	8.00
❏ 3-42836	Sooner or Later/In Wisconsin	1963	5.00	10.00	20.00
—"Columbia Single 33"; small hole					
❏ 42916	I'll Search My Heart/All the Sad Young Men	1963	2.00	4.00	8.00
❏ 42916 [DJ]	I'll Search My Heart (same on both sides)	1963	5.00	10.00	20.00
—Promo only on red vinyl					
❏ 44266	Misty Roses/Don't Talk to Me	1967	—	2.50	5.00
❏ 44357	Among the First to Know/Long Winter Nights	1967	—	2.50	5.00
❏ 44517	Venus/Don't Go Breakin' My Heart	1968	—	2.50	5.00
❏ 44637	You Make Me Think About You/Night Dreams	1968	—	2.50	5.00
❏ 44728	The End of the World/The 59th Street Bridge Song (Feelin' Groovy)	1968	—	2.50	5.00
❏ 44837	I'll Never Fall in Love Again/Whoever You Are, I Love You	1969	—	2.50	5.00
❏ 44915	Love Theme from Romeo and Juliet (A Time for Us)/The World I Threw Away	1969	—	2.50	5.00
❏ JZSP 44991 [DJ]	The Christmas Song (Merry Christmas to You)/What Child Is This?	1958	5.00	10.00	20.00
❏ 45022	Midnight Cowboy/We	1969	—	2.50	5.00
❏ 45035	Give Me Your Love for Christmas/Calypso Noel	1969	—	3.00	6.00
❏ 45035 [PS]	Give Me Your Love for Christmas/Calypso Noel	1969	2.00	4.00	8.00
❏ 45100 [DJ]	Give Me Your Love for Christmas/Calypso Noel	1969	2.00	4.00	8.00
❏ 45100 [PS]	Give Me Your Love for Christmas/Calypso Noel	1969	2.50	5.00	10.00
—The above sleeve and record were the 1969 Christmas Seals promo					
❏ 45104	For All We Know/Odds and Ends	1970	—	2.50	5.00
❏ 45183	The Last Time I Saw Her/Wherefore and Why	1970	—	2.50	5.00
❏ 45223	Darling Lili/Pieces of Dreams	1970	—	2.50	5.00
❏ 45263	Until It's Time for You to Go/Evil Ways	1970	—	2.50	5.00
❏ JZSP 45265 [DJ]	An Open Fire/I Concentrate on You	1959	5.00	10.00	20.00
❏ 45281	Christmas Is/Sign of the Dove	1970	—	2.50	5.00
❏ 45323	I Was There/Ten Times Forever More	1971	—	2.50	5.00
❏ 45371	Evie/Think About Things	1971	—	2.50	5.00
❏ 45415	Long Ago and Far Away/For All We Know	1971	—	2.50	5.00
❏ 45470	How Can You Mend a Broken Heart/If We Only Have Love	1971	—	2.50	5.00
❏ 45513	Christmas Is/Sign of the Dove	1971	—	2.50	5.00
❏ 45559	If We Only Have Love/This Way, Mary	1972	—	2.50	5.00
❏ 45635	Make It Easy on Yourself/Sometimes	1972	—	2.50	5.00
❏ 45729	Soul and Inspiration-Just Once in My Life/I	1972	—	2.50	5.00
❏ 45777	Walking Tall (Theme)/Take Good Care of Her	1973	—	2.50	5.00
❏ 45835	Show and Tell/Happy (Theme from Lady Sings the Blues)	1973	—	2.50	5.00
❏ 45908	I'm Coming Home/Stop, Look, and Listen to Your Heart	1973	—	2.50	5.00
❏ 45975	Life Is a Song Worth Singing/I Just Wanted to Be Me	1973	—	2.50	5.00
❏ 46048	I'm Stone in Love with You/Sweet Child	1974	—	2.50	5.00
❏ JZSP 55369 [DJ]	Maria/Tonight	1959	5.00	10.00	20.00
❏ 38-69092	In the Still of the Night/True Love Ways	1989	—	2.00	4.00
—A-side with Take 6					

Number	Title (A Side/B Side)	Yr	VG	VG+	NM
MERCURY					
❏ DJ-72 [DJ]	Chim Chim Cheree (same on both sides?)	1964	3.75	7.50	15.00
❏ 72184	Come Back/Your Teenage Dreams	1963	—	3.00	6.00
❏ 72184 [PS]	Come Back/Your Teenage Dreams	1963	2.50	5.00	10.00
❏ 72217	The Little Drummer Boy/Have Reindeer, Will Travel	1963	2.50	5.00	10.00
❏ 72217 [PS]	The Little Drummer Boy/Have Reindeer, Will Travel	1963	5.00	10.00	20.00
❏ 72229	Bye Bye Barbara/A Great Night for Cryin'	1964	—	3.00	6.00
❏ 72229 [PS]	Bye Bye Barbara/A Great Night for Cryin'	1964	2.50	5.00	10.00
❏ 72263	No More/The Fall of Love	1964	—	3.00	6.00
❏ 72287	Taste of Tears/White Roses from a Blue Valentine	1964	—	3.00	6.00
❏ 72339	Listen Lonely Girl/All I Wanted	1964	—	3.00	6.00
❏ 72339 [PS]	Listen Lonely Girl/All I Wanted	1964	2.50	5.00	10.00
❏ 72432	Dianacita/Take the Time	1965	—	3.00	6.00
❏ 72432 [PS]	Dianacita/Take the Time	1965	2.50	5.00	10.00
❏ 72464	Mirage/The Sweetheart Tree	1965	—	3.00	6.00
❏ 72464 [PS]	Mirage/The Sweetheart Tree	1965	2.50	5.00	10.00
❏ 72493	On a Clear Day You Can See Forever/Come Back to Me	1965	—	3.00	6.00
❏ 72539	Moment to Moment/Glass Mountain	1966	—	3.00	6.00
❏ 72568	The Shadow of Your Smile (Love Theme from "The Sandpiper")/The Sweetheart Tree	1966	—	3.00	6.00
❏ 72610	The Impossible Dream/So Nice	1966	—	3.00	6.00
❏ 72610 [PS]	The Impossible Dream/So Nice	1966	2.50	5.00	10.00
❏ 72653	Saturday Sunshine/Two Tickets and a Candy Heart	1967	—	3.00	6.00
❏ 72653 [PS]	Saturday Sunshine/Two Tickets and a Candy Heart	1967	2.50	5.00	10.00
7-Inch Extended Plays					
COLUMBIA					
❏ B-2129	*It's Not for Me to Say/Warm and Tender/Wonderful, Wonderful/Babalu	1957	3.75	7.50	15.00
❏ B-2129 [PS]	Songs from "Lizzie" and Other Favorites	1957	3.75	7.50	15.00
❏ B-2143	*Come to Me/Wild Is the Wind/No Love/When I Am with You	1957	3.75	7.50	15.00
❏ B-2143 [PS]	Johnny Mathis Sings	1957	3.75	7.50	15.00
❏ B-2537	The Twelfth of Never/Chances Are//Wonderful, Wonderful/It's Not for Me to Say	1959	3.00	6.00	12.00
❏ B-2537 [PS]	Johnny Mathis (Hall of Fame Series)	1959	3.00	6.00	12.00
❏ B-2626	*Call Me/A Certain Smile/All the Time/When Sunny Gets Blue	195?	3.00	6.00	12.00
❏ B-2626 [PS]	Johnny Mathis (Hall of Fame Series)	195?	3.00	6.00	12.00
❏ B-2640	*Come to Me/Wild Is the Wind/Someone/You Are Beautiful	195?	3.00	6.00	12.00
❏ B-2640 [PS]	Johnny Mathis (Hall of Fame Series)	195?	3.00	6.00	12.00
❏ B-8871	*Autumn in Rome/Love, Your Magic Spell Is Everywhere/Cabin in the Sky/In Other Words	1957	3.75	7.50	15.00
❏ B-8871 [PS]	Johnny Mathis, Vol. 1	1957	3.75	7.50	15.00
❏ B-8872	*Caravan/Star Eyes/It Might As Well Be Spring/Street of Dreams	1957	3.75	7.50	15.00
❏ B-8872 [PS]	Johnny Mathis, Vol. 2	1957	3.75	7.50	15.00
❏ B-8873	*Easy to Love/Prelude to a Kiss/Babalu/Angel Eyes	1957	3.75	7.50	15.00
❏ B-8873 [PS]	Johnny Mathis, Vol. 3	1957	3.75	7.50	15.00
❏ B-10281	Will I Find My Love Today/Looking at You//Let Me Love You/All Through the Night	1957	3.00	6.00	12.00
❏ B-10281 [PS]	Looking at You	1957	3.00	6.00	12.00
—Same contents, different title					
❏ B-10281 [PS]	Will I Find My Love Today	1957	3.00	6.00	12.00
❏ B-10282	*It Could Happen to You/That Old Black Magic/Too Close for Comfort/In the Wee Small Hours of the Morning	1957	3.00	6.00	12.00
❏ B-10282 [PS]	Too Close for Comfort	1957	3.00	6.00	12.00
❏ B-10283	*Year After Year/Early Autumn/You Stepped Out of a Dream/Day In, Day Out	1957	3.00	6.00	12.00
❏ B-10283 [PS]	Day In, Day Out	1957	3.00	6.00	12.00
❏ B-10781	Warm/A Handful of Stars//My One and Only Love/While We're Young	1958	3.00	6.00	12.00
❏ B-10781 [PS]	Warm, Vol. 1	1958	3.00	6.00	12.00
❏ B-10782	*By Myself/I've Grown Accustomed to Her Face/Baby, Baby, Baby/What'll I Do	1958	3.00	6.00	12.00
❏ B-10782 [PS]	Warm, Vol. 2	1958	3.00	6.00	12.00
❏ B-10783	*I'm Glad There Is You/The Lovely Things You Do/There Goes My Heart/Then I'll Be Tired of You	1958	3.00	6.00	12.00
❏ B-10783 [PS]	Warm, Vol. 3	1958	3.00	6.00	12.00
❏ B-11191	*Good Night, Dear Lord/I Heard a Forest Praying/Deep River/Swing Low, Sweet Chariot	1958	2.50	5.00	10.00
❏ B-11191 [PS]	Good Night, Dear Lord	1958	2.50	5.00	10.00
❏ B-11192	*Eli Eli/Kol Nidre/Where Can I Go?/One God	1958	2.50	5.00	10.00
❏ B-11192 [PS]	Eli Eli	1958	2.50	5.00	10.00
❏ B-11193	*Ave Maria (Bach-Gounod)/The Rosary/May the Good Lord Bless and Keep You/Ave Maria (Schubert)	1958	2.50	5.00	10.00
❏ B-11193 [PS]	Ave Maria	1958	2.50	5.00	10.00
❏ B-11651	To Be in Love/You'd Be So Nice to Come Home To//It's De-Lovely/I've Got the World on a String	1958	3.00	6.00	12.00
❏ B-11651 [PS]	Swing Softly, Vol. 1	1958	3.00	6.00	12.00
❏ B-11652	*Sweet Lorraine/Can't Get Out of This Mood/You Hit the Spot/Get Me to the Church on Time	1958	3.00	6.00	12.00
❏ B-11652 [PS]	Swing Softly, Vol. 2	1958	3.00	6.00	12.00
❏ B-11653	*Love Walked In/Easy to Say/This Heart of Mine/Like Someone in Love	1958	3.00	6.00	12.00
❏ B-11653 [PS]	Swing Softly, Vol. 3	1958	3.00	6.00	12.00
❏ B-11951	Winter Wonderland/Blue Christmas//White Christmas/Sleigh Ride	1958	3.00	6.00	12.00
❏ B-11951 [PS]	Merry Christmas, Vol. 1	1958	3.00	6.00	12.00
❏ B-11952	I'll Be Home for Christmas/Oh Holy Night/The Christmas Song/Silver Bells	1958	3.00	6.00	12.00
❏ B-11952 [PS]	Merry Christmas, Vol. 2	1958	3.00	6.00	12.00
❏ B-11953	The First Noel/It Came Upon a Midnight Clear//What Child Is This?/Silent Night, Holy Night	1958	3.00	6.00	12.00
❏ B-11953 [PS]	Merry Christmas, Vol. 3	1958	3.00	6.00	12.00

M

Number	Title (A Side/B Side)	Yr	VG	VG+	NM
B-12701	*Open Fire/Please Be Kind/ Bye Bye Blackbird/Tenderly	1959	2.50	5.00	10.00
B-12701 [PS]	Open Fire, Two Guitars, Vol. 1	1959	2.50	5.00	10.00
B-12702	*Embraceable You/My Funny Valentine/I'll Be Seeing You/I'm Just a Boy in Love	1959	2.50	5.00	10.00
B-12702 [PS]	Open Fire, Two Guitars, Vol. 2	1959	2.50	5.00	10.00
B-12703	I Concentrate on You/You'll Never Know//When I Fall in Love/In the Still of the Night	1959	2.50	5.00	10.00
B-12703 [PS]	Open Fire, Two Guitars, Vol. 3	1959	2.50	5.00	10.00
B-13511	*Heavenly/Misty/Hello, Young Lovers/I'll Be Easy to Find	1959	2.50	5.00	10.00
B-13511 [PS]	Heavenly, Vol. 1	1959	2.50	5.00	10.00
B-13512	*Something I Dreamed Last Night/Moonlight Becomes You/They Say It's Wonderful/More Than You Know	1959	2.50	5.00	10.00
B-13512 [PS]	Heavenly, Vol. 2	1959	2.50	5.00	10.00
B-13513	A Lovely Way to Spend an Evening/That's All// A Ride on a Rainbow/Stranger in Paradise	1959	2.50	5.00	10.00
B-13513 [PS]	Heavenly, Vol. 3	1959	2.50	5.00	10.00
B-14221	Secret Love/Where Are You//Maria/Where Do You Think You're Going	1959	2.50	5.00	10.00
B-14221 [PS]	Faithfully, Vol. 1	1959	2.50	5.00	10.00
B-14222	*Faithfully/One Starry Night/Nobody Knows/You Better Go Now	1959	2.50	5.00	10.00
B-14222 [PS]	Faithfully, Vol. 2	1959	2.50	5.00	10.00
B-14223	And This Is My Beloved/Tonight//Follow Me/ Blue Gardenia	1959	2.50	5.00	10.00
B-14223 [PS]	Faithfully, Vol. 3	1959	2.50	5.00	10.00
B-15261	Goodnight My Love/There's No You// Once/I'm So Lost	1960	2.50	5.00	10.00
B-15261 [PS]	Johnny's Mood, Vol. 1	1960	2.50	5.00	10.00
B-15262	*Corner to Corner/The Folks Who Live on the Hill/I'm in the Mood for Love/Stay Warm	1960	2.50	5.00	10.00
B-15262 [PS]	Johnny's Mood, Vol. 2	1960	2.50	5.00	10.00
B-15263	*I'm Gonna Laugh You Right Out of My Life/How High the Moon/April in Paris/In Return	1960	2.50	5.00	10.00
B-15263 [PS]	Johnny's Mood, Vol. 3	1960	2.50	5.00	10.00

Albums

COLUMBIA

Number	Title (A Side/B Side)	Yr	VG	VG+	NM
GP 2 [(2)]	Warm/Open Fire, Two Guitars	1969	3.75	7.50	15.00
C2L 17 [(2)M]	The Rhythms and Ballads of Broadway	1960	6.25	12.50	25.00
	—Red and black label with six "eye" logos				
C2L 17 [(2)M]	The Rhythms and Ballads of Broadway	1962	5.00	10.00	20.00
	—Red label with either "Guaranteed High Fidelity" or "360 Sound Mono"				
C2L 34 [(2)M]	The Great Years	1964	3.75	7.50	15.00
C2S 803 [(2)S]	The Rhythms and Ballads of Broadway	1960	7.50	15.00	30.00
	—Red and black label with six "eye" logos				
C2S 803 [(2)S]	The Rhythms and Ballads of Broadway	1962	6.25	12.50	25.00
	—Red "360 Sound" label				
C2S 834 [(2)S]	The Great Years	1964	5.00	10.00	20.00
	—Red "360 Sound" label				
CL 887 [M]	Johnny Mathis	1957	12.50	25.00	50.00
CS 1005	Raindrops Keep Fallin' on My Head	1970	3.00	6.00	12.00
CL 1028 [M]	Wonderful Wonderful	1957	7.50	15.00	30.00
	—Red and black label with six "eye" logos				
CL 1028 [M]	Wonderful Wonderful	1962	3.75	7.50	15.00
	—Red label with either "Guaranteed High Fidelity" or "360 Sound Mono"				
CL 1078 [M]	Warm	1957	7.50	15.00	30.00
	—Red and black label with six "eye" logos				
CL 1078 [M]	Warm	1962	3.75	7.50	15.00
	—Red label with either "Guaranteed High Fidelity" or "360 Sound Mono"				
CL 1119 [M]	Good Night, Dear Lord	1958	7.50	15.00	30.00
	—Red and black label with six "eye" logos				
CL 1119 [M]	Good Night, Dear Lord	1962	3.75	7.50	15.00
	—Red label with either "Guaranteed High Fidelity" or "360 Sound Mono"				
CL 1133 [M]	Johnny's Greatest Hits	1958	7.50	15.00	30.00
	—Red and black label with six "eye" logos				
CL 1133 [M]	Johnny's Greatest Hits	1962	3.75	7.50	15.00
	—Red label with either "Guaranteed High Fidelity" or "360 Sound Mono"				
CL 1165 [M]	Swing Softly	1958	7.50	15.00	30.00
	—Red and black label with six "eye" logos				
CL 1165 [M]	Swing Softly	1962	3.75	7.50	15.00
	—Red label with either "Guaranteed High Fidelity" or "360 Sound Mono"				
CL 1195 [M]	Merry Christmas	1958	10.00	20.00	40.00
	—Original cover has Johnny standing, holding skis and poles				
CL 1195 [M]	Merry Christmas	196?	7.50	15.00	30.00
	—Second cover has Johnny sitting, with skis and poles in snow				
CL 1270 [M]	Open Fire, Two Guitars	1959	7.50	15.00	30.00
	—Red and black label with six "eye" logos				
CL 1270 [M]	Open Fire, Two Guitars	1962	3.75	7.50	15.00
	—Red label with either "Guaranteed High Fidelity" or "360 Sound Mono"				
CL 1344 [M]	More Johnny's Greatest Hits	1959	6.25	12.50	25.00
	—Red and black label with six "eye" logos				
CL 1344 [M]	More Johnny's Greatest Hits	1962	3.75	7.50	15.00
	—Red label with either "Guaranteed High Fidelity" or "360 Sound Mono"				
CL 1351 [M]	Heavenly	1959	5.00	10.00	20.00
	—Red and black label with six "eye" logos				
CL 1351 [M]	Heavenly	1962	3.75	7.50	15.00
	—Red label with either "Guaranteed High Fidelity" or "360 Sound Mono"				
CL 1422 [M]	Faithfully	1959	5.00	10.00	20.00
	—Red and black label with six "eye" logos				
CL 1422 [M]	Faithfully	1962	3.75	7.50	15.00
	—Red label with either "Guaranteed High Fidelity" or "360 Sound Mono"				
CL 1526 [M]	Johnny's Mood	1960	5.00	10.00	20.00
	—Red and black label with six "eye" logos				
CL 1526 [M]	Johnny's Mood	1962	3.75	7.50	15.00
	—Red label with either "Guaranteed High Fidelity" or "360 Sound Mono"				
CL 1623 [M]	I'll Buy You a Star	1961	3.75	7.50	15.00
	—Red and black label with six "eye" logos				
CL 1623 [M]	I'll Buy You a Star	1962	3.00	6.00	12.00
	—Red label with either "Guaranteed High Fidelity" or "360 Sound Mono"				
CL 1644 [M]	Portrait of Johnny	1961	3.75	7.50	15.00
	—Red and black label with six "eye" logos; add 1/3 if portrait is there				
CL 1644 [M]	Portrait of Johnny	1962	3.00	6.00	12.00
	—Red label with either "Guaranteed High Fidelity" or "360 Sound Mono"				
CL 1711 [M]	Live It Up!	1962	3.00	6.00	12.00
	—Red label with either "Guaranteed High Fidelity" or "360 Sound Mono"				
CL 1711 [M]	Live It Up!	1962	3.75	7.50	15.00
	—Red and black label with six "eye" logos				
CL 1915 [M]	Rapture	1962	3.00	6.00	12.00
CL 2016 [M]	Johnny's Newest Hits	1963	3.00	6.00	12.00
CL 2044 [M]	Johnny	1963	3.00	6.00	12.00
CL 2098 [M]	Romantically	1963	3.00	6.00	12.00
CL 2143 [M]	I'll Search My Heart and Other Great Hits	1964	3.00	6.00	12.00
CL 2223 [M]	The Ballads of Broadway	1964	3.00	6.00	12.00
CL 2224 [M]	The Rhythms of Broadway	1964	3.00	6.00	12.00
CL 2726 [M]	Up, Up and Away	1967	3.75	7.50	15.00
CL 2837 [M]	Love Is Blue	1968	6.25	12.50	25.00
CL 2905 [M]	Those Were the Days	1968	10.00	20.00	40.00
CS 8012 [S]	Good Night, Dear Lord	1958	10.00	20.00	40.00
	—Red and black label with six "eye" logos				
CS 8012 [S]	Good Night, Dear Lord	1962	5.00	10.00	20.00
	—Red "360 Sound" label				
CS 8021 [S]	Merry Christmas	1959	6.25	12.50	25.00
	—Original cover has Johnny standing, holding skis and poles				
CS 8021 [S]	Merry Christmas	196?	5.00	10.00	20.00
	—Second cover has Johnny sitting, with skis and poles in snow				
CS 8023 [S]	Swing Softly	1958	10.00	20.00	40.00
	—Red and black label with six "eye" logos				
CS 8039 [S]	Warm	1958	10.00	20.00	40.00
	—Red and black label with six "eye" logos				
CS 8039 [S]	Warm	1962	5.00	10.00	20.00
	—Red "360 Sound" label				
CS 8056 [S]	Open Fire, Two Guitars	1959	10.00	20.00	40.00
	—Red and black label with six "eye" logos				
CS 8056 [S]	Open Fire, Two Guitars	1962	5.00	10.00	20.00
	—Red "360 Sound" label				
CS 8150 [S]	More Johnny's Greatest Hits	1959	7.50	15.00	30.00
	—Red and black label with six "eye" logos				
CS 8150 [S]	More Johnny's Greatest Hits	1962	5.00	10.00	20.00
	—Red "360 Sound" label				
CS 8150 [S]	More Johnny's Greatest Hits	1971	2.50	5.00	10.00
	—Orange label				
PC 8150 [S]	More Johnny's Greatest Hits	198?	—	3.00	6.00
	—Reissue with new prefix				
CS 8152 [S]	Heavenly	1959	7.50	15.00	30.00
	—Red and black label with six "eye" logos				
CS 8152 [S]	Heavenly	1962	5.00	10.00	20.00
	—Red "360 Sound" label				
CS 8152 [S]	Heavenly	1971	2.50	5.00	10.00
	—Orange label				
PC 8152 [S]	Heavenly	198?	—	3.00	6.00
	—Reissue with new prefix				
CS 8219 [S]	Faithfully	1959	6.25	12.50	25.00
	—Red and black label with six "eye" logos				
CS 8219 [S]	Faithfully	1962	5.00	10.00	20.00
	—Red "360 Sound" label				
CS 8326 [S]	Johnny's Mood	1960	6.25	12.50	25.00
	—Red and black label with six "eye" logos				
CS 8326 [S]	Johnny's Mood	1962	5.00	10.00	20.00
	—Red "360 Sound" label				
CS 8423 [S]	I'll Buy You a Star	1961	5.00	10.00	20.00
	—Red and black label with six "eye" logos				
CS 8423 [S]	I'll Buy You a Star	1962	3.75	7.50	15.00
	—Red "360 Sound" label				
CS 8444 [S]	Portrait of Johnny	1961	5.00	10.00	20.00
	—Red and black label with six "eye" logos; add 1/3 if portrait is there				
CS 8444 [S]	Portrait of Johnny	1962	3.75	7.50	15.00
	—Red "360 Sound" label				
CS 8511 [S]	Live It Up!	1962	3.75	7.50	15.00
	—Red "360 Sound" label				
CS 8511 [S]	Live It Up!	1962	5.00	10.00	20.00
	—Red and black label with six "eye" logos; add 1/3 if portrait is there				
CS 8634 [R]	Johnny's Greatest Hits	1963	3.00	6.00	12.00
CS 8715 [S]	Rapture	1962	3.75	7.50	15.00
	—Red "360 Sound" label				
CS 8816 [S]	Johnny's Newest Hits	1963	3.75	7.50	15.00
	—Red "360 Sound" label				
CS 8844 [S]	Johnny	1963	3.75	7.50	15.00
	—Red "360 Sound" label				
CS 8898 [S]	Romantically	1963	3.75	7.50	15.00
	—Red "360 Sound" label				
CS 8943 [S]	I'll Search My Heart and Other Great Hits	1964	3.75	7.50	15.00
	—Red "360 Sound" label				
CS 9023 [S]	The Ballads of Broadway	1964	3.75	7.50	15.00
	—Red "360 Sound" label				
CS 9024 [S]	The Ballads of Broadway	1964	3.75	7.50	15.00
	—Red "360 Sound" label				
CS 9046 [R]	Wonderful Wonderful	1964	3.00	6.00	12.00
CS 9526 [S]	Up, Up and Away	1967	3.75	7.50	15.00
CS 9637 [S]	Love Is Blue	1968	3.75	7.50	15.00
CS 9705 [S]	Those Were the Days	1968	3.75	7.50	15.00
CS 9871	People	1969	3.75	7.50	15.00
CS 9872	The Impossible Dream	1969	3.75	7.50	15.00
CS 9872	The Impossible Dream	1971	2.50	5.00	10.00
	—Orange label				
PC 9872	The Impossible Dream	198?	—	3.00	6.00
	—Reissue with new prefix				
CS 9909	Love Theme from "Romeo and Juliet"	1969	3.75	7.50	15.00
	—Red "360 Sound" label				
CS 9909	Love Theme from "Romeo and Juliet"	1971	2.50	5.00	10.00
	—Orange label				
PC 9909	Love Theme from "Romeo and Juliet"	198?	—	3.00	6.00
	—Reissue with new prefix				
CS 9923	Give Me Your Love for Christmas	1969	3.00	6.00	12.00
C 30210	Close to You	1970	3.00	6.00	12.00
G 30350 [(2)]	Johnny Mathis Sings the Music of Bacharach & Kaempfert	1970	3.75	7.50	15.00
C 30499	Love Story	1971	3.00	6.00	12.00
PC 30499	Love Story	198?	2.00	4.00	8.00
	—Budget-line reissue				
C 30740	You've Got a Friend	1971	3.00	6.00	12.00
CQ 30740 [Q]	You've Got a Friend	1972	5.00	10.00	20.00
PC 30740	You've Got a Friend	198?	2.00	4.00	8.00
	—Budget-line reissue				

The Mamas and the Papas, "Dancing Bear," Dunhill 4113, picture sleeve, $6-$12.

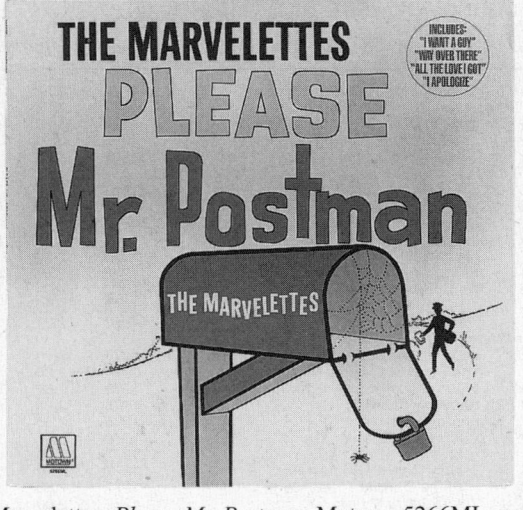

The Marvelettes, *Please Mr. Postman*, Motown 5266ML, mono LP, reissue, $5-$10.

Manfred Mann, *The Manfred Mann Album,* Ascot AM-13015, mono LP, $20-$40.

Dean Martin, *Everybody Loves Somebody,* Reprise RS-6130, stereo LP, $7.50-$15.

George Martin, "A Hard Day's Night," United Artists 750, picture sleeve, $1,000-$2,000.

Johnny Mathis, *Love Is Blue*, Columbia CS 9637, stereo LP, "360 Sound Stereo" on red label, $7.50-$15.

M

Number	Title (A Side/B Side)	Yr	VG	VG+	NM
☐ 2CQ 30979 [(2)Q]	Johnny Mathis In Person	1972	6.25	12.50	25.00
☐ KG 30979 [(2)]	Johnny Mathis In Person	1972	3.75	7.50	15.00
☐ CQ 31342 [Q]	The First Time Ever (I Saw Your Face)	1972	5.00	10.00	20.00
☐ KC 31342	The First Time Ever (I Saw Your Face)	1972	3.00	6.00	12.00
☐ PC 31342	The First Time Ever (I Saw Your Face)	198?	2.00	4.00	8.00
—Budget-line reissue					
☐ KG 31345 [(2)]	Johnny Mathis' All-Time Greatest Hits	1972	3.75	7.50	15.00
☐ CQ 31626 [Q]	Song Sung Blue	1972	5.00	10.00	20.00
☐ KC 31626	Song Sung Blue	1972	3.00	6.00	12.00
☐ CQ 32114 [Q]	Me and Mrs. Jones	1973	4.50	9.00	18.00
☐ KC 32114	Me and Mrs. Jones	1973	2.50	5.00	10.00
☐ KC 32258	Killing Me Softly with Her Song	1973	2.50	5.00	10.00
☐ CQ 32435 [Q]	I'm Coming Home	1973	4.50	9.00	18.00
☐ KC 32435	I'm Coming Home	1973	2.50	5.00	10.00
☐ PC 32435	I'm Coming Home	198?	2.00	4.00	8.00
—Budget-line reissue					
☐ C 32963	What'll I Do	1974	2.50	5.00	10.00
☐ KC 33251	The Heart of a Woman	1974	2.50	5.00	10.00
☐ PC 33420	When Will I See You Again	1975	2.50	5.00	10.00
☐ CG 33621 [(2)]	Heavenly/Faithfully	1975	3.00	6.00	12.00
☐ PC 33887	Feelings	1975	2.50	5.00	10.00
☐ PC 34117	I Only Have Eyes for You	1976	2.50	5.00	10.00
☐ PC 34441	Mathis Is…	1977	2.50	5.00	10.00
☐ PC 34667	Johnny Mathis' Greatest Hits	1977	2.50	5.00	10.00
☐ PC 34872	Hold Me, Thrill Me, Kiss Me	1977	2.50	5.00	10.00
☐ PC 35259	You Light Up My Life	1986	2.00	4.00	8.00
—Budget-line reissue					
☐ JC 35359	You Light Up My Life	1978	2.50	5.00	10.00
☐ C 35578	Romantically	1978	2.00	4.00	8.00
☐ JC 35649	The Best Days of My Life	1979	2.50	5.00	10.00
☐ PC 35649	The Best Days of My Life	1985	2.00	4.00	8.00
—Budget-line reissue					
☐ JC 36216	Mathis Magic	1979	2.50	5.00	10.00
☐ JC 36505	Different Kinda Different	1980	2.50	5.00	10.00
☐ JC 36871	The Best of Johnny Mathis 1975-1980	1980	2.50	5.00	10.00
☐ C2X 37440 [(2)]	The First 25 Years — The Silver Anniversary Album	1981	3.00	6.00	12.00
☐ FC 37748	Friends in Love	1982	2.50	5.00	10.00
☐ 3C 38306	Christmas with Johnny Mathis	1982	2.00	4.00	8.00
—Reissue of Columbia LE 10196 with same contents					
☐ FC 38699	Johnny Mathis Live	1983	2.50	5.00	10.00
☐ FC 38718	A Special Part of Me	1984	2.50	5.00	10.00
☐ PC 39468	For Christmas	1984	2.00	4.00	8.00
☐ FC 39601	Right from the Heart	1985	2.50	5.00	10.00
☐ FC 40372	The Hollywood Musicals	1986	2.50	5.00	10.00
—With Henry Mancini					
☐ FC 40447	Christmas Eve with Johnny Mathis	1986	2.50	5.00	10.00
☐ OC 44156	Once in a While	1988	2.50	5.00	10.00
☐ OC 44336	In the Still of the Night	1989	3.00	6.00	12.00
COLUMBIA LIMITED EDITION					
☐ LE 10003	Portrait of Johnny	197?	2.50	5.00	10.00
☐ LE 10196	Christmas with Johnny Mathis	1976	2.50	5.00	10.00
—Reissue of Harmony KH 30684 with same contents					
COLUMBIA MUSICAL TREASURY					
☐ 6P 6030 [(6)]	The Johnny Mathis Treasury	197?	7.50	15.00	30.00
COLUMBIA SPECIAL PRODUCTS					
☐ C 10896	Merry Christmas	1972	3.00	6.00	12.00
—Reissue					
☐ P 11477	Romantically, Johnny Mathis	197?	3.00	6.00	12.00
☐ P3 11837 [(3)]	Romantically, Johnny Mathis	197?	6.25	12.50	25.00
☐ P6 14628 [(6)]	Misty Memories: The Complete Johnny Mathis Treasury	197?	7.50	15.00	30.00
—Maunfactured for Candelite Music					
☐ P 14658	Holidays at the Fireside	197?	5.00	10.00	20.00
—Bonus album with box set 14628					
☐ P 14908	The Heart of Johnny Mathis	197?	3.75	7.50	15.00
—Bonus album with box set 14628					
☐ P4 14971 [(4)]	Johnny	197?	6.25	12.50	25.00
HARMONY					
☐ KH 30017	Johnny Mathis	1970	2.50	5.00	10.00
☐ KH 30684	Christmas with Johnny Mathis	1971	3.00	6.00	12.00
—Reissue of Mercury SR 60837 with two fewer tracks					
☐ KH 31935	Something for Everyone	1973	2.50	5.00	10.00
MERCURY					
☐ MG 20837 [M]	Sounds of Christmas	1963	3.00	6.00	12.00
☐ MG-20890 [M]	Tender Is the Night	1964	3.00	6.00	12.00
☐ MG-20913 [M]	The Wonderful World of Make Believe	1964	3.00	6.00	12.00
☐ MG-20942 [M]	This Is Love	1964	3.00	6.00	12.00
☐ MG-20988 [M]	Johnny Mathis Ole	1965	3.00	6.00	12.00
☐ MG-20991 [M]	Love Is Everything	1965	3.00	6.00	12.00
☐ MG-21041 [M]	The Sweetheart Tree	1965	3.00	6.00	12.00
☐ MG-21073 [M]	The Shadow of Your Smile	1966	3.00	6.00	12.00
☐ MG-21093 [M]	So Nice	1966	3.00	6.00	12.00
☐ MG-21107 [M]	Johnny Mathis Sings	1966	3.75	7.50	15.00
☐ SR 60837 [S]	Sounds of Christmas	1963	3.75	7.50	15.00
☐ SR-60890 [S]	Tender Is the Night	1964	3.75	7.50	15.00
☐ SR-60913 [S]	The Wonderful World of Make Believe	1964	3.75	7.50	15.00
☐ SR-60942 [S]	This Is Love	1964	3.75	7.50	15.00
☐ SR-60988 [S]	Johnny Mathis Ole	1965	3.75	7.50	15.00
☐ SR-60991 [S]	Love Is Everything	1965	3.75	7.50	15.00
☐ SR-61041 [S]	The Sweetheart Tree	1965	3.75	7.50	15.00
☐ SR-61073 [S]	The Shadow of Your Smile	1966	3.75	7.50	15.00
☐ SR-61093 [S]	So Nice	1966	3.75	7.50	15.00
☐ SR-61107 [S]	Johnny Mathis Sings	1967	3.75	7.50	15.00
MOBILE FIDELITY					
☐ 1-171	Heavenly	1985	6.25	12.50	25.00
—Audiophile vinyl					
READER'S DIGEST					
☐ RB4-097 [(6)]	His Greatest Hits and Finest Performances	198?	6.25	12.50	25.00
TIME-LIFE					
☐ SLGD-08 [(2)]	Legendary Singers: Johnny Mathis	1985	3.75	7.50	15.00

MATHIS, JOHNNY/DENIECE WILLIAMS Also see each artist's individual listings.
45s
COLUMBIA

Number	Title (A Side/B Side)	Yr	VG	VG+	NM
☐ 38-04379	Love Won't Let Me Wait/Lead Me to Your Love	1984	—	—	3.00
☐ 3-10693	Too Much, Too Little, Too Late/Emotion	1978	—	2.50	5.00

Number	Title (A Side/B Side)	Yr	VG	VG+	NM
☐ 3-10693	Too Much, Too Little, Too Late/ I Wrote a Symphony on My Guitar	1978	2.50	5.00	10.00
—B-side by Johnny Mathis solo					
☐ 3-10772	You're All I Need to Get By/You're a Special Part of My Life	1978	—	2.50	5.00
☐ 3-10772 [PS]	You're All I Need to Get By	1978	2.50	5.00	10.00
—Sleeve is promo only					
☐ 3-10826	That's What Friends Are For/I Just Can't Get Over You	1978	—	2.50	5.00
☐ 33360	Too Much, Too Little, Too Late/You're All I Need to Get By	198?	—	—	3.00
—Gray label					
☐ 33360	Too Much, Too Little, Too Late/You're All I Need to Get By	198?	—	2.00	4.00
—Red label					
Albums					
COLUMBIA					
☐ JC 35435	That's What Friends Are For	1978	2.50	5.00	10.00
☐ PC 35435	That's What Friends Are For	198?	2.00	4.00	8.00
—Budget-line reissue					

MATHIS BROTHERS, THE See DEAN AND MARK; THE NEWBEATS.

MATTHEWS, FAT MAN
45s
BAYOU

Number	Title (A Side/B Side)	Yr	VG	VG+	NM
☐ 016	I'm Thankful/Goin' Down	1952	37.50	75.00	150.00
IMPERIAL					
☐ 5211	When Boy Meets Girl/Later Baby	1952	1000.	1500.	2000.
☐ 5235	Down the Line/You Know It	1953	25.00	50.00	100.00

MATTHEWS, IAN Also see MATTHEWS' SOUTHERN COMFORT.
45s
COLUMBIA

Number	Title (A Side/B Side)	Yr	VG	VG+	NM
☐ 10374	Brown Eyed Girl/Steamboat	1976	—	2.50	5.00
☐ 10553	Tigers Will Survive/Times	1977	—	2.50	5.00
ELEKTRA					
☐ 45851	These Days/Same Old Man	1973	—	2.50	5.00
☐ 45871	Seven Bridges Road/You Fell Through My Mind	1973	—	2.50	5.00
☐ 45892	Dirty Work/A Wailing Goodbye	1974	—	2.50	5.00
MUSHROOM					
☐ 7039	Shake It/Stealin' Home	1978	—	2.00	4.00
☐ 7040	Give Me an Inch/Let There Be Blues	1979	—	2.00	4.00
☐ 7041	Don't Hang Up Your Dancing Shoes/Slip Away	1979	—	2.00	4.00
☐ 7045	Anna/You Don't See Me	1980	—	2.00	4.00
VERTIGO					
☐ 101	If You Saw Through My Eyes/Hearts	1971	—	3.00	6.00
☐ 102	Reno, Nevada/Desert Inn	1971	—	3.00	6.00
☐ 103	Da Doo Ron Ron/House of Un-American Blues Activity Dream	1972	—	3.00	6.00
☐ 105	Tigers Will Survive/Hope You Know	1972	—	3.00	6.00
Albums					
COLUMBIA					
☐ PC 34102	Go for Broke	1976	2.50	5.00	10.00
☐ PC 34671	Hit and Run	1977	2.50	5.00	10.00
ELEKTRA					
☐ EKS-75051	Valley Hi	1973	3.00	6.00	12.00
☐ EKS-75078	Some Days You Eat the Bear	1974	3.00	6.00	12.00
MUSHROOM					
☐ MRS-5012	Stealin' Home	1978	2.50	5.00	10.00
☐ MRS-5014	Siamese Friends	1979	2.50	5.00	10.00
RSO					
☐ RS-1-3092	A Spot of Interference	1980	2.50	5.00	10.00
VERTIGO					
☐ VEL-1002	If You Saw Thro' My Eyes	1971	3.00	6.00	12.00
☐ VEL-1010	Tigers Will Survive	1972	3.00	6.00	12.00
WINDHAM HILL					
☐ WD-1070	Walking a Changing Line: The Songs of Jules Shear	1987	2.50	5.00	10.00

MATTHEWS' SOUTHERN COMFORT
45s
DECCA

Number	Title (A Side/B Side)	Yr	VG	VG+	NM
☐ 32664	Colorado Springs Eternal/The Watch	1970	—	2.50	5.00
☐ 32774	Woodstock/Ballad of Obray Ramsey	1971	—	3.00	6.00
☐ 32845	Mare, Take Me Home/Brand New Tennessee Waltz	1971	—	2.50	5.00
☐ 32874	Tell Me Why/To Love	1971	—	2.50	5.00
Albums					
DECCA					
☐ DL 75191	Matthews' Southern Comfort	1970	3.00	6.00	12.00
☐ DL 75242	Second Spring	1970	3.00	6.00	12.00
☐ DL 75264	Later That Same Year	1971	3.00	6.00	12.00
PICKWICK					
☐ SPC-3698	Later That Same Year	197?	2.00	4.00	8.00

MATTY, JAY
45s
ERA

Number	Title (A Side/B Side)	Yr	VG	VG+	NM
☐ 3008	Janie My Lover/Tall Tale	1959	3.75	7.50	15.00
LUTE					
☐ 6021	Merry Twist Mas/Teenage Monster	1961	5.00	10.00	20.00

MAUDS, THE
45s
DUNWICH

Number	Title (A Side/B Side)	Yr	VG	VG+	NM
☐ 160	Hold On/C'mon and Move	1967	3.00	6.00	12.00
MERCURY					
☐ 72694	Hold On/C'mon and Move	1967	2.00	4.00	8.00
☐ 72720	When Something Is Wrong (With My Baby)/You Make Me Feel So Bad	1967	2.00	4.00	8.00
☐ 72760	He Will Break Your Heart/You Must Believe Me	1967	2.00	4.00	8.00
☐ 72832	Forever Gone/Soul Drippin'	1968	2.00	4.00	8.00
☐ 72877	Only Love Can Save You/Sergeant Sunshine	1968	2.00	4.00	8.00
☐ 72919	Brother Chickie/Satisfy My Hunger	1969	2.00	4.00	8.00

Number	Title (A Side/B Side)	Yr	VG	VG+	NM
RCA VICTOR					
❑ 74-0377	Forget It, I've Got It/A Man Without a Dream	1970	—	3.00	6.00
Albums					
MERCURY					
❑ MG-21135 [M]	The Mauds Hold On	1967	5.00	10.00	20.00
❑ SR-61135 [S]	The Mauds Hold On	1967	6.25	12.50	25.00

MAURIAT, PAUL
45s
Number	Title (A Side/B Side)	Yr	VG	VG+	NM
MGM					
❑ 14378	Love Theme from "The Godfather"/Butterfly	1972	—	2.00	4.00
PHILIPS					
❑ 40348	I Know a Place/I Tried and I Tried	1966	—	3.00	6.00
❑ 40426	You Don't Have to Say You Love Me/Kiss Tomorrow Goodbye	1967	—	3.00	6.00
❑ 40440	Black Is Black/Reach Out I'll Be There	1967	—	3.00	6.00
❑ 40462	This Is My Song/Puppet on a String	1967	—	3.00	6.00
❑ 40495	Love Is Blue/Alone in the World	1967	—	3.00	6.00
❑ 40495	Love Is Blue/Sunny	1967	—	3.00	6.00
❑ 40530	Love in Every Room/The English Nightingale	1968	—	3.00	6.00
❑ 40530 [PS]	Love in Every Room/The English Nightingale	1968	2.50	5.00	10.00
❑ 40550	San Francisco (Be Sure to Wear Flowers in Your Hair)/I Waited for You	1968	—	3.00	6.00
❑ 40574	Chitty Chitty Bang Bang/Come Un Carcon	1968	—	3.00	6.00
❑ 40594	Hey Jude/Those Were the Days	1969	—	2.50	5.00
❑ 40595	Sweet Charity/Irresistible	1969	—	2.50	5.00
❑ 40642	Get Back/Goodbye	1969	—	2.50	5.00
❑ 40647	Je T'Aime…Moi Non Plus/I Want to Love	1969	—	2.50	5.00
❑ 40683	Gone Is Love/She Is a Little Bit Sweeter	1970	—	2.50	5.00
❑ 40700	Etude in the Form of Rhythm and Blues/El Condor Pasa	1971	—	2.50	5.00
❑ 40707	Valerie's Theme/To Be the One You Love	1971	—	2.50	5.00
VERVE					
❑ 10682	Apres Toi (Come What May)/Theme from " A Summer Place"	1972	—	2.00	4.00
Albums					
FANTASY					
❑ 8380	Paris by Night	1968	3.00	6.00	12.00
❑ 8389	Joyeux Noel	1968	3.00	6.00	12.00
❑ 8394	Latin Style	1969	3.00	6.00	12.00
MERCURY					
❑ SRM-1-3746	Overseas	1978	2.50	5.00	10.00
MGM					
❑ SE-4838	Love Theme from "The Godfather"	1972	2.50	5.00	10.00
❑ M3G-4999	Have You Never Been Mellow	1975	2.50	5.00	10.00
PHILIPS					
❑ PHM 200197 [M]	Listen Too	1965	3.00	6.00	12.00
❑ PHM 200215 [M]	Of Vodka and Caviar	1966	3.00	6.00	12.00
❑ PHM 200226 [M]	More Mauriat	1967	3.75	7.50	15.00
❑ PHM 200248 [M]	Blooming Hits	1967	5.00	10.00	20.00
❑ PHM 200255 [M]	The Christmas Album	1967	5.00	10.00	20.00
❑ PHS 600197 [S]	Listen Too	1965	3.75	7.50	15.00
❑ PHS 600215 [S]	Of Vodka and Caviar	1966	3.75	7.50	15.00
❑ PHS 600226 [S]	More Mauriat	1967	3.75	7.50	15.00
❑ PHS 600248 [S]	Blooming Hits	1967	3.75	7.50	15.00
—Original copies have no "blurb" for "Love Is Blue" on front cover					
❑ PHS 600248 [S]	Blooming Hits	1968	3.00	6.00	12.00
—With blurb for "Love Is Blue" on front cover					
❑ PHS 600255 [S]	The Christmas Album	1967	3.75	7.50	15.00
❑ PHS 600270	Mauriat Magic	1968	3.75	7.50	15.00
❑ PHS 600280	Prevailing Airs	1968	3.75	7.50	15.00
❑ PHS 600292	Doing My Thing	1969	3.75	7.50	15.00
❑ PHS 600299	The Soul of Paul Mauriat	1969	3.75	7.50	15.00
❑ PHS 600320	L-O-V-E	1969	3.75	7.50	15.00
❑ PHS 600337	Midnight Cowboy/Let the Sunshine In	1970	3.00	6.00	12.00
❑ PHS 600345	Gone Is Love	1970	3.00	6.00	12.00
❑ PHS 600352	El Condor Pasa	1970	3.00	6.00	12.00
VERVE					
❑ V6-5087	Theme from "A Summer Place"	1973	2.50	5.00	10.00

MAXIMILLIAN
Organist/keyboard player on DEL SHANNON's biggest hit records of the early 1960s.
45s
Number	Title (A Side/B Side)	Yr	VG	VG+	NM
BIG TOP					
❑ 3068	The Wanderer/The Snake	1961	5.00	10.00	20.00
❑ 3095	The Twistin' Ghost/The Breeze and I-Peter Gunn Theme	1961	5.00	10.00	20.00
CUB					
❑ 9046	Gee Baby, You're the Utmost/Blowing My Brains Out (Over You)	1959	6.25	12.50	25.00
Albums					
ABC					
❑ S-696	Maximillian	1969	10.00	20.00	40.00

MAXWELL, HOLLY
45s
Number	Title (A Side/B Side)	Yr	VG	VG+	NM
CONSTELLATION					
❑ 152	One Thin Dime/It's Impossible	1965	6.25	12.50	25.00
❑ 162	Let Him Go for Himself/Only When You're Lonely	1965	6.25	12.50	25.00
CURTOM					
❑ 1942	No One Else/Suffer	1969	3.00	6.00	12.00

MAXWELL, ROBERT
45s
Number	Title (A Side/B Side)	Yr	VG	VG+	NM
DECCA					
❑ 25622	Shangri-La/That Old Black Magic	1964	2.00	4.00	8.00
❑ 25637	Peg o' My Heart/Little Dipper	1964	—	3.00	6.00
❑ 25671	A Summer Song/Summertime	1965	—	3.00	6.00
❑ 31668	One O'Clock Jump/Rosebud	1964	—	3.00	6.00
❑ 31734	April in Portugal/The Right to Love	1965	—	3.00	6.00
❑ 31839	Song of the Nairobi Trio/Theme from "Morituri"	1965	—	3.00	6.00
MERCURY					
❑ 5773	Chinatown, My Chinatown/Shuffle Off to Buffalo	1952	3.75	7.50	15.00
—As "Bobby Maxwell"					
❑ 5844	Limehouse Blues/Plink, Plank, Plunk	1952	3.75	7.50	15.00

Number	Title (A Side/B Side)	Yr	VG	VG+	NM
❑ 70033	Shangri-La/Mary Lou	1953	5.00	10.00	20.00
—As "Bobby Maxwell"					
❑ 70159	Hindustan/Bobble, Bobble, Bobble	1953	3.75	7.50	15.00
❑ 70177	Rose Marie/Ebb Tide	1953	3.75	7.50	15.00
MGM					
❑ 12215	The Nearness of You/Midnight Breeze	1956	3.00	6.00	12.00
❑ 12254	Spaghetti Rag/Can't Keep Running	1956	3.00	6.00	12.00
❑ 12293	Hot Tamale/Freckles	1956	3.00	6.00	12.00
❑ 12351	Injury Music for Football Games/Cumana	1956	3.00	6.00	12.00
❑ 12410	Song of the Nairobi Trio/Accidental Slip on an Oriental Rug	1957	3.00	6.00	12.00
❑ 12488	Mary Lou/Open Your Mouth and Sing	1957	3.00	6.00	12.00
❑ 12546	I've Told Every Little Star/Come Follow Me Baby	1957	3.00	6.00	12.00
ROULETTE					
❑ 4148	Little Dipper/Mexican Hop	1959	2.50	5.00	10.00
❑ 4180	Pink Parfait/Flower of Budapest	1959	2.50	5.00	10.00
❑ 4241	The Man with the Monocle/Ver Boten Liebe	1960	2.50	5.00	10.00
❑ 4338	Bazaar in Barcelona/Little Dipper	1961	2.50	5.00	10.00
—Roulette titles as "Mickey Mozart"					
Albums					
COMMAND					
❑ 33-913 [M]	Anytime	1967	3.75	7.50	15.00
❑ SD 913 [S]	Anytime	1967	3.00	6.00	12.00
DECCA					
❑ DL 4421 [M]	Shangri-La	1964	3.00	6.00	12.00
❑ DL 4563 [M]	Peg o' My Heart	1964	3.00	6.00	12.00
❑ DL 4609 [M]	Songs for All Seasons	1965	3.00	6.00	12.00
❑ DL 4723 [M]	Let's Get Away from It All	1966	3.00	6.00	12.00
❑ DL 74421 [S]	Shangri-La	1964	3.75	7.50	15.00
❑ DL 74563 [S]	Peg o' My Heart	1964	3.75	7.50	15.00
❑ DL 74609 [S]	Songs for All Seasons	1965	3.75	7.50	15.00
❑ DL 74723 [S]	Let's Get Away from It All	1966	3.75	7.50	15.00
MGM					
❑ E-4246 [M]	The Very Best of Robert Maxwell	1964	3.00	6.00	12.00
❑ SE-4246 [S]	The Very Best of Robert Maxwell	1964	3.75	7.50	15.00

MAY, BILLY
45s
Number	Title (A Side/B Side)	Yr	VG	VG+	NM
CAPITOL					
❑ KCF 329 [PS]	Big Band Bash	1952	2.50	5.00	10.00
—Empty box for 15859, 15860 and 15861					
❑ CCF 349 [PS]	A Band Is Born!	1952	2.50	5.00	10.00
—Empty box for 15905, 15906 and 15907					
❑ F1793	All of Me/Lean, Baby	1951	3.75	7.50	15.00
❑ F1794	Fat Man Boogie/My Silent Love	1951	3.75	7.50	15.00
❑ F1795	When My Sugar Walks Down the Street/I Guess I'll Have to Change My Plans	1951	3.75	7.50	15.00
❑ F1919	Charmaine/When I Take My Sugar to Tea	1952	3.75	7.50	15.00
❑ F1955	Unforgettable/Silver and Gold	1952	3.75	7.50	15.00
❑ F1995	Always/There Is No Greater Love	1952	3.75	7.50	15.00
❑ F2054	Honest and Truly/When the Swallows Come Back to Capistrano	1952	3.75	7.50	15.00
❑ F2113	Easy Street/Mayhem	1952	3.75	7.50	15.00
❑ F2157	Love Is Just Around the Corner/Gin and Tonic	1952	3.75	7.50	15.00
❑ F2227	Orchids in the Moonlight/Fat Man Mambo	1952	3.75	7.50	15.00
❑ F2284	High Noon/Do You Ever Think of Me	1952	3.75	7.50	15.00
❑ F2297	A Cute Piece of Property/Driftwood	1952	3.75	7.50	15.00
❑ F2364	Cocktails for Two/Little Brown Jug	1953	3.75	7.50	15.00
❑ F2474	Good Grief/From the Land of the Sky Blue Water	1953	3.75	7.50	15.00
❑ F2575	Gone with the Wind/Romance	1953	3.75	7.50	15.00
❑ F2653	Cool Water/Dixieland Band	1953	3.75	7.50	15.00
❑ F2721	The Breeze and I/Whistle Stop	1954	3.75	7.50	15.00
❑ F2759	Rose Marie/Bill and Sam	1954	3.75	7.50	15.00
❑ F2802	Young at Heart/Lemon Twist	1954	3.75	7.50	15.00
❑ F2840	Hernando's Hideaway/Anything Can Happen Mambo	1954	3.75	7.50	15.00
❑ F2849	Hi Fi/The Song Is You	1954	3.75	7.50	15.00
❑ F3066	How Important Can It Be?/Let It Happen	1955	3.00	6.00	12.00
❑ F3104	Whatever Lola Wants/Just Between Friends	1955	3.00	6.00	12.00
❑ F3123	Cha Cha Cha/Shaner Maidel	1955	3.00	6.00	12.00
❑ F3221	Oklahoma!/Por Favor	1955	3.00	6.00	12.00
❑ F3297	Street of Dreams/Suzette	1955	3.00	6.00	12.00
❑ F3372	Main Title — Theme from "The Man with the Golden Arm"/Our Melody	1956	3.00	6.00	12.00
❑ F3486	Nightmare/The Beat	1956	3.00	6.00	12.00
❑ F3598	Christopher Columbus/Floater	1956	3.00	6.00	12.00
❑ F3697	Theme from "The Strange One"/Laurel's Theme	1957	3.00	6.00	12.00
❑ F3846	Seventy-Six Trombones/Young and Dangerous	1957	3.00	6.00	12.00
❑ 4752	Love Makes the World Go Round/The Sweetest Sounds	1962	2.50	5.00	10.00
❑ F15731	If I Had You/All of Me	1951	3.00	6.00	12.00
❑ 6F15859	You're Driving Me Crazy/Tenderly	1952	2.50	5.00	10.00
❑ 6F15860	When Your Lover Has Gone/Please Be Kind	1952	2.50	5.00	10.00
❑ 6F15861	Perfidia/Diane	1952	2.50	5.00	10.00
—Above three comprise box set KCF-329, "Big Band Bash"					
❑ 6F15905	When My Sugar Walks Down the Street/I Guess I'll Have to Change My Plans	1952	2.50	5.00	10.00
❑ 6F15906	Charmaine/Lean, Baby	1952	2.50	5.00	10.00
❑ 6F15907	The Fat Man Boogie/There Is No Greater Love	1952	2.50	5.00	10.00
—Above three comprise box set CCF-349, "A Band Is Born!"					
MCA					
❑ 40352	Front Page Rag/Reunion	1974	2.00	4.00	8.00
REPRISE					
❑ 20054	Ballad of the Sergeants 3/Sergeant Boswell's Rock	1962	2.50	5.00	10.00
❑ 20062	Sergeants 3 March/Girls from the Antler Bar	1962	2.50	5.00	10.00
TIME					
❑ 1050	Advise and Consent/Bashful Billie	1962	2.50	5.00	10.00

7-Inch Extended Plays
Number	Title (A Side/B Side)	Yr	VG	VG+	NM
CAPITOL					
❑ EAP 1-562	(contents unknown)	195?	3.00	6.00	12.00
❑ EAP 1-562 [PS]	Sorta-May, Part 1	195?	3.00	6.00	12.00
❑ EAP 2-562	(contents unknown)	195?	3.00	6.00	12.00
❑ EAP 2-562 [PS]	Sorta-May, Part 2	195?	3.00	6.00	12.00
❑ EAP 3-562	You Go to My Head/In a Persian Market//Just One of Those Things	195?	3.00	6.00	12.00

M

Number	Title (A Side/B Side)	Yr	VG	VG+	NM
❏ EAP 3-562 [PS]	Sorta-May, Part 3	195?	3.00	6.00	12.00
❏ EAP 1-1043	(contents unknown)	1958	2.50	5.00	10.00
❏ EAP 1-1043	Big Fat Brass, Part 1	1958	2.50	5.00	10.00
Albums					
BAINBRIDGE					
❏ ST 1001	I Believe in You	197?	3.00	6.00	12.00
CAPITOL					
❏ H 237 [10]	Join the Band	1951	10.00	20.00	40.00
❏ L 329 [10]	Big Band Bash	1952	10.00	20.00	40.00
❏ T 329 [M]	Big Band Bash	195?	6.25	12.50	25.00
—Turquoise label original					
❏ H 349 [10]	A Band Is Born!	1952	10.00	20.00	40.00
❏ T 349 [M]	A Band Is Born!	195?	6.25	12.50	25.00
—Turquoise label original					
❏ H 374 [10]	Bacchanalia!	1953	10.00	20.00	40.00
❏ T 374 [M]	Bacchanalia!	195?	7.50	15.00	30.00
—Turquoise label original					
❏ H 487 [10]	Billy May's Naughty Operetta!	1953	10.00	20.00	40.00
❏ T 487 [M]	Billy May's Naughty Operetta!	195?	6.25	12.50	25.00
—Turquoise label original					
❏ M 562 [M]	Sorta-May	197?	2.50	5.00	10.00
—Reissue with new prefix					
❏ T 562 [M]	Sorta-May	195?	6.25	12.50	25.00
—Turquoise label original					
❏ T 677 [M]	Sorta-Dixie!	195?	6.25	12.50	25.00
—Turquoise label original					
❏ T 771 [M]	Billy May Plays for Fancy Dancin'	1956	6.25	12.50	25.00
—Turquoise label original					
❏ STAO 924 [S]	Jimmie Lunceford in Hi-Fi: Authentic Re-Creations of the Lunceford Style	1958	10.00	20.00	40.00
—Black colorband label, Capitol logo at left					
❏ ST 1043 [S]	Big Fat Brass	1958	7.50	15.00	30.00
—Black colorband label, Capitol logo at left					
❏ T 1043 [M]	Big Fat Brass	1958	5.00	10.00	20.00
—Black colorband label, Capitol logo at left					
❏ ST 1329 [S]	Cha Cha!	1959	6.25	12.50	25.00
—Black colorband label, Capitol logo at left					
❏ T 1329 [M]	Cha Cha!	1959	5.00	10.00	20.00
—Black colorband label, Capitol logo at left					
❏ T 1367 [M]	Cha Cha Mambos	1959	5.00	10.00	20.00
—Black colorband label, logo at left					
❏ T 1377 [M]	Pow!	1959	5.00	10.00	20.00
—Gold "The Star Line" label					
❏ ST 1417 [S]	The Girls and Boys on Broadway	1960	5.00	10.00	20.00
—Black colorband label, Capitol logo at left					
❏ T 1417 [M]	The Girls and Boys on Broadway	1960	3.75	7.50	15.00
—Black colorband label, Capitol logo at left					
❏ ST 1581 [S]	The Great Jimmie Lunceford: Authentic Re-Creations of the Lunceford Style by Billy May	1961	5.00	10.00	20.00
—Gold "The Star Line" label					
❏ T 1581 [M]	The Great Jimmie Lunceford: Authentic Re-Creations of the Lunceford Style by Billy May	1961	3.75	7.50	15.00
—Gold "The Star Line" label					
❏ ST 1709 [S]	The Sweetest Swingin' Sounds of No Strings	196?	5.00	10.00	20.00
❏ T 1709 [M]	The Sweetest Swingin' Sounds of No Strings	196?	3.75	7.50	15.00
❏ ST 1888 [S]	Bill's Bag	1963	5.00	10.00	20.00
❏ T 1888 [M]	Bill's Bag	1963	3.75	7.50	15.00
❏ ST 2560 [S]	Billy May Today	1965	3.75	7.50	15.00
❏ T 2560 [M]	Billy May Today	1965	3.00	6.00	12.00
❏ M 11885 [M]	Sorta-Dixie!	197?	2.50	5.00	10.00
—Reissue of Capitol 677					
CREATIVE WORLD					
❏ ST-1051 [M]	Sorta-May	197?	3.00	6.00	12.00
❏ ST-1054	Sorta-Dixie!	197?	3.00	6.00	12.00
IMPERIAL					
❏ LP-9042 [M]	Fuzzy Pink Nightgown	1957	12.50	25.00	50.00
—Movie soundtrack					
PAUSA					
❏ PR 9035	A Band Is Born!	198?	2.50	5.00	10.00
—Reissue of Capitol T 349					
PICKWICK					
❏ PC- 3010 [M]	Hey It's May	196?	3.75	7.50	15.00
❏ SPC- 3010 [R]	Hey It's May	196?	2.00	4.00	8.00
STEREO SOUNDS					
❏ SA-12	Music for Uptight Guys	196?	3.75	7.50	15.00
TIME					
❏ S-2064 [S]	Billy May and His Orchestra	1962	5.00	10.00	20.00
❏ 52064 [M]	Billy May and His Orchestra	1962	3.75	7.50	15.00
TIME-LIFE					
❏ STL-340 [(3)]	The Swing Era: 1930-1936	197?	5.00	10.00	20.00
—Box set with hardcover book; re-creations of original big-band charts, with some contributions by the Glenn Gray Orchestra					
❏ STL-341 [(3)]	The Swing Era: 1936-1937	197?	5.00	10.00	20.00
—Box set with hardcover book; re-creations of original big-band charts, with some contributions by the Glenn Gray Orchestra					
❏ STL-342 [(3)]	The Swing Era: 1937-1938	197?	5.00	10.00	20.00
—Box set with hardcover book; re-creations of original big-band charts, with some contributions by the Glenn Gray Orchestra					
❏ STL-343 [(3)]	The Swing Era: 1938-1939	197?	5.00	10.00	20.00
—Box set with hardcover book; re-creations of original big-band charts, with some contributions by the Glenn Gray Orchestra					
❏ STL-344 [(3)]	The Swing Era: 1939-1940	197?	5.00	10.00	20.00
—Box set with hardcover book; re-creations of original big-band charts, with some contributions by the Glenn Gray Orchestra					
❏ STL-345 [(3)]	The Swing Era: 1940-1941	197?	5.00	10.00	20.00
—Box set with hardcover book; re-creations of original big-band charts, with some contributions by the Glenn Gray Orchestra					
❏ STL-346 [(3)]	The Swing Era: 1941-1942	197?	5.00	10.00	20.00
—Box set with hardcover book; re-creations of original big-band charts, with some contributions by the Glenn Gray Orchestra					
❏ STL-347 [(3)]	The Swing Era: 1942-1944	197?	5.00	10.00	20.00
—Box set with hardcover book; re-creations of original big-band charts, with some contributions by the Glenn Gray Orchestra					
❏ STL-348 [(3)]	The Swing Era: 1944-1945	197?	5.00	10.00	20.00
—Box set with hardcover book; re-creations of original big-band charts, with some contributions by the Glenn Gray Orchestra					

Number	Title (A Side/B Side)	Yr	VG	VG+	NM
❏ STL-349 [(3)]	The Swing Era: The Postwar Years	197?	5.00	10.00	20.00
—Box set with hardcover book; re-creations of original big-band charts, with some contributions by the Glenn Gray Orchestra					
❏ STL-350 [(3)]	The Swing Era: Into the '50s	197?	5.00	10.00	20.00
—Box set with hardcover book; re-creations of original big-band charts, with some contributions by the Glenn Gray Orchestra					
❏ STL-351 [(3)]	The Swing Era: Encore!	197?	5.00	10.00	20.00
—Box set with hardcover book; re-creations of original big-band charts, with some contributions by the Glenn Gray Orchestra					
❏ STL-352 [(3)]	The Swing Era: Curtain Call	197?	5.00	10.00	20.00
—Box set with hardcover book; re-creations of original big-band charts, with some contributions by the Glenn Gray Orchestra					
❏ STL-353 [(3)]	The Swing Era: One More Time	197?	5.00	10.00	20.00
—Box set with hardcover book; re-creations of original big-band charts, with some contributions by the Glenn Gray Orchestra					

MAY BLITZ
Albums
PARAMOUNT

Number	Title (A Side/B Side)	Yr	VG	VG+	NM
❏ PAS-5020	May Blitz	1970	5.00	10.00	20.00

MAYALL, JOHN
12-Inch Singles
ISLAND

Number	Title (A Side/B Side)	Yr	VG	VG+	NM
❏ PR 2490 [DJ]	The Last Time (same on both sides)	1988	2.00	4.00	8.00
❏ PR 2595 [DJ]	Fascinatin' Lover/Interview (22:33)	1989	3.00	6.00	12.00
45s					
ABC					
❏ 12216	Sunshine/Turn Me Loose	1976	—	2.50	5.00
BLUE THUMB					
❏ 264	Step in the Sun/Al Goldstein Blues	1975	—	2.50	5.00
IMMEDIATE					
❏ 502	Telephone Blues/I'm Your Witch Doctor	1967	2.00	4.00	8.00
LONDON					
❏ 20016	Key to Love/Parchman Farm	1966	2.50	5.00	10.00
❏ 20024	All Your Love/Hideaway	1966	2.50	5.00	10.00
❏ 20035	Oh, Pretty Woman/Suspicions	1967	2.00	4.00	8.00
❏ 20037	Jenny/Picture on the Wall	1967	2.00	4.00	8.00
❏ 20039	Broken Wings/Sonny Boy Blue	1967	2.00	4.00	8.00
❏ 20042	Living Alone/Walking on Sunset	1968	2.00	4.00	8.00
POLYDOR					
❏ 14004	Don't Waste My Time/Don't Pick a Flower	1969	—	3.00	6.00
❏ 14010	Room to Move/Saw Mill Gulch Road	1969	—	3.00	6.00
❏ 14051	Nature's Disappearing/My Pretty Girl	1970	—	3.00	6.00
❏ 14051 [PS]	Nature's Disappearing/My Pretty Girl	1970	3.75	7.50	15.00
❏ 14117	Nobody Cares/Play the Harp	1972	—	3.00	6.00
❏ 14151	Moving On/Keep Our Country Green	1972	—	3.00	6.00
❏ 14243	The 1974 Gasoline Blues/Brand New Band	1974	—	3.00	6.00
❏ 14253	Let Me Give/Passing Through	1974	—	3.00	6.00
Albums					
ABC					
❏ ABCD-926	Notice to Appear	1976	2.50	5.00	10.00
❏ D-958	A Banquet in Blues	1976	2.50	5.00	10.00
❏ D-992	Lots of People	1977	2.50	5.00	10.00
❏ D-1039	A Hard Core Package	1977	2.50	5.00	10.00
❏ D-1086	Last of the British Blues	1978	2.50	5.00	10.00
ACCORD					
❏ SN-7209	Roadshow Blues Band	1982	2.50	5.00	10.00
BLUE THUMB					
❏ BTS-6019	New Year, New Band, New Company	1975	2.50	5.00	10.00
DECAL					
❏ LIK-1	Some of My Best Friends Are Blues	1986	2.50	5.00	10.00
DJM					
❏ 23	The Bottom Line	1979	2.50	5.00	10.00
❏ 29	No More Interviews	1979	2.50	5.00	10.00
GNP CRESCENDO					
❏ 2184	Behind the Iron Curtain	1986	2.50	5.00	10.00
ISLAND					
❏ 91005	Chicago Line	1988	2.50	5.00	10.00
❏ 842795-1	A Sense of Place	1990	3.00	6.00	12.00
LONDON					
❏ PS 492 [S]	Blues Breakers with Eric Clapton	1966	10.00	20.00	40.00
❏ PS 502 [S]	A Hard Road	1967	5.00	10.00	20.00
❏ PS 529 [S]	Crusade	1967	5.00	10.00	20.00
❏ PS 534	The Blues Alone	1968	3.75	7.50	15.00
❏ PS 537	Bare Wires	1968	3.75	7.50	15.00
❏ PS 543	Raw Blues	1968	3.75	7.50	15.00
❏ PS 545	Blues from Laurel Canyon	1969	3.75	7.50	15.00
❏ PS 562	Looking Back	1969	3.75	7.50	15.00
❏ PS 570	The Diary of a Band	1970	3.00	6.00	12.00
❏ PS 589	Live in Europe	1971	3.00	6.00	12.00
❏ 2PS 600 [(2)]	Through the Years	1971	3.00	6.00	12.00
❏ 2PS 618 [(2)]	Down the Line	1973	2.50	5.00	10.00
❏ LL 3492 [M]	Blues Breakers with Eric Clapton	1966	7.50	15.00	30.00
❏ LL 3502 [M]	A Hard Road	1967	5.00	10.00	20.00
❏ LL 3529 [M]	Crusade	1967	5.00	10.00	20.00
❏ LC-50009	Blues Breakers with Eric Clapton	1977	2.50	5.00	10.00
—Reissue of London PS 492					
❏ 800086-1	Blues Breakers with Eric Clapton	1983	2.00	4.00	8.00
—Reissue of London 50009					
❏ 820320-1	Primal Solos	1985	2.00	4.00	8.00
❏ 820331-1	Looking Back	1985	2.00	4.00	8.00
—Reissue of London PS 562					
❏ 820342-1	Raw Blues	1985	2.00	4.00	8.00
—Reissue of London PS 543					
MCA					
❏ 716	Last of the British Blues	1980	2.00	4.00	8.00
—Reissue of ABC 1086					
❏ 795	Hard Core	1980	2.00	4.00	8.00
—Reissue of ABC 1039					
MOBILE FIDELITY					
❏ 1-183	Blues Breakers Featuring Eric Clapton	1985	10.00	20.00	40.00
—Audiophile vinyl					
❏ 1-246	The Blues Alone	1996	7.50	15.00	30.00
—Audiophile vinyl					

Number	Title (A Side/B Side)	Yr	VG	VG+	NM
POLYDOR					
❏ 25-3002 [(2)]	Back to the Roots	1971	3.00	6.00	12.00
❏ PD2-3005 [(2)]	Ten Years Are Gone	1973	3.00	6.00	12.00
❏ PD2-3006 [(2)]	The Best of John Mayall	1973	3.00	6.00	12.00
❏ 24-4004	The Turning Point	1970	2.50	5.00	10.00
❏ 24-4010	Empty Rooms	1970	2.50	5.00	10.00
❏ 24-4022	U.S.A. Union	1970	2.50	5.00	10.00
❏ PD-5012	Memories	1971	2.50	5.00	10.00
❏ PD-5027	Jazz-Blues Fusion	1972	2.50	5.00	10.00
❏ PD-5036	Moving On	1972	2.50	5.00	10.00
❏ PD-6030	The Latest Edition	1974	3.00	6.00	12.00
❏ SKAO-93398	U.S.A. Union	1970	3.75	7.50	15.00
—Capitol Record Club edition					
❏ 823305-1	The Turning Point	1985	2.00	4.00	8.00
—Reissue of Polydor 24-4004					
❏ 837127-1	Archive to the Eighties	1988	2.00	4.00	8.00

MAYE, LEE Also recorded as "Arthur Lee Maye."
45s

Number	Title (A Side/B Side)	Yr	VG	VG+	NM
ABC					
❏ 11028	If You Leave Me/ The Greatest Love I've Ever Known	1967	2.00	4.00	8.00
BUDDAH					
❏ 141	He'll Have to Go/Jus' Lookin'	1969	—	3.00	6.00
CASH					
❏ 1063	Will You Be Mine/Honey Honey	1958	37.50	75.00	150.00
❏ 1065	All I Want Is Someone to Love/Pounding	1958	30.00	60.00	120.00
DIG					
❏ 124	This Is the Night for Love/(B-side unknown)	1956	62.50	125.00	250.00
❏ 133	A Fool's Prayer/(B-side unknown)	1957	37.50	75.00	150.00
FLIP					
❏ 330	Hey Pretty Baby/'Cause You're Mine Alone	1958	20.00	40.00	80.00
—As "Arthur Lee Maye"					
IMPERIAL					
❏ 5790	Will You Be Mine/Honey Honey	1961	5.00	10.00	20.00
JAMIE					
❏ 1272	Who Made You What You Are/Loving Fool	1964	2.50	5.00	10.00
❏ 1276	How's the World Treating You?/Loving Fool	1964	2.50	5.00	10.00
—As "Lee Maye of the Milwaukee Braves"					
❏ 1284	Only a Dream/The Breaks of Life	1964	2.50	5.00	10.00
❏ 1287	Even a Nobody/Who Made You What You Are	1964	2.50	5.00	10.00
❏ 1295	(Don't Pretend) Just Lay It on the Line/ Careless Hands	1965	2.00	4.00	8.00
—With Barbara Lynn					
LENOX					
❏ 5566	Half Way (Out of Love with You)/ I Can't Please You	1963	3.00	6.00	12.00
MODERN					
❏ 944	Set My Heart Free/I Wanna Love	1954	150.00	300.00	600.00
—As "Arthur Lee Maye and the Crowns"					
RPM					
❏ 424	Truly/Oochie Pachie	1955	50.00	100.00	200.00
—As "Arthur Lee Maye and the Crowns"					
❏ 429	Loop De Loop/Love Me Always	1955	30.00	60.00	120.00
—As "Arthur Lee Maye"					
❏ 438	Do the Bop/Please Don't Leave Me	1955	37.50	75.00	150.00
—As "Arthur Lee Maye and the Crowns"					
SPECIALTY					
❏ 573	Gloria/Oo-Rooba-Lee	1956	15.00	30.00	60.00
—As "Arthur Lee Maye and the Crowns"					
TOWER					
❏ 243	When My Heart Hurts No More/At the Party	1966	2.00	4.00	8.00

MAYER, NATHANIEL
45s

Number	Title (A Side/B Side)	Yr	VG	VG+	NM
FORTUNE					
❏ 449	Village of Love/I Want a Woman	1962	6.25	12.50	25.00
❏ 487	Hurting Love/Leave Me Alone	1962	7.50	15.00	30.00
—Fortune 449 and 487 were part of the United Artists numbering system					
❏ 542	My Last Dance with You/My Little Darling	1962	5.00	10.00	20.00
❏ 545	Village of Love/I Want a Woman	1962	5.00	10.00	20.00
❏ 547	Hurting Love/Leave Me Alone	1962	5.00	10.00	20.00
❏ 550	Work It Out/Well, I've Got News	1962	3.75	7.50	15.00
❏ 550	Mr. Santa Claus/(B-side unknown)	1962	7.50	15.00	30.00
❏ 554	I Had a Dream/I'm Not Gonna Cry	1963	3.75	7.50	15.00
❏ 557	Going Back to the Village of Love/ My Last Dance with You	1963	3.75	7.50	15.00
❏ 562	The Place I Know/Don't Come Back	196?	3.75	7.50	15.00
❏ 563	Village of Love/I Want a Woman	196?	3.00	6.00	12.00
❏ 567	From Now On/I Want Love and Affection	196?	3.00	6.00	12.00
Albums					
FORTUNE					
❏ 8014 [M]	Goin' Back to the Village of Love	196?	15.00	30.00	60.00
—Yellow label					
❏ 8014 [M]	Goin' Back to the Village of Love	196?	37.50	75.00	150.00
—Purple label					
❏ 8014 [M]	Goin' Back to the Village of Love	1964	75.00	150.00	300.00
—Light blue label					
❏ 8014 [M]	Goin' Back to the Village of Love	197?	3.75	7.50	15.00
—Bluish purple label, with much more flexible vinyl than earlier pressings					

MAYFIELD, CURTIS Also see THE IMPRESSIONS.
12-Inch Singles

Number	Title (A Side/B Side)	Yr	VG	VG+	NM
CAPITOL					
❏ V-15602	Superfly 1990 (6 versions)	1990	2.00	4.00	8.00
—With Ice-T					
CURTOM					
❏ 12-PO-22 [DJ]	I Mo Git U Sucka/He's a Fly Guy	198?	2.50	5.00	10.00
❏ 12-PO-52 [DJ]	Got to Be Real/On and On	198?	2.50	5.00	10.00
RSO/CURTOM					
❏ 1016 [DJ]	Tell Me, Tell Me (7:16)/Heartbeat/ Over the Hump	1979	2.50	5.00	10.00

45s

Number	Title (A Side/B Side)	Yr	VG	VG+	NM
ARISTA					
❏ 9806	He's a Flyguy/(Instrumental)	1989	—	—	2.00
❏ 9806 [PS]	He's a Flyguy/(Instrumental)	1989	—	—	3.00
—With Fishbone					
BOARDWALK					
❏ NB7-11-122	She Don't Let Nobody (But Me)/You Get All My Love	1981	—	2.00	4.00
❏ NB7-11-132	Toot An'Toot An'Toot/Come Free Your People	1981	—	2.00	4.00
❏ NB7-11-155	Hey Baby (Give It All to Me)/Summer Hot	1982	—	2.00	4.00
❏ NB7-11-169	Dirty Laundry/Nobody But You	1982	—	2.00	4.00
COLUMBIA					
❏ 10147	Stash That Butt, Sucker/Zanzibar	1975	—	2.50	5.00
CRC					
❏ 001	Baby It's You/Breakin' in the Streets	1985	—	3.00	6.00
CURTOM					
❏ 0105	So in Love/Hard Times	1975	—	2.50	5.00
❏ 0118	Only You Babe/Love to the People	1976	—	2.50	5.00
❏ 0122	Party Night/P.S. I Love You	1976	—	2.50	5.00
❏ 0125	Show Me Love/Just Want to Be with You	1977	—	2.50	5.00
❏ 0131	Do Do Wap Is Strong in Here/ Need Someone to Love	1977	—	2.50	5.00
❏ 0135	You Are, You Are/Get a Little Bit (Give, Get, Take and Have)	1978	—	2.50	5.00
❏ 0135 [PS]	You Are, You Are/Get a Little Bit (Give, Get, Take and Have)	1978	—	3.00	6.00
❏ 0141	Do It All Night/Party Party	1978	—	2.50	5.00
❏ 0142	In Love, In Love, In Love/Keeps Me Loving You	1978	—	2.50	5.00
❏ 1955	(Don't Worry) If There's a Hell Below We're All Going to Go/The Makings of You	1970	—	3.00	6.00
❏ 1960	Beautiful Brother of Mine/Give It Up	1971	—	3.00	6.00
❏ 1963	Mighty Mighty (Spade and Whitey)/(B-side unknown)	1971	—	3.00	6.00
❏ 1966	Get Down/We're a Winner	1971	—	3.00	6.00
❏ 1968	We Got to Have Peace/We're a Winner	1972	—	3.00	6.00
❏ 1968 [PS]	We Got to Have Peace/We're a Winner	1972	2.00	4.00	8.00
❏ 1972	Beautiful Brother of Mine/Love to Keep You In My Mind	1972	—	3.00	6.00
❏ 1974	Move On Up/Underground	1972	—	3.00	6.00
❏ 1975	Freddie's Dead (Theme from "Superfly")/ Underground	1972	—	3.00	6.00
❏ 1978	Superfly/Underground	1972	—	3.00	6.00
❏ 1978 [PS]	Superfly/Underground	1972	2.00	4.00	8.00
❏ 1987	Future Shock/The Other Side of Town	1973	—	3.00	6.00
❏ 1991	If I Were Only a Child Again/Think	1973	—	3.00	6.00
❏ 1993	Can't Say Nothin'/Future Song	1973	—	3.00	6.00
❏ 1999	Kung Fu/Right On for the Darkness	1974	—	3.00	6.00
❏ 1999 [PS]	Kung Fu/Right On for the Darkness	1974	2.00	4.00	8.00
❏ 2005	Sweet Exorcist/Suffer	1974	—	3.00	6.00
❏ 2006	Mother's Son/Love Me	1974	—	3.00	6.00
RSO/CURTOM					
❏ 919	This Year/(Instrumental)	1979	—	2.50	5.00
❏ 941	You're So Good to Me/ Between You, Babe, and Me	1979	—	2.50	5.00
—With Linda Clifford					
❏ 1029	Love's Sweet Sensation/(Instrumental)	1980	—	2.50	5.00
—With Linda Clifford					
❏ 1036	Love Me, Love Me Now/It's Alright	1980	—	2.50	5.00
❏ 1046	Tripping Out/Never Stop Loving	1980	—	2.50	5.00
Albums					
BOARDWALK					
❏ NB1-33239	Love Is the Place	1981	2.50	5.00	10.00
❏ NB1-33256	Honesty	1982	2.50	5.00	10.00
CRC					
❏ 2001	We Come in Peace with a Message of Love	1985	3.00	6.00	12.00
CURTOM					
❏ CUR-2003	There's No Place Like America Today	198?	2.00	4.00	8.00
—Reissue of 5001					
❏ CUR-2005	Something to Believe In	198?	2.00	4.00	8.00
—Reissue of RSO 3077					
❏ CUR-2008	Take It to the Street	198?	2.50	5.00	10.00
❏ CUR-2901 [(2)]	Live in Europe	198?	3.00	6.00	12.00
❏ CUR-2902 [(2)]	Greatest Hits of All Time (Classic Collection)	198?	3.00	6.00	12.00
❏ CU.5001	There's No Place Like America Today	1975	3.00	6.00	12.00
❏ CU 5007	Give, Get, Take and Have	1976	3.00	6.00	12.00
❏ CU 5013	Never Say You Can't Survive	1977	3.00	6.00	12.00
❏ CUK 5022	Do It All Night	1978	3.00	6.00	12.00
❏ CRS-8005	Curtis	1970	3.75	7.50	15.00
❏ CRS-8008 [(2)]	Curtis/Live!	1971	5.00	10.00	20.00
❏ CRS-8009	Roots	1971	3.75	7.50	15.00
❏ CRS-8014	Superfly	1972	5.00	10.00	20.00
❏ CRS-8015	Back to the World	1973	3.75	7.50	15.00
❏ CRS-8018	Curtis in Chicago	1973	3.75	7.50	15.00
❏ CRS-8601	Sweet Exorcist	1974	3.00	6.00	12.00
❏ CRS-8604	Got to Find a Way	1974	3.00	6.00	12.00
RSO					
❏ RS-1-3053	Heartbeat	1979	2.50	5.00	10.00
❏ RS-1-3077	Something to Believe In	1980	2.50	5.00	10.00

MAYFIELD, PERCY
45s

Number	Title (A Side/B Side)	Yr	VG	VG+	NM
ATLANTIC					
❏ 3207	I Don't Want to Be President/ Nothin' Stays the Same Forever	1974	—	2.50	5.00
BRUNSWICK					
❏ 55390	Walking on a Tightrope/P.M. Blues	1968	2.00	4.00	8.00
CHESS					
❏ 1599	Double Dealing/Are You Out There	1955	15.00	30.00	60.00
IMPERIAL					
❏ 5577	One Love/My Reward	1959	3.75	7.50	15.00
❏ 5620	My Heart Is a Prisoner/My Memories	1959	3.75	7.50	15.00
KING					
❏ 4480	Two Years of Torture/Half Awake	1951	15.00	30.00	60.00
RCA VICTOR					
❏ 74-0307	To Live the Past/Lying Woman (Not Trustworthy)	1970	—	3.00	6.00
❏ 74-0348	A Highway Is Like a Woman/ You Wear Your Hair Too Long	1970	—	3.00	6.00

M

Number	Title (A Side/B Side)	Yr	VG	VG+	NM
❏ 74-0379	Daddy Wants You to Come Home/Weakness Is a Thing Called Man	1970	—	3.00	6.00
❏ 74-0462	The Flirt/California Blues	1971	—	3.00	6.00
SPECIALTY					
❏ 375	Please Send Me Someone to Love/Strange Things Happening	1950	20.00	40.00	80.00
❏ 390	Lost Love/Life Is Suicide	1951	15.00	30.00	60.00
❏ 400	What a Fool I Was/Nightless Lover	1951	15.00	30.00	60.00
❏ 408	Prayin' For Your Return/My Blues	1951	15.00	30.00	60.00
❏ 416	Cry Baby/Hopeless	1952	10.00	20.00	40.00
❏ 425	The Big Question/The Hurt Is On	1952	10.00	20.00	40.00
❏ 432	Louisiana/Two Hearts Are Greater Than One	1952	10.00	20.00	40.00
❏ 439	Lonesome Highway/My Heart	1952	10.00	20.00	40.00
❏ 460	Lost Mind/Lonely One	1953	10.00	20.00	40.00
—Black vinyl					
❏ 460	Lost Mind/Lonely One	1953	20.00	40.00	80.00
—Colored vinyl					
❏ 473	The Bachelor Blues/How Deep Is the Well	1953	10.00	20.00	40.00
—Black vinyl					
❏ 473	The Bachelor Blues/How Deep Is the Well	1953	20.00	40.00	80.00
—Colored vinyl					
❏ 485	I Need Love So Bad/Loose Lips	1954	10.00	20.00	40.00
❏ 499	You Don't Exist No More/Sugar Mama, Peach Papa	1954	10.00	20.00	40.00
❏ 537	My Heart Is Cryin'/You Were Lyin' to Me	1954	10.00	20.00	40.00
❏ 544	Baby You're Rich/The Voice Within	1955	7.50	15.00	30.00
❏ 607	Diggin' the Moonglow/Please Believe Me	1956	7.50	15.00	30.00
❏ 690	When Did You Leave Heaven/What Must I Do	1960	5.00	10.00	20.00
❏ 723	Lost Mind/River's Invitation	1973	—	3.00	6.00
TANGERINE					
❏ 923	Never No More/I Reached for a Tear	1962	3.00	6.00	12.00
❏ 927	Never Say Now/Life Is Suicide	1963	2.50	5.00	10.00
❏ 931	River's Invitation/Baby Please	1963	2.50	5.00	10.00
❏ 934	The Hunt Is On/Cookin' in Style	1963	2.50	5.00	10.00
❏ 935	You Don't Exist No More/Memory Pain	1964	2.50	5.00	10.00
❏ 941	Stranger in My Own Home Town/Maybe It's Because of Love	1964	2.50	5.00	10.00
❏ 950	Fading Love/Stand By	1965	2.00	4.00	8.00
❏ 957	Give Me Time to Explain/My Jug and I	1965	2.00	4.00	8.00
❏ 966	It's Time to Make a Change/We Both Must Cry	1966	2.00	4.00	8.00
❏ 973	My Love/My Bottle Is My Companion	1966	2.00	4.00	8.00
❏ 977	As Long As You're Mine/Ha Ha in the Daytime	1967	2.00	4.00	8.00
❏ 979	Don't Start Lyin' to Me/Pretty Eyed Baby	1967	2.00	4.00	8.00
Albums					
BRUNSWICK					
❏ BL 754145	Walking on a Tightrope	1968	5.00	10.00	20.00
INTERMEDIA					
❏ QS-5010	Please Send Me Someone to Love	198?	2.50	5.00	10.00
RCA VICTOR					
❏ LSP-4269	Percy Mayfield Sings Percy Mayfield	1970	3.75	7.50	15.00
❏ LSP-4444	Weakness Is a Thing Called Man	1970	3.75	7.50	15.00
❏ LSP-4558	Blues And Then Some	1971	3.75	7.50	15.00
SPECIALTY					
❏ SPS-2126	The Best of Percy Mayfield	1970	5.00	10.00	20.00
❏ SP-7001	Poet of the Blues	1990	3.75	7.50	15.00
TANGERINE					
❏ TRC-1505 [M]	My Jug and I	1966	5.00	10.00	20.00
❏ TRCS-1505 [S]	My Jug and I	1966	6.25	12.50	25.00
❏ TRC-1510 [M]	Bought Blues	1967	5.00	10.00	20.00
❏ TRCS-1510 [S]	Bought Blues	1967	6.25	12.50	25.00

MAYO, DAVID
45s
TMI

Number	Title (A Side/B Side)	Yr	VG	VG+	NM
❏ ZS7 9001	Beautiful/Plain Old Gone	1971	—	3.50	7.00
❏ ZS7 9007	One Woman Man/(B-side unknown)	1971	—	3.50	7.00

MAYO, FRANKIE, AND THE FALCONS
45s
RCA VICTOR

Number	Title (A Side/B Side)	Yr	VG	VG+	NM
❏ 47-7076	Stepping Stone/Jigsaw Puzzle	1957	6.25	12.50	25.00

MAYPOLE
Albums
COLOSSUS

Number	Title (A Side/B Side)	Yr	VG	VG+	NM
❏ CS-1007	Maypole	1971	15.00	30.00	60.00

MAYS, WILLIE
45s
DUKE

Number	Title (A Side/B Side)	Yr	VG	VG+	NM
❏ 350	My Sad Heart/If You Love Me	1962	2.50	5.00	10.00
❏ 418	My Sad Heart/If You Love Me	1967	2.00	4.00	8.00
EPIC					
❏ 9066	Say Hey (The Willie Mays Song)/Out of the Bushes	1954	6.25	12.50	25.00
—With the Treniers					

MC5
45s
A-SQUARE

Number	Title (A Side/B Side)	Yr	VG	VG+	NM
❏ 333	Looking at You/Borderline	1967	20.00	40.00	80.00
—500 copies of this record were pressed					
❏ 333 [PS]	Looking at You/Borderline	1967	10.00	20.00	40.00
ALIVE/TOTAL ENERGY					
❏ NER 3012	Looking at You/Borderline	1998	—	—	2.00
—30th anniversary reissue					
❏ NER 3012 [PS]	Looking at You/Borderline	1998	—	—	2.00
AMG					
❏ 1000 [DJ]	I Can Only Give You Everything (same on both sides)	1966	12.50	25.00	50.00
❏ 1001	I Can Only Give You Everything/ I Just Don't Know	1969	12.50	25.00	50.00
—Black label					
❏ 1001	I Can Only Give You Everything/One of the Guys	1969	12.50	25.00	50.00
—Yellow label					
ATLANTIC					
❏ 2678	Tonight/Looking at You	1969	3.75	7.50	15.00
❏ 2724	The American Ruse/Shakin' Street	1970	3.75	7.50	15.00

ELEKTRA

Number	Title (A Side/B Side)	Yr	VG	VG+	NM
❏ MC5-1 [DJ]	Kick Out the Jams/Motor City Is Burning	1968	17.50	35.00	70.00
—Distributed free at Fillmore East concert 12/12/68; A-side is an alternate take					
❏ 45648	Kick Out the Jams/Motor City Is Burning	1969	5.00	10.00	20.00
Albums					
ALIVE					
❏ 0005 [10]	Power Trip	1994	—	3.00	6.00
❏ 0008 [10]	Ice Pick Slim/Mad Like Eldridge Cleaver	1994	—	3.00	6.00
ATLANTIC					
❏ SD 8247	Back in the USA	1970	12.50	25.00	50.00
❏ SD 8285	High Time	1971	12.50	25.00	50.00
ELEKTRA					
❏ EKS-74042	Kick Out the Jams	1969	5.00	10.00	20.00
—All other editions					
❏ EKS-74042	Kick Out the Jams	1969	12.50	25.00	50.00
—Gatefold cover with John Sinclair liner notes in center spread; brownish label					
SUNDAZED					
❏ LP 5092	Kick Out the Jams	2001	3.75	7.50	15.00
—Reissue of original Elektra album, complete with uncensored liner notes					
❏ LP 5093	Back in the USA	2002	3.00	6.00	12.00
—Reissue on 180-gram vinyl					
❏ LP 5094	High Time	2002	3.00	6.00	12.00
—Reissue on 180-gram vinyl					
TOTAL ENERGY					
❏ 2001 [10]	The American Ruse	1994	—	3.00	6.00

MCCALL, C.W.
45s
AMERICAN GRAMAPHONE

Number	Title (A Side/B Side)	Yr	VG	VG+	NM
❏ 351	Old Home Filler-Up An' Keep On-a-Truckin' Café/Old 30	1974	3.75	7.50	15.00
MGM					
❏ 14738	Old Home Filler-Up An' Keep On-a-Truckin' Café/Old 30	1974	—	2.00	4.00
❏ 14764	Wolf Creek Pass/Sloan	1974	—	2.00	4.00
❏ 14801	Classified/I've Trucked All Over This Land	1975	—	2.00	4.00
❏ 14825	Black Bear Road/Four Wheel Drive	1975	—	2.00	4.00
❏ 14839	Convoy/Long Lonesome Road	1975	—	2.50	5.00
POLYDOR					
❏ 14310	There Won't Be No Country Music (There Won't Be No Rock 'n' Roll)/Green River	1976	—	2.00	4.00
❏ 14331	Crispy Critters/Jackson Hole	1976	—	2.00	4.00
❏ 14352	Four Wheel Cowboy/Aurora Borealis	1976	—	2.00	4.00
❏ 14365	'Round the World with the Rubber Duck/ Night Rider	1976	—	2.00	4.00
❏ 14377	Audubon/Ratchetjaw	1977	—	2.00	4.00
❏ 14420	Roses for Mama/Columbine	1977	—	2.00	4.00
❏ 14445	Sing Silent Night/Old Glory	1977	—	2.50	5.00
❏ 14458	Old Glory/Watch the Wildwood Flowers	1978	—	2.00	4.00
❏ 14527	Outlaws and Lone Star Beer/Silver Cloud Breakdown	1978	—	2.00	4.00
❏ 14550	Milton/The Little Things in Life	1979	—	2.00	4.00
Albums					
MGM					
❏ M3G-4989	Wolf Creek Pass	1975	2.50	5.00	10.00
❏ M3G-5008	Black Bear Road	1975	2.50	5.00	10.00
POLYDOR					
❏ PD-1-6069	Wilderness	1976	2.50	5.00	10.00
❏ PD-1-6094	Rubber Duck	1977	2.50	5.00	10.00
❏ PD-1-6125	Roses for Mama	1978	2.50	5.00	10.00
❏ PD-1-6156	Greatest Hits	1978	2.50	5.00	10.00
❏ PD-1-6190	C.W. McCall & Co.	1979	2.50	5.00	10.00
❏ 825793-1	Greatest Hits	198?	2.00	4.00	8.00
—Reissue of 6156					

MCCALL, DARRELL
45s
ATLANTIC

Number	Title (A Side/B Side)	Yr	VG	VG+	NM
❏ 4019	There's Still a Lot of Love in San Antone/A Texas Honky Tonk	1974	—	2.50	5.00
❏ 4200	If You Don't Know Your Roses/Where Is All That Love You Talked About	1974	—	2.50	5.00
AVCO					
❏ 609	Cold Beer Signs and Country Music/ Face to the Wall	1975	—	3.00	6.00
❏ 615	Helpless/If You Don't Believe I Love You	1975	—	3.00	6.00
CAPITOL					
❏ 4543	My Kind of Lovin'/Beyond Imagination	1961	3.00	6.00	12.00
❏ 4609	Call the Zoo/Lonesome	1961	3.00	6.00	12.00
COLUMBIA					
❏ 3-10296	Pins and Needles (In My Heart)/Every Girl I See	1976	—	2.50	5.00
❏ 3-10410	I Come Home to Face the Music/ It's Been So Long, Darlin'	1976	—	2.50	5.00
❏ 3-10480	Lily Dale/Please Don't Leave Me	1976	—	2.50	5.00
—A-side with Willie Nelson					
❏ 3-10576	Dreams of a Dreamer/Sad Songs and Waltzes	1977	—	2.50	5.00
❏ 3-10653	Down the Roads of Daddy's Dreams/ An Old Memory's Arms	1977	—	2.50	5.00
❏ 3-10723	The Weeds Outlived the Roses/Love Didn't Drive My Good Woman Wild	1978	—	2.50	5.00
INDIGO					
❏ 304	Memphis in May/(B-side unknown)	1984	—	3.00	6.00
PHILIPS					
❏ 40053	I Can Take His Baby Away/A Man Can Change	1962	2.50	5.00	10.00
❏ 40079	A Stranger Was Here/I'm a Little Bit Lonely	1962	2.50	5.00	10.00
❏ 40116	No Place to Hide/Hud	1963	2.50	5.00	10.00
❏ 40154	Keeping My Feet on the Ground/Got My Baby on My Mind	1963	2.50	5.00	10.00
RCA					
❏ PB-12033	Long Line of Empties/I Wonder Which One of Us Is to Blame	1980	—	2.00	4.00
WAYSIDE					
❏ 003	Hurry Up/Wedding Band	1969	—	3.00	6.00
❏ 005	Hide and Go Cheat/Tiny Ribbons	1969	—	3.00	6.00
❏ 008	The Arms of My Weakness/Big Oak Tree	1970	—	3.00	6.00
❏ 011	Sally Bryson/(B-side unknown)	1970	—	3.00	6.00
❏ 1011	I'd Love to Live with You Again/I Love You Baby	1968	—	3.50	7.00
❏ 1021	Wall of Pictures/I'd Die to See You Smile	1968	—	3.50	7.00

Number	Title (A Side/B Side)	Yr	VG	VG+	NM

Albums
COLUMBIA

Number	Title (A Side/B Side)	Yr	VG	VG+	NM
☐ KC 34718	Lily Dale	1977	3.00	6.00	12.00

WAYSIDE

| ☐ 1030 | Meet Darrell McCall | 1969 | 5.00 | 10.00 | 20.00 |

MCCALLS, THE
45s
HIT

Number	Title (A Side/B Side)	Yr	VG	VG+	NM
☐ 236	Five O'Clock World/As Tears Go By	1966	3.00	6.00	12.00

—B-side by the Chords (2)

| ☐ 244 | Daydream/19th Nervous Breakdown | 1966 | 2.50 | 5.00 | 10.00 |
| ☐ 260 | Hanky Panky/Hungry | 1966 | 2.50 | 5.00 | 10.00 |

—B-side by the Gallicos

MCCALLUM, DAVID
45s
CAPITOL

Number	Title (A Side/B Side)	Yr	VG	VG+	NM
☐ 5571	My Carousel/Communications	1966	2.00	4.00	8.00
☐ 5571 [PS]	My Carousel/Communications	1966	3.00	6.00	12.00
☐ 5721	Three Bites of the Apple/House on Breckinridge Lane	1966	2.00	4.00	8.00
☐ 5721 [PS]	Three Bites of the Apple/House on Breckinridge Lane	1966	3.00	6.00	12.00
☐ 5802	A Man and a Woman/House of Mirrors	1966	2.00	4.00	8.00

Albums
CAPITOL

☐ ST 2432 [S]	Music — A Part of Me	1966	3.75	7.50	15.00
☐ T 2432 [M]	Music — A Part of Me	1966	3.00	6.00	12.00
☐ ST 2498 [S]	Music: A Bit More of Me	1966	3.75	7.50	15.00
☐ T 2498 [M]	Music: A Bit More of Me	1966	3.00	6.00	12.00
☐ ST 2651 [S]	Music: It's Happening Now	1967	3.75	7.50	15.00
☐ T 2651 [M]	Music: It's Happening Now	1967	3.75	7.50	15.00
☐ ST 2748 [S]	McCallum	1967	3.75	7.50	15.00
☐ T 2748 [M]	McCallum	1967	3.75	7.50	15.00

MCCANNON, GEORGE, III
45s
AMOS

Number	Title (A Side/B Side)	Yr	VG	VG+	NM
☐ 135	I Fall to Pieces/Birds of All Nations	1970	2.00	4.00	8.00
☐ 151	Tall Oak Tree/No Love at All	1970	2.00	4.00	8.00

BELL

| ☐ 702 | I Miss Her/Without Your Sweet Lips on Mine | 1968 | 3.00 | 6.00 | 12.00 |

MERCURY

| ☐ 72011 | Sigma Alpha Lonely/Shy Boy | 1962 | 3.00 | 6.00 | 12.00 |
| ☐ 72072 | Thumblin'/Candle in the Wind | 1963 | 3.00 | 6.00 | 12.00 |

PARKWAY

| ☐ 883 | Lana/What Am I Gonna Do | 1963 | 3.75 | 7.50 | 15.00 |

PHI-DAN

| ☐ 5007 | Seven Million People/You Can't Grow Peaches on a Cherry Tree | 1965 | 6.25 | 12.50 | 25.00 |

TOWER

| ☐ 198 | Look for the Rainbow/She Only Makes Me Love You More | 1966 | 3.00 | 6.00 | 12.00 |

MCCANTS, JUNIOR
45s
KING

Number	Title (A Side/B Side)	Yr	VG	VG+	NM
☐ 6076	A Boy Needs a Girl/Help My Love	1967	5.00	10.00	20.00
☐ 6106	Try Me for Your New Love/She Wrote It — I Read It	1967	2000.	3000.	4000.

MCCARTNEY, LINDA See PAUL McCARTNEY; SUZY AND THE RED STRIPES.

MCCARTNEY, PAUL Includes duets with Linda McCartney plus his work with Wings. Also see THE BEATLES; MICHAEL JACKSON AND PAUL McCARTNEY.
12-Inch Singles
ATLANTIC

Number	Title (A Side/B Side)	Yr	VG	VG+	NM
☐ PR 388 [DJ]	Every Night/Lucille	1981	62.50	125.00	250.00

CAPITOL

| ☐ SPRO-8574 [DJ] | Maybe I'm Amazed (mono/stereo) | 1976 | 20.00 | 40.00 | 80.00 |

—As "Wings"

☐ SPRO-9556/7 [DJ]	Spies Like Us (4:40) (3:46)	1985	7.50	15.00	30.00
☐ SPRO-9763 [DJ]	Press (same on both sides)	1986	5.00	10.00	20.00
☐ SPRO-9797 [DJ]	Angry (same on both sides)	1986	7.50	15.00	30.00
☐ SPRO-9860/1 [DJ]	Stranglehold/Angry	1986	6.25	12.50	25.00
☐ SPRO-9928 [DJ]	Pretty Little Head (same on both sides)	1986	12.50	25.00	50.00
☐ V-15212	Spies Like Us (Party Mix)/(Alternative Mix)//(DJ Version)/My Carnival	1985	3.75	7.50	15.00

—"MLP" on label instead of "MPL"

| ☐ V-15212 | Spies Like Us (Party Mix)/(Alternative Mix)//(DJ Version)/My Carnival | 1985 | 5.00 | 10.00 | 20.00 |

—"MPL" correct on label

| ☐ V-15235 | Press (Video Mix 4:41)/It's Not True (5:51)//Hanglide (5:18)/Press (Dub Mix 6:28) | 1986 | 3.00 | 6.00 | 12.00 |
| ☐ V-15499 | Ou Est Le Soleil? (7:10)/(Tub Dub Mix 4:27) (Instrumental 4:25) | 1989 | 3.00 | 6.00 | 12.00 |

COLUMBIA

| ☐ AS 775 [DJ] | Coming Up/Coming Up (Live at Glasgow) | 1980 | 12.50 | 25.00 | 50.00 |

—White label

| ☐ AS 775 [DJ] | Coming Up/Coming Up (Live at Glasgow) | 1980 | 15.00 | 30.00 | 60.00 |

—Red label

☐ AS 1444 [DJ]	Ebony and Ivory//Ballroom Dancing/The Pound Is Sinking	1982	7.50	15.00	30.00
☐ AS 1940 [DJ]	No More Lonely Nights (Ballad) (same on both sides)	1984	5.00	10.00	20.00
☐ AS 1990 [DJ]	No More Lonely Nights (Special Dance Mix) (same on both sides)	1984	5.00	10.00	20.00
☐ 44-03019	Take It Away/I'll Give You a Ring/Dress Me Up as a Robber	1982	3.00	6.00	12.00
☐ 44-05077	No More Lonely Nights (Playout Version)//Silly Love Songs/No More Lonely Nights (Ballad)	1984	3.00	6.00	12.00
☐ 44-05077	No More Lonely Nights (Special Dance Mix)//Silly Love Songs/No More Lonely Nights (Ballad)	1984	7.50	15.00	30.00
☐ 23-10940	Goodnight Tonight (7:25)/Daytime Nighttime Suffering	1979	2.50	5.00	10.00

—Credited to "Wings"; generic white cover, no picture cover or sticker

Number	Title (A Side/B Side)	Yr	VG	VG+	NM
☐ 23-10940	Goodnight Tonight (7:25)/Daytime Nighttime Suffering	1979	3.75	7.50	15.00

—Credited to "Wings"; with picture cover

| ☐ 23-10940 | Goodnight Tonight (7:25)/Daytime Nighttime Suffering | 1979 | 20.00 | 40.00 | 80.00 |

—Credited to "Wings"; generic white cover with large blue and white sticker

| ☐ 23-10940 [DJ] | Goodnight Tonight (7:25)/(4:18) | 1979 | 6.25 | 12.50 | 25.00 |

—Credited to "Wings"; promo issue with two versions of the A-side

| ☐ 8C8 39927 [PD] | No More Lonely Nights (Extended Version)//Silly Love Songs/No More Lonely Nights (Ballad) | 1984 | 5.00 | 10.00 | 20.00 |

—Picture disc; despite having only the above three tracks, its number is in the CBS album (not singles) numbering system

45s
APPLE

| ☐ 1829 | Another Day/Oh Woman, Oh Why | 1971 | 2.00 | 4.00 | 8.00 |
| ☐ 1829 | Another Day/Oh Woman, Oh Why | 1971 | 3.00 | 6.00 | 12.00 |

—With star on A-side label

| ☐ 1837 | Uncle Albert/Admiral Halsey//Too Many People | 1971 | 2.00 | 4.00 | 8.00 |

—Paul and Linda McCartney; with no misspelling

| ☐ 1837 | Uncle Albert/Admiral Halsey//Too Many People | 1971 | 3.75 | 7.50 | 15.00 |

—Paul and Linda McCartney; with "Pual" misspelling on producer credit

| ☐ 1837 | Uncle Albert/Admiral Halsey//Too Many People | 1971 | 12.50 | 25.00 | 50.00 |

—Paul and Linda McCartney; with unsliced apple on B-side label

| ☐ 1837 | Uncle Albert/Admiral Halsey//Too Many People | 1975 | 7.50 | 15.00 | 30.00 |

—Paul and Linda McCartney; with "All rights reserved" on label

| ☐ 1847 | Give Ireland Back to the Irish/Give Ireland Back to the Irish (Version) | 1972 | 2.50 | 5.00 | 10.00 |

—Wings

| ☐ 1847 [PS] | Give Ireland Back to the Irish/Give Ireland Back to the Irish (Version) | 1972 | 7.50 | 15.00 | 30.00 |

—Wings; title sleeve with large center hole

| ☐ 1851 | Mary Had a Little Lamb/Little Woman Love | 1972 | 2.50 | 5.00 | 10.00 |

—Wings

| ☐ 1851 [DJ] | Mary Had a Little Lamb/Little Woman Love | 1972 | 75.00 | 150.00 | 300.00 |

—White label promo, lists artist as Paul McCartney

| ☐ 1851 [PS] | Mary Had a Little Lamb/Little Woman Love | 1972 | 6.25 | 12.50 | 25.00 |

—Wings; without "Little Woman Love" on sleeve

| ☐ 1851 [PS] | Mary Had a Little Lamb/Little Woman Love | 1972 | 10.00 | 20.00 | 40.00 |

—Wings; with "Little Woman Love" on sleeve

| ☐ 1857 | Hi Hi Hi/C Moon | 1972 | 2.50 | 5.00 | 10.00 |

—Wings; red label

| ☐ 1861 | My Love/The Mess | 1973 | 2.00 | 4.00 | 8.00 |

—Paul McCartney and Wings; custom "Red Rose Speedway" label

| ☐ 1861 [DJ] | My Love/The Mess | 1973 | 50.00 | 100.00 | 200.00 |

—Paul McCartney and Wings; white label

| ☐ 1863 | Live and Let Die/I Lie Around | 1973 | 2.00 | 4.00 | 8.00 |

—Wings

| ☐ 1869 | Helen Wheels/Country Dreamer | 1973 | 2.00 | 4.00 | 8.00 |

—Paul McCartney and Wings

| ☐ P-1869 [DJ] | Helen Wheels/Country Dreamer | 1973 | 500.00 | 1000. | 2000. |

—Paul McCartney and Wings; a very rare promo, as most promos have the same song on both sides (see 6786 and 6787 below)

| ☐ 1871 | Jet/Let Me Roll It | 1974 | 2.00 | 4.00 | 8.00 |

—Paul McCartney and Wings

| ☐ 1871 | Jet/Mamunia | 1974 | 2.50 | 5.00 | 10.00 |

—Paul McCartney and Wings

| ☐ 1871 | Jet/Mamunia | 1974 | 25.00 | 50.00 | 100.00 |

—Paul McCartney and Wings; A-side incorrectly listed as playing for 2:49

| ☐ P-1871 [DJ] | Jet (Edited Mono)/Jet (Stereo) | 1974 | 12.50 | 25.00 | 50.00 |

—Paul McCartney and Wings

| ☐ 1873 | Band on the Run/Nineteen Hundred and Eighty-Five | 1974 | 2.00 | 4.00 | 8.00 |

—Paul McCartney and Wings

| ☐ P-1873 [DJ] | Band on the Run (Edited Mono)/Band on the Run (Full-length Stereo) | 1974 | 10.00 | 20.00 | 40.00 |

—Paul McCartney and Wings

| ☐ P-1873 [DJ] | Band on the Run (mono/stereo, both edits) | 1974 | 25.00 | 50.00 | 100.00 |

—Paul McCartney and Wings

| ☐ 1875 | Junior's Farm/Sally G | 1974 | 2.00 | 4.00 | 8.00 |

—Paul McCartney and Wings

| ☐ 1875 | Junior's Farm/Sally G | 1975 | 20.00 | 40.00 | 80.00 |

—Paul McCartney and Wings; with "All Rights Reserved" on label

| ☐ P-1875 [DJ] | Junior's Farm (Edited Mono)/Junior's Farm (Full-length Stereo) | 1974 | 12.50 | 25.00 | 50.00 |

—Paul McCartney and Wings

| ☐ P-1875 [DJ] | Sally G (mono/stereo) | 1974 | 20.00 | 40.00 | 80.00 |

—Paul McCartney and Wings

| ☐ PRO-6193/4 [DJ] | Another Day/Oh Woman, Oh Why | 1971 | 20.00 | 40.00 | 80.00 |
| ☐ PRO-6786 [DJ] | Helen Wheels (mono/stereo) | 1973 | 12.50 | 25.00 | 50.00 |

—Paul McCartney and Wings

| ☐ PRO-6787 [DJ] | Country Dreamer (mono/stereo) | 1973 | 100.00 | 200.00 | 400.00 |

—Paul McCartney and Wings

CAPITOL

| ☐ 1829 | Another Day/Oh Woman, Oh Why | 1976 | 3.75 | 7.50 | 15.00 |

—Black label

| ☐ 1837 | Uncle Albert/Admiral Halsey//Too Many People | 1976 | 3.75 | 7.50 | 15.00 |

—Credited to "Paul and Linda McCartney"; black label

| ☐ 1847 | Give Ireland Back to the Irish/Give Ireland Back to the Irish | 1976 | 5.00 | 10.00 | 20.00 |

—Credited to "Wings"; black label

| ☐ 1851 | Mary Had a Little Lamb/Little Woman Love | 1976 | 3.00 | 6.00 | 12.00 |

—Credited to "Wings"; black label

| ☐ 1857 | Hi Hi Hi/C Moon | 1976 | 3.75 | 7.50 | 15.00 |

—Credited to "Wings"; black label

| ☐ 1861 | My Love/The Mess | 1976 | 5.00 | 10.00 | 20.00 |

—Credited to "Paul McCartney and Wings"; black label; "The Mess" plays normally

| ☐ 1861 | My Love/The Mess | 1976 | 5.00 | 10.00 | 20.00 |

—Credited to "Paul McCartney and Wings"; black label; "The Mess" plays too fast

| ☐ 1863 | Live and Let Die/I Lie Around | 1976 | 3.00 | 6.00 | 12.00 |

—Credited to "Wings"; black label

| ☐ 1869 | Helen Wheels/Country Dreamer | 1976 | 3.75 | 7.50 | 15.00 |

—Credited to "Paul McCartney and Wings"; black label

| ☐ 1871 | Jet/Let Me Roll It | 1976 | 3.75 | 7.50 | 15.00 |

—Credited to "Paul McCartney and Wings"; black label

M

Number	Title (A Side/B Side)	Yr	VG	VG+	NM
❑ 1873	Band on the Run/Nineteen Hundred and Eighty-Five	1976	3.75	7.50	15.00

—Credited to "Paul McCartney and Wings"; black label

❑ 1875	Junior's Farm/Sally G	1976	3.75	7.50	15.00

—Credited to "Paul McCartney and Wings"; black label

❑ 4091	Listen to What the Man Said/Love in Song	1975	—	2.50	5.00

—Credited to "Wings"

❑ 4091 [PS]	Listen to What the Man Said/Love in Song	1975	3.00	6.00	12.00

—Credited to "Wings"

❑ 4145	Letting Go/You Gave Me the Answer	1975	—	2.50	5.00
❑ 4175	Venus and Mars Rock Show/Magneto and Titanium Man	1975	—	2.50	5.00

—Credited to "Wings"

❑ 4256	Silly Love Songs/Cook of the House	1976	—	2.00	4.00

—Credited to "Wings"; "Speed of Sound" label (more common version)

❑ 4256	Silly Love Songs/Cook of the House	1976	2.00	4.00	8.00

—Credited to "Wings"; black label

❑ 4293	Let 'Em In/Beware My Love	1976	—	2.00	4.00

—Credited to "Wings"; "Speed of Sound" label

❑ 4293	Let 'Em In/Beware My Love	1976	—	3.00	6.00

—Credited to "Wings"; black label (more common version)

❑ 4385	Maybe I'm Amazed/Soily	1976	—	2.00	4.00

—Credited to "Wings"; custom label (more common version)

❑ 4385	Maybe I'm Amazed/Soily	1976	5.00	10.00	20.00

—Credited to "Wings"; black label

❑ 4504	Girls' School/Mull of Kintyre	1977	—	2.50	5.00

—Credited to "Wings"; black label (more common version)

❑ 4504 [PS]	Girls' School/Mull of Kintyre	1977	3.00	6.00	12.00
❑ 4504	Girls' School/Mull of Kintyre	1978	30.00	60.00	120.00

—Credited to "Wings"; purple label, label has reeded edge

❑ 4559	With a Little Luck/Backwards Traveller-Cuff Link	1978	—	2.00	4.00

—Credited to "Wings"

❑ 4594	I've Had Enough/Deliver Your Children	1978	—	2.00	4.00

—Credited to "Wings"

❑ 4625	London Town/I'm Carrying	1978	—	2.00	4.00

—Credited to "Wings"

❑ B-5537	Spies Like Us/My Carnival	1985	—	—	3.00
❑ B-5537 [PS]	Spies Like Us/My Carnival	1985	—	3.00	6.00
❑ B-5597	Press/It's Not True	1986	—	2.50	5.00
❑ B-5597 [PS]	Press/It's Not True	1986	—	2.50	5.00
❑ B-5636	Stranglehold/Angry	1986	—	2.50	5.00
❑ B-5636 [PS]	Stranglehold/Angry	1986	—	2.50	5.00
❑ B-5672	Only Love Remains/Tough on a Tightrope	1987	—	2.50	5.00
❑ B-5672 [PS]	Only Love Remains/Tough on a Tightrope	1987	—	2.50	5.00
❑ SPRO-8570/1 [DJ]	Maybe I'm Amazed (3:43) (stereo/mono)	1977	7.50	15.00	30.00

—As "Wings"

❑ 7PRO-9552/3 [DJ]	Spies Like Us (4:40)/(3:46)	1985	5.00	10.00	20.00
❑ S7-17318	Off the Ground/Cosmically Conscious	1993	—	3.00	6.00

—Black vinyl "error" issue

❑ S7-17318	Off the Ground/Cosmically Conscious	1993	—	3.00	6.00

—White vinyl standard issue

❑ S7-17319	Biker Like an Icon/Things We Said Today	1993	—	3.00	6.00

—Black vinyl "error" issue

❑ S7-17319	Biker Like an Icon/Things We Said Today	1993	—	3.00	6.00

—White vinyl standard issue

❑ S7-17489	C'mon People/Down to the River	1993	2.00	4.00	8.00

—All copies on white vinyl

❑ S7-17643	Wonderful Christmastime/Rudolph, the Red-Nosed Reggae	1993	—	3.00	6.00

—Credited to "Paul McCartney & Wings"; red vinyl

❑ B-44367	My Brave Face/Flying to My Home	1989	—	2.50	5.00

—Version 3: Same as Version 2, time of A-side is "3:16"

❑ B-44367	My Brave Face/Flying to My Home	1989	2.00	4.00	8.00

—Version 2: Artist in custom print, title in block print, time of A-side is "3:17"

❑ B-44367	My Brave Face/Flying to My Home	1989	2.50	5.00	10.00

—Version 1: Both title and artist in block print, time of A-side is "3:17"

❑ B-44367 [PS]	My Brave Face/Flying to My Home	1989	—	2.50	5.00
❑ 50291	Freedom/From a Lover to a Friend	2001	—	2.00	4.00
❑ S7-56946	Hope of Deliverance/Long Leather Coat	1993	—	3.00	6.00
❑ 58823	No Other Baby/Try Not to Cry	1999	—	2.00	4.00
❑ 58995	Maybe I'm Amazed/Band on the Run	2001	—	2.50	5.00

—Credited to "Wings"; gold vinyl; both sides feature spoken introductions by Paul

❑ 77730	Your Loving Flame/Lonely Road	2002	—	2.00	4.00
❑ 7PRO-79700 [DJ]	This One (same on both sides)	1989	100.00	200.00	400.00

—Vinyl is promo only

❑ 7PRO-79889 [DJ]	Figure of Eight (same on both sides)	1989	25.00	50.00	100.00

—Test pressings with blank label; most known copies come in a Capitol sleeve; number taken from dead wax

COLUMBIA

❑ AE7 1204 [DJ]	Coming Up (Live at Glasgow)/(B-side blank)	1980	2.00	4.00	8.00

—Small hole, plays at 33 1/3 rpm; this was the bonus single included with most early pressings of the "McCartney II" LP (Columbia FC 36511) and was not distributed separately

❑ 18-02171	Silly Love Songs/Cook of the House	1981	6.25	12.50	25.00

—Credited to "Wings"; despite label information, this has an edited version of A-side

❑ 18-03018	Take It Away/I'll Give You a Ring	1982	—	—	3.00
❑ 18-03018 [PS]	Take It Away/I'll Give You a Ring	1982	—	—	3.00
❑ 38-03235	Tug of War/Get It	1982	3.00	6.00	12.00
❑ 38-04127	Wonderful Christmastime/Rudolph the Red-Nosed Reggae	1983	7.50	15.00	30.00

—Scarce reissue with B-side in stereo

❑ 38-04296	So Bad/Pipes of Peace	1983	—	2.50	5.00
❑ 38-04296 [PS]	So Bad/Pipes of Peace	1983	—	2.50	5.00
❑ 38-04581	No More Lonely Nights/(playout version)	1984	—	2.00	4.00
❑ 38-04581	No More Lonely Nights/(Special Dance Version)	1984	10.00	20.00	40.00
❑ 38-04581 [PS]	No More Lonely Nights/(playout version)	1984	—	2.50	5.00

—Title print in white, credit print in gray

❑ 38-04581 [PS]	No More Lonely Nights/(playout version)	1984	7.50	15.00	30.00

—Title print in gray, credit print in white

❑ 3-10939	Goodnight Tonight/Daytime Nighttime Suffering	1979	—	3.00	6.00

—Credited to "Wings"

❑ 3-11020	Getting Closer/Spin It On	1979	—	3.00	6.00

—Credited to "Wings"

❑ 3-11020 [PS]	Getting Closer/Spin It On	1979	7.50	15.00	30.00

—Title sleeve with large center hole

❑ 1-11070	Arrow Through Me/Old Siam, Sir	1979	—	3.00	6.00

—Credited to "Wings"

Number	Title (A Side/B Side)	Yr	VG	VG+	NM
❑ 1-11162	Wonderful Christmastime/Rudolph the Red-Nosed Reggae	1979	2.50	5.00	10.00
❑ 1-11162 [PS]	Wonderful Christmastime/Rudolph the Red-Nosed Reggae	1979	3.75	7.50	15.00
❑ 1-11263	Coming Up//Coming Up (Live at Glasgow)/Lunch Box-Odd Sox	1980	—	2.00	4.00

—The first song on side 2 is credited to "Paul McCartney & Wings"

❑ 1-11263 [PS]	Coming Up//Coming Up (Live at Glasgow)/Lunch Box-Odd Sox	1980	—	2.50	5.00
❑ 1-11335	Waterfalls/Check My Machine	1980	—	3.00	6.00
❑ 1-11335 [PS]	Waterfalls/Check My Machine	1980	5.00	10.00	20.00
❑ 13-33405	Goodnight Tonight/Getting Closer	1980	2.50	5.00	10.00

—Credited to "Wings"; red label "Hall of Fame" series

❑ 13-33407	My Love/Maybe I'm Amazed	1980	2.50	5.00	10.00

—Credited to "Paul McCartney and Wings"; red label "Hall of Fame" series; B-side is the studio version, making its first appearance on U.S. 45 here

❑ 13-33407	My Love/Maybe I'm Amazed	1985	7.50	15.00	30.00

—Credited to "Paul McCartney and Wings"; briefly available grayish label reissue

❑ 13-33408	Jet//Uncle Albert/Admiral Halsey	1980	2.50	5.00	10.00

—Credited to "Paul McCartney and Wings"; red label "Hall of Fame" series

❑ 13-33408	Jet//Uncle Albert/Admiral Halsey	1985	7.50	15.00	30.00

—Credited to "Paul McCartney and Wings"; briefly available grayish label reissue

❑ 13-33409	Band on the Run/Helen Wheels	1980	2.50	5.00	10.00

—Credited to "Paul McCartney and Wings"; red label "Hall of Fame" series

❑ 13-33409	Band on the Run/Helen Wheels	1985	7.50	15.00	30.00

—Credited to "Paul McCartney and Wings"; briefly available grayish label reissue

EMI

❑ 3977	Walking in the Park with Eloise/Bridge on the River Suite	1974	15.00	30.00	60.00
❑ 3977 [PS]	Walking in the Park with Eloise/Bridge on the River Suite	1974	20.00	40.00	80.00

—As "The Country Hams"

Albums

APPLE

❑ SMAS-3363	McCartney	197?	5.00	10.00	20.00

—New prefix on label

❑ SMAS-3363	McCartney	1975	25.00	50.00	100.00

—With "All Rights Reserved" on label

❑ STAO-3363	McCartney	1970	5.00	10.00	20.00

—Only "McCartney" on label; back cover does NOT say "An Abkco managed company"

❑ STAO-3363	McCartney	1970	6.25	12.50	25.00

—"McCartney" and "Paul McCartney" on separate lines on label; New York address on back cover

❑ STAO-3363	McCartney	1970	6.25	12.50	25.00

—Only "McCartney" on label; back cover says "An Abkco managed company"

❑ STAO-3363	McCartney	1970	7.50	15.00	30.00

—"McCartney" and "Paul McCartney" on separate lines on label; California address on back cover

❑ STAO-3363	McCartney	1970	20.00	40.00	80.00

—Apple label with small Capitol logo on B-side

❑ MAS-3375 [M]	Ram	1971	1000.	2000.	4000.

—Credited to "Paul and Linda McCartney"; mono record in stereo cover for radio station use only

❑ SMAS-3375	Ram	1971	3.75	7.50	15.00

—Credited to "Paul and Linda McCartney"; unsliced apple on one label, sliced apple on other

❑ SMAS-3375	Ram	1971	7.50	15.00	30.00

—Credited to "Paul and Linda McCartney"; unsliced apple on both labels

❑ SMAS-3375	Ram	1971	12.50	25.00	50.00

—Credited to "Paul and Linda McCartney"; Apple label with small Capitol logo on B-side

❑ SMAS-3375	Ram	1975	25.00	50.00	100.00

—Credited to "Paul and Linda McCartney"; with "All Rights Reserved" on label

❑ SW-3386	Wild Life	1971	3.75	7.50	15.00

—Credited to "Wings"

❑ SMAL-3409	Red Rose Speedway	1973	5.00	10.00	20.00

—Credited to "Paul McCartney and Wings"; with bound-in booklet

❑ SO-3415	Band on the Run	1973	5.00	10.00	20.00

—Credited to "Paul McCartney and Wings"; with photo innersleeve and poster

❑ SPRO-6210 [DJ]	Brung to Ewe By	1971	100.00	200.00	400.00

—Promo-only radio spots for "Ram"; counterfeits have uneven spacing between tracks

CAPITOL

❑ SMAS-3363	McCartney	1976	5.00	10.00	20.00

—Black label, "Manufactured by MPL Communications Inc" at top

❑ SMAS-3363	McCartney	1976	6.25	12.50	25.00

—Black label, "Manufactured by McCartney Music Inc" at top

❑ SMAS-3375	Ram	197?	5.00	10.00	20.00

—Credited to "Paul and Linda McCartney"; black label, "Manufactured by MPL Communications Inc" at top

❑ SMAS-3375	Ram	197?	10.00	20.00	40.00

—Credited to "Paul and Linda McCartney"; black label, "Manufactured by Capitol RecordsÖ" on label

❑ SMAS-3375	Ram	1976	7.50	15.00	30.00

—Credited to "Paul and Linda McCartney"; black label, "Manufactured by McCartney Music Inc" at top

❑ SW-3386	Wild Life	197?	5.00	10.00	20.00

—Credited to "Wings"; black label, "Manufactured by MPL Communications Inc" at top

❑ SW-3386	Wild Life	1976	7.50	15.00	30.00

—Credited to "Wings"; black label, "Manufactured by McCartney Music Inc" at top

❑ SMAL-3409	Red Rose Speedway	197?	6.25	12.50	25.00

—Credited to "Paul McCartney and Wings"; black label, "Manufactured by MPL Communications Inc" at top

❑ SMAL-3409	Red Rose Speedway	1976	7.50	15.00	30.00

—Credited to "Paul McCartney and Wings"; black label, "Manufactured by McCartney Music Inc" at top

❑ SO-3415	Band on the Run	197?	5.00	10.00	20.00

—Credited to "Paul McCartney and Wings"; black label, "Maunfactured by MPL Communications Inc." at top

❑ SO-3415	Band on the Run	197?	12.50	25.00	50.00

—Credited to "Paul McCartney and Wings"; black label, "Manufactured by Capitol Records..."

❑ SO-3415	Band on the Run	1975	5.00	10.00	20.00

—Credited to "Paul McCartney and Wings"; custom label with MPL logo

❑ SMAS-11419	Venus and Mars	1975	3.75	7.50	15.00

—Credited to "Wings"; with two posters and two stickers

❑ SW-11525	Wings at the Speed of Sound	1976	2.50	5.00	10.00

—Credited to "Wings"; custom label

❑ SW-11525 [DJ]	Wings at the Speed of Sound	1976	75.00	150.00	300.00

—Credited to "Wings"; white label advance promo

❑ SWCO-11593 [(3)]	Wings Over America	1976	6.25	12.50	25.00

—Credited to "Wings"; custom labels with poster

❑ ST-11642	Thrillington	1977	25.00	50.00	100.00

—Credited to "Percy 'Thrills' Thrillington"; instrumental versions of songs from Ram LP

Number	Title (A Side/B Side)	Yr	VG	VG+	NM
❑ SW-11777	London Town	1978	3.75	7.50	15.00

—Credited to "Wings"; custom label with poster

❑ SEAX-11901 [PD]	Band on the Run	1978	10.00	20.00	40.00

—Credited to "Paul McCartney and Wings"; picture disc

❑ SOO-11905	Wings Greatest	1978	3.75	7.50	15.00

—Credited to "Wings"; custom label with poster

❑ SOO-11905 [DJ]	Wings Greatest	1978	100.00	200.00	400.00

—Credited to "Wings"; white label advance promo/test pressing

❑ PJAS-12475	Press to Play	1986	3.00	6.00	12.00
❑ CLW-48287 [(2)]	All the Best!	1987	5.00	10.00	20.00
❑ C1-56500	Flaming Pie	1997	3.75	7.50	15.00
❑ C1-91653	Flowers in the Dirt	1989	5.00	10.00	20.00
❑ C1-94778 [(3)]	Tripping the Live Fantastic	1990	15.00	30.00	60.00
❑ 99176 [(2)]	Band on the Run	1999	10.00	20.00	40.00

—Limited-edition 180-gram reissue with original LP on one record and interviews and "The Making of..." on the second

❑ C1-595379	Tripping the Live Fantastic — Highlights!	1990	6.25	12.50	25.00

—Released on vinyl only through Columbia House; with Canada address on back cover, this was sold in the U.S. by Columbia House

❑ C1-595379	Tripping the Live Fantastic — Highlights!	1990	6.25	12.50	25.00

—Released on vinyl only through Columbia House; with U.S. address on back cover

COLUMBIA

❑ A2S 821 [(2)][DJ]	The McCartney Interview	1980	10.00	20.00	40.00

—Promo-only set; one LP is the entire interview, the other is banded for airplay; white labels with black print; counterfeits have blank white labels

❑ FC 36057	Back to the Egg	1979	2.50	5.00	10.00

—Credited to "Wings"; custom label

❑ FC 36057 [DJ]	Back to the Egg	1979	10.00	20.00	40.00

—Credited to "Wings"; "Demonstration -- Not for Sale" on custom label

❑ PC 36057	Back to the Egg	1984	7.50	15.00	30.00

—Credited to "Wings"; "PC" cover with "FC" label

❑ PC 36057	Back to the Egg	1984	10.00	20.00	40.00

—Credited to "Wings"; "PC" cover with "PC" label

❑ JC 36478	McCartney	1979	3.75	7.50	15.00
❑ PC 36478	McCartney	1984	3.75	7.50	15.00

—Budget-line reissue

❑ JC 36479	Ram	1980	3.75	7.50	15.00

—Credited to "Paul and Linda McCartney"

❑ PC 36479	Ram	1984	3.75	7.50	15.00

—Credited to "Paul and Linda McCartney"; budget-line reissue

❑ JC 36480	Wild Life	1980	3.75	7.50	15.00

—Credited to "Wings"

❑ PC 36480	Wild Life	1982	3.75	7.50	15.00

—Credited to "Wings"; budget-line reissue

❑ JC 36481	Red Rose Speedway	1980	3.75	7.50	15.00

—Credited to "Paul McCartney and Wings"; flat or glossy cover

❑ PC 36481	Red Rose Speedway	198?	3.75	7.50	15.00

—Credited to "Paul McCartney and Wings"; not issued with booklet

❑ JC 36482	Band on the Run	198?	25.00	50.00	100.00

—Credited to "Paul McCartney and Wings"; white "MPL" logo on lower left front cover

❑ JC 36482	Band on the Run	1980	3.75	7.50	15.00

—Credited to "Paul McCartney and Wings"; custom label

❑ PC 36482	Band on the Run	198?	5.00	10.00	20.00

—Credited to "Paul McCartney and Wings"; "PC" cover with "JC" label

❑ PC 36482	Band on the Run	198?	7.50	15.00	30.00

—Credited to "Paul McCartney and Wings"; "PC" cover with "PC" label

❑ FC 36511	McCartney II	1980	2.50	5.00	10.00

—Add 80% if bonus single of "Coming Up (Live at Glasgow)" (AE7 1204) is with package

❑ FC 36511 [DJ]	McCartney II	1980	7.50	15.00	30.00

—White label promo

❑ PC 36511	McCartney II	1984	6.25	12.50	25.00

—"PC" cover with "FC" label

❑ PC 36511	McCartney II	1984	25.00	50.00	100.00

—"PC" cover with "PC" label

❑ JC 36801	Venus and Mars	1980	3.75	7.50	15.00

—Credited to "Wings"; with one poster and two stickers

❑ PC 36801	Venus and Mars	1982	3.75	7.50	15.00

—Credited to "Wings"; budget-line reissue, not issued with inserts

❑ PC 36987	The McCartney Interview	1980	3.00	6.00	12.00

—Stock release of interview originally intended for promotional use only

❑ FC 37409	Wings at the Speed of Sound	1981	3.75	7.50	15.00

—Credited to "Wings"; custom label

❑ PC 37409	Wings at the Speed of Sound	1982	3.75	7.50	15.00

—Credited to "Wings"; regular Columbia label, budget-line reissue

❑ PC 37462	Tug of War	1984	7.50	15.00	30.00

—Custom label; "PC" cover with "TC" label

❑ PC 37462	Tug of War	1984	25.00	50.00	100.00

—Regular Columbia label; "PC" cover with "PC" label

❑ TC 37462	Tug of War	1982	2.50	5.00	10.00
❑ C3X 37990 [(3)]	Wings Over America	1982	12.50	25.00	50.00

—Credited to "Wings"; custom labels, no poster

❑ QC 39149	Pipes of Peace	1983	3.00	6.00	12.00
❑ SC 39613	Give My Regards to Broad Street	1984	3.75	7.50	15.00
❑ HC 46382	Band on the Run	1981	12.50	25.00	50.00

—Credited to "Paul McCartney and Wings"; half-speed mastered edition

MPL/PARLOPHONE

❑ 96413	Unplugged (The Official Bootleg)	1991	18.75	37.50	75.00

—No U.S. pressings; "American" copies were U.K. imports with liner notes in Spanish!

NATIONAL FEATURES CORP.

❑ 2955/6	Band on the Run Radio Interview Special	1973	375.00	750.00	1500.

—Promo-only interview disc

MCCARTNEY, PAUL, AND STEVIE WONDER Also see each artist's individual listings.
12-Inch Singles
COLUMBIA

❑ 44-02878	Ebony and Ivory//Rainclouds/Ebony and Ivory (Solo)	1982	3.00	6.00	12.00

—B-side by McCartney solo

45s
COLUMBIA

❑ 18-02860	Ebony and Ivory/Rainclouds	1982	—	2.00	4.00

—B-side by McCartney solo

❑ 18-02860 [PS]	Ebony and Ivory/Rainclouds	1982	—	2.00	4.00

Number	Title (A Side/B Side)	Yr	VG	VG+	NM

MCCLAY, YUL, AND THE MONDELLOS See THE MONDELLOS.

MCCORD, SYLVESTER
45s
HIT

❑ 72	Tie Me Kangaroo Down, Sport/Sukiyaki	1963	2.00	4.00	8.00

—B-side by the Music City Five

MCCORMICK, GAYLE Also see SMITH.
45s
ABC DUNHILL

❑ 4281	Gonna Be Alright Now/Save Me	1971	—	2.50	5.00
❑ 4288	It's a Cryin' Shame/If Only You Believe	1971	—	2.50	5.00
❑ 4298	You Really Got a Hold on Me/C'est La Vie	1972	—	2.50	5.00

DECCA

❑ 33030	Near You/Take Me Back	1972	—	2.50	5.00

MCA

❑ 40007	Sweet Feelings/Take Me Back	1973	—	2.00	4.00

SHADYBROOK

❑ 45017	Coming In Out of the Rain/Simon Said	1977	2.50	5.00	10.00

Albums
ABC DUNHILL

❑ DS-50109	Gayle McCormick	1971	3.00	6.00	12.00

DECCA

❑ DL 75364	Flesh and Blood	1972	3.00	6.00	12.00

FANTASY

❑ 9467	One More Hour	1974	3.00	6.00	12.00

MCCORMICK, MAUREEN Also see THE BRADY BUNCH; CHRIS KNIGHT AND MAUREEN McCORMICK.
45s
PARAMOUNT

❑ 0292	Love's in the Roses/Harmonize	1974	3.75	7.50	15.00

MCCOY, CHARLIE
45s
CADENCE

❑ 1390	Cherry Berry Wine/My Little Woman	1960	2.50	5.00	10.00
❑ 1415	I Just Want to Make Love to You/Rooster Blues	1962	2.50	5.00	10.00

MONUMENT

❑ 45-210	Summit Ridge Drive/Play It Again Charlie	1977	—	2.50	5.00
❑ 45-224	Amazing Grace/Squeezing	1977	—	2.50	5.00
❑ 45-239	Foggy River/Last Letter	1977	—	2.50	5.00
❑ 45-258	Fair and Tender Ladies/18th Century Rosewood Clock	1978	—	2.50	5.00
❑ 45-272	Drifting Lovers/West Virginia Mountain Melody	1978	—	2.50	5.00
❑ 45-282	Midnight Flyer/Cripple Creek	1979	—	2.50	5.00
❑ 45-289	Ramblin' Music Man/Red Haired Boy	1979	—	2.50	5.00
❑ 45-292	Carolina Morning/Appalachian Fever	1979	—	2.50	5.00
❑ 45-296	Cold, Cold Heart/Station Break	1980	—	2.50	5.00
❑ 842	My Babe/Will You Love Me Tomorrow	1964	3.00	6.00	12.00
❑ 870	I'm Ready/Harpoon Man	1965	2.00	4.00	8.00
❑ 893	Girl (Those Were the Good Old Days)/It's a Man Down There	1965	2.00	4.00	8.00
❑ 926	Let Him Go/Screamin', Shoutin', Beggin', Pleadin'	1966	2.00	4.00	8.00
❑ 975	Stubborn Kind of Fellow/My Baby's Back Again	1966	2.00	4.00	8.00
❑ 998	Cold Cold World/You've Got to Face Life	1967	2.00	4.00	8.00
❑ 1076	Gimme Some Lovin'/Boy from England	1968	—	3.00	6.00
❑ 1093	Harper Valley P.T.A./Juke	1968	—	3.00	6.00
❑ 1938	Blue Christmas/Christmas Cheer	1976	—	—	3.00

—"Golden Series" reissue

❑ 03518	The State of Our Union/Just Doin' Nothin' with You (Is Really Somethin')	1983	—	2.00	4.00

—With Laney Hicks

❑ 8529	I Started Loving You Again/The Real McCoy	1971	—	2.50	5.00
❑ 8546	I'm So Lonesome I Could Cry/Grade A	1972	—	2.50	5.00
❑ 8554	I Really Don't Want to Know/Minor, Minor	1972	—	2.50	5.00
❑ 8566	Orange Blossom Special/Hangin' On	1973	—	2.50	5.00
❑ 8576	Shenandoah/John Henry	1973	—	2.50	5.00
❑ 8589	Release Me/Fastest Harp in the South	1973	—	2.50	5.00
❑ 8600	Silver Threads and Golden Needles/I Just Can't Stand to See You Cry	1974	—	2.00	4.00
❑ 8611	Boogie Woogie (A/K/A T.D.'s Boogie Woogie)/Keep On Harpin'	1974	—	2.00	4.00

—With Barefoot Jerry

❑ 8625	The Way We Were/I Can't Help It	1974	—	2.00	4.00
❑ 8633	Blue Christmas/Christmas Cheer	1974	—	2.50	5.00
❑ 8638	Everybody Stand Up and Holler for the Union/New River Gorge	1975	—	2.00	4.00
❑ 8650	Please Don't Tell Me How the Story Ends/Juke	1975	—	2.00	4.00
❑ 8660	Blues Stay Away from Me/Pots and Pans	1975	—	2.00	4.00
❑ 8672	Columbus Stockade Blues/(I Heard That) Lonesome Whistle	1975	—	2.00	4.00
❑ 8683	The Star-Spangled Banner/Silver Wings	1976	—	2.00	4.00
❑ 8703	Wabash Cannonball/Ode to Billie Joe	1976	—	2.00	4.00
❑ 21001	Until the Nights/I Love the Way You Love Me	1981	—	2.50	5.00

—With Laney Smallwood

7-Inch Extended Plays
MONUMENT

❑ AEZ-00001 [DJ]	Jackson/Today I Started Loving You Again/Easy Lovin'//To Get to You/Rocky Top/I'm So Lonesome I Could Cry	1973	2.50	5.00	10.00

—Label calls this "Bonus Record"; contains excerpts of the above songs plus an interview with Frank Jones; small hole, plays at 33 1/3 rpm

❑ AEZ-00001 [PS]	Free Bonus 7"	1973	2.50	5.00	10.00

—Sleeve with large flap at left; may have been included with purchase of certain Charlie McCoy LPs in 1973

Albums
CMH

❑ 9030 [(2)]	Flat-Picking Spectacular	1984	3.00	6.00	12.00

MONUMENT

❑ 6623	The Real McCoy	1976	2.50	5.00	10.00

—Reissue of 31329

❑ 6624	Charlie McCoy	1976	2.50	5.00	10.00

—Reissue of 31910

M

Number	Title (A Side/B Side)	Yr	VG	VG+	NM
❑ 6625	Good Time Charlie	1976	2.50	5.00	10.00
—Reissue of 32215					
❑ 6626	The Fastest Harp in the South	1976	2.50	5.00	10.00
—Reissue of 32749					
❑ 6627	The Nashville Hit Man	1976	2.50	5.00	10.00
—Reissue of 32922					
❑ 6628	Charlie My Boy!	1976	2.50	5.00	10.00
—Reissue of 33384					
❑ 6629	Harpin' the Blues	1976	2.50	5.00	10.00
—Reissue of 33802					
❑ 6630	Play It Again Charlie	1976	2.50	5.00	10.00
❑ 7612	Cookin'	1977	2.50	5.00	10.00
❑ 7622	Greatest Hits	1978	2.50	5.00	10.00
❑ 7632	Appalachian Fever	1979	2.50	5.00	10.00
❑ SLP-18097	The World of Charlie McCoy	1968	3.75	7.50	15.00
❑ Z 31329	The Real McCoy	1971	3.00	6.00	12.00
❑ KZ 31910	Charlie McCoy	1972	3.00	6.00	12.00
❑ KZ 32215	Good Time Charlie	1973	3.00	6.00	12.00
❑ KZ 32749	The Fastest Harp in the South	1974	3.00	6.00	12.00
❑ KZ 32922	The Nashville Hit Man	1974	3.00	6.00	12.00
❑ PZ 33384	Charlie My Boy!	1975	3.00	6.00	12.00
❑ PZ 33802	Harpin' the Blues	1975	3.00	6.00	12.00
❑ PW 38387	The Greatest Hits of Charlie McCoy	1982	2.00	4.00	8.00

MCCOY, VAN

12-Inch Singles
H&L

Number	Title (A Side/B Side)	Yr	VG	VG+	NM
❑ 2002	Rhythms of the World (10:12)//Soul Cha Cha/				
	That's the Joint	1976	5.00	10.00	20.00

45s
AVCO

Number	Title (A Side/B Side)	Yr	VG	VG+	NM
❑ 4639	Love Is the Answer/Killing Me Softly	1974	—	2.50	5.00
❑ 4648	Boogie Down/Rainy Night in Georgia	1975	—	2.50	5.00
❑ 4653	The Hustle/Hey Girl, Come and Get It	1975	—	2.00	4.00
❑ 4660	Change with the Times/Goodnight Baby	1975	—	2.00	4.00
COLUMBIA					
❑ 43415	Keep Loving Me/Butterfly	1965	3.00	6.00	12.00
❑ 43495	Starlight Starbright/				
	This Is the Way We Fall in Love	1965	2.00	4.00	8.00
❑ 43694	I Will Wait for You/The House That Love Built	1966	2.00	4.00	8.00
EPIC					
❑ 10470	I Started a Joke/Toney's Theme	1969	—	3.50	7.00
H&L					
❑ 4653	The Hustle/Hey Girl, Come and Get It	197?	—	2.50	5.00
—Reissue of Avco 4653, but harder to find					
❑ 4667	Night Walk/Love Child	1976	—	2.00	4.00
❑ 4670	Party/The Disco Kid	1976	—	2.00	4.00
❑ 4677	The Shuffle/That's the Joint	1976	—	2.00	4.00
❑ 4682	Soul Cha Cha/Oriental Boogie	1977	—	2.00	4.00
LIBERTY					
❑ 55457	Follow Your Heart/Lonely	1962	3.00	6.00	12.00
MCA					
❑ 40885	My Favorite Fantasy/You're So Right for Me	1978	—	2.00	4.00
❑ 40938	Trying to Make the Best of It/Two Points	1978	—	2.00	4.00
❑ 40984	Lonely Dancer/Decisions	1979	—	2.00	4.00
ROCK'N					
❑ 101	Mr. D.J./Never Trust a Friend	1961	12.50	25.00	50.00

Albums
AVCO

Number	Title (A Side/B Side)	Yr	VG	VG+	NM
❑ AV-69002	Love Is the Answer	1974	2.50	5.00	10.00
❑ AV-69006	Disco Baby	1975	2.50	5.00	10.00
❑ AV-69009	The Disco Kid	1975	2.50	5.00	10.00
BUDDAH					
❑ BDS-5103	Soul Improvisations	1971	3.75	7.50	15.00
❑ BDS-5648	From Disco to Love	1975	2.50	5.00	10.00
—Retitled reissue of 5103					
COLUMBIA					
❑ CL 2497 [M]	Night Time Is the Lonely Time	1966	5.00	10.00	20.00
❑ CS 9297 [S]	Night Time Is the Lonely Time	1966	6.25	12.50	25.00
H&L					
❑ HL-69002	Love Is the Answer	1976	2.00	4.00	8.00
—Reissue of Avco 69002					
❑ HL-69006	Disco Baby	1976	2.00	4.00	8.00
—Reissue of Avco 69006					
❑ HL-69009	The Disco Kid	1976	2.00	4.00	8.00
—Reissue of Avco 69009					
❑ HL-69012	The Real McCoy	1976	2.50	5.00	10.00
❑ HL-69014	Rhythms of the World	1976	2.50	5.00	10.00
❑ HL-69016	The Hustle and Best of Van McCoy	1976	2.50	5.00	10.00
❑ HL-69022	Van McCoy and His Magnificent Movie Machine	1977	2.50	5.00	10.00
MCA					
❑ 3036	My Favorite Fantasy	1978	2.50	5.00	10.00
❑ 3054	A Woman Called Moses	1978	2.50	5.00	10.00
❑ 3071	Lovely Dancer	1979	2.50	5.00	10.00

MCCOYS, THE Also see RICK DERRINGER.

45s
BANG

Number	Title (A Side/B Side)	Yr	VG	VG+	NM
❑ 506	Hang On Sloopy/I Can't Explain It	1965	3.75	7.50	15.00
❑ 511	Fever/Sorrow	1965	2.50	5.00	10.00
❑ 516	Up and Down/If You Tell a Lie	1966	2.50	5.00	10.00
❑ 522	Come On Let's Go/Little People	1966	2.50	5.00	10.00
❑ 527	(You Make Me Feel) So Good/Runaway	1966	2.50	5.00	10.00
❑ 532	Don't Worry Mother, Your Son's Heart Is Pure/				
	Ko-Ko	1966	2.50	5.00	10.00
❑ 538	I Got to Go Back (And Watch That Little Girl				
	Dance)/Dynamite	1966	2.50	5.00	10.00
❑ 543	Beat the Clock/Like You Do to Me	1967	2.50	5.00	10.00
❑ 549	I Wonder If She Remembers Me/Say Those				
	Magic Words	1967	2.50	5.00	10.00
MERCURY					
❑ 72843	Jesse Brady/Resurrection	1968	2.00	4.00	8.00
❑ 72897	Daybreak/Epilogue	1969	2.00	4.00	8.00
❑ 72967	Don't Fight It/Rosa Rodriguez	1969	3.75	7.50	15.00

PHILCO-FORD

Number	Title (A Side/B Side)	Yr	VG	VG+	NM
❑ HP-6	Fever/Hang On Sloopy	1967	5.00	10.00	20.00
—4-inch plastic "Hip Pocket Record" with color sleeve					
RCA VICTOR					
❑ 47-7204	Daddy's Geisha Girl/Our Love Goes On and On	1958	5.00	10.00	20.00
❑ 47-7354	Full Grown Cat/Throwing Kisses	1958	6.25	12.50	25.00

Albums
BANG

Number	Title (A Side/B Side)	Yr	VG	VG+	NM
❑ BLP-212 [M]	Hang On Sloopy	1965	7.50	15.00	30.00
❑ BLPS-212 [S]	Hang On Sloopy	1965	10.00	20.00	40.00
❑ BLP-213 [M]	You Make Me Feel So Good	1966	7.50	15.00	30.00
❑ BLPS-213 [S]	You Make Me Feel So Good	1966	10.00	20.00	40.00
MERCURY					
❑ SR-61163	Infinite McCoys	1968	6.25	12.50	25.00
❑ SR-61207	Human Ball	1969	6.25	12.50	25.00

MCCRACKEN, HUGH

45s
CONGRESS

Number	Title (A Side/B Side)	Yr	VG	VG+	NM
❑ 257	Buzz in My Head/You Blow My Mind	1965	6.25	12.50	25.00
❑ 261	Runnin', Runnin'/What I Gotta Do to Satisfy You	1966	6.25	12.50	25.00

MCCRACKLIN, JIMMY

45s
ART-TONE

Number	Title (A Side/B Side)	Yr	VG	VG+	NM
❑ 825	Just Got to Know/The Drag	1961	3.00	6.00	12.00
❑ 826	Christmas Time (Part 1)/Christmas Time (Part 2)	1961	3.00	6.00	12.00
❑ 827	Shame, Shame, Shame/I'm the One	1962	3.00	6.00	12.00
❑ 831	That's No Big Thing/Susie and Pat	1962	3.00	6.00	12.00
CHECKER					
❑ 885	The Walk/I'm to Blame	1958	6.25	12.50	25.00
❑ 893	Everybody Rock/Get Tough	1958	3.75	7.50	15.00
CHESS					
❑ 1809	I Know/Later On	1961	2.50	5.00	10.00
❑ 1826	One Track Love/Trottin'	1962	2.50	5.00	10.00
HI					
❑ 2023	Things I Meant to Say/				
	Here Today and Gone Tomorrow	1960	3.00	6.00	12.00
HOLLYWOOD					
❑ 1054	It's All Right/Fare You Well	1955	12.50	25.00	50.00
IMPERIAL					
❑ 5892	Bitter Pill/Head Over Flip	1962	2.50	5.00	10.00
❑ 5906	I Don't Care/Just Got to Know	1963	2.50	5.00	10.00
❑ 5911	Advice/No No	1963	2.50	5.00	10.00
❑ 5926	The Bitter and the Sweet/Just Pretending	1963	2.50	5.00	10.00
❑ 5955	That's the Way (It Goes)/I'll See It Through	1963	2.50	5.00	10.00
❑ 5977	Every Night/The Slightest Idea	1963	2.50	5.00	10.00
❑ 5982	Sooner or Later/Looking for a Woman	1963	2.50	5.00	10.00
❑ 66010	I Did Wrong/Someone	1964	2.00	4.00	8.00
❑ 66035	Just Like It Is/Let's Do It All	1964	2.00	4.00	8.00
❑ 66067	Believe in Me/Set Six	1964	2.00	4.00	8.00
❑ 66094	Every Night, Every Day/Can't Raise Me	1965	2.00	4.00	8.00
❑ 66116	Arkansas (Part 1)/Arkansas (Part 2)	1965	2.00	4.00	8.00
❑ 66129	Think/Steppin' Up in Class	1965	2.00	4.00	8.00
❑ 66147	My Answer/Beulah	1966	2.00	4.00	8.00
❑ 66168	Come On Home (Back Where You Belong)/				
	Something That Belongs to Me	1966	2.00	4.00	8.00
❑ 66180	Just Let Me Cry/				
	These Boots Are Made for Walkin'	1966	2.00	4.00	8.00
❑ 66207	It's Got to Be Love/Sorry	1966	2.00	4.00	8.00
IRMA					
❑ 102	You're the One/I Wanna Make Love to You	1956	7.50	15.00	30.00
❑ 103	Take a Chance/Fare Well	1956	7.50	15.00	30.00
❑ 107	I'm the One/Savoy's Jump	1957	7.50	15.00	30.00
❑ 109	Beer Tavern Girl/Love for You	1957	7.50	15.00	30.00
KENT					
❑ 369	I've Got Eyes for You/				
	I'm Gonna Tell Your Mother	1962	2.50	5.00	10.00
LIBERTY					
❑ 56198	Believe Me/I Never Thought	1970	—	2.50	5.00
MERCURY					
❑ 71412	The Wobble/With Your Love	1959	3.75	7.50	15.00
❑ 71516	Let's Do It (The Chicken Scratch)/Georgia Slop	1959	3.75	7.50	15.00
❑ 71613	Doomed Lover/By Myself	1960	3.00	6.00	12.00
❑ 71666	You Rascal You/No One to Love Me	1960	3.00	6.00	12.00
❑ 71747	What's That (Part 1)/The Bridge	1961	3.00	6.00	12.00
❑ 71766	No One to Love Me/(B-side unknown)	1961	3.00	6.00	12.00
MINIT					
❑ 32018	Let the Door Hit You/This Thing	1967	—	3.00	6.00
❑ 32022	Dog (Part 1)/Dog (Part 2)	1967	—	3.00	6.00
❑ 32033	Get Together/How You Like Your Love	1967	—	3.00	6.00
❑ 32044	Pretty Little Sweet Thing/A & I	1968	—	3.00	6.00
❑ 32052	Love, Love, Love/Married Life	1968	—	3.00	6.00
❑ 32064	Drown in My Own Tears/What's Going On	1969	—	3.00	6.00
❑ 32086	I Had to Get With It/You Ain't Nothin' But a Devil	1969	—	3.00	6.00
❑ 32092	Stick to My Mind/I Just Live by the Rules	1970	—	3.00	6.00
MODERN					
❑ 926	Blues Blasters' Boogie/The Panic's On	1954	10.00	20.00	40.00
❑ 934	Darlin' Share Your Love/Give My Heart a Break	1954	10.00	20.00	40.00
❑ 951	Please Forgive Me Baby/Couldn't Be a Dream	1954	10.00	20.00	40.00
❑ 967	Gonna Tell Your Mother/That Ain't Right	1955	10.00	20.00	40.00
PEACOCK					
❑ 1605	My Days Are Limited/She's Gone	1952	15.00	30.00	60.00
❑ 1615	She Felt Too Good/Share and Share Alike	1953	15.00	30.00	60.00
❑ 1634	I Cried/The End	1953	15.00	30.00	60.00
❑ 1639	The Cheater/My Story	1954	15.00	30.00	60.00
❑ 1683	I Need Your Loving/The Swinging Thing	1958	6.25	12.50	25.00

Albums
CHESS

Number	Title (A Side/B Side)	Yr	VG	VG+	NM
❑ LP-1464 [M]	Jimmy McCracklin Sings	1961	30.00	60.00	120.00
CROWN					
❑ CLP-5244 [M]	Twist with Jimmy McCracklin	196?	3.75	7.50	15.00
—Black label, multi-color "Crown"					
❑ CLP-5244 [M]	Twist with Jimmy McCracklin	1962	6.25	12.50	25.00
—Gray label					

Number	Title (A Side/B Side)	Yr	VG	VG+	NM
❑ CLP-5244 [M]	Twist with Jimmy McCracklin	1962	12.50	25.00	50.00
—Black label, silver "Crown"					
EVEJIM					
❑ EJR-4013	Same Lovin'	198?	3.00	6.00	12.00
IMPERIAL					
❑ LP-9219 [M]	I Just Gotta Know	1964	6.25	12.50	25.00
❑ LP-9285 [M]	Every Night, Every Day	1965	6.25	12.50	25.00
❑ LP-9297 [M]	Think	1965	6.25	12.50	25.00
❑ LP-9306 [M]	My Answer	1966	6.25	12.50	25.00
❑ LP-9316 [M]	The New Soul of Jimmy McCracklin	1966	6.25	12.50	25.00
❑ LP-12219 [S]	I Just Gotta Know	1964	7.50	15.00	30.00
❑ LP-12285 [S]	Every Night, Every Day	1965	7.50	15.00	30.00
❑ LP-12297 [S]	Think	1965	7.50	15.00	30.00
❑ LP-12306 [S]	My Answer	1966	7.50	15.00	30.00
❑ LP-12316 [S]	The New Soul of Jimmy McCracklin	1966	7.50	15.00	30.00
MINIT					
❑ LP-4009 [M]	The Best of Jimmy McCracklin	1967	7.50	15.00	30.00
❑ LP-24009 [S]	The Best of Jimmy McCracklin	1967	6.25	12.50	25.00
❑ LP-24011	Let's Get Together	1968	6.25	12.50	25.00
❑ LP-24017	Stinger Man	1969	6.25	12.50	25.00
STAX					
❑ STS-2047	Yesterday Is Gone	1972	5.00	10.00	20.00
❑ MPS-8506	High on the Blues	1980	2.50	5.00	10.00

MCCRAE, GEORGE
12-Inch Singles
GOLD MOUNTAIN

Number	Title (A Side/B Side)	Yr	VG	VG+	NM
❑ 81205	Own the Night/Own the Night (Dub)	1984	2.00	4.00	8.00
T.K. DISCO					
❑ 22	Love in Motion (5:00)/Givin' Back the Feeling (5:31)	1977	3.00	6.00	12.00
❑ 62	Kiss Me (The Way I Like It) (3:42) (5:47)	1977	3.00	6.00	12.00
❑ 91	Let's Dance (6:10)/Hey Sexy Dancer	1978	3.00	6.00	12.00
45s					
SOUL CITY					
❑ XW456	Taking It All Off/Please Help Me Find My Baby	1974	—	3.00	6.00
T.K.					
❑ 1004	Rock Your Baby (Part 1)/Rock Your Baby (Part 2)	1974	—	2.50	5.00
❑ 1006	I Get Lifted/I Can't Leave You Alone	1974	—	2.50	5.00
❑ 1011	Look At You/I Need Someone Like You	1975	—	2.50	5.00
❑ 1014	I Ain't Lyin'/You Don't Know	1975	—	2.50	5.00
❑ 1016	Honey I/Sing a Happy Song	1975	—	2.50	5.00
❑ 1021	I'm Gonna Stay with My Baby Tonight/Love in Motion	1977	—	2.50	5.00
❑ 1024	Kiss Me (The Way I Like It) Part 1/Kiss Me (The Way I Like It) Part 2	1977	—	2.50	5.00
❑ 1029	Let's Dance (People All Over the World)/Let George Do It	1978	—	2.50	5.00
❑ 1032	I Want You Around Me/Are You Looking for Love	1979	—	2.50	5.00
❑ 1034	Don't You Feel My Love/You Got Me Going Crazy	1979	—	2.50	5.00
UNITED ARTISTS					
❑ 50811	Taking It All Off/Please Help Me Find My Baby	1971	2.50	5.00	10.00
Albums					
GOLD MOUNTAIN					
❑ GM 80008	Own the Night	1984	2.50	5.00	10.00
T.K.					
❑ 501	Rock Your Baby	1974	2.50	5.00	10.00
❑ 602	George McCrae	1975	2.50	5.00	10.00
❑ 606	Diamond Touch	1977	2.50	5.00	10.00

MCCRAE, GEORGE AND GWEN Also see each artist's individual listings.
45s
CAT

Number	Title (A Side/B Side)	Yr	VG	VG+	NM
❑ 2002	Winners Together or Losers Apart/Homesick Lovesick	1976	—	2.50	5.00
❑ 2004	I'll Do the Rockin'/Mechanical Body	1976	—	2.50	5.00
Albums					
CAT					
❑ 2606	Together	1976	2.50	5.00	10.00

MCCRAE, GWEN
12-Inch Singles
ATLANTIC

Number	Title (A Side/B Side)	Yr	VG	VG+	NM
❑ PR 387 [DJ]	Keep the Fire Burning (same on both sides)	1982	—	3.00	6.00
BLACK JACK					
❑ 0021	Do You Know What I Mean (Long Version) (Short Version) (Dub)	1984	2.00	4.00	8.00
45s					
ATLANTIC					
❑ 3853	Funky Sensation/Have a Good Time	1981	—	2.00	4.00
❑ 3881	Poison/(B-side unknown)	1981	—	2.00	4.00
❑ 89910	Keep the Fire Burning/Hang On	1982	—	2.00	4.00
❑ 89961	I Need to Be with You/(B-side unknown)	1982	—	2.00	4.00
CAT					
❑ 1987	He Keeps Something Groovy Goin' On/Your Love Is Worse Than a Cold Love	1973	—	2.50	5.00
❑ 1989	For Your Love/Your Love	1973	—	2.50	5.00
❑ 1992	It's Worth the Hurt/90% of Me Is You	1974	—	2.50	5.00
❑ 1994	Move Me Baby/He Don't Ever Lose His Groove	1974	—	2.50	5.00
❑ 1996	Rockin' Chair/It Keeps On Raining	1975	—	2.50	5.00
❑ 1999	Love Insurance/He Keeps Something Groovy Goin' On	1975	—	2.50	5.00
❑ 2000	Cradle of Love/Easy Rock	1976	—	2.50	5.00
❑ 2005	Damn Right It's Good/Love Without Sex	1976	—	2.50	5.00
❑ 2011	Starting All Over Again/At Bedtime	1977	—	2.50	5.00
❑ 2014	The Melody of Life/The Joy	197?	—	2.50	5.00
❑ 2015	Maybe I'll Find Somebody New/All This Love That I'm Givin'	197?	—	2.50	5.00
COLUMBIA					
❑ 45214	Lead Me On/Lay It On Me	1970	—	2.50	5.00
❑ 45320	Been So Long/Lay It On Me	1971	—	2.50	5.00
❑ 45448	Ain't Nothing You Can Do/Goin' Down the Road Feelin' Bad	1971	—	2.50	5.00
❑ 45578	You Were Always on My Mind/He's Not You	1972	—	2.50	5.00
❑ 45684	I'm Losing the Feeling/Leave the Driving to Us	1972	—	2.50	5.00

Albums
ATLANTIC

Number	Title (A Side/B Side)	Yr	VG	VG+	NM
❑ 80014	On My Way	1982	2.50	5.00	10.00
CAT					
❑ 2603	Gwen McCrae	1974	2.50	5.00	10.00
❑ 2605	Rockin' Chair	1975	2.50	5.00	10.00
❑ 2608	Something So Right	1976	2.50	5.00	10.00

MCCREA, DARLENE
45s
JUBILEE

Number	Title (A Side/B Side)	Yr	VG	VG+	NM
❑ 5524	I Feel a Little Bit Better/Soulful Feeling	1965	2.50	5.00	10.00
ROULETTE					
❑ 4173	You/You Made a Fool of Me	1959	3.00	6.00	12.00
TOWER					
❑ 104	Don't Worry Baby/Heart's Not In It	1964	2.50	5.00	10.00

MCCULLERS, MICKEY
45s
TAMLA

Number	Title (A Side/B Side)	Yr	VG	VG+	NM
❑ 54064	Same Old Story/I'll Cry a Million Tears	1962	10.00	20.00	40.00
V.I.P.					
❑ 25009	Same Old Story/Who You Gonna Run To	1964	12.50	25.00	50.00

MCCULLOCH, DANNY
45s
CAPITOL

Number	Title (A Side/B Side)	Yr	VG	VG+	NM
❑ 2363	Wings of a Man/Orange and Red Beans	1968	2.00	4.00	8.00
❑ 2488	Hold On/Hope	1969	2.00	4.00	8.00
Albums					
CAPITOL					
❑ ST-174	Wings of a Man	1969	5.00	10.00	20.00

MCCULLOUGH, CHARLES
45s
DOOTO

Number	Title (A Side/B Side)	Yr	VG	VG+	NM
❑ 462	My Girl/Zorro	1961	3.00	6.00	12.00
❑ 465	You're Not Too Young/That's Alright	1962	3.00	6.00	12.00

MCDANIELS, GENE
45s
ATLANTIC

Number	Title (A Side/B Side)	Yr	VG	VG+	NM
❑ 2805	The Lord Is Back/Tell Me Mr. President	1971	—	3.00	6.00
—As "Eugene McDaniels"					
COLUMBIA					
❑ 43800	Something Blue/Cause I Love You So	1966	2.50	5.00	10.00
❑ 44010	Touch of Your Lips/Sweet Lover No More	1967	2.50	5.00	10.00
LIBERTY					
❑ 55231	In Times Like These/Once Before	1959	3.75	7.50	15.00
❑ 55265	The Green Door/Facts of Life	1960	3.75	7.50	15.00
❑ 55308	A Hundred Pounds of Clay/Take a Chance on Love	1961	4.00	8.00	16.00
❑ 55344	A Tear/She's Come Back	1961	3.75	7.50	15.00
❑ 55371	Tower of Strength/The Secret	1961	4.00	8.00	16.00
❑ 55405	Chip Chip/Another Tear Falls	1962	3.75	7.50	15.00
❑ 55444	Funny/Chapel of Tears	1962	3.75	7.50	15.00
❑ 55480	Point of No Return/Warmer Than a Whisper	1962	3.75	7.50	15.00
❑ 55510	Spanish Lace/Somebody's Waiting	1962	3.75	7.50	15.00
❑ 55541	The Puzzle/Cry Baby Cry	1963	3.00	6.00	12.00
❑ 55597	It's a Lonely Town/False Friends	1963	3.00	6.00	12.00
❑ 55637	Old Country/Anyone Else	1963	3.00	6.00	12.00
❑ 55723	Make Me a Present of You/In Times Like These	1964	3.00	6.00	12.00
❑ 55752	Emily/Forgotten Man	1964	3.00	6.00	12.00
❑ 55805	A Miracle/Walk with a Winner	1965	2.50	5.00	10.00
❑ 55834	Hang On/Will It Last Forever	1965	2.50	5.00	10.00
MGM					
❑ 14613	Ol' Heartbreak Top Ten/River	1973	—	2.50	5.00
ODE					
❑ 66107	Lady Fair/Natural Juices	1975	—	2.00	4.00
UNITED ARTISTS					
❑ 0053	A Hundred Pounds of Clay/Tower of Strength	1973	—	2.00	4.00
—"Silver Spotlight Series" reissue					
❑ 0054	Chip Chip/Point of No Return	1973	—	2.00	4.00
—"Silver Spotlight Series" reissue					

Albums
ATLANTIC

Number	Title (A Side/B Side)	Yr	VG	VG+	NM
❑ SD 8259	Outlaw	1970	3.75	7.50	15.00
❑ SD 8281	Headless Heroes	1971	3.75	7.50	15.00
LIBERTY					
❑ LRP-3146 [M]	In Times Like These	1960	7.50	15.00	30.00
❑ LRP-3175 [M]	Sometimes I'm Happy, Sometimes I'm Blue	1960	7.50	15.00	30.00
❑ LRP-3191 [M]	100 Lbs. of Clay!	1961	7.50	15.00	30.00
❑ LRP-3204 [M]	Gene McDaniels Sings Movie Memories	1962	7.50	15.00	30.00
❑ LRP-3215 [M]	Tower of Strength	1962	7.50	15.00	30.00
❑ LRP-3258 [M]	Hit After Hit	1962	7.50	15.00	30.00
❑ LRP-3275 [M]	Spanish Lace	1963	6.25	12.50	25.00
❑ LRP-3311 [M]	The Wonderful World of Gene McDaniels	1963	6.25	12.50	25.00
❑ LST-7146 [S]	In Times Like These	1960	10.00	20.00	40.00
—Black vinyl					
❑ LST-7146 [S]	In Times Like These	1960	50.00	100.00	200.00
—Blue vinyl					
❑ LST-7175 [S]	Sometimes I'm Happy, Sometimes I'm Blue	1960	10.00	20.00	40.00
❑ LST-7191 [S]	100 Lbs. of Clay!	1961	10.00	20.00	40.00
❑ LST-7204 [S]	Gene McDaniels Sings Movie Memories	1962	10.00	20.00	40.00
❑ LST-7215 [S]	Tower of Strength	1962	10.00	20.00	40.00
❑ LST-7258 [S]	Hit After Hit	1962	10.00	20.00	40.00
❑ LST-7275 [S]	Spanish Lace	1963	7.50	15.00	30.00
❑ LST-7311 [S]	The Wonderful World of Gene McDaniels	1963	7.50	15.00	30.00
ODE					
❑ SP-77028	Natural Juices	1975	3.00	6.00	12.00
SUNSET					
❑ SUM-1122 [M]	Facts of Life	1967	3.00	6.00	12.00
❑ SUS-5122 [S]	Facts of Life	1967	3.75	7.50	15.00
UNITED ARTISTS					
❑ UA-LA447-E	The Very Best of Gene McDaniels	1975	2.50	5.00	10.00

M

Number	Title (A Side/B Side)	Yr	VG	VG+	NM
MCDEVITT, CHAS., AND HIS SKIFFLE GROUP					
45s					
CHIC					
❏ 1008	Freight Train/The Cotton Song	1957	3.75	7.50	15.00
EPIC					
❏ 9244	Face in the Rain/Sporting Life	1957	3.75	7.50	15.00
KAPP					
❏ 216	Sing, Sing, Sing/Johnny-O	1958	3.75	7.50	15.00
❏ 238	Stack-O-Lee/Real Love	1958	3.75	7.50	15.00
MCDONALD, COUNTRY JOE See COUNTRY JOE AND THE FISH.					
MCDONALD, KATHI					
45s					
CAPITOL					
❏ 3835	Freak Lover/Bogart to Bowie	1974	2.50	5.00	10.00
❏ 3880	Heat Wave/Bogart to Bowie	1974	2.50	5.00	10.00
Albums					
CAPITOL					
❏ ST-11224	Insane Asylum	1974	7.50	15.00	30.00
MCDONALD, MICHAEL Also see THE DOOBIE BROTHERS; THE REGENTS (5).					
12-Inch Singles					
MCA					
❏ 23641	Sweet Freedom (4 versions)	1986	2.00	4.00	8.00
REPRISE					
❏ PRO-A-4395 [DJ]All We Got (4 versions)		1990	2.50	5.00	10.00
❏ PRO-A-4398 [DJ]Tear It Up (same on both sides)		1990	2.00	4.00	8.00
❏ PRO-A-6538 [DJ]Hey Girl (Edit) (LP Version) (Radio Remix)		1993	2.00	4.00	8.00
❏ 21734	All We Got (5 versions)/Show Me	1990	2.00	4.00	8.00
WARNER BROS.					
❏ PRO-A-2325 [DJ]No Lookin' Back (same on both sides)		1985	2.00	4.00	8.00
45s					
BELL					
❏ 45182	Dear Me/I Think I Love You Again	1972	2.00	4.00	8.00
—All Bell records as "Mike McDonald"					
❏ 45219	Good Old Time Love Song/When I'm Home	1972	2.00	4.00	8.00
❏ 45259 [DJ]	Drivin' Wheel/(B-side unknown)	1972	2.00	4.00	8.00
—Stock copy may not exist					
❏ 45308 [DJ]	Where Do I Go from Here/(B-side unknown)	1973	2.00	4.00	8.00
—Stock copy may not exist					
MCA					
❏ 52857	Sweet Freedom/The Freedom Eights	1986	—	—	3.00
❏ 52857 [PS]	Sweet Freedom/The Freedom Eights	1986	—	—	3.00
QWEST					
❏ 29394	Yah Mo B There/Come in Da Machine	1983	—	2.00	4.00
—A-side with James Ingram; B-side: James Ingram solo					
RCA VICTOR					
❏ 74-0405	God Knows/If You Won't, I Will	1970	3.75	7.50	15.00
—As "Mike McDonald"					
REPRISE					
❏ 18469	I Stand for You/East of Eden	1993	—	—	3.00
WARNER BROS.					
❏ 28596	Our Love (Theme from "No Mercy")/Don't Let Me Down	1986	—	—	3.00
❏ 28596 [PS]	Our Love (Theme from "No Mercy")/Don't Let Me Down	1986	—	—	3.00
❏ 28847	Lost in the Parade/By Heart	1985	—	2.00	4.00
❏ 28847 [PS]	Lost in the Parade/By Heart	1985	—	2.00	4.00
❏ 28960	No Lookin' Back/Don't Let Me Down	1985	—	—	3.00
❏ 28960 [PS]	No Lookin' Back/Don't Let Me Down	1985	—	—	3.00
❏ 29743	Believe in It/Playin' by the Rules	1983	—	2.00	4.00
❏ 29862	I Gotta Try/Believe in It	1982	—	2.00	4.00
❏ 29862 [PS]	I Gotta Try/Believe in It	1982	—	2.00	4.00
❏ 29933	I Keep Forgettin' (Every Time You're Near)/Losin' End	1982	—	2.00	4.00
—Second pressing has subtitle on A-side					
❏ 29933	I Keep Forgettin'/Losin' End	1982	—	2.50	5.00
—First pressing has no subtitle on A-side					
❏ 29933 [PS]	I Keep Forgettin' (Every Time You're Near)/Losin' End	1982	—	2.00	4.00
—Second pressing has subtitle on A-side					
❏ 29933 [PS]	I Keep Forgettin'/Losin' End	1982	—	2.50	5.00
—First pressing has no subtitle on A-side					
Albums					
MOBILE FIDELITY					
❏ 1-149	If That's What It Takes	1985	5.00	10.00	20.00
—Audiophile vinyl					
REPRISE					
❏ 25979	Take It to Heart	1990	3.00	6.00	12.00
WARNER BROS.					
❏ 23703	If That's What It Takes	1982	2.50	5.00	10.00
❏ 25291	No Lookin' Back	1985	2.50	5.00	10.00
MCDOWELL, MISSISSIPPI FRED					
Albums					
ARHOOLIE					
❏ F-1021 [M]	Delta Blues	1964	12.50	25.00	50.00
❏ F-1027 [M]	Delta Blues, Volume 2	1966	12.50	25.00	50.00
❏ F-1046	Mississippi Fred McDowell and His Blues Boys	1970	7.50	15.00	30.00
❏ F-1068	Keep Your Lamp Trimmed and Burning	1973	5.00	10.00	20.00
CAPITOL					
❏ ST-403	I Do Not Play No Rock and Roll	1970	6.25	12.50	25.00
JUST SUNSHINE					
❏ JSS-4	Mississippi Fred McDowell 1904-1972	1973	3.75	7.50	15.00
MILESTONE					
❏ MLP-3003 [M]	Long Way from Home	1966	7.50	15.00	30.00
❏ MLS-93003 [S]	Long Way from Home	1966	10.00	20.00	40.00
SIRE					
❏ SES-97018	Mississippi Fred McDowell in London	1970	7.50	15.00	30.00
MCFADDEN, BOB					
45s					
BRUNSWICK					
❏ 55120	Frankie and Igor at a Rock and Roll Party/Children Cross the Bridge	1959	6.25	12.50	25.00

Number	Title (A Side/B Side)	Yr	VG	VG+	NM
❏ 55140	The Mummy/The Beat Generation	1959	6.25	12.50	25.00
—As "Bob McFadden and Dor"					
❏ 55140 [PS]	The Mummy/The Beat Generation	1959	10.00	20.00	40.00
—As "Bob McFadden and Dor"					
❏ 55156	Bingo/Shake, Rattle and Roll	1959	6.25	12.50	25.00
CORAL					
❏ 62209	Dracula Cha-Cha/Transylvania Polka	1959	7.50	5.00	30.00
Albums					
BRUNSWICK					
❏ BL 54056 [M]	Songs Our Mummy Taught Us	1959	50.00	100.00	200.00
❏ BL 754056 [S]	Songs Our Mummy Taught Us	1959	75.00	150.00	300.00
MCGHEE, BROWNIE					
45s					
DOT					
❏ 1184	Cheatin' and Lyin'/Need Someone to Love	1954	62.50	125.00	250.00
HARLEM					
❏ 2323	Worrying Over You/Christina	1954	15.00	30.00	60.00
❏ 2329	My Confession (I Want to Thank You)/Bluebird, Bluebird	1954	15.00	30.00	60.00
JAX					
❏ 302	Smiling and Crying Blues/A Letter to Lightnin' Hopkins	1951	30.00	60.00	120.00
❏ 304	I Feel So Good/Key to the Highway	1952	30.00	60.00	120.00
❏ 307	Meet You in the Morning/Brownie's Blues	1952	30.00	60.00	120.00
❏ 310	Guitar Strangers Blues/Dissatisfied Woman	1952	30.00	60.00	120.00
❏ 312	I'm 10,000 Years Old/Cherry Red	1952	30.00	60.00	120.00
❏ 322	New Bad Blood Blues/Pawnshop Blues	1953	30.00	60.00	120.00
RED ROBIN					
❏ 111	Don't Dog Your Woman/Daisy	1953	62.50	125.00	250.00
SAVOY					
❏ 835	Diamond Ring/So Much Trouble	1952	7.50	15.00	30.00
❏ 872	Tell Me Baby/Bad Nerves	1952	7.50	15.00	30.00
❏ 899	Sweet Baby Blues/4 O'Clock in the Morning	1953	7.50	15.00	30.00
❏ 1177	I'd Love to Love You/Anna Mae	1955	5.00	10.00	20.00
❏ 1185	When It's Love Time/My Fault	1956	5.00	10.00	20.00
❏ 1564	Living with the Blues/Be My Friend	1959	3.75	7.50	15.00
Albums					
BLUESVILLE					
❏ BVLP-1042 [M]	Brownie's Blues	1962	20.00	40.00	80.00
—Blue label, silver print					
❏ BVLP-1042 [M]	Brownie's Blues	1964	6.25	12.50	25.00
—Blue label, trident logo at right					
FANTASY					
❏ OBC-505	Brownie's Blues	198?	3.00	6.00	12.00
FOLKWAYS					
❏ FP-30 [10]	Brownie McGhee Blues	1951	30.00	60.00	120.00
❏ FA-2030 [10]	Brownie McGhee Blues	1951	25.00	50.00	100.00
❏ 2421/2 [(2)]	Traditional Blues Vol. 1 and 2	197?	3.75	7.50	15.00
❏ 3557	Brownie McGhee Sings the Blues	197?	3.00	6.00	12.00
SAVOY JAZZ					
❏ SJL-1204	Jumpin' the Blues	1989	3.00	6.00	12.00
MCGHEE, BROWNIE, AND SONNY TERRY See SONNY TERRY AND BROWNIE McGHEE.					
MCGHEE, STICK					
45s					
ATLANTIC					
❏ 873	Drinkin' Wine Spo-Dee-O-Dee/Blues Mixture (I'd Rather Drink Muddy Water)	1971	5.00	10.00	20.00
—Yellow label, "fan" logo at lower left; first issue of this number on 45					
❏ 955	Wee Wee Hours (Part 1)/Wee Wee Hours (Part 2)	1952	25.00	50.00	100.00
—Note: Stick McGhee records on Atlantic before 955 are unconfirmed on 45 rpm					
❏ 991	New Found Love/Meet You in the Morning	1953	20.00	40.00	80.00
HERALD					
❏ 553	Money Fever/Sleep-In Job	1960	3.75	7.50	15.00
KING					
❏ 4610	Little Things We Used to Do/Head Happy with Wine	1953	25.00	50.00	100.00
❏ 4628	Whiskey, Women and Loaded Dice/Blues in My Heart and Tears in My Eyes	1953	25.00	50.00	100.00
❏ 4672	Jungle Juice/Dealing from the Bottom	1953	25.00	50.00	100.00
❏ 4700	I'm Doin' All This Time/Wiggle Waggin' Woo	1954	25.00	50.00	100.00
❏ 4783	Double Crossin' Liquor/Six to Eight	1955	30.00	60.00	120.00
❏ 4800	Get Your Mind Out the Gutter/Sad, Bad, Glad	1955	25.00	50.00	100.00
LONDON					
❏ 978	You Gotta Have Something on the Ball/(B-side unknown)	1951	62.50	125.00	250.00
SAVOY					
❏ 1148	Things Have Changed/Help Me Baby	1955	7.50	15.00	30.00
MCGHEE, STICK, AND JOHN LEE HOOKER Also see each artist's individual listings.					
Albums					
AUDIO LAB					
❏ AL-1520 [M]	Highway of Blues	1959	87.50	175.00	350.00
MCGILL, JERRY					
45s					
SUN					
❏ 326	Love Struck/I Wanna Make Sweet Love	1959	7.50	15.00	30.00
MCGONNIGLE, MEL					
45s					
ROCKET					
❏ 101	Rattle Shakin' Mama/I Want You	1958	175.00	350.00	700.00
MCGOVERN, MAUREEN					
45s					
CBS					
❏ 39-07689	The Same Moon/Why Can't I Forget	1988	—	2.00	4.00
❏ 39-07689 [PS]	The Same Moon/Why Can't I Forget	1988	—	2.00	4.00
20TH CENTURY					
❏ 2010	The Morning After (Song from The Poseidon Adventure)/Midnight Storm	1973	—	2.00	4.00
❏ 2051	I Won't Last a Day Without You/Darlene	1973	—	2.00	4.00

Number	Title (A Side/B Side)	Yr	VG	VG+	NM
❏ 2072	Nice to Be Around/If I Wrote You a Song	1974	—	2.00	4.00
❏ 2107	Give Me a Reason to Be Gone/Love Knots	1974	—	2.00	4.00
❏ 2158	We May Never Love Like This Again/				
	Wherever Love Takes Me	1974	—	2.00	4.00
❏ 2213	Even Better Than I Know Myself/				
	All I Want (All I Need)	1975	—	2.00	4.00
❏ 2234	Love Songs Are Getting Harder to Sing/Stop Me	1975	—	2.00	4.00
❏ 2234 [PS]	Love Songs Are Getting Harder to Sing/Stop Me	1975	2.00	4.00	8.00

—No titles on sleeve, but catalog number is on it plus the words "The new Maureen McGovern in more ways than one!"

WARNER BROS.

Number	Title (A Side/B Side)	Yr	VG	VG+	NM
❏ 8750	Can You Read My Mind/You Love Me Too Late	1979	—	2.00	4.00
❏ 8835	Different Worlds/Carolina Moon	1979	—	2.00	4.00
❏ 49129	Can't Take My Eyes Off You/A Very Special Love	1979	—	2.00	4.00
❏ 49177	We Could Have It All/Don't Stop Now	1980	—	2.00	4.00
❏ 49525	Bottom Line/Don't Stop Now	1980	—	2.00	4.00

Albums
CBS

❏ BFM 42314	Another Woman in Love	1987	2.50	5.00	10.00

20TH CENTURY

❏ T-419	The Morning After	1973	3.00	6.00	12.00
❏ T-439	Nice to Be Around	1974	3.00	6.00	12.00
❏ T-474	Academy Award Performances	1975	3.00	6.00	12.00

WARNER BROS.

❏ BSK 3329	Maureen McGovern	1979	2.50	5.00	10.00

MCGRATH, BAT, AND DON POTTER
45s
EPIC

❏ 5-10562	Mr. Cadillac/Walking Bird	1969	2.00	4.00	8.00
❏ 5-10582	Me and Bobby McGee/Jefferson Queen	1970	2.50	5.00	10.00

Albums
EPIC

❏ BN 26499	Introducing	1969	3.75	7.50	15.00

MCGRIFF, JIMMY
12-Inch Singles
T.K. DISCO

❏ 79	Sky Hawk/Tailgunner	1976	3.00	6.00	12.00

45s
BLUE NOTE

❏ 1968	Black Pearl/Groove Alley	1971	—	2.50	5.00

CAPITOL

❏ 2875	Sugar Sugar/Fat Cakes	1970	—	2.50	5.00
❏ 3019	The Bird/Plain Brown Bag	1971	—	2.50	5.00

GROOVE MERCHANT

❏ 1003	Groove Grease/Mr. Lucky	1972	—	2.50	5.00
❏ 1006	Theme from Shaft/Let's Stay Together	1972	—	2.50	5.00
❏ 1014	Everyday I Have the Blues/It's You I Adore	1973	—	2.50	5.00
❏ 1025	If You're Ready (Come Go with Me)/				
	(B-side unknown)	1974	—	2.50	5.00
❏ 1029	Main Squeeze/The Sermon	1975	—	2.50	5.00
❏ 1033	Stump Juice/The Worm Turns	1976	—	2.50	5.00

JELL

❏ 503	Soul Song Of Christmas (Silent Nite)/Chip! Chip!	1965	2.00	4.00	8.00

MILESTONE

❏ 313	I'm Walkin'/(B-side unknown)	1984	—	2.00	4.00

SOLID STATE

❏ 2501	I Cover the Waterfront/Slow But Sure	1966	2.00	4.00	8.00
❏ 2502	Cherry/The Comeback	1966	2.00	4.00	8.00
❏ 2510	I Can't Give You Anything But Love, Baby/(I				
	Can't Get No) Satisfaction	1967	2.00	4.00	8.00
❏ 2515	Tennessee Waltz/Swingin' Shepherd Blues	1967	2.00	4.00	8.00
❏ 2516	Days of Wine and Roses/You Are My Sunshine	1967	2.00	4.00	8.00
❏ 2520	I've Got a Woman/Kiko	1968	—	3.00	6.00
❏ 2522	Honey/Since You've Been Gone	1968	—	3.00	6.00
❏ 2524	The Worm/Keep Loose	1968	—	3.00	6.00
❏ 2528	Step One/South Wes	1969	—	3.00	6.00
❏ 2531	Charlotte/Trying to Come By	1969	—	3.00	6.00
❏ 2534	Back on the Street/Chris Cross	1970	—	3.00	6.00

SUE

❏ 105	Hello Betty/Close Your Eyes	1964	2.00	4.00	8.00
❏ 110	All Day Long/When You're Smiling	1964	2.00	4.00	8.00
❏ 112	Topkapi/Theme from				
	"The Man with the Golden Arm"	1964	2.00	4.00	8.00
❏ 120	Sho 'Nuff/Bilbo	1965	2.00	4.00	8.00
❏ 123	Discoteque U.S.A./People	1965	2.00	4.00	8.00
❏ 128	Turn Blue/Bump De Bump	1965	2.00	4.00	8.00
❏ 770	I've Got a Woman (Part 1)/I've Got a Woman				
	(Part 2)	1962	2.50	5.00	10.00
❏ 777	All About My Girl/M.G. Blues	1963	2.00	4.00	8.00
❏ 786	The Last Minute (Part 1)/The Last Minute (Part 2)	1963	2.00	4.00	8.00
❏ 791	One of Mine/Broadway	1963	2.00	4.00	8.00
❏ 802	Lonely Avenue (Part 1)/Lonely Avenue (Part 2)	1963	2.00	4.00	8.00
❏ 804	Winter with McGriff Pt. 1/Winter with McGriff Pt. 2	1963	2.50	5.00	10.00
❏ 804	Christmas with McGriff Part 1/Part 2	1963	3.00	6.00	12.00
❏ 10001	Kiko/Jumpin' at the Woodside	1964	2.00	4.00	8.00

UNITED ARTISTS

❏ 50826	Pretty Baby/I Need Love So Bad	1971	—	2.50	5.00

—With Junior Parker

7-Inch Extended Plays
SOLID STATE

❏ SSLP 9-18002	I Cover the Waterfront/Hallelujah//See See				
	Rider/Boston Bust Out	196?	3.00	6.00	12.00

—Jukebox issue; small hole, plays at 33 1/3 rpm

❏ SSLP 9-18002 [PS]	A Bag Full of Soul	196?	3.00	6.00	12.00

Albums
BLUE NOTE

❏ BST-84350	Electric Funk	1970	3.75	7.50	15.00
❏ BST-84364	Something to Listen To	1971	3.75	7.50	15.00
❏ BST-84374	Black Pearl	1971	3.75	7.50	15.00

CAPITOL

❏ ST-616	Soul Sugar	1970	3.75	7.50	15.00

COLLECTABLES

❏ COL-5147	Blues for Mr. Jimmy	198?	2.50	5.00	10.00

GROOVE MERCHANT

Number	Title (A Side/B Side)	Yr	VG	VG+	NM
❏ 503	Groove Grease	1972	3.75	7.50	15.00
❏ 506	Let's Stay Together	1972	3.75	7.50	15.00
❏ 509	Fly Dude	1973	3.75	7.50	15.00
❏ 520	Come Together	1973	3.00	6.00	12.00
❏ 529	If You're Ready Come Go with Me	1974	3.00	6.00	12.00
❏ 534	Main Squeeze	1975	3.00	6.00	12.00
❏ 2203	Black and Blues	1971	3.75	7.50	15.00
❏ 2205	Good Things Don't Happen Every Day	1971	3.75	7.50	15.00
❏ 3300 [(2)]	Giants of the Organ In Concert	1974	3.75	7.50	15.00
❏ 3309	Stump Juice	1976	3.00	6.00	12.00
❏ 3311	Mean Machine	1976	3.00	6.00	12.00
❏ 4403 [(2)]	Flyin' Time	197?	3.75	7.50	15.00

JAM

❏ 002	City Lights	1982	3.00	6.00	12.00
❏ 005	Movin' Upside the Blues	1983	3.00	6.00	12.00

LRC

❏ 9316	Tailgunner	1977	3.75	7.50	15.00
❏ 9320	Outside Looking In	1978	3.75	7.50	15.00

MILESTONE

❏ M-9116	Countdown	1984	2.50	5.00	10.00
❏ M-9126	Skywalk	1985	2.50	5.00	10.00
❏ M-9135	State of the Art	1986	2.50	5.00	10.00
❏ M-9148	The Starting Five	1987	2.50	5.00	10.00
❏ M-9163	Blue to the 'Bone	1988	2.50	5.00	10.00

QUINTESSENCE

❏ 25061	Soul	1978	3.00	6.00	12.00

SOLID STATE

❏ SM-17001 [M]	The Big Band of Jimmy McGriff	1966	3.75	7.50	15.00
❏ SM-17002 [M]	A Bag Full of Soul	1966	3.75	7.50	15.00
❏ SM-17006 [M]	Cherry	1967	5.00	10.00	20.00
❏ SS-18001 [S]	The Big Band of Jimmy McGriff	1966	5.00	10.00	20.00
❏ SS-18002 [S]	A Bag Full of Soul	1966	5.00	10.00	20.00
❏ SS-18006 [S]	Cherry	1967	5.00	10.00	20.00
❏ SS-18017	A Bag Full of Blues	1968	5.00	10.00	20.00
❏ SS-18030	I've Got a New Woman	1968	5.00	10.00	20.00
❏ SS-18036	Honey	1968	5.00	10.00	20.00
❏ SS-18045	The Worm	1968	5.00	10.00	20.00
❏ SS-18053	Step I	1969	5.00	10.00	20.00
❏ SS-18060	A Thing to Come By	1969	5.00	10.00	20.00
❏ SS-18063	The Way You Look Tonight	1970	5.00	10.00	20.00

SUE

❏ LP-1012 [M]	I've Got a Woman	1962	7.50	15.00	30.00
❏ STLP-1012 [S]	I've Got a Woman	1962	10.00	20.00	40.00
❏ LP-1013 [M]	One of Mine	1963	7.50	15.00	30.00
❏ STLP-1013 [S]	One of Mine	1963	10.00	20.00	40.00
❏ LP-1017 [M]	Jimmy McGriff at the Apollo	1963	7.50	15.00	30.00
❏ STLP-1017 [S]	Jimmy McGriff at the Apollo	1963	10.00	20.00	40.00
❏ LP-1018 [M]	Christmas with McGriff	1963	7.50	15.00	30.00
❏ STLP-1018 [S]	Christmas with McGriff	1963	10.00	20.00	40.00
❏ LP-1020 [M]	Jimmy McGriff at the Organ	1963	7.50	15.00	30.00
❏ STLP-1020 [S]	Jimmy McGriff at the Organ	1963	10.00	20.00	40.00
❏ LP-1033 [M]	Topkapi	1964	7.50	15.00	30.00
❏ STLP-1033 [S]	Topkapi	1964	10.00	20.00	40.00
❏ LP-1039 [M]	Blues for Mister Jimmy	1965	7.50	15.00	30.00
❏ STLP-1039 [S]	Blues for Mister Jimmy	1965	10.00	20.00	40.00
❏ LP-1043 [M]	Toast to Greatest Hits	1966	5.00	10.00	20.00
❏ STLP-1043 [S]	Toast to Greatest Hits	1966	6.25	12.50	25.00

SUNSET

❏ SUS-5264	The Great Jimmy McGriff	1969	2.50	5.00	10.00

VEEP

❏ VP-13515 [M]	Live Where the Action Is	1966	5.00	10.00	20.00
❏ VP-13522 [M]	Greatest Organ Hits	1967	6.25	12.50	25.00
❏ VPS-16515 [S]	Live Where the Action Is	1966	6.25	12.50	25.00
❏ VPS-16522 [S]	Greatest Organ Hits	1967	5.00	10.00	20.00

MCGRIFF, JIMMY, AND JUNIOR PARKER Also see each artist's individual listings.
Albums
CAPITOL

❏ ST-569	Dudes Doin' Business	1971	3.75	7.50	15.00

UNITED ARTISTS

❏ UAS-5597	Jimmy McGriff and Junior Parker	1972	3.75	7.50	15.00
❏ UAS-6814	100 Proof Black Magic	1971	3.75	7.50	15.00

MCGUINN, ROGER Also see THE BYRDS.
45s
COLUMBIA

❏ 10019	Gate of Horn/Same Old Sound	1974	—	3.00	6.00
❏ 10181	Somebody Loves You/Easy Does It	1975	—	3.00	6.00
❏ 10201	Lover of the Bayou/Easy Does It	1975	—	3.00	6.00
❏ 10385	Take Me Away/Friend	1976	—	3.00	6.00
❏ 10543	American Girl/I'm Not Lonely Anymore	1977	—	3.00	6.00
❏ 45931	Draggin'/Time Cube	1973	—	3.00	6.00

Albums
ARISTA

❏ AL 8648	Back from Rio	1991	3.75	7.50	15.00

COLUMBIA

❏ AS 353 [DJ]	The Roger McGuinn Airplay Anthology	1977	7.50	15.00	30.00

—Promo only; also includes Byrds tracks

❏ KC 31946	Roger McGuinn	1973	3.00	6.00	12.00
❏ KC 32956	Peace On You	1974	3.00	6.00	12.00
❏ PC 33541	Roger McGuinn & Band	1975	3.00	6.00	12.00
❏ PC 34154	Cardiff Rose	1976	3.00	6.00	12.00
❏ PC 34656	Thunderbyrd	1977	3.00	6.00	12.00

MCGUINNESS FLINT
45s
CAPITOL

❏ 3014	When I'm Dead and Gone/Lazy Afternoon	1971	—	3.00	6.00
❏ 3139	Rock On/Malt and Barley Blues	1971	—	3.00	6.00
❏ 3186	Friends of Mine/Happy Birthday, Ruthy Baby	1971	—	3.00	6.00

Albums
CAPITOL

❏ SMAS-625	McGuinness Flint	1971	3.00	6.00	12.00
❏ ST-794	Happy Birthday, Ruthy Baby	1971	3.00	6.00	12.00

SIRE

❏ SAS-7405	Lo and Behold	1972	3.00	6.00	12.00

M

MCGUIRE, BARRY Also see THE NEW CHRISTY MINSTRELS.

45s

Number	Title (A Side/B Side)	Yr	VG	VG+	NM
DUNHILL					
4009	Eve of Destruction/What Exactly's the Matter with Me	1965	3.00	6.00	12.00
4014	Child of Our Times/Upon a Painted Ocean	1965	2.50	5.00	10.00
4014 [PS]	Child of Our Times/Upon a Painted Ocean	1965	3.75	7.50	15.00
4019	This Precious Time/Don't You Wonder Where It's At	1966	3.00	6.00	12.00
—A-side backing group: The Mamas and The Papas					
4028	Cloudy Summer Afternoon (Raindrops)/I'd Have to Be Outta My Mind	1966	2.50	5.00	10.00
4048	There's Nothing Else on My Mind/Why Not Stop and Dig It	1966	2.50	5.00	10.00
4098	Masters of War/Stop Now and Dig It While You Can	1967	2.00	4.00	8.00
4116	Lollipop Train/Inner-Manipulations	1968	2.00	4.00	8.00
4124	Grasshopper Song/Top o' the Hill	1968	2.50	5.00	10.00
4124 [PS]	Grasshopper Song/Top o' the Hill	1968	3.75	7.50	15.00
HORIZON					
4	One by One/Town and Country	1963	3.00	6.00	12.00
8	Oh, Miss Mary/So Long, Stay Well	1963	3.00	6.00	12.00
MIRA					
205	Greenback Dollar/Oh, Miss Mary	1965	2.50	5.00	10.00
MOSAIC					
1001	The Three/Theme from The Tree	1961	3.00	6.00	12.00
1004	I've Got a Secret/Cindy and Johnny	1962	3.00	6.00	12.00
MYRRH					
119	Love Is/David and Goliath	1973	—	2.50	5.00
ODE					
66010	Old Farm/South of the Border	1970	—	3.00	6.00
SPARROW					
1023	Cosmic Cowboy/What Good Would It Do	197?	—	3.00	6.00

Albums

Number	Title (A Side/B Side)	Yr	VG	VG+	NM
ABC DUNHILL					
DS-50033	The World's Last Private Citizen	1968	6.25	12.50	25.00
DUNHILL					
D-50003 [M]	Eve of Destruction	1965	7.50	15.00	30.00
DS-50003 [S]	Eve of Destruction	1965	10.00	20.00	40.00
D-50005 [M]	This Precious Time	1966	6.25	12.50	25.00
DS-50005 [S]	This Precious Time	1966	7.50	15.00	30.00
HORIZON					
ST-1636 [S]	The Barry McGuire Album	1963	10.00	20.00	40.00
WP-1636 [M]	The Barry McGuire Album	1963	7.50	15.00	30.00
MIRA					
LP-3000 [M]	The Barry McGuire Album	1965	5.00	10.00	20.00
—Reissue of Horizon LP					
LPS-3000 [S]	The Barry McGuire Album	1965	6.25	12.50	25.00
—Reissue of Horizon LP					
MYRRH					
MSA-6519	Seeds	1974	3.00	6.00	12.00
MSA-6531	Lighten Up	1975	3.00	6.00	12.00
ODE					
SP-77004	Barry McGuire with the Doctor	1970	3.75	7.50	15.00

MCGUIRE, BARRY, AND BARRY KANE

45s

Number	Title (A Side/B Side)	Yr	VG	VG+	NM
HORIZON					
354	Another Man/Bull 'Gine Run	1962	3.00	6.00	12.00

Albums

Number	Title (A Side/B Side)	Yr	VG	VG+	NM
HORIZON					
SWP-1608 [S]	Barry and Barry: Here and Now!	1962	7.50	15.00	30.00
WP-1608 [M]	Barry and Barry: Here and Now!	1962	6.25	12.50	25.00

MCGUIRE, PHYLLIS Also see THE McGUIRE SISTERS.

45s

Number	Title (A Side/B Side)	Yr	VG	VG+	NM
ABC-PARAMOUNT					
10826	My Happiness/Vaya Con Dios	1966	—	3.00	6.00
ORPHEUM					
4502	Just a Little Lovin'/You Don't Have the Heart to Tell Me	1968	—	3.00	6.00
REPRISE					
0310	I Don't Want to Walk Without You/That's Life	1964	—	3.00	6.00
0354	Run to My Arms/Someone Else Is Taking My Place	1965	—	3.00	6.00

Albums

Number	Title (A Side/B Side)	Yr	VG	VG+	NM
ABC-PARAMOUNT					
552 [M]	Phyllis McGuire Sings	1966	3.75	7.50	15.00
S-552 [S]	Phyllis McGuire Sings	1966	5.00	10.00	20.00

MCGUIRE SISTERS, THE Also see PHYLLIS McGUIRE.

45s

Number	Title (A Side/B Side)	Yr	VG	VG+	NM
ABC-PARAMOUNT					
10776	Grazia/Truer Than You Are	1966	—	3.00	6.00
CORAL					
60917	Picking Sweethearts/One, Two, Three, Four	1953	3.00	6.00	12.00
60969	Miss You/Tootle-Ooh Siana	1953	3.00	6.00	12.00
61002	Hey, Mister Cotton Picker/Where Good Times Are	1954	3.00	6.00	12.00
61073	Are You Looking for a Sweetheart/You'll Never Know Till Monday	1953	3.00	6.00	12.00
61126	Cling to Me/Pine Tree, Pine Over Me	1954	3.00	6.00	12.00
—With Johnny Desmond and Eileen Barton					
61187	Goodnight, Sweetheart, Goodnight/Heavenly Feeling	1954	3.00	6.00	12.00
61239	Uno, Duo, Tre/Lonesome Polecat	1954	3.00	6.00	12.00
61258	Muskrat Ramble/Not as a Stranger	1954	3.00	6.00	12.00
61278	Muskrat Ramble/Lonesome Polecat	1954	3.00	6.00	12.00
61303	Christmas Alphabet/Give Me Your Heart for Christmas	1954	3.00	6.00	12.00
61323	Sincerely/No More	1954	3.00	6.00	12.00
61334	Open Up Your Heart (And Let the Sun Shine In)/Melody of Love	1955	3.00	6.00	12.00
61335	Hearts of Stone/The Naughty Lady of Shady Lane	1955	3.00	6.00	12.00
61369	It May Sound Silly/Doesn't Anybody Love Me?	1955	3.00	6.00	12.00
61423	Something's Gotta Give/Rhythm 'N' Blues (Mama's Got the Rhythm — Papa's Got the Blues)	1955	3.00	6.00	12.00
61494	Give Me Love/Sweet Song of India	1955	3.00	6.00	12.00
61501	He/If You Believe	1955	3.00	6.00	12.00
61531	The Littlest Angel/I'd Like to Trim a Tree with You	1955	3.00	6.00	12.00
61532	My Baby's Got Such Lovin' Ways/(Baby, Baby) Be Good to Me	1955	3.00	6.00	12.00
61587	Missing/Tell Me Now	1956	2.50	5.00	10.00
61627	Picnic/Delilah Jones	1956	2.50	5.00	10.00
61703	Every Day of My Life/Endless	1956	2.50	5.00	10.00
61748	Goodnight My Love, Pleasant Dreams/Mommy	1956	2.50	5.00	10.00
61771	Kid Stuff/Without Him	1957	2.50	5.00	10.00
61798	He's Got Time/Blue Skies	1957	2.50	5.00	10.00
61815	Drownin' in Memories/Please Don't Do That to Me	1957	2.50	5.00	10.00
61842	Rock Bottom/Beginning to Miss You	1957	2.50	5.00	10.00
61856	Around the World in 80 Days/Interlude	1957	2.50	5.00	10.00
61888	Forgive Me/Kiss Them for Me	1957	2.50	5.00	10.00
61911	Santa Claus Is Comin' to Town/Honorable Congratulations	1957	2.50	5.00	10.00
61924	Sugartime/Banana Split	1958	3.00	6.00	12.00
61991	Ding Dong/Since You Went Away to School	1958	2.50	5.00	10.00
62021	Volare (Nel Blu, Dipinto Di Blue)/Do You Love Me Like You Kiss Me	1958	2.50	5.00	10.00
62047	Sweetie Pie/I'll Think of You	1958	2.50	5.00	10.00
62059	May You Always/Achoo Cha Cha	1958	2.50	5.00	10.00
62106	Summer Dreams/Peace	1959	2.50	5.00	10.00
62135	Red River Valley/Compromise	1959	2.50	5.00	10.00
62155	Some of These Days/Have a Nice Weekend	1959	2.50	5.00	10.00
62162	Livin' Dangerously/Lover's Lullaby	1960	2.00	4.00	8.00
62162 [PS]	Livin' Dangerously/Lover's Lullaby	1960	2.50	5.00	10.00
62196	The Unforgiven/I Give Thanks	1960	2.00	4.00	8.00
62216	The Last Dance/Nine O'Clock	1960	2.00	4.00	8.00
62235	To Be Loved/I Don't Know Why	1960	2.00	4.00	8.00
62249	Just for Old Times' Sake/Really Neat	1961	2.00	4.00	8.00
62249 [PS]	Just for Old Times' Sake/Really Neat	1961	2.50	5.00	10.00
62276	Tears on My Pillow/Will There Be Room in the Space Ship	1961	2.00	4.00	8.00
62276 [PS]	Tears on My Pillow/Will There Be Room in the Space Ship	1961	2.50	5.00	10.00
62288	Just Because/I Do, I Do	1961	2.00	4.00	8.00
62296	I Can Dream, Can't I/I'm Just Taking My Time	1961	2.00	4.00	8.00
62305	Sugartime Twist/More Hearts Are Broken That Way	1962	2.00	4.00	8.00
62333	I Really Don't Want to Know/Mama's Gone, Goodbye	1962	2.00	4.00	8.00
REPRISE					
0256	Now and Forever/Never	1964	—	3.00	6.00
0330	Dear Heart/Candy Heart	1964	—	3.00	6.00
0338	I'll Walk Alone/Ticket to Anywhere	1965	—	3.00	6.00
20197	Summertime (Is the Time for Love)/Cordially Invited	1963	—	3.00	6.00

7-Inch Extended Plays

Number	Title (A Side/B Side)	Yr	VG	VG+	NM
CORAL					
EC 81074	One Two Three Four/Tootle-Loo-Siana//Picking Sweethearts/Miss You	195?	3.75	7.50	15.00
EC 81074 [PS]	The Three McGuire Sisters	195?	3.75	7.50	15.00
EC 81082	(contents unknown)	195?	3.75	7.50	15.00
EC 81082 [PS]	Sweethearts on Broadway	195?	3.75	7.50	15.00
EC 81090	(contents unknown)	195?	3.75	7.50	15.00
EC 81090 [PS]	TV Favorites	195?	3.75	7.50	15.00
EC 81098	Melody of Love/Hearts of Stone//Open Up Your Heart/The Naughty Lady of Shady Lane	1955	3.75	7.50	15.00
EC 81098 [PS]	By Request	1955	3.75	7.50	15.00
EC 81127	(contents unknown)	195?	3.00	6.00	12.00
EC 81127 [PS]	'S Wonderful	195?	3.00	6.00	12.00
EC 81145	Sugartime/Banana Split//I Tried/Lullaby of Birdland	1958	3.00	6.00	12.00
EC 81145 [PS]	The McGuire Sisters	1958	3.00	6.00	12.00
EC 81165	(contents unknown)	1958	3.00	6.00	12.00
EC 81165 [PS]	While the Lights Are Low	1958	3.00	6.00	12.00
EC 81174	Summer Dreams/Ding Dong//Since You Went Away to School/Think of Me Kindly	1958	3.00	6.00	12.00
EC 81174 [PS]	Four by Three	1958	3.00	6.00	12.00
EC 81184 [M]	(contents unknown)	1959	3.00	6.00	12.00
EC 81184 [PS]	I'll Think of You	1959	3.00	6.00	12.00
EC 7-81184 [PS]	I'll Think of You	1959	5.00	10.00	20.00
EC 7-81184 [S]	(contents unknown)	1959	5.00	10.00	20.00
EC 81507	(contents unknown)	1959	3.00	6.00	12.00
EC 81507 [PS]	The McGuire Sisters	1959	3.00	6.00	12.00
EC 82022 [PS]	Do You Remember When?	195?	3.00	6.00	12.00
—Cover for 2-record set (83050 and 83051)					
EC 82031	(contents unknown)	195?	3.00	6.00	12.00
EC 82031 [PS]	Children's Holiday	195?	3.00	6.00	12.00
83050	Do You Remember When/Sometimes I'm Happy//June Night/Tip Toe Through the Tulips with Me	195?	3.00	6.00	12.00
—"Side 1" and "Side 2" of EC 82022					
83051	Them There Eyes/Cuddle Up a Little Closer, Lovey Mine//Does Your Heart Beat for Me?/Blue Skies	195?	3.00	6.00	12.00
—"Side 3" and "Side 4" of EC 82022					

Albums

Number	Title (A Side/B Side)	Yr	VG	VG+	NM
ABC-PARAMOUNT					
530 [M]	The McGuire Sisters Today	1966	3.75	7.50	15.00
S-530 [S]	The McGuire Sisters Today	1966	5.00	10.00	20.00
CORAL					
7CXB 6 [(2)P]	The Best of the McGuire Sisters	1965	6.25	12.50	25.00
CXB 6 [(2)M]	The Best of the McGuire Sisters	1965	6.25	12.50	25.00
CRL 56123 [10]	By Request	1955	12.50	25.00	50.00
CRL 57026 [M]	Do You Remember When	1956	10.00	20.00	40.00
CRL 57028 [M]	'S Wonderful	1956	10.00	20.00	40.00
CRL 57033 [M]	He	1956	10.00	20.00	40.00
CRL 57052 [M]	Sincerely	1956	10.00	20.00	40.00
CRL 57097 [M]	Children's Holiday	1956	10.00	20.00	40.00

Number	Title (A Side/B Side)	Yr	VG	VG+	NM
❏ CRL 57134 [M]	Teenage Party	1957	7.50	15.00	30.00
❏ CRL 57145 [M]	While the Lights Are Low	1957	7.50	15.00	30.00
❏ CRL 57180 [M]	Musical Magic	1957	7.50	15.00	30.00
❏ CRL 57217 [M]	Sugartime	1958	7.50	15.00	30.00
❏ CRL 57225 [M]	Greetings from the McGuire Sisters	1958	7.50	15.00	30.00
❏ CRL 57296 [M]	May You Always	1959	5.00	10.00	20.00
❏ CRL 57303 [M]	In Harmony with Him	1959	6.25	12.50	25.00
❏ CRL 57337 [M]	His and Hers	1960	5.00	10.00	20.00
❏ CRL 57349 [M]	Our Golden Favorites	1961	5.00	10.00	20.00
❏ CRL 57385 [M]	Just for Old Times' Sake	1961	5.00	10.00	20.00
❏ CRL 57398 [M]	Subways Are for Sleeping	1961	3.75	7.50	15.00
❏ CRL 57415 [M]	Songs Everybody Knows	1962	3.75	7.50	15.00
❏ CRL 57443 [M]	Showcase	196?	5.00	10.00	20.00
❏ CRL 757296 [S]	May You Always	1959	7.50	15.00	30.00
❏ CRL 757303 [S]	In Harmony with Him	1959	10.00	20.00	40.00
❏ CRL 757337 [S]	His and Hers	1960	7.50	15.00	30.00
❏ CRL 757349 [R]	Our Golden Favorites	196?	3.00	6.00	12.00
❏ CRL 757385 [S]	Just for Old Times' Sake	1961	7.50	15.00	30.00
❏ CRL 757398 [S]	Subways Are for Sleeping	1961	5.00	10.00	20.00
❏ CRL 757415 [S]	Songs Everybody Knows	1962	5.00	10.00	20.00
❏ CRL 757443 [R]	Showcase	196?	3.00	6.00	12.00
MCA					
❏ 4119 [(2)]	The Best of the McGuire Sisters	1978	3.00	6.00	12.00
—Reissue of Coral 6					
VOCALION					
❏ VL 3685 [M]	Children's Holiday	1960	5.00	10.00	20.00
❏ VL 3798 [M]	The McGuire Sisters	1967	3.75	7.50	15.00
❏ VL 73798 [R]	The McGuire Sisters	1967	3.00	6.00	12.00

MCKAY, SCOTTY

45s

Number	Title (A Side/B Side)	Yr	VG	VG+	NM
ACE					
❏ 603	Let the Good Times Roll/Little Liza Jane	1960	12.50	25.00	50.00
❏ 608	Brown Eyed Handsome Man/Cry Me a River	1960	15.00	30.00	60.00
❏ 623	Ole King Cole/Pull Down the Sky	1961	12.50	25.00	50.00
❏ 636	I've Got My Eyes on You/Shattered Dreams	1961	10.00	20.00	40.00
❏ 652	Olive Learned to Pop-Eye/Shame	1962	10.00	20.00	40.00
❏ 8003	Half a Heartache/Little Miss Blue	1962	7.50	15.00	30.00
CLARIDGE					
❏ 309	Batman/All Around the World	1966	6.25	12.50	25.00
EVENT					
❏ 4295	Rollin' Dynamite/Evenin' Time	1959	12.50	25.00	50.00
HANNA-BARBERA					
❏ 495	I'm Gonna Love Ya/Waikiki Beach	1966	6.25	12.50	25.00
LAWN					
❏ 102	I've Been Thinkin'/It's a Fun Thing	1960	6.25	12.50	25.00
PARKWAY					
❏ 806	Rollin' Dynamite/Evenin' Time	1959	10.00	20.00	40.00
PHILIPS					
❏ 40109	Mess Around/Sittin' Down and Cryin'	1963	5.00	10.00	20.00
SAVANNAH SOUND					
❏ 501	Here Comes Batman/All Around the World	196?	10.00	20.00	40.00
SWAN					
❏ 4049	Little Lump of Sugar/Midnight Cryin' Time	1960	15.00	30.00	60.00
UNI					
❏ 55205	High on Life/If You Really Want Me To, I'll Go	1970	3.00	6.00	12.00

MCKENDREE SPRING

45s

Number	Title (A Side/B Side)	Yr	VG	VG+	NM
DECCA					
❏ 32510	If the Sun Should Rise/ What Will We Do with the Child	1969	—	3.00	6.00
❏ 32773	Because It's Time/Oh, Now My Friend	1971	—	3.00	6.00
❏ 32961	Down by the River/Flying Dutchmen	1972	—	3.00	6.00
❏ 33000	God Bless the Conspiracy/Flying Dutchmen	1972	—	3.00	6.00
MCA					
❏ 40024	Underground Railroad/Watch Those Pennies	1973	—	2.50	5.00
PYE					
❏ 71023	Easier Things Have Been Done/(B-side unknown)	1975	—	2.50	5.00
❏ 71060	Too Young to Feel This Old/I'm Gonna Lose That Game Again	1976	—	2.50	5.00

Albums

Number	Title (A Side/B Side)	Yr	VG	VG+	NM
DECCA					
❏ DL 75104	McKendree Spring	1969	3.75	7.50	15.00
❏ DL 75230	Second Thoughts	1970	3.75	7.50	15.00
❏ DL 75332	McKendree Spring 3	1972	3.75	7.50	15.00
❏ DL 75385	Tracks	1972	3.75	7.50	15.00
MCA					
❏ 44	McKendree Spring 3	1973	2.50	5.00	10.00
—Reissue of Decca 75332					
❏ 50	Tracks	1973	2.50	5.00	10.00
—Reissue of Decca 75385					
❏ 277	McKendree Spring	1973	2.50	5.00	10.00
—Reissue of Decca 75104					
❏ 370	Spring Suite	1973	3.00	6.00	12.00
PYE					
❏ 12108	Get Me to the Country	1975	3.00	6.00	12.00
❏ 12124	Too Young to Feel This Old	1976	3.00	6.00	12.00

MCKENZIE, SCOTT Also see THE JOURNEYMEN (1); THE SMOOTHIES.

45s

Number	Title (A Side/B Side)	Yr	VG	VG+	NM
CAPITOL					
❏ 5348	All I Want Is You/Look in Your Eyes	1965	2.50	5.00	10.00
❏ 5500	There Stands the Glass/Wipe the Tears (From Your Face)	1965	2.50	5.00	10.00
❏ 5961	All I Want Is You/Look in Your Eyes	1967	—	3.00	6.00
EPIC					
❏ 10124	No, No, No, No, No/I Want to Be Alone	1967	2.00	4.00	8.00
—B-side by McKenzie's Musicians					
ODE					
❏ 103	San Francisco (Be Sure to Wear Flowers in Your Hair)/What's the Difference	1967	2.00	4.00	8.00
—Revised title and revised mix					

Number	Title (A Side/B Side)	Yr	VG	VG+	NM
❏ 103	San Francisco "Wear Some Flowers in Your Hair"/What's the Difference	1967	3.75	7.50	15.00
—Original title; also has a different mix (echoey bass drum in bridge) than the later, more common version					
❏ 105	Like and Old Time Movie/ What's the Difference, Chapter II	1967	—	3.00	6.00
❏ 107	Holy Man/What's the Difference, Chapter III	1968	—	3.00	6.00
❏ 66012	Going Home Again/Take a Moment	1970	—	2.50	5.00

Albums

Number	Title (A Side/B Side)	Yr	VG	VG+	NM
ODE					
❏ Z12 44001 [M]	The Voice of Scott McKenzie	1967	10.00	20.00	40.00
❏ Z12 44002 [S]	The Voice of Scott McKenzie	1967	6.25	12.50	25.00
❏ SP-77007	Stained Glass Morning	1970	3.75	7.50	15.00

MCKINLEYS, THE

45s

Number	Title (A Side/B Side)	Yr	VG	VG+	NM
SWAN					
❏ 4185	A Million Miles Away/Someone Cares for Me	1964	3.75	7.50	15.00

MCKUEN, ROD

45s

Number	Title (A Side/B Side)	Yr	VG	VG+	NM
A&M					
❏ 712	Hi Lonesome/Ballad of Hollywood	1963	2.50	5.00	10.00
BUDDAH					
❏ 372	Cycles/I Have Loved You	1973	—	2.00	4.00
❏ 401	Seasons in the Sun/(B-side unknown)	1974	—	2.00	4.00
BUENA VISTA					
❏ 482	Pastures Green/Scandalous John	1971	—	2.50	5.00
❏ 482 [PS]	Pastures Green/Scandalous John	1971	3.75	7.50	15.00
DECCA					
❏ 30660	Two Brothers/Jump Up	1958	3.75	7.50	15.00
❏ 30840	Lonesome Boy/Time's A-Gettin' Hard	1959	3.75	7.50	15.00
❏ 30902	Sure/Take It Like a Man	1959	3.75	7.50	15.00
HORIZON					
❏ 3	Advice to Folk Singers/There's a Hoot Tonight	1963	2.50	5.00	10.00
JUBILEE					
❏ 5420	Oliver Twist Meets the Duke of Oil/Steel Men	1962	3.00	6.00	12.00
KAPP					
❏ 366	In a Lonely Place/Marie, Marie	1961	3.00	6.00	12.00
LIBERTY					
❏ 55019	Rock Island Line/Head Like a Rock	1956	3.00	6.00	12.00
❏ 55034	Happy Is a Boy Named Me/Repeat After Me	1956	3.00	6.00	12.00
RCA VICTOR					
❏ 47-8613	Summer in My Eye/So Many Others	1965	2.00	4.00	8.00
❏ 47-8772	So Long, San Francisco/Some Trust in Chariots	1965	2.00	4.00	8.00
❏ 47-9139	The Ever Constant Sea/Baby Be My Love	1967	2.00	4.00	8.00
❏ 47-9376	Listen to the Warm/A Cat Named Sloopy	1967	2.00	4.00	8.00
❏ 47-9478	The Importance of the Rose/The Single Man	1968	2.00	4.00	8.00
SPIRAL					
❏ 1407	Oliver Twist/Celebrity Twist	1962	3.75	7.50	15.00
STANYAN					
❏ 34	Simple Christmas/A Hand To Hold At Christmas	1974	—	2.50	5.00
—B-side by Glenn Yarbrough					
WARNER BROS.					
❏ 7243	Seasons in the Sun/To Watch the Trains	1968	—	3.00	6.00
❏ 7259	Ivy That Clings to the Wall/Kaleidoscope	1969	—	3.00	6.00
❏ 7274	Boat Ride/I'll Catch the Sun	1969	—	3.00	6.00
❏ 7288	Look Away/Trashy	1969	—	3.00	6.00
❏ 7332	The Things Men Do/ The Time It Takes to Love You	1969	—	3.00	6.00
❏ 7346	Bring Her a Rose/Mister Kelly-Kelly and Me	1969	—	3.00	6.00
❏ 7389	I Think It's Going to Rain Today/London	1970	—	2.50	5.00
❏ 7420	My Mother's Eyes/Soldiers Want to Be Heroes	1970	—	2.50	5.00
❏ 7454	Champion Charlie Brown/Something for Snoopy	1971	—	3.00	6.00
❏ 7533	Hit 'Em in the Head with Love/ Soldiers Want to Be Heroes	1971	—	2.50	5.00
❏ 7542	The Carols of Christmas/ So My Sheep May Safely Graze	1971	—	2.50	5.00
❏ 7542 [PS]	The Carols of Christmas/ So My Sheep May Safely Graze	1971	—	3.00	6.00
❏ 7620	Time to Sing My Song/ Minute-Thirty-Second Waltz	1972	—	2.50	5.00
❏ 7699	Good for Nothin' Bill/The World I Used to Know	1973	—	2.00	4.00

7-Inch Extended Plays

Number	Title (A Side/B Side)	Yr	VG	VG+	NM
WARNER BROS.					
❏ PRO 298 [DJ]	A Personal Message from Rod McKuen// The Language of Hello/Concerto for 4 Hands/ Boat Ride	1968	3.75	7.50	15.00
—Promo-only item; small hole, plays at 33 1/3 rpm					
❏ PRO 298 [PS]	Lonesome Cities	1968	5.00	10.00	20.00

Albums

Number	Title (A Side/B Side)	Yr	VG	VG+	NM
BUDDAH					
❏ BDS-5138	Cycles	197?	3.00	6.00	12.00
CAPITOL					
❏ ST 2079 [S]	Rod McKuen Sings Rod McKuen	1964	5.00	10.00	20.00
❏ T 2079 [M]	Rod McKuen Sings Rod McKuen	1964	3.75	7.50	15.00
❏ ST 2838 [S]	Love Movement	1968	3.75	7.50	15.00
❏ T 2838 [M]	Love Movement	1968	6.25	12.50	25.00
DECCA					
❏ DL 4969 [M]	Very Warm	1968	5.00	10.00	20.00
❏ DL 8882 [M]	Anywhere I Wander	1958	5.00	10.00	20.00
❏ DL 8946 [M]	Alone After Dark	1959	5.00	10.00	20.00
❏ DL 74969 [S]	Very Warm	1968	3.75	7.50	15.00
❏ DL 78882 [S]	Anywhere I Wander	1958	7.50	15.00	30.00
❏ DL 78946 [S]	Alone After Dark	1959	7.50	15.00	30.00
EPIC					
❏ BN 26370 [M]	In Search of Eros	1968	7.50	15.00	30.00
—White label promo only; in stereo cover with "Epic Mono" sticker					
❏ BN 26370 [S]	In Search of Eros	1968	3.75	7.50	15.00
EVEREST					
❏ 3208	Desire Has No Special Time	1968	3.75	7.50	15.00
❏ 3267	Life Is	197?	3.75	7.50	15.00
HIFI					
❏ R 407 [M]	Time of Desire	1958	5.00	10.00	20.00
❏ SR 407 [S]	Time of Desire	1958	6.25	12.50	25.00

M

Number	Title (A Side/B Side)	Yr	VG	VG+	NM
❏ R 419 [M]	Beatsville	1960	5.00	10.00	20.00
❏ SR 419 [S]	Beatsville	1960	6.25	12.50	25.00
HORIZON					
❏ ST-1612 [S]	New Sounds in Folk Music	1963	6.25	12.50	25.00
❏ WP-1612 [M]	New Sounds in Folk Music	1963	5.00	10.00	20.00
❏ WPLP-1632 [M]	There's a Hoot Tonight	1963	5.00	10.00	20.00
❏ WPLP-1632 [S]	There's a Hoot Tonight	1963	6.25	12.50	25.00
IN					
❏ 1003 [M]	Seasons in the Sun	1964	5.00	10.00	20.00
❏ S-1003 [S]	Seasons in the Sun	1964	6.25	12.50	25.00
JUBILEE					
❏ J-5013 [M]	Mr. Oliver Twist	1962	5.00	10.00	20.00
❏ SJ-5013 [S]	Mr. Oliver Twist	1962	6.25	12.50	25.00
KAPP					
❏ KL-1538 [M]	In a Lonely Place	1967	5.00	10.00	20.00
❏ KS-3538 [S]	In a Lonely Place	1967	3.75	7.50	15.00
LIBERTY					
❏ LRP-3011 [M]	Lazy Afternoon	1956	10.00	20.00	40.00
RCA VICTOR					
❏ LPM-3424 [M]	Rod McKuen Sings His Own	1965	3.75	7.50	15.00
❏ LSP-3424 [S]	Rod McKuen Sings His Own	1965	5.00	10.00	20.00
❏ LPM-3508 [M]	The Loner	1966	3.75	7.50	15.00
❏ LSP-3508 [S]	The Loner	1966	5.00	10.00	20.00
❏ LPM-3635 [M]	Other Kinds of Songs	1966	3.75	7.50	15.00
❏ LSP-3635 [S]	Other Kinds of Songs	1966	5.00	10.00	20.00
❏ LPM-3786 [M]	Through European Windows	1967	5.00	10.00	20.00
❏ LSP-3786 [S]	Through European Windows	1967	3.75	7.50	15.00
❏ LPM-3863 [M]	Listen to the Warm	1967	5.00	10.00	20.00
❏ LSP-3863 [S]	Listen to the Warm	1967	3.75	7.50	15.00
❏ LSP-4010	A Single Man	1968	3.75	7.50	15.00
❏ LSP-4127	The Best of Rod McKuen	1969	3.75	7.50	15.00
STANYAN					
❏ STS-001	In Concert	197?	3.75	7.50	15.00
—Originals are numbered, limited editions					
❏ STS-003	Seasons in the Sun	197?	3.75	7.50	15.00
❏ 1894 [(2)]	Pastorale	197?	3.00	6.00	12.00
❏ 2560	Rod McKuen's Greatest Hits 2	197?	2.50	5.00	10.00
❏ 2688	Rod McKuen's Greatest Hits, Vol. 4	197?	2.50	5.00	10.00
❏ 4010	A Single Man	197?	2.50	5.00	10.00
❏ 5004	Seasons in the Sun Vol. 2	197?	3.00	6.00	12.00
❏ 5005	Blessings in Shades of Green	1970	3.00	6.00	12.00
❏ 5006	Folk Album	1970	3.00	6.00	12.00
❏ 5009	Love's Been Good to Me	1970	3.00	6.00	12.00
❏ 5010	A Boy Named Charlie Brown	1970	3.75	7.50	15.00
❏ 5016 [(2)]	Live in London!	1971	3.75	7.50	15.00
❏ 5020	Try Rod McKuen in Your Own Home	197?	3.00	6.00	12.00
❏ 5022	Rod McKuen Sings Jacques Brel	197?	3.00	6.00	12.00
❏ 5025	Rod	197?	3.00	6.00	12.00
❏ 5031	Rod McKuen's Greatest Hits, Vol. 3	197?	3.00	6.00	12.00
❏ 5032	Have a Nice Day	1973	3.00	6.00	12.00
❏ 5040	Evening in Vienna	1972	3.00	6.00	12.00
❏ 5042	Rod McKuen Grand Tour, Vol. 3	1972	3.00	6.00	12.00
❏ 5046 [(2)]	Seasons in the Sun Vols. 1 and 2	197?	3.75	7.50	15.00
❏ 5047	Pastures Green	197?	3.00	6.00	12.00
❏ 5048 [(2)]	Listen to the Warm	197?	3.75	7.50	15.00
❏ 5051 [(2)]	Amsterdam Concert	1972	3.75	7.50	15.00
❏ 5072	A Portrait of Rod McKuen	1972	3.00	6.00	12.00
❏ 5075	Live at the Sydney Opera House	197?	3.00	6.00	12.00
❏ 9001	Concerto No. 1 for Four Harpsichords and Orchestra	197?	3.00	6.00	12.00
❏ 9005	Symphony No. 1: "All Men Love Something"	197?	3.00	6.00	12.00
❏ 9006	Concerto No. 2 for Guitar and Orchestra; Five Pieces	197?	3.00	6.00	12.00
❏ 9008	Piano Variations	197?	3.00	6.00	12.00
❏ 9010	McKuen Conducts McKuen	1972	3.00	6.00	12.00
❏ 9012	Concerto No. 3 for Piano and Orchestra	1972	3.00	6.00	12.00
❏ 9015	Seascapes; Plains of My Country	197?	3.00	6.00	12.00
❏ 10009	Concerto No. 1; Four Statements	197?	3.00	6.00	12.00
SUNSET					
❏ SUS-5273	In the Beginning	1970	2.50	5.00	10.00
TRADITION					
❏ 2063 [M]	A San Francisco Hippie Trip	1967	6.25	12.50	25.00
WARNER BROS.					
❏ WS 1722	Beautiful Strangers	1968	3.75	7.50	15.00
❏ WS 1758	Lonesome Cities	1968	3.75	7.50	15.00
❏ WS 1772	Greatest Hits of Rod McKuen	1969	3.75	7.50	15.00
❏ 2WS 1794 [(2)]	Rod McKuen at Carnegie Hall	1969	5.00	10.00	20.00
❏ WS 1837	New Ballads	1970	3.00	6.00	12.00
❏ 2WS 1894 [(2)]	Pastorale	1971	3.75	7.50	15.00
❏ 2WS 1947 [(2)]	Rod McKuen Grand Tour	1971	3.75	7.50	15.00
❏ BS 2560	Rod McKuen's Greatest Hits 2	1970	3.00	6.00	12.00
❏ BS 2638	Odyssey	1973	3.00	6.00	12.00
❏ BS 2688	Rod McKuen's Greatest Hits, Vol. 4	1973	3.00	6.00	12.00
❏ 2WS 2731 [(2)]	Back to Carnegie Hall	1973	3.75	7.50	15.00
❏ BS 2785	Seasons in the Sun	1974	3.00	6.00	12.00
❏ BS 2817	Alone	1974	3.00	6.00	12.00
❏ BS 2931	McKuen Country	1976	2.50	5.00	10.00
❏ ST-92042	Greatest Hits of Rod McKuen	1969	5.00	10.00	20.00
—Capitol Record Club edition					

MCKUEN, ROD; TAK SHINDO; JULIE MEREDITH
Albums

Number	Title (A Side/B Side)	Yr	VG	VG+	NM
IMPERIAL					
❏ LP-9092 [M]	The Yellow Unicorn	1960	10.00	20.00	40.00
❏ LP-12036 [S]	The Yellow Unicorn	1960	12.50	25.00	50.00

MCLAIN, DENNY
45s

Number	Title (A Side/B Side)	Yr	VG	VG+	NM
CAPITOL					
❏ 2282	Extra Innings/Lonely Is the Name	1968	3.00	6.00	12.00
Albums					
CAPITOL					
❏ ST-204	Denny McLain In Las Vegas	1969	6.25	12.50	25.00
❏ ST 2881	Denny McLain at the Organ	1968	6.25	12.50	25.00

MCLAWLER, SARAH
45s

Number	Title (A Side/B Side)	Yr	VG	VG+	NM
KING					
❏ 4549	Please Try to Love Me/Ready, Willing, and Able	1952	25.00	50.00	100.00
❏ 4561	Romance in the Dark/I'm Just Another One	1952	25.00	50.00	100.00
VEE JAY					
❏ 199	Babe in the Woods/Flamingo	1956	7.50	15.00	30.00
❏ 239	Snowfall/Relax Miss Frisky	1957	7.50	15.00	30.00
—With Richard Otto					
Albums					
VEE JAY					
❏ LP-1030 [M]	At the Break of Day	1961	10.00	20.00	40.00
—With Richard Otto					

MCLEAN, DON
45s

Number	Title (A Side/B Side)	Yr	VG	VG+	NM
ARISTA					
❏ 0284	Prime Time/The Statue	1977	—	2.00	4.00
❏ 0379	It Doesn't Matter Anymore/If We Try	1978	—	2.00	4.00
CAPITOL					
❏ B-44098	Perfect Love/Can't Blame the Train	1987	—	—	3.00
❏ B-44186	Love in the Heart/Every Day's a Miracle	1988	—	—	3.00
❏ B-44258	Eventually/It's Not Your Fault	1988	—	—	3.00
EMI					
❏ 9100	American Pie/Vincent	1992	2.00	4.00	8.00
—Scarce reissue with entire 8:30 version of "American Pie" on one side					
EMI AMERICA					
❏ 8375	He's Got You/To Have and To Hold	1987	—	—	3.00
❏ 43025	Superman's Ghost/(B-side unknown)	1987	—	—	3.00
MEDIARTS					
❏ 108	And I Love You So/Castles in the Air	1970	2.50	5.00	10.00
MILLENNIUM					
❏ YB-11799	Crying/Genesis (In the Beginning)	1980	—	2.00	4.00
❏ YB-11803	Lloras "Crying"/Genesis (In the Beginning)	1981	—	—	—
—Unreleased					
❏ YB-11804	Since I Don't Have You/Your Cheating Heart	1981	—	2.00	4.00
❏ YB-11809	It's Just the Sun/Words and Music	1981	—	2.00	4.00
❏ YB-11819	Castles in the Air/Crazy Eyes	1981	—	2.00	4.00
❏ YB-13106	Jerusalem/Left for Dead on the Road of Love	1982	—	2.00	4.00
❏ GB-13477	Crying/Since I Don't Have You	1983	—	—	3.00
—Gold Standard Series					
UNITED ARTISTS					
❏ XW206	If We Try/The More You Pay	1973	—	2.00	4.00
❏ XW363	Fool's Paradise/Happy Trails	1973	—	2.00	4.00
❏ XW519	Vincent/Dreidel	1974	—	2.00	4.00
—Reissue					
❏ XW520	American Pie (Part 1)/American Pie (Part 2)	1974	—	2.00	4.00
—Reissue					
❏ XW541	Sitting on Top of the World/Mule Skinner Blues	1974	—	2.00	4.00
❏ XW579	Homeless Brothers/La La Love You	1974	—	2.00	4.00
❏ XW614	Wonderful Baby/Birthday Song	1975	—	2.00	4.00
❏ 50796	And I Love You So/Castles in the Air	1971	—	3.00	6.00
❏ 50856	American Pie/Empty Chairs	1971	—	—	—
—Unreleased?					
❏ 50856	American Pie — Part 1/American Pie — Part 2	1971	—	2.50	5.00
❏ 50856 [DJ]	American Pie (mono/stereo)	1971	2.00	4.00	8.00
—With a different edit than the Part 1/Part 2 stock copy					
❏ 50856 [PS]	American Pie	1971	2.50	5.00	10.00
—Comes with both promos and stock copies					
❏ 50887	Vincent/Castles in the Air	1972	—	2.50	5.00
❏ 50887 [PS]	Vincent/Castles in the Air	1972	2.50	5.00	10.00
❏ 51100	Dreidel/Bronco Bill's Lament	1973	—	2.00	4.00
Albums					
ARISTA					
❏ AL 4149	Prime Time	1978	2.50	5.00	10.00
CAPITOL					
❏ C1-48080	Love Tracks	1988	2.50	5.00	10.00
CASABLANCA					
❏ NBLP 7173	Chain Lightning	1979	—	—	—
—Canceled					
EMI AMERICA					
❏ ST-17255	Don McLean's Greatest Hits, Then and Now	1987	2.50	5.00	10.00
LIBERTY					
❏ LN-10037	American Pie	1980	2.00	4.00	8.00
—Reissue of United Artists 5535					
❏ LN-10157	Tapestry	1982	2.00	4.00	8.00
—Reissue of United Artists 5522					
❏ LN-10211	Homeless Brother	198?	2.00	4.00	8.00
—Reissue of United Artists 315					
MEDIARTS					
❏ 41-4	Tapestry	1970	5.00	10.00	20.00
MILLENNIUM					
❏ BXL1-7756	Chain Lightning	1981	2.50	5.00	10.00
❏ BXL1-7762	Believers	1981	2.50	5.00	10.00
UNITED ARTISTS					
❏ UA-LA161-F	Playin' Favorites	1973	3.00	6.00	12.00
❏ UA-LA315-G	Homeless Brother	1974	3.00	6.00	12.00
❏ UA-LA652-H2 [(2)]	Solo	1976	3.75	7.50	15.00
❏ UAS-5522	Tapestry	1971	3.00	6.00	12.00
—Reissue of Mediarts LP					
❏ UAS-5535	American Pie	1971	3.00	6.00	12.00
❏ UAS-5651	Don McLean	1972	3.00	6.00	12.00

MCLOLLIE, OSCAR
45s

Number	Title (A Side/B Side)	Yr	VG	VG+	NM
CLASS					
❏ 206	Here I Am/Say	1957	3.75	7.50	15.00
❏ 228	Hey Girl — Hey Boy/Let Me Know Let Me Know	1958	3.75	7.50	15.00
—With Jeanette Baker					
❏ 238	Let's Get Together/Rock-a-Cha	1958	3.75	7.50	15.00
—With Jeanette Baker					
❏ 243	Convicted/My Heart Speaks	1959	3.75	7.50	15.00
❏ 265	The Honey Jump/Call It Love	1960	3.75	7.50	15.00
❏ 503	Rain/Casino	1956	5.00	10.00	20.00

Number	Title (A Side/B Side)	Yr	VG	VG+	NM
MERCURY					
❑ 70964	Blue Velvet/The Penalty	1956	6.25	12.50	25.00
MODERN					
❑ 902	The Honey Jump (Part 1)/ The Honey Jump (Part 2)	1952	15.00	30.00	60.00
❑ 915	Be Cool My Heart/All the Oil in Texas	1952	12.50	25.00	50.00
❑ 920	Falling in Love with You/Lolly Pop	1953	12.50	25.00	50.00
❑ 938	Hot Banana/Wiggle Toe	1954	10.00	20.00	40.00
❑ 943	God Gave Us Christmas/ Dig That Crazy Santa Claus	1954	10.00	20.00	40.00
❑ 950	Pretty Girl/Hey Lolly Lolly	1955	10.00	20.00	40.00
❑ 955	Pagliacci (With a Broken Heart)/Eternal Love	1955	10.00	20.00	40.00
❑ 970	Roll, Hot Rod, Roll/Convicted	1955	10.00	20.00	40.00
❑ 976	God Gave Us Christmas/(B-side unknown)	1955	7.50	15.00	30.00
WING					
❑ 90083	God's Green Earth/Got Your Love in My Heart	1956	6.25	12.50	25.00
Albums					
CROWN					
❑ CLP-5016 [M]	Oscar McLollie and His Honey Jumpers	1956	100.00	200.00	400.00
—Opinions differ as to whether this LP actually exists. Value is probably conservative.					

MCLUHAN

Albums

BRUNSWICK

Number	Title (A Side/B Side)	Yr	VG	VG+	NM
❑ BL 754177	Anomaly	1972	5.00	10.00	20.00

MCLUHAN, MARSHALL

Albums

COLUMBIA

Number	Title (A Side/B Side)	Yr	VG	VG+	NM
❑ CL 2701 [M]	The Medium Is the Message	1967	6.25	12.50	25.00
❑ CS 9501 [S]	The Medium Is the Message	1967	6.25	12.50	25.00

MCMANUS, ROSS

45s

IMPERIAL

Number	Title (A Side/B Side)	Yr	VG	VG+	NM
❑ 66042	Patsy Girl/I'm the Greatest	1964	3.00	6.00	12.00

MCNABB, CECIL

45s

KING

Number	Title (A Side/B Side)	Yr	VG	VG+	NM
❑ 5116	Clock Tickin' Rhythm/Nothing Like This	1958	62.50	125.00	250.00

MCNAIR, BARBARA

45s

AUDIO FIDELITY

Number	Title (A Side/B Side)	Yr	VG	VG+	NM
❑ 153	Love Has a Way/(B-side unknown)	1969	2.50	5.00	10.00
❑ 162	After St. Francis/I Can Tell	1969	2.50	5.00	10.00
CORAL					
❑ 61923	Till There Was You/Bobby	1958	6.25	12.50	25.00
❑ 61972	He's Got the Whole World in His Hands/Flipped Over You	1958	7.50	15.00	30.00
❑ 61996	Indiscreet/Waltz Me Around	1958	6.25	12.50	25.00
❑ 62020	Too Late This Spring/See If I Care	1958	6.25	12.50	25.00
❑ 62071	Goin' Steady with the Moon/I Feel a Feeling	1959	6.25	12.50	25.00
❑ 62116	Lover's Prayer/Old Devil Moon	1959	6.25	12.50	25.00
KC					
❑ 109	Cross Over the Bridge/Gloryland	1962	12.50	25.00	50.00
❑ 112	A Little Bird Told Me/Nobody Rings My Bell	1963	10.00	20.00	40.00
MOTOWN					
❑ 1087	Touch of Time/You're Gonna Love My Baby	1965	6.25	12.50	25.00
❑ 1099	What a Day/Everything Is Good About You	1966	6.25	12.50	25.00
❑ 1106	Here I Am Baby/My World Is Empty Without You	1966	6.25	12.50	25.00
❑ 1112	Steal Away Tonight/For Once in My Life	1967	125.00	250.00	500.00
❑ 1123	Where Would I Be Without You/ For Once in My Life	1968	6.25	12.50	25.00
❑ 1133	You Could Never Love Him/Fancy Passes	1968	6.25	12.50	25.00
SIGNATURE					
❑ 12024	He's a King/Murray, What's Your Hurry	1960	5.00	10.00	20.00
❑ 12033	All About Love/You Done Me Wrong	1960	5.00	10.00	20.00
❑ 12049	Kansas City/Love Talk	1960	5.00	10.00	20.00
WARNER BROS.					
❑ 5633	Wanted Me/It Was Never Like This	1965	7.50	15.00	30.00
Albums					
AUDIO FIDELITY					
❑ AFSD-6222	More Today Than Yesterday	1969	5.00	10.00	20.00
❑ ST-92074	More Today Than Yesterday	1969	6.25	12.50	25.00
—Capitol Record Club edition					
MOTOWN					
❑ 644 [M]	Here I Am	1966	12.50	25.00	50.00
❑ S-644 [S]	Here I Am	1966	15.00	30.00	60.00
❑ S-680	The Real Barbara McNair	1969	7.50	15.00	30.00
SIGNATURE					
❑ SM 1042 [M]	Love Talk	1960	10.00	20.00	40.00
❑ SS 1042 [S]	Love Talk	1960	12.50	25.00	50.00
WARNER BROS.					
❑ W 1541 [M]	I Enjoy Being a Girl	1964	6.25	12.50	25.00
❑ WS 1541 [S]	I Enjoy Being a Girl	1964	7.50	15.00	30.00
❑ W 1570 [M]	The Livin' End	1964	6.25	12.50	25.00
❑ WS 1570 [S]	The Livin' End	1964	7.50	15.00	30.00

MCNAUGHTON, BYRON, AND HIS ALL NEWS ORCHESTRA

45s

JAMIE

Number	Title (A Side/B Side)	Yr	VG	VG+	NM
❑ 1427	Right from the Shark's Jaws (The Jaws Interview)/Jaws Jam	1975	2.50	5.00	10.00

MCNEELY, BIG JAY

45s

ALADDIN

Number	Title (A Side/B Side)	Yr	VG	VG+	NM
❑ 3242	Real Crazy Cool/Let's Split	1954	7.50	15.00	30.00
BAYOU					
❑ 014	Hometown Jamboree/Teenage Hop	1953	20.00	40.00	80.00
❑ 018	Catastrophe/Calamity	1953	20.00	40.00	80.00
FEDERAL					
❑ 12102	The Goof/Big Jay Shuffle	1952	10.00	20.00	40.00
❑ 12111	Just Crazy/Penthouse Serenade	1952	10.00	20.00	40.00

Number	Title (A Side/B Side)	Yr	VG	VG+	NM
❑ 12141	Nervous Man, Nervous/Rock Candy	1953	10.00	20.00	40.00
❑ 12151	3-D/Texas Turkey	1953	10.00	20.00	40.00
❑ 12168	Mule Walk/Ice Water	1954	10.00	20.00	40.00
❑ 12179	Hot Cinders/Whipped Cream	1954	10.00	20.00	40.00
❑ 12186	Let's Work/Hard Tack	1954	10.00	20.00	40.00
❑ 12191	Beachcomber/Strip Tease Swing	1954	10.00	20.00	40.00
IMPERIAL					
❑ 5219	Deacon's Express/Jet Fury	1953	12.50	25.00	50.00
—Note: Earlier Big Jay McNeely releases on Imperial are unknown on 45 rpm					
SAVOY					
❑ 1143	Deacon Hop/The Hucklebuck	1955	7.50	15.00	30.00
—With Paul Williams					
SWINGIN'					
❑ 614	There Is Something on Your Mind/ Back...Shack...Track	1959	6.25	12.50	25.00
❑ 618	I Got the Message/Psycho Serenade	1959	3.75	7.50	15.00
❑ 622	Minnie/My Darling Dear	1960	3.75	7.50	15.00
❑ 627	I Love You, Oh Darling/Oh, What a Fool	1960	3.75	7.50	15.00
❑ 629	After Midnight/Before Midnight	1961	3.75	7.50	15.00
❑ 637	Without a Love/The Squat	1962	3.75	7.50	15.00
VEE JAY					
❑ 142	Big Jay's Hop/Three Blind Mice	1955	10.00	20.00	40.00
❑ 212	Jay's Rock/The Convention	1956	15.00	30.00	60.00
—B-side by the Delegates					
WARNER BROS.					
❑ 5401	You Don't Have to Go/Big Jay's Count	1963	3.00	6.00	12.00
7-Inch Extended Plays					
FEDERAL					
❑ EP-246	Big Jake Shuffle/3-D//Nervous Man Nervous/ The Goof	1953	75.00	150.00	300.00
❑ EP-246 [PS]	Go! Go! Go! With Big Jay McNeely	1953	75.00	150.00	300.00
❑ EP-301	*Mule Milk/Hot Cinders/Ice Water/Whipped Cream	1954	50.00	100.00	200.00
❑ EP-301 [PS]	Big Jay McNeely, Volume 2	1954	50.00	100.00	200.00
❑ EP-332	(contents unknown)	1954	50.00	100.00	200.00
❑ EP-332 [PS]	Wild Man of the Saxophone	1954	50.00	100.00	200.00
❑ EP-373	(contents unknown)	1955	25.00	50.00	100.00
❑ EP-373 [PS]	Just Crazy	1955	25.00	50.00	100.00
Albums					
COLLECTABLES					
❑ COL-5133	Golden Classics	198?	2.50	5.00	10.00
FEDERAL					
❑ 295-96 [10]	Big Jay McNeely	1955	750.00	1500.	3000.
❑ 395-530 [M]	Big Jay McNeely in 3-D	1956	200.00	400.00	800.00
KING					
❑ 650 [M]	Big Jay McNeely in 3-D	1959	125.00	250.00	500.00
SAVOY					
❑ MG-15045 [10]	A Rhythm and Blues Concert	1955	1000.	1500.	2000.
WARNER BROS.					
❑ W 1533 [M]	Big Jay McNeely	1963	20.00	40.00	80.00
❑ WS 1533 [S]	Big Jay McNeely	1963	25.00	50.00	100.00

MCPHATTER, CLYDE Also see THE DRIFTERS.

45s

AMY

Number	Title (A Side/B Side)	Yr	VG	VG+	NM
❑ 941	Everybody's Somebody's Fool/I Belong to You	1965	3.75	7.50	15.00
❑ 950	Little Bit of Sunshine/ Everybody Loves a Good Time	1966	3.00	6.00	12.00
❑ 968	A Shot of Rhythm and Blues/ I'm Not Going to Work Today	1966	3.00	6.00	12.00
❑ 975	Sweet and Innocent/Lavender Lace	1966	3.00	6.00	12.00
❑ 993	I Dreamt I Died/Lonely People Can't Afford to Cry	1967	3.00	6.00	12.00
ATLANTIC					
❑ 1070	Everybody's Laughing/Hot Ziggity	1955	7.50	15.00	30.00
❑ 1077	Love Has Joined Us Together/I Gotta Have You	1955	7.50	15.00	30.00
—With Ruth Brown					
❑ 1081	Seven Days/I'm Not Worthy	1956	7.50	15.00	30.00
❑ 1092	Treasure of Love/When You're Sincere	1956	10.00	20.00	40.00
❑ 1106	Thirty Days/I'm Lonely Tonight	1956	7.50	15.00	30.00
❑ 1117	Without Love (There Is Nothing)/I Make Believe	1956	7.50	15.00	30.00
❑ 1133	No Matter What/Just to Hold My Hand	1957	6.25	12.50	25.00
❑ 1149	Long Lonely Nights/Heartaches	1957	6.25	12.50	25.00
❑ 1158	You'll Be There/Rock and Cry	1957	6.25	12.50	25.00
❑ 1170	That's Enough for Me/No Love Like Her Love	1958	6.25	12.50	25.00
❑ 1185	Come What May/Let Me Know	1958	6.25	12.50	25.00
❑ 1199	A Lover's Question/I Can't Stand Up Long	1958	6.25	12.50	25.00
❑ 2018	Lovey Dovey/My Island of Dreams	1959	5.00	10.00	20.00
❑ 2028	Since You've Been Gone/Try, Try Baby	1959	5.00	10.00	20.00
—B-side actually the "old" Drifters (uncredited)					
❑ 2038	You Went Back on Your Word/There You Go	1959	5.00	10.00	20.00
—B-side actually the "old" Drifters (uncredited)					
❑ 2049	Just Give Me a Ring/Don't Dog Me	1960	5.00	10.00	20.00
—B-side actually the "old" Drifters (uncredited)					
❑ 2060	Deep Sea Ball/Let the Boogie-Woogie Roll	1960	5.00	10.00	20.00
—B-side actually the "old" Drifters (uncredited)					
❑ 2082	If I Didn't Love You Like I Do/Go! Yes Go!	1960	5.00	10.00	20.00
—B-side actually the "old" Drifters (uncredited)					
DECCA					
❑ 32719	Book of Memories/I'll Belong to You	1970	2.00	4.00	8.00
❑ 32753	Why Can't We Get Together/Mixed-Up Cup	1970	2.00	4.00	8.00
DERAM					
❑ 85032	Thank You Love/Only a Fool	1968	2.50	5.00	10.00
❑ 85039	Baby You've Got It/ Baby I Could Be So Good at Loving You	1969	2.50	5.00	10.00
MERCURY					
❑ 71660	Ta Ta/I Ain't Givin' Up Nothin'	1960	3.75	7.50	15.00
❑ 71692	I Just Want to Love You/You're for Me	1960	3.75	7.50	15.00
❑ 71692 [PS]	I Just Want to Love You/You're for Me	1960	7.50	15.00	30.00
❑ 71740	One More Chance/Before I Fall in Love Again	1960	3.75	7.50	15.00
❑ 71740 [PS]	One More Chance/Before I Fall in Love Again	1960	7.50	15.00	30.00
❑ 71783	Tomorrow Is a-Comin'/ I'll Love You Till the Cows Come Home	1961	3.75	7.50	15.00
❑ 71783 [PS]	Tomorrow Is a-Comin'/ I'll Love You Till the Cows Come Home	1961	7.50	15.00	30.00
❑ 71809	A Whole Heap o'Love/You're Movin' Me	1961	3.75	7.50	15.00
❑ 71809 [PS]	A Whole Heap o'Love/You're Movin' Me	1961	7.50	15.00	30.00

M

Number	Title (A Side/B Side)	Yr	VG	VG+	NM
❏ 71841	I Never Knew/Happiness	1961	3.75	7.50	15.00
❏ 71841 [PS]	I Never Knew/Happiness	1961	6.25	12.50	25.00
❏ 71868	Same Time, Same Place/Your Second Choice	1961	3.75	7.50	15.00
❏ 71868 [PS]	Same Time, Same Place/Your Second Choice	1961	7.50	15.00	30.00
❏ 71941	Lover Please/Let's Forget About the Past	1962	5.00	10.00	20.00
❏ 71941 [PS]	Lover Please/Let's Forget About the Past	1962	10.00	20.00	40.00
❏ 71987	Little Bitty Pretty One/Next to Me	1962	3.75	7.50	15.00
❏ 71987 [PS]	Little Bitty Pretty One/Next to Me	1962	10.00	20.00	40.00
❏ 72025	Maybe/I Do Believe	1962	3.75	7.50	15.00
❏ 72025 [PS]	Maybe/I Do Believe	1962	7.50	15.00	30.00
❏ 72051	The Best Man Cried/Stop	1962	3.75	7.50	15.00
❏ 72051 [PS]	The Best Man Cried/Stop	1962	7.50	15.00	30.00
❏ 72166	So Close to Being in Love/From One to One	1963	3.75	7.50	15.00
❏ 72166 [PS]	So Close to Being in Love/From One to One	1963	7.50	15.00	30.00
❏ 72220	Deep in the Heart of Harlem/Happy Good Times	1963	3.75	7.50	15.00
❏ 72220 [PS]	Deep in the Heart of Harlem/Happy Good Times	1963	7.50	15.00	30.00
❏ 72253	Second Window, Second Floor/In My Tenement	1964	3.75	7.50	15.00
❏ 72317	Lucille/Baby, Baby	1964	3.75	7.50	15.00
❏ 72407	Crying Won't Help You Now/I Found My Love	1965	3.75	7.50	15.00
❏ 72407 [PS]	Crying Won't Help You Now/I Found My Love	1965	7.50	15.00	30.00
MGM					
❏ 12780	I Told Myself a Lie/The Masquerade Over	1959	5.00	10.00	20.00
❏ 12816	Twice As Nice/Where Did I Make My Mistake	1959	5.00	10.00	20.00
❏ 12843 [M]	Let's Try Again/Bless You	1959	5.00	10.00	20.00
❏ 12877	Think Me a Kiss/When the Right Time Comes Along	1960	5.00	10.00	20.00
❏ 12949	One Right After Another/This Is Not Goodbye	1960	5.00	10.00	20.00
❏ 12988	The Glory of Love/Take a Step	1961	5.00	10.00	20.00
❏ SK-50134 [S]	Let's Try Again/Bless You	1959	10.00	20.00	40.00
7-Inch Extended Plays					
ATLANTIC					
❏ EP 584	*Without Love (There Is Nothing)/Thirty Days/I Make Believe/Treasure of Love	1958	62.50	125.00	250.00
❏ EP 584 [PS]	Clyde McPhatter	1958	62.50	125.00	250.00
❏ EP 605	*Honey Love/What'cha Gonna Do/Seven Days/Long Lonely Nights	1958	62.50	125.00	250.00
❏ EP 605 [PS]	Rock with Clyde McPhatter	1958	62.50	125.00	250.00
❏ EP 618	A Lover's Question/I Can't Stand Up Alone//Lovey Dovey/My Island of Dreams	1959	62.50	125.00	250.00
❏ EP 618 [PS]	Clyde McPhatter	1959	62.50	125.00	250.00
Albums					
ALLEGIANCE					
❏ AV-5029	The Pretty One	198?	2.50	5.00	10.00
ATLANTIC					
❏ 8024 [M]	Love Ballads	1958	125.00	250.00	500.00
—Black label					
❏ 8024 [M]	Love Ballads	1960	50.00	100.00	200.00
—Brown and purple label					
❏ 8024 [M]	Love Ballads	1960	100.00	200.00	400.00
—White "bullseye" label					
❏ 8031 [M]	Clyde	1959	125.00	250.00	500.00
—Black label					
❏ 8031 [M]	Clyde	1960	50.00	100.00	200.00
—Brown and purple label					
❏ 8031 [M]	Clyde	1960	100.00	200.00	400.00
—White "bullseye" label					
❏ 8077 [M]	The Best of Clyde McPhatter	1963	50.00	100.00	200.00
DECCA					
❏ DL 75231	Welcome Home	1970	6.25	12.50	25.00
MERCURY					
❏ MG-20597 [M]	Ta Ta	1960	12.50	25.00	50.00
❏ MG-20655 [M]	Golden Blues Hits	1961	12.50	25.00	50.00
❏ MG-20711 [M]	Lover Please	1962	12.50	25.00	50.00
❏ MG-20750 [M]	Rhythm and Soul	1962	12.50	25.00	50.00
❏ MG-20783 [M]	Clyde McPhatter's Greatest Hits	1963	7.50	15.00	30.00
❏ MG-20902 [M]	Songs of the Big City	1964	7.50	15.00	30.00
❏ MG-20915 [M]	Live at the Apollo	1964	7.50	15.00	30.00
❏ SR-60262 [S]	Ta Ta	1960	17.50	35.00	70.00
❏ SR-60655 [S]	Golden Blues Hits	1961	17.50	35.00	70.00
❏ SR-60711 [S]	Lover Please	1962	17.50	35.00	70.00
❏ SR-60750 [S]	Rhythm and Soul	1962	17.50	35.00	70.00
❏ SR-60783 [S]	Clyde McPhatter's Greatest Hits	1963	10.00	20.00	40.00
❏ SR-60902 [S]	Songs of the Big City	1964	10.00	20.00	40.00
❏ SR-60915 [S]	Live at the Apollo	1964	10.00	20.00	40.00
MGM					
❏ E-3775 [M]	Let's Start Over Again	1959	37.50	75.00	150.00
❏ SE-3775 [S]	Let's Start Over Again	1959	50.00	100.00	200.00
❏ E-3866 [M]	Clyde McPhatter's Greatest Hits	1960	17.50	35.00	70.00
❏ SE-3866 [S]	Clyde McPhatter's Greatest Hits	1960	20.00	40.00	80.00
WING					
❏ MGW-12224 [M]	May I Sing for You?	1962	6.25	12.50	25.00
❏ SRW-16224 [S]	May I Sing for You?	1962	7.50	15.00	30.00

MCRAE, CARMEN

45s

Number	Title (A Side/B Side)	Yr	VG	VG+	NM
ATLANTIC					
❏ 2421	For Once in My Life/Got to Get You Into My Life	1967	—	3.00	6.00
❏ 2485	Elusive Butterfly/I'm Always Drunk in San Francisco	1968	—	3.00	6.00
❏ 2581	Gloomy Sunday/My Heart Reminds Me	1968	—	3.00	6.00
❏ 2691	I Love You More Than You'll Ever Know/Just a Dream Ago	1969	—	2.50	5.00
❏ 2736	I Want You/Just a Little Lovin'	1970	—	2.50	5.00
❏ 2776	Carry That Weight/Goodbye Joe	1971	—	2.50	5.00
❏ 2807	Silent Spring/I Love the Life I Lead	1971	—	2.50	5.00
BETHLEHEM					
❏ 11009	If I'm Lucky/Tip Toe Gently	1958	3.00	6.00	12.00
COLUMBIA					
❏ 42292	Take Five/Easy As You Go	1962	2.50	5.00	10.00
❏ 42376	How Does the Wine Taste/Nightlife	1962	2.50	5.00	10.00
❏ 42642	Am I Going Out of Your Mind/Baby, Baby	1962	2.50	5.00	10.00
DECCA					
❏ 29324	Ooh (What'cha Doin' to Me)/If I'm Lucky	1954	3.75	7.50	15.00
❏ 29398	Keep Me in Mind/They All Laughed	1954	3.75	7.50	15.00
❏ 29472	Whatever Lola Wants/Am I the One to Blame	1955	3.00	6.00	12.00
❏ 29555	Get Set/You Don't Have to Tell Me	1955	3.00	6.00	12.00

Number	Title (A Side/B Side)	Yr	VG	VG+	NM
❏ 29620	I Go for You/A Fine Romance	1955	3.00	6.00	12.00
—With Sammy Davis, Jr.					
❏ 29675	Love Is Here to Stay/This Will Make You Laugh	1955	3.00	6.00	12.00
❏ 29749	The Next Time It Happens/Come On, Come In	1955	3.00	6.00	12.00
❏ 29793	Come Down to Earth, Mr. Smith/I Guess I'll Dress for the Blues	1956	3.00	6.00	12.00
❏ 29890	Star Eyes/Tonight He's Out to Break Another Heart	1956	3.00	6.00	12.00
❏ 29949	You Don't Know Me/Never Loved Him Anyhow	1956	3.00	6.00	12.00
❏ 30004	Skyliner/If You Should Leave Me	1956	3.00	6.00	12.00
❏ 30075	I'm Putting All My Eggs in One Basket/Namely You	1956	3.00	6.00	12.00
❏ 30112	The Party's Over/I'm a Dreamer, Aren't We All	1956	3.00	6.00	12.00
❏ 30274	How Many Stars Have to Shine/It's Like Gettin' a Donkey	1957	3.00	6.00	12.00
❏ 30468	Rich Man, Poor Man/Coax Me	1957	3.00	6.00	12.00
❏ 30540	Passing Fancy/As I Love You	1958	3.00	6.00	12.00
❏ 30618	Invitation/Lo and Behold	1958	3.00	6.00	12.00
❏ 30667	So Nice to Be Wrong/Moon Ray	1958	3.00	6.00	12.00
❏ 30727	I Love the Ground You Walk On/I'll Love You	1958	3.00	6.00	12.00
GROOVE MERCHANT					
❏ 1018	It Takes a Whole Lot of Human Feeling/Straighten Up and Fly Right	1973	—	2.50	5.00
❏ 1022	The Good Life/How Could I Settle for Less	1973	—	2.50	5.00
KAPP					
❏ 259	Which Way Is Love/Play for Keeps	1959	2.50	5.00	10.00
❏ 290	Talk to Me/Show Me the Way	1959	2.50	5.00	10.00
❏ 302	The More I See You/Don't Cry Joe	1959	2.50	5.00	10.00
❏ 327	Big Town/What Has She Got	1960	2.50	5.00	10.00
MAINSTREAM					
❏ 613	Haven't We Met?/Life Is Just a Bowl of Cherries	1965	2.00	4.00	8.00
❏ 630	Go and Buy Yourself a Dream/(B-side unknown)	1965	2.00	4.00	8.00
❏ 650	Alfie/Modesty	1966	2.00	4.00	8.00
7-Inch Extended Plays					
ATLANTIC					
❏ EP-8165 [DJ]	Elusive Butterfly/I'm Always Drunk in San Francisco//Ask Any Woman/My Very Own Person	1968	3.75	7.50	15.00
—White label, large hole					
❏ EP-8165 [PS]	Portrait of Carmen	1968	3.75	7.50	15.00
DECCA					
❏ ED 2279	(contents unknown)	195?	3.00	6.00	12.00
❏ ED 2279 [PS]	By Special Request, Part 1	195?	3.00	6.00	12.00
❏ ED 2280	I Can't Get Started/Yardbird Suite//Just One of Those Things/This Will Make You Laugh	195?	3.00	6.00	12.00
❏ ED 2280 [PS]	By Special Request, Part 2	195?	3.00	6.00	12.00
❏ ED 2341	(contents unknown)	1956	3.00	6.00	12.00
❏ ED 2341 [PS]	Torchy! Part 1	1956	3.00	6.00	12.00
❏ ED 2342	But Beautiful/If You'd Stay the Way I Dream About You//I'm a Dreamer Aren't We All/Good Morning Heartache	1956	3.00	6.00	12.00
❏ ED 2342 [PS]	Torchy! Part 2	1956	3.00	6.00	12.00
❏ ED 2343	(contents unknown)	1956	3.00	6.00	12.00
❏ ED 2343 [PS]	Torchy! Part 3	1956	3.00	6.00	12.00
Albums					
ACCORD					
❏ SN-7152	Love Songs	1981	2.50	5.00	10.00
ATLANTIC					
❏ SD 2-904 [(2)]	The Great American Songbook	1971	5.00	10.00	20.00
❏ SD 1568	Just a Little Lovin'	1971	3.00	6.00	12.00
❏ 8143 [M]	For Once in My Life	1967	5.00	10.00	20.00
❏ SD 8143 [S]	For Once in My Life	1967	3.75	7.50	15.00
❏ 8165 [M]	Portrait of Carmen	1968	7.50	15.00	30.00
❏ SD 8165 [S]	Portrait of Carmen	1968	3.75	7.50	15.00
❏ SD 8200	The Sound of Silence	1968	3.75	7.50	15.00
BAINBRIDGE					
❏ 6221	The Sound of Silence	198?	2.50	5.00	10.00
BETHLEHEM					
❏ BCP-1023 [10]	Carmen McRae	1955	25.00	50.00	100.00
BLUE NOTE					
❏ BN-LA462-G	I Am Music	1975	—	3.00	6.00
❏ BN-LA635-G	Can't Hide Love	1976	—	3.00	6.00
❏ BN-LA709-H2 [(2)]	The Great Music Hall	1977	3.75	7.50	15.00
❏ LWB-709 [(2)]	The Great Music Hall	1981	3.00	6.00	12.00
—Reissue of BN-LA709-H2					
BUDDAH					
❏ B2D-6501 [(2)]	I'm Coming Home Again	1980	3.75	7.50	15.00
CATALYST					
❏ 7904	As Time Goes By	197?	3.00	6.00	12.00
COLUMBIA					
❏ CL 1730 [M]	Lover Man	1962	5.00	10.00	20.00
❏ CL 1943 [M]	Something Wonderful	1962	5.00	10.00	20.00
❏ CS 8530 [S]	Lover Man	1962	6.25	12.50	25.00
❏ CS 8743 [S]	Something Wonderful	1962	6.25	12.50	25.00
CONCORD JAZZ					
❏ CJ-128	Two for the Road	1980	2.50	5.00	10.00
❏ CJ-235	You're Looking at Me: A Collection of Nat King Cole Songs	1984	2.50	5.00	10.00
❏ CJ-342	Fine and Mellow	1988	2.50	5.00	10.00
DECCA					
❏ DL 8173 [M]	By Special Request	1955	12.50	25.00	50.00
—Black label, silver print					
❏ DL 8173 [M]	By Special Request	1960	5.00	10.00	20.00
—Black label with color bars					
❏ DL 8267 [M]	Torchy!	1956	12.50	25.00	50.00
—Black label, silver print					
❏ DL 8267 [M]	Torchy!	1960	5.00	10.00	20.00
—Black label with color bars					
❏ DL 8347 [M]	Blue Moon	1957	12.50	25.00	50.00
—Black label, silver print					
❏ DL 8347 [M]	Blue Moon	1960	5.00	10.00	20.00
—Black label with color bars					
❏ DL 8583 [M]	After Glow	1957	12.50	25.00	50.00
—Black label, silver print					
❏ DL 8583 [M]	After Glow	1960	5.00	10.00	20.00
—Black label with color bars					

Number	Title (A Side/B Side)	Yr	VG	VG+	NM
❑ DL 8662 [M]	Mad About the Man	1958	12.50	25.00	50.00
—Black label, silver print					
❑ DL 8662 [M]	Mad About the Man	1960	5.00	10.00	20.00
—Black label with color bars					
❑ DL 8738 [M]	Carmen for Cool Ones	1958	12.50	25.00	50.00
—Black label, silver print					
❑ DL 8738 [M]	Carmen for Cool Ones	1960	5.00	10.00	20.00
—Black label with color bars					
❑ DL 8815 [M]	Birds of a Feather	1959	12.50	25.00	50.00
—Black label, silver print					
❑ DL 8815 [M]	Birds of a Feather	1960	5.00	10.00	20.00
—Black label with color bars					
FOCUS					
❑ FL-334 [M]	Bittersweet	1964	3.75	7.50	15.00
❑ FS-334 [S]	Bittersweet	1964	5.00	10.00	20.00
GROOVE MERCHANT					
❑ 522	A Whole Lot of Human Feeling	1973	3.00	6.00	12.00
❑ 531	Ms. Jazz	1974	3.00	6.00	12.00
❑ 4401 [(2)]	Velvet Soul	197?	3.75	7.50	15.00
HARMONY					
❑ HL 7452 [M]	Yesterdays	1968	5.00	10.00	20.00
❑ HS 11252 [S]	Yesterdays	1968	3.00	6.00	12.00
❑ KH 32177	Carmen McRae Sings Billie Holiday	1972	2.50	5.00	10.00
JAZZ MAN					
❑ 5004	Carmen McRae and the Kenny Clarke/Francy Boland Big Band	198?	2.50	5.00	10.00
KAPP					
❑ KL-1117 [M]	Book of Ballads	1958	6.25	12.50	25.00
❑ KL-1135 [M]	When You're Away	1959	6.25	12.50	25.00
❑ KL-1169 [M]	Something to Swing About	1960	6.25	12.50	25.00
❑ KL-1541 [M]	This Is Carmen McRae	1967	5.00	10.00	20.00
❑ KS-3000 [S]	Book of Ballads	1958	7.50	15.00	30.00
❑ KS-3018 [S]	When You're Away	1959	7.50	15.00	30.00
❑ KS-3053 [S]	Something to Swing About	1960	7.50	15.00	30.00
❑ KS-3541 [S]	This Is Carmen McRae	1967	3.75	7.50	15.00
MAINSTREAM					
❑ 309	Carmen McRae	1971	3.00	6.00	12.00
❑ 338	Carmen's Gold	1972	3.00	6.00	12.00
❑ 352	Carmen McRae In Person	1972	3.00	6.00	12.00
❑ 387	I Want You	1972	3.00	6.00	12.00
❑ 403	Live and Doin' It	1974	3.00	6.00	12.00
❑ 800 [(2)]	Alive!	1974	3.75	7.50	15.00
❑ S-6028 [S]	Second to None	1965	5.00	10.00	20.00
❑ S-6044 [S]	Haven't We Met?	1965	5.00	10.00	20.00
❑ S-6065 [S]	Woman Talk	1966	5.00	10.00	20.00
❑ S-6084 [S]	Alfie	1966	5.00	10.00	20.00
❑ S-6091 [S]	In Person/San Francisco	1967	3.75	7.50	15.00
❑ S-6110	Live & Wailin'	1968	3.75	7.50	15.00
❑ 56028 [M]	Second to None	1965	3.75	7.50	15.00
❑ 56044 [M]	Haven't We Met?	1965	3.75	7.50	15.00
❑ 56065 [M]	Woman Talk	1966	3.75	7.50	15.00
❑ 56084 [M]	Alfie	1966	3.75	7.50	15.00
❑ 56091 [M]	In Person/San Francisco	1967	5.00	10.00	20.00
MCA					
❑ 4111 [(2)]	The Greatest of Carmen McRae	197?	3.00	6.00	12.00
NOVUS					
❑ 3086-1-N	Carmen Sings Monk	1990	3.00	6.00	12.00
PAUSA					
❑ 9003	Can't Hide Love	198?	2.50	5.00	10.00
QUINTESSENCE					
❑ 25021	Ms. Jazz	1978	2.50	5.00	10.00
—Reissue of Groove Merchant 531					
STANYAN					
❑ 10115	Mad About the Man	197?	3.00	6.00	12.00
TEMPONIC					
❑ 29562	Carmen	1972	3.00	6.00	12.00
TIME					
❑ S-2104 [S]	Live at Sugar Hill	1960	6.25	12.50	25.00
❑ 52104 [M]	Live at Sugar Hill	1960	5.00	10.00	20.00
VOCALION					
❑ VL 3697 [M]	Carmen McRae	1963	3.75	7.50	15.00
❑ VL 73828	My Foolish Heart	1969	3.00	6.00	12.00

MCVIE, CHRISTINE Also see CHICKEN SHACK; FLEETWOOD MAC.

45s

Number	Title (A Side/B Side)	Yr	VG	VG+	NM
EPIC					
❑ 10536	I'd Rather Go Blind/Get Like You Used to Be	1969	3.00	6.00	12.00
—As "Christine Perfect"					
SIRE					
❑ 732	I'd Rather Go Blind/Close to Me	1976	2.00	4.00	8.00
WARNER BROS.					
❑ GWB 0488	Got a Hold on Me/Love Will Show Us How	1986	—	—	3.00
—"Back to Back Hits" series					
❑ 29160	I'm the One/The Challenge	1984	—	—	3.00
❑ 29313	Love Will Show Us How/The Challenge	1984	—	—	3.00
❑ 29313 [PS]	Love Will Show Us How/The Challenge	1984	—	—	3.00
❑ 29372	Got a Hold on Me/Who's Dreaming This Dream	1984	—	—	3.00
❑ 29372 [PS]	Got a Hold on Me/Who's Dreaming This Dream	1984	—	—	3.00
Albums					
SIRE					
❑ SR 6022	The Legendary Christine Perfect Album	1978	2.50	5.00	10.00
—Reissue with Warner Bros. distribution					
❑ SASD-7522	The Legendary Christine Perfect Album	1976	3.75	7.50	15.00
—Original with ABC distribution					
WARNER BROS.					
❑ 25059	Christine McVie	1984	2.00	4.00	8.00
❑ 25059 [DJ]	Christine McVie	1984	3.75	7.50	15.00
—Promo on Quiex II vinyl					

MCWILLIAMS, DAVID

45s

Number	Title (A Side/B Side)	Yr	VG	VG+	NM
COLUMBIA					
❑ 4-43793	Blue Eyes/God and My Country	1966	3.00	6.00	12.00
KAPP					
❑ 896	Days of Pearly Spencer/There's No Lock Upon My Door	1968	2.50	5.00	10.00
❑ 952	This Side of Heaven/Can I Get There by Candlelight?	1968	2.00	4.00	8.00

Number	Title (A Side/B Side)	Yr	VG	VG+	NM
Albums					
KAPP					
❑ KS-3547	Days of Pearly Spencer	1968	6.25	12.50	25.00

ME & YOU

45s

Number	Title (A Side/B Side)	Yr	VG	VG+	NM
PARKWAY					
❑ 121	Let the World In/I've Got My Time Baby	1966	5.00	10.00	20.00

ME AND THEM

45s

Number	Title (A Side/B Side)	Yr	VG	VG+	NM
U.S. SONGS					
❑ 601	Everything I Do Is Wrong/Show You Mean It Too	1964	3.75	7.50	15.00

MEADER, VAUGHN

45s

Number	Title (A Side/B Side)	Yr	VG	VG+	NM
VERVE					
❑ 10309	St. Nick Visits the White House/'Twas the Night Before Christmas	1963	5.00	10.00	20.00
Albums					
CADENCE					
❑ CLP 3060 [M]	The First Family	1962	2.50	5.00	10.00
❑ CLP 3065 [M]	The First Family, Volume Two	1963	5.00	10.00	20.00
❑ CLP 25065 [S]	The First Family, Volume Two	1963	7.50	15.00	30.00
KAMA SUTRA					
❑ KSBS-2038	The Second Coming	1971	3.75	7.50	15.00
LAURIE					
❑ LLP-2035 [M]	Take That!	1966	3.75	7.50	15.00
VERVE					
❑ V-15042 [M]	Have Some Nuts	1964	3.75	7.50	15.00
❑ V6-15042 [S]	Have Some Nuts	1964	5.00	10.00	20.00
❑ V-15050 [M]	If the Shoe Fits	1965	3.75	7.50	15.00

MEADOW Supposedly, Laura Branigan was in this group.

45s

Number	Title (A Side/B Side)	Yr	VG	VG+	NM
PARAMOUNT					
❑ 0187	Here I Am/Something Borrowed, Something Blue	1973	2.00	4.00	8.00
❑ 0208	Cane and Able/Something Borrowed, Something Blue	1973	2.00	4.00	8.00
Albums					
PARAMOUNT					
❑ PAS-6066	The Friend Ship	1973	5.00	10.00	20.00

MEADOWLARKS, THE See DON JULIAN AND THE MEADOWLARKS.

MEAT LOAF Also see THE POPCORN BLIZZARD; STONEY AND MEATLOAF.

12-Inch Singles

Number	Title (A Side/B Side)	Yr	VG	VG+	NM
ATLANTIC					
❑ PR 966 [DJ]	Getting Away with Murder (same on both sides)	1986	2.00	4.00	8.00
❑ PR 997 [DJ]	Rock and Roll Mercenaries (same on both sides)	1986	2.00	4.00	8.00
CLEVELAND INT'L.					
❑ AS 1277 [DJ]	I'm Gonna Love Her for Both of Us/Peel Out	1981	2.00	4.00	8.00
EPIC					
❑ AS 477 [DJ]	Paradise by the Dashboard Light (7:55)//same (6:58 with play-by-play)/same (6:58 without play-by-play)	1978	5.00	10.00	20.00
—With "Bat Out of Hell" picture cover					
RCA					
❑ JD-14050 [DJ]	(Give Me the Future with a) Modern Girl (LP Version) (7" Version)	1984	2.50	5.00	10.00
❑ JW-14141 [DJ]	Surf's Up (LP Version)//Surf's Up (Edit)/Bad Attitude	1984	3.75	7.50	15.00

45s

Number	Title (A Side/B Side)	Yr	VG	VG+	NM
ATLANTIC					
❑ 89303	Rock 'N' Roll Mercenaries/Execution Day	1987	—	—	3.00
—A-side with John Parr					
❑ 89303 [PS]	Rock 'N' Roll Mercenaries/Execution Day	1987	—	—	3.00
❑ 89340	Getting Away with Murder/Rock 'N' Roll Hero	1986	—	—	3.00
CLEVELAND INT'L.					
❑ 02490	I'm Gonna Love Her for Both of Us/Peel Out	1981	—	2.00	4.00
❑ 02607	Read 'Em and Weep/Peel Out	1981	—	2.00	4.00
❑ 04028	The Razor's Edge/You Never Can Be Too Sure About the Girl	1983	—	2.00	4.00
EPIC					
❑ 50467	You Took the Words Right Out of My Mouth/For Crying Out Loud	1977	2.00	4.00	8.00
❑ 50513	Two Out of Three Ain't Bad (3:50)/For Crying Out Loud	1978	—	2.50	5.00
❑ 50513	Two Out of Three Ain't Bad (5:12)/For Crying Out Loud	1978	—	3.00	6.00
❑ 50588	Paradise by the Dashboard Light/"Bat" Overture	1978	—	2.50	5.00
❑ 50634	You Took the Words Right Out of My Mouth/Paradise by the Dashboard Light	1978	—	2.50	5.00
MCA					
❑ 54626	I'd Do Anything for Love (But I Won't Do That) (Single Edit)/I'd Do Anything for Love (But I Won't Do That) (Edit)	1993	—	2.00	4.00
❑ 54757	Rock and Roll Dreams Come Through/I'd Do Anything for Love (But I Won't Do That) (Live)	1993	—	2.00	4.00
❑ 54848	Objects in the Rear View Mirror May Appear Closer Than They Are/Two Out of Three Ain't Bad (Live)	1994	—	2.00	4.00
RCA					
❑ PB-14101	(Give Me the Future with a) Modern Girl/Sailor to a Siren	1985	—	—	3.00
❑ PB-14101 [PS]	(Give Me the Future with a) Modern Girl/Sailor to a Siren	1985	—	—	3.00
❑ PB-14149	Surf's Up/Jumpin' the Sun	1985	—	—	3.00
RSO					
❑ 407	More Than You Deserve/Presence of the Lord	1974	3.00	6.00	12.00
Albums					
ATLANTIC					
❑ 81698	Blind Before I Stop	1986	2.00	4.00	8.00
CLEVELAND INT'L.					
❑ FE 36007	Dead Ringer	1981	2.00	4.00	8.00
❑ PE 36007	Dead Ringer	198?	—	3.00	6.00
—Budget-line reissue					

M

Number	Title (A Side/B Side)	Yr	VG	VG+	NM
EPIC					
❑ E99 34974 [PD]	Bat Out of Hell	1978	5.00	10.00	20.00
❑ JE 34974	Bat Out of Hell	1979	2.00	4.00	8.00
—Dark blue label					
❑ PE 34974	Bat Out of Hell	1977	2.50	5.00	10.00
—Orange label; originals do not have bar code on back cover					
❑ PE 34974	Bat Out of Hell	1985	—	3.00	6.00
—Dark blue label; bar code on cover					
❑ FE 38444	Midnight at the Lost and Found	1983	2.00	4.00	8.00
❑ HE 44974	Bat Out of Hell	1981	10.00	20.00	40.00
—Half-speed mastered edition					
RCA VICTOR					
❑ AFL1-5451	Bad Attitude	1985	2.00	4.00	8.00

MEDALLIONS, THE (1)
45s
Number	Title (A Side/B Side)	Yr	VG	VG+	NM
DOOTO					
❑ 419	For Better or For Worse/I Wonder, Wonder, Wonder	1957	7.50	15.00	30.00
—As "Vernon Green and the Medallions"					
❑ 425	A Lover's Prayer/Unseen	1957	7.50	15.00	30.00
—As "Vernon Green and the Medallions"					
❑ 446	Magic Mountain/59 Volvo	1959	6.25	12.50	25.00
—As "Vernon Green and the Medallions"					
❑ 454	Behind the Door/Rocket Ship	1959	6.25	12.50	25.00
—As "Vernon Green and the Medallions"					
DOOTONE					
❑ 347	The Letter/Buick 59	1955	15.00	30.00	60.00
—Black label					
❑ 347	The Letter/Buick 59	1955	50.00	100.00	200.00
—Red label					
❑ 357	The Telegram/Coupe de Ville Baby	1955	15.00	30.00	60.00
—Maroon label					
❑ 357	The Telegram/Coupe de Ville Baby	1955	37.50	75.00	150.00
—Blue label					
❑ 364	Edna/Speeding	1955	15.00	30.00	60.00
❑ 373	My Pretty Baby/I'll Never Love Again	1955	15.00	30.00	60.00
—As "Johnny Twovoice and the Medallions"					
❑ 379	Dear Darling/Don't Shoot Baby	1955	17.50	35.00	70.00
❑ 393	I Want a Love/Dance and Swing	1956	12.50	25.00	50.00
❑ 400	Shedding Tears for You/Push Button Automobile	1956	15.00	30.00	60.00
—As "Vernon Green and the Medallions"					
❑ 407	My Mary Lou/Did You Have Fun	1956	15.00	30.00	60.00
—As "Vernon Green and the Medallions"					
❑ 479	Can You Talk/You Don't Know	1964	3.75	7.50	15.00
MINIT					
❑ 32034	Look at Me, Look at Me/Am I Ever Gonna See My Baby	1968	5.00	10.00	20.00
—As "Vernon Green and the Medallions"					
PAN WORLD					
❑ 71	Dear Ann/Shimmy Shimmy Shake	1962	12.50	25.00	50.00
—As "Vernon Green and the Medallions"					

7-Inch Extended Plays
Number	Title (A Side/B Side)	Yr	VG	VG+	NM
DOOTONE					
❑ 202	(contents unknown)	1958	25.00	50.00	100.00
❑ 202 [PS]	Rhythm and Blues	1958	37.50	75.00	150.00

MEDALLIONS, THE (2)
45s
Number	Title (A Side/B Side)	Yr	VG	VG+	NM
ESSEX					
❑ 901	I Know/Laki-Lani	1955	100.00	200.00	400.00

MEDALLIONS, THE (3)
45s
Number	Title (A Side/B Side)	Yr	VG	VG+	NM
LENOX					
❑ 5556	You Are Irresistible/Why Do You Look at Me	1962	6.25	12.50	25.00

MEDALLIONS, THE (4)
45s
Number	Title (A Side/B Side)	Yr	VG	VG+	NM
SINGULAR					
❑ 1002	A Broken Heart/Lolo Baby	1957	12.50	25.00	50.00
SULTAN					
❑ 4004	Love That Girl/Carachi	1959	20.00	40.00	80.00

MEDALLIONS, THE (U) Could be group (1), (3) or (4), or a totally different group.
45s
Number	Title (A Side/B Side)	Yr	VG	VG+	NM
SARG					
❑ 191	I Love You True/My Baby's Gone	1961	10.00	20.00	40.00
❑ 194	Lovin' Time/Home Town	1961	10.00	20.00	40.00

MEDIUM
Albums
Number	Title (A Side/B Side)	Yr	VG	VG+	NM
GAMMA					
❑ GS-503	Medium	196?	25.00	50.00	100.00

MEDLEY, BILL Also see THE RIGHTEOUS BROTHERS.
45s
Number	Title (A Side/B Side)	Yr	VG	VG+	NM
A&M					
❑ 1285	A Song for You/We've Only Just Begun	1971	—	2.50	5.00
❑ 1309	You've Lost That Lovin' Feeling/We've Only Just Begun	1971	—	2.50	5.00
❑ 1311	A Song for You/We've Only Just Begun	1971	—	2.00	4.00
❑ 1336	Help Me Make It Through the Night/Hung on You	1972	—	2.00	4.00
❑ 1350	Freedom for the Stallion/Damn Good Friend	1972	—	2.00	4.00
❑ 1371	A Simple Man/Missing You Too Long	1972	—	2.00	4.00
❑ 1434	Put a Little Love Away/It's Not Easy	1973	—	2.00	4.00
CURB					
❑ 10542	Most of All You/I'm Gonna Be Strong	1989	—	—	3.00
❑ 76890	Don't Let Go/Bridge Over Troubled Water	1990	—	—	3.00
ELEKTRA					
❑ 69281	Rude Awakening/Leave Love Behind	1989	—	—	3.00
—B-side by Jonathan Elias					
LIBERTY					
❑ 1402	Don't Know Much/Woman	1981	—	2.00	4.00
❑ 1412	Stay the Night/Grandma and Grandpa	1981	—	2.00	4.00

Number	Title (A Side/B Side)	Yr	VG	VG+	NM
MCA					
❑ 53443	Brown Eyed Woman/You've Lost That Lovin' Feelin'	1988	—	—	3.00
MGM					
❑ 13931	I Can't Make It Alone/One Day Girl	1968	2.00	4.00	8.00
❑ 13959	Brown Eyed Woman/Let the Good Times Roll	1968	2.00	4.00	8.00
❑ 14000	Peace Brother Peace/Winter Won't Come This Year	1968	2.00	4.00	8.00
❑ 14025	Something's So Wrong/This Is a Love Song	1969	2.00	4.00	8.00
❑ 14081	Reaching Back/Someone Is Standing Outside	1969	2.00	4.00	8.00
❑ 14099	Evie/Let Me Love Again	1969	2.00	4.00	8.00
❑ 14119	Hold On, I'm Comin'/Makin' My Way	1970	—	3.00	6.00
❑ 14145	Nobody Knows/Something's So Wrong	1970	—	3.00	6.00
❑ 14179	Gone/What Have You Got to Lose	1970	—	3.00	6.00
❑ 14202	Wasn't It Easy/Gone	1970	—	3.00	6.00
PARAMOUNT					
❑ 0089	Swing Low, Sweet Chariot/(B-side unknown)	1971	—	3.00	6.00
PLANET					
❑ YB-13317	Right Here and Now/The Best of My Life	1982	—	2.00	4.00
❑ YB-13425	I'm No Angel/I Need You in My Life	1983	—	—	3.00
❑ YB-13474	For You/I Need You in My Life	1983	—	—	3.00
RCA					
❑ 5224-7-RX	(I've Had) The Time of My Life/Love Is Strange	1987	—	—	3.00
—A-side: With Jennifer Warnes; b-side by Mickey and Sylvia					
❑ 5224-7-RX [PS]	(I've Had) The Time of My Life/Love Is Strange	1987	—	2.00	4.00
—A-side: With Jennifer Warnes; B-side by Mickey and Sylvia					
❑ PB-13692	I've Got Dreams to Remember/Till Your Memory's Gone	1983	—	—	3.00
❑ PB-13753	I Still Do/I've Got Dreams to Remember	1984	—	—	3.00
❑ PB-13851	Turn It Loose/I've Always Got the Heart to Sing the Blues	1984	—	—	3.00
❑ PB-13962	She Keeps Me in One Piece/Old Friend	1984	—	—	—
—Unreleased					
❑ PB-14021	Is There Anything I Can Do/Old Friend	1985	—	—	3.00
❑ PB-14081	Women in Love/Stand Up	1985	—	—	3.00
REPRISE					
❑ 0413	I Surrender to Your Touch/Leavin' Town	1965	3.75	7.50	15.00
SCOTTI BROTHERS					
❑ ZS4-07938	He Ain't Heavy, He's My Brother/The Bridge	1988	—	—	3.00
—B-side by Georgio Moroder					
❑ ZS4-07938 [PS]	He Ain't Heavy, He's My Brother/The Bridge	1988	—	—	3.00
UNITED ARTISTS					
❑ XW1256	Lay a Little Lovin' On Me/Wasn't That You Last Night	1978	—	2.00	4.00
❑ XW1270	Statue of a Fool/Wasn't That You Last Night	1978	—	2.00	4.00
❑ 1349	Hello Rock & Roll/Still a Fool	1980	—	2.00	4.00
VERVE					
❑ 10569	That Lucky Old Sun/My Darling Clementine	1967	2.50	5.00	10.00

Albums
Number	Title (A Side/B Side)	Yr	VG	VG+	NM
A&M					
❑ SP-3505	A Song for You	1971	3.00	6.00	12.00
❑ SP-3517	Smile	1972	3.00	6.00	12.00
LIBERTY					
❑ LT-1097	Sweet Thunder	1981	2.00	4.00	8.00
—Reissue of United Artists 1097					
MGM					
❑ E-4583 [M]	Bill Medley 100%	1968	12.50	25.00	50.00
—Mono is yellow label promo only					
❑ SE-4583 [S]	Bill Medley 100%	1968	5.00	10.00	20.00
❑ SE-4603	Soft and Soulful	1969	5.00	10.00	20.00
❑ SE-4640	Someone Is Standing Outside	1969	5.00	10.00	20.00
❑ SE-4702	Nobody Knows	1970	3.75	7.50	15.00
❑ SE-4741	Gone	1970	3.75	7.50	15.00
RCA VICTOR					
❑ BXL1-4434	Right Here and Now	1982	2.50	5.00	10.00
❑ CPL1-5352	Still Hung Up on You	1984	2.50	5.00	10.00
❑ MHL1-8519 [EP]	I Still Do	1985	2.00	4.00	8.00
UNITED ARTISTS					
❑ UA-LA929-H	Lay a Little Lovin' on Me	1978	2.50	5.00	10.00
❑ LT-1097	Sweet Thunder	1980	2.50	5.00	10.00

MEEHAN, DON
45s
Number	Title (A Side/B Side)	Yr	VG	VG+	NM
DATE					
❑ 2-1654	Sir, My Men Refuse to Go/That's the Reason Why	1969	2.50	5.00	10.00

MEEK, JOE
45s
Number	Title (A Side/B Side)	Yr	VG	VG+	NM
LONDON					
❑ 9634	Kennedy March/Theme of Freedom	1964	5.00	10.00	20.00

MEGATRONS, THE
45s
Number	Title (A Side/B Side)	Yr	VG	VG+	NM
ACOUSTICON					
❑ 101	Velvet Waters/The Merry Piper	1959	3.75	7.50	15.00
AUDICON					
❑ 101	Velvet Waters/The Merry Piper	1959	3.00	6.00	12.00
❑ 104	Whispering Winds/Tootie Flutie	1960	2.50	5.00	10.00
❑ 107	Dance of the Silhouettes/Ranchero	1960	2.50	5.00	10.00
❑ 110	Julienne/By the Waters of the Minnetonka	1960	2.50	5.00	10.00
LAURIE					
❑ 3291	Velvet Waters/The Merry Piper	1965	2.00	4.00	8.00
❑ 3310	A Love That Will Last Forever/The Detroit Sound	1965	2.00	4.00	8.00

MEL AND TIM
45s
Number	Title (A Side/B Side)	Yr	VG	VG+	NM
BAMBOO					
❑ 106	I've Got Puredee/(Instrumental)	1969	—	3.00	6.00
❑ 107	Backfield in Motion/Do It Right Baby	1969	—	3.00	6.00
—Multicolor label					
❑ 107	Backfield in Motion/Do It Right Baby	1969	2.00	4.00	8.00
—White label, not a promo					
❑ 109	Good Guys Only Win in the Movies/I Found That I Was Wrong	1970	—	3.00	6.00
❑ 112	Feeling Bad/I've Got Puredee	1970	—	3.00	6.00
❑ 114	Mail Call Time/Forget It, I've Got It	1970	—	3.00	6.00

Number	Title (A Side/B Side)	Yr	VG	VG+	NM
❑ 116	We've Got a Groove to Move On/Never on Time	1970	—	3.00	6.00
❑ 118	I'm the One/Put An Extra Plus to Your Love	1971	—	3.00	6.00

STAX

Number	Title (A Side/B Side)	Yr	VG	VG+	NM
❑ 0127	Starting All Over Again/It Hurts to Want It So Bad	1972	—	2.50	5.00
❑ 0154	I May Not Be What You Want/Too Much Wheelin' and Dealin'	1973	—	2.50	5.00
❑ 0160	Heaven Knows/Don't Mess with My Money, My Honey, Oh My Woman	1973	—	2.50	5.00
❑ 0202	Those Little Things That Count/The Same Folks	1974	—	2.50	5.00
❑ 0224	Forever and a Day/That's the Way I Want to Live My Life	1974	—	2.50	5.00

Albums

BAMBOO

Number	Title (A Side/B Side)	Yr	VG	VG+	NM
❑ BMS-8001	Good Guys Only Win in the Movies	1970	6.25	12.50	25.00

STAX

Number	Title (A Side/B Side)	Yr	VG	VG+	NM
❑ STS-3007	Starting All Over Again	1972	5.00	10.00	20.00
❑ STS-5501	Mel and Tim	1974	5.00	10.00	20.00

MEL-O-DOTS, THE
45s
APOLLO

Number	Title (A Side/B Side)	Yr	VG	VG+	NM
❑ 1192	One More Time/Just How Long	1952	750.00	1500.	3000.

MELA, DENNY
45s
PARKWAY

Number	Title (A Side/B Side)	Yr	VG	VG+	NM
❑ 802	Forget My Past/Blondie	1959	3.75	7.50	15.00

MELANIE
45s
AMHERST

Number	Title (A Side/B Side)	Yr	VG	VG+	NM
❑ 300	Who's Been Sleeping in My Bed (Edited)/Who's Been Sleeping in My Bed	1985	—	2.00	4.00

ATLANTIC

Number	Title (A Side/B Side)	Yr	VG	VG+	NM
❑ 3380	If I Needed You/Cyclone	1977	—	2.50	5.00

BLANCHE

Number	Title (A Side/B Side)	Yr	VG	VG+	NM
❑ 1	Imaginary Heroes/Detroit or Buffalo	1982	—	2.00	4.00
❑ 110	When You're Dead and Gone/Detroit or Buffalo	1982	—	2.00	4.00

BUDDAH

Number	Title (A Side/B Side)	Yr	VG	VG+	NM
❑ 113	Bo Bo's Party/I'm Back in Town	1969	—	3.00	6.00
❑ 135	Beautiful People/Any Guy	1969	—	3.00	6.00
❑ 161 [DJ]	Take Me Home (mono/stereo)	1970	—	3.00	6.00
—May be promo only					
❑ 167	Lay Down (Candles in the Rain)/Candles in the Rain	1970	—	3.00	6.00
❑ 167 [PS]	Lay Down (Candles in the Rain)/Candles in the Rain	1970	2.00	4.00	8.00
❑ 186	Peace Will Come (According to Plan)/Close to It All	1970	—	2.50	5.00
❑ 186	Peace Will Come (According to Plan)/Stop (I Don't Want to Hear It Anymore)	1970	—	2.50	5.00
❑ 186 [PS]	Peace Will Come (According to Plan)/Stop (I Don't Want to Hear It Anymore)	1970	—	3.00	6.00
❑ 202	Ruby Tuesday/Merry Christmas	1970	—	2.50	5.00
❑ 202	Ruby Tuesday/Lovin Baby Girl	1971	—	3.00	6.00
—Scarcer than the original B-side					
❑ 224	We Don't Know Where We're Going/The Good Book	1971	—	2.50	5.00
❑ 268	The Nickel Song/What Have They Done to My Song Ma	1971	—	2.50	5.00
❑ 268 [DJ]	The Nickel Song (stereo/mono)	1971	2.50	5.00	10.00
—Promo edition; custom light blue label with "Melanie" repeated seven times in white along the outer border					
❑ 268 [PS]	The Nickel Song/What Have They Done to My Song Ma	1971	—	3.00	6.00
❑ 304	I'm Back in Town/Johnny Boy	1972	—	2.50	5.00

COLUMBIA

Number	Title (A Side/B Side)	Yr	VG	VG+	NM
❑ 44349	My Beautiful People/God's Only Daughter	1967	2.50	5.00	10.00
❑ 44349 [PS]	My Beautiful People/God's Only Daughter	1967	5.00	10.00	20.00
❑ 44524	Garden in the City/Why Didn't My Mother Tell Me	1968	2.50	5.00	10.00
❑ 44524 [PS]	Garden in the City/Why Didn't My Mother Tell Me	1968	5.00	10.00	20.00

GORDIAN

Number	Title (A Side/B Side)	Yr	VG	VG+	NM
❑ 1947	Rag Doll/(B-side unknown)	1985	—	2.00	4.00

MIDSONG INT'L.

Number	Title (A Side/B Side)	Yr	VG	VG+	NM
❑ 40858	I'd Rather Leave While I'm in Love/Record People	1978	—	2.50	5.00
❑ 40903	Knock on Wood/Record People	1978	—	2.50	5.00

NEIGHBORHOOD

Number	Title (A Side/B Side)	Yr	VG	VG+	NM
❑ 4201	Brand New Key/Some Say (I Got Devil)	1971	—	2.50	5.00
—Multicolor label					
❑ 4201	Brand New Key/Some Say (I Got Devil)	1971	—	3.00	6.00
—White label (not a promo)					
❑ 4202	Ring the Living Bell/Railroad	1972	—	2.00	4.00
❑ 4202 [PS]	Ring the Living Bell/Railroad	1972	—	2.50	5.00
❑ 4204	Steppin'/Someday I'll Be a Farmer	1972	—	2.00	4.00
❑ 4204 [PS]	Steppin'/Someday I'll Be a Farmer	1972	2.00	4.00	8.00
❑ 4207	Together Alone/Center of the Circle	1972	—	2.00	4.00
❑ 4207 [PS]	Together Alone/Center of the Circle	1972	—	2.50	5.00
❑ 4209	Stoneground Woman/Do You Believe	1972	—	2.00	4.00
❑ 4210	Bitter Bad/Do You Believe	1973	—	2.00	4.00
❑ 4212	Seeds/Some Say (I Got Devil)	1973	—	2.00	4.00
❑ 4213	Will You Love Me Tomorrow/Here I Am	1973	—	2.00	4.00
❑ 4213 [PS]	Will You Love Me Tomorrow/Here I Am	1973	—	2.50	5.00
❑ 4214	Love to Love Again/Fine and Feather	1974	—	2.00	4.00
❑ 4214 [PS]	Love to Love Again/Fine and Feather	1974	—	3.00	6.00
❑ 4215	Lover's Cross/Holding Out	1974	—	2.00	4.00
❑ 10000	You're Not a Bad Ghost, Just an Old Song/Eyes of Man	1975	—	2.00	4.00
❑ 10001	Sweet Misery/Record Machine	1975	—	2.00	4.00

PORTRAIT

Number	Title (A Side/B Side)	Yr	VG	VG+	NM
❑ 51001	One More Try/Apathy	1981	—	2.00	4.00

STORK

Number	Title (A Side/B Side)	Yr	VG	VG+	NM
❑ (no #)	Timothy Scott Bogart	1970	3.00	6.00	12.00
—One-sided promo of "Christopher Robin" to celebrate the birth of Neil Bogart's son					

TOMATO

Number	Title (A Side/B Side)	Yr	VG	VG+	NM
❑ 10007	Running After Love/Holding Out	1979	—	2.50	5.00

WORLD UNITED

Number	Title (A Side/B Side)	Yr	VG	VG+	NM
❑ 1947	Oh Boy/Brand New Key	1978	—	2.50	5.00

7-Inch Extended Plays
BUDDAH

Number	Title (A Side/B Side)	Yr	VG	VG+	NM
❑ SP 2 [DJ]	Merry Christmas/Christopher Robin//I'm Back In Town/I Really Loved Harold	1971	2.50	5.00	10.00
❑ SP 2 [PS]	I'm Back in Town	1971	2.50	5.00	10.00

Albums

ABC

Number	Title (A Side/B Side)	Yr	VG	VG+	NM
❑ ABND-879	From the Beginning/Twelve Great Performances	1975	2.50	5.00	10.00

ACCORD

Number	Title (A Side/B Side)	Yr	VG	VG+	NM
❑ SN-7109	What Have They Done to My Song Ma	1981	2.50	5.00	10.00
❑ SN-7191	Beautiful People	1982	2.50	5.00	10.00

AMHERST

Number	Title (A Side/B Side)	Yr	VG	VG+	NM
❑ AMH-3302	Am I Real or What	1985	2.50	5.00	10.00

ATLANTIC

Number	Title (A Side/B Side)	Yr	VG	VG+	NM
❑ SD 18190	Photograph	1976	2.50	5.00	10.00

BLANCHE

Number	Title (A Side/B Side)	Yr	VG	VG+	NM
❑ BL 6177	Arabesque	1982	2.50	5.00	10.00

BUDDAH

Number	Title (A Side/B Side)	Yr	VG	VG+	NM
❑ BDS-5024	Born to Be	1969	3.75	7.50	15.00
❑ BDS-5041	Melanie	1969	3.75	7.50	15.00
❑ BDS-5060	Candles in the Rain	1970	3.75	7.50	15.00
❑ BDS-5066	Leftover Wine	1970	3.75	7.50	15.00
❑ BDS-5074	My First Album	1971	3.00	6.00	12.00
❑ BDS-5095	Garden in the City	1971	3.00	6.00	12.00
❑ BDS-5132	Please Love Me	1973	3.00	6.00	12.00
❑ B2D-5664 [(2)]	The Best…Melanie	197?	3.75	7.50	15.00
❑ BDS-95000	The Good Book	1971	3.75	7.50	15.00
❑ BDS-95005 [(2)]	Four Sides of Melanie	1972	3.75	7.50	15.00

MIDSONG

Number	Title (A Side/B Side)	Yr	VG	VG+	NM
❑ MCA-3033	Phonogenic: Not Just Another Pretty Face	1978	2.50	5.00	10.00

NEIGHBORHOOD

Number	Title (A Side/B Side)	Yr	VG	VG+	NM
❑ 3000	As I See It Now	1974	3.00	6.00	12.00
❑ 3001	Sunsets and Other Beginnings	1975	3.00	6.00	12.00
❑ 47001	Gather Me	1971	3.00	6.00	12.00
❑ 47005	Stoneground Words	1972	3.00	6.00	12.00
❑ 48001	Madrugada	1974	3.00	6.00	12.00
❑ 49001 [(2)]	Melanie at Carnegie Hall	1973	3.75	7.50	15.00

PICKWICK

Number	Title (A Side/B Side)	Yr	VG	VG+	NM
❑ SPC-3317	Try the Real Thing	197?	2.50	5.00	10.00

TOMATO

Number	Title (A Side/B Side)	Yr	VG	VG+	NM
❑ TOM-2-9003 [(2)]	Ballroom Streets	1979	3.00	6.00	12.00

MELCHER, TERRY   Also see BRUCE AND TERRY.
45s
COLUMBIA

Number	Title (A Side/B Side)	Yr	VG	VG+	NM
❑ 42427	I Waited Too Long/That's All I Want	1962	5.00	10.00	20.00
—As "Terry Day"					
❑ 42427 [PS]	I Waited Too Long/That's All I Want	1962	10.00	20.00	40.00
—As "Terry Day"					
❑ 42678	Be a Soldier/I Love You Betty	1963	5.00	10.00	20.00
—As "Terry Day"					
❑ 42678 [PS]	Be a Soldier/I Love You Betty	1963	10.00	20.00	40.00

RCA VICTOR

Number	Title (A Side/B Side)	Yr	VG	VG+	NM
❑ PB-10587	Fire in a Rainstorm/So Right Tonight	1976	2.50	5.00	10.00

Albums

REPRISE

Number	Title (A Side/B Side)	Yr	VG	VG+	NM
❑ MS 2185	Terry Melcher	1974	3.75	7.50	15.00

MELLO-HARPS, THE
45s
CASINO

Number	Title (A Side/B Side)	Yr	VG	VG+	NM
❑ 104	Gumma Gumma/No Good	1959	15.00	30.00	60.00

DO-RE-MI

Number	Title (A Side/B Side)	Yr	VG	VG+	NM
❑ 203	Love Is a Vow/Valerie	1956	4000.	6000.	8000.

TIN PAN ALLEY

Number	Title (A Side/B Side)	Yr	VG	VG+	NM
❑ 145/6	I Love Only You/Ain't Got the Money	1955	100.00	200.00	400.00
❑ 157/8	What Good Are My Dreams/Gone	1956	150.00	300.00	600.00
❑ 159	I Couldn't Believe/My Bleeding Heart	1956	150.00	300.00	600.00

MELLO-KINGS, THE
45s
HERALD

Number	Title (A Side/B Side)	Yr	VG	VG+	NM
❑ 502	Tonite Tonite/Do Baby Do	1957	12.50	25.00	50.00
—Label corrected to "The Mello-Kings"; script print inside flag					
❑ 502	Tonite Tonite/Do Baby Do	1957	125.00	250.00	500.00
—First pressing credits "The Mellotones"					
❑ 502	Tonite Tonite/Do Baby Do	1961	6.50	12.50	25.00
—Reissue; block print inside flag					
❑ 507	Chapel on the Hill/Sassafras	1957	7.50	15.00	30.00
❑ 511	Baby Tell Me Why Why Why/The Only Girl I'll Ever Know	1958	7.50	15.00	30.00
❑ 518	Valerie/She's Real Cool	1958	7.50	15.00	30.00
❑ 536	Chip Chip/Running to You	1959	7.50	15.00	30.00
—Both sides play as labeled					
❑ 536	Chip Chip/Running to You	1959	37.50	75.00	150.00
—Mispressing; plays "Rockin' at the Bandstand"/"Down in Cuba" by the Royal Holidays					
❑ 548	Our Love Is Beautiful/Dear Mr. Jock	1960	6.25	12.50	25.00
❑ 554	Kid Stuff/I Promise	1960	6.25	12.50	25.00
❑ 561	Penny/Till There Were None	1961	6.25	12.50	25.00
❑ 567	Love at First Sight/She's Real Cool	1961	6.25	12.50	25.00

LANA

Number	Title (A Side/B Side)	Yr	VG	VG+	NM
❑ 124	Tonite Tonite/Chip Chip	196?	2.50	5.00	10.00

LESCAY

Number	Title (A Side/B Side)	Yr	VG	VG+	NM
❑ 3009	Walk Softly/But You Lied	1962	7.50	15.00	30.00

LOST-NITE

Number	Title (A Side/B Side)	Yr	VG	VG+	NM
❑ 415	Tonite Tonite/Do Baby Do	197?	—	2.50	5.00
—Reissue					

7-Inch Extended Plays
HERALD

Number	Title (A Side/B Side)	Yr	VG	VG+	NM
❑ HEP-451	Tonite, Tonite/She's Real Cool//The Only Girl/Do Baby Do	1957	75.00	150.00	300.00
❑ HEP-451 [PS]	The Fabulous Mello-Kings	1957	100.00	200.00	400.00

M

Number	Title (A Side/B Side)	Yr	VG	VG+	NM
Albums					
COLLECTABLES					
❏ COL-5020	Greatest Hits	198?	2.50	5.00	10.00
HERALD					
❏ H-1013 [M]	Tonight-Tonight	196?	62.50	125.00	250.00
—Multi-color label					
❏ H-1013 [M]	Tonight-Tonight	1960	125.00	250.00	500.00
—Yellow label					
RELIC					
❏ LP-5035	Greatest Hits	198?	3.00	6.00	12.00

MELLO-MOODS, THE
45s

Number	Title (A Side/B Side)	Yr	VG	VG+	NM
GAMBLE					
❏ 2512	Stop Taking My Love for Granted/Inspirational Pleasure	1972	2.50	5.00	10.00
HAMILTON					
❏ 143	I'm Lost/I Woke Up This Morning	1953	25.00	50.00	100.00
LOST-NITE					
❏ 332	I Couldn't Sleep a Wink Last Night/And You Just Can't Go Through Life Alone	197?	—	2.50	5.00
—Reissue					
❏ 337	Where Are You (Now That I Need You)/How Could You	197?	—	2.50	5.00
—Reissue					
PRESTIGE					
❏ 799	Call on Me/I Tried and Tried and Tried	1953	175.00	350.00	700.00
❏ 856	I'm Lost/I Woke Up This Morning	1953	175.00	350.00	700.00
RED ROBIN					
❏ 104	I Couldn't Sleep a Wink Last Night/And You Just Can't Go Through Life Alone	1952	250.00	500.00	1000.
—Despite the lower number, this came out after Robin/Red Robin 105					
ROBIN					
❏ 105	Where Are You (Now That I Need You)/How Could You	1951	1250.	2500.	5000.
—Despite the higher number, this record pre-dates both of the Red Robin releases					

MELLO-TONES, THE   More than one group.
45s

Number	Title (A Side/B Side)	Yr	VG	VG+	NM
COLUMBIA					
❏ 1-904	When the Rain Gates Unfold/What Are They Doing in Heaven	1950	100.00	200.00	400.00
—Microgroove 33 1/3 rpm 7-inch record, small hole					
❏ 6-904	When the Rain Gates Unfold/What Are They Doing in Heaven	1950	100.00	200.00	400.00
—Originally released on Columbia's short-lived special numbering system for 7-inch records					
❏ 39051	When the Rain Gates Unfold/What Are They Doing in Heaven	1950	75.00	150.00	300.00
❏ 39215	Looking for a City/Flysing Saucers	1951	75.00	150.00	300.00
DECCA					
❏ 48318	Winos on Parade/Man Loves Woman	1954	100.00	200.00	400.00
❏ 48319	I'm Just Another One in Love with You/I'm Gonna Get	1954	100.00	200.00	400.00
FASCINATION					
❏ 1001	Rosie Lee/I'll Never Fall in Love Again	1957	37.50	75.00	150.00
GEE					
❏ 1037	Rosie Lee/I'll Never Fall in Love Again	1957	10.00	20.00	40.00
❏ 1040	Ca-Sandra/Rattle Shake Roll	1957	10.00	20.00	40.00
OKEH					
❏ 6828	Rough and Rocky Road/Cool by the River Banks	1951	75.00	150.00	300.00

MELLOW DROPS, THE
45s

Number	Title (A Side/B Side)	Yr	VG	VG+	NM
IMPERIAL					
❏ 5324	When I Grow Too Old to Dream/The Crazy Song	1955	50.00	100.00	200.00

MELLOWLARKS, THE
45s

Number	Title (A Side/B Side)	Yr	VG	VG+	NM
ARGO					
❏ 5285	Sing a Silly Sing Song/Farewell to You, My Nancy	1958	6.25	12.50	25.00

MELLOWS, THE
45s

Number	Title (A Side/B Side)	Yr	VG	VG+	NM
CANDLELIGHT					
❏ 1011	Moon of Silver/You're Gone	1956	37.50	75.00	150.00
❏ 1012	Farewell Farewell/No More Loneliness	1956	37.50	75.00	150.00
CELESTE					
❏ 3002	Lucky Guy/My Darling	1956	30.00	60.00	120.00
❏ 3004	I'm Yours/Sweet Lorraine	1956	150.00	300.00	600.00
JAY DEE					
❏ 793	How Sentimental Can I Be/Nothin' to Do	1954	50.00	100.00	200.00
❏ 797	Smoke from Your Cigarette/Pretty Baby	1954	62.50	125.00	250.00
❏ 801	I Was a Fool to Let You Go/I Still Care	1955	50.00	100.00	200.00
❏ 807	Yesterday's Memories/Loveable Lilly	1955	37.50	75.00	150.00

MELO GENTS, THE
45s

Number	Title (A Side/B Side)	Yr	VG	VG+	NM
WARNER BROS.					
❏ 5056	Baby Be Mine/Get Off My Back	1959	12.50	25.00	50.00

MELODEARS, THE
45s

Number	Title (A Side/B Side)	Yr	VG	VG+	NM
GONE					
❏ 5033	Summer Romance/Charock	1958	3.75	7.50	15.00
❏ 5040	It's Love Because/They Don't Say	1958	3.75	7.50	15.00

MELODY MAKERS, THE
45s

Number	Title (A Side/B Side)	Yr	VG	VG+	NM
HOLLIS					
❏ 1001	Carolina Moon/Let's Make Love Worthwhile	1957	25.00	50.00	100.00
❏ 1002	The Nearnes of You/Gotta Go	1957	37.50	75.00	150.00

MELVIN, HAROLD, AND THE BLUE NOTES   Also see THE BLUE NOTES (1).
12-Inch Singles

Number	Title (A Side/B Side)	Yr	VG	VG+	NM
PHILLY WORLD					
❏ PR 751 [DJ]	Today's Your Lucky Day (6:20) (7:07)	1984	2.00	4.00	8.00

Number	Title (A Side/B Side)	Yr	VG	VG+	NM
SOURCE					
❏ 13950	Prayin' (5:56)/Your Love Is Takin' Me on a Journey (5:55)	1979	3.00	6.00	12.00
45s					
ABC					
❏ 12240	Reaching for the World/Stay Together	1976	—	2.50	5.00
❏ 12268	After You Love Me, Why Do You Leave Me/Big Singing Star	1977	—	2.50	5.00
—With Sharon Paige					
❏ 12327	Baby, You Got My Nose Open/Try to Live a Day	1978	—	2.50	5.00
❏ 12368	Power of Love/Now Is the Time	1978	—	2.50	5.00
ARCTIC					
❏ 135	Go Away/What Can a Man Do	1967	2.50	5.00	10.00
LANDA					
❏ 703	Get Out (And Let Me Cry)/You May Not Love Me	1964	4.00	8.00	16.00
—As "The Blue Notes"					
MCA					
❏ 41291	Tonight's the Night/If You're Looking for Someone to Love	1980	—	2.00	4.00
—With Sharon Paige					
❏ 51190	Hang On In There/If You Love Me, Really Love Me	1982	—	2.00	4.00
PHILADELPHIA INT'L.					
❏ 3516	I Miss You (Part I)/I Miss You (Part II)	1972	—	2.50	5.00
❏ 3520	If You Don't Know Me By Now/Let Me Into Your World	1972	—	2.50	5.00
❏ 3525	Yesterday I Had the Blues/Ebony Woman	1973	—	2.50	5.00
❏ 3525 [PS]	Yesterday I Had the Blues/Ebony Woman	1973	—	3.00	6.00
❏ 3533	The Love I Lost (Part 1)/The Love I Lost (Part 2)	1973	—	2.50	5.00
❏ 3543	Satisfaction Guaranteed (Or Take Your Love Back)/I'm Weak for You	1974	—	2.50	5.00
❏ 3552	Where Are All My Friends/Let It Be You	1974	—	2.50	5.00
❏ 3562	Bad Luck (Part 1)/Bad Luck (Part 2)	1975	—	2.50	5.00
❏ 3569	Hope That We Can Be Together Soon/Be for Real	1975	—	2.50	5.00
—With Sharon Paige					
❏ 3579	Wake Up Everybody (Part 1)/Wake Up Everybody (Part 2)	1975	—	2.50	5.00
❏ 3588	Tell the World How I Feel About 'Cha Baby/You Know How to Make Me Feel So Good	1976	—	2.50	5.00
PHILLY WORLD					
❏ 99709	I Really Love You/I Can't Let Go	1984	—	2.00	4.00
❏ 99735	Today's Your Lucky Day (Long)/Today's Your Lucky Day (Short)	1984	—	2.00	4.00
❏ 99761	Don't Give Me Up/(Instrumental)	1984	—	2.00	4.00
SOURCE					
❏ 41156	Prayin' (Part 1)/Prayin' (Part 2)	1979	—	2.00	4.00
❏ 41157	Tonight's the Night/Your Love Is Taking Me on a Journey	1979	—	2.00	4.00
❏ 41231	I Should Be Your Lover (Part 1)/I Should Be Your Lover (Part 2)	1980	—	2.00	4.00
Albums					
ABC					
❏ AB-969	Reaching for the World	1977	2.50	5.00	10.00
❏ AB-1041	Now Is the Time	1978	2.50	5.00	10.00
MCA					
❏ 5261	All Things Happen in Time	1981	2.50	5.00	10.00
PHILADELPHIA INT'L.					
❏ KZ 31648	Harold Melvin and the Blue Notes	1972	3.00	6.00	12.00
❏ KZ 32407	Black & Blue	1973	3.00	6.00	12.00
❏ ZQ 32407 [Q]	Black & Blue	1973	5.00	10.00	20.00
❏ PZ 33148	To Be True	1975	3.00	6.00	12.00
❏ PZ 33808	Wake Up Everybody	1975	3.00	6.00	12.00
❏ PZQ 33808 [Q]	Wake Up Everybody	1975	5.00	10.00	20.00
❏ PZ 34232	Collector's Item — All Their Greatest Hits!	1976	3.00	6.00	12.00
PHILLY WORLD					
❏ 90187	Talk It Up (Tell Everybody)	1985	2.50	5.00	10.00
SOURCE					
❏ 3197	The Blue Album	1980	2.50	5.00	10.00

MEMORIES, THE
45s

Number	Title (A Side/B Side)	Yr	VG	VG+	NM
WAY-LIN					
❏ 101	Love Bells/I Promise	1959	100.00	200.00	400.00

MEMPHIS MINNIE
45s

Number	Title (A Side/B Side)	Yr	VG	VG+	NM
CHECKER					
❏ 771	Broken Heart/Me and My Chauffeur	1953	1000.	2000.	3000.
J.O.B.					
❏ 1101	Kissing in the Dark/World of Trouble	1952	250.00	500.00	1000.
Albums					
MCA					
❏ 1370	Moanin' the Blues	198?	3.75	7.50	15.00
PORTRAIT					
❏ RJ 44072	I Ain't No Bad Gal	1988	3.75	7.50	15.00

MEMPHIS SLIM
45s

Number	Title (A Side/B Side)	Yr	VG	VG+	NM
JOSIE					
❏ 973	Come Again/Little Lonely Girl	1967	2.50	5.00	10.00
KING					
❏ 6301	Messin' Around with the Blues/Mistake in Life	1970	2.00	4.00	8.00
MERCURY					
❏ 8251x45	Train Time/Blue Evening	1951	12.50	25.00	50.00
❏ 8266x45	No Mail Blues/Gonna Need My Help Some Day	1952	12.50	25.00	50.00
❏ 8281x45	The Question/Never Let Me Love	1952	12.50	25.00	50.00
❏ 70063x45	The Train Is Coming/Drivin' Me Mad	1953	10.00	20.00	40.00
MONEY					
❏ 212	My Country Gal/Treat Me Like I Treat You	1955	10.00	20.00	40.00
PEACOCK					
❏ 1602	Sitting and Thinking/Living Like a King	1952	12.50	25.00	50.00
STRAND					
❏ 25041	Four Walls/Lonesome	1961	6.25	12.50	25.00

Number	Title (A Side/B Side)	Yr	VG	VG+	NM
UNITED					
❏ 138	Back Alley/Living the Life I Love	1952	15.00	30.00	60.00
❏ 156	The Come Back/Five O'Clock Blues	1953	15.00	30.00	60.00
—Black vinyl					
❏ 156	The Come Back/Five O'Clock Blues	1953	37.50	75.00	150.00
—Red vinyl					
❏ 166	Call Before You Go Home/This Is My Lucky Day	1953	15.00	30.00	60.00
—Black vinyl					
❏ 166	Call Before You Go Home/This Is My Lucky Day	1953	37.50	75.00	150.00
—Red vinyl					
❏ 176	Wish Me Well/Sassy Mae	1954	15.00	30.00	60.00
—Black vinyl					
❏ 176	Wish Me Well/Sassy Mae	1954	37.50	75.00	150.00
—Red vinyl					
❏ 182	I Love My Baby/Four Years of Torment	1954	12.50	25.00	50.00
❏ 186	Memphis Slim U.S.A./Blues All Around My Head	1954	12.50	25.00	50.00
❏ 189	She's Alright/Two of a Kind	1955	12.50	25.00	50.00
❏ 201	Go to Find My Baby/Blue and Lonesome	1956	10.00	20.00	40.00
VEE JAY					
❏ 271	Stroll On Little Girl/Guitar Cha Cha Cha	1958	5.00	10.00	20.00
❏ 294	This Time I'm Through/What's the Matter	1958	5.00	10.00	20.00
❏ 330	Steppin' Out/My Gal Keeps Me Crying	1959	5.00	10.00	20.00
❏ 343	The Come Back/Slim's Blues	1960	3.75	7.50	15.00
WARNER BROS.					
❏ 7500	Chicago Seven/Boogie Woogie 1-9-7-0	1971	2.00	4.00	8.00
Albums					
BATTLE					
❏ BM-6118 [M]	Alone with My Friends	1963	12.50	25.00	50.00
❏ BM-6122 [M]	Baby Please Come Home	1963	12.50	25.00	50.00
BLUESVILLE					
❏ BVLP-1018 [M] Just Blues		1961	30.00	60.00	120.00
—Blue label, silver print					
❏ BVLP-1018 [M] Just Blues		1964	7.50	15.00	30.00
—Blue label, trident logo at right					
❏ BVLP-1031 [M] No Strain		1961	30.00	60.00	120.00
—Blue label, silver print					
❏ BVLP-1031 [M] No Strain		1964	7.50	15.00	30.00
—Blue label, trident logo at right					
❏ BVLP-1053 [M] All Kinds of Blues		1962	25.00	50.00	100.00
—Blue label, silver print					
❏ BVLP-1053 [M] All Kinds of Blues		1964	7.50	15.00	30.00
—Blue label, trident logo at right					
❏ BVLP-1075 [M] Steady Rollin' Blues		1963	25.00	50.00	100.00
—Blue label, silver print					
❏ BVLP-1075 [M] Steady Rollin' Blues		1964	7.50	15.00	30.00
—Blue label, trident logo at right					
BUDDAH					
❏ BDS-7505	Mother Earth	1969	5.00	10.00	20.00
CANDID					
❏ CM-8023 [M]	Slim's Tribute to Big Bill Broonzy	1961	15.00	30.00	60.00
❏ CM-8024 [M]	Memphis Slim U.S.A.	1962	15.00	30.00	60.00
❏ CS-9023 [S]	Slim's Tribute to Big Bill Broonzy	1961	20.00	40.00	80.00
❏ CS-9024 [S]	Memphis Slim U.S.A.	1962	20.00	40.00	80.00
CHESS					
❏ LP-1455 [M]	Memphis Slim	1961	37.50	75.00	150.00
—Black label					
❏ LP-1510 [M]	The Real Folk Blues	1966	20.00	40.00	80.00
DISC					
❏ D-105 [M]	If the Rabbit Had a Gun	1964	10.00	20.00	40.00
FOLKWAYS					
❏ FG-3524 [M]	The Real Boogie Woogie	1959	25.00	50.00	100.00
❏ FG-3535 [M]	Memphis Slim…And the Real Honky Tonk	1960	25.00	50.00	100.00
❏ FG-3536 [M]	Chicago Blues	1961	25.00	50.00	100.00
JUBILEE					
❏ JGM-8003 [M]	Legend of the Blues	1967	6.25	12.50	25.00
❏ JGS-8003 [S]	Legend of the Blues	1967	6.25	12.50	25.00
KING					
❏ 885 [M]	Memphis Slim Sings Folk Blues	1964	12.50	25.00	50.00
SCEPTER					
❏ SM-535 [M]	Self Portrait	1966	5.00	10.00	20.00
❏ SMS-535 [S]	Self Portrait	1966	6.25	12.50	25.00
SPIN-O-RAMA					
❏ 149 [M]	Lonesome Blues	196?	5.00	10.00	20.00
STRAND					
❏ SL-1046 [M]	The World's Foremost Blues Singer	1962	10.00	20.00	40.00
❏ SLS-1046 [S]	The World's Foremost Blues Singer	1962	12.50	25.00	50.00
UNITED ARTISTS					
❏ UAL-3137 [M]	Broken Soul Blues	1961	15.00	30.00	60.00
❏ UAS-6137 [S]	Broken Soul Blues	1961	20.00	40.00	80.00
VEE JAY					
❏ LP-1012 [M]	Memphis Slim at the Gate of the Horn	1959	50.00	100.00	200.00
—Maroon label					
❏ LP-1012 [M]	Memphis Slim at the Gate of the Horn	1961	30.00	60.00	120.00
—Black rainbow label, oval logo					

MENDEL, ED

45s

Number	Title (A Side/B Side)	Yr	VG	VG+	NM
HIT					
❏ 32	I Remember You/Green Onions	1962	2.00	4.00	8.00
—B-side by the Dave Grundy Combo					

MENDES, SERGIO Includes Brasil '66, '77, '86, '88, etc.

12-Inch Singles

Number	Title (A Side/B Side)	Yr	VG	VG+	NM
A&M					
❏ 12103	Dance Attack (Club Mix)/Dance Attack (Dub)	1984	—	3.00	6.00
❏ 12195	Nonstop (Remix)/(Instrumental)	1986	—	3.00	6.00
ELEKTRA					
❏ ED 5602 [DJ]	What Is This?/Fanfarra	1992	2.00	4.00	8.00
45s					
A&M					
❏ 807	Mas Que nada/The Joker	1966	—	3.00	6.00
❏ 814	Day Tripper/Slow Hot Wind	1966	—	3.00	6.00
❏ 825	Constant Rain (Chove Chuva)	1966	—	3.00	6.00
❏ 836	For Me/Gente	1967	—	3.00	6.00
❏ 853	Night and Day/Cinnamon and Clove	1967	—	2.50	5.00

Number	Title (A Side/B Side)	Yr	VG	VG+	NM
❏ 872	Watch What Happens/The Frog	1967	—	2.50	5.00
❏ 872 [PS]	Watch What Happens/The Frog	1967	2.50	5.00	10.00
❏ 910	Look Around/With a Little Help from My Friends	1968	—	2.50	5.00
❏ 924	The Look of Love/Like a Lover	1968	—	2.50	5.00
❏ 924 [PS]	The Look of Love/Like a Lover	1968	2.00	4.00	8.00
❏ 961	The Fool on the Hill/So Many Stars	1968	—	2.50	5.00
❏ 961 [PS]	The Fool on the Hill/So Many Stars	1968	2.00	4.00	8.00
❏ 986	Scarborough Fair/Canto Triste	1968	—	2.50	5.00
❏ 986 [PS]	Scarborough Fair/Canto Triste	1968	2.00	4.00	8.00
❏ 1049	Pretty World/Fiesta	1969	—	2.50	5.00
❏ 1049 [PS]	Pretty World/Fiesta	1969	—	3.00	6.00
❏ 1073	(Sittin' On) The Dock of the Bay/Song of No Regrets	1969	—	2.50	5.00
❏ 1073 [PS]	(Sittin' On) The Dock of the Bay/Song of No Regrets	1969	—	3.00	6.00
❏ 1132	Wichita Lineman/Ye Me Le	1969	—	2.50	5.00
❏ 1164	Norwegian Wood/Masquerade	1970	—	2.00	4.00
❏ 1164 [PS]	Norwegian Wood/Masquerade	1970	2.00	4.00	8.00
❏ 1209	For What It's Worth/Vira Mundo	1970	—	2.00	4.00
❏ 1226	Chelsea Morning/Where Are You Coming From	1970	—	2.00	4.00
❏ 1245	Lost in Paradise/Righteous Life	1971	—	2.00	4.00
❏ 1257	Aza Branca/Sometimes in Winter	1971	—	2.00	4.00
❏ 1279	Zanzibar/So Many People	1971	—	2.00	4.00
❏ 1313	After Midnight/Morro Velho	1971	—	2.00	4.00
❏ 1346	After Sunrise/The Grab	1972	—	2.00	4.00
❏ 2429	Summer Love/Life in the Movies	1982	—	2.00	4.00
❏ 2540	Never Gonna Let You Go/Carnival	1983	—	—	3.00
❏ 2563	Rainbow's End/Carnival	1983	—	—	3.00
❏ 2623	Olympia/Carnival	1984	—	—	3.00
❏ 2623 [PS]	Olympia/Carnival	1984	—	2.00	4.00
❏ 2639	Alibis/Confetti	1984	—	—	3.00
❏ 2662	Let's Give a Little More This Time/Confetti	1984	—	—	3.00
❏ 2672	Real Life/Confetti	1984	—	—	3.00
❏ 2706	Let's Give a Little More This Time/Confetti	1985	—	—	3.00
❏ 2859	Non-Stop/Flower of Bahia (Flor de Bahia)	1986	—	—	3.00
❏ 2875	Take This Love/Your Smile	1986	—	—	3.00
❏ 2917	What Do We Mean to Each Other/Flower of Bahia (Flor de Bahia)	1987	—	—	3.00
ATLANTIC					
❏ 2472	I Say a Little Prayer/Comin' Home Baby	1968	—	3.00	6.00
❏ 2502	My Favorite Things/Tempo Feliz	1968	—	3.00	6.00
❏ 5056	All My Loving/The Telephone Song	1967	—	3.00	6.00
❏ 5076	The Great Arrival/Monday, Monday	1969	—	3.00	6.00
BELL					
❏ 45335	Love Music/Walk the Way You Walk	1973	—	2.00	4.00
❏ 45372	Where Is the Love/Hey, Look at the Sun	1973	—	2.00	4.00
❏ 45410	Put a Little Love Away/They Look at the Sun	1973	—	2.50	5.00
ELEKTRA					
❏ 45235	If I Ever Lose This Heaven/You Been Away Too Long	1975	—	2.00	4.00
❏ 45249	The Trouble With Hello Is Goodbye/Davy	1975	—	2.00	4.00
❏ 45283	Someday We'll Be Free/Emerio	1975	—	2.00	4.00
❏ 45310	Sunny Day/Tell Me in a Whisper	1976	—	2.00	4.00
❏ 45360	Home Cooking/Real Thing	1976	—	2.00	4.00
❏ 45405	Love Me Tomorrow/Peninsula	1977	—	2.00	4.00
❏ 45416	The Real Thing/Peninsula	1977	—	2.00	4.00
❏ 45453	Love City/Peninsula	1978	—	2.00	4.00
❏ 45494	Midnight Lovers/Misturada	1978	—	2.00	4.00
❏ 45512	Waters of March/Misturada	1978	—	2.00	4.00
❏ 46064	Summer Dream/Lonely Woman	1979	—	2.00	4.00
❏ 46567	I'll Tell You/Lonely Woman	1979	—	2.00	4.00
❏ 46618	Let It Go/Magic Lady	1980	—	2.00	4.00
7-Inch Extended Plays					
A&M					
❏ SP 437	With a Little Help from My Friends/Roda/The Frog//The Look of Love/Batucuda/Look Around	1968	3.00	6.00	12.00
—Jukebox issue; small hole, plays at 33 1/3 rpm					
❏ SP 437 [PS]	Look Around	1968	3.00	6.00	12.00
Albums					
A&M					
❏ LP-116 [M]	Sergio Mendes and Brasil '66	1966	3.00	6.00	12.00
❏ LP-122 [M]	Equinox	1967	3.75	7.50	15.00
❏ SP-3108	Fool on the Hill	198?	2.00	4.00	8.00
—Budget-line reissue					
❏ SP-3258	Greatest Hits	198?	2.00	4.00	8.00
—Budget-line reissue					
❏ SP-3522 [(2)]	The Sergio Mendes Foursider	1973	3.75	7.50	15.00
❏ SP-4116 [S]	Sergio Mendes and Brasil '66	1966	3.75	7.50	15.00
❏ SP-4122 [S]	Equinox	1967	3.75	7.50	15.00
❏ SP-4137	Look Around	1968	3.75	7.50	15.00
❏ SP-4160	Fool on the Hill	1968	3.75	7.50	15.00
❏ SP-4197	Crystal Illusions	1969	3.75	7.50	15.00
❏ SP-4236	Ye-Me-Le	1969	3.75	7.50	15.00
❏ SP-4252	Greatest Hits	1970	3.75	7.50	15.00
❏ SP-4284	Stillness	1970	3.75	7.50	15.00
❏ SP-4315	Pais Tropical	1971	3.00	6.00	12.00
❏ SP-4353	Primal Roots	1972	3.00	6.00	12.00
❏ SP-4937	Sergio Mendes	1983	2.50	5.00	10.00
❏ SP-4984	Confetti	1984	2.50	5.00	10.00
❏ SP-5135	Sergio Mendes and Brasil '86	1986	2.50	5.00	10.00
❏ SP-5250	Arara	1989	3.00	6.00	12.00
❏ SP-6012 [(2)]	The Sergio Mendes Foursider	198?	2.50	5.00	10.00
—Budget-line reissue					
ATLANTIC					
❏ 1434 [M]	The Swinger from Rio	1965	3.75	7.50	15.00
❏ SD 1434 [S]	The Swinger from Rio	1965	5.00	10.00	20.00
❏ 1466 [M]	Great Arrival	1966	3.75	7.50	15.00
❏ SD 1466 [S]	Great Arrival	1966	5.00	10.00	20.00
❏ 1480 [M]	The Beat of Brazil	1967	5.00	10.00	20.00
❏ SD 1480 [S]	The Beat of Brazil	1967	3.75	7.50	15.00
❏ 8112 [M]	Sergio Mendes In Person at the El Matador	1967	5.00	10.00	20.00
❏ SD 8112 [S]	Sergio Mendes In Person at the El Matador	1967	3.75	7.50	15.00
❏ 8177 [M]	Sergio Mendes' Favorite Things	1968	10.00	20.00	40.00
—White label promo only					
❏ SD 8177 [S]	Sergio Mendes' Favorite Things	1968	5.00	10.00	20.00
BELL					
❏ 1119	Love Music	1973	2.50	5.00	10.00
❏ 1305	Vintage 74	1974	2.50	5.00	10.00

Number	Title (A Side/B Side)	Yr	VG	VG+	NM
CAPITOL					
❑ ST 2294 [S]	In a Brazilan Bag	1965	15.00	30.00	60.00
❑ T 2294 [M]	In a Brazilan Bag	1965	12.50	25.00	50.00
ELEKTRA					
❑ 6E-134	Sergio Mendes and Brasil '88	1978	2.50	5.00	10.00
❑ 6E-214	Magic Lady	1980	2.50	5.00	10.00
❑ 7E-1027	Sergio Mendes	1975	2.50	5.00	10.00
❑ EQ-1027 [Q]	Sergio Mendes	1975	3.75	7.50	15.00
❑ 7E-1055	Homecooking	1976	2.50	5.00	10.00
❑ 7E-1102	Sergio Mendes and the New Brasil '77	1977	2.50	5.00	10.00
MOBILE FIDELITY					
❑ 1-118	Sergio Mendes and Brasil '66	1984	12.50	25.00	50.00
—Audiophile vinyl					
PHILIPS					
❑ PHM 200263 [M]	Quiet Nights	1968	5.00	10.00	20.00
❑ PHS 600263 [S]	Quiet Nights	1968	3.75	7.50	15.00
PICKWICK					
❑ SPC-3149	So Nice	1972	2.50	5.00	10.00
TOWER					
❑ ST 5052 [S]	In a Brazilan Bag	1966	12.50	25.00	50.00
—Reissue of Capitol 2294					
❑ T 5052 [M]	In a Brazilan Bag	1966	10.00	20.00	40.00
—Reissue of Capitol 2294					

MEPHISTOPHELES
45s
REPRISE

❑ 0832	Cricket Song/Take a Jet	1969	3.00	6.00	12.00
Albums					
REPRISE					
❑ RS 6355	In Frustration I Hear Singing	1969	10.00	20.00	40.00

MERCED BLUE NOTES, THE
45s
ACCENT

❑ 1069	Rufus/Your Tender Lips	1961	10.00	20.00	40.00
GALAXY					
❑ 738	Rufus Jr./Thumping	1965	7.50	15.00	30.00
❑ 744	Mama Rufus/Bad Bad Whiskey	1965	7.50	15.00	30.00
SOUL					
❑ 35007	Do the Pig/Thumping	1965	250.00	500.00	1000.
TRI-PHI					
❑ 1011	Midnight Sessions (Part 1)/Midnight Sessions (Part 2)	1962	12.50	25.00	50.00
❑ 1023	Whole Lotta Nothin'/Fragile	1963	10.00	20.00	40.00

MERCER, JOHNNY
45s
CAPITOL

❑ 54-582	Baby It's Cold Outside/I Never Heard You Say	1949	7.50	15.00	30.00
—With Margaret Whiting					
❑ F853	Jamboree Jones/Dixieland Band	1950	5.00	10.00	20.00
❑ F982	She's Shimmyun on the Beach Again/At the Jazzland Ball	1950	5.00	10.00	20.00
❑ F1261	Jingle Bells/Santa Claus Is Comin' to Town	1950	3.75	7.50	15.00
❑ F1285	Winter Wonderland/Goofus	1950	3.75	7.50	15.00
❑ F1618	One for My Baby/St. Louis Blues	1951	3.75	7.50	15.00
—Reissue of material first issued on 78					
❑ F1641	Sugar Blues/Goofus	1951	3.75	7.50	15.00
—Reissue of material first issued on 78					
❑ F2248	The Glow-Worm/New Ashmolean	1952	3.75	7.50	15.00
❑ F15512	Candy/Ac-Cent-Tchu-Ate the Positive	1950	3.75	7.50	15.00
❑ F15513	G.I. Jive/I Lost My Sugar in Salt Lake City	1950	3.75	7.50	15.00
❑ F15514	On the Atchison, Topeka and the Santa Fe/Strip Polka	1950	3.75	7.50	15.00
—The above three comprise CCF-214; all are reissues of hits that charted from 1942-45					
❑ 54-90041	Jingle Bells/Santa Claus Is Coming to Town	1949	7.50	15.00	30.00
Albums					
CAPITOL					
❑ H 210 [10]	Music of Jerome Kern	1950	20.00	40.00	80.00
❑ H 214 [10]	Johnny Mercer Sings	1950	20.00	40.00	80.00
❑ T 907 [M]	Ac-Cent-Tchu-Ate the Positive	1957	12.50	25.00	50.00
JUPITER					
❑ JLP-1001 [M]	Johnny Mercer Sings Just for Fun	1956	12.50	25.00	50.00

MERCER, WILL
45s
CONSTELLATION

❑ 109	Penny Candy/Willowy Billowy Land	1963	3.75	7.50	15.00
SUN					
❑ 329	You're Just My Kind/Ballad of St. Mark's	1959	6.25	12.50	25.00

MERCHANTS OF DREAM, THE
45s
A&M

❑ 989	Sing Me Life/Dorothy the Fairy Queen	1968	2.50	5.00	10.00
Albums					
A&M					
❑ SP-4149	Strange Night Voyage	1969	6.25	12.50	25.00

MERCURY, ERIC
45s
AVCO EMBASSY

❑ 4516	Hurdy Gurdy Man/Enter My Love	1969	5.00	10.00	20.00
❑ 4523	Everybody Has the Right to Know/You Bring Me to My Knees	1969	5.00	10.00	20.00
ENTERPRISE					
❑ 9041	I Can Smell That Funky Music/Listen with Your Eyes	1971	3.75	7.50	15.00
❑ 9047	The Truth Will Set You Free/What's Usual Seems Natural	1972	3.75	7.50	15.00
❑ 9080	Love Is Taking Over/Take a Walk Down My Street	1973	3.00	6.00	12.00
❑ 9089	Sweet Sara/Don't Lose Faith in Me Lord	1973	3.00	6.00	12.00
SACK					
❑ 001	Lonely Girl/(B-side unknown)	196?	1000.	1750.	2500.

MERCURY, FREDDIE   Also see QUEEN.
12-Inch Singles
COLUMBIA

❑ AS 1928 [DJ]	Love Kills (same on both sides)	1984	2.50	5.00	10.00
❑ 05314	Living on My Own (Extended Version) (7" Version)	1985	2.00	4.00	8.00
45s					
ANTHEM					
❑ 104	I Can Hear Music/Going Back	1973	25.00	50.00	100.00
—As "Larry Lurex"; A-side matrix number on label is "A-0009-REMIX"					
❑ 104	I Can Hear Music/Going Back	1973	37.50	75.00	150.00
—As "Larry Lurex"; A-side matrix number on label is "A-0009"					
CAPITOL					
❑ B-5696	The Great Pretender/Exercises in Free Love	1987	—	—	3.00
❑ B-5696 [PS]	The Great Pretender/Exercises in Free Love	1987	—	2.00	4.00
COLUMBIA					
❑ 04606	Love Kills/Rotwang's Party (Robot Dance)	1984	—	2.00	4.00
❑ 04606 [PS]	Love Kills/Rotwang's Party (Robot Dance)	1984	—	2.00	4.00
❑ 04869	I Was Born to Love You/.Stop All the Fighting	1985	—	2.00	4.00
❑ 04869 [PS]	I Was Born to Love You/.Stop All the Fighting	1985	—	2.00	4.00
❑ 05455	Living on My Own/She Blows Hot and Cold	1985	—	2.00	4.00
Albums					
COLUMBIA					
❑ FC 40071	Mr. Bad Guy	1985	3.00	6.00	12.00

MERCY
45s
SUNDI

❑ 6811	Love (Can Make You Happy)/Fire Ball	1969	2.00	4.00	8.00
WARNER BROS.					
❑ 7291	Love Can Make You Happy/Happy As Can Be, La La La	1969	3.75	7.50	15.00
—Pressed in U.S. for export only; A-side is a re-recording of the hit on Sundi					
❑ 7297	Forever/The Morning's Come	1969	—	3.00	6.00
❑ 7331	Hello Baby/Heard You Went Away	1969	—	3.00	6.00
Albums					
SUNDI					
❑ SRLP-803	The Mercy & Love (Can Make You Happy)	1969	5.00	10.00	20.00
—Has the original version of the title song plus filler instrumentals					
WARNER BROS.					
❑ WS 1799	Love (Can Make You Happy)	1969	3.75	7.50	15.00
—"Love (Can Make You Happy)" was re-recorded for this LP					

MERKIN
Albums
WINDI

❑ 1004/5	Music from Merkin	1972	100.00	200.00	400.00

MERMAIDS, THE   See THE MURMAIDS.

MERRI-MEN, THE   Another group containing former members of BILL HALEY AND HIS COMETS.
45s
APT

❑ 25051	Big Daddy/St, Louis Blues	1960	6.25	12.50	25.00

MERRY ELVES, THE
45s
ARGUS

❑ 250	Rock & Roll Around the Christmas Tree/ I Love Christmas	1964	2.50	5.00	10.00

MERRY-GO-ROUND, THE   Also see EMMITT RHODES.
45s
A&M

❑ 834	Live/Time Will Show the Wiser	1967	2.50	5.00	10.00
❑ 857	Gonna Fight the World/We're in Love	1967	2.50	5.00	10.00
❑ 863	You're a Very Lovely Woman/ Where Have You Been All My Life	1967	2.50	5.00	10.00
❑ 886	Had to Run Around/She Laughed Loud	1967	2.50	5.00	10.00
❑ 920	Missing You/Listen, Listen	1968	2.50	5.00	10.00
❑ 957	Highway/'Til the Day After	1968	2.50	5.00	10.00
Albums					
A&M					
❑ LP-132 [M]	The Merry-Go-Round	1967	10.00	20.00	40.00
❑ SP-4132 [S]	The Merry-Go-Round	1967	7.50	15.00	30.00
RHINO					
❑ RNLP 126	The Best of the Merry-Go-Round	1985	2.50	5.00	10.00

MERRYWEATHER, NEIL
45s
CAPITOL

❑ 2537	Curiosity/Feeling of Freedom	1969	2.00	4.00	8.00
MERCURY					
❑ 73619	Hollywood Boulevard/ High Altitude Hide and Seek	1974	—	2.50	5.00
Albums					
CAPITOL					
❑ SKAO-220	Merryweather	1969	3.75	7.50	15.00
❑ STBB-278 [(2)]	Word of Mouth	1969	5.00	10.00	20.00
KENT					
❑ KST-546	Neil Merryweather and the Boers	197?	3.75	7.50	15.00
MERCURY					
❑ SRM-1-1007	Space Rangers	1974	3.00	6.00	12.00
❑ SRM-1-1024	Kryptonite	1975	3.00	6.00	12.00

MERRYWEATHER AND CAREY
45s
RCA VICTOR

❑ 74-0429	Shop Around/If I Were You	1971	—	3.00	6.00
Albums					
RCA VICTOR					
❑ LSP-4442	Ivar Avenue Reunion	1970	3.75	7.50	15.00
❑ LSP-4485	Vacuum Cleaner	1971	3.75	7.50	15.00

Number	Title (A Side/B Side)	Yr	VG	VG+	NM

MERSEY LADS, THE
45s
MGM
| ❏ 13481 | Johnny No Love/What 'Cha Gonna Do Baby | 1966 | 3.75 | 7.50 | 15.00 |

MERSEYBEATS, THE
45s
FONTANA
❏ 1513	It Would Take a Long Time/ Don't Let It Happen to Us	1965	3.75	7.50	15.00
❏ 1532	I Love You, Yes I Do/See Me Back	1965	3.75	7.50	15.00
❏ 1882	Mr. Moonlight/I Think of You	1964	3.75	7.50	15.00
❏ 1905	Don't Turn Around/Really Mystified	1964	3.75	7.50	15.00
❏ 1950	See Me Back/Last Night	1964	3.75	7.50	15.00
Albums
ARC INTERNATIONAL
| ❏ 834 [M] | England's Best Sellers | 1964 | 10.00 | 20.00 | 40.00 |

MERSEYBOYS, THE
Albums
VEE JAY
| ❏ VJ-1101 [DJ] | The 15 Greatest Songs of the Beatles | 1964 | 37.50 | 75.00 | 150.00 |
—White label, all-blue print; without typographical error on label: "Saluting Their Return to America"
| ❏ VJ-1101 [DJ] | The 15 Greatest Songs of the Beatles | 1964 | 37.50 | 75.00 | 150.00 |
—White label, blue and black print; with typographical error on label: "Saluting Their Return to Amercia"
| ❏ VJ-1101 [M] | The 15 Greatest Songs of the Beatles | 1964 | 25.00 | 50.00 | 100.00 |
—With typographical error on label "Saluting Their Return to Amercia"; this album is not known to exist in stereo
| ❏ VJ-1101 [M] | The 15 Greatest Songs of the Beatles | 1964 | 25.00 | 50.00 | 100.00 |
—Without typographical error on label "Saluting Their Return To America"; this album is not known to exist in stereo

MERSEYS, THE
45s
MERCURY
| ❏ 72582 | Sorrow/Some Other Day | 1966 | 5.00 | 10.00 | 20.00 |

MESHEL, BILLY
45s
OLD TOWN
| ❏ 1181 | My Little Angel/Tiger and the 71st Street Sharks | 1965 | 3.00 | 6.00 | 12.00 |
PROBE
| ❏ 459 | I Say Hello When I'm Leaving/(It Ain't Easy
Being) Shirley Newman's Boyfriend | 1969 | 2.50 | 5.00 | 10.00 |
| ❏ 462 | Today Has Been Cancelled/That's What Sends
Him to the Bowery | 1969 | 2.50 | 5.00 | 10.00 |
Albums
PROBE
| ❏ CPLP-4502 | The Love Songs of A. Wilbur Meshel | 1969 | 5.00 | 10.00 | 20.00 |

MESMERIZING EYE, THE
Albums
SMASH
| ❏ MGS-27090 [M] | Psychedelia — A Musical Light Show | 1967 | 12.50 | 25.00 | 50.00 |
| ❏ SRS-67090 [S] | Psychedelia — A Musical Light Show | 1967 | 15.00 | 30.00 | 60.00 |

MESSENGERS, THE (1) Milwaukee-based rock group.
45s
RARE EARTH
| ❏ 5032 | That's the Way a Woman Is/In the Jungle | 1971 | — | 2.50 | 5.00 |
SOUL
| ❏ 35037 | Window Shopping/California Soul | 1967 | 2.50 | 5.00 | 10.00 |
U.S.A.
| ❏ 866 | Midnight Hour/Up 'Til Now | 1967 | 3.00 | 6.00 | 12.00 |
—As "Michael and the Messengers"
| ❏ 866 | Midnight Hour/Hard Hard Year | 1967 | 3.75 | 7.50 | 15.00 |
—As "The Messengers"
| ❏ 874 | Romeo and Juliet/Lies | 1967 | 3.75 | 7.50 | 15.00 |
—As "Michael and the Messengers"
Albums
RARE EARTH
| ❏ RS-509 | The Messengers | 1969 | 5.00 | 10.00 | 20.00 |

MESSENGERS, THE (2)
45s
ERA
| ❏ 3143 | Let Me Be Your Man/You've Got Me Cryin' | 1964 | 3.00 | 6.00 | 12.00 |

MESSENGERS, THE (3) British group.
45s
MGM
| ❏ 13293 | I'm Stealin' Back/This Little Light of Mine | 1964 | 3.00 | 6.00 | 12.00 |
| ❏ 13346 | When Did You Leave Heaven/More Pretty Girls
Than One | 1965 | 3.00 | 6.00 | 12.00 |

MESSENGERS, THE (4) Chicago group; after THE MESSENGERS (1) changed record labels, this group recorded as "Michael and the Messengers" on U.S.A.
45s
U.S.A.
| ❏ 889 | Run and Hide/She Was the Girl | 1967 | 2.00 | 4.00 | 8.00 |
—As "Michael and the Messengers"
| ❏ 897 | Gotta Take It Easy/I Need Her Here | 1968 | 2.00 | 4.00 | 8.00 |
—As "Michael and the Messengers"

MESSINA, JIM Also see BUFFALO SPRINGFIELD; LOGGINS AND MESSINA; POCO.
45s
AUDIO FIDELITY
| ❏ 098 | The Breeze and I/Straight Man | 1964 | 7.50 | 15.00 | 30.00 |
COLUMBIA
| ❏ 11094 | New and Different Way/(Is This) Lovin' You Lady | 1979 | — | 2.00 | 4.00 |
| ❏ 11182 | Do You Want to Dance/Seeing You
(For the First Time) | 1980 | — | 2.00 | 4.00 |
FEATURE
| ❏ 101 | Panther Pounce/Tiger Tail | 1964 | 7.50 | 15.00 | 30.00 |
ULTIMA
| ❏ 705 | Drag Bike Boogie/A-Rab | 1964 | 7.50 | 15.00 | 30.00 |

VIV
| ❏ 1000 | Side Track/Sherrie | 1965 | 6.25 | 12.50 | 25.00 |
WARNER BROS.
❏ 29278	Big Tease/The Island	1984	—	2.00	4.00
❏ 29457	Forever My Love/One More Mile	1983	—	2.00	4.00
❏ 49784	Move Into Your Heart/Stay the Night	1981	—	2.00	4.00
—With Pauline Wilson
| ❏ 49839 | It's All Right Here/Move Into Your Heart | 1981 | — | 2.00 | 4.00 |
Albums
AUDIO FIDELITY
| ❏ DFM-3037 [M] | The Dragsters | 1964 | 20.00 | 40.00 | 80.00 |
| ❏ DFS-7037 [S] | The Dragsters | 1964 | 25.00 | 50.00 | 100.00 |
COLUMBIA
| ❏ JC 36141 | Oasis | 1979 | 2.50 | 5.00 | 10.00 |
THIMBLE
| ❏ TLP-3 | Jim Messina | 197? | 3.75 | 7.50 | 15.00 |
WARNER BROS.
| ❏ BSK 3559 | Messina | 1981 | 2.50 | 5.00 | 10.00 |
| ❏ BSK 3559 [DJ] | Messina | 1981 | 5.00 | 10.00 | 20.00 |
—Promo-only version on Quiex II vinyl
| ❏ 23825 | One More Mile | 1983 | 2.50 | 5.00 | 10.00 |

METERS, THE Also see AARON NEVILLE.
45s
JOSIE
❏ 1001	Sophisticated Cissy/Sehorn's Farm	1968	2.50	5.00	10.00
❏ 1005	Cissy Strut/Here Comes the Meter Man	1969	2.50	5.00	10.00
❏ 1008	Ease Back/Ann	1969	2.50	5.00	10.00
❏ 1013	Dry Spell/Look-Ka Py Py	1969	2.50	5.00	10.00
❏ 1015	Look-Ka Py Py/This Is My Last Affair	1970	2.50	5.00	10.00
❏ 1018	Chicken Strut/Hey! Last Minute	1970	2.50	5.00	10.00
❏ 1021	Hand Clapping Song/Joog	1970	2.50	5.00	10.00
❏ 1024	A Message from the Meters/Zony Mash	1970	2.50	5.00	10.00
❏ 1026	Stretch Your Rubber Band/Groovy Lady	1971	2.50	5.00	10.00
❏ 1029	(The World Is a Bit Under the Weather) Doodle-Oop/I Need More Time	1971	2.50	5.00	10.00
❏ 1031	Good Old Funky Music/Sassy Lady	1971	2.50	5.00	10.00
REPRISE
❏ 1086	Do the Dirt/Smiling	1972	2.00	4.00	8.00
❏ 1106	Cabbage Alley/The Flower Song	1972	2.00	4.00	8.00
❏ 1135	Chug Chug Chug-A-Lug (Part 1)/Chug Chug Chug-A-Lug (Part 2)	1972	2.00	4.00	8.00
❏ 1307	Hey Pocky A-Way/Africa	1974	—	3.00	6.00
❏ 1314	People Say/Loving You Is On My Mind	1974	—	3.00	6.00
❏ 1338	Running Fast/They All Ask'd for You	1975	—	3.00	6.00
❏ 1357	Disco Is the Thing Today/Mister Moon	1976	—	3.00	6.00
❏ 1372	Trick Bag/Find Yourself	1976	—	3.00	6.00
WARNER BROS.
❏ 8434	Be My Lady/No More Okey Doke	1977	—	2.50	5.00
Albums
JOSIE
❏ JOS-4010	The Meters	1969	17.50	35.00	70.00
❏ JOS-4011	Look-Ka Py Py	1970	17.50	35.00	70.00
❏ JOS-4012	Struttin'	1970	17.50	35.00	70.00
REPRISE
❏ MS 2076	Cabbage Alley	1972	17.50	35.00	70.00
❏ MS 2200	Rejuvenation	1974	12.50	25.00	50.00
❏ MS 2228	Fire on the Bayou	1975	12.50	25.00	50.00
❏ MS 2252	Trick Bag	1976	12.50	25.00	50.00
ROUNDER
❏ 2103	Look-Ka Py Py	1990	5.00	10.00	20.00
—Reissue of Josie 4011
| ❏ 2104 | Good Old Funky Music | 1990 | 5.00 | 10.00 | 20.00 |
SUNDAZED
| ❏ LP 5081 | Kickback | 2001 | 3.00 | 6.00 | 12.00 |
VIRGO
| ❏ 12002 | The Best of the Meters | 1972 | 12.50 | 25.00 | 50.00 |
WARNER BROS.
| ❏ BS 3042 | New Directions | 1977 | 12.50 | 25.00 | 50.00 |

METRONOMES, THE (1)
45s
CADENCE
| ❏ 1310 | I Love My Girl/I'm Gonna Get Me a Girl Somehow | 1957 | 25.00 | 50.00 | 100.00 |
| ❏ 1339 | How Much I Love You/Dear Don | 1957 | 30.00 | 60.00 | 120.00 |

METRONOMES, THE (2)
45s
CHALLENGE
| ❏ 9157 | Hot Time/Tears, Tears, Tears | 1962 | 3.75 | 7.50 | 15.00 |
MAUREEN
| ❏ 1000 | My Dearest Darling/The Chickie-Goo | 1962 | 12.50 | 25.00 | 50.00 |

METRONOMES, THE (U) Could be completely different groups.
Albums
STRAND
| ❏ SL-1057 [M] | The Fabulous Metronomes
Sing the Standard Hits | 1962 | 7.50 | 15.00 | 30.00 |
| ❏ SLS-1057 [S] | The Fabulous Metronomes
Sing the Standard Hits | 1962 | 10.00 | 20.00 | 40.00 |
WYNNE
| ❏ 106 [M] | And Now... The Metronomes | 1960 | 30.00 | 60.00 | 120.00 |

METROS, THE (1)
45s
1-2-3
| ❏ 1720 | If You Can Feel/The Dampness from Your Kiss | 1969 | 2.50 | 5.00 | 10.00 |
RCA VICTOR
❏ 47-8994	Sweetest One/Time Changes Things	1966	3.75	7.50	15.00
❏ 47-9159	Since I Found My Baby/No Baby	1967	20.00	40.00	80.00
❏ 47-9331	Let's Groove/The Replacer	1967	6.25	12.50	25.00
Albums
RCA VICTOR
| ❏ LPM-3776 [M] | Sweetest One | 1967 | 20.00 | 40.00 | 80.00 |
| ❏ LSP-3776 [S] | Sweetest One | 1967 | 25.00 | 50.00 | 100.00 |

M

Number	Title (A Side/B Side)	Yr	VG	VG+	NM

METROS, THE (2)
45s
JUST
| ❏ 1502 | All of My Life/Lookin' | 1959 | 100.00 | 200.00 | 400.00 |

METROTONES, THE
45s
COLUMBIA
| ❏ 40420 | A-Ting-a-Ling/Tonight | 1955 | 5.00 | 10.00 | 20.00 |
| ❏ 40486 | Write Me Baby/Even Though | 1955 | 5.00 | 10.00 | 20.00 |
RESERVE
| ❏ 116 | Please Come Back/Skitter Skatter | 1957 | 62.50 | 125.00 | 250.00 |
7-Inch Extended Plays
COLUMBIA
❏ B-2026	(contents unknown)	1955	5.00	10.00	20.00
❏ B-2026 [PS]	Tops in Rock and Roll, Vol. 1	1955	5.00	10.00	20.00
❏ B-2027	(contents unknown)	1955	5.00	10.00	20.00
❏ B-2027 [PS]	Tops in Rock and Roll, Vol. 2	1955	5.00	10.00	20.00
Albums
COLUMBIA
| ❏ CL 6341 [10] | Tops in Rock and Roll | 1955 | 62.50 | 125.00 | 250.00 |

MFSB
45s
PHILADELPHIA INT'L.
❏ 3528	Family Affair/Layin' Low	1973	—	2.50	5.00
❏ 3540	TSOP (The Sound of Philadelphia)/ Something for Nothing	1974	—	2.50	5.00
❏ 3547	Love Is the Message/My One and Only Love	1974	—	2.50	5.00
❏ 3567	Sexy/Human Machine	1975	—	2.50	5.00
❏ 3576	T.L.C. (Tender Lovin' Care)/ Love Has No Time or Place	1975	—	2.50	5.00
❏ 3578	The Zip/My Mood	1975	—	2.50	5.00
❏ 3583	Smile Happy/When Your Love Is Gone	1976	—	2.50	5.00
❏ 3589	Philadelphia Freedom/South Philly	1976	—	2.50	5.00
❏ 3600	Summertime And I'm Feelin' Mellow/Hot Summer Nights	1976	—	2.50	5.00
❏ 3607	We Got the Time/(B-side unknown)	1976	—	2.50	5.00
❏ 3626	I'm On Your Side/Picnic in the Park	1977	—	2.50	5.00
❏ 3641	K-Jee/My Mood	1978	—	2.50	5.00
❏ 3650	Use Ta Be My Guy/Redwood Beach	1978	—	2.50	5.00
❏ 3663	Let's Party Down/To Be in Love	1978	—	2.50	5.00
❏ 3668	Dance with Me Tonight/Is It Something I Said	1979	—	2.50	5.00
TSOP
❏ 02022	Mysteries of the World/Thank You Miss Scott	1981	—	2.00	4.00
❏ 4797	Manhattan Skyline/Metamorphosis	1980	—	2.00	4.00
Albums
PHILADELPHIA INT'L.
❏ KZ 32046	MFSB	1973	2.50	5.00	10.00
❏ KZ 32707	Love Is the Message	1974	2.50	5.00	10.00
❏ ZQ 32707 [Q]	Love Is the Message	1974	4.50	9.00	18.00
❏ PZ 33158	Universal Love	1975	2.50	5.00	10.00
❏ PZ 33845	Philadelphia Freedom	1975	2.50	5.00	10.00
❏ PZQ 33845 [Q]	Philadelphia Freedom	1975	4.50	9.00	18.00
❏ PZ 34238	Summertime	1976	2.50	5.00	10.00
❏ PZ 34658	The End of Phase One	1977	2.50	5.00	10.00
❏ JZ 35516	The Gamble-Huff Orchestra	1978	2.50	5.00	10.00
TSOP
❏ JZ 36405	Mysteries of the World	1980	2.50	5.00	10.00

MICHAEL AND THE MESSENGERS See THE MESSENGERS (1); THE MESSENGERS (4).

MICHAELS, LEE
45s
A&M
❏ 911	Sounding the Sleep/Love	1968	—	3.00	6.00
❏ 912	Tomorrow/Sounding the Sleep	1968	—	3.00	6.00
❏ 942	If I Lose You/My Friends	1968	—	3.00	6.00
❏ 1048	Goodbye, Goodbye/The War	1969	—	2.50	5.00
❏ 1095	Heighty Ho/Want My Baby	1969	—	2.50	5.00
❏ 1219	Uummmm My Lady/What Now America	1970	—	2.50	5.00
❏ 1262	Do You Know What I Mean/Keep the Circle Turning	1971	—	2.50	5.00
❏ 1262 [PS]	Do You Know What I Mean/Keep the Circle Turning	1971	2.50	5.00	10.00
❏ 1303	Can I Get a Witness/You Are What You Do	1971	—	2.00	4.00
❏ 1303 [PS]	Can I Get a Witness/You Are What You Do	1971	2.50	5.00	10.00
❏ 1326	Hold On to Freedom/Own Special Way	1972	—	2.00	4.00
❏ 1448	Rock Me Baby/Heighty Ho	1973	—	2.00	4.00
COLUMBIA
❏ 45874	Same Old Song/Rock and Roll Community	1973	—	2.50	5.00
Albums
A&M
| ❏ SP-3158 | Lee Michaels | 198? | 2.00 | 4.00 | 8.00 |
—Budget-line reissue
❏ SP-3518	Live	1973	3.75	7.50	15.00
❏ SP-4140	Carnival of Life	1968	10.00	20.00	40.00
❏ SP-4152	Recital	1968	5.00	10.00	20.00
❏ SP-4199	Lee Michaels	1969	3.75	7.50	15.00
❏ SP-4249	Barrel	1970	3.75	7.50	15.00
❏ SP-4302	5th	1971	3.75	7.50	15.00
❏ SP-4336	Space and First Takes	1972	3.75	7.50	15.00
COLUMBIA
❏ CQ 32275 [Q]	Nice Day for Something	1973	5.00	10.00	20.00
❏ KC 32275	Nice Day for Something	1973	3.00	6.00	12.00
❏ KC 32846	Tailface	1974	3.00	6.00	12.00

MICHAELS, MARILYN
45s
RCA VICTOR
| ❏ 47-7771 | Tell Tommy I Miss Him/ Everyone Was There But You | 1960 | 5.00 | 10.00 | 20.00 |
| ❏ 47-7831 | Past the Age of Innocence/Danny | 1961 | 3.75 | 7.50 | 15.00 |

MICKEY AND KITTY MICKEY BAKER (ex-MICKEY AND SYLVIA) and Kitty Noble.
45s
ATLANTIC
❏ 2024	Ooh-Sha-Lala/The Kid Brother	1959	3.75	7.50	15.00
❏ 2036	First Love/St. Louis Blues	1959	3.75	7.50	15.00
❏ 2046	My Reverie/Buttercup	1959	3.75	7.50	15.00

MICKEY AND SYLVIA Also see MICKEY BAKER; SYLVIA (1).
45s
ALL PLATINUM
| ❏ 2307 | Lovedrops/Because You Do It to Me | 1969 | — | 3.00 | 6.00 |
| ❏ 2310 | Anytime/Souling with Mickey and Sylvia | 1969 | — | 3.00 | 6.00 |
CAT
| ❏ 102 | Fine Love/Speedy Life | 1954 | 10.00 | 20.00 | 40.00 |
—As "Little" Sylvia Vanderpool and Mickey Baker
GROOVE
| ❏ 0164 | No Good Lover/Walkin' in the Rain | 1956 | 7.50 | 15.00 | 30.00 |
| ❏ 0175 | Love Is Strange/I'm Going Home | 1956 | 7.50 | 15.00 | 30.00 |
KING
| ❏ 5737 | Baby, Let's Dance/Oh Yea, Ah Ah | 1963 | 3.00 | 6.00 | 12.00 |
| ❏ 6006 | Love Is Strange/Darling | 1965 | 2.50 | 5.00 | 10.00 |
RAINBOW
| ❏ 316 | I'm So Glad/Se De Boom Run Dun | 1955 | 7.50 | 15.00 | 30.00 |
| ❏ 318 | Forever and a Day/Ride, Sally, Ride | 1955 | 7.50 | 15.00 | 30.00 |
RCA
| ❏ 5224-7-RX | Love Is Strange/(I've Had) The Time of My Life | 1987 | — | — | 3.00 |
—B-side by Bill Medley and Jennifer Warnes
RCA VICTOR
| ❏ 37-7877 | Love Is the Only Thing/Love Lesson | 1961 | 12.50 | 25.00 | 50.00 |
—"Compact Single 33" (small hole, plays at LP speed)
❏ 47-7403	To the Valley/Oh Yeah! Uh-Huh	1958	10.00	—	20.00
❏ 47-7774 [M]	Sweeter As the Days Go By/Mommy Out De Light	1960	3.75	7.50	15.00
❏ 47-7811 [M]	What Would I Do/This Is My Story	1960	5.00	10.00	20.00
❏ 47-7877	Love Is the Only Thing/Love Lesson	1961	3.75	7.50	15.00
❏ 47-8517	Let's Shake Some More/Gypsy	1965	3.00	6.00	12.00
❏ 47-8582	Fallin' in Love/From the Beginning of Time	1965	3.00	6.00	12.00
❏ 61-7774 [S]	Sweeter As the Days Go By/Mommy Out De Light	1960	10.00	20.00	40.00
—"Living Stereo" (large hole, plays at 45 rpm)
| ❏ 61-7811 [S] | What Would I Do/This Is My Story | 1960 | 10.00 | 20.00 | 40.00 |
—"Living Stereo" (large hole, plays at 45 rpm)
| ❏ APAO-0080 | Love Is Strange/Dearest | 1973 | — | 3.00 | 6.00 |
STANG
| ❏ 5004 | Rocky Raccoon/Souling with Mickey and Sylvia | 1969 | 2.00 | 4.00 | 8.00 |
| ❏ 5047 | Baby You're So Fine/Anytime You Want To | 1973 | — | 3.00 | 6.00 |
VIK
❏ 0252	Love Is Strange/I'm Going Home	1957	7.50	15.00	30.00
❏ 0267	There Oughta Be a Law/Dearest	1957	6.25	12.50	25.00
❏ 0280	Two Shadows on Your Window/Love Will Make You Fail in School	1957	6.25	12.50	25.00
❏ 0290	Love Is a Treasure/Let's Have a Picnic	1957	6.25	12.50	25.00
❏ 0297	There'll Be No Backin' Out/Where Is My Honey	1957	6.25	12.50	25.00
❏ 0324	Rock and Stroll Room/Bewildered	1958	5.00	10.00	20.00
❏ 0334	It's You I Love/True, True Love	1958	5.00	10.00	20.00
WILLOW
❏ 23000	Baby, You're So Fine/Lovedrops	1961	3.75	7.50	15.00
❏ 23002	Darling (I Miss You So)/I'm Guilty	1961	3.75	7.50	15.00
❏ 23004	Since I Fell for You/He Gave Me Everything	1962	3.75	7.50	15.00
❏ 23006	Love Is Strange/Walking in the Rain	1962	3.75	7.50	15.00
7-Inch Extended Plays
GROOVE
| ❏ EGA-18 | Love Is Strange/I'm Going Home//Walkin' in the Rain/No Good Lover | 1957 | 37.50 | 75.00 | 150.00 |
| ❏ EGA-18 [PS] | Love Is Strange | 1957 | 37.50 | 75.00 | 150.00 |
VIK
| ❏ 262 | *There Oughta Be a Law/I'm So Glad/Dearest/ Se De Boom Run Dun | 1957 | 20.00 | 40.00 | 80.00 |
| ❏ 262 [PS] | Love Is Strange | 1957 | 20.00 | 40.00 | 80.00 |
Albums
RCA CAMDEN
| ❏ CAL-863 [M] | Love Is Strange | 1965 | 12.50 | 25.00 | 50.00 |
| ❏ CAS-863(e) [R] | Love Is Strange | 1965 | 7.50 | 15.00 | 30.00 |
RCA VICTOR
| ❏ APM1-0327 | Do It Again | 1973 | 3.00 | 6.00 | 12.00 |
VIK
| ❏ LX-1102 [M] | New Sounds | 1957 | 100.00 | 200.00 | 400.00 |

MIDDLE OF THE ROAD
45s
RCA VICTOR
❏ 74-0407	Chirpy Chirpy Cheep Cheep/Rainin' 'N Painin'	1970	—	2.50	5.00
❏ 74-0539	Tweedle Dee, Tweedle Dum/Give It Time	1971	—	2.00	4.00
❏ 74-0612	Soley Soley/To Remind Me	1971	—	2.00	4.00
❏ 74-0732	On This Land/Talk of All the U.S.A.	1972	—	2.00	4.00
Albums
RCA VICTOR
| ❏ LSP-4674 | Acceleration | 1972 | 3.00 | 6.00 | 12.00 |

MIDDLETON, TONY Also see THE WILLOWS.
45s
A&M
| ❏ 1084 | Angela/Keep On Dancing | 1969 | 5.00 | 10.00 | 20.00 |
| ❏ 1124 | Harlem Lady/Sound of Goodbye | 1969 | 3.75 | 7.50 | 15.00 |
ABC-PARAMOUNT
| ❏ 10695 | You Spoiled My Reputation/ If I Could Write a Song | 1965 | 7.50 | 15.00 | 30.00 |
ALFA
| ❏ 113 | My Home Town/Please Take Me | 1962 | 3.00 | 6.00 | 12.00 |
ALTO
| ❏ 2001 | Untouchable/I Need You | 1960 | 3.00 | 6.00 | 12.00 |
BIG TOP
| ❏ 3037 | Unchained Melody/Sweet Baby of Mine | 1960 | 7.50 | 15.00 | 30.00 |
ELDORADO
| ❏ 508 | First Taste of Love/Only My Heart | 1957 | 7.50 | 15.00 | 30.00 |

Number	Title (A Side/B Side)	Yr	VG	VG+	NM
GONE					
☐ 5015	Let's Fall in Love/Say Yeah	1957	15.00	30.00	60.00
MALA					
☐ 544	Out of This World/My Baby Likes to Boogaloo	1966	6.25	12.50	25.00
MGM					
☐ 13493	Don't Ever Leave Me/To the Ends of the Earth	1966	10.00	20.00	40.00
MR. G					
☐ 811	Let Me Down Easy (Part 1)/Let Me Down Easy (Part 2)	1968	3.00	6.00	12.00
☐ 815	Good Morning World/(B-side unknown)	1968	3.00	6.00	12.00
PHILIPS					
☐ 40151	I Need You Tonight/Send Me Away	1963	3.00	6.00	12.00
☐ 40184	Too Hot to Handle/I Just Couldn't Help Myself	1964	3.00	6.00	12.00
ROULETTE					
☐ 4345	Is It This or Is It That/I'm Gonna Try Love One More Time	1961	6.25	12.50	25.00
ROYAL FLUSH					
☐ 102	Lady Fingers/A Garden in the Ghetto	1976	—	3.00	6.00
SAXONY					
☐ 104	I'm On My Way/(B-side unknown)	1958	12.50	25.00	50.00
SCEPTER					
☐ 12290	Border Song (Holy Moses)/Silliest People	1970	2.50	5.00	10.00
TOY					
☐ 3803	Rock and Roll Lullaby/Sittin' in the Sunshine	1972	2.00	4.00	8.00
TRIUMPH					
☐ 600	Count Your Blessings (See What Love Has Done)/I Just Want Somebody	1959	6.25	12.50	25.00
☐ 605	The Universe/Blackjack	1959	6.25	12.50	25.00
UNITED ARTISTS					
☐ 410	Drifting/Memories Are Made of This	1962	3.75	7.50	15.00

MIDLER, BETTE
12-Inch Singles

Number	Title (A Side/B Side)	Yr	VG	VG+	NM
ATLANTIC					
☐ DSKO 187 [DJ]	Married Men (7:58) (5:32)	1979	3.00	6.00	12.00
☐ 218 [DJ]	Big Noise from Winnetka (same on both sides)	1979	2.50	5.00	10.00
☐ 548 [DJ]	Favorite Waste of Time/Only in Miami	1983	2.50	5.00	10.00
☐ 578 [DJ]	Beast of Burden (same on both sides)	1983	2.50	5.00	10.00
☐ 1655 [DJ]	Moonlight Dancing (3 versions)	1990	—	2.50	5.00
☐ DK 4800	Married Men/Bang You're Dead	1979	3.00	6.00	12.00

45s

Number	Title (A Side/B Side)	Yr	VG	VG+	NM
ATLANTIC					
☐ 2928	Do You Want to Dance/Superstar	1972	—	2.50	5.00
☐ 2964	Boogie Woogie Bugle Boy/Delta Dawn	1973	—	2.50	5.00
☐ 2980	Friends/Chapel of Love	1973	—	2.50	5.00
☐ 3004	In the Mood/Drinking Again	1974	—	2.50	5.00
☐ 3319	Stranger in the Night/Somedi It Vendredi	1976	—	2.00	4.00
☐ 3325	Old Cape Cod/Tragedy	1976	—	2.00	4.00
☐ 3379	Let Me Just Follow Behind/You're Movin' Out Today	1976	—	2.00	4.00
☐ 3431	Storybook Children/Empty Bed Blues	1977	—	2.00	4.00
☐ 3475	Paradise/Red	1978	—	2.00	4.00
☐ 3582	Married Men/Bang, You're Dead	1979	—	2.00	4.00
☐ 3616	Hang On In There Baby/Cradle Days	1979	—	2.00	4.00
☐ 3628	Rain/Big Noise from Winnetka	1979	—	2.00	4.00
☐ 3643	When a Man Loves a Woman/Love Me with a Feeling	1980	—	2.00	4.00
☐ 3656	The Rose/Stay with Me	1980	—	2.00	4.00
☐ 3656 [PS]	The Rose/Stay with Me	1980	—	2.50	5.00
☐ 3771	My Mother's Eyes/Chapel of Love	1980	—	2.00	4.00
☐ 87572	Every Road Leads Back to You/I Remember You're-Dixie's Dream	1991	—	—	3.00
☐ 87820	From a Distance/One More Round	1990	—	2.00	4.00
☐ 87825	Night and Day/The Girl Is On to You	1990	—	—	3.00
☐ 88972	Wind Beneath My Wings/Oh Industry	1989	—	—	3.00
☐ 88972 [PS]	Wind Beneath My Wings/Oh Industry	1989	—	2.50	5.00
☐ 88976	Under the Boardwalk/The Friendship Theme	1989	—	—	3.00
☐ 88976	Under the Boardwalk/Otto Titsling	1989	—	2.00	4.00
☐ 88976 [PS]	Under the Boardwalk/The Friendship Theme	1989	—	2.00	4.00
☐ 89712	Beast of Burden/Come Back Jimmy Dean	1984	—	—	3.00
☐ 89761	Favorite Waste of Time/My Eye on You	1983	—	—	3.00
☐ 89789	All I Need to Know/My Eye on You	1983	—	—	3.00
☐ 89789 [PS]	All I Need to Know/My Eye on You	1983	—	2.00	4.00

Albums

Number	Title (A Side/B Side)	Yr	VG	VG+	NM
ATLANTIC					
☐ 7238 [M]	The Divine Miss M	1972	7.50	15.00	30.00
—Mono is promo only; white label, "dj copy monaural" sticker on stereo cover					
☐ QD 7238 [Q]	The Divine Miss M	1973	4.50	9.00	18.00
☐ SD 7238 [S]	The Divine Miss M	1972	2.50	5.00	10.00
☐ SD 7270	Bette Midler	1973	2.50	5.00	10.00
☐ SD 2-9000 [(2)]	Live! At Last	1977	3.00	6.00	12.00
☐ SD 16004	Thighs and Whispers	1979	2.50	5.00	10.00
☐ SD 16010	The Rose	1979	2.50	5.00	10.00
☐ SD 16022	Divine Madness	1980	2.50	5.00	10.00
☐ SD 18155	Songs for the New Depression	1976	2.50	5.00	10.00
☐ SD 19155	Broken Blossom	1977	2.50	5.00	10.00
☐ 80070	No Frills	1983	2.50	5.00	10.00
☐ 81291	Mud Will Be Flung Tonight	1985	2.50	5.00	10.00
☐ 81933	Beaches	1988	2.50	5.00	10.00
☐ 82129	Some People's Lives	1990	3.00	6.00	12.00

MIDNIGHT ANGELS, THE
45s

Number	Title (A Side/B Side)	Yr	VG	VG+	NM
APEX					
☐ 77073	I'm Sufferin'/In the Moonlight	1967	7.50	15.00	30.00
☐ 77073 [PS]	I'm Sufferin'/In the Moonlight	1967	10.00	20.00	40.00

MIDNIGHT STRING QUARTET
45s

Number	Title (A Side/B Side)	Yr	VG	VG+	NM
VIVA					
☐ 606	You Don't Have to Say You Love Me/The Lonely Bull	1966	—	3.00	6.00
☐ 616	Prophesy of Love/I Hear a Smyphony	1967	—	3.00	6.00
☐ 622	The Little Drummer Boy/Silent Night	1967	—	3.00	6.00
☐ 628	Midnight Memories/Classical Gas	1968	—	3.00	6.00

Albums

Number	Title (A Side/B Side)	Yr	VG	VG+	NM
VIVA					
☐ 2571 [(2)]	Best of the Midnight String Quartet	1971	3.00	6.00	12.00
☐ V-6001 [M]	Rhapsodies for Young Lovers	1966	3.00	6.00	12.00
☐ VS-6001 [S]	Rhapsodies for Young Lovers	1966	2.50	5.00	10.00
☐ V-6004 [M]	Spanish Rhapsodies for Young Lovers	1967	3.00	6.00	12.00
☐ V-6008 [M]	Rhapsodies for Young Lovers, Volume Two	1967	3.00	6.00	12.00
☐ V-6010 [M]	Christmas Rhapsodies for Young Lovers	1967	3.75	7.50	15.00
☐ V-6013 [M]	Love Rhapsodies	1968	3.75	7.50	15.00
☐ V-36004 [S]	Spanish Rhapsodies for Young Lovers	1967	2.50	5.00	10.00
☐ V-36008 [S]	Rhapsodies for Young Lovers, Volume Two	1967	2.50	5.00	10.00
☐ V-36010 [S]	Christmas Rhapsodies for Young Lovers	1967	2.50	5.00	10.00
☐ V-36013 [S]	Love Rhapsodies	1968	2.50	5.00	10.00
☐ V-36015	The Look of Love and Other Rhapsodies for Young Lovers	1968	2.50	5.00	10.00
☐ V-36019	Goodnight My Love and Other Rhapsodies for Young Lovers	1969	2.50	5.00	10.00
☐ V-36022	Rhapsodies for Young Lovers, Volume Three	1969	2.50	5.00	10.00
☐ V-36024	Chamber Music for Young Lovers	1969	2.50	5.00	10.00

MIDNIGHTERS, THE Also see HANK BALLARD AND THE MIDNIGHTERS; THE ROYALS (1).
45s

Number	Title (A Side/B Side)	Yr	VG	VG+	NM
FEDERAL					
☐ 12169	Work With Me Annie/Until I Die	1954	10.00	20.00	40.00
—All-green label; as "The Midnighters (Formerly Known As the Royals)"					
☐ 12169	Work With Me Annie/Until I Die	1954	25.00	50.00	100.00
—Silver top label; as " The Midnighters (Formerly Known As the Royals)"					
☐ 12177	Give It Up/That Woman	1954	20.00	40.00	80.00
—As "The Midnighters Formerly the Royals"					
☐ 12185	Sexy Ways/Don't Say Your Last Goodbye	1954	20.00	40.00	80.00
—As "The Midnighters Formerly the Royals"					
☐ 12195	Annie Had a Baby/She's the One	1954	15.00	30.00	60.00
☐ 12200	Annie's Aunt Fanny/Crazy Loving	1954	15.00	30.00	60.00
☐ 12202	Tell Them/Stingy Little Thing	1954	15.00	30.00	60.00
☐ 12205	She's the One/Moonrise	1955	15.00	30.00	60.00
☐ 12210	Ashamed of Myself/Ring-a-Ling-Ling	1955	15.00	30.00	60.00
☐ 12220	Why Are We Apart/Switchie, Witchie, Titchie	1955	15.00	30.00	60.00
☐ 12224	Henry's Got Flat Feet (Can't Dance No More)/Whatsoever You Do	1955	15.00	30.00	60.00
☐ 12227	It's Love Baby (24 Hours a Day)/Looka Here	1955	15.00	30.00	60.00
☐ 12230	Give It Up/That Woman	1955	15.00	30.00	60.00
☐ 12240	Rock and Roll Wedding/That House on the Hill	1955	15.00	30.00	60.00
☐ 12243	Don't Change Your Pretty Ways/We'll Never Meet Again	1955	15.00	30.00	60.00
☐ 12251	Partners for Life/Sweet Mama, Do Right	1956	15.00	30.00	60.00
☐ 12260	Rock Granny Roll/Open Up the Back Door	1956	15.00	30.00	60.00
☐ 12270	Tore Up Over You/Early One Morning	1956	12.50	25.00	50.00
☐ 12285	I'll Be Home Some Day/Come On and Get It	1957	12.50	25.00	50.00
☐ 12288	Let Me Hold Your Hand/Oh Bah Baby	1957	12.50	25.00	50.00
☐ 12293	E Basta Cosi/In the Doorway Crying	1957	12.50	25.00	50.00
☐ 12299	Oh, So Happy/Is Your Love for Real	1957	10.00	20.00	40.00
☐ 12305	Let 'Em Roll/What Made You Change Your Mind	1957	10.00	20.00	40.00
☐ 12317	Stay By My Side/Daddy's Little Baby	1958	10.00	20.00	40.00
☐ 12339	Baby Please/Ow-Wow-Oo-Wee	1958	10.00	20.00	40.00

7-Inch Extended Plays

Number	Title (A Side/B Side)	Yr	VG	VG+	NM
FEDERAL					
☐ 333	Work with Me Annie/Moonrise// Sexy Ways/Get It	1955	37.50	75.00	150.00
—All-green label					
☐ 333	Work with Me Annie/Moonrise// Sexy Ways/Get It	1955	75.00	150.00	300.00
—Green label, silver top					
☐ 333 [PS]	The Midnighters Sing Their Greatest Hits	1955	50.00	100.00	200.00
—Pink cover					
☐ 333 [PS]	The Midnighters Sing Their Greatest Hits	1955	50.00	100.00	200.00
—Purple cover					

Albums

Number	Title (A Side/B Side)	Yr	VG	VG+	NM
FEDERAL					
☐ 295-90 [10]	Their Greatest Hits	1954	4000.	6000.	8000.
☐ 541 [M]	Their Greatest Hits	1955	250.00	500.00	1000.
—Yellow cover					
☐ 541 [M]	Their Greatest Hits	1955	375.00	750.00	1500.
—Red cover					
☐ 581 [M]	The Midnighters, Volume 2	1955	300.00	600.00	1200.
KING					
☐ 541 [M]	Their Greatest Jukebox Hits	1958	100.00	200.00	400.00
—Crownless black label, "King" is two inches wide on label					
☐ 541 [M]	Their Greatest Jukebox Hits	196?	50.00	100.00	200.00
—Reissue with Hank Ballard on cover					
☐ 541 [M]	Their Greatest Jukebox Hits	196?	75.00	150.00	300.00
—Crownless black label, "King" is three inches wide on label. Above two have a girl on the cover.					
☐ 581 [M]	The Midnighters, Volume 2	1958	75.00	150.00	300.00
—Crownless black label, "King" is two inches wide on label					
☐ 581 [M]	The Midnighters, Volume 2	196?	50.00	100.00	200.00
—Crownless black label, "King" is three inches wide on label					

MIDNIGHTERS, THE (2)
45s

Number	Title (A Side/B Side)	Yr	VG	VG+	NM
20TH FOX					
☐ 182	The Road Home/Taco	1960	3.00	6.00	12.00

MIGHTY AVENGERS, THE
45s

Number	Title (A Side/B Side)	Yr	VG	VG+	NM
PRESS					
☐ 9746	Blue Turns to Grey/I'm Lost Without You	1965	2.50	5.00	10.00

MIGHTY BABY
Albums

Number	Title (A Side/B Side)	Yr	VG	VG+	NM
HEAD					
☐ LPS-025	Mighty Baby	1969	15.00	30.00	60.00

MIGHTY CLOUDS OF JOY
12-Inch Singles

Number	Title (A Side/B Side)	Yr	VG	VG+	NM
EPIC					
☐ 50693	Joy in These Changing Times/(Instrumental)	1979	3.00	6.00	12.00

M

Number	Title (A Side/B Side)	Yr	VG	VG+	NM
45s					
ABC					
❏ 12164	Mighty High/Touch My Soul	1976	—	2.00	4.00
❏ 12196	You Are So Beautiful/Everything Is All	1976	—	2.00	4.00
❏ 12241	There's Love in the World (Tell the Lonely People)/(B-side unknown)	1976	—	2.00	4.00
❏ 12281	God Is Not Dead/Music Is My Way of Life	1977	—	2.00	4.00
❏ 12322	Look on the Bright Side/(B-side unknown)	1978	—	2.00	4.00
ABC DUNHILL					
❏ 15012	Time/(B-side unknown)	1974	—	2.50	5.00
❏ 15025	Mighty Cloud of Joy/Everything Is Going Up	1974	—	2.50	5.00
EPIC					
❏ 50690	Joy in These Changing Times/We're Gonna Have a Good Time	1979	—	2.00	4.00
❏ 50691	I've Been in the Storm Too Long/We're Blessed	1979	—	2.00	4.00
❏ 50788	I Get a Blessing Every Day/Rainy Day Friend	1979	—	2.00	4.00
❏ 50875	What a Difference You've Made in My Life/We're Blessed	1980	—	2.00	4.00
MYRRH					
❏ 241	Glow Love/(B-side unknown)	1982	—	2.00	4.00
PEACOCK					
❏ 1823	Jesus Lead Us Safely/Ain't Got Long Here	1961	3.00	6.00	12.00
❏ 1839	I'll Be Alright/My Religion	1961	3.00	6.00	12.00
❏ 1857	Time Has Changed/I Love Jesus	1962	2.50	5.00	10.00
❏ 1869	Family Circle/None But the Righteous	1962	2.50	5.00	10.00
❏ 1895	Glory Hallelujah/Lord Hold My Hand	1962	2.50	5.00	10.00
❏ 1896	Nearer to Thee/You'll Never Know	1962	2.50	5.00	10.00
❏ 3025	I'll Go (Part 1)/I'll Go (Part 2)	1964	2.50	5.00	10.00
❏ 3050	A Friend in Jesus/Two Wings	1965	2.50	5.00	10.00
❏ 3064	He's Able/Swing Low	1965	2.50	5.00	10.00
❏ 3077	See How They Done My Lord/Look for Me in Heaven	1966	2.50	5.00	10.00
❏ 3080	Nobody Can Turn Me Around/Touch Me Lord	1966	2.50	5.00	10.00
❏ 3099	I'm Glad About It/Let Jesus Lead You	1966	2.50	5.00	10.00
❏ 3132	Somewhere Around God's Throne/The Holy Ghost	1967	2.00	4.00	8.00
❏ 3144	Pray for Me/Call Him Up	1968	2.00	4.00	8.00
❏ 3167	How Far Have I Strayed/Just to Behold His Face	1969	2.00	4.00	8.00
❏ 3175	In This World Alone/Why Do Men Treat the Lord	1970	2.00	4.00	8.00
❏ 3189	Heavy Load/I'll Be Alright Someday	1972	—	3.00	6.00
Albums					
ABC					
❏ D-899	Kickin'	1975	2.50	5.00	10.00
❏ D-986	The Truth Is the Power	1976	2.50	5.00	10.00
❏ D-1038	Live and Direct	1977	2.50	5.00	10.00
ABC DUNHILL					
❏ DSX-50177	It's Time	1974	2.50	5.00	10.00
HOB					
❏ 288	"Live" Zion Songs	196?	3.75	7.50	15.00
KING					
❏ SG3-1107	Out Talking to Yourself	1970	3.75	7.50	15.00
MCA					
❏ 1091 [(2)]	The Very Best of Mighty Clouds of Joy	198?	2.50	5.00	10.00
❏ 28008	Family Circle	198?	2.00	4.00	8.00
—Reissue of Peacock 114					
❏ 28012	The Bright Side	198?	2.00	4.00	8.00
—Reissue of Peacock 121					
❏ 28017	Mighty Clouds of Joy At the Music Hall	198?	2.00	4.00	8.00
—Reissue of Peacock 134					
❏ 28019	The Best of Mighty Clouds of Joy	198?	2.00	4.00	8.00
—Reissue of Peacock 136					
❏ 28025	The Untouchables	198?	2.00	4.00	8.00
—Reissue of Peacock 151					
❏ 28028	Songs of Rev. Julius Cheeks and the Nightingales	198?	2.00	4.00	8.00
—Reissue of Peacock 163					
❏ 28030	God Bless America	198?	2.00	4.00	8.00
—Reissue of Peacock 170					
❏ 28032	Live at the Apollo	198?	2.00	4.00	8.00
—Reissue of Peacock 173					
❏ 28040	The Best of Mighty Clouds of Joy — Volume 2	198?	2.00	4.00	8.00
MYRRH					
❏ MSB-6663	Cloudburst	1980	2.50	5.00	10.00
❏ MSB-6681	The Truth Is the Power	1981	2.50	5.00	10.00
❏ MSB-6694	Miracle Man	1982	2.50	5.00	10.00
❏ MSB-6712	Request Line	1983	2.50	5.00	10.00
❏ WR-8121	Mighty Clouds Alive	1984	2.50	5.00	10.00
❏ WR-8122	Sing and Shout	1984	2.50	5.00	10.00
PEACOCK					
❏ 114	Family Circle	196?	5.00	10.00	20.00
❏ 121	The Bright Side	196?	5.00	10.00	20.00
❏ 134	Mighty Clouds of Joy At the Music Hall	196?	5.00	10.00	20.00
❏ 136	The Best of Mighty Clouds of Joy	196?	5.00	10.00	20.00
❏ 151	The Untouchables	196?	5.00	10.00	20.00
❏ 161	Out Talking to Yourself	196?	5.00	10.00	20.00
❏ 163	Songs of Rev. Julius Cheeks and the Nightingales	196?	5.00	10.00	20.00
❏ 170	God Bless America	1971	3.75	7.50	15.00
❏ 173	Live at the Apollo	1972	3.75	7.50	15.00
PRIORITY					
❏ RV 37707	Changing Times	1982	2.50	5.00	10.00

MIGHTY MARVELOWS, THE See THE MARVELOWS.

MIGIL FIVE, THE

Number	Title (A Side/B Side)	Yr	VG	VG+	NM
45s					
CAMEO					
❏ 316	Mockin' Bird Hill/Long Ago (And Far Away)	1964	2.50	5.00	10.00
HICKORY					
❏ 1292	Your Cheatin' Heart/Boys and Girls	1965	2.50	5.00	10.00
❏ 1334	I'm in Love Again/One Hundred Years	1965	2.50	5.00	10.00
MERCURY					
❏ 72301	Near You/Don't Wanna Go On Shaking	1964	2.50	5.00	10.00

Number	Title (A Side/B Side)	Yr	VG	VG+	NM
MIKE AND THE JAYS					
45s					
DOYL					
❏ 1001	My Only Girl/Dingle Dangle Doll	1960	20.00	40.00	80.00
MIKE AND THE MODIFIERS					
45s					
GORDY					
❏ 7006	I Found Myself a Brand New Baby/It's Too Bad	1962	15.00	30.00	60.00
MIKE AND THE UTOPIANS					
45s					
CEE JAY					
❏ 574	Erlene/I Found a Penny	1958	37.50	75.00	150.00
❏ 574	Erlene/I Wish	1958	75.00	150.00	300.00

MIKE, JOHN AND BILL "Mike" is MICHAEL NESMITH, later of THE MONKEES.

Number	Title (A Side/B Side)	Yr	VG	VG+	NM
45s					
OMNIBUS					
❏ 239	How Can You Kiss Me/Just a Little Love	1963	75.00	150.00	300.00
MILANO, BOBBY					
45s					
CAPITOL					
❏ F-3012	A King or a Slave/If You Cared	1955	5.00	10.00	20.00
CHALLENGE					
❏ 59005	Life Begins at 4 O'Clock/Double Talking Baby	1958	25.00	50.00	100.00
TIME					
❏ 1019	Ruby/Do I Love You	1960	5.00	10.00	20.00
WARNER BROS.					
❏ 5027	Water Under the Bridge/My Yiddishe Momma	1959	3.00	6.00	12.00
MILBURN, AMOS					
45s					
ALADDIN					
❏ 3014	Chicken Shack Boogie/It Took a Long, Long Time	1950	50.00	100.00	200.00
—78 originally released in 1948					
❏ 3018	Bewildered/A and M Blues	1950	30.00	60.00	120.00
—78 originally released in 1948					
❏ 3068	Bad, Bad Whiskey/I'm Going to Tell My Mama	1950	125.00	250.00	500.00
—Note: Amos Milburn singles on Aladdin before 3068 are unconfirmed on 45 rpm except those listed					
❏ 3080	Let's Rock a While/Tears, Tears, Tears	1951	20.00	40.00	80.00
❏ 3090	Everybody Clap Hands/That Was Your Last Mistake	1951	20.00	40.00	80.00
❏ 3093	Ain't Nothin' Shaking/Just One More Drink	1951	20.00	40.00	80.00
❏ 3105	She's Gone Again/Boogie Woogie	1951	20.00	40.00	80.00
❏ 3124	Thinking and Drinking/Trouble in Mind	1952	20.00	40.00	80.00
❏ 3125	Flying Home/Put Something in My Hand	1952	20.00	40.00	80.00
❏ 3133	I Won't Be Your Fool Anymore/Roll Mr. Jelly	1952	20.00	40.00	80.00
❏ 3146	Button Your Lip/Everything I Do Is Wrong	1952	20.00	40.00	80.00
❏ 3150	Kiss Me Again/Greyhound	1952	20.00	40.00	80.00
❏ 3159	Rock, Rock, Rock/Boo Hoo	1952	15.00	30.00	60.00
❏ 3164	Let Me Go Home, Whiskey/Three Times a Fool	1953	15.00	30.00	60.00
❏ 3168	Long, Long Day/Please Mr. Johnson	1953	15.00	30.00	60.00
❏ 3197	One Scotch, One Bourbon, One Beer/What Can I Do	1953	25.00	50.00	100.00
❏ 3218	Good, Good Whiskey/Let's Have a Party	1954	20.00	40.00	80.00
❏ 3226	How Could You Hurt Me So/Rocky Mountain	1954	15.00	30.00	60.00
❏ 3240	Milk and Water/I'm Still a Fool for You	1954	15.00	30.00	60.00
❏ 3248	Glory of Love/Baby, Baby All the Time	1954	15.00	30.00	60.00
❏ 3253	Vicious, Vicious Vodka/I Done Done It	1954	15.00	30.00	60.00
❏ 3269	That's It/One, Two, Three Everybody	1954	15.00	30.00	60.00
❏ 3281	Why Don't You Do Right/I Love You Anyway	1955	10.00	20.00	40.00
❏ 3293	All Is Well/My Happiness Depends on You	1955	10.00	20.00	40.00
❏ 3306	House Party/I Guess I'll Go	1955	10.00	20.00	40.00
❏ 3320	French Fried Potatoes and Ketchup/I Need Someone	1956	10.00	20.00	40.00
❏ 3332	Chicken Shack Boogie/Juice, Juice, Juice	1956	10.00	20.00	40.00
❏ 3340	Girl of My Dreams/Everyday of the Week	1956	10.00	20.00	40.00
❏ 3363	Rum and Coca-Cola/Soft Pollow	1957	7.50	15.00	30.00
❏ 3370	Greyhound/Dear Angel	1957	7.50	15.00	30.00
❏ 3383	Thinking of You Baby/If I Could Be with You	1957	7.50	15.00	30.00
IMPERIAL					
❏ 5831	I'm Still a Fool for You/Rocky Mountain	1962	3.00	6.00	12.00
KING					
❏ 5405	Christmas (Comes But Once a Year)/Please Come Home for Christmas	1960	3.00	6.00	12.00
—B-side by Charles Brown					
❏ 5464	I Wanna Go Back Home/My Little Baby	1961	3.00	6.00	12.00
—With Charles Brown					
❏ 5483	My Sweet Baby's Love/Heartaches That Make You Cry	1961	3.00	6.00	12.00
❏ 5529	Movin' Time/The Hammer	1961	3.00	6.00	12.00
❏ 6095	Whiz O Shoo Pepi/Same Old Thing	1967	2.50	5.00	10.00
MOTOWN					
❏ 1038	I'll Make It Up to You Somehow/My Baby Gave Me Another Chance	1963	7.50	15.00	30.00
❏ 1046	My Daily Prayer/(B-side unknown)	1963	7.50	15.00	30.00
UNITED ARTISTS					
❏ 0149	Chicken Shack Boogie/Revitalized	1973	—	2.00	4.00
—"Silver Spotlight Series" reissue					
Albums					
ALADDIN					
❏ LP-704 [10]	Rockin' the Boogie	1952	1000.	2000.	4000.
—Black vinyl					
❏ LP-704 [10]	Rockin' the Boogie	1952	200.00	4000.	8000.
—Red vinyl, blue cover					
❏ LP-810 [M]	Rockin' the Boogie	1957	—	—	—
—Canceled					
IMPERIAL					
❏ LP-9176 [M]	Million Sellers	1962	125.00	250.00	500.00
MOSAIC					
❏ MQ10-155 [(10)]	The Complete Aladdin Recordings of Amos Milburn	199?	45.00	90.00	180.00
—Limited editon of 3,500					

Number	Title (A Side/B Side)	Yr	VG	VG+	NM
MOTOWN					
❑ 608 [M]	The Return of Amos Milburn, "The" Blues Boss	1963	225.00	450.00	900.00
SCORE					
❑ LP-4012 [M]	Let's Have a Party	1957	200.00	400.00	800.00
❑ LP-4035 [M]	Amos Milburn Sings the Blues	1958	—	—	—
—Canceled					

MILBURN, AMOS/WYNONIE HARRIS/ETC.
Albums

Number	Title (A Side/B Side)	Yr	VG	VG+	NM
ALADDIN					
❑ LP-703 [10]	Party After Hours	1952	1000.	2000.	4000.
—Black vinyl					
❑ LP-703 [10]	Party After Hours	1952	2000.	4000.	8000.
—Red vinyl, blue cover					

MILES, BUDDY
45s

Number	Title (A Side/B Side)	Yr	VG	VG+	NM
ATLANTIC					
❑ 3852 [DJ]	Can You Hold Me (same on both sides)	1981	—	2.00	4.00
—May be promo only					
❑ 4006 [DJ]	Sunshine of Your Love (same on both sides)	1982	—	2.00	4.00
—May be promo only					
CASABLANCA					
❑ 839	Rockin' and Rollin' on the Streets of Hollywood/ Livin' in the Right Space	1975	—	2.00	4.00
❑ 849	Nasty Disposition/Do It to Me	1975	—	2.00	4.00
❑ 859	Reuben "The Hurricane"/ Where You Gonna Run To Lady	1976	—	2.00	4.00
COLUMBIA					
❑ 10030	Pain/We Get Love	1974	—	2.50	5.00
❑ 10089	Pull Yourself Together/I'm Just a Kiss Away	1975	—	2.50	5.00
❑ 45826	Love Affair/Life Is What You Make It	1973	—	2.50	5.00
❑ 45876	Elvira/Hear No Evil	1973	—	2.50	5.00
❑ 45969	Crazy Love/Thinking of You	1973	—	2.50	5.00
MERCURY					
❑ 72860	The Train (Part 1)/The Train (Part 2)	1968	2.00	4.00	8.00
❑ 72903	This Lady/'69 Freedom Special	1969	2.00	4.00	8.00
❑ 72945	Memphis Train/My Chant	1969	—	3.00	6.00
❑ 73008	Them Changes/Spot on the Wall	1970	—	3.00	6.00
❑ 73086	Down By the River/Hearts Delight	1970	—	3.00	6.00
❑ 73119	Dreams/Your Feeling Is Mine	1970	—	3.00	6.00
❑ 73159	We Got to Live Together (Part 1)/ We Got to Live Together (Part 2)	1970	—	3.00	6.00
❑ 73170	Runaway Child/(B-side unknown)	1970	—	3.00	6.00
❑ 73205	Wholesale Love/That's the Way Life Is	1971	—	2.50	5.00
❑ 73238	Them Changes/The Way I Feel Tonight	1971	—	2.50	5.00
❑ 73261	Give Away None of My Love/ Take It Off Him and Put It On Me	1972	—	2.50	5.00
❑ 73277	Life Is What You Make It (Part 1)/ Life Is What You Make It (Part 2)	1972	—	2.50	5.00

Albums

Number	Title (A Side/B Side)	Yr	VG	VG+	NM
ATLANTIC					
❑ SD 2-4000 [(2)]	Sneak Attack	1982	3.00	6.00	12.00
CASABLANCA					
❑ NBLP 7019	More Miles Per Gallon	1975	2.50	5.00	10.00
❑ NBLP 7024	Bicentennial Gathering of the Tribes	1976	2.50	5.00	10.00
COLUMBIA					
❑ CQ 32048 [Q]	Chapter VII	1973	5.00	10.00	20.00
❑ KC 32048	Chapter VII	1973	3.00	6.00	12.00
❑ CQ 32694 [Q]	Booger Bear	1973	5.00	10.00	20.00
❑ KC 32694	Booger Bear	1973	3.00	6.00	12.00
❑ KC 33089	All the Faces	1974	3.00	6.00	12.00
MERCURY					
❑ SRM-1-608	A Message to the People	1971	3.75	7.50	15.00
❑ SRM-2-7500 [(2)]	Buddy Miles Live	1971	3.75	7.50	15.00
❑ SR-61196	Expressway to Your Skull	1968	5.00	10.00	20.00
❑ SR-61222	Electric Church	1969	5.00	10.00	20.00
❑ SR-61280	Them Changes	1970	3.75	7.50	15.00
❑ SR-61313	We Got to Live Together	1970	3.75	7.50	15.00

MILES, GARRY
45s

Number	Title (A Side/B Side)	Yr	VG	VG+	NM
LIBERTY					
❑ 55261	Look for a Star/Afraid of Love	1960	3.75	7.50	15.00
❑ 55261 [PS]	Look for a Star/Afraid of Love	1960	7.50	15.00	30.00
❑ 55279	Wishing Well/Dream Girl	1960	3.00	6.00	12.00
❑ 55596	Candy/Do the Bug	1963	3.00	6.00	12.00
❑ 55685	What Kind of Girl Are You/What's New	1964	2.50	5.00	10.00
❑ 55714	Here Goes a Fool/Ecstasy	1964	2.50	5.00	10.00
❑ 55738	How Are Things in Paradise/Please Take the Time	1964	2.50	5.00	10.00
UNITED ARTISTS					
❑ 0099	Look for a Star/Look for a Star	1973	—	2.50	5.00
—"Silver Spotlight Series" reissue; B-side by Garry Mills					

7-Inch Extended Plays

Number	Title (A Side/B Side)	Yr	VG	VG+	NM
LIBERTY					
❑ LSX-1005	Look for a Star/Wishing Well//I Miss You So/ Afraid of Love	1960	12.50	25.00	50.00
❑ LSX-1005 [PS]	Look for a Star	1960	12.50	25.00	50.00

MILES, LENNY
45s

Number	Title (A Side/B Side)	Yr	VG	VG+	NM
GROOVE					
❑ 58-0001	Stay with Me/Hercules	1963	2.50	5.00	10.00
❑ 58-0010	I Wouldn't Be Here/Mind Your Own Biz	1963	2.50	5.00	10.00
SCEPTER					
❑ 1212	Don't Believe Him Donna/Invisible	1960	3.00	6.00	12.00
❑ 1218	I Know Love/In Between Tears	1961	3.00	6.00	12.00

MILKWOOD (1)
Albums

Number	Title (A Side/B Side)	Yr	VG	VG+	NM
A&M					
❑ SP-4226	Under Milkwood	1969	75.00	150.00	300.00

MILKWOOD (2)
Albums

Number	Title (A Side/B Side)	Yr	VG	VG+	NM
PARAMOUNT					
❑ PAS-6046	How's the Weather?	1973	10.00	20.00	40.00

MILKWOOD TAPESTRY
Albums

Number	Title (A Side/B Side)	Yr	VG	VG+	NM
METROMEDIA					
❑ MD-1007	Milkwood Tapestry	1969	12.50	25.00	50.00

MILLARD & DYCE
Albums

Number	Title (A Side/B Side)	Yr	VG	VG+	NM
KAYMAR					
❑ KS-7-265	Open	1973	15.00	30.00	60.00

MILLENNIUM
45s

Number	Title (A Side/B Side)	Yr	VG	VG+	NM
COLUMBIA					
❑ 4-44546	I Just Want to Be Your Friend/It's You	1968	2.50	5.00	10.00
❑ 4-44607	5 A.M./Prelude	1968	2.50	5.00	10.00

MILLER, BOBBY
45s

Number	Title (A Side/B Side)	Yr	VG	VG+	NM
CONSTELLATION					
❑ 103	The Big Question/I Don't Believe You	1963	5.00	10.00	20.00
❑ 111	The Big Question/Uncle Willie Time	1963	5.00	10.00	20.00
❑ 116	Whoa (She's All Mine)/Take It in Stride	1964	5.00	10.00	20.00
❑ 127	This Is My Dance/Simon Says	1964	5.00	10.00	20.00
❑ 134	I'm For the Girls/Love Take the Case	1964	7.50	15.00	30.00

MILLER, CHUCK
45s

Number	Title (A Side/B Side)	Yr	VG	VG+	NM
CAPITOL					
❑ F2613	Am I to Blame/Count Your Blessings	1953	5.00	10.00	20.00
❑ F2700	The Pucker-Nut Free/After All	1954	5.00	10.00	20.00
❑ F2766	Idaho Red/The Joker (In the Card Game of Life)	1954	5.00	10.00	20.00
—With Dave Cavanaugh					
❑ F2841	Hopahula Boogie/I'll Know My Love	1954	5.00	10.00	20.00
❑ F3187	No Baby Like You/Rouge River Valley	1955	3.75	7.50	15.00
MERCURY					
❑ 70627	The House of Blue Lights/Can't Help Wonderin'	1955	5.00	10.00	20.00
❑ 70697	Hawk Eye/Something to Live For	1955	3.75	7.50	15.00
❑ 70767	Boogie Along/Lookout Mountain	1955	3.75	7.50	15.00
❑ 70842	Bright Red Convertible/Baltimore Jones	1956	3.75	7.50	15.00
❑ 70942	Vim Vam Vamoose/Cool It Baby!	1956	3.75	7.50	15.00
❑ 71001	The Auctioneer/Baby Doll	1956	3.75	7.50	15.00
❑ 71056	Me Head in De Barrel/Good Mornin' Darlin'	1957	3.00	6.00	12.00
❑ 71118	Rang Tang Ding Dong/Bye Bye Love	1957	3.00	6.00	12.00
❑ 71173	Plaything/After Yesterday	1957	3.00	6.00	12.00
❑ 71308	Down the Road Apiece/Mad About Her Blues	1958	3.00	6.00	12.00

Albums

Number	Title (A Side/B Side)	Yr	VG	VG+	NM
MERCURY					
❑ MG-20195 [M]	After Hours	1956	20.00	40.00	80.00

MILLER, CLINT
45s

Number	Title (A Side/B Side)	Yr	VG	VG+	NM
ABC-PARAMOUNT					
❑ 9878	Bertha Lou/Doggone It Baby, I'm in Love	1957	12.50	25.00	50.00
❑ 9938	Polka Dotted Poliwampus/Teenage Dance	1958	7.50	15.00	30.00
❑ 9938 [PS]	Polka Dotted Poliwampus/Teenage Dance	1958	15.00	30.00	60.00
❑ 9979	A Lover's Prayer/No, Never, My Love	1958	5.00	10.00	20.00
BIG TOP					
❑ 3013	Lonely Traveler/You Must Have Read My Mind	1959	5.00	10.00	20.00
HEADLINE					
❑ 1010	Silly Billy Boy/Do You Remember	1960	12.50	25.00	50.00
❑ 1011	London Town/Till the End of the World Rolls Around	1961	7.50	15.00	30.00
❑ 1013	I Still Write Your Name in the Sand/The Girl with a Ribbon in Her Hand	1961	7.50	15.00	30.00
LENOX					
❑ 5557	Forget Me Nots/Drummer Boy of Shiloh	1962	3.00	6.00	12.00
❑ 5574	Bridge Across the River/Crabs Walk Sideways	1963	3.00	6.00	12.00

MILLER, DREW, AND THE BEL-AIRES
45s

Number	Title (A Side/B Side)	Yr	VG	VG+	NM
MGM					
❑ 11627	When Christmas Angels Sing/Mystery Trail	1953	5.00	10.00	20.00

MILLER, GLENN Not included are later incarnations of the Glenn Miller Orchestra without Glenn Miller.
45s

Number	Title (A Side/B Side)	Yr	VG	VG+	NM
RCA VICTOR					
❑ 27-0026	Chattanooga Choo Choo//(I've Got a Gal in) Kalamazoo	1951	3.75	7.50	15.00
—Silver label, red print					
❑ 27-0152	On Army Team/Anchors Aweigh	195?	3.75	7.50	15.00
—Silver label, red print; part of WPT 39					
❑ 27-0155	Vilia/I Dream of Jeanie with the Light Brown Hair	195?	3.75	7.50	15.00
—Silver label, red print					
❑ 47-2852	American Patrol/Song of the Volga Boatmen	1949	5.00	10.00	20.00
—Aqua label					
❑ 47-2852	American Patrol/Song of the Volga Boatmen	1951	3.75	7.50	15.00
—Black label, outline of dog at right					
❑ 47-2853	In the Mood/Little Brown Jug	1949	5.00	10.00	20.00
—Aqua label					
❑ 47-2853	In the Mood/Little Brown Jug	1951	3.75	7.50	15.00
—Black label, outline of dog at right					
❑ 47-2854	Star Dust/Pennsylvania Six-Five Thousand	1949	5.00	10.00	20.00
—Aqua label					
❑ 47-2854	Star Dust/Pennsylvania Six-Five Thousand	1951	3.75	7.50	15.00
—Black label, outline of dog at right					
❑ 47-2858	A String of Pearls/Chattanooga Choo Choo	1949	5.00	10.00	20.00
❑ 47-2877	Bugle Call Rag/Runnin' Wild	1949	5.00	10.00	20.00
❑ 47-4086	In the Mood/A String of Pearls	1951	3.75	7.50	15.00
❑ 27-0028	Sunrise Serenade/Moonlight Serenade	1951	3.75	7.50	15.00
—Silver label, red print					
❑ 27-0158	Perfidia/At Last	195?	3.75	7.50	15.00
—Silver label, red print					

M

Number	Title (A Side/B Side)	Yr	VG	VG+	NM
❑ 447-0026	Holiday for Strings/Flyin' Home	195?	3.75	7.50	15.00
❑ 447-0027	Farewell Blues/Stormy Weather	195?	3.75	7.50	15.00
❑ 447-0028	St. Louis Blues March/ In an Eighteenth Century Drawing Room	195?	3.75	7.50	15.00
❑ 447-0029	Poinciana/It Must Be Jelly	1956	3.75	7.50	15.00
❑ 447-0030	My Blue Heaven/Begin the Beguine	195?	3.75	7.50	15.00
❑ 447-0031	Little Brown Jug/Adios	195?	3.75	7.50	15.00
❑ 447-0032	Alice Blue Gown/My Isle of Golden Dreams	195?	3.75	7.50	15.00
❑ 447-0033	American Patrol/Song of the Volga Boatmen	195?	3.00	6.00	12.00
❑ 447-0034	Anvil Chorus/By the Waters of the Minnetonka	195?	3.75	7.50	15.00
❑ 447-0035	Perfidia/At Last	195?	3.75	7.50	15.00
❑ 447-0036	Beautiful Ohio/Missouri Waltz	195?	3.75	7.50	15.00
❑ 447-0037	Blue Evening/Serenade in Blue	195?	3.75	7.50	15.00
❑ 447-0038	Runnin' Wild/Bugle Call Rag	195?	3.75	7.50	15.00
❑ 447-0039	Chattanooga Choo Choo/(I've Got a Gal in) Kalamazoo	195?	3.00	6.00	12.00
❑ 447-0040	Danny Boy/Ida! Sweet As Apple Cider	195?	3.75	7.50	15.00
❑ 447-0041	Elmer's Tune/Johnson Rag	195?	3.75	7.50	15.00
❑ 447-0042	Pavanne/Don't Sit Under the Apple Tree (With Anyone Else But Me)	195?	3.75	7.50	15.00
❑ 447-0043	In the Mood/A String of Pearls	195?	3.00	6.00	12.00
❑ 447-0044	That Old Black Magic/Juke Box Saturday Night	195?	3.75	7.50	15.00
❑ 447-0045	Sunrise Serenade/Moonlight Serenade	195?	3.75	7.50	15.00
❑ 447-0046	Pennsylvania Six-Five Thousand/ Moonlight Cocktail	195?	3.75	7.50	15.00
❑ 447-0047	Star Dust/Tuxedo Junction	195?	3.75	7.50	15.00

20TH FOX

Number	Title (A Side/B Side)	Yr	VG	VG+	NM
❑ 122	Boom Shot/You Say the Sweetest Things	1959	2.50	5.00	10.00

UNITED STATES ARMY

Number	Title (A Side/B Side)	Yr	VG	VG+	NM
❑ HO7H-1760/1 [DJ]	In the Mood/American Patrol	1958	10.00	20.00	40.00

—Promo-only "Recruiting Service" record; white label with red and blue print

7-Inch Extended Plays

EPIC

Number	Title (A Side/B Side)	Yr	VG	VG+	NM
❑ EG-7012	Time on My Hands/I Got Rhythm//Sleepy Time Gal/Sold American	195?	5.00	10.00	20.00
❑ EG-7012 [PS]	(title unknown)	195?	5.00	10.00	20.00

RCA VICTOR

Number	Title (A Side/B Side)	Yr	VG	VG+	NM
❑ SPD 18 [PS]	(title unknown)	1956	37.50	75.00	150.00

—Includes 10 records (599-9105 through 599-9114) plus box and booklet insert

Number	Title (A Side/B Side)	Yr	VG	VG+	NM
❑ 947-0024	One O'Clock Jump/Going Home//St. Louis Blues/Tiger Rag	195?	5.00	10.00	20.00

—One record of 2-EP set EPBT 3025

Number	Title (A Side/B Side)	Yr	VG	VG+	NM
❑ 947-0025	Everybody Loves My Baby/Georgia on My Mind/ /Jersey Bounce/My Blue Heaven	195?	5.00	10.00	20.00

—One record of 2-EP set EPBT 3025

Number	Title (A Side/B Side)	Yr	VG	VG+	NM
❑ 947-0026	Anchors Aweigh/My Buddy//I Got Rhythm/I Dream of Jeanie with the Light Brown Hair	195?	5.00	10.00	20.00

—Silver label, red print; one record of 2-EP set EPBT 3026

Number	Title (A Side/B Side)	Yr	VG	VG+	NM
❑ 947-0027	Vilia/Limehouse Blues//On the Alamo/ On Army Team	195?	5.00	10.00	20.00

—Silver label, red print; one record of 2-EP set EPBT 3026

Number	Title (A Side/B Side)	Yr	VG	VG+	NM
❑ 947-0038	Johnson Rag/My Isle of Golden Dreams// Anvil Chorus	195?	5.00	10.00	20.00

—Silver label, red print; one record of 2-EP set EPBT 3002

Number	Title (A Side/B Side)	Yr	VG	VG+	NM
❑ 947-0039	Beautiful Ohio/Pavanne//Danny Boy/Adios	195?	5.00	10.00	20.00

—Silver label, red print; one record of 2-EP set EPBT 3002

Number	Title (A Side/B Side)	Yr	VG	VG+	NM
❑ LPC-101	Serenade in Blue/In the Mood//Moonlight Serenade/Sunrise Serenade	1961	3.00	6.00	12.00

—"Compact Double 33"; small hole, plays at 33 1/3 rpm

Number	Title (A Side/B Side)	Yr	VG	VG+	NM
❑ LPC-101 [PS]	Glenn Miller Serenade	1961	3.00	6.00	12.00

—Cover for "Compact Double 33"

Number	Title (A Side/B Side)	Yr	VG	VG+	NM
❑ 947-0116	Moonlight Serenade-Perfidia/Wonderful One// The Lamplighter's Serenade/Farewell Blues	1953	2.50	5.00	10.00

—Sides 1 and 28 of EPNT 6700

Number	Title (A Side/B Side)	Yr	VG	VG+	NM
❑ 947-0117	Weekend of a Private Secretary/Always in My Heart//Mister Meadowlark/Just a Little Bit South of North Carolina/Under a Blanket of Blue	1953	2.50	5.00	10.00

—Side 2 and 27 of EPNT 6700

Number	Title (A Side/B Side)	Yr	VG	VG+	NM
❑ 947-0118	Boulder Bluff/Caribbean Clipper//Sliphorn Jive/ Here We Go Again	1953	2.50	5.00	10.00

—Side 3 and 26 of EPNT 6700

Number	Title (A Side/B Side)	Yr	VG	VG+	NM
❑ 947-0119	Make Believe/Say Si Si//Introduction to a Waltz/ /Sweet Eloise/Rhapsody in Blue	1953	2.50	5.00	10.00

—Side 4 and 25 of EPNT 6700

Number	Title (A Side/B Side)	Yr	VG	VG+	NM
❑ 947-0120	Japanese Sandman-What's the Matter with Me-Let's Dance-Blue Room/Down for the Count// Naughty Sweety Blues/Bless You	1953	2.50	5.00	10.00

—Side 5 and 24 of EPNT 6700

Number	Title (A Side/B Side)	Yr	VG	VG+	NM
❑ 947-0121	Rainbow Rhapsody/Little Brown Jug//The Hop/ Careless	1953	2.50	5.00	10.00

—Side 6 and 23 of EPNT 6700

Number	Title (A Side/B Side)	Yr	VG	VG+	NM
❑ 947-0122	Imagination/It Must Be Jelly//Fools Rush In/ Twenty-Four Robbers	1953	2.50	5.00	10.00

—Side 7 and 22 of EPNT 6700

Number	Title (A Side/B Side)	Yr	VG	VG+	NM
❑ 947-0123	Devil may Care/Chip Off the Old Block//Don't Sit Under the Apple Tree/Lady Be Good	1953	2.50	5.00	10.00

—Side 8 and 21 of EPNT 6700

Number	Title (A Side/B Side)	Yr	VG	VG+	NM
❑ 947-0124	American Patrol/Ida//Flagwaver/One O'Clock Jump	1953	2.50	5.00	10.00

—Side 9 and 20 of EPNT 6700

Number	Title (A Side/B Side)	Yr	VG	VG+	NM
❑ 947-0125	Guess I'll Have to Change My Plan/Glen Island Special//Sleepy Town Train/My Devotion/ Fresh as a Daisy	1953	2.50	5.00	10.00

—Side 10 and 19 of EPNT 6700

Number	Title (A Side/B Side)	Yr	VG	VG+	NM
❑ 947-0126	My Darling-Blueberry Hill-Can't Get Started/ Bugle Call Rag//Chattanooga Choo Choo/My Melancholy Baby-Moon Love-Stompin' at the Savoy-Blue Moon	1953	2.50	5.00	10.00

—Side 11 and 18 of EPNT 6700

Number	Title (A Side/B Side)	Yr	VG	VG+	NM
❑ 947-0127	On a Little Street in Singapore/Oh So Good// Angel Child/King Porter Stomp	1953	2.50	5.00	10.00

—Side 12 and 17 of EPNT 6700

Number	Title (A Side/B Side)	Yr	VG	VG+	NM
❑ 947-0128	Baby Me/There'll Be Some Changes Made// Wishing Will Make It So/Rug Cutter's Swing	1953	2.50	5.00	10.00

—Side 13 and 16 of EPNT 6700

Number	Title (A Side/B Side)	Yr	VG	VG+	NM
❑ 947-0129	Moon Over Miami-A Million Dreams Ago-Aloha/ Sun Valley Jump//String of Pearls/Love with a Capital "You"	1953	2.50	5.00	10.00

—Side 14 and 15 of EPNT 6700

Number	Title (A Side/B Side)	Yr	VG	VG+	NM
❑ 947-0136	Moonlight Serenade/American Patrol// Pennsylvania Six-Five Thousand/In the Mood	1954	5.00	10.00	20.00

—Silver label, red print; part of 2-EP set EPBT 3057

Number	Title (A Side/B Side)	Yr	VG	VG+	NM
❑ 947-0137	Tuxedo Junction/St. Louis Blues//String of Pearls/Little Brown Jug	1954	5.00	10.00	20.00

—Silver label, red print; part of 2-EP set EPBT 3057

Number	Title (A Side/B Side)	Yr	VG	VG+	NM
❑ EPA 148	American Patrol/Song of the Volga Boatmen//In the Mood/Little Brown Jug	195?	3.75	7.50	15.00
❑ EPA 148 [PS]	Glenn Miller: An Album of Outstanding Arrangements	195?	3.75	7.50	15.00
❑ 947-0178	Along the Santa Fe Trail/Swingin' at the Seance/ /I'll Never Smile Again/V for Victory Hop	1954	2.50	5.00	10.00

—Side 1 and 30 of 15-EP set EPOT 6701

Number	Title (A Side/B Side)	Yr	VG	VG+	NM
❑ 947-0179	In a Sentimental Mood/Frenesi//Dancing in a Dream/Sophisticated Lady	1954	2.50	5.00	10.00

—Side 2 and 29 of 15-EP set EPOT 6701

Number	Title (A Side/B Side)	Yr	VG	VG+	NM
❑ 947-0180	Isn't That Just Like Love/I Dreamt I Dwelt in Harlem//On the Alamo/April in Paris	1954	2.50	5.00	10.00

—Side 3 and 28 of 15-EP set EPOT 6701

Number	Title (A Side/B Side)	Yr	VG	VG+	NM
❑ 947-0181	You Walk By/Are You Jumpin' Jack?//How Deep Is the Ocean/Measure for Measure	1954	2.50	5.00	10.00

—Side 4 and 27 of 15-EP set EPOT 6701

Number	Title (A Side/B Side)	Yr	VG	VG+	NM
❑ 947-0182	A Million Dreams Ago/Daisy Mae//Let's Have Another Cup of Coffee/The Rhumba Jumps	1954	2.50	5.00	10.00

—Side 5 and 26 of 15-EP set EPOT 6701

Number	Title (A Side/B Side)	Yr	VG	VG+	NM
❑ 947-0183	Falling Leaves/Crosstown//Anchors Aweigh/ Body and Soul	1954	2.50	5.00	10.00

—Side 6 and 25 of 15-EP set EPOT 6701

Number	Title (A Side/B Side)	Yr	VG	VG+	NM
❑ 947-0184	At Sundown/My Last Goodbye//So Little Time/ Down South Camp Meetin'	1954	2.50	5.00	10.00

—Side 7 and 24 of 15-EP set EPOT 6701

Number	Title (A Side/B Side)	Yr	VG	VG+	NM
❑ 947-0185	Hallelujah/I'm Sorry for Myself//A Stone's Throw from Heaven/Humoresque	1954	2.50	5.00	10.00

—Side 8 and 23 of 15-EP set EPOT 6701

Number	Title (A Side/B Side)	Yr	VG	VG+	NM
❑ 947-0186	The Hour of Parting/The Jumpin' Jive//Doin' the Jive/This Can't Be Love	1954	2.50	5.00	10.00

—Side 9 and 22 of 15-EP set EPOT 6701

Number	Title (A Side/B Side)	Yr	VG	VG+	NM
❑ 947-0187	Twilight Interlude/And the Angels Sing//Daddy/ Deep in the Heart of Texas	1954	2.50	5.00	10.00

—Side 10 and 21 of 15-EP set EPOT 6701

Number	Title (A Side/B Side)	Yr	VG	VG+	NM
❑ 947-0188	Sunrise Serenade/Blue Orchids//I Don't Want to Walk Without You/Limehouse Blues	1954	2.50	5.00	10.00

—Side 11 and 20 of 15-EP set EPOT 6701

Number	Title (A Side/B Side)	Yr	VG	VG+	NM
❑ 947-0189	We Can Live on Love/Pagan Love Song// Georgia on My Mind/Be Happy	1954	2.50	5.00	10.00

—Side 12 and 19 of 15-EP set EPOT 6701

Number	Title (A Side/B Side)	Yr	VG	VG+	NM
❑ 947-0190	We've Come a Long Way Together/Get Out of Town//Indian Summer/Tiger Rag	1954	2.50	5.00	10.00

—Side 13 and 18 of 15-EP set EPOT 6701

Number	Title (A Side/B Side)	Yr	VG	VG+	NM
❑ 947-0191	Blue Skies/Heaven Can Wait//After All/ St. Louis Blues	1954	2.50	5.00	10.00

—Side 14 and 17 of 15-EP set EPOT 6701

Number	Title (A Side/B Side)	Yr	VG	VG+	NM
❑ 947-0192	Bluebirds in the Moonlight/I Want to Be Happy/ /My Heart Belongs to Daddy/Deep Purple	1954	2.50	5.00	10.00

—Side 15 and 16 of 15-EP set EPOT 6701

Number	Title (A Side/B Side)	Yr	VG	VG+	NM
❑ EPAT 401	Chattanooga Choo Choo/Kalamazoo//Juke Box Saturday Night/That Old Black Magic	195?	5.00	10.00	20.00
❑ EPAT 401 [PS]	Juke Box Saturday Night	195?	5.00	10.00	20.00
❑ EPAT 426	April Played the Fiddle/Blue Rain//Vagabond Dreams/The Story of a Starry Night	1954	5.00	10.00	20.00

—Silver label, red print

Number	Title (A Side/B Side)	Yr	VG	VG+	NM
❑ EPAT 426 [PS]	Ah! Spring	1954	5.00	10.00	20.00
❑ EPAT 427	The Nearness of You/To You//Moonlight Becomes You/Faithful to You	1954	5.00	10.00	20.00

—Silver label, red print

Number	Title (A Side/B Side)	Yr	VG	VG+	NM
❑ EPAT 427 [PS]	The Nearness of You	1954	5.00	10.00	20.00
❑ EPAT 428	The Spirit Is Willing/Long Tall Mama//Rainbow Rhapsody/Take the "A" Train	1954	5.00	10.00	20.00

—Silver label, red print

Number	Title (A Side/B Side)	Yr	VG	VG+	NM
❑ EPAT 428 [PS]	The Spirit Is Willing	1954	5.00	10.00	20.00
❑ EPAT 429	At Last/Blue Evening//Delilah/Elmer's Tune	1954	5.00	10.00	20.00

—Silver label, red print

Number	Title (A Side/B Side)	Yr	VG	VG+	NM
❑ EPAT 429 [PS]	Elmer's Tune	1954	5.00	10.00	20.00
❑ EPAT 430	Moonlight Cocktail/Perfidia//Serenade in Blue/It Happened in Hawaii	1954	5.00	10.00	20.00

—Silver label, red print

Number	Title (A Side/B Side)	Yr	VG	VG+	NM
❑ EPAT 430 [PS]	Moonlight Cocktail	1954	5.00	10.00	20.00
❑ EPA 727	Beautiful Ohio/Adios//Serenade in Blue/Bugle Call Rag	1956	3.75	7.50	15.00
❑ EPA 727 [PS]	This Is Glenn Miller	1956	3.75	7.50	15.00
❑ EPA 729	Going Home/April in Paris//Everybody Loves My Baby/Georgia on My Mind	1956	3.75	7.50	15.00
❑ EPA 729 [PS]	Glenn Miller Concert	1956	3.75	7.50	15.00
❑ EPA-733	Moonlight Serenade/In the Mood//Tuxedo Junction/String of Pearls	1956	3.75	7.50	15.00
❑ EPA-733 [PS]	Glenn Miller Plays Selections from The Glenn Miller Story	1956	3.75	7.50	15.00
❑ 547-1100	Moonlight Serenade/Running Wild/ Londonderry Air (Danny Boy)// One O'Clock Jump	1957	3.75	7.50	15.00

—"Side 1" and "Side 6" of EPC 1506

Number	Title (A Side/B Side)	Yr	VG	VG+	NM
❑ 547-1101	Stairway to the Stars/To You/Little Brown Jug// Jim Jam Jump/For Jones/Hold Tight	1957	3.75	7.50	15.00

—"Side 2" and "Side 5" of EPC 1506

Number	Title (A Side/B Side)	Yr	VG	VG+	NM
❑ 547-1102	In the Mood/Sunrise Serenade//Bugle Call Rag/ Moonlight Serenade	1957	3.75	7.50	15.00

—"Side 3" and "Side 4" of EPC 1506

Number	Title (A Side/B Side)	Yr	VG	VG+	NM
❑ EPA 1-1494	*Star Dust/A Lovely Way to Spend an Evening/ Long Ago and Far Away/My Ideal	1957	3.00	6.00	12.00
❑ EPA 1-1494 [PS]	Marvelous Miller Moods, Vol. 1	1957	3.00	6.00	12.00
❑ EPC-1506 [PS]	The Glenn Miller Carnegie Hall Concert	1957	3.75	7.50	15.00

—Cover for 3-EP set (547-1100, 547-1101, 547-1102)

Number	Title (A Side/B Side)	Yr	VG	VG+	NM
❑ EPBT 3002 [PS]This Is Glenn Miller		195?	5.00	10.00	20.00
—Cover for 2-EP set (947-0038, 947-0039)					
❑ EPBT 3025 [PS]Glenn Miller Concert		195?	5.00	10.00	20.00
—Cover for 2-EP set (947-0024, 947-0025)					
❑ EPBT 3026 [PS]Glenn Miller Concert, Vol. 2		195?	5.00	10.00	20.00
—Cover for 2-EP set (947-0026, 947-0027)					
❑ EPBT 3057 [PS]Selections from the Film					
"The Glenn Miller Story"		1954	5.00	10.00	20.00
—Cover for 2-EP set (947-0136, 947-0137)					
❑ E3CW-3349/50 [DJ]Highlights from the Great Glenn Miller					
Limited Edition 1953		1953	12.50	25.00	50.00
—Promo-only sampler from the limited box sets					
❑ EPA 5035	Make Believe Ballroom Time/I Guess I'll Have to Dream the Rest//Juke Box Saturday Night/It Happened in Sun Valley	1958	3.00	6.00	12.00
❑ EPA 5035 [PS] Glenn Miller (Gold Standard Series)		1958	3.00	6.00	12.00
❑ EPA 5049	Serenade in Blue/Little Brown Jug//Don't Sit Under the Apple Tree (With Anyone Else But Me)/Pennsylvania Six-Five Thousand	1958	3.00	6.00	12.00
❑ EPA 5049 [PS] Serenade in Blue		1958	3.00	6.00	12.00
❑ EPA 5081	Chattanooga Choo Choo/American Patrol//Tuxedo Junction/(I've Got a Gal in) Kalamazoo	1958	3.00	6.00	12.00
❑ EPA 5081 [PS] Chattanooga Choo Choo		1958	3.00	6.00	12.00
❑ EPA-5149	Rhapsody in Blue/Sun Valley Jump//Danny Boy (Londonderry Air)/Anvil Chorus	1959	3.00	6.00	12.00
❑ EPA-5149 [PS] Rhapsody in Blue		1959	3.00	6.00	12.00
❑ EPNT 6700 [(14)]Glenn Miller and His Orchestra — Limited Edition		1953	50.00	100.00	200.00
—With 14 records (947-0116 through 947-0129), white loose-leaf folder and numbered booklet					
❑ EPOT 6701 [(15)]Glenn Miller and His Orchestra — Limited Edition, Volume Two		1954	50.00	100.00	200.00
—With 15 records (947-0178 through 947-0192), gold loose-leaf folder and numbered booklet					
❑ 599-9103	Moonlight Serenade/Perfidia//Love with a Capital "You"/Down for the Count	1956	3.00	6.00	12.00
—Side 1 and 20 of 10-EP set SPD 18; gray label					
❑ 599-9103	Moonlight Serenade/Perfidia//Love with a Capital "You"/Down for the Count	1956	3.00	6.00	12.00
—Side 1 and 20 of 10-EP set SPD 18; pink label					
❑ 599-9104	Just a Little Bit South of North Carolina/My Devotion/Weekend of a Private Secretary//Always in My Heart/Introduction to a Waltz/Make Believe	1956	3.00	6.00	12.00
—Side 2 and 19 of 10-EP set SPD 18; gray label					
❑ 599-9104	Just a Little Bit South of North Carolina/My Devotion/Weekend of a Private Secretary//Always in My Heart/Introduction to a Waltz/Make Believe	1956	3.00	6.00	12.00
—Side 2 and 19 of 10-EP set SPD 18; pink label					
❑ 599-9105	Japanese Sandman-What's the Matter with Me-Let's Dance-Blue Room-Bugle Call Rag-Naughty Sweetie Blues//My Melancholy Baby-Moon Love-Stomping at the Savoy-Blue Moon-The Lamplighter's Serenade-Under a Blanket of Blue	1956	3.00	6.00	12.00
—Side 3 and 18 of 10-EP set SPD 18; gray label					
❑ 599-9105	Japanese Sandman-What's the Matter with Me-Let's Dance-Blue Room-Bugle Call Rag-Naughty Sweetie Blues//My Melancholy Baby-Moon Love-Stomping at the Savoy-Blue Moon-The Lamplighter's Serenade-Under a Blanket of Blue	1956	3.00	6.00	12.00
—Side 3 and 18 of 10-EP set SPD 18; pink label					
❑ 599-9106	On a Little Street in Singapore/Fools Rush In/The Hop//Ida/Fresh As a Daisy/Careless	1956	3.00	6.00	12.00
—Side 4 and 17 of 10-EP set SPD 18; gray label					
❑ 599-9106	On a Little Street in Singapore/Fools Rush In/The Hop//Ida/Fresh As a Daisy/Careless	1956	3.00	6.00	12.00
—Side 4 and 17 of 10-EP set SPD 18; pink label					
❑ 599-9107	I Guess I'll Have to Change My Plan/Twenty-Four Robbers/Lady Be Good//Wishing Will Make it So/Say Si Si/Mister Meadowlark	1956	3.00	6.00	12.00
—Side 5 and 16 of 10-EP set SPD 18; gray label					
❑ 599-9107	I Guess I'll Have to Change My Plan/Twenty-Four Robbers/Lady Be Good//Wishing Will Make it So/Say Si Si/Mister Meadowlark	1956	3.00	6.00	12.00
—Side 5 and 16 of 10-EP set SPD 18; pink label					
❑ 599-9108	Moon Over Miami-A Million Dreams Ago-Aloha Baby Me-Rainbow Rhapsody//Boulder Buff/Sweet Eloise/Caribbean Clipper	1956	3.00	6.00	12.00
—Side 6 and 15 of 10-EP set SPD 18; gray label					
❑ 599-9108	Moon Over Miami-A Million Dreams Ago-Aloha Baby Me-Rainbow Rhapsody//Boulder Buff/Sweet Eloise/Caribbean Clipper	1956	3.00	6.00	12.00
—Side 6 and 15 of 10-EP set SPD 18; pink label					
❑ 599-9109	My Darling-Blueberry Hill-I Can't Get Started-Don't Sit Under the Apple Tree-There'll Be Some Changes Made//Here We Go Again/Imagination/Angel Child	1956	3.00	6.00	12.00
—Side 7 and 14 of 10-EP set SPD 18; gray label					
❑ 599-9109	My Darling-Blueberry Hill-I Can't Get Started-Don't Sit Under the Apple Tree-There'll Be Some Changes Made//Here We Go Again/Imagination/Angel Child	1956	3.00	6.00	12.00
—Side 7 and 14 of 10-EP set SPD 18; pink label					
❑ 599-9110	Chattanooga Choo Choo/American Patrol/Oh So Good//Rhapsody in Blue/Rug Cutter's Swing/King Porter Stomp	1956	3.00	6.00	12.00
—Side 8 and 13 of 10-EP set SPD 18; gray label					
❑ 599-9110	Chattanooga Choo Choo/American Patrol/Oh So Good//Rhapsody in Blue/Rug Cutter's Swing/King Porter Stomp	1956	3.00	6.00	12.00
—Side 8 and 13 of 10-EP set SPD 18; pink label					
❑ 599-9111	Devil May Care/Sleepy Town Train/One O'Clock Jump//Sun Valley Jump/String of Pearls/Flagwaver	1956	3.00	6.00	12.00

Number	Title (A Side/B Side)	Yr	VG	VG+	NM
❑ 599-9111	Devil May Care/Sleepy Town Train/One O'Clock Jump//Sun Valley Jump/String of Pearls/Flagwaver	1956	3.00	6.00	12.00
—Side 9 and 12 of 10-EP set SPD 18; pink label					
❑ 599-9112	Sliphorn Jive/Little Brown Jug/Farewell Blues//It Must Be Jelly/Chip Off the Old Block/Glen Island Special	1956	3.00	6.00	12.00
—Side 10 and 11 of 10-EP set SPD 18; gray label					
❑ 599-9112	Sliphorn Jive/Little Brown Jug/Farewell Blues//It Must Be Jelly/Chip Off the Old Block/Glen Island Special	1956	3.00	6.00	12.00
—Side 10 and 11 of 10-EP set SPD 18; pink label					

Albums

BANDSTAND

Number	Title	Yr	VG	VG+	NM
❑ BS-7136	A Million Dreams Ago	198?	2.50	5.00	10.00

BLUEBIRD

Number	Title	Yr	VG	VG+	NM
❑ AXM2-5512 [(2)]The Complete Glenn Miller Volume 1, 1938-39	1975	3.00	6.00	12.00
❑ AXM2-5514 [(2)]The Complete Glenn Miller Volume 2, 1939	1976	3.00	6.00	12.00
❑ AXM2-5534 [(2)]The Complete Glenn Miller Volume 3, 1939-40	1976	3.00	6.00	12.00
❑ AXM2-5558 [(2)]The Complete Glenn Miller Volume 4, 1940	1978	3.00	6.00	12.00
❑ AXM2-5565 [(2)]The Complete Glenn Miller Volume 5, 1940	1979	3.00	6.00	12.00
❑ AXM2-5569 [(2)]The Complete Glenn Miller Volume 6, 1940-41	1980	3.00	6.00	12.00
❑ AXM2-5570 [(2)]The Complete Glenn Miller Volume 7, 1941	1980	3.00	6.00	12.00
❑ AXM2-5571 [(2)]The Complete Glenn Miller Volume 8, 1941-42	1980	3.00	6.00	12.00
❑ AXM2-5574 [(2)]The Complete Glenn Miller Volume 9, 1939-42	1980	3.00	6.00	12.00
❑ 6360-1-RB	Maj. Glenn Miller and the Army Air Force Band	1987	2.50	5.00	10.00
❑ 9785-1-RB [(4)]The Popular Recordings 1938-1942	1989	6.25	12.50	25.00

EPIC

| ❑ LA 16002 [M] | Glenn Miller | 1960 | 5.00 | 10.00 | 20.00 |

EVEREST

| ❑ 4005/5 [(5)] | His Complete Recordings on Columbia (1928-1938) As Player and Conductor | 1982 | 6.25 | 12.50 | 25.00 |
| —Box set with 8-page booklet | | | | | |

HARMONY

| ❑ HS 11393 [R] | Collector's Choice | 1970 | 3.00 | 6.00 | 12.00 |

INTERMEDIA

| ❑ QS-5045 | A String of Pearls | 198? | 2.00 | 4.00 | 8.00 |

KOALA

| ❑ AW 14186 | Chattanooga Choo Choo | 1979 | 3.00 | 6.00 | 12.00 |

MERCURY

| ❑ 826635-1 [(2)] | Glenn Miller In Hollywood | 1986 | 3.00 | 6.00 | 12.00 |
| —Reissue of material formerly on 20th Century | | | | | |

MOVIETONE

❑ MTM-1003 [M]	Glenn Miller's Shindig	1965	3.75	7.50	15.00
❑ MTS-72003 [R]	Glenn Miller's Shindig	1965	2.50	5.00	10.00
❑ MTS-72018 [R]	The Glenn Miller Years	1967	3.00	6.00	12.00

PAIR

| ❑ PDL2-1003 [(2)]Original Recordings, Volume 1 | 1986 | 3.00 | 6.00 | 12.00 |
| ❑ PDL2-1036 [(2)]Original Recordings, Volume 2 | 1986 | 3.00 | 6.00 | 12.00 |

PICKWICK

❑ DL2-0168 [(2)]	A String of Pearls	197?	2.50	5.00	10.00
—Reissue of RCA Camden ACL2-0168					
❑ ACL-7009	Parade of Hits	1976	2.00	4.00	8.00

RCA

| ❑ 7648-1-R | Pure Gold | 1988 | — | 3.00 | 6.00 |
| ❑ 7652-1-R | The Best of Glenn Miller | 1988 | — | 3.00 | 6.00 |

RCA CAMDEN

❑ ACL2-0168 [(2)]A String of Pearls	1973	3.00	6.00	12.00
❑ ACL-0503	This Time the Dream's On Me	1974	2.00	4.00	8.00
❑ CAL-751 [M]	The Great Glenn Miller	1963	3.75	7.50	15.00
❑ CAS-751(e) [R]	The Great Glenn Miller	1963	3.00	6.00	12.00
❑ CAL-829 [M]	The Original Recordings	1964	3.75	7.50	15.00
❑ CAS-829(e) [R]	The Original Recordings	1964	3.00	6.00	12.00
❑ CAL-2128 [M]	The Nearness of You and Others	1967	3.75	7.50	15.00
❑ CAS-2128 [R]	The Nearness of You and Others	1967	3.00	6.00	12.00
❑ CAS-2267	The One and Only Glenn Miller	1968	2.50	5.00	10.00
❑ CXS-9004 [(2)]	Sunrise Serenade	197?	3.00	6.00	12.00

RCA SPECIAL PRODUCTS

| ❑ DMM4-0322 [(4)]Glenn Miller | 1978 | 5.00 | 10.00 | 20.00 |
| —Box set; mail-order offer | | | | | |

RCA VICTOR

❑ LPT-16 [10]	Glenn Miller Concert — Volume 1	1951	15.00	30.00	60.00
❑ LPT-30 [10]	Glenn Miller Concert — Volume 2	1951	15.00	30.00	60.00
❑ LPT-31 [10]	Glenn Miller	1951	15.00	30.00	60.00
❑ PR-114 [M]	Glenn Miller Originals	1962	5.00	10.00	20.00
—Promotional item for Salada Foods Inc.					
❑ PRM-181 [M]	Moonlight Serenade	1965	3.75	7.50	15.00
❑ CPM2-0693 [(2)]A Legendary Performer	1974	3.00	6.00	12.00
❑ ANL1-0974	Pure Gold	1975	2.00	4.00	8.00
❑ LOP-1005 [M]	The Marvelous Miller Medleys	1958	10.00	20.00	40.00
❑ LPT-1016 [M]	Juke Box Saturday Night	1955	10.00	20.00	40.00
❑ LPT-1031 [M]	The Nearness of You	1955	10.00	20.00	40.00
❑ ANL1-1139	The Chesterfield Broadcasts, Volume 1	1975	2.00	4.00	8.00
❑ LPM-1189 [M]	The Sound of Glenn Miller	1956	10.00	20.00	40.00
❑ LPM-1190 [M]	This Is Glenn Miller	1956	10.00	20.00	40.00
❑ AFL1-1192	Selections from "The Glenn Miller Story" and Other Hits	1977	2.00	4.00	8.00
❑ LPM-1192 [M]	Selections from "The Glenn Miller Story" and Other Hits	1956	10.00	20.00	40.00
❑ LSP-1192 [R]	Selections from "The Glenn Miller Story" and Other Hits	196?	3.75	7.50	15.00
❑ LPM-1193 [M]	Glenn Miller Concert	1956	10.00	20.00	40.00
❑ LPM-1494 [M]	Marvelous Miller Moods	1957	10.00	20.00	40.00
❑ LPM-1506 [M]	The Glenn Miller Carnegie Hall Concert	1957	10.00	20.00	40.00
❑ LPM-1973 [M]	The Marvelous Miller Medleys	1959	7.50	15.00	30.00
❑ LSP-1973 [R]	The Marvelous Miller Medleys	196?	3.75	7.50	15.00
❑ CPL1-2080	A Legendary Performer, Volume 2	1976	2.50	5.00	10.00
❑ CPL1-2495	A Legendary Performer, Volume 3	1977	2.50	5.00	10.00
❑ LPM-2767 [M]	Glenn Miller On the Air Volume 1	1963	3.75	7.50	15.00
❑ LSP-2767 [R]	Glenn Miller On the Air Volume 1	1963	2.50	5.00	10.00
❑ LPM-2768 [M]	Glenn Miller On the Air Volume 2	1963	3.75	7.50	15.00
❑ LSP-2768 [R]	Glenn Miller On the Air Volume 2	1963	2.50	5.00	10.00
❑ LPM-2769 [M]	Glenn Miller On the Air Volume 3	1963	3.75	7.50	15.00
❑ LSP-2769 [R]	Glenn Miller On the Air Volume 3	1963	2.50	5.00	10.00
❑ AFL1-2825	The Best of Glenn Miller Volume 3	1978	2.00	4.00	8.00
❑ LPT-3001 [10]	Glenn Miller Concert — Volume 3	195?	15.00	30.00	60.00

M

Number	Title (A Side/B Side)	Yr	VG	VG+	NM
❏ LPT-3002 [10]	This Is Glenn Miller	195?	15.00	30.00	60.00
❏ LPT-3036 [10]	This Is Glenn Miller — Volume 2	195?	15.00	30.00	60.00
❏ LPT-3057 [10]	Selections from the Film "The Glenn Miller Story"	1954	15.00	30.00	60.00
❏ LPT-3067 [10]	Sunrise Serenade	1954	15.00	30.00	60.00
❏ LPM-3377 [M]	The Best of Glenn Miller	1965	3.75	7.50	15.00
❏ LSP-3377(e) [R]	The Best of Glenn Miller	1965	2.50	5.00	10.00
—Black label					
❏ LSP-3377(e) [R]	The Best of Glenn Miller	1969	2.00	4.00	8.00
—Orange label					
❏ LPM-3564 [M]	The Best of Glenn Miller Volume 2	1966	3.75	7.50	15.00
❏ LSP-3564 [R]	The Best of Glenn Miller Volume 2	1966	2.50	5.00	10.00
❏ LPM-3657 [M]	Blue Moonlight	1966	3.75	7.50	15.00
❏ LSP-3657 [R]	Blue Moonlight	1966	2.50	5.00	10.00
❏ AYL1-3666	Pure Gold	1980	—	3.00	6.00
❏ AYL1-3759	Selections from "The Glenn Miller Story" and Other Hits	1981	—	3.00	6.00
❏ AYL1-3809	The Best of Glenn Miller Volume 2	1981	—	3.00	6.00
❏ AYL1-3810	The Best of Glenn Miller Volume 3	1981	—	3.00	6.00
❏ AYL1-3871	The Best of Glenn Miller	1981	—	3.00	6.00
❏ LPM-3873 [M]	The Chesterfield Broadcasts, Volume 1	1967	3.75	7.50	15.00
❏ LSP-3873 [R]	The Chesterfield Broadcasts, Volume 1	1967	2.50	5.00	10.00
❏ LSP-3981 [R]	The Chesterfield Broadcasts, Volume 2	1968	3.00	6.00	12.00
❏ LSP-4125 [R]	The Best of Glenn Miller Volume 3	1969	3.00	6.00	12.00
❏ VPM-6019 [(2)]	Glenn Miller: A Memorial 1944-1969	1969	3.75	7.50	15.00
❏ VPM-6080 [(2)]	This Is Glenn Miller's Army Air Force Band	1972	3.75	7.50	15.00
❏ LPM-6100 [(3)M]	For the Very First Time…	195?	12.50	25.00	50.00
—Black "Long Play" labels in leatherette spiral-bound binder					
❏ LPM-6101 [(3)M]	Glenn Miller On the Air	1963	10.00	20.00	40.00
❏ LSP-6101 [(3)R]	Glenn Miller On the Air	1963	6.25	12.50	25.00
❏ LPT-6700 [(5)M]	Glenn Miller and His Orchestra Limited Edition — Second Pressing	195?	15.00	30.00	60.00
—Black "Long Play" labels in leatherette spiral-bound binder					
❏ LPT-6700 [(5)M]	Glenn Miller and His Orchestra Limited Edition	1953	37.50	75.00	150.00
—Silver labels with red print in leatherette spiral-bound binder					
❏ LPT-6701 [(5)M]	Glenn Miller and His Orchestra Limited Edition Volume Two — Second Pressing	195?	15.00	30.00	60.00
—Black "Long Play" labels in leatherette spiral-bound binder; identified as "Second Pressing" throughout					
❏ LPT-6701 [(5)M]	Glenn Miller and His Orchestra Limited Edition Volume Two	1954	30.00	60.00	120.00
—Black "Long Play" labels in leatherette spiral-bound binder					
❏ LPT-6702 [(4)M]	Glenn Miller Army Air Force Band	195?	15.00	30.00	60.00
—Same as above, but in box rather than in binder					
❏ LPT-6702 [(4)M]	Glenn Miller Army Air Force Band	1955	30.00	60.00	120.00
—Black "Long Play" labels in leatherette spiral-bound binder					
READER'S DIGEST					
❏ RD4-64 [(6)R]	The Unforgettable Glenn Miller	1968	5.00	10.00	20.00
SANDY HOOK					
❏ SH 2055	Uncle Sam Presents the Band of the Army Air Forces Training Command	1981	2.50	5.00	10.00
SPRINGBOARD					
❏ SPX-6013 [(2)]	Remember Glenn	1973	3.00	6.00	12.00
SUNBEAM					
❏ SB-232	Glenn Miller and His Chesterfield Orchestra	1984	2.50	5.00	10.00
TIME-LIFE					
❏ STBB-01 [(2)]	Big Bands: Glenn Miller	1983	3.75	7.50	15.00
❏ STBB-17 [(2)]	Big Bands: Major Glenn Miller	1985	3.75	7.50	15.00
❏ STBB-29 [(2)]	Big Bands: Glenn Miller: Take Two	1986	3.75	7.50	15.00
20TH CENTURY					
❏ T2-904 [(2)]	Remember Glenn	197?	3.75	7.50	15.00
20TH CENTURY FOX					
❏ TFM-3159 [M]	This Is Glenn Miller and His Greatest Orchestra, Volume 1	1964	3.75	7.50	15.00
❏ TFM-3160 [M]	This Is Glenn Miller and His Greatest Orchestra, Volume 2	1964	3.75	7.50	15.00
❏ TFS-4159 [R]	This Is Glenn Miller and His Greatest Orchestra, Volume 1	1964	2.50	5.00	10.00
❏ TFS-4160 [R]	This Is Glenn Miller and His Greatest Orchestra, Volume 2	1964	2.50	5.00	10.00
20TH FOX					
❏ TCF-100-2 [(2)M]	Glenn Miller and His Orchestra Original Film Sound Tracks	1958	7.50	15.00	30.00
❏ TCF-100-2S [(2)R]	Glenn Miller and His Orchestra Original Film Sound Tracks	1961	5.00	10.00	20.00
❏ FOX 3020 [M]	Glenn Miller's Original Film Soundtracks, Volume 1	1958	5.00	10.00	20.00
—Half of 101					
❏ FOX 3021 [M]	Glenn Miller's Original Film Soundtracks, Volume 2	1958	5.00	10.00	20.00
—Half of 101					

MILLER, HAL, AND THE RAYS "The Rays" actually are the future FOUR SEASONS.

45s

Number	Title (A Side/B Side)	Yr	VG	VG+	NM
AMY					
❏ 909	I Still Care/On My Own Two Feet	1964	25.00	50.00	100.00
❏ 920	A Blessing in Disguise/Cry Like the Rain	1965	20.00	40.00	80.00
TOPIX					
❏ 6003	An Angel Cried/Faith, Hope, Dreams	1961	10.00	20.00	40.00

MILLER, JODY

45s

Number	Title (A Side/B Side)	Yr	VG	VG+	NM
CAPITOL					
❏ 2005	To Sir, With Love/Only When You're Lonely	1967	2.00	4.00	8.00
❏ 2066	I Knew You Well/ I'm Into Lookin' for Someone to Love Me	1967	2.00	4.00	8.00
❏ 2187	It's My Time/Over the Edge	1968	2.00	4.00	8.00
❏ 2290	Long Black Limousine/Back in the Race	1968	2.00	4.00	8.00
❏ 2398	All the Crying in the World/Bon Soir Cher	1969	—	3.00	6.00
❏ 2558	Times to Come/My Daddy's Thousand Dollars	1969	—	3.00	6.00
❏ 5090	He Walks Like a Man/Looking at the World Through a Tear	1963	2.50	5.00	10.00
❏ 5162	They Call My Guy a Tiger/ Wonderful Round of Indifference	1964	2.50	5.00	10.00
❏ 5192	In My Room/Fever	1964	2.50	5.00	10.00
❏ 5269	My Baby's Gone/Warm Is the Love	1964	2.50	5.00	10.00
❏ 5298	This Is the Life/Look for Small Pleasures	1964	2.50	5.00	10.00
❏ 5353	Be My Man/Never Let Him Go	1965	2.50	5.00	10.00

Number	Title (A Side/B Side)	Yr	VG	VG+	NM
❏ 5402	Queen of the House/The Greatest Actor	1965	2.00	4.00	8.00
❏ 5429	Silver Threads and Golden Needles/ Melody for Robin	1965	2.00	4.00	8.00
❏ 5429 [PS]	Silver Threads and Golden Needles/ Melody for Robin	1965	3.00	6.00	12.00
❏ 5483	Home of the Brave/This Is the Life	1965	2.00	4.00	8.00
❏ 5483 [PS]	Home of the Brave/This Is the Life	1965	3.00	6.00	12.00
❏ 5541	Magic Town/A Lonely Queen	1965	2.00	4.00	8.00
❏ 5594	We're Gonna Let the Good Times Roll/ I Don't Care	1966	2.00	4.00	8.00
❏ 5671	I Remember Mama/Something in My Eye	1966	2.00	4.00	8.00
❏ 5743	Things/Quite a Long, Long Time	1966	2.00	4.00	8.00
❏ 5768	If You Were a Carpenter/Let Me Walk with You	1966	2.00	4.00	8.00
❏ 5846	Crazy/How Do You Say Goodbye	1967	2.00	4.00	8.00
❏ 5911	Shutters and Boards/Kiss Me	1967	2.00	4.00	8.00
EPIC					
❏ 5-10641	Look at Mine/Safe in These Lovin' Arms of Mine	1970	—	3.00	6.00
❏ 5-10692	If You Think I Love You Now (I've Just Started)/ Looking Out My Back Door	1970	—	3.00	6.00
❏ 5-10734	He's So Fine/You're Number Two	1971	—	3.00	6.00
❏ 5-10785	Baby I'm Yours/Good Lovin'	1971	—	3.00	6.00
❏ 5-10835	Be My Baby/ Your Love's Been a Long Time Comin'	1972	—	2.50	5.00
❏ 5-10878	There's a Party Goin' On/Love's the Answer	1972	—	2.50	5.00
❏ 5-10916	To Know Him Is to Love Him/Make Me Your Kind of Woman	1972	—	2.50	5.00
❏ 5-10960	Good News/Soul Song	1973	—	2.50	5.00
❏ 5-11016	Darling, You Can Always Come Back Home/ We'll Sing Our Song Together	1973	—	2.50	5.00
❏ 5-11056	The House of the Rising Sun/ In the Name of Love	1973	—	2.50	5.00
❏ 5-11076	Silent Night, Lonely Night/(B-side unknown)	1973	—	3.00	6.00
❏ 5-11094	Reflections/One More Chance	1974	—	2.50	5.00
❏ 5-11134	Natural Woman/Jimmy's Roses	1974	—	2.50	5.00
❏ 50042	Country Girl/Safe in These Lovin' Arms of Mine	1974	—	2.00	4.00
❏ 50079	The Best in Me/I'm Alright 'Til I See	1975	—	2.00	4.00
❏ 50117	Don't Take It Away/Long, Long Time	1975	—	2.00	4.00
❏ 50158	Will You Love Me Tomorrow/ Love, You Never Had It So Good	1975	—	2.00	4.00
❏ 50203	Ashes of Love/She Calls Me Baby	1976	—	2.00	4.00
❏ 50304	When the New Wears Off Our Love/ Silver and Gold	1976	—	2.00	4.00
❏ 50360	Spread a Little Love Around/Montana Cowboy	1977	—	2.00	4.00
❏ 50432	Another Lonely Night/All Night Long	1977	—	2.00	4.00
❏ 50512	Soft Lights and Slow Sexy Music/Home	1978	—	2.00	4.00
❏ 50568	(I Wanna) Love My Life Away/ I'm Gonna Write a Song	1978	—	2.00	4.00
❏ 50612	Kiss Away/Hold Me, Thrill Me, Kiss Me	1978	—	2.00	4.00
❏ 50673	I'm Gonna Make You Mine/I Don't Want Nobody (To Lead Me On)	1979	—	2.00	4.00
❏ 50734	Lay a Little Lovin' On Me/Crazy on You	1979	—	2.00	4.00

Albums

Number	Title (A Side/B Side)	Yr	VG	VG+	NM
CAPITOL					
❏ ST 1913 [S]	Wednesday's Child Is Full of Woe	1963	10.00	20.00	40.00
❏ T 1913 [M]	Wednesday's Child Is Full of Woe	1963	7.50	15.00	30.00
❏ ST 2349 [S]	Queen of the House	1965	5.00	10.00	20.00
❏ T 2349 [M]	Queen of the House	1965	3.75	7.50	15.00
❏ ST 2412 [S]	Home of the Brave	1965	5.00	10.00	20.00
❏ T 2412 [M]	Home of the Brave	1965	3.75	7.50	15.00
❏ ST 2446 [S]	Jody Miller Sings the Great Hits of Buck Owens	1966	5.00	10.00	20.00
❏ T 2446 [M]	Jody Miller Sings the Great Hits of Buck Owens	1966	3.75	7.50	15.00
❏ ST 2996	The Nashville Sound of Jody Miller	1968	3.75	7.50	15.00
❏ ST-11169	The Best of Jody Miller	1973	3.00	6.00	12.00
EPIC					
❏ E 30282	Look at Mine	1971	3.00	6.00	12.00
❏ E 30659	He's So Fine	1971	3.00	6.00	12.00
❏ KE 31706	There's a Party Goin' On	1972	3.00	6.00	12.00
❏ KE 32386	Good News!	1973	3.00	6.00	12.00
❏ KE 32569	House of the Rising Sun	1974	3.00	6.00	12.00
❏ KE 33349	Country Girl	1975	3.00	6.00	12.00
❏ KE 33934	Will You Love Me Tomorrow?	1976	3.00	6.00	12.00
❏ PE 34446	Here's Jody	1977	3.00	6.00	12.00

MILLER, JODY, AND JOHNNY PAYCHECK Also see each artist's individual listings.

45s

Number	Title (A Side/B Side)	Yr	VG	VG+	NM
EPIC					
❏ 5-10863	Let's All Go Down to the River/In the Garden	1972	—	3.50	7.00

MILLER, MICKEY

Albums

Number	Title (A Side/B Side)	Yr	VG	VG+	NM
FOLKWAYS					
❏ FA-2393 [M]	American Folk Songs	1959	7.50	15.00	30.00

MILLER, MITCH

45s

Number	Title (A Side/B Side)	Yr	VG	VG+	NM
COLUMBIA					
❏ B-315 [PS]	Mmmmitch!	1952	2.50	5.00	10.00
—Box for 4-record set					
❏ 1-706	Tzena, Tzena, Tzena/The Sleigh	1950	6.25	12.50	25.00
—Microgroove 33 1/3 rpm 7-inch single					
❏ 6-706	Tzena, Tzena, Tzena/The Sleigh	1950	5.00	10.00	20.00
❏ 1-789	In My Arms/Au Revoir Again	1950	6.25	12.50	25.00
—Microgroove 33 1/3 rpm 7-inch single					
❏ 6-789	In My Arms/Au Revoir Again	1950	5.00	10.00	20.00
❏ 1-790 (?)	Autumn Leaves/Song of Delilah	1950	6.25	12.50	25.00
—Microgroove 33 1/3 rpm 7-inch single					
❏ 6-790 (?)	Autumn Leaves/Song of Delilah	1950	5.00	10.00	20.00
❏ S7 30441 [S]	Goodnight Irene/On Top of Old Smoky	1960	2.50	5.00	10.00
—"Stereo Seven" 33 1/3 single, small hole					
❏ 31020 [S]	titles unknown	1961	2.50	5.00	10.00
❏ 31021 [S]	titles unknown	1961	2.50	5.00	10.00
❏ 31022 [S]	titles unknown	1961	2.50	5.00	10.00
❏ 31023 [S]	titles unknown	1961	2.50	5.00	10.00
❏ 31024 [S]	titles unknown	1961	2.50	5.00	10.00
❏ S7 31079 [S]	Cecelia/When the Red, Red Robin Comes Bob, Bob, Bobbin' Along	1961	2.50	5.00	10.00
❏ 31080 [S]	titles unknown	1961	2.50	5.00	10.00

Number	Title (A Side/B Side)	Yr	VG	VG+	NM
❏ 31081 [S]	titles unknown	1961	2.50	5.00	10.00
❏ 31082 [S]	titles unknown	1961	2.50	5.00	10.00
❏ 31083 [S]	titles unknown	1961	2.50	5.00	10.00
❏ 31364 [S]	titles unknown	1962	2.50	5.00	10.00
❏ 31365 [S]	titles unknown	1962	2.50	5.00	10.00
❏ 31366 [S]	titles unknown	1962	2.50	5.00	10.00
❏ 31367 [S]	titles unknown	1962	2.50	5.00	10.00
❏ 31368 [S]	titles unknown	1962	2.50	5.00	10.00
❏ 31565 [S]	titles unknown	1962	2.50	5.00	10.00
❏ 31566 [S]	titles unknown	1962	2.50	5.00	10.00
❏ 31567 [S]	titles unknown	1962	2.50	5.00	10.00
❏ 31568 [S]	titles unknown	1962	2.50	5.00	10.00
❏ 31569 [S]	titles unknown	1962	2.50	5.00	10.00

—The above 20 all are Columbia "Stereo 7" singles

Number	Title (A Side/B Side)	Yr	VG	VG+	NM
❏ 39053	The Sea of the Moon/Smile, Smile, Smile	1950	3.75	7.50	15.00
❏ 39111	Keep Me in Mind/The Winter Waltz	1950	3.75	7.50	15.00
❏ 39300	Cider Night/By the Moonlight	1951	3.75	7.50	15.00
❏ 39617	Greensleeves/Love Makes the World Go Round	1951	3.75	7.50	15.00
❏ 39679	Kalamazoo to Timbuktu/Sing Our Song	1952	3.00	6.00	12.00
❏ 39727	Serenade for Horns/Horn Belt Boogie	1952	3.00	6.00	12.00
❏ 39742	Cuban Nightingale/Bunk House Boogie	1952	3.00	6.00	12.00
❏ 39832	Kalamazoo to Timbuktu/Keep Me in Mind	1952	2.50	5.00	10.00
❏ 39833	The Sea of the Moon/Greensleeves	1952	2.50	5.00	10.00
❏ 39834	Tzena, Tzena, Tzena/Autumn Leaves	1952	2.50	5.00	10.00
❏ 39835	Au Revoir Again/Song of Delilah	1952	2.50	5.00	10.00

—The above four comprise box set B-315

Number	Title (A Side/B Side)	Yr	VG	VG+	NM
❏ 39851	Meet Mister Callaghan/How Strange	1952	3.00	6.00	12.00
❏ 39875	Zulu Warrior/Johnny Goggabie	1952	3.00	6.00	12.00
❏ 39901	Without My Love/Just Dreaming	1952	3.00	6.00	12.00
❏ 39982	Oriental Polka/Tira Lira Madeira	1953	3.00	6.00	12.00
❏ 40100	Under Paris Skies/Farewell	1953	3.00	6.00	12.00
❏ 40244	Frou! Frou!/Sail! Sail!	1954	3.00	6.00	12.00
❏ 40261	Napoleon/Monday Serenade	1954	3.00	6.00	12.00
❏ 40302	Sabrina/Wooden Shoes and Happy Hearts	1954	3.00	6.00	12.00
❏ 40409	Follow Me/The Singing Lesson	1955	2.50	5.00	10.00
❏ 40493	Theme from "I Am a Camera"/On Honolulu Bay	1955	2.50	5.00	10.00
❏ 40540	The Yellow Rose of Texas/Blackberry Winter	1955	2.50	5.00	10.00
❏ 40575	The Bonnie Blue Gal/Bel Sante	1955	2.50	5.00	10.00
❏ 40635	Lisbon Antigua (In Old Lisbon)/Willy Can	1956	2.50	5.00	10.00
❏ 40655	Madeira/Bolero Gaucho	1956	2.50	5.00	10.00
❏ 40683	That Girl/St. Lawrence River	1956	2.50	5.00	10.00
❏ 40715	The President on the Dollar/Trapeze	1956	2.50	5.00	10.00
❏ 40730	Theme Song from "Song for a Summer Night" (Vocal)/(Instrumental)	1956	2.50	5.00	10.00
❏ 40750	Jubilation T. Cornpone/War and Peace	1956	2.50	5.00	10.00
❏ 40772	Song of the Sparrow/(Instrumental)	1956	2.50	5.00	10.00
❏ 40831	A Very Special Love (Song for the Ninth Day)/ Song for the Ninth Day (A Very Special Love)	1957	2.50	5.00	10.00
❏ 40871	Just How Much I Love You/(Instrumental)	1957	2.50	5.00	10.00
❏ 40947	Java/Who Will Kiss Your Ruby Lips	1957	2.50	5.00	10.00
❏ 40999	Whistle Stop/The Bowery Grenadiers	1957	2.50	5.00	10.00
❏ 41066	March from the River Kwai and Coloney Bogey/ Hey Little Baby	1957	2.50	5.00	10.00
❏ 41128	Ginny, My Joy/Bonnie Eloise	1958	2.00	4.00	8.00
❏ 41203	Rockabye in Birdland/The Key to Your Heart	1958	2.00	4.00	8.00
❏ 41235	Bluebell/It Seems Like Only Yesterday	1958	2.00	4.00	8.00
❏ 41301	Lover's Gold/Moonlight and Roses	1958	2.00	4.00	8.00
❏ 41317	The Children's Marching Song/Carolina in the Morning	1959	2.00	4.00	8.00
❏ 41317 [PS]	The Children's Marching Song/Carolina in the Morning	1959	3.00	6.00	12.00
❏ 41375	Holiday for Lovers/This Here Goat	1959	2.00	4.00	8.00
❏ 41424	Join the Cavalry/Hey Betty Martin	1959	2.00	4.00	8.00
❏ 41499	Do-Re-Mi/Alouette March	1959	2.00	4.00	8.00
❏ 41499 [PS]	Do-Re-Mi/Alouette March	1959	3.00	6.00	12.00
❏ 41616	Sing Along/Pink Polemoniums	1960	2.00	4.00	8.00
❏ 41716	Silly Little Tune/Walkin' Down to Washington	1960	2.00	4.00	8.00
❏ 41789	The Zasu Zasu Tree/Sing-Song Girl	1960	2.00	4.00	8.00
❏ 41814	Must Be Santa/Christmas Spirit	1960	2.50	5.00	10.00
❏ 41941	Tunes of Glory/Shlub-a-Dubba-Due	1961	2.00	4.00	8.00
❏ 41941 [PS]	Tunes of Glory/Shlub-a-Dubba-Due	1961	2.50	5.00	10.00
❏ 41988	The Whiffenpoof Song/Sweet Adeline/Let Me Call You Sweetheart	1961	2.00	4.00	8.00
❏ 41989	Shine On Harvest Moon/For Me and My Gal/My Wild Irish Rose/When Irish Eyes Are Smiling	1961	2.00	4.00	8.00
❏ 41990	There Is a Tavern in the Town/Show Me the Way to Go Home/That Old Gang of Mine	1961	2.00	4.00	8.00
❏ 41991	The Prisoner's Song/Where Do You Work/Yes! We Have No Bananas	1961			
❏ 41992	Poor Butterfly/ I'm Looking Over a Four-Leaf Clover	1961	2.00	4.00	8.00
❏ 42016	The Guns of Navarone/Bye Bye Blackbird	1961	2.00	4.00	8.00
❏ 42210	Sleigh Ride/The Christmas Song	1961	2.00	4.00	8.00
❏ 42211	Rudolph the Red-Nosed Reindeer/The Twelve Days of Christmas	1961	2.00	4.00	8.00
❏ 42212	Jingle Bells/White Christmas	1961	2.00	4.00	8.00
❏ 42213	Silent Night, Holy Night/ Deck The Halls With Boughs Of Holly	1961	2.00	4.00	8.00
❏ 42214	God Rest Ye Merry Gentlemen/ O Come, All Ye Faithful	1961	2.00	4.00	8.00
❏ 42215	Aura Lee/The Fog and the Grog	1961	2.00	4.00	8.00
❏ 42240	Must Be Santa/Be a Santa	1961	2.00	4.00	8.00
❏ 3-42240	Must Be Santa/Be a Santa	1961	3.00	6.00	12.00

—"Columbia Single 33"; small hole

Number	Title (A Side/B Side)	Yr	VG	VG+	NM
❏ 42305	Happy Whistlin' Blues/(Instrumental)	1962	—	3.00	6.00
❏ 42397	Jeepers Creepers/Swanee	1962	—	3.00	6.00
❏ 42398	We're In the Money/Chinatown, My Chinatown	1962	—	3.00	6.00
❏ 42399	Ain't We Got Fun/You're An Old Smoothie	1962	—	3.00	6.00
❏ 42400	I Wanna Be Happy/Tea for Two	1962	—	3.00	6.00
❏ 42401	Black Bottom/Bidin' My Time	1962	—	3.00	6.00
❏ 42484	Rosa Linda/Sweet Evelina	1962	—	3.00	6.00
❏ 42585	The Longest Day/(Instrumental)	1962	—	3.00	6.00
❏ 42797	The House Is Haunted/It's a Darn Good Thing	1963	—	3.00	6.00
❏ 42813	The Great Escape March/Shenandoah	1963	—	3.00	6.00
❏ 42914	Pine Cones and Holly Berries/Whispering Hope	1963	2.00	4.00	8.00
❏ 42914 [PS]	Pine Cones and Holly Berries/Whispering Hope	1963	2.50	5.00	10.00
❏ 43053	Whip Out Your Ukulele/Song for a Summer Night	1964	—	3.00	6.00
❏ 43149	Youngblood Hawk Theme/(Instrumental)	1964	—	3.00	6.00

Number	Title (A Side/B Side)	Yr	VG	VG+	NM
❏ 43247	To Be with You/Major Dundee March	1965	—	3.00	6.00
❏ 50033	Autumn Leaves/(B-side unknown)	1955	2.50	5.00	10.00

—Early "Hall of Fame Series" reissue, this charted with this number in 1955

DECCA

Number	Title (A Side/B Side)	Yr	VG	VG+	NM
❏ 25701	Red Wing/Get Me to the Church On Time	1965	—	3.00	6.00
❏ 31883	Ballad from Vietnam/That's All for Now	1965	—	3.00	6.00
❏ 31934	Into Each Life Some Rain Must Fall/He Who Hesitates Is Lost	1966	—	3.00	6.00

DIAMOND

Number	Title (A Side/B Side)	Yr	VG	VG+	NM
❏ 251	Dear World/One Person	1968	—	2.50	5.00

UNITED ARTISTS

Number	Title (A Side/B Side)	Yr	VG	VG+	NM
❏ 50260	Soft Is the Sparrow/Waking Up Son	1968	—	2.50	5.00

7-Inch Extended Plays

COLUMBIA

Number	Title (A Side/B Side)	Yr	VG	VG+	NM
❏ B-2528	*The Yellow Rose of Texas/Green Sleeves/ Autumn Leaves/Under Paris Skies	195?	2.50	5.00	10.00
❏ B-2528 [PS]	Mitch Miller (Hall of Fame Series)	195?	2.50	5.00	10.00
❏ B-2644	Anchors Aweigh/From the Halls of Montezuma (The Marines Hymn)//U.S. Air Force Blues/ U.S. Field Artillery March	195?	2.50	5.00	10.00
❏ B-2644 [PS]	Mitch Miller (Hall of Fame Series)	195?	2.50	5.00	10.00
❏ C 7791	The Blizzard Song/Frosty The Snow Man//Let It Snow/Sleigh Ride	1966	—	3.00	6.00
❏ C 7791 [PS]	Singin' Up a Blizzard	1966	2.00	4.00	8.00

—Free with a 6-pack of Fresca (sleeve is designed to slip over the neck of a bottle)

Number	Title (A Side/B Side)	Yr	VG	VG+	NM
❏ B-11601	*That Old Gang of Mine/Down by the Old Mill Stream/You Are My Sunshine/By the Light of the Silvery Moon	1958	2.00	4.00	8.00
❏ B-11601 [PS]	Sing Along with Mitch, Vol. 1	1958	2.00	4.00	8.00
❏ B-11602	(contents unknown)	1958	2.00	4.00	8.00
❏ B-11602 [PS]	Sing Along with Mitch, Vol. 2	1958	2.00	4.00	8.00
❏ B-11603	(contents unknown)	1958	2.00	4.00	8.00
❏ B-11603 [PS]	Sing Along with Mitch, Vol. 3	1958	2.00	4.00	8.00
❏ B-12051	*Joy to the World/We Three Kings of Orient Are/ Hark! The Herald Angels Sing/It Came Upon a Midnight Clear	1958	2.00	4.00	8.00
❏ B-12051 [PS]	Christmas Sing Along with Mitch, Vol. 1	1958	2.00	4.00	8.00
❏ B-12052	What Child Is This/Silent Night, Holy Night//Deck the Halls with Boughs of Holly/THe First Noel	1958	2.00	4.00	8.00
❏ B-12052 [PS]	Christmas Sing Along with Mitch, Vol. 2	1958	2.00	4.00	8.00
❏ B-12053	(contents unknown)	1958	2.00	4.00	8.00
❏ B-12053 [PS]	Christmas Sing Along with Mitch, Vol. 3	1958	2.00	4.00	8.00
❏ B-12431	Pretty Baby-Be My Little Baby Bumble Bee/ Moonlight and Roses//Sweet Adeline-Let Me Call You Sweetheart/The Whiffenpoof Song	1958	2.00	4.00	8.00
❏ B-12431 [PS]	More Sing Along with Mitch, Vol. 1	1958	2.00	4.00	8.00
❏ B-12432	(contents unknown)	1958	2.00	4.00	8.00
❏ B-12432 [PS]	More Sing Along with Mitch, Vol. 2	1958	2.00	4.00	8.00
❏ B-12433	(contents unknown)	1958	2.00	4.00	8.00
❏ B-12433 [PS]	More Sing Along with Mitch, Vol. 3	1958	2.00	4.00	8.00
❏ B-12831	*In a Shanty in Old Shanty Town/Smiles/Beer Barrel Polka/Hinky Dinky Parlez-Vous - She'll Be Coming 'Round the Mountain	1959	2.00	4.00	8.00
❏ B-12831 [PS]	Still More! Sing Along with Mitch	1959	2.00	4.00	8.00
❏ B-13161	On Top of Old Smokey/Medley: Camptown Races-Oh, Susanna//Down in the Valley/ Blue Tail Fly	1960	2.00	4.00	8.00
❏ B-13161 [PS]	Folk Songs Sing Along with Mitch, Vol. I	1960	2.00	4.00	8.00
❏ B-13162	(contents unknown)	1960	2.00	4.00	8.00
❏ B-13162 [PS]	Folk Songs Sing Along with Mitch, Vol. II	1960	2.00	4.00	8.00
❏ B-13163 [PS]	Folk Songs Sing Along with Mitch, Vol. III	1960	2.00	4.00	8.00
❏ B-13163	(contents unknown)	1960	2.00	4.00	8.00
❏ B-13311	*I Love You Truly/Meet Me Tonight in Dreamland/The Sweetest Story Ever Told/I Wonder Who's Kissing Her Now	1960	2.00	4.00	8.00
❏ B-13311 [PS]	Party Sing Along with Mitch, Volume 1	1960	2.00	4.00	8.00
❏ B-13312	(contents unknown)	1960	2.00	4.00	8.00
❏ B-13312 [PS]	Party Sing Along with Mitch, Volume 2	1960	2.00	4.00	8.00
❏ B-13313	(contents unknown)	1960	2.00	4.00	8.00
❏ B-13313 [PS]	Party Sing Along with Mitch, Volume 3	1960	2.00	4.00	8.00
❏ B-13891	*Polly Wolly Doodle-Wait for the Wagon-The Old Gray Mare/Juanita-Sweet Genevieve/Drink to Me Only with Thine Eyes-Vive L'Amour/ Drunk Last Night	1960	2.00	4.00	8.00
❏ B-13891 [PS]	Fireside Sing Along with Mitch, Vol. 1	1960	2.00	4.00	8.00
❏ B-13892	(contents unknown)	1960	2.00	4.00	8.00
❏ B-13892 [PS]	Fireside Sing Along with Mitch, Vol. 2	1960	2.00	4.00	8.00
❏ B-13893	(contents unknown)	1960	2.00	4.00	8.00
❏ B-13893 [PS]	Fireside Sing Along with Mitch, Vol. 3	1960	2.00	4.00	8.00
❏ B-14751	The Bandit/The Whistler and His Dog//Loch Lomond March/The Little Shepherd's March	196?	2.00	4.00	8.00
❏ B-14751 [PS]	March Along with Mitch, Vol. I	196?	2.00	4.00	8.00

Albums

ATLANTIC

Number	Title (A Side/B Side)	Yr	VG	VG+	NM
❏ SD 8277	Peace Sing Along with Mitch	1970	3.00	6.00	12.00

COLUMBIA

Number	Title (A Side/B Side)	Yr	VG	VG+	NM
❏ CL 601 [M]	Mmmmitch!	1954	5.00	10.00	20.00

—Maroon label, gold print

Number	Title (A Side/B Side)	Yr	VG	VG+	NM
❏ CL 779 [M]	It's So Peaceful in the Country	1956	5.00	10.00	20.00

—Red and black label with 6 "eye" logos

Number	Title (A Side/B Side)	Yr	VG	VG+	NM
❏ CL 1102 [M]	Mitch's Marches	1957	3.75	7.50	15.00
❏ CL 1160 [M]	Sing Along with Mitch	1958	3.75	7.50	15.00
❏ CL 1205 [M]	Christmas Sing Along with Mitch	1958	3.75	7.50	15.00

—Originals have gatefold cover with eight detachable lyric sheets inside

Number	Title (A Side/B Side)	Yr	VG	VG+	NM
❏ CL 1243 [M]	More Sing Along with Mitch	1958	3.75	7.50	15.00
❏ CL 1283 [M]	Still More! Sing Along with Mitch	1959	3.75	7.50	15.00
❏ CL 1316 [M]	Folk Songs Sing Along with Mitch	1959	3.75	7.50	15.00
❏ CL 1331 [M]	Party Sing Along with Mitch	1959	3.75	7.50	15.00
❏ CL 1389 [M]	Fireside Sing Along with Mitch	1959	3.75	7.50	15.00
❏ CL 1414 [M]	Saturday Night Sing Along with Mitch	1960	3.00	6.00	12.00
❏ CL 1457 [M]	Sentimental Sing Along with Mitch	1960	3.00	6.00	12.00
❏ CL 1475 [M]	March Along with Mitch	1960	3.00	6.00	12.00
❏ CL 1542 [M]	Memories Sing Along with Mitch	1960	3.00	6.00	12.00
❏ CL 1544 [M]	Mitch's Greatest Hits	1961	3.00	6.00	12.00
❏ CL 1568 [M]	Happy Times! Sing Along with Mitch	1961	3.00	6.00	12.00
❏ CL 1628 [M]	TV Sing Along with Mitch	1961	3.00	6.00	12.00
❏ CL 1671 [M]	Your Request Sing Along with Mitch	1961	3.00	6.00	12.00

M

Number	Title (A Side/B Side)	Yr	VG	VG+	NM
❑ CL 1701 [M]	Holiday Sing Along with Mitch	1961	3.00	6.00	12.00
❑ CL 1727 [M]	Rhythm Sing Along with Mitch	1962	3.00	6.00	12.00
❑ CL 1773 [M]	Family Sing Along with Mitch	1962	3.00	6.00	12.00
❑ CL 1864 [M]	Night Time Sing Along with Mitch	1963	3.00	6.00	12.00
❑ CL 2063 [M]	Hymn Sing Along with Mitch	1963	3.00	6.00	12.00
❑ CL 6222 [10]	Mitch Miller with Horns and Chorus	195?	7.50	15.00	30.00
❑ CS 8004 [S]	Sing Along with Mitch	1959	5.00	10.00	20.00
—Red and black label with 6 "eye" logos					
❑ CS 8004	Sing Along with Mitch	1963	3.00	6.00	12.00
—Red label					
❑ CS 8004	Sing Along with Mitch	1970	2.00	4.00	8.00
—Orange label					
❑ PC 8004	Sing Along with Mitch	198?	—	3.00	6.00
—Reissue with new prefix					
❑ CS 8027 [S]	Christmas Sing Along with Mitch	1959	5.00	10.00	20.00
—Originals have gatefold cover with eight detachable lyric sheets inside					
❑ CS 8043 [S]	More Sing Along with Mitch	1959	5.00	10.00	20.00
❑ CS 8099 [S]	Still More! Sing Along with Mitch	1959	5.00	10.00	20.00
❑ CS 8118 [S]	Folk Songs Sing Along with Mitch	1959	5.00	10.00	20.00
❑ CS 8138 [S]	Party Sing Along with Mitch	1959	5.00	10.00	20.00
❑ CS 8184 [S]	Fireside Sing Along with Mitch	1959	5.00	10.00	20.00
❑ CS 8211 [S]	Saturday Night Sing Along with Mitch	1960	3.75	7.50	15.00
❑ CS 8251 [S]	Sentimental Sing Along with Mitch	1960	3.75	7.50	15.00
❑ CS 8342 [S]	Memories Sing Along with Mitch	1960	3.75	7.50	15.00
❑ CS 8368 [S]	Happy Times! Sing Along with Mitch	1961	3.75	7.50	15.00
❑ CS 8428 [S]	TV Sing Along with Mitch	1961	3.75	7.50	15.00
❑ CS 8471 [S]	Your Request Sing Along with Mitch	1961	3.75	7.50	15.00
❑ CS 8501 [S]	Holiday Sing Along with Mitch	1961	3.75	7.50	15.00
❑ CS 8527 [S]	Rhythm Sing Along with Mitch	1962	3.75	7.50	15.00
❑ CS 8573 [S]	Family Sing Along with Mitch	1962	3.75	7.50	15.00
❑ CS 8638 [R]	Mitch's Greatest Hits	1963	2.50	5.00	10.00
❑ CS 8664 [S]	Night Time Sing Along with Mitch	1963	3.75	7.50	15.00
❑ CS 8863 [S]	Hymn Sing Along with Mitch	1963	3.75	7.50	15.00
❑ G 30250 [(2)]	34 All Time Great Sing Along Selections	1970	3.00	6.00	12.00
❑ 3C 39297	Holiday Sing Along with Mitch	1984	2.00	4.00	8.00
❑ PC 39298	Christmas Sing Along with Mitch	1984	2.00	4.00	8.00
DECCA					
❑ DL 4777 [M]	Dance and Sing Along with Mitch	1966	2.50	5.00	10.00
❑ DL 74777 [S]	Dance and Sing Along with Mitch	1966	3.00	6.00	12.00
HARMONY					
❑ HL 7404 [M]	March Along with Mitch	1967	2.50	5.00	10.00
❑ HS 11204 [S]	March Along with Mitch	1967	3.00	6.00	12.00
❑ HS 11241	Fireside Sing Along with Mitch	1968	2.50	5.00	10.00
❑ HS 11242	Memories Sing Along with Mitch	1968	2.50	5.00	10.00
❑ HS 11273	Everybody Sing Along with Mitch	1968	2.50	5.00	10.00
❑ HS 11354	Night Time Sing Along with Mitch	1970	2.50	5.00	10.00

MILLER, MRS.
45s
AMARET

Number	Title (A Side/B Side)	Yr	VG	VG+	NM
❑ 101	Up, Up and Away/Green Thumb	1969	2.00	4.00	8.00
❑ 114	I've Gotta Be Me/Renaissance of Smut	1970	2.00	4.00	8.00
CAPITOL					
❑ 5640	Downtown/A Lover's Concerto	1966	2.50	5.00	10.00

Albums
AMARET

Number	Title (A Side/B Side)	Yr	VG	VG+	NM
❑ 5000	Mrs. Miller Does Her Thing	1969	5.00	10.00	20.00
CAPITOL					
❑ ST 2494 [S]	Mrs. Miller's Greatest Hits	1966	7.50	15.00	30.00
❑ T 2494 [M]	Mrs. Miller's Greatest Hits	1966	6.25	12.50	25.00
❑ ST 2579 [S]	Will Success Spoil Mrs. Miller?	1966	7.50	15.00	30.00
❑ T 2579 [M]	Will Success Spoil Mrs. Miller?	1966	6.25	12.50	25.00
❑ ST 2734 [S]	The Country Soul of Mrs. Miller	1967	6.25	12.50	25.00
❑ T 2734 [M]	The Country Soul of Mrs. Miller	1967	6.25	12.50	25.00

MILLER, NED
45s
CAPITOL

Number	Title (A Side/B Side)	Yr	VG	VG+	NM
❑ 2074	Endless/Only a Fool	1968	—	3.00	6.00
❑ 4607	My Heart Waits at the Door/Cold Gray Bars	1961	3.00	6.00	12.00
❑ 4652	Dark Moon/Go On Back, You Fool	1961	3.00	6.00	12.00
❑ 5431	Whistle Walkin'/Two Voices, Two Shadows, Two Faces	1965	2.00	4.00	8.00
❑ 5502	Fall of the King/Down the Street	1965	2.00	4.00	8.00
❑ 5568	Lovin' Pains/If the World Turned Into Ashes	1965	2.00	4.00	8.00
❑ 5661	Right Behind These Lips/Summer Roses	1966	2.00	4.00	8.00
❑ 5742	Lorraine/Teardrop Lane	1966	2.00	4.00	8.00
❑ 5868	The Hobo/Echo of the Pines	1967	2.00	4.00	8.00
DOT					
❑ 15601	From a Jack to a King/Parade of Broken Hearts	1957	10.00	20.00	40.00
❑ 15651	Turn Back/Lights in the Street	1957	3.75	7.50	15.00
FABOR					
❑ 114	From a Jack to a King/Parade of Broken Hearts	1962	3.00	6.00	12.00
❑ 116	One Among the Many/Man Behind the Gun	1963	2.50	5.00	10.00
❑ 121	Another Fool Like Me/Magic Moon	1963	2.50	5.00	10.00
❑ 125	Big Love/Sunday Morning Tears	1964	2.50	5.00	10.00
❑ 128	Invisible Tears/Old Restless Ocean	1964	2.50	5.00	10.00
❑ 137	Do What You Do Do Well/Dusty Guitar	1964	2.00	4.00	8.00
❑ 139	What I Know/Lights in the Street	1965	2.00	4.00	8.00
JACKPOT					
❑ 48020	Girl from the Second World/Ring the Bell for Johnny	1960	3.00	6.00	12.00
—With Jan Howard					
RADIO					
❑ 105	Gypsy/With Enough Love	1958	6.25	12.50	25.00
REPUBLIC					
❑ 1404	Autumn Winds/My Last Go-Round	1969	—	2.50	5.00
❑ 1410	Breakin'/Just Walkin' in the Rain	1970	—	2.50	5.00
❑ 1411	The Lover's Song/Cold Gray Bars	1970	—	2.50	5.00
❑ 1416	Back to Oklahoma/I Hang My Head and Cry	1970	—	2.50	5.00

Albums
CAPITOL

Number	Title (A Side/B Side)	Yr	VG	VG+	NM
❑ ST 2330 [S]	Ned Miller Sings the Songs of Ned Miller	1965	6.25	12.50	25.00
❑ T 2330 [M]	Ned Miller Sings the Songs of Ned Miller	1965	5.00	10.00	20.00
❑ ST 2414 [S]	The Best of Ned Miller	1966	5.00	10.00	20.00
❑ T 2414 [M]	The Best of Ned Miller	1966	3.75	7.50	15.00

Number	Title (A Side/B Side)	Yr	VG	VG+	NM
❑ ST 2586 [S]	Teardrop Lane	1967	5.00	10.00	20.00
❑ T 2586 [M]	Teardrop Lane	1967	5.00	10.00	20.00
❑ ST 2914	In the Name of Love	1968	3.75	7.50	15.00
FABOR					
❑ FLP-1001 [M]	From a Jack to a King	1963	10.00	20.00	40.00
—Black vinyl					
❑ FLP-1001 [M]	From a Jack to a King	1963	25.00	50.00	100.00
—Colored vinyl					

MILLER, ROGER
45s
BUENA VISTA

Number	Title (A Side/B Side)	Yr	VG	VG+	NM
❑ 493	Whistle Stop/Not in Nottingham	1973	—	2.50	5.00
❑ 493 [PS]	Whistle Stop/Not in Nottingham	1973	—	2.50	5.00
COLUMBIA					
❑ 02681	Old Friends/When a House Is Not a Home	1982	—	2.00	4.00
—Roger Miller/Willie Nelson/Ray Price					
❑ 10052	Our Love/Yester Waltz	1974	—	2.50	5.00
❑ 10107	I Love a Rodeo/Lovin' You Is Always on My Mind	1975	—	2.50	5.00
❑ 45873	Open Up Your Heart/Qua La Linta	1973	—	2.50	5.00
❑ 45948	I Believe in the Sunrise/Shannon's Song	1973	—	2.50	5.00
❑ 46000	Whistle Stop/The 4th of July	1974	—	2.50	5.00
DECCA					
❑ 30838	Wrong Kind of Girl/A Man Like Me	1959	3.75	7.50	15.00
❑ 30953	Sweet Ramona/Jason Fleming	1959	3.75	7.50	15.00
ELEKTRA					
❑ 47192	Everyone Gets Crazy Now and Then/Aladam Bama	1981		2.00	4.00
MCA					
❑ 52663	River in the Rain/Hand for the Hog	1985	—	—	3.00
❑ 52855	Some Hearts Get All the Breaks/Arkansas	1986	—	—	3.00
MERCURY					
❑ 71212	Poor Little John/My Fellow	1957	6.25	12.50	25.00
❑ 73102	South/Don't We All Have the Right	1970	—	2.50	5.00
❑ 73190	Tomorrow Night in Baltimore/A Million Years or So	1971	—	2.50	5.00
❑ 73230	Loving Her Was Easier (Than Anything I'll Ever Do Again)/Que La Linta	1971	—	2.50	5.00
❑ 73268	We Found It in Each Other's Arms/Sunny Side of My Life	1972	—	2.50	5.00
❑ 73321	Rings for Sale/Conversations	1972	—	2.50	5.00
❑ 73354	Hoppy's Gone/I Jumped from Uncle Harvey's Plane	1972	—	2.50	5.00
MUSICOR					
❑ 1102	Can't Stop Loving You/You're Forgetting Me	1965	2.50	5.00	10.00
RCA VICTOR					
❑ 47-7776	Footprints in the Snow/You Don't Want My Love	1960	3.75	7.50	15.00
❑ 47-7878	When Two Worlds Collide/Every Which-A-Way	1961	3.75	7.50	15.00
❑ 47-7958	Burma Shave/Fair Swiss Maiden	1961	3.75	7.50	15.00
❑ 47-8028	Sorry, Willie/Hitch-Hiker	1962	3.00	6.00	12.00
❑ 47-8091	Trouble on the Turnpike/Hey Little Star	1962	3.00	6.00	12.00
❑ 47-8175	Lock, Stock and Teardrops/I Know Who It Is	1963	3.00	6.00	12.00
❑ 47-8651	If You Want Me To/Hey Little Star	1965	2.50	5.00	10.00
SMASH					
❑ 1876	Less and Less/Got Two Again	1964	—	—	—
—Canceled?					
❑ 1881	Dang Me/Got Two Again	1964	2.50	5.00	10.00
❑ 1881 [PS]	Dang Me/Got Two Again	1964	3.75	7.50	15.00
—Red sleeve					
❑ 1881 [PS]	Dang Me/Got Two Again	1964	5.00	10.00	20.00
—Yellow sleeve					
❑ 1926	Chug-a-Lug/Reincarnation	1964	2.50	5.00	10.00
❑ 1947	Do-Wacka-Do/Love Is Not for Me	1964	2.50	5.00	10.00
❑ 1947 [PS]	Do-Wacka-Do/Love Is Not for Me	1964	3.75	7.50	15.00
❑ 1965	King of the Road/Atta Boy Girl	1965	3.00	6.00	12.00
❑ 1983	Engine, Engine #9/The Last Word in Lonesome Is Me	1965	2.00	4.00	8.00
❑ 1994	One Dyin' and a-Buryin'/It Happened Just That Way	1965	2.00	4.00	8.00
❑ 1994 [PS]	One Dyin' and a-Buryin'/It Happened Just That Way	1965	3.75	7.50	15.00
❑ 1998	Kansas City Star/Guess I'll Pack Up My Heart (And Go Home)	1965	2.00	4.00	8.00
❑ 2010	England Swings/Good Old Days	1965	2.00	4.00	8.00
❑ 2024	Husbands and Wives/I've Been a Long Time Leavin'	1966	2.00	4.00	8.00
❑ 2043	You Can't Roller Skate in a Buffalo Herd/Train of Life	1966	2.00	4.00	8.00
❑ 2055	My Uncle Used to Love Me But She Died/You're My Kingdom	1966	2.00	4.00	8.00
❑ 2066	Heartbreak Hotel/Less and Less	1966	2.00	4.00	8.00
❑ 2081	Walkin' in the Sunshine/Home	1967	2.00	4.00	8.00
❑ 2121	The Ballad of Waterhole #3 (Code of the West)/Rainbow Valley	1967	2.00	4.00	8.00
❑ 2121 [PS]	The Ballad of Waterhole #3 (Code of the West)/Rainbow Valley	1967	3.75	7.50	15.00
❑ 2130	Old Toy Trains/Silent Night	1967	2.50	5.00	10.00
❑ 2130 [PS]	Old Toy Trains/Silent Night	1967	3.00	6.00	12.00
❑ 2148	Little Green Apples/Our Little Love	1968	2.00	4.00	8.00
❑ 2148 [PS]	Little Green Apples/Our Little Love	1968	3.00	6.00	12.00
❑ 2183	What I'd Give (To Be the Wind)/Toliver	1968	2.00	4.00	8.00
❑ 2197	Vance/Little Children Run and Play	1968	2.00	4.00	8.00
❑ 2230	Me and Bobby McGee/I'm Gonna Teach My Heart to Bend (Instead of Break)	1969	—	3.00	6.00
❑ 2246	Where Have All the Average People Gone/Boeing Boeing 707	1969	—	3.00	6.00
❑ 2258	The Tom Green County Fair/I Know Who It Is	1970	—	3.00	6.00
STARDAY					
❑ 356	Can't Stop Loving You/You're Forgetting Me	1958	5.00	10.00	20.00
❑ 718	Playboy/Poor Little John	1965	2.50	5.00	10.00
❑ 7029	Under Your Spell Again/I Ain't Never	197?	—	2.50	5.00
❑ 7032	Country Girl/Jimmy Brown, The Newsboy	197?	—	2.50	5.00
❑ 7038	Tip of My Fingers/I Wish I Could Fall in Love Today	197?	—	2.50	5.00
20TH CENTURY					
❑ 2421	The Hat/Pleasing the Crowd	1979	—	2.00	4.00

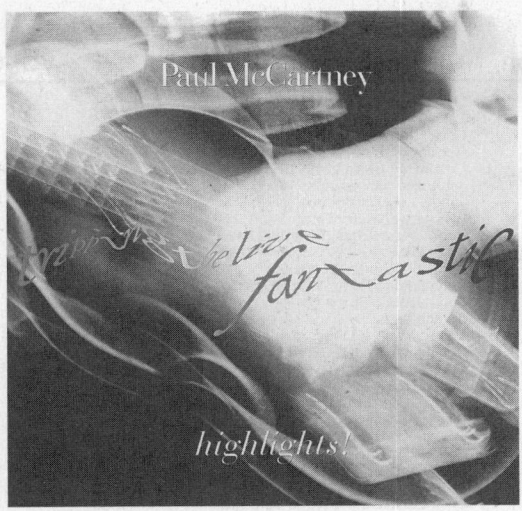

Paul McCartney, *Tripping the Live Fantastic… Highlights!*, Capitol C1-595379, stereo LP, Columbia House record club edition only, $12.50-$25.

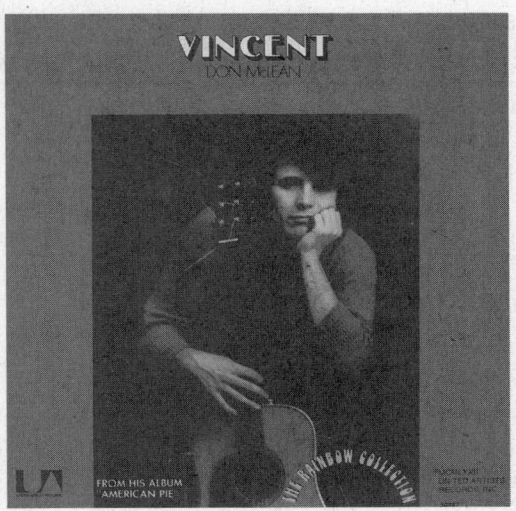

Don McLean, "Vincent," United Artists 50887, picture sleeve, $5-$10.

Vaughn Meader, *The First Family*, Cadence CLP-3060, mono LP, $5-$10.

Mercy, *Love Can Make You Happy*, Warner Bros. WS 1799, stereo LP, $7.50-$15.

The Midnighters, *Their Greatest Hits*, Federal 295-90, 10-inch LP, $6,000-$8,000.

The Steve Miller Band, *Sailor*, Capitol ST 2984, stereo LP, black label with rainbow ring along outer edge, $12.50-$25.

M

Number	Title (A Side/B Side)	Yr	VG	VG+	NM
WINDSONG					
CB-11072	Baby Me Baby/Dark Side of the Moon	1977	—	2.00	4.00
CB-11166	Oklahoma Woman/There's Nobody Like You	1977	—	2.00	4.00
Albums					
COLUMBIA					
KC 32449	Dear Folks Sorry I Haven't Written Lately	1973	3.75	7.50	15.00
KC 33472	Supersongs	1975	3.75	7.50	15.00
HILLTOP					
6109	King of the Road	197?	2.50	5.00	10.00
6131	Little Green Apples	197?	2.50	5.00	10.00
MCA					
5722	Roger Miller	1986	2.50	5.00	10.00
MERCURY					
SR-61297	A Trip in the Country	1970	3.75	7.50	15.00
SR-61361	The Best of Roger Miller	1971	3.75	7.50	15.00
826261-1	Golden Hits	198?	2.00	4.00	8.00
—Reissue of Smash 67073					
NASHVILLE					
2046	The Amazing Roger Miller	196?	3.00	6.00	12.00
PICKWICK					
PTP-2057 [(2)]	King High	1973	3.00	6.00	12.00
SPC-3226	Engine #9	197?	2.50	5.00	10.00
RCA CAMDEN					
CAL-851 [M]	Roger Miller	1964	3.00	6.00	12.00
CAS-851 [S]	Roger Miller	1964	3.75	7.50	15.00
CAL-903 [M]	The One and Only Roger Miller	1965	3.00	6.00	12.00
CAS-903 [S]	The One and Only Roger Miller	1965	3.75	7.50	15.00
SMASH					
MGS-27049 [M]	Dang Me	196?	3.00	6.00	12.00
—Yet another retitled version of "Roger and Out"					
MGS-27049 [M]	Dang Me/Chug-a-Lug	196?	3.00	6.00	12.00
—Retitled version of "Roger and Out"					
MGS-27049 [M]	Roger and Out	1964	3.75	7.50	15.00
MGS-27061 [M]	The Return of Roger Miller	1965	3.75	7.50	15.00
MGS-27068 [M]	The 3rd Time Around	1965	3.75	7.50	15.00
MGS-27073 [M]	Golden Hits	1965	3.75	7.50	15.00
MGS-27075 [M]	Words and Music	1966	3.75	7.50	15.00
MGS-27092 [M]	Walkin' in the Sunshine	1967	5.00	10.00	20.00
MGS-27096 [M]	Waterhole #3	1967	6.25	12.50	25.00
SRS-67049 [S]	Dang Me	196?	3.75	7.50	15.00
—Yet another retitled version of "Roger and Out"					
SRS-67049 [S]	Dang Me/Chug-a-Lug	196?	3.75	7.50	15.00
—Retitled version of "Roger and Out"					
SRS-67049 [S]	Roger and Out	1964	5.00	10.00	20.00
SRS-67061 [S]	The Return of Roger Miller	1965	5.00	10.00	20.00
SRS-67068 [S]	The 3rd Time Around	1965	5.00	10.00	20.00
SRS-67073 [S]	Golden Hits	1965	5.00	10.00	20.00
SRS-67075 [S]	Words and Music	1966	5.00	10.00	20.00
SRS-67092 [S]	Walkin' in the Sunshine	1967	5.00	10.00	20.00
SRS-67096 [S]	Waterhole #3	1967	5.00	10.00	20.00
SRS-67103	A Tender Look at Love	1968	5.00	10.00	20.00
SRS-67123	Roger Miller	1969	5.00	10.00	20.00
SRS-67129	Roger Miller 1970	1970	5.00	10.00	20.00
STARDAY					
SLP-318 [M]	The Country Side of Roger Miller	196?	6.25	12.50	25.00
—Retitled version of "Wild Child"					
SLP-318 [M]	Wild Child Roger Miller	1965	7.50	15.00	30.00
3011	Painted Poetry	1978	2.50	5.00	10.00
DT-90241 [R]	Wild Child Roger Miller	1965	10.00	20.00	40.00
—Capitol Record Club edition					
T-90241 [M]	Wild Child Roger Miller	1965	10.00	20.00	40.00
—Capitol Record Club edition					
20TH CENTURY					
T-592	Making a Name for Myself	1979	3.00	6.00	12.00
WINDSONG					
BHL1-2337	Off the Wall	1977	3.00	6.00	12.00

MILLER, STEVE   As far as we know, no relation to the Steve Miller Band.
45s
HIT

Number	Title (A Side/B Side)	Yr	VG	VG+	NM
313	Everlasting Love/In and Out of Love	1967	2.00	4.00	8.00
—B-side by Jenny and the Jewels					
330	This Guy's in Love with You/The Good, the Bad, and the Ugly	1968	2.00	4.00	8.00
—B-side by the New Society Group					

MILLER, STEVE, BAND   Also see THE GOLDBERG-MILLER BLUES BAND; BOZ SCAGGS.
12-Inch Singles
CAPITOL

Number	Title (A Side/B Side)	Yr	VG	VG+	NM
V-8613	Shangri-La (Extended)//Shangri-La (Dub)/Abracadabra	1984	2.50	5.00	10.00
V-8632	Bongo Bongo (Born to Dance Mix)/Get On Home	1985	2.00	4.00	8.00
V-8644	Italian X-Rays (Extended Version) (Edit)/Who Do You Love	1985	2.00	4.00	8.00
SPRO 9008/10 [DJ]	True Fine Love/Dance, Dance, Dance	1977	3.75	7.50	15.00
SPRO-9250/1 [DJ]	Shangri-La (Long Version) (Short Version)	1984	2.50	5.00	10.00
SPRO 9252/3 [DJ]	Shangri-La (Extended) (7" Version) (Dub Version)	1984	2.00	4.00	8.00
SPRO-9992 [DJ]	I Wanna Be Loved (same on both sides)	1986	3.75	7.50	15.00
—Promo only on blue vinyl					
V-15270	I Want to Make the World Turn Around (3 versions)/Slinky	1986	—	3.00	6.00

45s
CAPITOL

Number	Title (A Side/B Side)	Yr	VG	VG+	NM
2156	Roll With It/Sittin' in Circles	1968	3.00	6.00	12.00
2156 [PS]	Roll With It/Sittin' in Circles	1968	6.25	12.50	25.00
2287	Living in the U.S.A./Quicksilver Girl	1968	3.00	6.00	12.00
2447	Rock Love (B-side unknown)	1969	2.50	5.00	10.00
2520	My Dark Hour/Song for Our Ancestors	1969	2.00	4.00	8.00
2638	Don't Let Nobody Turn You Around/Little Girl	1969	2.00	4.00	8.00
2878	Going to the Country/Never Kill Another Man	1970	—	3.00	6.00
2945	Going to Mexico/Steve Miller's Midnight Tango	1970	—	3.00	6.00
3228	Rock Love/Let Me Serve You	1971	—	3.00	6.00
3344	Fandango/Love's Riddle	1972	—	3.00	6.00
3732	The Joker/Something to Believe In	1973	—	2.50	5.00
3837	Your Cash Ain't Nothin' But Trash/Evil	1974	—	2.50	5.00

Number	Title (A Side/B Side)	Yr	VG	VG+	NM
3884	Living in the U.S.A./Kow Kow Calqulator	1974	—	2.50	5.00
4260	Take the Money and Run/Sweet Maree	1976	—	2.00	4.00
4323	Rock'n Me/Shu Ba Da Du Ma Ma Ma Ma	1976	—	2.00	4.00
4323	Rockin' Me/Living in the U.S.A.	1976	—	2.50	5.00
4372	Fly Like an Eagle/Lovin' Cup	1976	—	2.00	4.00
4424	Jet Airliner/Babes in the Wood	1977	—	2.00	4.00
4466	Jungle Love/Wish Upon a Star	1977	—	2.00	4.00
4496	Swingtown/Winter Time	1977	—	2.00	4.00
A-5068	Heart Like a Wheel/True Fine Love	1981	—	—	3.00
A-5068 [PS]	Heart Like a Wheel/True Fine Love	1981	—	2.00	4.00
A-5086	Circle of Love/(Instrumental)	1982	—	—	3.00
B-5126	Abracadabra/Baby Wanna Dance	1982	—	—	3.00
B-5126	Abracadabra/Give It Up	1982	—	2.00	4.00
B-5126 [PS]	Abracadabra	1982	—	2.00	4.00
—Same sleeve has been found with record of either B-side					
B-5162	Cool Magic/Young Girl's Heart	1982	—	—	3.00
B-5162 [PS]	Cool Magic/Young Girl's Heart	1982	—	2.00	4.00
B-5194	Give It Up/Heart Like a Wheel	1982	—	—	3.00
B-5223	Buffalo's Serenade/Living in the U.S.A.	1983	—	—	3.00
B-5407	Shangri-La/Circle of Love	1984	—	—	3.00
B-5407 [PS]	Shangri-La/Circle of Love	1984	—	—	3.00
B-5442	Bongo Bongo/Get On Home	1985	—	—	3.00
B-5442 [PS]	Bongo Bongo/Get On Home	1985	—	—	3.00
B-5476	Italian X-Rays/Who Do You Love	1985	—	—	3.00
B-5646	I Want to Make the World Turn Around/Slinky	1986	—	—	3.00
B-5646 [PS]	I Want to Make the World Turn Around/Slinky	1986	—	—	3.00
B-5671	Nobody But You Baby/Maelstrom	1987	—	—	3.00
B-5704	I Wanna Be Loved/I Wanna Be Loved	1987	—	—	3.00
B-5704 [PS]	I Wanna Be Loved/I Wanna Be Loved	1987	—	—	3.00
B-44222	Ya Ya/Filthy McNasty	1988	—	—	3.00
B-44222 [PS]	Ya Ya/Filthy McNasty	1988	—	—	3.00
Albums					
CAPITOL					
SKAO-184	Brave New World	1969	5.00	10.00	20.00
—Black label with colorband					
SKAO-184	Brave New World	1970	3.75	7.50	15.00
—Green label					
SKAO-8-0184	Brave New World	1969	6.25	12.50	25.00
—Capitol Record Club edition; black label with colorband					
ST-331	Your Saving Grace	1969	3.75	7.50	15.00
SKAO-436	Number 5	1970	3.75	7.50	15.00
STBB-717 [(2)]	Children of the Future/Living in the U.S.A.	1971	3.75	7.50	15.00
—Repackage of 2920 and 2984 (with new title for the latter)					
SW-748	Rock Love	1971	3.75	7.50	15.00
SKAO 2920	Children of the Future	1968	6.25	12.50	25.00
—Black label with colorband					
SKAO 2920	Children of the Future	1970	3.75	7.50	15.00
—Green label					
ST 2984	Sailor	1968	6.25	12.50	25.00
—Black label with colorband					
ST 2984	Sailor	1970	3.75	7.50	15.00
—Green label					
SMAS-11022	Recall the Beginning…A Journey from Eden	1972	3.75	7.50	15.00
SVBB-11114 [(2)]	Anthology	1972	3.75	7.50	15.00
SMAS-11235	The Joker	1973	2.50	5.00	10.00
ST-11497	Fly Like an Eagle	1976	2.50	5.00	10.00
SO-11630	Book of Dreams	1977	2.50	5.00	10.00
SOO-11872	Greatest Hits 1974-1978	1978	2.50	5.00	10.00
SOO-11872 [DJ]	Greatest Hits 1974-1978	1978	7.50	15.00	30.00
—Promo only on blue vinyl					
SEAX-11903 [PD]	Book of Dreams	1978	3.75	7.50	15.00
ST-12121	Circle of Love	1981	2.50	5.00	10.00
ST-12216	Abracadabra	1982	2.50	5.00	10.00
ST-12263	Steve Miller Live	1983	2.50	5.00	10.00
SJ-12339	Italian X-Rays	1985	2.50	5.00	10.00
PJ-12445	Living in the 20th Century	1987	2.50	5.00	10.00
SN-16078	Brave New World	1980	2.00	4.00	8.00
SN-16079	Your Saving Grace	1980	2.00	4.00	8.00
SN-16262	Children of the Future	1982	2.00	4.00	8.00
SN-16263	Sailor	1982	2.00	4.00	8.00
SN-16321	Greatest Hits 1974-1978	1984	2.00	4.00	8.00
SN-16323	Book of Dreams	1984	2.00	4.00	8.00
SN-16339	Fly Like an Eagle	1984	2.00	4.00	8.00
SN-16357	Circle of Love	1985	2.00	4.00	8.00
21185	Fly Like an Eagle	1999	5.00	10.00	20.00
—Limited-edition reissue on 180-gram vinyl					
C1-48303	Born 2 B Blue	1988	2.50	5.00	10.00
SKAO-80436	Number 5	1970	5.00	10.00	20.00
—Capitol Record Club edition					
R 223186 [(2)]	Anthology	197?	3.75	7.50	15.00
—RCA Music Service edition					
DCC COMPACT CLASSICS					
LPZ-2028	Greatest Hits 1974-1978	1996	10.00	20.00	40.00
—Audiophile vinyl					
MOBILE FIDELITY					
1-021	Fly Like an Eagle	1979	10.00	20.00	40.00
—Audiophile vinyl					

MILLER, STEVE, BAND/QUICKSILVER MESSENGER SERVICE/THE BAND
Albums
CAPITOL

Number	Title (A Side/B Side)	Yr	VG	VG+	NM
STCR-288 [(3)]	Sailor/Quicksilver Messenger Service/Music from Big Pink	1969	10.00	20.00	40.00
—Special 3-LP box set combining these three LPs, also listed separately in each group's listing, in one package					

MILLER SISTERS, THE
45s
ACME

Number	Title (A Side/B Side)	Yr	VG	VG+	NM
111	Let's Start Anew/The Flip Skip	1957	12.50	25.00	50.00
717	You Made Me a Promise/Crazy Billboard Song	1957	10.00	20.00	40.00
721	Let's Start Anew/The Flip Skip	1958	10.00	20.00	40.00
EMBER					
1004	Guess Who/How Am I to Know	1956	7.50	15.00	30.00
FLIP					
504	Someday You Will Pay/I Knew You Would	1955	50.00	100.00	200.00

Number	Title (A Side/B Side)	Yr	VG	VG+	NM
GLODIS					
❑ 1003	Pop Your Finger/				
	You Got to Reap What You Sow	1961	3.75	7.50	15.00
GMC					
❑ 10006	I'm Telling It Like It Is/				
	Until You Come Home I'll Walk Alone	1967	2.50	5.00	10.00
HERALD					
❑ 455	Hippity Ha/Until You're Mine	1955	12.50	25.00	50.00
❑ 527	Hippity Ha/Until You're Mine	1958	5.00	10.00	20.00
HULL					
❑ 718	Please Don't Leave/Do You Wanna Go	1956	10.00	20.00	40.00
❑ 736	Just Wait and See/Black Pepper	1960	6.25	12.50	25.00
—B-side by Leo Price and Band					
❑ 750	Roll Back the Rug (And Twist)/Don't You Forget	1962	6.25	12.50	25.00
❑ 752	I Cried All Night/Hully Gully Reel	1962	5.00	10.00	20.00
MILLER					
❑ 1140	Oh Lover/Remember That	1960	5.00	10.00	20.00
❑ 1141	Pony Dance/Give Me Some Old Fashioned Love	1960	5.00	10.00	20.00
❑ 1143	Please Mr. D.J./(B-side unknown)	1960	5.00	10.00	20.00
ONYX					
❑ 507	Sugar Candy/My Own	1957	12.50	25.00	50.00
RAYNA					
❑ 5001	I Miss You So/Dance Little Sister	1962	3.75	7.50	15.00
❑ 5004	Oh Why/Walk On	1962	3.75	7.50	15.00
RIVERSIDE					
❑ 4535	Dance Close/Tell Him	1962	5.00	10.00	20.00
ROULETTE					
❑ 4491	Baby Your Baby/Silly Girl	1963	3.00	6.00	12.00
STARDUST					
❑ 3001	Feel Good/Cooncha	1964	2.50	5.00	10.00
SUN					
❑ 230	There's No Right Way to Do Me Wrong/				
	You Can Tell Me	1956	12.50	25.00	50.00
❑ 255	Finders Keepers/Ten Cats Down	1956	12.50	25.00	50.00
❑ 504	Someday You Will Pay/I Knew You Would	1955	37.50	75.00	150.00
YORKTOWN					
❑ 75	Looking Over My Life/Si Senor	1965	2.50	5.00	10.00

MILLINDER, LUCKY
45s

Number	Title (A Side/B Side)	Yr	VG	VG+	NM
KING					
❑ 4449	Chew Tobacco Rag/Georgia Rose	1951	15.00	30.00	60.00
❑ 4453	I'm Waiting Just for You/Bongo Boogie	1951	15.00	30.00	60.00
❑ 4476	The Grape Vine/No One Else Could Be	1951	15.00	30.00	60.00
❑ 4496	The Right Kind of Love/				
	It's Been a Long, Long Time	1951	15.00	30.00	60.00
❑ 4534	Ram-Bunk-Shush/Loaded with Love	1952	15.00	30.00	60.00
❑ 4545	When I Have You My Love/Please Be Careful	1952	25.00	50.00	100.00
❑ 4557	Lord Knows I Tried/Heavy Sugar	1952	25.00	50.00	100.00
❑ 4571	Backslider's Ball/Please Be Careful	1952	25.00	50.00	100.00
❑ 4792	It's a Sad, Sad Feeling/Ow	1955	20.00	40.00	80.00
—With the Admirals					
❑ 4803	Goody Good Love/I'm Here, Love	1955	7.50	15.00	30.00
❑ 5240	Heavy Sugar/Honeydripper	1959	3.00	6.00	12.00
RCA VICTOR					
❑ 47-2961	Tomorrow/I Ain't Got Nothin' to Lose	1949	12.50	25.00	50.00
❑ 47-3005	Awful Natural/In the Middle of the Night	1949	12.50	25.00	50.00
❑ 47-3128	I'll Never Be Free/Journey's End	1949	12.50	25.00	50.00
❑ 50-0054	D Natural Blues/Little Girl, Don't Cry	1949	15.00	30.00	60.00
—Gray label, orange vinyl					
❑ 50-0088	Let It Be/Sweet Slumber	1950	12.50	25.00	50.00
WARWICK					
❑ 582	Big Fat Mama/Slide My Trombone	1960	3.00	6.00	12.00
Albums					
ALAMAC					
❑ QSR-2425	Lucky Millinder and His Orchestra 1941-43	198?	2.50	5.00	10.00
HINDSIGHT					
❑ HSR-233	The Uncollected Lucky Millinder and His				
	Orchestra 1942	198?	2.50	5.00	10.00
MCA					
❑ 1357	Let It Roll	198?	3.00	6.00	12.00

MILLS, GARRY
45s

Number	Title (A Side/B Side)	Yr	VG	VG+	NM
IMPERIAL					
❑ 5674	Look for a Star — Part 1/Look for a Star — Part 2	1960	3.75	7.50	15.00
LONDON					
❑ 9504	I'll Step Down/Treasure Island	1962	3.75	7.50	15.00
TOP RANK					
❑ 2071	Top Teen Baby/Don't Forget	1960	3.75	7.50	15.00
UNITED ARTISTS					
❑ 0099	Look for a Star/Look for a Star	1973	—	2.50	5.00
—"Silver Spotlight Series" reissue; B-side by Gary Miles					

MILLS, HAYLEY
45s

Number	Title (A Side/B Side)	Yr	VG	VG+	NM
BUENA VISTA					
❑ 385	Let's Get Together/Cobbler, Cobbler	1961	3.00	6.00	12.00
❑ 385 [PS]	Let's Get Together/Cobbler, Cobbler	1961	6.25	12.50	25.00
❑ 395	Johnny Jingo/Jeepers Creepers	1962	2.50	5.00	10.00
❑ 395 [PS]	Johnny Jingo/Jeepers Creepers	1962	6.25	12.50	25.00
❑ 401	Side by Side/Ching Ching and a Ring Ding Ding	1962	2.50	5.00	10.00
❑ 401 [PS]	Side by Side/Ching Ching and a Ring Ding Ding	1962	6.25	12.50	25.00
❑ 408	Castaway/Sweet River	1962	2.50	5.00	10.00
❑ 408 [PS]	Castaway/Sweet River	1962	6.25	12.50	25.00
❑ 409	Let's Climb/Enjoy It	1962	2.50	5.00	10.00
—With Maurice Chevalier					
❑ 409 [PS]	Let's Climb/Enjoy It	1962	6.25	12.50	25.00
❑ 420	Flitterin'/Beautiful Beulah	1963	2.50	5.00	10.00
—With Eddie Hodges					
❑ 420 [PS]	Flitterin'/Beautiful Beulah	1963	6.25	12.50	25.00
MAINSTREAM					
❑ 656	Gypsy Girl/Younger Than Seventeen	1966	2.00	4.00	8.00

Number	Title (A Side/B Side)	Yr	VG	VG+	NM
Albums					
BUENA VISTA					
❑ BV-3311 [M]	Let's Get Together	1962	6.25	12.50	25.00
❑ STER-3311 [S]	Let's Get Together	1962	10.00	20.00	40.00

MILLS, MRS.
45s

Number	Title (A Side/B Side)	Yr	VG	VG+	NM
CAPITOL					
❑ 4758	Bobbikins/Popcorn	1962	3.00	6.00	12.00
Albums					
LIBERTY					
❑ LRP-3359 [M]	My Mother — The Ragtime Piano Player	1964	3.00	6.00	12.00
❑ LST-7359 [S]	My Mother — The Ragtime Piano Player	1964	3.75	7.50	15.00

MILLS BROTHERS, THE
45s

Number	Title (A Side/B Side)	Yr	VG	VG+	NM
DECCA					
❑ 9-33 [PS]	Famous Barber Shop Ballads, Volume One	1950	3.75	7.50	15.00
—Box for 24761, 24762 and 24763					
❑ 9-11051 T	Paper Doll/Tiger Rag	195?	5.00	10.00	20.00
—"Collectors' Classics" reissue on maroon label; part of "Curtain Call," 1-707					
❑ 23930	You Always Hurt the One You Love/Till Then	1960	2.00	4.00	8.00
—Black label with color bar					
❑ 9-23930	You Always Hurt the One You Love/Till Then	1955	5.00	10.00	20.00
—Reissue of 78 from 1944; black label with lines on either side of "Decca"					
❑ 9-23930	You Always Hurt the One You Love/Till Then	1955	3.00	6.00	12.00
—Black label with star under "Decca"					
❑ 9-24694	Someday/On a Chinese Honeymoon	1950	5.00	10.00	20.00
❑ 9-24756	If I Had My Way/Sweet Genevieve	1950	5.00	10.00	20.00
❑ 9-24761	You Tell Me Your Dreams, I'll Tell You Mine/				
	Sweet Adeline	1950	3.75	7.50	15.00
❑ 9-24762	My Gal Sal/Just a Dream of You, Dear	1950	3.75	7.50	15.00
❑ 9-24763	Meet Me Tonight in Dreamland/Can't You Hear				
	Me Callin', Caroline	1950	3.75	7.50	15.00
—The above three comprise "Album 9-33"					
❑ 9-24872	Daddy's Little Girl/If I Live to Be a Hundred	1950	5.00	10.00	20.00
❑ 9-25046	Lazy River/Cielito Lindo	1950	5.00	10.00	20.00
❑ 25516	Across the Alley from the Alamo/Don't Be a				
	Baby, Baby	1961	2.00	4.00	8.00
❑ 27157	Paper Doll/I'll Be Around	1960	2.00	4.00	8.00
—Black label with color bar					
❑ 9-27157	Paper Doll/I'll Be Around	1950	5.00	10.00	20.00
—Reissue of 78 from 1943; black label with lines on either side of "Decca"					
❑ 9-27157	Paper Doll/I'll Be Around	1955	3.00	6.00	12.00
—Black label with star under "Decca"					
❑ 9-27184	A Star for Everyone/I'm Afraid to Love You	1950	5.00	10.00	20.00
❑ 9-27236	Daddy's Little Boy/I Still Love You	1950	5.00	10.00	20.00
❑ 9-27253	Nevertheless (I'm in Love with You)/Thirsty for				
	Your Kisses	1950	5.00	10.00	20.00
❑ 9-27267	Funny Feelin'/I Don't Mind Being Alone	1950	5.00	10.00	20.00
❑ 9-27400	Around the World/You Don't Have to Drop a				
	Heart to Break It	1951	3.75	7.50	15.00
❑ 9-27447	Please Don't Talk About Me When I'm Gone/You				
	Know You Belong to Someone Else	1951	3.75	7.50	15.00
—With Tommy Dorsey					
❑ 9-27579	Mister and Mississippi/Wonderful, Wasn't It	1951	3.75	7.50	15.00
❑ 9-27615	Love Me/Who Knows Love	1951	3.75	7.50	15.00
❑ 9-27683	Lord Ups an' Downs/A Cottage with a Prayer	1951	5.00	10.00	20.00
❑ 9-27762	I Ran All the Way Home/Get Her Off My Hands	1951	3.75	7.50	15.00
❑ 9-27889	Be My Life's Companion/Love Lies	1951	3.75	7.50	15.00
❑ 9-28021	High and Dry/You're Not Worth My Tears	1952	3.75	7.50	15.00
❑ 9-28180	Pretty As a Picture/When You Come Back to Me	1952	3.75	7.50	15.00
❑ 9-28309	Just When We're Falling in Love/Blue and				
	Sentimental	1952	3.75	7.50	15.00
❑ 9-28384	The Glow-Worm/After All	1952	3.75	7.50	15.00
❑ 9-28458	Lazy River/Wish Me Good Luck, Amigo	1952	3.75	7.50	15.00
❑ 9-28459	Someone Loved Someone/				
	A Shoulder to Weep On	1952	3.75	7.50	15.00
❑ 9-28586	Twice As Much/I Want Someone to Care For	1953	3.00	6.00	12.00
❑ 9-28670	Say Si Si/I'm With You	1953	3.00	6.00	12.00
❑ 9-28736	Pretty Butterfly/Don't Let Me Dream	1953	3.00	6.00	12.00
❑ 9-28818	Who Put the Devil in Evelyn's Eyes/Beware	1953	3.00	6.00	12.00
❑ 9-28945	The Jones Boy/She Was Five and He Was Ten	1953	3.00	6.00	12.00
❑ 9-29019	I Had to Call You Up to Say I'm Sorry/You Didn't				
	Want Me When You Had Me	1954	3.00	6.00	12.00
❑ 9-29115	A Carnival in Venice/Go In and Out the Window	1954	3.00	6.00	12.00
❑ 9-29185	How Blue/Why Do I Keep Lovin' You	1954	3.00	6.00	12.00
❑ 9-29276	You're Nobody 'Til Somebody Loves You/Every				
	Second of Every Day	1954	3.00	6.00	12.00
❑ 9-29382	Paper Valentine/The Urge	1954	3.00	6.00	12.00
❑ 9-29496	Opus One/There You Are	1955	3.00	6.00	12.00
❑ 9-29511	Smack Dab in the Middle/Kiss Me and Kill Me				
	with Love	1955	3.00	6.00	12.00
❑ 9-29564	Daddy's Little Girl/Daddy's Little Boy	1955	3.00	6.00	12.00
❑ 9-29686	Suddenly There's a Valley/Gum Drop	1955	3.00	6.00	12.00
❑ 9-29754	I Believe in Santa Claus/You Don't Have to Be				
	a Santa Claus	1955	3.00	6.00	12.00
❑ 9-29781	All the Way 'Round the World/I've Changed My				
	Mind a Thousand Times	1956	2.50	5.00	10.00
❑ 9-29853	Dream of You/In a Mellow Tone	1956	2.50	5.00	10.00
❑ 9-29897	Standing on the Corner/King Porter Stomp	1956	2.50	5.00	10.00
❑ 9-30024	Don't Get Caught (Short on Love)/That's Right	1956	2.50	5.00	10.00
❑ 9-30136	That's All I Need/Tell Me More	1956	2.50	5.00	10.00
❑ 9-30224	In De Banana Tree/Knocked-Out Nightingale	1957	2.50	5.00	10.00
❑ 9-30299	Queen of the Senior Prom/My Troubled Mind	1957	2.50	5.00	10.00
❑ 30430	Two Minute Tango/Change for a Penny	1957	2.50	5.00	10.00
❑ 30546	The Barbershop Quartet/You Only Told Me Half	1958	2.50	5.00	10.00
DOT					
❑ 15695	Get a Job/I Found a Million Dollar Baby	1958	3.75	7.50	15.00
❑ 15827	Me and My Shadow/Music, Maestro, Please	1958	2.50	5.00	10.00
❑ 15858	Yellow Bird/Baby Clementine	1958	2.00	4.00	8.00
❑ 15909	You Can't Be True Dear/Beaver	1959	2.50	5.00	10.00
❑ 15950	Lullaby in Ragtime/Te Quiero	1959	2.50	5.00	10.00
❑ 15987	You Always Hurt the One You Love/				
	(B-side unknown)	1959	2.50	5.00	10.00
❑ 16037	Paper Doll/The Glow-Worm	1960	2.00	4.00	8.00
❑ 16049	I Miss You So/Oh Ma Ma	1960	2.00	4.00	8.00

Number	Title (A Side/B Side)	Yr	VG	VG+	NM
❏ 16091	Highways Are Happy Ways/I Got You	1960	2.00	4.00	8.00
❏ 16234	Yellow Bird/Baby Clementine	1961	2.00	4.00	8.00
❏ 16258	I'll Take Care of Your Cares/Ballerina	1961	2.00	4.00	8.00
❏ 16360	I Found the Only Girl for Me/				
	Queen of the Senior Prom	1961	2.00	4.00	8.00
❏ 16432	Tonight You Belong to Me/You Broke the Only				
	Heart That Ever Loved You	1963	—	3.50	7.00
❏ 16451	The End of the World/Big City	1963	—	3.50	7.00
❏ 16579	Don't Blame Me/				
	It Hurts Me More Than It Hurts You	1964	—	3.50	7.00
❏ 16703	Welcome Home/Chum Chum Chittilum Chum	1965	—	3.50	7.00
❏ 16733	Bye Bye Blackbird/Chum Chum Chittilum Chum	1965	—	3.50	7.00
❏ 16972	Smack Dab in the Middle/Honeysuckle Rose				
	Blues Bossa Nova	1967	—	3.00	6.00
❏ 17041	Cab Driver/Fortuosity	1967	—	3.00	6.00
❏ 17096	My Shy Violet/Flower Road	1968	—	3.00	6.00
❏ 17162	The Ol' Race Track/But for Love	1968	—	3.00	6.00
❏ 17198	Dream/Jimtown Road	1969	—	3.00	6.00
❏ 17235	A Guy on the Go/				
	What Have I Done for Her Lately	1969	—	3.00	6.00
❏ 17285	I'll Never Forgive Myself/Up to Maggie Jones	1969	—	3.00	6.00
❏ 17321	It Ain't No Big Thing/				
	Help Yourself to Some Tomorrow	1969	—	3.00	6.00
PARAMOUNT					
❏ 0046	Smile Away Every Rainy Day/Between Winston-				
	Salem and Nashville, Tennessee	1970	—	2.50	5.00
❏ 0095	Happy Songs of Love/I'm Sorry I Answered the				
	Phone	1971	—	2.50	5.00
❏ 0117	L-O-V-E/Strollin'	1971	—	2.50	5.00
❏ 0147	Come Summer/Sally Sunshine	1972	—	2.50	5.00
❏ 0181	There's No Life on the Moon/				
	A Donut and a Dream	1972	—	2.50	5.00
RANWOOD					
❏ 961	Truck Stop/He Gives Me Love	1973	—	2.00	4.00
❏ 1003	Tiger Rag/On a Chinese Honeymoon	1974	—	2.00	4.00
❏ 1020	You Are My Sunshine/Between Winston-Salem				
	and Nashville, Tennessee	1974	—	2.00	4.00
❏ 1040	El Paso/Till Then	197?	—	2.00	4.00
❏ 1042	Daisies Never Tell/Sawdust Heart	197?	—	2.00	4.00
❏ 1054	Coney Island Washboard/Nevertheless	197?	—	2.00	4.00
7-Inch Extended Plays					
DECCA					
❏ ED 582 [PS]	Souvenir Album	195?	3.00	6.00	12.00
—Cover for 2-EP set (91176, 91177)					
❏ ED 2010	Lazy River/I'm Afraid to Love You//Blue and				
	Sentimental/I've Got My Love to Keep Me				
	Warm	195?	3.75	7.50	15.00
❏ ED 2010 [PS]	The Mills Brothers, Volume 1	195?	3.75	7.50	15.00
❏ ED 2044	*Caravan/Solitude/It Don't Mean a Thing/				
	Georgia on My Mind	195?	3.75	7.50	15.00
❏ ED 2044 [PS]	The Mills Brothers, Vol. 2	195?	3.75	7.50	15.00
❏ ED 2513	One Dozen Roses/Rose Room//Mexicali Rose/				
	Honeysuckle Rose	195?	3.75	7.50	15.00
❏ ED 2513 [PS]	One Dozen Roses	195?	3.75	7.50	15.00
❏ ED 2573	Oh How I Miss You Tonight/You Only Told Me				
	Half the Story//When I Lost You/Will ❏ You				
	Remember Tomorrow	195?	3.75	7.50	15.00
❏ ED 2573 [PS]	Mills Brothers in Hi-Fi: Barbershop Ballads	195?	3.75	7.50	15.00
❏ ED 2742	Daddy's Little Girl/Daddy's Little Boy//You're				
	Nobody 'Til Somebody Loves You/Queen of				
	the Senior Prom	195?	3.00	6.00	12.00
❏ ED 2742 [PS]	The Mills Brothers	195?	3.00	6.00	12.00
❏ 91176	Paper Doll/I'll Be Around//You Always Hurt the				
	One You Love/Till Then	195?	3.00	6.00	12.00
—Part of 2-EP set ED 582					
❏ 91177	Too Many Irons in the Fire/I Guess I'll Get the				
	Papers and Go Home//You Never Miss the				
	Water Till the Well Runs Dry/After You	195?	3.00	6.00	12.00
—Part of 2-EP set ED 582					
DOT					
❏ DLP 592	Say Si Si/Time Was/It Happened in Monterey//				
	Perfidia/Yours/South of the Border	196?	3.00	6.00	12.00
—Jukebox issue; small hole, plays at 33 1/3 rpm					
❏ DLP 592 [PS]	Say Si Si and Other Great Latin Hits	196?	3.00	6.00	12.00
❏ DEP-1087	Glow Worm/Lazy River//Till Then/Paper Doll	195?	2.50	5.00	10.00
❏ DEP-1087 [PS]	Great Hits	195?	2.50	5.00	10.00
Albums					
ABC					
❏ 1027 [(2)]	The Best of the Mills Brothers, Volume 2	1978	3.00	6.00	12.00
❏ 4004	16 Great Performances	1975	2.50	5.00	10.00
ABC SONGBIRD					
❏ SBDP-255	Inspiration	1974	2.50	5.00	10.00
DECCA					
❏ DXB 193 [(2)M]	The Best of the Mills Brothers	1965	5.00	10.00	20.00
❏ DL 4084 [M]	Our Golden Favorites	1960	5.00	10.00	20.00
❏ DL 5050 [10]	Barber Shop Ballads	1950	12.50	25.00	50.00
❏ DL 5051 [10]	Barber Shop Ballads	1950	12.50	25.00	50.00
❏ DL 5102 [10]	Souvenir Album	1950	12.50	25.00	50.00
❏ DL 5337 [10]	Wonderful Words	1951	12.50	25.00	50.00
❏ DL 5506 [10]	Meet the Mills Brothers	1954	12.50	25.00	50.00
❏ DL 5516 [10]	Four Boys and a Guitar	1954	12.50	25.00	50.00
❏ DXSB 7193 [(2)R]	The Best of the Mills Brothers	1965	3.75	7.50	15.00
❏ DL 8148 [M]	Souvenir Album	1955	7.50	15.00	30.00
❏ DL 8209 [M]	Singin' and Swingin'	1956	7.50	15.00	30.00
❏ DL 8219 [M]	Memory Lane	1956	7.50	15.00	30.00
❏ DL 8491 [M]	One Dozen Roses	1957	7.50	15.00	30.00
❏ DL 8664 [M]	The Mills Brothers in Hi-Fi	1958	7.50	15.00	30.00
❏ DL 8827 [M]	Glow with the Mills Brothers	1958	7.50	15.00	30.00
❏ DL 8890 [M]	Barber Shop Harmony	1959	7.50	15.00	30.00
❏ DL 8892 [M]	Harmonizin' with the Mills Brothers	1959	7.50	15.00	30.00
❏ DL 74084 [R]	Our Golden Favorites	196?	3.00	6.00	12.00
❏ DL 75174 [R]	Golden Favorites, Volume 2	1970	2.50	5.00	10.00
DOT					
❏ DLP-3103 [M]	Mmmm, The Mills Brothers	1958	5.00	10.00	20.00
❏ DLP-3157 [M]	The Mills Brothers' Great Hits	1958	5.00	10.00	20.00
❏ DLP-3208 [M]	Great Barbershop Hits	1959	5.00	10.00	20.00

Number	Title (A Side/B Side)	Yr	VG	VG+	NM
❏ DLP-3232 [M]	Merry Christmas	1959	5.00	10.00	20.00
❏ DLP-3237 [M]	The Mills Brothers Sing	1960	5.00	10.00	20.00
❏ DLP-3308 [M]	The Mills Brothers' Great Hits, Volume 2	1960	3.75	7.50	15.00
❏ DLP-3338 [M]	Yellow Bird	1960	3.75	7.50	15.00
❏ DLP-3363 [M]	San Antonio Rose	1961	3.75	7.50	15.00
❏ DLP-3368 [M]	Great Hawaiian Hits	1961	3.75	7.50	15.00
❏ DLP-3465 [M]	Beer Barrel Polka and Other Hits	1962	3.00	6.00	12.00
❏ DLP-3508 [M]	The End of the World	1963	3.00	6.00	12.00
❏ DLP-3565 [M]	Gems by the Mills Brothers	1964	3.00	6.00	12.00
❏ DLP-3568 [M]	Hymns We Love	1964	3.00	6.00	12.00
❏ DLP-3592 [M]	Say Si Si and Other Great Latin Hits	1964	3.00	6.00	12.00
❏ DLP-3652 [M]	Ten Years of Hits 1954-1964	1965	3.00	6.00	12.00
❏ DLP-3699 [M]	These Are the Mills Brothers	1966	3.00	6.00	12.00
❏ DLP-3744 [M]	That Country Feeling	1966	3.00	6.00	12.00
❏ DL-3766 [M]	The Mills Brothers Today	1966	3.00	6.00	12.00
❏ DLP-3783 [M]	The Mills Brothers Live	1967	3.75	7.50	15.00
❏ DLP-25103 [S]	Mmmm, The Mills Brothers	1958	7.50	15.00	30.00
❏ DLP-25157 [S]	The Mills Brothers' Great Hits	195?	15.00	30.00	60.00
—Blue vinyl					
❏ DLP-25157 [S]	The Mills Brothers' Great Hits	1958	7.50	15.00	30.00
—Black vinyl					
❏ DLP-25208 [S]	Great Barbershop Hits	1959	7.50	15.00	30.00
❏ DLP-25232 [S]	Merry Christmas	1959	7.50	15.00	30.00
—Same as above, but in stereo; with cursive "Dot" logo					
❏ DLP-25232 [S]	Merry Christmas	1968	3.00	6.00	12.00
—With "Dot"/"Paramount" logo					
❏ DLP-25237 [S]	The Mills Brothers Sing	1960	7.50	15.00	30.00
❏ DLP-25308 [S]	The Mills Brothers' Great Hits, Volume 2	1960	5.00	10.00	20.00
❏ DLP-25338 [S]	Yellow Bird	1960	5.00	10.00	20.00
❏ DLP-25363 [S]	San Antonio Rose	1961	5.00	10.00	20.00
❏ DLP-25368 [S]	Great Hawaiian Hits	1961	5.00	10.00	20.00
❏ DLP-25465 [S]	Beer Barrel Polka and Other Hits	1962	3.75	7.50	15.00
❏ DLP-25508 [S]	The End of the World	1963	3.75	7.50	15.00
❏ DLP-25565 [S]	Gems by the Mills Brothers	1964	3.75	7.50	15.00
❏ DLP-25568 [S]	Hymns We Love	1964	3.75	7.50	15.00
❏ DLP-25592 [S]	Say Si Si and Other Great Latin Hits	1964	3.75	7.50	15.00
❏ DLP-25652 [S]	Ten Years of Hits 1954-1964	1965	3.75	7.50	15.00
❏ DLP-25699 [S]	These Are the Mills Brothers	1966	3.75	7.50	15.00
❏ DLP-25744 [S]	That Country Feeling	1966	3.75	7.50	15.00
❏ DLP-25766 [S]	The Mills Brothers Today	1966	3.75	7.50	15.00
❏ DLP-25783 [S]	The Mills Brothers Live	1967	3.75	7.50	15.00
❏ DLP-25809	Fortuosity	1968	3.75	7.50	15.00
❏ DLP-25872	My Shy Violet	1968	3.75	7.50	15.00
❏ DLP-25927	Dream	1969	3.75	7.50	15.00
❏ DLP-25960	The Mills Brothers In Motion	1970	3.75	7.50	15.00
EVEREST ARCHIVE OF FOLK & JAZZ					
❏ 300	The Mills Brothers	197?	2.50	5.00	10.00
❏ 328	The Mills Brothers, Volume 2	197?	2.50	5.00	10.00
GNP CRESCENDO					
❏ GNP-9106	Four Boys and a Guitar	197?	2.50	5.00	10.00
HAMILTON					
❏ HL-116 [M]	The Mills Brothers Sing for You	1964	3.00	6.00	12.00
❏ HS-12116 [S]	The Mills Brothers Sing for You	1964	3.00	6.00	12.00
MARK 56					
❏ 709	Original Radio Broadcasts	197?	2.50	5.00	10.00
MCA					
❏ 132	Golden Favorites, Volume 2	1973	2.50	5.00	10.00
❏ 188	Old Golden Favorites	1973	2.50	5.00	10.00
❏ 717	16 Great Performances	1980	2.00	4.00	8.00
❏ 1556	The Mills Brothers	198?	2.50	5.00	10.00
❏ 4039 [(2)]	The Best of the Mills Brothers	197?	3.00	6.00	12.00
❏ 15029	Merry Christmas	198?	2.50	5.00	10.00
❏ 27083	The Mills Brothers Great Hits	1980	2.00	4.00	8.00
❏ 28116	Were You There	198?	2.00	4.00	8.00
MCA SPECIAL MARKETS					
❏ MSM2-35067 [(2)]	Classic Mills Brothers	198?	2.50	5.00	10.00
PARAMOUNT					
❏ PAS-1010	The Best of the Mills Brothers	1973	3.00	6.00	12.00
❏ PAS-1027 [(2)]	The Best of the Mills Brothers, Volume 2	1974	3.75	7.50	15.00
❏ PAS-5025	No Turnin' Back	1971	3.00	6.00	12.00
❏ PAS-6024	What a Wonderful World	1972	3.00	6.00	12.00
❏ PAS-6038	A Donut and a Dream	1973	3.00	6.00	12.00
PICKWICK					
❏ SPC-1025	Merry Christmas	1979	2.50	5.00	10.00
—Reissue of Dot album with one fewer track					
❏ 2008	Songs You Remember	197?	2.50	5.00	10.00
❏ 2030	The Mills Brothers	1973	2.50	5.00	10.00
❏ SPC-3076	14 Karat Gold	196?	2.50	5.00	10.00
❏ SPC-3107	Anytime	197?	2.50	5.00	10.00
❏ SPC-3137	Dream a Little Dream	197?	2.50	5.00	10.00
❏ SPC-3158	Till We Meet Again	197?	2.50	5.00	10.00
❏ SPC-3220	Cab Driver	197?	2.50	5.00	10.00
❏ SPC-3556	The Mills Brothers	1976	2.00	4.00	8.00
RANWOOD					
❏ 7035 [(2)]	22 Great Hits	1985	2.50	5.00	10.00
❏ 8123	Cab Driver	197?	2.50	5.00	10.00
❏ 8133	The Mills Brothers Story	197?	2.50	5.00	10.00
❏ 8139	Country's Greatest Hits	197?	2.50	5.00	10.00
❏ 8152	50th Anniversary	197?	2.50	5.00	10.00
❏ 8198	Command Performance	198?	2.00	4.00	8.00
SUNNYVALE					
❏ 1023	Timeless	1978	2.50	5.00	10.00
VOCALION					
❏ VL 3607 [M]	In a Mellow Tone	196?	3.00	6.00	12.00
❏ VL 73607 [R]	In a Mellow Tone	196?	2.50	5.00	10.00
❏ VL 73859 [R]	Such Sweet Singing	1969	2.50	5.00	10.00

MILLS BROTHERS, THE, AND LOUIS ARMSTRONG See ARMSTRONG, LOUIS, AND THE MILLS BROTHERS.

MILSAP, RONNIE

12-Inch Singles

RCA

Number	Title (A Side/B Side)	Yr	VG	VG+	NM
❏ JD-11683 [DJ]	Get It Up/Hi-Heel Sneakers	1979	5.00	10.00	20.00
—Promo only on green vinyl					

Number	Title (A Side/B Side)	Yr	VG	VG+	NM
45s					
BOBLO					
524	Make Love Sweet/(B-side unknown)	1977	—	2.50	5.00
CAPITOL NASHVILLE					
S7-18909	The Christmas Song/Till the Season Comes 'Round Again	1995			3.00
CHIPS					
2889	Loving You Is a Natural Thing/So Hung Up on Sylvia	1970	2.00	4.00	8.00
2987	A Rose by Any Other Name (Is Still a Rose)/Sermonette	1970	2.00	4.00	8.00
FESTIVAL					
5002	Wishing You Were Here/Your Tears Leave Me Cold	1977	—	2.50	5.00
LIBERTY					
S7-17595	True Believer/These Foolish Things (Remind Me of You)	1993	—	2.00	4.00
—Red vinyl					
S7-17640	I'm Playing for You/Better Off with the Blues	1993	—	2.00	4.00
PACEMAKER					
245	Wishing You Were Here/A Loving Background	1967	2.00	4.00	8.00
RCA					
2509-7-R	Are You Loving Me Like I'm Loving You/Back to the Grindstone	1990			3.00
2848-7-R	Since I Don't Have You/I Ain't Gonna Cry No More	1991	—	—	3.00
5033-7-R	How Do I Turn You On/Don't Take It Tonight	1986	—	—	3.00
5049-7-R	Only One Night of the Year/It's Just Not Christmas (If I Can't Spend It With You)	1986	—	—	3.00
5169-7-R	Snap Your Fingers/This Time Last Year	1987	—	—	3.00
5209-7-R	Make No Mistake, She's Mine/You're My Love	1987	—	—	3.00
—With Kenny Rogers					
5209-7-R [PS]	Make No Mistake, She's Mine/You're My Love	1987	—	2.00	4.00
5259-7-R	Where Do the Nights Go/If You Don't Want Me To	1987	—	—	3.00
5351-7-R	Christmas Medley: Carol of the Bells/O Come, O Come Emmanuel/Silent Night/Joy to the World//I'll Be Home for Christmas	1987	—	—	3.00
6896-7-R	Old Folks/Earthquake	1988	—	—	3.00
—A-side with Mike Reid					
6896-7-R [PS]	Old Folks/Earthquake	1988	—	2.50	5.00
—A-side with Mike Reid					
8389-7-R	Button Off My Shirt/One Night	1988	—	—	3.00
8746-7-R	Don't You Ever Get Tired (Of Hurtin' Me)/I Never Expected to See You	1988	—	—	3.00
8868-7-R	Houston Solution/If You Don't Want Me To	1989	—	—	3.00
9027-7-R	A Woman in Love/Starting Today	1989	—	—	3.00
9071-7-R	I'll Be Home for Christrmas/We're Here to Love	1989	—	—	3.00
9120-7-R	Stranger Things Have Happened/Southern Roots	1989	—	—	3.00
PB-10843	Let My Love Be Your Pillow/Busy Makin' Plans	1976	—	2.00	4.00
GB-10931	(I'm a) Stand By My Woman Man/What Goes On When the Sun Goes Down	1977	—	2.00	4.00
—Gold Standard Series					
PB-10976	It Was Almost Like a Song/It Don't Hurt to Dream	1977	—	2.00	4.00
PB-11146	What a Difference You've Made in My Life/Selfish	1977	—	2.00	4.00
PB-11270	Only One Live in My Life/Back on My Mind Again	1978	—	2.00	4.00
PB-11333	Let My Love Be Your Pillow/Busy Makin' Plans	1978	—	2.00	4.00
PB-11369	Let's Take the Long Way Around the World/Not Trying to Forget	1978	—	2.00	4.00
PB-11421	Back on My Mind Again/Santa Barbara	1978	—	2.00	4.00
GB-11496	It Was Almost Like a Song/Only One Love in My Life	1979	—	2.00	4.00
—Gold Standard Series					
PB-11553	Nobody Likes Sad Songs/Just Because It Feels Good	1979	—	2.00	4.00
PB-11695	In No Time at All/Get It Up	1979	—	2.00	4.00
PB-11909	Why Don't You Spend the Night/Heads I Go, Hearts I Stay	1980	—	2.00	4.00
PB-11952	My Heart/Silent Night (After the Fight)	1980	—	2.00	4.00
GB-11987	What a Difference You've Made in My Life/Let's Take the Long Way Around the World	1980	—	2.00	4.00
—Gold Standard Series					
GB-11994	Back on My Mind Again/Nobody Likes Sad Songs	1980	—	2.00	4.00
—Gold Standard Series					
PB-12006	Cowboys and Clowns/Misery Loves Company	1980	—	2.00	4.00
PB-12006 [PS]	Cowboys and Clowns/Misery Loves Company	1980	—	2.50	5.00
PB-12084	Smoky Mountain Rain/Crystal Fallin' Rain	1980	—	2.00	4.00
PB-12194	Am I Losing You/He'll Have to Go	1981	—	2.00	4.00
PB-12264	(There's) No Gettin' Over Me/I Live My Whole Life at Night	1981	—	2.00	4.00
GB-12314	Why Don't You Spend the Night/Smoky Mountain Rain	1981	—	—	3.00
—Gold Standard Series					
GB-12315	My Heart/Silent Night (After the Fight)	1981	—	—	3.00
—Gold Standard Series					
PB-12342	I Wouldn't Have Missed It For the World/It Happens Every Time (I Think of You)	1981	—	2.00	4.00
PB-13216	Any Day Now/It's Just a Room	1982	—	2.00	4.00
PB-13286	He Got You/I Love New Orleans Music	1982	—	2.00	4.00
PB-13362	Inside/Carolina Dreams	1982	—	2.00	4.00
PB-13470	Stranger in My House/Is It Over	1983	—	2.00	4.00
GB-13491	(There's) No Gettin' Over Me/I Wouldn't Have Missed It for the World	1983	—	—	3.00
—Gold Standard Series					
PB-13564	Don't You Know How Much I Love You/Feelings Change	1983	—	2.00	4.00
PB-13658	Show Her/Watch Out for the Other Guy	1983	—	2.00	4.00
PB-13665	It's Christmas/We're Here to Love	1983	—	2.00	4.00
GB-13784	Don't You Know How Much I Love You/Show Her	1984	—	—	3.00
—Gold Standard Series					
GB-13785	Any Day Now/Stranger in My House	1984	—	—	3.00
—Gold Standard Series					
PB-13805	Still Losing You/I'll Take Care of You	1984	—	—	3.00
PB-13847	She Loves My Car/Prisoner of the Highway	1984	—	—	3.00
JD-13869 [DJ]	She Loves My Car/(Instrumental)	1984	2.00	4.00	8.00
PB-13955	She's Always in Love/I Might Have Said	1984	—	—	—
—Unreleased					
PB-14034	She Keeps the Home Fires Burning/Is It Over	1985	—	—	3.00
PB-14135	Lost in the Fifties Tonight (In the Still of the Night)/I Might Have Said	1985	—	2.00	4.00
PB-14135 [PS]	Lost in the Fifties Tonight (In the Still of the Night)/I Might Have Said	1985	—	2.00	4.00
PB-14286	Happy Happy Birthday Baby/I'll Take Care of You	1986	—	—	3.00
GB-14349	Lost in the Fifties Tonight (In the Still of the Night)/She Keeps the Home Fires Burning	1986	—	—	3.00
—Gold Standard Series					
PB-14365	In Love/Old Fashioned Girl Like You	1986	—	—	3.00
62104	Turn That Radio On/Old Habits Are Hard to Break	1991	—	—	3.00
62217	All Is Fair in Love and War/Back to the Grindstone	1992	—	—	3.00
62332	L.A. to the Moon/When the Hurt Comes Down	1992	—	—	3.00
62370	Still Losing You/If You Really Don't Want Me	1992	—	—	3.00
RCA VICTOR					
74-0969	I Hate You/(All Together Now) Let's Fall Apart	1973	—	3.00	6.00
APBO-0097	That Girl Who Waits on Tables/You're Drivin' Me Out of My Mind	1973	—	3.00	6.00
APBO-0237	Pure Love/Love the Second Time Around	1974	—	3.00	6.00
APBO-0313	Please Don't Tell Me How the Story Ends/Streets of Gold	1974	—	3.00	6.00
PB-10112	(I'd Be) A Legend in My Time/The Biggest Lie	1974	—	2.50	5.00
PB-10112 [PS]	(I'd Be) A Legend in My Time/The Biggest Lie	1974	2.00	4.00	8.00
GB-10167	That Girl Who Waits on Tables/I Hate You	1975	—	2.00	4.00
—Gold Standard Series					
PB-10228	Too Late to Worry, Too Blue to Cry/Country Cookin'	1975	—	2.50	5.00
PB-10335	Daydreams About Night Things/Play Born to Lose	1975	—	2.50	5.00
PB-10420	Just In Case/Remember to Remind Me (I'm Leaving)	1975	—	2.50	5.00
GB-10500	Please Don't Tell Me How the Story Ends/Streets of Gold	1975	—	2.00	4.00
—Gold Standard Series					
GB-10501	Too Late to Worry, Too Blue to Cry/Country Cookin'	1975	—	2.00	4.00
—Gold Standard Series					
GB-10502	(I'd Be) A Legend in My Time/The Biggest Lie	1975	—	2.00	4.00
GB-10503	Pure Love/Love the Second Time Around	1975	—	2.00	4.00
—Gold Standard Series					
PB-10593	What Goes On When the Sun Goes Down/Love Takes a Long Time to Die	1976	—	2.50	5.00
GB-10672	Daydreams About Night Things/Just in Case	1976	—	2.00	4.00
—Gold Standard Series					
PB-10724	(I'm a) Stand By My Woman Man/Lovers, Friends and Strangers	1976	—	2.50	5.00
SCEPTER					
12109	Let's Go Get Stoned/Never Had It So Good	1965	3.00	6.00	12.00
12127	A Thousand Miles from Nowhere/When It Comes to My Baby	1966	3.00	6.00	12.00
12145	The End of the World/I Saw Pity in the Face of a Friend	1966	3.00	6.00	12.00
12161	When the Boys Talk About the Girls/Ain't No Sole in These Old Shoes	1966	3.00	6.00	12.00
12161	When the Boys Talk About the Girls/Another Branch from the Old Branch	1966	3.00	6.00	12.00
12206	House of the Rising Sun/I Can't Tell a Lie	1967	2.50	5.00	10.00
12228	Do What You Gotta Do/Mr. Mailman	1968	2.00	4.00	8.00
12246	Nothing Is As Good As It Used to Be/Denver	1969	2.00	4.00	8.00
12272	What's Your Game/Love Will Never Pass Us By	1970	2.00	4.00	8.00
VIRGIN					
58853	Time, Love and Money/Livin' on Love	2000	—	—	3.00
WARNER BROS.					
5405	Total Disaster/It Went to Your Head	1963	3.75	7.50	15.00
7540	Sunday Rain/Why	1971	—	3.00	6.00
7629	Magic Me Again/Me and You, You and Me	1972	—	3.00	6.00
8127	She Even Woke Me Up to Say Goodbye/Loving You's a Natural Thing	1975	—	2.00	4.00
8160	A Rose by Any Other Name/Please Don't Tell Me How the Story Ends	1975	—	2.00	4.00
8218	Crying/Why	1976	—	2.00	4.00
Albums					
PAIR					
PDL2-1031 [(2)]	Believe It!	1986	3.00	6.00	12.00
PDL2-1105 [(2)]	Back on My Mind Again	1986	3.00	6.00	12.00
PICKWICK					
JS-6179	Plain and Simple	197?	2.50	5.00	10.00
RCA					
9588-1-R	Stranger Things Have Happened	1989	2.50	5.00	10.00
R 183710	Back to the Grindstone	1991	5.00	10.00	20.00
—Only released on vinyl through BMG Direct Marketing					
RCA VICTOR					
APL1-0338	Where My Heart Is	1973	5.00	10.00	20.00
APD1-0500 [Q]	Pure Love	1974	5.00	10.00	20.00
APL1-0500	Pure Love	1974	3.75	7.50	15.00
APD1-0846 [Q]	A Legend in My Time	1975	5.00	10.00	20.00
APL1-0846	A Legend in My Time	1975	3.75	7.50	15.00
APL1-1223	Night Things	1975	3.75	7.50	15.00
APL1-1666	20-20 Vision	1976	3.00	6.00	12.00
APL1-2043	Ronnie Milsap Live	1976	3.00	6.00	12.00
AFL1-2439	It Was Almost Like a Song	1977	3.00	6.00	12.00
AFL1-2780	Only One Love in My Life	1978	3.00	6.00	12.00
AHL1-3346	Images	1979	3.00	6.00	12.00
AHL1-3563	Milsap Magic	1980	2.50	5.00	10.00
AYL1-3760	Where My Heart Is	1980	2.00	4.00	8.00
—"Best Buy Series" reissue					
AHL1-3772	Greatest Hits	1980	2.50	5.00	10.00

M

Number	Title (A Side/B Side)	Yr	VG	VG+	NM
❏ AYL1-3899	Pure Love	1981	2.00	4.00	8.00
—"Best Buy Series" reissue					
❏ AAL1-3932	Out Where the Bright Lights Are Glowing	1981	2.50	5.00	10.00
❏ AHL1-4060	There's No Gettin' Over Me	1981	2.50	5.00	10.00
❏ AYL1-4171	Images	1981	2.00	4.00	8.00
—"Best Buy Series" reissue					
❏ AYL1-4255	Ronnie Milsap Live	1982	2.00	4.00	8.00
—"Best Buy Series" reissue					
❏ AHL1-4311	Inside Ronnie Milsap	1982	2.50	5.00	10.00
❏ AHL1-4670	Keyed Up	1983	2.50	5.00	10.00
❏ AHL1-5016	One More Try for Love	1984	2.50	5.00	10.00
❏ AYL1-5139	It Was Almost Like a Song	1984	2.00	4.00	8.00
—"Best Buy Series" reissue					
❏ AYL1-5140	There's No Gettin' Over Me	1984	2.00	4.00	8.00
—"Best Buy Series" reissue					
❏ AYL1-5142	Inside Ronnie Milsap	1984	2.00	4.00	8.00
—"Best Buy Series" reissue					
❏ AHL1-5425	Greatest Hits, Vol. 2	1985	2.50	5.00	10.00
❏ AYL1-5435	Keyed Up	1985	2.00	4.00	8.00
—"Best Buy Series" reissue					
❏ 5624-1-R	Christmas with Ronnie Milsap	1986	2.50	5.00	10.00
❏ 6425-1-R	Heart and Soul	1987	2.50	5.00	10.00
❏ CPL1-7166	Collector's Series	1986	2.00	4.00	8.00
❏ AHL1-7194	Lost in the Fifties Tonight	1986	2.50	5.00	10.00
❏ 7618-1-R	Heart and Soul	1988	2.00	4.00	8.00
—Reissue of 6245					
TIME-LIFE					
❏ STW-110	Country Music	1981	2.50	5.00	10.00
WARNER BROS.					
❏ WS 1934	Ronnie Milsap	1971	5.00	10.00	20.00
❏ BS 2870	A Rose By Any Other Name	1975	3.75	7.50	15.00

MIMMS, GARNET, AND THE ENCHANTERS Includes Garnet Mimms credited alone. Also see THE ENCHANTERS (2).

45s

Number	Title (A Side/B Side)	Yr	VG	VG+	NM
ARISTA					
❏ 0239	What It Is (Part 1)/What It Is (Part 2)	1977	—	2.00	4.00
❏ 0289	Johnny Perter/Tail Snatcher	1977	—	2.00	4.00
❏ 0332	Right Here in the Palm of My Hand/Tail Snatcher	1978	—	2.00	4.00
GSF					
❏ 6874	Another Place/Stop and Check Yourself	1972	—	3.00	6.00
❏ 6887	I'll Keep On Loving/Somebody, Someplace	1972	—	3.00	6.00
UNITED ARTISTS					
❏ 0109	Cry Baby/For Your Precious Love	1973	—	2.00	4.00
—"Silver Spotlight Series" reissue					
❏ 629	Cry Baby/Don't Change Your Heart	1963	3.75	7.50	15.00
❏ 658	Baby Don't You Weep/For Your Precious Love	1963	3.00	6.00	12.00
❏ 658 [PS]	Baby Don't You Weep/For Your Precious Love	1963	15.00	30.00	60.00
❏ 694	Tell Me Baby/Anytime You Want Me	1964	3.00	6.00	12.00
❏ 715	One Girl/A Quiet Place	1964	3.00	6.00	12.00
❏ 773	One Woman Man/Look Away	1964	3.00	6.00	12.00
❏ 796	A Little Bit of Soap/I'll Make It Up to You	1964	3.00	6.00	12.00
❏ 848	So Close/It Was Easier to Hurt Her	1965	3.00	6.00	12.00
❏ 868	Welcome Home/The Adventures of Moll Flanders	1965	3.00	6.00	12.00
❏ 887	Everytime/That Goes to Show You	1965	3.00	6.00	12.00
❏ 951	Looking for You/More Than a Miracle	1965	3.00	6.00	12.00
❏ 995	Prove It to Me/I'll Take Good Care of You	1966	3.00	6.00	12.00
❏ 50058	My Baby/Keep On Smilin'	1966	—	—	—
—Unreleased					
VEEP					
❏ 1232	Thinkin'/It's Been Such a Long Time Comin'	1966	2.00	4.00	8.00
❏ 1234	My Baby/Keep On Smilin'	1966	2.00	4.00	8.00
❏ 1252	All About Love/The Truth Hurts	1967	2.00	4.00	8.00
VERVE					
❏ 10596	Stop and Think It Over/I Can Hear My Baby Crying	1968	2.00	4.00	8.00
❏ 10624	Can You Top This/We Can Find That Love	1968	2.00	4.00	8.00
❏ 10642	Take Me/Happy Landing	1969	2.00	4.00	8.00
❏ 10650	Sad Song/Get It While You Can	1970	2.00	4.00	8.00
Albums					
ARISTA					
❏ AL 4153	Garnet Mimms Has It All	1978	3.00	6.00	12.00
UNITED ARTISTS					
❏ UAL 3305 [M]	Cry Baby and 11 Other Hits	1963	20.00	40.00	80.00
❏ UAL 3396 [M]	As Long As I Have You	1964	12.50	25.00	50.00
❏ UAL 3498 [M]	I'll Take Good Care of You	1966	12.50	25.00	50.00
❏ UAS 6305 [S]	Cry Baby and 11 Other Hits	1963	25.00	50.00	100.00
❏ UAS 6396 [S]	As Long As I Have You	1964	17.50	35.00	70.00
❏ UAS 6498 [S]	I'll Take Good Care of You	1966	17.50	35.00	70.00

MIND EXPANDERS, THE
Albums

Number	Title (A Side/B Side)	Yr	VG	VG+	NM
DOT					
❏ DLP-3773 [M]	What's Happening	1967	25.00	50.00	100.00
❏ DLP-25773 [S]	What's Happening	1967	20.00	40.00	80.00

MIND GARAGE, THE
45s

Number	Title (A Side/B Side)	Yr	VG	VG+	NM
RCA VICTOR					
❏ 47-9755	There Was a Time/What's Behind Those Eyes	1969	2.00	4.00	8.00
❏ 47-9812	Jailhouse Rock/Tobacco Road	1969	2.00	4.00	8.00
Albums					
RCA VICTOR					
❏ LSP-4218	The Mind Garage	1969	5.00	10.00	20.00
❏ LSP-4319	The Mind Garage Again!	1970	5.00	10.00	20.00

MINDBENDERS, THE Also see WAYNE FONTANA AND THE MINDBENDERS.
45s

Number	Title (A Side/B Side)	Yr	VG	VG+	NM
FONTANA					
❏ 1541	A Groovy Kind of Love/Love Is Good	1966	3.00	6.00	12.00
❏ 1555	Ashes to Ashes/Don't Know About Love	1966	2.00	4.00	8.00
❏ 1571	I Want Her, She Wants Me/Morning After	1967	2.00	4.00	8.00
❏ 1595	It's Getting Harder All the Time/Off and Running	1967	2.00	4.00	8.00
❏ 1620	Yellow Brick Road/Blessed Are the Lonely	1968	2.00	4.00	8.00
❏ 1628	Uncle Joe the Ice Cream Man/The Man Who Loved Trees	1968	2.00	4.00	8.00

Number	Title (A Side/B Side)	Yr	VG	VG+	NM
Albums					
FONTANA					
❏ MGF-27554 [M]	A Groovy Kind of Love	1966	6.25	12.50	25.00
—With "Ashes to Ashes"					
❏ MGF-27554 [M]	A Groovy Kind of Love	1966	7.50	15.00	30.00
—With "Don't Cry No More"					
❏ SRF-67554 [R]	A Groovy Kind of Love	1966	5.00	10.00	20.00
—With "Ashes to Ashes"					
❏ SRF-67554 [R]	A Groovy Kind of Love	1966	6.25	12.50	25.00
—With "Don't Cry No More"					

MINEO, SAL
45s

Number	Title (A Side/B Side)	Yr	VG	VG+	NM
DECCA					
❏ 31692	Why Don't You Love Me/A Girl Across the Way	1964	3.00	6.00	12.00
EPIC					
❏ 9216	Start Movin' (In My Direction)/Love Affair	1957	6.25	12.50	25.00
❏ 9216 [PS]	Start Movin' (In My Direction)/Love Affair	1957	10.00	20.00	40.00
❏ 9227	Lasting Love/You Shouldn't Do That	1957	5.00	10.00	20.00
❏ 9227 [PS]	Lasting Love/You Shouldn't Do That	1957	7.50	15.00	30.00
❏ 9246	Party Time/The Words That I Whisper	1957	5.00	10.00	20.00
❏ 9246 [PS]	Party Time/The Words That I Whisper	1957	7.50	15.00	30.00
❏ 9260	Little Pigeon/Cuttin' In	1958	5.00	10.00	20.00
❏ 9260 [PS]	Little Pigeon/Cuttin' In	1958			
—Rumored to exist, but without conclusive evidence, we will delete this from future editions					
❏ 9271	Seven Steps to Love/A Couple of Crazy Kids	1958	5.00	10.00	20.00
❏ 9287	Baby Face/Souvenirs of Summertime	1958	5.00	10.00	20.00
❏ 9327	Young As We Are/Make Believe Baby	1959	5.00	10.00	20.00
❏ 9327 [PS]	Young As We Are/Make Believe Baby	1959	7.50	15.00	30.00
❏ 9345	I'll Never Be Myself Again/The Words That I Whisper	1959	5.00	10.00	20.00
FONTANA					
❏ 1504	Save the Last Dance for Me/Take Me Back	1965	3.00	6.00	12.00

7-Inch Extended Plays

Number	Title (A Side/B Side)	Yr	VG	VG+	NM
EPIC					
❏ EG-7187	(contents unknown)	1958	12.50	25.00	50.00
❏ EG-7187 [PS]	Sal Mineo	1958	12.50	25.00	50.00
❏ EG-7194	Baby Face/Too Young//The Words That I Whisper/Blue-Eyed Baby	1958	10.00	20.00	40.00
❏ EG-7194 [PS]	Sal	1958	10.00	20.00	40.00
❏ EG-7195	(contents unknown)	1958	10.00	20.00	40.00
❏ EG-7195 [PS]	Sal	1958	10.00	20.00	40.00
❏ EG-7204	Souvenirs of Summertime/Seven Steps to Love//A Couple of Crazy Kids/Secret Doorway	1959	12.50	25.00	50.00
❏ EG-7204 [PS]	Souvenirs of Summertime	1959	12.50	25.00	50.00
❏ ZTEP 27283/4	Too Young/Start Movin'//Baby Face/Little Pigeon	195?	15.00	30.00	60.00
—Special item for Scotch cellophane tape					
❏ ZTEP 27283/4 [PS]	Sal Sings	195?	20.00	40.00	80.00
Albums					
EPIC					
❏ LN 3405 [M]	Sal	1958	37.50	75.00	150.00

MINNELLI, LIZA Also see JUDY GARLAND AND LIZA MINNELLI.
12-Inch Singles

Number	Title (A Side/B Side)	Yr	VG	VG+	NM
EPIC					
❏ 68858	Losing My Mind (4 versions)	1989	2.50	5.00	10.00
❏ 73166	Love Pains (5 versions)	1989	2.50	5.00	10.00
45s					
A&M					
❏ 915	Married/You Better Sit Down Kids//Waiting for My Friends	1968	—	3.00	6.00
❏ 1018	Raggedy Ann and Raggedy Andy/Frank Mills	1969	—	3.00	6.00
❏ 1173	Come Saturday Morning/Wherefore and Why	1970	—	3.00	6.00
❏ 1244	(I Wonder Where My) Easy Rider's Gone/The Man I Love	1971	—	3.00	6.00
CADENCE					
❏ 1436	What Do You Think I Am/You Are For Living	1963	3.00	6.00	12.00
CAPITOL					
❏ 4994	One Summer Love/How Much Do I Love You	1963	2.50	5.00	10.00
❏ 5103	Day Dreaming/His Woman	1964	2.50	5.00	10.00
❏ 5473	Did I Hurt Your Feelings/Imprevu	1965	2.00	4.00	8.00
❏ 5761	I Who Have Nothing/Middle of the Street	1966	2.00	4.00	8.00
COLUMBIA					
❏ 10178	All That Jazz/My Own Best Friend	1975	—	2.00	4.00
❏ 45715	Ring Them Bells/It Was a Good Time	1972	—	2.50	5.00
❏ 45746	The Singer/Mr. Emery Won't Be Home	1972	—	2.50	5.00
❏ 45846	Don't Let Me Be Lonely Tonight/Mr. Emery Won't Be Home	1973	—	2.50	5.00
❏ 45995	Harbour/More Than I Like You	1974	—	2.50	5.00
EPIC					
❏ 73011	Losing My Mind/Tonight Is Forever	1989	—	2.50	5.00
UNITED ARTISTS					
❏ XW1014	Theme from "New York, New York"/Hazy	1977	—	2.50	5.00
Albums					
A&M					
❏ SP-3524 [(2)]	Liza Minnelli Foursider	1973	3.75	7.50	15.00
❏ SP-4141 [M]	Liza Minnelli	1968	6.25	12.50	25.00
—Mono copies have stereo numbers, but the labels are mono white label promos					
❏ SP-4141 [S]	Liza Minnelli	1968	3.75	7.50	15.00
❏ SP-4164	Come Saturday Morning	1969	3.75	7.50	15.00
❏ SP-4272	New Feelin'	1970	3.75	7.50	15.00
❏ SP-4345	Live at the Olympia	1971	3.75	7.50	15.00
❏ SP-6013 [(2)]	Liza Minnelli Foursider	198?	2.50	5.00	10.00
—Reissue of 3524					
CAPITOL					
❏ ST 2174 [S]	Liza! Liza!	1964	6.25	12.50	25.00
❏ T 2174 [M]	Liza! Liza!	1964	5.00	10.00	20.00
❏ SM-2271	It Amazes Me	1976	2.50	5.00	10.00
—Reissue with new prefix					
❏ ST 2271 [S]	It Amazes Me	1965	6.25	12.50	25.00
❏ T 2271 [M]	It Amazes Me	1965	5.00	10.00	20.00
❏ ST 2448 [S]	There Is a Time	1966	6.25	12.50	25.00
❏ T 2448 [M]	There Is a Time	1966	5.00	10.00	20.00
❏ SM-11080	Maybe This Time	197?	2.50	5.00	10.00
—Reissue with new prefix					
❏ ST-11080	Maybe This Time	1972	3.00	6.00	12.00

Number	Title (A Side/B Side)	Yr	VG	VG+	NM
❑ SM-11803	There Is a Time	1978	2.50	5.00	10.00
—Reissue of ST 2448					
COLUMBIA					
❑ KC 31762	Liza with a "Z"	1972	3.75	7.50	15.00
❑ PC 31762	Liza with a "Z"	198?	2.00	4.00	8.00
—Budget-line reissue					
❑ CQ 32149 [Q]	Liza Minnelli The Singer	1973	5.00	10.00	20.00
❑ KC 32149	Liza Minnelli The Singer	1973	3.75	7.50	15.00
❑ PC 32149	Liza Minnelli The Singer	198?	2.00	4.00	8.00
—Budget-line reissue					
❑ PC 32854	Live at the Winter Garden	1974	3.75	7.50	15.00
❑ PC 34887	Tropical Nights	1977	3.00	6.00	12.00
EPIC					
❑ OE 45098	Results	1989	3.75	7.50	15.00
TELARC					
❑ 15502 [(2)]	Liza Minnelli at Carnegie Hall	1987	3.75	7.50	15.00

MINORBOPS, THE
45s
LAMP

Number	Title (A Side/B Side)	Yr	VG	VG+	NM
❑ 2012	Need You Tonight/Want You for My Own	1957	62.50	125.00	250.00

MINT JULEPS, THE
45s
HERALD

Number	Title (A Side/B Side)	Yr	VG	VG+	NM
❑ 481	Bells of Love/Vip-a-Dip	1956	6.25	12.50	25.00
—With block logo inside flag					
❑ 481	Bells of Love/Vip-a-Dip	1956	25.00	50.00	100.00
—With script logo inside flag					
LOST-NITE					
❑ 424	Bells of Love/Vip-a-Dip	197?	—	2.50	5.00
—Reissue					

MINT TATTOO
45s
DOT

Number	Title (A Side/B Side)	Yr	VG	VG+	NM
❑ 17242	Mark of the Beast/When Talking About You	1969	2.50	5.00	10.00

Albums
DOT

Number	Title (A Side/B Side)	Yr	VG	VG+	NM
❑ DLP-25918	Mint Tattoo	1969	7.50	15.00	30.00

MINTS, THE   See KEN COPELAND.

MINUTE MEN, THE
45s
ARGO

Number	Title (A Side/B Side)	Yr	VG	VG+	NM
❑ 5469	Please Keep the Beatles in England/My Love Is Gone	1964	3.75	7.50	15.00

MIRABAI
45s
ATLANTIC

Number	Title (A Side/B Side)	Yr	VG	VG+	NM
❑ 3300	Cosmic Overload/To Be Young	1975	—	2.50	5.00

Albums
ATLANTIC

Number	Title (A Side/B Side)	Yr	VG	VG+	NM
❑ SD 18144	Mirabai	1975	2.50	5.00	10.00

MIRACLES, THE   Includes records as "Smokey Robinson and the Miracles." Also see SMOKEY ROBINSON.
12-Inch Singles
COLUMBIA

Number	Title (A Side/B Side)	Yr	VG	VG+	NM
❑ AS 283 [DJ]	Spy for Brotherhood (6:04) (same on both sides)	1976	5.00	10.00	20.00
❑ 23-10515	Spy for Brotherhood (6:04)/Women (Make the World Go 'Round) (4:50)	1977	5.00	10.00	20.00
MOTOWN					
❑ PR-129 [DJ]	The Tracks of My Tears/I Second That Emotion//I Heard It Through the Grapevine (5:03)	1983	2.50	5.00	10.00

—As "Smokey Robinson and the Miracles"; B-side by Marvin Gaye; promo-only item issued in conjunction with the movie "The Big Chill"

45s
CHESS

Number	Title (A Side/B Side)	Yr	VG	VG+	NM
❑ 1734	Bad Girl/I Love Your Baby	1959	15.00	30.00	60.00
—Blue label with vertical Chess logo (original)					
❑ 1734	Bad Girl/I Love Your Baby	1963	6.25	12.50	25.00
—Black label					
❑ 1734	Bad Girl/I Love Your Baby	1966	5.00	10.00	20.00
—Blue label with "Chess" at top					
❑ 1768	I Need a Change/All I Want (Is You)	1960	10.00	20.00	40.00
COLUMBIA					
❑ 3-10464	Spy for Brotherhood/The Bird Must Fly Away	1976	—	2.50	5.00
❑ 3-10517	Women (Make the World Go 'Round)/I Can Touch the Sky	1977	—	2.50	5.00
❑ 3-10706	Mean Machine/The Magic of Your Eyes (Laura's Eyes)	1978	—	2.50	5.00
END					
❑ 1016	Got a Job/My Mama Done Told Me	1958	15.00	30.00	60.00
❑ 1029	Money/I Cry	1958	10.00	20.00	40.00
—Multicolor label with "A Division of Roulette Records Inc." on label					
❑ 1029	Money/I Cry	1958	12.50	25.00	50.00
—Mostly gray-white label, no mention of Roulette Records					
❑ 1084	Money/I Cry	1961	6.25	12.50	25.00
MOTOWN					
❑ G 1/G 2	Bad Girl/I Love Your Baby	1959	1250.	1875.	2500.
❑ TLX-2207	Bad Girl/I Love Your Baby	1959	1250.	1875.	2500.
STANDARD GROOVE					
❑ 13090 [DJ]	I Care About Detroit	1968	37.50	75.00	150.00
—With no Tamla logo on label					
❑ 13090 [DJ]	I Care About Detroit	1968	50.00	100.00	200.00
—With Tamla globe logo on label					
TAMLA					
❑ EX-009 [DJ]	The Christmas Song/Christmas Everyday	1963	50.00	100.00	200.00
❑ 54028	Way Over There/Depend On Me	1960	15.00	30.00	60.00
—With overdubbed strings on A-side					
❑ 54028	Way Over There/Depend On Me	1960	37.50	75.00	150.00
—No strings on A-side recording					
❑ 54028	The Feeling Is So Fine/You Can Depend On Me	1960	100.00	200.00	400.00

Number	Title (A Side/B Side)	Yr	VG	VG+	NM
❑ 54028	The Feeling Is So Fine/You Can Depend On Me	1960	125.00	250.00	500.00
—With alternate take of B-side; matrix number followed by "A" in trail-off wax					
❑ 54034	Shop Around/Who's Lovin' You	196?	3.00	6.00	12.00
—Hit take; "L-1" in trail-off wax; globe label					
❑ 54034	Shop Around/Who's Lovin' You	1960	7.50	15.00	30.00
—Hit take; "L-1" in trail-off wax; horizontal lines label					
❑ 54034	Shop Around/Who's Lovin' You	1960	10.00	20.00	40.00
—Hit take; "ZTSC-67018" on label and in trail-off wax of Side 1 and "ZTSC-67019" on label and in trail-off wax of Side 2; horizontal lines label					
❑ 54034	Shop Around/Who's Lovin' You	1960	45.00	90.00	180.00
—Original take, withdrawn shortly after release; "H55518A" in trail-off wax					
❑ 54036	Ain't It Baby/The Only One I Love	1961	37.50	75.00	150.00
❑ 54044	Mighty Good Lovin'/Broken Hearted	1961	12.50	25.00	50.00
❑ 54044 [PS]	Mighty Good Lovin'/Broken Hearted	1961	37.50	75.00	150.00
❑ 54048	Everybody's Gotta Pay Some Dues/I Can't Believe	1961	12.50	25.00	50.00
❑ 54048	You Gotta Pay Some Dues/I Can't Believe	1961	25.00	50.00	100.00
—Alternate A-side title					
❑ 54048 [PS]	Everybody's Gotta Pay Some Dues/I Can't Believe	1961	50.00	100.00	200.00
❑ 54053	What's So Good About Good-By/I've Been Good to You	1962	7.50	15.00	30.00
❑ 54053 [PS]	What's So Good About Good-By/I've Been Good to You	1962	30.00	60.00	120.00
❑ 54059	I'll Try Something New/You Never Miss a Good Thing	1962	5.00	10.00	20.00
❑ 54059 [PS]	I'll Try Something New/You Never Miss a Good Thing	1962	30.00	60.00	120.00
❑ 54069	Way Over There/If Your Mother Only Knew	1962	5.00	10.00	20.00
❑ 54073	You've Really Got a Hold on Me/Happy Landing	1962	5.00	10.00	20.00
❑ 54078	A Love She Can Count On/I Can Take a Hint	1963	5.00	10.00	20.00
❑ 54083	Mickey's Monkey/Whatever Makes You Happy	1963	5.00	10.00	20.00
❑ 54089	I Gotta Dance to Keep from Crying/Such Is Love, Such Is Life	1963	3.75	7.50	15.00
❑ 54092	(You Can't Let the Boy Overpower) The Man in You/Heartbreak Road	1964	3.75	7.50	15.00
❑ 54098	I Like It Like That/You're So Fine and Sweet	1964	3.75	7.50	15.00
❑ 54098 [PS]	I Like It Like That/You're So Fine and Sweet	1964	30.00	60.00	120.00
❑ 54102	That's What Love Is Made Of/Would I Love You	1964	3.75	7.50	15.00
❑ 54109	Come On Do the Jerk/Baby Don't You Go	1964	3.75	7.50	15.00
❑ 54113	Ooo Baby Baby/All That's Good	1965	3.75	7.50	15.00
❑ 54118	The Tracks of My Tears/A Fork in the Road	1965	3.75	7.50	15.00
❑ 54123	My Girl Has Gone/Since You Won My Heart	1965	3.75	7.50	15.00
❑ 54127	Going to A-Go-Go/Choosey Beggar	1965	3.75	7.50	15.00
❑ 54127 [PS]	Going to A-Go-Go/Choosey Beggar	1965	25.00	50.00	100.00
❑ 54134	Whole Lot of Shakin' in My Heart (Since I Met You)/Oh Be My Lover	1966	2.50	5.00	10.00
❑ 54140	Come 'Round Here — I'm the One You Need/Save Me	1966	2.50	5.00	10.00
❑ 54140 [PS]	Come 'Round Here — I'm the One You Need/Save Me	1966	25.00	50.00	100.00
❑ 54145	The Love I Saw in You Was Just a Mirage/Come Spy with Me	1967	2.00	4.00	8.00
—Starting here, through Tamla 54225, as "Smokey Robinson and the Miracles"					
❑ 54152	More Love/Swept for You Baby	1967	2.00	4.00	8.00
❑ 54159	I Second That Emotion/You Must Be Love	1967	2.00	4.00	8.00
❑ 54162	If You Can Want/When the Words from Your Heart Get Caught Up in Your Throat	1968	2.00	4.00	8.00
—"Tamla" in box on label					
❑ 54162	If You Can Want/When the Words from Your Heart Get Caught Up in Your Throat	1968	3.75	7.50	15.00
—"Tamla" in globe on label					
❑ 54167	Yester Love/Much Better Off	1968	2.00	4.00	8.00
❑ 54172	Special Occasion/Give Her Up	1968	2.00	4.00	8.00
❑ 54178	Baby, Baby Don't Cry/Your Mother's Only Daughter	1968	2.00	4.00	8.00
❑ 54183	Here I Go Again/Doggone Right	1969	2.00	4.00	8.00
❑ 54184	Abraham, Martin, and John/Much Better Off	1969	2.00	4.00	8.00
❑ 54189	Point It Out/Darling Dear	1969	2.00	4.00	8.00
❑ 54194	Who's Gonna Take the Blame/I Gotta Thing For You	1970	2.00	4.00	8.00
❑ 54199	The Tears of a Clown/Promise Me	1970	—	3.00	6.00
❑ 54205	I Don't Blame You at All/That Girl	1971	—	3.00	6.00
❑ 54206	Crazy About the La La La/Oh Baby Baby I Love You	1971	—	3.00	6.00
❑ 54211	Satisfaction/Flower Girl	1971	—	3.00	6.00
❑ 54220	We've Come Too Far to End It Now/When Sundown Comes	1972	—	3.00	6.00
❑ 54225	I Can't Stand to See You Cry/With Your Love Came	1972	—	3.00	6.00
❑ 54237	Don't Let It End (Til You Let It Begin)/Wigs and Lashes	1973	—	2.50	5.00
—Starting here, name reverts to The Miracles					
❑ 54240	Give Me Just Another Day/I Wanna Be with You	1973	—	2.50	5.00
❑ 54248	Do It Baby/I Wanna Be with You	1974	—	2.50	5.00
❑ 54256	Don't Cha Love It/Up Again	1974	—	2.50	5.00
❑ 54259	You Are Love/Gemini	1975	—	2.50	5.00
❑ 54262	Love Machine (Part 1)/Love Machine (Part 2)	1975	—	2.50	5.00
❑ 54268	Night Life/Smog	1976	—	2.50	5.00
TOPPS/MOTOWN					
❑ 11	Shop Around	1967	18.75	37.50	75.00
—Cardboard record					

Albums
COLUMBIA

Number	Title (A Side/B Side)	Yr	VG	VG+	NM
❑ PC 34460	Love Crazy	1977	3.00	6.00	12.00
❑ PCQ 34460 [Q]	Love Crazy	1977	5.00	10.00	20.00
❑ JC 34910	The Miracles	1978	3.00	6.00	12.00
MOTOWN					
❑ M5-133V1	Do It Baby	1981	2.00	4.00	8.00
—Reissue of Tamla 334					
❑ M5-136V1	Away We a Go-Go	1981	2.00	4.00	8.00
—Reissue of Tamla 271					
❑ M5-156V1	The Tears of a Clown	1981	2.00	4.00	8.00
—Reissue of Tamla 276					
❑ M5-160V1	Hi, We're the Miracles	1981	2.00	4.00	8.00
—Reissue of Tamla 220					

M

Number	Title (A Side/B Side)	Yr	VG	VG+	NM
❏ M5-210V1	Greatest Hits, Vol. 2	1981	2.00	4.00	8.00
—Reissue of Tamla 280					
❏ M5-217V1	Doin' Mickey's Monkey	1981	2.00	4.00	8.00
—Reissue of Tamla 245					
❏ M5-220V1	Recorded Live on Stage	1981	2.00	4.00	8.00
—Reissue of Tamla 241					
❏ M8-238M2 [(2)]	Greatest Hits from the Beginning	1982	3.00	6.00	12.00
—Reissue of Tamla 254					
❏ M 793R3 [(3)]	Smokey Robinson and the Miracles Anthology	1974	5.00	10.00	20.00
❏ 5253 ML	The Season for Miracles	1982	2.00	4.00	8.00
—Reissue of Tamla 307					
❏ 5254 ML	Christmas with the Miracles	1982	2.00	4.00	8.00
—Reissue of Tamla 236					
TAMLA					
❏ T 220 [M]	Hi We're the Miracles	1961	150.00	300.00	600.00
—White label					
❏ T 223 [M]	Cookin' with the Miracles	1962	200.00	400.00	800.00
—White label					
❏ T 230 [M]	I'll Try Something New	1962	150.00	300.00	600.00
—White label					
❏ T 236 [M]	Christmas with the Miracles	1963	75.00	150.00	300.00
—Originals have two globes on the top of the label					
❏ T 238 [M]	You've Really Got a Hold on Me	1963	50.00	100.00	200.00
—Retitled version of "The Fabulous Miracles"					
❏ T 238 [M]	The Fabulous Miracles	1963	75.00	150.00	300.00
❏ T 241 [M]	The Miracles On Stage	1963	50.00	100.00	200.00
❏ T 245 [M]	Doin' Mickey's Monkey	1963	50.00	100.00	200.00
❏ TS 245 [S]	Doin' Mickey's Monkey	1963	75.00	150.00	300.00
❏ T 254 [(2)M]	Greatest Hits from the Beginning	1965	12.50	25.00	50.00
❏ TS 254 [(2)P]	Greatest Hits from the Beginning	1965	10.00	20.00	40.00
❏ T 267 [M]	Going to a Go-Go	1966	7.50	15.00	30.00
❏ TS 267 [S]	Going to a Go-Go	1966	10.00	20.00	40.00
❏ T 271 [M]	Away We a Go-Go	1966	6.25	12.50	25.00
❏ TS 271 [S]	Away We a Go-Go	1966	7.50	15.00	30.00
❏ T 276 [M]	Make It Happen	1967	6.25	12.50	25.00
❏ TS 276 [S]	Make It Happen	1967	7.50	15.00	30.00
❏ TS 276 [S]	The Tears of a Clown	1970	3.75	7.50	15.00
—Retitled version of "Make It Happen"					
❏ TS 280	Greatest Hits, Vol. 2	1968	6.25	12.50	25.00
❏ TS 289	Live!	1969	5.00	10.00	20.00
❏ T 290 [M]	Special Occasion	1968	12.50	25.00	50.00
❏ TS 290 [S]	Special Occasion	1968	5.00	10.00	20.00
❏ TS 295	Time Out for Smokey Robinson & the Miracles	1969	5.00	10.00	20.00
❏ TS 297	Four in Blue	1969	5.00	10.00	20.00
❏ TS 301	What Love Has…Joined Together	1970	3.75	7.50	15.00
❏ TS 306	A Pocket Full of Miracles	1970	3.75	7.50	15.00
❏ TS 307	The Season for Miracles	1970	3.75	7.50	15.00
❏ TS 312	One Dozen Roses	1971	3.75	7.50	15.00
❏ TS 318	Flying High Together	1972	3.75	7.50	15.00
❏ TS 320 [(2)]	1957-1972	1972	5.00	10.00	20.00
❏ T 325F	Renaissance	1973	3.00	6.00	12.00
❏ T6-334	Do It Baby	1974	3.00	6.00	12.00
❏ T6-336	Don't Cha Love It	1975	3.00	6.00	12.00
❏ T6-339	City of Angels	1975	3.00	6.00	12.00
❏ T6-344	The Power of Music	1976	3.00	6.00	12.00
❏ T7-357	Greatest Hits	1977	3.00	6.00	12.00

MIRACLES, THE (2) No relation to the more famous group above.
45s

Number	Title (A Side/B Side)	Yr	VG	VG+	NM
BATON					
❏ 210	A Lover's Chant/Come Home with Me	1955	37.50	75.00	150.00
CASH					
❏ 1008	You're An Angel/A Gal Named Jo	1955	50.00	100.00	200.00

MIRANDA, BOB Of THE HAPPENINGS.
45s

Number	Title (A Side/B Side)	Yr	VG	VG+	NM
B.T. PUPPY					
❏ 544	Girl on a Swing/When I Lock My Door	1968	2.50	5.00	10.00
JUBILEE					
❏ 5709	Everybody Is a Star/Evergreen	1971	2.00	4.00	8.00

MIRETTES, THE Also see THE IKETTES.
45s

Number	Title (A Side/B Side)	Yr	VG	VG+	NM
MINIT					
❏ 32045	Help Wanted/Play Fair	1968	2.50	5.00	10.00
MIRWOOD					
❏ 5514	He's Alright with Me/Your Kind Ain't No Good	1966	3.00	6.00	12.00
❏ 5531	He's Alright with Me/Now That I Found You Baby	1967	2.50	5.00	10.00
REVUE					
❏ 11004	In the Midnight Hour/To Love Somebody	1968	2.50	5.00	10.00
❏ 11017	Take Me for a Little While/Real Thing	1968	2.00	4.00	8.00
❏ 11029	First Love/I'm a Whole New Thing	1968	2.00	4.00	8.00
UNI					
❏ 55110	Stand By Your Man/If Everybody'd Help Somebody	1969	—	3.00	6.00
❏ 55126	Heart Full of Gladness/You Ain't Trying to Cross Over	1969	—	3.00	6.00
❏ 55147	Whirlpool/You Ain't Trying to Cross Over	1969	—	3.00	6.00
❏ 55161	Rap Run It On Down/Sweet Soul Sister	1969	—	3.00	6.00
—A-side: Nate Turner and the Mirettes; B-side: Venetta Fields and the Mirettes					
Albums					
REVUE					
❏ RS-7205	In the Midnight Hour	1968	3.75	7.50	15.00
UNI					
❏ 73062	Whirlpool	1969	3.75	7.50	15.00

MISFITS, THE (U) More than one group. The punk band is outside the scope of this book and is not included.
45s

Number	Title (A Side/B Side)	Yr	VG	VG+	NM
ARIES					
❏ 3	Midnight Star/I Don't Know	1961	50.00	100.00	200.00
HUSH					
❏ 105	Give Me Your Heart/My Mother-in-Law	1960	100.00	200.00	400.00
IMPERIAL					
❏ 66054	This Little Piggy (I'm a Hog for You)/Lost Love	1964	6.25	12.50	25.00
JOEY					
❏ 117	Naughty Rooster/Chicago Confidential	1961	3.00	6.00	12.00

Number	Title (A Side/B Side)	Yr	VG	VG+	NM
SOUND STAGE 7					
❏ 2538	It's Up to You/Skiing Time	1965	6.25	12.50	25.00
TROY					
❏ 227	The Uncle Willie/Big Bad Wolf	196?	6.25	12.50	25.00

MR. CLEAN
45s

Number	Title (A Side/B Side)	Yr	VG	VG+	NM
ORIGINAL SOUND					
❏ 40	Mr. Clean/Jessie Lee	1964	37.50	75.00	150.00
—Written, produced and performed on by Frank Zappa					

MR. GASSER AND THE WEIRDOS
Albums

Number	Title (A Side/B Side)	Yr	VG	VG+	NM
CAPITOL					
❏ ST 2010 [S]	Hot Rod Hootenanny	1963	30.00	60.00	120.00
❏ T 2010 [M]	Hot Rod Hootenanny	1963	25.00	50.00	100.00
❏ ST 2057 [S]	Rods n' Ratfinks	1963	30.00	60.00	120.00
—Add 25% if ratfink decal is enclosed					
❏ T 2057 [M]	Rods n' Ratfinks	1963	25.00	50.00	100.00
—Add 25% if ratfink decal is enclosed					
❏ ST 2114 [S]	Surfink!	1964	37.50	75.00	150.00
—Without bonus single					
❏ ST 2114 [S]	Surfink!	1964	50.00	100.00	200.00
—With bonus single in pocket on cover: "Santa Barbara"/"Midnight Run" by the Super Stocks					
❏ T 2114 [M]	Surfink!	1964	25.00	50.00	100.00
—Without bonus single					
❏ T 2114 [M]	Surfink!	1964	37.50	75.00	150.00
—With bonus single in pocket on cover: "Santa Barbara"/"Midnight Run" by the Super Stocks					

MR. LUCKY AND THE GAMBLERS
45s

Number	Title (A Side/B Side)	Yr	VG	VG+	NM
DOT					
❏ 16930	Take a Look at Me/I Told You (Once Before)	1966	5.00	10.00	20.00
PANORAMA					
❏ 37	Take a Look at Me/I Told You (Once Before)	1966	5.00	10.00	20.00
❏ 52	Alice Designs/You Don't Need Me	1967	3.75	7.50	15.00
UNITED INT'L.					
❏ 1001	New Orleans/Searching	1965	5.00	10.00	20.00
❏ 4404	Koko Joe/I Told You (Once Before)	1966	5.00	10.00	20.00

MR. SHORT STUFF
Albums

Number	Title (A Side/B Side)	Yr	VG	VG+	NM
SPIVEY					
❏ 1005	Mr. Short Stuff	196?	5.00	10.00	20.00

MR. SOUL
45s

Number	Title (A Side/B Side)	Yr	VG	VG+	NM
GENUINE					
❏ 150	What Happened to Yesterday/(B-side unknown)	196?	450.00	900.00	1800.

MR. SOUL BOWL
45s

Number	Title (A Side/B Side)	Yr	VG	VG+	NM
ATLANTIC					
❏ 2823	Answer to the Want Ads/H-L-I-C	1971	—	3.00	6.00

MR. WIGGLES
45s

Number	Title (A Side/B Side)	Yr	VG	VG+	NM
PARKWAY					
❏ 104	Fat Back Part 1/Part 2	1966	12.50	25.00	50.00

MITCHELL, BILLY
45s

Number	Title (A Side/B Side)	Yr	VG	VG+	NM
ATLANTIC					
❏ 933	My Love, My Desire/Pack Up All Your Bags	1951	75.00	150.00	300.00
❏ 950	If I Had Known/Verna Lee	1951	50.00	100.00	200.00
❏ 954	Let's Have a Ball Tonight/Someday You'll Be Sorry	1952	50.00	100.00	200.00
❏ 974	Ghost Train/Bald Headed Woman	1952	50.00	100.00	200.00
—With Joe Morris					
CALLA					
❏ 165	Oh Happy Day/The Chokin' Kind	1969	2.00	4.00	8.00
❏ 167	Too Busy Thinking 'Bout My Baby/Crystal Blue Persuasion	1969	2.00	4.00	8.00
IMPERIAL					
❏ 5520	Satellite Be-Bop/Pickin' on the Wrong Chicken	1958	5.00	10.00	20.00
JUBILEE					
❏ 5400	Short Skirts/You Know I Do	1961	3.75	7.50	15.00
UNITED ARTISTS					
❏ 235	Call to Me (I'll Be Here)/Where	1960	3.75	7.50	15.00
WARWICK					
❏ 501	It Doesn't Matter to Me/Stop a Little While	1959	3.75	7.50	15.00

MITCHELL, BOBBY
45s

Number	Title (A Side/B Side)	Yr	VG	VG+	NM
IMPERIAL					
❏ 5236	I'm Cryin'/Rack 'Em Back	1953	50.00	100.00	200.00
❏ 5250	One Friday Morning/Four-Eleven-Forty-Four	1953	50.00	100.00	200.00
❏ 5270	Baby's Gone/Sister Lucy	1954	30.00	60.00	120.00
❏ 5282	Angel Child/School Boy Blues	1954	30.00	60.00	120.00
❏ 5295	The Wedding Bells Are Ringing/Meant for Me	1954	30.00	60.00	120.00
❏ 5309	I'm a Young Man/She Couldn't Be Found	1954	30.00	60.00	120.00
❏ 5326	I Wish I Knew/Nothing Sweet As You	1955	20.00	40.00	80.00
❏ 5346	I Cried/I'm in Love	1955	15.00	30.00	60.00
❏ 5378	Try Rock and Roll/No, No, No	1956	12.50	25.00	50.00
❏ 5392	Goin' Round in Circles/I Try So Hard	1956	12.50	25.00	50.00
❏ 5412	You Are My Angel/I've Got My Fingers Crossed	1956	12.50	25.00	50.00
❏ 5440	You Always Hurt the One You Love/I Would Like to Know	1957	10.00	20.00	40.00
❏ 5475	I'm Gonna Be a Wheel Someday/You Better Go Home	1957	12.50	25.00	50.00
❏ 5511	I Love to Hold You/64 Hours	1958	10.00	20.00	40.00
❏ 5558	Hearts of Fire/You're Going to Be Sorry	1959	10.00	20.00	40.00
❏ 5882	My Southern Bell/When First We Met	1962	3.00	6.00	12.00
❏ 5923	I Don't Want to Be a Wheel No More/I Got to Call That Number	1963	3.00	6.00	12.00
RON					
❏ 337	Sand Me Your Picture/You're Doing Me Wrong	1961	3.00	6.00	12.00
❏ 342	Mama Don't Allow/There's Only One of You	1961	3.00	6.00	12.00

Number	Title (A Side/B Side)	Yr	VG	VG+	NM
MITCHELL, CHAD Also see THE CHAD MITCHELL TRIO.					
45s					
AMY					
❏ 11043	For What It's Worth/Follow	1968	—	2.50	5.00
❏ 11054	The Bus Song/What's That Got to Do with Me	1969	—	2.50	5.00
WARNER BROS.					
❏ 5880	Quiet Room/Violets of Dawn	1966	—	3.00	6.00
❏ 7043	Suzanne/Marieka	1967	—	3.00	6.00
Albums					
BELL					
❏ 6028	Chad	1969	3.75	7.50	15.00
WARNER BROS.					
❏ W 1667 [M]	Chad Mitchell Himself	1966	3.75	7.50	15.00
❏ WS 1667 [S]	Chad Mitchell Himself	1966	5.00	10.00	20.00
❏ W 1706 [M]	A Feeling of Love	1967	5.00	10.00	20.00
❏ WS 1706 [S]	A Feeling of Love	1967	3.75	7.50	15.00
MITCHELL, CHAD, TRIO					
45s					
COLPIX					
❏ 133	Sally Ann/Vaya Con Dios	1959	3.00	6.00	12.00
❏ 136	Up On the Mountain/Walkin' on the Green Grasses	1959	3.00	6.00	12.00
❏ 144	I Do Adore Her/The Gallows Tree	1960	3.00	6.00	12.00
❏ 154	The Ballad of Herbie Spear/Pretty Saro	1960	3.00	6.00	12.00
❏ 157	Devil Road/Paddy West	1960	3.00	6.00	12.00
❏ 610	Six Men/I'm Going Home	1961	2.50	5.00	10.00
—B-side by Eugene Lamarr					
KAPP					
❏ 439	Lizzie Borden/Super Skier	1961	3.00	6.00	12.00
❏ 439 [PS]	Lizzie Borden/Super Skier	1961	5.00	10.00	20.00
❏ 457	John Birch Society/Golden Vanity	1962	2.50	5.00	10.00
❏ 481	Alberta/Come Along Home	1962	2.50	5.00	10.00
❏ 485	You Can Tell the World/Hello, Susan Brown	1962	2.50	5.00	10.00
❏ 510	Blowing in the Wind/Adios, Mi Corazon	1963	2.50	5.00	10.00
❏ 518	Green Grow the Lilacs/Leave Me If You Want To	1963	2.50	5.00	10.00
MAY					
❏ 116	The Ballad of Herbie Spear/Sally Ann	1962	2.50	5.00	10.00
MERCURY					
❏ 72197	The Marvelous Toy/Bonny Streets of Fyve-10	1963	2.50	5.00	10.00
❏ 72197 [PS]	The Marvelous Toy/Bonny Streets of Fyve-10	1963	3.75	7.50	15.00
❏ 72234	The Tarrier's Song/Tell Old Billy	1964	2.00	4.00	8.00
❏ 72234 [PS]	The Tarrier's Song/Tell Old Billy	1964	3.75	7.50	15.00
❏ 72257	What Did You Learn in School Today/Barry's Boys	1964	2.00	4.00	8.00
Albums					
COLPIX					
❏ CP-411 [M]	The Chad Mitchell Trio	1961	5.00	10.00	20.00
❏ SCP-411 [S]	The Chad Mitchell Trio	1961	7.50	15.00	30.00
❏ CP-463 [M]	Everybody's Listening	1964	5.00	10.00	20.00
❏ SCP-463 [S]	Everybody's Listening	1964	7.50	15.00	30.00
KAPP					
❏ KGP-102 BI [(3)M]	My Gift to You	196?	12.50	25.00	50.00
—Three-record boxed set containing KL-1262, KL-1281 and KL-1313 on mid-1960s reissue labels (black with white circle and "Kapp" vertical logo at top)					
❏ KL-1262 [M]	Mighty Day on Campus	1962	5.00	10.00	20.00
❏ KL-1281 [M]	The Chad Mitchell Trio at the Bitter End	1962	5.00	10.00	20.00
❏ KL-1313 [M]	Chad Mitchell Trio In Action	1963	5.00	10.00	20.00
❏ KL-1334 [M]	The Best of Chad Mitchell Trio	1963	5.00	10.00	20.00
❏ KS-3262 [S]	Mighty Day on Campus	1962	6.25	12.50	25.00
❏ KS-3281 [S]	The Chad Mitchell Trio at the Bitter End	1962	6.25	12.50	25.00
❏ KS-3313 [S]	Chad Mitchell Trio In Action	1963	6.25	12.50	25.00
❏ KS-3334 [S]	The Best of Chad Mitchell Trio	1963	6.25	12.50	25.00
MERCURY					
❏ MG-20838 [M]	Singin' Our Mind	1963	3.75	7.50	15.00
❏ MG-20891 [M]	Reflecting	1964	3.75	7.50	15.00
❏ SR-60838 [S]	Singin' Our Mind	1963	5.00	10.00	20.00
❏ SR-60891 [S]	Reflecting	1964	5.00	10.00	20.00
MITCHELL, GUY					
45s					
CHALICE					
❏ 711	My Angel/Bit of Love	1963	7.50	15.00	30.00
❏ 711	My Angel/Mr. Hobo	1963	7.50	15.00	30.00
❏ 712	Take Your Time/(B-side unknown)	1963	7.50	15.00	30.00
❏ 713	Your Imagination/(B-side unknown)	1963	7.50	15.00	30.00
COLUMBIA					
❏ 1-640 (?)	Giddy Up/Where in the World	1950	7.50	15.00	30.00
—Microgroove 33 1/3 rpm 7-inch single					
❏ 1-680 (?)	Me and My Imagination/To Me You're a Song	1950	7.50	15.00	30.00
—Microgroove 33 1/3 rpm 7-inch single					
❏ 1-760 (?)	Angels Cry/You're Not in My Arms Tonight	1950	7.50	15.00	30.00
—Microgroove 33 1/3 rpm 7-inch single					
❏ 6-760 (?)	Angels Cry/You're Not in My Arms Tonight	1950	6.25	12.50	25.00
❏ 1-918	My Heart Cries for You/The Roving Kind	1950	7.50	15.00	30.00
—Microgroove 33 1/3 rpm 7-inch single					
❏ 6-918	My Heart Cries for You/The Roving Kind	1950	6.25	12.50	25.00
❏ 39067	My Heart Cries for You/The Roving Kind	1950	3.75	7.50	15.00
❏ 39190	Sparrow in the Tree Top/Christopher Columbus	1951	3.75	7.50	15.00
❏ 3-39190	Sparrow in the Tree Top/Christopher Columbus	1951	7.50	15.00	30.00
—Microgroove 33 1/3 rpm 7-inch single					
❏ 39331	Unless/A Beggar in Love	1951	3.75	7.50	15.00
❏ 39415	My Truly, Truly Fair/Who Knows Love	1951	3.75	7.50	15.00
❏ 39512	Belle, Belle, My Liberty Belle/Sweetheart of Yesterday	1951	3.75	7.50	15.00
❏ 39595	There's Always Room at Our House/I Can't Help It (If I'm Still in Love with You)	1951	3.75	7.50	15.00
❏ 39639	Wimmin'/We Don't Live in a Castle	1952	5.00	10.00	20.00
❏ 39663	Pittsburgh, Pennsylvania/Doll with a Sawdust Heart	1952	3.75	7.50	15.00
❏ 39753	The Day of Jubilo/You'll Never Be Mine	1952	5.00	10.00	20.00
❏ 39822	Feet Up (Pat Him on the Po-Po)/Jenny Kissed Me	1952	3.75	7.50	15.00
❏ 39879	('Cause I Love You) That's-a Why/Train of Love	1952	3.75	7.50	15.00
—With Mindy Carson					

Number	Title (A Side/B Side)	Yr	VG	VG+	NM
❏ 39886	Don't Rob Another Man's Castle/Why Should I Go Home	1952	3.75	7.50	15.00
❏ 39909	She Wears Red Feathers/Pretty Little Blackeyed Susie	1952	3.75	7.50	15.00
❏ 39950	I Want You for a Sunbeam/So Am I	1953	3.00	6.00	12.00
❏ 39992	There's Nothing As Sweet As My Baby/Tell Us Where the Good Times Are	1953	3.00	6.00	12.00
—With Mindy Carson					
❏ 40008	Hannah Lee/Look at That Girl	1953	3.00	6.00	12.00
❏ 40035	Cloud Lucky Seven/Chicka-Boom	1953	3.00	6.00	12.00
❏ 40077	Sippin' Soda/Strollin' Blues	1953	3.00	6.00	12.00
❏ 40128	Got a Hole in My Sweater/The Cuff of My Shirt	1953	3.00	6.00	12.00
❏ 40175	Tear Down the Mountains/A Dime and a Dollar	1954	3.00	6.00	12.00
❏ 40240	There Once Was a Man/My Heaven on Earth	1954	3.00	6.00	12.00
❏ 40278	What Am I Doin' in Kansas City/You've Ruined Me	1954	3.00	6.00	12.00
❏ 40389	I Met the Cutest Little Eyeful (At the Eiffel Tower)/Gee But You Gotta Come Home	1954	3.00	6.00	12.00
❏ 40468	Nobody Home/Zoo Baby	1955	2.50	5.00	10.00
❏ 40507	Otto's Gotta Go (Otto Drives Me Crazy)/Man Overboard	1955	3.00	6.00	12.00
❏ 40531	Let Us Be Sweethearts Again/Too Late	1955	2.50	5.00	10.00
❏ 40560	When Binky Blows/Belonging	1955	2.50	5.00	10.00
❏ 40631	Ninety Nine Years (Dead or Alive)/Perfume, Candy and Flowers	1955	2.50	5.00	10.00
❏ 40672	Solo/Green Grows the Grass	1956	2.50	5.00	10.00
❏ 40700	Give Me a Carriage with Eight White Horses/I Used to Hate Ya	1956	2.50	5.00	10.00
❏ 40724	Finders Keepers/I'd Like to Say a Few Words About Texas	1956	2.50	5.00	10.00
❏ 40769	Singing the Blues/Crazy with Love	1956	2.50	5.00	10.00
❏ 40769 [PS]	Singing the Blues/Crazy with Love	1956	5.00	10.00	20.00
❏ 40820	Knee Deep in the Blues/Take Me Back Baby	1957	2.50	5.00	10.00
❏ 40820 [PS]	Knee Deep in the Blues/Take Me Back Baby	1957	3.75	7.50	15.00
❏ 40877	Rock-a-Billy/Hoot Owl	1957	2.50	5.00	10.00
❏ 40877 [PS]	Rock-a-Billy/Hoot Owl	1957	3.75	7.50	15.00
❏ 40940	Sweet Stuff/In the Middle of a Dark, Dark Night	1957	2.50	5.00	10.00
❏ 40987	A Cure for the Blues/Call Rosie on the Phone	1957	2.50	5.00	10.00
❏ 41033	C'mon Let's Go/The Unbeliever	1957	2.50	5.00	10.00
❏ 41075	One Way Street/The Lord Made a Peanut	1957	2.50	5.00	10.00
❏ 41146	Hey, Madame/Till We're Engaged	1958	2.00	4.00	8.00
❏ 41177	Hangin' Around/Honey Brown Eyes	1958	2.00	4.00	8.00
❏ 41215	Let It Shine, Let It Shine/Butterfly Doll	1958	2.00	4.00	8.00
❏ 41274	My Heart Cries for You/Under the Rainbow	1958	2.00	4.00	8.00
❏ 41311	Guilty Heart/Half As Much	1958	2.00	4.00	8.00
❏ 41359	Alias Jesse James/Pride o' Dixie	1959	2.00	4.00	8.00
❏ 41397	Loosen Up, Lucy/I'm Gonna Leave You Now	1959	2.00	4.00	8.00
❏ 41476	Heartaches By the Number/Two	1959	2.50	5.00	10.00
❏ 41476 [PS]	Heartaches By the Number/Two	1959	3.75	7.50	15.00
❏ 41576	The Same Old Me/Build Up My Gallows High	1960	2.00	4.00	8.00
❏ 41653	Symphony of Spring/Cry Hurtin' Heart	1960	2.00	4.00	8.00
❏ 41725	My Shoes Keep Walking Back to You/Silver Moon Upon the Golden Sands	1960	2.00	4.00	8.00
❏ 41853	Sunshine Guitar/Ridin' Around in the Rain	1960	2.00	4.00	8.00
❏ 41853 [PS]	Sunshine Guitar/Ridin' Around in the Rain	1960	3.00	6.00	12.00
❏ 41970	Follow Me/Your Goodnight Kiss	1961	2.00	4.00	8.00
❏ 42143	Divorce/I'll Just Pretend	1961	2.00	4.00	8.00
❏ 42231	Soft Rain/Big Big Chance	1961	2.00	4.00	8.00
❏ 42231 [PS]	Soft Rain/Big Big Chance	1961	3.00	6.00	12.00
JOY					
❏ 264	Rusty Old Halo/Charlie's Shoes	1962	2.00	4.00	8.00
❏ 270	Go Tiger Go/If You Ever Go Away	1962	2.00	4.00	8.00
❏ 273	Have I Told You Lately That I Love You/Blue Violet	1963	2.00	4.00	8.00
REPRISE					
❏ 0477	Best Thing That Ever Happened to Me/If I Had My Life to Live Over	1966	—	3.00	6.00
❏ 0513	Run to the Door/Foreign Love Affair	1966	—	3.00	6.00
STARDAY					
❏ 819	Traveling Shoes/Every Night Is a Lifetime	1967	—	3.00	6.00
❏ 828	Alabam/Irene Good-By	1968	—	3.00	6.00
❏ 846	Frisco Line/Singing the Blues	1968	—	3.00	6.00
❏ 866	Get It Over/Just Wish You'd Change Your Mind	1969	—	3.00	6.00
❏ 878	Smokey Blue Eyes/Heartaches by the Number	1969	—	3.00	6.00
7-Inch Extended Plays					
COLUMBIA					
❏ 5-1328	My Truly, Truly Fair/The Roving Kind//Sparrow in the Treetop/My Heart Cries for You	195?	5.00	10.00	20.00
—Alternate number is B-1585					
❏ B-1585 [PS]	Guy Mitchell Spotlite	195?	5.00	10.00	20.00
❏ B-2133	*Rock-A-Billy/Finders Keepers/Hoot Owl/A House Without Love	1957	3.00	6.00	12.00
❏ B-2133 [PS]	Rock-A-Billy and Other Hits	1957	3.00	6.00	12.00
❏ B-2502	*My Heart Cries for You/The Roving Kind/My Truly, Truly Fair/Pittsburgh, Pennsylvania	1957	3.00	6.00	12.00
❏ B-2502 [PS]	Guy Mitchell (Hall of Fame Series)	1957	3.00	6.00	12.00
Albums					
COLUMBIA					
❏ CL 1211 [M]	Guy in Love	1958	10.00	20.00	40.00
❏ CL 1226 [M]	Guy's Greatest Hits	1959	12.50	25.00	50.00
—Red and black label with six "eye" logos					
❏ CL 1226 [M]	Guy's Greatest Hits	1962	7.50	15.00	30.00
—"Guaranteed High Fidelity" on red label					
❏ CL 1226 [M]	Guy's Greatest Hits	1965	5.00	10.00	20.00
—"360 Sound Mono" on red label					
❏ CL 1552 [M]	Sunshine Guitar	1960	7.50	15.00	30.00
❏ CL 6231 [10]	Open Spaces	1953	17.50	35.00	70.00
❏ CS 8011 [S]	Guy in Love	1959	12.50	25.00	50.00
❏ CS 8352 [S]	Sunshine Guitar	1960	10.00	20.00	40.00
KING					
❏ 644 [M]	Sincerely Yours	1959	75.00	150.00	300.00
NASHVILLE					
❏ 2074	Heartaches	1970	3.00	6.00	12.00
STARDAY					
❏ 412	Traveling Shoes	1968	5.00	10.00	20.00
❏ 432	Singin' Up a Storm	1969	5.00	10.00	20.00

M

Number	Title (A Side/B Side)	Yr	VG	VG+	NM

MITCHELL, GUY, AND ROSEMARY CLOONEY Also see each artist's individual listings.
45s
COLUMBIA

Number	Title (A Side/B Side)	Yr	VG	VG+	NM
❏ 39052	You're Just in Love/Marrying for Love	1950	3.75	7.50	15.00

MITCHELL, JONI
12-Inch Singles
GEFFEN

Number	Title (A Side/B Side)	Yr	VG	VG+	NM
❏ PRO-A-2386	[DJ]Good Friends (same on both sides)	1985	—	3.00	6.00
❏ PRO-A-2441	[DJ]Shiny Toys (same on both sides)	1986	—	3.00	6.00
❏ PRO-A-3018	[DJ]Snakes and Ladders (same on both sides)	1988	—	3.00	6.00
❏ PRO-A-3116	[DJ]My Secret Place (Edit Version) (LP Version)	1988	—	3.00	6.00

45s
ASYLUM

Number	Title (A Side/B Side)	Yr	VG	VG+	NM
❏ 11010	You Turn Me On, I'm a Radio/Urge for Going	1972	—	2.50	5.00
❏ 11029	Raised on Robbery/Court and Spark	1973	—	2.50	5.00
❏ 11034	Help Me/Just Like This Train	1974	—	2.50	5.00
❏ 11041	Free Man in Paris/People's Parties	1974	—	2.50	5.00
❏ 45221	Big Yellow Taxi/Rainy Night House	1974	—	2.00	4.00
❏ 45244	Jericho/Carey	1975	—	2.00	4.00
❏ 45298	In France They Kiss on Main Street/Boho Dance	1976	—	2.00	4.00
❏ 45377	Coyote/Blue Motel Room	1976	—	2.00	4.00
❏ 45467	Dreamland/Jericho	1978	—	2.00	4.00
❏ 46506	The Dry Cleaner from Des Moines/God Must Be a Boogie Man	1979	—	2.00	4.00
❏ 47038	Why Do Fools Fall in Love/Black Crow	1980	—	2.00	4.00

GEFFEN

Number	Title (A Side/B Side)	Yr	VG	VG+	NM
❏ 27887	My Secret Place/Lakota	1988	—	2.00	4.00
❏ 28675	Shiny Toys/Three Great Stimulants	1986	—	2.00	4.00
❏ 28840	Good Friends/Smokin' Empty (Try Another)	1985	—	2.00	4.00
❏ 28840 [PS]	Good Friends/Smokin' Empty (Try Another)	1985	—	2.50	5.00
❏ 29757	Underneath the Streetlight/Be Cool	1983	—	2.00	4.00
❏ 29849	(You're So Square) Baby I Don't Care/Love	1982	—	2.00	4.00
❏ 29849 [PS]	(You're So Square) Baby I Don't Care/Love	1982	—	2.50	5.00

REPRISE

Number	Title (A Side/B Side)	Yr	VG	VG+	NM
❏ 0694	I Had a King/Night in the City	1968	2.00	4.00	8.00
❏ 0906	Big Yellow Taxi/Woodstock	1970	2.00	4.00	8.00
❏ 1029	Carey/This Flight Tonight	1971	2.00	4.00	8.00
❏ 1049	Case of You/California	1971	—	3.00	6.00
❏ 1154	Both Sides Now/Chelsea Morning	1972	—	2.50	5.00
—"Back to Back Hits" series					
❏ 1155	Big Yellow Taxi/Carey	1972	—	2.50	5.00
—"Back to Back Hits" series					

Albums
ASYLUM

Number	Title (A Side/B Side)	Yr	VG	VG+	NM
❏ AB-202	Miles of Aisles	1974	2.50	5.00	10.00
❏ 5E-505	Mingus	1979	2.50	5.00	10.00
❏ BB-701 [(2)]	Don Juan's Reckless Daughter	1977	3.00	6.00	12.00
❏ BB-704 [(2)]	Shadows and Light	1980	3.00	6.00	12.00
❏ 7E-1001	Court and Spark	1974	2.50	5.00	10.00
❏ EQ-1001 [Q]	Court and Spark	1974	5.00	10.00	20.00
❏ 7E-1051	The Hissing of Summer Lawns	1975	2.50	5.00	10.00
❏ EQ-1051 [Q]	The Hissing of Summer Lawns	1975	5.00	10.00	20.00
❏ 7E-1087	Hejira	1976	2.50	5.00	10.00
❏ SD 5057	For the Roses	1972	2.50	5.00	10.00

DCC COMPACT CLASSICS

Number	Title (A Side/B Side)	Yr	VG	VG+	NM
❏ LPZ-2044	Court and Spark	1997	30.00	60.00	120.00
—Audiophile vinyl					
❏ LPZ-2069	Blue	2000	—	—	—
—Audiophile vinyl; canceled					

GEFFEN

Number	Title (A Side/B Side)	Yr	VG	VG+	NM
❏ PRO-A-1081	[DJ]Wild Things Run Fast Sampler	1982	3.00	6.00	12.00
—Promo-only 4-song EP					
❏ GHS 2019	Wild Things Run Fast	1982	2.00	4.00	8.00
❏ GHS 24074	Dog Eat Dog	1985	2.00	4.00	8.00
❏ GHS 24172	Chalk Mark in a Rain Storm	1988	2.00	4.00	8.00
❏ GEF 24302	Night Ride Home	1991	3.75	7.50	15.00

NAUTILUS

Number	Title (A Side/B Side)	Yr	VG	VG+	NM
❏ NR-11	Court and Spark	1980	12.50	25.00	50.00
—Audiophile vinyl					

REPRISE

Number	Title (A Side/B Side)	Yr	VG	VG+	NM
❏ MS 2038	Blue	1970	3.75	7.50	15.00
❏ R 6293 [M]	Joni Mitchell	1968	10.00	20.00	40.00
—White label promo; evidently, no stock copies were issued in mono					
❏ RS 6293 [S]	Joni Mitchell	1968	5.00	10.00	20.00
—With "W7" and "r:" logos on two-tone orange label					
❏ RS 6293 [S]	Joni Mitchell	1970	3.00	6.00	12.00
—With only "r:" logo on all-orange (tan) label					
❏ RS 6341	Clouds	1969	5.00	10.00	20.00
—With "W7" and "r:" logos on two-tone orange label					
❏ RS 6341	Clouds	1970	3.00	6.00	12.00
—With only "r:" logo on all-orange (tan) label					
❏ RS 6376	Ladies of the Canyon	1970	3.00	6.00	12.00
—With only "r:" logo on all-orange (tan) label					
❏ RS 6376	Ladies of the Canyon	1970	5.00	10.00	20.00
—With "W7" and "r:" logos on two-tone orange label					

MITCHELL, LEE
45s
PHILLIPS INT'L.

Number	Title (A Side/B Side)	Yr	VG	VG+	NM
❏ 3530	The Frog/A Little Bird Told Me	1958	3.75	7.50	15.00

SHARP

Number	Title (A Side/B Side)	Yr	VG	VG+	NM
❏ 0862	Rootie Tootie Baby/Who's That Big Man	1959	75.00	150.00	300.00

MITCHELL, MARLON
45s
VENA

Number	Title (A Side/B Side)	Yr	VG	VG+	NM
❏ 100	Ice Cold Baby/Bermuda Shorts	1957	30.00	60.00	120.00

MITCHELL, ROSE
45s
IMPERIAL

Number	Title (A Side/B Side)	Yr	VG	VG+	NM
❏ 5243	Slipping In/I'm Searching	1953	15.00	30.00	60.00
❏ 5260	Live My Life/Baby Please Don't Go	1954	15.00	30.00	60.00

Number	Title (A Side/B Side)	Yr	VG	VG+	NM

MITCHELL, STAN
45s
GONE

Number	Title (A Side/B Side)	Yr	VG	VG+	NM
❏ 5106	Devil in Disguise/Lovin' Man	1961	7.50	15.00	30.00

MITCHELL, WILLIE
45s
HI

Number	Title (A Side/B Side)	Yr	VG	VG+	NM
❏ 2044	The Crawl (Part 1)/The Crawl (Part 2)	1962	2.50	5.00	10.00
❏ 2053	Drippin'/Buddy Bear	1962	2.50	5.00	10.00
❏ 2058	Easy Now/Sunrise Serenade	1962	2.50	5.00	10.00
❏ 2066	Percolatin'/Empty Rooms	1963	2.50	5.00	10.00
❏ 2075	20-75/Secret Home	1964	2.00	4.00	8.00
❏ 2083	Percolatin'/Check Me	1964	2.00	4.00	8.00
❏ 2091	Buster Browne/Woodchopper's Ball	1965	2.00	4.00	8.00
❏ 2097	That Driving Beat/Everything Is Gonna Be Alright	1965	2.00	4.00	8.00
❏ 2103	Bad Eye/Sugar T	1966	—	3.00	6.00
❏ 2112	Mercy/Sticks and Stones	1966	—	3.00	6.00
❏ 2119	Misty/Barefootin'	1967	—	3.00	6.00
❏ 2125	Au Shucks/Slippin' and Slidin'	1967	—	3.00	6.00
❏ 2132	Lucky/Ooh Baby, You Turn Me On	1967	—	3.00	6.00
❏ 2140	Soul Serenade/Mercy, Mercy	1968	—	3.00	6.00
❏ 2147	Prayer Meetin'/Run Daddy	1968	—	3.00	6.00
❏ 2151	Up-Hard/Beale Street Mood	1968	—	3.00	6.00
❏ 2151	Up-Hard/Red Light	1968	—	3.00	6.00
❏ 2151 [PS]	Up-Hard/Beale Street Mood	1968	2.50	5.00	10.00
❏ 2154	30-60-90/Take Five	1969	—	3.00	6.00
❏ 2158	Young People/Kitten Korner	1969	—	3.00	6.00
❏ 2167	My Babe/Teenie's Dream	1969	—	3.00	6.00
❏ 2175	Six to Go/Robin's Nest	1970	—	2.50	5.00
❏ 2181	Wade in the Water/Tails Out	1970	—	2.50	5.00
❏ 2190	Too Sweet/Restless	1971	—	2.50	5.00
❏ 2196	Breaking Point/Roadhouse	1971	—	2.50	5.00
❏ 2237	Last Tango in Paris/Six to Go	1973	—	2.00	4.00

HOME OF THE BLUES

Number	Title (A Side/B Side)	Yr	VG	VG+	NM
❏ 111	Thirty-Five Thirty/Yvonne	1960	3.00	6.00	12.00
❏ 119	One Mint Julep/I've Got a Right	1961	3.00	6.00	12.00
❏ 123	I Like It/Willie's House Party	1961	3.00	6.00	12.00

Albums
BEARSVILLE

Number	Title (A Side/B Side)	Yr	VG	VG+	NM
❏ BRK 3520	... Listen ... Dance	1980	2.50	5.00	10.00

HI

Number	Title (A Side/B Side)	Yr	VG	VG+	NM
❏ 8002	Willie Mitchell Live	1977	2.50	5.00	10.00
❏ HL-32010 [M]	Sunrise Serenade	1963	10.00	20.00	40.00
❏ SHL-32010 [S]	Sunrise Serenade	1963	6.25	12.50	25.00
❏ HL-32021 [M]	Hold It	1964	6.25	12.50	25.00
❏ SHL-32021 [S]	Hold It	1964	7.50	15.00	30.00
❏ HL-32026 [M]	It's Dance Time	1965	6.25	12.50	25.00
❏ HL-32029 [M]	Driving Beat	1966	6.25	12.50	25.00
❏ SHL-32029 [S]	Driving Beat	1966	7.50	15.00	30.00
❏ HL-32034 [M]	The Hit Sound of Willie Mitchell	1967	7.50	15.00	30.00
❏ SHL-32034 [S]	The Hit Sound of Willie Mitchell	1967	6.25	12.50	25.00
❏ SHL-32036 [S]	It's Dance Time	1965	7.50	15.00	30.00
❏ HL-32039 [M]	Ooh Baby, You Turn Me On	1967	7.50	15.00	30.00
❏ SHL-32039 [S]	Ooh Baby, You Turn Me On	1967	6.25	12.50	25.00
❏ SHL-32042	Willie Mitchell Live	1968	6.25	12.50	25.00
❏ SHL-32045	Solid Soul	1968	6.25	12.50	25.00
❏ SHL-32048	On Top	1969	6.25	12.50	25.00
❏ SHL-32050	Soul Bag	1969	6.25	12.50	25.00
❏ SHL-32056	The Many Moods of Willie Mitchell	1970	6.25	12.50	25.00
❏ SHL-32058	Robin's Nest	1970	6.25	12.50	25.00
❏ SHL-32068/9 [(2)]	The Best of Willie Mitchell	1971	7.50	15.00	30.00

MITCHELL TRIO, THE Records issued after JOHN DENVER replaced CHAD MITCHELL in THE CHAD MITCHELL TRIO.
45s
MERCURY

Number	Title (A Side/B Side)	Yr	VG	VG+	NM
❏ 72340	I Can't Help But Wonder/Stewball and Griselda	1964	2.00	4.00	8.00
❏ 72340 [PS]	I Can't Help But Wonder/Stewball and Griselda	1964	3.75	7.50	15.00
❏ 72400	You Were On My Mind/My Name Is Morgan	1965	2.00	4.00	8.00
❏ 72518	That's the Way It's Gonna Be/Violets of Dawn	1966	2.00	4.00	8.00
❏ 72544	Your Friendly, Liberal, Neighborhood Ku Klux Klan/Violets of Dawn	1966	2.00	4.00	8.00
❏ 72591	Dark Shadows and Empty Hallways/ Stay with Me	1966	2.00	4.00	8.00

REPRISE

Number	Title (A Side/B Side)	Yr	VG	VG+	NM
❏ 0588	Leaving on a Jet Plane/Baby, That's Where It Is	1967	—	3.00	6.00
❏ 0630	She Loves You/Like to Deal with the Ladies	1967	—	3.00	6.00

Albums
MERCURY

Number	Title (A Side/B Side)	Yr	VG	VG+	NM
❏ MG-20944 [M]	The Slightly Irreverent Mitchell Trio	1964	3.75	7.50	15.00
❏ MG-20992 [M]	Typical American Boys	1965	3.75	7.50	15.00
❏ MG-21049 [M]	That's the Way It's Gonna Be	1965	3.75	7.50	15.00
❏ MG-21067 [M]	Violets of Dawn	1966	3.75	7.50	15.00
❏ SR-60944 [S]	The Slightly Irreverent Mitchell Trio	1964	5.00	10.00	20.00
❏ SR-60992 [S]	Typical American Boys	1965	5.00	10.00	20.00
❏ SR-61049 [S]	That's the Way It's Gonna Be	1965	5.00	10.00	20.00
❏ SR-61067 [S]	Violets of Dawn	1966	5.00	10.00	20.00

REPRISE

Number	Title (A Side/B Side)	Yr	VG	VG+	NM
❏ R-6258 [M]	Alive	1967	5.00	10.00	20.00
❏ RS-6258 [S]	Alive	1967	3.75	7.50	15.00

MITCHUM, ROBERT
45s
CAPITOL

Number	Title (A Side/B Side)	Yr	VG	VG+	NM
❏ F3672	What Is This Generation Coming To/ Mama Looka Boo Boo	1957	3.75	7.50	15.00
❏ 3741	The Ballad of Thunder Road/ My Baby's Lovin' Arms	1973	—	3.00	6.00
❏ 3986	The Ballad of Thunder Road/ My Honey's Lovin' Arms	1960	2.50	5.00	10.00
—Purple label, Capitol logo at left, no "F" prefix					
❏ 3986	The Ballad of Thunder Road/ My Honey's Lovin' Arms	1962	2.00	4.00	8.00
—Orange and yellow swirl label, no "F" prefix					

Number	Title (A Side/B Side)	Yr	VG	VG+	NM
❏ 3986	The Ballad of Thunder Road/ My Honey's Lovin' Arms	1969	—	3.00	6.00

—*Red and orange "target" label*

Number	Title (A Side/B Side)	Yr	VG	VG+	NM
❏ 3986	The Ballad of Thunder Road/ My Honey's Lovin' Arms	1973	—	2.00	4.00

—*Orange label, "Capitol" at bottom*

Number	Title (A Side/B Side)	Yr	VG	VG+	NM
❏ F3986	The Ballad of Thunder Road/ My Honey's Lovin' Arms	1958	3.75	7.50	15.00

—*Purple label with "F" prefix*

Number	Title (A Side/B Side)	Yr	VG	VG+	NM
❏ F3986 [PS]	The Ballad of Thunder Road/ My Honey's Lovin' Arms	1958	6.25	12.50	25.00
COLUMBIA					
❏ 03483	The Ballad of Thunder Road/ That Little Ole Wine Drinker Me	1983	—	2.50	5.00
MONUMENT					
❏ 1006	Little Old Wine Drinker Me/Walker's Woods	1967	—	3.50	7.00
❏ 1025	You Deserve Each Other/That Man Right There	1967	—	3.50	7.00
Albums					
CAPITOL					
❏ T 853 [M]	Calypso — Is Like So…	1957	25.00	50.00	100.00
MONUMENT					
❏ MLP-8066 [M]	That Man, Robert Mitchum, Sings	1967	6.25	12.50	25.00
❏ SLP-18066 [S]	That Man, Robert Mitchum, Sings	1967	6.25	12.50	25.00

MIXTURES, THE (1)
45s

Number	Title (A Side/B Side)	Yr	VG	VG+	NM
LINDA					
❏ 104	Rainbow Stomp (Part 1)/ Rainbow Stomp (Part 2)	1962	2.50	5.00	10.00
❏ 106	Jawbone/It's Gonna Work Out Fine	1962	2.50	5.00	10.00
❏ 108	Olive Oyl/Canadian Sunset	1963	2.50	5.00	10.00
❏ 109	Tiki/Poochum	1963	2.50	5.00	10.00
❏ 113	Chinese Checkers/Dig These Blues	1963	2.50	5.00	10.00
❏ 115	Sen-Say-Shun/The Last Minute	1964	2.50	5.00	10.00
Albums					
LINDA					
❏ 3301 [M]	Stompin' at the Rainbow	1962	25.00	50.00	100.00

MIXTURES, THE (2)
45s

Number	Title (A Side/B Side)	Yr	VG	VG+	NM
SIRE					
❏ 350	The Pushbike Song/Who Loves Ya	1971	—	3.00	6.00

MIZELL, HANK
45s

Number	Title (A Side/B Side)	Yr	VG	VG+	NM
AMAZON					
❏ 711	Jungle Rock/Then I'm In Your Arms	1963	12.50	25.00	50.00
EKO					
❏ 506	Jungle Rock/Then I'm In Your Arms	1958	150.00	300.00	600.00

—*Issued as "Jim Bobo" on A-side and "Jim Bobo and Hank Mizell" on B-side*

Number	Title (A Side/B Side)	Yr	VG	VG+	NM
KING					
❏ 5236	Jungle Rock/Then I'm In Your Arms	1959	75.00	150.00	300.00

MOB, THE (1)
45s

Number	Title (A Side/B Side)	Yr	VG	VG+	NM
COLOSSUS					
❏ 130	I Dig Everything About You/ Love Had a Hold on Me	1970	—	3.00	6.00
❏ 134	Give It to Me/I'd Like to See More of You	1971	—	3.00	6.00
❏ 134 [PS]	Give It to Me/I'd Like to See More of You	1971	2.00	4.00	8.00
❏ 145	Money/Once a Man, Twice a Child	1971	—	3.00	6.00
MGM					
❏ 14406	Feel Like Dancin'/You Give Me the Strength	1972	—	3.00	6.00
Albums					
COLOSSUS					
❏ CS-1006	The Mob	1971	5.00	10.00	20.00
MGM					
❏ SE-4839	The Mob	1972	3.75	7.50	15.00

MOB, THE (U)   These may or may not be group (1).
45s

Number	Title (A Side/B Side)	Yr	VG	VG+	NM
MERCURY					
❏ 72791	Disappear/I Wish You'd Leave Me Alone	1968	2.00	4.00	8.00
PRIVATE STOCK					
❏ 45,016	Rock and Roller/(B-side unknown)	1975	—	2.50	5.00
❏ 45,031	Hot Music/I Can't Stop This Love Song	1975	—	2.50	5.00
❏ 45,053	All the Dudes Are Dancing/(B-side unknown)	1975	—	2.50	5.00
❏ 45,084	Don't Let It Get You Down/(B-side unknown)	1976	—	2.50	5.00
❏ 45,159	Love Connection/(B-side unknown)	1977	—	2.50	5.00
Albums					
PRIVATE STOCK					
❏ PS-2005	The Mob	1975	3.00	6.00	12.00

MOBY GRAPE   Also see ALEXANDER "SKIP" SPENCE.
45s

Number	Title (A Side/B Side)	Yr	VG	VG+	NM
COLUMBIA					
❏ 44170	Changes/Fall on You	1967	2.00	4.00	8.00
❏ 44170 [PS]	Changes/Fall on You	1967	5.00	10.00	20.00
❏ 44171	Sitting by the Window/Indifference	1967	2.00	4.00	8.00
❏ 44171 [PS]	Sitting by the Window/Indifference	1967	5.00	10.00	20.00
❏ 44172	8:05/Mister Blues	1967	2.00	4.00	8.00
❏ 44172 [PS]	8:05/Mister Blues	1967	5.00	10.00	20.00
❏ 44173	Omaha/Someday	1967	2.00	4.00	8.00
❏ 44173 [PS]	Omaha/Someday	1967	5.00	10.00	20.00
❏ 44174	Hey Grandma/Come in the Morning	1967	2.00	4.00	8.00
❏ 44174 [PS]	Hey Grandma/Come in the Morning	1967	5.00	10.00	20.00
❏ 44567	Can't Be So Bad/Bitter Wind	1968	—	3.00	6.00
❏ 44789	If You Can't Learn From My Mistakes/ Trucking Man	1969	—	3.00	6.00
❏ 44885	Ooh Mama Ooh/It's a Beautiful Day Today	1969	—	3.00	6.00
❏ JZSP 118972 [DJ]	Omaha/8:05	1967	3.00	6.00	12.00

—*Yellow label promo; "Rush Reservice"*

Number	Title (A Side/B Side)	Yr	VG	VG+	NM
REPRISE					
❏ 1040	Gypsy Wedding/Apocalypse	1971	—	2.50	5.00
❏ 1055	Goin' Down to Texas/About Time	1971	—	2.50	5.00
❏ 1096	Gone Fishin'/Gypsy Wedding	1972	—	2.50	5.00

Number	Title (A Side/B Side)	Yr	VG	VG+	NM
Albums					
COLUMBIA					
❏ MGS 1	Grape Jam	1968	5.00	10.00	20.00
❏ CXS 3 [(2)]	Wow/Grape Jam	1968	7.50	15.00	30.00

—*Joint release of the two albums under one cover*

Number	Title (A Side/B Side)	Yr	VG	VG+	NM
❏ CXS 3 [(2)]	Wow/Grape Jam	1971	3.75	7.50	15.00

—*Orange labels*

Number	Title (A Side/B Side)	Yr	VG	VG+	NM
❏ 2698/9498	Moby Grape Poster	1967	2.00	4.00	8.00

—*Poster has offending finger airbrushed out*

Number	Title (A Side/B Side)	Yr	VG	VG+	NM
❏ 2698/9498	Moby Grape Poster	1967	3.75	7.50	15.00

—*Poster has Don Stephenson "giving the finger" on his washboard*

Number	Title (A Side/B Side)	Yr	VG	VG+	NM
❏ CL 2698 [M]	Moby Grape	1967	5.00	10.00	20.00

—*Cover has offending finger airbrushed out*

Number	Title (A Side/B Side)	Yr	VG	VG+	NM
❏ CL 2698 [M]	Moby Grape	1967	10.00	20.00	40.00

—*Cover has Don Stephenson "giving the finger" on his washboard*

Number	Title (A Side/B Side)	Yr	VG	VG+	NM
❏ CS 9498 [S]	Moby Grape	1967	5.00	10.00	20.00

—*Cover has offending finger airbrushed out*

Number	Title (A Side/B Side)	Yr	VG	VG+	NM
❏ CS 9498 [S]	Moby Grape	1967	10.00	20.00	40.00

—*Cover has Don Stephenson "giving the finger" on his washboard*

Number	Title (A Side/B Side)	Yr	VG	VG+	NM
❏ CS 9498	Moby Grape	1971	3.00	6.00	12.00

—*Orange label; with poster*

Number	Title (A Side/B Side)	Yr	VG	VG+	NM
❏ CS 9613	Wow	1968	5.00	10.00	20.00
❏ CS 9613 [M]	Wow	1968	10.00	20.00	40.00

—*"Special Mono Radio Station Copy" with white label*

Number	Title (A Side/B Side)	Yr	VG	VG+	NM
❏ CS 9696	Moby Grape '69	1969	5.00	10.00	20.00
❏ CS 9912	Truly Fine Citizen	1969	5.00	10.00	20.00
❏ C 31098	Great Grape	1972	3.75	7.50	15.00
ESCAPE					
❏ ESA 1	Live Grape	1978	3.75	7.50	15.00
HARMONY					
❏ KH 30392	Omaha	1971	3.75	7.50	15.00
REPRISE					
❏ RS 6460	20 Granite Creek	1971	5.00	10.00	20.00

MOCEDADES
45s

Number	Title (A Side/B Side)	Yr	VG	VG+	NM
TARA					
❏ 100	Eres Tu (Touch the Wind)/Touch the Wind (Eres Tu)	1973	—	2.50	5.00
❏ 105	Dime Senor/I Ask the Lord	1974	—	2.00	4.00
❏ 105 [PS]	Dime Senor/I Ask the Lord	1974	—	3.00	6.00
Albums					
TARA					
❏ 53000	Eres Tu "Touch the Wind"	1974	3.00	6.00	12.00

MOCKINGBIRDS, THE   With GRAHAM GOULDMAN and Kevin Godley, later of 10CC.
45s

Number	Title (A Side/B Side)	Yr	VG	VG+	NM
ABC-PARAMOUNT					
❏ 10653	That's How/I Never Should Have Kissed You	1965	3.75	7.50	15.00

MOD AND THE ROCKERS
Albums

Number	Title (A Side/B Side)	Yr	VG	VG+	NM
JUSTICE					
❏ JLP-153	Mod and the Rockers Now!	1967	100.00	200.00	400.00

MODELS, THE
45s

Number	Title (A Side/B Side)	Yr	VG	VG+	NM
MGM					
❏ 13775	Bend Me, Shape Me/In a World of Pretty Faces	1967	5.00	10.00	20.00

MODUGNO, DOMENICO
45s

Number	Title (A Side/B Side)	Yr	VG	VG+	NM
DECCA					
❏ 30677	Nel Blu Dipinto Di Blu (Volare)/Mariti in Citta	1958	3.00	6.00	12.00
❏ 30747	Stay Here with Me/Io	1958	2.50	5.00	10.00
❏ 30777	Coma Prima/Strada 'Nfosa	1958	2.50	5.00	10.00
❏ 30845	Piove (Ciao, Ciao Bambino)/Farfalle	1959	2.50	5.00	10.00
❏ 30950	The Bandit/Lunga Notte	1959	2.50	5.00	10.00
❏ 31071	Olympia/O Solo Mio	1960	2.00	4.00	8.00
❏ 31171	Ciao Ciao Bambino/Si, Si, Si	1960	2.00	4.00	8.00
❏ 31359	La Novia/Se Dio Vorra	1962	2.00	4.00	8.00
❏ 31401	Addio...Addio/Lupi E Percorelle	1962	2.00	4.00	8.00
❏ 31718	Tu Si' 'Na Casa Grande/Tu Si O' Mare	1964	—	3.00	6.00
JUBILEE					
❏ 5339	La Petit Reveil/Cavudduzzu	1958	2.50	5.00	10.00
MGM					
❏ 13487	Dio, Come Ti Amo (English Version)/Dio, Come Ti Amo (Italian Version)	1966	—	3.00	6.00
RCA VICTOR					
❏ 47-7321	Musetto/Io Mammeta E Tu	1958	2.50	5.00	10.00
❏ 47-9502	Meraviglioso (Part 1)/Meraviglioso (Part 2)	1968	—	2.50	5.00
❏ 48-1022	Love Is Like the Wind/How Did You	1972	—	2.00	4.00
7-Inch Extended Plays					
DECCA					
❏ ED 2633	*Nel Blu Dipinto Di Blu (Volare)/Mariti in Citta/A Pizza C' 'A Pummarola/Ventu D'Estati	1958	3.75	7.50	15.00
❏ ED 2633 [PS]	Nel Blu Dipinto Di Blu (Volare) and Other Italian Favorites	1958	3.75	7.50	15.00
Albums					
DECCA					
❏ DL 4133 [M]	Viva Italia	1961	7.50	15.00	30.00
❏ DL 8808 [M]	Nel Blu Dipinto Di Blu (Volare) and Other Italian Favorites	1958	12.50	25.00	50.00
❏ DL 8853 [M]	Encore	1959	10.00	20.00	40.00

MOGEN DAVID AND THE GRAPES OF WRATH
45s

Number	Title (A Side/B Side)	Yr	VG	VG+	NM
CHA CHA					
❏ 757	Little Girl Gone/Go Away Girl	1967	2000.	3000.	4000.

MOJO MEN, THE
45s

Number	Title (A Side/B Side)	Yr	VG	VG+	NM
AUTUMN					
❏ 11	Mama's Little Baby/Off the Hook	1965	3.75	7.50	15.00
❏ 19	Dance with Me/The Loneliest Boy in Town	1965	3.75	7.50	15.00
❏ 27	She's My Baby/Fire in My Heart	1966	3.75	7.50	15.00

M

Number	Title (A Side/B Side)	Yr	VG	VG+	NM
GRT					
❑ 5	Flower of Love/I Can't Let Go	1969	2.50	5.00	10.00
❑ 8	Candle to Burn/Make You at Home	1969	2.50	5.00	10.00
❑ 16	Everyday Love/There Goes My Mind	1969	2.50	5.00	10.00
REPRISE					
❑ 0486	She's My Baby/Do the Hanky Panky	1966	5.00	10.00	20.00
❑ 0539	Sit Down, I Think I Love You/Don't Leave Me Crying Like Before	1966	2.50	5.00	10.00
❑ 0580	Me About You/When You're in Love	1967	2.50	5.00	10.00
❑ 0617	Whatever Happened to Happy/Make You at Home	1967	2.50	5.00	10.00
❑ 0661	Not Too Old to Start Crying/New York City	1968	2.50	5.00	10.00
❑ 0689	Should I Cry/You to Me	1968	2.50	5.00	10.00
❑ 0707	Sit Down, I Think I Love You/Me About You	1968	—	3.00	6.00
—"Back to Back Hits" series					
❑ 0759	Don't Be Cruel/Let It Be Him	1968	2.50	5.00	10.00
TIDE					
❑ 2000	Surfin' Fat Man/Paula	1964	10.00	20.00	40.00
Albums					
GRT					
❑ 10003	Mojo Magic	1969	6.25	12.50	25.00

MOJOS, THE
45s
Number	Title (A Side/B Side)	Yr	VG	VG+	NM
PARROT					
❑ 9707	Seven Daffodils/Nothin' at All	1964	2.50	5.00	10.00
❑ 45001	Everything's Alright/Give Your Loving to Me	1964	3.00	6.00	12.00
❑ 45002	Why Not Tonight/Don't Do It Anymore	1964	3.00	6.00	12.00

MOLES, GENE
45s
Number	Title (A Side/B Side)	Yr	VG	VG+	NM
CHALLENGE					
❑ 59249	Burning Rubber/Twin Pipes	1964	6.25	12.50	25.00
GARPAX					
❑ 44176	Kaha Huna (Goddess of Surfing)/Maria (The Wind)	1963	6.25	12.50	25.00

MOLLERN, RONNIE
45s
Number	Title (A Side/B Side)	Yr	VG	VG+	NM
KING					
❑ 5365	Rockin' Up/Fat Mama	1960	37.50	75.00	150.00

MOLOCH
Albums
Number	Title (A Side/B Side)	Yr	VG	VG+	NM
ENTERPRISE					
❑ ENS-1002	Moloch	1969	5.00	10.00	20.00

MOM & DADS, THE
45s
Number	Title (A Side/B Side)	Yr	VG	VG+	NM
GNP CRESCENDO					
❑ 439	The Rangers Waltz/Quentin's E Flat Boogie	1971	—	2.50	5.00
❑ 451	In the Blue Canadian Rockies/Blue Skirt Waltz	1972	—	2.50	5.00
❑ 455	Amazing Grace/Rippling River Waltz	1972	—	2.50	5.00
❑ 460	Jingle Bell Rock/Auld Lang Syne	1972	—	2.50	5.00
❑ 461	Angry/Anniversary Waltz	1973	—	2.00	4.00
❑ 466	The Waltz You Saved for Me/When the Saints Go Marching In	1973	—	2.00	4.00
❑ 472	Somewhere My Love/My Happiness	1973	—	2.00	4.00
❑ 478	My Blue Heaven/Your Cheatin' Heart	1974	—	2.00	4.00
❑ 485	Maiden's Prayer/Wabash Cannonball	1974	—	2.00	4.00
❑ 496	Kentucky Waltz/(B-side unknown)	1975	—	2.00	4.00
❑ 803	Silver Bells/Bill Bailey	1975	—	2.00	4.00
Albums					
GNP CRESCENDO					
❑ GNP-2061	The Rangers Waltz	1971	2.50	5.00	10.00
❑ GNP-2063	In the Blue Canadian Rockies	1972	2.50	5.00	10.00
❑ GNP-2065	Souvenirs	1972	2.50	5.00	10.00
❑ GNP-2068	Again!	1973	2.50	5.00	10.00
❑ GNP-2072	Reminiscing	1973	2.50	5.00	10.00
❑ GNP-2078	Dance with the Mom & Dads	1974	2.50	5.00	10.00
❑ GNP-2082	The Mom & Dads Play Your Favorite Hymns	1974	2.50	5.00	10.00
❑ GNP-2084	Love Is a Beautiful Song	1974	2.50	5.00	10.00
❑ GNP-2087	The Best of the Mom & Dads	1975	2.50	5.00	10.00
❑ GNP-2092	Dream	1975	2.50	5.00	10.00
❑ GNP-2096	Memories	1976	2.50	5.00	10.00
❑ GNP-2102	Summertime	1976	2.50	5.00	10.00
❑ GNP-2106	Down the River of Golden Dreams	1977	2.50	5.00	10.00
❑ GNP-2108	Whispering Hope	1977	2.50	5.00	10.00
❑ GNP-2110	One Dozen Roses	1977	2.50	5.00	10.00
❑ GNP-2121	Gratefully Yours	1978	2.50	5.00	10.00
❑ 2GNP-2123 [(2)]	Golden Country	1979	3.00	6.00	12.00
❑ GNP-2125	Love Letters in the Sand	1979	2.50	5.00	10.00
❑ 2GNP-2129 [(2)]	The Very Best of the Mom & Dads	1980	3.00	6.00	12.00
❑ GNP-2130	Blue Hawaii	1980	2.50	5.00	10.00
❑ GNP-2136	To Mom & Dad With Love from the Mom & Dads	1980	2.50	5.00	10.00
❑ GNP-2139	Waltz Across Texas	1981	2.50	5.00	10.00
❑ GNP-2150	Good Night Sweetheart	1985	2.00	4.00	8.00
❑ GNP-2173	20 Favorite Waltzes	1986	2.00	4.00	8.00
❑ GNP-2189	Red Sails in the Sunset	1987	2.00	4.00	8.00

MOM'S APPLE PIE
45s
Number	Title (A Side/B Side)	Yr	VG	VG+	NM
BROWN BAG					
❑ XW192	Love Plays a Song/Can You Help Me	1973	2.50	5.00	10.00
Albums					
BROWN BAG					
❑ BB-LA073-F	Mom's Apple Pie #2	1973	3.75	7.50	15.00
❑ 14200	Mom's Apple Pie	1972	5.00	10.00	20.00

—With barbed wire wall covering the former opening. This is much rarer than the first version, though less sought-after

Number	Title (A Side/B Side)	Yr	VG	VG+	NM
❑ 14200	Mom's Apple Pie	1972	5.00	10.00	20.00

—With vulva showing in the apple pie

MOMENTS, THE
R&B trio. For legal reasons, their records on EMI America, EMI Manhattan, Panoramic and Polydor were issued under the name "Ray, Goodman and Brown."
45s
Number	Title (A Side/B Side)	Yr	VG	VG+	NM
ALL PLATINUM					
❑ 2350	Sho Nuff Boogie (Part 1)/Sho Nuff Boogie (Part 2)	1974	—	2.50	5.00
—With Sylvia					
EMI AMERICA					
❑ 8365	Take It to the Limit/(Instrumental)	1986	—	—	3.00
❑ 8365 [PS]	Take It to the Limit/(Instrumental)	1986	—	—	3.00
❑ 8378	Celebrate Our Love/(Instrumental)	1987	—	—	3.00
❑ 8378 [PS]	Celebrate Our Love/(Instrumental)	1987	—	—	3.00
❑ 43022	Tonight (Baby)/Good Love	1987	—	—	3.00
EMI MANHATTAN					
❑ 50155	Where Did You Get That Body, (Baby)?/Where Are You Now	1988	—	—	3.00
❑ 50155 [PS]	Where Did You Get That Body, (Baby)?/Where Are You Now	1988	—	—	3.00
HOG					
❑ 1000	Baby I Want You/(B-side unknown)	196?	500.00	1000.	2000.
PANORAMIC					
❑ 201	Who's Gonna Make the First Move/Look Like Lovers	1984	—	2.00	4.00
POLYDOR					
❑ 2033	Special Lady/Deja Vu	1979	—	2.50	5.00
❑ 2077	Inside of You/Treat Her Right	1980	—	2.00	4.00
❑ 2116	My Prayer/The Way It Should Be	1980	—	2.00	4.00
❑ 2135	Happy Anniversary/You	1980	—	2.00	4.00
❑ 2159	Shoestrings/Me	1981	—	2.00	4.00
❑ 2191	How Can Love Be So Right (Yet So Wrong)/Each Time Is Like the First Time	1981	—	2.00	4.00
❑ 2203	Stay/Good Ole Days	1982	—	2.00	4.00
❑ 2208	Till the Right One Comes Along/Heaven in the Rain	1982	—	2.00	4.00
❑ 2222	Gambled on Your Love/Pool of Love	1982	—	2.00	4.00
❑ 2227	After All/Love Minus-One	1982	—	2.00	4.00
❑ 810056-7	Special Lady/My Prayer	1983	—	—	3.00
—Reissue					
STANG					
❑ 5000	Not on the Outside/Understanding	1968	2.00	4.00	8.00
❑ 5003	Sunday/Everybody Loves My Baby	1969	—	3.00	6.00
❑ 5005	I Do/Pocketful of Heartbreaks	1969	—	3.00	6.00
❑ 5008	I'm So Lost/Where	1969	—	3.00	6.00
❑ 5009	Lovely Way She Loves/I've Got to Keep On Loving, Love	1969	—	3.00	6.00
❑ 5012	Love on a Two-Way Street/I Won't Do Anything	1970	2.00	4.00	8.00
❑ 5016	If I Didn't Care/You Make Me Feel Good	1970	—	3.00	6.00
❑ 5017	All I Have/The Hurt's On Me	1970	—	3.00	6.00
❑ 5020	I Can't Help It/To You with Love	1971	—	3.00	6.00
❑ 5024	That's How It Feels/That's How It Feels (Long)	1971	—	3.00	6.00
❑ 5031	Lucky Me/I Lost One Bird in the Hand (Reaching Out for Two in the Bush)	1971	—	3.00	6.00
❑ 5033	To You with Love/Key to My Happiness	1971	—	3.00	6.00
❑ 5036	Thanks a Lot/I Lost One Bird in the Hand (Reaching Out for Two in the Bush)	1972	—	3.00	6.00
❑ 5041	Just Because He Wants to Make Love (Doesn't Mean He Loves You)/So This Is Our Goodbye	1972	—	3.00	6.00
❑ 5045	My Thing/Thanks a Lot	1972	—	3.00	6.00
❑ 5048	Girl I'm Gonna Miss You/I Think So	1973	—	2.50	5.00
❑ 5050	Gotta Find a Way/Sweeter As the Days Go By	1973	—	2.50	5.00
❑ 5052	Sexy Mama/Where Can I Find Her	1973	—	3.00	6.00
❑ 5054	Sweet Sweet Lady/Next Time I See You	1974	—	2.50	5.00
❑ 5056	What's Your Name/Mama I Miss You	1974	—	2.50	5.00
❑ 5057	Girls (Part 1)/Girls (Part 2)	1974	—	2.50	5.00
—With the Whatnauts					
❑ 5060	Look at Me (I'm in Love)/You've Come a Long Way	1975	—	2.50	5.00
❑ 5064	Got to Get to Know You/I Feel So Bad	1975	—	2.50	5.00
❑ 5066	Nine Times/When the Morning Comes	1976	—	2.50	5.00
❑ 5068	With You/The Next Time I See You	1976	—	2.50	5.00
❑ 5071	We Don't Cry Out Loud/Come In Girl	1977	—	2.50	5.00
❑ 5073	I Don't Wanna Go/Oh I Could Have Loved You	1977	—	2.50	5.00
❑ 5075	I Could Have Loved You/Jack in the Box	1978	—	2.50	5.00
❑ 5076	Rain in My Backyard/Disco Man	1978	—	2.50	5.00
SUGAR HILL					
❑ 758	Baby Let's Rap Now (Part 1)/Baby Let's Rap Now (Part 2)	1980	—	2.50	5.00
❑ 769	Record Breakin' Love Affair/(B-side unknown)	1981	—	2.50	5.00
Albums					
CHESS					
❑ CH2-92517 [(2)]	Greatest Hits	198?	3.00	6.00	12.00
POLYDOR					
❑ PD-1-6240	Ray, Goodman & Brown	1979	2.50	5.00	10.00
❑ PD-1-6299	Ray, Goodman & Brown II	1980	2.50	5.00	10.00
❑ PD-1-6341	Stay	1981	2.50	5.00	10.00
STANG					
❑ ST-1000	Not On the Outside, But On the Inside Strong	1969	7.50	15.00	30.00
❑ ST-1002	The Moments On Top	1970	7.50	15.00	30.00
❑ ST-1003	A Moment with the Moments	1970	7.50	15.00	30.00
❑ ST-1004	Moments Greatest Hits	1971	5.00	10.00	20.00
❑ ST-1006	The Moments Live at the New York State Womans Prison	1971	6.25	12.50	25.00
❑ ST-1009	The Other Side of the Moments	1972	6.25	12.50	25.00
❑ ST-1015	Live at the Miss Black America Pageant	1972	5.00	10.00	20.00
❑ ST-1019	The Best of the Moments	1975	3.75	7.50	15.00
❑ ST-1022	My Thing	1973	3.75	7.50	15.00
❑ ST-1023	The Sexy Moments	1974	3.75	7.50	15.00
❑ ST-1026	Look at Me	1975	3.75	7.50	15.00
❑ ST-1030	Moments With You	1976	3.75	7.50	15.00
❑ 2ST-1033 [(2)]	Greatest Hits	1977	5.00	10.00	20.00
❑ ST-1034	Sharp	1978	3.75	7.50	15.00

MOMENTS, THE (2)
California studio group.
45s
Number	Title (A Side/B Side)	Yr	VG	VG+	NM
ERA					
❑ 3099	Walk Right In/(Instrumental)	1963	2.50	5.00	10.00

Number	Title (A Side/B Side)	Yr	VG	VG+	NM
❏ 3104	Homework/Big Bound Wheel	1963	2.50	5.00	10.00
❏ 3114	Surfin' Train/Mamu Zey	1963	3.00	6.00	12.00
❏ 3128	In the Phonograph Booth/Blues at Sandy Cove	1964	2.50	5.00	10.00

MOMENTS, THE (3) Steve Marriott, later of SMALL FACES and HUMBLE PIE, was in this group.
45s
WORLD ARTISTS

❏ 1032	You Really Got Me/Money, Money	1964	2.50	5.00	10.00

MONARCHS, THE (1)
45s
MONUMENT

❏ 03484	Look Homeward, Angel/This Old Heart	1983	—	2.50	5.00

SOUND STAGE 7

❏ 2502	This Old Heart/'Til I Hear It From You	1963	3.00	6.00	12.00
❏ 2516	Look Homeward, Angel/What Made You Change Your Mind	1964	3.00	6.00	12.00
❏ 2530	Climb Every Mountain/Take Me Home	1964	3.00	6.00	12.00

MONARCHS, THE (2)
45s
DOT

❏ 15228	Gravy/Caravan Mambo	1954	10.00	20.00	40.00

MONARCHS, THE (3)
45s
LOST-NITE

❏ 120	Always Be Faithful/How Are You	196?	2.00	4.00	8.00

—Reissue
MELBA

❏ 101	Pretty Little Girl/In My Younger Days	1956	20.00	40.00	80.00

NEIL

❏ 101	Pretty Little Girl/In My Younger Days	1956	37.50	75.00	150.00
❏ 103	Always Be Faithful/How Are You	1956	30.00	60.00	120.00

MONARCHS, THE (U) Some of these could be by the above groups.
45s
LIBAN

❏ 1002	Love You That's Why/Coming Home	1959	500.00	1000.	2000.

WING

❏ 90040	Angels in the Sky/Wanna Go Home	1955	20.00	40.00	80.00

YUCCA

❏ 172	Forever Lost/Cuckoo	1964	12.50	25.00	50.00

ZONE

❏ 1067	Friday Night/El Bandito	1963	3.75	7.50	15.00

MONDAY BLUES
45s
VAULT

❏ 963	Be My Baby/Do I Love You	1970	2.00	4.00	8.00

Albums
VAULT

❏ 133	The Phil Spector Song Book	1970	5.00	10.00	20.00

MONDAY MORNING QUARTERBACK, THE
45s
WARNER BROS.

❏ 7664	The Twelve Days of Christmas (The Game Plan to Beat Miami)//Santa Claus Medley: Santa Claus Is Comin' to Town/ Here Comes Santa Claus	1972	2.50	5.00	10.00
❏ 7664 [PS]	The Twelve Days of Christmas (The Game Plan to Beat Miami)//Santa Claus Medley: Santa Claus Is Comin' to Town/ Here Comes Santa Claus	1972	3.75	7.50	15.00

—Picture sleeve is a slick pasted onto a plain white sleeve

MONDELLOS, THE
45s
RHYTHM

❏ 102	Come Back Home/100 Years from Today	1956	50.00	100.00	200.00

—As "Alice Jean and the Mondellos"

❏ 105	Over the Rainbow/Never Leave Me Alone	1956	37.50	75.00	150.00

—As "Yul McClay and the Mondellos"

❏ 106	That's What I Call Love/Daylight Saving Time	1956	37.50	75.00	150.00
❏ 109	Hard to Please/Happiness Street	1957	37.50	75.00	150.00
❏ 114	My Heart/That's What I Call Love	1957	37.50	75.00	150.00

—As "Rudy Lambert and the Mondellos"

❏ 128	That Old Feeling/Sunday Kind of Love	1957	37.50	75.00	150.00

—As "Rudy Lambert and the Mondellos"

MONEY, ZOOT
45s
EPIC

❏ 10077	Big Time Operator/Zoot's Sermon	1966	2.50	5.00	10.00

Albums
EPIC

❏ LN 24241 [M]	All Happening Zoot Money's Big Roll Band at Klooks Kleek	1966	5.00	10.00	20.00

MONITORS, THE (1)
45s
SOUL

❏ 35049	Step by Step (Hand in Hand)/Time Is Passing By	1968	3.75	7.50	15.00

V.I.P.

❏ 25028	Say You/All for Someone	1965	5.00	10.00	20.00
❏ 25032	Greetings (This Is Uncle Sam)/ Number One in Your Heart	1965	5.00	10.00	20.00
❏ 25039	Since I Lost You Girl/Don't Put Off Till Tomorrow What You Can Do Today	1966	5.00	10.00	20.00
❏ 25046	Bring Back the Love/The Further You Look, The Less You See	1967	5.00	10.00	20.00
❏ 25049	Step by Step (Hand in Hand)/Time Is Passing By	1968	12.50	25.00	50.00

Albums
SOUL

❏ SS-714	Greetings, We're the Monitors	1969	15.00	30.00	60.00

Number	Title (A Side/B Side)	Yr	VG	VG+	NM

MONITORS, THE (2)
45s
ALADDIN

❏ 3309	Tonight's the Night/Candy Coated Kisses	1955	25.00	50.00	100.00

MONITORS, THE (U) Some of these may be groups (1) or (2).
45s
BUDDAH

❏ 278	Fence Around Your Heart/Have You Seen Her	1972	—	2.50	5.00

CIRCUS

❏ 219	A Boyfriend's Prayer/Nita	1957	37.50	75.00	150.00

SPECIALTY

❏ 595	Our Schooldays/I've Got a Dream	1957	20.00	40.00	80.00
❏ 622	Closer to Heaven/Rock 'N' Roll Forever	1957	50.00	100.00	200.00
❏ 636	Mamma Linda/Hop Scotch	1958	15.00	30.00	60.00

MONK, THELONIOUS
45s
BLUE NOTE

❏ 542	Thelonious/Suburban Eyes	195?	5.00	10.00	20.00
❏ 543	Round About Midnight/Well You Needn't	195?	5.00	10.00	20.00
❏ 547	Evonce/Off Minor	195?	5.00	10.00	20.00
❏ 548	In Walked Bud/Epistrophy	195?	5.00	10.00	20.00
❏ 549	Evidence/Ruby My Dear	195?	5.00	10.00	20.00
❏ 1565	Monk's Mood/Who Knows	195?	3.75	7.50	15.00
❏ 1575	April in Paris/Nice Work	195?	3.75	7.50	15.00
❏ 1589	Straight No Chaser/Four in One	195?	3.75	7.50	15.00
❏ 1590	Criss Cross/Ebonel	195?	3.75	7.50	15.00
❏ 1602	Skippy/Let's Cool One	195?	3.75	7.50	15.00
❏ 1603	Carolina Moon/Hornin' In	195?	3.75	7.50	15.00
❏ 1664	'Round Midnight/In Walked Bud	195?	3.75	7.50	15.00

COLUMBIA

❏ 42825	Bye-Ya/Hackensack	1963	2.50	5.00	10.00
❏ 44780	Just a Glance at Love/Consecutive Seconds	1969	—	3.00	6.00

PRESTIGE

❏ 162	Blue Monk/Bye-Ya	196?	2.50	5.00	10.00
❏ 795	Sweet and Lovely/Bye-Ya	195?	3.00	6.00	12.00
❏ 838	These Foolish Things/Trinkle Tinkle	195?	3.00	6.00	12.00
❏ 850	Monk's Dream/Little Rootie Tootie	195?	3.00	6.00	12.00

RIVERSIDE

❏ 421	Coming on the Hudson/(B-side unknown)	195?	3.00	6.00	12.00
❏ 434	Blue Monk/(B-side unknown)	195?	3.00	6.00	12.00

Albums
ANALOGUE PRODUCTIONS

❏ AP-37 [(7)]	The Riverside Tenor Sessions	1999	62.50	125.00	250.00

BANDSTAND

❏ BDLP-1505	Blue Monk	1992	3.00	6.00	12.00
❏ BDLP-1516	April in Paris	1992	3.00	6.00	12.00

BLACK LION

❏ 152	Something in Blue	1972	3.00	6.00	12.00
❏ 197	The Man I Love	1973	3.00	6.00	12.00

BLUE NOTE

❏ BN-LA579-H2 [(2)]	The Complete Genius	1976	3.75	7.50	15.00
❏ LWB-579 [(2)]	The Complete Genius	1981	3.00	6.00	12.00

—Reissue of BN-LA579-H2

❏ BLP-1510 [M]	Genius of Modern Music, Vol. 1	1956	37.50	75.00	150.00

—Regular edition, Lexington Ave. address on label

❏ BLP-1510 [M]	Genius of Modern Music, Vol. 1	1956	50.00	100.00	200.00

—"Deep groove" version (deep indentation under label on both sides)

❏ BLP-1510 [M]	Genius of Modern Music, Vol. 1	1963	6.25	12.50	25.00

—"New York, USA" address on label

❏ BLP-1511 [M]	Genius of Modern Music, Vol. 2	1956	37.50	75.00	150.00

—Regular edition, Lexington Ave. address on label

❏ BLP-1511 [M]	Genius of Modern Music, Vol. 2	1956	50.00	100.00	200.00

—"Deep groove" version (deep indentation under label on both sides)

❏ BLP-1511 [M]	Genius of Modern Music, Vol. 2	1963	6.25	12.50	25.00

—"New York, USA" address on label

❏ BLP-5002 [10]	Genius of Modern Music, Vol. 1	1952	100.00	200.00	400.00
❏ BLP-5009 [10]	Genius of Modern Music, Vol. 1	1952	100.00	200.00	400.00
❏ BLP-81510 [R]	Genius of Modern Music, Vol. 1	1968	2.50	5.00	10.00
❏ BST-81510	Genius of Modern Music, Vol. 1	1985	2.50	5.00	10.00

—"The Finest in Jazz Since 1939" reissue

❏ BLP-81511 [R]	Genius of Modern Music, Vol. 2	1968	2.50	5.00	10.00
❏ BST-81511	Genius of Modern Music, Vol. 2	1985	2.50	5.00	10.00

—"The Finest in Jazz Since 1939" reissue
COLUMBIA

❏ CL 1965 [M]	Monk's Dream	1963	5.00	10.00	20.00
❏ CL 2038 [M]	Criss-Cross	1963	5.00	10.00	20.00
❏ CL 2164 [M]	Monk Big Band and Quartet In Concert	1964	5.00	10.00	20.00
❏ CL 2184 [M]	It's Monk's Time	1964	5.00	10.00	20.00
❏ CL 2291 [M]	Monk	1965	5.00	10.00	20.00
❏ CL 2349 [M]	Solo Monk	1965	5.00	10.00	20.00
❏ CL 2416 [M]	Misterioso	1966	5.00	10.00	20.00
❏ CL 2651 [M]	Straight No Chaser	1967	7.50	15.00	50.00
❏ CS 8765 [S]	Monk's Dream	1963	6.25	12.50	25.00
❏ CS 8838 [S]	Criss-Cross	1963	6.25	12.50	25.00
❏ CS 8964 [S]	Monk Big Band and Quartet In Concert	1964	6.25	12.50	25.00
❏ CS 8984 [S]	It's Monk's Time	1964	6.25	12.50	25.00
❏ CS 9091 [S]	Monk	1965	6.25	12.50	25.00
❏ CS 9149 [S]	Solo Monk	1965	6.25	12.50	25.00

—Red "360 Sound" label

❏ CS 9149	Solo Monk	1971	3.00	6.00	12.00

—Orange label

❏ PC 9149	Solo Monk	198?	2.00	4.00	8.00

—Reissue with new prefix

❏ CS 9216 [S]	Misterioso	1966	6.25	12.50	25.00
❏ CS 9451 [S]	Straight No Chaser	1967	5.00	10.00	20.00

—Red "360 Sound" label

❏ CS 9451	Straight No Chaser	1971	3.00	6.00	12.00

—Orange label

❏ PC 9451	Straight No Chaser	198?	2.00	4.00	8.00

—Reissue with new prefix

❏ CS 9632 [M]	Underground	1968	12.50	25.00	50.00

—White label promo only with stereo number; "Special Mono Radio Station Copy" sticker on stereo cover

M

Number	Title (A Side/B Side)	Yr	VG	VG+	NM
❑ CS 9632 [S]	Underground	1968	5.00	10.00	20.00
—Red "360 Sound" label					
❑ CS 9632	Underground	1971	3.00	6.00	12.00
—Orange label					
❑ PC 9632	Underground	198?	2.00	4.00	8.00
—Reissue with new prefix					
❑ CS 9775	Greatest Hits	1969	3.75	7.50	15.00
—Red "360 Sound" label					
❑ CS 9775	Greatest Hits	1971	3.00	6.00	12.00
—Orange label					
❑ PC 9775	Greatest Hits	198?	2.00	4.00	8.00
—Reissue with new prefix					
❑ CS 9806	Monk's Blues	1969	5.00	10.00	20.00
—Red "360 Sound" label					
❑ CS 9806	Monk's Blues	1971	3.00	6.00	12.00
—Orange label					
❑ PC 9806	Monk's Blues	198?	2.00	4.00	8.00
—Reissue with new prefix					
❑ KG 32892 [(2)]	Who's Afraid of the Big Band Monk	1974	3.75	7.50	15.00
❑ JG 35720 [(2)]	Always Know	1979	3.75	7.50	15.00
❑ C2 38030 [(2)]	Live at the It Club	1983	3.00	6.00	12.00
❑ C2 38269 [(2)]	Live at the Jazz Workshop	1983	3.00	6.00	12.00
❑ C2 38510 [(2)]	The Tokyo Concerts	1984	3.00	6.00	12.00
COLUMBIA JAZZ MASTERPIECES					
❑ CJ 40785	Underground	1987	2.50	5.00	10.00
❑ CJ 40786	Monk's Dream	1987	2.50	5.00	10.00
❑ CJ 44297	The Composer	1988	2.50	5.00	10.00
COLUMBIA MUSICAL TREASURY					
❑ DS 338	Monk's Miracles	1967	6.25	12.50	25.00
—Columbia Record Club exclusive					
EVEREST ARCHIVE OF FOLK & JAZZ					
❑ 336	Piano Solos	198?	2.50	5.00	10.00
FANTASY					
❑ OJC-010	Thelonious Monk Trio	198?	2.50	5.00	10.00
❑ OJC-016	Monk	198?	2.50	5.00	10.00
❑ OJC-024	Thelonious Monk Plays Duke Ellington	198?	2.50	5.00	10.00
❑ OJC-026	Brilliant Corners	198?	2.50	5.00	10.00
❑ OJC-059	Thelonious Monk/Sonny Rollins	198?	2.50	5.00	10.00
❑ OJC-064	The Unique Thelonious Monk	198?	2.50	5.00	10.00
❑ OJC-084	Monk's Music	198?	2.50	5.00	10.00
❑ OJC-103	Thelonious in Action	198?	2.50	5.00	10.00
❑ OJC-135	Thelonious Monk at Town Hall	198?	2.50	5.00	10.00
❑ OJC-206	Misterioso	1985	2.50	5.00	10.00
❑ OJC-231	Alone in San Francisco	1987	2.50	5.00	10.00
❑ OJC-254	Thelonious Himself	1987	2.50	5.00	10.00
❑ OJC-301	Mulligan Meets Monk	1988	2.50	5.00	10.00
❑ OJC-305	Thelonious Monk at the Blackhawk	1988	2.50	5.00	10.00
❑ OJC-362	5 By Monk By 5	1989	2.50	5.00	10.00
❑ OJC-488	Monk in Italy	1991	2.50	5.00	10.00
GATEWAY					
❑ 7023	Monk's Music	197?	3.00	6.00	12.00
GNP CRESCENDO					
❑ 9008 [(2)]	Thelonious Monk	197?	3.75	7.50	15.00
JAZZ MAN					
❑ 5017	Something in Blue	198?	2.50	5.00	10.00
MILESTONE					
❑ 9115	Evidence	198?	2.50	5.00	10.00
❑ 9124	Blues Five Spot	198?	2.50	5.00	10.00
❑ 47004 [(2)]	Pure Monk	1972	3.75	7.50	15.00
❑ 47023 [(2)]	Brilliance	197?	3.75	7.50	15.00
❑ 47033 [(2)]	Thelonious Monk In Person	197?	3.75	7.50	15.00
❑ 47043 [(2)]	Thelonious Monk at the Five Spot	1978	3.75	7.50	15.00
❑ 47052 [(2)]	The Riverside Trios	1980	3.75	7.50	15.00
❑ 47060 [(2)]	April in Paris/Live	198?	3.75	7.50	15.00
❑ 47064 [(2)]	Memorial Album	1982	3.00	6.00	12.00
❑ 47067 [(2)]	'Round Midnight	198?	3.00	6.00	12.00
MOSAIC					
❑ MR4-101 [(4)]	The Complete Blue Note Recordings of Thelonious Monk	198?	30.00	60.00	120.00
—Limited edition of 7,500					
❑ MR4-112 [(4)]	The Complete Black Lion and Vogue Recordings	199?	50.00	100.00	200.00
PICCADILLY					
❑ 3521	Monkisms	198?	2.50	5.00	10.00
PRESTIGE					
❑ PRLP-142 [10]	Thelonious Monk Trio	1953	50.00	100.00	200.00
❑ PRLP-166 [10]	Thelonious Monk Quintet with Sonny Rollins and Julius Watkins	1953	50.00	100.00	200.00
❑ PRLP-180 [10]	Thelonious Monk Quintet	1954	50.00	100.00	200.00
❑ PRLP-189 [10]	Thelonious Monk Trio	1954	50.00	100.00	200.00
❑ PRLP-7027 [M]	Thelonious Monk	1956	25.00	50.00	100.00
—Reissue of 142 and 189 on one 12-inch record					
❑ PRLP-7053 [M]	Monk	1956	25.00	50.00	100.00
—Reissue of 150					
❑ PRLP-7075 [M]	Thelonious Monk/Sonny Rollins	1957	25.00	50.00	100.00
—Reissue of 166					
❑ PRLP-7159 [M]	Monk's Moods	1959	18.75	37.50	75.00
—Reissue of 7027					
❑ PRLP-7169 [M]	Work	1959	18.75	37.50	75.00
—Reissue of 7075					
❑ PRLP-7245 [M]	We See	1962	18.75	37.50	75.00
—Reissue of 7053					
❑ PRLP-7363 [M]	The Golden Monk	1965	7.50	5.00	30.00
—Reissue of 7245					
❑ PRST-7363 [R]	The Golden Monk	1965	3.75	7.50	15.00
❑ PRLP-7508 [M]	The High Priest	1967	7.50	15.00	30.00
—Reissue of 7159					
❑ PRST-7508 [R]	The High Priest	1967	3.75	7.50	15.00
❑ PRST-7656	The Genius	1969	3.00	6.00	12.00
❑ PRST-7751	Reflections, Volume 1	1970	3.00	6.00	12.00
❑ PRST-7848	Blue Monk, Volume 2	197?	3.00	6.00	12.00
❑ 24006 [(2)]	Thelonious Monk	1971	3.75	7.50	15.00
RIVERSIDE					
❑ R-022 [(22)]	The Complete Riverside Recordings	1987	100.00	200.00	400.00
❑ RLP 12-201 [M]	Thelonious Monk Plays Duke Ellington	1955	100.00	200.00	400.00
—White label with blue print					

Number	Title (A Side/B Side)	Yr	VG	VG+	NM
❑ RLP 12-201 [M]	Thelonious Monk Plays Duke Ellington	1958	10.00	20.00	40.00
—Blue label with reel and microphone logo					
❑ RLP 12-209 [M]	The Unique Thelonious Monk	1956	25.00	50.00	100.00
—White label with blue print					
❑ RLP 12-209 [M]	The Unique Thelonious Monk	1958	10.00	20.00	40.00
—Blue label with reel and microphone logo					
❑ RLP 12-226 [M]	Brilliant Corners	1957	25.00	50.00	100.00
—White label with blue print					
❑ RLP 12-226 [M]	Brilliant Corners	1958	10.00	20.00	40.00
—Blue label with reel and microphone logo					
❑ RLP 12-235 [M]	Thelonious Himself	1957	25.00	50.00	100.00
—White label with blue print					
❑ RLP 12-235 [M]	Thelonious Himself	1958	10.00	20.00	40.00
—Blue label with reel and microphone logo					
❑ RLP 12-242 [M]	Monk's Music	1957	25.00	50.00	100.00
—White label with blue print					
❑ RLP 12-242 [M]	Monk's Music	1958	10.00	20.00	40.00
—Blue label with reel and microphone logo					
❑ RLP 12-247 [M]	Mulligan Meets Monk	1957	25.00	50.00	100.00
—White label with blue print					
❑ RLP 12-247 [M]	Mulligan Meets Monk	1958	10.00	20.00	40.00
—Blue label with reel and microphone logo					
❑ RLP 12-262 [M]	Thelonious in Action Recorded at the Five Spot Café, New York, With Johnny Griffn	1958	10.00	20.00	40.00
❑ RLP 12-279 [M]	Misterioso	1958	10.00	20.00	40.00
❑ RLP 12-300 [M]	The Thelonious Monk Orchestra at Town Hall	1959	10.00	20.00	40.00
❑ RLP 12-305 [M]	5 By Monk By 5	1959	10.00	20.00	40.00
❑ RLP 12-312 [M]	Thelonious Alone in San Francisco	1959	10.00	20.00	40.00
❑ RLP 12-323 [M]	Thelonious Monk Quartet Plus Two at the Blackhawk	1960	10.00	20.00	40.00
❑ RLP-421 [M]	Thelonious Monk's Greatest Hits	1962	5.00	10.00	20.00
❑ RLP-443 [M]	Thelonious Monk in Italy	1963	5.00	10.00	20.00
❑ RLP-460/1 [(2)M]	April in Paris	1963	10.00	20.00	40.00
❑ RLP-483 [M]	The Thelonious Monk Story, Volume 1	1965	5.00	10.00	20.00
❑ RLP-484 [M]	The Thelonious Monk Story, Volume 2	1965	5.00	10.00	20.00
❑ RLP-491 [M]	Monk in France	1965	5.00	10.00	20.00
❑ RLP 1101 [S]	Monk's Music	1959	10.00	20.00	40.00
—Black label with reel and microphone logo					
❑ RLP 1106 [S]	Mulligan Meets Monk	1959	10.00	20.00	40.00
—Black label with reel and microphone logo					
❑ RLP 1133 [S]	Misterioso	1958	12.50	25.00	50.00
❑ RLP 1138 [S]	The Thelonious Monk Orchestra at Town Hall	1959	12.50	25.00	50.00
❑ RLP 1150 [S]	5 By Monk By 5	1959	12.50	25.00	50.00
❑ RLP 1158 [S]	Thelonious Alone in San Francisco	1959	12.50	25.00	50.00
❑ RLP 1171 [S]	Thelonious Monk Quartet Plus Two at the Blackhawk	1960	12.50	25.00	50.00
❑ RLP 1190 [S]	Thelonious in Action Recorded at the Five Spot Café, New York, With Johnny Griffn	1960	12.50	25.00	50.00
❑ RM-3000 [M]	Mighty Monk	1967	5.00	10.00	20.00
❑ RS-3000 [S]	Mighty Monk	1967	3.75	7.50	15.00
❑ RM-3004 [M]	Monk's Music	1967	5.00	10.00	20.00
❑ RS-3004 [S]	Monk's Music	1967	3.75	7.50	15.00
❑ RS-3009 [R]	CT Meets Monk	1968	3.00	6.00	12.00
❑ RS-3015 [R]	Monk Plays Duke	1968	3.00	6.00	12.00
❑ RS-3020X [(2)R]	Two Hours with Thelonious Monk	1969	3.75	7.50	15.00
❑ RS-3037	Best of Thelonious Monk	1969	3.00	6.00	12.00
❑ RS-3047	Panorama!	1970	3.00	6.00	12.00
❑ 6039 [M]	Thelonious Monk Plays Duke Ellington	197?	3.00	6.00	12.00
❑ 6053 [M]	Thelonious Himself	197?	3.00	6.00	12.00
❑ 6068 [M]	The Unique Thelonious Monk	197?	3.00	6.00	12.00
❑ 6086	5 By Monk By 5	197?	3.00	6.00	12.00
❑ 6102	Thelonious in Action	197?	3.00	6.00	12.00
❑ 6107	Meet Thelonious Monk and Gerry Mulligan	197?	3.00	6.00	12.00
❑ 6119	Misterioso	197?	3.00	6.00	12.00
❑ 6163	Alone in San Francisco	198?	3.00	6.00	12.00
❑ 6183	Thelonious Monk at Town Hall	198?	3.00	6.00	12.00
❑ 6198	Thelonious Monk at the Blackhawk	198?	3.00	6.00	12.00
❑ 6207	Monk's Music	1983	2.50	5.00	10.00
❑ RS-9421 [S]	Thelonious Monk's Greatest Hits	1962	6.25	12.50	25.00
❑ RS-9443 [S]	Monk in Italy	1963	6.25	12.50	25.00
❑ RS-9460/1 [(2)S]	April in Paris	1963	12.50	25.00	250.00
❑ RS-9483 [S]	The Thelonious Monk Story, Volume 1	1965	6.25	12.50	25.00
❑ RS-9484 [S]	The Thelonious Monk Story, Volume 2	1965	6.25	12.50	25.00
❑ RS-9491 [S]	Monk in France	1965	6.25	12.50	25.00
TRIP					
❑ 5022	Pure Monk	1974	2.50	5.00	10.00
XANADU					
❑ 202	Live at the Village Gate	1985	2.50	5.00	10.00

MONK, THELONIOUS, AND JOHN COLTRANE Also see each artist's individual listings.

Albums

Number	Title (A Side/B Side)	Yr	VG	VG+	NM
FANTASY					
❑ OJC-039	Thelonious Monk with John Coltrane	198?	2.50	5.00	10.00
JAZZLAND					
❑ JLP-46 [M]	Thelonious Monk with John Coltrane	1961	10.00	20.00	40.00
❑ JLP-946 [S]	Thelonious Monk with John Coltrane	1961	12.50	25.00	50.00
MILESTONE					
❑ 47011 [(2)]	Monk/Trane	1973	3.75	7.50	15.00
RIVERSIDE					
❑ RLP-490 [M]	Thelonious Monk with John Coltrane	1965	6.25	12.50	25.00
—Reissue of Jazzland 46					
❑ RS-9490 [S]	Thelonious Monk with John Coltrane	1965	7.50	15.00	30.00
—Reissue of Jazzland 946					

MONKEES, THE Also see DOLENZ, JONES & TORK; DOLENZ, JONES, BOYCE & HART; MICKEY DOLENZ; DAVY JONES; MICHAEL NESMITH.

12-Inch Singles

Number	Title (A Side/B Side)	Yr	VG	VG+	NM
ARISTA					
❑ 9518	That Was Then, This Is Now/(Theme from) The Monkees	1986	2.00	4.00	8.00

45s

Number	Title (A Side/B Side)	Yr	VG	VG+	NM
ARISTA					
❑ 0201	Daydream Believer/Monkee's Theme	1976	2.50	5.00	10.00
❑ 9505	That Was Then, This Is Now/(Theme from) The Monkees	1986	—	—	3.00
—With A-side artist listed as " Mickey Dolenz and Peter Tork (of the Monkees)"					

Number	Title (A Side/B Side)	Yr	VG	VG+	NM
❑ 9505	That Was Then, This Is Now/(Theme from) The Monkees	1986	2.50	5.00	10.00

—*First pressings list both sides' artist as "The Monkees"*

❑ 9505 [PS]	That Was Then, This Is Now/(Theme from) The Monkees	1986	—	—	3.00

—*With "By Mickey Dolenz and Peter Tork (of the Monkees)" on sleeve*

❑ 9505 [PS]	That Was Then, This Is Now/(Theme from) The Monkees	1986	2.50	5.00	10.00

—*Without "By Mickey Dolenz and Peter Tork (of the Monkees)" on sleeve*

❑ 9532	Daydream Believer/Randy Scouse Git	1986	—	2.00	4.00
❑ 9532 [PS]	Daydream Believer/Randy Scouse Git	1986	—	2.00	4.00

COLGEMS

❑ 66-1001	Last Train to Clarksville/Take a Giant Step	1966	3.75	7.50	15.00
❑ 66-1001 [PS]	Last Train to Clarksville/Take a Giant Step	1966	5.00	10.00	20.00

—*Version 3: Color photo, white strip at bottom of each side. Side 1 type reads "Ask For The Monkees LP Album"; Side 2 has "Write To Monkees." Note: At least one source claims that there are seven (7) different variations of the "Last Train to Clarksville" picture sleeve, but these are the ones we know about*

❑ 66-1001 [PS]	Last Train to Clarksville/Take a Giant Step	1966	6.25	12.50	25.00

—*Version 2: Black & white photo, red strip at bottom with "Ask For The Monkees LP Album" in white*

❑ 66-1001 [PS]	Last Train to Clarksville/Take a Giant Step	1966	7.50	15.00	30.00

—*Version 1: Black & white photo, no red strip at bottom*

❑ 66-1002	I'm a Believer/(I'm Not Your) Steppin' Stone	1966	3.75	7.50	15.00
❑ 66-1002 [PS]	I'm a Believer/(I'm Not Your) Steppin' Stone	1966	7.50	15.00	30.00
❑ 66-1003	A Little Bit Me, A Little Bit You/She Hangs Out	1967	—	—	—

—*Unreleased*

❑ 66-1003 [PS]	A Little Bit Me, A Little Bit You/She Hangs Out	1967	250.00	500.00	1000.

—*Though the record does not exist, this picture sleeve does. It uses the same photo that appears on the "Pleasant Valley Sunday" sleeve.*

❑ 66-1004	A Little Bit Me, A Little Bit You/The Girl I Knew Somewhere	1967	3.75	7.50	15.00
❑ 66-1007	Pleasant Valley Sunday/Words	1967	3.75	7.50	15.00
❑ 66-1007 [PS]	Pleasant Valley Sunday/Words	1967	7.50	15.00	30.00
❑ 66-1012	Daydream Believer/Goin' Down	1967	3.75	7.50	15.00
❑ 66-1012 [PS]	Daydream Believer/Goin' Down	1967	7.50	15.00	30.00
❑ 66-1019	Valleri/Tapioca Tundra	1968	2.50	5.00	10.00
❑ 66-1023	D.W. Washburn/It's Nice to Be with You	1968	2.50	5.00	10.00
❑ 66-1023 [PS]	D.W. Washburn/It's Nice to Be with You	1968	7.50	15.00	30.00
❑ 66-1031	Porpoise Song/As We Go Along	1968	2.50	5.00	10.00
❑ 66-1031 [PS]	Porpoise Song/As We Go Along	1968	5.00	10.00	20.00
❑ 66-5000	Tear Drop City/A Man Without a Dream	1969	2.50	5.00	10.00
❑ 66-5000 [PS]	Tear Drop City/A Man Without a Dream	1969	6.25	12.50	25.00
❑ 66-5004	Listen to the Band/Someday Man	1969	2.50	5.00	10.00
❑ 66-5004 [PS]	Someday Man/Listen to the Band	1969	5.00	10.00	20.00

—*"Someday Man" listed first*

❑ 66-5004 [PS]	Listen to the Band/Someday Man	1969	6.25	12.50	25.00

—*"Listen to the Band" listed first*

❑ 66-5005	Good Clean Fun/Mommy and Daddy	1969	3.75	7.50	15.00
❑ 66-5005 [PS]	Good Clean Fun/Mommy and Daddy	1969	6.25	12.50	25.00
❑ 66-5011	Oh My My/I Love You Better	1970	3.75	7.50	15.00
❑ 66-5011 [PS]	Oh My My/I Love You Better	1970	7.50	15.00	30.00

RHINO

❑ 74408	Heart and Soul/M.G.B.G.T.	1987	—	—	3.00

—*Black vinyl*

❑ 74408	Heart and Soul/M.G.B.G.T.	1987	2.50	5.00	10.00

—*Pink vinyl*

❑ 74408 [PS]	Heart and Soul/M.G.B.G.T.	1987	—	2.00	4.00
❑ 74410	Every Step of the Way/(I'll) Love You Forever	1987	—	—	3.00
❑ 74410 [PS]	Every Step of the Way/(I'll) Love You Forever	1987	—	2.00	4.00
❑ RNSI 74411	Every Step of the Way/(I'll) Love You Forever	1987	2.50	5.00	10.00

—*Picture disc in plastic sleeve with small hole*

7-Inch Extended Plays

COLGEMS

❑ CGLP-101 [DJ]	Theme from The Monkees/I Wanna Be Free/Take a Giant Step//Last Train to Clarksville/Saturday's Child/Tomorrow's Gonna Be Another Day	1966	37.50	75.00	150.00

—*Jukebox mini-LP, small hole, plays at 33 1/3 rpm*

❑ CGLP-101 [PS]	The Monkees	1966	37.50	75.00	150.00

Albums

ARISTA

❑ AL 4089	The Monkees' Greatest Hits	1976	3.00	6.00	12.00

—*Reissue of Bell LP*

❑ AL8-8313	The Monkees' Greatest Hits	198?	2.00	4.00	8.00

—*Reissue of Arista 4089*

❑ AL9-8432	Then & Now...The Best of the Monkees	1986	3.00	6.00	12.00
❑ AL-8524	The Monkees	1988	3.00	6.00	12.00
❑ AL-8525	More of the Monkees	1988	3.00	6.00	12.00

BELL

❑ 6081	Re-Focus	1972	7.50	15.00	30.00

COLGEMS

❑ COM-101 [M]	The Monkees	1966	5.00	10.00	20.00

—*Second pressing: Side 1, Song 5 listed as "Papa Gene's Blues" (RE after number on upper right back cover)*

❑ COM-101 [M]	The Monkees	1966	6.25	12.50	25.00

—*First pressing: Side 1, Song 5 listed as "Papa Jean's Blues"*

❑ COS-101 [S]	The Monkees	1966	5.00	10.00	20.00

—*Second pressing: Side 1, Song 5 listed as "Papa Gene's Blues" (RE after number on upper right back cover)*

❑ COS-101 [S]	The Monkees	1966	6.25	12.50	25.00

—*First pressing: Side 1, Song 5 listed as "Papa Jean's Blues"*

❑ COM-102 [M]	More of the Monkees	1966	5.00	10.00	20.00
❑ COS-102 [S]	More of the Monkees	1966	5.00	10.00	20.00
❑ COM-103 [M]	The Monkees' Headquarters	1967	5.00	10.00	20.00

—*First pressing: Back cover, center bottom photo is of two of the LP's producers*

❑ COM-103 [M]	The Monkees' Headquarters	1967	7.50	15.00	30.00

—*Second pressing: Back cover, center bottom photo is of producers plus the Monkees with beards; "RE" on upper right back cover*

❑ COS-103 [S]	The Monkees' Headquarters	1967	5.00	10.00	20.00

—*First pressing: Back cover, center bottom photo is of two of the LP's producers*

❑ COS-103 [S]	The Monkees' Headquarters	1967	7.50	15.00	30.00

—*Second pressing: Back cover, center bottom photo is of producers plus the Monkees with beards; "RE" on upper right back cover*

❑ COM-104 [M]	Pisces, Aquarius, Capricorn & Jones Ltd.	1967	10.00	20.00	40.00
❑ COS-104 [S]	Pisces, Aquarius, Capricorn & Jones Ltd.	1967	5.00	10.00	20.00
❑ COM-109 [M]	The Birds, the Bees & the Monkees	1968	25.00	50.00	100.00

Number	Title (A Side/B Side)	Yr	VG	VG+	NM
❑ COS-109 [S]	The Birds, the Bees & the Monkees	1968	5.00	10.00	20.00
❑ COS-113	Instant Replay	1969	10.00	20.00	40.00
❑ COS-115	The Monkees Greatest Hits	1969	10.00	20.00	40.00
❑ COS-117	The Monkees Present	1969	12.50	25.00	50.00
❑ COS-119	Changes	1970	20.00	40.00	80.00
❑ PRS-329	The Monkees' Golden Hits	1971	25.00	50.00	100.00

—*RCA Special Products edition*

❑ SCOS-1001 [(2)]	A Barrel Full of Monkees	1971	18.75	37.50	75.00
❑ COSO-5008	Head	1968	12.50	25.00	50.00

FSH

❑ 71110	Live, 20th Anniversary Tour	1987	5.00	10.00	20.00

—*Live album sold at tour stops*

LAURIE HOUSE

❑ LH-8009	The Monkees	1974	5.00	10.00	20.00

—*TV mail-order offer*

PAIR

❑ ARPDL2-1109 [(2)]	Hit Factory	1986	5.00	10.00	20.00

RCA SPECIAL PRODUCTS

❑ DPL2-0188 [(2)]	The Monkees	1976	6.25	12.50	25.00

—*TV mail-order offer*

RHINO

❑ RNLP-113	Monkee Flips	1984	3.00	6.00	12.00
❑ RNLP-144	The Birds, the Bees and the Monkees	1985	3.00	6.00	12.00
❑ RNLP-145	Head	1985	3.00	6.00	12.00
❑ RNLP-146	Instant Replay	1985	3.00	6.00	12.00
❑ RNLP-147	The Monkees Present	1985	3.00	6.00	12.00
❑ RNLP-701 [PD]	Monkee Business	1982	3.75	7.50	15.00
❑ RNLP-70139	Live 1967	1987	3.00	6.00	12.00
❑ RNLP-70140	The Monkees	1986	3.00	6.00	12.00
❑ RNLP-70141	Pisces, Aquarius, Capricorn & Jones Ltd.	1986	3.00	6.00	12.00
❑ RNLP-70142	More of the Monkees	1986	3.00	6.00	12.00
❑ RNLP-70143	The Monkees' Headquarters	1986	3.00	6.00	12.00
❑ RNLP-70148	Changes	1986	3.00	6.00	12.00
❑ RNLP-70150	Missing Links	1987	3.00	6.00	12.00
❑ RNIN-70706	Pool It!	1987	2.50	5.00	10.00

SILHOUETTE

❑ SM-10012 [PD]	Tails of the Monkees	1983	3.75	7.50	15.00

SILVER EAGLE

❑ SE-1048 [(2)]	The Best of the Monkees	1986	3.75	7.50	15.00

—*TV mail-order offer*

SUNDAZED

❑ LP 5045	The Monkees	1996	2.50	5.00	10.00
❑ LP 5046	More of the Monkees	1996	2.50	5.00	10.00
❑ LP 5047	The Monkees Headquarters	1996	2.50	5.00	10.00
❑ LP 5048	Pisces, Aquarius, Capricorn & Jones Ltd.	1996	2.50	5.00	10.00
❑ LP 5049	The Birds, the Bees, and the Monkees	1996	2.50	5.00	10.00

—*All of the above are on colored vinyl with bonus tracks and posters*

MONORAYS, THE *More than one group?*
45s
ASTRA

❑ 1018	Face in the Crowd/Step Right Up	196?	3.75	7.50	15.00

—*Yellow vinyl*

RED ROCKET

❑ 476	Guardian Angel/Five Minutes to Love You	1959	10.00	20.00	40.00

TAMMY

❑ 1005	Guardian Angel/Five Minutes to Love You	1959	50.00	100.00	200.00

20TH CENTURY FOX

❑ 594	You're No Good/Love	1965	12.50	25.00	50.00

MONOTONES, THE (1) *Male vocal group from New Jersey.*
45s
ARGO

❑ 5290	Book of Love/You Never Loved Me	1958	7.50	15.00	30.00
❑ 5301	Tom Foolery/Zombi	1958	7.50	15.00	30.00
❑ 5321	The Legend of Sleepy Hollow/Soft Shadows	1958	7.50	15.00	30.00
❑ 5339	Tell It to the Judge/Fools Will Be Fools	1959	12.50	25.00	50.00

HULL

❑ 735	Reading the Book of Love/Dream	1960	12.50	25.00	50.00
❑ 743	Daddy's Home, But Momma's Gone/Tattle Tale	1961	12.50	25.00	50.00

MASCOT

❑ 124	Book of Love/You Never Loved Me	1957	200.00	400.00	800.00

MONOTONES, THE (2) *British group.*
45s
HICKORY

❑ 1250	Is It Right/What Would You Do	1964	5.00	10.00	20.00
❑ 1306	When Will I Be Loved/If You Can't Give Me All	1965	5.00	10.00	20.00

MONOTONES, THE (U) *Could be group (2); it's doubtful that it's group (1).*
45s
ABC-PARAMOUNT

❑ 10796	Crystal Ball/A Thousand Faces	1966	5.00	10.00	20.00

MONRO, MATT
45s
CAPITOL

❑ 2058	Only the Night Wind Knows/Fourth Blue Monday	1967	—	3.00	6.00
❑ 2103	Don't Answer Me/Pretty Polly	1968	—	2.50	5.00
❑ 2207	Yours Alone/The Music Played	1968	—	2.50	5.00
❑ 2318	Alguien Canto/De Repente Un Dea	1968	—	2.50	5.00
❑ 2390	Real Live Girl/When Joanna Loved Me	1969	—	2.50	5.00
❑ 2455	Love Song/Try to Remember	1969	—	2.50	5.00
❑ 2509	People/Southern Star	1969	—	2.50	5.00
❑ 2588	On Days Like These/Lily M'Lady	1969	—	2.50	5.00
❑ 2879	He Ain't Heavy, He's My Brother/We're Gonna Change the World	1970	—	2.00	4.00
❑ 3274	This Way Mary/Wish Now Was Then	1972	—	2.00	4.00
❑ 5623	Born Free/Other People	1966	—	3.00	6.00
❑ 5669	Honey on the Vine/Merci, Cherie	1966	—	3.00	6.00
❑ 5823	Wednesday's Child/The Lady Smiles	1967	—	3.00	6.00
❑ 5947	These Years/What to Do	1967	—	3.00	6.00

LIBERTY

❑ 55449	Softly, As I Leave You/Is There Anything I Can Do	1962	2.50	5.00	10.00
❑ 55573	The Girl I Love/Leave Me Now	1963	2.00	4.00	8.00
❑ 55682	From Russia with Love/Here and Now	1964	2.00	4.00	8.00

Number	Title (A Side/B Side)	Yr	VG	VG+	NM
❏ 55725	Softly, As I Leave You/I Love You Too	1964	2.00	4.00	8.00
❏ 55745	Walk Away/April Fool	1964	2.00	4.00	8.00
❏ 55763	For Mama/Going Places	1965	2.00	4.00	8.00
❏ 55786	Without You/Start Living	1965	2.00	4.00	8.00
❏ 55847	Yesterday/Just Yesterday	1965	2.00	4.00	8.00
❏ 55863	Beyond the Hill/Till Then My Love	1966	—	3.00	6.00

UNITED ARTISTS

Number	Title (A Side/B Side)	Yr	VG	VG+	NM
❏ XW521	Softly, As I Leave You/Walk Away	1974	—	2.00	4.00

—Reissue

WARWICK

Number	Title (A Side/B Side)	Yr	VG	VG+	NM
❏ 624	Portrait of My Love/You're the Top of My Parade	1961	2.50	5.00	10.00
❏ 636	My Kind of Girl/This Time	1961	3.00	6.00	12.00
❏ 669	Why Not Now/Love Is the Same Anywhere	1961	2.50	5.00	10.00

Albums

CAPITOL

Number	Title (A Side/B Side)	Yr	VG	VG+	NM
❏ SKAO-152	Best of Matt Monro	1969	2.50	5.00	10.00
❏ ST 2540 [S]	This Is the Life	1966	3.75	7.50	15.00
❏ T 2540 [M]	This Is the Life	1966	3.00	6.00	12.00
❏ ST 2608 [S]	Here's to My Lady	1966	3.75	7.50	15.00
❏ T 2608 [M]	Here's to My Lady	1966	3.00	6.00	12.00
❏ ST 2683 [S]	Invitation to Broadway	1967	3.75	7.50	15.00
❏ T 2683 [M]	Invitation to Broadway	1967	3.00	6.00	12.00
❏ ST 2730 [S]	Invitation to the Movies/Born Free	1967	3.00	6.00	12.00
❏ T 2730 [M]	Invitation to the Movies/Born Free	1967	3.75	7.50	15.00
❏ ST 2801 [S]	These Years	1968	3.00	6.00	12.00
❏ T 2801 [M]	These Years	1968	3.75	7.50	15.00

LIBERTY

Number	Title (A Side/B Side)	Yr	VG	VG+	NM
❏ LRP-3240 [M]	Matt Monro	1962	3.75	7.50	15.00
❏ LRP-3256 [M]	From Hollywood With Love	1962	3.75	7.50	15.00
❏ LRP-3402 [M]	Walk Away	1965	3.00	6.00	12.00
❏ LRP-3423 [M]	All My Loving	1965	3.00	6.00	12.00
❏ LRP-3437 [M]	Yesterday	1966	3.00	6.00	12.00
❏ LRP-3459 [M]	Matt Monro's Best	1966	3.00	6.00	12.00
❏ LST-7240 [S]	Matt Monro	1962	5.00	10.00	20.00
❏ LST-7256 [S]	From Hollywood With Love	1962	5.00	10.00	20.00
❏ LST-7402 [S]	Walk Away	1965	3.75	7.50	15.00
❏ LST-7423 [S]	All My Loving	1965	3.75	7.50	15.00
❏ LST-7437 [S]	Yesterday	1966	3.75	7.50	15.00
❏ LST-7459 [S]	Matt Monro's Best	1966	3.75	7.50	15.00

LONDON

Number	Title (A Side/B Side)	Yr	VG	VG+	NM
❏ LL 1611 [M]	Blue and Sentimental	1957	7.50	15.00	30.00

PICKWICK

Number	Title (A Side/B Side)	Yr	VG	VG+	NM
❏ SPC-3147	This Is All I Ask	197?	2.50	5.00	10.00

WARWICK

Number	Title (A Side/B Side)	Yr	VG	VG+	NM
❏ W 2045 [M]	My Kind of Girl	1961	7.50	15.00	30.00
❏ WST 2045 [S]	My Kind of Girl	1961	12.50	25.00	50.00

MONROE, MARILYN

45s

RCA VICTOR

Number	Title (A Side/B Side)	Yr	VG	VG+	NM
❏ 47-5745	River of No Return/I'm Gonna File My Claim	1954	12.50	25.00	50.00
❏ 47-5745 [DJ]	River of No Return/I'm Gonna File My Claim	1954	30.00	60.00	120.00

—Promo only with Marilyn Monroe's picture on label

Number	Title (A Side/B Side)	Yr	VG	VG+	NM
❏ 47-5745 [PS]	River of No Return/I'm Gonna File My Claim	1954	30.00	60.00	120.00
❏ 47-6033	Heat Wave/After You Get What You Want	1955	7.50	15.00	30.00
❏ 47-6033 [PS]	Heat Wave/After You Get What You Want	1955	30.00	60.00	120.00

20TH FOX

Number	Title (A Side/B Side)	Yr	VG	VG+	NM
❏ 311	River of No Return/One Silver Dollar	1962	5.00	10.00	20.00
❏ 311 [PS]	River of No Return/One Silver Dollar	1962	20.00	40.00	80.00

UNITED ARTISTS

Number	Title (A Side/B Side)	Yr	VG	VG+	NM
❏ 161	I Wanna Be Loved By You/I'm Through with Love	1959	5.00	10.00	20.00

Albums

ASCOT

Number	Title (A Side/B Side)	Yr	VG	VG+	NM
❏ AM-13008 [M]	Marilyn Monroe	1963	10.00	20.00	40.00
❏ AS-16008 [S]	Marilyn Monroe	1963	12.50	25.00	50.00

MOVIETONE

Number	Title (A Side/B Side)	Yr	VG	VG+	NM
❏ 1016 [M]	The Unforgettable Marilyn Monroe	1967	6.25	12.50	25.00
❏ 72016 [R]	The Unforgettable Marilyn Monroe	1967	5.00	10.00	20.00

SANDY HOOK

Number	Title (A Side/B Side)	Yr	VG	VG+	NM
❏ SH-2013 [PD]	Rare Recordings 1948-1962	1980	6.25	12.50	25.00

STET

Number	Title (A Side/B Side)	Yr	VG	VG+	NM
❏ DS-15005	Never Before and Never Again	1980	3.75	7.50	15.00

20TH CENTURY

Number	Title (A Side/B Side)	Yr	VG	VG+	NM
❏ T-901	Remember Marilyn	1973	6.25	12.50	25.00

20TH FOX

Number	Title (A Side/B Side)	Yr	VG	VG+	NM
❏ F/SXG-5000	Marilyn Bonus Photo	1962	12.50	25.00	50.00
❏ FXG-5000 [M]	Marilyn	1962	37.50	75.00	150.00
❏ SXG-5000 [R]	Marilyn	1962	25.00	50.00	100.00

MONROE, VAUGHN

45s

DOT

Number	Title (A Side/B Side)	Yr	VG	VG+	NM
❏ 16434	There! I've Said It Again/I Really Love You	1963	—	3.00	6.00
❏ 16482	Pee Wee Valley/Valley Forge	1963	—	3.00	6.00
❏ 16536	Desert Flower/Ballad of Shadow Mountain	1963	—	3.00	6.00

JUBILEE

Number	Title (A Side/B Side)	Yr	VG	VG+	NM
❏ 5412	Bye Bye Blackbird/One Hour Before the Posse	1961	2.00	4.00	8.00

MGM

Number	Title (A Side/B Side)	Yr	VG	VG+	NM
❏ 12968	Learn to Ski by Mail/Song of the Skier	1960	2.00	4.00	8.00

RCA VICTOR

Number	Title (A Side/B Side)	Yr	VG	VG+	NM
❏ 47-2791	Memory Lane/Memories	1949	3.75	7.50	15.00
❏ 47-2792	Just a Memory/Memories of You	1949	3.75	7.50	15.00
❏ 47-2793	Thanks for the Memory/Remember	1949	3.75	7.50	15.00
❏ 47-2794	Easy to Remember/Roses for Remembrance	1949	3.75	7.50	15.00
❏ 47-2799	Racing with the Moon/Tchaikovsky Piano Concerto No. 1	1949	3.75	7.50	15.00

—B-side by Freddie Martin; part of a various artists 4-record box set

Number	Title (A Side/B Side)	Yr	VG	VG+	NM
❏ 47-2804	I've Got a Pocketful of Dreams/Did You Ever See a Dream Walking	1949	5.00	10.00	20.00
❏ 47-2830	It's Only a Paper Moon/Moonlight and Roses	1949	3.75	7.50	15.00
❏ 47-2831	Moon of Manakoora/Moonglow	1949	3.75	7.50	15.00
❏ 47-2832	Racing with the Moon/Moon Over Miami	1949	3.75	7.50	15.00

—The above three comprise a box set

Number	Title (A Side/B Side)	Yr	VG	VG+	NM
❏ 47-2833	Drifting and Dreaming/I'll See You in My Dreams	1949	3.75	7.50	15.00
❏ 47-2834	Meet Me Tonight in Dreamland/My Isle of Golden Dreams	1949	3.75	7.50	15.00

Number	Title (A Side/B Side)	Yr	VG	VG+	NM
❏ 47-2835	Dream/My Dreams Are Getting Better All the Time	1949	3.75	7.50	15.00

—The above three comprise a box set

Number	Title (A Side/B Side)	Yr	VG	VG+	NM
❏ 47-2883	Anniversary Song/Something Special	1949	3.75	7.50	15.00
❏ 47-2884	Because/Oh, Promise Me	1949	3.75	7.50	15.00
❏ 47-2885	The Whiffenpoof Song/Without a Song	1949	3.75	7.50	15.00

—The above three comprise a box set

Number	Title (A Side/B Side)	Yr	VG	VG+	NM
❏ 47-2889	Red Roses for a Blue Lady/Melancholy Minstrel	1949	5.00	10.00	20.00
❏ 47-2902	Riders in the Sky (A Cowboy Legend)/Single Saddle	1949	6.25	12.50	25.00
❏ 47-2934	Telephone No Ring/It Looked So Good in De Window	1949	5.00	10.00	20.00
❏ 47-2944	Look for the Silver Lining/Kiss in the Night	1949	3.75	7.50	15.00
❏ 47-2945	Shine On Harvest Moon/Who	1949	3.75	7.50	15.00
❏ 47-2946	Time on My Hands/Avalon	1949	3.75	7.50	15.00
❏ 47-2986	Someday (You'll Want Me to Want You)/And It Still Goes	1949	5.00	10.00	20.00
❏ 47-3018	That Lucky Old Sun (Just Rolls Around Heaven All Day)/Make Believe	1949	5.00	10.00	20.00
❏ 47-3031	My Hot Tamale Want Chilly On Me/Gee, It's Tough to Be a Skunk	1949	5.00	10.00	20.00
❏ 47-3042	Vieni Su (Say You Love Me Too)/Blue for a Boy, Pink for a Girl	1949	5.00	10.00	20.00
❏ 47-3068	Sonny Boy/I Only Have Eyes for You	1949	5.00	10.00	20.00
❏ 47-3070	The Jolly Old Man in the Bright Red Suit/Auld Lang Syne	1949	5.00	10.00	20.00
❏ 47-3106	Mule Train/Singing My Way Back Home	1949	5.00	10.00	20.00
❏ 47-3112	So This Is Love/There's No One Here But Me	1949	5.00	10.00	20.00
❏ 47-3143	Bamboo/A Little Golden Cross	1949	5.00	10.00	20.00
❏ 47-3162	Toyland/Ah! Sweet Mystery of Life	1949	3.75	7.50	15.00
❏ 47-3163	Kiss Me/Indian Summer	1949	3.75	7.50	15.00
❏ 47-3164	Gypsy Love Song/I'm Falling in Love with Someone	1949	3.75	7.50	15.00
❏ 47-3257	Ballerina/The Stars Will Remember	1949	5.00	10.00	20.00
❏ 47-3711	Over and Over/It's Easter Time	1950	3.75	7.50	15.00
❏ 47-3773	Thanks, Mr. Florist/Tell Her You Love Her	1950	3.75	7.50	15.00
❏ 47-3806	Our Very Own/Violins from Nowhere	1950	3.75	7.50	15.00
❏ 47-3810	The Phantom Stagecoach/Gonna Ride 'n' Ride	1950	3.00	6.00	12.00
❏ 47-3811	While I'm Smokin' My Last Cigarette/No Range to Ride Anymore	1950	3.00	6.00	12.00
❏ 47-3812	The Pony Express/Rounded Up in Glory	1950	3.00	6.00	12.00

—The above three comprise a box set

Number	Title (A Side/B Side)	Yr	VG	VG+	NM
❏ 47-3818	The Phantom Stagecoach/Mexicali Trail	1950	3.75	7.50	15.00
❏ 47-3880	The Beer That I Left on the Bar/Why Fight the Feeling	1950	3.75	7.50	15.00
❏ 47-3907	This Is My Country/The Great American Dream	1950	3.75	7.50	15.00
❏ 47-3915	Frosty the Snowman/Could Be	1950	3.75	7.50	15.00
❏ 47-3929	Dream a Little Dream of Me/Dream Awhile	1950	3.75	7.50	15.00
❏ 47-3942	A Marshmallow World/Snowy White Snow and Jingle Bells	1950	3.75	7.50	15.00
❏ 47-4007	The Night Is Young/From This Moment On	1950	3.75	7.50	15.00
❏ 47-4059	Faithful/They're Playing Our Song	1951	3.75	7.50	15.00
❏ 47-4074	You Are the One/Strawberry Moon	1951	3.75	7.50	15.00
❏ 47-4113	Sound Off (The Duckworth Chant)/Oh Marry, Marry Me	1951	3.75	7.50	15.00
❏ 47-4114	On Top of Old Smoky/Shall We Dance	1951	3.75	7.50	15.00
❏ 47-4138	Where or When/The Most Beautiful Girl in the World	1951	3.75	7.50	15.00
❏ 47-4146	Old Soldiers Never Die/Love and Devotion	1951	3.75	7.50	15.00
❏ 47-4171	So in Love/I Concentrate on You	1951	3.00	6.00	12.00
❏ 47-4172	I Get a Kick Out of You/Easy to Love	1951	3.00	6.00	12.00
❏ 47-4173	Don't Fence Me In/What Is This Thing Called Love	1951	3.00	6.00	12.00
❏ 47-4180	Dark Is the Night/Wonder Why	1951	3.75	7.50	15.00
❏ 47-4194	Red Sails in the Sunset/Everlasting	1951	3.75	7.50	15.00
❏ 47-4218	Laura Lee/Got Her Off My Hands	1951	3.75	7.50	15.00
❏ 47-4271	Meanderin'/They Call the Wind Maria	1951	3.75	7.50	15.00
❏ 47-4299	Frosty the Snowman/The Jolly Old Man in the Bright Red Suit	1951	3.75	7.50	15.00
❏ 47-4375	Charmaine/Once	1951	3.75	7.50	15.00
❏ 47-4403	Tenderly/I Like It, I Like It	1951	3.75	7.50	15.00
❏ 47-4479	Mountain Laurel/Ooh What You Did	1952	3.00	6.00	12.00
❏ 47-4611	Lady Love/Idaho State Fair	1952	3.00	6.00	12.00
❏ 47-4638	Marionette/California Rose	1952	3.00	6.00	12.00
❏ 47-4726	On Top of Old Smoky/Ballerina	1952	2.50	5.00	10.00
❏ 47-4727	Riders in the Sky (A Cowboy Legend)/Red Roses for a Blue Lady	1952	2.50	5.00	10.00
❏ 47-4760	Do You Care/Faith	1952	3.00	6.00	12.00
❏ 47-4838	Man on the Misty Mountain/When My Love Comes Back to Me	1952	3.00	6.00	12.00
❏ 47-4850	Learn to Lose/Dancing Girl	1952	3.00	6.00	12.00
❏ 47-4942	Hound Dog/A Man Don't Life Who Can Die Alone	1952	3.75	7.50	15.00
❏ 47-4942	A Man's Best Friend Is His Horse/You'll Never Get Away	1952	3.00	6.00	12.00
❏ 47-5007	Voters on Parade/Man on Misty Mountain	1952	3.00	6.00	12.00
❏ 47-5030	Yours/I	1952	3.00	6.00	12.00
❏ 47-5145	Small World/Lonely Eyes	1953	3.00	6.00	12.00
❏ 47-5236	Co-Ed/Don't Build Your Dreams Too High	1953	3.00	6.00	12.00
❏ 47-5286	Ruby/Less Than Tomorrow	1953	3.00	6.00	12.00
❏ 47-5329	Don't Care/My Good Girl	1953	3.00	6.00	12.00
❏ 47-5490	I Know for Sure/Fiesta	1953	3.00	6.00	12.00
❏ 47-5608	Redwood Smoke/Guessing	1953	3.00	6.00	12.00
❏ 47-5767	Always, Always in My Dreams/Talkin' to a Sparrow	1954	2.50	5.00	10.00
❏ 47-5851	They Were Doin' the Mambo/Mister Sandman	1954	2.50	5.00	10.00
❏ 47-5943	Julie's Rainbow/Lila	1954	2.50	5.00	10.00
❏ 47-5970	Butterscotch Hop/Goodnight Mrs. Jones	1954	2.50	5.00	10.00
❏ 47-6002	The Holy Bible/The Ten Commandments	1954	3.00	6.00	12.00
❏ 47-6118	What a Diff'rence a Day Made/The Main Event	1955	2.50	5.00	10.00
❏ 47-6216	Roses and Revolvers/I Turned It Down	1955	2.50	5.00	10.00
❏ 47-6260	The Moon Was Yellow/You Could Hear a Pin Drop	1955	2.50	5.00	10.00
❏ 47-6358	Black Denim Trousers and Motorcycle Boots/All By Myself	1955	2.50	5.00	10.00
❏ 47-6501	Don't Go to Strangers/Steel Guitar	1955	2.50	5.00	10.00
❏ 47-6619	The Rock 'n' Roll Express/There She Goes	1956	3.00	6.00	12.00
	In the Middle of the House/Rollin' Heart	1956	2.50	5.00	10.00

Number	Title (A Side/B Side)	Yr	VG	VG+	NM
☐ 47-6895	The Ride Back!/Away Out West	1957	2.50	5.00	10.00
☐ 47-6895 [PS]	The Ride Back!/Away Out West	1957	3.75	7.50	15.00
☐ 47-7019	Tomorrow, Tomorrow/Miss You	1957	2.50	5.00	10.00
☐ 47-7093	The Best Dream of All/Stargazer	1957	2.50	5.00	10.00
☐ 47-7193	There's No Piano in This House/Somebody Else				
	Is Taking My Place	1958	2.50	5.00	10.00
☐ 47-7345	Ghost Train/Ten Chaperones	1958	2.50	5.00	10.00
☐ 47-7443	The Clown/There! I've Said It Again	1959	2.00	4.00	8.00
☐ 47-7495	The Battle of New Orleans/Hercules	1959	2.00	4.00	8.00
☐ 447-0200	Riders in the Sky/Racing with the Moon	195?	2.50	5.00	10.00

—Black label, dog on top

Number	Title (A Side/B Side)	Yr	VG	VG+	NM
☐ WBY-56	Westward Ho, the Wagons/Wringle Wrangle	1957	5.00	10.00	20.00

—From the "Bluebird Children's Records" series

UNITED ARTISTS

Number	Title (A Side/B Side)	Yr	VG	VG+	NM
☐ 214	Love Me Forever/Ballerina	1960	2.00	4.00	8.00
☐ 254	Reveille/The Locket	1960	—		

—Canceled

7-Inch Extended Plays

RCA VICTOR

Number	Title (A Side/B Side)	Yr	VG	VG+	NM
☐ EPA-450	Blue Tail Fly/Billy Boy, Billy Boy//Skip to My Lou/				
	Shoot the Buffalo	195?	5.00	10.00	20.00
☐ EPA-450 [PS]	Blue Tail Fly and Other Folk Favorites	195?	5.00	10.00	20.00

Albums

DOT

Number	Title (A Side/B Side)	Yr	VG	VG+	NM
☐ DLP-3419 [M]	Surfer's Stomp	1962	7.50	15.00	30.00
☐ DLP-3431 [M]	His Greatest Hits	1962	3.00	6.00	12.00
☐ DLP-3470 [M]	Great Themes of Famous				
	Bands and Famous Singers	1962	3.00	6.00	12.00
☐ DLP-3548 [M]	Great Gospels — Great Hymns	1963	3.00	6.00	12.00
☐ DLP-3584 [M]	His Greatest Hits, Volume 2	1964	3.00	6.00	12.00
☐ DLP-25419 [S]	Surfer's Stomp	1962	10.00	20.00	40.00
☐ DLP-25431 [S]	His Greatest Hits	1962	3.75	7.50	15.00
☐ DLP-25470 [S]	Great Themes of Famous Bands				
	and Famous Singers	1962	3.75	7.50	15.00
☐ DLP-25548 [S]	Great Gospels — Great Hymns	1963	3.75	7.50	15.00
☐ DLP-25584 [S]	His Greatest Hits, Volume 2	1964	3.75	7.50	15.00

HAMILTON

Number	Title (A Side/B Side)	Yr	VG	VG+	NM
☐ HLP-137 [M]	Racing with the Moon	1965	2.50	5.00	10.00
☐ HLP-12137 [S]	Racing with the Moon	1965	3.00	6.00	12.00

RCA CAMDEN

Number	Title (A Side/B Side)	Yr	VG	VG+	NM
☐ CAL-329 [M]	Dance with Me	1956	5.00	10.00	20.00
☐ CAL-354 [M]	Dreamland Special	1956	5.00	10.00	20.00

RCA VICTOR

Number	Title (A Side/B Side)	Yr	VG	VG+	NM
☐ LPM-13 [10]	Vaughn Monroe Plays Victor Herbert for				
	Dancing	1952	10.00	20.00	40.00
☐ ANL1-1140	The Best of Vaughn Monroe	1976	2.00	4.00	8.00
☐ LPM-1493 [M]	House Party	1957	7.50	15.00	30.00
☐ LPM-1799 [M]	There I Sing, Swing It Again	1958	5.00	10.00	20.00
☐ LSP-1799 [S]	There I Sing, Swing It Again	1958	7.50	15.00	30.00
☐ LPM-3048 [10]	Vaughn Monroe Caravan	1952	10.00	20.00	40.00
☐ LPM-3817 [M]	The Best of Vaughn Monroe	1967	5.00	10.00	20.00
☐ LSP-3817 [R]	The Best of Vaughn Monroe	1967	3.00	6.00	12.00
☐ VPM-6073 [(2)]	This Is Vaughn Monroe	1972	3.75	7.50	15.00

MONTAGE

45s

LAURIE

Number	Title (A Side/B Side)	Yr	VG	VG+	NM
☐ 3438	I Shall Call Her Mary/				
	An Audience with Miss Priscilla Gray	1968	2.00	4.00	8.00
☐ 3453	Wake Up Jimmy/Tinsel and Ivy	1968	2.00	4.00	8.00

Albums

LAURIE

Number	Title (A Side/B Side)	Yr	VG	VG+	NM
☐ SLP-2049	Montage	1969	5.00	10.00	20.00

MONTANA SLIM Also recorded extensively under his real name, "Wilf Carter." Other records are billed to both names.

45s

DECCA

Number	Title (A Side/B Side)	Yr	VG	VG+	NM
☐ 9-29384	My Mountain High Yodel Song/				
	Shoo Shoo Shoo Sh'La La	1954	6.25	12.50	25.00
☐ 9-29535	The Sunshine Bird/Maple Leaf Rag	1955	5.00	10.00	20.00
☐ 9-29585	A Strawberry Roan/Dynamite Trail	1955	5.00	10.00	20.00
☐ 9-29671	The Alpine Milkman/				
	There's a Tree on Every Road	1955	5.00	10.00	20.00
☐ 9-29942	I'm Ragged But I'm Right/Yodeling Song	1956	5.00	10.00	20.00
☐ 9-30079	My Little Lady/Silver Bell Yodel	1956	5.00	10.00	20.00
☐ 9-30340	Away Out on the Mountain/				
	Padlock on Your Heart	1957	5.00	10.00	20.00
☐ 9-30633	X's from Down in Texas/				
	Let a Little Sunshine in Your Heart	1958	5.00	10.00	20.00
☐ 9-30907	My French Canadian Girl/My Prairie Rose	1959	3.75	7.50	15.00
☐ 9-31034	Blind Boy's Prayer/				
	There's a Bluebird on Your Windowsill	1959	3.75	7.50	15.00

RCA VICTOR

Number	Title (A Side/B Side)	Yr	VG	VG+	NM
☐ 45-5322	The Night Before Christmas/Punkinhead	1951	7.50	15.00	30.00
☐ 47-4252	Wha' Hoppen/Tears Don't Always	1951	6.25	12.50	25.00
☐ 47-4303	The Night Before Christmas/Punkinhead	1951	6.25	12.50	25.00
☐ 47-4446	My Oklahoma Rose/I Wish There Were Three				
	Days in the Year	1952	6.25	12.50	25.00
☐ 47-4523	Goodbye Maria/Driftwood on the River	1952	6.25	12.50	25.00
☐ 47-4846	Alabama Saturday Night/Manhunt	1952	6.25	12.50	25.00
☐ 47-5045	Huggin' Squeezin' Kissin' Teasin'/				
	Sweet Little Love	1952	6.25	12.50	25.00
☐ 47-5276	Sleep, Little One, Sleep/Mockingbird Love	1953	6.25	12.50	25.00
☐ 47-8205	32 Wonderful Years/A Cashbox for a Heartache	1963	3.00	6.00	12.00
☐ 48-0054	Bluebird on Your Windowsill/				
	All I Need Is Some More Lovin'	1949	10.00	20.00	40.00

—Originals on green vinyl

Number	Title (A Side/B Side)	Yr	VG	VG+	NM
☐ 48-0090	Streamlined Yodel Song/				
	My Swiss Moonlight Lullaby	1949	10.00	20.00	40.00

—Originals on green vinyl

Number	Title (A Side/B Side)	Yr	VG	VG+	NM
☐ 48-0139	When the Ice Warms Next Again/				
	Shackles and Chains	1950	10.00	20.00	40.00

—Originals on green vinyl

Number	Title (A Side/B Side)	Yr	VG	VG+	NM
☐ 48-0180	Unfaithful One/Give a Little, Take a Little	1950	10.00	20.00	40.00

—Originals on green vinyl

Number	Title (A Side/B Side)	Yr	VG	VG+	NM
☐ 48-0316	No, No, Don't Ring/				
	A Little Shirt Mama Made for Me	1950	7.50	15.00	30.00

—Originals on green vinyl

Number	Title (A Side/B Side)	Yr	VG	VG+	NM
☐ 48-0352	Take It Easy Blues/				
	Apple, Cherry, Mince, Chocolate	1950	7.50	15.00	30.00

—Originals on green vinyl

Number	Title (A Side/B Side)	Yr	VG	VG+	NM
☐ 48-0392	Jolly Old St. Nicholas/				
	Rudolph the Red-Nosed Reindeer	1950	10.00	20.00	40.00

—Originals on green vinyl

Number	Title (A Side/B Side)	Yr	VG	VG+	NM
☐ 48-0397	The K.P. Blues/When That Love Bug Bites You	1950	7.50	15.00	30.00

—Originals on green vinyl

Number	Title (A Side/B Side)	Yr	VG	VG+	NM
☐ 48-0419	My Heart's Closed for Repairs/				
	Just a Woman's Smile	1951	7.50	15.00	30.00
☐ 48-0457	Let's Go Back to the Bible/She'll Be There	1951	7.50	15.00	30.00
☐ 48-0477	My Wife Is On a Diet/Sick, Sober and Sorry	1951	7.50	15.00	30.00

STARDAY

Number	Title (A Side/B Side)	Yr	VG	VG+	NM
☐ 686	Grandad's Yodeling Song/				
	The Little Shirt My Mother Made for Me	1964	3.00	6.00	12.00

Albums

DECCA

Number	Title (A Side/B Side)	Yr	VG	VG+	NM
☐ DL 4092 [M]	The Dynamite Trail	1960	12.50	25.00	50.00
☐ DL 8917 [M]	I'm Ragged But I'm Right	1959	15.00	30.00	60.00
☐ DL 74092 [S]	The Dynamite Trail	1960	15.00	30.00	60.00

RCA CAMDEN

Number	Title (A Side/B Side)	Yr	VG	VG+	NM
☐ CAL-527 [M]	Wilf Carter/Montana Slim	1958	10.00	20.00	40.00
☐ CAL-668 [M]	Reminiscin' with Montana Slim	1962	6.25	12.50	25.00
☐ CAL-846 [M]	32 Wonderful Years	1965	5.00	10.00	20.00
☐ CAS-846 [R]	32 Wonderful Years	1965	3.00	6.00	12.00

STARDAY

Number	Title (A Side/B Side)	Yr	VG	VG+	NM
☐ SLP-300 [M]	Wilf Carter As Montana Slim	1964	7.50	15.00	30.00
☐ SLP-389 [M]	Wilf Carter	1966	7.50	15.00	30.00

MONTCLAIRS, THE (1)

45s

PAULA

Number	Title (A Side/B Side)	Yr	VG	VG+	NM
☐ 345	Is This for Real/All I Really Care About Is You	1971	—	2.50	5.00
☐ 363	Dreaming Out of Season/I Just Can't Get Away	1972	—	2.50	5.00
☐ 375	Beggin' Is Hard to Do/Unwanted Love	1973	—	2.50	5.00
☐ 381	Make Up for Lost Time/How Can One Man Live	1973	—	2.50	5.00
☐ 382	I Need You More Than Ever/				
	Prelude to a Heartbreak	1973	—	2.50	5.00
☐ 390	I'm Calling You/Hung Up on Your Love	1973	—	2.50	5.00
☐ 409	Baby, You Know I'm Gonna Miss You (Part 1)/				
	Baby, You Know I'm Gonna Miss You (Part 2)	1974	—	2.50	5.00

MONTCLAIRS, THE (2)

45s

ABC-PARAMOUNT

Number	Title (A Side/B Side)	Yr	VG	VG+	NM
☐ 10463	I Believe (In Your Love)/No Baby	1963	3.75	7.50	15.00

MONTCLAIRS, THE (3)

45s

AUDICON

Number	Title (A Side/B Side)	Yr	VG	VG+	NM
☐ 111	Goodnight, Well, It's Time to Go/				
	A Broken Promise	1961	7.50	15.00	30.00

MONTCLAIRS, THE (4)

45s

HI-Q

Number	Title (A Side/B Side)	Yr	VG	VG+	NM
☐ 5001	Golden Angel/Don Juan	1957	75.00	150.00	300.00

PREMIUM

Number	Title (A Side/B Side)	Yr	VG	VG+	NM
☐ 404	Give Me a Chance/My Every Dream	1956	100.00	200.00	400.00

SONIC

Number	Title (A Side/B Side)	Yr	VG	VG+	NM
☐ 104	All I Want Is Love/I've Heard About You	1956	200.00	400.00	800.00

MONTCLAIRS, THE (U) Some of these could be group (2) or (3).

45s

SUNBURST

Number	Title (A Side/B Side)	Yr	VG	VG+	NM
☐ 106	Wait for Me/Happy Feet Time	1965	3.00	6.00	12.00
☐ 115	Poopsie/Sore Feet	1965	3.00	6.00	12.00

UNITED INT'L.

Number	Title (A Side/B Side)	Yr	VG	VG+	NM
☐ 1007	Lisa/Tap Tap Daisy	1963	6.25	12.50	25.00
☐ 1013	Young Wings Can Fly/Come On and Hold Me	1964	5.00	10.00	20.00

WICKWIRE

Number	Title (A Side/B Side)	Yr	VG	VG+	NM
☐ 13009	It's Gonna Work Out Fine/If You Need Me	196?	3.00	6.00	12.00

MONTE, LOU

45s

AFE

Number	Title (A Side/B Side)	Yr	VG	VG+	NM
☐ 102	Darktown Strutters Ball/The Sheik of Araby	1981	—	2.00	4.00

GWP

Number	Title (A Side/B Side)	Yr	VG	VG+	NM
☐ 530	I Really Don't Want to Know/				
	I Have an Angel in Heaven	1972	—	2.50	5.00

LAURIE

Number	Title (A Side/B Side)	Yr	VG	VG+	NM
☐ 3643	Paul Revere's Ride/Jerusalem, Jerusalem	1976	—	2.00	4.00
☐ 3652	Crabs Walk Sideways/Nicolena	1977	—	2.00	4.00

RCA VICTOR

Number	Title (A Side/B Side)	Yr	VG	VG+	NM
☐ 47-5382	Jealous of You/Angelina	1953	3.00	6.00	12.00
☐ 47-5496	Baby Cried/One Moment More	1953	3.00	6.00	12.00
☐ 47-5611	Darktown Strutters Ball/I Know How You Feel	1954	3.75	7.50	15.00
☐ 47-5691	Somewhere There Is Someone/Won't You				
	Forgive Me	1954	3.00	6.00	12.00
☐ 47-5778	Veras Veranda/Chain Reaction	1954	3.00	6.00	12.00
☐ 47-5832	Italian Hucklebuck/Just Like Before	1954	3.00	6.00	12.00
☐ 47-5883	When I Hold You in My Arms/In My Dreams	1954	3.00	6.00	12.00
☐ 47-5963	Cat's Whiskers/Roulette	1954	3.00	6.00	12.00
☐ 47-5993	How Important Can It Be/Truly Yours	1955	2.50	5.00	10.00
☐ 47-6072	The Italian Wallflower/Dreamboat	1955	2.50	5.00	10.00
☐ 47-6133	Bella Notte/With You Beside Me	1955	2.50	5.00	10.00
☐ 47-6246	King of the River/Yaller Yaller Gold	1955	2.50	5.00	10.00
☐ 47-6287	Tombolee-Tombola/Rosina	1955	2.50	5.00	10.00
☐ 47-6350	Santo Natale/Italian Jingle Bells	1955	3.00	6.00	12.00
☐ 47-6403	Nina, the Queen of the Teeners/Pony Tail	1956	2.50	5.00	10.00
☐ 47-6522	If I Knew You Were Comin' I'd've Baked a Cake/				
	Ask Your Heart	1956	2.50	5.00	10.00
☐ 47-6704	Elvis Presley for President/If I Were a Millionaire	1956	7.50	15.00	30.00
☐ 47-6769	Roman Guitar/Some Cloud Above	1956	2.50	5.00	10.00

Number	Title (A Side/B Side)	Yr	VG	VG+	NM
47-6848	Calypso Italiano/Someone Else Is Taking You Home	1957	2.50	5.00	10.00
47-6951	The Wife/Musica Bella	1957	2.50	5.00	10.00
47-7061	Ha! Ha! Ha!/Round and Round in My Heart	1957	2.50	5.00	10.00
47-7160	Lazy Mary/Angelique	1958	2.50	5.00	10.00
47-7265	Eh, Marie, Eh, Marie/The Shiek of Araby	1958	2.00	4.00	8.00
47-7346	Marianne/Strada 'Nfosa	1958	2.00	4.00	8.00
47-7423	Where Do You Work, Marie/Skinny Lena	1958	2.00	4.00	8.00
47-7467	The Italian Cowboy Song/Pizza Boy U.S.A.	1959	2.00	4.00	8.00
47-7523	The Angel in the Fountain/Sole Per Te (Only for You)	1959	2.00	4.00	8.00
47-7554	Pistol Packin' Mama/Have Another	1959	2.00	4.00	8.00
47-7641	Santa Nicola/All Because It's Christmas	1959	3.00	6.00	12.00
47-7689	Remember This Cumba/Guardo Che Luna	1960	2.00	4.00	8.00
47-8716	Mama Get the Hammer (There's a Fly on Papa's Head)/Six O'Clock Supper	1965	—	3.00	6.00
47-8754	Paul Revere's Horse (Ba-Cha-Ca-Loop)/Oh Lonesome Me	1965	—	3.00	6.00
47-8831	Cheech the Cat/Makin' Whoopee	1966	—	3.00	6.00
47-9021	Oh How I Miss You Tonight/Seventeen	1966	—	3.00	6.00
47-9216	When You Get What You Want/There'll Be Some Changes Made	1967	—	3.00	6.00
47-9328	Digga Digga Baby/A Girl, A Girl	1967	—	3.00	6.00
47-9405	I Don't Play with Matches Anymore/All for the Kids	1967	—	3.00	6.00
REGALIA					
6600	Goombar Custer's Last Stand/Tattooed Susie	1969	—	3.00	6.00
REPRISE					
0241	Down Little Doggie/La Luna Si Vuola Sposane	1963	—	3.00	6.00
0267	A Baby Cried/The Rooster and the Hen	1964	—	3.00	6.00
0284	Hello Dolly/Jungle Louie	1964	—	3.00	6.00
0302	You're So Bella, Isabella/Too Fat Polka	1964	—	3.00	6.00
0326	I Want to Hold Your Hand/My Parson's Across the Way	1964	2.00	4.00	8.00
0352	The Mixed-Up Bull from Palermo/I Know How You Feel	1965	—	3.00	6.00
0384	Don't Wish Your Heartbreak on Me/No, No, Don't Cry, My Love	1965	—	3.00	6.00
0724	Pepino the Italian Mouse/What Did Washington Say (When He Crossed the Delaware)	1968	—	2.00	4.00
—"Back to Back Hits" series					
20015	A Good Man Is Hard to Find/Sixteen Tons	1961	2.50	5.00	10.00
20037	Oh Mein Papa (Oh Mio Papa)/Tici Ti Tici To Tici Ti	1961	2.50	5.00	10.00
20044	Twist Italiano/Oh Tessie	1962	2.50	5.00	10.00
20085	Please Mr. Columbus (Turn the Ship Around)/Addio, Addio (Good-Bye)	1962	2.50	5.00	10.00
20106	Pepino the Italian Mouse/What Did Washington Say (When He Crossed the Delaware)	1962	2.00	4.00	8.00
20106 [PS]	Pepino the Italian Mouse/What Did Washington Say (When He Crossed the Delaware)	1962	3.00	6.00	12.00
20146	Pepino's Friend Pasqual (The Italian Pussy-Cat)/I Like You, You Like Me, Eh, Paisan?	1963	2.00	4.00	8.00
20146 [PS]	Pepino's Friend Pasqual (The Italian Pussy-Cat)/I Like You, You Like Me, Eh, Paisan?	1963	3.00	6.00	12.00
20171	Limbo Italiano/Bossa Nova Italiano	1963	2.00	4.00	8.00
20193	You're So Smart, You're So Smart Eh Papa/Paulucci	1963	2.00	4.00	8.00
20219	Hootenanny Italian Style/Who Stole My Provolone	1963	2.00	4.00	8.00
ROULETTE					
4253	The Darktown Strutter's Ball/Half a Love	1960	2.00	4.00	8.00
4266	Bim Bam Bu/Oh, Oh, Rosie	1960	2.00	4.00	8.00
4294	The Huckle-Buck/Always You	1960	2.00	4.00	8.00
4308	Christmas at Our House/Dominick the Donkey	1960	3.00	6.00	12.00
4366	The Sheriff of Sicily/Katareena	1961	2.00	4.00	8.00
Albums					
RCA CAMDEN					
CAL-455 [M]	Here's Lou Monte	195?	3.00	6.00	12.00
RCA VICTOR					
LPM-1651 [M]	Lou Monte Sings for You	1957	6.25	12.50	25.00
LPM-1877 [M]	Songs for Pizza Lovers	1958	6.25	12.50	25.00
LPM-1976 [M]	Italian House Party	1959	5.00	10.00	20.00
LSP-1976 [S]	Italian House Party	1959	6.25	12.50	25.00
LPM-3672 [M]	The Best of Lou Monte	1966	3.75	7.50	15.00
LSP-3672 [S]	The Best of Lou Monte	1966	3.00	6.00	12.00
LPM-3705 [M]	Good Time Songs	1967	3.75	7.50	15.00
LSP-3705 [S]	Good Time Songs	1967	3.00	6.00	12.00
REPRISE					
R-6005 [M]	Great Italian-American Hits	1961	5.00	10.00	20.00
R9-6005 [S]	Great Italian-American Hits	1961	6.25	12.50	25.00
R-6014 [M]	Live in Person	1961	5.00	10.00	20.00
R9-6014 [S]	Live in Person	1961	6.25	12.50	25.00
R-6058 [M]	Pepino The Italian Mouse & Other Italian Fun Songs	1962	5.00	10.00	20.00
R9-6058 [S]	Pepino The Italian Mouse & Other Italian Fun Songs	1962	6.25	12.50	25.00
R-6099 [M]	More Italian Fun Songs	1963	5.00	10.00	20.00
R9-6099 [S]	More Italian Fun Songs	1963	6.25	12.50	25.00
R-6118 [M]	The Golden Hits of Lou Monte	1964	3.75	7.50	15.00
RS-6118 [S]	The Golden Hits of Lou Monte	1964	5.00	10.00	20.00
ROULETTE					
R-25126 [M]	Italiano U.S.A.	1960	5.00	10.00	20.00
SR-25126 [S]	Italiano U.S.A.	1960	6.25	12.50	25.00
R-25257 [M]	The Magic World of Italy	1963	3.75	7.50	15.00
SR-25257 [S]	The Magic World of Italy	1963	5.00	10.00	20.00

MONTENEGRO, HUGO
45s

Number	Title (A Side/B Side)	Yr	VG	VG+	NM
GWP					
520	Lay Lady Lay/Blowin' in the Wind	1970	—	2.50	5.00
RCA VICTOR					
47-8369	Theme from The Long Ships/Good Neighbor Sam	1964	—	3.00	6.00
47-8522	Candy's Theme/Polly	1965	—	3.00	6.00
47-8707	Theme from "Bunny Lake Is Missing"/Space Safari	1965	—	3.00	6.00
47-8747	Our Man Flint/Judith	1965	—	3.00	6.00
47-8847	Theme from "The Man from U.N.C.L.E."/Solo Busanova	1966	2.50	5.00	10.00
47-9050	Theme from The Professionals/Jeannie	1966	—	3.00	6.00
47-9074	Hurry Sundown/Charlie's Trip	1967	—	3.00	6.00
47-9224	For a Few Dollars More/The Gentle Rain	1967	—	3.00	6.00
47-9423	The Good, the Bad and The Ugly/March with Hope	1967	2.00	4.00	8.00
47-9554	Hang 'Em High/Tomorrow;'s Love	1968	—	3.00	6.00
47-9638	Theme from "The Fox"/There's Got to Be a Better Way	1968	—	3.00	6.00
47-9712	Tony's Theme/Good Vibrations	1969	—	3.00	6.00
74-0160	Lady in Cement/Happy Together	1969	—	2.50	5.00
74-0302	Viva Max March/Don't Turn Back	1969	—	2.50	5.00
—With Al Hirt					
74-0515	Come Again/Lordy	1971	—	2.50	5.00
74-0607	Peace Train/Mammy Blue	1971	—	2.50	5.00
74-0690	Love Theme from "The Godfather"/Movin' On	1972	—	2.50	5.00
74-0875	Lost Horizon/Learn to Say Goodbye	1973	—	2.50	5.00
74-0954	Tara's Theme/Porcupine Pie	1973	—	2.50	5.00
PB-10059	Living for the City/You Are the Sunshine of My Life	1974	—	2.00	4.00
PB-10153	Love Said Goodbye/Shoo-Be-Doo-Be-Doo-Da-Day	1975	—	2.00	4.00
TIME					
1035	I Ain't Down Yet/If I Knew	1961	2.00	4.00	8.00
1040	The Young Savages/Majorca	1961	2.00	4.00	8.00
1043	Little Dutch Boy/Verdeales	1961	2.00	4.00	8.00
1048	Tarantella Twist/Nenella Bella	1962	2.00	4.00	8.00
1052	Palm Canyon Drive/Dark Eyes	1962	2.00	4.00	8.00
1058	Sherry/Get Off the Moon	1962	2.00	4.00	8.00
1062	Swanee River Boogie/Hot Crawfish	1963	2.00	4.00	8.00
1064	How the West Was Won/To Kill a Mockingbird	1963	2.50	5.00	10.00
—B-side by Dom Sebeskey					
1065	Have I Told You Lately/Mom and Dad's Waltz	1963	2.00	4.00	8.00
1079	Be My Love/I Concentrate on You	1964	2.00	4.00	8.00
20TH FOX					
133	April Showers/La Primavera	1959	2.50	5.00	10.00
161	St. Louis Blues/Vaya Con Dios	1959	2.50	5.00	10.00
Albums					
BAINBRIDGE					
1002	American Musical Theatre, Volume 1 (1924-1935)	198?	2.00	4.00	8.00
1003	American Musical Theatre, Volume 2 (1935-1945)	198?	2.00	4.00	8.00
1004	American Musical Theatre, Volume 3 (1946-1952)	198?	2.00	4.00	8.00
1005	American Musical Theatre, Volume 4 (1953-1960)	198?	2.00	4.00	8.00
1009	Big Band Boogie	198?	2.00	4.00	8.00
1021	Camelot	198?	2.00	4.00	8.00
1028	Hugo Montenegro Plays the Movies	198?	2.00	4.00	8.00
GWP					
2003	The Dawn of Dylan	1971	3.75	7.50	15.00
MAINSTREAM					
S-6101 [S]	Camelot	1967	3.00	6.00	12.00
56101 [M]	Camelot	1967	3.75	7.50	15.00
RCA CAMDEN					
CAL-729 [M]	In a Sentimental Mood	196?	3.00	6.00	12.00
CAS-729 [S]	In a Sentimental Mood	196?	3.00	6.00	12.00
CAS-2309	Hawaiian Wedding Song	1969	2.50	5.00	10.00
RCA VICTOR					
ARD1-0001 [Q]	Love Theme from "The Godfather"	1972	3.00	6.00	12.00
APD1-0025 [Q]	Scenes and Themes	1973	5.00	10.00	20.00
ARD1-0132 [Q]	Neil's Diamonds	1973	3.75	7.50	15.00
APL1-0413	Hugo in Wonderland	1974	3.00	6.00	12.00
ARD1-0413 [Q]	Hugo in Wonderland	1974	3.75	7.50	15.00
ARD1-0784 [Q]	Others by Brothers	1974	3.75	7.50	15.00
APD1-1024 [Q]	Rocket Man	1975	5.00	10.00	20.00
APL1-1024	Rocket Man	1975	3.00	6.00	12.00
ANL1-1094	Music from A Fistful of Dollars & For a Few Dollars More & The Good, The Bad and The Ugly	1975	2.50	5.00	10.00
ANL1-2348	The Neil Diamond Songbook	1977	2.50	5.00	10.00
LPM-3540 [M]	Come Spy with Me	1966	3.00	6.00	12.00
LSP-3540 [S]	Come Spy with Me	1966	3.75	7.50	15.00
LPM-3927 [M]	Music from A Fistful of Dollars & For a Few Dollars More & The Good, The Bad and The Ugly	1968	5.00	10.00	20.00
LSP-3927 [S]	Music from A Fistful of Dollars & For a Few Dollars More & The Good, The Bad and The Ugly	1968	3.75	7.50	15.00
LPM-4022 [M]	Hang 'Em High	1968	10.00	20.00	40.00
LSP-4022 [S]	Hang 'Em High	1968	3.75	7.50	15.00
LSP-4104	Good Vibrations	1969	3.75	7.50	15.00
LSP-4170	Moog Power	1969	5.00	10.00	20.00
LSP-4273	Colours of Love	1970	3.00	6.00	12.00
AFL1-4361	The Best of Hugo Montenegro	1977	2.50	5.00	10.00
LSP-4361	The Best of Hugo Montenegro	1970	3.00	6.00	12.00
LSP-4537	People…One to One	1971	3.00	6.00	12.00
LSP-4631	Mammy Blue	1971	3.00	6.00	12.00
VPS-6036 [(2)]	This Is Hugo Montenegro	1971	3.75	7.50	15.00
TIME					
S-2018 [S]	Cha Chas for Dancing	196?	5.00	10.00	20.00
S-2020 [S]	Boogie Woogie and Bongos	196?	5.00	10.00	20.00
S-2030 [S]	Arriba	196?	5.00	10.00	20.00
S-2035 [S]	American Musical Theatre, Volume 1 (1924-1935)	196?	3.75	7.50	15.00
S-2036 [S]	American Musical Theatre, Volume 2 (1935-1945)	196?	3.75	7.50	15.00
S-2037 [S]	American Musical Theatre, Volume 3 (1946-1952)	1961	3.75	7.50	15.00
S-2038 [S]	American Musical Theatre, Volume 4 (1953-1960)	1961	3.75	7.50	15.00
S-2044 [S]	Great Songs from Motion Pictures Vol. 1 (1927-1937)	1961	3.75	7.50	15.00

Number	Title (A Side/B Side)	Yr	VG	VG+	NM
❑ S-2045 [S]	Great Songs from Motion Pictures Vol. 2 (1938-1944)	1961	3.75	7.50	15.00
❑ S-2046 [S]	Great Songs from Motion Pictures Vol. 3 (1945-1960)	1961	3.75	7.50	15.00
❑ S-2051 [S]	Montenegro in Italy	196?	3.75	7.50	15.00
❑ 52018 [M]	Cha Chas for Dancing	196?	3.75	7.50	15.00
❑ 52020 [M]	Boogie Woogie and Bongos	196?	3.75	7.50	15.00
❑ 52030 [M]	Arriba	196?	3.75	7.50	15.00
❑ 52035 [M]	American Musical Theatre, Volume 1 (1924-1935)	196?	3.00	6.00	12.00
❑ 52036 [M]	American Musical Theatre, Volume 2 (1935-1945)	196?	3.00	6.00	12.00
❑ 52037 [M]	American Musical Theatre, Volume 3 (1946-1952)	1961	3.00	6.00	12.00
❑ 52038 [M]	American Musical Theatre, Volume 4 (1953-1960)	1961	3.00	6.00	12.00
❑ 52044 [M]	Great Songs from Motion Pictures Vol. 1 (1927-1937)	1961	3.00	6.00	12.00
❑ 52045 [M]	Great Songs from Motion Pictures Vol. 2 (1938-1944)	1961	3.00	6.00	12.00
❑ 52046 [M]	Great Songs from Motion Pictures Vol. 3 (1945-1960)	1961	3.00	6.00	12.00
❑ 52051 [M]	Montenegro in Italy	196?	3.00	6.00	12.00

20TH CENTURY FOX

Number	Title (A Side/B Side)	Yr	VG	VG+	NM
❑ S-4204	Lady in Cement	1968	5.00	10.00	20.00

20TH FOX

❑ 3018 [M]	The 20th Century Strings, Volume 1	1959	5.00	10.00	20.00

VIK

❑ LX-1089 [M]	Loves of My Life	1957	6.25	12.50	25.00
❑ LX-1106 [M]	Ellington Fantasy	1957	6.25	12.50	25.00

MONTEREYS, THE More than one group.
45s
ARWIN

❑ 130	Goodbye My Love/It Hurts Me So	1961	10.00	20.00	40.00

BLAST

❑ 219	Face in the Crowd/Step Right Up	1965	100.00	200.00	400.00

DOMINION

❑ 1019	First Kiss/Just One More Kiss	1964	10.00	20.00	40.00

EASTWEST

❑ 121	I'll Love You Again/The American Teens	1958	6.25	12.50	25.00

GNP CRESCENDO

❑ 314	For Sentimental Reasons/I Still Love You	1964	6.25	12.50	25.00

IMPALA

❑ 213	Without a Girl/So Deep	1959	30.00	60.00	120.00

MAJOR

❑ 1009	A Crowded Room/You Said That You Loved Me	1959	17.50	35.00	70.00

PRINCE

❑ 5060	Rita/Billy Bud	1960	3.75	7.50	15.00

ROSE

❑ 109	You're the Girl for Me/Ape Shape	1958	25.00	50.00	100.00

SATURN

❑ 1002	My Girl/With You	1956	10.00	20.00	40.00

TRANS AMERICAN

❑ 1000/1	Darlin' Send Me a Letter/Late Darlin'	1960	150.00	300.00	600.00

MONTEZ, CHRIS
45s
A&M

❑ 780	Call Me/Go Head On	1965	2.00	4.00	8.00
❑ 796	The More I See You/You, I Love You	1966	2.50	5.00	10.00
❑ 810	There Will Never Be Another You/You Can Hurt the One You Love	1966	2.00	4.00	8.00
❑ 822	Keep Talkin'/Time After Time	1966	2.00	4.00	8.00
❑ 839	Because of You/Elena	1967	2.00	4.00	8.00
❑ 852	Just Friends/Twiggy	1967	—	3.00	6.00
❑ 855	Foolin' Around/Dindi (Jin-Jee)	1967	—	3.00	6.00
❑ 906	Once in a While/The Face I Love	1968	—	3.00	6.00
❑ 958	Love Is Here to Stay/Nothing to Hide	1968	—	3.00	6.00
❑ 985	Where Are You Now/Watch What Happens	1968	—	3.00	6.00

JAMIE

❑ 1410	Let's Dance/Somebody Loves You	1973	—	2.50	5.00

MONOGRAM

❑ 500	All You Had to Do (Was Tell Me)/Love Me	1962	3.00	6.00	12.00
❑ 505	Let's Dance/You're the One	1962	5.00	10.00	20.00
❑ 507	Some Kinda Fun/Tell Me	1962	3.00	6.00	12.00
❑ 508	Rockin' Blues/(Let's Do the) Limbo	1963	3.75	7.50	15.00
❑ 513	In An English Towne/My Baby Loves to Dance	1963	3.00	6.00	12.00
❑ 516	No, No, No/Monkey Fever	1963	3.00	6.00	12.00
❑ 517	You're the One/All You Had to Do Was Tell Me	1964	3.00	6.00	12.00
—With Kathy Young					
❑ 520	It Takes Two/To Shoot the Curl	1964	3.00	6.00	12.00
—With Kathy Young					
❑ 522	(It's Not) Puppy Love/He's Been Leading You On	1964	3.00	6.00	12.00

PARAMOUNT

❑ 0109	We Can Make the World a Whole Lot Brighter/The End of the Line	1971	—	2.50	5.00

Albums
A&M

❑ LP-115 [M]	The More I See You/Call Me	1966	5.00	10.00	20.00
❑ LP-120 [M]	Time After Time	1966	3.75	7.50	15.00
❑ LP-128 [M]	Foolin' Around	1967	3.75	7.50	15.00
❑ LP-157 [M]	Watch What Happens	1967	3.75	7.50	15.00
❑ ST-4115 [S]	The More I See You/Call Me	1966	6.25	12.50	25.00
❑ SP-4120 [S]	Time After Time	1966	5.00	10.00	20.00
❑ SP-4128 [S]	Foolin' Around	1967	5.00	10.00	20.00
❑ SP-4157 [S]	Watch What Happens	1967	5.00	10.00	20.00

MONOGRAM

❑ M-100 [M]	Let's Dance and Have Some Kinda' Fun!!!	1963	100.00	200.00	400.00

MONTGOMERY, BOB
45s
BRUNSWICK

❑ 55157	Because I Love You/Taste of the Blues	1959	10.00	20.00	40.00

MONTGOMERY, CHRISTOPHER
45s
DOLTON

Number	Title (A Side/B Side)	Yr	VG	VG+	NM
❑ 84	My Paradise/Giants of Bombora	1963	7.50	15.00	30.00

MONTGOMERY, JACK
45s
SCEPTER

❑ 12152	Do You Believe It/My Dearly Beloved	1966	12.50	25.00	50.00

MONTGOMERY, MELBA
45s
CAPITOL

❑ 2513	As Far As My Forgetting's Got/You Let Me Win	1969	2.00	4.00	8.00
❑ 2758	The Closer She Gets/Where Do We Go from Here	1970	2.00	4.00	8.00
❑ 2825	Together Again/Eloy Crossing	1970	2.00	4.00	8.00
❑ 3091	He's My Man/We Don't Live Here Anymore	1971	2.00	4.00	8.00
❑ 3297	Hope I Never Love That Way Again/Say You'll Never Leave Me	1972	2.00	4.00	8.00
❑ 4290	He Called Me Baby/Country Child	1976	—	2.00	4.00

COMPASS

❑ 45-7	Straight Talkin'/(B-side unknown)	1986	—	3.00	6.00

ELEKTRA

❑ 45211	If You Want the Rainbow/Love, I Need You	1974	—	2.50	5.00
❑ 45229	Don't Let the Good Times Fool You/It Sure Gets Lonely	1975	—	2.50	5.00
❑ 45247	Searchin' (For Someone Like You)/Hiding in the Darkness of My Mind	1975	—	2.50	5.00
❑ 45272	If I Ever Needed Someone/He Loved You Right Out of My Mind	1975	—	2.50	5.00
❑ 45296	Love Was the Wind/I Never Dreamed That Love Could Be This Good	1975	—	2.50	5.00
❑ 45866	Wrap Your Love Around Me/Let Me Show You How I Can	1973	—	3.00	6.00
❑ 45875	He'll Come Home/Country Written Up and Down Your Face	1973	—	3.00	6.00
❑ 45883	No Charge/I Love Him Because He's That Way	1974	—	3.00	6.00
❑ 45883	No Charge/Wrap Your Love Around Me	1974	—	3.00	6.00
❑ 45894	Your Pretty Roses Came Too Late/My Feel Good Sure Feels Fine	1974	—	3.00	6.00

KARI

❑ 111	The Star/Carolina in My Mind	1980	—	3.00	6.00

MUSICOR

❑ 1157	Don't Keep Me Lonely Too Long/I'm Looking for the Man	1966	2.50	5.00	10.00
❑ 1175	Crossing Over Jordan/The Dead Shall Live Again	1966	2.50	5.00	10.00
❑ 1182	He's Out There With Her Somewhere/My Tiny Music Box	1966	2.50	5.00	10.00
❑ 1209	He Stayed Away (Long As He Could)/Won't Take Long	1966	2.50	5.00	10.00
❑ 1241	What Can I Tell the Folks Back Home/The Right Time to Lose My Mind	1967	2.50	5.00	10.00
❑ 1278	The Day Your Memory Came to Town/Twilight Years	1967	2.50	5.00	10.00
❑ 1291	He Wrote Forgive Me/You Put Me Here	1968	2.50	5.00	10.00
❑ 1311	Our Little Man/Tell Me Your Troubles	1968	2.50	5.00	10.00
❑ 1324	Hallelujah Road/Life Beyond Death	1968	2.50	5.00	10.00
❑ 1344	What's to Become of What's Left of Me/Every Day's a Happy Day for Fools	1969	2.50	5.00	10.00

UNITED ARTISTS

❑ 576	Hall of Shame/What's Bad for You Is Good for Me	1963	3.00	6.00	12.00
❑ 652	The Greatest One of All/Lies Can't Hide What's On My Mind	1963	3.00	6.00	12.00
❑ 705	The Face/I Will Always Love Loving You	1964	3.00	6.00	12.00
❑ 768	Big City Heartaches/Why Does the Lady Cry	1964	3.00	6.00	12.00
❑ 803	I Can't Change Overnight/I Can't Get Used to Being Lonely	1965	3.00	6.00	12.00
❑ 850	White Lightning/I Saw It	1965	3.00	6.00	12.00
❑ 900	Yearning/I'll Wait Till Seven	1965	3.00	6.00	12.00
❑ 964	Big Joke/Constantly	1965	3.00	6.00	12.00
❑ XW1008	Never Ending Love Affair/You	1977	—	2.50	5.00
❑ XW1115	Angel of the Morning/Pinkerton's Flowers	1977	—	2.50	5.00
❑ XW1175	Leavin' Me in Your Mind/We've Been Lyin' Here Too Long	1978	—	2.50	5.00

Albums
CAPITOL

❑ ST-328	The Big, Wonderful Country World of Melba Montgomery	1969	3.75	7.50	15.00

—This is the title on the cover; the label calls this "The Big, Beautiful Country World of Melba Montgomery"

❑ ST-468	Don't Keep Me Lonely Too Long	1970	3.75	7.50	15.00

ELEKTRA

❑ CM-2	Don't Let the Good Times Fool You	1975	2.50	5.00	10.00
❑ CM-6	The Greatest Gift of All	1975	2.50	5.00	10.00
❑ EKS-75069	Melba Montgomery	1973	3.00	6.00	12.00
❑ EKS-75079	No Charge	1974	2.50	5.00	10.00

HILLTOP

❑ JS-6031	Miss Country Music	196?	3.00	6.00	12.00

MUSICOR

❑ MM-2074 [M]	Country Girl	1966	3.75	7.50	15.00
❑ MM-2097 [M]	The Hallelujah Road	1966	3.75	7.50	15.00
❑ MM-2113 [M]	Melba Toast	1967	5.00	10.00	20.00
❑ MM-2114 [M]	Don't Keep Me Lonely Too Long	1967	5.00	10.00	20.00
❑ MS-3074 [S]	Country Girl	1966	5.00	10.00	20.00
❑ MS-3097 [S]	The Hallelujah Road	1966	5.00	10.00	20.00
❑ MS-3113 [S]	Melba Toast	1967	5.00	10.00	20.00
❑ MS-3114 [S]	Don't Keep Me Lonely Too Long	1967	5.00	10.00	20.00

STARDAY

❑ SLP-352 [M]	Queen of Country Music	1965	6.25	12.50	25.00

UNITED ARTISTS

❑ UAL-3341 [M]	America's Number One Country and Western Girl Singer	1964	5.00	10.00	20.00
❑ UAL-3369 [M]	Down Home	1964	5.00	10.00	20.00

M

Number	Title (A Side/B Side)	Yr	VG	VG+	NM
❑ UAL-3391 [M]	I Can't Get Used to Being Lonely	1965	5.00	10.00	20.00
❑ UAS-6341 [S]	America's Number One Country and Western Girl Singer	1964	6.25	12.50	25.00
❑ UAS-6369 [S]	Down Home	1964	6.25	12.50	25.00
❑ UAS-6391 [S]	I Can't Get Used to Being Lonely	1965	6.25	12.50	25.00

MONTGOMERY, TAMMY Later known as TAMMI TERRELL.
45s
CHECKER

Number	Title (A Side/B Side)	Yr	VG	VG+	NM
❑ 1072	If I Would Marry You/This Time Tomorrow	1964	6.25	12.50	25.00
—Mostly blue label with red and black checkers					
❑ 1072	If I Would Marry You/This Time Tomorrow	1964	10.00	20.00	40.00
—Maroon label					
SCEPTER					
❑ 1224	If You See Bill/It's Mine	1961	15.00	30.00	60.00
TRY ME					
❑ 28001	I Cried/If You Don't Think	1962	7.50	15.00	30.00
—As "Tana Montgomery"					
WAND					
❑ 123	Voice of Experience/I Wancha' to Be Sure	1962	7.50	15.00	30.00

MONTGOMERYS, THE
45s
AMY

Number	Title (A Side/B Side)	Yr	VG	VG+	NM
❑ 883	Promise of Love/Gotta Make a Hit Record	1963	62.50	125.00	250.00

MONTROSE
45s
WARNER BROS.

Number	Title (A Side/B Side)	Yr	VG	VG+	NM
❑ 7776	Rock the Nation/One Thing on My Mind	1974	—	2.50	5.00
❑ 7814	Make It Last/Space Station No. 5	1974	—	2.50	5.00
❑ 8063	The Dreamer/Paper Money	1975	—	2.50	5.00
❑ 8080	Connection/We're Going Home	1975	—	2.50	5.00
❑ 8172	Clown Woman/Matriarch	1976	—	2.50	5.00
❑ 8281	Music Man/Tuft-Sedge	1976	—	2.50	5.00
❑ 8351	Let's Go/(B-side unknown)	1977	—	2.50	5.00
Albums					
ENIGMA					
❑ ST-73264	Mean	1987	2.50	5.00	10.00
❑ D1-73323	Speed of Sound	1988	2.50	5.00	10.00
WARNER BROS.					
❑ BS 2740	Montrose	1974	3.00	6.00	12.00
❑ BS 2823	Paper Money	1974	3.00	6.00	12.00
❑ BS 2892	Warner Bros. Presents Montrose!	1975	3.00	6.00	12.00
❑ BS 2963	Jump On It	1976	3.00	6.00	12.00
❑ BSK 3106	Montrose	1978	2.00	4.00	8.00
—Reissue of 2740					

MONTY PYTHON
45s
ARISTA

Number	Title (A Side/B Side)	Yr	VG	VG+	NM
❑ 0130	The Single/(B-side unknown)	1975	2.00	4.00	8.00
❑ 0578	They Won't Play This Song on the Radio/Sit on My Face-Farewell to John Denver	1980	2.00	4.00	8.00
WARNER BROS.					
❑ 49112	Always Look on the Bright Side of Life/Brian	1979	2.50	5.00	10.00
Albums					
ARISTA					
❑ SP-101 [DJ]	Monty Python's Contractural Obligation Sampler	1980	7.50	15.00	30.00
—One side is censored, the other is uncensored					
❑ AL 4039	Matching Tie & Handkerchief	1975	5.00	10.00	20.00
—Side 2 is "trick tracked," with two different routines depending on where you place the needle at the start					
❑ AL 4050	The Album of the Soundtrack of the Trailer of the Film of "Monty Python and the Holy Grail"	1975	5.00	10.00	20.00
❑ AL 4073	Monty Python Live! At City Center	1976	5.00	10.00	20.00
❑ AL 8296	The Monty Python Instant Record Collection	198?	2.00	4.00	8.00
—Reissue					
❑ AL 8343	Monty Python's Contractual Obligation Album	198?	2.00	4.00	8.00
—Reissue					
❑ AL 8353	Monty Python Live! At City Center	198?	2.00	4.00	8.00
—Reissue					
❑ AL 8355	The Album of the Soundtrack of the Trailer of the Film of "Monty Python and the Holy Grail"	198?	2.00	4.00	8.00
—Reissue					
❑ AL 8357	Matching Tie and Handkerchief	198?	2.00	4.00	8.00
—Reissue; we don't know whether Side 2 maintains the trick groove on this issue					
❑ AB 9536	Monty Python's Contractual Obligation Album	1980	5.00	10.00	20.00
❑ AB 9580	The Monty Python Instant Record Collection	1981	3.75	7.50	15.00
BBC					
❑ 22073	Monty Python's Flying Circus	198?	5.00	10.00	20.00
—Excerpts from TV shows; pressed by Columbia, possibly for exclusive use by the record club					
BUDDAH					
❑ BDS 5656 [(2)]	The Worst of Monty Python	1976	5.00	10.00	20.00
—Repackage of the two Charisma LPs					
CHARISMA					
❑ CAS 1049	Another Monty Python Record	1972	6.25	12.50	25.00
❑ CAS 1063	Monty Python's Previous Record	1972	6.25	12.50	25.00
MCA					
❑ 6121	Monty Python and the Meaning of Life	1983	3.00	6.00	12.00
PYE					
❑ 12116	Monty Python's Flying Circus	1975	5.00	10.00	20.00
VIRGIN					
❑ 90865 [(2)]	The Final Rip Off	1988	5.00	10.00	20.00
WARNER BROS.					
❑ BSK 3396	Life of Brian	1979	3.75	7.50	15.00

MOODS, THE (1)
45s
BANG

Number	Title (A Side/B Side)	Yr	VG	VG+	NM
❑ 555	Gotta Figure Out/Genuine Jade	1968	2.00	4.00	8.00
WAND					
❑ 11224	Rainmaker/Lady Rain	1970	2.00	4.00	8.00

MOODS, THE (2)
45s
KOOL

Number	Title (A Side/B Side)	Yr	VG	VG+	NM
❑ 1024	High School Days/The Broken Hip	1964	2.50	5.00	10.00
❑ 1028	Oop-Sy-Do/Stay with Me	1965	2.50	5.00	10.00
❑ 1032	Only the Young/(B-side unknown)	1965	2.50	5.00	10.00

MOODS, THE (3)
45s
SARG

Number	Title (A Side/B Side)	Yr	VG	VG+	NM
❑ 162	Little Alice/Lady of the Sea	1959	20.00	40.00	80.00
❑ 176	Easy Going/Duck Walk	1959	10.00	20.00	40.00
❑ 179	Let Me Have Your Love/Broke Up	1959	12.50	25.00	50.00
❑ 184	Rockin' Santa Claus/Teenager's Past	1959	10.00	20.00	40.00
❑ 185	On the Move/Teenager's Past	1960	10.00	20.00	40.00

MOODY BLUES, THE Also see GRAEME EDGE; JUSTIN HAYWARD; DENNY LAINE; RAY THOMAS.
12-Inch Singles
POLYDOR

Number	Title (A Side/B Side)	Yr	VG	VG+	NM
❑ 431 [DJ]	The Other Side of Life (Edit) (LP Version)	1986	2.00	4.00	8.00
❑ 449 [DJ]	Running Out of Love (same on both sides)	1986	2.00	4.00	8.00
THRESHOLD					
❑ 174 [DJ]	Gemini Dream (same on both sides)	1981	2.00	4.00	8.00
❑ 224 [DJ]	Sitting at the Wheel (Edit) (LP Version)	1983	2.00	4.00	8.00

45s
DERAM

Number	Title (A Side/B Side)	Yr	VG	VG+	NM
❑ 5N-67012	I'm Just a Singer (In a Rock and Roll Band)/For My Lady	197?	—	2.00	4.00
—Reissue of Threshold 67012					
❑ 85023	Nights in White Satin/Cities	1968	2.00	4.00	8.00
—Composer of "Nights in White Satin" listed as "Justin Hayward"					
❑ 85023	Nights in White Satin/Cities	1968	2.00	4.00	8.00
—Composers of "Nights in White Satin" listed as "Redwave-Hayward"					
❑ 85023	Nights in White Satin/Cities	1968	2.50	5.00	10.00
—Composer of "Nights in White Satin" listed as "Redwave"					
❑ 85028	Tuesday Afternoon (Forever Afternoon)/Another Morning	1968	2.00	4.00	8.00
❑ 85033	Ride My See-Saw/Voices in the Sky	1968	2.00	4.00	8.00
❑ 85044	Never Comes the Day/So Deep Within You	1969	2.00	4.00	8.00
LONDON					
❑ 270	Steppin' in a Slide Zone/I'll Be Level with You	1978	—	2.00	4.00
❑ 273	Driftwood/I'm Your Man	1978	—	2.50	5.00
❑ 1005	This Is My House (But Nobody Calls)/Boulevard de la Madelaine	1967	3.00	6.00	12.00
❑ 9726	Go Now!/Lose Your Money	1965	2.00	4.00	8.00
—Blue swirl label, "London" in black					
❑ 9726	Go Now!/Lose Your Money	1965	3.00	6.00	12.00
—Blue swirl label, "London" in white					
❑ 9726	Go Now!/Lose Your Money	1965	5.00	10.00	20.00
—White, purple and blue label					
❑ 9726	Go Now!/Lose Your Money	197?	—	3.00	6.00
—"Sunrise" label					
❑ 9726V [DJ]	Go Now!/It's Easy Child	1965	5.00	10.00	20.00
—Orange and brown swirl label; may be promo only					
❑ 9764	From the Bottom of My Heart (I Love You)/And My Baby's Gone	1965	3.75	7.50	15.00
❑ 9799	Ev'ry Day/You Don't	1965	3.75	7.50	15.00
❑ 9810	Stop!/Bye Bye Bird	1966	3.75	7.50	15.00
❑ 20030	Fly Me High/I Really Haven't Got the Time	1967	3.00	6.00	12.00
POLYDOR					
❑ 870990-7	No More Lies/River of Endless Love	1988	—	—	3.00
❑ 870990-7 [PS]	No More Lies/River of Endless Love	1988	—	—	3.00
❑ 871270-7	Al Fin Voy a Encontrarte (I Know You're Out There Somewhere — Spanish Version)/I Know You're Out There Somewhere	1989	—	2.50	5.00
❑ 883906-7	Your Wildest Dreams/Talkin' Talkin'	1986	—	—	3.00
❑ 883906-7 [PS]	Your Wildest Dreams/Talkin' Talkin'	1986	—	—	3.00
❑ 885201-7	The Other Side of Life/The Spirit	1986	—	2.50	5.00
—Blue vinyl					
❑ 885201-7 [PS]	The Other Side of Life/The Spirit	1986	—	2.50	5.00
—Special sleeve for blue vinyl version					
❑ 885212-7	The Other Side of Life/The Spirit	1986	—	—	3.00
❑ 885212-7 [PS]	The Other Side of Life/The Spirit	1986	—	—	3.00
❑ 887600-7	I Know You're Out There Somewhere/Miracle	1988	—	—	3.00
❑ 887600-7 [PS]	I Know You're Out There Somewhere/Miracle	1988	—	—	3.00
❑ 887815-7	Here Comes the Weekend/River of Endless Love	1988	—	—	3.00
THRESHOLD					
❑ 601	Gemini Dream/Painted Smile	1981	—	2.00	4.00
❑ 602	The Voice/22,000 Days	1981	—	2.00	4.00
❑ 602 [PS]	The Voice/22,000 Days	1981	—	3.00	6.00
❑ 603	Talking Out of Turn/Veteran Cosmic Rocker	1981	—	2.00	4.00
❑ 604	Sitting at the Wheel/Going Nowhere	1983	—	2.00	4.00
❑ 604 [PS]	Sitting at the Wheel/Going Nowhere	1983	—	3.00	6.00
❑ 605	Blue World/Sorry	1983	—	2.00	4.00
❑ 606	Running Water/Under My Feet	1983	—	2.00	4.00
❑ 67004	Question/Candle of Life	1970	—	3.00	6.00
❑ 67006	The Story in Your Eyes/Melancholy Man	1971	—	3.00	6.00
❑ 67006 [PS]	The Story in Your Eyes/Melancholy Man	1971	3.00	6.00	12.00
❑ 67009	Isn't Life Strange/After You Came	1972	—	2.50	5.00
❑ 67012	I'm Just a Singer (In a Rock and Roll Band)/For My Lady	1973	—	2.50	5.00
Albums					
COMPLEAT					
❑ 672008 [(2)]	Early Blues	1985	3.75	7.50	15.00
—Reissue of London 1964-66 material					
DERAM					
❑ DE 16012 [M]	Days of Future Passed	1968	62.50	125.00	250.00
❑ DES 18012 [S]	Days of Future Passed	1968	5.00	10.00	20.00
—With large "DERAM" on top half of label					
❑ DES 18012 [S]	Days of Future Passed	1968	7.50	15.00	30.00
—With "LONDON" under "DERAM" on top half of label					
❑ DES 18017	In Search of the Lost Chord	1968	5.00	10.00	20.00
—Originals have gatefold covers					

Number	Title (A Side/B Side)	Yr	VG	VG+	NM
❏ DES 18025	On the Threshold of a Dream	1969	5.00	10.00	20.00
—Originals have gatefold covers and lyric booklet					
❏ DES 18051 [R]	In the Beginning	1971	5.00	10.00	20.00
❏ 820006-1 [S]	Days of Future Passed	1985	2.00	4.00	8.00
❏ 820168-1	In Search of the Lost Chord	1985	2.00	4.00	8.00
❏ 820170-1	On the Threshold of a Dream	1985	2.00	4.00	8.00
LONDON					
❏ PS 428 [R]	Go Now — The Moody Blues #1	1965	10.00	20.00	40.00
❏ PS 690/1 [(2)]	Caught Live + 5	1977	3.00	6.00	12.00
❏ PS 708	Octave	1978	2.50	5.00	10.00
❏ PS 708 [DJ]	Octave	1978	7.50	15.00	30.00
—Promo only on blue vinyl					
❏ LL 3428 [M]	Go Now — The Moody Blues #1	1965	12.50	25.00	50.00
❏ 820161-1 [(2)]	Caught Live + 5	1985	2.00	4.00	8.00
❏ 820329-1	Octave	1986	2.00	4.00	8.00
MOBILE FIDELITY					
❏ 1-042	Days of Future Passed	1980	15.00	30.00	60.00
—Audiophile vinyl					
❏ 1-151	Seventh Sojourn	1984	17.50	35.00	70.00
—Audiophile vinyl					
❏ 1-215	On the Threshold of a Dream	1994	6.25	12.50	25.00
—Audiophile vinyl					
❏ 1-232	Every Good Boy Deserves Favour	1995	6.25	12.50	25.00
—Audiophile vinyl					
❏ 1-253	To Our Children's Children's Children	1996	15.00	30.00	60.00
—Audiophile vinyl					
NAUTILUS					
❏ NR-21	On the Threshold of a Dream	1981	12.50	25.00	50.00
—Audiophile vinyl; DBX-encoded version					
❏ NR-21	On the Threshold of a Dream	1981	15.00	30.00	60.00
—Audiophile vinyl					
POLYDOR					
❏ 829 179-1	The Other Side of Life	1986	2.50	5.00	10.00
❏ 835 756-1	Sur La Mer	1988	3.00	6.00	12.00
❏ 840 659-1	Greatest Hits (1967-1988)	1989	3.75	7.50	15.00
THRESHOLD					
❏ THS 1	To Our Children's Children's Children	1969	3.75	7.50	15.00
—White label with purple logo; gatefold cover					
❏ THS 1	To Our Children's Children's Children	197?	2.50	5.00	10.00
—Blue label; no gatefold					
❏ THS 3	A Question of Balance	197?	2.50	5.00	10.00
—Blue label; no gatefold					
❏ THS 3	A Question of Balance	1970	3.75	7.50	15.00
—White label with purple logo; gatefold cover					
❏ THS 5	Every Good Boy Deserves Favour	197?	2.50	5.00	10.00
—Blue label; no gatefold					
❏ THS 5	Every Good Boy Deserves Favour	197?	3.00	6.00	12.00
—Blue label; gatefold cover					
❏ THS 5	Every Good Boy Deserves Favour	1971	3.75	7.50	15.00
—White label with purple logo; gatefold cover					
❏ THS 7	Seventh Sojourn	197?	2.50	5.00	10.00
—Blue label; no gatefold					
❏ THS 7	Seventh Sojourn	197?	3.00	6.00	12.00
—Blue label; gatefold cover					
❏ THS 7	Seventh Sojourn	1972	3.75	7.50	15.00
—White label with purple logo; gatefold cover					
❏ THS 12/13 [(2)]	This Is the Moody Blues	1974	3.75	7.50	15.00
❏ THX-100 [DJ]	Special Interview Kit	1971	37.50	75.00	150.00
—Includes script					
❏ TR-1-2901	Long Distance Voyager	1981	2.50	5.00	10.00
❏ TR-1-2902	The Present	1982	2.50	5.00	10.00
❏ SMAS-93329	A Question of Balance	1971	5.00	10.00	20.00
—Capitol Record Club edition					
❏ 810119-1	The Present	1983	2.00	4.00	8.00
❏ 820007-1 [(2)]	This Is the Moody Blues	1985	2.00	4.00	8.00
❏ 820105-1	Long Distance Voyager	1985	2.00	4.00	8.00
❏ 820155-1	Voices in the Sky/The Best of the Moody Blues	1985	2.50	5.00	10.00
❏ 820159-1	Seventh Sojourn	1985	2.00	4.00	8.00
❏ 820160-1	Every Good Boy Deserves Favour	1985	2.00	4.00	8.00
❏ 820211-1	A Question of Balance	1985	2.00	4.00	8.00

MOOG MACHINE, THE
Albums
COLUMBIA

Number	Title (A Side/B Side)	Yr	VG	VG+	NM
❏ CS 9921	Switched-On Rock	1969	5.00	10.00	20.00
❏ CS 9959	Christmas Becomes Electric	1969	5.00	10.00	20.00

MOON, KEITH Also see THE WHO.
45s
TRACK

Number	Title (A Side/B Side)	Yr	VG	VG+	NM
❏ 40316	Teenage Idol/Don't Worry Baby	1974	3.75	7.50	15.00
❏ 40387	Solid Gold/Move Over Ms. L.	1975	3.75	7.50	15.00
❏ 40435	In My Life/Crazy Like a Fox	1975	3.75	7.50	15.00

Albums
TRACK/MCA

Number	Title (A Side/B Side)	Yr	VG	VG+	NM
❏ 2136	Two Sides of the Moon	1975	10.00	20.00	40.00

MOON, THE With David Marks, ex-BEACH BOYS.
45s
IMPERIAL

Number	Title (A Side/B Side)	Yr	VG	VG+	NM
❏ 66285	Mothers and Fathers/Someday Girl	1968	7.50	15.00	30.00
❏ 66330	Faces/John Automaton	1968	6.25	12.50	25.00
❏ 66415	Not to Know/Pirate	1969	6.25	12.50	25.00

Albums
IMPERIAL

Number	Title (A Side/B Side)	Yr	VG	VG+	NM
❏ LP-12381	Without Earth	1968	10.00	20.00	40.00
❏ LP-12444	The Moon	1969	10.00	20.00	40.00

MOON BEAMS, THE
45s
GRATE

Number	Title (A Side/B Side)	Yr	VG	VG+	NM
❏ 100	A Lover's Plea/Don't Go Away	1959	37.50	75.00	150.00

MOONGLOWS, THE Also see HARVEY.
45s
BIG P

Number	Title (A Side/B Side)	Yr	VG	VG+	NM
❏ 101	Sincerely '72/You've Chosen Me	1972	2.50	5.00	10.00

CHAMPAGNE

Number	Title (A Side/B Side)	Yr	VG	VG+	NM
❏ 7500	I Just Can't Tell No Lie/I've Been Your Dog (Ever Since I've Been Your Man)	1952	375.00	750.00	1500.

CHANCE

Number	Title (A Side/B Side)	Yr	VG	VG+	NM
❏ 1147	Baby Please/Whistle My Love	1953	250.00	500.00	1000.
—Black vinyl					
❏ 1147	Baby Please/Whistle My Love	1953	1500.	2250.	3000.
—Red vinyl					
❏ 1150	Just a Lonely Christmas/Hey, Santa Claus	1953	1500.	2250.	3000.
—Red vinyl (this may not exist legitimately on black vinyl)					
❏ 1152	Secret Love/Real Gone Mama	1954	250.00	500.00	1000.
—Yellow and black label					
❏ 1152	Secret Love/Real Gone Mama	1954	375.00	750.00	1500.
—Silver and blue label					
❏ 1156	I Was Wrong/Ooh Rockin' Daddy	1954	150.00	300.00	600.00
—Black and white label					
❏ 1156	I Was Wrong/Ooh Rockin' Daddy	1954	150.00	300.00	600.00
—Yellow and black label					
❏ 1161	My Gal/219 Train	1954	2500.	3750.	5000.

CHESS

Number	Title (A Side/B Side)	Yr	VG	VG+	NM
❏ 1581	Sincerely/Tempting	1954	15.00	30.00	60.00
—Blue label, silver top					
❏ 1589	Most of All/She's Gone	1955	15.00	30.00	60.00
—Blue label, silver top					
❏ 1598	Foolish Me/Slow Down	1955	15.00	30.00	60.00
—Blue label, silver top					
❏ 1605	Starlite/In Love	1955	15.00	30.00	60.00
—Blue label, silver top					
❏ 1611	In My Diary/Lover, Love Me	1955	15.00	30.00	60.00
—Blue label, silver top					
❏ 1619	We Go Together/Chickie Um Bah	1956	12.50	25.00	50.00
—Blue label, silver top					
❏ 1629	See Saw/When I'm With You	1956	12.50	25.00	50.00
—Blue label, silver top					
❏ 1646	Over and Over Again/I Knew from the Start	1957	12.50	25.00	50.00
—With normal version of A-side; blue label, silver top					
❏ 1646	Over and Over Again/I Knew from the Start	1957	15.00	30.00	60.00
—With slower version of A-side; "8189A" in the run-off area					
❏ 1651	I'm Afraid the Masquerade Is Over/Don't Say Goodbye	1957	12.50	25.00	50.00
—Blue label, silver top					
❏ 1661	Please Send Me Someone to Love/Mr. Engineer (Bring Her Back to Me)	1957	12.50	25.00	50.00
—Blue label, silver top					
❏ 1669 [PS]	The Beating of My Heart/Confess It to Your Heart	1957	12.50	25.00	50.00

—In general, for the above singles, the blue label with vertical "Chess" versions are 60% of the above values; yellow early-1960s label versions and black mid-1960s versions are 40% of above; and blue late-1960s versions, with "Chess" on top, are about 20%

Number	Title (A Side/B Side)	Yr	VG	VG+	NM
❏ 1681	Too Late/Here I Am	1958	7.50	15.00	30.00
❏ 1689	In the Middle of the Night/Soda Pop	1958	7.50	15.00	30.00
❏ 1701	This Love/Sweeter Than Words	1958	7.50	15.00	30.00
❏ 1705	Ten Commandments of Love/Mean Old Blues	1958	7.50	15.00	30.00
—As "Harvey and the Moonglows"					
❏ 1717	Love Is a River/I'll Never Stop Wanting You	1959	6.25	12.50	25.00
❏ 1738	Mama Loocie/Unemployment	1959	6.25	12.50	25.00
—As "Harvey and the Moonglows"					
❏ 1770	Beatnick/Junior	1960	6.25	12.50	25.00
❏ 1811	Blue Velvet/Penny Arcade	1962	6.25	12.50	25.00
—As "Bobby Lester and the Moonglows"					

CRIMSON

Number	Title (A Side/B Side)	Yr	VG	VG+	NM
❏ 1003	My Imagination/Gee	1964	5.00	10.00	20.00

LANA

Number	Title (A Side/B Side)	Yr	VG	VG+	NM
❏ 130	Sincerely/Time After Time	196?	2.00	4.00	8.00
❏ 131	Most of All/What a Diffrence a Day Makes	196?	2.00	4.00	8.00
❏ 132	Blue Velvet/In My Diary	196?	2.00	4.00	8.00
❏ 133	See Saw/Love Is a River	196?	2.00	4.00	8.00
❏ 134	We Go Together/Shoo Doo Be Doo	196?	2.00	4.00	8.00
❏ 135	Ten Commandments of Love/Half a Heart	196?	2.00	4.00	8.00

LOST-NITE

Number	Title (A Side/B Side)	Yr	VG	VG+	NM
❏ 275	Just a Lonely Christmas/Baby Please	197?	—	3.00	6.00
—Reissue					
❏ 288	I Was Wrong/My Gal	197?	—	2.50	5.00
—Reissue					
❏ 294	Secret Love/Golden Teardrops	197?	—	2.50	5.00
—B-side by the Flamingos; reissue					

MELLO

Number	Title (A Side/B Side)	Yr	VG	VG+	NM
❏ 69	Just a Lonely Christmas/Hey, Santa Claus	19??	2.00	4.00	8.00
—Reissue					

RCA VICTOR

Number	Title (A Side/B Side)	Yr	VG	VG+	NM
❏ 74-0759	Sincerely/I Was Wrong	1972	—	2.50	5.00
❏ 74-0839	When I'm With You/You've Chosen Me	1972	—	2.50	5.00

VEE JAY

Number	Title (A Side/B Side)	Yr	VG	VG+	NM
❏ 423	Secret Love/Real Gone Mama	1962	6.25	12.50	25.00

7-Inch Extended Plays
CHESS

Number	Title (A Side/B Side)	Yr	VG	VG+	NM
❏ 5122	(contents unknown)	1959	62.50	125.00	250.00
❏ 5122 [PS]	Look! It's the Moonglows	1959	62.50	125.00	250.00
❏ 5123	True Love/Penny Arcade//I'll Stop Waiting/Sweeter Than Words	1959	62.50	125.00	250.00
❏ 5123 [PS]	Look! It's the Moonglows, Vol. 2	1959	62.50	125.00	250.00

Albums
CHESS

Number	Title (A Side/B Side)	Yr	VG	VG+	NM
❏ LP 1430 [M]	Look! It's the Moonglows	1959	125.00	250.00	500.00
❏ LP 1471 [M]	The Best of Bobby Lester & the Moonglows	1962	75.00	150.00	300.00
—Black label					
❏ LP 1471 [M]	The Best of Bobby Lester & the Moonglows	1966	12.50	25.00	50.00
—Blue, fading to white label					
❏ CH-9111	Their Greatest Sides	1986	3.00	6.00	12.00
❏ CH-9193	Look! It's the Moonglows	1987	3.00	6.00	12.00
—Reissue of 1430					

CONSTELLATION

Number	Title (A Side/B Side)	Yr	VG	VG+	NM
❏ C-2 [M]	Collectors Showcase — The Moonglows	1964	12.50	25.00	50.00
—Dark blue lettering					
❏ C-2 [M]	Collectors Showcase — The Moonglows	1964	25.00	50.00	100.00
—Light blue lettering					

Number	Title (A Side/B Side)	Yr	VG	VG+	NM
LOST-NITE					
❏ LP-23 [10]	The Moonglows	1981	3.00	6.00	12.00
RCA VICTOR					
❏ LSP-4722	The Return of the Moonglows	1972	3.75	7.50	15.00
MOORE, BOB					
45s					
HICKORY					
❏ 1357	Only the Lonely/Skokiaan	1965	—	3.00	6.00
❏ 1372	Hell's Angels/I Can't Stop Loving You	1966	—	3.00	6.00
❏ 1407	Spanish Eyes/Elephant Rock	1966	—	3.00	6.00
❏ 1426	Acapulco/Parade of the Matadors	1966	—	3.00	6.00
❏ 1437	A White Sport Coat/Amigo No. 1	1967	—	3.00	6.00
❏ 1480	The Fastest Guitar Alive/The River	1967	—	3.00	6.00
❏ 1521	You Sit Around All Day/Amigo No. 1	1968	—	3.00	6.00
MONUMENT					
❏ 406	Theme from My Three Sons/Mais Oui	1959	3.75	7.50	15.00
❏ 437	Theme from My Three Sons/Mais Oui	1961	2.50	5.00	10.00
❏ 446	Mexico/Hot Spot	1961	2.00	4.00	8.00
❏ 457	Auf Wiederseh'n Marlene/Ooh La La	1962	2.00	4.00	8.00
❏ 457 [PS]	Auf Wiederseh'n Marlene/Ooh La La	1962	3.75	7.50	15.00
❏ 800	Flea Circus/Autumn Souvenirs	1962	2.00	4.00	8.00
❏ 814	Kentucky/Flowers of Florence	1963	2.00	4.00	8.00
❏ 834	Cologne/Hooten Trumpet	1964	2.00	4.00	8.00
Albums					
HICKORY					
❏ LP-131 [M]	Viva Bob Moore	1965	3.75	7.50	15.00
❏ LPS-131 [S]	Viva Bob Moore	1965	5.00	10.00	20.00
MONUMENT					
❏ MLP-4005 [M]	Mexico and Other Great Hits!	1961	5.00	10.00	20.00
❏ SLP-4005 [S]	Mexico and Other Great Hits!	1961	6.25	12.50	25.00
❏ MLP-8008 [M]	Mexico	1967	3.00	6.00	12.00
❏ SLP-18008 [S]	Mexico	1967	3.75	7.50	15.00
MOORE, BOBBY, AND THE RHYTHM ACES					
45s					
CHECKER					
❏ 1129	Searching for My Love/Hey Mr. D.J.	1966	2.50	5.00	10.00
—Blue label					
❏ 1129	Searching for My Love/Hey Mr. D.J.	1966	3.75	7.50	15.00
—Maroon label, vertical "Checker"					
❏ 1156	Try My Love Again/Go Ahead and Burn Baby	1966	2.50	5.00	10.00
❏ 1180	Reaching Out/Chained to Your Heart	1967	2.50	5.00	10.00
Albums					
CHECKER					
❏ LP-3000 [M]	Searching for My Love	1966	7.50	15.00	30.00
❏ LPS-3000 [R]	Searching for My Love	1966	5.00	10.00	20.00
MOORE, DOROTHY					
12-Inch Singles					
STREETKING					
❏ SKDS-1120	Just Another Broken Heart (Vocal 7:05) (Dub 4:41) (Edit 3:25)	1984	3.00	6.00	12.00
VOLT					
❏ 3106	Can't Get Over You (Once Again I'm Misty Blue) (4:24)/Don't Hold Your Breath	1988	3.00	6.00	12.00
45s					
AVCO					
❏ 4590	See How They've Done My Love/ (B-side unknown)	1972	3.00	6.00	12.00
❏ 4599	Same Old Feeling/(B-side unknown)	1972	3.00	6.00	12.00
CHIMNEYVILLE					
❏ 10204	Don't Let Go/Two of a Kind	1975	—	3.00	6.00
❏ 10207	We Can Love/Making Love	1975	—	3.00	6.00
—With King Floyd					
GSF					
❏ 6908	Cry Like a Baby/ Just the One I've Been Looking For	1973	3.75	7.50	15.00
—B-side is sought by Northern Soul aficionados					
HANDSHAKE					
❏ WS9-02879	What's Forever For/Someone's Lover Before (But Never Someone's Girl)	1982	—	2.50	5.00
MALACO					
❏ 1029	Misty Blue/Here It Is	1976	—	3.00	6.00
❏ 1033	Funny How Time Slips Away/ Ain't That a Mother's Luck	1976	—	3.00	6.00
❏ 1037	For Old Time Sake/Daddy's Eyes	1976	—	3.00	6.00
❏ 1040	We Should Really Be in Love/I'll Never Be Loved	1977	—	2.50	5.00
—With Eddie Floyd					
❏ 1042	I Believe You/Love Me	1977	—	3.00	6.00
❏ 1047	With Pen in Hand/Too Blind to See	1977	—	2.50	5.00
❏ 1048	Let the Music Play/1-2-3 (You and Me)	1978	—	2.50	5.00
❏ 1052	Special Occasion/Girl Overboard	1978	3.75	7.50	15.00
—B-side is sought by Northern Soul aficionados					
❏ 1054	(We Need More) Loving Time/ Write a Little Prayer	1978	—	2.50	5.00
❏ 1059	Once or Twice/Love Me	1979	—	2.50	5.00
❏ 2062	Talk to Me-Every Beat of My Heart/Lonely	1980	—	2.50	5.00
❏ 2064	Angel of the Morning/Make It Soon	1980	—	2.50	5.00
❏ 2168	All Night Blue/Talk to Me	1990	—	2.50	5.00
❏ 2172	Be Strong Enough to Hold On/If You'll Give Me Your Heart	1991	—	2.00	4.00
❏ 2192	Read Me My Rights/Stay Close to Home	199?	—	2.00	4.00
PRELUDE					
❏ 8094	Just Came Apart at the Dreams/(Instrumental)	1984	2.50	5.00	10.00
STREETKING					
❏ SK-7120	Just Another Broken Heart/(Instrumental)	1984	—	2.50	5.00
VOLT					
❏ 301	Endless Summer Nights/Walk Through This Pain	1988	—	2.50	5.00
❏ 990	Can't Get Over You (Once Again I'm Misty Blue)/ Don't Hold Your Breath	1988	—	2.50	5.00
Albums					
MALACO					
❏ 6351	Misty Blue	1976	3.00	6.00	12.00
❏ 6353	Dorothy Moore	1977	3.75	7.50	15.00

Number	Title (A Side/B Side)	Yr	VG	VG+	NM
❏ 6356	Once More with Feeling	1978	3.00	6.00	12.00
❏ 6359	Definitely Dorothy	1979	3.00	6.00	12.00
❏ 7363	Talk to Me	1980	3.75	7.50	15.00
❏ 7455	Feel the Love	1990	3.00	6.00	12.00
REJOICE/A&M					
❏ WR 8326	Givin' It Straight to You	1986	3.75	7.50	15.00
VOLT					
❏ 3401	Time Out for Me	1988	3.00	6.00	12.00
❏ 3405	Winner	1989	3.00	6.00	12.00
MOORE, DUDLEY					
Albums					
ATLANTIC					
❏ 1403 [M]	Beyond the Fringe and All That Jazz	1963	6.25	12.50	25.00
❏ SD 1403 [S]	Beyond the Fringe and All That Jazz	1963	7.50	15.00	30.00
LONDON					
❏ PS 558	Dudley Moore Trio	1969	6.25	12.50	25.00
MOORE, GATEMOUTH					
45s					
KING					
❏ 4492	Christmas Blues/Happy New Year, Darling	1951	12.50	25.00	50.00
—B-side by Lonnie Johnson					
Albums					
AUDIO FIDELITY					
❏ AFLP-1921 [M] Revival!		196?	15.00	30.00	60.00
❏ AFSD-5921 [S] Revival!		196?	20.00	40.00	80.00
BLUESWAY					
❏ BLS 6074	After 21 Years	1973	5.00	10.00	20.00
KING					
❏ 684 [M]	Gatemouth Moore Sings Blues	1960	1250.	2500.	5000.
MOORE, HARV					
45s					
AMERICAN ARTS					
❏ 20	Interview of the Fab Four/I Feel So Fine	1964	75.00	150.00	300.00
MOORE, JACKIE					
12-Inch Singles					
COLUMBIA					
❏ 10994	This Time Baby/Let's Go Somewhere and Make Love	1979	2.50	5.00	10.00
❏ 11136	How's Your Love Life Baby/(Instrumental)	1979	2.50	5.00	10.00
❏ 11293	With Your Love/Helpless	1980	2.50	5.00	10.00
DIVA					
❏ 004	This Old Heart of Mine (4 versions)	198?	2.00	4.00	8.00
SUNNYVIEW					
❏ 421	Love Is the Answer (4:23) (6:03)	1985	—	3.00	6.00
45s					
ATLANTIC					
❏ 2681	Precious Precious/Will Power	1969	—	2.50	5.00
❏ 2798	Sometimes It's Got to Rain (In Your Love Life)/ Wonderful Marvelous	1971	—	2.50	5.00
❏ 2830	Time/Cover Me	1971	—	2.50	5.00
❏ 2861	Darling Baby/Something in a Love	1972	—	2.50	5.00
❏ 2902	It Ain't Who You Know/ They Tell Me of an Uncloudy Day	1972	—	2.50	5.00
❏ 2956	Sweet Charlie Babe/If	1973	—	2.50	5.00
❏ 2989	Both Ends Against the Middle/ Clean Up Your Own Yard	1973	—	2.50	5.00
CATAWBA					
❏ 1010	Holding Back/(B-side unknown)	1983	—	2.00	4.00
COLUMBIA					
❏ 04599	This Time Baby/ Let's Go Somewhere and Make Love	1984	—	—	3.00
❏ 10779	Personally/Ain't No Trouble Like Love Trouble	1978	—	2.00	4.00
❏ 10993	This Time Baby/Let's Go Somewhere and Make Love	1979	—	2.00	4.00
❏ 11140	How's Your Love Life Baby/ Do Ya Got What It Takes	1979	—	2.00	4.00
❏ 11288	Helpless/With Your Love	1980	—	2.00	4.00
❏ 11363	Love Won't Let Me Wait/With Your Love	1980	—	2.00	4.00
KAYVETTE					
❏ 5122	Make Me Feel Like a Woman/ Singin' Funky Music Turns Me On	1975	—	2.50	5.00
❏ 5124	Puttin' It Down to You/Never Is Forever	1975	—	2.50	5.00
❏ 5125	It's Harder to Leave/(B-side unknown)	1976	—	2.50	5.00
❏ 5127	Disco Body (Shake It to the East, Shake It to the West)/Tired of Hiding	1976	—	2.50	5.00
❏ 5129	Make Me Yours/Somebody Loves You	1977	—	2.50	5.00
❏ 5139	Heart Be Still/Singin' Funky Music Turns Me On	1981	—	2.00	4.00
❏ 5140	Who's Next/Singin' Funky Music Turns Me On	1981	—	2.00	4.00
SHOUT					
❏ 232	Dear John/Here I Am	1968	2.00	4.00	8.00
❏ 239	Why Don't You Call on Me/(B-side unknown)	1968	2.00	4.00	8.00
Albums					
ATLANTIC					
❏ SD 7285	Sweet Charlie Babe	1973	3.75	7.50	15.00
COLUMBIA					
❏ JC 35991	On My Way	1979	2.50	5.00	10.00
❏ JC 36455	With Your Love	1980	2.50	5.00	10.00
KAYVETTE					
❏ 801	Make Me Feel Like a Woman	1975	3.75	7.50	15.00
MOORE, LATTIE					
45s					
ARC					
❏ 8005	Juke Box Johnnie/Pretty Woman Blues	1952	50.00	100.00	200.00
KING					
❏ 1194	Foolish Castles/I'm Gonna Tell You Something	1953	12.50	25.00	50.00
❏ 1250	I Gotta Go Home/A Brand New Case of Love	1953	12.50	25.00	50.00
❏ 1327	They're Not Worth the Paper They're Printed On/ Under a Mexico Moon	1954	12.50	25.00	50.00
❏ 1350	Pull Down the Blinds/What Am I Supposed to Do	1954	12.50	25.00	50.00
❏ 4955	100,000 Women Can't Be Wrong/ Lonesome Man Blues	1956	12.50	25.00	50.00

Number	Title (A Side/B Side)	Yr	VG	VG+	NM
❏ 5370	Cajun Doll/Mine Again	1960	10.00	20.00	40.00
❏ 5413	Drunk Again/Driving Nails	1960	6.25	12.50	25.00
❏ 5526	Sundown and Sorrow/If the Good Lord's Willing	1961	5.00	10.00	20.00
❏ 5685	I Told You So/Heaven All Around Me	1962	3.75	7.50	15.00
❏ 5723	Out of Control/Just About Then	1963	3.75	7.50	15.00
❏ 5762	Honky Tonk Heaven/Lonesome Man Blues	1963	3.75	7.50	15.00
SPEED					
❏ 101	Juke Joint Johnny/It's Good Enough for You	1952	100.00	200.00	400.00
STARDAY					
❏ 403	You Never Looked Sweeter/ Why Did You Lie to Me	1958	7.50	15.00	30.00
❏ 441	Too Hot to Handle/Just a-Waitin'	1959	7.50	15.00	30.00
WPL					
❏ 1001	Old Ex-Husbands/Beat Years of Your Life	1970	25.00	50.00	100.00
Albums					
AUDIO LAB					
❏ AL-1555 [M]	The Best of Lattie Moore	1960	50.00	100.00	200.00
❏ AL-1573 [M]	Country Side	1962	37.50	75.00	150.00
DERBYTOWN					
❏ 102 [M]	Lattie Moore	196?	10.00	20.00	40.00

MOORE, MELBA
12-Inch Singles

Number	Title (A Side/B Side)	Yr	VG	VG+	NM
CAPITOL					
❏ 8543	Mind Up Tonight (Extended) (Instrumental)	1982	—	3.00	6.00
❏ 8586	Love Me Right (Extended) (Instrumental)	1983	—	3.00	6.00
❏ 8627	Read My Lips/Got to Have Your Love	1985	2.00	4.00	8.00
❏ 8647	When You Love Me Like This/Winner (Instrumental Edit)	1985	—	3.00	6.00
❏ SPRO-9335/6 [DJ]	Read My Lips (Special Mix) (Single Version)	1985	—	3.00	6.00
❏ SPRO-9381/2 [DJ]	Read My Lips (Remix) (Extended Version)	1985	—	3.00	6.00
❏ SPRO-9446/7 [DJ]	When You Love Me Like This (Club Mix) (Monster Groove Mix)	1985	2.00	4.00	8.00
❏ SPRO-9500 [DJ]	I Can't Believe (It's Over) (Extended Version) (Edit Version)	1985	2.00	4.00	8.00
❏ SPRO-9717 [DJ]	Love the One I'm With (5:44) (same on both sides)	1986	—	3.00	6.00
❏ SPRO-9776 [DJ]	Love the One I'm With (3 versions)	1986	—	3.00	6.00
❏ SPRO-9858/9980 [DJ]	Falling (Single Version) (LP Version)	1986	2.00	4.00	8.00
❏ V-15236	Love the One I'm With (5:44)/Don't Go Away	1986	—	3.00	6.00
❏ V-15256	A Little Bit More (4:54) (4:15)/When We Touch	1986	—	3.00	6.00
—With Freddie Jackson					
❏ V-15280	It's Been So Long (2 versions)/Don't Go Away	1987	—	3.00	6.00
❏ V-15426	Love and Kisses (3 versions)/I'm in Love	1988	—	3.00	6.00
❏ V-15561	Do You Really Want My Love (4 versions)	1990	—	3.00	6.00
EMI AMERICA					
❏ SPRO-9817 [DJ]	Love's Comin' At Ya (7" Version) (LP Version)	1981	2.00	4.00	8.00
EPIC					
❏ AS 660 [DJ]	Miss Thing (same on both sides)	1979	2.00	4.00	8.00
❏ 50665	Pick Me Up, I'll Dance/(Instrumental)	1979	3.00	6.00	12.00
❏ 50771	Miss Thing/Need Love	1979	3.00	6.00	12.00
❏ 50807	Hot and Tasty/Night People	1979	3.00	6.00	12.00
45s					
BUDDAH					
❏ 452	I Am His Lady/If I Lose You	1975	—	2.50	5.00
❏ 469	Natural Part of Everything/Must Be Dues	1975	—	2.50	5.00
❏ 496	Starting to Fall/Must Be Dues	1975	—	2.50	5.00
—With Jo Ellen Cohn					
❏ 519	This Is It/Stay Awhile	1976	—	2.50	5.00
❏ 519 [PS]	This Is It/Stay Awhile	1976	2.00	4.00	8.00
❏ 535	Lean On Me/One Less Morning	1976	—	2.50	5.00
❏ 562	The Way You Make Me Feel/ So Many Mountains	1977	—	2.50	5.00
❏ 568	The Long and Winding Road/Ain't No Love Lost	1977	—	2.50	5.00
❏ 572	My Sensitive, Passionate Man/ The Greatest Feeling	1977	—	2.50	5.00
❏ 572 [PS]	My Sensitive, Passionate Man/ The Greatest Feeling	1977	—	3.50	7.00
❏ 589	Standing Right Here/Living Free	1977	—	2.50	5.00
❏ 596	I Don't Know No One Else to Turn To/Just Another Link	1978	—	2.50	5.00
CAPITOL					
❏ B-5180	Mind Up Tonight/(Instrumental)	1982	—	—	3.00
❏ B-5208	Underlove/(Instrumental)	1983	—	—	3.00
❏ B-5288	Keepin' My Lover Satisfied/(Instrumental)	1983	—	—	3.00
❏ B-5288 [PS]	Keepin' My Lover Satisfied/(Instrumental)	1983	—	2.00	4.00
❏ B-5308	Livin' for Your Love/Got to Have Your Love	1984	—	—	3.00
❏ B-5308 [PS]	Livin' for Your Love/Got to Have Your Love	1984	—	2.00	4.00
❏ B-5343	Love Me Right/Never Say Never	1984	—	—	3.00
❏ B-5343 [PS]	Love Me Right/Never Say Never	1984	—	2.00	4.00
❏ B-5415	(Can't Take Half) All of You/Let Me Be Yours	1984	—	—	3.00
—With Lillo Thomas					
❏ B-5415 [PS]	(Can't Take Half) All of You/Let Me Be Yours	1984	—	2.00	4.00
❏ B-5437	Read My Lips/Got to Have Your Love	1985	—	—	3.00
❏ B-5437 [PS]	Read My Lips/Got to Have Your Love	1985	—	2.00	4.00
❏ B-5484	When You Love Me Like This/Winner	1985	—	—	3.00
❏ B-5484 [PS]	When You Love Me Like This/Winner	1985	—	2.00	4.00
❏ B-5520	I Can't Believe It (It's Over)/King of No Heart	1985	—	—	3.00
❏ B-5577	Love the One I'm With (A Lot of Love)/ Don't Go Away	1986	—	—	3.00
—With Kashif					
❏ B-5577 [PS]	Love the One I'm With (A Lot of Love)/ Don't Go Away	1986	—	—	3.00
❏ B-5632	A Little Bit More/When We Touch	1986	—	—	3.00
—A-side with Freddie Jackson					
❏ B-5651	Falling/(B-side unknown)	1986	—	—	3.00
❏ B-5681	It's Been So Long/Don't Go Away	1987	—	—	3.00
❏ B-5681 [PS]	It's Been So Long/Don't Go Away	1987	—	—	3.00
❏ B-44012	I'm Not Gonna Let You Go/Dreams	1987	—	—	3.00
❏ B-44012 [PS]	I'm Not Gonna Let You Go/Dreams	1987	—	—	3.00
❏ B-44148	I Can't Complain/ There I Go Falling in Love Again	1988	—	—	3.00
—A-side with Freddie Jackson					
❏ B-44148 [PS]	I Can't Complain/ There I Go Falling in Love Again	1988	—	—	3.00

Number	Title (A Side/B Side)	Yr	VG	VG+	NM
❏ B-44195	I'm in Love/Stay	1988	—	—	3.00
—With Kashif					
❏ B-44195 [PS]	I'm in Love/Stay	1988	—	—	3.00
❏ B-44265	Love and Kisses/I'm in Love	1988	—	—	3.00
EMI AMERICA					
❏ 8092	Take My Love/Just You, Just Me	1981	—	2.00	4.00
❏ 8104	Let's Stand Together/What a Woman Needs	1981	—	2.00	4.00
❏ 8114	Piece of the Rock/(Instrumental)	1982	—	2.00	4.00
❏ 8126	Love's Comin' At Ya/(Instrumental)	1982	—	2.00	4.00
EPIC					
❏ 50600	You Stepped Into My Life/There's No Other Like You	1978	—	2.00	4.00
❏ 50663	Pick Me Up, I'll Dance/Where Did You Ever Go	1979	—	2.00	4.00
❏ 50762	Miss Thing/Need Love	1979	—	2.00	4.00
❏ 50805	Hot and Tasty/Night People	1979	—	2.00	4.00
❏ 50909	Everything So Good About You/Next to You	1980	—	2.00	4.00
❏ 50954	Rest Inside My Love/Something on My Mind	1980	—	2.00	4.00
MERCURY					
❏ 72942	I Messed Up a Good Thing/ I'll Do It All Over Again	1969	2.00	4.00	8.00
❏ 72989	We're Living to Give (Each Other)/ (B-side unknown)	1969	2.00	4.00	8.00
❏ 73040	Time and Love/(B-side unknown)	1970	2.00	4.00	8.00
❏ 73072	I Got Love/I Love Making Love to You	1970	2.00	4.00	8.00
❏ 73134	Look What You're Doing to the Man/Patience Is Rewarded	1970	2.00	4.00	8.00
❏ 73183	If I Had a Million/Loving You Comes So Easy	1971	2.00	4.00	8.00
❏ 73217	He Ain't Heavy, He's My Brother/Take Up a Course in Happiness	1971	2.00	4.00	8.00
❏ 73289	Love Letters/I Ain't Got to Love Nobody Else	1972	2.00	4.00	8.00
MUSICOR					
❏ 1189	Does Love Believe in Me/Don't Cry, Sing Along with the Music	1966	2.50	5.00	10.00
Albums					
ACCORD					
❏ SN-7129	Sweet Melba	1981	2.50	5.00	10.00
BUDDAH					
❏ BDS-5629	Peach Melba	1975	2.50	5.00	10.00
❏ BDS-5657	This Is It	1976	2.50	5.00	10.00
❏ BDS-5677	Melba	1976	2.50	5.00	10.00
❏ BDS-5695	Portrait of Melba Moore	1977	2.50	5.00	10.00
❏ BDS-5720	Dancin' with Melba	1979	2.50	5.00	10.00
CAPITOL					
❏ ST-12243	The Other Side of the Rainbow	1982	2.50	5.00	10.00
❏ ST-12305	Never Say Never	1983	2.50	5.00	10.00
❏ ST-12382	Read My Lips	1985	2.50	5.00	10.00
❏ ST-12471	A Lot of Love	1986	2.50	5.00	10.00
❏ C1-92355	Soul Exposed	1990	3.00	6.00	12.00
EMI AMERICA					
❏ ST-17060	What a Woman Needs	1981	2.50	5.00	10.00
EPIC					
❏ JE 35507	Melba	1978	2.50	5.00	10.00
❏ JE 36128	Burn	1979	2.50	5.00	10.00
❏ JE 36412	Closer	1980	2.50	5.00	10.00
MERCURY					
❏ SRM-1-622	Live!	1972	3.00	6.00	12.00
❏ SR-61255	Living to Give	1970	3.75	7.50	15.00
❏ SR-61287	I Got Love	1970	3.75	7.50	15.00
❏ SR-61321	Look What You're Doing to the Man	1971	3.75	7.50	15.00

MOORE, MELVIN
45s

Number	Title (A Side/B Side)	Yr	VG	VG+	NM
KING					
❏ 4539	Possessed/Hold Me, Kiss Me, Squeeze Me	1952	25.00	50.00	100.00

MOORE, RUDY
45s

Number	Title (A Side/B Side)	Yr	VG	VG+	NM
FEDERAL					
❏ 12253	My Little Angel/I'm Mad with You	1956	12.50	25.00	50.00
❏ 12259	The Buggy Ride/Ring-a-Ling-Dong	1956	12.50	25.00	50.00
❏ 12276	Step It Up and Go/Let Me Come Home	1956	25.00	50.00	100.00
❏ 12280	Bobbie Dobbie/I'll Be Home to See You Tomorrow Night	1956	12.50	25.00	50.00

MOORE, SAM Also see SAM AND DAVE.
45s

Number	Title (A Side/B Side)	Yr	VG	VG+	NM
ATLANTIC					
❏ 2762	Give You Plenty Lovin'/Tennessee Waltz	1970	—	3.00	6.00
❏ 2791	Keep On Sockin' It To Me/Stop	1971	—	3.00	6.00
❏ 2814	Shop Around/If I Should Lose Your Love	1971	—	3.00	6.00

MOORE, SAMMIE
45s

Number	Title (A Side/B Side)	Yr	VG	VG+	NM
HIT					
❏ 125	No Particular Place to Go/Once Upon a Time	1964	2.00	4.00	8.00
—B-side by Sam Baker and Nancy Cohen					

MOORE, SCOTTY Original guitarist in ELVIS PRESLEY's backup band.
45s

Number	Title (A Side/B Side)	Yr	VG	VG+	NM
FERNWOOD					
❏ 107	Have Guitar Will Travel/Rest	1958	7.50	15.00	30.00
Albums					
EPIC					
❏ LN 24103 [M]	The Guitar That Changed the World	1964	20.00	40.00	80.00
❏ BN 26103 [S]	The Guitar That Changed the World	1964	25.00	50.00	100.00
GUINNESS					
❏ GNS-36038	What's Left	1977	3.75	7.50	15.00

MOORE, TIM
45s

Number	Title (A Side/B Side)	Yr	VG	VG+	NM
A SMALL RECORD COMPANY					
❏ 0601	Second Avenue/(B-side unknown)	1974	2.50	5.00	10.00
ABC DUNHILL					
❏ 4337	Fool Like You/Thinking About You	1973	—	2.50	5.00
ASYLUM					
❏ 45208	Second Avenue/Aviation Man	1974	—	2.00	4.00
❏ 45214	Charmer/I'll Be Your Time	1974	—	2.00	4.00

M

Number	Title (A Side/B Side)	Yr	VG	VG+	NM
❏ 45214 [PS]	Charmer/I'll Be Your Time	1974	—	3.00	6.00
❏ 45265	If Somebody Needs It/Sweet Navel Lightning	1975	—	2.00	4.00
❏ 45276	Rock and Roll Love Letter/	1975			
	Sweet Navel Lightning	1975	—	2.00	4.00
❏ 45287	Lay Down the Line to Me/Sweet Navel Lightning	1975	—	2.00	4.00
❏ 45394	In the Middle/Strengthen My Love	1977	—	2.00	4.00
❏ 45427	Second Avenue/Strengthen My Love	1977	—	2.00	4.00
❏ 46047	Fallen Angel/Crisis in the Finyard	1979	—	2.00	4.00

Albums

A SMALL RECORD COMPANY

Number	Title (A Side/B Side)	Yr	VG	VG+	NM
❏ SRS-10001	Tim Moore	1974	7.50	15.00	30.00

ABC DUNHILL

❏ DSX-50132	Of Woodstock and Other Places	1973	3.00	6.00	12.00

ASYLUM

❏ 6E-179	High Contrast	1979	2.50	5.00	10.00
❏ 7E-1019	Tim Moore	1974	2.50	5.00	10.00
❏ 7E-1042	Behind the Eyes	1975	2.50	5.00	10.00
❏ 7E-1088	White Shadows	1977	2.50	5.00	10.00

ELEKTRA

❏ 60463	Flash Forward	1985	2.50	5.00	10.00

MORGAN, JANE

45s

ABC

Number	Title (A Side/B Side)	Yr	VG	VG+	NM
❏ 10969	Somebody Someplace/				
	This Is My World Without You	1967	—	3.00	6.00
❏ 11002	Him's a Dope/I Promise You	1967	—	3.00	6.00
❏ 11024	The Marvelous Toy/Smile	1967	—	3.00	6.00
❏ 11034	Masquerade/Smile	1968	—	2.50	5.00
❏ 11054	My Funny Valentine/A Child	1968	—	2.50	5.00
❏ 11092	Look What You've Done to Me/				
	There's Nothing Else in My Mind	1968	—	2.50	5.00

COLPIX

❏ 713	Does Goodnight Mean Goodbye/Bless 'Em All	1963	2.00	4.00	8.00
❏ 713 [PS]	Does Goodnight Mean Goodbye/Bless 'Em All	1963	3.00	6.00	12.00
❏ 727	Frum Russia with Love/The Song from Moulin				
	Rouge (Where Is Your Heart)	1964	2.00	4.00	8.00
❏ 734	C'est Si Bon/Once Upon a Summertime	1964	2.00	4.00	8.00
❏ 754	Dominique/Funny World	1964	2.00	4.00	8.00
❏ 755	The Poor People of Paris/Funny World	1964	2.00	4.00	8.00
❏ 761	After the Fall/Oh, How I Lie	1965	2.00	4.00	8.00

EPIC

❏ 9819	Maybe/Walking the Streets in the Rain	1965	2.00	4.00	8.00
❏ 9847	Side by Side/Till I Waltz Again with You	1965	2.00	4.00	8.00
❏ 9881	Little Hands/Everyone Come to My Party	1965	2.00	4.00	8.00
❏ 10012	I Will Wait for You/Love Me True	1966	—	3.00	6.00
❏ 10032	Kiss Away/1-2-3	1966	—	3.00	6.00
❏ 10058	Elusive Butterfly/Good Lovin'	1966	—	3.00	6.00
❏ 10113	Kiss Tomorrow Goodbye/Now and Forever	1966	—	3.00	6.00
❏ 10159	The Three Bells/I Want to Be with You	1967	—	3.00	6.00

KAPP

❏ KJB-12	Love Makes the World Go 'Round/				
	Fly Me to the Moon	196?	—	3.50	7.00
❏ KJB-14	Fascination/The Day the Rains Came	196?	—	3.00	6.00

—"Winners Circle Series" reissue

❏ KJB-14 [PS]	Fascination/The Day the Rains Came	196?	2.50	5.00	10.00
❏ 104	Baseball, Baseball/Fairweather Friends	1954	3.75	7.50	15.00
❏ 111	I Try to Forget You/				
	Why Don't They Leave Us Alone	1955	3.00	6.00	12.00
❏ 115	Flyin' High/Give Me Your World	1955	3.00	6.00	12.00
❏ 121	In Paree/Take Me Away	1955	3.00	6.00	12.00
❏ 140	Let's Go Steady/Take Care	1956	3.00	6.00	12.00
❏ 148	La Ronde/Midnight Blues	1956	3.00	6.00	12.00
❏ 161	Two Different Worlds/Nights in Verona	1956	2.50	5.00	10.00

—With Roger Williams

❏ 172	Come Home, Come Home, Come Home/From				
	the First Hello to Our Last Goodbye	1957	2.50	5.00	10.00
❏ 185	It's Not for Me to Say/Around the World	1957	2.50	5.00	10.00
❏ 191	Fascination/(Instrumental)	1957	2.50	5.00	10.00
❏ 191 [PS]	Fascination/(Instrumental)	1957	5.00	10.00	20.00
❏ 191 [PS]	Fascination/(Instrumental)	1957	7.50	15.00	30.00

—With photos of Gary Cooper, Audrey Hepburn and Jane Morgan on sleeve

❏ 200	It's Been a Long, Long Time/I'm New at the				
	Game of Romance	1957	2.50	5.00	10.00
❏ 214	Only One Love/I've Got Bells on My Heart	1958	2.50	5.00	10.00
❏ 221	Enchanted Island/				
	Once More, My Love, Once More	1958	2.50	5.00	10.00
❏ 235	The Day the Rains Came/The Day the Rains				
	Came (French Version)	1958	2.50	5.00	10.00
❏ 236	You'll Never Walk Alone/I May Never Pass This				
	Way Again	1958	2.50	5.00	10.00
❏ 253	To Love and Be Loved/If Only I Could Live My				
	Life Again	1958	2.50	5.00	10.00
❏ 264	To Each His Own/Love Is Like Champagne	1959	2.50	5.00	10.00
❏ 284	With Open Arms/I Can't Begin to Tell You	1959	2.50	5.00	10.00
❏ 284 [PS]	With Open Arms/I Can't Begin to Tell You	1959	3.75	7.50	15.00
❏ 304	I'm in Love/Was It Day, Was It Night	1959	2.50	5.00	10.00
❏ 305	Happy Anniversary/C'est La Vie, C'est L'Amour	1959	2.50	5.00	10.00
❏ 305 [PS]	Happy Anniversary/C'est La Vie, C'est L'Amour	1959	3.75	7.50	15.00
❏ 317	The Bells of St. Mary's/Ballad of Lady Jane	1960	2.50	5.00	10.00
❏ 332	I Am a Heart/Romantica	1960	2.50	5.00	10.00
❏ 351	Lord and Master/Where's the Boy (I Never Met)	1960	2.50	5.00	10.00
❏ 358	The Angry Sea/Somebody	1960	2.50	5.00	10.00
❏ 369	Jerusalem/Jerusalem (French Version)	1961	2.00	4.00	8.00
❏ 390	Love Makes the World Go 'Round/				
	He Makes Me Feel I'm Lonely	1961	2.00	4.00	8.00
❏ 418	It Takes Love/Homesick for New England	1961	2.00	4.00	8.00
❏ 431	Moon River/Blue Hawaii	1961	2.00	4.00	8.00
❏ 450	What Now My Love/Forever My Love	1962	2.00	4.00	8.00
❏ 478	Ask Me to Dance/				
	Waiting for Charlie to Come Home	1962	2.00	4.00	8.00
❏ AS-924X [DJ]	The Second Time Around (same on both sides)	1961	5.00	10.00	20.00
❏ AS-928X [DJ]	Black Coffee/Guess I'll Hang My Tears Out to				
	Dry	1962	5.00	10.00	20.00

—"Special Disc Jockey Record" and "Album Sample"

RCA VICTOR

❏ 47-9727	Congratulations, I Guess/All of My Laughter	1969	—	2.50	5.00

Number	Title (A Side/B Side)	Yr	VG	VG+	NM
❏ 47-9839	A Girl Named Johnny Cash/Charley	1970	—	2.50	5.00
❏ 47-9901	The First Day/I'm Only a Woman	1970	—	2.50	5.00
❏ 74-0153	Marry Me, Marry Me/Three Rest Stops	1969	—	2.50	5.00
❏ 74-0194	Traces/Where Do I Go	1969	—	2.50	5.00
❏ 74-0316	He Gives Me Love/He's Never Too Busy	1970	—	2.50	5.00
❏ 74-0395	Jamie Boy/Things of Life	1970	—	2.50	5.00

7-Inch Extended Plays

EPIC

❏ 5-26166 [PS]	In My Style	1965	2.50	5.00	10.00
❏ 5-26166 [S]	I'm Sorry/You Belong to Me/Downtown//				
	Fascination/Why Don't You Believe Me/We'll				
	Sing in the Sunshine	1965	2.50	5.00	10.00

—33 1/3 rpm, small hole, "For Jukebox Use Only"

KAPP

❏ SE-405	The Day the Rains Came/Everybody Loves a				
	Lover//It's All in the Game/Wrap Your Troubles				
	in Dreams	1959	6.25	12.50	25.00

—Stereo, large hole

❏ SE-405 [PS]	(title unknown)	1959	6.25	12.50	25.00
❏ SE-406	You'll Never Walk Alone/Dancing in the Dark//				
	Catch a Falling Star/Melodie d'Amour	1959	6.25	12.50	25.00

—Stereo, large hole

❏ SE-406 [PS]	(title unknown)	1959	6.25	12.50	25.00
❏ KE-731	From the First Hello to the Last Goodbye/Come				
	Home, Come Home, Come Home//I'll Be				
	Seeing You/Thanks for the Memory	1957	3.75	7.50	15.00
❏ KE-731 [PS]	From the First Hello to the Last Goodbye	1957	3.75	7.50	15.00
❏ KE-747	Fascination/It's Not for Me to Say//My Heart				
	Reminds Me/An Affair to Remember	1957	3.75	7.50	15.00
❏ KE-747 [PS]	Fascination	1957	3.75	7.50	15.00
❏ KE-752	All the Way/Till//Melodie d'Amour				
	(Song of Love)/Tammy	1958	3.75	7.50	15.00
❏ KE-752 [PS]	All the Way	1958	3.75	7.50	15.00
❏ KE-758	The Day the Rains Came/Volare//It's All in the				
	Game/Everybody Loves a Lover	1958	3.75	7.50	15.00
❏ KE-758 [PS]	Jane Morgan	1958	3.75	7.50	15.00
❏ KBS 958	Moon River/With Open Arms/Wrap Your				
	Troubles in Dreams//The Day the Rains Came/				
	Blue Hawaii/The Second Time Around	196?	3.75	7.50	15.00

—Jukebox edition; small hole, plays at 33 1/3 rpm

❏ KBS 958 [PS]	More Golden Hits	196?	3.75	7.50	15.00

Albums

ABC

❏ S-638	A Jane Morgan Happening	1968	3.00	6.00	12.00

COLPIX

❏ CP 469 [M]	The Last Time I Saw Paris	1964	5.00	10.00	20.00
❏ SCP 469 [S]	The Last Time I Saw Paris	1964	6.25	12.50	25.00
❏ CP 497 [M]	The Jane Morgan Album	1966	3.75	7.50	15.00
❏ SCP 497 [S]	The Jane Morgan Album	1966	5.00	10.00	20.00

EPIC

❏ LN 24166 [M]	In My Style	1965	3.00	6.00	12.00
❏ LN 24190 [M]	Today's Hits…Tomorrow's Golden Favorites	1966	3.00	6.00	12.00
❏ LN 24211 [M]	Fresh Flavor	1966	3.00	6.00	12.00
❏ LN 24247 [M]	Kiss Tomorrow Goodbye	1967	3.75	7.50	15.00
❏ BN 26166 [S]	In My Style	1965	3.75	7.50	15.00
❏ BN 26190 [S]	Today's Hits…Tomorrow's Golden Favorites	1966	3.75	7.50	15.00
❏ BN 26211 [S]	Fresh Flavor	1966	3.75	7.50	15.00
❏ BN 26247 [S]	Kiss Tomorrow Goodbye	1967	3.00	6.00	12.00

HARMONY

❏ HS 11398	Sounds of Silence	1970	2.50	5.00	10.00

KAPP

❏ KJM-1 [DJ]	Radio Station Sampler	196?	6.25	12.50	25.00

—Promo only, gatefold cover

❏ KL-1023 [M]	Jane Morgan	1956	7.50	15.00	30.00
❏ KL-1066 [M]	Fascination	1957	7.50	15.00	30.00
❏ KL-1080 [M]	All the Way	1958	7.50	15.00	30.00
❏ KL-1089 [M]	Something Old, New, Borrowed, Blue	1958	7.50	15.00	30.00
❏ KL-1089S [S]	Something Old, New, Borrowed, Blue	1958	10.00	20.00	40.00
❏ KL-1093 [M]	Jane Morgan	1958	7.50	15.00	30.00
❏ KL-1105 [M]	The Day the Rains Came	1958	7.50	15.00	30.00
❏ KL-1105S [S]	The Day the Rains Came	1958	10.00	20.00	40.00
❏ KL-1129 [M]	Jane in Spain	1959	6.25	12.50	25.00
❏ KL-1170 [M]	Jane Morgan Time	1959	5.00	10.00	20.00
❏ KL-1191 [M]	Ballads of Lady Jane	1960	3.75	7.50	15.00
❏ KL-1239 [M]	Second Time Around	1961	3.75	7.50	15.00
❏ KL-1246 [M]	The Great Golden Hits	1961	3.75	7.50	15.00
❏ KL-1247 [M]	Big Hits from Broadway	1961	3.75	7.50	15.00
❏ KL-1250 [M]	Love Makes the World Go 'Round	1961	3.75	7.50	15.00
❏ KL-1268 [M]	Jane Morgan at the Cocoanut Grove	1962	3.75	7.50	15.00
❏ KL-1275 [M]	More Golden Hits	1962	3.75	7.50	15.00
❏ KL-1296 [M]	What Now My Love	1962	3.75	7.50	15.00
❏ KL-1329 [M]	Jane Morgan's Greatest Hits	1963	3.00	6.00	12.00
❏ KS-3001 [S]	Broadway in Stereo	1959	7.50	15.00	30.00
❏ KS-3014 [S]	Jane in Spain	1959	7.50	15.00	30.00
❏ KS-3017 [S]	Fascination	1959	7.50	15.00	30.00
❏ KS-3054 [S]	Jane Morgan Time	1959	6.25	12.50	25.00
❏ KS-3066 [S]	Fascination	1962	5.00	10.00	20.00
❏ KS-3191 [S]	Ballads of Lady Jane	1960	5.00	10.00	20.00
❏ KS-3239 [S]	Second Time Around	1961	5.00	10.00	20.00
❏ KS-3246 [S]	The Great Golden Hits	1961	5.00	10.00	20.00
❏ KS-3247 [S]	Big Hits from Broadway	1961	5.00	10.00	20.00
❏ KS-3250 [S]	Love Makes the World Go 'Round	1961	5.00	10.00	20.00
❏ KS-3268 [S]	Jane Morgan at the Cocoanut Grove	1962	5.00	10.00	20.00
❏ KS-3275 [S]	More Golden Hits	1962	5.00	10.00	20.00
❏ KS-3296 [S]	What Now My Love	1962	5.00	10.00	20.00
❏ KS-3329 [S]	Jane Morgan's Greatest Hits	1963	3.75	7.50	15.00
❏ UXL-5006 [(2)M]	Great Songs from the				
	Great Shows of the Century	195?	10.00	20.00	40.00

MCA

❏ 537	Jane Morgan's Greatest Hits	197?	2.50	5.00	10.00

RCA VICTOR

❏ LSP-4171	Traces of Love	1969	3.00	6.00	12.00
❏ LSP-4322	Jane Morgan in Nashville	1970	3.00	6.00	12.00

Number	Title (A Side/B Side)	Yr	VG	VG+	NM

MORGAN, LOUMELL
45s
ATLANTIC

| ❏ 953 | Charmaine/Jock-O-Mo | 1952 | 50.00 | 100.00 | 200.00 |

MORGAN TWINS, THE
45s
RCA VICTOR

| ❏ 47-7300 | TV Hop/This Feeling's Bound to Be Love | 1958 | 6.25 | 12.50 | 25.00 |
| ❏ 47-7373 | Let's Get Goin'/While It Lasted | 1958 | 6.25 | 12.50 | 25.00 |

MORGEN
45s
PROBE

| ❏ 474 | Of Dreams/She's the Nighttime | 1969 | 5.00 | 10.00 | 20.00 |

Albums
PROBE

| ❏ CPLP-4507 | Morgen | 1969 | 37.50 | 75.00 | 150.00 |

MORLEY, COZY
45s
ABC-PARAMOUNT

| ❏ 9811 | I Love My Girl/Why Don't You Fall in Love | 1957 | 6.25 | 12.50 | 25.00 |

MORLY GREY
Albums
STARSHINE

| ❏ 69000 | The Only Truth | 1969 | 50.00 | 100.00 | 200.00 |

MORNING DEW, THE
Albums
ROULETTE

| ❏ SR-42049 | The Morning Dew | 1970 | 75.00 | 150.00 | 300.00 |

MORNING GLORY
45s
FONTANA

| ❏ 1613 | Need Someone/I See a Light | 1968 | 2.50 | 5.00 | 10.00 |

Albums
FONTANA

| ❏ SRF-67573 | Two Suns Worth | 1968 | 6.25 | 12.50 | 25.00 |

MORNINGLORY
Albums
TOYA

| ❏ STLP-003 | Growing | 1972 | 10.00 | 20.00 | 40.00 |

MORRIS, JOE
45s
ATLANTIC

| ❏ 914 | Any Time, Any Place, Any Where/Come Back Daddy Daddy | 1950 | 125.00 | 250.00 | 500.00 |

—With Laura Tate; Atlantic's earliest number on 45; Morris' 78s on Atlantic before 914 were not issued on 45

| ❏ 985 | I'm Goin' to Leave You/That's What Makes My Baby Fat | 1953 | 25.00 | 50.00 | 100.00 |
| ❏ 1160 | Going, Going, Gone/Sinner Woman | 1957 | 5.00 | 10.00 | 20.00 |

HERALD

| ❏ 420 | Travelin' Man/No, It Can't Be Done | 1954 | 10.00 | 20.00 | 40.00 |

—Black vinyl

| ❏ 420 | Travelin' Man/No, It Can't Be Done | 1954 | 20.00 | 40.00 | 80.00 |

—Red vinyl

| ❏ 446 | Be Careful/Way Down Yonder | 1955 | 7.50 | 15.00 | 30.00 |

MORRISON, VAN
12-Inch Singles
MERCURY

| ❏ 447 [DJ] | Got to Go Back (same on both sides) | 1986 | — | 3.00 | 6.00 |

WARNER BROS.

| ❏ PRO-A-755 [DJ] | Wavelength (6:07) (3:57) | 1978 | 3.75 | 7.50 | 15.00 |
| ❏ PRO-A-911 [DJ] | Summertime in England (Edit)/Haunts | 1980 | 2.50 | 5.00 | 10.00 |

45s
BANG

❏ 545	Brown Eyed Girl/Goodbye, Baby	1967	3.00	6.00	12.00
❏ 552	Chick-a-Boom/Ro Ro Rosey	1967	2.50	5.00	10.00
❏ 585	Spanish Rose/Midnight Special	1971	2.00	4.00	8.00

MERCURY

❏ 880669-7	Haunts of Ancient Peace/Tore Down A La Rimbaud	1985	—	2.00	4.00
❏ 884841-7	Ivory Tower/New Kind of Man	1986	—	2.00	4.00
❏ 884841-7 [PS]	Ivory Tower/New Kind of Man	1986	—	2.00	4.00

PHILCO-FORD

| ❏ HP-16 | Brown Eyed Girl/Midnight Special | 1968 | 5.00 | 10.00 | 20.00 |

—4-inch plastic "Hip Pocket Record" with color sleeve

POINTBLANK

| ❏ 38655 | Precious Time/Jackie Wilson Said (I'm in Heaven When You Smile) (Live) | 1999 | — | 2.00 | 4.00 |

POINTBLANK/VIRGIN/EXILE

| ❏ 38754 | No Way Pedro/Let's Talk About Us | 2000 | — | 2.00 | 4.00 |

—With Linda Gail Lewis

WARNER BROS.

❏ 7383	Come Running/Crazy Love	1970	—	3.00	6.00
❏ 7434	Domino/Sweet Janine	1970	—	3.00	6.00
❏ 7462	Blue Money/Sweet Thing	1971	—	3.00	6.00
❏ 7488	Call Me Up in Dreamland/Street Choir	1971	—	3.00	6.00
❏ 7518	Wild Night/When That Evening Sun Goes Down	1971	—	3.00	6.00
❏ 7543	Tupelo Honey/Starting a New Life	1971	—	3.00	6.00
❏ 7573	Straight to My Heart Like a Cannonball/Old Old Woodstock	1972	—	2.50	5.00
❏ 7616	Jackie Wilson Said (I'm in Heaven When You Smile)/You've Got the Power	1972	—	2.50	5.00
❏ 7638	Redwood Tree/Saint Dominic's Preview	1972	—	2.50	5.00
❏ 7665	Gypsy/Saint Dominic's Preview	1972	—	2.50	5.00
❏ 7706	Warm Love/I Will Be There	1973	—	2.50	5.00
❏ 7744	Green/Wild Children	1973	—	2.50	5.00
❏ 7786	Gloria/(B-side unknown)	1973	—	2.50	5.00
❏ 7797	Ain't Nothin' You Can Do/Wild Children	1974	—	2.50	5.00

Number	Title (A Side/B Side)	Yr	VG	VG+	NM

❏ 8029	Bulbs/Cul-De-Sac	1974	—	2.50	5.00
❏ 8411	Joyous Sound/Mechanical Bliss	1977	—	2.50	5.00
❏ 8450	Moondance/Cold Wind in August	1977	—	2.50	5.00
❏ 8661	Wavelength/Checkin' It Out	1978	—	2.50	5.00
❏ 8743	Lifetimes/Natalia	1979	—	2.00	4.00
❏ 8805	Checkin' It Out/Kingdom Hall	1979	—	2.00	4.00
❏ 49086	Rolling Hills/Bright Side of the Road	1979	—	2.00	4.00
❏ 49162	Full Force Gale/You Make Me Feel So Free	1980	—	2.00	4.00
❏ 50031	Scandinavia/Cleaning Windows	1982	—	2.00	4.00

Albums
BANG

| ❏ BLB-218 [M] | Blowin' Your Mind | 1968 | 12.50 | 25.00 | 50.00 |

—With the censored "Brown Eyed Girl" lyric, "Laughin' and a-runnin', hey hey, behind the stadium with you," part of which was spliced in from another part of the song. This has been confirmed to exist in mono.

| ❏ BLBS-218 [S] | Blowin' Your Mind | 1968 | 5.00 | 10.00 | 20.00 |

—With the censored "Brown Eyed Girl" lyric, "Laughin' and a-runnin', hey hey, behind the stadium with you," part of which was spliced in from another part of the song!

| ❏ BLP-218 [M] | Blowin' Your Mind | 1967 | 7.50 | 15.00 | 30.00 |

—With the true "Brown Eyed Girl" lyric, "Makin' love in the green grass behind the stadium with you."

| ❏ BLPS-218 [S] | Blowin' Your Mind | 1967 | 10.00 | 20.00 | 40.00 |

—With the true "Brown Eyed Girl" lyric, "Makin' love in the green grass behind the stadium with you."

| ❏ BLPS-222 | The Best of Van Morrison | 1970 | 3.75 | 7.50 | 15.00 |
| ❏ BLPS-400 | T.B. Sheets | 1973 | 5.00 | 10.00 | 20.00 |

DIRECT DISK

| ❏ SD-16604 | Moondance | 1981 | 25.00 | 50.00 | 100.00 |

—Audiophile vinyl

MERCURY

❏ 818336-1	Live at the Grand Opera House, Belfast	1985	2.50	5.00	10.00
❏ 822895-1	A Sense of Wonder	1985	2.00	4.00	8.00
❏ 830077-1	No Guru, No Method, No Teacher	1986	2.00	4.00	8.00
❏ 832585-1	Poetic Champions Compose	1987	2.00	4.00	8.00
❏ 834496-1	Irish Heartbeat	1988	2.00	4.00	8.00

—With the Chieftains

❏ 839262-1	Avalon Sunset	1989	2.50	5.00	10.00
❏ 841970-1	The Best of Van Morrison	1990	3.75	7.50	15.00
❏ 847100-1	Enlightenment	1990	3.75	7.50	15.00

WARNER BROS.

| ❏ WBMS-102 [DJ] | Live at the Roxy | 1978 | 12.50 | 25.00 | 50.00 |
| ❏ WS 1768 | Astral Weeks | 1968 | 6.25 | 12.50 | 25.00 |

—With "W7" logo on green label

| ❏ WS 1768 | Astral Weeks | 1970 | 3.00 | 6.00 | 12.00 |

—With "WB" logo on green label

| ❏ WS 1768 | Astral Weeks | 1973 | 2.50 | 5.00 | 10.00 |

—"Burbank" palm-tree label

| ❏ WS 1768 | Astral Weeks | 1979 | 2.00 | 4.00 | 8.00 |

—Later white or tan label

| ❏ WS 1835 | Moondance | 1969 | 5.00 | 10.00 | 20.00 |

—With "W7" logo on green label

| ❏ WS 1835 | Moondance | 1970 | 3.00 | 6.00 | 12.00 |

—With "WB" logo on green label

| ❏ WS 1835 | Moondance | 1973 | 2.50 | 5.00 | 10.00 |

—"Burbank" palm-tree label

| ❏ WS 1884 | His Band and the Street Choir | 1970 | 3.75 | 7.50 | 15.00 |

—With "WB" logo on green label

| ❏ WS 1884 | His Band and the Street Choir | 1973 | 2.50 | 5.00 | 10.00 |

—"Burbank" palm-tree label

| ❏ WS 1884 | His Band and the Street Choir | 1979 | 2.00 | 4.00 | 8.00 |

—Later white or tan label

| ❏ WS 1950 | Tupelo Honey | 1971 | 3.75 | 7.50 | 15.00 |

—With "WB" logo on green label, plus poster

| ❏ WS 1950 | Tupelo Honey | 1973 | 2.50 | 5.00 | 10.00 |

—"Burbank" palm-tree label

| ❏ WS 1950 | Tupelo Honey | 1979 | 2.00 | 4.00 | 8.00 |

—Later white or tan label

| ❏ WS 2633 | Saint Dominic's Preview | 1972 | 3.75 | 7.50 | 15.00 |

—With "WB" logo on green label

| ❏ WS 2633 | Saint Dominic's Preview | 1973 | 2.50 | 5.00 | 10.00 |

—"Burbank" palm-tree label

| ❏ WS 2633 | Saint Dominic's Preview | 1979 | 2.00 | 4.00 | 8.00 |

—Later white or tan label

| ❏ BS 2712 | Hard Nose the Highway | 1973 | 3.00 | 6.00 | 12.00 |

—"Burbank" palm-tree label

| ❏ BS 2712 | Hard Nose the Highway | 1979 | 2.00 | 4.00 | 8.00 |

—Later white or tan label

| ❏ 2BS 2760 [(2)] | It's Too Late to Stop Now | 1974 | 3.75 | 7.50 | 15.00 |

—"Burbank" palm-tree labels

| ❏ 2BS 2760 [(2)] | It's Too Late to Stop Now | 1979 | 2.00 | 4.00 | 8.00 |

—Later white or tan label

| ❏ BS 2805 | Veedon Fleece | 1974 | 3.00 | 6.00 | 12.00 |

—"Burbank" palm-tree labels

| ❏ BS 2805 | Veedon Fleece | 1979 | 2.00 | 4.00 | 8.00 |

—Later white or tan label

| ❏ BS 2987 | A Period of Transition | 1977 | 3.00 | 6.00 | 12.00 |

—"Burbank" palm-tree label

| ❏ BS 2987 | A Period of Transition | 1979 | 2.00 | 4.00 | 8.00 |

—Later white or tan label

| ❏ BSK 3103 | Moondance | 1977 | 2.50 | 5.00 | 10.00 |

—Reissue with new number; "Burbank" palm-tree label

| ❏ BSK 3103 | Moondance | 1979 | 2.00 | 4.00 | 8.00 |

—Later white or tan label

❏ BSK 3212	Wavelength	1978	3.00	6.00	12.00
❏ HS 3390	Into the Music	1979	3.00	6.00	12.00
❏ BSK 3462	Common One	1980	3.00	6.00	12.00
❏ BSK 3652	Beautiful Vision	1981	3.00	6.00	12.00
❏ 23802	Inarticulate Speech of the Heart	1983	3.00	6.00	12.00

MORTIMER
45s
PHILIPS

❏ 40524	Dedicated Music Man/To Understand Someone	1968	2.00	4.00	8.00
❏ 40524 [PS]	Dedicated Music Man/To Understand Someone	1968	3.00	6.00	12.00
❏ 40567	Ingenue's Theme/Slicker Beauty Hints	1968	2.00	4.00	8.00

Albums
PHILIPS

| ❏ PHS 600267 | Mortimer | 1969 | 6.25 | 12.50 | 25.00 |

M

Number	Title (A Side/B Side)	Yr	VG	VG+	NM
MORTIMER, AZIE					
45s					
BIG TOP					
❏ 3041	Lips/Wrapped Up in a Dream	1960	100.00	200.00	400.00
EPIC					
❏ 5-9584	Cry Me a River/Little Boy (I Keep On Changing My Mind)	1963	5.00	10.00	20.00
OKEH					
❏ 4-7336	You Can't Take It Away/ A One Way Love (Is a Wrong Way Love)	1970	3.00	6.00	12.00
❏ 4-7337	I Don't Care/Prove It	1970	3.00	6.00	12.00
PALETTE					
❏ 5097	Mama, What Should I Do/ When You're Talking Love	1962	5.00	10.00	20.00
—As "A.Z. Mortimer"					
RCA VICTOR					
❏ 47-8985	Little Miss Everything/Best Years	1966	3.75	7.50	15.00
REGATTA					
❏ 2002	Brother Love/Treat Me Like You Love Me	1961	6.25	12.50	25.00
SWAN					
❏ 4158	Put Yourself in My Place/Bring Back Your Love	1963	3.75	7.50	15.00
TROY					
❏ 103	Little Soldier/Battle Hymn of the Republic	196?	6.25	12.50	25.00
❏ 104	Forever Kind of Love/Little Playboy	196?	6.25	12.50	25.00
❏ 105	Untouched by Human Love/Bring Back Your Love	196?	6.25	12.50	25.00
❏ 106	Little Old Lady/Cool It	196?	6.25	12.50	25.00
UNITED ARTISTS					
❏ 826	The Other Half of Me/Next Time	1965	—	—	—
—Canceled					
❏ 838	(I Get the Feeling) You're Ashamed of Me/ Deeper in My Heart	1965	—	—	—
—Canceled					
❏ 847	The Other Half of Me/(I Get the Feeling) You're Ashamed of Me	1965	10.00	20.00	40.00
MOSBY, JOHNNY AND JONIE					
45s					
CAPITOL					
❏ 2087	Mr. and Mrs. John Smith/Hello There Stranger	1968	—	3.00	6.00
❏ 2179	Our Golden Wedding Day/Two Dollar Honeymoon Room	1968	—	3.00	6.00
❏ 2258	Come In the Back Door (Go 'Round, Go 'Round)/ You Be the Mama, I'll Be the Papa	1968	—	3.00	6.00
❏ 2384	Just Hold My Hand/Walkin' Papers	1969	—	3.00	6.00
❏ 2505	Hold Me, Thrill Me, Kiss Me/ Comparing Him with You	1969	—	3.00	6.00
❏ 2608	I'll Never Be Free/Pattern of Our Lives	1969	—	3.00	6.00
❏ 2730	Third World/You Go Back to Your World (I'll Go Back to Mine)	1970	—	3.00	6.00
❏ 2796	I'm Leavin' It Up to You/If It's Left Up to Me	1970	—	3.00	6.00
❏ 2865	My Happiness/Let Your Sun Shine on Me	1970	—	3.00	6.00
❏ 2865 [PS]	My Happiness/Let Your Sun Shine on Me	1970	2.50	5.00	10.00
❏ 2978	A Little of Me, A Little of You/ Someone to Take My Place	1970	—	3.00	6.00
❏ 3039	Oh, Love of Mine/Closing Time Till Dawn	1971	—	3.00	6.00
❏ 3141	Let's Get This Show on the Road/ Souvenirs of Love	1971	—	3.00	6.00
❏ 3219	Just One More Time/Meet Me Tonight	1971	—	3.00	6.00
❏ 3277	Music to My Ears/I'll Say It Again	1972	—	3.00	6.00
❏ 3332	My Ecstasy/Ain't You Ever	1972	—	3.00	6.00
❏ 3613	Let's Try Love Again/It's All Because of You	1973	—	3.00	6.00
❏ 5980	Make a Left and Then a Right/ Take Back the World	1967	—	3.00	6.00
CHALLENGE					
❏ 59088	He Wouldn't Take Me Home to Meet His Mother/ Hard Luck and Misery	1960	3.75	7.50	15.00
COLUMBIA					
❏ 42668	Don't Call Me from a Honky Tonk/ Wrong Side of Town	1963	2.50	5.00	10.00
❏ 42841	Trouble in My Arms/Who's Been Cheatin' Who	1963	2.50	5.00	10.00
❏ 43005	Keep Those Cards and Letters Coming In/ Take Me Home	1964	2.50	5.00	10.00
❏ 43100	How the Other Half Lives/Stolen Paradise	1964	2.50	5.00	10.00
❏ 43218	Strawberry Wine/Wrong Company	1965	2.00	4.00	8.00
❏ 43344	The High Cost of Loving/ The Home She's Tearing Down	1965	2.00	4.00	8.00
❏ 43631	Heartbreak U.S.A./Identity	1966	2.00	4.00	8.00
TOPPA					
❏ 1034	Unreceived, Address Unknown/A Cup of Coffee	1961	3.75	7.50	15.00
❏ 1039	Making Believe/Ain't You Ever	1961	3.75	7.50	15.00
❏ 1047	Dear Okie/You Can't Hurt Me Anymore	1962	3.75	7.50	15.00
Albums					
CAPITOL					
❏ ST-170	Just Hold My Hand	1969	3.75	7.50	15.00
❏ ST-286	Hold Me	1969	3.75	7.50	15.00
❏ ST-414	I'll Never Be Free	1970	3.75	7.50	15.00
❏ ST-556	My Happiness	1970	3.75	7.50	15.00
❏ ST-737	Oh, Love of Mine	1971	3.75	7.50	15.00
❏ ST 2903	Make a Left and Then a Right	1968	3.75	7.50	15.00
COLUMBIA					
❏ CL 2297 [M]	Mr. & Mrs. Country Music	1965	3.75	7.50	15.00
❏ CS 9097 [S]	Mr. & Mrs. Country Music	1965	5.00	10.00	20.00
HARMONY					
❏ HS 11389	Mr. & Mrs. Country Music	1970	2.50	5.00	10.00
STARDAY					
❏ SLP-328 [M]	The New Sweethearts of Country Music	1965	7.50	15.00	30.00
MOSES, JOHNNY					
45s					
IMPERIAL					
❏ 5329	You're Torturing Me/Do You Love Me? Do You?	1955	10.00	20.00	40.00
MOSES, LEE					
45s					
FRONT PAGE					
❏ 2301	Time and Place/I Can't Take No Chances	1970	5.00	10.00	20.00
GATES					
❏ 1502	Bad Girl/Dark End of the Street	1967	20.00	40.00	80.00
MUSICOR					
❏ 1242	Bad Girl (Part 1)/(Part 2)	1967	7.50	15.00	30.00
MOSLEY, BOB					
Albums					
REPRISE					
❏ MS 2068	Bob Mosley	1972	5.00	10.00	20.00
MOSS, ROY					
45s					
FASCINATION					
❏ 1002	Wiggle Walkin' Baby/(B-side unknown)	1957	50.00	100.00	200.00
MERCURY					
❏ 70770	You're My Big Baby Now/ You Nearly Lost Your Mind	1955	50.00	100.00	200.00
❏ 70858	Corinne, Corrina/You Don't Know My Mind	1956	50.00	100.00	200.00
MOST, MICKIE					
45s					
LAWN					
❏ 236	Sea Cruise/It's a Little Bit Hot	1964	5.00	10.00	20.00
MOTHER EARTH Also see TRACY NELSON.					
45s					
MERCURY					
❏ 72878	Down So Long/Goodbye Nelda Greeby	1968	2.00	4.00	8.00
❏ 72909	Mother Earth/I Did My Part	1969	2.00	4.00	8.00
❏ 72943	Painted Girls and Wine/Your Time's Comin'	1969	2.00	4.00	8.00
REPRISE					
❏ 1019	Soul of Sadness/ Temptation Took Control of Me and I Fell	1971	—	3.00	6.00
❏ 1041	I'll Be Long Gone/Bring Me Home	1971	—	3.00	6.00
UNITED ARTISTS					
❏ 50303	Revolution/Stranger in My Own Home	1968	2.50	5.00	10.00
Albums					
MERCURY					
❏ SR-61194	Living with the Animals	1968	6.25	12.50	25.00
❏ SR-61226	Make a Joyful Noise	1969	5.00	10.00	20.00
❏ SR-61230	Tracy Nelson Country	1969	5.00	10.00	20.00
❏ SR-61270	Satisfied	1970	5.00	10.00	20.00
REPRISE					
❏ MS 2054	Tracy Nelson/Mother Earth	1972	3.75	7.50	15.00
❏ RS 6431	Bring Me Home	1971	3.75	7.50	15.00
MOTHERLODE					
45s					
BUDDAH					
❏ 131	When I Die/Hard Life	1969	2.00	4.00	8.00
❏ 144	What Does It Take (To Win Your Love)/ Memories of a Broken Promise	1969	—	3.00	6.00
❏ 185	I'm So Glad You're You, Not Me/Whippoorwill	1970	—	3.00	6.00
Albums					
BUDDAH					
❏ BDS-5046	When I Die	1969	3.75	7.50	15.00
❏ BDS-5108	Tapped Out	1970	3.75	7.50	15.00
MOTHERS OF INVENTION, THE See FRANK ZAPPA.					
MOTIONS, THE (1)					
45s					
ABC-PARAMOUNT					
❏ 10529	Big Chief/Where Is Your Heart	1964	3.00	6.00	12.00
CONGRESS					
❏ 237	It's Gone/I've Got Money	1965	3.00	6.00	12.00
MERCURY					
❏ 72297	Beatle Drums/Long Hair	1964	6.25	12.50	25.00
❏ 72368	I Can Dance/Land Beyond the Moon	1964	5.00	10.00	20.00
❏ 72413	Bumble Bee '65/Motions	1965	5.00	10.00	20.00
MOTIONS, THE (2)					
45s					
LAURIE					
❏ 3112	Make Me a Love/Mr. Night	1961	30.00	60.00	120.00
MOTIONS, THE (3)					
45s					
PHILIPS					
❏ 40624	Freedom/What's Your Name	1969	2.00	4.00	8.00
Albums					
PHILIPS					
❏ PHS 600317	Electric Baby	1969	5.00	10.00	20.00
MOTT THE HOOPLE Also see IAN HUNTER.					
45s					
ATLANTIC					
❏ 2749	Rock and Roll Queen/Backsliding Fearlessly	1970	2.00	4.00	8.00
COLUMBIA					
❏ 3-10091	All the Young Dudes/Rose	1975	—	2.50	5.00
❏ 4-45673	All the Young Dudes/One of the Boys	1972	—	3.00	6.00
—A-side is the British single version with "unlocked cars" lyric; matrix number in dead wax ends in "1" plus a letter					
❏ 4-45673	All the Young Dudes/One of the Boys	1972	2.00	4.00	8.00
—A-side is the LP version with "Marks and Sparks" lyric; matrix number in dead wax ends in the number "2" plus a letter					
❏ 4-45673 [PS]	All the Young Dudes/One of the Boys	1972	5.00	10.00	20.00
❏ 45754	One of the Boys/Sucker	1973	—	2.50	5.00
❏ 45784	Sweet Jane/Jerkin' Crocus	1973	—	2.50	5.00
❏ 45882	Honaloochie Boogie/Rose	1973	—	2.50	5.00

Number	Title (A Side/B Side)	Yr	VG	VG+	NM
❏ 45920	All the Way from Memphis/				
	I Wish I Was Your Mother	1973	—	2.50	5.00
❏ 46035	The Golden Age of Rock 'N' Roll/Rest in Peace	1974	—	2.50	5.00
❏ 46076	Roll Away the Stone/Looking Glass	1974	—	2.50	5.00
❏ 74712	All the Young Dudes/Hanoloochie Boogie	1992	—	—	3.00

—Reissue

Albums

ATLANTIC

❏ SD 7297	Rock and Roll Queen	1974	5.00	10.00	20.00
❏ SD 8258	Mott the Hoople	1970	5.00	10.00	20.00

—With "1841 Broadway" address and no mention of Warner Communications on label

❏ SD 8258	Mott the Hoople	198?	2.00	4.00	8.00

—With Warner Communications "W" logo on label

❏ SD 8272	Mad Shadows	1970	5.00	10.00	20.00
❏ SD 8284	Wildlife	1971	5.00	10.00	20.00
❏ SD 8304	Brain Capers	1972	5.00	10.00	20.00

COLUMBIA

❏ KC 31750	All the Young Dudes	1972	3.75	7.50	15.00
❏ PC 31750	All the Young Dudes	198?	2.00	4.00	8.00

—Budget-line reissue

❏ KC 32425	Mott	1973	3.75	7.50	15.00
❏ PC 32425	Mott	198?	2.00	4.00	8.00

—Budget-line reissue

❏ PC 32871	The Hoople	1974	3.75	7.50	15.00
❏ PCQ 32871 [Q]	The Hoople	1974	6.25	12.50	25.00
❏ PC 33282	Mott the Hoople Live	1974	3.75	7.50	15.00

—No bar code on cover

❏ PC 33282	Mott the Hoople Live	198?	2.00	4.00	8.00

—Reissue with bar code on cover

❏ PC 33705	Drive On	1975	3.75	7.50	15.00
❏ PC 34236	Shouting and Pointing	1976	3.75	7.50	15.00
❏ PC 34368	Mott the Hoople's Greatest Hits	1976	3.00	6.00	12.00

—No bar code on cover

❏ PC 34368	Mott the Hoople's Greatest Hits	198?	2.00	4.00	8.00

—Reissue with bar code on cover

MOTTOLA, TONY

45s

COMMAND

❏ 4024	Nina/Tra Vegila E Sonno	1962	2.00	4.00	8.00
❏ 4058	Michelle/Boulevard of Broken Dreams	1964	2.00	4.00	8.00
❏ 4076	Brasilia/Sabor A Mi	1965	2.00	4.00	8.00

PROJECT 3

❏ 1303	The Gang That Sang Heart of My Heart/				
	Georgia on My Mind	1967	—	3.00	6.00
❏ 1318	Call Me/The World of Your Embrace	1967	—	3.00	6.00
❏ 1323	Spanish Harlem/I Love, I Live, I Love	1968	—	3.00	6.00
❏ 1329	Somethin' Stupid/Lush and Lovely	1968	—	3.00	6.00
❏ 1337	Love in Every Room/This Guy's in Love with You	1968	—	3.00	6.00
❏ 1352	I've Gotta Be Me/Guitar Underground	1969	—	2.50	5.00
❏ 1355	I'll Never Fall in Love Again/				
	Those Were the Days	1969	—	2.50	5.00
❏ 1378	Something/Chewy Chewy Gum Gum	1970	—	2.50	5.00
❏ 1381	Tequila/Bluesette	1970	—	2.50	5.00
❏ 1402	It's Too Late/(B-side unknown)	1971	—	2.00	4.00
❏ 1413	Love/I Don't Know How to Love Him	1971	—	2.00	4.00
❏ 1430	Classical Gas/Galloping Guitars	197?	—	2.00	4.00
❏ 1431	Sugar Blues/Chicken A La Spring	197?	—	2.00	4.00
❏ 1437	Jelly Bean/One	197?	—	2.00	4.00
❏ 1438	Nadia's Theme/I Love My Wife	1976	—	2.00	4.00

Albums

ABC

❏ S-738	16 Great Performances	1972	2.50	5.00	10.00
❏ X-770	Mister Guitar	1973	2.50	5.00	10.00

COMMAND

❏ 33-807 [M]	Mr. Big	1961	3.00	6.00	12.00
❏ SD 807 [S]	Mr. Big	1961	3.75	7.50	15.00
❏ 33-816 [M]	Roman Guitar	1962	3.00	6.00	12.00
❏ SD 816 [S]	Roman Guitar	1962	3.75	7.50	15.00
❏ 33-823 [M]	Country and Western Folk Songs	1962	3.00	6.00	12.00
❏ SD 823 [S]	Country and Western Folk Songs	1962	3.75	7.50	15.00
❏ 33-828 [M]	String Band Strum-Along	1962	3.00	6.00	12.00
❏ SD 828 [S]	String Band Strum-Along	1962	3.75	7.50	15.00
❏ 33-836 [M]	Roman Guitar, Volume Two	1962	3.00	6.00	12.00
❏ SD 836 [S]	Roman Guitar, Volume Two	1962	3.75	7.50	15.00
❏ 33-841 [M]	Spanish Guitar	1963	3.00	6.00	12.00
❏ SD 841 [S]	Spanish Guitar	1963	3.75	7.50	15.00
❏ 33-847 [M]	Romantic Guitar	1963	3.00	6.00	12.00
❏ SD 847 [S]	Romantic Guitar	1963	3.75	7.50	15.00
❏ 33-864 [M]	Sentimental Guitar	1964	3.00	6.00	12.00
❏ SD 864 [S]	Sentimental Guitar	1964	3.75	7.50	15.00
❏ 33-877 [M]	Guitar — Paris	1964	3.00	6.00	12.00
❏ SD 877 [S]	Guitar — Paris	1964	3.75	7.50	15.00
❏ 33-885 [M]	Command Performance	1965	3.00	6.00	12.00
❏ SD 885 [S]	Command Performance	1965	3.75	7.50	15.00
❏ 33-889 [M]	Love Songs — Mexico/S.A.	1965	3.00	6.00	12.00
❏ SD 889 [S]	Love Songs — Mexico/S.A.	1965	3.75	7.50	15.00
❏ 33-900 [M]	Amor — Mexico/S.A.	1966	3.00	6.00	12.00
❏ SD 900 [S]	Amor — Mexico/S.A.	1966	3.75	7.50	15.00
❏ 33-908 [M]	Guitar — U.S.A.	1967	3.75	7.50	15.00
❏ SD 908 [S]	Guitar — U.S.A.	1967	3.00	6.00	12.00
❏ QD-40001 [Q]	Guitar — Paris	1972	5.00	10.00	20.00

PICKWICK

❏ SPC-3610	Spanish Guitar	1978	2.00	4.00	8.00

PROJECT 3

❏ PR-5003	Heart and Soul	1967	3.00	6.00	12.00
❏ PR-5010	A Latin Love-In	1967	3.00	6.00	12.00
❏ PR4C-5010 [Q]	A Latin Love-In	1973	4.50	9.00	18.00
❏ PR-5020	Lush, Latin & Lovely	1968	3.00	6.00	12.00
❏ PR4C-5020 [Q]	Lush, Latin & Lovely	1973	4.50	9.00	18.00
❏ PR-5025	Warm, Wild & Wonderful	1968	3.00	6.00	12.00
❏ PR4C-5025 [Q]	Warm, Wild & Wonderful	1973	4.50	9.00	18.00
❏ PR-5032	Roma Oggi/Rome Today	1969	3.00	6.00	12.00
❏ PR4C-5032 [Q]	Roma Oggi/Rome Today	1973	4.50	9.00	18.00
❏ PR-5035	Tony Mottola Joins the Guitar Underground	1969	3.00	6.00	12.00
❏ PR-5041	The Tony Touch	1970	3.00	6.00	12.00
❏ PR4C-5041 [Q]	The Tony Touch	1973	4.50	9.00	18.00

Number	Title (A Side/B Side)	Yr	VG	VG+	NM
❏ PR-5044	Tony Mottola's Guitar Factory	1970	3.00	6.00	12.00
❏ PR-5050	Close to You	1971	3.00	6.00	12.00
❏ PR-5058	Warm Feelings	1971	3.00	6.00	12.00
❏ PR-5062	Superstar Guitar	1972	3.00	6.00	12.00
❏ PR4C-5062 [Q]	Superstar Guitar	1973	3.75	7.50	15.00
❏ PR-5069	Tony and Strings	1973	3.00	6.00	12.00
❏ PR4C-5069 [Q]	Tony and Strings	1973	4.50	9.00	18.00
❏ PR-5074	Two Guitars	1974	2.50	5.00	10.00
❏ PR4C-5078 [Q]	Tony Mottola with the Quad Guitars	1974	3.75	7.50	15.00
❏ PR-5082	Tony Mottola with the Brass Menagerie	1974	3.00	6.00	12.00
❏ PR-5094	I Only Have Eyes for You	197?	2.50	5.00	10.00
❏ PR-5101	Goin' Out of My Head	197?	2.50	5.00	10.00
❏ PR-6007/8 [(2)]	Favorite Things: The Best of Tony Mottola	1975	3.75	7.50	15.00
❏ PR-6025/6 [(2)]	Feelings	198?	3.00	6.00	12.00
❏ PR-6031/2 [(2)]	The Best of Tony Mottola	198?	3.00	6.00	12.00

MOULTRY, MARY

45s

KING

❏ 6038	Last Year's Senior Prom/				
	They're Trying to Tear Us Apart	1966	7.50	15.00	30.00

MOUNT RUSHMORE

45s

DOT

❏ 17158	Stone Free/She's So Good to Me	1968	2.00	4.00	8.00

Albums

DOT

❏ DLP-25898	High on Mount Rushmore	1968	5.00	10.00	20.00
❏ DLP-25934	Mount Rushmore '69	1969	5.00	10.00	20.00

MOUNTAIN Also see FELIX PAPPALARDI; LESLIE WEST; WEST, BRUCE AND LAING.

45s

COLUMBIA

❏ 38-74711	Mississippi Queen/				
	The Animal Trainer and the Toad	1992	—	2.00	4.00

—Reissue

WINDFALL

❏ 532	Mississippi Queen/The Laird	1970	2.00	4.00	8.00
❏ 533	For Yasgur's Farm/To My Friend	1970	2.00	4.00	8.00
❏ 534	The Animal Trainer and the Toad/Tired Angels	1971	3.00	6.00	12.00
❏ 535	Silver Paper/Travelin' in the Dark	1971	2.50	5.00	10.00
❏ 536	Roll Over Beethoven/Crossroader	1971	2.50	5.00	10.00
❏ 537	Waiting to Take You Away/(B-side unknown)	1972	2.50	5.00	10.00

Albums

COLUMBIA

❏ CQ 32079 [Q]	The Best of Mountain	1973	5.00	10.00	20.00
❏ KC 32079	The Best of Mountain	1973	3.00	6.00	12.00
❏ PC 32079	The Best of Mountain	198?	2.00	4.00	8.00

—Budget-line reissue

❏ CG 32818 [(2)]	Twin Peaks	1974	3.75	7.50	15.00
❏ PG 32818 [(2)]	Twin Peaks	198?	2.50	5.00	10.00

—Budget-line reissue

❏ CQ 33008 [Q]	Avalanche	1974	5.00	10.00	20.00
❏ KC 33008	Avalanche	1974	3.00	6.00	12.00
❏ PC 33008	Avalanche	197?	2.00	4.00	8.00

—Budget-line reissue

SCOTTI BROTHERS

❏ FZ 40006	Go for Your Life	1985	2.50	5.00	10.00

WINDFALL

❏ 4501	Mountain Climbing!	1970	3.75	7.50	15.00
❏ 5500	Nantucket Sleighride	1971	3.75	7.50	15.00

—Deduct 20% if inserts are missing

❏ 5501	Flowers of Evil	1971	3.75	7.50	15.00
❏ 5502	Mountain Live (The Road Goes Ever On)	1972	3.75	7.50	15.00

MOUNTAIN BUS

Albums

GOOD

❏ 101	Sundance	1971	37.50	75.00	150.00

MOURNING REIGN, THE

45s

CONTOUR

❏ 601	Evil Hearted You/Get Out of My Life, Woman	1967	6.25	12.50	25.00

LINK

❏ 1	Satisfaction Guaranteed/Our Fate	1966	7.50	15.00	30.00
❏ 1 [PS]	Satisfaction Guaranteed/Our Fate	1966	150.00	300.00	600.00
❏ 2	Evil Hearted You/Get Out of My Life, Woman	1966	7.50	15.00	30.00

7-Inch Extended Plays

SUNDAZED

❏ SEP 115	*Satisfaction Guaranteed/Our Fate/Light				
	Switch/Cut Back	199?	—	—	2.00
❏ SEP 115 [PS]	The Mourning Reign	199?	—	—	2.00

Albums

BEAT ROCKET

❏ BR 102	The Mourning Reign	1999	3.00	6.00	12.00

MOUSE AND THE TRAPS

45s

CAPITOL

❏ 2460	Streets of a Dusty Town/Mouse	1969	2.50	5.00	10.00

FRATERNITY

❏ 956	A Public Execution/All for You	1966	5.00	10.00	20.00
❏ 966	Mad of Sugar/I Am the One	1966	3.75	7.50	15.00
❏ 971	Would You Believe/Like I Know You Do	1966	3.75	7.50	15.00
❏ 973	Promises, Promises/Do the Best You Can	1966	3.75	7.50	15.00
❏ 989	Ya Ya/Cryin' Inside	1967	3.75	7.50	15.00
❏ 1000	Beg, Borrow, and Steal/L.O.V.E. Love	1967	3.75	7.50	15.00
❏ 1005	Sometimes You Just Can't Win/Cryin' Inside	1968	3.75	7.50	15.00
❏ 1005 [PS]	Sometimes You Just Can't Win/Cryin' Inside	1968	20.00	40.00	80.00
❏ 1011	I Satisfy/Good Times	1968	3.75	7.50	15.00
❏ 1015	Look at the Sun/Requiem for Sarah	1968	3.75	7.50	15.00

SMUDGE

❏ 0703	Bottom Line/Gypsy Girl	1981	3.00	6.00	12.00

M

Number	Title (A Side/B Side)	Yr	VG	VG+	NM

MOUTH AND MACNEIL
45s
PHILIPS

Number	Title (A Side/B Side)	Yr	VG	VG+	NM
❏ 40715	How Do You Do?/Land of Milk and Honey	1972	—	2.00	4.00
—Dark blue label					
❏ 40715	How Do You Do?/Land of Milk and Honey	1972	—	2.50	5.00
—Light blue label					
❏ 40717	Why Did You, Why?/Hey, You Love	1972	—	2.00	4.00
❏ 40721	Sing Along/Hello	1973	—	2.00	4.00
❏ 40721 [PS]	Sing Along/Hello	1973	3.00	6.00	12.00
❏ 40724	You-Kou-La-La-Lou-Pi/ Let Your Life Lead by Love	1973	—	2.00	4.00

TARA

Number	Title (A Side/B Side)	Yr	VG	VG+	NM
❏ 110	I See a Star/My Friends	1974	—	2.00	4.00

Albums
PHILIPS

Number	Title (A Side/B Side)	Yr	VG	VG+	NM
❏ PHS 700000	How Do You Do?	1972	3.00	6.00	12.00
❏ PHS 700003	Mouth & MacNeil II	1973	3.00	6.00	12.00

MOVE, THE Also see ELECTRIC LIGHT ORCHESTRA; ROY WOOD.
45s
A&M

Number	Title (A Side/B Side)	Yr	VG	VG+	NM
❏ 884	Flowers in the Rain/(Here We Go Round the) Lemon Tree	1967	3.00	6.00	12.00
❏ 914	Walk Upon the Water/Fire Brigade	1968	3.75	7.50	15.00
❏ 966	Yellow Rainbow/Something	1968	3.00	6.00	12.00
❏ 1020	Blackberry Way/Something	1969	3.00	6.00	12.00
❏ 1119	This Time Tomorrow/Curly	1969	3.00	6.00	12.00
❏ 1197	Brontosaurus/Lightning Never Strikes Twice	1970	3.00	6.00	12.00
❏ 1239	When Alice Comes Back to the Farm/What?	1971	3.00	6.00	12.00
❏ 1546	Zing Went the Strings of My Heart/ Wild Tiger Woman	1974	2.50	5.00	10.00

CAPITOL

Number	Title (A Side/B Side)	Yr	VG	VG+	NM
❏ 3126	Tonight/Don't Mess Me Up	1971	5.00	10.00	20.00

DERAM

Number	Title (A Side/B Side)	Yr	VG	VG+	NM
❏ 7504	The Disturbance/Night of Fear	1967	3.75	7.50	15.00
❏ 7506	I Can Hear the Grass Grow/Wave the Flag and Stop the Train	1967	3.75	7.50	15.00

MGM

Number	Title (A Side/B Side)	Yr	VG	VG+	NM
❏ 14332 [DJ]	Chinatown/Down by the Bay	1971	5.00	10.00	20.00
—Evidently not released as stock copy					

UNITED ARTISTS

Number	Title (A Side/B Side)	Yr	VG	VG+	NM
❏ XW202	Tonight/My Marge	1973	—	3.00	6.00
❏ 50876	Chinatown/Down on the Bay	1972	2.00	4.00	8.00
❏ 50928	Do Ya/California Man	1972	2.00	4.00	8.00

Albums
A&M

Number	Title (A Side/B Side)	Yr	VG	VG+	NM
❏ SP-3181	Shazam	1982	2.50	5.00	10.00
—Budget-line reissue of 4259					
❏ SP-3625 [(2)]	The Best of the Move	1974	3.75	7.50	15.00
❏ SP-4259	Shazam	1969	7.50	15.00	30.00

CAPITOL

Number	Title (A Side/B Side)	Yr	VG	VG+	NM
❏ ST-658	Looking On	1971	5.00	10.00	20.00
❏ ST-811	Message from the Country	1971	5.00	10.00	20.00

UNITED ARTISTS

Number	Title (A Side/B Side)	Yr	VG	VG+	NM
❏ UAS-5666	Split Ends	1972	3.75	7.50	15.00

MOVING SIDEWALKS, THE With Billy Gibbons, later of ZZ TOP.
45s
TANTARA

Number	Title (A Side/B Side)	Yr	VG	VG+	NM
❏ 3101	99th Floor/What Are You Going to Do	1967	10.00	20.00	40.00
❏ 3103	I Want to Hold Your Hand/Joe Blues	1968	10.00	20.00	40.00
❏ 3113	Flashback/(B-side unknown)	1969	7.50	15.00	30.00

WAND

Number	Title (A Side/B Side)	Yr	VG	VG+	NM
❏ 1156	99th Floor/What Are You Going to Do	1967	6.25	12.50	25.00
❏ 1167	Need Me/Every Night a New Surprise	1968	6.25	12.50	25.00

Albums
TANTARA

Number	Title (A Side/B Side)	Yr	VG	VG+	NM
❏ 6919	Flash	1968	75.00	150.00	300.00

MOZART, MICKEY See ROBERT MAXWELL.

MUDCRUTCH Early Tom Petty and the Heartbreakers.
45s
PEPPER

Number	Title (A Side/B Side)	Yr	VG	VG+	NM
❏ 9449	Up in Mississippi/Cause Is Understood	1971	100.00	200.00	400.00

SHELTER

Number	Title (A Side/B Side)	Yr	VG	VG+	NM
❏ 40357	Depot Street/Wild Eyes	1975	7.50	15.00	30.00

MUDLARKS, THE
45s
ROULETTE

Number	Title (A Side/B Side)	Yr	VG	VG+	NM
❏ 4143	Love Game/My Grandfather's Clock	1959	3.00	6.00	12.00

MUDSLINGER, ROGER
45s
RED BIRD

Number	Title (A Side/B Side)	Yr	VG	VG+	NM
❏ 10-013	The Election Year 1964 (Part 1)/The Election Year 1964 (Part 2)	1964	5.00	10.00	20.00

MUEHLEISEN, MAURY Lead guitarist for JIM CROCE on most, if not all, of his hits.
45s
CAPITOL

Number	Title (A Side/B Side)	Yr	VG	VG+	NM
❏ 3076	I Have No Time/Just a Passing Thing	1971	—	3.00	6.00

MUGWUMPS, THE Also see DENNY DOHERTY; CASS ELLIOT; ZALMAN YANOVSKY.
45s
SIDEWALK

Number	Title (A Side/B Side)	Yr	VG	VG+	NM
❏ 900	Bald Headed Woman/Jug Band Music	1966	6.25	12.50	25.00
❏ 909	Season of the Witch/My Gal	1967	5.00	10.00	20.00

WARNER BROS.

Number	Title (A Side/B Side)	Yr	VG	VG+	NM
❏ 5471	I'll Remember Tonight/I Don't Wanna Know	1964	3.75	7.50	15.00
❏ 7018	Searchin'/Here It Is, Another Day	1967	2.50	5.00	10.00

Albums
WARNER BROS.

Number	Title (A Side/B Side)	Yr	VG	VG+	NM
❏ W 1697 [M]	The Mugwumps	1967	6.25	12.50	25.00
❏ WS 1697 [S]	The Mugwumps	1967	7.50	15.00	30.00

MULBERRY FRUIT BAND, THE
45s
BUDDAH

Number	Title (A Side/B Side)	Yr	VG	VG+	NM
❏ 1	Yes, We Have No Bananas/The Audition	1967	3.00	6.00	12.00

MULDAUR, GEOFF
Albums
FOLKLORE

Number	Title (A Side/B Side)	Yr	VG	VG+	NM
❏ FRLP-14004 [M]	Sleepy Man Blues	1964	7.50	15.00	30.00
❏ FRST-14004 [S]	Sleepy Man Blues	1964	10.00	20.00	40.00

PRESTIGE

Number	Title (A Side/B Side)	Yr	VG	VG+	NM
❏ PRST-7727	Sleepy Man Blues	1969	5.00	10.00	20.00
—Reissue of Folklore LP					

MULDAUR, GEOFF & MARIA
45s
REPRISE

Number	Title (A Side/B Side)	Yr	VG	VG+	NM
❏ 0807	Open Up Your Soul/Sittin' Alone in the Moonlight	1969	2.00	4.00	8.00

Albums
CARTHAGE

Number	Title (A Side/B Side)	Yr	VG	VG+	NM
❏ CGLP-4428	Pottery Pie	198?	2.50	5.00	10.00

REPRISE

Number	Title (A Side/B Side)	Yr	VG	VG+	NM
❏ MS 2073	Sweet Potatoes	1972	3.00	6.00	12.00

MULDAUR, MARIA
45s
REPRISE

Number	Title (A Side/B Side)	Yr	VG	VG+	NM
❏ 1183	Midnight at the Oasis/Any Old Time	1973	—	2.50	5.00
❏ 1319	I'm a Woman/Cool River	1974	—	2.00	4.00
❏ 1331	Oh Papa/Gringo de Mexico	1975	—	2.00	4.00
❏ 1352	Sad Eyes/Wild Bird	1976	—	2.00	4.00
❏ 1362	Sweet Harmony/Jon the Generator	1976	—	2.00	4.00

WARNER BROS.

Number	Title (A Side/B Side)	Yr	VG	VG+	NM
❏ 8580	Make Love to the Music/ I'll Keep My Light in My Window	1978	—	2.00	4.00
❏ 49058	Dancin' in the Street/Birds Fly South (When Winter Comes)	1979	—	2.00	4.00
❏ 49131	Fall in Love Again/Love Is Everything	1979	—	2.00	4.00

Albums
MYRRH

Number	Title (A Side/B Side)	Yr	VG	VG+	NM
❏ MSB-6685	There Is a Love	1984	2.50	5.00	10.00

REPRISE

Number	Title (A Side/B Side)	Yr	VG	VG+	NM
❏ MS 2148	Maria Muldaur	1973	3.00	6.00	12.00
❏ MS 2194	Waitress in a Donut Shop	1974	3.00	6.00	12.00
❏ MS4-2194 [Q]	Waitress in a Donut Shop	1974	5.00	10.00	20.00
❏ MS 2235	Sweet Harmony	1976	3.00	6.00	12.00

TAKOMA

Number	Title (A Side/B Side)	Yr	VG	VG+	NM
❏ 7084	Gospel Nights	1980	2.50	5.00	10.00

TUDOR

Number	Title (A Side/B Side)	Yr	VG	VG+	NM
❏ 109902	Sweet & Sour	1983	2.50	5.00	10.00

WARNER BROS.

Number	Title (A Side/B Side)	Yr	VG	VG+	NM
❏ BSK 3162	Southern Winds	1978	2.50	5.00	10.00
❏ BSK 3305	Open Your Eyes	1979	2.50	5.00	10.00

MULL, MARTIN
45s
ABC

Number	Title (A Side/B Side)	Yr	VG	VG+	NM
❏ 12251	Boogie Man/Bombed Away	1977	—	2.50	5.00
❏ 12304	Humming Song/Get Up, Get Down	1977	—	2.50	5.00

CAPRICORN

Number	Title (A Side/B Side)	Yr	VG	VG+	NM
❏ 0019	Dueling Tubas/2001 Polkas	1973	2.00	4.00	8.00
❏ 0024	In the Eyes of My Dog (Part 1)/ In the Eyes of My Dog (Part 2)	1973	2.00	4.00	8.00
❏ 0037	Santafly/Santa Doesn't Cop Out On Dope	1973	3.00	6.00	12.00
❏ 0241	Do the Dog/Thousands of Girls	1975	2.00	4.00	8.00
❏ 0282	Santafly/Santa Doesn't Cop Out On Dope	1977	2.50	5.00	10.00

ELEKTRA

Number	Title (A Side/B Side)	Yr	VG	VG+	NM
❏ 46056	The Fruit Song/Pig in a Blanket	1979	—	2.50	5.00
❏ 46057	Bernie Don't Disco/Bun and Run Part 1 and 3	1979	—	2.50	5.00

Albums
ABC

Number	Title (A Side/B Side)	Yr	VG	VG+	NM
❏ AB-997	I'm Everyone I've Ever Loved	1977	2.50	5.00	10.00
❏ AA-1064	Sex and Violins	1978	2.50	5.00	10.00

CAPRICORN

Number	Title (A Side/B Side)	Yr	VG	VG+	NM
❏ CP 0106	Martin Mull	1972	3.00	6.00	12.00
❏ CP 0117	Martin Mull and His Fabulous Furniture	1973	3.00	6.00	12.00
❏ CP 0126	Normal	1974	3.00	6.00	12.00
❏ CP 0155	Days of Wine and Neurosis	1975	3.00	6.00	12.00
❏ CP 0195	No Hits Four Errors	1977	2.50	5.00	10.00

ELEKTRA

Number	Title (A Side/B Side)	Yr	VG	VG+	NM
❏ 6E-200	Near Perfect	1979	2.50	5.00	10.00

MCA

Number	Title (A Side/B Side)	Yr	VG	VG+	NM
❏ 795	I'm Everyone I've Ever Loved	1980	2.00	4.00	8.00
—Reissue of ABC 997					

MULTIPLICATION ROCK (SOUNDTRACK)
45s
CAPITOL

Number	Title (A Side/B Side)	Yr	VG	VG+	NM
❏ 3693	Naughty Number Nine/I Got Six	1973	3.75	7.50	15.00

Albums
CAPITOL

Number	Title (A Side/B Side)	Yr	VG	VG+	NM
❏ SJA-11174	Multiplication Rock	1973	10.00	20.00	40.00

MUMMIES, THE
45s
HIT

Number	Title (A Side/B Side)	Yr	VG	VG+	NM
❏ 193	Tell Her No/For Me	1965	3.00	6.00	12.00
—B-side by Wayne Harris					

MUNGO JERRY
45s
BELL

Number	Title (A Side/B Side)	Yr	VG	VG+	NM
❏ 45123	Lady Rose/Little Louis	1971	—	2.00	4.00
❏ 45383	Alright, Alright, Alright/Little Miss Hipshake	1973	—	2.00	4.00
❏ 45427	Wild Love/Glad I'm a Rocker	1973	—	2.00	4.00

Number	Title (A Side/B Side)	Yr	VG	VG+	NM
❏ 45451	Long Legged Woman Dressed in Black/ Gonna Bop Till I Drop	1974	—	2.00	4.00
JANUS					
❏ 125	In the Summertime/Mighty Man	1970	—	3.00	6.00
❏ 128	Johnny B. Badde/My Friend	1970	—	2.50	5.00
❏ 148	Baby Jump/The Man Beside the Piano	1971	—	2.50	5.00
PYE					
❏ 65003	You Don't Have to Be in the Army/O'Reilly	1972	—	2.00	4.00
❏ 65009	Going Back Home/Open Up	1972	—	2.00	4.00
❏ 71032	In the Summertime/(B-side unknown)	1975	—	2.00	4.00
Albums					
JANUS					
❏ JLS-3027	Memoirs of a Stockbroker	1972	3.75	7.50	15.00
❏ JXS-7000	Mungo Jerry	1970	3.75	7.50	15.00

MUNSTERS, THE
45s
DECCA

Number	Title (A Side/B Side)	Yr	VG	VG+	NM
❏ 31670	Munster Creep/Make It Go Away	1964	5.00	10.00	20.00
Albums					
DECCA					
❏ DL 4588 [M]	The Munsters	1964	25.00	50.00	100.00
❏ DL 74588 [S]	The Munsters	1964	37.50	75.00	150.00

MURE, BILLY
45s
DANCO

Number	Title (A Side/B Side)	Yr	VG	VG+	NM
❏ 506	Mon Coeur Brise (My Broken Heart)/Rose of Cherry Bay	1965	2.00	4.00	8.00
EVEREST					
❏ 19335	Jambalaya (On the Bayou)/Kaw-Liga	1960	2.50	5.00	10.00
FORD					
❏ 2552	See the Fait from the Air/See Lanny Ross	1963	2.50	5.00	10.00
MGM					
❏ K13161	Maria Elena/In the Cool of the Day	1963	2.00	4.00	8.00
❏ K13190	Fascination/Mona Lisa	1963	2.00	4.00	8.00
❏ K13252	Ma, What Time Is It/Sticky Fingers	1964	2.00	4.00	8.00
—With Benny Mure					
❏ K13565	Five Foot Two, Eyes of Blue/ Yes Sir, That's My Baby	1966	2.00	4.00	8.00
PARIS					
❏ 545	Theme for the Lonely/Ambush	1960	2.50	5.00	10.00
RCA VICTOR					
❏ 47-7394	Haggis Baggis/Tara Lara	1958	3.75	7.50	15.00
RIVERSIDE					
❏ 4547	Diamonds/String of Guitars	1963	2.50	5.00	10.00
SPLASH					
❏ 800	A String of Trumpets/Tea and Trumpets	1959	3.00	6.00	12.00
—As "Billy Mure and the Trumpeteers"					
❏ 800	A String of Trumpets/Tea and Trumpets	1959	3.00	6.00	12.00
—As "The Trumpeteers"					
SRG					
❏ 102	Theme for the Lonely/Little Reuben	1960	3.75	7.50	15.00
STRAND					
❏ 25037	Hawaiian Drums/Pink Hawaii	1961	2.00	4.00	8.00

7-Inch Extended Plays
RCA VICTOR

Number	Title (A Side/B Side)	Yr	VG	VG+	NM
❏ EPA-4271	(contents unknown)	1958	3.00	6.00	12.00
❏ EPA-4271 [PS]	The Big Guitar	1958	3.00	6.00	12.00

Albums
EVEREST

Number	Title (A Side/B Side)	Yr	VG	VG+	NM
❏ SDBR-1067 [S]	A String of Trumpets	1960	7.50	15.00	30.00
❏ SDBR-1072 [S]	Songs of Hank Williams	1960	7.50	15.00	30.00
❏ SDBR-1120 [S]	Strictly Cha-Cha-Cha	1961	7.50	15.00	30.00
❏ LPBR-5067 [M]	A String of Trumpets	1960	5.00	10.00	20.00
❏ LPBR-5072 [M]	Songs of Hank Williams	1960	5.00	10.00	20.00
❏ LPBR-5120 [M]	Strictly Cha-Cha-Cha	1961	5.00	10.00	20.00
KAPP					
❏ KL-1253 [M]	Tough Strings	1961	5.00	10.00	20.00
❏ KS-3253 [S]	Tough Strings	1961	7.50	15.00	30.00
MGM					
❏ E-3780 [M]	Supersonic Guitars	1959	7.50	15.00	30.00
❏ SE-3780 [S]	Supersonic Guitars	1959	12.50	25.00	50.00
❏ E-3807 [M]	Supersonic Guitars, Vol. 2	1959	7.50	15.00	30.00
❏ SE-3807 [S]	Supersonic Guitars, Vol. 2	1959	12.50	25.00	50.00
❏ E-4131 [M]	Teen Bossa Nova	1963	5.00	10.00	20.00
❏ SE-4131 [S]	Teen Bossa Nova	1963	7.50	15.00	30.00
❏ E-4189 [M]	Maria Elena and Other Great Songs	1964	5.00	10.00	20.00
❏ SE-4189 [S]	Maria Elena and Other Great Songs	1964	7.50	15.00	30.00
❏ E-4406 [M]	Happy Guitars	1966	5.00	10.00	20.00
❏ SE-4406 [S]	Happy Guitars	1966	6.25	12.50	25.00
PREMIER					
❏ PM-9014 [M]	Blue Hawaii	196?	2.50	5.00	10.00
—Side 1 by Billy Mure; Side 2 by Harry Kaapuni and His Royal Hawaiians					
RCA VICTOR					
❏ LPM-1536 [M]	Supersonic Guitars in Hi-Fi	1957	10.00	20.00	40.00
❏ LPM-1694 [M]	Fireworks	1958	7.50	15.00	30.00
❏ LSP-1694 [S]	Fireworks	1958	10.00	20.00	40.00
❏ LPM-1869 [M]	Supersonic in Flight	1959	7.50	15.00	30.00
❏ LSP-1869 [S]	Supersonic in Flight	1959	12.50	25.00	50.00
SPIN-O-RAMA					
❏ S 147 [M]	Blue Hawaii	196?	2.50	5.00	10.00
—Side 1 by Billy Mure; Side 2 by Harry Kaapuni and His Royal Hawaiians					
❏ S 157 [M]	Hawaiian Moods	196?	2.50	5.00	10.00
—One side by Billy Mure; one side by Luke Leilani					
STRAND					
❏ SL-1010 [M]	Hawaiian Percussion	1961	6.25	12.50	25.00
❏ SLS-1010 [S]	Hawaiian Percussion	1961	10.00	20.00	40.00
❏ SL-1021 [M]	'Round the World in Percussion	1961	6.25	12.50	25.00
❏ SLS-1021 [S]	'Round the World in Percussion	1961	10.00	20.00	40.00
❏ SL-1070 [M]	Pink Hawaii	1962	5.00	10.00	20.00
❏ SLS-1070 [S]	Pink Hawaii	1962	7.50	15.00	30.00
SUNSET					
❏ SUS-5173	Songs of Hank Williams	196?	3.00	6.00	12.00
—Reissue of Everest SDBR-1072 with fewer tracks					

UNITED ARTISTS

Number	Title (A Side/B Side)	Yr	VG	VG+	NM
❏ UAL-3031 [M]	Bandstand Record Hop	1959	10.00	20.00	40.00
❏ UAS-6031 [S]	Bandstand Record Hop	1959	15.00	30.00	60.00

MURMAIDS, THE
45s
CHATTAHOOCHIE

Number	Title (A Side/B Side)	Yr	VG	VG+	NM
❏ 628	Popsicles and Icicles/Bunny Stomp	1963	3.75	7.50	15.00
❏ 628	Popsicles and Icicles/Comedy and Tragedy	1963	3.75	7.50	15.00
❏ 628	Popsicles and Icicles/Huntington Flats	1963	3.75	7.50	15.00
❏ 628	Popsicles and Icicles/Blue Dress	1963	5.00	10.00	20.00
❏ 636	Heartbreak Ahead/He's Good to Me	1964	2.50	5.00	10.00
❏ 641	Wild and Wonderful/Bull Talk	1964	2.50	5.00	10.00
❏ 668	Stuffed Animals/Little White Lies	1965	2.50	5.00	10.00
❏ 711	Little Boys/Go Away	1966	2.50	5.00	10.00
LIBERTY					
❏ 56069	Paper Sun/Song Through Perception	1968	—	—	—
—Unreleased					
❏ 56078	Paper Sun/Song Through Perception	1968	2.50	5.00	10.00
Albums					
CHATTAHOOCHEE					
❏ CHLP-628 [M]	The Mermaids Resurface!	1981	7.50	15.00	30.00

MURPHEY, MICHAEL   Also includes records as "Michael Martin Murphey."
45s
A&M

Number	Title (A Side/B Side)	Yr	VG	VG+	NM
❏ 1368	Geronimo's Cadillac/Boy from the Country	1972	—	2.50	5.00
❏ 1368 [PS]	Geronimo's Cadillac/Boy from the Country	1972	—	3.00	6.00
❏ 1447	Cosmic Cowboy/Temperature Train	1973	—	2.50	5.00
❏ 1459	Calico Silver/Blessing in Disguise	1973	—	2.50	5.00
❏ 1712	Geronimo's Cadillac/Blessing in Disguise	1975	—	2.00	4.00
EMI AMERICA					
❏ 8243	What She Wants/Still Taking Chances	1984	—	—	3.00
❏ 8243 [PS]	What She Wants/Still Taking Chances	1984	—	—	3.00
❏ 8265	Carolina in the Pines/Cherokee Fiddle	1985	—	—	3.00
EPIC					
❏ 02075	Take It As It Comes/Hard Country	1981	—	2.00	4.00
—A-side with Katy Moffatt					
❏ 11130	Holy Roller/Rye By-The-Sea	1974	—	2.00	4.00
❏ 11130 [PS]	Holy Roller/Rye By-The-Sea	1974	—	3.00	6.00
❏ 50014	You Can Only Say So Much/ Fort Worth, I Love You	1974	—	2.00	4.00
❏ 50084	Wildfire/Night Thunder	1975	—	2.50	5.00
❏ 50131	Carolina in the Pines/Without My Lady There	1975	—	2.00	4.00
❏ 50184	Mansion on the Hill/Renegade	1976	—	2.00	4.00
❏ 50214	Rhythm of the Road/Swans Against the Sun	1976	—	2.00	4.00
❏ 50319	Cherokee Fiddler/Running Wide Open	1976	—	2.00	4.00
❏ 50369	Changing Woman/ A North Wind and a New Moon	1977	—	2.00	4.00
❏ 50540	Nothing Is Your Own/Song Day	1978	—	2.00	4.00
❏ 50572	Paradise Tonight/Song Dog	1978	—	2.00	4.00
❏ 50686	Lightning/Chain Gang	1979	—	2.00	4.00
❏ 50739	South Coast/Backsliders Wine	1979	—	2.00	4.00
LIBERTY					
❏ 1455	Lost River/The Two-Step Is Easy	1982	—	—	3.00
❏ 1466	What's Forever For/Crystal	1982	—	—	3.00
❏ 1486	Still Taking Chances/Lost River	1982	—	—	3.00
❏ 1494	Crystal/Love Affairs	1983	—	—	3.00
❏ 1505	The Heart Never Lies/ Don't Count the Rainy Days	1983	—	—	3.00
❏ 1505 [PS]	The Heart Never Lies/ Don't Count the Rainy Days	1983	—	2.00	4.00
❏ 1514	Will It Be Love by Morning/ Goodbye Money Mountain	1983	—	—	3.00
❏ 1514 [PS]	Will It Be Love by Morning/ Goodbye Money Mountain	1983	—	2.00	4.00
❏ 1517	Disenchanted/Sacred Heart	1984	—	—	3.00
—Starting here, as "Michael Martin Murphey"					
❏ 1523	Radio Land/The Heart Never Lies	1984	—	—	3.00
WARNER BROS.					
❏ PRO-S-2869 [DJ]	Colorado Christmas/The Cowboy's Christmas Ball	1987	—	3.00	6.00
—B-side by Nitty Gritty Dirt Band					
❏ 7-18321	Big Iron/Cowboy Logic	1993	—	2.00	4.00
❏ 18928	I Don't Do Floors/I'm Gonna Miss You Girl	1992	—	—	3.00
❏ 19290	What Am I Doin' Here/Where Do Cowboys Go When They Die-Reincarnation	1991	—	—	3.00
❏ 19412	Let the Cowboy Dance/Red River Valley	1991	—	—	3.00
❏ 19724	Cowboy Logic/Spanish Is the Lovin' Tongue	1990	—	—	3.00
❏ 22666	Route 66/Juke Box	1990	—	—	3.00
❏ 22765	Family Tree/Wood Smoke in the Wind	1989	—	—	3.00
❏ 22970	Never Givin' Up on Love/Desperation Road	1989	—	—	3.00
❏ 22970 [PS]	Never Givin' Up on Love/Desperation Road	1989	—	2.00	4.00
❏ 27668	From the Word Go/Vanishing Breed	1989	—	—	3.00
❏ 27810	Pilgrims on the Way (Matthew's Song)/ Still Got the Fire	1988	—	—	3.00
❏ 27947	Talkin' to the Wrong Man/ What Am I Doin' Hangin' 'Round	1988	—	—	3.00
❏ 27947 [PS]	Talkin' to the Wrong Man/ What Am I Doin' Hangin' 'Round	1988	—	—	3.00
❏ 28168	I'm Gonna Miss You, Girl/Running Blood	1987	—	—	3.00
❏ 28370	A Long Line of Love/Worlds Apart	1987	—	—	3.00
❏ 28471	A Face in a Crowd/You're History	1987	—	—	3.00
—With Holly Dunn					
❏ 28598	Fiddlin' Man/Ghost Town (Messages from the Ghost Ranch)	1986	—	—	3.00
❏ 28694	Rollin' Nowhere/Face-2-Face with the Night	1986	—	—	3.00
❏ 28797	Tonight We Ride/Santa Fe Cantina	1986	—	—	3.00
Albums					
A&M					
❏ SP-3134	Geronimo's Cadillac	198?	2.00	4.00	8.00
—Budget-line reissue					
❏ SP-3137	Cosmic Cowboy Souvenir	198?	2.00	4.00	8.00
—Budget-line reissue					
❏ SP-4358	Geronimo's Cadillac	1972	3.00	6.00	12.00
❏ SP-4388	Cosmic Cowboy Souvenir	1973	3.00	6.00	12.00

M

Number	Title (A Side/B Side)	Yr	VG	VG+	NM
EMI AMERICA					
❏ LN-10310	The Heart Never Lies	1986	2.00	4.00	8.00
—Budget-line reissue					
❏ ST-17143	The Best of Michael Martin Murphey	1984	2.50	5.00	10.00
EPIC					
❏ KE 32835	Michael Murphey	1974	3.00	6.00	12.00
❏ KE 33290	Blue Sky — Night Thunder	1975	2.50	5.00	10.00
❏ PE 33290	Blue Sky — Night Thunder	197?	2.00	4.00	8.00
—Reissue with new prefix & dark blue label					
❏ PE 33851	Swans Against the Sun	1975	2.50	5.00	10.00
❏ PEQ 33851 [Q]	Swans Against the Sun	1975	4.00	8.00	16.00
❏ PE 34220	Flowing Free Forever	1976	2.50	5.00	10.00
❏ JE 35013	Lonewolf	1978	2.50	5.00	10.00
❏ JE 35742	Peaks, Valleys, Honky-Tonks & Alleys	1979	2.50	5.00	10.00
LIBERTY					
❏ LT-51120	Michael Martin Murphey	1982	2.50	5.00	10.00
❏ LT-51150	The Heart Never Lies	1983	2.50	5.00	10.00
WARNER BROS.					
❏ 25369	Tonight We Ride	1986	2.50	5.00	10.00
❏ 25500	Americana	1987	2.50	5.00	10.00
❏ 25644	River of Time	1988	2.50	5.00	10.00
❏ 25894	Land of Enchantment	1989	3.00	6.00	12.00

MURPHY, BILL
45s

Number	Title (A Side/B Side)	Yr	VG	VG+	NM
HIT					
❏ 28	Devil Woman/Little Diane	1962	2.00	4.00	8.00
—B-side by Ed Van Zandt					

MURPHY, KEITH, AND THE DAZE
45s

Number	Title (A Side/B Side)	Yr	VG	VG+	NM
KING					
❏ 6171	Dirty Ol' Sam/Slightly Reminiscent of Her	1968	25.00	50.00	100.00

MURRAY, ANNE
45s

Number	Title (A Side/B Side)	Yr	VG	VG+	NM
CAPITOL					
❏ 2738	Snowbird/Just Bidin' My Time	1970	—	3.00	6.00
❏ 2988	Sing High — Sing Low/Days of the Looking Glass	1970	—	2.50	5.00
❏ 3059	A Stranger in My Place/Sycamore Slick	1971	—	2.50	5.00
❏ 3082	Put Your Hand in the Hand/It Takes Time	1971	—	2.50	5.00
❏ 3159	Talk It Over in the Morning/Head Above the Water	1971	—	2.50	5.00
❏ 3260	Cotton Jenny/Destiny	1972	—	2.50	5.00
❏ 3352	Bobbie's Song for Jesus/You Can't Have a Hand on Me	1972	—	2.50	5.00
❏ 3481	Danny's Song/Drown Me	1972	—	2.00	4.00
❏ 3600	What About Me/Let Sunshine Have Its Day	1973	—	2.00	4.00
❏ 3648	Send a Little Love My Way/Head Above the Water	1973	—	2.00	4.00
❏ 3776	Love Song/You Can't Go Back	1973	—	2.00	4.00
❏ 3867	You Won't See Me/He Thinks I Still Care	1974	—	2.50	5.00
❏ 3955	Just One Look/Son of a Rotten Gambler	1974	—	2.00	4.00
❏ 4000	Day Tripper/Lullaby	1974	—	2.00	4.00
❏ 4025	Uproar/Lift Your Hearts to the Sun	1975	—	2.00	4.00
❏ 4072	A Stranger in My Place/Dream Lover	1975	—	2.00	4.00
❏ 4142	Sunday Sunrise/Out on the Road Again	1975	—	2.00	4.00
❏ 4207	The Call/Lady Bug	1976	—	2.00	4.00
❏ 4265	Golden Oldie/Together	1976	—	2.00	4.00
❏ 4329	Things/Caress Me Pretty Music	1976	—	2.00	4.00
❏ 4375	Sunday School to Broadway/Dancin' All Night Long	1976	—	2.00	4.00
❏ 4402	Canterbury Song/Shilo Song	1977	—	2.00	4.00
—With Gene MacLellan					
❏ 4527	Walk Right Back/A Million More	1978	—	2.00	4.00
❏ 4574	You Needed Me/I Still Wish the Very Best for You	1978	—	2.00	4.00
❏ 4675	I Just Fall in Love Again/Just to Feel This Love from You	1979	—	2.00	4.00
❏ 4675 [PS]	I Just Fall in Love Again/Just to Feel This Love from You	1979	—	2.50	5.00
❏ 4716	Shadows in the Moonlight/Yucatan Cafe	1979	—	2.00	4.00
❏ 4773	Broken Hearted Me/Why Don't You Stick Around	1979	—	2.00	4.00
❏ 4813	Daydream Believer/Do You Think of Me	1979	—	2.00	4.00
❏ 4848	Lucky Me/Somebody's Waiting	1980	—	2.00	4.00
❏ 4878	I'm Happy Just to Dance with You/What's Forever For	1980	—	2.00	4.00
❏ 4920	Could I Have This Dance/Somebody's Waiting	1980	—	2.00	4.00
❏ 4920 [PS]	Could I Have This Dance/Somebody's Waiting	1980	—	2.50	5.00
❏ 4987	Blessed Are the Believers/Only Love	1981	—	2.00	4.00
❏ 4987 [PS]	Blessed Are the Believers/Only Love	1981	—	2.50	5.00
❏ A-5013	We Don't Have to Hold Out/Call Me with the News	1981	—	2.00	4.00
❏ A-5013 [PS]	We Don't Have to Hold Out/Call Me with the News	1981	—	2.00	4.00
❏ A-5023	It's All I Can Do/If a Heart Must Be Broken	1981	—	2.00	4.00
❏ A-5083	Another Sleepless Night/It Should Have Been Easy	1982	—	2.00	4.00
❏ B-5145	Hey! Baby!/Song for the Mira	1982	—	—	3.00
❏ B-5145 [PS]	Hey! Baby!/Song for the Mira	1982	—	—	3.00
❏ B-5183	Somebody's Always Saying Goodbye/That'll Keep Me Dreamin'	1982	—	—	3.00
❏ B-5183 [PS]	Somebody's Always Saying Goodbye/That'll Keep Me Dreamin'	1982	—	—	3.00
❏ B-5264	A Little Good News/I'm Not Afraid Anymore	1983	—	—	3.00
❏ B-5264 [PS]	A Little Good News/I'm Not Afraid Anymore	1983	—	2.50	5.00
❏ B-5305	That's Not the Way (It's S'posed to Be)/The More We Try	1983	—	—	3.00
❏ B-5344	Just Another Woman in Love/Heart Stealer	1984	—	—	3.00
❏ B-5344 [PS]	Just Another Woman in Love/Heart Stealer	1984	—	—	3.00
❏ B-5384	Let Your Heart Do the Talking/I Don't Think I'm Ready for You	1984	—	—	3.00
❏ B-5401	Nobody Loves Me Like You Do/Love You Out of Your Mind	1984	—	—	3.00
—A-side with Dave Loggins					
❏ B-5401 [PS]	Nobody Loves Me Like You Do/Love You Out of Your Mind	1984	—	2.00	4.00
❏ B-5436	Time Don't Run Out on Me/Let Your Heart Do the Talking	1985	—	—	3.00
❏ B-5436 [PS]	Time Don't Run Out on Me/Let Your Heart Do the Talking	1985	—	—	3.00
❏ B-5472	I Don't Think I'm Ready for You/Take Good Care of My Baby	1985	—	—	3.00
❏ B-5472 [PS]	I Don't Think I'm Ready for You/Take Good Care of My Baby	1985	—	2.00	4.00
❏ B-5536	Go Tell It On the Mountain/O Holy Night	1985	—	2.00	4.00
❏ B-5536 [PS]	Go Tell It On the Mountain/O Holy Night	1985	—	2.50	5.00
❏ B-5547	Now and Forever (You and Me)/I Don't Wanna Spend Another Night Without You	1986	—	—	3.00
❏ B-5547 [PS]	Now and Forever (You and Me)/I Don't Wanna Spend Another Night Without You	1986	—	2.00	4.00
❏ B-5576	Who's Leaving Who/Reach for Me	1986	—	—	3.00
❏ B-5576 [PS]	Who's Leaving Who/Reach for Me	1986	—	—	3.00
❏ B-5610	My Life's a Dance/Call Us Fools	1986	—	—	3.00
❏ B-5655	On and On/Gotcha	1986	—	—	3.00
❏ SPRO-9723 [DJ]	Christmas Medley: Silver Bells/I'll Be Home for Christmas/Winter Wonderland (same on both sides)	1981	2.00	4.00	8.00
❏ B-44005	Are You Still in Love with Me/Give Me Your Love	1987	—	—	3.00
❏ B-44053	Anyone Can Do the Heartbreak/Without You	1987	—	—	3.00
❏ B-44134	Perfect Strangers/It Happens All the Time	1988	—	—	3.00
—With Doug Mallory					
❏ B-44219	Flying On Your Own/Slow All Night	1988	—	—	3.00
❏ B-44219 [PS]	Flying On Your Own/Slow All Night	1988	—	—	3.00
❏ B-44272	Slow Passin' Time/Flying on Your Own	1989	—	—	3.00
❏ B-44341	Who But You/You Make Me Curious	1989	—	—	3.00
❏ B-44432	If I Ever Fall in Love Again/Just Another Woman in Love	1989	—	—	3.00
—A-side: With Kenny Rogers					
❏ B-44495	I'd Fall in Love Tonight/Now and Forever (You and Me)	1989	—	—	3.00
CAPITOL NASHVILLE					
❏ 7PRO-79189	Feed This Fire (same on both sides)	1990	2.00	4.00	8.00
—Vinyl is promo only					
SBK					
❏ S7-18912	Winter Wonderland/The Little Drummer Boy	1995	—	—	3.00
Albums					
CAPITOL					
❏ ST-579	Snowbird	1970	3.00	6.00	12.00
❏ ST-667	Anne Murray	1971	3.00	6.00	12.00
❏ ST-821	Talk It Over in the Morning	1971	3.00	6.00	12.00
❏ ST-11024	Annie	1972	2.50	5.00	10.00
❏ ST-11172	Danny's Song	1973	2.50	5.00	10.00
❏ ST-11266	Love Song	1974	2.50	5.00	10.00
❏ ST-11324	Country	1974	2.50	5.00	10.00
❏ ST-11354	Highly Prized Possession	1974	2.50	5.00	10.00
❏ ST-11433	Together	1975	2.50	5.00	10.00
❏ ST-11559	Keeping in Touch	1976	2.50	5.00	10.00
❏ ST-11743	Let's Keep It That Way	1978	2.50	5.00	10.00
❏ SW-11849	New Kind of Feeling	1979	2.50	5.00	10.00
❏ SOO-12012	I'll Always Love You	1979	2.50	5.00	10.00
❏ ST-12039	A Country Collection	1980	2.50	5.00	10.00
❏ SOO-12064	Somebody's Waiting	1980	2.50	5.00	10.00
❏ SOO-12110	Anne Murray's Greatest Hits	1980	2.50	5.00	10.00
❏ SOO-12144	Where Do You Go When You Dream	1981	2.50	5.00	10.00
❏ ST-12225	The Hottest Night of the Year	1982	2.50	5.00	10.00
❏ ST-12301	A Little Good News	1983	2.50	5.00	10.00
❏ SJ-12363	Heart Over Mind	1984	2.50	5.00	10.00
❏ SJ-12466	Something to Talk About	1986	2.50	5.00	10.00
❏ PJ-12562	Harmony	1987	2.50	5.00	10.00
❏ SN-16080	Talk It Over in the Morning	1980	2.00	4.00	8.00
—Budget-line reissue					
❏ SN-16081	Highly Prized Possession	1980	2.00	4.00	8.00
—Budget-line reissue					
❏ SN-16082	Keeping in Touch	1980	2.00	4.00	8.00
—Budget-line reissue					
❏ SN-16211	Danny's Song	1981	2.00	4.00	8.00
—Budget-line reissue					
❏ SN-16212	Love Song	1981	2.00	4.00	8.00
—Budget-line reissue					
❏ SN-16213	Country	1981	2.00	4.00	8.00
—Budget-line reissue					
❏ SN-16232	Christmas Wishes	1981	2.50	5.00	10.00
—Original issue was on the budget-line series					
❏ SN-16233	There's a Hippo in My Tub	1981	2.50	5.00	10.00
—Original issue was on the budget-line series					
❏ SN-16282	Together	1982	2.00	4.00	8.00
—Budget-line reissue					
❏ SN-16283	New Kind of Feeling	1982	2.00	4.00	8.00
—Budget-line reissue					
❏ SN-16338	A Country Collection	198?	2.00	4.00	8.00
—Budget-line reissue					
❏ SN-16341	Let's Keep It That Way	198?	2.00	4.00	8.00
—Budget-line reissue					
❏ C1-48764	As I Am	1988	2.50	5.00	10.00
❏ C1-90886	Christmas	1987	2.00	4.00	8.00
❏ C1-92072	Greatest Hits Volume II	1989	3.00	6.00	12.00
CAPITOL NASHVILLE					
❏ R 173232	You Will	1990	5.00	10.00	20.00
—Only released on vinyl through BMG Direct Marketing					
PICKWICK					
❏ SPC-3350	What About Me	197?	2.00	4.00	8.00

MURRAY, ANNE, AND GLEN CAMPBELL Also see each artist's individual listings.
45s

Number	Title (A Side/B Side)	Yr	VG	VG+	NM
CAPITOL					
❏ 3200	I Say a Little Prayer-By the Time I Get to Phoenix/All Through the Night	1971	—	2.50	5.00
❏ 3287	United We Stand/Ease Your Pain	1972	—	2.50	5.00
Albums					
CAPITOL					
❏ SW-869	Anne Murray/Glen Campbell	1971	3.00	6.00	12.00
❏ SN-16144	Anne Murray/Glen Campbell	1980	2.00	4.00	8.00
—Budget-line reissue					

MURRAY, JACK
45s

Number	Title (A Side/B Side)	Yr	VG	VG+	NM
LAURIE					
❏ 3199	Surfin' with Me/What Do You Think of Me Baby	1963	3.75	7.50	15.00

The Mindbenders, *A Groovy Kind of Love,* Fontana MGF-27554, mono LP, with "Don't Cry No More" on the record, $15-$30.

The Miracles, *Away We A Go Go,* Tamla TS 271, stereo LP, $15-$30.

Guy Mitchell, *Sincerely Yours*, King 644, mono LP, $150-$300.

The Monkees, *The Birds, the Bees and the Monkees,* Colgems COS-109, stereo LP, $10-$20.

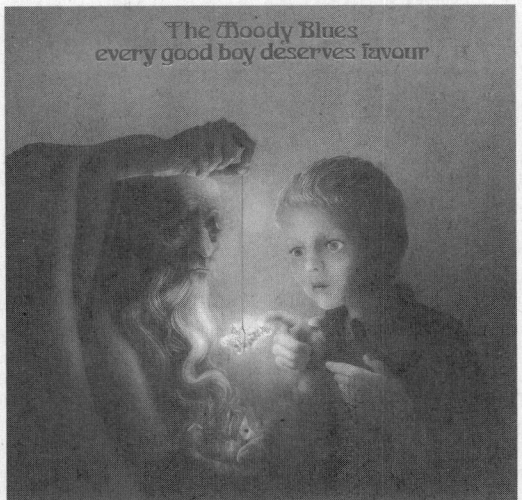

The Moody Blues, *Every Good Boy Deserves Favour,* Threshold THS 5, stereo LP, gatefold cover, white label with purple logo, $7.50-$15.

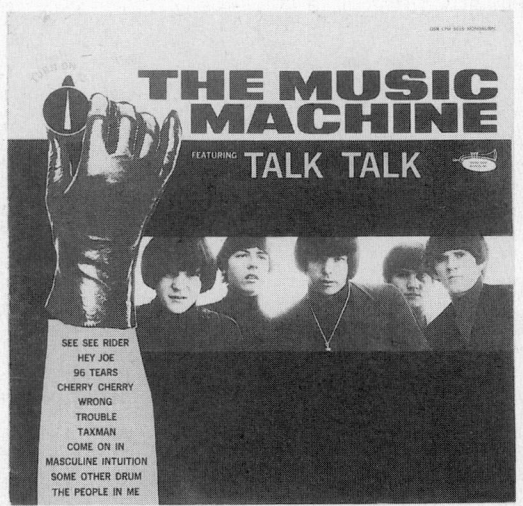

The Music Machine, *(Turn On) The Music Machine featuring Talk Talk,* Original Sound 5015, mono LP, $20-$40.

Number	Title (A Side/B Side)	Yr	VG	VG+	NM

MURRAY, RAY, AND THE DYNAMICS
45s
ARBO
| ❑ 222 | With All My Love/Baby, What You Want Me to Do | 1960 | 25.00 | 50.00 | 100.00 |

MURRAY THE "K" Also see VARIOUS ARTISTS COLLECTIONS.
45s
BRS
| ❑ 1/2 | Murray the "K" and The Beatles As It Happened | 1964 | 10.00 | 20.00 | 40.00 |
| ❑ 1/2 [PS] | Murray the "K" and The Beatles As It Happened | 1964 | 30.00 | 60.00 | 120.00 |
IBC
| ❑ F4KM-0082/3 | Murray "K" and The Beatles As It Happened | 1976 | 2.50 | 5.00 | 10.00 |
| ❑ F4KM-0082/3 [PS] | Murray the "K" and The Beatles As It Happened | 1976 | 2.50 | 5.00 | 10.00 |
RED BIRD
| ❑ 10-045 | It's What's Happening, Baby/Sins of a Family | 1966 | 3.75 | 7.50 | 15.00 |

MUSIC ASYLUM, THE
45s
ASCOT
| ❑ 2238 | Yesterday's Children/ I Need Someone (The Painter) | 1967 | 2.50 | 5.00 | 10.00 |
Albums
UNITED ARTISTS
| ❑ UAS-6778 | Commit Thyself | 1970 | 5.00 | 10.00 | 20.00 |

MUSIC CITY FIVE, THE
45s
HIT
❑ 62	Pipeline/Don't Say Nothin' Bad About My Baby	1963	2.00	4.00	8.00
—B-side by Clara Wilson					
❑ 72	Sukiyaki/Tie Me Kangaroo Down, Sport	1963	2.00	4.00	8.00
—B-side by Sylvester McCord					
❑ 76	Wipe Out/Judy's Turn to Cry	1963	2.00	4.00	8.00
—B-side by Katy Richards					
❑ 87	Washington Square/Donna the Prima Donna	1963	2.00	4.00	8.00
—As "The Music City Five & Ten"; B-side by Ed Hardin					
❑ 91	Maria Elena/The Matador	1963	2.00	4.00	8.00
—B-side by Harvey Frolic					

MUSIC CITY ORCHESTRA, THE
45s
HIT
❑ 20	The Stripper/Speedy Gonzales	1962	2.00	4.00	8.00
—B-side by Tom Walls					
❑ 49	Walk Right In/From a Jack to a King	1963	2.00	4.00	8.00
—B-side by Jackie Ott					
❑ 70	Sukiyaki/Hello Stranger	1963	2.00	4.00	8.00
—As "The Music City Chorus and Orchestra featuring Samayami"; B-side by Alpha Zoe					
❑ 195	Berlin Melody/Ferry Cross the Mersey	1965	2.00	4.00	8.00
—B-side by Johnny LaFlore					
❑ 210	Supercalifragilisticexpialidocious/ Chim Chim Cheree	1965	2.00	4.00	8.00
—As "The Music City Orchestra and Chorus"					

MUSIC CITY SINGERS, THE
45s
HIT
❑ 112	Don't Let the Rain Come Down/Suspicion	1964	2.00	4.00	8.00
—B-side by Ed Hardin					
❑ 119	Love Me with All Your Heart/Cotton Candy	1964	2.00	4.00	8.00
—B-side by the Nashville Five					
❑ 129	Today/Beans in My Ears	1964	2.00	4.00	8.00

MUSIC COMPANY, THE
Albums
CRESTVIEW
| ❑ CRS-3057 | Hard and Heavy | 196? | 6.25 | 12.50 | 25.00 |
MIRWOOD
| ❑ M-7002 [M] | Rubber Soul Jazz | 1966 | 5.00 | 10.00 | 20.00 |
| ❑ MS-7002 [S] | Rubber Soul Jazz | 1966 | 6.25 | 12.50 | 25.00 |

MUSIC EXPLOSION, THE
45s
ATTACK
| ❑ 1404 | The Little Black Egg/Stay By My Side | 1966 | 6.25 | 12.50 | 25.00 |
LAURIE
❑ 3380	Little Bit O'Soul/I See the Light	1967	3.00	6.00	12.00
❑ 3400	Can't Stop Now/Sunshine Games	1967	2.00	4.00	8.00
❑ 3414	We Gotta Go Home/Hearts and Flowers	1967	2.00	4.00	8.00
❑ 3429	What You Want/Road Runner	1968	2.00	4.00	8.00
❑ 3440	Where Are We Going/Flash	1968	2.00	4.00	8.00
❑ 3454	Yes Sir/Dazzling	1968	2.00	4.00	8.00
❑ 3466	Jack in the Box/Rewind	1968	2.00	4.00	8.00
❑ 3479	What's Your Name/Call Me Anything	1969	2.00	4.00	8.00
❑ 3500	The Little Black Egg/Stay By My Side	1969	2.00	4.00	8.00
Albums
LAURIE
| ❑ LLP-2040 [M] | Little Bit O'Soul | 1967 | 5.00 | 10.00 | 20.00 |
| ❑ SLLP-2040 [S] | Little Bit O'Soul | 1967 | 6.25 | 12.50 | 25.00 |

MUSIC MACHINE, THE Also see T.S. BONNIWELL.
45s
BELL
| ❑ 764 | Mother Nature—Father Earth/Advise and Consent | 1969 | 2.00 | 4.00 | 8.00 |
ORIGINAL SOUND
❑ (no #) [PS]	The Music Machine	1967	2.50	5.00	10.00
—Custom sleeve, large center hole, not assigned to any one record, with pictures of band members on front and ads for "Oldies But Goodies" LPs on back					
❑ 61	Talk Talk/Come On In	1966	3.00	6.00	12.00
❑ 67	The People in Me/Masculine Institution	1967	2.50	5.00	10.00
❑ 71	Double Yellow Line/Absolutely Positive	1967	2.50	5.00	10.00
❑ 75	I've Loved You/The Eagle Never Hunts the Fly	1967	2.50	5.00	10.00
❑ 82	Hey Joe/Wrong	1968	2.50	5.00	10.00
SUNDAZED
❑ 131	Point of No Return/King Mixer	199?	—	—	2.00
❑ 131 [PS]	Point of No Return/King Mixer	199?	—	—	2.00

WARNER BROS.
❑ 7093	Bottom of the Soul/Astrologically Incompatible	1968	2.00	4.00	8.00
❑ 7093 [PS]	Bottom of the Soul/Astrologically Incompatible	1968	3.75	7.50	15.00
❑ 7199	To the Light/You'll Love Me Again	1968	2.00	4.00	8.00
Albums
ORIGINAL SOUND
| ❑ 5015 [M] | (Turn On) The Music Machine | 1966 | 10.00 | 20.00 | 40.00 |
| ❑ 8875 [S] | (Turn On) The Music Machine | 1966 | 12.50 | 25.00 | 50.00 |
SUNDAZED
| ❑ LP 5038 | Ignition | 2000 | 3.00 | 6.00 | 12.00 |
WARNER BROS.
| ❑ W 1732 [M] | Bonniwell's Music Machine | 1967 | 6.25 | 12.50 | 25.00 |
| ❑ WS 1732 [S] | Bonniwell's Music Machine | 1967 | 10.00 | 20.00 | 40.00 |

MYDDLE CLASS, THE
45s
BUDDAH
| ❑ 150 | I Happen to Love You/ Don't Let Me Sleep Too Long | 1969 | 2.50 | 5.00 | 10.00 |
TOMORROW
❑ 912	Don't Look Back/Wind Chimes Laughter	1966	5.00	10.00	20.00
❑ 7501	Gates of Eden/Free As the Wind	1966	5.00	10.00	20.00
❑ 7503	I Happen to Love You/ Don't Let Me Sleep Too Long	1966	6.25	12.50	25.00

MYLES, BILLY
45s
DOT
| ❑ 15809 | King of Clowns/So In Need of You | 1958 | 5.00 | 10.00 | 20.00 |
EMBER
❑ 1026	The Joker (That's What They Call Me)/Honey Bee	1957	7.50	15.00	30.00
❑ 1040	Price of Your Love/I'm Too Sentimental	1958	6.25	12.50	25.00
❑ 1046	I'm Gonna Walk/Price of Your Love	1958	6.25	12.50	25.00
KING
❑ 5395	Dance Little Girlie/Two Empty Arms	1960	3.75	7.50	15.00
LOST-NITE
❑ 425	The Joker (That's What They Call Me)/Honey Bee	197?	—	2.50	5.00
—Reissue					

MYSTERY TOUR, THE
45s
MGM
| ❑ 14097 | The Ballad of Paul/The Ballad of Paul (Follow the Bouncing Ball) | 1969 | 6.25 | 12.50 | 25.00 |

MYSTIC ASTROLOGICAL CRYSTAL BAND, THE
45s
CAROLE
| ❑ 1004 | Flowers Never Cry/(B-side unknown) | 1967 | 6.25 | 12.50 | 25.00 |
Albums
CAROLE
❑ 8001 [M]	Mystic Astrological Crystal Band	1967	6.25	12.50	25.00
❑ S-8001 [S]	Mystic Astrological Crystal Band	1967	7.50	15.00	30.00
❑ S-8003	Clip Out, Put On Book	1968	7.50	15.00	30.00

MYSTIC MOODS ORCHESTRA, THE
45s
PHILIPS
❑ 40366	Fire Island/A Dream	1966	—	3.00	6.00
❑ 40419	Theme from "The Sand Pebbles"/Wednesday's Child	1966	—	3.00	6.00
❑ 40581	Medley: Sounds of Silence-Canticle-Scarborough Fair/Homeward Bound	1969	—	2.50	5.00
❑ 40623	Early Morning Rain/Lalena	1969	—	2.50	5.00
❑ 40623 [PS]	Early Morning Rain/Lalena	1969	2.50	5.00	10.00
❑ 40659	Love Token/Green, Green Grass of Home	1970	—	2.50	5.00
❑ 40696	Love Grows (Where My Rosemary Goes)/ Early in the Morning	1971	—	2.00	4.00
SOUNDBIRD
❑ 5002	Honeytrippin'/Midnight Snack	197?	—	2.00	4.00
WARNER BROS.
❑ 7686	Awakening/Cosmic Sea	1973	—	2.00	4.00
❑ 7743	Astral Trip/Drifting Thought	1973	—	2.00	4.00
❑ 7817	Your Place or Mine/Any Way You Want It	1974	—	2.00	4.00
Albums
BAINBRIDGE
❑ 6201	More Than Music	1982	—	3.00	6.00
❑ 6202	Moods for a Stormy Night	1982	—	3.00	6.00
—Reissue of Sound Bird 7504					
❑ 6203	Mexico!	1982	—	3.00	6.00
❑ 6204	Nightide	1982	—	3.00	6.00
—Reissue of Sound Bird 7502					
❑ 6205	One Stormy Night	1982	—	3.00	6.00
—Reissue of Sound Bird 7501					
❑ 6206	Emotions	1982	—	3.00	6.00
—Reissue of Sound Bird 7505					
❑ 6207	Love Token	1982	—	3.00	6.00
❑ 6208	Stormy Weekend	1982	—	3.00	6.00
—Reissue of Sound Bird 7506					
❑ 6209	Highway One	1982	—	3.00	6.00
❑ 6210	English Muffins	1982	—	3.00	6.00
❑ 6211	Country Lovin' Folk	1982	—	3.00	6.00
—Reissue of Sound Bird 8512					
❑ 6212	Extensions	1982	—	3.00	6.00
❑ 6215	Erogenous	1982	—	3.00	6.00
—Reissue of Sound Bird 7509					
❑ 6216	Another Stormy Night	1983	2.00	4.00	8.00
❑ 6219	Summer Moods	1985	2.00	4.00	8.00
MOBILE FIDELITY
❑ 1-001	Emotions	1979	6.25	12.50	25.00
—Audiophile vinyl					
❑ 1-002	Cosmic Forces	1979	6.25	12.50	25.00
—Audiophile vinyl					
❑ 1-003	Stormy Weekend	1979	6.25	12.50	25.00
—Audiophile vinyl					

Number	Title (A Side/B Side)	Yr	VG	VG+	NM
PHILIPS					
❏ PHM 200205 [M]	One Stormy Night	1966	3.00	6.00	12.00
❏ PHM 200213 [M]	Nightide	1966	3.00	6.00	12.00
❏ PHM 200231 [M]	More Than Music	1967	3.75	7.50	15.00
❏ PHM 200250 [M]	Mexican Trip	1967	3.75	7.50	15.00
❏ PHM 200260 [M]	The Mystic Moods of Love	1968	3.75	7.50	15.00
❏ PHS 600205 [S]	One Stormy Night	1966	3.75	7.50	15.00
❏ PHS 600213 [S]	Nightide	1966	3.75	7.50	15.00
❏ PHS 600231 [S]	More Than Music	1967	3.00	6.00	12.00
❏ PHS 600250 [S]	Mexican Trip	1967	3.00	6.00	12.00
❏ PHS 600260 [S]	The Mystic Moods of Love	1968	3.00	6.00	12.00
❏ PHS 600277	Emotions	1968	3.00	6.00	12.00
❏ PHS 600301	Extensions	1969	3.00	6.00	12.00
❏ PHS 600321	Love Token	1969	3.00	6.00	12.00
❏ PHS 600342	Stormy Weekend	1970	3.00	6.00	12.00
❏ PHS 600349	English Muffins	1970	3.00	6.00	12.00
❏ PHS 600351	Country Lovin' Folk	1971	3.00	6.00	12.00
SOUND BIRD					
❏ 7501	One Stormy Night	1975	2.00	4.00	8.00
—Reissue of Warner Bros. 2594					
❏ 7502	Nightide	1975	2.00	4.00	8.00
—Reissue of Warner Bros. 2593					
❏ 7503	Man and…	1975	2.00	4.00	8.00
❏ 7504	Moods for a Stormy Night	1975	2.00	4.00	8.00
❏ 7505	Emotions	1975	2.00	4.00	8.00
❏ 7506	Stormy Weekend	1975	2.00	4.00	8.00
—Reissue of Warner Bros. 2596					
❏ 7507	Touch	1975	2.00	4.00	8.00
❏ SQ 7507 [Q]	Touch	1975	3.00	6.00	12.00
❏ 7508	Love the One You're With	1975	2.00	4.00	8.00
—Reissue of Warner Bros. 2577					
❏ SQ 7508 [Q]	Love the One You're With	1975	3.00	6.00	12.00
—Reissue of Warner Bros. BS4 2577					
❏ 7509	Erogenous	1975	2.00	4.00	8.00
—Reissue of Warner Bros. 2786					
❏ SQ 7509 [Q]	Erogenous	1975	3.00	6.00	12.00
—Reissue of Warner Bros. BS4 2786					
❏ 7510	Being with You	1976	2.50	5.00	10.00
❏ SQ 7510 [Q]	Being with You	1976	4.00	8.00	16.00
❏ 8503	Misty	1978	2.00	4.00	8.00
❏ 8505	Midnight	1978	2.00	4.00	8.00
❏ 8508	Alone Together	1978	2.00	4.00	8.00
❏ 8510	Being with You	1978	2.00	4.00	8.00
—Reissue of Sound Bird 7510					
❏ 8511	Cosmic Forces	1978	2.00	4.00	8.00
❏ 8512	Country Lovin' Folk	1978	2.00	4.00	8.00
❏ 8514	Simple	1978	2.00	4.00	8.00
WARNER BROS.					
❏ BS 2577	Love the One You're With	1972	3.00	6.00	12.00
❏ BS4 2577 [Q]	Love the One You're With	1974	4.00	8.00	16.00
❏ BS 2593	Nightide	1972	2.50	5.00	10.00
—Reissue of Philips 600-213					
❏ BS 2594	One Stormy Night	1972	2.50	5.00	10.00
—Reissue of Philips 600-205					
❏ BS 2595	Love Token	1972	2.50	5.00	10.00
—Reissue of Philips 600-321					
❏ BS 2596	Stormy Weekend	1972	2.50	5.00	10.00
—Reissue of Philips 600-342					
❏ BS 2597	Emotions	1972	2.50	5.00	10.00
—Reissue of Philips 600-277					
❏ BS 2598	The Mystic Moods of Love	1972	2.50	5.00	10.00
—Reissue of Philips 600-260					
❏ BS 2648	Highway One	1973	3.00	6.00	12.00
❏ BS4 2648 [Q]	Highway One	1974	4.00	8.00	16.00
❏ BS 2690	Awakening	1973	3.00	6.00	12.00
❏ BS4 2690 [Q]	Awakening	1974	4.00	8.00	16.00
❏ BS 2745	Clear Light	1974	3.00	6.00	12.00
❏ BS4 2745 [Q]	Clear Light	1974	4.00	8.00	16.00
❏ BS 2786	Erogenous	1974	2.50	5.00	10.00
❏ BS4 2786 [Q]	Erogenous	1974	4.00	8.00	16.00

MYSTIC NUMBER NATIONAL BANK, THE
Albums

Number	Title (A Side/B Side)	Yr	VG	VG+	NM
PROBE					
❏ CPLP-4501	The Mystic Number National Bank	1969	5.00	10.00	20.00

MYSTIC SIVA
Albums

Number	Title (A Side/B Side)	Yr	VG	VG+	NM
VO					
❏ 19713	Mystic Siva	1971	250.00	500.00	1000.

MYSTICS, THE
45s

Number	Title (A Side/B Side)	Yr	VG	VG+	NM
AMBIENT SOUND					
❏ 02871	Now That Summer Is Here/Prayer to An Angel	1982	—	2.50	5.00
BLACK CAT					
❏ 101	Snoopy/Ooh Poo Pah Doo	1966	10.00	20.00	40.00
CONSTELLATION					
❏ 138	She's Got Everything/Just a Loser	1964	3.00	6.00	12.00
DOT					
❏ 16862	Now and For Always/Didn't We Have a Good Time	1966	2.50	5.00	10.00
KING					
❏ 5678	Mashed Potatoes With Me/The Hoppy Hop	1962	3.75	7.50	15.00
❏ 5735	The Jumpin' Bean/Just For Your Love	1963	3.75	7.50	15.00
LAURIE					
❏ 3028 [M]	Hushabye/Adam and Eve	1959	7.50	15.00	30.00
❏ S-3028 [S]	Hushabye/Adam and Eve	1959	30.00	60.00	120.00
❏ 3038	Don't Take the Stars/So Tenderly	1959	6.25	12.50	25.00
❏ 3047	All Through the Night/To Think of You Again	1960	6.25	12.50	25.00
❏ 3058	White Cliffs of Dover/Blue Star	1960	6.25	12.50	25.00
❏ 3086	Star Crossed Lovers/Goodbye Mr. Blue	1961	6.25	12.50	25.00
❏ 3104	Sunday Kind of Love/Darling I Know How	1961	7.50	15.00	30.00
NOLTA					
❏ 353	The Fox/Dan	1963	3.75	7.50	15.00
Albums					
AMBIENT SOUND					
❏ FZ 37716	Crazy for You	1982	2.50	5.00	10.00
COLLECTABLES					
❏ COL-5043	16 Golden Classics	198?	2.50	5.00	10.00

N

Number	Title (A Side/B Side)	Yr	VG	VG+	NM
NABAY					
45s					
IMPACT					
❏ 1032	Believe It or Not/(Instrumental)	1967	100.00	200.00	400.00
NABORS, JIM					
45s					
COLUMBIA					
❏ AE 1028 [DJ]	Ave Maria/How Great Thou Art	1971	—	3.00	6.00
❏ 10035	That's What Friends Are For/Lena the Queen of the Honky-Tonk Angels	1974	—	2.00	4.00
❏ 43395	Shazam!/Old Blue	1965	3.00	6.00	12.00
❏ 43553	Love Me with All Your Heart/Rock-a-Bye	1966	2.00	4.00	8.00
❏ 43751	You Don't Know Me/You're Gonna Hear from Me	1966	2.00	4.00	8.00
❏ 44114	You Know You Don't Want Me/It Hurts to Say Goodbye	1967	—	3.00	6.00
❏ 44241	You Don't Have to Say You Love Me/Time After Time	1967	—	3.00	6.00
❏ 44359	White Christmas/In A Humble Place	1967	—	3.00	6.00
❏ 44462	The Impossible Dream/Time After Time	1968	—	3.00	6.00
❏ 44537	To Give (The Reason I Live)/I Must Have Been Out of My Mind	1968	—	3.00	6.00
❏ 44965	It's My Life/Young Hearts	1969	—	3.00	6.00
❏ 45053	O Holy Night/I Was a King at Jesus' Birth	1969	—	3.00	6.00
❏ 45126	Tomorrow Never Comes/It's My Life	1970	—	2.50	5.00
❏ 45126 [PS]	Tomorrow Never Comes/It's My Life	1970	2.00	4.00	8.00
❏ 45271	I'll Begin Again/Louisiana Lady	1970	—	2.50	5.00
❏ 45321	God Bless America/The Star-Spangled Banner	1971	—	2.50	5.00
❏ 45636	(At) The End (Of a Rainbow)/It Won't Hurt to Try It	1972	—	2.50	5.00
❏ 45932	Oh Babe, What Would You Say/Cardboards, Crayons and Clay	1973	—	2.50	5.00
RANWOOD					
❏ 1081	Always Leave 'Em Laughing/Sing me a Love Song	1977	—	2.00	4.00
ROULETTE					
❏ 4105	There's No Tomorrow/I'm Working	1958	6.25	12.50	25.00
—As "Jimmy Nabors"					
Albums					
CAPITOL SPECIAL MARKETS					
❏ SL-8136	20 All-Time Favorites	1977	2.50	5.00	10.00
COLUMBIA					
❏ CS 1020	The Jim Nabors Hour	1970	3.00	6.00	12.00
❏ CL 2368 [M]	Shazam! (Gomer Pyle, U.S.M.C.)	1965	5.00	10.00	20.00
❏ CL 2558 [M]	Jim Nabors Sings Love Me with All Your Heart	1966	3.00	6.00	12.00
❏ CL 2665 [M]	Jim Nabors By Request	1967	3.00	6.00	12.00
❏ CL 2703 [M]	The Things I Love	1967	3.00	6.00	12.00
❏ CL 2731 [M]	Jim Nabors' Christmas Album	1967	3.00	6.00	12.00
❏ CS 9168 [S]	Shazam! (Gomer Pyle, U.S.M.C.)	1965	6.25	12.50	25.00
❏ CS 9358 [S]	Jim Nabors Sings Love Me with All Your Heart	1966	3.75	7.50	15.00
❏ CS 9465 [S]	Jim Nabors By Request	1967	3.75	7.50	15.00
❏ CS 9503 [S]	The Things I Love	1967	3.75	7.50	15.00
❏ CS 9531 [S]	Jim Nabors' Christmas Album	1967	3.00	6.00	12.00
—Originals with "360 Sound" label					
❏ CS 9531	Jim Nabors' Christmas Album	1970	2.50	5.00	10.00
—Later editions with orange label					
❏ CS 9620	Kiss Me Goodbye	1968	3.00	6.00	12.00
❏ CS 9716	The Lord's Prayer and Other Sacred Songs	1968	3.00	6.00	12.00
❏ PC 9716	The Lord's Prayer	1979	2.00	4.00	8.00
—Budget-line reissue					
❏ CS 9817	Galveston	1969	3.00	6.00	12.00
❏ C 30129	Everything Is Beautiful	1970	3.00	6.00	12.00
❏ C 30449	For the Good Times/The Jim Nabors Hour	1971	3.00	6.00	12.00
❏ 3C 30671	How Great Thou Art	198?	2.00	4.00	8.00
—Budget-line reissue					
❏ C 30671	How Great Thou Art	1971	3.00	6.00	12.00
❏ C 30810	Help Me Make It Through the Night	1971	3.00	6.00	12.00
❏ CQ 30810 [Q]	Help Me Make It Through the Night	1971	5.00	10.00	20.00
❏ KC 31336	The Way of Love	1972	3.00	6.00	12.00
❏ KG 31591 [(2)]	Great Love Songs	1972	3.75	7.50	15.00
❏ PG 31591 [(2)]	Great Love Songs	198?	2.50	5.00	10.00
—Budget-line reissue					
❏ C 31630	Merry Christmas	1972	2.50	5.00	10.00
❏ KG 31973 [(2)]	The World of Jim Nabors	1972	3.75	7.50	15.00
❏ PG 31973 [(2)]	The World of Jim Nabors	1979	2.50	5.00	10.00
—Budget-line reissue					
❏ KC 32377	The Twelfth of Never	1972	3.00	6.00	12.00
❏ KC 32909	Peace in the Valley	1973	3.00	6.00	12.00
❏ PC 32909	Peace in the Valley	1979	2.00	4.00	8.00
—Budget-line reissue					
❏ KC 32950	It's My Life	1973	3.00	6.00	12.00
❏ KC 33401	A Very Special Love Song	1974	3.00	6.00	12.00
❏ PC 33401	A Very Special Love Song	1979	2.00	4.00	8.00
—Budget-line reissue					
❏ CG 33618 [(2)]	The Lord's Prayer/How Great Thou Art	1975	3.75	7.50	15.00
COLUMBIA SPECIAL PRODUCTS					
❏ P 13507	Somewhere My Love	1977	2.50	5.00	10.00
HARMONY					
❏ KH 30398	More	1971	2.50	5.00	10.00
PAIR					
❏ PDL2-1077 [(2)]	The Very Special Warmth of Jim Nabors	1986	3.00	6.00	12.00
❏ PDL2-1097 [(2)]	On the Country Side	1986	3.00	6.00	12.00
RANWOOD					
❏ R-7017 [(2)]	22 Great Hymn and Country Favorites	1984	3.00	6.00	12.00
❏ R-8157	Old Time Religion	1976	2.50	5.00	10.00
❏ R-8164	Town & Country	1976	2.50	5.00	10.00
❏ R-8176	Sincerely	1977	2.50	5.00	10.00
❏ R-8178	I See God	1977	2.50	5.00	10.00
REALM					
❏ 1V-8170	Christmas with Jim Nabors	1982	2.00	4.00	8.00

N

Number	Title (A Side/B Side)	Yr	VG	VG+	NM

NADER, RICHARD See VARIOUS ARTISTS COLLECTIONS.

NAGLE, RON
Albums
WARNER BROS.

❑ WS 1902	Bad Rice	1970	5.00	10.00	20.00

NAPOLEON XIV
45s
WARNER BROS.

❑ 5831	They're Coming to Take Me Away, Ha-Haaa!/ Yawa Em Ekat ot Gnimoc Er'yeht, !Aaah-Ah	1966	3.00	6.00	12.00
❑ 5853	I'm in Love with My Little Red Tricycle/Doin' the Napoleon	1966	2.50	5.00	10.00
❑ 7726	They're Coming to Take Me Away, Ha-Haaa!/ !Aaah-Ah, Yawa Em Ekat ot Gnimoc Er'yeht	1973	2.00	4.00	8.00

Albums
RHINO

❑ RNLP 816	They're Coming to Take Me Away, Ha-Haaa!	1985	3.00	6.00	12.00
WARNER BROS.					
❑ W 1661 [M]	They're Coming to Take Me Away, Ha-Haaa!	1966	15.00	30.00	60.00
❑ WS 1661 [S]	They're Coming to Take Me Away, Ha-Haaa!	1966	25.00	50.00	100.00

NARZ, JACK
Albums
DOT

❑ DLP-3244 [M]	Sing the Folk Hits with Jack Narz	1960	6.25	12.50	25.00
❑ DLP-25244 [S]	Sing the Folk Hits with Jack Narz	1960	7.50	15.00	30.00

NASH, GRAHAM Also see CROSBY, STILLS AND NASH; CROSBY, STILLS, NASH & YOUNG; THE HOLLIES.
45s
ATLANTIC

❑ 2804	Chicago/Simple Man	1971	—	3.00	6.00
❑ 2827	Military Madness/Sleep Song	1971	—	2.50	5.00
❑ 2840	Used to Be a King/Wounded Bird	1971	—	2.50	5.00
❑ 2990	Prison Song/Hey You (Looking at the Moon)	1973	—	2.50	5.00
❑ 89373	Chippin' Away/Newday	1986	—	—	3.00
❑ 89396	Sad Eyes/Newday	1986	—	—	3.00
❑ 89434	Innocent Eyes/I Got a Rock	1986	—	—	3.00
❑ 89434 [PS]	Innocent Eyes/I Got a Rock	1986	—	2.00	4.00
CAPITOL					
❑ 4812	In the 80's/T.V. Guide	1979	—	2.00	4.00
❑ 4849	Helicopter Song/Out on the Island	1980	—	2.00	4.00
❑ 4879	Earth and Sky/Magical Child	1980	—	2.00	4.00

Albums
ATLANTIC

❑ SD 7204	Songs for Beginners	1971	3.00	6.00	12.00
❑ SD 7288	Wild Tales	1974	2.50	5.00	10.00
❑ 81633	Innocent Eyes	1986	2.00	4.00	8.00
CAPITOL					
❑ SWAK-12014	Earth & Sky	1980	2.50	5.00	10.00

NASH, GRAHAM, AND DAVID CROSBY Also see each artist's individual listings.
45s
ABC

❑ 12140	Carry Me/Mama Lion	1975	—	2.00	4.00
❑ 12165	Bittersweet/Take the Money and Run	1976	—	2.00	4.00
❑ 12185	Love Workout/Bittersweet	1976	—	2.00	4.00
❑ 12199	Out of the Darkness/Broken Bird	1976	—	2.00	4.00
❑ 12217	Foolish Man/Spotlight	1976	—	2.00	4.00
ATLANTIC					
❑ 2873	Immigration Man/Whole Cloth	1972	—	2.50	5.00
❑ 2892	Southbound Train/The Wall Song	1972	—	2.50	5.00

Albums
ABC

❑ ABCD-902	Wind on the Water	1975	2.50	5.00	10.00
❑ ABCD-956	Whistling Down the Wire	1976	2.50	5.00	10.00
❑ AA-1042	Crosby/Nash — Live	1977	2.50	5.00	10.00
❑ AA-1102	The Best of Crosby/Nash	1978	2.50	5.00	10.00
ATLANTIC					
❑ SD 7220	Graham Nash/David Crosby	1972	3.00	6.00	12.00
MCA					
❑ 37007	Wind on the Water	198?	2.00	4.00	8.00
—Reissue of ABC 902					
❑ 37008	The Best of Crosby/Nash	198?	2.00	4.00	8.00
—Reissue of ABC 1102					

NASH, JOHNNY Also see PAUL ANKA/GEORGE HAMILTON IV/JOHNNY NASH.
45s
ABC-PARAMOUNT

❑ 9743	Out of Town/A Teenager Sings the Blues	1956	5.00	10.00	20.00
❑ 9844	The Ladder of Love/I'll Walk Alone	1957	5.00	10.00	20.00
❑ 9874	A Very Special Love/Won't You Let Me Share My Love with You	1957	5.00	10.00	20.00
❑ 9894	My Pledge to You/It's So Easy to Say	1958	5.00	10.00	20.00
❑ 9927	Please Don't Go/I Lost My Love Last Night	1958	5.00	10.00	20.00
❑ 9942	Truly Love/You're Looking at Me	1958	5.00	10.00	20.00
❑ 9960	Almost in Your Arms/Midnight Moonlight	1958	5.00	10.00	20.00
❑ 9989	Roots of Heaven/Walk with Faith in Your Heart	1958	5.00	10.00	20.00
❑ 9996	As Time Goes By/The Voice of Love	1959	5.00	10.00	20.00
❑ 9996 [PS]	As Time Goes By/The Voice of Love	1959	10.00	20.00	40.00
❑ 10026	And the Angels Sing/Baby, Baby, Baby	1959	5.00	10.00	20.00
❑ 10046	Take a Giant Step/But Not for Me	1959	5.00	10.00	20.00
❑ 10060	The Wish/Too Proud	1959	5.00	10.00	20.00
❑ 10076	A Place in the Sun/Goodbye	1960	3.75	7.50	15.00
❑ 10095	Never My Love/(You've Got the) Love I Love	1960	3.75	7.50	15.00
❑ 10112	Let the Rest of the World Go By/Music of Love	1960	3.75	7.50	15.00
❑ 10137	(Looks Like) The End of the World/We Kissed	1960	3.75	7.50	15.00
❑ 10160	Kisses/Somebody	1960	3.75	7.50	15.00
❑ 10181	World of Tears/Some of Your Lovin'	1961	3.00	6.00	12.00
❑ 10205	I Need Someone to Stand By/A House on the Hill	1961	3.00	6.00	12.00
❑ 10212	A Thousand Miles Away/I Need Someone to Stand By Me	1961	3.00	6.00	12.00
❑ 10230	I'm Counting on You/I Lost My Baby	1961	3.00	6.00	12.00
❑ 10251	Too Much Love/Love's Young Dream	1961	3.00	6.00	12.00

ARGO

❑ 5471	Talk to Me/Love Ain't Nothin'	1964	2.00	4.00	8.00
❑ 5479	Then You Can Tell Me Goodbye/Always	1964	2.00	4.00	8.00
❑ 5492	Spring Is Here/Strange Feeling	1965	2.00	4.00	8.00
❑ 5501	Teardrops in the Rain/I Know What I Want	1965	2.00	4.00	8.00
ATLANTIC					
❑ 2344	Big City/Somewhere	1966	2.00	4.00	8.00
CADET					
❑ 5528	Teardrops in the Rain/Get Myself Together	1966	5.00	10.00	20.00
EPIC					
❑ 10873	Stir It Up/Cream Puff	1972	—	3.50	7.00
❑ 10902	I Can See Clearly Now/How Good It Is	1972	—	3.00	6.00
❑ 10949	Stir It Up/Ooh Baby You've Been Good to Me	1973	—	3.00	6.00
❑ 11003	My Merry-Go-Round/ We're Trying to Get Back to You	1973	—	2.50	5.00
❑ 11034	Ooh What a Feeling/Yellow House	1973	—	2.50	5.00
❑ 11070	Loving You/Gonna Open Up My Heart Again	1973	—	2.50	5.00
❑ 50021	You Can't Go Halfway/The Very First Time	1974	—	2.50	5.00
❑ 50051	Beautiful Baby/Celebrate Life	1974	—	2.50	5.00
❑ 50091	Good Vibrations/The Very First Time	1975	—	2.50	5.00
❑ 50138	Tears on My Pillow (I Can't Take It)/ Beautiful Baby	1975	—	2.50	5.00
❑ 50219	(What a) Wonderful World/Rock It Baby (We've Got a Date)	1976	—	2.50	5.00
❑ 50386	Back in Time/That Woman	1977	—	2.00	4.00
❑ 50737	Closer/Mr. Sea	1979	—	2.00	4.00
❑ 50821	You're the One/Don't Forget	1980	—	2.00	4.00
GROOVE					
❑ 58-0018	Helpless/I've Got a Lot to Offer, Darling	1963	2.50	5.00	10.00
❑ 58-0018 [PS]	Helpless/I've Got a Lot to Offer, Darling	1963	7.50	15.00	30.00
❑ 58-0021	Deep in the Heart of Harlem/What Kind of Love Is This	1963	10.00	20.00	40.00
❑ 58-0021 [PS]	Deep in the Heart of Harlem/ What Kind of Love Is This	1963	12.50	25.00	50.00
❑ 58-0026	It's No Good for Me/Town of Lonely Hearts	1963	2.50	5.00	10.00
❑ 58-0030	I'm Leaving/Oh Mary Don't You Weep	1964	2.50	5.00	10.00
JAD					
❑ 207	Hold Me Tight/Cupid	1968	2.00	4.00	8.00
—Mostly light green label with purple trim					
❑ 209	You Got Soul/Don't Cry	1968	2.00	4.00	8.00
❑ 214	Lovey Dovey/You Got Soul	1969	—	3.00	6.00
❑ 215	Sweet Charity/People in Love	1969	—	3.00	6.00
❑ 218	Love and Peace/People in Love	1969	—	3.00	6.00
❑ 220	Cupid/Hold Me Tight	1969	—	3.00	6.00
❑ 223	What a Groovy Feeling/You Got Soul (Part 1)	1970	—	3.00	6.00
JANUS					
❑ 136	Falling In and Out of Love/ You've Got to Change Your Ways	1970	—	3.00	6.00
JODA					
❑ 102	Let's Move and Groove (Together)/ Understanding	1965	2.50	5.00	10.00
❑ 105	One More Time/Got to Find Her	1965	2.50	5.00	10.00
❑ 106	Somewhere/Big City	1966	2.50	5.00	10.00
MGM					
❑ 13637	Amen/Perfumed Flower	1966	2.00	4.00	8.00
❑ 13683	Good Goodness/You Never Know	1967	2.00	4.00	8.00
❑ 13805	Stormy/(I'm So) Glad You're My Baby	1967	2.00	4.00	8.00
WARNER BROS.					
❑ 5270	Don't Take Your Love Away/Moment of Weakness	1962	3.00	6.00	12.00
❑ 5301	Ol' Man River/My Dear Little Sweetheart	1962	3.00	6.00	12.00
❑ 5336	Cigarettes, Whiskey and Wild, Wild Women/ I'm Movin' On	1963	3.00	6.00	12.00

Albums
ABC-PARAMOUNT

❑ 244 [M]	Johnny Nash	1958	7.50	15.00	30.00
❑ S-244 [S]	Johnny Nash	1959	10.00	20.00	40.00
❑ 276 [M]	Quiet Hour	1959	7.50	15.00	30.00
❑ S-276 [S]	Quiet Hour	1959	10.00	20.00	40.00
❑ 299 [M]	I Got Rhythm	1959	7.50	15.00	30.00
❑ S-299 [S]	I Got Rhythm	1959	10.00	20.00	40.00
❑ 344 [M]	Let's Get Lost	1960	7.50	15.00	30.00
❑ S-344 [S]	Let's Get Lost	1960	10.00	20.00	40.00
❑ 383 [M]	Studio Time	1961	7.50	15.00	30.00
❑ S-383 [S]	Studio Time	1961	10.00	20.00	40.00
ARGO					
❑ LP-4038 [M]	Composer's Choice	1964	5.00	10.00	20.00
❑ LPS-4038 [S]	Composer's Choice	1964	6.25	12.50	25.00
EPIC					
❑ KE 31607	I Can See Clearly Now	1972	3.75	7.50	15.00
—Yellow label					
❑ KE 31607	I Can See Clearly Now	1973	3.00	6.00	12.00
—Orange label					
❑ KE 32158	My Merry-Go-Round	1973	3.75	7.50	15.00
❑ PE 32828	Celebrate Life	1974	3.75	7.50	15.00
JAD					
❑ JS-1001	Prince of Peace	1969	6.25	12.50	25.00
❑ JS-1006	Folk Soul	1970	6.25	12.50	25.00
❑ JS-1207	Hold Me Tight	1968	7.50	15.00	30.00

NASHVILLE FIVE, THE
45s
HIT

❑ 119	Cotton Candy/Love Me with All Your Heart	1964	2.00	4.00	8.00
—B-side by the Music City Singers					
❑ 135	Walk Don't Run '64/Because	1964	2.50	5.00	10.00
—B-side by the Roamers					
❑ 231	A Taste of Honey/England Swings	1965	2.00	4.00	8.00
—B-side by Bobby Brooks					
❑ 243	Batman Theme/Husbands and Wives	1966	2.00	4.00	8.00

NASHVILLE GUITARS, THE
Albums
MONUMENT

❑ MLP-8058 [M]	The Nashville Guitars	1966	3.75	7.50	15.00
❑ SLP-18058 [S]	The Nashville Guitars	1966	5.00	10.00	20.00
❑ MLP-18093	The Nashville Guitars at Home	1968	3.75	7.50	15.00

Number	Title (A Side/B Side)	Yr	VG	VG+	NM
NASHVILLE TEENS, THE					
45s					
LONDON					
❏ 9689	Tobacco Road/I Like It Like That	1964	3.75	7.50	15.00
❏ 9712	T.N.T./Google Eyes	1964	3.00	6.00	12.00
❏ 9736	Devil-in-Law/Find My Way Back Home	1965	3.00	6.00	12.00
MGM					
❏ 13357	Little Bird/Whatcha Gonna Do	1965	2.50	5.00	10.00
❏ 13406	I Know How It Feels to Be Loved/Soon Forgotten	1965	2.50	5.00	10.00
❏ 13483	The Hard Way/Upside Down	1966	2.50	5.00	10.00
❏ 13678	That's My Woman/Words	1967	2.50	5.00	10.00
UNITED ARTISTS					
❏ 50880	Tennessee Woman/Ella James	1972	5.00	10.00	20.00
Albums					
LONDON					
❏ PS 407 [R]	Tobacco Road	1964	20.00	40.00	80.00
❏ LL 3407 [M]	Tobacco Road	1964	25.00	50.00	100.00
NATIONAL GALLERY, THE					
Albums					
PHILIPS					
❏ PHS 600266	The National Gallery (Performing Musical Interpretations of the Paintings of Paul Klee)	1968	7.50	15.00	30.00
NATIONAL LAMPOON Also see MELISSA MANCHESTER.					
45s					
BANANA					
❏ 218	Deteriorata/Thise Fabulous Sixties	1972	2.00	4.00	8.00
❏ 233	Pizza Man/Lemmings Lament	1974	2.00	4.00	8.00
❏ 240	The Watergate Tapes/The Silent Majority	1973	2.00	4.00	8.00
LABEL 21					
❏ 202	What Were You Expecting — Rock 'n Roll?/(B-side unknown)	197?	—	3.00	6.00
❏ 202 [PS]	What Were You Expecting — Rock 'n Roll?/(B-side unknown)	197?	2.50	5.00	10.00
Albums					
BANANA					
❏ BTS 38	Radio Dinner	1972	3.75	7.50	15.00
❏ BTS 6006	Lemmings	1973	3.75	7.50	15.00
❏ BTS 6008	Missing White House Tapes	1974	3.75	7.50	15.00
EPIC					
❏ PE 33410	Gold Turkey	1974	3.00	6.00	12.00
—Orange label					
❏ PE 33410	Gold Turkey	1979	2.00	4.00	8.00
—Dark blue label					
❏ PE 33956	Goodbye Pop	1975	3.00	6.00	12.00
—Orange label					
❏ PE 33956	Goodbye Pop	1979	2.00	4.00	8.00
—Dark blue label					
LABEL 21					
❏ IMP-2001	That's Not Funny, That's Sick!	1978	2.50	5.00	10.00
❏ PIC-2001 [PD]	That's Not Funny, That's Sick!	1978	5.00	10.00	20.00
❏ IMP-2002	The White Album	1979	2.50	5.00	10.00
MCA					
❏ 27023	Lemmings	198?	2.00	4.00	8.00
❏ 27024	Radio Dinner	198?	2.00	4.00	8.00
PASSPORT					
❏ PB 6018	Sex, Drugs, Rock and Roll and the End of the World	1982	2.50	5.00	10.00
VISA					
❏ 2001	That's Not Funny, That's Sick!	198?	2.00	4.00	8.00
❏ 2002	The White Album	198?	2.00	4.00	8.00
❏ 7008	Greatest Hits of the National Lampoon	1978	3.00	6.00	12.00
NATIVE BOYS, THE					
45s					
COMBO					
❏ 113	Strange Love/Cherrlyn	1956	15.00	30.00	60.00
❏ 115	Tears/When I Met You	1956	17.50	35.00	70.00
❏ 119	Laughing Love/Valley of Lovers	1956	17.50	35.00	70.00
❏ 120	Oh Let Me Dream/I've Got a Feeling	1956	15.00	30.00	60.00
LOST-NITE					
❏ 366	Strange Love/Cherrlyn	197?	—	2.50	5.00
—Reissue					
❏ 369	Tears/When I Met You	197?	—	2.50	5.00
—Reissue					
❏ 372	Laughing Love/Valley of Lovers	197?	—	2.50	5.00
—Reissue					
❏ 375	Oh Let Me Dream/I've Got a Feeling	197?	—	2.50	5.00
—Reissue					
MODERN					
❏ 939	Native Girl/It Won't Take Long	1954	100.00	200.00	400.00
NATURAL FOUR, THE					
45s					
ABC					
❏ 11205	Why Should We Stop Now/You Did This for Me	1969	2.00	4.00	8.00
❏ 11236	Same Thing in Mind/The Situation Needs No Explanation	1969	3.00	6.00	12.00
❏ 11253	Hurt/I Thought You Were Mine	1969	6.25	12.50	25.00
❏ 11257	Message from a Black Man/Stepping On Up	1970	3.00	6.00	12.00
CURTOM					
❏ 0101	Heaven Right Here on Earth/While We're Away	1975	—	2.50	5.00
❏ 0104	Love's So Wonderful/What's Happening Here	1975	—	2.50	5.00
❏ 0114	It's the Music/It's the Music (Disco Version)	1976	—	2.50	5.00
❏ 0119	Free/Nothing Beats a Failure (But a Try)	1976	—	2.50	5.00
❏ 1981	Things Will Be Better Tomorrow/Eddie, You Should Know Better	1973	—	2.50	5.00
❏ 1984	Try Love Again/Eddie, You Should Know Better	1973	—	2.50	5.00
❏ 1990	Can This Be Real/Try Love Again	1973	—	2.50	5.00
❏ 1995	Love That Really Counts/Love's Society	1974	—	2.50	5.00
❏ 2000	You Bring Out the Best in Me/You Can't Keep Running Away	1974	—	2.50	5.00
Albums					
CURTOM					
❏ CU 5004	Heaven Right Here on Earth	1975	5.00	10.00	20.00
❏ CRT-8600	The Natural Four	1974	5.00	10.00	20.00

Number	Title (A Side/B Side)	Yr	VG	VG+	NM
NATURALS, THE (1)					
45s					
CALLA					
❏ 181	I Can't Share You/Young Generation	1972	—	3.00	6.00
MOTOWN					
❏ 1208	Good Things/Where Was I When Love Came By	1972	—	3.00	6.00
SHOUT					
❏ 307	Color Him Father/Crystal Blue Persuasion	197?	—	3.00	6.00
❏ 310	Cold Day in Hell/(B-side unknown)	197?	—	3.00	6.00
NATURALS, THE (2)					
45s					
BEACON					
❏ 462	You Give Me So Much/What a Shape I'm In	1958	10.00	20.00	40.00
NATURALS, THE (3)					
45s					
CHATTAHOOCHIE					
❏ 633	Just in Case You Change Your Mind/Why Don't They Understand	1963	3.00	6.00	12.00
NATURALS, THE (4)					
45s					
ERA					
❏ 1089	The Mummy/Don't Send Me Away	1959	3.75	7.50	15.00
NATURALS, THE (5) Also see THE FOUR NATURALS.					
45s					
HUNT					
❏ 325	Blue Moon/How Strange	1959	3.75	7.50	15.00
RED TOP					
❏ 113	Blue Moon/How Strange	1959	7.50	15.00	30.00
NATURALS, THE (6) British group.					
45s					
LIBERTY					
❏ 55741	I Should Have Known Better/Didn't I	1964	3.00	6.00	12.00
❏ 55758	It Was You/Look at Me Now	1964	3.00	6.00	12.00
NATURALS, THE (7)					
45s					
MGM					
❏ K11970	Marty/The Jitterbug Waltz	1955	3.75	7.50	15.00
❏ K11970 [PS]	Marty/The Jitterbug Waltz	1955	20.00	40.00	80.00
—With photos of Ernest Borgnine and Betsy Blair, plus a synopsis of the play					
❏ K12576	Patti Ann/Missing	1957	3.00	6.00	12.00
❏ K12576 [PS]	Patti Ann/Missing	1957	5.00	10.00	20.00
NATURALS, THE (8)					
45s					
SMASH					
❏ 1925	Different Girls/Hey Fellas	1964	3.00	6.00	12.00
NATURALS, THE (U) We're not sure if this is a ninth different group.					
45s					
CUB					
❏ 9026	The Flower Song/Three Young Men	1959	3.75	7.50	15.00
—B-side by Lee Davis					
20TH CENTURY FOX					
❏ 545	Caravan/Whole Lotta Rockin'	1964	3.00	6.00	12.00
NATURE BOY & FRIENDS					
45s					
BERTRAM INT'L.					
❏ 255	Surfer John/John John	1964	10.00	20.00	40.00
NAYLOR, JERRY					
45s					
COLUMBIA					
❏ 4-44809	The Chokin' Kind/Helga	1969	2.00	4.00	8.00
❏ 4-44874	Gotta Travel On/Posters on the Wall	1969	2.00	4.00	8.00
❏ 4-45106	But for Love/Angeline	1970	—	3.50	7.00
❏ 4-45170	Broken-Hearted Man/Mind Excursion	1970	—	3.50	7.00
❏ 4-45212	If I Promise/Marie	1970	—	3.50	7.00
❏ 4-45292	Come On Love/Las Virgenes Road	1970	—	3.50	7.00
HITSVILLE					
❏ 6041	The Bad Part of Me/I Hate to Drink Alone	1976	—	2.50	5.00
❏ 6046	The Last Time You Love Me/Born to Fool Around	1976	—	2.50	5.00
MC					
❏ 5004	If You Don't Want to Love Her/Love Away Her Memory Tonight	1978	—	2.50	5.00
❏ 5010	Rave On/Lady, Would You Like to Dance	1978	—	2.50	5.00
MELODYLAND					
❏ 6003	Is This All There Is to a Honky Tonk?/You're the One	1974	—	2.50	5.00
❏ 6012	He'll Have to Go/Once Again	1975	—	2.50	5.00
❏ 6020	What's a Nice Girl Like You Doing in a Honky Tonk/Prayin' for My Mind	1975	—	2.50	5.00
MGM					
❏ 14312	With This Ring/Goodtime Charlie	1971	—	3.00	6.00
❏ 14393	That'll Be the Day/Hands	1972	—	3.00	6.00
❏ 14439	Continental Highway/In This World	1972	—	3.00	6.00
❏ 14497	Bitter Memories/Love You Most of All	1973	—	3.00	6.00
❏ 14546	If You Don't Know Me by Now/Bitter Memories	1973	—	3.00	6.00
❏ 14637	Honky Tonk Women/You Are a Song	1973	—	3.00	6.00
OAK					
❏ 1014	Cheating Eyes/America, I'm Coming Home to You	1980	—	3.00	6.00
SKYLA					
❏ 1118	You're Thirteen/Stop Your Crying	1961	5.00	10.00	20.00
❏ 1123	Judee Malone/I'm Tired	1962	5.00	10.00	20.00
SMASH					
❏ 1971	I'll Take You Home/I Found You	1965	3.75	7.50	15.00
TOWER					
❏ 139	It's Only Make Believe/Leave Him and Come to My Loving Arms	1965	3.75	7.50	15.00
❏ 162	City Lights/Life	1965	3.75	7.50	15.00

N

Number	Title (A Side/B Side)	Yr	VG	VG+	NM
❏ 214	My Special Angel/Would You Believe	1966	3.00	6.00	12.00
❏ 264	Almost Persuaded/				
	I'll Get My Life the Way I Want It	1966	3.00	6.00	12.00
❏ 280	Drinkin' and Thinkin'/Johnny Brown	1966	3.00	6.00	12.00
❏ 327	Sweet Violets/Temptation Leads Me	1967	3.00	6.00	12.00
❏ 365	High on Happiness/Today and Tomorrow	1967	3.00	6.00	12.00

WARNER BROS.

❏ 8767	But for Love/Part Time Lover, Full Time Fool	1979	—	2.50	5.00
❏ 8881	She Wears It Well/				
	Part Time Lover, Full Time Fool	1979	—	2.50	5.00

WEST

❏ 723	For Old Time Sake/I Want to Be Loved	1986	—	3.00	6.00
❏ 726	Lean on Me/I Wanna Be Loved	1987	—	3.00	6.00

NAZARETH
45s
A&M

❏ 1453	Broken Down Angel/Hard Living	1973	—	2.50	5.00
❏ 1469	Bad Bad Boy/Razamanaz	1973	—	2.50	5.00
❏ 1511	Go Down Fighting/This Flight Tonight	1974	—	2.50	5.00
❏ 1548	Sunshine/This Flight Tonight	1974	—	2.50	5.00
❏ 1671	Love Hurts/Hair of the Dog	1975	—	2.00	4.00
❏ 1671 [PS]	Love Hurts/Hair of the Dog	1975	—	3.00	6.00
❏ 1854	Loretta/Lift the Lid	1976	—	2.00	4.00
❏ 1895	I Want To (Do Everything for You)/I Don't Want				
	to Go On Without You	1976	—	2.00	4.00
❏ 1936	Somebody to Roll/This Flight Tonight	1976	—	2.00	4.00
❏ 2009	Kentucky Fried Blues/Shot Me Down	1978	—	2.00	4.00
❏ 2029	Gone Dead Train/Kentucky Fried Blues	1978	—	2.00	4.00
❏ 2116	Expect No Mercy/May the Sunshine	1979	—	2.00	4.00
❏ 2130	Whatever You Want Babe/Expect No Mercy	1979	—	2.00	4.00
❏ 2158	Star/Expect No Mercy	1979	—	2.00	4.00
❏ 2219	Holiday/Ship of Dreams	1980	—	2.00	4.00
❏ 2237	Hearts Grown Cold/Ship of Dreams	1980	—	2.00	4.00
❏ 2324	Dressed to Kill/Pop the Silo	1981	—	2.00	4.00
❏ 2378	Juicy Lucy/Morning Dew	1981	—	2.00	4.00
❏ 2389	Hair of the Dog/Holiday	1982	—	2.00	4.00
❏ 2421	Love Leads to Madness/Take the Rap	1982	—	2.00	4.00
❏ 2444	Dream On/Take the Rap	1982	—	2.00	4.00

WARNER BROS.

❏ 7599	Morning Dew (Take Me for a Walk)/Dear John	1972	2.00	4.00	8.00

Albums
A&M

❏ SP-3109	Close Enough for Rock 'N' Roll	1981	2.00	4.00	8.00

—Budget-line reissue

❏ SP-3168	Exercises	1982	2.00	4.00	8.00

—Reissue of Warner Bros. 2639

❏ SP-3169	Nazareth	1982	2.00	4.00	8.00

—Reissue of Warner Bros. 2615

❏ SP-3225	Hair of the Dog	1984	2.00	4.00	8.00

—Budget-line reissue

❏ SP-3226	Hot Tracks	1984	2.00	4.00	8.00

—Budget-line reissue

❏ SP-3609	Loud 'N' Proud	1974	2.50	5.00	10.00
❏ SP-3641	Rampant	1974	2.50	5.00	10.00
❏ SP-4396	Razamanaz	1973	3.75	7.50	15.00

—First edition with brown label

❏ SP-4396	Razamanaz	1974	2.50	5.00	10.00
❏ SP-4511	Hair of the Dog	1975	2.50	5.00	10.00
❏ SP-4562	Close Enough for Rock 'N' Roll	1976	2.50	5.00	10.00
❏ SP-4610	Play 'N' the Game	1976	2.50	5.00	10.00
❏ SP-4643	Hot Tracks	1977	2.50	5.00	10.00
❏ SP-4666	Expect No Mercy	1977	2.50	5.00	10.00
❏ SP-4741	No Mean City	1979	2.50	5.00	10.00
❏ SP-4799	Malice in Wonderland	1980	2.50	5.00	10.00
❏ SP-4844	The Fool Circle	1981	2.50	5.00	10.00
❏ SP-4901	2XS	1982	2.50	5.00	10.00
❏ SP-6703 [(2)]	'Snaz	1981	3.00	6.00	12.00

MCA

❏ 5458	Sound Elixir	1983	2.50	5.00	10.00

WARNER BROS.

❏ BS 2615	Nazareth	1972	5.00	10.00	20.00
❏ BS 2639	Exercises	1972	5.00	10.00	20.00

NAZZ (1) Also see TODD RUNDGREN.
45s
SGC

❏ 001	Hello It's Me/Open My Eyes	1969	2.00	4.00	8.00

—Third printing: Mostly green label with some yellow. Red vinyl copies on any label are bootlegs.

❏ 001	Hello It's Me/Open My Eyes	1969	3.00	6.00	12.00

—Second pressing: Darker yellow label with horizontal lines

❏ 001	Hello It's Me/Open My Eyes	1969	5.00	10.00	20.00

—First pressing: Light yellow label, no horizontal lines on label

❏ 001 [PS]	Hello It's Me/Open My Eyes	1969	5.00	10.00	20.00

—Legitimate sleeves are paper, not cardboard

❏ 006	Not Wrong Long/Under the Ice	1969	3.00	6.00	12.00
❏ 006 [PS]	Not Wrong Long/Under the Ice	1969	5.00	10.00	20.00
❏ 009	Magic Me/Some People	1970	3.00	6.00	12.00
❏ 009	Magic Me/Kicks	1970	6.25	12.50	25.00

Albums
RHINO

❏ RNLP 109	Nazz	1984	2.50	5.00	10.00
❏ RNLP 110	Nazz Nazz	1984	2.50	5.00	10.00
❏ RNLP 111	Nazz III	1984	2.50	5.00	10.00
❏ RNLP 116	The Best of Nazz	1984	2.50	5.00	10.00
❏ R1 70116	The Best of Nazz	1987	2.00	4.00	8.00

SGC

❏ SD 5001	Nazz	1968	10.00	20.00	40.00
❏ 5002 [M]	Nazz Nazz	1969	20.00	40.00	80.00

—Promo-only mono pressing on red vinyl

❏ SD 5002 [S]	Nazz Nazz	1969	10.00	20.00	40.00

—Red vinyl

❏ SD 5002 [S]	Nazz Nazz	1969	20.00	40.00	80.00

—Black vinyl

❏ SD 5004	Nazz III	1970	10.00	20.00	40.00

NAZZ (2) Early ALICE COOPER.
45s
VERY

❏ 001	Lay Down and Die, Goodbye/				
	Wonder Who's Loving Her Now	1967	1000.	1500.	2000.

—Warning! Reproductions of this record were made in the 1990s with white promo labels and picture sleeves. They are NOT the real thing.

NEAL, JERRY
45s
DOT

❏ 15810	I Hates Rabbits/Scratchin'	1958	20.00	40.00	80.00

—With Eddie Cochran on guitar on B-side

NED AND GARY
45s
LIBERTY

❏ 55160	Lovin'/I Bust My Seams	1958	15.00	30.00	60.00

NED AND NELDA FRANK ZAPPA and Ray Collins.
45s
VIGAH

❏ 002	Hey Nelda/Surf Along	1963	37.50	75.00	150.00

NEELY, SAM
45s
A&M

❏ 1523	Come a Little Bit Closer/Sadie Take a Lover	1974	—	2.00	4.00
❏ 1612	You Can Have Her/It's a Fine Morning	1974	—	2.00	4.00
❏ 1651	I Fought the Law/Guitar Man	1974	—	2.00	4.00
❏ 1694	Sanctuary/Cajun Man	1975	—	2.00	4.00

CAPITOL

❏ 3235	Long Road to Texas/				
	Change a Sad to a Happy Song	1971	—	3.00	6.00
❏ 3358	Blue Time/Cry Me a Song	1972	—	3.00	6.00
❏ 3381	Loving You Just Crossed My Mind/Everyday Is				
	the Same As Today	1972	—	2.50	5.00
❏ 3510	Rosalie/Try to Reason Why	1973	—	2.50	5.00
❏ 3586	Blue Time/Kiss the Morning Sunshine	1973	—	2.50	5.00

ELEKTRA

❏ 45419	Sail Away/My Lover and My Friend	1977	—	2.00	4.00
❏ 45484	Your Love Is In Good Hands/				
	Things That Lovers Do	1978	—	2.00	4.00

MCA

❏ 52194	The Party's Over (Everybody's Gone)/What Do				
	I Tell My Heart	1983	—	—	3.00
❏ 52226	When You Leave That Way You Can Never Go				
	Back/Music Made Me Do It	1983	—	—	3.00
❏ 52269	Let's Fall in Love Again Tonight/You're No				
	Ordinary Memory	1983	—	—	3.00
❏ 52323	Old Photographs/Somebody's Leaving	1983	—	—	3.00

Albums
A&M

❏ SP-3626	Sam Neely	1974	3.00	6.00	12.00

CAPITOL

❏ ST-873	Long Road to Texas	1972	3.75	7.50	15.00
❏ ST-11097	Loving You Just Crossed My Mind	1972	3.00	6.00	12.00

—Reissued version of ST-873

❏ SMAS-11143	Sam Neely — 2	1973	3.00	6.00	12.00

NEIGHB'RHOOD CHILDREN
45s
ACTA

❏ 813	Maintain/Just No Way	1967	5.00	10.00	20.00

—As "Neighborhood"

❏ 823	Happy Child/Please Leave Me Alone	1968	3.75	7.50	15.00
❏ 828	Behold the Lilies/I Want Action	1968	5.00	10.00	20.00

DOT

❏ 17238	On Our Way/Woman Thing	1969	3.75	7.50	15.00

NAM

❏ 2014	Dancing in the Street/(B-side unknown)	196?	3.75	7.50	15.00

Albums
ACTA

❏ 8005 [M]	The Neighb'rhood Children	1968	20.00	40.00	80.00
❏ 38005 [S]	The Neighb'rhood Children	1968	25.00	50.00	100.00

SUNDAZED

❏ LP 5023 [(2)]	Long Years in Space	199?	3.75	7.50	15.00

NEIGHBORHOOD, THE
45s
BIG TREE

❏ 102	Big Yellow Taxi/You Could Be Born Again	1970	—	2.00	4.00

—Later pressings have red and yellow labels

❏ 102	Big Yellow Taxi/You Could Be Born Again	1970	—	2.50	5.00

—Originals have white labels

❏ 106	Laugh/Now's the Time for Love	1970	—	2.50	5.00

Albums
BIG TREE

❏ 2001	Debut	1970	3.75	7.50	15.00

NEIGHBORHOOD KIDS, THE
45s
BRUNSWICK

❏ 55466	The Christmas Party of the Eighth Reindeer/				
	Christmas Is for Everyone	1971	2.00	4.00	8.00

NEIL, FRED Also see VINCE MARTIN AND FRED NEIL.
45s
BRUNSWICK

❏ 55117	Listen Kitten/Take Me Back Again	1959	7.50	15.00	30.00

—As "Freddie Neil"

CAPITOL

❏ 2047	The Dolphins/I've Got a Secret	1967	7.50	15.00	30.00
❏ 2091	Felicity/Please Send Me Someone to Love	1968	7.50	15.00	30.00
❏ 2256	Everybody's Talkin'/That's the Bag I'm In	1968	7.50	15.00	30.00
❏ 2604	Everybody's Talkin'/Badi-Da	1969	6.25	12.50	25.00

Number	Title (A Side/B Side)	Yr	VG	VG+	NM
EPIC					
❏ 5-9334	Love's Funny/Secret, Secret	1959	5.00	10.00	20.00
❏ 5-9403	Slippin' Around/				
	You Don't Have to Be a Baby to Cry	1960	5.00	10.00	20.00
❏ 5-9435	Four Chaplains/The Rainbow and the Rose	1961	5.00	10.00	20.00
LOOK					
❏ 1002	You Ain't Treatin' Me Right/(B-side unknown)	1958	15.00	30.00	60.00
—As "Freddie Neil"					
Albums					
CAPITOL					
❏ ST-294	Everybody's Talkin'	1969	6.25	12.50	25.00
❏ ST 2665 [S]	Fred Neil	1966	10.00	20.00	40.00
—With color photo on back					
❏ ST 2665 [S]	Fred Neil	1967	7.50	15.00	30.00
—With black & white photo on back					
❏ T 2665 [M]	Fred Neil	1966	7.50	15.00	30.00
❏ ST 2862 [S]	Fred Neil Sessions	1968	7.50	15.00	30.00
❏ T 2862 [M]	Fred Neil Sessions	1968	10.00	20.00	40.00
ELEKTRA					
❏ EKL-293 [M]	Bleecker and MacDougal	1965	7.50	15.00	30.00
❏ EKS-7293 [S]	Bleecker and MacDougal	1965	10.00	20.00	40.00
❏ EKS-74073	Little Bit of Rain	1970	5.00	10.00	20.00
—Reissue of 7293					
SUNDAZED					
❏ LP 5107	Bleecker and MacDougal	2002	3.00	6.00	12.00

NEIL AND JACK   NEIL DIAMOND and Jack Parker.
45s

Number	Title (A Side/B Side)	Yr	VG	VG+	NM
DUEL					
❏ 508	What Will I Do/You Are My Love at Last	1962	100.00	200.00	400.00
❏ 517	I'm Afraid/Till You've Tried Love	1962	100.00	200.00	400.00

NEKTAR
45s

Number	Title (A Side/B Side)	Yr	VG	VG+	NM
PASSPORT					
❏ 7902	Remember the Future/Confusion	1974	—	3.00	6.00
❏ 7904	Astral Man/Nelly the Elephant	1975	—	2.50	5.00
Albums					
PASSPORT					
❏ PPS-98002	Remember the Future	1974	3.00	6.00	12.00
❏ PPSD-98005	Down to Earth	1975	3.00	6.00	12.00
❏ PPSD-98011	Recycled	1976	2.50	5.00	10.00
❏ PPSD-98017	A Tab in the Ocean	1976	2.50	5.00	10.00
POLYDOR					
❏ PD-1-6115	Magic Is a Child	1977	2.50	5.00	10.00
VISA					
❏ IMP 9001 [(2)]	Thru the Ears	1979	3.00	6.00	12.00

NELSON, KATHY
45s

Number	Title (A Side/B Side)	Yr	VG	VG+	NM
LIBERTY					
❏ 55115	Santa Dear/Gimmie a Little Kiss, Will Ya Huh?	1957	5.00	10.00	20.00

NELSON, RICKY   Includes records as "Rick Nelson."
45s

Number	Title (A Side/B Side)	Yr	VG	VG+	NM
CAPITOL					
❏ 4962	Almost Saturday Night/The Loser Babe Is You	1981	—	2.50	5.00
❏ 4974	Call It What You Want/It Hasn't Happened Yet	1981	—	2.50	5.00
❏ 4988	Believe What You Say/The Loser Babe Is You	1981	—	2.50	5.00
❏ B-5178	No Fair Falling in Love/Give 'Em My Number	1982	—	2.50	5.00
❏ 89574	The Christmas Song (Chestnuts Roasting on an Open Fire)/Jingle Bells	2000	2.00	4.00	8.00
—Red vinyl					
COLLECTABLES					
❏ 4471	I'm Walking/A Teenager's Romance	1992	—	—	3.00
❏ 6022	Hello Mary Lou/Poor Little Fool	1992	—	—	3.00
❏ 6102	Sweeter Than You/It's Late	1993	—	—	3.00
❏ 6125	Be Bop Baby/Lonesome Town	1993	—	—	3.00
❏ 6126	Travelin' Man/It's Up to You	1993	—	—	3.00
—A-side is probably the "cold ending" version that has become the common version on reissues since the start of the compact disc era					
❏ 6127	Stood Up/Teenage Idol	1993	—	—	3.00
❏ 6210	Believe What You Say/Never Be Anyone Else But You	1994	—	—	3.00
❏ 6211	Waitin' in School/Just a Little Too Much	1994	—	—	3.00
❏ 6212	Young Emotions/Everlovin'	1994	—	—	3.00
❏ 90000	For You/Who Put the Bomp	199?	—	—	3.00
—B-side by Barry Mann					
❏ 90052	Garden Party/So Long Mama	199?	—	—	3.00
❏ 90106	Fools Rush In (Where Angels Fear to Tread)/For You	199?	—	—	3.00
DECCA					
❏ 31475	You Don't Love Me Anymore (And I Can Tell)/I Got a Woman	1963	3.75	7.50	15.00
❏ 31475 [PS]	You Don't Love Me Anymore (And I Can Tell)/I Got a Woman	1963	7.50	15.00	30.00
❏ 31495	String Along/Gypsy Woman	1963	3.75	7.50	15.00
❏ 31495 [PS]	String Along/Gypsy Woman	1963	7.50	15.00	30.00
❏ 31533	Fools Rush In/Down Home	1963	3.75	7.50	15.00
❏ 31533 [PS]	Fools Rush In/Down Home	1963	7.50	15.00	30.00
❏ 31574	For You/That's All She Wrote	1963	3.75	7.50	15.00
❏ 31574 [PS]	For You/That's All She Wrote	1963	7.50	15.00	30.00
❏ 31612	The Very Thought of You/I Wonder (If Your Love Will Ever Belong to Me)	1964	3.00	6.00	12.00
❏ 31612 [PS]	The Very Thought of You/I Wonder (If Your Love Will Ever Belong to Me)	1964	7.50	15.00	30.00
❏ 31656	There's Nothing I Can Say/Lonely Corner	1964	3.00	6.00	12.00
❏ 31656 [PS]	There's Nothing I Can Say/Lonely Corner	1964	7.50	15.00	30.00
❏ 31703	A Happy Guy/Don't Breathe a Word	1964	3.00	6.00	12.00
❏ 31703 [PS]	A Happy Guy/Don't Breathe a Word	1964	7.50	15.00	30.00
❏ 31756	Mean Old World/When the Chips Are Down	1965	3.00	6.00	12.00
❏ 31756 [PS]	Mean Old World/When the Chips Are Down	1965	7.50	15.00	30.00
❏ 31800	Yesterday's Love/Come Out Dancin'	1965	3.00	6.00	12.00
❏ 31800 [PS]	Yesterday's Love/Come Out Dancin'	1965	7.50	15.00	30.00
❏ 31845	Love and Kisses/Say You Love Me	1965	3.00	6.00	12.00
❏ 31845 [PS]	Love and Kisses/Say You Love Me	1965	10.00	20.00	40.00
❏ 31900	Your Kind of Lovin'/Fire Breathin' Dragon	1966	3.00	6.00	12.00

Number	Title (A Side/B Side)	Yr	VG	VG+	NM
❏ 31900 [PS]	Your Kind of Lovin'/Fire Breathin' Dragon	1966	37.50	75.00	150.00
❏ 31956	Louisiana Man/You Just Can't Quit	1966	3.00	6.00	12.00
❏ 31956 [PS]	Louisiana Man/You Just Can't Quit	1966	15.00	30.00	60.00
❏ 32026	Alone/Things You Gave Me	1966	3.00	6.00	12.00
❏ 32026 [PS]	Alone/Things You Gave Me	1966	20.00	40.00	80.00
❏ 32055	They Don't Give Medals (To Yesterday's Heroes)/Take a Broken Heart	1966	3.00	6.00	12.00
❏ 32120	Take a City Bride/I'm Called Lonely	1967	2.50	5.00	10.00
❏ 32120 [PS]	Take a City Bride/I'm Called Lonely	1967	15.00	30.00	60.00
❏ 32176	Moonshine/Suzanne on a Sunday Morning	1967	2.50	5.00	10.00
❏ 32222	Dream Weaver/Baby Close Your Eyes	1967	2.50	5.00	10.00
❏ 32284	Don't Blame It on Your Wife/Promenade in Green	1968	2.50	5.00	10.00
❏ 32298	Barefoot Boy/Don't Make Promises	1968	2.50	5.00	10.00
❏ 32550	She Belongs to Me/Promises	1969	2.00	4.00	8.00
❏ 32635	Easy to Be Free/Come On In	1970	2.00	4.00	8.00
❏ 32635 [PS]	Easy to Be Free/Come On In	1970	3.75	7.50	15.00
❏ 32676	I Shall Be Released/If You Gotta Go, Go Now	1970	2.00	4.00	8.00
❏ 32711	Look at Mary/We Got Such a Long Way to Go	1970	2.00	4.00	8.00
❏ 32739	How Long/Down Along the Bayou Country	1970	2.00	4.00	8.00
❏ 32779	Life/California	1971	2.00	4.00	8.00
❏ 32860	Thank You Lord/Sing Me a Song	1971	2.00	4.00	8.00
❏ 32906	Love Minus Zero-No Limit/Gypsy Pilot	1971	2.00	4.00	8.00
❏ 32980	Garden Party/So Long Mama	1972	2.50	5.00	10.00
❏ 34193 [S]	Gypsy Woman/For Your Sweet Love	1963	25.00	50.00	100.00
❏ 34193/7 [PS]	Envelope, bonus photo and intact jukebox title strips for these 5 singles	1963	25.00	50.00	100.00
❏ 34194 [S]	Pick Up the Pieces/Every Time I See You Smilin'	1963	25.00	50.00	100.00
❏ 34195 [S]	One Boy Too Late/Everytime I Think About You	1963	25.00	50.00	100.00
❏ 34196 [S]	Let's Talk the Whole Thing Over/I Got a Woman	1963	25.00	50.00	100.00
❏ 34197 [S]	I Will Follow You/What Comes Next	1963	25.00	50.00	100.00
—34193-34197 are 33 1/3 rpm, small hole jukebox singles. The set came with a package, priced separately.					
EPIC					
❏ 34-06066	Dream Lover/Rave On	1986	—	2.00	4.00
❏ 34-06066 [PS]	Dream Lover/Rave On	1986	—	2.00	4.00
❏ 50458	It's Another Day/You Can't Dance	1977	—	2.50	5.00
❏ 50501	Gimme A Little Sign/Something You Can't Buy	1978	—	2.50	5.00
❏ 50674	Dream Lover/That Ain't the Way Love's Supposed to Be	1979	—	2.50	5.00
IMPERIAL					
❏ 5463	Be-Bop Baby/Have I Told You Lately That I Love You	1957	6.25	12.50	25.00
—Black label					
❏ 5463	Be-Bop Baby/Have I Told You Lately That I Love You	1957	12.50	25.00	50.00
—Red label					
❏ 5463 [PS]	Be-Bop Baby/Have I Told You Lately That I Love You	1957	20.00	40.00	80.00
❏ 5483	Stood Up/Waitin' in School	1957	6.25	12.50	25.00
—Black label					
❏ 5483	Stood Up/Waitin' in School	1957	10.00	20.00	40.00
—Red label					
❏ 5483 [PS]	Stood Up/Waitin' in School	1957	17.50	35.00	70.00
❏ 5503	Believe What You Say/My Bucket's Got a Hole in It	1958	7.50	15.00	30.00
—Black label					
❏ 5503	Believe What You Say/My Bucket's Got a Hole in It	1958	12.50	25.00	50.00
—Red label					
❏ 5503 [PS]	Believe What You Say/My Bucket's Got a Hole in It	1958	17.50	35.00	70.00
❏ 5528	Poor Little Fool/Don't Leave Me This Way	1958	7.50	15.00	30.00
❏ 5545	Lonesome Town/I Got a Feeling	1958	7.50	15.00	30.00
❏ 5545	Lonesome Town/I Got a Feeling	1958	150.00	300.00	600.00
—Red vinyl					
❏ 5545 [PS]	Lonesome Town/I Got a Feeling	1958	17.50	35.00	70.00
❏ 5565	Never Be Anyone Else But You/It's Late	1959	6.25	12.50	25.00
—Black label					
❏ 5565	Never Be Anyone Else But You/It's Late	1959	10.00	20.00	40.00
—Red label					
❏ 5565 [PS]	Never Be Anyone Else But You/It's Late	1959	20.00	40.00	80.00
❏ 5595	Just a Little Too Much/Sweeter Than You	1959	6.25	12.50	25.00
❏ 5595 [PS]	Just a Little Too Much/Sweeter Than You	1959	17.50	35.00	70.00
❏ 5614	I Wanna Be Loved/Mighty Good	1959	6.25	12.50	25.00
❏ 5614 [PS]	I Wanna Be Loved/Mighty Good	1959	17.50	35.00	70.00
❏ 5663	Young Emotions/Right By My Side	1960	6.25	12.50	25.00
❏ 5663 [PS]	Young Emotions/Right By My Side	1960	17.50	35.00	70.00
❏ 5685	I'm Not Afraid/Yes Sir, That's My Baby	1960	6.25	12.50	25.00
❏ 5685 [PS]	I'm Not Afraid/Yes Sir, That's My Baby	1960	17.50	35.00	70.00
❏ 5707	You Are the Only One/Milk Cow Blues	1960	6.25	12.50	25.00
❏ 5707 [PS]	You Are the Only One/Milk Cow Blues	1960	17.50	35.00	70.00
❏ 5741	Travelin' Man/Hello Mary Lou	1961	6.25	12.50	25.00
—Black vinyl					
❏ 5741	Travelin' Man/Hello Mary Lou	1961	200.00	400.00	800.00
—Red vinyl					
❏ 5741 [PS]	Travelin' Man/Hello Mary Lou	1961	17.50	35.00	70.00
❏ 5770	A Wonder Like You/Everlovin'	1961	5.00	10.00	20.00
—Starting here, Imperial singles by "Rick Nelson"					
❏ 5770	A Wonder Like You/Everlovin'	1961	10.00	20.00	40.00
❏ 5805	Young World/Summertime	1962	5.00	10.00	20.00
❏ 5805 [PS]	Young World/Summertime	1962	10.00	20.00	40.00
❏ 5864	Teen Age Idol/I've Got My Eyes on You	1962	5.00	10.00	20.00
❏ 5864 [PS]	Teen Age Idol/I've Got My Eyes on You	1962	10.00	20.00	40.00
❏ 5901	It's Up to You/I Need You	1962	5.00	10.00	20.00
❏ 5901 [PS]	It's Up to You/I Need You	1962	10.00	20.00	40.00
❏ 5910	That's All/I'm in Love Again	1963	6.25	12.50	25.00
❏ 5935	Old Enough to Love/If You Can't Rock Me	1963	5.00	10.00	20.00
❏ 5935	Old Enough to Love/If You Can't Rock Me	1963	125.00	250.00	500.00
—Red vinyl					
❏ 5935 [PS]	Old Enough to Love/If You Can't Rock Me	1963	10.00	20.00	40.00
❏ 5958	A Long Vacation/Mad Mad World	1963	5.00	10.00	20.00
❏ 5958	A Long Vacation/Mad Mad World	1963	75.00	150.00	300.00
—Red vinyl					
❏ 5985	Time After Time/There's Not a Minute	1963	5.00	10.00	20.00
❏ 58896	Young World/A Wonder Like You	2000	—	2.50	5.00
—EMI-Capitol jukebox issue with Imperial logo at top					

N

Number	Title (A Side/B Side)	Yr	VG	VG+	NM
❑ 66004	Today's Teardrops/Thank You Darlin'	1963	3.75	7.50	15.00
❑ 66004 [PS]	Today's Teardrops/Thank You Darlin'	1963	10.00	20.00	40.00
❑ 66017	Congratulations/One Minute to One	1964	3.75	7.50	15.00
❑ 66039	Everybody But Me/Lucky Star	1964	3.75	7.50	15.00

MCA

Number	Title (A Side/B Side)	Yr	VG	VG+	NM
❑ 40001	Palace Guard/A Flower Opens Gently By	1973	—	3.00	6.00
❑ 40130	Evil Woman Child/Lifestream	1973	—	3.00	6.00
❑ 40187	Windfall/Legacy	1974	—	3.00	6.00
❑ 40214	One Night Stand/Lifestream	1974	—	3.00	6.00
❑ 40392	Louisiana Belle/Try (Try to Fall in Love)	1975	—	3.00	6.00
❑ 40458	Rock and Roll Lady/Fadeaway	1975	—	3.00	6.00
❑ 52781	You Know What I Mean/ Don't Leave Me This Way	1986	—	2.50	5.00
❑ 52781 [PS]	You Know What I Mean/ Don't Leave Me This Way	1986	—	2.50	5.00

UNITED ARTISTS

Number	Title (A Side/B Side)	Yr	VG	VG+	NM
❑ 0071	Be-Bop Baby/Stood Up	1973	—	2.50	5.00
❑ 0072	Lonesome Town/It's Up to You	1973	—	2.50	5.00
❑ 0073	Poor Little Fool/My Bucket's Got a Hole in It	1973	—	2.50	5.00
❑ 0074	Travelin' Man/Believe What You Say	1973	—	2.50	5.00
❑ 0075	Teen Age Idol/Young Emotions	1973	—	2.50	5.00
❑ 0076	Never Be Anyone Else But You/That's All	1973	—	2.50	5.00
❑ 0077	Young World/It's Late	1973	—	2.50	5.00
❑ 0078	Just a Little Too Much/Waitin' in School	1973	—	2.50	5.00
❑ 0079	Hello Mary Lou/Sweeter Than You	1973	—	2.50	5.00
❑ 0080	A Wonder Like You/Everlovin'	1973	—	2.50	5.00

—0071 through 0080 are "Silver Spotlight Series" reissues

VERVE

Number	Title (A Side/B Side)	Yr	VG	VG+	NM
❑ 10047	I'm Walkin'/A Teenager's Romance	1957	10.00	20.00	40.00

—Black and white label

| ❑ 10047 | I'm Walkin'/A Teenager's Romance | 1957 | 12.50 | 25.00 | 50.00 |

—Orange and yellow label

| ❑ 10070 | You're My One and Only Love/Honey Rock | 1957 | 10.00 | 20.00 | 40.00 |

—B-side by Barney Kessel

7-Inch Extended Plays

DECCA

Number	Title (A Side/B Side)	Yr	VG	VG+	NM
❑ ED 2760	I Will Follow You/Pick Up the Pieces//One Boy Too Late/Let's Talk the Whole Thing Over	1963	37.50	75.00	150.00
❑ ED 2760 [PS]	One Boy Too Late	1963	37.50	75.00	150.00
❑ 7-34319 [PS]	Best Always	1965	7.50	15.00	30.00

—With title strips

| ❑ 7-34319 [S] | I'm Not Ready for You Yet/Lonely Corner/Mean Old World/I Know a Place/It's Beginning to Hurt/When the Chips Are Down | 1965 | 7.50 | 15.00 | 30.00 |

—33 1/3 rpm, small hole jukebox edition

IMPERIAL

Number	Title (A Side/B Side)	Yr	VG	VG+	NM
❑ IMP 153	Be-Bop Baby/Have I Told You Lately That I Love You//Honeycomb/Boppin' the Blues	1957	12.50	25.00	50.00
❑ IMP 153 [PS]	Ricky (Honeycomb)	1957	12.50	25.00	50.00
❑ IMP 154	Teenage Doll/If You Can't Rock Me//Whole Lotta Shakin' Goin' On/Baby I'm Sorry	1957	12.50	25.00	50.00
❑ IMP 154 [PS]	Ricky, Volume 2	1957	12.50	25.00	50.00
❑ IMP 155	Your True Love/True Love//Am I Blue/I'm Confessin'	1957	12.50	25.00	50.00
❑ IMP 155 [PS]	Ricky (True Love)	1957	12.50	25.00	50.00
❑ IMP 156	Shirley Lee/There's Good Rockin' Tonight//Someday/I'm Feelin' Sorry	1958	12.50	25.00	50.00
❑ IMP 156 [PS]	Ricky Nelson (Someday)	1958	12.50	25.00	50.00
❑ IMP 157	Down the Line/Don't Leave Me This Way//I'm in Love Again/My Babe	1958	12.50	25.00	50.00
❑ IMP 157 [PS]	Ricky Nelson (Down the Line)	1958	12.50	25.00	50.00
❑ IMP 158	Unchained Melody/I'll Walk Alone//There Goes My Baby/Poor Little Fool	1958	12.50	25.00	50.00
❑ IMP 158 [PS]	Ricky Nelson (Unchained Melody)	1958	12.50	25.00	50.00
❑ IMP 159	Be True to Me/One of These Mornings//Lonesome Town/It's Late	1959	12.50	25.00	50.00
❑ IMP 159 [PS]	Ricky Sings Again (Be True to Me)	1959	12.50	25.00	50.00
❑ IMP 160	Restless Kid/It's All in the Game//Believe What You Say/You Tear Me Up	1959	12.50	25.00	50.00
❑ IMP 160 [PS]	Ricky Sings Again (Restless Kid)	1959	12.50	25.00	50.00
❑ IMP 161	Old Enough to Love/Tryin' to Get to You//Never Be Anyone Else But You/I Can't Help It	1959	12.50	25.00	50.00
❑ IMP 161 [PS]	Ricky Sings Again (Old Enough to Love)	1959	12.50	25.00	50.00
❑ IMP 162	You'll Never Know What You're Missin'/I've Been Thinkin'//So Long/You're So Fine	1959	12.50	25.00	50.00
❑ IMP 162 [PS]	Songs by Ricky (You'll Never Know What You're Missin')	1959	12.50	25.00	50.00
❑ IMP 163	One Minute To One/Blood from a Stone//Half Breed/Just a Little Too Much	1959	12.50	25.00	50.00
❑ IMP 163 [PS]	Songs by Ricky (One Minute to One)	1959	12.50	25.00	50.00
❑ IMP 164	Don't Leave Me/That's All//Sweeter Than You/A Long Vacation	1959	12.50	25.00	50.00

—Original track order

| ❑ IMP 164 | Don't Leave Me/That's All//A Long Vacation/Sweeter Than You | 1959 | 15.00 | 30.00 | 60.00 |

—Revised track order; "RE" before master number at 3 o'clock on label

❑ IMP 164 [PS]	Songs by Ricky (Don't Leave Me)	1959	12.50	25.00	50.00
❑ IMP 165	Glory Train/I Bowed My Head in Shame//March with the Band of the Lord/If You Believe It	1959	25.00	50.00	100.00
❑ IMP 165 [PS]	Ricky Sings Spirituals	1959	25.00	50.00	100.00
❑ LP 4-2232 [PS]	Million Sellers	1964	20.00	40.00	80.00
❑ LP 4-2232 [S]	Travelin' Man/Never Be Anyone Else But You/It's Late//Young Emotions/Hello Mary Lou/Yes Sir, That's My Baby	1964	20.00	40.00	80.00

—33 1/3 rpm, small hole, jukebox edition

VERVE

Number	Title (A Side/B Side)	Yr	VG	VG+	NM
❑ 5048	I'm Walkin'/A Teenager's Romance//You're My One and Only Love/Honey Rock	1957	37.50	75.00	150.00
❑ 5048 [PS]	Ricky	1957	50.00	100.00	200.00

Albums

CAPITOL

Number	Title (A Side/B Side)	Yr	VG	VG+	NM
❑ SOO-12109	Playing to Win	1981	2.50	5.00	10.00

DECCA

Number	Title (A Side/B Side)	Yr	VG	VG+	NM
❑ DL 4419 [M]	For Your Sweet Love	1963	7.50	15.00	30.00
❑ DL 4479 [M]	Rick Nelson Sings "For You"	1963	7.50	15.00	30.00
❑ DL 4559 [M]	The Very Thought of You	1964	7.50	15.00	30.00
❑ DL 4608 [M]	Spotlight on Rick	1964	7.50	15.00	30.00

Number	Title (A Side/B Side)	Yr	VG	VG+	NM
❑ DL 4660 [M]	Best Always	1965	7.50	15.00	30.00
❑ DL 4678 [M]	Love and Kisses	1965	7.50	15.00	30.00
❑ DL 4779 [M]	Bright Lights and Country Music	1966	6.25	12.50	25.00
❑ DL 4827 [M]	Country Fever	1967	6.25	12.50	25.00
❑ DL 4944 [M]	Another Side of Rick	1967	6.25	12.50	25.00
❑ DL 5014 [M]	Perspective	1968	12.50	25.00	50.00

—Mono copies are promo only

❑ DL 74419 [S]	For Your Sweet Love	1963	10.00	2.00	40.00
❑ DL 74479 [S]	Rick Nelson Sings "For You"	1963	10.00	20.00	40.00
❑ DL 74559 [S]	The Very Thought of You	1964	10.00	20.00	40.00
❑ DL 74608 [S]	Spotlight on Rick	1964	10.00	20.00	40.00
❑ DL 74660 [S]	Best Always	1965	10.00	20.00	40.00
❑ DL 74678 [S]	Love and Kisses	1965	10.00	20.00	40.00
❑ DL 74779 [S]	Bright Lights and Country Music	1966	7.50	15.00	30.00
❑ DL 74827 [S]	Country Fever	1967	7.50	15.00	30.00
❑ DL 74944 [S]	Another Side of Rick	1967	7.50	15.00	30.00
❑ DL 75014 [S]	Perspective	1968	7.50	15.00	30.00
❑ DL 75162	Rick Nelson In Concert	1970	6.25	12.50	25.00
❑ DL 75236	Rick Sings Nelson	1970	6.25	12.50	25.00

—Deduct 20 percent if poster is missing

| ❑ DL 75297 | Rudy the Fifth | 1971 | 6.25 | 12.50 | 25.00 |
| ❑ DL 75391 | Garden Party | 1972 | 6.25 | 12.50 | 25.00 |

EMI AMERICA

Number	Title (A Side/B Side)	Yr	VG	VG+	NM
❑ SQ-17192	The Very Best of Rick Nelson	1986	2.50	5.00	10.00

—Reissue of United Artists UA-LA330

EPIC

Number	Title (A Side/B Side)	Yr	VG	VG+	NM
❑ JE 34420	Intakes	1977	3.00	6.00	12.00
❑ FE 40388	The Memphis Sessions	1986	2.50	5.00	10.00

EPIC/NU-DISK

Number	Title (A Side/B Side)	Yr	VG	VG+	NM
❑ 3E 36868 [10]	Four You	1981	3.00	6.00	12.00

IMPERIAL

Number	Title (A Side/B Side)	Yr	VG	VG+	NM
❑ LP 9048 [M]	Ricky	1957	25.00	50.00	100.00

—Black label with stars

| ❑ LP 9048 [M] | Ricky | 1964 | 6.25 | 12.50 | 25.00 |

—Black label with pink and white at left

| ❑ LP 9048 [M] | Ricky | 1966 | 5.00 | 10.00 | 20.00 |

—Black label with green and white at left

| ❑ LP 9050 [M] | Ricky Nelson | 1958 | 25.00 | 50.00 | 100.00 |

—Black label with stars

| ❑ LP 9050 [M] | Ricky Nelson | 1964 | 6.25 | 12.50 | 25.00 |

—Black label with pink and white at left

| ❑ LP 9050 [M] | Ricky Nelson | 1966 | 5.00 | 10.00 | 20.00 |

—Black label with green and white at left

| ❑ LP 9061 [M] | Ricky Sings Again | 1959 | 25.00 | 50.00 | 100.00 |

—Black label with stars

| ❑ LP 9061 [M] | Ricky Sings Again | 1964 | 6.25 | 12.50 | 25.00 |

—Black label with pink and white at left

| ❑ LP 9061 [M] | Ricky Sings Again | 1966 | 5.00 | 10.00 | 20.00 |

—Black label with green and white at left

| ❑ LP 9082 [M] | Songs by Ricky | 1959 | 18.75 | 37.50 | 75.00 |

—Black label with stars

| ❑ LP 9082 [M] | Songs by Ricky | 1964 | 6.25 | 12.50 | 25.00 |

—Black label with pink and white at left

| ❑ LP 9082 [M] | Songs by Ricky | 1966 | 5.00 | 10.00 | 20.00 |

—Black label with green and white at left

| ❑ LP 9122 [M] | More Songs by Ricky | 1960 | 18.75 | 37.50 | 75.00 |

—Black label with stars

| ❑ LP 9122 [M] | More Songs by Ricky | 1964 | 6.25 | 12.50 | 25.00 |

—Black label with pink and white at left

| ❑ LP 9122 [M] | More Songs by Ricky | 1966 | 5.00 | 10.00 | 20.00 |

—Black label with green and white at left

| ❑ LP 9152 [M] | Rick Is 21 | 1961 | 10.00 | 20.00 | 40.00 |

—Black label with stars

| ❑ LP 9152 [M] | Rick Is 21 | 1964 | 6.25 | 12.50 | 25.00 |

—Black label with pink and white at left

| ❑ LP 9152 [M] | Rick Is 21 | 1966 | 5.00 | 10.00 | 20.00 |

—Black label with green and white at left

| ❑ LP 9167 [M] | Album Seven by Rick | 1962 | 10.00 | 20.00 | 40.00 |

—Black label with stars

| ❑ LP 9167 [M] | Album Seven by Rick | 1964 | 6.25 | 12.50 | 25.00 |

—Black label with pink and white at left

| ❑ LP 9167 [M] | Album Seven by Rick | 1966 | 5.00 | 10.00 | 20.00 |

—Black label with green and white at left

| ❑ LP 9218 [M] | Best Sellers by Rick Nelson | 1963 | 10.00 | 20.00 | 40.00 |

—Black label with stars

| ❑ LP 9218 [M] | Best Sellers by Rick Nelson | 1964 | 6.25 | 12.50 | 25.00 |

—Black label with pink and white at left

| ❑ LP 9218 [M] | Best Sellers by Rick Nelson | 1966 | 5.00 | 10.00 | 20.00 |

—Black label with green and white at left

| ❑ LP 9223 [M] | It's Up to You | 1963 | 10.00 | 20.00 | 40.00 |

—Black label with stars

| ❑ LP 9223 [M] | It's Up to You | 1964 | 6.25 | 12.50 | 25.00 |

—Black label with pink and white at left

| ❑ LP 9223 [M] | It's Up to You | 1966 | 5.00 | 10.00 | 20.00 |

—Black label with green and white at left

| ❑ LP 9232 [M] | Million Sellers | 1963 | 10.00 | 20.00 | 40.00 |

—Black label with stars

| ❑ LP 9232 [M] | Million Sellers | 1964 | 6.25 | 12.50 | 25.00 |

—Black label with pink and white at left

| ❑ LP 9232 [M] | Million Sellers | 1966 | 5.00 | 10.00 | 20.00 |

—Black label with green and white at left

| ❑ LP 9244 [M] | A Long Vacation | 1963 | 10.00 | 20.00 | 40.00 |

—Black label with stars

| ❑ LP 9244 [M] | A Long Vacation | 1964 | 6.25 | 12.50 | 25.00 |

—Black label with pink and white at left

| ❑ LP 9244 [M] | A Long Vacation | 1966 | 5.00 | 10.00 | 20.00 |

—Black label with green and white at left

| ❑ LP 9251 [M] | Rick Nelson Sings for You | 1964 | 6.25 | 12.50 | 25.00 |

—Black label with pink and white at left

| ❑ LP 9251 [M] | Rick Nelson Sings for You | 1964 | 10.00 | 20.00 | 40.00 |

—Black label with stars

| ❑ LP 9251 [M] | Rick Nelson Sings for You | 1966 | 5.00 | 10.00 | 20.00 |

—Black label with green and white at left

| ❑ LP 12030 [S] | Songs by Ricky | 1959 | 50.00 | 100.00 | 200.00 |

—Black label with silver print

| ❑ LP 12030 [S] | Songs by Ricky | 1964 | 10.00 | 20.00 | 40.00 |

—Black label with pink and white at left

Number	Title (A Side/B Side)	Yr	VG	VG+	NM
❏ LP 12030 [S]	Songs by Ricky	1966	6.25	12.50	25.00
—Black label with green and white at left					
❏ LP 12059 [DJ]	More Songs by Ricky	1960	250.00	500.00	1000.
—Promo copy on blue vinyl. Add 20 percent for enclosed poster.					
❏ LP 12059 [S]	More Songs by Ricky	1960	25.00	50.00	100.00
—Black label with silver print					
❏ LP 12059 [S]	More Songs by Ricky	1964	10.00	20.00	40.00
—Black label with pink and white at left					
❏ LP 12059 [S]	More Songs by Ricky	1966	6.25	12.50	25.00
—Black label with green and white at left					
❏ LP 12071 [S]	Rick Is 21	1961	25.00	50.00	100.00
—Black label with silver print					
❏ LP 12071 [S]	Rick Is 21	1964	10.00	20.00	40.00
—Black label with pink and white at left					
❏ LP 12071 [S]	Rick Is 21	1966	6.25	12.50	25.00
—Black label with green and white at left					
❏ LP 12082 [S]	Album Seven by Rick	1962	25.00	50.00	100.00
—Black label with silver print					
❏ LP 12082 [S]	Album Seven by Rick	1964	10.00	20.00	40.00
—Black label with pink and white at left					
❏ LP 12082 [S]	Album Seven by Rick	1966	6.25	12.50	25.00
—Black label with green and white at left					
❏ LP 12090 [S]	Ricky Sings Again	1962	37.50	75.00	150.00
—Black label with silver print					
❏ LP 12090 [S]	Ricky Sings Again	1964	10.00	20.00	40.00
—Black label with pink and white at left					
❏ LP 12090 [S]	Ricky Sings Again	1966	6.25	12.50	25.00
—Black label with green and white at left					
❏ LP 12218 [R]	Best Sellers	1964	5.00	10.00	20.00
—Black label with pink and white at left					
❏ LP 12218 [R]	Best Sellers	1966	3.75	7.50	15.00
—Black label with green and white at left					
❏ LP 12232 [R]	Million Sellers	1964	5.00	10.00	20.00
—Black label with pink and white at left					
❏ LP 12232 [R]	Million Sellers	1966	3.75	7.50	15.00
—Black label with green and white at left					
❏ LP 12244 [R]	A Long Vacation	1964	5.00	10.00	20.00
—Black label with pink and white at left					
❏ LP 12244 [R]	A Long Vacation	1966	3.75	7.50	15.00
—Black label with green and white at left					
❏ LP 12251 [R]	Rick Nelson Sings for You	1964	5.00	10.00	20.00
—Black label with pink and white at left					
❏ LP 12251 [R]	Rick Nelson Sings for You	1964	6.25	12.50	25.00
—Black label with silver print					
❏ LP 12251 [R]	Rick Nelson Sings for You	1966	3.75	7.50	15.00
—Black label with green and white at left					
❏ LP 12392 [R]	Ricky	1968	3.75	7.50	15.00
—Rechanneled reissue of 9048					
❏ LP 12393 [R]	Ricky Nelson	1968	3.75	7.50	15.00
—Rechanneled reissue of 9050					
LIBERTY					
❏ LM-1004	Ricky	1981	2.00	4.00	8.00
—Reissue of United Artists 1004					
❏ LXB-9960 [(2)]	Legendary Masters	198?	3.00	6.00	12.00
—Reissue of United Artists 9960					
❏ LN-10134	Ricky Sings Again	1982	2.50	5.00	10.00
—Reissue of Imperial 12090					
❏ LN-10205	Souvenirs	1983	2.00	4.00	8.00
❏ LN-10253	Teen Age Idol	1984	2.00	4.00	8.00
❏ LN-10304	I Need You	1986	2.00	4.00	8.00
—Reissue of Sunset 5205					
❏ LN-10305	Ricky Nelson	1986	2.00	4.00	8.00
—Another reissue					
❏ LM-51004	Ricky	1983	2.00	4.00	8.00
—Reissue of Liberty 1004					
MCA					
❏ 3	Rick Nelson In Concert	1973	3.00	6.00	12.00
—Reissue of Decca 75162					
❏ 20	Rick Sings Nelson	1973	3.00	6.00	12.00
—Reissue of Decca 75236					
❏ 37	Rudy the Fifth	1973	3.00	6.00	12.00
—Reissue of Decca 75297					
❏ 62	Garden Party	1973	3.00	6.00	12.00
—Reissue of Decca 75391					
❏ 383	Windfall	1974	3.75	7.50	15.00
❏ 1517	The Decca Years	1982	2.00	4.00	8.00
❏ 2-4004 [(2)]	Rick Nelson Country	1973	3.75	7.50	15.00
❏ 6163	All My Best	1986	2.50	5.00	10.00
❏ 25983	Rick Nelson In Concert The Troubadour, 1969	1987	2.50	5.00	10.00
—Reissue of MCA 3 with revised title					
RHINO					
❏ RNLP 215	Greatest Hits	1985	3.00	6.00	12.00
❏ RNDF 259 [PD]	Greatest Hits	1985	3.75	7.50	15.00
❏ R1-70215	Greatest Hits	1987	2.50	5.00	10.00
❏ R1-71114	Live 1983-1985	1989	3.00	6.00	12.00
SUNSET					
❏ SUM-1118 [M]	Ricky Nelson	1966	3.75	7.50	15.00
❏ SUS-5118 [P]	Ricky Nelson	1966	5.00	10.00	20.00
❏ SUS-5205	I Need You	1968	3.75	7.50	15.00
TIME-LIFE					
❏ SRNR 31 [(2)]	Rick Nelson: 1957-1972	1989	3.75	7.50	15.00
UNITED ARTISTS					
❏ UA-LA330-E	The Very Best of Rick Nelson	1974	3.00	6.00	12.00
❏ LM-1004	Ricky	1980	2.50	5.00	10.00
—Reissue of Imperial 9048					
❏ UAS-9960 [(2)]	Legendary Masters	1971	6.25	12.50	25.00
VERVE					
❏ V 2083 [M]	Teen Time	1957	125.00	250.00	500.00
—Has three Ricky Nelson songs plus tracks by four others; usually treated as Rick's LP because of his prominence on the cover					

Number	Title (A Side/B Side)	Yr	VG	VG+	NM
NELSON, SANDY Also see THE GAMBLERS.					
45s					
IMPERIAL					
❏ 5630	Drum Party/Big Noise from Winnetka	1959	3.00	6.00	12.00
❏ 5648	Party Time/The Wiggle	1960	3.00	6.00	12.00
❏ 5672	Bouncy/Lost Dreams	1960	3.00	6.00	12.00
❏ 5708	Cool Operator/Jive Talk	1960	3.00	6.00	12.00
❏ 5745	Big Noise from the Jungle/Get With It	1961	3.00	6.00	12.00
❏ 5775	Let There Be Drums/Quite a Beat	1961	3.75	7.50	15.00
❏ 5809	Drums Are My Beat/The Birth of the Beat	1962	3.00	6.00	12.00
❏ 5829	Drummin' Up a Storm/Drum Stomp	1962	3.00	6.00	12.00
❏ 5860	All Night Long/Rompin' and Stompin'	1962	3.00	6.00	12.00
❏ 5870	And Then There Were Drums/Live It Up	1962	3.00	6.00	12.00
❏ 5884	Teenage House Party/Day Train	1962	3.00	6.00	12.00
❏ 5904	Be-Bop Baby/Let the Four Winds Blow	1962	3.00	6.00	12.00
❏ 5932	Ooh Poo Pah Doo/Feel So Good	1963	3.00	6.00	12.00
❏ 5940	You Name It/Alexis	1963	3.00	6.00	12.00
❏ 5965	Here We Go Again/Just Bill	1963	3.00	6.00	12.00
❏ 5988	Caravan/Sandy	1963	3.00	6.00	12.00
❏ 66019	Drum Shack/Kitty's Theme	1964	2.50	5.00	10.00
❏ 66034	Castle Rock/You Don't Say	1964	2.50	5.00	10.00
❏ 66060	Teen Beat '65/Kitty's Theme	1964	3.00	6.00	12.00
❏ 66093	Chop Chop/Reach for a Star	1965	2.50	5.00	10.00
❏ 66107	Land of 1000 Dances/Let There Be Drums	1965	2.50	5.00	10.00
❏ 66127	Drums A-Go-Go/Caesar	1965	2.50	5.00	10.00
❏ 66146	A Lover's Concerto/Treat Her Right	1965	2.50	5.00	10.00
❏ 66193	Rock It To 'Em J.B./The Charge	1966	2.50	5.00	10.00
❏ 66209	Let's Go Trippin'/Pipeline	1966	3.00	6.00	12.00
❏ 66246	The Drums Go On/Lawdy Miss Clawdy	1967	2.50	5.00	10.00
❏ 66253	Peter Gunn/You Got Me Hummin'	1967	2.50	5.00	10.00
❏ 66284	Alligator Boogaloo/Midnight Magic	1968	2.50	5.00	10.00
❏ 66350	Rebirth of the Beat/Lion in Winter	1969	2.50	5.00	10.00
❏ 66375	Manhattan Spiritual/The Stripper	1969	2.50	5.00	10.00
❏ 66402	Let There Be Drums and Brass/Leap Frog	1969	2.50	5.00	10.00
ORIGINAL SOUND					
❏ 5	Teen Beat/Big Jump	1959	6.25	12.50	25.00
UNITED ARTISTS					
❏ 0082	Teen Beat/Let There Be Drums	1973	—	2.50	5.00
—"Silver Spotlight Series" reissue					
❏ XW383	You Are the Sunshine of My Life/Dance with the Devil	1974	2.50	5.00	10.00
❏ 50830	Sapporo '72	1971	—	—	—
—Unreleased					
VEEBLETRONICS					
❏ 1	Drum Tunnel/Boogie #5	198?	—	2.50	5.00
❏ 2	Hunk of Drums/Witch Hunt	198?	—	2.50	5.00
❏ 3	A Drum Is a Woman/Boogie #5	198?	—	2.50	5.00
Albums					
IMPERIAL					
❏ LP 9105 [M]	Sandy Nelson Plays Teen Beat	1960	7.50	15.00	30.00
❏ LP 9136 [M]	He's a Drummer Boy	1961	7.50	15.00	30.00
❏ LP 9159 [M]	Let There Be Drums	1962	7.50	15.00	30.00
❏ LP 9168 [M]	Drums Are My Beat!	1962	5.00	10.00	20.00
❏ LP 9189 [M]	Drummin' Up a Storm	1962	5.00	10.00	20.00
❏ LP 9202 [M]	Golden Hits	1962	5.00	10.00	20.00
❏ LP 9203 [M]	Country Style	1962	5.00	10.00	20.00
❏ LP 9203 [M]	On the Wild Side	1966	3.75	7.50	15.00
—Same LP as above, but new title on cover					
❏ LP 9204 [M]	Compelling Percussion	1962	5.00	10.00	20.00
❏ LP 9215 [M]	Teenage House Party	1963	5.00	10.00	20.00
❏ LP 9224 [M]	The Best of the Beats	1963	3.75	7.50	15.00
❏ LP 9237 [M]	Beat That Drum	1963	3.75	7.50	15.00
❏ LP 9249 [M]	Sandy Nelson Plays	1963	3.75	7.50	15.00
❏ LP 9258 [M]	Be True to Your School	1964	3.75	7.50	15.00
❏ LP 9272 [M]	Live! In Las Vegas	1964	5.00	10.00	20.00
❏ LP 9278 [M]	Teen Beat '65	1965	3.75	7.50	15.00
❏ LP 9283 [M]	Drum Discotheque	1965	3.75	7.50	15.00
❏ LP 9287 [M]	Drums A Go-Go	1965	3.75	7.50	15.00
❏ LP 9298 [M]	Boss Beat	1965	3.75	7.50	15.00
❏ LP 9305 [M]	"In" Beat	1966	3.75	7.50	15.00
❏ LP 9314 [M]	Super Drums	1966	3.75	7.50	15.00
❏ LP 9329 [M]	Beat That #!!@* Drum	1966	3.00	6.00	12.00
❏ LP 9340 [M]	Cheetah Beat	1967	3.00	6.00	12.00
❏ LP 9345 [M]	The Beat Goes On	1967	3.00	6.00	12.00
❏ LP 9362 [M]	Soul Drums	1967	3.75	7.50	15.00
❏ LP 12044 [S]	Sandy Nelson Plays Teen Beat	1960	10.00	20.00	40.00
❏ LP 12080 [R]	Let There Be Drums	1962	6.25	12.50	25.00
❏ LP 12083 [S]	Drums Are My Beat!	1962	6.25	12.50	25.00
❏ LP 12089 [R]	He's a Drummer Boy	1962	6.25	12.50	25.00
❏ LP 12189 [S]	Drummin' Up a Storm	1962	6.25	12.50	25.00
❏ LP 12202 [P]	Golden Hits	1962	6.25	12.50	25.00
❏ LP 12203 [S]	Country Style	1962	6.25	12.50	25.00
❏ LP 12203 [S]	On the Wild Side	1966	5.00	10.00	20.00
—Same LP as above, but new title on cover					
❏ LP 12204 [S]	Compelling Percussion	1962	6.25	12.50	25.00
❏ LP 12215 [S]	Teenage House Party	1963	6.25	12.50	25.00
❏ LP 12224 [S]	The Best of the Beats	1963	5.00	10.00	20.00
❏ LP 12237 [S]	Beat That Drum	1963	5.00	10.00	20.00
❏ LP 12249 [S]	Sandy Nelson Plays	1963	5.00	10.00	20.00
❏ LP 12258 [S]	Be True to Your School	1964	5.00	10.00	20.00
❏ LP 12272 [R]	Live! In Las Vegas	1964	3.75	7.50	15.00
❏ LP 12278 [S]	Teen Beat '65	1965	5.00	10.00	20.00
❏ LP 12283 [S]	Drum Discotheque	1965	5.00	10.00	20.00
❏ LP 12287 [S]	Drums A Go-Go	1965	5.00	10.00	20.00
❏ LP 12298 [S]	Boss Beat	1965	5.00	10.00	20.00
❏ LP 12305 [S]	"In" Beat	1966	5.00	10.00	20.00
❏ LP 12314 [S]	Super Drums	1966	5.00	10.00	20.00
❏ LP 12329 [S]	Beat That #!!@* Drum	1966	3.75	7.50	15.00
❏ LP 12340 [S]	Cheetah Beat	1967	3.75	7.50	15.00
❏ LP 12345 [S]	The Beat Goes On	1967	3.75	7.50	15.00
❏ LP 12362 [S]	Soul Drums	1967	3.00	6.00	12.00
❏ LP 12367	Boogaloo Beat	1968	3.00	6.00	12.00
❏ LP 12400	Rock and Roll Revival	1968	3.00	6.00	12.00
❏ LP 12424	Rebirth of the Beat	1969	3.00	6.00	12.00
❏ LP 12439	Manhattan Spiritual	1969	3.00	6.00	12.00
❏ LP 12451	Groovy	1970	3.00	6.00	12.00

N

Number	Title (A Side/B Side)	Yr	VG	VG+	NM

LIBERTY

Number	Title (A Side/B Side)	Yr	VG	VG+	NM
❏ LN-10172	The Very Best of Sandy Nelson	1982	2.00	4.00	8.00
❏ LN-10209	Collectors' Gems, Vol. 2	1983	2.00	4.00	8.00

SUNSET

❏ SUM-1114 [M]	Walking Beat	1966	2.50	5.00	10.00
❏ SUM-1166 [M]	Teen Drums	1967	2.50	5.00	10.00
❏ SUS-5114 [S]	Walking Beat	1966	3.00	6.00	12.00
❏ SUS-5166 [S]	Teen Drums	1967	3.00	6.00	12.00
❏ SUS-5224	And There Were Drums (Drums and More Drums)	1968	2.50	5.00	10.00
❏ SUS-5261	Heavy Drums	1969	2.50	5.00	10.00
❏ SUS-5291	Sandy Nelson Plays Fats Domino Hits	1970	2.50	5.00	10.00

UNITED ARTISTS

❏ UA-LA440-E	The Very Best of Sandy Nelson	1975	3.00	6.00	12.00

NELSON, TERI, GROUP

45s

KAMA SUTRA

❏ 245	Sweet Talkin' Willie/Back Side	1968	2.50	5.00	10.00

NELSON, TRACY Also see MOTHER EARTH; TRACY AND WILLIE NELSON.

45s

ATLANTIC

❏ 3235	It Takes a Lot to Laugh, It Takes a Train to Cry/ Lean On Me	1975	—	2.50	5.00

CAPITOL

❏ 4442	Sad Situation/Let's Get Down to the Truth	1977	—	2.00	4.00
—With Larry Ballard					

MCA

❏ 40479	Sweet Soul Music/Nothing I Can't Handle	1975	—	2.00	4.00

MERCURY

❏ 72995	Sad Situation/Stay As Sweet As You Are	1970	2.00	4.00	8.00

Albums

ADELPHI

❏ 4119	Doin' It My Way	1981	2.50	5.00	10.00

ATLANTIC

❏ SD 7310	Tracy Nelson	1974	3.00	6.00	12.00

COLUMBIA

❏ KC 31759	Poor Man's Paradise	1973	3.00	6.00	12.00

FLYING FISH

❏ FF-052	Homemade Songs	1978	2.50	5.00	10.00
❏ FF-209	Come See About Me	1980	2.50	5.00	10.00

MCA

❏ 494	Sweet Soul Music	1975	3.00	6.00	12.00
❏ 2203	Time Is On My Side	1976	3.00	6.00	12.00

PRESTIGE

❏ PRLP 7393 [M]	Deep Are the Roots	1965	6.25	12.50	25.00
❏ PRST 7393 [S]	Deep Are the Roots	1965	7.50	15.00	30.00
❏ PRST 7726	Deep Are the Roots	1969	3.75	7.50	15.00

NELSON, TRACY AND WILLIE Also see each artist's individual listings.

45s

ATLANTIC

❏ 4028	After the Fire Is Gone/Whiskey River	1976	—	2.50	5.00

NELSON, WILLIE Includes many duets not listed separately below. Also see HANK COCHRAN; DANNY DAVIS; MERLE HAGGARD; WAYLON JENNINGS; TRACY NELSON; WAYLON AND WILLIE.

45s

AMERICAN GOLD

❏ 7601	Night Life/Rainy Day Blues	1976	—	2.50	5.00

ATLANTIC

❏ 2968	Shotgun Willie/Sad Songs and Waltzes	1973	—	2.50	5.00
❏ 2979	Devil in a Sleepin' Bag/Stay All Night	1973	—	2.50	5.00
❏ 3008	Heaven and Hell/ I Still Can't Believe You're Gone	1974	—	2.50	5.00
❏ 3020	Phases and Stages/Bloody Mary Morning	1974	—	2.50	5.00
❏ 3228	Sister's Coming Home/Pick Up the Tempo	1974	—	2.50	5.00
❏ 3334	Heaven and Hell/ I Still Can't Believe You're Gone	1976	—	2.50	5.00

BELLAIRE

❏ 107	Night Life/Rainy Day Blues	1963	7.50	15.00	30.00
❏ 107	Night Life/Rainy Day Blues	1963	15.00	30.00	60.00
—Colored vinyl					
❏ 5000	Night Life '76/Man with the Blues	1976	—	2.50	5.00

BETTY

❏ 5702	What a Way to Love/Misery Mansion	1964	5.00	10.00	20.00
❏ 5703	Man with the Blues/The Storm Has Just Begun	1964	5.00	10.00	20.00

CHALLENGE

❏ 59280	I'm Talking About Love/I'm in Love with a Dancing Girl Working at Metropole	1965	3.75	7.50	15.00

COLUMBIA

❏ AE7 1182 [DJ]	White Christmas/Blue Christmas	1979	6.25	12.50	25.00
—Green vinyl					
❏ AE7 1183 [DJ]	Pretty Paper/Rudolph the Red-Nosed Reindeer	1979	6.25	12.50	25.00
—Red vinyl					
❏ AE7 1775 [DJ]	Pretty Paper/White Christmas	1982	—	3.00	6.00
❏ 02000	Mona Lisa/Twinkle, Twinkle Little Star	1981	—	2.00	4.00
❏ 02166	On the Road Again/September Song	1981	—	—	3.00
—Reissue					
❏ 02187	I'm Gonna Sit Right Down and Write Myself a Letter/Over the Rainbow	1981	—	2.00	4.00
❏ 02558	Heartaches of a Fool/Uncloudy Day	1981	—	2.00	4.00
❏ 02741	Always on My Mind/The Party's Over	1982	—	2.00	4.00
❏ 03073	Let It Be Me/Permanently Lonely	1982	—	2.00	4.00
❏ 03123	Angel Flying Too Close to the Ground/Mona Lisa	1982	—	—	3.00
—Reissue					
❏ 03124	Heartache of a Fool/Midnight Rider	1982	—	—	3.00
—Reissue					
❏ 03385	Last Thing I Needed First Thing This Morning/ Old Fords and a Natural Stone	1982	—	2.00	4.00
❏ 03476	Pretty Paper/White Christmas	1982	—	2.50	5.00
❏ 03674	Beer Barrel Polka/Little Old Fashioned Karma	1983	—	2.00	4.00
❏ 03965	Why Do I Have to Choose/ Would You Lay with Me (In a Field of Stone)	1983	—	2.00	4.00

❏ 04217	To All the Girls I've Loved Before/ I Don't Want to Wake You	1984	—	—	3.00
—Julio Iglesias & Willie Nelson; B-side by Julio Iglesias solo					
❏ 04217 [PS]	To All the Girls I've Loved Before/I Don't Want to Wake You	1984	—	2.00	4.00
—Julio Iglesias & Willie Nelson; second sleeve has artists' names in all capital letters					
❏ 04217 [PS]	To All the Girls I've Loved Before/I Don't Want to Wake You	1984	—	2.50	5.00
—Julio Iglesias & Willie Nelson; first sleeve has artists' names in both capital and small letters					
❏ 04263	Without a Song/I Can't Begin to Tell You	1983	—	—	3.00
❏ 04495	As Time Goes By/You'll Never Know	1984	6.25	12.50	25.00
—Willie Nelson and Julio Iglesias; withdrawn immediately upon release					
❏ 04495 [PS]	As Time Goes By/You'll Never Know	1984	6.25	12.50	25.00
—Willie Nelson and Julio Iglesias; withdrawn immediately upon release					
❏ 04568	City of New Orleans/Why Are You Pickin' On Me	1984	—	—	3.00
❏ 04568 [PS]	City of New Orleans/Why Are You Pickin' On Me	1984	—	2.00	4.00
❏ 04715	Seven Spanish Angels/Who Cares	1984	—	—	3.00
—A-side: Ray Charles and Willie Nelson; B-side: Ray Charles and Janie Frickie					
❏ 04847	Forgiving You Was Easy/You Wouldn't Cross the Street (To Say Goodbye)	1985	—	—	3.00
❏ 04881	Highwayman/The Human Condition	1985	—	—	3.00
—A-side: Willie Nelson/Waylon Jennings/Johnny Cash/Kris Kristofferson; B-side: Nelson, Cash					
❏ 04881 [PS]	Highwayman/The Human Condition	1985	—	2.00	4.00
—A-side: Willie Nelson/Waylon Jennings/Johnny Cash/Kris Kristofferson; B-side: Nelson, Cash					
❏ 05566	Are There Any More Real Cowboys/ I'm a Memory	1985	—	—	3.00
—A-side with Neil Young					
❏ 05594	Desperados Waiting for a Train/The Twentieth Century Is Almost Over	1985	—	—	3.00
—A-side: Willie Nelson/Waylon Jennings/Johnny Cash/Kris Kristofferson; B-side: Nelson, Cash					
❏ 05597	Me and Paul/I Let My Mind Wander	1985	—	—	3.00
❏ 05677	Slow Movin' Outlaw/They All Went to Mexico	1985	—	—	3.00
—A-side with Lacy J. Dalton; B-side with Carlos Santana					
❏ 05749	I Told a Lie to My Heart/Slow Movin' Outlaw	1986	—	—	3.00
—A-side with Hank Williams, Jr.; B-side: with Lacy J. Dalton					
❏ 05834	Living in the Promiseland/Bach Minuet in G	1986	—	—	3.00
❏ 06246	I'm Not Trying to Forget You/ I've Got the Craziest Feeling	1986	—	—	3.00
❏ 06530	Partners After All/Home Away from Home	1986	—	—	3.00
❏ 07007	Heart of Gold/So Much Like My Dad	1987	—	—	3.00
❏ 07202	Island in the Sun/There Is No Easy Way (But There Is a Way)	1987	—	—	3.00
❏ 07636	Nobody There But Me/Wake Me When It's Over	1987	—	—	3.00
❏ 08044	Spanish Eyes/Ole Buttermilk Sky	1988	—	—	3.00
—With Julio Iglesias					
❏ 08395	Living in the Promiseland/ Forgiving You Was Easy	1988	—	—	3.00
—Reissue					
❏ 08406	Highwayman/Desperados Waiting for a Train	1988	—	—	3.00
—Waylon Jennings/Willie Nelson/Johnny Cash/Kris Kristofferson; reissue					
❏ 08541	Twilight Time/Ac-Cent-Tchu-Ate the Positive	1989	—	—	3.00
❏ 10176	Blue Eyes Cryin' in the Rain/Bandera	1975	—	2.50	5.00
❏ 10275	Remember Me/Time of the Preacher	1975	—	2.50	5.00
❏ 10327	I'd Have to Be Crazy/Amazing Grace	1976	—	2.50	5.00
❏ 10383	If You've Got the Money, I've Got the Time/The Sound in Your Mind	1976	—	2.50	5.00
❏ 10453	Uncloudy Day/Precious Memories	1976	—	2.50	5.00
❏ 10588	I Love You a Thousand Ways/ Mom and Dad's Waltz	1977	—	2.50	5.00
❏ 10644	Something to Brag About/Anybody's Darlin' (Anybody But Mine)	1977	—	2.50	5.00
—With Mary Kay Place					
❏ 10704	Georgia on My Mind/ On the Sunny Side of the Street	1978	—	2.50	5.00
❏ 10784	Blue Skies/Moonlight in Vermont	1978	—	2.50	5.00
❏ 10834	All of Me/Unchained Melody	1978	—	2.50	5.00
❏ 10877	Whiskey River/Under the Double Eagle	1978	—	2.50	5.00
❏ 10929	September Song/ Don't Get Around Much Anymore	1979	—	2.00	4.00
❏ 11126	Help Me Make It Through the Night/ The Pilgrim: Chapter 33	1979	—	2.00	4.00
❏ 11186	My Heroes Have Always Been Cowboys/Rising Star (Love Theme)	1980	—	2.00	4.00
❏ 11257	Midnight Rider/Do You Think You're a Cowboy	1980	—	2.00	4.00
❏ 11351	On the Road Again/Jumpin' Cotton-Eyed Joe	1980	—	2.00	4.00
—B-side by Johnny Gimble					
❏ 11418	Angel Flying Too Close to the Ground/I Guess I've Come to Live Here in Your Eyes	1981	—	2.00	4.00
❏ 68923	Nothing I Can Do About It Now/If I Were a Painting	1989	—	—	3.00
❏ 73015	There You Are/Spirit	1989	—	—	3.00
❏ 73233	Silver Stallion/America Remains	1990	—	—	3.00
—Waylon Jennings/Willie Nelson/Johnny Cash/Kris Kristofferson					
❏ 73249	The Highway/Spirit	1990	—	—	3.00
❏ 73374	Is the Better Part Over/Mr. Record Man	1990	—	—	3.00
❏ 73381	Born and Raised in Black and White/Texas	1990	—	—	3.00
—The Highwaymen (Waylon Jennings/Willie Nelson/Johnny Cash/Kris Kristofferson)					
❏ 73518	It Ain't Necessarily So/I Never Cared for You	1990	—	—	3.00
❏ 73572	American Remains/Texas	1990	—	—	3.00
—The Highwaymen (Waylon Jennings/Willie Nelson/Johnny Cash/Kris Kristofferson)					
❏ 73655	The Piper Came Today/(I Don't Have a Reason) To Go to California Anymore	1991	—	—	3.00
❏ 73749	Ten with a Two/You Decide	1991	—	—	3.00
❏ 77184	Still Is Still Moving to Me/Valentine	1993	—	—	3.00

D

❏ 1084	Man with the Blues/The Storm Has Just Begun	1959	7.50	15.00	30.00
❏ 1131	What a Way to Love/Misery Mansion	1960	7.50	15.00	30.00

ISLAND

❏ 572414-7	The Maker/I Never Cared for You	1998	—	—	3.00

LIBERTY

❏ S7-18486	It Is What It Is/The Devil's Right Hand	1995	—	—	3.00
—By The Highwaymen					
❏ S7-18584	One After 909/Yesterday	1995	—	—	3.00
—B-side by Billy Dean					
❏ 55386	Mr. Record Man/The Part Where I Cry	1961	5.00	10.00	20.00
❏ 55403	Willingly/Chain of Love	1962	3.75	7.50	15.00
—A-side with Shirley Collie					

Number	Title (A Side/B Side)	Yr	VG	VG+	NM
55439	Touch Me/Where My House Lives	1962	3.75	7.50	15.00
55468	You Dream About Me/Is This My Destiny	1962	3.75	7.50	15.00
—A-side with Shirley Collie					
55494	Wake Me When It's Over/There's Gonna Be Love in My House	1962	3.75	7.50	15.00
55532	Half a Man/The Last Letter	1963	3.00	6.00	12.00
55591	Take My Word/Feed It a Memory	1963	3.00	6.00	12.00
55638	How Long Is Forever/You Took My Happy Away	1963	3.00	6.00	12.00
55661	Am I Blue/There'll Be No Teardrops Tonight	1964	2.50	5.00	10.00
55697	River Boy/Opportunity to Cry	1964	2.50	5.00	10.00
56143	Right or Wrong/I Hope So	1969	—	3.00	6.00

LONE STAR

Number	Title (A Side/B Side)	Yr	VG	VG+	NM
703	The End of Understanding/Will You Remember Mine	1978	—	2.50	5.00

MERCURY

Number	Title (A Side/B Side)	Yr	VG	VG+	NM
088 172243-7	Mendocino County Line/Maria (Shut Up and Kiss Me)	2002	—	—	3.00
—A-side with Lee Ann Womack					

MONUMENT

Number	Title (A Side/B Side)	Yr	VG	VG+	NM
855	I Never Cared for You/You Left Me	1964	3.75	7.50	15.00
03408	Everything Is Beautiful (In Its Own Way)/Put It Off Until Tomorrow	1982	—	2.00	4.00
—A-side: Willie Nelson and Dolly Parton; B-side: Dolly Parton and Kris Kristofferson					
03781	You're Gonna Love Yourself (In the Morning)/What Do You Think About Lovin'	1983	—	2.00	4.00
—A-side: Willie Nelson and Brenda Lee; B-side: Dolly Parton and Brenda Lee					

PARADISE

Number	Title (A Side/B Side)	Yr	VG	VG+	NM
629	Wabash Cannonball/Tennessee Waltz	1984	—	2.00	4.00
—A-side with Hank Wilson (a.k.a. Leon Russell); B-side by Wilson solo					

RCA

Number	Title (A Side/B Side)	Yr	VG	VG+	NM
PB-10969	I'm a Memory/It Should Be Easier Now	1977	—	2.50	5.00
—With Darrell McCall					
PB-11061	You Ought to Hear Me Cry/One in a Row	1977	—	2.50	5.00
PB-11235	If You Can Touch Her at All/Rainy Day Blues	1978	—	2.50	5.00
PB-11465	Sweet Memories/Little Things	1979	—	2.50	5.00
PB-11673	Crazy Arms/Hurricane Shirley	1979	—	2.50	5.00
—B-side by Bobby Bare					
GB-11995	Sweet Memories/If You Can Touch Her At All	1980	—	—	3.00
—Gold Standard Series					
PB-12254	Good Times/Where Do You Stand	1981	—	2.00	4.00
PB-12254 [PS]	Good Times/Where Do You Stand	1981	—	2.50	5.00
PB-12328	Mountain Dew/Laying My Burdens Down	1981	—	2.00	4.00

RCA VICTOR

Number	Title (A Side/B Side)	Yr	VG	VG+	NM
47-8484	Pretty Paper/What a Merry Christmas This Could Be	1964	3.75	7.50	15.00
47-8519	She's Not for You/Permanently Lonely	1965	3.00	6.00	12.00
47-8594	Healing Hands of Time/One Day at a Time	1965	3.00	6.00	12.00
47-8682	I Just Can't Let You Say Goodbye/And So Will You, My Love	1965	3.00	6.00	12.00
47-8801	Columbus Stockade Blues/He Sits at My Table	1966	3.00	6.00	12.00
47-8852	I'm Still Not Over You/I Love You Because	1966	3.00	6.00	12.00
47-8933	One in a Row/San Antonio Rose	1966	3.00	6.00	12.00
47-9029	Pretty Paper/What a Merry Christmas This Could Be	1966	3.00	6.00	12.00
47-9100	The Party's Over/Make Way for a Better Man	1967	2.50	5.00	10.00
47-9202	Blackjack County Chain/Some Other World	1967	2.50	5.00	10.00
47-9324	San Antonio/To Make a Long Story Short	1967	2.50	5.00	10.00
47-9427	Little Things/I'll Stay Around	1968	2.50	5.00	10.00
47-9536	Good Times/Don't You Ever Get Tired	1968	2.50	5.00	10.00
47-9605	Johnny One Time/She's Still Gone	1968	2.50	5.00	10.00
47-9684	Bring Me Sunshine/Don't Say Love or Nothing	1968	2.50	5.00	10.00
47-9778	Pretty Paper/What a Merry Christmas This Could Be	1969	—	—	—
—Unreleased					
47-9798	Who Do I Know in Dallas/Once More with Feeling	1969	2.00	4.00	8.00
47-9903	Laying My Burdens Down/Truth Number One	1970	2.00	4.00	8.00
47-9931	Pretty Paper/What a Merry Christmas This Could Be	1970	2.00	4.00	8.00
47-9951	I'm a Memory/I'm So Lonesome I Could Cry	1971	—	3.00	6.00
47-9984	Kneel at the Feet of Jesus/What Can You Do to Me Now	1971	—	3.00	6.00
74-0162	Jimmy's Road/Natural to Be Gone	1969	2.00	4.00	8.00
74-0542	Yesterday's Wine/Me and Paul	1971	—	3.00	6.00
74-0635	A Moment Isn't Very Long/Words Don't Fit the Picture	1972	—	3.00	6.00
74-0816	Mountain Dew/Phases, Stages, Circles, Cycles, and Scenes	1972	—	3.00	6.00
PB-10429	I'm a Memory/Fire and Rain	1975	—	2.50	5.00
PB-10461	Pretty Paper/What a Merry Christmas This Could Be	1975	2.00	4.00	8.00
PB-10591	Summer of Roses/I Gotta Get Drunk	1976	—	2.50	5.00

SARG

Number	Title (A Side/B Side)	Yr	VG	VG+	NM
260	A Storm Has Just Begun/When I Sang My Last Hillbilly Song	196?	12.50	25.00	50.00
—Some sources say this came out in 1955, but that doesn't coincide with this label's history					

SONGBIRD

Number	Title (A Side/B Side)	Yr	VG	VG+	NM
41313	Family Bible/In God's Eyes	1980	—	2.00	4.00

UNITED ARTISTS

Number	Title (A Side/B Side)	Yr	VG	VG+	NM
641	Night Life/Rainy Day Blues	1963	3.75	7.50	15.00
XW771	The Last Letter/There Goes a Man	1976	—	2.50	5.00
XW1165	Hello Walls/The Last Letter	1978	—	2.50	5.00
XW1254	There'll Be Teardrops Tonight/Blue Must Be the Color of the Blues	1978	—	2.50	5.00

WILLIE NELSON

Number	Title (A Side/B Side)	Yr	VG	VG+	NM
628	No Place for Me/The Lumberjack	1957	75.00	150.00	300.00

Albums

ALLEGIANCE

Number	Title (A Side/B Side)	Yr	VG	VG+	NM
AV-5005	Willie or Won't He	1983	2.50	5.00	10.00
AV-5010	Wild & Willie	1983	2.50	5.00	10.00

ATLANTIC

Number	Title (A Side/B Side)	Yr	VG	VG+	NM
SD 7262	Shotgun Willie	1973	5.00	10.00	20.00
SD 7291	Phases and Stages	1974	5.00	10.00	20.00

COLUMBIA

Number	Title (A Side/B Side)	Yr	VG	VG+	NM
KC 33482	Red Headed Stranger	1975	3.75	7.50	15.00
—No bar code on back cover					
PC 33482	Red Headed Stranger	1979	2.00	4.00	8.00
—With bar code on back cover; budget-line reissue					
PC 34092	The Sound in Your Mind	1976	3.00	6.00	12.00
—No bar code on back cover					
PC 34092	The Sound in Your Mind	1979	2.00	4.00	8.00
—With bar code on back cover; budget-line reissue					
KC 34112	The Troublemaker	1976	3.00	6.00	12.00
—No bar code on back cover					
PC 34112	The Troublemaker	1979	2.00	4.00	8.00
—With bar code on back cover; budget-line reissue					
JC 34695	To Lefty From Willie	1977	3.00	6.00	12.00
PC 34695	To Lefty From Willie	1979	2.00	4.00	8.00
—Budget-line reissue					
JC 35305	Stardust	1978	2.50	5.00	10.00
JC 35305	Stardust	2000	6.25	12.50	25.00
—Classic Records reissue on audiophile vinyl					
KC2 35642 [(2)]	Willie and Family Live	1978	3.75	7.50	15.00
JC 36188	Willie Nelson Sings Kristofferson	1979	2.50	5.00	10.00
PC 36188	Willie Nelson Sings Kristofferson	1980	2.00	4.00	8.00
—Budget-line reissue					
JC 36189	Pretty Paper	1979	2.50	5.00	10.00
JS 36327	The Electric Horseman	1979	2.50	5.00	10.00
—Side 2 by Dave Grusin					
S2 36752 [(2)]	Honeysuckle Rose	1980	3.00	6.00	12.00
—Over half of the LP is by Willie					
FC 36883	Somewhere Over the Rainbow	1981	2.50	5.00	10.00
KC2 37542 [(2)]	Willie Nelson's Greatest Hits (& Some That Will Be)	1981	3.00	6.00	12.00
FC 37951	Always on My Mind	1982	2.50	5.00	10.00
PC 37951	Always on My Mind	1984	2.00	4.00	8.00
—Budget-line reissue					
PC 38248	Tougher Than Leather	1984	2.00	4.00	8.00
—Budget-line reissue					
QC 38248	Tougher Than Leather	1983	2.50	5.00	10.00
CX 38250 [(10)]	Willie Nelson	1983	30.00	60.00	120.00
FC 39110	Without a Song	1983	2.50	5.00	10.00
PC 39110	Without a Song	1984	2.00	4.00	8.00
—Budget-line reissue					
FC 39145	City of New Orleans	1984	2.50	5.00	10.00
PC 39145	City of New Orleans	1985	2.00	4.00	8.00
—Budget-line reissue					
FC 39363	Angel Eyes	1984	2.50	5.00	10.00
PC 39363	Angel Eyes	1985	2.00	4.00	8.00
—Budget-line reissue					
FC 39894	Partners	1986	2.50	5.00	10.00
PC 39894	Partners	1987	2.00	4.00	8.00
—Budget-line reissue					
9C9 39943 [PD]	Always on My Mind	1985	5.00	10.00	20.00
FC 39990	Half Nelson	1985	2.50	5.00	10.00
—Duets with 10 different artists					
PC 39990	Half Nelson	1986	2.00	4.00	8.00
—Budget-line reissue					
FC 40008	Me and Paul	1985	2.50	5.00	10.00
PC 40008	Me and Paul	1986	2.00	4.00	8.00
—Budget-line reissue					
FC 40056	Highwayman	1985	2.50	5.00	10.00
—Waylon Jennings/Willie Nelson/Johnny Cash/Kris Kristofferson					
FC 40327	The Promiseland	1986	2.50	5.00	10.00
FC 40487	Island in the Sea	1987	2.50	5.00	10.00
HC 43482	Red Headed Stranger	1982	10.00	20.00	40.00
—Half-speed mastered edition					
FC 44431	What a Wonderful World	1988	2.50	5.00	10.00
FC 45046	A Horse Called Music	1989	2.50	5.00	10.00
C 45240	Highwayman 2	1990	3.75	7.50	15.00
—Waylon Jennings/Willie Nelson/Johnny Cash/Kris Kristofferson					
HC 45305	Stardust	1981	17.50	35.00	70.00
—Half-speed mastered edition					
HC 47951	Always on My Mind	1982	12.50	25.00	50.00
—Half-speed mastered edition					
HC 48248	Tougher Than Leather	1983	12.50	25.00	50.00
—Half-speed mastered edition					

HEARTLAND

Number	Title (A Side/B Side)	Yr	VG	VG+	NM
HL 1038/9 [(2)]	The Best of Willie Nelson	1987	3.75	7.50	15.00

LIBERTY

Number	Title (A Side/B Side)	Yr	VG	VG+	NM
LRP-3239 [M]	...And Then I Wrote	1962	10.00	20.00	40.00
LRP-3308 [M]	Here's Willie Nelson	1963	10.00	20.00	40.00
LST-7239 [S]	...And Then I Wrote	1962	12.50	25.00	50.00
LST-7308 [S]	Here's Willie Nelson	1963	12.50	25.00	50.00
LN-10013	Country Willie	1980	2.00	4.00	8.00
—Budget-line reissue					
LN-10118	The Best of Willie Nelson	1982	2.00	4.00	8.00
—Budget-line reissue					

PAIR

Number	Title (A Side/B Side)	Yr	VG	VG+	NM
PDL2-1007 [(2)]	Country Winners	1986	3.00	6.00	12.00
PDL2-1032 [(2)]	Once More with Feeling	1986	3.00	6.00	12.00
PDL2-1114 [(2)]	Good Hearted Woman	1986	3.00	6.00	12.00

PICKWICK

Number	Title (A Side/B Side)	Yr	VG	VG+	NM
ACL1-0326	Country Winners	1976	2.00	4.00	8.00
ACL1-0705	Spotlight on Willie Nelson	1976	2.00	4.00	8.00
SPC-3584	Hello Walls	1978	2.50	5.00	10.00
ACL1-7018	Columbus Stockade Blues	1976	2.00	4.00	8.00

PLANTATION

Number	Title (A Side/B Side)	Yr	VG	VG+	NM
PLP-24	The Longhorn Jamboree Presents: Willie Nelson & His Friends	1976	2.50	5.00	10.00
—Also includes tracks by David Allan Coe, Jerry Lee Lewis and Carl Perkins					

RCA CAMDEN

Number	Title (A Side/B Side)	Yr	VG	VG+	NM
ACL1-0326	Country Winners	1973	3.00	6.00	12.00
ACL1-0705	Spotlight on Willie Nelson	1974	3.00	6.00	12.00
CAS-2444	Columbus Stockade Blues	1970	3.75	7.50	15.00
ACL1-7018	Columbus Stockade Blues	1975	2.50	5.00	10.00

RCA VICTOR

Number	Title (A Side/B Side)	Yr	VG	VG+	NM
ANL1-1102	Yesterday's Wine	1975	2.50	5.00	10.00
APL1-1234	What Can You Do to Me Now	1975	3.00	6.00	12.00
APL1-1487	Willie Nelson Live	1976	3.00	6.00	12.00
APL1-2210	Before His Time	1977	2.50	5.00	10.00
AHL1-3243	Sweet Memories	1979	2.50	5.00	10.00
LPM-3418 [M]	Country Willie — His Own Songs	1965	5.00	10.00	20.00

N

Number	Title (A Side/B Side)	Yr	VG	VG+	NM
❏ LSP-3418 [S]	Country Willie — His Own Songs	1965	6.25	12.50	25.00
❏ LPM-3528 [M]	Country Favorites, Willie Nelson Style	1966	5.00	10.00	20.00
❏ LSP-3528 [S]	Country Favorites, Willie Nelson Style	1966	6.25	12.50	25.00
❏ AHL1-3549	Danny Davis & Willie Nelson ❏ with the Nashville Brass	1980	2.50	5.00	10.00
❏ LPM-3659 [M]	Country Music Concert	1966	5.00	10.00	20.00
❏ LSP-3659 [S]	Country Music Concert	1966	6.25	12.50	25.00
❏ AYL1-3671	Before His Time	1980	2.00	4.00	8.00
—"Best Buy Series" reissue					
❏ LPM-3748 [M]	Make Way for Willie Nelson	1967	5.00	10.00	20.00
❏ LSP-3748 [S]	Make Way for Willie Nelson	1967	6.25	12.50	25.00
❏ AYL1-3800	Yesterday's Wine	1980	2.00	4.00	8.00
—"Best Buy Series" reissue					
❏ LPM-3858 [M]	The Party's Over and Other Great Willie Nelson Songs	1967	6.25	12.50	25.00
❏ LSP-3858 [S]	The Party's Over and Other Great Willie Nelson Songs	1967	5.00	10.00	20.00
❏ LPM-3937 [M]	Texas in My Soul	1968	25.00	50.00	100.00
❏ LSP-3937 [S]	Texas in My Soul	1968	5.00	10.00	20.00
❏ AYL1-3958	What Can You Do to Me Now	1981	2.00	4.00	8.00
—"Best Buy Series" reissue					
❏ AHL1-4045	The Minstrel Man	1981	2.50	5.00	10.00
❏ LSP-4057	Good Times	1968	5.00	10.00	20.00
❏ LSP-4111	My Own Peculiar Way	1969	5.00	10.00	20.00
❏ AYL1-4165	Willie Nelson Live	1981	2.00	4.00	8.00
—"Best Buy Series" reissue					
❏ LSP-4294	Both Sides Now	1970	5.00	10.00	20.00
❏ AYL1-4300	Sweet Memories	1982	2.00	4.00	8.00
—"Best Buy Series" reissue					
❏ LSP-4404	Laying My Burdens Down	1970	5.00	10.00	20.00
❏ AHL1-4420	The Best of Willie Nelson	1982	2.50	5.00	10.00
❏ LSP-4489	Willie Nelson & Family	1971	5.00	10.00	20.00
❏ LSP-4568	Yesterday's Wine	1971	5.00	10.00	20.00
❏ LSP-4653	The Picture	1972	5.00	10.00	20.00
❏ LSP-4760	The Willie Way	1972	5.00	10.00	20.00
❏ AHL1-4819	My Own Way	1983	2.50	5.00	10.00
❏ AYL1-5143	The Best of Willie Nelson	1984	2.00	4.00	8.00
—"Best Buy Series" reissue					
❏ CPL1-5174	Don't You Ever Get Tired of Hurting Me	1984	2.50	5.00	10.00
❏ AYL1-5438	My Own Way	1985	2.00	4.00	8.00
—"Best Buy Series" reissue					
❏ AHL1-5470	Collector's Series	1985	2.50	5.00	10.00
❏ CPL1-7158	Willie	1986	2.50	5.00	10.00
SONGBIRD					
❏ 3258	Family Bible	1980	2.50	5.00	10.00
SUNSET					
❏ SUM-1138 [M]	Hello Walls	1966	3.75	7.50	15.00
❏ SUS-5138 [S]	Hello Walls	1966	5.00	10.00	20.00
TAKOMA					
❏ TAK-7104	The Legend Begins	1983	2.50	5.00	10.00
TIME-LIFE					
❏ P 16946 [(3)]	Country and Western Classics	1983	5.00	10.00	20.00
UNITED ARTISTS					
❏ UA-LA086-E	The Best of Willie Nelson	1973	3.75	7.50	15.00
—Reissue of Liberty tracks					
❏ UA-LA410-G	Country Willie	1975	3.75	7.50	15.00
❏ UA-LA574-H2 [(2)]	Texas Country	1975	4.50	9.00	18.00
❏ UA-LA930-G	There'll Be No Teardrops Tonight	1978	3.75	7.50	15.00

NELSON, WILLIE, AND DAVID ALLAN COE
Albums
PLANTATION

Number	Title (A Side/B Side)	Yr	VG	VG+	NM
❏ PLP 41	Willie and David	1980	2.50	5.00	10.00

—One side is solo songs by Willie Nelson, the other side solo songs by David Allan Coe

NELSON, WILLIE, AND KRIS KRISTOFFERSON Also see each artist's individual listings.
45s
COLUMBIA

Number	Title (A Side/B Side)	Yr	VG	VG+	NM
❏ 38-04652	How Do You Feel About Foolin' Around/Eye of the Storm	1984	—	—	3.00

Albums
COLUMBIA

| ❏ FC 39531 | Music from Songwriter | 1984 | 2.50 | 5.00 | 10.00 |

NELSON, WILLIE, AND ROGER MILLER Also see each artist's individual listings.
45s
COLUMBIA

Number	Title (A Side/B Side)	Yr	VG	VG+	NM
❏ 02681	Old Friends/When a House Is Not a Home	1982	—	2.00	4.00

—With Ray Price
Albums
COLUMBIA

| ❏ FC 38013 | Old Friends | 1982 | 2.50 | 5.00 | 10.00 |
| ❏ PC 38013 | Old Friends | 198? | 2.00 | 4.00 | 8.00 |

—Budget-line reissue

NELSON, WILLIE, AND WEBB PIERCE Also see each artist's individual listings.
45s
COLUMBIA

Number	Title (A Side/B Side)	Yr	VG	VG+	NM
❏ 03231	In the Jailhouse Now/Back Street Affair	1982	—	2.00	4.00

Albums
COLUMBIA

| ❏ FC 38095 | In the Jailhouse Now | 1982 | 2.50 | 5.00 | 10.00 |
| ❏ PC 38095 | In the Jailhouse Now | 198? | 2.00 | 4.00 | 8.00 |

—Budget-line reissue

NELSON, WILLIE, AND RAY PRICE Also see each artist's individual listings.
45s
COLUMBIA

Number	Title (A Side/B Side)	Yr	VG	VG+	NM
❏ 11329	Faded Love/This Cold World with You	1980	—	2.00	4.00
❏ 11405	Don't You Ever Get Tired (Of Loving Me)/Funny How Time Slips Away	1980	—	2.00	4.00

Albums
COLUMBIA

| ❏ JC 36476 | San Antonio Rose | 1980 | 2.50 | 5.00 | 10.00 |
| ❏ PC 36476 | San Antonio Rose | 198? | 2.00 | 4.00 | 8.00 |

—Budget-line reissue

NELSON, WILLIE, AND LEON RUSSELL Also see each artist's individual listings.
45s
COLUMBIA

Number	Title (A Side/B Side)	Yr	VG	VG+	NM
❏ 11023	Heartbreak Hotel/Sioux City Sue	1979	—	2.00	4.00
❏ 11119	Trouble in Mind/One for My Baby (And One More for the Road)	1979	—	2.00	4.00

Albums
COLUMBIA

| ❏ KC2 36064 [(2)] | One for the Road | 1979 | 3.75 | 7.50 | 15.00 |

NELSON, WILLIE, AND HANK SNOW
Albums
COLUMBIA

| ❏ FC 39977 | Brand on My Heart | 1984 | 2.50 | 5.00 | 10.00 |
| ❏ PC 39977 | Brand on My Heart | 1985 | 2.00 | 4.00 | 8.00 |

—Budget-line reissue

NELSON, WILLIE, AND FARON YOUNG
Albums
COLUMBIA

| ❏ FC 39484 | Funny How Time Slips Away | 1984 | 2.50 | 5.00 | 10.00 |
| ❏ PC 39484 | Funny How Time Slips Away | 1985 | 2.00 | 4.00 | 8.00 |

—Budget-line reissue

NELSON, WILLY Cousin of RICKY NELSON, this isn't the famous country singer. It's confusing enough that he recorded for Liberty, for which the "other" Willie recorded in the early 1960s, but some pressings of this record were spelled "Willie"!
45s
LIBERTY

Number	Title (A Side/B Side)	Yr	VG	VG+	NM
❏ 55155	Susie/No Dough	1958	6.25	12.50	25.00
—As "Willy Nelson"					
❏ 55155	Susie/No Dough	1958	7.50	15.00	30.00
—As "Willie Nelson"					

NEON PHILHARMONIC, THE
45s
MCA

❏ 40518	So Glad You're a Woman/Making Out the Best You Can	1976	—	2.50	5.00
TRX					
❏ 5039	Annie Poor/Love Will Find a Way	1972	—	2.50	5.00
WARNER BROS.					
❏ 7261	Morning Girl/Brilliant Colors	1969	2.00	4.00	8.00
❏ 7311	No One Is Going to Hurt You/You Lied	1969	—	3.00	6.00
❏ 7355	Clouds/Snow	1969	—	3.00	6.00
❏ 7380	Heighdy-Ho Princess/Don't Know My Way Around My Soul	1970	—	3.00	6.00
❏ 7419	Flowers for Your Pillow/To Be Continued	1970	—	3.00	6.00
❏ 7457	Something to Believe In/A Little Love	1971	—	3.00	6.00
❏ 7497	Gotta Feeling in My Bones/Keep the Faith in Me	1971	—	3.00	6.00

Albums
WARNER BROS.

| ❏ WS 1769 | The Moth Confesses | 1968 | 6.25 | 12.50 | 25.00 |
| ❏ WS 1804 | The Neon Philharmonic | 1969 | 3.75 | 7.50 | 15.00 |

NEONS, THE (1)
45s
CHALLENGE

| ❏ 9147 | Magic Moment/Fat Girls | 1962 | 25.00 | 50.00 | 100.00 |
| ❏ 59147 | Magic Moment/Fat Girls | 1962 | 12.50 | 25.00 | 50.00 |

NEONS, THE (2)
45s
GONE

❏ 5090	Angel Face/Golden Dreams	1960	10.00	20.00	40.00
TETRA					
❏ 4444	Angel Face/Kiss Me Quickly	1956	20.00	40.00	80.00
❏ 4449	Road of Romance/My Chickadee	1957	20.00	40.00	80.00
VINTAGE					
❏ 1016	Honey Bun/Golden Dreams	1974	—	2.50	5.00

NEONS, THE (3)
45s
WALDON

| ❏ 1001 | My Lover/Tucson | 1961 | 175.00 | 350.00 | 700.00 |

NEP-TUNES, THE
Albums
FAMILY

| ❏ FLP-152 [M] | Surfer's Holiday | 1963 | 50.00 | 100.00 | 200.00 |
| ❏ SFLP-152 [S] | Surfer's Holiday | 1963 | 75.00 | 150.00 | 300.00 |

NEPTUNES, THE Several different groups.
45s
CHECKER

❏ 967	She'll Understand/So Little Time	1960	3.00	6.00	12.00
GEM					
❏ 100	Turn Around/(B-side unknown)	196?	6.25	12.50	25.00
GLORY					
❏ 269	Fraidy Cat/As Long As	1959	5.00	10.00	20.00
INSTANT					
❏ 3255	Make a Memory/House of Heartaches	1963	6.25	12.50	25.00
PAYSON					
❏ 101/2	If You Care/She Went That-a-Way	1958	5.00	10.00	20.00
RCA VICTOR					
❏ 47-7931	Curiosity Killed the Cat/This Is Love	1961	3.00	6.00	12.00
VICTORIA					
❏ 102	I'm Coming Home/I Don't Cry Anymore	1964	6.25	12.50	25.00
WARNER BROS.					
❏ 5453	Shame Girl/I've Got Plans	1964	3.00	6.00	12.00

NERO, FRANCES
45s
SOUL

| ❏ 35020 | Keep On Lovin' Me/Fight Off Fire with Fire | 1966 | 12.50 | 25.00 | 50.00 |

Number	Title (A Side/B Side)	Yr	VG	VG+	NM

NERO, PETER
45s
ARIOLA AMERICA

❏ 7635	There'll Be Time/Always Lovely Times	1976	—	2.00	4.00
❏ 7650	Tara's Theme/Always Lovely Times	1976	—	2.00	4.00

ARISTA

❏ 0112	Emmanuelle/Soul Ballet	1975	—	2.00	4.00
❏ 0125	Theme from "The Young and the Restless"/Superstition	1975	—	2.00	4.00

COLUMBIA

❏ 44846	Soulful Strut/For Once in My Life	1969	—	2.50	5.00
❏ 44934	Be-In/Theme from Picasso Summer	1969	—	2.50	5.00
❏ 45077	Come Saturday Morning/Maybe Tomorrow	1970	—	2.00	4.00
❏ 45167	Company/Raindrops Keep Fallin' on My Head	1970	—	2.00	4.00
❏ 45198	The Great Hits of Summer Medley/Something	1970	—	2.00	4.00
❏ 45279	Theme from "Love Story"/El Condor Pasa	1970	—	2.00	4.00
❏ 45399	Theme from "Summer of '42"/Theme from "Jesus Christ Superstar"	1971	—	2.00	4.00
❏ 45544	Brian's Song/Just for Her	1972	—	2.00	4.00
❏ 45651	Love Theme from "The Godfather"/A Love That Never Ends	1972	—	2.00	4.00
❏ 45731	Ben (Theme from "Ben")/His World	1972	—	2.00	4.00
❏ 45756	Lady Sings the Blues/Love Is Waiting	1973	—	2.00	4.00
❏ 45756 [PS]	Lady Sings the Blues/Love Is Waiting	1973	—	2.50	5.00
❏ 45825	Theme from "Baxter"/Love Is Waiting	1973	—	2.00	4.00
❏ 45959	The Morning After/Daydream	1973	—	2.00	4.00

RCA VICTOR

❏ 47-7932	Maria/On the Street Where You Live	1961	2.00	4.00	8.00
❏ 47-7956	Theme from "Summer and Smoke"/Maria	1961	2.00	4.00	8.00
❏ 47-7956 [PS]	Theme from "Summer and Smoke"/Maria	1961	3.00	6.00	12.00
❏ 47-8161	Space Flight/It's a Darn Good Thing	1963	2.00	4.00	8.00
❏ 47-8322	Sunday in New York/More in Love	1964	—	3.00	6.00
❏ 47-8503	Theme from "36 Hours"/If You've Got a Heart	1965	—	3.00	6.00
❏ 47-8620	Ship of Fools/Why Did I Choose You	1965	—	3.00	6.00
❏ 47-8715	Thunderball/Theme from "The Spy Who Came In from the Cold"	1965	—	3.00	6.00
❏ 47-8892	Born Free/Who's Afraid	1966	—	3.00	6.00
❏ 47-9125	Theme from The Quiller Memorandum/Amy's Theme	1967	—	3.00	6.00
❏ 47-9247	Guantanamera/Xochimilco	1967	—	3.00	6.00
❏ 47-9423	Theme from The Fox/Who Will Answer	1968	—	3.00	6.00
❏ 47-9556	Elvira/A Heart Without Love	1968	—	3.00	6.00

Albums
ARISTA

❏ AL 4034	Disco, Dance and Love Themes	1976	2.50	5.00	10.00

BAINBRIDGE

❏ BT-6268	The Sounds of Love	1987	2.50	5.00	10.00

COLUMBIA

❏ CS 1009	I'll Never Fall in Love Again	1970	2.50	5.00	10.00
❏ CS 9800	I've Gotta Be Me	1969	3.00	6.00	12.00
❏ C 30586	Love Story	1971	2.50	5.00	10.00
❏ CQ 31105 [Q]	Summer of '42	1971	3.75	7.50	15.00
❏ KC 31105	Summer of '42	1971	2.50	5.00	10.00
❏ KC 31335	The First Time Ever (I Saw Your Face)	1972	2.50	5.00	10.00
❏ C2 31982 [(2)]	The World of Peter Nero	1972	3.00	6.00	12.00
❏ KC 32689	Say, Has Anybody Seen My Sweet Gypsy Rose	1973	2.50	5.00	10.00
❏ PC 33136	Greatest Hits	1974	2.50	5.00	10.00

CONCORD JAZZ

❏ CJ-48	Now	1978	2.50	5.00	10.00

CRYSTAL CLEAR

❏ 6001	The Wiz	198?	5.00	10.00	20.00
—Direct-to-disc recording					

MODE

❏ LP-117 [M]	Bernie Nerow Trio	1957	20.00	40.00	80.00
—As "Bernie Nerow"					

PREMIER

❏ PM-2011 [M]	Just for You	1963	5.00	10.00	20.00
❏ PS-2011 [R]	Just for You	1963	3.00	6.00	12.00

RCA CAMDEN

❏ CAL-2139 [M]	Peter Nero Plays Born Free and Others	1967	3.75	7.50	15.00
❏ CAS-2139 [S]	Peter Nero Plays Born Free and Others	1967	3.00	6.00	12.00
❏ CAL-2228 [M]	If Ever I Would Leave You	1968	3.75	7.50	15.00
❏ CAS-2228 [S]	If Ever I Would Leave You	1968	3.00	6.00	12.00

RCA VICTOR

❏ PRM-241 [M]	Tender Is the Night	1967	3.75	7.50	15.00
❏ PRS-241 [S]	Tender Is the Night	1967	5.00	10.00	20.00
—Special-products release					
❏ ADL1-0284 [(2)]	Music Festival of Hits	1973	3.00	6.00	12.00
❏ LPM-2334 [M]	Piano Forte	1961	3.75	7.50	15.00
❏ LSP-2334 [S]	Piano Forte	1961	5.00	10.00	20.00
❏ LPM-2383 [M]	New Piano in Town	1961	3.75	7.50	15.00
❏ LSP-2383 [S]	New Piano in Town	1961	5.00	10.00	20.00
❏ LPM-2484 [M]	Young and Warm and Wonderful	1962	3.75	7.50	15.00
❏ LSP-2484 [S]	Young and Warm and Wonderful	1962	5.00	10.00	20.00
❏ LPM-2536 [M]	For the Nero-Minded	1962	3.75	7.50	15.00
❏ LSP-2536 [S]	For the Nero-Minded	1962	5.00	10.00	20.00
❏ LPM-2618 [M]	The Colorful Peter Nero	1963	3.75	7.50	15.00
❏ LSP-2618 [S]	The Colorful Peter Nero	1963	5.00	10.00	20.00
❏ LPM-2638 [M]	Hail the Conquering Nero	1963	3.75	7.50	15.00
❏ LSP-2638 [S]	Hail the Conquering Nero	1963	5.00	10.00	20.00
❏ LPM-2710 [M]	Peter Nero in Person	1963	3.75	7.50	15.00
❏ LSP-2710 [S]	Peter Nero in Person	1963	5.00	10.00	20.00
❏ LPM-2827 [M]	Sunday in New York	1964	3.75	7.50	15.00
❏ LSP-2827 [S]	Sunday in New York	1964	5.00	10.00	20.00
❏ LPM-2853 [M]	Reflections	1964	3.75	7.50	15.00
❏ LSP-2853 [S]	Reflections	1964	5.00	10.00	20.00
❏ LPM-2935 [M]	Songs You Won't Forget	1964	3.75	7.50	15.00
❏ LSP-2935 [S]	Songs You Won't Forget	1964	5.00	10.00	20.00
❏ LPM-2978 [M]	The Best of Peter Nero	1965	3.75	7.50	15.00
❏ LSP-2978 [S]	The Best of Peter Nero	1965	5.00	10.00	20.00
❏ LPM-3313 [M]	Career Girls	1965	3.75	7.50	15.00
❏ LSP-3313 [S]	Career Girls	1965	5.00	10.00	20.00
❏ LPM-3496 [M]	The Screen Scene	1966	3.00	6.00	12.00
❏ LSP-3496 [S]	The Screen Scene	1966	3.75	7.50	15.00
❏ LPM-3550 [M]	Peter Nero — Up Close	1966	3.00	6.00	12.00
❏ LSP-3550 [S]	Peter Nero — Up Close	1966	3.75	7.50	15.00
❏ LPM-3610 [M]	Peter Nero On Tour	1966	3.00	6.00	12.00
❏ LSP-3610 [S]	Peter Nero On Tour	1966	3.75	7.50	15.00
❏ LPM-3720 [M]	Plays a Salute to Herb Alpert and the Tijuana Brass	1967	3.75	7.50	15.00
❏ LSP-3720 [S]	Plays a Salute to Herb Alpert and the Tijuana Brass	1967	3.00	6.00	12.00
❏ LPM-3814 [M]	Xochimilico	1967	3.75	7.50	15.00
❏ LSP-3814 [S]	Xochimilico	1967	3.00	6.00	12.00
❏ LPM-3871 [M]	Nero-ing In on the Hits	1968	3.75	7.50	15.00
❏ LSP-3871 [S]	Nero-ing In on the Hits	1968	3.00	6.00	12.00
❏ LPM-3936 [M]	Peter Nero Plays Love Is Blue and Ten Other Great Songs	1968	3.75	7.50	15.00
❏ LSP-3936 [S]	Peter Nero Plays Love Is Blue and Ten Other Great Songs	1968	3.00	6.00	12.00
❏ LSP-4072	Impressions (Great Songs of Burt Bacharach and Hal David)	1968	3.00	6.00	12.00
❏ LSP-4205	Love Trip	1969	3.00	6.00	12.00

NEROW, BERNIE See PETER NERO.

NERVOUS NORVUS
45s
BIG BEN

❏ 101	Pure Gold/Let's Worship God Each Sunday	1960	6.25	12.50	25.00

DOT

❏ 15470	Transfusion/Dig	1956	7.50	15.00	30.00
—Second pressings have black labels					
❏ 15470	Transfusion/Dig	1956	12.50	25.00	50.00
—Originals have maroon labels					
❏ 15485	Ape Call/Wild Dog of Kentucky	1956	5.00	10.00	20.00
—Second pressings have black labels					
❏ 15485	Ape Call/Wild Dog of Kentucky	1956	7.50	15.00	30.00
—Originals have maroon labels					
❏ 15500	The Fang/The Bullfrog	1956	5.00	10.00	20.00
—Second pressings have black labels					
❏ 15500	The Fang/The Bullfrog	1956	7.50	15.00	30.00
—Originals have maroon labels					
❏ 16765	Transfusion/Ape Call	1965	3.00	6.00	12.00

EMBEE

❏ 117	I Like Girls/Stone Age Woo	1959	5.00	10.00	20.00

NESMITH, MICHAEL Also see MIKE, JOHN AND BILL; THE MONKEES.
45s
COLPIX

❏ 787	The New Recruit/A Journey	1965	37.50	75.00	150.00
—As "Michael Blessing"					
❏ 792	Until It's Time for You to Go/What's the Trouble, Officer	1965	37.50	75.00	150.00
—As "Michael Blessing"					

EDAN

❏ 1001	Just a Little Love/Curson Terrace	1965	30.00	60.00	120.00

HIGHNESS

❏ HN-13	Wanderin'/Well Well Well	1963	100.00	200.00	400.00
—As "Mike Nesmith"					

PACIFIC ARTS

❏ 084	Life, the Unsuspecting Captive/Rio	1977	2.00	4.00	8.00
❏ 101	Roll with the Flow/I've Just Begun to Care	1978	—	3.00	6.00
❏ PAC45-104	Rio/Casablanca Moonlight	1978	—	3.00	6.00
❏ PAC45-104 [PS]	Rio/Casablanca Moonlight	1978	3.00	6.00	12.00
❏ 106	Magic (This Night Is Magic)/Dance	1979	—	3.00	6.00
❏ 108	Cruisin'/Horserace	1979	—	3.00	6.00
❏ 6373	Life, the Unsuspecting Captive/Rio	1976	2.50	5.00	10.00
❏ 6398	Navajo Trail/Love's First Kiss	1976	2.50	5.00	10.00

RCA VICTOR

❏ 47-9853	Rose City Chimes/Little Red Rider	1970	2.50	5.00	10.00
❏ 74-0368	Joanne/One Rose	1970	3.00	6.00	12.00
❏ 74-0399	Silver Moon/Lady of the Valley	1970	2.50	5.00	10.00
❏ 74-0453	Nevada Fighter/Here I Am	1971	2.00	4.00	8.00
❏ 74-0453 [PS]	Nevada Fighter/Here I Am	1971	5.00	10.00	20.00
❏ 74-0491	Tumbling Tumbleweeds/Texas Morning	1971	2.00	4.00	8.00
❏ 74-0540	Only Bound/Propinquity	1971	2.00	4.00	8.00
❏ 74-0629	Lazy Lady/Mama Rocker	1971	2.00	4.00	8.00
❏ 74-0804	Roll with the Flow/Keep On	1972	2.00	4.00	8.00

Albums
PACIFIC ARTS

❏ (no #) [DJ]	The Michael Nesmith Radio Special	1979	10.00	20.00	40.00
❏ 11-101A	The Prison	197?	12.50	25.00	50.00
—Boxed set with booklet					
❏ 7-101	The Prison	197?	5.00	10.00	20.00
—Standard cover					
❏ 7-106	Compilation	1976	5.00	10.00	20.00
❏ 7-107	From a Radio Engine to the Photon Wing	1977	3.00	6.00	12.00
❏ 7-116	And the Hits Just Keep On Comin'	1978	3.75	7.50	15.00
—Reissue of RCA 4695					
❏ 7-117	Pretty Much Your Standard Ranch Stash	1978	3.75	7.50	15.00
—Reissue of RCA APL1-0164					
❏ 7-118	Live at the Palais	1978	3.75	7.50	15.00
❏ 7-130	Infinite Rider on the Big Dogma	1979	3.75	7.50	15.00
❏ ILPA-9486	From a Radio Engine to the Photon Wing	1977	3.75	7.50	15.00
—Original issue					

RCA VICTOR

❏ APL1-0164	Pretty Much Your Standard Ranch Stash	1973	6.25	12.50	25.00
❏ LSP-4371	Magnetic South	1970	7.50	15.00	30.00
❏ LSP-4415	Loose Salute	1970	7.50	15.00	30.00
❏ LSP-4497	Nevada Fighter	1971	6.25	12.50	25.00
❏ LSP-4563	Tantamount to Treason	1971	6.25	12.50	25.00
❏ LSP-4695	And the Hits Just Keep On Comin'	1972	6.25	12.50	25.00

RHINO

❏ R1-70168	The Newer Stuff	1989	3.00	6.00	12.00

N

Number	Title (A Side/B Side)	Yr	VG	VG+	NM

NETHERWORLD
Albums
R.E.M.

Number	Title (A Side/B Side)	Yr	VG	VG+	NM
❏ 4441	Netherworld	196?	15.00	30.00	60.00

NEUMAN, ALFRED E., AND THE FURSHLUGGINER FIVE
45s
ABC-PARAMOUNT

Number	Title (A Side/B Side)	Yr	VG	VG+	NM
❏ 10013	What — Me Worry?/Potrzebie	1959	10.00	20.00	40.00
❏ 10013 [PS]	What — Me Worry?/Potrzebie	1959	15.00	30.00	60.00

NEVILLE, AARON Also see THE METERS; LINDA RONSTADT.
45s
A&M

Number	Title (A Side/B Side)	Yr	VG	VG+	NM
❏ 31458 0312 7	The Grand Tour/Don't Take Away My Heaven	1993	—	2.00	4.00
❏ 31458 0442 7	Please Come Home for Christmas/Louisiana Christmas Day	1993	—	2.50	5.00
❏ 31458 1112 7	For the Good Times/Crying in the Chapel	1995	—	2.00	4.00
❏ 75021 1563 7	Everybody Plays the Fool/House on a Hill	1991	—	2.00	4.00
BELL					
❏ 746	You Can Give, But You Can't Take/Where Is My Baby	1968	2.00	4.00	8.00
❏ 781	Speak to Me/You Don't Love Me Anymore	1969	2.00	4.00	8.00
❏ 834	All These Things/She's On My Mind	1969	2.00	4.00	8.00
MERCURY					
❏ 73310	Baby I'm-a Want You/Mojo Hannah	1972	—	3.00	6.00
❏ 73387	Hercules/Going Home	1973	—	3.00	6.00
MINIT					
❏ 612	Over You/Every Day	1960	3.75	7.50	15.00
—As "Arron Neville"					
❏ 618	Show Me the Way/Get Out of My Life	1960	3.00	6.00	12.00
❏ 624	Don't Cry/Reality	1961	3.00	6.00	12.00
❏ 631	Let's Live/I Found Another Love	1961	3.00	6.00	12.00
❏ 639	How Many Times/I'm Waitin' at the Station	1962	3.00	6.00	12.00
❏ 650	Humdinger/Sweet Little Mama	1962	3.00	6.00	12.00
❏ 657	Wrong Number/How Could I Help But Love You	1963	3.00	6.00	12.00
PAR-LO					
❏ 101	Tell It Like It Is/Why Worry	1966	5.00	10.00	20.00
—Black and white label					
❏ 101	Tell It Like It Is/Why Worry	1966	6.25	12.50	25.00
—Turquoise label, silver print					
❏ 101	Tell It Like It Is/Why Worry	1966	6.25	12.50	25.00
—Yellow label, red and black print					
❏ 103	She Took You for a Ride/Space Man	1967	2.00	4.00	8.00
POLYDOR					
❏ 14426	Greatest Love/Performance	1977	—	2.00	4.00
SAFARI					
❏ 201	Forever More/Ape Man	1967	2.50	5.00	10.00
WHO DAT?					
❏ VPAG-4476/7	Who Dat? (The History of the Saints)/(Extended Version)	1987	2.00	4.00	8.00
Albums					
MINIT					
❏ LP 24007 [R]	Like It 'Tis	1967	7.50	15.00	30.00
❏ LP 40007 [M]	Like It 'Tis	1967	10.00	20.00	40.00
PAR-LO					
❏ 1 [M]	Tell It Like It Is	1967	20.00	40.00	80.00
❏ 1 [S]	Tell It Like It Is	1967	50.00	100.00	200.00

NEVILLE, AARON, AND TRISHA YEARWOOD
45s
MCA

Number	Title (A Side/B Side)	Yr	VG	VG+	NM
❏ 54836	I Fall to Pieces/(Instrumental)	1994	—	2.00	4.00

NEW BIRTH, THE Also see LOVE, PEACE AND HAPPINESS; THE NITE-LITERS.
45s
ARIOLA AMERICA

Number	Title (A Side/B Side)	Yr	VG	VG+	NM
❏ 7760	I Love You/Fastest Gun	1979	—	2.00	4.00
BUDDAH					
❏ 464	Granddaddy (Part 1)/Granddaddy (Part 2)	1975	—	2.00	4.00
❏ 470	Dream Merchant/Why Did It	1975	—	2.00	4.00
RCA VICTOR					
❏ 74-0400	What'll I Do/One Way Bus	1970	—	3.00	6.00
❏ 74-0520	It's Impossible/Honeybee	1971	—	2.50	5.00
❏ 74-0657	Unh Song/Two Kinds of People	1972	—	2.50	5.00
❏ 74-0774	Come Back in My Life (Part 1)/Come Back in My Life (Part 2)	1972	—	2.50	5.00
❏ 74-0912	I Can Understand It/Oh Baby, I Love the Way	1973	—	2.50	5.00
❏ APBO-0003	Until It's Time for You to Go/You Are What I'm All About	1973	—	2.50	5.00
❏ APBO-0185	It's Been a Long Time/Keep On Doin' It	1973	—	2.50	5.00
❏ APBO-0265	Wildflower/Got to Get a Knutt	1974	—	2.50	5.00
❏ PB-10017	I Wash My Hands of the Whole Damn Deal Part 1/Part 2	1974	—	2.50	5.00
❏ PB-10110	Comin' From All Sides/Patiently	1974	—	2.50	5.00
❏ PB-10242	Do It Again/Pretty Music	1975	—	2.50	5.00
WARNER BROS.					
❏ 8217	The Long and Winding Road/Hurry Hurry	1976	—	2.00	4.00
❏ 8256	Fallin' in Love — Part I/Fallin' in Love — Part II	1976	—	2.00	4.00
❏ 8292	We Are All God's Children — Part I/We Are All God's Children — Part II	1976	—	2.00	4.00
❏ 8422	Deeper/Deeper (Part 2)	1977	—	2.00	4.00
❏ 8499	The Mighty Army/Hurry Hurry	1977	—	2.00	4.00
❏ 8536	How Will I Live/Squeezing Too Much Living	1978	—	2.00	4.00
Albums					
ARIOLA AMERICA					
❏ SW-50062	Platinum City	1979	2.50	5.00	10.00
BUDDAH					
❏ BDS-5636	Blind Baby	1975	2.50	5.00	10.00
COLLECTABLES					
❏ COL-5100	Golden Classics	1988	2.50	5.00	10.00
RCA VICTOR					
❏ APD1-0285 [Q]	It's Been a Long Time	1974	5.00	10.00	20.00
❏ APL1-0285	It's Been a Long Time	1974	2.50	5.00	10.00
❏ APL1-0494	Comin' From All Ends	1974	2.50	5.00	10.00
❏ APL1-1021	The Best of the New Birth	1975	2.50	5.00	10.00

Number	Title (A Side/B Side)	Yr	VG	VG+	NM
❏ ANL1-2145	Birth Day	1977	2.50	5.00	10.00
—Reissue of 4797					
❏ AFL1-4411	I'm Back	1982	2.50	5.00	10.00
❏ LSP-4450	The New Birth	1970	3.75	7.50	15.00
❏ LSP-4526	Ain't No Big Thing, But It's Growing	1971	3.75	7.50	15.00
❏ LSP-4697	Coming Together	1972	3.75	7.50	15.00
❏ LSP-4797	Birth Day	1973	3.00	6.00	12.00
WARNER BROS.					
❏ BS 2953	Love Potion	1976	2.50	5.00	10.00
❏ BSK 3071	Behold the Mighty Army	1977	2.50	5.00	10.00

NEW CHRISTY MINSTRELS, THE Also see BARRY McGUIRE; KENNY ROGERS.
45s
COLUMBIA

Number	Title (A Side/B Side)	Yr	VG	VG+	NM
❏ 42592	This Land Is Your Land/Don't Cry, Suzanne	1962	2.50	5.00	10.00
❏ 42592 [PS]	This Land Is Your Land/Don't Cry, Suzanne	1962	3.75	7.50	15.00
❏ 42673	Denver/Liza Lee	1963	2.50	5.00	10.00
❏ 42805	Green, Green/The Banjo	1963	2.50	5.00	10.00
❏ 42887	Saturday Night/The Wheeler-Dealers	1963	2.50	5.00	10.00
❏ 43000	Today/Miss Katy Cruel	1964	2.00	4.00	8.00
❏ 43092	Silly Ol' Summertime/The Far Side of the Hill	1964	2.00	4.00	8.00
❏ 43137	Same Ol' Huckleberry Finn/The Ol' Riverboat	1964	2.00	4.00	8.00
❏ 43178	Down the Road I Go/Gotta Get a-Goin'	1964	2.00	4.00	8.00
❏ 43215	Chim Chim Cheree/They Gotta Quit Kickin' My Dog Around	1965	2.00	4.00	8.00
❏ 43281	The River/Se Paingi, Se Ridi	1965	2.00	4.00	8.00
❏ 43347	Jim 'n' I, Him 'n' I, Flying in the Gemini/A Little Bit of Happiness	1965	2.00	4.00	8.00
❏ 43470	Born to Be Free/Everybody Loves Saturday Night	1965	2.00	4.00	8.00
❏ 43533	Dance My Troubles Away (Zorba's Dance)/There But for Fortune	1966	—	3.00	6.00
❏ 43644	If I Could Start My Life Again/The Music of the World a-Turnin'	1966	—	3.00	6.00
❏ 43822	A Corner in the Sun/Beautiful, Beautiful World	1966	—	3.00	6.00
❏ 43940	We Need a Little Christmas/Oh Holy Night	1966	2.50	5.00	10.00
❏ 43961	It Should Have Been You/Sleep Comes Easy	1967	—	3.00	6.00
❏ 44176	I'll Coat Your Mind with Honey/Night and Day	1967	—	3.00	6.00
❏ 44355	The Clown/No Matter What People	1967	—	3.00	6.00
❏ 44528	Ballad for Americans/Gallant Men	1968	—	2.50	5.00
❏ 44577	Alice's Restaurant/Summertime Love	1968	—	2.50	5.00
❏ 4-44631	Chitty Chitty Bang Bang/Me Old Bam-Boo	1968	—	3.00	6.00
❏ JZSP 116417/8 [DJ]	We Need a Little Christmas/Sleigh Ride	1966	3.00	6.00	12.00
—White label					
❏ JZSP 116417/8 [DJ]	We Need a Little Christmas/Sleigh Ride	1966	3.00	6.00	12.00
—Yellow label					
GREGAR					
❏ 71-0102	You Need Someone to Love/South American Getaway	1970	—	2.00	4.00
❏ 71-0106	Brother/I Still Do	1970	—	2.00	4.00
❏ 71-0109	You Are Always On My Mind/Where Are You Then	1971	—	2.00	4.00
❏ 71-0114	The Age of Not Believing/Love It Along	1972	—	2.00	4.00
Albums					
COLUMBIA					
❏ CL 1872 [M]	The New Christy Minstrels	1962	5.00	10.00	20.00
❏ CL 1941 [M]	The New Christy Minstrels In Person	1963	5.00	10.00	20.00
❏ CL 2017 [M]	Tall Tales! Legends & Nonsense	1963	5.00	10.00	20.00
❏ CL 2055 [M]	Ramblin' Feturing Green, Green	1963	5.00	10.00	20.00
❏ CL 2096 [M]	Merry Christmas	1963	5.00	10.00	20.00
❏ CL 2159 [M]	Today	1964	5.00	10.00	20.00
❏ CL 2187 [M]	Land of Giants	1964	5.00	10.00	20.00
❏ CL 2280 [M]	The Quiet Sides of the New Christy Minstrels	1965	5.00	10.00	20.00
❏ CL 2303 [M]	Cowboys and Indians	1965	5.00	10.00	20.00
❏ CL 2369 [M]	Chim Chim Cher-ee	1965	5.00	10.00	20.00
❏ CL 2384 [M]	The Wandering Minstrels	1965	5.00	10.00	20.00
❏ CL 2479 [M]	Greatest Hits	1966	5.00	10.00	20.00
❏ CL 2531 [M]	In Italy…In Italian	1966	5.00	10.00	20.00
❏ CL 2542 [M]	New Kick	1967	5.00	10.00	20.00
❏ CL 2556 [M]	Christmas with the Christies	1966	5.00	10.00	20.00
❏ CS 8672 [S]	The New Christy Minstrels	1962	6.25	12.50	25.00
❏ CS 8741 [S]	The New Christy Minstrels In Person	1963	6.25	12.50	25.00
❏ CS 8817 [S]	Tall Tales! Legends & Nonsense	1963	6.25	12.50	25.00
❏ CS 8855 [S]	Ramblin' Feturing Green, Green	1963	6.25	12.50	25.00
❏ CS 8896 [S]	Merry Christmas	1963	6.25	12.50	25.00
❏ CS 8959 [S]	Today	1964	6.25	12.50	25.00
❏ CS 8987 [S]	Land of Giants	1964	6.25	12.50	25.00
❏ CS 9080 [S]	The Quiet Sides of the New Christy Minstrels	1965	6.25	12.50	25.00
❏ CS 9103 [S]	Cowboys and Indians	1965	6.25	12.50	25.00
❏ CS 9169 [S]	Chim Chim Cher-ee	1965	6.25	12.50	25.00
❏ CS 9184 [S]	The Wandering Minstrels	1965	6.25	12.50	25.00
❏ CS 9279 [S]	Greatest Hits	1966	6.25	12.50	25.00
❏ CS 9331 [S]	In Italy…In Italian	1966	6.25	12.50	25.00
❏ CS 9342 [S]	New Kick	1967	6.25	12.50	25.00
❏ CS 9356 [S]	Christmas with the Christies	1966	6.25	12.50	25.00
❏ CS 9616 [S]	On Tour Through Motortown	1968	12.50	25.00	50.00
—White label promo only; "Special Mono Radio Station Copy" sticker on front					
❏ CS 9616 [S]	On Tour Through Motortown	1968	5.00	10.00	20.00
❏ CS 9709	Chitty Chitty Bang Bang	1969	5.00	10.00	20.00
GREGAR					
❏ 102	You Need Someone to Love	1970	3.75	7.50	15.00

NEW COLONY SIX, THE
45s
CENTAUR

Number	Title (A Side/B Side)	Yr	VG	VG+	NM
❏ 1201	I Confess/Dawn Is Breaking	1966	3.75	7.50	15.00
❏ 1202	I Like Awake/At the River's Edge	1966	3.75	7.50	15.00
MCA					
❏ 40215	Never Be Lonely/Long Time to Be Alone	1974	6.25	12.50	25.00
❏ 40288	I Really Don't Want to Go/Run	1974	7.50	15.00	30.00
MERCURY					
❏ 72737	Treat Her Groovy/Rap-a-Tap	1967	2.50	5.00	10.00
—Orange and red swirl label					
❏ 72737	Treat Her Groovy/Rap-a-Tap	1967	3.00	6.00	12.00
—Red label with "Mercury" logo in all capital letters					
❏ 72737 [PS]	Treat Her Groovy/Rap-a-Tap	1967	3.75	7.50	15.00

Number	Title (A Side/B Side)	Yr	VG	VG+	NM
❏ 72775	I Will Always Think About You/ Hold Me with Your Eyes	1968	2.50	5.00	10.00
—Orange and red swirl label					
❏ 72775	I Will Always Think About You/ Hold Me with Your Eyes	1968	3.00	6.00	12.00
—Red label with "Mercury" logo in all capital letters					
❏ 72817	Can't You See Me Cry/ Summertime's Another Name for Love	1968	2.00	4.00	8.00
❏ 72817 [PS]	Can't You See Me Cry/ Summertime's Another Name for Love	1968	3.75	7.50	15.00
❏ 72858	Things I'd Like to Say/ Come and Give Your Love to Me	1968	2.50	5.00	10.00
—Red label with "Mercury" logo in an oval					
❏ 72858	Things I'd Like to Say/ Come and Give Your Love to Me	1968	3.00	6.00	12.00
—Orange and red swirl label					
❏ 72920	I Could Never Lie to You/Just Feel Worse	1969	2.00	4.00	8.00
❏ 72961	I Want You to Know/Free	1969	2.00	4.00	8.00
❏ 73004	Barbara, I Love You/Prairie Grey	1970	2.00	4.00	8.00
❏ 73063	People and Me/Ride the Wicked Wind	1970	3.75	7.50	15.00
❏ 73093	Close Your Eyes Little Girl/ Love, That's the Best I Can Do	1970	5.00	10.00	20.00
—Promo copies go for less					
SENTAR					
❏ 1203	Cadillac/Sunshine	1966	3.75	7.50	15.00
❏ 1204	(Ballad of the) Wingbat Marmaduke/ Power of Love	1966	3.75	7.50	15.00
❏ 1205	Love You So Much/Let Me Love You	1967	3.75	7.50	15.00
❏ 1206	You're Gonna Be Mine/Woman	1967	3.75	7.50	15.00
❏ 1207	I'm Just Waiting Anticipating for Her to Show Up/ Hello Lonely	1967	3.75	7.50	15.00
SENTAUR					
❏ 1202	I Like Awake/At the River's Edge	1966	5.00	10.00	20.00
—Reissue of Centaur 1202, but harder to find					
SUNLIGHT					
❏ 1001	Roll On/If You Could See	1971	—	3.00	6.00
❏ 1004	Long Time to Be Alone/Never Be Lonely	1971	—	3.00	6.00
❏ 1005	Someone, Sometime/Come On Down	1972	2.00	4.00	8.00
TWILIGHT					
❏ 1004	Long Time to Be Alone/Never Be Lonely	1973	—	—	—
—The existence of this record as a US pressing has not been confirmed					
Albums					
MERCURY					
❏ SR-61165	Revelations	1968	7.50	15.00	30.00
❏ SR-61228	Attacking a Straw Man	1969	7.50	15.00	30.00
SENTAR					
❏ LP-101 [M]	Breakthrough	1966	125.00	250.00	500.00
❏ SST-3001 [S]	Colonization	1967	15.00	30.00	60.00
❏ ST-3001 [M]	Colonization	1967	12.50	25.00	50.00
SUNDAZED					
❏ LP 5007	At the River's Edge	1995	2.50	5.00	10.00

NEW DAWN, THE
45s

Number	Title (A Side/B Side)	Yr	VG	VG+	NM
GARLAND					
❏ 2020	Why Did You Go/Tears	1970	6.25	12.50	25.00
IMPERIAL					
❏ 66397	Melody Fair/Sometimes in the Morning	1969	2.00	4.00	8.00
MAINSTREAM					
❏ 652	If I Can't Have Your Love/Loser	1966	6.25	12.50	25.00
❏ 664	Slave of Desire/Funny Feeling	1966	6.25	12.50	25.00
RCA VICTOR					
❏ 47-9569	Listen to the Music/Someday	1968	2.00	4.00	8.00
Albums					
HOOT					
❏ GR 704569	There's a New Dawn	1970	250.00	500.00	1000.

NEW ESTABLISHMENT, THE   May be more than one group.
45s

Number	Title (A Side/B Side)	Yr	VG	VG+	NM
COLGEMS					
❏ 66-5006	(One of These Days) Sunday's Gonna Come on Tuesday/Baby, the Rain Must Fall	1969	2.00	4.00	8.00
❏ 66-5009	I'll Build a Bridge/Seattle	1969	2.00	4.00	8.00
MERCURY					
❏ 72705	And We Were Strangers/A Time for Everything	1967	2.50	5.00	10.00
UNITED WORLD					
❏ 1001	Slums of the City/Riding High	197?	50.00	100.00	200.00
Albums					
COLGEMS					
❏ COS-118	The New Establishment	1970	—	—	—
—Scheduled but never released					

NEW GROUP, THE
45s

Number	Title (A Side/B Side)	Yr	VG	VG+	NM
ROULETTE					
❏ R-4557	A World to Win/Lulu's Back in Town	1964	2.50	5.00	10.00

NEW HOPE See THE KIT KATS.

NEW KINGSTON TRIO, THE See THE KINGSTON TRIO.

NEW MARKETTS, THE See THE MARKETTS.

NEW MIX, THE
Albums

Number	Title (A Side/B Side)	Yr	VG	VG+	NM
UNITED ARTISTS					
❏ UAS-6678	The New Mix	1968	5.00	10.00	20.00

NEW ORDER, THE
45s

Number	Title (A Side/B Side)	Yr	VG	VG+	NM
WARNER BROS.					
❏ 5816	You've Got Me High/Meet Your Match	1966	7.50	15.00	30.00
❏ 5836	Why Can't I?/Pucci Girl	1966	5.00	10.00	20.00
❏ 5870	Sailing Ship/Had I Loved Her Less	1966	3.00	6.00	12.00

NEW ORLEANS BAND, THE
45s

Number	Title (A Side/B Side)	Yr	VG	VG+	NM
HIT					
❏ 275	Winchester Cathedral/Born Free	1966	2.00	4.00	8.00
—B-side by Floyd Tiller					

NEW RENAISSANCE SOCIETY, THE
Albums

Number	Title (A Side/B Side)	Yr	VG	VG+	NM
HANNA-BARBERA					
❏ HLP-9504 [M]	Baroque n' Stones	1966	5.00	10.00	20.00
❏ HST-9504 [S]	Baroque n' Stones	1966	6.25	12.50	25.00

NEW RIDERS OF THE PURPLE SAGE JERRY GARCIA was briefly in this group.
45s

Number	Title (A Side/B Side)	Yr	VG	VG+	NM
A&M					
❏ 2327	Fly Right/Night for Making Love	1981	—	2.00	4.00
❏ 2352	Full Moon at Midnite/No Other Love	1981	—	2.00	4.00
COLUMBIA					
❏ 10067	You Angel You/Parson Brown	1974	—	2.50	5.00
❏ 45469	Louisiana Lady/The Last Lonely Eagle	1971	—	3.00	6.00
❏ 45526	Garden of Eden/I Don't Know You	1972	—	2.50	5.00
❏ 45607	I Don't Need No Doctor/Runnin' Back to You	1972	—	2.50	5.00
❏ 45682	Rainbow/Dim Lights, Thick Smoke	1972	—	2.50	5.00
❏ 45763	Groupie/She's No Angel	1973	—	2.50	5.00
❏ 45976	Panama Red/Cement, Clay, and Glass	1973	—	3.00	6.00
MCA					
❏ 40564	Don't Put Her Down/ Fifteen Days Under the Hood	1976	—	2.00	4.00
❏ 40591	Dead Flowers/She's Looking Better Every Beer	1976	—	2.00	4.00
❏ 40686	Red Hot Women and Ice Cold Beer/Love Has Strange Ways	1977	—	2.00	4.00
❏ 40715	(Just) Another Night in Reno/Home Grown	1977	—	2.00	4.00
Albums					
A&M					
❏ SP-4818	Feelin' All Right	1981	2.50	5.00	10.00
COLUMBIA					
❏ KC 30888	New Riders of the Purple Sage	1971	3.75	7.50	15.00
❏ PC 30888	New Riders of the Purple Sage	1979	2.00	4.00	8.00
—Budget-line reissue					
❏ KC 31284	Powerglide	1972	3.75	7.50	15.00
❏ PC 31284	Powerglide	1979	2.00	4.00	8.00
—Budget-line reissue					
❏ KC 31930	Gypsy Cowboy	1972	3.75	7.50	15.00
❏ PC 31930	Gypsy Cowboy	1979	2.00	4.00	8.00
—Budget-line reissue					
❏ CQ 32450 [Q]	The Adventures of Panama Red	1974	5.00	10.00	20.00
❏ KC 32450	The Adventures of Panama Red	1973	3.75	7.50	15.00
❏ PC 32450	The Adventures of Panama Red	1979	2.00	4.00	8.00
—Budget-line reissue					
❏ PC 32870	Home, Home on the Road	1974	3.75	7.50	15.00
—Originals have no bar code					
❏ PC 33145	Brujo	1974	3.75	7.50	15.00
—Originals have no bar code					
❏ PC 33688	Oh, What a Mighty Time	1975	3.75	7.50	15.00
—Originals have no bar code					
❏ PC 34367	The Best of New Riders of the Purple Sage	1976	3.00	6.00	12.00
—Originals have no bar code					
❏ PC 34367	The Best of New Riders of the Purple Sage	1979	2.00	4.00	8.00
—Budget-line reissue with bar code					
MCA					
❏ 632	Marin County Line	1980	2.00	4.00	8.00
—Reissue of 2307					
❏ 2196	New Riders	1976	3.00	6.00	12.00
❏ 2248	Who Are These Guys	1977	3.00	6.00	12.00
❏ 2307	Marin County Line	1977	3.00	6.00	12.00
RELIX					
❏ RRLP-2024	Before Time Began	1986	2.00	4.00	8.00
❏ RRLP-2025	Vintage NRPS	1987	2.00	4.00	8.00

NEW SEEKERS, THE
45s

Number	Title (A Side/B Side)	Yr	VG	VG+	NM
COCA-COLA					
❏ (no #) [DJ]	Buy the World a Coke//Bring a Little Sunshine/ It's the Real Thing	1971	3.00	6.00	12.00
—All three songs are Coca-Coca jingles. The A-side became "I'd Like to Teach the World to Sing"					
COLUMBIA					
❏ 10559	You Never Can Tell/Give Me Love Your Way	1977	—	2.50	5.00
ELEKTRA					
❏ 45699	Look What They've Done to My Song, Ma/It's a Beautiful Day	1970	—	3.00	6.00
❏ 45710	Beautiful People/When There's No Love Left	1970	—	2.50	5.00
❏ 45719	The Nickel Song/Cincinnati	1971	—	2.50	5.00
❏ 45734	Never Ending Song of Love/All Right My Love	1971	—	—	—
—Unreleased					
❏ 45747	Tonight/Sweet Louise	1971	—	2.50	5.00
❏ 45762	I'd Like to Teach the World to Sing/Boom Town	1971	—	3.00	6.00
❏ 45780	Beg, Steal or Borrow/Mystic Queen	1972	—	2.50	5.00
❏ 45787	Circles/I Can Say You're Beautiful	1972	—	2.50	5.00
❏ 45805	Dance, Dance, Dance/ I Can Say You're Beautiful	1972	—	2.50	5.00
MGM					
❏ 14586	The Greatest Song I've Ever Heard/ Woman Grows	1973	—	2.50	5.00
❏ 14683	Reach Out I'll Be There/ You Won't Find Another Fool Like Me	1973	—	2.50	5.00
❏ 14691	Song for You and Me/ You Won't Find Another Fool Like Me	1974	—	2.50	5.00
MGM VERVE					
❏ 10698	Come Softly to Me/Unwithered Rose	1972	—	2.50	5.00
❏ 10698 [PS]	Come Softly to Me/Unwithered Rose	1972	—	2.50	5.00
❏ 10709	Pinball Wizard-See Me, Feel Me/ Come Softly to Me	1973	—	2.50	5.00
❏ 10709	Pinball Wizard-See Me, Feel Me/Time Limit	1973	—	3.00	6.00
Albums					
ELEKTRA					
❏ EQ-5051 [Q]	The Best of the New Seekers	1973	5.00	10.00	20.00
❏ EKS-74088	Beautiful People	1971	3.00	6.00	12.00

N

Number	Title (A Side/B Side)	Yr	VG	VG+	NM
❏ EKS-74108	New Colours	1971	3.00	6.00	12.00
❏ EKS-74115	We'd Like to Teach the World to Sing	1971	3.00	6.00	12.00
❏ EKS-75034	Circles	1972	3.00	6.00	12.00
❏ EKS-75051	The Best of the New Seekers	1973	3.00	6.00	12.00

MGM VERVE

Number	Title (A Side/B Side)	Yr	VG	VG+	NM
❏ V 5090	Come Softly to Me	1972	2.50	5.00	10.00
❏ V 5095	The History of the New Seekers	1973	2.50	5.00	10.00
❏ V 5098	Pinball Wizards	1973	2.50	5.00	10.00

NEW SOCIETY GROUP, THE
45s
HIT

Number	Title (A Side/B Side)	Yr	VG	VG+	NM
❏ 280	Mercy, Mercy, Mercy/ Green, Green Grass of Home	1967	2.00	4.00	8.00

—B-side by Ed Hardin

| ❏ 319 | Love Is Blue/I Can Take or Leave Your Loving | 1968 | 2.00 | 4.00 | 8.00 |

—B-side by the Chords (2)

| ❏ 330 | The Good, the Bad, and the Ugly/ This Guy's in Love with You | 1968 | 2.00 | 4.00 | 8.00 |

—B-side by Steve Miller

| ❏ 355 | Soulful Strut/You Showed Me | 1969 | 2.00 | 4.00 | 8.00 |

—B-side by the Fantastics

NEW THINGS, THE
45s
ACCENT

Number	Title (A Side/B Side)	Yr	VG	VG+	NM
❏ 1228	Dumbo/I Want You Back	1967	10.00	20.00	40.00

NEW TWEEDY BROTHERS, THE
45s
DOT

Number	Title (A Side/B Side)	Yr	VG	VG+	NM
❏ 16910	Good Time Car/Terms of You Love Me	1966	10.00	20.00	40.00

Albums
RIDON

| ❏ 234 | The New Tweedy Brothers | 1968 | 100.00 | 200.00 | 400.00 |

—With plain white cover

| ❏ 234 | The New Tweedy Brothers | 1968 | 500.00 | 1000. | 2000. |

—With oversized hexagonal cover designed to look like a sugar cube

NEW VAUDEVILLE BAND, THE
45s
FONTANA

Number	Title (A Side/B Side)	Yr	VG	VG+	NM
❏ 1562	Winchester Cathedral/Wait for Me Baby	1966	2.00	4.00	8.00
❏ 1573	Peek-A-Boo/Amy	1967	—	3.00	6.00
❏ 1589	Finchley Central/Sadie Moonshine	1967	—	3.00	6.00
❏ 1589 [PS]	Finchley Central/Sadie Moonshine	1967	2.50	5.00	10.00
❏ 1598	Green Street Green/Fourteen Lovely Women	1967	—	3.00	6.00
❏ 1612	Bonnie and Clyde/Anniversary Song	1968	—	3.00	6.00

7-Inch Extended Plays
FONTANA

| ❏ SRF-752-C | Winchester Cathedral/Tap Your Feet/A Nightingale Sang in Berkeley Square// Whispering/That's All for Now Sugar Baby/ Lili Marlene | 1966 | 3.75 | 7.50 | 15.00 |
| ❏ SRF-752-C [PS] | Winchester Cathedral | 1966 | 3.75 | 7.50 | 15.00 |

Albums
FONTANA

| ❏ MGF-27560 [M] | Winchester Cathedral | 1966 | 3.75 | 7.50 | 15.00 |

—With "Oh, Donna Clara"; record has mono number and actually plays in mono; the number "27560" is in the trail-off

| ❏ MGF-27560 [M] | Winchester Cathedral | 1966 | 3.75 | 7.50 | 15.00 |

—With "Whatever Happened to Phyllis Puke" and "Diana Goodbye"

| ❏ MGF-27560 [P] | Winchester Cathedral | 1966 | 3.00 | 6.00 | 12.00 |

—With "Oh, Donna Clara"; record has mono number, but plays stereo; the number "2/67560" is in trail-off area

| ❏ MGF-27688 [M] | The New Vaudeville Band on Tour | 1967 | 3.00 | 6.00 | 12.00 |
| ❏ SRF-67560 [P] | Winchester Cathedral | 1966 | 3.00 | 6.00 | 12.00 |

—With "Oh, Donna Clara"

| ❏ SRF-67560 [P] | Winchester Cathedral | 1966 | 3.75 | 7.50 | 15.00 |

—With "Whatever Happened to Phyllis Puke" and "Diana Goodbye"

| ❏ SRF-67688 [P] | The New Vaudeville Band on Tour | 1967 | 3.00 | 6.00 | 12.00 |

NEW WANDERERS, THE
45s
READY

Number	Title (A Side/B Side)	Yr	VG	VG+	NM
❏ 1001	Let Me Render My Service to You/ (B-side unknown)	196?	250.00	500.00	1000.
❏ 1006	This Man in Love/(B-side unknown)	196?	25.00	50.00	100.00

NEW WAVE, THE
45s
CANTERBURY

| ❏ 503 | Where Do We Go from Here/Not from You | 1967 | 2.50 | 5.00 | 10.00 |
| ❏ 512 | Little Dreams/Autre Fois | 1967 | 2.50 | 5.00 | 10.00 |

Albums
CANTERBURY

| ❏ CLPS-1501 | The New Wave | 1967 | 6.25 | 12.50 | 25.00 |

NEW WORLD
45s
RAK

Number	Title (A Side/B Side)	Yr	VG	VG+	NM
❏ ZS7 4505	Tom Tom Turnaround/Lay Me Down	1972	—	3.50	7.00
❏ ZS7 4509	First Steps/Sister Jane	1972	—	3.50	7.00
❏ ZS7 4514	Living Next Door to Alice/Something to Say	1973	2.00	4.00	8.00

NEW YORK CITY
45s
CHELSEA

❏ BCBO-0025	Make Me Twice the Man/Uncle James	1973	—	2.50	5.00
❏ 78-0113	I'm Doin' Fine Now/Ain't It So	1973	—	2.50	5.00
❏ BCBO-0150	Quick, Fast, In a Hurry/Set the Record Straight	1973	—	2.50	5.00
❏ 3000	Happiness Is/Darling Take Me Back	1974	—	2.50	5.00
❏ 3008	Love Is What You Make It/ Do You Remember Yesterday	1974	—	2.50	5.00
❏ 3010	Got to Get You Back In My Life/Reach Out	1975	—	2.50	5.00
❏ 3031	Can't Survive Without My Sweets/Take My Hand	1975	—	2.50	5.00

Albums
CHELSEA

Number	Title (A Side/B Side)	Yr	VG	VG+	NM
❏ BCL1-0198	I'm Doin' Fine Now	1973	3.75	7.50	15.00
❏ CHL 500	Soulful Road	1974	3.75	7.50	15.00
❏ CHL 514	The Best of New York City	1977	3.00	6.00	12.00

NEW YORK DOLLS
45s
MERCURY

| ❏ DJ-378 [DJ] | Trash (mono/stereo) | 1973 | 3.75 | 7.50 | 15.00 |
| ❏ DJ-378 [PS] | Trash (mono/stereo) | 1973 | 18.75 | 37.50 | 75.00 |

—Promo-only numbered sleeve

❏ DJ-387 [DJ]	Personality Crisis (mono/stereo)	1973	3.75	7.50	15.00
❏ 73414 [DJ]	Trash/Personality Crisis	1973	15.00	30.00	60.00
❏ 73414 [PS]	Trash/Personality Crisis	1973	3.75	7.50	15.00
❏ 73478	Stranded in the Jungle/ Who Are the Mystery Girls	1974	3.75	7.50	15.00
❏ 73615	Puss 'N' Boots/Showmen	1974	5.00	10.00	20.00

Albums
MERCURY

❏ SRM-1-675	New York Dolls	1973	10.00	20.00	40.00
❏ SRM-1-1001	In Too Much Too Soon	1974	10.00	20.00	40.00
❏ 826094-1	Night of the Living Dolls	1985	3.00	6.00	12.00

NEW YORK ROCK ENSEMBLE, THE Includes records as "The New York Rock and Roll Ensemble."
45s
ATCO

| ❏ AT-305X [DJ] | Beautiful/Beautiful Too | 1968 | 5.00 | 10.00 | 20.00 |

—"Composed and Recorded For The Bell System Film 'Operator' (Nell Cox Films)" on bottom of both sides' labels; possibly a Bell System promo item

❏ 6467	Biji/Biji Rock	1967	2.50	5.00	10.00
❏ 6501	Kiss Her Once/Suddenly	1967	2.50	5.00	10.00
❏ 6584	The Thing to Do/Pick Up in the Morning	1968	2.50	5.00	10.00
❏ 6671	Wait Until Tomorrow/The Brandenburg	1969	2.50	5.00	10.00

COLUMBIA

❏ 45242	Running Down the Highway/Law and Order	1970	—	2.50	5.00
❏ 45288	The King Is Dead/Beside You	1970	—	2.50	5.00
❏ 45367	Fields of Joy/Ride, Ride My Lady	1971	—	2.50	5.00
❏ 45574	Roll Over/A Whiter Shade of Pale	1972	—	2.50	5.00

Albums
ATCO

❏ SD 33-240	The New York Rock 'n' Roll Ensemble	1968	3.75	7.50	15.00
❏ SD 33-294	Faithful Friends	1969	3.75	7.50	15.00
❏ SD 33-312	Reflections	1970	3.75	7.50	15.00

COLUMBIA

| ❏ C 30033 | Roll Over | 1970 | 3.75 | 7.50 | 15.00 |
| ❏ KC 31317 | Freedomburger | 1972 | 3.75 | 7.50 | 15.00 |

NEW YORK SOUNDS, THE
45s
RED BIRD

Number	Title (A Side/B Side)	Yr	VG	VG+	NM
❏ 10-060	Drag Street/Good Lovin'	1966	5.00	10.00	20.00

NEW YORKERS, THE (1) With FRED PARRIS of THE FIVE SATINS.
45s
WALL

| ❏ 547 | Miss Fine/Dream a Little Dream | 1961 | 7.50 | 15.00 | 30.00 |
| ❏ 548 | Tears in My Eyes/A Little Bit | 1961 | 7.50 | 15.00 | 30.00 |

NEW YORKERS, THE (2) Early version of THE HUDSON BROTHERS.
45s
DECCA

| ❏ 32569 | I Guess the Lord Must Be in New York City/ Do Wah Diddy | 1969 | 2.50 | 5.00 | 10.00 |

JERDEN

| ❏ 906 | Adrienne/Ice Cream World | 1968 | 3.00 | 6.00 | 12.00 |
| ❏ 908 | Land of Ur/Michael Glover | 1969 | 3.00 | 6.00 | 12.00 |

SCEPTER

❏ 12190	You're Not My Girl/When I'm Gone	1967	3.75	7.50	15.00
❏ 12199	Mr. Kirby/Seeds of Spring	1967	3.75	7.50	15.00
❏ 12207	Again/Show Me the Way to Love	1968	3.00	6.00	12.00

WARNER BROS.

| ❏ 7318 | Lonely/There'll Come a Time | 1969 | 2.50 | 5.00 | 10.00 |

NEW YORKERS, THE (3)
45s
TAC-FUL

| ❏ 101 | You Should Have Told Me/ Don't Want to Be Your Fool | 1964 | 12.50 | 25.00 | 50.00 |

NEW YORKERS FIVE, THE
45s
DANICE

| ❏ 801 | Gloria My Darling/Cha Cha Baby | 1955 | 100.00 | 200.00 | 400.00 |

NEWBAG, JOHNNY
45s
ATLANTIC

| ❏ 2355 | The Poorer the Man (The Higher His Love)/ Got to Get You Back | 1966 | 3.00 | 6.00 | 12.00 |

PORT

| ❏ 3008 | Sweet Thing/Little Samson | 1965 | 6.25 | 12.50 | 25.00 |

NEWBEATS, THE Also see DEAN AND MARC.
45s
BUDDAH

| ❏ 390 | The Way You Do the Things You Do/ Does Your Body Need Lovin' | 1973 | 2.00 | 4.00 | 8.00 |

HICKORY

❏ 326	Bread and Butter/Tough Little Buggy	1974	—	3.00	6.00
❏ 1269	Bread and Butter/Tough Little Buggy	1964	3.75	7.50	15.00
❏ 1282	Everything's All Right/Pink Dally Rue	1964	3.00	6.00	12.00
❏ 1290	Break Away (From That Boy)/Hey-O Daddy-O	1965	2.50	5.00	10.00
❏ 1305	(The Bees Are For the Birds) The Birds Are For the Bees/Better Watch Your Step	1965	2.50	5.00	10.00
❏ 1320	Little Child/I Can't Hear You No More	1965	2.50	5.00	10.00

Number	Title (A Side/B Side)	Yr	VG	VG+	NM
❏ 1332	Run, Baby, Run (Back Into My Arms)/ Mean Wooly Willie	1965	3.00	6.00	12.00
❏ 1366	Shake Hands (And Come Out Crying)/ Too Sweet to Be Forgotten	1966	2.50	5.00	10.00
❏ 1387	Short on Love/Crying My Heart Out	1966	2.00	4.00	8.00
❏ 1408	Bird Dog/Evil Eva	1966	2.00	4.00	8.00
❏ 1422	My Yesterday Love/Patent on Love	1966	2.00	4.00	8.00
❏ 1436	So Fine/Top Secret	1967	2.00	4.00	8.00
❏ 1467	Hide the Moon/It's Really Goodbye	1967	2.00	4.00	8.00
❏ 1485	Don't Turn Me Loose/You and Me and Happiness	1967	2.00	4.00	8.00
❏ 1496	Bad Dreams/Swinger	1968	2.00	4.00	8.00
❏ 1510	I've Been a Long Time Loving You/ Michelle de Ann	1968	2.00	4.00	8.00
❏ 1522	Ain't That Lovin' You/The Girls and the Boys	1968	2.00	4.00	8.00
❏ 1539	Great Balls of Fire/Thou Shalt Not Steal	1969	2.00	4.00	8.00
❏ 1552	Groovin' (Out on Life)/Bread and Butter	1969	2.50	5.00	10.00
❏ 1562	Laura (What's He Got That I Ain't Got)/Break Away (From That Boy)	1970	—	3.00	6.00
❏ 1569	I'm a Teardrop/She Won't Hang Her Love (Out on the Line)	1970	—	3.00	6.00
❏ 1600	Am I Not My Brother's Keeper/Run, Baby, Run (Back Into My Arms)	1971	2.50	5.00	10.00
❏ 1624	Oh, Pretty Woman/Remember Love	1972	2.50	5.00	10.00
❏ 1637	Love Gets Sweeter/Eveything's All Right	1972	2.50	5.00	10.00
PLAYBOY					
❏ 6013	I Believe I'm in Love with You/I Know (You Don't Want Me No More)	1974	—	3.00	6.00

Albums

Number	Title (A Side/B Side)	Yr	VG	VG+	NM
HICKORY					
❏ LPM 120 [M]	Bread and Butter	1964	12.50	25.00	50.00
❏ LPS 120 [S]	Bread and Butter	1964	37.50	75.00	150.00
❏ LPM 122 [M]	Big Beat Sounds by the Newbeats	1965	12.50	25.00	50.00
❏ LPS 122 [S]	Big Beat Sounds by the Newbeats	1965	25.00	50.00	100.00
❏ LPM 128 [M]	Run Baby Run	1965	12.50	25.00	50.00
❏ LPS 128 [S]	Run Baby Run	1965	25.00	50.00	100.00
❏ DT 90701 [R]	Bread and Butter	1965	37.50	75.00	150.00
—Capitol Record Club edition					
❏ ST 90701 [S]	Bread and Butter	1965	50.00	100.00	200.00
—Capitol Record Club edition					
❏ T 90701 [M]	Bread and Butter	1965	37.50	75.00	150.00
—Capitol Record Club edition					

NEWBURY, MICKEY
45s

Number	Title (A Side/B Side)	Yr	VG	VG+	NM
ABC HICKORY					
❏ 54006	Hand Me Another of Those/Leavin' Kentucky	1977	—	2.50	5.00
❏ 54015	Makes Me Wonder If I Ever Said Goodbye/ Shenandoah	1977	—	2.50	5.00
❏ 54025	Gone to Alabama/Westphalia Texas Blues	1978	—	2.50	5.00
❏ 54034	It Don't Matter Anymore/Wish I Was	1978	—	2.50	5.00
❏ 54042	Looking for the Sunshine/A Weed Is a Weed	1979	—	2.50	5.00
AIRBORNE					
❏ 10005	An American Trilogy/San Francisco Mabel Joy	1988	—	2.50	5.00
ELEKTRA					
❏ 45206	You Only Live Once (In a While)/ Baby's Not Home	1974	—	2.50	5.00
❏ 45238	Lovers/Good Night	1975	—	2.50	5.00
❏ 45256	Sail Away/If You Ever Get to Houston	1975	—	2.50	5.00
❏ 45329	An American Trilogy/Sunshine	1976	—	2.50	5.00
❏ 45750	An American Trilogy/San Francisco Mable Joy	1971	2.50	5.00	10.00
❏ 45771	Mobile Blue/Frisco Depot	1972	—	3.00	6.00
❏ 45789	How I Love Them Old Songs/ Remember the Good	1972	—	3.00	6.00
❏ 45840	Heaven Help the Child/Good Morning Dear	1973	—	2.50	5.00
❏ 45853	Sunshine/Song for Susan	1973	—	2.50	5.00
❏ 45889	If I Could Be/Love Look	1974	—	2.50	5.00
HICKORY					
❏ 1312	Lonely Place/Well I Did (Last Night)	1965	2.50	5.00	10.00
❏ 1344	There Is a Time to Die/Travelin' Man	1965	2.50	5.00	10.00
❏ 1370	Anyway You Want Me/ (It May Not Take) Too Much	1966	2.50	5.00	10.00
❏ 1419	After the Rains/Baby Just Said Goodbye	1966	2.50	5.00	10.00
❏ 1463	Dreamin' in the Rain/ Leavin' Makes the Rain Come Down	1967	2.50	5.00	10.00
❏ 1673	America the Beautiful/Freedom	1980	—	2.50	5.00
MCA					
❏ 41032	Blue Sky Shinin'/Darlin' Take Care of Yourself	1979	—	2.50	5.00
MERCURY					
❏ 57061	Country Boy Saturday Night/ Let's Say Goodbye One More Time	1981	—	2.50	5.00
❏ 72975	Ten Tottle Tommy/San Francisco Mable Joy	1969	—	3.50	7.00
❏ 73036	Sunshine/Sad Satin Rhyme	1970	—	3.50	7.00
RCA VICTOR					
❏ 47-9570	Weeping Annaleah/Are My Thoughts with You	1968	2.00	4.00	8.00
❏ 47-9632	Got Down on Saturday/Sweet Memories	1968	2.00	4.00	8.00
❏ 47-9690	Organized Noise/The Queen	1968	2.00	4.00	8.00

Albums

Number	Title (A Side/B Side)	Yr	VG	VG+	NM
ABC HICKORY					
❏ HA-44002	Rusty Tracks	1977	2.50	5.00	10.00
❏ HA-44011	Eye on the Sparrow	1978	2.50	5.00	10.00
❏ HB-44017	The Sailor	1979	2.50	5.00	10.00
ELEKTRA					
❏ EK-PROMO 20 [DJ]	Recorded Live at Montezuma Hall, San Diego State University, March 6, 1973	1973	10.00	20.00	40.00
❏ 7E-1007	I Came to Hear the Music	1974	2.50	5.00	10.00
❏ 7E-1030	Lovers	1975	2.50	5.00	10.00
❏ EQ-4107 [Q]	'Frisco Mabel Joy	1974	5.00	10.00	20.00
❏ EKS-74107	'Frisco Mabel Joy	1971	2.50	5.00	10.00
❏ EKS-75055	Heaven Help the Child	1973	2.50	5.00	10.00
MCA					
❏ 802	Rusty Tracks	198?	2.00	4.00	8.00
—Reissue					
❏ 803	Eye on the Sparrow	198?	2.00	4.00	8.00
—Reissue					
❏ 804	The Sailor	198?	2.00	4.00	8.00
—Reissue					

Number	Title (A Side/B Side)	Yr	VG	VG+	NM
❏ 945	Sweet Memories	1985	2.50	5.00	10.00
MERCURY					
❏ SR 61236	Looks Like Rain	1969	3.75	7.50	15.00
RCA VICTOR					
❏ LSP-4043	Harlequin Melodies	1968	3.75	7.50	15.00

NEWCOMERS, THE
45s

Number	Title (A Side/B Side)	Yr	VG	VG+	NM
MERCURY					
❏ 74011	Do Yourself a Favor/That's When You Know Your Woman Wants to Be Free	1978	7.50	15.00	30.00
STAX					
❏ 0099	Pin the Tail on the Donkey/Mannish Boy	1971	2.00	4.00	8.00
TRUTH					
❏ 3204	Keep an Eye on Your Close Friends/ (Instrumental)	1974	3.75	7.50	15.00
❏ 3213	(Too Much in Common to Be Lovers) Too Much Going to Say Good-Bye/The Whole World's a Picture Show	1974	7.50	15.00	30.00
VOLT					
❏ 4022	Open Up Your Heart/Girl, This Boy Loves You	1969	7.50	15.00	30.00
❏ 4049	You Put the Sunshine Back in My World/ Still a Boy in My Heart	1971	7.50	15.00	30.00

NEWHART, BOB
Albums

Number	Title (A Side/B Side)	Yr	VG	VG+	NM
HARMONY					
❏ HS 11344	The Very Funny Bob Newhart	196?	3.00	6.00	12.00
MURRAY HILL					
❏ OP 2529 [(2)]	The Best of the Button-Down Mind	197?	5.00	10.00	20.00
WARNER BROS.					
❏ W 1379 [M]	The Button-Down Mind of Bob Newhart	1960	7.50	15.00	30.00
❏ WS 1379 [S]	The Button-Down Mind of Bob Newhart	1960	6.25	12.50	25.00
❏ W 1393 [M]	The Button-Down Mind Strikes Back!	1960	7.50	15.00	30.00
❏ WS 1393 [S]	The Button-Down Mind Strikes Back!	1960	6.25	12.50	25.00
❏ 2N 1399 [(2)M]	The Bob Newhart Deluxe Edition	1961	12.50	25.00	50.00
❏ 2NS 1399 [(2)S]	The Bob Newhart Deluxe Edition	1961	10.00	20.00	40.00
❏ W 1417 [M]	Behind the Button-Down Mind of Bob Newhart	1961	6.25	12.50	25.00
❏ WS 1417 [S]	Behind the Button-Down Mind of Bob Newhart	1961	5.00	10.00	20.00
❏ W 1467 [M]	The Button-Down Mind on TV	1962	6.25	12.50	25.00
❏ WS 1467 [S]	The Button-Down Mind on TV	1962	5.00	10.00	20.00
❏ W 1517 [M]	Bob Newhart Faces Bob Newhart (Faces Bob Newhart)	1964	6.25	12.50	25.00
❏ W 1588 [M]	The Windmills Are Weakening	1965	7.50	15.00	30.00
❏ W 1672 [M]	The Best of Bob Newhart	1966	7.50	15.00	30.00
❏ WS 1672 [S]	The Best of Bob Newhart	1966	6.25	12.50	25.00
—Gold label					
❏ WS 1672 [S]	The Best of Bob Newhart	1968	5.00	10.00	20.00
—Green "W7" label					
❏ WS 1672 [S]	The Best of Bob Newhart	1970	3.75	7.50	15.00
—Green "WB" label					
❏ WS 1672 [S]	The Best of Bob Newhart	1973	3.00	6.00	12.00
—"Burbank" palm-trees label					
❏ WS 1672 [S]	The Best of Bob Newhart	1979	2.00	4.00	8.00
—White or tan label					
❏ W 1717 [M]	This Is It	1967	7.50	15.00	30.00

NEWLEY, ANTHONY
45s

Number	Title (A Side/B Side)	Yr	VG	VG+	NM
ACAPELLA					
❏ 778	Tribute/Lament for a Hero	1964	3.00	6.00	12.00
KAPP					
❏ 984	I'm All I Need/When You Gotta Go	1969	—	3.00	6.00
LONDON					
❏ 1871	I've Waited So Long/Sat'day Night Rock-a-Boogie	1959	3.00	6.00	12.00
❏ 1882	My Blue Angel/Idle Rock	1959	2.50	5.00	10.00
❏ 1918	Do You Mind/Girls Were Made to Love and Kiss	1960	2.50	5.00	10.00
❏ 1929	If She Should Come to You/ A Lifetime of Happiness	1960	2.50	5.00	10.00
❏ 1972	And the Heavens Cried/ Lonely Boy and Pretty Girl	1961	2.50	5.00	10.00
❏ 5201	There's No Such Thing/She's Just Another Girl	1963	2.50	5.00	10.00
❏ 5202	I Saw Her Standing There/ I Love Everything About Her	1963	5.00	10.00	20.00
—One of the first cover versions of a Beatles song to be released in the U.S.					
❏ 5205	Father of Girls/Young Only Yesterday	1963	2.50	5.00	10.00
❏ 9501	Gone with the Wind/Pop Goes the Weasel	1961	2.50	5.00	10.00
❏ 9512	When Your Lover Has Gone/ Yes, We Have No Bananas	1961	2.50	5.00	10.00
❏ 9518	What Now My Love/Why	1961	2.50	5.00	10.00
❏ 9531	Deep River/Letters to My Love	1962	2.50	5.00	10.00
❏ 9546	What Kind of Fool Am I/Gonna Build a Mountain	1962	3.00	6.00	12.00
MGM					
❏ 14220	Pure Imagination/Love Story (Where Do I Begin)	1971	—	2.50	5.00
❏ 14252	The Candy Man/Pure Imagination	1971	—	2.50	5.00
❏ 14307	Cheer Up Charlie/Pop Goes the Weasel	1971	—	2.50	5.00
❏ 14479	A Fool Who Dared to Dream/Ain't It Funny	1973	—	2.00	4.00
❏ 14627	Good Old Bad Old Days/Ain't It Funny	1973	—	2.00	4.00
❏ 14724	If I Were Free/Long Live Hope	1974	—	2.00	4.00
RCA VICTOR					
❏ 47-8485	Who Can I Turn To/The Joker	1964	2.00	4.00	8.00
❏ 47-8785	Is There a Way Back to Your Arms/ Why Can't You Try to Didgeridoo	1966	2.00	4.00	8.00
❏ 47-9310	I Think I Love You/Something in Your Smile	1967	2.00	4.00	8.00
UNITED ARTISTS					
❏ XW825	Shelby/Teach the Children	1976	—	2.00	4.00
❏ XW1012	The Hollywood Seven/Lunch with a Friend	1977	—	2.00	4.00
WARNER BROS.					
❏ 7174	Sweet November/Sara's Theme	1968	—	3.00	6.00
—B-side by Michel Legrand					

Albums

Number	Title (A Side/B Side)	Yr	VG	VG+	NM
LONDON					
❏ PS 244 [S]	Tony	1962	6.25	12.50	25.00
❏ PS 461 [S]	Genius	1966	3.75	7.50	15.00
❏ LL 3156 [M]	Love Is a Now and Then Thing	1960	5.00	10.00	20.00
❏ LL 3252 [M]	Tony	1962	3.75	7.50	15.00

N

Number	Title (A Side/B Side)	Yr	VG	VG+	NM
❏ LL 3262 [M]	This Is Tony Newley	1962	3.75	7.50	15.00
❏ LL 3461 [M]	Genius	1966	3.00	6.00	12.00
RCA VICTOR					
❏ LPM-2925 [M]	In My Solitude	1964	3.75	7.50	15.00
❏ LSP-2925 [S]	In My Solitude	1964	5.00	10.00	20.00
❏ LPM-3347 [M]	Who Can I Turn To	1965	3.00	6.00	12.00
❏ LSP-3347 [S]	Who Can I Turn To	1965	3.75	7.50	15.00
❏ LPM-3614 [M]	Newly Recorded	1966	3.00	6.00	12.00
❏ LSP-3614 [S]	Newly Recorded	1966	3.75	7.50	15.00
❏ LPM-3839 [M]	Doctor Dolittle	1967	3.00	6.00	12.00
❏ LSP-3839 [S]	Doctor Dolittle	1967	3.75	7.50	15.00
❏ LSP-4163	The Best of Anthony Newley	1969	3.00	6.00	12.00

NEWLYWEDS, THE
45s
HOMOGENIZED SOUL

Number	Title (A Side/B Side)	Yr	VG	VG+	NM
❏ 601	Love Walked Out/The Quarrel	1961	1500.	2250.	3000.

NEWMAN, RANDY
12-Inch Singles
WARNER BROS.

Number	Title (A Side/B Side)	Yr	VG	VG+	NM
❏ PRO-A-860 [DJ]	Political Science/Spys	1979	2.00	4.00	8.00

45s
DOT

Number	Title (A Side/B Side)	Yr	VG	VG+	NM
❏ 16411	Golden Gridiron Boy/Country Boy	1962	12.50	25.00	50.00

—*May be promo only*
REPRISE

Number	Title (A Side/B Side)	Yr	VG	VG+	NM
❏ 0692	I Think It's Going to Rain Today/				
	The Beehive State	1968	3.75	7.50	15.00
❏ 0771	Last Night I Had a Dream/I Think He's Hiding	1968	6.25	12.50	25.00

—*May be promo only*

Number	Title (A Side/B Side)	Yr	VG	VG+	NM
❏ 0917	Have You Seen My Baby/Hold On	1970	3.75	7.50	15.00
❏ 0945	Gone Dead Train/Harry Flowers	1970	3.75	7.50	15.00
❏ 1102	Sail Away/Political Science	1972	—	3.00	6.00
❏ 1123	You Can Leave Your Hat On/Memo to My Son	1972	—	3.00	6.00
❏ 1324	Guilty/Naked Man	1975	—	2.50	5.00
❏ 1387	Louisiana 1927/Marie	1977	—	2.50	5.00
❏ 22798	I'd Love to See You Smile/End Title				
	(I'd Love to See You Smile)	1989	—	—	3.00
❏ 27709	It's Money That Matters/Roll with the Punches	1988	—	—	3.00
❏ 27709 [PS]	It's Money That Matters/Roll with the Punches	1988	—	—	3.00
❏ 27856	Falling in Love/Bad News from Home	1989	—	—	3.00
WARNER BROS.					
❏ 8492	Short People/Old Man on the Farm	1977	—	2.50	5.00
❏ 8550	Baltimore/You Can't Fool the Fat Man	1978	—	2.00	4.00
❏ 8630	Rider in the Rain/Sigmund Freud's				
	Impersonation of Albert Einstein in America	1978	—	2.00	4.00
❏ 29241	The Natural/The Natural (Final Game)	1984	—	2.00	4.00
❏ 29687	I Love L.A./Song for the Dead	1983	—	2.00	4.00
❏ 29803	The Blues/The Same Girl	1983	—	2.00	4.00

—*A-side: With Paul Simon*

Number	Title (A Side/B Side)	Yr	VG	VG+	NM
❏ 29803 [PS]	The Blues/The Same Girl	1983	—	2.00	4.00
❏ 49088	It's Money That I Love/Ghosts	1979	—	2.00	4.00
❏ 49149	Half a Man/The Story of a Rock and Roll Band	1979	—	2.00	4.00
❏ 49223	Spies/Political Science (Let's Drop the Big One)	1980	—	2.00	4.00

Albums
REPRISE

Number	Title (A Side/B Side)	Yr	VG	VG+	NM
❏ MS 2064	Sail Away	1972	2.50	5.00	10.00

—*With song titles listed on back*

Number	Title (A Side/B Side)	Yr	VG	VG+	NM
❏ MS 2064	Sail Away	1972	3.75	7.50	15.00

—*With no song titles listed on back*

Number	Title (A Side/B Side)	Yr	VG	VG+	NM
❏ MS 2193	Good Old Boys	1974	2.50	5.00	10.00
❏ MS4 2193 [Q]	Good Old Boys	1974	3.75	7.50	15.00
❏ RS 6286	Randy Newman	1968	3.75	7.50	15.00

—*Cover with close-up of Randy's face; "W7" and "r:" logos on two-tone orange label*

Number	Title (A Side/B Side)	Yr	VG	VG+	NM
❏ RS 6286	Randy Newman	1968	5.00	10.00	20.00

—*Cover with Randy standing in the clouds*

Number	Title (A Side/B Side)	Yr	VG	VG+	NM
❏ RS 6286	Randy Newman	1970	3.00	6.00	12.00

—*With only "r:" logo on all-orange (tan) label*

Number	Title (A Side/B Side)	Yr	VG	VG+	NM
❏ RS 6373	12 Songs	1970	2.50	5.00	10.00

—*With only "r:" logo on all-orange (tan) label*

Number	Title (A Side/B Side)	Yr	VG	VG+	NM
❏ RS 6373	12 Songs	1970	3.75	7.50	15.00

—*With "W7" and "r:" logos on two-tone orange label*

Number	Title (A Side/B Side)	Yr	VG	VG+	NM
❏ RS 6459	Randy Newman/Live	1971	2.50	5.00	10.00
❏ 25773	Land of Dreams	1988	2.50	5.00	10.00
WARNER BROS.					
❏ BSK 3079	Little Criminals	1977	2.50	5.00	10.00
❏ HS 3346	Born Again	1979	2.50	5.00	10.00
❏ 23755	Trouble in Paradise	1983	2.50	5.00	10.00

NEWMAN, TED
45s
RCA VICTOR

Number	Title (A Side/B Side)	Yr	VG	VG+	NM
❏ 47-7197	It's Hot in Here/Why Did You Break My Heart	1958	3.75	7.50	15.00
❏ 47-7251	Hey Little Freshman/Brigette	1958	3.75	7.50	15.00
REV					
❏ 3505	Plaything/Unlucky Me	1957	5.00	10.00	20.00
❏ 3511	I Double Dare You/None of Your Tears	1957	3.75	7.50	15.00

NEWPORTS, THE (1)
45s
CRYSTAL BALL

Number	Title (A Side/B Side)	Yr	VG	VG+	NM
❏ 129	Jingle Bells/My Juanita	1979	2.00	4.00	8.00
GUYDEN					
❏ 2067	If I Could Tonight/A Fellow Needs a Girl	1962	7.50	15.00	30.00
❏ 2116	Tears/Disillusioned Love	1964	7.50	15.00	30.00

NEWPORTS, THE (2)
45s
KENT

Number	Title (A Side/B Side)	Yr	VG	VG+	NM
❏ 380	The Wonder of Love/Dixie Women	1962	7.50	15.00	30.00

NEWPORTS, THE (3)
45s
LAURIE

Number	Title (A Side/B Side)	Yr	VG	VG+	NM
❏ 3327	The Trouble Is You/I Want You	1966	6.25	12.50	25.00

NEWPORTS, THE (U) May be group (3), may be completely different.
45s
PARROT

Number	Title (A Side/B Side)	Yr	VG	VG+	NM
❏ 45008	Party Night/Listen to Your Big Brother	1966	3.75	7.50	15.00

NEWTON, JUICE
45s
CAPITOL

Number	Title (A Side/B Side)	Yr	VG	VG+	NM
❏ 4499	Come to Me/Save a Heart	1977	—	3.00	6.00
❏ 4552	It's a Heartache/Wouldn't Mind the Rain	1978	—	3.00	6.00
❏ 4611	Hey Baby/It's Not Impossible	1978	—	3.00	6.00
❏ 4679	Let's Keep It That Way/Tell My Baby Goodbye	1979	—	2.50	5.00
❏ 4714	Lay Back in the Arms of Someone/				
	It's Not Impossible	1979	—	2.50	5.00
❏ 4768	Any Way That You Want Me/				
	A Dream Never Dies	1979	—	2.50	5.00
❏ 4793	Until Tonight/Lay Back in the Arms of Someone	1979	—	2.50	5.00
❏ 4818	Sunshine/Go Easy on Me	1980	—	2.00	4.00
❏ 4856	You Fill My Life/Tear It Up	1980	—	2.00	4.00
❏ 4976	Angel of the Morning/Headin' for a Heartache	1981	—	—	3.00
❏ 4976 [PS]	Angel of the Morning/Headin' for a Heartache	1981	—	—	3.00
❏ 4997	Queen of Hearts/River of Love	1981	—	—	3.00
❏ 4997 [PS]	Queen of Hearts/River of Love	1981	—	2.00	4.00
❏ A-5046	The Sweetest Thing (I've Ever Known)/				
	Ride 'Em Cowboy	1981	—	—	3.00
❏ A-5046 [PS]	The Sweetest Thing (I've Ever Known)/				
	Ride 'Em Cowboy	1981	—	2.00	4.00
❏ B-5120	Love's Been a Little Bit Hard on Me/Ever True	1982	—	—	3.00
❏ B-5120 [PS]	Love's Been a Little Bit Hard on Me/Ever True	1982	—	2.00	4.00
❏ B-5148	Break It to Me Gently/Adios Mi Corazon	1982	—	—	3.00
❏ B-5148 [PS]	Break It to Me Gently/Adios Mi Corazon	1982	—	2.00	4.00
❏ B-5192	Heart of the Night/Love Sail Away	1982	—	—	3.00
❏ B-5192 [PS]	Heart of the Night/Love Sail Away	1982	—	2.00	4.00
❏ B-5265	Tell Her No/Stranger at My Door	1983	—	—	3.00
❏ B-5265 [PS]	Tell Her No/Stranger at My Door	1983	—	2.00	4.00
❏ B-5289	Dirty Looks/20 Years Ago	1983	—	—	3.00
❏ B-5289 [PS]	Dirty Looks/20 Years Ago	1983	—	2.00	4.00
❏ B-5379	Ride 'Em Cowboy/Love Sail Away	1984	—	—	3.00
RCA					
❏ 5068-7-R	What Can I Do with My Heart/				
	Let Your Woman Take Care of You	1986	—	—	3.00
❏ 5170-7-R	First Time Caller/Til You Cry	1987	—	—	3.00
❏ 5283-7-R	Tell Me True/If I Didn't Love You	1987	—	—	3.00
❏ 8815-7-R	When Love Comes Around the Bend/				
	(B-side unknown)	1989	—	—	3.00
❏ PB-10828	If I Ever/Bye, Bye Baby	1976	2.00	4.00	—
❏ PB-13823	A Little Love/Waiting for the Sun	1984	—	—	3.00
❏ PB-13823 [PS]	A Little Love/Waiting for the Sun	1984	—	2.00	4.00
❏ PB-13863	Can't Wait All Night/Restless Heart	1984	—	—	3.00
❏ PB-13863 [PS]	Can't Wait All Night/Restless Heart	1984	—	2.00	4.00
❏ PB-13907	Restless Heart/Eye of a Hurricane	1984	—	—	3.00
❏ PB-14139	You Make Me Want to Make You Mine/				
	Waiting for the Sun	1985	—	—	3.00
❏ PB-14139 [PS]	You Make Me Want to Make You Mine/				
	Waiting for the Sun	1985	—	2.00	4.00
❏ PB-14199	Hurt/Eye of a Hurricane	1985	—	—	3.00
❏ PB-14295	Old Flame/One Touch	1986	—	—	3.00
❏ GB-14355	Hurt/You Make Me Want to Make You Mine	1986	—	—	3.00
❏ PB-14377	Both to Each Other (Friends and Lovers)/				
	A World Without Love	1986	—	—	3.00

—*With Eddie Rabbitt*

Number	Title (A Side/B Side)	Yr	VG	VG+	NM
❏ PB-14377 [PS]	Both to Each Other (Friends and Lovers)/				
	A World Without Love	1986	—	2.50	5.00
❏ PB-14417	Cheap Love/Old Flame	1986	—	—	3.00
RCA VICTOR					
❏ PB-10354	Catwillow River/It's High Time	1975	2.00	4.00	8.00

—*With Silver Spur*

Number	Title (A Side/B Side)	Yr	VG	VG+	NM
❏ PB-10412	The Sweetest Thing (I've Ever Known)/				
	The Shelter of Your Love	1975	2.00	4.00	8.00

—*With Silver Spur*

Number	Title (A Side/B Side)	Yr	VG	VG+	NM
❏ PB-10538	Love Is a Word/The Sweetest Thing				
	(I've Ever Known)	1976	2.00	4.00	8.00

—*With Silver Spur*
Albums
CAPITOL

Number	Title (A Side/B Side)	Yr	VG	VG+	NM
❏ ST-11682	Come to Me	1977	3.75	7.50	15.00
❏ ST-11811	Well-Kept Secret	1978	3.75	7.50	15.00
❏ ST-12000	Take Heart	1980	3.75	7.50	15.00
❏ ST-12136	Juice	1981	2.50	5.00	10.00
❏ ST-12210	Quiet Lies	1982	2.50	5.00	10.00
❏ ST-12294	Dirty Looks	1983	2.50	5.00	10.00
❏ SJ-12353	Greatest Hits	1984	2.50	5.00	10.00
❏ SN-16242	Come to Me	1982	2.00	4.00	8.00

—*Budget-line reissue*

Number	Title (A Side/B Side)	Yr	VG	VG+	NM
❏ SN-16243	Well-Kept Secret	1982	2.00	4.00	8.00

—*Budget-line reissue*

Number	Title (A Side/B Side)	Yr	VG	VG+	NM
❏ SN-16244	Take Heart	1982	2.00	4.00	8.00

—*Budget-line reissue*

Number	Title (A Side/B Side)	Yr	VG	VG+	NM
❏ SN-16313	Juice	1984	2.00	4.00	8.00

—*Budget-line reissue*

Number	Title (A Side/B Side)	Yr	VG	VG+	NM
❏ SN-16314	Quiet Lies	1984	2.00	4.00	8.00

—*Budget-line reissue*

Number	Title (A Side/B Side)	Yr	VG	VG+	NM
❏ SN-16356	Dirty Looks	1985	2.00	4.00	8.00

—*Budget-line reissue*

Number	Title (A Side/B Side)	Yr	VG	VG+	NM
❏ SN-16471	Greatest Hits	1987	2.00	4.00	8.00

—*Budget-line reissue*
RCA

Number	Title (A Side/B Side)	Yr	VG	VG+	NM
❏ 5646-1-R	Old Flame	1986	2.50	5.00	10.00

—*Reissue of 5493 with slightly different lineup*

Number	Title (A Side/B Side)	Yr	VG	VG+	NM
❏ 6371-1-R	Emotion	1987	2.50	5.00	10.00
❏ 8376-1-R	Ain't Gonna Cry	1989	2.50	5.00	10.00
RCA VICTOR					
❏ APL1-1004	Juice Newton and Silver Spur	1975	5.00	10.00	20.00
❏ APL1-1722	After Dust Settled	1977	3.75	7.50	15.00
❏ AYL1-4037	Juice Newton and Silver Spur	1982	2.00	4.00	8.00

—*"Best Buy Series" reissue*

Number	Title (A Side/B Side)	Yr	VG	VG+	NM
AYL1-4038	After Dust Settled	1982	2.00	4.00	8.00

—"Best Buy Series" reissue

Number	Title (A Side/B Side)	Yr	VG	VG+	NM
AFL1-4995	Can't Wait All Night	1984	2.50	5.00	10.00
AFL1-5493	Old Flame	1985	3.00	6.00	12.00

NEWTON, WAYNE Also see THE NEWTON BROTHERS.

45s

ARIES II

Number	Title (A Side/B Side)	Yr	VG	VG+	NM
101	You Stepped Into My Life/She Believes in Me	1979	—	2.00	4.00
107	I Apologize/It's Nice to Be with You	1979	—	2.00	4.00
108	Years/Rhythm Rhapsody	1980	—	2.00	4.00

CAPITOL

Number	Title (A Side/B Side)	Yr	VG	VG+	NM
2016	Love of the Common People/It's Still Loving You	1967	—	3.00	6.00
2917	Up Here in a Tree/Fallin'	1970	—	2.50	5.00
2980	For the Good Times/Little Dreamer	1970	—	2.50	5.00
3044	Apartment 21/Me and Bobby McGee	1971	—	2.50	5.00
3118	Remember the Good Times/Good Morning Dear	1971	—	2.50	5.00
3189	I Ain't That Easy to Love/Leavin' Ya Going My Way	1971	—	2.50	5.00
3241	Just a Memory/Higher Ground	1971	—	2.50	5.00
4920	Heart! (I Hear You Beating)/So Long Lucy	1963	2.50	5.00	10.00
4920	Heart/So Long Lucy	1963	3.00	6.00	12.00

—Original pressing has no subtitle on A-side

Number	Title (A Side/B Side)	Yr	VG	VG+	NM
4989	Danke Schoen/Better Now Than Later	1963	3.00	6.00	12.00
5058	Shirl Girl/Someone's Ahead of You	1963	2.50	5.00	10.00
5124	Dream Baby (How Long Must I Dream)/I'm Looking Over a Four-Leaf Clover	1964	2.50	5.00	10.00
5171	Bill Bailey/When the Saints Go Marching In	1964	2.50	5.00	10.00
5203	Only You/Too Late to Meet	1964	2.50	5.00	10.00
5338	Comin' On Too Strong/Lookin' Through a Tear	1965	6.25	12.50	25.00

—Bruce Johnston and Terry Melcher help out on this record

Number	Title (A Side/B Side)	Yr	VG	VG+	NM
5366	Red Roses for a Blue Lady/One More Memory	1965	2.00	4.00	8.00
5419	I'll Be With You in Apple Blossom Time/Laura Lee	1965	2.00	4.00	8.00
5470	Summer Wind/I'll Be Standing By	1965	2.00	4.00	8.00
5514	Keep the Lovin' Feelin'/Remember When	1965	2.00	4.00	8.00
5553	A Little Bit of Heaven/Some Sunday Morning	1965	2.00	4.00	8.00
5578	You Just Don't Know/After the Laughter	1966	2.00	4.00	8.00
5578 [PS]	You Just Don't Know/After the Laughter	1966	3.75	7.50	15.00
5643	Somebody to Love/Stagecoach to Cheyenne	1966	2.00	4.00	8.00
5643 [PS]	Somebody to Love/Stagecoach to Cheyenne	1966	3.75	7.50	15.00
5692	Excuse Me/How Loud a Sound	1966	2.00	4.00	8.00
5754	The Games That Lovers Play/Half a World Away	1966	2.00	4.00	8.00
5793	Happy Is Gone/How D'Ya Talk to a Girl	1966	2.00	4.00	8.00
5842	If I Only Had a Song to Sing/Sunny Day Girl	1967	—	3.00	6.00
5954	Dream Street Rose/Summer Colors	1967	—	3.00	6.00
5993	Through the Eyes of Love/Just a Memory	1967	—	3.00	6.00

CHALLENGE

Number	Title (A Side/B Side)	Yr	VG	VG+	NM
59228	I Want to Mean Everything to You/I Still Love You	1964	2.50	5.00	10.00
59238	The Little White Cloud That Cried/Born When You Kissed Me	1964	2.50	5.00	10.00
59238	The Little White Cloud That Cried/Calorie Date	1964	2.50	5.00	10.00

CHELSEA

Number	Title (A Side/B Side)	Yr	VG	VG+	NM
BCBO-0091	May the Road Rise to Meet You/Pour Me a Little More Wine	1973	—	2.00	4.00
78-0100	Daddy Don't You Walk So Fast/Echo Valley 2-6809	1972	—	2.50	5.00

—Mostly pink label

Number	Title (A Side/B Side)	Yr	VG	VG+	NM
78-0100	Daddy Don't You Walk So Fast/Echo Valley 2-6809	1972	—	3.00	6.00

—White label (not a promo)

Number	Title (A Side/B Side)	Yr	VG	VG+	NM
78-0105	Can't You Hear the Song?/You Don't Have to Ask	1972	—	2.00	4.00
78-0109	Anthem/Fool	1972	—	2.00	4.00
78-0116	Just Yesterday/While We're Still Young	1973	—	2.00	4.00
78-0124	Help Me Help You/We Didn't Know the Time of Day	1973	—	2.00	4.00
AMBO-0126	Daddy Don't You Walk So Fast/Fool	1973	—	2.00	4.00

—Gold Standard Series reissue

Number	Title (A Side/B Side)	Yr	VG	VG+	NM
3003	Lay Lady Lay/Walking in the Sand	1974	—	2.00	4.00
3018	All Alone Am I/You Don't Have to Ask	1975	—	2.00	4.00
3028	Run to Me/Lady Lonely	1975	—	2.00	4.00
3041	The Hungry Years/In Dreams	1976	—	2.00	4.00
3058	It Could Have Been a Wonderful Christmas/Jingle Bell Hustle	1976	—	2.50	5.00

CURB

Number	Title (A Side/B Side)	Yr	VG	VG+	NM
10520	Cowboy's Christmas/(B-side unknown)	1988	—	—	3.00
10559	While the Feeling's Good/Our Wedding Band	1989	—	—	3.00

—A-side with Tammy Wynette

GEORGE

Number	Title (A Side/B Side)	Yr	VG	VG+	NM
7777	The Little White Cloud That Cried/(B-side unknown)	1962	5.00	10.00	20.00

MGM

Number	Title (A Side/B Side)	Yr	VG	VG+	NM
13891	All the Time/Like Everything Else	1968	—	2.50	5.00
13936	Remembering/Angelica	1968	—	2.50	5.00
13955	Dreams of the Everyday Housewife/The Tip of My Fingers	1968	—	2.50	5.00
13993	Silence Says/Town and Country	1968	—	2.50	5.00
14014	I Just Can't Help Believin'/Husbands and Wives	1968	—	2.50	5.00
14019	Christmas Prayer/Santa Claus Is Comin' to Town	1968	—	2.50	5.00
14046	Everything's in Love Today/The Silence Says	1969	—	2.50	5.00
14083	New York City/For the First Time	1969	—	2.50	5.00
14098	It's Such a Lonely Time of the Year/The Country	1969	—	2.50	5.00
14430	With Pen in Hand/Town and Country	1972	—	2.00	4.00

20TH CENTURY

Number	Title (A Side/B Side)	Yr	VG	VG+	NM
2393	Hold Me Like You Never Had Me/Housewife	1978	—	2.00	4.00

WARNER BROS.

Number	Title (A Side/B Side)	Yr	VG	VG+	NM
8415	I Want You with Me/Midnight Sun	1977	—	2.00	4.00

7-Inch Extended Plays

ARIES II

Number	Title (A Side/B Side)	Yr	VG	VG+	NM
102	White Christmas/It's the Season//I'll Be Home for Christmas/Blue Snow at Christmas	1979	—	2.00	4.00

Albums

ARIES II

Number	Title (A Side/B Side)	Yr	VG	VG+	NM
WY 201	Wayne Newton Christmas	1979	2.50	5.00	10.00

CAPITOL

Number	Title (A Side/B Side)	Yr	VG	VG+	NM
SKAO-137	The Best of Wayne Newton, Volume 2	1968	3.75	7.50	15.00
STBB-487 [(2)]	Merry Christmas to You	1970	3.75	7.50	15.00
ST 1973 [S]	Danke Schoen	1963	5.00	10.00	20.00
T 1973 [M]	Danke Schoen	1963	3.75	7.50	15.00
ST 2029 [S]	Wayne Newton In Person	1964	5.00	10.00	20.00
T 2029 [M]	Wayne Newton In Person	1964	3.75	7.50	15.00
ST 2130 [S]	Wayne Newton Sings Hit Songs	1964	5.00	10.00	20.00
T 2130 [M]	Wayne Newton Sings Hit Songs	1964	3.75	7.50	15.00
SM-2335	Red Roses for a Blue Lady	197?	2.50	5.00	10.00

—Reissue

Number	Title (A Side/B Side)	Yr	VG	VG+	NM
ST 2335 [S]	Red Roses for a Blue Lady	1965	5.00	10.00	20.00
T 2335 [M]	Red Roses for a Blue Lady	1965	3.75	7.50	15.00
ST 2389 [S]	Summer Wind	1965	5.00	10.00	20.00
T 2389 [M]	Summer Wind	1965	3.75	7.50	15.00
ST 2445 [S]	Wayne Newton — Now!	1966	5.00	10.00	20.00
T 2445 [M]	Wayne Newton — Now!	1966	3.75	7.50	15.00
SM-2563	The Old Rugged Cross	197?	2.50	5.00	10.00

—Reissue

Number	Title (A Side/B Side)	Yr	VG	VG+	NM
ST 2563 [S]	The Old Rugged Cross	1966	5.00	10.00	20.00
T 2563 [M]	The Old Rugged Cross	1966	3.75	7.50	15.00
ST 2588 [S]	Songs for a Merry Christmas	1966	3.75	7.50	15.00
T 2588 [M]	Songs for a Merry Christmas	1966	3.00	6.00	12.00
ST 2635 [S]	It's Only the Good Times	1967	5.00	10.00	20.00
T 2635 [M]	It's Only the Good Times	1967	3.75	7.50	15.00
ST 2714 [S]	Song of the Year...Wayne Newton Style	1967	3.75	7.50	15.00
T 2714 [M]	Song of the Year...Wayne Newton Style	1967	5.00	10.00	20.00
ST 2797 [S]	The Best of Wayne Newton	1967	3.75	7.50	15.00
T 2797 [M]	The Best of Wayne Newton	1967	5.00	10.00	20.00
ST 2832 [S]	God Is Alive	1968	3.75	7.50	15.00
T 2832 [M]	God Is Alive	1968	5.00	10.00	20.00
ST 2847 [S]	Wayne Newton — The Greatest	1968	3.75	7.50	15.00
T 2847 [M]	Wayne Newton — The Greatest	1968	5.00	10.00	20.00
SM-11972	Danke Schoen	1979	2.50	5.00	10.00

—Reissue

Number	Title (A Side/B Side)	Yr	VG	VG+	NM
SN-16083	The Best of Wayne Newton	1980	2.00	4.00	8.00

—Budget-line reissue

CAPITOL PICKWICK SERIES

Number	Title (A Side/B Side)	Yr	VG	VG+	NM
PC-3455 [M]	Somewhere My Love	196?	2.50	5.00	10.00
SPC-3455 [S]	Somewhere My Love	196?	2.50	5.00	10.00
PC-3459 [M]	Everybody Loves Somebody	196?	2.50	5.00	10.00
SPC-3459 [S]	Everybody Loves Somebody	196?	2.50	5.00	10.00
PC-3461 [M]	Michelle	196?	2.50	5.00	10.00
SPC-3461 [S]	Michelle	196?	2.50	5.00	10.00
PC-3464 [M]	Wow! Wayne Newton Live	196?	2.50	5.00	10.00
SPC-3464 [S]	Wow! Wayne Newton Live	196?	2.50	5.00	10.00

CHELSEA

Number	Title (A Side/B Side)	Yr	VG	VG+	NM
BCL1-0367	Pour Me a Little More Wine	1973	3.00	6.00	12.00
CHL-504	The Best of Wayne Newton Live	1974	2.50	5.00	10.00
CHL-507	Midnight Idol	1975	2.50	5.00	10.00
CHL-512	Tomorrow	1976	2.50	5.00	10.00
CHL-513	Daddy Don't You Walk So Fast	1976	2.50	5.00	10.00

—Reissue of 1001

Number	Title (A Side/B Side)	Yr	VG	VG+	NM
CHE 1001	Daddy Don't You Walk So Fast	1972	3.00	6.00	12.00
CHE 1003	Can't You Hear the Song?	1972	3.00	6.00	12.00
CHE 1006	While We're Still Young	1973	3.00	6.00	12.00

CURB

Number	Title (A Side/B Side)	Yr	VG	VG+	NM
10607	Coming Home	1989	3.00	6.00	12.00

MGM

Number	Title (A Side/B Side)	Yr	VG	VG+	NM
E-4523 [M]	Walking on New Grass	1968	5.00	10.00	20.00
SE-4523 [S]	Walking on New Grass	1968	3.00	6.00	12.00
E-4549 [M]	One More Time	1968	5.00	10.00	20.00
SE-4549 [S]	One More Time	1968	3.00	6.00	12.00
SE-4593	Christmas Isn't Christmas Without You	1968	3.00	6.00	12.00
SE-4594	Dreams of the Everyday Housewife/Town and Country	1969	3.00	6.00	12.00

20TH CENTURY

Number	Title (A Side/B Side)	Yr	VG	VG+	NM
T-576	Change of Heart	1979	2.50	5.00	10.00

WORD

Number	Title (A Side/B Side)	Yr	VG	VG+	NM
WST-8586	Only Believe	1972	3.00	6.00	12.00

NEWTON BROTHERS, THE With WAYNE NEWTON.

45s

CAPITOL

Number	Title (A Side/B Side)	Yr	VG	VG+	NM
F-4236	The Real Thing/I Spy	1959	20.00	40.00	80.00

NEWTON-JOHN, OLIVIA

12-Inch Singles

MCA

Number	Title (A Side/B Side)	Yr	VG	VG+	NM
L33-1150 [DJ]	Twist of Fate (2 versions)	1983	5.00	10.00	20.00
13987	Livin' in Desperate Times/Twist of Fate	1984	5.00	10.00	20.00
23593	Soul Kiss (Extended Dance Mix) (Dub Mix) (Instrumental Mix)	1985	2.00	4.00	8.00
23606	Toughen Up (Dance Remix) (Instrumental)	1986	2.00	4.00	8.00
23890	The Rumour (4 versions)	1988	2.00	4.00	8.00

45s

ATLANTIC

Number	Title (A Side/B Side)	Yr	VG	VG+	NM
89420	The Best of Me/Sage	1986	—	—	3.00

—With David Foster

Number	Title (A Side/B Side)	Yr	VG	VG+	NM
89420 [PS]	The Best of Me/Sage	1986	—	—	3.00

MCA

Number	Title (A Side/B Side)	Yr	VG	VG+	NM
40043	Take Me Home, Country Roads/Sail Into Tomorrow	1973	7.50	15.00	30.00

—This has (finally) been proven to exist

Number	Title (A Side/B Side)	Yr	VG	VG+	NM
40043 [DJ]	Take Me Home, Country Roads (mono/stereo)	1973	5.00	10.00	20.00
40101	Let Me Be There/Maybe Then I'll Think of You	1973	—	2.50	5.00
40209	If You Love Me (Let Me Know)/Brotherly Love	1974	—	2.50	5.00
40280	I Honestly Love You/Home Ain't Home Anymore	1974	—	2.50	5.00
40349	Have You Never Been Mellow/Water Under the Bridge	1974	—	2.50	5.00
40418	Please Mr. Please/And In the Morning	1975	—	2.50	5.00
40418 [PS]	Please Mr. Please/And In the Morning	1975	2.50	5.00	10.00
40459	Something Better to Do/He's My Rock	1975	—	2.50	5.00
40459 [PS]	Something Better to Do/He's My Rock	1975	—	3.00	6.00
40495	Let It Shine/He Ain't Heavy, He's My Brother	1975	—	2.50	5.00
40525	Come On Over/Small Talk and Pride	1976	—	2.00	4.00
40600	Don't Stop Believin'/Greensleeves	1976	—	2.00	4.00

Number	Title (A Side/B Side)	Yr	VG	VG+	NM
❑ 40600 [PS]	Don't Stop Believin'/Greensleeves	1976	—	2.50	5.00
❑ 40642	Every Face Tells a Story/Love You Hold the Key	1976	—	2.00	4.00
❑ 40670	Sam/I'll Bet You a Kangaroo	1976	—	2.00	4.00
❑ 40737	Making a Good Thing Better/ I Think I'll Say Goodbye	1977	—	2.00	4.00
❑ 40811	I Honestly Love You/Don't Cry for Me Argentina	1977	—	2.50	5.00
❑ 40811 [PS]	I Honestly Love You/Don't Cry for Me Argentina	1977	2.50	5.00	10.00
❑ 40975	A Little More Love/Borrowed Time	1978	—	2.00	4.00
❑ 40975 [PS]	A Little More Love/Borrowed Time	1978	—	2.50	5.00
❑ 41009	Deeper Than the Night/ Please Don't Keep Me Waiting	1979	—	2.00	4.00
❑ 41074	Totally Hot/Dancing Round and Round	1979	—	2.00	4.00
❑ 41074 [PS]	Totally Hot/Dancing Round and Round	1979	—	2.50	5.00
❑ 41247	Magic/Fool Country	1980	—	2.00	4.00
—Standard blue rainbow label					
❑ 41247	Magic/Fool Country	1980	—	2.50	5.00
—Custom pink "Xanadu" label					
❑ 41247 [PS]	Magic/Fool Country	1980	—	2.50	5.00
❑ 41285	Xanadu/Whenever You're Away from Me	1980	—	2.00	4.00
—A-side with Electric Light Orchestra; B-side with Gene Kelly. Persistent rumors claim existence of a U.S. picture sleeve for this record, but we've never seen one.					
❑ 41286	Suddenly/You Made Me Love You	1980	—	2.50	5.00
—A-side with Cliff Richard					
❑ 51007	Suddenly/You Made Me Love You	1980	—	2.00	4.00
—A-side with Cliff Richard					
❑ 51007 [PS]	Suddenly/You Made Me Love You	1980	—	2.50	5.00
❑ 51182	Physical/The Promise (The Dolphin Song)	1981	—	—	3.00
❑ 51182 [PS]	Physical/The Promise (The Dolphin Song)	1981	—	2.00	4.00
❑ 52000	Make a Move on Me/Falling	1982	—	—	3.00
❑ 52000 [PS]	Make a Move on Me/Falling	1982	—	2.50	5.00
❑ 52069	Landslide/Recovery	1982	—	—	3.00
❑ 52069 [PS]	Landslide/Recovery	1982	—	2.00	4.00
❑ 52100	Heart Attack/Strangers Touch	1982	—	—	3.00
❑ 52100 [PS]	Heart Attack/Strangers Touch	1982	—	—	3.00
❑ 52155	Tied Up/Silvery Rain	1983	—	—	3.00
❑ 52155 [PS]	Tied Up/Silvery Rain	1983	—	—	3.00
❑ 52284	Twist of Fate/Take a Chance	1983	—	—	3.00
❑ 52284 [PS]	Twist of Fate/Take a Chance	1983	—	—	3.00
❑ 52341	Livin' in Desperate Times/Landslide	1984	—	—	3.00
❑ 52341 [PS]	Livin' in Desperate Times/Landslide	1984	—	—	3.00
❑ 52686	Soul Kiss/Electric	1985	—	—	3.00
❑ 52686 [PS]	Soul Kiss/Electric	1985	—	—	3.00
❑ 52757	Toughen Up/Driving Music	1986	—	—	3.00
❑ 52757 [PS]	Toughen Up/Driving Music	1986	—	—	3.00
❑ 53294	The Rumour/Winter Angel	1988	—	—	3.00
❑ 53294 [PS]	The Rumour/Winter Angel	1988	—	—	3.00
❑ 53438	Can't We Talk It Over in Bed/Get Out	1988	—	—	3.00
❑ 53438 [PS]	Can't We Talk It Over in Bed/Get Out	1988	—	2.00	4.00
❑ 72053	I Honestly Love You/ I Honestly Love You (Remix)	1998	—	—	3.00
—New recordings					
MCA NASHVILLE					
❑ 72074	Back with a Heart/Under My Skin	1998	—	—	3.00
RSO					
❑ 903	Hopelessly Devoted to You/ Love Is a Many-Splendored Thing	1978	—	2.00	4.00
UNI					
❑ 55281	If Not for You/The Biggest Clown	1971	2.50	5.00	10.00
❑ 55304	Banks of the Ohio/It's So Hard to Say Goodbye	1971	2.00	4.00	8.00
❑ 55317	What Is Life/I'm a Small and Lonely Light	1972	2.00	4.00	8.00
❑ 55348	Just a Little Too Much/My Old Man's Gotta Gun	1972	3.00	6.00	12.00
Albums					
GEFFEN					
❑ GHS 24257	Warm and Tender	1989	3.00	6.00	12.00
MCA					
❑ 389	Let Me Be There	1973	3.75	7.50	15.00
❑ 411	If You Love Me Let Me Know	1974	2.50	5.00	10.00
—With corrected song title: "I Honestly Love You"					
❑ 411	If You Love Me Let Me Know	1974	3.75	7.50	15.00
—Originals have incorrect song title: "I Love You, I Honestly Love You"					
❑ 2133	Have You Never Been Mellow	1975	2.50	5.00	10.00
❑ 2148	Clearly Love	1975	2.50	5.00	10.00
❑ 2186	Come On Over	1976	2.50	5.00	10.00
❑ 2223	Don't Stop Believin'	1976	2.50	5.00	10.00
❑ 2280	Making a Good Thing Better	1977	2.50	5.00	10.00
❑ 3012	Let Me Be There	1977	2.00	4.00	8.00
—Reissue					
❑ 3013	If You Love Me Let Me Know	1977	2.00	4.00	8.00
—Reissue					
❑ 3014	Have You Never Been Mellow	1977	2.00	4.00	8.00
—Reissue					
❑ 3015	Clearly Love	1977	2.00	4.00	8.00
—Reissue					
❑ 3016	Come On Over	1977	2.00	4.00	8.00
—Reissue					
❑ 3017	Don't Stop Believin'	1977	2.00	4.00	8.00
—Reissue					
❑ 3018	Making a Good Thing Better	1977	2.00	4.00	8.00
—Reissue					
❑ 3028	Olivia Newton-John's Greatest Hits	1977	2.50	5.00	10.00
❑ 3067	Totally Hot	1978	2.50	5.00	10.00
❑ 5229	Physical	1981	2.00	4.00	8.00
❑ 5347	Olivia's Greatest Hits, Vol. 2	1982	2.00	4.00	8.00
❑ 6151	Soul Kiss	1985	2.00	4.00	8.00
❑ 6245	The Rumour	1988	2.00	4.00	8.00
❑ 16011	Physical	1982	6.25	12.50	25.00
—Audiophile edition					
❑ 37061	Clearly Love	1980	2.00	4.00	8.00
—Reissue					
❑ 37062	Come On Over	1980	2.00	4.00	8.00
—Reissue					
❑ 37063	Don't Stop Believin'	1980	2.00	4.00	8.00
—Reissue					
❑ 37123	Totally Hot	1981	2.00	4.00	8.00
—Reissue					

Number	Title (A Side/B Side)	Yr	VG	VG+	NM
MOBILE FIDELITY					
❑ 1-040	Totally Hot	1980	5.00	15.00	20.00
—Audiophile vinyl					
UNI					
❑ 73117	If Not for You	1971	20.00	40.00	80.00

NEXT MORNING, THE
Albums

Number	Title (A Side/B Side)	Yr	VG	VG+	NM
CALLA					
❑ SC-2002	The Next Morning	1972	25.00	50.00	100.00

NIC NACS, THE
45s

Number	Title (A Side/B Side)	Yr	VG	VG+	NM
RPM					
❑ 342	Gonna Have a Merry Christmas/Found Me a Sugar Daddy	1951	50.00	100.00	200.00

NICE, THE Keith Emerson, later of EMERSON, LAKE AND PALMER, was in this group.
45s

Number	Title (A Side/B Side)	Yr	VG	VG+	NM
IMMEDIATE					
❑ 5004	Azrial (Angel of Death)/ Thoughts of Emerlist Davjack	1968	3.00	6.00	12.00
❑ 5008	America/Diamnd Hard Apples of the Moon	1968	3.00	6.00	12.00
MERCURY					
❑ 73114	Country Pie/(B-side unknown)	1970	2.00	4.00	8.00
❑ 73272	Country Pie-Brandenburg Concerto No. 6 (Part 1)/Finale-5th Bridge	1972	—	3.00	6.00
Albums					
COLUMBIA SPECIAL PRODUCTS					
❑ P 11633	Thoughts of Emerlist Davjack	1973	3.00	6.00	12.00
❑ P 11634	Ars Longa Vita Brevis	1973	3.00	6.00	12.00
❑ P 11635	The Nice	1973	3.00	6.00	12.00
IMMEDIATE					
❑ Z12 52004	Thoughts of Emerlist Davjack	1968	5.00	10.00	20.00
❑ Z12-52020	Ars Longa Vita Brevis	1969	5.00	10.00	20.00
❑ Z12-52022	The Nice	1969	3.75	7.50	15.00
MERCURY					
❑ SRM-2-6500 [(2)]	Keith Emerson with The Nice	1972	3.75	7.50	15.00
❑ SR 61295	Five Bridges	1970	3.00	6.00	12.00
❑ SR 61324	Elegy	1971	3.00	6.00	12.00
SIRE					
❑ SASH-3710 [(2)]	The Vintage Years	1975	3.75	7.50	15.00

NICHOLAS, PAUL
45s

Number	Title (A Side/B Side)	Yr	VG	VG+	NM
COLUMBIA					
❑ 46050	D.J. Saturday Night/Lovely Lady	1974	—	2.50	5.00
RSO					
❑ 851	Reggae Like It Used to Be/Heat of the Night	1976	—	2.00	4.00
❑ 878	Heaven on the 7th Floor/Do You Want My Love	1977	—	2.00	4.00
❑ 887	On the Strip/Beauty Queen	1978	—	2.00	4.00
Albums					
RSO					
❑ RS-1-3028	Paul Nicholas	1977	3.00	6.00	12.00

NICHOLS, MIKE, AND ELAINE MAY
Albums

Number	Title (A Side/B Side)	Yr	VG	VG+	NM
MERCURY					
❑ SRM-2-628 [(2)]	Retrospect	1972	5.00	10.00	20.00
❑ OCM 2200 [M]	An Evening with Mike Nichols and Elaine May	1961	7.50	15.00	30.00
❑ OCS 6200 [S]	An Evening with Mike Nichols and Elaine May	1961	10.00	20.00	40.00
❑ MG 20376 [M]	Improvisations to Music	1959	7.50	15.00	30.00
❑ MG 20680 [M]	Nichols and May Examine Doctors	1962	6.25	12.50	25.00
❑ MG 20997 [M]	The Best of Nichols and May	1965	5.00	10.00	20.00
❑ SR 60040 [S]	Improvisations to Music	1959	10.00	20.00	40.00
❑ SR 60680 [S]	Nichols and May Examine Doctors	1962	7.50	15.00	30.00
❑ SR 60997 [S]	The Best of Nichols and May	1965	6.25	12.50	25.00

NICHOLS, NICHELLE
Albums

Number	Title (A Side/B Side)	Yr	VG	VG+	NM
EPIC					
❑ LN 24351 [M]	Down to Earth	1968	20.00	40.00	80.00
—White label promo only; in stereo cover with "Mono" sticker					
❑ BN 26351 [S]	Down to Earth	1968	10.00	20.00	40.00

NICK AND THE JAGUARS
45s

Number	Title (A Side/B Side)	Yr	VG	VG+	NM
TAMLA					
❑ 5501F	Ich-I-Bon #1/Cool and Crazy	1960	75.00	150.00	300.00

NICK AND THE NACKS
45s

Number	Title (A Side/B Side)	Yr	VG	VG+	NM
BARRY					
❑ 108	The Night/That Old Black Magic	1964	100.00	200.00	400.00

NICK AND THE STINGRAYS
45s

Number	Title (A Side/B Side)	Yr	VG	VG+	NM
MILL-MONT					
❑ 1628	You Are So Beautiful/Broken Hearted Baby	196?	50.00	100.00	200.00

NICKEL BAG, THE
Albums

Number	Title (A Side/B Side)	Yr	VG	VG+	NM
KAMA SUTRA					
❑ KLPS-8066	Doing Their Love Thing	1968	6.25	12.50	25.00

NICKIE AND THE NITELITES With Nick Massi, later of THE FOUR SEASONS.
45s

Number	Title (A Side/B Side)	Yr	VG	VG+	NM
BRUNSWICK					
❑ 55155	I'm Lonely/Tell Me You Care	1959	25.00	50.00	100.00

NICKY AND THE NOBLES

45s

Number	Title (A Side/B Side)	Yr	VG	VG+	NM
END					
1021	Schoolhouse Rock/A Way to Tell Her	1958	12.50	25.00	50.00
1098	School Bells/School Day Crush	1961	6.25	12.50	25.00
GONE					
5039	School Bells/School Day Crush	1958	6.25	12.50	25.00
—Multicolor label					
5039	School Bells/School Day Crush	1958	15.00	30.00	60.00
—Black label					
5039	School Bells/School Days	1958	25.00	50.00	100.00
—With B-side title variation					

NICO Also see THE VELVET UNDERGROUND.

Albums

Number	Title (A Side/B Side)	Yr	VG	VG+	NM
ELEKTRA					
EKS-74029	The Marble Index	1968	6.25	12.50	25.00
ISLAND					
ILPS-9311	The End	1975	3.75	7.50	15.00
PVC					
8938	Camera Obscura	198?	3.00	6.00	12.00
REPRISE					
RS 6424	Desert Shore	1970	5.00	10.00	20.00
VERVE					
V-5032 [M]	Chelsea Girl	1967	7.50	15.00	30.00
V6-5032 [S]	Chelsea Girl	1967	10.00	20.00	40.00

NICOL, JIMMY His 15 minutes of fame came from his brief stint filling in for an ailing Ringo Starr on a 1964 Beatles tour.

45s

Number	Title (A Side/B Side)	Yr	VG	VG+	NM
ARGO					
5464	Night Train/Humpty Dumpty	1964	—	—	—
—Unreleased					
MAR MAR					
313	Night Train/Humpty Dumpty	1965	37.50	75.00	150.00
PARROT					
9752	Sweet Clementine/Roaring Blue	1965	6.25	12.50	25.00

NIGHT WATCH, THE

45s

Number	Title (A Side/B Side)	Yr	VG	VG+	NM
ABC					
10862	Closed Time/Lips to Your Heart	1966	6.25	12.50	25.00

NIGHTCRAWLERS, THE

45s

Number	Title (A Side/B Side)	Yr	VG	VG+	NM
KAPP					
KE-110	The Little Black Egg/You're Running Wild	1966	2.50	5.00	10.00
709	The Little Black Egg/You're Running Wild	1965	3.75	7.50	15.00
746	A Basket of Flowers/Washboard	1966	3.75	7.50	15.00
826	My Butterfly/Today I'm Happy	1967	7.50	15.00	30.00
LEE					
101	Cry/Marie	1964	15.00	30.00	60.00
1012	The Little Black Egg/You're Running Wild	1965	12.50	25.00	50.00
MARLIN					
1904	A Basket of Flowers/Washboard	1966	5.00	10.00	20.00

Albums

Number	Title (A Side/B Side)	Yr	VG	VG+	NM
KAPP					
KL-1520 [M]	The Little Black Egg	1967	15.00	30.00	60.00
KS-3520 [S]	The Little Black Egg	1967	10.00	20.00	40.00

NIGHTHAWK, ROBERT

45s

Number	Title (A Side/B Side)	Yr	VG	VG+	NM
STATES					
131	The Moon Is Rising/Maggie Campbell	1954	75.00	150.00	300.00

NILSSON Also see THE FOTO-FI FOUR; THE RIC-A-SHAYS.

45s

Number	Title (A Side/B Side)	Yr	VG	VG+	NM
CRUSADER					
103	Baa Baa Black Sheep/Baa Baa Black Sheep (Part 2)	1964	7.50	15.00	30.00
—As "Bo Pete"					
MUSICOR					
6308	Please Mr. Music Man/Foolish Clock	1977	—	2.00	4.00
POLYDOR					
881177-7	Silver Horse/Loneliness	1984	—	2.00	4.00
RCA					
PB-10759	Just One Look-Baby I'm Yours/That Is All	1976	—	2.00	4.00
—With Lynda Lawrence					
PB-11059	Perfect Day/Who Done It	1977	—	2.00	4.00
PB-11059 [PS]	Perfect Day/Who Done It	1977	—	2.50	5.00
PB-11144	All I Think About Is You/I Never Thought I'd Get This Lonely	1977	—	2.00	4.00
PB-11193	Ain't It Kinda Wonderful/I'm Bringing a Red, Red Rose	1978	—	2.00	4.00
PB-11318	Spaceman/Me and My Arrow	1978	—	2.00	4.00
RCA VICTOR					
47-9206	Without Her/Freckles	1967	2.00	4.00	8.00
47-9298	You Can't Do That/Ten Little Indians	1967	2.50	5.00	10.00
47-9383	River Deep Mountain High/She Sang Hymns Out of Tune	1967	2.00	4.00	8.00
47-9442	One/Sister Marie	1968	2.00	4.00	8.00
47-9544	Everybody's Talkin'/Don't Leave Me	1968	3.00	6.00	12.00
47-9675	Rainmaker/I Will Take You There	1968	2.00	4.00	8.00
74-0161	Everybody's Talkin'/Rainmaker	1969	2.50	5.00	10.00
74-0207	Maybe/Marchin' Down Broadway	1969	2.00	4.00	8.00
74-0261	I Guess the Lord Must Be in New York City/Maybe	1969	2.00	4.00	8.00
74-0310	I'll Be Home/Waiting	1970	—	3.00	6.00
74-0336	Caroline/Yellow Man	1970	—	3.00	6.00
74-0362	Down to the Valley/Buy My Album	1970	—	3.00	6.00
74-0443	Me and My Arrow/Are You Sleeping	1971	—	3.00	6.00
74-0524	Without Her/Good Old Desk	1971	—	2.50	5.00
74-0604	Without You/Gotta Get Up	1971	—	2.50	5.00
74-0673	Jump Into the Fire/The Moonbeam Song	1972	—	2.50	5.00
74-0718	Coconut/Down	1972	—	2.50	5.00
74-0788	Spaceman/Turn On Your Radio	1972	—	2.50	5.00
74-0855	Remember (Christmas)/The Lottery Song	1972	—	2.50	5.00
APBO-0039	As Time Goes By/Lullabye in Ragtime	1973	—	3.00	6.00
APBO-0246	Daybreak/Down	1974	—	2.00	4.00
APBO-0246 [PS]	Daybreak/Down	1974	—	3.00	6.00
SP-45-304 [DJ]	Jump Into the Fire (mono/stereo)	1972	2.50	5.00	10.00
—Promo-only number					
PB-10001	Many Rivers to Cross/Don't Forget Me	1974	2.00	4.00	8.00
PB-10078	Subterranean Homesick Blues/Mucho Mungo	1974	2.00	4.00	8.00
PB-10130	Remember (Christmas)/The Lottery Song	1974	—	2.00	4.00
PB-10139	Loop De Loop/Don't Forget Me	1974	—	2.00	4.00
PB-10183	Kojak Columbo/Turn Out the Light	1975	—	2.00	4.00
PB-10183 [PS]	Kojak Columbo/Turn Out the Light	1975	—	2.50	5.00
PB-10634	Sail Away/Moonshine Bandit	1976	—	2.00	4.00
TOWER					
103	Sixteen Tons/I'm Gonna Lose My Mind	1964	3.75	7.50	15.00
136	You Can't Take Your Love Away from Me/Born in Grenada	1965	3.75	7.50	15.00
244	She's Yours/Growing Up	1966	3.75	7.50	15.00
518	Good Time/Growin' Up	1969	3.75	7.50	15.00
TRY					
501	Do You Wanna/Groovy Little Suzie	1964	10.00	20.00	40.00
—As "Bo Pete"					

Albums

Number	Title (A Side/B Side)	Yr	VG	VG+	NM
MUSICOR					
MUS-2505 [S]	Early Tymes	1977	3.75	7.50	15.00
PICKWICK					
SPC-3321	Rock 'N' Roll	1977	2.50	5.00	10.00
RAPPLE					
ABL1-0220	Son of Dracula	1974	3.00	6.00	12.00
RCA VICTOR					
(no #)	The True One	1967	50.00	100.00	200.00
—Boxed set with mono copy of RCA Victor 3874, two photos, button, poster, sticker, bios					
APL1-0097	A Little Touch of Schmilsson in the Night	1973	3.00	6.00	12.00
APL1-0203	Nilsson Sings Newman	1974	2.50	5.00	10.00
—Reissue of LSP-4289					
APD1-0319 [Q]	Nilsson Schmilsson	1974	5.00	10.00	20.00
SPS-33-567 [DJ]	Scatalogue	197?	25.00	50.00	100.00
APD1-0570 [Q]	Pussy Cats	1974	7.50	15.00	30.00
CPL1-0570	Pussy Cats	1974	5.00	10.00	20.00
APD1-0817 [Q]	Duit On Mon Dei	1975	5.00	10.00	20.00
APL1-0817	Duit On Mon Dei	1975	3.00	6.00	12.00
LSPX-1003	The Point!	1971	3.00	6.00	12.00
APD1-1031 [Q]	Sandman	1976	5.00	10.00	20.00
APL1-1031	Sandman	1976	3.00	6.00	12.00
APL1-1119	That's the Way It Is	1976	3.00	6.00	12.00
AFL1-2276	Knnillssonn	1977	3.00	6.00	12.00
AFL1-2798	Greatest Hits	1978	3.00	6.00	12.00
ANL1-3464	Nilsson Schmilsson	1979	2.00	4.00	8.00
AYL1-3761	A Little Touch of Schmilsson in the Night	1980	2.00	4.00	8.00
—"Best Buy Series" reissue					
AYL1-3811	The Point!	1980	2.00	4.00	8.00
—"Best Buy Series" reissue					
AYL1-3812	Son of Schmilsson	1980	2.00	4.00	8.00
—"Best Buy Series" reissue					
LPM-3874 [M]	Pandemonium Shadow Show	1967	10.00	20.00	40.00
LSP-3874 [S]	Pandemonium Shadow Show	1967	5.00	10.00	20.00
—"Stereo" on black label					
LSP-3874 [S]	Pandemonium Shadow Show	1969	3.75	7.50	15.00
—Orange label					
LPM-3956 [M]	Aerial Ballet	1968	12.50	25.00	50.00
LSP-3956 [S]	Aerial Ballet	1968	5.00	10.00	20.00
—"Stereo" on black label					
LSP-3956 [S]	Aerial Ballet	1969	3.75	7.50	15.00
—Orange label, non-flexible vinyl					
LSP-4197	Harry	1969	3.75	7.50	15.00
—Orange label, non-flexible vinyl					
LSP-4289	Nilsson Sings Newman	1970	3.00	6.00	12.00
—Orange label, non-flexible vinyl					
LSP-4417	The Point!	1971	2.50	5.00	10.00
—Reissue of LSPX-1003					
LSP-4515	Nilsson Schmilsson	1971	3.00	6.00	12.00
LSP-4543	Aerial Pandemonium Ballet	1971	3.00	6.00	12.00
—Collection of tracks from 3874 and 3956, remixed with, in some cases, new vocals					
LSP-4717	Son of Schmilsson	1972	3.00	6.00	12.00
—With custom black "Victor" label					
TOWER					
ST 5095 [S]	Spotlight on Nilsson	1967	5.00	10.00	20.00
T 5095 [M]	Spotlight on Nilsson	1967	5.00	10.00	20.00
DT 5165 [R]	Spotlight on Nilsson	1969	3.75	7.50	15.00

NIMBLE, JACK B. AND THE QUICKS

45s

Number	Title (A Side/B Side)	Yr	VG	VG+	NM
DEL RIO					
2303/4	Like Keyed/Babes in Toyland	1962	6.25	12.50	25.00
2305	Nut Rocker/Never on Sunday	1962	7.50	15.00	30.00
DOT					
16319	Nut Rocker/Never on Sunday	1962	3.75	7.50	15.00

NIMOY, LEONARD

45s

Number	Title (A Side/B Side)	Yr	VG	VG+	NM
DOT					
17028	The Ballad of Bilbo Baggins/Cotton Candy	1967	3.75	7.50	15.00
17038	Theme from "Star Trek"/Visit to a Sad Planet	1967	5.00	10.00	20.00
17125	I'd Love Making Love to You/Please Don't Try to Change My Mind	1968	3.75	7.50	15.00
17175	Consilium/Here We Go 'Round Again	1968	3.75	7.50	15.00
17330	The Sun Will Rise/Time to Get It Together	1969	3.75	7.50	15.00

Albums

Number	Title (A Side/B Side)	Yr	VG	VG+	NM
CAEDMON					
TC-1466	The Martian Chronicles	1976	7.50	15.00	30.00
TC-1479	The Illustrated Man	1976	7.50	15.00	30.00
TC-1520	War of the Worlds	1977	7.50	15.00	30.00
TC-1526	Green Hills of Earth	1977	7.50	15.00	30.00
DOT					
DLP 3794 [M]	Mr. Spock's Music from Outer Space	1967	12.50	25.00	50.00
DLP 3835 [M]	Two Sides of Leonard Nimoy	1968	12.50	25.00	50.00

N

Number	Title (A Side/B Side)	Yr	VG	VG+	NM
☐ DLP 3883 [M]	The Way I Feel	1968	20.00	40.00	80.00
—Stereo cover with "Monaural" sticker; label is black stock copy					
☐ DLP 25794 [S]	Mr. Spock's Music from Outer Space	1967	20.00	40.00	80.00
☐ DLP 25835 [S]	Two Sides of Leonard Nimoy	1968	20.00	40.00	80.00
☐ DLP 25883 [S]	The Way I Feel	1968	15.00	30.00	60.00
☐ DLP 25910	The Touch of Leonard Nimoy	1969	15.00	30.00	60.00
☐ DLP 25966	The New World of Leonard Nimoy	1969	15.00	30.00	60.00
JRT					
☐ (# unknown)	The Mysterious Golem	1982	10.00	20.00	40.00
PARAMOUNT					
☐ PAS-1030 [(2)]	Outer Space/Inner Mind	1970	12.50	25.00	50.00
PICKWICK					
☐ SPC-3199	Space Odyssey	197?	12.50	25.00	50.00
SEARS					
☐ SPS-491	Leonard Nimoy	196?	20.00	40.00	80.00

1910 FRUITGUM COMPANY Also see KASENETZ-KATZ SINGING ORCHESTRAL CIRCUS.
45s

Number	Title (A Side/B Side)	Yr	VG	VG+	NM
ATTACK					
☐ 10293	Lawdy, Lawdy/The Clock	1970	3.00	6.00	12.00
BUDDAH					
☐ 24	Simon Says/Reflections from the Looking Glass	1968	2.50	5.00	10.00
☐ 39	May I Take a Giant Step (Into Your Heart)/ (Poor Old) Mr. Jensen	1968	2.00	4.00	8.00
☐ 54	1,2,3, Red Light/Sticky, Sticky	1968	2.50	5.00	10.00
☐ 71	Goody Goody Gumdrops/Candy Kisses	1968	2.00	4.00	8.00
☐ 91	Indian Giver/Pow Wow	1969	2.50	5.00	10.00
☐ 114	Special Delivery/No Good Annie	1969	2.00	4.00	8.00
☐ 130	The Train/Eternal Light	1969	2.00	4.00	8.00
☐ 146	When We Get Married/Baby Sweet	1969	2.00	4.00	8.00
SUPER K					
☐ 115	Go Away/The Track	1970	3.00	6.00	12.00
Albums					
BUDDAH					
☐ BDM-5010 [M]	Simon Says	1968	12.50	25.00	50.00
—Appears to be promo only; "Mono" sticker on stereo cover					
☐ BDS-5010 [S]	Simon Says	1968	6.25	12.50	25.00
☐ BDS-5022	1,2,3 Red Light	1968	6.25	12.50	25.00
☐ BDS-5027	Goody, Goody Gumdrops	1969	6.25	12.50	25.00
☐ BDS-5036	Indian Giver	1969	6.25	12.50	25.00
☐ BDS-5043	Hard Ride	1969	6.25	12.50	25.00
☐ BDS-5057	Juiciest Fruitgum	1970	6.25	12.50	25.00

NINO AND THE EBB TIDES
45s

Number	Title (A Side/B Side)	Yr	VG	VG+	NM
ACME					
☐ 720	Franny Franny/Darling I'll Love Only You	1958	75.00	150.00	300.00
MADISON					
☐ 162	Those Oldies But Goodies (Remind Me of You)/ Don't Run Away	1961	10.00	20.00	40.00
☐ 166	Juke Box Saturday Night/(Someday) I'll Fall in Love	1961	7.50	15.00	30.00
MALA					
☐ 480	Automatic Reaction/Linda Lou Garrett Like 24 Karat	1964	5.00	10.00	20.00
MARCO					
☐ 105	Little Miss Blue/Someday	1961	12.50	25.00	50.00
MR. PEACOCK					
☐ 102	Wished I Was Home/Happy Guy	1961	6.25	12.50	25.00
☐ 117	Lovin' Time/Stamps, Baby, Stamps	1962	6.25	12.50	25.00
MR. PEEKE					
☐ 123	Tonight I'll Be Lonely/Nursery Rhymes	1963	6.25	12.50	25.00
RECORTE					
☐ 405	Puppy Love/You Make Me Rock 'N' Roll	1958	12.50	25.00	50.00
☐ 408	The Real Meaning of Christmas/Two Purple Shadows in the Snow	1958	75.00	150.00	300.00
☐ 409	I'm Confessin'/Tell the World I Do	1959	12.50	25.00	50.00
☐ 413	Don't Look Around/I Love Girls	1959	25.00	50.00	100.00

NIRVANA (1)
45s

Number	Title (A Side/B Side)	Yr	VG	VG+	NM
BELL					
☐ 715	We Can Help You/Pentecost Hotel	1968	2.50	5.00	10.00
☐ 730	You Are Just the One/Girl in the Park	1968	2.50	5.00	10.00
☐ 739	Trapeze/The Touchables	1968	2.50	5.00	10.00
Albums					
BELL					
☐ 6015	The Story of Simon Simopath	1968	6.25	12.50	25.00
☐ 6024	All of Us	1969	6.25	12.50	25.00

NIRVANA (2)
Albums

Number	Title (A Side/B Side)	Yr	VG	VG+	NM
METROMEDIA					
☐ MD-1018	Nirvana	1970	6.25	12.50	25.00

NITE RIDERS, THE Possibly two different groups.
45s

Number	Title (A Side/B Side)	Yr	VG	VG+	NM
MGM					
☐ 12487	Sippin' Coffee/Tank Town	1957	7.50	15.00	30.00
TEEN					
☐ 116	Starlight and You/I Know You're In There	1955	10.00	20.00	40.00
☐ 118	Got Me a Six-Button Benny/Don't Hang Up the Phone	1955	10.00	20.00	40.00
☐ 120	When a Man Cries/Waiting in the Schoolroom	1955	10.00	20.00	40.00

NITE ROCKERS, THE
45s

Number	Title (A Side/B Side)	Yr	VG	VG+	NM
RCA VICTOR					
☐ 47-7323	Nite Rock/Oh! Baby	1958	7.50	15.00	30.00

NITE-LITERS, THE Also see LOVE, PEACE AND HAPPINESS; THE NEW BIRTH.
45s

Number	Title (A Side/B Side)	Yr	VG	VG+	NM
RCA VICTOR					
☐ 74-0374	Con-Funk-Shun/Down and Dirty	1970	—	3.00	6.00
☐ 74-0461	K-Jee/Tanga Boo Gonk	1971	—	2.50	5.00
☐ 74-0591	Afro-Strut/(We've Got to) Pull Together	1971	—	2.50	5.00
☐ 74-0714	Cherish Every Precious Moment/I've Got Dreams to Remember	1972	—	2.50	5.00
☐ 74-0812	Funky-Doo/Do the Granny	1972	—	2.50	5.00
☐ APBO-0244	Pe-Foul/Serenade for a Jive Turkey	1974	—	2.50	5.00
Albums					
RCA VICTOR					
☐ LSP-4493	Morning, Noon & The Nite-Liters	1971	3.75	7.50	15.00
☐ LSP-4580	Instrumental Directions	1972	3.75	7.50	15.00

NITTY GRITTY DIRT BAND Includes The Dirt Band. Also see JOHN DENVER.
45s

Number	Title (A Side/B Side)	Yr	VG	VG+	NM
DECCA					
☐ 55206	Maybe Baby/Crying, Waiting, Hoping	1996	—	—	3.00
—B-side by Marty Stuart and Steve Earle					
LIBERTY					
☐ 1389	High School Yearbook/Too Good to Be True	1980	—	2.00	4.00
—As "The Dirt Band"					
☐ 1398	Nazamas Nuestra Magic (Make a Little Magic)/ Jas' Moon	1981	—	2.00	4.00
—As "The Dirt Band"					
☐ 1429	Fire in the Sky/EZ Slow	1981	—	2.00	4.00
—As "The Dirt Band"					
☐ 1449	Badlands/Jealousy	1982	—	2.00	4.00
—As "The Dirt Band"					
☐ 1467	Too Close for Comfort/Circular Man	1982	—	2.00	4.00
—As "The Dirt Band"					
☐ 1499	Let's Go/Shot Full of Love	1983	—	2.00	4.00
☐ 1507	Mary Anne/Dance Little Jean	1983	—	2.00	4.00
☐ 1513	Colorado Christmas/Mr. Bojangles	1983	—	3.00	6.00
☐ 55948	Buy for Me the Rain/Candy Man	1967	2.50	5.00	10.00
☐ 55982	The Teddy Bear's Picnic/Truly Right	1967	2.00	4.00	8.00
☐ 55982 [PS]	The Teddy Bear's Picnic/Truly Right	1967	3.75	7.50	15.00
☐ 56054	These Days/Collegiana	1968	2.00	4.00	8.00
☐ 56134	Some of Shelley's Blues/Yukon Railroad	1969	—	3.00	6.00
☐ 56159	Rave On/The Cure	1970	—	3.00	6.00
☐ 56197	Mr. Bojangles/Mr. Bojangles (Prelude: Uncle Charlie and His Dog Teddy)	1970	—	3.00	6.00
☐ 56197	Mr. Bojangles (Prelude: Uncle Charlie and His Dog Teddy)/Spanish Fandango	1970	2.00	4.00	8.00
☐ S7-57766	I Fought the Law/Mr. Bojangles	1992	—	—	3.00
MCA					
☐ 53795	One Step Over the Line/Riding Along	1990	—	—	3.00
—A-side: With Roseanne Cash; B-side: With Emmylou Harris					
☐ 53964	The Rest of the Dream/Snowballs	1990	—	—	3.00
☐ 55182	You Believed in Me/Atlanta Reel '96	1996	—	—	3.00
—A-side by Karla Bonoff and the Nitty Gritty Dirt Band; B-side by Michael Omartian					
☐ 79013	From Small Things (Big Things One Day Come)/ Blues Berry Hill	1990	—	—	3.00
☐ 79075	You Make Life Good Again/Snowballs	1990	—	—	3.00
UNITED ARTISTS					
☐ 0061	Mr. Bojangles/Buy for Me the Rain	1973	—	2.00	4.00
—"Silver Spotlight Series" reissue					
☐ XW177	Will the Circle Be Unbroken/Honky Tonkin'	1973	—	2.50	5.00
☐ XW177 [PS]	Will the Circle Be Unbroken/Honky Tonkin'	1973	2.00	4.00	8.00
☐ XW247	Grand Ole Opry Song/Orange Blossom Special	1973	—	2.50	5.00
☐ XW263	Cosmic Cowboy (Part 1)/ Cosmic Cowboy (Part 2)	1973	—	2.50	5.00
☐ XW321	Tennessee Stud/Way Down Town	1973	—	2.50	5.00
—With Doc Watson					
☐ XW544	The Battle of New Orleans/Mountain Whipporwill	1974	—	2.50	5.00
☐ XW544 [PS]	The Battle of New Orleans/Mountain Whipporwill	1974	—	3.00	6.00
☐ XW655	(All I Have to Do Is) Dream/Raleigh-Durham Reel	1975	—	2.50	5.00
☐ XW741	Mother of Love/The Moon Just Turned Blue	1975	—	2.50	5.00
☐ XW830	Cosmic Cowboy/Stars and Stripes Forever	1976	—	2.00	4.00
—As "The Dirt Band"					
☐ XW889	Jamaica Lady/Bayou Jubilee- Sally Was a Goodun	1976	—	2.00	4.00
—As "The Dirt Band"					
☐ XW936	Buy for Me the Rain/Mother Earth (Provides for Me)	1976	—	2.00	4.00
—As "The Dirt Band"					
☐ XW1164	Orange Blossom Special/ Will the Circle Be Unbroken	1978	—	2.00	4.00
☐ XW1228	Wild Nights/In for the Night	1978	—	2.00	4.00
—As "The Dirt Band"					
☐ XW1268	For a Little While/On the Loose	1978	—	2.00	4.00
—As "The Dirt Band"					
☐ 1312	In Her Eyes/Jas' Moon	1979	—	2.00	4.00
☐ 1330	An American Dream/Take Me Back	1979	—	2.50	5.00
—As "The Dirt Band"					
☐ 1356	Make a Little Magic/Jas' Moon	1980	—	2.00	4.00
—As "The Dirt Band"					
☐ 1378	Badlands/Too Good to Be True	1980	—	2.00	4.00
—As "The Dirt Band"					
☐ 50769	House at Pooh Corner/Travelin' Mood	1971	—	3.00	6.00
☐ 50769 [PS]	House at Pooh Corner/Travelin' Mood	1971	2.00	4.00	8.00
☐ 50817	The Cure/Some of Shelly's Blues	1971	—	3.00	6.00
☐ 50849	Precious Jewel/I Saw the Light	1971	—	3.00	6.00
—With Roy Acuff					
☐ 50861	I Saw the Light/Sixteen Tracks	1971	—	3.00	6.00
☐ 50890	Jambalaya (On the Bayou)/Hoping to Say	1972	—	3.00	6.00
☐ 50890 [PS]	Jambalaya (On the Bayou)/Hoping to Say	1972	2.00	4.00	8.00
☐ 50921	Baltimore/Fish Song	1972	—	3.00	6.00
☐ 50965	Honky Tonkin'/Jamaica	1972	—	3.00	6.00
UNIVERSAL					
☐ UVL-66009	Turn of the Century/Blueberry Hill	1989	—	—	3.00
☐ UVL-66023	When It's Gone/I'm Sittin' on Top of the World	1989	—	2.00	4.00
WARNER BROS.					
☐ PRO-S-2869 [DJ]	Colorado Christmas/ The Cowboy's Christmas Ball	1987	—	3.00	6.00
—B-side by Michael Martin Murphey					
WARNER BROS.					
☐ 27679	Down That Road Tonight/A Lot Like Me	1989	—	—	3.00

Number	Title (A Side/B Side)	Yr	VG	VG+	NM
❏ 28173	Oh What a Love/America, My Sweetheart	1987	—	—	3.00
❏ 28173 [PS]	Oh What a Love/America, My Sweetheart	1987	—	2.00	4.00
❏ 28311	Fishin' in the Dark/Keepin' the Road Hot	1987	—	—	3.00
❏ 28443	Baby's Got a Hold on Me/Oleanna	1987	—	—	3.00
❏ 28547	Cadillac Ranch/Fire in the Sky	1986	—	—	3.00
❏ 28690	Stand a Little Rain/Miner's Night Out	1986	—	—	3.00
❏ 28780	Partners, Brothers and Friends/Redneck Riviera	1986	—	—	3.00
❏ 28897	Home Again in My Heart/Telluride	1985	—	2.00	4.00
❏ 29027	Modern Day Romance/Queen of the Road	1985	—	2.00	4.00
❏ 29099	High Horse/Must Be Love	1985	—	2.00	4.00
❏ 29203	I Love Only You/Face on the Cutting Room Floor	1984	—	2.00	4.00
❏ 29282	Long Hard Road (The Sharecropper's Dream)/ Video Tape	1984	—	2.00	4.00

Albums
LIBERTY

Number	Title (A Side/B Side)	Yr	VG	VG+	NM
❏ LWB-184 [(2)]	Stars and Stripes Forever	1981	2.50	5.00	10.00
❏ LKCL-670 [(3)]	Dirt, Silver and Gold	1981	3.00	6.00	12.00
❏ LO-974	An American Dream	1981	2.00	4.00	8.00
❏ LT-1042	Make a Little Magic	1981	2.00	4.00	8.00
❏ LRP-3501 [M]	The Nitty Gritty Dirt Band	1967	6.25	12.50	25.00
❏ LRP-3516 [M]	Ricochet	1967	6.25	12.50	25.00
❏ LMAS-5553	All the Good Times	1981	2.00	4.00	8.00
❏ LST-7501 [S]	The Nitty Gritty Dirt Band	1967	7.50	15.00	30.00
❏ LST-7516 [S]	Ricochet	1967	7.50	15.00	30.00
❏ LST-7540	Rare Junk	1968	6.25	12.50	25.00
❏ LST-7611	Alive	1969	6.25	12.50	25.00
❏ LST-7642	Uncle Charlie and His Dog Teddy	1970	6.25	12.50	25.00
—Standard issue of LP					
❏ LST-7642 [DJ]	Uncle Charlie and His Dog Teddy	1970	30.00	60.00	120.00
—Leatherette promo pack with LP, two other discs, photos, booklet					
❏ LTAO-7642	Uncle Charlie and His Dog Teddy	1981	2.00	4.00	8.00
❏ LT-51146	Let's Go	1982	2.50	5.00	10.00
❏ LWCL-51158 [(3)]	Will the Circle Be Unbroken	1986	3.75	7.50	15.00
MCA					
❏ 6407	The Rest of the Dream	1990	3.00	6.00	12.00
UNITED ARTISTS					
❏ UA-LA184-J2 [(2)]	Stars and Stripes Forever	1974	3.75	7.50	15.00
❏ UA-LA469-G	Dream	1975	3.00	6.00	12.00
❏ UA-LA670-L3 [(3)]	Dirt, Silver and Gold	1976	5.00	10.00	20.00
❏ UA-LA830-H	The Chicken Chronicles	1978	2.50	5.00	10.00
❏ UA-LA854-H	The Dirt Band	1978	2.50	5.00	10.00
❏ UA-LA974-H	An American Dream	1979	2.50	5.00	10.00
❏ LT-1042	Make a Little Magic	1980	2.50	5.00	10.00
❏ LW-1106	Jealousy	1981	2.50	5.00	10.00
❏ UAS-5553	All the Good Times	1972	3.75	7.50	15.00
❏ UAS-9801 [(3)]	Will the Circle Be Unbroken	1972	7.50	15.00	30.00
UNIVERSAL					
❏ UVL2-12500 [(2)]	Will the Circle Be Unbroken, Volume Two	1989	5.00	10.00	20.00
WARNER BROS.					
❏ 25113	Plain Dirt Fashion	1984	2.00	4.00	8.00
❏ 25304	Partners, Brothers and Friends	1985	2.00	4.00	8.00
❏ 25382	Twenty Years of Dirt: The Best of the Nitty Gritty Dirt Band	1986	2.00	4.00	8.00
❏ 25573	Hold On	1987	2.00	4.00	8.00
❏ 25722	Workin' Band	1988	2.00	4.00	8.00
❏ 25830	More Great Dirt: The Best of the Nitty Gritty Dirt Band, Vol. 2	1989	2.50	5.00	10.00

NITZINGER
45s
CAPITOL

Number	Title (A Side/B Side)	Yr	VG	VG+	NM
❏ 3359	Earth Eater/One Foot in History	1973	—	2.50	5.00
20TH CENTURY					
❏ 2311	Yellow Dog/Are You With Me	1976	—	2.00	4.00

Albums
CAPITOL

Number	Title (A Side/B Side)	Yr	VG	VG+	NM
❏ SMAS-11091	Nitzinger	1972	3.75	7.50	15.00
❏ SMAS-11122	One Foot in History	1973	3.75	7.50	15.00
20TH CENTURY					
❏ T-518	Live Better Electrically	1976	3.00	6.00	12.00

NITZSCHE, JACK
45s
FANTASY

Number	Title (A Side/B Side)	Yr	VG	VG+	NM
❏ 760	One Flew Over the Cuckoo's Next/The Last Dance	1976	—	3.00	6.00
❏ 760 [PS]	One Flew Over the Cuckoo's Next/The Last Dance	1976	2.50	5.00	10.00
—Jack Nicholson is pictured on the sleeve					
MCA					
❏ 40897	Coke Machine/Hard Workin' Man	1978	—	2.00	4.00
REPRISE					
❏ 0262	The Last Race/Man with the Golden Arm	1964	5.00	10.00	20.00
❏ 0285	Theme from The Long Ships/Zapata	1964	5.00	10.00	20.00
❏ 0337	The Green Grass of Texas/Night Walker	1965	5.00	10.00	20.00
❏ 0364	Senorita from Detroit/Puerto Vallarta	1965	5.00	10.00	20.00
❏ 20202	The Lonely Surfer/Song for a Summer Night	1963	7.50	15.00	30.00
❏ 20202 [PS]	The Lonely Surfer/Song for a Summer Night	1963	25.00	50.00	100.00
❏ 20225	Rumble/Theme for a Broken Heart	1963	5.00	10.00	20.00

Albums
REPRISE

Number	Title (A Side/B Side)	Yr	VG	VG+	NM
❏ MS 2092	St. Giles Cripplegate	1972	5.00	10.00	20.00
❏ R 6101 [M]	The Lonely Surfer	1963	25.00	50.00	100.00
❏ R9-6101 [S]	The Lonely Surfer	1963	50.00	100.00	200.00
—Pink, gold and green label					
❏ RS 6101 [S]	The Lonely Surfer	197?	5.00	10.00	20.00
—With only "r:" logo on all-orange (tan) label					
❏ R 6115 [M]	Dance to the Hits of the Beatles	1964	12.50	25.00	50.00
❏ RS 6115 [S]	Dance to the Hits of the Beatles	1964	15.00	30.00	60.00
❏ R 6200 [M]	Chopin '66	1966	6.25	12.50	25.00
❏ RS 6200 [S]	Chopin '66	1966	7.50	15.00	30.00

NIX, DON
45s
CREAM

Number	Title (A Side/B Side)	Yr	VG	VG+	NM
❏ 7604	A Demain (Until Tomorrow)/A Demain (Until Tomorrow) (Edited Version)	1976	—	2.00	4.00
❏ 7608	Rollin' in My Dreams/(B-side unknown)	1976	—	2.00	4.00
ELEKTRA					
❏ 45746	Olena/Riding the Blinds	1971	—	2.50	5.00
❏ 45776	Going Down/She Don't Want a Lover, She Just Needs a Friend	1972	—	2.50	5.00
ENTERPRISE					
❏ 9067	Black Cat Moan/ The Train Don't Stop Here No More	1973	—	2.50	5.00
❏ 9083	She's a Friend of Mine/ When I Lay My Burden Down	1973	—	2.50	5.00

Albums
CREAM

Number	Title (A Side/B Side)	Yr	VG	VG+	NM
❏ 1001	Gone Too Long	1979	2.50	5.00	10.00
ELEKTRA					
❏ EKS-74101	Living by the Days	1971	3.00	6.00	12.00
ENTERPRISE					
❏ ENS-1032	Hobos, Heroes and Street Corner Clowns	1974	3.00	6.00	12.00

NIX, WILLIE
45s
CHANCE

Number	Title (A Side/B Side)	Yr	VG	VG+	NM
❏ 1163	Nervous Wreck/No More Love	1954	750.00	1500.	3000.
SABRE					
❏ 104	All By Myself/Just Can't Stay	1953	500.00	1000.	2000.

NO NAMES, THE
45s
GUYDEN

Number	Title (A Side/B Side)	Yr	VG	VG+	NM
❏ 2114	Love/Jam	1964	12.50	25.00	50.00

NOBELLS, THE
45s
MAR

Number	Title (A Side/B Side)	Yr	VG	VG+	NM
❏ 101	Searchin' for My Love/Crying Over You	1962	25.00	50.00	100.00

NOBLE, NICK
45s
CAPITOL

Number	Title (A Side/B Side)	Yr	VG	VG+	NM
❏ 3677	It's All Up to You/Let Me Be a Man	1973	—	2.50	5.00
CHESS					
❏ 1876	Sleep Walk/Flying Over Rainbows	1963	2.50	5.00	10.00
❏ 1879	Stay with Me/Flying Over Rainbows	1963	2.00	4.00	8.00
❏ 1909	Don't Forget/Not Like I Used to Be	1964	2.00	4.00	8.00
CHURCHILL					
❏ 7701	May God Be With You/(B-side unknown)	1978	—	3.00	6.00
❏ 7713	Stay with Me/My Country Kind of Girl	1978	—	3.00	6.00
❏ 7755	Big Man's Cafe/My Country Kind of Girl	1980	—	3.00	6.00
COLUMBIA					
❏ 4-44887	I'm Gonna Make You Love Me/I'm So Busy Being Broken Hearted	1969	—	3.00	6.00
CORAL					
❏ 9-62075	How Much Can a Heart Take/ My Darling's Earrings	1959	2.50	5.00	10.00
❏ 9-62124	I Need Someone/Thank Heaven for Little Girls	1959	2.50	5.00	10.00
❏ 9-62144	Somethin' Cha Cha/I Surrender Dear	1959	2.50	5.00	10.00
❏ 62169	Violino/Lemons and Cloves	1960	2.50	5.00	10.00
❏ 62213	The Tip of My Fingers/Sweet Love	1960	3.00	6.00	12.00
❏ 62233	Excuse Me (I Think I've Got a Heartache)/ Island Farewell	1960	2.50	5.00	10.00
❏ 62246	Someplace to Cry/Over Someone's Shoulder	1961	2.50	5.00	10.00
❏ 62262	(I'm Gonna) Cry Some Tears/ They Call Me the Fool	1961	2.50	5.00	10.00
❏ 62280	For Just a Little While Tonight/ The Beat of My Soul	1961	2.50	5.00	10.00
❏ 62495	The Tip of My Fingers/Someplace to Cry	1966	2.00	4.00	8.00
DATE					
❏ 2-1582	Until It's Time for You to Go/ You're the Right One for Me	1967	—	3.50	7.00
❏ 2-1616	My Marie/It Hurts to Say Goodbye	1968	—	3.50	7.00
❏ 2-1629	Lovely As I Leave You/Take Me Back	1968	—	3.50	7.00
EPIC					
❏ 50327	Forgetting Someone/ If We Could Live Our Life Away	1977	—	2.00	4.00
FRATERNITY					
❏ 817	Fountains Cry/There's a Church in Your Heart	1958	2.50	5.00	10.00
❏ 825	One Track Mind/Lonely Star	1958	2.50	5.00	10.00
LIBERTY					
❏ 55442	The Twelfth Dark Hour/My Heart Came Running Back to You	1962	2.00	4.00	8.00
❏ 55488	Hello Out There/We Could	1962	2.00	4.00	8.00
❏ 55534	A Legend in My Time/Closer to Heaven	1963	2.00	4.00	8.00
❏ 55576	Gee Little Girl/A Rose and a Star	1963	2.00	4.00	8.00
MERCURY					
❏ 70397	Right or Wrong/Maybe Today	1954	3.75	7.50	15.00
❏ 70496	Tara's Theme/Please Don't Break My Heart	1954	3.75	7.50	15.00
❏ 70821	To You, My Love/You Are My Only Love	1956	3.00	6.00	12.00
❏ 70897	Keeping Cool (With Lemonade)/You're Sensational	1956	3.00	6.00	12.00
❏ 70959	Autumn Concerto/Mom, Oh Mom	1956	3.00	6.00	12.00
❏ 71031	No One Sweeter Than You/I'm a Visitor	1957	3.00	6.00	12.00
❏ 71117	A Fallen Star/They're Playing Our Song	1957	3.00	6.00	12.00
❏ 71124	A Fallen Star/Let Me Hold You in My Arms	1957	2.50	5.00	10.00
❏ 71169	Moonlight Swim/Lucy Lou	1957	2.50	5.00	10.00
❏ 71233	Halo of Love/Sweet Treat	1957	2.50	5.00	10.00
TMS					
❏ 601	The Girl on the Other Side/ Why Don't You Believe Me	1979	—	3.00	6.00
❏ 612	I Wanna Go Back/(B-side unknown)	1979	—	3.00	6.00
20TH CENTURY FOX					
❏ 6612	The Girl with the Long Red Hair/Simple, Simple	1965	2.00	4.00	8.00

N

Number	Title (A Side/B Side)	Yr	VG	VG+	NM

WING
❏ 90003	The Bible Tells Me So/Army of the Lord	1955	3.00	6.00	12.00
❏ 90028	The Best Is Yet to Come/If It Happened to You	1955	3.00	6.00	12.00
❏ 90042	Lovely Lies/Bella Bella Perzicella	1955	3.00	6.00	12.00
❏ 90045	To You My Love/You Are My Only Love	1955	3.75	7.50	15.00

Albums
COLUMBIA
| ❏ CS 9810 | I'm Gonna Make You Love Me | 1969 | 3.75 | 7.50 | 15.00 |
LIBERTY
| ❏ LRP-3302 [M] | Relax | 1963 | 5.00 | 10.00 | 20.00 |
| ❏ LST-7302 [M] | Relax | 1963 | 6.25 | 12.50 | 25.00 |
MERCURY
| ❏ MG-20182 [M] | You Don't Know What Love Is | 1956 | 6.25 | 12.50 | 25.00 |
WING
| ❏ MGW-12184 [M] | Music for Lovers | 196? | 3.75 | 7.50 | 15.00 |

NOBLES, CLIFF
45s
ATLANTIC
| ❏ 2352 | My Love Is Getting Stronger/Too Fond of You | 1966 | 2.00 | 4.00 | 8.00 |
| ❏ 2380 | Your Love Is All I Need/Everybody Is Weak for Somebody | 1967 | 2.00 | 4.00 | 8.00 |
JAMIE
| ❏ 1406 | The Horse/If You Don't | 1972 | — | 3.00 | 6.00 |
MOON SHOT
| ❏ 6710 | Pony the Horse/Little Claudie | 1969 | 2.00 | 4.00 | 8.00 |
PHIL-L.A. OF SOUL
❏ 310	The More I Do for You Baby/This Love Will Last	1968	2.00	4.00	8.00
❏ 313	The Horse/Love Is All Right	1968	2.50	5.00	10.00
❏ 318	Horse Fever/Judge Baby, I'm Back	1968	2.00	4.00	8.00
❏ 324	Switch It On/Burning Desire	1969	2.00	4.00	8.00
❏ 329	The Camel/Goin' Away	1969	2.00	4.00	8.00
ROULETTE
| ❏ 7142 | This Feeling of Loneliness/We Got Our Thing Together | 1973 | — | 3.00 | 6.00 |

Albums
MOON SHOT
| ❏ 601 | Pony the Horse | 1969 | 10.00 | 20.00 | 40.00 |
PHIL-L.A. OF SOUL
| ❏ 4001 | The Horse | 1968 | 15.00 | 30.00 | 60.00 |

NOBLES, THE (1)
45s
ABC-PARAMOUNT
| ❏ 9984 | Till the End of Time/Standing Loose | 1958 | 6.25 | 12.50 | 25.00 |
| ❏ 10012 | Just for Me/To Me | 1959 | 6.25 | 12.50 | 25.00 |

NOBLES, THE (2)
45s
KLIK
| ❏ 305 | Poor Rock and Roll/Ting-a-Ling | 1958 | 50.00 | 100.00 | 200.00 |
LOST-NITE
| ❏ 153 | Poor Rock and Roll/Ting-a-Ling | 196? | — | 3.00 | 6.00 |
—Reissue
TIMES SQUARE
| ❏ 1 | Poor Rock and Roll/Ting-a-Ling | 1963 | 6.25 | 12.50 | 25.00 |
—Green vinyl
| ❏ 1 | Poor Rock and Roll/Ting-a-Ling | 1963 | 7.50 | 15.00 | 30.00 |
—Blue vinyl
| ❏ 12 | Crime Doesn't Pay/Darkness | 1963 | 5.00 | 10.00 | 20.00 |
—All copies on blue vinyl
| ❏ 33 | Why Be a Fool/The Search | 1964 | 5.00 | 10.00 | 20.00 |

NOBLES, THE (3)
45s
SELBON
| ❏ 1005 | Black Widow/Jaguar | 1963 | 10.00 | 20.00 | 40.00 |

NOBLES, THE (4)
45s
STACY
| ❏ 926 | Serenade/You Ain't Right | 1962 | 10.00 | 20.00 | 40.00 |

NOBLES, THE (5)
45s
U.S.A.
| ❏ 788 | Marlene/That Special One | 1965 | 6.25 | 12.50 | 25.00 |

NOBLES, THE (U)
45s
TEE GEE
| ❏ 101 | Oops Oh Lawdy/Stop Crying | 1958 | 12.50 | 25.00 | 50.00 |

NOCTURNES, THE
45s
CARLSON INT'L
| ❏ 4105 | My Christmas Star/(B-side unknown) | 1964 | 15.00 | 30.00 | 60.00 |

NODAENS, THE With Dave Nowlen, formerly of THE SURVIVORS.
45s
GOLD
| ❏ 1001 | Beach Girl/Gypsy | 196? | 20.00 | 40.00 | 80.00 |

NOEL, SID
45s
ALADDIN
| ❏ 3331 | The Flying Saucer (Part 1)/The Flying Saucer (Part 2) | 1956 | 10.00 | 20.00 | 40.00 |
—Cover version of the Buchanan and Goodman break-in record

NOGUEZ, JACKY
45s
JAMIE
❏ 1127	Ciao, Ciao Bambina (Chiow, Chiow, Bambeena)/De Serait Dommage	1959	3.00	6.00	12.00
❏ 1137	Marina/Adonis	1959	3.00	6.00	12.00
❏ 1148	Amapola/Mahzel	1959	3.00	6.00	12.00
❏ 1148 [PS]	Amapola/Mahzel	1959	3.75	7.50	15.00

Albums
JAMIE
❏ JLP-3007 [M]	Chow Chow Bambina	1959	5.00	10.00	20.00
❏ JLPS-3007 [S]	Chow Chow Bambina	1959	7.50	15.00	30.00
❏ JLP-3012 [M]	Jacky Noguez	1960	5.00	10.00	20.00
❏ JLPS-3012 [S]	Jacky Noguez	1960	7.50	15.00	30.00
❏ JLP-3013 [M]	Dance Along with Jacky Noguez	1960	5.00	10.00	20.00
❏ JLPS-3013 [S]	Dance Along with Jacky Noguez	1960	7.50	15.00	30.00

NOLAN, FRANKIE
45s
ABC-PARAMOUNT
| ❏ 10231 | I Still Care/(I Wish It Were) Summer All Year Round | 1961 | 10.00 | 20.00 | 40.00 |
—Frankie Valli also appears on this record

NOLAND, TERRY
45s
APT
| ❏ 25065 | There Goes a Girl/Long Gone Baby | 1962 | 3.75 | 7.50 | 15.00 |
BRUNSWICK
❏ 55010	Hypnotized/Ten Little Women	1957	7.50	15.00	30.00
❏ 55036	Patty Baby/Don't Do Me This Way	1957	7.50	15.00	30.00
❏ 55054	Puppy Love/Oh Baby, Look at Me	1958	7.50	15.00	30.00
❏ 55069	Crazy Dream/Everyone But One	1958	7.50	15.00	30.00
❏ 55092	There Was a Fungus Among Us/Sugar Drop	1958	10.00	20.00	40.00
❏ 55122	Guess I'm Gonna Fall/Teenage Teardrops	1959	7.50	15.00	30.00
CORAL
| ❏ 62274 | There Was a Fungus Among Us/Sugar Drop | 1961 | 5.00 | 10.00 | 20.00 |
Albums
BRUNSWICK
| ❏ BL 54041 [M] | Terry Noland | 1958 | 150.00 | 300.00 | 600.00 |
—Buddy Holly plays guitar

NON-CONFORMISTS, THE
45s
SCEPTER
| ❏ 12184 | Two-Legged Big Eyed Yellow Haired Crying Canary/Bird Walk | 1967 | 7.50 | 15.00 | 30.00 |

NOONE, PETER Also see HERMAN'S HERMITS.
45s
BELL
| ❏ 45131 | Oh You Pretty Thing/Because You're There | 1971 | 12.50 | 25.00 | 50.00 |
—Allegedly features David Bowie on A-side piano
| ❏ 45266 | Should I/(B-side unknown) | 1972 | 2.00 | 4.00 | 8.00 |
CASABLANCA
❏ 0017	Meet Me at the Corner Down at Joe's Cafe/(Blame It)On the Pony Express	1974	—	2.50	5.00
❏ 0106	Meet Me at the Corner Down at Joe's Cafe/(Blame It)On the Pony Express	1974	—	2.00	4.00
❏ 802	Meet Me at the Corner Down at Joe's Cafe/(Blame It)On the Pony Express	1974	—	2.00	4.00
❏ 823	Something Old, Something New/(B-side unknown)	1975	—	2.00	4.00
JOHNSTON
| ❏ 02838 | (I Don't Wanna Love You But) You Got Me Anyway/I'm One of the Glory Boys | 1982 | — | 2.00 | 4.00 |
PHILIPS
| ❏ 40730 | All SIng Together/Getting Over You | 1974 | — | 2.50 | 5.00 |
Albums
JOHNSTON
| ❏ ARZ 37369 | One of the Glory Boys | 1982 | 2.50 | 5.00 | 10.00 |

NORMAN, GENE, AND THE ROCKIN' ROCKETS
45s
SNAG
| ❏ 101 | Snaggle Tooth Ann/Long Gone Night Train | 1958 | 250.00 | 500.00 | 1000. |

NORMAN, JIMMY
45s
BUDDAH
| ❏ 439 | Funk Don't Mean a Scent/In the Palm of Another's Hand | 1974 | 3.75 | 7.50 | 15.00 |
| ❏ 504 | I Wanna Make Love to You/Fallin' in Love | 1975 | 3.00 | 6.00 | 12.00 |
DOT
| ❏ 16016 | Green Stamps/Just to Get to You | 1959 | 7.50 | 15.00 | 30.00 |
JOSIE
| ❏ 994 | Gangster of Love/Gangster of Love Pt. 2 | 1968 | 6.25 | 12.50 | 25.00 |
LITTLE STAR
❏ 113	I Don't Love You No More (I Don't Care About You)/Tell Her for Me	1962	5.00	10.00	20.00
❏ 121	You Crack Me Up/I Know I'm in Love	1962	10.00	20.00	40.00
❏ 126	Love Is Wonderful/What's the Word, Do the Bird	1963	7.50	15.00	30.00
MUN-RAB
| ❏ 102 | You Win Again/Thank Him | 1959 | 10.00 | 20.00 | 40.00 |
POLO
| ❏ 211 | Dotted Line/You Crack Me Up | 1964 | 15.00 | 30.00 | 60.00 |
RAY STAR
| ❏ 781 | I'll Never Be Free/Lovesick Feeling | 1961 | 10.00 | 20.00 | 40.00 |
| ❏ 783 | One of These Days/Someone to Care For | 1962 | 10.00 | 20.00 | 40.00 |
SAMAR
| ❏ 112 | You're Only Hurting Yourself/That Little Old Groovemaker | 1966 | 50.00 | 100.00 | 200.00 |
—Jimi Hendrix played guitar on these two sides
| ❏ 116 | Can You Blame Me/This I Beg of You | 1966 | 6.25 | 12.50 | 25.00 |

NORMAN, LARRY A founding father of Christian rock. Also see PEOPLE.
45s
CAPITOL
| ❏ 2766 | Sweet Sweet Song of Salvation/Walking Backwards Down the Stairs | 1970 | 5.00 | 10.00 | 20.00 |
MGM
❏ 14351	Righteous Rocker, Holy Rocker/Peace, Pollution, Revolution	1972	3.75	7.50	15.00
❏ 14676	Christmas Time/The Same Old Story	1973	3.75	7.50	15.00
❏ 14703	Nightmare/Baroquen Spirits	1974	3.75	7.50	15.00

Number	Title (A Side/B Side)	Yr	VG	VG+	NM
SOLID ROCK					
❑ 202	Christmas Time/The Christmas Song	1976	2.00	4.00	8.00
VERVE					
❑ 10718	I've Got to Learn to Live Without You/Readers Digest	1973	5.00	10.00	20.00
❑ 10720	I've Got to Learn to Live Without You/The Outlaw	1973	5.00	10.00	20.00
Albums					
AB					
❑ 777	Streams of White Light Into Darkened Corners	1977	6.25	12.50	25.00
CAPITOL					
❑ ST-446	Upon This Rock	1970	7.50	15.00	30.00
IMPACT					
❑ 3121	Upon This Rock	197?	5.00	10.00	20.00
MGM					
❑ SE-4942	So Long Ago the Garden	1974	10.00	20.00	40.00
ONE WAY					
❑ 900	Bootleg	1972	7.50	15.00	30.00
—Regular cover					
❑ 4847	Bootleg	1972	10.00	20.00	40.00
—Gatefold cover					
❑ 7397	Street Level	1971	7.50	15.00	30.00
PHYDEAUX					
❑ ARF-777-6	Almost So Long Ago the Garden	1984	3.00	6.00	12.00
❑ BONE-777-6	Almost So Long Ago the Garden	1981	3.75	7.50	15.00
SOLID ROCK					
❑ 2001	In Another Land	1976	3.75	7.50	15.00
❑ 2007	Something New Under the Son	1981	3.75	7.50	15.00
STREET LEVEL					
❑ ROCK-888-5	Only Visiting This Planet	1978	3.00	6.00	12.00
—Regular cover					
❑ ROCK-888-5	Only Visiting This Planet	1978	3.75	7.50	15.00
—Gatefold cover					
VERVE					
❑ V6-5092	Only Visiting This Planet	1973	7.50	15.00	30.00
—Tri-fold cover					
❑ V6-5092	Only Visiting This Planet	1973	10.00	20.00	40.00
—Gatefold cover					

NORMANAIRES, THE
45s

Number	Title (A Side/B Side)	Yr	VG	VG+	NM
MGM					
❑ 11622	My Greatest Sin/Wrap It Up	1953	20.00	40.00	80.00

NORRIS, CHARLES
45s

Number	Title (A Side/B Side)	Yr	VG	VG+	NM
ATLANTIC					
❑ 994	Messin' Up/Let Me Know	1953	15.00	30.00	60.00

NORTH, FREDDIE
45s

Number	Title (A Side/B Side)	Yr	VG	VG+	NM
A-BET					
❑ 9418	Don't Make Me Look So Bad/Hold Back	1967	3.00	6.00	12.00
❑ 9430	I Have a Dream/(Instrumental)	1968	2.50	5.00	10.00
❑ 9436	Oh Lord, What Are You Doing to Me/Long Hard Road	1968	2.50	5.00	10.00
❑ 9439	Love to Hate/Thank That Woman	1969	2.50	5.00	10.00
❑ 9440	Follow the Lamb/From the Blind Side	1969	2.50	5.00	10.00
CAPITOL					
❑ 4832	Just to Please You/Ninety-Pound Woman	1962	3.75	7.50	15.00
❑ 4873	Just to Please You/Ninety-Pound Woman	1962	3.75	7.50	15.00
MANKIND					
❑ 12004	She's All I Got/Ain't Nothin' in the News (But the Blues)	1971	2.00	4.00	8.00
❑ 12009	You and Me Together Forever/Did I Come Back Too Soon (Or Stay Away Too Long)	1972	2.00	4.00	8.00
❑ 12011	Sweeter Than Sweetness/I Did the Woman Wrong	1972	2.00	4.00	8.00
❑ 12014	Roll Over (Play Like Love Ain't Dead)/Are You Thinking of Him	1972	2.00	4.00	8.00
❑ 12016	Song #29 (I'm Your Man)/Laid Back and Easy	1972	2.00	4.00	8.00
❑ 12018	You're Killing Me Slowly But Surely/It's So Groovy Doing What You Want to Do	1973	2.00	4.00	8.00
❑ 12019	Lovin' on Back Streets/Love to Hate	1973	2.00	4.00	8.00
❑ 12020	Taking Her Love Ain't Gonna Be Easy/Raining on a Sunny Day	1973	2.00	4.00	8.00
❑ 12022	Love to Hate/Cuss the Wind	197?	2.50	5.00	10.00
❑ 12025	I Loved Another Woman/Rainy Night in Georgia	197?	2.00	4.00	8.00
PHILLIPS INT'L.					
❑ 3574	Don't Make Me Cry/Sometime She'll Come Along	1962	6.25	12.50	25.00
RIC					
❑ 119	The Hurt/It's No Good for Me	1964	50.00	100.00	200.00
UNIVERSITY					
❑ 605	How to Cry/OK, So What?	1960	7.50	15.00	30.00
Albums					
MANKIND					
❑ 204	Friend	1971	6.25	12.50	25.00
❑ 205	Cuss the Wind	1973	10.00	20.00	40.00

NORTH, JAY
45s

Number	Title (A Side/B Side)	Yr	VG	VG+	NM
KEM					
❑ 2756	The Cat And The Christmas Tree/Christmas For Tommy	1960	3.75	7.50	15.00
Albums					
KEM					
❑ 27	Look Who's Singing!	1960	25.00	50.00	100.00

NORTHCOTT, TOM
45s

Number	Title (A Side/B Side)	Yr	VG	VG+	NM
UNI					
❑ 55267	I Think It's Going to Rain Today/It's True	1971	—	3.50	7.00
❑ 55288	Suzanne/Spaceship Races	1971	—	3.50	7.00
WARNER BROS.					
❑ 7051	Sunny Goodge Street/Who Planted Thorns in Miss Alice's Garden	1967	2.50	5.00	10.00

Number	Title (A Side/B Side)	Yr	VG	VG+	NM
❑ 7160	1941/Other Times	1968	2.00	4.00	8.00
❑ 7212	Girl from the north Country/Landscape Grown Cold	1968	3.00	6.00	12.00
❑ 7283	Make Me an Island/High Hope	1969	3.00	6.00	12.00
❑ 7330	The Rainmaker/Cities Make the Country Colder	1969	3.00	6.00	12.00

NORTHERN LIGHT
45s

Number	Title (A Side/B Side)	Yr	VG	VG+	NM
COLUMBIA					
❑ 3-10136	Minnesota/Theme from Minnesota	1975	—	2.50	5.00
GLACIER					
❑ 4501	Minnesota/Theme from Minnesota	1974	2.00	4.00	8.00
❑ 4504	Runnin'/The Runner	197?	—	3.00	6.00

NORTHERN LIGHTS, THE With Bjorn Ulvaeus, later of ABBA.
45s

Number	Title (A Side/B Side)	Yr	VG	VG+	NM
UNITED ARTISTS					
❑ 991	Time to Move Along/No Time	1966	5.00	10.00	20.00

NORWOOD, DOROTHY
45s

Number	Title (A Side/B Side)	Yr	VG	VG+	NM
GRC					
❑ 1011	There's Got to Be Rain in Your Life (To Appreciate the Sunshine)/Get Aboard the Soul Train	1973	2.00	4.00	8.00
❑ 2009	Mama Loves Her Children All the Time (Part 1)/(Part 2)	1974	2.00	4.00	8.00
❑ 2057	Let Your Feet Down Easy/What a Beautiful World	1975	—	3.50	7.00
JEWEL					
❑ 262	He's a Friend/There Is Someone Who Cares for You	1978	—	3.00	6.00
SAVOY					
❑ 4204	Johnny and Jesus/Failure Is Not in God, It's in Me	1963	3.75	7.50	15.00
❑ 4223	I'm Thine, Oh Lord/The Old Lady's House	1964	3.75	7.50	15.00
❑ 4261	A Boy and His Kite/(B-side unknown)	1966	3.00	6.00	12.00
❑ 4282	The Singing Slave/(B-side unknown)	1967	3.00	6.00	12.00
❑ 4301	In That Little Town/Prescription	1969	2.50	5.00	10.00
❑ 4325	Jesus Is a Soul Man/Our Prayer	1969	2.50	5.00	10.00
❑ 4338	Precious Lord/(B-side unknown)	1970	2.50	5.00	10.00
Albums					
I AM					
❑ 4002-1-M	A Wonderful Day	1990	3.75	7.50	15.00
JEWEL					
❑ 0134	He's a Friend	1978	3.75	7.50	15.00
SAVOY					
❑ SL-7042 [(2)]	The Mountain Climbers	1979	5.00	10.00	20.00
❑ MG 14083 [M]	Johnny and Jesus	196?	6.25	12.50	25.00
❑ MG 14093 [M]	The Old Lady's House	196?	6.25	12.50	25.00
❑ MG 14107 [M]	The Bell Didn't Toll	196?	6.25	12.50	25.00
❑ MG 14127 [M]	He Will Never Let Go My Hand	196?	6.25	12.50	25.00
❑ MG 14140 [M]	Denied Mother	196?	6.25	12.50	25.00
❑ MG 14157 [M]	Soldier from Vietnam	196?	6.25	12.50	25.00
❑ MG 14169 [M]	The Dorothy Norwood Singers	196?	6.25	12.50	25.00
❑ MG 14175 [M]	The Singing Slave	196?	6.25	12.50	25.00
❑ MG 14190 [M]	Bereaved Child	196?	6.25	12.50	25.00
❑ MG 14212	The Stories Behind the Songs	196?	6.25	12.50	25.00
❑ MG 14217	Just in Time	196?	6.25	12.50	25.00
❑ MG 14244	Brother Came Too Late	196?	6.25	12.50	25.00
❑ MG 14259	Jesus Picked Up the Pieces	196?	6.25	12.50	25.00
❑ MG 14266	Despondent Wife	196?	6.25	12.50	25.00
❑ MG 14282	Three Little Pigs	197?	6.25	12.50	25.00
—With Lois Snead					
❑ MG 14295	Just the Two of Us	1972	6.25	12.50	25.00
—With Lois Snead					
❑ MG 14309	Come By Here	1973	6.25	12.50	25.00
❑ SL-14515	Faithful Daughter	198?	3.75	7.50	15.00
❑ SL-14557	God Can	198?	3.75	7.50	15.00
❑ SL-14598	Answer Me Dear Jesus	198?	3.75	7.50	15.00
❑ SL-14630	Look What They've Done to My Child	198?	3.75	7.50	15.00
❑ SL-14651	Somebody Here	198?	3.75	7.50	15.00
—With the Allen Darling Ensemble					
❑ SL-14716	Up Where We Belong	1983	3.75	7.50	15.00
WORD					
❑ WR-8420	Mother's Son	1988	2.50	5.00	10.00

NOSY PARKER
Albums

Number	Title (A Side/B Side)	Yr	VG	VG+	NM
(NO LABEL)					
❑ (no #)	Nosy Parker	1975	62.50	125.00	250.00

NOTE-TORIALS, THE
45s

Number	Title (A Side/B Side)	Yr	VG	VG+	NM
IMPALA					
❑ 201	Valerie/Loved and Lost	1958	250.00	500.00	1000.
SUNBEAM					
❑ 119	Valerie/Loved and Lost	1958	50.00	100.00	200.00

NOTES, THE
45s

Number	Title (A Side/B Side)	Yr	VG	VG+	NM
CAPITOL					
❑ F3332	Don't Leave Me Now/Cha Jezebel	1956	75.00	150.00	300.00
MGM					
❑ 12338	Trust in Me/Round and Round	1956	50.00	100.00	200.00
SARG					
❑ 177	Little Girl/G.I. Blues	1959	12.50	25.00	50.00

NOVA LOCAL, THE
45s

Number	Title (A Side/B Side)	Yr	VG	VG+	NM
DECCA					
❑ 32138	Games/If You Only Had the Time	1967	5.00	10.00	20.00
❑ 32194	Other Girls/John Knight's Body (I Wanna Get Out)	1967	5.00	10.00	20.00
Albums					
DECCA					
❑ DL 74977	Nova 1	1968	17.50	35.00	70.00

N

Number	Title (A Side/B Side)	Yr	VG	VG+	NM

NOVAS, THE
45s
PARROT

Number	Title (A Side/B Side)	Yr	VG	VG+	NM
❏ 45005	The Crusher/Take 7	1964	20.00	40.00	80.00

TWIN TOWN

Number	Title (A Side/B Side)	Yr	VG	VG+	NM
❏ 713	Novas Coaster/On the Road Again	1965	10.00	20.00	40.00

NOVELLS, THE
Albums
MOTHER'S

Number	Title (A Side/B Side)	Yr	VG	VG+	NM
❏ MLPS-73	A Happening	1968	12.50	25.00	50.00

NRBQ
45s
BEARSVILLE

Number	Title (A Side/B Side)	Yr	VG	VG+	NM
❏ 29588	Rain at the Drive-In/Shackaroo	1983	—	2.50	5.00

BUTTON

Number	Title (A Side/B Side)	Yr	VG	VG+	NM
❏ 037	Froggy Went a-Courtin'/ Bless Your Beautiful Hide	1975	12.50	25.00	50.00

COLUMBIA

Number	Title (A Side/B Side)	Yr	VG	VG+	NM
❏ 44865	Stomp/I Didn't Know Myself	1969	—	3.00	6.00
❏ 44937	C'mon Everybody/Rocket No. 9	1969	—	3.00	6.00
❏ 45019	Sure to Fall (In Love With You)/Down in My Heart	1969	—	3.00	6.00

KAMA SUTRA

Number	Title (A Side/B Side)	Yr	VG	VG+	NM
❏ 544	Howard Johnson's Got His Hojo Workin'/ Do You Feel It	1972	—	3.00	6.00
❏ 549	Only You/Magnet	1972	—	3.00	6.00
❏ 575	C'mon If You're Comin'/RC Cola and a Moon Pie	1973	—	3.00	6.00
❏ 586	Get That Gasoline Blues/Mona	1974	—	3.00	6.00

MERCURY

Number	Title (A Side/B Side)	Yr	VG	VG+	NM
❏ 73991	Green Lights/I Love Her, She Loves Me	1978	—	2.50	5.00

RED ROOSTER

Number	Title (A Side/B Side)	Yr	VG	VG+	NM
❏ 1001	Ridin' in My Car/Do the Bump	1977	2.50	5.00	10.00
❏ 1002	I Got a Rocket in My Pocket/Tapdancin' Bats	1977	—	3.00	6.00
❏ 1002 [PS]	I Got a Rocket in My Pocket/Tapdancin' Bats	1977	2.50	5.00	10.00
❏ 1006	Christmas Wish/Jolly Old St. Nicholas	1978	2.50	5.00	10.00
❏ 1006 [PS]	Christmas Wish/Jolly Old St. Nicholas	1978	2.50	5.00	10.00

ROUNDER

Number	Title (A Side/B Side)	Yr	VG	VG+	NM
❏ 1010	Captain Lou!/Boardin' House Pie	1982	—	2.00	4.00
❏ 1010 [PS]	Captain Lou!/Boardin' House Pie	1982	—	2.00	4.00
❏ 4521	Hot Biscuits and Sweet Marie/ She Don't Look Good	1979	—	2.50	5.00
❏ 4522	Get That Gasoline Blues/Wacky Tobacky	1979	—	2.50	5.00
❏ 4525	Christmas Wish/Jolly Old St. Nicholas	1979	—	2.50	5.00
❏ 4525 [PS]	Christmas Wish/Jolly Old St. Nicholas	1979	—	3.00	6.00
❏ 4531	Me and the Boys/People	1980	—	2.50	5.00
❏ 4531 [PS]	Me and the Boys/People	1980	2.50	5.00	10.00
❏ 4539	Never Take the Place of You/ Captain Lou Albano for Tiddlywinks	1980	—	2.50	5.00
❏ 4556	Things to Do/I Can't Stop Loving You Now	1985	—	2.00	4.00

—With Skeeter Davis

SCEPTER

Number	Title (A Side/B Side)	Yr	VG	VG+	NM
❏ 12322	Sho' Need Love/Don't Talk About My Music1	1971	12.50	25.00	50.00

—As "The Dickens"

SELECT-O-HIT

Number	Title (A Side/B Side)	Yr	VG	VG+	NM
❏ 022	Sourpuss/Rumors	1974	12.50	25.00	50.00

VIRGIN

Number	Title (A Side/B Side)	Yr	VG	VG+	NM
❏ 99130	If I Don't Have You/Boozoo, That's Who	1989	—	2.00	4.00
❏ 99161 [DJ]	Wild Weekend/This Love Is True	1989	—	2.00	4.00

7-Inch Extended Plays
RED ROOSTER

Number	Title (A Side/B Side)	Yr	VG	VG+	NM
❏ EP-1	Christmas Wish/Here Comes Santa Claus// God Rest Ye Merry Gentlemen/Message from the North Pole	1979	3.75	7.50	15.00

—Called "Merry Christmas from NRBQ"; not issued with cover

Albums
ANNUIT COEPTIS

Number	Title (A Side/B Side)	Yr	VG	VG+	NM
❏ 1001/2 [(2)]	Scraps/Workshop	1976	5.00	10.00	20.00

—Reissue of Kama Sutra LPs

BEARSVILLE

Number	Title (A Side/B Side)	Yr	VG	VG+	NM
❏ 23817	Grooves in Orbit	1983	2.50	5.00	10.00

COLUMBIA

Number	Title (A Side/B Side)	Yr	VG	VG+	NM
❏ CS 9858	NRBQ	1969	6.25	12.50	25.00

—"360 Sound Stereo" label

Number	Title (A Side/B Side)	Yr	VG	VG+	NM
❏ CS 9858	NRBQ	1970	3.00	6.00	12.00

—Orange label

Number	Title (A Side/B Side)	Yr	VG	VG+	NM
❏ PC 9858	NRBQ	198?	2.00	4.00	8.00

—Budget-line reissue

KAMA SUTRA

Number	Title (A Side/B Side)	Yr	VG	VG+	NM
❏ KSBS-2045	Scraps	1972	7.50	15.00	30.00
❏ KSBS-2065	Workshop	1973	10.00	20.00	40.00

MERCURY

Number	Title (A Side/B Side)	Yr	VG	VG+	NM
❏ SRM-1-3712	NRBQ at Yankee Stadium	1978	3.75	7.50	15.00
❏ 824462-1	NRBQ at Yankee Stadium	1984	2.50	5.00	10.00

—Reissue

RED ROOSTER

Number	Title (A Side/B Side)	Yr	VG	VG+	NM
❏ 101	All Hopped Up	1977	3.75	7.50	15.00

ROUNDER

Number	Title (A Side/B Side)	Yr	VG	VG+	NM
❏ EP-2501 [EP]	Christmas Wish	1985	3.00	6.00	12.00
❏ 3029	All Hopped Up	1979	3.00	6.00	12.00
❏ 3030	Kick Me Hard	1979	3.00	6.00	12.00
❏ 3048	Tiddlywinks	1980	3.00	6.00	12.00
❏ 3055	Scraps	1982	2.50	5.00	10.00
❏ 3066	Tapdancin' Bats	1983	2.50	5.00	10.00
❏ 3090	RC Cola & a Moon Pie	1987	2.50	5.00	10.00
❏ 3098	Lou and the Q	1986	2.50	5.00	10.00

—With pro wrestler Captain Lou Albano

Number	Title (A Side/B Side)	Yr	VG	VG+	NM
❏ 3108	God Bless Us All	1988	2.50	5.00	10.00
❏ 3109	Live! Diggin' Uncle Q	1988	2.50	5.00	10.00

SUNDAZED

Number	Title (A Side/B Side)	Yr	VG	VG+	NM
❏ LP-5162	Atsa My Band	2003	3.75	7.50	15.00

VIRGIN

Number	Title (A Side/B Side)	Yr	VG	VG+	NM
❏ 91291	Wild Weekend	1989	2.50	5.00	10.00

NU-TONES, THE
45s
COMBO

Number	Title (A Side/B Side)	Yr	VG	VG+	NM
❏ 127	At Midnight/Beans 'N' Greens	1957	37.50	75.00	150.00

HOLLYWOOD STAR

Number	Title (A Side/B Side)	Yr	VG	VG+	NM
❏ 798	You're No Barking Dog/Believe	1955	150.00	300.00	600.00
❏ 798	Annie Kicked the Bucket/Believe	1955	2000.	4000.	8000.

NU TORNADOS, THE
45s
CARLTON

Number	Title (A Side/B Side)	Yr	VG	VG+	NM
❏ 492	Philadelphia, U.S.A./Magic Record	1959	6.25	12.50	25.00
❏ 497	The "Ole Mummers" Strut/Let's Have a Party	1959	5.00	10.00	20.00

FELSTED

Number	Title (A Side/B Side)	Yr	VG	VG+	NM
❏ 8577	Cry Baby Cry/Keep a Flower Growing in Your Heart	1959	5.00	10.00	20.00

NUGENT, TED   Also see THE AMBOY DUKES.
45s
ATLANTIC

Number	Title (A Side/B Side)	Yr	VG	VG+	NM
❏ 89436	Little Miss Dangerous/Angry Young Man	1986	—	—	3.00
❏ 89442	High Heels in Motion/Angry Young Man	1986	—	—	3.00
❏ 89442 [PS]	High Heels in Motion/Angry Young Man	1986	—	2.00	4.00
❏ 89661	Lean Mean R&R Machine/(Where Do You) Draw the Line	1984	—	—	3.00
❏ 89705	Tied Up in Love/Lean Mean R&R Machine	1984	—	2.50	5.00

—Promo copies, with "Tied Up in Love" on both sides, go for less

Number	Title (A Side/B Side)	Yr	VG	VG+	NM
❏ 89705 [PS]	Tied Up in Love/Lean Mean R&R Machine	1984	—	2.50	5.00
❏ 89978	No, No, No/Habitual Offender	1982	—	—	3.00
❏ 89998	Bound and Gagged/Habitual Offender	1982	—	—	3.00
❏ 89998 [PS]	Bound and Gagged/Habitual Offender	1982	—	2.50	5.00

EPIC

Number	Title (A Side/B Side)	Yr	VG	VG+	NM
❏ 01046	Land of a Thousand Dances/The TNT Overture	1981	—	2.00	4.00
❏ 50172	Motor City Madness/ Where Have You Been All My Life	1975	—	2.50	5.00
❏ 50197	Hey Baby/Stormtroopin'	1976	—	2.50	5.00
❏ 50301	Dog Eat Dog/Light My Way	1976	—	2.50	5.00
❏ 50363	Free-for-All/Street Rags	1977	—	2.00	4.00
❏ 50425	Cat Scratch Fever/Wang Dang Sweet Poontang	1977	—	2.50	5.00
❏ 50493	Death by Misadventure/Home Bound	1977	—	2.00	4.00
❏ 50533	Yank Me, Crank Me/Cat Scratch Fever	1978	—	2.00	4.00
❏ 50648	Need You Bad/Need to Get the Feelin'	1979	—	2.00	4.00
❏ 50713	I Want to Tell You/Bite Down Hard	1979	—	2.00	4.00
❏ 50907	Wango Tango/Scream Dream	1980	—	2.00	4.00

Albums
ATLANTIC

Number	Title (A Side/B Side)	Yr	VG	VG+	NM
❏ SD 19365	Nugent	1982	2.50	5.00	10.00
❏ 80125	Penetrator	1984	2.50	5.00	10.00
❏ 81632	Little Miss Dangerous	1986	2.50	5.00	10.00
❏ 81812	If You Can't Lick 'Em...Lick 'Em	1988	2.50	5.00	10.00

EPIC

Number	Title (A Side/B Side)	Yr	VG	VG+	NM
❏ AS99-607 [PD]	State of Shock	1979	10.00	20.00	40.00

—Promo-only picture disc

Number	Title (A Side/B Side)	Yr	VG	VG+	NM
❏ PE 33692	Ted Nugent	1975	3.00	6.00	12.00

—Orange label

Number	Title (A Side/B Side)	Yr	VG	VG+	NM
❏ PE 33692	Ted Nugent	1979	2.00	4.00	8.00

—Reissue with dark blue label and bar code

Number	Title (A Side/B Side)	Yr	VG	VG+	NM
❏ PE 34121	Free-for-All	1976	3.00	6.00	12.00

—Orange label

Number	Title (A Side/B Side)	Yr	VG	VG+	NM
❏ PE 34121	Free-for-All	1979	2.00	4.00	8.00

—Reissue with dark blue label and bar code

Number	Title (A Side/B Side)	Yr	VG	VG+	NM
❏ PEQ 34121 [Q]	Free-for-All	1976	5.00	10.00	20.00
❏ JE 34700	Cat Scratch Fever	1977	3.00	6.00	12.00

—Orange label

Number	Title (A Side/B Side)	Yr	VG	VG+	NM
❏ PE 34700	Cat Scratch Fever	198?	2.00	4.00	8.00

—Reissue with dark blue label and bar code

Number	Title (A Side/B Side)	Yr	VG	VG+	NM
❏ KE2 35069 [(2)]	Double Live Gonzo!	1978	3.75	7.50	15.00

—Orange labels

Number	Title (A Side/B Side)	Yr	VG	VG+	NM
❏ FE 35551	Weekend Warriors	1978	3.00	6.00	12.00

—Orange label

Number	Title (A Side/B Side)	Yr	VG	VG+	NM
❏ PE 35551	Weekend Warriors	198?	2.00	4.00	8.00

—Reissue with dark blue label and bar code

Number	Title (A Side/B Side)	Yr	VG	VG+	NM
❏ FE 36000	State of Shock	1979	2.50	5.00	10.00
❏ PE 36000	State of Shock	198?	2.00	4.00	8.00

—Budget-line reissue

Number	Title (A Side/B Side)	Yr	VG	VG+	NM
❏ FE 36404	Scream Dream	1980	2.50	5.00	10.00
❏ FE 37084	Intensities in 10 Cities	1981	2.50	5.00	10.00
❏ PE 37084	Intensities in 10 Cities	198?	2.00	4.00	8.00

—Budget-line reissue

Number	Title (A Side/B Side)	Yr	VG	VG+	NM
❏ FE 37667	Great Gonzos! The Best of Ted Nugent	1981	2.50	5.00	10.00
❏ PE 37667	Great Gonzos! The Best of Ted Nugent	198?	2.00	4.00	8.00

—Budget-line reissue

NUGGETS, THE (1)
45s
CAPITOL

Number	Title (A Side/B Side)	Yr	VG	VG+	NM
❏ F-2989	So Help Me I Love You/Quirl Up in My Arms	1954	5.00	10.00	20.00
❏ F-3052	Anxious Heart/Shtiggy Boom	1955	3.75	7.50	15.00

NUGGETS, THE (2)
45s
RCA VICTOR

Number	Title (A Side/B Side)	Yr	VG	VG+	NM
❏ 47-7930	Before We Say Goodnight/Angel on the Dance Floor	1961	7.50	5.00	30.00
❏ 47-8031	Just a Friend/Cat Snapper	1962	3.75	7.50	15.00

NUMBERS, THE
45s
BONNEVILLE

Number	Title (A Side/B Side)	Yr	VG	VG+	NM
❏ 101	Big Red/My Pillow	1962	50.00	100.00	200.00

DORE

Number	Title (A Side/B Side)	Yr	VG	VG+	NM
❏ 641	Big Red/My Pillow	1962	12.50	25.00	50.00

NUTMEGS, THE
45s
BABY GRAND

Number	Title (A Side/B Side)	Yr	VG	VG+	NM
❏ 800	Story Untold '72/Tell Me	1972	2.00	4.00	8.00

Nazareth, *Hair of the Dog*, A&M SP-4511, stereo LP, $5-$10.

Ricky Nelson, *Songs by Ricky,* Imperial LP 9082, mono LP, black label with stars, $37.50-$75.

Willie Nelson, *Always on My Mind*, Columbia FC 37951, stereo LP, $5-$10.

Olivia Newton-John, "Please Mr. Please," MCA 40418, picture sleeve, $5-$10.

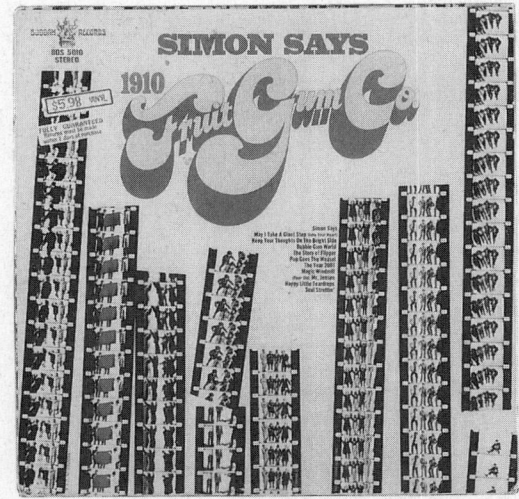

1910 Fruitgum Company, *Simon Says,* Buddah BDS-5010, stereo LP, $12.50-$25.

Ted Nugent, *Weekend Warriors*, Epic FE 35551, stereo LP, orange label, no bar code, $6-$12.

Number	Title (A Side/B Side)	Yr	VG	VG+	NM
HERALD					
❏ 452	Story Untold/Make Me Lose My Mind	1955	17.50	35.00	70.00
❏ 459	Ship of Love/Rock Me	1955	10.00	20.00	40.00
❏ 466	Whispering Sorrows/Betty Lou	1955	12.50	25.00	50.00
❏ 475	Key to the Kingdom (Of Your Heart)/				
	Gift O' Gabbin' Woman	1956	12.50	25.00	50.00
❏ 492	Love So True/Comin' Home	1956	10.00	20.00	40.00
❏ 538	My Sweet Dream/My Story	1959	10.00	20.00	40.00
❏ 574	Rip Van Winkle/Crazy 'Bout You	1962	6.25	12.50	25.00
LANA					
❏ 128	Story Untold/Beautiful Dreamer	196?	2.50	5.00	10.00
❏ 129	Tingaling/Ship of Love	196?	2.50	5.00	10.00
LOST-NITE					
❏ 412	Story Untold/Make Me Lose My Mind	197?	—	2.50	5.00
—Reissue					
❏ 430	Ship of Love/Rock Me	197?	—	2.50	5.00
—Reissue					
❏ 445	Love So True/Comin' Home	197?	—	2.50	5.00
—Reissue					
NIGHTRAIN					
❏ 905	Shifting Sands/Take Me and Make Me	1973	2.00	4.00	8.00
TEL					
❏ 1014	A Dream of Love/				
	Someone, Somewhere (Help Me)	1960	25.00	50.00	100.00
TIMES SQUARE					
❏ 6	Let Me Tell You/Hello	1963	6.25	12.50	25.00
—Blue vinyl					
❏ 14	The Way Love Should Be/Wide Hoop Skirts	1963	5.00	10.00	20.00
❏ 19	Down to Earth/Coo Coo Cuddle Coo	1963	5.00	10.00	20.00
—B-side by the Admirations					
❏ 22	Why Must We Go to School/				
	Ink Dries Quicker Than Tears	1963	5.00	10.00	20.00
—B-side by the Volumes					
❏ 27	Down in Mexico/My Sweet Dreams	1964	5.00	10.00	20.00
❏ 103	You're Crying/Wa-Do-Wa	1964	5.00	10.00	20.00
7-Inch Extended Plays					
HERALD					
❏ 452	*Story Untold/Betty Lou/Comin' Home/				
	Whispering Sorrows	1960	25.00	50.00	100.00
❏ 452 [PS]	Story Untold	1960	30.00	60.00	120.00
Albums					
COLLECTABLES					
❏ COL-5018	Greatest Hits	198?	2.50	5.00	10.00
QUICKSILVER					
❏ QS-1001	Shoo-Wop-a-Doo-Wop	198?	2.50	5.00	10.00
RELIC					
❏ LP-5002	The Nutmegs Featuring Leroy Griffin	198?	2.50	5.00	10.00
❏ LP-5011	Greatest Hits (1955-1959)	198?	2.50	5.00	10.00

NUTTY SQUIRRELS, THE
45s

Number	Title (A Side/B Side)	Yr	VG	VG+	NM
COLUMBIA					
❏ 41818	Please Don't Take Our Tree for Christmas/Nutty				
	Noel	1960	5.00	10.00	20.00
❏ 41818 [PS]	Please Don't Take Our Tree for Christmas/Nutty				
	Noel	1960	10.00	20.00	40.00
HANOVER					
❏ 4540	Uh! Oh! (Part 1)/Uh! Oh! (Part 2)	1959	6.25	12.50	25.00
❏ 4540 [PS]	Uh! Oh! (Part 1)/Uh! Oh! (Part 2)	1959	12.50	25.00	50.00
❏ 4551	Eager Beaver/Zowee	1960	5.00	10.00	20.00
RCA VICTOR					
❏ 47-8287	Hello Again/Bluesette	1963	3.75	7.50	15.00
7-Inch Extended Plays					
HANOVER					
❏ 301	Uh-Huh/Ding Dong//Salt Peanuts/Zowee	1960	10.00	20.00	40.00
❏ 301 [PS]	(title unknown)	1960	15.00	30.00	60.00
—Paper sleeve (not cardboard)					
Albums					
COLUMBIA					
❏ CL 1589 [M]	Bird Watching	1961	7.50	15.00	30.00
❏ CS 8389 [S]	Bird Watching	1961	10.00	20.00	40.00
HANOVER					
❏ HML-8014 [M]	The Nutty Squirrels	1960	12.50	25.00	50.00
MGM					
❏ E-4272 [M]	A Hard Day's Night	1964	6.25	12.50	25.00
❏ SE-4272 [S]	A Hard Day's Night	1964	7.50	15.00	30.00

NYRO, LAURA
45s

Number	Title (A Side/B Side)	Yr	VG	VG+	NM
COLUMBIA					
❏ 44531	Sweet Blindness/Eli's Comin'	1968	2.00	4.00	8.00
❏ 44786	Once It Was Alright (Farmer Joe)/Lu	1969	—	3.00	6.00
❏ 45041	Time and Love/A Man Who Sends Me Home	1969	—	3.00	6.00
❏ 45089	Save the Country/New York Tendaberry	1970	—	3.00	6.00
❏ 45230	Up On the Roof/Captain Saint Lucifer	1970	—	3.00	6.00
❏ 45298	When I Was a Freeport and You Were the Main				
	Drag/Been On a Train	1971	—	3.00	6.00
❏ JZSP139152/3 [DJ]	Sweet Blindness/Stoned Soul Picnic	1968	3.75	7.50	15.00
VERVE FOLKWAYS					
❏ 5024	Wedding Bell Blues/Stoney End	1966	2.50	5.00	10.00
❏ 5038	Billie's Blues/Goodbye Joe	1967	2.50	5.00	10.00
❏ 5051	And When I Die/Flim Flam Man	1967	2.50	5.00	10.00
VERVE FORECAST					
❏ 5095	Stoney End/Flim Flam Man	1968	2.00	4.00	8.00
❏ 5104	And When I Die/I Never Meant to Hurt You	1969	2.00	4.00	8.00
❏ 5112	Goodbye Joe/I Never Meant to Hurt You	1969	2.00	4.00	8.00
Albums					
COLUMBIA					
❏ CL 2826 [M]	Eli and the Thirteenth Confession	1968	10.00	20.00	40.00
❏ CS 9626 [S]	Eli and the Thirteenth Confession	1968	3.75	7.50	15.00
—"360 Sound Stereo" label					
❏ CS 9626	Eli and the Thirteenth Confession	1970	2.50	5.00	10.00
—Orange label					
❏ PC 9626	Eli and the Thirteenth Confession	198?	2.00	4.00	8.00
—Budget-line reissue					
❏ CS 9737	New York Tendaberry	1969	3.75	7.50	15.00
—"360 Sound Stereo" label					
❏ CS 9737	New York Tendaberry	1970	2.50	5.00	10.00
—Orange label					
❏ PC 9737	New York Tendaberry	198?	2.00	4.00	8.00
—Budget-line reissue					
❏ KC 30259	Christmas and the Beads of Sweat	1970	2.50	5.00	10.00
—Orange label					
❏ KC 30259	Christmas and the Beads of Sweat	1970	3.75	7.50	15.00
—"360 Sound Stereo" label					
❏ PC 30259	Christmas and the Beads of Sweat	198?	2.00	4.00	8.00
—Budget-line reissue					
❏ KC 30987	Gonna Take a Miracle	1971	3.75	7.50	15.00
❏ PC 30987	Gonna Take a Miracle	197?	2.00	4.00	8.00
—Budget-line reissue					
❏ KC 31410	The First Songs	1973	3.75	7.50	15.00
—Reissue of Verve Forecast 3020					
❏ PC 31410	The First Songs	197?	2.00	4.00	8.00
—Budget-line reissue					
❏ PC 33912	Smile	1976	3.00	6.00	12.00
—No bar code on cover					
❏ PC2 34331 [(2)DJ]	Season of Lights…Laura Nyro in Concert	1977	12.50	25.00	50.00
—Promo only in plain cardboard jacket; this LP was edited to one LP for release					
❏ JC 34786	Season of Lights…Laura Nyro in Concert	1977	3.00	6.00	12.00
—Edited version of above					
❏ JC 35449	Nested	1978	3.00	6.00	12.00
❏ PC 35449	Nested	198?	2.00	4.00	8.00
—Budget-line reissue					
❏ FC 39215	Mother's Spiritual	1984	2.50	5.00	10.00
VERVE FOLKWAYS					
❏ FT-3020 [M]	Laura Nyro — More Than a New Discovery	1967	7.50	15.00	30.00
❏ FTS-3020 [S]	Laura Nyro — More Than a New Discovery	1967	7.50	15.00	30.00
VERVE FORECAST					
❏ FTS-3020 [S]	Laura Nyro — More Than a New Discovery	1967	5.00	10.00	20.00
❏ FTS-3029	Laura Nyro	1968	—	—	—
—Canceled					
❏ ST 93036	Laura Nyro — More Than a New Discovery	1968	6.25	12.50	25.00
—Capitol Record Club edition					

Number	Title (A Side/B Side)	Yr	VG	VG+	NM

O

O'BRIAN, HUGH
7-Inch Extended Plays
ABC-PARAMOUNT

Number	Title (A Side/B Side)	Yr	VG	VG+	NM
❏ A-203	(contents unknown)	1957	5.00	10.00	20.00
❏ A-203 [PS]	Hugh O'Brian (TV's Wyatt Earp) Sings, Vol. I	1957	5.00	10.00	20.00
❏ B-203	(contents unknown)	1957	5.00	10.00	20.00
❏ B-203 [PS]	Hugh O'Brian (TV's Wyatt Earp) Sings, Vol. II	1957	5.00	10.00	20.00
❏ C-203	Don't Move/Timothy//I'm Walkin' Away/ Down in the Meadow	1957	5.00	10.00	20.00
❏ C-203 [PS]	Hugh O'Brian (TV's Wyatt Earp) Sings, Vol. III	1957	5.00	10.00	20.00

Albums
ABC-PARAMOUNT

Number	Title	Yr	VG	VG+	NM
❏ ABC-203 [M]	TV's Wyatt Earp Sings	1957	15.00	30.00	60.00

O'BRIEN, RHYS
45s
MGM

Number	Title	Yr	VG	VG+	NM
❏ 13862	The Word Called Love/Christmas Morning	1967	2.00	4.00	8.00

O'BRIEN, TIMMY
45s
RASON

Number	Title	Yr	VG	VG+	NM
❏ 1001	Just In Time For Christmas/I Been A Good Boy	1959	3.00	6.00	12.00

O'CONNOR, CARROLL
Albums
A&M

Number	Title	Yr	VG	VG+	NM
❏ SP-4340	Remembering You	1972	6.25	12.50	25.00

AUDIO FIDELITY

Number	Title	Yr	VG	VG+	NM
❏ AFSD-6727	Carroll O'Connor Sings for Old P.F.A.R.T.S.	1976	6.25	12.50	25.00

O'CONNOR, CARROLL, AND JEAN STAPLETON
45s
ATLANTIC

Number	Title	Yr	VG	VG+	NM
❏ 2847	Those Were the Days/Those Were the Days	1971	—	2.50	5.00
❏ 2847 [PS]	Those Were the Days/Those Were the Days	1971	2.00	4.00	8.00

O'DELL, KENNY
45s
CAPRICORN

Number	Title	Yr	VG	VG+	NM
❏ 0020	Rock and Roll Man/Ain't Gonna Study No More	1973	—	2.50	5.00
❏ 0038	You Bet Your Sweet. Sweet Love/Let's Go Find Some Country Music	1973	—	2.50	5.00
❏ 0203	I Take It On Home/I'll Find Another Way	1974	—	2.00	4.00
❏ 0219	Soulful Woman/Let's Get On the Road	1975	—	2.00	4.00
❏ 0233	My Honky Tonk Ways/Behind Closed Doors	1975	—	2.00	4.00
❏ 0247	Together This Christmas/I Can't Think When You're Doing That to Me	1975	—	2.00	4.00
❏ 0301	Let's Shake Hands and Come Out Lovin'/ We Might Be All Night	1978	—	2.00	4.00
❏ 0309	As Long As I Can Wake Up in Your Arms/ Soulful Woman	1978	—	2.00	4.00
❏ 0317	Medicine Woman/Who Do I Know in Denver	1979	—	2.00	4.00

EPIC

Number	Title	Yr	VG	VG+	NM
❏ 10693	If I Was a Rambler/High on Life	1971	—	2.50	5.00
❏ 10730	I Was a Loser (But Now I've Got You)/Jubal	1971	—	2.50	5.00
❏ 10791	I Was a Loser (But Now I've Got You)/Jubal	1971	—	2.50	5.00

KAPP

Number	Title	Yr	VG	VG+	NM
❏ 2169	Two for the Road/ Why Don't We Go Somewhere and Love	1972	—	2.50	5.00
❏ 2178	Lizzie and the Rainman/Homecoming Queen	1972	—	2.50	5.00

MAR-KAY

Number	Title	Yr	VG	VG+	NM
❏ 3696	Old Time Lovin'/Take Another Look	1966	2.50	5.00	10.00

VEGAS

Number	Title	Yr	VG	VG+	NM
❏ 718	Beautiful People/Flower Girl	1967	2.00	4.00	8.00
❏ 722	Springfield Plane/I'm Gonna Take It	1968	—	3.00	6.00
❏ 724	Happy with You/Couldn't Love You	1968	—	3.00	6.00

WHITE WHALE

Number	Title	Yr	VG	VG+	NM
❏ 319	No Obligation/(B-side unknown)	1969	—	3.00	6.00
❏ 331	Groovy Relationship/(B-side unknown)	1969	—	3.00	6.00

Albums
CAPRICORN

Number	Title	Yr	VG	VG+	NM
❏ CP 0140	Kenny O'Dell	1974	3.00	6.00	12.00
❏ CP 0211	Let's Shake Hands and Come Out Lovin'	1978	3.00	6.00	12.00

VEGAS

Number	Title	Yr	VG	VG+	NM
❏ 401	Beautiful People	1968	6.25	12.50	25.00

O'HENRY, LENNY
45s
ABC-PARAMOUNT

Number	Title	Yr	VG	VG+	NM
❏ 10222	Billy the Continental Kid/Cheated Heart	1961	3.75	7.50	15.00
❏ 10272	Goin' to a Party/Touch of You	1961	3.75	7.50	15.00

ATCO

Number	Title	Yr	VG	VG+	NM
❏ 6291	Across the Street/Saturday Angel	1964	3.00	6.00	12.00
❏ 6312	Sweet Young Love/Savin' All My Love	1964	3.00	6.00	12.00
❏ 6525	Across the Street/Saturday Angel	1967	2.00	4.00	8.00

SMASH

Number	Title	Yr	VG	VG+	NM
❏ 1800	Burning Memories/Mr. Moonlight	1963	3.00	6.00	12.00

O'JAYS, THE
12-Inch Singles
EMI

Number	Title	Yr	VG	VG+	NM
❏ SPRO-04305/24 [DJ]	Have You Had Your Love Today (2 versions)/Lovin' You	1989	2.50	5.00	10.00
❏ 4853/4 [DJ]	Merry Christmas Baby/The Christmas Song	1991	2.50	5.00	10.00
❏ V-56127	Have You Had Your Love Today (4 versions)	1989	—	3.00	6.00
❏ V-56207	Don't Let Me Down (6 versions)	1990	2.00	4.00	8.00

PHILADELPHIA INT'L.

Number	Title	Yr	VG	VG+	NM
❏ 4Z8-3708	Sing a Happy Song (5:00)/ Get On Out and Party (5:02)	1979	3.75	7.50	15.00
❏ 4Z8-3713	I Love Music (6:33)/Livin' for the Weekend (6:29)	1979	6.25	12.50	25.00

—First issue of these two dance hits on a 12-inch single

Number	Title	Yr	VG	VG+	NM
❏ 4Z9-05000	Extraordinary Girl (5:18)/(Instrumental)	1984	2.50	5.00	10.00
❏ 4Z9-05040	Let Me Show You (How Much I Really Love You) (unknown versions)	1984	2.50	5.00	10.00
❏ V-56049	Don't Take Your Love Away (3 versions)/ I Just Want Somebody to Love Me	1987	2.00	4.00	8.00
❏ SPRO-79129/30 [DJ]	Lovin' You (5:15)/ Don't Let the Dream Get Away (4:16)	1987	2.50	5.00	10.00

VOLCANO

Number	Title	Yr	VG	VG+	NM
❏ 34272	What's Stopping You (4 versions)	1997	—	3.00	6.00
❏ 37226	Pay the Bills (Main Mix) (Instrumental)/ (same on both sides)	1997	2.50	5.00	10.00

45s
APOLLO

Number	Title	Yr	VG	VG+	NM
❏ 759	Miracles/Can't Take It	1961	7.50	15.00	30.00

ASTROSCOPE

Number	Title	Yr	VG	VG+	NM
❏ 106	Wisdom of a Child/Peace	1974	2.00	4.00	8.00
❏ 110	Peace/Don't You Know a True Love (When You See Her)	1974	2.00	4.00	8.00

BELL

Number	Title	Yr	VG	VG+	NM
❏ 691	I'll Be Sweeter Tomorrow (Than I Was Today)/I Dig Your Act	1967	2.50	5.00	10.00
❏ 704	Look Over Your Shoulder/ I'm So Glad I Found You	1968	2.50	5.00	10.00
❏ 737	The Choice/Going, Going, Gone	1968	2.50	5.00	10.00
❏ 749	I Miss You/Now That I Found You	1968	2.50	5.00	10.00
❏ 770	Don't You Know a True Love/That's All Right	1969	2.00	4.00	8.00
❏ 45378	Look Over Your Shoulder/Four for the Price of One	1973	—	2.50	5.00

EMI

Number	Title	Yr	VG	VG+	NM
❏ S7-17491	Somebody Else Will/Decisions	1993	—	2.00	4.00
❏ S7-18914	Have Yourself a Merry Little Christmas/I Can Hardly Wait 'Til Christmas	1995	—	2.00	4.00
❏ B-50180	Have You Had Your Love Today/Pot Can't Call the Kettle Black	1989	—	—	3.00
❏ B-50212	Out of My Mind (Radio Mix)/(Soul 2 Mix)	1989	—	—	3.00
❏ B-50230	Serious Hold on Me/(Instrumental)	1989	—	2.00	4.00

IMPERIAL

Number	Title	Yr	VG	VG+	NM
❏ 5942	How Does It Feel/Crack Up Laughing	1963	3.75	7.50	15.00
❏ 5976	Lonely Drifter/That's Enough	1963	2.50	5.00	10.00
❏ 66007	Stand Tall/The Storm Is Over	1963	2.50	5.00	10.00
❏ 66025	I'll Never Stop Loving You/My Dearest Beloved	1964	2.50	5.00	10.00
❏ 66037	You're on Top/Lovely Dee	1964	2.50	5.00	10.00
❏ 66076	Girl Machine/Oh How You Hurt Me	1964	2.50	5.00	10.00
❏ 66102	Lipstick Traces/Think It Over, Baby	1965	2.50	5.00	10.00
❏ 66121	Whip It On Me Baby/I've Cried My Last Tear	1965	2.50	5.00	10.00
❏ 66131	You're the One (You're the Only One)/ Let It All Come Out	1965	2.50	5.00	10.00
❏ 66145	I'll Never Let You Go/It Won't Hurt	1965	2.50	5.00	10.00
❏ 66162	I'll Never Forget You/Pretty Words	1966	20.00	40.00	80.00
❏ 66177	No Time for You/It's a Blowin' Wind	1966	2.50	5.00	10.00
❏ 66197	Friday Night/Stand In for Love	1966	2.50	5.00	10.00
❏ 66200	Lonely Drifter/That's Enough	1966	2.50	5.00	10.00

LITTLE STAR

Number	Title	Yr	VG	VG+	NM
❏ 124	How Does It Feel/Crack Up Laughing	1963	6.25	12.50	25.00
❏ 125	Dream Girl/Joey St. Vincent	1963	6.25	12.50	25.00
❏ 1401	Now He's Home/Just to Be with You	1962	6.25	12.50	25.00

MINIT

Number	Title	Yr	VG	VG+	NM
❏ 32015	Hold On/Working on Your Case	1967	2.50	5.00	10.00

NEPTUNE

Number	Title	Yr	VG	VG+	NM
❏ 12	One Night Affair/There's Someone (Waiting Back Home)	1969	2.00	4.00	8.00
❏ 18	Branded Bad/ You're the Best Thing Since Candy	1969	2.00	4.00	8.00
❏ 20	Christmas Ain't Christmas New Year's Ain't New Year's Without the One You Love/ There's Someone Waiting	1969	2.50	5.00	10.00
❏ 22	Deeper (In Love with You)/I've Got the Groove	1970	2.00	4.00	8.00
❏ 31	Looky Looky (Look at Me Girl)/ Let Me in Your World	1970	2.00	4.00	8.00
❏ 33	Christmas Ain't Christmas New Year's Ain't Year's Without the One You Love/ Just Can't Get Enough	1970	2.00	4.00	8.00

PHILADELPHIA INT'L.

Number	Title	Yr	VG	VG+	NM
❏ ZS8-02096	Forever Mine/Girl, Don't Let It Get You Down	1981	—	—	3.00
—Reissue					
❏ ZS5-02834	I Just Want to Satisfy/Don't Walk Away Mad	1982	—	2.00	4.00
❏ ZS4-02982	My Favorite Person/One by One	1982	—	2.00	4.00
❏ ZS5-03009	Your Body's Here with Me (But Your Mind's on the Other Side of Town)/Out in the Real World	1982	—	2.00	4.00
❏ 3101	Hurry Up and Come Back/Identify	1979	—	2.50	5.00
❏ 3517	Back Stabbers/Sunshine	1972	—	2.50	5.00
❏ 3522	992 Arguments/Listen to the Clock on the Wall	1972	—	2.50	5.00
❏ 3524	Love Train/Who Am I	1973	—	2.50	5.00
❏ 3531	Time to Get Down/Shiftless, Shady, Jealous Kind of People	1973	—	2.50	5.00
❏ 3535	Put Your Hands Together/ You Got Your Hooks in Me	1973	—	2.50	5.00
❏ 3537	Christmas Ain't Christmas New Year's Ain't New Year's Without the One You Love/ Just Can't Get Enough	1973	—	3.00	6.00
❏ 3544	For the Love of Money/People Keep Tellin' Me	1974	—	2.50	5.00
❏ 3558	Sunshine (Part 1)/Sunshine (Part 2)	1974	—	2.50	5.00
❏ 3565	Give the People What They Want/ What Am I Waiting For	1975	—	2.50	5.00
❏ 3573	Let Me Make Love to You/Survival	1975	—	2.50	5.00
❏ 3577	I Love Music (Part 1)/I Love Music (Part 2)	1975	—	2.50	5.00
❏ 3581	Christmas Ain't Christmas New Year's Ain't New Year's Without the One You Love/ Just Can't Get Enough	1975	—	2.50	5.00
❏ 3587	Livin' for the Weekend/Stairway to Heaven	1976	—	2.50	5.00
❏ 3596	Family Reunion/Unity	1976	—	2.50	5.00
❏ 3601	Message in Our Music/She's Only a Woman	1976	—	2.50	5.00
❏ 3610	Darlin' Darlin' Baby (Sweet, Tender, Love)/ A Prayer	1976	—	2.50	5.00
❏ 3631	Work On Me/Let's Spend Some Time Together	1977	—	2.50	5.00
❏ 3642	Use Ta Be My Girl/This Time Baby	1978	—	2.50	5.00
❏ 3652	Brandy/Take Me to the Stars	1978	—	2.50	5.00
❏ 3666	Cry Together/Strokety Stroke	1978	—	2.50	5.00

Number	Title (A Side/B Side)	Yr	VG	VG+	NM
❏ 3707	Sing a Happy Song/One in a Million (Girl)	1979	—	2.50	5.00
❏ 3726	I Want You Here with Me/Get On Out and Party	1979	—	2.50	5.00
❏ 3727	Forever Mine/Get On Out and Party	1979	—	2.50	5.00
❏ ZS4-03892	I Can't Stand the Pain/A Letter to My Friends	1983	—	2.00	4.00
❏ ZS4-04069	Put Our Heads Together/Nice and Easy	1983	—	2.00	4.00
❏ ZS4-04437	Extraordinary Girl/I Really Need You Now	1984	—	2.00	4.00
❏ ZS4-04535	Let Me Show You (How Much I Really Love You)/Love You Direct	1984	—	2.00	4.00
❏ B-50013	Just Another Lonely Night/What Good Are These Arms of Mine	1985	—	—	3.00
❏ B-50021	What a Woman/I Love America	1985	—	—	3.00
❏ B-50067	Don't Take Your Love Away/I Just Want Somebody to Love Me	1987	—	—	3.00
❏ B-50084	Lovin' You/Don't Let the Dream Get Away	1987	—	—	3.00
❏ B-50104	Let Me Touch You/Undercover Lover	1987	—	—	3.00
❏ B-50122	I Just Want Someone to Love Me/Lovin' You	1988	—	—	3.00

SARU

Number	Title (A Side/B Side)	Yr	VG	VG+	NM
❏ 1220	Shattered Man/La De Da (Means I'm Out to Get You)	1971	—	3.00	6.00

TSOP

Number	Title (A Side/B Side)	Yr	VG	VG+	NM
❏ 3771	Christmas Ain't Christmas New Year's Ain't New Year's Without the One You Love/Just Can't Get Enough	1980	—	2.50	5.00
❏ 4790	Girl, Don't Let It Get You Down/You're the Girl of My Dreams	1980	—	2.00	4.00
❏ 4791	Once Is Not Enough/To Prove I Love You	1980	—	2.00	4.00
❏ 70050	You Won't Fall/You'll Never Know (All There Is to Know 'Bout Love)	1981	—	2.00	4.00

Albums

BELL

Number	Title	Yr	VG	VG+	NM
❏ 6014	Back on Top	1968	5.00	10.00	20.00
❏ 6082	The O'Jays	1973	3.00	6.00	12.00

EMI

❏ E1-90921	Serious	1989	2.50	5.00	10.00
❏ E1-93390	Emotionally Yours	1991	3.75	7.50	15.00
❏ E1-96420	Home for Christmas	1991	3.75	7.50	15.00

IMPERIAL

| ❏ LP 9290 [M] | Comin' Through | 1965 | 10.00 | 20.00 | 40.00 |
| ❏ LP 12290 [S] | Comin' Through | 1965 | 12.50 | 25.00 | 50.00 |

KORY

| ❏ 1006 | The O'Jays | 1977 | 2.50 | 5.00 | 10.00 |

LIBERTY

| ❏ LN-10119 | Greatest Hits | 1980 | 2.00 | 4.00 | 8.00 |

—Budget-line reissue of Imperial material

MINIT

| ❏ LP-24008 [S] | Soul Sounds | 1967 | 12.50 | 25.00 | 50.00 |
| ❏ LP-40008 [M] | Soul Sounds | 1967 | 10.00 | 20.00 | 40.00 |

NEPTUNE

| ❏ 202 | The O'Jays in Philadelphia | 1969 | 7.50 | 15.00 | 30.00 |

PHILADELPHIA INT'L.

❏ ASZ 140 [DJ]	Everything You Always Wanted to Hear by the O'Jays But Were Afraid to Ask For	1975	3.75	7.50	15.00
❏ KZ 31712	Back Stabbers	1972	3.00	6.00	12.00
❏ KZ 32120	The O'Jays in Philadelphia	1973	3.00	6.00	12.00

—Reissue of Neptune LP

| ❏ KZ 32408 | Ship Ahoy | 1973 | 2.50 | 5.00 | 10.00 |
| ❏ PZ 32408 | Ship Ahoy | 198? | 2.00 | 4.00 | 8.00 |

—Budget-line reissue

❏ PZQ 32408 [Q]	Ship Ahoy	1974	3.75	7.50	15.00
❏ KZ 32953	The O'Jays Live in London	1974	2.50	5.00	10.00
❏ PZQ 32953 [Q]	The O'Jays Live in London	1974	3.75	7.50	15.00
❏ PZ 33150	Survival	1975	2.50	5.00	10.00
❏ PZ 33807	Family Reunion	1975	2.50	5.00	10.00

—No bar code on back cover

| ❏ PZ 33807 | Family Reunion | 198? | 2.00 | 4.00 | 8.00 |

—Budget-line reissue with bar code

❏ PZQ 33807 [Q]	Family Reunion	1975	3.75	7.50	15.00
❏ PZ 34245	Message in the Music	1976	2.50	5.00	10.00
❏ PZ 34684	Travelin' at the Speed of Thought	1977	2.50	5.00	10.00
❏ PZG 35024 [(2)]	The O'Jays: Collector's Items	1978	3.00	6.00	12.00
❏ Z2 35024 [(2)]	The O'Jays: Collector's Items	198?	2.50	5.00	10.00

—Reissue

| ❏ JZ 35355 | So Full of Love | 1978 | 2.50 | 5.00 | 10.00 |
| ❏ PZ 35355 | So Full of Love | 198? | 2.00 | 4.00 | 8.00 |

—Budget-line reissue

❏ FZ 36027	Identify Yourself	1979	2.50	5.00	10.00
❏ FZ 37999	My Favorite Person	1982	2.50	5.00	10.00
❏ FZ 38518	When Will I See You Again	1983	2.50	5.00	10.00
❏ PZ 38518	When Will I See You Again	1985	2.00	4.00	8.00

—Budget-line reissue

❏ FZ 39251	Greatest Hits	1984	2.50	5.00	10.00
❏ 53015	Love Fever	1985	2.50	5.00	10.00
❏ 53036	Let Me Touch You	1987	2.50	5.00	10.00

SUNSET

| ❏ SUS-5222 | Full of Soul | 1968 | 3.75 | 7.50 | 15.00 |

—Reissue of Imperial LP

TSOP

| ❏ FZ 36416 | The Year 2000 | 1980 | 2.50 | 5.00 | 10.00 |

UNITED ARTISTS

| ❏ UAS-5655 | The O'Jays Greatest Hits | 1972 | 3.00 | 6.00 | 12.00 |

VOLCANO

| ❏ 31149 | Love You to Tears | 1997 | 3.75 | 7.50 | 15.00 |

O'KAYSIONS, THE

45s

ABC

Number	Title (A Side/B Side)	Yr	VG	VG+	NM
❏ 11094	Girl Watcher/Deal Me In	1968	2.00	4.00	8.00
❏ 11153	Love Machine/Dedicated to the One I Love	1968	—	3.00	6.00
❏ 11207	Twenty-Four Hours from Tulsa/Colors	1969	—	3.00	6.00

COTILLION

| ❏ 44089 | Happiness/Watch Out Girl | 1970 | — | 2.50 | 5.00 |
| ❏ 44134 | Life and Things/Travelin' Life | 1971 | — | 2.50 | 5.00 |

NORTH STATE

| ❏ 1001 | Girl Watcher/Deal Me In | 1968 | 25.00 | 50.00 | 100.00 |
| ❏ 1001 [PS] | Girl Watcher/Deal Me In | 1968 | 75.00 | 150.00 | 300.00 |

Albums

ABC

Number	Title	Yr	VG	VG+	NM
❏ S-664	Girl Watcher	1968	10.00	20.00	40.00

O'KEEFE, DANNY

45s

ATLANTIC

Number	Title (A Side/B Side)	Yr	VG	VG+	NM
❏ 2978	Angel, Spread Your Wings/Mad Ruth the Babe	1973	—	2.50	5.00
❏ 3267	The Delta Queen/Quits	1975	—	2.50	5.00

JERDEN

| ❏ 806 | Don't Wake Me in the Morning/That Old Sweet Song | 1966 | 2.50 | 5.00 | 10.00 |

PICCADILLY

| ❏ 228 | Don't Wake Me in the Morning/That Old Sweet Song | 1967 | 2.00 | 4.00 | 8.00 |
| ❏ 237 | Today One Day Later/Baby | 1967 | 2.00 | 4.00 | 8.00 |

SIGNPOST

| ❏ 70006 | Good Time Charlie's Got the Blues/The Valentine Pieces | 1972 | — | 3.00 | 6.00 |
| ❏ 70012 | The Road/I'm Sober Now | 1972 | — | 2.50 | 5.00 |

WARNER BROS.

| ❏ 8435 | You Look Just Like a Girl Again/On Discovering a Missing Person | 1977 | — | 2.50 | 5.00 |
| ❏ 8489 | The Runaway/Just Jones | 1977 | — | 2.50 | 5.00 |

Albums

ATLANTIC

| ❏ SD 7264 | Breezy Stories | 1973 | 3.00 | 6.00 | 12.00 |
| ❏ SD 18125 | So Long, Harry Truman | 1975 | 3.00 | 6.00 | 12.00 |

COTILLION

| ❏ SD 9036 | Danny O'Keefe | 1971 | 3.75 | 7.50 | 15.00 |

FIRST AMERICAN

| ❏ 7700 | The Seattle Tapes | 1977 | 3.00 | 6.00 | 12.00 |
| ❏ 7721 | The Seattle Tapes, Volume 2 | 1979 | 3.00 | 6.00 | 12.00 |

PANORAMA

| ❏ 105 | Introducing Danny O'Keefe | 1966 | 10.00 | 20.00 | 40.00 |

SIGNPOST

| ❏ SD 8404 | O'Keefe | 1972 | 3.00 | 6.00 | 12.00 |

WARNER BROS.

❏ PRO 760 [DJ]	The O'Keefe File	1977	3.75	7.50	15.00
❏ BS 3050	American Roulette	1977	2.50	5.00	10.00
❏ BSK 3314	Global Blues	1978	2.50	5.00	10.00

O'KEEFE, JOHNNY

45s

BRUNSWICK

Number	Title (A Side/B Side)	Yr	VG	VG+	NM
❏ 55067	Real Wild Child/Shake Baby Shake	1958	50.00	100.00	200.00

LIBERTY

❏ 55223	She's My Baby/Own True Self	1959	10.00	20.00	40.00
❏ 55228	She's My Baby/It's Too Late	1959	7.50	15.00	30.00
❏ 55228 [PS]	She's My Baby/It's Too Late	1959	12.50	25.00	50.00
❏ 55262	Come On and Take My Hand/Don't You Know Little Baby	1960	10.00	20.00	40.00

MR. PEACOCK

| ❏ 111 | I'm Counting on You/The Steady Game | 1962 | 10.00 | 20.00 | 40.00 |

SIMS

| ❏ 337 | So Why/Cryin' Is the One Thing I Do Very Well | 1968 | 2.00 | 4.00 | 8.00 |

O'KEEFE, PAUL

45s

EVEREST

| ❏ 19322 | (Santa Claus) What Would You Like for Christmas?/A Baby in a Basket | 1959 | 3.00 | 6.00 | 12.00 |
| ❏ 19322 [PS] | (Santa Claus) What Would You Like for Christmas?/A Baby in a Basket | 1959 | 3.75 | 7.50 | 15.00 |

O'SULLIVAN, GILBERT

45s

EPIC

Number	Title (A Side/B Side)	Yr	VG	VG+	NM
❏ 50415	You Got Me Going/Call On Me	1977	—	2.00	4.00
❏ 50967	What's in a Kiss/Down, Down, Down	1981	—	2.00	4.00

MAM

❏ 3602	Nothing Rhymed/Everybody Knows	1971	—	3.00	6.00
❏ 3607	Underneath the Blanket Go/(B-side unknown)	1971	—	3.00	6.00
❏ 3613	We Will/I Didn't Know What to Do	1971	—	3.00	6.00
❏ 3617	No Matter How I Try/If I Don't Get You Back	1972	—	2.50	5.00
❏ 3619	Alone Again (Naturally)/Save It	1972	—	3.00	6.00
❏ 3626	Clair/Ooh Wakka Doo Wakka Day	1972	—	2.50	5.00
❏ 3626 [PS]	Clair/Ooh Wakka Doo Wakka Day	1972	—	3.00	6.00
❏ 3628	Out of the Question/Everybody Knows	1973	—	2.50	5.00
❏ 3629	Get Down/A Very Extraordinary Sort of Girl	1973	—	2.50	5.00
❏ 3633	Ooh Baby/Good Company	1973	—	2.00	4.00
❏ 3636	Happiness Is Me and You/Breakfast, Dinner and Tea	1974	—	2.00	4.00
❏ 3641	A Woman's Place/Too Bad	1974	—	2.00	4.00
❏ 3642	You Are You/To Cut a Long Story Short	1974	—	2.00	4.00
❏ 3643	Marriage Machine/Tell Me Why	1975	—	2.00	4.00
❏ 3644	I Don't Love You But I Think I Like You/That's a Fact	1975	—	2.00	4.00
❏ 3645	Christmas Song/Just As You Are	1975	—	2.50	5.00

Albums

EPIC

| ❏ JE 37013 | Off Centre | 1981 | 2.50 | 5.00 | 10.00 |

MAM

❏ 4	Gilbert O'Sullivan — Himself	1972	3.75	7.50	15.00
❏ 5	Back to Front	1972	3.75	7.50	15.00
❏ 7	I'm a Writer, Not a Fighter	1973	3.75	7.50	15.00
❏ 10	Stranger in My Own Backyard	1974	3.75	7.50	15.00

OAK RIDGE BOYS, THE

45s

ABC

Number	Title (A Side/B Side)	Yr	VG	VG+	NM
❏ 12350	I'll Be True to You/Old Time Family Bluegrass Band	1978	—	2.00	4.00
❏ 12397	Cryin' Again/I Can Love You	1978	—	2.00	4.00
❏ 12434	Come On In/Morning Glory Do	1978	—	2.00	4.00
❏ 12463	Sail Away/Only One	1979	—	2.00	4.00

Number	Title (A Side/B Side)	Yr	VG	VG+	NM
ABC/DOT					
❑ 17710	Y'All Come Back Saloon/Emmylou	1977	—	2.00	4.00
❑ 17732	You're the One/Morning Glory Do	1977	—	2.00	4.00
CADENCE					
❑ 1362	The Mocking Bird/The House of the Lord	1959	6.25	12.50	25.00
—As "The Oak Ridge Quartet"					
CAPITOL					
❑ F2181	A Mother's Prayer/My Lord's Gonna Move This Wicked Race	1952	7.50	15.00	30.00
❑ F2182	Give Me That Old Time Religion/No Tears in Heaven	1952	7.50	15.00	30.00
❑ F2183	Her Mansion Is Higher Than Mine/I've Found a Hidin' Place	1952	7.50	15.00	30.00
—The above three as "The Oak Ridge Quartet"					
CAPITOL NASHVILLE					
❑ S7-19345	Blue Christmas/I Still Believe in Christmas	1996	—	—	3.00
—B-side by Billy Dean					
COLUMBIA					
❑ 10083	Rhythm Guitar/There Must Be a Better Way	1975	—	2.50	5.00
❑ 10226	Heaven Bound/Look Away Mama	1975	—	2.50	5.00
❑ 10320	Where the Soul Never Dies/No Earthly Good	1976	—	2.50	5.00
❑ 10349	Family Reunion/Don't Be Late	1976	—	2.50	5.00
❑ 10419	All Our Favorite Songs/Whoever Finds This, I Love You	1976	—	2.50	5.00
❑ 11009	Rhythm Guitar/All Our Favorite Songs	1979	—	2.00	4.00
❑ 46001	He's Gonna Shine on Me/Put Your Arms Around Me, Blessed Jesus	1974	—	2.50	5.00
❑ 46044	Loves Me Like a Rock/He	1974	—	2.50	5.00
HEARTWARMING					
❑ 5067	How Much Farther Can We Go/(B-side unknown)	197?	2.00	4.00	8.00
❑ 5103	Jesus Christ, What a Man/God Is Beautiful	197?	2.00	4.00	8.00
❑ 5119	The Flowers Kissed the Shoes/(B-side unknown)	197?	2.00	4.00	8.00
IMPACT					
❑ 5093	Jesus Is a Soul Man/Jesus Is Coming Soon	197?	2.00	4.00	8.00
❑ 5094	Talk About the Good Times/Get Together	197?	2.00	4.00	8.00
MCA					
❑ S45-1154 [DJ]	Santa's Song/Happy Christmas Eve	1982	3.00	6.00	12.00
❑ S45-1250 [DJ]	Thank God for Kids/Jesus Is Born Today	1982	3.00	6.00	12.00
❑ S45-1705 [DJ]	Star Spangled Banner (stereo/mono)	1980	2.50	5.00	10.00
❑ S45-1741 [DJ]	The Boy Scout Way/Check Out the Boy Scouts	1981	3.75	7.50	15.00
—Label calls this a "Public Service Recording (Not for Sale)"					
❑ 12463	Sail Away/Only One	1979	—	—	3.00
❑ S45-17233 [DJ]	When You Give It Away/The Voices Of Rejoicing Love	1986	3.75	7.50	15.00
—Promo only on green vinyl					
❑ S45-17450 [DJ]	There's A New Kid In Town/From a Distance	1986	2.50	5.00	10.00
—B-side by Nanci Griffith					
❑ 41078	Dream On/Sometimes the Rain Won't Let Me Sleep	1979	—	2.00	4.00
❑ 41154	Leaving Louisiana in the Broad Daylight/I Gotta Get Over This	1979	—	2.00	4.00
❑ 41217	Trying to Love Two Women/Hold On 'Til Sunday	1980	—	2.00	4.00
❑ 41280	Love Takes Two/Heart of Mine	1980	—	2.00	4.00
❑ 51022	Ready to Take My Chances/Beautiful You	1980	—	2.00	4.00
❑ 51084	Elvira/A Woman Like You	1981	—	2.00	4.00
❑ 51169	Fancy Free/How Long Has It Been	1981	—	2.00	4.00
❑ 51231	Bobbie Sue/Live In Love	1982	—	2.00	4.00
❑ 52006	Bobbie Sue/Live In Love	1982	—	2.00	4.00
❑ 52065	So Fine/I Wish You Were Here	1982	—	2.00	4.00
❑ 52095	Back in Your Arms Again/I Wish I Could Have Turned My Head	1982	—	2.00	4.00
❑ 52145	Thank God for Kids/Christmas Is Paintin' the Town	1982	—	2.00	4.00
❑ 52179	American Made/The Cure for My Broken Heart	1983	—	2.00	4.00
❑ 52224	Love Song/Heart on the Line	1983	—	2.00	4.00
❑ 52288	Ozark Mountain Jubilee/Down Deep Inside	1983	—	2.00	4.00
❑ 52342	I Guess It Never Hurts to Hurt Sometimes/Through My Eyes	1984	—	—	3.00
❑ 52419	Everyday/Ain't No Cure for the Rock 'N' Roll	1984	—	—	3.00
❑ 52488	Make My Life with You/Break My Mind	1984	—	—	3.00
❑ 52556	Little Things/Secret of Love	1985	—	—	3.00
❑ 52646	Touch a Hand, Make a Friend/Only One I Love	1985	—	—	3.00
❑ 52722	Come On In (You Did the Best You Could Do)/Roll Tennessee River	1985	—	—	3.00
❑ 52722 [DJ]	Come On In (You Did the Best You Could Do) (same on both sides)	1985	2.50	5.00	10.00
—Promo only on blue vinyl					
❑ 52722 [PS]	Come On In (You Did the Best You Could Do)/Roll Tennessee River	1985	—	2.00	4.00
❑ 52801	Juliet/Everybody Wins	1986	—	—	3.00
❑ 52801 [DJ]	Juliet (same on both sides)	1986	3.00	6.00	12.00
—Promo only on green vinyl					
❑ 52873	You Made a Rock Out of a Rolling Stone/Hidin' Place	1986	—	—	3.00
❑ 53010	It Takes a Little Rain (To Make Love Grow)/Looking for Love	1987	—	—	3.00
❑ 53023	This Crazy Love/Where the Fast Lane Ends	1987	—	—	3.00
❑ 53023 [DJ]	This Crazy Love (same on both sides)	1987	2.50	5.00	10.00
—Promo only on blue vinyl					
❑ 53175	Time In/A Little More Coal on the Fire	1987	—	—	3.00
❑ 53272	True Heart/Love Without Mercy	1988	—	—	3.00
❑ 53381	Gonna Take a Lot of River/Private Lives	1988	—	—	3.00
❑ 53460	Bridges and Walls/Never Together (But Close Sometimes)	1988	—	—	3.00
❑ 53625	Beyond Those Years/Too Many Heartaches	1989	—	—	3.00
❑ 53705	An American Family/Too Many Heartaches	1989	—	—	3.00
❑ 53757	No Matter How High/Bed of Roses	1989	—	—	3.00
❑ 79006	Baby, You'll Be My Baby/Cajun Girl	1990	—	—	3.00
RCA					
❑ 2665-7-R	Soul and Inspiration/(B-side unknown)	1990	—	2.00	4.00
❑ 2779-7-R	Lucky Moon/Walkin' After Midnight	1991	—	2.00	4.00
❑ 62013	Change My Mind/Our Love Is Here to Stay	1991	—	2.00	4.00
❑ 62099	Baby On Board/When It Comes to You	1991	—	2.00	4.00
❑ 62228	Fall/Wait Until You're Back in My Arms Again	1992	—	2.00	4.00

Number	Title (A Side/B Side)	Yr	VG	VG+	NM
WARNER BROS.					
❑ 5359	This Ole House/Early in the Morning	1963	5.00	10.00	20.00
Albums					
ABC					
❑ AA-1065	Room Service	1978	2.50	5.00	10.00
❑ AA-1135	Have Arrived	1979	3.00	6.00	12.00
ABC/DOT					
❑ DA-2093	Y'all Come Back Saloon	1977	2.50	5.00	10.00
ACCORD					
❑ SN-7138	Spiritual Jubilee	198?	2.50	5.00	10.00
❑ SN-7159	Spiritual Jubilee — Volume 2	198?	2.50	5.00	10.00
❑ SN-7199	Spiritual Jubilee — Volume 3	198?	2.50	5.00	10.00
CADENCE					
❑ CLP-3019 [M]	The Oak Ridge Quartet	1958	15.00	30.00	60.00
CANAAN					
❑ 9625	Together	1966	5.00	10.00	20.00
—With the Harvesters					
COLUMBIA					
❑ KC 32742	The Oak Ridge Boys	1974	3.00	6.00	12.00
❑ PC 32742	The Oak Ridge Boys	197?	2.00	4.00	8.00
—Reissue					
❑ KC 33057	Sky High	1975	3.00	6.00	12.00
❑ PC 33057	Sky High	197?	2.00	4.00	8.00
—Reissue					
❑ KC 33935	Old Fashioned, Down Home, Hand Clappin', Foot Stompin', Southern Style, Gospel Quartet Music	1976	3.00	6.00	12.00
❑ PC 35202	The Best of the Oak Ridge Boys	1978	2.50	5.00	10.00
❑ PC 37711	Old Fashoned Gospel Quartet Music	1984	2.00	4.00	8.00
❑ FC 37737	All Our Favorite Songs	1981	2.50	5.00	10.00
❑ PC 38467	Smoky Mountain Gospel	1984	2.00	4.00	8.00
HEARTWARMING					
❑ HWS 3036	Thanks	1971	3.75	7.50	15.00
❑ HWS 3091	International	1971	3.75	7.50	15.00
❑ HWS 3159	The Light	1972	3.75	7.50	15.00
INTERMEDIA					
❑ QS-5012	Glory Train	198?	2.50	5.00	10.00
LIBERTY					
❑ LN-10046	The Oak Ridge Boys at Their Best	1981	2.00	4.00	8.00
MCA					
❑ AA-1135	Have Arrived	1979	2.50	5.00	10.00
❑ L33-2-1276 [(2)DJ]	"Step On Out" World Premiere	1985	6.25	12.50	25.00
—Promo-only interview and music LP with no script or cover					
❑ 1446	Deliver	1985	2.00	4.00	8.00
—Budget-line reissue					
❑ 1447	American Made	1985	2.00	4.00	8.00
—Budget-line reissue					
❑ 3220	Together	1980	2.50	5.00	10.00
❑ 5150	Greatest Hits	1980	2.50	5.00	10.00
❑ 5209	Fancy Free	1981	2.50	5.00	10.00
❑ 5294	Bobbie Sue	1982	2.50	5.00	10.00
❑ 5365	Christmas	1982	2.50	5.00	10.00
❑ 5390	American Made	1983	2.50	5.00	10.00
❑ 5455	Deliver	1983	2.50	5.00	10.00
❑ 5496	Greatest Hits 2	1984	2.50	5.00	10.00
❑ 5555	Step On Out	1985	2.50	5.00	10.00
❑ 5714	Seasons	1986	2.50	5.00	10.00
❑ 5799	Christmas Again	1986	2.50	5.00	10.00
❑ 5945	Where the Fast Lane Ends	1987	2.50	5.00	10.00
❑ 37153	Room Service	198?	2.00	4.00	8.00
—Budget-line reissue					
❑ 37221	Have Arrived	1984	2.00	4.00	8.00
—Budget-line reissue					
❑ 37222	Y'all Come Back Saloon	1984	2.00	4.00	8.00
—Budget-line reissue					
❑ 37223	Together	1984	2.00	4.00	8.00
—Budget-line reissue					
❑ 42036	Heartbeat	1987	2.50	5.00	10.00
❑ 42205	Monongahela	1988	2.50	5.00	10.00
❑ 42311	American Dreams	1989	2.50	5.00	10.00
NASHVILLE					
❑ 2086	Higher Power	1970	3.75	7.50	15.00
POWER PAK					
❑ 716	The Oak Ridge Boys	197?	2.50	5.00	10.00
PRIORITY					
❑ PU 37711	Old Fashoned Gospel Quartet Music	1981	2.50	5.00	10.00
❑ PU 38467	Smoky Mountain Gospel	1983	2.50	5.00	10.00
RCA					
❑ R 164223	Unstoppable	1991	3.75	7.50	15.00
—Only released on vinyl through BMG Direct Marketing					
SKYLITE					
❑ RLP-6020 [M]	The Oak Ridge Boys Sing for You	1964	5.00	10.00	20.00
❑ SRLP-6020 [S]	The Oak Ridge Boys Sing for You	1964	6.25	12.50	25.00
❑ RLP-6030 [M]	I Wouldn't Take Nothing for My Journey Now	1965	5.00	10.00	20.00
❑ SRLP-6030 [S]	I Wouldn't Take Nothing for My Journey Now	1965	6.25	12.50	25.00
❑ RLP-6040 [M]	The Solid Gospel Sound of the Oak Ridge Boys	1966	5.00	10.00	20.00
❑ SRLP-6040 [S]	The Solid Gospel Sound of the Oak Ridge Boys	1966	6.25	12.50	25.00
❑ RLP-6045 [M]	River of Love	1967	5.00	10.00	20.00
❑ SRLP-6045 [S]	River of Love	1967	6.25	12.50	25.00
STARDAY					
❑ SLP-356 [M]	The Sensational Oak Ridge Boys	1965	6.25	12.50	25.00
UNITED ARTISTS					
❑ UAL 3554 [M]	The Oak Ridge Boys at Their Best	1966	5.00	10.00	20.00
❑ UAS 6554 [S]	The Oak Ridge Boys at Their Best	1966	6.25	12.50	25.00
❑ LN-10046	The Oak Ridge Boys at Their Best	1979	2.50	5.00	10.00
WARNER BROS.					
❑ W 1497 [M]	With Sounds of Nashville	1963	5.00	10.00	20.00
❑ WS 1497 [S]	With Sounds of Nashville	1963	6.25	12.50	25.00
❑ W 1521 [M]	Folk-Minded Spirituals for Spiritual-Minded Folks	1963	5.00	10.00	20.00
❑ WS 1521 [S]	Folk-Minded Spirituals for Spiritual-Minded Folks	1963	6.25	12.50	25.00

O

Number	Title (A Side/B Side)	Yr	VG	VG+	NM
OBOLER, ARCH					
Albums					
CAPITOL					
❏ ST 1763 [S]	Drop Dead! An Exercise in Horror	1962	7.50	15.00	30.00
❏ T 1763 [M]	Drop Dead! An Exercise in Horror	1962	6.25	12.50	25.00
OBSESSIONS, THE					
45s					
ACCENT					
❏ 1182	Love Always/A Fool	1964	50.00	100.00	200.00
OCEAN					
45s					
KAMA SUTRA					
❏ 519	Put Your Hand in the Hand/Tear Down the Fences	1971	—	2.50	5.00
❏ 525	Deep Enough for Me/No Other Woman	1971	—	2.00	4.00
❏ 529	We Got a Dream/Will the Circle Be Unbroken	1971	—	2.00	4.00
❏ 556	One More Chance/Will the Circle Be Unbroken	1972	—	2.00	4.00
Albums					
KAMA SUTRA					
❏ KSBS-2033	Put Your Hand in the Hand	1971	3.00	6.00	12.00
❏ KSBS-2064	Give Tomorrow's Children One More Chance	1972	3.00	6.00	12.00
OCHS, PHIL					
45s					
A&M					
❏ 881	Flower Lady/Cross My Heart	1967	2.50	5.00	10.00
❏ 891	Outside of a Small Circle of Friends/Miranda	1967	2.50	5.00	10.00
❏ 932	The War Is Over/The Harder They Fall	1968	2.00	4.00	8.00
❏ 1070	My Life/The World Began in Eden and Ended in Los Angeles	1969	2.00	4.00	8.00
❏ 1180	My Kingdom for a Car/One Way Ticket Home	1970	2.00	4.00	8.00
❏ 1376	Kansas City Bomber/Gas Station Woman	1972	2.00	4.00	8.00
❏ 1509	Here's to the State of Richard Nixon/Power and Glory	1974	2.00	4.00	8.00
Albums					
A&M					
❏ (# unknown)	Gunfight at Carnegie Hall	197?	5.00	10.00	20.00
❏ LP-133 [M]	Pleasures of the Harbor	1967	6.25	12.50	25.00
❏ SP-3125	Phil Ochs Greatest Hits	198?	2.00	4.00	8.00
—Budget-line reissue					
❏ SP-4133 [S]	Pleasures of the Harbor	1967	5.00	10.00	20.00
❏ SP-4148	Tape from California	1968	5.00	10.00	20.00
❏ SP-4181	Rehearsals for Retirement	1969	5.00	10.00	20.00
❏ SP-4253	Phil Ochs Greatest Hits	1970	5.00	10.00	20.00
❏ SP-6511 [(2)]	Chords of Fame	1976	5.00	10.00	20.00
CARTHAGE					
❏ CGLP-4422	I Ain't Marching Anymore	198?	2.50	5.00	10.00
❏ CGLP-4427	All the News That's Fit to Sing	198?	2.50	5.00	10.00
ELEKTRA					
❏ EKL-269 [M]	All the News That's Fit to Sing	1964	7.50	15.00	30.00
—Gold label with "guitar player" logo					
❏ EKL-269 [M]	All the News That's Fit to Sing	1966	5.00	10.00	20.00
—Gold label with stylized "E" logo					
❏ EKL-287 [M]	I Ain't Marching Anymore	1965	7.50	15.00	30.00
—Gold label with "guitar player" logo					
❏ EKL-287 [M]	I Ain't Marching Anymore	1966	5.00	10.00	20.00
—Gold label with stylized "E" logo					
❏ EKL-310 [M]	Phil Ochs in Concert	1966	5.00	10.00	20.00
❏ EKS-7269 [S]	All the News That's Fit to Sing	1964	10.00	20.00	40.00
—Gold label with "guitar player" logo					
❏ EKS-7269 [S]	All the News That's Fit to Sing	1966	6.25	12.50	25.00
—Gold label with stylized "E" logo					
❏ EKS-7287 [S]	I Ain't Marching Anymore	1965	10.00	20.00	40.00
—Gold label with "guitar player" logo					
❏ EKS-7287 [S]	I Ain't Marching Anymore	1966	6.25	12.50	25.00
—Gold label with stylized "E" logo					
❏ EKS-7310 [S]	Phil Ochs in Concert	1966	6.25	12.50	25.00
FOLKWAYS					
❏ FB-5320	Phil Ochs Sings Songs for Broadside (#10)	197?	3.00	6.00	12.00
❏ FB-5321	Phil Ochs Interviews	197?	3.00	6.00	12.00
❏ FD-5362	Broadside Tapes 1 (#14)	1979	3.00	6.00	12.00
PICKWICK					
❏ SPC-3707	Rehearsals for Retirement	197?	2.50	5.00	10.00
RHINO					
❏ RNLP-70080	A Toast to Those Who Are Gone	1986	2.50	5.00	10.00
SMITHSONIAN/FOLKWAYS					
❏ SF-40008	Broadside Tapes 1 (#14)	1989	3.00	6.00	12.00
OCTAVES, THE					
45s					
VAL					
❏ 1001	You're Too Young/Mambo Carolyn	1958	18.75	37.50	75.00
OCTOBER COUNTRY					
45s					
EPIC					
❏ 5-10252	October Country/Baby What I Mean	1967	2.50	5.00	10.00
❏ 5-10320	My Girlfriend Is a Witch/I Just Don't Know	1968	2.50	5.00	10.00
Albums					
EPIC					
❏ BN 26381	October Country	1968	5.00	10.00	20.00
ODA					
Albums					
LOUD					
❏ A 0011	Oda	1973	50.00	100.00	200.00
ODDIS, RAY					
45s					
V.I.P.					
❏ 25012	Happy Ghoul Tide/Ray the Newspaper Boy	1964	5.00	10.00	20.00

Number	Title (A Side/B Side)	Yr	VG	VG+	NM
ODDS AND ENDS					
45s					
RED BIRD					
❏ 10-083	Before You Go (Hey Little Girl)/Never Learn	1967	3.00	6.00	12.00
ODETTA					
45s					
ABC DUNHILL					
❏ 4213	Ballad of Easy Rider/Visa Versa	1969	—	3.00	6.00
POLYDOR					
❏ 14045	Take Me to the Pilot/Hit or Miss	1970	—	2.50	5.00
RCA VICTOR					
❏ 47-8262	Got My Mind on Freedom/It's a Mighty World	1963	2.50	5.00	10.00
RIVERSIDE					
❏ 4524	Make Me a Pallet on Your Floor/Oh, My Babe	1962	2.50	5.00	10.00
VANGUARD					
❏ 35007	Motherless Children/The Ox-Driver Song	1959	3.00	6.00	12.00
VERVE FOLKWAYS					
❏ 5030	Until It's Time for You to Go/Clown Town	1966	2.00	4.00	8.00
VERVE FORECAST					
❏ 5087	Peace and Harmony/Until It's Time for You to Go	1968	—	3.00	6.00
Albums					
ALCAZAR					
❏ ALC-104	Christmas Spirituals	198?	2.50	5.00	10.00
EVEREST ARCHIVE OF FOLK & JAZZ					
❏ 273	Odetta	1973	3.00	6.00	12.00
FANTASY					
❏ 3-15 [10]	Odetta and Larry	1955	12.50	25.00	50.00
❏ OBC-509	Odetta and the Blues	198?	2.50	5.00	10.00
—Reissue of Riverside LP					
❏ F-3252 [M]	Odetta and Larry	1957	12.50	25.00	50.00
—Dark red vinyl					
❏ F-3252 [M]	Odetta and Larry	1958	7.50	15.00	30.00
❏ F-8345	Odetta and Larry	1963	3.00	6.00	12.00
—Reissue of 3252					
RCA VICTOR					
❏ LPM-2573 [M]	Sometimes I Feel Like Crying	1962	5.00	10.00	20.00
❏ LSP-2573 [S]	Sometimes I Feel Like Crying	1962	6.25	12.50	25.00
❏ LPM-2643 [M]	Odetta Sings Folk Songs	1963	5.00	10.00	20.00
❏ LSP-2643 [S]	Odetta Sings Folk Songs	1963	6.25	12.50	25.00
❏ LPM-2792 [M]	It's a Mighty World	1964	3.75	7.50	15.00
❏ LSP-2792 [S]	It's a Mighty World	1964	5.00	10.00	20.00
❏ LPM-2923 [M]	Odetta Sings of Many Things	1964	3.75	7.50	15.00
❏ LSP-2923 [S]	Odetta Sings of Many Things	1964	5.00	10.00	20.00
❏ LPM-3324 [M]	Odetta Sings Dylan	1965	3.75	7.50	15.00
❏ LSP-3324 [S]	Odetta Sings Dylan	1965	5.00	10.00	20.00
❏ LPM-3457 [M]	Odetta in Japan	1965	3.75	7.50	15.00
❏ LSP-3457 [S]	Odetta in Japan	1965	5.00	10.00	20.00
RIVERSIDE					
❏ RLP-417 [M]	Odetta and the Blues	1962	6.25	12.50	25.00
❏ RS-9417 [S]	Odetta and the Blues	1962	7.50	15.00	30.00
ROSE QUARTZ					
❏ RQ-101	Movin' It On	1987	2.50	5.00	10.00
TRADITION					
❏ TRP-1010 [M]	Odetta Sings Ballads and Blues	1957	7.50	15.00	30.00
❏ TRP-1025 [M]	Odetta at the Gate of Horn	1958	7.50	15.00	30.00
❏ TRP-1052 [M]	The Best of Odetta	1967	5.00	10.00	20.00
❏ TRS-2052 [R]	The Best of Odetta	1967	3.75	7.50	15.00
VANGUARD					
❏ VSD-43/44 [(2)]	Essential Odetta	1973	3.75	7.50	15.00
❏ VSD-2046 [S]	My Eyes Have Seen	1960	6.25	12.50	25.00
❏ VSD-2057 [S]	Ballads for Americans	1960	6.25	12.50	25.00
❏ VSD-2072 [S]	Odetta at Carnegie Hall	1961	6.25	12.50	25.00
❏ VSD-2079 [S]	Christmas Spirituals	1961	6.25	12.50	25.00
❏ VSD-2109 [S]	Odetta at Town Hall	1962	6.25	12.50	25.00
❏ VSD-2153 [S]	One Grain of Sand	1963	6.25	12.50	25.00
❏ VRS-3003 [M]	Odetta at Carnegie Hall	1967	3.75	7.50	15.00
❏ VRS-9059 [M]	My Eyes Have Seen	1960	5.00	10.00	20.00
❏ VRS-9066 [M]	Ballads for Americans	1960	5.00	10.00	20.00
❏ VRS-9076 [M]	Odetta at Carnegie Hall	1961	5.00	10.00	20.00
❏ VRS-9079 [M]	Christmas Spirituals	1961	5.00	10.00	20.00
❏ VRS-9103 [M]	Odetta at Town Hall	1962	5.00	10.00	20.00
❏ VRS-9137 [M]	One Grain of Sand	1963	5.00	10.00	20.00
❏ VSD-73003 [S]	Odetta at Carnegie Hall	1967	5.00	10.00	20.00
OFF KEYS, THE					
45s					
ROWE					
❏ 003	Our Wedding Day/Singing Bells	1962	25.00	50.00	100.00
TECHNICHORD					
❏ 1001	Our Wedding Day/Singing Bells	1962	6.25	12.50	25.00
—Flat maroon label					
❏ 1001	Our Wedding Day/Singing Bells	1962	12.50	25.00	50.00
—Glossy red label					
OGNIR AND THE NIGHT PEOPLE					
45s					
SAMRON					
❏ 102	I Found a New Love/All My Heart	1965	10.00	20.00	40.00
WARNER BROS.					
❏ 5687	I Found a New Love/All My Heart	1965	6.25	12.50	25.00
OHIO EXPRESS, THE Also see THE RARE BREED.					
45s					
BUDDAH					
❏ 38	Yummy Yummy Yummy/Zig Zag	1968	2.50	5.00	10.00
❏ 56	Down at Lulu's/She's Not Coming Home	1968	2.00	4.00	8.00
❏ 70	Chewy Chewy/Firebird	1968	2.50	5.00	10.00
❏ 92	Sweeter Than Sugar/Bitter Than Lemon	1969	2.00	4.00	8.00
❏ 102	Mercy/Roll It Up	1969	2.00	4.00	8.00
❏ 117	Pinch Me (Baby, Convince Me)/Peanuts	1969	2.00	4.00	8.00
❏ 129	Sausalito (Is the Place to Go)/Make Love Not War	1969	2.00	4.00	8.00
—With Graham Gouldman, later of 10CC, on lead vocal					
❏ 147	Cowboy Convention/The Race (That Took Place)	1970	2.00	4.00	8.00
❏ 160	Love Equals Love/Peanuts	1970	2.00	4.00	8.00

Number	Title (A Side/B Side)	Yr	VG	VG+	NM
❏ 386	Wham Bam/Slow and Steady	1973	3.75	7.50	15.00
—As "Ohio Ltd."					

CAMEO

Number	Title (A Side/B Side)	Yr	VG	VG+	NM
❏ 483	Beg, Borrow and Steal/Maybe	1967	3.00	6.00	12.00
❏ 2001	Try It/Soul Struttin'	1967	3.00	6.00	12.00

SUPER K

Number	Title (A Side/B Side)	Yr	VG	VG+	NM
❏ 114	Hot Dog/Ooh La La	1970	2.50	5.00	10.00

Albums

BUDDAH

Number	Title (A Side/B Side)	Yr	VG	VG+	NM
❏ BDM 1018 [M]	The Ohio Express	1968	10.00	20.00	40.00
—Stereo cover with "mono" sticker attached; white label promo					
❏ BDS 5018 [S]	The Ohio Express	1968	5.00	10.00	20.00
❏ BDS 5026	Chewy, Chewy	1969	5.00	10.00	20.00
❏ BDS 5037	Mercy	1969	5.00	10.00	20.00
❏ BDS 5058	The Very Best of the Ohio Express	1970	5.00	10.00	20.00

CAMEO

Number	Title (A Side/B Side)	Yr	VG	VG+	NM
❏ C 20000 [M]	Beg, Borrow and Steal	1967	7.50	15.00	30.00
❏ CS 20000 [S]	Beg, Borrow and Steal	1967	10.00	20.00	40.00

OHIO PLAYERS, THE Also see THE OHIO UNTOUCHABLES.

12-Inch Singles

AIR CITY

Number	Title (A Side/B Side)	Yr	VG	VG+	NM
❏ A-402	Sight for Sore Eyes/(Instrumental)	1984	—	3.00	6.00

ARISTA

Number	Title (A Side/B Side)	Yr	VG	VG+	NM
❏ SP-46 [DJ]	Everybody Up (9:32) (3:57)	1979	3.00	6.00	12.00

BOARDWALK

Number	Title (A Side/B Side)	Yr	VG	VG+	NM
❏ AS 941 [DJ]	Try a Little Tenderness/DDDDDDDance	1981	3.75	7.50	15.00
—B-side by Rox					

MERCURY

Number	Title (A Side/B Side)	Yr	VG	VG+	NM
❏ MK-43 [DJ]	Magic Trick/Good Luck Charm	1976	3.75	7.50	15.00

TRACK

Number	Title (A Side/B Side)	Yr	VG	VG+	NM
❏ 58813	Sweat (3 versions)/Rock the House	1988	—	3.00	6.00

45s

AIR CITY

Number	Title (A Side/B Side)	Yr	VG	VG+	NM
❏ 402	Sight for Sore Eyes/(Instrumental)	1984	—	2.00	4.00
❏ 402 [PS]	Sight for Sore Eyes/(Instrumental)	1984	—	2.00	4.00
❏ 1007	Follow Me/(B-side unknown)	1984	—	2.50	5.00

ARISTA

Number	Title (A Side/B Side)	Yr	VG	VG+	NM
❏ 0408	Everybody Up/Take De Funk Off, Fly	1979	—	2.00	4.00
❏ 0440	Don't Say Goodbye/Say It	1979	—	2.00	4.00

BOARDWALK

Number	Title (A Side/B Side)	Yr	VG	VG+	NM
❏ NB7-11-133	Star of the Party/I Better Take a Coffee Break	1981	—	2.00	4.00
❏ WS8-02063	Skinny/Call Me	1981	—	2.00	4.00
❏ 5708	Try a Little Tenderness/Try to Be a Man	1981	—	2.00	4.00

CAPITOL

Number	Title (A Side/B Side)	Yr	VG	VG+	NM
❏ 2385	Bad Bargain/Here Today and Gone Tomorrow	1969	2.50	5.00	10.00
❏ 2523	Find Someone to Love/Over the Rainbow	1969	2.50	5.00	10.00

COMPASS

Number	Title (A Side/B Side)	Yr	VG	VG+	NM
❏ 7015	Tresspassin'/You Don't Mean It	1967	3.00	6.00	12.00
❏ 7018	It's a Crying Shame/I've Got to Hold On	1968	3.00	6.00	12.00

MERCURY

Number	Title (A Side/B Side)	Yr	VG	VG+	NM
❏ 73480	Jive Turkey (Part 1)/Streakin' Cheek to Cheek	1974	—	2.50	5.00
❏ 73609	Skin Tight/Heaven Must Be Like This	1974	—	2.50	5.00
❏ 73643	Fire/Together	1974	—	2.50	5.00
❏ 73675	I Want to Be Free/Smoke	1975	—	2.50	5.00
❏ 73713	Sweet Sticky Thing/Alone	1975	—	2.50	5.00
❏ 73734	Love Rollercoaster/It's All Over	1975	—	2.50	5.00
❏ 73753	Happy Holidays (Part 1)/Happy Holidays (Part 2)	1975	—	3.00	6.00
❏ 73775	Fopp/Let's Love	1976	—	2.50	5.00
❏ 73814	Who'd She Coo?/Bi-Centennial	1976	—	2.50	5.00
❏ 73860	Far East Mississippi/Only a Child Can Love	1976	—	2.50	5.00
❏ 73881	Feel the Beat (Everybody Disco)/Contradiction	1976	—	2.50	5.00
❏ 73913	Body Vibes/Don't Fight My Love	1977	—	2.50	5.00
❏ 73932	O-H-I-O/Can You Still Love Me	1977	—	2.50	5.00
❏ 73956	Merry Go Round/Angel	1977	—	2.50	5.00
❏ 73974	Good Luck Charm (Part 1)/				
	Good Luck Charm (Part 2)	1977	—	2.50	5.00
❏ 73983	Magic Trick/Mr. Mean	1978	—	2.50	5.00
❏ 74014	Funk-O-Nots/Sleepwalkin'	1978	—	2.50	5.00
❏ 74031	Time Slips Away/Nott Enuff	1978	—	2.50	5.00

TANGERINE

Number	Title (A Side/B Side)	Yr	VG	VG+	NM
❏ 978	Neighbors/A Thing Called Love	1967	3.00	6.00	12.00

TRACK

Number	Title (A Side/B Side)	Yr	VG	VG+	NM
❏ 58812	Let's Play (From Now On)/Show Off	1988	—	—	3.00
❏ 58815	Sweat/Rock the House	1988	—	—	3.00

WESTBOUND

Number	Title (A Side/B Side)	Yr	VG	VG+	NM
❏ 188	Pain (Part 1)/Pain (Part 2)	1971	—	3.00	6.00
❏ 204	Pleasure/I Wanna Hear from You	1972	—	3.00	6.00
❏ 208	Walt's First Trip/Varce Is Love	1972	—	3.00	6.00
❏ 214	Funky Worm/Paint Me	1973	—	3.00	6.00
❏ 216	Ecstasy/Not So Sad and Lonely	1973	—	3.00	6.00
❏ 228	Sleep Talk/Food Stamps Y'All	1974	—	3.00	6.00
❏ 5018	Rattlesnake/Gone Forever	1976	—	3.00	6.00

Albums

ACCORD

Number	Title (A Side/B Side)	Yr	VG	VG+	NM
❏ SN-7102	Young and Ready	1981	2.00	4.00	8.00

ARISTA

Number	Title (A Side/B Side)	Yr	VG	VG+	NM
❏ AB 4226	Everybody Up	1979	2.00	4.00	8.00

BOARDWALK

Number	Title (A Side/B Side)	Yr	VG	VG+	NM
❏ FW 37090	Tenderness	1981	2.00	4.00	8.00

CAPITOL

Number	Title (A Side/B Side)	Yr	VG	VG+	NM
❏ ST-192	Observations in Time	1969	12.50	25.00	50.00
❏ ST-11291	The Ohio Players	1974	3.00	6.00	12.00
—Reissue of 192					

MERCURY

Number	Title (A Side/B Side)	Yr	VG	VG+	NM
❏ SRM-1-705	Skin Tight	1974	2.50	5.00	10.00
—Chicago skyline label					
❏ SRM-1-705	Skin Tight	1974	3.00	6.00	12.00
—Red label					
❏ SRM-1-1013	Fire	1974	2.50	5.00	10.00
❏ SRM-1-1038	Honey	1975	2.50	5.00	10.00
❏ SRM-1-1088	Contradiction	1976	2.50	5.00	10.00
❏ SRM-1-1122	Ohio Players Gold	1976	2.50	5.00	10.00
❏ SRM-1-3701	Angel	1977	2.50	5.00	10.00
❏ SRM-1-3707	Mr. Mean	1977	2.50	5.00	10.00
❏ SRM-1-3730	Jass-Ay-Lay-Dee	1978	2.50	5.00	10.00
❏ 824461-1	Ohio Players Gold	198?	2.00	4.00	8.00
—Reissue of 1122					

TRACK

Number	Title (A Side/B Side)	Yr	VG	VG+	NM
❏ TRK 58810	Back	1988	2.50	5.00	10.00

TRIP

Number	Title (A Side/B Side)	Yr	VG	VG+	NM
❏ 8029	First Impression	1972	3.00	6.00	12.00

UNITED ARTISTS

Number	Title (A Side/B Side)	Yr	VG	VG+	NM
❏ UA-LA502-E	The Very Best of The Ohio Players	1975	3.00	6.00	12.00

WESTBOUND

Number	Title (A Side/B Side)	Yr	VG	VG+	NM
❏ 211	Rattlesnake	1975	3.00	6.00	12.00
❏ 219	Pain	1976	3.00	6.00	12.00
—Reissue of 2015					
❏ 220	Pleasure	1976	3.00	6.00	12.00
—Reissue of 2017					
❏ 222	Ecstasy	1976	3.00	6.00	12.00
—Reissue of 2021					
❏ 304	The Best of the Early Years	1977	3.75	7.50	15.00
❏ 1003	Climax	1974	3.75	7.50	15.00
❏ 1005	Ohio Players Greatest Hits	1975	3.75	7.50	15.00
❏ 2015	Pain	1972	5.00	10.00	20.00
❏ 2017	Pleasure	1973	5.00	10.00	20.00
❏ 2021	Ecstasy	1973	5.00	10.00	20.00

OHIO UNTOUCHABLES, THE Early version of THE OHIO PLAYERS.

45s

LUPINE

Number	Title (A Side/B Side)	Yr	VG	VG+	NM
❏ 109	She's My Heart's Desire/What to Do	1962	12.50	25.00	50.00
❏ 110	Love Is Amazing/Forgive Me Darling	1962	12.50	25.00	50.00
❏ 116/7	I'm Tired/Uptown	1962	10.00	20.00	40.00
❏ 1009	She's My Heart's Desire/What to Do	1964	5.00	10.00	20.00
❏ 1010	Love Is Amazing/Forgive Me Darling	1964	5.00	10.00	20.00
❏ 1011	I'm Tired/Uptown	1964	3.75	7.50	15.00

OKLAHOMA WRANGLERS, THE

45s

RCA VICTOR

Number	Title (A Side/B Side)	Yr	VG	VG+	NM
❏ 47-4376	Unhappy New Year/Savannah River Rag	1951	3.75	7.50	15.00

OLA AND THE JANGLERS

45s

GNP CRESCENDO

Number	Title (A Side/B Side)	Yr	VG	VG+	NM
❏ 423	Let's Dance/Strolling Along	1969	2.00	4.00	8.00
❏ 427	What a Way to Die/That's Why I Cry	1969	2.00	4.00	8.00
❏ 432	California Sun/Baby, Baby, Baby	1970	2.00	4.00	8.00

LONDON

Number	Title (A Side/B Side)	Yr	VG	VG+	NM
❏ 20034	Eeny Meeny Miney Moe/I Can Wait	1967	2.50	5.00	10.00

Albums

GNP CRESCENDO

Number	Title (A Side/B Side)	Yr	VG	VG+	NM
❏ GNPS-2050	Let's Dance/What a Way to Die	1969	5.00	10.00	20.00

OLD & IN THE WAY JERRY GARCIA heads a bluegrass band!

Albums

ROUND

Number	Title (A Side/B Side)	Yr	VG	VG+	NM
❏ RX-103	Old & In the Way	1975	6.25	12.50	25.00

SUGAR HILL

Number	Title (A Side/B Side)	Yr	VG	VG+	NM
❏ SH-3746	Old & In the Way	1987	2.50	5.00	10.00
—Reissue of Round LP					

OLDFIELD, MIKE

10-Inch Singles

VIRGIN

Number	Title (A Side/B Side)	Yr	VG	VG+	NM
❏ PR 361 [DJ]	Guilty//North Star/Platinum Finale	1979	25.00	50.00	100.00

12-Inch Singles

KINETIC

Number	Title (A Side/B Side)	Yr	VG	VG+	NM
❏ PRO-A-9752 [DJ]	Far Above the Clouds (Jam & Spoon Mix) (Timewriters Big Bag of Secrets Mix) (Jam & Spoon Deep Inside Club) (Far Below the Bass)	1999	7.50	15.00	30.00
❏ 44669	Far Above the Clouds (Jam & Spoon Mix) (Timewriters Big Bag of Secrets Mix) (Jam & Spoon Deep Inside Club) (Far Below the Bass)	1999	3.00	6.00	12.00

REPRISE

Number	Title (A Side/B Side)	Yr	VG	VG+	NM
❏ PRO-A-7992 [(2)DJ]	Let There Be Light (BT's Pure Luminescence Remix)/(The Ultraviolet Mix Edit)//(Hardfloor Remix) (Hardfloor Dub)/(BT's Entropic Dub)	1995	6.25	12.50	25.00
❏ 40749	Sentinel Restructure (Trance Mix) (Tubular Beats)/The Bell (Edit)//Sentinel Restructure (Satoshi Tomii Interpretation) (Global Lust Mix)	1992	5.00	10.00	20.00
❏ 43561	Let There Be Light (BT's Pure Luminescense Remix) (BT's Entropic Dub)	1995	3.75	7.50	15.00

VIRGIN

Number	Title (A Side/B Side)	Yr	VG	VG+	NM
❏ PR 2113 [DJ]	Magic Touch (same on both sides)	1988	5.00	10.00	20.00
❏ PR 2181 [DJ]	Wind Chimes Part 2/North Point	1988	12.50	25.00	50.00

VIRGIN/EPIC

Number	Title (A Side/B Side)	Yr	VG	VG+	NM
❏ AS 1424 [DJ]	Five Miles Out/Family Man	1982	7.50	15.00	30.00

45s

VIRGIN

Number	Title (A Side/B Side)	Yr	VG	VG+	NM
❏ PR 199 [DJ]	Tubular Bells (same on both sides?)	1974	6.25	12.50	25.00
❏ PR 223 [DJ]	Hergest Ridge (two different edits?)	1974	5.00	10.00	20.00
❏ 9505	Theme: From Ommadawn/On Horseback	1975	—	3.00	6.00
❏ 9510	Portsmouth/Argiers	1975	—	3.00	6.00
❏ 55100	Tubular Bells (Now the Original Theme from the Movie "The Exorcist")/Tubular Bells	1973	2.00	4.00	8.00
❏ 99402	Magic Touch/Wind Chimes Part 1	1987	—	2.00	4.00
❏ 99402 [PS]	Magic Touch/Wind Chimes Part 1	1987	—	2.00	4.00

VIRGIN/EPIC

Number	Title (A Side/B Side)	Yr	VG	VG+	NM
❏ 14-02877	Family Man/Mount Teidi	1982	—	3.00	6.00

7-Inch Extended Plays

VIRGIN

Number	Title (A Side/B Side)	Yr	VG	VG+	NM
❏ PR 196 [DJ]	Tubular Bells Excerpts	1974	6.25	12.50	25.00
—Six different edits; promo only					

Albums

VIRGIN

Number	Title (A Side/B Side)	Yr	VG	VG+	NM
❏ QD 13-105 [Q]	Tubular Bells	1974	6.25	12.50	25.00
❏ VR 13-105	Tubular Bells	1973	3.75	7.50	15.00
—First stereo issue of this album					

Number	Title (A Side/B Side)	Yr	VG	VG+	NM
❏ VR 13-109	Hergest Ridge	1974	3.00	6.00	12.00
—First issue of this album					
❏ VR 13-109 [DJ]	Hergest Ridge	1974	5.00	10.00	20.00
—Promo only; banded for airplay					
❏ VR 13-115	The Orchestral Tubular Bells	1975	3.00	6.00	12.00
❏ VR 13135	Tubular Bells	1979	2.50	5.00	10.00
—Third stereo issue of this album					
❏ VR 13143 [(2)]	Airborn	1980	3.75	7.50	15.00
—U.S.-only compilation, which may make it much more valuable overseas					
❏ PZ 33913	Ommadawn	1975	3.00	6.00	12.00
—Original U.S. issue of this album					
❏ PZ 33913 [DJ]	Ommadawn	1975	5.00	10.00	20.00
—Promo only; banded for airplay					
❏ PZQ 33913 [Q]	Ommadawn	1975	5.00	10.00	20.00
❏ PZ 34116	Tubular Bells	1976	3.00	6.00	12.00
—Second stereo issue of this album (note the "PZ" prefix)					
❏ 90589	Tubular Bells	1987	2.00	4.00	8.00
—Fifth stereo issue of this album					
❏ 90590	Hergest Ridge	1987	2.00	4.00	8.00
—Reissue of Virgin International 2013					
❏ 90591	The Killing Fields	1987	2.50	5.00	10.00
❏ 90645	Islands	1988	2.50	5.00	10.00
❏ 90894	The Orchestral Tubular Bells	1989	2.50	5.00	10.00
—Reissue of 13-115					
❏ 91270	Earth Moving	1990	3.00	6.00	12.00
VIRGIN INTERNATIONAL					
❏ VI-2013	Hergest Ridge	1979	2.50	5.00	10.00
—Reissue of 13-109; not to be confused with UK pressings that have only a "V" prefix					
❏ VI-2043	Ommadawn	1979	2.50	5.00	10.00
—Reissue of 33913; not to be confused with UK pressings that have only a "V" prefix					
VIRGIN/EPIC					
❏ PE 34116	Tubular Bells	1982	2.00	4.00	8.00
—Fourth stereo issue of this album (note the "PE" prefix)					
❏ FE 37358	QE2	1981	2.50	5.00	10.00
❏ ARE 37983	Five Miles Out	1982	2.50	5.00	10.00
❏ HE 44116	Tubular Bells	1982	7.50	15.00	30.00
—Half-speed mastered edition					

OLDHAM, ANDREW
45s
PARROT

Number	Title (A Side/B Side)	Yr	VG	VG+	NM
❏ 9684	Theme from The Dick Van Dyke Show/I'd Like to See Me on the "B" Side	1964	7.50	15.00	30.00
❏ 9745	I Get Around/Save It For Me	1965	7.50	15.00	30.00
Albums					
LONDON					
❏ PS 457 [S]	The Rolling Stones Songbook	1965	37.50	75.00	150.00
❏ LL 3457 [M]	The Rolling Stones Songbook	1965	25.00	50.00	100.00
PARROT					
❏ PA 61003 [M]	East Meets West	1965	20.00	40.00	80.00
❏ PAS 71003 [S]	East Meets West	1965	25.00	50.00	100.00

OLENN, JOHNNY
45s
ANTLER

Number	Title (A Side/B Side)	Yr	VG	VG+	NM
❏ 1101	My Sweetie Pie/For the First Time	1959	10.00	20.00	40.00
❏ 1105	Born Reckless/You, Loveable You	1959	10.00	20.00	40.00
❏ 4009	My Sweetie Pie/Smile	1957	10.00	20.00	40.00
❏ 4018	The Magic Touch/Football Freddy	1957	10.00	20.00	40.00
LIBERTY					
❏ 55053	Candy Kisses/My Idea of Love	1957	6.25	12.50	25.00
PERSONALITY					
❏ 1002	Teenie/Devil Darling	1959	12.50	25.00	50.00
TNT					
❏ 1016	Candy Kisses/Sally Let Your Bangs Hang Down	1955	12.50	25.00	50.00
❏ 1018	I Ain't Gonna Cry No More/ Blues Stay Away from Me	1955	12.50	25.00	50.00
Albums					
LIBERTY					
❏ LRP-3029 [M]	Just Rollin' with Johnny Olenn	1956	75.00	150.00	300.00

OLIVA, TONY
Albums
KUBANY

Number	Title (A Side/B Side)	Yr	VG	VG+	NM
❏ SD-600	My Favorite Music	1966	7.50	15.00	30.00

OLIVER
45s
CREWE

Number	Title (A Side/B Side)	Yr	VG	VG+	NM
❏ 334	Jean/The Arrangement	1969	2.00	4.00	8.00
❏ 334 [PS]	Jean/The Arrangement	1969	3.75	7.50	15.00
❏ 337	Sunday Mornin'/Let Me Kiss You with a Dream	1969	—	3.00	6.00
❏ 341	Angelica/Anna	1970	—	3.00	6.00
❏ 346	I Can Remember/Where There's a Heartache There Must Be a Heart	1970	—	3.00	6.00
JUBILEE					
❏ 5659	Good Morning Starshine/Can't You See	1969	2.00	4.00	8.00
MCA					
❏ 52063	Don't Take Your Love Away/Everybody Wants to Be the Boss	1982	—	—	3.00
❏ 52113	I Want Your Love, I Need Your Love/Make Up Your Mind	1982	—	—	3.00
PARAMOUNT					
❏ 0198	Everybody I Love You/I Am Reaching	1973	—	2.00	4.00
UNITED ARTISTS					
❏ 0130	Good Morning Starshine/Jean	1973	—	2.00	4.00
—"Silver Spotlight Series" reissue					
❏ 50735	Sweet Kindness/Light the Way	1970	—	2.50	5.00
❏ 50750	Dedicated to the One I Love/Light the Way	1971	—	—	—
—Unreleased					
❏ 50762	Early Morning Rain/Catch Me If You Can	1971	—	2.50	5.00
❏ 50814	Walkin' Down the Line/Firelight	1971	—	2.50	5.00
❏ 50862	Why You Been Gone So Long/Please	1971	—	2.50	5.00
Albums					
CREWE					
❏ CR-1333	Good Morning Starshine	1969	3.75	7.50	15.00
❏ CR-1344	Oliver Again	1970	3.75	7.50	15.00

UNITED ARTISTS

Number	Title (A Side/B Side)	Yr	VG	VG+	NM
❏ UAS-5511	Prisms	1971	3.75	7.50	15.00

OLIVER, WARD
45s
HIT

Number	Title (A Side/B Side)	Yr	VG	VG+	NM
❏ 36	Next Door to an Angel/He's a Rebel	1962	2.50	5.00	10.00
—B-side by the Gleams					

OLIVER AND THE TWISTERS
45s
COLPIX

Number	Title (A Side/B Side)	Yr	VG	VG+	NM
❏ 615	Mother Goose Twist/Locomotion Twist	1961	3.00	6.00	12.00
❏ 615 [PS]	Mother Goose Twist/Locomotion Twist	1961	6.25	12.50	25.00
Albums					
COLPIX					
❏ CP-423 [M]	Look Who's Twistin' Everybody	1961	10.00	20.00	40.00

OLIVERS, THE
45s
PHALANX

Number	Title (A Side/B Side)	Yr	VG	VG+	NM
❏ 1022	Bleecker Street/I Saw What You Did	1967	15.00	30.00	60.00
RCA VICTOR					
❏ 47-9113	Bleecker Street/I Saw What You Did	1967	5.00	10.00	20.00

OLIVES, THE
45s
HIT

Number	Title (A Side/B Side)	Yr	VG	VG+	NM
❏ 306	How Can I Be Sure/Come Back When You Grow Up	1967	2.00	4.00	8.00
—B-side by Jimmy Lewis and the Elfs					

OLLIE AND THE NIGHTINGALES
45s
STAX

Number	Title (A Side/B Side)	Yr	VG	VG+	NM
❏ 0014	You're Leaving Me/Showered with Love	1968	—	3.00	6.00
❏ 0027	The Mellow Way You Treat Your Man/ Don't Do What I Did	1969	—	3.00	6.00
❏ 0045	I've Got a Feeling/You'll Never Do Wrong	1969	—	3.00	6.00
❏ 0065	I'll Be Your Anything/Bracing Myself for the Fall	1970	—	3.00	6.00
❏ 245	I Got a Sure Thing/ Girl You Have My Heart Singing	1968	2.00	4.00	8.00
Albums					
STAX					
❏ STS-2021	Ollie and the Nightingales	1969	12.50	25.00	50.00

OLSEN, DOROTHY
45s
RCA VICTOR

Number	Title (A Side/B Side)	Yr	VG	VG+	NM
❏ 47-7654	The Christmas Spirit/Little Donkey	1959	3.75	7.50	15.00

OLSSON, NIGEL Drummer in ELTON JOHN's band.
12-Inch Singles
BANG

Number	Title (A Side/B Side)	Yr	VG	VG+	NM
❏ 2Z8-4801	Little Bit of Soap (5:28)/ Cassey Blue-Au Revoir (6:24)	1979	3.75	7.50	15.00
45s					
BANG					
❏ 740	Dancin' Shoes/Living in a Fantasy	1978	—	2.50	5.00
❏ 4800	Little Bit of Soap/Thinking of You	1979	—	2.00	4.00
❏ 4803	Part of the Chosen Few/All It Takes	1979	—	2.00	4.00
COLUMBIA					
❏ 10733	Rainy Day/Right or Wrong	1978	—	2.50	5.00
ROCKET					
❏ 40337	Only One Woman/In Good Time	1974	—	2.50	5.00
❏ 40455	Something Lacking in Me/Songs I Sing	1975	—	2.50	5.00
❏ 40491	A Girl Like You/Girl, We've Got to Keep On	1975	—	2.50	5.00
UNI					
❏ 55291	Some Sweet Day/Weirdhouse	1971	—	3.00	6.00
—As "Nigel Olsson's Drum Orchestra"					
❏ 55308	And I Know in My Heart/Sunshine Looks Like Rain	1971	—	3.00	6.00
Albums					
BANG					
❏ JZ 35792	Nigel	1979	2.50	5.00	10.00
❏ JZ 36491	Changing Tides	1980	2.50	5.00	10.00
ROCKET					
❏ L33-1962 [DJ]	Drummers Can Sing Too!	1975	5.00	10.00	20.00
—Promo-only interview album					
❏ PIG-2158	Nigel Olsson	1975	3.00	6.00	12.00
UNI					
❏ 73113	Nigel Olsson's Drum Orchestra	1971	3.75	7.50	15.00

OLYMPIC RUNNERS PETE WINGFIELD was in this group.
45s
LONDON

Number	Title (A Side/B Side)	Yr	VG	VG+	NM
❏ 202	Do It Over/Put the Music Where Your Mouth Is	1974	—	2.50	5.00
❏ 216	Grab It/Let Your Fingers Do the Talking	1974	—	2.50	5.00
❏ 217	Sproutin' Out/Be My Main Squeeze	1975	—	2.50	5.00
❏ 219	Drag It Over Here/Mac B. Coolie	1975	—	2.50	5.00
❏ 227	Dump the Bump/Exit City	1976	—	2.50	5.00
❏ 233	Party Time Is Here to Stay/'Til the Sun Comes Up	1976	—	2.50	5.00
❏ 247	Say What You Wanna But It Sure Is Funny/ It's Only Love	1976	—	2.50	5.00
❏ 261	Keep It Up/The Kool Gent	1977	—	2.50	5.00
POLYDOR					
❏ 2008	The Bitch/Onya	1979	—	2.00	4.00
❏ 2030	God Bless You/The Bitch	1979	—	2.00	4.00
Albums					
LONDON					
❏ PS 653	Put the Music Where Your Mouth Is	1974	3.75	7.50	15.00
❏ PS 658	Out in Front	1975	3.75	7.50	15.00
❏ PS 668	Don't Let Up	1975	3.75	7.50	15.00
❏ PS 678	Hot to Trot	1977	3.75	7.50	15.00
POLYDOR					
❏ PD-1-6196	Dancealot	1979	3.00	6.00	12.00

Number	Title (A Side/B Side)	Yr	VG	VG+	NM

OLYMPICS, THE Also see THE CHALLENGERS (3); WALTER WARD AND THE CHALLENGERS.
45s
ARVEE

Number	Title (A Side/B Side)	Yr	VG	VG+	NM
❑ 562	(Baby) Hully Gully/Private Eye	1959	6.25	12.50	25.00
❑ 595	Big Boy Pete/The Slop	1960	6.25	12.50	25.00
❑ 5006	Shimmy Like Kate/Workin' Hard	1960	5.00	10.00	20.00
❑ 5020	Dance by the Light of the Moon/Dodge City	1960	5.00	10.00	20.00
❑ 5023	Little Pedro/The Bullfight	1961	5.00	10.00	20.00
❑ 5031	Stay Where You Are/Dooley	1961	10.00	20.00	40.00
❑ 5044	Mash Them 'Taters/The Stomp	1961	5.00	10.00	20.00
❑ 5051	Everybody Likes to Cha Cha Cha/The Twist	1962	3.75	7.50	15.00
❑ 5056	Baby It's Hot/The Scotch	1962	3.75	7.50	15.00
❑ 5073	What'd I Say (Part 1)/What'd I Say (Part 2)	1963	3.75	7.50	15.00
❑ 6501	Big Boy Pete '65/Stay Where You Are	1965	3.00	6.00	12.00

DEMON

Number	Title (A Side/B Side)	Yr	VG	VG+	NM
❑ 1508	Western Movies/Well!	1958	7.50	15.00	30.00
❑ 1512	Dance with the Teacher/Everybody Needs Love	1958	6.25	12.50	25.00
❑ 1514	Your Love/The Chicken	1959	6.25	12.50	25.00

DUO DISC

Number	Title (A Side/B Side)	Yr	VG	VG+	NM
❑ 104	The Boogler (Part 1)/The Boogler (Part 2)	1964	3.00	6.00	12.00
❑ 105	Return of Big Boy Pete/Return of the Watusi	1964	3.00	6.00	12.00

JUBILEE

Number	Title (A Side/B Side)	Yr	VG	VG+	NM
❑ 5674	The Cartoon Song/Things That Make Me Laugh	1969	2.00	4.00	8.00

LOMA

Number	Title (A Side/B Side)	Yr	VG	VG+	NM
❑ 2010	I'm Comin' Home/Rainin' in My Heart	1965	2.50	5.00	10.00
❑ 2013	Good Lovin'/Olympic Shuffle	1965	2.50	5.00	10.00
❑ 2017	Baby I'm Yours/No More Will I Cry	1965	2.50	5.00	10.00

LOST-NITE

Number	Title (A Side/B Side)	Yr	VG	VG+	NM
❑ 311	Big Boy Pete/Mine Exclusively	197?	—	2.50	5.00

MGM

Number	Title (A Side/B Side)	Yr	VG	VG+	NM
❑ 14505	Worm in Your Wheatgerm/The Apartment	1973	—	2.50	5.00

MIRWOOD

Number	Title (A Side/B Side)	Yr	VG	VG+	NM
❑ 5504	We Go Together (Pretty Baby)/Secret Agents	1966	2.00	4.00	8.00
❑ 5513	Mine Exclusively/Secret Agents	1966	2.00	4.00	8.00
❑ 5523	Baby Do the Philly Dog/Western Movies	1966	2.00	4.00	8.00
❑ 5525	The Bounce/The Duck	1966	2.00	4.00	8.00
❑ 5529	The Same Old Thing/I'll Do a Little Bit More	1967	2.00	4.00	8.00
❑ 5533	Big Boy Pete/(Baby) Hully Gully	1967	2.00	4.00	8.00

PARKWAY

Number	Title (A Side/B Side)	Yr	VG	VG+	NM
❑ 6003	Lookin' for a Love/Good Things	1968	2.00	4.00	8.00

TITAN

Number	Title (A Side/B Side)	Yr	VG	VG+	NM
❑ 1718	The Chicken/Cool Short	1961	6.25	12.50	25.00

TRI DISC

Number	Title (A Side/B Side)	Yr	VG	VG+	NM
❑ 105	Return of Big Boy Pete/Return of the Watusi	1962	3.75	7.50	15.00
❑ 106	The Bounce/Fireworks	1963	3.75	7.50	15.00
❑ 107	Dancin' Holiday/Do the Slauson Shuffle	1963	3.75	7.50	15.00
❑ 110	Bounce Again/A New Dancin' Partner	1963	3.75	7.50	15.00
❑ 112	The Broken Hip/So Goodbye	1963	3.75	7.50	15.00

WARNER BROS.

Number	Title (A Side/B Side)	Yr	VG	VG+	NM
❑ 7369	Girl, You're My Kind of People/Please, Please, Please	1970	—	3.00	6.00

7-Inch Extended Plays
ARVEE

Number	Title (A Side/B Side)	Yr	VG	VG+	NM
❑ 423	(contents unknown)	1960	50.00	100.00	200.00
❑ 423 [PS]	Doin' the Hully Gully	1960	50.00	100.00	200.00

Albums
ARVEE

Number	Title (A Side/B Side)	Yr	VG	VG+	NM
❑ A-423 [M]	Doin' the Hully Gully	1960	40.00	80.00	160.00
❑ A-424 [M]	Dance by the Light of the Moon	1961	30.00	60.00	120.00
❑ A-429 [M]	Party Time	1961	30.00	60.00	120.00

EVEREST

Number	Title (A Side/B Side)	Yr	VG	VG+	NM
❑ 4109	The Olympics	1981	2.50	5.00	10.00

MIRWOOD

Number	Title (A Side/B Side)	Yr	VG	VG+	NM
❑ MS-7003 [S]	Something Old, Something New	1966	12.50	25.00	50.00
❑ MW-7003 [M]	Something Old, Something New	1966	10.00	20.00	40.00

POST

Number	Title (A Side/B Side)	Yr	VG	VG+	NM
❑ 8000	The Olympics Sing	196?	6.25	12.50	25.00

RHINO

Number	Title (A Side/B Side)	Yr	VG	VG+	NM
❑ RNDF-207	The Official Record Album of the Olympics	1983	3.00	6.00	12.00

TRI-DISC

Number	Title (A Side/B Side)	Yr	VG	VG+	NM
❑ 1001 [M]	Do the Bounce	1963	20.00	40.00	80.00

OMEGAS, THE (1)
45s
DECCA

Number	Title (A Side/B Side)	Yr	VG	VG+	NM
❑ 31008	When You Touch Me/Froze	1959	5.00	10.00	20.00
❑ 31094	So How Come (No One Loves Me)/Study Hall	1960	5.00	10.00	20.00
❑ 31138	Falling in Love/No One Will Ever Know	1960	5.00	10.00	20.00

GROOVE

Number	Title (A Side/B Side)	Yr	VG	VG+	NM
❑ 4	I Wanna Go Home/Midnight Run	1961	3.75	7.50	15.00

OMEGAS, THE (2)
45s
UNITED ARTISTS

Number	Title (A Side/B Side)	Yr	VG	VG+	NM
❑ 50247	I Can't Believe/Mr. Yates	1968	7.50	15.00	30.00

OMNIBUS
45s
UNITED ARTISTS

Number	Title (A Side/B Side)	Yr	VG	VG+	NM
❑ 50631	It's All in Your Heart/The Man Song	1970	2.00	4.00	8.00

Albums
UNITED ARTISTS

Number	Title (A Side/B Side)	Yr	VG	VG+	NM
❑ UAS-6743	Omnibus	1970	10.00	20.00	40.00

ONCOMERS, THE
45s
GATEWAY CUSTOM

Number	Title (A Side/B Side)	Yr	VG	VG+	NM
❑ 103	Every Day Now/You Let Me Down	196?	10.00	20.00	40.00

100 PROOF AGED IN SOUL
45s
HOT WAX

Number	Title (A Side/B Side)	Yr	VG	VG+	NM
❑ 6904	Too Many Cooks (Spoil the Soup)/Not Enough Love to Satisfy	1969	—	3.00	6.00

—Later pressings as "100 Proof Aged in Soul"

Number	Title (A Side/B Side)	Yr	VG	VG+	NM
❑ 6904	Too Many Cooks (Spoil the Soup)/Not Enough Love to Satisfy	1969	3.00	6.00	12.00

—First pressings as "Aged in Soul"

Number	Title (A Side/B Side)	Yr	VG	VG+	NM
❑ 7004	Somebody's Been Sleeping/I've Come to Save You	1970	—	3.00	6.00
❑ 7009	One Man's Leftovers (Is Another Man's Feast)/If I Could See the Light in the Window	1970	—	3.00	6.00
❑ 7104	Driveway/Love Is Sweeter	1971	—	3.00	6.00
❑ 7108	90 Day Freeze (On Her Love)/Not Enough Love to Satisfy	1971	—	3.00	6.00
❑ 7202	Everything Good Is Bad/I'd Rather Fight Than Switch	1972	—	3.00	6.00
❑ 7206	Don't Scratch/If I Could See the Light in the Window	1972	—	3.00	6.00
❑ 7211	Nothing Sweeter Than Love/Since You've Been Gone	1972	—	3.00	6.00

Albums
HOT WAX

Number	Title (A Side/B Side)	Yr	VG	VG+	NM
❑ 704	Somebody's Been Sleeping in My Bed	1970	3.75	7.50	15.00
❑ 712	100 Proof Aged in Soul	1971	3.75	7.50	15.00

ONO, YOKO Also see JOHN LENNON.
12-Inch Singles
GEFFEN

Number	Title (A Side/B Side)	Yr	VG	VG+	NM
❑ PRO-A-934 [DJ]	Walking on Thin Ice (3:23) (5:58)	1981	3.75	7.50	15.00
❑ PRO-A-975 [DJ]	No, No, No/Dogtown/I Don't Know Why/She Gets Down on Her Knees	1981	5.00	10.00	20.00

POLYDOR

Number	Title (A Side/B Side)	Yr	VG	VG+	NM
❑ PRO 192 [DJ]	My Man/Let the Tears Dry	1982	2.50	5.00	10.00
❑ 810575-1	Never Say Goodbye (Remix)/Loneliness (Remix)	1983	3.75	7.50	15.00
❑ 883455-1	Hell in Paradise (Club Version) (Dub Version) (Single Version)	1985	2.00	4.00	8.00
❑ 883872-1 [DJ]	Walking on Thin Ice (Remix 7:17)/Cape Clear (2 versions)	1986	3.75	7.50	15.00

45s
APPLE

Number	Title (A Side/B Side)	Yr	VG	VG+	NM
❑ GM/OYB-1 [DJ]	Greenfield Morning/Open Your Box	1971	200.00	400.00	800.00

—Exactly six copies made for the personal use of Yoko Ono.

Number	Title (A Side/B Side)	Yr	VG	VG+	NM
❑ 1839	Mrs. Lennon/Midsummer New York	1971	—	3.50	7.00

—As "Yoko Ono/Plastic Ono Band"

Number	Title (A Side/B Side)	Yr	VG	VG+	NM
❑ 1853	Now or Never/Move On Fast	1972	—	3.50	7.00
❑ 1853 [PS]	Now or Never/Move On Fast	1972	2.00	4.00	8.00
❑ 1859	Death of Samantha/Yang Yang	1973	—	3.50	7.00
❑ 1867	Woman Power/Men, Men, Men	1973	—	3.50	7.00

CAPITOL

Number	Title (A Side/B Side)	Yr	VG	VG+	NM
❑ S7-18550	Never Say Goodbye/We're All Water	1995	—	2.00	4.00

GEFFEN

Number	Title (A Side/B Side)	Yr	VG	VG+	NM
❑ PRO-S-935 [DJ]	Walking on Thin Ice (3:23) (5:58)	1981	3.00	6.00	12.00
❑ 49683	Walking on Thin Ice/It Happened	1981	—	2.50	5.00
❑ 49683 [PS]	Walking on Thin Ice/It Happened	1981	—	2.50	5.00

—Includes picture sleeve and lyric insert

Number	Title (A Side/B Side)	Yr	VG	VG+	NM
❑ 49802	No, No, No/Will You Touch Me	1981	—	2.50	5.00
❑ 49802 [PS]	No, No, No/Will You Touch Me	1981	—	2.50	5.00
❑ 49849	Goodbye Sadness/I Don't Know Why	1981	—	2.50	5.00

POLYDOR

Number	Title (A Side/B Side)	Yr	VG	VG+	NM
❑ 2224	My Man/Let the Tears Dry	1982	—	2.00	4.00
❑ 2224 [PS]	My Man/Let the Tears Dry	1982	—	2.00	4.00
❑ 883455-7	Hell in Paradise/(Instrumental)	1985	—	2.00	4.00
❑ 883455-7 [PS]	Hell in Paradise/(Instrumental)	1985	—	2.00	4.00

Albums
APPLE

Number	Title (A Side/B Side)	Yr	VG	VG+	NM
❑ SW-3373	Yoko Ono Plastic Ono Band	1970	5.00	10.00	20.00
❑ SVBB-3380 [(2)]	Fly	1971	6.50	12.50	25.00
❑ SVBB-3399 [(2)]	Approximately Infinite Universe	1973	6.25	12.50	25.00
❑ SW-3412	Feeling the Space	1973	5.00	10.00	20.00

CAPITOL

Number	Title (A Side/B Side)	Yr	VG	VG+	NM
❑ SPRO-11219 [DJ]	Rising Mixes	1996	3.00	6.00	12.00

—Promo-only vinyl EP of six remixes from the CD "Rising"
GEFFEN

Number	Title (A Side/B Side)	Yr	VG	VG+	NM
❑ GHS 2004	Season of Glass	1981	3.00	6.00	12.00

POLYDOR

Number	Title (A Side/B Side)	Yr	VG	VG+	NM
❑ PD-1-6364	It's Alright (I See Rainbows)	1982	2.50	5.00	10.00
❑ 823289-1	It's Alright (I See Rainbows)	1984	2.00	4.00	8.00

—Reissue

Number	Title (A Side/B Side)	Yr	VG	VG+	NM
❑ 827530-1	Starpeace	1985	3.00	6.00	12.00

OPALS, THE (1)
45s
APOLLO

Number	Title (A Side/B Side)	Yr	VG	VG+	NM
❑ 462	My Heart's Desire/Oh But She Did	1954	50.00	100.00	200.00

—Original with flat (non-glossy) label

Number	Title (A Side/B Side)	Yr	VG	VG+	NM
❑ 462	My Heart's Desire/Oh But She Did	1958	10.00	20.00	40.00

—Reissue with glossy label

OPALS, THE (2)
45s
BELTONE

Number	Title (A Side/B Side)	Yr	VG	VG+	NM
❑ 2025	Love/Two-Sided Love	1962	6.25	12.50	25.00

OPALS, THE (3)
45s
OKEH

Number	Title (A Side/B Side)	Yr	VG	VG+	NM
❑ 7188	Does It Matter/Tender Lover	1964	6.25	12.50	25.00
❑ 7202	You Can't Hurt Me No More/Rhythm	1964	6.25	12.50	25.00
❑ 7224	I'm So Afraid/Restless Lover	1965	6.25	12.50	25.00

O

Number	Title (A Side/B Side)	Yr	VG	VG+	NM
OPALS, THE (U) May be group (3); could be a different group.					
45s					
LAURIE					
❑ 3288	No, No, Never Again/Just Like a Little Bitty Baby	1965	3.00	6.00	12.00
ORANG UTAN					
Albums					
BELL					
❑ 6054	Orang Utan	1971	10.00	20.00	40.00
ORANGE COLORED SKY					
45s					
UNI					
❑ 55088	Orange Colored Sky/The Shadow of Summer	1968	3.00	6.00	12.00
❑ 55115	Happiness Is/Another Sky	1969	3.00	6.00	12.00
❑ 55156	The Sun and I/Sweet Potato	1969	3.00	6.00	12.00
Albums					
UNI					
❑ 73031	Orange Colored Sky	1968	12.50	25.00	50.00
ORANGE WEDGE					
Albums					
(NO LABEL)					
❑ (no #)	No One Left But Me	1975	75.00	150.00	300.00
❑ (no #)	Wedge	1975	75.00	150.00	300.00
ORBISON, ROY					
12-Inch Singles					
VIRGIN					
❑ PR 2593 [DJ]	You Got It (same on both sides)	1989	3.00	6.00	12.00
❑ PR 2667 [DJ]	She's a Mystery to Me (same on both sides)	1989	3.75	7.50	15.00
45s					
ASYLUM					
❑ 46048	Tears/Easy Way Out	1979	—	2.50	5.00
❑ 46541	Poor Baby/Lay It Down	1979	—	2.50	5.00
ERIC					
❑ 7101	Pretty Paper/Oh Pretty Woman	197?	—	2.00	4.00
JE-WEL					
❑ 101	Ooby Dooby/Tryin' to Get to You	1956	1500.	2750.	4000.
—As "The Teen Kings"; with "Vocal: Roy Oribson" credit (spelled incorrectly)					
❑ 101	Ooby Dooby/Tryin' to Get to You	1956	1500.	2750.	4000.
—As "The Teen Kings"; with "Vocal: Roy Orbison" credit (spelled correctly)					
MERCURY					
❑ 73610	Sweet Mama Blue/Heartache	1974	2.00	4.00	8.00
❑ 73652	Hung Up onYou/Spanish Nights	1975	—	3.00	6.00
❑ 73705	It's Lonely/Still	1975	—	3.00	6.00
MGM					
❑ CS9-5	Celebrity Scene: Roy Orbison	1967	25.00	50.00	100.00
—Box set of five singles (13756-13760). Price includes box, all 5 singles, jukebox title strips, bio. Records are sometimes found by themselves, so they are also listed separately.					
❑ 13386	Ride Away/Wonderin'	1965	2.50	5.00	10.00
❑ 13386 [PS]	Ride Away/Wonderin'	1965	5.00	10.00	20.00
❑ 13410	Crawling Back/If You Can't Say Something Nice	1965	2.50	5.00	10.00
❑ 13410 [PS]	Crawling Back/If You Can't Say Something Nice	1965	5.00	10.00	20.00
❑ 13446	Breakin' Up Is Breakin' My Heart/Wait	1966	2.50	5.00	10.00
❑ 13446 [PS]	Breakin' Up Is Breakin' My Heart/Wait	1966	5.00	10.00	20.00
❑ 13498	Twinkle Toes/Where Is Tomorrow	1966	2.50	5.00	10.00
❑ 13498 [PS]	Twinkle Toes/Where Is Tomorrow	1966	5.00	10.00	20.00
❑ 13549	Too Soon to Know/ You'll Never Be Sixteen Again	1966	2.50	5.00	10.00
❑ 13549 [PS]	Too Soon to Know/ You'll Never Be Sixteen Again	1966	25.00	50.00	100.00
❑ 13634	Communication Breakdown/ Going Back to Gloria	1966	2.50	5.00	10.00
❑ 13685	So Good/Memories	1967	2.50	5.00	10.00
❑ 13756	Ride Away/Crawlin' Back	1967	3.75	7.50	15.00
—Part of Celebrity Scene CS9-5					
❑ 13757	Breakin' Up Is Breakin' My Heart/ Too Soon to Know	1967	3.75	7.50	15.00
—Part of Celebrity Scene CS9-5					
❑ 13758	Twinkle Toes/Where Is Tomorrow?	1967	3.75	7.50	15.00
—Part of Celebrity Scene CS9-5					
❑ 13759	Sweet Dreams/Going Back to Gloria	1967	3.75	7.50	15.00
—Part of Celebrity Scene CS9-5					
❑ 13760	You'll Never Be Sixteen Again/There Won't Be Many Coming Home	1967	3.75	7.50	15.00
—Part of Celebrity Scene CS9-5					
❑ 13764	Cry Softly Lonely One/Pistolero	1967	2.50	5.00	10.00
❑ 13764 [PS]	Cry Softly Lonely One/Pistolero	1967	5.00	10.00	20.00
❑ 13817	She/Here Comes the Rain Baby	1967	2.50	5.00	10.00
❑ 13889	Shy Away/Born to Be Loved by You	1968	2.50	5.00	10.00
❑ 13950	Flowers/Walk On	1968	2.50	5.00	10.00
❑ 13991	Heartache/Sugar Man	1968	2.50	5.00	10.00
❑ 14039	Southbound Jericho Parkway/My Friend	1969	2.50	5.00	10.00
❑ 14079	Penny Arcade/Tennessee Own My Soul	1969	2.50	5.00	10.00
❑ 14105	How Do You Start Over/She Cheats on Me	1970	2.50	5.00	10.00
❑ 14121	So Young/If I Had a Woman Like You	1970	2.50	5.00	10.00
❑ 14293	Close Again/Last Night	1971	2.50	5.00	10.00
❑ 14358	Changes/God Loves You	1972	2.50	5.00	10.00
❑ 14413	Remember the Good/Harlem Woman	1972	2.50	5.00	10.00
❑ 14413	Remember the Good/If Only for a While	1972	2.50	5.00	10.00
❑ 14441	I Can Read Between the Lines/ Memphis, Tennessee	1972	2.50	5.00	10.00
❑ 14552	Rain Rain (Coming Down)/Sooner or Later	1973	2.50	5.00	10.00
❑ 14626	I Wanna Live/You Lay So Easy on My Mind	1973	2.50	5.00	10.00
MONUMENT					
❑ 45-200	(I'm a) Southern Man/Born to Love Me	1976	—	2.50	5.00
❑ 45-215	Drifting Away/Under Suspicion	1977	—	2.50	5.00
❑ 409	Paper Boy/With the Bug	1959	20.00	40.00	80.00
—White label with vertical lines					
❑ 412	Uptown/Pretty One	1959	7.50	15.00	30.00
❑ 421	Only the Lonely (Know the Way I Feel)/Here Comes That Song Again	1960	6.25	12.50	25.00
❑ 425	Blue Angel/Today's Teardrops	1960	5.00	10.00	20.00
❑ 433	I'm Hurtin'/I Can't Stop Loving You	1960	5.00	10.00	20.00
❑ 433 [PS]	I'm Hurtin'/I Can't Stop Loving You	1960	30.00	60.00	120.00

Number	Title (A Side/B Side)	Yr	VG	VG+	NM
❑ 438	Running Scared/Love Hurts	1961	5.00	10.00	20.00
❑ 438 [PS]	Running Scared/Love Hurts	1961	10.00	20.00	40.00
❑ 447	Crying/Candy Man	1961	5.00	10.00	20.00
❑ 447 [PS]	Crying/Candy Man	1961	10.00	20.00	40.00
❑ 456	Dream Baby (How Long Must I Dream)/ The Actress	1962	5.00	10.00	20.00
❑ 456 [PS]	Dream Baby (How Long Must I Dream)/ The Actress	1962	10.00	20.00	40.00
❑ 461	The Crowd/Mama	1962	5.00	10.00	20.00
❑ 461 [PS]	The Crowd/Mama	1962	10.00	20.00	40.00
❑ 467	Leah/Workin' for the Man	1962	5.00	10.00	20.00
❑ 467 [PS]	Leah/Workin' for the Man	1962	10.00	20.00	40.00
❑ 503	Paper Boy/With the Bug	196?	3.00	6.00	12.00
—Reissue of 409					
❑ 505	Uptown/Pretty One	196?	3.00	6.00	12.00
—Reissue of 412					
❑ 508	Only the Lonely (Know the Way I Feel)/ Here Comes That Song Again	196?	3.00	6.00	12.00
—Reissue of 421					
❑ 509	Blue Angel/Today's Teardrops	196?	3.00	6.00	12.00
—Reissue of 425					
❑ 510	I'm Hurtin'/I Can't Stop Loving You	196?	3.00	6.00	12.00
—Reissue of 433					
❑ 514	Running Scared/Love Hurts	196?	3.00	6.00	12.00
—Reissue of 438					
❑ 517	Crying/Candy Man	196?	3.00	6.00	12.00
—Reissue of 447					
❑ 519	Dream Baby (How Long Must I Dream)/ The Actress	196?	3.00	6.00	12.00
—Reissue of 456					
❑ 520	The Crowd/Mama	196?	3.00	6.00	12.00
—Reissue of 461					
❑ 521	Leah/Working for the Man	196?	3.00	6.00	12.00
—Reissue of 467; note that the B-side title is slightly different here than on 467					
❑ 526	In Dreams/Shahdaroba	196?	3.00	6.00	12.00
—Reissue of 806					
❑ 527	Falling/Distant Drums	196?	3.00	6.00	12.00
—Reissue of 815					
❑ 530	Mean Woman Blues/Blue Bayou	196?	3.00	6.00	12.00
—Reissue of 824					
❑ 531	Pretty Paper/Beautiful Dreamer	196?	3.00	6.00	12.00
—Reissue of 830					
❑ 533	It's Over/Indian Wedding	196?	3.00	6.00	12.00
—Reissue of 837					
❑ 806	In Dreams/Shahdaroba	1963	5.00	10.00	20.00
❑ 806 [PS]	In Dreams/Shahdaroba	1963	10.00	20.00	40.00
❑ 815	Falling/Distant Drums	1963	5.00	10.00	20.00
❑ 815 [PS]	Falling/Distant Drums	1963	12.50	25.00	50.00
❑ 824	Mean Woman Blues/Blue Bayou	1963	5.00	10.00	20.00
❑ 830	Pretty Paper/Beautiful Dreamer	1963	5.00	10.00	20.00
❑ 837	It's Over/Indian Wedding	1964	5.00	10.00	20.00
❑ 837 [PS]	It's Over/Indian Wedding	1964	10.00	20.00	40.00
❑ 851	Oh Pretty Woman/Yo Te Amo Maria	1964	5.00	10.00	20.00
—Revised title					
❑ 851	Pretty Woman/Yo Te Amo Maria	1964	7.50	15.00	30.00
—Original title					
❑ 873	Goodnight/Only with You	1965	3.75	7.50	15.00
❑ 891	(Say) You're My Girl/Sleepy Hollow	1965	3.75	7.50	15.00
❑ 906	Let the Good Times Roll/Distant Drums	1965	3.75	7.50	15.00
❑ 939	Lana/Our Summer Song	1966	3.75	7.50	15.00
❑ 1900	Running Scared/Love Hurts	197?	—	2.00	4.00
—"Golden Series" reissue					
❑ 1901	Crying/Candy Man	197?	—	2.00	4.00
—"Golden Series" reissue					
❑ 1902	Leah/Workin' for the Man	197?	—	2.00	4.00
—"Golden Series" reissue					
❑ 1903	Mean Woman Blues/Blue Bayou	197?	—	2.00	4.00
—"Golden Series" reissue					
❑ 1904	Falling/Distant Drums	197?	—	2.00	4.00
—"Golden Series" reissue					
❑ 1906	Only the Lonely (Know the Way I Feel)/Uptown	197?	—	2.00	4.00
—"Golden Series" reissue					
❑ 1907	Dream Baby (How Long Must I Dream)/I'm Hurtin'	197?	—	2.00	4.00
—"Golden Series" reissue					
❑ 1908	In Dreams/The Crowd	197?	—	2.00	4.00
—"Golden Series" reissue					
❑ 1910	Oh Pretty Woman/It's Over	197?	—	2.00	4.00
—"Golden Series" reissue					
❑ 1915	Blue Angel/Paper Boy	197?	—	2.00	4.00
—"Golden Series" reissue					
❑ 1936	Pretty Paper/Beautiful Dreamer	1976	—	2.00	4.00
—"Golden Series" reissue					
❑ 8690	Belinda/All These Chains	1976	—	2.50	5.00
NORTON					
❑ 45-846	Domino/Everybody's Tryin' to Kiss My Baby	2001	—	2.00	4.00
—B-side by Gene Ross; includes custom company sleeve; Sun Records outtakes					
RCA VICTOR					
❑ 47-7381	Sweet and Innocent/Seems to Me	1958	10.00	20.00	40.00
❑ 47-7447	Almost Eighteen/Julie	1959	10.00	20.00	40.00
SUN					
❑ 242	Ooby Dooby/Go! Go! Go!	1956	25.00	50.00	100.00
❑ 251	Rockhouse/You're My Baby	1956	15.00	30.00	60.00
❑ 265	Devil Doll/Sweet and Easy to Love	1957	20.00	40.00	80.00
❑ 284	Chicken Hearted/I Like Love	1958	12.50	25.00	50.00
❑ 353	Devil Doll/Sweet and Easy to Love	1960	62.50	125.00	250.00
VIRGIN					
❑ 99159	Oh Pretty Woman/Claudette	1989	—	—	3.00
❑ 99159 [PS]	Oh Pretty Woman/Claudette	1989	—	—	3.00
❑ 99202	California Blue/In Dreams	1989	—	—	3.00
❑ 99202 [PS]	California Blue/In Dreams	1989	—	—	3.00
❑ 99227	She's a Mystery to Me/Dream Baby	1989	—	—	3.00
❑ 99227 [PS]	She's a Mystery to Me/Dream Baby	1989	—	—	3.00
❑ 99245	You Got It/Crying	1989	—	2.00	4.00
—B-side with k.d. lang					
❑ 99245	You Got It/The Only One	1989	—	—	3.00

Number	Title (A Side/B Side)	Yr	VG	VG+	NM
❏ 99245 [PS]	You Got It	1989	—	—	3.00
—The same sleeve may have come with both issues of the 45					
❏ 99388	Crying/Falling	1988	—	—	3.00
—A-side with k.d. lang					
❏ 99388 [PS]	Crying/Falling	1988	—	—	3.00
❏ 99434	In Dreams/Leah	1987	—	—	3.00
❏ 99434 [PS]	In Dreams/Leah	1987	—	2.00	4.00
WARNER BROS.					
❏ 49262	That Lovin' You Feeling Again/Lola	1980	—	2.50	5.00
—A-side with Emmylou Harris; B-side by Craig Hundley					

7-Inch Extended Plays
MONUMENT

Number	Title (A Side/B Side)	Yr	VG	VG+	NM
❏ MSP-2	Crying/Our Summer Song/Let's Make a Memory//Lana/Loneliness/Night Life	1962	25.00	50.00	100.00
—Probably a jukebox single; small hole, plays at 33 1/3 rpm; picture sleeve is unconfirmed					
❏ SSP-512	Oh, Pretty Woman/Dance/Let the Good Times Roll//(I Get So) Sentimental/Wedding Day/I'd Be a Legend in My Time	1965	10.00	20.00	40.00
—Jukebox issue; small hole, plays at 33 1/3 rpm					
❏ SSP-512 [PS]	Orbisongs, Volume One	1965	10.00	20.00	40.00

Albums
ACCORD

Number	Title (A Side/B Side)	Yr	VG	VG+	NM
❏ SN-7150	Ooby Dooby	1981	2.00	4.00	8.00
ASYLUM					
❏ 6E-198	Laminar Flow	1979	3.00	6.00	12.00
BUCKBOARD					
❏ BBS-1015	Roy Orbison's Golden Hits	197?	2.50	5.00	10.00
CANDELITE					
❏ P2 12946 [(2)]	The Living Legend of Roy Orbison	1976	3.75	7.50	15.00
DCC COMPACT CLASSICS					
❏ LPZ-2042 [(2)]	The All-Time Greatest Hits of Roy Orbison	1997	30.00	60.00	120.00
—Audiophile vinyl					
DESIGN					
❏ DLP-164 [M]	Orbiting with Roy Orbison	196?	3.75	7.50	15.00
❏ DLPS-164 [R]	Orbiting with Roy Orbison	196?	2.50	5.00	10.00
HALLMARK					
❏ SHM-824	The Exciting Roy Orbison	197?	2.00	4.00	8.00
HITS UNLIMITED					
❏ 233-0	My Spell on You	1982	2.00	4.00	8.00
MERCURY					
❏ SRM-1-1045	I'm Still in Love with You	1975	3.00	6.00	12.00
MGM					
❏ E-4308 [M]	There Is Only One Roy Orbison	1965	6.25	12.50	25.00
❏ SE-4308 [S]	There Is Only One Roy Orbison	1965	8.75	17.50	35.00
❏ E-4322 [M]	The Orbison Way	1965	6.25	12.50	25.00
❏ SE-4322 [S]	The Orbison Way	1965	8.75	17.50	35.00
❏ E-4379 [M]	The Classic Roy Orbison	1966	6.25	12.50	25.00
❏ SE-4379 [S]	The Classic Roy Orbison	1966	8.75	17.50	35.00
❏ E-4424 [M]	Roy Orbison Sings Don Gibson	1967	6.25	12.50	25.00
❏ SE-4424 [S]	Roy Orbison Sings Don Gibson	1967	8.75	17.50	35.00
❏ E-4514 [M]	Cry Softly, Lonely One	1967	6.25	12.50	25.00
❏ SE-4514 [S]	Cry Softly, Lonely One	1967	8.75	17.50	35.00
❏ SE-4636	The Many Moods of Roy Orbison	1969	6.25	12.50	25.00
❏ SE-4659	The Great Songs of Roy Orbison	1970	6.25	12.50	25.00
❏ SE-4683	Hank Williams the Roy Orbison Way	1970	6.25	12.50	25.00
❏ SE-4835	Roy Orbison Sings	1972	3.75	7.50	15.00
❏ SE-4867	Memphis	1972	3.75	7.50	15.00
❏ SE-4934	Milestones	1973	3.75	7.50	15.00
❏ ST 90454 [S]	There Is Only One Roy Orbison	1965	10.00	20.00	40.00
—Capitol Record Club edition					
❏ T 90454 [M]	There Is Only One Roy Orbison	1965	10.00	20.00	40.00
—Capitol Record Club edition					
❏ ST-90631 [S]	The Orbison Way	1965	8.75	17.50	35.00
—Capitol Record Club edition					
❏ T-90631 [M]	The Orbison Way	1965	8.75	17.50	35.00
—Capitol Record Club edition					
❏ ST-90928 [S]	The Classic Roy Orbison	1966	8.75	17.50	35.00
—Capitol Record Club edition					
❏ T-90928 [M]	The Classic Roy Orbison	1966	8.75	17.50	35.00
—Capitol Record Club edition					
❏ ST-91173 [S]	Roy Orbison Sings Don Gibson	1967	8.75	17.50	35.00
—Capitol Record Club edition					
❏ T-91173 [M]	Roy Orbison Sings Don Gibson	1967	8.75	17.50	35.00
—Capitol Record Club edition					
MONUMENT					
❏ M-4002 [M]	Lonely and Blue	1961	37.50	75.00	150.00
❏ M-4007 [M]	Crying	1962	30.00	60.00	120.00
❏ M-4009 [M]	Roy Orbison's Greatest Hits	1962	12.50	25.00	50.00
❏ MC-6619	Roy Orbison's Greatest Hits	1977	3.00	6.00	12.00
❏ MC-6620	In Dreams	1977	3.00	6.00	12.00
❏ MC-6621	More of Roy Orbison's Greatest Hits	1977	3.00	6.00	12.00
❏ MC-6622	The Very Best of Roy Orbison	1977	3.00	6.00	12.00
❏ MG-7600	Regeneration	1976	3.75	7.50	15.00
❏ MLP-8000 [M]	Roy Orbison's Greatest Hits	1963	7.50	15.00	30.00
❏ MLP-8003 [M]	In Dreams	1963	12.50	25.00	50.00
—White and rainbow label					
❏ MLP-8003 [M]	In Dreams	1964	7.50	15.00	30.00
—Green and gold label					
❏ MLP-8023 [M]	Early Orbison	1964	7.50	15.00	30.00
❏ MLP-8024 [M]	More of Roy Orbison's Greatest Hits	1964	7.50	15.00	30.00
❏ MLP-8035 [M]	Orbisongs	1965	6.25	12.50	25.00
❏ MLP-8045 [M]	The Very Best of Roy Orbison	1966	6.25	12.50	25.00
❏ MP-8600 [(2)]	The All-Time Greatest Hits of Roy Orbison	1977	4.00	8.00	16.00
❏ SM-14002 [S]	Lonely and Blue	1961	150.00	300.00	600.00
❏ SM-14007 [S]	Crying	1962	150.00	300.00	600.00
❏ SM-14009 [S]	Roy Orbison's Greatest Hits	1962	20.00	40.00	80.00
❏ SLP-18000 [S]	Roy Orbison's Greatest Hits	1963	10.00	20.00	40.00
❏ SLP-18003 [S]	In Dreams	1963	25.00	50.00	100.00
—White and rainbow label					
❏ SLP-18003 [S]	In Dreams	1964	12.50	25.00	50.00
—Green and gold label					
❏ SLP-18023 [S]	Early Orbison	1964	12.50	25.00	50.00
❏ SLP-18024 [S]	More of Roy Orbison's Greatest Hits	1964	10.00	20.00	40.00
❏ SLP-18035 [S]	Orbisongs	1965	8.75	17.50	35.00
❏ SLP-18045 [P]	The Very Best of Roy Orbison	1966	8.75	17.50	35.00
—"It's Over" is rechanneled					

Number	Title (A Side/B Side)	Yr	VG	VG+	NM
❏ KZG 31484 [(2)]	The All-Time Greatest Hits of Roy Orbison	1972	6.25	12.50	25.00
❏ KWG 38384 [(2)]	The All-Time Greatest Hits of Roy Orbison	1982	2.50	5.00	10.00
RHINO					
❏ R1 70711	The Classic Roy Orbison	1989	3.00	6.00	12.00
❏ R1 70916	The Sun Years	1989	3.75	7.50	15.00
❏ R1 71493 [(2)]	For the Lonely: A Roy Orbison Anthology	1988	3.00	6.00	12.00
SUN					
❏ 113	The Original Sound	1969	3.00	6.00	12.00
❏ LP-1260 [M]	Roy Orbison at the Rock House	1961	150.00	300.00	600.00
TIME-LIFE					
❏ SRNR 34 [(2)]	Roy Orbison 1960-1965	1990	5.00	10.00	20.00
—Box set in "The Rock 'n' Roll Era" series					
TRIP					
❏ TLX-8505	The Best of Roy Orbison	197?	2.00	4.00	8.00
VIRGIN					
❏ 90604 [(2)]	In Dreams: The Greatest Hits	1987	3.00	6.00	12.00
—Re-recordings of his original hits					
❏ 91058	Mystery Girl	1989	2.50	5.00	10.00
❏ 91295	A Black and White Night	1990	3.75	7.50	15.00

ORBITS, THE More than one group.
45s
ARGO

Number	Title (A Side/B Side)	Yr	VG	VG+	NM
❏ 5286	Who Are You/Mr. Bad Luck	1958	10.00	20.00	40.00
DOOTO					
❏ 601	Tell Me Baby/Two Crazy Scientists	196?	5.00	10.00	20.00
FLAIR-X					
❏ 5000	Message of Love/I Really Do	1956	7.50	15.00	30.00
NU-KAT					
❏ 116/7	Knock Her Down/My Love	1959	7.50	15.00	30.00
SPACE					
❏ 1116	Queen Bee/Darlin'	1960	100.00	200.00	400.00

ORCHIDS, THE (1)
45s
COLUMBIA

Number	Title (A Side/B Side)	Yr	VG	VG+	NM
❏ 42913	That Boy Is Messin' Up My Mind/Harlem Tango	1963	5.00	10.00	20.00
❏ 43066	Tell Me a Story/From Bad to Worse	1964	5.00	10.00	20.00
❏ 43175	Christmas Is the Time to Be With Your Baby/It Doesn't Matter	1964	5.00	10.00	20.00

ORCHIDS, THE (2)
45s
HARLOW

Number	Title (A Side/B Side)	Yr	VG	VG+	NM
❏ 101	I Don't Think You Missed Me/We're in Love	1962	5.00	10.00	20.00

ORCHIDS, THE (3)
45s
KING

Number	Title (A Side/B Side)	Yr	VG	VG+	NM
❏ 4661	Oh Why/All Night Baby	1953	100.00	200.00	400.00
❏ 4663	I've Been a Fool from the Start/Beginning to Miss You	1953	100.00	200.00	400.00
LOST-NITE					
❏ 150	I Can't Refuse/You Said You Loved Me	196?	—	3.00	6.00
—Reissue					
❏ 159	Newly Wed/You're Everything to Me	196?	—	3.00	6.00
—Reissue					
PARROT					
❏ 815	Newly Wed/You're Everything to Me	1955	100.00	200.00	400.00
❏ 819	I Can't Refuse/You Said You Loved Me	1955	62.50	125.00	250.00

ORCHIDS, THE (U) Some of these could be group (1) or (2).
45s
ROULETTE

Number	Title (A Side/B Side)	Yr	VG	VG+	NM
❏ 4412	Pony Walk/Good Time Stomp	1962	5.00	10.00	20.00
❏ 4633	Good Good Time/Love Is What You Make It	1965	3.00	6.00	12.00
UNITED ARTISTS					
❏ 375	You'll Never Know/Say Yes	1961	5.00	10.00	20.00
WALL					
❏ 549	Soft Shadows/Good Gully	1961	5.00	10.00	20.00

Albums
ROULETTE

Number	Title (A Side/B Side)	Yr	VG	VG+	NM
❏ R-25169 [M]	Twistin' at the Roundtable	1962	5.00	10.00	20.00
❏ SR-25169 [S]	Twistin' at the Roundtable	1962	6.25	12.50	25.00

ORGAN GRINDERS, THE
45s
SMASH

Number	Title (A Side/B Side)	Yr	VG	VG+	NM
❏ 2242	Babylon/Precious Time	1969	2.50	5.00	10.00

Albums
MERCURY

Number	Title (A Side/B Side)	Yr	VG	VG+	NM
❏ SR-61282	Out of the Egg	1970	7.50	15.00	30.00

ORIENT EXPRESS, THE
Albums
MAINSTREAN

Number	Title (A Side/B Side)	Yr	VG	VG+	NM
❏ S-6117	The Orient Express	1969	20.00	40.00	80.00

ORIENTS, THE
45s
LAURIE

Number	Title (A Side/B Side)	Yr	VG	VG+	NM
❏ 3232	Queen of the Angels/Shouldn't I	1964	10.00	20.00	40.00

ORIGINAL CADILLACS, THE See THE CADILLACS.

ORIGINAL CASTE, THE
45s
DOT

Number	Title (A Side/B Side)	Yr	VG	VG+	NM
❏ 17071	Just Like Tom Thumb's Blues/I Can't Make It Anymore	1968	3.75	7.50	15.00
❏ 17138	Snakes and Ladders/I'm So Much in Love	1968	3.75	7.50	15.00
T-A					
❏ 186	One Tin Soldier/Live for Tomorrow	1969	3.00	6.00	12.00
❏ 186 [PS]	One Tin Soldier/Live for Tomorrow	1969	3.00	6.00	12.00
❏ 192	Mr. Monday/Highway	1970	2.50	5.00	10.00
❏ 197	Nothing Can Touch Me/Country Song	1970	2.50	5.00	10.00
❏ 204	Sweet Chicago/Ain't That Tellin' You People	1970	2.50	5.00	10.00
❏ 211	Sault Ste. Marie/When Love Is Near	1971	2.50	5.00	10.00

O

Number	Title (A Side/B Side)	Yr	VG	VG+	NM
Albums					
T-A					
❏ 5003	One Tin Soldier	1970	3.75	7.50	15.00
ORIGINAL CASUALS, THE					
45s					
BACK BEAT					
❏ 503	So Tough/I Love My Darling	1958	6.25	12.50	25.00
❏ 503	So Tough/I Love My Darling	1958	10.00	20.00	40.00
—Original pressings by "The Casuals"					
❏ 510	Ju-Judy/Don't Pass Me By	1958	6.25	12.50	25.00
❏ 514	Three Kisses Past Midnight/ It's Been a Long Time	1958	6.25	12.50	25.00

ORIGINAL LAST POETS, THE See THE LAST POETS.

ORIGINAL SURFARIS, THE See THE SURFARIS (2).

Number	Title (A Side/B Side)	Yr	VG	VG+	NM
ORIGINAL TWISTERS, THE					
Albums					
WING					
❏ MGW-12217 [M]	Come On and Twist	1962	5.00	10.00	20.00
❏ SRW-16217 [S]	Come On and Twist	1962	6.25	12.50	25.00
ORIGINALS, THE (1)					
12-Inch Singles					
FANTASY					
❏ D-118	Blue Moon (8:27)/While the Cat's Away (7:34)	1979	3.00	6.00	12.00
❏ D-130	J-E-A-L-O-U-S (Means I Love You)/Jezebel (You've Got Me Under Your Spell)	1979	3.00	6.00	12.00
PHASE II					
❏ AS 917 [DJ]	Waitin' on a Letter/Mr. Postman (8:40) (Instrumental 8:56)	1981	2.50	5.00	10.00
❏ 4W8-5655	Waitin' on a Letter/Mr. Postman (8:40)//The Magic Is You (5:00)	1981	2.00	4.00	8.00
SOUL					
❏ M 00001D1	Down to Love Town (5:55)/Let's Be Young Tonight (5:07)	1976	5.00	10.00	20.00
—B-side by Jermaine Jackson on Motown					
45s					
FANTASY					
❏ 820	Take This Love/Ladies (We Need You)	1978	—	2.50	5.00
❏ 847	Blue Moon/Ladies (We Need You)	1979	—	2.50	5.00
❏ 856	J-E-A-L-O-U-S (Means I Love You)/Jezebel (You've Got Me Under Your Spell)	1979	—	2.50	5.00
MOTOWN					
❏ PR-1 [DJ]	Young Train (same on both sides?)	1973	50.00	100.00	200.00
❏ 1355	Good Lovin' Is Just a Dime Away/Nothing Can Take the Place (Of Your Love)	1975	—	3.00	6.00
❏ 1370	50 Years/Financial Affair	1975	—	3.00	6.00
❏ 1379	Everybody's Got to Do Something/ (Instrumental)	1975	—	3.00	6.00
PHASE II					
❏ WS8-02061	Baby I'm for Real/Share Your Love with Me	1981	—	2.00	4.00
❏ WS8-02147	The Magic Is You/Let Me Dance	1981	—	2.00	4.00
❏ ZS5-02724	Baby I'm for Real/The Magic Is You	1982	—	2.00	4.00
—As "Hank Dixon and the Originals"					
❏ 5653	Waitin' on a Letter/Mr. Postman//(B-side unknown)	1981	—	2.50	5.00
SOUL					
❏ 35029	Goodnight Irene/Need Your Loving (Want It Back)	1967	3.00	6.00	12.00
❏ 35056	We've Got a Way Out Love/You're the One	1969	3.00	6.00	12.00
❏ 35061	Green Grow the Lilacs/You're the One	1969	3.00	6.00	12.00
❏ 35066	Baby I'm for Real/The Moment of Truth	1969	2.00	4.00	8.00
❏ 35069	The Bells/I'll Wait for You	1970	2.00	4.00	8.00
❏ 35074	We Can Make It Baby/I Like Your Style	1970	2.00	4.00	8.00
❏ 35074	We Can Make It/I Like Your Style	1970	3.00	6.00	12.00
❏ 35079	God Bless Whoever Sent You/Desperate Young Man	1970	2.00	4.00	8.00
❏ 35085	Keep Me/A Man Without Love	1971	—	3.00	6.00
❏ 35093	I'm Someone Who Cares/Once I Have You	1972	—	3.00	6.00
❏ 35102	Be My Love/Endlessly Love	1973	—	3.00	6.00
❏ 35109	First Lady (Sweet Mother's Love)/There's a Chance When You Love, You Love	1973	—	3.00	6.00
❏ 35112	Supernatural Voodoo Woman (Part 1)/ Supernatural Voodoo Woman (Part 2)	1974	—	3.00	6.00
❏ 35113	Game Called Love/Ooh You Put a Spell on Me	1974	—	3.00	6.00
❏ 35115	You're My Only World (And Yet So Far)	1974	—	3.00	6.00
❏ 35117	Touch/Ooh You Put a Spell on Me	1975	—	3.00	6.00
❏ 35119	Down to Love Town/Just to Be Closer to You	1976	—	3.00	6.00
❏ 35121 [DJ]	Call On Your Six Million Dollar Man (mono/ stereo)	1977	—	3.00	6.00
Albums					
FANTASY					
❏ F-9546	Another Time, Another Place	1978	2.50	5.00	10.00
❏ F-9577	Come Away with Me	1979	2.50	5.00	10.00
MOTOWN					
❏ M5-110V	Motown Superstar Series, Vol. 10	1982	2.50	5.00	10.00
❏ M7-826	California Sunset	1975	3.75	7.50	15.00
PHASE II					
❏ JW 37075	Yesterday and Today	1981	3.00	6.00	12.00
SOUL					
❏ SS-716	Baby I'm for Real	1969	10.00	20.00	40.00
❏ SS-724	Portrait of the Originals	1970	6.25	12.50	25.00
❏ SS-729	Naturally Together	1971	6.25	12.50	25.00
❏ SS-734	Definitions	1971	5.00	10.00	20.00
❏ SS-740	The Game Called…	1973	3.75	7.50	15.00
❏ SS-743	California Sunset		—	—	—
—Unreleased					
❏ S7-746	Communique	1976	3.75	7.50	15.00
❏ S7-749	Down to Love Town	1977	3.75	7.50	15.00

Number	Title (A Side/B Side)	Yr	VG	VG+	NM
ORIGINALS, THE (2)					
45s					
DIAMOND					
❏ 102	At Times Like These/Gimme a Little Kiss, Will Ya, Huh?	1961	10.00	20.00	40.00
❏ 116	Summer Schoo/You and I	1962	10.00	20.00	40.00

ORIGINALS, THE (3) CHUCK RIO was in this group.

Number	Title (A Side/B Side)	Yr	VG	VG+	NM
45s					
JACKPOT					
❏ 48007	The Whip/The Blue Kat	1959	7.50	15.00	30.00
❏ 48012	Anna/Sleepless Nights	1959	7.50	15.00	30.00

ORIGINALS, THE (4) TONY ALLEN was in this group.

Number	Title (A Side/B Side)	Yr	VG	VG+	NM
45s					
ORIGINAL SOUND					
❏ 10	Wishing Star/Let Me Hear You Say Yeah	1960	7.50	15.00	30.00
❏ 13	Little Lonely Girl/I Still Love You	1960	5.00	10.00	20.00
—As "Tony Allan and the Originals"					

ORIOLES, THE Also see SONNY TIL.

Number	Title (A Side/B Side)	Yr	VG	VG+	NM
45s					
ABNER					
❏ 1016	Sugar Girl/Didn't I Say	1958	15.00	30.00	60.00
CHARLIE PARKER					
❏ 211	Secret Love/The Wobble	1962	5.00	10.00	20.00
❏ 212	In the Chapel in the Moonlight/Hey! Little Woman	1962	5.00	10.00	20.00
❏ 213	Back to the Chapel Again/(It's Gonna Be a) Lonely Christmas	1962	5.00	10.00	20.00
❏ 214	What Are You Doing New Year's Eve/Don't Mess Around with My Love	1962	5.00	10.00	20.00
❏ 215	It's Too Soon to Know/I Miss You So	1963	3.75	7.50	15.00
❏ 216	Write and Tell Me Why/Don't Tell Her What Happens to Me	1963	3.75	7.50	15.00
❏ 219	I Miss You So/Hey! Little Woman	1963	3.75	7.50	15.00
HARLEM SOUND					
❏ 1001	Lonely Christmas/ What Are You Doing New Year's Eve	19??	—	2.50	5.00
JUBILEE					
❏ 5000	It's Too Soon to Know/Barbara Lee	1951	1000.	2000.	4000.
❏ 5005	Tell Me So/Deacon Jones	1951	500.00	1000.	2000.
❏ 5016	So Much/Forgive and Forget	1951	500.00	1000.	2000.
❏ 5017	What Are You Doing New Year's Eve/ Lonely Christmas	1951	200.00	400.00	800.00
❏ 5017 [PS]	What Are You Doing New Year's Eve/ Lonely Christmas	1954	250.00	500.00	1000.
❏ 5025	At Night/Every Dog-Gone Time	1951	250.00	500.00	1000.
❏ 5040	I Cross My Fingers/Can't Seem to Laugh Anymore	1951	500.00	1000.	2000.
❏ 5045	Oh Holy Night/The Lord's Prayer	1951	150.00	300.00	600.00
—Original on blue label					
❏ 5045 [PS]	Oh Holy Night/The Lord's Prayer	1954	150.00	300.00	600.00
❏ 5045	Oh Holy Night/The Lord's Prayer	196?	6.25	12.50	25.00
—Reissue on black label					
❏ 5051	I Miss You So/You Are My First Love	1951	200.00	400.00	800.00
❏ 5051	I Miss You So/You Are My First Love	1951	1000.	1500.	2000.
—Red vinyl					
❏ 5055	Pal of Mine/Happy Go Lucky Local Blues	1951	200.00	400.00	800.00
❏ 5061	I'm Just a Fool in Love/Hold Me, Squeeze Me	1951	200.00	400.00	800.00
❏ 5065	Baby, Please Don't Go/ Don't Tell Her What's Happened to Me	1951	150.00	300.00	600.00
—Black vinyl					
❏ 5065	Baby, Please Don't Go/Don't Tell Her What's Happened to Me	1951	1000.	1500.	2000.
—Red vinyl					
❏ 5071	When You're Not Around/How Blind Can You Be	1952	150.00	300.00	600.00
❏ 5074	Trust in Me/Shrimp Boats	1952	125.00	250.00	500.00
❏ 5076	Proud of You/You Never Cared for Me	1952	125.00	250.00	500.00
❏ 5082	It's All Over Because You're Through/Waiting	1952	125.00	250.00	500.00
❏ 5084	Barfly/Getting Tired, Tired, Tired	1952	100.00	200.00	400.00
❏ 5092	Don't Cry Baby/See See Rider	1952	100.00	200.00	400.00
❏ 5092	Don't Cry Baby/See See Rider	1952	375.00	750.00	1500.
—Red vinyl					
❏ 5102	You Belong to Me/I Don't Want to Take a Chance	1952	125.00	250.00	500.00
❏ 5107	I Miss You So/Till Then	1952	100.00	200.00	400.00
❏ 5107	I Miss You So/Till Then	1952	375.00	750.00	1500.
—Red vinyl					
❏ 5107	I Miss You So/Till Then	1963	6.25	12.50	25.00
—Reissue, credited to "Sonny Til and the Orioles"					
❏ 5108	Teardrops on My Pillow/ Hold Me, Thrill Me, Kiss Me	1953	100.00	200.00	400.00
❏ 5108	Teardrops on My Pillow/ Hold Me, Thrill Me, Kiss Me	1953	375.00	750.00	1500.
—Red vinyl					
❏ 5115	Bad Little Girl/Dem Days	1953	100.00	200.00	400.00
❏ 5120	I Cover the Waterfront/One More Time	1953	100.00	200.00	400.00
❏ 5120	I Cover the Waterfront/One More Time	1953	300.00	600.00	1200.
—Red vinyl					
❏ 5122	Crying in the Chapel/ Don't You Think I Ought to Know	1953	20.00	40.00	80.00
❏ 5127	In the Mission of St. Augustine/ Write and Tell Me Why	1953	12.50	25.00	50.00
❏ 5134	There's No One But You/Rose of Calvary	1954	12.50	25.00	50.00
❏ 5137	Secret Love/Don't Go to Strangers	1954	12.50	25.00	50.00
❏ 5143	Maybe You'll Be There/ Drowning Every Hope I Ever Had	1954	20.00	40.00	80.00
❏ 5154	In the Chapel in the Moonlight/T hank the Lord, Thank the Lord	1954	12.50	25.00	50.00
❏ 5161	If You Believe/Longing	1954	12.50	25.00	50.00
❏ 5172	Runaround/ Count Your Blessings Instead of Sheep	1954	12.50	25.00	50.00
❏ 5177	I Love You Mostly/Fair Exchange	1955	10.00	20.00	40.00
❏ 5189	I Need You Baby/The Good Lord Will Smile	1955	10.00	20.00	40.00
❏ 5221	Please Sing My Blues Tonight/Moody Over You	1955	10.00	20.00	40.00
❏ 5231	Angel/Don't Go to Strangers	1956	15.00	30.00	60.00
❏ 5363	Tell Me So/At Night	1959	3.75	7.50	15.00
—As "Sonny Til and the Orioles"					

Number	Title (A Side/B Side)	Yr	VG	VG+	NM
❏ 5384	Come On Home/The First of Summer	1960	3.75	7.50	15.00
—As "Sonny Til and the Orioles"					
❏ 6001	Crying in the Chapel/Forgive and Forget	1959	3.75	7.50	15.00
—As "Sonny Til and the Orioles"					
LANA					
❏ 109	What Are You Doing New Year's Eve/Crying in the Chapel	196?	2.00	4.00	8.00
—Oldies reissue					
VEE JAY					
❏ 196	I Just Got Lucky/Happy 'Til the Letter	1956	7.50	15.00	30.00
❏ 228	For All We Know/Never Leave Me Baby	1956	7.50	15.00	30.00
❏ 244	Sugar Girl/Didn't I Say	1957	10.00	20.00	40.00
VIRGO					
❏ 6017	What Are You Doing New Year's Eve/Crying in the Chapel	1972	—	2.00	4.00
7-Inch Extended Plays					
JUBILEE					
❏ 5000	Too Soon to Know/Forgive and Forget//Tell Me So/At Night	1954	250.00	500.00	1000.
❏ 5000 [PS]	The Orioles Sing	1954	250.00	500.00	1000.
Albums					
BIG A					
❏ LP-2001	The Orioles' Greatest All-Time Hits	1969	7.50	15.00	30.00
CHARLIE PARKER					
❏ PLP-816 [M]	Modern Sounds of the Orioles	1962	20.00	40.00	80.00
❏ PLP-816S [S]	Modern Sounds of the Orioles	1962	25.00	50.00	100.00
COLLECTABLES					
❏ COL-5014	Sonny Til and the Orioles' Greatest Hits	198?	3.00	6.00	12.00
MURRAY HILL					
❏ M 61234 [(5)]	For Collectors Only	1983	10.00	20.00	40.00

ORION Also see JIMMY ELLIS.
45s

Number	Title (A Side/B Side)	Yr	VG	VG+	NM
KRISTAL					
❏ 2292/2308	I'm Saving Up My Pennies/I'm Starting Over	1985	—	2.00	4.00
❏ 2338	100 Pounds of Clay/Because He Lived	1986	—	2.00	4.00
RADIOACTIVE					
❏ 18772-1 [DJ]	Unchained Melody (same on both sides)	1987	—	2.50	5.00
STARGEM					
❏ 2465 [DJ]	Only a Woman Like You (same on both sides)	1990	—	2.50	5.00
❏ 2469	I Want You, I Need You, I Love You/Plastic Saddle	1990	—	2.50	5.00
❏ 2502	Love It Back Together/If That Isn't Love	1990	—	2.50	5.00
—Red vinyl					
❏ 2502 [PS]	Love It Back Together/If That Isn't Love	1990	—	2.50	5.00
SUN					
❏ 1142	Honey/Ebony Eyes	1979	—	2.00	4.00
❏ 1147	Before the Next Teardrop Falls/Washing Machine	1979	—	2.00	4.00
❏ 1148	Remember Bethlehem/Silent Night	1979	—	2.00	4.00
❏ 1148 [DJ]	Remember Bethlehem (same on both sides)	1979	2.50	5.00	10.00
—Yellow vinyl promo					
❏ 1151	Be-Bop-a-Lula/The Breakup	1980	—	2.00	4.00
—A-side with Jerry Lee Lewis; B-side with Charlie Rich					
❏ 1152	It Ain't No Mystery/Stranger in My Place	1980	—	2.00	4.00
❏ 1152 [DJ]	It Ain't No Mystery (same on both sides)	1980	2.50	5.00	10.00
—Yellow vinyl promo					
❏ 1153	Texas Tea/Faded Love	1980	—	2.00	4.00
❏ 1153 [DJ]	Texas Tea (same on both sides)	1980	2.50	5.00	10.00
—Yellow vinyl promo					
❏ 1156	Am I That Easy to Forget/Crazy Arms	1980	—	2.00	4.00
❏ 1156 [DJ]	Am I That Easy to Forget (same on both sides)	1980	2.50	5.00	10.00
—Yellow vinyl promo					
❏ 1159	Rockabilly Rebel/Memphis Sun	1980	—	2.00	4.00
❏ 1159 [DJ]	Rockabilly Rebel (same on both sides)	1980	2.50	5.00	10.00
—Yellow vinyl promo					
❏ 1162	Crazy Little Thing Called Love/Matchbox	1981	—	2.00	4.00
❏ 1165	Born/If I Can't Have You	1981	—	2.00	4.00
❏ 1165 [DJ]	Born (same on both sides)	1981	2.50	5.00	10.00
—Yellow vinyl promo					
❏ 1170	Some You Win, Some You Lose/Ain't No Good	1981	—	2.00	4.00
❏ 1170 [DJ]	Some You Win, Some You Lose (same on both sides)	1981	2.50	5.00	10.00
—Yellow vinyl promo					
❏ 1172	Baby Please Say Yes/Feelings	1982	—	2.00	4.00
❏ 1175	Honky Tonk Heaven/Morning, Noon and Night	1982	—	2.00	4.00
❏ 1175 [DJ]	Honky Tonk Heaven (same on both sides)	1982	2.50	5.00	10.00
—Yellow vinyl promo					
7-Inch Extended Plays					
SUN					
❏ 1152 [DJ]	Stranger in My Place Greetings: Wedding Anniversary/Good Music/Great Station//Favorite Station/Best Music/Birthday	1981	10.00	20.00	40.00
—Came with insert but no cover					
Albums					
SUN					
❏ 1012	Orion Reborn	1978	2.50	5.00	10.00
—Blue cover					
❏ 1012	Orion Reborn	1978	7.50	15.00	30.00
—White cover, also known as the "coffin cover"					
❏ 1017	Sunrise	1979	2.50	5.00	10.00
❏ 1019	Orion Country	1980	2.50	5.00	10.00
❏ 1021	Rockabilly	1981	2.50	5.00	10.00
❏ 1025	Glory	1982	2.50	5.00	10.00
❏ 1028	Fresh	1983	2.50	5.00	10.00

ORION, P.J., AND THE MAGNATES
Albums

Number	Title (A Side/B Side)	Yr	VG	VG+	NM
MAGNATE					
❏ 122459	P.J. Orion and the Magnates	196?	37.50	75.00	150.00

ORLANDO, TONY Also see BERTELL DACHE; DAWN (1).
12-Inch Singles

Number	Title (A Side/B Side)	Yr	VG	VG+	NM
CASABLANCA					
❏ NBD 20158	They're Playing Our Song (8:06)/(B-side blank)	1979	2.50	5.00	10.00

Number	Title (A Side/B Side)	Yr	VG	VG+	NM
45s					
ATCO					
❏ 6376	Think Before You Act/She Loves Me (For What I Am)	1965	2.50	5.00	10.00
CAMEO					
❏ 471	Sweet Sweet/Manuelito (Little Manuel	1967	2.50	5.00	10.00
CASABLANCA					
❏ 967	They're Playing Our Song (Medley)/Moonlight	1979	—	2.00	4.00
❏ 991	Sweets for My Sweet/High Steppin'	1979	—	2.00	4.00
❏ 2229	San Pedros Children/High Steppin'	1979	—	2.00	4.00
❏ 2249	Pullin' Together/She Always Knew	1980	—	2.00	4.00
EPIC					
❏ 9441	Halfway to Paradise/Lonely Tomorrows	1961	3.75	7.50	15.00
❏ 9441 [PS]	Halfway to Paradise/Lonely Tomorrows	1961	6.25	12.50	25.00
❏ 9452	Bless You/Am I the Guy	1961	3.75	7.50	15.00
❏ 9452 [PS]	Bless You/Am I the Guy	1961	6.25	12.50	25.00
❏ 9476	Hapy Times (Are Here to Stay)/Lonely Am I	1961	3.00	6.00	12.00
❏ 9476 [PS]	Hapy Times (Are Here to Stay)/Lonely Am I	1961	6.25	12.50	25.00
❏ 9491	My Baby's a Starnger/Talkin' About You	1962	3.00	6.00	12.00
❏ 9491 [PS]	My Baby's a Starnger/Talkin' About You	1962	6.25	12.50	25.00
❏ 9502	I'd Never Find Another You/Love on Your Lips	1962	3.00	6.00	12.00
❏ 9519	At the Edge of Tears/Chills	1962	3.00	6.00	12.00
❏ 9519 [PS]	At the Edge of Tears/Chills	1962	6.25	12.50	25.00
❏ 9562	Beautiful Dreamer/The Loneliest	1962	2.50	5.00	10.00
❏ 9570	Joanie/Shirley	1963	2.50	5.00	10.00
❏ 9622	I'll Be There/What Am I Gonna Do	1963	2.50	5.00	10.00
❏ 9668	She Doesn't Know It/Tell Me What I Can Do	1964	2.50	5.00	10.00
❏ 9715	To Wait for Love/Accept It	1964	2.50	5.00	10.00
Albums					
CASABLANCA					
❏ NBLP 7153	I Got Rhythm	1979	2.50	5.00	10.00
❏ NBLP 7209	Living for the Music	1980	2.50	5.00	10.00
EPIC					
❏ BN 611 [S]	Bless You and 11 Other Great Hits	1961	10.00	20.00	40.00
❏ LN 3808 [M]	Bless You and 11 Other Great Hits	1961	7.50	15.00	30.00
❏ BG 33785 [(2)]	Before Dawn	1975	3.75	7.50	15.00

ORLANDO, TONY (2) This is not by the same singer as the rest.
45s

Number	Title (A Side/B Side)	Yr	VG	VG+	NM
MILO					
❏ 101	Ding Dong/You and Only You	1959	25.00	50.00	100.00

ORLANDO, TONY, AND DAWN See DAWN (1).

ORLEANS
12-Inch Singles

Number	Title (A Side/B Side)	Yr	VG	VG+	NM
INFINITY					
❏ L33-1004 [DJ]	Love Takes Time (same on both sides)	1979	2.50	5.00	10.00
45s					
ABC					
❏ 11408	Please Be There/Mountains	1973	—	2.50	5.00
❏ 11420	If/Stoned	1974	—	2.50	5.00
ASYLUM					
❏ 45243	Let There Be Music/Give One Heart	1975	—	2.00	4.00
❏ 45261	Dance with Me/Ending of a Song	1975	—	2.50	5.00
❏ 45336	Still the One/Siam Sam	1976	—	2.50	5.00
—Clouds label					
❏ 45336	Still the One/Siam Sam	1976	—	3.00	6.00
—Dark blue label with white stylized "a" at top					
❏ 45375	Reach/Sweet Destiny	1976	—	2.00	4.00
❏ 45391	The Bum/Spring Fever	1977	—	2.00	4.00
❏ 45447	Business As Usual/Time Passes On	1977	—	2.00	4.00
ATLANTIC AMERICA					
❏ 99981	One of a Kind/Beatin' Around the Bush	1982	—	2.00	4.00
INFINITY					
❏ 50006	Love Takes Time/Isn't It Easy	1979	—	2.00	4.00
❏ 50017	Don't Throw Our Love Away/The Flame and the Moth	1979	—	2.00	4.00
❏ 50036	Forever/Keep On Rollin'	1979	—	2.00	4.00
MCA					
❏ 41228	Change Your Mind/When Are You Coming Home	1980	—	2.00	4.00
❏ 41283	No Ordinary Lady/Dukie's Tune	1980	—	2.00	4.00
❏ 52862	Lady Liberty/On Hold	1986	—	—	3.00
❏ 52909	Grown-Up Children/On Hold	1986	—	—	3.00
❏ 52963	You're Mine/Language of Love	1986	—	—	3.00
Albums					
ABC					
❏ ABCX-795	Orleans	1973	3.75	7.50	15.00
❏ AA-1058-2 [(2)]	Before the Dance	1977	3.00	6.00	12.00
❏ AC-30011	The ABC Collection	1976	2.50	5.00	10.00
ASYLUM					
❏ 7E-1029	Let There Be Music	1975	2.50	5.00	10.00
❏ 7E-1070	Waking and Dreaming	1976	2.50	5.00	10.00
INFINITY					
❏ INF-9006	Forever	1979	2.50	5.00	10.00
MCA					
❏ 5110	Orleans	1980	2.50	5.00	10.00
❏ 5767	Grown Up Children	1986	2.00	4.00	8.00
RADIO					
❏ 90012	One of a Kind	1982	2.50	5.00	10.00

ORLONS, THE
45s

Number	Title (A Side/B Side)	Yr	VG	VG+	NM
ABC					
❏ 10894	Everything/Keep Your Hands Off My Baby	1967	2.50	5.00	10.00
❏ 10948	Kissin' Time/Once Upon a Time	1967	2.50	5.00	10.00
CALLA					
❏ 113	Spinnin' Top/Anyone Who Had a Heart	1966	2.50	5.00	10.00
CAMEO					
❏ 105 [DJ]	Big Girls Don't Cry/Pop Pop Pop-Pie	1962	10.00	20.00	40.00
—Yellow label, black print, promo only					
❏ 198	I'll Be True/Heart Darling Angel	1961	12.50	25.00	50.00
❏ 211	Mr. 21/Please Let It Be Me	1961	12.50	25.00	50.00
❏ 218	The Wah-Watusi/Holiday Hill	1962	5.00	10.00	20.00
❏ 231	Don't Hang Up/The Conservative	1962	5.00	10.00	20.00

Number	Title (A Side/B Side)	Yr	VG	VG+	NM
☐ 231 [PS]	Don't Hang Up/The Conservative	1962	10.00	20.00	40.00
☐ 243	South Street/Them Terrible Boots	1963	5.00	10.00	20.00
☐ 243 [PS]	South Street/Them Terrible Boots	1963	10.00	20.00	40.00
☐ 257	Not Me/My Best Friend	1963	5.00	10.00	20.00
☐ 257 [PS]	Not Me/My Best Friend	1963	7.50	15.00	30.00
☐ 273	Cross Fire!/It's No Big Thing	1963	5.00	10.00	20.00
☐ 273 [PS]	Cross Fire!/It's No Big Thing	1963	7.50	15.00	30.00
☐ 287	Bon-Doo-Wah/Don't Throw Your Love Away	1963	3.75	7.50	15.00
☐ 287 [PS]	Bon-Doo-Wah/Don't Throw Your Love Away	1963	7.50	15.00	30.00
☐ 295	Shimmy Shimmy/Everything Nice	1964	3.75	7.50	15.00
☐ 295 [PS]	Shimmy Shimmy/Everything Nice	1964	6.25	12.50	25.00
☐ 319	Rules of Love/Heartbreak Hotel	1964	3.75	7.50	15.00
☐ 319 [PS]	Rules of Love/Heartbreak Hotel	1964	6.25	12.50	25.00
☐ 332	Knock! Knock! (Who's There)/Goin' Places	1964	3.75	7.50	15.00
☐ 332 [PS]	Knock! Knock! (Who's There)/Goin' Places	1964	6.25	12.50	25.00
☐ 346	I Ain't Coming Back/Envy (In My Eyes)	1965	3.00	6.00	12.00
☐ 352	Come On Down Baby/I Ain't Coming Back	1965	3.00	6.00	12.00
☐ 372	Don't You Want My Lovin'/I Can't Take It	1965	3.00	6.00	12.00
☐ 384	No Love But Your Love/Envy (In My Eyes)	1965	10.00	20.00	40.00
Albums					
CAMEO					
☐ C 1020 [M]	The Wah-Watusi	1962	15.00	30.00	60.00
☐ C 1033 [M]	All the Hits by the Orlons	1962	15.00	30.00	60.00
☐ C 1041 [M]	South Street	1963	15.00	30.00	60.00
☐ C 1054 [M]	Not Me	1963	12.50	25.00	50.00
☐ C 1061 [M]	The Orlons' Biggest Hits	1964	12.50	25.00	50.00
☐ C 1073 [M]	Down Memory Lane with the Orlons	1964	12.50	25.00	50.00

ORLONS, THE / THE DOVELLS Also see each artist's individual listings.
Albums
CAMEO

Number	Title (A Side/B Side)	Yr	VG	VG+	NM
☐ C 1067 [M]	Golden Hits of the Orlons and the Dovells	1964	12.50	25.00	50.00

ORPHAN EGG
Albums
CAROLE

Number	Title (A Side/B Side)	Yr	VG	VG+	NM
☐ CARS-8004	Orphan Egg	1968	10.00	20.00	40.00

ORPHANS, THE
45s
EPIC

Number	Title (A Side/B Side)	Yr	VG	VG+	NM
☐ 10288	There's No Flowers in My Garden/One Spoken Word	1968	2.50	5.00	10.00
☐ 10348	This Is the Time/Deserted	1968	2.50	5.00	10.00

ORPHEUS
45s
BELL

Number	Title (A Side/B Side)	Yr	VG	VG+	NM
☐ 45128	Big Green Pearl/Sweet Life	1971	—	2.50	5.00
MGM					
☐ 13882	Can't Find the Time/Lesley's Girl	1967	2.50	5.00	10.00
—Originals have black labels					
☐ 13882	Can't Find the Time/Lesley's Girl	1969	—	3.00	6.00
—Reissues (same number) have blue and gold labels					
☐ 13947	I've Never Seen Love Like This/Congress Alley	1968	—	3.00	6.00
☐ 14022	Brown Arms in Houston/I Can Make the Sun Rise	1969	—	3.00	6.00
☐ 14022 [PS]	Brown Arms in Houston/I Can Make the Sun Rise	1969	2.50	5.00	10.00
☐ 14139	Joyful/By the Size of My Shoes	1970	—	3.00	6.00
RED BIRD					
☐ 10-041	My Life/Music Minus Orpheus	1965	3.75	7.50	15.00
Albums					
MGM					
☐ E-4524 [M]	Orpheus	1968	6.25	12.50	25.00
☐ SE-4524 [S]	Orpheus	1968	5.00	10.00	20.00
☐ E-4569 [M]	Ascending	1968	10.00	20.00	40.00
—Known copies are yellow label promos with "DJ Monaural" sticker on stereo cover					
☐ SE-4569 [S]	Ascending	1968	5.00	10.00	20.00
☐ SE-4599 [S]	Joyful	1969	5.00	10.00	20.00

ORR, J.D.
45s
SUMMIT

Number	Title (A Side/B Side)	Yr	VG	VG+	NM
☐ 105	Hula-Hoop Boogie/Lonesome Hearted Blues	1958	100.00	200.00	400.00

ORSI, PHIL, AND THE LITTLE KINGS
45s
LUCKY

Number	Title (A Side/B Side)	Yr	VG	VG+	NM
☐ 1009	Come On Everybody/Oh My Darling	1963	18.75	37.50	75.00
☐ 1015	Don't You Just Know It/(B-side unknown)	1964	6.25	12.50	25.00
U.S.A.					
☐ 837	Stay/Whoever He May Be	1965	6.25	12.50	25.00
☐ 841	Sorry (I Ran All the Way Home)/Whoever He May Be	1965	6.25	12.50	25.00

OSBORNE, ARTHUR
45s
BRUNSWICK

Number	Title (A Side/B Side)	Yr	VG	VG+	NM
☐ 55068	Hey Ruby/Don't Give Me Heartaches	1958	15.00	30.00	60.00

OSBORNE, KELL, AND THE CHICKS
45s
CLASS

Number	Title (A Side/B Side)	Yr	VG	VG+	NM
☐ 302	Little Chick-A-Dee/Do You Mind	1962	3.75	7.50	15.00
HIGHLAND					
☐ (# unknown)	Law Against a Heartbreaker/(B-side unknown)	196?	1000.	1750.	2500.
LOMA					
☐ 2023	That's What's Happening/You Can't Outsmart a Woman	1965	2.50	5.00	10.00
TITANIC					
☐ 5008	Quicksand/Lonely Boy Song	1963	25.00	50.00	100.00
TREY					
☐ 3006	The Bells of St. Mary's/That's All Right, Baby	1960	6.25	12.50	25.00

OSBORNE BROTHERS, THE
45s
CMH

Number	Title (A Side/B Side)	Yr	VG	VG+	NM
☐ 1522	Shackles and Chains//(B-side unknown)	1979	—	2.00	4.00
—With Mac Wiseman					
☐ 1524	I Can Hear Kentucky Calling Me//(B-side unknown)	1980	—	2.00	4.00
DECCA					
☐ 31546	Take This Hammer/Don't Even Look at Me	1963	2.00	4.00	8.00
☐ 31595	Bluegrass Express/Cuckoo Bird	1964	2.00	4.00	8.00
☐ 31655	Charlie Cotton/This Heart of Mine	1964	2.00	4.00	8.00
☐ 31751	Hey, Hey, Bartender/Me and My Old Banjo	1965	2.00	4.00	8.00
☐ 31823	Lonesome Day/I'll Be Alright Tomorrow	1965	2.00	4.00	8.00
☐ 31886	Up This Hill and Down/Memories	1965	2.00	4.00	8.00
☐ 31977	Hard Times/A World of Unwanted	1966	2.00	4.00	8.00
☐ 32052	The Kind of Woman I Got/One Tear	1966	2.00	4.00	8.00
☐ 32137	Roll Muddy River/Making Plans	1967	2.00	4.00	8.00
☐ 32242	Rocky Top/My Favorite Memory	1967	2.00	4.00	8.00
☐ 32325	Cut the Cornbread, Mama/If I Could Count on You	1968	2.00	4.00	8.00
☐ 32382	Son of a Sawmill Man/That Was Yesterday	1968	2.00	4.00	8.00
☐ 32451	Working Man/World of Forgotten	1969	2.00	4.00	8.00
☐ 32516	Tennessee Hound Dog/Thanks for All the Yesterdays	1969	2.00	4.00	8.00
☐ 32598	Ruby, Are You Mad/Sempre	1969	2.00	4.00	8.00
☐ 32680	Listen to the Rain/Midnight Angel	1970	2.00	4.00	8.00
☐ 32746	My Old Kentucky Home (Turpentine and Dandelion Wine)/No Good Son of a Gun	1970	2.00	4.00	8.00
☐ 32794	Georgia Pineywoods/Searching for Yesterday	1971	2.00	4.00	8.00
☐ 32864	Muddy Bottom/Beneath Still Waters	1971	2.00	4.00	8.00
☐ 32908	Take Me Home, Country Roads/Tears Are No Stranger	1971	2.00	4.00	8.00
☐ 32942	Windy City/Shelly's Winter Love	1972	2.00	4.00	8.00
☐ 32979	Miss You Mississippi/Today I Started Loving You Again	1972	2.00	4.00	8.00
☐ 33028	Midnight Flyer/Tears Will Kiss the Morning Dew	1972	2.00	4.00	8.00
☐ 55274	Rocky Top (Radio Mix)/Rocky Top (Original Version)	1996	—	2.00	4.00
MCA					
☐ 40028	Lizzie Lou/Tears	1973	—	2.00	4.00
☐ 40113	Blue Heartache/You're Heavy on My Mind	1973	—	2.00	4.00
☐ 40169	Sled Ridin'/Fastest Grass Alive	1973	—	2.00	4.00
☐ 40226	Bluegrass Melodies/The Seventh of December	1974	—	2.00	4.00
☐ 40346	El Rancho/A Heartache Looking for a Home	1974	—	2.00	4.00
☐ 40509	Don't Let Smokey Mountain Smoke Get In Your Eyes/Born a Ramblin' Man	1976	—	2.00	4.00
MGM					
☐ 12308	My Aching Heart/Ruby Are You Mad	1956	3.75	7.50	15.00
—With Red Allen					
☐ 12383	Whu Dun It/Teardrops in My Eyes	1956	3.75	7.50	15.00
—With Red Allen					
☐ 12420	Ho Honey Ho/Down in the Willow Garden	1957	3.00	6.00	12.00
—With Red Allen					
☐ 12527	Della Mae/Wild Mountain Honey	1957	3.00	6.00	12.00
—With Red Allen					
☐ 12583	Once More/She's No Angel	1957	3.00	6.00	12.00
—With Red Allen					
☐ 12633	My Destiny/If You Don't Somebody Else Will	1958	3.00	6.00	12.00
—With Red Allen					
☐ 12689	Love Pains/It Hurts to Know	1958	3.00	6.00	12.00
☐ 12762	I Love You Only/Give This Message to Your Heart	1959	3.00	6.00	12.00
☐ 12805	Lost Highway/You'll Never Know	1959	3.00	6.00	12.00
☐ 12839	Sweethearts Again/There's a Woman Behind Every Man	1959	3.00	6.00	12.00
☐ 12930	Blame Me/Lonely, Lonely Me	1960	2.50	5.00	10.00
☐ 12970	At the First Fall of Snow/Fair and Tender Ladies	1960	2.50	5.00	10.00
☐ 13045	Black Sheep Returned to the Fold/Each Season Changes You	1961	2.50	5.00	10.00
☐ 13073	Five Days of Heaven/It Ain't Gonna Rain No Mo'	1962	2.50	5.00	10.00
☐ 13098	Banjo Boys/Poor Old Cora	1962	2.50	5.00	10.00
☐ 13126	Mule Skinner Blues/Lovey Told Me Goodbye	1963	2.50	5.00	10.00
RCA					
☐ PB-13097	Rocky Top/Old Flames Can't Hold a Candle to You	1982	—	2.00	4.00
Albums					
CMH					
☐ 4501	Greatest Bluegrass Hits, Vol. 1	198?	3.00	6.00	12.00
☐ 6206	#1	197?	3.00	6.00	12.00
☐ 6231	Bluegrass Concerto	197?	3.00	6.00	12.00
☐ 6244	Kentucky Calling Me	1980	3.00	6.00	12.00
☐ 6256	Bobby and His Mandolin	1981	3.00	6.00	12.00
☐ 9008 [(2)]	From Rocky Top to Muddy Bottom	1977	3.75	7.50	15.00
☐ 9011 [(2)]	Bluegrass Collection	1978	3.75	7.50	15.00
☐ 9016 [(2)]	The Essential Bluegrass Album	1979	3.75	7.50	15.00
—With MacWiseman					
DECCA					
☐ DL 4602 [M]	Voices in the Bluegrass	1965	3.75	7.50	15.00
☐ DL 4767 [M]	Up This Hill and Down	1966	3.75	7.50	15.00
☐ DL 4903 [M]	Modern Sounds of Bluegrass Music	1967	3.75	7.50	15.00
☐ DL 4993 [M]	Yesterday, Today and The Osborne Brothers	1968	6.25	12.50	25.00
☐ DL 74602 [S]	Voices in the Bluegrass	1965	5.00	10.00	20.00
☐ DL 74767 [S]	Up This Hill and Down	1966	5.00	10.00	20.00
☐ DL 74903 [S]	Modern Sounds of Bluegrass Music	1967	5.00	10.00	20.00
☐ DL 74993 [S]	Yesterday, Today and The Osborne Brothers	1968	5.00	10.00	20.00
☐ DL 75079	Favorite Hymns by the Osborne Brothers	1969	5.00	10.00	20.00
☐ DL 75128	Up to Date and Down to Earth	1969	5.00	10.00	20.00
☐ DL 75204	Ru-Beeeee	1970	5.00	10.00	20.00
☐ DL 75271	The Osborne Brothers	1971	3.75	7.50	15.00
☐ DL 75321	Country Roads	1971	3.75	7.50	15.00
☐ DL 75356	Bobby & Sonny	1972	3.75	7.50	15.00
MCA					
☐ 105	Voices in the Bluegrass	1973	3.00	6.00	12.00
—Reissue of Decca 74602					
☐ 119	Yesterday, Today and The Osborne Brothers	1973	3.00	6.00	12.00
—Reissue of Decca 74993					

Number	Title (A Side/B Side)	Yr	VG	VG+	NM
❑ 125	Favorite Hymns by the Osborne Brothers	1973	3.00	6.00	12.00
—Reissue of Decca 75079					
❑ 135	Ru-Beeeee	1973	3.00	6.00	12.00
—Reissue of Decca 75204					
❑ 4086 [(2)]	The Best of the Osborne Brothers	1974	3.75	7.50	15.00
MGM					
❑ GAS 140	The Osborne Brothers (Golden Archives Series)	1970	5.00	10.00	20.00
❑ E-3734 [M]	Country Pickin' and Hillside Singin'	1959	12.50	25.00	50.00
❑ E-4018 [M]	Bluegrass Music	1962	6.25	12.50	25.00
❑ SE-4018 [S]	Bluegrass Music	1962	7.50	15.00	30.00
❑ E-4090 [M]	Bluegrass Instrumentals	1962	6.25	12.50	25.00
❑ SE-4090 [S]	Bluegrass Instrumentals	1962	7.50	15.00	30.00
❑ E-4149 [M]	Cuttin' Grass	1963	6.25	12.50	25.00
❑ SE-4149 [S]	Cuttin' Grass	1963	7.50	15.00	30.00
RCA VICTOR					
❑ AHL1-4324	Bluegrass Spectacular	1982	2.50	5.00	10.00
❑ AYL1-5436	Bluegrass Spectacular	1985	2.00	4.00	8.00
—"Best Buy Series" reissue					
ROUNDER					
❑ SS-03	The Osborne Brothers with Red Allen	1981	3.00	6.00	12.00
❑ SS-04	The Osborne Brothers	198?	3.00	6.00	12.00
SUGAR HILL					
❑ SH-3740	Some Things I Want to Sing About	1984	2.50	5.00	10.00
❑ SH-3754	Once More, Vol. 1	1986	2.50	5.00	10.00
❑ SH-3758	Once More, Vol. 2	1987	2.50	5.00	10.00
❑ SH-3764	Singing, Shouting Praises	1988	2.50	5.00	10.00

OSCAR See CARROLL SPINNEY.

OSHINS, MILT
45s

Number	Title (A Side/B Side)	Yr	VG	VG+	NM
PELVIS					
❑ 169	All About Elvis/All About Elvis (Part 2)	1956	18.75	37.50	75.00

OSIBISA
45s

Number	Title (A Side/B Side)	Yr	VG	VG+	NM
DECCA					
❑ 32920	Woyaya/Music for Gong Gong	1972	—	2.50	5.00
❑ 32957	Move On/Survival	1972	—	2.50	5.00
❑ 32994	Ana-Bo/Wango Wango	1972	—	2.50	5.00
ISLAND					
❑ 053	Sunshine Day/Bum to Bum	1976	—	2.00	4.00
❑ 064	Dance the Body Music/Right Now	1976	—	2.00	4.00
❑ 080	The Coffee Song/The Warrior	1977	—	2.00	4.00
WARNER BROS.					
❑ 7770	Adwoa/Fire	1974	—	2.50	5.00
❑ 8031	Rokoto/Who's Got the Paper	1974	—	2.50	5.00
Albums					
ANTILLES					
❑ 7051	Welcome Home	1978	2.50	5.00	10.00
❑ 7058	Ojah Awake	1978	2.50	5.00	10.00
BUDDAH					
❑ BDS-5136	Super Fly T.N.T.	1973	7.50	15.00	30.00
DECCA					
❑ DL 75285	Osibisa	1971	3.75	7.50	15.00
❑ DL 75327	Woyaya	1972	3.75	7.50	15.00
❑ DL 75368	Heads	1972	3.75	7.50	15.00
ISLAND					
❑ ILPS 9355	Welcome Home	1976	2.50	5.00	10.00
❑ ILPS 9411	Ojah Awake	1977	2.50	5.00	10.00
MCA					
❑ 32	Osibisa	1973	2.50	5.00	10.00
—Reissue of Decca 75285					
❑ 43	Woyaya	1973	2.50	5.00	10.00
—Reissue of Decca 75327					
WARNER BROS.					
❑ BS 2732	Happy Children	1973	2.50	5.00	10.00
❑ BS 2802	Osibirock	1974	2.50	5.00	10.00

OSMOND, DONNY Also see DONNY AND MARIE OSMOND; THE OSMONDS.
12-Inch Singles

Number	Title (A Side/B Side)	Yr	VG	VG+	NM
CAPITOL					
❑ V-15505	Hold On (5 versions)	1989	—	3.00	6.00
❑ V-15642	My Love Is a Fire (3 versions)	1990	—	3.00	6.00
❑ V-15666	Sure Lookin' (5 versions)	1990	2.50	5.00	10.00
❑ SPRO-79419 [DJ]	My Love Is a Fire (3 versions)	1990	2.00	4.00	8.00
45s					
CAPITOL					
❑ B-44369	Soldier of Love/My Secret Touch	1989	—	—	3.00
❑ B-44369 [PS]	Soldier of Love/My Secret Touch	1989	—	2.50	5.00
❑ B-44379	Sacred Emotion/Groove	1989	—	—	3.00
❑ 7PRO-79585	Soldier of Love (same on both sides)	1989	2.00	4.00	8.00
—Promo-only pressing					
❑ 7PRO-79608	Sacred Emotion (same on both sides)	1989	—	2.50	5.00
—7-inch vinyl originally was promo only					
❑ 7PRO-79608 [PS]	Sacred Emotion (same on both sides)	1989	—	2.50	5.00
—Picture sleeve appears to have been released only with promo copies					
❑ 7PRO-79683	Hold On (same on both sides)	1989	—	3.00	6.00
—7-inch vinyl is promo only					
❑ 7PRO-79912/3	I'll Be Good to You (1/2 Guitar Solo)/(Extended Guitar Mix)	1990	—	3.00	6.00
—7-inch vinyl is promo only					
MGM					
❑ 14227	Sweet and Innocent/Flirtin'	1971	—	3.00	6.00
❑ 14227 [PS]	Sweet and Innocent/Flirtin'	1971	2.00	4.00	8.00
❑ 14285	Go Away Little Girl/The Wild Rover (Time to Ride)	1971	—	2.50	5.00
—Altered B-side title					
❑ 14285	Go Away Little Girl/Time to Ride	1971	—	3.00	6.00
❑ 14322	Hey Girl/I Knew You When	1971	—	3.00	6.00
❑ 14367	Puppy Love/Let My People Go	1972	—	3.00	6.00
❑ 14407	Too Young/Love Me	1972	—	3.00	6.00
❑ 14424	Lonely Boy/Why	1972	—	3.00	6.00
❑ 14503	The Twelfth of Never/Life Is Just What You Make It	1973	—	2.50	5.00
❑ 14503 [PS]	The Twelfth of Never/Life Is Just What You Make It	1973	2.00	4.00	8.00
❑ 14583	A Million to One/Young Love	1973	—	2.50	5.00

Number	Title (A Side/B Side)	Yr	VG	VG+	NM
❑ 14677	Are You Lonesome Tonight/When I Fall in Love	1973	—	2.50	5.00
❑ 14781	I Have a Dream/I'm Dyin'	1975	—	2.00	4.00
POLYDOR					
❑ 14320	C'mon Marianne/Ol' Man Auctioneer	1976	—	2.00	4.00
❑ 14417	You Got Me Dangling on a String/I'm Sorry	1977	—	2.00	4.00
Albums					
CAPITOL					
❑ C1-92354	Donny Osmond	1989	3.00	6.00	12.00
❑ C1-94051	Eyes Don't Lie	1990	3.75	7.50	15.00
MGM					
❑ SE-4782	The Donny Osmond Album	1971	3.00	6.00	12.00
❑ SE-4797	To You with Love, Donny	1971	2.50	5.00	10.00
❑ SE-4820	Portrait of Donny	1972	2.50	5.00	10.00
❑ SE-4854	Too Young	1972	2.50	5.00	10.00
❑ SE-4872	My Best to You	1972	2.50	5.00	10.00
❑ SE-4886	Alone Together	1973	6.25	12.50	25.00
—With tear-off 10x10 photo intact; deduct 60 percent if missing					
❑ M3G-4930	A Time for Us	1973	2.50	5.00	10.00
❑ M3G-4978	Donny	1974	2.50	5.00	10.00
POLYDOR					
❑ PD-1-6067	Disco Train	1976	2.00	4.00	8.00
❑ PD-1-6109	Donald Clark Osmond	1977	2.00	4.00	8.00

OSMOND, DONNY AND MARIE Also see DONNY OSMOND; MARIE OSMOND; THE OSMONDS.
45s

Number	Title (A Side/B Side)	Yr	VG	VG+	NM
MGM					
❑ 14735	I'm Leaving It (All) Up to You/The Umbrella Song	1974	—	2.50	5.00
❑ 14765	Morning Side of the Mountain/One of These Days	1974	—	2.00	4.00
❑ 14807	Make the World Go Away/Living on My Suspicion	1975	—	2.00	4.00
❑ 14840	Deep Purple/Take Me Back Again	1975	—	2.00	4.00
POLYDOR					
❑ 14363	Ain't Nothin' Like the Real Thing/Sing	1976	—	2.00	4.00
❑ 14439	(You're My) Soul and Inspiration/Now We're Together	1977	—	2.00	4.00
❑ 14456	Baby, I'm Sold on You/Sure Would Be Nice	1978	—	2.00	4.00
❑ 14474	May Tomorrow Be a Perfect Day/I Want to Give You My Everything	1978	—	2.00	4.00
❑ 14510	On the Shelf/Certified Honey	1978	—	2.00	4.00
Albums					
MGM					
❑ M3G-4968	I'm Leaving It All Up to You	1974	2.50	5.00	10.00
❑ M3G-4996	Make the World Go Away	1975	2.50	5.00	10.00
POLYDOR					
❑ PD-1-6068	Donny & Marie — Featuring Songs from Their Television Show	1976	2.00	4.00	8.00
❑ PD-1-6083	Donny & Marie — New Season	1976	2.00	4.00	8.00
❑ PD-1-6127	Winning Combination	1978	2.00	4.00	8.00
❑ PD-1-6169	Goin' Coconuts	1978	2.00	4.00	8.00

OSMOND, JIMMY Youngest of the first generation of singing Osmonds.
45s

Number	Title (A Side/B Side)	Yr	VG	VG+	NM
MERCURY					
❑ 74005	Life Is Just What You Make It/Theme from "The Great Brain"	1978	—	2.00	4.00
MGM					
❑ 14199	Santa, No Chimney/I Hope You Have a Merry Christmas	1970	—	3.00	6.00
❑ 14328	If Santa Were My Daddy/Silent Night	1971	—	3.00	6.00
—As "Little Jimmy Osmond"					
❑ 14328 [PS]	If Santa Were My Daddy/Silent Night	1971	2.00	4.00	8.00
❑ 14376	Long Haired Lover from Liverpool/Mother of Mine	1972	—	2.50	5.00
❑ 14468	Tweedlee Dee/Mama'd Know What to Do	1972	—	2.50	5.00
❑ 14687	I'm Gonna Knock on Your Door/Give Me a Good Old Mammy Song	1973	—	2.50	5.00
❑ 14770	Yes Virginia, There Is a Santa Claus/If Santa Were My Daddy	1974	—	3.00	6.00
❑ 14771	Don't You Remember/Little Arrows	1974	—	2.50	5.00
Albums					
MGM					
❑ SE-4855	Killer Joe	1972	2.50	5.00	10.00
❑ M3G-4916	Little Arrows	1975	3.00	6.00	12.00

OSMOND, MARIE Also see DONNY AND MARIE OSMOND.
45s

Number	Title (A Side/B Side)	Yr	VG	VG+	NM
CAPITOL					
❑ B-5445	Until I Fall in Love Again/I Don't Want to Go Too Far	1985	—	—	3.00
❑ B-5478	Meet Me in Montana/What Do Lonely People Do	1985	—	—	3.00
—With Dan Seals					
❑ B-5478 [PS]	Meet Me in Montana/What Do Lonely People Do	1985	—	2.00	4.00
❑ B-5521	There's No Stopping Your Heart/Blue Sky Shinin'	1985	—	—	3.00
❑ B-5563	Read My Lips/That Old Devil Moon	1986	—	—	3.00
❑ B-5613	You're Still New to Me/New Love	1986	—	—	3.00
—With Paul Davis					
❑ B-5613 [PS]	You're Still New to Me/New Love	1986	—	2.00	4.00
❑ B-5663	I Only Wanted You/We're Gonna Need a Love Song	1986	—	—	3.00
❑ B-5703	Everybody's Crazy 'Bout My Baby/Making Music	1987	—	—	3.00
❑ B-44044	Cry Just a Little/More Than Dancing	1987	—	—	3.00
❑ B-44176	Without a Trace/Baby's Blue Eyes	1988	—	—	3.00
❑ B-44215	Sweet Life/My Home Town Boy	1988	—	—	3.00
—A-side: With Paul Davis					
❑ B-44269	I'm in Love and He's in Dallas/My Home Town Boy	1989	—	—	3.00
❑ B-44412	Steppin' Stone/What Would You Do About Me If You Were Me	1989	—	—	3.00
❑ B-44468	Slowly But Surely/What Would You Do About You	1989	—	2.00	4.00
❑ NR-44505	Let Me Be the First/What's a Little Lovin' Between Friends	1990	—	2.50	5.00

Number	Title (A Side/B Side)	Yr	VG	VG+	NM
❑ 7PRO-79808	Slowly But Surely (same on both sides)	1989	—	2.50	5.00
—Vinyl originally was promo only					
CURB					
❑ 76840	Like a Hurricane/I'll Be Faithful to You	1990	—	2.00	4.00
❑ 76851	Paper Roses/Think with Your Heart	1990	—	2.00	4.00
ELEKTRA					
❑ 69882	I'm Learning/Look Who's Getting Over Who	1982	—	2.00	4.00
❑ 69995	Back to Believing Again/Look Who's Getting Over Who	1982	—	2.00	4.00
MGM					
❑ 14609	Paper Roses/Least of All You	1973	—	2.50	5.00
❑ 14609 [PS]	Paper Roses/Least of All You	1973	2.00	4.00	8.00
❑ 14694	My Little Corner of the World/It's Just the Other Way Around	1974	—	2.00	4.00
❑ 14786	Who's Sorry Now/This I Promise You	1975	—	2.00	4.00
POLYDOR					
❑ 14333	"A" My Name Is Alice/Weeping Willow	1976	—	2.00	4.00
❑ 14385	This Is the Way That I Feel/Play the Music Loud	1977	—	2.00	4.00
❑ 14385 [PS]	This Is the Way That I Feel/Play the Music Loud	1977	—	2.50	5.00
❑ 14405	Cry, Baby, Cry/Please Tell Him I Said Hello	1977	—	2.00	4.00
RCA					
❑ PB-13680	Who's Counting/'Til the Best Comes Along	1983	—	2.00	4.00
Albums					
CAPITOL					
❑ ST-12414	There's No Stopping Your Heart	1985	2.00	4.00	8.00
❑ ST-12516	I Only Wanted You	1986	2.00	4.00	8.00
❑ C1-48968	All in Love	1988	2.00	4.00	8.00
❑ C1-91781	Steppin' Stone	1989	2.50	5.00	10.00
MGM					
❑ SE-4910	Paper Roses	1973	3.00	6.00	12.00
❑ M3G-4944	In My Little Corner of the World	1974	3.00	6.00	12.00
❑ M3G-4979	Who's Sorry Now	1975	3.00	6.00	12.00
POLYDOR					
❑ PD-1-6099	This Is the Way That I Feel	1977	2.00	4.00	8.00

OSMONDS, THE Includes records as "The Osmond Brothers." (Most of these were pre-1970, before Donny was a member of the group.) Also see DONNY OSMOND.

45s

Number	Title (A Side/B Side)	Yr	VG	VG+	NM
BARNABY					
❑ 2002	Mary Elizabeth/Speak Like a Child	1968	2.50	5.00	10.00
❑ 2004	I've Got Loving on My Mind/Mollie-"A"	1968	2.50	5.00	10.00
❑ 2005	Taking a Chance on Love/Groove With What You Got	1969	2.50	5.00	10.00
ELEKTRA					
❑ 47438	I Think About Your Lovin'/Working Man's Blues	1982	—	2.00	4.00
❑ 69883	Never Ending Song of Love/You'll Be Seeing Me	1982	—	2.00	4.00
❑ 69969	It's Like Falling in Love/Your Leaving Was the Last Thing on My Mind	1982	—	2.00	4.00
EMI AMERICA					
❑ 8298	Baby When Your Heart Breaks Down/Love Burning Down	1985	—	—	3.00
❑ 8313	Baby Wants/Lovin' Proof	1986	—	—	3.00
❑ 8325	You Look Like the One I Love/It's Only a Heartache	1986	—	—	3.00
❑ 8360	Looking for Suzanne/Back in Your Arms	1986	—	—	3.00
❑ 43033	Slow Ride/Heartbreak Radio	1987	—	—	3.00
MERCURY					
❑ 74056	Love on the Line/You're Mine	1979	—	2.00	4.00
❑ 74079	Emily/Rainin'	1979	—	2.00	4.00
MGM					
❑ 13162	Be My Little Baby Bumble Bee/I Wouldn't Trade the Silver in My Mother's Hair	1963	3.75	7.50	15.00
❑ 13174	Theme from "The Travels of Jamie McPheeters"/Aura Lee	1963	3.75	7.50	15.00
❑ 13174 [PS]	Theme from "The Travels of Jamie McPheeters"/Aura Lee	1963	7.50	15.00	30.00
❑ 13281	Mr. Sandman/My Mom	1964	5.00	10.00	20.00
❑ 13281 [PS]	Mr. Sandman/My Mom	1964	12.50	25.00	50.00
❑ 14159	Movin' Along/Open Up Your Heart	1970	2.00	4.00	8.00
❑ 14193	One Bad Apple/He Ain't Heavy, He's My Brother	1970	—	3.00	6.00
❑ 14193 [PS]	One Bad Apple/He Ain't Heavy, He's My Brother	1970	12.50	25.00	50.00
—Sleeve calls the group "The Osmond Brothers," rather than "The Osmonds" as the 45 does, which may explain its rarity					
❑ 14259	Double Lovin'/Chilly Winds	1971	—	3.00	6.00
❑ 14295	Yo-Yo/Keep on My Side	1971	—	3.00	6.00
❑ 14324	Down by the Lazy River/He's the Light of the World	1971	—	3.00	6.00
❑ 14405	Hold Her Tight/Love Is	1972	—	2.50	5.00
❑ 14450	Crazy Horses/That's My Girl	1972	—	2.50	5.00
❑ 14562	Goin' Home/Are You Up There	1973	—	2.50	5.00
❑ 14617	Let Me In/One Way Ticket to Anywhere	1973	—	2.50	5.00
❑ 14617 [PS]	Let Me In/One Way Ticket to Anywhere	1973	2.00	4.00	8.00
❑ 14746	Love Me for a Reason/Fever	1974	—	2.50	5.00
❑ 14791	The Proud One/The Last Day Is Coming	1975	—	2.50	5.00
❑ 14831	Thank You/I'm Still Gonna Need You	1975	—	2.50	5.00
❑ 14831 [PS]	Thank You/I'm Still Gonna Need You	1975	—	3.00	6.00
POLYDOR					
❑ 14348	Check It Out/I Can't Live a Dream	1976	—	2.00	4.00
UNI					
❑ 55015	I Can't Stop/Flower Music	1967	2.50	5.00	10.00
❑ 55276	I Can't Stop/Flower Music	1971	—	3.00	6.00
WARNER BROS.					
❑ 28982	Any Time/Desperately	1985	—	—	3.00
❑ 29312	If Every Man Had a Woman Like You/Come Back to Me	1984	—	2.00	4.00
❑ 29387	Where Does An Angel Go When She Cries/One More for Lovers	1984	—	2.00	4.00
❑ 29594	She's Ready for Someone to Love Her/You Make the Long Road Shorter with Your Love	1983	—	2.00	4.00
Albums					
ELEKTRA					
❑ 60180	The Osmond Brothers	1982	2.50	5.00	10.00
MERCURY					
❑ SRM-1-3766	Steppin' Out	1979	2.50	5.00	10.00

Number	Title (A Side/B Side)	Yr	VG	VG+	NM
METRO					
❑ M 543 [M]	We Sing You a Merry Christmas	1965	3.75	7.50	15.00
—Reissue of 4187 with one track missing and remaining contents rearranged					
❑ MS 543 [S]	We Sing You a Merry Christmas	1965	5.00	10.00	20.00
MGM					
❑ PM-7 [M]	The Travels of Jaimie McPheeters	1963	12.50	25.00	50.00
—Side 1: Dialogue from TV show; Side 2: Osmond Brothers tracks. AC Spark Plugs promo.					
❑ PM-9 [M]	We Sing You a Merry Christmas	1963	10.00	20.00	40.00
—Special-products issue for AC Spark Plug dealers					
❑ E-4146 [M]	Songs We Sang on the Andy Williams Show	1963	6.25	12.50	25.00
❑ SE-4146 [S]	Songs We Sang on the Andy Williams Show	1963	7.50	15.00	30.00
—As "The Osmond Brothers"					
❑ E-4187 [M]	We Sing You a Merry Christmas	1963	6.25	12.50	25.00
—As "The Osmond Brothers"					
❑ SE-4187 [S]	We Sing You a Merry Christmas	1963	7.50	15.00	30.00
❑ E-4235 [M]	The Osmond Brothers Sing the All-Time Hymn Favorites	1964	5.00	10.00	20.00
❑ SE-4235 [S]	The Osmond Brothers Sing the All-Time Hymn Favorites	1964	6.25	12.50	25.00
❑ E-4291 [M]	The New Sound of the Osmond Brothers	1965	5.00	10.00	20.00
❑ SE-4291 [S]	The New Sound of the Osmond Brothers	1965	6.25	12.50	25.00
❑ SE-4724	Osmonds	1971	3.00	6.00	12.00
❑ SE-4770	Homemade	1971	7.50	15.00	30.00
—With tear-off poster intact; deduct 60 percent if poster is not attached					
❑ SE-4796	Phase-III	1972	3.00	6.00	12.00
❑ SE-4826 [(2)]	The Osmonds "Live"	1972	3.75	7.50	15.00
❑ SE-4851	Crazy Horses	1972	3.00	6.00	12.00
❑ SE-4902	The Plan	1973	2.50	5.00	10.00
❑ M3G-4939	Love Me for a Reason	1974	2.50	5.00	10.00
❑ M3G-4993	The Proud One	1975	2.50	5.00	10.00
❑ MG-2-5012 [(2)]	Around the World — Live in Concert	1975	3.00	6.00	12.00
❑ ST 90403 [S]	The New Sound of the Osmond Brothers	1965	10.00	20.00	40.00
—Capitol Record Club edition					
❑ T 90403 [M]	The New Sound of the Osmond Brothers	1965	10.00	20.00	40.00
—Capitol Record Club edition					
POLYDOR					
❑ PD-1-6077	Brainstorm	1976	2.50	5.00	10.00
❑ PD-2-8001 [(2)]	The Osmond Christmas Album	1976	3.75	7.50	15.00
—Includes group, solo and duet recordings					
❑ PD-2-9005	The Osmonds Greatest Hits	1977	3.00	6.00	12.00
WARNER BROS.					
❑ 25070	One Way Rider	1984	2.00	4.00	8.00

OSWALD, LEE HARVEY

Albums

Number	Title (A Side/B Side)	Yr	VG	VG+	NM
EYEWITNESS					
❑ 1002	Lee Harvey Oswald Speaks	1967	20.00	40.00	80.00
INCA					
❑ 1001	Oswald: Self Portrait in Red	1965	25.00	50.00	100.00
KEY					
❑ 880	The President's Assassin Speaks	1964	25.00	50.00	100.00

OTHER HALF, THE (1)

45s

Number	Title (A Side/B Side)	Yr	VG	VG+	NM
ACTA					
❑ 801	Flight of the Dragon Lady/Wonderful Day	1967	5.00	10.00	20.00
❑ 806	I Need You/No Doubt About It	1967	5.00	10.00	20.00
❑ 819	What Can I Do for You/Bad Day	1968	3.75	7.50	15.00
❑ 825	Morning Fire/Ozlee Eaves Drop	1968	3.75	7.50	15.00
GNP CRESCENDO					
❑ 378	I've Come So Far/Mr. Pharmacist	1966	5.00	10.00	20.00
Albums					
ACTA					
❑ 38004	The Other Half	1968	25.00	50.00	100.00

OTHER HALF, THE (2)

Albums

Number	Title (A Side/B Side)	Yr	VG	VG+	NM
7/2					
❑ (no #)	The Other Half	1966	375.00	750.00	1500.
—Album has been counterfeited, but those records are translucent when held to a light, originals are not					

OTHER ONES, THE

45s

Number	Title (A Side/B Side)	Yr	VG	VG+	NM
ABC-PARAMOUNT					
❑ 10793	Stop/Dreaming Out Loud	1966	3.00	6.00	12.00

OTHER TIKIS, THE See THE TIKIS.

OTHERS, THE (1) British group.

45s

Number	Title (A Side/B Side)	Yr	VG	VG+	NM
FONTANA					
❑ 1944	Oh Yeah!/I'm Taking Her Home	1964	7.50	15.00	30.00

OTHERS, THE (2)

45s

Number	Title (A Side/B Side)	Yr	VG	VG+	NM
MERCURY					
❑ 72602	Revenge/I'm in Need	1966	7.50	15.00	30.00

OTHERS, THE (U)

45s

Number	Title (A Side/B Side)	Yr	VG	VG+	NM
RCA VICTOR					
❑ 47-8669	I Can't Stand This Love, Goodbye/Until I Heard It From You	1965	7.50	15.00	30.00
❑ 47-8776	Lonely Street/(I Remember) The First Time I Saw You	1965	3.75	7.50	15.00

OTIS, JOHNNY

45s

Number	Title (A Side/B Side)	Yr	VG	VG+	NM
ATLANTIC					
❑ 2409	Keep the Faith — Part I/Keep the Faith — Part II	1967	3.00	6.00	12.00
CAPITOL					
❑ F3799	Can't You Hear Me Callin'/My Ding-a-Ling	1957	12.50	25.00	50.00
❑ F3799/3802	The Johnny Otis Show	1957	100.00	200.00	400.00
—Four-record set with four-pocket cover. Price is for entire set. Records alone are valued separately below.					
❑ F3800	Ma, He's Makin' Eyes at Me/In the Dark	1957	12.50	25.00	50.00

Number	Title (A Side/B Side)	Yr	VG	VG+	NM
❏ F3801	Stay with Me/Tell Me So	1957	12.50	25.00	50.00
❏ F3802	It's Too Soon to Know/Star of Love	1957	12.50	25.00	50.00
❏ F3852	Bye Bye Baby/Good Golly	1957	6.25	12.50	25.00
❏ F3889	Well, Well, Well/You Just Kissed Me Goodbye	1958	6.25	12.50	25.00
❏ F3966	Willie and the Hand Jive/Ring-a-Ling	1958	7.50	15.00	30.00
❏ F4060	Willie Did the Cha Cha/Crazy Country Hop	1958	6.25	12.50	25.00
❏ F4156	My Dear/You	1959	5.00	10.00	20.00
❏ F4168 [M]	Castin' My Spell/Telephone Baby	1959	5.00	10.00	20.00
❏ F4168 [S]	Castin' My Spell/Telephone Baby	1959	12.50	25.00	50.00
❏ F4226	Three Girls Named Molly (Doin' the Hully Gully)/ I'll Do the Same for You	1959	5.00	10.00	20.00
❏ F4260	Let the Sun Shine in My Life/Baby, Just You	1959	5.00	10.00	20.00
❏ 4326	Mumblin' Mosie/Hey Baby, Don't You Know	1960	3.75	7.50	15.00
DIG					
❏ 119	Hey! Hey! Hey! Hey!/ Let the Sunshine in My Heart	1956	7.50	15.00	30.00
❏ 122	The Midnite Creeper (Part 1)/The Midnite Creeper (Part 2)	1956	7.50	15.00	30.00
❏ 132	My Eyes Are Full of Tears/Turtle Dove	1957	7.50	15.00	30.00
❏ 134	Wa Wa (Part 1)/Wa Wa (Part 2)	1957	7.50	15.00	30.00
❏ 139	Stop, Look and Love Me/The Night Is Young	1957	7.50	15.00	30.00
ELDO					
❏ 106	The New Bo Diddley/The Jelly Roll	1960	3.75	7.50	15.00
❏ 152	Keep the Faith (Part 1)/Keep the Faith (Part 2)	1968	2.00	4.00	8.00
❏ 153	Long Distance/Banana Peels	1968	2.00	4.00	8.00
EPIC					
❏ 5-10606	You Can Depend on Me/The Watts Breakaway	1970	—	3.00	6.00
❏ 5-10757	Willie and the Hand Jive/Goin' Back to L.A.	1971	—	3.00	6.00
—B-side with Delmar Evans					
HAWK SOUND					
❏ 1003	Jaws/Good to the Last Drop	1975	—	2.50	5.00
KENT					
❏ 506	Country Girl/Bye Bye Baby	1969	2.00	4.00	8.00
❏ 4521	Shuggie's Blues/Cool Ade	1969	2.00	4.00	8.00
KING					
❏ 5581	Hand Jive One More Time/Baby I Got News for You	1961	3.75	7.50	15.00
❏ 5606	She's All Right/It Must Be Love	1962	3.75	7.50	15.00
❏ 5634	Queen of the Twist/I Know My Love Is True	1962	3.75	7.50	15.00
❏ 5690	The Hey Hey Hey Song/Early in the Morning Blues	1962	3.75	7.50	15.00
❏ 5707	Somebody Call the Station/Yes	1963	3.00	6.00	12.00
❏ 5790	Bye, Bye Baby/The Hash	1963	3.00	6.00	12.00
MERCURY					
❏ 8263	Oopy Doo/Stardust	1952	12.50	25.00	50.00
❏ 8273	One-Nighter Blues/Goomp Blues	1952	12.50	25.00	50.00
❏ 8289	Call Operator 210/Baby Baby Blues	1952	12.50	25.00	50.00
❏ 8295	Gypsy Blues/The Candle's Burning Low	1952	12.50	25.00	50.00
❏ 70038	Why Don't You Believe Me/Wishing Well	1953	12.50	25.00	50.00
❏ 70050	Love Bug Boogie/Brown Skin Butterball	1953	12.50	25.00	50.00
OKEH					
❏ 7332	Watts Breakaway/You Can Depend On Me	1969	—	3.00	6.00
PEACOCK					
❏ 1625	Young Girl/Rock Me Baby	1953	20.00	40.00	80.00
❏ 1636	Shake It/I Won't Be Your Fool No More	1954	12.50	25.00	50.00
❏ 1648	Sittin' Here Drinkin'/You Got Me Crying	1955	12.50	25.00	50.00
❏ 1675	Butter Ball/Dandy's Boogie	1957	12.50	25.00	50.00
SAVOY					
❏ 731	Double Crossing Blues/Back Alley Blues	1950	25.00	50.00	100.00
—B-side by the Beale Street Gang					
❏ 731	Double Crossing Blues/Ain't Nothin' Shakin'	1950	30.00	60.00	120.00
❏ 750	Cupid Boogie/Just Can't Get Free	1950	15.00	30.00	60.00
❏ 764	Wedding Blues/Far Away Blues (Xmas Blues)	1950	15.00	30.00	60.00
❏ 766	Rockin' Blues/My Heart Tells Me	1950	15.00	30.00	60.00
❏ 777	Gee Baby/Mambo Boogie	1951	12.50	25.00	50.00
❏ 780	Doggin' Blues/Living and Loving You	1951	12.50	25.00	50.00
❏ 787	I Dream/Hangover Blues	1951	12.50	25.00	50.00
❏ 788	All Nite Long/New Love	1951	12.50	25.00	50.00
❏ 812	Warning Blues/I'll Ask My Heart	1951	12.50	25.00	50.00
❏ 815	Harlem Nocturne/Midnight in the Barrelhouse	1951	12.50	25.00	50.00
❏ 824	Get Together Blues/Chittlin' Switch	1951	12.50	25.00	50.00
❏ 855	It Ain't the Beauty/Gonna Take a Train	1952	12.50	25.00	50.00

7-Inch Extended Plays

Number	Title (A Side/B Side)	Yr	VG	VG+	NM
CAPITOL					
❏ EAP 1-940	Hum Ding a Ling/It's Too Soon to Know//Stay with Me/Ma (He's Makin' Eyes at Me)	1958	37.50	75.00	150.00
❏ EAP 1-940 [PS]	The Johnny Otis Show	1958	37.50	75.00	150.00

Albums

Number	Title (A Side/B Side)	Yr	VG	VG+	NM
ALLIGATOR					
❏ AL-4726	The New Johnny Otis Show	1982	2.50	5.00	10.00
CAPITOL					
❏ T 940 [M]	The Johnny Otis Show	1958	62.50	125.00	250.00
❏ C1-92858 [(2)]	The Capitol Years	1989	3.75	7.50	15.00
DIG					
❏ 104 [M]	Rock and Roll Hit Parade, Volume 1	1957	300.00	600.00	900.00
—Gold cover with thick cardboard and thick vinyl records. Counterfeits have noticeably thinner vinyl.					
❏ 104 [M]	Rock and Roll Hit Parade, Volume 1	1958	150.00	300.00	600.00
—Yellow cover with thick cardboard and thick vinyl records. Counterfeits have noticeably thinner vinyl.					
EPIC					
❏ BN 26524	Cuttin' Up	1970	6.25	12.50	25.00
❏ EG 30473 [(2)]	The Johnny Otis Show Live at Monterey	1971	7.50	15.00	30.00
KENT					
❏ KST-534	Cold Shot	1968	6.25	12.50	25.00
SAVOY					
❏ SJL-2230 [(2)]	The Original Johnny Otis Show	1978	3.75	7.50	15.00
❏ SJL-2252 [(2)]	The Original Johnny Otis Show, Vol. 2	1980	3.75	7.50	15.00

OTIS, SHUGGIE
45s

Number	Title (A Side/B Side)	Yr	VG	VG+	NM
EPIC					
❏ 10603	Hurricane/Jennie Lee	1970	—	3.00	6.00
❏ 10798	Strawberry Letter 23/Ice Cold Daydream	1971	2.00	4.00	8.00
❏ 10978	Purple (Part 1)/Purple (Part 2)	1973	—	3.00	6.00
❏ 50054	Inspiration Information/Aht Uh Mi Hed	1975	—	3.00	6.00
LUAKA BOP					
❏ 77666	Aht Uh Mi Hed/Strawberry Letter 23	2001	—	2.00	4.00

Albums

Number	Title (A Side/B Side)	Yr	VG	VG+	NM
EPIC					
❏ BN 26511	Here Comes Shuggie Otis	1970	3.75	7.50	15.00
❏ KE 30752	Freedom Flight	1971	3.75	7.50	15.00
❏ PE 33059	Inspiration Information	1975	3.75	7.50	15.00

OTIS AND CARLA
45s

Number	Title (A Side/B Side)	Yr	VG	VG+	NM
ATCO					
❏ 6665	When Something Is Wrong with My Baby/ Ooh Carla, Ooh Otis	1968	2.50	5.00	10.00
STAX					
❏ 216	Tramp/Tell It Like It Is	1967	2.50	5.00	10.00
❏ 228	Knock on Wood/Let Me Be Good to You	1967	2.50	5.00	10.00
❏ 244	Lovey Dovey/New Year's Resolution	1968	2.50	5.00	10.00

Albums

Number	Title (A Side/B Side)	Yr	VG	VG+	NM
STAX					
❏ ST-716 [M]	King and Queen	1967	8.75	17.50	35.00
❏ STS-716 [S]	King and Queen	1967	12.50	25.00	50.00
SUNDAZED					
❏ LP 5069 [S]	King and Queen	2001	3.00	6.00	12.00
—Reissue on 180-gram vinyl					

OTT, JACKIE
45s

Number	Title (A Side/B Side)	Yr	VG	VG+	NM
HIT					
❏ 49	From a Jack to a King/Walk Right In	1963	2.00	4.00	8.00
—B-side by the Music City Orchestra					
❏ 58	Out of My Mind/Young Lovers	1963	2.00	4.00	8.00
—B-side by Bob and Bobbie					

OUR GANG
45s

Number	Title (A Side/B Side)	Yr	VG	VG+	NM
BR'ER BIRD					
❏ 001	Summertime Summertime/ Theme from Leon's Garage	1966	50.00	100.00	200.00

OUTLAW BLUES BAND, THE
Albums

Number	Title (A Side/B Side)	Yr	VG	VG+	NM
BLUESWAY					
❏ BLS-6020	Breakin' In	1969	6.25	12.50	25.00
❏ BLS-6021	The Outlaw Blues Band	1968	6.25	12.50	25.00

OUTLAWS
"Southern rock" band; few, if any, of their releases used the word "The" before their name.

12-Inch Singles

Number	Title (A Side/B Side)	Yr	VG	VG+	NM
ARISTA					
❏ SP-39 [DJ]	You Are the Show/If Dreams Came True	1979	3.75	7.50	15.00
PASHA					
❏ AS 2513 [DJ]	Soldiers of Fortune (2 versions?)	1986	5.00	10.00	20.00
❏ AS 2570 [DJ]	One Last Ride (2 versions?)	1987	3.75	7.50	15.00

45s

Number	Title (A Side/B Side)	Yr	VG	VG+	NM
ARISTA					
❏ 0150	There Goes Another Love Song/Keep Prayin'	1975	—	2.00	4.00
❏ 0188	Breaker-Breaker/South Carolina	1976	—	2.00	4.00
❏ 0213	Green Grass and High Tides/Prisoner	1976	—	2.50	5.00
❏ 0258	Hurry Sundown/So Afraid	1977	—	2.00	4.00
❏ 0282	Hearin' My Heart Talkin'/Holiday	1977	—	2.00	4.00
❏ 0338	Green Grass and High Tides/Holiday	1978	—	2.00	4.00
❏ 0378	Take It Anyway You Want It/Cry Some More	1978	—	2.00	4.00
❏ 0397	You Are the Show/If Dreams Came True	1979	—	2.00	4.00
❏ 0582	(Ghost) Riders in the Sky/Devil's Road	1981	—	2.00	4.00
❏ 0597	Wishing Well/I Can't Stop Loving You	1981	—	2.00	4.00
❏ 0678	Running/(B-side unknown)	1982	—	2.00	4.00
PASHA					
❏ ZS4-06550	One Last Ride/Saved by the Bell	1987	—	—	3.00

Albums

Number	Title (A Side/B Side)	Yr	VG	VG+	NM
ARISTA					
❏ SP-132 [EP]	Radio Remixes	1982	3.00	6.00	12.00
—Promo-only four-song sampler					
❏ AL 4042	Outlaws	1975	2.50	5.00	10.00
❏ AL 4070	Lady in Waiting	1976	2.50	5.00	10.00
❏ AQ 4070 [Q]	Lady in Waiting	1976	3.75	7.50	15.00
❏ AL 4135	Hurry Sundown	1977	2.50	5.00	10.00
❏ AB 4205	Playin' to Win	1978	2.50	5.00	10.00
❏ A2L 8114 [(2)]	Bring It Back Alive	198?	2.50	5.00	10.00
—Second reissue					
❏ A2L 8300 [(2)]	Bring It Back Alive	1978	3.00	6.00	12.00
❏ AL 8301	Outlaws	198?	2.00	4.00	8.00
—Reissue					
❏ AL 8319	Greatest Hits of the Outlaws/High Tides Forever	198?	2.00	4.00	8.00
—Reissue					
❏ AL 8369	Hurry Sundown	198?	2.00	4.00	8.00
—Reissue					
❏ A2L 8608 [(2)]	Bring It Back Alive	198?	2.50	5.00	10.00
—Reissue					
❏ AL 9507	In the Eye of the Storm	1979	2.50	5.00	10.00
❏ AL 9542	Ghost Riders	1980	2.50	5.00	10.00
❏ AL 9584	Los Hombres Malo	1982	2.50	5.00	10.00
❏ AL 9614	Greatest Hits of the Outlaws/High Tides Forever	1982	2.50	5.00	10.00
DIRECT DISC					
❏ SD 16617	Outlaws	198?	12.50	25.00	50.00
—Audiophile vinyl					
PAIR					
❏ PDL2-1050 [(2)]	The Outlaws	1986	3.00	6.00	12.00
PASHA					
❏ BFZ 40512	Soldiers of Fortune	1986	2.00	4.00	8.00

OUTLAWS, THE (2)
45s

Number	Title (A Side/B Side)	Yr	VG	VG+	NM
CRUSADE					
❏ 92765	Chains/(B-side unknown)	1965	7.50	15.00	30.00

Number	Title (A Side/B Side)	Yr	VG	VG+	NM

OUTLAWS, THE (3)
45s
DOT

Number	Title (A Side/B Side)	Yr	VG	VG+	NM
❏ 16512	Hold-Up/Somethin' Else	1963	10.00	20.00	40.00

OUTLAWS, THE (U) Could be group (2); could be a completely different group.
45s
SMASH

❏ 2025	Don't Cry/Only for You	1966	3.00	6.00	12.00

OUTSIDERS, THE Lead singer Sonny Geraci later sang with CLIMAX.
45s
BELL

❏ 904	Changes/Lost in My World	1970	—	3.00	6.00

CAPITOL

❏ 2055	Little Bit of Lovin'/I Will Love You	1967	2.00	4.00	8.00
❏ 2216	Oh How It Hurts/We Ain't Gonna Make It	1968	2.00	4.00	8.00
❏ 5573	Time Won't Let Me/Was It Really Real	1966	3.00	6.00	12.00
❏ 5646	Girl in Love/What Makes You So Bad	1966	2.50	5.00	10.00
❏ 5646 [PS]	Girl in Love/What Makes You So Bad	1966	5.00	10.00	20.00
❏ 5701	Respectable/Lost in My World	1966	2.50	5.00	10.00
❏ 5759	Help Me Girl/You Gotta Look	1966	2.50	5.00	10.00
❏ 5759 [PS]	Help Me Girl/You Gotta Look	1966	5.00	10.00	20.00
❏ 5843	I'll Give You Time/I'm Not Trying to Hurt You	1967	2.00	4.00	8.00
❏ 5843 [PS]	I'll Give You Time/I'm Not Trying to Hurt You	1967	5.00	10.00	20.00
❏ 5892	I Just Can't See You Anymore/ Gotta Leave Us Alone	1967	2.00	4.00	8.00
❏ 5955	I'll See You in the Summertime/ And Now You Want My Sympathy	1967	2.00	4.00	8.00
❏ 5955 [PS]	I'll See You in the Summertime/ And Now You Want My Sympathy	1967	5.00	10.00	20.00

ELLEN

❏ 503	Rickity-Boom-Bal-Aye/The Bird Rattle	196?	3.75	7.50	15.00

KAPP

❏ 2104	Tinker, Tailor/Oh You're Not So Pretty	1970	—	3.00	6.00

Albums
CAPITOL

❏ ST 2501 [S]	Time Won't Let Me	1966	7.50	15.00	30.00
❏ T 2501 [M]	Time Won't Let Me	1966	6.25	12.50	25.00
❏ ST 2558 [S]	The Outsiders Album #2	1966	7.50	15.00	30.00
❏ T 2568 [M]	The Outsiders Album #2	1966	6.25	12.50	25.00
❏ ST 2636 [S]	In	1967	6.25	12.50	25.00
❏ T 2636 [M]	In	1967	7.50	15.00	30.00
❏ ST 2745 [S]	Happening "Live!"	1967	6.25	12.50	25.00
❏ T 2745 [M]	Happening "Live!"	1967	7.50	15.00	30.00

RHINO

❏ RNLP-70132	The Best of the Outsiders (1965-1968)	1986	2.50	5.00	10.00

OUTSIDERS, THE (U) Probably not the same group as above.
45s
KARATE

❏ 505	The Guy with the Long Liverpool Hair/Outsider	1964	5.00	10.00	20.00

OVATIONS, THE (1) R&B vocal group. In essence this is two versions of the same group; the later records featured former members of OLLIE AND THE NIGHTINGALES.
45s
GOLDWAX

❏ 110	Pretty Little Angel/Won't You Call	1964	3.75	7.50	15.00
❏ 113	It's Wonderful to Be in Love/Dance Party	1965	3.75	7.50	15.00
❏ 117	I'm Living Good/Recipe for Love	1965	3.75	7.50	15.00
❏ 300	Don't Cry/I Need a Lot of Loving	1966	3.75	7.50	15.00
❏ 306	I Believe I'll Go Back Home/Qualifications	1966	3.75	7.50	15.00
❏ 314	Me and My Imagination/They Say	1967	3.75	7.50	15.00
❏ 322	I've Gotta Go/Kiss My Troubles and Blues Away	1967	3.75	7.50	15.00
❏ 341	Happiness/Rockin' Chair	1969	3.75	7.50	15.00
❏ 342	You Had Your Choice/I'm Living Good	1969	3.75	7.50	15.00

MGM

❏ 14623	"Having a Party" Medley/ Just Too Good to Be True	1973	2.00	4.00	8.00
❏ 14705	I'm in Love/Don't Say You Love Me	1974	2.00	4.00	8.00

—As "Louis Williams and the Ovations"
SOUNDS OF MEMPHIS

❏ 708	Touching Me/Don't Break Your Promise	1972	2.00	4.00	8.00
❏ 712	Hooked on a Feeling/ Take It From One Who Knows	1972	2.00	4.00	8.00
❏ 717	One in a Million/So Nice to Be Loved by You	1973	2.00	4.00	8.00

Albums
MGM

❏ SE-4945	Having a Party	1973	3.75	7.50	15.00

SOUNDS OF MEMPHIS

❏ 7001	Hooked on a Feeling	1972	5.00	10.00	20.00

OVATIONS, THE (2)
45s
ANDIE

❏ 5017	My Lullaby/Whole Wide World	1960	10.00	20.00	40.00

BARRY

❏ 101	My Lullaby/The Day We Fell in Love	1961	10.00	20.00	40.00

EPIC

❏ 9470	Oh, What a Day/Real True Love	1961	10.00	20.00	40.00

OVATIONS, THE (3)
45s
CAPITOL

❏ 5082	I Don't Wanna Cry/ Loneliness Never Entered My Mind	1963	7.50	15.00	30.00

OVATIONS, THE (U) Each of these could be by one of the above groups.
45s
HAWK

❏ 153	I Still Love You/Runaround	1963	50.00	100.00	200.00

JOSIE

❏ 916	Who Needs Love/Remembering	1964	6.25	12.50	25.00

OVERLANDERS, THE
45s
HICKORY

Number	Title (A Side/B Side)	Yr	VG	VG+	NM
❏ 1258	Yesterday's Gone/Gone the Rainbow	1964	3.00	6.00	12.00
❏ 1275	Movin'/Don't It Make You Feel Good	1964	3.00	6.00	12.00
❏ 1295	January/Leaves Are Falling	1965	3.00	6.00	12.00
❏ 1327	Rainbow/Take the Bucket to the Well	1965	3.00	6.00	12.00
❏ 1362	Michelle/Cradle of Love	1965	3.00	6.00	12.00
❏ 1384	My Life/Girl from Indiana	1966	3.00	6.00	12.00
❏ 1427	Shanghai Rooster/Leaves Are Falling	1966	3.00	6.00	12.00

MERCURY

❏ 72165	Call of the Wild/ Summer Skies and Golden Sands	1963	3.75	7.50	15.00

OVERMAN, RUNE
45s
PARKWAY

❏ 859	Madison Piano/Big Bass Boogie	1962	3.75	7.50	15.00

STACY

❏ 970	Beatnik Walk/Smorgasbord	1964	2.50	5.00	10.00

OWEN, MACK
45s
SUN

❏ 336	Walkin' and Talkin'/Somebody Like You	1960	5.00	10.00	20.00

OWEN-B
Albums
MUS-I-COL

❏ 101209	Owen-B	1970	15.00	30.00	60.00

OWENS, BONNIE
45s
CAPITOL

❏ 2029	Don't Tell Me/Somewhere Between	1967	2.00	4.00	8.00
❏ 2210	How Can Our Cheatin' Be Wrong/ Yes I Love You Only	1968	2.00	4.00	8.00
❏ 2340	Lead Me On/ I'll Always Be Glad to Take You Back	1968	2.00	4.00	8.00
❏ 2586	It Don't Take Much to Make Me Cry/ My Hi-Fi to Cry By	1969	2.00	4.00	8.00
❏ 2716	Philadelphia Lawyer/That Little Boy of Mine	1970	2.00	4.00	8.00
❏ 5459	Number One Heel/The Longer You Wait	1965	2.50	5.00	10.00
❏ 5529	Excuse Me for Living/Souvenirs	1965	2.50	5.00	10.00
❏ 5618	Merry-Go-Round/Livin' on Your Love	1966	2.50	5.00	10.00
❏ 5688	You Don't Even Try/What's It Gonna Cost Me	1966	2.50	5.00	10.00
❏ 5755	Consider the Children/I Know He Loves Me	1966	2.50	5.00	10.00
❏ 5847	Someone Else You've Known/ The Best Part of Me	1967	2.50	5.00	10.00
❏ 5977	I'd Be More of a Woman/Everything That's Fastened Down Is Coming Loose	1967	2.50	5.00	10.00

MAR-VEL

❏ 102	A Dear John Letter/Wonderful World	1953	12.50	25.00	50.00

—With Fuzzy Owens
TALLY

❏ 149	Why Don't Daddy Live Here Anymore/ Waggin' Tongues	1963	6.25	12.50	25.00
❏ 156	Don't Take Advantage of Me/Stop the World	1964	6.25	12.50	25.00
❏ 184	Lie a Little/I'll Try Again Tomorrow	1964	6.25	12.50	25.00

"X"

❏ 0028	I Traded My Heart for His Gold/Take Me	1954	10.00	20.00	40.00
❏ 0065	No Tomorrow/Just a Love for Someone to Steal	1954	10.00	20.00	40.00

Albums
CAPITOL

❏ ST-195	Lead Me On	1969	6.25	12.50	25.00
❏ ST-341	Hi-Fi to Cry By	1969	6.25	12.50	25.00
❏ ST-557	Mother's Favorite Hymns	1970	6.25	12.50	25.00
❏ ST 2403 [S]	Don't Take Advantage of Me	1965	6.25	12.50	25.00
❏ T 2403 [M]	Don't Take Advantage of Me	1965	5.00	10.00	20.00
❏ ST 2600 [S]	All of Me Belongs to You	1967	6.25	12.50	25.00
❏ T 2600 [M]	All of Me Belongs to You	1967	6.25	12.50	25.00
❏ ST 2861	Somewhere Between	1968	6.25	12.50	25.00

OWENS, BUCK
45s
CAPITOL

❏ 2001	It Takes People Like You (To Make People Like Me)/You Left Her Lonely Too Long	1967	2.00	4.00	8.00
❏ 2001 [PS]	It Takes People Like You (To Make People Like Me)/You Left Her Lonely Too Long	1967	3.00	6.00	12.00
❏ 2080	How Long Will My Baby Be Gone/ Everybody Needs Somebody	1968	2.00	4.00	8.00
❏ 2080 [PS]	How Long Will My Baby Be Gone/ Everybody Needs Somebody	1968	3.00	6.00	12.00
❏ 2142	Sweet Rosie Jones/ Happy Times Are Here Again	1968	2.00	4.00	8.00
❏ 2142 [PS]	Sweet Rosie Jones/ Happy Times Are Here Again	1968	3.00	6.00	12.00
❏ 2237	Let the World Keep On a-Turnin'/ I'll Love You Forever and Ever	1968	2.00	4.00	8.00

—With Buddy Alan

❏ 2237 [PS]	Let the World Keep On a-Turnin'/I'll Love You Forever and Ever	1968	3.00	6.00	12.00

—As "Buck Owens and Buddy Alan and the Buckaroos"

❏ 2300	I've Got You on My Mind Again/That's All Right with Me (If It's All Right with You)	1968	2.00	4.00	8.00
❏ 2300 [PS]	I've Got You on My Mind Again/That's All Right with Me (If It's All Right with You)	1968	3.00	6.00	12.00
❏ 2328	Christmas Shopping/One of Everything You Got	1968	2.00	4.00	8.00
❏ 2330	Turkish Holiday/ Things I Saw Happening at the Fountain	1968	2.00	4.00	8.00
❏ 2377	Who's Gonna Mow Your Grass/ There's Gotta Be Some Chances Made	1969	2.00	4.00	8.00
❏ 2377 [PS]	Who's Gonna Mow Your Grass/ There's Gotta Be Some Chances Made	1969	3.00	6.00	12.00
❏ 2485	Johnny B. Goode/Maybe If I Close My Eyes (It'll Go Away)	1969	2.00	4.00	8.00

Number	Title (A Side/B Side)	Yr	VG	VG+	NM
❏ 2485 [PS]	Johnny B. Goode/				
	Maybe If I Close My Eyes (It'll Go Away)	1969	3.00	6.00	12.00
❏ 2570	Tall Dark Stranger/Sing That Kind of Song	1969	2.00	4.00	8.00
❏ 2570 [PS]	Tall Dark Stranger/Sing That Kind of Song	1969	3.00	6.00	12.00
❏ 2646	Big in Vegas/White Satin Bed	1969	2.00	4.00	8.00
❏ 2646 [PS]	Big in Vegas/White Satin Bed	1969	3.00	6.00	12.00
❏ 2783	The Kansas City Song/I'd Love to Be Your Man	1970	2.00	4.00	8.00
❏ 2783 [PS]	The Kansas City Song/I'd Love to Be Your Man	1970	2.50	5.00	10.00
❏ 2947	I Wouldn't Live in New York City (If They Gave Me the Whole Dang Town)/No Milk and Honey in Baltimore	1970	2.00	4.00	8.00
❏ 2947 [PS]	I Wouldn't Live in New York City (If They Gave Me the Whole Dang Town)/No Milk and Honey in Baltimore	1970	2.50	5.00	10.00
❏ 2962	Buckaroo/Okie from Muskogee	1970	3.00	6.00	12.00
—As "Buck Owens' Bakersfield Brass"					
❏ 3011	Act Naturally/My Heart Skips a Beat	1971	3.00	6.00	12.00
—As "Buck Owens' Bakersfield Brass"					
❏ 3023	Bridge Over Troubled Water/(I'm Goin') Home	1971	—	3.00	6.00
❏ 3023 [PS]	Bridge Over Troubled Water/(I'm Goin') Home	1971	2.50	5.00	10.00
❏ 3066	Cajun Brass/Waitin' in Your Welfare Line	1971	2.50	5.00	10.00
—As "Buck Owens' Bakersfield Brass"					
❏ 3096	Ruby (Are You Mad)/Heartbreak Mountain	1971	—	3.00	6.00
❏ 3164	Rollin' in My Sweet Baby's Arms/Corn Likker	1971	—	3.00	6.00
❏ 3164 [PS]	Rollin' in My Sweet Baby's Arms/Corn Likker	1971	2.50	5.00	10.00
❏ 3215	Too Old to Cut the Mustard/Wham Bam	1971	—	3.00	6.00
—As "Buck and Buddy" (Buck Owens and BUDDY ALAN)					
❏ 3215 [PS]	Too Old to Cut the Mustard/Wham Bam	1971	2.50	5.00	10.00
❏ 3262	I'll Still Be Waiting for You/Full Time Daddy	1972	—	3.00	6.00
❏ 3314	Made in Japan/Black Texas Dirt	1972	—	3.00	6.00
❏ 3429	You Ain't Gonna Have Ol' Buck to Kick Around No More/I Love You So Much It Hurts	1972	—	3.00	6.00
❏ 3504	In the Palm of Your Hand/Get Out of Town Before Sundown	1972	—	3.00	6.00
❏ 3563	Ain't It Amazing, Gracie/The Good Old Days	1973	—	3.00	6.00
❏ 3688	Arms Full of Empty/Songwriter's Lament	1973	—	3.00	6.00
❏ 3769	Big Game Hunter/That Loving Feeling	1973	—	3.00	6.00
❏ F3824	Come Back/I Know What It Means	1957	5.00	10.00	20.00
❏ 3841	On the Cover of the Music City News/Stony Mountain, West Virginia	1974	—	3.00	6.00
❏ 3907	(It's a) Monsters' Holiday/Great Expectations	1974	—	3.00	6.00
❏ F3957	Sweet Thing/I Only Know That I Love You So	1957	5.00	10.00	20.00
❏ 3976	Great Expectations/Let the Fun Begin	1974	—	3.00	6.00
❏ 4043	41st Street Lonely Hearts Club/Weekend Daddy	1975	—	3.00	6.00
❏ F4090	I'll Take a Chance on Loving You/Walk the Floor	1958	5.00	10.00	20.00
❏ 4138	The Battle of New Orleans/Run Him to the Roundhouse Nellie	1975	—	3.00	6.00
❏ F4172	Second Fiddle/Everlasting Love	1959	5.00	10.00	20.00
❏ 4181	Meanwhile Back at the Ranch/Country Singer's Prayer	1976	—	3.00	6.00
❏ F4245	Under Your Spell Again/Tired of Livin'	1959	5.00	10.00	20.00
❏ 4337	Above and Beyond/Till These Dreams Come True	1960	3.75	7.50	15.00
❏ 4412	Excuse Me (I Think I've Got a Heartache)/I've Got a Right to Know	1960	3.75	7.50	15.00
❏ 4496	Foolin' Around/High As the Mountains	1961	3.75	7.50	15.00
❏ 4602	Under the Influence of Love/Bad Bad Dream	1961	3.75	7.50	15.00
❏ 4679	Nobody's Fool But Yours/Mirror Mirror on the Wall	1962	3.75	7.50	15.00
❏ 4765	Save the Last Dance for Me/King of Fools	1962	3.75	7.50	15.00
❏ 4826	Kickin' Our Hearts Around/I Can't Stop (My Lovin' You)	1962	3.75	7.50	15.00
❏ 4872	You're for Me/House Down the Block	1962	3.75	7.50	15.00
❏ 4937	Act Naturally/Over and Over Again	1963	3.75	7.50	15.00
❏ 5025	Love's Gonna Live Here/Getting Used to Losing You	1963	3.00	6.00	12.00
❏ 5136	My Heart Skips a Beat/Together Again	1964	3.00	6.00	12.00
❏ 5240	I Don't Care (Just As Long As You Love Me)/Don't Let Her Know	1964	3.00	6.00	12.00
❏ 5336	I've Got a Tiger by the Tail/Cryin' Time	1965	2.50	5.00	10.00
❏ 5336 [PS]	I've Got a Tiger by the Tail/Cryin' Time	1965	3.75	7.50	15.00
❏ 5410	Before You Go/No One But You	1965	2.50	5.00	10.00
❏ 5410 [PS]	Before You Go/No One But You	1965	3.75	7.50	15.00
❏ 5465	Only You (Can Break My Heart)/Gonna Have Love	1965	2.50	5.00	10.00
❏ 5465 [PS]	Only You (Can Break My Heart)/Gonna Have Love	1965	3.75	7.50	15.00
❏ 5517	Buckaroo/If You Want a Love	1965	2.50	5.00	10.00
❏ 5537	Santa Looked a Lot Like Daddy/All I Want for Christmas Dear Is You	1965	2.50	5.00	10.00
❏ 5537 [PS]	Santa Looked a Lot Like Daddy/All I Want for Christmas Dear Is You	1965	3.75	7.50	15.00
❏ 5537	Santa Looked a Lot Like Daddy/All I Want for Christmas Dear Is You	1973	—	2.00	4.00
—Orange label, "Capitol" at bottom					
❏ 5566	Waitin' in Your Welfare Line/In the Palm of Your Hand	1965	2.50	5.00	10.00
❏ 5647	Think of Me/Heart of Glass	1966	2.50	5.00	10.00
❏ 5647 [PS]	Think of Me/Heart of Glass	1966	3.75	7.50	15.00
❏ 5705	Open Up Your Heart/No More Me and You	1966	2.50	5.00	10.00
❏ 5705 [PS]	Open Up Your Heart/No More Me and You	1966	3.75	7.50	15.00
❏ 5811	Where Does the Good Times Go/The Way That I Love You	1967	2.00	4.00	8.00
❏ 5811 [PS]	Where Does the Good Times Go/The Way That I Love You	1967	3.00	6.00	12.00
❏ 5865	Sam's Place/Don't Ever Tell Me Goodbye	1967	2.00	4.00	8.00
❏ 5865 [PS]	Sam's Place/Don't Ever Tell Me Goodbye	1967	3.00	6.00	12.00
❏ 5942	Your Tender Loving Care/What a Liar I Am	1967	2.00	4.00	8.00
❏ 5942 [PS]	Your Tender Loving Care/What a Liar I Am	1967	3.00	6.00	12.00
❏ B-44248	Hot Dog/Second Fiddle	1988	—	2.00	4.00
❏ B-44248 [PS]	Hot Dog/Second Fiddle	1988	—	2.50	5.00
❏ B-44295	A-11/Sweethearts in Heaven	1988	—	2.00	4.00
❏ B-44356	Put a Quarter in the Jukebox/Don't Let Her Know	1989	—	2.00	4.00
❏ B-44409	Act Naturally/The Key's in the Mailbox	1989	3.75	7.50	15.00
—A-side with Ringo Starr					
❏ 7PRO-79805 [DJ]	Gonna Have Love (same on both sides)	1989	2.50	5.00	10.00
—Vinyl is promo only					

Number	Title (A Side/B Side)	Yr	VG	VG+	NM
DIXIE					
❏ 505	Hot Dog/Rhythm and Booze	1956	100.00	200.00	400.00
—As "Corky Jones"					
PEP					
❏ 105	It Don't Show on Me/Down on the Corner of Love	1956	12.50	25.00	50.00
❏ 106	The House Down the Block/Right After the Dance	1956	12.50	25.00	50.00
❏ 107	Hot Dog/Rhythm and Booze	1956	62.50	125.00	250.00
—As "Corky Jones"					
❏ 109	There Goes My Love/Sweethearts in Heaven	1957	12.50	25.00	50.00
REPRISE					
❏ 27964	Streets of Bakersfield/One More Name	1988	—	—	3.00
—With Dwight Yoakam					
❏ 27964 [PS]	Streets of Bakersfield/One More Name	1988	—	2.00	4.00
STARDAY					
❏ 571	There Goes My Love/It Don't Show on Me	1961	3.75	7.50	15.00
❏ 588	Down on the Corner of Love/Right After the Dance	1962	3.75	7.50	15.00
❏ 7010	Sweethearts in Heaven/Down on the Corner of Love	196?	—	2.50	5.00
❏ 8004	Sweethearts in Heaven/Down on the Corner of Love	197?	—	2.00	4.00
WARNER BROS.					
❏ 8223	Hollywood Waltz/Rain on Your Parade	1976	—	2.50	5.00
❏ 8255	California Okie/Child Support	1976	—	2.50	5.00
❏ 8316	World Famous Paradise Inn/He Don't Deserve You Anymore	1977	—	2.50	5.00
❏ 8316	World Famous Holiday Inn/He Don't Deserve You Anymore	1977	2.50	5.00	10.00
❏ 8395	It's Been a Long, Long Time/Rain on Your Parade	1977	—	2.50	5.00
❏ 8433	Our Old Mansion/How Come My God Don't Bark	1977	—	2.50	5.00
❏ 8486	Let the Good Times Roll/Texas Tornado	1977	—	2.50	5.00
❏ 8614	Nights Are Forever Without You/When I Need You	1978	—	2.00	4.00
❏ 8701	Do You Wanna Make Love/Seasons of My Heart	1978	—	2.00	4.00
❏ 8830	Play Together Again Again/He Don't Deserve You Anymore	1979	—	2.00	4.00
—A-side with Emmylou Harris					
❏ 49046	Hangin' In and Hangin' On/Sweet Molly Brown's	1979	—	2.00	4.00
❏ 49118	Let Jesse Rob the Train/Victim of Life's Circumstances	1979	—	2.00	4.00
❏ 49200	Love Is a Warm Cowboy/I Don't Want to Live in San Francisco	1980	—	2.00	4.00
❏ 49278	Moonlight and Magnolia/Nickels and Dimes	1980	—	2.00	4.00
❏ 49651	Without You/Love Don't Make the Bars	1981	—	2.00	4.00
7-Inch Extended Plays					
CAPITOL					
❏ SXA-1777	You're for Me/Down on the Corner of Love/Fool Me Again//Country Polka/Under the Influence of Love/Nobody's Fool But Yours	196?	5.00	10.00	20.00
—Jukebox issue; small hole, plays at 33 1/3 rpm					
❏ SXA-1777 [PS]	You're for Me	196?	5.00	10.00	20.00
❏ SXA-2186	I Don't Care/Don't Let Her Know/Playboy//You're Welcome Anytime/Bud's Bounce/Understand Your Man	196?	5.00	10.00	20.00
—Jukebox issue; small hole, plays at 33 1/3 rpm					
❏ SXA-2186 [PS]	I Don't Care	196?	5.00	10.00	20.00
❏ SU-2353	No Fool Like an Old Fool/Steel Guitar Rag/I Betcha Didn't Know//There's Gonna Come a Day/Raz-Ma-Taz Polka/Charlie Brown	196?	5.00	10.00	20.00
—Jukebox issue; small hole, plays at 33 1/3 rpm					
❏ SU-2353 [PS]	Before You Go/No One But You	196?	5.00	10.00	20.00
❏ R-5446	Memphis/Let the Bad Times Roll On//Fallin' for You/If You Fall Out of Love	1965	3.75	7.50	15.00
❏ R-5446 [PS]	4-By Buck Owens	1965	6.25	12.50	25.00
Albums					
CAPITOL					
❏ ST-131	I've Got You on My Mind Again	1969	5.00	10.00	20.00
❏ SKAO-145	The Best of Buck Owens, Volume 3	1969	5.00	10.00	20.00
❏ ST-194	Anywhere U.S.A.	1969	5.00	10.00	20.00
❏ ST-212	Tall Dark Stranger	1969	5.00	10.00	20.00
❏ ST 8-0232	Buck Owens in London	1969	6.25	12.50	25.00
—Capitol Record Club edition					
❏ ST-232	Buck Owens in London	1969	5.00	10.00	20.00
❏ SWBB-257 [(2)]	Close-Up	1969	5.00	10.00	20.00
—Reissue of "Together Again" and "No One But You"					
❏ ST-439	Your Mother's Prayer	1970	5.00	10.00	20.00
❏ ST-476	The Kansas City Song	1970	5.00	10.00	20.00
❏ STBB-486 [(2)]	A Merry "Hee Haw" Christmas	1970	6.25	12.50	25.00
❏ STCL-574 [(3)]	Buck Owens	1970	10.00	20.00	40.00
❏ ST-628	I Wouldn't Live in New York City	1970	5.00	10.00	20.00
❏ ST-685	Bridge Over Troubled Water	1971	3.75	7.50	15.00
❏ ST-830	The Best of Buck Owens, Vol. 4	1971	3.75	7.50	15.00
❏ ST 1482 [S]	Buck Owens Sings Harlan Howard	1961	12.50	25.00	50.00
❏ T 1482 [M]	Buck Owens Sings Harlan Howard	1961	10.00	20.00	40.00
❏ DT 1489 [R]	Under Your Spell Again	1968	6.25	12.50	25.00
—"Duophonic" reissue of mono original with new title					
❏ T 1489 [M]	Buck Owens	1961	10.00	20.00	40.00
—Black colorband label, Capitol logo at left					
❏ T 1489 [M]	Buck Owens	1962	7.50	15.00	30.00
—Black colorband label, Capitol logo at top					
❏ ST 1777 [S]	You're for Me	1962	12.50	25.00	50.00
❏ T 1777 [M]	You're for Me	1962	10.00	20.00	40.00
❏ ST 1879 [S]	On the Bandstand	1963	12.50	25.00	50.00
❏ T 1879 [M]	On the Bandstand	1963	10.00	20.00	40.00
❏ ST 1989 [S]	Buck Owens Sings Tommy Collins	1963	12.50	25.00	50.00
❏ T 1989 [M]	Buck Owens Sings Tommy Collins	1963	10.00	20.00	40.00
❏ ST 2105 [S]	The Best of Buck Owens	1964	7.50	15.00	30.00
❏ T 2105 [M]	The Best of Buck Owens	1964	6.25	12.50	25.00
❏ ST 2135 [S]	Together Again/My Heart Skips a Beat	1964	7.50	15.00	30.00
❏ T 2135 [M]	Together Again/My Heart Skips a Beat	1964	6.25	12.50	25.00
❏ ST 2186 [S]	I Don't Care	1964	7.50	15.00	30.00
❏ T 2186 [M]	I Don't Care	1964	6.25	12.50	25.00
❏ ST 2283 [S]	I've Got a Tiger by the Tail	1965	7.50	15.00	30.00
❏ T 2283 [M]	I've Got a Tiger by the Tail	1965	6.25	12.50	25.00

O

Number	Title (A Side/B Side)	Yr	VG	VG+	NM
❏ ST 2353 [S]	Before You Go/No One But You	1965	7.50	15.00	30.00
❏ T 2353 [M]	Before You Go/No One But You	1965	6.25	12.50	25.00
❏ ST 2367 [S]	The Instrumental Hits of Buck Owens & the Buckaroos	1965	7.50	15.00	30.00
❏ T 2367 [M]	The Instrumental Hits of Buck Owens & the Buckaroos	1965	6.25	12.50	25.00
❏ ST 2396 [S]	Christmas with Buck Owens and His Buckaroos	1965	7.50	15.00	30.00
❏ T 2396 [M]	Christmas with Buck Owens and His Buckaroos	1965	5.00	10.00	20.00
❏ ST 2443 [S]	Roll Out the Red Carpet for Buck Owens & The Buckaroos	1966	6.25	12.50	25.00
❏ T 2443 [M]	Roll Out the Red Carpet for Buck Owens & The Buckaroos	1966	5.00	10.00	20.00
❏ ST 2497 [S]	Dust on Mother's Bible	1966	6.25	12.50	25.00
❏ T 2497 [M]	Dust on Mother's Bible	1966	5.00	10.00	20.00
❏ ST 2556 [S]	Carnegie Hall Concert	1966	6.25	12.50	25.00
❏ T 2556 [M]	Carnegie Hall Concert	1966	5.00	10.00	20.00
❏ ST 2650 [S]	Open Up Your Heart	1967	6.25	12.50	25.00
❏ T 2650 [M]	Open Up Your Heart	1967	5.00	10.00	20.00
❏ ST 2715 [S]	Buck Owens and His Buckaroos in Japan	1967	6.25	12.50	25.00
❏ T 2715 [M]	Buck Owens and His Buckaroos in Japan	1967	5.00	10.00	20.00
❏ ST 2760 [S]	Your Tender Loving Care	1967	6.25	12.50	25.00
❏ T 2760 [M]	Your Tender Loving Care	1967	6.25	12.50	25.00
❏ ST 2841 [S]	It Takes People Like You to Make People Like Me	1968	6.25	12.50	25.00
❏ T 2841 [M]	It Takes People Like You to Make People Like Me	1968	10.00	20.00	40.00
❏ ST 2897	The Best of Buck Owens, Vol. 2	1968	6.25	12.50	25.00
❏ ST 2902	A Night on the Town	1968	6.25	12.50	25.00
❏ ST 2962	Sweet Rosie Jones	1968	6.25	12.50	25.00
❏ ST 2977	Christmas Shopping	1968	6.25	12.50	25.00
❏ SPRO 2980/1 [DJ]	Minute Masters	1966	12.50	25.00	50.00
—Promo-only excerpts of 24 songs					
❏ ST 2994	Buck Owens, The Guitar Player	1968	6.25	12.50	25.00
❏ ST-11105	Live at the White House	1972	3.75	7.50	15.00
❏ ST-11136	In the Palm of Your Hand	1973	3.75	7.50	15.00
❏ SMAS-11180	Ain't It Amazing, Gracie	1973	3.75	7.50	15.00
❏ ST-11222	Arms Full of Empty	1972	3.75	7.50	15.00
❏ ST-11273	The Best of Buck Owens Volume 5	1973	3.75	7.50	15.00
❏ ST-11332	Monster's Holiday	1974	3.75	7.50	15.00
❏ ST-11390	Weekend Daddy	1974	3.75	7.50	15.00
❏ ST-11471	The Best of Buck Owens, Volume 6	1976	3.75	7.50	15.00
❏ C1-91132	Hot Dog!	1988	3.00	6.00	12.00
❏ C1-92893	Act Naturally	1989	3.75	7.50	15.00
COUNTRY MUSIC FOUNDATION					
❏ CMF-012	Live at Carnegie Hall	198?	3.00	6.00	12.00
LABREA					
❏ 1017 [M]	Buck Owens	1961	25.00	50.00	100.00
❏ 8017 [S]	Buck Owens	1961	37.50	75.00	150.00
STARDAY					
❏ SLP-172	The Fabulous Country Music Sound of Buck Owens	1962	12.50	25.00	50.00
❏ SLP-324	Coutnry Hit Maker #1	1964	6.25	12.50	25.00
TIME-LIFE					
❏ STW-114	Country Music	1981	2.50	5.00	10.00
WARNER BROS.					
❏ BS 2952	Buck 'Em	1976	3.00	6.00	12.00
❏ BS 3087	Our Old Mansion	1977	3.00	6.00	12.00

OWENS, BUCK, AND ROSE MADDOX
45s
CAPITOL

Number	Title (A Side/B Side)	Yr	VG	VG+	NM
❏ 4550	Mental Cruelty/Loose Talk	1961	3.75	7.50	15.00
❏ 4992	We're the Talk of the Town/ Sweethearts in Heaven	1963	3.75	7.50	15.00

OWENS, BUCK, AND SUSAN RAYE Also see each artist's individual listings.
45s
CAPITOL

Number	Title (A Side/B Side)	Yr	VG	VG+	NM
❏ 2731	We're Gonna Get Together/ Everybody Needs Somebody	1970	2.00	4.00	8.00
❏ 2731 [PS]	We're Gonna Get Together/ Everybody Needs Somebody	1970	2.50	5.00	10.00
❏ 2791	Togetherness/Fallin' for You	1970	2.00	4.00	8.00
❏ 2791 [PS]	Togetherness/Fallin' for You	1970	2.50	5.00	10.00
❏ 2871	The Great White Horse/ Your Tender Loving Care	1970	2.00	4.00	8.00
❏ 2871 [PS]	The Great White Horse/ Your Tender Loving Care	1970	2.50	5.00	10.00
❏ 3225	Santa's Gonna Come in a Stagecoach/ One of Everything You Got	1971	2.00	4.00	8.00
❏ 3368	Looking Back to See/Cryin' Time	1972	—	3.00	6.00
❏ 3368 [PS]	Looking Back to See/Cryin' Time	1972	2.50	5.00	10.00
❏ 3601	The Good Old Days (Are Here Again)/When You Get to Heaven (I'll Be There)	1973	—	3.00	6.00
❏ 4100	Love Is Strange/Sweethearts in Heaven	1975	—	3.00	6.00

Albums
CAPITOL

Number	Title (A Side/B Side)	Yr	VG	VG+	NM
❏ ST-448	We're Gonna Get Together	1970	5.00	10.00	20.00
❏ ST-558	Great White Horse	1970	3.75	7.50	15.00
❏ ST-837	Merry Christmas from Buck Owens and Susan Raye	1971	3.75	7.50	15.00
❏ ST-11084	The Best of Buck Owens and Susan Raye	1972	3.75	7.50	15.00
❏ ST-11204	The Good Old Days (Are Here Again)	1973	3.75	7.50	15.00

OWENS BROTHERS, THE
45s
ABC-PARAMOUNT

Number	Title (A Side/B Side)	Yr	VG	VG+	NM
❏ 9775	Night Train/Don't Cry	1956	10.00	20.00	40.00
—Also released on Sheraton by the Four Chaps.					

OXFORD CIRCLE, THE
45s
WORLD UNITED

Number	Title (A Side/B Side)	Yr	VG	VG+	NM
❏ 002	Mind Destruction/Foolsih Woman	196?	12.50	25.00	50.00

OXFORD CIRCUS, THE
45s
ZIG ZAG

Number	Title (A Side/B Side)	Yr	VG	VG+	NM
❏ 101	Tracy/4th Street Carnival	1967	10.00	20.00	40.00

OZ KNOZZ
Albums
OZONE

Number	Title (A Side/B Side)	Yr	VG	VG+	NM
❏ O2-1000	Ruff Mix	1975	125.00	250.00	500.00

OZARK MOUNTAIN DAREDEVILS
12-Inch Singles
COLUMBIA

Number	Title (A Side/B Side)	Yr	VG	VG+	NM
❏ AS 766 [DJ]	Take You Tonight (same on both sides)	1980	3.75	7.50	15.00

45s
A&M

Number	Title (A Side/B Side)	Yr	VG	VG+	NM
❏ 1477	Country Girl/Within Without	1973	—	2.50	5.00
❏ 1515	If You Wanna Get to Heaven/Spaceship Orion	1974	—	2.50	5.00
❏ 1623	Look Away/It Probably Always Will	1974	—	2.00	4.00
❏ 1654	Jackie Blue/Better Days	1974	—	2.00	4.00
❏ 1654 [PS]	Jackie Blue/Better Days	1974	—	3.00	6.00
❏ 1709	Colorado Song/Thin Ice	1975	—	2.00	4.00
❏ 1772	If I Only Knew/Dreams	1975	—	2.00	4.00
❏ 1808	Keep On Churnin'/Time Warp	1976	—	2.00	4.00
❏ 1809	You Make It Right/Dreams	1976	—	2.00	4.00
❏ 1842	Journey to the Center of Your Heart/Chicken Train Stomp	1976	—	2.00	4.00
❏ 1880	Noah (Let It Rain)/Red Plum	1976	—	2.00	4.00
❏ 1888	You Know Like I Know/Arroyo	1976	—	2.00	4.00
❏ 1888 [PS]	You Know Like I Know/Arroyo	1976	—	3.00	6.00
❏ 1989	Crazy Lovin'/Stinghead	1977	—	2.00	4.00
❏ 2016	Following (The Way That I Feel)/Snowbound	1978	—	2.00	4.00
COLUMBIA					
❏ 1-11247	Take You Tonight/Runnin' Out	1980	—	2.00	4.00
❏ 1-11357	Oh Darlin'/Sailin' Around the World	1980	—	2.00	4.00

Albums
A&M

Number	Title (A Side/B Side)	Yr	VG	VG+	NM
❏ SP-3110	The Ozark Mountain Daredevils	198?	2.00	4.00	8.00
—Budget-line reissue					
❏ SP-3192	It'll Shine When It Shines	198?	2.00	4.00	8.00
—Budget-line reissue					
❏ SP-3202	The Best of Ozark Mountain Daredevils	1982	2.50	5.00	10.00
❏ SP-3654	It'll Shine When It Shines	1974	3.00	6.00	12.00
❏ SP-4411	The Ozark Mountain Daredevils	1973	3.00	6.00	12.00
❏ SP-4549	The Car Over the Lake Album	1975	3.00	6.00	12.00
❏ SP-4601	Men from Earth	1976	3.00	6.00	12.00
❏ SP-4662	Don't Look Down	1977	3.00	6.00	12.00
❏ SP-6006 [(2)]	It's Alive	1978	3.75	7.50	15.00
COLUMBIA					
❏ JC 36375	Ozark Mountain Daredevils	1980	2.50	5.00	10.00
SOUNDS GREAT					
❏ SG-5004	The Lost Cabin Sessions	1985	2.50	5.00	10.00

Ohio Players, *Fire*, Mercury SRM-1-1013, stereo LP, $5-$10.

Roy Orbison, "I'm Hurtin'," Monument 45-433, picture sleeve, $60-$120.

The Orlons, "Don't Hang Up," Cameo 231, picture sleeve, $20-$40.

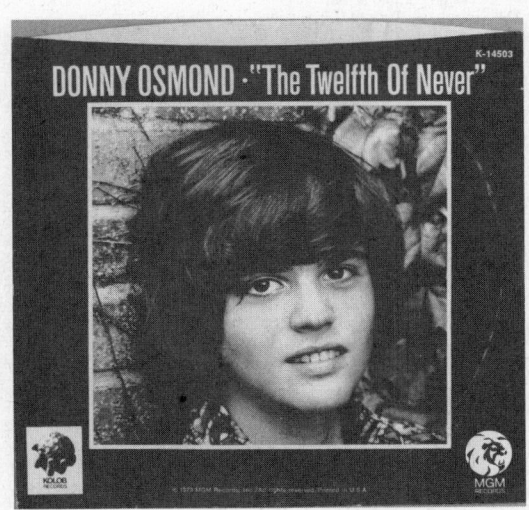

Donny Osmond, "The Twelfth of Never," MGM 14503, picture sleeve, $4-$8.

The Outsiders, "Help Me Girl," Capitol 5759, picture sleeve, $10-$20.

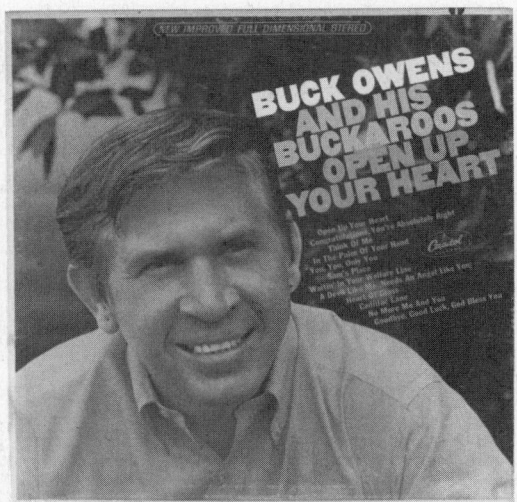

Buck Owens, *Open Up Your Heart,* Capitol ST 2650, stereo LP, $12.50-$25.

O

Number	Title (A Side/B Side)	Yr	VG	VG+	NM

P

P.F.M.
45s
MANTICORE

Number	Title (A Side/B Side)	Yr	VG	VG+	NM
❑ 2002	Celebration/(B-side unknown)	1973	—	3.00	6.00
❑ 7003	Mr. Nine Til Five/Celebration	1974	—	2.50	5.00

Albums
ASYLUM

| ❑ 7E-1071 | Chocolate Kings | 1976 | 2.50 | 5.00 | 10.00 |
| ❑ 7E-1101 | Jet Lag | 1977 | 2.50 | 5.00 | 10.00 |

MANTICORE

❑ MA6-502	P.F.M. 'Cook'	1974	3.00	6.00	12.00
❑ MC 66668	Photos of Ghosts	1973	3.00	6.00	12.00
❑ MC 66673	The World Became the World	1974	3.00	6.00	12.00

P.J.
45s
TAMLA

| ❑ 54215 | T.L.C./It Takes a Man to Teach a Woman How to Love | 1972 | 6.25 | 12.50 | 25.00 |

V.I.P.

| ❑ 25062 | It Takes a Man to Teach a Woman How to Love/The Best Years of My Life | 1970 | 10.00 | 20.00 | 40.00 |

PABLO CRUISE
12-Inch Singles
A&M

❑ SP-17050 [DJ]	Don't Want to Live Without It (Disco Version) (same on both sides)	1978	2.50	5.00	10.00
❑ SP-17105 [DJ]	I Want You Tonight (LP Version)/I Want You Tonight (Edit)	1979	2.00	4.00	8.00
❑ SP-17161 [DJ]	Cool Love/This Time	1981	2.00	4.00	8.00
❑ SP-17244 [DJ]	Will You, Won't You (LP Version)/Will You, Won't You (Edit)	1983	2.00	4.00	8.00

45s
A&M

❑ 1695	Island Woman/Denny	1975	—	2.50	5.00
❑ 1742	What Does It Take/In My Own Quiet Way	1975	—	2.50	5.00
❑ 1815	(I Think) It's Finally Over/Look to the Sky	1976	—	2.50	5.00
❑ 1834	Don't Believe It/Look to the Sky	1976	—	2.50	5.00
❑ 1876	Crystal/Look to the Sky	1976	—	2.50	5.00
❑ 1910	A Place in the Sun/El Verano	1977	—	2.50	5.00
❑ 1920	Whatcha Gonna Do?/Atlanta June	1977	—	2.00	4.00
❑ 1920 [PS]	Whatcha Gonna Do?/Atlanta June	1977	—	3.00	6.00
❑ 1976	A Place in the Sun/El Verano	1977	—	2.00	4.00
❑ 1999	Atlanta June/Never Had a Love	1977	—	2.00	4.00
❑ 2048	Love Will Find a Way/Always Be Together	1978	—	2.00	4.00
❑ 2048 [PS]	Love Will Find a Way/Always Be Together	1978	—	2.50	5.00
❑ 2076	Don't Want to Live Without It/Raging Fire	1978	—	2.00	4.00
❑ 2112	I Go to Rio/Raging Fire	1979	—	2.00	4.00
❑ 2195	I Want You Tonight/Family Man	1979	—	2.00	4.00
❑ 2217 [DJ]	Part of the Game (mono/stereo)	1980	—	2.50	5.00
—No stock copies known					
❑ 2349	Cool Love/Jenny	1981	—	2.00	4.00
❑ 2373	Slip Away/That's When	1981	—	2.00	4.00
❑ 2373 [PS]	Slip Away/That's When	1981	—	2.00	4.00
❑ 2570	Another World/Will You, Won't You	1983	—	—	3.00

Albums
A&M

❑ SP-3111	Pablo Cruise	198?	2.00	4.00	8.00
—Budget-line reissue of 4528					
❑ SP-3198	Worlds Away	198?	2.00	4.00	8.00
—Budget-line reissue of 4697					
❑ SP-3236	A Place in the Sun	198?	2.00	4.00	8.00
—Budget-line reissue of 4625					
❑ SP-3712	Part of the Game	1979	2.50	5.00	10.00
❑ SP-3726	Reflector	1981	2.50	5.00	10.00
❑ SP-4528	Pablo Cruise	1975	2.50	5.00	10.00
❑ SP-4575	Lifeline	1976	2.50	5.00	10.00
❑ SP-4625	A Place in the Sun	1977	2.50	5.00	10.00
❑ SP-4697	Worlds Away	1978	2.50	5.00	10.00
❑ SP-4909	Out of Our Hands	1983	2.50	5.00	10.00

MOBILE FIDELITY

| ❑ 1-029 | A Place in the Sun | 1979 | 5.00 | 10.00 | 20.00 |
| —Audiophile vinyl | | | | | |

NAUTILUS

❑ NR-6	Lifeline	1980	5.00	10.00	20.00
—Audiophile vinyl					
❑ NR-28	Worlds Away	1981	5.00	10.00	20.00
—Audiophile vinyl					

PACERS, THE More than one group.
45s
CALICO

| ❑ 101/2 | I Found a Dream/I Wanna Dance with You | 1958 | 7.50 | 15.00 | 30.00 |

CORAL

| ❑ 62398 | Sassy Sue/You Got Me Bugged | 1964 | 2.50 | 5.00 | 10.00 |

GUYDEN

| ❑ 2064 | How Sweet/No Wonder | 1962 | 375.00 | 750.00 | 1500. |

RAZORBACK

❑ 103	Fright Street/Sooie	1958	6.25	12.50	25.00
❑ 108	Confound It/Skeeter Dape	1960	6.25	12.50	25.00
❑ 112	Don't Get Around Much/Sad Sad	1962	6.25	12.50	25.00
❑ 115	West Memphis/Dollar, Two Ninety-Eight	1963	6.25	12.50	25.00
❑ 118	Tennessee Stud/Beautiful Debbie	1964	5.00	10.00	20.00
❑ 123	The Pit/Pace Setter	1965	5.00	10.00	20.00
❑ 125	Batman/Gotham City	1966	5.00	10.00	20.00
❑ 137	Short Squashed Texan/Sock It To 'Em Soobey	1967	5.00	10.00	20.00

Albums
RAZORBACK

| ❑ 121 [M] | You Asked For It | 1965 | 25.00 | 50.00 | 100.00 |

PACIFIC DRIFT
45s
DERAM

Number	Title (A Side/B Side)	Yr	VG	VG+	NM
❑ 85063	Tomorrow Morning Brings/Yes You Do	1970	2.00	4.00	8.00

Albums
DERAM

| ❑ DES 18040 | Feelin' Free | 1970 | 5.00 | 10.00 | 20.00 |

PACIFIC GAS & ELECTRIC
45s
COLUMBIA

❑ 45009	Redneck/Bluebuster	1969	—	3.00	6.00
❑ 45158	Are You Ready?/Staggolee	1970	—	3.00	6.00
—Available with at least three different label variations, all equal in value					
❑ 45221	Elvira/Father Come On Home	1970	—	2.50	5.00
❑ 45304	The Time Has Come/Death Row No. 172	1971	—	2.50	5.00
❑ 45444	One More River to Cross/Rocky Roller's Lament	1971	—	2.50	5.00
❑ 45519	Thank God for You Baby/See the Monkey Run	1971	—	2.50	5.00
❑ 45621	Heat Wave/We Did What We Could	1972	—	2.50	5.00

KENT

| ❑ 4538 | The Hunter/Long Handled Shovel | 1971 | 3.00 | 6.00 | 12.00 |

POWER

| ❑ 1701 | Wade in the Water/Live Love | 1969 | 2.50 | 5.00 | 10.00 |

Albums
ABC DUNHILL

| ❑ DSX-50157 | Pacific Gas and Electric Starring Charlie Allen | 1974 | 3.00 | 6.00 | 12.00 |

BRIGHT ORANGE

| ❑ 701 | Get It On | 1968 | 10.00 | 20.00 | 40.00 |

COLUMBIA

❑ CS 1017	Are You Ready	1970	3.00	6.00	12.00
—Orange label					
❑ CS 1017	Are You Ready	1970	3.75	7.50	15.00
—"360 Sound" label					
❑ CS 9900	Pacific Gas and Electric	1969	3.75	7.50	15.00
—"360 Sound" label					
❑ CS 9900	Pacific Gas and Electric	1970	3.00	6.00	12.00
—Orange label					
❑ C 30362	PG&E	1971	3.00	6.00	12.00
❑ C 32019	The Best of Pacific Gas & Electric	1972	3.00	6.00	12.00

POWER

| ❑ 701 | Get It On | 1969 | 6.25 | 12.50 | 25.00 |

PACKARDS, THE
45s
PARADISE

| ❑ 105 | Dream of Love/Ding Dong | 1956 | 100.00 | 200.00 | 400.00 |

PLA-BAC

| ❑ 106 | Ladise/My Doctor of Love | 1956 | 500.00 | 1000. | 2000. |

PADDY, KLAUS AND GIBSON
45s
CHESS

| ❑ 1956 | No Good Without You Baby/Rejected | 1966 | 2.00 | 4.00 | 8.00 |

PAGE, GENE
12-Inch Singles
ARISTA

| ❑ SP-13 [DJ] | Close Encounters of the Third Kind (6:00) (3:38) | 1978 | 2.50 | 5.00 | 10.00 |

ATLANTIC

| ❑ DSKO 69 [DJ] | Wild Cherry (6:00) (same on both sides) | 1976 | 3.00 | 6.00 | 12.00 |

45s
ARISTA

❑ 0302	Close Encounters of the Third Kind/When You Wish Upon a Star	1978	—	2.50	5.00
❑ 0322	Theme from "Star Trek"/Sho Like to Ride on a Star	1978	—	2.50	5.00
❑ 0337	Moonglow-Love Theme/Beyond the Hole in Space	1978	—	2.50	5.00
❑ 0492	Love Starts After Dark/I Wanna Dance	1980	—	2.00	4.00
❑ 0516	Put a Little Love in Your Lovin'/With You in the Night	1980	—	2.00	4.00

ATLANTIC

❑ 3247	All My Dreams Are Coming True/Cream Corner	1975	—	2.50	5.00
❑ 3322	Wild Cherry/Fantasy Woman	1976	—	2.50	5.00
❑ 3338	Into My Thing/Organ Grinder	1976	—	2.50	5.00

Albums
ARISTA

| ❑ AL 4174 | Close Encounters | 1978 | 2.50 | 5.00 | 10.00 |
| ❑ AL 4262 | Love Starts After Dark | 1980 | 2.50 | 5.00 | 10.00 |

ATLANTIC

| ❑ SD 18111 | Hot City | 1974 | 3.00 | 6.00 | 12.00 |
| ❑ SD 18161 | Lovelock! | 1975 | 3.00 | 6.00 | 12.00 |

PAGE, HOT LIPS
45s
KING

❑ 1404	Cadillac Song/Ain't Nothing Wrong	1954	25.00	50.00	100.00
❑ 4584	Last Call for Alcohol/Old Parie	1952	75.00	150.00	300.00
❑ 4594	I Bongo You/Ruby	1953	50.00	100.00	200.00
❑ 4616	Jungle King/What Shall I Do	1953	37.50	75.00	150.00

RCA VICTOR

| ❑ 50-0120 | Let Me In/That's the One for Me | 1951 | 25.00 | 50.00 | 100.00 |
| ❑ 50-0129 | Strike While the Iron's Hot/I Wanna Ride Like the Cowboys Do | 1951 | 25.00 | 50.00 | 100.00 |

Albums
CONTINENTAL

| ❑ 16007 [M] | Hot and Cozy | 1962 | 7.50 | 15.00 | 30.00 |

ONYX

| ❑ 207 | After Hours | 197? | 3.00 | 6.00 | 12.00 |

XANADU

| ❑ 107 | Trumpet at Minton's | 197? | 3.00 | 6.00 | 12.00 |

Number	Title (A Side/B Side)	Yr	VG	VG+	NM
PAGE, LARRY, ORCHESTRA					
45s					
CALLA					
☐ 126	Jo Jo/Waltzing to Jazz	1966	3.00	6.00	12.00
☐ 144	Girl on a Swing/The Last Waltz	1967	2.50	5.00	10.00
LONDON					
☐ 259	I'm Hooked on You/Erotic Soul	1977	—	2.00	4.00
PAGE ONE					
☐ 21010	Hey Jude/Those Were the Days	1969	2.00	4.00	8.00
☐ 21018	Promises, Promises/Wichita Lineman	1969	2.00	4.00	8.00
Albums					
RHINO					
☐ RNLP-058	Kinky Music	1984	2.50	5.00	10.00
☐ RNDF-257 [PD]Kinky Music		1984	3.00	6.00	12.00
PAGE, PATTI Also see FRANKIE LAINE.					
45s					
AVCO					
☐ 603	I May Not Be Lovin' You/ Whoever Finds This, I Love You	1974	—	2.00	4.00
☐ 607	Pour Your Lovin' on Me/Big Wind from Dallas	1975	—	2.00	4.00
☐ 613	Less Than the Song/Did He Ask About Me	1975	—	2.00	4.00
COLUMBIA					
☐ 4-42671	Pretty Boy Lonely/Just a Simple Melody	1963	2.00	4.00	8.00
☐ 4-42791	Say Wonderful Things/ I Knew I Would See Him Again	1963	2.00	4.00	8.00
☐ 4-42857	Nobody/Maybe He'll Come Back to Me	1963	2.00	4.00	8.00
☐ 4-42902	Love Letters/If and When	1963	2.00	4.00	8.00
☐ 4-42963	I Adore You/I Wonder, I Wonder, I Wonder	1964	—	3.00	6.00
☐ 4-43019	Drive-In Movie/I'd Rather Be Sorry	1964	—	3.00	6.00
☐ 4-43078	Drina (Little Soldier Boy)/Promises	1964	—	3.00	6.00
☐ 4-43183	Don't You Pass Me By/Days of the Waltz	1964	—	3.00	6.00
☐ 4-43251	Hush, Hush, Sweet Charlotte/ Longing to Hold You Again	1965	2.00	4.00	8.00
☐ 4-43345	You Can't Be True, Dear/ Who's Gonna Shoe My Pretty Little Feet	1965	—	3.00	6.00
☐ 4-43429	Ribbons and Roses/That's What I Tell Him	1965	—	3.00	6.00
☐ 4-43447	Happy Birthday, Jesus (A Child's Prayer)/ Christmas Bells	1965	2.00	4.00	8.00
☐ 4-43447 [PS]	Happy Birthday, Jesus (A Child's Prayer)/ Christmas Bells	1965	2.50	5.00	10.00
☐ 4-43517	Till You Come Back to Me/Custody	1966	—	3.00	6.00
☐ 4-43647	Can I Trust You?/In This Day and Age	1966	—	3.00	6.00
☐ 4-43761	It's the World Outside/Detour	1966	—	3.00	6.00
☐ 4-43794	Almost Persuaded/It's the World Outside	1966	—	3.00	6.00
☐ 4-43909	The Wishing Doll/Music and Memories	1966	—	3.00	6.00
☐ 4-43990	Wish Me a Rainbow/This Is the Sunday	1967	—	2.50	5.00
☐ 4-44115	Walkin' — Just Walkin'/Same Old You	1967	—	2.50	5.00
☐ 4-44242	What's She Got That I Ain't Got (Darlin')/ Pretty Bluebird	1967	—	2.50	5.00
☐ 4-44257	All the Time/Pretty Bluebird	1967	—	2.50	5.00
☐ 4-44353	Gentle on My Mind/Excuse Me	1967	—	2.50	5.00
☐ 4-44556	Little Green Apples/This House	1968	—	2.50	5.00
☐ 4-44666	Stand By Your Man/Red Summer Roses	1968	—	2.50	5.00
☐ 4-44778	A Mighty Fortress Is Our Love/The Love Song	1969	—	2.50	5.00
☐ 4-44989	Boy from the Country/You Don't Need a Heart	1969	—	2.50	5.00
☐ 4-45059	Pickin' Up the Pieces/Tied Down	1969	—	2.50	5.00
☐ 4-45159	I Wish I Had a Mommy Like You/ He'll Never Take the Place of You	1970	—	2.50	5.00
☐ JZSP 111907/8 [DJ]Happy Birthday, Jesus (A Child's Prayer)/ Christmas Bells		1965	2.00	4.00	8.00
—Black vinyl					
☐ JZSP 111907/8 [DJ]Happy Birthday, Jesus (A Child's Prayer)/ Christmas Bells		1965	2.50	5.00	10.00
—Green vinyl					
EPIC					
☐ 11032	Love Lives Again/I Can't Sit Still	1973	—	2.00	4.00
☐ 11072	You're Gonna Hurt Me/Mama Take Me Home	1973	—	2.00	4.00
☐ 11109	Someone Came to See Me/One Final Stand	1974	—	2.00	4.00
MERCURY					
☐ 505	Confess/Money, Marbles and Chalk	1950	7.50	15.00	30.00
—Reissue of her first hit from 1948					
☐ 5396	I Don't Care If the Sun Don't Shine/I'm Gonna Paper All My Walls with Your Love Letters	1950	5.00	10.00	20.00
☐ 5455	All My Love (Bolero)/Roses Remind Me of You	1950	5.00	10.00	20.00
☐ 5463	Back in Your Own Backyard/Right Kind of Love	1950	5.00	10.00	20.00
☐ 5511	Confess/That Old Feeling	1950	5.00	10.00	20.00
☐ 5512	All My Love (Bolero)/Back in Your Own Backyard	1950	5.00	10.00	20.00
☐ 5521	So in Love/Why Can't You Behave	1950	5.00	10.00	20.00
☐ 5534	The Tennessee Waltz/ Boogie Woogie Santa Claus	1950	5.00	10.00	20.00
☐ 5534	The Tennessee Waltz/Long, Long Ago	1951	3.75	7.50	15.00
☐ 5571	Would I Love You (Love You, Love You)/ Sentimental Music	1951	3.75	7.50	15.00
☐ 5579	Down the Trail of Achin' Hearts/ Ever True Ever More	1951	3.75	7.50	15.00
☐ 5592	Tag-a-Long/Soft and Tenderly	1951	5.00	10.00	20.00
—With Rex Allen					
☐ 5595	Mockin' Bird Hill/I Love You Because	1951	3.75	7.50	15.00
☐ 5645	Mister and Mississippi/These Things I Offer You	1951	3.75	7.50	15.00
—Black vinyl					
☐ 5645	Mister and Mississippi/These Things I Offer You	1951	10.00	20.00	40.00
—Red vinyl					
☐ 5682	Detour/Who's Gonna Shoe My Pretty Little Feet	1951	3.75	7.50	15.00
☐ 5706	And So to Sleep Again/One Sweet Letter	1951	3.75	7.50	15.00
☐ 5707	Whispering/Cabaret	1951	3.75	7.50	15.00
☐ 5715	That's All I Ask of You/I'm Glad You're Happy with Someone Else	1951	3.75	7.50	15.00
☐ 5729	Boogie Woogie Santa Claus/Christmas Bells	1951	3.75	7.50	15.00
☐ 5730-X45	Jingle Bells/Christmas Choir	195?	2.50	5.00	10.00
—Reissue with black label and no reference to an album on label					
☐ 5730-X45	Jingle Bells/Christmas Choir	1951	3.75	7.50	15.00
—Original with maroon label and "From Album 'Christmas with Patti Page'" on label					
☐ 5731	Santa Claus Is Coming to Town/Silent Night	1951	3.75	7.50	15.00
☐ 5732	White Christmas/The Christmas Song	1951	3.75	7.50	15.00
—The above four comprise a box set					

Number	Title (A Side/B Side)	Yr	VG	VG+	NM
☐ 5751	Down in the Valley/ I Want to Be a Cowboy's Sweetheart	1951	3.75	7.50	15.00
☐ 5772	Come What May/Retreat (Cries My Heart)	1952	3.75	7.50	15.00
☐ 5816	Whispering Winds/Love Where You Are	1952	3.75	7.50	15.00
☐ 5867	Once in Awhile/I'm Glad You're Happy with Someone Else	1952	3.75	7.50	15.00
☐ 5895	Release Me/Wedding Bells Will Soon Be Ringing	1952	3.75	7.50	15.00
—With Rusty Draper					
☐ 5899	I Went to Your Wedding/You Belong to Me	1952	3.75	7.50	15.00
☐ 70025	Why Don't You Believe Me?/Conquest	1952	3.75	7.50	15.00
☐ 70070	The Doggie in the Window/My Jealous Eyes	1953	3.75	7.50	15.00
☐ 70127	Oo What You Do to Me/Now That I'm in Love	1953	3.75	7.50	15.00
☐ 70137	Tell Me Why/Big Mamou	1953	3.75	7.50	15.00
—With Rusty Draper					
☐ 70183	Butterflies/This Is My Song	1953	3.75	7.50	15.00
☐ 70190	Arfie, the Doggie in the Window/ Arfie Goes to School	1953	5.00	10.00	20.00
☐ 70222	Father, Father/The Lord's Prayer	1953	5.00	10.00	20.00
☐ 70230	My World Is Yours/Milwaukee Polka	1953	3.75	7.50	15.00
☐ 70260	Changing Partners/Where Did My Snowman Go	1953	3.75	7.50	15.00
☐ 70295	Changing Partners/ Don't Get Around Much Anymore	1954	3.75	7.50	15.00
☐ 70302	Cross Over the Bridge/My Restless Lover	1954	3.75	7.50	15.00
☐ 70380	Steam Heat/Lonely Days	1954	3.75	7.50	15.00
☐ 70416	What a Dream/I Cried	1954	3.75	7.50	15.00
☐ 70458	The Mama Doll Song/ I Can't Tell a Waltz from a Tango	1954	3.75		15.00
☐ 70506	Pretty Snowflakes/ I Wanna Go Dancing with Willie	1954	3.75	7.50	15.00
☐ 70511	Let Me Go, Lover!/Hocus Pocus	1954	3.75	7.50	15.00
☐ 70528	Everlovin'/You Too Can Be a Dreamer	1955	3.00	6.00	12.00
☐ 70532	I Got It Bad/Don't Get Around Much Anymore	1955	3.00	6.00	12.00
☐ 70579	Little Crazy Quilt/Keep Me in Mind	1955	3.00	6.00	12.00
☐ 70607	Near to You/I Love to Dance with You	1955	3.00	6.00	12.00
☐ 70657	Piddily Patter Patter/Every Day	1955	3.00	6.00	12.00
☐ 70713	Croce di Oro (Cross of Gold)/Search My Heart	1955	3.00	6.00	12.00
☐ 70766	Go On with the Wedding/The Voice Inside	1955	3.00	6.00	12.00
☐ 70820	Too Young to Go Steady/My First Formal Gown	1956	3.00	6.00	12.00
☐ 70878	Allegheny Moon/The Strangest Romance	1956	3.00	6.00	12.00
☐ 70971	Mama from the Train/Every Time (I Feel His Spirit)	1956	3.00	6.00	12.00
☐ 71015	Repeat After Me/Learnin' My Latin	1956	3.00	6.00	12.00
☐ 71059	A Poor Man's Roses (Or a Rich Man's Gold)/ The Wall	1957	2.50	5.00	10.00
☐ 71101	Old Cape Cod/Wondering	1957	2.50	5.00	10.00
☐ 71177	No One to Cry To/Money, Marbles and Chalk	1957	2.50	5.00	10.00
☐ 71189	I'll Remember Today/My How the Time Goes By	1957	2.50	5.00	10.00
☐ 71247	Belonging to Someone/Bring Up Together	1957	2.50	5.00	10.00
☐ 71294	Another Time, Another Place/ These Worldly Wonders	1958	2.50	5.00	10.00
☐ 71331	Left Right Out of Your Heart (Hi Lee Hi Lo Hi Lup Up Up)/Longing to Hold You Again	1958	2.50	5.00	10.00
☐ 71355	Fibbin'/You Will Find Your Love (In Paris)	1958	2.50	5.00	10.00
☐ 71355 [PS]	Fibbin'/You Will Find Your Love (In Paris)	1958	5.00	10.00	20.00
☐ 71400	Trust in Me/Under the Sun Valley Moon	1958	2.50	5.00	10.00
☐ 71428	The Walls Have Ears/My Promise	1959	2.50	5.00	10.00
☐ 71469	With My Eyes Wide Open I'm Dreaming/ My Mother's Eyes	1959	2.50	5.00	10.00
☐ 71510	Goodbye Charlie/Because Him Is a Baby	1959	2.50	5.00	10.00
☐ 71555	The Sound of Music/Little Donkey	1959	2.50	5.00	10.00
☐ 71597	Two Thousand, Two Hundred, Twenty-Three Miles/Promise Me, Thomas	1960	2.00	4.00	8.00
☐ 71639	One of Us (Will Weep Tonight)/ What Will My Future Be	1960	2.00	4.00	8.00
☐ 71639 [PS]	One of Us (Will Weep Tonight)/ What Will My Future Be	1960	3.75	7.50	15.00
☐ 71695	I Wish I'd Never Been Born/I Need You	1960	2.00	4.00	8.00
☐ 71695 [PS]	I Wish I'd Never Been Born/I Need You	1960	3.75	7.50	15.00
☐ 71745	Don't Read the Letter/That's All I Need to Know	1960	2.00	4.00	8.00
☐ 71745 [PS]	Don't Read the Letter/That's All I Need to Know	1960	3.75	7.50	15.00
☐ 71792	A City Girl Stole My Country Boy/Dondi	1961	2.00	4.00	8.00
☐ 71792 [PS]	A City Girl Stole My Country Boy/Dondi	1961	3.75	7.50	15.00
☐ 71823	You'll Answer to Me/Mom and Dad's Waltz	1961	2.00	4.00	8.00
☐ 71823 [PS]	You'll Answer to Me/Mom and Dad's Waltz	1961	3.75	7.50	15.00
☐ 71870	Broken Heart and a Pillow Filled with Tears/ Dark Moon	1961	2.00	4.00	8.00
☐ 71870 [PS]	Broken Heart and a Pillow Filled with Tears/ Dark Moon	1961	3.75	7.50	15.00
☐ 71906	Go On Home/Too Late to Cry	1961	2.00	4.00	8.00
☐ 71906 [PS]	Go On Home/Too Late to Cry	1961	3.75	7.50	15.00
☐ 71950	Most People Get Married/You Don't Know Me	1962	2.00	4.00	8.00
☐ 71950 [PS]	Most People Get Married/You Don't Know Me	1962	3.00	6.00	12.00
☐ 72013	The Boys' Night Out/Three Fools	1962	2.00	4.00	8.00
☐ 72013 [PS]	The Boys' Night Out/Three Fools	1962	3.00	6.00	12.00
☐ 72044	Everytime I Hear Your Name/Let's Cry Together	1962	2.00	4.00	8.00
☐ 72078	High on the Hill of Hope/By a Long Shot	1963	2.00	4.00	8.00
☐ 72123	I'm Walkin'/Invitation to the Blues	1963	2.00	4.00	8.00
☐ 73162	Give Him Love/ Wish I Could Take That Little Boy Home	1970	—	2.50	5.00
☐ 73199	Make Me Your Kind of Woman/ I Wish I Was a Little Boy Again	1971	—	2.50	5.00
☐ 73222	I'd Rather Be Sorry/Words	1971	—	2.50	5.00
☐ 73249	Think Again/A Woman Left Lonely	1971	—	2.50	5.00
☐ 73280	Jody and the Kid/Things We Care About	1972	—	2.50	5.00
☐ 73306	Come What May/Love Is a Friend of Mine	1972	—	2.50	5.00
PLANTATION					
☐ 197	No Aces/Everytime You Touch Me	1981	—	2.00	4.00
☐ 199	Wasn't It Good/Detour	1981	—	2.00	4.00
☐ 201	On the Inside/A Poor Man's Roses	1981	—	2.00	4.00
☐ 208	My Man Friday/Tennessee Waltz	1982	—	2.00	4.00
☐ 212	Barbara's Daughter/(B-side unknown)	1982	—	2.00	4.00
7-Inch Extended Plays					
MERCURY					
☐ EP-1-3008	The Tennessee Waltz/ And So to Sleep Again//Come What May/ Down the Trail of Aching Hearts	195?	3.00	6.00	12.00

P

Number	Title (A Side/B Side)	Yr	VG	VG+	NM
❑ EP-1-3008 [PS]	Tennessee Waltz	195?	3.00	6.00	12.00
❑ EP-1-3038	The Christmas Song/The First Noel//Christmas Choir/Christmas Bells	1956	3.00	6.00	12.00
❑ EP-1-3038 [PS]	Christmas with Patti Page	1956	3.00	6.00	12.00
❑ EP-1-3080	*Lonely Wine/This Is My Song/I'll Never Be Free/When You're Smiling	195?	3.00	6.00	12.00
❑ EP-1-3080 [PS]	This Is My Song	195?	3.00	6.00	12.00
❑ EP-1-3307	Come Rain or Come Shine/I Wished on the Moon//Stay As Sweet As You Are/When Your Lover Has Gone	195?	2.50	5.00	10.00
❑ EP-1-3307 [PS]	(title unknown)	195?	2.50	5.00	10.00
❑ EP-1-3346	Once Upon a Dream/Never Leave Me//Indian Giver/The Party (Noah)	195?	2.50	5.00	10.00
❑ EP-1-3346 [PS]	More Selections from Manhattan Tower	195?	2.50	5.00	10.00
❑ EP-1-3398	Tennessee Waltz/Cross Over the Bridge//(How Much Is) That Doggie in the Window/I Went to Your Wedding	195?	2.50	5.00	10.00
❑ EP-1-3398 [PS]	(title unknown)	195?	2.50	5.00	10.00
❑ EP-1-4007	Everlovin' (A One Way Love)/You Too Can Be a Dreamer//Hocus-Pocus/When Your Lover Has Gone	195?	3.00	6.00	12.00
❑ EP-1-4007 [PS]	Tops in Pops	195?	3.00	6.00	12.00

Albums

ACCORD

Number	Title	Yr	VG	VG+	NM
❑ SN-7206	Special Thoughts	1982	2.50	5.00	10.00

COLUMBIA

Number	Title	Yr	VG	VG+	NM
❑ CL 2049 [M]	Say Wonderful Things	1963	3.75	7.50	15.00
❑ CL 2132 [M]	Love After Midnight	1964	3.75	7.50	15.00
❑ CL 2353 [M]	Hush, Hush, Sweet Charlotte	1965	3.75	7.50	15.00
❑ CL 2414 [M]	Christmas with Patti Page	1965	3.00	6.00	12.00
❑ CL 2505 [M]	America's Favorite Hymns	1966	3.00	6.00	12.00
❑ CL 2526 [M]	Patti Page's Greatest Hits	1966	3.00	6.00	12.00
❑ CL 2761 [M]	Today My Way	1967	5.00	10.00	20.00
❑ CS 8849 [S]	Say Wonderful Things	1963	5.00	10.00	20.00
❑ CS 8932 [S]	Love After Midnight	1964	5.00	10.00	20.00
❑ CS 9153 [S]	Hush, Hush, Sweet Charlotte	1965	5.00	10.00	20.00
❑ CS 9214 [S]	Christmas with Patti Page	1965	3.75	7.50	15.00
❑ CS 9305 [S]	America's Favorite Hymns	1966	3.75	7.50	15.00
❑ CS 9326 [S]	Patti Page's Greatest Hits	1966	3.75	7.50	15.00
—"360 Sound" label					
❑ CS 9326	Patti Page's Greatest Hits	1970	2.50	5.00	10.00
—Orange label					
❑ PC 9326	Patti Page's Greatest Hits	198?	2.00	4.00	8.00
—Budget-line reissue					
❑ CS 9561 [S]	Today My Way	1967	3.75	7.50	15.00
❑ CS 9666	Gentle on My Mind	1968	3.75	7.50	15.00
❑ CS 9999	Honey Come Back	1970	3.00	6.00	12.00

EMARCY

Number	Title	Yr	VG	VG+	NM
❑ MG-36074 [M]	In the Land of Hi-Fi	1956	12.50	25.00	50.00
❑ MG-36116 [M]	The East Side	1957	12.50	25.00	50.00
❑ MG-36136 [M]	The West Side	1957	12.50	25.00	50.00
❑ SR-60013 [S]	The West Side	1959	12.50	25.00	50.00
❑ SR-60014 [S]	The East Side	1959	12.50	25.00	50.00
❑ SR-80000 [S]	In the Land of Hi-Fi	1959	12.50	25.00	50.00

HARMONY

Number	Title	Yr	VG	VG+	NM
❑ HS 11381	Stand By Your Man	1970	2.50	5.00	10.00
❑ KH 30407	Green, Green Grass of Home	1971	2.50	5.00	10.00

MERCURY

Number	Title	Yr	VG	VG+	NM
❑ PKW-118 [(2)]	The Most	1969	3.75	7.50	15.00
❑ MG-20076 [M]	Romance on the Range	1955	7.50	15.00	30.00
❑ MG-20093 [M]	Christmas with Patti Page	1956	7.50	15.00	30.00
❑ MG-20095 [M]	Page I	1955	7.50	15.00	30.00
❑ MG-20096 [M]	Page II	1955	7.50	15.00	30.00
❑ MG-20097 [M]	Page III	1955	7.50	15.00	30.00
❑ MG-20098 [M]	You Go to My Head	1955	7.50	15.00	30.00
❑ MG-20099 [M]	Music for Two in Love	1955	7.50	15.00	30.00
❑ MG-20100 [M]	The Voice of Patti Page	1955	7.50	15.00	30.00
❑ MG-20101 [M]	Page IV	1955	7.50	15.00	30.00
❑ MG-20102 [M]	This Is My Song	1955	7.50	15.00	30.00
❑ MG-20226 [M]	Manhattan Tower	1956	7.50	15.00	30.00
❑ MG-20318 [M]	The Waltz Queen	1957	10.00	20.00	40.00
—With one image of Patti Page on cover; "Custom High Fidelity" and Mercury logo at upper right of front cover					
❑ MG-20318 [M]	The Waltz Queen	1959	7.50	15.00	30.00
—With two images of Patti Page on cover; Mercury logo at upper left of front cover, "High Custom Fidelity" in white strip along bottom front cover					
❑ MG-20387 [M]	Let's Get Away from It All	1957	7.50	15.00	30.00
❑ MG-20388 [M]	I've Heard That Song Before	1957	7.50	15.00	30.00
❑ MG-20398 [M]	Patti Page On Camera	1958	7.50	15.00	30.00
❑ MG-20405 [M]	Indiscretion	1959	7.50	15.00	30.00
❑ MG-20406 [M]	I'll Remember April	1959	7.50	15.00	30.00
❑ MG-20417 [M]	Three Little Words	1960	7.50	15.00	30.00
❑ MG-20495 [M]	Patti Page's Golden Hits	1960	7.50	15.00	30.00
❑ MG-20573 [M]	Just a Closer Walk with Thee	1960	7.50	15.00	30.00
❑ MG-20599 [M]	Patti Page Sings and Stars In "Elmer Gantry"	1960	6.25	12.50	25.00
❑ MG-20615 [M]	Country & Western Golden Hits	1961	5.00	10.00	20.00
❑ MG-20689 [M]	Go On Home	1962	5.00	10.00	20.00
❑ MG-20712 [M]	Golden Hits of the Boys	1962	5.00	10.00	20.00
❑ MG-20758 [M]	Patti Page On Stage	1963	5.00	10.00	20.00
❑ MG-20794 [M]	Patti Page's Golden Hits, Volume 2	1963	5.00	10.00	20.00
❑ MG-20819 [M]	The Singing Rage	1963	5.00	10.00	20.00
❑ MG-20909 [M]	Blue Dream Street	1964	5.00	10.00	20.00
❑ MG-20952 [M]	The Nearness of You	1965	3.75	7.50	15.00
❑ MG-25059 [10]	Songs	1950	10.00	20.00	40.00
❑ MG-25101 [10]	Folksong Favorites	1951	10.00	20.00	40.00
❑ MG-25109 [10]	Christmas	1951	10.00	20.00	40.00
❑ MG-25154 [10]	Tennessee Waltz	1952	10.00	20.00	40.00
❑ MG-25185 [10]	Patti Sings for Romance	1954	10.00	20.00	40.00
❑ MG-25187 [10]	Song Souvenirs	1954	10.00	20.00	40.00
❑ MG-25196 [10]	Just Patti	1954	10.00	20.00	40.00
❑ MG-25197 [10]	Patti's Songs	1954	10.00	20.00	40.00
❑ MG-25209 [10]	And I Thought About You	1954	10.00	20.00	40.00
❑ MG-25210 [10]	So Many Memories	1954	10.00	20.00	40.00
❑ SR-60010 [S]	Let's Get Away from It All	1959	10.00	20.00	40.00
❑ SR-60011 [S]	I've Heard That Song Before	1959	10.00	20.00	40.00
❑ SR-60025 [S]	Patti Page On Camera	1959	10.00	20.00	40.00
❑ SR-60037 [S]	Three Little Words	1960	10.00	20.00	40.00
❑ SR-60049 [S]	The Waltz Queen	1959	10.00	20.00	40.00
❑ SR-60059 [S]	Indiscretion	1959	10.00	20.00	40.00
❑ SR-60081 [S]	I'll Remember April	1959	10.00	20.00	40.00
❑ SR-60233 [S]	Just a Closer Walk with Thee	1960	10.00	20.00	40.00
❑ SR-60260 [S]	Patti Page Sings and Stars In "Elmer Gantry"	1960	7.50	15.00	30.00
❑ SR-60495 [S]	Patti Page's Golden Hits	196?	6.25	12.50	25.00
❑ SR-60615 [S]	Country & Western Golden Hits	1961	6.25	12.50	25.00
❑ SR-60689 [S]	Go On Home	1962	6.25	12.50	25.00
❑ SR-60712 [S]	Golden Hits of the Boys	1962	6.25	12.50	25.00
❑ SR-60758 [S]	Patti Page On Stage	1963	6.25	12.50	25.00
❑ SR-60794 [S]	Patti Page's Golden Hits, Volume 2	1963	6.25	12.50	25.00
❑ SR-60819 [S]	The Singing Rage	1963	6.25	12.50	25.00
❑ SR-60909 [S]	Blue Dream Street	1964	6.25	12.50	25.00
❑ SR-60952 [S]	The Nearness of You	1965	5.00	10.00	20.00
❑ SR-61344	I'd Rather Be Sorry	1971	3.00	6.00	12.00
❑ 822740-1	Christmas with Patti Page	1987	2.50	5.00	10.00
—Reissue					

PLANTATION

Number	Title	Yr	VG	VG+	NM
❑ 548	Aces	1981	2.50	5.00	10.00

WING

Number	Title	Yr	VG	VG+	NM
❑ MGW 12121 [M]	The Waltz Queen	196?	3.00	6.00	12.00
❑ MGW 12174 [M]	Christmas with Patti Page	196?	5.00	10.00	20.00
—Same contents and order as Mercury 20093					
❑ MGW 12250 [M]	Let's Get Away from It All	196?	3.00	6.00	12.00
❑ SRW 16121 [S]	The Waltz Queen	196?	3.75	7.50	15.00
❑ SRW 16250 [S]	Let's Get Away from It All	196?	3.75	7.50	15.00

PAGE, PATTI, AND TOM T. HALL Also see each artist's individual listings.

45s

MERCURY

Number	Title (A Side/B Side)	Yr	VG	VG+	NM
❑ 73347	Hello We're Lonely/We're Not Getting Older	1972	—	2.50	5.00

PAGE BOYS, THE Probably more than one group.

45s

ABC-PARAMOUNT

Number	Title (A Side/B Side)	Yr	VG	VG+	NM
❑ 10323	Lonely Sea/Road of Life	1962	2.50	5.00	10.00

BIG B

Number	Title (A Side/B Side)	Yr	VG	VG+	NM
❑ 1017	Santa's Snowdeer/White Wonderland	19??	2.00	4.00	8.00

DECCA

Number	Title (A Side/B Side)	Yr	VG	VG+	NM
❑ 31505	If Tears Could Speak/Ole Buttermilk Skies	1963	3.00	6.00	12.00

HAMILTON

Number	Title (A Side/B Side)	Yr	VG	VG+	NM
❑ 50025	Barracuda/Peter Gunn	1960	3.00	6.00	12.00

PREP

Number	Title (A Side/B Side)	Yr	VG	VG+	NM
❑ 117	Waiting/This I Give to You	1957	6.25	12.50	25.00

PAGENTS, THE

45s

BAMBOO

Number	Title (A Side/B Side)	Yr	VG	VG+	NM
❑ 525	Pa-Cha/Sad and Lonely	1963	12.50	25.00	50.00

ERA

Number	Title (A Side/B Side)	Yr	VG	VG+	NM
❑ 3119	Enchanted/The Big Daddy	1963	7.50	15.00	30.00
❑ 3124	Glenda/Shake	1964	7.50	15.00	30.00
❑ 3134	Pa-Cha/Sad and Lonely	1964	6.25	12.50	25.00

IKE

Number	Title (A Side/B Side)	Yr	VG	VG+	NM
❑ 631	Enchanted Surf/The Big Daddy	1963	25.00	50.00	100.00

PAIGE, HAL

45s

ATLANTIC

Number	Title (A Side/B Side)	Yr	VG	VG+	NM
❑ 996	Drive It Home/Break of Day Blues	1953	37.50	75.00	150.00
❑ 1032	Big Foot May/Please Say You Do	1954	37.50	75.00	150.00

CHECKER

Number	Title (A Side/B Side)	Yr	VG	VG+	NM
❑ 873	Don't Have to Cry No More/Pour the Corn	1957	5.00	10.00	20.00

FURY

Number	Title (A Side/B Side)	Yr	VG	VG+	NM
❑ 1002	Don't Have to Cry No More/Pour the Corn	1957	20.00	40.00	80.00
❑ 1024	After Hours Blues/Going Back to My Home Town	1959	5.00	10.00	20.00

J&S

Number	Title (A Side/B Side)	Yr	VG	VG+	NM
❑ 1601	Thunderbird/Sugar Bare	1957	7.50	15.00	30.00

PAIR, THE

45s

LIBERTY

Number	Title (A Side/B Side)	Yr	VG	VG+	NM
❑ 55820	Get Up Off It Baby/Donna Lee	1965	—	—	—
—Canceled					
❑ 55910	Run for Your Life/Girl, I Think I Love You	1966	2.00	4.00	8.00

Albums

LIBERTY

Number	Title	Yr	VG	VG+	NM
❑ LRP-3410 [M]	The Pair Live! At the Ice House	1965	5.00	10.00	20.00
❑ LRP-3440 [M]	The Pair Extraordinaire	1966	3.75	7.50	15.00
❑ LRP-3461 [M]	"In"-Citement	1966	3.75	7.50	15.00
❑ LRP-3504 [M]	It's a Wonderful World	1967	3.75	7.50	15.00
❑ LST-7410 [S]	The Pair Live! At the Ice House	1965	6.25	12.50	25.00
❑ LST-7440 [S]	The Pair Extraordinaire	1966	5.00	10.00	20.00
❑ LST-7461 [S]	"In"-Citement	1966	5.00	10.00	20.00
❑ LST-7504 [S]	It's a Wonderful World	1967	5.00	10.00	20.00

PAISLEYS, THE

Albums

AUDIO CITY

Number	Title	Yr	VG	VG+	NM
❑ 70	Cosmic Mind at Play	1970	50.00	100.00	200.00

PALACE GUARD, THE

45s

ORANGE EMPIRE

Number	Title (A Side/B Side)	Yr	VG	VG+	NM
❑ 331	All Night Long/Playgirl	1965	3.75	7.50	15.00
❑ 332	A Girl You Can Depend On/If You Need Me	1965	3.75	7.50	15.00
❑ 400	Falling Sugar/Oh Blue	1965	3.75	7.50	15.00

PARKWAY

Number	Title (A Side/B Side)	Yr	VG	VG+	NM
❑ 111	Saturday's Child/Party Lights	1966	3.00	6.00	12.00
❑ 124	Calliope/Creed	1966	3.00	6.00	12.00

VERVE

Number	Title (A Side/B Side)	Yr	VG	VG+	NM
❑ 10410	Falling Sugar/Oh Blue	1966	2.50	5.00	10.00

PALANCE, JACK

Albums

WARNER BROS.

Number	Title	Yr	VG	VG+	NM
❑ WS 1865	Palance	1970	7.50	15.00	30.00

Number	Title (A Side/B Side)	Yr	VG	VG+	NM

PALISADES, THE More than one group.
45s
CALICO
| ❑ 113 | Close Your Eyes/I Can't Quit | 1960 | 5.00 | 10.00 | 20.00 |

CHAIRMAN
| ❑ 4401 | Heaven Is Being with You/ | | | | |
| | Make the Night a Little Longer | 1963 | 6.25 | 12.50 | 25.00 |

—With Carole King
DEBRA
| ❑ 1003 | Chapel Bells/She Can't Stop Dancing | 1963 | 37.50 | 75.00 | 150.00 |

—Also released credited to "The Magics"
DORE
| ❑ 609 | Hometown Girl/Oh My Love | 1961 | 3.75 | 7.50 | 15.00 |

LEADER
| ❑ 806 | Dear Joan/The Shrine | 1960 | 5.00 | 10.00 | 20.00 |

MEDIEVAL
| ❑ 205 | This Is the Night/Relic Rock | 1962 | 5.00 | 10.00 | 20.00 |

PALM BEACH BAND BOYS, THE
45s
RCA VICTOR
❑ 47-9003	Bend It/Gypsy Caravan	1966	—	3.00	6.00
❑ 47-9026	I'm Gonna Sit Right Down and Write Myself a				
	Letter/I Don't Want to Set the World on Fire	1966	—	3.00	6.00
❑ 47-9207	More and More/Fernanda's Theme	1967	—	3.00	6.00
❑ 47-9141	The Object of My Affection/Strangers in the Night	1967	—	3.00	6.00

Albums
RCA VICTOR
❑ LPM-3734 [M]	Winchester Cathedral	1966	3.00	6.00	12.00
❑ LSP-3734 [S]	Winchester Cathedral	1966	2.50	5.00	10.00
❑ LPM-3808 [M]	The Palm Beach Band Boys Strike Again	1967	3.75	7.50	15.00
❑ LSP-3808 [S]	The Palm Beach Band Boys Strike Again	1967	2.50	5.00	10.00

PALMER, BRUCE
Albums
VERVE FORECAST
| ❑ FTS-3086 | The Cycle Is Complete | 1970 | 5.00 | 10.00 | 20.00 |

PALMER, ROBERT Also see VINEGAR JOE.
12-Inch Singles
EMI
❑ SPRO 4739/45 [DJ]	Mercy Mercy Me (The Ecology)-I Want You				
	(4 versions)	1991	2.00	4.00	8.00
❑ V-56140	Tell Me I'm Not Dreaming (5 versions)	1989	—	3.00	6.00

EMI MANHATTAN
❑ SPRO 04074 [DJ]	Simply Irresistible (same on both sides)	1988	—	3.00	6.00
❑ SPRO 04192 [DJ]	More Than Ever (LP Version)/				
	More Than Ever (Live)	1988	—	3.00	6.00
❑ 56113	Early in the Morning (3 versions)/				
	Disturbing Behavior	1988	—	3.00	6.00

ISLAND
❑ PR 635 [DJ]	You Are in My System (6:06) (2:57)	1983	—	3.00	6.00
❑ PR 678 [DJ]	Pride (3 versions)	1983	2.00	4.00	8.00
❑ PR 791 [DJ]	Discipline of Love (6:44) (3:20)	1985	—	3.00	6.00
❑ PR 827 [DJ]	Addicted to Love (6:01) (same on both sides)	1986	2.00	4.00	8.00
❑ PR 830 [DJ]	Addicted to Love (Edit 4:04) (same on both				
	sides)	1986	3.75	7.50	15.00
❑ PR 879 [DJ]	Hyperactive (same on both sides)	1986	—	3.00	6.00
❑ PR 891 [DJ]	I Didn't Mean to Turn You On				
	(same on both sides)	1986	—	3.00	6.00
❑ PRO-A-906 [DJ]	Johnny and Mary	1980	2.00	4.00	8.00

—B-side is blank
❑ PRO-A-922 [DJ]	Looking for Clues (same on both sides)	1980	2.00	4.00	8.00
❑ PR 969 [DJ]	I Didn't Mean to Turn You On (3 versions)/				
	Addicted to Love	1986	2.50	5.00	10.00
❑ 2236 [DJ]	Sweet Lies (same on both sides)	1988	—	3.00	6.00
❑ 96804	I Didn't Mean to Turn You On (3 versions)/				
	Addicted to Love	1986	2.00	4.00	8.00
❑ 96840	Discipline of Love//				
	Woke Up Laughing/Dance for Me	1985	—	3.00	6.00
❑ 96984	Pride (Remix)/Pride (Dub)	1983	2.00	4.00	8.00

45s
EMI
| ❑ 7PRO-04311 [DJ] | Tell Me I'm Not Dreaming/Tell Me I'm Not | | | | |
| | Dreaming (12" Edit) | 1989 | — | 2.50 | 5.00 |

—Vinyl is promo only
❑ S7-18129	Know By Now/In the Stars	1994	—	—	3.00
❑ 50183	She Makes My Day/Casting a Spell	1989	—	—	3.00
❑ 50183 [PS]	She Makes My Day/Casting a Spell	1989	—	—	3.00

EMI MANHATTAN
❑ 50133	Simply Irresistible/Nova	1988	—	—	3.00
❑ 50133 [PS]	Simply Irresistible/Nova	1988	—	—	3.00
❑ 50157	Early in the Morning/Disturbing Behavior	1988	—	—	3.00
❑ 50157 [PS]	Early in the Morning/Disturbing Behavior	1988	—	—	3.00

ISLAND
❑ 006	Sneakin' Sally Through the Alley/Epidemic	1974	—	2.50	5.00
❑ 015	Get Ta Steppin'/Get Right On Down	1975	—	2.50	5.00
❑ 042	Which One of Us Is the Fool/Get Outside	1975	—	2.50	5.00
❑ 049	Pressure Drop/Give Me an Inch Girl	1976	—	2.50	5.00
❑ 075	Man Smart, Woman Smarter/Keep in Touch	1976	—	2.50	5.00
❑ 081	One Last Look/Some People Can Do What They				
	Want	1977	—	2.50	5.00
❑ 100	Every Kinda People/How Much Fun	1978	—	2.00	4.00
❑ 105	You Overwhelm Me/Come Over	1978	—	2.00	4.00
❑ 8697	Where Can It Go/You're Gonna Get What's				
	Coming	1978	—	2.00	4.00
❑ 49016	Bad Case of Loving You (Doctor, Doctor)/Love				
	Can Run Faster	1979	—	2.00	4.00
❑ 49094	In Walks Love Again/Jealous	1979	—	2.00	4.00
❑ 49137	Can We Still Be Friends/Remember to				
	Remember	1979	—	2.00	4.00
❑ 49554	Style Kills/Johnny and Mary	1980	—	2.00	4.00
❑ 49620	Looking for Clues/Woke Up Laughing	1980	—	2.00	4.00
❑ 50042	Some Guys Have All the Luck/				
	Too Good to Be True	1982	—	2.00	4.00
❑ 99139	Bad Case of Loving You/Sweet Lies	1989	—	—	3.00

❑ 99139 [PS]	Bad Case of Loving You/Sweet Lies	1989	—	2.00	4.00
❑ 99377	Sweet Lies/Want You More	1988	—	—	3.00
❑ 99377 [PS]	Sweet Lies/Want You More	1988	—	—	3.00
❑ 99537	I Didn't Mean to Turn You On/				
	Get It Through Your Heart	1986	—	—	3.00
❑ 99537 [PS]	I Didn't Mean to Turn You On/				
	Get It Through Your Heart	1986	—	—	3.00
❑ 99545	Hyperactive/Woke Up Laughing	1986	—	—	3.00
❑ 99570	Addicted to Love/Let's Fall in Love Tonight	1986	—	—	3.00
❑ 99570 [PS]	Addicted to Love/Let's Fall in Love Tonight	1986	—	2.00	4.00

—First version: Close-up photo of Robert Palmer
| ❑ 99570 [PS] | Addicted to Love/Let's Fall in Love Tonight | 1986 | — | 2.00 | 4.00 |

—Second version: Photo of "models" band from video
❑ 99597	Discipline of Love (Why Did You Do It)/				
	Dance for Me	1985	—	—	3.00
❑ 99597 [PS]	Discipline of Love (Why Did You Do It)/				
	Dance for Me	1985	—	—	3.00
❑ 99835	Pride/(B-side unknown)	1983	—	—	3.00
❑ 99835 [PS]	Pride/(B-side unknown)	1983	—	2.00	4.00
❑ 99866	You Are In My System/Deadline	1983	—	—	3.00
❑ 99866 [PS]	You Are In My System/Deadline	1983	—	—	3.00

MCA
| ❑ 52643 | All Around the World/It's Not Difficult | 1985 | — | — | 3.00 |

Albums
EMI MANHATTAN
| ❑ E1-48057 | Heavy Nova | 1988 | 2.50 | 5.00 | 10.00 |

ISLAND
| ❑ PRO-819 [DJ] | Secrets | 1979 | 7.50 | 15.00 | 30.00 |

—Promo-only picture disc
❑ ILPS 9294	Sneakin' Sally Through the Alley	1975	3.00	6.00	12.00
❑ ILPS 9372	Pressure Drop	1976	3.00	6.00	12.00
❑ ILPS 9420	Some People Can Do What They Like	1977	3.00	6.00	12.00
❑ ILPS 9476	Double Fun	1978	3.00	6.00	12.00

—Original copies of the above four albums were NOT distributed by Warner Bros.
❑ ILPS 9544	Secrets	1979	2.50	5.00	10.00
❑ ILPS 9595	Clues	1980	2.50	5.00	10.00
❑ ILPS 9665	Maybe It's Live	1982	2.50	5.00	10.00
❑ 90065	Pride	1983	2.50	5.00	10.00
❑ 90086	Sneakin' Sally Through the Alley	1984	2.00	4.00	8.00
❑ 90087	Pressure Drop	1984	2.00	4.00	8.00
❑ 90089	Secrets	1984	2.00	4.00	8.00
❑ 90471	Riptide	1985	2.50	5.00	10.00
❑ 90493	Clues	1986	2.00	4.00	8.00
❑ 90494	Double Fun	1986	2.00	4.00	8.00
❑ 91318	Addictions Volume I	1989	3.00	6.00	12.00

—Original pressing available only for a short time
| ❑ 842301-1 | Addictions Volume I | 1990 | 2.50 | 5.00 | 10.00 |

WARNER BROS.
| ❑ WBMS-111 [DJ] | Live in Boston | 1979 | 7.50 | 15.00 | 30.00 |

—Part of "The Warner Bros. Music Show"

PALS, THE
45s
GUYDEN
| ❑ 2019 | My Baby Likes to Rock/Summer Is Here | 1959 | 5.00 | 10.00 | 20.00 |

TURF
| ❑ 1000 | My Baby Likes to Rock/Summer Is Here | 1958 | 10.00 | 20.00 | 40.00 |

PANDIT, KORLA
45s
FANTASY
| ❑ 545 | Turkish Dance/Brazilian Brion | 195? | 3.75 | 7.50 | 15.00 |

VITA
❑ V-1	White Christmas/Merry Christmas	195?	3.75	7.50	15.00
❑ V-2	Ave Maria/Bist Du Bi Mir	195?	3.75	7.50	15.00
❑ V-3	Adeste Fideles//Jesu Bambino/Silent Night	195?	3.75	7.50	15.00
❑ V-4	Joy to the World/Hark! The Herald Angels Sing	195?	3.75	7.50	15.00
❑ 220	Remembering/They Say	195?	5.00	10.00	20.00

Albums
FANTASY
| ❑ 3272 [M] | Music of the Exotic East | 1958 | 6.25 | 12.50 | 25.00 |
—Black vinyl
| ❑ 3272 [M] | Music of the Exotic East | 1958 | 10.00 | 20.00 | 40.00 |
—Red vinyl
| ❑ 3284 [M] | Latin Holiday | 1959 | 6.25 | 12.50 | 25.00 |
—Black vinyl
| ❑ 3284 [M] | Latin Holiday | 1959 | 10.00 | 20.00 | 40.00 |
—Red vinyl
| ❑ 3286 [M] | Korla Pandit at the Pipe Organ | 1959 | 6.25 | 12.50 | 25.00 |
—Black vinyl
| ❑ 3286 [M] | Korla Pandit at the Pipe Organ | 1959 | 10.00 | 20.00 | 40.00 |
—Red vinyl
| ❑ 3288 [M] | Tropical Magic | 1959 | 6.25 | 12.50 | 25.00 |
—Black vinyl
| ❑ 3288 [M] | Tropical Magic | 1959 | 10.00 | 20.00 | 40.00 |
—Red vinyl
| ❑ 3293 [M] | Speak to Me of Love | 1959 | 6.25 | 12.50 | 25.00 |
—Black vinyl
| ❑ 3293 [M] | Speak to Me of Love | 1959 | 10.00 | 20.00 | 40.00 |
—Red vinyl
| ❑ 3304 [M] | Korla Pandit in Concert | 1960 | 6.25 | 12.50 | 25.00 |
—Black vinyl
| ❑ 3304 [M] | Korla Pandit in Concert | 1960 | 10.00 | 20.00 | 40.00 |
—Red vinyl
| ❑ 3320 [M] | Music of Mystery and Romance | 1961 | 6.25 | 12.50 | 25.00 |
—Black vinyl
| ❑ 3320 [M] | Music of Mystery and Romance | 1961 | 10.00 | 20.00 | 40.00 |
—Red vinyl
| ❑ 3327 [M] | Love Letters | 1961 | 6.25 | 12.50 | 25.00 |
—Black vinyl
| ❑ 3327 [M] | Love Letters | 1961 | 10.00 | 20.00 | 40.00 |
—Red vinyl
| ❑ 3329 [M] | Hypnotique | 1961 | 6.25 | 12.50 | 25.00 |
—Black vinyl
| ❑ 3329 [M] | Hypnotique | 1961 | 10.00 | 20.00 | 40.00 |
—Red vinyl

P

Number	Title (A Side/B Side)	Yr	VG	VG+	NM
❑ 3334 [M]	Music of Hollywood	1962	6.25	12.50	25.00
—Black vinyl					
❑ 3334 [M]	Music of Hollywood	1962	10.00	20.00	40.00
—Red vinyl					
❑ 3342 [M]	Music for Meditation	1962	6.25	12.50	25.00
—Black vinyl					
❑ 3342 [M]	Music for Meditation	1962	10.00	20.00	40.00
—Red vinyl					
❑ 3347 [M]	Korla Pandit in Paris	1962	6.25	12.50	25.00
❑ 3350 [M]	Christmas with Korla Pandit	1962	6.25	12.00	25.00
—Black vinyl					
❑ 3350 [M]	Christmas with Korla Pandit	1962	10.00	20.00	40.00
—Red vinyl					
❑ 8013 [S]	Music of the Exotic East	1960	7.50	15.00	30.00
—Black vinyl					
❑ 8013 [S]	Music of the Exotic East	1960	12.50	25.00	50.00
—Blue vinyl					
❑ 8018 [S]	Korla Pandit at the Pipe Organ	1960	7.50	15.00	30.00
—Black vinyl					
❑ 8018 [S]	Korla Pandit at the Pipe Organ	1960	12.50	25.00	50.00
—Blue vinyl					
❑ 8027 [S]	Latin Holiday	1960	7.50	15.00	30.00
—Black vinyl					
❑ 8027 [S]	Latin Holiday	1960	12.50	25.00	50.00
—Blue vinyl					
❑ 8034 [S]	Tropical Magic	1960	7.50	15.00	30.00
—Black vinyl					
❑ 8034 [S]	Tropical Magic	1960	12.50	25.00	50.00
—Blue vinyl					
❑ 8039 [S]	Speak to Me of Love	1960	7.50	15.00	30.00
—Black vinyl					
❑ 8039 [S]	Speak to Me of Love	1960	12.50	25.00	50.00
—Blue vinyl					
❑ 8049 [S]	Korla Pandit in Concert	1960	7.50	15.00	30.00
—Black vinyl					
❑ 8049 [S]	Korla Pandit in Concert	1960	12.50	25.00	50.00
—Blue vinyl					
❑ 8061 [S]	Music of Mystery and Romance	1961	7.50	15.00	30.00
—Black vinyl					
❑ 8061 [S]	Music of Mystery and Romance	1961	12.50	25.00	50.00
—Blue vinyl					
❑ 8070 [S]	Love Letters	1961	7.50	15.00	30.00
—Black vinyl					
❑ 8070 [S]	Love Letters	1961	12.50	25.00	50.00
—Blue vinyl					
❑ 8075 [S]	Hypnotique	1961	7.50	15.00	30.00
—Black vinyl					
❑ 8075 [S]	Hypnotique	1961	12.50	25.00	50.00
—Blue vinyl					
❑ 8086 [S]	Music of Hollywood	1962	7.50	15.00	30.00
—Black vinyl					
❑ 8086 [S]	Music of Hollywood	1962	12.50	25.00	50.00
—Blue vinyl					
❑ 8342 [S]	Music for Meditation	1962	7.50	15.00	30.00
—Black vinyl					
❑ 8342 [S]	Music for Meditation	1962	12.50	25.00	50.00
—Blue vinyl					
❑ 8347 [S]	Korla Pandit in Paris	1962	7.50	15.00	30.00
❑ 8350 [S]	Christmas with Korla Pandit	1962	7.50	15.00	30.00
—Black vinyl					
❑ 8350 [S]	Christmas with Korla Pandit	1962	12.50	25.00	50.00
—Blue vinyl					
NATIONAL CUSTOM					
❑ NCR 12-574	Fantastique!	196?	7.50	15.00	30.00
SYMPATHY FOR THE RECORD INDUSTRY					
❑ SFTRI 387	Exotica 2000	1996	3.00	6.00	12.00
VITA					
❑ VLP-14 [10]	Rememb'ring with Korla Pandit	195?	20.00	40.00	80.00

PANICS, THE
45s

Number	Title (A Side/B Side)	Yr	VG	VG+	NM
ABC-PARAMOUNT					
❑ 10072	Heartaches/You're Driving Me Crazy	1959	3.75	7.50	15.00
CHANCELLOR					
❑ 1109	Panicsville/Bony Moronie	1962	3.75	7.50	15.00
❑ 1127	Skinnie Minnie Olive Oil/Voodoo Walk	1962	3.75	7.50	15.00
PHILIPS					
❑ 40230	The Kangaroo/It Ain't What You Got	1964	3.00	6.00	12.00
SHOESTRING					
❑ 107	No More/I Pretend	196?	2.50	5.00	10.00
SWAN					
❑ 4247	Beans/Show Her You Care	1966	3.00	6.00	12.00
Albums					
CHANCELLOR					
❑ CHL-5026 [M]	Panicsville	1962	7.50	15.00	30.00
❑ CHLS-5026 [S]	Panicsville	1962	10.00	20.00	40.00
PHILIPS					
❑ PHM 200159 [M]	Discotheque Dance Party	1964	3.75	7.50	15.00
❑ PHS 600159 [S]	Discotheque Dance Party	1964	5.00	10.00	20.00

PAPA DOO RUN RUN With BRUCE JOHNSTON.
45s

Number	Title (A Side/B Side)	Yr	VG	VG+	NM
BLUE PACIFIC					
❑ 1-001	Lady Love/Slow Down	197?	—	2.00	4.00
❑ 1-001 [PS]	Lady Love/Slow Down	197?	—	2.00	4.00
EQUINOX					
❑ PB-10404	Disney Girls/Be True to Your School	1975	2.50	5.00	10.00
Albums					
TELARC					
❑ 70501	California Project	1985	2.50	5.00	10.00

PAPER DOLLS, THE
45s

Number	Title (A Side/B Side)	Yr	VG	VG+	NM
MGM					
❑ 13766	'Cause I Love You/You're the Boy I Want to Marry	1967	3.00	6.00	12.00
UNI					
❑ 55104	Someday/Any Old Time You're Lonely and Sad	1969	2.50	5.00	10.00

Number	Title (A Side/B Side)	Yr	VG	VG+	NM
WARNER BROS.					
❑ 7191	All the Time in the World/Something Here in My Heart (Keeps a-Tellin' Me No)	1968	2.50	5.00	10.00

PAPER GARDEN, THE
Albums

Number	Title (A Side/B Side)	Yr	VG	VG+	NM
MUSICOR					
❑ MS-(# unknown)	The Paper Garden	1968	10.00	20.00	40.00

PAPER LACE
45s

Number	Title (A Side/B Side)	Yr	VG	VG+	NM
BANG					
❑ 700	Martha/You Can't Touch Me	1972	—	2.50	5.00
❑ 704	Ragamuffin Man/Elsie	1973	—	2.50	5.00
❑ 711	Ragamuffin Man/Elsie	1974	—	—	—
—Canceled					
MERCURY					
❑ 73479	Billy, Don't Be a Hero/Celia	1974	—	3.00	6.00
❑ 73492	The Night Chicago Died/Can You Get It When You Want It	1974	—	2.00	4.00
—Chicago skyline label					
❑ 73492	The Night Chicago Died/Can You Get It When You Want It	1974	—	3.00	6.00
—Red label					
❑ 73620	The Black-Eyed Boys/Jean	1974	—	2.00	4.00
❑ 73694	So What If I Am/Himalayan Lullaby	1975	—	2.00	4.00
Albums					
MERCURY					
❑ SRM-1-1008	Paper Lace	1974	3.00	6.00	12.00

PAPPALARDI, FELIX Also see MOUNTAIN.
45s

Number	Title (A Side/B Side)	Yr	VG	VG+	NM
COLUMBIA					
❑ 43773	Love Someday/You Lie to Me	1966	6.25	12.50	25.00
Albums					
A&M					
❑ SP-4586	Creation	1976	2.50	5.00	10.00
❑ SP-4729	Don't Worry Me	1979	2.50	5.00	10.00

PARADE, THE
45s

Number	Title (A Side/B Side)	Yr	VG	VG+	NM
A&M					
❑ 841	Sunshine Girl/This Old Melody	1967	2.50	5.00	10.00
❑ 867	She's Got the Magic/Welcome, You're in Love	1967	—	3.00	6.00
❑ 887	Frog Prince/Hallelujah Rocket	1967	—	3.00	6.00
❑ 904	I Can See Love/Radio Song	1968	—	3.00	6.00
❑ 950	A.C.-D.C./She Sleeps Alone	1968	—	3.00	6.00
❑ 970	Laughing Lady/Hallelujah Rocket	1968	—	3.00	6.00

PARADONS, THE
45s

Number	Title (A Side/B Side)	Yr	VG	VG+	NM
MILESTONE					
❑ 2003	Diamonds and Pearls/I Want Love	1960	5.00	10.00	20.00
—Green label					
❑ 2003	Diamonds and Pearls/I Want Love	1960	7.50	15.00	30.00
—Red label					
❑ 2003	Diamonds and Pearls/I Want Love	1960	12.50	25.00	50.00
—Maroon label					
❑ 2005	Bells Ring/Please Tell Me	1960	7.50	15.00	30.00
❑ 2015	I Had a Dream/Never, Never	1962	10.00	20.00	40.00
TUFFEST					
❑ 102	Never Again/This Is Love	1961	37.50	75.00	150.00
WARNER BROS.					
❑ 5186	Take All of Me/So Fine, So Fine, So Fine	1960	5.00	10.00	20.00

PARAGONS, THE
45s

Number	Title (A Side/B Side)	Yr	VG	VG+	NM
BUDDAH					
❑ 478	Oh Lovin' You/Con Me	1975	—	3.00	6.00
LOST-NITE					
❑ 121	The Vows of Love/Stick with Me Baby	196?	2.00	4.00	8.00
❑ 125	Let's Start All Over Again/Stick With Me Baby	196?	2.00	4.00	8.00
—Reissue					
❑ 128	Hey Little School Girl/Florence	196?	2.00	4.00	8.00
—Reissue					
❑ 130	Two Hearts Are Better Than One/Give Me Love	196?	2.00	4.00	8.00
—Reissue					
❑ 133	Twilight/Stick with Me Baby	196?	2.00	4.00	8.00
❑ 160	So You Will Know/Don't Cry Baby	196?	2.00	4.00	8.00
—Reissue					
MUSIC CLEF					
❑ 3001/2	Time After Time/Baby, Take My Hand	1963	5.00	10.00	20.00
MUSICRAFT					
❑ 1102	Wedding Bells/Blue Velvet	1960	6.25	12.50	25.00
TAP					
❑ 500	If/Hey Baby	1961	12.50	25.00	50.00
❑ 503	In the Midst of the Night/Begin the Beguine	1961	10.00	20.00	40.00
❑ 504	These Are the Things I Love/If You Love Me	1961	10.00	20.00	40.00
TIMES SQUARE					
❑ 9	So You Will Know/Don't Cry Baby	1963	5.00	10.00	20.00
WINLEY					
❑ 215	Hey Little School Girl/Florence	1957	12.50	25.00	50.00
❑ 220	Let's Start All Over Again/Stick with Me Baby	1957	12.50	25.00	50.00
❑ 223	Two Hearts Are Better Than One/Give Me Love	1958	10.00	20.00	40.00
❑ 227	The Vows of Love/Twilight	1958	10.00	20.00	40.00
❑ 227	The Wows of Love/Twilight	1958	250.00	500.00	1000.
—With misspelled A-side title					
❑ 228	Don't Cry Baby/So You Will Know	1958	10.00	20.00	40.00
❑ 236	Darling, I Love You/Doll Baby	1959	10.00	20.00	40.00
❑ 240	So You Will Know/Doll Baby	1959	7.50	15.00	30.00
❑ 250	Kneel and Pray/Just a Moment	1961	7.50	15.00	30.00
Albums					
COLLECTABLES					
❑ COL-5035	The Best of the Paragons	198?	2.50	5.00	10.00

Number	Title (A Side/B Side)	Yr	VG	VG+	NM

LOST-NITE
| ❏ LLP-4 [10] | The Best of the Paragons | 1981 | 2.50 | 5.00 | 10.00 |

—Red vinyl; in die-cut cover with sticker

PARAGONS, THE & THE HARPTONES
Albums
MUSICTONE
| ❏ M-8001 [M] | The Paragons vs. the Harptones | 1964 | 10.00 | 20.00 | 40.00 |

PARAGONS, THE & THE JESTERS
Albums
JOSIE
| ❏ 4008 [M] | The Paragons Meet the Jesters | 1962 | 50.00 | 100.00 | 200.00 |

JUBILEE
| ❏ JLP-1098 [M] | The Paragons Meet the Jesters | 1959 | 75.00 | 150.00 | 300.00 |

—Blue label, black vinyl
| ❏ JLP-1098 [M] | The Paragons Meet the Jesters | 1959 | 750.00 | 1125. | 1500. |

—Multi-color splash vinyl
| ❏ JLP-1098 [M] | The Paragons Meet the Jesters | 196? | 15.00 | 30.00 | 60.00 |

—Black label with multi-color logo
| ❏ JLP-1098 [M] | The Paragons Meet the Jesters | 196? | 37.50 | 75.00 | 150.00 |

—Flat black label
WINLEY
| ❏ LP-6003 [M] | War! The Jesters vs. the Paragons | 195? | 125.00 | 250.00 | 500.00 |

PARAGONS, THE (2) Not the same group as the others.
45s
CENTURY CUSTOM
| ❏ 19317 | Surf Drums/Sunday Morning | 196? | 15.00 | 30.00 | 60.00 |

—B-side by the Samohi Serenaders

PARAKEETS, THE (1)
45s
BIG TOP
| ❏ 3130 | I Love You Like I Do/I Want You Right Now | 1962 | 5.00 | 10.00 | 20.00 |

JUBILEE
| ❏ 5407 | Come Back/Shangri-La | 1961 | 6.25 | 12.50 | 25.00 |

PARAKEETS, THE (2)
45s
GEM
| ❏ 218 | Give Me Time/I'm Losing My Mind Over You | 1954 | 100.00 | 200.00 | 400.00 |

PARAMOR, NORRIE
45s
CAPITOL
❏ F3629	Every Street's a Boulevard/Magic Banjo	1957	2.50	5.00	10.00
❏ F3714	Taurus Tango/Gemini Waltz	1957	2.50	5.00	10.00
❏ F4266	Waltzing Matilda/Barcelona	1959	2.50	5.00	10.00

ESSEX
| ❏ 337 | Callahan's Monkey/Melodia | 1953 | 3.75 | 7.50 | 15.00 |
| ❏ 356 | Wedding Day/Luxembourg Polka | 1954 | 3.00 | 6.00 | 12.00 |

Albums
CAPITOL
❏ ST 2071 [S]	In London…In Love Again	1964	3.75	7.50	15.00
❏ T 2071 [M]	In London…In Love Again	1964	3.00	6.00	12.00
❏ ST 2357 [S]	Warm and Willing	1965	3.75	7.50	15.00
❏ T 2357 [M]	Warm and Willing	1965	3.00	6.00	12.00
❏ ST 2526 [S]	In Tokyo — In Love	1966	3.75	7.50	15.00
❏ T 2526 [M]	In Tokyo — In Love	1966	3.00	6.00	12.00
❏ ST 10025 [S]	In London…In Love	196?	3.75	7.50	15.00
❏ T 10025 [M]	In London…In Love	196?	3.00	6.00	12.00
❏ T 10052 [M]	London After Dark	196?	3.00	6.00	12.00
❏ T 10130 [M]	Norrie Paramor's Moods	196?	3.00	6.00	12.00
❏ ST 10212 [S]	Autumn	196?	3.75	7.50	15.00
❏ T 10212 [M]	Autumn	196?	3.00	6.00	12.00
❏ ST 10238 [S]	Amor Amor	196?	3.75	7.50	15.00
❏ T 10238 [M]	Amor Amor	196?	3.00	6.00	12.00

POLYDOR
| ❏ 24-6006 | Love at First Sight | 1970 | 2.50 | 5.00 | 10.00 |

PARAMOUNTS, THE (1)
45s
CARLTON
| ❏ 524 | Girl Friend/Trying | 1960 | 10.00 | 20.00 | 40.00 |

PARAMOUNTS, THE (2)
45s
CENTAUR
| ❏ 103 | When I Dream/Where's Carolyn Tonight | 1963 | 15.00 | 30.00 | 60.00 |

PARAMOUNTS, THE (3) ROBERT KNIGHT was in this group.
45s
DOT
| ❏ 16175 | Why Do You Have to Go/Congratulations | 1961 | 6.25 | 12.50 | 25.00 |
| ❏ 16201 | When You Dance/Year 17 | 1961 | 6.25 | 12.50 | 25.00 |

PARAMOUNTS, THE (4) British group; an early incarnation of PROCOL HARUM.
45s
LIVERPOOL SOUND
| ❏ 903 | Poison Ivy/I Feel Good All Over | 1964 | 12.50 | 25.00 | 50.00 |

PARAMOUNTS, THE (U) Could be any of the above groups except (4), or they could be entirely different.
45s
COMBO
| ❏ 156 | Take My Heart/Thunderbird Baby | 1960 | 30.00 | 60.00 | 120.00 |

FLEETWOOD
| ❏ 1014 | I Know You'll Be My Love/Christopher Columbus | 1960 | 25.00 | 50.00 | 100.00 |

LAURIE
| ❏ 3201 | Just to Be with You/One More for the Road | 1963 | 7.50 | 15.00 | 30.00 |

LOST-NITE
| ❏ 374 | Take My Heart/Thunderbird Baby | 197? | — | 2.50 | 5.00 |

—Reissue
MAGNUM
| ❏ 722 | Time Will Bring a Change/Under Your Spell | 1964 | 7.50 | 15.00 | 30.00 |

MERCURY
| ❏ 72429 | Girl with the Big Black Boots/I Won't Share Your Love | 1965 | 3.00 | 6.00 | 12.00 |

PARAMOURS, THE BIL MEDLEY and BOBBY HATFIELD, later THE RIGHTEOUS BROTHERS.
45s
MOONGLOW
| ❏ 214 | That's All I Want Tonight/There She Goes | 1962 | 5.00 | 10.00 | 20.00 |
| ❏ 214 | That's All I Want Tonight/There She Goes | 1962 | 10.00 | 20.00 | 40.00 |

—Red vinyl
SMASH
| ❏ 1701 | That's the Way We Love/Prison Break | 1961 | 5.00 | 10.00 | 20.00 |
| ❏ 1718 | Cutie Cutie/Miss Social Climber | 1961 | 5.00 | 10.00 | 20.00 |

PARFAYS, THE
45s
FONTANA
| ❏ 1526 | You've Got a Good Thing Goin' Boy/In the Beginning | 1965 | 7.50 | 15.00 | 30.00 |

PARIS With Bob Welch, ex-FLEETWOOD MAC.
45s
CAPITOL
| ❏ 4356 | Blue Robin/Big Towne, 2061 | 1976 | — | 2.50 | 5.00 |

Albums
CAPITOL
| ❏ ST-11464 | Paris | 1975 | 3.00 | 6.00 | 12.00 |
| ❏ ST-11560 | Big Towne, 2061 | 1976 | 3.00 | 6.00 | 12.00 |

PARIS, FREDDIE No relation to FRED PARRIS.
45s
RCA VICTOR
❏ 47-9232	Take Me As I Am/It's Okay to Cry Now	1967	2.50	5.00	10.00
❏ 47-9358	Little Things Can Make a Woman Cry/Face It, Boy, It's Over	1967	2.50	5.00	10.00
❏ 47-9571	There She Goes/Young Hearts, Young Hands	1968	5.00	10.00	20.00

Albums
RCA VICTOR
| ❏ LSP-4064 | Lovin' Mood | 1968 | 5.00 | 10.00 | 20.00 |

PARIS BROTHERS, THE
45s
BRUNSWICK
| ❏ 55132 | This Is It/Our Love Is Here to Stay | 1959 | 7.50 | 15.00 | 30.00 |

CORAL
| ❏ 62220 | Funny Feeling/(B-side unknown) | 1959 | 5.00 | 10.00 | 20.00 |

PARIS PILOT
Albums
HIP
| ❏ 7004 | Paris Pilot | 1970 | 6.25 | 12.50 | 25.00 |

PARIS SISTERS, THE
45s
CAPITOL
| ❏ 2081 | Golden Days/Greener Days | 1968 | 2.00 | 4.00 | 8.00 |

CAVALIER
| ❏ 828 | Christmas in My Home Town/Man with the Mistletoe Moustache | 197? | — | 3.00 | 6.00 |

DECCA
❏ 29372	Ooh La La/Whose Arms Are You Missing	1954	6.25	12.50	25.00
❏ 29488	Baby, Honey, Baby/Huckleberry Pie	1955	6.25	12.50	25.00
❏ 29527	His and Hers/Truly Do	1955	6.25	12.50	25.00

—With Gary Crosby
❏ 29574	The Know How/I Wanna	1955	6.25	12.50	25.00
❏ 29744	Lover Boy/Oh Yes You Do	1955	6.25	12.50	25.00
❏ 29891	I Love You Dear/Mistaken	1956	6.25	12.50	25.00
❏ 29970	Daughter! Daughter!/So Much — So Very Much	1956	6.25	12.50	25.00
❏ 30554	Don't Tell Anybody/Mind Reader	1958	5.00	10.00	20.00

GNP CRESCENDO
| ❏ 410 | Stand Naked Clown/Ugliest Girl in Town | 1968 | 2.00 | 4.00 | 8.00 |

GREGMARK
❏ 2	Be My Boy/I'll Be Crying Tomorrow	1961	5.00	10.00	20.00
❏ 6	I Love How You Love Me/All Through the Night	1961	6.25	12.50	25.00
❏ 10	He Knows I Love Him Too Much/Lonely Girl's Prayer	1962	5.00	10.00	20.00
❏ 12	Let Me Be the One/What Am I to Do	1962	5.00	10.00	20.00
❏ 13	Yes I Love You/Once Upon a While Ago	1962	5.00	10.00	20.00

—All the Gregmark records were Phil Spector productions
IMPERIAL
| ❏ 5465 | Old Enough to Cry/Tell Me More | 1957 | 5.00 | 10.00 | 20.00 |
| ❏ 5487 | Some Day/My Original Love | 1958 | 5.00 | 10.00 | 20.00 |

MERCURY
❏ 72320	Once Upon a Time/When I Fall in Love	1964	2.50	5.00	10.00
❏ 72320 [PS]	Once Upon a Time/When I Fall in Love	1964	5.00	10.00	20.00
❏ 72468	Always Waitin'/Why Do I Take It from You	1965	2.50	5.00	10.00
❏ 72468 [PS]	Always Waitin'/Why Do I Take It from You	1965	5.00	10.00	20.00

MGM
| ❏ 13236 | Dream Lover/Lonely Girl | 1964 | 3.75 | 7.50 | 15.00 |
| ❏ 13236 [PS] | Dream Lover/Lonely Girl | 1964 | 6.25 | 12.50 | 25.00 |

REPRISE
❏ 0440	Sincerely/Too Good to Be True	1965	2.50	5.00	10.00
❏ 0472	I'm Me/You	1966	2.50	5.00	10.00
❏ 0511	It's My Party/My Good Friend	1966	2.50	5.00	10.00
❏ 0548	Some of Your Lovin'/Long After Tonight Is All Over	1967	2.50	5.00	10.00

Albums
REPRISE
| ❏ R-6259 [M] | Everything Under the Sun | 1967 | 10.00 | 20.00 | 40.00 |
| ❏ RS-6359 [S] | Everything Under the Sun | 1967 | 15.00 | 30.00 | 60.00 |

SIDEWALK
| ❏ DT 5906 [R] | Golden Hits of the Paris Sisters | 1967 | 7.50 | 15.00 | 30.00 |
| ❏ T 5906 [M] | Golden Hits of the Paris Sisters | 1967 | 12.50 | 25.00 | 50.00 |

UNIFILMS
| ❏ 505 [M] | The Paris Sisters Sing Songs from Glass House | 1966 | 10.00 | 20.00 | 40.00 |
| ❏ S-505 [S] | The Paris Sisters Sing Songs from Glass House | 1966 | 12.50 | 25.00 | 50.00 |

P

Number	Title (A Side/B Side)	Yr	VG	VG+	NM

PARISH HALL
Albums
FANTASY

Number	Title (A Side/B Side)	Yr	VG	VG+	NM
❑ 8398	Parish Hall	1969	5.00	10.00	20.00

PARKER, BILLY (1)
45s
SOUNDWAVES

❑ 4686	Too Many Irons in the Fire/Honky Tonk Girl	1982	—	2.50	5.00

—A-side with Cal Smith

PARKER, BOBBY
45s
V-TONE

❑ 223	Watch Your Step/Steal Your Heart Away	1961	3.75	7.50	15.00

—"223-AAX" in hit side trail-off area

❑ 223	Watch Your Step/Steal Your Heart Away	1961	5.00	10.00	20.00

—"45-V Tone 223-A" in hit side trail-off area
VEE JAY

❑ 279	You Got What It Takes/Blues Get Off My Shoulder	1958	7.50	15.00	30.00

PARKER, CHARLIE
45s
CLEF

❑ 89129	Cosmic Rays/Kim	1955	6.25	12.50	25.00
❑ 89138	I Remember You/Chi Chi	1955	6.25	12.50	25.00
❑ 89144	I Hear Music/Laird Baird	1955	6.25	12.50	25.00

MERCURY

❑ 11070	You Came Along from Out of Nowhere/ East of the Sun	195?	25.00	50.00	100.00

—Red vinyl; part of Album C-509, which means there must be others like it, but this is the only one we've confirmed

7-Inch Extended Plays
CLEF

❑ EP 255	Summertime/I Didn't Know What Time It Was// Bloom Dido/Melancholy Baby	195?	12.50	25.00	50.00
❑ EP 255 [PS]	(title unknown)	195?	12.50	25.00	50.00

Albums
ALAMAC

❑ QSR 2430	Charlie Parker's All Stars 1950	198?	3.00	6.00	12.00

AMERICAN RECORDING SOCIETY

❑ G-441 [M]	Now's the Time	1957	12.50	25.00	50.00

BARONET

❑ B-105 [M]	A Handful of Modern Jazz	1962	5.00	10.00	20.00
❑ BS-105 [R]	A Handful of Modern Jazz	1962	3.00	6.00	12.00
❑ B-107 [M]	The Early Bird	1962	5.00	10.00	20.00
❑ BS-107 [R]	The Early Bird	1962	3.00	6.00	12.00

BIRDLAND

❑ 425 [10]	A Night at Carnegie Hall	1956	75.00	150.00	300.00

BLUE NOTE

❑ BT-85108	Charlie Parker at Storyville	198?	3.00	6.00	12.00

BLUE RIBBON

❑ 8011 [M]	The Early Bird	1962	5.00	10.00	20.00
❑ S-8011 [R]	The Early Bird	1962	3.00	6.00	12.00

CHARLIE PARKER

❑ PLP-401 [M]	Bird Is Free	1961	10.00	20.00	40.00
❑ PLP-404 [M]	The Happy Bird	1961	10.00	20.00	40.00
❑ PLP-406 [M]	Charlie Parker	1961	10.00	20.00	40.00
❑ PLP-407 [M]	Bird Symbols	1961	10.00	20.00	40.00
❑ PLP-408 [M]	Once There Was Bird	1961	10.00	20.00	40.00
❑ CP-2-502 [(2)M]	Live at Rockland Palace, September 26, 1952	1961	12.50	25.00	50.00
❑ CP-513 [M]	Charlie Parker Plus Strings	196?	10.00	20.00	40.00
❑ PLP-701 [(3)]	Historical Masterpieces	196?	15.00	30.00	60.00

CLEF

❑ MGC-101 [10]	Charlie Parker with Strings	1958	—	—	—

—Canceled

❑ MGC-157 [10]	Charlie Parker	1954	100.00	200.00	400.00
❑ MGC-501 [10]	Charlie Parker with Strings	1954	100.00	200.00	400.00

—Reissue of Mercury 501

❑ MGC-509 [10]	Charlie Parker with Strings, No. 2	1954	100.00	200.00	400.00

—Reissue of Mercury 509

❑ MGC-512 [10]	Bird and Diz	1954	100.00	200.00	400.00

—Reissue of Mercury 512

❑ MGC-513 [10]	South of the Border	1954	100.00	200.00	400.00

—Reissue of Mercury 513

❑ MGC-609 [M]	Charlie Parker Big Band	1954	100.00	200.00	400.00
❑ MGC-646 [M]	The Magnificent Charlie Parker	1955	100.00	200.00	400.00
❑ MGC-675 [M]	Charlie Parker with Strings	1955	100.00	200.00	400.00
❑ MGC-725 [M]	Night and Day	1956	30.00	60.00	120.00

COLUMBIA

❑ C2 34808 [(2)]	One Night in Birdland	198?	3.00	6.00	12.00

—Reissue with new prefix

❑ JG 34808 [(2)]	One Night in Birdland	1977	3.75	7.50	15.00
❑ JC 34831	Summit Meeting	1977	3.00	6.00	12.00
❑ JC 34832	Bird with Strings Live	1977	3.00	6.00	12.00

CONCERT HALL JAZZ

❑ 1004 [10]	The Fabulous Bird	1955	15.00	30.00	60.00
❑ 1017 [10]	The Art of Charlie Parker, Vol. 2	1955	15.00	30.00	60.00

CONTINENTAL

❑ 16004 [M]	Bird Lives	1962	10.00	20.00	40.00

DEBUT

❑ DEB-611 [M]	Bird on 52nd Street	196?	12.50	25.00	50.00

DIAL

❑ LP-1 [M]	The Bird Blows the Blues	1949	1000.	2000.	4000.

—Mail-order offer

❑ LP-201 [10]	Charlie Parker Quintet	1949	200.00	400.00	800.00
❑ LP-202 [10]	Charlie Parker Quintet	1949	200.00	400.00	800.00
❑ LP-203 [10]	Charlie Parker	1949	200.00	400.00	800.00
❑ LP-207 [10]	Charlie Parker Sextet	1949	200.00	400.00	800.00
❑ LP-901 [M]	The Bird Blows the Blues	1950	150.00	300.00	600.00
❑ LP-904 [M]	Alternate Masters	1951	150.00	300.00	600.00
❑ LP-905 [M]	Alternate Masters	1951	150.00	300.00	600.00

ELEKTRA/MUSICIAN

❑ 60019	One Night in Washington	1982	2.50	5.00	10.00

ESP-DISK'

❑ ESP-BIRD-2	Broadcast Performances 1948-1949, Vol. 2	1973	5.00	10.00	20.00

EVEREST ARCHIVE OF FOLK & JAZZ

❑ 214	Charlie Parker	1969	3.00	6.00	12.00
❑ 232	Charlie Parker, Volume 2	1970	2.50	5.00	10.00
❑ 254	Charlie Parker, Vol. 3	197?	2.50	5.00	10.00
❑ 295	Charlie Parker, Vol. 4	197?	2.50	5.00	10.00
❑ 315	Charlie Parker, Vol. 5	197?	2.50	5.00	10.00

FANTASY

❑ OJC-041	Bird at St. Nick's	198?	2.50	5.00	10.00
❑ OJC-044	Jazz at Massey Hall	198?	2.50	5.00	10.00
❑ OJC-114	Bird on 52nd St.	198?	2.50	5.00	10.00
❑ 6011 [M]	Bird on 52nd St.	1964	7.50	15.00	30.00
❑ 6012 [M]	Bird at St. Nick's	1964	7.50	15.00	30.00
❑ 86011 [R]	Bird on 52nd St.	1964	3.75	7.50	15.00
❑ 86012 [R]	Bird at St. Nick's	1964	3.75	7.50	15.00

HALL OF FAME

❑ 617	Giants of Jazz	197?	2.50	5.00	10.00
❑ 620	Takin' Off	197?	2.50	5.00	10.00

JAZZ WORKSHOP

❑ JWS-500 [M]	Bird at St. Nick's	1958	30.00	60.00	120.00
❑ JWS-501 [M]	Bird on 52nd Street	1958	30.00	60.00	120.00

JAZZTONE

❑ J-(# unk) [M]	The Art of Charlie Parker, Vol. 2	1955	12.50	25.00	50.00
❑ J-1204 [M]	Giants of Modern Jazz	1955	12.50	25.00	50.00
❑ J-1214 [M]	The Fabulous Bird	1955	12.50	25.00	50.00
❑ J-1240 [M]	The Saxes of Stan Getz and Charlie Parker	1957	12.50	25.00	50.00

LES JAZZ COOL

❑ 101 [M]	Les Jazz Cool, Volume 1	1960	12.50	25.00	50.00
❑ 102 [M]	Les Jazz Cool, Volume 2	1960	12.50	25.00	50.00
❑ 103 [M]	Les Jazz Cool, Volume 3	1960	12.50	25.00	50.00

MERCURY

❑ MGC-101 [10]	Charlie Parker with Strings	1950	125.00	250.00	500.00

—Reissue of 35010

❑ MGC-109 [10]	Charlie Parker with Strings, Volume 2	1950	125.00	250.00	500.00
❑ MGC-501 [10]	Charlie Parker with Strings	1951	125.00	250.00	500.00

—Reissue of 101 with new number

❑ MGC-509 [10]	Charlie Parker with Strings, Volume 2	1952	125.00	250.00	500.00

—Reissue of 109 with new number

❑ MGC-512 [10]	Bird and Diz	1952	125.00	250.00	500.00
❑ MGC-513 [10]	South of the Border	1952	125.00	250.00	500.00
❑ MG-35010 [10]	Charlie Parker with Strings	1950	150.00	300.00	600.00

MGM

❑ M3G-4949	Archetypes	1974	3.00	6.00	12.00

MOSAIC

❑ MR10-129 [(10)]	The Complete Dean Benedetti Recordings of Charlie Parker	199?	25.00	50.00	100.00

ONYX

❑ 221	First Recordings with Jay McShann	197?	3.00	6.00	12.00

PHOENIX

❑ 10	New Bird	197?	2.50	5.00	10.00
❑ 12	New Bird, Vol. 2	197?	2.50	5.00	10.00
❑ 17	Yardbird in Lotusland	197?	2.50	5.00	10.00

PICKWICK

❑ PC-3054 [M]	Yardbird	196?	3.00	6.00	12.00
❑ SPC-3054 [R]	Yardbird	196?	2.50	5.00	10.00

PRESTIGE

❑ 24009 [(2)]	Charlie Parker	197?	3.75	7.50	15.00
❑ 24024 [(2)]	Parker/Powell/Mingus/Roach	197?	3.75	7.50	15.00

ROOST

❑ LP-2210 [M]	All Star Sextet	1958	30.00	60.00	120.00
❑ LP-2257 [M]	The World of Charlie Parker	1963	10.00	20.00	40.00

SAVOY

❑ MG-9000 [10]	Charlie Parker	1950	125.00	250.00	500.00
❑ MG-9001 [10]	Charlie Parker, Volume 2	1951	125.00	250.00	500.00
❑ MG-9010 [10]	Charlie Parker, Volume 3	1952	125.00	250.00	500.00
❑ MG-9011 [10]	Charlie Parker, Volume 4	1952	125.00	250.00	500.00
❑ MG-12000 [M]	Charlie Parker Memorial	1955	25.00	50.00	100.00
❑ MG-12001 [M]	The Immortal Charlie Parker	1955	25.00	50.00	100.00
❑ MG-12009 [M]	Charlie Parker Memorial, Volume 2	1955	25.00	50.00	100.00
❑ MG-12014 [M]	The Genius of Charlie Parker	1955	25.00	50.00	100.00
❑ MG-12079 [M]	The Charlie Parker Story	1956	25.00	50.00	100.00
❑ MG-12138 [M]	Bird's Night	1960	10.00	20.00	40.00
❑ MG-12152 [M]	An Evening at Home with the Bird	196?	10.00	20.00	40.00
❑ MG-12179 [M]	The "Bird" Returns	196?	7.50	15.00	30.00
❑ MG-12186 [M]	Newly Discovered Sides by the Immortal Charlie Parker	1966	7.50	15.00	30.00

SAVOY JAZZ

❑ SJL-1107	Encores	197?	3.00	6.00	12.00
❑ SJL-1108	Bird at the Roost	197?	3.00	6.00	12.00
❑ SJL-1129	Encores, Vol. 2	198?	2.50	5.00	10.00
❑ SJL-1132	One Night in Chicago	198?	2.50	5.00	10.00
❑ SJL-1173	Bird at the Roost, Vol. 3	1987	2.50	5.00	10.00
❑ SJL-1208	Original Bird: The Best on Savoy	198?	2.50	5.00	10.00
❑ SJL-2201 [(2)]	Bird: The Savoy Recordings	1976	3.75	7.50	15.00
❑ SJL-2259 [(2)]	Bird at the Roost: The Complete Royal Roost Performances, Vol. 1	198?	3.75	7.50	15.00
❑ SJL-2260 [(2)]	Bird at the Roost: The Complete Royal Roost Performances, Vol. 2	1986	3.75	7.50	15.00
❑ SJL-5500 [(5)]	The Complete Savoy Studio Sessions	197?	7.50	15.00	30.00

SPOTLITE

❑ 101	Charlie Parker on Dial, Vol. 1	197?	2.50	5.00	10.00
❑ 102	Charlie Parker on Dial, Vol. 2	197?	2.50	5.00	10.00
❑ 103	Charlie Parker on Dial, Vol. 3	197?	2.50	5.00	10.00
❑ 104	Charlie Parker on Dial, Vol. 4	197?	2.50	5.00	10.00
❑ 105	Charlie Parker on Dial, Vol. 5	197?	2.50	5.00	10.00
❑ 106	Charlie Parker on Dial, Vol. 6	197?	2.50	5.00	10.00

STASH

❑ ST-260	Birth of the Bebop	1986	2.50	5.00	10.00
❑ ST-280	The Bird You Never Heard	1988	2.50	5.00	10.00

TRIP

❑ 5035 [(2)]	The Master	197?	3.00	6.00	12.00
❑ 5039 [(2)]	Birdology	197?	3.75	7.50	15.00

VERVE

❑ VSP-23 [M]	Bird Wings	1966	5.00	10.00	20.00
❑ VSPS-23 [R]	Bird Wings	1966	3.00	6.00	12.00

Number	Title (A Side/B Side)	Yr	VG	VG+	NM
❑ UMV-2029	Now's the Time	198?	2.50	5.00	10.00
❑ UMV-2030	Swedish Schnapps	198?	2.50	5.00	10.00
❑ VE-2-2501 [(2)]	The Verve Years 1948-50	197?	3.75	7.50	15.00
❑ VE-2-2508 [(2)]	Charlie Parker Sides	197?	3.75	7.50	15.00
❑ VE-2-2512 [(2)]	The Verve Years 1950-51	197?	3.75	7.50	15.00
❑ VE-2-2523 [(2)]	The Verve Years 1952-54	197?	3.75	7.50	15.00
❑ UMV-2562	Charlie Parker with Strings	198?	2.50	5.00	10.00
❑ UMV-2617	Jazz Perennial	198?	2.50	5.00	10.00
❑ 50-5263 [M]	April in Paris (The Genius of Charlie Parker #2)	197?	3.75	7.50	15.00
—Book-of-the-Month Club edition of 8004					
❑ MGV-8000 [M]	The Charlie Parker Story, Volume 1	1957	20.00	40.00	80.00
❑ V-8000 [M]	The Charlie Parker Story, Volume 1	1961	6.25	12.50	25.00
❑ V6-8000 [R]	The Charlie Parker Story, Volume 1	196?	3.00	6.00	12.00
❑ MGV-8001 [M]	The Charlie Parker Story, Volume 2	1957	20.00	40.00	80.00
❑ V-8001 [M]	The Charlie Parker Story, Volume 2	1961	6.25	12.50	25.00
❑ V6-8001 [R]	The Charlie Parker Story, Volume 2	196?	3.00	6.00	12.00
❑ MGV-8002 [M]	The Charlie Parker Story, Volume 3	1957	20.00	40.00	80.00
❑ V-8002 [M]	The Charlie Parker Story, Volume 3	1961	6.25	12.50	25.00
❑ V6-8002 [R]	The Charlie Parker Story, Volume 3	196?	3.00	6.00	12.00
❑ MGV-8003 [M]	Night and Day (The Genius of Charlie Parker #1)	1957	20.00	40.00	80.00
❑ V-8003 [M]	Night and Day (The Genius of Charlie Parker #1)	1961	6.25	12.50	25.00
❑ V6-8003 [R]	Night and Day (The Genius of Charlie Parker #1)	196?	3.00	6.00	12.00
❑ MGV-8004 [M]	April in Paris (The Genius of Charlie Parker #2)	1957	20.00	40.00	80.00
❑ V-8004 [M]	April in Paris (The Genius of Charlie Parker #2)	1961	6.25	12.50	25.00
❑ V6-8004 [R]	April in Paris (The Genius of Charlie Parker #2)	196?	3.00	6.00	12.00
❑ MGV-8005 [M]	Now's the Time (The Genius of Charlie Parker #3)	1957	20.00	40.00	80.00
❑ V-8005 [M]	Now's the Time (The Genius of Charlie Parker #3)	1961	6.25	12.50	25.00
❑ V6-8005 [R]	Now's the Time (The Genius of Charlie Parker #3)	196?	3.00	6.00	12.00
❑ MGV-8006 [M]	Bird and Diz (The Genius of Charlie Parker #4)	1957	20.00	40.00	80.00
❑ V-8006 [M]	Bird and Diz (The Genius of Charlie Parker #4)	1961	6.25	12.50	25.00
❑ V6-8006 [R]	Bird and Diz (The Genius of Charlie Parker #4)	196?	3.00	6.00	12.00
❑ MGV-8007 [M]	Charlie Parker Plays Cole Porter (The Genius of Charlie Parker #5)	1957	20.00	40.00	80.00
❑ V-8007 [M]	Charlie Parker Plays Cole Porter (The Genius of Charlie Parker #5)	1961	6.25	12.50	25.00
❑ V6-8007 [R]	Charlie Parker Plays Cole Porter (The Genius of Charlie Parker #5)	196?	3.00	6.00	12.00
❑ MGV-8008 [M]	Fiesta (The Genius of Charlie Parker #6)	1957	20.00	40.00	80.00
❑ V-8008 [M]	Fiesta (The Genius of Charlie Parker #6)	1961	6.25	12.50	25.00
❑ V6-8008 [R]	Fiesta (The Genius of Charlie Parker #6)	196?	3.00	6.00	12.00
❑ MGV-8009 [M]	Jazz Perennial (The Genius of Charlie Parker #7)	1957	20.00	40.00	80.00
❑ V-8009 [M]	Jazz Perennial (The Genius of Charlie Parker #7)	1961	6.25	12.50	25.00
❑ V6-8009 [R]	Jazz Perennial (The Genius of Charlie Parker #7)	196?	3.00	6.00	12.00
❑ MGV-8010 [M]	Swedish Schnapps (The Genius of Charlie Parker #8)	1957	20.00	40.00	80.00
❑ V-8010 [M]	Swedish Schnapps (The Genius of Charlie Parker #8)	1961	6.25	12.50	25.00
❑ V6-8010 [R]	Swedish Schnapps (The Genius of Charlie Parker #8)	196?	3.00	6.00	12.00
❑ MGV-8100-3 [(3)M]	The Charlie Parker Story	1957	37.50	75.00	150.00
—Combines 8000, 8001 and 8002 in a box set					
❑ V-8100-3 [(3)M]	The Charlie Parker Story	1961	15.00	30.00	60.00
—Combines 8000, 8001 and 8002 in a box set					
❑ V-8409 [M]	The Essential Charlie Parker	1961	6.25	12.50	25.00
❑ V6-8409 [R]	The Essential Charlie Parker	196?	3.00	6.00	12.00
❑ V6-8787 [R]	Bird Set	1969	3.75	7.50	15.00
❑ V3HB-8840 [(2)]	Return Engagement	197?	3.75	7.50	15.00
❑ 817442-1	Bird on Verve, Vol. 1: Charlie Parker with Strings	1985	2.50	5.00	10.00
❑ 817443-1	Bird on Verve, Vol. 2: Bird and Diz	1985	2.50	5.00	10.00
❑ 817444-1	Bird on Verve, Vol. 3: More Charlie Parker with Strings	1985	2.50	5.00	10.00
❑ 817445-1	Bird on Verve, Vol. 4: Afro-Cuban Jazz	1985	2.50	5.00	10.00
❑ 817446-1	Bird on Verve, Vol. 5: Charlie Parker	1985	2.50	5.00	10.00
❑ 817447-1	Bird on Verve, Vol. 6: South of the Border	1985	2.50	5.00	10.00
❑ 817448-1	Bird on Verve, Vol. 7: Big Band	1985	2.50	5.00	10.00
❑ 817449-1	Bird on Verve, Vol. 8: Charlie Parker in Hi-Fi	1985	2.50	5.00	10.00
❑ 823250-1	The Cole Porter Songbook	1986	2.50	5.00	10.00
❑ 833564-1	Charlie Parker Sides	198?	2.50	5.00	10.00
❑ 837176-1	Bird: The Original Recordings of Charlie Parker	1987	2.50	5.00	10.00
VOGUE					
❑ LAE-12002 [M]	Memorial Album	1955	37.50	75.00	150.00
WARNER BROS.					
❑ 6BS 3159 [(6)]	The Complete Dial Recordings	1977	20.00	40.00	80.00
—Limited edition of 4,000 box sets					
❑ 2WB 3198 [(2)]	The Very Best of Bird	1977	5.00	10.00	20.00
ZIM					
❑ 1001	Lullaby in Rhythm	197?	3.00	6.00	12.00
❑ 1003	At the Pershing Ballroom, Chicago, 1950	197?	3.00	6.00	12.00
❑ 1006	Apartment Jam	197?	3.00	6.00	12.00

PARKER, CHARLIE/STAN GETZ/WARDELL GRAY

Albums

DESIGN

Number	Title (A Side/B Side)	Yr	VG	VG+	NM
❑ DLP-183 [M]	Charlie Parker/Stan Getz/Wardell Gray	196?	3.75	7.50	15.00

PARKER, CHARLIE/DIZZY GILLESPIE

Albums

EMUS

Number	Title (A Side/B Side)	Yr	VG	VG+	NM
❑ ES-12027 [R]	Charlie Parker / Dizzy Gillespie	197?	3.00	6.00	12.00

PARKER, CHARLIE; DIZZY GILLESPIE; RED NORVO

Albums

DIAL

Number	Title (A Side/B Side)	Yr	VG	VG+	NM
❑ LP-903 [M]	Fabulous Jam Session	1951	150.00	300.00	600.00

PARKER, CHARLIE/DIZZY GILLESPIE/BUD POWELL/MAX ROACH

Albums

SAVOY

Number	Title (A Side/B Side)	Yr	VG	VG+	NM
❑ MG-9034 [10]	Bird, Diz, Bud, Max	1953	150.00	300.00	600.00

PARKER, CHARLIE/COLEMAN HAWKINS/GEORGIE AULD

Albums

JAM

Number	Title (A Side/B Side)	Yr	VG	VG+	NM
❑ 5006	Unearthed Masters, Vol. 1	198?	2.50	5.00	10.00

PARKER, JUNIOR

Also includes records as "Little Junior Parker." Also see JIMMY McGRIFF AND JUNIOR PARKER.

45s

Number	Title (A Side/B Side)	Yr	VG	VG+	NM
BLUE ROCK					
❑ 4064	I Got Money/Lover to Friend	1968	2.00	4.00	8.00
❑ 4067	Reconsider Baby/Lovin' Man on Your Hands	1968	2.00	4.00	8.00
❑ 4080	Ain't Gon' Be No Cuttin' Loose/I'm So Satisfied	1969	2.00	4.00	8.00
❑ 4088	Easy Lovin'/You Can't Keep a Good Woman Down	1969	2.00	4.00	8.00
CAPITOL					
❑ 2857	The Outside Man/Darling, Depend on Me	1970	—	3.00	6.00
❑ 2951	Lady Madonna/Tomorrow Never Knows	1970	2.50	5.00	10.00
❑ 2997	Drownin' on Dry Land/River's Invitation	1970	—	3.00	6.00
DUKE					
❑ 120	Dirty Friend Blues/Can't Understand	1954	15.00	30.00	60.00
❑ 127	Please Baby Please/Sittin', Drinkin' and Thinkin'	1954	15.00	30.00	60.00
❑ 137	Backtracking/I Wanna Ramble	1954	17.50	35.00	70.00
❑ 147	Driving Me/There Better Not Be No Feel	1956	12.50	25.00	50.00
❑ 157	Mother-in-Law Blues/That's My Baby	1956	12.50	25.00	50.00
❑ 164	Next Time You See Me/My Dolly Bee	1957	7.50	15.00	30.00
❑ 168	That's Alright/Pretty Baby	1957	7.50	15.00	30.00
❑ 177	Peaches/Pretty Little Doll	1957	7.50	15.00	30.00
❑ 184	Wondering/Sitting and Thinking	1958	6.25	12.50	25.00
❑ 193	Barefoot Rock/What Did I Do	1958	6.25	12.50	25.00
❑ 301	Sweet Home Chicago/Sometimes	1959	5.00	10.00	20.00
❑ 306	Five Long Years/I'm Holding On	1959	5.00	10.00	20.00
❑ 309	Stranded/Blue Letter	1959	5.00	10.00	20.00
❑ 315	Dangerous Woman/Belinda Marie	1960	3.75	7.50	15.00
❑ 317	The Next Time/You're On My Mind	1960	3.75	7.50	15.00
❑ 326	I'll Learn to Love Again/That's Just Alright	1960	3.75	7.50	15.00
❑ 330	Stand By Me/I'll Forget About You	1960	3.75	7.50	15.00
❑ 335	Driving Wheel/Seven Days	1961	6.25	12.50	25.00
❑ 341	In the Dark/How Long Can This Go On	1961	3.00	6.00	12.00
❑ 345	Annie Get Your Yo-Yo/Mary Jo	1961	3.00	6.00	12.00
❑ 351	I Feel Alright Again/Sweeter As the Days Go By	1962	3.00	6.00	12.00
❑ 357	Foxy Devil/Someone Somewhere	1962	3.00	6.00	12.00
❑ 362	It's a Pity/Last Night	1963	3.00	6.00	12.00
❑ 364	If You Don't Love Me/I Can't Forget About You	1963	3.00	6.00	12.00
❑ 367	The Tables Have Turned/Yonders Wall	1963	3.00	6.00	12.00
❑ 371	Strange Things Happening/I'm Gonna Stop	1964	3.00	6.00	12.00
❑ 376	Things I Used to Do/That's Why I'm Always Crying	1964	3.00	6.00	12.00
❑ 384	I'm in Love/Jivin' Woman	1964	3.00	6.00	12.00
❑ 389	Crying for My Baby/Guess You Don't Know (The Golden Rule)	1965	3.00	6.00	12.00
❑ 394	These Kind of Blues (Part 1)/These Kind of Blues (Part 2)	1966	3.00	6.00	12.00
❑ 398	Walking the Floor Over You/Goodbye Little Girl	1966	3.00	6.00	12.00
❑ 406	Get Away Blues/Why Do You Make Me Cry	1966	3.00	6.00	12.00
❑ 413	Man or Mouse/Wait for Another Day	1966	3.00	6.00	12.00
GROOVE MERCHANT					
❑ 1002	Way Back Home/(B-side unknown)	1971	3.00	6.00	12.00
❑ 1004	I Like Your Style/I Need Love So Bad	1972	2.50	5.00	10.00
❑ 1010	Love Ain't Nothin' But a Business Goin' On/Losing Battle	1972	2.50	5.00	10.00
MERCURY					
❑ 72620	Baby Please/Just Like a Fish	1966	2.50	5.00	10.00
❑ 72651	You Can Make It If You Care/Ooh Wee Baby, That's the Way You Make Me Feel	1967	2.50	5.00	10.00
❑ 72672	Country Girl/Sometimes I Wonder	1967	2.50	5.00	10.00
❑ 72699	I Can't Put My Finger On It/If I Had Your Love	1967	2.50	5.00	10.00
❑ 72733	Hurtin' Inside/What a Fool I Was	1967	2.50	5.00	10.00
❑ 72793	It Must Be Love/Your Love's All Over	1968	2.00	4.00	8.00
MINIT					
❑ 32080	Worried Life Blues/Let the Good Times Roll	1969	—	3.00	6.00
SUN					
❑ 187	Feelin' Good/Fussin' and Fightin' Blues	1953	100.00	200.00	400.00
—As "Little Junior's Blue Flames"					
❑ 192	Mystery Train/Love My Baby	1954	75.00	150.00	300.00
—As "Little Junior's Blue Flames"					
UNITED ARTISTS					
❑ 50855	Funny How Time Slips Away/No One Knows	1971	2.50	5.00	10.00

Albums

Number	Title (A Side/B Side)	Yr	VG	VG+	NM
ABC					
❑ AC-30010	The ABC Collection	1976	3.75	7.50	15.00
ABC DUKE					
❑ DLP-76	Driving Wheel	1974	3.75	7.50	15.00
❑ DLP-83	The Best of Junior Parker	1974	3.75	7.50	15.00
BLUE ROCK					
❑ SRB-64004	Honey-Drippin' Blues	1969	3.75	7.50	15.00
BLUESWAY					
❑ BLS-6066	Sometime Tomorrow	1973	3.75	7.50	15.00
CAPITOL					
❑ ST-564	Outside Man	1970	3.75	7.50	15.00
DUKE					
❑ DLP-76 [M]	Driving Wheel	196?	25.00	50.00	100.00
—With Wagon Wheel on front cover					
❑ DLP-76 [M]	Driving Wheel	1962	37.50	75.00	150.00
—With Cadillac on front cover					
❑ DLP-83 [M]	The Best of Junior Parker	1967	12.50	25.00	50.00
❑ DLPS-83 [P]	The Best of Junior Parker	1967	10.00	20.00	40.00
GROOVE MERCHANT					
❑ 513	Love Ain't Nothin'	1974	3.75	7.50	15.00
MCA					
❑ 27046	The Best of Junior Parker	1980	2.50	5.00	10.00
MERCURY					
❑ MG-21101 [M]	Like It Is	1967	7.50	15.00	30.00
❑ SR-61101 [S]	Like It Is	1967	6.25	12.50	25.00
MINIT					
❑ 24024	Blues Man	1969	6.25	12.50	25.00
UNITED ARTISTS					
❑ UAS-6823	I Tell Stories Sad and True	1971	3.75	7.50	15.00

P

Number	Title (A Side/B Side)	Yr	VG	VG+	NM

PARKER, JUNIOR, AND BOBBY BLAND Also see each artist's individual listings.
Albums
ABC DUKE
| ❏ DLP-72 | Blues Consolidated | 1974 | 3.75 | 7.50 | 15.00 |

DUKE
| ❏ DLP-72 [M] | Blues Consolidated | 1961 | 37.50 | 75.00 | 150.00 |

PARKER, ROBERT
45s
IMPERIAL
❏ 5842	Mash Potatoes All Night Long/				
	Twistin' Out of Space	1962	3.00	6.00	12.00
❏ 5889	You're Lookin' Good/Little Things Mean a Lot	1962	3.00	6.00	12.00
❏ 5916	Please Forgive Me/You Got It	1963	3.00	6.00	12.00

ISLAND
❏ 044	Give Me the Country Side of Life/				
	It's Hard But It's Fair	1975	—	2.00	4.00
❏ 074	A Little Bit Something/Better Luck in the Summer	1976	—	2.00	4.00

NOLA
❏ 721	Barefootin'/Let's Go Baby (Where the Action Is)	1966	5.00	10.00	20.00
❏ 724	Ring Around the Roses/She's Coming Home	1966	3.00	6.00	12.00
❏ 726	Happy Feet/The Scratch	1966	3.00	6.00	12.00
❏ 729	Tip Toe/Soul Kind of Loving	1966	3.00	6.00	12.00
❏ 730	A Letter To Santa/C.C. Rider	1966	3.00	6.00	12.00
❏ 733	Yak Yak Yak/Secret Agents	1967	3.00	6.00	12.00
❏ 735	Everybody's Hip-Hugging/Foxy Mama	1967	3.00	6.00	12.00
❏ 738	I Caught You in a Lie/Holdin' Out	1967	3.00	6.00	12.00
❏ 739	Barefootin' Boogaloo/Soul Sister	196?	3.75	7.50	15.00

RON
| ❏ 327 | All Nite Long (Part 1)/All Nite Long (Part 2) | 1959 | 3.75 | 7.50 | 15.00 |
| ❏ 331 | Walkin'/Across the Track | 1960 | 3.75 | 7.50 | 15.00 |

SILVER FOX
| ❏ 12 | You Shakin' Things Up/You See Me | 1969 | — | 3.00 | 6.00 |

Albums
NOLA
| ❏ LP-1001 [M] | Barefootin' | 1966 | 7.50 | 15.00 | 30.00 |

PARKER, BILLIE JEAN
Albums
RCA VICTOR
| ❏ LPM-3967 [M] | The Truth About Bonnie and Clyde | 1968 | 10.00 | 20.00 | 40.00 |
| ❏ LSP-3967 [S] | The Truth About Bonnie and Clyde | 1968 | 3.75 | 7.50 | 15.00 |

PARKS, GINO
45s
CRAZY HORSE
| ❏ 1303 | Nerves of Steel/Help Me Somebody | 1968 | 7.50 | 15.00 | 30.00 |

FORTUNE
| ❏ 528 | Last Night I Cried/Just Go | 1957 | 20.00 | 40.00 | 80.00 |

GOLDEN WORLD
| ❏ 32 | My Sophisticated Lady/Talkin' About My Baby | 1966 | 5.00 | 10.00 | 20.00 |

MIRACLE
| ❏ 3 | Don't Say Bye Bye/(B-side unknown) | 1960 | 200.00 | 400.00 | 800.00 |

TAMLA
| ❏ 54042 | That's No Lie/Same Thing | 1961 | 15.00 | 30.00 | 60.00 |
| ❏ 54066 | For This I Thank You/Fire | 1962 | 15.00 | 30.00 | 60.00 |

PARKS, MICHAEL
45s
MGM
❏ 14092	Tie Me to Your Apron Strings Again/Won't You				
	Ride in My Little Red Wagon	1969	—	2.50	5.00
❏ 14104	Long Lonesome Highway/Mountain High	1970	—	3.00	6.00
❏ 14154	Sally/Save a Little, Spend a Little	1970	—	2.50	5.00
❏ 14363	Won't You Ride in My Little Red Wagon/				
	Big "T" Water	1972	—	2.50	5.00

VERVE
| ❏ 10653 | Drownin' on Dry Land/River's Invitation | 1971 | — | 2.50 | 5.00 |

Albums
FIRST AMERICAN
| ❏ 7781 | You Don't Know Me | 1983 | 2.50 | 5.00 | 10.00 |

MGM
❏ SE-4646	Closing the Gap	1969	3.75	7.50	15.00
❏ SE-4662	Long Lonesome Highway	1970	3.75	7.50	15.00
❏ SE-4717	Blue	1970	3.75	7.50	15.00
❏ SE-4784	The Best of Michael Parks	1971	3.75	7.50	15.00

VERVE
| ❏ V6-5079 | Lost and Found | 1971 | 3.75 | 7.50 | 15.00 |

PARKS, RAY
45s
CAPITOL
| ❏ F3580 | You're Gonna Have to Bawl, That's All/ | | | | |
| | Just a-Hangin' Around | 1956 | 17.50 | 35.00 | 70.00 |

PARKS, VAN DYKE
45s
MGM
| ❏ 13441 | Do What You Wanta/Number Nine | 1966 | 3.00 | 6.00 | 12.00 |
| ❏ 13570 | Come to the Sunshine/Farther Along | 1966 | 3.00 | 6.00 | 12.00 |

WARNER BROS.
| ❏ 7026 | Donovan's Colors Part 1/Part 2 | 1967 | 3.00 | 6.00 | 12.00 |
—As "George Washington Brown"
❏ 7409	On the Rolling Sea When Jesus Speaks to Me/				
	The Eagle and Me	1970	2.50	5.00	10.00
❏ 7609	Occapella/Ode to Tobago	1972	—	3.00	6.00
❏ 7632	Riverboat/John Jones	1972	—	3.00	6.00

Albums
SUNDAZED
| ❏ LP- 5140 | Song Cycle | 2002 | 3.75 | 7.50 | 15.00 |
—Reissue on 180-gram vinyl
| ❏ LP-5141 | Discover America | 2002 | 3.75 | 7.50 | 15.00 |
—Reissue on 180-gram vinyl

WARNER BROS.
| ❏ WS 1727 | Song Cycle | 1968 | 3.75 | 7.50 | 15.00 |
—Green label with "W7" box logo

| ❏ WS 1727 | Song Cycle | 1968 | 6.25 | 12.50 | 25.00 |
—Gold label
| ❏ WS 1727 | Song Cycle | 1970 | 3.00 | 6.00 | 12.00 |
—Green label with "WB" shield logo
❏ BS 2589	Discover America	1972	3.00	6.00	12.00
❏ BS 2878	Clang of the Yankee Reaper	1975	3.00	6.00	12.00
❏ 23829	Jump!	1984	3.00	6.00	12.00
❏ 25968	Tokyo Rose	1989	3.00	6.00	12.00

PARLETTES, THE
45s
JUBILEE
| ❏ 5467 | Tonight I Met An Angel/ | | | | |
| | Because We're Very Young | 1964 | 3.00 | 6.00 | 12.00 |

PARLIAMENT Also see GEORGE CLINTON; FUNKADELIC; THE PARLIAMENTS.
12-Inch Singles
CASABLANCA
❏ NBD 20113	Flash Light (10:31)/(B-side blank)	1977	10.00	20.00	40.00
❏ NBD 20208	Theme from The Black Hole/Big Bang Theory//				
	(B-side blank)	1979	5.00	10.00	20.00
❏ 876585-1	Flash Light (10:31)/P-Funk (Wants to Get				
	Funked Up) (7:34)	198?	2.50	5.00	10.00
—"Timepieces" reissue

45s
CASABLANCA
❏ 0003	The Goose (Part 1)/The Goose (Part 2)	1974	—	3.00	6.00
❏ 0013	Up for the Down Stroke/Presence of a Brain	1974	—	3.00	6.00
❏ 0104	Up for the Down Stroke/Presence of a Brain	1974	—	2.50	5.00
❏ 803	Up for the Down Stroke/Presence of a Brain	1974	—	2.50	5.00
❏ 811	Testify/I Can Move You	1974	—	2.50	5.00
❏ 831	Chocolate City/Chocolate City (Part 2)	1975	—	2.50	5.00
❏ 843	Ride On/Big Footin'	1975	—	2.50	5.00
❏ 852	P. Funk (Wants to Get Funked Up)/Night of the				
	Tempasaurus Peoples	1976	—	2.50	5.00
❏ 856	Tear the Roof Off the Sucker (Give Up the Funk)/				
	P-Funk	1976	—	2.00	4.00
—Tan label
| ❏ 856 | Tear the Roof Off the Sucker (Give Up the Funk)/ | | | | |
| | P-Funk | 1976 | — | 2.50 | 5.00 |
—Blue label
❏ 864	Star Child (Mothership Connection)/				
	Supergroovealistic	1976	—	2.50	5.00
❏ 871	Do That Stuff/Handcuffs	1976	—	2.50	5.00
❏ 875	Dr. Funkenstein/Children of Production	1977	—	2.50	5.00
❏ 892	Fantasy Is Reality/The Landing (Of the				
	Mothership)	1977	—	2.50	5.00
❏ 900	Bop Gun (Endangered Species)/I've Been				
	Watchin' You	1977	—	2.50	5.00
❏ 909	Flash Light/Swing Down, Sweet Chariot	1978	—	2.50	5.00
❏ 921	Funkentelechy/Funkentelechy (Part 2)	1978	—	2.50	5.00
❏ 950	Aqua Boogie (A				
	Psychoalphadiscobetabioaquadoloop)/				
	(You're a Fish and I'm a) Water Sign	1978	—	2.50	5.00
❏ 950 [PS]	Aqua Boogie (A				
	Psychoalphadiscobetabioaquadoloop)/				
	(You're a Fish and I'm a) Water Sign	1978	2.50	5.00	10.00
❏ 976	Rumpofsteelskin/Liquid Sunshine	1979	—	2.50	5.00
❏ 2222	Party People/Party People (Part 2)	1979	—	2.50	5.00
❏ 2235	Theme from The Black Hole/(You're a Fish and				
	I'm a) Water Sign	1980	—	2.50	5.00
❏ 2250	The Big Bang Theory/The Big Bang Theory (Part 2)	1980	—	2.50	5.00
❏ 2317	Agony of DeFeet/The Freeze	1980	—	2.50	5.00
❏ 2330	Crush It/Body Language	1981	—	2.50	5.00

INVICTUS
❏ 9077	I Call My Baby Pussy Cat/Little Ole Country Boy	1970	2.50	5.00	10.00
❏ 9091	Red Hot Mama/Little Ole Country Boy	1971	2.50	5.00	10.00
❏ 9095	Breakdown/Little Ole Country Boy	1971	2.50	5.00	10.00
❏ 9123	Come In Out of the Rain/Little Ole Country Boy	1972	2.00	4.00	8.00

Albums
CASABLANCA
❏ NBLP 7002	Up for the Down Stroke	1974	10.00	20.00	40.00
❏ NBLP 7014	Chocolate City	1975	10.00	20.00	40.00
❏ NBLP 7022	Mothership Connection	1976	7.50	15.00	30.00
❏ NBLP 7034	The Clones of Dr. Funkenstein	1976	7.50	15.00	30.00
❏ NBLP 7053 [(2)]Parliament Live/P. Funk Earth Tour	1977	10.00	20.00	40.00
❏ NBLP 7084	Funkentelechy vs. the Placebo Syndrome	1977	7.50	15.00	30.00
❏ NBLP 7125	Motor-Booty Affair	1978	7.50	15.00	30.00
❏ NBPIX 7125 [PD]Motor-Booty Affair	1978	10.00	20.00	40.00
❏ NBLP 7195	Gloryhallastoopid (Or Pin the Tale on the Funky)	1979	7.50	15.00	30.00
❏ NBLP 7249	Trombipulation	1980	7.50	15.00	30.00
❏ NBLP 9003	Up for the Down Stroke	1974	12.50	25.00	50.00
—Original pressing, distributed by Warner Bros.
❏ 822637-1	Greatest Hits	1984	3.75	7.50	15.00
❏ 824501-1	Funkentelechy vs. the Placebo Syndrome	1985	3.75	7.50	15.00
❏ 824502-1	Mothership Connection	1985	3.75	7.50	15.00

INVICTUS
| ❏ ST-7302 | Osmium | 1970 | 25.00 | 50.00 | 100.00 |

PARLIAMENTS, THE All of the below are probably the same group, a Detroit-based R&B group led by GEORGE CLINTON that evolved into PARLIAMENT and FUNKADELIC.
45s
APT
| ❏ 25036 | Poor Willie/Party Boys | 1959 | 10.00 | 20.00 | 40.00 |

ATCO
| ❏ 6675 | A New Day Begins/I'll Wait | 1969 | 5.00 | 10.00 | 20.00 |

FLIPP
| ❏ 100/1 | Lonely Island/You Make Me Wanna Cry | 1960 | 7.50 | 15.00 | 30.00 |
—Yellow label
| ❏ 100/1 | Lonely Island/You Make Me Wanna Cry | 1960 | 10.00 | 20.00 | 40.00 |
—Red label

GOLDEN WORLD
| ❏ 46 | Heart Trouble/That Was My Girl | 1966 | 12.50 | 25.00 | 50.00 |

LEN
| ❏ 101 | Don't Need You Anymore/ | | | | |
| | Honey, Take Me Home with You | 1958 | 20.00 | 40.00 | 80.00 |

Number	Title (A Side/B Side)	Yr	VG	VG+	NM
REVILOT					
207	(I Wanna) Testify/I Can Feel the Ice Melting	1967	3.75	7.50	15.00
211	All Your Goodies Are Gone (The Loser's Seat)/Don't Be Sore at Me	1967	3.75	7.50	15.00
214	Little Man/The Goose (That Laid the Golden Egg)	1968	3.75	7.50	15.00
217	Look at What I Almost Missed/What You Been Growing	1968	3.75	7.50	15.00
223	Good Old Music/Time	1968	3.75	7.50	15.00
228	A New Day Begins/I'll Wait	1968	7.50	15.00	30.00
SYMBOL					
917	You're Cute/I'll Get You Yet	1962	6.25	12.50	25.00
U.S.A.					
719	My Only Love/To Be Alone	1961	5.00	10.00	20.00

PARRIS, FRED Not to be confused with FREDDIE PARIS. Also see THE CHAMPLAINS; THE CHEROKEES (5); THE FIVE SATINS; THE NEW YORKERS (1).

45s

Number	Title (A Side/B Side)	Yr	VG	VG+	NM
ATCO					
6439	Land of the Broken Hearts/Bring It Home to Daddy	1966	2.50	5.00	10.00
BIRTH					
101	Dark at the Top of My Heart/Benediction	196?	2.00	4.00	8.00
CHECKER					
1108	No Use in Crying/Walk a Little Faster	1965	2.50	5.00	10.00
GREEN SEA					
106	Blushing Bride/Giving My Love to You	1966	2.50	5.00	10.00
107	I'll Be Hangin' On/I Can Really Satisfy	1966	2.50	5.00	10.00
KLIK					
7905	The Voice/She's Gone (With the Wind)	1958	50.00	100.00	200.00
—With the Scarlets and Passionettes					
MAMA SADIE					
1001	In the Still of the Nite "67"/Heck No	1967	2.50	5.00	10.00

PARROTS, THE (1)

45s

Number	Title (A Side/B Side)	Yr	VG	VG+	NM
CHECKER					
772	Don't Leave Me/Weep, Weep, Weep	1953	125.00	250.00	500.00

PARROTS, THE (2)

45s

Number	Title (A Side/B Side)	Yr	VG	VG+	NM
MALA					
558	They All Got Carried Away/Hey, Put the Clock Back on the Wall	1967	3.00	6.00	12.00

PARSONS, BILL Also see BOBBY BARE.

45s

Number	Title (A Side/B Side)	Yr	VG	VG+	NM
FRATERNITY					
835	The All American Boy/Rubber Dolly	1959	10.00	20.00	40.00
—This record is actually by Bobby Bare miscredited					
838	Educated Rock and Roll/Carefree Wanderer	1959	7.50	15.00	30.00
STARDAY					
526	Hod Rod Volkswagen/Guitar Blues	1960	7.50	15.00	30.00
544	The Price We Pay for Livin'/A-Waitin'	1960	5.00	10.00	20.00

PARSONS, GRAM Also see THE BYRDS; THE FLYING BURRITO BROTHERS; THE INTERNATIONAL SUBMARINE BAND.

45s

Number	Title (A Side/B Side)	Yr	VG	VG+	NM
REPRISE					
1139	That's All It Took/She	1972	—	3.00	6.00
1192	Love Hurts/In My Hour of Darkness	1974	—	3.00	6.00
SIERRA					
104	Medley (Bony Moronie/40 Days/Almost Grown)//Conversations/Hot Burrito #1	1982	—	2.50	5.00
—Second song on side 2 by Gene Parsons					
104 [PS]	Gram Parsons and the Fallen Angels	1982	—	2.50	5.00
105	Love Hurts/The New Soft Shoe	1982	—	2.50	5.00
WARNER BROS.					
50013	Return of the Grievous Angel/Hearts on Fire	1982	—	2.50	5.00
Albums					
REPRISE					
MS 2123	G.P.	1973	3.75	7.50	15.00
MS 2171	Grievous Angel	1974	3.75	7.50	15.00
SIERRA					
SP-1963	Early Years, Volume 1 (1963-65)	198?	2.00	4.00	8.00
—Reissue of 8702					
GP-1973	Gram Parsons and the Fallen Angels Live '73	1982	2.50	5.00	10.00
8702	Early Years, Volume 1 (1963-65)	1979	2.50	5.00	10.00
SUNDAZED					
LP 5076	Another Side of This Life	2000	3.00	6.00	12.00

PARTON, DOLLY Also see KENNY ROGERS AND DOLLY PARTON; PORTER WAGONER AND DOLLY PARTON.

12-Inch Singles

Number	Title (A Side/B Side)	Yr	VG	VG+	NM
RCA					
JD-11425 [DJ]	Baby I'm Burning/I Wanna Fall in Love	1978	2.50	5.00	10.00
—Promo version on black vinyl					
PD-11425	Baby I'm Burnin'/I Wanna Fall in Love	1978	3.75	7.50	15.00
—Pink vinyl					
PW-13545 [DJ]	Potential New Boyfriend (Long Version)/(Instrumental)	1983	2.50	5.00	10.00
PW-13712 [DJ]	Save the Last Dance for Me (Long Version)/(Instrumetnal) (Short Version)	1983	2.00	4.00	8.00
45s					
COLUMBIA					
07665	The River Unbroken/More Than I Can Say	1988	—	—	3.00
07665 [PS]	The River Unbroken/More Than I Can Say	1988	—	—	3.00
07727	I Know You by Heart/Could I Have Your Autograph	1988	—	—	3.00
—With Smokey Robinson					
07727 [PS]	I Know You by Heart/Could I Have Your Autograph	1988	—	—	3.00
07995	Make Love Mine/Two Lovers	1988	—	—	3.00
68760	Why'd You Come In Here Lookin' Like That/Wait Til I Get You Home	1989	—	—	3.00
69040	Yellow Roses/Wait Til I Get You Home	1989	—	—	3.00

Number	Title (A Side/B Side)	Yr	VG	VG+	NM
73200	He's Alive/What Is It We Love	1990	—	—	3.00
73226	Time for Me to Fly/The Moon, the Stars, and Me	1990	—	—	3.00
73341	White Limozeen/The Moon, the Stars, and Me	1990	—	—	3.00
73498	Slow Healin' Heart/Take Me Back to the Country	1990	—	—	3.00
73711	Rockin' Years/What a Heartache	1991	—	—	3.00
—A-side with Ricky Van Shelton					
73826	Silver and Gold/Runaway Feelin'	1991	—	—	3.00
74011	Eagle When She Flies/Wildest Dreams	1991	—	—	3.00
74183	The Best Woman Wins/Country Road	1992	—	—	3.00
—A-side with Lorrie Morgan					
74876	Romeo/The High and the Mighty	1993	—	—	3.00
—A-side: "Dolly Parton and Friends"					
74954	More Where That Came From/I'll Make Your Bed	1993	—	—	3.00
77083	Full Circle/What Will Baby Be	1993	—	—	3.00
77294	Silver Threads and Golden Needles/Let Her Fly	1993	—	—	3.00
—Dolly Parton/Tammy Wynette/Loretta Lynn					
77723	To Daddy/PMS Blues	1994	—	—	3.00
78079	I Will Always Love You/Speakin' of the Devil	1995	—	—	3.00
—A-side: "With Special Guest Vince Gill"					
DECCA					
72061	Honky Tonk Songs/Paradise Road	1998	—	—	3.00
72080	The Salt in My Tears/Hungry Again	1998	—	—	3.00
GOLDBAND					
1086	Puppy Love/Girl Left Alone	1959	150.00	300.00	600.00
—Originals have a red label					
1086	Puppy Love/Girl Left Alone	198?	—	.3.00	6.00
—Reissue; has a white label with a photo of Dolly					
MERCURY					
71982	It's Sure Gonna Hurt/The Love You Gave	1962	75.00	150.00	300.00
MONUMENT					
869	I Wasted My Tears/What Do You Think About Lovin'	1965	3.75	7.50	15.00
897	Old Enough to Know Better (Too Young to Resist)/Happy, Happy Birthday Baby	1965	3.75	7.50	15.00
913	Busy Signal/I Took Him for Granted	1965	3.75	7.50	15.00
922	Control Yourself/Don't Drop Out	1966	3.75	7.50	15.00
948	Little Things/I'll Put It Off Until Tomorrow	1966	3.75	7.50	15.00
982	Dumb Blonde/The Giving and the Taking	1967	2.50	5.00	10.00
1007	Something Fishy/I've Lived My Life	1967	2.50	5.00	10.00
1032	Why, Why, Why/I Couldn't Wait Forever	1967	2.50	5.00	10.00
1047	I'm Not Worth the Tears/Ping Pong	1968	2.00	4.00	8.00
03408	Everything Is Beautiful (In Its Own Way)/Put It Off Until Tomorrow	1982	—	2.00	4.00
—A-side with Willie Nelson; B-side with Kris Kristofferson					
03781	What Do You Think About Lovin'/You're Gonna Love Yourself (In the Morning)	1983	—	2.00	4.00
—A-side: Dolly Parton and Brenda Lee; B-side: Willie Nelson and Brenda Lee					
RCA					
5001-7-R	Do I Ever Cross Your Mind/We Had It All	1986	—	—	3.00
PB-10935	Light of a Clear Blue Morning/There	1977	—	2.00	4.00
PB-11123	Here You Come Again/Me and Little Andy	1977	—	2.00	4.00
PB-11240	Two Doors Down/It's All Wrong, But It's All Right	1978	—	2.00	4.00
JB-11296 [DJ]	Heartbreaker (same on both sides)	1978	2.50	5.00	10.00
—Promo only on red vinyl					
PB-11296	Heartbreaker/Sure Thing	1978	—	2.00	4.00
JB-11420 [DJ]	Baby I'm Burning (same on both sides)	1978	2.50	5.00	10.00
—Promo only on red vinyl					
PB-11420	Baby I'm Burnin'/I Really Got the Feeling	1978	—	2.00	4.00
GB-11505	Here You Come Again/Two Doors Down	1979	—	—	3.00
—Gold Standard Series					
PB-11577	You're the Only One/Down	1979	—	2.00	4.00
JB-11705 [DJ]	Great Balls of Fire (same on both sides)	1979	2.50	5.00	10.00
—Promo only on red vinyl					
PB-11705	Sweet Summer Lovin'/Great Balls of Fire	1979	—	2.00	4.00
JH-11926 [DJ]	Starting Over Again (same on both sides)	1980	3.00	6.00	12.00
—Promo only on green vinyl					
PB-11926	Starting Over Again/Sweet Agony	1980	—	2.00	4.00
GB-11993	Baby I'm Burnin'/Heartbreaker	1980	—	—	3.00
—Gold Standard Series					
PB-12040	Old Flames Can't Hold a Candle to You/I Knew You When	1980	—	2.00	4.00
JH-12133 [DJ]	9 to 5 (same on both sides)	1980	3.75	7.50	15.00
—Promo only on blue vinyl					
PB-12133	9 to 5/Sing for the Common Man	1980	—	2.00	4.00
PB-12133 [PS]	9 to 5/Sing for the Common Man	1980	—	2.50	5.00
PB-12200	But You Know I Love You/Poor Folks' Town	1981	—	2.00	4.00
PB-12282	The House of the Rising Sun/Working Girl	1981	—	2.00	4.00
GB-12316	9 to 5/Old Flames Can't Hold a Candle to You	1981	—	—	3.00
—Gold Standard Series					
JK-13057 [DJ]	Single Women (same on both sides)	1982	3.00	6.00	12.00
—Promo only on red vinyl					
PB-13057	Single Women/Barbara on Your Mind	1982	—	2.00	4.00
PB-13234	Heartbreak Express/Act Like a Fool	1982	—	2.00	4.00
PB-13260	I Will Always Love You/Do I Ever Cross Your Mind	1982	—	2.00	4.00
—A-side is the same song, but a different recording than that on APBO-0234					
PB-13260 [PS]	I Will Always Love You/Do I Ever Cross Your Mind	1982	—	2.50	5.00
JK-13361 [DJ]	Hard Candy Christmas (same on both sides)	1982	3.00	6.00	12.00
—Promo only on red vinyl					
PB-13361	Hard Candy Christmas/Me and Little Andy	1982	—	2.00	4.00
JK-13514 [DJ]	Potential New Boyfriend (Short) (same on both sides)	1983	3.00	6.00	12.00
—Promo only on yellow vinyl					
JK-13514 [DJ]	Potential New Boyfriend (same on both sides)	1983	3.00	6.00	12.00
—Promo only on blue vinyl					
PB-13514	Potential New Boyfriend/One of Those Days	1983	—	—	3.00
PB-13619	Tennessee Homesick Blues/Butterflies	1984	—	—	3.00
JK-13703 [DJ]	Save the Last Dance for Me (same on both sides)	1983	2.50	5.00	10.00
—Promo only on green vinyl					
PB-13703	Save the Last Dance for Me/Elusive Butterfly	1983	—	—	3.00
PB-13756	The Great Pretender/Downtown	1984	—	—	3.00
PB-13756 [PS]	The Great Pretender/Downtown	1984	—	—	3.00
PB-13856	Sweet Lovin' Friends/Too Much Water	1984	—	—	3.00
—Unreleased					
PB-13883	Sweet Lovin' Friends/God Won't Get You	1984	—	—	3.00
—With Sylvester Stallone					

Number	Title (A Side/B Side)	Yr	VG	VG+	NM
❏ JK-13944 [DJ]	Medley: Winter Wonderland/				
	Sleigh Ride (same on both sides)	1984	—	2.00	4.00
❏ PB-13944	Medley: Winter Wonderland-Sleigh Ride/The				
	Christmas Song	1984	—	—	3.00
—B-side by Kenny Rogers					
❏ PB-13987	Don't Call It Love/We Got Too Much	1985	—	—	3.00
❏ GB-14070	Tennessee Homesick Blues/Hard Candy				
	Christmas	1985	—	—	3.00
—Gold Standard Series					
❏ PB-14218	Think About Love/Come Back to Me	1985	—	—	3.00
❏ PB-14297	Tie Our Love (In a Double Knot)/				
	I Hope You're Never Happy	1986	—	—	3.00
❏ GB-14346	Don't Call It Love/Real Love	1986	—	—	3.00
—Gold Standard Series					
RCA VICTOR					
❏ 47-9548	Just Because I'm a Woman/I Wish I Felt This				
	Way at Home	1968	2.00	4.00	8.00
❏ 47-9657	In the Good Old Days (When Times Were Bad)/				
	Try Being Lonely	1968	2.00	4.00	8.00
❏ 47-9784	Daddy Come and Get Me/Chas	1969	—	3.00	6.00
❏ 47-9863	Mule Skinner Blues/More Than Their Share	1970	—	3.00	6.00
❏ 47-9928	Joshua/I'm Doing This for Your Sake	1970	—	3.00	6.00
❏ 47-9971	Comin' For to Carry Me Home/				
	Golden Streets of Glory	1971	2.50	5.00	10.00
❏ 47-9999	My Blue Tears/The Mystery of the Mystery	1971	—	3.00	6.00
❏ 74-0132	Daddy/He's a Go-Getter	1969	—	3.00	6.00
❏ 74-0192	In the Ghetto/Bridge	1969	—	3.00	6.00
❏ 74-0243	My Blue Ridge Mountain Boy/				
	'Til Death Do Us Part	1969	—	3.00	6.00
❏ 74-0538	Coat of Many Colors/Here I Am	1971	—	3.00	6.00
❏ 74-0538 [PS]	Coat of Many Colors/Here I Am	1971	2.50	5.00	10.00
❏ 74-0662	Touch Your Woman/Mission Chapel Memories	1972	—	2.50	5.00
❏ 74-0757	Washday Blues/Just As Good As Gone	1972	2.50	5.00	10.00
❏ 74-0797	Lord, Hold My Hand/When I Sing for Him	1972	—	2.50	5.00
❏ 74-0868	My Tennessee Mountain Home/				
	Better Part of Life	1973	—	2.50	5.00
❏ 74-0950	Traveling Man/I Remember	1973	—	2.50	5.00
❏ APBO-0145	Jolene/Love, You're So Beautiful Tonight	1973	—	2.50	5.00
❏ APBO-0234	I Will Always Love You/Lonely Comin' Down	1974	—	2.50	5.00
❏ PB-10031	Love Is Like a Butterfly/Sacred Memories	1974	—	2.00	4.00
❏ PB-10164	The Bargain Store/I'll Never Forget	1975	—	2.00	4.00
❏ GB-10165	Jolene/My Tennessee Mountain Home	1975	—	—	3.00
—Gold Standard Series					
❏ PB-10310	The Seeker/Love with Feeling	1975	2.00	4.00	8.00
❏ PB-10396	We Used To/My Heart Started Breaking	1975	—	2.00	4.00
❏ GB-10504	Love Is Like a Butterfly/Sacred Memories	1975	—	—	3.00
—Gold Standard Series					
❏ GB-10505	I Will Always Love You/Lovely Comin' Down	1975	—	—	3.00
—Gold Standard Series					
❏ PB-10564	Hey, Lucky Lady/Most of All, Why	1976	—	2.00	4.00
❏ GB-10676	The Bargain Store/The Seeker	1976	—	—	3.00
—Gold Standard Series					
❏ PB-10730	All I Can Do/Falling Out of Love with Me	1976	—	2.00	4.00
RISING TIDE					
❏ 56041	Just When I Needed You Most/				
	For the Good Times	1996	—	—	3.00
Albums					
COLUMBIA					
❏ FC 40968	Rainbow	1987	2.50	5.00	10.00
❏ FC 44384	White Limozeen	1989	3.00	6.00	12.00
❏ C 46882	Eagle When She Flies	1991	5.00	10.00	20.00
—Available on vinyl only through Columbia House					
MONUMENT					
❏ 7623	In the Beginning	197?	3.00	6.00	12.00
❏ MLP-8085 [M]	Hello, I'm Dolly	1967	7.50	15.00	30.00
❏ SLP-18085 [S]	Hello, I'm Dolly	1967	10.00	20.00	40.00
❏ SLP-18136	As Long As I Love	1970	5.00	10.00	20.00
❏ KZG 31913 [(2)]	The World of Dolly	1972	5.00	10.00	20.00
❏ KZG 33876 [(2)]	Hello, I'm Dolly	1975	5.00	10.00	20.00
PAIR					
❏ PDL2-1009 [(2)]	Just the Way I Am	1986	3.00	6.00	12.00
❏ PDL2-1116 [(2)]	Portrait	1986	3.00	6.00	12.00
RCA					
❏ 5706-1-R	The Best of Dolly Parton, Vol. 3	1987	2.50	5.00	10.00
❏ 6497-1-R	The Best There Is	1987	2.50	5.00	10.00
RCA CAMDEN					
❏ ACL1-0307	Mine	1973	2.50	5.00	10.00
❏ CAS-2583	Just the Way I Am	1972	2.50	5.00	10.00
RCA VICTOR					
❏ APL1-0033	My Tennessee Mountain Home	1973	3.00	6.00	12.00
❏ APD1-0286 [Q]	Bubbling Over	1974	5.00	10.00	20.00
❏ APL1-0286	Bubbling Over	1973	3.00	6.00	12.00
❏ APL1-0473	Jolene	1974	3.00	6.00	12.00
❏ APL1-0712	Love Is Like a Butterfly	1974	3.00	6.00	12.00
❏ APL1-0950	The Bargain Store	1975	3.00	6.00	12.00
❏ APL1-1117	The Best of Dolly Parton	1975	3.00	6.00	12.00
❏ APL1-1221	Dolly	1975	3.00	6.00	12.00
❏ APL1-1665	All I Can Do	1976	3.00	6.00	12.00
❏ APL1-2188	New Harvest...First Gathering	1977	3.00	6.00	12.00
❏ DJL1-2314 [DJ]	Personal Music Dialogue with Dolly Parton	1976	6.25	12.50	25.00
❏ AFL1-2544	Here You Come Again	1977	3.00	6.00	12.00
❏ AFL1-2797	Heartbreaker	1978	3.00	6.00	12.00
❏ AHL1-3361	Great Balls of Fire	1979	3.00	6.00	12.00
❏ AHL1-3546	Dolly Dolly Dolly	1980	3.00	6.00	12.00
❏ AYL1-3665	Heartbreaker	1980	2.00	4.00	8.00
—"Best Buy Series" reissue					
❏ AYL1-3764	My Tennessee Mountain Home	1980	2.00	4.00	8.00
—"Best Buy Series" reissue					
❏ AHL1-3852	9 to 5 and Odd Jobs	1980	3.00	6.00	12.00
❏ AYL1-3898	Jolene	1981	2.00	4.00	8.00
—"Best Buy Series" reissue					
❏ LPM-3949 [M]	Just Because I'm a Woman	1968	25.00	50.00	100.00
❏ LSP-3949 [S]	Just Because I'm a Woman	1968	5.00	10.00	20.00
—Orange label					
❏ LSP-3949 [S]	Just Because I'm a Woman	1968	7.50	15.00	30.00
—"Stereo" on black label					

Number	Title (A Side/B Side)	Yr	VG	VG+	NM
❏ AYL1-3980	New Harvest	1981	2.00	4.00	8.00
—"Best Buy Series" reissue					
❏ LSP-4099	In the Good Old Days	1969	5.00	10.00	20.00
❏ LSP-4188	My Blue Ridge Mountain Boy	1969	5.00	10.00	20.00
❏ LSP-4288	The Fairest of Them All	1970	5.00	10.00	20.00
❏ AHL1-4289	Heartbreak Express	1982	3.00	6.00	12.00
❏ LSP-4387	A Real Live Dolly	1970	6.25	12.50	25.00
—Four songs feature Porter Wagoner					
❏ LSP-4398	Golden Streets of Glory	1971	5.00	10.00	20.00
❏ AHL1-4422	Greatest Hits	1982	3.00	6.00	12.00
❏ LSP-4449	The Best of Dolly Parton	1970	5.00	10.00	20.00
❏ LSP-4507	Joshua	1971	5.00	10.00	20.00
❏ LSP-4603	Coat of Many Colors	1971	5.00	10.00	20.00
❏ LSP-4686	Touch Your Woman	1972	5.00	10.00	20.00
❏ AHL1-4691	Burlap & Satin	1983	2.50	5.00	10.00
❏ LSP-4752	My Favorite Song Writer: Porter Wagoner	1972	5.00	10.00	20.00
❏ LSP-4762	Dolly Parton Sings	1972	3.75	7.50	15.00
❏ AYL1-4829	Here You Come Again	1984	2.00	4.00	8.00
—"Best Buy Series" reissue					
❏ AYL1-4830	9 to 5 and Odd Jobs	1984	2.00	4.00	8.00
—"Best Buy Series" reissue					
❏ AHL1-4940	The Great Pretender	1984	2.50	5.00	10.00
❏ AYL1-5146	The Best of Dolly Parton	1984	2.00	4.00	8.00
—"Best Buy Series" reissue					
❏ AHL1-5414	Real Love	1985	2.50	5.00	10.00
❏ AYL1-5437	Burlap & Satin	1985	2.00	4.00	8.00
—"Best Buy Series" reissue					
❏ AHL1-5471	Collector's Series	1985	2.50	5.00	10.00
❏ AHL1-9508	Think About Love	1986	2.50	5.00	10.00
TIME-LIFE					
❏ STW-107	Country Music	1981	2.50	5.00	10.00

PARTON, DOLLY/GEORGE JONES
Albums
STARDAY

Number	Title (A Side/B Side)	Yr	VG	VG+	NM
❏ LP 429 [P]	Dolly Parton and George Jones	1968	10.00	20.00	40.00
—One side of Dolly in stereo, one side of "Possum" in rechanneled stereo					

PARTON, DOLLY/FAYE TUCKER
Albums
SOMERSET

Number	Title (A Side/B Side)	Yr	VG	VG+	NM
❏ S-9700 [M]	Hits Made Famous by Country Queens	1963	6.25	12.50	25.00
❏ SF-19700 [S]	Hits Made Famous by Country Queens	1963	7.50	15.00	30.00
—Dolly Parton sings songs made famous by Kitty Wells					
❏ SF-29400	Dolly Parton Sings Country Oldies	1968	3.75	7.50	15.00
TIME					
❏ 2108	Country & Western Soul	1963	10.00	20.00	40.00

PARTRIDGE FAMILY, THE Also see DANNY BONADUCE; DAVID CASSIDY.
45s
BELL

Number	Title (A Side/B Side)	Yr	VG	VG+	NM
❏ 910	I Think I Love You/Somebody Wants to Love You	1970	—	2.50	5.00
❏ 910 [PS]	I Think I Love You/Somebody Wants to Love You	1970	—	3.00	6.00
❏ 963	Doesn't Somebody Want to Be Wanted/You Are				
	Always on My Mind	1971	—	2.50	5.00
❏ 963 [PS]	Doesn't Somebody Want to Be Wanted/				
	You Are Always on My Mind	1971	—	3.00	6.00
❏ 996	I'll Meet You Halfway/Morning Rider on the Road	1971	—	2.50	5.00
❏ 45130	I Woke Up in Love This Morning/				
	Twenty-Four Hours a Day	1971	—	2.50	5.00
❏ 45160	It's One of Those Nights (Yes Love)/				
	One Night Stand	1971	—	2.50	5.00
❏ 45200	Am I Losing You/If You Ever Go	1972	—	2.00	4.00
❏ 45235	Breaking Up Is Hard to Do/I'm Here, You're Here	1972	—	2.00	4.00
❏ 45301	Looking Through the Eyes of Love/				
	Storybook Love	1972	—	2.00	4.00
❏ 45336	Friend and a Lover/Something's Wrong	1973	—	2.00	4.00
❏ 45414	Lookin' for a Good Time/Money Money	1973	10.00	20.00	40.00
—Extremely rare as a stock copy					
❏ 45414 [PS]	Lookin' for a Good Time/Money Money	1973	10.00	20.00	40.00
Albums					
BELL					
❏ 1107	The Partridge Family				
	At Home with Their Greatest Hits	1972	5.00	10.00	20.00
❏ 1111	The Partridge Family Notebook	1972	6.25	12.50	25.00
❏ 1122	Crossword Puzzle	1973	7.50	15.00	30.00
❏ 1137	Bulletin Board	1973	12.50	25.00	50.00
❏ 1319 [(2)]	The World of the Partridge Family	1974	10.00	20.00	40.00
❏ 6050	The Partridge Family Album Bonus Photo	1970	2.50	5.00	10.00
❏ 6050	The Partridge Family Album	1970	5.00	10.00	20.00
❏ 6059	Up to Date Book Cover	1971	2.50	5.00	10.00
❏ 6059	Up to Date	1971	5.00	10.00	20.00
❏ 6064	The Partridge Family Sound Magazine	1971	5.00	10.00	20.00
❏ 6066	A Partridge Family Christmas Card	1971	3.75	7.50	15.00
—Without Christmas card					
❏ 6066	A Partridge Family Christmas Card	1971	6.25	12.50	25.00
—With attached Christmas card					
❏ 6066	A Partridge Family Christmas Card	1971	10.00	20.00	40.00
—With Christmas card printed on the cover (later pressing)					
❏ 6072	The Partridge Family Shopping Bag Bonus				
	Shopping Bag	1972	2.50	5.00	10.00
❏ 6072	The Partridge Family Shopping Bag	1972	5.00	10.00	20.00
LAURIE HOUSE					
❏ H-8014 [(2)]	The Partridge Family	197?	12.50	25.00	50.00

PASSIONS, THE (1)
45s
ABC-PARAMOUNT

Number	Title (A Side/B Side)	Yr	VG	VG+	NM
❏ 10436	The Bully/The Empty Seat	1963	6.25	12.50	25.00
AUDICON					
❏ 102	Just to Be with You/Oh Melancholy Me	1959	10.00	20.00	40.00
❏ 105	I Only Want You/This Is My Love	1960	5.00	10.00	20.00
—Red, black and white label					
❏ 105	I Only Want You/This Is My Love	1960	7.50	15.00	30.00
—Red label					
❏ 106	Gloria/Jungle Drums	1960	7.50	15.00	30.00
❏ 108	Beautiful Dreamer/One Look Is All It Took	1960	7.50	15.00	30.00

Number	Title (A Side/B Side)	Yr	VG	VG+	NM
❏ 112	Made for Lovers/You Don't Have Me Anymore	1961	10.00	20.00	40.00
DIAMOND					
❏ 146	Sixteen Candles/The Third Floor	1963	10.00	20.00	40.00
JUBILEE					
❏ 5406	Lonely Road/One Look Is All It Took	1961	5.00	10.00	20.00
OCTAVIA					
❏ 8005	Aphrodite/I've Gotta Know	1962	200.00	400.00	800.00

PASSIONS, THE (2)
45s
BACK BEAT

Number	Title (A Side/B Side)	Yr	VG	VG+	NM
❏ 573	Baby I Do/Man About Town	1966	2.50	5.00	10.00
TOWER					
❏ 424	Without a Warning/Just Like a Rolling Seal	1968	2.00	4.00	8.00
❏ 443	I Can See My Way Through/Just Another Reason	1968	2.00	4.00	8.00
❏ 443	I Can See My Way Through/Without a Warning	1968	2.00	4.00	8.00
❏ 474	Just Like a Rolling Stone/Just Another	1969	2.00	4.00	8.00
❏ 485	Hijacked/Hijacked	1969	2.00	4.00	8.00

PASSIONS, THE (3)
45s
CAPITOL

Number	Title (A Side/B Side)	Yr	VG	VG+	NM
❏ F3963	Jackie Brown/My Aching Heart	1958	7.50	15.00	30.00
ERA					
❏ 1063	Jackie Brown/My Aching Heart	1957	10.00	20.00	40.00

PASSIONS, THE (U) Could be group (1) or (3), or a completely different group.
45s
DORE

Number	Title (A Side/B Side)	Yr	VG	VG+	NM
❏ 505	Nervous About Sally/Tango of Love	1958	7.50	15.00	30.00
GSF					
❏ 6880	One Night Affair/A Toast (May There Be No Last Time)	1972	7.50	15.00	30.00
TOPAZ					
❏ 1317	It Ain't Fair/I'm So Afraid	196?	2.50	5.00	10.00

PASSPORT
12-Inch Singles
ATLANTIC

Number	Title (A Side/B Side)	Yr	VG	VG+	NM
❏ DMD 843 [DJ]	Running in Real Time (Extended Mix 7:24) (Dub Mix 6:33) (7 Inch Edit 3:19)	1986	2.00	4.00	8.00

45s
ATCO

Number	Title (A Side/B Side)	Yr	VG	VG+	NM
❏ 7054	Ju-Ju Man/(B-side unknown)	1976	—	2.00	4.00
ATLANTIC					
❏ 3487	Loco-Motive/Mandrake	1978	—	2.50	5.00
❏ 3659	Departure/(B-side unknown)	1979	—	2.50	5.00
❏ 3857	Rambling/Riding on a Cloud	1981	—	2.50	5.00
❏ 89558	Running in Real Time/(B-side unknown)	1986	—	2.50	5.00
❏ 89697	Man in the Mirror/(B-side unknown)	1983	—	2.50	5.00
❏ 89925	New Moon/(B-side unknown)	1982	—	2.50	5.00

Albums
ATCO

Number	Title (A Side/B Side)	Yr	VG	VG+	NM
❏ SD 36-107	Cross-Collateral	1975	3.00	6.00	12.00
❏ SD 36-132	Infinity Machine	1976	3.00	6.00	12.00
❏ SD 36-149	Iguacu	1977	3.00	6.00	12.00
❏ SD 7042	Looking Through	1974	3.75	7.50	15.00
ATLANTIC					
❏ SD 18162	Doldinger Jubilee '75	1976	3.00	6.00	12.00
❏ SD 19177	Sky Blue	1978	2.50	5.00	10.00
❏ SD 19233	Garden of Eden	1979	2.50	5.00	10.00
❏ SD 19265	Oceanliner	1980	2.50	5.00	10.00
❏ SD 19304	Blue Tattoo	1981	2.50	5.00	10.00
❏ 80034	Earthborn	1982	2.50	5.00	10.00
❏ 80144	Man in the Mirror	1983	2.50	5.00	10.00
❏ 81251	Running in Real Time	1985	2.50	5.00	10.00
❏ 81727	Heavy Nights	1986	2.50	5.00	10.00
❏ 81937	Talk Back	1989	2.50	5.00	10.00

PASTEL SIX, THE
45s
CHATTAHOOCHIE

Number	Title (A Side/B Side)	Yr	VG	VG+	NM
❏ 696	I Can't Dance/Red River Quetzal	1966	2.50	5.00	10.00
DOWNEY					
❏ 101	Twitchin'/Open House at the Cinder	1962	7.50	15.00	30.00
❏ 101	Twitchin'/Wino Stomp	1962	7.50	15.00	30.00
❏ 102	Braum's Nightmare/Open House at the Cinder	1962	6.25	12.50	25.00
ZEN					
❏ 102	The Cinnamon Cinder (It's a Very Nice Dance)/Bandido	1962	6.25	12.50	25.00
❏ 105	Sing Along Song/The Strange Ghost	1963	6.25	12.50	25.00
❏ 108	The Milkshake/Parchman Farm	1963	6.25	12.50	25.00
❏ 111	Miss Sue/Baby Please Don't Go	1963	6.25	12.50	25.00

Albums
ZEN

Number	Title (A Side/B Side)	Yr	VG	VG+	NM
❏ 1001 [M]	The Cinnamon Cinder	1963	25.00	50.00	100.00

PASTELS, THE
45s
ARGO

Number	Title (A Side/B Side)	Yr	VG	VG+	NM
❏ 5287	Been So Long/My One and Only Dream	1958	6.25	12.50	25.00
❏ 5297	You Don't Love Me Anymore/Let's Go to the Rock 'N' Roll Ball	1958	7.50	15.00	30.00
❏ 5314	So Far Away/Don't Knock	1958	6.25	12.50	25.00
ARK					
❏ 298	Jungle Run/K-Nif	196?	12.50	25.00	50.00
JUBILEE					
❏ 5495	First Star/Tokyo Melody	1965	3.00	6.00	12.00
MASCOT					
❏ 123	Been So Long/My One and Only Dream	1957	75.00	150.00	300.00
UNITED					
❏ 196	Put Your Arms Around Me/Boom De De Boom	1957	20.00	40.00	80.00

PATCHETT, TOM, AND JAY TARSES
45s
DECCA

Number	Title (A Side/B Side)	Yr	VG	VG+	NM
❏ 32892	Howard Hardsell/Run to Daylight	1971	—	2.50	5.00
—B-side by H.B. Barnum					

Albums
DECCA

Number	Title (A Side/B Side)	Yr	VG	VG+	NM
❏ DL 75300	Instant Replay (Two Sides of Football)	1971	3.75	7.50	15.00

PATIENCE AND PRUDENCE
45s
CHATATHOOCHIE

Number	Title (A Side/B Side)	Yr	VG	VG+	NM
❏ 665	Tonight You Belong to Me (New Version)/How Can I Tell Him	1965	2.50	5.00	10.00
LIBERTY					
❏ 55022	Tonight You Belong to Me/A Smile and a Ribbon	1956	7.50	15.00	30.00
❏ 55040	Gonna Get Along Without Ya Now/The Money Tree	1956	6.25	12.50	25.00
—Blue-green label, silver print					
❏ 55040	Gonna Get Along Without Ya Now/The Money Tree	1956	10.00	20.00	40.00
—Maroon label, gold print					
❏ 55058	Dreamer's Bay/We Can't Sing Rhythm and Blues	1957	6.25	12.50	25.00
❏ 55084	You Tattletale/Very Nice in Bali Bali	1957	6.25	12.50	25.00
❏ 55084 [PS]	You Tattletale/Very Nice in Bali Bali	1957	12.50	25.00	50.00
❏ 55107	Witchcraft/Over Here	1957	6.25	12.50	25.00
❏ 55125	Heavenly Angel/Little Wheel	1958	6.25	12.50	25.00
❏ 55154	All I Do Is Dream of You/Your Careless Love	1958	6.25	12.50	25.00
❏ 55169	Golly Oh Gee/Tom Thumb's Tune	1958	6.25	12.50	25.00
❏ 55207	Should I/Whisper Whisper	1959	3.75	7.50	15.00
—With Mike Clifford					
UNITED ARTISTS					
❏ 0012	Tonight You Belong to Me/Gonna Get Along Without You Now	1973	—	2.50	5.00
—"Silver Spotlight Series" reissue					

PATRICK, MILT
45s
CAPITOL

Number	Title (A Side/B Side)	Yr	VG	VG+	NM
❏ 4634	Up to My Ears in Tears/When I Met You	1961	2.50	5.00	10.00
DEMON					
❏ 1518	A Fountain of Love/You Are My Inspiration	1959	3.00	6.00	12.00
EVEREST					
❏ 2014	I Don't Think I Wanna Do It/No Fool Like an Old Fool	1963	2.00	4.00	8.00
TERRI-ANN					
❏ 101	Merry Twistmas/Just A Doggone Dream	1962	2.50	5.00	10.00

PATRON SAINTS, THE
Albums
(NO LABEL)

Number	Title (A Side/B Side)	Yr	VG	VG+	NM
❏ JT-1001	Fohhob Bohob	1969	1000.	2000.	3000.
—100 copies were pressed					
PATRON SAINT					
❏ JT-1001	Fohhob Bohob	1997	6.25	12.50	25.00
—Authorized reissue with bonus 7-inch single; numbered edition of 500					

PATTERSON, MIKE, AND THE FUGITIVES
45s
IMPERIAL

Number	Title (A Side/B Side)	Yr	VG	VG+	NM
❏ 66083	Cookin' Beans/Jerky	1965	3.00	6.00	12.00
❏ 66118	Don't You Just Know It/Righteous Theme	1965	3.00	6.00	12.00

PATTO Also see SPOOKY TOOTH.
45s
ISLAND

Number	Title (A Side/B Side)	Yr	VG	VG+	NM
❏ 1208	Mummy/Singing the Blues on Reds	1972	—	3.00	6.00

Albums
ISLAND

Number	Title (A Side/B Side)	Yr	VG	VG+	NM
❏ SW-9322	Roll 'Em, Smoke 'Em, Put Another Line Out	1972	7.50	15.00	30.00
VERTIGO					
❏ VEL-1001	Patto	1971	3.75	7.50	15.00
❏ VEL-1008	Hold Your Fire	1972	3.75	7.50	15.00

PATTON, JIMMY
45s
SAGE AND SAND

Number	Title (A Side/B Side)	Yr	VG	VG+	NM
❏ 261	Call Me/Forty-Nine Women	1958	30.00	60.00	120.00
❏ 282	Ocean Full of Tears/Twinklin' Teardrops	1959	10.00	20.00	40.00
SIMS					
❏ 103	Careful/Guilty	1955	12.50	25.00	50.00
—With Ann Jones					
❏ 104	Teenage Haert/Jalopy	1955	12.50	25.00	50.00
❏ 105	Ocean of Tears/I Don't Want It	1955	12.50	25.00	50.00
❏ 117	Okie's in the Pokie/Lonely Nights	1960	50.00	100.00	200.00
❏ 227	Blue Darling/Preacher and a Girl in the Night	1965	3.00	6.00	12.00
❏ 256	Can't Shake the Blues/(B-side unknown)	1965	3.00	6.00	12.00

Albums
MOON

Number	Title (A Side/B Side)	Yr	VG	VG+	NM
❏ 101 [M]	Make Room for the Blues	1966	10.00	20.00	40.00
SIMS					
❏ 127 [M]	Blue Darlin'	1965	10.00	20.00	40.00
SOURDOUGH					
❏ 127 [M]	Blue Darlin'	1965	12.50	25.00	50.00
STEREOPHONIC					
❏ LP-1002 [S]	Take 30 Minutes with Jimmy Patton	196?	30.00	60.00	120.00

PATTY AND THE EMBLEMS
45s
CONGRESS

Number	Title (A Side/B Side)	Yr	VG	VG+	NM
❏ 263	Easy Come, Easy Go/It's the Little Things	1966	5.00	10.00	20.00
HERALD					
❏ 590	Mixed-Up, Shook-Up, Girl/Ordinary Guy	1964	5.00	10.00	20.00
❏ 593	The Sound of Music Makes Me Want to Dance/You Took Advantage of a Good Thing	1964	3.75	7.50	15.00

P

Number	Title (A Side/B Side)	Yr	VG	VG+	NM
❑ 595	And We Danced/You Can't Get Away from Me	1964	3.75	7.50	15.00
KAPP					
❑ 791	Let Him Go Little Heart/Try It, You Won't Forget It	1966	5.00	10.00	20.00
❑ 850	Please Don't Ever Leave Me/				
	All My Tomorrows Are Gone	1967	5.00	10.00	20.00
❑ 870	I'll Cry Later/One Man Woman	1967	5.00	10.00	20.00
❑ 897	I'm Gonna Love You a Long, Long Time/My				
	Heart's So Full of You	1968	3.75	7.50	15.00
LOST-NITE					
❑ 420	Mixed-Up, Shook-Up, Girl/Ordinary Guy	197?	—	2.50	5.00
—Reissue					

PATTY FLABBIE'S COUGHED ENGINE
45s
DIAMOND

Number	Title (A Side/B Side)	Yr	VG	VG+	NM
❑ 252	Billy Got a Goat/Tin Can Eater	1968	6.25	12.50	25.00

PAUL See RAY HILDEBRAND.

PAUL, BILLY
12-Inch Singles
PHILADELPHIA INT'L.

Number	Title (A Side/B Side)	Yr	VG	VG+	NM
❑ 3678	Bring the Family Back (5:53)/It's Critical (6:33)	1979	3.00	6.00	12.00
❑ 3706	False Faces (6:52)/(B-side unknown)	1979	3.00	6.00	12.00
45s					
GAMBLE					
❑ 232	Somewhere/Bluesette	1968	3.00	6.00	12.00
JUBILEE					
❑ 5081	That's Why I Dream/Why Am I	1952	7.50	15.00	30.00
❑ 5086	You Didn't Know/The Stars Are Mine	1952	7.50	15.00	30.00
NEPTUNE					
❑ 30	Mrs. Robinson/Let's Fall in Love All Over	1970	2.50	5.00	10.00
PHILADELPHIA INT'L.					
❑ 3120	Jesus Boy (You Only Look Like a Man)/				
	Love Buddies	1980	—	2.50	5.00
❑ 3509	Love Buddies/Magic Carpet Ride	1971	—	3.00	6.00
❑ 3515	This Is Your Life/I Wish It Were Yesterday	1972	—	3.00	6.00
❑ 3521	Me and Mrs. Jones/Your Song	1972	—	2.50	5.00
❑ 3526	Am I Black Enough for You/I'm Gonna Make It				
	This Time	1973	—	2.50	5.00
❑ 3538	Thanks for Saving My Life/I Was Married	1974	—	2.50	5.00
❑ 3551	Be Truthful to Me/I Wish It Was Yesterday	1974	—	2.50	5.00
❑ 3563	Billy's Back Home/I've Got So Much to Live For	1975	—	2.50	5.00
❑ 3572	When It's Your Turn to Go/July, July, July, July	1975	—	2.50	5.00
❑ 3584	Let's Make a Baby/My Head's On Straight	1976	—	2.50	5.00
❑ 3593	People Power/I Want Cha Baby	1976	—	2.50	5.00
❑ 3613	How Good Is Your Game/				
	I Think I'll Stay Home Today	1977	—	2.50	5.00
❑ 3621	Let 'Em In/We All Got a Mission	1977	—	2.50	5.00
❑ 3630	I Trust You/Love Won't Come Easy	1977	—	2.50	5.00
❑ 3635	Only the Strong Survive/Where I Belong	1977	—	2.50	5.00
❑ 3639	Everybody's Breakin' Up/Sooner or Later	1978	—	2.50	5.00
❑ 3645	One Man's Junk/Don't Give Up on Love	1978	—	2.50	5.00
❑ 3676	Bring the Family Back/It's Critical	1979	—	2.50	5.00
❑ 3699	False Faces/I Gotta Put This Life Down	1979	—	2.50	5.00
❑ 3736	You're My Sweetness/(B-side unknown)	1979	—	2.50	5.00
❑ ZS9 3737	Jesus Boy (You Only Look Like a Man)/				
	(B-side unknown)	1979	—	3.00	6.00
TOTAL EXPERIENCE					
❑ 2419	Lately/(Instrumental)	1985	—	2.50	5.00
❑ 2434	Sexual Therapy/Hot Date	1986	—	2.50	5.00
Albums					
GAMBLE					
❑ SG-5002	Feeling Good at the Cadillac Club	1968	7.50	15.00	30.00
ICHIBAN					
❑ ICH-1025	Wide Open	198?	2.50	5.00	10.00
NEPTUNE					
❑ 201	Ebony Woman	1970	5.00	10.00	20.00
PHILADELPHIA INT'L.					
❑ Z 30580	Going East	1971	3.00	6.00	12.00
❑ KZ 31793	360 Degrees of Billy Paul	1972	3.00	6.00	12.00
❑ ZQ 31793 [Q]	360 Degrees of Billy Paul	1972	5.00	10.00	20.00
❑ KZ 32118	Ebony Woman	1973	3.00	6.00	12.00
❑ KZ 32119	Feeling Good at the Cadillac Club	1973	3.00	6.00	12.00
—Reissue of Neptune LP					
❑ KZ 32119	Feeling Good at the Cadillac Club	1973	3.00	6.00	12.00
—Reissue of Gamble LP					
❑ KZ 32409	War of the Gods	1973	2.50	5.00	10.00
❑ ZQ 32409 [Q]	War of the Gods	1973	5.00	10.00	20.00
❑ KZ 32952	Live in Europe	1974	2.50	5.00	10.00
❑ ZQ 32952 [Q]	Live in Europe	1974	5.00	10.00	20.00
❑ PZ 33157	Got My Head On Straight	1975	2.50	5.00	10.00
❑ PZ 33843	When Love Is New	1975	2.50	5.00	10.00
❑ PZ 34389	Let 'Em In	1976	2.50	5.00	10.00
❑ PZ 34923	Only the Strong Survive	1977	2.50	5.00	10.00
❑ JZ 35756	First Class	1979	2.50	5.00	10.00
❑ Z2 36314 [(2)]	The Best of Billy Paul	1980	3.75	7.50	15.00
TOTAL EXPERIENCE					
❑ TEL8-5711	Lately	1985	2.50	5.00	10.00

PAUL, BUNNY
45s
BRUNSWICK

Number	Title (A Side/B Side)	Yr	VG	VG+	NM
❑ 55003	Poor Joe/Buzz Me	1957	3.75	7.50	15.00
❑ 55022	Breedle-Lump-Bump/The One You Love	1957	3.75	7.50	15.00
CAPITOL					
❑ F3074	Please Have Mercy/				
	These Are the Things We'll Share	1955	3.75	7.50	15.00
❑ F3109	Two Castanets/Leave My Heart Alone	1955	3.75	7.50	15.00
❑ F3178	Song of the Dreamer/For the Very First Time	1955	3.75	7.50	15.00
❑ F3224	Take a Chance/Tell the Man	1955	3.75	7.50	15.00
❑ F3288	Open the Door/Who Am I Foolin'	1955	3.75	7.50	15.00
DOT					
❑ 15107	Magic Guitar/Never Let Me Go	1953	6.25	12.50	25.00
ESSEX					
❑ 344	New Love/You'll Never Leave My Side	1954	25.00	50.00	100.00
❑ 352	Such a Night/I'm Gonna Have Some Fun	1954	15.00	30.00	60.00

Number	Title (A Side/B Side)	Yr	VG	VG+	NM
❑ 359	Lovey Dovey/Answer the Call	1954	15.00	30.00	60.00
❑ 364	Honey Love/I'll Never Tell	1954	25.00	50.00	100.00
❑ 371	You Are Always in My Heart/				
	You Came a Long Way from St. Louis	1954	15.00	30.00	60.00
❑ 385	Brown Jug/Pam-Poo-Dey	1955	15.00	30.00	60.00
GORDY					
❑ 7017	We're Only Young Once/I'm Hooked	1963	5.00	10.00	20.00
POINT					
❑ 5	Sweet Talk/History	1956	10.00	20.00	40.00
ROULETTE					
❑ 4186	Such a Night/A Million Miles from Nowhere	1959	3.75	7.50	15.00

PAUL, LES See note under LES PAUL AND MARY FORD.
45s
DECCA

Number	Title (A Side/B Side)	Yr	VG	VG+	NM
❑ 27903	Blue Skies/Dark Eyes	1951	3.75	7.50	15.00
❑ 29013	Steel Guitar Rag/Guitar Boogie	1954	3.75	7.50	15.00
LONDON					
❑ 120	Los Angeles/The System	1969	—	3.00	6.00
Albums					
CAPITOL					
❑ N-16286	Early Les Paul	1982	2.00	4.00	8.00
DECCA					
❑ DL-5018 [10]	Hawaiian Paradise	1949	25.00	50.00	100.00
❑ DL-5376 [10]	Galloping Guitars	1952	25.00	50.00	100.00
❑ DL 8589 [M]	More of Les	1957	10.00	20.00	40.00
GLENDALE					
❑ 6014	The Les Paul Trio	198?	2.50	5.00	10.00
LONDON					
❑ 50016	Multi-Trackin'	1979	3.00	6.00	12.00
LONDON PHASE 4					
❑ SP-44101	Les Paul Now!	1968	3.75	7.50	15.00
VOCALION					
❑ VL 3849 [M]	The Guitar Artistry of Les Paul	196?	3.00	6.00	12.00
❑ VL 73849 [R]	The Guitar Artistry of Les Paul	196?	2.50	5.00	10.00

PAUL, LES, AND MARY FORD Included in the Capitol listings are LES PAUL solo works.
Some of these appear on B-sides of duet hits.
45s
CAPITOL

Number	Title (A Side/B Side)	Yr	VG	VG+	NM
❑ PRO 233/4 [DJ]	Magic Melody/Magic Melody — Part II	1955	7.50	15.00	30.00
—Promo-only release; B-side's running time listed as "One Second"!					
❑ CCF-286 [PS]	The New Sound! Vol. II	1951	3.75	7.50	15.00
—Box for 3-record set (F15748, F15749, F15750)					
❑ F1014	Nola/Jealous	1950	5.00	10.00	20.00
❑ F1088	Dry My Tears/Cryin'	1950	5.00	10.00	20.00
❑ F1192	Goofus/Sugar Sweet	1950	5.00	10.00	20.00
❑ F1316	Tennessee Waltz/Little Rock Getaway	1950	5.00	10.00	20.00
❑ F1373	Mockin' Bird Hill/Chicken Reel	1951	5.00	10.00	20.00
❑ F1451	How High the Moon/Walkin' Whistlin' Blues	1951	6.25	12.50	25.00
❑ F1592	Josephine/I Wish I Had Never Seen Sunshine	1951	3.75	7.50	15.00
❑ F1600	Brazil/Lover	1951	3.00	6.00	12.00
—As "Les Paul"					
❑ F1621	Nola/Jealous	1951	3.00	6.00	12.00
—Reissue					
❑ F1675	How High the Moon/Josephine	195?	3.00	6.00	12.00
—Reissue					
❑ F1676	Tennessee Waltz/Mockin' Bird Hill	195?	3.00	6.00	12.00
—Reissue					
❑ F1690	Meet Mister Callaghan/My Baby's Comin' Home	195?	3.00	6.00	12.00
—Reissue					
❑ F1748	The World Is Waiting for the Sunrise/Whispering	1951	3.75	7.50	15.00
❑ F1825	Just One More Chance/Jazz Me Blues	1951	3.75	7.50	15.00
❑ F1881	Jingle Bells/Silent Night	1951	3.75	7.50	15.00
❑ F1920	Tiger Rag/It's a Lonesome Old Town	1951	3.75	7.50	15.00
❑ F2080	I'm Confessin' (That I Love You)/Carioca	1952	3.75	7.50	15.00
❑ F2123	Smoke Rings/In the Good Old Summertime	1952	3.75	7.50	15.00
❑ F2193	Meet Mister Callaghan/				
	Take Me in Your Arms and Hold Me	1952	3.75	7.50	15.00
❑ F2265	My Baby's Coming Home/Lady of Spain	1952	3.75	7.50	15.00
❑ F2316	Bye Bye Blues/Mammy's Boogie	1953	3.75	7.50	15.00
❑ F2400	I'm Sitting on Top of the World/Sleep	1953	3.75	7.50	15.00
❑ F2486	Vaya Con Dios (May God Be With You)/				
	Johnny (Is the Boy for Me)	1953	3.75	7.50	15.00
❑ F2614	Don'cha Hear Them Bells/The Kangaroo	1953	3.75	7.50	15.00
❑ F2617	Jungle Bells (Dingo-Dango-Day)/				
	White Chirstmas	1953	3.75	7.50	15.00
❑ F2735	I Really Don't Want to Know/South	1954	3.00	6.00	12.00
❑ F2839	I'm a Fool to Care/Auctioneer	1954	3.00	6.00	12.00
❑ F2928	Whither Thou Goest/Mandolino	1954	3.00	6.00	12.00
❑ F3015	Someday Sweetheart/Song in Blue	1955	3.00	6.00	12.00
❑ F3108	No Letter Today/Genuine Love	1955	3.00	6.00	12.00
❑ F3165	Hummingbird/Goodbye My Love	1955	3.00	6.00	12.00
❑ F3248	Amukiriki (The Lord Willing)/Magic Melody	1955	3.00	6.00	12.00
❑ F3301	Texas Lady/Alabamy Bound	1955	3.00	6.00	12.00
❑ F3302	Rudolph the Red-Nosed Reindeer/Santa Claus				
	Is Comin' to Town	1955	3.00	6.00	12.00
❑ F3329	Moritat (Theme from Threepenny Opera)/				
	Nuevo Laredo	1956	2.50	5.00	10.00
❑ F3389	Say the Words I Love to Hear/				
	Send Me Some Money	1956	2.50	5.00	10.00
❑ F3444	Cimarron/San Antonio Rose	1956	2.50	5.00	10.00
❑ F3570	Blow the Smoke Away/Running Wild	1956	2.50	5.00	10.00
❑ F3612	Cinco Robles (Five Oaks)/Ro-Ro-Robinson	1957	2.50	5.00	10.00
❑ F3725	Tuxedos and Flowers/Hummin' and Waltzin'	1957	2.50	5.00	10.00
❑ F3776	I Don't Want You No More/Strollin' Blues	1957	2.50	5.00	10.00
❑ F3825	A Pair of Fools/Fire	1957	2.50	5.00	10.00
❑ F3858	Goodnight My Someone/The Night of the Fourth	1957	2.50	5.00	10.00
❑ F3934	More and More Each Day/A Small Island	1958	2.50	5.00	10.00
❑ F15748	In the Good Old Summertime/La Rosita	1951	3.75	7.50	15.00
—"Part 1" and "Part 6" of CCF-286					
❑ F15749	Three Little Words/Moon Over Manakoora	1951	3.75	7.50	15.00
—"Part 2" and "Part 5" of CCF-286					
❑ F15750	I'm Forever Blowing Bubbles/				
	The Lonesome Road	1951	3.75	7.50	15.00
—"Part 3" and "Part 4" of CCF-286					

Number	Title (A Side/B Side)	Yr	VG	VG+	NM

COLUMBIA

Number	Title (A Side/B Side)	Yr	VG	VG+	NM
S7 31385 [S]	'Deed I Do/Makin' Whoopee!	1962	3.00	6.00	12.00
S7 31386 [S]	A Cottage for Sale/Chasing Shadows	1962	3.00	6.00	12.00
S7 31387 [S]	It's Been a Long, Long Time/After You've Gone	1962	3.00	6.00	12.00
S7 31388 [S]	Am I Blue/You Brought a New Kind of Love to Me	1962	3.00	6.00	12.00
S7 31389 [S]	(titles unknown)	1962	3.00	6.00	12.00

—The above five are "Stereo Seven" 33 1/3 rpm jukebox singles from "JS7-52"

Number	Title (A Side/B Side)	Yr	VG	VG+	NM
41222	Put a Ring on My Finger/Fantasy	1958	2.50	5.00	10.00
41222 [PS]	Put a Ring on My Finger/Fantasy	1958	3.75	7.50	15.00
41278	Jealous Heart/Big Eyed Gal	1958	2.50	5.00	10.00
41350	All I Need Is You/At the Save-a-Penny Super Store	1959	2.50	5.00	10.00
41592	The Poor People of Paris/All Night Long	1960	2.00	4.00	8.00
41660	Wonderful Rain/Take a Warning	1960	2.00	4.00	8.00
41994	Jura (I Swear I Love You)/It's Been a Long, Long Time	1961	2.00	4.00	8.00
41994 [PS]	Jura (I Swear I Love You)/It's Been a Long, Long Time	1961	3.00	6.00	12.00
42179	It's Too Late/Mountain Railroad	1961	2.00	4.00	8.00
42241	Goodnight Irene/Lonely Guitar	1961	2.00	4.00	8.00
42241 [PS]	Goodnight Irene/Lonely Guitar	1961	3.00	6.00	12.00
42419	Your Cheatin' Heart/Another Town, Another Time	1962	2.00	4.00	8.00
42419 [PS]	Your Cheatin' Heart/Another Town, Another Time	1962	3.00	6.00	12.00
42602	Playing Make Believe/I Just Don't Understand	1962	2.00	4.00	8.00
42602 [PS]	Playing Make Believe/I Just Don't Understand	1962	3.00	6.00	12.00
42754	Gentle Is Your Love/Move Along Baby (Don't Waste My Time)	1963	2.00	4.00	8.00
42754 [PS]	Gentle Is Your Love/Move Along Baby (Don't Waste My Time)	1963	3.00	6.00	12.00

7-Inch Extended Plays

CAPITOL

Number	Title (A Side/B Side)	Yr	VG	VG+	NM
1-286	In the Good Old Summertime/Three Little Words//La Rosita/Just One More Chance	195?	5.00	10.00	20.00
2-286	The Lonesome Road/Jazz Me Blues//I'm Forever Blowing Bubbles/Moon of Manakoora	195?	5.00	10.00	20.00
EBF-286 [PS]	Les Paul's New Sound, Vol. 2	195?	7.50	15.00	30.00

—Gatefold sleeve for 1-286 and 2-286 (we don't know if the EP records also were issued individually with separate "Part 1" and "Part 2" sleeves)

Number	Title (A Side/B Side)	Yr	VG	VG+	NM
1-356	(contents unknown)	195?	5.00	10.00	20.00
2-356	(contents unknown)	195?	5.00	10.00	20.00
EBF-356 [PS]	Bye Bye Blues	195?	7.50	15.00	30.00

—Gatefold sleeve for 1-356 and 2-356 (we don't know if the EP records also were issued individually with separate "Part 1" and "Part 2" sleeves)

Number	Title (A Side/B Side)	Yr	VG	VG+	NM
EAP 1-416	How High the Moon/Josephine//Mockin' Bird Hill/Whispering	195?	5.00	10.00	20.00
EAP 1-416 [PS]	The Hit Makers, Part 1	195?	5.00	10.00	20.00
EAP 2-416	*Meet Mister Callaghan/Tiger Rag/Tennessee Waltz/The World Is Waiting for the Sunrise	195?	5.00	10.00	20.00
EAP 2-416 [PS]	The Hit Makers, Part 2	195?	5.00	10.00	20.00
EAP 1-495	Vaya Con Dios (May God Be With You)/Sleep//Lady of Spain/My Baby's Comin' Home	195?	5.00	10.00	20.00
EAP 1-495 [PS]	Vaya Con Dios	195?	5.00	10.00	20.00
EAP 1-540	I'm Sitting on Top of the World/South//Smoke Rings/Jazz Me Blues	195?	5.00	10.00	20.00
EAP 1-540 [PS]	Sitting on Top of the World	195?	5.00	10.00	20.00
EAP 1-543	Jingle Bells/White Christmas//Santa Claus Is Comin' to Town/Silent Night	195?	5.00	10.00	20.00
EAP 1-543 [PS]	Christmas Cheer	195?	5.00	10.00	20.00
EAP 1-554	I'm a Fool to Care/I Really Don't Want to Know//Auctioneer/It's a Lonesome Old Town	1956	3.75	7.50	15.00
EAP 1-554 [PS]	I'm a Fool to Care	1956	3.75	7.50	15.00
EAP 1-559	Whither Thou Goest/Nola//Take Me in Your Arms and Hold Me/Mandolino	1955	5.00	10.00	20.00
EAP 1-559 [PS]	Whither Thou Goest	1955	5.00	10.00	20.00
EAP 1-577	Falling in Love with Love/On the Sunny Side of the Street//Just One of Those Things/Twelfth Street Rag	1955	3.75	7.50	15.00
EAP 1-577 [PS]	Les and Mary, Part 1	1955	3.75	7.50	15.00
EAP 2-577	Lies/Turista//Swing Low Sweet Chariot/Nuevo Laredo	1955	3.75	7.50	15.00
EAP 2-577 [PS]	Les and Mary, Part 2	1955	3.75	7.50	15.00
EAP 3-577	The Best Things in Life Are Free/Theme from "Laughing Eyes"//Some of These Days/Tico Tico	1955	3.75	7.50	15.00
EAP 3-577 [PS]	Les and Mary, Part 3	1955	3.75	7.50	15.00
EAP 4-577 [PS]	Les and Mary, Part 4	195?	3.75	7.50	15.00
EAP 4-577	Baby Won't You Please Come Home/Dangerous Curves//I'm Movin' On/Farewell for Just Awhile	1955	3.75	7.50	15.00
EBF 1-577 [PS]	Les and Mary, Parts 1 and 2	1955	5.00	10.00	20.00
EBF 2-577 [PS]	Les and Mary, Parts 3 and 4	1955	5.00	10.00	20.00

—Gatefold cover for some editions of 3-577 and 4-577

Number	Title (A Side/B Side)	Yr	VG	VG+	NM
EAP 1-695	(contents unknown)	195?	3.75	7.50	15.00
EAP 1-695 [PS]	Songs for Today	195?	3.75	7.50	15.00
EAP 1-802	(contents unknown)	1956	3.75	7.50	15.00
EAP 1-802 [PS]	Time to Dream, Volume 1	1956	3.75	7.50	15.00
EAP 2-802	(contents unknown)	1956	3.75	7.50	15.00
EAP 2-802 [PS]	Time to Dream, Volume 2	1956	3.75	7.50	15.00
EAP 3-802	(contents unknown)	1956	3.75	7.50	15.00
EAP 3-802 [PS]	Time to Dream, Volume 3	1956	3.75	7.50	15.00
EAP 1-9121	Mister Sandman/That's What I Like/I Need You Now/The Things I Didn't Do	1955	3.75	7.50	15.00
EAP 1-9121 [PS]	Les Paul and Mary Ford	1955	3.75	7.50	15.00

Albums

CAPITOL

Number	Title (A Side/B Side)	Yr	VG	VG+	NM
H 226 [10]	The New Sound, Volume 1	1950	20.00	40.00	80.00
T 226 [M]	The New Sound, Volume 1	1955	12.50	25.00	50.00
H 286 [10]	The New Sound, Volume 2	1951	20.00	40.00	80.00
SM-286	The New Sound, Volume 2	197?	2.50	5.00	10.00
T 286 [M]	The New Sound, Volume 2	1955	12.50	25.00	50.00
H 356 [10]	Bye Bye Blues	1952	20.00	40.00	80.00
T 356 [M]	Bye Bye Blues	1955	12.50	25.00	50.00
H 416 [10]	The Hit Makers	1953	20.00	40.00	80.00
T 416 [M]	The Hit Makers	1955	12.50	25.00	50.00
H 577 [10]	Les and Mary	1955	20.00	40.00	80.00
W 577 [M]	Les and Mary	1955	12.50	25.00	50.00
T 802 [M]	Time to Dream	1956	12.50	25.00	50.00
DT 1476 [R]	The Hits of Les and Mary	1960	5.00	10.00	20.00
T 1476 [M]	The Hits of Les and Mary	1960	6.25	12.50	25.00
SM-11308	The World Is Still Waiting for the Sunrise	197?	2.50	5.00	10.00

—Reissue with new prefix

Number	Title (A Side/B Side)	Yr	VG	VG+	NM
ST-11308	The World Is Still Waiting for the Sunrise	1974	3.00	6.00	12.00

CAPITOL SPECIAL MARKETS

Number	Title (A Side/B Side)	Yr	VG	VG+	NM
SLCR-8130 [(3)]	The All-Time Greatest Hits of Les Paul and Mary Ford	1980	5.00	10.00	20.00

—Produced for Murray Hill Records (979462)

COLUMBIA

Number	Title (A Side/B Side)	Yr	VG	VG+	NM
CL 1276 [M]	Lovers' Luau	1959	5.00	10.00	20.00
CL 1688 [M]	Warm and Wonderful	1962	5.00	10.00	20.00
CL 1821 [M]	Bouquet of Roses	1962	5.00	10.00	20.00
CL 1928 [M]	Swingin' South	1963	3.75	7.50	15.00
CS 8086 [S]	Lovers' Luau	1959	7.50	15.00	30.00
CS 8488 [S]	Warm and Wonderful	1962	6.25	12.50	25.00
CS 8621 [S]	Bouquet of Roses	1962	6.25	12.50	25.00
CS 8728 [S]	Swingin' South	1963	5.00	10.00	20.00

HARMONY

Number	Title (A Side/B Side)	Yr	VG	VG+	NM
HL 7333 [M]	The Fabulous Les Paul and Mary Ford	1965	3.00	6.00	12.00
HS 11133 [S]	The Fabulous Les Paul and Mary Ford	1965	3.00	6.00	12.00

PICKWICK

Number	Title (A Side/B Side)	Yr	VG	VG+	NM
SPC-3122	Brazil	197?	2.50	5.00	10.00

PAUL, LOUIS

45s

COTILLION

Number	Title (A Side/B Side)	Yr	VG	VG+	NM
44064	Annie Mae/Railroad Man	1970	2.50	5.00	10.00

ENTERPRISE

Number	Title (A Side/B Side)	Yr	VG	VG+	NM
9056	Gotta Get Away/With a Little Bit of Love	1972	—	3.00	6.00
9060	It's Christmas Time/Santa Claus Is on His Way Again	1972	—	3.00	6.00
9077	Merry-Go-Round/Mister Crystal	1973	—	3.00	6.00
9094	I Like Rock and Roll/My Dream	1974	—	3.00	6.00

Albums

ENTERPRISE

Number	Title (A Side/B Side)	Yr	VG	VG+	NM
ENS-1034	Reflections of the Way It Really Is	1971	3.75	7.50	15.00

PAUL AND PAULA Also see RAY HILDEBRAND; JILL JACKSON.

45s

LE CAM

Number	Title (A Side/B Side)	Yr	VG	VG+	NM
99	The Beginning of Love/All I Want Is You	1963	5.00	10.00	20.00
305	From the Top of the World/All I Want Is You	197?	—	2.00	4.00

—As "Jill and Ray"

Number	Title (A Side/B Side)	Yr	VG	VG+	NM
315	Hey Paula ('77 Disco)/(Instrumental)	1977	—	2.00	4.00
321	Hey Paula/Paula (My Love)	1978	—	2.00	4.00

—Reissued in 1982 with the same catalog number

Number	Title (A Side/B Side)	Yr	VG	VG+	NM
354	Hey Paula/Elmer's Tune	198?	—	2.00	4.00
979	Hey Paula/Bobbie Is the One	1962	12.50	25.00	50.00

—As "Jill and Ray"

PHILIPS

Number	Title (A Side/B Side)	Yr	VG	VG+	NM
40084	Hey Paula/Bobby Is the One	1962	3.75	7.50	15.00
40096	Young Lovers/Ba-Hey-Be	1963	3.00	6.00	12.00
40096 [PS]	Young Lovers/Ba-Hey-Be	1963	5.00	10.00	20.00
40114	First Quarrel/School Is Thru	1963	3.00	6.00	12.00
40114 [PS]	First Quarrel/School Is Thru	1963	5.00	10.00	20.00
40130	Something Old, Something New/Flipped Over You	1963	3.00	6.00	12.00
40142	First Day Back at School/A Perfect Pair	1963	3.00	6.00	12.00
40158	Holiday for Teens/Holiday Hootenanny	1963	3.00	6.00	12.00
40168	We'll Never Break Up for Good/Crazy Little Things	1964	2.50	5.00	10.00
40209	The Young Years/Darlin'	1964	2.50	5.00	10.00
40234	No Other Baby/Too Dark to See	1964	2.50	5.00	10.00
40268	True Love/Any Way You Want Me	1965	2.00	4.00	8.00
40296	Dear Paula/All the Love	1965	2.00	4.00	8.00
40352	All I Want Is You/The Beginning of Love	1966	2.50	5.00	10.00

UNI

Number	Title (A Side/B Side)	Yr	VG	VG+	NM
55052	All These Things/Wedding	1968	2.00	4.00	8.00

UNITED ARTISTS

Number	Title (A Side/B Side)	Yr	VG	VG+	NM
50712	Moments Like These/Mrs. Bean	1970	—	3.00	6.00

Albums

PHILIPS

Number	Title (A Side/B Side)	Yr	VG	VG+	NM
PHM 200078 [M]	Paul and Paula Sing for Young Lovers	1963	7.50	15.00	30.00
PHM 200089 [M]	We Go Together	1963	7.50	15.00	30.00
PHM 200101 [M]	Holiday for Teens	1963	7.50	15.00	30.00
PHS 600078 [S]	Paul and Paula Sing for Young Lovers	1963	10.00	20.00	40.00
PHS 600089 [S]	We Go Together	1963	10.00	20.00	40.00
PHS 600101 [S]	Holiday for Teens	1963	10.00	20.00	40.00

PAULA, MARLENA

45s

REGENT

Number	Title (A Side/B Side)	Yr	VG	VG+	NM
7506	I Wanna Spend Christmas with Elvis/Once More It's Christmas	1956	12.50	25.00	50.00

PAULSON, BUTCH

45s

VIRGELLE

Number	Title (A Side/B Side)	Yr	VG	VG+	NM
708	Man from Mars/My Own Brother	195?	25.00	50.00	100.00
718	Candy Lou/Today Was Blue Tomorrow	195?	12.50	25.00	50.00

PAULSON, PAT

Albums

RUBICON/MERCURY

Number	Title (A Side/B Side)	Yr	VG	VG+	NM
SR 61179	Pat Paulson for President	1968	5.00	10.00	20.00
SR 61251	Live at the Ice House	1970	3.75	7.50	15.00

PAUPERS, THE

45s

VERVE FOLKWAYS

Number	Title (A Side/B Side)	Yr	VG	VG+	NM
5033	Copper Penny/If I Call You by Some Other Name	1966	2.50	5.00	10.00
5043	Let Me Be/Simple Deed	1967	2.50	5.00	10.00

VERVE FORECAST

Number	Title (A Side/B Side)	Yr	VG	VG+	NM
5056	One Rainy Day/Tudor Impressions	1967	2.50	5.00	10.00
5062	Magic People/Black Thank You Package	1967	2.50	5.00	10.00

P

Number	Title (A Side/B Side)	Yr	VG	VG+	NM
❏ 5074	Think I Care/White Song	1967	2.50	5.00	10.00
❏ 5094	Another Man's Hair on My Razor/Cairo Hotel	1968	2.50	5.00	10.00
Albums					
VERVE FORECAST					
❏ FT-3026 [M]	Magic People	1967	5.00	10.00	20.00
❏ FTS-3026 [S]	Magic People	1967	5.00	10.00	20.00
❏ FTS-3051	Ellis Island	1968	3.75	7.50	15.00

PAVLOV'S DOG
45s
ABC

Number	Title (A Side/B Side)	Yr	VG	VG+	NM
❏ 12086	Episode/Julia	1975	2.50	5.00	10.00
Albums					
ABC					
❏ D-866	Pampered Menial	1975	6.25	12.50	25.00
COLUMBIA					
❏ PC 33552	Pampered Menial	1976	3.00	6.00	12.00
—*Reissue of ABC album*					
❏ PC 33964	At the Sound of the Bell	1976	3.00	6.00	12.00

PAVONE, RITA
45s
POLYDOR

Number	Title (A Side/B Side)	Yr	VG	VG+	NM
❏ 15011	'Til Tomorrow/Try It and See	1970	—	3.00	6.00
RCA VICTOR					
❏ 47-8212	Cuore/Ballo del Mattone	1963	2.00	4.00	8.00
❏ 47-8365	Remember Me/Just One More	1964	2.00	4.00	8.00
❏ 47-8365 [PS]	Remember Me/Just One More	1964	2.50	5.00	10.00
❏ 47-8420	Wait for Me/It's Not Easy	1964	2.00	4.00	8.00
❏ 47-8420 [PS]	Wait for Me/It's Not Easy	1964	2.50	5.00	10.00
❏ 47-8538	I Don't Wanna Be Hurt/Eyes of Mine	1965	2.00	4.00	8.00
❏ 47-8612	Oh My Mama/Right Now	1965	2.00	4.00	8.00
❏ 47-9485	Okay, Okay/Wenn Ich Ein Junge War	1968	2.50	5.00	10.00
Albums					
RCA VICTOR					
❏ LPM-2900 [M]	Rita Pavone	1964	3.75	7.50	15.00
❏ LSP-2900 [S]	Rita Pavone	1964	5.00	10.00	20.00
❏ LPM-2996 [M]	Small Wonder	1965	3.75	7.50	15.00
❏ LSP-2996 [S]	Small Wonder	1965	5.00	10.00	20.00

PAXTON, GARY Also see THE HOLLYWOOD ARGYLES; THE PLEDGES; SKIP AND FLIP.
45s
CAPITOL

Number	Title (A Side/B Side)	Yr	VG	VG+	NM
❏ 5467	My Heart Won't Let My Lips Say Goodbye/It's My Way (Of Lovin' You)	1965	3.75	7.50	15.00
❏ 5707	Goin' Through the Motions/You Got to Do the Best You Can	1966	3.75	7.50	15.00
❏ 5975	Mother-in-Law/Miles and Cities	1967	3.75	7.50	15.00
FELSTED					
❏ 8691	Sweet Senorita from Santa Fe/Kansas City	1964	5.00	10.00	20.00
GARPAX					
❏ 44172	It Had to Be You/We're Going Back Together	1963	5.00	10.00	20.00
❏ 44177	The Scavenger/How to Be a Fool (In Six Easy Lessons)	1963	5.00	10.00	20.00
❏ 44180	Two Duel Bump Camel Named Robert E. Lee/Your Past Is Back Again	1964	5.00	10.00	20.00
LIBERTY					
❏ 55407	Teen Age Crush/It's So Funny I Could Cry	1962	5.00	10.00	20.00
❏ 55485	Stop Twistin' Baby/Alley Oop Was a Two Dab Man	1962	5.00	10.00	20.00
❏ 55584	Spooky Movies (Part 1)/Spooky Movies (Part 2)	1963	5.00	10.00	20.00
LONDON					
❏ 5208	Super Torque/Cute Little Coly	1964	5.00	10.00	20.00
LUTE					
❏ 5801	You're Ruinin' My Gladness/The Way I See It	1960	5.00	10.00	20.00
MGM					
❏ 14306	Carin' for Karen/Out on a Limb	1971	—	3.00	6.00
❏ 14362	Rocky Top/Parchman Farm	1972	—	3.00	6.00
NEW PAX					
❏ 6	Different World/(B-side unknown)	1976	2.00	4.00	8.00
❏ 5349	Lord I Need You Right Now/(B-side unknown)	197?	2.00	4.00	8.00
PAX					
❏ 2406	The Big A/The Big M	197?	—	3.00	6.00
—*Red vinyl*					
PRIVATE STOCK					
❏ 45,007	The Clone Affair/(B-side unknown)	1975	—	2.50	5.00
RCA VICTOR					
❏ 74-0916	Shadow of Your Memory/This Little Light of Mine	1973	—	2.50	5.00
❏ APBO-0081	It's Hard to Be a Rock and Roll Star When You're Old and Fat/White Tornado Alias Gary S. Paxton	1973	—	2.50	5.00
❏ PB-10449	Too Far Gone (To Care What You Do to Me)/Freedom Lives in a Country Song	1975	—	2.50	5.00
W.I.N.					
❏ 28	The Race Driver's Song/Someday Darling I'll Give You	197?	3.75	7.50	15.00
❏ 28 [PS]	The Race Driver's Song/Someday Darling I'll Give You	197?	6.25	12.50	25.00
—*Sponsored by NAPA*					
Albums					
NEW PAX					
❏ NP-33005	The Astonishing, Outrageous, Amazing, Incredible, Unbelievably Different World of Gary S. Paxton	1976	3.00	6.00	12.00
❏ NP-33033	More from the Astonishing, Outrageous, Amazing, Incredible, Unbelievable World of Gary S. Paxton	1977	3.00	6.00	12.00
❏ NP-33048	The Gospel According to Gary S.	1979	3.00	6.00	12.00
❏ NP-33080	(Some of) The Best of Gary S. Paxton (So Far)	1980	3.00	6.00	12.00
PAX					
❏ R-2406	Terminally Weird but Godly Right/Anchored in the Rock of Ages	1978	3.00	6.00	12.00
❏ R-2411	Gary Sanford Paxton	1979	3.00	6.00	12.00

PAXTON, TOM
45s
ELEKTRA

Number	Title (A Side/B Side)	Yr	VG	VG+	NM
❏ 45667	Crazy John/Things I Notice Now	1969	—	3.00	6.00
❏ 45674	Jimmy Newman/Forest Lawn	1970	—	3.00	6.00
❏ 45703	Whose Garden Was This/Annie's Going to Sing Her Song	1970	—	3.00	6.00
REPRISE					
❏ 1110	Peace Will Come (According to Plan)/Jesus Christ S.R.O.	1972	—	2.50	5.00
VANGUARD					
❏ 35206	The Death of Stephen Biko/Anita O.J.	1977	—	2.50	5.00
Albums					
ELEKTRA					
❏ EKL-277 [M]	Ramblin' Boy	1964	5.00	10.00	20.00
❏ EKL-298 [M]	Ain't That News	1965	5.00	10.00	20.00
❏ EKL-317 [M]	Outward Bound	1966	5.00	10.00	20.00
❏ 7E-2003 [(2)]	The Compleat Tom Paxton	1971	5.00	10.00	20.00
❏ EKS-7277 [S]	Ramblin' Boy	1964	6.25	12.50	25.00
❏ EKS-7298 [S]	Ain't That News	1965	6.25	12.50	25.00
❏ EKS-7317 [S]	Outward Bound	1966	6.25	12.50	25.00
❏ EKS-74019	Morning Again	1968	5.00	10.00	20.00
❏ EKS-74043	The Things I Notice Now	1969	3.75	7.50	15.00
❏ EKS-74066	Tom Paxton 6	1970	3.75	7.50	15.00
FLYING FISH					
❏ FF-280	Even a Gray Day	1983	2.50	5.00	10.00
❏ FF-356	One Million Lawyers...And Other Disasters	1986	2.50	5.00	10.00
❏ FF-408	The Marvellous Toy and Other Gallimaufry	1987	2.50	5.00	10.00
❏ FF-414	And Loving You	1987	2.50	5.00	10.00
❏ FF-486	Politics	199?	3.00	6.00	12.00
❏ FF-519	The Very Best of Tom Paxton	199?	3.00	6.00	12.00
GASLIGHT					
❏ GV-116 [M]	I'm the Man Who Built the Bridges	1962	20.00	40.00	80.00
HOGEYE					
❏ 004	Bulletin...We Interrupt This Record	198?	2.50	5.00	10.00
MOUNTAIN RAILROAD					
❏ 52792	Up and Up	1980	3.00	6.00	12.00
❏ 52796	The Paxton Report	198?	3.00	6.00	12.00
PRIVATE STOCK					
❏ PS-2002	Something in My Life	1975	3.00	6.00	12.00
REPRISE					
❏ MS 2096	Peace Will Come	1972	3.75	7.50	15.00
❏ MS 2144	New Songs for Old Friends	1973	3.75	7.50	15.00
❏ RS 6443	How Come the Sun	1971	3.75	7.50	15.00
VANGUARD					
❏ VSD-79395	New Songs from the Briarpatch	1977	3.00	6.00	12.00
❏ VSD-79411	Heroes	1978	3.00	6.00	12.00

PAYCHECK, JOHNNY
45s
AMI

Number	Title (A Side/B Side)	Yr	VG	VG+	NM
❏ 1322	I Never Got Over You/Ole Pay Ain't Checked Out Yet	1984	—	2.50	5.00
❏ 1323	You're Every Step I Take/I Can't Stop Drinking	1985	—	2.50	5.00
❏ 1327	Everything Is Changing/Palimony	1985	—	2.50	5.00
BIG A					
❏ A-100	Nothing Lasts Forever/No One Ever Lost More	1967	3.00	6.00	12.00
CERTRON					
❏ 10003	Forever Ended Yesterday/It's For Sure I Can't Go On	1970	2.00	4.00	8.00
DAMASCUS					
❏ 2001	Scars/(B-side unknown)	1989	—	3.00	6.00
DECCA					
❏ 9-30763	On This Mountaintop/It's Been a Long, Long Time for Me	1958	7.50	15.00	30.00
—*A-side as "Donny Young and Roger Miller"; B-side as "Donny Young"*					
❏ 9-30881	The Old Man and the River/Pictures Can't Talk Back	1959	6.25	12.50	25.00
—*As "Donny Young"*					
❏ 31077	Shakin' the Blues/Miracle of Love	1960	10.00	20.00	40.00
—*As "Donny Young"*					
❏ 31283	Go Ring the Bells/I Guess I Had It Coming	1961	6.25	12.50	25.00
—*As "Donny Young"*					
DESPERADO					
❏ 1001	Out of Beer/Oklahoma Lady	1988	—	3.00	6.00
EPIC					
❏ 19-02144	Yesterday's News (Just Hit Home Today)/Someone Told My Story	1981	—	2.00	4.00
❏ 14-02684	The Highlight of '81/Sharon Rae	1982	—	2.00	4.00
❏ 14-02817	No Way Out/We've All Gone Crazy	1982	—	2.00	4.00
❏ 14-03052	D.O.A. (Drunk On Arrival)/Gonna Get Right (And Do Something Wrong)	1982	—	2.00	4.00
❏ 5-10783	She's All I Got/You Touched My Life	1971	—	3.50	7.00
❏ 5-10836	Someone to Give My Love To/Love Sure Is Beautiful	1972	—	3.50	7.00
❏ 5-10876	Love Is a Good Thing/High on the Thought of You	1972	—	3.50	7.00
❏ 5-10912	Somebody Loves Me/Without You	1972	—	3.50	7.00
❏ 5-10947	Something About You I Love/Your Love Is the Key to It All	1973	—	3.00	6.00
❏ 5-10999	Mr. Lovemaker/Once You've Had the Best	1973	—	3.00	6.00
❏ 5-11046	Song and Dance Man/Love Is a Strange and Wonderful Thing	1973	—	3.00	6.00
❏ 5-11090	My Part of Forever/If Love Gets Any Better	1974	—	3.00	6.00
❏ 5-11142	Keep On Lovin' Me/The Ballad of Thunder Road	1974	—	3.00	6.00
❏ 8-50040	For a Minute There/She's All I Live For	1974	—	3.00	6.00
❏ 8-50073	Loving You Beats All I've Ever Seen/Touch of the Master's Hand	1975	—	3.00	6.00
❏ 8-50111	I Didn't Love Her Anymore/Loving Her Is All I Thought It Would Be	1975	—	3.00	6.00
❏ 8-50146	All-American Man/The Fool Strikes Again	1975	—	3.00	6.00
❏ 8-50193	The Feminine Touch/Rhythm Guitar	1976	—	3.00	6.00
❏ 8-50215	Gone at Last/Live with Me	1976	—	3.00	6.00
❏ 8-50249	11 Months and 29 Days/Live with Me (Till I Can Learn to Live Again)	1976	—	3.00	6.00

Number	Title (A Side/B Side)	Yr	VG	VG+	NM
❏ 8-50291	I Can See Me Lovin' You Again/I Sleep with Her Memory Every Night	1976	—	3.00	6.00
❏ 8-50334	Slide Off of Your Satin Sheets/That's What the Outlaws in Texas Want to Hear	1977	—	3.00	6.00
❏ 8-50391	I'm the Only Hell (Mama Ever Raised)/She's Still Lookin' Good	1977	—	3.00	6.00
❏ 8-50469	Take This Job and Shove It/Colorado Kool-Aid	1977	2.00	4.00	8.00
❏ 8-50539	Georgia in a Jug/Me and the I.R.S.	1978	—	3.00	6.00
❏ 8-50621	Friend, Lover, Wife/Leave It to Me	1978	—	3.00	6.00
❏ 8-50655	The Outlaw's Prayer/Armed and Crazy	1979	—	3.00	6.00
❏ 9-50777	(Stay Away From) The Cocaine Train/Billy Bardo	1979	—	2.50	5.00
❏ 9-50818	Drinkin' and Drivin'/Just Makin' Love Don't Make It Love	1979	—	2.50	5.00
❏ 9-50863	Fifteen Beers/Who Was That Man Who Beat Me So	1980	—	2.50	5.00
❏ 9-50923	In Memory of a Memory/New York Town	1980	—	2.50	5.00
HILLTOP					
❏ 3002	Don't Start Countin' on Me/I'd Rather Be Your Fool	1964	5.00	10.00	20.00
❏ 3006	For Those Who Think Young/The Girl They Talk About	1965	3.75	7.50	15.00
❏ 3007	A-11/Where (In the World)	1965	3.75	7.50	15.00
❏ 3009	Heartbreak Tennessee/Help Me Hank, I'm Fallin'	1966	3.75	7.50	15.00
❏ 3015	I'm Barely Hangin' On to Me/The Real Mr. Heartache	1966	3.75	7.50	15.00
LITTLE DARLIN'					
❏ 008	The Lovin' Machine/Pride Covered Ears	1966	2.50	5.00	10.00
❏ 0011	The Ballad of the Green Berets/A Dying Hero	1966	2.50	5.00	10.00
❏ 0014	Right Back Where We Parted/The Way Things Were Going	1966	2.50	5.00	10.00
—With Micki Evans					
❏ 0016	Motel Time Again/If You Should Come Back Today	1966	2.50	5.00	10.00
❏ 0020	Jukebox Charlie/Something in Your World	1967	2.50	5.00	10.00
❏ 0032	The Cave/Then Love Dies	1967	2.50	5.00	10.00
❏ 0035	Don't Monkey with Another Monkey's Monkey/You'll Recover in Time	1967	2.50	5.00	10.00
❏ 0042	(It Won't Be Long) And I'll Be Hating You/Fools Hall of Fame	1968	2.50	5.00	10.00
❏ 0043	The Old Year Is Gone/According to the Bible	1968	2.50	5.00	10.00
❏ 0046	My Heart Keeps Running to You/Yesterday, Today and Tomorrow	1968	2.50	5.00	10.00
❏ 0052	If I'm Gonna Sink/The Loser	1968	2.50	5.00	10.00
❏ 0055	Jingle Bells/The Old Year Is Gone	1968	2.50	5.00	10.00
❏ 0057	My World of Memories/(B-side unknown)	1969	2.50	5.00	10.00
❏ 0060	Wherever You Are/I Can't Promise You Won't Get Lonely	1969	2.50	5.00	10.00
❏ 0072	Wildfire/Basin Street Mama	1969	2.50	5.00	10.00
❏ 7804	It Won't Be Long/If I'm Gonna Sink (Might As Well Go to the Bottom)	1978	—	3.00	6.00
❏ 7808	Down on the Corner at a Bar Named Kelly's/Something He'll Have to Learn	1978	—	3.00	6.00
❏ 7810	I'll Place My Order Early/The Old Year Is Gone	1978	—	3.00	6.00
❏ 7918	California Dreams/The Loser	1979	—	3.00	6.00
❏ 7923	Gentle on My Mind/Everything You Touch Turns to Hurt	1979	—	3.00	6.00
MERCURY					
❏ 71900	On Second Thought/One Day a Week	1962	5.00	10.00	20.00
—As "Donny Young"					
❏ 71981	Not Much I Don't/I'd Come Back to Me	1962	5.00	10.00	20.00
—As "Donny Young"					
❏ 884720-7	Old Violin/Comin' Home to Baby	1986	—	2.00	4.00
❏ 888088-7	Don't Bury Me 'Til I'm Ready/Ex-Wives and Lovers	1986	—	2.00	4.00
❏ 888341-7	Come to Me/Ragtime Redneck	1987	—	2.00	4.00
❏ 888651-7	I Grow Old Too Fast (And Smart Too Slow)/Caught Between a Rock and a Soft Place	1987	—	2.00	4.00
❏ 888925-7	Modern Times/She Don't Love Me All the Time	1987	—	2.00	4.00
TODD					
❏ 1098	Don't You Get Lonesome Without Me/I'm Glad to Have Her Back Again	1964	5.00	10.00	20.00
—As "Donny Young"					
Albums					
ACCORD					
❏ SN-7173	Extra Special	1981	2.50	5.00	10.00
ALLEGIANCE					
❏ AV-435	I Don't Need to Know That Right Now	198?	2.00	4.00	8.00
CERTRON					
❏ 7002	Johnny Paycheck Again	1970	3.75	7.50	15.00
EPIC					
❏ E 31141	She's All I Got	1971	3.00	6.00	12.00
❏ KE 31449	Someone to Give My Love To	1972	3.00	6.00	12.00
❏ KE 31702	Somebody Loves Me	1972	3.00	6.00	12.00
❏ KE 32387	Something About You I Love	1973	3.00	6.00	12.00
❏ KE 32570	Song and Dance Man	1973	3.00	6.00	12.00
❏ KE 33091	Greatest Hits	1974	2.50	5.00	10.00
❏ PE 33091	Greatest Hits	198?	2.00	4.00	8.00
—Budget-line reissue					
❏ KE 33354	Loving You Beats All I've Ever Seen	1975	2.50	5.00	10.00
❏ KE 33943	11 Months and 29 Days	1975	2.50	5.00	10.00
❏ PE 34693	Slide Off of Your Satin Sheets	1976	2.50	5.00	10.00
❏ KE 35045	Take This Job and Shove It	1977	2.50	5.00	10.00
❏ PE 35045	Take This Job and Shove It	198?	2.00	4.00	8.00
—Budget-line reissue					
❏ KE 35444	Armed and Crazy	1978	2.50	5.00	10.00
❏ KE 35623	Greatest Hits, Volume 2	1978	2.50	5.00	10.00
❏ PE 35623	Greatest Hits, Volume 2	198?	2.00	4.00	8.00
—Budget-line reissue					
❏ JE 36200	Everybody's Got a Family — Meet Mine	1979	2.50	5.00	10.00
❏ JE 36496	New York Town	1980	2.50	5.00	10.00
❏ FE 36761	Mr. Hag Told My Story	1981	2.50	5.00	10.00
❏ PE 36761	Mr. Hag Told My Story	1981	2.00	4.00	8.00
—Budget-line reissue					
❏ FE 37345	Encore	1981	2.50	5.00	10.00

Number	Title (A Side/B Side)	Yr	VG	VG+	NM
❏ PE 37345	Encore	198?	2.00	4.00	8.00
—Budget-line reissue					
❏ FE 37933	Lovers and Losers	1982	2.50	5.00	10.00
❏ FE 38322	Johnny Paycheck's Biggest Hits	1983	2.50	5.00	10.00
❏ PE 39943	John Austin Paycheck	1984	2.00	4.00	8.00
INTERMEDIA					
❏ QS-5018	Back On the Job	198?	2.00	4.00	8.00
LITTLE DARLIN'					
❏ LD-4001 [M]	Johnny Paycheck at Carnegie Hall	1966	5.00	10.00	20.00
❏ LD-4003 [M]	The Lovin' Machine	1966	5.00	10.00	20.00
❏ LD-4004 [M]	Gospeltime in My Fashion	1967	5.00	10.00	20.00
❏ LD-4006 [M]	Johnny Paycheck Sings Jukebox Charlie	1967	6.25	12.50	25.00
❏ SLD-8001 [S]	Johnny Paycheck at Carnegie Hall	1966	6.25	12.50	25.00
❏ SLD-8003 [S]	The Lovin' Machine	1966	6.25	12.50	25.00
❏ SLD-8004 [S]	Gospeltime in My Fashion	1967	6.25	12.50	25.00
❏ SLD-8006 [S]	Johnny Paycheck Sings Jukebox Charlie	1967	6.25	12.50	25.00
❏ SLD-8010	Country Soul	1968	6.25	12.50	25.00
❏ SLD-8012	Johnny Paycheck's Greatest Hits	1968	6.25	12.50	25.00
❏ SLD-8023	Wherever You Are	1969	6.25	12.50	25.00
MERCURY					
❏ 830404-1	Modern Times	1987	2.50	5.00	10.00
POWER PAK					
❏ PO-284	Johnny Paycheck At His Best	197?	2.00	4.00	8.00

PAYCHECK, JOHNNY, AND MERLE HAGGARD Also see each artist's individual listings.
45s

Number	Title (A Side/B Side)	Yr	VG	VG+	NM
EPIC					
❏ 19-51012	I Can't Hold Myself in Line/Carolyn	1981	—	2.00	4.00

PAYNE, FREDA
12-Inch Singles

Number	Title (A Side/B Side)	Yr	VG	VG+	NM
CAPITOL					
❏ 8509	I'll Do Anything for You (7:40)/(Instrumental)	1978	3.00	6.00	12.00
❏ SPRO-8922/3 [DJ]	Happy Days Are Here Again-Happy Music/I'll Do Anything for You	1978	3.75	7.50	15.00
❏ SPRO-9219 [DJ]	Red Hot (7:01) (same on both sides)	1979	2.50	5.00	10.00
SUTRA					
❏ SUD 009	In Motion (5:35)/(Instrumental)	1982	3.75	7.50	15.00
45s					
ABC					
❏ 12079	Shadows on the Wall/I Get Carried Away	1975	—	2.50	5.00
❏ 12139	Lost in Love/You	1975	—	2.50	5.00
ABC DUNHILL					
❏ 15018	It's Yours to Have/Run for Life	1974	—	2.50	5.00
ABC-PARAMOUNT					
❏ 10366	Desafinado/He Who Laughs Last	1962	5.00	10.00	20.00
❏ 10437	Pretty Baby/Grin and Bear It	1963	5.00	10.00	20.00
CAPITOL					
❏ 4383	I Can't Live on a Memory/I Get High (On Your Memory)	1976	—	2.50	5.00
❏ 4431	Baby, You've Got What It Takes/Bring Back the Joy	1977	—	2.50	5.00
❏ 4494	Love Magnet/Loving You Means So Much to Me	1977	—	2.50	5.00
❏ 4537	Feed Me Your Love/Stares and Whispers	1978	—	2.50	5.00
❏ 4631	Happy Days Are Here Again-Happy Music (Dance the Night Away)/Falling in Love	1978	—	2.50	5.00
❏ 4695	I'll Do Anything for You (Part 1)/I'll Do Anything for You (Part 2)	1979	—	2.50	5.00
❏ 4775	Red Hot/Longest Night	1979	—	2.50	5.00
❏ 4805	Can't Wait/Longest Night	1979	—	2.50	5.00
IMPULSE!					
❏ 221	It's Time/Sweet September	1963	5.00	10.00	20.00
INVICTUS					
❏ 1255	Two Wrongs Don't Make a Right/We've Gotta Find a Way Back to Love	1973	—	3.00	6.00
❏ 1257	For No Reason/Mother Misery's Favorite Child	1973	—	3.00	6.00
❏ 9073	The Unhooked Generation/Easiest Way to Fall	1969	—	3.00	6.00
❏ 9075	Band of Gold/Easiest Way to Fall	1970	—	3.00	6.00
❏ 9080	Deeper and Deeper/The Unhooked Genration	1970	—	3.00	6.00
❏ 9085	Cherish What Is Dear to You (While It Is Near to You)/They Don't Owe Me a Thing	1971	—	3.00	6.00
❏ 9085 [PS]	Cherish What Is Dear to You (While It Is Near to You)/They Don't Owe Me a Thing	1971	2.50	5.00	10.00
❏ 9092	Bring the Boys Home/I Shall Not Be Moved	1971	—	3.00	6.00
❏ 9100	You Brought the Joy/Suddenly It's Yesterday	1971	—	3.00	6.00
❏ 9109	I'm Not Getting Any Better/The Road We Didn't Take	1972	—	3.00	6.00
❏ 9128	She's in My Life/Through the Memory of My Mind	1972	—	3.00	6.00
MGM					
❏ 13509	You've Lost That Lovin' Feelin'/Sad Sad September	1966	5.00	10.00	20.00
SUTRA					
❏ 117	In Motion/(Instrumental)	1982	—	2.50	5.00
Albums					
ABC					
❏ D-901	Out of Payne Comes Love	1976	3.00	6.00	12.00
ABC DUNHILL					
❏ DSX-50176	Payne and Pleasure	1974	3.75	7.50	15.00
ABC IMPULSE!					
❏ AS-53 [S]	After the Lights Go Down Low…And Much More	1968	3.75	7.50	15.00
CAPITOL					
❏ ST-11700	Stares and Whispers	1977	3.00	6.00	12.00
❏ ST-11864	Supernatural	1978	3.00	6.00	12.00
❏ ST-12003	Hot	1979	3.00	6.00	12.00
IMPULSE!					
❏ A-53 [M]	After the Lights Go Down Low…And Much More	1964	7.50	15.00	30.00
❏ AS-53 [S]	After the Lights Go Down Low…And Much More	1964	10.00	20.00	40.00
INVICTUS					
❏ ST-7301	Band of Gold	1970	3.75	7.50	15.00
❏ SMAS-7307	Contact	1971	3.75	7.50	15.00
❏ ST-9804	The Best of Freda Payne	1972	3.75	7.50	15.00
❏ Z 32493	Reaching Out	1973	3.75	7.50	15.00
MGM					
❏ GAS-128	Freda Payne (Golden Archive Series)	1970	3.75	7.50	15.00
❏ E-4370 [M]	How Do You Say I Don't Love You Anymore	1966	5.00	10.00	20.00
❏ SE-4370 [S]	How Do You Say I Don't Love You Anymore	1966	6.25	12.50	25.00

P

Number	Title (A Side/B Side)	Yr	VG	VG+	NM

PEACE, JOE
Albums
RITE
❑ 29917 — Finding Peace — 1972 — 50.00 — 100.00 — 200.00

PEACHEROOS, THE
45s
EXCELLO
❑ 2044 — Be-Bop Baby/Everyday My Love Is True — 1954 — 100.00 — 200.00 — 400.00

PEACHES AND HERB Herb Fame with at least three different female singers who were "Peaches."
12-Inch Singles
POLYDOR
❑ PRO 165 [DJ] — Freeway (6:03) (same on both sides) — 1981 — 3.00 — 6.00 — 12.00
45s
COLUMBIA

Number	Title (A Side/B Side)	Yr	VG	VG+	NM
❑ 03872	Remember/Come to Me	1983	—	2.00	4.00
❑ 04081	In My World/Keep On Smiling	1983	—	2.00	4.00
❑ 45386	The Sound of Silence/The Two of Us	1971	—	2.50	5.00
❑ 45554	God Save This World/ I Can't Forget the One I Love	1972	—	2.50	5.00

DATE

Number	Title (A Side/B Side)	Yr	VG	VG+	NM
❑ 1523	Let's Fall in Love/We're In This Thing Together	1966	2.50	5.00	10.00
❑ 1549	Close Your Eyes/I Will Watch Over You	1967	2.50	5.00	10.00
❑ 1549 [PS]	Close Your Eyes/I Will Watch Over You	1967	3.75	7.50	15.00
❑ 1555	Cupid-Venus/Darling, How Long	1967	3.75	7.50	15.00
❑ 1563	For Your Love/I Need Your Love So Desperately	1967	2.50	5.00	10.00
❑ 1563 [PS]	For Your Love/I Need Your Love So Desperately	1967	3.75	7.50	15.00
❑ 1574	Love Is Strange/It's True I Love You	1967	2.50	5.00	10.00
❑ 1574 [PS]	Love Is Strange/It's True I Love You	1967	3.75	7.50	15.00
❑ 1586	Two Little Kids/We've Got to Love One Another	1967	2.00	4.00	8.00
❑ 1592	The Ten Commandments of Love/What a Lovely Way (To Say Goodnight)	1968	2.00	4.00	8.00
❑ 1603	United/Thank You	1968	2.00	4.00	8.00
❑ 1603 [PS]	United/Thank You	1968	3.75	7.50	15.00
❑ 1623	Let's Make a Promise/Me and You	1968	2.00	4.00	8.00
❑ 1623 [PS]	Let's Make a Promise/Me and You	1968	3.75	7.50	15.00
❑ 1633	We've Got to Love One Another/So True	1968	2.50	5.00	10.00
❑ 1637	When He Touches Me (Nothing Else Matters)/ Thank You	1969	2.00	4.00	8.00
❑ 1649	Let Me Be the One/ I Need Your Love So Desperately	1969	2.00	4.00	8.00
❑ 1655	Cupid/Darling, How Long	1969	2.00	4.00	8.00
❑ 1669	It's Just a Game, Love/Satisfy My Hunger	1970	2.00	4.00	8.00
❑ 1676	Soothe Me with Your Love/ We're So Much in Love	1970	2.00	4.00	8.00

MCA

Number	Title (A Side/B Side)	Yr	VG	VG+	NM
❑ 40701	We're Still Together/Love Is Here Beside Us	1977	—	2.50	5.00
❑ 40782	It Will Never Be the Same Again/ I'm Counting on You	1977	—	2.50	5.00

MERCURY

Number	Title (A Side/B Side)	Yr	VG	VG+	NM
❑ 73350	Keep It Coming/I'm a-Hurtin' Inside	1973	—	2.50	5.00
❑ 73388	Can't It Wait/Thank Heaven for You	1973	—	2.50	5.00

POLYDOR

Number	Title (A Side/B Side)	Yr	VG	VG+	NM
❑ 2031	Roller-Skatin' Mate (Part 1)/Roller-Skatin' Mate (Part 2)	1979	—	2.00	4.00
❑ 2053	I Pledge My Love/(I Want Us) Back Together	1980	—	2.00	4.00
❑ 2115	Funtime (Part 1)/Funtime (Part 2)	1980	—	2.00	4.00
❑ 2140	One Child of Love/Hearsay	1980	—	2.00	4.00
❑ 2157	Surrender/Love Stealers	1981	—	2.00	4.00
❑ 2178	Freeway/Pickin' Up the Pieces	1981	—	2.00	4.00
❑ 2187	Bluer Than Blue/Go with the Flow	1981	—	2.00	4.00
❑ 14514	Shake Your Groove Thing/All Your Love (Get It Here)	1978	—	2.00	4.00
❑ 14547	Reunited/Easy as Pie	1979	—	2.00	4.00
❑ 14577	We've Got Love/Four's a Traffic Jam	1979	—	2.00	4.00

Albums
COLUMBIA
❑ FC 38746 — Remember — 1983 — 2.50 — 5.00 — 10.00
DATE

Number	Title (A Side/B Side)	Yr	VG	VG+	NM
❑ TEM 3004 [M]	Let's Fall in Love	1967	5.00	10.00	20.00
❑ TEM 3005 [M]	For Your Love	1967	6.25	12.50	25.00
❑ TEM 3007 [M]	Golden Duets	1968	7.50	15.00	30.00
❑ TES 4004 [S]	Let's Fall in Love	1967	6.25	12.50	25.00
❑ TES 4005 [S]	For Your Love	1967	5.00	10.00	20.00
❑ TES 4007 [S]	Golden Duets	1968	5.00	10.00	20.00
❑ TES 4012	Peaches and Herb's Greatest Hits	1968	5.00	10.00	20.00

EPIC
❑ E 36089 — Love Is Strange — 1979 — 2.50 — 5.00 — 10.00
—Reissue of Date material
❑ JE 36099 — Peaches and Herb's Greatest Hits — 1979 — 2.50 — 5.00 — 10.00
—Reissue of Date 4012
MCA
❑ 2261 — Peaches and Herb — 1977 — 3.00 — 6.00 — 12.00
POLYDOR

Number	Title (A Side/B Side)	Yr	VG	VG+	NM
❑ PD-1-6172	2 Hot!	1978	2.50	5.00	10.00
❑ PD-1-6239	Twice the Fire	1979	2.50	5.00	10.00
❑ PD-1-6298	Worth the Wait	1980	2.50	5.00	10.00
❑ PD-1-6332	Sayin' Something!	1981	2.50	5.00	10.00

PEANUT BUTTER CONSPIRACY, THE
45s
CHALLENGE

Number	Title (A Side/B Side)	Yr	VG	VG+	NM
❑ 500	Back in L.A./Have a Little Faith	1969	2.00	4.00	8.00
❑ 500 [PS]	Back in L.A./Have a Little Faith	1969	12.50	25.00	50.00

COLUMBIA

Number	Title (A Side/B Side)	Yr	VG	VG+	NM
❑ 43985	It's a Happening Thing/Twice Is Life	1967	2.50	5.00	10.00
❑ 43985 [PS]	It's a Happening Thing/Twice Is Life	1967	10.00	20.00	40.00
❑ 44063	Then Came Love/Dark on You Now	1967	2.00	4.00	8.00
❑ 44356	Turn On a Friend (To the Good Life)/ Captain Sandwich	1967	2.00	4.00	8.00
❑ 44667	I'm a Fool/It's So Hard	1968	2.00	4.00	8.00

VAULT
❑ 933 — Time Is After You/Floating Dream — 1966 — 3.75 — 7.50 — 15.00

Albums
CHALLENGE
❑ 2000 — For Children of All Ages — 1969 — 7.50 — 15.00 — 30.00
COLUMBIA

Number	Title (A Side/B Side)	Yr	VG	VG+	NM
❑ CL 2654 [M]	The Peanut Butter Conspiracy Is Spreading	1967	7.50	15.00	30.00
❑ CL 2790 [M]	The Great Conspiracy	1968	10.00	20.00	40.00
❑ CS 9454 [S]	The Peanut Butter Conspiracy Is Spreading	1967	7.50	15.00	30.00
❑ CS 9590 [S]	The Great Conspiracy	1968	7.50	15.00	30.00

PEARLS, THE (1)
45s
AMBER
❑ 2003 — I Cried/It Must Be Love — 1961 — 125.00 — 250.00 — 500.00
—Originals have matrix muber stamped into trail-off wax

PEARLS, THE (2)
45s
ATCO

Number	Title (A Side/B Side)	Yr	VG	VG+	NM
❑ 6057	Shadows of Love/Yum Yummy	1956	7.50	15.00	30.00
❑ 6066	Bells of Love/Come On Home	1956	10.00	20.00	40.00

LOST-NITE
❑ 393 — Let's You and I Go Steady/Zippidy Zippidy Zoom — 197? — — — 2.50 — 5.00
—Reissue
ON THE SQUARE
❑ 320 — Band of Angels/Ugly Face — 1959 — 5.00 — 10.00 — 20.00
ONYX

Number	Title (A Side/B Side)	Yr	VG	VG+	NM
❑ 503	Let's You and I Go Steady/Zippidy Zippidy Zoom	1956	15.00	30.00	60.00
❑ 506	My Oh My/Tree in the Meadow	1956	37.50	75.00	150.00
❑ 510	Your Cheatin' Heart/I Sure Need You	1957	15.00	30.00	60.00
❑ 511	Ice Cream Baby/Yuz-a-Ma-Tuz	1957	15.00	30.00	60.00
❑ 516	The Wheel of Love/It's Love, Love, Love	1957	30.00	60.00	120.00

PEARLS, THE (3)
45s
BELL
❑ 45342 — You Came, You Saw, You Conquered/(B-side unknown) — 1973 — — — 2.50 — 5.00
PRIVATE STOCK
❑ 45-060 — Pearly/I'll See You in My Dreams — 1975 — — — 2.50 — 5.00

PEARLS, THE (4)
45s
WARNER BROS.
❑ 5300 — Happy Over You/If I Had a Choice — 1962 — 5.00 — 10.00 — 20.00

PEARLS BEFORE SWINE
45s
ESP-DISK'

Number	Title (A Side/B Side)	Yr	VG	VG+	NM
❑ 4554	Morning Song/Drop Out	1967	10.00	20.00	40.00
❑ 4575	Images of April/There Was a Man	1968	10.00	20.00	40.00
❑ 4576	I Saw the World/(B-side unknown)	1968	10.00	20.00	40.00

REPRISE

Number	Title (A Side/B Side)	Yr	VG	VG+	NM
❑ 0873	If You Don't Want To/These Things Too	1969	3.00	6.00	12.00
❑ 0916	God Save the Child/Rocket Man	1970	3.00	6.00	12.00
❑ 0949	The Jeweler/Rocket Man	1970	3.00	6.00	12.00

Albums
ADELPHI
❑ 4111 [(2)] — The Best of Pearls Before Swine — 198? — 3.75 — 7.50 — 15.00
ESP-DISK

Number	Title (A Side/B Side)	Yr	VG	VG+	NM
❑ 1054	One Nation Under Ground Bonus Poster	1967	6.25	12.50	25.00
❑ 1054 [M]	One Nation Under Ground	1967	12.50	25.00	50.00
❑ 1054 [S]	One Nation Under Ground	1967	12.50	25.00	50.00
—Black and white cover					
❑ 1054 [S]	One Nation Under Ground	1967	12.50	25.00	50.00
—Sepia-tone cover with no border					
❑ 1054 [S]	One Nation Under Ground	1967	12.50	25.00	50.00
—Sepia-tone cover with white border					
❑ 1054 [S]	One Nation Under Ground	1968	7.50	15.00	30.00
—Full-color cover					
❑ 1075	Balaklava	1968	10.00	20.00	40.00

REPRISE

Number	Title (A Side/B Side)	Yr	VG	VG+	NM
❑ RS 6364	These Things Too	1969	7.50	15.00	30.00
❑ RS 6405	The Use of Ashes	1970	7.50	15.00	30.00
❑ RS 6442	City of Gold	1971	10.00	20.00	40.00
❑ RS 6467	Beautiful Lies You Could Live In	1971	10.00	20.00	40.00

PEBBLES AND BAMM BAMM
45s
HANNA-BARBERA

Number	Title (A Side/B Side)	Yr	VG	VG+	NM
❑ 449	Open Up Your Heart/ The Lord Is Counting on You	1965	6.25	12.50	25.00
❑ 449 [PS]	Open Up Your Heart/ The Lord Is Counting on You	1965	12.50	25.00	50.00
❑ 484	The World Is Full of Toys/Daddy	1966	6.25	12.50	25.00

7-Inch Extended Plays
HANNA-BARBERA

Number	Title (A Side/B Side)	Yr	VG	VG+	NM
❑ CS 7044	Little Drummer Boy/We Three Kings//Silent Night/It Came Upon a Midnight Clear	1965	12.50	25.00	50.00
❑ CS 7044 [PS]	We Wish You a Merry Christmas	1965	25.00	50.00	100.00

Albums
HANNA-BARBERA

Number	Title (A Side/B Side)	Yr	VG	VG+	NM
❑ HLP-2033 [M]	Pebbles and Bamm-Bamm Sing Songs of Christmas	1965	30.00	60.00	120.00
❑ HLP-2040 [M]	On the Good Ship Lollipop	1966	25.00	50.00	100.00

PEDICIN, MIKE
45s
ABC-PARAMOUNT
❑ 10303 — Gotta Twist/When the Cats Come Twistin' In — 1962 — 3.00 — 6.00 — 12.00
APOLLO
❑ 534 — Hey Pop, Give Me the Keys/St. James Infirmary — 1959 — 10.00 — 20.00 — 40.00
CAMEO
❑ 125 — Shake a Hand/The Dickie Doo — 1957 — 6.25 — 12.50 — 25.00
FEDERAL
❑ 12417 — Burnt Toast/You Gotta Go, You Gotta Go — 1961 — 3.75 — 7.50 — 15.00

Number	Title (A Side/B Side)	Yr	VG	VG+	NM
MALVERN					
❏ 101	The Dickie Doo/(B-side unknown)	1957	7.50	15.00	30.00
RCA VICTOR					
❏ 47-6043	I'm Hip/				
	I Wanna Hug You, Kiss You, Squeeze You	1955	6.25	12.50	25.00
❏ 47-6051	Mambo Rock/D-E-V-I-L	1955	6.25	12.50	25.00
❏ 47-6150	Fe-Fi-Fo-Fum/The Hot Barcarolle	1955	6.25	12.50	25.00
❏ 47-6235	You Gotta Go/The Banjo Rock	1955	6.25	12.50	25.00
❏ 47-6285	Jackpot/When the Cats Come Marching In	1955	6.25	12.50	25.00
❏ 47-6369	The Large, Large House/Hotter Than a Pistol	1955	6.25	12.50	25.00
❏ 47-6546	The Beat/Save Us, Preacher Davis	1956	6.25	12.50	25.00
❏ 47-6676	Teenage Fairy Tales/Close All the Doors	1956	6.25	12.50	25.00
❏ 47-6847	The Hucklebuck/Calypso Rock	1957	6.25	12.50	25.00
20TH CENTURY					
❏ 75006	My Heart Is Breaking/I'll Always Love You Some	195?	7.50	15.00	30.00
❏ 75009	Kiss, Kiss, Kiss/Love Every Moment	195?	7.50	15.00	30.00
❏ 75012	Never Mind/M-m-Boy	195?	7.50	15.00	30.00
❏ 75019	I've Got a Feeling It's Love/				
	Is That What You Call Love	195?	7.50	15.00	30.00
❏ 75021	Disc Jockey's Boogie/Tiger Rag	195?	7.50	15.00	30.00
❏ 75023	It's My Heart to Give/				
	Kiss Me Before You Say Goodbye	195?	7.50	15.00	30.00
❏ 75027	Shake a Hand!/Disc Jockey's Boogie	195?	10.00	20.00	40.00
❏ 75027	Shake a Hand!/When We Met	195?	10.00	20.00	40.00
❏ 75029	Not Somebody Else Just Me/				
	Sweet Georgia Brown	195?	7.50	15.00	30.00
Albums					
APOLLO					
❏ LP-484 [M]	Musical Medicine	1957	37.50	75.00	150.00

PEDRICK, BOBBY, JR. See ROBERT JOHN.

PEEBLES, ANN

12-Inch Singles					
HI					
❏ 78519	I Didn't Take Your Man/(B-side unknown)	1978	3.00	6.00	12.00
45s					
HI					
❏ 2157	Walk Away/I Can't Let You Go	1969	—	3.00	6.00
❏ 2165	Give Me Some Credit/Solid Foundation	1969	—	3.00	6.00
❏ 2173	Generation Gap Between Us/I'll Get Along	1970	—	3.00	6.00
❏ 2178	Part Time Love/I Still Love You	1970	—	3.00	6.00
❏ 2186	I Pity the Fool/Heartaches, Heartaches	1971	—	3.00	6.00
❏ 2198	Slipped, Tripped and Fell in Love/99 Lbs.	1971	—	3.00	6.00
❏ 2205	Breaking Up Somebody's Home/Troubles,				
	Heartaches and Sadness	1972	—	3.00	6.00
❏ 2219	Somebody's On Your Case/				
	I've Been There Before	1972	—	3.00	6.00
❏ 2232	I'm Gonna Tear Your Playhouse Down/				
	One Way Street	1973	—	3.00	6.00
❏ 2248	I Can't Stand the Rain/I've Been There Before	1973	—	3.00	6.00
❏ 2265	(You Keep Me) Hangin' On/				
	Heartaches, Heartaches	1974	—	3.00	6.00
❏ 2271	Do I Need You/Love Vibration	1974	—	3.00	6.00
❏ 2278	Until You Came Into My Life/				
	Put Yourself in My Place	1974	—	3.00	6.00
❏ 2284	Beware/You Got to Feed the Fire	1975	—	3.00	6.00
❏ 2294	Come to Mama/I'm Leaving You	1975	—	3.00	6.00
❏ 2302	Dr. Love Power/I Still Love You	1976	—	3.00	6.00
❏ 2309	I Don't Lend My Man/I Need Somebody	1976	—	3.00	6.00
❏ 2320	Fill This World with Love/It Was Jealousy	1976	—	3.00	6.00
❏ 77502	If This Is Heaven/Sailing	1977	—	2.50	5.00
❏ 78509	Old Man with Young Ideas/A Good Day for Lovin'	1978	—	2.50	5.00
❏ 78518	I Didn't Take Your Man/Being Here with You	1978	—	2.50	5.00
❏ 79528	If You've Got the Time (I've Got the Love)/Let				
	Your Lovelight Shine	1979	—	2.50	5.00
❏ 80533	I'd Rather Leave While I'm in Love/Heartaches	1980	—	2.50	5.00
❏ 81534	Mon Belle-Amour/(B-side unknown)	1981	—	2.50	5.00
Albums					
HI					
❏ HLP-6002	If This Is Heaven	1977	3.00	6.00	12.00
❏ HLP-6007	The Handwriting Is On the Wall	1978	3.00	6.00	12.00
❏ HLP-8005	Part Time Love	197?	3.00	6.00	12.00
—Reissue of 32059					
❏ HLP-8009	Straight from the Heart	197?	3.00	6.00	12.00
—Reissue of 32065					
❏ SHL-32059	Part Time Love	1971	5.00	10.00	20.00
❏ SHL-32065	Straight from the Heart	1972	5.00	10.00	20.00
❏ XSHL-32079	I Can't Stand the Rain	1974	5.00	10.00	20.00
❏ SHL-32091	Tellin' It	1975	5.00	10.00	20.00

PEEL, DAVID

45s					
APPLE					
❏ PRO-6498/9 [DJ]	F Is Not a Dirty Word/				
	The Ballad of New York City	1972	30.00	60.00	120.00
❏ PRO-6545/6 [DJ]	Hippie from New York City/				
	The Ballad of New York City	1972	30.00	60.00	120.00
ORANGE					
❏ 1001	Bring Back the Beatles/Imagine	1977	2.50	5.00	10.00
Albums					
APPLE					
❏ SW-3391	The Pope Smokes Dope	1972	18.75	37.50	75.00
ELEKTRA					
❏ EKS-74032	Have a Marijuana	1968	10.00	20.00	40.00
❏ EKS-74069	The American Revolution	1970	7.50	15.00	30.00

PEELS, THE

45s					
KARATE					
❏ 522	Juanita Banana/Fun	1966	3.00	6.00	12.00
❏ 527	Scrooey Mooey/Time Marches On	1966	2.00	4.00	8.00
❏ 533	Juanita Banana II/Rosita Tomato	1966	2.50	5.00	10.00
Albums					
KARATE					
❏ 5402 [M]	Juanita Banana	1966	20.00	40.00	80.00

Number	Title (A Side/B Side)	Yr	VG	VG+	NM
PEEPS, THE					
45s					
PHILIPS					
❏ 40315	Now Is the Time/Got Plenty of Love	1965	2.50	5.00	10.00
PEIL, DANNY					
45s					
RAYNARD					
❏ 602	Jingle Jump/Flip Side	1964	3.75	7.50	15.00
—As "Danny Peil and the Apollos" with the B-side credited to "The Apollos"					
❏ 602	Jingle Jump/Flip Side	1964	3.75	7.50	15.00
—As "Danny Peil and the Tigers"					
PEJOE, MORRIS					
45s					
CHECKER					
❏ 766	Tired of Crying Over You/				
	Gonna Buy Me a Telephone	1953	125.00	250.00	500.00
—Black vinyl					
❏ 766	Tired of Crying Over You/				
	Gonna Buy Me a Telephone	1953	1500.	2250.	3000.
—Red vinyl					
❏ 781	Can't Get Along/It'll Plumb Get It	1953	100.00	200.00	400.00
—Black vinyl					
❏ 781	Can't Get Along/It'll Plumb Get It	1953	250.00	500.00	1000.
—Red vinyl					
VEE JAY					
❏ 148	You're Gonna Need Me/Hurt My Feelings	1955	15.00	30.00	60.00
PELICANS, THE					
45s					
IMPERIAL					
❏ 5307	Chimes/Ain't Gonna Do It	1954	250.00	500.00	1000.
LOST-NITE					
❏ 155	White Cliffs of Dover/Aurelia	196?	2.00	4.00	8.00
—Reissue					
PARROT					
❏ 793	White Cliffs of Dover/Aurelia	1954	750.00	1500.	3000.
—Black vinyl					
❏ 793	White Cliffs of Dover/Aurelia	1954	3000.	4500.	6000.
—Red vinyl					
PENDARVIS, TRACY					
45s					
SUN					
❏ 335	A Thousand Guitars/Is It Too Late	1960	5.00	10.00	20.00
❏ 345	Is It Me/South Bound Line	1960	6.25	12.50	25.00
❏ 359	Eternally/Belle of the Swanee	1961	5.00	10.00	20.00
PENDLETONS, THE					
45s					
DOT					
❏ 16511	Board Party/Barefoot Adventure	1963	25.00	50.00	100.00
RENDEZVOUS					
❏ 194	The Waddle/Itchy Bon Mash	1962	10.00	20.00	40.00
PENETRATIONS, THE					
45s					
ICON					
❏ 1002	Bring 'Em Back Alive/Fackin' Out	196?	7.50	15.00	30.00
—Black vinyl; note slightly different A-side title					
❏ 1002	Bring 'Em In/Fackin' Out	196?	15.00	30.00	60.00
—Blue vinyl					
PENGUINS, THE					
45s					
ATLANTIC					
❏ 1132	Pledge of Love/I Knew I'd Fall in Love	1957	7.50	15.00	30.00
DOOTO					
❏ 348	Earth Angel/Hey Senorita	1959	5.00	10.00	20.00
—Reissue on altered label name and yellow label					
❏ 428	That's How Much I Need You/Be My Lovin' Baby	1957	10.00	20.00	40.00
❏ 432	Sweet Love/Let Me Make Up Your Mind	1958	7.50	15.00	30.00
❏ 435	Do Not Pretend/If You're Mine	1958	7.50	15.00	30.00
DOOTONE					
❏ 345	No There Ain't No News Today/When I Am Gone	1954	75.00	150.00	300.00
—B-side by Dootsie Williams Orchestra					
❏ 348	Earth Angel/Hey Senorita	1954	37.50	75.00	150.00
—First pressings on glossy red labels					
❏ 348	Earth Angel/Hey Senorita	1955	7.50	15.00	30.00
—Black label					
❏ 348	Earth Angel/Hey Senorita	1955	10.00	20.00	40.00
—Blue label					
❏ 348	Earth Angel/Hey Senorita	1955	12.50	25.00	50.00
—Maroon label					
❏ 353	Love Will Make Your Mind Go Wild/Ookey Ook	1954	17.50	35.00	70.00
—First pressings on glossy red label					
❏ 353	Love Will Make Your Mind Go Wild/Ookey Ook	1955	7.50	15.00	30.00
—Black label					
❏ 353	Love Will Make Your Mind Go Wild/Ookey Ook	1955	10.00	20.00	40.00
—Blue label					
❏ 353	Love Will Make Your Mind Go Wild/Ookey Ook	1955	12.50	25.00	50.00
—Maroon label					
❏ 362	Baby, Let's Make Some Love/				
	Kiss a Fool Goodbye	1955	12.50	25.00	50.00
ELDO					
❏ 119	Universal Twist/To Keep Our Love	1962	5.00	10.00	20.00
GLENVILLE					
❏ 101	Earth Angel/Hey Senorita	197?	—	3.00	6.00
—Reissue					
MERCURY					
❏ 70610	Don't Do It/Be Mine or Be a Fool	1955	12.50	25.00	50.00
—Black vinyl					
❏ 70610	Don't Do It/Be Mine or Be a Fool	1955	50.00	100.00	200.00
—Red vinyl					
❏ 70654	Walkin' Down Broadway/				
	It Only Happens with You	1955	12.50	25.00	50.00

P

Number	Title (A Side/B Side)	Yr	VG	VG+	NM
❏ 70703	Promises, Promises, Promises/				
	The Devil That I See	1955	12.50	25.00	50.00
❏ 70762	A Christmas Prayer/Jingle Jangle	1955	20.00	40.00	80.00
❏ 70799	My Troubles Are Not At an End/				
	She's Gone, Gone	1956	6.25	12.50	25.00
—Black label					
❏ 70799	My Troubles Are Not At an End/				
	She's Gone, Gone	1956	12.50	25.00	50.00
—Maroon label					
❏ 70943	Earth Angel/Ice	1956	10.00	20.00	40.00
—Not the same recording as the hit on Dootone					
❏ 71033	Cool Baby Cool/Will You Be Mine	1957	10.00	20.00	40.00
ORIGINAL SOUND					
❏ 27	Memories of El Monte/Be Mine	1963	12.50	25.00	50.00
—Black and silver label; A-side written by Frank Zappa					
❏ 27	Memories of El Monte/Be Mine	1963	25.00	50.00	100.00
—Black and red label					
❏ 54	Heavenly Angel/Big Bobo's Party Train	1965	6.25	12.50	25.00
POWER					
❏ 7023	Earth Angel/Hey Senorita	195?	2.00	4.00	8.00
—Reissue from "S.P.C. Newark, N.J."					
❏ 7023 [PS]	Earth Angel/Hey Senorita	195?	3.00	6.00	12.00
SUN STATE					
❏ 001	Believe Me/The Pony Rock	1962	6.25	12.50	25.00
WING					
❏ 90076	Dealer of Dreams/Peace of Mind	1956	7.50	15.00	30.00
7-Inch Extended Plays					
DOOTO					
❏ 241	Butterball/Heart of a Fool//Money Talks/				
	Lover or Fool	1959	30.00	60.00	120.00
❏ 241 [PS]	The Cool, Cool Penguins Vol. 1	1959	30.00	60.00	120.00
❏ 243	(contents unknown)	1959	30.00	60.00	120.00
❏ 243 [PS]	The Cool, Cool Penguins, Vol. 2	1959	30.00	60.00	120.00
❏ 244	(contents unknown)	1959	30.00	60.00	120.00
❏ 244 [PS]	The Cool, Cool Penguins, Vol. 3	1959	30.00	60.00	120.00
DOOTONE					
❏ 101	Earth Angel/I Ain't Gonna Cry No More//Love				
	Will Make Your Mind Go Wild/				
	Baby Let's Make Some Love	1955	62.50	125.00	250.00
❏ 101 [PS]	The Penguins	1955	62.50	125.00	250.00
—Issued in "Dootone" jacket rather than custom jacket					
Albums					
COLLECTABLES					
❏ COL-5045	Golden Classics	198?	2.50	5.00	10.00
DOOTO					
❏ DTL-204 [M]	The Best Vocal Groups…Rhythm and Blues	1959	50.00	100.00	200.00
—Reissue of Dootone 204; blue and yellow label					
❏ DTL-204 [M]	The Best Vocal Groups…Rhythm and Blues	196?	25.00	50.00	100.00
—Black label with gold/orange/blue ring. This is NOT a counterfeit.					
❏ DTL-242 [M]	The Cool, Cool Penguins	1959	175.00	350.00	700.00
—Blue and yellow label					
❏ DTL-242 [M]	The Cool, Cool Penguins	1959	175.00	350.00	700.00
—Red and yellow label					
❏ DTL-242 [M]	The Cool, Cool Penguins	196?	50.00	100.00	200.00
—Black label with gold/orange/blue ring. This is NOT a counterfeit.					
DOOTONE					
❏ DTL-204 [M]	The Best Vocal Groups…Rhythm and Blues	195?	125.00	250.00	500.00
—As above; glossy maroon label					
❏ DTL-204 [M]	The Best Vocal Groups…Rhythm and Blues	1957	375.00	750.00	1500.
—Also includes tracks by the Medallions, Don Julian and the Meadowlarks, and the Dootones. Flat maroon label.					

PENN, LITTLE "LAMBSIE"
45s
ATCO

Number	Title (A Side/B Side)	Yr	VG	VG+	NM
❏ 6082	I Wanna Spend Christmas With Elvis/Painted				
	Lips and Pigtails	1956	12.50	25.00	50.00

PENN, WILLIAM, AND THE QUAKERS
45s
DUANE

Number	Title (A Side/B Side)	Yr	VG	VG+	NM
❏ 104	Coming Up My Way/Care Free	196?	10.00	20.00	40.00
HUSH					
❏ 230	Little Girl/Somebody's Dum Dum	196?	12.50	25.00	50.00
MELRON					
❏ 5013	California Sun/No More Love	1966	12.50	25.00	50.00
❏ 5024	Santa Needs Ear Muffs on His Nose/Philly	1966	15.00	30.00	60.00
❏ 5024	Santa Needs Ear Muffs on His Nose/Sweet				
	Caroline	1966	15.00	30.00	60.00
THUNDERBIRD					
❏ 502	Blow My Mind/Swami	1966	10.00	20.00	40.00
—As the "William Penn Fyve"					
TWILIGHT					
❏ 410	Ghost of the Monks/Goodbye My Love	1967	7.50	15.00	30.00
UPTOWN					
❏ 745	Chrome Dome Wheeler Dealer/Scrapped	1967	10.00	20.00	40.00

PENNANTS, THE
45s
WORLD

Number	Title (A Side/B Side)	Yr	VG	VG+	NM
❏ 102	Don't Go/Workin' Man	1961	25.00	50.00	100.00

PENNER, DICK
45s
SUN

Number	Title (A Side/B Side)	Yr	VG	VG+	NM
❏ 282	Cindy Lou/Your Honey Love	1958	12.50	25.00	50.00

PENNINGTON, RAY
45s
CAPITOL

Number	Title (A Side/B Side)	Yr	VG	VG+	NM
❏ 2006	Who's Gonna Walk the Dog (And Put Out the				
	Cat)/You Turned the Lights On	1967	2.00	4.00	8.00
❏ 2118	Hush, Hush, Sweet Charlotte/Someday You'll				
	Fall Back to Me	1968	2.00	4.00	8.00
❏ 5751	Who's Been Mowing the Lawn (While I Was				
	Gone)/I Don't Feel at Home	1966	2.00	4.00	8.00

Number	Title (A Side/B Side)	Yr	VG	VG+	NM
❏ 5855	Ramblin' Man/Let Go	1967	2.00	4.00	8.00
DIMENSION					
❏ 1039	For Christmas/Don't Let Me Lie Again	1982	—	2.50	5.00
❏ 1043	While I Was Slippin' In (She Was Steppin' Out)/				
	I Can Forget About You	1983	—	2.50	5.00
EMH					
❏ 0022	The Memories That Last/Nothing to Go On	1983	—	2.50	5.00
❏ 0027	For Christmas/Dark Haired Woman	1983	—	2.50	5.00
❏ 0029	Drowning My Troubles (Till They've Learned				
	How to Swim)/Till the Fear Slips Away	1984	—	2.50	5.00
❏ 0033	Nothing's Changed, Nothing's New/				
	The Devil's Den	1984	—	2.50	5.00
KING					
❏ 5783	The First Step Down Is the Longest/Your Diary	1963	3.00	6.00	12.00
LEE					
❏ 502	Boogie Woogie Country Girl/(B-side unknown)	1958	62.50	125.00	250.00
❏ 504	My Steady Baby/(B-side unknown)	1958	37.50	75.00	150.00
MONUMENT					
❏ 1109	Raining in My Heart/My Mind Is No Match for				
	Your Memory	1968	—	3.50	7.00
❏ 1134	After I'm Number One/Cold, Gray Light of Dawn	1969	—	3.50	7.00
❏ 1145	What Eva Doesn't Have/Denver	1969	—	3.50	7.00
❏ 1170	This Song Don't Care Who Sings It/I Wouldn't				
	Treat a Doggone Dog				
	(The Way You're Treatin' Me)	1969	—	3.50	7.00
❏ 1194	You Don't Know Me/Country Blues	1970	—	3.50	7.00
❏ 1208	The Other Woman/I Know Love	1970	—	3.50	7.00
❏ 1231	Bubbles in My Beer/				
	Don't Build No Fences for Me	1970	—	3.50	7.00
❏ 8527	The Best Worst Thing/				
	My Daddy Was a Travelin' Man	1971	—	3.00	6.00
❏ 8537	My Church/This Song Don't Care Who Sings It	1971	—	3.00	6.00
❏ 8540	Woman Go On Home/Dark Haired Woman	1972	—	3.00	6.00
❏ 8553	Let Them Talk/Happy Times	1972	—	3.00	6.00
MRC					
❏ 1022	She Wanted a Little Bit More/(B-side unknown)	1978	—	2.50	5.00
RUBY					
❏ 290	Fancy Free/				
	You'll Want Me Back But I Won't Care	1957	15.00	30.00	60.00
STEP ONE					
❏ 340	Deep Water/Faded Love	198?	—	2.50	5.00
❏ 343	Cincinnati Blues/Before You Turn Me Down	198?	—	2.50	5.00
❏ 403	Blue of a Kind/Fat Boy Rag	1989	—	2.50	5.00
ZODIAC					
❏ 1003	I Can't Get Up Myself/(B-side unknown)	1976	—	3.00	6.00
❏ 1010	Steppin' Aside Just Ain't My Style/The Good Old				
	Days Are Right Now	1976	—	3.00	6.00
Albums					
DIMENSION					
❏ DLP-5007	Memories	1983	3.00	6.00	12.00
MONUMENT					
❏ SLP-18145	Ray Pennington Sings for the Other Woman	1970	3.75	7.50	15.00

PENNSYLVANIA PLAYERS, THE See DICKIE GOODMAN.

PENNY AND JEAN
45s
RCA VICTOR

Number	Title (A Side/B Side)	Yr	VG	VG+	NM
❏ 47-7844	I Forgot More Than You'll Ever Know/				
	How Come I'm Crying Now?	1961	3.00	6.00	12.00
Albums					
RCA VICTOR					
❏ LPM-2244 [M]	Two for the Road	1961	5.00	10.00	20.00
❏ LSP-2244 [S]	Two for the Road	1961	6.25	12.50	25.00

PENNY AND THE OVERTONES
45s
RIM

Number	Title (A Side/B Side)	Yr	VG	VG+	NM
❏ 2021	What Made You Forget/(B-side unknown)	1958	25.00	50.00	100.00

PENTAGONS, THE
45s
DONNA

Number	Title (A Side/B Side)	Yr	VG	VG+	NM
❏ 1337	To Be Loved (Forever)/Down at the Beach	1961	7.50	15.00	30.00
❏ 1344	I Like the Way You Look (At Me)/For a Love That				
	Is Mine	1961	7.50	15.00	30.00
FLEET INT'L.					
❏ 100	Down at the Beach/To Be Loved (Forever)	1960	50.00	100.00	200.00
—Original record has "Down at the Beach" labeled as "100-1" and "To Be Loved (Forever)" as "100-2"					
JAMIE					
❏ 1201	I Wonder/She's Mine	1961	3.75	7.50	15.00
❏ 1210	Until Then/I'm in Love	1962	3.75	7.50	15.00
LOST-NITE					
❏ 210	To Be Loved (Forever)/Down at the Beach	196?	—	2.50	5.00
—Reissue					

PENTANGLE, THE
45s
REPRISE

Number	Title (A Side/B Side)	Yr	VG	VG+	NM
❏ PRO 391 [DJ]	Light Flight/Sally Go 'Round the Roses	1969	2.50	5.00	10.00
❏ 0784	Let No Man Steal Your Throne/				
	Way Behind the Sun	1968	2.00	4.00	8.00
❏ 0843	I Saw an Angel/Once I Had a Sweetheart	1969	2.00	4.00	8.00
Albums					
GREEN LINNET					
❏ SIF-3048	So Early in the Spring	1990	3.00	6.00	12.00
REPRISE					
❏ MS 2100	Solomon's Seal	1972	3.75	7.50	15.00
❏ RS 6315	The Pentangle	1968	5.00	10.00	20.00
—With "W7" and "r:" logos on two-tone orange label					
❏ RS 6315	The Pentangle	1970	3.75	7.50	15.00
—With only "r:" logo on all-orange (tan) label					
❏ 2RS 6334 [(2)]	Sweet Child	1969	6.25	12.50	25.00
—With "W7" and "r:" logos on two-tone orange label					

Number	Title (A Side/B Side)	Yr	VG	VG+	NM
❑ 2RS 6334 [(2)]	Sweet Child	1970	4.50	9.00	18.00
—With only "r:" logo on all-orange (tan) label					
❑ RS 6372	Basket of Light	1969	5.00	10.00	20.00
—With "W7" and "r:" logos on two-tone orange label					
❑ RS 6372	Basket of Light	1970	3.75	7.50	15.00
—With only "r:" logo on all-orange (tan) label					
❑ RS 6430	Cruel Sister	1971	3.75	7.50	15.00
❑ RS 6463	Reflection	1971	3.75	7.50	15.00
SHANACHIE					
❑ 79066	A Maid That's Deep in Love	198?	2.50	5.00	10.00
VARRICK					
❑ VR-017	Open the Door	1985	2.50	5.00	10.00
❑ VR-026	In the Round	1986	2.50	5.00	10.00

PEOPLE   Also see LARRY NORMAN.
45s
CAPITOL

Number	Title (A Side/B Side)	Yr	VG	VG+	NM
❑ 2078	I Love You/Somebody Tell Me My Name	1968	3.00	6.00	12.00
❑ 2251	Apple Cider/Ashes of Me	1968	2.50	5.00	10.00
❑ 2499	Turnin' Me In/Ulla	1969	2.50	5.00	10.00
❑ 5920	Organ Grinder/Riding High	1967	2.50	5.00	10.00
PARAMOUNT					
❑ 0005	Love Will Take Us Higher and Higher/Livin' It Up	1969	—	3.00	6.00
❑ 0011	Sunshine Lady/Crosstown Bus	1969	—	3.00	6.00
❑ 0019	For What It's Worth/Maple Street	1970	—	3.00	6.00
❑ 0028	One Chain Don't Make No Prison/Keep It Alive	1970	—	3.00	6.00
POLYDOR					
❑ 14087	Chant for Peace/I Don't Carry No Guns	1971	—	3.00	6.00
ZEBRA					
❑ 102	Come Back Beatles (same on both sides)	1978	2.50	5.00	10.00
Albums					
CAPITOL					
❑ ST-151	Both Sides of People	1969	10.00	20.00	40.00
❑ ST 2924	I Love You	1968	10.00	20.00	40.00
PARAMOUNT					
❑ PAS-5013	There Are People	1970	5.00	10.00	20.00

PEOPLE'S CHOICE
45s
CASABLANCA

Number	Title (A Side/B Side)	Yr	VG	VG+	NM
❑ 2322	My Feet Won't Move, But My Shoes Did the Boogie/You Ought to Be Dancin'	1980	—	2.00	4.00
PALMER					
❑ 5020	Easy to Be True/Savin' My Love for You	1967	62.50	125.00	250.00
PHIL-L.A. OF SOUL					
❑ 349	I Likes to Do It/Big Ladies Man	1971	—	3.00	6.00
❑ 352	Wootie-T-Woo/'Cause That's the Way I Know	1971	—	3.00	6.00
❑ 356	Magic/Oh How I Love It	1972	—	3.00	6.00
❑ 358	Let Me Do My Thing/On a Cloudy Day	1972	—	3.00	6.00
PHILADELPHIA INT'L.					
❑ 3649	Turn Me Loose/Soft and Tender	1978	—	2.00	4.00
❑ 3658	Rough-Ride/Stay with Me	1978	—	2.00	4.00
PHILIPS					
❑ 40653	Keep On Holding On/Just Look What You've Done	1969	3.00	6.00	12.00
TSOP					
❑ 4751	Love Shot/The Big Hurt	1973	—	2.50	5.00
❑ 4759	Party Is a Groovy Thing/Asking for Trouble	1974	—	2.50	5.00
❑ 4769	Do It Any Way You Wanna/The Big Hurt	1975	—	2.50	5.00
❑ 4773	Nursery Rhymes (Part 1)/Nursery Rhymes (Part 2)	1975	—	2.50	5.00
❑ 4781	Here We Go Again/Mickey D's	1976	—	2.50	5.00
❑ 4782	Movin' In All Directions/Mellow Hood	1976	—	2.50	5.00
❑ 4784	Cold Blooded & Down-Right Funky/Jam, Jam, Jam (All Night Long)	1976	—	2.50	5.00
❑ 4786	If You Gonna Do It (Put Your Mind To It) (Part I)/If You Gonna Do It (Put Your Mind To It) (Part II)	1977	—	2.50	5.00
Albums					
PHILADELPHIA INT'L.					
❑ JZ 35363	Turn Me Loose	1978	2.50	5.00	10.00
TSOP					
❑ KZ 33154	Boogie Down U.S.A.	1975	2.50	5.00	10.00
❑ PZ 34124	We Got the Rhythm	1976	2.50	5.00	10.00

PEPE AND THE ASTROS
45s
SWAMI

Number	Title (A Side/B Side)	Yr	VG	VG+	NM
❑ 553/4	Judy My Love/Now, Ain't That a Shame	1961	12.50	25.00	50.00

PEPP, GEORGE
45s
COLEMAN

Number	Title (A Side/B Side)	Yr	VG	VG+	NM
❑ 80	The Feeling Is Real/(B-side unknown)	196?	300.00	600.00	1200.

PEPPERMINT RAINBOW, THE
45s
DECCA

Number	Title (A Side/B Side)	Yr	VG	VG+	NM
❑ 32316	Pink Lemonade/Walking in Different Circles	1968	2.00	4.00	8.00
❑ 32410	Will You Be Staying After Sunday/And I'll Be There	1968	2.50	5.00	10.00
❑ 32498	Don't Wake Me Up in the Morning, Michael/Rosemary	1969	2.00	4.00	8.00
❑ 32498 [PS]	Don't Wake Me Up in the Morning, Michael/Rosemary	1969	3.00	6.00	12.00
❑ 32562	You're the Sound of Love/Jamais	1969	2.00	4.00	8.00
❑ 32601	Good Morning Means Goodbye/Don't Love Me Unless It's Forever	1969	2.00	4.00	8.00
Albums					
DECCA					
❑ DL 75129	Will You Be Staying After Sunday	1969	5.00	10.00	20.00

PEPPERMINT TROLLEY COMPANY, THE
45s
ACTA

Number	Title (A Side/B Side)	Yr	VG	VG+	NM
❑ 807	She's the Kind of Girl/Little Miss Sunshine	1967	2.00	4.00	8.00
❑ 809	It's a Lazy Summer Day/Blue Eyes	1967	2.00	4.00	8.00

Number	Title (A Side/B Side)	Yr	VG	VG+	NM
❑ 815	Baby You Come Rollin' Across My Mind/9 O'Clock Business Man	1968	2.50	5.00	10.00
❑ 829	Trust/I Remember Long Along	1968	2.00	4.00	8.00
❑ 834	The Last Thing on My Mind/Memphis City Letter	1969	2.00	4.00	8.00
❑ 835	Spinnin' 'n' Whirlin' Around/New York City	1969	2.00	4.00	8.00
VALIANT					
❑ 752	Lollipop Train/Bored to Tears	1966	3.75	7.50	15.00
Albums					
ACTA					
❑ A-8007 [M]	The Peppermint Trolley Company	1968	12.50	25.00	50.00
—In stereo cover with "Monaural" sticker					
❑ A-38007 [S]	The Peppermint Trolley Company	1968	6.25	12.50	25.00

PEPS, THE   See THE FABULOUS PEPS.

PERENNIALS, THE
45s
BALL

Number	Title (A Side/B Side)	Yr	VG	VG+	NM
❑ 1016	My Big Mistake/I'm Yours 'Til the End	1963	100.00	200.00	400.00

PERFECT, CHRISTINE   See CHRISTINE McVIE.

PERFIDIANS, THE
45s
HUSKY

Number	Title (A Side/B Side)	Yr	VG	VG+	NM
❑ 1	La Paz/Whiplash	1962	10.00	20.00	40.00
—Black vinyl					
❑ 1	La Paz/Whiplash	1962	20.00	40.00	80.00
—Red vinyl					

PERHACS, LINDA
Albums
KAPP

Number	Title (A Side/B Side)	Yr	VG	VG+	NM
❑ KS-3636	Parallelograms	1970	50.00	100.00	200.00

PERKINS, CARL
45s
COLUMBIA

Number	Title (A Side/B Side)	Yr	VG	VG+	NM
❑ 41131	Pink Pedal Pushers/Jive After Five	1958	7.50	15.00	30.00
❑ 41131 [PS]	Pink Pedal Pushers/Jive After Five	1958	30.00	60.00	120.00
❑ 41207	Levi Jacket/Pop, Let Me Have the Car	1958	6.25	12.50	25.00
❑ 41296	Y-O-U/This Life I Live	1958	6.25	12.50	25.00
❑ 41379	Pointed Toe Shoes/Highway of Love	1959	6.25	12.50	25.00
❑ 41449	One Ticket to Loneliness/I Don't See Me in Your Eyes Anymore	1959	6.25	12.50	25.00
❑ 41651	L-O-V-E-V-I-L-L-E/Too Much for a Man to Understand	1960	6.25	12.50	25.00
❑ 41825	Honey, 'Cause I Love You/Just for You	1960	6.25	12.50	25.00
❑ 42061	Anyway the Wind Blows/The Unhappy Girls	1961	6.25	12.50	25.00
❑ 42403	Hollywood City/Forget Me Next Time Around	1962	—	—	—
—Unreleased?					
❑ 42405 [PS]	Hollywood City/The Fool I Used to Be	1962	30.00	60.00	120.00
❑ 42405	Hollywood City/The Fool I Used to Be	1962	6.25	12.50	25.00
❑ 42514	Sister Twister/Hambone	1962	6.25	12.50	25.00
❑ 42514 [PS]	Sister Twister/Hambone	1962	100.00	200.00	400.00
❑ 42753	I Just Got Back from There/Forget Me Next Time Around	1963	6.25	12.50	25.00
❑ 44723	Restless/1143	1968	2.00	4.00	8.00
❑ 44883	For Your Love/Four Letter Word	1969	2.00	4.00	8.00
❑ 44993	C.C. Rider/Soul Beat	1969	2.00	4.00	8.00
❑ 45107	All Mama's Children/Step Aside	1970	2.00	4.00	8.00
—With NRBQ					
❑ 45132	State of Confusion/My Son, My Son	1970	—	3.00	6.00
❑ 45253	What Every Little Boy Ought to Know/Just As Long	1970	—	2.50	5.00
❑ 45347	Me Without You/Red Headed Woman	1971	—	2.50	5.00
❑ 45466	Cotton Top/About All I Can Give You Is My Love	1971	—	2.50	5.00
❑ 45582	High on Love/Take Me Back to Memphis	1972	—	2.50	5.00
❑ 45694	Someday/The Trip	1972	—	2.50	5.00
DECCA					
❑ 31548	Help Me Find My Baby/For a Little While	1963	3.75	7.50	15.00
❑ 31591	After Sundown/I Wouldn't Have Told You	1964	3.75	7.50	15.00
❑ 31709	The Monkeyshine/Let My Baby Be	1964	3.75	7.50	15.00
❑ 31786	One of These Days/Mama of My Song	1965	3.75	7.50	15.00
DOLLIE					
❑ 505	Country Boy's Dream/If I Could Come Back	1966	3.00	6.00	12.00
❑ 508	Shine, Shine, Shine/Almost Love	1967	3.00	6.00	12.00
❑ 512	Without You/You Can Take the Boy Out of the Country	1967	3.00	6.00	12.00
❑ 514	My Old Home Town/Back to Tennessee	1967	3.00	6.00	12.00
❑ 516	It's You/Lake County Cotton Country	1968	3.00	6.00	12.00
FLIP					
❑ 501	Movie Magg/Turn Around	1955	250.00	500.00	1000.
JET					
❑ 5054	Blue Suede Shoes/Rock Around the World	1979	—	2.00	4.00
MERCURY					
❑ 55009	The E.P. Express/Big Bad Blues	1977	—	2.00	4.00
❑ 73425	(Let's Get) Dixiefried/One More Loser Goin' Home	1973	—	3.00	6.00
❑ 73489	Ruby, Don't Take Your Love to Town/Sing My Song	1974	—	2.50	5.00
❑ 73653	You'll Always Be a Lady to Me/Low Class	1974	—	2.50	5.00
❑ 73690	The E.P. Express/Big Bad Blues	1975	—	2.50	5.00
❑ 73993	Help Me Dream/You Tore My Heaven All to Hell	1973	—	3.00	6.00
MMI					
❑ 1016	Don't Get Off Gettin' It On/Georgia Court Room	1977	—	2.00	4.00
❑ 1019	Standing in the Need of Love/Georgia Court Room	1977	—	2.00	4.00
MUSIC MILL					
❑ 1007	Born to Boogie/Take Me Back	1976	—	2.00	4.00
SMASH					
❑ 884760-7	Birth of Rock and Roll/Rock and Roll (Fais-Do-Do)	1986	—	2.00	4.00
—B-side with Jerry Lee Lewis, Roy Orbison and Johnny Cash					
❑ 884760-7 [PS]	Birth of Rock and Roll/Rock and Roll (Fais-Do-Do)	1986	—	2.00	4.00
—B-side with Jerry Lee Lewis, Roy Orbison and Johnny Cash					

P

Number	Title (A Side/B Side)	Yr	VG	VG+	NM
❑ 884934-7	Sixteen Candles/Rock & Roll (Fais-Do-Do)	1986	—	2.00	4.00
—B-side with Jerry Lee Lewis, Roy Orbison and Johnny Cash; A-side by Jerry Lee Lewis					
❑ 888142-7	Class of '55/We Remember the King	1987	—	2.00	4.00
—B-side with Jerry Lee Lewis, Roy Orbison and Johnny Cash					
SUEDE					
❑ 101	I Don't Want to Fall in Love Again/We Did It in '54	1978	—	2.00	4.00
❑ 102	Rock-a-Billy Fever/Till You Get Through with Me	1978	—	2.00	4.00
❑ 6777	Little Teardrops/Green Grass of Home	1977	—	2.00	4.00
SUN					
❑ 224	Gone, Gone, Gone/				
	Let the Jukebox Keep On Playing	1955	25.00	50.00	100.00
❑ 234	Blue Suede Shoes/Honey Don't	1956	15.00	30.00	60.00
❑ 235	Sure to Fall/Tennessee	1956	—	—	—
—Unreleased					
❑ 243	Boppin' the Blues/All Mama's Children	1956	10.00	20.00	40.00
❑ 249	Dixie Fried/I'm Sorry, I'm Not Sorry	1956	7.50	15.00	30.00
❑ 261	Matchbox/Your True Love	1957	7.50	15.00	30.00
❑ 274	That's Right/Forever Yours	1957	7.50	15.00	30.00
❑ 287	Glad All Over/Lend Me Your Comb	1958	7.50	15.00	30.00
UNIVERSAL					
❑ UVL-66002	Charlene/Love Makes Dreams Come True	1989	—	2.00	4.00
❑ UVL-66019	Hambone/Love Makes Dreams Come True	1989	—	2.00	4.00
7-Inch Extended Plays					
COLUMBIA					
❑ B-12341	Whole Lotta Shakin' Goin' On/That's All Right//				
	Tutti Frutti/I Got a Woman	1958	50.00	100.00	200.00
❑ B-12341 [PS]	Whole Lotta Shakin'	1958	50.00	100.00	200.00
SUN					
❑ EPA-115	Blue Suede Shoes/Movie Magg//Sure to Fall/				
	Gone, Gone, Gone	1958	100.00	200.00	400.00
❑ EPA-115 [PS]	Carl Perkins	1958	100.00	200.00	400.00
Albums					
ACCORD					
❑ SN-7169	Presenting Carl Perkins	1982	2.50	5.00	10.00
ALBUM GLOBE					
❑ 8118	Country Soul	1980	2.50	5.00	10.00
❑ 9037	Goin' Back to Memphis	1980	2.50	5.00	10.00
ALLEGIANCE					
❑ AV-5001	The Heart and Soul of Carl Perkins	198?	2.50	5.00	10.00
BULLDOG					
❑ BDL-2034	Twenty Golden Pieces	198?	2.50	5.00	10.00
COLUMBIA					
❑ CL 1234 [DJ]	Whole Lotta Shakin'	1958	200.00	400.00	800.00
—White label promo					
❑ CL 1234 [M]	Whole Lotta Shakin'	1958	100.00	200.00	400.00
❑ CS 9833	Carl Perkins' Greatest Hits	1969	6.25	12.50	25.00
—Red "360 Sound Stereo" label					
❑ CS 9931	Carl Perkins On Top	1969	6.25	12.50	25.00
—Red "360 Sound Stereo" label					
❑ CS 9981	Boppin' the Blues	1970	3.00	6.00	12.00
—Orange label					
❑ CS 9981	Boppin' the Blues	1970	6.25	12.50	25.00
—Red "360 Sound Stereo" label					
❑ PC 9981	Boppin' the Blues	198?	2.00	4.00	8.00
—Budget-line reissue					
❑ FC 37961	The Survivors	1982	2.50	5.00	10.00
—With Johnny Cash and Jerry Lee Lewis					
❑ PC 37961	The Survivors	198?	2.00	4.00	8.00
—Budget-line reissue					
COLUMBIA LIMITED EDITION					
❑ LE 10117	Carl Perkins' Greatest Hits	1974	3.00	6.00	12.00
—"Limited Edition" brown label					
DESIGN					
❑ DLP-611 [M]	Tennessee	1963	7.50	15.00	30.00
❑ SDLP-611 [R]	Tennessee	1963	5.00	10.00	20.00
DOLLIE					
❑ 4001	Country Boy's Dream	1967	7.50	15.00	30.00
❑ ST-91428	Country Boy's Dream	1967	10.00	20.00	40.00
—Capitol Record Club edition					
HARMONY					
❑ HS 11385	Carl Perkins	1970	3.75	7.50	15.00
❑ KH 31179	Brown Eyed Handsome Man	1971	3.00	6.00	12.00
❑ KH 31792	Greatest Hits	1972	3.00	6.00	12.00
HILLTOP					
❑ 6103	Matchbox	197?	3.00	6.00	12.00
JET					
❑ JT-LA856-H	Ol' Blue Suede's Back	1978	3.75	7.50	15.00
❑ JZ 35604	Ol' Blue Suede's Back	1978	2.50	5.00	10.00
KOALA					
❑ AW 14164	Country Soul	198?	2.50	5.00	10.00
MCA DOT					
❑ 39035	Carl Perkins	1985	2.50	5.00	10.00
MERCURY					
❑ SRM-1-691	My Kind of Country	1973	3.00	6.00	12.00
RHINO					
❑ RNLP-70221	Original Sun Greatest Hits (1955-1957)	1986	3.00	6.00	12.00
ROUNDER					
❑ SS-27	Honky Tonk Gal: Rare and Unissued Sun Masters	1989	3.00	6.00	12.00
SMASH					
❑ 830002-1	Class of '55	1986	3.00	6.00	12.00
—With Jerry Lee Lewis, Roy Orbison and Johnny Cash					
SUEDE					
❑ 002	Live at Austin City Limits	1981	2.50	5.00	10.00
SUN					
❑ LP-111	Original Golden Hits	1969	3.00	6.00	12.00
❑ LP-112	Blue Suede Shoes	1969	3.00	6.00	12.00
❑ SLP-1225 [M]	The Dance Album of Carl Perkins	1957	300.00	600.00	1200.
❑ SLP-1225 [M]	Teen Beat — The Best of Carl Perkins	1961	125.00	250.00	500.00
—Reissue with new title					
SUNNYVALE					
❑ 9330803	The Sun Story, Vol. 3	1977	3.00	6.00	12.00
TRIP					
❑ TLP-8503 [(2)]	The Best of Carl Perkins	1974	3.00	6.00	12.00
UNIVERSAL					
❑ UVL-76001	Born to Rock	1989	3.75	7.50	15.00

Number	Title (A Side/B Side)	Yr	VG	VG+	NM
PERKINS, LAURA LEE					
45s					
IMPERIAL					
❑ 5493	Kiss Me Baby/I Just Don't Like This Kind of Lovin'	1958	10.00	20.00	40.00
❑ 5507	Don't Wait Up/Oh La Baby	1958	10.00	20.00	40.00
PERKINS, ROY					
45s					
MELADEE					
❑ 111	Bye Bye Baby/You're on My Mind	1958	25.00	50.00	100.00
❑ 112	You're Gone/Here Am I	1958	150.00	300.00	600.00
MERCURY					
❑ 71278	Drop Top/That's What the Mailman Had to Say	1958	10.00	20.00	40.00
PERKINS, TONY					
45s					
EPIC					
❑ 9165	If You'll Be Mine/A Little Love Can Go a Long Way	1956	5.00	10.00	20.00
—As "Anthony Perkins"					
❑ 9181	Friendly Persuasion/If You Were the Only Girl	1956	5.00	10.00	20.00
—As "Anthony Perkins"					
❑ 9201	A Fool in Love/Melody for Lovers	1957	5.00	10.00	20.00
—As "Anthony Perkins"					
RCA VICTOR					
❑ 47-7020	Moon-Light Swim/First Romance	1957	3.00	6.00	12.00
❑ 47-7078	When School Starts Again/Rocket to the Moon	1957	3.00	6.00	12.00
❑ 47-7155	Indian Giver/Just Being of Age	1958	3.00	6.00	12.00
❑ 47-7155 [PS]	Indian Giver/Just Being of Age	1958	6.25	12.50	25.00
❑ 47-7244	The Prettiest Girl in School/No, No, No	1958	3.00	6.00	12.00
❑ 47-7295	Moonlight Swim/She Used to Be My Girl	1958	3.00	6.00	12.00
❑ 47-7415	Treasure Island/Gonna Get Some Lovin'	1958	3.00	6.00	12.00
Albums					
EPIC					
❑ LN 3394 [M]	Tony Perkins	1957	12.50	25.00	50.00
RCA VICTOR					
❑ LPM-1679 [M]	From My Heart	1958	10.00	20.00	40.00
❑ LSP-1679 [S]	From My Heart	1958	15.00	30.00	60.00
❑ LPM-1853 [M]	On a Rainy Afternoon	1958	10.00	20.00	40.00
❑ LSP-1853 [S]	On a Rainy Afternoon	1958	15.00	30.00	60.00
PERPETUAL MOTION					
45s					
DIAL					
❑ 4078	Neckin' Don't Make It/Get Ready	1968	3.00	6.00	12.00
PERRINE, PEP					
Albums					
HIDEOUT					
❑ 1003 [M]	Pep Perrine Live and In Person	196?	30.00	60.00	120.00
PERSIANS, THE (1)					
45s					
ABC					
❑ 11087	Too Much Pride/That's If You Want Me To	1968	2.00	4.00	8.00
❑ 11145	I Only Have Eyes for You/The Sun's Gotta Shine				
	in Your Heart	1968	2.00	4.00	8.00
CAPITOL					
❑ 3230	Your Love/Keep On Moving	1971	—	3.00	6.00
❑ 3333	I Want to Go Home/Baby Come Back Home	1972	—	3.00	6.00
❑ 3414	Give Me a Little Tune/				
	I Won't Cry for You Anymore	1972	—	3.00	6.00
GWP					
❑ 509	I Don't Know How (To Fall Out of Love)/				
	Here It Comes	1969	—	3.50	7.00
GWP'S GRAPEVINE					
❑ 201	Detour/(B-side unknown)	1970	—	3.50	7.00
PERSIANS, THE (2)					
45s					
GOLD EAGLE					
❑ 1813	Love Me Tonight/Gee What a Girl	1962	6.25	12.50	25.00
GOLDISC					
❑ 1	Teardrops Are Falling/Vault of Memories	1963	15.00	30.00	60.00
❑ 17	Let's Monkey Again/When You Said				
	Let's Get Married	1963	7.50	15.00	30.00
MUSIC WORLD					
❑ 102	Let's Monkey Again/When You Said				
	Let's Get Married	1963	3.00	6.00	12.00
PAGEANT					
❑ 601	Get a Hold of Yourself/The Steady Kind	1963	3.75	7.50	15.00
RSVP					
❑ 114	Tears of Love/Dance Now	1962	7.50	15.00	30.00
RTO					
❑ 100	Sunday Kind of Love/When We Get Married	1963	3.75	7.50	15.00
PERSONALITIES, THE					
45s					
SAFARI					
❑ 1002	Woe Woe Baby/Yours to Command	1957	12.50	25.00	50.00
—No giraffe on label					
❑ 1002	Woe Woe Baby/Yours to Command	1957	50.00	100.00	200.00
—With giraffe on label					
PERSUADERS, THE More than one group?					
45s					
ATCO					
❑ 6822	Thin Line Between Love and Hate/Thigh Spy	1971	2.50	5.00	10.00
❑ 6919	Bad, Bold and Beautiful Girl/Please Stay	1973	—	3.50	7.00
❑ 6943	Some Guys Have All the Luck/Love Attack	1973	2.00	4.00	8.00
❑ 6956	Best Thing That Ever Happened to Me/				
	The Way She Is	1974	—	3.50	7.00
❑ 6964	All Strung Out on You/Once in a Lifetime Thing	1974	—	3.50	7.00
❑ 7012	I've Been Through This Before/Stay with Me	1975	—	3.50	7.00
BUM BUM					
❑ 701	Miserlou/World of Wonder	196?	7.50	15.00	30.00

Patti Page, *Tennessee Waltz,* Mercury MG-25154, 10-inch LP, $20-$40.

Van Dyke Parks, *Jump!,* Warner Bros. 23829, stereo LP, $6-$12.

The Partridge Family, "I Think I Love You," Bell 910, picture sleeve, $3-$6.

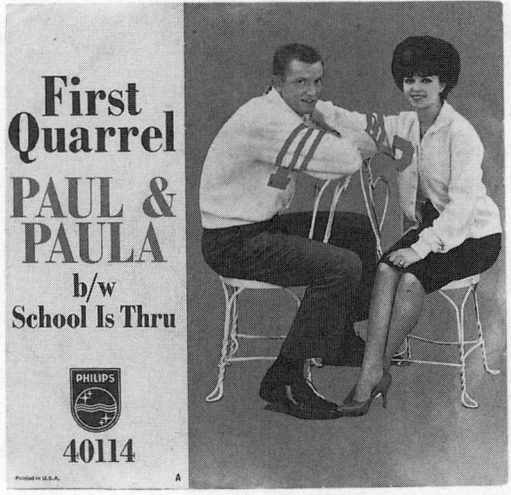

Paul and Paula, "First Quarrel," Philips 40114, picture sleeve, $10-$20.

Peter and Gordon, "Nobody I Know," Capitol 5211, picture sleeve, $8-$16.

Peter, Paul and Mary, *Peter, Paul and Mary,* Warner Bros. WS 1449, stereo LP, gold label, $12.50-$25.

Number	Title (A Side/B Side)	Yr	VG	VG+	NM
CALLA					
3006	I Need Love/Sure Shot	1977	—	3.00	6.00
3007	Trying to Love Two Women/Quickest Way Out	1977	—	3.00	6.00
CARLTON					
568	Arabella/Viva El Matador	1962	3.75	7.50	15.00
WIN OR LOSE					
220	Love Gonna Pack Up (And Walk Out)/You Musta Put Something In Your Love	1971	2.00	4.00	8.00
222	If This Is What You Call Love (I Don't Want No Part of It)/Thanks for Loving Me	1972	2.00	4.00	8.00
225	Peace in the Valley of Love/What Is the Definition of Love	1972	2.00	4.00	8.00
WINLEY					
235	Tears/What Could It Be	1959	37.50	75.00	150.00
Albums					
ATCO					
SD 7021	The Persuaders	1973	5.00	10.00	20.00
SD 7046	Best Thing That Ever Happened to Me	1974	5.00	10.00	20.00
CALLA					
PZ 34802	It's All About Love	1977	3.75	7.50	15.00
COLLECTABLES					
COL-5139	Thin Line Between Love and Hate (Golden Classics)	198?	2.50	5.00	10.00
WIN OR LOSE					
SD 33-387	Thin Line Between Love and Hate	1972	6.25	12.50	25.00

PERSUADERS, THE (2)
45s

Number	Title (A Side/B Side)	Yr	VG	VG+	NM
SATURN					
404	Surfing Strip/Hanging Ten	1963	7.50	15.00	30.00
405	Caught in the Soup/Gremmie Bread	1963	7.50	15.00	30.00
Albums					
SATURN					
SAT-5000 [M]	Surfer's Nightmare	1963	75.00	150.00	300.00
SATS-5000 [S]	Surfer's Nightmare	1963	100.00	200.00	400.00

PERSUASIONS, THE
45s

Number	Title (A Side/B Side)	Yr	VG	VG+	NM
A&M					
1531	I Really Got It Bad for You/We're All Goin' Home	1974	—	3.00	6.00
1631	With This Ring/Somewhere to Lay My Head	1974	—	3.00	6.00
1658	I Just Want to Sing with My Friends/Somewhere to Lay My Head	1975	—	3.00	6.00
1698	One Thing on My Mind/Darlin'	1975	—	3.00	6.00
CAPITOL					
3162	Let It Be/It's You That I Need	1971	2.00	4.00	8.00
3242	Don't Know Why I Love You/Tempts Jam	1971	2.00	4.00	8.00
3317	People Get Ready/Buffalo Soldier	1972	2.00	4.00	8.00
3425	The Ten Commandments of Love/Good Times	1972	2.00	4.00	8.00
3492	Three Angels (Part 1)/Three Angels (Part 2)	1972	2.00	4.00	8.00
ELEKTRA					
45396	Papa-Oom-Mow-Mow/Women and Drinkin'	1977	—	2.50	5.00
MCA					
40080	Good Old Accapella/You Must Believe in Me	1973	—	3.00	6.00
40118	Chapel of Love/Love You Most of All	1973	—	3.00	6.00
REPRISE					
0977	Since I Fell for You/Without a Song	1970	2.00	4.00	8.00
TOWER					
146	Try Me/I'll Go Crazy	1965	2.50	5.00	10.00
197	Big Brother/Deep Down Love	1966	2.50	5.00	10.00
Albums					
A&M					
SP-3635	More Than Before	1974	3.00	6.00	12.00
SP-3656	I Just Want to Sing with My Friends	1974	3.00	6.00	12.00
CAPITOL					
SM-791	We Came to Play	197?	2.50	5.00	10.00
—Reissue with new prefix					
ST-791	We Came to Play	1971	6.25	12.50	25.00
ST-872	Street Corner Symphony	1972	6.25	12.50	25.00
ST-11101	Spread the Word	1972	6.25	12.50	25.00
CATAMOUNT					
905	Stardust	197?	10.00	20.00	40.00
ELEKTRA					
7E-1099	Chirpin'	1977	3.00	6.00	12.00
FLYING FISH					
FF-093	Comin' At Ya	1979	3.00	6.00	12.00
MCA					
326	We Still Ain't Got No Band	1973	3.75	7.50	15.00
REPRISE					
RS 6394	Acapella	1970	7.50	15.00	30.00
ROUNDER					
3053	Good News	1981	2.50	5.00	10.00
3083	No Frills	1984	2.50	5.00	10.00

PETER AND GORDON Also see GORDON WALLER.
45s

Number	Title (A Side/B Side)	Yr	VG	VG+	NM
CAPITOL					
2071	Greener Days/Never Ever	1968	2.50	5.00	10.00
2214	You've Had Better Times/Sipping My Wine	1968	2.50	5.00	10.00
2544	I Can Remember (Not Too Long Ago)/Hard Time, Rainy Day	1969	2.50	5.00	10.00
5175	A World Without Love/If I Were You	1964	3.00	6.00	12.00
5211	Nobody I Know/You Don't Have to Tell Me	1964	3.00	6.00	12.00
5211 [PS]	Nobody I Know/You Don't Have to Tell Me	1964	4.00	8.00	16.00
5272	I Don't Want to See You Again/I Would Buy You Presents	1964	3.00	6.00	12.00
5272 [PS]	I Don't Want to See You Again/I Would Buy You Presents	1964	4.00	8.00	16.00
5335	I Go to Pieces/Love Me, Baby	1965	3.00	6.00	12.00
5335 [PS]	I Go to Pieces/Love Me, Baby	1965	4.00	8.00	16.00
5406	True Love Ways/If You Wish	1965	3.00	6.00	12.00
5406 [PS]	True Love Ways/If You Wish	1965	4.00	8.00	16.00
5461	To Know You Is to Love You/I Told You So	1965	2.50	5.00	10.00
5461 [PS]	To Know You Is to Love You/I Told You So	1965	3.75	7.50	15.00
5532	Don't Pity Me/Crying in the Rain	1965	2.50	5.00	10.00

Number	Title (A Side/B Side)	Yr	VG	VG+	NM
5579	Woman/Wrong from the Start	1966	2.50	5.00	10.00
—A-side composer listed as "A. Smith"					
5579	Woman/Wrong from the Start	1966	3.00	6.00	12.00
—A-side composer listed as "Bernard Webb"					
5650	There's No Living Without Your Loving/A Stranger with a Black Dove	1966	2.50	5.00	10.00
5650 [PS]	There's No Living Without Your Loving/A Stranger with a Black Dove	1966	3.75	7.50	15.00
5684	To Show I Love You/Start Trying Someone Else	1966	2.50	5.00	10.00
5684 [PS]	To Show I Love You/Start Trying Someone Else	1966	3.75	7.50	15.00
5740	Lady Godiva/Morning's Calling	1966	2.50	5.00	10.00
5740	Lady Godiva/The House I Live In	1966	3.75	7.50	15.00
5808	Knight in Rusty Armour/Flower Lady	1966	2.50	5.00	10.00
5808 [PS]	Knight in Rusty Armour/Flower Lady	1966	3.75	7.50	15.00
5864	Sunday for Tea/Hurtin' Is Lovin'	1967	2.50	5.00	10.00
5864 [PS]	Sunday for Tea/Hurtin' Is Lovin'	1967	3.75	7.50	15.00
5919	The Jokers/Red Cream and Velvet	1967	2.50	5.00	10.00
CAPITOL CREATIVE PRODUCTS					
51 [DJ]	Wrong from the Start/You've Lost That Lovin' Feelin'	1966	3.00	6.00	12.00
—B-side by the Lettermen					
CAPITOL STARLINE					
6076	A World Without Love/Nobody I Know	1965	2.00	4.00	8.00
—Green swirl label original					
6103	I Go to Pieces/Love Me Baby	1966	2.00	4.00	8.00
—Green swirl label original					
6104	There's No Living Without Your Loving/Stranger with a Black Dove	1966	2.00	4.00	8.00
—Green swirl label original					
6155	I Don't Want to See You Again/Woman	197?	—	3.00	6.00
—Red and white "bullseye" label original					
6156	Lady Godiva/You've Had Better Times	197?	—	3.00	6.00
—Red and white "bullseye" label original					
Albums					
CAPITOL					
ST 2115 [S]	A World Without Love	1964	6.25	12.50	25.00
T 2115 [M]	A World Without Love	1964	5.00	10.00	20.00
ST 2220 [S]	I Don't Want to See You Again	1964	6.25	12.50	25.00
T 2220 [M]	I Don't Want to See You Again	1964	5.00	10.00	20.00
ST 2324 [S]	I Go to Pieces	1965	6.25	12.50	25.00
T 2324 [M]	I Go to Pieces	1965	5.00	10.00	20.00
ST 2368 [S]	True Love Ways	1965	6.25	12.50	25.00
T 2368 [M]	True Love Ways	1965	5.00	10.00	20.00
ST 2430 [S]	Peter and Gordon Sing the Hits of Nashville	1966	6.25	12.50	25.00
T 2430 [M]	Peter and Gordon Sing the Hits of Nashville	1966	5.00	10.00	20.00
ST 2477 [P]	Woman	1966	6.25	12.50	25.00
—"Woman" is rechanneled					
T 2477 [M]	Woman	1966	5.00	10.00	20.00
ST 2549 [P]	The Best of Peter and Gordon	1966	4.50	9.00	18.00
—Black label with colorband; "Woman" is rechanneled					
ST 2549 [P]	The Best of Peter and Gordon	1967	3.75	7.50	15.00
—"Starline" label					
T 2549 [M]	The Best of Peter and Gordon	1966	3.75	7.50	15.00
—Black label with colorband					
T 2549 [M]	The Best of Peter and Gordon	1967	3.00	6.00	12.00
—"Starline" label					
ST 2664 [S]	Lady Godiva	1967	5.00	10.00	20.00
T 2664 [M]	Lady Godiva	1967	3.75	7.50	15.00
ST 2729 [S]	Knight in Rusty Armour	1967	5.00	10.00	20.00
T 2729 [M]	Knight in Rusty Armour	1967	3.75	7.50	15.00
ST 2747 [S]	In London for Tea	1967	5.00	10.00	20.00
T 2747 [M]	In London for Tea	1967	3.75	7.50	15.00
ST 2882 [S]	Hot, Cold and Custard	1968	6.25	12.50	25.00
SN-16084 [S]	The Best of Peter and Gordon	1979	2.00	4.00	8.00

PETER, PAUL AND MARY Also see PAUL STOOKEY; MARY TRAVERS; PETER YARROW.
45s

Number	Title (A Side/B Side)	Yr	VG	VG+	NM
(NO LABEL)					
(no #) [DJ]	Eugene McCarthy for President	1968	6.25	12.50	25.00
WARNER BROS.					
(no #)	A-Soalin' (mono/stereo)	196?	3.00	6.00	12.00
—Green custom label					
(no #) [PS]	A-Soalin' (mono/stereo)	196?	5.00	10.00	20.00
—Illustrated book with lyrics					
PRO 149 [DJ]	Morning Train/Gone the Rainbow	1963	3.75	7.50	15.00
—Stereo 33 1/3 rpm, 7-inch single with small hole; "Promotion" at 10 o'clock on label					
S 155 [DJ]	Quit Your Low Down Ways/Freight Train	1963	3.75	7.50	15.00
—Stereo 33 1/3 rpm, 7-inch single with small hole; "Promotion" at bottom of label					
5274	Lemon Tree/Early in the Morning	1962	2.50	5.00	10.00
5296	If I Had a Hammer/Gone the Rainbow	1962	2.50	5.00	10.00
5325	Big Boat/Tiny Sparrow	1962	2.50	5.00	10.00
5325 [PS]	Big Boat/Tiny Sparrow	1962	5.00	10.00	20.00
5334	Settle Down (Goin' Down That Highway)/500 Miles	1963	2.50	5.00	10.00
5348	Puff (The Magic Dragon)/Pretty Mary	1963	2.50	5.00	10.00
—Later pressings add subtitle					
5348	Puff/Pretty Mary	1963	3.00	6.00	12.00
—First pressings have no subtitle on A-side					
5368	Blowin' in the Wind/Flora	1963	2.50	5.00	10.00
5385	Don't Think Twice, It's All Right/Autumn to May	1963	2.50	5.00	10.00
5399	Stewball/The Cruel War	1963	2.50	5.00	10.00
5402	A-Soalin'/High-A-Bye	1963	3.00	6.00	12.00
5402 [PS]	A-Soalin'/High-A-Bye	1963	5.00	10.00	20.00
5418	Tell It on the Mountain/Old Coat	1964	2.50	5.00	10.00
5442	Oh, Rock My Soul (Part 1)/Oh, Rock My Soul (Part 2)	1964	2.50	5.00	10.00
5496	For Lovin' Me/Monday Morning	1965	2.00	4.00	8.00
5625	When the Ship Comes In/The Times They Are a-Changin'	1965	2.00	4.00	8.00
5659	Early Morning Rain/The Rising of the Moon	1965	2.00	4.00	8.00
5809	The Cruel War/Mon Vrai Destin	1966	2.00	4.00	8.00
5842	Hurry Sundown/Sometime Lover	1966	—	—	8.00
—Unreleased?					
5849	The Other Side of This Life/Sometime Lover	1966	2.00	4.00	8.00
5883	For Baby (For Bobbie)/Hurry Sundown	1966	2.00	4.00	8.00
7067	I Dig Rock and Roll Music/The Great Mandella (The Wheel of Life)	1967	2.50	5.00	10.00
7092	Too Much of Nothing/The House Song	1967	2.00	4.00	8.00

Number	Title (A Side/B Side)	Yr	VG	VG+	NM
❑ 7232	Yesterday's Tomorrow/Love City				
	(Postcards to Duluth)	1968	2.00	4.00	8.00
❑ 7279	Day Is Done/Make Believe Town	1969	2.00	4.00	8.00
❑ 7340	Leaving on a Jet Plane/The House Song	1969	2.50	5.00	10.00
❑ 7359	Christmas Dinner/The Marvelous Toy	1969	2.50	5.00	10.00
❑ 8684	Like the First Time/Best of Friends	1978	—	2.00	4.00
❑ 8728	Forever Young/Best of Friends	1978	—	2.00	4.00

7-Inch Extended Plays
WARNER BROS.

Number	Title (A Side/B Side)	Yr	VG	VG+	NM
❑ S 1473	(Moving)	196?	3.00	6.00	12.00
❑ S 1473	Settle Down/Gone the Rainbow/Pretty Mary//				
	This Land Is Your Land/Man Come Into Egypt/				
	Morning Train	196?	3.00	6.00	12.00
—Jukebox issue; small hole, plays at 33 1/3 rpm					
❑ S 1507	Very Last Day/Tell It on the Mountain/Freight				
	Train//Rocky Road/Quit Your Low Down				
	Ways/Stewball	196?	3.00	6.00	12.00
—Jukebox issue; small hole, plays at 33 1/3 rpm, "Promotion" on label					
❑ S 1507-1	Tell It on the Mountain/Blowin' in the Wind/Very				
	Last Day//Freight Train/All My Trials/Quit Your				
	Low Down Ways	196?	3.00	6.00	12.00
—Jukebox issue; small hole, plays at 33 1/3 rpm, "Promotion" on label					
❑ S 1507-1 [PS]	In the Wind	196?	3.00	6.00	12.00
❑ S 1751	Moments of Soft Persuasion/Too Much of				
	Nothing/Reason to Believe//She Dreams/				
	Hymn/I Shall Be Released	1968	2.50	5.00	10.00
—Jukebox issue; small hole, plays at 33 1/3 rpm					
❑ S 1751 [PS]	Late Again	1968	2.50	5.00	10.00

Albums
GOLD CASTLE

Number	Title (A Side/B Side)	Yr	VG	VG+	NM
❑ D1-71301	No Easy Walk to Freedom	1988	2.50	5.00	10.00
—Reissue of 171001					
❑ D1-71316	A Holiday Celebration	1988	2.50	5.00	10.00
❑ R 164086	A Holiday Celebration	1988	3.00	6.00	12.00
—Same as above, except BMG Direct Marketing edition					
❑ 171001	No Easy Walk to Freedom	1987	3.00	6.00	12.00

PETER, PAUL AND MARY

Number	Title (A Side/B Side)	Yr	VG	VG+	NM
❑ 830331	Such Is Love	1983	5.00	10.00	20.00

WARNER BROS.

Number	Title (A Side/B Side)	Yr	VG	VG+	NM
❑ W 1449 [M]	Peter, Paul and Mary	1962	5.00	10.00	20.00
❑ WS 1449 [S]	Peter, Paul and Mary	1962	6.25	12.50	25.00
—Gold label					
❑ WS 1449 [S]	Peter, Paul and Mary	1968	3.00	6.00	12.00
—Green "W7" label					
❑ WS 1449 [S]	Peter, Paul and Mary	1970	2.50	5.00	10.00
—Any later Warner Bros. label (green "WB", palm trees, white label)					
❑ W 1473 [M]	(Moving)	1963	5.00	10.00	20.00
❑ WS 1473 [S]	(Moving)	1963	6.25	12.50	25.00
—Gold label					
❑ WS 1473 [S]	(Moving)	1968	2.50	5.00	10.00
—Any later Warner Bros. label (green "W7", green "WB", palm trees, white label)					
❑ W 1507 [M]	In the Wind	1963	5.00	10.00	20.00
❑ WS 1507 [S]	In the Wind	1963	6.25	12.50	25.00
—Gold label					
❑ WS 1507 [S]	In the Wind	1968	2.50	5.00	10.00
—Any later Warner Bros. label					
❑ 2W 1555 [(2)M]	Peter, Paul and Mary In Concert	1964	6.25	12.50	25.00
❑ 2WS 1555 [(2)S]	Peter, Paul and Mary In Concert	1964	7.50	15.00	30.00
—Gold labels					
❑ 2WS 1555 [(2)S]	Peter, Paul and Mary In Concert	1968	3.00	6.00	12.00
—Any later Warner Bros. label					
❑ W 1589 [M]	A Song Will Rise	1965	5.00	10.00	20.00
❑ WS 1589 [S]	A Song Will Rise	1965	6.25	12.50	25.00
—Gold label					
❑ WS 1589 [S]	A Song Will Rise	1968	2.50	5.00	10.00
—Any later Warner Bros. label					
❑ W 1615 [M]	See What Tomorrow Brings	1965	5.00	10.00	20.00
❑ WS 1615 [S]	See What Tomorrow Brings	1965	6.25	12.50	25.00
—Gold label					
❑ WS 1615 [S]	See What Tomorrow Brings	1968	2.50	5.00	10.00
—Any later Warner Bros. label					
❑ W 1648 [M]	Peter, Paul and Mary Album	1966	5.00	10.00	20.00
❑ WS 1648 [S]	Peter, Paul and Mary Album	1966	6.25	12.50	25.00
—Gold label					
❑ WS 1648 [S]	Peter, Paul and Mary Album	1968	2.50	5.00	10.00
—Any later Warner Bros. label					
❑ W 1700 [M]	Album 1700	1967	6.25	12.50	25.00
❑ WS 1700 [S]	Album 1700	1967	6.25	12.50	25.00
—Gold label					
❑ WS 1700 [S]	Album 1700	1968	3.00	6.00	12.00
—Green "W7" label					
❑ WS 1700 [S]	Album 1700	1970	2.50	5.00	10.00
—Any later Warner Bros. label					
❑ WS 1751	Late Again	1968	3.75	7.50	15.00
—Green "W7" label					
❑ WS 1751	Late Again	1970	2.50	5.00	10.00
—Any later Warner Bros. label					
❑ WS 1785	Peter, Paul and Mommy	1969	3.75	7.50	15.00
—Green "W7" label					
❑ WS 1785	Peter, Paul and Mommy	1970	2.50	5.00	10.00
—Any later Warner Bros. label					
❑ BS 2552	(Ten) Years Together —				
	The Best of Peter, Paul and Mary	1970	3.75	7.50	15.00
—Green "WB" label					
❑ BS 2552	(Ten) Years Together —				
	The Best of Peter, Paul and Mary	1973	3.00	6.00	12.00
—"Burbank" palm-trees label					
❑ BSK 3105	(Ten) Years Together —				
	The Best of Peter, Paul and Mary	1977	2.50	5.00	10.00
—"Burbank" palm-trees label					
❑ BSK 3105	(Ten) Years Together —				
	The Best of Peter, Paul and Mary	1979	2.00	4.00	8.00
—White or tan label					
❑ BSK 3231	Reunion	1978	2.50	5.00	10.00

PETERSEN, PAUL Also see JAMES DARREN/SHELLEY FABARES/PAUL PETERSEN.
45s
COLPIX

Number	Title (A Side/B Side)	Yr	VG	VG+	NM
❑ 620	She Can't Find Her Keys/Very Likely	1962	3.75	7.50	15.00
❑ 620 [PS]	She Can't Find Her Keys/Very Likely	1962	7.50	15.00	30.00
—Sleeve spells his last name "Peterson" in error					
❑ 631	What Did They Do Before Rock and Roll/				
	Very Unlikely	1962	5.00	10.00	20.00
—With Shelly Fabares					
❑ 631 [PS]	What Did They Do Before Rock and Roll/				
	Very Unlikely	1962	100.00	200.00	400.00
❑ 632	Keep Your Love Locked (Deep in Your Heart)/				
	Be Everything to Anyone You Love	1962	3.00	6.00	12.00
❑ 632 [PS]	Keep Your Love Locked (Deep in Your Heart)/				
	Be Everything to Anyone You Love	1962	7.50	15.00	30.00
❑ 649	Lollipops and Roses/Please Mr. Sun	1962	3.00	6.00	12.00
❑ 663	My Dad/Little Boy Sad	1962	3.75	7.50	15.00
❑ 663 [PS]	My Dad/Little Boy Sad	1962	7.50	15.00	30.00
❑ 676	Amy/Goody Goody	1963	3.00	6.00	12.00
❑ 676	Amy/I Only Have Eyes for You	1963	3.00	6.00	12.00
❑ 697	Girls in the Summertime/				
	Mama, Your Little Boy Fell	1963	3.00	6.00	12.00
❑ 707	The Cheer Leader/Polka Dots and Moonbeams	1963	3.00	6.00	12.00
❑ 720	She Rides with Me/Poorest Boy in Town	1964	20.00	40.00	80.00
—A-side produced by Brian Wilson					
❑ 730	Where Is She/Hey There Beautiful	1964	3.00	6.00	12.00
❑ 763	Happy/Little Dreamer	1965	3.00	6.00	12.00
❑ 785	The Ring/You Don't Need Money	1965	3.00	6.00	12.00

MOTOWN

Number	Title (A Side/B Side)	Yr	VG	VG+	NM
❑ 1108	Chained/Don't Let It Happen	1967	5.00	10.00	20.00
❑ 1129	A Little Bit for Sandy/Your Love's Got Me Runnin'	1968	5.00	10.00	20.00

Albums
COLPIX

Number	Title (A Side/B Side)	Yr	VG	VG+	NM
❑ CP-429 [M]	Lollipops and Roses	1962	12.50	25.00	50.00
❑ SCP-429 [S]	Lollipops and Roses	1962	15.00	30.00	60.00
❑ CP-442 [M]	My Dad	1963	12.50	25.00	50.00
❑ SCP-442 [S]	My Dad	1963	15.00	30.00	60.00

PETERSON, EARL
45s
COLUMBIA

Number	Title (A Side/B Side)	Yr	VG	VG+	NM
❑ 21364	Boogie Blues/Believe Me	1955	12.50	25.00	50.00
❑ 21406	Be Careful of the Heart You're Going to Break/				
	I'm Not Buying Baby	1955	12.50	25.00	50.00
❑ 21467	I Ain't Gonna Fall in Love/I'll Live My Life Alone	1955	12.50	25.00	50.00
❑ 21540	You Gotta Be My Baby/World of Make Believe	1956	10.00	20.00	40.00

SUN

Number	Title (A Side/B Side)	Yr	VG	VG+	NM
❑ 197	Boogie Blues/In the Dark	1954	125.00	250.00	500.00

PETERSON, RAY
45s
CLOUD 9

Number	Title (A Side/B Side)	Yr	VG	VG+	NM
❑ 134	Nobody But Me/(B-side unknown)	1975	—	2.50	5.00

DECCA

Number	Title (A Side/B Side)	Yr	VG	VG+	NM
❑ 32861	Stamp Out Loneliness/There's a Better Way	1971	—	2.50	5.00

DUNES

Number	Title (A Side/B Side)	Yr	VG	VG+	NM
❑ 2002	Corrina, Corrina/Be My Girl	1960	6.25	12.50	25.00
—Produced by Phil Spector					
❑ 2002 [PS]	Corrina, Corrina/Be My Girl	1960	15.00	30.00	60.00
❑ 2004	Sweet Little Kathy/You Didn't Care	1961	3.75	7.50	15.00
❑ 2006	Missing You/You Thrill Me	1961	3.75	7.50	15.00
❑ 2009	I Could Have Loved You So Well/Why Don't You				
	Write Me	1961	5.00	10.00	20.00
—Produced by Phil Spector					
❑ 2013	You Know Me Much Too Well/You Didn't Care	1962	3.75	7.50	15.00
❑ 2018	If Only Tomorrow/You Didn't Care	1962	3.75	7.50	15.00
❑ 2019	Is It Wrong/Slowly	1963	3.75	7.50	15.00
❑ 2022	A Love to Remember/I'm Not Jimmy	1963	3.75	7.50	15.00
❑ 2024	Where Are You/Deep Are the Roots	1963	3.75	7.50	15.00
❑ 2025	Give Us Your Blessing/Without Love (There Is				
	Nothing)	1963	3.75	7.50	15.00
❑ 2027	I Forgot What It Was Like/Be My Girl	1963	3.75	7.50	15.00
❑ 2030	Promises/Sweet Little Kathy	1963	3.75	7.50	15.00

MGM

Number	Title (A Side/B Side)	Yr	VG	VG+	NM
❑ 13269	If You Were Here/Oh No	1964	2.50	5.00	10.00
❑ 13269 [PS]	If You Were Here/Oh No	1964	3.75	7.50	15.00
❑ 13299	Across the Street (Is a Million Miles Away)/When				
	I Stop Dreaming	1964	2.50	5.00	10.00
❑ 13330	Unchained Melody/That's All	1965	2.00	4.00	8.00
❑ 13336	A House Without WIndows/				
	Wish I Could Say No to You	1965	2.00	4.00	8.00
❑ 13388	I'm Only Human/One Lonesome Rose	1965	2.00	4.00	8.00
❑ 13436	Love Hurts/Everybody	1966	2.00	4.00	8.00
❑ 13508	Amanda/I'm Gonna Change Everything	1966	2.00	4.00	8.00
❑ 13564	Just One Smile/The Whole World's Goin' Crazy	1966	2.00	4.00	8.00

RCA

Number	Title (A Side/B Side)	Yr	VG	VG+	NM
❑ GB-11758	Tell Laura I Love Her/The Wonder of You	1979	—	—	3.00
—Gold Standard Series					

RCA VICTOR

Number	Title (A Side/B Side)	Yr	VG	VG+	NM
❑ 37-7845	My Blue Angel/I'm Tired	1961	12.50	25.00	50.00
—"Compact Single 33" (small hole, plays at LP speed)					
❑ 47-7087	Fever/We're Old Enough to Cry	1957	6.25	12.50	25.00
❑ 47-7165	Let's Try Romance/Shirley Purley	1958	5.00	10.00	20.00
❑ 47-7255	Suddenly/Tall Light	1958	5.00	10.00	20.00
❑ 47-7303	Patricia/The Blue-Eyed Baby	1958	5.00	10.00	20.00
❑ 47-7336	Dream Way/I'll Always Want You Near	1958	5.00	10.00	20.00
❑ 47-7404	Richer Than I/Love Is a Woman	1958	5.00	10.00	20.00
❑ 47-7513	The Wonder of You/I'm Gone	1959	6.25	12.50	25.00
❑ 47-7578	My Blue Angel/Come and Get It	1959	5.00	10.00	20.00
❑ 47-7635	Goodnight My Love (Pleasant Dreams)/Till Then	1959	5.00	10.00	20.00
❑ 47-7635 [PS]	Goodnight My Love (Pleasant Dreams)/Till Then	1959	7.50	15.00	30.00
❑ 47-7703	Answer Me, My Love/What Do You Want to				
	Make Those Eyes At Me For	1960	5.00	10.00	20.00
❑ 47-7745	Tell Laura I Love Her/Wedding Days	1960	6.25	12.50	25.00
❑ 47-7779	Teenage Heartache/I'll Always Want You Near	1960	5.00	10.00	20.00
❑ 47-7845	My Blue Angel/I'm Tired	1961	5.00	10.00	20.00

P

Number	Title (A Side/B Side)	Yr	VG	VG+	NM
❏ 47-8333	The Wonder of You/Goodnight My Love	1964	2.50	5.00	10.00
❏ 61-7578 [S]	My Blue Angel/Come and Get It	1959	20.00	40.00	80.00
—"Living Stereo" (large hole, plays at 45 rpm)					
❏ 61-7745 [S]	Tell Laura I Love Her/Wedding Days	1960	25.00	50.00	100.00
—"Living Stereo" (large hole, plays at 45 rpm)					
REPRISE					
❏ 0811	Love Rules the World/Together	1969	2.00	4.00	8.00
UNI					
❏ 55249	Love the Understanding Way/Oklahoma City Rimes	1970	2.00	4.00	8.00
❏ 55268	Tell Laura I Love Her/To Wait for Love	1971	—	3.00	6.00
❏ 55275	Fever/Changes	1971	—	3.00	6.00
7-Inch Extended Plays					
RCA VICTOR					
❏ EPA-4367	Tell Laura I Love Her/Suddenly//Fever/The Wonder of You	1960	30.00	60.00	120.00
❏ EPA-4367 [PS]	Tell Laura I Love Her	1960	30.00	60.00	120.00
Albums					
DECCA					
❏ DL 75307	Ray Peterson Country	1971	5.00	10.00	20.00
MGM					
❏ E-4250 [M]	The Very Best of Ray Peterson	1964	6.25	12.50	25.00
❏ SE-4250 [S]	The Very Best of Ray Peterson	1964	7.50	15.00	30.00
❏ E-4277 [M]	The Other Side of Ray Peterson	1965	6.25	12.50	25.00
❏ SE-4277 [S]	The Other Side of Ray Peterson	1965	7.50	15.00	30.00
RCA CAMDEN					
❏ CAL-2119 [M]	Goodnight My Love	1966	3.00	6.00	12.00
❏ CAS-2119 [S]	Goodnight My Love	1966	3.00	6.00	12.00
RCA VICTOR					
❏ LPM-2297 [M]	Tell Laura I Love Her	1960	25.00	50.00	100.00
❏ LSP-2297 [S]	Tell Laura I Love Her	1960	37.50	75.00	150.00
UNI					
❏ 73078	Missing You/Featuring His Greatest Hits!	1969	5.00	10.00	20.00

PETRIFIED FOREST, THE
45s
FONTANA

Number	Title (A Side/B Side)	Yr	VG	VG+	NM
❏ 1596	So Mystifying/She's the Only Thing That's Kept Me Going	1967	3.75	7.50	15.00

PETS, THE
45s
ARWIN

Number	Title (A Side/B Side)	Yr	VG	VG+	NM
❏ 109	Cha-Hua-Hua/Cha-Kow-Ski	1958	3.75	7.50	15.00
❏ 112	Wow-Ee!!!/Beyond the Sea	1958	3.75	7.50	15.00
❏ 116	Guitarro/Whatever Will Be, Will Be	1958	3.75	7.50	15.00

PETTICOATS, THE (1)
45s
CHALLENGE

Number	Title (A Side/B Side)	Yr	VG	VG+	NM
❏ 9211	Surfin' Sally/Why Does Billy Play in Your Yard	1963	6.25	12.50	25.00

PETTICOATS, THE (2)
45s
DOT

Number	Title (A Side/B Side)	Yr	VG	VG+	NM
❏ 16052	By the Light of the Silvery Moon/Troubadour	1960	5.00	10.00	20.00
❏ 16155	For Sentimental Reasons/Cincinnati	1960	5.00	10.00	20.00

PETTICOATS, THE (3)
45s
PREP

Number	Title (A Side/B Side)	Yr	VG	VG+	NM
❏ 125	I Ain't Gonna Do It No More/Manhattan Mountains	1957	5.00	10.00	20.00
UNIQUE					
❏ 344	The Motorboat Song/The First One	1956	5.00	10.00	20.00
❏ 363	High Heels/I'll Go Along with You	1956	5.00	10.00	20.00
❏ 387	In My Loving Heart/Michigan Bankroll	1957	5.00	10.00	20.00

PETTY, NORMAN, TRIO Also see THE PICKS.
45s
ABC-PARAMOUNT

Number	Title (A Side/B Side)	Yr	VG	VG+	NM
❏ 9787	Almost Paradise/It's Been a Long, Long Time	1957	3.00	6.00	12.00
COLUMBIA					
❏ 40929	The First Kiss/(Instrumental)	1957	3.00	6.00	12.00
❏ 41039	Moondreams/Toy Boy	1957	25.00	50.00	100.00
—With Buddy Holly on guitar					
FELSTED					
❏ 8647	Mood Indigo/On the Alamo	1962	2.50	5.00	10.00
JARO					
❏ 77027	Ditty Dum/Bring Your Heart	1960	3.00	6.00	12.00
"X"					
❏ 0040	Mood Indigo/Petty's Little Polka	1954	3.00	6.00	12.00
❏ 0071	On the Alamo/Echo Polka	1954	3.00	6.00	12.00
❏ 0104	I Wonder Why/Three Little Kisses	1955	3.00	6.00	12.00
❏ 0130	Oh! You Pretty Woman/Hey! Good Lookin'	1955	3.00	6.00	12.00
❏ 0167	Solitude/When It's Darkness on the Delta	1955	3.00	6.00	12.00
7-Inch Extended Plays					
COLUMBIA					
❏ B-10921	(contents unknown)	1958	25.00	50.00	100.00
❏ B-10921 [PS]	Moondreams	1958	25.00	50.00	100.00
"X"					
❏ EXA-82	(contents unknown)	1955	5.00	10.00	20.00
❏ EXA-82 [PS]	The Norman Petty Trio In Full Fidelity	1955	5.00	10.00	20.00
Albums					
COLUMBIA					
❏ CL 1092 [M]	Moondreams	1958	37.50	75.00	150.00
TOP RANK					
❏ R-639 [M]	Petty for Your Thoughts	1960	7.50	15.00	30.00
❏ RS-639 [S]	Petty for Your Thoughts	1960	10.00	20.00	40.00
VIK					
❏ LX-1073 [M]	Corsage	1957	17.50	35.00	70.00

PHAETONS, THE
45s
HI-Q

Number	Title (A Side/B Side)	Yr	VG	VG+	NM
❏ 5012	Fling/Homemade	1959	5.00	10.00	20.00

SAHARA

Number	Title (A Side/B Side)	Yr	VG	VG+	NM
❏ 102	I'm So Lonely/Road of Blues	1963	5.00	10.00	20.00
❏ 103	The Beatle Walk/Frantic	1964	12.50	25.00	50.00
—B-side by the Premiers					
VIN					
❏ 1015	I Love My Baby/As You Know	1959	15.00	30.00	60.00
WARNER BROS.					
❏ 7082	She Came Like the Rain/Three Weeks, Four Days and Fifteen Hours	1967	2.50	5.00	10.00
❏ 7205	Leave It to Me/You'd Better Come Home	1968	2.50	5.00	10.00

PHAFNER
45s
DRAGON

Number	Title (A Side/B Side)	Yr	VG	VG+	NM
❏ 1001	Overdrive/Plea from the Soul	1971	50.00	100.00	200.00
Albums					
DRAGON					
❏ LP-101	Overdrive	1971	1000.	2000.	3000.

PHANTOM, THE (1)
45s
CAPITOL

Number	Title (A Side/B Side)	Yr	VG	VG+	NM
❏ F3427	Whispering/Five Foot Two, Eyes of Blue	1956	5.00	10.00	20.00

PHANTOM, THE (2)
45s
CAPITOL

Number	Title (A Side/B Side)	Yr	VG	VG+	NM
❏ 3857	Calm Before the Storm/Black Magic, White Magic	1974	3.00	6.00	12.00
HIDEOUT					
❏ 1080	Calm Before the Storm/Black Magic, White Magic	1974	5.00	10.00	20.00
Albums					
CAPITOL					
❏ ST-11313	The Phantom's Divine Comedy, Part One	1974	15.00	30.00	60.00

PHANTOM, THE (3)
45s
DOT

Number	Title (A Side/B Side)	Yr	VG	VG+	NM
❏ 16056	Love Me/Whisper Your Love	1960	37.50	75.00	150.00
❏ 16056 [PS]	Love Me/Whisper Your Love	1960	75.00	150.00	300.00

PHELPS, JAMES
45s
ARGO

Number	Title (A Side/B Side)	Yr	VG	VG+	NM
❏ 5499	Love Is a Five-Letter Word/I'll Do the Best I Can	1965	2.00	4.00	8.00
❏ 5509	La De Da, I'm a Fool in Love/Wasting Time	1965	2.00	4.00	8.00
CADET					
❏ 5534	Oh, What a Feeling/Action	1966	2.00	4.00	8.00
FONTANA					
❏ 1581	Don't Be a Cry Baby/Walking the Floor Over You	1967	—	3.00	6.00
❏ 1600	Fabulous One/The Wrong Number	1967	—	3.00	6.00
PARAMOUNT					
❏ 0136	My Lover's Prayer/Check Yourself	1971	—	2.50	5.00

PHIL AND DEL
45s
LINDA

Number	Title (A Side/B Side)	Yr	VG	VG+	NM
❏ 105	My Girl/Don't Play with Love	1962	3.00	6.00	12.00
RAMPART					
❏ 656	It Hurts Me/These Feelings	196?	2.50	5.00	10.00

PHIL AND HARV
45s
RAMPART

Number	Title (A Side/B Side)	Yr	VG	VG+	NM
❏ 611	Darling (Please Bring Your Love)/Friendship	196?	3.00	6.00	12.00
❏ 612	Sweeter Than Candy/The Facts of Love	196?	3.00	6.00	12.00

PHILADELPHIA STRUMMERS, THE
45s
PARKWAY

Number	Title (A Side/B Side)	Yr	VG	VG+	NM
❏ 816	I Ain't Down Yet/Every Moment You Live	1961	2.50	5.00	10.00

PHILBIN, REGIS
Albums
MERCURY

Number	Title (A Side/B Side)	Yr	VG	VG+	NM
❏ SR-61169	It's Time for Regis!	1968	6.25	12.50	25.00

PHILIP AND STEPHAN P.F. SLOAN and STEVE BARRI, again.
45s
INTERPHON

Number	Title (A Side/B Side)	Yr	VG	VG+	NM
❏ 7711	Meet Me Tonight Little Girl/When You're Near, You're So Far Away	1964	3.75	7.50	15.00

PHILIPS, TERRY
45s
CORAL

Number	Title (A Side/B Side)	Yr	VG	VG+	NM
❏ 62247	Fear/Find a Horseshoe	1961	3.75	7.50	15.00
UNITED ARTISTS					
❏ 351	My Foolish Ways/Hands of a Fool	1961	20.00	40.00	80.00

PHILLIPS, CHARLIE
45s
ARA

Number	Title (A Side/B Side)	Yr	VG	VG+	NM
❏ 1001	Rambling Guitar Man/Kiss Her Once for Me	196?	3.00	6.00	12.00
COLUMBIA					
❏ 42035	No More Sugartime/Welcome to the Wedding	1961	3.00	6.00	12.00
❏ 42289	I Guess I'll Never Learn/Now That It's Over	1962	2.50	5.00	10.00
❏ 42526	Cancel the Call/You're Moving Away	1962	2.50	5.00	10.00
❏ 42691	No One to Love/'Til Sunday	1963	2.50	5.00	10.00
❏ 42851	Later Tonight/This Is the House	1963	2.50	5.00	10.00
❏ 43014	Street of Loneliness/Please Help Me Believe	1964	2.50	5.00	10.00
CORAL					
❏ 61908	Sugartime/One Faded Rose	1958	6.25	12.50	25.00
❏ 61970	Be My Bride/Too Many Tears	1958	6.25	12.50	25.00
K-ARK					
❏ 874	Your Going Is Coming/Just Let the Flowers Grow	197?	2.00	4.00	8.00

Number	Title (A Side/B Side)	Yr	VG	VG+	NM
LONGHORN					
❏ 574	Rainbow in the Valley/The Big Ball Is in Cowtown	1966	2.50	5.00	10.00
—As "Charlie 'Sugartime' Phillips"					
REPRISE					
❏ 0581	Be Careful, Go Easy, Go Slow/				
	Souvenirs of Sorrow	1967	2.00	4.00	8.00

PHILLIPS, ESTHER Includes records as "Little Esther" and "Little Esther Phillips."

12-Inch Singles

Number	Title (A Side/B Side)	Yr	VG	VG+	NM
MERCURY					
❏ 90 [DJ]	Oo-Oop-Oo-Oop (Long Version)/				
	Oo-Oop-Oo-Oop (Edit)	1979	3.00	6.00	12.00
❏ 101 [DJ]	Our Day Will Come (same on both sides)	1979	3.00	6.00	12.00
WINNING					
❏ 1002	Turn Me Out (4:39) (5:51)	1983	2.50	5.00	10.00

45s

Number	Title (A Side/B Side)	Yr	VG	VG+	NM
ATLANTIC					
❏ 2223	Hello Walls/Double Crossing Blues	1964	3.75	7.50	15.00
—With Jimmy Ricks					
❏ 2229	No Headstone on My Grave/Mo Jo Hannah	1964	3.75	7.50	15.00
❏ 2251	It's Too Soon to Know/				
	You're the Reason I'm Living	1964	3.75	7.50	15.00
❏ 2265	Half a Heart/				
	Some Things You Never Get Used To	1964	3.75	7.50	15.00
❏ 2281	And I Love Him/Shangri-La	1965	3.00	6.00	12.00
❏ 2294	Moonglow & Theme from Picnic/Makin'				
	Whoopee	1965	3.00	6.00	12.00
❏ 2304	Let Me Know When It's Over/I Saw Me	1965	3.00	6.00	12.00
❏ 2324	Just Say Goodbye/I Could Have Told You	1966	3.00	6.00	12.00
❏ 2335	When a Woman Loves a Man/Ups and Downs	1966	3.00	6.00	12.00
❏ 2360	Somebody Else Is Taking My Place/When Love				
	Comes to the Human Race	1966	3.00	6.00	12.00
❏ 2370	Fever/Try Me	1966	3.00	6.00	12.00
❏ 2411	Release Me/Don't Feel Rained	1967	2.50	5.00	10.00
❏ 2417	I'm Sorry/Cheater Man	1967	2.50	5.00	10.00
❏ 2745	Brand New Day/Set Me Free	1970	—	3.00	6.00
❏ 2775	Crazy Love/All God Has Is Us	1970	—	3.00	6.00
❏ 2783	Catch Me I'm Falling/Woman Will Do Wrong	1971	—	3.00	6.00
❏ 2800	Cry Me a River Blues/I'm Getting 'Long Alright	1971	—	3.00	6.00
DECCA					
❏ 28804	If You Want Me/Talkin' All Out of My Head	1953	10.00	20.00	40.00
❏ 48305	Please Don't Send Me/Stop Crying	1953	10.00	20.00	40.00
❏ 48314	Sit Back Down/He's a No Good Man	1954	15.00	30.00	60.00
FEDERAL					
❏ 12023	I'm a Bad, Bad Girl/Don't Make a Fool Out of Me	1951	20.00	40.00	80.00
❏ 12036	Heart to Heart/				
	Looking for a Man to Satisfy My Soul	1951	125.00	250.00	500.00
—With the Dominoes					
❏ 12042	Cryin' and Singin' the Blues/				
	Tell Him That I Need Him	1951	20.00	40.00	80.00
❏ 12055	Ring-a-Ding-Doo/The Crying Blues	1952	17.50	35.00	70.00
❏ 12063	Summertime/The Storm	1952	17.50	35.00	70.00
❏ 12065	Better Beware/I'll Be There	1952	17.50	35.00	70.00
❏ 12078	Aged and Mellow/Bring My Lovin' Back to Me	1952	17.50	35.00	70.00
❏ 12090	Somebody New/Ramblin' Blues	1952	17.50	35.00	70.00
❏ 12100	Saturday Night Daddy/Mainliner	1952	75.00	150.00	300.00
—With Bobby Nunn					
❏ 12108	Last Laugh Blues/Flesh, Blood and Bones	1952	17.50	35.00	70.00
—With Little Willie Littlefield					
❏ 12115	Hollerin' and Screamin'/				
	Turn the Lamp Down Low	1953	17.50	35.00	70.00
—With Little Willie Littlefield					
❏ 12122	You Took My Love Too Fast/Street Lights	1953	75.00	150.00	300.00
—With Bobby Nunn					
❏ 12126	Hound Dog/Sweet Lips	1953	17.50	35.00	70.00
❏ 12142	Cherry Wine/Love Oh Love	1953	17.50	35.00	70.00
KUDU					
❏ 904	Home Is Where the Hatred Is/Til My Back Ain't				
	Got No Bone	1972	—	2.50	5.00
❏ 906	Baby I'm for Real/That's All Right with Me	1972	—	2.50	5.00
❏ 910	I've Never Found a Man (To Love Me Like You				
	Do)/Cherry Red	1972	—	2.50	5.00
❏ 915	Use Me/Let Me in Your Life	1973	—	2.50	5.00
❏ 917	Justified/Too Many Roads	1973	—	2.50	5.00
❏ 921	Such a Night/Can't Trust Your Neighbor	1974	—	2.50	5.00
❏ 922	Disposable Society/(B-side unknown)	1974	—	2.50	5.00
❏ 925	What a Difference a Day Makes/Turn Around,				
	Look at Me	1975	—	2.50	5.00
❏ 929	For All We Know/Fever	1976	—	2.50	5.00
❏ 936	Boy I Really Tied One On/Magic's in the Air	1976	—	2.50	5.00
❏ 938	Higher and Higher/All the Way Down	1976	—	2.50	5.00
LENOX					
❏ 5555	Release Me/Don't Feel Rained On	1962	7.50	15.00	30.00
❏ 5560	Am I That Easy to Forget/				
	I Really Don't Want to Know	1963	5.00	10.00	20.00
❏ 5565	You Never Miss Your Water (Till the Well Runs				
	Dry)/If You Want It (I've Got It)	1963	5.00	10.00	20.00
—As "Little Esther Phillips and Big Al Downing"					
❏ 5570	Why Should We Try Anymore/While It Lasted	1963	5.00	10.00	20.00
❏ 5575	Don't Let Me Go/Why Was I Born	1963	5.00	10.00	20.00
❏ 5577	A Lover's Hymn/				
	God Bless the Child Who's Got His Own	1963	5.00	10.00	20.00
MERCURY					
❏ 73967	Love Addict/I've Never Been a Woman Before	1977	—	2.00	4.00
❏ 74030	There You Go Again (There She Goes Again)/				
	Stormy Weather	1978	—	2.00	4.00
❏ 74060	Oo-Oop-Oo-Oop/I'll Close My Eyes	1979	—	2.00	4.00
❏ 74077	Our Day Will Come/Mr. Melody	1979	—	2.00	4.00
ROULETTE					
❏ 7031	Too Late to Worry, Too Blue to Cry/I'm in the				
	Mood for Love	1969	—	3.50	7.00
❏ 7049	Tonight I'll Be Staying Here with You/				
	Sweet Dreams	1969	—	3.50	7.00
❏ 7059	Nobody But You/Too Much of a Man	1969	—	3.50	7.00

Number	Title (A Side/B Side)	Yr	VG	VG+	NM
SAVOY					
❏ 1193	You Can Bet Your Life/				
	'Tain't Whatcha Say It's Whatcha Do	1956	6.25	12.50	25.00
❏ 1516	Longing in My Heart/If It's News to Me	1957	5.00	10.00	20.00
❏ 1563	It's So Good/Do You Ever Think of Me	1959	3.75	7.50	15.00
WARWICK					
❏ 610	Gee Baby/Wild Child	1961	3.75	7.50	15.00
WINNING					
❏ 1001	Turn Me Out/(B-side unknown)	1983	—	2.50	5.00
Albums					
ATLANTIC					
❏ SD 1565	Burnin'	1970	6.25	12.50	25.00
❏ SD 1680	Confessin' the Blues	1975	3.75	7.50	15.00
❏ 8102 [M]	And I Love Him	1965	12.50	25.00	50.00
—Cover has a pink Cupid on it					
❏ 8102 [M]	And I Love Him	1966	7.50	15.00	30.00
—Cover has a black photo on it					
❏ SD 8102 [S]	And I Love Him	1965	20.00	40.00	80.00
—Cover has a pink Cupid on it					
❏ SD 8102 [S]	And I Love Him	1966	10.00	20.00	40.00
—Cover has a black photo on it					
❏ 8122 [M]	Esther	1966	7.50	15.00	30.00
❏ SD 8122 [S]	Esther	1966	10.00	20.00	40.00
❏ 8130 [M]	The Country Side of Esther Phillips	1966	7.50	15.00	30.00
—Reissue of Lenox 227					
❏ SD 8130 [S]	The Country Side of Esther Phillips	1966	10.00	20.00	40.00
—Reissue of Lenox S-227					
❏ 90670	Confessin' the Blues	1987	2.50	5.00	10.00
—Reissue of 1680					
CBS ASSOCIATED					
❏ PZ 40710	What a Diff'rence a Day Makes	1987	2.00	4.00	8.00
—Reissue of Kudu 23					
❏ PZ 40935	From a Whisper to a Scream	1988	2.00	4.00	8.00
—Reissue of Kudu 05					
KING					
❏ 622 [M]	Memory Lane	1959	1000.	2000.	4000.
KUDU					
❏ 05	From a Whisper to a Scream	1972	3.00	6.00	12.00
❏ 09	Alone Again, Naturally	1972	3.00	6.00	12.00
❏ 14	Black-Eyed Blues	1973	3.00	6.00	12.00
❏ 18	Performance	1974	3.00	6.00	12.00
❏ 23	What a Diff'rence a Day Makes	1975	3.00	6.00	12.00
❏ 28	For All We Know	1976	3.00	6.00	12.00
❏ 31	Capricorn Princess	1976	3.00	6.00	12.00
LENOX					
❏ 227 [M]	Release Me	1962	25.00	50.00	100.00
❏ S-227 [S]	Release Me	1962	50.00	100.00	200.00
MERCURY					
❏ SRM-1-1187	You've Come a Long Way, Baby	1977	2.50	5.00	10.00
❏ SRM-1-3733	All About Esther Phillips	1978	2.50	5.00	10.00
❏ SRM-1-3769	Here's Esther — Are You Ready?	1979	2.50	5.00	10.00
❏ SRM-1-4005	A Good Black Is Hard to Crack	1981	2.50	5.00	10.00
MUSE					
❏ MR-5302	A Way to Say Goodbye	1986	3.00	6.00	12.00
SAVOY JAZZ					
❏ SJL-2258	The Complete Savoy Recordings	1984	2.50	5.00	10.00

PHILLIPS, GENE

Albums

Number	Title (A Side/B Side)	Yr	VG	VG+	NM
CROWN					
❏ CLP-5375 [M]	Gene Phillips and the Rockers	1963	7.50	15.00	30.00

PHILLIPS, JOHN Also see THE JOURNEYMEN; THE MAMAS AND THE PAPAS; THE SMOOTHIES.

45s

Number	Title (A Side/B Side)	Yr	VG	VG+	NM
ABC DUNHILL					
❏ 4236	Mississippi/April Anne	1970	—	3.00	6.00
ATCO					
❏ 6960	Green-Eyed Lady/Lion	1974	—	3.00	6.00
COLUMBIA					
❏ 45737	Revolution on Vacation/Cup of Tea	1972	—	2.50	5.00
Albums					
ABC DUNHILL					
❏ DS-50077	John Phillips (John the Wolfking of L.A.)	1970	3.75	7.50	15.00

PHILLIPS, MICHELLE Also see THE MAMAS AND THE PAPAS.

45s

Number	Title (A Side/B Side)	Yr	VG	VG+	NM
A&M					
❏ 1740	There She Goes/Aloha Louie	1975	—	2.50	5.00
❏ 1824	No Love Today/Aloha Louie	1976	—	2.00	4.00
❏ 1824 [PS]	No Love Today/Aloha Louie	1976	—	3.00	6.00
❏ 1996	The Aching Kind/Lady of Fantasy	1977	—	2.50	5.00
❏ 2021	There She Goes/Victim of Romance	1978	—	2.50	5.00
Albums					
A&M					
❏ SP-4651	Victim of Romance	1977	3.75	7.50	15.00

PHILLIPS, PHIL

45s

Number	Title (A Side/B Side)	Yr	VG	VG+	NM
KHOURY'S					
❏ 711	Sea of Love/Juella	1959	375.00	750.00	1500.
MERCURY					
❏ 10021 [S]	Take This Heart/Verdie Mae	1959	12.50	25.00	50.00
❏ 71465	Sea of Love/Juella	1959	6.25	12.50	25.00
❏ 71531 [M]	Take This Heart/Verdie Mae	1959	5.00	10.00	20.00
❏ 71550	Providing/Don't Leave Me	1960	5.00	10.00	20.00
❏ 71611	What Will I Tell My Heart/				
	Your True Love Once More	1960	5.00	10.00	20.00
❏ 71649	Stormy Weather/Don't Cry Baby	1960	5.00	10.00	20.00
❏ 71657	Come Back My Darling/				
	Nobody Knows-Nobody Cares	1960	5.00	10.00	20.00
❏ 71817	Sweet Affection/Betray	1961	6.25	12.50	25.00

P

Number	Title (A Side/B Side)	Yr	VG	VG+	NM
PHILLIPS, RICHARD					
45s					
HIT					
❏ 225	Kansas City Star/Yesterday	1965	3.00	6.00	12.00
—B-side by the Jalopy Five					
PHILLIPS, SHAWN					
45s					
A&M					
❏ 1238	A Christmas Song/Lovely Lady	1970	2.50	5.00	10.00
❏ 1238 [PS]	A Christmas Song/Lovely Lady	1970	2.50	5.00	10.00
❏ 1402	We/"L" Ballade	1972	—	2.50	5.00
❏ 1405	Lost Horizon/Landscape	1973	—	2.50	5.00
❏ 1435	Anella/Hey Miss Lonely	1973	—	2.50	5.00
❏ 1482	Dream Queen/Bright White	1973	—	2.50	5.00
❏ 1507	All the Kings and Castles/Salty Tears	1974	—	2.50	5.00
❏ 1750	Do You Wonder/Summer Vignette	1975	—	2.50	5.00
ASCOT					
❏ 2152	The New Frankie and Johnny Song/Cloudy Summer Afternoon	1964	3.00	6.00	12.00
Albums					
A&M					
❏ SP-3128	Second Contribution	198?	2.00	4.00	8.00
—Budget-line reissue					
❏ SP-3135	Faces	198?	2.00	4.00	8.00
—Budget-line reissue					
❏ SP-3662	Furthermore	1974	3.00	6.00	12.00
❏ SP-4241	Contribution	1970	3.75	7.50	15.00
❏ SP-4282	Second Contribution	1971	3.75	7.50	15.00
❏ SP-4324	Collaboration	1972	3.75	7.50	15.00
❏ SP-4363	Faces	1972	3.00	6.00	12.00
❏ SP-4402	Bright White	1973	3.00	6.00	12.00
❏ SP-4539	Do You Wonder	1975	3.00	6.00	12.00
❏ SP-4582	Rumpelstiltskin's Resolve	1976	3.00	6.00	12.00
❏ SP-4650	Spaced	1977	3.00	6.00	12.00
CHAMELEON					
❏ D1-74764	Beyond Here Be Dragons	1988	2.50	5.00	10.00
RCA VICTOR					
❏ AFL1-3028	Transcendence	1978	2.50	5.00	10.00
❏ AYL1-3873	Transcendence	1981	2.00	4.00	8.00
—"Best Buy Series" reissue					
PHILOSOPHERS, THE					
Albums					
PHILO					
❏ 1001	After Sundown	1969	37.50	75.00	150.00
PHLUPH					
45s					
VERVE					
❏ 10564	Another Day/Doctor Mind	1967	3.75	7.50	15.00
❏ 10575	Patterns/In Her Way	1967	5.00	10.00	20.00
Albums					
VERVE					
❏ V6-5054	Phluph	1968	7.50	15.00	30.00
PIANO RED Also see DR. FEELGOOD AND THE INTERNS.					
45s					
CHECKER					
❏ 911	Get Up Mare/So Worried	1958	7.50	15.00	30.00
GROOVE					
❏ 0023	Decatur Street Blues/Big Rock Joe from Kokomo	1954	7.50	15.00	30.00
❏ 0101	Pay It No Mind/Jump, Man, Jump	1955	7.50	15.00	30.00
❏ 0118	Six O'Clock Bounce/Goodbye	1955	7.50	15.00	30.00
❏ 0126	Red's Blues/Gordy's Rock	1955	7.50	15.00	30.00
❏ 0136	Jumpin' with Daddy/She Knocks Me Out	1956	7.50	15.00	30.00
❏ 0145	I'm Nobody's Fool/That's My Desire	1956	7.50	15.00	30.00
❏ 0169	Woo-Ee/You Were Mine for Awhile	1956	7.50	15.00	30.00
JAX					
❏ 1000	This Old World/I Feel Good	1959	3.75	7.50	15.00
❏ 1006	Guitar Walk/I've Been Walkin'	1959	3.75	7.50	15.00
KING					
❏ 6330	I Want a Bowlegged Woman/Underground Atlanta	1970	—	2.50	5.00
RCA VICTOR					
❏ 47-4265	Diggin' the Boogie/ Let's Have a Good Time Tonight	1951	15.00	30.00	60.00
❏ 47-4380	Hey Good Lookin'/It Makes No Difference Now	1951	15.00	30.00	60.00
❏ 47-4524	Bouncin' with Red/Count the Days I'm Gone	1952	15.00	30.00	60.00
❏ 47-4766	She Walks Right In/Sales Tax Boogie	1952	15.00	30.00	60.00
❏ 47-4957	Yoo Doopee Doo/Daybreak	1952	15.00	30.00	60.00
❏ 47-5101	I'm Gonna Rock Some More/ Everybody's Boogie	1952	12.50	25.00	50.00
❏ 47-5224	She's Dynamite/I'm Gonna Tell Everybody	1953	10.00	20.00	40.00
❏ 47-5337	Decatur Street Boogie/ Your Mouth's Got a Hole In It	1953	10.00	20.00	40.00
❏ 47-5544	Right and Read, Taxi, Taxi 6963	1953	10.00	20.00	40.00
❏ 47-6856	Wild Fire/Rock Baby	1957	5.00	10.00	20.00
❏ 47-6953	Peachtree Parade/Please Don't Talk About Me	1957	5.00	10.00	20.00
❏ 47-7065	South/Coo Cha	1957	5.00	10.00	20.00
❏ 47-7217	Comin' On/One Glimpse of Heaven	1958	5.00	10.00	20.00
❏ 50-0090	Rockin' with Red/Red's Boogie	1950	37.50	75.00	150.00
—Gray label, orange vinyl					
❏ 50-0106	The Wrong Yo-Yo/My Gal Jo	1951	15.00	30.00	60.00
❏ 50-0118	Jumpin' the Boogie/Just Right Bounce	1951	15.00	30.00	60.00
❏ 50-0130	Layin' the Boogie/Baby What's Wrong	1951	15.00	30.00	60.00
7-Inch Extended Plays					
GROOVE					
❏ EGA-3	(contents unknown)	1956	25.00	50.00	100.00
❏ EGA-3 [PS]	Jump, Man, Jump	1956	25.00	50.00	100.00
❏ EGA-26	(contents unknown)	1956	15.00	30.00	60.00
❏ EGA-26 [PS]	Piano Red In Concert, Vol. 1	1956	15.00	30.00	60.00
❏ EGA-27	(contents unknown)	1956	15.00	30.00	60.00
❏ EGA-27 [PS]	Piano Red In Concert, Vol. 2	1956	15.00	30.00	60.00
❏ EGA-28	(contents unknown)	1956	15.00	30.00	60.00
❏ EGA-28 [PS]	Piano Red In Concert, Vol. 3	1956	15.00	30.00	60.00

Number	Title (A Side/B Side)	Yr	VG	VG+	NM
RCA VICTOR					
❏ EPA-587	Rockin' with Red/I'm Gonna Rock Some More// Red's Boogie/Diggin' the Boogie	1954	25.00	50.00	100.00
❏ EPA-587 [PS]	Rockin' with Red	1954	25.00	50.00	100.00
❏ EPA-5091	(contents unknown)	1959	12.50	25.00	50.00
—Black label					
❏ EPA-5091	(contents unknown)	1959	25.00	50.00	100.00
—Maroon label					
❏ EPA-5091 [PS]	Rockin' with Red	1959	12.50	25.00	50.00
Albums					
ARHOOLIE					
❏ 1064	William Perryman (Alone with Piano)	197?	3.00	6.00	12.00
EUPHONIC					
❏ 1212	Percussive Piano	198?	2.50	5.00	10.00
GROOVE					
❏ LG-1001 [M]	Jump Man, Jump	1956	—	—	—
—The existence of this LP has not been confirmed					
❏ LG-1002 [M]	Piano Red in Concert	1956	150.00	300.00	600.00
KING					
❏ KS-1117	Happiness Is Piano Red	1970	5.00	10.00	20.00
RCA CAMDEN					
❏ ACL1-0547	Rockin' with Red	1974	3.00	6.00	12.00
SOUTHLAND					
❏ 8	Willie Perryman-Piano Red-Dr. Feelgood	1983	3.75	7.50	15.00
PICKETT, BOBBY "BORIS"					
45s					
ANTHEM					
❏ 205	Monster Concert/Am I	1973	—	3.00	6.00
CAPITOL					
❏ 5063	Simon the Sensible Surfer/Simon Says So What	1963	6.25	12.50	25.00
GARPAX					
❏ P-1	Monster Mash/Monster's Mash Party	1962	7.50	15.00	30.00
—Orange label, first release of 44167?					
❏ 724	I'm Down to My Last Heartbreak/I Can't Stop	1962	6.25	12.50	25.00
❏ 44167	Monster Mash/Monster's Mash Party	1962	6.25	12.50	25.00
❏ 44167 [PS]	Monster Mash/Monster's Mash Party	1962	15.00	30.00	60.00
❏ 44171	Monster's Holiday/Monster's Motion	1962	6.25	12.50	25.00
❏ 44171 [PS]	Monster's Holiday/Monster's Motion	1962	10.00	20.00	40.00
❏ 44175	Graduation Day/The Humpty Dumpty	1963	6.25	12.50	25.00
❏ 44175 [PS]	Graduation Day/The Humpty Dumpty	1963	10.00	20.00	40.00
❏ 44185	Blood Bank Blues/Me and My Mummy	1965	6.25	12.50	25.00
METROMEDIA					
❏ BMBO-0089	Me and My Mummy /It's Not the Same Without You	1973	2.50	5.00	10.00
—B-side by Pickett and Payne					
PARROT					
❏ 348	Monster Mash/Monster's Mash Party	1970	2.50	5.00	10.00
—Reissued in 1973 with the same number and label design					
❏ 366	Monster's Holiday/Monster Minuet	1971	2.50	5.00	10.00
PIZZERIA					
❏ 1	Star Drek/Mangy Old Sidewinder	1977	2.00	5.00	10.00
—With Peter Ferrara; originals are autographed on the label by both					
POLYDOR					
❏ 14361	King Kong (Your Song)/Disco Kong	1976	—	2.50	5.00
—With Peter Ferrara					
RCA VICTOR					
❏ 47-8312	Smoke! Smoke! Smoke! (That Cigarette)/Gotta Leave This Town	1964	3.75	7.50	15.00
❏ 47-8459	The Werewolf Watusi/Monster Swim	1964	3.75	7.50	15.00
WHITE WHALE					
❏ 363	Monster Man Jam/Am I	1970	6.25	12.50	25.00
—B-side by Bobby and Joan Pickett					
❏ 365	Monster Concert/(B-side unknown)	1970	6.25	12.50	25.00
Albums					
GARPAX					
❏ GPX 57001 [M]	The Original Monster Mash	1962	37.50	75.00	150.00
❏ SGP 67001 [S]	The Original Monster Mash	1962	62.50	125.00	250.00
PARROT					
❏ XPAS 71063 [R]	The Original Monster Mash	1973	6.25	12.50	25.00
—Reissue of Garpax LP with four tracks deleted and one added					
PICKETT, WILSON Also see THE FALCONS.					
12-Inch Singles					
MOTOWN					
❏ 217	Land of a Thousand Dances (4 versions)/ Just Let Her Know	1987	2.00	4.00	8.00
45s					
ATLANTIC					
❏ 2233	I'm Gonna Cry/For Better or Worse	1964	3.75	7.50	15.00
❏ 2271	Come Home Baby/Take a Little Love	1965	3.75	7.50	15.00
❏ 2289	In the Midnight Hour/I'm Not Tired	1965	3.75	7.50	15.00
❏ 2306	Don't Fight It/It's All Over	1965	3.75	7.50	15.00
❏ 2320	634-5789 (Soulsville, U.S.A.)/That's a Man's Way	1966	3.75	7.50	15.00
❏ 2334	Ninety-Nine and a Half (Won't Do)/Danger Zone	1966	3.75	7.50	15.00
❏ 2348	Land of 1000 Dances/You're So Fine	1966	3.75	7.50	15.00
❏ 2365	Mustang Sally/Three Time Loser	1966	3.75	7.50	15.00
❏ 2381	Everybody Needs Somebody to Love/Nothing You Can Do	1967	3.00	6.00	12.00
❏ 2394	I Found a Love — Part I/I Found a Love — Part II	1967	3.00	6.00	12.00
❏ 2412	Soul Dance Number Three/ You Can't Stand Alone	1967	3.00	6.00	12.00
❏ 2430	Funky Broadway/I'm Sorry About That	1967	3.00	6.00	12.00
❏ 2448	Stag-O-Lee/I'm In Love	1967	3.00	6.00	12.00
❏ 2484	Jealous Love/I've Come a Long Way	1968	2.50	5.00	10.00
❏ 2504	She's Lookin' Good/We've Got to Have Love	1968	2.50	5.00	10.00
❏ 2528	I'm a Midnight Mover/Deborah	1968	2.50	5.00	10.00
❏ 2558	I Found a True Love/For Better or Worse	1968	2.50	5.00	10.00
❏ 2575	A Man and a Half/People Make the World (What It Is)	1968	2.50	5.00	10.00
❏ 2591	Hey Jude/Search Your Heart	1969	2.50	5.00	10.00
❏ 2611	Mini-Skirt Minnie/Back in Your Arms	1969	2.00	4.00	8.00
❏ 2631	Born to Be Wild/Toe Hold	1969	2.00	4.00	8.00
❏ 2648	Hey Joe/Night Owl	1969	2.00	4.00	8.00

7-Inch Extended Play Singles

From about 1953 to the early 1960s, most record labels issued extended play singles, or EPs for short. Few of these were big sellers, and some are quite collectible today. The values below include the record and the sleeve together.

Harry Belafonte, *Calypso*, RCA Victor EPA-768, $12-$25.

Johnny Cash, *Johnny Cash Sings Hank Williams*, Sun EPA-111, $50-$100.

Fats Domino, *Here Stands Fats Domino*, Imperial IMP-148, record with maroon label, $75-$150.

Duane Eddy, *Yep!*, Jamie JEP 302, $50-$100.

Ricky Nelson, *Ricky Sings Again*, Imperial IMP-161, $50-$100.

Elvis Presley, *Elvis by Request*, RCA Victor LPC-128, $40-$80.

Colored Vinyl Albums

In the history of pop music, relatively few popular albums have been issued on colors of vinyl other than black. Curiously, two noteworthy exceptions both were Top 10 chart hits in 1973.

J. Geils Band, *Bloodshot*, **Atlantic SD 7260, red vinyl, $10-$20.**

Grand Funk, *We're An American Band,* **Capitol SMAS-11207, gold vinyl, $15-$30.**

Colored Vinyl 45s

Many more colored vinyl 45s than LPs exist. In fact, when RCA Victor first started making 45s in 1949, they were color-coded by genre. Two of those are pictured here, as are two others that came later.

Eddy Arnold, *"Bouquet of Roses,"* RCA Victor 48-0001,
green vinyl, $25-$50.

Piano Red, *"Rockin' with Red,"* RCA Victor 50-0099,
cerise (orange-like) vinyl, $75-$150.

The Prisonaires, *"Just Walkin' in the Rain,"* Sun 186, red
vinyl, $2,500-$5,000.

Chubby Checker, *"Let's Twist Again,"* Parkway 824,
orange vinyl, $100-$200.

Original Labels and Hit Labels

Especially in the 1950s and 1960s, many hit songs were first issued on one label, then became a hit for another label. In nearly all cases, the original release is more valuable than the "hit" release. Here are some examples.

The Tune Weavers, *"Happy Happy Birthday Baby,"* Casa Grande 4037, original, $75-$150.

The Tune Weavers, *"Happy Happy Birthday Baby,"* Checker 872, hit, $12.50-$25.

Danny and the Juniors, *"At the Hop,"* Singular 711, original, $500-$1,000.

Danny and the Juniors, *"At the Hop,"* ABC-Paramount 9871, hit, $15-$30.

Danleers, *"One Summer Night,"* AMP 3 #2115, original, $20-$40.

Danleers, *"One Summer Night,"* Mercury 71322, hit, $10-$20.

The Shields, *"You Cheated,"* Tender 513, original, no reference to Dot Records on label, $75-$150.

The Shields, *"You Cheated,"* Dot 15805, hit, $12.50-$25.

The Electric Indian, *"Keem-O-Sabe,"* Marmaduke 4001, original, $10-$20.

The Electric Indian, *"Keem-O-Sabe,"* United Artists 50563, hit, $3-$6.

David Bowie, *"Space Oddity,"* Mercury 72949, original, $25-$50.

David Bowie, *"Space Oddity,"* RCA Victor 74-0876, hit, $3-$6.

10-Inch LPs

From 1948 until the mid-1950s, most pop albums were issued as 10-inch records, the same size as 78s. Once the 12-inch disc became standard, the 10-inchers were phased out. They are difficult to find in top-notch condition. Here are some examples.

Doris Day and Harry James, *Young Man with a Horn*, Columbia CL 6106, $50-$100.

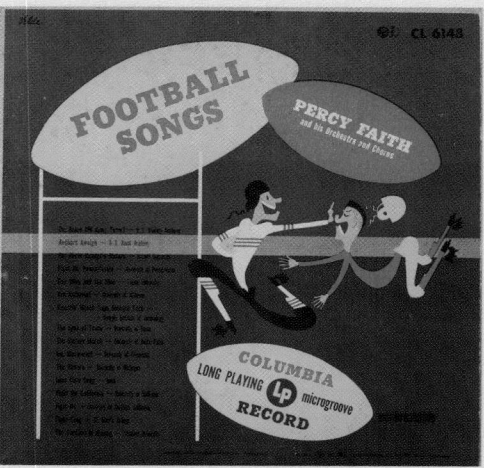

Percy Faith, *Football Songs*, Columbia CL 6148, $20-$40.

Burl Ives, *Ballads and Folk Songs, Volume II*, Decca DL 5013, $25-$50.

Vaughn Monroe, *Vaughn Monroe Caravan*, RCA Victor LPM-3048, $20-$40.

Billy Ward and His Dominoes, *Billy Ward and His Dominoes*, Federal 295-94, $9,500-$13,000.

Tony Bennett, Because of You, Columbia CL 2550, *"House Party Series"* issue, $30-$60.

Elvis Presley Sun 45s

Elvis Presley's first five singles were on the Sun label in Memphis. Though there are plenty of copies around compared to other records in the same price range, there is high demand for them, thus the prices remain lofty.

"That's All Right," Sun 209, $4,000-$6,000.

"Good Rockin' Tonight," Sun 210, $2,500-$3,500.

"Milkcow Blues Boogie," Sun 215, $3,500-$5,000.

"Baby Let's Play House," Sun 217, $2,000-$3,000.

"Mystery Train," Sun 223, $1,250-$2,500.

"I Forgot to Remember to Forget" was the "other" side of Sun 223. It was Elvis' first #1 hit on any national chart when it topped the Billboard country chart in early 1956.

1960s Motown Picture Sleeves

Most of the big hits from the Motown family of labels are easy to find. Most of the accompanying picture sleeves are not. Here are some of those sleeves; the price is for the sleeve by itself.

The Four Tops, "Reach Out I'll Be There,"
Motown 1098, $40-$80.

The Marvelettes, "You're My Remedy," Tamla
54097, $30-$60.

The Miracles, "(Come 'Round Here) I'm the
One You Need," Tamla 54140, $50-$100.

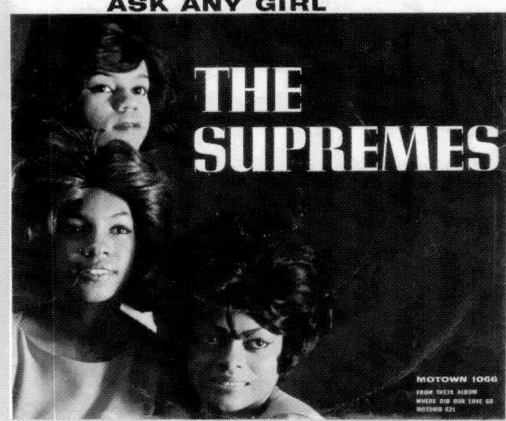

The Supremes, "Baby Love," Motown 1066,
$15-$30.

The Temptations, "Beauty Is Only Skin Deep,"
Gordy 7055, $20-$40.

Mary Wells, "The One Who Really Loves You,"
Motown 1024, $40-$80.

Number	Title (A Side/B Side)	Yr	VG	VG+	NM
❑ 2682	You Keep Me Hangin' On/ Now You See Me, Now You Don't	1969	2.00	4.00	8.00
❑ 2722	Sugar, Sugar/Cole, Cooke, and Redding	1970	2.00	4.00	8.00
❑ 2753	She Said Yes/It's Still Good	1970	—	3.00	6.00
❑ 2765	Engine Number Nine/International Playboy	1970	—	3.00	6.00
❑ 2781	Don't Let the Green Grass Fool You/Ain't No Doubt About It	1971	—	3.00	6.00
❑ 2797	Don't Knock My Love (Part 1)/Don't Knock My Love (Part 2)	1971	—	3.00	6.00
❑ 2824	Call My Name, I'll Be There/Woman Let Me Down Home	1971	—	3.00	6.00
❑ 2852	Fire and Water/Pledging My Love	1971	—	3.00	6.00
❑ 2878	Funk Factory/One Step Away	1972	—	3.00	6.00
❑ 2909	Mama Told Me Not to Come/ Covering the Same Old Ground	1972	—	3.00	6.00
❑ 2961	Come Right Here/International Playboy	1973	—	3.00	6.00
BIG TREE					
❑ 16121	Who Turned You On/Dance You Down	1978	—	2.50	5.00
❑ 16129	Groovin'/Time to Let the Sun Shine In	1978	—	2.50	5.00
CORREC-TONE					
❑ 501	Let Me Be Your Boy/My Heart Belongs to You	1962	15.00	30.00	60.00
CUB					
❑ 9113	Let Me Be Your Boy/My Heart Belongs to You	1962	7.50	15.00	30.00
DOUBLE L					
❑ 713	If You Need Me/Baby Call on Me	1963	5.00	10.00	20.00
❑ 717	It's Too Late/I'm Gonna Love You	1963	5.00	10.00	20.00
❑ 724	I'm Down to My Last Heartbreak/I Can't Stop	1963	3.75	7.50	15.00
EMI AMERICA					
❑ 8027	I Want You/Love of My Life	1979	—	2.50	5.00
❑ 8034	Live with Me/Granny	1980	—	2.50	5.00
❑ 8070	Ain't Gonna Give You No More/Don't Underestimate the Power of Love	1981	—	2.50	5.00
❑ 8082	Back on the Right Track/It's You	1981	—	2.50	5.00
ERVA					
❑ 318	Love Dagger/Time to Let the Sun Shine on Me	1977	—	2.50	5.00
MOTOWN					
❑ 1898	Don't Turn Away/Can't Stop Now	1987	—	2.00	4.00
❑ 1916	In the Midnight Hour/Just Let Her Know	1987	—	2.00	4.00
❑ 1938	Love Never Let Me Down/Just Let Her Know	1988	—	2.00	4.00
❑ 53407	Love Never Let Me Down/Just Let Her Know	1988	—	2.00	4.00
PHILCO-FORD					
❑ HP-11	Land of a 1000 Dances/Midnight Hour	1967	3.75	7.50	15.00
—4-inch plastic "Hip Pocket Record" with color sleeve					
RCA VICTOR					
❑ 74-0908	Mr. Magic Man/I Sho' Love You	1973	—	3.00	6.00
❑ APBO-0049	Take a Closer Look at the Woman You're With/ Two Woman and a Wife	1973	—	3.00	6.00
❑ APBO-0174	Soft Soul Boogie Woogie/Take That Pollution Out of Your Throat	1973	—	3.00	6.00
❑ APBO-0309	Take Your Pleasure Where You Find It/ What Good Is a Lie	1974	—	3.00	6.00
❑ PB-10067	I Was Too Nice/Isn't That So	1974	—	3.00	6.00
VERVE					
❑ 10378	Let Me Be Your Boy/My Heart Belongs to You	1966	5.00	10.00	20.00
WICKED					
❑ 8101	The Best Part of a Man/How Will I Ever Know	1975	—	3.00	6.00
❑ 8102	Love Will Keep Us Together/It's Gonna Be Good	1976	—	3.00	6.00
7-Inch Extended Plays					
ATLANTIC					
❑ SD 8129	Something You Got/Barefootin'/Land of 1000 Dances//In the Midnight Hour/Ninety-Nine and a Half (Won't Do)/I'm Drifting	1966	3.75	7.50	15.00
—Jukebox issue; small hole, plays at 33 1/3 rpm					
❑ SD 8129 [PS]	The Exciting Wilson Pickett	1966	3.75	7.50	15.00
❑ SD 7-8250	Groovy Little Woman/Funky Way/It's Still Good/ /This Old Town/You Keep Me Hangin' On	1970	3.00	6.00	12.00
—Jukebox issue; small hole, plays at 33 1/3 rpm					
❑ SD 7-8250 [PS]	Right On	1970	3.00	6.00	12.00
Albums					
ATLANTIC					
❑ SD 2-501 [(2)]	Wilson Pickett's Greatest Hits	1973	5.00	10.00	20.00
❑ 8114 [M]	In the Midnight Hour	1965	10.00	20.00	40.00
❑ SD 8114 [R]	In the Midnight Hour	1965	7.50	15.00	30.00
❑ 8129 [M]	The Exciting Wilson Pickett	1966	10.00	20.00	40.00
❑ SD 8129 [R]	The Exciting Wilson Pickett	1966	7.50	15.00	30.00
❑ 8136 [M]	The Wicked Pickett	1967	10.00	20.00	40.00
❑ SD 8136 [R]	The Wicked Pickett	1967	7.50	15.00	30.00
❑ 8145 [M]	The Sound of Wilson Pickett	1967	10.00	20.00	40.00
❑ SD 8145 [P]	The Sound of Wilson Pickett	1967	10.00	20.00	40.00
❑ 8151 [M]	The Best of Wilson Pickett	1967	10.00	20.00	40.00
❑ SD 8151 [R]	The Best of Wilson Pickett	1967	5.00	10.00	20.00
❑ SD 8175	I'm in Love	1968	6.25	12.50	25.00
❑ SD 8183	The Midnight Mover	1968	6.25	12.50	25.00
❑ SD 8215	Hey Jude	1969	5.00	10.00	20.00
❑ SD 8250	Right On	1970	5.00	10.00	20.00
❑ SD 8270	Wilson Pickett in Philadelphia	1970	5.00	10.00	20.00
❑ 8290 [M]	The Best of Wilson Pickett, Vol. II	1971	6.25	12.50	25.00
—Mono copies are promo only					
❑ SD 8290 [S]	The Best of Wilson Pickett, Vol. II	1971	3.75	7.50	15.00
❑ SD 8300	Don't Knock My Love	1971	3.75	7.50	15.00
❑ 81283	The Best of Wilson Pickett	1985	2.50	5.00	10.00
BIG TREE					
❑ SD 76011	Funky Situation	1978	3.00	6.00	12.00
DOUBLE-L					
❑ DL-2300 [M]	It's Too Late	1963	12.50	25.00	50.00
❑ SDL-8300 [S]	It's Too Late	1963	17.50	35.00	70.00
EMI AMERICA					
❑ SW-17019	I Want You	1979	3.00	6.00	12.00
❑ SW-17043	Right Track	1981	3.00	6.00	12.00
MOTOWN					
❑ 6244 ML	American Soul Man	1987	2.50	5.00	10.00
RCA VICTOR					
❑ APL1-0312	Miz Lena's Boy	1973	3.75	7.50	15.00
❑ APL1-0495	Pickett in the Pocket	1974	3.75	7.50	15.00
❑ APL1-0856	Join Me and Let's Be Free	1975	3.75	7.50	15.00

Number	Title (A Side/B Side)	Yr	VG	VG+	NM
❑ ANL1-2149	Join Me and Let's Be Free	1977	2.50	5.00	10.00
—Reissue					
❑ LSP-4858	Mr. Magic Man	1973	3.75	7.50	15.00
TRIP					
❑ 8010	Wickedness	1972	2.50	5.00	10.00
UPFRONT					
❑ UPF-127 [S]	It's Too Late	197?	2.50	5.00	10.00
WAND					
❑ WD-672 [M]	Great Wilson Pickett Hits	1966	7.50	15.00	30.00
❑ WDS-672 [R]	Great Wilson Pickett Hits	1966	5.00	10.00	20.00
WICKED					
❑ 9001	Chocolate Mountain	1976	6.25	12.50	25.00

PICKS, THE Also see NORMAN PETTY TRIO.
45s

Number	Title (A Side/B Side)	Yr	VG	VG+	NM
COLUMBIA					
❑ 41096	Moondreams/Look to the Future	1958	12.50	25.00	50.00

PICKWICKS, THE
45s

Number	Title (A Side/B Side)	Yr	VG	VG+	NM
PARROT					
❑ 9679	Apple Blossom Time/ I Don't Want to Tell You Again	1964	3.75	7.50	15.00
WARNER BROS.					
❑ 5492	Little by Little/I Took My Baby Home	1965	3.75	7.50	15.00

PIERCE, WEBB
45s

Number	Title (A Side/B Side)	Yr	VG	VG+	NM
DECCA					
❑ 9-28091	That Heart Belongs to Me/So Used to Loving You	1952	6.25	12.50	25.00
❑ 9-28369	Back Street Affair/I'll Always Take Care of You	1952	6.25	12.50	25.00
❑ 9-28431	Bow Thy Head/The Country Church	1952	7.50	15.00	30.00
❑ 9-28534	I'll Go On Alone/That's Me Without You	1953	6.25	12.50	25.00
❑ 9-28594	The Last Waltz/I Haven't Got the Heart	1953	6.25	12.50	25.00
❑ 9-28725	It's Been So Long/Don't Throw Your Life Away	1953	6.25	12.50	25.00
❑ 9-28834	There Stands the Glass/I'm Walking the Dog	1953	6.25	12.50	25.00
❑ 9-28991	Slowly/You Just Can't Be True	1954	6.25	12.50	25.00
❑ 9-29107	Even Tho/Sparkling Brown Eyes	1954	6.25	12.50	25.00
❑ 9-29155	Mother Calling My Name in Prayer/ Bugle Call from Heaven	1954	7.50	15.00	30.00
❑ 9-29252	More and More/You're Not Mine Anymore	1954	6.25	12.50	25.00
❑ 9-29391	In the Jailhouse Now/ I'm Gonna Fall Out of Love with You	1955	5.00	10.00	20.00
❑ 9-29480	I Don't Care/Your Good for Nothing Heart	1955	5.00	10.00	20.00
❑ 9-29662	Love, Love, Love/If You Were Me	1955	5.00	10.00	20.00
❑ 9-29805	Yes, I Know Why/'Cause I Love You	1956	5.00	10.00	20.00
❑ 9-29974	Any Old Time/We'll Find a Way	1956	5.00	10.00	20.00
❑ 9-30045	Teenage Boogie/I'm Really Glad You Hurt Me	1956	10.00	20.00	40.00
❑ 9-30155	I'm Tired/It's My Way	1956	5.00	10.00	20.00
❑ 9-30255	Honky Tonk Song/Someday	1957	5.00	10.00	20.00
❑ 9-30321	Bye Bye, Love/Missing You	1957	3.75	7.50	15.00
❑ 9-30419	Holiday for Love/Don't Do It Darlin'	1957	3.75	7.50	15.00
❑ 9-30550	New Panhandle Rag/How Long?	1958	3.75	7.50	15.00
❑ 9-30623	Cryin' Over You/You'll Come Back	1958	3.75	7.50	15.00
❑ 9-30711	Tupelo County Jail/Falling Back to You	1958	3.75	7.50	15.00
❑ 9-30789	I'm Letting You Go/Sittin' Alone	1958	3.75	7.50	15.00
❑ 9-30858	A Thousand Miles Ago/ What Goes On in Your Heart	1959	3.75	7.50	15.00
❑ 9-30923	I Ain't Never/Shanghaied	1959	3.75	7.50	15.00
❑ 9-31021	No Love Have I/Whirlpool of Love	1959	3.75	7.50	15.00
❑ 31058	Is It Wrong (For Loving You)/ (Doin' the) Lovers Leap	1960	3.00	6.00	12.00
❑ 31118	Drifting Texas Sand/All I Need Is You	1960	3.00	6.00	12.00
❑ 31165	Fallen Angel/Truck Driver's Blues	1960	3.00	6.00	12.00
❑ 31197	Let Forgiveness In/There's More Pretty Girls Than One	1961	3.00	6.00	12.00
❑ 31249	Sweet Lips/Last Night	1961	3.00	6.00	12.00
❑ 31298	Walking the Streets/How Do You Talk to a Baby	1961	3.00	6.00	12.00
❑ 31347	Alla My Love/You Are My Life	1962	3.00	6.00	12.00
❑ 31380	Take Time/Crazy Wild Desire	1962	3.00	6.00	12.00
❑ 31421	Cow Town/Sooner or Later	1962	3.00	6.00	12.00
❑ 31451	Sawmill/If I Could Come Back	1963	2.50	5.00	10.00
❑ 31488	Sands of Gold/Nobody's Darlin' But Mine	1963	2.50	5.00	10.00
❑ 31544	Those Wonderful Years/If the Back Door Could Talk	1963	2.50	5.00	10.00
❑ 31582	Waiting a Lifetime/Love Come to Me	1964	2.50	5.00	10.00
❑ 31617	Memory No. 1/French Riviera	1964	2.50	5.00	10.00
❑ 31704	That's Where My Money Goes/Broken Engagement	1964	2.50	5.00	10.00
❑ 31737	Loving You Then Losing You/Let Me Live a Little	1965	2.50	5.00	10.00
❑ 31816	Who Do I Think I Am/Hobo and the Rose	1965	2.50	5.00	10.00
❑ 31867	Christmas at Home/Sweet Memories	1965	3.00	6.00	12.00
❑ 31924	You Ain't No Better Than Me/The Champ	1966	2.50	5.00	10.00
❑ 31982	Love's Something (I Can't Understand)/A Loner	1966	2.50	5.00	10.00
❑ 32033	Where'd Ya Stay Last Night/She's Twenty-One	1966	2.50	5.00	10.00
❑ 32098	Goodbye City, Goodbye Girl/That Same Old Street	1967	2.00	4.00	8.00
❑ 32167	Fool Fool Fool/Bottles and Babies	1967	2.00	4.00	8.00
❑ 32246	Luzianna/Somebody Please Kiss My Sweet Thing	1967	2.00	4.00	8.00
❑ 32339	Stranger in a Strange, Strange City/ In Another World	1968	2.00	4.00	8.00
❑ 32388	Saturday Night/I Tried Everything to Please	1968	2.00	4.00	8.00
❑ 32438	If I Had Last Night to Live Over/No Tears Tonight	1969	2.00	4.00	8.00
❑ 32508	This Thing/Does My Memory Ever Cross Your Mind	1969	2.00	4.00	8.00
❑ 32577	Love Ain't Never Gonna Be No Better❑ /The Other Side of You	1969	2.00	4.00	8.00
❑ 32641	Merry-Go-Round World/Fools Night Out	1970	2.00	4.00	8.00
❑ 32694	The Man You Want Me to Be/Too Long	1970	2.00	4.00	8.00
❑ 32762	Showing His Dollar/The Way We Were Back Then	1970	2.00	4.00	8.00
❑ 32787	Tell Him That You Love Him/Heartaches Are for Lovers, Not for Friends	1971	2.00	4.00	8.00
❑ 32855	Someone Stepped In (And Stole Me Blind)/I Miss the Little Things	1971	2.00	4.00	8.00

P

Number	Title (A Side/B Side)	Yr	VG	VG+	NM
❏ 32924	Hey Good Lookin'/Wonderful, Wonderful, Wonderful	1972	2.00	4.00	8.00
❏ 32973	I'm Gonna Be a Swinger/Someday	1972	2.00	4.00	8.00
❏ 33015	There Stands the Glass/Valentino of the Hobos	1972	2.00	4.00	8.00
❏ 33044	Let the Children Pick the Flowers/You're Letting Me Go	1973	2.00	4.00	8.00
❏ 7-34014 [S]	Hideaway Heart/(B-side unknown)	1962	3.75	7.50	15.00
—33 1/3 rpm jukebox single, small hole					
❏ 7-34015 [S]	Cow Town/(B-side unknown)	1962	3.75	7.50	15.00
—33 1/3 rpm jukebox single, small hole					
❏ 7-34016 [S]	First to Have a Second Chance//(B-side unknown)	1962	3.75	7.50	15.00
—33 1/3 rpm jukebox single, small hole					
❏ 7-34017 [S]	Tennessee Waltz/(B-side unknown)	1962	3.75	7.50	15.00
—33 1/3 rpm jukebox single, small hole					
❏ 7-34018 [S]	I'm Walking Behind You/(B-side unknown)	1962	3.75	7.50	15.00
—33 1/3 rpm jukebox single, small hole					
❏ 7-34076 [S]	Waterloo/Cry, Cry Darling	1962	3.75	7.50	15.00
—33 1/3 rpm jukebox single, small hole					
❏ 7-34135 [S]	I've Got a New Heartache/(B-side unknown)	1963	3.75	7.50	15.00
—33 1/3 rpm jukebox single, small hole					
❏ 7-34136 [S]	What Good Will It Do/One More Time	1963	3.75	7.50	15.00
—33 1/3 rpm jukebox single, small hole					
❏ 7-34137 [S]	Are You Sincere?/(B-side unknown)	1963	3.75	7.50	15.00
—33 1/3 rpm jukebox single, small hole					
❏ 7-34138 [S]	I Can't Stop Loving You/(B-side unknown)	1963	3.75	7.50	15.00
—33 1/3 rpm jukebox single, small hole					
❏ 7-34139 [S]	If I Lost Your Love/(B-side unknown)	1963	3.75	7.50	15.00
—33 1/3 rpm jukebox single, small hole					
❏ 7-38223 [S]	Drinkin' My Blues Away/Let Me Be the First to Know	196?	5.00	10.00	20.00
—33 1/3 rpm jukebox single, small hole					
❏ 7-38224 [S]	I Think of You/You Make Love to Everyone	196?	5.00	10.00	20.00
—33 1/3 rpm jukebox single, small hole					
❏ 9-46322	If Crying Would Make You Care/Drifting Texas Sand	1951	7.50	15.00	30.00
❏ 9-46332	California Blues/You Scared the Love Right Out of Me	1951	7.50	15.00	30.00
❏ 9-46364	Wondering/New Silver Bells	1951	6.25	12.50	25.00
❏ 9-46385	I'm Gonna See My Baby/You Know I'm Still in Love	1952	6.25	12.50	25.00
4 STAR					
❏ 1601	Heebie Jeebie Blues/High Geared Daddy	1952	7.50	15.00	30.00
❏ 1610	Hawaiian Echoes/I Saw Your Face in the Moon	1952	7.50	15.00	30.00
❏ 1616	Georgia Rag/Lucky Lee	1952	7.50	15.00	30.00
❏ 1629	Jilted Love/I'm Happy You Hurt Me	1953	7.50	15.00	30.00
KING					
❏ 5366	New Panhandle Rag/It's All Between the Lines	1960	3.00	6.00	12.00
❏ 5429	Jilted Love/Georgia Rag	1960	3.00	6.00	12.00
MCA					
❏ 40128	Lo-Lenna/When You're Living in Hell	1973	—	3.00	6.00
❏ 40181	I'd Be Number One/You Better Treat Her Right	1974	—	3.00	6.00
❏ 40255	Honey (Open That Door)/Take the Time It Takes	1974	—	3.00	6.00
❏ 40310	I Know, I Know, I Know/I'm Ashamed to Be Here	1974	—	3.00	6.00
PLANTATION					
❏ 131	The Good Lord Giveth (And Uncle Sam Taketh Away)/Send My Love to Me	1975	—	3.00	6.00
❏ 136	I've Got Leaving on My Mind/Shame, Shame, Shame	1976	—	3.00	6.00
❏ 141	That's Me Without You/Appleton	1976	—	3.00	6.00
❏ 145	Christmas Time's a Coming/The Family Christmas Tree	1976	—	3.00	6.00
❏ 149	Got You on My Mind/Love Brought Us Together	1977	—	2.50	5.00
—With Carol Channing					
❏ 154	Rhinestone Cowboy Club/Sparkling Brown Eyes	1977	—	3.00	6.00
7-Inch Extended Plays					
DECCA					
❏ ED 2144	The Wondering Boy, Part 1	195?	5.00	10.00	20.00
❏ ED 2144	Wondering/There Stands the Glass//That's Me Without You/Don't Throw Your Life Away	195?	5.00	10.00	20.00
❏ ED 2145	Back Street Affair/It's Been So Long//Slowly/That Heart Belongs to Me	195?	5.00	10.00	20.00
❏ ED 2145	The Wondering Boy, Part 2	195?	5.00	10.00	20.00
❏ ED 2241	(contents unknown)	195?	5.00	10.00	20.00
❏ ED 2241 [PS]	Webb Pierce, Vol. 1	195?	5.00	10.00	20.00
❏ ED 2242	(contents unknown)	195?	5.00	10.00	20.00
❏ ED 2242 [PS]	Webb Pierce, Vol. 2	195?	5.00	10.00	20.00
❏ ED 2243	(contents unknown)	195?	5.00	10.00	20.00
❏ ED 2243 [PS]	Webb Pierce, Vol. 3	195?	5.00	10.00	20.00
❏ ED 2355	(contents unknown)	1956	5.00	10.00	20.00
❏ ED 2355 [PS]	The Country Church	1956	5.00	10.00	20.00
❏ ED 2364	(contents unknown)	1956	5.00	10.00	20.00
❏ ED 2364 [PS]	The Wondering Boy, Vol. 3	1956	5.00	10.00	20.00
❏ ED 2581	*New Love Affair/I Care No More/Just Imagination/I Love	1958	5.00	10.00	20.00
❏ ED 2581 [PS]	Just Imagination	1958	5.00	10.00	20.00
❏ ED 2653 [M]	*After the Boy Gets the Girl/My Shoes Keep Walking Back to You/Life to Go	1959	5.00	10.00	20.00
❏ ED 2653 [PS]	Webb	1959	5.00	10.00	20.00
❏ ED 7-2653 [PS]	Webb	1959	7.50	15.00	30.00
❏ ED 7-2653 [S]	*After the Boy Gets the Girl/My Shoes Keep Walking Back to You/Life to Go	1959	7.50	15.00	30.00
❏ ED 2668 [M]	*I Ain't Never/Shanghaied/A Thousand Miles Ago/What Goes On in Your Heart	1959	5.00	10.00	20.00
❏ ED 2668 [PS]	I Ain't Never	1959	5.00	10.00	20.00
❏ ED 7-2668 [PS]	I Ain't Never	1959	7.50	15.00	30.00
❏ ED 7-2668 [S]	*I Ain't Never/Shanghaied/A Thousand Miles Ago/What Goes On in Your Heart	1959	7.50	15.00	30.00
❏ ED 2685	*Walking the Streets/All I Need Is You/Drifting Texas Sand/Drinking My Blues Away	1960	6.25	12.50	25.00
❏ ED 2685 [PS]	Walking the Streets	1960	6.25	12.50	25.00
❏ ED 2694	*Is It Wrong/Lover's Leap/No Love Have I/Whirlpool of Love	1961	6.25	12.50	25.00
❏ ED 2694 [PS]	Is It Wrong	1961	6.25	12.50	25.00
❏ ED 2709	*Hideaway Heart/Tender Years/Pictures on the Wall/First to Have a Second Chance	1962	6.25	12.50	25.00
❏ ED 2709 [PS]	Hideaway Heart	1962	6.25	12.50	25.00
❏ ED 2715	Alla My Love/You Are My Life//Sweet Lips/How Do You Talk to a Baby	1962	6.25	12.50	25.00
❏ ED 2715 [PS]	Alla My Love	1962	6.25	12.50	25.00
❏ ED 2719	(contents unknown)	1962	6.25	12.50	25.00
❏ ED 2719 [PS]	Webb Pierce	1962	6.25	12.50	25.00
❏ ED 2734	*Crazy Wild Desire/Take Time/I'm Falling in Love with You/There's More Pretty Girls Than One	1962	6.25	12.50	25.00
❏ ED 2734 [PS]	Crazy Wild Desire	1962	6.25	12.50	25.00
❏ ED 2748	(contents unknown)	1963	7.50	15.00	30.00
❏ ED 2748 [PS]	Fallen Angel	1963	7.50	15.00	30.00
❏ ED 2761	*Cow Town/If I Could Come Back/Sooner or Later/Sawmill	1964	7.50	15.00	30.00
❏ ED 2761 [PS]	Cow Town	1964	7.50	15.00	30.00
❏ ED 2785	(contents unknown)	1965	10.00	20.00	40.00
❏ ED 2785 [PS]	Nobody's Darling But Mine	1965	10.00	20.00	40.00
❏ ED 2786	Softly and Tenderly/If Jesus Came to Your House//What Would You Give in Exchange for Your Soul/Bow Thy Head	1965	10.00	20.00	40.00
❏ ED 2786 [PS]	Softly and Tenderly	1965	10.00	20.00	40.00
❏ ED 2799	(contents unknown)	1966	10.00	20.00	40.00
❏ ED 2799 [PS]	Loving You Then Losing You	1966	10.00	20.00	40.00
❏ 7-34110	Walk On By/Are You Sincere/I've Got a New Heartache//Little Bitty Tear/If I Could Come Back/One More Time	196?	3.75	7.50	15.00
—Jukebox issue; small hole, plays at 33 1/3 rpm					
❏ 7-34110 [PS]	I've Got a New Heartache	196?	3.75	7.50	15.00
Albums					
DECCA					
❏ DXB 181 [(2)M]	The Webb Pierce Story	1964	7.50	15.00	30.00
—Deduct 25% if booklet is missing					
❏ DL 4015 [M]	Webb with a Beat	1960	7.50	15.00	30.00
❏ DL 4079 [M]	Walking the Streets	1960	7.50	15.00	30.00
❏ DL 4110 [M]	Golden Favorites	1961	7.50	15.00	30.00
❏ DL 4144 [M]	Fallen Angel	1961	7.50	15.00	30.00
❏ DL 4218 [M]	Hideaway Heart	1962	7.50	15.00	30.00
❏ DL 4294 [M]	Cross Country	1962	7.50	15.00	30.00
❏ DL 4358 [M]	I've Got a New Heartache	1963	6.25	12.50	25.00
❏ DL 4384 [M]	Bow Thy Head	1963	6.25	12.50	25.00
❏ DL 4486 [M]	Sands of Gold	1964	6.25	12.50	25.00
❏ DL 4604 [M]	Memory #1	1965	6.25	12.50	25.00
❏ DL 4659 [M]	Country Music Time	1965	6.25	12.50	25.00
❏ DL 4739 [M]	Sweet Memories	1966	6.25	12.50	25.00
❏ DL 4782 [M]	Webb's Choice	1966	6.25	12.50	25.00
❏ DL 4844 [M]	Where'd Ya Stay Last Night	1967	7.50	15.00	30.00
❏ DL 4964 [M]	Fool, Fool, Fool	1968	12.50	25.00	50.00
❏ DL 5536 [10]	That Wondering Boy	1954	30.00	60.00	120.00
❏ DXSB 7181 [(2)S]	The Webb Pierce Story	1964	10.00	20.00	40.00
—Deduct 25% if booklet is missing					
❏ DL 8129 [M]	Webb Pierce	1955	15.00	30.00	60.00
—Black label, silver print					
❏ DL 8129 [M]	Webb Pierce	196?	7.50	15.00	30.00
—Black label with color bar					
❏ DL 8295 [M]	That Wondering Boy	1956	15.00	30.00	60.00
—Black label, silver print					
❏ DL 8295 [M]	That Wondering Boy	196?	7.50	15.00	30.00
—Black label with color bar					
❏ DL 8728 [M]	Just Imagination	1957	12.50	25.00	50.00
—Black label, silver print					
❏ DL 8728 [M]	Just Imagination	196?	7.50	15.00	30.00
—Black label with color bar					
❏ DL 8889 [M]	Bound for the Kingdom	1959	10.00	20.00	40.00
—Black label, silver print					
❏ DL 8889 [M]	Bound for the Kingdom	196?	6.25	12.50	25.00
—Black label with color bar					
❏ DL 8899 [M]	Webb!	1959	10.00	20.00	40.00
—Black label, silver print					
❏ DL 8899 [M]	Webb!	196?	6.25	12.50	25.00
—Black label with color bar					
❏ DL 74015 [S]	Webb with a Beat	1960	10.00	20.00	40.00
❏ DL 74079 [S]	Walking the Streets	1960	10.00	20.00	40.00
❏ DL 74110 [S]	Golden Favorites	1961	10.00	20.00	40.00
❏ DL 74144 [S]	Fallen Angel	1961	10.00	20.00	40.00
❏ DL 74218 [S]	Hideaway Heart	1962	10.00	20.00	40.00
❏ DL 74294 [S]	Cross Country	1962	10.00	20.00	40.00
❏ DL 74358 [S]	I've Got a New Heartache	1963	7.50	15.00	30.00
❏ DL 74384 [S]	Bow Thy Head	1963	7.50	15.00	30.00
❏ DL 74486 [S]	Sands of Gold	1964	7.50	15.00	30.00
❏ DL 74604 [S]	Memory #1	1965	7.50	15.00	30.00
❏ DL 74659 [S]	Country Music Time	1965	7.50	15.00	30.00
❏ DL 74739 [S]	Sweet Memories	1966	7.50	15.00	30.00
❏ DL 74782 [S]	Webb's Choice	1966	7.50	15.00	30.00
❏ DL 74844 [S]	Where'd Ya Stay Last Night	1967	6.25	12.50	25.00
❏ DL 74964 [S]	Fool, Fool, Fool	1968	6.25	12.50	25.00
❏ DL 74999 [S]	Webb Pierce's Greatest Hits	1968	6.25	12.50	25.00
❏ DL 75071	Saturday Night	1969	6.25	12.50	25.00
❏ DL 75132	Webb Pierce Sings This Thing	1969	6.25	12.50	25.00
❏ DL 75168	Love Ain't Never Gonna Be No Better	1970	6.25	12.50	25.00
❏ DL 75210	Merry-Go-Round World	1970	5.00	10.00	20.00
❏ DL 75280	The Webb Pierce Road Show	1971	5.00	10.00	20.00
❏ DL 75393	I'm Gonna Be a Swinger	1972	5.00	10.00	20.00
❏ DL 78889 [S]	Bound for the Kingdom	1959	12.50	25.00	50.00
—Black label, silver print					
❏ DL 78889 [S]	Bound for the Kingdom	196?	7.50	15.00	30.00
—Black label with color bar					
❏ DL 78899 [S]	Webb!	1959	12.50	25.00	50.00
—Black label, silver print					
❏ DL 78899 [M]	Webb!	196?	7.50	15.00	30.00
—Black label with color bar					
KING					
❏ 648 [M]	The One and Only Webb Pierce	1959	17.50	35.00	70.00
MCA					
❏ 130	Greatest Hits	1973	3.00	6.00	12.00
❏ 513	I'm Gonna Be a Swinger	197?	3.00	6.00	12.00
—Reissue of Decca 75393					
❏ 4087 [(2)]	The Best of Webb Pierce	1974	3.75	7.50	15.00
VOCALION					
❏ VL 73830	Country Songs	1968	3.00	6.00	12.00
❏ VL 73911	Country Favorites	1970	3.75	7.50	15.00

PIERCE, WEBB AND DEBBIE

45s

Number	Title (A Side/B Side)	Yr	VG	VG+	NM
MCA					
❏ 40048	Foreign Girl/What the People Say	1973	—	3.00	6.00
PLANTATION					
❏ 189	On My Way Out/I'm Coming Home Again	1980	—	2.50	5.00
❏ 191	Reality of Life/My Memory Remembers	1980	—	2.50	5.00
❏ 196	Happy Birthday Jesus/(B-side unknown)	1980	—	3.00	6.00

PIERCE, WEBB, AND NANCY DEE

45s

Number	Title (A Side/B Side)	Yr	VG	VG+	NM
DECCA					
❏ 32884	Above Suspicion/I Owe It to My Heart	1971	2.00	4.00	8.00

PILOT (1)

45s

Number	Title (A Side/B Side)	Yr	VG	VG+	NM
ARISTA					
❏ AS 0259	One Good Reason Why/Get Up and Go	1977	—	2.00	4.00
EMI					
❏ 3992	Magic/Just Let Me Be	1974	—	2.50	5.00
❏ 4135	Don't Speak Loudly/Just a Smile	1975	—	2.00	4.00
❏ 4202	January/Do Me Good	1975	—	2.00	4.00
❏ 4305	Canada/Mover	1976	—	2.00	4.00
Albums					
EMI					
❏ ST-11368	Pilot	1975	2.50	5.00	10.00
❏ ST-11488	January	1976	2.50	5.00	10.00

PILOT (2)

45s

Number	Title (A Side/B Side)	Yr	VG	VG+	NM
RCA VICTOR					
❏ 74-0770	Rider/Miss Sandy	1972	—	3.00	6.00
Albums					
RCA VICTOR					
❏ LSP-4730	Pilot	1972	3.00	6.00	12.00
❏ LSP-4825	Point of View	1973	5.00	10.00	20.00

PILTDOWN MEN, THE

45s

Number	Title (A Side/B Side)	Yr	VG	VG+	NM
CAPITOL					
❏ 4414	Brontosaurus Stomp/McDonald's Cave	1960	5.00	10.00	20.00
❏ 4460	Piltdown Rides Again/Bubbles in the Tar	1960	3.75	7.50	15.00
❏ 4501	Goodnight Mrs. Flintstone/The Great Impostor	1961	3.75	7.50	15.00
❏ 4581	Fossil Rock/Gargantua	1961	3.75	7.50	15.00
❏ 4703	Big Lizard/A Pretty Girl Is Like a Melody	1962	3.75	7.50	15.00
❏ 4875	Tequila Bossa Nova/Night Surfin'	1962	3.75	7.50	15.00

PIN-UPS, THE

45s

Number	Title (A Side/B Side)	Yr	VG	VG+	NM
STORK					
❏ STK-1	Lookin' for Boys/Kenny	1964	3.75	7.50	15.00

PING PONGS, THE

45s

Number	Title (A Side/B Side)	Yr	VG	VG+	NM
CUB					
❏ 9062	Big Ben/In the Chapel in the Moonlight	1960	5.00	10.00	20.00
UNITED ARTISTS					
❏ 236	Zyzzle/Summer Reverie	1960	5.00	10.00	20.00

PINK CLOUD, THE

45s

Number	Title (A Side/B Side)	Yr	VG	VG+	NM
TOWER					
❏ 376	Midnight Sun (Vocal)/Midnight Sun (Instrumental)	1967	5.00	10.00	20.00

PINK FLOYD Also see SYD BARRETT.

12-Inch Singles

Number	Title (A Side/B Side)	Yr	VG	VG+	NM
COLUMBIA					
❏ AS 777 [DJ]	Run Like Hell/Don't Leave Me Now	1980	5.00	10.00	20.00
❏ AS 1334 [DJ]	Money/Another Brick in the Wall, Part 2	1981	6.25	12.50	25.00
—Pink vinyl					
❏ AS 1541 [DJ]	When the Tigers Broke Free/Bring the Boys Back Home	1982	3.00	6.00	12.00
❏ AS 1635 [DJ]	Your Possible Pasts/The Final Cut	1982	3.00	6.00	12.00
❏ CAS 2775 [DJ]	Learning to Fly (Edit)/Learning to Fly (LP)	1987	3.00	6.00	12.00
❏ CAS 2878 [DJ]	On the Turning Away (7" Edit)/On the Turning Away (Live)	1987	3.00	6.00	12.00

45s

Number	Title (A Side/B Side)	Yr	VG	VG+	NM
CAPITOL					
❏ 58884	Money (Single Edit)/Time (Single Edit)	2000	—	2.00	4.00
❏ 58885	Wish You Were Here/Have a Cigar	2000	—	2.00	4.00
COLUMBIA					
❏ AE7 1653 [DJ]	Not Now John (Obscured Version) (same on both sides)	1983	2.50	5.00	10.00
❏ AE7 1653 [PS]	Not Now John (Obscured Version) (same on both sides)	1983	2.50	5.00	10.00
❏ 02165	Run Like Hell/Comfortably Numb	1981	—	—	3.00
—Reissue					
❏ 03118	Another Brick in the Wall, Part 2/One of My Turns	1982	—	—	3.00
—Reissue					
❏ 03142	When the Tigers Broke Free/Bring the Boys Back Home	1982	—	2.00	4.00
❏ 03142 [PS]	When the Tigers Broke Free/Bring the Boys Back Home	1982	—	2.50	5.00
—Fold-open cardboard sleeve					
❏ X18-03176	When the Tigers Broke Free/Bring the Boys Back Home	1982	2.50	5.00	10.00
❏ X18-03176 [PS]	When the Tigers Broke Free/Bring the Boys Back Home	1982	2.50	5.00	10.00
—Fold-open cardboard sleeve					
❏ 03905	Not Now John (Obscured Version)/The Heroes Return	1983	—	2.00	4.00
❏ 03905 [PS]	Not Now John (Obscured Version)/The Heroes Return	1983	—	2.50	5.00
❏ 07363	Learning to Fly/Terminal Frost	1987	—	2.00	4.00
❏ 07363 [PS]	Learning to Fly/Terminal Frost	1987	—	2.00	4.00
❏ 07660	On the Turning Away/Run Like Hell	1987	—	2.00	4.00
❏ 07660 [PS]	On the Turning Away/Run Like Hell	1987	—	2.00	4.00
❏ 10248	Have a Cigar/Welcome to the Machine	1975	3.00	6.00	12.00
❏ 11187	Another Brick in the Wall (Part 2)/One of My Turns	1980	—	2.00	4.00
—Regular Columbia orange label					
❏ 11187	Another Brick in the Wall (Part 2)/One of My Turns	1980	—	2.50	5.00
—Custom "wall" label					
❏ 11187 [PS]	Another Brick in the Wall (Part 2)/One of My Turns	1980	2.00	4.00	8.00
❏ 11265	Run Like Hell/Don't Leave Me Now	1980	—	2.00	4.00
❏ 11311	Comfortably Numb/Hey You	1980	—	2.00	4.00
❏ 77493	Take It Back/Astronomy Domine (Live)	1994	—	2.00	4.00
HARVEST					
❏ 3240	Fearless/One of These Days	1971	5.00	10.00	20.00
❏ 3391	Stay/Free Four	1972	5.00	10.00	20.00
❏ 3609	Money/Any Colour You Like	1973	3.75	7.50	15.00
❏ P-3609 [DJ]	Money (Edited Mono)/Money (Edited Stereo)	1973	5.00	10.00	20.00
❏ 3832	Time/Us and Them	1974	5.00	10.00	20.00
❏ SPRO-6669 [DJ]	Money (Censored Edited Mono)/Money (Censored Edited Stereo)	1973	3.75	7.50	15.00
—This promo was sent to radio stations with a frantic note telling them to disregard the first promo					
TOWER					
❏ 333	Arnold Layne/Candy and a Currant Bun	1967	50.00	100.00	200.00
❏ 333 [PS]	Arnold Layne/Candy and a Currant Bun	1967	175.00	350.00	700.00
—Only issued with promotional copies					
❏ 356	See Emily Play/Scarecrow	1967	50.00	100.00	200.00
❏ 356 [PS]	See Emily Play/Scarecrow	1967	175.00	350.00	700.00
—Title sleeve; only issued with some promotional copies					
❏ 356 [PS]	See Emily Play/Scarecrow	1967	200.00	400.00	800.00
—Photo sleeve; only issued with some promotional copies					
❏ 378	The Gnome/Flaming	1967	37.50	75.00	150.00
❏ 426	It Would Be So Nice/Julia Dream	1968	62.50	125.00	250.00
❏ 440	Let There Be More Light/Remember a Day	1968	75.00	150.00	300.00

Albums

Number	Title (A Side/B Side)	Yr	VG	VG+	NM
CAPITOL					
❏ SPRO-8116/7 [DJ]	Pink Floyd Tour '75	1975	20.00	40.00	80.00
❏ SEAX-11902 [PD]	The Dark Side of the Moon	1978	7.50	15.00	30.00
❏ ST-12276	Works	1983	2.50	5.00	10.00
❏ SN-16230	More	1982	2.00	4.00	8.00
—Budget-line reissue					
❏ SN-16234	Relics	1982	2.00	4.00	8.00
—Budget-line reissue					
❏ SN-16330	Obscured by Clouds	1985	2.00	4.00	8.00
—Budget-line reissue					
❏ SN-16337	Atom Heart Mother	1985	2.00	4.00	8.00
—Budget-line reissue					
COLUMBIA					
❏ AP-1 [DJ]	Animals	1977	37.50	75.00	150.00
—White cover, with the song "Pigs" edited for airplay					
❏ AS 736 [DJ]	Off the Wall	1979	37.50	75.00	150.00
—Sampler from 2-LP set					
❏ AS 1636 [DJ]	The Final Cut	1983	6.25	12.50	25.00
—White label, record banded for airplay					
❏ HC 33453	Wish You Were Here	1981	15.00	30.00	60.00
—Half-speed mastered edition (original)					
❏ PC 33453	Wish You Were Here	1975	3.00	6.00	12.00
—Standard copy (no blue wraparound) without bar code					
❏ PC 33453	Wish You Were Here	1975	6.25	12.50	25.00
—Original copies had a blue wraparound with title/artist sticker. Most buyers threw this out upon opening the LP!					
❏ PC 33453 [DJ]	Wish You Were Here	1975	62.50	125.00	250.00
—White cover, "Special DJ Copy"; banded for airplay					
❏ PC 33453 [DJ]	Wish You Were Here	1975	75.00	150.00	300.00
—Blue cover with photo and title on jacket; unbanded record					
❏ PCQ 33453 [Q]	Wish You Were Here	1975	50.00	100.00	200.00
❏ JC 34474	Animals	1977	2.50	5.00	10.00
❏ JC 34474 [DJ]	Animals	1977	25.00	50.00	100.00
—"Demonstration Not for Sale" on label; also has insert					
❏ PC2 36183 [(2)]	The Wall	1979	3.75	7.50	15.00
❏ PC 37680	A Collection of Great Dance Songs	198?	2.00	4.00	8.00
—Budget-line reissue					
❏ TC 37680	A Collection of Great Dance Songs	1981	2.50	5.00	10.00
❏ QC 38243	The Final Cut	1983	2.50	5.00	10.00
❏ OC 40599	A Momentary Lapse of Reason	1987	2.50	5.00	10.00
❏ HC 43453	Wish You Were Here	1982	10.00	20.00	40.00
—Half-speed mastered edition (reissue)					
❏ PC2 44484 [(2)]	Delicate Sound of Thunder	1988	5.00	10.00	20.00
❏ HC2 46183 [(2)]	The Wall	1983	62.50	125.00	250.00
—Half-speed mastered edition					
❏ HC 47680	A Collection of Great Dance Songs	1982	12.50	25.00	50.00
—Half-speed mastered edition					
❏ C 64200	The Division Bell	1994	5.00	10.00	20.00
—U.S. pressings on blue vinyl					
EMI					
❏ 32700 [(4)]	Pulse	1995	15.00	30.00	60.00
—Pressed in U.K. for U.S. release; box set with 12x12 hardback book; identical to British pressings except for American bar code (67065) on shrink wrap					
HARVEST					
❏ SKAO-382	Atom Heart Mother	197?	3.75	7.50	15.00
—With title on front cover					
❏ SKAO-382	Atom Heart Mother	1970	6.25	12.50	25.00
—Without title on front cover					
❏ SKBB-388 [(2)]	Ummagumma	1969	10.00	20.00	40.00
—With the soundtrack LP from "Gigi" leaning against wall on front cover					
❏ SKBB-388 [(2)]	Ummagumma	1970	5.00	10.00	20.00
—With white LP cover leaning against wall on front cover					
❏ SW-759	Relics	1971	3.75	7.50	15.00
❏ SMAS-832	Meddle	1971	3.75	7.50	15.00
❏ ST-11078	Obscured by Clouds	1972	3.75	7.50	15.00
❏ SMAS-11163	The Dark Side of the Moon	1973	3.00	6.00	12.00
—With no inserts					
❏ SMAS-11163	The Dark Side of the Moon	1973	6.25	12.50	25.00
—With poster and two stickers					
❏ ST-11198	More	1973	3.00	6.00	12.00
—Reissue of Tower 5169					
❏ SABB-11257 [(2)]	A Nice Pair	1973	3.75	7.50	15.00

P

Number	Title (A Side/B Side)	Yr	VG	VG+	NM
MOBILE FIDELITY					
❏ 1-017	The Dark Side of the Moon	1980	12.50	25.00	50.00
—Audiophile vinyl					
❏ MFQR-017	The Dark Side of the Moon	1982	75.00	150.00	300.00
—Audiophile vinyl; "Ultra High Quality Recording" in box					
❏ 1-190	Meddle	1987	12.50	25.00	50.00
—Audiophile vinyl					
❏ 1-202	Atom Heart Mother	1994	7.50	15.00	30.00
—Audiophile vinyl					
TOWER					
❏ ST 5093 [S]	Pink Floyd (The Piper at the Gates of Dawn)	1967	20.00	40.00	80.00
—Orange label					
❏ ST 5093 [S]	Pink Floyd (The Piper at the Gates of Dawn)	1968	10.00	20.00	40.00
—Multi-color striped label					
❏ T 5093 [M]	Pink Floyd (The Piper at the Gates of Dawn)	1967	62.50	125.00	250.00
❏ ST 5131	A Saucerful of Secrets	1968	10.00	20.00	40.00
—Multi-color striped label					
❏ ST 5131	A Saucerful of Secrets	1968	20.00	40.00	80.00
—Orange label					
❏ ST 5169	More	1968	12.50	25.00	50.00

PINKERTON'S ASSORTED COLOURS
45s

Number	Title (A Side/B Side)	Yr	VG	VG+	NM
LONDON					
❏ 9820	Mirror, Mirror/She Don't Care	1966	5.00	10.00	20.00
PARROT					
❏ 40001	Don't Stop Loving Me Baby/Will You	1966	5.00	10.00	20.00

PINKNEY, BILL Also see THE DRIFTERS.
45s

Number	Title (A Side/B Side)	Yr	VG	VG+	NM
FONTANA					
❏ 1956	Don't Call Me/I Do the Jerk	1964	3.00	6.00	12.00
GAME					
❏ 394	Ol' Man River/Millionaire	196?	12.50	25.00	50.00
PHILLIPS INT'L.					
❏ 3524	After the Hop/Sally's Got a Sister	1958	5.00	10.00	20.00
—As "Bill Pinky"					
VEEP					
❏ 1264	I Found Some Lovin'/The Masquerade Is Over	1967	2.50	5.00	10.00

PIPES, THE (1)
45s

Number	Title (A Side/B Side)	Yr	VG	VG+	NM
CARLTON					
❏ 575	Teamwork/Soon I Will Be Done	1962	5.00	10.00	20.00

PIPES, THE (2)
45s

Number	Title (A Side/B Side)	Yr	VG	VG+	NM
DOOTO					
❏ 388	Be Fair/Let Me Give You Money	1958	6.25	12.50	25.00
❏ 401	You Are An Angel/I Love the Life I Live	1958	6.25	12.50	25.00
DOOTONE					
❏ 388	Be Fair/Let Me Give You Money	1956	75.00	150.00	300.00
❏ 401	You Are An Angel/I Love the Life I Live	1956	75.00	150.00	300.00

PIPKINS, THE
45s

Number	Title (A Side/B Side)	Yr	VG	VG+	NM
CAPITOL					
❏ 2819	Gimme Dat Ding/To Love You	1970	—	3.00	6.00
❏ 2874	Sugar and Spice-Are You Cookin' Goose/				
	Yakety Yak	1970	—	2.50	5.00
Albums					
CAPITOL					
❏ ST-483	Gimme Dat Ding	1970	6.25	12.50	25.00

PIPS, THE See GLADYS KNIGHT AND THE PIPS.

PIPSQUEEKS, THE
45s

Number	Title (A Side/B Side)	Yr	VG	VG+	NM
WARNER BROS.					
❏ 5878	Santa's Little Helpers/Santa's Magic Flute	1966	2.50	5.00	10.00

PIRANHAS, THE
Albums

Number	Title (A Side/B Side)	Yr	VG	VG+	NM
CUSTOM FIDELITY					
❏ 1452	Somethin' Fishy	1969	37.50	75.00	150.00

PIRATES, THE Early version of THE TEMPTATIONS.
45s

Number	Title (A Side/B Side)	Yr	VG	VG+	NM
MEL-O-DY					
❏ 105	Mind Over Matter (I'm Gonna Make You Mine)/				
	I'll Love You Till I Die	1962	25.00	50.00	100.00

PISTILLI, GENE Also see CASHMAN, PISTILLI & WEST; MANHATTAN TRANSFER.
45s

Number	Title (A Side/B Side)	Yr	VG	VG+	NM
ATCO					
❏ 6850	Benn Down So Long It Looks Like Up to Me/				
	Lettin' Down an Old Friend	1971	—	2.50	5.00
CAPITOL					
❏ 2627	Mr. Bojangles/Ruby Tuesday	1969	—	2.50	5.00

PITNEY, GENE
45s

Number	Title (A Side/B Side)	Yr	VG	VG+	NM
BLAZE					
❏ 351	Going Back to My Love/Cradle of My Arms	1958	7.50	15.00	30.00
—As "Billy Bryan"					
EPIC					
❏ 50332	Dedication AKA This Song I Want to Dedicate				
	to You/Sandman	1977	—	2.50	5.00
❏ 50461	It's Over, It's Over/Walkin' in the Sun	1977	—	2.50	5.00
FESTIVAL					
❏ 25002	Please Come Back/I'll Find You	1960	7.50	15.00	30.00
MUSICOR					
❏ 1002	(I Wanna) Love My Life Away/				
	I Laughed So Hard I Cried	1960	3.75	7.50	15.00
❏ 1002 [PS]	(I Wanna) Love My Life Away/				
	I Laughed So Hard I Cried	1960	10.00	20.00	40.00
❏ 1006	Louisiana Mama/Take Me Tonight	1961	3.75	7.50	15.00

Number	Title (A Side/B Side)	Yr	VG	VG+	NM
❏ 1006 [PS]	Louisiana Mama/Take Me Tonight	1961	7.50	15.00	30.00
❏ 1009	Town Without Pity/Air Mail Special Delivery	1961	3.75	7.50	15.00
❏ 1011	Every Breath I Take/Mr. Moon, Mr. Cupid and I	1961	5.00	10.00	20.00
—Produced by Phil Spector; mostly brown label					
❏ 1011	Every Breath I Take/Mr. Moon, Mr. Cupid and I	1961	7.50	15.00	30.00
—Produced by Phil Spector; mostly gunmetal gray label with color inserts					
❏ 1011 [PS]	Every Breath I Take/Mr. Moon, Mr. Cupid and I	1961	6.25	12.50	25.00
❏ 1020	(The Man Who Shot) Liberty Valance/				
	Take It Like a Man	1962	3.75	7.50	15.00
—Mostly brown label					
❏ 1022	Only Love Can Break a Heart/If				
	I Didn't Have a Dime	1962	3.75	7.50	15.00
—Mostly brown label					
❏ 1026	Half Heaven-Half Heartache/Tower Tall	1962	3.75	7.50	15.00
—Mostly black label					
❏ 1026	Half Heaven-Half Heartache/Tower Tall	1962	6.25	12.50	25.00
—Mostly brown label					
❏ 1028	Mecca/Teardrop by Teardrop	1963	3.75	7.50	15.00
❏ 1028 [PS]	Mecca/Teardrop by Teardrop	1963	5.00	10.00	20.00
❏ 1032	True Love Never Runs Smooth/Donna Means				
	Heartbreak	1963	3.75	7.50	15.00
❏ 1034	Twenty-Four Hours from Tulsa/				
	Lonely Night Dream	1963	3.75	7.50	15.00
❏ 1034 [PS]	Twenty-Four Hours from Tulsa/				
	Lonely Night Dream	1963	5.00	10.00	20.00
❏ 1036	That Girl Belongs to Yesterday/Who Needs It	1964	5.00	10.00	20.00
—A-side written by Mick Jagger and Keith Richards and produced by Andrew Oldham					
❏ 1036 [PS]	That Girl Belongs to Yesterday/Who Needs It	1964	6.25	12.50	25.00
❏ 1038	Yesterday's Hero/Cornflower Blue	1964	3.75	7.50	15.00
❏ 1039	I'm Gonna Find Myself a Girl/Lips Are Redder	1964	—	—	—
—Unreleased?					
❏ 1040	It Hurts to Be in Love/Hawaii	1964	3.75	7.50	15.00
❏ 1040 [PS]	It Hurts to Be in Love/Hawaii	1964	5.00	10.00	20.00
❏ 1045	I'm Gonna Be Strong/E Se Domani	1964	3.75	7.50	15.00
❏ 1045	I'm Gonna Be Strong/Aladdin's Lamp	1964	5.00	10.00	20.00
❏ 1045 [PS]	I'm Gonna Be Strong/E Se Domani	1964	5.00	10.00	20.00
❏ 1065	Amici Miri/I Tuoi Anni Piu Belli	1965	—	—	—
—Unreleased?					
❏ 1070	I Must Be Seeing Things/Marianne	1965	3.00	6.00	12.00
❏ 1070 [PS]	I Must Be Seeing Things/Marianne	1965	3.75	7.50	15.00
❏ 1093	Last Chance to Turn Around/Save Your Love	1965	3.00	6.00	12.00
❏ 1103	Looking Through the Eyes of Love/There's No				
	Living Without Your Loving	1965	3.00	6.00	12.00
❏ 1130	Princess in Rags/Amore Mio	1965	3.00	6.00	12.00
❏ 1150	Me Voy Para El Compo/Hojas Muertas	1966	—	—	—
—Unreleased?					
❏ 1155	Lei Mi Aspetta/Nessuno Mi Puo' Guidcare	1966	3.75	7.50	15.00
❏ 1171	Backstage/Blue Color	1966	2.50	5.00	10.00
❏ 1171 [PS]	Backstage/Blue Color	1966	3.75	7.50	15.00
❏ 1200	(In the) Cold Light of Day/The Boss' Daughter	1966	2.50	5.00	10.00
❏ 1200 [PS]	(In the) Cold Light of Day/The Boss' Daughter	1966	3.75	7.50	15.00
❏ 1219	Just One Smile/Innamorato	1966	2.50	5.00	10.00
❏ 1233	For Me, This Is Happy/I'm Gonna Listen to Me	1967	2.50	5.00	10.00
❏ 1235	Don't Mean to Be a Preacher/Animal Crackers				
	(In Cellophane Boxes)	1967	2.50	5.00	10.00
❏ 1245	Tremblin'/Where Did the Magic Go	1967	2.50	5.00	10.00
❏ 1252	Somethin' Gotten Hold of My Heart/				
	Building Up My Dream World	1967	2.50	5.00	10.00
❏ 1299	The More I Saw of Her/Won't Take Long	1968	2.00	4.00	8.00
❏ 1306	She's a Heartbreaker/Conquistador	1968	2.50	5.00	10.00
❏ 1308	Somewhere in the Country/Lonely Drifter	1968	2.00	4.00	8.00
❏ 1331	Billy, You're My Friend/Lonely Drifter	1968	2.00	4.00	8.00
❏ 1331	Billy, You're My Friend/She Believes in Me	1968	2.00	4.00	8.00
❏ 1331 [PS]	Billy, You're My Friend/Lonely Drifter	1968	3.00	6.00	12.00
❏ 1348	Baby, You're My Kind of Woman/Hate	1969	2.00	4.00	8.00
❏ 1358	Maria Elena/The French Horn	1969	2.00	4.00	8.00
❏ 1361	Playing Games of Love/California	1969	2.00	4.00	8.00
❏ 1384	She Lets Her Hair Down (Early in the Morning)/				
	I Remember	1969	2.00	4.00	8.00
❏ 1394	All the Young Women/I Remember	1970	—	3.00	6.00
❏ 1405	A Street Called Hope/Think of Us	1970	—	3.00	6.00
❏ 1419	Shady Lady/Billy, You're My Friend	1970	—	3.00	6.00
❏ 1439	Higher and Higher/Beautiful Sounds	1971	—	3.00	6.00
❏ 1442	A Thousand Arms (Five Hundred Hearts)/Gene,				
	Are You There?	1971	—	3.00	6.00
❏ 1453	I Just Can't Help Myself/Beautiful Sounds	1972	—	3.00	6.00
❏ 1461	Summertime Dreaming/A Thousand Arms				
	(Five Hundred Hearts)	1972	—	3.00	6.00
❏ 1474	Shady Lady/Run, Run Roadrunner	1973	—	3.00	6.00
Albums					
MUSIC DISC					
❏ MDS 1003	The Man Who Shot Liberty Valance	1969	3.00	6.00	12.00
❏ MDS 1005	Town Without Pity	1969	3.00	6.00	12.00
❏ MDS 1006	America's Greatest Country Songs	1969	3.00	6.00	12.00
❏ MDS 1008	Twenty Four Hours from Tulsa	1969	3.00	6.00	12.00
❏ MDS 1014	Baby, I Need Your Lovin'	1969	3.00	6.00	12.00
MUSICOR					
❏ MM-2001 [M]	The Many Sides of Gene Pitney	1962	12.50	25.00	50.00
—Brown label					
❏ MM-2001 [M]	The Many Sides of Gene Pitney	1963	6.25	12.50	25.00
—Black label					
❏ MM-2003 [M]	Only Love Can Break a Heart	1962	10.00	20.00	40.00
—Brown label					
❏ MM-2003 [M]	Only Love Can Break a Heart	1963	6.25	12.50	25.00
—Black label					
❏ MM-2004 [M]	Gene Pitney Sings Just for You	1963	7.50	15.00	30.00
❏ MM-2005 [M]	World-Wide Winners	1963	7.50	15.00	30.00
❏ MM-2006 [M]	Blue Gene	1963	7.50	15.00	30.00
❏ MM-2007 [M]	Gene Pitney Meets the Fair Young Ladies of				
	Folkland	1964	7.50	15.00	30.00
❏ MM-2008 [M]	Gene Pitney's Big Sixteen	1964	7.50	15.00	30.00
❏ MM-2015 [M]	Gene Italiano	1964	6.25	12.50	25.00
❏ MM-2019 [M]	It Hurts to Be in Love	1964	6.25	12.50	25.00
❏ MM-2043 [M]	Gene Pitney's More Big Sixteen	1965	6.25	12.50	25.00
❏ MM-2056 [M]	I Must Be Seeing Things	1965	6.25	12.50	25.00
❏ MM-2069 [M]	Looking Through the Eyes of Love	1965	6.25	12.50	25.00
❏ MM-2072 [M]	Gene Pitney En Espanol	1965	6.25	12.50	25.00

Number	Title (A Side/B Side)	Yr	VG	VG+	NM
❏ MM-2085 [M]	Big Sixteen, Vol. 3	1966	5.00	10.00	20.00
❏ MM-2095 [M]	Backstage I'm Lonely	1966	5.00	10.00	20.00
❏ MM-2100 [M]	Messumo Mi Puo Giudicare	1966	5.00	10.00	20.00
❏ MM-2101 [M]	The Gene Pitney Show	1966	5.00	10.00	20.00
❏ MM-2102 [M]	Greatest Hits of All Times	1966	5.00	10.00	20.00
❏ MM-2104 [M]	The Country Side of Gene Pitney	1967	5.00	10.00	20.00
❏ MM-2108 [M]	Young and Warm and Wonderful	1967	5.00	10.00	20.00
❏ MM-2117 [M]	Just One Smile	1967	5.00	10.00	20.00
❏ MM-2134 [M]	Golden Greats	1967	6.25	12.50	25.00
❏ MS-3001 [R]	The Many Sides of Gene Pitney	1962	7.50	15.00	30.00
—Brown label					
❏ MS-3001 [R]	The Many Sides of Gene Pitney	1963	5.00	10.00	20.00
—Black label					
❏ MS-3003 [S]	Only Love Can Break a Heart	1962	12.50	25.00	50.00
—Brown label					
❏ MS-3003 [S]	Only Love Can Break a Heart	1963	7.50	15.00	30.00
—Black label					
❏ MS-3004 [S]	Gene Pitney Sings Just for You	1963	10.00	20.00	40.00
❏ MS-3005 [P]	World-Wide Winners	1963	10.00	20.00	40.00
❏ MS-3006 [S]	Blue Gene	1963	10.00	20.00	40.00
❏ MS-3007 [S]	Gene Pitney Meets the Fair Young Ladies of Folkland	1964	10.00	20.00	40.00
❏ MS-3008 [P]	Gene Pitney's Big Sixteen	1964	10.00	20.00	40.00
❏ MS-3015 [S]	Gene Italiano	1964	7.50	15.00	30.00
❏ MS-3019 [P]	It Hurts to Be in Love	1964	7.50	15.00	30.00
❏ MS-3043 [S]	Gene Pitney's More Big Sixteen	1965	7.50	15.00	30.00
❏ MS-3056 [S]	I Must Be Seeing Things	1965	7.50	15.00	30.00
❏ MS-3069 [S]	Looking Through the Eyes of Love	1965	7.50	15.00	30.00
❏ MS-3072 [S]	Gene Pitney En Espanol	1965	7.50	15.00	30.00
❏ MS-3085 [S]	Big Sixteen, Vol. 3	1966	6.25	12.50	25.00
❏ MS-3095 [S]	Backstage I'm Lonely	1966	6.25	12.50	25.00
❏ MS-3100 [S]	Messumo Mi Puo Giudicare	1966	6.25	12.50	25.00
❏ MS-3101 [S]	The Gene Pitney Show	1966	6.25	12.50	25.00
❏ MS-3102 [P]	Greatest Hits of All Times	1966	6.25	12.50	25.00
❏ MS-3104 [S]	The Country Side of Gene Pitney	1967	6.25	12.50	25.00
❏ MS-3108 [S]	Young and Warm and Wonderful	1967	6.25	12.50	25.00
❏ MS-3117 [S]	Just One Smile	1967	6.25	12.50	25.00
❏ MS-3134 [S]	Golden Greats	1967	5.00	10.00	20.00
❏ M2-3148 [(2)]M] The Gene Pitney Story		1968	10.00	20.00	40.00
—Mono is promo only					
❏ M2S-3148 [(2)S] The Gene Pitney Story		1968	6.25	12.50	25.00
—Add 40% if bonus photo is enclosed					
❏ MS-3161	Gene Pitney Sings Burt Bacharach	1968	5.00	10.00	20.00
❏ MS-3164	She's a Heartbreaker	1968	5.00	10.00	20.00
❏ MS-3174	The Greatest Hits of Gene Pitney	1969	5.00	10.00	20.00
❏ MS-3183	Gene Pitney Sings the Platters' Golden Platters	1970	3.75	7.50	15.00
❏ MS-3193	Gene Pitney Super Star	1971	3.75	7.50	15.00
❏ MS-3206	Ten Years After	1971	3.75	7.50	15.00
❏ MS-3233	Golden Hour	1972	3.75	7.50	15.00
❏ MUX-4600 [(2)]	The Best of Gene Pitney (Double Gold Series)	1977	3.75	7.50	15.00
RHINO					
❏ RNDA-1102 [(2)]	Anthology (1961-1968)	1984	3.00	6.00	12.00
SPRINGBOARD					
❏ SPB-4057	Gene Pitney	1975	2.50	5.00	10.00

PITNEY, GENE, AND GEORGE JONES Also see each artist's individual listings.
45s
MUSICOR

Number	Title (A Side/B Side)	Yr	VG	VG+	NM
❏ 1066	I've Got Five Dollars and It's Saturday Night/ Wreck on the Highway	1965	3.00	6.00	12.00
❏ 1071	I've Got a New Heartache/My Shoes Keep Walking Back to You	1965	—	—	—
—Unreleased?					
❏ 1097	I'm a Fool to Care/Louisiana Man	1965	3.00	6.00	12.00
❏ 1097 [PS]	I'm a Fool to Care/Louisiana Man	1965	3.75	7.50	15.00
❏ 1115	Your Old Standby/Big Job	1965	3.00	6.00	12.00
❏ 1115 [PS]	Your Old Standby/Big Job	1965	3.75	7.50	15.00
❏ 1165	Y'All Come/That's All It Took	1966	2.50	5.00	10.00

Albums
MUSICOR

Number	Title (A Side/B Side)	Yr	VG	VG+	NM
❏ MM-2044 [M]	For the First Time! Two Great Singers Together: George Jones and Gene Pitney	1965	6.25	12.50	25.00
❏ MM-2065 [M]	It's Country Time Again	1965	6.25	12.50	25.00
❏ MS-3044 [S]	For the First Time! Two Great Singers Together: George Jones and Gene Pitney	1965	7.50	15.00	30.00
❏ MS-3065 [S]	It's Country Time Again	1965	7.50	15.00	30.00

PITNEY, GENE, AND MELBA MONTGOMERY Also see each artist's individual listings.
45s
MUSICOR

Number	Title (A Side/B Side)	Yr	VG	VG+	NM
❏ 1135	Baby, Ain't That Fine/ Everybody Knows But You and Me	1965	3.00	6.00	12.00
❏ 1173	King and Queen/Being Together	1966	2.50	5.00	10.00

Albums
MUSICOR

Number	Title (A Side/B Side)	Yr	VG	VG+	NM
❏ MM-2077 [M]	Being Together	1966	6.25	12.50	25.00
❏ MS-3077 [S]	Being Together	1966	7.50	15.00	30.00

PITTMAN, BARBARA
45s
PHILLIPS INT'L.

Number	Title (A Side/B Side)	Yr	VG	VG+	NM
❏ 3518	Two Young Fools in Love/ I'm Getting Better All the Time	1957	10.00	20.00	40.00
❏ 3527	Cold, Cold Heart/Everlasting Love	1958	10.00	20.00	40.00
❏ 3553	Handsome Man/The Eleventh Commandment	1960	5.00	10.00	20.00
SUN					
❏ 253	I Need a Man/No Matter Who's to Blame	1956	37.50	75.00	150.00

PITTS, GLORIA JEAN
45s
IMPERIAL

Number	Title (A Side/B Side)	Yr	VG	VG+	NM
❏ 5406	I Don't Stand No Quittin'/ Things You Should Know	1956	12.50	25.00	50.00

PIXIES THREE, THE
45s
MERCURY

Number	Title (A Side/B Side)	Yr	VG	VG+	NM
❏ 72130	Birthday Party/Our Love	1963	3.75	7.50	15.00
❏ 72130 [PS]	Birthday Party/Our Love	1963	6.25	12.50	25.00
❏ 72208	Cold, Cold Winter/442 Glenwood Avenue	1963	3.75	7.50	15.00
❏ 72208 [PS]	Cold, Cold Winter/442 Glenwood Avenue	1963	6.25	12.50	25.00
❏ 72250	Gee/After the Party	1964	3.75	7.50	15.00
❏ 72250 [PS]	Gee/After the Party	1964	7.50	15.00	30.00
❏ 72288	It's Summertime U.S.A./The Hootch	1964	3.75	7.50	15.00
❏ 72288 [PS]	It's Summertime U.S.A./The Hootch	1964	6.25	12.50	25.00
❏ 72331	Love Walked In/Orphan Boy	1964	3.75	7.50	15.00
❏ 72357	Love Me, Love Me/Your Way	1964	3.75	7.50	15.00

Albums
MERCURY

Number	Title (A Side/B Side)	Yr	VG	VG+	NM
❏ MG-20912 [M]	Party with the Pixies Three	1964	37.50	75.00	150.00
❏ SR-60912 [S]	Party with the Pixies Three	1964	50.00	100.00	200.00

PLAIDS, THE
45s
DARL

Number	Title (A Side/B Side)	Yr	VG	VG+	NM
❏ 1001	Keeper of My Heart/I Sing for You	1956	5.00	10.00	20.00
❏ 1003	Halfway to Heaven/Al-Lee-O, Al-Lee-Ay	1956	5.00	10.00	20.00
ERA					
❏ 3002	Around the Corner/He Stole Flo	1959	5.00	10.00	20.00
LIBERTY					
❏ 55167	Hungry for Your Love/Chit-Chat	1958	100.00	200.00	400.00
NASCO					
❏ 6011	Till the End of the Dance/My Pretty Baby	1958	5.00	10.00	20.00

PLANETS, THE (1)
45s
ALJON

Number	Title (A Side/B Side)	Yr	VG	VG+	NM
❏ 1244	Be Sure/Once Upon a Lifetime	1962	75.00	150.00	300.00

PLANETS, THE (2)
45s
ERA

Number	Title (A Side/B Side)	Yr	VG	VG+	NM
❏ 1038	Never Again/Stand There Mountain	1957	12.50	25.00	50.00
❏ 1049	Be Sure/Wild Leaves	1957	12.50	25.00	50.00
NU-CLEAR					
❏ 7422	I Need You So/Sharin' Lockers	1959	15.00	30.00	60.00

PLANETS, THE (3)
45s
ROULETTE

Number	Title (A Side/B Side)	Yr	VG	VG+	NM
❏ 4551	You Are My Sunshine/Mr. Moon	1964	3.75	7.50	15.00

PLANT & SEE
45s
WHITE WHALE

Number	Title (A Side/B Side)	Yr	VG	VG+	NM
❏ 309	Henrietta/Put Out the Fire	1969	3.00	6.00	12.00

Albums
WHITE WHALE

Number	Title (A Side/B Side)	Yr	VG	VG+	NM
❏ WWS-7120	Plant & See	1969	6.25	12.50	25.00

PLANT LIFE
45s
DATE

Number	Title (A Side/B Side)	Yr	VG	VG+	NM
❏ 1572	Flower Girl/Say It Over Again	1967	2.50	5.00	10.00

PLANTS, THE
45s
J&S

Number	Title (A Side/B Side)	Yr	VG	VG+	NM
❏ 248/9	I Searched the Seven Seas/ I Took a Trip Way Over the Sea	1956	100.00	200.00	400.00
❏ 1602	Dear, I Swear/It's You	1957	10.00	20.00	40.00
—No address under label name					
❏ 1602	Dear, I Swear/It's You	1957	100.00	200.00	400.00
—Address under label name					

PLASTER CASTERS, THE
Albums
BLUESTIME

Number	Title (A Side/B Side)	Yr	VG	VG+	NM
❏ BTS-9001	The Plaster Casters Blues Band	1969	12.50	25.00	50.00

PLASTIC COW, THE
45s
DOT

Number	Title (A Side/B Side)	Yr	VG	VG+	NM
❏ 17284	The Plastic Cow/Medicine Man	1969	2.50	5.00	10.00
❏ 17300	Lady Jane/One Many, One Vault	1969	2.50	5.00	10.00

Albums
DOT

Number	Title (A Side/B Side)	Yr	VG	VG+	NM
❏ DLP 25961	The Plastic Cow Goes Mooooog	1969	5.00	10.00	20.00

PLASTIC ONO BAND See JOHN LENNON; YOKO ONO.

PLATO
45s
PARKWAY

Number	Title (A Side/B Side)	Yr	VG	VG+	NM
❏ 914	Copy Cat/Claude's Theme	1964	2.50	5.00	10.00

PLATTERS, THE More than one group has used this name over the years, but all are related. Also see TONY WILLIAMS.
45s
ANTLER

Number	Title (A Side/B Side)	Yr	VG	VG+	NM
❏ 3000/1	I Do It All the Time/ Shake What Your Mama Gave You	1982	—	3.00	6.00
AVALANCHE					
❏ XW224	Sunday with You/If the World Loved	1973	2.00	4.00	8.00
—As "The Buck Ram Platters"					
ENTREE					
❏ 107	Won't You Be My Friend/Run While It's Dark	1965	2.00	4.00	8.00
—As "The Platters 1965"					
FEDERAL					
❏ 12153	Give Thanks/Hey Now	1953	100.00	200.00	400.00
—As "Tony Williams and the Platters"					

P

Number	Title (A Side/B Side)	Yr	VG	VG+	NM
❑ 12164	I'll Cry When You're Gone/I Need You All the Time	1954	250.00	500.00	1000.
❑ 12181	Roses of Picardy/Beer Barrel Polka	1954	75.00	150.00	300.00
❑ 12188	Tell the World/Love All Night	1954	50.00	100.00	200.00
❑ 12198	Voo-Vee-Ah-Bee/Shake It Up Mambo	1954	50.00	100.00	200.00
❑ 12204	Maggie Doesn't Work Here Anymore/Take Me Back, Take Me Back	1955	50.00	100.00	200.00
❑ 12244	Only You (And You Alone)/You Made Me Cry	1955	75.00	150.00	300.00
❑ 12250	Tell the World/I Need You All the Time	1955	30.00	60.00	120.00
❑ 12271	Give Thanks/I Need You All the Time	1956	20.00	40.00	80.00
MERCURY					
❑ 10001 [S]	Smoke Gets In Your Eyes/No Matter What You Are	1959	12.50	25.00	50.00
❑ 10007 [S]	Remember When/Love of a Lifetime	1959	10.00	20.00	40.00
❑ 70633	Only You (And You Alone)/Bark, Battle and Ball	1955	10.00	20.00	40.00
—Black label					
❑ 70633	Only You (And You Alone)/Bark, Battle and Ball	1955	12.50	25.00	50.00
—Earliest pressings have pink labels					
❑ 70753	The Great Pretender/I'm Just a Dancing Partner	1955	5.00	10.00	20.00
—Black label					
❑ 70753	The Great Pretender/I'm Just a Dancing Partner	1955	10.00	20.00	40.00
—Maroon label					
❑ 70819	(You've Got) The Magic Touch/Winner Take All	1956	5.00	10.00	20.00
—Black label					
❑ 70819	(You've Got) The Magic Touch/Winner Take All	1956	10.00	20.00	40.00
—Maroon label					
❑ 70893	My Prayer/Heaven on Earth	1956	5.00	10.00	20.00
—Black label					
❑ 70893	My Prayer/Heaven on Earth	1956	10.00	20.00	40.00
—Maroon label					
❑ 70948	You'll Never Never Know/It Isn't Right	1956	5.00	10.00	20.00
—Black label					
❑ 70948	You'll Never Never Know/It Isn't Right	1956	7.50	15.00	30.00
—Maroon label					
❑ 71011	One in a Million/On My Word of Honor	1956	7.50	15.00	30.00
❑ 71032	I'm Sorry/He's Mine	1957	5.00	10.00	20.00
—Black label					
❑ 71032	I'm Sorry/He's Mine	1957	7.50	15.00	30.00
—Maroon label					
❑ 71093	My Dream/I Wanna	1957	5.00	10.00	20.00
—Black label					
❑ 71093	My Dream/I Wanna	1957	7.50	15.00	30.00
—Maroon label					
❑ 71184	Only Because/The Mystery of You	1957	6.25	12.50	25.00
❑ 71246	Helpless/Indifferent	1957	6.25	12.50	25.00
❑ 71289	Twilight Time/Out of My Mind	1958	6.25	12.50	25.00
❑ 71320	You're Making a Mistake/My Old Flame	1958	6.25	12.50	25.00
❑ 71353	I Wish/It's Raining Outside	1958	6.25	12.50	25.00
—Black label					
❑ 71353	I Wish/It's Raining Outside	1958	7.50	15.00	30.00
—Blue label					
❑ 71383	Smoke Gets In Your Eyes/No Matter What You Are	1958	6.25	12.50	25.00
—Black label					
❑ 71383	Smoke Gets In Your Eyes/No Matter What You Are	1958	7.50	15.00	30.00
—Blue label					
❑ 71427	Enchanted/The Sound and the Fury	1959	5.00	10.00	20.00
❑ 71467 [M]	Remember When/Love of a Lifetime	1959	5.00	10.00	20.00
❑ 71502	Where/Wish It Were Me	1959	5.00	10.00	20.00
❑ 71538	My Secret/What Does It Matter	1959	5.00	10.00	20.00
❑ 71563	Harbor Lights/Sleepy Lagoon	1960	5.00	10.00	20.00
❑ 71563 [PS]	Harbor Lights/Sleepy Lagoon	1960	10.00	20.00	40.00
❑ 71624	Ebb Tide/(I'll Be With You) In Apple Blossom Time	1960	5.00	10.00	20.00
❑ 71656	Red Sails in the Sunset/Sad River	1960	5.00	10.00	20.00
❑ 71656 [PS]	Red Sails in the Sunset/Sad River	1960	7.50	15.00	30.00
❑ 71697	To Each His Own/Down the River of Golden Dreams	1960	5.00	10.00	20.00
❑ 71697 [PS]	To Each His Own/Down the River of Golden Dreams	1960	7.50	15.00	30.00
❑ 71749	If I Didn't Care/True Lover	1961	3.75	7.50	15.00
❑ 71749 [PS]	If I Didn't Care/True Lover	1961	7.50	15.00	30.00
❑ 71791	Trees/Immortal Love	1961	3.75	7.50	15.00
❑ 71791 [PS]	Trees/Immortal Love	1961	7.50	15.00	30.00
❑ 71847	I'll Never Smile Again/You Don't Say	1961	3.75	7.50	15.00
❑ 71847 [PS]	I'll Never Smile Again/You Don't Say	1961	7.50	15.00	30.00
❑ 71904	Song for the Lonely/You'll Never Know	1961	3.75	7.50	15.00
❑ 71904 [PS]	Song for the Lonely/You'll Never Know	1961	7.50	15.00	30.00
❑ 71921	It's Magic/Reaching for a Star	1962	3.75	7.50	15.00
❑ 71921 [PS]	It's Magic/Reaching for a Star	1962	7.50	15.00	30.00
❑ 71986	More Than You Know/Every Little Moment	1962	3.00	6.00	12.00
❑ 72060	Memories/Heartbreak	1962	3.00	6.00	12.00
❑ 72107	Once in a While/I'll See You in My Dreams	1963	2.50	5.00	10.00
❑ 72129	Strangers/Here Comes Heaven Again	1963	2.50	5.00	10.00
❑ 72194	Viva Ju Joy/Quando Caliente El Sol	1963	2.50	5.00	10.00
❑ 72242	Java Jive/Michael Row the Boat Ashore	1964	2.50	5.00	10.00
❑ 72305	Sincerely/P.S. I Love You	1964	2.50	5.00	10.00
❑ 72359	Love Me Tender/Little Things Mean a Lot	1964	2.50	5.00	10.00
❑ 76160	Platterama Medley/Red Sails in the Sunset	1982	—	3.00	6.00
MUSICOR					
❑ 1166	I Love You 1000 Times/Don't Hear, Speak, See No Evil	1966	2.00	4.00	8.00
❑ 1195	Alone in the Light (Without You)/Devri	1966	2.00	4.00	8.00
❑ 1211	I'll Be Home/(You've Got) The Magic Touch	1966	2.00	4.00	8.00
❑ 1229	With This Ring/If I Had a Love	1967	2.50	5.00	10.00
❑ 1251	Washed Ashore (On a Lonely Island in the Sea)/One in a Million	1967	2.00	4.00	8.00
❑ 1251	Washed Ashore (On a Lonely Island in the Sea)/What Name Shall I Give You, My Love	1967	2.00	4.00	8.00
❑ 1262	On Top of My Mind/Shing-a-Ling-a-Loo	1967	2.00	4.00	8.00
❑ 1275	Sweet, Sweet Lovin'/Sonata	1967	2.00	4.00	8.00
❑ 1288	Love Must Go On/How Beautiful Our Love Is	1968	2.00	4.00	8.00
❑ 1302	So Many Tears/Think Before You Walk Away	1968	2.00	4.00	8.00
❑ 1322	Hard to Get a Thing Called Love/Why	1968	2.00	4.00	8.00
❑ 1341	Fear of Loving You/Sonata	1968	2.00	4.00	8.00
❑ 1443	Be My Love/Sweet Sweet Lovin'	1971	2.00	4.00	8.00

Number	Title (A Side/B Side)	Yr	VG	VG+	NM
OWL					
❑ 320	Sixteen Tons/Are You Sincere	1973	2.00	4.00	8.00
POWER					
❑ 7012	Only You/Voo Vee Ah Bee	195?	2.00	4.00	8.00
—Reissue from "S.P.C. Newark, N.J."					
RAM					
❑ 1002	Only You/Here Comes the Boogie Man	1977	2.00	4.00	8.00
❑ 1004/5	My Ship Is Coming In/Guilty	1977	2.00	4.00	8.00
❑ 4852	Personality/Who's Sorry Now	1978	2.00	4.00	8.00
7-Inch Extended Plays					
FEDERAL					
❑ EP-378	*Only You (And You Alone)/I Need You All the Time/Tell the World/Give Thanks	1956	100.00	200.00	400.00
❑ EP-378 [PS]	The Platters Sing for Only You	1956	100.00	200.00	400.00
KING					
❑ 378	(contents unknown)	1956	37.50	75.00	150.00
❑ 378 [PS]	The Platters	1956	37.50	75.00	150.00
—Reissue of Federal EP					
❑ 651	(contents unknown)	1956	40.00	80.00	160.00
—"Federal" 651 is a counterfeit; all originals are on King					
❑ 651 [PS]	The Platters	1956	40.00	80.00	160.00
MERCURY					
❑ SR 621	Summertime/People Will Say We're in Love/More Than You Know//Stormy Weather/Every Little Movement/Poor Butterfly	196?	7.50	15.00	30.00
—Jukebox issue; small hole, plays at 33 1/3 rpm					
❑ SR 621 [PS]	Encore of Broadway Golden Hits	196?	7.50	15.00	30.00
❑ EP 1-3336	My Prayer/Have Mercy//On My Word of Honor/I'm Sorry	1957	10.00	20.00	40.00
❑ EP 1-3336 [PS]	The Platters	1957	10.00	20.00	40.00
❑ EP 1-3343	Heart of Stone/I'd Climb the Highest Mountain//September in the Rain/You've Changed	1957	10.00	20.00	40.00
❑ EP 1-3343 [PS]	The Platters (Part 1)	1957	10.00	20.00	40.00
❑ EP 1-3344	I'll Get By/I'll Give You My Word//In the Still of the Night/Wagon Wheels	1957	10.00	20.00	40.00
❑ EP 1-3344 [PS]	The Platters (Part 2)	1957	10.00	20.00	40.00
❑ EP 1-3345	Take Me in Your Arms/You Can Depend on Me//Temptation/I Don't Know Why	1957	10.00	20.00	40.00
❑ EP 1-3345 [PS]	The Platters (Part 3)	1957	10.00	20.00	40.00
❑ EP 1-3353	No Power on Earth/You Are Too Beautiful//Darktown Strutter's Ball/Sweet Sixteen	1958	10.00	20.00	40.00
❑ EP 1-3353 [PS]	The Flying Platters (Part 1)	1958	10.00	20.00	40.00
❑ EP 1-3354	Only Because/Love, You Funny Thing/I'm Gonna Sit Right Down and Write Myself a Letter/In the Middle of Nowhere	1958	10.00	20.00	40.00
❑ EP 1-3354 [PS]	The Flying Platters (Part 2)	1958	10.00	20.00	40.00
❑ EP 1-3355	Mean to Me/Oh Promise Me//Time and Tide/Don't Forget	1958	10.00	20.00	40.00
❑ EP 1-3355 [PS]	The Flying Platters	1958	10.00	20.00	40.00
❑ EP 1-3393	Twilight Time/For the First Time//Don't Blame Me/But Not Like You	1958	10.00	20.00	40.00
❑ EP 1-3393 [PS]	Twilight Time	1958	10.00	20.00	40.00
❑ EP1-4029	Twilight Time/My Prayer//Smoke Gets in Your Eyes/Remember When	196?	7.50	15.00	30.00
❑ EP1-4029 [PS]	Encore of Golden Hits - Vol. 1	196?	7.50	15.00	30.00
Albums					
CANDELITE MUSIC					
❑ CMI 1000 [(5)]	The 50 Golden Hits of the Platters	197?	10.00	20.00	40.00
COLUMBIA SPECIAL PRODUCTS					
❑ P 11834 [S]	Christmas with the Platters	1973	3.75	7.50	15.00
—Reissue of Mercury SR-60841 with fewer tracks					
FEDERAL					
❑ 549 [M]	The Platters	1957	400.00	800.00	1600.
KING					
❑ 651 [M]	The Platters	1959	200.00	400.00	800.00
❑ KLP-651 [M]	The Platters	1987	2.50	5.00	10.00
—Reissue with "Highland Records" on label					
❑ 5002	19 Hits of the Platters	197?	3.00	6.00	12.00
MERCURY					
❑ SRM-1-4050	Platterama	1982	2.50	5.00	10.00
❑ MG-20146 [M]	The Platters	1956	25.00	50.00	100.00
❑ MG-20216 [M]	The Platters, Volume Two	1956	25.00	50.00	100.00
❑ MG-20298 [M]	The Flying Platters	1957	25.00	50.00	100.00
❑ MG-20366 [M]	The Flying Platters Around the World	1958	7.50	15.00	30.00
❑ MG-20410 [M]	Remember When?	1959	7.50	15.00	30.00
❑ MG-20472 [M]	Encore of Golden Hits	1960	7.50	15.00	30.00
❑ MG-20481 [M]	Reflections	1960	6.25	12.50	25.00
❑ MG-20589 [M]	Life Is Just a Bowl of Cherries	1960	6.25	12.50	25.00
❑ MG-20591 [M]	More Encore of Golden Hits	1960	6.25	12.50	25.00
❑ MG-20613 [M]	Encore of Broadway Golden Hits	1961	5.00	10.00	20.00
❑ MG-20669 [M]	Song for the Lonely	1962	5.00	10.00	20.00
❑ MG-20759 [M]	Moonlight Memories	1963	5.00	10.00	20.00
❑ MG-20782 [M]	The Platters Present All-Time Movie Hits	1963	5.00	10.00	20.00
❑ MG-20808 [M]	The Platters Sing Latino	1963	5.00	10.00	20.00
❑ MG-20841 [M]	Christmas with the Platters	1963	7.50	15.00	30.00
❑ MG-20893 [M]	Encore of Golden Hits of the Groups	1964	5.00	10.00	20.00
❑ MG-20933 [M]	10th Anniversary Album	1964	5.00	10.00	20.00
❑ MG-20983 [M]	The New Soul of the Platters	1965	3.75	7.50	15.00
❑ SR-60043 [S]	The Flying Platters Around the World	1959	12.50	25.00	50.00
❑ SR-60087 [S]	Remember When?	1959	12.50	25.00	50.00
❑ SR-60160 [S]	Reflections	1960	7.50	15.00	30.00
❑ SR-60243 [P]	Encore of Golden Hits	1960	10.00	20.00	40.00
—Original: Black label, silver print; 12 songs on LP					
❑ SR-60243 [P]	Encore of Golden Hits	1965	6.25	12.50	25.00
—Second edition: Red label, "MERCURY" in white across top; may or may not have "Gold Record Award" insignia on back cover; 12 songs on LP					
❑ SR-60243 [P]	Encore of Golden Hits	1975	3.00	6.00	12.00
—Chicago skyline label; album has 10 songs					
❑ SR-60245 [S]	Life Is Just a Bowl of Cherries	1960	7.50	15.00	30.00
❑ SR-60252 [S]	More Encore of Golden Hits	1960	7.50	15.00	30.00
❑ SR-60613 [S]	Encore of Broadway Golden Hits	1961	6.25	12.50	25.00
❑ SR-60669 [S]	Song for the Lonely	1962	6.25	12.50	25.00
❑ SR-60759 [S]	Moonlight Memories	1963	6.25	12.50	25.00
❑ SR-60782 [S]	The Platters Present All-Time Movie Hits	1963	6.25	12.50	25.00
❑ SR-60808 [S]	The Platters Sing Latino	1963	6.25	12.50	25.00
❑ SR-60841 [S]	Christmas with the Platters	1963	10.00	20.00	40.00
—Same as above, but in stereo					

Number	Title (A Side/B Side)	Yr	VG	VG+	NM
❏ SR-60893 [S]	Encore of Golden Hits of the Groups	1964	6.25	12.50	25.00
❏ SR-60933 [S]	10th Anniversary Album	1964	6.25	12.50	25.00
❏ SR-60983 [S]	The New Soul of the Platters	1965	5.00	10.00	20.00
❏ 828246-1	More Encore of Golden Hits	198?	2.00	4.00	8.00
—Reissue					
❏ 828254-1	Encore of Golden Hits	198?	2.00	4.00	8.00
—Reissue					
MUSIC DISC					
❏ MDS-1002	Only You	1969	3.00	6.00	12.00
MUSICOR					
❏ MM-2091 [M]	I Love You 1,000 Times	1966	3.75	7.50	15.00
❏ MM-2111 [M]	The Platters Have the Magic Touch	1966	3.75	7.50	15.00
❏ MM-2125 [M]	Going Back to Detroit	1967	3.75	7.50	15.00
❏ MM-2141 [M]	New Golden Hits of the Platters	1967	5.00	10.00	20.00
❏ MS-3091 [S]	I Love You 1,000 Times	1966	5.00	10.00	20.00
❏ MS-3111 [S]	The Platters Have the Magic Touch	1966	5.00	10.00	20.00
❏ MS-3125 [S]	Going Back to Detroit	1967	3.75	7.50	15.00
❏ MS-3141 [S]	New Golden Hits of the Platters	1967	3.75	7.50	15.00
❏ MS-3156	Sweet, Sweet Lovin'	1968	3.75	7.50	15.00
❏ MS-3171	I Get the Sweetest Feeling	1968	3.75	7.50	15.00
❏ MS-3185	Singing the Great Hits Our Way	1969	3.75	7.50	15.00
❏ MS-3231	Golden Hour	1973	3.00	6.00	12.00
❏ MS-3254	The Golden Hits of the Platters	1973	3.00	6.00	12.00
PICKWICK					
❏ PTP-2083 [(2)]	Only You	1973	3.00	6.00	12.00
❏ SPC-3236	Super Hits	197?	2.50	5.00	10.00
RHINO					
❏ RNFP-71495 [(2)]	Anthology (1955-1967)	1986	3.00	6.00	12.00
SPRINGBOARD					
❏ SPB-4059	The Platters	197?	2.50	5.00	10.00
WING					
❏ MGW-12112 [M]	Encores!	1959	7.50	15.00	30.00
—With liner notes on back cover					
❏ MGW-12112 [M]	Encores!	196?	3.75	7.50	15.00
—With photos of other Wing LPs on back cover					
❏ MGW-12226 [M]	Flying Platters	1963	3.00	6.00	12.00
❏ MGW-12272 [M]	Reflections	1964	3.00	6.00	12.00
❏ MGW-12346 [M]	10th Anniversary Album	196?	3.00	6.00	12.00
❏ SRW-16112 [R]	Encores!	196?	3.00	6.00	12.00
❏ SRW-16226 [S]	Flying Platters	1963	3.00	6.00	12.00
❏ SRW-16272 [S]	Reflections	1964	3.00	6.00	12.00
❏ SRW-16346 [S]	10th Anniversary Album	196?	3.00	6.00	12.00

PLAYBOYS, THE (1) The only of the many Playboys groups to have a national hit (other than Gary Lewis' or John Fred's bands).
45s

Number	Title (A Side/B Side)	Yr	VG	VG+	NM
CAMEO					
❏ 142	Over the Weekend/Double Talk	1958	5.00	10.00	20.00
MARTINIQUE					
❏ 101	Over the Weekend/Double Talk	1958	12.50	25.00	50.00
❏ 400	Please Forgive Me/Sing Along	1959	10.00	20.00	40.00

PLAYBOYS, THE (2)
45s

Number	Title (A Side/B Side)	Yr	VG	VG+	NM
ABC-PARAMOUNT					
❏ 10070	You're All I See/Memories	1959	5.00	10.00	20.00

PLAYBOYS, THE (3)
45s

Number	Title (A Side/B Side)	Yr	VG	VG+	NM
ACE					
❏ 670	Gotta Feelin'/How Could You Forget	1963	3.00	6.00	12.00

PLAYBOYS, THE (4)
45s

Number	Title (A Side/B Side)	Yr	VG	VG+	NM
CAT					
❏ 108	Tell Me/Rock, Moan and Cry	1954	12.50	25.00	50.00
❏ 115	Good Golly Miss Molly/Honey Run	1955	12.50	25.00	50.00

PLAYBOYS, THE (5)
45s

Number	Title (A Side/B Side)	Yr	VG	VG+	NM
CATALINA					
❏ 1069	Shortnin' Bread/Cheater Stomp	1964	7.50	15.00	30.00

PLAYBOYS, THE (6)
45s

Number	Title (A Side/B Side)	Yr	VG	VG+	NM
TETRA					
❏ 4447	One Question/So Good	1956	37.50	75.00	150.00

PLAYBOYS, THE (U) Many of these could be by the above groups; many probably are not.
45s

Number	Title (A Side/B Side)	Yr	VG	VG+	NM
CHANCELLOR					
❏ 1074	Boston Hop/What'd I Say	1961	3.75	7.50	15.00
—B-side by the Cousins					
❏ 1106	Duck Walk/If I Had My Way	1962	3.75	7.50	15.00
COTTON					
❏ 1008	Careful with My Heart/Girl of My Dreams	1962	6.25	12.50	25.00
DOLTON					
❏ 8	Party Ice/Icy Fingers	1959	5.00	10.00	20.00
HEARTBEAT					
❏ 60	Harlem Nocturne/Blue Moon	1963	5.00	10.00	20.00
IMPERIAL					
❏ 5586	Sweet Talk/Crazy Daisy	1959	5.00	10.00	20.00
LEGATO					
❏ 101	Mope De Mope/The Night Before Christmas	1963	7.50	15.00	30.00
MERCURY					
❏ 71228	Why Do I Love You, Why Do I Care/ Don't Do Me Wrong	1957	6.25	12.50	25.00
RIK					
❏ 572	Jungle Fever/Shotgun	1959	6.25	12.50	25.00
SOUVENIR					
❏ 1001	Believe It or Not/Hawaiian War Chant	1959	3.75	7.50	15.00
TITAN					
❏ 1732	The Scramble/Cat Walk	1963	5.00	10.00	20.00
ZIPP					
❏ 101	Sweet Talk/Crazy Daisy	1959	10.00	20.00	40.00

PLAYMATES, THE
45s

Number	Title (A Side/B Side)	Yr	VG	VG+	NM
ABC-PARAMOUNT					
❏ 10422	"A" My Name Is Alice/Just a Little Bit	1963	2.50	5.00	10.00
❏ 10468	She Never Looked Better/ But Not Through Tears	1963	2.50	5.00	10.00
❏ 10492	I Cross My Fingers/I'll Never Get Over You	1963	2.50	5.00	10.00
❏ 10522	Guy Behind the Wheel/ One Guy Left on the Corner	1964	2.50	5.00	10.00
BELL					
❏ 45149	Foundation of Love/Davenu	1971	—	3.00	6.00
COLPIX					
❏ 760	Fiddler on the Roof/Piece of the Sky	1964	2.00	4.00	8.00
❏ 769	One by One the Roses Died/Spanish Perfume	1965	2.00	4.00	8.00
CONGRESS					
❏ 245	Ballad of Stanley the Lifeguard/ Should I Ask Someone Else to Tell Her	1965	2.00	4.00	8.00
RAINBOW					
❏ 360	Nickelodeon Rag/I Have Only Myself to Blame	1956	7.50	15.00	30.00
ROULETTE					
❏ 4003	Barefoot Girl/Pretty Woman	1957	3.75	7.50	15.00
❏ 4022	Darling It's Wonderful/Island Girl	1957	3.75	7.50	15.00
❏ 4022	Darling It's Wonderful/Magic Shoes	1957	3.75	7.50	15.00
❏ 4037	Jo-Ann/You Can't Stop Me from Dreaming	1957	6.25	12.50	25.00
❏ 4056	Let's Be Lovers/Give Me Another Chance	1958	3.75	7.50	15.00
❏ 4072	Don't Go Home/ Can't You Get It Through Your Head	1958	3.75	7.50	15.00
❏ 4100	The Day I Died/While the Record Goes Around	1958	3.75	7.50	15.00
❏ 4115	Beep Beep/Your Love	1958	6.25	12.50	25.00
❏ 4136	Star Love/The Thing-A-Ma-Jig	1959	3.00	6.00	12.00
❏ 4160	What Is Love/I Am	1959	3.00	6.00	12.00
❏ 4200	First Love/A-Ciu-E	1959	3.00	6.00	12.00
❏ 4211	On the Beach/The Song Everybody's Singing	1959	3.00	6.00	12.00
❏ 4227	Second Chance/These Things I Offer You	1960	3.00	6.00	12.00
❏ 4252	Parade of Pretty Girls/Our Wedding Day	1960	3.00	6.00	12.00
❏ 4276	Wait for Me/Eyes of Angel	1960	3.00	6.00	12.00
❏ 4322	Little Mis Stuck-Up/Real Life	1961	3.00	6.00	12.00
❏ 4370	Tell Me What She Said/Cowboys Never Cry	1961	3.00	6.00	12.00
❏ 4393	Wimoweh/One Little Kiss	1961	3.00	6.00	12.00
❏ 4417	A Rose and a Star/Bachelor Flat	1962	2.50	5.00	10.00
❏ 4432	Keep Your Hands in Your Pocket/ The Cop on the Beat	1962	2.50	5.00	10.00
❏ 4464	What a Funny Way to Show It/Petticoats Fly	1962	2.50	5.00	10.00
Albums					
FORUM					
❏ F-9012 [M]	At Play with the Playmates	196?	3.00	6.00	12.00
❏ SF-9012 [S]	At Play with the Playmates	196?	3.75	7.50	15.00
❏ F-9021 [M]	Broadway Show Stoppers	196?	3.00	6.00	12.00
❏ SF-9021 [S]	Broadway Show Stoppers	196?	3.75	7.50	15.00
❏ F-16001 [M]	The Playmates Visit West of the Indies	1960	3.75	7.50	15.00
❏ SF-16001 [S]	The Playmates Visit West of the Indies	1960	5.00	10.00	20.00
ROULETTE					
❏ R-25001 [M]	Calypso	1957	6.25	12.50	25.00
❏ R-25043 [M]	At Play with the Playmates	1958	6.25	12.50	25.00
❏ SR-25043 [S]	At Play with the Playmates	1958	7.50	15.00	30.00
❏ R-25059 [M]	Rock and Roll Record Hop	1959	5.00	10.00	20.00
❏ SR-25059 [S]	Rock and Roll Record Hop	1959	6.25	12.50	25.00
❏ R-25068 [M]	Cuttin' Capers	1960	5.00	10.00	20.00
❏ SR-25068 [S]	Cuttin' Capers	1960	6.25	12.50	25.00
❏ R-25084 [M]	Broadway Show Stoppers	1961	5.00	10.00	20.00
❏ SR-25084 [S]	Broadway Show Stoppers	1961	6.25	12.50	25.00

PLEASE, BOBBY
45s

Number	Title (A Side/B Side)	Yr	VG	VG+	NM
ERA					
❏ 1044	Heartache Street/Your Driver's License Please	1957	3.75	7.50	15.00
IMPERIAL					
❏ 5508	I'm Girl Crazy/My Tummy Flip	1958	3.75	7.50	15.00
JAMIE					
❏ 1118	The Monster/The Switch	1959	3.75	7.50	15.00

PLEASURE FAIR, THE With Robb Royer, later of BREAD.
45s

Number	Title (A Side/B Side)	Yr	VG	VG+	NM
UNI					
❏ 55016	Morning Glory Days/Fade In, Fade Out	1967	2.00	4.00	8.00
❏ 55078	Today/I'm Gonna Hafta Let You Go	1968	2.00	4.00	8.00
Albums					
UNI					
❏ 3008 [M]	The Pleasure Fair	1967	5.00	10.00	20.00
❏ 73008 [S]	The Pleasure Fair	1967	5.00	10.00	20.00

PLEASURE SEEKERS SUZI QUATRO was in this group.
45s

Number	Title (A Side/B Side)	Yr	VG	VG+	NM
CAPITOL					
❏ 2050	(Theme from) Valley of the Dolls/ If You Climb on the Tiger's Back	1967	5.00	10.00	20.00
HIDEOUT					
❏ 1006	Never Thought You'd Leave Me/ What a Way to Die	1967	25.00	50.00	100.00
MERCURY					
❏ 72800	Good Kind of Hurt/Light of Love	1968	6.25	12.50	25.00

PLEBS, THE
45s

Number	Title (A Side/B Side)	Yr	VG	VG+	NM
MGM					
❏ 13320	Bad Blood/Babe I'm Gonna Leave You	1965	3.00	6.00	12.00

PLEDGES, THE Actually Clyde Battin and GARY PAXTON, who recorded as SKIP AND FLIP.
45s

Number	Title (A Side/B Side)	Yr	VG	VG+	NM
REV					
❏ 3517	Betty Jean/Her Bermuda Shorts	1958	6.25	12.50	25.00

PLUM NELLY
Albums

Number	Title (A Side/B Side)	Yr	VG	VG+	NM
CAPITOL					
❏ ST-692	Deceptive Lines	1971	5.00	10.00	20.00

P

Number	Title (A Side/B Side)	Yr	VG	VG+	NM

PLUMB, EVE "Jan Brady" of THE BRADY BUNCH.
45s
RCA VICTOR

Number	Title (A Side/B Side)	Yr	VG	VG+	NM
❑ 74-0409	How Will It Be/Fortune Cookie Song	1970	3.75	7.50	15.00
❑ 74-0409 [PS]	How Will It Be/Fortune Cookie Song	1970	5.00	10.00	20.00

PLUMMER, DAVE, AND THE PLUNGERS
45s
MAYBROOK

Number	Title (A Side/B Side)	Yr	VG	VG+	NM
❑ 320	Surfin' Monster/King of the Road	196?	10.00	20.00	40.00

POCO Also see JIM MESSINA.
12-Inch Singles
MCA

Number	Title (A Side/B Side)	Yr	VG	VG+	NM
❑ 2314 [DJ]	Under the Gun (same on both sides)	1980	2.00	4.00	8.00

RCA

Number	Title (A Side/B Side)	Yr	VG	VG+	NM
❑ 9039-1-RAB [DJ]	Call It Love (Edit)/Call It Love (LP)	1989	—	3.00	6.00

45s
ABC

Number	Title (A Side/B Side)	Yr	VG	VG+	NM
❑ 12126	Keep On Tryin'/Georgia, Bind My Ties	1975	—	2.50	5.00
❑ 12159	Makin' Love/Flyin' Solo	1976	—	2.50	5.00
❑ 12204	Rose of Cimarron/Tulsa Turnaround	1976	—	2.50	5.00
❑ 12295	Indian Summer/Me and You	1977	—	2.50	5.00
❑ 12439	Crazy Love/Barbados	1978	—	2.50	5.00

ATLANTIC

Number	Title (A Side/B Side)	Yr	VG	VG+	NM
❑ 89629	Save a Corner of Your Heart/The Storm	1984	—	2.50	5.00
❑ 89650	This Old Flame/The Storm	1984	—	—	3.00
❑ 89674	Days Gone By/Daylight	1984	—	—	3.00
❑ 89851	Break of Hearts/Love's So Cruel	1983	—	2.50	5.00
❑ 89919	Shoot for the Moon/The Midnight Rodeo	1982	—	—	3.00
❑ 89970	Ghostown/High Sierra	1982	—	—	3.00
❑ 89970 [PS]	Ghostown/High Sierra	1982	—	2.00	4.00

EPIC

Number	Title (A Side/B Side)	Yr	VG	VG+	NM
❑ 10501	Pickin' Up the Pieces/First Love	1969	2.50	5.00	10.00
❑ 10543	My Kind of Love/Hard Luck	1969	2.50	5.00	10.00
❑ 10636	You Better Think Twice/Anyway, Bye Bye	1970	2.00	4.00	8.00
❑ 10714	C'Mon/I Guess You Made It	1971	2.00	4.00	8.00
❑ 10804	Just for Me and You/Ol' Forgiver	1971	2.00	4.00	8.00
❑ 10816	You Are the One/Railroad Days	1971	2.00	4.00	8.00
❑ 10890	Good Feeling to Know/Early Times	1972	—	3.00	6.00
❑ 10958	I Can See Everything/Go and Say Goodbye	1973	—	3.00	6.00
❑ 11055	Here We Go Again/Fools Gold	1973	—	3.00	6.00
❑ 11092	Magnolia/Blue Water	1974	—	3.00	6.00
❑ 11141	Rocky Mountain Breakdown/ Faith in the Families	1974	—	3.00	6.00
❑ 50076	Bitter Blue/High and Dry	1975	—	3.00	6.00

MCA

Number	Title (A Side/B Side)	Yr	VG	VG+	NM
❑ 41023	Heart of the Night/Last Goodbye	1979	—	2.00	4.00
❑ 41103	Legend/Indian Summer	1979	—	2.00	4.00
❑ 41269	Under the Gun/Reputation	1980	—	2.00	4.00
❑ 41269 [PS]	Under the Gun/Reputation	1980	—	3.00	6.00
❑ 41326	Midnight Rain/Fool's Paradise	1980	—	2.00	4.00
❑ 51034	Everlasting Kind/Friends in the Distance	1980	—	2.00	4.00
❑ 51172	Down on the River Again/Widowmaker	1981	—	2.00	4.00
❑ 52001	Seas of Heartbreaks/Feudin'	1982	—	2.00	4.00

RCA

Number	Title (A Side/B Side)	Yr	VG	VG+	NM
❑ 9038-7-R	Call It Love/Lovin' You Every Minute	1989	—	—	3.00
❑ 9038-7-R [PS]	Call It Love/Lovin' You Every Minute	1989	—	—	3.00
❑ 9131-7-R	Nothin' to Hide/If It Wasn't for You	1989	—	—	3.00
❑ 9131-7-R [PS]	Nothin' to Hide/If It Wasn't for You	1989	—	—	3.00

Albums
ABC

Number	Title (A Side/B Side)	Yr	VG	VG+	NM
❑ D-890	Head Over Heels	1975	2.50	5.00	10.00
❑ D-946	Rose of Cimarron	1976	2.50	5.00	10.00
❑ D-989	Indian Summer	1977	2.50	5.00	10.00
❑ AA-1099	Legend	1978	3.00	6.00	12.00

ATLANTIC

Number	Title (A Side/B Side)	Yr	VG	VG+	NM
❑ 80008	Ghost Town	1982	2.50	5.00	10.00
❑ 80148	Inamorata	1984	2.50	5.00	10.00

EPIC

Number	Title (A Side/B Side)	Yr	VG	VG+	NM
❑ BN 26460	Pickin' Up the Pieces	1969	3.75	7.50	15.00
—Yellow label					
❑ BN 26460	Pickin' Up the Pieces	1973	2.50	5.00	10.00
—Orange label					
❑ BN 26522	Poco	1970	3.75	7.50	15.00
—Yellow label					
❑ BN 26522	Poco	1973	2.50	5.00	10.00
—Orange label					
❑ EQ 30209 [Q]	Deliverin'	1972	5.00	10.00	20.00
❑ KE 30209	Deliverin'	1971	3.75	7.50	15.00
—Yellow label					
❑ KE 30209	Deliverin'	1973	2.50	5.00	10.00
—Orange label					
❑ E 30753	From the Inside	1973	2.50	5.00	10.00
—Reissue with new prefix					
❑ KE 30753	From the Inside	1971	3.75	7.50	15.00
—Yellow label					
❑ KE 30753	From the Inside	1973	2.50	5.00	10.00
—Orange label					
❑ KE 31601	A Good Feelin' to Know	1972	3.75	7.50	15.00
—Yellow label					
❑ KE 31601	A Good Feelin' to Know	1973	2.50	5.00	10.00
—Orange label					
❑ PE 31601	A Good Feelin' to Know	198?	2.00	4.00	8.00
—Budget-line reissue					
❑ EQ 32354 [Q]	Crazy Eyes	1973	5.00	10.00	20.00
❑ KE 32354	Crazy Eyes	1973	3.00	6.00	12.00
—Orange label					
❑ PE 32354	Crazy Eyes	1979	2.00	4.00	8.00
—Blue label					
❑ EQ 32895 [Q]	Seven	1974	5.00	10.00	20.00
❑ KE 32895	Seven	1974	3.00	6.00	12.00
—Orange label					
❑ PCQ 33192 [Q]	Cantamos	1974	5.00	10.00	20.00
❑ PE 33192	Cantamos	1974	3.00	6.00	12.00
—Orange label					

Number	Title (A Side/B Side)	Yr	VG	VG+	NM
❑ PE 33336	Live	1976	3.00	6.00	12.00
—Orange label					
❑ PEG 33537 [(2)]	The Very Best of Poco	1975	3.75	7.50	15.00
—Orange labels					
❑ JE 36210	The Songs of Paul Cotton	1980	2.50	5.00	10.00
❑ JE 36211	The Songs of Richie Furay	1980	2.50	5.00	10.00

MCA

Number	Title (A Side/B Side)	Yr	VG	VG+	NM
❑ AA-1099	Legend	1979	2.50	5.00	10.00
—Reissue of ABC 1099					
❑ 5132	Under the Gun	1980	2.50	5.00	10.00
❑ 5227	Blue and Gray	1981	2.50	5.00	10.00
❑ 5288	Cowboys & Englishmen	1982	2.50	5.00	10.00
❑ 5363	Backtracks	1983	2.50	5.00	10.00
❑ 37009	Head Over Heels	1980	2.00	4.00	8.00
—Budget-line reissue					
❑ 37010	Rose of Cimarron	1980	2.00	4.00	8.00
—Budget-line reissue					
❑ 37011	Indian Summer	1980	2.00	4.00	8.00
—Budget-line reissue					
❑ 37117	Legend	1981	2.00	4.00	8.00
—Budget-line reissue					
❑ 37160	Under the Gun	198?	2.00	4.00	8.00
—Budget-line reissue					

MOBILE FIDELITY

Number	Title (A Side/B Side)	Yr	VG	VG+	NM
❑ 1-020	Legend	1979	5.00	10.00	20.00
—Audiophile vinyl					

RCA

Number	Title (A Side/B Side)	Yr	VG	VG+	NM
❑ 9694-1-R	Legacy	1989	2.50	5.00	10.00

POETS, THE (1)
45s
SYMBOL

Number	Title (A Side/B Side)	Yr	VG	VG+	NM
❑ 214	She Blew a Good Thing/Out to Lunch	1966	3.75	7.50	15.00
❑ 216	So Young (And So Innocent)/A Sure Thing	1966	3.00	6.00	12.00
❑ 219	I'm Particular/I've Only Two Hearts	1966	3.00	6.00	12.00

VEEP

Number	Title (A Side/B Side)	Yr	VG	VG+	NM
❑ 1286	The Hustler/Soul Brothers Holiday	1968	5.00	10.00	20.00

POETS, THE (2) British group.
45s
DYNO VOX

Number	Title (A Side/B Side)	Yr	VG	VG+	NM
❑ 201	Now We're Thru/There Are Some	1965	2.50	5.00	10.00

POETS, THE (3)
45s
FLASH

Number	Title (A Side/B Side)	Yr	VG	VG+	NM
❑ 129	Vowels of Love/Dead	1958	15.00	30.00	60.00
—Maroon label					
❑ 129	Vowels of Love/Dead	1958	50.00	100.00	200.00
—Black label					

POETS, THE (4)
45s
IMPERIAL

Number	Title (A Side/B Side)	Yr	VG	VG+	NM
❑ 5664	Honey Chile/I'm in Love	1960	3.75	7.50	15.00

POETS, THE (U) These could be group (1) or (2).
45s
CHAIRMAN

Number	Title (A Side/B Side)	Yr	VG	VG+	NM
❑ 4408	Coffee House/Number One (More Time)	1963	3.00	6.00	12.00

J-2

Number	Title (A Side/B Side)	Yr	VG	VG+	NM
❑ 1302	Wrapped Around Your Finger/(B-side unknown)	196?	250.00	500.00	1000.

RED BIRD

Number	Title (A Side/B Side)	Yr	VG	VG+	NM
❑ 10-046	Merry Christmas Baby/I'm Stuck on You	1965	3.00	6.00	12.00

TRY ME

Number	Title (A Side/B Side)	Yr	VG	VG+	NM
❑ 28006	Devil's Den (Part 1)/(Part 2)	196?	5.00	10.00	20.00

POINDEXTER, DON, AND THE STARLITE WRANGLERS
45s
SUN

Number	Title (A Side/B Side)	Yr	VG	VG+	NM
❑ 202	Now She Cares No More for Me/My Kind of Love	1954	500.00	1000.	2000.

POINTER SISTERS, THE
12-Inch Singles
COLUMBIA

Number	Title (A Side/B Side)	Yr	VG	VG+	NM
❑ 07883	Power of Persuasion (3 versions)	1988	—	3.00	6.00

MCA

Number	Title (A Side/B Side)	Yr	VG	VG+	NM
❑ 23769	Be There (4 versions)	1987	—	3.00	6.00

MOTOWN

Number	Title (A Side/B Side)	Yr	VG	VG+	NM
❑ 4661	Friend's Advice (Don't Take It) (3 versions)	1990	—	3.00	6.00
❑ L33-17922 [DJ]	Friend's Advice (Don't Take It) (5 versions)	1990	2.00	4.00	8.00

PLANET

Number	Title (A Side/B Side)	Yr	VG	VG+	NM
❑ 11403 [DJ]	Happiness (same on both sides)	1979	2.00	4.00	8.00
❑ 11406 [DJ]	Come and Get Your Love/Dirty Work/ Echoes of Love/Hypnotized	1979	3.00	6.00	12.00
❑ 11407 [DJ]	Fire/Happiness	1979	3.00	6.00	12.00
—Red vinyl					
❑ JD-13328 [DJ]	I'm So Excited	1982	2.50	5.00	10.00
—One-sided promo					
❑ YD-13429	I'm So Excited/If You Wanna Get Back My Love	1983	2.50	5.00	10.00
❑ YD-13721	Automatic (4:48) (6:06)	1984	2.00	4.00	8.00
❑ YD-13781	Jump (For My Love) (6:24)/(Instrumental)/ Heartbeat	1984	2.00	4.00	8.00
❑ JR-13858 [DJ]	I'm So Excited (same on both sides)	1984	2.50	5.00	10.00
❑ YD-13952	Neutron Dance (4:59)/Telegraph Your Love	1984	2.00	4.00	8.00
❑ YD-14042	Baby Come and Get It (7:14)/Operator	1985	2.00	4.00	8.00

RCA

Number	Title (A Side/B Side)	Yr	VG	VG+	NM
❑ 5774-1-RDAC [DJ]	Goldmine (2 versions)/Sexual Power	1986	—	3.00	6.00
❑ 6491-1-RDAC [DJ]	Mercury Rising (3 versions)	1986	—	3.00	6.00
❑ 6865-1-RD	He Turned Me Out (4 versions)	1988	—	3.00	6.00
❑ PD-14127	Dare Me (Long) (Instrumental)/I'll Be There	1985	—	3.00	6.00
❑ PD-14196	Twist My Arm (Dance Mix)/ (Instrumental)/Easy Persuasion	1985	2.00	4.00	8.00
❑ PD-14225	Freedom (4:18) (6:21)	1985	—	3.00	6.00

45s
ATLANTIC

Number	Title (A Side/B Side)	Yr	VG	VG+	NM
❑ 2845	Don't Try to Take the Fifth/Tulsa County	1971	5.00	10.00	20.00
❑ 2893	Destination No More Heartaches/Send Him Back	1972	10.00	20.00	40.00

Number	Title (A Side/B Side)	Yr	VG	VG+	NM
BLUE THUMB					
❑ 229	Yes We Can Can/Jada	1973	—	3.00	6.00
❑ 243	Wang Dang Doodle/Cloudburst	1973	—	3.00	6.00
❑ 248	Steam Heat/Shaky Flat Blues	1974	—	3.00	6.00
❑ 254	Fairytale/Love In Them Thar Hills	1974	—	2.50	5.00
—Second pressing has a multicolor label with ABC logo					
❑ 254	Fairytale/Love In Them Thar Hills	1974	2.50	5.00	10.00
—First pressing has a gray to white label and no reference to ABC					
❑ 262	Live Your Life Before You Die/Shaky Flat Blues	1975	—	2.50	5.00
❑ 265	How Long (Betcha' Got a Chick on the Side)/ Easy Days	1975	—	2.50	5.00
❑ 268	Going Down Slowly/Sleeping Alone	1975	—	2.50	5.00
❑ 271	You Gotta Believe/Shaky Flat Blues	1976	—	2.50	5.00
❑ 275	Having a Party/Lonely Gal	1977	—	2.50	5.00
❑ 277	I Need a Man/I'll Get By Without You	1978	—	2.50	5.00
COLUMBIA					
❑ 08015	Power of Persuasion/(Instrumental)	1988	—	—	3.00
❑ 08015 [PS]	Power of Persuasion/(Instrumental)	1988	—	—	3.00
MCA					
❑ 53120	Be There/(Instrumental)	1987	—	—	3.00
❑ 53120 [PS]	Be There/(Instrumental)	1987	—	—	3.00
MOTOWN					
❑ 902	Friends' Advice (Don't Take It)/Friends' Advice (Don't Take It) (Dub)	1990	—	2.00	4.00
PLANET					
❑ YB-13254	American Music/I Want to Do It with You	1982	—	2.00	4.00
❑ YB-13327	I'm So Excited/Nothing But a Heartache (Live)	1982	—	2.00	4.00
❑ YB-13430	If You Wanna Get Back Your Lady/I'm So Excited	1983	—	2.00	4.00
❑ GB-13485	American Music/I'm So Excited	1983	—	—	3.00
—Gold Standard Series					
❑ YB-13639	I Need You/If You Wanna Get Back Your Lady	1983	—	2.00	4.00
❑ YB-13730	Automatic/Nightline	1984	—	2.00	4.00
❑ YB-13780	Jump (For My Love)/Heart Beat	1984	—	2.00	4.00
❑ GB-13795	I Need You/If You Wanna Get Back Your Lady	1984	—	—	3.00
—Gold Standard Series					
❑ YB-13857	I'm So Excited/Dance Electric	1984	—	2.00	4.00
❑ YB-13951	Neutron Dance/Telegraph Your Love	1984	—	2.00	4.00
❑ YB-14041	Baby Come and Get It/Operator	1985	—	2.00	4.00
❑ YB-14041 [PS]	Baby Come and Get It/Operator	1985	—	2.00	4.00
❑ GB-14072	Jump (For My Love)/Automatic	1985	—	—	3.00
—Gold Standard Series					
❑ GB-14076	Fire/He's So Shy	1985	—	—	3.00
—Gold Standard Series					
❑ GB-14077	Slow Hand/Should I Do It	1985	—	—	3.00
—Gold Standard Series					
❑ 45901	Fire/Love Is Like a Rolling Stone	1978	—	2.00	4.00
❑ 45901 [PS]	Fire/Love Is Like a Rolling Stone	1978	—	3.00	6.00
❑ 45902	Happiness/Too Late	1979	—	2.00	4.00
❑ 45906	Blind Faith/The Shape I'm In	1979	—	2.00	4.00
❑ 47916	He's So Shy/Movin' On	1980	—	2.00	4.00
❑ 47918	Es Tan Timido/Cosas Especiales	1980	—	3.00	6.00
❑ 47920	Could I Be Dreaming/Evil	1980	—	2.00	4.00
❑ 47925	Where Did the Time Go/Special Things	1981	—	2.00	4.00
❑ 47929	Slow Hand/Holdin' Out for Love	1981	—	2.00	4.00
❑ 47937	What a Surprise/Fall in Love Again	1981	—	2.00	4.00
❑ 47945	Sweet Lover Man/Got to Find Love	1981	—	2.00	4.00
❑ 47960	Should I Do It/We're Gonna Make It	1982	—	2.00	4.00
RCA					
❑ 5062-7-R	Goldmine/Sexual Power	1986	—	—	3.00
❑ 5062-7-R [PS]	Goldmine/Sexual Power	1986	—	—	3.00
❑ 5112-7-R	All I Know Is the Way I Feel/Translation	1987	—	—	3.00
❑ 5230-7-R	Mercury Rising/Say the Word	1987	—	—	3.00
❑ 6865-7-R	He Turned Me Out/Translation	1988	—	—	3.00
❑ 6865-7-R [PS]	He Turned Me Out/Translation	1988	—	—	3.00
❑ 8378-7-R	I'm in Love/Uh-Oh	1988	—	—	3.00
❑ PB-14126	Dare Me/I'll Be There	1985	—	—	3.00
❑ PB-14126 [PS]	Dare Me/I'll Be There	1985	—	—	3.00
❑ PB-14197	Twist My Arm/Easy Persuasion	1986	—	—	3.00
❑ PB-14197 [PS]	Twist My Arm/Easy Persuasion	1986	—	—	3.00
❑ PB-14224	Freedom/Telegraph Your Love	1985	—	—	3.00
❑ PB-14224 [PS]	Freedom/Telegraph Your Love	1985	—	—	3.00
❑ GB-14354	Neutron Dance/Baby Come and Get It	1986	—	—	3.00
—Gold Standard Series					
SBK					
❑ S7-17637	Don't Walk Away/Tell It to My Heart	1993	—	2.00	4.00
Albums					
ABC BLUE THUMB					
❑ BT-6021	Steppin	1975	3.00	6.00	12.00
❑ BT-6023	Having a Party	1977	3.00	6.00	12.00
❑ BTSY-6026 [(2)]	The Best of the Pointer Sisters	1976	3.75	7.50	15.00
BLUE THUMB					
❑ BTS-48	The Pointer Sisters	1973	3.00	6.00	12.00
❑ BTS-6009	That's a Plenty	1974	3.00	6.00	12.00
❑ BTS-8002 [(2)]	Live at the Opera House	1974	3.75	7.50	15.00
MCA					
❑ 3275	Retrospect	1981	2.50	5.00	10.00
—Reissue of Blue Thumb material					
MOTOWN					
❑ 6287 ML	Right Rhythm	1990	3.00	6.00	12.00
PLANET					
❑ P-1	Energy	1978	2.50	5.00	10.00
❑ P-9	Special Things	1980	2.50	5.00	10.00
❑ P-18	Black and White	1981	2.50	5.00	10.00
❑ BXL1-4355	So Excited!	1982	2.50	5.00	10.00
❑ BEL1-4705A	Break Out	1984	2.00	4.00	8.00
—Reissue has "I'm So Excited" plus a remix of "Jump (For My Love)"					
❑ BXL1-4705	Break Out	1983	2.50	5.00	10.00
—Original does not have "I'm So Excited"					
❑ P-9003	Priority	1979	2.50	5.00	10.00
❑ 60203	Pointer Sisters' Greatest Hits	1982	2.50	5.00	10.00
RCA					
❑ 5609-1-R	Hot Together	1986	2.50	5.00	10.00
❑ 6562-1-R	Serious Slammin'	1988	2.50	5.00	10.00

Number	Title (A Side/B Side)	Yr	VG	VG+	NM
RCA VICTOR					
❑ AYL1-5088	Special Things	1985	2.00	4.00	8.00
—Budget-line reissue					
❑ AYL1-5089	Priority	1985	2.00	4.00	8.00
—Budget-line reissue					
❑ AYL1-5091	Energy	1985	2.00	4.00	8.00
—Budget-line reissue					
❑ AYL1-5092	Black and White	1985	2.00	4.00	8.00
—Budget-line reissue					
❑ AJL1-5487	Contact	1985	2.50	5.00	10.00
POITIER, SIDNEY					
Albums					
WARNER BROS.					
❑ W 1561 [M]	Poitier Meets Plato	1965	6.25	12.50	25.00
❑ WS 1561 [S]	Poitier Meets Plato	1965	7.50	15.00	30.00
POLLARD, RAY					
45s					
DECCA					
❑ 32111	Lie, Lips, Lie/This Is My Song	1967	10.00	20.00	40.00
❑ 32189	This Is No Laughing Matter/Wanderlust	1967	30.00	60.00	120.00
OMNIPOTENT					
❑ 1001	Soulmate?/(B-side unknown)	1973	200.00	400.00	800.00
SHRINE					
❑ 0103	No One Likes Me/This Time (I'm Gonna Be True)	1965	200.00	400.00	800.00
UNITED ARTISTS					
❑ 856	Darling Take Me Back/My Girl and I	1965	20.00	40.00	80.00
❑ 916	The Drifter/Let Him Go (And Let Me Love You)	1965	20.00	40.00	80.00
❑ 50012	All the Things You Are/It's a Sad Thing	1966	25.00	50.00	100.00
POLLUTION					
45s					
CAPITOL					
❑ 2458	Getting Together/Angela Jerome	1969	2.50	5.00	10.00
PROPHECY					
❑ 55001	Do You Really Have a Heart/(B-side unknown)	1971	2.00	4.00	8.00
❑ 55003	The River/(B-side unknown)	1972	2.00	4.00	8.00
Albums					
CAPITOL					
❑ ST-205	Heir: Pollution	1969	5.00	10.00	20.00
PROPHECY					
❑ SD 6051	Pollution	1971	5.00	10.00	20.00
❑ SD 6067	Pollution II	1972	5.00	10.00	20.00
POLNAREFF, MICHEL					
45s					
ATLANTIC					
❑ 3314	Since I Saw You/If You Only Believe	1976	—	2.50	5.00
❑ 3330	Lipstick (Part 1)/Lipstick (Part 2)	1976	—	2.50	5.00
4 CORNERS OF THE WORLD					
❑ 141	Time Will Tell/Under What Star Was I Born	1967	3.75	7.50	15.00
KAPP					
❑ 786	Love Me, Please Love Me/No, No, No, No, No	1966	2.00	4.00	8.00
Albums					
ATLANTIC					
❑ SD 18153	Michel Polnareff	1976	2.50	5.00	10.00
4 CORNERS OF THE WORLD					
❑ FCL-4240 [M]	French Rock-Blues	1967	3.00	6.00	12.00
❑ FCS-4240 [S]	French Rock-Blues	1967	3.75	7.50	15.00
PONCHER, JERRY					
45s					
HIT					
❑ 124	What'd I Say/Every Little Bit Hurts	1964	2.00	4.00	8.00
—B-side by Peggy Gaines					
PONI-TAILS, THE					
45s					
ABC-PARAMOUNT					
❑ 9846	Wild Eyes and Tender Lips/It's Just My Luck to Be Fifteen	1957	5.00	10.00	20.00
❑ 9934	Born Too Late/Come On Joey Dance With Me	1958	6.25	12.50	25.00
❑ 9934 [DJ]	Born Too Late/Come On Joey Dance With Me	1958	12.50	25.00	50.00
—White label promo with artist's name spelled "Pony-Tails"					
❑ 9969	Close Friends/Seven Minutes in Heaven	1958	5.00	10.00	20.00
❑ 9995	Early to Bed/Father Time	1959	5.00	10.00	20.00
❑ 10027	Moody/Ooh-Pah Polka	1959	5.00	10.00	20.00
❑ 10047	I'll Be Seeing You/I'll Keep Tryin'	1959	5.00	10.00	20.00
❑ 10077	Before We Say Goodnight/Come Be My Love	1960	5.00	10.00	20.00
❑ 10114	Who, When and Why/Oh My, You	1960	5.00	10.00	20.00
MARC					
❑ 1001	Can I Be Sure/Still in Your Teens	1957	6.25	12.50	25.00
POINT					
❑ 8	Your Wild Heart/Que La Bozena	1957	6.25	12.50	25.00
POOBAH					
Albums					
A.E.I.					
❑ A-LP-1	U.S. Rock	1976	62.50	125.00	250.00
PEPPERMINT					
❑ PP-1180	Steamroller	1979	37.50	75.00	150.00
RITE					
❑ (no #)	Let Me In	1972	150.00	300.00	600.00
POOH AND THE HEFFALUMPS					
45s					
LAURIE					
❑ 3281	Lady Godiva/Rooty Toot	1965	3.00	6.00	12.00
POOLE, BRIAN Also see BRIAN POOLE AND THE TREMELOES.					
45s					
DATE					
❑ 1539	Everything I Touch Turns to Tears/ I Need Her Tonight	1966	2.50	5.00	10.00

P

Number	Title (A Side/B Side)	Yr	VG	VG+	NM

POOLE, BRIAN, AND THE TREMELOES Also see BRIAN POOLE; THE TREMELOES.
45s
AUDIO FIDELITY

| ❏ 112 | I Go Crazy/Love Me Baby | 1965 | 2.50 | 5.00 | 10.00 |
| ❏ 121 | Good Lovin'/Could It Be You | 1966 | 2.50 | 5.00 | 10.00 |

LONDON

| ❏ 9600 | Keep On Dancing/Blue | 1963 | 3.75 | 7.50 | 15.00 |
| ❏ 9625 | Do You Love Me/Why Can't I Love You | 1964 | 3.75 | 7.50 | 15.00 |

MONUMENT

❏ 840	Candy Man/I Can Dream	1964	3.00	6.00	12.00
❏ 846	Someone, Someone/(Meet Me) Where We Used to Meet	1964	3.00	6.00	12.00
❏ 882	After a While/Don't Cry	1965	3.00	6.00	12.00

Albums
AUDIO FIDELITY

❏ AFLP 2151 [M]	Brian Poole Is Here	1966	12.50	25.00	50.00
❏ AFSD 2151 [R]	Brian Poole Is Here	1966	10.00	20.00	40.00
❏ AFLP 2177 [M]	The Tremeloes Are Here	1967	10.00	20.00	40.00

—Reissue of above album with new title

| ❏ AFSD 2177 [R] | The Tremeloes Are Here | 1967 | 7.50 | 15.00 | 30.00 |

—Reissue of above album with new title

POPCORN AND THE MOHAWKS
45s
MOTOWN

| ❏ 1002 | Custer's Last Man/Shimmy Gully | 1960 | 15.00 | 30.00 | 60.00 |

POPCORN BLIZZARD, THE Possibly two different groups. The Magenda 45 features the first recorded performance by MEAT LOAF.
45s
DE-LITE

| ❏ 516 | Good Thing Going/My Suzanne | 1969 | 5.00 | 10.00 | 20.00 |
| ❏ 522 | Good Good Day/I Just Saw a Face | 1969 | 5.00 | 10.00 | 20.00 |

MAGENDA

| ❏ 7411 | Once Upon a Time/Hello! | 1967 | 25.00 | 50.00 | 100.00 |

Albums
DE-LITE

| ❏ DE-2004 | Explode! | 1969 | 10.00 | 20.00 | 40.00 |

POPE, RAYMOND, AND THE LOVETONES
45s
SQUALOR

| ❏ 1313 | I Love Nadine/Star | 1962 | 37.50 | 75.00 | 150.00 |

POPE JOHN XXIII
Albums
MERCURY

| ❏ 200 [M] | Pope John XXIII | 1963 | 3.75 | 7.50 | 15.00 |

—Tribute album released after his death

POPPIES, THE Dorothy Moore of "Misty Blue" fame was in this group.
45s
EPIC

❏ 9893	I Wonder Why/Lullaby of Love	1966	2.50	5.00	10.00
❏ 10019	He's Ready/He's Got Real Love	1966	2.50	5.00	10.00
❏ 10019 [PS]	He's Ready/He's Got Real Love	1966	5.00	10.00	20.00
❏ 10059	Do It with Soul/He Means So Much to Me	1966	3.00	6.00	12.00
❏ 10086	There's a Pain in My Heart/My Love and I	1966	6.25	12.50	25.00

TUFF

| ❏ 372 | Johnny Don't Cry/(Instrumental) | 1964 | 3.75 | 7.50 | 15.00 |

Albums
EPIC

| ❏ LN 24200 [M] | Lullaby of Love | 1966 | 10.00 | 20.00 | 40.00 |
| ❏ BN 26200 [S] | Lullaby of Love | 1966 | 12.50 | 25.00 | 50.00 |

POPPY FAMILY, THE Also see TERRY JACKS.
45s
LONDON

| ❏ 128 | Another Year, Another Day/You Don't Know What Love Is | 1970 | 2.50 | 5.00 | 10.00 |

—Deleted quickly; a more common Margaret Whiting single was also issued as London 128

❏ 129	Which Way You Goin' Billy/Endless Sleep	1970	—	3.00	6.00
❏ 139	That's When I Went Wrong/Shadows on My Wall	1970	—	2.50	5.00
❏ 148	I Was Wondering/Where Evil Grows	1971	—	2.50	5.00
❏ 164	No Good to Cry/I'll See You There	1971	—	2.50	5.00
❏ 172	Good Friends/Tryin'	1972	—	2.50	5.00

Albums
LONDON

| ❏ PS 574 | Which Way You Goin' Billy? | 1970 | 3.75 | 7.50 | 15.00 |
| ❏ PS 599 | Seeds | 1971 | 3.75 | 7.50 | 15.00 |

POPSICLES, THE (1)
45s
GNP CRESCENDO

| ❏ 336 | I Don't Want to Be Your Baby Anymore/Baby I Miss You | 1965 | 2.50 | 5.00 | 10.00 |

POPSICLES, THE (2)
45s
KNIGHT

| ❏ 2002 | Thumb Print/This Is the End | 1958 | 10.00 | 20.00 | 40.00 |

POPULAIRES, THE
45s
MARVELLO

| ❏ 5001 | Island of Paradise/I Lost My Heart | 1957 | 50.00 | 100.00 | 200.00 |

PORCELAIN BEARMEAT
Albums
DILL PICKLE

| ❏ 3468 | Free Love, Free Sex, Free Music | 1971 | 5.00 | 10.00 | 20.00 |

PORTER, DAVID
45s
ENTERPRISE

| ❏ 9014 | Can't See You When I Want To/One Part, Two Parts | 1970 | — | 3.00 | 6.00 |
| ❏ 9049 | Ain't That Loving You (For More Reasons Than One)/Baby I'm-a Want You | 1972 | — | 2.50 | 5.00 |

—With Isaac Hayes

❏ 9050	I'm Afraid the Masquerade Is Over/Sloopy	1972	—	2.50	5.00
❏ 9055	Wanna Be Your Somebody/When the Chips Are Down	1972	—	2.50	5.00
❏ 9071	As Long As You're the One Somebody in the World/When You Have to Sneak	1973	—	2.50	5.00
❏ 9090	Falling Out, Falling In/I Got You and I'm Glad	1973	—	2.50	5.00

STAX

| ❏ 163 | Can't See You When I Want To/Win You Over | 1965 | 5.00 | 10.00 | 20.00 |

Albums
ENTERPRISE

❏ ENS-1009	Gritty, Groovy, & Gettin' It	1970	5.00	10.00	20.00
❏ ENS-1012	David Porter…Into a Real Thing	1971	5.00	10.00	20.00
❏ ENS-1019	Victim of the Joke?	1972	5.00	10.00	20.00
❏ ENS-1026	Sweat and Love	1973	5.00	10.00	20.00

PORTER, JIM
45s
HIT

| ❏ 05 | Dr. Feelgood/Shout | 1962 | 2.00 | 4.00 | 8.00 |

—B-side by Bill Austin

PORTER, ROYCE
45s
D

| ❏ 1026 | Lookin'/I Still Belong to You | 1958 | 25.00 | 50.00 | 100.00 |

LOOK

| ❏ 1001 | Yes I Do/(B-side unknown) | 1957 | 62.50 | 125.00 | 250.00 |

MERCURY

| ❏ 71314 | Good Time/Beach of Love | 1958 | 25.00 | 50.00 | 100.00 |

PORTRAITS, THE (1)
45s
CAPITOL

| ❏ F-4181 | Close to You/Easy Cash | 1959 | 7.50 | 15.00 | 30.00 |

PORTRAITS, THE (2)
45s
SIDEWALK

| ❏ 928 | A Million to One/Let's Tell the World | 1967 | 3.75 | 7.50 | 15.00 |
| ❏ 935 | Over the Rainbow/Runaround Girl | 1968 | 5.00 | 10.00 | 20.00 |

PORTRAITS, THE (3)
45s
TRI-DISC

| ❏ 109 | We're Gonna Party/Three Blind Mice | 1963 | 3.75 | 7.50 | 15.00 |

PORTRAITS, THE (U) Could be group (1) or (3).
45s
RCA VICTOR

| ❏ 47-7900 | Yo-Yo Girl/My Big Brother's Friend | 1961 | 3.75 | 7.50 | 15.00 |

POSEY, SANDY
45s
AUDIOGRAPH

| ❏ 449 | Can't Get Used to Sleeping Without You/(B-side unknown) | 1983 | — | 2.00 | 4.00 |

COLUMBIA

❏ 45360	Losing Out on You/You Say Beautiful Things to Me	1971	—	2.50	5.00
❏ 45458	Bring Him Safely Home To Me/A Man in Need of Love	1971	—	2.50	5.00
❏ 45596	Why Don't We Go Somewhere and Love/Together	1972	—	2.50	5.00
❏ 45703	Happy Happy Birthday Baby/Thank the Lord for New York City	1972	—	2.50	5.00
❏ 45828	Don't/Thank the Lord for New York City	1973	—	2.50	5.00

MGM

❏ 13501	Born a Woman/Caution to the Wind	1967	2.00	4.00	8.00
❏ 13612	Single Girl/Blue Is My Best Color	1966	2.00	4.00	8.00
❏ 13612 [PS]	Single Girl/Blue Is My Best Color	1966	3.00	6.00	12.00
❏ 13702	What a Woman in Love Won't Do/Shattered	1967	2.00	4.00	8.00
❏ 13744	I Take It Back/The Boy I Love	1967	2.00	4.00	8.00
❏ 13744 [PS]	I Take It Back/The Boy I Love	1967	3.00	6.00	12.00
❏ 13824	Are You Never Coming Home/I Can Show You How to Live	1967	2.00	4.00	8.00
❏ 13892	Silly Girl, Silly Boy/Something I'll Remember	1968	—	3.00	6.00
❏ 13967	Ways of the World/Wonderful World of Summer	1968	—	3.00	6.00
❏ 14006	All Hung Up in Your Green Eyes/Your Conception of Love	1968	—	3.00	6.00

MONUMENT

| ❏ 8698 | Trying to Live Without You Kind of Days/Why Do We Carry On | 1976 | — | 2.50 | 5.00 |

WARNER BROS.

❏ 8289	It's Midnight (Do You Know Where Your Baby Is)/Long Distance Kissing	1976	—	2.00	4.00
❏ 8540	Born to Be with You/It's Not Too Late	1978	—	2.00	4.00
❏ 8610	Love, Love, Love-Chapel of Love/I Believe in Love	1978	—	2.00	4.00
❏ 8731	Love Is Sometimes Easy/I Believe in Love	1979	—	2.00	4.00
❏ 8852	Try Home/Love Is Sometimes Easy	1979	—	2.00	4.00
❏ 49104	Black Is the Night/Best Things in My Life	1979	—	2.00	4.00

Albums
COLUMBIA

| ❏ KC 31594 | Why Don't We Go Somewhere and Love | 1972 | 3.00 | 6.00 | 12.00 |

MGM

❏ GAS-125	Sandy Posey (Golden Archive Series)	1970	3.75	7.50	15.00
❏ E-4418 [M]	Born a Woman	1966	3.75	7.50	15.00
❏ SE-4418 [S]	Born a Woman	1966	5.00	10.00	20.00
❏ E-4455 [M]	Single Girl	1967	5.00	10.00	20.00
❏ SE-4455 [S]	Single Girl	1967	5.00	10.00	20.00
❏ E-4480 [M]	I Take It Back	1967	5.00	10.00	20.00
❏ SE-4480 [S]	I Take It Back	1967	5.00	10.00	20.00
❏ E-4509 [M]	The Best of Sandy Posey	1967	6.25	12.50	25.00
❏ SE-4509 [S]	The Best of Sandy Posey	1967	5.00	10.00	20.00

Number	Title (A Side/B Side)	Yr	VG	VG+	NM
❑ E-4525 [M]	Looking at You	1968	6.25	12.50	25.00
❑ SE-4525 [S]	Looking at You	1968	3.75	7.50	15.00
❑ ST-91110	Single Girl	1967	6.25	12.50	25.00
—Capitol Record Club issue					

POSEY, SANDY/ SKEETER DAVIS Also see each artist's individual listings.
Albums
GUSTO
| ❑ 0005 | The Best of Sandy Posey/Skeeter Davis | 198? | 2.00 | 4.00 | 8.00 |

POSITIVELY 13 O'CLOCK
45s
HANNA-BARBERA
| ❑ 500 | Psychotic Reaction/ 13 O'Clock Theme for Psychotics | 1966 | 10.00 | 20.00 | 40.00 |

POSSESSIONS, THE
45s
BRITTON
❑ 1003	No More Love/You and Your Lies	1964	10.00	20.00	40.00
❑ 1003	No More Love/You and Your Lies	1964	17.50	35.00	70.00
—Blue vinyl					
PARKWAY
❑ 930	No More Love/You and Your Lies	1964	5.00	10.00	20.00

POSSUM Possibly two different groups.
45s
HIGHLAND
| ❑ 10 | The Cockroach That Ate Cincinnati/Chula Vista | 1966 | 3.75 | 7.50 | 15.00 |
Albums
CAPITOL
| ❑ ST-648 | Possum | 1970 | 3.00 | 6.00 | 12.00 |

POSSUM HUNTERS, THE
Albums
TAKOMA
| ❑ C-1010 | Death on Lee Highway | 1970 | 5.00 | 10.00 | 20.00 |

POST, MIKE
45s
BELL
| ❑ 45155 | Nicholas and Alexandra's Theme/Kotch | 1971 | — | 2.50 | 5.00 |
ELEKTRA
❑ 47186	The Theme from Hill Street Blues/Aaron's Tune	1981	—	2.00	4.00
❑ 47186 [PS]	The Theme from Hill Street Blues/Aaron's Tune	1981	—	2.00	4.00
❑ 47400	Theme from Magnum, P.I./Gumbus Bed	1982	—	2.00	4.00
❑ 47400 [PS]	Theme from Magnum, P.I./Gumbus Bed	1982	—	2.00	4.00
❑ 47477	School's Out/Aaron's Tune	1982	—	2.00	4.00
EPIC
❑ 50325	Theme from "Baa Baa Black Sheep"/ Southbound	1976	—	2.00	4.00
MGM
❑ 14772	The Rockford Files/Dixie Lullabye	1974	—	2.50	5.00
❑ 14829	Manhattan Spiritual/Lay Back Lafayette	1975	—	2.00	4.00
MUSIC FACTORY
❑ 419	Harper Valley P.T.A./Walking to San Francisco	1968	2.00	4.00	8.00
POLYDOR
❑ 887145-7	Theme from "L.A. Law"/Jenny's Ayre	1987	—	2.00	4.00
❑ 887145-7 [PS]	Theme from "L.A. Law"/Jenny's Ayre	1987	—	2.00	4.00
RCA
❑ PB-13859	The A Team//6/24	1984	—	2.50	5.00
REPRISE
❑ 0406	For My Home/Long Time Alone	1965	2.50	5.00	10.00
❑ 0468	Hard Times/Louisiana Man	1966	2.50	5.00	10.00
WARNER BROS.
❑ 7357	Bubble Gum Breakthrough/Not a Blade of Grass	1969	2.00	4.00	8.00
Albums
ELEKTRA
| ❑ 60028 [EP] | Television Theme Songs | 1982 | 2.00 | 4.00 | 8.00 |
MGM
| ❑ M3G-5005 | Railhead Overture | 1975 | 2.50 | 5.00 | 10.00 |
POLYDOR
| ❑ 833985-1 | Theme from L.A. Law and Otherwise | 1987 | 2.00 | 4.00 | 8.00 |
RCA VICTOR
| ❑ AFL1-5415 | Mike Post | 1985 | 2.50 | 5.00 | 10.00 |

POSTA, ADRIENNE
45s
LONDON
| ❑ 9782 | When a Girl Really Loves You/Winds That Bloe | 1966 | 2.50 | 5.00 | 10.00 |

POTLIQUOR
45s
CAPITOL
| ❑ 4795 | Misery/Oh So Long | 1979 | — | 2.00 | 4.00 |
| ❑ 4819 | Boy Oh Boy/Red Stick | 1980 | — | 2.00 | 4.00 |
JANUS
❑ 139	Down the River Boogie/Riverboat	1970	—	2.50	5.00
❑ 179	Cheer/Chattanooga	1972	—	2.50	5.00
❑ 186	Beyond the River Jordan/(B-side unknown)	1972	—	2.50	5.00
❑ 195	Waitin' for Me at the River/(B-side unknown)	1972	—	2.50	5.00
Albums
CAPITOL
| ❑ ST-11998 | Potliquor | 1979 | 2.50 | 5.00 | 10.00 |
JANUS
❑ JLS-3002	Potliquor	1970	3.75	7.50	15.00
❑ JLS-3033	Levee Blues	1972	3.75	7.50	15.00
❑ JLS-3036	Louisiana Rock and Roll	1973	3.75	7.50	15.00

POWDER PUFFS, THE
45s
IMPERIAL
| ❑ 66014 | (You Can't Take) My Boyfriend's Woody/ Woody Wagon | 1964 | 6.25 | 12.50 | 25.00 |

POWELL, ADAM CLAYTON
Albums
JUBILEE
| ❑ JGM 2062 [M] | Keep the Faith, Baby! | 1967 | 3.75 | 7.50 | 15.00 |

POWELL, AUSTIN
45s
ATLANTIC
| ❑ 968 | Wrong Again/What More Can I Ask | 1952 | 50.00 | 100.00 | 200.00 |
DECCA
| ❑ 48206 | All This Can't Be True/Some Other Spring | 1951 | 20.00 | 40.00 | 80.00 |

POWELL, CHRIS, AND THE FIVE BLUE FLAMES
45s
COLUMBIA
| ❑ 39272 | Country Girl Blues/Man with a Horn | 1951 | 37.50 | 75.00 | 150.00 |
| ❑ 39407 | My Love Has Gone/In the Cool of the Evening | 1951 | 125.00 | 250.00 | 500.00 |
GRAND
❑ 108	Sweet Sue Mambo/Uh Uh Baby	1953	12.50	25.00	50.00
❑ 112	Secret Love Mambo/I Love Paris Mambo	1954	12.50	25.00	50.00
❑ 116	Dinah/Song of the Vagabond	1954	12.50	25.00	50.00
❑ 120	Mr. Sandman/Mambo Gunch	1954	12.50	25.00	50.00
❑ 124	Anniversary Waltz/Sweet Georgia Brown	1955	10.00	20.00	40.00
❑ 127	Mandolin Mambo/The Whiffenpoof Song	1955	10.00	20.00	40.00
GROOVE
❑ 0105	Break It Up/Love Ya Like Crazy	1955	5.00	10.00	20.00
❑ 0111	Unchained Melody/Something's Gotta Give	1955	5.00	10.00	20.00
❑ 0128	Goodbye Little Girl/Chinatown	1955	5.00	10.00	20.00
❑ 0144	Moritat/The Poor People of Paris	1956	5.00	10.00	20.00
OKEH
❑ 6818	The Masquerade Is Over/Talkin'	1951	75.00	150.00	300.00
❑ 6850	October Twilight/That's Right	1952	25.00	50.00	100.00
❑ 6875	Ida Red/Darn That Dream	1952	25.00	50.00	100.00
❑ 6900	Blue Boy/I Come from Jamaica	1952	25.00	50.00	100.00

POWELL, JEROME
45s
PARKWAY
| ❑ 927 | Home to Stay/Live and Let Live | 1964 | 3.00 | 6.00 | 12.00 |

POWELL, JIMMY (1) British singer.
45s
DECCA
| ❑ 32685 | Stranger on a Train/Sugar Man | 1970 | — | 3.00 | 6.00 |
LONDON
| ❑ 9545 | I Love You/Dance Her By Me (One More Time) | 1962 | 2.50 | 5.00 | 10.00 |

POWELL, JIMMY (2) American instrumentalist.
45s
JUBILEE
| ❑ 5533 | The Shadow of Your Smile/On a Clear Day You Can See Forever | 1966 | 2.00 | 4.00 | 8.00 |
Albums
JUBILEE
| ❑ JGM 8001 [M] | In a Sentimental Mood | 1966 | 3.75 | 7.50 | 15.00 |

POWELL, MEL
Albums
METRO
| ❑ M-577 [M] | Mickey Most Presents English In-Groups | 1966 | 5.00 | 10.00 | 20.00 |

POWELL, SANDY
45s
HERALD
| ❑ 557 | Bon Bon/Pistol-Packin' Mama | 1961 | 25.00 | 50.00 | 100.00 |
IMPALA
| ❑ 211 | Bon Bon/Pistol-Packin' Mama | 1961 | 75.00 | 150.00 | 300.00 |
SINGULAR
| ❑ 714 | My Jimmie/Next Thing to Paradise | 1958 | 6.25 | 12.50 | 25.00 |

POWELL, WILLIAM
45s
POWERHOUSE
| ❑ 101 | Heartache Souvenirs/(B-side unknown) | 196? | 375.00 | 750.00 | 1500. |

POWER, DUFFY
45s
EPIC
| ❑ 10650 | Hellhound/Hummingbird | 1970 | — | 3.00 | 6.00 |
VEEP
| ❑ 1204 | Where Am I/I Don't Care | 1964 | 3.00 | 6.00 | 12.00 |
Albums
GSF
| ❑ 1005 | Duffy Power | 1973 | 2.50 | 5.00 | 10.00 |

POWERS, JETT See P.J. PROBY.

POWERS, JOEY
45s
AMY
❑ 892	Midnight Mary/Where Do You Want the World Delivered	1963	3.00	6.00	12.00
❑ 898	Billy Old Buddy/In the Morning Gloria	1964	2.50	5.00	10.00
❑ 903	Love Is a Season/You Comb Her Hair	1964	2.50	5.00	10.00
❑ 914	Tears Keep Falling/Where Did the Summer Go	1964	2.50	5.00	10.00
❑ 986	Gimmie Gimmie/Baila Maria	1967	2.00	4.00	8.00
MGM
❑ 13421	I Love You/Leave Me Alone	1965	2.00	4.00	8.00
RCA VICTOR
❑ 47-8039	Two Tickets and a Candy Heart/Jenny, Won't You Walk Up?	1962	2.50	5.00	10.00
❑ 47-8119	Don't Envy Me/Me, Myself and I	1962	2.50	5.00	10.00
❑ 47-9790	Hard to Be Without You/You're in a Bad Way	1969	—	2.50	5.00
—As "Joey Powers' Flower"					
❑ 74-0326	Land of the Midnight Sun/So Sing the Children on the Avenue	1970	—	2.50	5.00
—As "Joey Powers' Flower"					

P

Number	Title (A Side/B Side)	Yr	VG	VG+	NM
Albums					
AMY					
❑ 8001 [M]	Midnight Mary	1964	7.50	15.00	30.00
POWERS, JOHNNY					
45s					
FORTUNE					
❑ 199	Honey Let's Go (To a Rock and Roll Show)/				
	Your Love	1955	50.00	100.00	200.00
FOX					
❑ 916	Rock Rock/Long Blonde Hair, Red Rose Lips	1957	125.00	250.00	500.00
HI-Q					
❑ 5044	Rock the Universe/Honey Let's Go				
	(To a Rock and Roll Show)	1958	25.00	50.00	100.00
SUN					
❑ 327	With Your Love, With Your Kiss/				
	Be Mine, All Mine	1959	12.50	25.00	50.00
TRIODEX					
❑ 103	A Teenage Prayer/A Young Boy's Heart	1960	6.25	12.50	25.00
POWERS, TINA					
45s					
PARKWAY					
❑ 847	Making Up Is Fun to Do/Back to School	1962	5.00	10.00	20.00
POWERS OF BLUE, THE					
45s					
MTA					
❑ 113	Good Lovin'/(I Can't Get No) Satisfaction	1966	2.50	5.00	10.00
❑ 118	Cool Jerk/You Blow My Mind	1967	2.00	4.00	8.00
Albums					
MTA					
❑ 1002 [M]	Flipout	1967	7.50	15.00	30.00
❑ 5002 [S]	Flipout	1967	7.50	15.00	30.00
POZO-SECO SINGERS, THE DON WILLIAMS was in this group.					
45s					
CERTRON					
❑ 10006	Apartment #9/Comin' Apart	1970	—	2.50	5.00
❑ 10020	Strawberry Fields & Something/				
	There's Never Been a Time	1970	—	2.50	5.00
❑ 10033	Bringing It Down to Me/He's a Friend of Mine	1971	—	2.50	5.00
COLUMBIA					
❑ 43437	Time/Down the Road I Go	1965	2.00	4.00	8.00
❑ 43646	I'll Be Gone/It Ain't Worth the Lonely Road Back	1966	2.00	4.00	8.00
❑ 43784	I Can Make It With You/Come a Little Bit Closer	1966	2.00	4.00	8.00
❑ 43927	Look What You've Done/Almost Persuaded	1966	2.00	4.00	8.00
❑ 44041	I Believed It All/Excuse Me Dear Martha	1967	2.00	4.00	8.00
❑ 44168	It's All Right/Morning Dew	1967	2.00	4.00	8.00
❑ 44263	Louisiana Man/Tomorrow Proper	1967	2.00	4.00	8.00
❑ 44598	Gotta Come Up with Something/The Renegade	1968	—	3.00	6.00
❑ 44690	Good Morning Today/Remember Suzie	1968	—	3.00	6.00
❑ 44841	Leavin'/Creole Woman	1969	—	3.00	6.00
❑ 44979	Woman in Love/God Save the Children	1969	—	3.00	6.00
—As "Susan Taylor and Pozo Seco"					
❑ 44980	Morning Mama Memories/				
	The Proper Mrs. Brown	1969	2.50	5.00	10.00
—As "Don Williams and Pozo Seco"; his first "solo" credit					
❑ 45065	High on Life/Till You Hear Your Mama Call	1970	—	3.00	6.00
EDMARK					
❑ 10017	Time/Down the Road I Go	1965	5.00	10.00	20.00
Albums					
CERTRON					
❑ CS-7007	Spend Some Time with Me	1970	3.75	7.50	15.00
COLUMBIA					
❑ CL 2515 [M]	Time/I'll Be Gone	1966	3.75	7.50	15.00
❑ CL 2600 [M]	I Can Make It with You	1967	5.00	10.00	20.00
❑ CS 9315 [S]	Time/I'll Be Gone	1966	5.00	10.00	20.00
❑ CS 9400 [S]	I Can Make It with You	1967	3.75	7.50	15.00
❑ CS 9656	Shades of Time	1968	3.75	7.50	15.00
POWER PAK					
❑ 285	The Pozo-Seco Singers with Don Williams	198?	2.50	5.00	10.00
PRADO, PEREZ					
45s					
RCA VICTOR					
❑ 47-3782	El Mambo/Mambo #5	1950	5.00	10.00	20.00
❑ 47-3873	Chattanoogie Shoe Shine Boy/More Mambo				
	Jambo	1950	3.75	7.50	15.00
❑ 47-3917	Mambo #8/Babarabatiri	1950	3.75	7.50	15.00
❑ 47-3918	Pachito E-Che/Mambo #5	1950	3.75	7.50	15.00
❑ 47-3988	Cuban Mambo/Mambo del Papelero	1950	3.75	7.50	15.00
❑ 47-4196	Syncopated Clock Mambo/Broadway Mambo	1951	3.75	7.50	15.00
❑ 47-4319	C'est Si Bon Mambo/				
	In a Little Spanish Town Mambo	1951	3.75	7.50	15.00
❑ 47-5281	A La Billy May/Beautiful	1953	3.00	6.00	12.00
❑ 47-5367	Anna/Silvana Mangano	1953	3.00	6.00	12.00
❑ 47-5738	Such a Night/Ballin' the Jack	1954	3.00	6.00	12.00
❑ 47-5820	St. Louis Blues Mambo/Tomcat Mambo	1954	3.00	6.00	12.00
❑ 47-5839	Skokiaan/The High and the Mighty	1954	3.00	6.00	12.00
❑ 47-5892	Marilyn Monroe Mambo/Steam Heat Mambo	1954	6.25	12.50	25.00
❑ 47-5965	Cherry Pink and Apple Blossom White/Rhythm				
	Sticks	1954	3.00	6.00	12.00
❑ 47-6085	Mood Indigo/Back Bay Shuffle (Mambo)	1955	2.50	5.00	10.00
❑ 47-6122	Whatever Lola Wants/Dilo (Mambo)	1955	2.50	5.00	10.00
❑ 47-6214	Crazy, Crazy/Monitor Mambo	1955	2.50	5.00	10.00
❑ 47-6277	Pretty Doll/La Macarena	1955	2.50	5.00	10.00
❑ 47-6375	Red River Valley Mambo/Black Horse Mambo	1955	2.50	5.00	10.00
❑ 47-6477	The Story of Love/Tomorrow I Will Live	1956	2.50	5.00	10.00
❑ 47-6538	Cuban Rock/Hawaiian War Chant	1956	3.00	6.00	12.00
❑ 47-6684	Petticoats of Portugal/Bandido	1956	2.50	5.00	10.00
❑ 47-6752	Bongo Bash/Donna	1956	2.50	5.00	10.00
❑ 47-6776	Hawaiian Cha Cha Cha/Mambo Japanese	1956	2.50	5.00	10.00
❑ 47-6882	Rum and Coca-Cola/Cose, Cose, Cose	1957	2.50	5.00	10.00
❑ 47-6960	Calypso Man/Cucara Cha Cha Cha	1957	2.50	5.00	10.00

Number	Title (A Side/B Side)	Yr	VG	VG+	NM
❑ 47-6990	Beautiful Margaret/Leyende Mexicana				
	(Legend of Mexico)	1957	2.50	5.00	10.00
❑ 47-7120	A Lo Loco/Kilindini Dance	1957	2.50	5.00	10.00
❑ 47-7245	Patricia/Why Wait	1958	2.50	5.00	10.00
❑ 47-7337	Guaglione/Paris	1958	2.00	4.00	8.00
❑ 47-7456	The Millionaire/Catalania	1959	2.00	4.00	8.00
❑ 47-7540	Tic Toc Polly Woc/My Roberta	1959	2.00	4.00	8.00
❑ 47-7630	Clap Hands/Divina	1959	2.00	4.00	8.00
❑ 47-7768	Oh, Oh, Rosie/Rockambo Baby	1960	2.00	4.00	8.00
❑ 47-7826	Julie Is Her Name/Be True to Me	1960	2.00	4.00	8.00
❑ 47-7873	Teresita La Chunga/Ritmo De Chunga	1961	2.00	4.00	8.00
❑ 47-7963	Arriverderci Roma/Moliendo Café	1961	2.00	4.00	8.00
❑ 47-8006	Patricia Twist/Ti-Pi-Tin Twist	1962	2.00	4.00	8.00
❑ 47-8077	La Raggaza (The Girl)/Via Veneto	1962	2.00	4.00	8.00
❑ 47-8204	Katanga/Teresita	1963	2.00	4.00	8.00
❑ 47-8259	Natalia Dengue/El Dengue	1963	2.00	4.00	8.00
❑ 47-8356	Caravan/Papa Mi	1964	2.00	4.00	8.00
❑ 61-8520 [S]	You're Driving Me Crazy! (What Did I Do?)/				
	Taking a Chance on Love	1960	6.25	12.50	25.00
—"Living Stereo" (large hole, plays at 45 rpm)					
UNITED ARTISTS					
❑ 765	The Girl with the Green Eyes/Woman of Straw	1964	2.00	4.00	8.00
7-Inch Extended Plays					
RCA VICTOR					
❑ LPC-114	Cherry Pink and Apple Blossom White/Mambo				
	No. 5//In a Little Spanish Town/Patricia	1961	3.00	6.00	12.00
—"Compact 33 Double"; small hole, plays at 33 1/3 rpm					
❑ LPC-114	Big Hits by Prado	1961	3.00	6.00	12.00
❑ EPA-404	Cuban Mambo/In a Little Spanish Town ('Twas				
	on a Night Like This)//Mambo Jambo/Perdido	195?	3.75	7.50	15.00
❑ EPA-404 [PS]	Perez Prado and His Orchestra	195?	3.75	7.50	15.00
❑ EPA-732	Mambo Jambo/Mambo No. 5//Perdido/				
	Mambo No. 8	1956	3.00	6.00	12.00
❑ EPA-732 [PS]	(title unknown)	1956	3.00	6.00	12.00
❑ EPA-4322	Patricia/Mood Indigo//Pretty Doll/Whistling Rock	1958	3.00	6.00	12.00
❑ EPA-4322 [PS]	Patricia	1958	3.00	6.00	12.00
❑ EPA-5022	Cherry Pink and Apple Blossom White/St. Louis				
	Blues Mambo//Mambo Jambo/Mambo No. 5	1958	3.00	6.00	12.00
❑ EPA-5022 [PS]	Perez Prado (Gold Standard Series)	1958	3.00	6.00	12.00
Albums					
RCA CAMDEN					
❑ CAL-409 [M]	Mambo Happy!	1957	5.00	10.00	20.00
❑ CAL-547 [M]	Latino!	1960	5.00	10.00	20.00
RCA VICTOR					
❑ LPM-21 [10]	Perez Prado Plays Mucho Mambo for Dancing	1951	15.00	30.00	60.00
❑ LPM-1075 [M]	Mambo Mania	1955	10.00	20.00	40.00
❑ LPM-1101 [M]	Voodoo Suite (and Six All-Time Greats)	1955	10.00	20.00	40.00
❑ LPM-1196 [M]	Mambo by the King	1956	10.00	20.00	40.00
❑ LPM-1257 [M]	Havana 3 A.M.	1956	10.00	20.00	40.00
❑ LPM-1459 [M]	Latin Satin	1957	10.00	20.00	40.00
❑ LPM-1556 [M]	"Prez"	1958	7.50	15.00	30.00
❑ LSP-1556 [S]	"Prez"	1959	10.00	20.00	40.00
❑ LPM-1883 [M]	Dilo (Ugh!)	1958	7.50	15.00	30.00
❑ LSP-1883 [S]	Dilo (Ugh!)	1959	10.00	20.00	40.00
❑ ANL1-1941	Pure Gold	1975	2.50	5.00	10.00
❑ LPM-2028 [M]	Pops and Prado	1959	7.50	15.00	30.00
❑ LSP-2028 [S]	Pops and Prado	1959	10.00	20.00	40.00
❑ LPM-2104 [M]	Big Hits by Prado	1959	7.50	15.00	30.00
❑ LSP-2104 [S]	Big Hits by Prado	1959	10.00	20.00	40.00
❑ LPM-2133 [M]	A Touch of Tabasco	1960	5.00	10.00	20.00
❑ LSP-2133 [S]	A Touch of Tabasco	1960	7.50	15.00	30.00
❑ LPM-2308 [M]	Rockambo	1961	5.00	10.00	20.00
❑ LSP-2308 [S]	Rockambo	1961	7.50	15.00	30.00
❑ LPM-2379 [M]	The New Dance La Chunga	1961	5.00	10.00	20.00
❑ LSP-2379 [S]	The New Dance La Chunga	1961	7.50	15.00	30.00
❑ LPM-2524 [M]	The Twist Goes Latin	1962	5.00	10.00	20.00
❑ LSP-2524 [S]	The Twist Goes Latin	1962	7.50	15.00	30.00
❑ LPM-2571 [M]	Exotic Suite	1962	5.00	10.00	20.00
❑ LSP-2571 [S]	Exotic Suite	1962	7.50	15.00	30.00
❑ LPM-2610 [M]	Our Man in Latin America	1963	5.00	10.00	20.00
❑ LSP-2610 [S]	Our Man in Latin America	1963	7.50	15.00	30.00
❑ LPM-3108 [10]	Mambo by the King	1953	15.00	30.00	60.00
❑ LPM-3330 [M]	Dance Latino	1965	3.75	7.50	15.00
❑ LSP-3330 [S]	Dance Latino	1965	5.00	10.00	20.00
❑ LPM-3732 [M]	The Best of Perez Prado	1967	5.00	10.00	20.00
❑ LSP-3732 [S]	The Best of Perez Prado	1967	3.75	7.50	15.00
❑ VPS-6066 [(2)]	This Is Perez Prado	1972	3.75	7.50	15.00
UNITED ARTISTS					
❑ LS-61032	Estas Si Viven (The Living End)	196?	3.75	7.50	15.00
PRATT, ANDY					
45s					
COLUMBIA					
❑ 45804	Avenging Annie/So Fine (It's Frightening)	1973	—	2.50	5.00
NEMPEROR					
❑ 007	If You Could See Yourself (Through My Eyes)/				
	(B-side unknown)	1976	—	2.00	4.00
❑ 008	Some Things Go On Forever/That's When				
	Miracles Occur	1976	—	2.00	4.00
❑ 013	All I Want Is You/(B-side unknown)	1977	—	2.00	4.00
Albums					
COLUMBIA					
❑ KC 31722	Andy Pratt	1973	2.50	5.00	10.00
NEMPEROR					
❑ SD 438	Resolution	1976	2.50	5.00	10.00
❑ SD 443	Shiver in the Night	1977	2.50	5.00	10.00
POLYDOR					
❑ 24-4015	Records Are Like Life	1970	3.00	6.00	12.00
PRATT & MCCLAIN					
45s					
ABC DUNHILL					
❑ 4387	Spirit of Love/When My Ship Comes In	1974	—	2.50	5.00
❑ 15004	Turn, Turn, Turn/Here I Am	1974	—	2.50	5.00
❑ 15024	We've Lost the Magic/When My Ship Comes In	1974	—	2.50	5.00

Number	Title (A Side/B Side)	Yr	VG	VG+	NM
REPRISE					
❏ 1351	Happy Days/Cruisin' with the Fonz	1976	—	2.50	5.00
❏ 1361	Devil with a Blue Dress/ Tonight We're Gonna Fall in Love	1976	—	2.00	4.00
❏ 1367	One Way or the Other/ Tonight We're Gonna Fall in Love	1976	—	—	—
—Canceled?					
❏ 1373	Whachersign/Who Needs It	1976	—	2.00	4.00
Albums					
ABC DUNHILL					
❏ DSX-50164	Pratt-McClain	1974	3.00	6.00	12.00
REPRISE					
❏ MS 2250	Pratt & McClain Featuring "Happy Days"	1976	2.50	5.00	10.00

PREACHERS, THE
45s
CHALLENGE

Number	Title (A Side/B Side)	Yr	VG	VG+	NM
❏ 501	Vitamin L.O.V.E./Till the Dawn	1969	3.00	6.00	12.00
MOONGLOW					
❏ 240	Who Do You Love/Chicken Poppa	1965	6.25	12.50	25.00
❏ 5006	Pain and Sorrow/Stay Out of My World	1965	5.00	10.00	20.00

PRECISIONS, THE (1)
45s
ATCO

Number	Title (A Side/B Side)	Yr	VG	VG+	NM
❏ 6643	Don't Double (With Trouble)/Into My Life	1969	3.00	6.00	12.00
❏ 6669	New York City/You're the Best (That Ever Did It)	1969	3.00	6.00	12.00
D-TOWN					
❏ 1033	My Lover Come Back/I Wanna Tell My Baby	1965	50.00	100.00	200.00
❏ 1055	Mexican Love Song/You're Sweet	1965	6.25	12.50	25.00
DREW					
❏ 1001	Such Misery/A Lover's Plea	1967	6.25	12.50	25.00
❏ 1002	Why Girl/What I Want	1967	3.75	7.50	15.00
❏ 1002	Why Girl/Sugar Ain't Sweet	1967	1000.	1750.	2500.
❏ 1003	If This Is Love (I'd Rather Be Lonely)/ You'll Soon Be Gone	1967	6.25	12.50	25.00
❏ 1004	Instant Heartbreak (Just Add Tears)/Dream Girl	1968	3.75	7.50	15.00
❏ 1005	Never Let Her Go/A Place	1968	3.75	7.50	15.00

PRECISIONS, THE (2)
45s
HIGHLAND

Number	Title (A Side/B Side)	Yr	VG	VG+	NM
❏ 300	Eight Reasons Why I Love You/(B-side unknown)	1962	100.00	200.00	400.00

PRECISIONS, THE (U) May be group (2); could be someone else.
45s
RAYNA

Number	Title (A Side/B Side)	Yr	VG	VG+	NM
❏ 1001	White Christmas/Silent Night	19??	25.00	50.00	100.00

PRELUDE
45s
ISLAND

Number	Title (A Side/B Side)	Yr	VG	VG+	NM
❏ IXPI 1 [DJ]	Christmas Message (same on both sides)	1974	2.50	5.00	10.00
❏ 002	After the Goldrush/Johnson Boy	1974	—	3.00	6.00
❏ 018	Fly/Lady from a Small Town	1975	—	2.50	5.00
PYE					
❏ 71045	For a Dancer/Best of a Bad Time	1975	—	2.50	5.00
Albums					
ISLAND					
❏ ILPS 9282	After the Gold Rush	1974	3.00	6.00	12.00
PYE					
❏ 12120	Owlcreek Incident	1975	3.00	6.00	12.00
❏ 12139	Back Into the Light	1976	3.00	6.00	12.00

PRELUDES, THE (1)
45s
ARLISS

Number	Title (A Side/B Side)	Yr	VG	VG+	NM
❏ 1004	Lorraine/Oh Please, Genie	1961	20.00	40.00	80.00
OCTAVIA					
❏ 8008	A Place for You (In My Heart)/That Would Be So Good	1962	10.00	20.00	40.00

PRELUDES, THE (2)
45s
CUB

Number	Title (A Side/B Side)	Yr	VG	VG+	NM
❏ 9005	Kingdom of Love/Vanishing Angel	1958	37.50	75.00	150.00

PRELUDES, THE (3)
45s
EMPIRE

Number	Title (A Side/B Side)	Yr	VG	VG+	NM
❏ 103	Don't Fall in Love Too Soon/I Want Your Arms Around Me (All the Time)	1956	25.00	50.00	100.00

PRELUDES FIVE, THE
45s
PIK

Number	Title (A Side/B Side)	Yr	VG	VG+	NM
❏ 231	Starlight/Don't You Know Love?	1961	6.25	12.50	25.00

PREMEERS, THE
45s
HERALD

Number	Title (A Side/B Side)	Yr	VG	VG+	NM
❏ 577	Diary of Our Love/Gee Oh Gee	1963	7.50	15.00	30.00

PREMIATA FORNERIA MARCONI See P.F.M.

PREMIERS, THE (1)
45s
FARO

Number	Title (A Side/B Side)	Yr	VG	VG+	NM
❏ 615	Farmer John/Duffy's Blues	1964	7.50	15.00	30.00
❏ 621	Get Your Baby/Little Ways	1965	3.00	6.00	12.00
❏ 624	Come On and Dance/Get On the Plane	1966	3.00	6.00	12.00
❏ 627	Ring Around My Rosie (Part 1)/ Ring Around My Rosie (Part 2)	1967	3.00	6.00	12.00
WARNER BROS.					
❏ 5443	Farmer John/Duffy's Blues	1964	3.75	7.50	15.00
❏ 5464	Annie Oakley/Blues for Arlene	1964	3.00	6.00	12.00

Number	Title (A Side/B Side)	Yr	VG	VG+	NM
Albums					
WARNER BROS.					
❏ W 1565 [M]	Farmer John	1964	10.00	20.00	40.00
❏ WS 1565 [S]	Farmer John	1964	12.50	25.00	50.00

PREMIERS, THE (2)
45s
ALERT

Number	Title (A Side/B Side)	Yr	VG	VG+	NM
❏ 706	Jolene/Oh, Theresa	1959	25.00	50.00	100.00
FURY					
❏ 1029	I Pray/Pigtails, Eyes Are Blue	1960	10.00	20.00	40.00
RUST					
❏ 5032	Falling Star/She Gives Me Fever	1961	25.00	50.00	100.00

PREMIERS, THE (3)
45s
CINDY

Number	Title (A Side/B Side)	Yr	VG	VG+	NM
❏ 3008	China Doll/Life Is Grand	1958	20.00	40.00	80.00
DIG					
❏ 106	New Moon/Baby	1956	37.50	75.00	150.00
❏ 113	My Darling/Have a Heart	1956	62.50	125.00	250.00
FORTUNE					
❏ 527	When You Are in Love/The Trap of Love	1956	20.00	40.00	80.00
GONE					
❏ 5009	Is It a Dream/Valerie	1957	50.00	100.00	200.00
—With "Let Me Share Your Dream" by The Deltas (Gone 5010) on Side 1 by mistake					
❏ 5009	Is It a Dream/Valerie	1957	125.00	250.00	500.00
—With correct track on side 1					
RCA VICTOR					
❏ 47-6958	Run Along Baby/Hey Miss Fancy	1957	20.00	40.00	80.00

PREMIERS, THE (4)
45s
KING

Number	Title (A Side/B Side)	Yr	VG	VG+	NM
❏ 6061	She's Always There/I'm Better Off Now	1966	5.00	10.00	20.00
STAX					
❏ 177	Make It Me/You Make a Strong Girl Weak	1965	7.50	15.00	30.00

PREMIERS, THE (5)
45s
MINK

Number	Title (A Side/B Side)	Yr	VG	VG+	NM
❏ 21	Tonight/I Think I Love You	1959	25.00	50.00	100.00
PARKWAY					
❏ 807	Tonight/I Think I Love You	1959	5.00	10.00	20.00

PREMIERS, THE (6)
45s
NU-PHI

Number	Title (A Side/B Side)	Yr	VG	VG+	NM
❏ 367/8	Cruisin'/(B-side unknown)	1959	7.50	15.00	30.00
❏ 701	Firewater/Younger Than You	1960	7.50	15.00	30.00

PREMIERS, THE (U) Could be one of the above groups; could be a completely different group.
45s
BOND

Number	Title (A Side/B Side)	Yr	VG	VG+	NM
❏ 5803/4	Hop and Skip/Uh-Huh	1958	5.00	10.00	20.00

PRESENT, THE
45s
PHILIPS

Number	Title (A Side/B Side)	Yr	VG	VG+	NM
❏ 40466	I Know/Many's the Slip Twixt the Cup and the Lip	1966	7.50	15.00	30.00

PRESIDENTS, THE (1)
45s
SUSSEX

Number	Title (A Side/B Side)	Yr	VG	VG+	NM
❏ 200	For You/Gotta Keep Movin'	1970	—	3.50	7.00
❏ 207	5-10-15-20 (25-30 Years of Love)/ I'm Still Dancing	1970	2.00	4.00	8.00
❏ 212	Triangle of Love (Hey Diddle Diddle)/ Sweet Magic	1971	—	3.50	7.00
❏ 217	The Sweetest Thing This Side of Heaven/ It's All Over Now	1971	—	3.50	7.00
Albums					
SUSSEX					
❏ SXBX-7005	5-10-15-20 (25-30 Years of Love)	1970	6.25	12.50	25.00

PRESIDENTS, THE (2) Not the same as group (1). The Sussex group's success forced this group to change its name, as reflected in the label credit on their final DeLuxe 45.
45s
DELUXE

Number	Title (A Side/B Side)	Yr	VG	VG+	NM
❏ 113	Gold Walk/I Want My Baby	1969	2.00	4.00	8.00
❏ 120	Snoopy/Stinky	1969	2.00	4.00	8.00
❏ 127	Which Way/Peter Rabbit	1970	2.00	4.00	8.00
❏ 134	Lover's Psalm/Our Meeting	1971	—	3.00	6.00
—As "The President's Band"					

PRESIDENTS, THE (3)
45s
MERCURY

Number	Title (A Side/B Side)	Yr	VG	VG+	NM
❏ 72016	Pots 'n' Pans/The Toasts	1962	5.00	10.00	20.00

PRESIDENTS, THE (U) The Hollywood record could be group (1) or (2); the Warner Bros. record could be group (3).
45s
HOLLYWOOD

Number	Title (A Side/B Side)	Yr	VG	VG+	NM
❏ 1137	Shoeshine (Part 1)/Shoeshine (Part 2)	1968	2.50	5.00	10.00
PLUM					
❏ 31	Mighty Fly Do/Love Pain	197?	2.50	5.00	10.00
WARNER BROS.					
❏ 5240	Hot Toddy March/I Do Love You (Do I Love You)	1961	3.75	7.50	15.00

PRESLEY, ELVIS
12-Inch Singles
RCA

Number	Title (A Side/B Side)	Yr	VG	VG+	NM
❏ EP-0517 [DJ]	Little Sister/Rip It Up	1983	25.00	50.00	100.00
❏ 60570	A Little Less Conversation (12" Extended Remix)/(Radio Remix Edit) (Original Version)	2002	3.00	6.00	12.00
—Credited to "Elvis vs JXL"					

P

Number	Title (A Side/B Side)	Yr	VG	VG+	NM

45s

BMG

Number	Title (A Side/B Side)	Yr	VG	VG+	NM
❑ 56193	Rubberneckin' (Paul Oakenfold Remix Radio Edit)/(Original)	2003	—	2.50	5.00

COLLECTABLES

Number	Title (A Side/B Side)	Yr	VG	VG+	NM
❑ COL-0103 [(23)]	Elvis #1 Hit Singles Collection	2001	25.00	50.00	100.00

—Contains reproductions, on red vinyl, of 18 RCA singles and all five Sun singles, using facsimiles of original labels and reproductions of original picture sleeves, and all-new sleeves for those songs not issued originally with picture sleeves; with poster and all in wooden box

Number	Title (A Side/B Side)	Yr	VG	VG+	NM
❑ COL-0134 [(23)]	Elvis Hit Singles Collection Volume 2	2002	25.00	50.00	100.00

—Contains reproductions, on red vinyl, of 23 RCA singles not in the first box, using facsimiles of original labels and reproductions of original picture sleeves, and all-new sleeves for those songs not issued originally with picture sleeves; with poster and all in wooden box

Number	Title (A Side/B Side)	Yr	VG	VG+	NM
❑ COL-4500	Good Rockin' Tonight/ I Don't Care If the Sun Don't Shine	1986	—	—	3.00
—Black vinyl					
❑ COL-4500	Good Rockin' Tonight/ I Don't Care If the Sun Don't Shine	1992	—	2.00	4.00
—Gold vinyl					
❑ COL-4501	You're a Heartbreaker/Milkcow Blues Boogie	1986	—	—	3.00
—Black vinyl					
❑ COL-4501	You're a Heartbreaker/Milkcow Blues Boogie	1992	—	2.00	4.00
—Gold vinyl					
❑ COL-4502	Baby Let's Play House/ I'm Left, You're Right, She's Gone	1986	—	—	3.00
—Black vinyl					
❑ COL-4502	Baby Let's Play House/ I'm Left, You're Right, She's Gone	1992	—	2.00	4.00
—Gold vinyl					
❑ COL-4503	I Got a Woman/I'm Counting on You	1986	—	—	3.00
—Black vinyl					
❑ COL-4503	I Got a Woman/I'm Counting on You	1992	—	2.00	4.00
—Gold vinyl					
❑ COL-4504	I'll Never Let You Go (Little Darlin')/I'm Gonna Sit Right Down and Cry (Over You)	1986	—	—	3.00
—Black vinyl					
❑ COL-4504	I'll Never Let You Go (Little Darlin')/I'm Gonna Sit Right Down and Cry (Over You)	1992	—	2.00	4.00
—Gold vinyl					
❑ COL-4505	Tryin' to Get to You/I Love You Because	1986	—	—	3.00
—Black vinyl					
❑ COL-4505	Tryin' to Get to You/I Love You Because	1992	—	2.00	4.00
—Gold vinyl					
❑ COL-4506	Money Honey/One-Sided Love Affair	1986	—	—	3.00
—Black vinyl					
❑ COL-4506	Money Honey/One-Sided Love Affair	1992	—	2.00	4.00
—Gold vinyl					
❑ COL-4507	Too Much/Playing for Keeps	1986	—	—	3.00
—Black vinyl					
❑ COL-4507	Too Much/Playing for Keeps	1992	—	2.00	4.00
—Gold vinyl					
❑ COL-4508	A Big Hunk o'Love/My Wish Came True	1986	—	—	3.00
—Black vinyl					
❑ COL-4508	A Big Hunk o'Love/My Wish Came True	1992	—	2.00	4.00
—Gold vinyl					
❑ COL-4509	Stuck on You/Fame and Fortune	1986	—	—	3.00
—Black vinyl					
❑ COL-4509	Stuck on You/Fame and Fortune	1992	—	2.00	4.00
—Gold vinyl					
❑ COL-4510	I Feel So Bad/Wild in the Country	1986	—	—	3.00
—Black vinyl					
❑ COL-4510	I Feel So Bad/Wild in the Country	1992	—	2.00	4.00
—Gold vinyl					
❑ COL-4511	She's Not You/Jailhouse Rock	1986	—	—	3.00
—Black vinyl					
❑ COL-4511	She's Not You/Jajlhouse Rock	1992	—	2.00	4.00
—Gold vinyl					
❑ COL-4512	One Broken Heart for Sale/Devil in Disguise	1986	—	—	3.00
—Black vinyl					
❑ COL-4512	One Broken Heart for Sale/Devil in Disguise	1992	—	2.00	4.00
—Gold vinyl					
❑ COL-4513	Bossa Nova Baby/Such a Night	1986	—	—	3.00
—Black vinyl					
❑ COL-4513	Bossa Nova Baby/Such a Night	1992	—	2.00	4.00
—Gold vinyl					
❑ COL-4514	Love Me/Flaming Star	1986	—	—	3.00
—Black vinyl					
❑ COL-4514	Love Me/Flaming Star	1992	—	2.00	4.00
—Gold vinyl					
❑ COL-4515	Follow That Dream/When My Blue Moon Turns to Gold Again	1986	—	—	3.00
—Black vinyl					
❑ COL-4515	Follow That Dream/When My Blue Moon Turns to Gold Again	1992	—	2.00	4.00
—Gold vinyl					
❑ COL-4516	Frankie and Johnny/Love Letters	1986	—	—	3.00
—Black vinyl					
❑ COL-4516	Frankie and Johnny/Love Letters	1992	—	2.00	4.00
—Gold vinyl					
❑ COL-4517	U.S. Male/Until It's Time for You to Go	1986	—	—	3.00
—Black vinyl					
❑ COL-4517	U.S. Male/Until It's Time for You to Go	1992	—	2.00	4.00
—Gold vinyl					
❑ COL-4518	Old Shep/You'll Never Walk Alone	1986	—	—	3.00
—Black vinyl					
❑ COL-4518	Old Shep/You'll Never Walk Alone	1992	—	2.00	4.00
—Gold vinyl					
❑ COL-4519	Poor Boy/An American Trilogy	1986	—	—	3.00
—Black vinyl					
❑ COL-4519	Poor Boy/An American Trilogy	1992	—	2.00	4.00
—Gold vinyl					
❑ COL-4520	How Great Thou Art/His Hand in Mine	1986	—	—	3.00
—Black vinyl					
❑ COL-4520	How Great Thou Art/His Hand in Mine	1992	—	2.00	4.00
—Gold vinyl					
❑ COL-4521	Big Boss Man/Paralyzed	1986	—	—	3.00
—Black vinyl					
❑ COL-4521	Big Boss Man/Paralyzed	1992	—	2.00	4.00
—Gold vinyl					
❑ COL-4522	Fools Fall in Love/Blue Suede Shoes	1986	—	—	3.00
—Black vinyl					
❑ COL-4522	Fools Fall in Love/Blue Suede Shoes	1992	—	2.00	4.00
—Gold vinyl					
❑ COL-4564	The Elvis Medley/Always on My Mind	1986	—	—	3.00
❑ COL-4738	Ask Me/The Girl of My Best Friend	1997	—	—	3.00
❑ COL-4743	Girls! Girls! Girls!/Ain't That Loving You Baby	1997	—	—	3.00
❑ COL-4744	It's Only Love/Beyond the Reef	1997	—	—	3.00
❑ 04764	Witchcraft/Spinout	1997	—	—	3.00
❑ 80000	(Now and Then There's) A Fool Such As I/I Need Your Love Tonight	1997	—	2.00	4.00
—Gray marbled vinyl					
❑ 80001	Separate Ways/Always on My Mind	1997	—	2.00	4.00
—Gray marbled vinyl					
❑ 80002	An American Trilogy/Until It's Time for You to Go	1997	—	2.00	4.00
—Gray marbled vinyl					
❑ 80003	Crying in the Chapel/ I Believe in the Man in the Sky	1997	—	2.00	4.00
—Gray marbled vinyl					
❑ 80004	Don't/I Beg of You	1997	—	2.00	4.00
—Gray marbled vinyl					
❑ 80005	Don't Cry Daddy/Rubberneckin'	1997	—	2.00	4.00
—Gray marbled vinyl					
❑ 80006	Good Luck Charm/Anything That's Part of You	1997	—	2.00	4.00
—Gray marbled vinyl					
❑ 80007	Guitar Man/Hi-Heel Sneakers	1997	—	2.00	4.00
—Gray marbled vinyl					
❑ 80008	Hard Headed Woman/Don't Ask Me Why	1997	—	2.00	4.00
—Gray marbled vinyl					
❑ 80009	Heartbreak Hotel/I Was the One	1997	—	2.00	4.00
—Gray marbled vinyl					
❑ 80010	Mystery Train/I Forgot to Remember to Forget	1997	—	2.00	4.00
—Gray marbled vinyl					
❑ 80011	One Night/I Got Stung	1997	—	2.00	4.00
—Gray marbled vinyl					
❑ 80012	I Really Don't Want to Know/ There Goes My Everything	1997	—	2.00	4.00
—Gray marbled vinyl					
❑ 80013	I Want You, I Need You, I Love You/ My Baby Left Me	1997	—	2.00	4.00
—Gray marbled vinyl					
❑ 80014	If I Can Dream/Edge of Reality	1997	—	2.00	4.00
—Gray marbled vinyl					
❑ 80015	Kentucky Rain/My Little Friend	1997	—	2.00	4.00
—Gray marbled vinyl					
❑ 80016	Kiss Me Quick/Suspicion	1997	—	2.00	4.00
—Gray marbled vinyl					
❑ 80017	Kissin' Cousins/It Hurts Me	1997	—	2.00	4.00
—Gray marbled vinyl					
❑ 80018	Marie's the Name His Latest Flame/Little Sister	1997	—	2.00	4.00
—Gray marbled vinyl					
❑ 80019	(Let Me Be You) Teddy Bear/Loving You	1997	—	2.00	4.00
—Gray marbled vinyl					
❑ 80020	The Wonder of You/Mama Liked the Roses	1997	—	2.00	4.00
—Gray marbled vinyl					
❑ 80021	Memories/Charro	1997	—	2.00	4.00
—Gray marbled vinyl					
❑ 80022	My Boy/Thinking About You	1997	—	2.00	4.00
—Gray marbled vinyl					
❑ 80023	Way Down/My Way	1997	—	2.00	4.00
—Gray marbled vinyl					
❑ 80024	Patch It Up/You Don't Have to Say You Love Me	1997	—	2.00	4.00
—Gray marbled vinyl					
❑ 80025	Surrender/Lonely Man	1997	—	2.00	4.00
—Gray marbled vinyl					
❑ 80026	That's All Right/Blue Moon of Kentucky	1997	—	2.00	4.00
—Gray marbled vinyl					
❑ 80027	Wear My Ring Around Your Neck/Doncha' Think It's Time	1997	—	2.00	4.00
—Gray marbled vinyl					
❑ 80028	Puppet on a String/Wooden Heart	1997	—	2.00	4.00
—Gray marbled vinyl					

RCA

Number	Title (A Side/B Side)	Yr	VG	VG+	NM
❑ 447-0600	I Forgot to Remember to Forget/Mystery Train	1977	—	2.00	4.00

—Note: All RCA releases with a "447" prefix are from the Gold Standard Series and are black label, dog near top

Number	Title (A Side/B Side)	Yr	VG	VG+	NM
❑ 447-0601	That's All Right/Blue Moon of Kentucky	1977	—	2.00	4.00
❑ 447-0602	Good Rockin' Tonight/I Don't Care If the Sun Don't Shine	1977	—	2.00	4.00
❑ 447-0603	Milkcow Blues Boogie/You're a Heartbreaker	1977	—	2.00	4.00
❑ 447-0604	Baby Let's Play House/I'm Left, You're Right, She's Gone	1977	—	2.00	4.00
❑ 447-0605	Heartbreak Hotel/I Was the One	1977	—	2.00	4.00
❑ 447-0607	I Want You, I Need You, I Love You/ My Baby Left Me	1977	—	2.00	4.00
❑ 447-0608	Hound Dog/Don't Be Cruel	1977	—	2.00	4.00
❑ 447-0609	Blue Suede Shoes/Tutti Frutti	1977	—	2.00	4.00
❑ 447-0613	Blue Moon/Just Because	1977	—	2.00	4.00
❑ 447-0614	Money Honey/One-Sided Love Affair	1977	—	2.00	4.00
❑ 447-0615	Lawdy Miss Clawdy/Shake, Rattle, and Roll	1977	—	2.00	4.00
❑ 447-0616	Love Me Tender/Anyway You Want Me (That's How I Will Be)	1977	—	2.00	4.00
❑ 447-0617	Too Much/Playing for Keeps	1977	—	2.00	4.00
❑ 447-0618	All Shook Up/That's When Your Heartaches Begin	1977	—	2.00	4.00
❑ 447-0619	Jailhouse Rock/Treat Me Nice	1977	—	2.00	4.00
❑ 447-0620	(Let Me Be Your) Teddy Bear/Loving You	1977	—	2.00	4.00
❑ 447-0621	Don't/I Beg of You	1977	—	2.00	4.00
❑ 447-0622	Wear My Ring Around Your Neck/Don'tcha Think It's Time	1977	—	2.00	4.00
❑ 447-0623	Hard Headed Woman/Don't Ask Me Why	1977	—	2.00	4.00
❑ 447-0624	One Night/I Got Stung	1977	—	2.00	4.00

Elvis Presley, *Elvis Presley,* RCA Victor SPD-23, three-record EP set, $3,000-$6,000 (cover and all three records together).

Elvis Presley, "Love Me Tender," RCA Victor 47-6643, picture sleeve, black and light pink print, $15-$30.

Elvis Presley, "Wear My Ring Around Your Neck," RCA Victor 47-7240, picture sleeve, $45-$90.

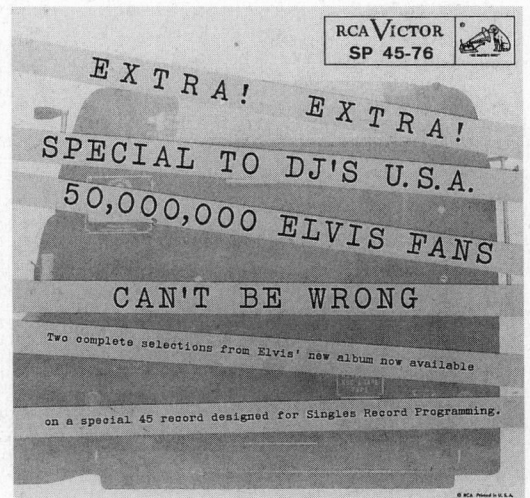

Elvis Presley, "Don't," RCA Victor SP-45-76, special promotional picture sleeve, $1,500-$2,000.

Elvis Presley, *A Touch of Gold, Volume 3,* RCA Victor EPA-5141, 7-inch EP, maroon label on record, $235-$470.

Elvis Presley, *Moody Blue,* RCA Victor, blue vinyl, $5-$10 or less.

Number	Title (A Side/B Side)	Yr	VG	VG+	NM
❏ 447-0625	(Now and Then There's) A Fool Such As I/I Need Your Love Tonight	1977	—	2.00	4.00
❏ 447-0626	A Big Hunk o'Love/My Wish Came True	1977	—	2.00	4.00
❏ 447-0627	Stuck on You/Fame and Fortune	1977	—	2.00	4.00
❏ 447-0628	It's Now or Never/A Mess of Blues	1977	—	2.00	4.00
❏ 447-0629	Are You Lonesome To-Night?/I Gotta Know	1977	—	2.00	4.00
❏ 447-0630	Surrender/Lonely Man	1977	—	2.00	4.00
❏ 447-0631	I Feel So Bad/Wild in the Country	1977	—	2.00	4.00
❏ 447-0634	(Marie's the Name) His Latest Flame/Little Sister	1977	—	2.00	4.00
❏ 447-0635	Can't Help Falling in Love/Rock-a-Hula Baby	1977	—	2.00	4.00
❏ 447-0636	Good Luck Charm/Anything That's Part of You	1977	—	2.00	4.00
❏ 447-0637	She's Not You/Just Tell Her Jim Said Hello	1977	—	2.00	4.00
❏ 447-0638	Return to Sender/Where Do You Come From	1977	—	2.00	4.00
❏ 447-0639	Kiss Me Quick/Suspicion	1977	—	2.00	4.00
❏ 447-0640	One Broken Heart for Sale/They Remind Me Too Much of You	1977	—	2.00	4.00
❏ 447-0641	(You're the) Devil in Disguise/Please Don't Drag That String Around	1977	—	2.00	4.00
❏ 447-0642	Bossa Nova Baby/Witchcraft	1977	—	2.00	4.00
❏ 447-0643	Crying in the Chapel/I Believe in the Man in the Sky	1977	—	2.00	4.00
❏ 447-0644	Kissin' Cousins/It Hurts Me	1977	—	2.00	4.00
❏ 447-0645	Such a Night/Never Ending	1977	—	2.00	4.00
❏ 447-0646	Viva Las Vegas/What'd I Say	1977	—	2.00	4.00
❏ 447-0647	Blue Christmas/Santa Claus Is Back in Town	1977	—	2.00	4.00
❏ 447-0647 [PS]	Blue Christmas/Santa Claus Is Back in Town	1977	2.50	5.00	10.00

—Does not mention "Gold Standard Series" on sleeve

Number	Title (A Side/B Side)	Yr	VG	VG+	NM
❏ 447-0648	Do the Clam/You'll Be Gone	1977	—	2.00	4.00
❏ 447-0649	Ain't That Loving You Baby/Ask Me	1977	—	2.00	4.00
❏ 447-0650	Puppet on a String/Wooden Heart	1977	—	2.00	4.00
❏ 447-0651	Joshua Fit the Battle/Known Only to Him	1977	—	2.00	4.00
❏ 447-0653	(Such An) Easy Question/It Feels So Right	1977	—	2.00	4.00
❏ 447-0654	I'm Yours/(It's a) Long, Lonely Highway	1977	—	2.00	4.00
❏ 447-0655	Tell Me Why/Blue River	1977	—	2.00	4.00
❏ 447-0656	Frankie and Johnny/Please Don't Stop Loving Me	1977	—	2.00	4.00
❏ 447-0657	Love Letters/Come What May	1977	—	2.00	4.00
❏ 447-0658	Spinout/All That I Am	1977	—	2.00	4.00
❏ 447-0659	Indescribably Blue/Fools Fall in Love	1977	—	2.00	4.00
❏ 447-0661	There's Always Me/Judy	1977	—	2.00	4.00
❏ 447-0662	Big Boss Man/You Don't Know Me	1977	—	2.00	4.00
❏ 447-0663	Guitar Man/High Heel Sneakers	1977	—	2.00	4.00
❏ 447-0664	U.S. Male/Stay Away	1977	—	2.50	5.00
❏ 447-0665	You'll Never Walk Alone/We Call on Him	1977	—	2.00	4.00
❏ 447-0666	Let Yourself Go/Your Time Hasn't Come Yet, Baby	1977	—	2.00	4.00
❏ 447-0667	A Little Less Conversation/Almost in Love	1977	—	2.00	4.00
❏ 447-0668	If I Can Dream/Edge of Reality	1977	—	2.00	4.00
❏ 447-0669	Memories/Charro	1977	—	2.00	4.00
❏ 447-0670	How Great Thou Art/His Hand in Mine	1977	—	2.00	4.00
❏ 447-0671	In the Ghetto/Any Day Now	1977	—	2.00	4.00
❏ 447-0672	Clean Up Your Own Back Yard/The Fair Is Moving On	1977	—	2.00	4.00
❏ 447-0673	Suspicious Minds/You'll Think of Me	1977	—	2.00	4.00
❏ 447-0674	Don't Cry Daddy/Rubberneckin'	1977	—	2.00	4.00
❏ 447-0675	Kentucky Rain/My Little Friend	1977	—	2.00	4.00
❏ 447-0676	The Wonder of You/Mama Liked the Roses	1976	—	2.00	4.00
❏ 447-0677	I've Lost You/The Next Step Is Love	1977	—	2.00	4.00
❏ 447-0678	You Don't Have to Say You Love Me/Patch It Up	1977	—	2.00	4.00
❏ 447-0679	I Really Don't Want to Know/There Goes My Everything	1977	—	2.00	4.00
❏ 447-0680	Where Did They Go, Lord/Rags to Riches	1977	—	2.00	4.00
❏ 447-0681	If Every Day Was Like Christmas/How Would You Like to Be	1977	—	2.00	4.00
❏ 447-0682	Life/Only Believe	1977	—	2.00	4.00
❏ 447-0683	I'm Leavin'/Heart of Rome	1977	—	2.00	4.00
❏ 447-0684	It's Only Love/The Sound of Your Cry	1977	—	2.00	4.00
❏ 447-0685	An American Trilogy/Until It's Time for You to Go	1977	—	2.00	4.00
❏ DME1-1803	King of the Whole Wide World/King Creole	1997	2.00	4.00	8.00

—Gold vinyl (about 7,000 pressed)

Number	Title (A Side/B Side)	Yr	VG	VG+	NM
❏ DME1-1803 [DJ]	King of the Whole Wide World/King Creole	1997	100.00	200.00	400.00

—Test pressings of above on green, blue, white and clear vinyl. Value is for any of them.

Number	Title (A Side/B Side)	Yr	VG	VG+	NM
❏ DME1-1803 [PS]	King of the Whole Wide World/King Creole	1997	2.00	4.00	8.00

—Same picture sleeve with either edition

Number	Title (A Side/B Side)	Yr	VG	VG+	NM
❏ DME1-1803R	King of the Whole Wide World/King Creole	1997	3.75	7.50	15.00

—Red vinyl, marked as a promotional copy (about 3,000 pressed)

Number	Title (A Side/B Side)	Yr	VG	VG+	NM
❏ 8760-7-R	Heartbreak Hotel/Heartbreak Hotel	1988	—	2.50	5.00

—B-side by David Keith

Number	Title (A Side/B Side)	Yr	VG	VG+	NM
❏ 8760-7-R [PS]	Heartbreak Hotel/Heartbreak Hotel	1988	—	3.00	6.00

—"Pink Cadillac" sleeve

Number	Title (A Side/B Side)	Yr	VG	VG+	NM
❏ 8760-7-R [PS]	Heartbreak Hotel/Heartbreak Hotel	1988	20.00	40.00	80.00

—Promo-only sleeve of RCA executive Butch Waugh dressed as Elvis

Number	Title (A Side/B Side)	Yr	VG	VG+	NM
❏ GB-10485	Take Good Care of Her/I've Got a Thing About You, Baby	1977	—	2.00	4.00

—Gold Standard Series; black label

Number	Title (A Side/B Side)	Yr	VG	VG+	NM
❏ GB-10486	Separate Ways/Always on My Mind	1977	—	2.00	4.00

—Gold Standard Series; black label

Number	Title (A Side/B Side)	Yr	VG	VG+	NM
❏ GB-10487	T-R-O-U-B-L-E/Mr. Songman	1977	—	2.00	4.00

—Gold Standard Series; black label

Number	Title (A Side/B Side)	Yr	VG	VG+	NM
❏ GB-10488	Promised Land/It's Midnight	1977	—	2.00	4.00

—Gold Standard Series; black label

Number	Title (A Side/B Side)	Yr	VG	VG+	NM
❏ GB-10489	My Boy/Thinking About You	1977	—	2.00	4.00

—Gold Standard Series; black label

Number	Title (A Side/B Side)	Yr	VG	VG+	NM
❏ PB-10601	Hurt/For the Heart	1976	25.00	50.00	100.00

—Second pressings (very rare) on the 1976-88 "dog near top" black label

Number	Title (A Side/B Side)	Yr	VG	VG+	NM
❏ JB-10857 [DJ]	Moody Blue/She Thinks I Still Care	1976	250.00	500.00	1000.

—Colored vinyl pressings exist in five different colors -- red, white, gold, blue, green. Value is for any of them.

Number	Title (A Side/B Side)	Yr	VG	VG+	NM
❏ PB-10857	Moody Blue/She Thinks I Still Care	1976	—	2.50	5.00
❏ PB-10857 [PS]	Moody Blue/She Thinks I Still Care	1976	2.50	5.00	10.00
❏ JH-10951 [DJ]	Let Me Be There (mono/stereo)	1977	50.00	100.00	200.00

—Promo only

Number	Title (A Side/B Side)	Yr	VG	VG+	NM
❏ PB-10998	Way Down/Pledging My Love	1977	—	2.50	5.00
❏ PB-10998 [PS]	Way Down/Pledging My Love	1977	2.50	5.00	10.00
❏ PB-11099	Hound Dog/Don't Be Cruel	1977	—	2.00	4.00
❏ PB-11099 [PS]	Hound Dog/Don't Be Cruel	1977	—	2.00	4.00

—From boxes "15 Golden Records, 30 Golden Hits" and "20 Golden Hits in Full Color Sleeves"

Number	Title (A Side/B Side)	Yr	VG	VG+	NM
❏ PB-11100	In the Ghetto/Any Day Now	1977	—	2.00	4.00
❏ PB-11100 [PS]	In the Ghetto/Any Day Now	1977	—	2.00	4.00

—From boxes "15 Golden Records, 30 Golden Hits" and "20 Golden Hits in Full Color Sleeves"

Number	Title (A Side/B Side)	Yr	VG	VG+	NM
❏ PB-11101	Jailhouse Rock/Treat Me Nice	1977	—	2.00	4.00
❏ PB-11101 [PS]	Jailhouse Rock/Treat Me Nice	1977	—	2.00	4.00

—From box "15 Golden Records, 30 Golden Hits"

Number	Title (A Side/B Side)	Yr	VG	VG+	NM
❏ PB-11102	Can't Help Falling in Love/Rock-a-Hula Baby	1977	—	2.00	4.00
❏ PB-11102 [PS]	Can't Help Falling in Love/Rock-a-Hula Baby	1977	—	2.00	4.00

—From boxes "15 Golden Records, 30 Golden Hits" and "20 Golden Hits in Full Color Sleeves"

Number	Title (A Side/B Side)	Yr	VG	VG+	NM
❏ PB-11103	Suspicious Minds/You'll Think of Me	1977	—	2.00	4.00
❏ PB-11103 [PS]	Suspicious Minds/You'll Think of Me	1977	—	2.00	4.00

—From box "15 Golden Records, 30 Golden Hits"

Number	Title (A Side/B Side)	Yr	VG	VG+	NM
❏ PB-11104	Are You Lonesome To-Night?/I Gotta Know	1977	—	2.00	4.00
❏ PB-11104 [PS]	Are You Lonesome To-Night?/I Gotta Know	1977	—	2.00	4.00

—From boxes "15 Golden Records, 30 Golden Hits" and "20 Golden Hits in Full Color Sleeves"

Number	Title (A Side/B Side)	Yr	VG	VG+	NM
❏ PB-11105	Heartbreak Hotel/I Was the One	1977	—	2.00	4.00
❏ PB-11105 [PS]	Heartbreak Hotel/I Was the One	1977	—	2.00	4.00

—From boxes "15 Golden Records, 30 Golden Hits" and "20 Golden Hits in Full Color Sleeves"

Number	Title (A Side/B Side)	Yr	VG	VG+	NM
❏ PB-11106	All Shook Up/That's When Your Heartaches Begin	1977	—	2.00	4.00
❏ PB-11106 [PS]	All Shook Up/That's When Your Heartaches Begin	1977	—	2.00	4.00

—From boxes "15 Golden Records, 30 Golden Hits" and "20 Golden Hits in Full Color Sleeves"

Number	Title (A Side/B Side)	Yr	VG	VG+	NM
❏ PB-11107	Blue Suede Shoes/Tutti Frutti	1977	—	2.00	4.00
❏ PB-11107 [PS]	Blue Suede Shoes/Tutti Frutti	1977	—	2.00	4.00

—From boxes "15 Golden Records, 30 Golden Hits" and "20 Golden Hits in Full Color Sleeves"

Number	Title (A Side/B Side)	Yr	VG	VG+	NM
❏ PB-11108	Love Me Tender/Any Way You Want Me (That's How I Will Be)	1977	—	2.00	4.00
❏ PB-11108 [PS]	Love Me Tender/Any Way You Want Me (That's How I Will Be)	1977	—	2.00	4.00

—From boxes "15 Golden Records, 30 Golden Hits" and "20 Golden Hits in Full Color Sleeves"

Number	Title (A Side/B Side)	Yr	VG	VG+	NM
❏ PB-11109	(Let Me Be Your) Teddy Bear/Loving You	1977	—	2.00	4.00
❏ PB-11109 [PS]	(Let Me Be Your) Teddy Bear/Loving You	1977	—	2.00	4.00

—From boxes "15 Golden Records, 30 Golden Hits" and "20 Golden Hits in Full Color Sleeves"

Number	Title (A Side/B Side)	Yr	VG	VG+	NM
❏ PB-11110	It's Now or Never/A Mess of Blues	1977	—	2.00	4.00
❏ PB-11110 [PS]	It's Now or Never/A Mess of Blues	1977	—	2.00	4.00

—From box "15 Golden Records, 30 Golden Hits"

Number	Title (A Side/B Side)	Yr	VG	VG+	NM
❏ PB-11111	Return to Sender/Where Do You Come From	1977	—	2.00	4.00
❏ PB-11111 [PS]	Return to Sender/Where Do You Come From	1977	—	2.00	4.00

—From boxes "15 Golden Records, 30 Golden Hits" and "20 Golden Hits in Full Color Sleeves"

Number	Title (A Side/B Side)	Yr	VG	VG+	NM
❏ PB-11112	One Night/I Got Stung	1977	—	2.00	4.00
❏ PB-11112 [PS]	One Night/I Got Stung	1977	—	2.00	4.00

—From box "15 Golden Records, 30 Golden Hits"

Number	Title (A Side/B Side)	Yr	VG	VG+	NM
❏ PB-11113	Crying in the Chapel/I Believe in the Man in the Sky	1977	—	2.00	4.00
❏ PB-11113 [PS]	Crying in the Chapel/I Believe in the Man in the Sky	1977	—	2.00	4.00

—From box "15 Golden Records, 30 Golden Hits"

Number	Title (A Side/B Side)	Yr	VG	VG+	NM
❏ PB-11165	My Way/America	1977	—	2.50	5.00
❏ PB-11165 [PS]	My Way/America	1977	5.00	10.00	20.00
❏ PB-11165	My Way/America the Beautiful	1977	2.50	5.00	10.00
❏ PB-11165 [PS]	My Way/America the Beautiful	1977	6.25	12.50	25.00
❏ PB-11212	Unchained Melody/Softly, As I Leave You	1978	—	2.50	5.00

—No credit to Sherrill Nielsen on the "Unchained Melody" side

Number	Title (A Side/B Side)	Yr	VG	VG+	NM
❏ PB-11212	Unchained Melody/Softly, As I Leave You	1978	2.50	5.00	10.00

—Erroneously states "Vocal Accompaniment by Sherrill Nielsen" on "Unchained Melody" side

Number	Title (A Side/B Side)	Yr	VG	VG+	NM
❏ PB-11212 [PS]	Unchained Melody/Softly, As I Leave You	1978	2.50	5.00	10.00
❏ PP-11301	15 Golden Records, 30 Golden Hits	1977	15.00	30.00	60.00

—Includes 15 records (11099-11113) and outer box

Number	Title (A Side/B Side)	Yr	VG	VG+	NM
❏ PB-11320	(Let Me Be Your) Teddy Bear/Puppet on a String	1978	—	2.50	5.00
❏ PB-11320 [PS]	(Let Me Be Your) Teddy Bear/Puppet on a String	1978	2.50	5.00	10.00
❏ GB-11326	Moody Blue/For the Heart	1978	—	2.00	4.00

—Gold Standard Series

Number	Title (A Side/B Side)	Yr	VG	VG+	NM
❏ PP-11340	20 Golden Hits in Full Color Sleeves	1977	20.00	40.00	80.00

—Includes 10 records (11099, 11100, 11102, 11104-11109, 11111) and outer box

Number	Title (A Side/B Side)	Yr	VG	VG+	NM
❏ GB-11504	Way Down/My Way	1979	—	2.00	4.00

—Gold Standard Series

Number	Title (A Side/B Side)	Yr	VG	VG+	NM
❏ PB-11533	Are You Sincere/Solitaire	1979	—	2.50	5.00
❏ PB-11533 [PS]	Are You Sincere/Solitaire	1979	2.50	5.00	10.00
❏ PB-11679	There's a Honky Tonk Angel (Who Will Take Me Back In)/I Got a Feelin' in My Body	1979	—	2.50	5.00

—Has production credits removed; no producers are listed

Number	Title (A Side/B Side)	Yr	VG	VG+	NM
❏ PB-11679	There's a Honky Tonk Angel (Who Will Take Me Back In)/I Got a Feelin' in My Body	1979	3.75	7.50	15.00

—Has full production credits (background vocals, strings) listed in error on both sides

Number	Title (A Side/B Side)	Yr	VG	VG+	NM
❏ PB-11679 [PS]	There's a Honky Tonk Angel (Who Will Take Me Back In)/I Got a Feelin' in My Body	1979	2.50	5.00	10.00
❏ GB-11988	Unchained Melody/Are You Sincere	1980	—	2.00	4.00

—Gold Standard Series

Number	Title (A Side/B Side)	Yr	VG	VG+	NM
❏ JH-12158 [DJ]	Guitar Man (mono/stereo)	1981	75.00	150.00	300.00

—Promo only on red vinyl

Number	Title (A Side/B Side)	Yr	VG	VG+	NM
❏ PB-12158	Guitar Man/Faded Love	1981	—	2.50	5.00
❏ PB-12158 [PS]	Guitar Man/Faded Love	1981	2.50	5.00	10.00
❏ JB-12205 [DJ]	Lovin' Arms/You Asked Me To	1981	75.00	150.00	300.00

—Promo only on green vinyl

Number	Title (A Side/B Side)	Yr	VG	VG+	NM
❏ PB-12205	Lovin' Arms/You Asked Me To	1981	—	3.00	6.00

—Not issued with picture sleeve (bootlegs exist)

Number	Title (A Side/B Side)	Yr	VG	VG+	NM
❏ PB-13058	There Goes My Everything/You'll Never Walk Alone	1982	—	2.50	5.00
❏ PB-13058 [PS]	There Goes My Everything/You'll Never Walk Alone	1982	2.50	5.00	10.00
❏ GB-13275	Suspicious Minds/You'll Think of Me	1982	—	2.00	4.00

—Gold Standard Series

Number	Title (A Side/B Side)	Yr	VG	VG+	NM
❏ JH-13302	The Impossible Dream (The Quest)/An American Trilogy	1982	25.00	50.00	100.00
❏ JH-13302 [PS]	The Impossible Dream (The Quest)/An American Trilogy	1982	25.00	50.00	100.00

—Promo only, distributed to visitors to Elvis' birthplace in Tupelo, Mississippi, in 1982.

Number	Title (A Side/B Side)	Yr	VG	VG+	NM
❏ JB-13351 [DJ]	The Elvis Medley (Long Version)/The Elvis Medley (Short Version)	1982	75.00	150.00	300.00

—Promo only on gold vinyl

Number	Title (A Side/B Side)	Yr	VG	VG+	NM
❏ PB-13351	The Elvis Medley/Always on My Mind	1982	—	2.50	5.00
❏ PB-13351 [PS]	The Elvis Medley/Always on My Mind	1982	2.50	5.00	10.00
❏ JB-13500 [DJ]	I Was the One/Wear My Ring Around Your Neck	1983	75.00	150.00	300.00

—Promo only on gold vinyl

Number	Title (A Side/B Side)	Yr	VG	VG+	NM
❏ PB-13500	I Was the One/Wear My Ring Around Your Neck	1983	—	2.50	5.00
❏ PB-13500 [PS]	I Was the One/Wear My Ring Around Your Neck	1983	2.50	5.00	10.00

Number	Title (A Side/B Side)	Yr	VG	VG+	NM
❏ JB-13547 [DJ]	Little Sister/Paralyzed	1983	75.00	150.00	300.00
—Promo only on blue vinyl					
❏ PB-13547	Little Sister/Paralyzed	1983	—	2.50	5.00
❏ PB-13547 [PS]	Little Sister/Paralyzed	1983	2.50	5.00	10.00
❏ JB-13875 [DJ]	Baby Let's Play House/Hound Dog	1984	50.00	100.00	200.00
—Gold vinyl, custom label					
❏ PB-13875	Baby Let's Play House/Hound Dog	1984	10.00	20.00	40.00
—Gold vinyl, custom label					
❏ PB-13875 [PS]	Baby Let's Play House/Hound Dog	1984	10.00	20.00	40.00
❏ PB-13885	Blue Suede Shoes/Tutti Frutti	1984	—	2.00	4.00
—From box "Elvis' Greatest Hits, Golden Singles, Volume 1"; gold vinyl					
❏ PB-13885 [PS]	Blue Suede Shoes/Tutti Frutti	1984	—	2.00	4.00
❏ PB-13886	Don't Be Cruel/Hound Dog	1984	—	2.00	4.00
—From box "Elvis' Greatest Hits, Golden Singles, Volume 1"; gold vinyl					
❏ PB-13886 [PS]	Don't Be Cruel/Hound Dog	1984	—	2.00	4.00
❏ PB-13887	I Want You, I Need You, I Love You/Love Me	1984	—	2.00	4.00
—From box "Elvis' Greatest Hits, Golden Singles, Volume 1"; gold vinyl					
❏ PB-13887 [PS]	I Want You, I Need You, I Love You/Love Me	1984	—	2.00	4.00
❏ PB-13888	All Shook Up/(Let Me Be Your) Teddy Bear	1984	—	2.00	4.00
—From box "Elvis' Greatest Hits, Golden Singles, Volume 1"; gold vinyl					
❏ PB-13888 [PS]	All Shook Up/(Let Me Be Your) Teddy Bear	1984	—	2.00	4.00
❏ PB-13889	It's Now or Never/Surrender	1984	—	2.00	4.00
—From box "Elvis' Greatest Hits, Golden Singles, Volume 1"; gold vinyl					
❏ PB-13889 [PS]	It's Now or Never/Surrender	1984	—	2.00	4.00
❏ PB-13890	In the Ghetto/If I Can Dream	1984	—	2.00	4.00
—From box "Elvis' Greatest Hits, Golden Singles, Volume 1"; gold vinyl					
❏ PB-13890 [PS]	In the Ghetto/If I Can Dream	1984	—	2.00	4.00
❏ PB-13891	That's All Right/Blue Moon of Kentucky	1984	—	2.00	4.00
—From box "Elvis' Greatest Hits, Golden Singles, Volume 2"; gold vinyl					
❏ PB-13891 [PS]	That's All Right/Blue Moon of Kentucky	1984	—	2.00	4.00
❏ PB-13892	Heartbreak Hotel/Jailhouse Rock	1984	—	2.00	4.00
—From box "Elvis' Greatest Hits, Golden Singles, Volume 2"; gold vinyl					
❏ PB-13892 [PS]	Heartbreak Hotel/Jailhouse Rock	1984	—	2.00	4.00
❏ PB-13893	Love Me Tender/Loving You	1984	—	2.00	4.00
—From box "Elvis' Greatest Hits, Golden Singles, Volume 2"; gold vinyl					
❏ PB-13893 [PS]	Love Me Tender/Loving You	1984	—	2.00	4.00
❏ PB-13894	(Marie's the Name) His Latest Flame/Little Sister	1984	—	2.00	4.00
—From box "Elvis' Greatest Hits, Golden Singles, Volume 2"; gold vinyl					
❏ PB-13894 [PS]	(Marie's the Name) His Latest Flame/Little Sister	1984	—	2.00	4.00
❏ PB-13895	Are You Lonesome Tonight?/Can't Help Falling in Love	1984	—	2.00	4.00
—From box "Elvis' Greatest Hits, Golden Singles, Volume 2"; gold vinyl					
❏ PB-13895 [PS]	Are You Lonesome Tonight?/Can't Help Falling in Love	1984	—	2.00	4.00
❏ PB-13896	Suspicious Minds/Burning Love	1984	—	2.00	4.00
—From box "Elvis' Greatest Hits, Golden Singles, Volume 2"; gold vinyl					
❏ PB-13896 [PS]	Suspicious Minds/Burning Love	1984	—	2.00	4.00
❏ PB-13897	Elvis' Greatest Hits, Golden Singles, Volume 1	1984	3.75	7.50	15.00
—Box set of six 45s with sleeves (13885-13890) with box					
❏ PB-13898	Elvis' Greatest Hits, Golden Singles, Volume 2	1984	3.75	7.50	15.00
—Box set of six 45s with sleeves (13891-13896) with box					
❏ PB-13929	Blue Suede Shoes/Promised Land	1984	3.00	6.00	12.00
—Blue vinyl; correct label -- "Blue Suede Shoes" side says "Mono" and "Promised Land" side says "Stereo"					
❏ PB-13929	Blue Suede Shoes/Promised Land	1984	3.75	7.50	15.00
—Blue vinyl; incorrect label -- "Blue Suede Shoes" side says "Stereo" and "Promised Land" side says "Mono"					
❏ PB-13929 [PS]	Blue Suede Shoes/Promised Land	1984	2.50	5.00	10.00
❏ PB-14090	Always on My Mind/My Boy	1985	2.50	5.00	10.00
—Purple vinyl					
❏ PB-14090 [PS]	Always on My Mind/My Boy	1985	2.50	5.00	10.00
❏ PB-14237	Merry Christmas Baby/Santa Claus Is Back in Town	1985	—	2.50	5.00
—Normal black RCA label					
❏ PB-14237	Merry Christmas Baby/Santa Claus Is Back in Town	1985	3.75	7.50	15.00
—"Elvis 50th Anniversary" label					
❏ PB-14237	Merry Christmas Baby/Santa Claus Is Back in Town	1985	3.75	7.50	15.00
—Green vinyl					
❏ PB-14237 [PS]	Merry Christmas Baby/Santa Claus Is Back in Town	1985	3.00	6.00	12.00
❏ 60575	A Little Less Conversation (JXL Radio Edit Remix)/(Original Version)	2002	2.00	4.00	8.00
—Credited to "Elvis Presley: Elvis vs JXL"					
❏ 62402	Don't Be Cruel/Ain't That Lovin' You Baby (Fast Version)	1992	—	2.50	5.00
❏ 62402 [PS]	Don't Be Cruel/Ain't That Lovin' You Baby (Fast Version)	1992	—	2.50	5.00
—Generic white sleeve with "Elvis -- The King of Rock 'n' Roll" sticker					
❏ 62403	Blue Christmas/Love Me Tender	1992	—	2.50	5.00
❏ 62403 [PS]	Blue Christmas/Love Me Tender	1992	—	2.50	5.00
—Generic white sleeve with "Elvis -- The King of Rock 'n' Roll" sticker					
❏ 62411	Silver Bells (Unreleased Version)/Silver Bells	1993	—	2.50	5.00
❏ 62449	Heartbreak Hotel/Hound Dog	1992	—	2.50	5.00
❏ 64476	Heartbreak Hotel/I Was the One//Heartbreak Hotel (Alternate Take 5)/I Was the One (Alternate Take 2)	1996	—	—	3.00
❏ 64476 [PS]	Heartbreak Hotel/I Was the One//Heartbreak Hotel (Alternate Take 5)/I Was the One (Alternate Take 2)	1996	—	—	3.00

RCA VICTOR

Number	Title (A Side/B Side)	Yr	VG	VG+	NM
❏ 37-7850	Surrender/Lonely Man	1961	150.00	300.00	600.00
—"Compact Single 33" (small hole, plays at LP speed)					
❏ 37-7850 [PS]	Surrender/Lonely Man	1961	250.00	500.00	1000.
—Special picture sleeve for above record					
❏ 37-7880	I Feel So Bad/Wild in the Country	1961	250.00	500.00	1000.
—"Compact Single 33" (small hole, plays at LP speed)					
❏ 37-7880 [PS]	I Feel So Bad/Wild in the Country	1961	300.00	600.00	1200.
—Special picture sleeve for above record					
❏ 37-7908	(Marie's the Name) His Latest Flame/Little Sister	1961	375.00	750.00	1500.
—"Compact Single 33" (small hole, plays at LP speed)					
❏ 37-7908 [PS]	(Marie's the Name) His Latest Flame/Little Sister	1961	1000.	1500.	2000.
—Special picture sleeve for above record					
❏ 37-7908 [PS]	(Marie's the Name) His Latest Flame/Little Sister	1961	1125.	1688.	2250.
—Special picture sleeve for above record; says "Stereo-Orthophonic" on sleeve in error					

Number	Title (A Side/B Side)	Yr	VG	VG+	NM
❏ 37-7968	Can't Help Falling in Love/Rock-a-Hula Baby	1961	1000.	1500.	2000.
—"Compact Single 33" (small hole, plays at LP speed)					
❏ 37-7968 [PS]	Can't Help Falling in Love/Rock-a-Hula Baby	1961	2000.	3000.	4000.
—Special picture sleeve for above record					
❏ 37-7992	Good Luck Charm/Anything That's Part of You	1962	1250.	1875.	2500.
—"Compact Single 33" (small hole, plays at LP speed)					
❏ 37-7992 [PS]	Good Luck Charm/Anything That's Part of You	1962	2500.	3750.	5000.
—Special picture sleeve for above record					
❏ 47-6357	I Forgot to Remember to Forget/Mystery Train	1955	15.00	30.00	60.00
—No horizontal line on label					
❏ 47-6357	I Forgot to Remember to Forget/Mystery Train	1955	15.00	30.00	60.00
—With horizontal line on label					
❏ 47-6357 [PS]	This Is His Life: Elvis Presley	1955	375.00	750.00	1500.
—Promo-only sleeve issued with above single; no stock picture sleeve was issued. This was formerly listed under "I Want You, I Need You, I Love You," as the sleeve does not have a number. Consensus opinion now places it with "Mystery Train."					
❏ 47-6380	That's All Right/Blue Moon of Kentucky	1955	15.00	30.00	60.00
—No horizontal line on label					
❏ 47-6380	That's All Right/Blue Moon of Kentucky	1955	15.00	30.00	60.00
—With horizontal line on label					
❏ 47-6381	Good Rockin' Tonight/I Don't Care If the Sun Don't Shine	1955	15.00	30.00	60.00
—No horizontal line on label					
❏ 47-6381	Good Rockin' Tonight/I Don't Care If the Sun Don't Shine	1955	15.00	30.00	60.00
—With horizontal line on label					
❏ 47-6382	Milkcow Blues Boogie/You're a Heartbreaker	1955	15.00	30.00	60.00
—No horizontal line on label					
❏ 47-6382	Milkcow Blues Boogie/You're a Heartbreaker	1955	15.00	30.00	60.00
—With horizontal line on label					
❏ 47-6383	Baby Let's Play House/I'm Left, You're Right, She's Gone	1955	15.00	30.00	60.00
—No horizontal line on label					
❏ 47-6383	Baby Let's Play House/I'm Left, You're Right, She's Gone	1955	15.00	30.00	60.00
—With horizontal line on label					
❏ 47-6420	Heartbreak Hotel/I Was the One	1956	10.00	20.00	40.00
—No horizontal line on label					
❏ 47-6420	Heartbreak Hotel/I Was the One	1956	10.00	20.00	40.00
—With horizontal line on label					
❏ 47-6540	I Want You, I Need You, I Love You/My Baby Left Me	1956	10.00	20.00	40.00
—No horizontal line on label					
❏ 47-6540	I Want You, I Need You, I Love You/My Baby Left Me	1956	10.00	20.00	40.00
—With horizontal line on label					
❏ 47-6604	Don't Be Cruel/Hound Dog	1956	7.50	15.00	30.00
—No horizontal line on label					
❏ 47-6604	Don't Be Cruel/Hound Dog	1956	7.50	15.00	30.00
—With horizontal line on label					
❏ 47-6604 [PS]	Don't Be Cruel/Hound Dog	1956	30.00	60.00	120.00
—"Hound Dog!" listed on top of "Don't Be Cruel"					
❏ 47-6604 [PS]	Don't Be Cruel/Hound Dog	1956	50.00	100.00	200.00
—"Don't Be Cruel" listed on top of "Hound Dog!"					
❏ 47-6636	Blue Suede Shoes/Tutti Frutti	1956	20.00	40.00	80.00
—No horizontal line on label					
❏ 47-6636	Blue Suede Shoes/Tutti Frutti	1956	20.00	40.00	80.00
—With horizontal line on label					
❏ 47-6637	I Got a Woman/I'm Countin' On You	1956	20.00	40.00	80.00
—No horizontal line on label					
❏ 47-6637	I Got a Woman/I'm Countin' On You	1956	20.00	40.00	80.00
—With horizontal line on label					
❏ 47-6638	I'm Gonna Sit Right Down and Cry (Over You)/I'll Never Let You Go (Little Darlin')	1956	17.50	35.00	70.00
—No horizontal line on label					
❏ 47-6638	I'm Gonna Sit Right Down and Cry (Over You)/I'll Never Let You Go (Little Darlin')	1956	17.50	35.00	70.00
—With horizontal line on label					
❏ 47-6639	Tryin' to Get to You/I Love You Because	1956	17.50	35.00	70.00
—No horizontal line on label					
❏ 47-6639	Tryin' to Get to You/I Love You Because	1956	17.50	35.00	70.00
—With horizontal line on label					
❏ 47-6640	Blue Moon/Just Because	1956	15.00	30.00	60.00
—No horizontal line on label					
❏ 47-6640	Blue Moon/Just Because	1956	15.00	30.00	60.00
—With horizontal line on label					
❏ 47-6641	Money Honey/One-Sided Love Affair	1956	12.50	25.00	50.00
—No horizontal line on label					
❏ 47-6641	Money Honey/One-Sided Love Affair	1956	12.50	25.00	50.00
—With horizontal line on label					
❏ 47-6642	Lawdy Miss Clawdy/Shake, Rattle, and Roll	1956	10.00	20.00	40.00
—No horizontal line on label					
❏ 47-6642	Lawdy Miss Clawdy/Shake, Rattle, and Roll	1956	10.00	20.00	40.00
—With horizontal line on label, dog on label as usual					
❏ 47-6642	Lawdy Miss Clawdy/Shake, Rattle, and Roll	1956	50.00	100.00	200.00
—With horizontal line on label, but with no dog					
❏ 47-6643	Love Me Tender/Anyway You Want Me (That's How I Will Be)	1956	7.50	15.00	30.00
—No horizontal line on label					
❏ 47-6643	Love Me Tender/Anyway You Want Me (That's How I Will Be)	1956	7.50	15.00	30:00
—With horizontal line on label					
❏ 47-6643	Love Me Tender/Anyway You Want Me (That's How I Will Be)	1956	10.00	20.00	40.00
—No reference to the movie "Love Me Tender" on label					
❏ 47-6643 [PS]	Love Me Tender/Anyway You Want Me (That's How I Will Be)	1956	7.50	15.00	30.00
—Black and light pink sleeve					
❏ 47-6643 [PS]	Love Me Tender/Anyway You Want Me (That's How I Will Be)	1956	10.00	20.00	40.00
—Black and dark pink sleeve					
❏ 47-6643 [PS]	Love Me Tender/Anyway You Want Me (That's How I Will Be)	1956	18.75	37.50	75.00
—Black and green sleeve					
❏ 47-6643 [PS]	Love Me Tender/Anyway You Want Me (That's How I Will Be)	1956	45.00	90.00	180.00
—Black and white sleeve					

Number	Title (A Side/B Side)	Yr	VG	VG+	NM
47-6800	Too Much/Playing for Keeps	1957	7.50	15.00	30.00

—No horizontal line on label

Number	Title (A Side/B Side)	Yr	VG	VG+	NM
47-6800	Too Much/Playing for Keeps	1957	7.50	15.00	30.00

—With horizontal line on label, dog on label as normal

| 47-6800 | Too Much/Playing for Keeps | 1957 | 50.00 | 100.00 | 200.00 |

—With horizontal line on label, but with no dog

| 47-6800 [PS] | Too Much/Playing for Keeps | 1957 | 22.50 | 45.00 | 90.00 |
| 47-6870 | All Shook Up/That's When Your Heartaches Begin | 1957 | 7.50 | 15.00 | 30.00 |

—No horizontal line on label

| 47-6870 | All Shook Up/That's When Your Heartaches Begin | 1957 | 7.50 | 15.00 | 30.00 |

—With horizontal line on label

| 47-6870 [PS] | All Shook Up/That's When Your Heartaches Begin | 1957 | 22.50 | 45.00 | 90.00 |
| 47-7000 | (Let Me Be Your) Teddy Bear/Loving You | 1957 | 7.50 | 15.00 | 30.00 |

—Parentheses around "Let Me Be Your", no horizontal line on label

| 47-7000 | (Let Me Be Your) Teddy Bear/Loving You | 1957 | 7.50 | 15.00 | 30.00 |

—Parentheses around "Let Me Be Your", with horizontal line on label

| 47-7000 | (Let Me Be Your) Teddy Bear/Loving You | 1957 | 10.00 | 20.00 | 40.00 |

—Label says "Let Me Be Your TEDDY BEAR" (no parentheses)

| 47-7000 [PS] | (Let Me Be Your) Teddy Bear/Loving You | 1957 | 30.00 | 60.00 | 120.00 |
| 47-7035 | Jailhouse Rock/Treat Me Nice | 1957 | 7.50 | 15.00 | 30.00 |

—No horizontal line on label

| 47-7035 | Jailhouse Rock/Treat Me Nice | 1957 | 7.50 | 15.00 | 30.00 |

—With horizontal line on label

| 47-7035 | Jailhouse Rock/Treat Me Nice | 1957 | 5000. | 7500. | 10000. |

—Gold label; gold vinyl

| 47-7035 [PS] | Jailhouse Rock/Treat Me Nice | 1957 | 25.00 | 50.00 | 100.00 |
| 47-7150 | Don't/I Beg of You | 1958 | 6.25 | 12.50 | 25.00 |

—No horizontal line on label

| 47-7150 | Don't/I Beg of You | 1958 | 6.25 | 12.50 | 25.00 |

—With horizontal line on label

47-7150 [PS]	Don't/I Beg of You	1958	22.50	45.00	90.00
47-7240	Wear My Ring Around Your Neck/Don'tcha Think It's Time	1958	6.25	12.50	25.00
47-7240 [PS]	Wear My Ring Around Your Neck/Don'tcha Think It's Time	1958	22.50	45.00	90.00
47-7280	Hard Headed Woman/Don't Ask Me Why	1958	6.25	12.50	25.00
47-7280 [PS]	Hard Headed Woman/Don't Ask Me Why	1958	17.50	35.00	70.00
47-7410	One Night/I Got Stung	1958	6.25	12.50	25.00
47-7410 [PS]	One Night/I Got Stung	1958	17.50	35.00	70.00
47-7506	(Now and Then There's) A Fool Such As I/I Need Your Love Tonight	1959	6.25	12.50	25.00
47-7506 [PS]	(Now and Then There's) A Fool Such As I/I Need Your Love Tonight	1959	15.00	30.00	60.00

—Sleeve lists Elvis' EPs and Gold Standard singles

| 47-7506 [PS] | (Now and Then There's) A Fool Such As I/I Need Your Love Tonight | 1959 | 250.00 | 500.00 | 1000. |

—Sleeve promotes the "Elvis Sails" EP

47-7600	A Big Hunk o'Love/My Wish Came True	1959	6.25	12.50	25.00
47-7600 [PS]	A Big Hunk o'Love/My Wish Came True	1959	17.50	35.00	70.00
47-7740	Stuck on You/Fame and Fortune	1960	5.00	10.00	20.00
47-7740 [PS]	Stuck on You/Fame and Fortune	1960	15.00	30.00	60.00
47-7777	It's Now or Never/A Mess of Blues	1960	5.00	10.00	20.00

—All other pressings with overdubbed piano

| 47-7777 | It's Now or Never/A Mess of Blues | 1960 | 250.00 | 500.00 | 1000. |

—An early mispress is missing the piano part on the A-side. Has the number "L2WW-0100-3S" or "L2WW-0100-4S" in trail-off wax.

47-7777 [PS]	It's Now or Never/A Mess of Blues	1960	15.00	30.00	60.00
47-7810	Are You Lonesome To-Night?/I Gotta Know	1960	5.00	10.00	20.00
47-7810 [PS]	Are You Lonesome To-Night?/I Gotta Know	1960	15.00	30.00	60.00
47-7850	Surrender/Lonely Man	1961	5.00	10.00	20.00
47-7850 [PS]	Surrender/Lonely Man	1961	15.00	30.00	60.00
47-7880	I Feel So Bad/Wild in the Country	1961	5.00	10.00	20.00
47-7880 [PS]	I Feel So Bad/Wild in the Country	1961	12.50	25.00	50.00
47-7908	(Marie's the Name) His Latest Flame/Little Sister	1961			

—All copies of this record actually read "Marie's the Name HIS LATEST FLAME" (no parentheses)

47-7908 [PS]	(Marie's the Name) His Latest Flame/Little Sister	1961	12.50	25.00	50.00
47-7968	Can't Help Falling in Love/Rock-a-Hula Baby	1961	5.00	10.00	20.00
47-7968 [PS]	Can't Help Falling in Love/Rock-a-Hula Baby	1961	10.00	20.00	40.00
47-7992	Good Luck Charm/Anything That's Part of You	1962	5.00	10.00	20.00
47-7992 [PS]	Good Luck Charm/Anything That's Part of You	1962	10.00	20.00	40.00

—Titles in blue and pink letters

| 47-7992 [PS] | Good Luck Charm/Anything That's Part of You | 1962 | 10.00 | 20.00 | 40.00 |

—Titles in rust and lavender letters

47-8041	She's Not You/Just Tell Her Jim Said Hello	1962	5.00	10.00	20.00
47-8041 [PS]	She's Not You/Just Tell Her Jim Said Hello	1962	10.00	20.00	40.00
47-8100	Return to Sender/Where Do You Come From	1962	5.00	10.00	20.00
47-8100 [PS]	Return to Sender/Where Do You Come From	1962	10.00	20.00	40.00
47-8134	One Broken Heart for Sale/They Remind Me Too Much of You	1963	3.00	6.00	12.00
47-8134 [PS]	One Broken Heart for Sale/They Remind Me Too Much of You	1963	7.50	15.00	30.00
47-8188	(You're the) Devil in Disguise/Please Don't Drag That String Around	1963	3.00	6.00	12.00

—Second pressing with correct B-side title

| 47-8188 | (You're the) Devil in Disguise/Please Don't Drag That String Along | 1963 | 50.00 | 100.00 | 200.00 |

—First pressing with incorrect B-side title

| 47-8188 [PS] | (You're the) Devil in Disguise/Please Don't Drag That String Around | 1963 | 7.50 | 15.00 | 30.00 |

—All sleeves have correct B-side title

| 47-8243 | Bossa Nova Baby/Witchcraft | 1963 | 3.00 | 6.00 | 12.00 |
| 47-8243 [PS] | Bossa Nova Baby/Witchcraft | 1963 | 7.50 | 15.00 | 30.00 |

—"Ask For" on sleeve

| 47-8243 [PS] | Bossa Nova Baby/Witchcraft | 1963 | 7.50 | 15.00 | 30.00 |

—"Coming Soon" on sleeve

| 47-8243 [PS] | Bossa Nova Baby/Witchcraft | 1963 | 7.50 | 15.00 | 30.00 |

—No reference to another album on sleeve

47-8307	Kissin' Cousins/It Hurts Me	1964	3.00	6.00	12.00
47-8307 [PS]	Kissin' Cousins/It Hurts Me	1964	6.25	12.50	25.00
47-8360	Viva Las Vegas/What'd I Say	1964	3.00	6.00	12.00
47-8360 [PS]	Viva Las Vegas/What'd I Say	1964	6.25	12.50	25.00

—"Coming Soon" on sleeve

| 47-8360 [PS] | Viva Las Vegas/What'd I Say | 1964 | 12.50 | 25.00 | 50.00 |

—"Ask For" on sleeve

| 47-8400 | Such a Night/Never Ending | 1964 | 3.00 | 6.00 | 12.00 |
| 47-8400 [DJ] | Such a Night/Never Ending | 1964 | 2500. | 3750. | 5000. |

—An inexplicably rare regular white label promo

47-8400 [PS]	Such a Night/Never Ending	1964	6.25	12.50	25.00
47-8440	Ain't That Loving You Baby/Ask Me	1964	2.50	5.00	10.00
47-8440 [PS]	Ain't That Loving You Baby/Ask Me	1964	6.25	12.50	25.00

—"Ask For" on sleeve

| 47-8440 [PS] | Ain't That Loving You Baby/Ask Me | 1964 | 6.25 | 12.50 | 25.00 |

—"Coming Soon" on sleeve

47-8500	Do the Clam/You'll Be Gone	1965	2.50	5.00	10.00
47-8500 [PS]	Do the Clam/You'll Be Gone	1965	6.25	12.50	25.00
47-8585	(Such An) Easy Question/It Feels So Right	1965	2.50	5.00	10.00
47-8585 [PS]	(Such An) Easy Question/It Feels So Right	1965	6.25	12.50	25.00

—"Ask For" on sleeve

| 47-8585 [PS] | (Such An) Easy Question/It Feels So Right | 1965 | 6.25 | 12.50 | 25.00 |

—"Coming Soon" on sleeve

47-8657	I'm Yours/(It's a) Long, Lonely Highway	1965	2.50	5.00	10.00
47-8657 [PS]	I'm Yours/(It's a) Long, Lonely Highway	1965	6.25	12.50	25.00
47-8740	Tell Me Why/Blue River	1965	2.50	5.00	10.00
47-8740 [PS]	Tell Me Why/Blue River	1965	6.25	12.50	25.00
47-8780	Frankie and Johnny/Please Don't Stop Loving Me	1966	2.50	5.00	10.00
47-8780 [PS]	Frankie and Johnny/Please Don't Stop Loving Me	1966	6.25	12.50	25.00
47-8870	Love Letters/Come What May	1966	2.50	5.00	10.00
47-8870 [PS]	Love Letters/Come What May	1966	6.25	12.50	25.00

—"Ask For" on sleeve

| 47-8870 [PS] | Love Letters/Come What May | 1966 | 6.25 | 12.50 | 25.00 |

—"Coming Soon" on sleeve

| 47-8941 | Spinout/All That I Am | 1966 | 2.50 | 5.00 | 10.00 |
| 47-8941 [PS] | Spinout/All That I Am | 1966 | 6.25 | 12.50 | 25.00 |

—"Ask For" on sleeve

| 47-8941 [PS] | Spinout/All That I Am | 1966 | 6.25 | 12.50 | 25.00 |

—"Watch For" on sleeve

47-8950	If Every Day Was Like Christmas/How Would You Like to Be	1966	5.00	10.00	20.00
47-8950 [PS]	If Every Day Was Like Christmas/How Would You Like to Be	1966	10.00	20.00	40.00
47-9056	Indescribably Blue/Fools Fall in Love	1966	2.50	5.00	10.00
47-9056 [PS]	Indescribably Blue/Fools Fall in Love	1966	6.25	12.50	25.00
47-9115	Long Legged Girl (With the Short Dress On)/That's Someone You Never Forget	1967	2.50	5.00	10.00
47-9115 [PS]	Long Legged Girl (With the Short Dress On)/That's Someone You Never Forget	1967	6.25	12.50	25.00

—"Ask For" on sleeve

| 47-9115 [PS] | Long Legged Girl (With the Short Dress On)/That's Someone You Never Forget | 1967 | 6.25 | 12.50 | 25.00 |

—"Coming Soon" on sleeve

47-9287	There's Always Me/Judy	1967	2.50	5.00	10.00
47-9287 [PS]	There's Always Me/Judy	1967	6.25	12.50	25.00
47-9341	Big Boss Man/You Don't Know Me	1967	2.50	5.00	10.00
47-9341 [PS]	Big Boss Man/You Don't Know Me	1967	6.25	12.50	25.00
47-9425	Guitar Man/High Heel Sneakers	1968	2.50	5.00	10.00
47-9425 [PS]	Guitar Man/High Heel Sneakers	1968	6.25	12.50	25.00

—"Ask For" on sleeve

| 47-9425 [PS] | Guitar Man/High Heel Sneakers | 1968 | 6.25 | 12.50 | 25.00 |

—"Coming Soon" on sleeve

47-9465	U.S. Male/Stay Away	1968	2.50	5.00	10.00
47-9465 [PS]	U.S. Male/Stay Away	1968	6.25	12.50	25.00
47-9547	Let Yourself Go/Your Time Hasn't Come Yet, Baby	1968	2.50	5.00	10.00
47-9547 [PS]	Let Yourself Go/Your Time Hasn't Come Yet, Baby	1968	6.25	12.50	25.00

—"Ask For" on sleeve

| 47-9547 [PS] | Let Yourself Go/Your Time Hasn't Come Yet, Baby | 1968 | 6.25 | 12.50 | 25.00 |

—"Coming Soon" on sleeve

47-9600	You'll Never Walk Alone/We Call on Him	1968	3.00	6.00	12.00
47-9600 [PS]	You'll Never Walk Alone/We Call on Him	1968	25.00	50.00	100.00
47-9610	A Little Less Conversation/Almost in Love	1968	2.50	5.00	10.00
47-9610 [PS]	A Little Less Conversation/Almost in Love	1968	6.25	12.50	25.00
47-9670	If I Can Dream/Edge of Reality	1968	2.00	4.00	8.00

—First Elvis single on orange label

| 47-9670 [PS] | If I Can Dream/Edge of Reality | 1968 | 5.00 | 10.00 | 20.00 |

—Does not mention his NBC-TV special on sleeve

| 47-9670 [PS] | If I Can Dream/Edge of Reality | 1968 | 5.00 | 10.00 | 20.00 |

—Mentions his NBC-TV special on sleeve

47-9731	Memories/Charro	1969	2.00	4.00	8.00
47-9731 [PS]	Memories/Charro	1969	5.00	10.00	20.00
47-9741	In the Ghetto/Any Day Now	1969	2.00	4.00	8.00
47-9741 [PS]	In the Ghetto/Any Day Now	1969	5.00	10.00	20.00

—"Ask For" on sleeve

| 47-9741 [PS] | In the Ghetto/Any Day Now | 1969 | 5.00 | 10.00 | 20.00 |

—"Coming Soon" on sleeve

47-9747	Clean Up Your Own Back Yard/The Fair Is Moving On	1969	2.00	4.00	8.00
47-9747 [PS]	Clean Up Your Own Back Yard/The Fair Is Moving On	1969	5.00	10.00	20.00
47-9764	Suspicious Minds/You'll Think of Me	1969	2.00	4.00	8.00
47-9764 [PS]	Suspicious Minds/You'll Think of Me	1969	5.00	10.00	20.00
47-9768	Don't Cry Daddy/Rubberneckin'	1969	2.00	4.00	8.00
47-9768 [PS]	Don't Cry Daddy/Rubberneckin'	1969	3.75	7.50	15.00
47-9791	Kentucky Rain/My Little Friend	1969	2.00	4.00	8.00
47-9791 [PS]	Kentucky Rain/My Little Friend	1969	3.75	7.50	15.00
47-9835	The Wonder of You/Mama Liked the Roses	1970	2.00	4.00	8.00
47-9835 [PS]	The Wonder of You/Mama Liked the Roses	1970	3.75	7.50	15.00
47-9873	I've Lost You/The Next Step Is Love	1970	—	3.00	6.00
47-9873 [PS]	I've Lost You/The Next Step Is Love	1970	3.75	7.50	15.00
47-9916	You Don't Have to Say You Love Me/Patch It Up	1970	—	3.00	6.00
47-9916 [PS]	You Don't Have to Say You Love Me/Patch It Up	1970	3.75	7.50	15.00
47-9960	I Really Don't Want to Know/There Goes My Everything	1971	—	3.00	6.00
47-9960 [PS]	I Really Don't Want to Know/There Goes My Everything	1971	3.75	7.50	15.00

—"Ask For" on sleeve

Number	Title (A Side/B Side)	Yr	VG	VG+	NM
47-9960 [PS]	I Really Don't Want to Know/There Goes My Everything	1971	3.75	7.50	15.00
—"Coming Soon" on sleeve					
47-9980	Where Did They Go, Lord/Rags to Riches	1971	—	3.00	6.00
47-9980 [PS]	Where Did They Go, Lord/Rags to Riches	1971	5.00	10.00	20.00
47-9985	Life/Only Believe	1971	—	3.00	6.00
47-9985 [PS]	Life/Only Believe	1971	7.50	15.00	30.00
47-9998	I'm Leavin'/Heart of Rome	1971	—	3.00	6.00
47-9998 [PS]	I'm Leavin'/Heart of Rome	1971	5.00	10.00	20.00
48-1017	It's Only Love/The Sound of Your Cry	1971	—	3.00	6.00
48-1017 [PS]	It's Only Love/The Sound of Your Cry	1971	3.75	7.50	15.00
61-7740 [S]	Stuck on You/Fame and Fortune	1960	100.00	200.00	400.00
—"Living Stereo" (large hole, plays at 45 rpm)					
61-7777 [S]	It's Now or Never/A Mess of Blues	1960	100.00	200.00	400.00
—"Living Stereo" (large hole, plays at 45 rpm)					
61-7810 [S]	Are You Lonesome To-Night?/I Gotta Know	1960	150.00	300.00	600.00
—"Living Stereo" (large hole, plays at 45 rpm)					
61-7850 [S]	Surrender/Lonely Man	1961	200.00	400.00	800.00
—"Living Stereo" (large hole, plays at 45 rpm)					
68-7850 [S]	Surrender/Lonely Man	1961	1000.	1500.	2000.
—"Compact Stereo 33" in "Living Stereo"					
74-0130	How Great Thou Art/His Hand in Mine	1969	6.25	12.50	25.00
74-0130 [PS]	How Great Thou Art/His Hand in Mine	1969	37.50	75.00	150.00
74-0572	Merry Christmas Baby/O Come All Ye Faithful	1971	3.75	7.50	15.00
74-0572 [PS]	Merry Christmas Baby/O Come All Ye Faithful	1971	10.00	20.00	40.00
74-0619	Until It's Time for You to Go/We Can Make the Morning	1971	—	3.00	6.00
74-0619 [PS]	Until It's Time for You to Go/We Can Make the Morning	1971	3.75	7.50	15.00
74-0651	He Touched Me/The Bosom of Abraham	1972	2.00	4.00	8.00
—"He Touched Me" plays correctly. A-side has "APKS-1277" stamped in trail-off wax.					
74-0651	He Touched Me/The Bosom of Abraham	1972	37.50	75.00	150.00
—"He Touched Me" actually plays at about 35 rpm in error. A-side has "AWKS-1277" stamped in trail-off wax.					
74-0651 [PS]	He Touched Me/The Bosom of Abraham	1972	30.00	60.00	120.00
74-0672	An American Trilogy/The First Time Ever I Saw Your Face	1972	5.00	10.00	20.00
74-0672 [PS]	An American Trilogy/The First Time Ever I Saw Your Face	1972	10.00	20.00	40.00
74-0769	Burning Love/It's a Matter of Time	1972	—	3.00	6.00
—Originals have orange labels					
74-0769 [PS]	Burning Love/It's a Matter of Time	1972	3.75	7.50	15.00
74-0769	Burning Love/It's a Matter of Time	1974	37.50	75.00	150.00
—Very rare reissues have gray labels					
74-0815	Separate Ways/Always on My Mind	1972	—	3.00	6.00
74-0815 [PS]	Separate Ways/Always on My Mind	1972	3.75	7.50	15.00
74-0910	Steamroller Blues/Fool	1973	—	3.00	6.00
74-0910 [PS]	Steamroller Blues/Fool	1973	3.75	7.50	15.00
447-0600	I Forgot to Remember to Forget/Mystery Train	1959	3.75	7.50	15.00
—Note: All RCA Victor releases with a "447" prefix are from the Gold Standard Series. Black label, dog on top					
447-0600	I Forgot to Remember to Forget/Mystery Train	1965	2.50	5.00	10.00
—Black label, dog on left					
447-0600	I Forgot to Remember to Forget/Mystery Train	1969	6.25	12.50	25.00
—Orange label					
447-0600	I Forgot to Remember to Forget/Mystery Train	1970	2.00	4.00	8.00
—Red label					
447-0601	That's All Right/Blue Moon of Kentucky	1959	3.75	7.50	15.00
—Black label, dog on top					
447-0601 [DJ]	That's All Right/Blue Moon of Kentucky	1964	25.00	50.00	100.00
447-0601 [PS]	That's All Right/Blue Moon of Kentucky	1964	50.00	100.00	200.00
447-0601	That's All Right/Blue Moon of Kentucky	1965	2.50	5.00	10.00
—Black label, dog on left					
447-0601	That's All Right/Blue Moon of Kentucky	1969	2.00	4.00	8.00
—Red label; B-side artist credit is misspelled "Elvis Presely"					
447-0602	Good Rockin' Tonight/I Don't Care If the Sun Don't Shine	1959	3.75	7.50	15.00
—Black label, dog on top					
447-0602	Good Rockin' Tonight/I Don't Care If the Sun Don't Shine	1959	2000.	4000.	6000.
—One-of-a-kind red vinyl pressing					
447-0602 [DJ]	Good Rockin' Tonight/I Don't Care If the Sun Don't Shine	1964	25.00	50.00	100.00
447-0602 [PS]	Good Rockin' Tonight/I Don't Care If the Sun Don't Shine	1964	50.00	100.00	200.00
447-0602	Good Rockin' Tonight/I Don't Care If the Sun Don't Shine	1965	2.50	5.00	10.00
—Black label, dog on left					
447-0602	Good Rockin' Tonight/I Don't Care If the Sun Don't Shine	1970	2.00	4.00	8.00
—Red label					
447-0603	Milkcow Blues Boogie/You're a Heartbreaker	1959	3.75	7.50	15.00
—Black label, dog on top					
447-0603	Milkcow Blues Boogie/You're a Heartbreaker	1965	2.50	5.00	10.00
—Black label, dog on left					
447-0603	Milkcow Blues Boogie/You're a Heartbreaker	1969	6.25	12.50	25.00
—Orange label					
447-0603	Milkcow Blues Boogie/You're a Heartbreaker	1970	2.00	4.00	8.00
—Red label					
447-0604	Baby Let's Play House/I'm Left, You're Right, She's Gone	1959	3.75	7.50	15.00
—Black label, dog on top					
447-0604	Baby Let's Play House/I'm Left, You're Right, She's Gone	1965	2.50	5.00	10.00
—Black label, dog on left					
447-0604	Baby Let's Play House/I'm Left, You're Right, She's Gone	1970	2.00	4.00	8.00
—Red label					
447-0605	Heartbreak Hotel/I Was the One	1959	3.75	7.50	15.00
—Black label, dog on top					
447-0605 [DJ]	Heartbreak Hotel/I Was the One	1964	25.00	50.00	100.00
447-0605 [PS]	Heartbreak Hotel/I Was the One	1964	50.00	100.00	200.00
447-0605	Heartbreak Hotel/I Was the One	1965	2.50	5.00	10.00
—Black label, dog on left					
447-0605	Heartbreak Hotel/I Was the One	1969	6.25	12.50	25.00
—Orange label					
447-0605	Heartbreak Hotel/I Was the One	1970	2.00	4.00	8.00
—Red label					
447-0607	I Want You, I Need You, I Love You/My Baby Left Me	1959	3.75	7.50	15.00
—Black label, dog on top					
447-0607	I Want You, I Need You, I Love You/My Baby Left Me	1965	2.50	5.00	10.00
—Black label, dog on left					
447-0607	I Want You, I Need You, I Love You/My Baby Left Me	1969	6.25	12.50	25.00
—Orange label					
447-0607	I Want You, I Need You, I Love You/My Baby Left Me	1970	2.00	4.00	8.00
—Red label					
447-0608	Hound Dog/Don't Be Cruel	1959	3.75	7.50	15.00
—Black label, dog on top					
447-0608 [DJ]	Hound Dog/Don't Be Cruel	1964	25.00	50.00	100.00
447-0608 [PS]	Hound Dog/Don't Be Cruel	1964	50.00	100.00	200.00
447-0608	Hound Dog/Don't Be Cruel	1965	2.50	5.00	10.00
—Black label, dog on left					
447-0608	Hound Dog/Don't Be Cruel	1969	6.25	12.50	25.00
—Orange label					
447-0608	Hound Dog/Don't Be Cruel	1970	2.00	4.00	8.00
—Red label					
447-0609	Blue Suede Shoes/Tutti Frutti	1959	3.75	7.50	15.00
—Black label, dog on top					
447-0609	Blue Suede Shoes/Tutti Frutti	1965	2.50	5.00	10.00
—Black label, dog on left					
447-0609	Blue Suede Shoes/Tutti Frutti	1969	6.25	12.50	25.00
—Orange label					
447-0609	Blue Suede Shoes/Tutti Frutti	1970	2.00	4.00	8.00
—Red label					
447-0610	I Got a Woman/I'm Countin' On You	1959	3.75	7.50	15.00
—Black label, dog on top					
447-0611	I'm Gonna Sit Right Down and Cry (Over You)/I'll Never Let You Go (Little Darlin')	1959	3.75	7.50	15.00
—Black label, dog on top					
447-0612	Tryin' to Get to You/I Love You Because	1959	3.75	7.50	15.00
—Black label, dog on top					
447-0613	Blue Moon/Just Because	1959	3.75	7.50	15.00
—Black label, dog on top					
447-0613	Blue Moon/Just Because	1965	2.50	5.00	10.00
—Black label, dog on left					
447-0613	Blue Moon/Just Because	1969	6.25	12.50	25.00
—Orange label					
447-0613	Blue Moon/Just Because	1970	2.00	4.00	8.00
—Red label					
447-0614	Money Honey/One-Sided Love Affair	1959	3.75	7.50	15.00
—Black label, dog on top					
447-0614	Money Honey/One-Sided Love Affair	1965	2.50	5.00	10.00
—Black label, dog on left					
447-0614	Money Honey/One-Sided Love Affair	1969	6.25	12.50	25.00
—Orange label					
447-0614	Money Honey/One-Sided Love Affair	1970	2.00	4.00	8.00
—Red label					
447-0615	Lawdy Miss Clawdy/Shake, Rattle, and Roll	1959	3.75	7.50	15.00
—Black label, dog on top					
447-0615	Lawdy Miss Clawdy/Shake, Rattle, and Roll	1965	2.50	5.00	10.00
—Black label, dog on left					
447-0615	Lawdy Miss Clawdy/Shake, Rattle, and Roll	1969	6.25	12.50	25.00
—Orange label					
447-0615	Lawdy Miss Clawdy/Shake, Rattle, and Roll	1970	2.00	4.00	8.00
—Red label					
447-0616	Love Me Tender/Anyway You Want Me (That's How I Will Be)	1959	3.75	7.50	15.00
—Black label, dog on top					
447-0616	Love Me Tender/Anyway You Want Me (That's How I Will Be)	1965	2.50	5.00	10.00
—Black label, dog on left					
447-0616	Love Me Tender/Anyway You Want Me (That's How I Will Be)	1969	6.25	12.50	25.00
—Orange label					
447-0616	Love Me Tender/Anyway You Want Me (That's How I Will Be)	1970	2.00	4.00	8.00
—Red label					
447-0617	Too Much/Playing for Keeps	1959	3.75	7.50	15.00
—Black label, dog on top					
447-0617	Too Much/Playing for Keeps	1965	2.50	5.00	10.00
—Black label, dog on left					
447-0617	Too Much/Playing for Keeps	1969	6.25	12.50	25.00
—Orange label					
447-0617	Too Much/Playing for Keeps	1970	2.00	4.00	8.00
—Red label					
447-0618	All Shook Up/That's When Your Heartaches Begin	1959	3.75	7.50	15.00
—Black label, dog on top					
447-0618 [DJ]	All Shook Up/That's When Your Heartaches Begin	1964	25.00	50.00	100.00
447-0618 [PS]	All Shook Up/That's When Your Heartaches Begin	1964	50.00	100.00	200.00
447-0618	All Shook Up/That's When Your Heartaches Begin	1965	2.50	5.00	10.00
—Black label, dog on left					
447-0618	All Shook Up/That's When Your Heartaches Begin	1969	6.25	12.50	25.00
—Orange label					
447-0618	All Shook Up/That's When Your Heartaches Begin	1970	2.00	4.00	8.00
—Red label					
447-0619	Jailhouse Rock/Treat Me Nice	1959	3.75	7.50	15.00
—Black label, dog on top					
447-0619	Jailhouse Rock/Treat Me Nice	1965	2.50	5.00	10.00
—Black label, dog on left					
447-0619	Jailhouse Rock/Treat Me Nice	1969	6.25	12.50	25.00
—Orange label					
447-0619	Jailhouse Rock/Treat Me Nice	1970	2.00	4.00	8.00
—Red label					

P

Number	Title (A Side/B Side)	Yr	VG	VG+	NM
❑ 447-0620	(Let Me Be Your) Teddy Bear/Loving You	1959	3.75	7.50	15.00
—Black label, dog on top					
❑ 447-0620	(Let Me Be Your) Teddy Bear/Loving You	1965	2.50	5.00	10.00
—Black label, dog on left					
❑ 447-0620	(Let Me Be Your) Teddy Bear/Loving You	1969	6.25	12.50	25.00
—Orange label					
❑ 447-0620	(Let Me Be Your) Teddy Bear/Loving You	1970	2.00	4.00	8.00
—Red label					
❑ 447-0621	Don't/I Beg of You	1961	3.00	6.00	12.00
—Black label, dog on top					
❑ 447-0621	Don't/I Beg of You	1965	2.50	5.00	10.00
—Black label, dog on left					
❑ 447-0621	Don't/I Beg of You	1969	6.25	12.50	25.00
—Orange label					
❑ 447-0621	Don't/I Beg of You	1970	2.00	4.00	8.00
—Red label					
❑ 447-0622	Wear My Ring Around Your Neck/Don'tcha Think It's Time	1961	3.00	6.00	12.00
—Black label, dog on top					
❑ 447-0622	Wear My Ring Around Your Neck/Don'tcha Think It's Time	1965	2.50	5.00	10.00
—Black label, dog on left					
❑ 447-0622	Wear My Ring Around Your Neck/Don'tcha Think It's Time	1969	6.25	12.50	25.00
—Orange label					
❑ 447-0622	Wear My Ring Around Your Neck/Don'tcha Think It's Time	1970	2.00	4.00	8.00
—Red label					
❑ 447-0623	Hard Headed Woman/Don't Ask Me Why	1961	3.75	7.50	15.00
—Black label, dog on top					
❑ 447-0623	Hard Headed Woman/Don't Ask Me Why	1965	2.50	5.00	10.00
—Black label, dog on left					
❑ 447-0623	Hard Headed Woman/Don't Ask Me Why	1969	6.25	12.50	25.00
—Orange label					
❑ 447-0623	Hard Headed Woman/Don't Ask Me Why	1970	2.00	4.00	8.00
—Red label					
❑ 447-0624	One Night/I Got Stung	1961	3.00	6.00	12.00
—Black label, dog on top					
❑ 447-0624	One Night/I Got Stung	1965	2.50	5.00	10.00
—Black label, dog on left					
❑ 447-0624	One Night/I Got Stung	1969	6.25	12.50	25.00
—Orange label					
❑ 447-0624	One Night/I Got Stung	1970	2.00	4.00	8.00
—Red label					
❑ 447-0625	(Now and Then There's) A Fool Such As I/I Need Your Love Tonight	1961	3.75	7.50	15.00
—Black label, dog on top					
❑ 447-0625	(Now and Then There's) A Fool Such As I/I Need Your Love Tonight	1965	2.50	5.00	10.00
—Black label, dog on left					
❑ 447-0625	(Now and Then There's) A Fool Such As I/I Need Your Love Tonight	1969	6.25	12.50	25.00
—Orange label					
❑ 447-0625	(Now and Then There's) A Fool Such As I/I Need Your Love Tonight	1970	2.00	4.00	8.00
—Red label					
❑ 447-0626	A Big Hunk o'Love/My Wish Came True	1962	3.75	7.50	15.00
—Black label, dog on top					
❑ 447-0626	A Big Hunk o'Love/My Wish Came True	1965	2.50	5.00	10.00
—Black label, dog on left					
❑ 447-0626	A Big Hunk o'Love/My Wish Came True	1969	6.25	12.50	25.00
—Orange label					
❑ 447-0626	A Big Hunk o'Love/My Wish Came True	1970	2.00	4.00	8.00
—Red label					
❑ 447-0627	Stuck on You/Fame and Fortune	1962	3.00	6.00	12.00
—Black label, dog on top					
❑ 447-0627	Stuck on You/Fame and Fortune	1965	2.50	5.00	10.00
—Black label, dog on left					
❑ 447-0627	Stuck on You/Fame and Fortune	1969	6.25	12.50	25.00
—Orange label					
❑ 447-0627	Stuck on You/Fame and Fortune	1970	2.00	4.00	8.00
—Red label					
❑ 447-0628	It's Now or Never/A Mess of Blues	1962	3.00	6.00	12.00
—Black label, dog on top					
❑ 447-0628	It's Now or Never/A Mess of Blues	1965	2.50	5.00	10.00
—Black label, dog on left					
❑ 447-0628	It's Now or Never/A Mess of Blues	1969	6.25	12.50	25.00
—Orange label					
❑ 447-0628	It's Now or Never/A Mess of Blues	1970	2.00	4.00	8.00
—Red label					
❑ 447-0629	Are You Lonesome To-Night?/I Gotta Know	1962	3.75	7.50	15.00
—Black label, dog on top					
❑ 447-0629	Are You Lonesome To-Night?/I Gotta Know	1965	2.50	5.00	10.00
—Black label, dog on top					
❑ 447-0629	Are You Lonesome To-Night?/I Gotta Know	1969	6.25	12.50	25.00
—Orange label					
❑ 447-0629	Are You Lonesome To-Night?/I Gotta Know	1970	2.00	4.00	8.00
—Red label					
❑ 447-0630	Surrender/Lonely Man	1962	6.25	12.50	25.00
—Black label, dog on top					
❑ 447-0630	Surrender/Lonely Man	1965	2.50	5.00	10.00
—Black label, dog on left					
❑ 447-0630	Surrender/Lonely Man	1969	6.25	12.50	25.00
—Orange label					
❑ 447-0630	Surrender/Lonely Man	1970	2.00	4.00	8.00
—Red label					
❑ 447-0631	I Feel So Bad/Wild in the Country	1962	3.00	6.00	12.00
—Black label, dog on top					
❑ 447-0631	I Feel So Bad/Wild in the Country	1965	2.50	5.00	10.00
—Black label, dog on left					
❑ 447-0631	I Feel So Bad/Wild in the Country	1970	2.00	4.00	8.00
—Red label					
❑ 447-0634	(Marie's the Name) His Latest Flame/Little Sister	1962	3.00	6.00	12.00
—Black label, dog on top					
❑ 447-0634	(Marie's the Name) His Latest Flame/Little Sister	1965	2.50	5.00	10.00
—Black label, dog on left					
❑ 447-0634	(Marie's the Name) His Latest Flame/Little Sister	1969	6.25	12.50	25.00
—Orange label					
❑ 447-0634	(Marie's the Name) His Latest Flame/Little Sister	1970	2.00	4.00	8.00
—Red label					
❑ 447-0635	Can't Help Falling in Love/Rock-a-Hula Baby	1962	3.00	6.00	12.00
—Black label, dog on top					
❑ 447-0635	Can't Help Falling in Love/Rock-a-Hula Baby	1965	2.50	5.00	10.00
—Black label, dog on left					
❑ 447-0635	Can't Help Falling in Love/Rock-a-Hula Baby	1969	6.25	12.50	25.00
—Orange label					
❑ 447-0635	Can't Help Falling in Love/Rock-a-Hula Baby	1970	2.00	4.00	8.00
—Red label					
❑ 447-0636	Good Luck Charm/Anything That's Part of You	1962	3.00	6.00	12.00
—Black label, dog on top					
❑ 447-0636	Good Luck Charm/Anything That's Part of You	1965	2.50	5.00	10.00
—Black label, dog on left					
❑ 447-0636	Good Luck Charm/Anything That's Part of You	1969	6.25	12.50	25.00
—Orange label					
❑ 447-0636	Good Luck Charm/Anything That's Part of You	1970	2.00	4.00	8.00
—Red label					
❑ 447-0637	She's Not You/Just Tell Her Jim Said Hello	1963	3.00	6.00	12.00
—Black label, dog on top					
❑ 447-0637	She's Not You/Just Tell Her Jim Said Hello	1965	2.50	5.00	10.00
—Black label, dog on left					
❑ 447-0637	She's Not You/Just Tell Her Jim Said Hello	1969	6.25	12.50	25.00
—Orange label					
❑ 447-0637	She's Not You/Just Tell Her Jim Said Hello	1970	2.00	4.00	8.00
—Red label					
❑ 447-0638	Return to Sender/Where Do You Come From	1963	3.00	6.00	12.00
—Black label, dog on top					
❑ 447-0638	Return to Sender/Where Do You Come From	1965	2.50	5.00	10.00
—Black label, dog on left					
❑ 447-0638	Return to Sender/Where Do You Come From	1969	6.25	12.50	25.00
—Orange label					
❑ 447-0638	Return to Sender/Where Do You Come From	1970	2.00	4.00	8.00
—Red label					
❑ 447-0639	Kiss Me Quick/Suspicion	1964	2.50	5.00	10.00
—Black label, dog on top					
❑ 447-0639 [PS]	Kiss Me Quick/Suspicion	1964	10.00	20.00	40.00
❑ 447-0639	Kiss Me Quick/Suspicion	1969	6.25	12.50	25.00
—Orange label					
❑ 447-0639	Kiss Me Quick/Suspicion	1970	2.00	4.00	8.00
—Red label					
❑ 447-0640	One Broken Heart for Sale/They Remind Me Too Much of You	1964	6.25	12.50	25.00
—Black label, dog on top					
❑ 447-0640	One Broken Heart for Sale/They Remind Me Too Much of You	1965	2.50	5.00	10.00
—Black label, dog on left					
❑ 447-0640	One Broken Heart for Sale/They Remind Me Too Much of You	1969	6.25	12.50	25.00
—Orange label					
❑ 447-0640	One Broken Heart for Sale/They Remind Me Too Much of You	1970	2.00	4.00	8.00
—Red label					
❑ 447-0641	(You're the) Devil in Disguise/Please Don't Drag That String Around	1964	6.25	12.50	25.00
—Black label, dog on top					
❑ 447-0641	(You're the) Devil in Disguise/Please Don't Drag That String Around	1965	2.50	5.00	10.00
—Black label, dog on left					
❑ 447-0641	(You're the) Devil in Disguise/Please Don't Drag That String Around	1970	2.00	4.00	8.00
—Red label					
❑ 447-0642	Bossa Nova Baby/Witchcraft	1964	6.25	12.50	25.00
—Black label, dog on top					
❑ 447-0642	Bossa Nova Baby/Witchcraft	1965	2.50	5.00	10.00
—Black label, dog on left					
❑ 447-0642	Bossa Nova Baby/Witchcraft	1969	6.25	12.50	25.00
—Orange label					
❑ 447-0642	Bossa Nova Baby/Witchcraft	1970	2.00	4.00	8.00
—Red label					
❑ 447-0643	Crying in the Chapel/I Believe in the Man in the Sky	1965	2.50	5.00	10.00
—Black label, dog on left					
❑ 447-0643 [PS]	Crying in the Chapel/I Believe in the Man in the Sky	1965	7.50	15.00	30.00
❑ 447-0643	Crying in the Chapel/I Believe in the Man in the Sky	1970	2.00	4.00	8.00
—Red label					
❑ 447-0644	Kissin' Cousins/It Hurts Me	1965	2.50	5.00	10.00
—Black label, dog on top					
❑ 447-0644	Kissin' Cousins/It Hurts Me	1969	6.25	12.50	25.00
—Orange label					
❑ 447-0644	Kissin' Cousins/It Hurts Me	1970	2.00	4.00	8.00
—Red label					
❑ 447-0645	Such a Night/Never Ending	1965	2.50	5.00	10.00
—Black label, dog on left					
❑ 447-0645	Such a Night/Never Ending	1965	10.00	20.00	40.00
—Black label, dog on top					
❑ 447-0645	Such a Night/Never Ending	1969	6.25	12.50	25.00
—Orange label					
❑ 447-0645	Such a Night/Never Ending	1970	2.00	4.00	8.00
—Red label					
❑ 447-0646	Viva Las Vegas/What'd I Say	1965	2.50	5.00	10.00
—Black label, dog on left					
❑ 447-0646	Viva Las Vegas/What'd I Say	1965	6.25	12.50	25.00
—Black label, dog on top					
❑ 447-0646	Viva Las Vegas/What'd I Say	1969	6.25	12.50	25.00
—Orange label					
❑ 447-0646	Viva Las Vegas/What'd I Say	1970	2.00	4.00	8.00
—Red label					
❑ 447-0647	Blue Christmas/Santa Claus Is Back in Town	1965	3.00	6.00	12.00
—Black label, dog on left					
❑ 447-0647 [PS]	Blue Christmas/Santa Claus Is Back in Town	1965	7.50	15.00	30.00
—Has "Gold Standard Series" on sleeve					

Number	Title (A Side/B Side)	Yr	VG	VG+	NM
❑ 447-0647	Blue Christmas/Santa Claus Is Back in Town	1969	6.25	12.50	25.00
—Orange label					
❑ 447-0647	Blue Christmas/Santa Claus Is Back in Town	1970	2.00	4.00	8.00
—Red label					
❑ 447-0648	Do the Clam/You'll Be Gone	1965	2.50	5.00	10.00
—Black label, dog on left					
❑ 447-0648	Do the Clam/You'll Be Gone	1970	2.50	5.00	10.00
—Red label					
❑ 447-0649	Ain't That Loving You Baby/Ask Me	1965	2.50	5.00	10.00
—Black label, dog on left					
❑ 447-0649	Ain't That Loving You Baby/Ask Me	1970	2.00	4.00	8.00
—Red label					
❑ 447-0650	Puppet on a String/Wooden Heart	1965	2.50	5.00	10.00
—Black label, dog on left					
❑ 447-0650 [PS]	Puppet on a String/Wooden Heart	1965	7.50	15.00	30.00
❑ 447-0650	Puppet on a String/Wooden Heart	1970	2.00	4.00	8.00
—Red label					
❑ 447-0651	Joshua Fit the Battle/Known Only to Him	1966	3.75	7.50	15.00
—Black label, dog on left					
❑ 447-0651 [PS]	Joshua Fit the Battle/Known Only to Him	1966	50.00	100.00	200.00
❑ 447-0651	Joshua Fit the Battle/Known Only to Him	1970	2.00	4.00	8.00
—Red label					
❑ 447-0652	Milky White Way/Swing Down Sweet Chariot	1966	3.75	7.50	15.00
—Black label, dog on left					
❑ 447-0652 [PS]	Milky White Way/Swing Down Sweet Chariot	1966	50.00	100.00	200.00
❑ 447-0652	Milky White Way/Swing Down Sweet Chariot	1970	2.00	4.00	8.00
—Red label					
❑ 447-0653	(Such An) Easy Question/It Feels So Right	1966	2.50	5.00	10.00
—Black label, dog on left					
❑ 447-0653	(Such An) Easy Question/It Feels So Right	1970	2.00	4.00	8.00
—Red label					
❑ 447-0654	I'm Yours/(It's a) Long, Lonely Highway	1966	2.50	5.00	10.00
—Black label, dog on left					
❑ 447-0654	I'm Yours/(It's a) Long, Lonely Highway	1970	2.00	4.00	8.00
—Red label					
❑ 447-0655	Tell Me Why/Blue River	1968	2.50	5.00	10.00
—Black label, dog on left					
❑ 447-0655	Tell Me Why/Blue River	1970	2.00	4.00	8.00
—Red label					
❑ 447-0656	Frankie and Johnny/Please Don't Stop Loving Me	1968	2.50	5.00	10.00
—Black label, dog on left					
❑ 447-0656	Frankie and Johnny/Please Don't Stop Loving Me	1969	6.25	12.50	25.00
—Orange label					
❑ 447-0656	Frankie and Johnny/Please Don't Stop Loving Me	1970	2.00	4.00	8.00
—Red label					
❑ 447-0657	Love Letters/Come What May	1968	2.50	5.00	10.00
—Black label, dog on left					
❑ 447-0657	Love Letters/Come What May	1970	2.00	4.00	8.00
—Red label					
❑ 447-0658	Spinout/All That I Am	1968	2.50	5.00	10.00
—Black label, dog on left					
❑ 447-0658	Spinout/All That I Am	1970	2.00	4.00	8.00
—Red label					
❑ 447-0659	Indescribably Blue/Fools Fall in Love	1969	6.25	12.50	25.00
—Orange label					
❑ 447-0659	Indescribably Blue/Fools Fall in Love	1970	2.00	4.00	8.00
—Red label					
❑ 447-0660	Long Legged Girl (With the Short Dress On)/That's Someone You Never Forget	1970	10.00	20.00	40.00
❑ 447-0661	There's Always Me/Judy	1970	3.75	7.50	15.00
❑ 447-0662	Big Boss Man/You Don't Know Me	1970	2.50	5.00	10.00
❑ 447-0663	Guitar Man/High Heel Sneakers	1970	2.00	4.00	8.00
❑ 447-0664	U.S. Male/Stay Away	1970	2.00	4.00	8.00
❑ 447-0665	You'll Never Walk Alone/We Call on Him	1970	2.50	5.00	10.00
❑ 447-0666	Let Yourself Go/Your Time Hasn't Come Yet, Baby	1970	2.00	4.00	8.00
❑ 447-0667	A Little Less Conversation/Almost in Love	1970	2.00	4.00	8.00
❑ 447-0668	If I Can Dream/Edge of Reality	1970	2.00	4.00	8.00
❑ 447-0669	Memories/Charro	1970	2.00	4.00	8.00
❑ 447-0670	How Great Thou Art/His Hand in Mine	1970	2.50	5.00	10.00
❑ 447-0671	In the Ghetto/Any Day Now	1970	2.00	4.00	8.00
❑ 447-0672	Clean Up Your Own Back Yard/The Fair Is Moving On	1970	2.00	4.00	8.00
❑ 447-0673	Suspicious Minds/You'll Think of Me	1970	2.00	4.00	8.00
❑ 447-0674	Don't Cry Daddy/Rubberneckin'	1970	2.00	4.00	8.00
❑ 447-0675	Kentucky Rain/My Little Friend	1971	2.00	4.00	8.00
❑ 447-0676	The Wonder of You/Mama Liked the Roses	1971	2.00	4.00	8.00
❑ 447-0677	I've Lost You/The Next Step Is Love	1971	2.00	4.00	8.00
❑ 447-0678	You Don't Have to Say You Love Me/Patch It Up	1972	2.00	4.00	8.00
❑ 447-0679	I Really Don't Want to Know/There Goes My Everything	1972	2.00	4.00	8.00
❑ 447-0680	Where Did They Go, Lord/Rags to Riches	1972	2.00	4.00	8.00
❑ 447-0681	If Every Day Was Like Christmas/How Would You Like to Be	1972	2.00	4.00	8.00
❑ 447-0682	Life/Only Believe	1972	2.50	5.00	8.00
❑ 447-0683	I'm Leavin'/Heart of Rome	1972	2.00	4.00	8.00
❑ 447-0684	It's Only Love/The Sound of Your Cry	1972	2.00	4.00	8.00
❑ 447-0685	An American Trilogy/Until It's Time for You to Go	1973	2.00	4.00	8.00
❑ 447-0720	Blue Christmas/Wooden Heart	1964	3.75	7.50	15.00
❑ 447-0720 [PS]	Blue Christmas/Wooden Heart	1964	15.00	30.00	60.00
❑ CR-15 [DJ]	Old Shep	1956	250.00	500.00	1000.
—One-sided promo					
❑ SP-45-76 [DJ]	Don't Wear My Ring Around Your Neck	1960	200.00	400.00	800.00
❑ SP-45-76 [PS]	Don't Wear My Ring Around Your Neck	1960	1000.	1500.	2000.
❑ APBO-0088	Raised on Rock/For Ol' Times Sake	1973	—	3.00	6.00
❑ APBO-0088 [PS]	Raised on Rock/For Ol' Times Sake	1973	3.75	7.50	15.00
❑ 4-834-115 [DJ]	I'll Be Back	1966	4000.	6000.	8000.
—One-sided promo with designation "For Special Academy Consideration Only"					
❑ SP-45-118 [DJ]	King of the Whole Wide World/Home Is Where the Heart Is	1962	50.00	100.00	200.00
❑ SP-45-118 [PS]	King of the Whole Wide World/Home Is Where the Heart Is	1962	75.00	150.00	300.00
❑ SP-45-139 [DJ]	Roustabout/One Track Heart	1964	75.00	150.00	300.00
❑ SP-45-162 [DJ]	How Great Thou Art/So High	1967	37.50	75.00	150.00

Number	Title (A Side/B Side)	Yr	VG	VG+	NM
❑ SP-45-162 [PS]	How Great Thou Art/So High	1967	50.00	100.00	200.00
❑ APBO-0196	Take Good Care of Her/I've Got a Thing About You, Baby	1973	—	3.00	6.00
❑ APBO-0196 [PS]	Take Good Care of Her/I've Got a Thing About You, Baby	1973	3.75	7.50	15.00
❑ APBO-0280	If You Talk in Your Sleep/Help Me	1974	—	3.00	6.00
—On label, the title "If You Talk" is on one line and "In Your Sleep" is on another line					
❑ APBO-0280	If You Talk in Your Sleep/Help Me	1974	3.00	6.00	12.00
—On label, the title "If You Talk in Your Sleep" is all on one line					
❑ APBO-0280 [PS]	If You Talk in Your Sleep/Help Me	1974	3.75	7.50	15.00
❑ HO7W-0808 [DJ]	Blue Christmas (same on both sides)	1957	375.00	750.00	1500.
❑ PB-10074	Promised Land/It's Midnight	1974	—	2.50	5.00
—Gray label (available at the same time as orange label)					
❑ PB-10074	Promised Land/It's Midnight	1974	—	2.50	5.00
—Orange label (available at the same time as gray label)					
❑ PB-10074	Promised Land/It's Midnight	1975	6.25	12.50	25.00
—Tan label (reissue)					
❑ PB-10074 [PS]	Promised Land/It's Midnight	1975	2.50	5.00	10.00
❑ GB-10156	Burning Love/Steamroller Blues	1975	2.00	4.00	8.00
—Gold Standard Series; red label					
❑ GB-10156	Burning Love/Steamroller Blues	1977	—	2.00	4.00
—Gold Standard Series; black label					
❑ GB-10157	Raised on Rock/If You Talk in Your Sleep	1975	2.00	4.00	8.00
—Gold Standard Series; red label					
❑ GB-10157	Raised on Rock/If You Talk in Your Sleep	1977	—	2.00	4.00
—Gold Standard Series; black label					
❑ PB-10191	My Boy/Thinking About You	1975	—	2.50	5.00
—Orange label					
❑ PB-10191	My Boy/Thinking About You	1975	—	2.50	5.00
—Tan label					
❑ PB-10191 [PS]	My Boy/Thinking About You	1975	2.50	5.00	10.00
❑ PB-10278	T-R-O-U-B-L-E/Mr. Songman	1975	—	2.50	5.00
—Orange label					
❑ PB-10278	T-R-O-U-B-L-E/Mr. Songman	1975	2.50	5.00	10.00
—Tan label					
❑ PB-10278	T-R-O-U-B-L-E/Mr. Songman	1975	25.00	50.00	100.00
—Gray label					
❑ PB-10278 [PS]	T-R-O-U-B-L-E/Mr. Songman	1975	2.50	5.00	10.00
❑ PB-10401	Bringing It Back/Pieces of My Life	1975	—	2.50	5.00
—Tan label					
❑ PB-10401	Bringing It Back/Pieces of My Life	1975	50.00	100.00	200.00
—Orange label					
❑ PB-10401 [PS]	Bringing It Back/Pieces of My Life	1975	2.50	5.00	10.00
❑ GB-10485	Take Good Care of Her/I've Got a Thing About You, Baby	1975	2.00	4.00	8.00
—Gold Standard Series; red label					
❑ GB-10486	Separate Ways/Always on My Mind	1975	2.00	4.00	8.00
—Gold Standard Series; red label					
❑ GB-10487	T-R-O-U-B-L-E/Mr. Songman	1975	2.00	4.00	8.00
—Gold Standard Series; red label					
❑ GB-10488	Promised Land/It's Midnight	1975	2.00	4.00	8.00
—Gold Standard Series; red label					
❑ GB-10489	My Boy/Thinking About You	1975	2.00	4.00	8.00
—Gold Standard Series; red label					
❑ PB-10601	Hurt/For the Heart	1976	—	2.50	5.00
—Originals on tan labels					
❑ PB-10601 [PS]	Hurt/For the Heart	1976	2.50	5.00	10.00

SUN

Number	Title (A Side/B Side)	Yr	VG	VG+	NM
❑ 209	That's All Right/Blue Moon of Kentucky	1954	2000.	4000.	6000.
—A mint copy of this has sold for over $17,000, but so far that is an aberration					
❑ 210	Good Rockin' Tonight/I Don't Care If the Sun Don't Shine	1954	1500.	2500.	3500.
❑ 215	Milkcow Blues Boogie/You're a Heartbreaker	1955	2000.	3500.	5000.
❑ 217	Baby Let's Play House/I'm Left, You're Right, She's Gone	1955	1000.	2000.	3000.
❑ 223	I Forgot to Remember to Forget/Mystery Train	1955	625.00	1250.	2500.

7-Inch Extended Plays

RCA

Number	Title (A Side/B Side)	Yr	VG	VG+	NM
❑ DTF0-2006 [PS]	Aloha from Hawaii Via Satellite	1973	25.00	50.00	100.00
❑ DTF0-2006 [S]	Something/You Gave Me a Mountain/I Can't Stop Loving You/My Way/What Now My Love/I'm So Lonesome I Could Cry	1973	20.00	40.00	80.00
—Jukebox issue; small hole, plays at 33 1/3 rpm					

RCA VICTOR

Number	Title (A Side/B Side)	Yr	VG	VG+	NM
❑ DJ-7 [DJ]	Love Me Tender/Anyway You Want Me (That's How I Will Be)//Welcome to the Club/I Won't Be Rockin' Tonight	1956	50.00	100.00	200.00
—B-side tracks by Jean Chapel; white label; each side is labeled with the corresponding nuimber for the regular 45 rpm issue					
❑ SPD-22 [(2)]	Elvis Presley	1956	100.00	200.00	400.00
—Value is for both discs together					
❑ SPD-22 [PS]	Elvis Presley	1956	100.00	200.00	400.00
—Bonus given to buyers of a Victrola					
❑ SPD-23 [(3)]	Elvis Presley	1956	1000.	2000.	3000.
—Value is for all three discs together					
❑ SPD-23 [PS]	Elvis Presley	1956	1000.	2000.	3000.
—Bonus given to buyers of a more expensive Victrola					
❑ SPA-7-37 [DJ]	Perfect for Parties	1956	15.00	30.00	60.00
—With horizontal line on label					
❑ SPA-7-37 [DJ]	Perfect for Parties	1956	15.00	30.00	60.00
—Without horizontal line on label					
❑ SPA-7-37 [PS]	Perfect for Parties	1956	15.00	30.00	60.00
❑ DJ-56 [DJ]	Too Much//Playing for Keeps//Chantez-Chantez/Honkytonk Heart	1956	50.00	100.00	200.00
—B-side tracks by Dinah Shore; white label; each side is labeled with the corresponding nuimber for the regular 45 rpm issue					
❑ LPC-128	Flaming Star/Summer Kisses, Winter Tears//Are You Lonesome To-Night?/It's Now or Never	1961	10.00	20.00	40.00
—"Compact 33 Double" with small hole					
❑ LPC-128 [PS]	Elvis By Request	1961	10.00	20.00	40.00
❑ EPA-747	Blue Suede Shoes/Tutti Frutti//I Got a Woman/Just Because	1956	12.50	25.00	50.00
—With horizontal line on label					
❑ EPA-747	Blue Suede Shoes/Tutti Frutti//I Got a Woman/Just Because	1956	12.50	25.00	50.00
—Without horizontal line on label					

Number	Title (A Side/B Side)	Yr	VG	VG+	NM
❏ EPA-747	Blue Suede Shoes/Tutti Frutti//I Got a Woman/ Just Because	1956	50.00	100.00	200.00

—With horizontal line on label, but with no dog

Number	Title (A Side/B Side)	Yr	VG	VG+	NM
❏ EPA-747	Blue Suede Shoes/Tutti Frutti//I Got a Woman/ Just Because	1956	50.00	100.00	200.00

—With incorrect label on Side 1 that lists, as song 3, "I'm Gonna Sit Right Down and Cry (Over You)," which does not appear on this record. Known copies of this version do not have horizontal line on label.

Number	Title (A Side/B Side)	Yr	VG	VG+	NM
❏ EPA-747 [PS]	Elvis Presley	1956	12.50	25.00	50.00

—Five different back covers exist, all with titles on front cover; any are of equal value

Number	Title (A Side/B Side)	Yr	VG	VG+	NM
❏ EPA-747 [PS]	Elvis Presley	1956	150.00	300.00	600.00

—Temporary envelope sleeve with black print, "Blue Suede Shoes by Elvis Presley" in big letters

Number	Title (A Side/B Side)	Yr	VG	VG+	NM
❏ EPA-747 [PS]	Elvis Presley	1956	250.00	500.00	1000.

—Temporary envelope sleeve with dark blue print, "Blue Suede Shoes by Elvis Presley" in big letters

Number	Title (A Side/B Side)	Yr	VG	VG+	NM
❏ EPA-747	Blue Suede Shoes/Tutti Frutti//I Got a Woman/ Just Because	1965	7.50	15.00	30.00

—Black label, dog on left

Number	Title (A Side/B Side)	Yr	VG	VG+	NM
❏ EPA-747 [PS]	Elvis Presley	1965	7.50	15.00	30.00

—No titles at top of front cover

Number	Title (A Side/B Side)	Yr	VG	VG+	NM
❏ EPA-747	Blue Suede Shoes/Tutti Frutti//I Got a Woman/ Just Because	1969	20.00	40.00	80.00

—Orange label

Number	Title (A Side/B Side)	Yr	VG	VG+	NM
❏ EPA-821	Heartbreak Hotel/I Was the One//Money Honey/ I Forgot to Remember to Forget	1956	12.50	25.00	50.00

—With horizontal line on label

Number	Title (A Side/B Side)	Yr	VG	VG+	NM
❏ EPA-821	Heartbreak Hotel/I Was the One//Money Honey/ I Forgot to Remember to Forget	1956	12.50	25.00	50.00

—Without horizontal line on label

Number	Title (A Side/B Side)	Yr	VG	VG+	NM
❏ EPA-821	Heartbreak Hotel/I Was the One//Money Honey/ I Forgot to Remember to Forget	1956	50.00	100.00	200.00

—With horizontal line on label, but with no dog

Number	Title (A Side/B Side)	Yr	VG	VG+	NM
❏ EPA-821 [PS]	Heartbreak Hotel	1956	12.50	25.00	50.00
❏ EPA-821	Heartbreak Hotel/I Was the One//Money Honey/ I Forgot to Remember to Forget	1965	7.50	15.00	30.00

—Black label, dog on left

Number	Title (A Side/B Side)	Yr	VG	VG+	NM
❏ EPA-821	Heartbreak Hotel/I Was the One//Money Honey/ I Forgot to Remember to Forget	1969	20.00	40.00	80.00

—Orange label

Number	Title (A Side/B Side)	Yr	VG	VG+	NM
❏ EPA-830	Shake, Rattle and Roll/I Love You Because// Blue Moon/Lawdy, Miss Clawdy	1956	12.50	25.00	50.00

—With horizontal line on label

Number	Title (A Side/B Side)	Yr	VG	VG+	NM
❏ EPA-830	Shake, Rattle and Roll/I Love You Because// Blue Moon/Lawdy, Miss Clawdy	1956	12.50	25.00	50.00

—Without horizontal line on label

Number	Title (A Side/B Side)	Yr	VG	VG+	NM
❏ EPA-830	Shake, Rattle and Roll/I Love You Because// Blue Moon/Lawdy, Miss Clawdy	1956	50.00	100.00	200.00

—With horizontal line on label, but with no dog

Number	Title (A Side/B Side)	Yr	VG	VG+	NM
❏ EPA-830 [PS]	Elvis Presley	1956	12.50	25.00	50.00
❏ EPA-830	Shake, Rattle and Roll/I Love You Because// Blue Moon/Lawdy, Miss Clawdy	1965	7.50	15.00	30.00

—Black label, dog on left

Number	Title (A Side/B Side)	Yr	VG	VG+	NM
❏ EPA-830	Shake, Rattle and Roll/I Love You Because// Blue Moon/Lawdy, Miss Clawdy	1969	20.00	40.00	80.00

—Orange label

Number	Title (A Side/B Side)	Yr	VG	VG+	NM
❏ EPA-940	Don't Be Cruel/I Want You, I Need You, I Love You//Hound Dog/My Baby Left Me	1956	12.50	25.00	50.00

—With horizontal line on label

Number	Title (A Side/B Side)	Yr	VG	VG+	NM
❏ EPA-940	Don't Be Cruel/I Want You, I Need You, I Love You//Hound Dog/My Baby Left Me	1956	12.50	25.00	50.00

—Without horizontal line on label

Number	Title (A Side/B Side)	Yr	VG	VG+	NM
❏ EPA-940	Don't Be Cruel/I Want You, I Need You, I Love You//Hound Dog/My Baby Left Me	1956	50.00	100.00	200.00

—With horizontal line on label, but with no dog

Number	Title (A Side/B Side)	Yr	VG	VG+	NM
❏ EPA-940 [PS]	The Real Elvis	1956	12.50	25.00	50.00
❏ EPA-965	Anyway You Want Me (That's How I Will Be)/I'm Left, You're Right, She's Gone/I Don't Care If the Sun Don't Shine/Mystery Train	1956	10.00	20.00	40.00

—With horizontal line on label

Number	Title (A Side/B Side)	Yr	VG	VG+	NM
❏ EPA-965	Anyway You Want Me (That's How I Will Be)/I'm Left, You're Right, She's Gone/I Don't Care If the Sun Don't Shine/Mystery Train	1956	10.00	20.00	40.00

—Without horizontal line on label

Number	Title (A Side/B Side)	Yr	VG	VG+	NM
❏ EPA-965	Anyway You Want Me (That's How I Will Be)/I'm Left, You're Right, She's Gone/I Don't Care If the Sun Don't Shine/Mystery Train	1956	50.00	100.00	200.00

—With horizontal line on label, but with no dog

Number	Title (A Side/B Side)	Yr	VG	VG+	NM
❏ EPA-965 [PS]	Anyway You Want Me	1956	12.50	25.00	50.00

—With song titles and catalog number on front

Number	Title (A Side/B Side)	Yr	VG	VG+	NM
❏ EPA-965 [PS]	Anyway You Want Me	196?	10.00	20.00	40.00

—Without song titles and catalog number on front

Number	Title (A Side/B Side)	Yr	VG	VG+	NM
❏ EPA-965	Anyway You Want Me (That's How I Will Be)/I'm Left, You're Right, She's Gone/I Don't Care If the Sun Don't Shine/Mystery Train	1965	7.50	15.00	30.00

—Black label, dog on left

Number	Title (A Side/B Side)	Yr	VG	VG+	NM
❏ EPA-965	Anyway You Want Me (That's How I Will Be)/I'm Left, You're Right, She's Gone/I Don't Care If the Sun Don't Shine/Mystery Train	1969	20.00	40.00	80.00

—Orange label

Number	Title (A Side/B Side)	Yr	VG	VG+	NM
❏ EPA-992	Rip It Up/Love Me//When My Blue Moon Turns to Gold Again/Paralyzed	1956	10.00	20.00	40.00

—With horizontal line on label

Number	Title (A Side/B Side)	Yr	VG	VG+	NM
❏ EPA-992	Rip It Up/Love Me//When My Blue Moon Turns to Gold Again/Paralyzed	1956	10.00	20.00	40.00

—Without horizontal line on label

Number	Title (A Side/B Side)	Yr	VG	VG+	NM
❏ EPA-992	Rip It Up/Love Me//When My Blue Moon Turns to Gold Again/Paralyzed	1956	50.00	100.00	200.00

—With horizontal line on label; but with no dog

Number	Title (A Side/B Side)	Yr	VG	VG+	NM
❏ EPA-992 [PS]	Elvis (Volume 1)	1956	12.50	25.00	50.00
❏ EPA-992	Rip It Up/Love Me//When My Blue Moon Turns to Gold Again/Paralyzed	1965	7.50	15.00	30.00

—Black label, dog on left

Number	Title (A Side/B Side)	Yr	VG	VG+	NM
❏ EPA-992	Rip It Up/Love Me//When My Blue Moon Turns to Gold Again/Paralyzed	1969	20.00	40.00	80.00

—Orange label

Number	Title (A Side/B Side)	Yr	VG	VG+	NM
❏ EPA-993	So Glad You're Mine/Old Shep//Ready Teddy/ Anyplace Is Paradise	1956	10.00	20.00	40.00

—With horizontal line on label

Number	Title (A Side/B Side)	Yr	VG	VG+	NM
❏ EPA-993	So Glad You're Mine/Old Shep//Ready Teddy/ Anyplace Is Paradise	1956	10.00	20.00	40.00

—Without horizontal line on label

Number	Title (A Side/B Side)	Yr	VG	VG+	NM
❏ EPA-993	So Glad You're Mine/Old Shep//Ready Teddy/ Anyplace Is Paradise	1956	50.00	100.00	200.00

—With horizontal line on label, but with no dog

Number	Title (A Side/B Side)	Yr	VG	VG+	NM
❏ EPA-993 [PS]	Elvis (Volume 2)	1956	12.50	25.00	50.00

—Titles at top of front cover

Number	Title (A Side/B Side)	Yr	VG	VG+	NM
❏ EPA-993	So Glad You're Mine/Old Shep//Ready Teddy/ Anyplace Is Paradise	1965	7.50	15.00	30.00

—Black label, dog on left

Number	Title (A Side/B Side)	Yr	VG	VG+	NM
❏ EPA-993 [PS]	Elvis (Volume 2)	1965	7.50	15.00	30.00

—No titles at top of front cover

Number	Title (A Side/B Side)	Yr	VG	VG+	NM
❏ EPA-993	So Glad You're Mine/Old Shep//Ready Teddy/ Anyplace Is Paradise	1969	20.00	40.00	80.00

—Orange label

Number	Title (A Side/B Side)	Yr	VG	VG+	NM
❏ EPA-994	Long Tall Sally/First in Line//How Do You Think I Feel/How's the World Treating You	1956	12.50	25.00	50.00

—With horizontal line on label

Number	Title (A Side/B Side)	Yr	VG	VG+	NM
❏ EPA-994	Long Tall Sally/First in Line//How Do You Think I Feel/How's the World Treating You	1956	12.50	25.00	50.00

—Without horizontal line on label

Number	Title (A Side/B Side)	Yr	VG	VG+	NM
❏ EPA-994	Long Tall Sally/First in Line//How Do You Think I Feel/How's the World Treating You	1956	50.00	100.00	200.00

—With horizontal line on label, but with no dog

Number	Title (A Side/B Side)	Yr	VG	VG+	NM
❏ EPA-994 [PS]	Strictly Elvis (Elvis, Vol. 3)	1956	12.50	25.00	50.00

—With titles listed on front cover

Number	Title (A Side/B Side)	Yr	VG	VG+	NM
❏ EPA-994	Long Tall Sally/First in Line//How Do You Think I Feel/How's the World Treating You	1965	7.50	15.00	30.00

—Black label, dog on left

Number	Title (A Side/B Side)	Yr	VG	VG+	NM
❏ EPA-994 [PS]	Strictly Elvis (Elvis, Vol. 3)	1965	7.50	15.00	30.00

—No titles listed on front cover

Number	Title (A Side/B Side)	Yr	VG	VG+	NM
❏ EPA-994	Long Tall Sally/First in Line//How Do You Think I Feel/How's the World Treating You	1969	20.00	40.00	80.00
❏ EPB-1254 [(2)]	Elvis Presley	1956	50.00	100.00	200.00

—With horizontal line on label; eight songs on two discs; value is for both discs together

Number	Title (A Side/B Side)	Yr	VG	VG+	NM
❏ EPB-1254 [(2)]	Elvis Presley	1956	50.00	100.00	200.00

—Without horizontal line on label; eight songs on two discs; value is for both discs together

Number	Title (A Side/B Side)	Yr	VG	VG+	NM
❏ EPB-1254 [(2)]	Elvis Presley	1956	375.00	750.00	1500.

—Two records have three songs on each side (12 total), as opposed to the two of the standard release

Number	Title (A Side/B Side)	Yr	VG	VG+	NM
❏ EPB-1254 [PS]	Elvis Presley	1956	37.50	75.00	150.00

—With no hype of other non-Elvis releases on back

Number	Title (A Side/B Side)	Yr	VG	VG+	NM
❏ EPB-1254 [PS]	Elvis Presley	1956	50.00	100.00	200.00

—Three different back covers exist hyping other non-Elvis RCA Victor releases; any are of equal value

Number	Title (A Side/B Side)	Yr	VG	VG+	NM
❏ EPB-1254 [PS]	Elvis Presley... the most talked-about new personality in the last ten years of recorded music	1956	375.00	750.00	1500.
❏ EPA-1-1515	Loving You/Party//(Let Me Be Your) Teddy Bear/ True Love	1957	10.00	20.00	40.00

—With horizontal line on label

Number	Title (A Side/B Side)	Yr	VG	VG+	NM
❏ EPA-1-1515	Loving You/Party//(Let Me Be Your) Teddy Bear/ True Love	1957	10.00	20.00	40.00

—Without horizontal line on label

Number	Title (A Side/B Side)	Yr	VG	VG+	NM
❏ EPA-1-1515 [PS]	Loving You, Vol. I	1957	10.00	20.00	40.00
❏ EPA-1-1515	Loving You/Party//(Let Me Be Your) Teddy Bear/ True Love	1965	7.50	15.00	30.00

—Black label, dog on left

Number	Title (A Side/B Side)	Yr	VG	VG+	NM
❏ EPA-1-1515	Loving You/Party//(Let Me Be Your) Teddy Bear/ True Love	1969	20.00	40.00	80.00

—Orange label

Number	Title (A Side/B Side)	Yr	VG	VG+	NM
❏ EPA-2-1515	Lonesome Cowboy/Hot Dog//Mean Woman Blues/Got a Lot of Livin' to Do	1957	10.00	20.00	40.00

—With horizontal line on label

Number	Title (A Side/B Side)	Yr	VG	VG+	NM
❏ EPA-2-1515	Lonesome Cowboy/Hot Dog//Mean Woman Blues/Got a Lot of Livin' to Do	1957	10.00	20.00	40.00

—Without horizontal line on label

Number	Title (A Side/B Side)	Yr	VG	VG+	NM
❏ EPA-2-1515 [PS]	Loving You, Vol. II	1957	10.00	20.00	40.00

—With song titles on top of front cover

Number	Title (A Side/B Side)	Yr	VG	VG+	NM
❏ EPA-2-1515	Lonesome Cowboy/Hot Dog//Mean Woman Blues/Got a Lot of Livin' to Do	1965	7.50	15.00	30.00

—Black label, dog on left

Number	Title (A Side/B Side)	Yr	VG	VG+	NM
❏ EPA-2-1515 [PS]	Loving You, Vol. II	1965	7.50	15.00	30.00

—No song titles on top of front cover

Number	Title (A Side/B Side)	Yr	VG	VG+	NM
❏ EPA-2-1515	Lonesome Cowboy/Hot Dog//Mean Woman Blues/Got a Lot of Livin' to Do	1969	20.00	40.00	80.00

—Orange label

Number	Title (A Side/B Side)	Yr	VG	VG+	NM
❏ EPA-4006	Love Me Tender/Let Me//Poor Boy/We're Gonna Move	1956	12.50	25.00	50.00

—With horizontal line on label

Number	Title (A Side/B Side)	Yr	VG	VG+	NM
❏ EPA-4006	Love Me Tender/Let Me//Poor Boy/We're Gonna Move	1956	12.50	25.00	50.00

—Without horizontal line on label

Number	Title (A Side/B Side)	Yr	VG	VG+	NM
❏ EPA-4006	Love Me Tender/Let Me//Poor Boy/We're Gonna Move	1956	50.00	100.00	200.00

—With horizontal line on label, but with no dog

Number	Title (A Side/B Side)	Yr	VG	VG+	NM
❏ EPA-4006 [PS]	Love Me Tender	1956	12.50	25.00	50.00

—With song titles on top of front cover

Number	Title (A Side/B Side)	Yr	VG	VG+	NM
❏ EPA-4006	Love Me Tender/Let Me//Poor Boy/We're Gonna Move	1965	7.50	15.00	30.00

—Black label, dog on left

Number	Title (A Side/B Side)	Yr	VG	VG+	NM
❏ EPA-4006 [PS]	Love Me Tender	1965	7.50	15.00	30.00

—No song titles on top of front cover

Number	Title (A Side/B Side)	Yr	VG	VG+	NM
❏ EPA-4006	Love Me Tender/Let Me//Poor Boy/We're Gonna Move	1969	20.00	40.00	80.00

—Orange label

Number	Title (A Side/B Side)	Yr	VG	VG+	NM
❏ EPA-4041	I Need You So/Have I Told You Lately//Blueberry Hill/Is It So Strange	1957	12.50	25.00	50.00

—With horizontal line on label

Number	Title (A Side/B Side)	Yr	VG	VG+	NM
❏ EPA-4041	I Need You So/Have I Told You Lately//Blueberry Hill/Is It So Strange	1957	12.50	25.00	50.00

—Without horizontal line on label

Number	Title (A Side/B Side)	Yr	VG	VG+	NM
❏ EPA-4041	I Need You So/Have I Told You Lately//Blueberry Hill/Is It So Strange	1957	50.00	100.00	200.00

—With horizontal line on label, but with no dog

Number	Title (A Side/B Side)	Yr	VG	VG+	NM
❏ EPA-4041 [PS]	Just for You (Elvis Presley)	1957	12.50	25.00	50.00
❏ EPA-4041	I Need You So/Have I Told You Lately//Blueberry Hill/Is It So Strange	1965	7.50	15.00	30.00

—Black label, dog on left

❏ EPA-4041	I Need You So/Have I Told You Lately//Blueberry Hill/Is It So Strange	1969	20.00	40.00	80.00

—Orange label

❏ EPA-4054	(There'll Be) Peace in the Valley (For Me)/It Is No Secret (What God Can Do)//I Believe/Take My Hand, Precious Lord	1957	10.00	20.00	40.00

—With horizontal line on label

❏ EPA-4054	(There'll Be) Peace in the Valley (For Me)/It Is No Secret (What God Can Do)//I Believe/Take My Hand, Precious Lord	1957	10.00	20.00	40.00

—Without horizontal line on label

❏ EPA-4054 [PS]	Peace in the Valley	1957	10.00	20.00	40.00
❏ EPA-4108	Santa Bring My Baby Back (To Me)/Blue Christmas//Santa Claus Is Back in Town/I'll Be Home for Christmas	1957	10.00	20.00	40.00

—Black label, dog on top

❏ EPA-4108 [PS]	Elvis Sings Christmas Songs	1957	10.00	20.00	40.00
❏ EPA-4108	Santa Bring My Baby Back (To Me)/Blue Christmas//Santa Claus Is Back in Town/I'll Be Home for Christmas	1965	7.50	15.00	30.00

—Black label, dog on left

❏ EPA-4108	Santa Bring My Baby Back (To Me)/Blue Christmas//Santa Claus Is Back in Town/I'll Be Home for Christmas	1969	20.00	40.00	80.00

—Orange label

❏ EPA-4114	Jailhouse Rock/Young and Beautiful//I Want to Be Free/Don't Leave Me Now//(You're So Square) Baby I Don't Care	1957	10.00	20.00	40.00

—Black label, dog on top

❏ EPA-4114 [PS]	Jailhouse Rock	1957	10.00	20.00	40.00
❏ EPA-4114	Jailhouse Rock/Young and Beautiful//I Want to Be Free/Don't Leave Me Now//(You're So Square) Baby I Don't Care	1965	7.50	15.00	30.00

—Black label, dog on left

❏ EPA-4114	Jailhouse Rock/Young and Beautiful//I Want to Be Free/Don't Leave Me Now//(You're So Square) Baby I Don't Care	1969	20.00	40.00	80.00

—Orange label

❏ EPA-4319	King Creole/New Orleans//As Long As I Have You/Lover Doll	1958	10.00	20.00	40.00
❏ EPA-4319 [PS]	King Creole	1958	10.00	20.00	40.00

—Without copyright notice on front cover

❏ EPA-4319 [PS]	King Creole	1958	12.50	25.00	50.00

—With copyright notice on front cover

❏ EPA-4321	Trouble/Young Dreams//Crawfish/Dixieland Rock	1958	10.00	20.00	40.00

—Black label, dog on top

❏ EPA-4321 [PS]	King Creole, Vol. 2	1958	10.00	20.00	40.00
❏ EPA-4321	Trouble/Young Dreams//Crawfish/Dixieland Rock	1965	7.50	15.00	30.00

—Black label, dog on left

❏ EPA-4321	Trouble/Young Dreams//Crawfish/Dixieland Rock	1969	20.00	40.00	80.00

—Orange label

❏ EPA-4325	Press Interview with Elvis Presley//Elvis Presley's Newsreel Interview/Pat Hernon Interviews Elvis...	1958	20.00	40.00	80.00
❏ EPA-4325 [PS]	Elvis Sails	1958	20.00	40.00	80.00

—With 1959 calendar and a hole to make it suitable for hanging

❏ EPA-4340	White Christmas/Here Comes Santa Claus//Oh Little Town of Bethlehem/Silent Night	1958	17.50	35.00	70.00

—Black label, dog on top

❏ EPA-4340 [PS]	Christmas with Elvis	1958	20.00	40.00	80.00

—With copyright notice and "Printed in U.S.A." at lower right

❏ EPA-4340	White Christmas/Here Comes Santa Claus//Oh Little Town of Bethlehem/Silent Night	1965	10.00	20.00	40.00

—Black label, dog on left

❏ EPA-4340 [PS]	Christmas with Elvis	1965	10.00	20.00	40.00

—Without copyright notice and "Printed in U.S.A." at lower right

❏ EPA-4340	White Christmas/Here Comes Santa Claus//Oh Little Town of Bethlehem/Silent Night	1969	10.00	40.00	80.00

—Orange label

❏ EPA-4368	Follow That Dream/Angel//What a Wonderful Life/I'm Not the Marrying Kind	1962	7.50	15.00	30.00

—Black label, dog on top, no playing times on label

❏ EPA-4368	Follow That Dream/Angel//What a Wonderful Life/I'm Not the Marrying Kind	1962	10.00	20.00	40.00

—Black label, dog on top, with playing times on label

❏ EPA-4368 [PS]	Follow That Dream	1962	10.00	20.00	40.00

—Incorrect playing times on back cover; "Follow That Dream" is listed as 1:35 but is actually 1:38, and two others are wrong also

❏ EPA-4368 [PS]	Follow That Dream	1962	37.50	75.00	150.00

—Paper sleeve with "Coin Operator -- DJ Prevue" at top; print is in red

❏ EPA-4368	Follow That Dream/Angel//What a Wonderful Life/I'm Not the Marrying Kind	1965	6.25	12.50	25.00

—Black label, dog on left

❏ EPA-4368 [PS]	Follow That Dream	1965	6.25	12.50	25.00

—Correct playing times on back cover

❏ EPA-4368	Follow That Dream/Angel//What a Wonderful Life/I'm Not the Marrying Kind	1969	20.00	40.00	80.00

—Orange label

❏ EPA-4371	King of the Whole Wide World/This Is Living/Riding the Rainbow//Home Is Where the Heart Is/I Got Lucky/A Whistling Tune	1962	10.00	20.00	40.00

—Black label, dog on top

❏ EPA-4371 [PS]	Kid Galahad	1962	10.00	20.00	40.00
❏ EPA-4371	King of the Whole Wide World/This Is Living/Riding the Rainbow//Home Is Where the Heart Is/I Got Lucky/A Whistling Tune	1965	7.50	15.00	30.00

—Black label, dog on left

❏ EPA-4371	King of the Whole Wide World/This Is Living/Riding the Rainbow//Home Is Where the Heart Is/I Got Lucky/A Whistling Tune	1969	20.00	40.00	80.00

—Orange label

❏ EPA-4382	If You Think I Don't Need You/I Need Somebody to Lean On//C'mon Everybody/Today, Tomorrow and Forever	1964	10.00	20.00	40.00

—Black label, dog on top

❏ EPA-4382 [PS]	Viva Las Vegas	1964	10.00	20.00	40.00
❏ EPA-4382	If You Think I Don't Need You/I Need Somebody to Lean On//C'mon Everybody/Today, Tomorrow and Forever	1965	7.50	15.00	30.00

—Black label, dog on left

❏ EPA-4382	If You Think I Don't Need You/I Need Somebody to Lean On//C'mon Everybody/Today, Tomorrow and Forever	1969	20.00	40.00	80.00

—Orange label

❏ EPA-4383	I Feel That I've Known You Forever/Slowly But Surely//Night Rider/Dirty Feeling	1965	7.50	15.00	30.00

—Black label, dog on left

❏ EPA-4383 [PS]	Tickle Me	1965	7.50	15.00	30.00

—"Ask For" on front cover

❏ EPA-4383 [PS]	Tickle Me	1965	7.50	15.00	30.00

—"Coming Soon" on front cover

❏ EPA-4383	I Feel That I've Known You Forever/Slowly But Surely//Night Rider/Dirty Feeling	1969	20.00	40.00	80.00

—Orange label

❏ EPA-4383 [PS]	Tickle Me	1969	8.75	17.50	35.00

—No blurb for new album on front cover

❏ EPA-4387	Easy Come, Easy Go/The Love Machine/Yoga Is As Yoga Does//You Gotta Shop/Sing You Children/I'll Take Love	1967	7.50	15.00	30.00

—All copies appear to be black label, dog on left

❏ EPA-4387 [PS]	Easy Come, Easy Go	1967	7.50	15.00	30.00
❏ EPA-5088	Hard Headed Woman/Good Rockin' Tonight//Don't/I Beg of You	1959	15.00	30.00	60.00

—Black label, dog on top

❏ EPA-5088	Hard Headed Woman/Good Rockin' Tonight//Don't/I Beg of You	1959	100.00	200.00	400.00

—Maroon label

❏ EPA-5088 [PS]	A Touch of Gold	1959	15.00	30.00	60.00
❏ EPA-5088	Hard Headed Woman/Good Rockin' Tonight//Don't/I Beg of You	1965	7.50	15.00	30.00

—Black label, dog on left

❏ EPA-5088	Hard Headed Woman/Good Rockin' Tonight//Don't/I Beg of You	1969	20.00	40.00	80.00

—Orange label

❏ EPA-5101	Wear My Ring Around Your Neck/Treat Me Nice//One Night/That's All Right	1959	15.00	30.00	60.00

—Black label, dog on top

❏ EPA-5101	Wear My Ring Around Your Neck/Treat Me Nice//One Night/That's All Right	1959	100.00	200.00	400.00

—Maroon label

❏ EPA-5101 [PS]	A Touch of Gold, Volume II	1959	15.00	30.00	60.00
❏ EPA-5101	Wear My Ring Around Your Neck/Treat Me Nice//One Night/That's All Right	1965	7.50	15.00	30.00

—Black label, dog on left

❏ EPA-5101	Wear My Ring Around Your Neck/Treat Me Nice//One Night/That's All Right	1969	20.00	40.00	80.00

—Orange label

❏ EPA-5120	Don't Be Cruel/I Want You, I Need You, I Love You//Hound Dog/My Baby Left Me	1959	15.00	30.00	60.00

—Black label, dog on top

❏ EPA-5120	Don't Be Cruel/I Want You, I Need You, I Love You//Hound Dog/My Baby Left Me	1959	150.00	300.00	600.00

—Maroon label

❏ EPA-5120 [PS]	The Real Elvis	1959	15.00	30.00	60.00
❏ EPA-5120	Don't Be Cruel/I Want You, I Need You, I Love You//Hound Dog/My Baby Left Me	1965	6.25	12.50	25.00

—Black label, dog on left

❏ EPA-5120	Don't Be Cruel/I Want You, I Need You, I Love You//Hound Dog/My Baby Left Me	1969	20.00	40.00	80.00

—Orange label

❏ EPA-5121	(There'll Be) Peace in the Valley (For Me)/It Is No Secret (What God Can Do)//I Believe/Take My Hand, Precious Lord	1959	7.50	15.00	30.00

—Black label, dog on top

❏ EPA-5121	(There'll Be) Peace in the Valley (For Me)/It Is No Secret (What God Can Do)//I Believe/Take My Hand, Precious Lord	1959	100.00	200.00	400.00

—Maroon label

❏ EPA-5121 [PS]	Peace in the Valley	1959	10.00	20.00	40.00

—Three slightly different cover variations with no difference in value

❏ EPA-5121	(There'll Be) Peace in the Valley (For Me)/It Is No Secret (What God Can Do)//I Believe/Take My Hand, Precious Lord	1965	6.25	12.50	25.00

—Black label, dog on left

❏ EPA-5121	(There'll Be) Peace in the Valley (For Me)/It Is No Secret (What God Can Do)//I Believe/Take My Hand, Precious Lord	1969	20.00	40.00	80.00

—Orange label

❏ EPA-5122	King Creole/New Orleans//As Long As I Have You/Lover Doll	1959	7.50	15.00	30.00

—Black label, dog on top

❏ EPA-5122	King Creole/New Orleans//As Long As I Have You/Lover Doll	1959	1000.	1500.	2000.

—Maroon label

❏ EPA-5122 [PS]	King Creole	1959	10.00	20.00	40.00

—With "Gold Standard Series" on front cover

❏ EPA-5122	King Creole/New Orleans//As Long As I Have You/Lover Doll	1965	6.25	12.50	25.00

—Black label, dog on left

❏ EPA-5122 [PS]	King Creole	1965	7.50	15.00	30.00

—Without "Gold Standard Series" on front cover

❏ EPA-5122	King Creole/New Orleans//As Long As I Have You/Lover Doll	1969	20.00	40.00	80.00

—Orange label

P

Number	Title (A Side/B Side)	Yr	VG	VG+	NM
❑ EPA-5141	All Shook Up/Don't Ask Me Why//Too Much/Blue Moon of Kentucky	1959	7.50	15.00	30.00

—Black label, dog on left

Number	Title (A Side/B Side)	Yr	VG	VG+	NM
❑ EPA-5141	All Shook Up/Don't Ask Me Why//Too Much/Blue Moon of Kentucky	1959	17.50	35.00	70.00

—Black label, dog on top

Number	Title (A Side/B Side)	Yr	VG	VG+	NM
❑ EPA-5141	All Shook Up/Don't Ask Me Why//Too Much/Blue Moon of Kentucky	1959	20.00	40.00	80.00

—Orange label

Number	Title (A Side/B Side)	Yr	VG	VG+	NM
❑ EPA-5141	All Shook Up/Don't Ask Me Why//Too Much/Blue Moon of Kentucky	1959	100.00	200.00	400.00

—Maroon label

Number	Title (A Side/B Side)	Yr	VG	VG+	NM
❑ EPA-5141 [PS]	A Touch of Gold, Volume 3	1959	17.50	35.00	70.00
❑ EPA-5157	Press Interview with Elvis Presley//Elvis Presley's Newsreel Interview/Pat Hernon Interviews Elvis...	1965	7.50	15.00	30.00

—Black label, dog on top

Number	Title (A Side/B Side)	Yr	VG	VG+	NM
❑ EPA-5157 [PS]	Elvis Sails	1965	7.50	15.00	30.00
❑ EPA-5157	Press Interview with Elvis Presley//Elvis Presley's Newsreel Interview/Pat Hernon Interviews Elvis...	1969	20.00	40.00	80.00

—Orange label

Number	Title (A Side/B Side)	Yr	VG	VG+	NM
❑ G8-MW-8705 [DJ]	TV Guide Presents Elvis Presley	1956	300.00	600.00	1200.

—Blue label, locked grooves (needle has to be lifted to play each of the four excerpts)

Number	Title (A Side/B Side)	Yr	VG	VG+	NM
❑ 599-9141	Blue Moon of Kentucky/Love Me Tender//Mystery Train/Milkcow Boogie Blues	1957	100.00	200.00	400.00

—This is "Side 6" and "Side 15" of various artists box set SPD-26, "Great Country/Western Hits"; notice the error in title on the second side

Albums

BOXCAR

Number	Title (A Side/B Side)	Yr	VG	VG+	NM
❑ (no #)	Having Fun with Elvis on Stage	1974	37.50	75.00	150.00

—All-talking record sold at Elvis concerts in 1974

DCC COMPACT CLASSICS

Number	Title (A Side/B Side)	Yr	VG	VG+	NM
❑ LPZ-2037 [S]	Elvis Is Back!	1997	30.00	60.00	120.00

—Audiophile vinyl

Number	Title (A Side/B Side)	Yr	VG	VG+	NM
❑ LPZ-2040 [(2)]	24 Karat Hits!	1997	30.00	60.00	120.00

—Audiophile vinyl

FOTOPLAY

Number	Title (A Side/B Side)	Yr	VG	VG+	NM
❑ FSP-1001 [PD]	To Elvis: Love Still Burning	1978	3.75	7.50	15.00

—In black cardboard cover with white printing

Number	Title (A Side/B Side)	Yr	VG	VG+	NM
❑ FSP-1001 [PD]	To Elvis: Love Still Burning	1978	6.25	12.50	25.00

—Tribute-song picture disc of Elvis; in plastic bag with 11x11 insert

Number	Title (A Side/B Side)	Yr	VG	VG+	NM
❑ FSP-1001 [PD]	To Elvis: Love Still Burning	1978	7.50	15.00	30.00

—In white cardboard cover with black printing

GOLDEN EDITIONS

Number	Title (A Side/B Side)	Yr	VG	VG+	NM
❑ KING-1	The First Year (Elvis, Scotty and Bill)	1979	3.75	7.50	15.00
❑ GEL-101	The First Year (Elvis, Scotty and Bill)	1979	5.00	10.00	20.00

GREAT NORTHWEST

Number	Title (A Side/B Side)	Yr	VG	VG+	NM
❑ GV-2004	The King Speaks (February 1961, Memphis, Tennessee)	1977	2.50	5.00	10.00

—Label says this is on "Green Valley" while sleeve says "Great Northwest"

Number	Title (A Side/B Side)	Yr	VG	VG+	NM
❑ GNW-4005	The Elvis Tapes	1977	3.00	6.00	12.00
❑ GNW-4006	The King Speaks (February 1961, Memphis, Tennessee)	1977	2.00	4.00	8.00

—Both label and sleeve say this is on "Great Northwest"

GREEN VALLEY

Number	Title (A Side/B Side)	Yr	VG	VG+	NM
❑ GV-2001	Elvis Exclusive Live Press Conference (Memphis, Tennessee, February 1961)	1977	10.00	20.00	40.00

—Issued with two slightly different covers

Number	Title (A Side/B Side)	Yr	VG	VG+	NM
❑ GV-2001/3 [(2)]	Elvis (Speaks to You)	1978	7.50	15.00	30.00

—Elvis interviews plus tracks by the Jordanaires

GUSTO

Number	Title (A Side/B Side)	Yr	VG	VG+	NM
❑ SD-995	Interviews with Elvis (Canada 1957)	1978	10.00	20.00	40.00

—Reissue of Great Northwest album

HALW

Number	Title (A Side/B Side)	Yr	VG	VG+	NM
❑ HALW-0001	The First Years	1978	5.00	10.00	20.00

—Without limited edition number

Number	Title (A Side/B Side)	Yr	VG	VG+	NM
❑ HALW-0001	The First Years	1978	7.50	15.00	30.00

—With stamped, limited edition number

K-TEL

Number	Title (A Side/B Side)	Yr	VG	VG+	NM
❑ NU 9900	Love Songs	1981	5.00	10.00	20.00

LOUISIANA HAYRIDE

Number	Title (A Side/B Side)	Yr	VG	VG+	NM
❑ LH-3061	Beginning Years	1984	5.00	10.00	20.00

—With booklet and facsimile contract

MARVENCO

Number	Title (A Side/B Side)	Yr	VG	VG+	NM
❑ 101	Beginning (1954-1955)	1988	3.75	7.50	15.00

—Pink vinyl with booklet and facsimile contract

MOBILE FIDELITY

Number	Title (A Side/B Side)	Yr	VG	VG+	NM
❑ 1-059	From Elvis in Memphis	1982	12.50	25.00	50.00

—Audiophile vinyl

MUSIC WORKS

Number	Title (A Side/B Side)	Yr	VG	VG+	NM
❑ PB-3601	The First Live Recordings	1984	3.75	7.50	15.00
❑ PB-3602	The Hillbilly Cat	1984	3.75	7.50	15.00

OAK

Number	Title (A Side/B Side)	Yr	VG	VG+	NM
❑ 1003	Vintage 1955 Elvis	1990	15.00	30.00	60.00

PAIR

Number	Title (A Side/B Side)	Yr	VG	VG+	NM
❑ PDL2-1010 [(2)]	Double Dynamite	1982	5.00	10.00	20.00
❑ PDL2-1037 [(2)]	Remembering	1983	7.50	15.00	30.00
❑ PDL2-1185 [(2)]	Elvis Aron Presley Forever	1988	5.00	10.00	20.00

PICKWICK

Number	Title (A Side/B Side)	Yr	VG	VG+	NM
❑ (no #) [(7)]	The Pickwick Pack (unofficial title)	1978	15.00	30.00	60.00

—Seven Pickwick albums in special package and cardboard wrapper; one of the LPs is Elvis' Christmas Album

Number	Title (A Side/B Side)	Yr	VG	VG+	NM
❑ (no #) [(7)]	The Pickwick Pack (unofficial title)	1979	15.00	30.00	60.00

—Seven Pickwick albums in special package and cardboard wrapper; one of the LPs is Frankie and Johnny

Number	Title (A Side/B Side)	Yr	VG	VG+	NM
❑ CAS-2304	Elvis Sings Flaming Star	1976	2.50	5.00	10.00
❑ CAS-2408	Let's Be Friends	1975	2.50	5.00	10.00
❑ CAS-2428 [M]	Elvis' Christmas Album	1975	3.00	6.00	12.00

—Same contents as RCA Camden LP; no Christmas trim on border; despite the "CAS" catalog number, this album is mono

Number	Title (A Side/B Side)	Yr	VG	VG+	NM
❑ CAS-2428 [M]	Elvis' Christmas Album	1976	2.50	5.00	10.00

—Same as above, but with Christmas trim on cover border; despite the "CAS" catalog number, this album is mono

Number	Title (A Side/B Side)	Yr	VG	VG+	NM
❑ CAS-2440	Almost in Love	1975	2.50	5.00	10.00

Number	Title (A Side/B Side)	Yr	VG	VG+	NM
❑ CAL-2472	You'll Never Walk Alone	1975	2.50	5.00	10.00
❑ CAL-2518	C'mon Everybody	1975	2.50	5.00	10.00
❑ CAS-2533	I Got Lucky	1975	2.50	5.00	10.00
❑ CAS-2567	Elvis Sings Hits from His Movies, Volume 1	1975	2.50	5.00	10.00
❑ CAS-2595	Burning Love And Hits from His Movies, Vol. 2	1975	3.00	6.00	12.00

—First cover contains a notice about the upcoming "Aloha from Hawaii" show

Number	Title (A Side/B Side)	Yr	VG	VG+	NM
❑ CAS-2595	Burning Love And Hits from His Movies, Vol. 2	1976	2.00	4.00	8.00

—Reissue deletes the "Aloha from Hawaii" notice

Number	Title (A Side/B Side)	Yr	VG	VG+	NM
❑ CAS-2611	Separate Ways	1975	2.50	5.00	10.00
❑ DL2-5001 [(2)]	Double Dynamite	1975	6.25	12.50	25.00
❑ ACL-7007	Frankie and Johnny	1976	2.50	5.00	10.00
❑ ACL-7064	Mahalo from Elvis	1978	5.00	10.00	20.00

PREMORE

Number	Title (A Side/B Side)	Yr	VG	VG+	NM
❑ PL-589	Early Elvis (1954-1956 Live at the Louisiana Hayride)	1989	7.50	15.00	30.00

RCA

Number	Title (A Side/B Side)	Yr	VG	VG+	NM
❑ 2023-1-R	The Million Dollar Quartet	1990	3.00	6.00	12.00

—With Jerry Lee Lewis, Carl Perkins, and perhaps Johnny Cash

Number	Title (A Side/B Side)	Yr	VG	VG+	NM
❑ 2227-1-R	The Great Performances	1990	10.00	20.00	40.00
❑ 3114-1-R [(3)]	Collectors Gold	1991	50.00	100.00	200.00
❑ 5600-1-R	Return of the Rocker	1986	5.00	10.00	20.00
❑ 6221-1-R [(2)]	The Memphis Record	1987	7.50	15.00	30.00
❑ 6313-1-R	Elvis Talks!	1987	7.50	15.00	30.00
❑ 6382-1-R	The Number One Hits	1987	7.50	15.00	30.00
❑ 6383-1-R [(2)]	The Top Ten Hits	1987	7.50	15.00	30.00
❑ 6414-1-R [(2)]	The Complete Sun Sessions	1987	7.50	15.00	30.00
❑ 6738-1-R	Essential Elvis: The First Movies	1988	6.25	12.50	25.00
❑ 6985-1-R	The Alternate Aloha	1988	5.00	10.00	20.00
❑ 8468-1-R	Elvis in Nashville (1956-1971)	1988	10.00	20.00	40.00
❑ 9586-1-R	Elvis Gospel 1957-1971 (Known Only to Him)	1989	10.00	20.00	40.00
❑ 9589-1-R	Essential Elvis, Vol. 2 (Stereo '57)	1989	6.25	12.50	25.00
❑ 07863-67642-1	Elvis' Golden Records	1997	7.50	15.00	30.00

—Reissue for the Tower Records chain with 6 bonus tracks

Number	Title (A Side/B Side)	Yr	VG	VG+	NM
❑ 07863-67643-1	Elvis' Gold Records Volume 2 — 50,000,000 Elvis Fans Can't Be Wrong	1997	7.50	15.00	30.00

—Reissue for the Tower Records chain with 10 bonus tracks

Number	Title (A Side/B Side)	Yr	VG	VG+	NM
❑ 07863-68079-1 [(2)]	30 #1 Hits	2002	5.00	10.00	20.00

RCA CAMDEN

Number	Title (A Side/B Side)	Yr	VG	VG+	NM
❑ CAS-2304	Elvis Sings Flaming Star	1969	7.50	15.00	30.00
❑ CAS-2408	Let's Be Friends	1970	7.50	15.00	30.00
❑ CAL-2428 [M]	Elvis' Christmas Album	1970	7.50	15.00	30.00

—Blue label, non-flexible vinyl

Number	Title (A Side/B Side)	Yr	VG	VG+	NM
❑ CAL-2428 [M]	Elvis' Christmas Album	1971	3.00	6.00	12.00

—Blue label, flexible vinyl

Number	Title (A Side/B Side)	Yr	VG	VG+	NM
❑ CAS-2440	Almost in Love	1970	10.00	20.00	40.00

—Last song on Side 2 is "Stay Away, Joe"

Number	Title (A Side/B Side)	Yr	VG	VG+	NM
❑ CAS-2440	Almost in Love	1973	6.25	12.50	25.00

—Last song on Side 2 is "Stay Away"

Number	Title (A Side/B Side)	Yr	VG	VG+	NM
❑ CAL-2472	You'll Never Walk Alone	1974	7.50	15.00	30.00
❑ CALX-2472	You'll Never Walk Alone	1971	3.75	7.50	15.00
❑ CAL-2518	C'mon Everybody	1971	5.00	10.00	20.00
❑ CAL-2533	I Got Lucky	1971	6.25	12.50	25.00
❑ CAS-2567	Elvis Sings Hits from His Movies, Volume 1	1972	5.00	10.00	20.00
❑ CAS-2595	Burning Love And Hits from His Movies, Vol. 2	1972	2.50	5.00	10.00

—No star on cover, no bonus photo

Number	Title (A Side/B Side)	Yr	VG	VG+	NM
❑ CAS-2595	Burning Love And Hits from His Movies, Vol. 2	1972	6.25	12.50	25.00

—With star on front cover advertising a bonus photo, the presence of which doubles the value of this LP

Number	Title (A Side/B Side)	Yr	VG	VG+	NM
❑ CAS-2611	Separate Ways	1973	7.50	15.00	30.00

RCA SPECIAL PRODUCTS

Number	Title (A Side/B Side)	Yr	VG	VG+	NM
❑ DPL2-0056(e) [(2)]	Elvis	1973	6.25	12.50	25.00

—Blue labels

Number	Title (A Side/B Side)	Yr	VG	VG+	NM
❑ DPL2-0056(e) [(2)]	Elvis	1973	12.50	25.00	50.00

—Mustard labels

Number	Title (A Side/B Side)	Yr	VG	VG+	NM
❑ DPL2-0056(e) [(2)]	Elvis Commemorative Album	1978	20.00	40.00	80.00

—Reissue of "Elvis" (same number) with new title and gold vinyl

Number	Title (A Side/B Side)	Yr	VG	VG+	NM
❑ DPL2-0168 [(2)]	Elvis in Hollywood	1976	15.00	30.00	60.00

—Blue labels; with 20-page booklet

Number	Title (A Side/B Side)	Yr	VG	VG+	NM
❑ DML5-0263 [(5)]	The Elvis Story	1977	15.00	30.00	60.00

—Available through Candelite Music via mail order

Number	Title (A Side/B Side)	Yr	VG	VG+	NM
❑ DML1-0264	His Songs of Inspiration	1977	3.75	7.50	15.00
❑ DPL5-0347 [(5)]	Memories of Elvis (A Lasting Tribute to the King of Rock 'N' Roll)	1978	20.00	40.00	80.00
❑ DML1-0348	The Greatest Show on Earth	1978	3.75	7.50	15.00
❑ DML6-0412 [(6)]	The Legendary Recordings of Elvis Presley	1979	25.00	50.00	100.00
❑ DML1-0413	The Greatest Moments in Music	1980	3.75	7.50	15.00
❑ DML1-0437	Rock 'N Roll Forever	1981	3.75	7.50	15.00
❑ DVL1-0461	The Legendary Magic of Elvis Presley	1980	3.75	7.50	15.00
❑ DML3-0632 [(3)]	The Elvis Presley Collection	1984	20.00	40.00	80.00

—Available through Candelite Music via mail order

Number	Title (A Side/B Side)	Yr	VG	VG+	NM
❑ DPL1-0647	Elvis Country	1984	7.50	15.00	30.00
❑ DVM1-0704	Elvis (One Night with You)	1984	15.00	30.00	60.00

—With poster (deduct 25% if missing)

Number	Title (A Side/B Side)	Yr	VG	VG+	NM
❑ SVL3-0710 [(3)]	50 Years — 50 Hits	1985	7.50	15.00	30.00
❑ DVL2-0728 [(2)]	His Songs of Faith and Inspiration	1986	12.50	25.00	50.00
❑ SVL2-0824 [(2)]	Good Rockin' Tonight	1988	5.00	10.00	20.00
❑ CAL-2428 [M]	Elvis' Christmas Album	1986	7.50	15.00	30.00

—Reissue for The Special Music Company

RCA VICTOR

Number	Title (A Side/B Side)	Yr	VG	VG+	NM
❑ (no #)	International Hotel, Las Vegas Nevada, Presents Elvis, 1969	1969	1250.	1875.	2500.

—Gift box to guests at Elvis' July 31-Aug, 1, 1969 shows. Includes LPM-4088 and LSP-4155; press release; 1969 catalog; three photos; and thank-you note from Elvis and the Colonel. Most of the value is for the box.

Number	Title (A Side/B Side)	Yr	VG	VG+	NM
❑ (no #)	International Hotel, Las Vegas Nevada, Presents Elvis, 1970	1970	1250.	1875.	2500.

—Gift box to guests at Elvis' Jan. 28, 1970 show. Includes LSP-6020 and 47-9791; press release; 1970 catalog; photo; booklet; and dinner menu. Most of the value is for the box.

Number	Title (A Side/B Side)	Yr	VG	VG+	NM
❑ PRS-279	Singer Presents Elvis Singing Flaming Star and Others	1968	25.00	50.00	100.00

—Sold only at Singer sewing machine dealers; reissued on RCA Camden 2304

Number	Title (A Side/B Side)	Yr	VG	VG+	NM
❑ APL1-0283	Elvis	1973	12.50	25.00	50.00
❑ CPL1-0341	A Legendary Performer, Volume 1	1974	6.25	12.50	25.00

—Includes booklet (deduct 40% if missing); with die-cut hole in front cover

Number	Title (A Side/B Side)	Yr	VG	VG+	NM
❑ CPL1-0341	A Legendary Performer, Volume 1	1986	3.75	7.50	15.00

—No die-cut hole in cover and no booklet

Number	Title (A Side/B Side)	Yr	VG	VG+	NM
❏ APL1-0388	Raised on Rock/For Ol' Times Sake	1973	7.50	15.00	30.00

—Orange label

❏ APL1-0388	Raised on Rock/For Ol' Times Sake	1975	7.50	15.00	30.00

—Tan label

| ❏ APL1-0388 | Raised on Rock/For Ol' Times Sake | 1977 | 3.00 | 6.00 | 12.00 |

—Black label, dog near top

| ❏ SP-33-461 [DJ] | Special Palm Sunday Programming | 1967 | 175.00 | 350.00 | 700.00 |

—White label promo. Add 25% for cue sheet.

| ❏ AFL1-0475 | Good Times | 1977 | 3.00 | 6.00 | 12.00 |

—Black label, dog near top; includes copies with sticker wrapped around spine with new number

| ❏ CPL1-0475 | Good Times | 1974 | 12.50 | 25.00 | 50.00 |

—Orange label

| ❏ CPL1-0475 | Good Times | 1976 | 3.00 | 6.00 | 12.00 |

—Black label, dog near top

| ❏ SPS-33-571 [DJ] | Elvis As Recorded at Madison Square Garden | 1972 | 75.00 | 150.00 | 300.00 |

—"Radio Station Banded Special Version"; came in plain white cover with stickers

| ❏ AFL1-0606 | Elvis Recorded Live on Stage in Memphis | 1977 | 3.00 | 6.00 | 12.00 |

—Black label, dog near top; includes copies with sticker wrapped around spine with new number

| ❏ APD1-0606 [Q] | Elvis Recorded Live on Stage in Memphis | 1974 | 50.00 | 100.00 | 200.00 |

—"RCA QuadraDisc" labels

| ❏ CPL1-0606 | Elvis Recorded Live on Stage in Memphis | 1974 | 6.25 | 12.50 | 25.00 |

—Orange label

| ❏ CPL1-0606 | Elvis Recorded Live on Stage in Memphis | 1975 | 6.25 | 12.50 | 25.00 |

—Tan label

| ❏ DJL1-0606 [DJ] | Elvis Recorded Live on Stage in Memphis | 1974 | 75.00 | 150.00 | 300.00 |

—Special banded version for radio airplay

| ❏ AFM1-0818 | Having Fun with Elvis on Stage | 1977 | 6.25 | 12.50 | 25.00 |

—Black label, dog near top

| ❏ CPM1-0818 | Having Fun with Elvis on Stage | 1974 | 7.50 | 15.00 | 30.00 |

—Commercial issue of Boxcar LP; orange label

| ❏ CPM1-0818 | Having Fun with Elvis on Stage | 1975 | 5.00 | 10.00 | 20.00 |

—Tan label

| ❏ DJM1-0835 [DJ] | Elvis Presley Interview Record: An Audio Self-Portrait | 1984 | 20.00 | 40.00 | 80.00 |

—Promotional item for "50th Anniversary" series; later issued as RCA 6313-1-R

| ❏ AFL1-0873 | Promised Land | 1977 | 3.75 | 7.50 | 15.00 |

—Black label, dog near top

| ❏ APD1-0873 [Q] | Promised Land | 1975 | 50.00 | 100.00 | 200.00 |

—"RCA QuadraDisc" label

| ❏ APD1-0873 [Q] | Promised Land | 1977 | 30.00 | 60.00 | 120.00 |

—Black label, dog near top; quadraphonic reissue

| ❏ APL1-0873 | Promised Land | 1975 | 5.00 | 10.00 | 20.00 |

—Tan label

| ❏ APL1-0873 | Promised Land | 1975 | 15.00 | 30.00 | 60.00 |

—Orange label

| ❏ ANL1-0971(e) | Pure Gold | 1975 | 3.75 | 7.50 | 15.00 |

—Orange label

| ❏ ANL1-0971(e) | Pure Gold | 1976 | 3.00 | 6.00 | 12.00 |

—Yellow label

| ❏ LOC-1035 [M] | Elvis' Christmas Album Sticker | 1957 | 37.50 | 75.00 | 150.00 |

—Gold sticker with "To_____" and "From_____" blanks

| ❏ LOC-1035 [M] | Elvis' Christmas Album | 1957 | 125.00 | 250.00 | 500.00 |

—Gatefold cover; title printed in gold on LP spine; includes bound-in booklet but not sticker

| ❏ LOC-1035 [M] | Elvis' Christmas Album | 1957 | 125.00 | 250.00 | 500.00 |

—Gatefold cover; title printed in silver on LP spine; includes bound-in booklet but not sticker

| ❏ LOC-1035 [M] | Elvis' Christmas Album | 1957 | 7500. | 11250. | 15000. |

—Red vinyl; unique

| ❏ AFL1-1039 | Elvis Today | 1977 | 3.00 | 6.00 | 12.00 |

—Black label, dog near top; includes copies with sticker wrapped around spine with new number

| ❏ APD1-1039 [Q] | Elvis Today | 1975 | 50.00 | 100.00 | 200.00 |

—"RCA QuadraDisc" labels

| ❏ APD1-1039 [Q] | Elvis Today | 1977 | 37.50 | 75.00 | 150.00 |

—Black label, dog near top; quadraphonic reissue

| ❏ APL1-1039 | Elvis Today | 1975 | 7.50 | 15.00 | 30.00 |

—Tan label

| ❏ APL1-1039 | Elvis Today | 1975 | 15.00 | 30.00 | 60.00 |

—Orange label

| ❏ AFL1-1254(e) | [R]Elvis Presley | 1977 | 3.00 | 6.00 | 12.00 |

—Black label, dog near top; includes copies with sticker wrapped around spine with new number

| ❏ LPM-1254 [M] | Elvis Presley | 1956 | 62.50 | 125.00 | 250.00 |

—Version 3: "Long Play" on label; "Elvis" in pale pink, "Presley" in neon green on cover; black logo box in upper right front cover

| ❏ LPM-1254 [M] | Elvis Presley | 1956 | 100.00 | 200.00 | 400.00 |

—Version 2: "Long Play" on label; "Elvis" in pale pink, "Presley" in neon green on cover; neon green logo box in upper right front cover

| ❏ LPM-1254 [M] | Elvis Presley | 1956 | 125.00 | 250.00 | 500.00 |

—Version 1: "Long Play" on label; "Elvis" in pale pink, "Presley" in pale green on cover; pale green logo box in upper right front cover

| ❏ LPM-1254 [M] | Elvis Presley | 1958 | 50.00 | 100.00 | 200.00 |

—Version 4: "Long Play" on label; "Elvis" in neon pink, almost red, "Presley" in neon green on cover; black logo box in upper right front cover

| ❏ LPM-1254 [M] | Elvis Presley | 1963 | 30.00 | 60.00 | 120.00 |

—"Mono" on label; cover photo is slightly left of center, otherwise same as Version 4 above

| ❏ LPM-1254 [M] | Elvis Presley | 1964 | 15.00 | 30.00 | 60.00 |

—"Monaural" on label

| ❏ LSP-1254(e) | [R]Elvis Presley | 1962 | 50.00 | 100.00 | 200.00 |

—"Stereo Electronically Reprocessed" and silver "RCA Victor" on label

| ❏ LSP-1254(e) | [R]Elvis Presley | 1965 | 10.00 | 20.00 | 40.00 |

—"Stereo Electronically Reprocessed" and white "RCA Victor" on label

| ❏ LSP-1254(e) | [R]Elvis Presley | 1968 | 7.50 | 15.00 | 30.00 |

—Orange label, non-flexible vinyl

| ❏ LSP-1254(e) | [R]Elvis Presley | 1975 | 3.75 | 7.50 | 15.00 |

—Tan label

| ❏ LSP-1254(e) | [R]Elvis Presley | 1976 | 3.00 | 6.00 | 12.00 |

—Black label, dog near top

| ❏ ANL1-1319 [S] | His Hand in Mine | 1976 | 3.75 | 7.50 | 15.00 |

—Reissue with more tightly cropped photo of Elvis on front cover

| ❏ CPL1-1349 | A Legendary Performer, Volume 2 | 1976 | 7.50 | 15.00 | 30.00 |

—Includes booklet (deduct 40% if missing); with die-cut hole in front cover

| ❏ CPL1-1349 | A Legendary Performer, Volume 2 | 1976 | 15.00 | 30.00 | 60.00 |

—Without false starts and outtakes of "Such a Night" and "Cane and a High Starched Collar," which are supposed to be there. End of matrix number may be "31."

| ❏ CPL1-1349 | A Legendary Performer, Volume 2 | 1986 | 3.75 | 7.50 | 15.00 |

—No die-cut hole in cover and no booklet

| ❏ AFL1-1382(e) | [R]Elvis | 1977 | 3.00 | 6.00 | 12.00 |

—Black label, dog near top; includes copies with sticker wrapped around spine with new number

| ❏ LPM-1382 [M] | Elvis | 1956 | 75.00 | 150.00 | 300.00 |

—Back cover has ads for other albums. At least 11 different variations of this are known, all of equal value.

| ❏ LPM-1382 [M] | Elvis | 1956 | 75.00 | 150.00 | 300.00 |

—Back cover has no ads for other albums. "Long Play" on label.

| ❏ LPM-1382 [M] | Elvis | 1956 | 100.00 | 200.00 | 400.00 |

—With tracks listed on labels as "Band 1" through "Band 6"

| ❏ LPM-1382 [M] | Elvis | 1956 | 200.00 | 400.00 | 800.00 |

—With alternate take of "Old Shep" on side 2. Matrix number on the "Old Shep" side ends in "15S," "17S" or "19S," but should be played for positive ID. On alternate take, Elvis sings "he grew old AND his eyes were growing dim" (no AND on standard press)

| ❏ LPM-1382 [M] | Elvis | 1963 | 20.00 | 40.00 | 80.00 |

—"Mono" on label

| ❏ LPM-1382 [M] | Elvis | 1965 | 15.00 | 30.00 | 60.00 |

—"Monaural" on label

| ❏ LSP-1382(e) | [R]Elvis | 1962 | 50.00 | 100.00 | 200.00 |

—"Stereo Electronically Reprocessed" and silver "RCA Victor" on label

| ❏ LSP-1382(e) | [R]Elvis | 1964 | 12.50 | 25.00 | 50.00 |

—"Stereo Electronically Reprocessed" and white "RCA Victor" on label

| ❏ LSP-1382(e) | [R]Elvis | 1968 | 7.50 | 15.00 | 30.00 |

—Orange label, non-flexible vinyl

| ❏ LSP-1382(e) | [R]Elvis | 1971 | 5.00 | 10.00 | 20.00 |

—Orange label, flexible vinyl

| ❏ LSP-1382(e) | [R]Elvis | 1975 | 3.75 | 7.50 | 15.00 |

—Tan label

| ❏ LSP-1382(e) | [R]Elvis | 1976 | 3.00 | 6.00 | 12.00 |

—Black label, dog near top

| ❏ AFL1-1506 | From Elvis Presley Boulevard, Memphis, Tennessee | 1977 | 2.50 | 5.00 | 10.00 |

—Black label, dog near top; new number is on cover and label

| ❏ AFL1-1506 | From Elvis Presley Boulevard, Memphis, Tennessee | 1977 | 3.00 | 6.00 | 12.00 |

—Black label, dog near top; with sticker wrapped around spine with new number (old number still on label)

| ❏ APL1-1506 | From Elvis Presley Boulevard, Memphis, Tennessee | 1976 | 7.50 | 15.00 | 30.00 |

—Tan label

| ❏ AFL1-1515(e) | [R]Loving You | 1977 | 3.00 | 6.00 | 12.00 |

—Black label, dog near top; includes copies with sticker wrapped around spine with new number

| ❏ LPM-1515 [M] | Loving You | 1957 | 75.00 | 150.00 | 300.00 |

—"Long Play" on label

| ❏ LPM-1515 [M] | Loving You | 1963 | 25.00 | 50.00 | 100.00 |

—"Mono" on label

| ❏ LPM-1515 [M] | Loving You | 1964 | 12.50 | 25.00 | 50.00 |

—"Monaural" on label

| ❏ LSP-1515(e) | [R]Loving You | 1962 | 37.50 | 75.00 | 150.00 |

—"Stereo Electronically Reprocessed" and silver "RCA Victor" on label

| ❏ LSP-1515(e) | [R]Loving You | 1964 | 12.50 | 25.00 | 50.00 |

—"Stereo Electronically Reprocessed" and white "RCA Victor" on label

| ❏ LSP-1515(e) | [R]Loving You | 1968 | 10.00 | 20.00 | 40.00 |

—Orange label, non-flexible vinyl

| ❏ LSP-1515(e) | [R]Loving You | 1971 | 5.00 | 10.00 | 20.00 |

—Orange label, flexible vinyl

| ❏ LSP-1515(e) | [R]Loving You | 1975 | 5.00 | 10.00 | 20.00 |

—Tan label

| ❏ LSP-1515(e) | [R]Loving You | 1976 | 3.00 | 6.00 | 12.00 |

—Black label, dog near top

| ❏ AFM1-1675 | The Sun Sessions | 1977 | 3.75 | 7.50 | 15.00 |

—Black label, dog near top; includes copies with sticker wrapped around spine with new number

| ❏ APM1-1675 | The Sun Sessions | 1976 | 3.00 | 6.00 | 12.00 |

—Black label, dog near top

| ❏ APM1-1675 | The Sun Sessions | 1976 | 5.00 | 10.00 | 20.00 |

—Tan label

| ❏ AFL1-1707(e) | [R]Elvis' Golden Records | 1977 | 3.00 | 6.00 | 12.00 |

—Black label, dog near top; includes copies with sticker wrapped around spine with new number

| ❏ AQL1-1707(e) | [R]Elvis' Golden Records | 1979 | 2.50 | 5.00 | 10.00 |

—Another reissue with new prefix

| ❏ LPM-1707 [M] | Elvis' Golden Records | 1958 | 37.50 | 75.00 | 150.00 |

—Title on cover in light blue letters; no song titles listed on front cover; "RE" on back cover

| ❏ LPM-1707 [M] | Elvis' Golden Records | 1958 | 62.50 | 125.00 | 250.00 |

—Title on cover in light blue letters; no song titles listed on front cover

| ❏ LPM-1707 [M] | Elvis' Golden Records | 1963 | 15.00 | 30.00 | 60.00 |

—"Mono" on label; title on cover in white letters; song titles added to front cover

| ❏ LPM-1707 [M] | Elvis' Golden Records | 1964 | 10.00 | 20.00 | 40.00 |

—"Monaural" on label; "RE2" on back cover

| ❏ LSP-1707(e) | [R]Elvis' Golden Records | 1962 | 50.00 | 100.00 | 200.00 |

—"Stereo Electronically Reprocessed" and silver "RCA Victor" on label

| ❏ LSP-1707(e) | [R]Elvis' Golden Records | 1964 | 12.50 | 25.00 | 50.00 |

—"Stereo Electronically Reprocessed" and white "RCA Victor" on label

| ❏ LSP-1707(e) | [R]Elvis' Golden Records | 1968 | 7.50 | 15.00 | 30.00 |

—Orange label, non-flexible vinyl

| ❏ LSP-1707(e) | [R]Elvis' Golden Records | 1971 | 5.00 | 10.00 | 20.00 |

—Orange label, flexible vinyl

| ❏ LSP-1707(e) | [R]Elvis' Golden Records | 1975 | 5.00 | 10.00 | 20.00 |

—Tan label

| ❏ LSP-1707(e) | [R]Elvis' Golden Records | 1976 | 3.00 | 6.00 | 12.00 |

—Black label, dog near top

| ❏ AFL1-1884(e) | [R]King Creole | 1977 | 3.00 | 6.00 | 12.00 |

—Black label, dog near top; includes copies with sticker wrapped around spine with new number

| ❏ LPM-1884 [M] | King Creole | 1958 | 50.00 | 100.00 | 200.00 |

—"Long Play" on label; contrary to some other sources, this was NOT issued with a bonus photo

| ❏ LPM-1884 [M] | King Creole | 1963 | 20.00 | 40.00 | 80.00 |

—"Mono" on label

| ❏ LPM-1884 [M] | King Creole | 1964 | 15.00 | 30.00 | 60.00 |

—"Monaural" on label

| ❏ LSP-1884(e) | [R]King Creole | 1962 | 37.50 | 75.00 | 150.00 |

—"Stereo Electronically Reprocessed" and silver "RCA Victor" on label

| ❏ LSP-1884(e) | [R]King Creole | 1964 | 15.00 | 30.00 | 60.00 |

—"Stereo Electronically Reprocessed" and white "RCA Victor" on label

| ❏ LSP-1884(e) | [R]King Creole | 1968 | 10.00 | 20.00 | 40.00 |

—Orange label, non-flexible vinyl

| ❏ LSP-1884(e) | [R]King Creole | 1971 | 5.00 | 10.00 | 20.00 |

—Orange label, flexible vinyl

| ❏ LSP-1884(e) | [R]King Creole | 1975 | 5.00 | 10.00 | 20.00 |

—Tan label

| ❏ LSP-1884(e) | [R]King Creole | 1976 | 3.00 | 6.00 | 12.00 |

—Black label, dog near top

P

Number	Title (A Side/B Side)	Yr	VG	VG+	NM
❏ ANL1-1936	Elvis Sings the Wonderful World of Christmas	1975	3.75	7.50	15.00
—New number; same contents as LSP-4579. Orange label.					
❏ ANL1-1936	Elvis Sings the Wonderful World of Christmas	1976	3.00	6.00	12.00
—Tan label					
❏ ANL1-1936	Elvis Sings the Wonderful World of Christmas	1977	2.50	5.00	10.00
—Black label, dog near top					
❏ LPM-1951 [M]	Elvis' Christmas Album	1958	37.50	75.00	150.00
—Same contents as LOC-1035, but with non-gatefold blue cover; "Long Play" at bottom of label					
❏ LPM-1951 [M]	Elvis' Christmas Album	1963	17.50	35.00	70.00
—"Mono" at bottom of label; "RE" on lower left front cover (photos on back were altered)					
❏ LPM-1951 [M]	Elvis' Christmas Album	1964	10.00	20.00	40.00
—"Monaural" at bottom of label; "RE" on lower left front cover					
❏ LSP-1951(e) [R]Elvis' Christmas Album		1964	12.50	25.00	50.00
—Black label, dog on top; "Stereo Electronically Reprocessed" at bottom of label					
❏ LSP-1951(e) [R]Elvis' Christmas Album		1968	15.00	30.00	60.00
—Orange label, non-flexible vinyl					
❏ AFL1-1990(e) [R]For LP Fans Only		1977	3.00	6.00	12.00
—Black label, dog near top; includes copies with sticker wrapped around spine with new number					
❏ LPM-1990 [M]	For LP Fans Only	1959	62.50	125.00	250.00
—"Long Play" on label					
❏ LPM-1990 [M]	For LP Fans Only	1963	20.00	40.00	80.00
—"Mono" on label					
❏ LPM-1990 [M]	For LP Fans Only	1964	12.50	25.00	50.00
—"Monaural" on label					
❏ LSP-1990(e) [R]For LP Fans Only		1965	12.50	25.00	50.00
—"Stereo Electronically Reprocessed" on label; normal cover with different front and back cover photos					
❏ LSP-1990(e) [R]For LP Fans Only		1965	75.00	150.00	300.00
—"Stereo Electronically Reprocessed" on label; error cover with same photo on both front and back					
❏ LSP-1990(e) [R]For LP Fans Only		1968	7.50	15.00	30.00
—Orange label, non-flexible vinyl					
❏ LSP-1990(e) [R]For LP Fans Only		1975	5.00	10.00	20.00
—Tan label					
❏ LSP-1990(e) [R]For LP Fans Only		1976	3.00	6.00	12.00
—Black label, dog near top					
❏ AFL1-2011(e) [R]A Date with Elvis		1977	3.00	6.00	12.00
—Black label, dog near top; includes copies with sticker wrapped around spine with new number					
❏ LPM-2011 [M]	A Date with Elvis	1959	100.00	200.00	400.00
—"Long Play" on label; gatefold cover, no sticker on cover					
❏ LPM-2011 [M]	A Date with Elvis	1959	125.00	250.00	500.00
—"Long Play" on label; gatefold cover, with sticker on cover					
❏ LPM-2011 [M]	A Date with Elvis	1963	25.00	50.00	100.00
—"Mono" on label; no gatefold cover					
❏ LPM-2011 [M]	A Date with Elvis	1965	12.50	25.00	50.00
—"Monaural" on label					
❏ LSP-2011(e) [R]A Date with Elvis		1965	12.50	25.00	50.00
—Black label, "Stereo Electronically Reprocessed" on label					
❏ LSP-2011(e) [R]A Date with Elvis		1968	7.50	15.00	30.00
—Orange label, non-flexible vinyl					
❏ LSP-2011(e) [R]A Date with Elvis		1971	5.00	10.00	20.00
—Orange label, flexible vinyl					
❏ LSP-2011(e) [R]A Date with Elvis		1975	5.00	10.00	20.00
—Tan label					
❏ LSP-2011(e) [R]A Date with Elvis		1977	3.00	6.00	12.00
—Black label, dog near top					
❏ AFL1-2075(e) [R]Elvis' Gold Records Volume 2 — 50,000,000 Elvis Fans Can't Be Wrong		1977	3.00	6.00	12.00
—Black label, dog near top; includes copies with sticker wrapped around spine with new number					
❏ LPM-2075 [M]	Elvis' Gold Records Volume 2 — 50,000,000 Elvis Fans Can't Be Wrong	1960	50.00	100.00	200.00
—"Long Play" on label; "Magic Millions" on upper right front cover with RCA Victor logo					
❏ LPM-2075 [M]	Elvis' Gold Records Volume 2 — 50,000,000 Elvis Fans Can't Be Wrong	1963	20.00	40.00	80.00
—"Mono" on label; "RE" on lower right front cover					
❏ LPM-2075 [M]	Elvis' Gold Records Volume 2 — 50,000,000 Elvis Fans Can't Be Wrong	1964	12.50	25.00	50.00
—"Monaural" on label; label has words "50,000,000 Elvis Presley Fans Can't Be Wrong"					
❏ LPM-2075 [M]	Elvis' Gold Records Volume 2 — 50,000,000 Elvis Fans Can't Be Wrong	1964	12.50	25.00	50.00
—"Monaural" on label; label only has "Elvis' Gold Records - Vol. 2"					
❏ LSP-2075(e) [R]Elvis' Gold Records Volume 2 — 50,000,000 Elvis Fans Can't Be Wrong		1962	37.50	75.00	150.00
—"Stereo Electronically Reprocessed" on label; label has words "50,000,000 Elvis Presley Fans Can't Be Wrong"					
❏ LSP-2075(e) [R]Elvis' Gold Records Volume 2 — 50,000,000 Elvis Fans Can't Be Wrong		1964	12.50	25.00	50.00
—"Stereo Electronically Reprocessed" and white "RCA Victor" on label					
❏ LSP-2075(e) [R]Elvis' Gold Records Volume 2 — 50,000,000 Elvis Fans Can't Be Wrong		1968	7.50	15.00	30.00
—Orange label, non-flexible vinyl					
❏ LSP-2075(e) [R]Elvis' Gold Records Volume 2 — 50,000,000 Elvis Fans Can't Be Wrong		1971	5.00	10.00	20.00
—Orange label, flexible vinyl					
❏ LSP-2075(e) [R]Elvis' Gold Records Volume 2 — 50,000,000 Elvis Fans Can't Be Wrong		1975	5.00	10.00	20.00
—Tan label					
❏ LSP-2075(e) [R]Elvis' Gold Records Volume 2 — 50,000,000 Elvis Fans Can't Be Wrong		1976	3.00	6.00	12.00
—Black label, dog near top					
❏ AFL1-2231 [S]	Elvis Is Back!	1977	3.00	6.00	12.00
—Black label, dog near top; includes copies with sticker wrapped around spine with new number					
❏ LPM-2231 [M]	Elvis Is Back!	1960	37.50	75.00	150.00
—With sticker attached to front cover. Side 2, Song 4 is listed as "The Girl Next Door Went a-Walking."					
❏ LPM-2231 [M]	Elvis Is Back!	1960	37.50	75.00	150.00
—With sticker attached to front cover. Side 2, Song 4 is listed as "The Girl Next Door."					
❏ LPM-2231 [M]	Elvis Is Back!	1960	50.00	100.00	200.00
—With no sticker attached to front cover. Side 2, Song 4 is listed as "The Girl Next Door Went a-Walking."					
❏ LPM-2231 [M]	Elvis Is Back!	1960	50.00	100.00	200.00
—With no sticker attached to front cover. Side 2, Song 4 is listed as "The Girl Next Door."					
❏ LPM-2231 [M]	Elvis Is Back!	1963	15.00	30.00	60.00
—"Mono" on label; song titles printed on front cover					
❏ LPM-2231 [M]	Elvis Is Back!	1964	15.00	30.00	60.00
—"Monaural" on label					
❏ LSP-2231 [S]	Elvis Is Back!	1960	75.00	150.00	300.00
—"Living Stereo" on label; with no sticker attached to front cover. Side 2, Song 4 is listed as "The Girl Next Door Went a-Walking."					
❏ LSP-2231 [S]	Elvis Is Back!	1960	75.00	150.00	300.00
—"Living Stereo" on label; with no sticker attached to front cover. Side 2, Song 4 is listed as "The Girl Next Door."					
❏ LSP-2231 [S]	Elvis Is Back!	1960	75.00	150.00	300.00
—"Living Stereo" on label; with sticker attached to front cover. Side 2, Song 4 is listed as "The Girl Next Door Went a-Walking."					
❏ LSP-2231 [S]	Elvis Is Back!	1960	75.00	150.00	300.00
—"Living Stereo" on label; with sticker attached to front cover. Side 2, Song 4 is listed as "The Girl Next Door."					
❏ LSP-2231 [S]	Elvis Is Back!	1964	15.00	30.00	60.00
—"Stereo" on label; song titles printed on front cover					
❏ LSP-2231 [S]	Elvis Is Back!	1968	10.00	20.00	40.00
—Orange label, non-flexible vinyl					
❏ LSP-2231 [S]	Elvis Is Back!	1975	5.00	10.00	20.00
—Tan label					
❏ LSP-2231 [S]	Elvis Is Back!	1976	3.75	7.50	15.00
—Black label, dog on top					
❏ AFL1-2256 [S]	G.I. Blues	1977	3.00	6.00	12.00
—Black label, dog near top; includes copies with sticker wrapped around spine with new number					
❏ LPM-2256 [M]	G.I. Blues	1960	30.00	60.00	120.00
—"Long Play" on label; with no sticker on front cover					
❏ LPM-2256 [M]	G.I. Blues	1960	125.00	250.00	500.00
—"Long Play" on label; with sticker on front cover advertising the presence of "Wooden Heart"					
❏ LPM-2256 [M]	G.I. Blues	1963	25.00	50.00	100.00
—"Mono" on label					
❏ LPM-2256 [M]	G.I. Blues	1964	12.50	25.00	50.00
—"Monaural" on label					
❏ LSP-2256 [S]	G.I. Blues	1960	25.00	50.00	100.00
—"Living Stereo" on label; with no sticker on front cover					
❏ LSP-2256 [S]	G.I. Blues	1960	150.00	300.00	600.00
—"Living Stereo" on label; with sticker on front cover advertising the presence of "Wooden Heart"					
❏ LSP-2256 [S]	G.I. Blues	1964	12.50	25.00	50.00
—"Stereo" on black label					
❏ LSP-2256 [S]	G.I. Blues	1968	10.00	20.00	40.00
—Orange label, non-flexible vinyl					
❏ LSP-2256 [S]	G.I. Blues	1971	5.00	10.00	20.00
—Orange label, flexible vinyl					
❏ LSP-2256 [S]	G.I. Blues	1975	6.25	12.50	25.00
—Tan label					
❏ LSP-2256 [S]	G.I. Blues	1976	3.00	6.00	12.00
—Black label, dog near top					
❏ AFL1-2274	Welcome to My World	1977	3.00	6.00	12.00
—Black label, dog near top; includes copies with sticker wrapped around spine with new number					
❏ APL1-2274	Welcome to My World	1977	5.00	10.00	20.00
—Black label, dog near top					
❏ AQL1-2274	Welcome to My World	1979	2.50	5.00	10.00
—Black label, dog near top; includes copies with sticker wrapped around spine with new number					
❏ LPM-2328 [M]	His Hand in Mine	1960	30.00	60.00	120.00
—"Long Play" on label					
❏ LPM-2328 [M]	His Hand in Mine	1963	15.00	30.00	60.00
—"Mono" on label					
❏ LPM-2328 [M]	His Hand in Mine	1964	12.50	25.00	50.00
—"Monaural" on label					
❏ LSP-2328 [S]	His Hand in Mine	1960	50.00	100.00	200.00
—"Living Stereo" on label					
❏ LSP-2328 [S]	His Hand in Mine	1964	25.00	50.00	100.00
—"Stereo" and white "RCA Victor" on black label					
❏ LSP-2328 [S]	His Hand in Mine	1964	150.00	300.00	600.00
—"Stereo" and silver "RCA Victor" on black label					
❏ LSP-2328 [S]	His Hand in Mine	1968	12.50	25.00	50.00
—Orange label, non-flexible vinyl					
❏ LSP-2328 [S]	His Hand in Mine	197?	5.00	10.00	20.00
—Orange label, flexible vinyl					
❏ LSP-2328 [S]	His Hand in Mine	1975	5.00	10.00	20.00
—Tan label					
❏ AHL1-2347	Greatest Hits, Volume One	1981	6.25	12.50	25.00
—With embossed cover					
❏ AHL1-2347	Greatest Hits, Volume One	1983	3.75	7.50	15.00
—Without embossed cover					
❏ AFL1-2370 [S]	Something for Everybody	1977	3.00	6.00	12.00
—Black label, dog near top; includes copies with sticker wrapped around spine with new number					
❏ LPM-2370 [M]	Something for Everybody	1961	30.00	60.00	120.00
—"Long Play" on label; back cover advertises RCA Compact 33 singles and doubles					
❏ LPM-2370 [M]	Something for Everybody	1963	20.00	40.00	80.00
—"Mono" on label; back cover advertises "Viva Las Vegas" EP					
❏ LPM-2370 [M]	Something for Everybody	1964	12.50	25.00	50.00
—"Monaural" on label; back cover advertises "Viva Las Vegas" EP					
❏ LSP-2370 [S]	Something for Everybody	1961	50.00	100.00	200.00
—"Living Stereo" on label; back cover advertises RCA Compact 33 singles and doubles					
❏ LSP-2370 [S]	Something for Everybody	1963	25.00	50.00	100.00
—"Stereo" and silver "RCA Victor" on black label; back cover advertises Elvis' Christmas Album and His Hand in Mine LPs and "Viva Las Vegas" EP					
❏ LSP-2370 [S]	Something for Everybody	1964	12.50	25.00	50.00
—"Stereo" and white "RCA Victor" on black label; back cover advertises "Viva Las Vegas" EP					
❏ LSP-2370 [S]	Something for Everybody	1968	10.00	20.00	40.00
—Orange label, non-flexible vinyl; final back cover change advertises Elvis (NBC-TV Special), Elvis' Christmas Album and His Hand in Mine LPs					
❏ LSP-2370 [S]	Something for Everybody	1971	5.00	10.00	20.00
—Orange label, flexible vinyl					
❏ LSP-2370 [S]	Something for Everybody	1975	5.00	10.00	20.00
—Tan label					
❏ LSP-2370 [S]	Something for Everybody	1976	3.00	6.00	12.00
—Black label, dog near top					
❏ AFL1-2426 [S]	Blue Hawaii	1977	3.00	6.00	12.00
—Black label, dog near top; with sticker wrapped around spine with new number					
❏ LPM-2426 [M]	Blue Hawaii	1961	25.00	50.00	100.00
—"Long Play" on label; with sticker on cover advertising the presence of "Can't Help Falling in Love" and "Rock-a-Hula Baby"					
❏ LPM-2426 [M]	Blue Hawaii	1962	15.00	30.00	60.00
—"Long Play" on label; no sticker on front cover					
❏ LPM-2426 [M]	Blue Hawaii	1963	12.50	25.00	50.00
—"Mono" on label					
❏ LPM-2426 [M]	Blue Hawaii	1964	10.00	20.00	40.00
—"Monaural" on label					

Number	Title (A Side/B Side)	Yr	VG	VG+	NM
❑ LSP-2426 [S] Blue Hawaii		1961	37.50	75.00	150.00

—"Living Stereo" on label and upper right front cover; with sticker on cover advertising the presence of "Can't Help Falling in Love" and "Rock-a-Hula Baby"

❑ LSP-2426 [S] Blue Hawaii		1962	20.00	40.00	80.00

—"Living Stereo" on label and upper right front cover; no sticker on front cover

❑ LSP-2426 [S] Blue Hawaii		1964	12.50	25.00	50.00

—"Stereo" on label; "Victor Stereo" on upper right front cover

❑ LSP-2426 [S] Blue Hawaii		1968	10.00	20.00	40.00

—Orange label, non-flexible vinyl

❑ LSP-2426 [S] Blue Hawaii		197?	250.00	500.00	1000.

—One-of-a-kind blue vinyl pressing with black label, dog near top

❑ LSP-2426 [S] Blue Hawaii		1971	50.00	10.00	20.00

—Orange label, flexible vinyl

❑ LSP-2426 [S] Blue Hawaii		1975	50.00	10.00	20.00

—Tan label

❑ LSP-2426 [S] Blue Hawaii		1977	3.00	6.00	12.00

—Black label, dog near top

❑ AFK1-2428 Moody Blue		1977	1500.	2250.	3000.

—Alternate cover slick (never put on an actual cover), with the words "Moody Blue" inside the large word "Elvis." See any late-1970s Elvis inner sleeve for a black and white photo of the scrapped cover.

❑ AFL1-2428 Moody Blue		1977	2.50	5.00	10.00

—Blue vinyl

❑ AFL1-2428 Moody Blue		1977	50.00	100.00	200.00

—Black vinyl

❑ AFL1-2428 [DJ]Moody Blue		1977	500.00	1000.	2000.

—Experimental colored vinyl pressings (with no cover), any color or combination except blue or black

❑ AQL1-2428 Moody Blue		1979	6.25	12.50	25.00

—Reissue with new prefix

❑ AFL1-2523 [S] Pot Luck with Elvis		1977	3.00	6.00	12.00

—Black label, dog near top; includes copies with sticker wrapped around spine with new number

❑ LPM-2523 [M] Pot Luck with Elvis		1962	25.00	50.00	100.00

—"Long Play" on label

❑ LPM-2523 [M] Pot Luck with Elvis		1964	30.00	60.00	120.00

—"Monaural" on label

❑ LSP-2523 [S] Pot Luck with Elvis		1962	37.50	75.00	150.00

—"Living Stereo" on label

❑ LSP-2523 [S] Pot Luck with Elvis		1964	15.00	30.00	60.00

—"Stereo" on black label

❑ LSP-2523 [S] Pot Luck with Elvis		1968	10.00	20.00	40.00

—Orange label, non-flexible vinyl

❑ LSP-2523 [S] Pot Luck with Elvis		1975	5.00	10.00	20.00

—Tan label

❑ LSP-2523 [S] Pot Luck with Elvis		1976	3.00	6.00	12.00

—Black label, dog near top

❑ APL1-2558 [S] Harum Scarum		1977	3.00	6.00	12.00

—Black label, dog near top

❑ APL1-2560 [S] Spinout		1977	3.00	6.00	12.00

—Black label, dog near top

❑ APL1-2564 [S] Double Trouble		1977	3.00	6.00	12.00

—Black label, dog near top; includes copies with sticker wrapped around spine with new number

❑ APL1-2565 Clambake		1977	3.00	6.00	12.00
❑ APL1-2568 [S] It Happened at the World's Fair		1977	3.00	6.00	12.00
❑ AFL2-2587 [(2)]Elvis in Concert		197?	250.00	500.00	1000.

—Both records on translucent blue vinyl; possibly an in-house demo at the RCA Indianapolis pressing plant

❑ APL2-2587 [(2)]Elvis in Concert		1977	6.25	12.50	25.00
❑ CPL2-2587 [(2)]Elvis in Concert		1982	10.00	20.00	40.00
❑ AFL1-2621 [S] Girls! Girls! Girls!		1977	3.00	6.00	12.00

—Black label, dog near top; includes copies with sticker wrapped around spine with new number

❑ LPM-2621 [M] Girls! Girls! Girls!		1962	20.00	40.00	80.00

—"Long Play" on label

❑ LPM-2621 [M] Girls! Girls! Girls!		1963	15.00	30.00	60.00

—"Mono" on label

❑ LPM-2621 [M] Girls! Girls! Girls!		1964	10.00	20.00	40.00

—"Monaural" on label

❑ LPM/LSP-2621 Girls! Girls! Girls! Bonus 1963 Calendar		1962	37.50	75.00	150.00

—With listing of other Elvis records on back

❑ LSP-2621 [S] Girls! Girls! Girls!		1962	37.50	75.00	150.00

—"Living Stereo" on label

❑ LSP-2621 [S] Girls! Girls! Girls!		1964	15.00	30.00	60.00

—"Stereo" on black label

❑ LSP-2621 [S] Girls! Girls! Girls!		1968	10.00	20.00	40.00

—Orange label, non-flexible vinyl

❑ LSP-2621 [S] Girls! Girls! Girls!		1971	5.00	10.00	20.00

—Orange label, flexible vinyl

❑ LSP-2621 [S] Girls! Girls! Girls!		1975	6.25	12.50	25.00

—Tan label

❑ LSP-2621 [S] Girls! Girls! Girls!		1976	3.00	6.00	12.00

—Black label, dog near top

❑ CPD2-2642 [(2)Q]Aloha from Hawaii Via Satellite		1975	7.50	15.00	30.00

—Orange labels

❑ CPD2-2642 [(2)Q]Aloha from Hawaii Via Satellite		1977	20.00	40.00	80.00

—Black labels, dog near top

❑ CPL2-2642 [(2)Q]Aloha from Hawaii Via Satellite		1984	3.00	6.00	12.00

—New prefix; single-pocket instead of gatefold jacket

❑ LPM-2697 [M] It Happened at the World's Fair		1963	30.00	60.00	120.00
❑ LPM/LSP-2697 It Happened at the World's Fair Photo		1963	62.50	125.00	250.00
❑ LSP-2697 [S] It Happened at the World's Fair		1963	50.00	100.00	200.00

—"Living Stereo" and silver "RCA Victor" on black label

❑ LSP-2697 [S] It Happened at the World's Fair		1964	20.00	40.00	80.00

—"Stereo" and white "RCA Victor" on black label

❑ AFL1-2756 [S] Fun in Acapulco		1977	3.00	6.00	12.00

—Black label, dog near top; includes copies with sticker wrapped around spine with new number

❑ LPM-2756 [M] Fun in Acapulco		1963	20.00	40.00	80.00

—"Mono" on label

❑ LPM-2756 [M] Fun in Acapulco		1964	12.50	25.00	50.00

—"Monaural" on label

❑ LSP-2756 [S] Fun in Acapulco		1963	25.00	50.00	100.00

—"Stereo" and silver "RCA Victor" on black label

❑ LSP-2756 [S] Fun in Acapulco		1964	15.00	30.00	60.00

—"Stereo" and white "RCA Victor" on black label

❑ LSP-2756 [S] Fun in Acapulco		1968	10.00	20.00	40.00

—Orange label, non-flexible vinyl

❑ LSP-2756 [S] Fun in Acapulco		1975	6.25	12.50	25.00

—Tan label

❑ LSP-2756 [S] Fun in Acapulco		1976	3.00	6.00	12.00

—Black label, dog near top

Number	Title (A Side/B Side)	Yr	VG	VG+	NM
❑ AFL1-2765 [S] Elvis' Golden Records, Volume 3		1977	3.00	6.00	12.00

—Black label, dog near top; includes copies with sticker wrapped around spine with new number

❑ LPM-2765 [M] Elvis' Golden Records, Volume 3		1963	25.00	50.00	100.00

—"Mono" on label

❑ LPM-2765 [M] Elvis' Golden Records, Volume 3		1964	15.00	30.00	60.00

—"Monaural" on label

❑ LSP-2765 [S] Elvis' Golden Records, Volume 3		1963	37.50	75.00	150.00

—"Stereo" and silver "RCA Victor" on black label

❑ LSP-2765 [S] Elvis' Golden Records, Volume 3		1964	12.50	25.00	50.00

—"Stereo" and white "RCA Victor" on black label

❑ LSP-2765 [S] Elvis' Golden Records, Volume 3		1968	10.00	20.00	40.00

—Orange label, non-flexible vinyl

❑ LSP-2765 [S] Elvis' Golden Records, Volume 3		1975	5.00	10.00	20.00

—Tan label

❑ LSP-2765 [S] Elvis' Golden Records, Volume 3		1976	3.00	6.00	12.00

—Black label, dog near top

❑ AFL1-2772 He Walks Beside Me		1978	6.25	12.50	25.00

—Includes 20-page photo booklet

❑ AFL1-2894 [S] Kissin' Cousins		1977	3.00	6.00	12.00

—Black label, dog near top; includes copies with sticker wrapped around spine with new number

❑ LPM-2894 [M] Kissin' Cousins		1964	20.00	40.00	80.00

—"Mono" on label; front cover has a small black and white photo of six cast members in lower right

❑ LPM-2894 [M] Kissin' Cousins		1964	25.00	50.00	100.00

—"Monaural" on label; front cover has a small black and white photo of six cast members in lower right

❑ LPM-2894 [M] Kissin' Cousins		1964	50.00	100.00	200.00

—"Monaural" on label; front cover does NOT have black and white photo in lower right

❑ LPM-2894 [M] Kissin' Cousins		1964	50.00	100.00	200.00

—"Mono" on label; front cover does NOT have black and white photo in lower right

❑ LSP-2894 [S] Kissin' Cousins		1964	15.00	30.00	60.00

—"Stereo" and white "RCA Victor" on black label; all front covers have the cast photo in lower right

❑ LSP-2894 [S] Kissin' Cousins		1964	30.00	60.00	120.00

—"Stereo" and silver "RCA Victor" on black label; front cover has a small black and white photo of six cast members in lower right

❑ LSP-2894 [S] Kissin' Cousins		1964	50.00	100.00	200.00

—"Stereo" and silver "RCA Victor" on black label; front cover does NOT have black and white photo in lower right

❑ LSP-2894 [S] Kissin' Cousins		1968	10.00	20.00	40.00

—Orange label, non-flexible vinyl

❑ LSP-2894 [S] Kissin' Cousins		1971	5.00	10.00	20.00

—Orange label, flexible vinyl

❑ LSP-2894 [S] Kissin' Cousins		1975	6.25	12.50	25.00

—Tan label

❑ LSP-2894 [S] Kissin' Cousins		1976	3.00	6.00	12.00

—Black label, dog near top

❑ LSP-2894 [S] Kissin' Cousins		1976	375.00	750.00	1500.

—Black label, dog near top; blue vinyl

❑ CPL1-2901 Elvis Sings for Children and Grownups Too!		1978	2.50	5.00	10.00

—With greeting card graphic printed on back cover, and no slits on back cover

❑ CPL1-2901 Elvis Sings for Children and Grownups Too!		1978	5.00	10.00	20.00

—With two slits for removable greeting card on back cover (card should be with package)

❑ AFL1-2999 [S] Roustabout		1977	3.00	6.00	12.00

—Black label, dog near top; includes copies with sticker wrapped around spine with new number

❑ LPM-2999 [M] Roustabout		1964	25.00	50.00	100.00

—"Mono" on label

❑ LPM-2999 [M] Roustabout		1965	15.00	30.00	60.00

—"Monaural" on label

❑ LSP-2999 [S] Roustabout		1964	15.00	30.00	60.00

—"Stereo" and white "RCA Victor" on black label

❑ LSP-2999 [S] Roustabout		1964	150.00	300.00	600.00

—"Stereo" and silver "RCA Victor" on black label

❑ LSP-2999 [S] Roustabout		1968	10.00	20.00	40.00

—Orange label, non-flexible vinyl

❑ LSP-2999 [S] Roustabout		1971	5.00	10.00	20.00

—Orange label, flexible vinyl

❑ LSP-2999 [S] Roustabout		1975	5.00	10.00	20.00

—Tan label

❑ LSP-2999 [S] Roustabout		1976	3.00	6.00	12.00

—Black label, dog near top

❑ CPL1-3078 [PD]A Legendary Performer, Volume 3		1978	6.25	12.50	25.00

—Picture disc applied to blue vinyl LP; with booklet (deduct 40% if missing)

❑ CPL1-3082 A Legendary Performer, Volume 3		1978	6.25	12.50	25.00

—Includes booklet (deduct 40% if missing); with die-cut hole in front cover

❑ CPL1-3082 A Legendary Performer, Volume 3		1986	2.00	4.00	8.00

—No die-cut hole in cover and no booklet

❑ AQL1-3279 Our Memories of Elvis		1979	5.00	10.00	20.00
❑ AFL1-3338 [S] Girl Happy		1977	3.00	6.00	12.00

—Black label, dog near top; includes copies with sticker wrapped around spine with new number

❑ LPM-3338 [M] Girl Happy		1965	15.00	30.00	60.00
❑ LSP-3338 [S] Girl Happy		1965	15.00	30.00	60.00

—"Stereo" on black label

❑ LSP-3338 [S] Girl Happy		1968	10.00	20.00	40.00

—Orange label, non-flexible vinyl

❑ LSP-3338 [S] Girl Happy		1971	5.00	10.00	20.00

—Orange label, flexible vinyl

❑ LSP-3338 [S] Girl Happy		1975	6.25	12.50	25.00

—Tan label

❑ LSP-3338 [S] Girl Happy		1976	3.00	6.00	12.00

—Black label, dog near top

❑ AQL1-3448 Our Memories of Elvis, Volume 2		1979	5.00	10.00	20.00
❑ AFL1-3450 [P] Elvis for Everyone		1977	3.00	6.00	12.00

—Black label, dog near top; includes copies with sticker wrapped around spine with new number

❑ LPM-3450 [P] Elvis for Everyone		1965	15.00	30.00	60.00
❑ LSP-3450 [P] Elvis for Everyone		1965	15.00	30.00	60.00

—Black label, "Stereo" on label

❑ LSP-3450 [P] Elvis for Everyone		1968	10.00	20.00	40.00

—Orange label, non-flexible vinyl

❑ LSP-3450 [P] Elvis for Everyone		1971	5.00	10.00	20.00

—Orange label, flexible vinyl

❑ LSP-3450 [P] Elvis for Everyone		1975	5.00	10.00	20.00

—Tan label

❑ LSP-3450 [P] Elvis for Everyone		1976	3.00	6.00	12.00

—Black label, dog near top

❑ DJL1-3455 [DJ]Pure Elvis		1979	150.00	300.00	600.00

—Promo-only item for Our Memories of Elvis, Volume 2; contains original version of five songs on one side, "unsweetened" versions of same songs on the other

❑ LPM-3468 [M] Harum Scarum		1965	15.00	30.00	60.00

P

Number	Title (A Side/B Side)	Yr	VG	VG+	NM
❑ LPM/LSP-3468 Harum Scarum Bonus Photo		1965	15.00	30.00	60.00
❑ LSP-3468 [S] Harum Scarum		1965	15.00	30.00	60.00
—"Stereo" on black label					
❑ LPM-3553 [M] Frankie and Johnny		1966	15.00	30.00	60.00
❑ LPM/LSP-3553 Frankie and Johnny Bonus Print		1966	15.00	30.00	60.00
❑ LSP-3553 [S] Frankie and Johnny		1966	15.00	30.00	60.00
—"Stereo" on black label					
❑ AFL1-3643 [S] Paradise, Hawaiian Style		1977	3.00	6.00	12.00
—Black label, dog near top; includes copies with sticker wrapped around spine with new number					
❑ LPM-3643 [M] Paradise, Hawaiian Style		1966	15.00	30.00	60.00
❑ LSP-3643 [S] Paradise, Hawaiian Style		1966	15.00	30.00	60.00
—"Stereo" on black label					
❑ LSP-3643 [S] Paradise, Hawaiian Style		1968	10.00	20.00	40.00
—Orange label, non-flexible vinyl					
❑ LSP-3643 [S] Paradise, Hawaiian Style		1971	5.00	10.00	20.00
—Orange label, flexible vinyl					
❑ LSP-3643 [S] Paradise, Hawaiian Style		1975	3.75	7.50	15.00
—Tan label					
❑ LSP-3643 [S] Paradise, Hawaiian Style		1976	3.00	6.00	12.00
—Black label, dog near top					
❑ AYL1-3683 [S] Blue Hawaii		1980	2.50	5.00	10.00
—"Best Buy Series" reissue					
❑ AYL1-3684 [S] Spinout		1980	2.00	4.00	8.00
—"Best Buy Series" reissue					
❑ CPL8-3699 [(8)]Elvis Aron Presley		1980	25.00	50.00	100.00
—Box set; regular issue with booklet					
❑ CPL8-3699 [(8)]Elvis Aron Presley		1980	62.50	125.00	250.00
—Box set; "Reviewer Series" edition (will be identified as such on the cover)					
❑ LPM-3702 [M] Spinout		1966	15.00	30.00	60.00
❑ LPM/LSP-3702 Spinout Bonus Photo		1966	15.00	30.00	60.00
❑ LSP-3702 [S] Spinout		1966	15.00	30.00	60.00
—"Stereo" on black label					
❑ DJL1-3729 [DJ]Elvis Aron Presley (Excerpts)		1980	30.00	60.00	120.00
—Promo-only excerpts of songs from box set					
❑ AYL1-3732 Pure Gold		1980	2.00	4.00	8.00
—"Best Buy Series" reissue					
❑ AYL1-3733 [R] King Creole		1980	2.00	4.00	8.00
—"Best Buy Series" reissue; includes copies with sticker wrapped around spine with new number					
❑ AYL1-3734 [S] Harum Scarum		1980	2.00	4.00	8.00
—"Best Buy Series" reissue					
❑ AYL1-3735 [S] G.I. Blues		1980	2.00	4.00	8.00
—"Best Buy Series" reissue					
❑ AFL1-3758 [S] How Great Thou Art		1977	3.00	6.00	12.00
—Black label, dog near top; includes copies with sticker wrapped around spine with new number					
❑ AQL1-3758 [S] How Great Thou Art		1979	2.50	5.00	10.00
—Reissue with new prefix					
❑ LPM-3758 [M] How Great Thou Art		1967	15.00	30.00	60.00
—"Mono Dynagroove" on label					
❑ LSP-3758 [S] How Great Thou Art		1967	15.00	30.00	60.00
—"Stereo Dynagroove" on black label					
❑ LSP-3758 [S] How Great Thou Art		1968	10.00	20.00	40.00
—Orange label, non-flexible vinyl					
❑ LSP-3758 [S] How Great Thou Art		1971	6.25	12.50	25.00
—Orange label, flexible vinyl					
❑ LSP-3758 [S] How Great Thou Art		1975	5.00	10.00	20.00
—Tan label					
❑ LSP-3758 [S] How Great Thou Art		1976	3.00	6.00	12.00
—Black label, dog near top					
❑ DJL1-3781 [DJ]Elvis Aron Presley (Selections)		1980	30.00	60.00	120.00
—Promo-only complete versions of songs from box set					
❑ LPM-3787 [M] Double Trouble		1967	15.00	30.00	60.00
—With bonus photo announcement on cover					
❑ LPM-3787 [M] Double Trouble		1967	20.00	40.00	80.00
—With no bonus photo announcement on cover					
❑ LPM/LSP-3787 Double Trouble Bonus Photo		1967	12.50	25.00	50.00
❑ LSP-3787 [S] Double Trouble		1967	15.00	30.00	60.00
—With bonus photo announcement on cover					
❑ LSP-3787 [S] Double Trouble		1967	17.50	35.00	70.00
—With no bonus photo announcement on cover; black label "Stereo"					
❑ LSP-3787 [S] Double Trouble		1968	10.00	20.00	40.00
—Orange label, non-flexible vinyl					
❑ LSP-3787 [S] Double Trouble		1975	5.00	10.00	20.00
—Tan label					
❑ LSP-3787 [S] Double Trouble		1977	3.00	6.00	12.00
—Black label, dog near top					
❑ AYL1-3892 Elvis in Person at the International Hotel, Las Vegas, Nevada		1981	2.00	4.00	8.00
—"Best Buy Series" reissue					
❑ AYM1-3893 The Sun Sessions		1981	2.00	4.00	8.00
—"Best Buy Series" reissue; includes copies with sticker wrapped around spine with new number					
❑ LPM-3893 [M] Clambake		1967	62.50	125.00	250.00
❑ LPM/LSP-3893 Clambake Bonus Photo		1967	12.50	25.00	50.00
❑ LSP-3893 [S] Clambake		1967	15.00	30.00	60.00
❑ AYM1-3894 Elvis (NBC-TV Special)		1981	2.00	4.00	8.00
—"Best Buy Series" reissue					
❑ AAL1-3917 Guitar Man		1981	7.50	15.00	30.00
❑ AFL1-3921 [P] Elvis' Gold Records, Volume 4		1976	3.75	7.50	15.00
—Tan label with new prefix					
❑ AFL1-3921 [P] Elvis' Gold Records, Volume 4		1977	3.00	6.00	12.00
—Black label, dog near top; includes copies with sticker wrapped around spine with new number					
❑ LPM-3921 [M] Elvis' Gold Records, Volume 4		1968	500.00	1000.	2000.
—"Monaural" on label					
❑ LSP-3921 [P] Elvis' Gold Records, Volume 4		1968	10.00	20.00	40.00
—Orange label, non-flexible vinyl					
❑ LSP-3921 [P] Elvis' Gold Records, Volume 4		1968	12.50	25.00	50.00
—"Stereo" and white "RCA Victor" on black label					
❑ LSP-3921 [P] Elvis' Gold Records, Volume 4		197?	5.00	10.00	20.00
—Orange label, flexible vinyl					
❑ LSP-3921 [P] Elvis' Gold Records, Volume 4		1975	6.25	12.50	25.00
—Tan label					
❑ LSP-3921 [P] Elvis' Gold Records, Volume 4		1976	3.00	6.00	12.00
—Black label, dog near top					
❑ AYL1-3935 [S] His Hand in Mine		1981	2.00	4.00	8.00
—"Best Buy Series" reissue; includes copies with sticker wrapped around spine with new number					
❑ AYL1-3956 Elvis Country ("I'm 10,000 Years Old")		1981	2.00	4.00	8.00
—"Best Buy Series" reissue					
❑ AFL1-3989 [S] Speedway		1977	3.00	6.00	12.00
—Black label, dog near top; includes copies with sticker wrapped around spine with new number					
❑ LPM-3989 [M] Speedway		1968	500.00	1000.	2000.
❑ LPM/LSP-3989 Speedway Bonus Photo		1968	12.50	25.00	50.00
❑ LSP-3989 [S] Speedway		1968	10.00	20.00	40.00
—Orange label, non-flexible vinyl					
❑ LSP-3989 [S] Speedway		1968	15.00	30.00	60.00
—"Stereo" on black label					
❑ LSP-3989 [S] Speedway		1971	5.00	10.00	20.00
—Orange label, flexible vinyl					
❑ LSP-3989 [S] Speedway		1975	5.00	10.00	20.00
—Tan label					
❑ LSP-3989 [S] Speedway		1976	3.00	6.00	12.00
—Black label, dog near top					
❑ CPL2-4031 [(2)]This Is Elvis		1980	3.75	7.50	15.00
❑ AFM1-4088 Elvis (NBC-TV Special)		1977	3.00	6.00	12.00
—Black label, dog near top; includes copies with sticker wrapped around spine with new number					
❑ LPM-4088 Elvis (NBC-TV Special)		1968	10.00	20.00	40.00
—Orange label, non-flexible vinyl					
❑ LPM-4088 Elvis (NBC-TV Special)		1971	7.50	15.00	30.00
—Orange label, flexible vinyl					
❑ LPM-4088 Elvis (NBC-TV Special)		1975	5.00	10.00	20.00
—Tan label					
❑ LPM-4088 Elvis (NBC-TV Special)		1976	3.75	7.50	15.00
—Black label, dog near top					
❑ AYL1-4114 That's the Way It Is		1981	2.00	4.00	8.00
—"Best Buy Series" reissue; includes copies with sticker wrapped around spine with new number					
❑ AYL1-4115 [S] Kissin' Cousins		1981	2.00	4.00	8.00
—"Best Buy Series" reissue; includes copies with sticker wrapped around spine with new number					
❑ AYL1-4116 [S] Something for Everybody		1981	2.00	4.00	8.00
—"Best Buy Series" reissue; includes copies with sticker wrapped around spine with new number					
❑ AFL1-4155 From Elvis in Memphis		1977	3.00	6.00	12.00
—Black label, dog near top; includes copies with sticker wrapped around spine with new number					
❑ LSP-4155 From Elvis in Memphis		1969	10.00	20.00	40.00
—Orange label, non-flexible vinyl					
❑ LSP-4155 From Elvis in Memphis Bonus Photo		1969	10.00	20.00	40.00
❑ LSP-4155 From Elvis in Memphis		1971	7.50	15.00	30.00
—Orange label, flexible vinyl					
❑ LSP-4155 From Elvis in Memphis		1975	6.25	12.50	25.00
—Tan label					
❑ LSP-4155 From Elvis in Memphis		1976	3.75	7.50	15.00
—Black label, dog near top					
❑ AYL1-4232 [P] Elvis for Everyone		1982	2.00	4.00	8.00
—"Best Buy Series" reissue					
❑ AFL1-4362 On Stage February, 1970		1977	3.00	6.00	12.00
—Black label, dog near top; includes copies with sticker wrapped around spine with new number					
❑ AQL1-4362 On Stage February, 1970		1983	2.00	4.00	8.00
—Reissue with some cover changes					
❑ LSP-4362 On Stage February, 1970		1970	10.00	20.00	40.00
—Orange label, non-flexible vinyl					
❑ LSP-4362 On Stage February, 1970		1971	6.25	12.50	25.00
—Orange label, flexible vinyl					
❑ LSP-4362 On Stage February, 1970		1975	6.25	12.50	25.00
—Tan label					
❑ LSP-4362 On Stage February, 1970		1976	7.50	15.00	30.00
—Black label, dog near top					
❑ CPL1-4395 Memories of Christmas		1982	3.75	7.50	15.00
—With greeting card (deduct 1/3 if missing)					
❑ AFL1-4428 Elvis in Person at the International Hotel, Las Vegas, Nevada		1977	3.00	6.00	12.00
—Black label, dog near top; includes copies with sticker wrapped around spine with new number					
❑ LSP-4428 Elvis in Person at the International Hotel, Las Vegas, Nevada		1970	12.50	25.00	50.00
—Orange label, non-flexible vinyl					
❑ LSP-4428 Elvis in Person at the International Hotel, Las Vegas, Nevada		1971	10.00	20.00	40.00
—Orange label, flexible vinyl					
❑ LSP-4428 Elvis in Person at the International Hotel, Las Vegas, Nevada		1975	6.25	12.50	25.00
—Tan label					
❑ LSP-4428 Elvis in Person at the International Hotel, Las Vegas, Nevada		1976	3.75	7.50	15.00
—Black label, dog near top					
❑ AFL1-4429 Back in Memphis		1977	3.00	6.00	12.00
—Black label, dog near top; with sticker wrapped around spine with new number					
❑ LSP-4429 Back in Memphis		1970	10.00	20.00	40.00
—Orange label, non-flexible vinyl					
❑ LSP-4429 Back in Memphis		1971	7.50	15.00	30.00
—Orange label, flexible vinyl					
❑ LSP-4429 Back in Memphis		1975	6.25	12.50	25.00
—Tan label					
❑ LSP-4429 Back in Memphis		1977	3.75	7.50	15.00
—Black label, dog near top					
❑ AFL1-4445 That's the Way It Is		1977	3.00	6.00	12.00
—Black label, dog near top; includes copies with sticker wrapped around spine with new number					
❑ LSP-4445 That's the Way It Is		1970	20.00	40.00	80.00
—Orange label, non-flexible vinyl					
❑ LSP-4445 That's the Way It Is		1971	6.25	12.50	25.00
—Orange label, flexible vinyl					
❑ LSP-4445 That's the Way It Is		1975	5.00	10.00	20.00
—Tan label					
❑ LSP-4445 That's the Way It Is		1976	3.75	7.50	15.00
—Black label, dog near top					
❑ AFL1-4460 Elvis Country ("I'm 10,000 Years Old")		1977	3.00	6.00	12.00
—Black label, dog near top; includes copies with sticker wrapped around spine with new number					
❑ LSP-4460 Elvis Country ("I'm 10,000 Years Old")		197?	500.00	1000.	2000.
—Green vinyl; black label, dog near top					
❑ LSP-4460 Elvis Country ("I'm 10,000 Years Old") Bonus Photo		1971	3.75	7.50	15.00
—Available in either orange-label pressing					
❑ LSP-4460 Elvis Country ("I'm 10,000 Years Old")		1971	6.25	12.50	25.00
—Orange label, flexible vinyl					
❑ LSP-4460 Elvis Country ("I'm 10,000 Years Old")		1971	10.00	20.00	40.00
—Orange label, non-flexible vinyl					
❑ LSP-4460 Elvis Country ("I'm 10,000 Years Old")		1975	6.25	12.50	25.00
—Tan label					

Number	Title (A Side/B Side)	Yr	VG	VG+	NM
❏ LSP-4460	Elvis Country ("I'm 10,000 Years Old")	1976	3.75	7.50	15.00
—Black label, dog near top					
❏ AFL1-4530	Love Letters from Elvis	1977	3.00	6.00	12.00
—Black label, dog near top; includes copies with sticker wrapped around spine with new number					
❏ AHL1-4530	The Elvis Medley	1982	3.00	6.00	12.00
❏ LSP-4530	Love Letters from Elvis	1971	7.50	15.00	30.00
—Orange label; "Love Letters" on one line of cover; "from" on a second line, "Elvis" on a third line					
❏ LSP-4530	Love Letters from Elvis	1971	10.00	20.00	40.00
—Orange label; "Love Letters from" on one line of cover, "Elvis" on a second line					
❏ LSP-4530	Love Letters from Elvis	1975	6.25	12.50	25.00
—Tan label; "Love Letters" on one line of cover; "from" on a second line, "Elvis" on a third line					
❏ LSP-4530	Love Letters from Elvis	1975	7.50	15.00	30.00
—Tan label; "Love Letters from" on one line of cover, "Elvis" on a second line					
❏ LSP-4530	Love Letters from Elvis	1976	5.00	10.00	20.00
—Black label, dog near top					
❏ LSP-4579	Elvis Sings the Wonderful World of Christmas Postcard	1971	5.00	10.00	20.00
❏ LSP-4579	Elvis Sings the Wonderful World of Christmas	1971	7.50	15.00	30.00
—Orange label. Bonus postcard is priced separately					
❏ AFL1-4671	Elvis Now	1977	3.00	6.00	12.00
—Black label, dog near top; includes copies with sticker wrapped around spine with new number					
❏ LSP-4671	Elvis Now	1972	7.50	15.00	30.00
—Orange label					
❏ LSP-4671 [DJ]	Elvis Now	1972	25.00	50.00	100.00
—Orange label; with white timing sticker on front cover					
❏ LSP-4671	Elvis Now	1975	6.25	12.50	25.00
—Tan label					
❏ LSP-4671	Elvis Now	1976	3.75	7.50	15.00
—Black label, dog near top					
❏ AHL1-4678	I Was the One	1983	2.50	5.00	10.00
❏ AFL1-4690	He Touched Me	1977	3.00	6.00	12.00
—Black label, dog near top; includes copies with sticker wrapped around spine with new number					
❏ LSP-4690	He Touched Me	1972	10.00	20.00	40.00
—Orange label					
❏ LSP-4690 [DJ]	He Touched Me	1972	25.00	50.00	100.00
—Orange label; with white timing sticker on front cover					
❏ LSP-4690	He Touched Me	1975	5.00	10.00	20.00
—Tan label					
❏ LSP-4690	He Touched Me	1976	3.75	7.50	15.00
—Black label, dog near top					
❏ AFL1-4776	Elvis As Recorded at Madison Square Garden	1977	3.00	6.00	12.00
—Black label, dog near top; includes copies with sticker wrapped around spine with new number					
❏ AQL1-4776	Elvis As Recorded at Madison Square Garden	1980	2.00	4.00	8.00
—Another reissue with new prefix					
❏ LSP-4776	Elvis As Recorded at Madison Square Garden	1972	7.50	15.00	30.00
—Orange label					
❏ LSP-4776 [DJ]	Elvis As Recorded at Madison Square Garden	1972	25.00	50.00	100.00
—Orange label; with white timing sticker on front cover					
❏ LSP-4776	Elvis As Recorded at Madison Square Garden	1975	5.00	10.00	20.00
—Tan label					
❏ LSP-4776	Elvis As Recorded at Madison Square Garden	1976	3.75	7.50	15.00
—Black label, dog near top					
❏ CPL1-4848	A Legendary Performer, Volume 4	1983	7.50	15.00	30.00
—Includes booklet (deduct 40% if missing); with die-cut hole in front cover					
❏ CPL1-4848	A Legendary Performer, Volume 4	1986	5.00	10.00	20.00
—No die-cut hole in cover					
❏ AFL1-4941	Elvis' Gold Records, Volume 5	1984	2.50	5.00	10.00
❏ CPM6-5172 [(6)]	A Golden Celebration	1984	25.00	50.00	100.00
❏ AFM1-5182	Rocker	1984	5.00	10.00	20.00
❏ AFM1-5196 [M]	Elvis' Golden Records	1984	5.00	10.00	20.00
—50th Anniversary reissue in mono with banner					
❏ AFM1-5197 [M]	Elvis' Gold Records Volume 2 — 50,000,000 Elvis Fans Can't Be Wrong	1984	5.00	10.00	20.00
—50th Anniversary reissue in mono with banner					
❏ AFM1-5198 [M]	Elvis Presley	1984	5.00	10.00	20.00
—50th Anniversary reissue in mono with banner					
❏ AFM1-5199 [M]	Elvis	1984	5.00	10.00	20.00
—50th Anniversary reissue in mono with banner					
❏ AFL1-5353	A Valentine Gift for You	1985	2.50	5.00	10.00
—Black vinyl					
❏ AFL1-5353	A Valentine Gift for You	1985	5.00	10.00	20.00
—Red vinyl					
❏ AFL1-5418	Reconsider Baby	1985	5.00	10.00	20.00
—All copies on blue vinyl					
❏ AFL1-5430	Always on My Mind	1985	5.00	10.00	20.00
—All copies on purple vinyl					
❏ AFM1-5486 [M]	Elvis' Christmas Album	1985	3.75	7.50	15.00
—Same as LOC-1035; black vinyl with booklet					
❏ AFM1-5486 [M]	Elvis' Christmas Album	1985	5.00	10.00	20.00
—Same as LOC-1035; green vinyl with booklet					
❏ UNRM-5697/8 [DJ]	Special Christmas Programming	1967	300.00	600.00	1200.
—White label promo. Add 25% for script.					
❏ LSP-6020	From Memphis to Vegas/From Vegas to Memphis Bonus Photos	1969	12.50	25.00	50.00
—Four different photos came with LP, but no more than two per set. Value is for any two different of the four photos.					
❏ LSP-6020 [(2)]	From Memphis to Vegas/From Vegas to Memphis	1969	25.00	50.00	100.00
—Orange labels, non-flexible vinyl; with composers of "Words" correctly listed as Barry, Robin and Maurice Gibb					
❏ LSP-6020 [(2)]	From Memphis to Vegas/From Vegas to Memphis	1969	37.50	75.00	150.00
—Orange labels, non-flexible vinyl; with composers of "Words" incorrectly listed as Tommy Boyce and Bobby Hart					
❏ LSP-6020 [(2)]	From Memphis to Vegas/From Vegas to Memphis	1971	10.00	20.00	40.00
—Orange labels, flexible vinyl					
❏ LSP-6020 [(2)]	From Memphis to Vegas/From Vegas to Memphis Bonus Photos	1975	7.50	15.00	30.00
—Tan labels					
❏ LSP-6020 [(2)]	From Memphis to Vegas/From Vegas to Memphis Bonus Photos	1976	5.00	10.00	20.00
—Black label, dog near top					
❏ VPSX-6089 [(2)Q] [DJ]	Aloha from Hawaii Via Satellite	1973	500.00	1000.	2000.
—Orange or dark orange label; with white timing sticker on front cover					
❏ VPSX-6089 [(2)Q]	Aloha from Hawaii Via Satellite	1973	10.00	20.00	40.00
—Lighter orange labels, "RCA" on side					

Number	Title (A Side/B Side)	Yr	VG	VG+	NM
❏ VPSX-6089 [(2)Q]	Aloha from Hawaii Via Satellite	1973	25.00	50.00	100.00
—Dark orange labels, "QuadraDisc" on top, "RCA" on bottom					
❏ VPSX-6089 [(2)Q]	Aloha from Hawaii Via Satellite	1973	2500.	3750.	5000.
—Stokely-Van Camp employee version with Saturn-shaped sticker on front cover with "Chicken of the Sea" and mermaid (beware: this has been counterfeited)					
❏ LPM-6401	Worldwide 50 Gold Award Hits, Vol. 1 Photo Book	1970	10.00	20.00	40.00
—Two different books have been found in this LP box; price is for either					
❏ LPM-6401 [(4)]	Worldwide 50 Gold Award Hits, Vol. 1	1970	20.00	40.00	80.00
—Orange labels, non-flexible vinyl; with blurb for photo book on cover					
❏ LPM-6401 [(4)]	Worldwide 50 Gold Award Hits, Vol. 1	1970	20.00	40.00	80.00
—Orange labels, flexible vinyl; with blurb for photo book on cover					
❏ LPM-6401 [(4)]	Worldwide 50 Gold Award Hits, Vol. 1	1975	10.00	20.00	40.00
—Tan labels					
❏ LPM-6401 [(4)]	Worldwide 50 Gold Award Hits, Vol. 1	1977	7.50	15.00	30.00
—Black labels, dog near top					
❏ LPM-6402	The Other Sides: Worldwide 50 Gold Award Hits, Vol. 2 Poster	1971	6.25	12.50	25.00
❏ LPM-6402	The Other Sides: Worldwide 50 Gold Award Hits, Vol. 2 Swatch and Envelope	1971	6.25	12.50	25.00
❏ LPM-6402 [(4)]	The Other Sides: Worldwide 50 Gold Award Hits, Vol. 2	1971	17.50	35.00	70.00
—Orange labels, flexible vinyl; with blurb for inserts on cover					
❏ LPM-6402 [(4)]	The Other Sides: Worldwide 50 Gold Award Hits, Vol. 2	1975	7.50	15.00	30.00
—Tan labels					
❏ LPM-6402 [(4)]	The Other Sides: Worldwide 50 Gold Award Hits, Vol. 2	1977	5.00	10.00	20.00
—Black labels, dog near top					
❏ KKL1-7065	A Canadian Tribute	1978	5.00	10.00	20.00
—Gold vinyl, embossed cover					
❏ R 213690 [(2)]	Worldwide Gold Award Hits, Parts 1 & 2	1974	10.00	20.00	40.00
—RCA Record Club version; tan labels					
❏ R 213690 [(2)]	Worldwide Gold Award Hits, Parts 1 & 2	1974	30.00	60.00	120.00
—RCA Record Club version; one label is orange, the other is tan (orange label on both records is unknown)					
❏ R 213690 [(2)]	Worldwide Gold Award Hits, Parts 1 & 2	1977	6.25	12.50	25.00
—RCA Record Club version; black labels, dog near top					
❏ R 213736 [(2)S]	Aloha from Hawaii Via Satellite	1973	17.50	35.00	70.00
—RCA Record Club edition in stereo instead of quadraphonic; orange labels					
❏ R 213736 [(2)S]	Aloha from Hawaii Via Satellite	1975	15.00	30.00	60.00
—RCA Record Club edition in stereo instead of quadraphonic; tan labels					
❏ R 213736 [(2)S]	Aloha from Hawaii Via Satellite	1977	7.50	15.00	30.00
—RCA Record Club edition in stereo instead of quadraphonic; black labels, dog near top					
❏ R 214657 [(2)]	Worldwide Gold Award Hits, Parts 3 & 4	1978	5.00	10.00	20.00
—RCA Record Club version; black labels, dog near top					
❏ R 233299(e) [(2)]	Country Classics	1980	10.00	20.00	40.00
—RCA Music Service exclusive					
❏ R 234340 [(2)]	From Elvis with Love	1978	10.00	20.00	40.00
—RCA Music Service exclusive					
❏ R 244657 [(2)]	The Legendary Concert Performances	1978	10.00	20.00	40.00
—RCA Music Service exclusive					
❏ R 244069 [(2)]	Country Memories	1978	10.00	20.00	40.00
—RCA Music Service exclusive					

READER'S DIGEST

❏ 010/A [(7)]	His Greatest Hits	1983	15.00	30.00	60.00
—Yellow box					
❏ 010/A [(7)]	His Greatest Hits	1990	10.00	20.00	40.00
—White box					
❏ RD-10/A [(8)]	His Greatest Hits	1979	100.00	200.00	400.00
—White box					
❏ RBA-072/D	Great Hits of 1956-57	1987	5.00	10.00	20.00
❏ RD4A-181/D	Elvis Sings Inspirational Favorites	1983	5.00	10.00	20.00
❏ RB4-191/A [(7)]	The Legend Lives On	1986	15.00	30.00	60.00
❏ RDA-242/D	Elvis Sings Country Favorites	1984	15.00	30.00	60.00

SHOW-LAND

❏ LP-2001	The First of Elvis	1979	25.00	50.00	100.00

SILHOUETTE

❏ 10001/2 [(2)]	Personally Elvis	1979	7.50	15.00	30.00
—Interview records; no music					

SUN

❏ 1001	The Sun Years — Interviews and Memories	1977	2.00	4.00	8.00
—With "Nashville, U.S.A." on label; white cover with brown print					
❏ 1001	The Sun Years — Interviews and Memories	1977	3.75	7.50	15.00
—With "Nashville, U.S.A." on label; dark yellow cover with brown print					
❏ 1001	The Sun Years — Interviews and Memories	1977	6.25	12.50	25.00
—With "Memphis, Tennessee" on label					

TIME-LIFE

❏ STL-106 [(2)]	Elvis Presley: 1954-1961	1986	7.50	15.00	30.00
❏ STW-106	Country Music	1981	5.00	10.00	20.00
❏ STL-126 [(2)]	Elvis the King: 1954-1965	1989	20.00	40.00	80.00

PRESTON, BILLY

12-Inch Singles

MEGATONE

❏ 124	And Dance (5:41)/Kick It (5:46)	1984	—	3.00	6.00

MOTOWN

❏ PR-64 [DJ]	Give It Up Hot/Sock-It, Rocket	1979	3.00	6.00	12.00
❏ 4570	Since I Held You Close (3 versions)/It Don't Get Better Than This	1986	—	3.00	6.00

45s

A&M

❏ 1320	Outa-Space/I Wrote a Simple Song	1972	—	2.50	5.00
❏ 1340	Should Have Known Better/The Bus	1972	—	2.50	5.00
❏ 1380	Slaughter/God Loves You	1972	—	2.50	5.00
❏ 1380 [PS]	Slaughter/God Loves You	1972	—	3.00	6.00
❏ 1411	Will It Go Round in Circles/Blackbird	1973	—	2.00	4.00
❏ 1463	Space Race/We're Gonna Make It	1973	—	2.00	4.00
❏ 1463 [PS]	Space Race/We're Gonna Make It	1973	—	3.00	6.00
❏ 1492	You're So Unique/ How Long Has the Train Been Gone	1973	—	2.00	4.00
❏ 1536	Creature Feature/My Soul Is a Witness	1974	—	2.00	4.00
❏ 1544	Nothing from Nothing/My Soul Is a Witness	1974	—	2.00	4.00
❏ 1544 [PS]	Nothing from Nothing/My Soul Is a Witness	1974	—	3.00	6.00
❏ 1644	Struttin'/You Are So Beautiful	1974	—	2.00	4.00
❏ 1735	Fancy Lady/Song of Joy	1975	—	2.00	4.00

Number	Title (A Side/B Side)	Yr	VG	VG+	NM
❑ 1735 [PS]	Fancy Lady/Song of Joy	1975	—	3.00	6.00
❑ 1768	Do It While You Can/Song of Joy	1975	—	2.00	4.00
❑ 1892	Do What You Want/I've Got the Spirit	1976	—	2.00	4.00
❑ 1925	Girl/Ecstasy	1977	—	2.00	4.00
❑ 1954	Wide Stride/When You Are Mine	1977	—	2.00	4.00
❑ 1980	A Whole New Thing/Wide Stride	1977	—	2.00	4.00
❑ 2012	I Really Miss You/Attitudes	1978	—	2.00	4.00
❑ 2071	Get Back/Space Race	1978	—	2.00	4.00

APPLE

Number	Title (A Side/B Side)	Yr	VG	VG+	NM
❑ 1808	That's the Way God Planned It/What About You	1969	2.00	4.00	8.00
❑ 1808 [PS]	That's the Way God Planned It/What About You	1969	2.50	5.00	10.00
❑ 1808	That's the Way God Planned It/What About You	1972	2.00	4.00	8.00
—With "Mono" on both sides of record and reference to LP					
❑ P-1808/PRO 6555 [DJ]	That's the Way God Planned It (Parts 1 & 2) (mono/stereo)	1969	15.00	30.00	60.00
❑ 1814	Everything's All Right/I Want to Thank You	1969	2.00	4.00	8.00
❑ 1817	All That I've Got (I'm Gonna Give It to You)/As I Get Older	1970	2.00	4.00	8.00
❑ 1817 [PS]	All That I've Got (I'm Gonna Give It to You)/As I Get Older	1970	3.75	7.50	15.00
❑ 1826	My Sweet Lord/Little Girl	1970	2.00	4.00	8.00
❑ 1826	My Sweet Lord/Little Girl	1970	3.00	6.00	12.00
—With star on A-side label					

APPLE/AMERICOM

Number	Title (A Side/B Side)	Yr	VG	VG+	NM
❑ 1808P/M-433	That's the Way God Planned It (Edit)/What About You	1969	100.00	200.00	400.00
—Four-inch flexi-disc sold from vending machines					

CAPITOL

Number	Title (A Side/B Side)	Yr	VG	VG+	NM
❑ 2309	Hey Brother (Part 1)/Hey Brother (Part 2)	1968	2.00	4.00	8.00
❑ 5611	The Girl's Got "It"/The Night	1966	2.00	4.00	8.00
❑ 5660	In the Midnight Hour/Advice	1966	2.00	4.00	8.00
❑ 5730	Sunny/Let the Music Play	1966	2.00	4.00	8.00
❑ 5797	Phony Friends/Can't She Tell	1966	2.00	4.00	8.00

DERBY

Number	Title (A Side/B Side)	Yr	VG	VG+	NM
❑ 1002	Greazee (Part 1)/(Part 2)	1963	6.25	12.50	25.00

MGM

Number	Title (A Side/B Side)	Yr	VG	VG+	NM
❑ 14001	The Split/It's Just a Love Game	1968	2.00	4.00	8.00

MOTOWN

Number	Title (A Side/B Side)	Yr	VG	VG+	NM
❑ 1470	It Will Come In Time/All I Wanted Was You	1979	—	2.00	4.00
❑ 1505	Sock-It Rocket/Hope	1981	—	2.00	4.00
❑ 1511	A Change Is Gonna Come/You	1981	—	2.00	4.00
❑ 1625	I'm Never Gonna Say Goodbye/Love You So	1982	—	2.00	4.00

MYRRH

Number	Title (A Side/B Side)	Yr	VG	VG+	NM
❑ 216	One with the Lord/Universal Love	1979	2.00	4.00	8.00

VEE JAY

Number	Title (A Side/B Side)	Yr	VG	VG+	NM
❑ 646	Don't Let the Sun Catch You Cryin'/(B-side unknown)	1965	—	—	—
—Canceled?					
❑ 653	Don't Let the Sun Catch You Cryin'/Billy's Bag	1965	2.50	5.00	10.00
❑ 692	Log Cabin/Drown in My Own Tears	1965	2.50	5.00	10.00

Albums

A&M

Number	Title (A Side/B Side)	Yr	VG	VG+	NM
❑ SP-3205	The Best of Billy Preston	1982	2.50	5.00	10.00
❑ SP-3507	I Wrote a Simple Song	1971	3.00	6.00	12.00
❑ SP-3516	Music Is My Life	1972	3.00	6.00	12.00
❑ SP-3526	Everybody Likes Some Kind of Music	1973	3.00	6.00	12.00
❑ SP-3637	Live European Tour	1974	3.00	6.00	12.00
❑ SP-3645	The Kids & Me	1974	3.00	6.00	12.00
❑ SP-4532	It's My Pleasure	1975	3.00	6.00	12.00
❑ SP-4587	Billy Preston	1976	3.00	6.00	12.00
❑ SP-4657	It's a Whole New Thing	1977	3.00	6.00	12.00

APPLE

Number	Title (A Side/B Side)	Yr	VG	VG+	NM
❑ ST-3359	That's the Way God Planned It	1969	12.50	25.00	50.00
—Cover has close-up of Billy Preston					
❑ ST-3359	That's the Way God Planned It	1972	5.00	10.00	20.00
—Cover has multiple images of Billy Preston					
❑ ST-3370	Encouraging Words	1970	5.00	10.00	20.00

BUDDAH

Number	Title (A Side/B Side)	Yr	VG	VG+	NM
❑ BDS-7502	Billy Preston	1969	3.75	7.50	15.00

CAPITOL

Number	Title (A Side/B Side)	Yr	VG	VG+	NM
❑ ST 2532 [S]	Wildest Organ in Town!	1966	10.00	20.00	40.00
❑ T 2532 [M]	Wildest Organ in Town!	1966	7.50	15.00	30.00
❑ DT 2607 [R]	Club Meetin'	1967	—	—	—
❑ T 2607 [M]	Club Meetin'	1967	—	—	—
—The above versions of Club Meetin' may not exist					

DERBY

Number	Title (A Side/B Side)	Yr	VG	VG+	NM
❑ LPM-701 [M]	16 Year Old Soul	1963	62.50	125.00	250.00

EXODUS

Number	Title (A Side/B Side)	Yr	VG	VG+	NM
❑ 304 [M]	Early Hits of 1965	1965	6.25	12.50	25.00

GNP CRESCENDO

Number	Title (A Side/B Side)	Yr	VG	VG+	NM
❑ GNPS-2071 [(2)]	Soul'd Out	1973	3.75	7.50	15.00

MCA

Number	Title (A Side/B Side)	Yr	VG	VG+	NM
❑ 28037	Gospel Soul	198?	2.00	4.00	8.00
—Reissue of Peacock LP					

MOTOWN

Number	Title (A Side/B Side)	Yr	VG	VG+	NM
❑ M7-925	Late at Night	1980	2.50	5.00	10.00
❑ M8-941	The Way I Am	1981	2.50	5.00	10.00
❑ M7-958	Billy Preston & Syreeta	1981	2.50	5.00	10.00
❑ 6020 ML	Pressin' On	1982	2.50	5.00	10.00

MYRRH

Number	Title (A Side/B Side)	Yr	VG	VG+	NM
❑ MSB-6605	Behold	1978	3.00	6.00	12.00
❑ MSB-6607	Universal Love	1979	3.00	6.00	12.00

PEACOCK

Number	Title (A Side/B Side)	Yr	VG	VG+	NM
❑ 179	Gospel Soul	197?	3.00	6.00	12.00

PICKWICK

Number	Title (A Side/B Side)	Yr	VG	VG+	NM
❑ SPC-3315	Organ Transplant	197?	2.50	5.00	10.00

VEE JAY

Number	Title (A Side/B Side)	Yr	VG	VG+	NM
❑ LP-1123 [M]	The Most Exciting Organ Ever	1965	7.50	15.00	30.00
❑ LPS-1123 [S]	The Most Exciting Organ Ever	1965	12.50	25.00	50.00
❑ LP-1142 [M]	Greatest Hits	1966	7.50	15.00	30.00
❑ LPS-1142 [S]	Greatest Hits	1966	12.50	25.00	50.00

PRESTON, BILLY, AND SYREETA Also see each artist's individual listings.
45s

MOTOWN

Number	Title (A Side/B Side)	Yr	VG	VG+	NM
❑ 1460	With You I'm Born Again/Go For It	1979	—	2.50	5.00
❑ 1477	With You I'm Born Again/All I Wanted Was You	1979	—	2.00	4.00
❑ 1520	Searchin'/Hey You	1981	—	2.00	4.00
❑ 1522	Just for You (Put the Boogie in Your Body)/Hey You	1981	—	2.00	4.00

TAMLA

Number	Title (A Side/B Side)	Yr	VG	VG+	NM
❑ 54312	Dance For Me Children/One More Time for Love	1980	—	2.00	4.00
❑ 54319	Please Stay/Signed, Sealed, Delivered (I'm Yours)	1980	—	2.00	4.00

PRESTON, JACKIE
45s

HIT

Number	Title (A Side/B Side)	Yr	VG	VG+	NM
❑ 144	Tottle-Dee Doodle, Dee Doo/We'll Sing in the Sunshine	1964	2.00	4.00	8.00
—B-side by Betty Coleson					

PRESTON, JOHN
45s

HIT

Number	Title (A Side/B Side)	Yr	VG	VG+	NM
❑ 69	Blue on Blue/Those Lazy-Hazy-Crazy Days of Summer	1963	2.00	4.00	8.00
—B-side by Frank Clark					
❑ 92	Walking Proud/500 Miles Away from Home	1963	2.00	4.00	8.00
—B-side by Mitch Wood					
❑ 155	Ringo/The Spirit of This Land	1964	2.00	4.00	8.00
—B-side by Charlie Rogers					
❑ 177	Speaking of Broken Hearts/You're Nobody Till Somebody Loves You	1965	2.00	4.00	8.00
—B-side by Marty Wood					
❑ 194	You Were Gone/Can't You Hear My Heartbeat	1965	2.00	4.00	8.00
—B-side by Jackie Harris					
❑ 207	Long Lonely Nights/Once You've Been in Love	1965	2.00	4.00	8.00

PRESTON, JOHNNY
45s

ABC

Number	Title (A Side/B Side)	Yr	VG	VG+	NM
❑ 11085	I'm Only Human/There's No One Like You	1968	2.50	5.00	10.00
❑ 11187	Kick the Can/I've Just Been Wasting My Time	1969	2.50	5.00	10.00

HALLWAY

Number	Title (A Side/B Side)	Yr	VG	VG+	NM
❑ 1201	All Around the World/Just Plain Hurt	1964	3.75	7.50	15.00
❑ 1204	Willie and the Hand Jive/I've Got My Eyes on You	1964	3.75	7.50	15.00
❑ 1927	Running Bear '65/Dedicated to the One I Love	1965	3.75	7.50	15.00

IMPERIAL

Number	Title (A Side/B Side)	Yr	VG	VG+	NM
❑ 5924	This Little Bitty Tear/The Day the World Stood Still	1963	2.50	5.00	10.00
❑ 5947	I've Got My Eyes on You/I Couldn't Take It Again	1963	2.50	5.00	10.00

MERCURY

Number	Title (A Side/B Side)	Yr	VG	VG+	NM
❑ 10027 [S]	Cradle of Love/City of Tears	1960	12.50	25.00	50.00
❑ 10036 [S]	Feel So Fine/I'm Starting to Go Steady	1960	15.00	30.00	60.00
❑ 71474	Running Bear/My Heart Knows	1959	6.25	12.50	25.00
❑ 71598 [M]	Cradle of Love/City of Tears	1960	5.00	10.00	20.00
❑ 71598 [PS]	Cradle of Love/City of Tears	1960	7.50	15.00	30.00
❑ 71651 [M]	Feel So Fine/I'm Starting to Go Steady	1960	5.00	10.00	20.00
❑ 71651 [PS]	Feel So Fine/I'm Starting to Go Steady	1960	7.50	15.00	30.00
❑ 71691	Charming Billy/Up in the Air	1960	5.00	10.00	20.00
❑ 71728	New Baby for Christmas/(I Want a) Rock and Roll Guitar	1960	5.00	10.00	20.00
❑ 71761	Leave My Kitten Alone/Token of Love	1961	5.00	10.00	20.00
❑ 71761 [PS]	Leave My Kitten Alone/Token of Love	1961	7.50	15.00	30.00
❑ 71803	I Feel Good/Willy Walk	1961	5.00	10.00	20.00
❑ 71803 [PS]	I Feel Good/Willy Walk	1961	10.00	20.00	40.00
❑ 71865	Let Them Talk/She Once Belonged to Me	1961	5.00	10.00	20.00
❑ 71908	Free Me/Kissin' Tree	1961	5.00	10.00	20.00
❑ 71908 [PS]	Free Me/Kissin' Tree	1961	7.50	15.00	30.00
❑ 71951	Let's Leave It That Way/Broken Hearts Anonymous	1962	3.75	7.50	15.00
❑ 72049	Let the Big Boss Man (Pull You Through)/The Day After Forever	1962	3.75	7.50	15.00

TCF HALL

Number	Title (A Side/B Side)	Yr	VG	VG+	NM
❑ 101	Running Bear '65/Dedicated to the One I Love	1965	2.50	5.00	10.00
❑ 110	Sounds Like Trouble/You Can Make It If You Try	1965	3.75	7.50	15.00
❑ 120	I'm Askin' Forgiveness/Good Good Lovin'	1965	2.50	5.00	10.00

Albums

MERCURY

Number	Title (A Side/B Side)	Yr	VG	VG+	NM
❑ MG-20592 [M]	Running Bear	1960	25.00	50.00	100.00
❑ MG-20609 [M]	Come Rock with Me	1960	25.00	50.00	100.00
❑ SR-60250 [S]	Running Bear	1960	37.50	75.00	150.00
—Black label					
❑ SR-60250 [S]	Running Bear	1981	3.00	6.00	12.00
—Reissue on Chicago skyline label					
❑ SR-60609 [S]	Come Rock with Me	1960	37.50	75.00	150.00

WING

Number	Title (A Side/B Side)	Yr	VG	VG+	NM
❑ MGW-12246 [M]	Running Bear	1963	5.00	10.00	20.00
❑ SRW-16246 [S]	Running Bear	1963	6.25	12.50	25.00

PRESTON, MIKE
45s

LONDON

Number	Title (A Side/B Side)	Yr	VG	VG+	NM
❑ 1834	A House, a Car and a Wedding Ring/My Lucky Love	1958	3.00	6.00	12.00
❑ 1865	Girl Without a Heart/In Surabaya	1959	2.50	5.00	10.00
❑ 1903	'Till Tomorrow/An Ordinary Couple	1960	2.50	5.00	10.00
❑ 1981	Girl Without a Heart/Marry Me	1960	2.50	5.00	10.00
❑ 9601	Careless Love/Little Grain of Sand	1963	2.50	5.00	10.00

PRESTON, TERRY See FERLIN HUSKY.

PRETENDERS, THE (2) Also see JIMMY JONES.
45s

APT

Number	Title (A Side/B Side)	Yr	VG	VG+	NM
❑ 25026	Blue and Lonely/Daddy Needs Baby	1959	125.00	250.00	500.00

CENTRAL

Number	Title (A Side/B Side)	Yr	VG	VG+	NM
❑ 2605	Blue and Lonely/Daddy Needs Baby	1958	375.00	750.00	1500.

Number	Title (A Side/B Side)	Yr	VG	VG+	NM

PRETENDERS, THE (3)
45s
BETHLEHEM

| ❑ 3050 | The Day You Are Mine/Ding Dong Bells | 1962 | 50.00 | 100.00 | 200.00 |

PRETENDERS, THE (4)
45s
CHATTAHOOCHIE

| ❑ 685 | Pepita's Theme/Tijuana Taxi | 1965 | 5.00 | 10.00 | 20.00 |

PRETENDERS, THE (U) The Rama and Whirlin' Disc records could be by group (2). None of these, or any of the above, are by the group fronted by Chrissie Hynde; they are outside the scope of this book.
45s
LOST-NITE

| ❑ 353 | Close Your Eyes/Part-Time Sweetheart | 197? | — | 2.50 | 5.00 |

—Reissue
POWER-MARTIN

| ❑ 1001 | Smile/I'm So Happy | 1961 | 25.00 | 50.00 | 100.00 |

RAMA

| ❑ 198 | Possessive Love/I've Got to Have You Baby | 1956 | 30.00 | 60.00 | 120.00 |

WHIRLIN' DISC

| ❑ 106 | Close Your Eyes/Part-Time Sweetheart | 1957 | 62.50 | 125.00 | 250.00 |

PRETTY BOY See DON COVAY.

PRETTY THINGS, THE
45s
FONTANA

❑ 1508	I Can Never Say/Honey, I Need	1965	3.75	7.50	15.00
❑ 1518	Cry to Me/I Can Never Say	1965	3.75	7.50	15.00
❑ 1518	Cry to Me/Judgment Day	1965	3.75	7.50	15.00
❑ 1540	Midnight to Six Man/Can't Stand Pain	1966	3.75	7.50	15.00
❑ 1550	Come See Me/Judgment Day	1966	3.75	7.50	15.00
❑ 1550	Come See Me/Progress	1966	3.75	7.50	15.00
❑ 1916	Big Boss Man/Rosalyn	1964	3.75	7.50	15.00
❑ 1941	Don't Bring Me Down/We'll Be Together	1964	3.75	7.50	15.00

LAURIE

| ❑ 3458 | Talkin' About the Good Times/Walking Through My Dreams | 1968 | 7.50 | 15.00 | 30.00 |

NORTON

❑ 45-084	All Light Up/Vivian Prince	1999	—	—	2.00
❑ 45-084 [PS]	All Light Up/Vivian Prince	1999	—	—	2.00
❑ PT 109	All Light Up/Pretty Beat	1999	—	2.00	4.00

—Red vinyl, small hole, called "The Pretty Things U.S. Tour 45"
RARE EARTH

| ❑ 5005 | Private Sorrow/Balloon Burning | 1969 | 3.75 | 7.50 | 15.00 |

SWAN SONG

| ❑ 70104 | Come Home Momma/Joey | 1975 | — | 2.50 | 5.00 |
| ❑ 70107 | It Isn't Rock & Roll/Remember That Boy | 1975 | — | 2.50 | 5.00 |

7-Inch Extended Plays
NORTON

❑ EP-501	Rosalyn/Judgement Day//Roadrunner/Don't Bring Me Down	1999	—	—	2.00
❑ EP-501 [PS]	Rosalyn	1999	—	—	2.00
❑ EP-502	Big City/I Can Never Say//Get Yourself Home/Honey I Need	1999	—	—	2.00
❑ EP-502 [PS]	Big City	1999	—	—	2.00
❑ EP-503	You Don't Believe Me/Buzz the Jerk//You'll Never Do It Baby/Come See Me	1999	—	—	2.00
❑ EP-503 [PS]	Buzz the Jerk	1999	—	—	2.00
❑ EP-504	Midnight to Six Man/Can't Stand the Pain//LSD/Me Needing You	1999	—	—	2.00
❑ EP-504 [PS]	Midnight to Six Man	1999	—	—	2.00
❑ EP-505	A House in the Country/Progress//Tripping/Photographer	1999	—	—	2.00
❑ EP-505 [PS]	A House in the Country	1999	—	—	2.00

Albums
BIG BEAT

| ❑ WIK-24 | Live at Heartbreak Hotel | 1985 | 2.50 | 5.00 | 10.00 |

FONTANA

| ❑ MGF-27544 [M] | The Pretty Things | 1965 | 20.00 | 40.00 | 80.00 |
| ❑ SRF-67544 [P] | The Pretty Things | 1965 | 20.00 | 40.00 | 80.00 |

NORTON

❑ 282	The Pretty Things	2000	3.00	6.00	12.00
❑ 283	Get the Picture?	2000	3.00	6.00	12.00
❑ 284	Midnight to Six	2000	3.00	6.00	12.00
❑ TED-1001 [10]	Defecting Grey	2000	2.00	4.00	8.00

RARE EARTH

| ❑ RS 506 | S.F. Sorrow | 1969 | 5.00 | 10.00 | 20.00 |

—Later copies are standard in shape

| ❑ RS 506 | S.F. Sorrow | 1969 | 12.50 | 25.00 | 50.00 |

—Original covers are rounded at top

| ❑ RS 515 | Parachute | 1970 | 5.00 | 10.00 | 20.00 |
| ❑ R 549R2 [(2)] | Real Pretty | 1976 | 3.75 | 7.50 | 15.00 |

—The two prior Rare Earth albums in one package
SIRE

| ❑ SASH-3713 [(2)] | The Vintage Years | 1976 | 3.75 | 7.50 | 15.00 |

SWAN SONG

| ❑ SS 8411 | Silk Torpedo | 1975 | 2.50 | 5.00 | 10.00 |
| ❑ SS 8414 | Savage Eye | 1976 | 2.50 | 5.00 | 10.00 |

WARNER BROS.

| ❑ BS 2680 | Freeway Madness | 1973 | 2.50 | 5.00 | 10.00 |
| ❑ BSK 3466 | Cross Talk | 1980 | 2.50 | 5.00 | 10.00 |

PREVIN, ANDRE
45s
COLUMBIA

❑ 30833 [S]	(titles unknown)	1960	2.50	5.00	10.00
❑ 30834 [S]	(titles unknown)	1960	2.50	5.00	10.00
❑ 30835 [S]	(titles unknown)	1960	2.50	5.00	10.00
❑ 30836 [S]	(titles unknown)	1960	2.50	5.00	10.00
❑ 30837 [S]	(titles unknown)	1960	2.50	5.00	10.00
❑ 31074 [S]	(titles unknown)	1961	2.50	5.00	10.00
❑ 31075 [S]	(titles unknown)	1961	2.50	5.00	10.00
❑ 31076 [S]	(titles unknown)	1961	2.50	5.00	10.00
❑ 31077 [S]	(titles unknown)	1961	2.50	5.00	10.00
❑ 31078 [S]	(titles unknown)	1961	2.50	5.00	10.00
❑ 31540 [S]	(titles unknown)	1962	2.50	5.00	10.00
❑ 31541 [S]	(titles unknown)	1962	2.50	5.00	10.00
❑ 31542 [S]	(titles unknown)	1962	2.50	5.00	10.00
❑ 31543 [S]	(titles unknown)	1962	2.50	5.00	10.00
❑ 31544 [S]	(titles unknown)	1962	2.50	5.00	10.00

—Anyone who can fill in these gaps -- the above 15 all are Columbia "Stereo 7" singles -- please let us know.

❑ 41683	Love Me or Leave Me/Like Love	1960	2.00	4.00	8.00
❑ 42596	Song from "Two for the Seesaw"/Song from "Long Day's Journey Into Night"	1962	2.00	4.00	8.00
❑ 43136	Goodbye, Charlie/Kiss Me, Stupid	1964	2.00	4.00	8.00
❑ JZSP 55071/0 [DJ]	God Rest Ye Merry, Gentlemen/Let No Walls Divide	1961	3.00	6.00	12.00

—B-side by Doris Day
DECCA

| ❑ 25529 | Moonlight Becomes You/Let's Fall in Love | 1961 | 2.00 | 4.00 | 8.00 |

MGM

| ❑ 12792 | Like Young/Young Man's Lament | 1959 | 2.50 | 5.00 | 10.00 |
| ❑ 12840 | Young and Tender/Too Young to Be True | 1959 | 2.50 | 5.00 | 10.00 |

RCA VICTOR

❑ 47-2764	But Not for Me/Hallelujah	1949	3.75	7.50	15.00
❑ 47-2765	My Shining Hour/This Can't Be Love	1949	3.75	7.50	15.00
❑ 47-2766	Mad About the Boy/Just One of Those Things	1949	3.75	7.50	15.00

—The above three comprise box set WP-214, "Andre Previn Plays the Piano"

❑ 47-2767	I Didn't Know What Time It Was/Should I	1949	3.75	7.50	15.00
❑ 47-3080	Dardanella/The Gypsy in My Soul	1949	3.75	7.50	15.00
❑ 47-3123	Anything Goes/Bewitched, Bothered and Bewildered	1949	3.75	7.50	15.00
❑ 47-3124	You're the Top/I'm Old Fashioned	1949	3.75	7.50	15.00
❑ 47-3125	Who Cares/Who	1949	3.75	7.50	15.00

—The above three comprise a box set

❑ 47-3263	I Didn't Know What Time It Was/Should I	1949	3.75	7.50	15.00
❑ 47-3836	Three Little Words/Thinking of You	1950	3.75	7.50	15.00
❑ 47-3837	Who's Sorry Now/All Alone	1950	3.75	7.50	15.00
❑ 47-4161	Skylark/You Took Advantage of Me	1951	3.75	7.50	15.00
❑ 47-4163	Dearly Beloved/Love Is Just Around the Corner	1951	3.75	7.50	15.00
❑ 47-4351	Lullaby of Broadway/I Only Have Eyes for You	1951	3.00	6.00	12.00
❑ 47-4352	This Head of Mine/September in the Rain	1951	3.00	6.00	12.00
❑ 47-4353	This Heart of Mine/I Know Why and So Do You	1951	3.00	6.00	12.00
❑ 47-4354	I'll String Along/Jeepers Creepers	1951	3.00	6.00	12.00

—The above four comprise a box set

❑ 47-4780	The Story of a Piano (Part 1)/Romance, Op. 28, No. 2	1952	3.00	6.00	12.00
❑ 47-4781	The Story of a Piano (Part 2)/Valse Brilliance in A Minor	1952	3.00	6.00	12.00
❑ 47-4782	The Story of a Piano (Part 3)/Traumere Op. 15	1952	3.00	6.00	12.00
❑ 47-4783	The Story of a Piano (Part 4)/Adagio Cantabile	1952	3.00	6.00	12.00

—The above four comprise a box set

| ❑ 47-9122 | Theme from Hotel/The Bad Guys | 1967 | — | 3.00 | 6.00 |
| ❑ WP 214 [PS] | Andre Previn Plays the Piano | 1949 | 3.75 | 7.50 | 15.00 |

—Empty box for 47-2764, 47-2765 and 47-2766
UNITED ARTISTS

| ❑ 50080 | Bad Guys/Waltz of the Fortune Cookie | 1966 | — | 3.00 | 6.00 |

Albums
ANGEL

| ❑ DS-37780 | A Different Kind of Blues | 1981 | 2.50 | 5.00 | 10.00 |
| ❑ S-1-37799 | It's a Breeze | 1981 | 2.50 | 5.00 | 10.00 |

COLUMBIA

| ❑ CL 1437 [M] | Like Love | 1960 | 3.75 | 7.50 | 15.00 |

—Red and black label with six "eye" logos

| ❑ CL 1437 [M] | Like Love | 1963 | 3.00 | 6.00 | 12.00 |

—Red label with "Guaranteed High Fidelity" or "360 Sound Mono" at bottom

| ❑ CL 1495 [M] | Rhapsody in Blue | 1960 | 3.75 | 7.50 | 15.00 |

—Red and black label with six "eye" logos

| ❑ CL 1495 [M] | Rhapsody in Blue | 1963 | 3.00 | 6.00 | 12.00 |

—Red label with "Guaranteed High Fidelity" or "360 Sound Mono" at bottom

| ❑ CL 1530 [M] | Give My Regards to Broadway | 1960 | 5.00 | 10.00 | 20.00 |

—Red and black label with six "eye" logos

| ❑ CL 1530 [M] | Give My Regards to Broadway | 1963 | 3.00 | 6.00 | 12.00 |

—Red label with "Guaranteed High Fidelity" or "360 Sound Mono" at bottom

| ❑ CL 1569 [M] | Camelot | 1961 | 5.00 | 10.00 | 20.00 |

—Red and black label with six "eye" logos

| ❑ CL 1569 [M] | Camelot | 1963 | 3.00 | 6.00 | 12.00 |

—Red label with "Guaranteed High Fidelity" or "360 Sound Mono" at bottom

| ❑ CL 1595 [M] | Thinking of You | 1961 | 5.00 | 10.00 | 20.00 |

—Red and black label with six "eye" logos

| ❑ CL 1595 [M] | Thinking of You | 1963 | 3.00 | 6.00 | 12.00 |

—Red label with "Guaranteed High Fidelity" or "360 Sound Mono" at bottom

| ❑ CL 1649 [M] | A Touch of Elegance | 1961 | 5.00 | 10.00 | 20.00 |

—Red and black label with six "eye" logos

| ❑ CL 1741 [M] | Mack the Knife and Other Kurt Weill Music | 1962 | 5.00 | 10.00 | 20.00 |

—Red and black label with six "eye" logos

| ❑ CL 1741 [M] | Mack the Knife and Other Kurt Weill Music | 1963 | 3.00 | 6.00 | 12.00 |

—Red label with "Guaranteed High Fidelity" or "360 Sound Mono" at bottom

| ❑ CL 1786 [M] | Faraway Part of Town | 1962 | 5.00 | 10.00 | 20.00 |

—Red and black label with six "eye" logos

| ❑ CL 1786 [M] | Faraway Part of Town | 1963 | 3.00 | 6.00 | 12.00 |

—Red label with "Guaranteed High Fidelity" or "360 Sound Mono" at bottom

| ❑ CL 1888 [M] | The Light Fantastic | 1962 | 5.00 | 10.00 | 20.00 |

—Red and black label with six "eye" logos

| ❑ CL 1888 [M] | The Light Fantastic | 1963 | 3.00 | 6.00 | 12.00 |

—Red label with "Guaranteed High Fidelity" or "360 Sound Mono" at bottom

| ❑ CL 2034 [M] | Andre Previn in Hollywood | 1963 | 3.75 | 7.50 | 15.00 |

—Red label with "Guaranteed High Fidelity" at bottom

| ❑ CL 2034 [M] | Andre Previn in Hollywood | 1966 | 3.00 | 6.00 | 12.00 |

—Red label with "360 Sound Mono" at bottom

| ❑ CL 2114 [M] | The Soft and Swinging Music of Jimmy McHugh | 1964 | 3.75 | 7.50 | 15.00 |

—Red label with "Guaranteed High Fidelity" at bottom

| ❑ CL 2114 [M] | The Soft and Swinging Music of Jimmy McHugh | 1966 | 3.00 | 6.00 | 12.00 |

—Red label with "360 Sound Mono" at bottom

| ❑ CL 2195 [M] | My Fair Lady | 1964 | 3.75 | 7.50 | 15.00 |

—Red label with "Guaranteed High Fidelity" at bottom

| ❑ CL 2195 [M] | My Fair Lady | 1966 | 3.00 | 6.00 | 12.00 |

—Red label with "360 Sound Mono" at bottom

P

Number	Title (A Side/B Side)	Yr	VG	VG+	NM
❑ CL 2294 [M]	Popular Previn	1965	3.75	7.50	15.00
—Red label with "Guaranteed High Fidelity" at bottom					
❑ CL 2294 [M]	Popular Previn	1966	3.00	6.00	12.00
—Red label with "360 Sound Mono" at bottom					
❑ CS 8233 [S]	Like Love	1960	5.00	10.00	20.00
—Red and black label with six "eye" logos					
❑ CS 8233 [S]	Like Love	1963	3.75	7.50	15.00
—Red label with "360 Sound Stereo" at bottom					
❑ CS 8286 [S]	Rhapsody in Blue	1960	5.00	10.00	20.00
—Red and black label with six "eye" logos					
❑ CS 8286 [S]	Rhapsody in Blue	1963	3.75	7.50	15.00
—Red label with "360 Sound Stereo" at bottom					
❑ CS 8330 [S]	Give My Regards to Broadway	1963	3.75	7.50	15.00
—Red label with "360 Sound Stereo" at bottom					
❑ CS 8330 [S]	Give My Regards to Broadway	1960	6.25	12.50	25.00
—Red and black label with six "eye" logos					
❑ CS 8369 [S]	Camelot	1961	6.25	12.50	25.00
—Red and black label with six "eye" logos					
❑ CS 8369 [S]	Camelot	1963	3.75	7.50	15.00
—Red label with "360 Sound Stereo" at bottom					
❑ CS 8395 [S]	Thinking of You	1961	6.25	12.50	25.00
—Red and black label with six "eye" logos					
❑ CS 8395 [S]	Thinking of You	1963	3.75	7.50	15.00
—Red label with "360 Sound Stereo" at bottom					
❑ CS 8449 [S]	A Touch of Elegance	1961	6.25	12.50	25.00
—Red and black label with six "eye" logos					
❑ CS 8541 [S]	Mack the Knife and Other Kurt Weill Music	1962	3.75	7.50	15.00
—Red label with "360 Sound Stereo" at bottom					
❑ CS 8541 [S]	Mack the Knife and Other Kurt Weill Music	1962	6.25	12.50	25.00
—Red and black label with six "eye" logos					
❑ CS 8586 [S]	Faraway Part of Town	1962	6.25	12.50	25.00
—Red and black label with six "eye" logos					
❑ CS 8586 [S]	Faraway Part of Town	1963	3.75	7.50	15.00
—Red label with "360 Sound Stereo" at bottom					
❑ CS 8688 [S]	The Light Fantastic	1962	6.25	12.50	25.00
—Red and black label with six "eye" logos					
❑ CS 8688 [S]	The Light Fantastic	1963	3.75	7.50	15.00
—Red label with "360 Sound Stereo" at bottom					
❑ CS 8834 [S]	Andre Previn in Hollywood	1963	5.00	10.00	20.00
—Red label with "360 Sound Stereo" in black at bottom					
❑ CS 8834 [S]	Andre Previn in Hollywood	1966	3.75	7.50	15.00
—Red label with "360 Sound Stereo" in white at bottom					
❑ CS 8914 [S]	The Soft and Swinging Music of Jimmy McHugh	1964	5.00	10.00	20.00
—Red label with "360 Sound Stereo" at bottom					
❑ CS 8914 [S]	The Soft and Swinging Music of Jimmy McHugh	1966	3.75	7.50	15.00
—Red label with "360 Sound Stereo" in white at bottom					
❑ CS 8995 [S]	My Fair Lady	1964	5.00	10.00	20.00
—Red label with "360 Sound Stereo" in black at bottom					
❑ CS 8995 [S]	My Fair Lady	1966	3.75	7.50	15.00
—Red label with "360 Sound Stereo" in white at bottom					
❑ CS 9094 [S]	Popular Previn	1965	5.00	10.00	20.00
—Red label with "360 Sound Stereo" in black at bottom					
❑ CS 9094 [S]	Popular Previn	1966	3.75	7.50	15.00
—Red label with "360 Sound Stereo" in white at bottom					
CONTEMPORARY					
❑ C-3543 [M]	Pal Joey	1957	12.50	25.00	50.00
❑ C-3548 [M]	Gigi	1958	12.50	25.00	50.00
❑ M-3558 [M]	Andre Previn Plays Vernon Duke	1959	12.50	25.00	50.00
❑ M-3567 [M]	Andre Previn Plays Jerome Kern	1959	12.50	25.00	50.00
❑ M-3570 [M]	Jazz Trio, King Size	1959	12.50	25.00	50.00
❑ M-3572 [M]	West Side Story	1960	10.00	20.00	40.00
❑ M-3575 [M]	Like Previn	1960	10.00	20.00	40.00
❑ M-3586 [M]	Andre Previn Plays Harold Arlen	1960	10.00	20.00	40.00
❑ S-7543 [S]	Pal Joey	1959	10.00	20.00	40.00
❑ S-7548 [S]	Gigi	1959	10.00	20.00	40.00
❑ S-7558 [S]	Andre Previn Plays Vernon Duke	1959	10.00	20.00	40.00
❑ S-7567 [S]	Andre Previn Plays Jerome Kern	1959	10.00	20.00	40.00
❑ S-7570 [S]	Jazz Trio, King Size	1959	10.00	20.00	40.00
❑ S-7572 [S]	West Side Story	1960	7.50	15.00	30.00
❑ S-7575 [S]	Like Previn	1960	7.50	15.00	30.00
❑ S-7586 [S]	Andre Previn Plays Harold Arlen	1960	7.50	15.00	30.00
CORONET					
❑ 170	Featuring Andre Previn	196?	3.00	6.00	12.00
❑ 181	The Magic Sounds of Andre Previn	196?	3.00	6.00	12.00
DECCA					
❑ DL 4115 [M]	Andre Previn Plays Pretty	1961	3.00	6.00	12.00
❑ DL 4350 [M]	But Beautiful	1963	3.00	6.00	12.00
❑ DL 8131 [M]	Let's Get Away from It All	1955	10.00	20.00	40.00
❑ DL 8341 [M]	Hollywood at Midnight	1957	10.00	20.00	40.00
❑ DL 74115 [S]	Andre Previn Plays Pretty	1961	3.75	7.50	15.00
❑ DL 74350 [S]	But Beautiful	1963	3.75	7.50	15.00
EVEREST ARCHIVE OF FOLK & JAZZ					
❑ 247	Early Years	1970	2.50	5.00	10.00
FANTASY					
❑ OJC-157	Double Play!	198?	2.50	5.00	10.00
—Reissue of Contemporary 7011					
❑ OJC-170	Like Previn	198?	2.50	5.00	10.00
—Reissue of Contemporary 7575					
❑ OJC-422	West Side Story	1990	2.50	5.00	10.00
❑ OJC-637	Pal Joey	1991	3.00	6.00	12.00
GUEST STAR					
❑ 1436	Piano Greats	196?	3.00	6.00	12.00
HARMONY					
❑ HL 7348 [M]	Misty	1965	3.00	6.00	12.00
❑ HL 7407 [M]	Starlight Piano	196?	3.00	6.00	12.00
❑ HL 7429 [M]	Camelot	1967	3.00	6.00	12.00
❑ HS 11148 [S]	Misty	1965	3.00	6.00	12.00
❑ HS 11207 [S]	Starlight Piano	196?	3.00	6.00	12.00
❑ HS 11229 [S]	Camelot	1967	3.00	6.00	12.00
JAZZ ODYSSEY					
❑ 32160260	Mack the Knife and Other Kurt Weill Music	196?	3.00	6.00	12.00
—Reissue of Columbia 8541					
MGM					
❑ E-3716 [M]	Secret Songs for Young Lovers	1959	5.00	10.00	20.00
❑ SE-3716 [S]	Secret Songs for Young Lovers	1959	6.25	12.50	25.00
❑ E-3811 [M]	Like Blue	1960	5.00	10.00	20.00

Number	Title (A Side/B Side)	Yr	VG	VG+	NM
❑ SE-3811 [S]	Like Blue	1960	6.25	12.50	25.00
❑ E-4186 [M]	Andre Previn — Composer, Conductor, Arranger, Pianist	1964	3.75	7.50	15.00
❑ SE-4186 [S]	Andre Previn — Composer, Conductor, Arranger, Pianist	1964	5.00	10.00	20.00
MOBILE FIDELITY					
❑ 1-095	West Side Story	1982	6.25	12.50	25.00
—Audiophile vinyl					
MONARCH					
❑ 203 [10]	All Star Jazz	1952	20.00	40.00	80.00
❑ 204 [10]	Andre Previn Plays Duke	1952	20.00	40.00	80.00
PRI					
❑ 3026 [S]	The World's Most Honored Pianist	1962	6.25	12.50	25.00
—Issued on yellow vinyl					
RCA CAMDEN					
❑ CAL-792 [M]	Love Walked In	1964	3.00	6.00	12.00
❑ CAS-792 [R]	Love Walked In	1964	2.50	5.00	10.00
RCA VICTOR					
❑ LPM-1011 [M]	Gershwin	1955	10.00	20.00	40.00
❑ LPM-1356 [M]	Three Little Words	1957	10.00	20.00	40.00
❑ ANL1-2805	Pure Gold	1978	2.50	5.00	10.00
❑ LPT-3002 [10]	Andre Previn Plays Harry Warren	1952	20.00	40.00	80.00
❑ LPM-3491 [M]	Andre Previn Plays Music of the Young Hollywood Composers	1966	3.00	6.00	12.00
❑ LSP-3491 [S]	Andre Previn Plays Music of the Young Hollywood Composers	1966	3.75	7.50	15.00
❑ LPM-3551 [M]	Andre Previn with Voices	1966	3.00	6.00	12.00
❑ LSP-3551 [S]	Andre Previn with Voices	1966	3.75	7.50	15.00
❑ LPM-3806 [M]	All Alone	1967	3.75	7.50	15.00
❑ LSP-3806 [S]	All Alone	1967	3.00	6.00	12.00
SPRINGBOARD					
❑ SPB-4053	After Dark	197?	2.50	5.00	10.00
STEREO RECORDS					
❑ S-7004 [S]	Pal Joey	1958	12.50	25.00	50.00
❑ S-7020 [S]	Gigi	1958	12.50	25.00	50.00
STRAND					
❑ SL 1074 [M]	Andre Previn Plays	1962	3.00	6.00	12.00
❑ SLS 1074 [S]	Andre Previn Plays	1962	3.75	7.50	15.00
VERVE					
❑ V-8565 [M]	The Essential Andre Previn	1963	3.00	6.00	12.00
❑ V6-8565 [S]	The Essential Andre Previn	1963	3.75	7.50	15.00

PREVIN, ANDRE; HERB ELLIS; SHELLY MANNE; RAY BROWN
Albums

Number	Title (A Side/B Side)	Yr	VG	VG+	NM
COLUMBIA					
❑ CL 2018 [M]	Four to Go	1963	3.75	7.50	15.00
❑ CS 8818 [S]	Four to Go	1963	5.00	10.00	20.00

PREVIN, ANDRE, AND RUSS FREEMAN
Albums

Number	Title (A Side/B Side)	Yr	VG	VG+	NM
CONTEMPORARY					
❑ C-3537 [M]	Double Play!	1957	12.50	25.00	50.00
❑ S-7011 [S]	Double Play!	1959	10.00	20.00	40.00
STEREO RECORDS					
❑ S-7011 [S]	Double Play!	1958	12.50	25.00	50.00

PRICE, ALAN Also see THE ANIMALS.
45s

Number	Title (A Side/B Side)	Yr	VG	VG+	NM
COTILLION					
❑ 44044	Falling in Love Again/Sly Sadie	1969	—	3.00	6.00
EPIC					
❑ 04319	I Don't Feel No Pain No More (Time and Tide)/ Rowf and Snitter Run to Sea	1984	—	2.00	4.00
JET					
❑ XW1119	I Wanna Dance/Just for You	1978	—	2.00	4.00
❑ 5056	This Is Your Lucky Day/Mama Don't Go Home	1979	—	2.00	4.00
PARROT					
❑ 3001	I Put a Spell on You/Iechyd-Da	1966	2.50	5.00	10.00
❑ 3007	Hi-Lili, Hi-Lo/Take Me Home	1966	2.50	5.00	10.00
❑ 3009	Tickle Me/Simon Smith and His Amazing Dancing Bears	1966	2.50	5.00	10.00
❑ 3013	Who Cares/The House That Jack Built	1967	2.00	4.00	8.00
❑ 3014	Shame/Don't Do That Again	1967	2.00	4.00	8.00
❑ 3019	Not Born to Follow/To Ramona	1968	2.00	4.00	8.00
WARNER BROS.					
❑ 7717	Poor People/O Lucky Man	1973	—	2.50	5.00
Albums					
ACCORD					
❑ SJA-7904	It's Priceless	1982	2.50	5.00	10.00
JET					
❑ JT-LA809-H	Alan Price	1977	2.50	5.00	10.00
—The "H" suffix is on the label, but the front and back cover, inner sleeve and spine have a "G" prefix; it's not known if any labels have a "G" prefix					
❑ JZ 35710	Lucky Day	1979	2.50	5.00	10.00
❑ NJZ 36510	Rising Sun	1980	2.50	5.00	10.00
PARROT					
❑ PAS 71018 [P]	The Price Is Right	1968	7.50	15.00	30.00
TOWNHOUSE					
❑ SN-7126	House of the Rising Sun	1981	2.50	5.00	10.00
WARNER BROS.					
❑ BS 2710	O Lucky Man	1973	3.00	6.00	12.00
❑ BS 2783	Between Today and Yesterday	1974	3.00	6.00	12.00

PRICE, LLOYD
45s

Number	Title (A Side/B Side)	Yr	VG	VG+	NM
ABC					
❑ 1237	Stagger Lee/Personality	1969	—	3.00	6.00
—"Golden Treasure Chest" reissue; contains the "samitized" version of "Stagger Lee" with Mr. Lee and Billy arguing over a woman					
❑ 11016	Personality/Just Because	1967	2.00	4.00	8.00
ABC-PARAMOUNT					
❑ 9792	Just Because/Why	1957	5.00	10.00	20.00
❑ 9972 [M]	Stagger Lee/You Need Love	1958	5.00	10.00	20.00
—Most, if not all, copies contain the "raunchy" version of "Stagger Lee" with Mr. Lee and Billy playing cards					
❑ S-9972 [S]	Stagger Lee/You Need Love	1958	10.00	20.00	40.00

Number	Title (A Side/B Side)	Yr	VG	VG+	NM
❏ 9997 [M]	Where Were You (On Our Wedding Day)?/ Is It Really Love	1959	5.00	10.00	20.00
❏ S-9997 [S]	Where Were You (On Our Wedding Day)?/ Is It Really Love	1959	10.00	20.00	40.00
❏ 10018 [M]	(You've Got) Personality/ Have You Ever Had the Blues	1959	5.00	10.00	20.00
—Note longer title					
❏ 10018 [M]	Personality/Have You Ever Had the Blues	1959	5.00	10.00	20.00
❏ S-10018 [S]	Personality/Have You Ever Had the Blues	1959	12.50	25.00	50.00
❏ 10032 [M]	I'm Gonna Get Married/Three Little Pigs	1959	5.00	10.00	20.00
❏ S-10032 [S]	I'm Gonna Get Married/Three Little Pigs	1959	12.50	25.00	50.00
❏ 10062	Come Into My Heart/Won't Cha Come Home	1959	3.75	7.50	15.00
❏ S-10062 [S]	Come Into My Heart/Won't Cha Come Home	1959	12.50	25.00	50.00
❏ 10075	Lady Luck/Never Let Me Go	1960	3.75	7.50	15.00
❏ 10102	No If's — No And's/For Love	1960	3.75	7.50	15.00
❏ 10123	Question/If I Look a Little Blue	1960	3.75	7.50	15.00
❏ 10139	Just Call Me (And I'll Understand)/ Who Could've Told You	1960	3.75	7.50	15.00
❏ 10162	(You Better) Know What You're Doin'/That's Why Tears Come and Go	1960	3.75	7.50	15.00
❏ 10177	Boo Hoo/I Made You Cry	1961	3.75	7.50	15.00
❏ 10197	One Hundred Percent/Say I'm the One	1961	3.75	7.50	15.00
❏ 10206	String of Pearls/Chantilly Lace	1961	3.75	7.50	15.00
❏ 10221	Mary and Man-O/I Ain't Givin' Up Nothin'	1961	3.75	7.50	15.00
❏ 10229	Talk to Me/I Cover the Waterfront	1961	3.75	7.50	15.00
❏ 10288	Be a Leader/'Nother Fairy Tale	1962	3.75	7.50	15.00
❏ 10299	Twistin' the Blues/Pop Eye's Irresistable You	1962	3.75	7.50	15.00
❏ 10342	Counterfeit Friends/Your Picture	1962	3.75	7.50	15.00
❏ 10372	Under Your Spell Again/Happy Birthday Mama	1962	3.75	7.50	15.00
❏ 10412	Who's Sorry Now/Hello Bill	1963	3.75	7.50	15.00
DOUBLE-L					
❏ 714	Pistol Packin' Mama/Tennessee Waltz	1963	2.50	5.00	10.00
❏ 722	Misty/Cry On	1963	2.50	5.00	10.00
❏ 728	Merry Christmas Mama/Auld Lang Syne	1963	3.00	6.00	12.00
❏ 729	Billie Baby/Try a Little Bit of Tenderness	1964	2.50	5.00	10.00
❏ 729 [PS]	Billie Baby/Try a Little Bit of Tenderness	1964	6.25	12.50	25.00
❏ 730	I'll Be a Fool for You/You're Nobody Till Somebody Loves You	1964	2.50	5.00	10.00
❏ 736	Go On Little Girl/You're Reading Me	1965	2.50	5.00	10.00
❏ 739	Every Night/Peeping and Hiding	1966	2.50	5.00	10.00
❏ 740	Send Me Some Loving/ Somewhere Along the Way	1966	2.50	5.00	10.00
GSF					
❏ 6882	Sing a Song/(B-side unknown)	1972	—	3.00	6.00
❏ 6894	Love Music/Just for Baby	1973	—	3.00	6.00
❏ 6904	Trying to Slip (Away)/They Get Down	1973	—	3.00	6.00
HURD					
❏ 82	Misty '66/Saturday Night	1966	2.00	4.00	8.00
JAD					
❏ 208	Luv, Luv, Luv/Take All	1968	2.00	4.00	8.00
❏ 212	Don't Stop Now/The Truth	1968	2.00	4.00	8.00
KRC					
❏ 301	Lonely Chair/The Chicken and the Bop	1957	12.50	25.00	50.00
❏ 303	Hello Little Girl/Georgianna	1957	6.25	12.50	25.00
❏ 305	How Many Times/To Love and Be Loved	1957	6.25	12.50	25.00
❏ 587	Just Because/Why	1957	20.00	40.00	80.00
❏ 5000	No Limit to Love/Such a Mess	195?	6.25	12.50	25.00
❏ 5002	Gonna Let You Come Back Home/Down by the River	195?	6.25	12.50	25.00
LPG					
❏ 111	What Did You Do with My Love/Love Music	1976	—	3.00	6.00
LUDIX					
❏ 4747	Feelin' Good/Cupid's Bandwagon	197?	—	3.00	6.00
MONUMENT					
❏ 856	Don't Cry/I Love You, I Just Love You	1964	2.50	5.00	10.00
❏ 865	Amen/I'd Fight the World	1964	2.50	5.00	10.00
❏ 877	Oh, Lady Luck/Woman	1965	2.50	5.00	10.00
❏ 887	If I Had My Life to Live Over/Two for Love	1965	2.50	5.00	10.00
PARAMOUNT					
❏ 0168	In the Eyes of God/ The Legend of Nigger Charley	1972	—	3.00	6.00
REPRISE					
❏ 0499	I Won't Cry Anymore/The Man Who Took the Valise Off the Floor at Grand Central Station at Noon	1966	2.00	4.00	8.00
SCEPTER					
❏ 12310	Hooked on a Feeling/If You Really Love Him	1971	—	3.00	6.00
❏ 12327	Mr. and Mrs. Untrue/Natural Sinner	1971	—	3.00	6.00
SPECIALTY					
❏ 428	Lawdy Miss Clawdy/Mailman Blues	1952	62.50	125.00	250.00
❏ 428	Lawdy Miss Clawdy/Mailman Blues	1952	375.00	750.00	1500.
—Red vinyl					
❏ 440	Oooh-Oooh-Oooh/Restless Heart	1952	25.00	50.00	100.00
❏ 452	Ain't It a Shame?/Tell Me Pretty Baby	1953	25.00	50.00	100.00
❏ 452	Ain't It a Shame?/Tell Me Pretty Baby	1953	50.00	100.00	200.00
—Red vinyl					
❏ 457	What's the Matter Now/So Long	1953	25.00	50.00	100.00
❏ 457	What's the Matter Now/So Long	1953	50.00	100.00	200.00
—Red vinyl					
❏ 463	Where You At?/Baby Don't Turn Your Back on Me	1953	25.00	50.00	100.00
❏ 463	Where You At?/Baby Don't Turn Your Back on Me	1953	50.00	100.00	200.00
—Red vinyl					
❏ 471	I Wish Your Picture Was You/Frog Legs	1953	25.00	50.00	100.00
❏ 483	Let Me Come Home, Baby/Too Late for Tears	1954	20.00	40.00	80.00
❏ 483	Let Me Come Home, Baby/Too Late for Tears	1954	50.00	100.00	200.00
—Red vinyl					
❏ 494	Walkin' the Track/Jimmie Lee	1954	20.00	40.00	80.00
❏ 535	Oo-Ee Baby/Chee-Koo Baby	1954	10.00	20.00	40.00
❏ 540	Trying to Find Someone to Love/ Lord, Lord, Amen!	1955	10.00	20.00	40.00
❏ 571	Woe Ho Ho/I Yi Yi Gomen-a-Sai (I'm Sorry)	1956	10.00	20.00	40.00
❏ 578	Country Boy Rock/Rock 'N' Dance	1956	12.50	25.00	50.00
❏ 582	Forgive Me, Clawdy/I'm Glad	1956	7.50	15.00	30.00
❏ 602	Baby Please Come Home/Breaking My Heart (All Over Again)	1957	7.50	15.00	30.00
❏ 661	Lawdy Miss Clawdy/Mailman Blues	1959	5.00	10.00	20.00

Number	Title (A Side/B Side)	Yr	VG	VG+	NM
TURNTABLE					
❏ 501	I Understand/The Grass Will Sing (For You)	1969	2.00	4.00	8.00
❏ 502	I Heard It Through the Grapevine/It's Your Thing	1969	2.00	4.00	8.00
❏ 506	Bad Conditions/The Truth	1969	2.00	4.00	8.00
❏ 509	Lawdy Miss Clawdy/Little Volcano	1969	2.00	4.00	8.00
7-Inch Extended Plays					
ABC-PARAMOUNT					
❏ A-277 [PS]	Lawdy Miss Clawdy/Just Because//You Need Love/Why	1959	25.00	50.00	100.00
❏ A-277 [PS]	The Exciting Lloyd Price	1959	25.00	50.00	100.00
❏ A-315	Ain't Nobody's Business/Just to Hold Your Hand/ /Talk to Me/I Cover the Waterfront	1960	25.00	50.00	100.00
❏ A-315 [PS]	Mr. Personality Sings the Blues	1960	25.00	50.00	100.00
❏ A-324	Lady Luck/Personality//Stagger Lee/I'm Gonna Get Married	1960	25.00	50.00	100.00
❏ A-324 [PS]	Mr. Personality's Big Hits	1960	25.00	50.00	100.00
Albums					
ABC					
❏ S-297	Mr. Personality	1967	3.75	7.50	15.00
—Reissue on revised label					
❏ S-324 [R]	Mr. Personality's Big 15	1968	3.75	7.50	15.00
—Reissue on revised label					
❏ X-763	16 Greatest Hits	1972	3.75	7.50	15.00
❏ AC-30006	The ABC Collection	1976	3.75	7.50	15.00
❏ DW-94842	16 Greatest Hits	1972	5.00	10.00	20.00
—Capitol Record Club edition					
ABC-PARAMOUNT					
❏ ABC-277 [M]	The Exciting Lloyd Price	1959	10.00	20.00	40.00
❏ ABCS-277 [S]	The Exciting Lloyd Price	1959	20.00	40.00	80.00
❏ ABC-297 [M]	Mr. Personality	1959	10.00	20.00	40.00
❏ ABCS-297 [S]	Mr. Personality	1959	20.00	40.00	80.00
❏ ABC-315 [M]	Mr. Personality Sings the Blues	1960	10.00	20.00	40.00
❏ ABCS-315 [S]	Mr. Personality Sings the Blues	1960	20.00	40.00	80.00
❏ ABC-324 [M]	Mr. Personality	1960	10.00	20.00	40.00
—Label calls this "Mr. Personality's Big Hits"					
❏ ABC-346 [M]	The Fantastic Lloyd Price	1960	10.00	20.00	40.00
❏ ABCS-346 [R]	The Fantastic Lloyd Price	196?	6.25	12.50	25.00
❏ ABC-366 [M]	Lloyd Price Sings the Million Sellers	1961	10.00	20.00	40.00
❏ ABCS-366 [S]	Lloyd Price Sings the Million Sellers	1961	12.50	25.00	50.00
❏ ABC-382 [M]	Cookin' with Lloyd Price	1961	10.00	20.00	40.00
❏ ABCS-382 [S]	Cookin' with Lloyd Price	1961	12.50	25.00	50.00
DOUBLE-L					
❏ DL-2301 [M]	The Lloyd Price Orchestra	1963	6.25	12.50	25.00
❏ DL-2303 [M]	Misty	1963	6.25	12.50	25.00
❏ SDL-8301 [S]	The Lloyd Price Orchestra	1963	10.00	20.00	40.00
❏ SDL-8303 [S]	Misty	1963	10.00	20.00	40.00
GRAND PRIX					
❏ 422 [M]	Mr. Rhythm and Blues	196?	3.00	6.00	12.00
❏ S-422 [R]	Mr. Rhythm and Blues	196?	2.50	5.00	10.00
GUEST STAR					
❏ G-1910 [M]	Come to Me	196?	3.00	6.00	12.00
❏ GS-1910 [R]	Come to Me	196?	2.50	5.00	10.00
JAD					
❏ 1002	Lloyd Price Now	1969	6.25	12.50	25.00
LPG					
❏ 001	Music…Music	1976	2.50	5.00	10.00
MCA					
❏ 1503	Greatest Hits	1982	2.00	4.00	8.00
MONUMENT					
❏ MLP-8032 [M]	Lloyd Swings for Sammy	1965	6.25	12.50	25.00
❏ SLP-18032 [S]	Lloyd Swings for Sammy	1965	10.00	20.00	40.00
PICKWICK					
❏ SPC-3518	Big Hits	197?	2.00	4.00	8.00
SCEPTER					
❏ CTN-18006	The Best of Lloyd Price	1972	2.50	5.00	10.00
SPECIALTY					
❏ SP-2105 [M]	Lloyd Price	1959	45.00	90.00	180.00
❏ SP-2105	Lloyd Price	198?	3.00	6.00	12.00
—1980s reissue					
TRIP					
❏ TOP 16-5	16 Greatest Hits	1976	2.50	5.00	10.00
TURNTABLE					
❏ TTS-5001	Lloyd Price Now	197?	3.75	7.50	15.00
UPFRONT					
❏ UPF-126	Misty	197?	3.00	6.00	12.00

PRICE, RAY Also see WILLIE NELSON.
45s

Number	Title (A Side/B Side)	Yr	VG	VG+	NM
ABC					
❏ 12084	Roses and Love Songs/The Closest Thing to Love	1975	—	2.00	4.00
❏ 12095	Farthest Thing from My Mind/ All That Keeps Me Going	1975	—	2.00	4.00
ABC DOT					
❏ 17588	Say I Do/I'll Still Love You	1975	—	2.00	4.00
❏ 17616	That's All She Wrote/I Didn't Feel Nothing	1976	—	2.00	4.00
❏ 17637	To Make a Long Story Short/ We're Getting There	1976	—	2.00	4.00
❏ 17666	A Mansion on the Hill/Hey, Good Lookin'	1976	—	2.00	4.00
❏ 17690	Different Kind of Flower/ Don't Let the Stars Get in Your Eyes	1977	—	2.00	4.00
❏ 17718	Born to Love Me/ The Only Way to Say Good Morning	1977	—	2.00	4.00
COLUMBIA					
❏ 10006	Like a First Time Thing/You Are the Song	1974	—	2.50	5.00
❏ 10150	If You Ever Change Your Mind/Just Enough to Make Me Stay	1975	—	2.00	4.00
❏ 10503	Help Me/Nobody Wins	1977	—	2.00	4.00
❏ 10631	Born to Love Me/ I'm Sorry for the Hateful Things I Did	1977	—	2.00	4.00
❏ 20810	You've Got My Troubles Now/If You've Ever Lonely Darling	1951	7.50	15.00	30.00
❏ 20833	I Saw My Castles Fall Today/Hey Lala	1951	7.50	15.00	30.00
❏ 20863	Heart Aching Blues/Till Death Do Us Part	1951	7.50	15.00	30.00
❏ 20883	I Made a Mistake and I'm Sorry/Weary Blues	1952	6.25	12.50	25.00
❏ 20913	Talk to Your Heart/I've Got to Hurry, Hurry, Hurry	1952	6.25	12.50	25.00

Number	Title (A Side/B Side)	Yr	VG	VG+	NM
❑ 20943	Hot Diggity Dog/I've Got to Hurry, Hurry, Hurry	1952	5.00	10.00	20.00
—With Jimmy Dickens					
❑ 20963	Road of No Return/I Know I'll Never Win Your Love Again	1952	5.00	10.00	20.00
❑ 21015	I Can't Escape from You/Won't You Please Be Mine	1952	5.00	10.00	20.00
❑ 21025	Don't Let the Stars Get In Your Eyes/I Lost the Only Love I Know	1952	5.00	10.00	20.00
❑ 21053	You're Under Arrest/My Old Scrapbook	1953	5.00	10.00	20.00
❑ 21089	Price for Loving You/That's What I Got for Loving You	1953	5.00	10.00	20.00
❑ 21117	Cold Shoulder/You Weren't Ashamed to Kiss Me	1953	5.00	10.00	20.00
❑ 21149	Wrong Side of Town/Who Stole That Train	1953	5.00	10.00	20.00
❑ 21173	Leave Her Alone/You Always Get By	1953	5.00	10.00	20.00
❑ 21214	I'll Be There (If You Ever Want Me)/Release Me	1954	5.00	10.00	20.00
❑ 21249	Much Too Young to Die/I Love You So Much	1954	5.00	10.00	20.00
❑ 21299	I Could Love You More/What If He Don't Love You	1954	5.00	10.00	20.00
❑ 21315	If You Don't, Somebody Else Will/Oh Yes Darling	1954	5.00	10.00	20.00
❑ 21354	One Broken Heart/I'm Alone Because I Love You	1955	3.75	7.50	15.00
❑ 21402	Sweet Little Miss Blue Eyes/Let Me Talk to You	1955	3.75	7.50	15.00
❑ 21404	A Man Called Peter/Call the Lord and He'll Be There	1955	5.00	10.00	20.00
❑ 21442	I Can't Go On Like This/I Don't Want It on My Conscience	1955	3.75	7.50	15.00
❑ 21474	Run Boy/You Never Will Be True	1955	3.75	7.50	15.00
❑ 21510	Crazy Arms/You Done Me Wrong	1956	3.75	7.50	15.00
❑ 21562	I've Got a New Heartache/Wasted Words	1956	3.75	7.50	15.00
❑ 31428 [S]	(titles unknown)	1962	3.75	7.50	15.00
❑ 31429 [S]	(titles unknown)	1962	3.75	7.50	15.00
❑ 31430 [S]	(titles unknown)	1962	3.75	7.50	15.00
❑ 31431 [S]	(titles unknown)	1962	3.75	7.50	15.00
❑ 31432 [S]	(titles unknown)	1962	3.75	7.50	15.00
—Anyone who can fill in these gaps -- the above 5 all are Columbia "Stereo 7" singles -- please let us know.					
❑ 40889	I'll Be There (When You Get Lonely)/Please Don't Leave Me	1957	3.75	7.50	15.00
❑ 40951	My Shoes Keep Walking Back to You/Don't Do This to Me	1957	3.75	7.50	15.00
❑ 41105	Curtain in the Window/It's All Your Fault	1958	3.00	6.00	12.00
❑ 41191	City Lights/Invitation to the Blues	1958	3.00	6.00	12.00
❑ 41309	That's What It's Like to Be Lonesome/Kissing Your Picture	1958	3.00	6.00	12.00
❑ 41374	Heartaches By the Number/Wall of Tears	1959	3.00	6.00	12.00
❑ 41477	The Same Old Me/Under Your Spell Again	1959	3.00	6.00	12.00
❑ 41590	One More Time/Who'll Be the First	1960	3.00	6.00	12.00
❑ 41767	I Wish I Could Fall in Love Today/I Can't Run Away from Myself	1960	3.00	6.00	12.00
❑ 41947	Heart Over Mind/The Twenty-Fourth Hour	1961	2.50	5.00	10.00
❑ 42132	Soft Rain/Here We Are Again	1961	2.50	5.00	10.00
❑ 42310	I've Just Destroyed the World (I'm Living In)/Big Shoes	1962	2.50	5.00	10.00
❑ 42518	Pride/I'm Walking Slow	1962	2.50	5.00	10.00
❑ 42658	Walk Me to the Door/You Took Her Off My Hands (Now Please Take Her Off My Mind)	1963	2.50	5.00	10.00
❑ 42827	Make the World Go Away/Night Life	1963	2.50	5.00	10.00
❑ 42971	Burning Memories/That's All That Matters	1964	2.50	5.00	10.00
❑ 43086	Please Talk to My Heart/I Don't Know Why	1964	2.50	5.00	10.00
❑ 43162	A Thing Called Sadness/Here Comes My Baby Back Again	1964	2.50	5.00	10.00
❑ 43264	The Other Woman/Tearful Earful	1965	2.00	4.00	8.00
❑ 43427	Don't You Ever Get Tired of Hurting Me/Unloved, Unwanted	1965	2.00	4.00	8.00
❑ 43560	A Way to Survive/I'm Not Crazy Yet	1966	2.00	4.00	8.00
❑ 43795	Touch My Heart/It Should Be Easier Now	1966	2.00	4.00	8.00
❑ 44042	Danny Boy/I'll Let My Mind Wander	1967	2.00	4.00	8.00
❑ 44042 [PS]	Danny Boy/I'll Let My Mind Wander	1967	3.00	6.00	12.00
❑ 44195	I'm Still Not Over You/Crazy	1967	2.00	4.00	8.00
❑ 44374	Take Me As I Am (Or Let Me Go)/In the Summer of My Life	1967	2.00	4.00	8.00
❑ 44505	I've Been There Before/Night Life	1968	2.00	4.00	8.00
❑ 44628	She Wears My Ring/Goin' Away	1968	2.00	4.00	8.00
❑ 44747	Set Me Free/Trouble	1969	—	3.00	6.00
❑ 44761	Sweetheart of the Year/How Can I Write on Paper (What I Feel in My Heart)	1969	—	3.00	6.00
❑ 44931	Raining in My Heart/I Know Love	1969	—	3.00	6.00
❑ 45005	April's Fool/Make It Rain	1969	—	3.00	6.00
❑ 45046	Jingle Bells/Happy Birthday to You, Our Lord	1969	—	3.00	6.00
❑ 45095	You Wouldn't Know Love/Everybody Wants to Get to Heaven	1970	—	3.00	6.00
❑ 45178	For the Good Times/Grazin' in Greener Pastures	1970	—	3.00	6.00
❑ 45329	I Won't Mention It Again/Kiss the World Goodbye	1971	—	2.50	5.00
❑ 45425	I'd Rather Be Sorry/When I Loved Her	1971	—	2.50	5.00
❑ 45583	The Lonesomest Lonesome/That's What Leaving's About	1972	—	2.50	5.00
❑ 45724	She's Got to Be a Saint/Oh Lonesome Me	1972	—	2.50	5.00
❑ 45889	You're the Best Thing That Ever Happened to Me/What Kind of Love Is This	1973	—	2.50	5.00
❑ 46015	Storms of Troubled Times/Some Things Never Change	1974	—	2.50	5.00

DIMENSION

Number	Title (A Side/B Side)	Yr	VG	VG+	NM
❑ 1018	Getting Over You Again/Circle Driveway	1981	—	2.00	4.00
❑ 1021	It Don't Hurt Me Half As Bad/She's the Right Kind of Woman (Loving the Wrong Kind of Man)	1981	—	2.00	4.00
❑ 1024	Diamonds in the Stars/Grazing in Greener Pastures	1981	—	2.00	4.00
❑ 1031	Forty and Fadin'/Something to Forget You By	1982	—	2.00	4.00
❑ 1035	Will Till Those Bridges Are Gone/Angel in My Heart (Devil in My Mind)	1982	—	2.00	4.00
❑ 1038	Somewhere in Texas/Getting Down and Getting High	1982	—	2.00	4.00

MONUMENT

Number	Title (A Side/B Side)	Yr	VG	VG+	NM
❑ 45-267	Feet/Let's Make a Nice Memory (Today)	1978	—	2.00	4.00
❑ 45-277	There's Always Me/If It All the Same to You (I'll Be Leaving in the Morning)	1979	—	2.00	4.00
❑ 45-283	That's the Only Way to Say Good Morning/All the Good Things Are Gone	1979	—	2.00	4.00
❑ 45-290	Misty Morning Rain/We Can't Build a Fire in the Rain	1979	—	2.00	4.00

MYRRH

Number	Title (A Side/B Side)	Yr	VG	VG+	NM
❑ 146	Like Old Times Again/My First Day Without Her	1974	—	2.50	5.00
❑ 150	Roses and Love Songs/The Closest Thing to Love	1975	—	2.50	5.00

STEP ONE

Number	Title (A Side/B Side)	Yr	VG	VG+	NM
❑ 341	(She Got a Hold of Me Where It Hurts) She Won't Let Go/Memories to Burn	1985	—	2.00	4.00
❑ 344	I'm Not Leaving (I'm Just Getting Out of Your Way)/Why Don't Love Just Go Away	1985	—	2.00	4.00
❑ 350	Five Fingers/Lonely Like a Rose	1985	—	2.00	4.00
❑ 352	You're Nobody Till Somebody Loves You/I'm In the Mood for Love	1986	—	2.00	4.00
❑ 355	All the Way/Bummin' Around	1986	—	2.00	4.00
❑ 361	Please Don't Talk About Me When I'm Gone/For the Good Times	1986	—	2.00	4.00
❑ 366	When You Gave Your Love to Me/Forty and Fadin'	1986	—	2.00	4.00
❑ 370	Sentimental Journey/Better Class of Loser	1987	—	2.00	4.00
❑ 378	Just Enough Love/Why Don't Love Just Go Away	1987	—	2.00	4.00
❑ 381	For Christmas/With Christmas Near	1987	—	2.00	4.00
❑ 383	Big Ole Teardrops/The Season for Missing You	1988	—	2.00	4.00
❑ 388	Don't the Morning Always Come Too Soon/All You Have to Do Is Come Back	1988	—	2.00	4.00
❑ 393	I'd Do It All Over Again/Wind Beneath My Wings	1988	—	2.00	4.00
❑ 410	Love Me Down to Size/(B-side unknown)	1989	—	2.00	4.00
❑ 436	Memories That Last/A Whole Lot of You	1991	—	2.00	4.00
—With Faron Young					

VIVA

Number	Title (A Side/B Side)	Yr	VG	VG+	NM
❑ 29147	What Am I Gonna Do Without You/You've Been Leaving Me for Years	1984	—	—	3.00
❑ 29217	Better Class of Loser/Everytime I Sing a Love Song	1984	—	—	3.00
❑ 29277	A New Place to Begin/Everyone Gets Crazy Now and Then	1984	—	—	3.00
❑ 29543	Scotch and Soda/I Love You Eyes	1983	—	—	3.00

WARNER BROS.

Number	Title (A Side/B Side)	Yr	VG	VG+	NM
❑ 29691	Willie, Write Me a Song/I Love You Eyes	1983	—	—	3.00
❑ 29830	One Fiddle, Two Fiddle/San Antonio Rose	1982	—	2.00	4.00

7-Inch Extended Plays

COLUMBIA

Number	Title (A Side/B Side)	Yr	VG	VG+	NM
❑ H-1786	You're Under Arrest (For Stealing My Heart)/Don't Let the Stars Get In Your Eyes//You Weren't Ashamed to Kiss Me Last Night/The Price for Loving You	195?	7.50	15.00	30.00
❑ H-1786 [PS]	Ray Price	195?	7.50	15.00	30.00
❑ B-2118	Wasted Words/I've Got a New Heartache//Crazy Arms/You Done Me Wrong	195?	5.00	10.00	20.00
❑ B-2118 [PS]	(title unknown)	195?	5.00	10.00	20.00
❑ B-2137	Four Walls/A Fallen Star//Gone/Bye Bye Love	195?	5.00	10.00	20.00
❑ B-2137 [PS]	(title unknown)	195?	5.00	10.00	20.00
❑ B-2809	*I'll Be There/Release Me/Don't Let the Stars Get In Your Eyes/I Lost the Only Love I Knew	195?	3.75	7.50	15.00
❑ B-2809 [PS]	Ray Price (Hall of Fame Series)	195?	3.75	7.50	15.00
❑ B-2812	The Last Letter/My Shoes Keep Walking Back to You//Crazy Arms/I'm Alone Because I Love You	195?	3.75	7.50	15.00
❑ B-2812 [PS]	Ray Price (Hall of Fame Series)	195?	3.75	7.50	15.00
❑ B-10151	I Love You Because/Let Me Talk to You//Blues, Stay Away from Me/Many Tears Ago	1957	3.75	7.50	15.00
❑ B-10151 [PS]	Ray Price Sings Heart Songs, Vol. 1	1957	3.75	7.50	15.00
❑ B-10152	Letters Have No Arms/Faded Love//Remember Me (I'm the One Who Loves You)/I Saw My Castles Fall Today	1957	3.75	7.50	15.00
❑ B-10152 [PS]	Ray Price Sings Heart Songs, Vol. 2	1957	3.75	7.50	15.00
❑ B-10153	I'll Sail My Ship Alone/I Can't Help It//A Mansion on the Hill/Pins and Needles in My Heart	1957	3.75	7.50	15.00
❑ B-10153 [PS]	Ray Price Sings Heart Songs, Vol. 3	1957	3.75	7.50	15.00

Albums

ABC DOT

Number	Title (A Side/B Side)	Yr	VG	VG+	NM
❑ DO-2037	Say I Do	1975	3.00	6.00	12.00
❑ DO-2053	Rainbows and Tears	1976	3.00	6.00	12.00
❑ DOSD-2062	Hank 'n Me	1976	3.00	6.00	12.00
❑ DO-2073	Reunited	1977	3.00	6.00	12.00

COLUMBIA

Number	Title (A Side/B Side)	Yr	VG	VG+	NM
❑ GP 28 [(2)]	The World of Ray Price	1970	3.75	7.50	15.00
❑ CL 1015 [M]	Ray Price Sings Heart Songs	1957	12.50	25.00	50.00
❑ CL 1148 [M]	Talk to Your Heart	1958	10.00	20.00	40.00
❑ CL 1494 [M]	Faith	1960	7.50	15.00	30.00
❑ CL 1566 [M]	Ray Price's Greatest Hits	1961	7.50	15.00	30.00
❑ CL 1756 [M]	San Antonio Rose	1962	5.00	10.00	20.00
❑ CL 1971 [M]	Night Life	1963	3.75	7.50	15.00
❑ CL 2189 [M]	Love Life	1964	3.75	7.50	15.00
❑ CL 2339 [M]	Burning Memories	1965	3.75	7.50	15.00
❑ CL 2382 [M]	Western Strings	1965	3.75	7.50	15.00
❑ CL 2528 [M]	The Other Woman	1965	3.75	7.50	15.00
❑ CL 2606 [M]	Another Bridge to Burn	1966	3.75	7.50	15.00
❑ CL 2670 [M]	Touch My Heart	1967	5.00	10.00	20.00
❑ CL 2677 [M]	Ray Price's Greatest Hits, Volume 2	1967	5.00	10.00	20.00
❑ CL 2677 [M]	Danny Boy	1967	5.00	10.00	20.00
❑ CL 2806 [M]	Take Me As I Am	1968	7.50	15.00	30.00
❑ CS 8285 [S]	Faith	1960	10.00	20.00	40.00
❑ CS 8556 [S]	San Antonio Rose	1962	7.50	15.00	30.00
❑ CS 8771 [S]	Night Life	1963	5.00	10.00	20.00
❑ CS 8866 [R]	Ray Price's Greatest Hits	1964	3.00	6.00	12.00
❑ PC 8866	Ray Price's Greatest Hits	198?	2.00	4.00	8.00
—Reissue with new prefix					
❑ CS 8989 [S]	Love Life	1964	5.00	10.00	20.00
❑ CS 9089 [S]	Burning Memories	1965	5.00	10.00	20.00
❑ CS 9139 [S]	Western Strings	1965	6.25	12.50	25.00
❑ CS 9182 [S]	The Other Woman	1965	5.00	10.00	20.00
❑ CS 9328 [S]	Another Bridge to Burn	1966	5.00	10.00	20.00
❑ CS 9406 [S]	Touch My Heart	1967	3.75	7.50	15.00
❑ CS 9470 [S]	Ray Price's Greatest Hits, Volume 2	1967	3.75	7.50	15.00

Bobby "Boris" Pickett, *Monster Mash,"* Garpax 44167, picture sleeve, $30-$60.

Pink Floyd, *The Piper at the Gates of Dawn,* Tower ST 5093, stereo LP, orange label, $40-$80.

Gene Pitney, "(I Wanna) Love My Life Away," Musicor 1002, picture sleeve, $20-$40.

The Platters, *More Encore of Golden Hits*, Mercury MG 20591, mono LP, black label, $12.50-$25.

The Pointer Sisters, *The Pointer Sisters*, Blue Thumb BTS 48, stereo LP, $6-$12.

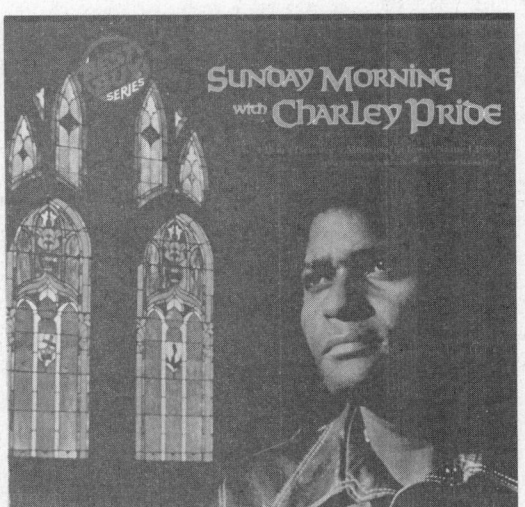

Charley Pride, *Sunday Morning with Charley Pride*, RCA Victor AYL1-3740, stereo LP, "Best Buy Series" reissue, $4-$8.

P

Number	Title (A Side/B Side)	Yr	VG	VG+	NM
❑ CS 9477 [S]	Danny Boy	1967	3.75	7.50	15.00
❑ CS 9606 [S]	Take Me As I Am	1968	3.75	7.50	15.00
❑ CS 9733	She Wears My Ring	1968	3.75	7.50	15.00
❑ CS 9822	Sweetheart of the Year	1969	3.75	7.50	15.00
❑ CS 9861	Ray Price's Christmas Album	1969	3.75	7.50	15.00
❑ CS 9918	You Wouldn't Know Love	1970	3.75	7.50	15.00
❑ C 30106	For the Good Times	1970	3.00	6.00	12.00
❑ CQ 30106 [Q]	For the Good Times	1972	5.00	10.00	20.00
❑ C 30510	I Won't Mention It Again	1971	3.00	6.00	12.00
❑ CG 30878 [(2)]	Welcome to My World	1971	3.75	7.50	15.00
❑ KG 31364 [(2)]	Ray Price's All-Time Greatest Hits	1972	3.75	7.50	15.00
❑ KC 31546	The Lonesomest Lonesome	1972	3.00	6.00	12.00
❑ KC 32033	She's Got to Be a Saint	1973	3.00	6.00	12.00
❑ PC 32033	She's Got to Be a Saint	197?	2.00	4.00	8.00
—Reissue with new prefix					
❑ KC 32777	You're the Best Thing That Ever Happened to Me	1973	3.00	6.00	12.00
❑ PC 32777	You're the Best Thing That Ever Happened to Me	197?	2.00	4.00	8.00
—Reissue with new prefix					
❑ PC 33560	If You Change Your Mind	1975	3.00	6.00	12.00
❑ CG 33633 [(2)]	For the Good Times/I Won't Mention It Again	1975	3.75	7.50	15.00
—Reissue of two LPs in one package					
❑ PC 34160	The Best of Ray Price	1976	3.00	6.00	12.00
❑ PC 34710	Help Me	1977	3.00	6.00	12.00
❑ JC 37061	A Tribute to Willie and Kris	1982	2.50	5.00	10.00
COLUMBIA LIMITED EDITION					
❑ LE 10142	Love Life	197?	2.50	5.00	10.00
—Reissue of Columbia CS 8989					
HARMONY					
❑ HL 7372 [M]	Collectors' Choice	196?	3.00	6.00	12.00
❑ HL 7440 [M]	Born to Lose	1967	3.00	6.00	12.00
❑ HS 11172 [R]	Collectors' Choice	196?	3.00	6.00	12.00
❑ HS 11240 [S]	Born to Lose	1967	3.00	6.00	12.00
❑ HS 11373	I Fall to Pieces	1969	2.50	5.00	10.00
❑ KH 30272	Make the World Go Away	1970	2.50	5.00	10.00
MONUMENT					
❑ 7633	Always Me	1979	2.50	5.00	10.00
MYRRH					
❑ 6532	This Time, Lord	1975	3.00	6.00	12.00
PAIR					
❑ PDL2-1044 [(2)]	Happens to Be the Best	1986	3.00	6.00	12.00
❑ PDL2-1044 [(2)]	Ray Price Happens to Be the Best!	1986	3.00	6.00	12.00
❑ PDL2-1096 [(2)]	Priceless	1986	3.00	6.00	12.00
ROUNDER					
❑ SS-22	The Honky Tonk Years	1986	2.50	5.00	10.00
WORD					
❑ 8723	Precious Memories	197?	3.00	6.00	12.00
❑ 8780	How Great Thou Art	1978	3.00	6.00	12.00

PRIDE
Albums
WARNER BROS.

Number	Title (A Side/B Side)	Yr	VG	VG+	NM
❑ WS 1848	Pride	1970	6.25	12.50	25.00

PRIDE, CHARLEY Includes releases as "Country Charley Pride."
45s
RCA

Number	Title (A Side/B Side)	Yr	VG	VG+	NM
❑ 2723-7-R	The Easy Part's Over/The Right to Do Wrong	1990	—	—	3.00
—"Gold Standard Series" reissue					
❑ PB-10757	A Whole Lotta Things to Sing About/ The Hardest Part of Livin' Lovin' Me	1976	—	2.00	4.00
❑ PB-10875	She's Just An Old Love Turned Memory/ Country Music	1977	—	2.00	4.00
❑ PB-10975	I'll Be Leaving Alone/We Need Lovin'	1977	—	2.00	4.00
❑ PB-11086	More to Me/ Heaven Watches Over Fools Like Me	1977	—	2.00	4.00
❑ PB-11201	Someone Loves You Honey/Days of Our Lives	1978	—	2.00	4.00
❑ PB-11287	When I Stop Leaving (I'll Be Gone)/I Can See the Lovin' in Your Eyes	1978	—	2.00	4.00
❑ GB-11331	My Eyes Can Only See As Far As You/A Whole Lotta Things to Sing About	1978	—	—	3.00
—"Gold Standard Series" reissue					
❑ PB-11391	Burgers and Fries/ Nothing's Prettier Than Rose Is	1978	—	2.00	4.00
❑ PB-11477	Where Do I Put Her Memory/ The Best in the World	1979	—	2.00	4.00
❑ GB-11498	Someone Loves You Honey/ When I Stop Leaving (I'll Be Gone)	1979	—	—	3.00
—"Gold Standard Series" reissue					
❑ PB-11655	You're My Jamaica/ Let Me Have a Chance to Love You	1979	—	2.00	4.00
❑ PB-11736	Dallas Cowboys/When I Stop Leaving	1979	—	3.00	6.00
—Regular black-label edition					
❑ PB-11736	Dallas Cowboys/When I Stop Leaving	1979	3.00	6.00	12.00
—Special blue and silver label edition					
❑ PB-11751	Missin' You/Heartbreak Mountain	1979	—	2.00	4.00
❑ PB-11912	Honky Tonk Blues/I'm So Lonesome I Could Cry	1980	—	—	3.00
❑ GB-11992	Burgers and Fries/Where Do I Put Her Memory	1980	—	—	3.00
—"Gold Standard Series" reissue					
❑ PB-12002	You Win Again/There's a Little Bit of Hank in Me	1980	—	—	3.00
❑ PB-12100	You Almost Slipped My Mind/Ghost Written Love Letters	1980	—	—	3.00
❑ PB-12178	Roll On Mississippi/Fall Back on Me	1981	—	—	3.00
❑ PB-12294	Never Been So Loved (In All My Life)/ I Call Her My Girl	1981	—	—	3.00
❑ GB-12371	Honky Tonk Blues/You Win Again	1981	—	—	3.00
—"Gold Standard Series" reissue					
❑ PB-13014	Mountain of Love/Love Is a Shadow	1981	—	—	3.00
❑ PB-13096	I Don't Think She's in Love Anymore/Oh What a Beautiful Love Song	1982	—	—	3.00
❑ PB-13293	You're So Good When You're Bad/I Haven't Loved This Way in Years	1982	—	—	3.00
❑ PB-13359	Let It Snow, Let It Snow, Let It Snow/ Peace on Earth	1982	—	2.50	5.00
—B-side by Razzy Bailey					
❑ PB-13397	Why Baby Why/It's So Good to Be Together	1982	—	—	3.00
❑ PB-13451	More and More/Radio Heroes	1983	—	—	3.00
❑ PB-13542	Night Games/I Could Let Her Get Close to Me	1983	—	—	3.00

Number	Title (A Side/B Side)	Yr	VG	VG+	NM
❑ PB-13648	Ev'ry Heart Should Have One/ Lovin' It Up (Livin' It Down)	1983	—	—	3.00
❑ PB-13667	Let It Snow, Let It Snow, Let It Snow/O Holy Night	1983	—	2.00	4.00
❑ PB-13732	The Late Show/Love on a Blue Rainy Day	1984	—	2.00	4.00
❑ JK-13754	Stagger Lee (same on both sides)	1984	2.50	5.00	10.00
—Promo on red vinyl					
❑ PB-13821	The Power of Love/Ellie	1984	—	—	3.00
❑ PB-13936	Missin' Mississippi/Falling in Love Again	1984	—	—	3.00
❑ PB-14045	Down on the Farm/Now and Then	1985	—	—	3.00
❑ PB-14134	Let a Little Love Come In/Night Games	1985	—	—	3.00
❑ PB-14265	The Best There Is/ The Tumbleweed and the Rose	1986	—	—	3.00
❑ PB-14296	Love on a Blue Rainy Day/I Used It All on You	1986	—	—	3.00
RCA VICTOR					
❑ 47-8738	Atlantic Coastal Line/Snakes Crawl at Night	1966	3.75	7.50	15.00
❑ 47-8862	Miller's Cave/Before I Met You	1966	3.75	7.50	15.00
❑ 47-9000	Just Between You and Me/Detroit City	1966	3.00	6.00	12.00
❑ 47-9162	I Know One/The Best Banjo Picker	1967	3.00	6.00	12.00
❑ 47-9281	Does My Ring Hurt Your Finger/ The Spell of the Freight Train	1967	3.00	6.00	12.00
—Above three labeled as "Country Charley Pride"					
❑ 47-9403	The Day the World Stood Still/Gone, On the Other Hand	1967	2.00	4.00	8.00
❑ 47-9514	The Easy Part's Over/Right to Do Wrong	1968	2.00	4.00	8.00
❑ 47-9622	Let the Chips Fall/She Made Me Go	1968	2.00	4.00	8.00
❑ 47-9716	Kaw-Liga/Little Folks	1969	2.00	4.00	8.00
❑ 47-9777	Wings of a Dove/They Stood in Silent Prayer	1969	3.00	6.00	12.00
❑ 47-9806	Is Anybody Goin' to San Antone/ Things Are Looking Up	1970	—	3.00	6.00
❑ 47-9855	Wonder Could I Live There Anymore/ Piroque Joe	1970	—	3.00	6.00
❑ 47-9902	I Can't Believe That You've Stopped Loving Me/ Time	1970	—	3.00	6.00
❑ 47-9933	Christmas in My Home Town/Santa and the Kids	1970	2.00	4.00	8.00
❑ 47-9952	I'd Rather Love You/You Don't Belong	1971	—	3.00	6.00
❑ 47-9974	Let Me Live/Did You Think to Pray	1971	2.00	4.00	8.00
❑ 47-9996	I'm Just Me/A Place for the Lonesome	1971	—	3.00	6.00
❑ 74-0167	All I Have to Offer You (Is Me)/ Brand New Bed of Roses	1969	2.00	4.00	8.00
❑ 74-0265	(I'm So) Afraid of Losing You Again/ Good Chance of Tear-Fall Tonight	1969	2.00	4.00	8.00
❑ 74-0550	Kiss an Angel Good Mornin'/ No One Could Ever Take Me from You	1971	—	3.00	6.00
❑ 74-0624	All His Children/You'll Still Be the One	1972	—	2.50	5.00
❑ 74-0707	It's Gonna Take a Little Bit Longer/You're Wanting Me to Stop Loving You	1972	—	2.50	5.00
❑ 74-0707 [PS]	It's Gonna Take a Little Bit Longer/You're Wanting Me to Stop Loving You	1972	2.00	4.00	8.00
❑ 74-0802	She's Too Good to Be True/She's That Kind	1972	—	2.50	5.00
❑ 74-0884	A Shoulder to Cry On/I'm Learning to Love Her	1973	—	2.50	5.00
❑ 74-0942	Don't Fight the Feelings of Love/Tennessee Girl	1973	—	2.50	5.00
❑ 447-0920	I'm Just Me/Jeanie Norman	1972	—	3.00	6.00
—Gold Standard Series on red label; B-side makes its first 45 rpm appearance here					
❑ 447-0921	You'll Still Be the One/Crystal Chandelier	1972	—	3.00	6.00
—Gold Standard Series on red label; B-side makes its first 45 rpm appearance here					
❑ 447-0935	Christmas in My Home Town/Santa and the Kids	1972	—	2.00	4.00
—Gold Standard Series					
❑ APBO-0073	Amazing Love/ Blue Ridge Mountains Turnin' Green	1973	—	2.50	5.00
❑ AMBO-0128	A Shoulder to Cry On/ Don't Fight the Feelings of Love	1973	—	2.00	4.00
—"Gold Standard Series" reissue					
❑ APBO-0257	We Could/Love Put a Song in My Heart	1974	—	2.50	5.00
❑ PB-10030	Mississippi Cotton Picking Delta Town/ Mary Go Round	1974	—	2.00	4.00
❑ PB-10126	Then Who Am I/Completely Helpless	1974	—	2.00	4.00
❑ PB-10236	I Ain't All Bad/Hard Times Will Be the Best Times	1975	—	2.00	4.00
❑ PB-10344	Hope You're Feelin' Me (Like I'm Feelin' You)/ Searching for the Morning Sun	1975	—	2.00	4.00
❑ PB-10455	The Happiness of Having You/Right Back Missing You Again	1975	—	2.00	4.00
❑ GB-10507	Then Who Am I/Completely Helpless	1975	—	—	3.00
—"Gold Standard Series" reissue					
❑ GB-10508	Mississippi Cotton Picking Delta Town/ Mary Go Round	1975	—	—	3.00
—"Gold Standard Series" reissue					
❑ GB-10509	Amazing Love/ Blue Ridge Mountains Turning Green	1975	—	—	3.00
—"Gold Standard Series" reissue					
❑ PB-10592	My Eyes Can Only See As Far As You/ Oklahoma Morning	1976	—	2.00	4.00
❑ PB-10643	In Jesus' Name I Pray/I Don't Deserve a Mansion	1976	—	3.00	6.00
❑ GB-10674	I Ain't All Bad/Hope You're Feelin' Me (Like I'm Feelin' You)	1976	—	2.00	4.00
—"Gold Standard Series" reissue					
16TH AVENUE					
❑ 70400	Have I Got Some Blues for You/Ever Knowin'	1987	—	2.00	4.00
❑ 70402	If You Still Want a Fool Around/ You Took Me There	1987	—	2.00	4.00
❑ 70408	Shouldn't It Be Easier Than This/ Look in Your Mirror	1987	—	2.00	4.00
❑ 70414	I'm Gonna Love Her on the Radio/ Shouldn't It Be Easier Than This	1988	—	2.00	4.00
❑ 70420	Where Was I/A Whole Lotta Lovin' (Goes a Long, Long Way)	1988	—	2.00	4.00
❑ 70425	White Houses/Shouldn't It Be Easier Than This	1989	—	2.00	4.00
❑ 70429	The More I Do/Heaven Help Us All	1989	—	2.00	4.00
❑ 70435	Amy's Eyes/I Made Love to You in My Mind	1989	—	2.00	4.00
❑ 70440	Moody Woman/Shouldn't It Be Easier Than This	1990	—	2.50	5.00
❑ 70446	Whole Lotta Love on the Line/Plenty Good Lovin'	1990	—	2.50	5.00
Albums					
PAIR					
❑ PDL2-1023 [(2)]	Country in My Soul	1986	3.00	6.00	12.00
RCA CAMDEN					
❑ CAS-2584	The Incomparable Charley Pride	1972	3.75	7.50	15.00
RCA VICTOR					
❑ APD1-0217 [Q]	Sweet Country	1973	6.25	12.50	25.00
❑ APL1-0217	Sweet Country	1973	3.75	7.50	15.00

Number	Title (A Side/B Side)	Yr	VG	VG+	NM
❏ APL1-0315	Charley Pride Presents the Pridesmen	1973	3.75	7.50	15.00
❏ APD1-0397 [Q]	Amazing Love	1974	6.25	12.50	25.00
❏ APL1-0397	Amazing Love	1974	8.75	7.50	15.00
❏ APL1-0534	Country Feelin'	1974	3.75	7.50	15.00
❏ APD1-0757 [Q]	Pride of America	1974	6.25	12.50	25.00
❏ APL1-0757	Pride of America	1974	3.75	7.50	15.00
❏ ANL1-0996	Charley Pride — In Person	1975	2.50	5.00	10.00
—Reissue of LSP-4094					
❏ APD1-1038 [Q]	Charley	1975	6.25	12.50	25.00
❏ APL1-1038	Charley	1975	3.75	7.50	15.00
❏ ANL1-1214	I'm Just Me	1975	2.50	5.00	10.00
—Reissue of LSP-4560					
❏ APD1-1241 [Q]	The Happiness of Having You	1975	6.25	12.50	25.00
❏ APL1-1241	The Happiness of Having You	1975	3.75	7.50	15.00
❏ APD1-1359 [Q]	Sunday Morning with Charley Pride	1976	6.25	12.50	25.00
❏ APL1-1359	Sunday Morning with Charley Pride	1976	3.75	7.50	15.00
❏ ANL1-1934	Christmas in My Home Town	1976	2.00	4.00	8.00
—Reissue of APL1-4406					
❏ APL1-2023	The Best of Charley Pride, Vol. III	1976	3.00	6.00	12.00
❏ APL1-2261	She's Just an Old Love Turned Memory	1977	3.00	6.00	12.00
❏ AHL1-2478	Someone Loves You Honey	1978	3.00	6.00	12.00
❏ AHL1-2963	Burgers and Fries	1978	3.00	6.00	12.00
❏ AHL1-3441	You're My Jamaica	1979	3.00	6.00	12.00
❏ AHL1-3548	There's a Little Bit of Hank in Me	1980	3.00	6.00	12.00
❏ LPM-3645 [M]	Country Charley Pride	1966	6.25	12.50	25.00
❏ LSP-3645 [S]	Country Charley Pride	1966	7.50	15.00	30.00
❏ AYL1-3676	Someone Loves You Honey	1980	2.00	4.00	8.00
—"Best Buy Series" reissue					
❏ AYL1-3740	Sunday Morning with Charley Pride	1980	2.00	4.00	8.00
—"Best Buy Series" reissue					
❏ LPM-3775 [M]	The Pride of Country Music	1967	6.25	12.50	25.00
❏ LSP-3775 [S]	The Pride of Country Music	1967	5.00	10.00	20.00
❏ AYL1-3874	I'm Just Me	1981	2.00	4.00	8.00
—"Best Buy Series" reissue					
❏ LPM-3895 [M]	The Country Way	1967	6.25	12.50	25.00
❏ LSP-3895 [S]	The Country Way	1967	5.00	10.00	20.00
❏ AHL1-3905	Roll On Mississippi	1981	2.50	5.00	10.00
❏ AYL1-3943	The Happiness of Having You	1981	2.00	4.00	8.00
—"Best Buy Series" reissue					
❏ LPM-3952 [M]	Make Mine Country	1968	15.00	30.00	60.00
❏ LSP-3952 [S]	Make Mine Country	1968	5.00	10.00	20.00
❏ LSP-4041	Songs of Pride — Charley, That Is	1968	5.00	10.00	20.00
❏ AYL1-4074	Amazing Love	1981	2.00	4.00	8.00
—"Best Buy Series" reissue					
❏ LSP-4094	Charley Pride — In Person	1969	5.00	10.00	20.00
❏ AHL1-4151	Greatest Hits	1981	2.50	5.00	10.00
❏ LSP-4153	The Sensational Charley Pride	1969	5.00	10.00	20.00
❏ AYL1-4166	She's Just an Old Love Turned Memory	1981	2.00	4.00	8.00
—"Best Buy Series" reissue					
❏ AHL1-4223	The Best of Charley Pride	198?	2.50	5.00	10.00
—Reissue of LSP-4223					
❏ LSP-4223	The Best of Charley Pride	1969	5.00	10.00	20.00
❏ AYL1-4252	Burgers and Fries	1982	2.00	4.00	8.00
—"Best Buy Series" reissue					
❏ AHL1-4287	Charley Pride Sings Everybody's Choice	1982	2.50	5.00	10.00
❏ LSP-4290	Just Plain Charley	1970	5.00	10.00	20.00
❏ LSP-4367	Charley Pride's 10th Album	1970	5.00	10.00	20.00
❏ LSP-4406	Christmas in My Home Town	1970	5.00	10.00	20.00
❏ LSP-4468	From Me to You	1971	5.00	10.00	20.00
❏ LSP-4513	Did You Think to Pray	1971	5.00	10.00	20.00
❏ AHL1-4524	Charley Pride Live	1983	2.50	5.00	10.00
❏ LSP-4560	I'm Just Me	1971	5.00	10.00	20.00
❏ LSP-4617	Charley Pride Sings Heart Songs	1971	5.00	10.00	20.00
❏ AHL1-4662	Country Classics	1983	2.50	5.00	10.00
❏ AHL1-4682	The Best of Charley Pride, Volume 2	198?	2.50	5.00	10.00
—Reissue of LSP-4682					
❏ LSP-4682	The Best of Charley Pride, Volume 2	1972	5.00	10.00	20.00
❏ LSP-4742	A Sunshiny Day with Charley Pride	1972	5.00	10.00	20.00
❏ AHL1-4822	Night Games	1983	2.50	5.00	10.00
❏ AYL1-4831	There's a Little Bit of Hank in Me	1983	2.00	4.00	8.00
—"Best Buy Series" reissue					
❏ LSP-4837	Songs of Love by Charley Pride	1973	3.75	7.50	15.00
❏ AHL1-5031	The Power of Love	1984	2.50	5.00	10.00
❏ AYL1-5147	Greatest Hits	1984	2.00	4.00	8.00
—"Best Buy Series" reissue					
❏ AYL1-5148	The Best of Charley Pride	1984	2.00	4.00	8.00
—"Best Buy Series" reissue					
❏ AHL1-5426	Greatest Hits, Volume 2	1985	2.50	5.00	10.00
❏ AHL1-5851	Back to the Country	1986	2.50	5.00	10.00
❏ CPL1-7049	Collector's Series	1985	2.50	5.00	10.00
❏ AHL1-7174	The Best There Is	1986	2.50	5.00	10.00
READER'S DIGEST					
❏ RDA-217 [(6)]	Charley Pride's Country	1979	10.00	20.00	40.00
16TH AVENUE					
❏ ST-70550	After All This Time	1987	3.00	6.00	12.00
❏ D1-70551	I'm Gonna Love Her on the Radio	1988	3.00	6.00	12.00
❏ D1-70554	Moody Woman	1989	3.00	6.00	12.00
TIME-LIFE					
❏ STW-101	Country Music	1981	2.50	5.00	10.00

PRIESMAN, MAGEL
45s

Number	Title (A Side/B Side)	Yr	VG	VG+	NM
SUN					
❏ 294	Memories of You/I Feel So Blue	1958	6.25	12.50	25.00

PRIMA, LOUIS
45s

Number	Title (A Side/B Side)	Yr	VG	VG+	NM
ABC					
❏ 11093	Almost Persuaded/Waitin' in Your Welfare Line	1968	—	3.00	6.00
❏ 11122	Joanna/You Can't Take the Country Out of the Boy	1968	—	3.00	6.00
❏ 11166	Flooby Dooby Doo/I Never Opened My Eyes	1969	—	3.00	6.00
❏ 12047	Time Heals Everything/When Hazel Comes in the Room	1974	—	2.00	4.00
BRUNSWICK					
❏ 55485	I Left My Heart in San Francisco/I Never Promised You a Rose Garden	1972	—	3.00	6.00

Number	Title (A Side/B Side)	Yr	VG	VG+	NM
BUENA VISTA					
❏ 446	Jolly Holiday/Supercalifragilisticexpialidocious	1965	3.75	7.50	15.00
—With Gia Maione					
❏ 454	Santa, How Come Your Eyes Are Green When Last Year They Were Blue/Senor Santa Claus	1966	3.00	6.00	12.00
CAPITOL					
❏ F3566	A Banana Spilt for My Baby/ Five Months, Two Weeks, Two Days	1956	3.00	6.00	12.00
—With Sam Butera					
❏ F3615	Whistle Stop/Be Mine	1957	3.00	6.00	12.00
—With Sam Butera					
❏ F3667	Midnight Melody/The Wild Ones	1957	3.00	6.00	12.00
—With Sam Butera					
❏ F3856	Beep Beep/Buona Sera	1957	3.00	6.00	12.00
❏ 4732	Twist All Night/Everybody Knows	1962	2.50	5.00	10.00
❏ 4805	Big Daddy/Ooh, Look What You've Done to Me	1962	2.50	5.00	10.00
—With Gia Maione					
❏ 58572	Jump, Jive, An' Wail/Just a Gigolo-I Ain't Got Nobody (Medley)	1998	—	—	3.00
❏ 58804	Buona Sera/Oh Marie	1999	—	—	3.00
COLUMBIA					
❏ 39614	Shake Hands with Santa/Eleanor	1951	5.00	10.00	20.00
❏ 39692	Basta/Ooh Dah Dilly Dah	1952	5.00	10.00	20.00
❏ 39735	The Bigger the Figure/Boney Bones	1952	5.00	10.00	20.00
❏ 39823	Chili Sauce/One Mint Julep	1952	5.00	10.00	20.00
❏ 39969	Oh Marie/Luigi	1953	5.00	10.00	20.00
❏ 40015	Paul Revere/It's As Good As New	1953	5.00	10.00	20.00
❏ 40064	Barncale Bill the Sailor/Shepherd Boy	1953	5.00	10.00	20.00
DECCA					
❏ 29128	Happy Wanderer/Until Sunrise	1954	3.75	7.50	15.00
❏ 29162	Paper Doll/The Dummy Song	1954	3.75	7.50	15.00
DOT					
❏ 15978	Confessin'/Night and Day	1959	2.50	5.00	10.00
❏ 16009	Hey Ba-Ba-Re-Bop/My Cucuzza	1959	2.50	5.00	10.00
❏ 16060	When My Baby Smiles at Me/Paradise	1960	2.50	5.00	10.00
❏ 16108	Don't You Know/Brooklyn Bridge	1960	2.50	5.00	10.00
❏ 16151	Wonderland by Night/Ol' Man Moses	1960	2.50	5.00	10.00
❏ 16193	Enchantment/Chapel by the Sea	1961	2.50	5.00	10.00
❏ 16211	My Prayer/You Can Depend on Me	1961	2.50	5.00	10.00
❏ 16273	Mod Indigo/Come Back to Sorrento	1961	2.50	5.00	10.00
❏ 16301	Continental Twist/Oh Ma Ma Twist	1962	2.50	5.00	10.00
❏ 16401	Josephine, Please No Lean on the Bell/ Brooklyn Bridge	1962	2.50	5.00	10.00
HANNA-BARBERA					
❏ 467	I'm Gonna Sit Right Down and Write Myself a Letter/Civilization (Bongo, Bongo, Bongo)	1966	2.50	5.00	10.00
KAMA SUTRA					
❏ 213	Jug Band Music/Bald-Headed Girl	1966	2.00	4.00	8.00
MERCURY					
❏ 5386	Over the Rainbow/Tears on My Tie	1950	7.50	15.00	30.00
—Note: Earlier Louis Prima 45s on Mercury may exist.					
❏ 5406	Francis, the Talking Mule/ A Good Time Was Had By All	1950	7.50	15.00	30.00
❏ 5451	Here, Pretty Kitty/Buona Sera	1950	7.50	15.00	30.00
PRIMA					
❏ 1013	I Ain't Got Nobody/Just a Gigolo	196?	2.50	5.00	10.00
❏ 22206	Judy/I'm Leavinf You	197?	2.00	4.00	8.00
❏ 22208	Oh Marie/Marie Yootch	197?	2.00	4.00	8.00
RCA VICTOR					
❏ 47-2960	Five Foot Two, Eyes of Blue/For Mari-Yooten	1949	5.00	10.00	20.00
ROBIN HOOD					
❏ 101	Oh Babe!/Piccolina Lena	1950	7.50	15.00	30.00
❏ 102	Goodbye Joe/My Conchetta	1950	7.50	15.00	30.00
SAVOY					
❏ 1111	Robin Hood/Brooklyn Boogie	1953	5.00	10.00	20.00
UNITED ARTISTS					
❏ 50175	Illya Darling/I Believe in You	1967	—	3.00	6.00
❏ 50200	My Cup Runneth Over/Cabaret	1967	—	3.00	6.00
❏ 50223	The Impossible Dream/Poor Old Marat	1967	—	3.00	6.00

7-Inch Extended Plays

Number	Title (A Side/B Side)	Yr	VG	VG+	NM
CAPITOL					
❏ EAP 1-755	Medley: Just a Gigolo-I Ain't Got Nobody-Nobody Cares for Me//Night Train/(I'll Be Glad When You're Dead) You Rascal You	1956	3.75	7.50	15.00
❏ EAP 1-755 [PS]	The Wildest! Part 1	1956			
❏ EAP 1-836	Medley: When You're Smiling (The Whole World Smiles with You)-The Shiek of Araby/Blow, Red, Blow//When the Saints Go Marching In	1957	3.75	7.50	15.00
❏ EAP 1-836 [PS]	The Call of the Wildest, Part 1	1957	3.75	7.50	15.00
❏ EAP 1-908	*On the Sunny Side of the Street/Exactly Like You//Robin Hood/Oh Babe	1957	3.75	7.50	15.00
❏ EAP 1-908 [PS]	The Wildest Show at Tahoe, Part 1	1957	3.75	7.50	15.00
❏ EAP 2-908	Foggy Day/How High the Moon//Come Back to Sorrento/I Gotta Right to Sing the Blues	1957	3.75	7.50	15.00
❏ EAP 2-908 [PS]	The Wildest Show at Tahoe, Part 2	1957	3.75	7.50	15.00
COLUMBIA					
❏ B-12061	*Chop Suey Chow Mein/Basta/ Barnacle Bill the Sailor/Shepherd Boy	1959	3.75	7.50	15.00
❏ B-12061 [PS]	Breakin' It Up!	1959	3.75	7.50	15.00

Albums

Number	Title (A Side/B Side)	Yr	VG	VG+	NM
BRUNSWICK					
❏ BL 754183	The Prima Generation '72	1972	20.00	40.00	80.00
CAPITOL					
❏ T 755 [M]	The Wildest	1956	12.50	25.00	50.00
❏ T 836 [M]	The Call of the Wildest	1957	12.50	25.00	50.00
❏ T 908 [M]	The Wildest Show at Tahoe	1957	12.50	25.00	50.00
❏ T 1010 [M]	Las Vegas Prima Style	1958	12.50	25.00	50.00
❏ T 1132 [M]	Strictly Prima	1959	7.50	15.00	30.00
❏ ST 1723 [S]	The Wildest Comes Home	1962	7.50	15.00	30.00
❏ T 1723 [M]	The Wildest Comes Home	1962	6.25	12.50	25.00
❏ ST 1797 [S]	Lake Tahoe Prima Style	1962	7.50	15.00	30.00
❏ T 1797 [M]	Lake Tahoe Prima Style	1962	6.25	12.50	25.00
COLUMBIA					
❏ CL 1206 [M]	Breakin' It Up!	1959	10.00	20.00	40.00

P

Number	Title (A Side/B Side)	Yr	VG	VG+	NM
DOT					
❑ DLP-3262 [M]	His Greatest Hits	1960	6.25	12.50	25.00
❑ DLP-3264 [M]	Pretty Music Prima Style	1960	6.25	12.50	25.00
❑ DLP-3272 [M]	The Wildest Clan	1960	6.25	12.50	25.00
❑ DLP-3352 [M]	Wonderland by Night	1960	6.25	12.50	25.00
❑ DLP-3385 [M]	Blue Moon	1961	6.25	12.50	25.00
❑ DLP-3392 [M]	Return of the Wildest!	1961	6.25	12.50	25.00
❑ DLP-3410 [M]	Doin' the Twist	1961	6.25	12.50	25.00
❑ DLP-25262 [S]	His Greatest Hits	1960	7.50	15.00	30.00
❑ DLP-25264 [S]	Pretty Music Prima Style	1960	7.50	15.00	30.00
❑ DLP-25272 [S]	The Wildest Clan	1960	7.50	15.00	30.00
❑ DLP-25352 [S]	Wonderland by Night	1960	7.50	15.00	30.00
❑ DLP-25385 [S]	Blue Moon	1961	7.50	15.00	30.00
❑ DLP-25392 [S]	Return of the Wildest!	1961	7.50	15.00	30.00
❑ DLP-25410 [S]	Doin' the Twist	1961	7.50	15.00	30.00
GOLDEN TONE					
❑ 326 [M]	Italian Favorites	196?	2.50	5.00	10.00
—Label calls this "Italian Songs"; one side is by Louis Prima, the other side by Phil Brito					
HANNA-BARBERA					
❑ HLP-8502 [M]	The Golden Hits of Louis Prima	1966	7.50	15.00	30.00
MERCURY					
❑ MG-25142 [10]	Louis Prima Plays	1953	20.00	40.00	80.00
PRIMA					
❑ ST 0072	The Prima Generation	1972	12.50	25.00	50.00
❑ ST 0074	Angelina	1973	6.25	12.50	25.00
❑ PM 3001 [M]	Prima Show in the Casbar	1963	10.00	20.00	40.00
❑ PS 3001 [S]	Prima Show in the Casbar	1963	15.00	30.00	60.00
❑ PM 3003 [M]	King of Clubs	1964	17.50	35.00	70.00
❑ PS 3003 [S]	King of Clubs	1964	25.00	50.00	100.00
RONDO-LETTE					
❑ A-9 [M]	Louis Prima in All His Moods	1959	7.50	15.00	30.00
❑ A-25 [M]	Louis Prima Entertains	1959	7.50	15.00	30.00
SAVOY JAZZ					
❑ SJL-2264 [(2)]	Play Pretty for the People	198?	3.00	6.00	12.00
TOPS					
❑ 9759 [M]	Italian Favorites	195?	3.75	7.50	15.00

PRIMA, LOUIS, AND KEELY SMITH Also see each artist's individual listings.
45s

Number	Title (A Side/B Side)	Yr	VG	VG+	NM
CAPITOL					
❑ F4063	That Old Black Magic/You Are My Love	1958	3.00	6.00	12.00
❑ F4140	I've Got You Under My Skin/ Don't Take Your Love from Me	1959	2.50	5.00	10.00
DOT					
❑ 15956	Bei Mir Bist Du Schoen/I Don't Know Why	1959	2.50	5.00	10.00
❑ 16042	Nyot! Nyot! Nyot! (The Pussycat Song)/Moshiya	1960	2.50	5.00	10.00
❑ 16192	Begin the Beguine/Surprise Package	1961	2.50	5.00	10.00
❑ 16221	Mustapha/The Shepard Man	1961	2.50	5.00	10.00
❑ 16249	Because of You/Absent Minded Lover	1961	2.50	5.00	10.00
TOD					
❑ 123	Oh Babe!/(B-side unknown)	196?	2.00	4.00	8.00
Albums					
CAPITOL					
❑ T 1160 [M]	Hey Boy! Hey Girl!	1959	12.50	25.00	50.00
❑ SM-1531	The Hits of Louis and Keely	197?	2.50	5.00	10.00
—Reissue with new prefix					
❑ ST 1531 [S]	The Hits of Louis and Keely	1961	7.50	15.00	30.00
❑ T 1531 [M]	The Hits of Louis and Keely	1961	6.25	12.50	25.00
CORONET					
❑ CX 121 [M]	Louis Prima Digs Keely Smith	196?	3.75	7.50	15.00
DOT					
❑ DLP-3210 [M]	Louis and Keely!	1959	7.50	15.00	30.00
❑ DLP-3263 [M]	Together	1960	6.25	12.50	25.00
❑ DLP-3266 [M]	Louis and Keely on Stage	1960	6.25	12.50	25.00
❑ DLP-25210 [S]	Louis and Keely!	1959	10.00	20.00	40.00
❑ DLP-25263 [S]	Together	1960	7.50	15.00	30.00
❑ DLP-25266 [S]	Louis and Keely on Stage	1960	7.50	15.00	30.00
FLEET					
❑ 101 [M]	Louis Prima Digs Keely Smith	196?	3.75	7.50	15.00
RHINO					
❑ RNLP-70225	Zooma Zooma: The Best of Louis Prima Featuring Keely Smith	1986	2.50	5.00	10.00
SPIN-O-RAMA					
❑ 74 [M]	Box of Oldies	196?	3.75	7.50	15.00

PRIMETTES, THE Early version of THE SUPREMES.
45s

Number	Title (A Side/B Side)	Yr	VG	VG+	NM
LUPINE					
❑ 120	Tears of Sorrow/Pretty	1962	75.00	150.00	300.00

PRIMITIVES, THE (1)
45s

Number	Title (A Side/B Side)	Yr	VG	VG+	NM
PARKWAY					
❑ 940	Help Me/Let Them Fall	1965	5.00	10.00	20.00

PRIMITIVES, THE (2) LOU REED was in this group.
45s

Number	Title (A Side/B Side)	Yr	VG	VG+	NM
PICKWICK					
❑ 1001	The Ostrich/Sneaky Pete	1964	75.00	150.00	300.00

PRINCE, BOBBY
45s

Number	Title (A Side/B Side)	Yr	VG	VG+	NM
CHANCE					
❑ 1128	Tell Me Why, Why, Why/I Want to Hold You	1953	125.00	250.00	500.00
❑ 1158	Better Think It Over/If You Only Knew	1954	100.00	200.00	400.00
EXCELLO					
❑ 2039	Too Many Keys/Please Give Me Your Love	1954	20.00	40.00	80.00

PRINCE BUSTER
45s

Number	Title (A Side/B Side)	Yr	VG	VG+	NM
AMY					
❑ 906	Everybody Ska/30 Pieces of Silver	1964	3.75	7.50	15.00
ATLANTIC					
❑ 2231	Don't Make Me Cry/That Lucky Old Sun	1964	3.75	7.50	15.00
PHILIPS					
❑ 40427	Ten Commandments/Don't Make Me Cry	1967	3.00	6.00	12.00

Number	Title (A Side/B Side)	Yr	VG	VG+	NM
RCA VICTOR					
❑ 47-9114	Ten Commandments from Woman to Man/ Ain't That Saying a Lot	1967	3.00	6.00	12.00
Albums					
RCA VICTOR					
❑ LPM-3792 [M]	Ten Commandments	1967	6.25	12.50	25.00
❑ LSP-3792 [S]	Ten Commandments	1967	7.50	15.00	30.00

PRINE, JOHN
45s

Number	Title (A Side/B Side)	Yr	VG	VG+	NM
ASYLUM					
❑ 45509	Fish and Whistle/ Sabu Visits the Twin Cities Alone	1978	—	2.00	4.00
❑ 45550	There She Goes/ That's the Way That the World Goes 'Round	1978	—	2.00	4.00
❑ 46562	Ubangi Stomp/Automobile	1979	—	2.00	4.00
ATLANTIC					
❑ 2815	Sam Stone/Blue Umbrella	1971	—	2.50	5.00
❑ 2857	Quiet Man/Illegal Smile	1972	—	2.50	5.00
❑ 2925	Clocks and Spoons/Everybody	1972	—	2.50	5.00
❑ 3013	Grandpa Was a Carpenter/Onomatopoeia	1974	—	2.00	4.00
❑ 3218	Quiet Man/Illegal Smile	1974	—	2.00	4.00
❑ 3276	Middle Man/Saddle in the Rain	1975	—	2.00	4.00
❑ 3297	Common Sense/Come Back to Us Barbara Lewis, Harre Krishna, Beauregard	1975	—	2.00	4.00
OH BOY					
❑ 001	I Saw Mommy Kissing Santa Claus/Silver Bells	198?	2.50	5.00	10.00
—Red vinyl					
❑ 001 [PS]	I Saw Mommy Kissing Santa Claus/Silver Bells	198?	3.00	6.00	12.00
Albums					
ASYLUM					
❑ 6E-139	Bruised Orange	1978	3.00	6.00	12.00
❑ 6E-222	Pink Cadillac	1979	3.00	6.00	12.00
❑ 6E-286	Storm Windows	1980	3.00	6.00	12.00
ATLANTIC					
❑ SD 7240	Diamonds in the Rough	1972	3.00	6.00	12.00
❑ SD 7274	Sweet Revenge	1973	3.00	6.00	12.00
❑ SD 8296	John Prine	1971	3.00	6.00	12.00
❑ SD 18127	Common Sense	1975	3.00	6.00	12.00
❑ SD 18202	Prime Prine — The Best of John Prine	1976	3.00	6.00	12.00
❑ SD 19156	John Prine	1978	2.50	5.00	10.00
—Reissue of 8296					
OH BOY					
❑ 002	Aimless Love	198?	2.50	5.00	10.00
❑ 003	German Afternoons	198?	2.50	5.00	10.00
❑ 005 [(2)]	John Prine Live	1986	3.75	7.50	15.00

PRISCO, TOMMY
45s

Number	Title (A Side/B Side)	Yr	VG	VG+	NM
EPIC					
❑ 5-9219	Maybe Someday/Teardrops in My Heart	1957	5.00	10.00	20.00
❑ 5-9239	I Don't Want to Love You/Hasty Words	1957	5.00	10.00	20.00
❑ 5-9267	Chewin' Gum/O Bella Mia	1958	5.00	10.00	20.00
❑ 5-9302	Till There Was You/For Me and My Girl	1959	5.00	10.00	20.00
❑ 5-9315	Stingaree/Only Once	1959	7.50	15.00	30.00

PRISONAIRES, THE
45s

Number	Title (A Side/B Side)	Yr	VG	VG+	NM
SUN					
❑ 186	Just Walking in the Rain/Baby Please	1953	125.00	250.00	500.00
❑ 186	Just Walking in the Rain/Baby Please	1953	2500.	3750.	5000.
—Red vinyl					
❑ 189	Softly and Tenderly/My God Is Real	1953	175.00	350.00	700.00
❑ 191	A Prisoner's Prayer/I Know	1953	125.00	250.00	500.00
❑ 207	There Is Love in You/What'll You Do Next	1954	5000.	8500.	12000.

PRIZES, THE
45s

Number	Title (A Side/B Side)	Yr	VG	VG+	NM
PARKWAY					
❑ 917	Summer's Here at Last/I Found Someone New	1964	2.50	5.00	10.00

PROBY, P.J.
45s

Number	Title (A Side/B Side)	Yr	VG	VG+	NM
BETA					
❑ 1008	Loud Perfume/(B-side unknown)	1958	50.00	100.00	200.00
—As "Jett Powers"					
DESIGN					
❑ 811	Go Girl Go/Teen-Age Quarrel	1957	75.00	150.00	300.00
—As "Jett Powers"					
IMPERIAL					
❑ 66079	Rocking Pneumonia/Just Call, I'll Be There	1964	3.75	7.50	15.00
❑ 66084	Somewhere/Just Like Him	1965	—	—	—
—Unreleased					
LIBERTY					
❑ 55367	There Stands the One/Try to Forget Her	1961	3.75	7.50	15.00
❑ 55505	The Other Side of Town/Watch Me Walk Away	1962	3.75	7.50	15.00
❑ 55588	So Do I/I Can't Take It Like You Can	1963	3.75	7.50	15.00
❑ 55757	Somewhere/Just Like Him	1964	3.00	6.00	12.00
❑ 55777	Rocking Pneumonia/I Apologize	1965	3.00	6.00	12.00
❑ 55791	Stagger Lee/Mission Bell	1965	3.00	6.00	12.00
❑ 55806	That Means a Lot/Let the Water Run Down	1965	3.00	6.00	12.00
—The A-side is a Lennon-McCartney song; the Beatles' own version was not released until 1996					
❑ 55850	Good Things Are Coming My Way/Maria	1965	3.00	6.00	12.00
❑ 55875	My Prayer/Wicked Woman	1966	3.00	6.00	12.00
❑ 55915	I Can't Make It Alone/If I Ruled the World	1966	3.00	6.00	12.00
❑ 55915 [PS]	I Can't Make It Alone/If I Ruled the World	1966	3.75	7.50	15.00
❑ 55936	Niki-Hoeky/Good Things Are Coming My Way	1966	2.50	5.00	10.00
❑ 55974	Work with Me Annie/You Can't Come Home Again (If You Leave Me Now)	1967	2.50	5.00	10.00
❑ 55974 [PS]	Work with Me Annie/You Can't Come Home Again (If You Leave Me Now)	1967	3.75	7.50	15.00
❑ 55989	Butterfly High/Just Holding On	1967	2.50	5.00	10.00
❑ 56031	It's Your Day Today/I Apologize	1968	2.00	4.00	8.00
❑ 56051	What's Wrong with My World/Turn Her Away	1968	2.00	4.00	8.00
LONDON					
❑ 9648	Hold Me/The Tip of My Fingers	1964	3.75	7.50	15.00
❑ 9688	Hold Me/The Tip of My Fingers	1964	3.75	7.50	15.00
❑ 9705	Sweet and Tender Romance/Together	1964	3.75	7.50	15.00

Number	Title (A Side/B Side)	Yr	VG	VG+	NM

SURFSIDE

Number	Title (A Side/B Side)	Yr	VG	VG+	NM
❏ 714	You Got Me Crying/I Need Love	1965	5.00	10.00	20.00

UNITED ARTISTS

Number	Title (A Side/B Side)	Yr	VG	VG+	NM
❏ 0070	Niki-Hoeky/Let the Water Run Down	1973	—	2.00	4.00

—"Silver Spotlight Series" reissue

Albums
LIBERTY

Number	Title	Yr	VG	VG+	NM
❏ LRP-3406 [M]	Somewhere/Go Go P.J. Proby	1965	5.00	10.00	20.00
❏ LRP-3421 [M]	P.J. Proby	1965	5.00	10.00	20.00
❏ LRP-3497 [M]	Enigma	1967	5.00	10.00	20.00
❏ LRP-3515 [M]	Phenomenon	1967	5.00	10.00	20.00
❏ LST-7406 [S]	Somewhere/Go Go P.J. Proby	1965	6.25	12.50	25.00
❏ LST-7421 [S]	P.J. Proby	1965	6.25	12.50	25.00
❏ LST-7497 [S]	Enigma	1967	6.25	12.50	25.00
❏ LST-7515 [S]	Phenomenon	1967	6.25	12.50	25.00
❏ LST-7561	What's Wrong with My World?	1968	6.25	12.50	25.00

PROCESSION

45s
SMASH

Number	Title	Yr	VG	VG+	NM
❏ 2225	Adelaide, Adelaide/One Day in Every Week	1969	2.00	4.00	8.00
❏ 2239	Every American Citizen/You-Me	1969	2.00	4.00	8.00

Albums
SMASH

Number	Title	Yr	VG	VG+	NM
❏ SRS-67122	Procession	1969	5.00	10.00	20.00

PROCOL HARUM Also see THE PARAMOUNTS (4); ROBIN TROWER.

45s
A&M

Number	Title	Yr	VG	VG+	NM
❏ 885	Homburg/Good Captain Clack	1967	3.00	6.00	12.00
❏ 927	In the Wee Small Hours of Sixpence/Quite Rightly So	1968	3.00	6.00	12.00
❏ 1069	A Salty Dog/Long Gone Geek	1969	2.00	4.00	8.00
❏ 1111	The Devil Came from Kansas/Boredom	1969	2.00	4.00	8.00
❏ 1218	Whiskey Train/About to Die	1970	—	3.00	6.00
❏ 1264	Power Failure/Broken Barricades	1971	—	3.00	6.00
❏ 1287	Song for a Dreamer/Simple Sister	1971	—	3.00	6.00
❏ 1287 [PS]	Song for a Dreamer/Simple Sister	1971	2.50	5.00	10.00
❏ 1347	Conquistador/A Salty Dog	1972	—	2.50	5.00
❏ 1347 [PS]	Conquistador/A Salty Dog	1972	2.00	4.00	8.00
❏ 1389	A Whiter Shade of Pale/Lime Street Blues	1972	—	2.50	5.00
❏ 1389 [PS]	A Whiter Shade of Pale/Lime Street Blues	1972	—	2.50	5.00

CHRYSALIS

Number	Title	Yr	VG	VG+	NM
❏ 2011 [DJ]	Bringing Home the Bacon (mono/stereo)	1973	2.00	4.00	8.00
—May be promo only					
❏ 2013	Grand Hotel/Fires	1973	—	2.50	5.00
❏ 2013 [PS]	Grand Hotel/Fires	1973	2.50	5.00	10.00
❏ 2032	Nothing But the Truth/Drunk Again	1973	—	2.50	5.00
❏ 2109	Pandora's Box/Piper's Tune	1975	—	2.50	5.00

DERAM

Number	Title	Yr	VG	VG+	NM
❏ 7507	A Whiter Shade of Pale/Lime Street Blues	1967	3.75	7.50	15.00

WARNER BROS.

Number	Title	Yr	VG	VG+	NM
❏ CRS 2115	Wizard Man/Something Magic	1977	—	3.00	6.00

—Warner Bros. label with Chrysalis number; possible factory mispress?

Albums
A&M

Number	Title	Yr	VG	VG+	NM
❏ SP-3123	A Salty Dog	1979	2.00	4.00	8.00
—Reissue of 4179					
❏ SP-3259	The Best of Procol Harum	198?	2.00	4.00	8.00
—Reissue of 4401					
❏ SP-4151	Shine On Brightly	1968	6.25	12.50	25.00
❏ SP-4179	A Salty Dog	1969	3.75	7.50	15.00
❏ SP-4261	Home	1970	3.00	6.00	12.00
❏ SP-4294	Broken Barricades	1971	3.00	6.00	12.00
❏ SP-4335	Procol Harum Live in Concert with the Edmonton Symphony Orchestra	1972	3.00	6.00	12.00
❏ SP-4373	A Whiter Shade of Pale	1972	3.00	6.00	12.00
—Reissue of Deram 18008 with one more track					
❏ SP-4401	The Best of Procol Harum	1973	3.00	6.00	12.00
❏ SP-8503 [DJ]	Procol Harum Lives	197?	12.50	25.00	50.00
—Interview LP alone					
❏ SP-8503 [DJ]	Procol Harum Lives	197?	75.00	150.00	300.00
—Promo-only box set with press kit, photos, keychain and interview LP					

CHRYSALIS

Number	Title	Yr	VG	VG+	NM
❏ CHR 1037	Grand Hotel	1973	3.00	6.00	12.00
—Green label with "3300 Warner Blvd." address					
❏ CHR 1037	Grand Hotel	1977	2.50	5.00	10.00
—Blue label with New York address					
❏ CHR 1058	Exotic Birds and Fruit	1974	3.00	6.00	12.00
—Green label with "3300 Warner Blvd." address					
❏ CHR 1058	Exotic Birds and Fruit	1977	2.50	5.00	10.00
—Blue label with New York address					
❏ CHR 1080	Procol's Ninth	1975	3.00	6.00	12.00
—Green label with "3300 Warner Blvd." address					
❏ CHR 1080	Procol's Ninth	1977	2.50	5.00	10.00
—Blue label with New York address					
❏ CHR 1130	Something Magic	1977	2.50	5.00	10.00
❏ PV 41037	Grand Hotel	1985	2.00	4.00	8.00
❏ PV 41058	Exotic Birds and Fruit	1985	2.00	4.00	8.00
❏ PV 41080	Procol's Ninth	1985	2.00	4.00	8.00

DERAM

Number	Title	Yr	VG	VG+	NM
❏ DE 16008 [M]	Procol Harum	1967	20.00	40.00	80.00
❏ DE/S 16008/18008	Procol Harum Poster	1967	6.25	12.50	25.00
❏ DES 18008 [R]	Procol Harum	1967	10.00	20.00	40.00

PROCTOR, BILLY

45s
EPIC

Number	Title	Yr	VG	VG+	NM
❏ 50160	(I'm Gonna) Chop Down That Oak Tree/Keeping Up with the Joneses	1975	—	2.50	5.00

SOUL

Number	Title	Yr	VG	VG+	NM
❏ 35099	What Is Black/I Can Take It All	1972	5.00	10.00	20.00

PROFESSOR MORRISON'S LOLLIPOP

45s
WHITE WHALE

Number	Title	Yr	VG	VG+	NM
❏ 275	Gypsy Lady/You Got the Love	1968	2.50	5.00	10.00
❏ 288	Angela/Duba Duba Doo	1968	2.50	5.00	10.00
❏ 293	Oo Poo Pah Susie/You Can Take It	1969	2.50	5.00	10.00

PROFFITT, RANDY, AND THE BEACHCOMBERS

45s
BETT-COE

Number	Title	Yr	VG	VG+	NM
❏ 103	Check That Baby Out One Time/Young Love in Spring	196?	12.50	25.00	50.00

PROFILES, THE (1)

45s
BAMBOO

Number	Title	Yr	VG	VG+	NM
❏ 104	Got to Be Love (Something Stupid)/You Don't Care About Me	1969	2.00	4.00	8.00
❏ 108	Be Careful/I Still Love You	1969	2.00	4.00	8.00
❏ 115	A Little Misunderstanding/Got to Be Love	1970	2.00	4.00	8.00

DUO

Number	Title	Yr	VG	VG+	NM
❏ 7449	If I Didn't Love You/(B-side unknown)	1968	2.50	5.00	10.00

PROFILES, THE (2)

45s
GAIT

Number	Title	Yr	VG	VG+	NM
❏ 1444	Never/Right By Her Side	1962	50.00	100.00	200.00

PROGRESSIVES, THE

45s
DOT

Number	Title	Yr	VG	VG+	NM
❏ 16514	Hot Cinders/Man of Mystery	1963	5.00	10.00	20.00

PROPHETS, THE

45s
DELPHI

Number	Title	Yr	VG	VG+	NM
❏ 007	Talk Don't Bother Me/Don't Look Back	1967	37.50	75.00	150.00
❏ 009	Don't You Think It's Time/I Don't Love You No More	1967	30.00	60.00	120.00

JUBILEE

Number	Title	Yr	VG	VG+	NM
❏ 5565	Talk Don't Bother Me/Don't Look Back	1967	6.25	12.50	25.00
❏ 5596	Don't You Think It's Time/I Don't Love You No More	1967	7.50	15.00	30.00

SHRINE

Number	Title	Yr	VG	VG+	NM
❏ 116	If I Had One Gold Piece/Huh Baby	1966	1500.	2250.	3000.

SMASH

Number	Title	Yr	VG	VG+	NM
❏ 2161	I Got the Fever/Soul Control	1967	2.50	5.00	10.00

STEPHANYE

Number	Title	Yr	VG	VG+	NM
❏ 335	My Kind of Girl/I Can't Make It	196?	7.50	15.00	30.00

PROVINE, DOROTHY

45s
WARNER BROS.

Number	Title	Yr	VG	VG+	NM
❏ 5202	Bye Bye Blackbird/Crazy Words-Crazy Tune	1961	3.00	6.00	12.00
❏ 5249	The Whisper Song/Don't Bring Lulu	1961	3.00	6.00	12.00

Albums
WARNER BROS.

Number	Title	Yr	VG	VG+	NM
❏ W 1394 [M]	The Roaring 20's	1961	5.00	10.00	20.00
❏ WS 1394 [S]	The Roaring 20's	1961	6.25	12.50	25.00
❏ W 1419 [M]	The Vamp of the Roaring 20's	1961	5.00	10.00	20.00
❏ WS 1419 [S]	The Vamp of the Roaring 20's	1961	6.25	12.50	25.00

PROVISOR, DENNY

45s
20TH CENTURY-FOX

Number	Title	Yr	VG	VG+	NM
❏ 506	Mickey Mouse/Walk On with Him	1964	3.00	6.00	12.00

VALIANT

Number	Title	Yr	VG	VG+	NM
❏ 717	Little Girl Lost/Dead Letter	1965	3.00	6.00	12.00
❏ 728	She's Not Mine Anymore/It Really Tears Me Up	1965	3.00	6.00	12.00

PROW, JIMMY LEE

45s
KING

Number	Title	Yr	VG	VG+	NM
❏ 4929	Shopping List/You Tell Her, I Stutter	1956	7.50	15.00	30.00

PRUETT, JEANNE

45s
AUDIOGRAPH

Number	Title	Yr	VG	VG+	NM
❏ 441	Star-Studded Nights/Wild Side of Life	1984	—	2.00	4.00
❏ 454	Love Me/Safely in the Arms of Jesus	1983	—	2.50	5.00
—A-side with Marty Robbins					
❏ 467	Lady of the Eighties/Ain't No Way to Make a Bad Love Grow	1983	—	2.00	4.00
❏ 477	We Came So Close/(B-side unknown)	1983	—	2.00	4.00

DECCA

Number	Title	Yr	VG	VG+	NM
❏ 32383	One Woman Man/One Day Ahead of My Tears	1968	2.00	4.00	8.00
❏ 32435	Make Me Feel Like a Woman Again/Don't Hold Your Breath	1969	2.00	4.00	8.00
❏ 32614	It Ain't Fair That It Ain't Right/At the Sight of You	1970	—	3.00	6.00
❏ 32703	King Size Bed/One Day Ahead of My Tears	1970	—	3.00	6.00
❏ 32857	Hold On to My Unchanging Love/He's Calling Me Baby Again	1971	—	3.00	6.00
❏ 32929	Love Me/I'm Out Looking for You	1972	—	3.00	6.00
❏ 32977	Call On Me/Stay on His Mind	1972	—	3.00	6.00
❏ 33013	I Forgot More Than You'll Ever Know (About Him)/Don't Hold Your Breath	1972	—	3.00	6.00

IBC

Number	Title	Yr	VG	VG+	NM
❏ 0002	Please Sing Satin Sheets for Me/Love All the Leavin' Out of You	1979	—	2.50	5.00
❏ 0005	Back to Back/Wild Side of Life	1979	—	2.50	5.00
❏ 0008	Temporarily Yours/Ain't We Sad Today	1980	—	2.50	5.00
❏ 00010	It's Too Late/I Can't Feel at Home	1980	—	2.50	5.00

MCA

Number	Title	Yr	VG	VG+	NM
❏ 40015	Satin Sheets/Sweet Sweetheart	1973	—	3.00	6.00
❏ 40116	I'm Your Woman/Your Memory's Comin' On	1973	—	2.00	4.00
❏ 40207	You Don't Need to Move a Mountain/Hopefully	1974	—	2.00	4.00

P

Number	Title (A Side/B Side)	Yr	VG	VG+	NM
❑ 40284	Welcome to the Sunshine (Sweet Baby Jane)/				
	What My Thoughts Do All the Time	1974	—	2.00	4.00
❑ 40340	Just Like Your Daddy/One More Time	1974	—	2.00	4.00
❑ 40395	Honey on His Hands/One of These Days	1975	—	2.00	4.00
❑ 40440	A Poor Man's Woman/Momma Let Me Find				
	Shelter (In Your Sweet Woman's Arms)	1975	—	2.00	4.00
❑ 40490	My Baby's Gone/But Not Today	1975	—	2.00	4.00
❑ 40527	Driftin' Too Far Away/Sweet Sorrow	1976	—	2.00	4.00
❑ 40569	It Doesn't Hurt to Ask/				
	If I'm Not Girl Enough to Hold You	1976	—	2.00	4.00
❑ 40605	I've Taken/Sweet and Warm and Right	1976	—	2.00	4.00
❑ 40678	I'm Living a Lie/My First Pay Day	1977	—	2.00	4.00
❑ 40723	She's Still All Over You/Fancy Place to Cry	1977	—	2.00	4.00
MERCURY					
❑ 55017	I'm a Woman/Midnight Exchange	1978	—	2.00	4.00
❑ 55034	I Guess I'm Not That Good at Being Bad/				
	Where Do You Draw the Line	1978	—	2.00	4.00
MSR					
❑ 1956	Rented Room/(B-side unknown)	1987	—	2.00	4.00
PAID					
❑ 118	Sad Ole Shade of Gray/When I Stop Dreaming	1981	—	2.00	4.00
❑ 136	I Ought to Feel Guilty/Who'll Turn Out the Lights				
	(In Your World)	1981	—	2.00	4.00
RCA VICTOR					
❑ 47-8157	Another Heart to Break/Just a Little After				
	Heartaches	1963	3.75	7.50	15.00
❑ 47-8232	Little Black Book/The Things I Don't Know	1963	3.75	7.50	15.00
❑ 47-8297	As a Matter of Fact/Sing Me a Song I Can Cry By	1963	3.75	7.50	15.00
Albums					
ALLEGIANCE					
❑ AV-5028	Stand By Your Man	1984	2.50	5.00	10.00
DECCA					
❑ DL 75360	Love Me	1972	3.75	7.50	15.00
DOT/MCA					
❑ 39031	Jeanne Pruett	1985	2.50	5.00	10.00
MCA					
❑ 338	Satin Sheets	1973	3.00	6.00	12.00
❑ 388	Jeanne Pruett	1974	3.00	6.00	12.00
❑ 479	Honey on His Hands	1975	3.00	6.00	12.00
❑ 503	Love Me	1975	3.00	6.00	12.00
—Reissue of Decca LP					

PRYOR, RICHARD
Albums
AUDIOFIDELITY

Number	Title (A Side/B Side)	Yr	VG	VG+	NM
❑ 349 [PD]	Richard Pryor Live	198?	3.75	7.50	15.00
DOVE					
❑ RS 6325	Richard Pryor	1968	5.00	10.00	20.00
LAFF					
❑ (# unknown)	Supernigger	198?	2.00	4.00	8.00
❑ A 146	Craps: After Hours	1971	3.00	6.00	12.00
❑ A 170	Pryor Goes Foxx Hunting	197?	3.00	6.00	12.00
❑ A 184	Down 'N' Dirty	197?	3.00	6.00	12.00
❑ A 188	Richard Pryor Meets Richard and Willie and the				
	S.L.A.	1976	3.00	6.00	12.00
❑ A 196	Are You Serious???	1977	3.00	6.00	12.00
❑ A 198	Who Me? I'm Not Him	1977	3.00	6.00	12.00
❑ A 200	Black Ben	1978	2.50	5.00	10.00
❑ A 202	Wizard of Comedy	1978	2.50	5.00	10.00
❑ A 206	Outrageous	1979	2.50	5.00	10.00
❑ A 209	Insane	1980	2.50	5.00	10.00
❑ A 212	Holy Smoke	1980	2.50	5.00	10.00
❑ A 216	Rev. Du Rite	1981	2.50	5.00	10.00
❑ A 221	The Very Best of Richard Pryor	1982	2.50	5.00	10.00
❑ 226	Blackjack	198?	2.00	4.00	8.00
—Reissue of 146					
❑ 227	Show Biz	198?	2.00	4.00	8.00
—Reissue of 200					
❑ 279	Richard Pryor Live	198?	2.00	4.00	8.00
PARTEE					
❑ PBS-2404	That Nigger's Crazy	1974	3.75	7.50	15.00
REPRISE					
❑ MS 2227	Is It Something I Said?	1975	3.00	6.00	12.00
❑ MS 2241	That Nigger's Crazy	197?	3.00	6.00	12.00
—Reissue of Partee LP					
❑ MSK 2285	Is It Something I Said?	1977	2.50	5.00	10.00
—Reissue of 2227					
❑ MSK 2287	That Nigger's Crazy	1977	2.50	5.00	10.00
—Reissue of Reprise 2241					
❑ RS 6325	Richard Pryor	197?	3.00	6.00	12.00
—Reissue of Dove LP					
TIGER LILY					
❑ TL 14023	L.A. Jail	1977	3.00	6.00	12.00
WARNER BROS.					
❑ BS 2960	Bicentennial Nigger	1976	3.00	6.00	12.00
❑ BSK 3057	Richard Pryor's Greatest Hits	1977	2.50	5.00	10.00
❑ BSK 3114	Bicentennial Nigger	1977	2.50	5.00	10.00
—Reissue of 2960					
❑ 2BSK 3364 [(2)]	Wanted	1978	3.00	6.00	12.00
❑ BSK 3660	Richard Pryor Live on the Sunset Strip	1982	2.50	5.00	10.00
❑ 23981	Richard Pryor: Here and Now	1983	2.50	5.00	10.00

PRYOR, SNOOKY
45s
J.O.B.

Number	Title (A Side/B Side)	Yr	VG	VG+	NM
❑ 1014	Cryin' Shame/Eight, Nine, Ten	1953	100.00	200.00	400.00
❑ 1126	Uncle Sam, Don't Take My Man/Boogie Twist	1963	50.00	100.00	200.00
PARROT					
❑ 807	Crosstown Blues/I Want You for Yourself	1954	375.00	750.00	1500.
—Black vinyl					
❑ 807	Crosstown Blues/I Want You for Yourself	1954	625.00	1250.	2500.
—Red vinyl					
VEE JAY					
❑ 215	Judgment Day/Someone to Love Me	1956	30.00	60.00	120.00

PRYSOCK, ARTHUR
45s
BETHLEHEM

Number	Title (A Side/B Side)	Yr	VG	VG+	NM
❑ 3100	The Girls I Never Kissed/Funny World	1972	—	3.00	6.00
DECCA					
❑ 25684	When Day Is Done/What Will I Tell My Heart	1965	2.00	4.00	8.00
❑ 27722	Blue Velvet/Morning Side Of the Mountain	1951	3.75	7.50	15.00
❑ 27769	Sin/The Love of a Gypsy	1951	3.75	7.50	15.00
❑ 27871	A Man Ain't Supposed to Cry/I Didn't Sleep a				
	Wink Last Night	1951	3.75	7.50	15.00
❑ 27967	Wheel of Fortune/'Til the Stars Fall in the Ocean	1952	3.75	7.50	15.00
❑ 27978	I Hear a Rhapsody/Am I to Blame	1952	3.75	7.50	15.00
❑ 28220	School of Love/Sentimental Fool	1952	3.75	7.50	15.00
❑ 28700	I'd Give Anything/This Is the Time	1953	3.75	7.50	15.00
❑ 28867	My Mood/Temptation	1953	3.75	7.50	15.00
❑ 28950	Nobody Cares/Jean	1953	3.75	7.50	15.00
❑ 29118	Baby Don't You Cry/My Last Goodbye	1954	3.75	7.50	15.00
❑ 31710	Wheel of Fortune/I Cover the Waterfront	1964	2.00	4.00	8.00
❑ 31775	Baby, Don't You Cry/				
	I Didn't Sleep a Wink Last Night	1965	2.00	4.00	8.00
GUSTO					
❑ 9023	Today I Started Loving You Again/				
	It Ain't No Big Thing	1979	—	3.00	6.00
KING					
❑ 6243	Soul Soliloquy/(I Wanna Go)				
	Where the Soul Trees Grow	1969	—	3.00	6.00
❑ 6271	The 23rd Psalm/I Believe	1969	—	3.00	6.00
❑ 6276	Save Your Love for Me/If I Were Young Again	1969	—	3.00	6.00
❑ 6279	Go Ahead and Fly/How Do I Tell Her	1969	—	3.00	6.00
❑ 6307	Have a Good Time/Frisco Line	1970	—	3.00	6.00
❑ 6315	Lord, Is That Me/My Home Is Not a Home				
	Without You	1970	—	3.00	6.00
❑ 6353	Cry/Unforgettable	1971	—	3.00	6.00
❑ 6354	It Ain't No Big Thing/Big Blue Diamonds	1971	—	3.00	6.00
❑ 6364	Precious Memories/				
	Just a Closer Walk with Thee	1971	—	3.00	6.00
MCA					
❑ 40943	Here's to Good Friends/All I Can Do Is Cry	1978	2.00	4.00	8.00
—The song that became the "Tonight, let it be Lowenbrau" commercial					
MERCURY					
❑ 70352	Take Care of Yourself/I'll Never Let You Cry	1954	3.75	7.50	15.00
❑ 70414	This I Know/If You Don't, Somebody Will	1954	3.75	7.50	15.00
❑ 70502	Show Me How to Mambo/I'm in Heaven Tonight	1954	3.75	7.50	15.00
❑ 70599	I Have Lied/Morning, Noon and Night	1955	3.75	7.50	15.00
OLD TOWN					
❑ 100	In the Rain/Thank Heaven for You	1973	—	2.50	5.00
❑ 103	Color My World/Good Morning News	1974	—	2.50	5.00
❑ 106	Hurt So Bad/Love Makes It Right	1974	—	2.50	5.00
❑ 108	I Wantcha Baby/One Broken Heart	1975	—	2.50	5.00
❑ 1000	When Love Is New/All I Need Is You	1976	—	2.50	5.00
❑ 1001	I Wantcha Baby/One Broken Heart	1977	—	2.50	5.00
❑ 1002	You Can Do It/You Can Do It (Part 2)	1977	—	2.50	5.00
❑ 1003	Since I Fell for You/Between Hello and Goodbye	1978	—	2.50	5.00
❑ 1055	I Love You So/The Greatest Gift	1958	3.00	6.00	12.00
❑ 1060	I Just Want to Make Love to You/				
	Keep a Light in the Window	1958	3.00	6.00	12.00
❑ 1073	I Worry About You/My Faith	1959	3.00	6.00	12.00
❑ 1079	The Very Thought of You/				
	If Ever I Should Fall in Love	1960	2.50	5.00	10.00
❑ 1087	This Is My Love/Do You Believe	1960	2.50	5.00	10.00
❑ 1092	Good Rockin' Tonight/My Everything	1960	2.50	5.00	10.00
❑ 1101	This Time/I Wonder Where Our Love Has Gone	1961	2.50	5.00	10.00
❑ 1106	One More Time/Speak to Me	1961	2.50	5.00	10.00
❑ 1115	April in Paris/When I Fall in Love	1962	2.50	5.00	10.00
❑ 1125	Where Can I Go/Pianissimo	1962	2.50	5.00	10.00
❑ 1132	Our Love Will Last/Come and See This Old Fool	1963	2.50	5.00	10.00
❑ 1138	My Special Prayer/You Can't Come In	1963	2.50	5.00	10.00
❑ 1144	There Will Never Be Another You/Crawdad	1963	2.50	5.00	10.00
❑ 1146	Stella by Starlight/My Wish	1963	2.50	5.00	10.00
❑ 1155	Ebb Tide/Are You Ready for a Laugh	1964	2.00	4.00	8.00
❑ 1163	Close Your Eyes/My Everlasting Love	1964	2.00	4.00	8.00
❑ 1170	Fly Me to the Moon/Without the One You Love	1964	2.00	4.00	8.00
❑ 1174	Full Moon and Empty Arms/You Always Hurt the				
	One You Love	1964	2.00	4.00	8.00
❑ 1177	Teardrops in the Rain/I'm Crossing Over	1965	2.00	4.00	8.00
❑ 1183	It's Too Late, Baby Too Late/Who Can I Turn To	1965	2.00	4.00	8.00
❑ 1185	Open Up Your Heart/				
	Only a Fool Breaks His Own Heart	1965	2.00	4.00	8.00
❑ 1188	Again/I Got the Blues So Bad	1965	2.00	4.00	8.00
❑ 1191	My Funny Valentine/				
	House by the Side of the Road	1966	2.00	4.00	8.00
❑ 1196	Because/Let It Be Me	1966	2.00	4.00	8.00
VERVE					
❑ 10470	You Don't Have to Say You Love Me/10,000				
	Kisses, 10,000 Hugs	1966	—	3.00	6.00
❑ 10515	Love Me/She's a Woman	1967	—	3.00	6.00
❑ 10544	Before You Break My Heart/Goodbye, So Long	1967	—	3.00	6.00
❑ 10574	A Working Man's Prayer/No More in Life	1967	—	3.00	6.00
❑ 10592	Madam/No Sun Today	1968	—	3.00	6.00
❑ 10620	I Must Be Doing Something Right/				
	Young Runaways	1968	—	3.00	6.00
❑ 10633	My Special Prayer/Pretty Girl	1969	—	3.00	6.00
Albums					
DECCA					
❑ DL 4581 [M]	Strictly Sentimental	1965	3.75	7.50	15.00
❑ DL 4628 [M]	Showcase	1965	3.75	7.50	15.00
❑ DL 74581 [S]	Strictly Sentimental	1965	5.00	10.00	20.00
❑ DL 74628 [S]	Showcase	1965	5.00	10.00	20.00
KING					
❑ KS-1064	The Country Side of Arthur Prysock	1969	3.00	6.00	12.00
❑ KS-1066	Where the Soul Trees Go	1970	3.00	6.00	12.00
❑ KS-1067	The Lord Is My Shepherd	1970	3.00	6.00	12.00
❑ KS-1088	Fly My Love	1970	3.00	6.00	12.00
❑ KS-1134	Unforgettable	1971	3.00	6.00	12.00
MCA					
❑ 3061	Here's To Good Friends	1978	2.50	5.00	10.00

Number	Title (A Side/B Side)	Yr	VG	VG+	NM

MGM
| ❏ GAS-134 | Arthur Prysock (Golden Archive Series) | 1970 | 3.00 | 6.00 | 12.00 |
| ❏ SE-4694 | Arthur Prysock | 1970 | 3.00 | 6.00 | 12.00 |

MILESTONE
❏ M-9139	A Rockin' Good Way	1986	2.50	5.00	10.00
❏ M-9146	This Guy's in Love with You	1987	2.50	5.00	10.00
❏ M-9157	Today's Love Songs, Tomorrow's Blues	1988	2.50	5.00	10.00

OLD TOWN
❏ 12-001	Arthur Prysock '74	1973	3.00	6.00	12.00
❏ 12-002	Love Makes It Right	1974	3.00	6.00	12.00
❏ 12-004	All My Life	1976	3.00	6.00	12.00
❏ LP-102 [M]	I Worry About You	1962	12.50	25.00	50.00
❏ LP-2004 [M]	Arthur Prysock Sings Only for You	1962	12.50	25.00	50.00
❏ LP-2005 [M]	Coast to Coast	1963	10.00	20.00	40.00
❏ LP-2006 [M]	A Portrait of Arthur Prysock	1963	10.00	20.00	40.00
❏ LP-2007 [M]	Everlasting Songs for Everlasting Lovers	1964	10.00	20.00	40.00
❏ LP-2008 [M]	Intimately Yours	1964	10.00	20.00	40.00
❏ LP-2009 [M]	A Double Header with Arthur Prysock	1965	10.00	20.00	40.00
❏ LP-2010 [M]	In a Mood	1965	10.00	20.00	40.00
❏ OT 12005	Arthur Prysock Does It Again	1977	3.00	6.00	12.00
❏ ST-90604 [S]	A Portrait of Arthur Prysock	1965	10.00	20.00	40.00
—Capitol Record Club edition					
❏ T-90604 [M]	A Portrait of Arthur Prysock	1965	10.00	20.00	40.00
—Capitol Record Club edition					

POLYDOR
| ❏ PD-2-8901 [(2)] | Silk and Satin | 1977 | 3.75 | 7.50 | 15.00 |

VERVE
❏ V6-650 [(2)]	24 Karat Hits	1969	3.75	7.50	15.00
❏ V-5009 [M]	Art and Soul	1966	3.00	6.00	12.00
❏ V6-5009 [S]	Art and Soul	1966	3.75	7.50	15.00
❏ V-5011 [M]	The Best of Arthur Prysock	1967	3.00	6.00	12.00
❏ V6-5011 [S]	The Best of Arthur Prysock	1967	3.75	7.50	15.00
❏ V-5012 [M]	A Portrait of Arthur Prysock	1967	3.75	7.50	15.00
❏ V6-5012 [S]	A Portrait of Arthur Prysock	1967	3.75	7.50	15.00
❏ V-5014 [M]	Mister Prysock	1967	3.00	6.00	12.00
❏ V6-5014 [S]	Mister Prysock	1967	3.75	7.50	15.00
❏ V-5029 [M]	Love Me	1968	3.75	7.50	15.00
❏ V6-5029 [S]	Love Me	1968	3.00	6.00	12.00
❏ V-5038 [M]	The Best of Arthur Prysock, Number 2	1968	5.00	10.00	20.00
—All mono copies appear to be yellow label promos					
❏ V6-5038 [S]	The Best of Arthur Prysock, Number 2	1968	3.00	6.00	12.00
❏ V-5048 [M]	To Love or Not to Love	1968	7.50	15.00	30.00
—May be promo only					
❏ V6-5048 [S]	To Love or Not to Love	1968	3.00	6.00	12.00
❏ V6-5059	I Must Be Doing Something Right	1968	3.00	6.00	12.00
❏ V6-5070	This Is My Beloved	1969	3.00	6.00	12.00

PRYSOCK, ARTHUR/COUNT BASIE Also see each artist's individual listings.
Albums
VERVE
❏ V-8646 [M]	Arthur Prysock/Count Basie	1966	3.75	7.50	15.00
❏ V6-8646 [S]	Arthur Prysock/Count Basie	1966	5.00	10.00	20.00
❏ 827011-1	Arthur Prysock/Count Basie	1985	2.00	4.00	8.00
—Reissue					

PRYSOCK, RED
45s
CHESS
| ❏ 2042 | I Heard It Through the Grapevine/Groovy Sax | 1968 | 2.00 | 4.00 | 8.00 |

KING
❏ 5595	Hand Clapping One More Time/Smokestack	1962	2.50	5.00	10.00
❏ 5644	Quick as a Flash/Old Folks	1962	2.50	5.00	10.00
❏ 5669	Harem Girl/Ride Away	1962	2.50	5.00	10.00
❏ 5704	Here We Go Again/Can't Sit Down	1963	2.50	5.00	10.00

MERCURY
❏ 70367	Jump Red Jump/Body and Soul	1954	5.00	10.00	20.00
❏ 70419	Happy Feet/Blow Your Horn	1954	5.00	10.00	20.00
❏ 70460	Hey There/Fats' Place	1954	5.00	10.00	20.00
❏ 70540	Rock 'n' Roll/Little Jamie	1955	5.00	10.00	20.00
❏ 70602	The Zonked/Horn Blows	1955	5.00	10.00	20.00
❏ 70674	Hand Clappin'/Shoe String	1955	5.00	10.00	20.00
❏ 70698	Jumbo/Hand Clappin'	1955	5.00	10.00	20.00
❏ 70733	Finger Tips/Short Circuit	1955	5.00	10.00	20.00
❏ 70787	Zip/Red Speaks	1956	3.75	7.50	15.00
❏ 70918	Rock and Roll Party/Rock and Roll Mambo	1956	3.75	7.50	15.00
❏ 70985	Teen-Age Rock/Paquino Walk	1956	3.75	7.50	15.00
❏ 71054	Head Snappin'/Pog Wog	1957	3.75	7.50	15.00
❏ 71175	Rooster Walk/Two Point Eight	1957	3.75	7.50	15.00
❏ 71214	What's the Word, Thunderbird/Satellite	1957	3.75	7.50	15.00
❏ 71358	Billie's Blues/Willow Weep for Me	1958	3.00	6.00	12.00
❏ 71471	Margie/Chop Suey	1959	3.00	6.00	12.00
❏ 71476	Riffin' with Red/And the Angels Sing	1959	3.00	6.00	12.00
❏ 71573	Deep Purple/Offshore	1960	3.00	6.00	12.00
❏ 71735	More Handclappin'/Twistin' 'n' Bendin'	1960	3.00	6.00	12.00
❏ 71786	Charleston Twist/Bony Maronie	1961	3.00	6.00	12.00

RED ROBIN
❏ 107	Wiggles/Crying My Heart Out	1952	30.00	60.00	120.00
❏ 117	Hard Rock/Jump for George	1953	25.00	50.00	100.00
❏ 139	Jackpot/The Hammer	1956	20.00	40.00	80.00

Albums
MERCURY
❏ MG-20088 [M]	Rock 'n' Roll	1955	50.00	100.00	200.00
❏ MG-20211 [M]	Fruit Boots	1957	30.00	60.00	120.00
❏ MG-20307 [M]	The Beat	1957	20.00	40.00	80.00
❏ MG-20512 [M]	Swing Softly Red	1958	12.50	25.00	50.00
❏ SR-60188 [S]	Swing Softly Red	1959	20.00	40.00	80.00

WING
❏ MGW-12007 [M]	Fruit Boots	1959	10.00	20.00	40.00
—Originals have liner notes on back cover					
❏ MGW-12007 [M]	Fruit Boots	196?	5.00	10.00	20.00
—Reissues have other LPs listed on back cover					
❏ SRW-16007 [R]	Fruit Boots	196?	3.00	6.00	12.00

PUCKETT, GARY, AND THE UNION GAP Includes Gary Puckett solo and records credited to "The Union Gap Featuring Gary Puckett."
45s
COLUMBIA
❏ 44297	Woman, Woman/Don't Make Promises	1967	2.00	4.00	8.00
❏ 44297 [PS]	Woman, Woman/Don't Make Promises	1967	3.00	6.00	12.00
—As "The Union Gap"					
❏ 44450	Young Girl/I'm Losing You	1968	2.00	4.00	8.00
—As "The Union Gap Featuring Gary Puckett"					
❏ 44450 [PS]	Young Girl/I'm Losing You	1968	3.00	6.00	12.00
—As "The Union Gap featuring Gary Puckett"					
❏ 44547	Lady Willpower/Daylight Strangers	1968	2.00	4.00	8.00
❏ 44547 [PS]	Lady Willpower/Daylight Strangers	1968	3.00	6.00	12.00
—As "The Union Gap"					
❏ 44644	Over You/If the Day Would Come	1968	—	3.00	6.00
❏ 44644 [PS]	Over You/If the Day Would Come	1968	3.00	6.00	12.00
❏ 44788	Don't Give In to Him/Could I	1969	—	3.00	6.00
❏ 44967	This Girl Is a Woman Now/His Other Woman	1969	—	3.00	6.00
❏ 45097	Let's Give Adam and Eve Another Chance/The Beggar	1970	—	3.00	6.00
❏ 45097 [PS]	Let's Give Adam and Eve Another Chance/The Beggar	1970	2.00	4.00	8.00
❏ 45249	I Just Don't Know What to Do With Myself/All That Matters	1970	—	2.50	5.00
❏ 45303	Keep the Customer Satisfied/No One Really Knows	1971	—	2.50	5.00
❏ 45358	Life Has Its Little Ups and Downs/Shimmering Eyes	1971	—	2.50	5.00
❏ 45438	Hello Morning/Gentle Woman	1971	—	2.50	5.00
❏ 45509	Hello Morning/I Can't Hold On	1971	—	2.50	5.00
❏ 45678	Bless the Child/Leavin' in the Morning	1972	—	2.50	5.00

Albums
COLUMBIA
❏ CS 1042	Gary Puckett and the Union Gap's Greatest Hits	1970	5.00	10.00	20.00
❏ CL 2812 [M]	Woman, Woman	1968	10.00	20.00	40.00
—As "The Union Gap Featuring Gary Puckett"					
❏ CL 2864 [M]	Young Girl	1968	12.50	25.00	50.00
—Red label stock copy with "Mono" on label; this has been confirmed to exist					
❏ CL 2915 [M]	Incredible	1968	15.00	30.00	60.00
—Red label stock copy with "Mono" on label; this has been confirmed to exist					
❏ CS 9612 [S]	Woman, Woman	1968	5.00	10.00	20.00
—As "The Union Gap Featuring Gary Puckett"					
❏ CS 9664 [S]	Young Girl	1968	5.00	10.00	20.00
❏ CS 9715 [S]	Incredible	1968	5.00	10.00	20.00
❏ CS 9935	The New Gary Puckett and the Union Gap Album	1969	5.00	10.00	20.00
❏ C 30862	The Gary Puckett Album	1971	3.75	7.50	15.00

HARMONY
| ❏ KH 31184 | Lady Willpower | 1972 | 2.50 | 5.00 | 10.00 |

PUFNSTUF
45s
DECCA
| ❏ 32702 | Pufnstuf/Nonsense | 1970 | 3.75 | 7.50 | 15.00 |

PUGSLEY MUNION
Albums
J&S
| ❏ SLP-001 | Just Like You | 1969 | 25.00 | 50.00 | 100.00 |

PULLEN, DWIGHT See WHITEY PULLEN.

PULLEN, WHITEY
45s
CARLTON
| ❏ 455 | Sunglasses After Dark/Teenage Bug | 1958 | 75.00 | 150.00 | 300.00 |
| —As "Dwight Pullen" | | | | | |

DELTA
| ❏ 1503 | Broke Waiting for a Break/I'm Beggin' Your Pardon | 196? | 12.50 | 25.00 | 50.00 |

ROLLIN' ROCK
❏ 005	Let's All Go Wild/Moonshine Liquor	1978	—	2.50	5.00
❏ 010	Drinkin' Wine/Everybody's Rockin'	1978	—	2.50	5.00
❏ 017	Tuscaloosa Lucy/Tight Slacks	1979	—	2.50	5.00

SAGE
❏ 274	Walk My Way Back Home/Don't Make Me Cry	1958	62.50	125.00	250.00
❏ 279	By You, By the Bayou/It's Over With	1959	50.00	100.00	200.00
—As "Dwight Pullen"					
❏ 283	I Live a Lifetime Last Night/You'll Get Yours Some Day	1959	50.00	100.00	200.00
—As "Dwight Pullen"					
❏ 294	Let's All Go Wild Tonight/Gently	1959	37.50	75.00	150.00
❏ 303	I'm Beggin' Your Pardon/Let Your Left Hand Know	1960	25.00	50.00	100.00
❏ 313	Tuscaloosa Lucy/Waltz of the Steel Guitar	1960	30.00	60.00	120.00
❏ 372	Crazy in Love/I Won the Day I Lost You	1962	10.00	20.00	40.00

PUMPKIN
45s
BRUNSWICK
| ❏ 55004 | Half Past Seventeen/Boom Boom | 1957 | 10.00 | 20.00 | 40.00 |

PURCELL, BOOTS, COMBO
45s
HIT
❏ 26	Rinky Dink/Vacation	1962	2.00	4.00	8.00
—B-side by Connie Landers					
❏ 39	Desafinado/Release Me	1962	2.00	4.00	8.00
—B-side by Lucille Johns					

PURE LOVE AND PLEASURE
45s
ABC DUNHILL
| ❏ 4232 | All in My Mind/What Cha Gonna Do | 1970 | 2.00 | 4.00 | 8.00 |

Albums
ABC DUNHILL
| ❏ DS-50076 | A Record of Pure Love and Pleasure | 1970 | 3.75 | 7.50 | 15.00 |

P

Number	Title (A Side/B Side)	Yr	VG	VG+	NM

PURE PRAIRIE LEAGUE
45s
CASABLANCA

❏ 2266	Let Me Love You Tonight/Janny Lou	1980	—	2.00	4.00
❏ 2294	I'm Almost Ready/You're My True Love	1980	—	2.00	4.00
❏ 2319	I Can't Stop the Feelin'/A Lifetime of Nightime	1980	—	2.00	4.00
❏ 2332	Still Right Here in My Heart/Don't Keep Me Hangin'	1981	—	2.00	4.00
❏ 2337	You're Mine Tonight. Do You Love Me Truly, Julie	1981	—	2.00	4.00

RCA

❏ PB-10829	Dance/Help Yourself	1976	—	2.00	4.00
❏ PB-10880	All the Way/Fade Away	1977	—	2.00	4.00
❏ PB-11148	The Sun Shone Lightly/Lucille Crawfield	1977	—	2.00	4.00
❏ PB-11260	Working in the Coal Mine/Bad Cream	1978	—	2.00	4.00
❏ PB-11282	Love Will Grow/Slim Pickin's	1978	—	2.00	4.00
❏ PB-11678	Can't Hold Back/Restless Woman	1979	—	2.00	4.00

RCA VICTOR

❏ 48-1028	Tears/You're Between Me	1972	—	3.00	6.00
❏ 74-0742	Woman/She Darked the Sun	1972	—	3.00	6.00
❏ 74-0794	Early Morning Riser/Angel #9	1972	—	3.00	6.00
❏ PB-10184	Amie/Memories	1975	—	2.50	5.00
❏ PB-10302	Two-Lane Highway/Sister's Keeper	1975	—	2.00	4.00
❏ PB-10382	Just Can't Believe It/Kentucky Moonshine	1975	—	2.00	4.00
❏ GB-10490	Amie/Memories	1975	—	—	3.00
—Gold Standard Series					
❏ PB-10580	Long Cold Winter/The Sun Shone Brightly	1976	—	2.00	4.00
❏ PB-10679	That'll Be the Day/I Can Only Dream of You	1976	—	2.00	4.00

Albums
CASABLANCA

| ❏ NBLP-7212 | Firin' Up | 1980 | 2.50 | 5.00 | 10.00 |
| ❏ NBLP-7255 | Something in the Night | 1981 | 2.50 | 5.00 | 10.00 |

PAIR

| ❏ PDL2-1034 [(2)] | Home on the Range | 1986 | 3.00 | 6.00 | 12.00 |

RCA VICTOR

❏ APD1-0933 [Q]	Two Lane Highway	1975	5.00	10.00	20.00
❏ APL1-0933	Two Lane Highway	1975	3.00	6.00	12.00
❏ APD1-1247 [Q]	If the Shoe Fits	1976	5.00	10.00	20.00
❏ APL1-1247	If the Shoe Fits	1976	3.00	6.00	12.00
❏ APL1-1924	Dance	1976	3.00	6.00	12.00
❏ CPL2-2404 [(2)]	Live!! Takin' the Stage	1977	3.75	7.50	15.00
❏ AFL1-2590	Just Fly	1978	3.00	6.00	12.00
❏ AFL1-3335	Can't Hold Back	1979	3.00	6.00	12.00
❏ AYL1-3669	Two Lane Highway	1980	2.00	4.00	8.00
—"Best Buy Series" reissue					
❏ AYL1-3717	If the Shoe Fits	1981	2.00	4.00	8.00
—"Best Buy Series" reissue					
❏ AYL1-3718	Just Fly	1981	2.00	4.00	8.00
—"Best Buy Series" reissue					
❏ AYL1-3719	Pure Prairie League	1981	2.00	4.00	8.00
—"Best Buy Series" reissue					
❏ AYL1-3723	Dance	1981	2.00	4.00	8.00
—"Best Buy Series" reissue					
❏ AFL1-4650	Pure Prairie League	1977	2.50	5.00	10.00
—Reissue of LSP-4650					
❏ LSP-4650	Pure Prairie League	1972	3.00	6.00	12.00
❏ AYL1-4656	Bustin' Out	1984	2.00	4.00	8.00
—"Best Buy Series" reissue					
❏ AFL1-4769	Bustin' Out	1977	2.50	5.00	10.00
—Reissue of LSP-4769					
❏ LSP-4769	Bustin' Out	1972	3.00	6.00	12.00

PURIFY, JAMES AND BOBBY
45s
BELL

❏ 648	I'm Your Puppet/So Many Reasons	1966	3.75	7.50	15.00
❏ 660	Wish You Didn't Have to Go/You Can't Keep a Good Man Down	1967	2.00	4.00	8.00
❏ 669	Shake a Tail Feather/Goodness Gracious	1967	3.00	6.00	12.00
❏ 680	I Take What I Want/Sixteen Tons	1967	2.00	4.00	8.00
❏ 685	Let Love Come Between Us/I Don't Want to Have to Wait	1967	2.00	4.00	8.00
❏ 700	Do Unto Me/Everybody Needs Somebody	1967	2.00	4.00	8.00
❏ 721	I Can Remember/I Was Born to Lose Out	1968	2.00	4.00	8.00
❏ 735	Help Yourself (To All of My Lovin')/Last Piece of Love	1968	2.00	4.00	8.00
❏ 751	Untie Me/We're Finally Gonna Make It	1968	2.00	4.00	8.00
❏ 774	I Don't Know What It Is You Got/Section C	1969	2.00	4.00	8.00

CASABLANCA

❏ 812	Do Your Thing/Why Love	1974	—	2.50	5.00
❏ 827	Man Can't Be a Man Without a Woman/You and Me Together Forever	1975	—	2.50	5.00
❏ 830	All the Love I Got/(B-side unknown)	1975	—	2.50	5.00

MERCURY

❏ 73767	I'm Your Puppet/Lay Me Down Easy	1976	—	2.50	5.00
❏ 73806	Morning Glory/Turning Back the Pages	1976	—	2.50	5.00
❏ 73884	I Ain't Got to Love Nobody Else/What's Better Than Love	1977	—	2.50	5.00
❏ 73893	Get Closer/What's Better Than Love	1977	—	2.50	5.00

PHILCO-FORD

| ❏ HP-28 | I'm Your Puppet/Goodnight Gracious | 1968 | 3.75 | 7.50 | 15.00 |
| —4-inch plastic "Hip Pocket Record" with color sleeve | | | | | |

SPHERE SOUND

| ❏ 77004 | I'm Your Puppet/Everybody Needs Somebody | 196? | 2.00 | 4.00 | 8.00 |

Albums
BELL

❏ 6003 [M]	James and Bobby Purify	1966	6.25	12.50	25.00
❏ S-6003 [S]	James and Bobby Purify	1966	7.50	15.00	30.00
❏ 6010 [M]	The Pure Sound of the Purifys	1967	6.25	12.50	25.00
❏ S-6010 [S]	The Pure Sound of the Purifys	1967	7.50	15.00	30.00

MERCURY

| ❏ SRM-1-1134 | The Purify Brothers | 1977 | 3.00 | 6.00 | 12.00 |

PURPLE GANG, THE
Albums
SIRE

| ❏ SES 97006 | The Purple Gang Strikes | 1969 | 5.00 | 10.00 | 20.00 |

PURPLE IMAGE
Albums
MAP CITY

| ❏ 3015 | Purple Image | 1971 | 12.50 | 25.00 | 50.00 |

PURSELL, BILL
45s
COLUMBIA

❏ 42619	Our Winter Love/A Wound Can't Erase	1962	2.00	4.00	8.00
❏ 42780	Loved/Stranger	1963	—	3.00	6.00
❏ 42832	Pride/Farewell to Adra	1963	—	3.00	6.00
❏ 42876	Dark Alley/Autumn Magic	1963	—	3.00	6.00
❏ 42970	The Theme from Captain Newman/Remember Me (I'm the One Who Loves You)	1964	—	3.00	6.00
❏ 43090	Crying/I'll Never Be Free	1964	—	3.00	6.00
❏ 43255	Madrilena/Remembered Love	1965	—	3.00	6.00
❏ 43380	You've Lost That Lovin' Feelin'/Quiet Nights of Quiet Stars	1965	—	3.00	6.00
❏ 43593	Love Theme from Superman/Soul Shall It Be	1966	2.50	5.00	10.00

DOT

| ❏ 17217 | Geary Street/Winter Waves | 1969 | — | 2.50 | 5.00 |

Albums
COLUMBIA

❏ CL 1992 [M]	Our Winter Love	1963	3.75	7.50	15.00
❏ CL 2077 [M]	Chasing a Dream	1964	3.75	7.50	15.00
❏ CL 2421 [M]	Remembered Love	1965	3.75	7.50	15.00
❏ CS 8792 [S]	Our Winter Love	1963	5.00	10.00	20.00
❏ CS 8877 [S]	Chasing a Dream	1964	5.00	10.00	20.00
❏ CS 9221 [S]	Remembered Love	1965	5.00	10.00	20.00

PUZZLE
45s
ABC

| ❏ 11181 | Hey Medusa/Make the Children Happy | 1969 | 2.00 | 4.00 | 8.00 |

Albums
ABC

| ❏ ABCS-671 | Puzzle | 1969 | 5.00 | 10.00 | 20.00 |

PYRAMIDS, THE (1) Surf instrumental group.
45s
BEST

❏ 1	Pyramid's Stomp/Paul	1963	7.50	15.00	30.00
❏ 102	Penetration/Here Comes Marsha	1963	10.00	20.00	40.00
❏ 13001	Pyramid's Stomp/Paul	1963	5.00	10.00	20.00
❏ 13002	Penetration/Here Comes Marsha	1964	3.75	7.50	15.00
—With "Dist. by London" or similar wording on label					
❏ 13002	Penetration/Here Comes Marsha	1964	5.00	10.00	20.00
—No mention of London Records on label					
❏ 13002 [PS]	Penetration/Here Comes Marsha	1964	10.00	20.00	40.00
—Black sleeve					
❏ 13002 [PS]	Penetration/Here Comes Marsha	1964	10.00	20.00	40.00
—Red sleeve					

CEDWICKE

| ❏ 13005 | Midnight Run/Custom Caravan | 1964 | 10.00 | 20.00 | 40.00 |
| ❏ 13006 | Contact/Pressure | 1964 | 10.00 | 20.00 | 40.00 |

Albums
BEST

❏ LPM-1001 [M]	The Original Penetration! And Other Favorites	1964	62.50	125.00	250.00
—Original issue with "Walkin' the Dog"					
❏ BR 16501 [M]	The Original Penetration! And Other Favorites	1964	50.00	100.00	200.00
—Reissue with "Road Runnah"					
❏ BS 36501 [R]	The Original Penetration! And Other Favorites	1964	30.00	60.00	120.00

SUNDAZED

| ❏ LP-5012 | Penetration! The Best of the Pyramids | 1995 | 2.50 | 5.00 | 10.00 |

PYRAMIDS, THE (2) Black vocal group.
45s
CUB

| ❏ 9112 | I'm the Playboy/Cryin' | 1962 | 5.00 | 10.00 | 20.00 |

SONBERT

| ❏ 82861 | I'm the Playboy/Cryin' | 1962 | 10.00 | 20.00 | 40.00 |

VEE JAY

| ❏ 489 | What Is Love/Shakin' Fit | 1963 | 6.25 | 12.50 | 25.00 |

PYRAMIDS, THE (U) Neither group (1) nor (2), but probably not all the same.
45s
DAVIS

| ❏ 453 | At Any Cost/Okay, Baby! | 1956 | 12.50 | 25.00 | 50.00 |
| ❏ 457 | Why Did You Go/Before It's Too Late | 1957 | 12.50 | 25.00 | 50.00 |

FEDERAL

| ❏ 12233 | Deep in My Heart for You/And I Need You | 1955 | 100.00 | 200.00 | 400.00 |

HOLLYWOOD

| ❏ 1047 | Someday/Bow Wow | 1955 | 125.00 | 250.00 | 500.00 |

RCA VICTOR

| ❏ 47-7556 | Long Long Time/Oh No You Won't (Oh Yes You Will) | 1959 | 3.75 | 7.50 | 15.00 |

SHELL

❏ 304	Ankle Bracelet/Hot Dog Dooly Wah	1961	6.25	12.50	25.00
—As "The Original Pyramids"					
❏ 711	Ankle Bracelet/Hot Dog Dooly Wah	1958	12.50	25.00	50.00

PYTHON LEE JACKSON With ROD STEWART on vocals.
45s
GNP CRESCENDO

❏ 449	In a Broken Dream/Doin' Fine	1972	—	3.00	6.00
❏ 449	In a Broken Dream/Turn the Music Down	1972	—	3.00	6.00
❏ 462	Cloud Nine/Rod's Blues	1973	—	3.00	6.00

Albums
GNP CRESCENDO

| ❏ GNPS-2066 | In a Broken Dream | 1972 | 3.75 | 7.50 | 15.00 |

Number	Title (A Side/B Side)	Yr	VG	VG+	NM

Q

QUADRANGLE, THE
45s
PHILIPS

Number	Title (A Side/B Side)	Yr	VG	VG+	NM
❏ 40408	She's Too Familiar Now/No More Time	1966	7.50	15.00	30.00

QUADRELLS, THE
45s
WHIRLIN' DISC

❏ 103	What Can the Matter Be/Come to Me	1957	17.50	35.00	70.00

QUADS, THE
45s
VAULT

❏ 907	Surfin' Hearse/Little Queenie	1963	10.00	20.00	40.00

QUAILS, THE (1) See BILL ROBINSON AND THE QUAILS.

QUAILS, THE (2)
45s
HARVEY

❏ 116	My Love/Never Felt Like This Before	1961	12.50	25.00	50.00
❏ 120	I Thought/Over the Hump	1963	12.50	25.00	50.00

QUAITE, CHRISTINE
45s
WORLD ARTISTS

❏ 1022	Tell Me Mamma/In the Middle of the Floor	1964	3.00	6.00	12.00
❏ 1028	Mr. Stuck Up/Will You Be the Same Tomorrow	1964	3.00	6.00	12.00

QUAKER CITY BOYS, THE
45s
SWAN

❏ 4023	Teasin'/Won't Ya Come Out Mary Ann	1958	3.00	6.00	12.00
❏ 4026	Everywhere You Go/Love Me Tonight	1959	2.50	5.00	10.00
❏ 4045	Goodbye 50's, Hello 60's/You Call Everybody Darlin'	1959	2.50	5.00	10.00

QUARTER NOTES, THE (1)
45s
BISON

❏ 757	Frantic Flip/Canadian Sunset	1960	7.50	15.00	30.00

IMPERIAL

❏ 5647	Frantic Flip/Canadian Sunset	1960	3.75	7.50	15.00

WIZZ

❏ 715	Record Hop Blues/Suki-Yaki-Rocki	1959	6.25	12.50	25.00

QUARTER NOTES, THE (2)
45s
BOOM

❏ 60018	Hey Little Girl/I've Been Loved	1966	3.75	7.50	15.00

QUARTER NOTES, THE (3)
45s
DELUXE

❏ 6116	Loneliness/Come De Nite	1957	6.25	12.50	25.00
❏ 6129	My Fantasy/Ten Minutes to Midnight	1957	6.25	12.50	25.00

QUARTER NOTES, THE (U) Some of these could be group (1) or (3).
45s
DOT

❏ 15685	Please Come Home/Like You Bug Me	1958	6.25	12.50	25.00

GUYDEN

❏ 2083	Pretty Pretty Eyes/I Don't Wanna Go Home	1963	5.00	10.00	20.00

RCA VICTOR

❏ 47-7327	The Interview/Punkanilla	1958	3.75	7.50	15.00

QUARTERMASS
Albums
HARVEST

❏ SKAO-314	Quartermass	1970	7.50	15.00	30.00

QUATEMAN, BILL
45s
COLUMBIA

❏ 4-45792	Only Love/Keep Dreaming	1973	—	2.50	5.00
❏ 4-45792 [PS]	Only Love/Keep Dreaming	1973	2.00	4.00	8.00
❏ 4-45858	Get It Right On Out There/Your Love Can Make It Real	1973	—	2.50	5.00

RCA

❏ PB-10912	Night After Night/Your Money or Your Life	1977	—	2.00	4.00
❏ PB-11180	Wait Until Tomorrow/Josephine	1977	—	2.00	4.00
❏ PB-11254	Shot in the Dark/All Over Now	1978	—	2.00	4.00
❏ PB-11588	Just Like You/It's Alright	1979	—	2.00	4.00

Albums
COLUMBIA

❏ KC 31761	Bill Quateman	1973	3.00	6.00	12.00

RCA VICTOR

❏ APL1-2027	Night After Night	1977	2.50	5.00	10.00
❏ APL1-2434	Shot in the Dark	1977	2.50	5.00	10.00

QUATRO, SUZI Also see THE PLEASURE SEEKERS.
12-Inch Singles
DREAMLAND

❏ DPR 1204 [DJ]	Rock Hard (same on both sides)	1980	2.50	5.00	10.00

45s
ARISTA

❏ 0106	Your Mama Won't Like Me/Peter Peter	1975	—	3.00	6.00

BELL

❏ 45401	48 Crash/Little Bitch Blue	1973	—	3.00	6.00
❏ 45416	Can the Can/Ain't Ya Somethin' Honey	1973	—	3.50	7.00
❏ 45477	All Shook Up/Glycerine Queen	1974	—	3.00	6.00
❏ 45609	Devil Gate Drive/In the Morning	1974	—	3.00	6.00
❏ 45615	Keep a-Knockin'/Cat Size	1974	—	3.00	6.00

BIG TREE

❏ 16053	Can the Can/Don't Mess Around	1975	—	3.00	6.00

DREAMLAND

❏ 104	Rock Hard/State of Mind	1980	—	2.00	4.00
❏ 104 [PS]	Rock Hard/State of Mind	1980	—	2.00	4.00
❏ 107	Lipstick/Woman Cry	1980	—	2.00	4.00

RAK

❏ 4512	Brain Confusion (For All the Lonely People)/Rolling Stone	1972	3.00	6.00	12.00

RSO

❏ 917	Stumblin' In/A Stranger to Paradise	1979	—	2.00	4.00

—With Chris Norman (lead singer of Smokie)

❏ 929	If You Can't Give Me Love/Non-Citizen	1979	—	2.00	4.00
❏ 1001	I've Never Been in Love/Space Cadets	1979	—	2.00	4.00
❏ 1014	She's in Love with You/Starlight Lady	1979	—	2.00	4.00

Albums
ARISTA

❏ AL 4035	Your Mama Won't Like Me	1975	3.00	6.00	12.00

BELL

❏ 1302	Suzi Quatro	1974	3.75	7.50	15.00
❏ 1313	Quatro	1974	3.75	7.50	15.00

DREAMLAND

❏ DL-1-5006	Rock Hard	1980	2.50	5.00	10.00

RSO

❏ RS-1-3044	If You Knew Suzi...	1979	2.50	5.00	10.00
❏ RS-1-3064	Suzi...And Other Four Letter Words	1980	2.50	5.00	10.00

QUATTLEBAUM, DOUG
45s
GOTHAM

❏ 519	Don't Be Funny Baby/Lizzie Lou	1953	25.00	50.00	100.00

Albums
BLUESVILLE

❏ BVLP-1065 [M]	Softee Man Blues	1963	15.00	30.00	60.00

—Blue label, silver print

❏ BVLP-1065 [M]	Softee Man Blues	1964	5.00	10.00	20.00

—Blue label, trident logo at right

QUEEN Also see FREDDIE MERCURY.
12-Inch Singles
CAPITOL

❏ V-8575	Radio Ga Ga (Vocal) (Instrumental)/I Go Crazy	1984	3.00	6.00	12.00
❏ V-8590	I Want to Break Free/Machines (Or Back to Humans)	1984	3.00	6.00	12.00

—We don't know if this 12-inch single has four different covers the way the 45 has four different picture sleeves

❏ V-8622	Thank God It's Christmas/Keep Passing the Open Windows (Extended)/Man on the Prowl (Extended)	1984	5.00	10.00	20.00
❏ SPRO-9064 [DJ]	Radio Ga Ga (same on both sides)	1984	3.75	7.50	15.00
❏ SPRO-9160 [DJ]	It's a Hard Life (same on both sides?)	1984	5.00	10.00	20.00
❏ SPRO-9271/6 [DJ]	Hammer to Fall (Headbanger Mix) (Single Edit)	1984	5.00	10.00	20.00
❏ SPRO-9537 [DJ]	One Vision (same on both sides)	1985	3.75	7.50	15.00
❏ SPRO-9649 [DJ]	Princes of the Universe (same on both sides)	1986	5.00	10.00	20.00
❏ SPRO-9714/5 [DJ]	A Kind of Magic (4:30) (6:30)	1986	3.75	7.50	15.00
❏ V-15210	One Vision (Extended Version)/Blurred Vision	1985	3.75	7.50	15.00
❏ V-15232	A Kind of Magic (Extended Version)/Gimme the Prize (Kurgan's Theme)	1986	3.75	7.50	15.00
❏ V-15260	Pain Is So Close to Pleasure (2 versions)/Don't Lose Your Head	1986	3.75	7.50	15.00

DREAMWORKS

❏ PRO-A-5105 [DJ]	Another One Bites the Dust (4 versions)	1998	3.00	6.00	12.00
❏ PRO-A-5113 [DJ]	Another One Bites the Dust (3 versions)	1998	3.75	7.50	15.00
❏ PRO-A-5118 [DJ]	Another One Bites the Dust (7 versions)	1998	3.75	7.50	15.00

ELEKTRA

❏ 12-77DJ [DJ]	We Are the Champions/We Will Rock You//We Will Rock You/We Are the Champions	1977	20.00	40.00	80.00
❏ AS 11401 [DJ]	Bicycle Race/Fat Bottomed Girls (both stereo)//same (both mono)	1978	6.25	12.50	25.00
❏ AS 11461 [DJ]	Another One Bites the Dust (same on both sides)	1980	3.75	7.50	15.00
❏ AS 11481 [DJ]	Flash's Theme AKA Flash (stereo/mono)	1980	3.75	7.50	15.00
❏ AS 11567 [DJ]	Body Language (stereo/mono)	1982	3.00	6.00	12.00
❏ 67954	Back Chat/Staying Power	1982	5.00	10.00	20.00

HOLLYWOOD

❏ ED 5529 [DJ]	We Will Rock You (7 versions)/We Are the Champions	1991	3.75	7.50	15.00
❏ ED 10607 [DJ]	You Don't Fool Me (3 versions)	1996	5.00	10.00	20.00
❏ HR-66003	You Don't Fool Me (4 versions)	1996	2.00	4.00	8.00

45s
CAPITOL

❏ B-5317	Radio Ga Ga/I Go Crazy	1984	—	2.00	4.00
❏ B-5317 [PS]	Radio Ga Ga/I Go Crazy	1984	—	2.00	4.00
❏ B-5350	I Want to Break Free/Machines (Or Back to Humans)	1984	—	2.00	4.00
❏ B-5350 [PS]	I Want to Break Free/Machines (Or Back to Humans)	1984	—	2.50	5.00

—With Brian May in center

❏ B-5350 [PS]	I Want to Break Free/Machines (Or Back to Humans)	1984	—	2.50	5.00

—With Freddie Mercury in center

❏ B-5350 [PS]	I Want to Break Free/Machines (Or Back to Humans)	1984	—	2.50	5.00

—With John Deacon in center

❏ B-5350 [PS]	I Want to Break Free/Machines (Or Back to Humans)	1984	—	2.50	5.00

—With Roger Taylor in center

❏ B-5372	It's a Hard Life/Is This the World We Created?	1984	—	2.50	5.00
❏ B-5372 [PS]	It's a Hard Life/Is This the World We Created?	1984	—	2.50	5.00
❏ B-5424	Hammer to Fall/Tear It Up	1984	—	2.50	5.00
❏ B-5424 [PS]	Hammer to Fall/Tear It Up	1984	—	2.50	5.00
❏ B-5530	One Vision/Blurred Vision	1985	—	2.00	4.00
❏ B-5530 [PS]	One Vision/Blurred Vision	1985	—	2.00	4.00
❏ B-5568	Princes of the Universe/A Dozen Red Roses for My Darling	1985	—	2.00	4.00

Number	Title (A Side/B Side)	Yr	VG	VG+	NM
❑ B-5568 [PS]	Princes of the Universe/				
	A Dozen Red Roses for My Darling	1985	—	2.00	4.00
❑ B-5590	A Kind of Magic/Gimme the Prize				
	(Kurgan's Theme)	1986	—	2.00	4.00
❑ B-5590 [PS]	A Kind of Magic/Gimme the Prize				
	(Kurgan's Theme)	1986	—	2.00	4.00

—*Later sleeves have either the correct B-side, or no B-side at all, listed*

❑ B-5590 [PS]	A Kind of Magic/				
	A Dozen Red Roses for My Darling	1986	—	3.00	6.00

—*First edition of sleeve has wrong B-side listed; this was the British pairing for this single, but we don't think this pairing was issued in the U.S.*

❑ B-5633	Pain Is So Close to Pleasure/				
	Don't Lose Your Head	1986	—	2.00	4.00
❑ B-5633 [PS]	Pain Is So Close to Pleasure/				
	Don't Lose Your Head	1986	—	2.00	4.00
❑ 7PRO-9114 [DJ]	I Want to Break Free (same on both sides)	1984	3.00	6.00	12.00

—*White label, no song title or name of group on label*

❑ 7PRO-9546/7 [DJ]	One Vision (4:00)/(3:46)	1985	3.00	6.00	12.00
❑ B-44372	I Want It All/Hang On In There	1989	—	2.50	5.00
❑ B-44372 [PS]	I Want It All/Hang On In There	1989	—	2.50	5.00
❑ 7PRO-79685	Breakthru (same on both sides)	1989	3.00	6.00	12.00

—*Vinyl is promo only*

❑ 7PRO-79779	Scandal (same on both sides)	1989	3.00	6.00	12.00

—*Vinyl is promo only*

ELEKTRA

❑ 45080	Killer Queen/Liar	1977	—	2.00	4.00

—*"Spun Gold" reissue*

❑ 45083	Bohemian Rhapsody/You're My Best Friend	1977	—	2.00	4.00

—*"Spun Gold" reissue*

❑ 45090	We Are the Champions/We Will Rock You	1979	—	2.00	4.00

—*"Spun Gold" reissue*

❑ 45103	Crazy Little Thing Called Love/Bicycle Race	1981	—	2.00	4.00

—*"Spun Gold" reissue*

❑ 45106	Another One Bites the Dust/Keep Yourself Alive	1981	—	2.00	4.00

—*"Spun Gold" reissue*

❑ 45226	Killer Queen/Flick of the Wrist	1975	2.00	4.00	8.00

—*Butterfly label*

❑ 45226	Killer Queen/Flick of the Wrist	1975	2.50	5.00	10.00

—*Caterpillar label*

❑ 45268	Keep Yourself Alive//Lily of the Valley/				
	God Save the Queen	1975	2.00	4.00	8.00
❑ 45297	Bohemian Rhapsody/I'm in Love with My Car	1975	2.00	4.00	8.00

—*Butterfly label*

❑ 45297	Bohemian Rhapsody/I'm in Love with My Car	1976	2.50	5.00	10.00

—*Red label, much scarcer than butterfly label*

❑ 45318	You're My Best Friend/'39	1976	—	3.00	6.00

—*Butterfly label*

❑ 45318	You're My Best Friend/'39	1976	2.50	5.00	10.00

—*Red label, much scarcer than butterfly label*

❑ 45362	Somebody to Love/White Man	1976	—	3.00	6.00

—*Butterfly label*

❑ 45362	Somebody to Love/White Man	1976	2.50	5.00	10.00

—*Red label, much scarcer than butterfly label*

❑ 45385	Tie Your Mother Down/Drowse	1977	—	3.00	6.00
❑ 45412	Long Away/You and I	1977	2.00	4.00	8.00
❑ 45441	We Are the Champions/We Will Rock You	1977	—	3.00	6.00
❑ 45441 [PS]	We Are the Champions/We Will Rock You	1977	2.50	5.00	10.00
❑ 45478	It's Late/Sheer Heart Attack	1978	—	3.00	6.00
❑ 45478 [PS]	It's Late/Sheer Heart Attack	1978	2.50	5.00	10.00
❑ 45541	Bicycle Race/Fat Bottomed Girls	1978	—	3.00	6.00
❑ 45541 [PS]	Bicycle Race/Fat Bottomed Girls	1978	3.00	6.00	12.00
❑ 45863	Keep Yourself Alive/Son and Daughter	1973	6.25	12.50	25.00
❑ 45884	Liar/Doing All Right	1974	5.00	10.00	20.00
❑ 45891	Seven Seas of Rhye/See What a Fool I've Been	1974	5.00	10.00	20.00
❑ 46008	Don't Stop Me Now/More of That Jazz	1979	—	3.00	6.00
❑ 46039	Jealousy/Fun It	1979	—	3.00	6.00
❑ 46532	We Will Rock You (Live)/Let Me Entertain You	1979	2.00	4.00	8.00
❑ 46579	Crazy Little Thing Called Love/				
	Spread Your Wings	1979	—	2.00	4.00
❑ 46652	Play the Game/A Human Body	1980	—	2.00	4.00
❑ 46652 [PS]	Play the Game/A Human Body	1980	—	2.50	5.00
❑ 47031	Another One Bites the Dust/Don't Try Suicide	1980	—	2.00	4.00
❑ 47086	Need Your Loving Tonight/Rock It (prime jive)	1980	—	2.00	4.00
❑ 47092	Flash's Theme AKA Flash/Football Fight	1980	—	2.00	4.00
❑ 47092 [PS]	Flash's Theme AKA Flash/Football Fight	1980	—	2.50	5.00
❑ 47235	Under Pressure/Soul Brother	1981	—	2.00	4.00

—*A-side with David Bowie*

❑ 47235 [PS]	Under Pressure/Soul Brother	1981	—	3.00	6.00
❑ 47452	Body Language/Life Is Real (Song for Lennon)	1982	—	2.00	4.00

—*Most copies of this did not come with picture sleeves*

❑ 47452 [PS]	Body Language/Life Is Real (Song for Lennon)	1982	2.50	5.00	10.00

—*All-white sleeve*

❑ 47452 [PS]	Body Language/Life Is Real (Song for Lennon)	1982	3.75	7.50	15.00

—*Nude bodies sleeve*

❑ 69941	Back Chat/Staying Power	1982	—	2.00	4.00
❑ 69941 [PS]	Back Chat/Staying Power	1982	—	2.50	5.00
❑ 69981	Calling All Girls/Put Out the Fire	1982	—	2.00	4.00
❑ 69981 [PS]	Calling All Girls/Put Out the Fire	1982	—	2.50	5.00

HOLLYWOOD

❑ 64725	We Are the Champions/				
	These Are the Days of Our Lives	1992	—	2.00	4.00
❑ 64794	Bohemian Rhapsody/The Show Must Go On	1992	—	2.00	4.00

Albums
CAPITOL

❑ ST-12322	The Works	1984	2.50	5.00	10.00
❑ SMAS-12476	A Kind of Magic	1986	2.50	5.00	10.00
❑ C1-92357	The Miracle	1989	3.75	7.50	15.00

DCC COMPACT CLASSICS

❑ LPZ-2072	A Night at the Opera	2000	6.25	12.50	25.00

—*Audiophile vinyl*

ELEKTRA

❑ 6E-101	A Day at the Races	1977	2.50	5.00	10.00

—*Butterfly, red, or red/black labels*

❑ 6E-112	News of the World	1977	2.50	5.00	10.00
❑ 6E-112 [DJ]	News of the World	1977	37.50	75.00	150.00

—*White label promo with oversize cover and press kit*

Number	Title (A Side/B Side)	Yr	VG	VG+	NM
❑ 6E-166	Jazz	1978	2.00	4.00	8.00

—*Without poster of the nude bicycle race. Some copies had a sticker on the shrink wrap with an address at which the poster was available free.*

❑ 6E-166	Jazz	1978	3.00	6.00	12.00

—*With poster of the nude bicycle race*

❑ 5E-513	The Game	1980	2.50	5.00	10.00

—*With dull gray cover; all copies have custom white labels*

❑ 5E-513	The Game	1980	3.75	7.50	15.00

—*With shiny, mirrorlike cover; all copies have custom white labels*

❑ 5E-564	Queen's Greatest Hits	1981	3.00	6.00	12.00
❑ BB-702 [(2)]	Live Killers	1979	3.00	6.00	12.00
❑ 7E-1026	Sheer Heart Attack	1974	2.50	5.00	10.00

—*Butterfly, red, or red/black labels*

❑ 7E-1026 [DJ]	Sheer Heart Attack	1974	12.50	25.00	50.00

—*White label promo*

❑ 7E-1053	A Night at the Opera	1975	2.50	5.00	10.00

—*Butterfly, red, or red/black labels*

❑ EQ-5064 [Q]	Queen	1973	10.00	20.00	40.00
❑ 60128	Hot Space	1982	2.50	5.00	10.00
❑ EKS-75064	Queen	1973	2.50	5.00	10.00

—*With "Queen" printed on the cover; butterfly, red, or red/black labels*

❑ EKS-75064	Queen	1973	7.50	15.00	30.00

—*With "Queen" gold-embossed on the cover*

❑ EKS-75064 [DJ]	Queen	1973	12.50	25.00	50.00

—*White label promo*

❑ EKS-75082	Queen II	1974	2.50	5.00	10.00

—*Butterfly, red, or red/black labels*

❑ EKS-75082 [DJ]	Queen II	1974	12.50	25.00	50.00

—*White label promo*

HOLLYWOOD

❑ ED-62005 [PD]	Queen at the BBC	1995	25.00	50.00	100.00

—*Promo-only picture disc (no U.S. stock vinyl)*

❑ 62017	Made in Heaven	1996	5.00	10.00	20.00

—*White vinyl; imported from Europe; the only distinguishing mark to make this a U.S. version is the Hollywood bar code, which was stuck to the shrink wrap*

MOBILE FIDELITY

❑ 1-067	A Night at the Opera	1980	20.00	40.00	80.00

—*Audiophile vinyl*

❑ 1-211	The Game	1995	7.50	15.00	30.00

—*Audiophile vinyl*

❑ 1-256	A Day at the Races	1996	12.50	25.00	50.00

—*Audiophile vinyl*

QUEEN, THE
45s
MERCURY

❑ 71389	Honky Tonky/Somewhere Along the Line	1958	5.00	10.00	20.00

QUEEN'S NECTORINE MACHINE, THE
45s
ABC

❑ 11172	I Got Trouble/Gypsy Lady	1969	3.75	7.50	15.00

Albums
ABC

❑ S-666	The Mystical Powers of Roving Tarot Gamble	1969	10.00	20.00	40.00

? (QUESTION MARK) AND THE MYSTERIANS
45s
ABKCO

❑ 4020	96 Tears/Can't Get Enough of You, Baby	1973	3.00	6.00	12.00

—*Reissue; contains full-length version of A-side (most Cameo singles are edited)*

❑ 4033	I Need Somebody/Girl (You Captivate Me)	1973	3.00	6.00	12.00

—*Reissue*

CAMEO

❑ 428	96 Tears/Midnight Hour	1966	3.75	7.50	15.00

—*Contains an early fade of the A-side and the LP version of the B-side; trail-off wax markings are "C 428 A R" and "C 428 B R"; composer of both songs listed as "The Mysterians"*

❑ 428	96 Tears/Midnight Hour	1966	5.00	10.00	20.00

—*Contains an early fade of the A-side and the LP version of the B-side; trail-off wax markings are "C 428 A R" and "C 428 B R"; composer of both songs listed as "Rudy Martinez"*

❑ 428	96 Tears/Midnight Hour	1966	7.50	15.00	30.00

—*Contains the LP version of the A-side and an alternate version (different vocal and words) of the B-side; trail-off wax markings are "C 428 A-1A" and "C 428 B-1B"*

❑ 428	96 Tears/Midnight Hour	1966	3.75	7.50	15.00

—*Label credit is "? and the Mysterians"; contains an early fade of the A-side (even though the time is listed as "2:53") and the LP version of the B-side; trail-off wax markings are "C 428 A" and "62831" on Side 1 and "C 428 B" and "62831-X" on Side 2; composer of both songs listed as "The Mysterians"*

❑ 441	I Need Somebody/"8" Teen	1966	3.75	7.50	15.00
❑ 467	Can't Get Enough of You, Baby/Smokes	1967	3.75	7.50	15.00
❑ 479	Girl (You Captivate Me)/Got To	1967	3.75	7.50	15.00
❑ 496	Do Something to Me/Love Me, Baby	1967	3.75	7.50	15.00

CAPITOL

❑ 2162	Make You Mine/I Love You, Baby (Like Nobody's Business)	1968	5.00	10.00	20.00

CHICORY

❑ 410	Talk Is Cheap/She Goes to Church on Sunday	1968	7.50	15.00	30.00

COLLECTABLES

❑ 4050	96 Tears/Midnight Hour	1997	—	2.00	4.00

—*Yellow-orange vinyl; new recordings by the original group*

LUV

❑ 159	Funky Lady/Hot N' Groovin'	1975	3.75	7.50	15.00

NORTON

❑ 45-083	Are You for Real?/I'll Be Back	1999	—	—	2.00

—*1966 demo recordings*

❑ 45-083 [PS]	Are You for Real?/I'll Be Back	1999	—	—	2.00
❑ 45-096	Sally Go Round the Roses/It's Not Easy	2000	—	—	2.00
❑ 45-096 [PS]	Sally Go Round the Roses/It's Not Easy	2000	—	—	2.00

PA-GO-GO

❑ 102	96 Tears/Midnight Hour	1965	175.00	350.00	700.00

SUPER K

❑ 102	Hang In/Sha La La	1969	3.75	7.50	15.00

QUICK, THE Featuring ERIC CARMEN.
45s
EPIC

❑ 10516	Ain't Nothing Gonna Stop Me/Southern Comfort	1969	6.25	12.50	25.00

Number	Title (A Side/B Side)	Yr	VG	VG+	NM

QUICKLY, TOMMY
45s
LIBERTY
| ❏ 55732 | It's As Simple As That/You Might As Well Forget Him | 1964 | 2.50 | 5.00 | 10.00 |
| ❏ 55753 | Wild Side of Life/Forget the Other Guy | 1964 | 2.50 | 5.00 | 10.00 |

QUICKSILVER MESSENGER SERVICE Includes records as "Quicksilver." Also see DINO VALENTI.
45s
CAPITOL
❏ 2194	Pride of Man/Dino's Song	1968	3.00	6.00	12.00
❏ 2320	Stand By Me/Bears	1968	3.00	6.00	12.00
❏ 2557	Who Do You Love/Which Do You Love	1969	3.00	6.00	12.00
❏ 2670	Words Can't Say/Holy Holy	1969	3.00	6.00	12.00
❏ 2800	Shady Grove/Three or Four Feet from Home	1970	2.50	5.00	10.00
❏ 2920	Fresh Air/Freeway Flyer	1970	2.50	5.00	10.00
❏ 3046	Good Old Rock and Roll/What About Me	1971	2.00	4.00	8.00
❏ 3233	Hope/I Found Love	1971	2.00	4.00	8.00
❏ 3349	Doin' Time in the U.S.A./Changes	1972	2.00	4.00	8.00
❏ 3417	Fresh Air/Freeway Flyer	1972	2.00	4.00	8.00
❏ 4206	Gypsy Lights/Witches' Moon	1976	—	3.00	6.00
Albums
CAPITOL
❏ ST-120	Happy Trails	1969	7.50	15.00	30.00
—Black label with colorband					
❏ ST-120	Happy Trails	1973	3.00	6.00	12.00
—Orange label					
❏ SKAO-391	Shady Grove	1969	6.25	12.50	25.00
—Lime green label					
❏ SKAO-391	Shady Grove	1973	3.00	6.00	12.00
—Orange label					
❏ SM-391	Shady Grove	1976	2.50	5.00	10.00
—Reissue on yellow label and new prefix					
❏ SMAS-498	Just for Love	1970	6.25	12.50	25.00
—Lime green label					
❏ SMAS-498	Just for Love	1973	3.00	6.00	12.00
—Orange label					
❏ SMAS-630	What About Me	1970	6.25	12.50	25.00
—Lime green label					
❏ SMAS-630	What About Me	1973	3.00	6.00	12.00
—Orange label					
❏ SW-819	Quicksilver	1971	6.25	12.50	25.00
—Red label with stylized "C" at top					
❏ SW-819	Quicksilver	1973	3.00	6.00	12.00
—Orange label					
❏ ST 2904	Quicksilver Messenger Service	1968	10.00	210.00	40.00
—Black label with colorband; glossy black cover with red and silver foil-like printing					
❏ ST-2904	Quicksilver Messenger Service	1969	5.00	10.00	20.00
—Lime green or red label					
❏ ST-2904	Quicksilver Messenger Service	1973	3.00	6.00	12.00
—Orange label					
❏ SMAS-11002	Comin' Thru	1972	3.75	7.50	15.00
❏ SVBB-11165 [(2)]Anthology		1973	5.00	10.00	20.00
❏ ST-11462	Solid Silver	1975	3.75	7.50	15.00
❏ SM-11820	Solid Silver	1978	2.50	5.00	10.00
—Reissue of 11462					
❏ ST-12496	Peace By Piece	1986	2.50	5.00	10.00
❏ SN-16089	Quicksilver Messenger Service	1980	2.00	4.00	8.00
—Budget-line reissue					
❏ SN-16090	Happy Trails	1980	2.00	4.00	8.00
—Budget-line reissue					
❏ SN-16091	Quicksilver	1980	2.00	4.00	8.00
—Budget-line reissue					
❏ SN-16092	What About Me	1980	2.00	4.00	8.00
—Budget-line reissue					
❏ SN-16093	Just for Love	1980	2.00	4.00	8.00
—Budget-line reissue					
❏ SN-16094	Shady Grove	1980	2.00	4.00	8.00
—Budget-line reissue					

QUILL
Albums
COTILLION
| ❏ SD 9017 | Quill | 1970 | 5.00 | 10.00 | 20.00 |

QUIN-TONES, THE
45s
HUNT
| ❏ 321 | Down the Aisle of Love/Please Dear | 1958 | 12.50 | 25.00 | 50.00 |
| ❏ 322 | There'll Be No Sorrow/What Am I to Do | 1958 | 15.00 | 30.00 | 60.00 |
RED TOP
| ❏ 108 | Down the Aisle of Love/Please Dear | 1958 | 10.00 | 20.00 | 40.00 |

Number	Title (A Side/B Side)	Yr	VG	VG+	NM

❏ 108	Down the Aisle of Love/Please Dear	1958	30.00	60.00	120.00
—Red label					
❏ 116	Heavenly Father/I Watch the Stars	1959	25.00	50.00	100.00

QUINN, CAROLE
45s
MGM
| ❏ K-13265 | Good Boy Gone Bad/What's So Sweet About Sweet Sixteen | 1964 | 2.50 | 5.00 | 10.00 |
| ❏ K-13326 | Do Those Little Things/I'll Do It for You | 1965 | 2.50 | 5.00 | 10.00 |

QUINNS, THE
45s
LOST-NITE
| ❏ 127 | Oh Starlight/Hong Kong | 196? | 2.00 | 4.00 | 8.00 |
| —Reissue | | | | | |

QUINTEROS, EDDIE
45s
BRENT
❏ 7009	Come Dance with Me/Vivian	1960	7.50	15.00	30.00
❏ 7012	Please Don't Go/Lookin' for My Baby	1960	8.75	17.50	35.00
❏ 7014	Slow Down Sandy/Lindy Lou	1960	12.50	25.00	50.00

QUINTESSENCE
Albums
ISLAND
| ❏ SMAS-9301 | Quintessence | 1971 | 6.25 | 12.50 | 25.00 |
| ❏ SW-9305 | Dive Deep | 1971 | 6.25 | 12.50 | 25.00 |

QUINTET, THE
Albums
UNITED ARTISTS
| ❏ UAS-5514 | Future Tense | 1971 | 3.75 | 7.50 | 15.00 |
| ❏ UAS-5599 | The Quintet | 1972 | 3.75 | 7.50 | 15.00 |

QUINTONES, THE (1)
45s
CHESS
| ❏ 1685 | I Try So Hard/Ding Dong | 1957 | 10.00 | 20.00 | 40.00 |

QUINTONES, THE (2)
45s
GEE
| ❏ 1009 | I'm Willing/Strange As It Seems | 1956 | 250.00 | 500.00 | 1000. |

QUINTONES, THE (3)
45s
PHILLIPS INT'L.
| ❏ 3586 | Times Sho' Gettin' Ruff/Softie | 1963 | 5.00 | 10.00 | 20.00 |

QUINTONES, THE (U)
45s
PARK
| ❏ 111/2 | South Sea Island/More Than a Notion | 1957 | 100.00 | 200.00 | 400.00 |

QUIVER Also see SUTHERLAND BROTHERS AND QUIVER.
Albums
WARNER BROS.
| ❏ WS 1939 | Quiver | 1971 | 3.75 | 7.50 | 15.00 |
| ❏ BS 2630 | Gone in the Morning | 1972 | 3.75 | 7.50 | 15.00 |

QUOTATIONS, THE Several different groups.
45s
ADMIRAL
| ❏ 753 | In the Night/Oh No, I Still Love Her | 1964 | 5.00 | 10.00 | 20.00 |
DEVENUS
| ❏ 107 | It Can Happen to You/You Don't Have to Worry | 1968 | 3.00 | 6.00 | 12.00 |
DOWNSTAIRS
| ❏ 1003 | Night/Why Do You Do Me Like You Do | 1970 | 2.00 | 4.00 | 8.00 |
IMPERIAL
| ❏ 66338 | Havin' a Good Time/Can I Have Someone | 1968 | 2.50 | 5.00 | 10.00 |
| ❏ 66368 | Havin' a Good Time (With My Baby)/Can I Have Someone (For Once) | 1969 | 2.50 | 5.00 | 10.00 |
LIBERTY
| ❏ 55527 | Listen, My Children, And You Shall Hear/Speak Softly and Carry a Big Horn | 1962 | 6.25 | 12.50 | 25.00 |
VERVE
❏ 10245	Imagination/Ala-Men-Say	1961	7.50	15.00	30.00
❏ 10252	This Love of Mine/We'll Reach Heaven Together	1962	7.50	15.00	30.00
❏ 10261	See You in September/Sumemrtime Goodbye	1962	12.50	25.00	50.00

Q

R

Number	Title (A Side/B Side)	Yr	VG	VG+	NM

R.P.S.
Albums
MARS

Number	Title (A Side/B Side)	Yr	VG	VG+	NM
❏ (# unknown)	R.P.S.	197?	20.00	40.00	80.00

RABBITT, EDDIE
45s
CAPITOL

Number	Title (A Side/B Side)	Yr	VG	VG+	NM
❏ NR-44527	On Second Thought/Only One Love in My Life	1990	—	—	—
—Reissue of Universal 66025; unreleased on vinyl?					
❏ NR-44538	Runnin' with the Wind/Feel Like a Stranger	1990	—	2.00	4.00
CAPITOL NASHVILLE					
❏ S7-19347	Rockin' Around the Christmas Tree/Have Yourself a Merry Little Christmas	1996	—	—	3.00
DATE					
❏ 2-1599	The Bed/Holding On	1968	3.00	6.00	12.00
❏ 2-1599 [PS]	The Bed/Holding On	1968	5.00	10.00	20.00
ELEKTRA					
❏ 378 [DJ]	Song of Ireland (same on both sides)	1978	3.75	7.50	15.00
—Promo only on green vinyl; small center hole					
❏ 45237	Forgive and Forget/Pure Love	1975	—	2.50	5.00
❏ 45269	I Should Have Married You/Sweet Janine	1975	—	2.50	5.00
❏ 45301	Drinkin' My Baby (Off My Mind)/When I Was Young	1976	—	2.50	5.00
❏ 45315	Rocky Mountian Music/Do You Right Tonight	1976	—	2.50	5.00
—Butterfly label; most, if not all, copies misspell "Mountain" as above					
❏ 45315	Rocky Mountian Music/Do You Right Tonight	1976	—	3.00	6.00
—Red label; most, if not all, copies misspell "Mountain" as above					
❏ 45357	Two Dollars in the Jukebox/Don't Wanna Make Love	1976	—	2.50	5.00
—Butterfly label					
❏ 45357	Two Dollars in the Jukebox/Don't Wanna Make Love	1976	—	3.00	6.00
—Red label					
❏ 45381	Could You Love a Poor Boy, Dolly/There's Someone She Lies To (To Lie Here with Me)	1977	—	3.00	6.00
❏ 45390	I Can't Help Myself/She Loves Me Like She Means It	1977	—	2.00	4.00
❏ 45418	We Can't Go On Living Like This/We Made Love Beautiful	1977	—	2.00	4.00
❏ 45461	Hearts on Fire/Girl on My Mind	1978	—	2.00	4.00
❏ 45488	You Don't Love Me Anymore/Caroline	1978	—	2.00	4.00
❏ 45531	I Just Want to Love You/Crossin' the Mississippi	1978	—	2.00	4.00
❏ 45554	Every Which Way But Loose/Under the Double Eagle	1978	—	2.00	4.00
❏ 45895	You Get to Me/Que Pasa	1974	—	2.50	5.00
❏ 46053	Suspicions/I Don't Want to Make Love (With Anyone But You)	1979	—	2.00	4.00
❏ 46558	Pour Me Another Tequila/I Will Never Let You Go	1979	—	2.00	4.00
❏ 46613	Gone Too Far/Loveline	1980	—	2.00	4.00
❏ 46656	Drivin' My Life Away/Pretty Lady	1980	—	2.00	4.00
❏ 47066	I Love a Rainy Night/Short Road to Love	1980	—	2.00	4.00
❏ 47174	Step By Step/My Only Wish	1981	—	2.00	4.00
❏ 47174 [PS]	Step By Step/My Only Wish	1981	—	3.00	6.00
❏ 47239	Someone Could Lose a Heart Tonight/Nobody Loves Me Like My Baby	1981	—	2.00	4.00
❏ 47435	I Don't Know Where to Start/Skip-A-Beat	1982	—	2.00	4.00
❏ 69936	You and I/All My Life, All My Love	1982	—	2.00	4.00
—A-side with Crystal Gayle					
RCA					
❏ 5012-7-R	Gotta Have You/Singing in the Subway	1986	—	—	3.00
❏ 5093-7-R	When We Make Love/(B-side unknown)	1987	—	—	3.00
❏ 5238-7-R	Wanna Dance with You/Gotta Have You	1987	—	—	3.00
❏ 8306-7-R	The Wanderer/Workin' Out	1988	—	—	3.00
❏ 8716-7-R	We Must Be Doing Something Right/He's a Cheater	1988	—	—	3.00
❏ 8819-7-R	That's Why I Fell in Love with You/She's An Old Cadillac	1988	—	—	3.00
❏ PB-14192	A World Without Love/1-2-3, You Really Got a Hold on Me (The Wrestling Song)	1985	—	—	3.00
❏ PB-14317	Repetitive Love/Letter from Home	1986	—	—	3.00
❏ PB-14377	Both to Each Other (Friends and Lovers)/A World Without Love	1986	—	—	3.00
—With Juice Newton					
❏ PB-14377 [PS]	Both to Each Other (Friends and Lovers)/A World Without Love	1986	—	2.50	5.00
20TH FOX					
❏ 474	Six Nights and Seven Days/Next to the Note	1964	5.00	10.00	20.00
UNIVERSAL					
❏ UVL-66025	On Second Thought/Only One Love in My Life	1989	—	2.00	4.00
WARNER BROS.					
❏ 28976	She's Comin' Back to Say Goodbye/Dial That Telephone	1985	—	2.00	4.00
❏ 29089	Warning Sign/Go to Sleep, Big Bertha	1985	—	2.00	4.00
❏ 29186	The Best Year of My Life/Over There	1984	—	2.00	4.00
❏ 29279	B-B-B-Burnin' Up with Love/747	1984	—	2.00	4.00
❏ 29431	Nothing Like Falling in Love/Gone Too Far	1983	—	2.00	4.00
❏ 29512	Our Love Will Survive/You Put the Beat in My Heart	1983	—	2.00	4.00
❏ 29712	You Can't Run from Love/You Got Me Now	1983	—	2.00	4.00
Albums					
ELEKTRA					
❏ CM-3	Eddie Rabbitt	1975	3.75	7.50	15.00
❏ 6E-127	Variations	1978	3.00	6.00	12.00
❏ 6E-181	Loveline	1979	2.50	5.00	10.00
❏ 6E-235	The Best of Eddie Rabbitt	1979	2.50	5.00	10.00
❏ 6E-276	Horizon	1980	2.50	5.00	10.00
❏ 5E-532	Step by Step	1981	2.50	5.00	10.00
❏ 7E-1065	Rocky Mountain Music	1976	3.75	7.50	15.00
—Butterfly label					
❏ 7E-1065	Rocky Mountain Music	198?	2.00	4.00	8.00
—Red label					

Number	Title (A Side/B Side)	Yr	VG	VG+	NM
❏ 7E-1105	Rabbitt	1977	3.75	7.50	15.00
—Butterfly label					
❏ 7E-1105	Rabbitt	198?	2.00	4.00	8.00
—Red label					
❏ 60160	Radio Romance	1982	2.50	5.00	10.00
RCA					
❏ 6373-1-R	I Wanna Dance with You	1988	2.00	4.00	8.00
RCA VICTOR					
❏ AHL1-7041	Rabbitt Trax	1986	2.00	4.00	8.00
WARNER BROS.					
❏ 6E-127	Variations	1983	2.00	4.00	8.00
—Reissue of Elektra LP					
❏ 6E-181	Loveline	1983	2.00	4.00	8.00
—Reissue of Elektra LP					
❏ 6E-235	The Best of Eddie Rabbitt	1983	2.00	4.00	8.00
—Reissue of Elektra LP					
❏ 6E-276	Horizon	1983	2.00	4.00	8.00
—Reissue of Elektra LP					
❏ 5E-532	Step by Step	1983	2.00	4.00	8.00
—Reissue of Elektra LP					
❏ 7E-1065	Rocky Mountain Music	1983	2.00	4.00	8.00
—Reissue of Elektra LP					
❏ 23925	Greatest Hits, Volume II	1983	2.50	5.00	10.00
❏ 25251	The Best Year of My Life	1984	2.50	5.00	10.00
❏ 25278	#1's	1985	2.50	5.00	10.00
❏ 60160	Radio Romance	1983	2.00	4.00	8.00
—Reissue of Elektra LP					

RABBLE, THE
Albums
ROULETTE

Number	Title (A Side/B Side)	Yr	VG	VG+	NM
❏ SR-42010	The Rabble	1968	37.50	75.00	150.00

RABIN, MIKE, AND THE DEMONS Also see FREDDIE AND THE DREAMERS.
45s
TOWER

Number	Title (A Side/B Side)	Yr	VG	VG+	NM
❏ 109	Head Over Heels/I'm Leaving You	1964	3.75	7.50	15.00

RACE MARBLES, THE
45s
TOWER

Number	Title (A Side/B Side)	Yr	VG	VG+	NM
❏ 194	Like a Dribbling Fram/Someday	1965	7.50	15.00	30.00

RACHEL AND THE REVOLVERS
45s
DOT

Number	Title (A Side/B Side)	Yr	VG	VG+	NM
❏ 16392	The Revo-Lution/Number One	1962	125.00	250.00	500.00
—Produced by Brian Wilson					

RACKET SQUAD, THE
45s
JUBILEE

Number	Title (A Side/B Side)	Yr	VG	VG+	NM
❏ 5591	Hung Up/Higher Than High	1967	7.50	15.00	30.00
❏ 5601	Little Red Wagon/(Just Like) Romeo and Juliet	1967	5.00	10.00	20.00
❏ 5613	The Loser/No Fair at All	1968	5.00	10.00	20.00
❏ 5623	Let's Dance to the Beat of My Heart/Higher Than High	1968	5.00	10.00	20.00
❏ 5628	That's How Much I Love My Baby/Movin' In	1968	5.00	10.00	20.00
❏ 5638	Suburban Life/The Loser	1968	5.00	10.00	20.00
❏ 5657	I'll Never Forget Your Love/(B-side unknown)	1969	5.00	10.00	20.00
❏ 5682	In Your Arms/(B-side unknown)	1969	7.50	15.00	30.00
❏ 5694	Roller Coaster Ride/Coal Town	1970	7.50	15.00	30.00
Albums					
JUBILEE					
❏ JGS-8015	The Racket Squad	1968	10.00	20.00	40.00
❏ JGS-8026	Corners of Your Mind	1969	10.00	20.00	40.00

RADHA KRISHNA TEMPLE
45s
APPLE

Number	Title (A Side/B Side)	Yr	VG	VG+	NM
❏ 1810	Hare Krishna Mantra/Prayer to the Spiritual Masters	1969	2.00	4.00	8.00
❏ 1810 [PS]	Hare Krishna Mantra/Prayer to the Spiritual Masters	1969	100.00	200.00	400.00
—Only one copy is known to exist. The price is highly speculative.					
❏ 1821	Govinda/Govinda Jai Jai	1970	2.00	4.00	8.00
❏ 1821	Govinda/Govinda Jai Jai	1970	2.50	5.00	10.00
—With Capitol logo on B-side label bottom					
❏ 1821 [PS]	Govinda/Govinda Jai Jai	1970	2.50	5.00	10.00
❏ PRO-5013/4 [DJ]	Govinda/Govinda Jai Jai	1970	6.25	12.50	25.00
—With an edit of the A-side					
❏ SPRO-5067/8 [DJ]	Govinda (Edit)/Govinda	1970	10.00	20.00	40.00
Albums					
APPLE					
❏ SKAO-3376	The Radha Krishna Temple	1971	5.00	10.00	20.00

RADIANTS, THE
45s
ABC

Number	Title (A Side/B Side)	Yr	VG	VG+	NM
❏ 12394	I Need a Vacation/Just Like You	1978	—	2.50	5.00
CHESS					
❏ 1832	Father Knows Best/One Day I'll SHow You	1962	3.75	7.50	15.00
❏ 1849	Please Don't Leave Me/Heartbreak Society	1963	3.75	7.50	15.00
❏ 1872	I'm in Love/Shy Guy	1963	3.75	7.50	15.00
❏ 1887	Noble the Bargain Man/I Got to Dance to Keep My Baby	1964	3.75	7.50	15.00
❏ 1904	Voice Your Choice/If I Only Had You	1964	3.00	6.00	12.00
❏ 1925	It Ain't No Big Thing/I Got a Girl	1965	3.00	6.00	12.00
❏ 1939	Whole Lot of Love/Tomorrow	1965	3.00	6.00	12.00
❏ 1954	I Want to Thank You, Baby/Baby You've Got It	1966	3.00	6.00	12.00
—As "Maurice and the Radiants"					
❏ 1986	(Don't It Make You) Feel Kind of Bad/Anything You Do Is Alright	1967	3.00	6.00	12.00
❏ 2021	Don't Take Your Love/The Clown Is Clever	1967	3.00	6.00	12.00
❏ 2037	Hold On/I'm Glad I'm the Loser	1968	3.00	6.00	12.00
❏ 2057	Tears of a Clown/I'm Just a Man	1968	3.00	6.00	12.00
❏ 2066	Choo Choo/Ida Mae Foster	1969	2.50	5.00	10.00

Number	Title (A Side/B Side)	Yr	VG	VG+	NM
❏ 2078	Book of Love/				
	Another Mule Is Kicking In Your Stall	1969	2.50	5.00	10.00
❏ 2083	I'm So Glad I'm the Loser/Shadow of a Doubt	1970	2.50	5.00	10.00
TWINIGHT					
❏ 153	My Sunshine Girl/Don't Wanna Face the Truth	1971	2.00	4.00	8.00

RAE, CHARLOTTE
Albums
VANGUARD

❏ VRS-9004 [M]	Songs I Taught My Mother	1956	10.00	20.00	40.00

RAELETTS, THE Backing vocalists for RAY CHARLES.
45s
TANGERINE

❏ 972	One Hurt Deserves Another/One Room Paradise	1967	2.00	4.00	8.00
❏ 976	Into Something Fine/Lover's Blues	1967	2.00	4.00	8.00
❏ 984	I'm Gett'n Long Alright/All I Need Is His Love	1968	2.00	4.00	8.00
❏ 986	I Want to Thank You/It's Almost Here	1968	2.00	4.00	8.00
❏ 1006	I Want To (Do Everything for You)/ Keep It to Yourself	1970	2.00	4.00	8.00
❏ 1014	Bad Water/That Goes to Show You	1970	2.00	4.00	8.00
❏ 1017	Here I Go Again/Leave My Man Alone	1971	2.00	4.00	8.00
❏ 1024	Come Get It, I Got It/Try a Little Kindness	197?	2.00	4.00	8.00
❏ 1029	You Must Be Doing Alright/ You Have a Way with Me	197?	2.00	4.00	8.00
❏ 1031	Many Rivers to Cross/If You Wanna Keep Him	197?	2.00	4.00	8.00
Albums					
TANGERINE					
❏ TRCS-1515	Yesterday, Today, Tomorrow	1972	3.75	7.50	15.00

RAFFERTY, GERRY Also see THE HUMBLEBUMS; STEALERS WHEEL
45s
BLUE THUMB

❏ 231	Can I Have My Money Back/ Sign on the Dotted Line	1973	2.00	4.00	8.00
LIBERTY					
❏ 1482	Good Intentions/Standing at the Gates	1982	—	2.00	4.00
SIGNPOST					
❏ 70001	Make You, Break You/Mary Skeffington	1972	2.50	5.00	10.00
UNITED ARTISTS					
❏ XW1098	Mattie's Rag/City to City	1977	—	2.50	5.00
❏ XW1192	Baker Street/Big Change in the Weather	1978	—	2.00	4.00
—Regular press with the edited, slightly sped-up version of "Baker Street" on A-side					
❏ XW1192	Baker Street/Big Change in the Weather	1978	2.00	4.00	8.00
—Mispress with the full-length album version of "Baker Street" on A-side There is no "E" in the trail-off wax.					
❏ XW1233	Right Down the Line/Waiting for the Day	1978	—	2.00	4.00
❏ XW1233 [PS]	Right Down the Line/Waiting for the Day	1978	—	2.50	5.00
❏ XW1266	Home and Dry/Mattie's Rag	1978	—	2.00	4.00
❏ XW1298	Days Gone Down (Still Got That Light in Your Eyes)/Why Won't You Talk to Me	1979	—	2.00	4.00
❏ 1316	Get It Right Next Time/ It's Gonna Be a Long Night	1979	—	2.00	4.00
❏ 1366	The Royal Mile/In Transit	1980	—	2.00	4.00
Albums					
ABC/BLUE THUMB					
❏ 6031	Can I Have My Money Back?	1978	3.00	6.00	12.00
BLUE THUMB					
❏ BTS-58	Can I Have My Money Back?	1973	5.00	10.00	20.00
LIBERTY					
❏ LO-840	City to City	1981	2.00	4.00	8.00
—Reissue of United Artists 840					
❏ LOO-958	Night and Day	1981	2.00	4.00	8.00
—Reissue of United Artists 958					
❏ LOO-1039	Snakes and Ladders	1981	2.00	4.00	8.00
—Reissue of United Artists 1039					
❏ LT-51132	Sleepwalking	1982	2.50	5.00	10.00
MOBILE FIDELITY					
❏ 1-058	City to City	1980	10.00	20.00	40.00
—Audiophile vinyl					
POLYDOR					
❏ 835449-1	North and South	1988	2.50	5.00	10.00
UNITED ARTISTS					
❏ UA-LA840-H	City to City	1978	2.50	5.00	10.00
❏ UA-LA958-I	Night Owl	1979	2.50	5.00	10.00
❏ LOO-1039	Snakes and Ladders	1980	2.50	5.00	10.00
VISA					
❏ 7006	Gerry Rafferty	1978	2.50	5.00	10.00
—Reissue of Blue Thumb material					

RAG DOLLS, THE
45s
MALA

❏ 493	Dusty/Hey Hoagy	1964	2.50	5.00	10.00
❏ 499	Baby's Gone/We Almost Made It	1965	2.50	5.00	10.00
❏ 506	Little Girl Tears/Put a Ring on My Finger	1965	2.50	5.00	10.00
PARKWAY					
❏ 921	Society Girl/Ragen (Society Girl Bossa Nova)	1964	3.00	6.00	12.00

RAGLAND, LOU
45s
AMY

❏ 988	Travel Alone/Big Wheel	1967	50.00	100.00	200.00

RAIDERS, THE (1) See PAUL REVERE AND THE RAIDERS.

RAIDERS, THE (2)
45s
ANDEX

❏ 4015	Yoo Hoo/Hocus Pocus	1958	30.00	60.00	120.00
ATCO					
❏ 6125	Raiders from Outer Space/The Castle of Love	1958	20.00	40.00	80.00
BRUNSWICK					
❏ 55090	Walking Through the Jungle/My Steady Girl	1958	10.00	20.00	40.00

RAIDERS, THE (3)
45s
LIBERTY

❏ 55393	Dardanella/What Time Is It	1961	7.50	15.00	30.00
Albums					
LIBERTY					
❏ LRP-3225 [M]	Twistin' the Country Classics	1962	6.25	12.50	25.00
❏ LST-7225 [S]	Twistin' the Country Classics	1962	7.50	15.00	30.00

RAIDERS, THE (4)
45s
SPRING-DALE

❏ 102	Raiders' Rhythm/Tall Texas Women	1964	12.50	25.00	50.00

RAIDERS, THE (5)
45s
VAN

❏ 00262	Stick Shift/Skipping Around	1962	12.50	25.00	50.00
❏ 00663	On a Straight Away/It's Motivation	1963	5.00	10.00	20.00
❏ 00763	Supercharger/Cruisin' Low	1963	5.00	10.00	20.00
❏ 01064	Raisin' Cain/Repetition	1964	5.00	10.00	20.00
VEE JAY					
❏ 504	Stick Shift/Skipping Around	1963	5.00	10.00	20.00

RAIN At least two different groups.
45s
A.P.I.

❏ 336	Outta My Life/E.S.P.	1967	10.00	20.00	40.00
❏ 337	Substitute/Hear You Cry	1967	10.00	20.00	40.00
BELL					
❏ 45206	Caught in the Middle of It/ Stop Me from Believing in You	1972	—	2.50	5.00
LONDON					
❏ 107	Outta My Life/E.S.P.	1967	6.25	12.50	25.00
❏ 111	Substitute/Hear You Cry	1967	7.50	15.00	30.00
MGM					
❏ 13622	Take It Away/City Lovin'	1966	6.25	12.50	25.00
PARAMOUNT					
❏ 0087	Show Me the Road Home/Funky Junky Blues	1971	5.00	10.00	20.00
Albums					
PROJECT 3					
❏ PR 5072 SD	New Rock Group	1972	6.25	12.50	25.00
WHAZOO					
❏ USR-3049	Live Christmas Night	1969	37.50	75.00	150.00
—Issued with no cover					

RAINBO Sissy Spacek is on this record.
45s
ROULETTE

❏ 7030	John You Went Too Far This Time/ C'mon Teach Me to Live	1969	5.00	10.00	20.00

RAINBOW
45s
MERCURY

❏ 76146	Stone Cold/Rock Fever	1982	—	2.00	4.00
❏ 76146 [PS]	Stone Cold/Rock Fever	1982	—	2.50	5.00
❏ 815660-7	Street of Dreams/Anybody There	1983	—	2.00	4.00
❏ 815660-7 [PS]	Street of Dreams/Anybody There	1983	—	2.00	4.00
POLYDOR					
❏ 2014	Since You Been Gone/Bad Girls	1979	—	2.00	4.00
❏ 2163	I Surrender/Vielleicht Das Nachster Leit	1981	—	2.00	4.00
❏ 14290	Snake Charmer/Man on the Silver Mountain	1975	—	3.00	6.00
—As "Blackmore's Rainbow"					
❏ 14481	Long Live Rock 'n Roll/Sensitive to Light	1978	—	2.00	4.00
Albums					
MERCURY					
❏ SRM-1-4041	Straight Between the Eyes	1982	2.50	5.00	10.00
❏ 815305-1	Bent Out of Shape	1983	2.50	5.00	10.00
❏ 827987-1 [(2)]	Finyl Vinyl	1986	3.00	6.00	12.00
OYSTER					
❏ OY-1-1601	Rainbow Rising	1976	3.00	6.00	12.00
❏ OY-2-1801 [(2)]	On Stage	1977	3.75	7.50	15.00
❏ OY-6049	Ritchie Blackmore's R-A-I-N-B-O-W	1975	3.00	6.00	12.00
POLYDOR					
❏ PX-1-502 [EP]	Jealous Lover	1981	2.00	4.00	8.00
❏ PD-1-6143	Long Live Rock 'n' Roll	1978	2.50	5.00	10.00
❏ PD-1-6221	Down to Earth	1979	2.50	5.00	10.00
❏ PD-1-6316	Difficult to Cure	1981	2.50	5.00	10.00
❏ 823655-1	Rainbow Rising	1985	2.00	4.00	8.00
—Reissue					
❏ 823656-1 [(2)]	On Stage	1985	2.50	5.00	10.00
—Reissue					
❏ 823705-1	Down to Earth	1985	2.00	4.00	8.00
—Reissue					
❏ 825089-1	Ritchie Blackmore's R-A-I-N-B-O-W	1985	2.00	4.00	8.00
—Reissue					
❏ 825090-1	Long Live Rock 'n' Roll	1985	2.00	4.00	8.00
—Reissue					
❏ 825383-1	Difficult to Cure	1985	2.00	4.00	8.00
—Reissue					
❏ 881516-1 [EP]	Jealous Lover	1985	—	3.00	6.00
—Reissue					

RAINBOW (2)
Albums
GNP CRESCENDO

❏ GNPS-2049	After the Storm	1969	6.25	12.50	25.00

RAINBOW PRESS, THE
45s
MR. G

❏ 817	There's a War On/Better Way	1968	3.75	7.50	15.00
❏ 821	Great White Whale/The Last Platoon	1969	3.75	7.50	15.00

R

Number	Title (A Side/B Side)	Yr	VG	VG+	NM
Albums					
MR. G					
❏ 9003	There's a War On	1968	7.50	15.00	30.00
❏ 9004	Sunday Funnies	1969	7.50	15.00	30.00
RAINBOW PROMISE, THE					
Albums					
NEW WINE					
❏ LPS-251-01	The Rainbow Promise	1970	75.00	150.00	300.00
RAINBOWS, THE (1)					
45s					
ARGYLE					
❏ 1012	Shirley/Stay	1962	6.25	12.50	25.00
FIRE					
❏ 1012	Mary Lee/Evening	1960	5.00	10.00	20.00
LOST-NITE					
❏ 340	Mary Lee/Evening	197?	—	2.50	5.00
—Reissue					
PILGRIM					
❏ 703	Mary Lee/Evening	1956	12.50	25.00	50.00
❏ 711	Shirley/Stay	1956	50.00	100.00	200.00
RAMA					
❏ 209	Minnie/They Say	1956	150.00	300.00	600.00
RED ROBIN					
❏ 134	Mary Lee/Evening	1955	150.00	300.00	600.00
—Note: Red Robin 141 is a bootleg					
RAINBOWS, THE (2)					
45s					
DAVE					
❏ 908	I Know/Only a Picture	1963	7.50	15.00	30.00
❏ 909	It Wouldn't Be Right/Family Monkey	1963	7.50	15.00	30.00
RAINBOWS, THE (3)					
45s					
DOT					
❏ 16612	My Ringo/He's Hooked on J's	1964	3.75	7.50	15.00
❏ 16920	Color of Love/Down the Block	1966	2.50	5.00	10.00
RAINBOWS, THE (4)					
45s					
EPIC					
❏ 9900	Balla Balla/Ju Ju Hand	1966	2.50	5.00	10.00
JAMIE					
❏ 1339	Balla Balla/Ju Ju Hand	1967	2.00	4.00	8.00
RAINBOWS, THE (U) Some of these could be by groups (2), (3) or (4).					
45s					
GRAMO					
❏ 5508	Till Tomorrow/Mama, Take Your Daughter Back	196?	5.00	10.00	20.00
MERCURY					
❏ 72068	Gonna Go Down/Dreamwalk	1962	3.75	7.50	15.00
MGM					
❏ 13058	Old Man's Twist/Straight Ahead	1962	5.00	10.00	20.00
RONNIE					
❏ 202	The Christmas Song/Love Me	19??	2.50	5.00	10.00
—B-side by the Mellow Moods					
RAINDROPS, THE (1) JEFF BARRY and ELLIE GREENWICH.					
45s					
JUBILEE					
❏ 5444	What a Guy/It's So Wonderful	1963	5.00	10.00	20.00
❏ 5455	The Kind of Boy You Can't Forget/Even Though You Can't Dance	1963	6.25	12.50	25.00
❏ 5466	That Boy John/Hanky Panky	1963	6.25	12.50	25.00
❏ 5469	Book of Love/I Won't Cry	1964	5.00	10.00	20.00
❏ 5475	Let;s Go Together/You Got What I Like	1964	5.00	10.00	20.00
❏ 5487	One More Tear/Another Boy Like Mine	1964	5.00	10.00	20.00
❏ 5497	Don't Let Go/My Mama Don't Like Him	1965	5.00	10.00	20.00
Albums					
JUBILEE					
❏ JGM-5023 [M]	The Raindrops	1963	37.50	75.00	150.00
❏ JGS-5023 [S]	The Raindrops	1963	75.00	150.00	300.00
RAINDROPS, THE (2)					
45s					
CAPITOL					
❏ F-4136	Rockababy Rock/Rain	1959	7.50	15.00	30.00
RAINDROPS, THE (3)					
45s					
CORSAIR					
❏ 104	Maybe/Love Is Like a Mountain	1960	20.00	40.00	80.00
DORE					
❏ 561	Maybe/Love Is Like a Mountain	1960	6.25	12.50	25.00
RAINDROPS, THE (4)					
45s					
IMPERIAL					
❏ 5785	I Remember in the Still of the Night/Sweet Song	1961	7.50	15.00	30.00
RAINDROPS, THE (5)					
45s					
SPIN-IT					
❏ 104	(I Found) Heaven in Love/I Prayed for Gold	1956	50.00	100.00	200.00
❏ 106	Little One/Rockin' on the Farm	1956	50.00	100.00	200.00
RAINDROPS, THE (U) Not sure which group this is.					
45s					
HAMILTON					
❏ 50021	Oh Why/Without Love, Love, Love	1960	5.00	10.00	20.00

Number	Title (A Side/B Side)	Yr	VG	VG+	NM
RAINWATER, MARVIN					
45s					
(NO LABEL)					
❏ MR 1 [DJ]	Hearts Hall of Fame//Gotta Go Get My Baby/ Albino Stallion	195?	25.00	50.00	100.00
—Called "Especially for Friends by Marvin Rainwater"; white label					
BRAVE					
❏ 1001	Part Time Lover/That Aching Heart	1963	2.50	5.00	10.00
—With Bill Guess					
❏ 1003	Love's Prison/These Thoughts of You	196?	2.50	5.00	10.00
—With Bill Guess					
❏ 1004	Bad Girl/I Saw Your New Love Today	196?	2.50	5.00	10.00
—With Bill Guess					
❏ 1017	The Old Gang's Gone/Run for Your Life Boy	196?	2.00	4.00	8.00
❏ 1028	Oklahoma Hills/Wedding Rings	196?	2.00	4.00	8.00
CORAL					
❏ 9-61342	I Gotta Go Get My Baby/ Daddy's Glad You Came Home	1955	5.00	10.00	20.00
HILLTOP					
❏ G-12	Tainted Gold/I Gotta Get to My Baby	196?	—	3.50	7.00
MGM					
❏ 12071	Sticks and Stones/Albino Stallion	1955	5.00	10.00	20.00
❏ 12090	Tennessee Houn' Dog Yodel/Tea Bag Romeo	1955	5.00	10.00	20.00
❏ 12152	Where Do We Go from Here/ Dem Low Down Blues	1955	5.00	10.00	20.00
❏ 12240	Hot and Cold/Mr. Blues	1956	10.00	20.00	40.00
❏ 12313	Why Did You Have to Go and Leave Me/What Am I Supposed to Do	1956	5.00	10.00	20.00
❏ 12370	Get Off the Stool/(Sometimes) I Feel Like Leaving Town	1956	7.50	15.00	30.00
❏ 12412	Gonna Find Me a Bluebird/ So You Think You've Got Troubles	1957	5.00	10.00	20.00
❏ 12511	My Brand of Blues/My Love Is Real	1957	5.00	10.00	20.00
❏ 12586	Lucky Star/Look for Me	1957	5.00	10.00	20.00
❏ 12609	Whole Lotta Woman/Baby Don't Go	1958	5.00	10.00	20.00
❏ 12653	Moanin' the Blues/Gamblin' Man	1958	6.25	12.50	25.00
❏ 12665	I Dig You Baby/Moanin' the Blues	1958	5.00	10.00	20.00
❏ 12701	Nothin' Needs Nothin' (Like I Need You)/(There's Always) A Need for Love	1958	5.00	10.00	20.00
❏ 12739	Lonely Island/Born to Be Lonesome	1958	5.00	10.00	20.00
❏ 12773	Love Me Baby (Like There's No Tomorrow)/ That's When I'll Stop Loving You	1959	5.00	10.00	20.00
❏ 12803	Half-Breed/A Song of Love	1959	5.00	10.00	20.00
❏ 12829	Young Girls/Valley of the Moon	1959	5.00	10.00	20.00
❏ 12865	Pale Faced Indian/Wayward Angel	1960	3.75	7.50	15.00
❏ 12891	Hard Luck Blues/She's Gone	1960	3.75	7.50	15.00
❏ 12938	You're Not Happy ('Til I'm Cryin')/ Yesterday's Kisses	1960	3.75	7.50	15.00
NU TRAYL					
❏ 902	Haircut/Looking Good	1976	—	3.00	6.00
RALPH HIMSELF					
❏ 17094	Little Ralph the Robot (Poem)/Little Ralph the Robot (Song)	197?	—	2.50	5.00
UNITED ARTISTS					
❏ 837	It Wasn't Enough/My Old Home Town	1965	2.50	5.00	10.00
❏ 917	Black Sheep/Indian Burial Ground	1965	2.50	5.00	10.00
❏ 50023	Sorrow Brings a Good Man Down/The Troubles My Little Boy Had	1966	2.50	5.00	10.00
WARNER BROS.					
❏ 7373	Let Me Live Again/I Love My Country	1970	—	3.50	7.00
WARWICK					
❏ 666	Boo Hoo/I Can't Forget	1961	10.00	20.00	40.00
❏ 674	Tough Top Cat/(There's a) Honky Tonk in Your Heart	1962	6.25	12.50	25.00
7-Inch Extended Plays					
MGM					
❏ X1464	(contents unknown)	1957	6.25	12.50	25.00
❏ X1464 [PS]	Songs by Marvin Rainwater, Vol. 1	1957	6.25	12.50	25.00
❏ X1465	Tennessee Houn' Dog Yodel/What Am I Supposed to Do//Why Did You Have to Go and Leave Me/Mr. Blues	1957	6.25	12.50	25.00
❏ X1465 [PS]	Songs by Marvin Rainwater Vol. 2	1957	6.25	12.50	25.00
❏ X1466	(contents unknown)	1957	6.25	12.50	25.00
❏ X1466 [PS]	Songs by Marvin Rainwater, Vol. 3	1957	6.25	12.50	25.00
Albums					
CROWN					
❏ CST-307 [R]	Marvin Rainwater	196?	3.00	6.00	12.00
❏ CLP-5307 [M]	Marvin Rainwater	196?	3.00	6.00	12.00
GUEST STAR					
❏ GS-1435 [M]	Country and Western Star	196?	3.00	6.00	12.00
MGM					
❏ E-3534 [M]	Songs by Marvin Rainwater	1957	37.50	75.00	150.00
❏ E-3721 [M]	Marvin Rainwater Sings with a Beat	1958	30.00	60.00	120.00
❏ E-4046 [M]	Gonna Find Me a Bluebird	1962	20.00	40.00	80.00
❏ SE-4046 [R]	Gonna Find Me a Bluebird	1962	12.50	25.00	50.00
SPIN-O-RAMA					
❏ SPM-109 [M]	Golden Country Hits	196?	3.00	6.00	12.00
RAINY DAYS, THE					
45s					
JUBILEE					
❏ 5517	He Was a Friend of Mine/Don't Want No Fool	1965	3.00	6.00	12.00
PANIK					
❏ 7542	Turn on Your Lovelight/Go On and Cry	1966	6.25	12.50	25.00
❏ 7566	I Can Only Give You Anything/(B-side unknown)	1966	6.25	12.50	25.00
RAINY DAZE, THE					
45s					
CHICORY					
❏ 404	That Acapulco Gold/In My Mind Lives a Forest	1967	3.75	7.50	15.00
UNI					
❏ 55002	That Acapulco Gold/In My Mind Lives a Forest	1967	2.50	5.00	10.00
❏ 55011	Discount City/Good Morning, Mr. Smith	1967	2.50	5.00	10.00
❏ 55026	Stop Sign/Blood of Oblivion	1967	2.50	5.00	10.00

Number	Title (A Side/B Side)	Yr	VG	VG+	NM

WHITE WHALE

| ❑ 279 | My Door Is Always Open/Make Me Laugh | 1968 | 2.50 | 5.00 | 10.00 |

Albums

UNI

| ❑ 3002 [M] | That Acapulco Gold | 1967 | 5.00 | 10.00 | 20.00 |
| ❑ 73002 [S] | That Acapulco Gold | 1967 | 6.25 | 12.50 | 25.00 |

RAITT, BONNIE

12-Inch Singles

WARNER BROS.

❑ PRO-A-1030 [DJ]	Me and the Boys (same on both sides)	1982	3.00	6.00	12.00
❑ PRO-A-2536 [DJ]	No Way to Treat a Lady (same on both sides)	1986	—	3.00	6.00
❑ PRO-A-2613 [DJ]	Who But a Fool (same on both sides)	1986	—	3.00	6.00
❑ PRO-A-2655 [DJ]	Crimes of Passion (same on both sides)	1986	—	3.00	6.00

45s

A&M

| ❑ 1249 | Baby Mine/Mickey Mouse March | 1988 | — | 2.00 | 4.00 |
| —A-side with Was (Not Was); B-side by Aaron Neville |
| ❑ 1249 [PS] | Baby Mine/Mickey Mouse March | 1988 | — | 2.00 | 4.00 |

ARISTA

| ❑ 12795 | You Got It/Feeling of Falling | 1995 | — | — | 3.00 |

CAPITOL

| ❑ S7-17818 | Love Sneakin' Up on You/Hell to Pay | 1994 | — | — | 3.00 |
| ❑ S7-18039 | You/Feeling of Falling | 1994 | — | 2.00 | 4.00 |
| —Red vinyl |
❑ S7-18299	Storm Warning/Longing in Their Hearts	1995	—	—	3.00
❑ B-44364	Nick of Time/The Road's My Middle Name	1989	—	2.00	4.00
❑ B-44365	Thing Called Love/The Road's My Middle Name	1989	—	2.00	4.00
❑ B-44365 [PS]	Thing Called Love/The Road's My Middle Name	1989	—	2.00	4.00
❑ NR-44729	I Can't Make You Love Me/Come to Me	1991	—	2.00	4.00
—White label, but not a promo
❑ S7-56799	All at Once/Come to Me	1992	—	2.00	4.00
❑ S7-57698	Not the Only One/All at Once	1992	—	2.00	4.00
❑ S7-57741	I Can't Make You Love Me/Something to Talk About	1992	—	2.00	4.00
❑ S7-57879	Good Man, Good Woman/Nick of Time	1992	—	2.00	4.00
—A-side: Duet with Delbert McClinton
❑ 58844	The Fundamental Things/Cold, Cold, Cold	2000	—	—	3.00
❑ 77731	I Can't Help You Now/Gnawin' On It	2002	—	2.00	4.00
❑ 7PRO-79940 [DJ]	Have a Heart (same on both sides)	1990	2.00	4.00	8.00
—Vinyl is promo only

FULL MOON

| ❑ 49612 | Once in a Lifetime/You're Only Lonely | 1980 | — | 2.00 | 4.00 |
| —B-side by J.D. Souther |

FULL MOON/ASYLUM

| ❑ 47033 | Don't It Make You Wanna Dance/Orange Blossom Special | 1980 | — | 2.50 | 5.00 |
| —B-side by Gilley's Urban Cowboy Band |
| ❑ 47033 [PS] | Don't It Make You Wanna Dance/Orange Blossom Special | 1980 | — | 3.00 | 6.00 |

REPRISE

| ❑ 1370 | When You Touch Me This Way/Since I've Been With You Babe | 1976 | — | 2.50 | 5.00 |
| —By Geoff Muldaur and Bonnie Raitt |

WARNER BROS.

❑ 7554	Bluebird/Women Be Wise	1972	2.00	4.00	8.00
❑ 7645	Too Long at the Fair/Under the Falling Sky	1972	2.00	4.00	8.00
❑ 7758	Everybody's Cryin' Mercy/You've Been in Love Too Long	1973	—	3.00	6.00
❑ 8044	I Got Plenty/You Got to Be Ready for Love	1974	—	3.00	6.00
❑ 8166	Good Enough/My First Night Alone Without You	1975	—	3.00	6.00
❑ 8189	Run Like a Thief/Walk Out the Front Door	1976	—	2.50	5.00
❑ 8382	Runaway/Louise	1977	—	2.50	5.00
❑ 8430	Two Lives/Three Time Loser	1977	—	2.50	5.00
❑ 8485	Gamblin' Man/About to Make Me Leave Home	1977	—	2.50	5.00
❑ 28450	Crimes of Passion/Stand Up to the Night	1987	—	2.00	4.00
❑ 28615	No Way to Treat a Lady/Stand Up to the Night	1986	—	2.00	4.00
❑ 29992	River of Tears/Me and the Boys	1982	—	2.00	4.00
❑ 49116	You're Gonna Get What's Comin'/The Glow	1979	—	2.00	4.00
❑ 49116 [PS]	You're Gonna Get What's Comin'/The Glow	1979	2.00	4.00	8.00
❑ 49185	Wild for You Baby/(I Could Have Been Your) Best Old Friend	1980	—	2.00	4.00
❑ 50022	Can't Get Enough/Keep This Heart in Mind	1982	—	2.00	4.00

Albums

CAPITOL

| ❑ C1-91268 | Nick of Time | 1989 | 3.00 | 6.00 | 12.00 |
| ❑ C1-96111 | Luck of the Draw | 1991 | 3.75 | 7.50 | 15.00 |

DCC COMPACT CLASSICS

| ❑ LPZ-2025 | Nick of Time | 1996 | 20.00 | 40.00 | 80.00 |
| —Audiophile vinyl |
| ❑ LPZ-2031 | Luck of the Draw | 1997 | 20.00 | 40.00 | 80.00 |
| —Audiophile vinyl |

WARNER BROS.

| ❑ WS 1953 | Bonnie Raitt | 1971 | 3.75 | 7.50 | 15.00 |
| —Green "WB" label |
| ❑ WS 1953 | Bonnie Raitt | 1973 | 3.00 | 6.00 | 12.00 |
| —"Burbank" palm trees label |
| ❑ WS 1953 | Bonnie Raitt | 1979 | 2.00 | 4.00 | 8.00 |
| —White or tan label |
| ❑ BS 2643 | Give It Up | 1972 | 3.75 | 7.50 | 15.00 |
| —Green "WB" label |
| ❑ BS 2643 | Give It Up | 1973 | 3.00 | 6.00 | 12.00 |
| —"Burbank" palm trees label |
| ❑ BS 2643 | Give It Up | 1979 | 2.00 | 4.00 | 8.00 |
| —White or tan label |
| ❑ BS 2729 | Takin' My Time | 1973 | 3.00 | 6.00 | 12.00 |
| —"Burbank" palm trees label |
| ❑ BS 2729 | Takin' My Time | 1979 | 2.00 | 4.00 | 8.00 |
| —White or tan label |
| ❑ BS 2818 | Streetlights | 1974 | 3.00 | 6.00 | 12.00 |
| —"Burbank" palm trees label |
| ❑ BS 2818 | Streetlights | 1979 | 2.00 | 4.00 | 8.00 |
| —White or tan label |
| ❑ BS 2864 | Home Plate | 1975 | 3.00 | 6.00 | 12.00 |
| —"Burbank" palm trees label |
| ❑ BS 2864 | Home Plate | 1979 | 2.00 | 4.00 | 8.00 |
| —White or tan label |
| ❑ BS 2990 | Sweet Forgiveness | 1977 | 3.00 | 6.00 | 12.00 |
| —"Burbank" palm trees label |
| ❑ BS 2990 | Sweet Forgiveness | 1979 | 2.00 | 4.00 | 8.00 |
| —White or tan label |
❑ HS 3369	The Glow	1979	3.00	6.00	12.00
❑ BSK 3630	Green Light	1982	3.00	6.00	12.00
❑ 25486	Nine Lives	1986	2.50	5.00	10.00

RAJAHS, THE

45s

KLIK

| ❑ 7805 | I Fell in Love/Shifting Sands | 1957 | 75.00 | 150.00 | 300.00 |

RALLY PACKS, THE STEVE BARRI and P.F. SLOAN with JAN AND DEAN.

45s

IMPERIAL

| ❑ 66036 | Move Out Little Mustang/Bucket Seats | 1964 | 15.00 | 30.00 | 60.00 |

RAM

45s

POLYDOR

| ❑ 14099 | The Want in You/Mother's Day Song | 1971 | 2.00 | 4.00 | 8.00 |

Albums

POLYDOR

| ❑ 24-5013 | Where (In Conclusion) | 1972 | 6.25 | 12.50 | 25.00 |

RAMAL, BILL

45s

MGM

| ❑ 13123 | Hard Times/Sax Fifth Ave. | 1963 | 2.50 | 5.00 | 10.00 |

20TH CENTURY FOX

| ❑ 432 | Exodus/Theme from "Dr. No" | 1963 | 2.50 | 5.00 | 10.00 |

RAMATAM

45s

ATLANTIC

| ❑ 2916 | Changing Days/Wild Like Wind | 1972 | — | 2.50 | 5.00 |

Albums

ATLANTIC

| ❑ SD 7236 | Ramatam | 1972 | 3.75 | 7.50 | 15.00 |
| ❑ SD 7261 | In April Came the Dawning of the Red Suns | 1973 | 3.75 | 7.50 | 15.00 |

RAMBEAU, EDDIE

45s

BELL

| ❑ 847 | Who Will Buy-Where Is Love/Solitary Man | 1969 | — | 3.00 | 6.00 |
| ❑ 873 | Don't Leave Me/Solitary Man | 1970 | — | 3.00 | 6.00 |

DYNO VOICE

❑ 204	Concrete and Clay/Don't Believe Him	1965	2.50	5.00	10.00
❑ 207	I Just Need Your Love/My Name Is Mud	1965	2.00	4.00	8.00
❑ 211	The Train/Yesterday's Newspapers	1966	2.00	4.00	8.00
❑ 217	I Just Need Your Love/I'm the Sky	1966	2.00	4.00	8.00
❑ 221	I Miss You/Thinkin' About You Baby	1966	2.00	4.00	8.00
❑ 225	The Clock/If I Were You	1966	2.00	4.00	8.00

SWAN

❑ 4077	Skin Divin'/Toni	1961	2.50	5.00	10.00
❑ 4105	My Four Leaf Clover/Anyone Want More Flowers	1962	2.50	5.00	10.00
❑ 4112	Summertime Guy/Last Night Was My Last Night with You	1962	2.50	5.00	10.00
❑ 4145	Lover's Medley/The Car Hop and the Hard Top	1963	2.50	5.00	10.00

20TH CENTURY FOX

| ❑ 491 | Come Closer/She's Smilin' at Me | 1964 | 2.50 | 5.00 | 10.00 |

Albums

DYNO VOICE

| ❑ 9001 [M] | Concrete and Clay | 1965 | 5.00 | 10.00 | 20.00 |
| ❑ DS-9001 [S] | Concrete and Clay | 1965 | 6.25 | 12.50 | 25.00 |

RAMBLERS, THE (1)

45s

ADDIT

| ❑ 1257 | Rambling/Devil Train | 1960 | 7.50 | 15.00 | 30.00 |

RAMBLERS, THE (2)

45s

ALMONT

❑ 311	Father Sebastian/Barbara (I Loved You)	1964	6.25	12.50	25.00
❑ 313	School Girl/Birdland Baby	1964	5.00	10.00	20.00
❑ 315	Surfin' Santa/Silly Little Boy	1964	6.25	12.50	25.00

RAMBLERS, THE (3)

45s

FEDERAL

| ❑ 12286 | Don't You Know?/The Heaven and Earth | 1957 | 37.50 | 75.00 | 150.00 |

RAMBLERS, THE (4)

45s

JAX

| ❑ 319 | Search My Heart/50-50 Love | 1953 | 125.00 | 250.00 | 500.00 |
| —Red vinyl |

RAMBLERS, THE (5)

45s

MGM

| ❑ 11850 | Vadunt-Un-Va-Da Song (Oui Oui Baby)/Please Bring Yourself Back Home | 1954 | 75.00 | 150.00 | 300.00 |
| ❑ 55006 | Bad Girl/Rickey-Do, Rickey-Do | 1955 | 37.50 | 75.00 | 150.00 |

RAMBLERS, THE (6)

45s

TRUMPET

| ❑ 102 | So Sad/Come On Back | 1963 | 250.00 | 500.00 | 1000. |

R

Number	Title (A Side/B Side)	Yr	VG	VG+	NM

RAMBLERS, THE (U) Some of these could be by some of the above groups.
45s
IMPACT

❑ 10	Yaba Daba Ah Doo/Funny Papers	1961	6.25	12.50	25.00

RCA VICTOR

❑ 47-5240	Mama He Treats Your Daughter Mean/ And the Bull Walked Around Olay	1953	100.00	200.00	400.00

SIDEWINDER

❑ 101	Ticonderoga/Mozart Stomp	1964	10.00	20.00	40.00

RAMISTELLA, JOHNNY See JOHNNY RIVERS.

RAMRODS
45s
AMY

❑ 813	(Ghost) Riders in the Sky/Zig Zag	1961	6.25	12.50	25.00
❑ 817	Loch Lomond Rock/ Take Me Back to My Boots and Saddle	1961	5.00	10.00	20.00
❑ 846	War Cry/Boing!	1962	5.00	10.00	20.00

QUEEN

❑ 240145	Slee-Zee/Slouchee	1962	5.00	10.00	20.00

R&H

❑ 1001	Moonlight Surf/Night Ride	1963	12.50	25.00	50.00

RAMS, THE
45s
FLAIR

❑ 1066	Sweet Thing/Rock Bottom	1955	37.50	75.00	150.00

RAN-DELLS, THE
45s
CHAIRMAN

❑ 4403	Martian Hop/Forgive Me, Darling (I Have Lied)	1963	5.00	10.00	20.00
❑ 4403 [PS]	Martian Hop/Forgive Me, Darling (I Have Lied)	1963	12.50	25.00	50.00
❑ 4407	Sound of the Sun/Come On and Love Me	1964	3.75	7.50	15.00

R.S.V.P.

❑ 1104	Beyond the Stars/Wintertime	1964	3.75	7.50	15.00

RANCHEROS, THE
45s
DOT

❑ 16572	Linda's Tune/Little Linda	1964	6.25	12.50	25.00

LONNIE

❑ 5005	Linda's Tune/Little Linda	1963	12.50	25.00	50.00

RANDAZZO, TEDDY Also see THE THREE CHUCKLES.
45s
ABC-PARAMOUNT

❑ 9998	Papito/You Are Always in My Heart	1959	3.00	6.00	12.00
❑ 10014	Laughing on the Outside/Awkward Age	1959	3.00	6.00	12.00
❑ 10043	Lies/I'm On a Merry-Go Round	1959	3.00	6.00	12.00
❑ 10068	How I Need You/You Don't Care Anymore	1959	3.00	6.00	12.00
❑ 10088	The Way of a Clown/Cherie	1960	3.00	6.00	12.00
❑ 10103	Triste Pagliaccio (The Way of a Clown)/Cherie	1960	3.75	7.50	15.00
❑ 10127	But You Broke My Heart/Misery	1960	3.00	6.00	12.00
❑ 10131	Journey of Love/Misery	1960	3.00	6.00	12.00
❑ 10193	Happy Ending/But You Broke My Heart	1961	2.50	5.00	10.00
❑ 10228	Broken Bell/Let the Sunshine In	1961	2.50	5.00	10.00
❑ 10247	Don't Go Away/One More Chance	1961	2.50	5.00	10.00
❑ 10287	Mother Goose Twist/It's a Pity to Say Goodbye	1961	2.50	5.00	10.00
❑ 10312	Teenage Senorita/Blue Hawaii Moon	1962	2.50	5.00	10.00
❑ 10350	Dance to the Locomotion/Cotton Fields	1962	2.50	5.00	10.00
❑ 10377	Echoes/It Wasn't a Dream	1962	2.50	5.00	10.00

COLPIX

❑ 662	Big Wide World/Be Sure My Love	1962	3.00	6.00	12.00
❑ 684	Dear Heart/Just Hold My Hand	1963	2.50	5.00	10.00

DCP

❑ 1003	Pretty Blue Eyes/Doo Dah	1964	2.00	4.00	8.00
❑ 1108	Less Than Tomorrow/Lost Without You	1964	2.00	4.00	8.00
❑ 1134	You Don't Need a Heart/As Long As I Live	1965	2.00	4.00	8.00
❑ 1153	You're Not That Girl Anymore/Soul	1966	2.00	4.00	8.00

MGM

❑ 13448	Lara's Theme/The Old and the New	1966	2.00	4.00	8.00
❑ 13449	Theme from "A Patch of Blue"/ The Old and the New	1966	2.00	4.00	8.00
❑ 13511	Watch What Happens/Per Un Pugno Di Dollari	1966	2.00	4.00	8.00
❑ 13648	I'm Losing You/Trick or Treat	1966	2.00	4.00	8.00
❑ 13682	A Fistful of Dollars/Take Me Back	1967	2.00	4.00	8.00

VERVE FOLKWAYS

❑ 5050	A World Without Love/Just One More Time	1967	2.00	4.00	8.00

VIK

❑ 0277	Next Stop Paradise/How Could You Know?	1957	3.00	6.00	12.00
❑ 0289	Kiddio/I Was the Last One to Know	1957	3.00	6.00	12.00
❑ 0310	I'll Never Smile Again/Red Ruby Lips	1957	3.00	6.00	12.00
❑ 0319	Dutch Treat/To Belong	1958	3.00	6.00	12.00
❑ 0330	Little Serenade/Be My Kitten, Little Chicken	1958	3.75	7.50	15.00

Albums
ABC-PARAMOUNT

❑ 352 [M]	Journey to Love	1961	7.50	15.00	30.00
❑ S-352 [S]	Journey to Love	1961	10.00	20.00	40.00
❑ 421 [M]	Teddy Randazzo Twists	1962	7.50	15.00	30.00
❑ S-421 [S]	Teddy Randazzo Twists	1962	10.00	20.00	40.00

COLPIX

❑ CP-445 [M]	Big Wide World	1963	7.50	15.00	30.00
❑ SCP-445 [S]	Big Wide World	1963	10.00	20.00	40.00

VIK

❑ LX-1121 [M]	I'm Confessin'	1958	50.00	100.00	200.00

RANDELL, BUDDY
45s
UNI

❑ 55209	Be My Baby/Randi Randi	1970	—	3.00	6.00

RANDELL, LYNNE
45s
ABC

❑ 11112	Open Letter/Right to Cry	1968	5.00	10.00	20.00

EPIC

❑ 10147	Stranger in My Arms/Ciao Baby	1967	7.50	15.00	30.00
❑ 10197	I Need You Boy/That's a Hoe-Down	1967	7.50	15.00	30.00

RANDOLPH, BARBARA
45s
SOUL

❑ 35038	I Got a Feeling/You Got Me Hurtin' All Over	1967	5.00	10.00	20.00
❑ 35050	Can I Get a Witness/You Got Me Hurtin' All Over	1968	5.00	10.00	20.00

RANDOLPH, BOOTS
45s
MONUMENT

❑ 45-209	Honky Tonk/Memphis	1977	—	2.00	4.00
❑ 45-227	Jive Talkin'/Blueberry Hill	1977	—	2.00	4.00
❑ 45-263	You Light Up My Life/Movin' On Up	1978	—	2.00	4.00
❑ 45-294	I Write the Songs/Motherland-Oluwa	1980	—	2.00	4.00
❑ 443	Fancy Dan/Hey, Daddy Daddy	1961	2.50	5.00	10.00
❑ 460	Bluebird of Happiness/Keep a Light in Your Window Tonight	1962	2.50	5.00	10.00
❑ 804	Yakety Sax/I Really Don't Want to Know	1963	2.50	5.00	10.00
❑ 821	Lonely Street/Windy and Warm	1963	2.00	4.00	8.00
❑ 835	Hey, Mr. Sax Man/Baby, Go to Sleep	1964	2.00	4.00	8.00
❑ 852	Mickey's Tune/ I'll Take You Home Again, Kathleen	1964	2.00	4.00	8.00
❑ 884	King of the Road/Theme from a Dream	1965	2.00	4.00	8.00
❑ 928	These Boots Are Made for Walking/ Honey in Your Heart	1966	2.00	4.00	8.00
❑ 950	Yodeling Sax/Miss You	1966	2.00	4.00	8.00
❑ 976	The Shadow of Your Smile/I'll Just Walk Away	1966	2.00	4.00	8.00
❑ 1009	Temptation/You've Lost That Lovin' Feelin'	1967	—	3.00	6.00
❑ 1038	Love Letters/Big Daddy	1967	—	3.00	6.00
❑ 1056	Wonderland by Night/Fred	1968	—	3.00	6.00
❑ 1081	Gentle on My Mind/Jackson	1968	—	3.00	6.00
❑ 1125	Games People Play/By the Time I Get to Phoenix	1969	—	3.00	6.00
❑ 1165	Hey Jude/Down Yonder	1969	—	3.00	6.00
❑ 1176	Sleigh Ride/White Christmas	1969	2.00	4.00	8.00
❑ 1199	Spanish Harlem/Anna	1970	—	2.50	5.00
❑ 1219	Sunday Morning Coming Down/ Those Were the Days	1970	—	2.50	5.00
❑ 1226	Proud Mary/Without Love (There Is Nothing)	1970	—	2.50	5.00
❑ 1233	Take a Letter Maria/See See Rider	1970	—	2.50	5.00
❑ 1937	Sleigh Ride/White Christmas		—	2.00	4.00

—Golden Series

❑ 8500	My Sweet Lord/(B-side unknown)	1971	—	2.50	5.00
❑ 8534	Lookin'/Alligator Annie	1972	—	2.50	5.00
❑ 8541	Lonesome Ladies/Mountain Minuet	1972	—	2.00	4.00
❑ 8552	Love Theme from "The Godfather"/Rocky Top	1972	—	2.00	4.00
❑ 8588	Marie/Sentimental Journey	1973	—	2.00	4.00
❑ 8616	Behind Closed Doors/Old Joe Clarke	1974	—	2.00	4.00
❑ 8632	Sleigh Ride/White Christmas	1974	—	2.50	5.00
❑ 8634	Sanford & Son Theme/Ebb Tide	1974	—	2.50	5.00

RCA VICTOR

❑ 47-7278	Difficult/I'm Getting Your Message Baby	1958	3.75	7.50	15.00
—As "Randy Randolph"					
❑ 47-7395	Yakety Sax/Percolator	1958	5.00	10.00	20.00
—As "Randy Randolph"					
❑ 47-7515	Blue Guitar/Greenback Dollar	1959	3.00	6.00	12.00
—As "Randy Randolph"					
❑ 47-7611	Temptation/Sweet Talk	1959	3.00	6.00	12.00
❑ 47-7721	Red Light/La Golondrina	1960	3.00	6.00	12.00
❑ 47-7835	Bog Daddy/Bongo Band	1961	3.00	6.00	12.00

7-Inch Extended Plays
MONUMENT

❑ SMN-361 [DJ]	Sleigh Ride/Rudolph The Red-Nosed Reindeer/ /White Christmas/I'll Be Home For Christmas	1969	5.00	10.00	20.00

Albums
MONUMENT

❑ DS 632	King of Yakety	197?	3.75	7.50	15.00
—Manufactured by CBS Direct Marketing Services					
❑ 6600	Boots Randolph's Yakety Sax	197?	2.50	5.00	10.00
—Reissue of 18002					
❑ 6601	Hip Boots	197?	2.50	5.00	10.00
—Reissue of 18015					
❑ 6602	Boots Randolph Plays More Yakety Sax	197?	2.50	5.00	10.00
—Reissue of 18037					
❑ 6603	The Fantastic Boots Randolph	197?	2.50	5.00	10.00
—Reissue of 18042					
❑ 6604	Boots with Strings	197?	2.50	5.00	10.00
—Reissue of 18066					
❑ MC 6605	Sax-Sational	1976	2.50	5.00	10.00
—Reissue of 18079					
❑ 6606	Boots Randolph with the Knightsbridge Strings & Voices	197?	2.50	5.00	10.00
—Reissue of 18082					
❑ 6607	Sunday Sax	197?	2.50	5.00	10.00
—Reissue of 18092					
❑ 6608	The Sound of Boots	197?	2.50	5.00	10.00
—Reissue of 18099					
❑ 6609	...With Love/The Seductive Sax of Boots Randolph	197?	2.50	5.00	10.00
—Reissue of 18111					
❑ 6610	Boots and Stockings	197?	2.50	5.00	10.00
—Reissue of 18127					
❑ 6611	Yakety Revisited	197?	2.50	5.00	10.00
—Reissue of 18128					
❑ 6612	Hit Boots 1970	197?	2.50	5.00	10.00
—Reissue of 18144					
❑ 6613	Boots with Brass	197?	2.50	5.00	10.00
—Reissue of 18147					
❑ 6614	Homer Louis Randolph, III	197?	2.50	5.00	10.00
—Reissue of 30678					
❑ 6615	Boots Randolph Plays the Great Hits of Today	197?	2.50	5.00	10.00
—Reissue of 31908					
❑ 6616	Sentimental Journey	197?	2.50	5.00	10.00
—Reissue of 32292					

Number	Title (A Side/B Side)	Yr	VG	VG+	NM
❏ 6617	Country Boots	197?	2.50	5.00	10.00
—Reissue of 32912					
❏ 6618	Cool Boots	197?	2.50	5.00	10.00
—Reissue of 33803					
❏ 7602	Greatest Hits	1977	2.50	5.00	10.00
❏ 7611	Sax Appeal	1977	2.50	5.00	10.00
❏ 7627	Put a Little Sax	1978	2.50	5.00	10.00
❏ MLP-8002 [M]	Boots Randolph's Yakety Sax	1963	5.00	10.00	20.00
❏ MLP-8015 [M]	Hip Boots	1964	3.75	7.50	15.00
❏ MLP-8029 [M]	12 Monstrous Sax Hits	1965	3.75	7.50	15.00
❏ MLP-8037 [M]	Boots Randolph Plays More Yakety Sax	1965	3.75	7.50	15.00
❏ MLP-8042 [M]	The Fantastic Boots Randolph	1966	3.75	7.50	15.00
❏ MLP-8066 [M]	Boots with Strings	1966	3.75	7.50	15.00
❏ MLP-8079 [M]	Sax-Sational	1967	5.00	10.00	20.00
❏ MLP-8082 [M]	Boots Randolph with the Knightsbridge Strings & Voices	1967	5.00	10.00	20.00
❏ 8604 [(2)]	Party Boots	197?	3.00	6.00	12.00
—Reissue of 34082					
❏ SLP-18002 [S]	Boots Randolph's Yakety Sax	1963	6.25	12.50	25.00
❏ SLP-18015 [S]	Hip Boots	1964	5.00	10.00	20.00
❏ SLP-18029 [S]	12 Monstrous Sax Hits	1965	5.00	10.00	20.00
❏ SLP-18037 [S]	Boots Randolph Plays More Yakety Sax	1965	5.00	10.00	20.00
❏ SLP-18042 [S]	The Fantastic Boots Randolph	1966	5.00	10.00	20.00
❏ SLP-18066 [S]	Boots with Strings	1966	5.00	10.00	20.00
❏ SLP-18079 [S]	Sax-Sational	1967	3.75	7.50	15.00
❏ SLP-18082 [S]	Boots Randolph with the Knightsbridge Strings & Voices	1967	3.75	7.50	15.00
❏ SLP-18092	Sunday Sax	1968	5.00	10.00	20.00
❏ SLP-18099	The Sound of Boots	1968	5.00	10.00	20.00
❏ SLP-18111	…With Love/The Seductive Sax of Boots Randolph	1969	3.75	7.50	15.00
❏ SLP 18127	Boots and Stockings	1969	3.75	7.50	15.00
❏ SLP-18128	Yakety Revisited	1969	3.75	7.50	15.00
❏ SLP-18144	Hit Boots 1970	1970	3.75	7.50	15.00
❏ SLP-18147	Boots with Brass	1970	3.75	7.50	15.00
❏ Z 30678	Homer Louis Randolph, III	1971	3.00	6.00	12.00
❏ Z2 30964 [(2)]	The World of Boots Randolph	1971	3.75	7.50	15.00
❏ KZ 31908	Boots Randolph Plays the Great Hits of Today	1972	3.00	6.00	12.00
❏ KZ 32292	Sentimental Journey	1973	3.00	6.00	12.00
❏ KZ 32912	Country Boots	1974	3.00	6.00	12.00
❏ KZ 33298	Boots Randolph's Yakety Sax	1974	3.00	6.00	12.00
❏ KZ 33803	Cool Boots	1975	3.00	6.00	12.00
❏ Z2 34082 [(2)]	Party Boots	1976	3.75	7.50	15.00
❏ PW 38388	Greatest Hits	1983	2.50	5.00	10.00
❏ JW 38396	Dedication	1983	2.50	5.00	10.00
RCA CAMDEN					
❏ CAL-825 [M]	Yakin' Sax Man	1964	3.75	7.50	15.00
❏ CAS-825 [S]	Yakin' Sax Man	1964	3.75	7.50	15.00
❏ CAL-865 [M]	Sweet Talk	1965	3.75	7.50	15.00
❏ CAS-865 [R]	Sweet Talk	1965	3.00	6.00	12.00
❏ ACL-9003 [(2)]	Yakety Sax	1972	3.00	6.00	12.00
RCA VICTOR					
❏ LPM-2165 [M]	Yakety Sax	1960	10.00	20.00	40.00
❏ LSP-2165 [S]	Yakety Sax	1960	12.50	25.00	50.00

RANDOLPH, WILLIAM
45s
HIT

❏ 173	Song of Love/The Wedding	1965	2.00	4.00	8.00
—B-side by Betty Coleson					
❏ 188	Swinging Spiritual/No Arms Can Ever Hold You	1965	2.00	4.00	8.00
—B-side by Danny Woods					
❏ 196	Madrid/Red Roses for a Blue Lady	1965	2.00	4.00	8.00
❏ 201	I'm in a Very Romantic Mood/I Know a Place	1965	2.00	4.00	8.00
—B-side by Betty Coleson					
❏ 205	Theme from "Peyton Place"/Tower Suite	1965	2.00	4.00	8.00
❏ 214	Come Back to Me/I'll Never Find Another You	1965	2.00	4.00	8.00
—B-side by the Broadway Singers					

RANDY AND THE RADIANTS
45s
SUN

❏ 395	The Mountain's High/Peek-a-Boo	1965	6.25	12.50	25.00
❏ 398	My Way of Thinking/Truth from My Eyes	1966	6.25	12.50	25.00

RANDY AND THE RAINBOWS
45s
AMBIENT SOUND

❏ 02872	Debbie/Try the Impossible	1982	—	2.50	5.00
B.T. PUPPY					
❏ 535	I'll Be Seeing You/Oh to Get Away	1967	2.50	5.00	10.00
MIKE					
❏ 4001	Lovely Lies/I'll Forget Her Tomorrow	1966	3.00	6.00	12.00
❏ 4004	Quarter to Three/He's a Fugitive	1966	3.00	6.00	12.00
❏ 4008	Bonnie's Part of Town/Can It Be	1966	3.00	6.00	12.00
RUST					
❏ 5059	Denise/Come Back	1963	5.00	10.00	20.00
—Mostly white label					
❏ 5059	Denise/Come Back	1963	7.50	15.00	30.00
—Blue label					
❏ 5073	She's My Angel/Why Do Kids Grow Up	1964	3.75	7.50	15.00
❏ 5080	Happy Teenager/Dry Your Eyes	1964	3.75	7.50	15.00
❏ 5091	Little Star/Sharin'	1964	3.75	7.50	15.00
❏ 5101	Joy Ride/Little Hot Rod Suzie	1965	3.75	7.50	15.00

Albums
AMBIENT SOUND

❏ ASR-601	Remember	1985	3.00	6.00	12.00
❏ FZ 37715	C'mon, Let's Go	1982	3.00	6.00	12.00

RANDY AND THE ROCKETS
45s
AZALEA

❏ 138	Over the Waves/New Chapel Hill	196?	5.00	10.00	20.00
JIN					
❏ 161	Let's Do the Cajun Twist/Rockets' Twist	196?	3.75	7.50	15.00
❏ 165	No More Trouble/Bye Bye Baby	196?	3.75	7.50	15.00

Number	Title (A Side/B Side)	Yr	VG	VG+	NM
VIKING					
❏ 1000	If You Really Care/Genevieve	1959	5.00	10.00	20.00
❏ 1003	Is It True/Crazy Notion	1959	5.00	10.00	20.00
❏ 1004	That's Life/Sweet Love	1959	5.00	10.00	20.00

RANGERS, THE
45s
CHALLENGE

❏ 59229	Snow Skiing/Mogul Monster	1964	5.00	10.00	20.00
❏ 59239	Justine/Reputation	1964	5.00	10.00	20.00
FTP					
❏ 404	Four on the Floor/Riders in the Sky	1961	7.50	15.00	30.00

RANGLIN, ERNEST
45s
STUDIO

❏ 1	Surfing (Part 1)/Surfing (Part 2)	196?	12.50	25.00	50.00

RANK, KEN
45s
FENTON

❏ 2194	Twin City Saucer/Ken's Thing	1968	7.50	15.00	30.00

RANKIN, KENNY
45s
ABC-PARAMOUNT

❏ 10268	Funny That's Love/Go Home Little Girl	1961	3.00	6.00	12.00
—As "Ken Rankin"					
ATLANTIC					
❏ 3663	Regrets/(B-side unknown)	1980	—	2.00	4.00
COLUMBIA					
❏ 42881	Soft Guitar/Baby Goodbye	1963	2.50	5.00	10.00
❏ 43036	Where Did My Little Girl Go/U.S. Mail	1964	2.50	5.00	10.00
❏ 4-43201	Knowing I Won't Go Back There/There'll Be No Other Love	1964	2.50	5.00	10.00
❏ 43885	Haven't We Met/In the Name of Love	1966	2.50	5.00	10.00
DECCA					
❏ 30485	Saturday After the Game/I'll Be Waiting	1957	5.00	10.00	20.00
❏ 30691	My Popular Baby/You Be the Judge	1958	3.75	7.50	15.00
❏ 30852	Cindy Loo/Catch Love	1959	3.75	7.50	15.00
❏ 30954	I Cry By Night/Have Pity Miss Kitty	1959	3.75	7.50	15.00
❏ 31054	What Do You Want to Make Those Eyes at Me For/Tonight I'm Speaking Love	1960	3.00	6.00	12.00
❏ 31124	Casey Jones/It Started in Naples	1960	3.00	6.00	12.00
❏ 31162	Sure As You're Born/Teasin' Heart	1960	3.00	6.00	12.00
LITTLE DAVID					
❏ 725	String Man/Comin' Down	1972	—	2.50	5.00
❏ 726	Peaceful/Sometimes	1973	—	2.50	5.00
❏ 727	Why Do Fools Fall in Love/(B-side unknown)	1973	—	2.50	5.00
❏ 728	Penny Lane/Killed a Cat	1974	—	2.50	5.00
❏ 729	Catfish/Silver Morning	1975	—	2.50	5.00
❏ 732	Sunday Kind of Love/Inside	1975	—	2.50	5.00
❏ 733	Creepin'/Lost Up in Loving You	1976	—	2.50	5.00
❏ 735	On and On/Through the Eyes of the Eagle	1977	—	2.50	5.00
❏ 737	When Sunny Gets Blue/I Love You	1977	—	2.50	5.00
❏ 8072	Penny Lane/Killed a Cat	1975	—	2.50	5.00
❏ 8093	Catfish/Silver Morning	1975	—	2.50	5.00
MERCURY					
❏ 72768	Peaceful/The Dolphin	1968	2.00	4.00	8.00
❏ 72768 [PS]	Peaceful/The Dolphin	1968	3.00	6.00	12.00
❏ 72956	Minuet/Peaceful	1969	2.00	4.00	8.00

Albums
ATLANTIC

❏ SD 19271	After the Roses	1980	2.50	5.00	10.00
LITTLE DAVID					
❏ LD 1003	Like a Seed	1972	2.50	5.00	10.00
❏ LD 1009	Inside	1975	2.50	5.00	10.00
❏ LD 1013	The Kenny Rankin Album	1977	2.50	5.00	10.00
❏ SD 3000	Silver Morning	1974	2.50	5.00	10.00
❏ 90131	Silver Morning	1984	2.00	4.00	8.00
—Reissue of 3000					
MERCURY					
❏ MG-21141 [M]	Mind Dusters	1967	3.75	7.50	15.00
❏ SR-61141 [S]	Mind Dusters	1967	3.00	6.00	12.00
❏ SR-61240	Family	1969	3.00	6.00	12.00

RARE BIRD
45s
ABC

❏ 11284	Hammerhead/What You Want to Know	1970	—	3.00	6.00
POLYDOR					
❏ 15079	Birdman (Part 1)/Birdman (Part 2)	1973	—	2.50	5.00
❏ 15081	The Darkest Hour/Hey Man	1973	—	2.50	5.00
❏ 15087	Somebody's Watching (Part 1)/Somebody's Watching (Part 2)	1974	—	2.50	5.00
❏ 15093	Body and Soul/(B-side unassigned)	1974	—	—	—
—Canceled					
PROBE					
❏ 477	Sympathy/Beautiful Scarlet	1970	2.00	4.00	8.00

Albums
ABC

❏ X-715	As Your Mind Flies	1972	3.75	7.50	15.00
POLYDOR					
❏ PD 5530	Epic Forest	1973	3.75	7.50	15.00
❏ PD 6502	Somebody's Watching	1974	3.75	7.50	15.00
❏ PD 6506	Born Again	1974	3.75	7.50	15.00
PROBE					
❏ 4514	Rare Bird	1970	6.25	12.50	25.00

RARE BREED, THE Later known as THE OHIO EXPRESS.
45s
ATTACK

❏ 1401	Beg, Borrow and Steal/Jeri's Theme	1966	7.50	15.00	30.00
❏ 1403	Come and Take a Ride in My Boat/Take Me to This World of Yours	1966	5.00	10.00	20.00

R

Number	Title (A Side/B Side)	Yr	VG	VG+	NM

RARE EARTH

45s

PRODIGAL

Number	Title (A Side/B Side)	Yr	VG	VG+	NM
❑ 0637	Crazy Love/Is Your Teacher Cool	1977	—	2.50	5.00
❑ 0640	Warm Ride/Would You Like to Come Along	1978	—	2.50	5.00
❑ 0643	I Can Feel My Love Risin'/S.O.S. (Stop Her On Sight)	1978	—	2.50	5.00

RARE EARTH

Number	Title (A Side/B Side)	Yr	VG	VG+	NM
❑ 960/961 [DJ]	What'd I Say (stereo/mono)	1972	6.25	12.50	25.00
—Blue vinyl, promo only, white label					
❑ 5010	Generation (Light of the Sky)/Magic Key	1969	3.00	6.00	12.00
❑ 5012	Get Ready/Magic Key	1970	—	3.00	6.00
❑ 5017	(I Know) I'm Losing You/When Joanie Smiles	1970	—	3.00	6.00
❑ 5021	Born to Wander/Here Comes the Night	1970	—	3.00	6.00
❑ 5031	I Just Want to Celebrate/The Seed	1971	—	3.00	6.00
❑ 5031 [PS]	I Just Want to Celebrate/The Seed	1971	2.50	5.00	10.00
❑ 5038	Hey Big Brother/Under God's Light	1971	—	3.00	6.00
❑ 5043	What'd I Say/Nice to Be with You	1972	—	3.00	6.00
❑ 5048	Good Time Sally/Love Shines Down	1972	—	3.00	6.00
❑ 5052	We're Gonna Have a Good Time/Would You Like to Come Along	1973	—	3.00	6.00
❑ 5053	Ma/(Instrumental)	1973	—	3.00	6.00
❑ 5054	Hum Along and Dance/Come with Me	1973	—	3.00	6.00
❑ 5056	Big John Is My Name/Ma	1974	—	3.00	6.00
❑ 5057	Chained/Fresh from the Can	1974	—	3.00	6.00
❑ 5058	It Makes You Happy (But It Ain't Gonna Last Too Long)/Boogie with Me Children	1975	—	3.00	6.00
❑ 5059	Let Me Be Your Sunshine/Keep Me Out of the Storm	1976	—	3.00	6.00
❑ 5060	Midnight Lady/Walking Shtick	1976	—	3.00	6.00

RCA

Number	Title (A Side/B Side)	Yr	VG	VG+	NM
❑ PB-13076	Howzabout Some Love/Let Me Take You Out	1982	—	—	—
—Unreleased					

VERVE

Number	Title (A Side/B Side)	Yr	VG	VG+	NM
❑ 10622	Stop-Where Did Our Love Go/Mother's Oats	1968	3.00	6.00	12.00

Albums

MOTOWN

Number	Title (A Side/B Side)	Yr	VG	VG+	NM
❑ M5-116V1	Motown Superstar Series, Vol. 16	1981	2.50	5.00	10.00
❑ M5-202V1	Ecology	1981	2.00	4.00	8.00
❑ 5229 ML	Get Ready	1982	2.00	4.00	8.00

PRODIGAL

Number	Title (A Side/B Side)	Yr	VG	VG+	NM
❑ P6-10019	Rare Earth	1977	2.50	5.00	10.00
❑ P7-10025	Band Together	1978	2.50	5.00	10.00
❑ P7-10027	Grand Slam	1979	2.50	5.00	10.00

RARE EARTH

Number	Title (A Side/B Side)	Yr	VG	VG+	NM
❑ RS 507	Get Ready	1969	7.50	15.00	30.00
—Original cover has a rounded top					
❑ RS 507	Get Ready	1970	3.00	6.00	12.00
—Regular square cover					
❑ RS 510	Generation	1970	—	—	—
—Canceled					
❑ RS 514	Ecology	1970	3.75	7.50	15.00
❑ RS 520	One World	1971	3.75	7.50	15.00
❑ R 534 [(2)]	Rare Earth in Concert	1971	3.75	7.50	15.00
❑ R 543	Willie Remembers	1972	3.00	6.00	12.00
❑ R6-546	Ma	1973	3.00	6.00	12.00
❑ R6-548	Back to Earth	1975	3.00	6.00	12.00
❑ R7-550	Midnight Lady	1976	3.00	6.00	12.00

VERVE

Number	Title (A Side/B Side)	Yr	VG	VG+	NM
❑ V6-5066	Dreams/Answers	1968	12.50	25.00	50.00

RASCALS, THE Includes "The Young Rascals." Also see FELIX CAVALIERE; GENE CORNISH; FELIX AND THE ESCORTS.

45s

ATLANTIC

Number	Title (A Side/B Side)	Yr	VG	VG+	NM
❑ 2312	I Ain't Gonna Eat Out My Heart Anymore/Slow Down	1965	3.75	7.50	15.00
—From here through Atlantic 2463, as "The Young Rascals"					
❑ 2321	Good Lovin'/Mustang Sally	1966	3.75	7.50	15.00
❑ 2338	You Better Run/Love Is a Beautiful Thing	1966	2.50	5.00	10.00
❑ 2338 [PS]	You Better Run/Love Is a Beautiful Thing	1966	5.00	10.00	20.00
❑ 2353	Come On Up/What Is the Reason	1966	2.50	5.00	10.00
❑ 2377	I've Been Lonely Too Long/If You Knew	1967	2.50	5.00	10.00
❑ 2377 [PS]	I've Been Lonely Too Long/If You Knew	1967	5.00	10.00	20.00
❑ 2401	Groovin'/Sueno	1967	2.00	4.00	8.00
❑ 2401 [PS]	Groovin'/Sueno	1967	5.00	10.00	20.00
❑ 2424	A Girl Like You/It's Love	1967	2.00	4.00	8.00
❑ 2424 [PS]	A Girl Like You/It's Love	1967	5.00	10.00	20.00
❑ 2428	Groovin' (Spanish)/Groovin' (Italian)	1967	5.00	10.00	20.00
❑ 2438	How Can I Be Sure/I'm So Happy Now	1967	2.00	4.00	8.00
❑ 2463	It's Wonderful/Of Course	1967	2.00	4.00	8.00
❑ 2493	A Beautiful Morning/Rainy Day	1968	—		3.00
—First record as "The Rascals"					
❑ 2493 [PS]	A Beautiful Morning/Rainy Day	1968	5.00	10.00	20.00
❑ 2537	People Got to Be Free/My World	1968	—		3.00	6.00
❑ 2537 [PS]	People Got to Be Free/My World	1968	3.00	6.00	12.00
❑ 2584	A Ray of Hope/Any Dance'll Do	1968	—	3.00	6.00
❑ 2584 [PS]	A Ray of Hope/Any Dance'll Do	1968	3.00	6.00	12.00
❑ 2599	Heaven/Baby I'm Blue	1969	—	3.00	6.00
❑ 2634	See/Away Away	1969	—	3.00	6.00
❑ 2634 [PS]	See/Away Away	1969	3.00	6.00	12.00
❑ 2664	Carry Me Back/Real Thing	1969	—	3.00	6.00
❑ 2664 [PS]	Carry Me Back/Real Thing	1969	3.00	6.00	12.00
❑ 2695	Hold On/I Believe	1969	—	3.00	6.00
❑ 2695 [PS]	Hold On/I Believe	1969	3.00	6.00	12.00
❑ 2743	Glory Glory/You Don't Know	1970	—	3.00	6.00
❑ 2743 [PS]	Glory Glory/You Don't Know	1970	3.00	6.00	12.00
❑ 2773	Right On/Almost Home	1970	—		3.00	6.00

COLUMBIA

Number	Title (A Side/B Side)	Yr	VG	VG+	NM
❑ 45400	Love Me/Happy Song	1971	—	3.00	6.00
❑ 45491	Lucky Day/Love Letter	1971	—	3.00	6.00
❑ 45568	Brother Tree/Saga of New York	1972	—	3.00	6.00
❑ 45600	Echoes/Hummin' Song	1972	—	3.00	6.00
❑ 45649	Jungle Walk/Saga of New York	1972	2.50	5.00	10.00

PHILCO-FORD

Number	Title (A Side/B Side)	Yr	VG	VG+	NM
❑ HP-18	A Girl Like You/I've Been Lonely Too Long	1967	3.75	7.50	15.00
—4-inch plastic "Hip Pocket Record" with color sleeve					

7-Inch Extended Plays

ATLANTIC

Number	Title (A Side/B Side)	Yr	VG	VG+	NM
❑ SD 7-8169	Please Love Me/It's Wonderful/I'm Gonna Love You//Easy Rollin'/Rainy Day	1968	5.00	10.00	20.00
—Jukebox issue; small hole, plays at 33 1/3 rpm					
❑ SD 7-8169 [PS]	Once Upon a Dream	1968	5.00	10.00	20.00

Albums

ATLANTIC

Number	Title (A Side/B Side)	Yr	VG	VG+	NM
❑ ST-137 [DJ]	Freedom Suite Sampler	1969	12.50	25.00	50.00
❑ SD 2-901 [(2)]	Freedom Suite	1969	5.00	10.00	20.00
❑ 8123 [M]	The Young Rascals	1966	7.50	15.00	30.00
❑ SD 8123 [S]	The Young Rascals	1966	10.00	20.00	40.00
—Green and blue label					
❑ SD 8123 [S]	The Young Rascals	1966	12.50	25.00	50.00
—Purple and green label					
❑ SD 8123 [S]	The Young Rascals	1969	3.00	6.00	12.00
—Red and green label					
❑ 8134 [M]	Collections	1967	6.25	12.50	25.00
❑ SD 8134 [S]	Collections	1967	7.50	15.00	30.00
—Green and blue label					
❑ SD 8134 [S]	Collections	1969	3.00	6.00	12.00
—Red and green label					
❑ 8148 [M]	Groovin'	1967	6.25	12.50	25.00
❑ SD 8148 [S]	Groovin'	1967	7.50	15.00	30.00
—Green and blue label					
❑ SD 8148 [S]	Groovin'	1969	3.00	6.00	12.00
—Red and green label					
❑ 8169 [M]	Once Upon a Dream	1968	10.00	20.00	40.00
❑ SD 8169 [S]	Once Upon a Dream	1968	6.25	12.50	25.00
—Green and blue label					
❑ SD 8169 [S]	Once Upon a Dream	1969	3.00	6.00	12.00
—Red and green label					
❑ 8190 [M]	Time Peace/The Rascals' Greatest Hits	1968	12.50	25.00	50.00
—Mono is promo only					
❑ SD 8190 [S]	Time Peace/The Rascals' Greatest Hits	1968	3.75	7.50	15.00
—Purple and gold label					
❑ SD 8190 [S]	Time Peace/The Rascals' Greatest Hits	1968	6.25	12.50	25.00
—Green and blue label					
❑ SD 8190 [S]	Time Peace/The Rascals' Greatest Hits	1969	3.00	6.00	12.00
—Red and green label					
❑ 8246 [M]	See	1969	12.50	25.00	50.00
—Mono is promo only; cover has "dj copy monaural" sticker on front					
❑ SD 8246 [S]	See	1969	3.75	7.50	15.00
❑ 8276 [M]	Search and Nearness	1970	12.50	25.00	50.00
—Mono is promo only; cover has "dj copy monaural" sticker on front					
❑ SD 8276 [S]	Search and Nearness	1970	3.75	7.50	15.00

COLUMBIA

Number	Title (A Side/B Side)	Yr	VG	VG+	NM
❑ G 30462 [(2)]	Peaceful World	1971	3.75	7.50	15.00
❑ KC 31103	The Island of Real	1972	3.00	6.00	12.00

PAIR

Number	Title (A Side/B Side)	Yr	VG	VG+	NM
❑ PDL2-1106 [(2)]	Rock and Roll Treasures	1986	3.75	7.50	15.00

RHINO

Number	Title (A Side/B Side)	Yr	VG	VG+	NM
❑ RNLP 70237	The Young Rascals	1988	2.50	5.00	10.00
❑ RNLP 70238	Collections	1988	2.50	5.00	10.00
❑ RNLP 70239	Groovin'	1988	2.50	5.00	10.00
❑ R1-70240	Once Upon a Dream	1988	2.50	5.00	10.00
❑ R1-70241	Freedom Suite	1988	2.50	5.00	10.00
❑ R1-70242	Searching for Ecstasy: The Rest of the Rascals 1969-1972	1988	2.50	5.00	10.00

SUNDAZED

Number	Title (A Side/B Side)	Yr	VG	VG+	NM
❑ LP 5116	The Young Rascals	2002	3.00	6.00	12.00
❑ LP 5117	Collections	2002	3.00	6.00	12.00
❑ LP 5118	Groovin'	2002	3.00	6.00	12.00
❑ LP 5119	Once Upon a Dream	2002	3.00	6.00	12.00

WARNER SPECIAL PRODUCTS

Number	Title (A Side/B Side)	Yr	VG	VG+	NM
❑ SP-2502 [(2)]	24 Greatest Hits	1971	5.00	10.00	20.00

WES FARRELL

Number	Title (A Side/B Side)	Yr	VG	VG+	NM
❑ PFT-1002 [DJ]	Songs from the Rascals	197?	6.25	12.50	25.00
—Promo-only publisher's demo					

RASPBERRIES Also see ERIC CARMEN; THE CHOIR.

45s

CAPITOL

Number	Title (A Side/B Side)	Yr	VG	VG+	NM
❑ 3280	Don't Want to Say Goodbye/Rock and Roll Mama	1972	2.00	4.00	8.00
❑ 3280 [PS]	Don't Want to Say Goodbye/Rock and Roll Mama	1972	6.25	12.50	25.00
❑ 3348	Go All the Way/With You in My Life	1972	—	3.00	6.00
❑ 3473	I Wanna Be with You/Goin' Nowhere Tonight	1972	—	3.00	6.00
❑ 3546	Let's Pretend/Every Way I Can	1973	—	3.00	6.00
❑ 3546 [PS]	Let's Pretend/Every Way I Can	1973	3.00	6.00	12.00
❑ 3610	Tonight/Had to Get Over a Heartbreak	1973	—	3.00	6.00
❑ 3765	I'm a Rocker/Money Down	1973	—	3.00	6.00
❑ 3826	Don't Want to Say Goodbye/Ecstasy	1974	—	3.00	6.00
❑ 3885	Drivin' Around/Might As Well	1974	—	3.00	6.00
❑ 3946	Overnight Sensation (Hit Record)/Hands on You	1974	—	3.00	6.00
❑ 4001	The Party's Over/Cruisin' Music	1974	—	3.00	6.00
❑ PRO-6426 [DJ]	Don't Want to Say Goodbye (3:48 Mono)/(5:00 Stereo)	1972	5.00	10.00	20.00

Albums

CAPITOL

Number	Title (A Side/B Side)	Yr	VG	VG+	NM
❑ SK-11036	Raspberries	1972	7.50	15.00	30.00
—Originals have red labels and a "scratch 'n' sniff" cover, the smell of which fades over time					
❑ ST-11036	Raspberries	1973	5.00	10.00	20.00
—Orange label, "Capitol" at bottom					
❑ ST-11123	Fresh	1972	5.00	10.00	20.00
❑ SMAS-11220	Side 3	1973	5.00	10.00	20.00
—With cover cut in the shape of a basket of raspberries					
❑ ST-11329	Starting Over	1974	5.00	10.00	20.00
❑ ST-11524	Raspberries' Best Featuring Eric Carmen	1976	3.75	7.50	15.00
❑ SN-16095	Raspberries' Best Featuring Eric Carmen	1979	2.50	5.00	10.00

Number	Title (A Side/B Side)	Yr	VG	VG+	NM

RATCHELL
45s
DECCA

Number	Title (A Side/B Side)	Yr	VG	VG+	NM
❏ 32893	Lazy Lady/Problems	1971	—	3.00	6.00
❏ 32958	Julie My Woman/Out of Hand	1972	—	2.50	5.00
❏ 32981	Peace of Mind/My My	1972	—	2.50	5.00

Albums
DECCA

Number	Title	Yr	VG	VG+	NM
❏ DL 75330	Ratchell	1972	3.75	7.50	15.00
❏ DL 75365	Ratchell 2	1972	3.75	7.50	15.00

RATIONALS, THE
45s
A-SQUARE

Number	Title (A Side/B Side)	Yr	VG	VG+	NM
❏ 101	Look What You're Doin'/Gave My Love	1966	6.25	12.50	25.00
❏ 103	Feelin' Lost/Little Girls Cry	1966	5.00	10.00	20.00
❏ 103	Feelin' Lost/Respect	1966	6.25	12.50	25.00
❏ 104	Leavin' Here/Respect	1966	7.50	15.00	30.00

—This is the original issue of this single

Number	Title (A Side/B Side)	Yr	VG	VG+	NM
❏ 104/3	Leavin' Here/Feelin' Lost	1966	6.25	12.50	25.00
❏ 107	I Need You/Out in the Streets	1968	5.00	10.00	20.00
❏ 402	I Need You/Get the Picture	1967	6.25	12.50	25.00

—B-side by SRC (Scott Richard Case)
CAMEO

Number	Title (A Side/B Side)	Yr	VG	VG+	NM
❏ 437	Respect/Feelin' Lost	1966	3.00	6.00	12.00
❏ 455	Hold On Baby/Sing	1967	3.75	7.50	15.00
❏ 481	Leavin' Here/Not Like It Is	1967	3.75	7.50	15.00

CAPITOL

Number	Title (A Side/B Side)	Yr	VG	VG+	NM
❏ 2124	I Need You/Out in the Streets	1968	3.00	6.00	12.00

CREWE

Number	Title (A Side/B Side)	Yr	VG	VG+	NM
❏ 340	Handbags and Gladrags/Guitar Army	1969	2.50	5.00	10.00

DANBY'S

Number	Title (A Side/B Side)	Yr	VG	VG+	NM
❏ (no #)	Turn On/Irrational	1966	12.50	25.00	50.00

—Made for Danby's clothiers
GENESIS

Number	Title (A Side/B Side)	Yr	VG	VG+	NM
❏ 1	Guitar Army/Sunset	1969	3.75	7.50	15.00

Albums
CREWE

Number	Title	Yr	VG	VG+	NM
❏ CR-1334	The Rationals	1969	10.00	20.00	40.00

RATS, THE
45s
LAURIE

Number	Title (A Side/B Side)	Yr	VG	VG+	NM
❏ 3276	Spoonful/I've Got My Eyes on You Baby	1964	3.00	6.00	12.00

RUST

Number	Title (A Side/B Side)	Yr	VG	VG+	NM
❏ TR-2	Spoonful/I've Got My Eyes on You Baby	1965	3.75	7.50	15.00

RATTLES, THE Also see THE SEARCHERS.
45s
LONDON

Number	Title (A Side/B Side)	Yr	VG	VG+	NM
❏ 1037	Devil's on the Loose/I Know You Don't Know	1972	—	2.50	5.00
❏ 1047	Devil's Sun/Why Do I Care	1973	—	2.50	5.00

MERCURY

Number	Title (A Side/B Side)	Yr	VG	VG+	NM
❏ 72403	Shame, Shame, Shame/Someone Who Is Just Like You	1965	3.00	6.00	12.00
❏ 72554	Sha La La La Lee/Dance	1966	3.00	6.00	12.00

PROBE

Number	Title (A Side/B Side)	Yr	VG	VG+	NM
❏ 480	The Witch/Geraldine	1970	2.00	4.00	8.00

Albums
MERCURY

Number	Title	Yr	VG	VG+	NM
❏ MG 21127 [M]	The Rattles' Greatest Hits	1967	20.00	40.00	80.00
❏ SR 61127 [R]	The Rattles' Greatest Hits	1967	12.50	25.00	50.00

RAVEN, PAUL See GARY GLITTER.

RAVENAIRS, THE
45s
ALGONQUIN

Number	Title (A Side/B Side)	Yr	VG	VG+	NM
❏ 718	A Night to Remember/Together Forever	1958	25.00	50.00	100.00

—Originally released as "The Rivieras"

RAVENS, THE Also see JIMMY RICKS.
45s
ARGO

Number	Title (A Side/B Side)	Yr	VG	VG+	NM
❏ 5255	Kneel and Pray/I Can't Believe	1956	10.00	20.00	40.00
❏ 5261	A Simple Prayer/Water Boy	1956	20.00	40.00	80.00
❏ 5276	That'll Be the Day/Dear One	1957	7.50	15.00	30.00
❏ 5284	Here Is My Heart/Lazy Mule	1957	7.50	15.00	30.00

CHECKER

Number	Title (A Side/B Side)	Yr	VG	VG+	NM
❏ 871	That'll Be the Day/Dear One	1957	5.00	10.00	20.00

COLUMBIA

Number	Title (A Side/B Side)	Yr	VG	VG+	NM
❏ 1-903	Don't Look Now/Time Takes Care of Everything	1950	375.00	750.00	1500.

—Microgroove 33 1/3 single

Number	Title (A Side/B Side)	Yr	VG	VG+	NM
❏ 6-903	Don't Look Now/Time Takes Care of Everything	1950	175.00	350.00	700.00
❏ 1-925	My Baby's Gone/I'm So Crazy for Love	1950	375.00	750.00	1500.

—Microgroove 33 1/3 single

Number	Title (A Side/B Side)	Yr	VG	VG+	NM
❏ 6-925	My Baby's Gone/I'm So Crazy for Love	1950	150.00	300.00	600.00
❏ 4-39112	You Don't Have to Drop a Heart/Midnight Blues	1950	500.00	1000.	2000.
❏ 4-39194	You're Always in My Dreams/Gotta Find My Baby	1951	500.00	1000.	2000.
❏ 4-39408	You Foolish Thing/Honey I Don't Want You	1951	500.00	1000.	2000.

JUBILEE

Number	Title (A Side/B Side)	Yr	VG	VG+	NM
❏ 45-5184	Bye Bye Baby Blues/Happy Go Lucky Baby	1955	7.50	15.00	30.00
❏ 45-5203	Green Eyes/The Bells of San Rafael	1955	7.50	15.00	30.00

—As "Jimmy Ricks and the Ravens"

Number	Title (A Side/B Side)	Yr	VG	VG+	NM
❏ 45-5217	On Chapel Hill/We'll Raise a Ruckus Tonight	1955	7.50	15.00	30.00
❏ 45-5237	I'll Always Be in Love with You/(Take Me Back To My) Boots and Saddles	1956	7.50	15.00	30.00

—As "Jimmy Ricks and the Ravens"
MERCURY

Number	Title (A Side/B Side)	Yr	VG	VG+	NM
❏ 5764x45	There's No Use Pretending/Wagon Wheels	1951	75.00	150.00	300.00
❏ 5800x45	Begin the Beguine/Looking for My Baby	1952	62.50	125.00	250.00
❏ 5853x45	Why Did You Leave Me/Chloe	1952	62.50	125.00	250.00
❏ 8259x45	There's No Use Pretending/Wagon Wheels	1951	100.00	200.00	400.00
❏ 8291x45	Rock Me All Night Long/One Sweet Letter	1952	37.50	75.00	150.00
❏ 70060x45	I'll Be Back/Don't Mention My Name	1953	50.00	100.00	200.00

Number	Title (A Side/B Side)	Yr	VG	VG+	NM
❏ 70119x45	Come a Little Bit Closer/She's Got to Go	1953	37.50	75.00	150.00
❏ 70213x45	Who'll Be the Fool/Rough Ridin'	1953	37.50	75.00	150.00
❏ 70240x45	Without a Song/Walkin' My Blues Away	1953	37.50	75.00	150.00
❏ 70307x45	September Song/Escortin' Or Courtin'	1954	37.50	75.00	150.00
❏ 70330x45	Going Home/Lonesome Road	1954	37.50	75.00	150.00
❏ 70413x45	I've Got You Under My Skin/Love Is No Dream	1954	25.00	50.00	100.00

—Black label

Number	Title (A Side/B Side)	Yr	VG	VG+	NM
❏ 70413x45	I've Got You Under My Skin/Love Is No Dream	1954	62.50	125.00	250.00

—Pink label

Number	Title (A Side/B Side)	Yr	VG	VG+	NM
❏ 70505x45	White Christmas/Silent Night	1954	25.00	50.00	100.00

—Black label

Number	Title (A Side/B Side)	Yr	VG	VG+	NM
❏ 70505x45	White Christmas/Silent Night	1954	50.00	100.00	200.00

—Pink label

Number	Title (A Side/B Side)	Yr	VG	VG+	NM
❏ 70554x45	Ol' Man River/Write Me a Letter	1955	25.00	50.00	100.00

—Black label

Number	Title (A Side/B Side)	Yr	VG	VG+	NM
❏ 70554x45	Ol' Man River/Write Me a Letter	1955	50.00	100.00	200.00

—Pink label
NATIONAL

Number	Title (A Side/B Side)	Yr	VG	VG+	NM
❏ 9111x45	Count Every Star/I'm Gonna Paper All My Walls with Your Love	1950	1500.	2250.	3000.

—The only known Ravens single on a National 45
OKEH

Number	Title (A Side/B Side)	Yr	VG	VG+	NM
❏ 6825	The Whiffenpoof Song/I Get All My Lovin' on a Saturday Night	1951	125.00	250.00	500.00
❏ 6843	That Old Gang of Mine/Everything But You	1951	125.00	250.00	500.00
❏ 6888	Mam'selle/Calypso Song	1952	100.00	200.00	400.00

SAVOY

Number	Title (A Side/B Side)	Yr	VG	VG+	NM
❏ 1540	White Christmas/Silent Night	1958	5.00	10.00	20.00

TOP RANK

Number	Title (A Side/B Side)	Yr	VG	VG+	NM
❏ 2003	Into the Shadows/The Rising Sun	1959	6.25	12.50	25.00
❏ 2016	Solitude/Hole in the Middle of the Moon	1959	6.25	12.50	25.00

7-Inch Extended Plays
KING

Number	Title (A Side/B Side)	Yr	VG	VG+	NM
❏ 310	*Honey/Bye Bye Baby Blues/Out of a Dream/My Sugar Is So Refined	1954	125.00	250.00	500.00
❏ 310 [PS]	The Ravens Featuring Jimmy Ricks	1954	125.00	250.00	500.00

RENDITION

Number	Title (A Side/B Side)	Yr	VG	VG+	NM
❏ 104	(contents unknown)	195?	375.00	750.00	1500.
❏ 104 [PS]	Ol' Man River	195?	500.00	1000.	2000.

Albums
HARLEM HIT PARADE

Number	Title	Yr	VG	VG+	NM
❏ 1007	The Ravens	1975	2.50	5.00	10.00

REGENT

Number	Title	Yr	VG	VG+	NM
❏ MG-6062 [M]	Write Me a Letter	195?	37.50	75.00	150.00

—Red label

Number	Title	Yr	VG	VG+	NM
❏ MG-6062 [M]	Write Me a Letter	1957	75.00	150.00	300.00

—Green label
SAVOY JAZZ

Number	Title	Yr	VG	VG+	NM
❏ SJL-2227 [(2)]	The Greatest Group of Them All	1978	3.00	6.00	12.00

RAW
Albums
CORAL

Number	Title	Yr	VG	VG+	NM
❏ CRL 757515	Raw Holly	1971	7.50	15.00	30.00

RAW SPITT
45s
UNITED ARTISTS

Number	Title (A Side/B Side)	Yr	VG	VG+	NM
❏ 50813	That Ain't My Wife/Song to Sing	1971	3.00	6.00	12.00

Albums
UNITED ARTISTS

Number	Title	Yr	VG	VG+	NM
❏ UAS-6795	Maybe You Ain't Black	1971	6.25	12.50	25.00

RAWLS, LOU
12-Inch Singles
PHILADELPHIA INT'L.

Number	Title (A Side/B Side)	Yr	VG	VG+	NM
❏ 2Z8 3686	Let Me Be Good to You/Lover's Holiday	1979	2.50	5.00	10.00

45s
ARISTA

Number	Title (A Side/B Side)	Yr	VG	VG+	NM
❏ 0103	Baby You Don't Know How Good You Are/Hour Glass	1975	—	3.00	6.00

BELL

Number	Title (A Side/B Side)	Yr	VG	VG+	NM
❏ 45608	She's Gone/Hour Glass	1974	—	3.00	6.00
❏ 45616	Who Can Tell Us Why?/Now You're Coming Back Michelle	1974	—	3.00	6.00

CANDIX

Number	Title (A Side/B Side)	Yr	VG	VG+	NM
❏ 305	In My Little Black Book/Just Thought You'd Like to Know	1960	5.00	10.00	20.00
❏ 312	When We Get Old/Eighty Ways	1961	5.00	10.00	20.00

CAPITOL

Number	Title (A Side/B Side)	Yr	VG	VG+	NM
❏ 2026	Little Drummer Boy/A Child with a Toy	1967	2.00	4.00	8.00
❏ 2084	Evil Woman/My Ancestors	1968	2.00	4.00	8.00
❏ 2172	Soul Serenade/You're Good for Me	1968	2.00	4.00	8.00
❏ 2252	Down Here on the Ground/I'm Satisfied (The Duffy Theme)	1968	2.00	4.00	8.00
❏ 2348	The Split/Why Can't I Speak	1968	2.00	4.00	8.00
❏ 2408	It's You/Sweet Charity	1969	2.00	4.00	8.00
❏ 2550	Your Good Thing (Is About to End)/Season of the Witch	1969	2.00	4.00	8.00
❏ 2668	I Can't Make It Alone/Make the World Go Away	1969	2.00	4.00	8.00
❏ 2734	You've Made Me So Very Happy/Let's Burn Down the Cornfield	1970	2.00	4.00	8.00
❏ 2856	Bring It On Home/Can You Dig It-Take Me for What I Am	1970	2.00	4.00	8.00
❏ 2942	Win Your Love for Me/Coppin' a Plea	1970	2.00	4.00	8.00
❏ 4622	That Lucky Old Sun/In My Heart	1961	3.75	7.50	15.00
❏ 4669	Nine-Pound Hammer/Above My Head	1961	3.75	7.50	15.00
❏ 4695	The Wedding (The Bride)/The Biggest Lover in Town	1962	3.00	6.00	12.00
❏ 4743	Trust Me/Please Let Me Be the First to Know	1962	3.00	6.00	12.00
❏ 4761	Save Your Love for Me/Trust Me	1962	3.00	6.00	12.00
❏ 4803	Stormy Monday/Sweet Lover	1962	3.00	6.00	12.00

—With Les McCann

Number	Title (A Side/B Side)	Yr	VG	VG+	NM
❏ 5049	Tobacco Road/Blues for Four-String Guitar	1963	3.00	6.00	12.00
❏ 5160	The House Next Door/Come On In, Mr. Blues	1964	3.00	6.00	12.00
❏ 5227	Love Is Blind/I Fell in Love	1964	3.00	6.00	12.00

R

Number	Title (A Side/B Side)	Yr	VG	VG+	NM
❑ 5424	Three O'Clock in the Morning/				
	Nothing Really Feels the Same	1965	3.00	6.00	12.00
❑ 5505	What'll I Do/Can I Please	1965	3.00	6.00	12.00
❑ 5655	The Shadow of Your Smile/Southside Blues	1966	2.50	5.00	10.00
❑ 5709	Love Is a Hurtin' Thing/Memory Lane	1966	2.50	5.00	10.00
❑ 5790	You Can Bring Me All Your Heartaches/A				
	Woman Who's a Woman	1966	2.50	5.00	10.00
❑ 5824	Trouble Down Here Below/The Life That I Lead	1967	2.50	5.00	10.00
❑ 5824 [PS]	Trouble Down Here Below/The Life That I Lead	1967	2.50	5.00	10.00
❑ 5869	Dead End Street/Yes It Hurts, Doesn't It	1967	2.50	5.00	10.00
❑ 5941	Show Business/When Love Goes Wrong	1967	2.50	5.00	10.00
❑ S7-18908	What Are You Doing New Year's Eve?/Have				
	Yourself a Merry Little Christmas	1995	—	—	3.00
EPIC					
❑ 02999	Now Is the Time for Love/				
	Will You Kiss Me One More Time	1982	—	2.00	4.00
❑ 03299	Together Again/Here Comes Garfield	1982	—	2.00	4.00
—Lou Rawls and Desiree Goyette					
❑ 03357	Let Me Show You How/Watch Your Back	1982	—	2.00	4.00
❑ 03758	Wind Beneath My Wings/Midnight Sun	1983	—	2.00	4.00
❑ 03944	Couple More Years/Upside Down	1983	—	2.00	4.00
❑ 04079	The One I Sing My Love Songs To/You Can't				
	Take It With You	1983	—	2.00	4.00
❑ 04550	All-Time Lover/When We Were Young	1984	—	2.00	4.00
❑ 04677	Close Company/The Lady in My Life	1984	—	2.00	4.00
❑ 04773	Close Company/Forever I Do	1985	—	2.00	4.00
❑ 05714	Learn to Love Again/Ready or Not	1985	—	2.00	4.00
❑ 05831	Are You With Me/(Instrumental)	1986	—	2.00	4.00
❑ 05831 [PS]	Are You With Me/(Instrumental)	1986	—	2.00	4.00
❑ 06145	Stop Me from Starting This Feeling/				
	Never Entered My Mind	1986	—	2.00	4.00
GAMBLE & HUFF					
❑ 310	I Wish You Belonged to Me/It's a Tough Job	1987	—	2.50	5.00
❑ 316	Two Happy Hearts/Jealous Lover	1988	—	2.50	5.00
MGM					
❑ 14262	A Natural Man/Believe in Me	1971	—	3.00	6.00
❑ 14262	A Natural Man/You Can't Hold On	1971	—	3.00	6.00
❑ 14349	His Song Shall Be Sung/I'm Waiting	1972	—	3.00	6.00
❑ 14428	Politician/Walk On In	1972	—	3.00	6.00
❑ 14489	Man of Value/Learning Cup	1973	—	3.00	6.00
❑ 14527	Star Spangled Banner/Just a Closer Walk with				
	Thee	1973	—	3.00	6.00
❑ 14574	Send for Me/Morning Comes Around	1973	—	3.00	6.00
❑ 14652	Dead End Street/Love Is a Hurtin' Thing	1973	—	3.00	6.00
PHILADELPHIA INT'L.					
❑ ZS9 3102	Ain't That Loving You (For More Reasons Than				
	One)/(B-side unknown)	1980	—	2.50	5.00
❑ ZS9 3114	I Go Crazy/Be Anything (But Be Mine)	1980	—	2.50	5.00
❑ ZS8 3592	You'll Never Find Another Love Like Mine/Let's				
	Fall in Love All Over Again	1976	—	2.50	5.00
❑ ZS8 3604	Groovy People/This Song Will Last Forever	1976	—	2.50	5.00
❑ ZS8 3623	See You When I Git There/Spring Again	1977	—	2.50	5.00
❑ ZS8 3634	Lady Love/Not the Staying Kind	1977	—	2.50	5.00
❑ ZS8 3643	One Life to Live/If I Coulda, Woulda, Shoulda	1978	—	2.50	5.00
❑ ZS8 3653	There Will Be Love/Unforgettable	1978	—	2.50	5.00
❑ ZS8 3672	Send In the Clowns/This Song Will Last Forever	1978	—	2.50	5.00
❑ ZS8 3684	Let Me Be Good to You/Lover's Holiday	1979	—	2.50	5.00
❑ ZS9 3715	What's the Matter with the World/Tomorrow	1979	—	2.50	5.00
❑ ZS9 3738	Sit Down and Talk to Me/When You Get Home	1979	—	2.50	5.00
❑ ZS9 3750	You're My Blessing/Heartaches	1980	—	2.50	5.00
❑ ZS8 3765	See You When I Git There/Groovy People	197?	—	2.00	4.00
—Reissue					
❑ ZS8 3770	You'll Never Find Another Love Like Mine/				
	One Life to Live	197?	—	2.00	4.00
—Reissue					
❑ ZS8 3775	Lady Love/Send In the Clowns	197?	—	2.00	4.00
—Reissue					
❑ 70051	Hoochie Coochie Man/				
	You've Lost That Lovin' Feelin'	1981	—	2.50	5.00
7-Inch Extended Plays					
CAPITOL					
❑ SU 1824	Black and Blue/Everyday I Have the Blues/				
	Kansas City//Roll 'Em Pete/Strange Fruit/How				
	Long, How Long Blues	196?	2.50	5.00	10.00
—Jukebox issue; small hole, plays at 33 1/3 rpm					
❑ SU 1824 [PS]	Black and Blue	196?	2.50	5.00	10.00
Albums					
ALLEGIANCE					
❑ AV-5016	Trying As Hard As I Can	198?	2.50	5.00	10.00
BELL					
❑ 1318	She's Gone	1974	3.00	6.00	12.00
BLUE NOTE					
❑ B1-91441	Stormy Monday	1990	3.00	6.00	12.00
—Reissue of Capitol 1714					
❑ B1-91937	At Last	1990	3.00	6.00	12.00
❑ B1-93841	It's Supposed to Be Fun	1990	3.75	7.50	15.00
CAPITOL					
❑ ST-122	The Way It Was	1969	3.75	7.50	15.00
❑ ST 8-0215	The Way It Was — The Way It Is	1969	5.00	10.00	20.00
—Capitol Record Club edition					
❑ ST-215	The Way It Was — The Way It Is	1969	3.75	7.50	15.00
❑ SWBB-261 [(2)]	Close-Up	1969	5.00	10.00	20.00
—Reissue of 1824 and 2042 in one package					
❑ ST-325	Your Good Thing	1969	3.75	7.50	15.00
❑ ST-427	You've Made Me So Very Happy	1970	3.75	7.50	15.00
❑ ST-479	Bring It on Home	1970	3.75	7.50	15.00
❑ STBB-720 [(2)]	Down Here on the Ground/I'd Rather Drink				
	Muddy Water	1971	5.00	10.00	20.00
❑ SM-1714	Stormy Monday	197?	2.50	5.00	10.00
—Reissue with new prefix					
❑ ST 1714 [S]	Stormy Monday	1962	6.25	12.50	25.00
❑ T 1714 [M]	Stormy Monday	1962	5.00	10.00	20.00
❑ ST 1824 [S]	Black and Blue	1963	6.25	12.50	25.00
❑ T 1824 [M]	Black and Blue	1963	5.00	10.00	20.00
❑ ST 2042 [S]	Tobacco Road	1964	6.25	12.50	25.00
❑ T 2042 [M]	Tobacco Road	1964	5.00	10.00	20.00

Number	Title (A Side/B Side)	Yr	VG	VG+	NM
❑ ST 2273 [S]	Nobody But Lou	1965	6.25	12.50	25.00
❑ T 2273 [M]	Nobody But Lou	1965	5.00	10.00	20.00
❑ ST 2401 [S]	Lou Rawls and Strings	1965	6.25	12.50	25.00
❑ T 2401 [M]	Lou Rawls and Strings	1965	5.00	10.00	20.00
❑ SM-2459	Lou Rawls Live!	197?	2.50	5.00	10.00
—Reissue with new prefix					
❑ ST 2459 [S]	Lou Rawls Live!	1966	5.00	10.00	20.00
❑ T 2459 [M]	Lou Rawls Live!	1966	3.75	7.50	15.00
❑ SM-2566	Lou Rawls Soulin'	197?	2.50	5.00	10.00
—Reissue with new prefix					
❑ ST 2566 [S]	Lou Rawls Soulin'	1966	5.00	10.00	20.00
❑ T 2566 [M]	Lou Rawls Soulin'	1966	3.75	7.50	15.00
❑ ST 2632 [S]	Lou Rawls Carryin' On!	1966	5.00	10.00	20.00
❑ T 2632 [M]	Lou Rawls Carryin' On!	1966	3.75	7.50	15.00
❑ ST 2713 [S]	Too Much!	1967	3.75	7.50	15.00
❑ T 2713 [M]	Too Much!	1967	5.00	10.00	20.00
❑ ST 2756 [S]	That's Lou	1967	3.75	7.50	15.00
❑ T 2756 [M]	That's Lou	1967	5.00	10.00	20.00
❑ ST 2790 [S]	Merry Christmas, Ho, Ho, Ho	1967	3.00	6.00	12.00
❑ T 2790 [M]	Merry Christmas, Ho, Ho, Ho	1967	3.75	7.50	15.00
❑ ST 2864 [S]	Feelin' Good	1968	3.75	7.50	15.00
❑ T 2864 [M]	Feelin' Good	1968	7.50	15.00	30.00
❑ ST 2927	You're Good for Me	1968	3.75	7.50	15.00
❑ SKAO 2948	The Best of Lou Rawls	1968	3.75	7.50	15.00
❑ SM-2948	The Best of Lou Rawls	197?	2.50	5.00	10.00
—Reissue with new prefix					
❑ SKBB-11585 [(2)]	The Best from Lou Rawls	1976	3.00	6.00	12.00
❑ SN-16096	The Best of Lou Rawls	1980	2.00	4.00	8.00
—Budget-line reissue					
❑ SN-16097	Lou Rawls Live!	1980	2.00	4.00	8.00
—Budget-line reissue					
EPIC					
❑ FE 37448	Now Is the Time	1982	2.50	5.00	10.00
❑ FE 38553	When the Night Comes	1983	2.50	5.00	10.00
❑ FE 39403	Close Company	1984	2.50	5.00	10.00
❑ FE 40210	Love All Your Blues Away	1986	2.50	5.00	10.00
MGM					
❑ SE-4771	Natural Man	1971	3.00	6.00	12.00
❑ SE-4809	Silk & Soul	1972	3.00	6.00	12.00
❑ SE-4861	A Man of Value	1973	3.00	6.00	12.00
❑ SE-4965	Live at the Century Plaza	1974	3.00	6.00	12.00
PHILADELPHIA INT'L.					
❑ PZ 33957	All Things in Time	1976	2.50	5.00	10.00
—No bar code on cover					
❑ PZ 33957	All Things in Time	198?	2.00	4.00	8.00
—With bar code on cover					
❑ PZ 34488	Unmistakably Lou	1977	2.50	5.00	10.00
❑ PZ 34488	Unmistakably Lou	1986	2.00	4.00	8.00
—Budget-line reissue					
❑ JZ 35036	When You Hear Lou, You've Heard It All	1977	2.50	5.00	10.00
❑ PZ2 35517 [(2)]	Lou Rawls Live	1978	3.00	6.00	12.00
❑ JZ 36006	Let Me Be Good to You	1979	2.50	5.00	10.00
❑ PZ 36006	Let Me Be Good to You	198?	2.00	4.00	8.00
—Budget-line reissue					
❑ JZ 36304	Sit Down and Talk to Me	1979	2.50	5.00	10.00
❑ PZ 36304	Sit Down and Talk to Me	198?	2.00	4.00	8.00
—Budget-line reissue					
❑ JZ 36774	Shades of Blue	1980	2.50	5.00	10.00
❑ FZ 39285	Classics	1984	2.50	5.00	10.00
PICKWICK					
❑ SPC-3156	Come On In, Mr. Blues	1971	2.50	5.00	10.00
❑ SPC-3228	Gee Baby	1972	2.50	5.00	10.00
POLYDOR					
❑ PD-1-6086	Naturally	1976	2.50	5.00	10.00

RAY, ALDER
45s
LIBERTY

Number	Title (A Side/B Side)	Yr	VG	VG+	NM
❑ 55715	'Cause I Love Him/A Little Love (Will Go a Long				
	Way)	1964	3.75	7.50	15.00
MINIT					
❑ 32005	I Need You Baby/My Heart Is in Danger	1966	2.50	5.00	10.00
REVUE					
❑ 11014	Love Will Let You Down/Run, Baby, Run	1968	2.00	4.00	8.00

RAY, DANNY
45s
VIN

Number	Title (A Side/B Side)	Yr	VG	VG+	NM
❑ 1025	Love Me/Gone	1960	25.00	50.00	100.00

RAY, DAVE
Albums
ELEKTRA

Number	Title (A Side/B Side)	Yr	VG	VG+	NM
❑ EKL-284 [M]	Snaker's Here	1965	5.00	10.00	20.00
❑ EKL-319 [M]	Fine Soft Land	1966	5.00	10.00	20.00
❑ EKS-7284 [S]	Snaker's Here	1965	6.25	12.50	25.00
❑ EKS-7319 [S]	Fine Soft Land	1966	6.25	12.50	25.00

RAY, DIANE
45s
MERCURY

Number	Title (A Side/B Side)	Yr	VG	VG+	NM
❑ 72117	Please Don't Talk to the Lifeguard/That's All I				
	Want from You	1963	3.75	7.50	15.00
❑ 72117 [PS]	Please Don't Talk to the Lifeguard/That's All I				
	Want from You	1963	25.00	50.00	100.00
❑ 72195	My Summer Love/Where Is the Boy	1963	3.75	7.50	15.00
❑ 72195 [PS]	My Summer Love/Where Is the Boy	1963	15.00	30.00	60.00
❑ 72223	Snow Man/Just So Bobby Can See	1963	3.75	7.50	15.00
❑ 72223 [PS]	Snow Man/Just So Bobby Can See	1963	15.00	30.00	60.00
❑ 72248	No Arms Can Ever Hold You/Tied Up with Mary	1964	3.75	7.50	15.00
❑ 72276	Happy Happy Birthday Baby/				
	That Boy's Gonna Be Mine	1964	3.75	7.50	15.00

Albums
MERCURY

Number	Title (A Side/B Side)	Yr	VG	VG+	NM
❑ MG-20903 [M]	The Exciting Years	1964	20.00	40.00	80.00
❑ SR-60903 [S]	The Exciting Years	1964	25.00	50.00	100.00

Number	Title (A Side/B Side)	Yr	VG	VG+	NM

RAY, JAMES
45s
CAPRICE
❏ 110	If You Gotta Make a Fool of Somebody/It's Been a Drag	1961	7.50	15.00	30.00
❏ 114	Itty Bitty Pieces/You Remember the Face	1962	6.25	12.50	25.00
❏ 117	Things Are Gonna Be Different/A Miracle	1962	6.25	12.50	25.00
CONGRESS
❏ 109	Marie/The Old Man and the Mule	1963	5.00	10.00	20.00
❏ 201	Do the Monkey/Put Me in Your Diary	1963	5.00	10.00	20.00
❏ 203	The Masquerade Is Over/One by One	1963	5.00	10.00	20.00
❏ 218	We Got a Thing Goin' On/On That Day	1964	5.00	10.00	20.00
DYNAMIC SOUND
❏ 503	I've Got My Mind Set on You/Always	1963	10.00	20.00	40.00
—The A-side was remade by George Harrison in 1987 as "Got My Mind Set on You"
7-Inch Extended Plays
CAPRICE
| ❏ 1002 | The Old Man & the Mule/Lazy Bones//Come Rain or Come Shine/St. James Infirmary | 1962 | 12.50 | 25.00 | 50.00 |
| ❏ 1002 [PS] | James Ray | 1962 | 12.50 | 25.00 | 50.00 |
Albums
CAPRICE
| ❏ LP-1002 [M] | James Ray | 1962 | 20.00 | 40.00 | 80.00 |
| ❏ SLP-1002 [S] | James Ray | 1962 | 30.00 | 60.00 | 120.00 |

RAY, JOHNNIE Also see DORIS DAY/JOHNNIE RAY.
45s
CADENCE
| ❏ 1387 | In the Heart of a Fool/Let's Forget It Now | 1960 | 3.00 | 6.00 | 12.00 |
COLUMBIA
| ❏ 39636 | Please Mr. Sun/Here Am I — Broken Hearted | 1952 | 3.75 | 7.50 | 15.00 |
| ❏ 39659 | Cry/Because of You | 1952 | 3.00 | 6.00 | 12.00 |
—B-side by Tony Bennett; early reissue
❏ 39698	What's the Use?/Mountains in Moonlight	1952	3.75	7.50	15.00
❏ 39700	Coffee and Cigarettes/Don't Blame Me	1952	3.00	6.00	12.00
❏ 39701	Walking My Baby Back Home/Out in the Cold Again	1952	3.00	6.00	12.00
❏ 39702	Don't Take Your Love from Me/The Lady Drinks Champagne	1952	3.00	6.00	12.00
❏ 39703	All of Me/Give Me Time	1952	3.00	6.00	12.00
—The above four comprise a box set
| ❏ 39729 | What's the Use?/A Guy Is a Guy | 1952 | 2.50 | 5.00 | 10.00 |
—B-side by Doris Day
❏ 39750	Walkin' My Baby Back Home/Give Me Time	1952	3.75	7.50	15.00
❏ 39788	All of Me/A Sinner Am I	1952	3.75	7.50	15.00
❏ 39814	Gee But I'm Lonesome/Don't Say Love Has Ended	1952	3.75	7.50	15.00
❏ 39837	Love Me (Baby Can't You Love Me)/Faith Can Move Mountains	1952	3.75	7.50	15.00
❏ 39897	The Thing I Might Have Been/The Commandments of Love	1952	3.75	7.50	15.00
❏ 39908	A Touch of God's Hand/I'm Gonna Walk and Talk with the Lord	1952	3.75	7.50	15.00
❏ 39939	Mr. Midnight/Oh, What a Sad, Sad Day	1953	3.00	6.00	12.00
❏ 39961	Somebody Stole My Gal/Glad Rag Doll	1953	3.00	6.00	12.00
❏ 40006	Satisfied/With These Hands	1953	3.00	6.00	12.00
❏ 40046	All I Do Is Dream of You/Tell the Lady I Said Goodbye	1953	3.00	6.00	12.00
❏ 40090	Please Don't Talk About Me When I'm Gone/An Orchid for the Lady	1953	3.00	6.00	12.00
❏ 40154	Why Should I Be Sorry?/You'd Be Surprised	1954	3.00	6.00	12.00
❏ 40200	Such a Night/Destiny	1954	3.75	7.50	15.00
❏ 40224	Hernando's Hideaway/Hey There	1954	3.00	6.00	12.00
❏ 40252	Going-Going-Gone/To Ev'ry Girl-To Ev'ry Boy	1954	3.00	6.00	12.00
❏ 40324	Papa Loves Mambo/The Only Girl I'll Ever Love	1954	3.00	6.00	12.00
❏ 40391	Alexander's Ragtime Band/If You Believe	1954	3.00	6.00	12.00
❏ 40392	As Time Goes By/Nobody's Sweetheart	1954	3.00	6.00	12.00
❏ 40435	Parade of Broken Hearts/Paths of Paradise	1955	3.00	6.00	12.00
❏ 40471	Flip, Flop and Fly/Thine Eyes Are As the Eyes of a Dove	1955	3.00	6.00	12.00
❏ 40528	Song of the Dreamer/I've Got So Many Million Miles	1955	3.00	6.00	12.00
❏ 40578	Johnnie's Comin' Home/Love, Love, Love	1955	3.00	6.00	12.00
❏ 40613	Who's Sorry Now/A Heart Comes In Handy	1955	3.00	6.00	12.00
❏ 40649	Ain't Misbehavin'/Walk Along with Kings	1956	3.00	6.00	12.00
❏ 40695	Because I Love You/Goodbye, Au Revoir, Adios	1956	3.00	6.00	12.00
❏ 40729	Just Walking in the Rain/In the Candlelight	1956	2.50	5.00	10.00
❏ 40803	You Don't Owe Me a Thing/Look Homeward, Angel	1956	2.50	5.00	10.00
❏ 40803 [PS]	You Don't Owe Me a Thing/Look Homeward, Angel	1956	6.25	12.50	25.00
❏ 40893	Yes Tonight, Josephine/No Wedding Today	1957	2.50	5.00	10.00
❏ 40942	Build Your Love (On a Strong Foundation)/Street of Memories	1957	2.50	5.00	10.00
❏ 41002	Pink Sweater Angel/Texas Tambourine	1957	2.50	5.00	10.00
❏ 41069	Miss Me Just a Little/Soliloquy of a Fool	1957	2.50	5.00	10.00
❏ 41124	Plant a Little Seed/Strollin' Girl	1958	2.50	5.00	10.00
❏ 41162	Endlessly/Lonely for a Letter	1958	2.50	5.00	10.00
❏ 41213	Up Until Now/No Regrets	1958	2.50	5.00	10.00
❏ 41280	What More Can I Say/You're the One Who Knows	1958	2.50	5.00	10.00
❏ 41327	One Man's Love Song Is Another Man's Blues/When's Your Birthday, Baby	1959	2.50	5.00	10.00
❏ 41372	Call Me Yours/Here and Now	1959	2.50	5.00	10.00
❏ 41438	I'll Never Fall in Love Again/You're All That I Live For	1959	2.50	5.00	10.00
❏ 41528	When It's Springtime in the Rockies/An Ordinary Couple	1959	2.50	5.00	10.00
❏ 41626	I'll Make You Mine/Before You	1959	2.50	5.00	10.00
❏ 41705	Don't Leave Me Now/Tell Me	1960	2.50	5.00	10.00
DECCA
❏ 31459	After My Laughter Came Tears/Lookout Chattanooga	1963	2.00	4.00	8.00
❏ 31507	Lonely Wine/I Can't Stop Crying for You	1963	2.00	4.00	8.00
❏ 31601	Can't I/Break My Heartbreak	1964	2.00	4.00	8.00
GROOVE
❏ 58-0044	One Life/Sometime Love	1964	2.00	4.00	8.00
LIBERTY
❏ 55400	I Believe/A Mother's Love	1961	2.50	5.00	10.00
—With Timi Yuro
| ❏ 55404 | A Lover's Question/Nothing Goes Up Without Coming Down | 1962 | 2.00 | 4.00 | 8.00 |
| ❏ 55431 | Cry/Scotch and Soda | 1962 | 2.00 | 4.00 | 8.00 |
OKEH
| ❏ 6809 | Whiskey and Gin/Tell the Lady I Said Goodbye | 1951 | 6.25 | 12.50 | 25.00 |
| ❏ 6840 | Cry/The Little White Cloud That Cried | 1951 | 5.00 | 10.00 | 20.00 |
—Label listed as "Okeh" at top
| ❏ 6840 | Cry/The Little White Cloud That Cried | 1951 | 7.50 | 15.00 | 30.00 |
—Label listed as "Okeh Rhythm and Blues" at top
UNITED ARTISTS
| ❏ 341 | How Many Nights, How Many Days/I'll Bring Along My Banjo | 1961 | 2.50 | 5.00 | 10.00 |
7-Inch Extended Plays
COLUMBIA
❏ B-2115	Just Walking in the Rain/All of Me//In the Candlelight/Weaker Than Wise	1956	5.00	10.00	20.00
❏ B-2115 [PS]	Just Walking in the Rain	1956	5.00	10.00	20.00
❏ B-2123	You Don't Owe Me a Thing/Look Homeward, Angel//Ain't Misbehavin'/Who's Sorry Now?	1957	3.75	7.50	15.00
❏ B-2123 [PS]	You Don't Owe Me a Thing	1957	3.75	7.50	15.00
❏ B-2536	*Walkin' My Baby Back Home/Somebody Stole My Gal/Nobody's Sweetheart/Please Don't Talk About Me When I'm Gone	195?	5.00	10.00	20.00
❏ B-2536 [PS]	Johnnie Ray (Hall of Fame Series)	195?	5.00	10.00	20.00
❏ B-2566	*Just Walking in the Rain/Please, Mr. Sun/All of Me/Tell the Lady I Said Goodbye	195?	5.00	10.00	20.00
❏ B-2566 [PS]	Johnnie Ray (Hall of Fame Series)	195?	5.00	10.00	20.00
❏ B-9611	Pretty-Eyed Baby/Lotus Blossom//Shake a Hand/I'll Never Be Free	1957	5.00	10.00	20.00
❏ B-9611 [PS]	The Big Beat, Part 1	1957	5.00	10.00	20.00
❏ B-9612	I'm Gonna Move to the Outskirts of Town/How Long, How Long Blues//I Miss You So/Trouble in Mind	1957	5.00	10.00	20.00
❏ B-9612 [PS]	The Big Beat, Part 2	1957	5.00	10.00	20.00
EPIC
❏ EG-7021	Cry/The Little White Cloud That Cried//Whiskey and Gin/Tell the Lady I Said Goodbye	1957	6.25	12.50	25.00
❏ EG-7021 [PS]	Johnnie Ray's Greatest	1957	6.25	12.50	25.00
Albums
COLUMBIA
❏ CL 961 [M]	The Big Beat	1957	12.50	25.00	50.00
❏ CL 1093 [M]	At the Desert Inn in Las Vegas	1957	12.50	25.00	50.00
❏ CL 1225 [M]	'Til Morning	1958	10.00	20.00	40.00
—Red and black label with six "eye" logos
| ❏ CL 1225 [M] | 'Til Morning | 1963 | 5.00 | 10.00 | 20.00 |
—Red label with either "Guraranteed High Fidelity" or "360 Sound Mono" at bottom
| ❏ CL 1227 [M] | Johnnie Ray's Greatest Hits | 1958 | 10.00 | 20.00 | 40.00 |
—Red and black label with 6 "eye" logos
| ❏ CL 1227 [M] | Johnnie Ray's Greatest Hits | 1962 | 6.25 | 12.50 | 25.00 |
—"Guaranteed High Fidelity" on label
| ❏ CL 1227 [M] | Johnnie Ray's Greatest Hits | 1965 | 3.75 | 7.50 | 15.00 |
—"360 Sound" label
| ❏ CL 1385 [M] | On the Trail | 1959 | 10.00 | 20.00 | 40.00 |
| ❏ CL 2510 [10] | I Cry for You | 1955 | 17.50 | 35.00 | 70.00 |
—"House Party Series" issue
| ❏ CL 6199 [10] | Johnnie Ray | 1951 | 20.00 | 40.00 | 80.00 |
| ❏ CS 8180 [S] | On the Trail | 1959 | 12.50 | 25.00 | 50.00 |
COLUMBIA SPECIAL PRODUCTS
| ❏ P 13086 | Greatest Hits | 197? | 2.50 | 5.00 | 10.00 |
EPIC
| ❏ LN 1120 [10] | Johnnie Ray | 1955 | 20.00 | 40.00 | 80.00 |
HARMONY
| ❏ H 30609 | The Best of Johnnie Ray | 1971 | 3.00 | 6.00 | 12.00 |
LIBERTY
| ❏ LRP-3221 [M] | Johnnie Ray | 1962 | 5.00 | 10.00 | 20.00 |
| ❏ LST-7221 [S] | Johnnie Ray | 1962 | 7.50 | 15.00 | 30.00 |
SUNSET
| ❏ SUM-1125 [M] | Mr. Cry | 196? | 3.00 | 6.00 | 12.00 |
| ❏ SUS-5125 [S] | Mr. Cry | 196? | 3.00 | 6.00 | 12.00 |

RAY AND THE DARCHAES
45s
ALJON
| ❏ 1249 | Carol/Little Girl So Fine | 1962 | 30.00 | 60.00 | 120.00 |
BUZZY
| ❏ 202 | Darling Forever/There Will Always Be | 1962 | 25.00 | 50.00 | 100.00 |

RAY, GOODMAN AND BROWN See THE MOMENTS.

RAY-O-VACS, THE
45s
ATCO
| ❏ 6085 | Party Time/Crying All Alone | 1957 | 6.25 | 12.50 | 25.00 |
DECCA
❏ 48162	Besame Mucho/You Gotta Love My Baby Too	1950	6.25	12.50	25.00
❏ 48181	A Kiss in the Dark/Got Two Arms	1950	6.25	12.50	25.00
❏ 48197	Goodnight My Love/Take Me Back to My Boots and Saddle	1951	6.25	12.50	25.00
❏ 48211	You Can Depend on Me/If You Ever Should Leave Me	1951	6.25	12.50	25.00
❏ 48221	My Baby's Gone/Let's	1951	6.25	12.50	25.00
❏ 48234	What's Mine Is Mine/I Still Love You Baby	1951	6.25	12.50	25.00
❏ 48260	Charmaine/Hands Across the Table	1951	6.25	12.50	25.00
❏ 48274	When the Swallows Come Back to Capistrano/She's a Real Lovin' Baby	1952	6.25	12.50	25.00
JOSIE
❏ 763	Darling/Ridin' High	1954	7.50	15.00	30.00
❏ 781	I Still Love You/Daddy	1955	7.50	15.00	30.00
JUBILEE
❏ 5098	What Can I Say/Start Lovin' Me	1952	7.50	15.00	30.00
❏ 5124	Outside of Paradise/You Know	1953	7.50	15.00	30.00

R

Number	Title (A Side/B Side)	Yr	VG	VG+	NM
KAISER					
❏ 384	Crying All Alone/Party Time	1956	7.50	15.00	30.00
❏ 389	Wine-O/Hong Kong	1956	7.50	15.00	30.00
SHARP					
❏ 103	I'll Always Be in Love with You/Little Boy	1960	5.00	10.00	20.00

RAY-VONS, THE
45s

Number	Title (A Side/B Side)	Yr	VG	VG+	NM
LAURIE					
❏ 3248	Judy/Regina	1964	20.00	40.00	80.00

RAYE, SUSAN Also see BUCK OWENS AND SUSAN RAYE.
45s

Number	Title (A Side/B Side)	Yr	VG	VG+	NM
CAPITOL					
❏ 2620	I Ain't Gonna Be Treated That-a-Way/Maybe If I Close My Eyes (It'll Go Away)	1969	—	3.00	6.00
❏ 2701	Put a Little Love in Your Heart/I've Carried This Torch Much Too Long	1969	—	3.00	6.00
❏ 2833	One Night Stand/She Don't Deserve You Anymore	1970	—	3.00	6.00
❏ 2950	Willy Jones/I'll Love You Forever (If You're Sure You'll Want Me Then)	1970	—	3.00	6.00
❏ 3035	L.A. International Airport/Merry-Go-Round of Love	1971	—	3.00	6.00
❏ 3129	Pitty, Pitty, Patter/I'll Be Gone	1971	—	3.00	6.00
❏ 3209	(I've Got a) Happy Heart/How Long Will My Baby Be Gone	1971	—	3.00	6.00
❏ 3289	A Song to Sing/Adios, Farewell, Goodbye, Good Luck, So Long	1972	—	2.50	5.00
❏ 3327	My Heart Has a Mind of Its Own/You'll Never Miss the Water	1972	—	2.50	5.00
❏ 3438	Wheel of Fortune/My Heart Skips a Beat	1972	—	2.50	5.00
❏ 3499	Love Sure Feels Good in My Heart/I've Got You on My Mind Again	1972	—	2.50	5.00
❏ 3569	Cheating Game/I'll Love You Forever and Ever	1973	—	2.50	5.00
❏ 3699	Plastic Trains, Paper Planes/I Won't Be Needing You	1973	—	2.50	5.00
❏ 3782	When You Get Back from Nashville/Nobody's Fool But Yours	1973	—	2.50	5.00
❏ 3850	Stop the World (And Let Me Off)/Love's Ups and Downs	1974	—	2.00	4.00
❏ 3927	You Can Sure See It from Here/I Wish I Was a Butterfly	1974	—	2.00	4.00
❏ 3980	Whatcha Gonna Do with a Dog Like That/That Loving Feeling	1974	—	2.00	4.00
❏ 4063	Ghost Story/Beginner's Luck	1975	—	2.00	4.00
❏ 4140	He Gives Me Something (To Forgive Him For)/You're the Piece That's Always Gone	1975	—	2.00	4.00
❏ 4197	Honey Toast and Sunshine/Only a Good Love Lasts Forever	1975	—	2.00	4.00
UNITED ARTISTS					
❏ XW870	Ozark Mountain Lullaby/Johnny Sunshine	1976	—	2.00	4.00
❏ XW934	Mr. Heartache/Turn Away	1977	—	2.00	4.00
❏ XW976	Saturday Night to Sunday Quiet/My Hiding Place	1977	—	2.00	4.00
❏ XW1026	It Didn't Have to Be a Diamond/My Hiding Place	1977	—	2.00	4.00
WESTEXAS AMERICA					
❏ 1	Put Another Notch in Your Belt/I Just Can't Take the Leaving Anymore	1984	—	2.00	4.00

Albums

Number	Title	Yr	VG	VG+	NM
CAPITOL					
❏ ST-543	One Night Stand	1970	3.75	7.50	15.00
❏ ST-736	Willy Jones	1971	3.75	7.50	15.00
❏ ST-807	Pitty, Pitty, Patter	1971	3.75	7.50	15.00
❏ ST-875	(I've Got a) Happy Heart	1972	3.75	7.50	15.00
❏ ST-11055	My Heart Has a Mind of Its Own	1972	3.00	6.00	12.00
❏ ST-11106	Wheel of Fortune	1972	3.00	6.00	12.00
❏ ST-11135	Love Sure Feels Good in My Heart	1973	3.00	6.00	12.00
❏ ST-11179	Cheating Game	1973	3.00	6.00	12.00
❏ ST-11223	Plastic Trains, Paper Planes	1973	3.00	6.00	12.00
❏ ST-11255	Hymns by Susan Raye	1974	3.00	6.00	12.00
❏ ST-11282	The Best of Susan Raye	1974	3.00	6.00	12.00
❏ ST-11333	Singing	1974	3.00	6.00	12.00
❏ ST-11393	Whatch Gonna Do with a Dog Like That	1975	3.00	6.00	12.00
UNITED ARTISTS					
❏ UA-LA764-G	Susan Raye	1977	3.00	6.00	12.00

RAYS, THE
45s

Number	Title (A Side/B Side)	Yr	VG	VG+	NM
AMY					
❏ 900	Love Another Girl/Sad Saturday	1964	2.00	4.00	8.00
CAMEO					
❏ 117	Silhouettes/Daddy Cool	1957	6.25	12.50	25.00
❏ 128	Rendezvous/Triangle	1958	7.50	15.00	30.00
❏ 133	Rags to Riches/The Man Above	1958	7.50	15.00	30.00
CHESS					
❏ 1613	Tippity Top/Moo-Goo-Gai-Pan	1956	6.25	12.50	25.00
❏ 1678	How Long Must I Wait/Second Fiddle	1957	6.25	12.50	25.00
UNART					
❏ 2001	Souvenirs of Summertime/Elevator Operator	1958	10.00	20.00	40.00
XYZ					
❏ 100	My Steady Girl/No One Loves You Like I Do	1957	15.00	30.00	60.00
❏ 102	Silhouettes/Daddy Cool	1957	15.00	30.00	60.00
—Blue label					
❏ 102	Silhouettes/Daddy Cool	1957	50.00	100.00	200.00
—Gray label					
❏ 106	Souvenirs of Summertime/Elevator Operator	1958	12.50	25.00	50.00
❏ 600	Why Do You Look the Other Way/Zimbo Lula	1959	12.50	25.00	50.00
❏ 605	It's a Cryin' Shame/Mediterranean Moon	1959	10.00	20.00	40.00
❏ 607	Magic Moon/Louie Hoo Hoo	1960	6.25	12.50	25.00
—Red label					
❏ 607	Magic Moon/Louie Hoo Hoo	1960	10.00	20.00	40.00
—Blue label					
❏ 608	Old Devil Moon/Silver Starlight	1960	6.25	12.50	25.00

7-Inch Extended Plays

Number	Title	Yr	VG	VG+	NM
CHESS					
❏ 5120	(contents unknown)	1958	100.00	200.00	400.00
❏ 5120 [PS]	The Rays	1958	100.00	200.00	400.00

RAYS, THE (2)
45s

Number	Title (A Side/B Side)	Yr	VG	VG+	NM
PERRI					
❏ 1004	Are You Happy Now/Bright Brown Eyes	1962	7.50	15.00	30.00
—Frankie Valli performed on this record					

RE'VELLS, THE

Number	Title (A Side/B Side)	Yr	VG	VG+	NM
ROMAN PRESS					
❏ 201	Let It Please Be You/Love Walked In	1962	25.00	50.00	100.00

RE-VELS, THE
45s

Number	Title (A Side/B Side)	Yr	VG	VG+	NM
ATLAS					
❏ 1035	My Lost Love/Love Me, Baby	1954	100.00	200.00	400.00
—As "The Re-Vels Quartette"					
CHESS					
❏ 1708	False Alarm/When You Come Back to Me	1958	37.50	75.00	150.00
SOUND					
❏ 129	You Lied to Me/Later, Later Baby	1956	37.50	75.00	150.00
❏ 135	Dream, My Darlin', Dream/Cha Cha Toni	1956	37.50	75.00	150.00
TEEN					
❏ 122	So in Love/It Happened to Me	1955	200.00	400.00	600.00

REAL ORIGINAL BEATLES, THE Yeah, right.
45s

Number	Title (A Side/B Side)	Yr	VG	VG+	NM
DOT					
❏ 16655	The Beatle Story (Part 1)/The Beatle Story (Part 2)	1964	5.00	10.00	20.00

REBECCA AND THE SUNNY BROOK FARMERS
Albums

Number	Title	Yr	VG	VG+	NM
MUSICOR					
❏ MS-3176	Rebecca and the Sunny Brook Farmers	1969	10.00	20.00	40.00

REBELS, THE (1) See ROCKIN' REBELS.

REBELS, THE (2)
45s

Number	Title (A Side/B Side)	Yr	VG	VG+	NM
KING'S X					
❏ 3362	In the Park/In My Heart	1959	250.00	500.00	1000.

REBELS, THE (3)
45s

Number	Title (A Side/B Side)	Yr	VG	VG+	NM
PEACOCK					
❏ 1909	The Donkey Step/Just Give Me Your Heart	1962	5.00	10.00	20.00

REBENACK, MAC See DR. JOHN.

REBIRTH
Albums

Number	Title	Yr	VG	VG+	NM
AVANT GARDE					
❏ AVS-135	Rebirth	1971	12.50	25.00	50.00

REBOUNDS, THE This is not the group that became the Stampeders, according to a former member of the band.
45s

Number	Title (A Side/B Side)	Yr	VG	VG+	NM
TOWER					
❏ 288	Since I Fell for You/I'm Not Your Steppin' Stone	1966	3.75	7.50	15.00

REBS, THE
Albums

Number	Title	Yr	VG	VG+	NM
FREDLO					
❏ 6830	1968 A.D. Break Through	1968	100.00	200.00	400.00

RECALLS, THE
45s

Number	Title (A Side/B Side)	Yr	VG	VG+	NM
ARROW					
❏ 2002	No Reason/Nobody's Guy	196?	20.00	40.00	80.00

RED CRAYOLA, THE
Albums

Number	Title	Yr	VG	VG+	NM
INTERNATIONAL ARTISTS					
❏ 2 [M]	Parable of the Arable Land	1968	25.00	50.00	100.00
❏ 2 [S]	Parable of the Arable Land	1968	15.00	30.00	60.00
❏ 2	Parable of the Arable Land	1979	3.75	7.50	15.00
—Reissue with "Masterfonics" in trail-off wax					
❏ 7	God Bless the Red Crayola	1968	15.00	30.00	60.00
❏ 7	God Bless the Red Crayola	1979	3.75	7.50	15.00
—Reissue with "Masterfonics" in trail-off wax					

REDBONE Also see PAT AND LOLLY VEGAS.
45s

Number	Title (A Side/B Side)	Yr	VG	VG+	NM
EPIC					
❏ 10597	Crazy Cajun Cade Walk Band/Night Come Down	1970	—	3.00	6.00
❏ 10670	Maggie/New Blue Sermonette	1970	—	3.00	6.00
❏ 10712	Who Can Say/Light as a Feather	1971	—	3.00	6.00
❏ 10749	The Witch Queen of New Orleans/Chant: 13th Hour	1971	—	3.00	6.00
❏ 10839	When You Got Trouble/(B-side unknown)	1972	—	2.50	5.00
❏ 10866	One Monkey (Don't Stop No Show)/Message from a Drum	1972	—	2.50	5.00
❏ 10910	Already Here/Fais-Do	1972	—	2.50	5.00
❏ 10946	Poison Ivy/Condition Your Condition	1973	—	2.50	5.00
❏ 10979	We Were All Wounded at Wounded Knee/Speakeasy	1973	—	2.50	5.00
❏ 11035	Come and Get Your Love/Day to Day Life	1973	—	2.50	5.00
❏ 11035	Come and Get Your Love/Your Miserable Face	1973	—	2.50	5.00
❏ 11131	Wovoka/Clouds in My Sunshine	1974	—	2.00	4.00
❏ 50015	Suzie Girl/Interstate Highway 101	1974	—	2.00	4.00
❏ 50043	One More Time/Blood, Sweat and Tears	1974	—	2.00	4.00
❏ 50074	Only You and Rock and Roll/Interstate Highway 101	1975	—	2.00	4.00
❏ 50107	Physical Attraction/I've Got to Find the Right Woman	1975	—	2.00	4.00
RCA					
❏ PB-11096	Give Our Love Another Try/Funny Silk	1977	—	2.00	4.00
❏ PB-11182	Checkin' It Out/Funky Silk	1977	—	2.00	4.00

P. J. Proby, *Somewhere,* Liberty LRP-3406, mono LP, $10-$20.

Gary Puckett and the Union Gap, "Over You," Columbia 4-44644, picture sleeve, $6-$12.

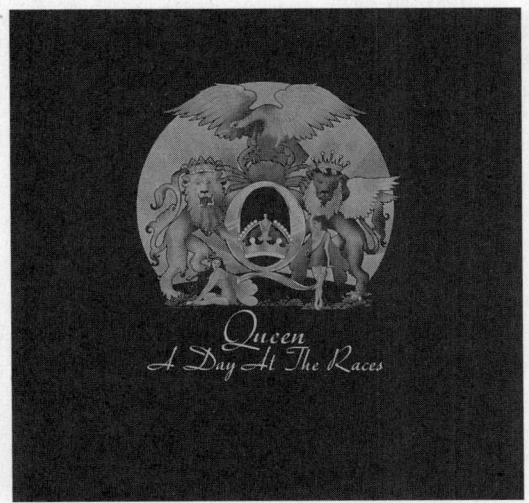

Queen, *A Day at the Races,* Elektra 6E-101, stereo LP, butterfly label, $5-$10.

The Rascals, *Time Peace – The Rascals Greatest Hits,* Atlantic SD 8190, stereo LP, green and blue label, $12.50-$25.

The Ravens, *Four Great Voices* (also known as *Ol' Man River),* Rendition 104, 7-inch EP, $1,750-$3,500 (cover and record together).

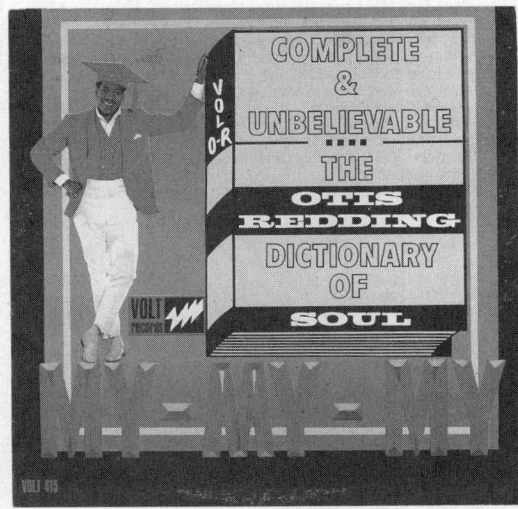

Otis Redding, *Complete and Unbelievable… The Otis Redding Dictionary of Soul,* Volt 415, mono LP, $20-$40.

R

Number	Title (A Side/B Side)	Yr	VG	VG+	NM
REDCOATS, THE					
Albums					
EPIC					
❏ EGP 501 [(2)]	Redbone	1970	5.00	10.00	20.00
❏ E 30109	Potlatch	1970	3.75	7.50	15.00
❏ EQ 30815 [Q]	Message from a Drum	1973	5.00	10.00	20.00
❏ KE 30815	Message from a Drum	1972	3.75	7.50	15.00
❏ KE 31598	Already Here	1972	3.75	7.50	15.00
❏ KE 32462	Wovoka	1974	3.75	7.50	15.00
❏ EQ 33053 [Q]	Bearded Dreams Through Turquoise Eyes	1974	5.00	10.00	20.00
❏ KE 33053	Bearded Dreams Through Turquoise Eyes	1974	3.75	7.50	15.00
❏ KEG 33456 [(2)]	Come & Get Your Redbone	1975	5.00	10.00	20.00
RCA VICTOR					
❏ AFL1-2352	Cycles	1977	3.00	6.00	12.00

REDCOATS, THE Also see STEVE ALAIMO.

Number	Title (A Side/B Side)	Yr	VG	VG+	NM
45s					
KITE					
❏ 2003	Perkin/Hi Ho	1957	12.50	25.00	50.00
❏ 2003	Perkins/Hi Ho	1957	12.50	25.00	50.00
—Note slight variation in A-side title					

REDDING, OTIS Also see OTIS AND CARLA; THE SHOOTERS.

Number	Title (A Side/B Side)	Yr	VG	VG+	NM
45s					
ATCO					
❏ 6592	Hard to Handle/Amen	1968	2.50	5.00	10.00
❏ 6612	I've Got Dreams to Remember/Nobody's Fault But Mine	1968	2.50	5.00	10.00
❏ 6631	White Christmas/Merry Christmas, Baby	1968	2.50	5.00	10.00
❏ 6636	Papa's Got a Brand New Bag/Direct Me	1968	2.50	5.00	10.00
❏ 6654	A Lover's Question/You Made a Man Out of Me	1969	2.50	5.00	10.00
❏ 6677	Love Man/I Can't Turn You Loose	1969	2.50	5.00	10.00
❏ 6700	Free Me/Higher and Higher	1969	2.50	5.00	10.00
❏ 6723	Look at the Girl/That's a Good Idea	1969	2.50	5.00	10.00
❏ 6742	Demonstration/Johnny's Heartbreak	1970	2.00	4.00	8.00
❏ 6766	Giving Away None of My Love/ Snatch a Little Piece	1970	2.00	4.00	8.00
❏ 6802	Try a Little Tenderness/ I've Been Loving You Too Long (To Stop Now)	1971	—	3.00	6.00
❏ 6907	My Girl/Good to Me	1972	—	2.50	5.00
❏ 7069	White Christmas/Merry Christmas, Baby	1976	—	2.50	5.00
❏ 7321	White Christmas/Merry Christmas, Baby	1980	—	2.00	4.00
❏ 99955	White Christmas/Merry Christmas, Baby	1982	—	2.00	4.00
BETHLEHEM					
❏ 3083	Shout Bamalama/Fat Girl	1964	5.00	10.00	20.00
CONFEDERATE					
❏ 135	Shout Bamalama/Fat Girl	1962	12.50	25.00	50.00
FINER ARTS					
❏ 2016	She's Alright/Tough Enuff	1961	12.50	25.00	50.00
—Originally released on Trans World by "The Shooters"					
KING					
❏ 6149	Shout Bamalama/Fat Girl	1968	2.50	5.00	10.00
ORBIT					
❏ 135	Shout Bamalama/Fat Girl	1961	75.00	150.00	300.00
PHILCO-FORD					
❏ HP-13	Shake/Fa-Fa-Fa-Fa-Fa	1967	5.00	10.00	20.00
—4-inch plastic "Hip Pocket Record" with color sleeve					
STONE					
❏ 209	You Left the Water Running/The Otis Jam	1976	3.00	6.00	12.00
—B-side by the Memphis Studio Band					
VOLT					
❏ 103	These Arms of Mine/Hey, Hey Baby	1962	5.00	10.00	20.00
❏ 109	That's What My Heart Needs/Mary's Little Lamb	1963	5.00	10.00	20.00
❏ 112	Pain in My Heart/Something Is Worrying Me	1963	5.00	10.00	20.00
❏ 116	Come to Me/Don't Leave Me This Way	1964	3.75	7.50	15.00
❏ 117	Security/I Want to Thank You	1964	3.75	7.50	15.00
❏ 121	Chained and Bound/Your One and Only Man	1964	3.75	7.50	15.00
❏ 124	Mr. Pitiful/That's How Strong My Love Is	1965	3.75	7.50	15.00
❏ 126	I've Been Loving You Too Long (To Stop Now)/ I'm Depending on You	1965	3.75	7.50	15.00
❏ 128	Respect/Ole Man Trouble	1965	3.75	7.50	15.00
❏ 130	I Can't Turn You Loose/Just One More Day	1965	3.75	7.50	15.00
❏ 132	Satisfaction/Any Ole Way	1966	3.75	7.50	15.00
❏ 136	My Lover's Prayer/Don't Mess with Cupid	1966	3.75	7.50	15.00
❏ 138	Fa-Fa-Fa-Fa-Fa (Sad Song)/Good to Me	1966	3.75	7.50	15.00
❏ 141	Try a Little Tenderness/I'm Sick Y'All	1966	3.75	7.50	15.00
❏ 146	I Love You More Than Words Can Say/ Let Me Come On Home	1967	3.00	6.00	12.00
❏ 149	Shake/You Don't Miss Your Water	1967	3.00	6.00	12.00
❏ 152	Glory of Love/I'm Coming Home	1967	3.00	6.00	12.00
❏ 157	(Sittin' On) The Dock of the Bay/Sweet Lorene	1968	2.50	5.00	10.00
—Multicolor (mostly brown) label					
❏ 157	(Sittin' On) The Dock of the Bay/Sweet Lorene	1968	3.00	6.00	12.00
—Black and red label					
❏ 163	The Happy Song (Dum-Dum)/Open That Door	1968	2.50	5.00	10.00
Albums					
ATCO					
❏ 33-161 [M]	Pain in My Heart	1964	62.50	125.00	250.00
❏ SD 33-161 [R]	Pain in My Heart	1968	62.50	125.00	250.00
❏ 33-252 [M]	The Immortal Otis Redding	1968	12.50	25.00	50.00
—Mono is white label promo only					
❏ SD 33-252 [S]	The Immortal Otis Redding	1968	3.75	7.50	15.00
❏ SD 33-261	History of Otis Redding	1968	3.75	7.50	15.00
—Reissue of Volt 418					
❏ SD 33-265	Otis Redding In Person at the Whiskey A-Go-Go	1968	3.75	7.50	15.00
❏ SD 33-284	Otis Blue/Otis Redding Sings Soul	1969	3.75	7.50	15.00
—Reissue of Volt 412					
❏ SD 33-285	The Soul Album	1969	3.75	7.50	15.00
—Reissue of Volt 413					
❏ SD 33-286	Otis Redding Live in Europe	1969	3.75	7.50	15.00
—Reissue of Volt 416					
❏ SD 33-287	Complete & Unbelievable…The Otis Redding Dictionary of Soul	1969	3.75	7.50	15.00
—Reissue of Volt 415					
❏ SD 33-288	The Dock of the Bay	1969	3.75	7.50	15.00
—Reissue of Volt 419					
❏ SD 33-289	Love Man	1969	3.75	7.50	15.00

Number	Title (A Side/B Side)	Yr	VG	VG+	NM
❏ SD 33-333	Tell the Truth	1970	3.75	7.50	15.00
❏ SD 2-801 [(2)]	The Best of Otis Redding	1972	5.00	10.00	20.00
ATLANTIC					
❏ SD 19346	Recorded Live	198?	2.50	5.00	10.00
❏ 81282	The Best of Otis Redding	1985	2.50	5.00	10.00
❏ 81762 [(4)]	The Otis Redding Story	1987	7.50	15.00	30.00
PAIR					
❏ PDL2-1062 [(2)]	The Legend of Otis Redding	1984	3.75	7.50	15.00
SUNDAZED					
❏ LP 5063 [M]	Complete & Unbelievable ... The Otis Redding Dictionary of Soul	2001	3.00	6.00	12.00
—Reissue on 180-gram vinyl					
❏ LP 5064 [M]	Otis Blue/Otis Redding Sings Soul	2001	3.00	6.00	12.00
—Reissue on 180-gram vinyl					
❏ LP 5132 [M]	The Soul Album	2003	3.00	6.00	12.00
—Reissue on 180-gram vinyl					
❏ LP 5133 [S]	Otis Redding In Person at the Whiskey A-Go-Go	2003	3.00	6.00	12.00
—Reissue on 180-gram vinyl					
❏ LP 5134 [S]	Otis Redding Live in Europe	2003	3.00	6.00	12.00
—Reissue on 180-gram vinyl					
❏ LP 5172 [S]	The Dock of the Bay	2003	3.00	6.00	12.00
—Reissue on 180-gram vinyl					
VOLT					
❏ 411 [M]	The Great Otis Redding Sings Soul Ballads	1965	22.50	45.00	90.00
❏ S-411 [R]	The Great Otis Redding Sings Soul Ballads	1968	27.50	55.00	110.00
❏ 412 [M]	Otis Blue/Otis Redding Sings Soul	1965	10.00	20.00	40.00
❏ S-412 [S]	Otis Blue/Otis Redding Sings Soul	1965	12.50	25.00	50.00
❏ 413 [M]	The Soul Album	1966	10.00	20.00	40.00
❏ S-413 [S]	The Soul Album	1966	12.50	25.00	50.00
❏ 415 [M]	Complete & Unbelievable…The Otis Redding Dictionary of Soul	1966	10.00	20.00	40.00
❏ S-415 [S]	Complete & Unbelievable…The Otis Redding Dictionary of Soul	1966	12.50	25.00	50.00
❏ 416 [M]	Otis Redding Live in Europe	1967	7.50	15.00	30.00
❏ S-416 [S]	Otis Redding Live in Europe	1967	10.00	20.00	40.00
❏ 418 [M]	History of Otis Redding	1967	10.00	20.00	40.00
❏ S-418 [S]	History of Otis Redding	1967	7.50	15.00	30.00
❏ S-419	The Dock of the Bay	1968	7.50	15.00	30.00

REDDY, HELEN

Number	Title (A Side/B Side)	Yr	VG	VG+	NM
45s					
CAPITOL					
❏ 3027	I Don't Know How to Love Him/I Believe in Music	1971	—	2.50	5.00
❏ 3138	Crazy Love/Best Friend	1971	—	2.50	5.00
❏ 3231	No Sad Song/More Than You Could Take	1971	—	2.50	5.00
❏ 3350	I Am Woman/More Than You Could Take	1972	—	2.00	4.00
—Orange label, "Capitol" at bottom					
❏ 3350	I Am Woman/More Than You Could Take	1972	—	2.50	5.00
—Red and orange "target" label					
❏ 3527	Peaceful/What Would They Say	1973	—	2.00	4.00
❏ 3645	Delta Dawn/If We Could Still Be Friends	1973	—	2.00	4.00
❏ 3768	Leave Me Alone (Ruby Red Dress)/The Old Fashioned Way	1973	—	2.00	4.00
❏ 3845	Keep On Singing/You're My Home	1974	—	2.00	4.00
❏ 3897	You and Me Against the World/ Love Song for Jeffrey	1974	—	2.00	4.00
❏ 3972	Angie Baby/I Think I'll Write a Song	1974	—	2.00	4.00
❏ 4021	Emotion/I've Been Waiting for You So Long	1974	—	2.00	4.00
❏ 4128	You Don't Need a Reason/Long Time Looking	1975	—	2.00	4.00
❏ 4128	Bluebird/You Don't Need a Reason	1975	—	2.00	4.00
❏ 4192	Somewhere in the Night/Ten to Eight	1975	—	2.00	4.00
❏ 4312	I Can't Hear You No More/Music Is My Life	1976	—	2.00	4.00
❏ 4350	You Make It So Easy/Gladiola	1976	—	2.00	4.00
❏ 4418	You're My World/Thank You	1977	—	2.00	4.00
❏ 4487	The Happy Girls/Laissez Les Bontemps Rouler	1977	—	2.00	4.00
❏ 4521	Candle on the Water/Brazzle Dazzle Day	1977	—	2.00	4.00
❏ 4521 [PS]	Candle on the Water/Brazzle Dazzle Day	1977	—	3.00	6.00
❏ 4555	We'll Sing in the Sunshine/I'd Rather Be Alone	1978	—	2.00	4.00
❏ 4582	Ready or Not/ If I Ever Had to Say Goodbye to You	1978	—	2.00	4.00
❏ 4628	Lady of the Night/Poor Little Fool	1978	—	2.00	4.00
❏ 4654	Mama/West Wind Circus	1978	—	2.00	4.00
❏ 4712	Make Love to Me/More Than You Could Take	1979	—	2.00	4.00
❏ 4786	Trying to Get to You/Let Me Be Your Woman	1979	—	2.00	4.00
❏ 4867	Love's Not the Question/Take What You Find	1980	—	2.00	4.00
❏ 4918	Way with the Ladies/Killer Barracuda	1980	—	2.00	4.00
FONTANA					
❏ 1611	One Way Ticket/Go	1968	3.75	7.50	15.00
MCA					
❏ 51106	I Can't Say Goodbye to You/Let's Just Stay Home Tonight	1981	—	2.00	4.00
❏ 51143	Stars Fell on California/When I Dream	1981	—	2.00	4.00
❏ 51186	Theme from "Continental Divide"/When I Dream	1981	—	2.00	4.00
❏ 52170	Don't Tell Me Tonight/Yesterday Can't Hurt Me	1983	—	2.00	4.00
❏ 52221	Imagination/The Way I Feel	1983	—	2.00	4.00
Albums					
CAPITOL					
❏ ST-762	I Don't Know How to Love Him	1971	3.75	7.50	15.00
❏ ST-857	Helen Reddy	1971	3.75	7.50	15.00
❏ ST-11068	I Am Woman	1972	2.50	5.00	10.00
❏ SMAS-11213	Long Hard Climb	1973	2.50	5.00	10.00
❏ SO-11284	Love Song for Jeffrey	1974	2.50	5.00	10.00
❏ ST-11348	Free and Easy	1974	2.50	5.00	10.00
❏ ST-11418	No Way to Treat a Lady	1975	2.50	5.00	10.00
❏ ST-11467	Helen Reddy's Greatest Hits	1975	2.50	5.00	10.00
—Orange label					
❏ SW-11467	Helen Reddy's Greatest Hits	1978	2.00	4.00	8.00
—Purple label					
❏ ST-11547	Music, Music	1976	2.50	5.00	10.00
❏ SO-11640	Ear Candy	1977	2.50	5.00	10.00
❏ SW-11759	We'll Sing in the Sunshine	1978	2.50	5.00	10.00
❏ SKBO-11873 [(2)]	Live	1979	3.00	6.00	12.00
❏ SO-11949	Reddy	1979	2.50	5.00	10.00
❏ SOO-12068	Take What You Find	1980	2.50	5.00	10.00
❏ SN-16098	Helen Reddy	1980	2.00	4.00	8.00
—Budget-line reissue					

| ❏ 4108 | Bluebird/You Don't Need a Reason | 1975 | — | 2.00 | 4.00 |
| ❏ 4128 | Ain't No Way to Treat a Lady/Long Time Looking | 1975 | — | 2.00 | 4.00 |

Number	Title (A Side/B Side)	Yr	VG	VG+	NM
❑ SN-16099	I Am Woman	1980	2.00	4.00	8.00
—Budget-line reissue					
❑ SN-16100	I Don't Know How to Love Him	1980	2.00	4.00	8.00
—Budget-line reissue					
❑ SN-16101	Long Hard Climb	1980	2.00	4.00	8.00
—Budget-line reissue					
❑ SN-16195	Love Song for Jeffrey	198?	2.00	4.00	8.00
—Budget-line reissue					
❑ SN-16196	No Way to Treat a Lady	1980	2.00	4.00	8.00
—Budget-line reissue					
❑ SN-16199	We'll Sing in the Sunshine	1980	2.00	4.00	8.00
—Budget-line reissue					
❑ SN-16200	Reddy	1980	2.00	4.00	8.00
—Budget-line reissue					
❑ SN-16248	Take What You Find	198?	2.00	4.00	8.00
—Budget-line reissue					
❑ SN-16249	Free and Easy	198?	2.00	4.00	8.00
—Budget-line reissue					
❑ SN-16250 [(2)]	Live	198?	2.00	4.00	8.00
—Budget-line reissue					
❑ SN-16333	Helen Reddy's Greatest Hits	1984	—	3.00	6.00
—Budget-line reissue					
MCA					
❑ 5376	Imagination	198?	2.00	4.00	8.00
PAIR					
❑ PDL2-1066 [(2)]	Lust for Life	1986	3.00	6.00	12.00

REDELL, TEDDY
45s
ATCO

Number	Title (A Side/B Side)	Yr	VG	VG+	NM
❑ 6162	Judy/Can't You See	1960	5.00	10.00	20.00
HI					
❑ 2024	Pipeliner/I Want to Hold You	1960	5.00	10.00	20.00
VADEN					
❑ 110	Knockin' on the Backside/Before It Began	1960	30.00	60.00	120.00
❑ 115	Goldust/Corrine, Corrina	1960	30.00	60.00	120.00
❑ 116	Judy/Can't You See	1960	30.00	60.00	120.00
❑ 117	Pipeliner/I Want to Hold You	1960	30.00	60.00	120.00
❑ 301	Pipeliner/I Want to Hold You	1961	20.00	40.00	80.00
❑ 305	I'll Sail My Ship Alone/Don't Grow Old Alone	1961	20.00	40.00	80.00

REDEYE
45s
PENTAGRAM

Number	Title (A Side/B Side)	Yr	VG	VG+	NM
❑ 202	Mississippi State Line/199 Thoughts Too Late	1970	—	3.00	6.00
❑ 204	Games/Collections of Yesterday and Now	1970	—	3.00	6.00
❑ 206	Red Eye Blues/Making of a Hero	1971	—	3.00	6.00
❑ 209	Homebound Feelin'/I'm Going Blind	1971	—	3.00	6.00
❑ 213	Mountain Annie/Just a Little More	1971	—	3.00	6.00

Albums
PENTAGRAM

Number	Title (A Side/B Side)	Yr	VG	VG+	NM
❑ PE-10003	Redeye	1970	3.75	7.50	15.00
❑ PR-10006	One Man's Poison	1971	3.75	7.50	15.00

REDJACKS, THE
45s
APT

Number	Title (A Side/B Side)	Yr	VG	VG+	NM
❑ 25006	Big Brown Eyes/To Make You Mine	1958	5.00	10.00	20.00
OKLAHOMA					
❑ 5005	Big Brown Eyes/To Make You Mine	1958	12.50	25.00	50.00

REDNOW, EIVETS See STEVIE WONDER.

REDWOODS, THE JEFF BARRY was involved with this group.
45s
EPIC

Number	Title (A Side/B Side)	Yr	VG	VG+	NM
❑ 9447	Shake, Shake Sherry/The Memory Lingers On	1961	7.50	15.00	30.00
—As "The Redwoods"					
❑ 9447	Shake, Shake Sherry/The Memory Lingers On	1961	10.00	20.00	40.00
—As "The Flairs"					
❑ 9473	Never Take It Away/Unemployment Insurance	1961	7.50	15.00	30.00
❑ 9505	Please, Mr. Scientist/Where You Need to Be	1962	10.00	20.00	40.00

REED, DEAN
45s
CAPITOL

Number	Title (A Side/B Side)	Yr	VG	VG+	NM
❑ F4121	The Search/Annabelle	1959	3.75	7.50	15.00
❑ F4198	A Pair of Scissors/I Kissed a Queen	1959	3.75	7.50	15.00
❑ F4273	Our Summer Romance/I Ain't Got You	1959	3.75	7.50	15.00
❑ 4384	Don't Let Her Go/No Wonder	1960	3.75	7.50	15.00
❑ 4438	Pistolero/Hummingbird	1960	3.75	7.50	15.00
IMPERIAL					
❑ 5733	I Forgot More Than You'll Ever Know/ Once Again	1961	3.00	6.00	12.00

REED, JAMES
45s
BIG TOWN

Number	Title (A Side/B Side)	Yr	VG	VG+	NM
❑ 117	Things Ain't What They Used to Be/ You Better Hold Me	1954	37.50	75.00	150.00
FLAIR					
❑ 1034	My Mama Told Me/This Is the End	1954	50.00	100.00	200.00
❑ 1042	Dr. Brown/You Better Hold Me	1954	50.00	100.00	200.00
MONEY					
❑ 201	Oh People/My Love Is Real	1954	50.00	100.00	200.00
RHYTHM					
❑ 1775	Tin Pan Alley/Biggest Place in Town	1954	125.00	250.00	500.00

REED, JERRY
45s
CAPITOL

Number	Title (A Side/B Side)	Yr	VG	VG+	NM
❑ F3294	If the Good Lord's Willing and the Creeks Don't Rise/Here I Am	1955	5.00	10.00	20.00
❑ F3381	I'm a Lover, Not a Fighter/Honey Chile	1956	5.00	10.00	20.00
❑ F3429	When I Found You/Mister Whiz	1956	5.00	10.00	20.00
❑ F3504	Just a Romeo/This Great Big Empty Room	1956	5.00	10.00	20.00
❑ F3592	Too Busy Cryin' the Blues/You're Braggin', Boy	1956	5.00	10.00	20.00

Number	Title (A Side/B Side)	Yr	VG	VG+	NM
❑ F3657	It's High Time/Forever	1957	3.75	7.50	15.00
❑ F3731	Rockin' in Bagdad/Oh Lonely Heart	1957	3.75	7.50	15.00
❑ F3823	In My Own Back Yard/Ba-Bee	1957	3.75	7.50	15.00
❑ F3882	Too Young to Be Blue/Bessie Baby	1958	3.75	7.50	15.00
❑ F3992	How Can I Go On This Way/ Your Money Makes You Purty	1958	3.75	7.50	15.00
❑ B-5531	Big Time Fool/What Comes Around	1985	—	—	3.00
❑ B-5556	Country's Alive and Doing Well/Let It Go	1986	—	—	3.00
❑ B-5612	This Missin' You's a Whole Lotta Fun/ There Was You	1986	—	—	3.00
❑ B-5660	You Can't Get the Hell Out of Texas/ Old Fashioned Heart	1986	—	—	3.00
COLUMBIA					
❑ 42047	Love and War (Ain't Much Difference in the Two)/ Love Is the Cause of It All	1961	2.50	5.00	10.00
❑ 42183	Hit and Run/Sure Is Blue Out Tonight	1961	2.50	5.00	10.00
❑ 42311	Pity the Fool/I've Got Everybody Fooled But Me	1962	2.50	5.00	10.00
❑ 42417	I'm Movin' On/Goodnight Irene	1962	2.50	5.00	10.00
❑ 42533	Twist-a-Roo/Hully Gully Guitar	1962	2.50	5.00	10.00
❑ 42639	Too Old to Cut the Mustard/ Overlooked and Underloved	1962	2.50	5.00	10.00
❑ 42704	I Want to Be Loved/I'll See You in My Dreams	1963	2.50	5.00	10.00
❑ 42808	The Shock/Let's Get Ready for the Summer	1963	2.50	5.00	10.00
❑ 42863	The Mountain Man/Love Don't Grow on Trees	1963	2.50	5.00	10.00
❑ 43052	June Night/Spilled Milk	1964	2.50	5.00	10.00
NRC					
❑ 014	Have Blues Will Travel/ This Can't Be Happening to Me	1958	3.75	7.50	15.00
❑ 032	Just Right/Stone Eternal	1959	3.00	6.00	12.00
❑ 5008	Little Lovin' Liza/Soldier's Joy	1959	3.00	6.00	12.00
RCA					
❑ PB-10784	Remembering/Babe	1976	—	2.00	4.00
❑ PB-10893	Semolita/Phantom of the Opry	1977	—	2.00	4.00
❑ PB-11008	With His Pants in His Hand/We Called It Everything Else	1977	—	2.00	4.00
❑ PB-11056	East Bound and Down/ (I'm Just A) Redneck in a Rock and Roll Bar	1977	—	2.00	4.00
❑ PB-11164	You Know What/Louisiana Lady	1977	—	2.00	4.00
—With Seidina					
❑ PB-11232	Sweet Love Feelings/You're Gonna Need Someone	1978	—	2.00	4.00
❑ PB-11281	(I Love You) What Can I Say/High Rollin'	1978	—	2.00	4.00
❑ PB-11281	(I Love You) What Can I Say/I Feel for You	1978	—	2.00	4.00
❑ PB-11370	Stars and Stripes Forever/Reedology	1978	—	2.00	4.00
❑ PB-11404	Gimme Back My Blues/Honkin'	1978	—	2.00	4.00
❑ PB-11472	Second-Hand Satin Lady (And a Bargain Basement Boy)/Jiffy Jam	1979	—	2.00	4.00
❑ PB-11638	(Who Was the Man Who Put) The Line in Gasoline/Piece of Cake	1979	—	2.00	4.00
❑ PB-11698	Hot Stuff/Nervous Breakdown	1979	—	2.00	4.00
❑ PB-11764	Sugar Foot Rag/ I Wanna Go Back Home to Georgia	1979	—	2.00	4.00
❑ PB-11944	Age/Workin' at the Car Wash Blues	1980	—	2.00	4.00
❑ GB-11986	East Bound and Down/ (I'm Just A) Redneck in a Rock and Roll Bar	1980	—	—	3.00
—Gold Standard Series					
❑ PB-12034	The Friendly Family Inn/Bandit	1980	—	2.00	4.00
❑ PB-12083	Texas Bound and Flyin'/Concrete Sailor	1980	—	2.00	4.00
❑ PB-12157	Caffein, Nicotine, Benzedrine (And Wish Me Luck)/If Love's Not Around the House	1981	—	2.00	4.00
❑ PB-12210	The Testimony of Soddy Hoe/ Dreaming Fairy Tales	1981	—	2.00	4.00
❑ PB-12253	Good Friends Make Good Lovers/The Devil Went Down to Georgia	1981	—	2.00	4.00
❑ JK-12318 [DJ]	Patches (same on both sides)	1981	2.50	5.00	10.00
—Promo only on blue vinyl					
❑ PB-12318	Patches/Stray Dogs and Stray Women	1981	—	2.00	4.00
❑ PB-13081	The Man with the Golden Thumb/ East Bound and Down	1982	—	2.00	4.00
❑ PB-13268	She Got the Goldmine (I Got the Shaft)/44	1982	—	2.50	5.00
❑ PB-13355	The Bird/The Hobo	1982	—	2.50	5.00
—As "Jerry Reed and Friends"					
❑ PB-13422	Down on the Corner/Good Times	1983	—	2.00	4.00
❑ PB-13527	Good Ole Boys/ She's Ready for Someone to Love Her	1983	—	2.00	4.00
❑ PB-13663	I'm a Slave/Nobody Ever Loved Me	1983	—	2.00	4.00
❑ JK-13666 [DJ]	Christmas Time's a-Coming (same on both sides)	1983	—	2.50	5.00
❑ PB-13666	Christmas Time's a-Coming/The Best I Ever Had	1983	—	2.50	5.00
❑ GB-14069	She Got the Goldmine (I Got the Shaft)/The Bird	1985	—	—	3.00
—Gold Standard Series					
RCA VICTOR					
❑ 47-8565	If I Don't Live Up to It/I Feel a Sin Coming On	1965	2.00	4.00	8.00
❑ 47-8667	Ain't That Just Like a Fool/Love's Battleground	1965	2.00	4.00	8.00
❑ 47-8730	Fighting for the U.S.A./Navy Blues	1965	2.00	4.00	8.00
❑ 47-8957	Woman Shy/I Feel for You	1966	2.00	4.00	8.00
❑ 47-9152	Guitar Man/It Don't Work That Way	1967	2.50	5.00	10.00
❑ 47-9334	Tupelo Mississippi Flash/Wabash Cannonball	1967	2.00	4.00	8.00
❑ 47-9493	Remembering/Fine on My Mind	1968	2.00	4.00	8.00
❑ 47-9623	Alabama Wild Man/Twelve Bar Midnight	1968	2.00	4.00	8.00
❑ 47-9701	Oh, What a Woman/Losing Your Love	1968	2.00	4.00	8.00
❑ 47-9754	Turn It Around in Your Mind/Long Gone	1969	—	—	—
—Unreleased					
❑ 47-9804	Talk About the Good Times/Alabama Jubilee	1969	—	3.00	6.00
❑ 47-9870	Georgia Sunshine/Swinging '69	1970	—	3.00	6.00
❑ 47-9890	Tennessee Stud/Cannonball Rag	1970	—	3.00	6.00
—With Chet Atkins					
❑ 47-9904	Amos Moses/The Preacher and the Bear	1970	—	3.00	6.00
❑ 47-9976	When You're Hot, You're Hot/You've Been Crying Again	1971	—	3.00	6.00
❑ 48-1011	Ko Ko Joe/I Feel for You	1971	—	3.00	6.00
❑ 74-0124	Blues Land/There's Better Things in Life	1969	—	3.00	6.00
❑ 74-0211	Are You From Dixie/A Worried Man	1969	—	3.00	6.00
❑ 74-0242	A Thing Called Love/Hallelujah I Love Her So	1969	—	—	—
—Unreleased					
❑ 74-0613	Another Puff/Love Man	1971	—	2.50	5.00
❑ 74-0667	Smell the Flowers/If It Comes to That	1972	—	2.50	5.00

R

Number	Title (A Side/B Side)	Yr	VG	VG+	NM
❏ 74-0738	Alabama Wildman/Take It Easy	1972	—	2.50	5.00
❏ 74-0775	Nashtownville/Jerry's Breakdown	1972	—	2.50	5.00
—With Chet Atkins					
❏ 74-0857	You Took All the Ramblin' Out of Me/I'm Not Playing Games	1972	—	2.50	5.00
❏ 74-0960	Lord, Mr. Ford/2-Timin'	1973	—	2.50	5.00
❏ APBO-0194	The Uptown Poker Club/Honkin'	1973	—	2.50	5.00
❏ APBO-0224	The Crude Oil Blues/Pickie, Pickie, Pickie	1974	—	2.50	5.00
❏ APBO-0273	A Good Woman's Love/Everybody Needs Someone	1974	—	2.50	5.00
❏ PB-10013	You've Got It/Lightning Rod	1974	—	2.50	5.00
❏ PB-10063	Boogie Woogie Rock and Roll/In Between	1974	—	2.50	5.00
❏ PB-10132	Let's Sing Our Song/Grab Bag	1974	—	2.50	5.00
❏ PB-10247	Mind Your Love/Struttin'	1975	—	2.50	5.00
❏ PB-10325	The Telephone/City of New Orleans	1975	—	2.50	5.00
❏ PB-10389	You Got a Lock on Me/Reedology	1975	—	2.50	5.00
❏ GB-10510	Lord, Mr. Ford/Two-Timin'	1975	—	—	3.00
—Gold Standard Series					
❏ PB-10717	Gator/Good for Him	1976	—	2.50	5.00
Albums					
CAPITOL					
❏ ST-12492	Lookin' at You	1986	2.00	4.00	8.00
HARMONY					
❏ H 30547	I'm Movin' On	1971	2.50	5.00	10.00
RCA CAMDEN					
❏ ACL1-0331	Tupelo Mississippi Flash	1973	2.50	5.00	10.00
❏ CAS-2585	Oh What a Woman!	1972	2.50	5.00	10.00
RCA VICTOR					
❏ APD1-0238 [Q]	Lord, Mr. Ford	1973	6.25	12.50	25.00
❏ APL1-0238	Lord, Mr. Ford	1973	3.00	6.00	12.00
❏ APL1-0356	The Uptown Poker Club	1973	3.00	6.00	12.00
❏ APL1-0544	A Good Woman's Love	1974	3.00	6.00	12.00
❏ APL1-0787	Mind Your Love	1974	3.00	6.00	12.00
❏ APL1-1226	Red Hot Picker	1975	3.00	6.00	12.00
❏ ANL1-1345	When You're Hot, You're Hot	1975	2.50	5.00	10.00
—Reissue of 4506					
❏ APL1-1861	Both Barrels	1976	3.00	6.00	12.00
❏ ANL1-2167	Me and Chet	1976	2.50	5.00	10.00
—Reissue of 4707					
❏ AHL1-2346	Jerry Reed Rides Again	1977	3.00	6.00	12.00
❏ AHL1-2516	East Bound and Down	1977	3.00	6.00	12.00
❏ AHL1-2764	Sweet Love Feelings	1978	3.00	6.00	12.00
❏ AHL1-3359	Half Singin' & Half Pickin'	1979	3.00	6.00	12.00
❏ AHL1-3453	Jerry Reed Live!	1979	3.00	6.00	12.00
❏ AHL1-3604	Jerry Reed Sings Jim Croce	1980	3.00	6.00	12.00
❏ AYL1-3677	East Bound and Down	1980	2.00	4.00	8.00
—"Best Buy Series" reissue					
❏ LPM-3756 [M]	The Unbelievable Guitar and Voice of Jerry Reed	1967	6.25	12.50	25.00
❏ LSP-3756 [S]	The Unbelievable Guitar and Voice of Jerry Reed	1967	5.00	10.00	20.00
❏ AHL1-3771	Texas Bound and Flyin'	1980	3.00	6.00	12.00
❏ LPM-3978 [M]	Nashville Underground	1968	12.50	25.00	50.00
❏ LSP-3978 [S]	Nashville Underground	1968	5.00	10.00	20.00
❏ AHL1-4021	Dixie Dreams	1981	3.00	6.00	12.00
❏ LSP-4069	Alabama Wild Man	1968	5.00	10.00	20.00
❏ LSP-4147	Better Things in Life	1969	5.00	10.00	20.00
❏ AYL1-4167	Jerry Reed Live!	1982	2.00	4.00	8.00
—"Best Buy Series" reissue					
❏ LSP-4204	Jerry Reed Explores Guitar Country	1969	5.00	10.00	20.00
❏ LSP-4293	Cookin'	1970	5.00	10.00	20.00
❏ AHL1-4315	The Man with the Golden Thumb	1982	2.50	5.00	10.00
❏ LSP-4391	Georgia Sunshine	1970	5.00	10.00	20.00
❏ AYL1-4394	Texas Bound and Flyin'	1982	2.00	4.00	8.00
—"Best Buy Series" reissue					
❏ LSP-4506	When You're Hot, You're Hot	1971	3.75	7.50	15.00
❏ AHL1-4529	The Bird	1982	2.50	5.00	10.00
❏ LSP-4596	Ko-Ko Joe	1971	3.75	7.50	15.00
❏ LSP-4660	Smell the Flowers	1972	3.75	7.50	15.00
❏ AHL1-4692	Ready	1983	2.50	5.00	10.00
❏ LSP-4707	Me and Chet	1972	3.75	7.50	15.00
—With Chet Atkins					
❏ LSP-4729	The Best of Jerry Reed	1972	3.75	7.50	15.00
❏ LSP-4750	Jerry Reed	1972	3.75	7.50	15.00
❏ LSP-4838	Hot A' Mighty!	1973	3.75	7.50	15.00
❏ AYL1-5151	The Bird	1984	2.00	4.00	8.00
—"Best Buy Series" reissue					
❏ AHL1-5176	Greatest Hits	1984	2.50	5.00	10.00
❏ AHL1-5472	Collector's Series	1985	2.50	5.00	10.00

REED, JIMMY
45s

Number	Title (A Side/B Side)	Yr	VG	VG+	NM
ABC					
❏ 10887	Got Nowhere to Go/Two Ways to Skin (A Cat)	1966	2.00	4.00	8.00
BLUESWAY					
❏ 61003	I Wanna Know/Two Heads Are Better Than One	1967	2.00	4.00	8.00
❏ 61006	Don't Press Your Luck Woman/Feel Like I Want to Ramble	1967	2.00	4.00	8.00
❏ 61013	Buy Me a Hound Dog/Crazy About Oklahoma	1968	2.00	4.00	8.00
❏ 61020	Peepin' and Hidin'/My Baby Told Me	1968	2.00	4.00	8.00
❏ 61025	Don't Light My Fire/The Judge Should Know	1969	2.00	4.00	8.00
CANYON					
❏ 38	Hard Walkin' Hannah (Part 1)/Hard Walkin' Hannah (Part 2)	196?	2.00	4.00	8.00
CHANCE					
❏ 1142	High and Lonesome/Roll and Rhumba	1953	700.00	1400.	2100.
EXODUS					
❏ 2005	Knockin' At Your Door/Dedication to Sonny	1966	2.50	5.00	10.00
❏ 2008	Cousin Peaches/Crazy 'Bout Oklahoma	1966	2.50	5.00	10.00
RRG					
❏ 44001	Christmas Present Blues/Crying Blind	19??	2.00	4.00	8.00
VEE JAY					
❏ 100	High and Lonesome/Roll and Rumba	1953	150.00	300.00	600.00
❏ 100	High and Lonesome/Roll and Rumba	1953	300.00	600.00	1200.
—Red vinyl					
❏ 105	I Found My Baby/Jimmy's Boogie	1953	50.00	100.00	200.00

Number	Title (A Side/B Side)	Yr	VG	VG+	NM
❏ 105	I Found My Baby/Jimmy's Boogie	1953	100.00	200.00	400.00
—Red vinyl					
❏ 119	You Don't Have to Go/Boogie in the Dark	1954	20.00	40.00	80.00
❏ 119	You Don't Have to Go/Boogie in the Dark	1954	75.00	150.00	300.00
—Red vinyl					
❏ 132	Pretty Thing/I'm Gonna Ruin You	1955	25.00	50.00	100.00
❏ 153	I Don't Go for That/She Don't Want Me No More	1955	12.50	25.00	50.00
❏ 168	Ain't That Lovin' You Baby/Baby, Don't Say That No More	1956	10.00	20.00	40.00
❏ 186	Can't Stand to See You Go/Rockin' with Reed	1956	10.00	20.00	40.00
❏ 203	I Love You Baby/My First Plea	1956	7.50	15.00	30.00
❏ 226	You've Got Me Dizzy/Honey, Don't Let Me Go	1956	7.50	15.00	30.00
❏ 237	Honey, Where You Going/Little Rain	1957	7.50	15.00	30.00
❏ 248	The Sun Is Shining/Baby, What's On Your Mind	1957	7.50	15.00	30.00
❏ 253	Honest I Do/Signals of Love	1957	7.50	15.00	30.00
❏ 270	You're Something Else/A String to My Heart	1958	7.50	15.00	30.00
❏ 275	You Got Me Crying/Go On to School	1958	7.50	15.00	30.00
❏ 287	I Know It's a Sin/Down in Virginia	1958	7.50	15.00	30.00
❏ 298	I'm Gonna Get My Baby/Odds and Ends	1958	7.50	15.00	30.00
❏ 304	I Told You Baby/Ends and Odds (Instrumental)	1958	7.50	15.00	30.00
❏ 314	Take Out Some Insurance/You Know I Love You	1959	7.50	15.00	30.00
❏ 326	I Wanna Be Loved/Going to New York	1959	7.50	15.00	30.00
❏ 333	Baby What You Want Me to Do/Caress Me, Baby	1959	7.50	15.00	30.00
❏ 347	Found Love/Where Can You Be	1960	6.25	12.50	25.00
❏ 357	Hush Hush/Going to the River, Part 2	1960	6.25	12.50	25.00
❏ 373	Laughing at the Blues/Close Together	1961	6.25	12.50	25.00
❏ 380	Big Boss Man/I'm a Love You	1961	6.25	12.50	25.00
❏ 398	Bright Lights, Big City/I'm Mr. Luck	1961	6.25	12.50	25.00
❏ 425	Aw, Shucks, Hush Your Mouth/Baby, What's Wrong	1962	5.00	10.00	20.00
❏ 449	Tell Me You Love Me/Good Lover	1962	5.00	10.00	20.00
❏ 459	I'll Change My Style/Too Much	1962	5.00	10.00	20.00
❏ 473	Let's Get Together/Oh, John	1962	5.00	10.00	20.00
❏ 509	There'll Be a Day/Shame, Shame, Shame	1963	3.75	7.50	15.00
❏ 552	Mary Mary/I'm Gonna Help You	1963	3.75	7.50	15.00
❏ 570	Outskirts of Town/St. Louis Blues	1963	3.75	7.50	15.00
❏ 584	See See Rider/Wee Wee Baby Blues	1964	3.75	7.50	15.00
❏ 593	Help Yourself/Heading for a Fall	1964	3.75	7.50	15.00
❏ 616	Oh John/Down in Mississippi	1964	3.75	7.50	15.00
❏ 622	I'm Going Upside Your Head/The Devil's Shoestring	1964	3.75	7.50	15.00
❏ 642	I Wanna Be Loved/A New Leaf	1965	3.75	7.50	15.00
❏ 702	I'm the Man Down There/Left Handed Woman	1965	3.75	7.50	15.00
❏ 709	Don't Think I'm Through/When Girls Do It	1966	3.75	7.50	15.00
Albums					
ANTILLES					
❏ 7007	Cold Chills	197?	3.75	7.50	15.00
BLUESVILLE					
❏ BLS-6054	I Ain't From Chicago	1973	3.75	7.50	15.00
❏ BLS-6067	The Ultimate Jimmy Reed	1973	3.75	7.50	15.00
❏ BLS-6073 [(2)]	Jimmy Reed at Carnegie Hall	1973	5.00	10.00	20.00
BLUESWAY					
❏ BL-6004 [M]	The New Jimmy Reed Album	1967	5.00	10.00	20.00
❏ BLS-6004 [S]	The New Jimmy Reed Album	1967	5.00	10.00	20.00
❏ BL-6009 [M]	Soulin'	1967	5.00	10.00	20.00
❏ BLS-6009 [S]	Soulin'	1967	5.00	10.00	20.00
❏ BLS-6015	Big Boss Man	1968	5.00	10.00	20.00
❏ BLS-6024	Down in Virginia	1969	5.00	10.00	20.00
BUDDAH					
❏ BDS-4003	The Very Best of Jimmy Reed	1969	3.75	7.50	15.00
—Reissue of Vee Jay 1039					
CHAMELEON					
❏ D1-74762	Bright Lights, Big City	1988	2.50	5.00	10.00
EVEREST ARCHIVE OF FOLK & JAZZ					
❏ 234	Jimmy Reed	197?	3.00	6.00	12.00
GNP CRESCENDO					
❏ GNPS-10006 [(2)]	The Best of Jimmy Reed	1974	3.75	7.50	15.00
SUNSET					
❏ SUS-5218	Somethin' Else	1968	3.00	6.00	12.00
TRADITION					
❏ 2069	Wailin' the Blues	1969	3.00	6.00	12.00
TRIP					
❏ 8012 [(2)]	History of Jimmy Reed	1971	3.75	7.50	15.00
VEE JAY					
❏ LP-1004 [M]	I'm Jimmy Reed	1958	55.00	110.00	220.00
—Maroon label					
❏ LP-1004 [M]	I'm Jimmy Reed	1961	20.00	40.00	80.00
—Black label with colorband					
❏ VJLP-1004	I'm Jimmy Reed	198?	2.50	5.00	10.00
—Reissue with glossy labels					
❏ LP-1008 [M]	Rockin' with Reed	1959	50.00	100.00	200.00
—Maroon label					
❏ LP-1008 [M]	Rockin' with Reed	1961	20.00	40.00	80.00
—Black label with colorband					
❏ VJLP-1008	Rockin' with Reed	198?	2.50	5.00	10.00
—Reissue with glossy labels					
❏ LP-1022 [M]	Found Love	1959	50.00	100.00	200.00
—Maroon label					
❏ LP-1022 [M]	Found Love	1961	20.00	40.00	80.00
—Black label with colorband					
❏ LP-1025 [M]	Now Appearing	1960	20.00	40.00	80.00
❏ VJLP-1025	Now Appearing	198?	2.50	5.00	10.00
—Reissue with glossy labels					
❏ 2LP-1035 [(2)M]	Jimmy Reed at Carnegie Hall	1961	12.50	25.00	50.00
❏ 2SR-1035 [(2)S]	Jimmy Reed at Carnegie Hall	1961	17.50	35.00	70.00
❏ VJLP2-1035 [(2)]	Jimmy Reed at Carnegie Hall	198?	3.00	6.00	12.00
—Reissue with glossy labels					
❏ LP-1039 [M]	The Best of Jimmy Reed	1962	10.00	20.00	40.00
❏ SR-1039 [S]	The Best of Jimmy Reed	1962	15.00	30.00	60.00
❏ VJLP-1039	The Best of Jimmy Reed	198?	2.50	5.00	10.00
—Reissue with glossy labels					
❏ LP-1050 [M]	Just Jimmy Reed	1962	10.00	20.00	40.00
❏ SR-1050 [S]	Just Jimmy Reed	1962	15.00	30.00	60.00
❏ LP-1067 [M]	T'Ain't No Big Thing…But He Is Jimmy Reed	1963	10.00	20.00	40.00
❏ SR-1067 [S]	T'Ain't No Big Thing…But He Is Jimmy Reed	1963	15.00	30.00	60.00
❏ LP-1072 [M]	The Best of the Blues	1963	10.00	20.00	40.00

Number	Title (A Side/B Side)	Yr	VG	VG+	NM
❏ LP-1073 [M]	The 12 String Guitar Blues	1963	10.00	20.00	40.00
❏ SR-1073 [S]	The 12 String Guitar Blues	1963	37.50	75.00	150.00
❏ LP-1080 [M]	More of the Best of Jimmy Reed	1964	10.00	20.00	40.00
❏ SR-1080 [S]	More of the Best of Jimmy Reed	1964	37.50	75.00	150.00
❏ LP-1095 [M]	Jimmy Reed at Soul City	1964	10.00	20.00	40.00
❏ VJLP-1095	Jimmy Reed at Soul City	198?	2.50	5.00	10.00
—Reissue with glossy labels					
❏ VJS-7303	Blues Is My Business	198?	2.50	5.00	10.00
❏ LP-8501 [M]	The Legend, The Man	1965	10.00	20.00	40.00
❏ VJLP-8501	The Legend, The Man	198?	2.50	5.00	10.00
—Reissue with glossy labels					
❏ VJS-8501 [S]	The Legend, The Man	1965	37.50	75.00	150.00

REED, LOU Also see THE PRMITIVES; THE VELVET UNDERGROUND.
12-Inch Singles
A&M

Number	Title (A Side/B Side)	Yr	VG	VG+	NM
❏ 17352 [DJ]	September Song/September Song (7" Version)	1986	—	3.00	6.00
ARISTA					
❏ SP-14 [DJ]	Street Hassle (stereo)/Street Hassle (mono)	1978	2.50	5.00	10.00
❏ SP-36 [DJ]	Walk on the Wild Side/Coney Island Baby/ Satellite of Love	1978	2.50	5.00	10.00
❏ SP-56 [DJ]	Disco Mystic/I Wanna Boogie with You	1979	2.50	5.00	10.00
❏ SP-84 [DJ]	How Do You Speak to An Angel/Keep Away/The Power of Positive Drinking/Standing on Ceremony	1980	3.75	7.50	15.00
❏ 9375 [DJ]	Hot Hips (same on both sides)	1985	2.50	5.00	10.00
ATLANTIC					
❏ 819 [DJ]	My Love Is Chemical (same on both sides)	1985	—	3.50	7.00
RCA					
❏ 5711-1	Original Wrapper (2 versions)/Video Violence (2 versions)	198?	2.00	4.00	8.00
❏ JR-13849 [DJ]	I Love You, Suzanne (same on both sides)	1984	—	3.50	7.00
❏ PD-13928	My Red Joystick (remix) (instrumental)/ I Love You Suzanne	1984	2.50	5.00	10.00
❏ JR-14343 [DJ]	No Money Down (same on both sides)	1986	3.00	6.00	12.00
—Green vinyl					
❏ PD-14388	No Money Down (Extended)/No Money Down (Dub)/Don't Hurt a Woman	1986	2.00	4.00	8.00
❏ JR-14420 [DJ]	Video Violence (same on both sides)	1986	2.00	4.00	8.00
❏ PD-14427	The Original Wrapper (3 mixes)/Video Violence	1986	2.00	4.00	8.00
SIRE					
❏ PRO-A-3359 [DJ]	Dirty Blvd. (Radio Edit)/Dirty Blvd. (LP Version)	1988	2.00	4.00	8.00

45s
A&M

Number	Title (A Side/B Side)	Yr	VG	VG+	NM
❏ 2781	September Song/Oh Heavenly Salvation	1985	—	2.00	4.00
—B-side by Mark Bingham/Johnny Adams/Aaron Neville					
❏ 2883	Soul Man/Sweet Sarah	1986	—	—	3.00
—With Sam Moore					
ARISTA					
❏ 0215	I Believe in Love/Senselessly Cruel	1976	—	2.00	4.00
❏ 0431	City Lights/I Want to Boogie with You	1979	—	2.00	4.00
❏ 0535	Growing Up in Public/ The Power of Positive Drinking	1980	—	2.00	4.00
ATLANTIC					
❏ 89468	My Love Is Chemical/People Have Got to Move	1985	—	—	3.00
—B-side by Jenny Burton					
❏ 89468 [PS]	My Love Is Chemical/People Have Got to Move	1985	—	—	3.00
RCA					
❏ JB-13558	Martial Law/Don't Talk to Me About Work	1983	—	—	3.00
❏ PB-13841	I Love You Suzanne/My Friend George	1984	—	—	3.00
❏ PB-14368	No Money Down/Don't Hurt a Woman	1986	—	—	3.00
RCA VICTOR					
❏ 74-0727	I Can't Stand It/Going Down	1972	—	3.00	6.00
❏ 74-0784	Walk and Talk It/Wild Child	1972	—	3.00	6.00
❏ 74-0887	Walk on the Wild Side/Perfect Day	1973	—	3.00	6.00
❏ 74-0964	Satellite of Love/Walk and Talk It	1973	—	3.00	6.00
❏ APBO-0054	Vicious/Good Night Ladies	1973	—	2.50	5.00
❏ APBO-0172	Lady Day/How Do You Think It Feels	1973	—	2.50	5.00
❏ APBO-0238	Sweet Jane/Lady Day	1974	7.50	15.00	30.00
—Part of U.S. numbering system, but pressed for export.					
❏ PB-10053	Sally Can't Dance/Vicious	1974	—	2.00	4.00
❏ PB-10081	Sally Can't Dance/Ennui	1974	—	2.00	4.00
❏ GB-10162	Walk on the Wild Side/Vicious	1975	—	—	3.00
—Gold Standard Series reissue					
❏ PB-10573	Charley's Girl/Nowhere At All	1976	—	2.00	4.00
❏ PB-10648	Crazy Feeling/Nowhere At All	1976	—	2.00	4.00
SIRE					
❏ 22876	Romeo Had Juliette/Busload of Faith	1989	—	—	3.00
❏ 22876 [PS]	Romeo Had Juliette/Busload of Faith	1989	—	—	3.00

7-Inch Extended Plays
NORTON

Number	Title (A Side/B Side)	Yr	VG	VG+	NM
❏ EP-097	Your Love/Merry Go Round//So Blue/ Leave Her for Me	2000	—	—	2.00
—Early recordings; Side 1 credited to "Lewis Reed"; Side 2 credited to "The Jades"					
❏ EP-097 [PS]	All Tomorrow's Dance Parties	2000	—	—	2.00

Albums
ARISTA

Number	Title (A Side/B Side)	Yr	VG	VG+	NM
❏ AL 4100	Rock and Roll Heart	1976	3.75	7.50	15.00
—Originals on light blue labels					
❏ AL 4169	Street Hassle	1978	3.75	7.50	15.00
❏ AL 4229	The Bells	1979	3.00	6.00	12.00
❏ ALB6-8390	City Lights — Classic Performances by Lou Reed	1985	2.50	5.00	10.00
❏ AL11 8434 [(2)]	Rock and Roll Diary 1967-1980	198?	4.00	8.00	16.00
—Reissue					
❏ AL 8502 [(2)]	Live! Take No Prisoners	1978	4.50	9.00	18.00
❏ A2L 8603 [(2)]	Rock and Roll Diary 1967-1980	1980	4.50	9.00	18.00
❏ AL 9522	Growing Up in Public	1980	3.00	6.00	12.00
❏ R 252506 [(2)]	Rock and Roll Diary 1967-1980	1980	4.50	9.00	18.00
—RCA Music Service reissue					
DIRECT DISK					
❏ (no #) [DJ]	The Blue Mask	1982	37.50	75.00	150.00
—Only exists on test pressings; no stock copies made					
RCA VICTOR					
❏ APL1-0207	Berlin	1973	3.00	6.00	12.00

Number	Title (A Side/B Side)	Yr	VG	VG+	NM
❏ AFL1-0472	Rock & Roll Animal	1977	2.00	4.00	8.00
—Reissue					
❏ APL1-0472	Rock & Roll Animal	1974	3.00	6.00	12.00
❏ AFL1-0611	Sally Can't Dance	1977	2.00	4.00	8.00
—Reissue					
❏ CPL1-0611	Sally Can't Dance	1974	5.00	10.00	20.00
❏ APL1-0915	Coney Island Baby	1976	4.00	8.00	16.00
❏ AFL1-0959	Lou Reed Live	1977	2.00	4.00	8.00
—Reissue					
❏ APL1-0959	Lou Reed Live	1975	3.75	7.50	15.00
❏ CPD2-1101 [(2)Q]	Metal Machine Music	1975	37.50	75.00	150.00
❏ CPL2-1101 [(2)]	Metal Machine Music	1975	12.50	25.00	50.00
—Orange or brown label					
❏ AFL1-2001	Walk on the Wild Side	1978	2.00	4.00	8.00
—Reissue					
❏ APL1-2001	Walk on the Wild Side	1977	3.00	6.00	12.00
❏ ANL1-2480	Coney Island Baby	1977	2.00	4.00	8.00
—Reissue					
❏ AYL1-3664	Rock & Roll Animal	1980	2.00	4.00	8.00
—Best Buy Series reissue					
❏ AYL1-3752	Lou Reed Live	1980	2.00	4.00	8.00
—Best Buy Series reissue					
❏ AYL1-3753	Walk on the Wild Side	1980	2.00	4.00	8.00
—Best Buy Series reissue					
❏ AYL1-3806	Transformer	1980	2.00	4.00	8.00
—Best Buy Series reissue					
❏ AYL1-3807	Coney Island Baby	1980	2.00	4.00	8.00
—Best Buy Series reissue					
❏ AFL1-4221	The Blue Mask	1982	2.50	5.00	10.00
❏ DJL1-4266 [DJ]	Special Radio Series, Vol. XVII	1980	6.25	12.50	25.00
—Promo-only with insert					
❏ DJL1-4267	The Blue Mask Interview Album	1982	10.00	20.00	40.00
❏ DJL1-4345 [DJ]	The Blue Mask Sampler	1982	3.00	6.00	12.00
—Three-song EP released to radio					
❏ AYL1-4388	Berlin	1983	2.00	4.00	8.00
—Best Buy Series reissue					
❏ AYL1-4555	Sally Can't Dance	1983	2.00	4.00	8.00
—Best Buy Series reissue					
❏ AFL1-4568	Legendary Hearts	1983	2.50	5.00	10.00
❏ LSP-4701	Lou Reed	1972	5.00	10.00	20.00
❏ AYL1-4780	The Blue Mask	1984	2.00	4.00	8.00
—Best Buy Series reissue					
❏ AFL1-4807	Transformer	1977	2.00	4.00	8.00
—Reissue					
❏ LSP-4807	Transformer	1972	5.00	10.00	20.00
❏ AFL1-4998	New Sensations	1984	2.00	4.00	8.00
❏ AFL1-7190	Mistrial	1986	3.00	6.00	12.00
SIRE					
❏ 25829	New York	1989	2.50	5.00	10.00
❏ R 101058	New York	1989	3.00	6.00	12.00
—BMG Music Service edition					

REED, LOU, AND JOHN CALE
Albums
SIRE

Number	Title (A Side/B Side)	Yr	VG	VG+	NM
❏ 26140	Songs for Drella	1990	2.50	5.00	10.00

REED, TAWNEY
45s
CONGRESS

Number	Title (A Side/B Side)	Yr	VG	VG+	NM
❏ 270	My Heart Cried/Can't Take It Away	1966	3.00	6.00	12.00
RED BIRD					
❏ 10-044	Needle in a Haystack/I Got a Feeling	1965	10.00	20.00	40.00

REED, URSULA
45s
OLD TOWN

Number	Title (A Side/B Side)	Yr	VG	VG+	NM
❏ 1001	Your're Laffin' "Cause I'm Cryin'/Ursula's Blues	1954	100.00	200.00	400.00

REEDER, BILL
45s
FERNWOOD

Number	Title (A Side/B Side)	Yr	VG	VG+	NM
❏ 121	You're My Baby/Where Were You Last Night	1960	20.00	40.00	80.00
HI					
❏ 2037	Till I Waltz Again with You/There Was a Time	1961	20.00	40.00	80.00
❏ 2041	Secret Love/Judy	1961	5.00	10.00	20.00
VOLL					
❏ 100	Till I Waltz Again with You/There Was a Time	1961	50.00	100.00	200.00

REEKERS, THE
45s
RY-JAC

Number	Title (A Side/B Side)	Yr	VG	VG+	NM
❏ 13	Grindin'/Don't Call Me Flyface	1964	12.50	25.00	50.00

REESE, DELLA
45s
ABC

Number	Title (A Side/B Side)	Yr	VG	VG+	NM
❏ 10815	Stranger on Earth/If It's the Last Thing I Do	1966	2.00	4.00	8.00
❏ 10841	It Was a Very Good Year/Solitary Woman	1966	2.00	4.00	8.00
❏ 10876	Sunny/That's Life	1966	2.00	4.00	8.00
❏ 10931	Soon/Every Other Day	1967	—	3.00	6.00
❏ 10962	I Heard You Cried Last Night/On the South Side of Chicago	1967	—	3.00	6.00
❏ 11017	Let's Make the Most of a Beautiful Thing/Sorry Baby	1967	—	3.00	6.00
❏ 11051	I Gotta Be Me/Never My Love	1968	—	3.00	6.00
ABC-PARAMOUNT					
❏ 10691	After Loving You/How Do You Keep from Crying	1965	2.00	4.00	8.00
❏ 10721	And That Reminds Me/I Only Want a Buddy, Not a Sweetheart	1965	2.00	4.00	8.00
❏ 10759	'T'Ain't Nobody's Bizness If I Do/ I Ain't Ready for That	1965	2.00	4.00	8.00
AVCO					
❏ 4521	Simple Song of Freedom/(B-side unknown)	1970	—	3.50	7.00
❏ 4586	If It Feels Good Do It/Good Lovin' Makes It Right	1972	—	2.50	5.00
AVCO EMBASSY					
❏ 4515	Games People Play/Compared to What	1969	—	3.00	6.00

Number	Title (A Side/B Side)	Yr	VG	VG+	NM
❏ 4545	Billy My Love/(B-side unknown)	1970	—	3.00	6.00
❏ 4566	The Troublemaker/				
	The Love I've Been Looking For	1971	—	3.00	6.00
CHI-SOUND					
❏ XW978	I'll Be Your Sunshine/Nothing But a True Love	1977	—	2.00	4.00
JUBILEE					
❏ 5198	In the Still of the Night/Kiss My Love Goodbye	1955	3.75	7.50	15.00
❏ 5214	Time After Time/Fine Sugar	1955	3.75	7.50	15.00
❏ 5233	I've Got My Love to Keep Me Warm/				
	Years from Now	1956	3.75	7.50	15.00
❏ 5247	Headin' Home/Daybreak Serenade	1956	3.75	7.50	15.00
❏ 5251	My Melancholy Baby/One for My Baby	1956	3.75	7.50	15.00
❏ 5263	In the Meantime/The More I See You	1956	3.75	7.50	15.00
❏ 5278	How About You/How Can You Not Believe	1957	3.75	7.50	15.00
❏ 5292	And That Reminds Me/I Cried for You	1957	3.00	6.00	12.00
❏ 5307	I Only Want to Love You/By Love Possessed	1957	3.00	6.00	12.00
❏ 5317	How Can You Lose (What You Never Had)/				
	If Not for You	1958	3.00	6.00	12.00
❏ 5323	I've Got a Feelin' You're Foolin'/C'mon, C'mon	1958	3.00	6.00	12.00
❏ 5332	I Wish/You Gotta Love Everybody	1958	3.00	6.00	12.00
❏ 5345	Sermonette/Dreams End at Dawn	1958	3.00	6.00	12.00
❏ 5346	When I Grow Too Old to Dream/				
	You're Just in Love	1958	3.00	6.00	12.00
—*Della Reese and Kirk Stuart*					
❏ 5369	Time Was/Once Upon a Dream	1959	3.00	6.00	12.00
❏ 5375	I Don't Want to Walk Without You/				
	I'm Nobody's Baby	1959	3.00	6.00	12.00
❏ 5453	Sermonette/You Gotta Love Somebody	1963	2.50	5.00	10.00
RCA VICTOR					
❏ 47-7591	Don't You Know/Soldier Won't You Marry Me	1959	2.50	5.00	10.00
❏ 47-7644	Not One Minute More/You're My Love	1959	2.50	5.00	10.00
❏ 47-7683	Someday/The Lady Is a Tramp	1960	2.50	5.00	10.00
❏ 47-7706	Someday You'll Want Me to Want You/Faraway				
	Boy	1960	2.50	5.00	10.00
❏ 47-7750	Everyday/There's No Two Ways About It	1960	2.50	5.00	10.00
❏ 47-7750 [PS]	Everyday/There's No Two Ways About It	1960	5.00	10.00	20.00
❏ 47-7784	And Now/There's Nothin' Like a Boy	1960	2.50	5.00	10.00
❏ 47-7784 [PS]	And Now/There's Nothin' Like a Boy	1960	5.00	10.00	20.00
❏ 47-7833	The Most Beautiful Words/				
	You Mean All the World to Me	1961	2.50	5.00	10.00
❏ 47-7867	The Touch of Your Lips/				
	Won'cha Come Home, Bill Bailey	1961	2.50	5.00	10.00
❏ 47-7884	I Possess/A Far, Far Better Thing	1961	2.50	5.00	10.00
❏ 47-7961	One/What Do You Think, Joe	1961	2.50	5.00	10.00
❏ 47-7996	Ninety-Nine and a Half Won't Do/You Don't				
	Know How Blessed You Are	1962	2.50	5.00	10.00
❏ 47-8021	Rome Adventure/Here's That Rainy Day	1962	2.50	5.00	10.00
❏ 47-8070	I Love You So Much It Hurts/Blow Out the Sun	1962	2.50	5.00	10.00
❏ 47-8093	As Long As He Needs Me/				
	It Makes No Difference Now	1962	2.50	5.00	10.00
❏ 47-8093 [PS]	As Long As He Needs Me/				
	It Makes No Difference Now	1962	3.75	7.50	15.00
❏ 47-8145	Be My Love/I Behold You	1963	2.50	5.00	10.00
❏ 47-8187	More/Serenade	1963	2.50	5.00	10.00
❏ 47-8260	Angel D'Amore/Forbidden Games	1963	2.50	5.00	10.00
❏ 47-8337	The Bottom of Old Smokey/				
	A Clock That's Got No Hands	1964	2.00	4.00	8.00
❏ 47-8394	If I Didn't Care/Wind in the Willows	1964	2.00	4.00	8.00
❏ 48-1018	Ninety-Nine and a Half Won't Do/And Now	1971	—	2.00	4.00
❏ 74-0558	You Came a Long Way from St. Louis/				
	Nobody's Sweetheart	1971	—	2.00	4.00
❏ 47-8145 [PS]	Be My Love/I Behold You	1963	3.75	7.50	15.00
7-Inch Extended Plays					
RCA VICTOR					
❏ EPA-4349	Don't You Know/Soldier, Won't You Marry Me//				
	Not One Minute More/You're My Love	1959	3.75	7.50	15.00
❏ EPA-4349 [PS]	Don't You Know	1959	3.75	7.50	15.00
Albums					
ABC					
❏ 569 [M]	Della Reese Live	1966	3.75	7.50	15.00
❏ S-569 [S]	Della Reese Live	1966	5.00	10.00	20.00
❏ 589 [M]	One More Time	1967	5.00	10.00	20.00
❏ S-589 [S]	One More Time	1967	3.75	7.50	15.00
❏ 612 [M]	Della on Strings of Blue	1967	5.00	10.00	20.00
❏ S-612 [S]	Della on Strings of Blue	1967	3.75	7.50	15.00
❏ S-636	I Gotta Be Me…This Trip Out	1968	3.75	7.50	15.00
❏ AC-30002	The ABC Collection	1976	3.75	7.50	15.00
ABC-PARAMOUNT					
❏ ABC-524 [M]	C'mon and Hear Della Reese	1965	3.75	7.50	15.00
❏ ABCS-524 [S]	C'mon and Hear Della Reese	1965	5.00	10.00	20.00
❏ ABC-540 [M]	I Like It Like Dat!	1966	3.75	7.50	15.00
❏ ABCS-540 [S]	I Like It Like Dat!	1966	5.00	10.00	20.00
AVCO EMBASSY					
❏ 33004	Black Is Beautiful	1969	3.75	7.50	15.00
❏ 33017	Right Now	1970	3.75	7.50	15.00
JAZZ A LA CARTE					
❏ 3	One of a Kind	1978	3.75	7.50	15.00
JUBILEE					
❏ JLP-1026 [M]	Melancholy Baby	1957	7.50	15.00	30.00
❏ JGM-1071 [M]	A Date with Della Reese at Mr. Kelly's in Chicago	196?	5.00	10.00	20.00
—*Black label with all-silver print*					
❏ JGM-1071 [M]	A Date with Della Reese at Mr. Kelly's in Chicago	1963	3.75	7.50	15.00
—*Black label, multi-colored spokes around "jubilee"*					
❏ JGS-1071 [S]	A Date with Della Reese at Mr. Kelly's in Chicago	1965	3.75	7.50	15.00
—*Black label, multi-colored spokes around "jubilee," yellow spoke goes nowhere near center hole; new prefix*					
❏ JLP-1071 [M]	A Date with Della Reese at Mr. Kelly's in Chicago	1959	6.25	12.50	25.00
—*Originals have blue labels*					
❏ SDJLP-1071 [S]	A Date with Della Reese at Mr. Kelly's in Chicago	1959	6.25	12.50	25.00
—*Black label with all-silver print*					
❏ SDJLP-1071 [S]	A Date with Della Reese at Mr. Kelly's in Chicago	1959	7.50	15.00	30.00
—*Originals have blue labels*					
❏ SDJLP-1071 [S]	A Date with Della Reese at Mr. Kelly's in Chicago	1962	5.00	10.00	20.00
—*Black label, multi-colored spokes around "jubilee," yellow spoke goes almost to center hole*					
❏ JLP-1083 [M]	Amen	1959	6.25	12.50	25.00
❏ SDJLP-1083 [S]	Amen	1959	7.50	15.00	30.00

Number	Title (A Side/B Side)	Yr	VG	VG+	NM
❏ JGM-1095 [M]	The Story of the Blues	1962	3.75	7.50	15.00
—*Black label, multi-colored spokes around "jubilee," yellow spoke goes almost to center hole; new prefix*					
❏ JGS-1095 [S]	The Story of the Blues	1964	3.75	7.50	15.00
—*Black label, multi-colored spokes around "jubilee," yellow spoke goes nowhere near center hole*					
❏ JLP-1095 [M]	The Story of the Blues	1960	5.00	10.00	20.00
—*Black label, multi-colored spokes around "jubilee," yellow spoke goes almost to center hole*					
❏ JLP-1095 [M]	The Story of the Blues	1960	6.25	12.50	25.00
—*Original labels are black with all-silver print*					
❏ SDJLP-1095 [S]	The Story of the Blues	1960	7.50	15.00	30.00
—*Original labels are black with all-silver print*					
❏ SDJLP-1095 [S]	The Story of the Blues	1962	6.25	12.50	25.00
—*Black label, multi-colored spokes around "jubilee," yellow spoke goes almost to center hole*					
❏ JLP-1109 [M]	What Do You Know About Love	1960	6.25	12.50	25.00
❏ JLP-1116 [M]	And That Reminds Me	1960	6.25	12.50	25.00
❏ JGM-5002 [M]	The Best of Della Reese	196?	3.75	7.50	15.00
❏ JGS-5002 [S]	The Best of Della Reese	196?	5.00	10.00	20.00
PICKWICK					
❏ SPC-3058	And That Reminds Me	196?	3.00	6.00	12.00
RCA VICTOR					
❏ LPM-2157 [M]	Della	1960	5.00	10.00	20.00
❏ LSP-2157 [S]	Della	1960	6.25	12.50	25.00
❏ LPM-2204 [M]	Della by Starlight	1960	5.00	10.00	20.00
❏ LSP-2204 [S]	Della by Starlight	1960	6.25	12.50	25.00
❏ LPM-2280 [M]	Della Della Cha-Cha-Cha	1961	5.00	10.00	20.00
❏ LSP-2280 [S]	Della Della Cha-Cha-Cha	1961	6.25	12.50	25.00
❏ LPM-2391 [M]	Special Delivery	1961	5.00	10.00	20.00
❏ LSP-2391 [S]	Special Delivery	1961	6.25	12.50	25.00
❏ LPM-2419 [M]	The Classic Della	1962	5.00	10.00	20.00
❏ LSP-2419 [S]	The Classic Della	1962	6.25	12.50	25.00
❏ LPM-2568 [M]	Della on Stage	1962	5.00	10.00	20.00
❏ LSP-2568 [S]	Della on Stage	1962	6.25	12.50	25.00
❏ LPM-2711 [M]	Waltz with Me	1963	5.00	10.00	20.00
❏ LSP-2711 [S]	Waltz with Me	1963	6.25	12.50	25.00
❏ LPM-2814 [M]	Moody	1963	5.00	10.00	20.00
❏ LSP-2814 [S]	Moody	1963	6.25	12.50	25.00
❏ LPM-2872 [M]	Della Reese at Basin Street East	1964	5.00	10.00	20.00
❏ LSP-2872 [S]	Della Reese at Basin Street East	1964	6.25	12.50	25.00
❏ LSP-4651	The Best of Della Reese	1972	3.00	6.00	12.00

REESE, JAXON May also be known as "Jackson Reese."
45s

Number	Title (A Side/B Side)	Yr	VG	VG+	NM
PARKWAY					
❏ 129	Hurry Sundown/How Do You Speak to an Angel	1967	10.00	20.00	40.00
❏ 142	Pretty Girl/Cry Me a River	1967	10.00	20.00	40.00

REEVES, DEL
45s

Number	Title (A Side/B Side)	Yr	VG	VG+	NM
CAPITOL					
❏ F3819	Love, Love, Love/You're Not the Changing Kind	1957	7.50	15.00	30.00
—*With Chester Smith*					
❏ F3979	The Trot/Cool Drool	1958	7.50	15.00	30.00
❏ F4045	Two Teen Hearts/Baby I Love You	1958	7.50	15.00	30.00
CHART					
❏ 5082	Stand In/Bad, Bad Tuesday	1970	2.00	4.00	8.00
COLUMBIA					
❏ 4-43044	Talking to the Night Lights/Not Since Adam	1964	2.50	5.00	10.00
DECCA					
❏ 31307	Be Quiet Mind/As Far As I Can See	1961	3.00	6.00	12.00
❏ 31417	He Stands Real Tall/Empty House	1962	3.00	6.00	12.00
KOALA					
❏ 324	Good Ole Girls/Doin' Soft Time	1980	—	2.50	5.00
❏ 329	White Christmas/White Christmas				
	(Second Version)	1980	—	2.50	5.00
❏ 333	Swinging Doors/				
	Who Left the Door to Heaven Open	1981	—	2.50	5.00
❏ 336	Slow Hand/Take Off Time	1981	—	2.50	5.00
❏ 339	Ain't Nobody Gonna Get My Body But You/Let's				
	Think About Livin'	1981	—	2.50	5.00
❏ 347	That's What I Like About the South/				
	(B-side unknown)	1982	—	2.50	5.00
❏ 584	Take Me to Your Heart/				
	What the Love of a Lady Can Do	1980	—	2.50	5.00
❏ 594	What Am I Gonna Do?/Night Out	1980	—	2.50	5.00
PEACH					
❏ 739	You Must Be an Angel/				
	I Watched You Walk Away	1960	6.25	12.50	25.00
❏ 746	Time After Time/I Don't Wonder	1961	5.00	10.00	20.00
❏ 748	You Must Be an Angel/				
	I Watched You Walk Away	1961	5.00	10.00	20.00
PLAYBACK					
❏ 1103	The Second Time Around/(B-side unknown)	1986	—	2.50	5.00
❏ 1301	Dear Dr. Ruth/Anywhere U.S.A.	1988	—	3.00	6.00
❏ 1302	Louisiana Legs/(B-side unknown)	1988	—	3.00	6.00
❏ 1303	I Used My Doodle-De-Doos/I Wish I Had Loved	1988	—	3.00	6.00
REPRISE					
❏ 20158	The Only Girl I Can't Forget/				
	The Love She Offered Me	1963	2.50	5.00	10.00
❏ 20228	I Closed My Eyes and Saw the Light/Once a Fool	1963	2.50	5.00	10.00
UNITED ARTISTS					
❏ 0141	Girl on the Billboard/Bar Room Talk	1973	—	2.00	4.00
—*"Silver Spotlight Series" reissue*					
❏ XW249	Mm-Mm Good/Bridge That Wouldn't Burn	1973	—	2.50	5.00
❏ XW308	Lay a Little Lovin' on Me/Lay Me to Sleep	1973	—	2.50	5.00
❏ XW378	What a Way to Go/Sometimes Woman	1973	—	2.50	5.00
❏ XW427	Prayer from a Mobile Home/Three Years Late	1974	—	2.50	5.00
❏ XW532	She Likes Country Bands/A Rose Is Hard to Beat	1974	—	2.50	5.00
❏ XW564	Pour It All on Me/Belles of Broadway	1974	—	2.50	5.00
❏ XW593	But I Do/One More Round of Gin	1975	—	2.50	5.00
❏ XW639	Puttin' In Overtime at Home/Homemade Love	1975	—	2.50	5.00
❏ XW702	You Comb Her Hair Every Morning/				
	Hell and Half of Georgia	1975	—	2.50	5.00
❏ XW760	I Ain't Got Nobody/I Would Like to See You Again	1976	—	2.50	5.00
❏ 824	Girl on the Billboard/				
	Eyes Don't Come Crying to Me	1965	2.00	4.00	8.00
❏ XW829	Nobody Touches My Baby/				
	She's the Best Thing I Ever Almost Had	1976	—	2.50	5.00

Number	Title (A Side/B Side)	Yr	VG	VG+	NM
❑ XW885	My Better Half/Dig a Little Deeper in the Well	1976	—	2.50	5.00
❑ 890	The Belles of Southern Bell/Nothing to Write Home About	1965	2.00	4.00	8.00
❑ 940	Women Do Funny Things to Me/My Half of Our Part	1965	2.00	4.00	8.00
❑ XW989	Ladies Night/Cryin' in Arkansas Tonight	1977	—	2.50	5.00
❑ XW1047	Am I in Heaven/Rita Ballow	1977	—	2.50	5.00
❑ XW1191	When My Angel Turns Into a Devil/How Can Anything That Feels So Good (Hurt So Bad)	1978	—	2.50	5.00
❑ XW1230	Dig Down Deep/Darlin' I Love You	1978	—	2.50	5.00
❑ 50001	One Bum Town/Dead and Gone	1966	2.00	4.00	8.00
❑ 50035	Gettin' Any Feed for Your Chickens/Plain as the Tears on My Face	1966	2.00	4.00	8.00
❑ 50081	This Must Be the Bottom/Laughter Keeps Running Down My Cheeks	1966	2.00	4.00	8.00
❑ 50115	Christmas Is Lonely/Sajo	1966	2.50	5.00	10.00
❑ 50128	Blame It On My Do Wrong/I Don't Have Sense Enough	1967	2.00	4.00	8.00
❑ 50157	The Private/Things Her Memory Makes	1967	2.00	4.00	8.00
❑ 50157 [PS]	The Private/Things Her Memory Makes	1967	5.00	10.00	20.00
❑ 50210	A Dime at a Time/So Much Got Lost	1967	2.00	4.00	8.00
❑ 50270	Wild Blood/Lest We Forget	1968	—	3.50	7.00
❑ 50332	Looking at the World Through a Windshield/If I Lived Here (I'd Be Home Now)	1968	—	3.50	7.00
❑ 50487	Good Time Charlie's/These Feet	1968	—	3.50	7.00
❑ 50531	Be Glad/Moccasin Branch	1969	—	3.50	7.00
❑ 50564	There Wouldn't Be a Lonely Heart in Town/Little Bit of Somethin' Else	1969	—	3.50	7.00
❑ 50622	A Lover's Question/Spare Me	1970	—	3.50	7.00
❑ 50667	Son of a Coal Man/The Chair That Rocked Us All	1970	—	3.50	7.00
❑ 50714	Right Back Loving You Again/Gardenia Brown	1970	—	3.50	7.00
❑ 50743	Bar Room Talk/I'm Not Through Loving You	1971	—	3.00	6.00
❑ 50763	Working Like the Devil (For the Lord)/Sidewalks of Chicago	1971	—	3.00	6.00
❑ 50802	The Philadelphia Fillies/Belles of Broadway	1971	—	3.00	6.00
❑ 50840	A Dozen Pairs of Boots/A Rose Is Hard to Beat	1971	—	3.00	6.00
❑ 50877	The Best Is Yet to Come/Truth Can Hurt a Woman	1972	—	3.00	6.00
❑ 50906	No Rings — No Strings/Hey, Anybody Here Seen Cupid	1972	—	3.00	6.00
❑ 50964	Before Goodbye/Buck Jones Guitar	1972	—	3.00	6.00
❑ 51106	Trucker's Paradise/Gathering of My Memories	1973	—	3.00	6.00

Albums

KOALA
Number	Title	Yr	VG	VG+	NM
❑ KO 14188	Del Reeves	1980	3.00	6.00	12.00

PLAYBACK
| ❑ 12002 | Here's Del Reeves | 1988 | 3.75 | 7.50 | 15.00 |

STARDAY
| ❑ 998 | Greatest Hits | 197? | 2.50 | 5.00 | 10.00 |

SUNSET
❑ SUS-5230	Wonderful World of Country Music	1968	3.00	6.00	12.00
❑ SUS-5279	Country Concert Live!	1969	3.00	6.00	12.00
❑ SUS-5321	Out in the Country	1970	3.00	6.00	12.00

UNITED ARTISTS
❑ UA-LA044-F	Trucker's Paradise	1973	3.75	7.50	15.00
❑ UA-LA204-G	Live at the Palomino Club	1974	3.75	7.50	15.00
❑ UA-LA235	The Very Best of Del Reeves	1974	3.75	7.50	15.00
❑ UA-LA364-G	Del Reeves with Strings and Things	1975	3.75	7.50	15.00
❑ UA-LA687-G	10th Anniversary	1977	3.00	6.00	12.00
❑ UAL-3441 [M]	Del Reeves Sings Girl on the Billboard	1965	6.25	12.50	25.00
❑ UAL-3458 [M]	Doodle-Oo-Doo-Doo	1965	5.00	10.00	20.00
❑ UAL-3468 [M]	Del Reeves Sings Jim Reeves	1966	5.00	10.00	20.00
❑ UAL-3488 [M]	Special Delivery	1966	5.00	10.00	20.00
❑ UAL-3528 [M]	Santa's Boy	1966	5.00	10.00	20.00
❑ UAL-3530 [M]	Gettin' Any Feed for Your Chickens?	1966	5.00	10.00	20.00
❑ UAL-3571 [M]	Struttin' My Stuff	1967	6.25	12.50	25.00
❑ UAL-3595 [M]	Six of One, Half a Dozen of the Other	1967	6.25	12.50	25.00
❑ UAL-3612 [M]	The Little Church in the Dell	1967	7.50	15.00	30.00
❑ UAS-6441 [S]	Del Reeves Sings Girl on the Billboard	1965	7.50	15.00	30.00
❑ UAS-6458 [S]	Doodle-Oo-Doo-Doo	1965	6.25	12.50	25.00
❑ UAS-6468 [S]	Del Reeves Sings Jim Reeves	1966	6.25	12.50	25.00
❑ UAS-6488 [S]	Special Delivery	1966	6.25	12.50	25.00
❑ UAS-6528 [S]	Santa's Boy	1966	6.25	12.50	25.00
❑ UAS-6530 [S]	Gettin' Any Feed for Your Chickens?	1966	6.25	12.50	25.00
❑ UAS-6571 [S]	Struttin' My Stuff	1967	5.00	10.00	20.00
❑ UAS-6595 [S]	Six of One, Half a Dozen of the Other	1967	5.00	10.00	20.00
❑ UAS-6612 [S]	The Little Church in the Dell	1967	6.25	12.50	25.00
❑ UAS-6635	The Best of Del Reeves	1968	5.00	10.00	20.00
❑ UAS-6643	Running Wild	1968	5.00	10.00	20.00
❑ UAS-6674	Looking at the World Through a Windshield	1968	5.00	10.00	20.00
❑ UAS-6705	Down at Good Time Charlie's	1969	5.00	10.00	20.00
❑ UAS-6733	Big Daddy Del	1970	5.00	10.00	20.00
❑ UAS-6758	The Best of Del Reeves, Vol. 2	1970	5.00	10.00	20.00
❑ UAS-6789	Friends and Neighbors	1971	5.00	10.00	20.00
❑ UAS-6820	The Del Reeves Album	1971	5.00	10.00	20.00
❑ UAS-6830	Before Goodbye	1972	5.00	10.00	20.00

REEVES, DEL, AND BOBBY GOLDSBORO Also see each artist's individual listings.

45s

UNITED ARTISTS
| ❑ 50591 | She Thinks I Still Care/Take a Little Good Will Home | 1969 | — | 3.50 | 7.00 |

Albums

UNITED ARTISTS
| ❑ UAL 3615 [M] | Our Way of Life | 1967 | 5.00 | 10.00 | 20.00 |
| ❑ UAS 6615 [S] | Our Way of Life | 1967 | 5.00 | 10.00 | 20.00 |

REEVES, JIM

45s

ABBOTT
❑ 115	Wagon Load of Love/What Were You Doing Last Nite	1953	6.25	12.50	25.00
❑ 115	Wagon Load of Love/What Were You Doing Last Nite	1953	15.00	30.00	60.00
—Red vinyl					
❑ 116	Mexican Joe/I Could Cry	1953	6.25	12.50	25.00

Number	Title (A Side/B Side)	Yr	VG	VG+	NM
❑ 116	Mexican Joe/I Could Cry	1953	15.00	30.00	60.00
—Red vinyl					
❑ 137	Let Me Love You Just a Little/Butterfly Love	1953	6.25	12.50	25.00
❑ 137	Let Me Love You Just a Little/Butterfly Love	1953	15.00	30.00	60.00
—Red vinyl					
❑ 143	El Rancho Del Rio/It's Hard to Love Just One	1953	6.25	12.50	25.00
❑ 143	El Rancho Del Rio/It's Hard to Love Just One	1953	15.00	30.00	60.00
—Red vinyl					
❑ 148	Bimbo/Gypsy Heart	1953	15.00	30.00	60.00
—Red vinyl					
❑ 148	Bimbo/Gypsy Heart	1953	6.25	12.50	25.00
—Black vinyl					
❑ 160	Echo Bonita/Then I'll Stop Loving You	1954	5.00	10.00	20.00
❑ 164	Ramblin' Heart/Beatin' on the Ding Dong	1954	5.00	10.00	20.00
❑ 168	Padre of Old San Antone/Mother Went A-Walkin'	1954	5.00	10.00	20.00
❑ 170	Penny Candy/I'll Follow You	1954	5.00	10.00	20.00
❑ 174	Where Does a Broken Heart Go/The Wilder Your Heart Beats, The Sweeter You Love	1954	5.00	10.00	20.00
❑ 178	Drinking Tequila/Red Eyed and Rowdy	1955	5.00	10.00	20.00
❑ 180	Give Me One More Kiss/Tahiti	1955	5.00	10.00	20.00
❑ 184	Are You the One/How Many	1955	5.00	10.00	20.00
—With Alvadean Coker					
❑ 186	Let Me Remember/Hillbilly Waltz	1956	5.00	10.00	20.00

RCA
❑ PB-10956	It's Nothin' to Me/I Won't Forget You	1977	—	2.00	4.00
❑ PB-11060	Little Ole Dime/A Letter to My Heart	1977	—	2.00	4.00
❑ PB-11187	You're the Only Good Thing (That's Happened to Me)/When You Are Gone	1978	—	2.00	4.00
❑ PB-11564	Don't Let Me Cross Over/I've Enjoyed As Much of This As I Can Stand	1979	—	2.00	4.00
❑ PB-11737	Oh, How I Miss You Tonight/The Talking Walls	1979	—	2.00	4.00
❑ PB-11946	Take Me in Your Arms and Hold Me/Missing Angel	1980	—	2.00	4.00
—A-side with Deborah Allen (overdubbed)					
❑ PB-12118	There's Always Me/Somewhere Along the Line	1980	—	2.00	4.00
❑ PB-13410	The Jim Reeves Medley/He'll Have to Go	1982	—	2.00	4.00
❑ PB-13693	The Image of Me/Won't Come In While He's There	1983	—	2.00	4.00

RCA VICTOR
❑ 47-6200	Yonder Comes a Sucker/I'm Hurtin' Inside	1955	5.00	10.00	20.00
❑ 47-6274	I've Lived a Lot in My Time/Jimbo Jenkins	1955	5.00	10.00	20.00
❑ 47-6401	If You Were Mine/That's a Sad Affair	1956	5.00	10.00	20.00
❑ 47-6517	My Lips Are Sealed/Pickin' a Chicken	1956	5.00	10.00	20.00
❑ 47-6620	According to My Heart/The Mother of a Honky Tonk Girl	1956	5.00	10.00	20.00
—With Carol Johnson					
❑ 47-6625	Bimbo/Penny Candy	1956	5.00	10.00	20.00
❑ 47-6626	Mexican Joe/How Many	1956	5.00	10.00	20.00
❑ 47-6627	Then I'll Stop Loving You/Drinking Tequila	1956	5.00	10.00	20.00
❑ 47-6749	Am I Losing You/Waitin' for a Train	1956	5.00	10.00	20.00
❑ 47-6874	Four Walls/I Know and You Know	1957	3.75	7.50	15.00
❑ 47-6973	Young Hearts/Two Shadows on Your Window	1957	3.75	7.50	15.00
❑ 47-7070	Anna Marie/Everywhere You Go	1957	3.75	7.50	15.00
❑ 47-7171	I Love You More/Overnight	1958	3.75	7.50	15.00
❑ 47-7266	Blue Boy/Theme of Love (I Love to Say I Love You)	1958	3.75	7.50	15.00
❑ 47-7380	Billy Bayou/I'd Like to Be	1958	3.75	7.50	15.00
❑ 47-7479	Home/If Heartache Is the Fashion	1959	3.75	7.50	15.00
❑ 47-7557	Partners/I'm Beginning to Forget You	1959	3.75	7.50	15.00
❑ 47-7643	He'll Have to Go/In a Mansion Stands My Love	1959	3.00	6.00	12.00
❑ 47-7756	I'm Gettin' Better/I Know One	1960	3.00	6.00	12.00
❑ 47-7756 [PS]	I'm Gettin' Better/I Know One	1960	5.00	10.00	20.00
❑ 47-7800	Am I Losing You/I Missed Me	1960	3.00	6.00	12.00
❑ 47-7800 [PS]	Am I Losing You/I Missed Me	1960	5.00	10.00	20.00
❑ 47-7855	The Blizzard/Danny Boy	1961	3.00	6.00	12.00
❑ 47-7905	What Would You Do?/Stand At Your Window	1961	3.00	6.00	12.00
❑ 47-7950	Losing Your Love/(How Can I Write on Paper) What I Feel in My Heart	1961	3.00	6.00	12.00
❑ 47-8019	Adios Amigo/A Letter to My Heart	1962	2.50	5.00	10.00
❑ 47-8080	I'm Gonna Change Everything/Pride Goes Before a Fall	1962	2.50	5.00	10.00
❑ 47-8127	Is This Me?/Missing Angel	1963	2.50	5.00	10.00
❑ 47-8127 [PS]	Is This Me?/Missing Angel	1963	6.25	12.50	25.00
❑ 47-8193	Guilty/Little Ole You	1963	2.50	5.00	10.00
❑ 47-8193 [PS]	Guilty/Little Ole You	1963	3.75	7.50	15.00
❑ 47-8252	An Old Christmas Card/Senor Santa Claus	1963	3.75	7.50	15.00
❑ 47-8252 [PS]	An Old Christmas Card/Senor Santa Claus	1963	10.00	20.00	40.00
❑ 47-8289	Welcome to My World/Good Morning Self	1963	2.50	5.00	10.00
❑ 47-8324	Love Is No Excuse/Look Who's Talking	1964	2.50	5.00	10.00
—With Dottie West					
❑ 47-8383	I Guess I'm Crazy/Not Until the Next Time	1964	2.50	5.00	10.00
❑ 47-8461	I Won't Forget You/Highway to Nowhere	1964	2.50	5.00	10.00
❑ 47-8508	This Is It/There's That Smile Again	1965	2.00	4.00	8.00
❑ 47-8625	Is It Really Over?/Rosa Rio	1965	2.00	4.00	8.00
❑ 47-8625 [PS]	Is It Really Over?/Rosa Rio	1965	3.00	6.00	12.00
❑ 47-8719	Snowflake/Take My Hand, Precious Lord	1965	2.00	4.00	8.00
❑ 47-8789	Distant Drums/Old Tige	1966	2.00	4.00	8.00
❑ 47-8902	Blue Side of Lonesome/It Hurts So Much (To See You Go)	1966	2.00	4.00	8.00
❑ 47-9057	I Won't Come In While He's There/Maureen	1966	2.00	4.00	8.00
❑ 47-9238	The Storm/Trying to Forget	1967	2.00	4.00	8.00
❑ 47-9343	I Heard a Heart Break Last Night/Golden Memories and Silver Tears	1967	2.00	4.00	8.00
❑ 47-9455	That's When I See the Blues (In Your Pretty Brown Eyes)/I've Lived a Lot in My Time	1968	2.00	4.00	8.00
❑ 47-9614	When You Are Gone/How Can I Write on Paper	1968	2.00	4.00	8.00
❑ 47-9880	Angels Don't Lie/You Kept Me Awake Last Night	1970	—	3.00	6.00
❑ 47-9969	Gypsy Feet/He Will	1971	—	3.00	6.00
❑ 74-0135	When Two Worlds Collide/Could I Be Falling in Love	1969	—	3.00	6.00
❑ 74-0286	Why Do I Love You (Melody of Love)/Nobody's Fool	1969	—	3.00	6.00
❑ 74-0626	The Writing on the Wall/You're Free to Go	1971	—	3.00	6.00
❑ 74-0744	Missing You/The Tie That Binds	1972	—	2.50	5.00
❑ 74-0859	Blue Christmas/Snowflake	1972	—	2.50	5.00
❑ 74-0963	Am I That Easy to Forget/Rosa Rio	1973	—	2.00	4.00

R

Number	Title (A Side/B Side)	Yr	VG	VG+	NM
❏ 447-0884	An Old Christmas Card/Senor Santa Claus	1972	—	2.00	4.00
—Gold Standard Series					
❏ 447-0885	Snowflake/Take My Hand, Precious Lord	1972	—	2.00	4.00
—Gold Standard Series					
❏ APBO-0255	I'd Fight the World/What's In It for Me	1974	—	2.00	4.00
❏ EP-10133	He Will/We Thank Thee	1974	—	2.00	4.00
❏ PB-10299	You Belong to Me/Maureen	1975	—	2.00	4.00
❏ PB-10418	You'll Never Know/There's That Smile Again	1975	—	2.00	4.00
❏ GB-10511	Missing You/I'd Fight the World	1975	—	2.00	4.00
—Gold Standard Series					

7-Inch Extended Plays

RCA VICTOR

Number	Title (A Side/B Side)	Yr	VG	VG+	NM
❏ EPA-757	Roly Poly/Have I Told You Lately That I Love You//Tweedle O'Twill/Each Time You Leave	1956	5.00	10.00	20.00
❏ EPA-757 [PS]	(title unknown)	1956	5.00	10.00	20.00
❏ VLP-3482	Welcome to My World/I Guess I'm Crazy/Is This Me?//My Lips Are Sealed/Mexican Joe/According to My Heart	196?	3.75	7.50	15.00
—Jukebox issue; small hole, plays at 33 1/3 rpm					
❏ VLP-3482 [PS]	The Best of Jim Reeves, Vol. II	196?	3.75	7.50	15.00
❏ VLP-3793	Blue Side of Lonesome/Trying to Forget/I Know One//I Won't Come In While He's There/Teardrops on the Rocks/Deep Dark Water	1967	3.75	7.50	15.00
—Stereo jukebox issue; small hole, plays at 33 1/3 rpm					
❏ VLP-3793 [PS]	Blue Side of Lonesome	1967	3.75	7.50	15.00
❏ EPA-4357	He'll Have to Go/Wishful Thinking//Please Come Home/After Awhile	1960	5.00	10.00	20.00
❏ EPA-4357 [PS]	He'll Have to Go	1960	5.00	10.00	20.00
❏ EPA-5124	Four Walls/Blue Boy//Bimbo/Mexican Joe	1958	3.75	7.50	15.00
❏ EPA-5124 [PS]	Jim Reeves' Hits (Gold Standard Series)	1958	3.75	7.50	15.00
❏ EPA-5145	Am I Losing You/Home//Billy Bayou/Partners	1958	3.75	7.50	15.00
❏ EPA-5145 [PS]	Am I Losing You (Gold Standard Series)	1958	3.75	7.50	15.00

Albums

ABBOTT

Number	Title (A Side/B Side)	Yr	VG	VG+	NM
❏ LP-5001 [M]	Jim Reeves Sings	1956	1000.	1500.	2000.

COUNTRY MUSIC FOUNDATION

Number	Title (A Side/B Side)	Yr	VG	VG+	NM
❏ CMF-008	Live at the Opry	198?	2.50	5.00	10.00

PAIR

Number	Title (A Side/B Side)	Yr	VG	VG+	NM
❏ PDL2-1002 [(2)]	The Country Side of Jim Reeves	1986	3.00	6.00	12.00

RCA CAMDEN

Number	Title (A Side/B Side)	Yr	VG	VG+	NM
❏ ACL1-0123	Kimberley Jim	1973	3.75	7.50	15.00
❏ CAL-583 [M]	According to My Heart	1960	5.00	10.00	20.00
❏ CAS-583 [R]	According to My Heart	1960	5.00	10.00	20.00
❏ CAL-686 [M]	The Country Side of Jim Reeves	1962	5.00	10.00	20.00
❏ CAS-686 [S]	The Country Side of Jim Reeves	1962	5.00	10.00	20.00
❏ CAL-784 [M]	Good 'N' Country	1963	5.00	10.00	20.00
❏ CAS-784 [S]	Good 'N' Country	1963	5.00	10.00	20.00
❏ CAL-842 [M]	Have I Told You Lately That I Love You?	1964	5.00	10.00	20.00
❏ CAS-842 [S]	Have I Told You Lately That I Love You?	1964	5.00	10.00	20.00
❏ CAS-2532	Young and Country	1971	3.75	7.50	15.00
❏ CAX-9001 [(2)]	Jim Reeves	1972	5.00	10.00	20.00

RCA VICTOR

Number	Title (A Side/B Side)	Yr	VG	VG+	NM
❏ APL1-0039	Am I That Easy to Forget	1973	5.00	10.00	20.00
❏ APL1-0330	Great Moments with Jim Reeves	1973	5.00	10.00	20.00
❏ APL1-0537	I'd Fight the World	1974	5.00	10.00	20.00
❏ APL1-0793	The Best of Jim Reeves Sacred Songs	1974	5.00	10.00	20.00
❏ APL1-1037	Songs of Love	1975	5.00	10.00	20.00
❏ APL1-1224	I Love You Because	1976	5.00	10.00	20.00
❏ LPM-1256 [M]	Singing Down the Lane	1956	50.00	100.00	200.00
❏ LPM-1410 [M]	Bimbo	1957	50.00	100.00	200.00
—Reissue of Abbott LP					
❏ LPM-1576 [M]	Jim Reeves	1957	20.00	40.00	80.00
❏ LPM-1685 [M]	Girls I Have Known	1958	15.00	30.00	60.00
❏ CPL1-1891	A Legendary Performer	1976	5.00	10.00	20.00
❏ ANL1-1927	Twelve Songs of Christmas	1976	2.00	4.00	8.00
—Reissue of LSP-2758					
❏ LPM-1950 [M]	God Be With You	1958	10.00	20.00	40.00
❏ LSP-1950 [S]	God Be With You	1958	12.50	25.00	50.00
❏ LPM-2001 [M]	Songs to Warm the Heart	1959	10.00	20.00	40.00
❏ LSP-2001 [S]	Songs to Warm the Heart	1959	12.50	25.00	50.00
❏ LPM-2216 [M]	The Intimate Jim Reeves	1960	7.50	15.00	30.00
❏ LSP-2216 [S]	The Intimate Jim Reeves	1960	10.00	20.00	40.00
❏ LPM-2223 [M]	Featuring He'll Have to Go and Other Favorites	1960	7.50	15.00	30.00
—Black and white cover (original)					
❏ LPM-2223 [M]	Featuring He'll Have to Go and Other Favorites	1962	5.00	10.00	20.00
—Color cover (reissue)					
❏ LSP-2223 [S]	Featuring He'll Have to Go and Other Favorites	1960	10.00	20.00	40.00
—Black and white cover (original)					
❏ LSP-2223 [S]	Featuring He'll Have to Go and Other Favorites	1962	6.25	12.50	25.00
—Color cover (reissue)					
❏ LPM-2284 [M]	Tall Tales and Short Tempers	1961	6.25	12.50	25.00
❏ LSP-2284 [S]	Tall Tales and Short Tempers	1961	7.50	15.00	30.00
❏ APL1-2309	It's Nothin' to Me	1977	3.75	7.50	15.00
❏ LPM-2339 [M]	Talkin' to Your Heart	1961	6.25	12.50	25.00
❏ LSP-2339 [S]	Talkin' to Your Heart	1961	7.50	15.00	30.00
❏ LPM-2487 [M]	A Touch of Velvet	1962	6.25	12.50	25.00
❏ LSP-2487 [S]	A Touch of Velvet	1962	7.50	15.00	30.00
❏ LPM-2552 [M]	We Thank Thee	1962	6.25	12.50	25.00
❏ LSP-2552 [S]	We Thank Thee	1962	7.50	15.00	30.00
❏ LPM-2605 [M]	Gentleman Jim	1963	6.25	12.50	25.00
❏ LSP-2605 [S]	Gentleman Jim	1963	7.50	15.00	30.00
❏ LPM-2704 [M]	The International Jim Reeves	1963	6.25	12.50	25.00
❏ LSP-2704 [S]	The International Jim Reeves	1963	7.50	15.00	30.00
❏ AHL1-2720	Jim Reeves	1978	3.75	7.50	15.00
❏ LPM-2758 [M]	Twelve Songs of Christmas	1963	6.25	12.50	25.00
❏ LSP-2758 [S]	Twelve Songs of Christmas	1963	7.50	15.00	30.00
❏ LPM-2780 [M]	Kimberley Jim	1964	6.25	12.50	25.00
❏ LSP-2780 [S]	Kimberley Jim	1964	7.50	15.00	30.00
❏ LPM-2854 [M]	Moonlight and Roses	1964	6.25	12.50	25.00
❏ LSP-2854 [S]	Moonlight and Roses	1964	7.50	15.00	30.00
❏ LPM-2890 [M]	The Best of Jim Reeves	1964	5.00	10.00	20.00
❏ LSP-2890 [S]	The Best of Jim Reeves	1964	6.25	12.50	25.00
❏ LPM-2968 [M]	The Jim Reeves Way	1965	5.00	10.00	20.00
❏ LSP-2968 [S]	The Jim Reeves Way	1965	6.25	12.50	25.00
❏ ANL1-3014	Pure Gold, Volume 1	1978	3.00	6.00	12.00
❏ AHL1-3271	The Best of Jim Reeves, Volume IV	1979	3.75	7.50	15.00
❏ LPM-3427 [M]	Up Through the Years	1965	5.00	10.00	20.00

Number	Title (A Side/B Side)	Yr	VG	VG+	NM
❏ LSP-3427 [S]	Up Through the Years	1965	6.25	12.50	25.00
❏ AHL1-3454	Don't Let Me Cross Over	1979	3.75	7.50	15.00
❏ LPM-3482 [M]	The Best of Jim Reeves, Vol. II	1966	5.00	10.00	20.00
❏ LSP-3482(e) [P]	The Best of Jim Reeves, Vol. II	1966	6.25	12.50	25.00
—This album is at least partially, and possibly entirely, in rechanneled stereo					
❏ LPM-3542 [M]	Distant Drums	1966	5.00	10.00	20.00
❏ LSP-3542 [P]	Distant Drums	1966	6.25	12.50	25.00
—"Overnight" and "The Gods Were Angry with Me" are rechanneled					
❏ AYL1-3678	The Best of Jim Reeves	1980	3.00	6.00	12.00
—"Best Buy Series" reissue					
❏ LPM-3709 [M]	Yours Sincerely, Jim Reeves	1966	5.00	10.00	20.00
❏ LSP-3709(e) [P]	Yours Sincerely, Jim Reeves	1966	6.25	12.50	25.00
—This album is at least partially, and possibly entirely, in rechanneled stereo					
❏ AYL1-3765	The Best of Jim Reeves Sacred Songs	1980	2.50	5.00	10.00
—"Best Buy Series" reissue					
❏ LPM-3793 [M]	Blue Side of Lonesome	1967	6.25	12.50	25.00
❏ LSP-3793 [S]	Blue Side of Lonesome	1967	5.00	10.00	20.00
❏ AHL1-3827	There's Always Me	1980	3.00	6.00	12.00
❏ LPM-3903 [M]	My Cathedral	1967	7.50	15.00	30.00
❏ LSP-3903 [S]	My Cathedral	1967	6.25	12.50	25.00
❏ AYL1-3936	Pure Gold, Volume 1	1980	2.50	5.00	10.00
—"Best Buy Series" reissue					
❏ LPM-3987 [M]	A Touch of Sadness	1968	15.00	30.00	60.00
❏ LSP-3987 [S]	A Touch of Sadness	1968	5.00	10.00	20.00
❏ LSP-4062	Jim Reeves On Stage	1968	5.00	10.00	20.00
❏ AYL1-4075	The Best of Jim Reeves, Volume IV	1981	2.50	5.00	10.00
—"Best Buy Series" reissue					
❏ LSP-4112	Jim Reeves and Some Friends	1969	5.00	10.00	20.00
❏ AYL1-4168	The Best of Jim Reeves, Vol. II	1981	2.50	5.00	10.00
—"Best Buy Series" reissue					
❏ LSP-4187	The Best of Jim Reeves Volume III	1969	5.00	10.00	20.00
❏ LSP-4475	Jim Reeves Writes You a Record	1971	5.00	10.00	20.00
❏ LSP-4528	Something Special	1971	5.00	10.00	20.00
❏ AHL1-4531	The Jim Reeves Medley	1983	2.50	5.00	10.00
❏ LSP-4646	My Friend	1972	5.00	10.00	20.00
❏ LSP-4749	Missing You	1972	5.00	10.00	20.00
❏ AYL1-4833	Don't Let Me Cross Over	1983	2.50	5.00	10.00
—"Best Buy Series" reissue					
❏ AYL1-4835	I Love You Because	1983	2.50	5.00	10.00
—"Best Buy Series" reissue					
❏ AYL1-4836	Songs of Love	1983	2.50	5.00	10.00
—"Best Buy Series" reissue					
❏ AYL1-4838	The Best of Jim Reeves Vol. III	1983	2.50	5.00	10.00
—"Best Buy Series" reissue					
❏ AYL1-4839	There's Always Me	1983	2.50	5.00	10.00
—"Best Buy Series" reissue					
❏ AYL1-4840	We Thank Thee	1983	2.50	5.00	10.00
—"Best Buy Series" reissue					
❏ AHL1-4865	A Special Collection	1983	3.00	6.00	12.00
❏ CPL2-5044 [(2)]	Just for You	1984	3.75	7.50	15.00
❏ AHL1-5424	Collector's Series	1985	3.00	6.00	12.00

TIME-LIFE

Number	Title (A Side/B Side)	Yr	VG	VG+	NM
❏ STW-113	Country Music	1981	2.50	5.00	10.00

REEVES, JIM, AND PATSY CLINE
Also see each artist's individual listings. Their duets were created electronically; they never actually recorded together.

45s

MCA

Number	Title (A Side/B Side)	Yr	VG	VG+	NM
❏ 52052	So Wrong/I Fall to Pieces	1982	—	2.00	4.00

RCA

Number	Title (A Side/B Side)	Yr	VG	VG+	NM
❏ PB-12346	Have You Ever Been Lonely (Have You Ever Been Blue)/Welcome to My World	1981	—	2.00	4.00

Albums

MCA

Number	Title (A Side/B Side)	Yr	VG	VG+	NM
❏ 5319	Remembering Jim Reeves and Patsy Cline	1982	3.75	7.50	15.00

RCA VICTOR

Number	Title (A Side/B Side)	Yr	VG	VG+	NM
❏ AHL1-4127	Greatest Hits	1981	3.75	7.50	15.00
❏ AYL1-5152	Greatest Hits	1984	2.50	5.00	10.00
—"Best Buy Series" reissue					

REEVES, MARTHA
Also see MARTHA AND THE VANDELLAS.

45s

ARISTA

Number	Title (A Side/B Side)	Yr	VG	VG+	NM
❏ 0124	Love Blind/This Time I'll Be Sweeter	1975	—	2.50	5.00
—Also see "Martha and the Vandellas"					
❏ 0160	Now That We Found Love/Higher and Higher	1975	—	2.00	4.00
❏ 0211	The Rest of My Life/Thank You	1976	—	2.00	4.00
❏ 0228	You've Lost That Lovin' Feelin'/Now That We Found Love	1977	—	2.00	4.00

FANTASY

Number	Title (A Side/B Side)	Yr	VG	VG+	NM
❏ 825	Love Don't Come No Stronger/You're Like Sunshine	1978	—	2.00	4.00
❏ 868	Dancin' in the Streets (Skatin' in the Streets)/When You Came	1979	—	2.00	4.00
❏ 887	Really Like Your Rap/That's What I Want	1979	—	2.00	4.00

MCA

Number	Title (A Side/B Side)	Yr	VG	VG+	NM
❏ 40194	Power of Love/Stand By Me	1974	—	2.50	5.00
❏ 40274	Stand By Me/Wild Night	1974	—	2.50	5.00
❏ 40329	My Man/Facsimile	1974	—	2.50	5.00

Albums

ARISTA

Number	Title (A Side/B Side)	Yr	VG	VG+	NM
❏ AL 4105	The Rest of My Life	1976	3.00	6.00	12.00

FANTASY

Number	Title (A Side/B Side)	Yr	VG	VG+	NM
❏ F-9549	We'll Meet Again	1978	3.00	6.00	12.00
❏ F-9591	Gotta Keep Moving	1980	3.00	6.00	12.00

MCA

Number	Title (A Side/B Side)	Yr	VG	VG+	NM
❏ 414	Martha Reeves	1974	3.00	6.00	12.00

REFLECTIONS, THE (1)
Detroit-based rock group.

45s

ABC

Number	Title (A Side/B Side)	Yr	VG	VG+	NM
❏ 10794	Like Adam and Eve/Vito's House	1966	6.25	12.50	25.00
❏ 10822	You're Gonna Find Out (You Love Me)/Long Cigarette	1966	7.50	15.00	30.00

Number	Title (A Side/B Side)	Yr	VG	VG+	NM
GOLDEN WORLD					
❑ 9	(Just Like) Romeo and Juliet/Can't You Tell By the Look in His Eyes	1964	5.00	10.00	20.00
❑ 12	Like Columbus Did/Lonely Girl	1964	3.75	7.50	15.00
❑ 15	Oowee Now/Talkin' 'Bout My Girl	1964	3.75	7.50	15.00
❑ 16	Henpecked Guy/Don't Do That to Me	1964	3.75	7.50	15.00
❑ 19	You're My Baby/Shabby Little Hut	1964	3.75	7.50	15.00
❑ 20	Poor Man's Son/Comin' At You	1965	3.75	7.50	15.00
❑ 22	Wheelin' and Dealin'/Deborah Ann	1965	3.75	7.50	15.00
❑ 24	June Bride/Out of the Picture	1965	3.75	7.50	15.00
❑ 29	Girl in the Candy Store/Your Kind of Love	1965	3.75	7.50	15.00
LANA					
❑ 140	(Just Like) Romeo and Juliet/ Can't You Tell by the Look in My Eyes	196?	—	3.00	6.00
—Oldies reissue					
Albums					
GOLDEN WORLD					
❑ 300 [M]	(Just Like) Romeo and Juliet	1964	37.50	75.00	150.00
REFLECTIONS, THE (2) R&B group from New York.					
45s					
CAPITOL					
❑ 4078	Three Steps from True Love/How Could We Let the Love Get Away	1975	—	3.00	6.00
❑ 4137	Love on Delivery/One Into One	1975	—	2.50	5.00
❑ 4222	Are You Ready (Here I Am)/Day After Day (Night After Night)	1976	—	2.50	5.00
❑ 4358	Gift Wrap My Love/She's My Summer Breeze	1976	—	2.50	5.00
RCA					
❑ PB-11408	Boogie City/I'm Gonna Let You Go This Time	1978	—	2.50	5.00
REFLECTIONS, THE (3)					
45s					
CROSSROADS					
❑ 401	I Really Must Know/Maybe Tomorrow	1961	15.00	30.00	60.00
❑ 402	Rocket to the Moon/Because of You	1962	20.00	40.00	80.00
REFLECTIONS, THE (U) These could be either group (1) or (3).					
45s					
KAY-KO					
❑ 1003	Helpless/You Said Goodbye	1963	50.00	100.00	200.00
TIGRE					
❑ 602	In the Still of the Night/Tic Toc	1962	10.00	20.00	40.00
REGALS, THE (1)					
45s					
ALADDIN					
❑ 3266	Run Pretty Baby/May the Good Lord Bless and Keep You	1954	30.00	60.00	120.00
ATLANTIC					
❑ 1062	I'm So Lonely/Got the Water Boiling	1955	15.00	30.00	60.00
MGM					
❑ 11869	There'll Always Be a Christmas/When You're Home with the Ones You Love	1954	10.00	20.00	40.00
REGALS, THE (2)					
45s					
LAST CHANCE					
❑ 109	See You in the Morning/Yes My Love	1961	2.50	5.00	10.00
LAVENDER					
❑ 1452	See You in the Morning/Yes My Love	1960	7.50	15.00	30.00
UNITED ARTISTS					
❑ 380	Icy Fingers/Tiger Tears	1961	7.50	15.00	30.00
REGAN, DENISE					
45s					
DEE GEE					
❑ 3005	A Date with Santa Claus/Hole in the Stocking	1965	2.50	5.00	10.00
❑ 3005 [PS]	A Date with Santa Claus/Hole in the Stocking	1965	5.00	10.00	20.00
REGAN, EDDIE					
45s					
ABC					
❑ 10795	Playin' Hide and Seek/Talk About Heartaches	1966	7.50	15.00	30.00
REGAN, RUSS					
45s					
ABC-PARAMOUNT					
❑ 9949	Junior, Junior, Junior/I Never Knew	1958	5.00	10.00	20.00
CAPITOL					
❑ F4169	Joan of Love/That's When I Ran	1959	3.00	6.00	12.00
❑ F4280	Adults Only/Just the Two of Us	1959	3.00	6.00	12.00
CORVETTE					
❑ 1002	Junior, Junior, Junior/I Never Knew	1958	12.50	25.00	50.00
REGAN, TOMMY					
45s					
COLPIX					
❑ 725	I'll Never Stop Loving You/ This Time I'm Losing You	1964	25.00	50.00	100.00
TELL STAR					
❑ 5001	Santa Twist/(B-side unknown)	1962	3.00	6.00	12.00
WORLD ARTISTS					
❑ 1049	I Adore You/9 to 5	1965	3.75	7.50	15.00
REGENTS, THE (1)					
45s					
COUSINS					
❑ 1002	Barbara-Ann/I'm So Lonely	1961	300.00	600.00	1200.
GEE					
❑ 1065	Barbara-Ann/I'm So Lonely	1961	7.50	15.00	30.00
❑ 1071	Runaround/Laura My Darling	1961	6.25	12.50	25.00
❑ 1073	Don't Be a Fool/Liar	1961	6.25	12.50	25.00
❑ 1075	Lonesome Boy/Oh Baby	1961	6.25	12.50	25.00
Albums					
GEE					
❑ GLP-706 [M]	Barbara Ann	1961	37.50	75.00	150.00
❑ SGLP-706 [S]	Barbara Ann	1961	62.50	125.00	250.00

Number	Title (A Side/B Side)	Yr	VG	VG+	NM
❑ SGLP-706	Barbara Ann	197?	6.25	12.50	25.00
—Reissue by Publishers Central Bureau (clearly marked as such on cover)					
REGENTS, THE (2)					
45s					
ARGO					
❑ 5268	Isle of Trinidad/Bamboo Tree	1957	6.25	12.50	25.00
REGENTS, THE (3)					
45s					
BLUE CAT					
❑ 110	Playmates/Me and You	1965	2.50	5.00	10.00
DOT					
❑ 16970	The Russian Spy and I/Bald Headed Woman	1966	2.50	5.00	10.00
PENTHOUSE					
❑ 502	Words/Worryin' Kind	1966	2.50	5.00	10.00
REGENTS, THE (4)					
45s					
KAYO					
❑ 101	(That's What I Call) A Real Good Time/ No Hard Feelings	1960	6.25	12.50	25.00
PEORIA					
❑ 8	Summertime Blues/(B-side unknown)	196?	3.75	7.50	15.00
REGENTS, THE (5) MICHAEL McDONALD, later of THE DOOBIE BROTHERS, was in this group.					
45s					
REPRISE					
❑ 0430	She's Got Her Own Way of Lovin'/ When I Die, Don't You Cry	1965	7.50	15.00	30.00
REGENTS, THE (U)					
Albums					
CAPITOL					
❑ KAO 2153 [M]	Live at the AM-PM Discotheque	1964	12.50	25.00	50.00
❑ SKAO 2153 [S]	Live at the AM-PM Discotheque	1964	15.00	30.00	60.00
REID, CLARENCE					
45s					
ALSTON					
❑ 3717	Baptize Me in Your Love/Whatever It Takes	1975	—	2.50	5.00
❑ 3720	Come On With It/Mr. Smith's Wife	1976	—	2.50	5.00
❑ 3723	Shake Your Butt/Caution! Love Ahead	1976	—	2.50	5.00
❑ 3733	Just Another Guy in the Band/I'm Excited	1977	—	2.50	5.00
❑ 3748	You Get Me Up/It's Hell Trying to Get to Heaven	1979	—	2.50	5.00
❑ 4572	Fools Are Not Born (They Are Made)/ Part-Time Lover	1969	2.00	4.00	8.00
❑ 4574	Nobody But You Babe/Send Me Back My Money	1969	2.00	4.00	8.00
❑ 4578	I'm a Man of My Word/I'm Gonna Tear You a New Heart	1969	2.00	4.00	8.00
❑ 4582	I've Been Trying/Don't Look Too Hard	1970	—	3.00	6.00
❑ 4584	Chicken Hawk/That's How It Is	1970	—	3.00	6.00
❑ 4588	Masterpiece/Down the Road of Love	1970	—	3.00	6.00
❑ 4592	Direct Me/You Knock Me Out	1971	—	3.00	6.00
❑ 4597	You Got to Fight/Three Is a Crowd	1971	—	3.00	6.00
❑ 4598	I Get My Kicks/Gotta Take It Home to Mother	1971	—	3.00	6.00
❑ 4602	Love Every Woman You Can/ Ten Tons of Dynamite	1971	—	3.00	6.00
❑ 4603	Good Old Days/Ten Tons of Dynamite	1972	—	3.00	6.00
❑ 4608	I'm Gonna Do Something Good to You/ Real Woman	1972	—	3.00	6.00
❑ 4613	Ruby/Two People in Love	1972	—	3.00	6.00
❑ 4616	Till I Get My Share/With Friends Like These	1973	—	3.00	6.00
❑ 4621	Funky Party/Winter Man	1974	—	3.00	6.00
ATCO					
❑ 7025	See Through/I Bet You Believe Me Now	1975	2.00	4.00	8.00
DIAL					
❑ 3018	I Got My Shake/There'll Come a Day	1964	3.75	7.50	15.00
❑ 4019	I Refuse to Give Up/Somebody Will	1965	3.00	6.00	12.00
❑ 4040	Gimmie a Try/Part of Your Love	1966	3.00	6.00	12.00
PHIL-L.A. OF SOUL					
❑ 301	Cadillac Annie/Tired Blood	1967	2.50	5.00	10.00
WAND					
❑ 1106	Somebody Will/I Refuse to Give Up	1966	6.25	12.50	25.00
❑ 1121	I'm Your Yes Man/ Your Love Is All the Help I Need	1966	50.00	100.00	200.00
Albums					
ATCO					
❑ SD 33-307	Dancin' with Nobody But You Babe	1969	7.50	15.00	30.00
REID, MATTHEW					
45s					
ABC-PARAMOUNT					
❑ 10259	Jane/Why Start	1961	6.25	12.50	25.00
❑ 10305	Tarzan Twist (Bwana Ungava)/ Through My Tears	1962	6.25	12.50	25.00
DECCA					
❑ 31662	One More Minute/Hurt Me	1964	3.00	6.00	12.00
PHILIPS					
❑ 40634	Outward Bound/Hey There Sweet Sue	1969	2.50	5.00	10.00
SCEPTER					
❑ 1238	Faded Roses/Tomorrow	1962	6.25	12.50	25.00
TOPIX					
❑ 6006	Cry Myself to Sleep/Lollipops Went Out of Style	1961	10.00	20.00	40.00
REID, TERRY					
45s					
ABC					
❑ 12209	Ooh Baby (Make Me Feel So Young)/ Brace Awakening	1976	—	2.50	5.00
EPIC					
❑ 10498	May Fly/Superlungs My Supergirl	1969	2.00	4.00	8.00
Albums					
ABC					
❑ X-935	Seed of Memory	1976	3.00	6.00	12.00

R

Number	Title (A Side/B Side)	Yr	VG	VG+	NM
ATLANTIC					
❑ SD 7259	River	1973	3.00	6.00	12.00
CAPITOL					
❑ SW-11857	Rogue Waves	1978	3.00	6.00	12.00
EPIC					
❑ BN 26427	Bang, Bang You're Terry Reid	1968	3.75	7.50	15.00
❑ BN 26477	Terry Reid	1969	3.75	7.50	15.00

REINER, CARL, AND MEL BROOKS
Albums

Number	Title (A Side/B Side)	Yr	VG	VG+	NM
CAPITOL					
❑ SW 1529 [S]	2000 Years	1961	5.00	10.00	20.00
❑ W 1529 [M]	2000 Years	1961	3.75	7.50	15.00
❑ SW 1618 [S]	2000 and One Years	1961	5.00	10.00	20.00
❑ W 1618 [M]	2000 and One Years	1961	3.75	7.50	15.00
❑ SW 1815 [S]	At the Cannes Film Festival	1962	5.00	10.00	20.00
❑ W 1815 [M]	At the Cannes Film Festival	1962	3.75	7.50	15.00
❑ ST 2981	The Best of the 2000 Year Old Man	1968	3.75	7.50	15.00
WARNER BROS.					
❑ BS 2741	2000 and Thirteen	1973	3.75	7.50	15.00
❑ 3XX 2744 [(3)]	The Incomplete Works of Reiner and Brooks	1973	6.25	12.50	25.00
WORLD PACIFIC					
❑ WP-1401 [M]	2000 Years	1960	7.50	15.00	30.00

RELATIVES, THE
45s

Number	Title (A Side/B Side)	Yr	VG	VG+	NM
ALMONT					
❑ 306	Never Will I Love You Again/I'm Just Looking for Love	1964	10.00	20.00	40.00
MUSICOR					
❑ 1063	Eternally/Hadn't Been for Baby	1965	2.50	5.00	10.00

RELF, KEITH Lead singer of THE YARDBIRDS. Also see ARMAGEDDON (2); RENAISSANCE.
45s

Number	Title (A Side/B Side)	Yr	VG	VG+	NM
EPIC					
❑ 10044	Mr. Zero/Knowing	1966	12.50	25.00	50.00
❑ 10044 [DJ]	Mr. Zero/Knowing	1966	37.50	75.00	150.00
—Promo on red vinyl... Reportedly, two promos were released for this single; the second, a different mix, was accompanied by a note telling the radio people not to play the first one, but to use the second one instead. This has not been confirmed.					
❑ 10110	Shapes in My Mind/Blue Sands	1966	12.50	25.00	50.00
❑ 10110 [DJ]	Shapes in My Mind (same on both sides)	1966	37.50	75.00	150.00
—Promo on red vinyl					
❑ 10110 [PS]	Shapes in My Mind/Blue Sands	1966	25.00	50.00	100.00
MCCM					
❑ 002	Together Now/All the Falling Angels	1989	—	2.50	5.00
—Purple marbled vinyl					
❑ 002 [PS]	Together Now/All the Falling Angels	1989	—	2.50	5.00

RELLA, CINDY
45s

Number	Title (A Side/B Side)	Yr	VG	VG+	NM
CARLTON					
❑ 583	He Don't Love Me Anymore/I Want Him to Come Back Home	1962	3.00	6.00	12.00
❑ 601	Phil Will/To Tommy with Love	1964	3.00	6.00	12.00
DRUM BOY					
❑ 112	Bring Me A Beatle for Christmas/Cla-wence	1964	3.00	6.00	12.00

REMAINS, THE
45s

Number	Title (A Side/B Side)	Yr	VG	VG+	NM
EPIC					
❑ 9777	You Say You're Sorry/I'm Talking About You	1965	20.00	40.00	80.00
❑ 9783	My Babe/Why Do I Cry	1965	20.00	40.00	80.00
❑ 9872	But I Ain't Got You/I Can't Get Away from You	1965	20.00	40.00	80.00
❑ 10001	Diddy Wah Diddy/Once Before	1966	20.00	40.00	80.00
❑ 10001 [DJ]	Diddy Wah Diddy/Once Before	1966	27.50	75.00	150.00
❑ 10001 [PS]	To Be Seen and Heard: Diddy Wah Diddy	1966	25.00	50.00	100.00
—Promo-only sleeve					
❑ 10060	Don't Look Back/Me Right Now	1966	20.00	40.00	80.00

Albums

Number	Title (A Side/B Side)	Yr	VG	VG+	NM
EPIC					
❑ LN 24214 [M]	The Remains	1966	50.00	100.00	200.00
❑ BN 26214 [S]	The Remains	1966	75.00	150.00	300.00
SPOONFED					
❑ SFD-3205	The Remains	1978	3.75	7.50	15.00
—Red vinyl					
SUNDAZED					
❑ SEP 10-162 [10]	The Remains	2000	2.00	4.00	8.00
❑ LP 5015	A Session with the Remains	199?	2.50	5.00	10.00
❑ LP 5055	The Remains	1999	3.00	6.00	12.00

REMARKABLES, THE
45s

Number	Title (A Side/B Side)	Yr	VG	VG+	NM
CHASE					
❑ 1600	Write Me/Whirl-A-Round	1964	62.50	125.00	250.00

REMINISCENTS, THE
45s

Number	Title (A Side/B Side)	Yr	VG	VG+	NM
DAY					
❑ 1000	Zoom Zoom Zoom/Oh Let Me Dream	1963	12.50	25.00	50.00
—Blue vinyl					
MARCEL					
❑ 1000	Cards of Love/Flames	1962	30.00	60.00	120.00

REMUS, EUGENE
45s

Number	Title (A Side/B Side)	Yr	VG	VG+	NM
MOTOWN					
❑ 1001	You Never Miss a Good Thing/Gotta Have Your Lovin'	1960	125.00	250.00	500.00
❑ 1001	You Never Miss a Good Thing/Hold Me Tight	1960	150.00	300.00	600.00

RENAISSANCE
Actually two diffferent groups, though treated by collectors as one. The first, on Elektra, featured KEITH RELF and other ex-YARDBIRDS. The later group was that group's spiritual heir, but had all new members.

45s

Number	Title (A Side/B Side)	Yr	VG	VG+	NM
CAPITOL					
❑ 3487	Prologue/Spare Some Love	1972	2.00	4.00	8.00
❑ 3715	Carpet of the Sun/Bound for Infinity	1973	2.00	4.00	8.00
I.R.S.					
❑ 9904	Remember/Bon Jour Swan Song	1982	—	2.50	5.00
❑ 9914	Richard IX/(B-side unknown)	1982	—	2.50	5.00
SIRE					
❑ 714	Mother Russia/I Think of You	1974	—	3.00	6.00
❑ 728	Carpet of the Sun/Kiev	1976	—	3.00	6.00
❑ 740	Midas Man/Captive Heart	1977	—	3.00	6.00
❑ 1022	Northern Lights/Opening Out	1978	—	2.50	5.00
❑ 1041	Northern Lights/Opening Out	1979	—	2.50	5.00
❑ 49041	Forever Changing/Jekyll and Hyde	1979	—	2.50	5.00

Albums

Number	Title (A Side/B Side)	Yr	VG	VG+	NM
CAPITOL/SOVEREIGN					
❑ SMAS-11116	Prologue	1972	3.75	7.50	15.00
❑ ST-11216	Ashes Are Burning	1973	3.75	7.50	15.00
❑ SWBC-11871 [(2)]	In the Beginning	1978	3.75	7.50	15.00
—Combines 11116 and 11216 in one package					
ELEKTRA					
❑ EKS-74068	Renaissance	1969	7.50	15.00	30.00
I.R.S.					
❑ SP-70019	Camera Camera	1981	2.50	5.00	10.00
❑ SP-70033	Time Line	1983	2.50	5.00	10.00
MOBILE FIDELITY					
❑ 1-099	Scheherazade and Other Stories	1982	12.50	25.00	50.00
—Audiophile vinyl					
SIRE					
❑ SASD-3902 [(2)]	Live at Carnegie Hall	1976	3.75	7.50	15.00
❑ SR 6015	Turn of the Cards	1977	2.50	5.00	10.00
—Reissue of 7502					
❑ SR 6017	Scheherazade and Other Stories	1977	2.50	5.00	10.00
—Reissue of 7510					
❑ SR 6024	Novella	1977	2.50	5.00	10.00
—Reissue of 7526					
❑ 2XS 6029 [(2)]	Live at Carnegie Hall	1977	3.00	6.00	12.00
—Reissue of 3902					
❑ SRK 6049	A Song for All Seasons	1978	3.00	6.00	12.00
❑ SRK 6068	Azure d'Or	1979	3.00	6.00	12.00
❑ SAS-7502	Turn of the Cards	1974	3.00	6.00	12.00
❑ SASD-7510	Scheherazade and Other Stories	1975	3.00	6.00	12.00
❑ SASD-7526	Novella	1977	3.00	6.00	12.00

RENAY, DIANE
45s

Number	Title (A Side/B Side)	Yr	VG	VG+	NM
ATCO					
❑ 6240	Falling Star/Little White Lies	1962	3.00	6.00	12.00
❑ 6262	Dime a Dozen/Tender	1963	3.00	6.00	12.00
FONTANA					
❑ 1679	Hold Me, Thrill Me, Kiss Me/Yesterday	1969	2.50	5.00	10.00
MGM					
❑ 13296	Billy Blue Eyes/Watch Out Sally	1964	2.50	5.00	10.00
❑ 13335	I Had a Dream/Troublemaker	1965	5.00	10.00	20.00
NEW VOICE					
❑ 800	Words/The Company You Keep	1965	2.50	5.00	10.00
❑ 803	Cross My Heart, Hope to Die/Happy Birthday, Broken Heart	1965	2.50	5.00	10.00
20TH CENTURY FOX					
❑ 456	Navy Blue/Unbelievable Boy	1964	3.75	7.50	15.00
❑ 477	Kiss Me Sailor/Soft Spoken Guy	1964	2.50	5.00	10.00
❑ 514	Growin' Up Too Fast/Waitin' for Joey	1964	2.50	5.00	10.00
❑ 533	It's In Your Tears/Present from Eddie	1964	2.50	5.00	10.00
UNITED ARTISTS					
❑ 50048	Dynamite/Please Gypsy	1966	3.75	7.50	15.00

Albums

Number	Title (A Side/B Side)	Yr	VG	VG+	NM
20TH CENTURY FOX					
❑ TF-3133 [M]	Navy Blue	1964	20.00	40.00	80.00
❑ TFS-4133 [S]	Navy Blue	1964	37.50	75.00	150.00

RENDEZVOUS
45s

Number	Title (A Side/B Side)	Yr	VG	VG+	NM
REPRISE					
❑ 20089	Congratulations Baby/Faithfully	1962	7.50	15.00	30.00
RUST					
❑ 5041	It Breaks My Heart/Take a Break	1961	10.00	20.00	40.00

RENDEZVOUS STOMPERS, THE
45s

Number	Title (A Side/B Side)	Yr	VG	VG+	NM
DORE					
❑ 626	Gremmies Unite/Rock Me Gently	1962	10.00	20.00	40.00

RENE AND RENE
45s

Number	Title (A Side/B Side)	Yr	VG	VG+	NM
ABC					
❑ 10699	Chantilly Lace/I'm Not the Only One (No Soy El Unico)	1965	2.00	4.00	8.00
ARV INTERNATIONAL					
❑ A-5011	Lo Mucho Que Te Quiero/Mornin'	1968	3.00	6.00	12.00
—Blue label					
❑ A-5011	Lo Mucho Que Te Quiero/Mornin'	1968	3.75	7.50	15.00
—Silver label					
❑ A-5022	Kiss Me One More Time/Should You Ever Leave Me	196?	2.50	5.00	10.00
CERTRON					
❑ 10011	My Amigo Jose/Good Old Days	1970	—	2.50	5.00
COLUMBIA					
❑ 43045	Angelito/Write Me Soon	1964	2.00	4.00	8.00
❑ 43045 [PS]	Angelito/Write Me Soon	1964	3.00	6.00	12.00
❑ 4-43140	Yo Te Lo Dije (I Could Have Told You)/Pretty Flowers Fade Away	1964	2.00	4.00	8.00
❑ 43163	Please Don't Bother/Undecided	1964	2.00	4.00	8.00

Number	Title (A Side/B Side)	Yr	VG	VG+	NM
EAST BEND					
❑ 209	Really Hurtin' This Guy/El Mexicano	196?	2.50	5.00	10.00
❑ 213	Put Me in Jail (Gastigueme Ya)/El Bandito	196?	2.50	5.00	10.00
EPIC					
❑ 10443	Muchachita/Our Day Will Come	1969	—	2.50	5.00
JOX					
❑ 017	Angelito/Write Me Soon	1964	3.00	6.00	12.00
❑ 025	Pretty Flowers/Fade Away	1965	2.50	5.00	10.00
❑ 032	Chantilly Lace/I'm Not the Only One	1965	2.50	5.00	10.00
❑ 041	Little Peanuts/Little Vagabond	1965	2.50	5.00	10.00
❑ 050	Loving You Could Hurt Me So/Little Diamonds	1966	2.50	5.00	10.00
WHITE WHALE					
❑ 281	Lo Mucho Que Te Quiero/Lloraras	1968	—	3.00	6.00
❑ 287	Lo Mucho Que Te Quiero/Mornin'	1968	—	2.50	5.00
❑ 298	Las Cosas/You Will Cry	1969	—	2.50	5.00
❑ 303	Enchilada Jose/Lloraras	1969	—	2.50	5.00
❑ 327	Love Is for the Two of Us/Sally Tosis	1969	—	2.50	5.00
Albums					
WHITE WHALE					
❑ WWS-7119	Lo Mucho Que Te Quiero	1968	3.75	7.50	15.00

RENEGADES, THE (1)
45s

Number	Title (A Side/B Side)	Yr	VG	VG+	NM
AMERICAN INT'L.					
❑ 537	Charge/Geronimo	1959	12.50	25.00	50.00

RENEGADES, THE (2)
45s

Number	Title (A Side/B Side)	Yr	VG	VG+	NM
CONGRESS					
❑ 241	Cadillac/Matelot (Sailor Boy)	1965	7.50	15.00	30.00

RENEGADES, THE (3)
45s

Number	Title (A Side/B Side)	Yr	VG	VG+	NM
DORSET					
❑ 5007	Stolen Angel/Keep Laughin'	1961	12.50	25.00	50.00

RENEGADES, THE (U) If these are any of the above, they are most likely group (2).
45s

Number	Title (A Side/B Side)	Yr	VG	VG+	NM
GARLAND					
❑ 2036	I'm a Loner/Travelin' Through This Countryside	196?	2.50	5.00	10.00
KARATE					
❑ 519	Take a Heart/If It Gets Lonesome	1966	3.75	7.50	15.00

RENO, AL
45s

Number	Title (A Side/B Side)	Yr	VG	VG+	NM
KAPP					
❑ 432	Cheryl/Congratulations	1961	10.00	20.00	40.00

REO SPEEDWAGON
12-Inch Singles

Number	Title (A Side/B Side)	Yr	VG	VG+	NM
EPIC					
❑ AE 314 [DJ]	Ridin' the Storm Out (mono/stereo)	1977	2.50	5.00	10.00
❑ AE 1489 [DJ]	Keep the Fire Burnin' (same on both sides)	1982	—	3.00	6.00
❑ EAS 2091 [DJ]	Gotta Feel More (3 versions)	1985	2.00	4.00	8.00
45s					
EPIC					
❑ 01054	Take It on the Run/Someone Tonight	1981	—	2.00	4.00
❑ 02127	Don't Let Him Go/I Wish You Were There	1981	—	2.00	4.00
❑ 02127 [PS]	Don't Let Him Go/I Wish You Were There	1981	—	2.50	5.00
❑ 02153	Keep On Loving You/Time for Me to Fly	1981	—	—	3.00
—Reissue					
❑ 02457	In Your Letter/Shakin' It Loose	1981	—	2.00	4.00
❑ 02967	Keep the Fire Burnin'/I'll Follow You	1982	—	2.00	4.00
❑ 03175	Sweet Time/Stillness of the Night	1982	—	2.50	4.00
❑ 03175 [PS]	Sweet Time/Stillness of the Night	1982	—	2.50	5.00
❑ ENR-03264	Sweet Time	1982	—	2.50	5.00
—One-sided budget release					
❑ 03400	Let's Be-Bop/The Key	1982	—	2.00	4.00
❑ 03846	Keep the Fire Burnin'/Take It on the Run	1983	—	—	3.00
—Reissue					
❑ 03847	In Your Letter/Don't Let Him Go	1983	—	—	3.00
—Reissue					
❑ 04659	I Do'Wanna Know/Rock 'N Roll Star	1984	—	—	3.00
❑ 04659 [PS]	I Do'Wanna Know/Rock 'N Roll Star	1984	—	2.00	4.00
❑ 04713	Can't Fight This Feeling/Break His Spell	1984	—	—	3.00
❑ 04713 [PS]	Can't Fight This Feeling/Break His Spell	1984	—	3.00	6.00
❑ 04848	One Lonely Night/Wheels Are Turnin'	1985	—	—	3.00
❑ 04848 [PS]	One Lonely Night/Wheels Are Turnin'	1985	—	2.00	4.00
❑ 05412	Live Every Moment/Gotta Feel More	1985	—	—	3.00
❑ 06656	That Ain't Love/Accidents Can Happen	1987	—	—	3.00
❑ 06656 [PS]	That Ain't Love/Accidents Can Happen	1987	—	—	3.00
❑ 07055	Variety Tonight/Tired of Gettin' Nowhere	1987	—	—	3.00
❑ 07055 [PS]	Variety Tonight/Tired of Gettin' Nowhere	1987	—	—	3.00
❑ 07255	In My Dreams/Over the Edge	1987	—	—	3.00
❑ 07255 [PS]	In My Dreams/Over the Edge	1987	—	—	3.00
❑ 07901	Here with Me/Wherever You're Goin' (It's Alright)	1988	—	—	3.00
❑ 07901 [PS]	Here with Me/Wherever You're Goin' (It's Alright)	1988	—	—	3.00
❑ 08030	I Don't Want to Lose You/On the Road Again	1988	—	—	3.00
❑ 10827	Sophisticated Lady/Prison Women	1972	3.00	6.00	12.00
❑ 10847	157 Riverside Avenue/ Five Men Were Killed Today	1972	3.00	6.00	12.00
❑ 10892	Lay Me Down/Gypsy Woman's Passion	1972	3.00	6.00	12.00
❑ 10975	Golden Country/Little Queenie	1973	3.00	6.00	12.00
❑ 11078	Ridin' the Storm Out/Whiskey Night	1974	3.00	6.00	12.00
❑ 11132	Start a New Life/Open Up	1974	2.50	5.00	10.00
❑ 50059	Sky Blues/Throw the Chains Away	1975	2.00	4.00	8.00
❑ 50120	Out of Control/Running Blind	1975	2.00	4.00	8.00
❑ 50180	Reelin'/Headed for a Fall	1975	2.00	4.00	8.00
❑ 50254	Tonight/Keep Pushin'	1976	—	3.00	6.00
❑ 50288	Flying Turkey Trot/Keep Pushin'	1976	—	3.00	6.00
❑ 50367	Ridin' the Storm Out/Being Kind	1977	—	3.00	6.00
❑ 50459	Flying Turkey Trot/Keep Pushin'	1977	—	3.00	6.00
❑ 50545	Roll with the Changes/ Unidentified Flying Tuna Trot	1978	—	2.50	5.00
❑ 50582	Time for Me to Fly/Runnin' Blind	1978	—	2.50	5.00
❑ 50764	I Need You Tonight/Easy Money	1979	—	2.50	5.00

Number	Title (A Side/B Side)	Yr	VG	VG+	NM
❑ 50790	Only the Strong Survive/ Drop It (An Old Disguise)	1979	—	2.50	5.00
❑ 50858	Time for Me to Fly/Lightning	1980	—	2.00	4.00
❑ 50953	Keep On Loving You/Follow My Heart	1980	—	2.00	4.00
❑ 51006	Take It on the Run/Someone Tonight	1981	—	—	—
—Unreleased?					
❑ 73499	Live It Up/All Heaven Broke Loose	1990	—	—	3.00
❑ 73540	Love Is a Rock/Go for Broke	1990	—	—	3.00
Albums					
EPIC					
❑ E 31089	REO Speedwagon	1972	3.75	7.50	15.00
—Yellow label original					
❑ KE 31089	REO Speedwagon	1973	3.00	6.00	12.00
—Orange label					
❑ PE 31089	REO Speedwagon	1979	2.00	4.00	8.00
—Dark blue label					
❑ KE 31745	R.E.O./T.W.O.	1972	3.75	7.50	15.00
—Yellow label original					
❑ KE 31745	R.E.O./T.W.O.	1973	3.00	6.00	12.00
—Orange label					
❑ PE 31745	R.E.O./T.W.O.	1979	2.00	4.00	8.00
—Dark blue label					
❑ KE 32378	Ridin' the Storm Out	1973	3.00	6.00	12.00
—Orange label					
❑ PE 32378	Ridin' the Storm Out	1979	2.00	4.00	8.00
—Dark blue label					
❑ PE 32948	Lost in a Dream	1974	3.00	6.00	12.00
—Orange label					
❑ PE 32948	Lost in a Dream	1979	2.00	4.00	8.00
—Dark blue label					
❑ PEQ 32948 [Q]	Lost in a Dream	1974	5.00	10.00	20.00
❑ PE 33338	This Time We Mean It	1975	3.00	6.00	12.00
—Orange label					
❑ PE 33338	This Time We Mean It	1979	2.00	4.00	8.00
—Dark blue label					
❑ PEQ 33338 [Q]	This Time We Mean It	1975	5.00	10.00	20.00
❑ PE 34143	R.E.O.	1976	3.00	6.00	12.00
—Orange label					
❑ PE 34143	R.E.O.	1979	2.00	4.00	8.00
—Dark blue label					
❑ PEG 34494 [(2)]	REO Speedwagon Live/ You Get What You Play For	1977	3.75	7.50	15.00
—Orange labels					
❑ PEG 34494 [(2)]	REO Speedwagon Live/ You Get What You Play For	1979	3.00	6.00	12.00
—Dark blue labels					
❑ JE 35082	You Can Tune a Piano, But You Can't Tuna Fish	1978	2.50	5.00	10.00
—Orange label; with bar code on back cover					
❑ JE 35082	You Can Tune a Piano, But You Can't Tuna Fish	1978	3.00	6.00	12.00
—Orange label; no bar code on back cover					
❑ JE 35082	You Can Tune a Piano, But You Can't Tuna Fish	1979	2.00	4.00	8.00
—Dark blue label					
❑ PE 35082	You Can Tune a Piano, But You Can't Tuna Fish	198?	2.00	4.00	8.00
❑ FE 35988	Nine Lives	1979	2.50	5.00	10.00
❑ PE 35988	Nine Lives	198?	2.00	4.00	8.00
—Budget-line reissue					
❑ KE2 36444 [(2)]	A Decade of Rock and Roll 1970 to 1980	1980	3.00	6.00	12.00
❑ FE 36844	Hi Infidelity	1980	2.00	4.00	8.00
❑ FE 38100	Good Trouble	1982	2.50	5.00	10.00
❑ PE 38100	Good Trouble	198?	2.00	4.00	8.00
—Budget-line reissue					
❑ QE 39593	Wheels Are Turnin'	1984	2.00	4.00	8.00
❑ FE 40444	Life As We Know It	1987	2.00	4.00	8.00
❑ OE 44202	The Hits	1988	2.50	5.00	10.00
❑ HE 45082	You Can Tune a Piano, But You Can't Tuna Fish	198?	10.00	20.00	40.00
—Half-speed mastered edition					
❑ E 45246	The Earth, a Small Man, His Dog and a Chicken	1990	3.00	6.00	12.00
❑ HE 46844	Hi Infidelity	1982	7.50	15.00	30.00
—Half-speed mastered edition					
❑ HE 48100	Good Trouble	1982	7.50	15.00	30.00
—Half-speed mastered edition					

REPARATA AND THE DELRONS
45s

Number	Title (A Side/B Side)	Yr	VG	VG+	NM
BIG TREE					
❑ 114	Just You/There's So Little Time	1971	—	2.50	5.00
KAPP					
❑ 989	(That's What Sends Men to) The Bowery/I've Got an Awful Lot of Losing to Do	1969	—	3.00	6.00
❑ 2010	San Juan/We're Gonna Hold the Night	1969	—	3.00	6.00
❑ 2050	Waking in the Rain/Got Fear of Losing You	1969	—	3.00	6.00
LAURIE					
❑ 3252	Your Big Mistake/Leave Us Alone	1964	7.50	15.00	30.00
—As "The Delrons"					
❑ 3589	Octopus' Garden/Your Life Is Gone	1972	—	2.50	5.00
—As "Reparata"					
MALA					
❑ 573	I Believe/It's Waiting There for You	1967	—	3.00	6.00
❑ 589	Captain of Your Ship/Toom Toom Is a Little Boy	1968	3.00	6.00	12.00
❑ 12000	Saturday Night Didn't Happen/Panic	1968	—	3.00	6.00
❑ 12016	You Can't Change a Young Boy's Mind/Weather Forecast	1968	—	3.00	6.00
❑ 12026	Heaven Only Knows/Summer Laughter	1968	—	3.00	6.00
POLYDOR					
❑ 14271	Shoes/Song for All	1975	—	2.00	4.00
—As "Reparata"					
❑ 14298	Jezebee Lancer the Belly Dancer/We Need You	1975	—	—	—
—Unreleased					
RCA VICTOR					
❑ 47-8721	I Can Tell/Take a Look Around You	1965	2.50	5.00	10.00
❑ 47-8820	I'm Nobody's Baby Now/ The Loneliest Girl in Town	1966	3.75	7.50	15.00
❑ 47-8921	Mama's Little Girl/He Don't Want You	1966	2.50	5.00	10.00
❑ 47-9123	Boys and Girls/That Kind of Trouble That I Love	1967	2.50	5.00	10.00
❑ 47-9185	I Can Hear the Rain/Always Waitin'	1967	2.50	5.00	10.00

R

Number	Title (A Side/B Side)	Yr	VG	VG+	NM
WORLD ARTISTS					
❑ 1036	Whenever a Teenager Cries/He's My Guy	1964	3.00	6.00	12.00
❑ 1051	Tommy/Mama Don't Allow	1965	3.00	6.00	12.00
❑ 1057	He's the Greatest/A Summer Thought	1965	3.00	6.00	12.00
❑ 1062	The Boy I Love/I Found My Place	1965	3.00	6.00	12.00
Albums					
AVCO EMBASSY					
❑ AVE-33008	Rock and Roll Revolution	1970	6.25	12.50	25.00
WORLD ARTISTS					
❑ WAM-2006 [M]	Whenever a Teenager Cries	1965	12.50	25.00	50.00
❑ WAS-3006 [S]	Whenever a Teenager Cries	1965	15.00	30.00	60.00

REPRISE REPERTORY THEATRE, THE Artists who were signed to Reprise Records at the time, including ROSEMARY CLOONEY, BING CROSBY, SAMMY DAVIS, JR., DEAN MARTIN, FRANK SINATRA and JO STAFFORD, perform new versions of famous musicals under this collective name.

Albums

REPRISE

Number	Title (A Side/B Side)	Yr	VG	VG+	NM
❑ F-2015 [M]	Finian's Rainbow	196?	5.00	10.00	20.00
—Standard cover					
❑ F-2015 [M]	Finian's Rainbow	1964	7.50	15.00	30.00
—Gatefold cover					
❑ FS-2015 [S]	Finian's Rainbow	196?	6.25	12.50	25.00
—Standard cover					
❑ FS-2015 [S]	Finian's Rainbow	1964	10.00	20.00	40.00
—Gatefold cover					
❑ F-2016 [M]	Guys and Dolls	196?	5.00	10.00	20.00
—Standard cover					
❑ F-2016 [M]	Guys and Dolls	1964	7.50	15.00	30.00
—Gatefold cover					
❑ FS-2016 [S]	Guys and Dolls	196?	6.25	12.50	25.00
—Standard cover					
❑ FS-2016 [S]	Guys and Dolls	1964	10.00	20.00	40.00
—Gatefold cover					
❑ F-2017 [M]	Kiss Me, Kate	196?	5.00	10.00	20.00
—Standard cover					
❑ F-2017 [M]	Kiss Me, Kate	1964	7.50	15.00	30.00
—Gatefold cover					
❑ FS-2017 [S]	Kiss Me, Kate	196?	6.25	12.50	25.00
—Standard cover					
❑ FS-2017 [S]	Kiss Me, Kate	1964	10.00	20.00	40.00
—Gatefold cover					
❑ F-2018 [M]	South Pacific	196?	5.00	10.00	20.00
—Standard cover					
❑ F-2018 [M]	South Pacific	1964	7.50	15.00	30.00
—Gatefold cover					
❑ FS-2018 [S]	South Pacific	196?	6.25	12.50	25.00
—Standard cover					
❑ FS-2018 [S]	South Pacific	1964	10.00	20.00	40.00
—Gatefold cover					
❑ F-2019 [(4)M]	The Reprise Repertory Theatre	1964	50.00	100.00	200.00
—Box set of all four of the above LPs in gatefold covers					
❑ FS-2019 [(4)S]	The Reprise Repertory Theatre	1964	75.00	150.00	300.00
—Box set of all four of the above LPs in gatefold covers					

RESIDENTS, THE

12-Inch Singles

RALPH

Number	Title (A Side/B Side)	Yr	VG	VG+	NM
❑ RZ 8006-D	Diskomo/Goosebump	1980	2.50	5.00	10.00
❑ RZ 8006-D	Diskomo/Goosebump	1980	5.00	10.00	20.00
—Green vinyl					
❑ RR 8721	Hit the Road Jack (Dance Mix)/Jambalaya-Firefly-The Big Bubble-Cry for the Fire	1987	2.00	4.00	8.00

45s

CRYPTIC

Number	Title (A Side/B Side)	Yr	VG	VG+	NM
❑ RZ-SP-1SP 1	Earth Vs. the Flying Saucers	1986	5.00	10.00	20.00
—Green vinyl, one-sided, bonus with collector's edition of book "The Cryptic Guide to the Residents"					

EVA-TONE

| ❑ 10371900-1 | Diskomo (Live) | 1988 | — | 2.50 | 5.00 |
| —Flexi-disc included with April 1988 issue of Reflex | | | | | |

RALPH

❑ RR 0577	Beyond the Valley of A Day in the Life/Flying	1977	37.50	75.00	150.00
❑ RR 0577 [PS]	Beyond the Valley of A Day in the Life/Flying	1977	37.50	75.00	150.00
—Also known as "The Residents Meet the Beatles and The Beatles Meet the Residents"					
❑ RR 0776	Satisfaction/Loser Is Congruent to Weed	1976	37.50	75.00	150.00
❑ RR 0776 [PS]	Satisfaction/Loser Is Congruent to Weed	1976	37.50	75.00	150.00
❑ RR 1272	Fire/Aircraft Damage	1972	50.00	100.00	200.00
—Part of "Santa Dog" two-7" single set					
❑ RR 1272	Lightning/Explosion	1972	50.00	100.00	200.00
—Part of "Santa Dog" two-7" single set					
❑ RR 1272 [PS]	Santa Dog: Fire/Aircraft Damage; Lightning/Explosion	1972	150.00	300.00	600.00
—Signed, intentionally misnumbered sleeve for above two records					
❑ RR 7803	Satisfaction/Loser Is Congruent to Weed	1978	—	2.00	4.00
❑ RR 7803 [PS]	Satisfaction/Loser Is Congruent to Weed	1978	—	2.00	4.00
❑ RR 7812	Santa Dog '78/Fire	1978	5.00	10.00	20.00
❑ RR 7812 [PS]	Santa Dog '78/Fire	1978	5.00	10.00	20.00
❑ RZ 8422	It's a Man's Man's Man's World/Safety Is a Cootie Wootie	1984	—	2.50	5.00
—Black vinyl					
❑ RZ 8422	It's a Man's Man's Man's World/Safety Is a Cootie Wootie	1984	3.75	7.50	15.00
—White vinyl; blue "iris" label and plastic sleeve with red lines; corrected labels					
❑ RZ 8422	It's a Man's Man's Man's World/Safety Is a Cootie Wootie	1984	5.00	10.00	20.00
—White vinyl; blue "iris" label and plastic sleeve with red lines; labels reversed					
❑ RZ 8422 [PS]	It's a Man's Man's Man's World/Safety Is a Cootie Wootie	1984	—	2.50	5.00
—Sleeve with black vinyl edition					
❑ RZ 8621	Kaw-Liga/Stars and Stripes Forever	1986	3.75	7.50	15.00
—Picture disc					
❑ RZ 8622	Kaw-Liga/Stars and Stripes Forever	1986	—	—	3.00
❑ RZ 8622	Kaw-Liga/Stars and Stripes Forever	1986	2.50	5.00	10.00
—White vinyl					
❑ RZ 8622 [PS]	Kaw-Liga/Stars and Stripes Forever	1986	—	—	3.00
❑ RR 8721 [PD]	Hit the Road Jack/For Elsie (Excerpt)	1987	3.75	7.50	15.00
—Picture disc					

Number	Title (A Side/B Side)	Yr	VG	VG+	NM
❑ RR 8722	Hit the Road Jack/For Elsie (Excerpt)	1987	—	—	3.00
❑ RR 8722 [PS]	Hit the Road Jack/For Elsie (Excerpt)	1987	—	—	3.00

7-Inch Extended Plays

RALPH

❑ WEIRD 1	Babyfingers	1981	5.00	10.00	20.00
—Pink vinyl on labels left over from fan club issue					
❑ WEIRD 1 [PS]	Babyfingers	1981	5.00	10.00	20.00
❑ RR 0377	*Monstrous Intro/Death in Barstow/Melon Collie Lassie/Flight of the Bumble Roach/Walter Westinghouse	1979	25.00	50.00	100.00
—Also known as "Babyfingers"; first edition not issued with picture sleeve					
❑ RR 0377	*Monstrous Intro/Death in Barstow/Melon Collie Lassie/Flight of the Bumble Roach/Walter Westinghouse	1979	50.00	100.00	200.00
—Label hand-decorated with felt-tip pens					
❑ RR 0377 [PS]	Babyfingers	1979	50.00	100.00	200.00
—Actually a modified "Santa Dog '78" sleeve; this was sent with the felt-tip decorated copies to 10 people who had been waiting two years for a limited-edition copy of "The Third Reich 'n' Roll" LP					
❑ RR 1177	*Laughing Song/Blue Rosebuds/Constantinople/The Booker Tease/Sinister Exaggerator/Bach Is Dead/Elvis and His Boss	1978	2.00	4.00	8.00
—Red label					
❑ RR 1177 [PS]	Duck Stab	1978	—	2.50	5.00
—Matte cover					
❑ RR 1177 [PS]	Duck Stab	1978	11.25	22.50	45.00
—Shiny cover					

W.E.I.R.D.

❑ WEIRD 1	Babyfingers	1981	5.00	10.00	20.00
—Fan club reissue					
❑ WEIRD 1 [PS]	Babyfingers	1981	5.00	10.00	20.00

Albums

CRYPTIC

| ❑ S-18335 SP-2 | For Elsie | 1987 | 25.00 | 50.00 | 100.00 |
| —Green vinyl one-sided LP | | | | | |

ENIGMA

| ❑ 73547 | The King & Eye | 1989 | 3.75 | 7.50 | 15.00 |

EPISODE

❑ ED 21	The Census Taker (Soundtrack)	1985	5.00	10.00	20.00
❑ ED 21	The Census Taker (Soundtrack)	1985	20.00	40.00	80.00
—Red vinyl					

RALPH

❑ Mole Show 001	The Mole Show (The Roxy)	1983	7.50	15.00	30.00
❑ C-002A	The Mole Show (The Roxy)	1983	10.00	20.00	40.00
—Picture disc					
❑ OP-011 [DJ]	Freak Show	1991	20.00	40.00	80.00
—Promo-only black vinyl pressing; 400 made					
❑ OP-011 [PD]	Freak Show	1991	10.00	20.00	40.00
—Picture disc					
❑ RR 0274	Meet the Residents	1974	50.00	100.00	200.00
—First version: "Meet the Beatles" LP parody cover and "First Edition" on back cover					
❑ RR 0278	Duck Stab	1978	2.50	5.00	10.00
—Second version: Yellow titles box on back					
❑ RR 0278	Duck Stab	1978	3.00	6.00	12.00
—First version: Green titles box on back					
❑ RR 0677	Meet the Residents	1977	3.00	6.00	12.00
—Fourth version: same cover as second version, modified and orange back cover					
❑ RR 0677	Meet the Residents	1977	3.75	7.50	15.00
—Third version: same cover as second version, black "a" Ralph logo					
❑ RR 0677	Meet the Residents	1977	5.00	10.00	20.00
—Second version: "She Loves You" picture sleeve parody cover, split "a" Ralph logo					
❑ RR 1075	The Third Reich 'N' Roll	1976	2.50	5.00	10.00
—Fourth version: Gray carrot, black "a" Ralph logo					
❑ RR 1075	The Third Reich 'N' Roll	1976	3.00	6.00	12.00
—Third version: Orange carrot, black "a" Ralph logo					
❑ RR 1075	The Third Reich 'N' Roll	1976	3.75	7.50	15.00
—Second version: Gray carrot, split "a" Ralph logo					
❑ RR 1075	The Third Reich 'N' Roll	1976	12.50	25.00	50.00
—Censored cover with swastikas obscured, pressed in U.S. for export to Germany					
❑ RR 1075	The Third Reich 'N' Roll	1976	12.50	25.00	50.00
—First version of 1,000: Liner notes inside, orange carrot					
❑ RR 1075	The Third Reich 'N' Roll	1976	375.00	750.00	1500.
—Numbered box set on marbled vinyl, silkscreened cover and lithographs inside					
❑ RR 1174	Not Available	1978	2.50	5.00	10.00
—Green label, address is "109 Minna"					
❑ RR 1174	Not Available	1978	3.00	6.00	12.00
—Green label, address is "444 Grove"					
❑ RR 1174	Not Available	1978	3.75	7.50	15.00
—Orange label, remastered, "Re-3" in trail-off vinyl					
❑ RR 1174	Not Available	1978	6.25	12.50	25.00
—Purple label, mis-mastered, "Re-1" in trail-off vinyl					
❑ RR 1276	Fingerprince	1977	2.50	5.00	10.00
—Third version: Color cover					
❑ RR 1276	Fingerprince	1977	5.00	10.00	20.00
—Second version: Lighter brown cover					
❑ RR 1276	Fingerprince	1977	20.00	40.00	80.00
—First version: Dark brown cover, "First Pressing" written on back cover					
❑ RZ 7707 [PD]	Meet the Residents	1986	7.50	15.00	30.00
—Picture disc, with original cover on one side, replacement cover on other					
❑ DJ 7901 [DJ]	Please Do Not Steal It!	1979	10.00	20.00	40.00
—Promo-only sampler					
❑ ESK 7906	Eskimo	1979	2.50	5.00	10.00
—Third version: Black vinyl, standard cover					
❑ ESK 7906	Eskimo	1979	3.75	7.50	15.00
—Second version: Black vinyl, gatefold					
❑ ESK 7906	Eskimo	1979	6.25	12.50	25.00
—First version: White vinyl, gatefold cover					
❑ RZ 7906 [PD]	Eskimo	1979	7.50	15.00	30.00
—Picture disc					
❑ RZ 8052	The Residents Commercial Album	1980	3.00	6.00	12.00
—Third version: Green vinyl					
❑ RZ 8052	The Residents Commercial Album	1980	3.75	7.50	15.00
—Second version: Corrected song order, green logo					
❑ RZ 8052	The Residents Commercial Album	1980	5.00	10.00	20.00
—First version: Purple Ralph logo, songs listed in wrong order					
❑ RZ 8152	Mark of the Mole	1981	2.50	5.00	10.00

Number	Title (A Side/B Side)	Yr	VG	VG+	NM
❏ RZ 8152	Mark of the Mole	1981	12.50	25.00	50.00
—Signed brown vinyl edition with lyrics					
❏ RZ 8202	The Tunes of Two Cities	1982	2.50	5.00	10.00
—Second edition: "109 Minna Street" address					
❏ RZ 8202	The Tunes of Two Cities	1982	3.00	6.00	12.00
—First edition: "444 Grove Street" address					
❏ RZ 8252	Intermission	1982	3.00	6.00	12.00
❏ RZ 8252	Intermission	1982	3.50	7.00	14.00
—Red vinyl					
❏ RZ 8302	Residue	1983	3.00	6.00	12.00
❏ RR 8315	Title in Limbo	1983	3.00	6.00	12.00
—With Renaldo and The Loaf					
❏ RZ 8402	George & James	1984	2.50	5.00	10.00
—Second edition: Approved mix with "Re-5" in trail-off					
❏ RZ 8402	George & James	1984	7.50	15.00	30.00
—First edition: Rejected mix with "Re-1" in trail-off					
❏ RZ 8402	George & James	1984	12.50	25.00	50.00
—"Re-5" in trail-off, clear vinyl					
❏ RZ 8452	Whatever Happened to Vileness Fats?	1984	3.00	6.00	12.00
❏ RZ 8452	Whatever Happened to Vileness Fats?	1984	20.00	40.00	80.00
—Red vinyl					
❏ RZ 8552	The Big Bubble	1985	3.00	6.00	12.00
❏ RZ 8552	The Big Bubble	1985	20.00	40.00	80.00
—Pink vinyl					
❏ RZ 8602	The Eyeball Show (The 13th Anniversary Show) Live in Japan	1986	2.50	5.00	10.00
❏ RZ 8602	The Eyeball Show (The 13th Anniversary Show) Live in Japan	1986	20.00	40.00	80.00
—White vinyl					
❏ RZ 8652	Stars & Hank Forever	1986	2.50	5.00	10.00
❏ RZ 8652	Stars & Hank Forever	1986	10.00	20.00	40.00
—Blue vinyl					
❏ RR 82761	Fingerprince	1988	2.50	5.00	10.00
—New number, black vinyl					
❏ RR 82761	Fingerprince	1988	3.00	6.00	12.00
—New number, purple vinyl					
❏ RR 87521	Duck Stab	1988	2.50	5.00	10.00
—New number, black vinyl					
❏ RR 87521	Duck Stab	1988	3.00	6.00	12.00
—New number, red vinyl					
❏ RR 88521	Meet the Residents	1988	3.00	6.00	12.00
—Original "Meet the Beatles" parody cover restored, black vinyl					
❏ RR 88521	Meet the Residents	1988	3.75	7.50	15.00
—Original "Meet the Beatles" parody cover restored, white vinyl					
RYKO ANALOGUE					
❏ RALP-0044-2 [(2)]God in Three Persons	1988	5.00	10.00	20.00
—Clear vinyl					
❏ RALP-0045-2	God in Three Persons Instrumental	1988	3.75	7.50	15.00
—Clear vinyl					
UWEB					
❏ 0011	Stranger Than Supper	1990	6.25	12.50	25.00
—Fan club issue					

RESTIVO, JOHNNY
45s
EPIC

Number	Title (A Side/B Side)	Yr	VG	VG+	NM
❏ 9537	My Reputation/You Can't Turn Back the Clock	1962	3.75	7.50	15.00
RCA VICTOR					
❏ 47-7559 [M]	The Shape I'm In/Ya Ya	1959	5.00	10.00	20.00
❏ 47-7559 [PS]	The Shape I'm In/Ya Ya	1959	12.50	25.00	50.00
❏ 47-7601	Dear Someone/I Like Girls	1959	3.75	7.50	15.00
❏ 47-7601 [PS]	Dear Someone/I Like Girls	1959	7.50	15.00	30.00
❏ 47-7636	Our Wedding Day/Come Closer	1959	5.00	10.00	20.00
❏ 47-7697	High School Play/But I Love You	1960	3.75	7.50	15.00
❏ 47-7758	That's Good That's Bad/I Can't Take It	1960	3.75	7.50	15.00
❏ 47-7818	Two Crazy Kids/Give Me a Little Whistle (And I'll Be There)	1960	3.75	7.50	15.00
❏ 61-7559 [S]	The Shape I'm In/Ya Ya	1959	12.50	25.00	50.00
—"Living Stereo" issue with large hole					
20TH FOX					
❏ 260	Sweet Lovin'/Looka Here Now	1961	3.75	7.50	15.00
❏ 279	Doctor Love/The Magic Age Is Seventeen	1961	3.75	7.50	15.00
❏ 279 [PS]	Doctor Love/The Magic Age Is Seventeen	1961	7.50	15.00	30.00
Albums					
RCA VICTOR					
❏ LPM-2149 [M]	Oh, Johnny!	1959	15.00	30.00	60.00
❏ LSP-2149 [S]	Oh, Johnny!	1959	25.00	50.00	100.00

RETURN TO FOREVER
45s
COLUMBIA

Number	Title (A Side/B Side)	Yr	VG	VG+	NM
❏ 10497	Musicmagic/When Love Is New	1977	—	2.00	4.00
POLYDOR					
❏ 15067	Spain/Captain Marvel	1973	—	3.00	6.00
—As "Chick Corea and Return to Forever"					
❏ 15094	Earth Juice/Beyond the Seventh Galaxy	1974	—	2.50	5.00
—As "Chick Corea and Return to Forever"					
❏ 15099	An Excerpt from the First Movement of Heavy Metal/Jungle Waterfall	1975	—	2.50	5.00
—As "Chick Corea and Return to Forever"					
Albums					
COLUMBIA					
❏ PC 34076	Romantic Warrior	1976	2.50	5.00	10.00
—No bar code on cover					
❏ PC 34076	Romantic Warrior	198?	2.00	4.00	8.00
—Reissue with bar code					
❏ PC 34682	Musicmagic	1977	2.50	5.00	10.00
—No bar code on cover					
❏ PC 34682	Musicmagic	1985	2.00	4.00	8.00
—Reissue with bar code					
❏ PCQ 34682 [Q]Musicmagic	1977	5.00	10.00	20.00
❏ JC 35281	Return to Forever Live	1979	2.50	5.00	10.00
❏ JC 36359	The Best of Return to Forever	1980	2.50	5.00	10.00
❏ PC 36359	The Best of Return to Forever	198?	2.00	4.00	8.00
—Budget-line reissue					

ECM

Number	Title (A Side/B Side)	Yr	VG	VG+	NM
❏ 1015	Return to Forever	197?	3.75	7.50	15.00
POLYDOR					
❏ PD-5525	Light as a Feather	1973	3.00	6.00	12.00
❏ PD-5536	Hymn of the Seventh Galaxy	1973	3.00	6.00	12.00
❏ PD-6509	Where Have I Known You Before	1974	3.00	6.00	12.00
❏ PD-6512	No Mystery	1975	3.00	6.00	12.00
❏ 825336-1	Hymn of the Seventh Galaxy	198?	2.00	4.00	8.00
—Reissue					

REUNION
45s
A&M

Number	Title (A Side/B Side)	Yr	VG	VG+	NM
❏ 1308	City Song/No Good Alone	1971	—	2.00	4.00
BELL					
❏ 45222	Smile (Theme from Modern Times)/Turn Back the Hands of Time (Gotta Have You Back)	1972	—	2.00	4.00
❏ 45287	Living Together, Growing Together/ Just Say Goodbye	1974	—	2.00	4.00
RCA VICTOR					
❏ PB-10056	Life Is a Rock (But the Radio Rolled Me)/ Are You Ready to Believe	1974	—	2.50	5.00
❏ PB-10150	Disco-Tekin/Goodstuff	1975	—	2.00	4.00
❏ PB-10252	They Don't Make 'Em Like That Anymore/ Goodstuff	1975	—	2.00	4.00
❏ GB-10491	Life Is a Rock (But the Radio Rolled Me)/Are You Ready to Believe	1975	—	—	3.00
—Gold Standard Series					

REV-LONS, THE
45s
GARPAX

Number	Title (A Side/B Side)	Yr	VG	VG+	NM
❏ 44168	Boy Trouble/Give Me One More Chance	1962	3.75	7.50	15.00
REPRISE					
❏ 0251	After Last Night/It's Gonna Happen Someday	1964	3.00	6.00	12.00
❏ 20200	I Can't Forget About You/Love Can't Be a One-Way Deal	1963	3.00	6.00	12.00

REVALONS, THE
45s
PET

Number	Title (A Side/B Side)	Yr	VG	VG+	NM
❏ 802	Dreams Are for Fools/This Is the Moment	1958	30.00	60.00	120.00

REVELLS, THE
Albums
REPRISE

Number	Title (A Side/B Side)	Yr	VG	VG+	NM
❏ R-6160 [M]	The Go Sound of the Slots	1965	37.50	75.00	150.00
❏ RS-6160 [S]	The Go Sound of the Slots	1965	50.00	100.00	200.00

REVELS, THE (1)
45s
NORGOLDE

Number	Title (A Side/B Side)	Yr	VG	VG+	NM
❏ 103	Midnight Stroll/Talking to My Heart	1959	6.25	12.50	25.00
—Same A-side as above, but with revised title					
❏ 103	Dead Man's Stroll/Talking to My Heart	1959	30.00	60.00	120.00
❏ 104	Tweedlee Dee/Foo Man Choo	1959	5.00	10.00	20.00

REVELS, THE (2)
45s
CT

Number	Title (A Side/B Side)	Yr	VG	VG+	NM
❏ 1	Church Key/Vesuvius	1960	25.00	50.00	100.00
DOWNEY					
❏ 123	Intoxica/Comanche	1964	6.25	12.50	25.00
IMPACT					
❏ 1	Church Key/Vesuvius	1960	6.25	12.50	25.00
—Black vinyl					
❏ 1	Church Key/Vesuvius	1960	12.50	25.00	50.00
—Red vinyl					
❏ 3	Intoxica/Tequila	1961	6.25	12.50	25.00
❏ 7	Comanche/Rampage	1961	6.25	12.50	25.00
—Black vinyl					
❏ 7	Comanche/Rampage	1961	12.50	25.00	50.00
—Yellow vinyl					
❏ 13	Party Time/Soft Top	1961	6.25	12.50	25.00
❏ 22	Conga Twist/Revellion	1962	6.25	12.50	25.00
—Black vinyl					
❏ 22	The Monkey Bird/Revellion	1962	6.25	12.50	25.00
—Black vinyl					
❏ 22	Conga Twist/Revellion	1962	12.50	25.00	50.00
—Yellow vinyl; Both A-sides of Impact 22 are the same song					
❏ 22	The Monkey Bird/Revellion	1962	12.50	25.00	50.00
—Yellow vinyl					
LYNN					
❏ 1302	Six Pak/Good Grief	1960	15.00	30.00	60.00
SWINGIN'					
❏ 620	Six Pak/Good Grief	1960	10.00	20.00	40.00
WESTCO					
❏ 3/4	Party Time/Soft Top	1963	12.50	25.00	50.00
—Red and yellow vinyl					
Albums					
IMPACT					
❏ LPM-1 [M]	Revels on a Rampage	1964	125.00	250.00	500.00
SUNDAZED					
❏ LP 5010	Intoxica! The Best of the Revels	1994	2.50	5.00	10.00

REVELS, THE (3)
45s
DIAMOND

Number	Title (A Side/B Side)	Yr	VG	VG+	NM
❏ 143	Lots of Luck/Gonna Have Some Fun	1963	3.75	7.50	15.00

REVELS, THE (4)
45s
JAMIE

Number	Title (A Side/B Side)	Yr	VG	VG+	NM
❏ 1318	True Love/ Everybody Can Do the New Dog But Me	1966	2.50	5.00	10.00

R

Number	Title (A Side/B Side)	Yr	VG	VG+	NM

REVELS, THE (U)

It's doubtful that any of these are group (2), and they probably aren't group (1), either. Group (3) and (4) are not out of the question, though.

45s
ANDIE

Number	Title (A Side/B Side)	Yr	VG	VG+	NM
❑ 5077	Please/Two Little Monkeys (In a Banana Tree)	1960	5.00	10.00	20.00

KAPP

| ❑ 621 | Downtown/Dollar Sign | 1964 | 7.50 | 15.00 | 30.00 |

PALETTE

| ❑ 5074 | O How I Love You/I Met My Lost Love | 1961 | 5.00 | 10.00 | 20.00 |

REVENGERS, THE
45s
MGM

| ❑ 13465 | Batman Theme/Back Side Blues | 1966 | 3.00 | 6.00 | 12.00 |

Albums
METRO

| ❑ M-565 [M] | Batman and Other Supermen | 1966 | 7.50 | 15.00 | 30.00 |
| ❑ MS-565 [S] | Batman and Other Supermen | 1966 | 10.00 | 20.00 | 40.00 |

REVERE, PAUL, AND THE RAIDERS

Includes records as "Raiders" in the early 1970s. Also see MARK LINDSAY; JIM VALLEY; FREDDY WELLER.

45s
COLUMBIA

Number	Title (A Side/B Side)	Yr	VG	VG+	NM
❑ CSP-262	SS 396/Corvair Baby	1965	6.25	12.50	25.00
❑ CSM-466	SS 396/Camaro	1967	6.25	12.50	25.00
—B-side by The Cyrkle					
❑ CSM-466 [PS]	SS 396/Camaro	1967	12.50	25.00	50.00
—B-side by The Cyrkle					
❑ 10126	Gonna Have a Good Time/Your Love (Is the Only Love)	1975	2.50	5.00	10.00
❑ 42814	Louie Louie/Night Train	1963	10.00	20.00	40.00
❑ 43008	Louie Go Home/Have Love Will Travel	1964	3.75	7.50	15.00
❑ 43114	Over You/Swim	1964	3.75	7.50	15.00
❑ 43273	Ooh Poo Pah Doo/Sometimes	1965	3.75	7.50	15.00
❑ 43375	Steppin' Out/Blue Fox	1965	2.50	5.00	10.00
❑ 43375 [DJ]	Steppin' Out (same on both sides)	1965	12.50	25.00	50.00
—Red vinyl promo					
❑ 43461	Just Like Me/B.F.R.D.F. Blues	1965	2.50	5.00	10.00
❑ 43461 [DJ]	Just Like Me (same on both sides)	1965	12.50	25.00	50.00
—Red vinyl promo					
❑ 43556	Kicks/Shake It Up	1966	2.50	5.00	10.00
❑ 43556 [DJ]	Kicks (same on both sides)	1966	12.50	25.00	50.00
—Red vinyl promo					
❑ 43678	Hungry/There She Goes	1966	2.50	5.00	10.00
❑ 43678 [DJ]	Hungry (same on both sides)	1966	12.50	25.00	50.00
—Red vinyl promo					
❑ 43678 [PS]	Hungry/There She Goes	1966	5.00	10.00	20.00
❑ 43810	The Great Airplane Strike/In My Community	1966	2.50	5.00	10.00
❑ 43810 [DJ]	The Great Airplane Strike (same on both sides)	1966	12.50	25.00	50.00
—Red vinyl promo					
❑ 43810 [PS]	The Great Airplane Strike/In My Community	1966	3.75	7.50	15.00
❑ 43907	Good Thing/Undecided Man	1966	2.50	5.00	10.00
❑ 43907 [PS]	Good Thing/Undecided Man	1966	5.00	10.00	20.00
❑ 44018	Ups and Downs/Leslie	1967	2.50	5.00	10.00
❑ 44018 [PS]	Ups and Downs/Leslie	1967	3.75	7.50	15.00
❑ 44094	Him or Me — What's It Gonna Be?/Legend of Paul Revere	1967	2.50	5.00	10.00
❑ 44094 [PS]	Him or Me — What's It Gonna Be?/Legend of Paul Revere	1967	3.75	7.50	15.00
❑ 44227	I Had a Dream/Upon Your Leaving	1967	2.00	4.00	8.00
❑ 44227 [PS]	I Had a Dream/Upon Your Leaving	1967	2.50	5.00	10.00
❑ 44335	Peace of Mind/Do Unto Others	1967	2.00	4.00	8.00
❑ 44335 [PS]	Peace of Mind/Do Unto Others	1967	2.50	5.00	10.00
❑ 44376	Rain, Sleet or Snow/Brotherly Love	1967	—	—	—
—Canceled					
❑ 44444	Too Much Talk/Happening '68	1968	2.00	4.00	8.00
❑ 44444 [PS]	Too Much Talk/Happening '68	1968	2.50	5.00	10.00
❑ 44553	Don't Take It Too Hard/Observation from Flight 285 (In 3/4 Time)	1968	—	3.00	6.00
❑ 44553 [PS]	Don't Take It Too Hard/Observation from Flight 285 (In 3/4 Time)	1968	2.50	5.00	10.00
❑ 44655	Cinderella Sunshine/It's Happening	1968	2.00	4.00	8.00
❑ 44744	Mr. Sun, Mr. Moon/Without You	1969	—	3.00	6.00
❑ 44744 [PS]	Mr. Sun, Mr. Moon/Without You	1969	2.50	5.00	10.00
❑ 44854	Let Me/I Don't Know	1969	—	3.00	6.00
❑ 44970	We Gotta All Get Together/Frankfort Side Street	1969	—	3.00	6.00
❑ 45082	Just Seventeen/Sorceress with Blue Eyes	1970	—	3.00	6.00
—As "Raiders"					
❑ 45150	Gone Movin' On/Interlude (To Be Forgotten)	1970	—	3.00	6.00
—As "Raiders"					
❑ 45332	Indian Reservation (The Lament of the Cherokee Reservation Indian)/Terry's Tune	1971	—	3.00	6.00
—As "Raiders"; orange label with "Columbia" background print					
❑ 45332	Indian Reservation (The Lament of the Cherokee Reservation Indian)/Terry's Tune	1971	2.00	4.00	8.00
—As "Raiders"; red label, black print					
❑ 45453	Birds of a Feather/The Turkey	1971	—	3.00	6.00
—As "Raiders"					
❑ 45535	Country Wine/It's So Hard Getting Up Today	1972	—	2.50	5.00
—As "The Raiders"; gray label					
❑ 45535	Country Wine/It's So Hard Getting Up Today	1972	—	3.00	6.00
—As "The Raiders"; orange label with "COLUMBIA" background					
❑ 45601	Powder Blue Mercedes Queen/Golden Girls Sometimes	1972	2.00	4.00	8.00
—As "Raiders"					
❑ 45688	Song Seller/A Simple Song	1972	2.00	4.00	8.00
—As "Raiders"					
❑ 45759	Love Music/Goodbye, No. 9	1973	2.00	4.00	8.00
—As "Raiders"					
❑ 45898	All Over You/Seaboard Line Boogie	1973	2.00	4.00	8.00
—As "Raiders"					

DRIVE

| ❑ 6248 | Ain't Nothing Wrong/You're Really Saying Something | 1976 | — | 2.50 | 5.00 |

GARDENA

| ❑ 106 | Beatnick Sticks/Orbit (The Spy) | 1960 | 7.50 | 15.00 | 30.00 |
| ❑ 115 | Paul Revere's Ride/Unfinished Fifth | 1960 | 10.00 | 20.00 | 40.00 |

Number	Title (A Side/B Side)	Yr	VG	VG+	NM
❑ 116	Like, Long Hair/Sharon	1961	7.50	15.00	30.00
❑ 118	Like, Charleston/Midnite Ride	1961	6.25	12.50	25.00
❑ 124	All Night Long/Groovey	1962	10.00	20.00	40.00
❑ 127	Like, Bluegrass/Leatherneck	1962	10.00	20.00	40.00
❑ 131	Shake It Up (Part 1)/Shake It Up (Part 2)	1962	10.00	20.00	40.00
❑ 137	Tall Cool One/Road Runner	1963	12.50	25.00	50.00

HITBOUND

❑ X-2	Jingle Bell Rock/Jingle Bells	1983	3.00	6.00	12.00
—B-side by Mike Love and Dean Torrence					
❑ X-2 [PS]	Jingle Bell Rock/Jingle Bells	1983	5.00	10.00	20.00
—B-side by Mike Love and Dean Torrence					

JERDEN

| ❑ 807 | So Fine/Blues Stay Away | 1966 | 6.25 | 12.50 | 25.00 |

SANDE

| ❑ 101 | Louie Louie/Night Train | 1963 | 62.50 | 125.00 | 250.00 |

20TH CENTURY

| ❑ 2283 | The British Are Coming/Surrender at Appomattox | 1976 | — | 3.00 | 6.00 |
| —B-side by Susie Allanson | | | | | |

7-Inch Extended Plays
COLUMBIA

❑ 7-9665	Happening '68/Communication Part 1/Communication Part 2//Happens Every Day/Love Makes the World Go Round (Don't You Let It Stop Now)/Free	1968	6.25	12.50	25.00
—Jukebox issue, small hole, plays at 33 1/3 rpm					
❑ 7-9665 [PS]	Happening '68	1968	6.25	12.50	25.00

Albums
COLUMBIA

❑ GP 12 [(2)]	Two All Time Great Selling LPs	1969	6.25	12.50	25.00
—Combines 9395 and 9521 in one package; red labels					
❑ GP 12	Two All Time Great Selling LPs	1971	5.00	10.00	20.00
—Combines 9395 and 9521 in one package; orange labels					
❑ CL 2307 [M]	Here They Come!	1965	5.00	10.00	20.00
—"360 Sound Mono" on label					
❑ CL 2307 [M]	Here They Come!	1965	7.50	15.00	30.00
—"Guaranteed High Fidelity" on label					
❑ CL 2451 [M]	Just Like Us!	1966	6.25	12.50	25.00
❑ CL 2508 [M]	Midnight Ride	1966	6.25	12.50	25.00
❑ CL 2595 [M]	The Spirit of '67	1966	6.25	12.50	25.00
❑ KCL 2662 [M]	Greatest Hits	1967	7.50	15.00	30.00
—Add 20% if booklet is included; at least some copies actually are stereo with the "XSS" prefix on the label's master numbers rather than "XLP," though we don't know if all of them are					
❑ CL 2721 [M]	Revolution!	1967	7.50	15.00	30.00
❑ CL 2755 [M]	A Christmas Present…And Past	1967	15.00	30.00	60.00
❑ CL 2805 [M]	Goin' to Memphis	1968	20.00	40.00	80.00
❑ CS 9107 [S]	Here They Come!	1965	6.25	12.50	25.00
—"360 Sound Stereo" in white on label					
❑ CS 9107 [S]	Here They Come!	1965	10.00	20.00	40.00
—"360 Sound Stereo" in black on label					
❑ CS 9251 [S]	Just Like Us!	1966	7.50	15.00	30.00
❑ CS 9308 [S]	Midnight Ride	1966	7.50	15.00	30.00
❑ CS 9395 [S]	The Spirit of '67	1966	7.50	15.00	30.00
❑ KCS 9462 [P]	Greatest Hits	1967	6.25	12.50	25.00
—Add 20% if booklet is included					
❑ CS 9521 [S]	Revolution!	1967	6.25	12.50	25.00
❑ CS 9555 [S]	A Christmas Present…And Past	1967	6.25	12.50	25.00
❑ CS 9605 [S]	Goin' to Memphis	1968	5.00	10.00	20.00
❑ CS 9665	Something Happening	1968	5.00	10.00	20.00
❑ CS 9753	Hard 'N' Heavy (With Marshmallow)	1969	5.00	10.00	20.00
—Black and white cover					
❑ CS 9753	Hard 'N' Heavy (With Marshmallow)	1969	7.50	15.00	30.00
—Color cover					
❑ CS 9905	Alias Pink Puzz	1969	5.00	10.00	20.00
❑ CS 9964	Collage	1970	5.00	10.00	20.00
❑ C 30386	Greatest Hits, Volume 2	1971	5.00	10.00	20.00
❑ C 30768	Indian Reservation	1971	3.75	7.50	15.00
❑ KC 31106	Country Wine	1972	3.75	7.50	15.00
❑ KG 31464 [(2)]	All-Time Greatest Hits	1972	5.00	10.00	20.00
❑ PC 35593	Greatest Hits	1978	2.50	5.00	10.00

COLUMBIA LIMITED EDITION

| ❑ LE 10170 [S] | Midnight Ride | 197? | 3.75 | 7.50 | 15.00 |
| —Reissue of 9308 | | | | | |

COLUMBIA SPECIAL PRODUCTS

| ❑ P 13512 | Goin' to Memphis | 197? | 3.75 | 7.50 | 15.00 |

ERA

| ❑ NU 5880 | The Great Raider Reunion | 1983 | 3.00 | 6.00 | 12.00 |
| —Re-recordings | | | | | |

GARDENA

| ❑ LP-G-1000 [M] | Like, Long Hair | 1961 | 150.00 | 300.00 | 600.00 |

HARMONY

❑ H 30089	Paul Revere and the Raiders Featuring Mark Lindsay	1970	3.00	6.00	12.00
❑ KH 30975	Good Thing	1971	3.00	6.00	12.00
❑ KH 31183	Movin' On	1972	3.00	6.00	12.00

JERDEN

❑ JRL-7004 [M]	Paul Revere and the Raiders In the Beginning	1966	15.00	30.00	60.00
❑ JRS-7004 [R]	Paul Revere and the Raiders In the Beginning	1966	7.50	15.00	30.00
❑ DT-90709 [R]	Paul Revere and the Raiders In the Beginning	1966	12.50	25.00	50.00
—Capitol Record Club edition					
❑ T-90709 [M]	Paul Revere and the Raiders In the Beginning	1966	17.50	35.00	70.00
—Capitol Record Club edition					

PICKWICK

| ❑ SPC-3176 [R] | Paul Revere and the Raiders | 1969 | 2.50 | 5.00 | 10.00 |

SANDE

❑ S-1001 [M]	Paul Revere and the Raiders	1963	300.00	600.00	1200.
—Original version with "Sande" and no mention of "Etiquette" in trail-off area					
❑ S-1001 [M]	Paul Revere and the Raiders	1979	6.25	12.50	25.00
—Legitimate reissue with "Sande" and "Etiquette" in trail-off area					

SEARS

| ❑ SPS-493 | Paul Revere and the Raiders | 1969 | 6.25 | 12.50 | 25.00 |

Jim Reeves, *Jim Reeves Sings*, Abbott LP-5001, mono LP, $1,500-$2,000.

The Regents, "Barbara-Ann," Cousins 1002, 45 rpm single, $600-$1,200.

Renaissance, *Renaissance*, Elektra EKS-74068, stereo LP, red label, $15-$30.

REO Speedwagon, *Live – You Get What You Play For*, Epic PEG 34494, stereo 2-LP set, orange labels, $7.50-$15.

Reparata and the Delrons, *Whenever a Teenager Cries*, World Artists WAS-3006, stereo LP, $30-$60.

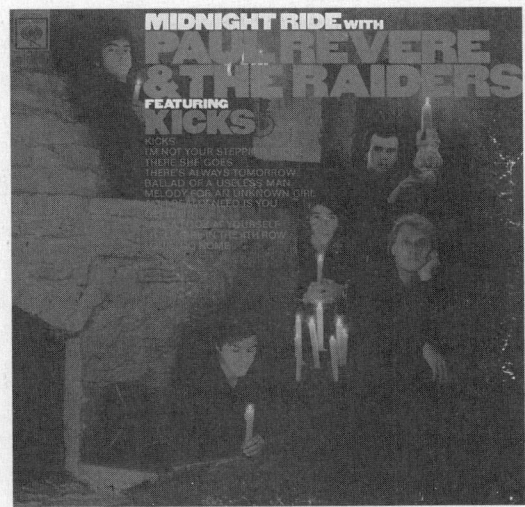

Paul Revere and the Raiders, *Midnight Ride*, Columbia CL 2508, mono LP, $12.50-$25.

R

Number	Title (A Side/B Side)	Yr	VG	VG+	NM

REVERES, THE (1)
45s
GLORY
| ❏ 272 | Leonore/Honeystroller | 1958 | 5.00 | 10.00 | 20.00 |

—B-side by the Honeystrollers

REVERES, THE (2)
45s
JUBILEE
| ❏ 5463 | Beyond the Sea/The Show Must Go On | 1963 | 6.25 | 12.50 | 25.00 |

REVERES, THE (3) BRUCE JOHNSTON appears on this record.
45s
VALIANT
| ❏ 6041 | Big "T"/Me and My Spider | 1964 | 12.50 | 25.00 | 50.00 |

REVLONS, THE More than one group.
45s
CAPITOL
❏ 4739	Dry Your Eyes/She'll Come to Me	1962	7.50	15.00	30.00
PARKWAY					
❏ 107	Ya Ya/It Could Happen to You	1966	3.00	6.00	12.00
RAE COX					
❏ 105	This Restless Heart/I Promise Love	1961	7.50	15.00	30.00
TIMES SQUARE					
❏ 15	Ride Awy/Betty	1963	6.25	12.50	25.00

—B-side by the Centuries
TOY
| ❏ 101 | What a Love This Is/Did I Make a Mistake | 1962 | 5.00 | 10.00 | 20.00 |

REYNOLDS, JODY
45s
BRENT
❏ 7042	Raggedy Ann/The Girl from King Marie	1963	2.50	5.00	10.00
DEMON					
❏ 1507	Endless Sleep/Tight Capris	1958	7.50	15.00	30.00
❏ 1509	Fire of Love/Daisy Mae	1958	6.25	12.50	25.00
❏ 1511	Closin' In/Elope with Me	1958	6.25	12.50	25.00
❏ 1515	Golden Idol/Beulah Lee	1959	6.25	12.50	25.00
❏ 1519	The Storm/Please Remember	1959	6.25	12.50	25.00
❏ 1523	Whipping Post/I Wanna Be with You Tonight	1960	6.25	12.50	25.00
❏ 1524	Stone Cold/(The Girl with) The Raven Hair	1960	6.25	12.50	25.00
INDIGO					
❏ 127	Tarantula/Thunder	1961	12.50	25.00	50.00
PULSAR					
❏ 2419	Endless Sleep/My Baby's Eyes	1969	—	3.00	6.00
SMASH					
❏ 1810	Don't Jmp/Stormy	1963	3.00	6.00	12.00
TITAN					
❏ 1734	Devil Girl/A Tear for Hesse	1963	3.75	7.50	15.00
❏ 1736	Requiem for Love/Stranger in the Mirror	1963	3.75	7.50	15.00

—With Bobbie Gentry
Albums
TRU-GEMS
| ❏ 1002 | Endless Sleep | 1978 | 3.00 | 6.00 | 12.00 |

RHINOCEROS
45s
ELEKTRA
❏ 45640	You're My Girl/I Will Serenade You	1968	—	3.00	6.00
❏ 45647	Apricot Brandy/When You Say You're Sorry	1969	2.00	4.00	8.00
❏ 45659	I Need Love/Velvuekus	1969	—	3.00	6.00
❏ 45677	Back Door/In a Little Room	1970	—	3.00	6.00
❏ 45691	Let's Party/Old Age	1970	—	3.00	6.00
❏ 45694	Better Times/It's a Groovy World	1970	—	3.00	6.00
Albums
ELEKTRA
❏ EKS-74030	Rhinoceros	1968	6.25	12.50	25.00
❏ EKS-74056	Satin Chickens	1969	5.00	10.00	20.00
❏ EKS-74075	Better Times Are Coming	1970	5.00	10.00	20.00

RHODES, EMITT Also see THE MERRY-GO-ROUND.
45s
A&M
| ❏ 1254 | Till the Day After/You're a Very Lovely Woman | 1971 | — | 3.00 | 6.00 |

—As "Emitt Rhodes with the Merry-Go-Round"
ABC DUNHILL
❏ 4267	Fresh as a Daisy/				
	You Take the Dark Out of the Night	1970	—	3.00	6.00
❏ 4274	Live Till You Die/Promises I've Made	1971	—	2.50	5.00
❏ 4280	A Lullaby/With My Face on the Floor	1971	—	2.50	5.00
❏ 4295	Really Wanted You/Love Will Stone You	1971	—	2.50	5.00
❏ 4303	Take You Far Away/Golden Child of God	1972	—	2.50	5.00
❏ 4315	Tame the Lion/Golden Child of God	1972	—	2.50	5.00
Albums
A&M
| ❏ SP-4254 | The American Dream | 1970 | 6.25 | 12.50 | 25.00 |

—Original album contains "You're a Very Lovely Woman" and has Rhodes in front of a paint-covered backdrop on cover
| ❏ SP-4254 | The American Dream | 1971 | 3.75 | 7.50 | 15.00 |

—Reissue contains "Saturday Night" and a framed photo of Rhodes on cover
ABC DUNHILL
❏ DS-50089	Emitt Rhodes	1970	3.00	6.00	12.00
❏ DS-50111	Mirror	1971	3.00	6.00	12.00
❏ DS-50122	Farewell to Paradise	1972	3.00	6.00	12.00

RHODES, SLIM
45s
RHODES
| ❏ 101 | Brothers Frank and Jesse James/ | | | | |
| | (B-side unknown) | 195? | 12.50 | 25.00 | 50.00 |
SUN
❏ 216	Don't Believe/Uncertain Blues	1955	25.00	50.00	100.00
❏ 225	Are You Ashamed of Me/The House of Sin	1955	75.00	150.00	300.00
❏ 238	Bad Girl/Gonna Romp and Stomp	1956	25.00	50.00	100.00
❏ 256	Do What I Do/Take and Give	1956	12.50	25.00	50.00

Number	Title (A Side/B Side)	Yr	VG	VG+	NM

RHODES, TODD
45s
KING
❏ 4469	Gin, Gin, Gin/I Shouldn't Cry But I Do	1951	25.00	50.00	100.00
❏ 4486	Good Man/Evening Breeze	1951	15.00	30.00	60.00
❏ 4509	Your Daddy's Doggin' Around/Red Boy Is Back	1952	15.00	30.00	60.00
❏ 4528	Rocket 69/Possessed	1952	12.50	25.00	50.00
❏ 4556	Snuff Dipper/Trying	1952	12.50	25.00	50.00

—B-side by La Vern Baker
| ❏ 4566 | Pig Latin Blues/Blue Autumn | 1952 | 12.50 | 25.00 | 50.00 |
| ❏ 4583 | Hog Maw and Cabbage Slaw/Must I Cry Again | 1952 | 12.50 | 25.00 | 50.00 |

—B-side by La Vern Baker
| ❏ 4601 | Thunderbolt Boogie/Lost Child | 1953 | 12.50 | 25.00 | 50.00 |

—B-side by La Vern Baker
❏ 4648	Your Mouth Got a Hole In It/Feathers	1953	10.00	20.00	40.00
❏ 4666	Let Down Blues/Beet Patch	1953	10.00	20.00	40.00
❏ 4736	Silver Sunset/Specks	1954	7.50	15.00	30.00
❏ 4755	Chicken Strut/Echoes	1954	7.50	15.00	30.00
Albums
KING
| ❏ 295-88 [10] | Todd Rhodes Playing His Greatest Hits | 1954 | 375.00 | 750.00 | 1500. |
| ❏ 658 [M] | Dance Music | 1960 | 200.00 | 400.00 | 800.00 |

RHYTHM, JOHNNY
45s
MGM
| ❏ 13043 | This Is It/Wouldn't It Be Nice | 1961 | 10.00 | 20.00 | 40.00 |

RHYTHM ACES, THE (1)
45s
ACE
| ❏ 518 | Rock and Roll March/Look What You've Done | 1956 | 10.00 | 20.00 | 40.00 |

—B-side by Bob Douglas
VEE JAY
| ❏ 124 | I Wonder Why/Get Lost | 1954 | 50.00 | 100.00 | 200.00 |

—Black vinyl
| ❏ 124 | I Wonder Why/Get Lost | 1954 | 500.00 | 1000. | 2000. |

—Red vinyl
| ❏ 138 | Whisper to Me/Olly, Olly, Oxsen Free | 1955 | 50.00 | 100.00 | 200.00 |

—Black vinyl
| ❏ 138 | Whisper to Me/Olly, Olly, Oxsen Free | 1955 | 500.00 | 1000. | 2000. |

—Red vinyl
| ❏ 160 | That's My Sugar/Flippety Flop | 1955 | 30.00 | 60.00 | 120.00 |

RHYTHM ACES, THE (2)
45s
MARK-X
| ❏ 8004 | Boppin' Sloppin' Baby/Crazy Jealousy | 1960 | 7.50 | 15.00 | 30.00 |

RHYTHM ACES, THE (3)
45s
ROULETTE
❏ 4268	Mohawk Rock/It'll Do	1960	3.75	7.50	15.00
❏ 4426	Raunchy Twist/Mockin' Bird Twist	1962	3.75	7.50	15.00
SIOUX					
❏ 82260	Allan's Rock/Go Get It	1960	7.50	15.00	30.00
❏ 102261	Yahma/What'd I Say Twist	1961	7.50	15.00	30.00
UNIVERSAL ARTISTS					
❏ 3160	Mohawk Rock/It'll Do	1960	10.00	20.00	40.00

RHYTHM CADETS, THE
45s
VESTA
| ❏ 501/2 | Dearest Doryce/Rocking Jimmy | 1957 | 200.00 | 400.00 | 800.00 |

RHYTHM HERITAGE
45s
ABC
| ❏ 12063 | Theme from "Young Frankenstein"/I Wouldn't Treat a Dog (The Way You Treated Me) | 1975 | — | 2.50 | 5.00 |
| ❏ 12135 | Theme from S.W.A.T./I Wouldn't Treat a Dog (The Way You Treated Me) | 1975 | — | 2.00 | 4.00 |

—Version 2: With long version of A-side; "RE-1" on label next to matrix number
| ❏ 12135 | Theme from S.W.A.T./I Wouldn't Treat a Dog (The Way You Treated Me) | 1975 | — | 2.50 | 5.00 |

—Version 1: With short version of A-side
❏ 12177	Baretta's Theme (Keep Your Eye on the Sparrow)/My Cherie Amour	1976	—	2.00	4.00
❏ 12205	Disco-Fied/(It's Time to) Boogie Down	1976	—	2.00	4.00
❏ 12243	Gonna Fly Now (Theme from "Rocky")/Last Night on Earth	1976	—	2.00	4.00
❏ 12273	Theme from "Starsky and Hutch"/Disco Queen	1977	—	2.00	4.00
❏ 12334 [DJ]	Holdin' Out for You Love (mono/stereo)	1978	—	2.00	4.00

—May be promo only
| ❏ 12378 | Language of Love/Sail Away with Me | 1978 | — | 2.00 | 4.00 |
Albums
ABC
❏ D-934	Disco-Fied	1976	2.50	5.00	10.00
❏ D-987	Last Night on Earth	1977	2.50	5.00	10.00
❏ AA-1037	The Sky's the Limit	1978	2.50	5.00	10.00

RHYTHM MASTERS, THE (1)
45s
ACE
| ❏ 610 | The Devil and His Old Suitcase/Holding My Savior's Hand | 1961 | 5.00 | 10.00 | 20.00 |
Albums
ACE
| ❏ LP-1010 [M] | Hymns and Spirituals | 1961 | 25.00 | 50.00 | 100.00 |

RHYTHM MASTERS, THE (2)
45s
FLIP
| ❏ 314 | Baby We Two/Patricia | 1956 | 75.00 | 150.00 | 300.00 |

Number	Title (A Side/B Side)	Yr	VG	VG+	NM
RHYTHM ROCKERS (1)					
45s					
CHALLENGE					
❏ 9196	Rendezvous Stomp/The Slide	1963	6.25	12.50	25.00
Albums					
CHALLENGE					
❏ CHL-617 [M]	Soul Surfin'	1963	22.50	45.00	90.00
RHYTHM ROCKERS (2)					
45s					
SATIN					
❏ 921	Oh Boy/We Belong Together	1960	15.00	30.00	60.00
❏ 921 [PS]	Oh Boy/We Belong Together	1960	25.00	50.00	100.00
RHYTHM ROCKERS (3)					
45s					
SUN					
❏ 248	Fiddle Bop/Juke Box, Help Me Find My Baby	1956	25.00	50.00	100.00
RHYTHM ROCKERS (U) These could be by group (1) or (2).					
45s					
FENTON					
❏ 944	Surf Around/Three Strikes	1962	12.50	25.00	50.00
WIPE OUT					
❏ 1001	Foot Cruising/Get It On	1962	10.00	20.00	40.00
RHYTHMETTES, THE					
45s					
BRUNSWICK					
❏ 55012	Mind Reader/Mister Love	1957	3.75	7.50	15.00
❏ 55050	That's a-Plenty/Till My Baby Comes Home	1958	3.00	6.00	12.00
❏ 55083	Elaine/Bow Legged Woman	1958	3.00	6.00	12.00
❏ 55097	I'll Be With You in Apple Blossom Time/ Page from the Future	1958	3.00	6.00	12.00
CORAL					
❏ 62186	High School Lovers/Snow Queen	1960	2.50	5.00	10.00
RCA VICTOR					
❏ 47-6089	Only You/Him	1955	5.00	10.00	20.00
❏ 47-6244	Show Me the Way/The Bridge of Love	1955	3.75	7.50	15.00
❏ 47-6349	Take My Hand, Show Me the Way/I've Got to Know	1955	3.75	7.50	15.00
❏ 47-6539	Homin' Pigeon/Boom-Boom	1956	3.75	7.50	15.00
❏ 47-6742	Winter Snow/Take a Look in the Mirror	1956	3.75	7.50	15.00
RIA AND THE REASONS					
45s					
AMY					
❏ 888	Memories Linger On/Sorry I Lied	1963	6.25	12.50	25.00
❏ 888	Memories Linger On/Sorry I Lied	1963	20.00	40.00	80.00
—Blue vinyl					
RSVP					
❏ 1110	He's Not There/She Fell in Love	1965	5.00	10.00	20.00
—As "Ria and the Revellons"					
RIALTOS, THE					
45s					
CB					
❏ 5009	Let Me In/It Hurts	1962	75.00	150.00	300.00
RIBBONS, THE					
45s					
MARSH					
❏ 202	Ain't Gonna Kiss Ya/My Baby Said	1963	3.75	7.50	15.00
❏ 203	After Last Night/This Is Our Melody	1963	3.00	6.00	12.00
PARKWAY					
❏ 912	Meoldie D'Amour/They Played a Sad Song	1964	3.00	6.00	12.00
RIC-A-SHAYS, THE Harry NILSSON was in this group.					
45s					
LOLA					
❏ 002	Groovy/Turn On	1964	6.25	12.50	25.00
RICARDOS, THE					
45s					
STAR-X					
❏ 512	Mary's Little Lamb/I Mean Really	1958	40.00	80.00	160.00
RICE, JIMMY					
45s					
RED BIRD					
❏ 10-022	The Grass Is Always Greener/Spanish Perfume	1965	5.00	10.00	20.00
❏ 10-027	Nobody But You/Or Not at All	1965	5.00	10.00	20.00
RICE, TONY					
45s					
ACTION					
❏ 100	My Darling Y-O-U/I Thank You Baby	1961	7.50	15.00	30.00
PRINCETON					
❏ 101	Summer's Love/Please Don't	1960	15.00	30.00	60.00
RAE COX					
❏ 106	Little School Girl/Blue Bird of Happiness	1961	5.00	10.00	20.00
RICH, CHARLIE					
45s					
ELEKTRA					
❏ 45553	I'll Wake You Up When I Get Home/ Salty Dog Blues	1978	—	2.00	4.00
❏ 47047	A Man Just Doesn't Know What a Woman Goes Through/Marie	1980	—	2.00	4.00
❏ 47104	Are We Dreamin' the Same Dream/Angelina	1981	—	2.00	4.00
EPIC					
❏ 02058	You Made It Beautiful/How Good It Used to Be	1981	—	2.00	4.00
❏ 03165	Try a Little Tenderness/As Time Goes By	1982	—	2.00	4.00
❏ 10287	Set Me Free/I'll Just Go Away	1968	—	3.00	6.00
❏ 10358	Raggedy Ann/Nothing in the World	1968	—	3.00	6.00
❏ 10492	Life's Little Ups and Downs/It Takes Time	1969	—	3.00	6.00
❏ 10585	July 12, 1939/I'm Flying to Nashville Tonight	1970	—	3.00	6.00

Number	Title (A Side/B Side)	Yr	VG	VG+	NM
❏ 10662	Nice 'N' Easy/I Can't Even Drink It Away	1970	—	3.00	6.00
❏ 10745	A Woman Left Lonely/Have a Heart	1971	—	2.50	5.00
❏ 10809	A Part of Your Life/A Sunday Kind of Woman	1971	—	2.50	5.00
❏ 10867	I Take It On Home/Peace on You	1972	—	2.50	5.00
❏ 10950	Behind Closed Doors/A Sunday Kind of Woman	1973	—	2.00	4.00
—Repressings have orange labels					
❏ 10950	Behind Closed Doors/A Sunday Kind of Woman	1973	—	2.50	5.00
—Originals have yellow labels					
❏ 11040	The Most Beautiful Girl/I Feel Like Going Home	1973	—	2.00	4.00
❏ 11091	A Very Special Love Song/ I Can't Even Drink It Away	1974	—	2.00	4.00
❏ 20006	I Love My Friend/Why Oh Why	1974	—	2.00	4.00
❏ 50064	My Elusive Dreams/Whatever Happened	1975	—	2.00	4.00
❏ 50103	Every Time You Touch Me (I Get High)/ Pass On By	1975	—	2.00	4.00
❏ 50142	All Over Me/You & I	1975	—	2.00	4.00
❏ 50182	Since I Fell for You/She	1975	—	2.00	4.00
❏ 50222	America the Beautiful (1976)/Down By the Riverside	1976	—	2.00	4.00
❏ 50268	Road Song/The Grass Is Always Greener	1976	—	2.00	4.00
❏ 50328	Easy Look/My Lady	1976	—	2.00	4.00
❏ 50392	Rollin' with the Flow/To Sing a Love Song	1977	—	2.00	4.00
❏ 50562	Beautiful Woman/Everybody Wrote That Song for Me	1978	—	2.00	4.00
❏ 50616	On My Knees/Mellow Melody	1978	—	2.00	4.00
❏ 50701	Spanish Eyes/I Do My Swingin' at Home	1979	—	2.00	4.00
❏ 50869	Even a Fool Would Let Go/Pretty People	1980	—	2.00	4.00
GROOVE					
❏ 58-0020	The Grass Is Always Greener/She Loved Everybody But Me	1963	3.75	7.50	15.00
❏ 58-0020 [PS]	The Grass Is Always Greener/She Loved Everybody But Me	1963	7.50	15.00	30.00
❏ 58-0025	Big Boss Man/Let Me Go My Merry Way	1963	3.75	7.50	15.00
❏ 58-0032	Lady Love/Why, Oh Why	1964	3.75	7.50	15.00
❏ 58-0035	The Ways of a Woman in Love/ My Mountain Dew	1964	3.75	7.50	15.00
❏ 58-0041	Nice 'N' Easy/Turn Around and Face Me	1964	3.75	7.50	15.00
HI					
❏ 2116	Love Is After Me/Pass On By	1966	2.50	5.00	10.00
❏ 2123	My Heart Would Know/ Nobody's Lonesome for Me	1967	2.50	5.00	10.00
❏ 2134	Hurry Up Freight Train/Only Me	1967	2.50	5.00	10.00
MERCURY					
❏ 73466	I Washed My Hands in Muddy Water/No Home	1974	—	2.50	5.00
❏ 73498	A Field of Yellow Daisies/Party Girl	1974	—	2.50	5.00
❏ 73646	Something Just Came Over Me/Best Years	1974	—	2.50	5.00
PHILLIPS INT'L.					
❏ 3532	Whirlwind/Philadelphia Baby	1959	6.25	12.50	25.00
❏ 3542	Rebound/Big Man	1959	6.25	12.50	25.00
❏ 3552	Lonely Weekends/Everything I Do Is Wrong	1960	6.25	12.50	25.00
❏ 3560	School Days/Gonna Be Waiting	1960	6.25	12.50	25.00
❏ 3562	On My Knees/Stay	1960	6.25	12.50	25.00
❏ 3566	Who Will the Next Fool Be/Caught in the Middle	1961	6.25	12.50	25.00
❏ 3572	Just a Little Sweet/It's Too Late	1962	5.00	10.00	20.00
❏ 3576	Easy Money/Midnight Blues	1962	5.00	10.00	20.00
❏ 3582	Sittin' and Thinkin'/Finally Found Out	1962	5.00	10.00	20.00
❏ 3584	There's Another Place I Can't Go/ I Need Your Love	1963	5.00	10.00	20.00
RCA					
❏ PB-10859	My Mountain Dew/Nice 'N Easy	1976	—	2.00	4.00
❏ PB-10966	Nice 'N Easy/It's All Over Now	1977	—	2.00	4.00
RCA VICTOR					
❏ 47-8468	It's All Over Now/Too Many Teardrops	1964	3.75	7.50	15.00
❏ 47-8536	There Won't Be Anymore/Gentleman Jim	1965	5.00	10.00	20.00
❏ 47-8817	Nice 'N' Easy/Ol' Man River	1966	3.00	6.00	12.00
❏ 74-0983	Tomorrow Night/The Ways of a Woman in Love	1973	—	2.00	4.00
❏ APBO-0195	There Won't Be Anymore/It's All Over Now	1973	—	2.50	5.00
❏ APBO-0260	I Don't See Me in Your Eyes Anymore/ No Room to Dance	1974	—	2.00	4.00
❏ PB-10062	She Called Me Baby/$10 and a Clean White Shirt	1974	—	2.00	4.00
❏ GB-10159	There Won't Be Anymore/Tomorrow Night	1975	—	—	3.00
—Gold Standard Series					
❏ PB-10256	It's All Over Now/Big Jack	1975	—	2.00	4.00
❏ PB-10458	Not Everybody Knows/ I've Got You Under My Skin	1975	—	2.00	4.00
❏ GB-10512	She Called Me Baby/ $10 and a Clean White Shirt	1975	—	—	3.00
—Gold Standard Series					
SMASH					
❏ 1993	Mohair Sam/ I Washed My Hands in Muddy Water	1965	5.00	10.00	20.00
❏ 2012	Dance of Love/I Can't Go On	1965	3.75	7.50	15.00
❏ 2022	Hawg Jaw/Something Just Came Over Me	1966	3.75	7.50	15.00
❏ 2038	No Home/Tears a-Go-Go	1966	3.75	7.50	15.00
❏ 2060	That's the Way/When My Baby Comes Home	1966	3.75	7.50	15.00
SUN					
❏ 1110	Who Will the Next Fool Be/Stay	1970	—	2.50	5.00
❏ 1151	The Breakup/Be-Bop-a-Lula	1980	—	2.00	4.00
—B-side by Jerry Lee Lewis; both sides are duets with Orion					
UNITED ARTISTS					
❏ XW1193	Puttin' In Overtime at Home/ Ghost of Another Man	1978	—	2.00	4.00
❏ XW1223	I Still Believe in Love/Wishful Thinking	1978	—	2.00	4.00
❏ XW1269	The Fool Strikes Again/I Loved You All the Way	1978	—	2.00	4.00
❏ XW1280	I Lost My Head/ She Knows Just How to Touch Me	1979	—	2.00	4.00
❏ XW1307	Life Goes On/Standing Tall	1979	—	2.00	4.00
❏ 1325	You're Gonna Love Yourself in the Morning/ Top of the Stairs	1979	—	2.00	4.00
❏ 1340	I'd Build a Bridge/ All You Ever Have to Do Is Touch Me	1980	—	2.00	4.00

R

Number	Title (A Side/B Side)	Yr	VG	VG+	NM
7-Inch Extended Plays					
EPIC					
❏ AE7 1065 [DJ]	Big Boss Man/Nice 'n' Easy//Life Has Its Little				
	Ups and Downs/I Take It on Home	1972	—	3.00	6.00
—Small hole, plays at 33 1/3 rpm; came as a bonus with some copies of KE 31933, "The Best of Charlie Rich"					
❏ AE7 1065 [PS]	The Best of Charlie Rich Bonus Record	1972	—	3.00	6.00
—Special sleeve for above disc; came as a bonus with some copies of KE 31933, "The Best of Charlie Rich"					
Albums					
BUCKBOARD					
❏ 1019	The Entertainer	197?	2.50	5.00	10.00
COLUMBIA SPECIAL PRODUCTS					
❏ P2 13663 [(2)]	Super Hits	197?	3.75	7.50	15.00
ELEKTRA					
❏ 6E-301	Once a Drifter	1981	2.50	5.00	10.00
EPIC					
❏ AS 50 [DJ]	Charlie Rich	1973	7.50	15.00	30.00
—Promo-only compilation					
❏ AS 139 [DJ]	Everything You Always Wanted to Hear by				
	Charlie Rich But Were Afraid to Ask For	1976	6.25	12.50	25.00
—Promo-only sampler					
❏ BN 26376	Set Me Free	1968	5.00	10.00	20.00
❏ BN 26516	The Fabulous Charlie Rich	1970	5.00	10.00	20.00
❏ E 30214	Boss Man	1970	5.00	10.00	20.00
❏ CQ 31933 [Q]	The Best of Charlie Rich	1972	5.00	10.00	20.00
❏ KE 31933	The Best of Charlie Rich	1972	3.75	7.50	15.00
—Yellow label; add 80 percent if bonus record AE7 1065 and its special sleeve are still there					
❏ KE 31933	The Best of Charlie Rich	1973	3.00	6.00	12.00
—Orange label					
❏ CQ 32247 [Q]	Behind Closed Doors	1973	5.00	10.00	20.00
❏ KE 32247	Behind Closed Doors	1973	3.00	6.00	12.00
❏ PE 32247	Behind Closed Doors	197?	2.00	4.00	8.00
—Reissue					
❏ PE 32531	Very Special Love Songs	1974	3.00	6.00	12.00
❏ PEQ 32531 [Q]	Very Special Love Songs	1974	5.00	10.00	20.00
❏ PE 33250	The Silver Fox	1974	3.00	6.00	12.00
❏ PEQ 33250 [Q]	The Silver Fox	1974	5.00	10.00	20.00
❏ PE 33455	Every Time You Touch Me (I Get High)	1975	3.00	6.00	12.00
❏ PEQ 33455 [Q]	Every Time You Touch Me (I Get High)	1975	5.00	10.00	20.00
❏ PE 33545	Silver Linings	1976	2.50	5.00	10.00
❏ PE 34240	Greatest Hits	1976	2.50	5.00	10.00
—Without bar code on cover					
❏ PE 34240	Greatest Hits	1979	2.00	4.00	8.00
—With bar code on cover					
❏ PE 34444	Take Me	1977	2.50	5.00	10.00
❏ PE 34444	Take Me	1977	2.50	5.00	10.00
❏ PE 34891	Rollin' with the Flow	1977	2.50	5.00	10.00
❏ JE 35394	Classic Rich, Vol. 1	1978	2.50	5.00	10.00
❏ JE 35624	Classic Rich, Vol. 2	1978	2.50	5.00	10.00
GROOVE					
❏ GM-1000 [M]	Charlie Rich	1964	37.50	75.00	150.00
❏ GS-1000 [S]	Charlie Rich	1964	75.00	150.00	300.00
HARMONY					
❏ KH 32166	I Do My Swingin' at Home	1973	3.00	6.00	12.00
HI					
❏ 8006	I'm So Lonesome I Could Cry	198?	2.00	4.00	8.00
—Reissue of Hi 32084					
❏ HL 12037 [M]	Charlie Rich Sings Country and Western	1967	7.50	15.00	30.00
❏ SHL 32037 [S]	Charlie Rich Sings Country and Western	1967	5.00	10.00	20.00
❏ SHL 32084	Charlie Rich Sings the Songs of Hank Williams				
	& Others	1974	3.00	6.00	12.00
—Reissue of 32037					
HILLTOP					
❏ 6139	Lonely Weekends	197?	2.50	5.00	10.00
❏ 6149	Songs for Beautiful Girls	1974	2.50	5.00	10.00
❏ 6160	Entertainer of the Year	197?	2.50	5.00	10.00
MERCURY					
❏ SRM-2-7505 [(2)]	Fully Realized	1974	3.75	7.50	15.00
PHILLIPS INTERNATIONAL					
❏ PLP-1970 [M]	Lonely Weekends	1960	150.00	300.00	600.00
PICKWICK					
❏ ACL-7001	Too Many Teardrops	1975	2.50	5.00	10.00
POWER PAK					
❏ PO-241	There Won't Be Anymore	197?	2.50	5.00	10.00
❏ PO-245	Arkansas Traveler	197?	2.50	5.00	10.00
❏ PO-252	The Silver Fox	197?	2.50	5.00	10.00
QUICKSILVER					
❏ QS-1005	Midnight Blue	198?	3.00	6.00	12.00
RCA CAMDEN					
❏ CAS-2417	The Versatile and Talented Charlie Rich	1970	2.50	5.00	10.00
RCA VICTOR					
❏ APL1-0258	Tomorrow Night	1973	3.00	6.00	12.00
❏ APL1-0433	There Won't Be Anymore	1974	3.00	6.00	12.00
❏ APL1-0686	She Called Me Baby	1974	3.00	6.00	12.00
❏ APL1-0857	Greatest Hits	1975	3.00	6.00	12.00
❏ APL1-1242	Now Everybody Knows	1975	3.00	6.00	12.00
❏ ANL1-1542	Tomorrow Night	1976	2.50	5.00	10.00
—Reissue					
❏ APL1-2260	Big Boss Man/My Mountain Dew	1977	3.00	6.00	12.00
❏ ANL1-2424	She Called Me Baby	1977	2.50	5.00	10.00
—Reissue of APL1-0686					
❏ LPM-3352 [M]	That's Rich	1965	10.00	20.00	40.00
❏ LSP-3352 [S]	That's Rich	1965	12.50	25.00	50.00
❏ LPM-3537 [M]	Big Boss Man	1966	10.00	20.00	40.00
❏ LSP-3557 [S]	Big Boss Man	1966	12.50	25.00	50.00
❏ AHL1-5496	Collector's Series	1985	2.00	4.00	8.00
SMASH					
❏ MGS-27070 [M]	The Many New Sides of Charlie Rich	1965	7.50	15.00	30.00
❏ MGS-27078 [M]	The Best Years	1966	7.50	15.00	30.00
❏ SRS-67070 [S]	The Many New Sides of Charlie Rich	1965	10.00	20.00	40.00
❏ SRS-67070 [S]	The Best Years	1966	10.00	20.00	40.00
SUN					
❏ LP 110	Lonely Weekend	1970	3.00	6.00	12.00
❏ LP 123	A Time for Tears	1971	3.00	6.00	12.00

Number	Title (A Side/B Side)	Yr	VG	VG+	NM
❏ LP 132	The Early Years	1974	3.00	6.00	12.00
❏ LP 133	The Memphis Sound of Charlie Rich	1974	3.00	6.00	12.00
❏ LP 134	Golden Treasures	1974	3.00	6.00	12.00
❏ LP 135	Sun's Best of Charlie Rich	1974	3.00	6.00	12.00
❏ 1003	20 Golden Hits	1979	2.50	5.00	10.00
—Gold vinyl					
❏ 1007	The Original Charlie Rich	1979	2.50	5.00	10.00
SUNNYVALE					
❏ 9330	The Sun Story Vol. 2	1977	2.50	5.00	10.00
TIME-LIFE					
❏ STW-115	Country Music	1981	2.50	5.00	10.00
TRIP					
❏ TLP-8502 [(2)]	The Best of Charlie Rich	1974	3.00	6.00	12.00
UNITED ARTISTS					
❏ UA-LA876-H	I Still Believe in Love	1978	3.00	6.00	12.00
❏ UA-LA925-H	The Fool Strikes Again	1978	2.50	5.00	10.00
WING					
❏ SRW-16375	A Lonely Weekend	1969	3.00	6.00	12.00
RICH, DAVE					
45s					
BRAGG					
❏ 210	Big Hands/Sin Pays	196?	3.75	7.50	15.00
DECCA					
❏ 31513	The Great Speckled Bird/				
	I Want to Know You Lord	1963	3.00	6.00	12.00
❏ 31573	It's Not for Me to Understand/When They Ring				
	Those Golden Bells	1963	3.00	6.00	12.00
MONUMENT					
❏ 918	The Runt/Hang On Till the Goin' On Comes On	1966	2.50	5.00	10.00
RCA VICTOR					
❏ 47-6327	I Forgot/I Think I'm Gonna Die	1955	7.50	15.00	30.00
❏ 47-6435	I'm Glad/Darling, I'm Lonesome	1956	7.50	15.00	30.00
❏ 47-6595	Your Pretty Blue Eyes/Ain't It Fine	1956	10.00	20.00	40.00
❏ 47-6687	I'm Sorry, Goodbye/I Love 'Em All	1956	7.50	15.00	30.00
❏ 47-6753	Lonely Street/Didn't Work Out, Did It	1956	7.50	15.00	30.00
❏ 47-6824	Tuggin' on My Heart Strings/				
	Our Last Night Together	1957	7.50	15.00	30.00
❏ 47-6926	The Key to My Heart/Red Sweater	1957	7.50	15.00	30.00
❏ 47-7045	Chicken House/I've Learned	1957	7.50	15.00	30.00
❏ 47-7141	School Blues/I've Thought It Over	1958	7.50	15.00	30.00
❏ 47-7247	City Lights/Burn On Love Fire	1958	7.50	15.00	30.00
❏ 47-7334	Rosie Let's Get Cozy/Sunshine in My Heart	1958	7.50	15.00	30.00
❏ 47-7656	Where Else Would I Want to Be/				
	Brand New Feeling	1959	6.25	12.50	25.00
REPUBLIC					
❏ 390	Because You're Gone/Cheatin', Stealin', Steel				
	Guitar Man	1977	—	2.50	5.00
STOP					
❏ 122	When I've Learned/I Don't Need Nobody Else	196?	2.00	4.00	8.00
❏ 132	I Never Gave Up/On the Battlefield	196?	2.00	4.00	8.00
❏ 171	I Believe/Peace On Earth Begins Today	196?	2.00	4.00	8.00
TRUE					
❏ 116	The Sea of Galilee/King Jesus	1978	—	3.00	6.00
❏ 118	Love Is Running Out of My Eyes/When I Need				
	Love	197?	—	3.00	6.00
❏ 201	I Come Apart/Don't You Ever Go Back	197?	—	3.00	6.00
Albums					
STOP					
❏ 10007	Soul Brother	196?	7.50	15.00	30.00
RICH KIDS, THE					
45s					
STEED					
❏ 702	Plastic Flowers/Got to Find a Woman	1967	2.50	5.00	10.00
❏ 706	You Made Me a Man/I Tried to Tell You	1968	2.50	5.00	10.00
RICHARD, CLIFF Also see THE SHADOWS.					
45s					
ABC-PARAMOUNT					
❏ 10042	Living Doll/Apron Strings	1959	6.25	12.50	25.00
❏ 10066	Travellin' Light/Dynamite	1959	5.00	10.00	20.00
❏ 10093	Voice in the Wilderness/Don't Be Mad at Me	1960	5.00	10.00	20.00
❏ 10109	Fall in Love with You/Choppin' 'N' Changin'	1960	5.00	10.00	20.00
❏ 10136	Please Don't Tease/Where Is My Heart	1960	5.00	10.00	20.00
❏ 10175	Catch Me, I'm Falling/"D" in Love	1961	5.00	10.00	20.00
❏ 10195	Theme for a Dream/Mumblin' Mosie	1961	10.00	20.00	40.00
BIG TOP					
❏ 3101	The Young Ones/We Say Yeah	1962	5.00	10.00	20.00
CAPITOL					
❏ F4096	Move It/High Class Baby	1958	10.00	20.00	40.00
❏ F4154	Livin' Lovin' Doll/Steady with You	1959	10.00	20.00	40.00
DOT					
❏ 16399	Wonderful to Be Young/Got a Funny Feeling	1962	5.00	10.00	20.00
EMI					
❏ S7-19767	Mistletoe and Wine/				
	Have Yourself a Merry Little Christmas	1997	—	2.00	4.00
EMI AMERICA					
❏ 8025	We Don't Talk Anymore/Count Me Out	1979	—	2.00	4.00
❏ 8035	Carrie/Language of Love	1980	—	2.00	4.00
❏ 8057	Dreaming/Dynamite	1980	—	2.00	4.00
—Gray label					
❏ 8057	Dreaming/Dynamite	1980	—	2.50	5.00
—Green label					
❏ 8068	A Little in Love/Everyman	1980	—	2.00	4.00
❏ 8076	Give a Little Bit More/Keep Lookin'	1981	—	2.00	4.00
❏ 8076 [PS]	Give a Little Bit More/Keep Lookin'	1981	—	2.50	5.00
❏ 8095	Wired for Sound/Hold On	1981	—	2.00	4.00
❏ 8103	Daddy's Home/Summer Rain	1982	—	2.00	4.00
❏ 8135	The Only Way Out/Be in My Heart	1982	—	2.00	4.00
❏ 8149	Little Town/Be in My Heart	1982	—	2.00	4.00
❏ 8180	Never Say Die (Give a Little Bit More)/				
	Front Page	1983	—	2.00	4.00
❏ 8193	Donna/Ocean Deep	1984	—	*2.00	4.00
EPIC					
❏ 9597	Lucky Lips/Next Time	1963	5.00	10.00	20.00

Number	Title (A Side/B Side)	Yr	VG	VG+	NM
❑ 9597 [PS]	Lucky Lips/Next Time	1963	6.25	12.50	25.00
❑ 9633	It's All in the Game/I'm Looking Out the Window	1963	5.00	10.00	20.00
❑ 9633 [PS]	It's All in the Game/I'm Looking Out the Window	1963	—	—	—

—Rumored to exist, but without conclusive evidence, we will delete this from future editions

Number	Title (A Side/B Side)	Yr	VG	VG+	NM
❑ 9670	I'm the Lonely One/I Only Have Eyes for You	1964	5.00	10.00	20.00
❑ 9670 [PS]	I'm the Lonely One/I Only Have Eyes for You	1964	6.25	12.50	25.00
❑ 9691	Bachelor Boy/True, True Lovin'	1964	5.00	10.00	20.00
❑ 9737	I Don't Wanna Love You/Look in My Eyes Maria	1964	3.75	7.50	15.00
❑ 9757	Again/The Minute You're Gone	1965	3.75	7.50	15.00
❑ 9810	I Could Easily Fall (In Love with You)/On My Word	1965	3.75	7.50	15.00
❑ 9839	The Twelfth of Never/Paradise Lost	1965	3.75	7.50	15.00
❑ 9866	Wind Me Up (and Let Me Go)/Eye of a Needle	1965	3.75	7.50	15.00
❑ 10018	Blue Turns to Grey/I'll Walk Alone	1966	3.75	7.50	15.00
❑ 10070	Visions/Quando, Quando, Quando	1966	3.75	7.50	15.00
❑ 10101	Time Drags By/The La La La Song	1966	3.75	7.50	15.00
❑ 10178	It's All Over/Heartbeat	1967	3.75	7.50	15.00

MONUMENT

❑ 1211	Goodbye Sam, Hello Samantha/You Never Can Tell	1970	—	3.00	6.00
❑ 1229	I Ain't Got Time Anymore/Morning Comes Too Soon	1970	—	3.00	6.00

POLYDOR

❑ 885336-7	All I Ask of You/Phantom of the Opera Overture, Act 2	1987	—	—	3.00

—With Sarah Brightman

❑ 885336-7 [PS]	All I Ask of You/Phantom of the Opera Overture, Act 2	1987	—	—	3.00

ROCKET

❑ YB-11463	Green Light/Needing a Friend	1979	—	2.00	4.00
❑ 40531	Miss You Nights/Love Enough	1976	—	2.00	4.00
❑ 40574	Devil Woman/Love On (Shine On)	1976	—	2.50	5.00
❑ 40652	Junior Cowboy/I Can't Ask for Anymore Than You	1976	—	2.00	4.00
❑ 40724	Don't Turn the Light Out/Nothing Left for Me to Say	1977	—	2.00	4.00
❑ 40771	You've Got Me Wondering/Try a Smile	1977	—	2.00	4.00

SIRE

❑ 703	Living in Harmony/Jesus	1973	—	2.50	5.00
❑ 707	Power to All Our Friends/Come Back Billie Joe	1973	—	2.50	5.00

STRIPED HORSE

❑ 7008	My Pretty One/Love Ya	1988	—	—	3.00
❑ 7008 [PS]	My Pretty One/Love Ya	1988	—	—	3.00
❑ 7011	Some People/Love Ya	1988	—	—	3.00
❑ 7011 [PS]	Some People/Love Ya	1988	—	—	3.00

UNI

❑ 55061	All My Love/Our Story Book	1968	2.50	5.00	10.00
❑ 55069	Congratulations/High 'N' Dry	1968	2.50	5.00	10.00
❑ 55145	The Day I Met Marie/Sweet Little Jesus Boy	1969	3.00	6.00	12.00

WARNER BROS.

❑ 7344	Throw Down a Line/Reflections	1969	2.00	4.00	8.00

—A-side by Cliff and Hank (Marvin)

Albums

ABC-PARAMOUNT

❑ 321 [M]	Cliff Sings	1960	20.00	40.00	80.00
❑ S-321 [S]	Cliff Sings	1960	25.00	50.00	100.00
❑ 391 [M]	Listen to Cliff	1961	20.00	40.00	80.00
❑ S-391 [S]	Listen to Cliff	1961	25.00	50.00	100.00

EMI AMERICA

❑ SN-16220	Green Light	1981	2.00	4.00	8.00
❑ SN-16221	I'm Nearly Famous	1981	2.00	4.00	8.00
❑ SN-16253	Every Face Tells a Story	1981	2.00	4.00	8.00
❑ SW-17018	We Don't Talk Anymore	1979	2.50	5.00	10.00
❑ SW-17039	I'm No Hero	1980	2.50	5.00	10.00
❑ SW-17059	Wired for Sound	1981	2.50	5.00	10.00
❑ ST-17081	Now You See Me, Now You Don't	1982	2.50	5.00	10.00
❑ ST-17105	Give a Little Bit More	1983	2.50	5.00	10.00

EPIC

❑ LN 24063 [M]	Summer Holiday	1963	10.00	20.00	40.00
❑ LN 24089 [M]	It's All in the Game	1964	7.50	15.00	30.00
❑ LN 24115 [M]	Cliff Richard in Spain	1965	7.50	15.00	30.00
❑ BN 26063 [S]	Summer Holiday	1963	12.50	25.00	50.00
❑ BN 26089 [S]	It's All in the Game	1964	10.00	20.00	40.00
❑ BN 26115 [S]	Cliff Richard in Spain	1965	10.00	20.00	40.00

ROCKET

❑ PIG-2210	I'm Nearly Famous	1976	3.00	6.00	12.00
❑ PIG-2268	Every Face Tells a Story	1977	3.00	6.00	12.00
❑ BXL1-2958	Green Light	1978	3.00	6.00	12.00

WORD

❑ WR-8306	Walking in the Light	1985	3.00	6.00	12.00

RICHARD AND THE YOUNG LIONS
45s

PHILIPS

❑ 40381	Open Up Your Door/Once Upon Your Smile	1966	2.50	5.00	10.00
❑ 40381 [PS]	Open Up Your Door/Once Upon Your Smile	1966	5.00	10.00	20.00
❑ 40414	Nasty/Lost and Found	1966	2.00	4.00	8.00
❑ 40438	To Have and to Hold/You Can Make It	1967	2.00	4.00	8.00

RICHARDS, BETTY
45s

HIT

❑ 241	These Boots Are Made for Walking/Working My Way Back to You	1966	2.00	4.00	8.00

—B-side by the Chellows

❑ 254	How Does That Grab You Darlin'/Leaning on the Lamp Post	1966	2.00	4.00	8.00

—B-side by the Chords (2)

RICHARDS, KATY
45s

HIT

❑ 34	All Alone Am I/He Thinks I Still Care	1962	2.00	4.00	8.00

—B-side by Connie Landers

❑ 66	Losing You/Still	1963	2.50	5.00	10.00

—B-side by Bobby Russell

❑ 76	Judy's Turn to Cry/Wipe Out	1963	2.00	4.00	8.00

—B-side by the Music City Five

RICHARDS, SYLVIA
45s

HIT

❑ 53	Blame It on the Bossa Nova/Let's Limbo Some More	1963	2.00	4.00	8.00

—B-side by Leroy Jones

RICHARDSON, JAPE See THE BIG BOPPER.

RICHARDSON, RUDI
45s

SUN

❑ 271	Fools Hall of Fame/Why Should I Cry	1957	7.50	15.00	30.00

RICHARDSON, WARREN S., JR.
Albums

COTILLION

❑ SD 9013	Warren S. Richardson, Jr.	1970	7.50	15.00	30.00

RICHEY, GEORGE
45s

ASCOT

❑ 2149	Silent Telephone/Lonely Part of Town	1964	2.50	5.00	10.00

RICHIE, LITTLE JOE See LITTLE JOE.

RICHIE AND THE ROYALS
45s

GOLDEN CREST

❑ 573	Be My Girl/We're Strollin'	1962	12.50	25.00	50.00

RELLO

❑ 1	And When I'm Near You/Goody Goody	1961	20.00	40.00	80.00
❑ 3	Be My Girl/We're Strollin'	1962	50.00	100.00	200.00

RICHIE AND THE SAXONS
45s

TIP

❑ 1020	Bottom of the Barrel/Easy Now	196?	12.50	25.00	50.00

RICHMAN, JONATHAN, AND THE MODERN LOVERS
45s

BESERKLEY

❑ 5701	Roadrunner/Friday on My Mind	1975	2.50	5.00	10.00

—B-side by Earth Quake

❑ 5701 [PS]	Roadrunner/Friday on My Mind	1975	2.50	5.00	10.00
❑ 5743	New England/Here Come the Martians	1976	2.50	5.00	10.00
❑ 5743 [PS]	New England/Here Come the Martians	1976	2.50	5.00	10.00

Albums

BESERKLEY

❑ BZ-0048	Jonathan Richman and the Modern Lovers	1976	7.50	15.00	30.00

—Distributed by GRT

❑ JBZ 0048	Jonathan Richman and the Modern Lovers	1976	6.25	12.50	25.00

—Distributed by Playboy/CBS

❑ BZ-0050	The Modern Lovers	1976	7.50	15.00	30.00

—Distributed by GRT

❑ JBZ 0050	The Modern Lovers	1978	6.25	12.50	25.00

—Distributed by Playboy/CBS

❑ BZ-0053	Rock 'N' Roll with the Modern Lovers	1977	4.50	9.00	18.00

—Distributed by Janus/GRT

❑ JBZ 0055	Modern Lovers "Live"	1978	3.50	7.00	14.00

—Distributed by Playboy/CBS

❑ JBZ 0060	Back in Your Life	1979	2.50	5.00	10.00

—Distributed by Playboy/CBS

❑ 10060	Back in Your Life	1980	3.00	6.00	12.00

—Reissue -- change in distributing label to Elektra

❑ PZ 34800	Rock 'N' Roll with the Modern Lovers	1977	3.50	7.00	14.00

—Distributed by Playboy/CBS

BOMP!

❑ 4021	The Original Modern Lovers	1981	5.00	10.00	20.00

—Same album as Mohawk releasse

HOME OF THE HITS

❑ HH-1910	The Modern Lovers	1975	12.50	25.00	50.00

MOHAWK

❑ SCALP 0002	The Original Modern Lovers	1981	6.25	12.50	25.00

RHINO

❑ RNLP 70091	The Modern Lovers	1986	3.00	6.00	12.00

—Reissue

❑ RNLP 70092	Jonathan Richman and the Modern Lovers	1986	3.00	6.00	12.00

—Reissue

❑ RNLP 70093	Rock 'N' Roll with the Modern Lovers	1986	3.00	6.00	12.00

—Reissue

❑ RNLP 70094	Modern Lovers "Live"	1986	3.00	6.00	12.00

—Reissue

❑ RNLP 70095	Back in Your Life	1986	3.00	6.00	12.00

—Reissue

ROUNDER

❑ 9014	Modern Lovers '88	1988	3.00	6.00	12.00
❑ 9021	Jonathan Richman	1989	3.00	6.00	12.00
❑ 9024	Jonathan Goes Country	1990	3.00	6.00	12.00

SIRE

❑ 23939	Jonathan Sings!	1983	3.00	6.00	12.00

VAPOR

❑ 47086	I'm So Confused	1998	3.75	7.50	15.00
❑ 48216	Her Mystery Not of High Heels and Eye Shadow	2001	3.75	7.50	15.00

RICHY, PAUL
45s

SUN

❑ 338	The Legend of the Big Steeple/Broken Hearted Willie	1960	5.00	10.00	20.00

RICK AND DONNA
45s

A&M

❑ 710	I'm a Losing Guy/Wedding Bells Will Ring	1963	3.00	6.00	12.00

TOWER

❑ 112	A.B.C./What Good Is Love	1965	2.50	5.00	10.00

R

Number	Title (A Side/B Side)	Yr	VG	VG+	NM
RICK AND THE KEENS					
45s					
AUSTIN					
❑ 303	Peanuts/I'll Be Home	1961	12.50	25.00	50.00
JAMIE					
❑ 1219	Your Turn ot Cry/Tender Years	1962	5.00	10.00	20.00
LE CAM					
❑ 133	Darla/Someone New	1964	7.50	15.00	30.00
❑ 721	Peanuts/I'll Be Home	1961	12.50	25.00	50.00
SMASH					
❑ 1705	Peanuts/I'll Be Home	1961	5.00	10.00	20.00
❑ 1722	Maybe/Popcorn	1961	5.00	10.00	20.00
TOLLIE					
❑ 9016	Darla/Someone New	1964	5.00	10.00	20.00
RICK AND THE MASTERS					
45s					
CAMEO					
❑ 226	Flame of Love/Here Come Nancy	1962	12.50	25.00	50.00
❑ 247	Let It Please Be You/I Don't Want Your Love	1963	12.50	25.00	50.00
HARAL					
❑ 776	Bewitched, Bothered and Bewildered/ A Kissin' Friend	1962	15.00	30.00	60.00
TABA					
❑ 101	Flame of Love/Here Come Nancy	1962	37.50	75.00	150.00
RICK AND THE RAIDERS Early version of THE McCOYS. Also see RICK DERRINGER.					
45s					
SONIC					
❑ 76234	You Know That I Love You/What Can I Do?	1963	12.50	25.00	50.00
RICK AND THE RANDELLS					
45s					
ABC-PARAMOUNT					
❑ 10055	Let It Be You/Honey Doll	1959	10.00	20.00	40.00
RICK AND THE RAVENS With RAY MANZAREK, later of THE DOORS.					
45s					
AURA					
❑ 4506	Henrietta/Just for Me	1965	15.00	30.00	60.00
❑ 4511	Soul Train/Geraldine	1965	12.50	25.00	50.00
POSAE					
❑ 101	Big Bucket "T"/Rampage	196?	20.00	40.00	80.00
RICK, ROBIN & HIM					
45s					
V.I.P.					
❑ 25035	Three Choruses of Despair/Cause You Know Me	1965	6.25	12.50	25.00
RICKIE AND THE HALLMARKS					
45s					
AMY					
❑ 877	Wherever You Are/Joanie Don't You Cry	1963	10.00	20.00	40.00
RICKLES, DON					
Albums					
WARNER BROS.					
❑ WS 1745	Hello Dummy!	1968	3.75	7.50	15.00
❑ WS 1779	Don Rickles Speaks!	1969	3.75	7.50	15.00
RICKS, JIMMY Also see THE RAVENS.					
45s					
ARNOLD					
❑ 1011	Canadian Sunset/Change of Heart	1961	3.75	7.50	15.00
ATCO					
❑ 6220	Daddy Rolling Stone/Homesick	1962	5.00	10.00	20.00
ATLANTIC					
❑ 2246	Trouble in Mind/Romance in the Dark	1964	3.75	7.50	15.00
BATON					
❑ 236	I'm a Fool to Want You/Bad Man of Missouri	1957	10.00	20.00	40.00
DECCA					
❑ 30443	What Have I Done/Lazy Mule	1957	6.25	12.50	25.00
FELSTED					
❑ 8560	Secret Love/If It Didn't Hurt So Much	1959	6.25	12.50	25.00
❑ 8582	Leaning On Your Love/ Here Come the Tears Again	1959	6.25	12.50	25.00
FURY					
❑ 1070	I Wonder/Let Me Down Easy	1962	5.00	10.00	20.00
JOSIE					
❑ 796	She's Fine, She's Mine/The Unbeliever	1956	10.00	20.00	40.00
JUBILEE					
❑ 5559	Lonely Man/If You Ever Loved Someone	1967	3.00	6.00	12.00
❑ 5561	Wigglin' and Gigglin'/Long, Long Arm of Love	1967	3.00	6.00	12.00
❑ 5579	Don't Go to Strangers/Lonely Man	1967	3.00	6.00	12.00
❑ 5608	It's All in the Game/Baby Don't Leave Me	1967	3.00	6.00	12.00
❑ 5619	Snap Your Fingers/Wigglin' and Gigglin'	1968	3.00	6.00	12.00
MAINSTREAM					
❑ 625	Girl of My Dreams/Glow Worm	1965	3.75	7.50	15.00
MERCURY					
❑ 8296	Love Is the Thing/Too Soon	1952	20.00	40.00	80.00
PARIS					
❑ 504	Do You Promise/The Sugar Man Song	1957	7.50	15.00	30.00
SIGNATURE					
❑ 12013	At Sunrise/Goodnight My Love	1959	6.25	12.50	25.00
❑ 12040	I Needed Your Love/Timber	1960	5.00	10.00	20.00
❑ 12051	The Christmas Song/Love Is the Thing	1960	5.00	10.00	20.00
Albums					
JUBILEE					
❑ JGS-8021	Tell Her You Love Her	1969	12.50	25.00	50.00
MAINSTREAM					
❑ S-6050 [S]	Vibrations	1965	15.00	30.00	60.00
❑ 56050 [M]	Vibrations	1965	12.50	25.00	50.00
SIGNATURE					
❑ SM-1032 [M]	Jimmy Ricks	1961	50.00	100.00	200.00
—White label promo					
❑ SM-1032 [M]	Jimmy Ricks	1961	75.00	150.00	300.00

Number	Title (A Side/B Side)	Yr	VG	VG+	NM
RICKY AND THE VACELS					
45s					
EXPRESS					
❑ 711	Lorraine/Bubble Gum	1962	7.50	15.00	30.00
FARGO					
❑ 1050	His Girl/Don't Want Your Love No More	1963	7.50	15.00	30.00
❑ 1050	His Girl/Don't Want Your Love No More	1963	20.00	40.00	80.00
—Blue vinyl					
RICO AND THE RAVENS					
45s					
AUTUMN					
❑ 6	Don't You Know/In My Heart	1965	3.75	7.50	15.00
RALLY					
❑ 1601	Don't You Know/In My Heart	1965	10.00	20.00	40.00
RIDDLE, NELSON					
45s					
CAPITOL					
❑ F2609	Martin Kane Theme/ Make Believe That You're in Love	1953	3.75	7.50	15.00
❑ F2648	You Won't Forget Me/Drive-In	1953	3.75	7.50	15.00
❑ F2744	Brother John/Deep Blue Sea	1954	3.75	7.50	15.00
❑ F2846	In the Chapel in the Moonlight/Shadow Waltz	1954	3.75	7.50	15.00
❑ F2893	Song from "The Caine Mutiny" (I Can't Believe That You're in Love)/Vilia	1954	3.75	7.50	15.00
❑ F2997	Never-Never Land/Vera Cruz	1954	3.75	7.50	15.00
❑ F3037	Run for Cover/Pendulum Song	1955	3.75	7.50	15.00
❑ F3206	Three Little Stars/Take It or Leave It	1955	3.75	7.50	15.00
❑ F3225	All Er Nothin'/Pore Jud Is Daid	1955	3.75	7.50	15.00
❑ F3287	Lisbon Antigua/Robin Hood	1955	3.75	7.50	15.00
❑ F3374	Port-au-Prince/Midnight Blues	1956	3.00	6.00	12.00
❑ F3472	Theme from "The Proud Ones"/ The Love of Genevieve	1956	3.00	6.00	12.00
❑ F3559	The Farmer's Tango/Could You	1956	3.00	6.00	12.00
❑ F3631	Accordion Willy/Holiday in Naples	1957	3.00	6.00	12.00
❑ F3717	Theme from "The New Girl in Town"/ Matinee Theatre	1957	3.00	6.00	12.00
❑ F3758	Tangi Tahiti/Rue Madeleine	1957	3.00	6.00	12.00
❑ F3794	Blame It on Paree/In a Small Forgotten Town	1957	3.00	6.00	12.00
❑ F3877	I'm Getting Sentimental Over You/ The Girl Most Likely	1958	3.00	6.00	12.00
❑ F3980	Love Theme from St. Louis Blues/The Seventh Voyage of Sinbad	1958	3.00	6.00	12.00
❑ F4005	Song from "Kings Go Forth"/Siesta in Sevilla	1958	3.00	6.00	12.00
❑ F4024	Nel Blu Dipinto Di Blu (Volare)/Walkin'	1958	3.00	6.00	12.00
❑ F4075	Birds of Paradise/Uma Casa Portugese	1958	3.00	6.00	12.00
❑ F4120	The Joy of Livin'/Something Special	1959	3.00	6.00	12.00
❑ F4175	De Guello/Blue Safari	1959	3.00	6.00	12.00
❑ F4244	Markham Theme/Ting-a-Lay-O	1959	3.00	6.00	12.00
❑ 4309	The Untouchables/Autumn in Rio	1959	3.75	7.50	15.00
❑ 4378	Theme — The Untouchables/ The Untouchables Strike Back	1960	3.75	7.50	15.00
❑ 4378 [PS]	Theme — The Untouchables/ The Untouchables Strike Back	1960	6.25	12.50	25.00
❑ 4448	The Green Leaves of Summer/De Guelle	1960	2.50	5.00	10.00
❑ 4521	Little Old New York/My Gentle Young Johnny	1961	2.50	5.00	10.00
❑ 4691	O Mein Liebchen/Come a-Wandering with Me	1962	2.50	5.00	10.00
❑ 4741	Route 66 Theme/Lolita Ya-Ya	1962	2.50	5.00	10.00
❑ 4843	Naked City Theme/The Defenders Theme	1962	2.50	5.00	10.00
❑ 4896	The Ballad of Jed Clampett/ Stoney Burke Theme	1962	2.50	5.00	10.00
EPIC					
❑ 5-10175	El Dorado (Vocal)/(Instrumental)	1967	—	3.50	7.00
❑ 5-10175 [PS]	El Dorado (Vocal)/(Instrumental)	1967	2.50	5.00	10.00
LIBERTY					
❑ 55952	Thoroughly Modern Millie/See the Cheetah	1967	—	3.50	7.00
REPRISE					
❑ 0270	Hello, Dolly!/My True Carrie Love	1964	2.00	4.00	8.00
❑ 0319	Fiddler on the Roof/Gabriel	1965	2.00	4.00	8.00
❑ 0348	John F. Kennedy March/Big Mr. C	1965	2.00	4.00	8.00
❑ 0386	Me and My Shadow/Melancholie	1965	2.00	4.00	8.00
❑ 0412	Marriage on the Rocks/Theme from "Skyscraper"	1965	2.00	4.00	8.00
❑ 0467	Time for Singing/Freddie's New Slacks	1966	2.00	4.00	8.00
❑ 0476	Don't Drink the Water/Freddie's New Slacks	1966	2.00	4.00	8.00
❑ 20169	Come Blow Your Horn/Connie's Theme	1963	2.00	4.00	8.00
20TH CENTURY FOX					
❑ 6626	Batman Theme/Nelson's Riddler	1966	3.75	7.50	15.00
VERVE					
❑ 10194	March of the Swiss Soldiers/Walking the Dog	1960	3.00	6.00	12.00
7-Inch Extended Plays					
CAPITOL					
❑ EAP 1-620	(contents unknown)	195?	3.00	6.00	12.00
❑ EAP 1-620 [PS]	Moonglow	195?	3.00	6.00	12.00
❑ EAP 1-814	(contents unknown)	1957	3.00	6.00	12.00
❑ EAP 1-814 [PS]	Hey, Let Yourself Go, Part 1	1957	3.00	6.00	12.00
❑ EAP 2-814	(contents unknown)	1957	3.00	6.00	12.00
❑ EAP 2-814 [PS]	Hey, Let Yourself Go, Part 2	1957	3.00	6.00	12.00
❑ EAP 3-814	(contents unknown)	1957	3.00	6.00	12.00
❑ EAP 3-814 [PS]	Hey, Let Yourself Go, Part 3	1957	3.00	6.00	12.00
Albums					
ALSHIRE					
❑ 5203	Bridge Over Troubled Water	197?	2.50	5.00	10.00
AVON					
❑ 10170	Avon Wishes You a Happy Holiday and a Joyous New Year	1970	3.75	7.50	15.00
—Given to Avon salespeople					
CAPITOL					
❑ T 753 [M]	The Tender Touch	1956	6.25	12.50	25.00
❑ T 813 [M]	Hey, Let Yourself Go	1957	6.25	12.50	25.00
❑ T 893 [M]	C'mon, Get Happy	1957	6.25	12.50	25.00
❑ T 915 [M]	Sea of Dreams	1958	6.25	12.50	25.00
❑ ST 1148 [S]	The Joy of Living	1959	6.25	12.50	25.00
❑ T 1148 [M]	The Joy of Living	1959	5.00	10.00	20.00
❑ STAO 1259 [S]	Sing a Song with Riddle	1960	6.25	12.50	25.00

Number	Title (A Side/B Side)	Yr	VG	VG+	NM
❑ TAO 1259 [M]	Sing a Song with Riddle	1960	5.00	10.00	20.00
❑ ST 1365 [S]	Can-Can	1961	6.25	12.50	25.00
❑ T 1365 [M]	Can-Can	1961	5.00	10.00	20.00
❑ ST 1571 [S]	Love Tide	1961	6.25	12.50	25.00
❑ T 1571 [M]	Love Tide	1961	5.00	10.00	20.00
❑ ST 1670 [S]	Magic Moments from "The Gay Life"	1962	6.25	12.50	25.00
❑ T 1670 [M]	Magic Moments from "The Gay Life"	1962	5.00	10.00	20.00
❑ ST 1771 [S]	Route 66 Theme and Other Great TV Themes	1962	7.50	15.00	30.00
❑ T 1771 [M]	Route 66 Theme and Other Great TV Themes	1962	6.25	12.50	25.00
❑ ST 1817 [S]	Love Is a Game of Poker	1962	6.25	12.50	25.00
❑ T 1817 [M]	Love Is a Game of Poker	1962	5.00	10.00	20.00
❑ ST 1869 [S]	More Hit TV Themes	1963	6.25	12.50	25.00
❑ T 1869 [M]	More Hit TV Themes	1963	5.00	10.00	20.00
❑ DT 1990 [P]	The Best of Nelson Riddle	1963	3.75	7.50	15.00
❑ T 1990 [M]	The Best of Nelson Riddle	1963	3.75	7.50	15.00
❑ SM-11764	The Best of Nelson Riddle	1976	2.50	5.00	10.00
DAYBREAK					
❑ DS 2015	Viva Legrand!	197?	5.00	10.00	20.00
HARMONY					
❑ HS 11320	Nelson Riddle and His Orchestra Play the Wonderful Nat King Cole Songs	1969	3.00	6.00	12.00
LIBERTY					
❑ LRP-3508 [M]	The Bright and the Beautiful	1967	3.75	7.50	15.00
❑ LST-3532 [M]	The Riddle of Today	1967	5.00	10.00	20.00
❑ LST-7508 [S]	The Bright and the Beautiful	1967	3.75	7.50	15.00
❑ LST-7532 [S]	The Riddle of Today	1967	3.75	7.50	15.00
PICKWICK					
❑ PC 3007 [M]	Witchcraft	1965	3.75	7.50	15.00
❑ SPC 3007 [R]	Witchcraft	1965	3.00	6.00	12.00
REPRISE					
❑ R-6071 [M]	Come Blow Your Horn	1963	3.75	7.50	15.00
❑ R9-6071 [S]	Come Blow Your Horn	1963	5.00	10.00	20.00
❑ R-6120 [M]	"White on White," "Shangri-La," "Charade" and Other Hits of 1964	1964	3.75	7.50	15.00
❑ RS-6120 [S]	"White on White," "Shangri-La," "Charade" and Other Hits of 1964	1964	5.00	10.00	20.00
❑ R-6138 [M]	Great Music, Great Films, Great Sounds	1964	3.75	7.50	15.00
❑ RS-6138 [S]	Great Music, Great Films, Great Sounds	1964	5.00	10.00	20.00
❑ R-6162 [M]	Nat	1965	3.75	7.50	15.00
❑ RS-6162 [S]	Nat	1965	5.00	10.00	20.00
SEARS					
❑ SP-406 [M]	Witchcraft	196?	3.75	7.50	15.00
❑ SPS-406 [R]	Witchcraft	196?	3.00	6.00	12.00
SOLID STATE					
❑ SS-18013	Music for Wives and Lovers	1967	5.00	10.00	20.00
❑ ST-91083	Music for Wives and Lovers	1967	6.25	12.50	25.00
—Capitol Record Club edition					
SUNSET					
❑ SUS-5233	The Riddle Touch	1968	3.00	6.00	12.00
UNITED ARTISTS					
❑ UAS 6670	The Contemporary Sound of Nelson Riddle	1968	5.00	10.00	20.00
❑ ST-91566	The Contemporary Sound of Nelson Riddle	1968	6.25	12.50	25.00
—Capitol Record Club edition					

RIDGLEY, TOMMY
45s
ATLANTIC

Number	Title (A Side/B Side)	Yr	VG	VG+	NM
❑ 1009	Ooh Lawdy My Baby/ I'm Gonna Cross That River	1953	15.00	30.00	60.00
❑ 1039	Jam Up/Wish I Had Never	1954	10.00	20.00	40.00
❑ 2136	Jam Up Twist/Wish I Had Never	1962	3.75	7.50	15.00
DECCA					
❑ 48226	Anything But Love/Once in a Lifetime	1951	20.00	40.00	80.00
HERALD					
❑ 501	When I Meet My Girl/Whatcha Gonna Do	1957	5.00	10.00	20.00
❑ 508	Baby Do Liddle/Just a Memory	1957	5.00	10.00	20.00
❑ 513	Come back Baby/Woncha Gone	1958	5.00	10.00	20.00
❑ 526	Mairzy Doats and Dozy Doats/ I've Heard That Story Before	1958	5.00	10.00	20.00
❑ 537	I'll Be True/Girl Across the Street	1959	5.00	10.00	20.00
❑ 540	Tina/How I Feel	1959	5.00	10.00	20.00
IMPERIAL					
❑ 5198	I Live My Life/Lavinia	1952	37.50	75.00	150.00
❑ 5203	Looped/Junie Mae	1952	37.50	75.00	150.00
❑ 5214	Monkey Man/Nobody Cares	1953	37.50	75.00	150.00
❑ 5223	Good Times/A Day Is Coming	1953	37.50	75.00	150.00
RIC					
❑ 968	Is It True/Let's Try and Talk It Over	1959	3.75	7.50	15.00
❑ 973	Do You Remember/Please Hurry Home	1960	3.75	7.50	15.00
❑ 978	Double Eye Whammy/Should I Ever Love Again	1961	3.75	7.50	15.00
❑ 982	Three Times/The Only Girl for Me	1961	3.75	7.50	15.00
❑ 984	The Girl from Kooka Monga/ In the Same Old Way	1961	3.75	7.50	15.00
❑ 990	My Ordinary Girl/She's Got What It Takes	1962	3.00	6.00	12.00
❑ 993	Heavenly/I Love You Yes I Do	1963	3.00	6.00	12.00
❑ 994	Honest I Do/I've Heard That Story Before	1963	3.00	6.00	12.00
RONN					
❑ 36	It's the Same Old Way/I'm Not the Same Person	1969	2.50	5.00	10.00
WHITE CLIFFS					
❑ 260	Hey Little Chick/Did You Tell Him	1967	2.50	5.00	10.00

RIFFS, THE
45s
JAMIE

Number	Title (A Side/B Side)	Yr	VG	VG+	NM
❑ 1296	Tell Her/I Been Thinkin'	1965	3.00	6.00	12.00
OLD TOWN					
❑ 1179	Tell Tale Friends/Why Are the Nights So Cold	1965	12.50	25.00	50.00
SUNNY					
❑ 22	Little Girl/Why Are the Nights So Cold	1964	50.00	100.00	200.00

RIG
45s
CAPITOL

Number	Title (A Side/B Side)	Yr	VG	VG+	NM
❑ 2855	Quiet Lady/Sister Liza Bookman	1970	3.00	6.00	12.00
❑ 2952	Last Time Around/Have a Cigar	1970	3.00	6.00	12.00

Number	Title (A Side/B Side)	Yr	VG	VG+	NM
Albums					
CAPITOL					
❑ ST-473	Rig	1970	5.00	10.00	20.00

RIGHTEOUS BROTHERS, THE Also see BOBBY HATFIELD; BILL MEDLEY; THE PARAMOURS; PHIL SPECTOR.
45s
HAVEN

Number	Title (A Side/B Side)	Yr	VG	VG+	NM
❑ 800	Hold On to What You Got/Let Me Make the Music	1976	—	2.00	4.00
❑ 7002	Rock and Roll Heaven/I Just Wanna Be Me	1974	—	2.50	5.00
❑ 7004	Give It to the People/Love Is Not a Dirty Word	1974	—	2.00	4.00
❑ 7006	Dream On/Dr. Rock and Roll	1974	—	2.00	4.00
❑ 7011	High Blood Pressure/Never Say I Love You	1975	—	2.00	4.00
❑ 7014	Young Blood/Substitute	1975	—	2.00	4.00
MOONGLOW					
❑ 215	Little Latin Lupe Lu/I'm So Lonely	1963	5.00	10.00	20.00
❑ 215 [DJ]	Little Latin Lupe Lu/I'm So Lonely	1963	12.50	25.00	50.00
—Red vinyl promo					
❑ 221	Gotta Tell You How I Feel/If You're Lying, You'll Be Crying	1963	5.00	10.00	20.00
❑ 223	My Babe/Fee-Fi-Fidily-I-Oh	1963	5.00	10.00	20.00
❑ 224	Ko Ko Joe/B-Flat Blues	1963	5.00	10.00	20.00
❑ 231	Try to Find Another Man/I Still Love You	1964	5.00	10.00	20.00
❑ 234	Bring Your Love to Me/ If You're Lying, You'll Be Crying	1964	5.00	10.00	20.00
❑ 235	This Little Girl of Mine/ If You're Lying, You'll Be Crying	1964	3.75	7.50	15.00
❑ 238	Bring Your Love to Me/Fannie Mae	1965	3.75	7.50	15.00
❑ 239	You Can Have Her/Love or Magic	1965	3.75	7.50	15.00
❑ 242	Justine/In That Great Gettin' Up Morning	1965	3.75	7.50	15.00
❑ 243	For Your Love/Gotta Tell You How I Feel	1965	3.75	7.50	15.00
❑ 244	Georgia on My Mind/My Tears Will Go Away	1966	3.75	7.50	15.00
❑ 245	I Need a Girl/Bring Your Love to Me	1966	3.75	7.50	15.00
PHILLES					
❑ 124	You've Lost That Lovin' Feelin'/ There's a Woman	1964	3.75	7.50	15.00
❑ 127	Just Once in My Life/The Blues	1965	3.75	7.50	15.00
❑ 127 [PS]	Just Once in My Life/The Blues	1965	7.50	15.00	30.00
❑ 129	Unchained Melody/Hung on You	1965	3.75	7.50	15.00
—With "Producer: Phil Spector" on the "Unchained Melody" side					
❑ 129	Unchained Melody/Hung on You	1965	7.50	15.00	30.00
—With no producer credit on the "Unchained Melody" side					
❑ 130	Ebb Tide/(I Love You) For Sentimental Reasons	1965	3.75	7.50	15.00
❑ 130 [PS]	Ebb Tide/(I Love You) For Sentimental Reasons	1965	7.50	15.00	30.00
❑ 132	The White Cliffs of Dover/She's Mine, All Mine	1966	5.00	10.00	20.00
❑ 132 [PS]	The White Cliffs of Dover/She's Mine, All Mine	1966	10.00	20.00	40.00
VERVE					
❑ CS8-5	Celebrity Scene: The Righteous Brothers	1967	15.00	30.00	60.00
—Box set of five singles (10520-10524). Price includes box, all 5 singles, jukebox title strips, bio. Records are sometimes found by themselves, so they are also listed separately.					
❑ 10383	(You're My) Soul and Inspiration/B Side Blues	1966	3.75	7.50	15.00
❑ 10383 [PS]	(You're My) Soul and Inspiration/B Side Blues	1966	7.50	15.00	30.00
❑ 10403	Rat Race/Green Onions	1966	3.75	7.50	15.00
❑ 10406	He/He Will Break Your Heart	1966	2.50	5.00	10.00
❑ 10406 [PS]	He/He Will Break Your Heart	1966	5.00	10.00	20.00
❑ 10430	Go Ahead and Cry/Things Didn't Go Your Way	1966	2.50	5.00	10.00
❑ 10449	On This Side of Goodbye/ A Man Without a Dream	1966	2.50	5.00	10.00
❑ 10479	Along Came Jones/Jimmy's Blues	1967	2.00	4.00	8.00
❑ 10507	Melancholy Music Man/Don't Give Up on Me	1967	2.00	4.00	8.00
❑ 10520	(You're My) Soul and Inspiration/ Go Ahead and Cry	1967	2.50	5.00	10.00
❑ 10521	Hold On, I'm Coming/He Will Break Your Heart	1967	2.50	5.00	10.00
❑ 10522	Melancholy Music Man/I Believe	1967	2.50	5.00	10.00
❑ 10523	I (Who Have Nothing)/Island in the Sun	1967	2.50	5.00	10.00
❑ 10524	My Girl/Something You Got	1967	2.50	5.00	10.00
❑ 10551	Stranded in the Middle of No Place/Been So Nice	1967	2.00	4.00	8.00
❑ 10551 [PS]	Stranded in the Middle of No Place/Been So Nice	1967	3.75	7.50	15.00
❑ 10577	Here I Am/So Many Lonely Nights Ahead	1968	2.00	4.00	8.00
❑ 10637	Let the Good Times Roll/ You've Lost That Lovin' Feelin'	1968	2.00	4.00	8.00
❑ 10648	And the Party Goes On/Woman, Man Needs Ya	1968	2.00	4.00	8.00
❑ 10649	Good N' Nuff/Po' Folks	1968	2.00	4.00	8.00
❑ 871882-7	Unchained Melody/Hung on You	1989	—	2.00	4.00
Albums					
HAVEN					
❑ ST-9201	Give It to the People	1974	3.75	7.50	15.00
❑ ST-9203	Sons of Mrs. Righteous	1975	3.75	7.50	15.00
MGM					
❑ GAS-102	The Righteous Brothers (Golden Archive Series)	1970	3.75	7.50	15.00
❑ SE-4885	The History of the Righteous Brothers	1973	3.75	7.50	15.00
MOONGLOW					
❑ MLP-1001 [M]	Right Now!	1963	10.00	20.00	40.00
❑ MSP-1001 [S]	Right Now!	1963	15.00	30.00	60.00
❑ MLP-1002 [M]	Some Blue-Eyed Soul	1964	10.00	20.00	40.00
❑ MSP-1002 [S]	Some Blue-Eyed Soul	1964	15.00	30.00	60.00
❑ MLP-1003 [M]	This Is New!	1965	10.00	20.00	40.00
❑ MSP-1003 [S]	This Is New!	1965	15.00	30.00	60.00
❑ MLP-1004 [M]	The Best of the Righteous Brothers	1966	6.25	12.50	25.00
❑ MSP-1004 [S]	The Best of the Righteous Brothers	1966	7.50	15.00	30.00
PHILLES					
❑ PHLP-4007 [M]	You've Lost That Lovin' Feelin'	1964	6.25	12.50	25.00
❑ PHLPS-4007 [S]	You've Lost That Lovin' Feelin'	1964	10.00	20.00	40.00
❑ PHLP-4008 [M]	Just Once in My Life	1965	6.25	12.50	25.00
❑ PHLPS-4008 [S]	Just Once in My Life	1965	10.00	20.00	40.00
❑ PHLP-4009 [M]	Back to Back	1965	6.25	12.50	25.00
❑ PHLPS-4009 [S]	Back to Back	1965	10.00	20.00	40.00
❑ ST-90677 [S]	Back to Back	1965	10.00	20.00	40.00
—Capitol Record Club edition					
❑ T-90677 [M]	Back to Back	1965	7.50	15.00	30.00
—Capitol Record Club edition					
❑ ST-90692 [S]	You've Lost That Lovin' Feelin'	1965	12.50	25.00	50.00
—Capitol Record Club edition					
❑ T-90692 [M]	You've Lost That Lovin' Feelin'	1965	12.50	25.00	50.00
—Capitol Record Club edition					

R

Number	Title (A Side/B Side)	Yr	VG	VG+	NM
RHINO					
☐ R1-71488 [(2)]	Anthology	1989	3.75	7.50	15.00
VERVE					
☐ V-5001 [M]	Soul and Inspiration	1966	5.00	10.00	20.00
☐ V6-5001 [S]	Soul and Inspiration	1966	6.25	12.50	25.00
☐ V-5004 [M]	Go Ahead and Cry	1966	5.00	10.00	20.00
☐ V6-5004 [S]	Go Ahead and Cry	1966	6.25	12.50	25.00
☐ V-5010 [M]	Sayin' Somethin'	1967	5.00	10.00	20.00
☐ V6-5010 [S]	Sayin' Somethin'	1967	6.25	12.50	25.00
☐ V-5020 [M]	Greatest Hits	1967	6.25	12.50	25.00
☐ V6-5020 [S]	Greatest Hits	1967	5.00	10.00	20.00
☐ V-5031 [M]	Souled Out	1967	7.50	15.00	30.00
☐ V6-5031 [S]	Souled Out	1967	5.00	10.00	20.00
☐ V6-5051	Standards	1968	5.00	10.00	20.00
☐ V6-5058	One for the Road	1968	5.00	10.00	20.00
—Without The Blossoms credited on the back cover					
☐ V6-5058	One for the Road	1968	7.50	15.00	30.00
—With The Blossoms credited on the back cover					
☐ V6-5071	Greatest Hits, Vol. 2	1969	5.00	10.00	20.00
☐ V6-5076	Re-Birth	1970	5.00	10.00	20.00
☐ ST-90669 [S]	Soul and Inspiration	1966	7.50	15.00	30.00
—Capitol Record Club edition					
☐ ST-90921 [S]	Go Ahead and Cry	1966	7.50	15.00	30.00
—Capitol Record Club edition					
☐ ST-91057 [S]	Sayin' Somethin'	1967	6.25	12.50	25.00
—Capitol Record Club edition					
☐ T-91057 [M]	Sayin' Somethin'	1967	7.50	15.00	30.00
—Capitol Record Club edition					
☐ 823662-1	Greatest Hits	198?	2.50	5.00	10.00

RILEY, BILLY LEE
45s

Number	Title (A Side/B Side)	Yr	VG	VG+	NM
ATLANTIC					
☐ 2525	Sittin' and a Waitin'/Happy Man	1968	2.00	4.00	8.00
BRUNSWICK					
☐ 55085	Rockin' on the Moon/Is That All to the Ball	1958	50.00	100.00	200.00
ENTRANCE					
☐ 7508	I Got a Thing About You Baby/You Don't Love Me	1972	—	2.50	5.00
GNP CRESCENDO					
☐ 371	Gonna Find a Cave/That's the Bag I'm In	1966	2.50	5.00	10.00
☐ 377	The Way I Feel/St. James Infirmary	1966	2.50	5.00	10.00
HIP					
☐ 8006	Family Portrait/Going Back to Memphis	1968	2.00	4.00	8.00
☐ 8011	Show Me Your Soul/Midnight Hour	1968	2.00	4.00	8.00
HOME OF THE BLUES					
☐ 233	Flip, Flop, and Fly/Teenage Letter	1961	7.50	15.00	30.00
MERCURY					
☐ 72314	Bo Diddley/Memphis	1964	3.75	7.50	15.00
☐ 72385	Mojo Workout/Charlene	1965	3.00	6.00	12.00
MOJO					
☐ 1933	Southern Soul/Midnight Hour	1967	2.50	5.00	10.00
SUN					
☐ 245	Trouble Bound/Rock with Me, Baby	1956	30.00	60.00	120.00
☐ 260	Flying Saucers Rock and Roll/I Want You Baby	1957	25.00	50.00	100.00
☐ 277	Red Hot/Pearly Lee	1957	15.00	30.00	60.00
☐ 289	Baby Please Don't Go/Wouldn't You Know	1958	12.50	25.00	50.00
☐ 313	Down by the Riverside/No Name Girl	1959	6.25	12.50	25.00
☐ 322	One More Time/Got the Water Boilin'	1959	12.50	25.00	50.00
☐ 1100	Kay/Looking for Her Heart	1969	—	3.00	6.00
☐ 1105	Pilot Town L.A./Workin' on the River	1969	—	3.00	6.00
☐ 1116	Tallahassee/Old Home Place	1970	—	2.50	5.00
Albums					
GNP CRESCENDO					
☐ GNP-2020 [M]	Billy Lee Riley	1966	3.75	7.50	15.00
☐ GNPS-2020 [S]	Billy Lee Riley	1966	5.00	10.00	20.00
MERCURY					
☐ MG-20958 [M]	The Whiskey A-Go-Go Presents Billy Lee Riley	1964	5.00	10.00	20.00
☐ MG-20965 [M]	Big Harmonica Special	1964	5.00	10.00	20.00
☐ MG-20974 [M]	Beatlemania Harmonica	1965	5.00	10.00	20.00
☐ SR-60958 [S]	The Whiskey A-Go-Go Presents Billy Lee Riley	1964	6.25	12.50	25.00
☐ SR-60965 [S]	Big Harmonica Special	1964	6.25	12.50	25.00
☐ SR-60974 [S]	Beatlemania Harmonica	1965	6.25	12.50	25.00

RILEY, BOB
45s

Number	Title (A Side/B Side)	Yr	VG	VG+	NM
CORAL					
☐ 62125	I Think It's a Shame/Blue Guitar Waltz	1959	5.00	10.00	20.00
DOT					
☐ 15625	Baby Sittin'/Without Your Love	1957	6.25	12.50	25.00
MGM					
☐ 12612	Wanda Jean/The Midnight Line	1958	37.50	75.00	150.00

RILEY, JEANNIE C.
45s

Number	Title (A Side/B Side)	Yr	VG	VG+	NM
CAPITOL					
☐ 2378	The Price I Pay to Stay/How Can Anything So Right Be So Wrong	1969	—	2.50	5.00
☐ 2449	I Don't Know What I'm Doing Here/You've Got Me Singing Nursery Rhymes	1969	—	2.50	5.00
LITTLE DARLIN'					
☐ 0031	What About Them/You Write the Music	1967	3.75	7.50	15.00
—As "Jean Riley"					
☐ 0048	I Don't Know What I'm Doing Here/I'll Be a Woman of the World	1968	—	3.00	6.00
MCA					
☐ 52018	From Harper Valley to the Mountain/I Don't Have to Die to Get Into Heaven	1982	—	—	3.00
MERCURY					
☐ 73616	Plain Vanilla/Country Girl	1974	—	2.00	4.00
MGM					
☐ 14310	Houston Blues/How Hard I'm Trying	1971	—	2.00	4.00
☐ 14341	Give Myself a Party/Why You Been Gone So Long	1972	—	2.00	4.00
☐ 14382	Good Morning Country Rain/This Is for You	1972	—	2.00	4.00
☐ 14427	One Night/Without You	1972	—	2.00	4.00
☐ 14495	When Love Has Gone Away/Thou Shalt Not Kill	1973	—	2.00	4.00

Number	Title (A Side/B Side)	Yr	VG	VG+	NM
☐ 14554	Hush/Not Looking Back	1973	—	2.00	4.00
☐ 14666	Another Football Year/Mother America	1973	—	2.00	4.00
☐ 14696	Missouri/Sing Jeannie Sing	1974	—	2.00	4.00
PLANTATION					
☐ 3	Harper Valley P.T.A./Yesterday All Day Long Today	1968	—	3.00	6.00
—Green and white label					
☐ 3	Harper Valley P.T.A./Yesterday All Day Long Today	1968	2.00	4.00	8.00
—Blue label					
☐ 3	Harper Valley P.T.A./Yesterday All Day Long Today	1968	2.00	4.00	8.00
—Yellow label					
☐ 7	The Girl Most Likely/My Scrapbook	1968	—	2.50	5.00
☐ 16	There Never Was a Time/Back to School	1969	—	2.50	5.00
☐ 22	The Rib/I'm the Woman	1969	—	2.50	5.00
☐ 29	The Back Side of Dallas/Things Go Better with Love	1969	—	2.50	5.00
☐ 44	Country Girl/We Were Raised on Love	1970	—	2.50	5.00
☐ 59	Duty Not Desire/Holdin' On	1970	—	2.50	5.00
☐ 65	My Man/The Generation Gap	1970	—	2.50	5.00
☐ 72	Oh, Singer/I'll Take What's Left of You	1971	—	2.50	5.00
☐ 75	Good Enough to Be Your Wife/Light Your Light	1971	—	2.50	5.00
☐ 79	Roses and Thorns/Shed Me No Tears	1971	—	2.50	5.00
☐ 85	The Lion's Club/Tell the Truth and Shame the Devil	1972	—	2.50	5.00
☐ 93	If You Could Read My Mind/Will the Real Jesus Please Stand Up	1972	—	2.50	5.00
☐ 173	Harper Valley P.T.A. (Soundtrack Version)/I've Done a Lot of Living Since Then	1979	—	3.00	6.00
PLAYBACK					
☐ 1350	Here's to the Cowboys/Free	1989	—	3.00	6.00
WARNER BROS.					
☐ 8226	The Best I've Ever Had/Thank You for Forgiving	1976	—	2.00	4.00
☐ 8290	Pure Gold/Take Time	1976	—	2.00	4.00
7-Inch Extended Plays					
PLANTATION					
☐ PEP-1	Harper Valley P.T.A./Shed Me No Tears/Widow Jones//No Brass Band/The Cotton Patch/The Little Town Square	1968	2.50	5.00	10.00
—Jukebox issue; small hole, plays at 33 1/3 rpm					
☐ PEP-1 [PS]	Harper Valley P.T.A.	1968	2.50	5.00	10.00
Albums					
ALLEGIANCE					
☐ AV-5026	Tears, Joys and Memories	198?	2.50	5.00	10.00
CAPITOL					
☐ ST-177	The Songs of Jeannie C. Riley	1969	3.75	7.50	15.00
MGM					
☐ SE-4805	Give Myself a Party	1972	3.00	6.00	12.00
☐ SE-4849	Down to Earth	1973	3.00	6.00	12.00
☐ SE-4891	When Love Has Gone Away	1973	3.00	6.00	12.00
☐ SE-4909	Just Jeannie C. Riley	1973	3.00	6.00	12.00
PICKWICK					
☐ 6098	The Girl Most Likely	197?	2.50	5.00	10.00
☐ 6119	The World of Country	197?	2.50	5.00	10.00
PLANTATION					
☐ PLP 1	Harper Valley P.T.A.	1968	5.00	10.00	20.00
☐ PLP 2	Yearbooks and Yesterdays	1969	3.75	7.50	15.00
☐ PLP 3	Things Go Better with Love	1969	3.75	7.50	15.00
☐ PLP 8	Country Girl	1970	3.75	7.50	15.00
☐ PLP 11	The Generation Gap	1970	3.75	7.50	15.00
☐ PLP 13	Jeannie C. Riley's Greatest Hits	1971	3.75	7.50	15.00
☐ PLP 16	Jeannie	1971	3.75	7.50	15.00
☐ 508	Country Queens	197?	3.00	6.00	12.00
POWER PAK					
☐ 250	Country Gold	197?	2.50	5.00	10.00

RINCON SURFSIDE BAND, THE
Another creation of P.F. SLOAN and STEVE BARRI.
Albums

Number	Title (A Side/B Side)	Yr	VG	VG+	NM
DUNHILL					
☐ D 50001 [M]	Surfing Songbook	1965	50.00	100.00	200.00
☐ DS 50001 [S]	Surfing Songbook	1965	75.00	150.00	300.00

RINGO, JIMMY
45s

Number	Title (A Side/B Side)	Yr	VG	VG+	NM
DOT					
☐ 15787	I Like This Kind of Music/No One Else	1958	7.50	15.00	30.00
☐ 15997	I Like This Kind of Music/No One Else	1959	5.00	10.00	20.00

RINKY-DINKS, THE
See BOBBY DARIN.

RIO, BOBBY
45s

Number	Title (A Side/B Side)	Yr	VG	VG+	NM
ABC-PARAMOUNT					
☐ 10656	Boy Meets Girl/Don't Break My Heart and Run Away	1965	3.75	7.50	15.00
LENOX					
☐ 5569	Don Diddley/I Got You	1963	3.75	7.50	15.00

RIO, CHUCK
Also see THE CHAMPS; THE ORIGINALS (3).
45s

Number	Title (A Side/B Side)	Yr	VG	VG+	NM
CHALLENGE					
☐ 59019	Bad Boy/Denise	1958	5.00	10.00	20.00
☐ 59073	Ramblin' Through Dixie/Akiko	1960	5.00	10.00	20.00
FLAIR					
☐ 103	You Don't Have to Be a Baby to Cry/Big Boy	1962	10.00	20.00	40.00
JACKPOT					
☐ 48016	Margarita/C'est La Vie	1960	7.50	15.00	30.00
KENT					
☐ 308	Bye Bye Baby/No Matter What You Do	1958	5.00	10.00	20.00
SATURN					
☐ 402	Kreschendo Stomp/Rock-A-Nova	1962	12.50	25.00	50.00
TEQUILA					
☐ 100	Caravan/El Bracero	1961	5.00	10.00	20.00
☐ 103	La Cha Cha Twist/If You Were the Only Girl in the World	1961	5.00	10.00	20.00

Number	Title (A Side/B Side)	Yr	VG	VG+	NM
RIOS, AUGIE					
45s					
METRO					
❏ 20010	Donde Esta Santa Claus?/Ol' Fatso	1958	10.00	20.00	40.00
❏ 20016	Run Rattler Run/Hop, Skip and Jump	1959	7.50	15.00	30.00
❏ 20027	Trip to the Island/				
	Teacher Walked Out of the Room	1959	7.50	15.00	30.00
MGM					
❏ 12966	Feliz Navidades/Gypsy Boy	1960	5.00	10.00	20.00
❏ 13292	Donde Esta Santa Claus?/Ol' Fatso	1964	3.00	6.00	12.00
SHELLEY					
❏ 181	I've Got a Girl/There's a Girl Down the Way	1963	10.00	20.00	40.00
❏ 186	When You Dance/No One	1963	7.50	15.00	30.00
❏ 192	Teach Me Tonight/Linda Lou	1964	5.00	10.00	20.00
RIOS, MIGUEL					
45s					
A&M					
❏ 1193	A Song of Joy (Himno A La Alegria)/El Rio	1970	—	2.50	5.00
❏ 1193 [PS]	A Song of Joy (Himno A La Alegria)/El Rio	1970	2.00	4.00	8.00
❏ 1203	Himno A La Alegria/El Rio	1970	—	3.00	6.00
Albums					
A&M					
❏ SPX-4267	A Song of Joy	1970	3.75	7.50	15.00
RIOS, WALDO DE LOS					
45s					
UNITED ARTISTS					
❏ 50772	Mozart Symphony No. 40 in G Minor, K.550, 1st				
	Movement/Ode to Joy	1971	—	2.50	5.00
❏ 50821	Serenata #13/Concerto Para Piano	1971	—	2.00	4.00
❏ 50871	Elvira Madigan Theme/A Night of Music	1972	—	2.00	4.00
VAULT					
❏ 952	Those Were the Days/Aranguez (Mon Amour)	1969	—	2.50	5.00
WARNER BROS.					
❏ 8034	Elixir de Amor/Nabucco	1974	—	2.00	4.00
Albums					
UNITED ARTISTS					
❏ UAS-5554	Mozartmania	1972	3.00	6.00	12.00
❏ UAS-6802	Sinfonias	1971	3.00	6.00	12.00
VAULT					
❏ VS-126	International Hits	1969	3.75	7.50	15.00
WARNER BROS.					
❏ BS 2801	Operas	1974	3.00	6.00	12.00
RIOT SQUAD, THE					
45s					
HANNA-BARBERA					
❏ 485	I Take It That We're Through/Working Man	1966	3.00	6.00	12.00
REPRISE					
❏ 0457	Cry, Cry, Cry/How Is It Done?	1966	2.50	5.00	10.00
ROULETTE					
❏ 4621	Gonna Make You Mine/I Wanna Talk About My				
	Baby	1965	3.00	6.00	12.00
RIP CHORDS, THE					
45s					
COLUMBIA					
❏ 42687	Here I Stand/Karen	1963	3.75	7.50	15.00
❏ 42687 [DJ]	Here I Stand (same on both sides)	1963	5.00	10.00	20.00
—Black vinyl promo					
❏ 42687 [DJ]	Here I Stand (same on both sides)	1963	12.50	25.00	50.00
—Green vinyl promo					
❏ 42687 [PS]	Here I Stand	1963	12.50	25.00	50.00
—Sleeve is promo only					
❏ 42812	Gone/She Thinks I Still Care	1963	3.75	7.50	15.00
❏ 42812 [DJ]	Gone (same on both sides)	1963	12.50	25.00	50.00
—Blue vinyl promo					
❏ 42812 [PS]	Gone (same on both sides)	1963	12.50	25.00	50.00
—Sleeve is promo only					
❏ 42921	Hey, Little Cobra/The Queen	1963	5.00	10.00	20.00
❏ 42921 [DJ]	Hey, Little Cobra (same on both sides)	1963	12.50	25.00	50.00
—Yellow vinyl promo					
❏ 43035	Three Window Coupe/Hot Rod U.S.A.	1964	3.75	7.50	15.00
❏ 43035 [DJ]	Three Window Coupe (same on both sides)	1964	12.50	25.00	50.00
—Red vinyl promo					
❏ 43093	One Piece Topless Bathing Suit/Wah-Wahini	1964	3.75	7.50	15.00
❏ 43221	Don't Be Scared/Bunny Hill	1965	3.75	7.50	15.00
Albums					
COLUMBIA					
❏ CL 2151 [M]	Hey Little Cobra and Other Hot Rod Hits	1964	10.00	20.00	40.00
❏ CL 2216 [M]	Three Window Coupe	1964	12.50	25.00	50.00
❏ CS 8951 [S]	Hey Little Cobra and Other Hot Rod Hits	1964	12.50	25.00	50.00
❏ CS 9016 [S]	Three Window Coupe	1964	17.50	35.00	70.00
RIP-CHORDS, THE					
45s					
ABCO					
❏ 105	I Love You the Most/Let's Do the Razzle Dazzle	1956	150.00	300.00	600.00
—Black vinyl					
❏ 105	I Love You the Most/Let's Do the Razzle Dazzle	1956	375.00	750.00	1500.
—Red vinyl					
RIPERTON, MINNIE Also see ROTARY CONNECTION.					
45s					
CAPITOL					
❏ 4706	Memory Lane/I'm a Woman	1979	—	2.00	4.00
❏ 4761	Lover and Friend/Return to Forever	1979	—	2.00	4.00
❏ 4902	Here We Go/Return to Forever	1980	—	2.00	4.00
❏ 4955	Give Me Time/Island in the Sun	1980	—	2.00	4.00
CHESS					
❏ 1980	Lonely Girl/You Gave Me Soul	1966	2.50	5.00	10.00
—As "Andrea Davis"					
EPIC					
❏ 11139	Every Time He Comes Around/Reasons	1974	—	2.50	5.00
❏ 50020	Edge of a Dream/Seeing You This Way	1974	—	2.50	5.00

Number	Title (A Side/B Side)	Yr	VG	VG+	NM
❏ 50057	Lovin' You/Edge of a Dream	1974	—	2.50	5.00
❏ 50128	Don't Let Anyone Bring You Down/				
	Inside My Love	1975	—	2.50	5.00
❏ 50155	When It Comes Down To It/Minnie's Lament	1975	—	2.50	5.00
❏ 50166	Simple Things/Minnie's Lament	1975	—	2.50	5.00
❏ 50190	Adventures in Paradise/				
	When It Comes Down To It	1976	—	2.50	5.00
❏ 50337	Stick Together (Part One)/				
	Stick Together (Part Two)	1977	—	2.50	5.00
❏ 50351	Young, Willing and Able/Stick Together	1977	—	2.50	5.00
❏ 50394	Wouldn't Matter Where You Are	1977	—	2.50	5.00
❏ 50427	How Could I Love You More/				
	Young, Willing and Able	1977	—	2.50	5.00
GRT					
❏ 42	Oh! By the Way/Le Fleur	1972	—	3.00	6.00
Albums					
ACCORD					
❏ SN-7205	Wistful Memories	1981	2.50	5.00	10.00
CAPITOL					
❏ SO-11936	Minnie	1979	2.50	5.00	10.00
❏ SN-12004	Perfect Angel	1979	2.50	5.00	10.00
—Reissue of Epic 32561					
❏ SN-12005	Adventures in Paradise	1979	2.50	5.00	10.00
—Reissue of Epic 33454					
❏ SN-12006	Stay in Love	1979	2.50	5.00	10.00
—Reissue of Epic 34191					
❏ SOO-12097	Love Lives Forever	1980	2.50	5.00	10.00
❏ ST-12189	The Best of Minnie Riperton	1981	2.50	5.00	10.00
❏ SN-16145	Perfect Angel	1980	2.00	4.00	8.00
—Budget-line reissue					
❏ SN-16146	Adventures in Paradise	1980	2.00	4.00	8.00
—Budget-line reissue					
❏ SN-16147	Stay in Love	1980	2.00	4.00	8.00
—Budget-line reissue					
EPIC					
❏ EQ 32561 [Q]	Perfect Angel	1974	5.00	10.00	20.00
❏ KE 32561	Perfect Angel	1974	3.00	6.00	12.00
❏ PE 33454	Adventures in Paradise	1975	3.00	6.00	12.00
❏ PEQ 33454 [Q]	Adventures in Paradise	1975	5.00	10.00	20.00
❏ PE 34191	Stay in Love	1977	3.00	6.00	12.00
GRT					
❏ 30001	Come To My Garden	1970	3.75	7.50	15.00
JANUS					
❏ 7011	Come To My Garden	1974	3.00	6.00	12.00
—Reissue of GRT LP					
RIPPLES AND WAVES PLUS MICHAEL, THE See THE JACKSONS.					
RIPPY, RODNEY ALLEN					
45s					
BELL					
❏ 45403	Take Life a Little Easier/World of Love	1973	2.00	4.00	8.00
Albums					
BELL					
❏ 1311	Take Life a Little Easier	1974	5.00	10.00	20.00
RISERS, THE					
Albums					
IMPERIAL					
❏ LP-9269 [M]	She's a Bad Motorcycle	1964	25.00	50.00	100.00
❏ LP-12269 [S]	She's a Bad Motorcycle	1964	37.50	75.00	150.00
RISING STORM, THE					
Albums					
ARF! ARF!					
❏ 007	Alive in Anover Again	1983	30.00	60.00	120.00
REMNANT					
❏ BBA-3571	Calm Before the Rising Storm	1968	600.00	900.00	1200.
STANTON PARK					
❏ 001	Calm Before the Rising Storm	1991	5.00	10.00	20.00
—Reissue of Remnant album					
RISING SUNS, THE Among the members of this group were RY COODER and TAJ MAHAL.					
45s					
COLUMBIA					
❏ 43534	Candy Man/The Devil's Got My Woman	1966	10.00	20.00	40.00
RITA MARIE					
45s					
SUN					
❏ 1106	Lottie's Lament/Trouble	1969	—	2.50	5.00
RITCHIE FAMILY, THE					
12-Inch Singles					
CASABLANCA					
❏ NBD 20192	Put Your Feet to the Beat (6:58)/				
	Bad Reputation (6:01)	1979	3.75	7.50	15.00
RCA					
❏ PD-13093	I'll Do My Best (For You Baby)/				
	You've Got Me Dancin'	1982	—	3.00	6.00
❏ PD-13551	All Night All Right/Fantasy	1983	—	3.00	6.00
45s					
CASABLANCA					
❏ 2206	Put Your Feet to the Beat/It's a Man's World	1979	—	2.00	4.00
❏ 2259	Give Me a Break/Bad Reputation	1980	—	2.00	4.00
❏ 2292	All My Love/I'll Never Be Able to Set You Free	1980	—	2.00	4.00
MARLIN					
❏ 3306	The Best Disco in Town/The Best Disco in Town				
	(Part 2)	1976	—	2.00	4.00
❏ 3309	Life Is Music/Lady Luck	1977	—	2.00	4.00
❏ 3316	Quiet Village/Voodoo	1977	—	2.00	4.00
❏ 3323	American Generation/Music Man	1978	—	2.00	4.00
RCA					
❏ PB-13092	I'll Do My Best (For You Baby)/You've Got Me				
	Dancin'	1982	—	—	3.00
❏ PB-13281	Walk with Me/Tonight I Need to Have Your Love	1982	—	—	3.00
❏ PB-13550	All Night All Right/Fantasy	1983	—	—	3.00

R

Number	Title (A Side/B Side)	Yr	VG	VG+	NM
20TH CENTURY					
❑ 2218	Brazil/Hot Trip	1975	—	2.00	4.00
❑ 2252	I Want to Dance with You (Dance with Me)/Lady Champagne	1975	—	2.00	4.00
Albums					
CASABLANCA					
❑ NBLP-7166	Bad Reputation	1979	2.50	5.00	10.00
❑ NBLP-7223	Give Me a Break	1980	2.50	5.00	10.00
MARLIN					
❑ 2201	Arabian Nights	1976	2.50	5.00	10.00
❑ 2203	Life Is Music	1977	2.50	5.00	10.00
❑ 2206	African Queens	1977	2.50	5.00	10.00
❑ 2215	American Generation	1978	2.50	5.00	10.00
RCA VICTOR					
❑ AFL1-4324	I'll Do My Best	1982	2.50	5.00	10.00
❑ AFL1-4601	All Night, All Night	1983	2.50	5.00	10.00
20TH CENTURY					
❑ T-498	Brazil	1975	2.50	5.00	10.00

RITES, THE
45s
DECCA

Number	Title (A Side/B Side)	Yr	VG	VG+	NM
❑ 32218	Things/Hour Glass	1967	6.25	12.50	25.00

RITES OF SPRING, THE
45s
PARKWAY

Number	Title (A Side/B Side)	Yr	VG	VG+	NM
❑ 109	Why/Comin' On to Me	1966	7.50	15.00	30.00

RITTER, TEX
45s
CAPITOL

Number	Title (A Side/B Side)	Yr	VG	VG+	NM
❑ F885	Deck of Cards/Rye Whiskey	1950	7.50	15.00	30.00
❑ F928	Boogie Woogie Cowboy/He's a Cowboy Auctioneer	1950	10.00	20.00	40.00
❑ F1058	Bad Brahma Bull/Blood on the Saddle	1950	7.50	15.00	30.00
❑ F1071	I've Got $5 and It's Saturday Night/Boiled Crawfish	1950	7.50	15.00	30.00
❑ F1098	Thief on the Cross/Beautiful Life	1950	7.50	15.00	30.00
❑ F1141	The Pledge of Allegiance/Fiery Bear	1950	7.50	15.00	30.00
❑ F1188	Coal Smoke, Valve Oil and Steam/Nobody's Fool	1950	7.50	15.00	30.00
❑ F1264	Merry Christmas Polka/Christmas Carols by the Old Corral	1950	7.50	15.00	30.00
❑ F1267	Daddy's Last Letter/Onward Christian Soldiers	1950	7.50	15.00	30.00
❑ F1334	Stay Away from My Heart/Big Blue Diamonds	1950	7.50	15.00	30.00
❑ F1388	You're Always Brand New/My Bucket's Been Fixed	1951	6.25	12.50	25.00
❑ F1453	If I Could Steal You/There's No One to Cry Over Me	1951	6.25	12.50	25.00
❑ F1581	Wearin' Out Your Walkin' Shoes/Coffee Pot	1951	6.25	12.50	25.00
❑ F1629	Jealous Heart/Green Grow the Lilacs	1951	6.25	12.50	25.00
—Reissue of 1940s material first issued on 78					
❑ F1631	Rye Whiskey/Blood on the Saddle	1951	6.25	12.50	25.00
—Reissue of 1940s material first issued on 78					
❑ F1665	Deck of Cards/Ol' Shorty	195?	6.25	12.50	25.00
—Reissue of 1940s material first issued on 78					
❑ F1698	High Noon (Do Not Forsake Me)/Let Me Go Devil	195?	3.75	7.50	15.00
—Reissue					
❑ F1783	Tennessee Blues/Rock All Babies	1951	6.25	12.50	25.00
❑ PRO.1886 [DJ]	The Pledge of Allegiance (same on both sides)	196?	5.00	10.00	20.00
—Promo only; light blue label, dark blue print					
❑ F1977	As Long As the River Flows On/When My Blue Moon Turns to Gold	1952	6.25	12.50	25.00
❑ F2034	The Letter Edged in Black/There Shall Be Showers	1952	6.25	12.50	25.00
❑ 2097	Bump Tiddle Dee Bum Bum/I Just Can't Get Away	1968	2.00	4.00	8.00
❑ F2120	High Noon (Do Not Forsake Me)/Go On! Get Out!	1952	7.50	15.00	30.00
❑ F2174	Boll Weevil Song/Have I Told You Lately That I Love You	1952	6.25	12.50	25.00
❑ 2232	Texas/Stranger on Boot Hill	1968	2.00	4.00	8.00
❑ F2368	My Woman Ain't Pretty/Buffalo Dream	1953	6.25	12.50	25.00
❑ 2388	A Funny Thing Happened (On the Way to Miami)/The Governor and the Kid	1969	2.00	4.00	8.00
❑ F2475	The Marshall's Daughter/The San Antone Story	1953	6.25	12.50	25.00
❑ 2541	Growin' Up/A Letter to My Sons	1969	2.00	4.00	8.00
❑ F2594	Let Me Go, Devil!/Long Black Rifle	1953	6.25	12.50	25.00
❑ 2677	Wand'rin' Star/Chuckwagon Son of a Gun	1969	2.00	4.00	8.00
❑ F2686	Red Deck of Cards/Lord Send Me an Angel	1953	6.25	12.50	25.00
❑ F2756	Brave Man/Turn Around Boy	1954	5.00	10.00	20.00
❑ 2815	Green Green Valley/God Bless America Again	1970	—	3.50	7.00
❑ F2836	Lovely Veil of White/The Best Time of All	1954	5.00	10.00	20.00
❑ F2916	Prairie Home (Theme from The Vanishing Prairie)/The Bandit	1954	5.00	10.00	20.00
❑ F2957	Is There a Santa Claus/Ole Tex Kringle	1954	5.00	10.00	20.00
❑ F3003	A Whale of a Tale/High on a Mountain Top	1954	6.25	12.50	25.00
❑ 3154	Fall Away/Looking Back	1971	—	3.50	7.00
❑ F3179	Wichita/September Song	1955	5.00	10.00	20.00
❑ F3230	Gunsmoke/Remember the Alamo	1955	6.25	12.50	25.00
❑ 3286	Bourbon Man/Little Peanut Shell (Gotta Make It Grow)	1972	—	3.50	7.00
❑ F3324	These Hands/The Last Frontier	1956	5.00	10.00	20.00
❑ 3357	Lorena/The Keeper of the Key	1972	—	3.50	7.00
❑ F3363	If Jesus Came to Your House/Touch of the Master's Hand	1956	5.00	10.00	20.00
❑ F3430	The Wayward Wind/The Searchers (Ride Away)	1956	5.00	10.00	20.00
❑ 3457	Comin' After Jinny/You Will Have to Pay for Your Yesterday	1972	—	3.50	7.00
❑ F3538	The Last Wagon/Paul Bunyan Love	1956	5.00	10.00	20.00
❑ 3570	One Night for Willie/Sweet Bird of Youth	1973	—	3.00	6.00
❑ F3589	Green Grow the Lilacs/He Is There	1956	5.00	10.00	20.00
❑ F3640	Children and Fools/I Leaned on a Man	1957	5.00	10.00	20.00
❑ 3705	Willie, the Wandering Gypsy, and Me/Wind of Oklahoma	1973	—	3.00	6.00

Number	Title (A Side/B Side)	Yr	VG	VG+	NM
❑ F3754	Trooper Hook (Chapter 1)/Trooper Hook (Chapter 2)	1957	5.00	10.00	20.00
❑ 3814	The Americans (A Canadian's Opinion)/He Who Is Without Sin	1974	—	3.00	6.00
❑ F3903	Here Was a Man/It Came Upon the Midnight Clear	1959	3.75	7.50	15.00
❑ F4006	Jealous Heart/Burning Sand	1958	3.75	7.50	15.00
❑ F4043	The History Song/I Look for a Love	1958	3.75	7.50	15.00
❑ F4217	Conversation with a Gun/Rye Whiskey	1959	3.75	7.50	15.00
❑ 4239	God Bless America Again/Lucy Let Your Lovelight Shine	1976	—	2.50	5.00
❑ F4285	Deck of Cards/Conversation with a Gun	1959	3.75	7.50	15.00
❑ 4364	The Vanishing American/The Gun, The Gold, and the Girl	1960	3.75	7.50	15.00
❑ 4567	I Dreamed of a Hill-Billy Heaven/The Wind and the Tree	1961	3.00	6.00	12.00
❑ 4644	Lonely Soldier Boy/Strange Little Melody	1961	3.00	6.00	12.00
❑ 4753	The Pledge of Allegiance/Ol' Shorty	1962	3.00	6.00	12.00
❑ 4849	Coo Se Coo/The Cookson Hills	1962	3.00	6.00	12.00
❑ 5004	The Gods Were Angry with Me/Will	1963	2.50	5.00	10.00
❑ 5159	That Son of a Saginaw Fisherman/Gallows Pole	1964	2.50	5.00	10.00
❑ 5224	Fool's Paradise/Gimme Some	1964	2.50	5.00	10.00
❑ 5347	She Loved This House/I Dreamed of a Hill-Billy Heaven	1965	2.50	5.00	10.00
❑ 5474	Bummin' Around/Take Him Fishin'	1965	2.50	5.00	10.00
❑ 5574	The Men in My Little Girl's Life/Custody	1966	2.00	4.00	8.00
❑ 5697	Mommy, Daddy, Tell Us/Remember Us	1966	2.00	4.00	8.00
❑ 5839	Just Beyond the Moon/Greedy Old Dog	1967	2.00	4.00	8.00
❑ 5966	A Working Man's Prayer/William Barrett Travis: A Message from the Alamo	1967	2.00	4.00	8.00
❑ 54-40179	The Chisholm Trail/San Antonio Rose	1949	7.50	15.00	30.00
❑ 54-40180	Try Me One More Time/Boll Weevil Song	1949	7.50	15.00	30.00
❑ 54-40181	Blood on the Saddle/Rounded Up in Glory	1949	7.50	15.00	30.00
❑ 54-40182	Rye Whiskey/Bad Brahma Bull	1949	7.50	15.00	30.00
—The above four comprise a box set					
❑ F40248	Never Mind My Tears/Some Sweet Day	1949	10.00	20.00	40.00

7-Inch Extended Plays
CAPITOL

Number	Title (A Side/B Side)	Yr	VG	VG+	NM
❑ EAP 1-431	*High Noon (Do Not Forsake Me)/Green Grow the Lilacs/I'm Wastin' My Tears on You/Jealous Heart	195?	5.00	10.00	20.00
❑ EAP 1-431 [PS]	Tex Ritter Sings	195?	5.00	10.00	20.00

Albums
BUCKBOARD

Number	Title	Yr	VG	VG+	NM
❑ BBS 1030	Tex Ritter	198?	2.50	5.00	10.00

CAPITOL

Number	Title	Yr	VG	VG+	NM
❑ ST-213	Chuck Wagon Days	1969	5.00	10.00	20.00
❑ ST-467	Green Green Valley	1970	5.00	10.00	20.00
❑ T 971 [M]	Songs from the Western Screen	1958	20.00	40.00	80.00
—Turquoise or gray label					
❑ T 971 [M]	Songs from the Western Screen	1959	10.00	20.00	40.00
—Black colorband label, logo at left					
❑ T 971 [M]	Songs from the Western Screen	1962	6.25	12.50	25.00
—Black colorband label, logo at top					
❑ T 1100 [M]	Psalms	1959	12.50	25.00	50.00
—Black colorband label, logo at left					
❑ T 1100 [M]	Psalms	1962	6.25	12.50	25.00
—Black colorband label, logo at top					
❑ ST 1292 [S]	Blood on the Saddle	1960	10.00	20.00	40.00
—Black colorband label, logo at left					
❑ ST 1292 [S]	Blood on the Saddle	1962	6.25	12.50	25.00
—Black colorband label, logo at top					
❑ T 1292 [M]	Blood on the Saddle	1960	7.50	15.00	30.00
—Black colorband label, logo at left					
❑ T 1292 [M]	Blood on the Saddle	1962	5.00	10.00	20.00
—Black colorband label, logo at top					
❑ SW 1562 [S]	The Lincoln Hymns	1961	10.00	20.00	40.00
❑ W 1562 [M]	The Lincoln Hymns	1961	7.50	15.00	30.00
❑ SM-1623	Hillbilly Heaven	1976	2.50	5.00	10.00
—Reissue with new prefix					
❑ ST 1623 [S]	Hillbilly Heaven	1961	10.00	20.00	40.00
—Black colorband label, logo at left					
❑ ST 1623 [S]	Hillbilly Heaven	1962	6.25	12.50	25.00
—Black colorband label, logo at top					
❑ T 1623 [M]	Hillbilly Heaven	1961	7.50	15.00	30.00
—Black colorband label, logo at left					
❑ T 1623 [M]	Hillbilly Heaven	1962	5.00	10.00	20.00
—Black colorband label, logo at top					
❑ ST 1910 [S]	Border Affair	1963	6.25	12.50	25.00
❑ T 1910 [M]	Border Affair	1963	5.00	10.00	20.00
❑ ST 2402 [S]	The Friendly Voice of Tex Ritter	1965	6.25	12.50	25.00
❑ T 2402 [M]	The Friendly Voice of Tex Ritter	1965	5.00	10.00	20.00
❑ DT 2595 [R]	The Best of Tex Ritter	1966	3.75	7.50	15.00
❑ T 2595 [M]	The Best of Tex Ritter	1966	6.25	12.50	25.00
❑ ST 2743 [S]	Sweet Land of Liberty	1967	6.25	12.50	25.00
❑ T 2743 [M]	Sweet Land of Liberty	1967	7.50	15.00	30.00
❑ ST 2786 [S]	Just Beyond the Moon	1967	6.25	12.50	25.00
❑ T 2786 [M]	Just Beyond the Moon	1967	7.50	15.00	30.00
❑ ST 2890 [S]	Bum Tiddil Dee Bum Bum!	1968	6.25	12.50	25.00
❑ T 2890 [M]	Bum Tiddil Dee Bum Bum!	1968	12.50	25.00	50.00
❑ ST 2974	Tex Ritter's Wild West	1968	6.25	12.50	25.00
❑ H 4004 [10]	Cowboy Favorites	195?	45.00	90.00	180.00
❑ ST-11037	Supercountrylegendary	1972	3.75	7.50	15.00
❑ SKC-11241 [(3)]	An American Legend	1973	7.50	15.00	30.00
❑ ST-11351	Fall Away	1974	3.75	7.50	15.00
❑ ST-11503	Comin' After Jinny	1976	3.75	7.50	15.00

HILLTOP

Number	Title	Yr	VG	VG+	NM
❑ PTP-2020 [(2)]	My Kinda Songs	197?	3.75	7.50	15.00
❑ JS-6043	Tex Ritter Sings His Hits	196?	3.00	6.00	12.00
❑ JS-6075	Love You As Big As Texas	196?	3.00	6.00	12.00
❑ JS-6138	High Noon	196?	3.00	6.00	12.00
❑ JS-6155	Tex	197?	3.00	6.00	12.00

LABREA

Number	Title	Yr	VG	VG+	NM
❑ L-8036 [M]	Jamboree, Nashville Style	196?	5.00	10.00	20.00
❑ LS-8036 [S]	Jamboree, Nashville Style	196?	6.25	12.50	25.00

PREMIER

Number	Title	Yr	VG	VG+	NM
❑ 9023	Tex Ritter and the Rio Grande River Boys	196?	3.00	6.00	12.00

Number	Title (A Side/B Side)	Yr	VG	VG+	NM
RITUALS, THE Featuring Arnie Ginsburg, formerly of JAN AND ARNIE.					
45s					
ARWIN					
□ 120	Girl in Zanzibar/Guitarro	1963	7.50	15.00	30.00
□ 127	This Is Paradise/Gone	1964	7.50	15.00	30.00
□ 128	Surfers Rule/Gone	1964	10.00	20.00	40.00
RIVERA, LUCY					
45s					
END					
□ 1041	Make Me Queen/Ific	1959	5.00	10.00	20.00
RIVERS, JOHNNY					
45s					
ATLANTIC					
□ 3011	Sitting in Limbo/Artists and Poets	1974	—	2.50	5.00
□ 3028	Six Days on the Road/Artists and Poets	1974	—	2.50	5.00
□ 3230	John Lee Hooker '74/Get It Up for Love	1974	—	2.50	5.00
BIG TREE					
□ 16094	Swayin' to the Music (Slow Dancin')/Outside Help	1977	—	2.00	4.00
□ 16106	Curious Mind (Um, Um, Um, Um, Um)/Ashes and Sand	1977	—	2.00	4.00
CAPITOL					
□ 4850	Long Black Veil/This Could Be the One	1962	3.75	7.50	15.00
□ 4913	If You Want It, I've Got It/My Heart Is In Your Hands	1963	3.75	7.50	15.00
□ 5232	Long Black Veil/Don't Look Now	1964	3.75	7.50	15.00
CHANCELLOR					
□ 1070	I Get So Doggone Lonesome/Knock Three Times	1961	5.00	10.00	20.00
□ 1108	To Be Loved/Too Good to Last	1962	5.00	10.00	20.00
CORAL					
□ 62425	That's My Baby/Your First and Last Love	1964	3.75	7.50	15.00
CUB					
□ 9047	Everyday/Darling Talk to Me	1959	6.25	12.50	25.00
□ 9058	Answer Me My Love/The Customary Thing	1960	5.00	10.00	20.00
DEE DEE					
□ 239	The White Cliffs of Dover/Your First and Last Love	1959	5.00	10.00	20.00
EPIC					
□ 50121	Help Me Rhonda/New Lovers and Old Friends	1975	—	2.50	5.00
—A-side features Brian Wilson on backing vocals					
□ 50150	Can I Change My Mind/John Lee Hooker	1975	—	2.00	4.00
□ 50208	Welcome Home/Outside Help	1976	—	2.00	4.00
□ 50248	Linda Lue/Outside Help	1976	—	2.00	4.00
ERA					
□ 3037	Call Me/Andersonville	1961	5.00	10.00	20.00
GONE					
□ 5026	Baby Come Back/Long Long Walk	1958	10.00	20.00	40.00
GUYDEN					
□ 2003	You're the One/A Hole in the Ground	1958	6.25	12.50	25.00
□ 2110	You're the One/A Hole in the Ground	1964	3.75	7.50	15.00
IMPERIAL					
□ 66032	Memphis/It Wouldn't Happen with Me	1964	3.00	6.00	12.00
□ 66056	Maybelline/Walk Myself On Home	1964	2.50	5.00	10.00
□ 66056 [PS]	Maybelline/Walk Myself On Home	1964	3.75	7.50	15.00
□ 66075	Mountain of Love/Moody River	1964	2.50	5.00	10.00
□ 66087	Midnight Special/Cupid	1965	2.50	5.00	10.00
□ 66112	Seventh Son/Unsquare Dance	1965	2.50	5.00	10.00
□ 66112 [PS]	Seventh Son/Unsquare Dance	1965	3.75	7.50	15.00
□ 66133	Where Have All the Flowers Gone/Love Me While You Can	1965	2.50	5.00	10.00
□ 66144	Under Your Spell Again/Long Time Man	1965	2.50	5.00	10.00
□ 66144 [PS]	Under Your Spell Again/Long Time Man	1965	3.75	7.50	15.00
□ 66159	Secret Agent Man/You Dig	1966	3.00	6.00	12.00
□ 66159 [PS]	Secret Agent Man/You Dig	1966	3.75	7.50	15.00
□ 66175	(I Washed My Hands In) Muddy Water/Roogalator	1966	2.50	5.00	10.00
□ 66205	Poor Side of Town/A Man Can Cry	1966	3.00	6.00	12.00
□ 66205 [PS]	Poor Side of Town/A Man Can Cry	1966	3.75	7.50	15.00
□ 66227	Baby I Need Your Lovin'/Gettin' Ready for Tomorrow	1967	2.50	5.00	10.00
□ 66227 [PS]	Baby I Need Your Lovin'/Gettin' Ready for Tomorrow	1967	3.75	7.50	15.00
□ 66244	The Tracks of My Tears/Rewind Medley	1967	2.50	5.00	10.00
□ 66244 [PS]	The Tracks of My Tears/Rewind Medley	1967	3.75	7.50	15.00
□ 66267	Summer Rain/Memory of the Coming Good	1967	2.50	5.00	10.00
□ 66286	Look To Your Soul/Something's Strange	1968	2.00	4.00	8.00
□ 66286 [PS]	Look To Your Soul/Something's Strange	1968	3.00	6.00	12.00
□ 66314	Everybody's Talkin'/The Way We Live	1968	—		
—Unreleased					
□ 66335	Right Relations/Better Life	1968	2.00	4.00	8.00
□ 66335 [PS]	Right Relations/Better Life	1968	3.00	6.00	12.00
□ 66360	These Are Not My People/Going Back to Big Sur	1969	2.00	4.00	8.00
□ 66386	Muddy River/Resurrection	1969	2.00	4.00	8.00
□ 66386 [PS]	Muddy River/Resurrection	1969	3.00	6.00	12.00
□ 66418	One Woman/Ode to John Lee	1969	2.00	4.00	8.00
□ 66448	Into the Mystic/Jesus Is a Soul Man	1970	2.00	4.00	8.00
□ 66453	Fire and Rain/Apple Tree	1970	2.00	4.00	8.00
MCA					
□ 52502	Heartbreak Love/Why Can't We Communicate	1984	—	2.00	4.00
MGM					
□ 13266	Answer Me, My Love/Customary Thing	1964	3.75	7.50	15.00
RIVERAIRE					
□ 1001	Don't Bug Me Baby/Haunting Black Eyes	1959	7.50	15.00	30.00
ROULETTE					
□ 4565	Baby Come Back/Long Long Walk	1964	5.00	10.00	20.00
RSO					
□ 1030	Romance (Give Me a Chance)/□ Don't Need No Other Now	1980	—	2.00	4.00
□ 1045	China/The Price	1980	—	2.00	4.00
SOUL CITY					
□ 007	Ashes and Sand/Outside Help	1977	—	2.50	5.00
□ 008	Swayin' to the Music (Slow Dancin')/Outside Help	1977	2.00	4.00	8.00

Number	Title (A Side/B Side)	Yr	VG	VG+	NM
□ 010	Little White Lie/Be My Baby	1980	—	2.50	5.00
□ 014	RSVP/The Price	1982	—	2.50	5.00
SUEDE					
□ 1401	Little Girl/Two by Two	1957	25.00	50.00	100.00
—As "Johnny Ramistella"					
UNITED ARTISTS					
□ 0101	Memphis/Secret Agent Man	1973	—	2.00	4.00
□ 0102	Mountain of Love/Maybellene	1973	—	2.00	4.00
□ 0103	Seventh Son/Midnight Special	1973	—	2.00	4.00
□ 0104	Poor Side of Town/Baby I Need Your Lovin'	1973	—	2.00	4.00
□ 0105	Summer Rain/The Tracks of My Tears	1973	—	2.00	4.00
—0101 through 0105 are "Silver Spotlight Series" reissues					
□ XW198	Blue Suede Shoes/Stories to a Child	1973	—	2.50	5.00
□ XW226	Searchin'-So Fine/New York City Dues	1973	—	2.50	5.00
□ XW310	I'll Feel a Whole Lot Better/Over the Line	1973	—	2.50	5.00
□ XW522	Rockin' Pneumonia-Boogie Woogie Flu/Blue Suede Shoes	1974	—	2.00	4.00
—Reissue					
□ XW523	Where Have All the Flowers Gone/(I Washed My Hands in) Muddy Water	1974	—	2.00	4.00
—Reissue					
□ 741	Oh What a Kiss/Knock Three Times	1964	3.00	6.00	12.00
□ 769	Dream Doll/To Be Loved	1964	3.00	6.00	12.00
□ 50778	Sea Cruise/Our Lady of the Well	1971	—	3.00	6.00
□ 50822	Think His Name/Permanent Change	1971	—	3.00	6.00
□ 50948	On the Borderline/Come Home America	1972	—	2.50	5.00
□ 50960	Rockin' Pneumonia-Boogie Woogie Flu/Come Home America	1972	—	3.00	6.00
—On some pressings, the intro of the A-side is not repeated (lasts about 20 seconds)					
□ 50960	Rockin' Pneumonia-Boogie Woogie Flu/Come Home America	1972	—	3.00	6.00
—On most pressings, the intro of the A-side lasts about 35 seconds					
Albums					
ATLANTIC					
□ SD 7301	The Road	1974	3.00	6.00	12.00
BIG TREE					
□ BT 76004	Outside Help	1977	3.00	6.00	12.00
CAPITOL					
□ ST 2161 [S]	The Sensational Johnny Rivers	1964	6.25	12.50	25.00
□ T 2161 [M]	The Sensational Johnny Rivers	1964	5.00	10.00	20.00
COLUMBIA					
□ FE 38429	Not a Through Street	1983	2.50	5.00	10.00
□ PE 38429	Not a Through Street	1985	2.00	4.00	8.00
—Budget-line reissue					
EPIC					
□ PE 33681	New Lovers and Old Friends	1975	3.00	6.00	12.00
IMPERIAL					
□ LP-9264 [M]	Johnny Rivers at the Whiskey A-Go-Go	1964	5.00	10.00	20.00
—Black label with pink and white at left					
□ LP-9264 [M]	Johnny Rivers at the Whiskey A-Go-Go	1966	3.00	6.00	12.00
—Black label with green and white at left					
□ LP-9274 [M]	Here We A-Go-Go Again!	1964	5.00	10.00	20.00
—Black label with pink and white at left					
□ LP-9274 [M]	Here We A-Go-Go Again!	1966	3.00	6.00	12.00
—Black label with green and white at left					
□ LP-9280 [M]	Johnny Rivers In Action!	1965	5.00	10.00	20.00
—Black label with pink and white at left					
□ LP-9280 [M]	Johnny Rivers In Action!	1966	3.00	6.00	12.00
—Black label with green and white at left					
□ LP-9284 [M]	Meanwhile Back at the Whiskey a-Go-Go	1965	5.00	10.00	20.00
—Black label with pink and white at left					
□ LP-9284 [M]	Meanwhile Back at the Whiskey a-Go-Go	1966	3.00	6.00	12.00
—Black label with green and white at left					
□ LP-9293 [M]	Johnny Rivers Rocks the Folk	1965	5.00	10.00	20.00
—Black label with pink and white at left					
□ LP-9293 [M]	Johnny Rivers Rocks the Folk	1966	3.00	6.00	12.00
—Black label with green and white at left					
□ LP-9307 [M]	...And I Know You Wanna Dance	1966	3.00	6.00	12.00
—Black label with green and white at left					
□ LP-9307 [M]	...And I Know You Wanna Dance	1966	5.00	10.00	20.00
—Black label with pink and white at left					
□ LP-9324 [M]	Johnny Rivers' Golden Hits	1966	3.75	7.50	15.00
□ LP-9334 [M]	Changes	1966	3.75	7.50	15.00
□ LP-9341 [M]	Rewind	1967	5.00	10.00	20.00
□ LP-9372 [M]	Realization	1968	10.00	20.00	40.00
□ LP-12264 [S]	Johnny Rivers at the Whiskey A-Go-Go	1964	6.25	12.50	25.00
—Black label with pink and white at left					
□ LP-12264 [S]	Johnny Rivers at the Whiskey A-Go-Go	1966	3.75	7.50	15.00
—Black label with green and white at left					
□ LP-12274 [S]	Here We A-Go-Go Again!	1964	6.25	12.50	25.00
—Black label with pink and white at left					
□ LP-12274 [S]	Here We A-Go-Go Again!	1966	3.75	7.50	15.00
—Black label with green and white at left					
□ LP-12280 [S]	Johnny Rivers In Action!	1965	6.25	12.50	25.00
—Black label with pink and white at left					
□ LP-12280 [S]	Johnny Rivers In Action!	1966	3.75	7.50	15.00
—Black label with green and white at left					
□ LP-12284 [S]	Meanwhile Back at the Whiskey a-Go-Go	1965	6.25	12.50	25.00
—Black label with pink and white at left					
□ LP-12284 [S]	Meanwhile Back at the Whiskey a-Go-Go	1966	3.75	7.50	15.00
—Black label with green and white at left					
□ LP-12293 [S]	Johnny Rivers Rocks the Folk	1965	6.25	12.50	25.00
—Black label with pink and white at left					
□ LP-12293 [S]	Johnny Rivers Rocks the Folk	1966	3.75	7.50	15.00
—Black label with green and white at left					
□ LP-12307 [S]	...And I Know You Wanna Dance	1966	3.75	7.50	15.00
—Black label with pink and white at left					
□ LP-12307 [S]	...And I Know You Wanna Dance	1966	6.25	12.50	25.00
—Black label with pink and white at left					
□ LP-12324 [S]	Johnny Rivers' Golden Hits	1966	5.00	10.00	20.00
□ LP-12334 [S]	Changes	1966	5.00	10.00	20.00
□ LP-12341 [S]	Rewind	1967	5.00	10.00	20.00
□ LP-12372 [S]	Realization	1968	5.00	10.00	20.00
□ LP-12427	A Touch of Gold	1969	5.00	10.00	20.00
□ LP-16001	Slim Slo Slider	1970	5.00	10.00	20.00

R

Number	Title (A Side/B Side)	Yr	VG	VG+	NM
LIBERTY					
❏ LN-10120	The Best of Johnny Rivers	1981	2.00	4.00	8.00
❏ LN-10121	Changes	1981	2.00	4.00	8.00
—Budget-line reissue					
❏ LN-10154	Blue Suede Shoes	1981	2.00	4.00	8.00
—Budget-line reissue					
❏ LO-12324	Johnny Rivers' Golden Hits	198?	2.00	4.00	8.00
—Budget-line reissue					
❏ LW-12427	A Touch of Gold	198?	2.00	4.00	8.00
—Budget-line reissue					
MCA					
❏ 917	Greatest Hits	1985	2.50	5.00	10.00
PICKWICK					
❏ PC-3022 [M]	Johnny Rivers	196?	3.75	7.50	15.00
❏ SPC-3022 [R]	Johnny Rivers	196?	2.50	5.00	10.00
—Later covers have "electronically enhanced for STEREO" at upper right					
❏ SPC-3022 [R]	Johnny Rivers	196?	3.00	6.00	12.00
—First pressing covers have no "electronically enhanced for STEREO" at upper right					
❏ SPC-3191	If You Want It, I Got It	196?	3.00	6.00	12.00
RSO					
❏ RS-1-3082	Borrowed Time	1980	2.50	5.00	10.00
SEARS					
❏ SPS-417	Mr. Teenage	196?	6.25	12.50	25.00
❏ SPS-487	Groovin'	1968	6.25	12.50	25.00
SOUL CITY					
❏ SC 1007-1	Greatest Hits	1998	5.00	10.00	20.00
—500 copies, each autographed by Johnny Rivers					
SUNSET					
❏ SUM-1157 [M]	Whiskey A-Go-Go Revisited	1967	3.00	6.00	12.00
❏ SUS-5157 [S]	Whiskey A-Go-Go Revisited	1967	2.50	5.00	10.00
❏ SUS-5251	The Early Years	1969	2.50	5.00	10.00
UNART					
❏ M-20007 [M]	The Great Johnny Rivers	1967	3.00	6.00	12.00
❏ S-21007 [S]	The Great Johnny Rivers	1967	3.00	6.00	12.00
UNITED ARTISTS					
❏ UA-LA075-F	Blue Suede Shoes	1973	3.00	6.00	12.00
❏ USX-93 [(2)]	Johnny Rivers Superpak	1971	5.00	10.00	20.00
❏ UA-LA253-G	The Very Best of Johnny Rivers	1974	3.00	6.00	12.00
❏ UA-LA387-E	The Very Best of Johnny Rivers	1975	3.00	6.00	12.00
❏ UA-LA486-G	Wild Night	1976	3.00	6.00	12.00
❏ UAL-3386 [M]	Go, Johnny, Go	1964	5.00	10.00	20.00
❏ UAS-5532	Home Grown	1971	3.75	7.50	15.00
❏ UAS-5650	L.A. Reggae	1972	3.75	7.50	15.00
❏ UAS-6386 [S]	Go, Johnny, Go	1964	6.25	12.50	25.00
❏ ST-90813 [S]	Go, Johnny, Go	1965	7.50	15.00	30.00
—Capitol Record Club edition					
❏ T-90813 [M]	Go, Johnny, Go	1965	6.25	12.50	25.00
—Capitol Record Club edition					
WARNER BROS.					
❏ R133498 [S]	Johnny Rivers' Golden Hits	197?	7.50	15.00	30.00
—RCA Music Service edition of Imperial LP-12324 on "Burbank" palm trees label; why this was pressed on Warner Bros. is anyone's guess, but it doesn't appear to be an error					

RIVERS, TONY, AND THE CASTAWAYS
45s
CONSTELLATION

Number	Title (A Side/B Side)	Yr	VG	VG+	NM
❏ 128	I Love the Way You Walk/I Love You	1964	3.75	7.50	15.00

RIVERAS, THE (1) R&B vocal group from northern New Jersey.
45s
COED

Number	Title (A Side/B Side)	Yr	VG	VG+	NM
❏ 503	Count Every Star/True Love Is Hard to Find	1958	12.50	25.00	50.00
❏ 508	Moonlight Serenade/Neither Rain Nor Snow	1959	10.00	20.00	40.00
❏ 513	Our Love/Midnight Flyer	1959	7.50	15.00	30.00
❏ 513	Our Love/True Love Is Hard to Find	1959	7.50	15.00	30.00
❏ 522	Since I Made You Cry/11th Hour Melody	1959	7.50	15.00	30.00
❏ 529	Blessing of Love/Moonlight Cocktails	1960	6.25	12.50	25.00
❏ 538	My Friend/Great Big Eyes	1960	6.25	12.50	25.00
❏ 542	Easy to Remember/Stay in My Heart	1960	6.25	12.50	25.00
❏ 551	El Doraado/Refrigerator	1961	6.25	12.50	25.00
❏ 592	Moonlight Cocktails/Midnight Flyer	1964	3.75	7.50	15.00
LOST-NITE					
❏ 162	Blessing of Love/Moonlight Cocktails	196?	—	3.00	6.00
—Reissue					
❏ 164	Count Every Star/True Love Is Hard to Find	196?	—	3.00	6.00
—Reissue					
❏ 167	Moonlight Serenade/Neither Rain Nor Snow	196?	—	3.00	6.00
—Reissue					
❏ 169	Our Love/True Love Is Hard to Find	196?	—	3.00	6.00
—Reissue					
❏ 170	Easy to Remember/Stay in My Heart	196?	—	3.00	6.00
—Reissue					
❏ 172	Since I Made You Cry/11th Hour Melody	196?	—	3.00	6.00
—Reissue					
Albums					
POST					
❏ 2000	The Riviras Sing	196?	10.00	20.00	40.00

RIVIERAS, THE (2) Surf-garage rock band from South Bend, Indiana.
45s
LANA

Number	Title (A Side/B Side)	Yr	VG	VG+	NM
❏ 136	California Sun/H.B. Goose Step	196?	2.00	4.00	8.00
—Oldies reissue					
RIVIERA					
❏ 1401	California Sun/H.B. Goose Step	1964	5.00	10.00	20.00
❏ 1401	California Sun/Played On	1964	10.00	20.00	40.00
—Possibly as few as 1,000 were pressed with this B-side					
❏ 1402	Little Donna/Let's Have a Party	1964	3.75	7.50	15.00
❏ 1403	Rockin' Robin/Battle Line	1964	3.75	7.50	15.00
❏ 1405	Whole Lotta Shakin'/Rip It Up	1965	3.75	7.50	15.00
❏ 1405	Whole Lotta Shakin'/Lakeview Lane	1965	5.00	10.00	20.00
❏ 1406	Let's Go to Hawaii/Lakeview Lane	1965	3.75	7.50	15.00
❏ 1407	Somebody Asked Me/Somebody New	1965	3.75	7.50	15.00
—Credited to the Rivieras, but actually by Bobby Whiteside					
❏ 1409	Bug Juice/Never Feel the Pain	1965	5.00	10.00	20.00

Number	Title (A Side/B Side)	Yr	VG	VG+	NM
Albums					
RIVIERA					
❏ 701 [M]	Campus Party	1964	62.50	125.00	250.00
U.S.A.					
❏ 102 [M]	Let's Have a Party	1964	37.50	75.00	150.00

RIVIERAS, THE (3)
45s
ALGONQUIN

Number	Title (A Side/B Side)	Yr	VG	VG+	NM
❏ 718	Together Forever/A Night to Remember	1958	50.00	100.00	200.00
—Reissued as "The Ravenairs"					

RIVILEERS, THE
45s
BATON

Number	Title (A Side/B Side)	Yr	VG	VG+	NM
❏ 200	A Thousand Stars/Hey Chiquita	1953	50.00	100.00	200.00
❏ 201	Forever/Darling Farewell	1954	30.00	60.00	120.00
❏ 205	Carolyn/Eternal Love	1954	30.00	60.00	120.00
❏ 207	(I Love You) For Sentimental Reasons/ I Want to See My Baby	1955	15.00	30.00	60.00
❏ 209	Little Girl/Don't Ever Leave Me	1955	15.00	30.00	60.00
❏ 241	A Thousand Stars/Who Is the Girl	1957	10.00	20.00	40.00

RIVINGTONS, THE
45s
A.R.E. AMERICAN

Number	Title (A Side/B Side)	Yr	VG	VG+	NM
❏ 100	All That Glitters/You Move Me Baby	1964	3.75	7.50	15.00
AGC					
❏ 5	I Lost the Love/Mind Your Man	1968	2.00	4.00	8.00
BATON MASTER					
❏ 202	Teach Me Tonight/Reach Our Goal	1967	2.00	4.00	8.00
COLUMBIA					
❏ 43581	A Rose Growing in the Ruins/Tend to Business	1966	3.00	6.00	12.00
❏ 43772	Yadi Yadi Yum Yum/Yadi Yadi Revisited	1966	3.00	6.00	12.00
J.D.					
❏ 122	Don't Hate Your Father (Part 1)/ Don't Hate Your Father (Part 2)	1976	—	2.50	5.00
LIBERTY					
❏ 1484 [DJ]	Papa-Oom-Mow-Mow (same on both sides)	1982	—	3.00	6.00
—Reissue; promo only					
❏ 55427	Papa-Oom-Mow-Mow/Deep Water	1962	6.25	12.50	25.00
❏ 55513	Kickapoo Joy Juice/My Reward	1962	3.75	7.50	15.00
❏ 55528	Mama-Oom-Mow-Mow/Waiting	1962	3.75	7.50	15.00
❏ 55553	The Bird's the Word/I'm Losing My Grip	1963	5.00	10.00	20.00
❏ 55585	The Shaky Bird (Part 1)/The Shaky Bird (Part 2)	1963	3.75	7.50	15.00
❏ 55610	Little Sally Walker/Cherry	1963	7.50	15.00	30.00
❏ 55671	Fairy Tales/Wee Jee Walk	1964	3.75	7.50	15.00
QUAN					
❏ 1379	I Don't Want a New Baby/You're Gonna Pay	1967	2.50	5.00	10.00
RCA VICTOR					
❏ 74-0301	Pop Your Corn (Part 1)/Pop Your Corn (Part 2)	1969	2.00	4.00	8.00
REPRISE					
❏ 0293	I Tried/One Monkey Don't Stop No Show	1964	3.00	6.00	12.00
UNITED ARTISTS					
❏ 0096	Papa-Oom-Mow-Mow/The Bird's the Word	1973	—	2.00	4.00
—"Silver Spotlight Series" reissue					
VEE JAY					
❏ 634	All That Glitters/You Move Me Baby	1964	3.00	6.00	12.00
❏ 649	I Love You Always/Years of Tears	1965	3.00	6.00	12.00
❏ 677	The Willy/Just Got to Be Mine	1965	3.00	6.00	12.00
WAND					
❏ 11253	Papa-Oom-Mow-Mow/I Don't Want a New Baby	1973		2.50	5.00
Albums					
LIBERTY					
❏ LRP-3282 [M]	Doin' the Bird	1963	25.00	50.00	100.00
❏ LST-7282 [S]	Doin' the Bird	1963	50.00	100.00	200.00

ROAD, THE
45s
BLUE ONION

Number	Title (A Side/B Side)	Yr	VG	VG+	NM
❏ 106	It's So Hard to Find/You Rub Me the Wrong Way	1969	7.50	15.00	30.00
KAMA SUTRA					
❏ 256	She's Not There/A Bummer	1968	2.00	4.00	8.00
❏ 266	The Grass Looks Greener on the Other Side/ In Love	1969	2.00	4.00	8.00
❏ 267	Mr. Soul/I Can Only Give You Everything	1969	2.00	4.00	8.00
❏ 504	Mr. Soul/The Grass Looks Greener on the Other Side	1970	—	3.00	6.00
❏ 531	Alone/If You Ever Needed a Woman	1971	—	3.00	6.00
Albums					
KAMA SUTRA					
❏ KSBS-2012	The Road	1970	3.75	7.50	15.00
—Reissue of 8075					
❏ KSBS-2032 [(2)]	Cognition	1970	5.00	10.00	20.00
❏ KLPS-8075	The Road	1969	5.00	10.00	20.00

ROAD RUNNERS, THE More than one group. Also see GARY PAXTON.
45s
CHALLENGE

Number	Title (A Side/B Side)	Yr	VG	VG+	NM
❏ 9197	Dead Man/Pretty Girls	1963	5.00	10.00	20.00
FELSTED					
❏ 8692	Quasimoto/Road Runnah	1964	10.00	20.00	40.00
MIRAMAR					
❏ 116	Take Me/I'll Make It Up to You	1965	3.75	7.50	15.00
MOROCCO					
❏ 001	Goodbye/Tell Her You Love Her	1966	5.00	10.00	20.00
REPRISE					
❏ 0418	Take Me/I'll Make It Up to You	1965	3.75	7.50	15.00
Albums					
LONDON					
❏ PS 381 [S]	The New Mustang (And Other Hot Rod Hits)	1964	75.00	150.00	300.00
❏ LL 3381 [M]	The New Mustang (And Other Hot Rod Hits)	1964	50.00	100.00	200.00

Number	Title (A Side/B Side)	Yr	VG	VG+	NM

ROAMERS, THE
45s
HIT

Number	Title (A Side/B Side)	Yr	VG	VG+	NM
❏ 94	Be True to Your School/Wonderful Summer	1963	2.00	4.00	8.00
—B-side by Joanne Kay					
❏ 102	Hey Little Cobra/Daisy Petal Pickin'	1964	2.00	4.00	8.00
—B-side by Ricky Dickens					
❏ 115	Dead Man's Curve/Ronnie	1964	2.00	4.00	8.00
—B-side by the Chellows					
❏ 118	Bits and Pieces/(Just Like) Romeo and Juliet	1964	2.50	5.00	10.00
❏ 126	I Get Around/Yesterday's Gone	1964	2.00	4.00	8.00
❏ 132	The Little Old Lady from Pasadena/Can't You See That She's Mine	1964	2.50	5.00	10.00
❏ 135	Because/Walk Don't Run '64	1964	2.50	5.00	10.00
—B-side by the Nashville Five					
❏ 140	G.T.O./In the Misty Moonlight	1964	2.00	4.00	8.00
—B-side by Marty Wood					
❏ 141	Save It for Me/Selfish One	1964	2.00	4.00	8.00
—B-side by Betty Wrigley					
❏ 147	When I Grow Up (To Be a Man)/Matchbox	1964	2.50	5.00	10.00
—B-side by the Jalopy Five					
❏ 151	Tobacco Road/I Know Johnny Loves Me	1964	2.50	5.00	10.00
—B-side by Amy and the Jarretts					
❏ 152	Ride the Wild Surf/You're the Only Girl for Me	1964	2.00	4.00	8.00
❏ 158	Everything's Alright/Dance, Dance, Dance	1964	3.00	6.00	12.00
—B-side by the Spartas					
❏ 160	We Build a 409/Big Man in Town	1964	3.00	6.00	12.00
—B-side by the Chellows					
❏ 172	Love Potion Number Nine/Never Forget Me	1965	3.00	6.00	12.00
❏ 217	I Want Candy/(I Can't Get No) Satisfaction	1965	3.00	6.00	12.00
—B-side by the Jalopy Five					
❏ 218	I Want Candy/I Like It Like That	1965	3.00	6.00	12.00
—B-side by the Jalopy Five					
❏ 221	Eve of Destruction/I Got You Babe	1965	3.00	6.00	12.00
—B-side by Wayne and Dee					
❏ 222	Hang On Sloopy/The "In" Crowd	1965	3.00	6.00	12.00
—B-side by Just Three					
❏ 224	You Were On My Mind/Baby Don't Go	1965	2.50	5.00	10.00
—B-side by Jimmy and Pat					
❏ 227	Treat Her Right/You're the One	1965	2.00	4.00	8.00
—As "Cal York and the Roamers"; B-side by the Crests (2)					
❏ 250	Be True to Your School/Wonderful Summer	1966	2.00	4.00	8.00
—B-side by Joanne Kay					

ROBB, DEE Later of THE ROBBS.
45s
ARGO

Number	Title (A Side/B Side)	Yr	VG	VG+	NM
❏ 5439	Bye Bye Baby/The Prom	1963	3.00	6.00	12.00
SCORE					
❏ 1006	He's Got the Whole World in His Hands/Say That Thing	1964	3.75	7.50	15.00

ROBBINS, EDDIE
45s
DAVID

Number	Title (A Side/B Side)	Yr	VG	VG+	NM
❏ 1001	Janice/It Was Fun	196?	6.25	12.50	25.00
DOT					
❏ 15702	A Girl Like You/Dear Parents	1958	10.00	20.00	40.00
POWER					
❏ 214	A Girl Like You/Dear Parents	1958	30.00	60.00	120.00

ROBBINS, MARTY
45s
COLUMBIA

Number	Title (A Side/B Side)	Yr	VG	VG+	NM
❏ 02444	Jumper Cable Man/Good Hearted Woman	1981	—	2.00	4.00
❏ 02575	Teardrops on My Heart/Honeycomb	1981	—	2.00	4.00
❏ 02854	Lover, Lover/Some Memories Just Won't Die	1982	—	2.00	4.00
❏ 03236	Tie Your Dream to Mine/That's All She Wrote	1982	—	2.00	4.00
❏ 03789	Change of Heart/Devil in a Cowboy Hat	1983	—	2.00	4.00
❏ 03927	Baby That's Love/What If I Said I Love You	1983	—	2.00	4.00
❏ 10305	El Paso City/When I'm Gone	1976	—	2.50	5.00
❏ 10396	Among My Souvenirs/She's Just a Drifter	1976	—	2.50	5.00
❏ 10472	Adios Amigo/Helen	1977	—	2.50	5.00
❏ 10536	I Don't Know Why (I Just Do)/Inspiration for a Song	1977	—	2.50	5.00
❏ 10629	Don't Let Me Touch You/Tomorrow, Tomorrow, Tomorrow	1977	—	2.50	5.00
❏ 10673	Return to Me/More Than Anything, I Miss You	1978	—	2.50	5.00
❏ 10821	Please Don't Play a Love Song/Jenny	1978	—	2.50	5.00
❏ 10905	Touch Me with Magic/Confused and Lonely	1979	—	2.50	5.00
❏ 11016	All Around Cowboy/The Dreamer	1979	—	2.50	5.00
❏ 11102	Buenos Dias Argentina/Ballad of a Small Man	1979	—	2.50	5.00
❏ 11240	She's Made of Faith/Misery in My Soul	1980	—	2.00	4.00
❏ 11291	One Man's Trash (Is Another Man's Treasure)/I Can't Wait Until Tomorrow	1980	—	2.00	4.00
❏ 11372	An Occasional Rose/Holding On to You	1980	—	2.00	4.00
❏ 11425	Completely Out of Love/Another Cup of Coffee	1981	—	2.00	4.00
❏ 20925	Tomorrow You'll Be Gone/Love Me or Leave Me Alone	1952	7.50	15.00	30.00
❏ 20965	Crying 'Cause I Love You/I Wish Somebody Loved Me	1952	7.50	15.00	30.00
❏ 21022	I'll Go On Alone/You're Breaking My Heart	1952	7.50	15.00	30.00
❏ 21032	My Isle of Golden Dreams/Sweet Hawaiian Dream	1952	—	—	—
—Unreleased					
❏ 21075	I Couldn't Keep from Crying/After You Leave	1953	7.50	15.00	30.00
❏ 21111	A Castle in the Sky/A Half-Way Chance with You	1953	7.50	15.00	30.00
❏ 21145	Sing Me Something Sentimental/At the End of Long, Lonely Days	1953	7.50	15.00	30.00
❏ 21172	Blessed Jesus Should I Fall Don't Let Me Lay/Kneel and Let the Lord Take Your Load	1953	7.50	15.00	30.00
❏ 21176	Don't Make Me Ashamed/It's a Long, Long Ride	1953	7.50	15.00	30.00
❏ 21213	My Isle of Golden Dreams/Aloha Oe	1954	7.50	15.00	30.00
❏ 21246	Pretty Words/Your Heart's Turn to Break	1954	7.50	15.00	30.00
❏ 21291	Call Me Up (And I'll Come Calling on You)/I'm Too Big to Cry	1954	7.50	15.00	30.00

Number	Title (A Side/B Side)	Yr	VG	VG+	NM
❏ 21324	Time Goes By/It's a Pity What Money Can Do	1954	7.50	15.00	30.00
❏ 21351	That's All Right/Gossip	1955	12.50	25.00	50.00
❏ 21352	God Understands/Have Thine Own Way, Lord	1955	6.25	12.50	25.00
❏ 21388	Daddy Loves You/Pray for Me, Mother of Mine	1955	6.25	12.50	25.00
❏ 21414	It Looks Like I'm Just in the Way/I'll Love You Till the Day I Die	1955	6.25	12.50	25.00
❏ 21446	Maybellene/This Broken Heart of Mine	1955	12.50	25.00	50.00
❏ 21461	Pretty Mama/Don't Let Me Hang Around	1955	12.50	25.00	50.00
❏ 21477	Tennessee Toddy/Mean Mama Blues	1955	12.50	25.00	50.00
❏ 21508	Singing the Blues/I Can't Quit (I've Gone Too Far)	1956	10.00	20.00	40.00
❏ 21525	I'll Know You're Gone/How Long Will It Be	1956	6.25	12.50	25.00
—With Lee Emerson					
❏ 21545	Singing the Blues/I Can't Quit (I've Gone Too Far)	1956	7.50	15.00	30.00
❏ S7 30511 [S]	El Paso/Running Gun	1959	7.50	15.00	30.00
—"Stereo Seven" (small hole, plays at 33 1/3 rpm)					
❏ S7 30589 [S]	Big Iron/Saddle Tramp	1960	7.50	15.00	30.00
—"Stereo Seven" single (small hole, plays at 33 1/3 rpm)					
❏ S7 30771 [S]	Five Brothers/Ride, Cowboy, Ride	1960	7.50	15.00	30.00
—"Stereo Seven" single (small hole, plays at 33 1/3 rpm)					
❏ S7 30809 [S]	Ballad of the Alamo/A Time and a Place for Everything	1960	7.50	15.00	30.00
—"Stereo Seven" single (small hole, plays at 33 1/3 rpm)					
❏ S7 31124 [S]	To Each His Own/I Can't Help It	1961	5.00	10.00	20.00
❏ S7 31125 [S]	Answer Me My Love/Clara	1961	5.00	10.00	20.00
❏ S7 31126 [S]	Half As Much/Unchained Melody	1961	5.00	10.00	20.00
❏ S7 31127 [S]	Are You Sincere?/Guess I'll Be Going	1961	5.00	10.00	20.00
❏ S7 31128 [S]	To Think You've Chosen Me/Too Young	1961	5.00	10.00	20.00
—The above five are "Stereo Seven" 33 1/3 rpm jukebox singles from set "JS7-32" entitled "Just a Little Sentimental"					
❏ S7 31190 [S]	Just a Little Sentimental/Hurt	1961	5.00	10.00	20.00
❏ S7 31191 [S]	To Each His Own/I Can't Help It	1961	5.00	10.00	20.00
❏ S7 31192 [S]	Answer Me My Love/Half As Much	1961	5.00	10.00	20.00
❏ S7 31193 [S]	Unchained Melody/Are You Sincere?	1961	5.00	10.00	20.00
❏ S7 31747 [S]	Devil Woman/Time Can't Make Me Forget	1963	5.00	10.00	20.00
—"Stereo Seven" single, small hole, plays at 33 1/3 rpm					
❏ S7 31748 [S]	In the Ashes of an Old Love Affair/The Hands You're Holding Now	1963	5.00	10.00	20.00
—"Stereo Seven" single, small hole, plays at 33 1/3 rpm					
❏ S7 31749 [S]	Worried/Little Rich Girl	1963	5.00	10.00	20.00
—"Stereo Seven" single, small hole, plays at 33 1/3 rpm					
❏ S7 31750 [S]	Progressive Love/Love Is a Hurting Thing	1963	5.00	10.00	20.00
—"Stereo Seven" single, small hole, plays at 33 1/3 rpm					
❏ S7 31751 [S]	Kinda Halfway Feel/The Wine Flowed Freely	1963	5.00	10.00	20.00
—The above five are "Stereo Seven" 33 1/3 rpm jukebox singles from set "JS7-78" entitled "Devil Woman"					
❏ 3-39020 [S]	Change That Dial/You Won't Have Her Long	1964	7.50	15.00	30.00
—Jukebox single, small hole, plays at 33 1/3 rpm; rather than the usual rainbow "target" label of Columbia "Stereo Seven" singles, this one has green labels					
❏ 40679	Long Tall Sally/Mr. Teardrop	1956	12.50	25.00	50.00
❏ 40706	Respectfully Miss Brooks/You Don't Owe Me a Thing	1956	12.50	25.00	50.00
❏ 40815	Knee Deep in the Blues/The Same Two Lips	1957	6.25	12.50	25.00
❏ 40864	A White Sport Coat (And a Pink Carnation)/Grown Up Tears	1957	6.25	12.50	25.00
❏ 40864 [PS]	A White Sport Coat (And a Pink Carnation)/Grown Up Tears	1957	10.00	20.00	40.00
❏ 40868	I Cried Like a Baby/Where D'Ja Go	1957	6.25	12.50	25.00
—With Lee Emerson					
❏ 40969	Please Don't Blame Me/Teen-Age Dream	1957	6.25	12.50	25.00
❏ 41013	The Story of My Life/Once-a-Week Date	1957	6.25	12.50	25.00
❏ 41013 [PS]	The Story of My Life/Once-a-Week Date	1957	10.00	20.00	40.00
❏ 41143	Just Married/Stairway of Love	1958	5.00	10.00	20.00
❏ 41208	She Was Only Seventeen (He Was One Year More)/Sittin' in a Tree House	1958	5.00	10.00	20.00
❏ 41208 [PS]	She Was Only Seventeen (He Was One Year More)/Sittin' in a Tree House	1958	10.00	20.00	40.00
❏ 41282	Ain't I the Lucky One/The Last Time I Saw My Heart	1958	5.00	10.00	20.00
❏ 41325	The Hanging Tree/The Blues, Country Style	1959	5.00	10.00	20.00
❏ 41325 [PS]	The Hanging Tree/The Blues, Country Style	1959	10.00	20.00	40.00
❏ 41408	Cap and Gown/Last Night About This Time	1959	5.00	10.00	20.00
❏ 41511 [M]	El Paso/Running Gun	1959	5.00	10.00	20.00
❏ 41511 [PS]	El Paso/Running Gun	1959	7.50	15.00	30.00
❏ 41589 [M]	Big Iron/Saddle Tramp	1960	3.75	7.50	15.00
❏ 41686	Is There Any Chance/I Told My Heart	1960	3.75	7.50	15.00
❏ 41766	Don't Worry/A Time and a Place for Everything	1960	—	—	—
—Unreleased					
❏ 41771 [M]	Five Brothers/Ride, Cowboy, Ride	1960	3.75	7.50	15.00
❏ 41809 [M]	Ballad of the Alamo/A Time and a Place for Everything	1960	3.75	7.50	15.00
❏ 41809 [PS]	Ballad of the Alamo/A Time and a Place for Everything	1960	7.50	15.00	30.00
❏ 41922	Don't Worry/Like All the Other Times	1961	3.75	7.50	15.00
❏ 41922 [PS]	Don't Worry/Like All the Other Times	1961	6.25	12.50	25.00
❏ 42008	Jimmy Martinez/Ghost Train	1961	3.75	7.50	15.00
❏ 42008 [PS]	Jimmy Martinez/Ghost Train	1961	6.25	12.50	25.00
❏ 42065	It's Your World/You Told Me So	1961	3.75	7.50	15.00
❏ 42065 [PS]	It's Your World/You Told Me So	1961	6.25	12.50	25.00
❏ 42246	I Told the Brook/Sometimes I'm Tempted	1961	3.75	7.50	15.00
❏ 42246 [PS]	I Told the Brook/Sometimes I'm Tempted	1961	6.25	12.50	25.00
❏ 42375	Love Can't Wait/Too Far Gone	1962	3.75	7.50	15.00
❏ 42375 [PS]	Love Can't Wait/Too Far Gone	1962	6.25	12.50	25.00
❏ 42486	Devil Woman/April Fool's Day	1962	3.75	7.50	15.00
❏ 42486 [PS]	Devil Woman/April Fool's Day	1962	6.25	12.50	25.00
❏ 42614	Ruby Ann/Won't You Forgive	1962	3.75	7.50	15.00
❏ 42614 [PS]	Ruby Ann/Won't You Forgive	1962	6.25	12.50	25.00
❏ 42672	Hawaii's Calling Me/Ka-Lu-A	1963	3.00	6.00	12.00
❏ 42701	Cigarettes and Coffee Blues/Teenager's Dad	1963	3.00	6.00	12.00
❏ 42701 [PS]	Cigarettes and Coffee Blues/Teenager's Dad	1963	6.25	12.50	25.00
❏ 42781	No Sign of Loneliness Here/I'm Not Ready Yet	1963	3.00	6.00	12.00
❏ 42781 [PS]	No Sign of Loneliness Here/I'm Not Ready Yet	1963	6.25	12.50	25.00
❏ 42831	Not So Long Ago/I Hope You Learn a Lot	1963	3.00	6.00	12.00
❏ 42890	Begging to You/Over High Mountain	1963	3.00	6.00	12.00
❏ 42968	Girl from Spanish Town/Kingston Girl	1964	2.50	5.00	10.00

R

Number	Title (A Side/B Side)	Yr	VG	VG+	NM
43049	The Cowboy in the Continental Suit/ Man Walks Among Us	1964	2.50	5.00	10.00
43134	One of These Days/Up in the Air	1964	2.50	5.00	10.00
43196	I Eish-Tay-Mah-Su (I Love You)/ A Whole Lot Easier	1964	2.50	5.00	10.00
43258	Ribbon of Darkness/Little Robin	1965	2.50	5.00	10.00
43377	Old Red/Matilda	1965	2.00	4.00	8.00
43428	While You're Dancing/Lonely Too Long	1965	2.00	4.00	8.00
43500	Count Me Out/Private Wilson White	1965	2.00	4.00	8.00
43651	Ain't I Right/My Own Native Land	1966	—	—	—
—Unreleased					
43680	The Shoe Goes On the Other Foot Tonight/It Kind of Reminds Me of You	1966	2.00	4.00	8.00
43845	No Tears Milady/Fly Butterfly Fly	1966	2.00	4.00	8.00
43870	Mr. Shorty/Tall Handsome Strangers	1966	2.00	4.00	8.00
44128	Tonight Carmen/Waiting in Reno	1967	—	3.00	6.00
44271	Gardenias in Her Hair/ In the Valley of the Rio Grande	1967	—	3.00	6.00
44509	Love Is in the Air/I've Been Leaving Everyday	1968	—	3.00	6.00
44633	I Walk Alone/Lily of the Valley	1968	—	3.00	6.00
44641	It Finally Happened/Big Mouthin' Around	1968	—	3.00	6.00
—By "Marty Robbins Jr. and Sr."					
44739	It's a Sin/I Feel Another Heartache Coming On	1969	—	2.50	5.00
44895	I Can't Say Goodbye/Hello Daily News	1969	—	2.50	5.00
44968	Girl from Spanish Town/Kingston Girl	1969	2.00	4.00	8.00
45024	Camelia/Virginia	1969	—	2.50	5.00
45091	My Woman, My Woman, My Wife/ Martha Ellen Jenkins	1970	—	2.50	5.00
45215	Jolie Girl/The City	1970	—	2.50	5.00
45273	Padre/At Times	1970	—	3.00	6.00
45346	Little Spot in Heaven/Wait a Little Longer Please, Jesus	1971	—	3.00	6.00
45377	The Chair/Seventeen Years	1971	—	2.50	5.00
45442	Early Morning Sunshine/ Another Day Has Gone By	1971	—	2.50	5.00
45520	The Best Part of Living/Gone with the Wind	1971	—	2.50	5.00
45668	I've Got a Woman's Love/A Little Spot in Heaven	1972	—	2.50	5.00
45775	Laura (What's He Got That I Ain't Got)/It Kind of Reminds Me of You	1973	—	2.50	5.00
JZSP 49158/48863 [DJ]	El Paso (2:58)/El Paso (4:37)	1959	10.00	20.00	40.00
DECCA					
33006	This Much a Man/ Guess I'll Stand Here Looking Dumb	1972	—	3.50	7.00
MCA					
40012	Franklin, Tennessee/Walking Piece of Heaven	1973	—	2.50	5.00
40067	A Man and a Train/Las Vegas, Nevada	1973	—	2.50	5.00
40134	Love Me/Crawling on My Knees	1973	—	2.50	5.00
40172	I'm Wanting To/Twentieth Century Drifter	1973	—	2.50	5.00
40236	Don't You Think/I Couldn't Believe It Was True	1974	—	2.50	5.00
40296	Two-Gun Daddy/Queen of the Big Rodeo	1974	—	2.50	5.00
40342	Life/It Takes Faith	1974	—	2.50	5.00
40425	These Are My Souvenirs/Shotgun Rider	1975	—	2.50	5.00
52197	Two Gun Daddy/Life	1983	—	2.50	5.00
WARNER BROS.					
29847	Honkytonk Man/Shotgun Rag	1982	—	2.00	4.00
—B-side by Johnny Gimble and the Texas Swing Band					

7-Inch Extended Plays

COLUMBIA

Number	Title (A Side/B Side)	Yr	VG	VG+	NM
H-1785	I'll Go On Alone/Crying 'Cause I Love You//I Couldn't Keep from Crying/A Half-Way Chance with You	1953	15.00	30.00	60.00
H-1785 [PS]	Marty Robbins	1953	15.00	30.00	60.00
B-2116	*Singing the Blues/I Can't Quit/Long Gone Lonesome Blues/Lorelei	1956	12.50	25.00	50.00
B-2116 [PS]	Singing the Blues	1956	12.50	25.00	50.00
B-2134	A White Sport Coat/Mean Mama Blues//Grown-Up Tears/Long Tall Sally	1957	10.00	20.00	40.00
B-2134 [PS]	A White Sport Coat	1957	10.00	20.00	40.00
B-2153	The Letter Edged in Black/The Little Rosewood Casket//The Dream of the Miner's Child/The Convict and the Rose	1957	7.50	15.00	30.00
B-2153 [PS]	Marty Robbins	1957	7.50	15.00	30.00
B-2808	I Couldn't Keep from Crying/Sing Me Something Sentimental//Tennessee Toddy/You Don't Owe Me a Thing	1957	12.50	25.00	50.00
B-2808 [PS]	Marty Robbins (Hall of Fame Series)	1957	12.50	25.00	50.00
B-2814	A White Sport Coat/Singing the Blues//The Story of My Life/I'm So Lonesome I Could Cry	1958	3.00	6.00	12.00
B-2814 [PS]	Marty Robbins	1958	3.00	6.00	12.00
7-8718	*The Wine Flowed Freely/Kinda Halfway Feel/ Worried/Love Is a Hurting Thing/Devil Woman/ In the Ashes of an Old Love Affair	196?	3.75	7.50	15.00
—Jukebox issue; small hole, plays at 33 1/3 rpm					
7-8718 [PS]	Devil Woman	196?	3.75	7.50	15.00
—Jukebox issue; small hole, plays at 33 1/3 rpm					
7-9020	*Everybody's Darling Plus Mine/Southern Dixie Flyer/Only a Picture Stops Time/Making Excuses/Rainbow/I Lived a Lifetime in a Day	196?	3.75	7.50	15.00
—Jukebox issue; small hole, plays at 33 1/3 rpm					
7-9020 [PS]	R.F.D.	196?	3.75	7.50	15.00
B-9761	Lovesick Blues/I'm So Lonesome I Could Cry// It's Too Late Now/Rose of Ol' Pawnee	1957	3.75	7.50	15.00
B-9761 [PS]	The Song of Robbins Vol. I	1957	3.75	7.50	15.00
B-9762	I Never Let You Cross My Mind/I Hang My Head and Cry//You Only Want Me When You're Lonely/Moanin' the Blues	1957	3.75	7.50	15.00
B-9762 [PS]	The Song of Robbins Vol. II	1957	3.75	7.50	15.00
B-9763	I'll Step Aside/All the World Is Lonely Now// Bouquet of Roses/Have I Told You Lately That I Love You?	1957	3.75	7.50	15.00
B-9763 [PS]	The Song of Robbins, Vol. III	1957	3.75	7.50	15.00
B-10871	*Song of the Islands/Now Is the Hour/Sweet Leilani/Aloha Oe	1957	3.75	7.50	15.00
B-10871 [PS]	Song of the Islands	1957	3.75	7.50	15.00
B-11891	Kaw-Liga/Waltz of the Wind//Then I Turned and Walked Slowly Away/A House with Everything But Love	1958	3.75	7.50	15.00

Number	Title (A Side/B Side)	Yr	VG	VG+	NM
B-11891 [PS]	Marty Robbins	1958	3.75	7.50	15.00
B-13491	El Paso/A Hundred and Sixty Acres//They're Hanging Me Tonight/The Strawberry Roan	1959	3.00	6.00	12.00
B-13491 [PS]	Gunfighter Ballads and Trail Songs, Vol. I	1959	3.00	6.00	12.00
B-13492	Big Iron/In the Valley//Running Gun/Utah Carol	1959	3.00	6.00	12.00
B-13492 [PS]	Gunfighter Ballads and Trail Songs, Vol. II	1959	3.00	6.00	12.00
B-13493	Cool Water/The Master's Call//Billy the Kid/The Little Green Valley	1959	3.75	7.50	15.00
B-13493 [PS]	Gunfighter Ballads and Trail Songs, Vol. III	1959	3.75	7.50	15.00
B-14811	*San Angelo/Prairie Fire/Streets of Laredo	1960	3.00	6.00	12.00
B-14811 [PS]	More Gunfighter Ballads and Trail Songs, Vol. I	1960	3.00	6.00	12.00
B-14812	*Five Brothers/Little Joe the Wrangler/Song of the Bandit/I've Got No Use for the Woman	1960	3.00	6.00	12.00
B-14812 [PS]	More Gunfighter Ballads and Trail Songs, Vol. II	1960	3.00	6.00	12.00
B-14813	*She Was Young and She Was Pretty/My Love/ Ride Cowboy Ride/This Peaceful Sod	1960	3.00	6.00	12.00
B-14813 [PS]	More Gunfighter Ballads and Trail Songs, Vol. III	1960	3.00	6.00	12.00

Albums

ARTCO

Number	Title (A Side/B Side)	Yr	VG	VG+	NM
110	The Best of Marty Robbins	1973	10.00	20.00	40.00
COLUMBIA					
GP 15 [(2)]	Marty's Country	1969	6.25	12.50	25.00
CL 976 [M]	The Song of Robbins	1957	25.00	50.00	100.00
—Red and black label with six "eye" logos					
CL 976 [M]	The Song of Robbins	1963	5.00	10.00	20.00
—Red label with "Guaranteed High Fidelity" or "360 Sound Mono"					
CL 1087 [M]	Song of the Islands	1957	30.00	60.00	120.00
—Red and black label with six "eye" logos					
CL 1087 [M]	Song of the Islands	1963	5.00	10.00	20.00
—Red label with "Guaranteed High Fidelity" or "360 Sound Mono"					
CL 1189 [M]	Marty Robbins	1958	20.00	40.00	80.00
—Red and black label with six "eye" logos					
CL 1189 [M]	Marty Robbins	1963	5.00	10.00	20.00
—Red label with "Guaranteed High Fidelity" or "360 Sound Mono"					
CL 1325 [M]	Marty's Greatest Hits	1959	20.00	40.00	80.00
—Red and black label with six "eye" logos					
CL 1325 [M]	Marty's Greatest Hits	1963	5.00	10.00	20.00
—Red label with "Guaranteed High Fidelity" or "360 Sound Mono"					
CL 1349 [M]	Gunfighter Ballads and Trail Songs	1959	7.50	15.00	30.00
—Red and black label with six "eye" logos					
CL 1349 [M]	Gunfighter Ballads and Trail Songs	1963	3.75	7.50	15.00
—Red label with "Guaranteed High Fidelity" or "360 Sound Mono"					
CL 1481 [M]	More Gunfighter Ballads and Trail Songs	1960	7.50	15.00	30.00
—Red and black label with six "eye" logos					
CL 1481 [M]	More Gunfighter Ballads and Trail Songs	1963	3.75	7.50	15.00
—Red label with "Guaranteed High Fidelity" or "360 Sound Mono"					
CL 1635 [M]	More Greatest Hits	1961	6.25	12.50	25.00
—Red and black label with six "eye" logos					
CL 1635 [M]	More Greatest Hits	1963	3.75	7.50	15.00
—Red label with "Guaranteed High Fidelity" or "360 Sound Mono"					
CL 1666 [M]	Just a Little Sentimental	1961	6.25	12.50	25.00
—Red and black label with six "eye" logos					
CL 1666 [M]	Just a Little Sentimental	1963	3.75	7.50	15.00
—Red label with "Guaranteed High Fidelity" or "360 Sound Mono"					
CL 1801 [M]	Marty After Midnight	1962	5.00	10.00	20.00
—Red label with "Guaranteed High Fidelity"					
CL 1801 [M]	Marty After Midnight	1962	12.50	25.00	50.00
—Red and black label with six "eye" logos					
CL 1801 [M]	Marty After Midnight	1965	3.75	7.50	15.00
—Red label with "360 Sound Mono"					
CL 1855 [M]	Portrait of Marty	1962	10.00	20.00	40.00
CL 1855/CS 8655	Portrait of Marty Bonus Photo	1962	7.50	15.00	30.00
CL 1918 [M]	Devil Woman	1962	6.25	12.50	25.00
—Red label with "Guaranteed High Fidelity"					
CL 1918 [M]	Devil Woman	1965	3.75	7.50	15.00
—Red label with "360 Sound Mono"					
CL 2040 [M]	Hawaii's Calling Me	1963	6.25	12.50	25.00
—Red label with "Guaranteed High Fidelity"					
CL 2040 [M]	Hawaii's Calling Me	1965	3.75	7.50	15.00
—Red label with "360 Sound Mono"					
CL 2072 [M]	Return of the Gunfighter	1963	5.00	10.00	20.00
—Red label with "Guaranteed High Fidelity"					
CL 2072 [M]	Return of the Gunfighter	1965	3.75	7.50	15.00
—Red label with "360 Sound Mono"					
CL 2176 [M]	Island Woman	1964	7.50	15.00	30.00
—Red label with "Guaranteed High Fidelity"					
CL 2176 [M]	Island Woman	1965	5.00	10.00	20.00
—Red label with "360 Sound Mono"					
CL 2220 [M]	R.F.D.	1964	5.00	10.00	20.00
—Red label with "Guaranteed High Fidelity"					
CL 2220 [M]	R.F.D.	1965	3.75	7.50	15.00
—Red label with "360 Sound Mono"					
CL 2304 [M]	Turn the Lights Down Low	1965	3.75	7.50	15.00
—Red label with "360 Sound Mono"					
CL 2304 [M]	Turn the Lights Down Low	1965	6.25	12.50	25.00
—Red label with "Guaranteed High Fidelity"					
CL 2448 [M]	What God Has Done	1966	3.75	7.50	15.00
CL 2527 [M]	The Drifter	1966	3.75	7.50	15.00
CL 2601 [10]	Rock 'N Roll 'N Robbins	1956	250.00	500.00	1000.
CL 2645 [M]	My Kind of Country	1967	6.25	12.50	25.00
CL 2725 [M]	Tonight Carmen	1967	7.50	15.00	30.00
CL 2735 [M]	Christmas with Marty Robbins	1967	12.50	25.00	50.00
CL 2817 [M]	By the Time I Get to Phoenix	1968	15.00	30.00	60.00
CS 8158 [S]	Gunfighter Ballads and Trail Songs	1959	10.00	20.00	40.00
—Red and black label with six "eye" logos					
CS 8158 [S]	Gunfighter Ballads and Trail Songs	1963	5.00	10.00	20.00
—Red label with "360 Sound Stereo"					
CS 8158 [S]	Gunfighter Ballads and Trail Songs	1971	2.50	5.00	10.00
—Orange label					
PC 8158	Gunfighter Ballads and Trail Songs	198?	2.00	4.00	8.00
—Reissue with new prefix					
CS 8272 [S]	More Gunfighter Ballads and Trail Songs	1960	10.00	20.00	40.00
—Red and black label with six "eye" logos					
CS 8272 [S]	More Gunfighter Ballads and Trail Songs	1963	5.00	10.00	20.00
—Red label with "360 Sound Stereo"					
CS 8272 [S]	More Gunfighter Ballads and Trail Songs	1971	2.50	5.00	10.00
—Orange label					

Number	Title (A Side/B Side)	Yr	VG	VG+	NM
❏ PC 8272	More Gunfighter Ballads and Trail Songs	198?	2.00	4.00	8.00
—Reissue with new prefix					
❏ CS 8435 [S]	More Greatest Hits	1961	7.50	15.00	30.00
—Red and black label with six "eye" logos					
❏ CS 8435 [S]	More Greatest Hits	1963	5.00	10.00	20.00
—Red label with "360 Sound Stereo"					
❏ CS 8435 [S]	More Greatest Hits	1971	2.50	5.00	10.00
—Orange label					
❏ PC 8435	More Greatest Hits	198?	2.00	4.00	8.00
—Reissue with new prefix					
❏ CS 8466 [S]	Just a Little Sentimental	1961	7.50	15.00	30.00
—Red and black label with six "eye" logos					
❏ CS 8466 [S]	Just a Little Sentimental	1963	5.00	10.00	20.00
—Red label with "360 Sound Stereo"					
❏ CS 8601 [S]	Marty After Midnight	1962	7.50	15.00	30.00
—Red label with "360 Sound Stereo" in black					
❏ CS 8601 [S]	Marty After Midnight	1962	20.00	40.00	80.00
—Red and black label with six "eye" logos					
❏ CS 8601 [S]	Marty After Midnight	1965	5.00	10.00	20.00
—Red label with "360 Sound Stereo" in white					
❏ CS 8639 [P]	Marty's Greatest Hits	1962	7.50	15.00	30.00
—Red label with "360 Sound Stereo" in black					
❏ CS 8639 [P]	Marty's Greatest Hits	1965	5.00	10.00	20.00
—Red label with "360 Sound Stereo" in white					
❏ CS 8639 [P]	Marty's Greatest Hits	1970	2.50	5.00	10.00
—Orange label					
❏ PC 8639	Marty's Greatest Hits	198?	2.00	4.00	8.00
—Reissue with new prefix					
❏ CS 8655 [S]	Portrait of Marty	1962	12.50	25.00	50.00
❏ CS 8718 [S]	Devil Woman	1962	7.50	15.00	30.00
—Red label with "360 Sound Stereo" in black					
❏ CS 8718 [S]	Devil Woman	1965	5.00	10.00	20.00
—Red label with "360 Sound Stereo" in white					
❏ CS 8718 [S]	Devil Woman	1970	2.50	5.00	10.00
—Orange label					
❏ CS 8840 [S]	Hawaii's Calling Me	1963	7.50	15.00	30.00
—Red label with "360 Sound Stereo" in black					
❏ CS 8840 [S]	Hawaii's Calling Me	1965	5.00	10.00	20.00
—Red label with "360 Sound Stereo" in white					
❏ CS 8872 [S]	Return of the Gunfighter	1963	6.25	12.50	25.00
—Red label with "360 Sound Stereo" in black					
❏ CS 8872 [S]	Return of the Gunfighter	1965	5.00	10.00	20.00
—Red label with "360 Sound Stereo" in white					
❏ CS 8872 [S]	Return of the Gunfighter	1970	2.50	5.00	10.00
—Orange label					
❏ CS 8976 [S]	Island Woman	1964	10.00	20.00	40.00
—Red label with "360 Sound Stereo" in black					
❏ CS 8976 [S]	Island Woman	1965	7.50	15.00	30.00
—Red label with "360 Sound Stereo" in white					
❏ CS 9020 [S]	R.F.D.	1964	6.25	12.50	25.00
—Red label with "360 Sound Stereo" in black					
❏ CS 9020 [S]	R.F.D.	1965	5.00	10.00	20.00
—Red label with "360 Sound Stereo" in white					
❏ CS 9104 [S]	Turn the Lights Down Low	1965	5.00	10.00	20.00
—Red label with "360 Sound Stereo" in white					
❏ CS 9104 [S]	Turn the Lights Down Low	1965	7.50	15.00	30.00
—Red label with "360 Sound Stereo" in black					
❏ CS 9248 [S]	What God Has Done	1966	5.00	10.00	20.00
—Red "360 Sound" label					
❏ CS 9248 [S]	What God Has Done	1970	2.50	5.00	10.00
—Orange label					
❏ CS 9327 [S]	The Drifter	1966	5.00	10.00	20.00
—Red "360 Sound" label					
❏ CS 9327 [S]	The Drifter	1970	2.50	5.00	10.00
—Orange label					
❏ CS 9421 [R]	The Song of Robbins	1967	3.75	7.50	15.00
—Red "360 Sound" label					
❏ CS 9421 [R]	The Song of Robbins	1970	2.50	5.00	10.00
—Orange label					
❏ CS 9425 [R]	Song of the Islands	1967	3.75	7.50	15.00
❏ CS 9445 [R]	My Kind of Country	1967	5.00	10.00	20.00
❏ CS 9525 [S]	Tonight Carmen	1967	5.00	10.00	20.00
—Red "360 Sound" label					
❏ CS 9525 [S]	Tonight Carmen	1970	2.50	5.00	10.00
—Orange label					
❏ 3C 9535	Christmas with Marty Robbins	198?	2.50	5.00	10.00
—Budget-line reissue					
❏ CS 9535 [S]	Christmas with Marty Robbins	1967	7.50	15.00	30.00
❏ CS 9617 [M]	By the Time I Get to Phoenix	1968	12.50	25.00	50.00
—"Special Mono Radio Station Copy" with stereo number and "Mono" on white label					
❏ CS 9617 [S]	By the Time I Get to Phoenix	1968	5.00	10.00	20.00
❏ CS 9725	I Walk Alone	1968	5.00	10.00	20.00
—Red "360 Sound" label					
❏ CS 9725	I Walk Alone	1970	2.50	5.00	10.00
—Orange label					
❏ CS 9811	It's a Sin	1969	5.00	10.00	20.00
—Red "360 Sound" label					
❏ CS 9811	It's a Sin	1970	2.50	5.00	10.00
—Orange label					
❏ CS 9978	My Woman, My Woman, My Wife	1970	3.75	7.50	15.00
—Orange label					
❏ CS 9978	My Woman, My Woman, My Wife	1970	5.00	10.00	20.00
—Red "360 Sound" label					
❏ PC 30316	El Paso	198?	2.00	4.00	8.00
—Reissue of Harmony 30316					
❏ C 30571	Marty Robbins' Greatest Hits Vol. III	1971	3.75	7.50	15.00
❏ PC 30571	Marty Robbins' Greatest Hits Vol. III	198?	2.00	4.00	8.00
—Budget-line reissue					
❏ C 30816	Today	1971	3.75	7.50	15.00
❏ G 30881 [(2)]	The World of Marty Robbins	1971	5.00	10.00	20.00
❏ KC 31341	Bound for Old Mexico (Great Hits from South of the Border)	1973	3.75	7.50	15.00
❏ CG 31361 [(2)]	All Time Greatest Hits	1972	4.50	9.00	18.00
❏ KG 31361 [(2)]	Marty Robbins' All-Time Greatest Hits	1972	5.00	10.00	20.00
❏ KC 31628	I've Got a Woman's Love	1972	3.75	7.50	15.00
❏ KC 32586	Have I Told You Lately That I Love You	1974	3.75	7.50	15.00

Number	Title (A Side/B Side)	Yr	VG	VG+	NM
❏ KC 33476	No Sign of Loneliness Here	1976	3.00	6.00	12.00
❏ CG 33630 [(2)]	Gunfighter Ballads and Trail Songs/My Woman, My Woman, My Wife	1976	3.75	7.50	15.00
❏ PC 34303	El Paso City	1976	3.00	6.00	12.00
—No bar code on cover					
❏ PC 34303	El Paso City	198?	2.00	4.00	8.00
—With bar code on cover					
❏ PC 34448	Adios Amigo	1977	3.00	6.00	12.00
—No bar code on cover					
❏ PC 34448	Adios Amigo	198?	2.00	4.00	8.00
—With bar code on cover					
❏ KC 35040	Don't Let Me Touch You	1977	3.00	6.00	12.00
❏ JC 35446	The Performer	1979	3.00	6.00	12.00
❏ KC 35629	Greatest Hits Vol. IV	1978	3.00	6.00	12.00
❏ JC 36085	All Around Cowboy	1979	3.00	6.00	12.00
❏ PC 36085	All Around Cowboy	198?	2.00	4.00	8.00
—Budget-line reissue					
❏ JC 36507	With Love	1980	3.00	6.00	12.00
❏ JC 36860	Everything I've Always Wanted	1981	3.00	6.00	12.00
❏ FC 37353	Encore	1981	3.00	6.00	12.00
❏ PC 37353	Encore	198?	2.00	4.00	8.00
—Budget-line reissue					
❏ FC 37541	The Legend	1982	3.00	6.00	12.00
❏ PC 37541	The Legend	1985	2.00	4.00	8.00
—Budget-line reissue					
❏ FC 37995	Come Back to Me	1982	3.00	6.00	12.00
❏ PC 37995	Come Back to Me	198?	2.00	4.00	8.00
—Budget-line reissue					
❏ FC 38309	Biggest Hits	1982	3.00	6.00	12.00
❏ FC 38603	Some Memories Just Won't Die	1983	3.00	6.00	12.00
❏ C2 38870 [(2)]	A Lifetime of Song 1951-1982	1983	3.75	7.50	15.00
❏ KC2 39575 [(2)]	Long, Long Ago	1984	3.75	7.50	15.00
COLUMBIA LIMITED EDITION					
❏ LE 10022	Portrait of Marty	197?	2.50	5.00	10.00
❏ LE 10030	It's a Sin	197?	2.50	5.00	10.00
❏ LE 10033	My Kind of Country	197?	2.50	5.00	10.00
❏ LE 10045	By the Time I Get to Phoenix	197?	2.50	5.00	10.00
❏ LE 10046	Today	197?	2.50	5.00	10.00
❏ LE 10144	R.F.D.	197?	2.50	5.00	10.00
❏ LE 10145	Turn the Lights Down Low	197?	2.50	5.00	10.00
❏ LE 10189	Tonight Carmen	197?	2.50	5.00	10.00
❏ LE 10575	From the Heart	197?	2.50	5.00	10.00
❏ LE 10576	Streets of Laredo	197?	2.50	5.00	10.00
❏ LE 10577	The Story of My Life	197?	2.50	5.00	10.00
❏ LE 10578	The Song of Robbins	197?	2.50	5.00	10.00
❏ LE 10579	Devil Woman	197?	2.50	5.00	10.00
COLUMBIA MUSICAL TREASURY					
❏ P5S 5812 [(5)]	Marty	1972	10.00	20.00	40.00
COLUMBIA RECORD CLUB					
❏ DS 445	Bend in the River	1968	10.00	20.00	40.00
COLUMBIA SPECIAL PRODUCTS					
❏ C 10980 [S]	Christmas with Marty Robbins	1972	3.75	7.50	15.00
—Stereo reissue; "Distributed by Apex Rendezvous, Inc." on back cover					
❏ C 11122	Marty's Greatest Hits	1972	3.00	6.00	12.00
❏ C 11311	By the Time I Get to Phoenix	1972	3.75	7.50	15.00
❏ C 11513	By the Time I Get to Phoenix	1973	3.75	7.50	15.00
❏ P 12416	Marty Robbins' Own Favorites	1974	3.75	7.50	15.00
❏ P 13358	Christmas with Marty Robbins	1976	3.00	6.00	12.00
❏ P 14035	Legendary Music Man	1977	3.00	6.00	12.00
❏ P 14613	The Best of Marty Robbins	1978	2.50	5.00	10.00
❏ P 15594	The Number One Cowboy	1981	2.50	5.00	10.00
❏ P 15812	Marty Robbins' Best	1982	2.50	5.00	10.00
❏ P 16561	Reflections	1982	2.50	5.00	10.00
❏ 3P 16578 [(3)]	Classics	1983	5.00	10.00	20.00
❏ P 16914	Country Classics	1983	2.50	5.00	10.00
❏ P 17120	Sincerely	1983	2.50	5.00	10.00
❏ P 17136	Forever Yours	1983	2.50	5.00	10.00
❏ P 17137	That Country Feeling	1983	2.50	5.00	10.00
❏ P 17138	Banquet of Songs	1983	2.50	5.00	10.00
❏ P 17159	The Great Marty Robbins	1983	2.50	5.00	10.00
❏ P 17206	The Legendary Marty Robbins	1983	2.50	5.00	10.00
❏ P 17209	Country Cowboy	1983	2.50	5.00	10.00
❏ P 17367	Song of the Islands	1983	2.50	5.00	10.00
DECCA					
❏ DL 75389	This Much a Man	1972	3.75	7.50	15.00
HARMONY					
❏ HS 11338	Singing the Blues	1969	3.75	7.50	15.00
❏ HS 11409	The Story of My Life	1970	3.75	7.50	15.00
❏ KH 30316	El Paso	1971	3.00	6.00	12.00
❏ KH 31257	Marty Robbins Favorites	1972	3.00	6.00	12.00
❏ H 31258	Songs of the Islands	1972	5.00	10.00	20.00
❏ KH 32286	Streets of Laredo	1973	3.00	6.00	12.00
MCA					
❏ 61	This Much a Man	1973	3.00	6.00	12.00
—Reissue of Decca LP					
❏ 342	Marty Robbins	1973	3.75	7.50	15.00
❏ 421	Good'n Country	1974	3.75	7.50	15.00
READER'S DIGEST					
❏ RDA-054/A [(5)]	His Greatest Hits and Finest Performances	1983	7.50	15.00	30.00
TIME-LIFE					
❏ STW-109	Country Music	1981	3.00	6.00	12.00

ROBBINS, MEL
45s
ARGO

Number	Title (A Side/B Side)	Yr	VG	VG+	NM
❏ 5340	Save It/To Know You	1959	25.00	50.00	100.00

ROBBS, THE   Also see DEE ROBB.
45s
ABC

Number	Title (A Side/B Side)	Yr	VG	VG+	NM
❏ 11270	I'll Never Get Enough/It All Comes Back	1970	—	3.00	6.00
ABC DUNHILL					
❏ 4208	Write to You/Movin'	1969	2.50	5.00	10.00
❏ 4233	Written in the Dust/Last of the Wine	1970	2.00	4.00	8.00
ATLANTIC					
❏ 2511	Castles in the Air/I Don't Want to Discuss It	1968	2.50	5.00	10.00
❏ 2578	A Good Time Song/Changin' Winds	1968	2.50	5.00	10.00

R

Number	Title (A Side/B Side)	Yr	VG	VG+	NM
MERCURY					
❏ 72579	Race with the Wind/In a Funny Sort of Way	1966	2.50	5.00	10.00
❏ 72616	I Don't Feel Alone/Next Time You Call Me	1966	2.50	5.00	10.00
❏ 72641	Bittersweet/End of the Week	1966	2.50	5.00	10.00
❏ 72641 [PS]	Bittersweet/End of the Week	1966	3.75	7.50	15.00
❏ 72678	Rapid Transit/Cynthia Loves	1967	2.50	5.00	10.00
❏ 72730	Girls, Girls/Violets of Dawn	1967	2.50	5.00	10.00
Albums					
MERCURY					
❏ MG-21130 [M]	The Robbs	1967	10.00	20.00	40.00
❏ SR-61130 [S]	The Robbs	1967	7.50	15.00	30.00
ROBBY AND THE ROBBINS					
45s					
TODD					
❏ 1089	Surfer's Life/She Cried	1963	10.00	20.00	40.00
ROBERT AND JOHNNY					
45s					
OLD TOWN					
❏ 1021	I Believe You/Train to Paradise	1956	12.50	25.00	50.00
❏ 1029	You're Mine/Million Dollar Bills	1956	10.00	20.00	40.00
❏ 1038	Don't Do It/Baby Come Home	1957	10.00	20.00	40.00
❏ 1043	Broken Hearted Man/Indian Marriage	1957	10.00	20.00	40.00
❏ 1047	We Belong Together/In the Rain	1958	12.50	25.00	50.00
❏ 1052	I Believe in You/Marry Me	1958	10.00	20.00	40.00
❏ 1052	I Know/Marry Me	1958	10.00	20.00	40.00
❏ 1058	Eternity with You/I'm Truly, Truly Yours	1958	7.50	15.00	30.00
❏ 1065	Give Me the Key to Your Heart/Truly in Love	1959	7.50	15.00	30.00
❏ 1068	Dream Girl/Oh My Love	1959	7.50	15.00	30.00
❏ 1072	Wear This Ring/Bad Dan	1959	7.50	15.00	30.00
❏ 1078	Hear My Heartbeat/Try Me Pretty Baby	1960	6.25	12.50	25.00
❏ 1086	We Belong Together/In the Rain	1960	6.25	12.50	25.00
❏ 1100	You're Mine/Please Me Please	1961	5.00	10.00	20.00
❏ 1108	Togetherness/I Got You	1961	5.00	10.00	20.00
❏ 1117	Wear This Ring/Broken Hearted Man	1962	5.00	10.00	20.00
SUE					
❏ 792	A Perfect Wife/Brown, Pretty Brown Eyes	1963	6.25	12.50	25.00
ROBERTINO					
45s					
4 CORNERS OF THE WORLD					
❏ 101	Santo Natale/Caro Gesu Bambino	1963	2.00	4.00	8.00
KAPP					
❏ 416	O Sole Mio/Romantica	1961	2.00	4.00	8.00
❏ 445	Ave Maria/Santa Lucia	1962	2.00	4.00	8.00
❏ 474	Papa/Parlami D'Amore	1962	2.00	4.00	8.00
Albums					
KAPP					
❏ KL-1252 [M]	O Sole Mio	1962	3.75	7.50	15.00
❏ KL-1293 [M]	The Young Italian Singing Sensation	1962	3.75	7.50	15.00
❏ KL-1338 [M]	Italia Mia	1963	3.75	7.50	15.00
❏ KL-1471 [M]	The Best of Robertino	1966	3.00	6.00	12.00
❏ KS-3252 [S]	O Sole Mio	1962	5.00	10.00	20.00
❏ KS-3293 [S]	The Young Italian Singing Sensation	1962	5.00	10.00	20.00
❏ KS-3338 [S]	Italia Mia	1963	5.00	10.00	20.00
❏ KS-3471 [S]	The Best of Robertino	1966	3.75	7.50	15.00
ROBERTS, ART					
45s					
IMPERIAL					
❏ 5504	Give Her the Ax, Max/Terrible Ivan	1958	6.25	12.50	25.00
ROBERTS, AUSTIN					
45s					
ABC					
❏ 11289	Live Is for Living/I Can Make It Better	1971	—	3.00	6.00
ARISTA					
❏ 0335	Don't Stop Me Baby/Question of Love	1978	—	2.00	4.00
CHELSEA					
❏ BCBO-0053	Baby Don't You Walk Out on Me/One Word	1973	—	2.00	4.00
❏ 78-0101	Something's Wrong with Me/My Song	1972	—	2.50	5.00
❏ 78-0110	Keep On Singing/Take Away the Sunshine	1973	—	2.50	5.00
❏ 78-0123	The Last Thing on My Mind/Losing You Is More Than I Can Stand	1973	—	2.50	5.00
❏ AMBO-0129	Something's Wrong with Me/Keep On Singing	1973	—	2.00	4.00
—Gold Standard Series reissue					
❏ BCBO-0219	Somethin' to Believe In/Nothing Seems the Same When You're Not Here	1974	—	2.00	4.00
PHILIPS					
❏ 40560	I'll Smile/Mary and Me	1968	—	3.00	6.00
❏ 40586	Ricky Ticky Ta Ta Ta/No Last Goodbyes	1969	—	3.00	6.00
❏ 40638	Runaway-Just a Little (Medley)/Sarah	1969	—	3.00	6.00
❏ 40649	Baltimore/Sarah	1969	—	3.00	6.00
❏ 40660	One Night Ann/The Other Side	1970	—	3.00	6.00
PRIVATE STOCK					
❏ 45,020	Rocky/You Got the Power	1975	—	2.00	4.00
❏ 45,051	Fool/Children of the Rain	1975	—	2.00	4.00
❏ 45,061	Is There Somethin' Goin' On/Just to Make You Mine	1975	—	2.00	4.00
❏ 45,080	This Time I'm In It for Love/Susannah	1976	—	2.00	4.00
Albums					
CHELSEA					
❏ BCL1-0199	The Last Thing on My Mind	1973	3.00	6.00	12.00
❏ CES-1004	Austin Roberts	1972	3.00	6.00	12.00
NEW PAX					
❏ NP-33016	8 Days (A Personal Journey)	1977	3.00	6.00	12.00
PRIVATE STOCK					
❏ PS-5000	Rocky	1975	3.00	6.00	12.00

Number	Title (A Side/B Side)	Yr	VG	VG+	NM
ROBERTS, DEREK					
45s					
ROULETTE					
❏ 4656	There Won't Be Any Snow (Christmas In The Jungle)/A World Without Sunshine	1965	2.50	5.00	10.00
ROBERTS, LANCE					
45s					
SUN					
❏ 348	The Good Guy Always Wins/The Time Is Right	1960	5.00	10.00	20.00
ROBERTS, LOU					
45s					
GENIE					
❏ 101	Rattle Snake Shake/(B-side unknown)	1965	20.00	40.00	80.00
MGM					
❏ 13347	Gettin' Ready/You Fooled Me	1965	7.50	15.00	30.00
❏ 13387	Don't Count on Me/Ten to One	1965	6.25	12.50	25.00
ROBERTS, ROCKY, AND THE AIREDALES					
45s					
BRUNSWICK					
❏ 55357	Buzz Buzz Buzz/Too Much	1967	2.50	5.00	10.00
❏ 55368	Tell Me/Gotta Thing Going	1968	2.50	5.00	10.00
Albums					
BRUNSWICK					
❏ BL 754133	Rocky Roberts and the Airedales	1968	5.00	10.00	20.00
ROBERTS, TINA					
45s					
SECURITY					
❏ 1366	One Way or the Other//(B-side unknown)	196?	250.00	500.00	1000.
ROBINS, THE (1) Vocal group from Los Angeles. Part of the group splintered off and became the core of THE COASTERS.					
45s					
ATCO					
❏ 6059	Smokey Joe's Cafe/Just Like a Fool	1956	12.50	25.00	50.00
CROWN					
❏ 106	I Made a Vow/Double Crossing Baby	1954	100.00	200.00	400.00
❏ 120	Key to My Heart/All I Do Is Rock	1954	75.00	150.00	300.00
KNIGHT					
❏ 2001	Quarter to Twelve/Pretty Little Dolly	1958	12.50	25.00	50.00
❏ 2008	It's Never Too Late/A Little Bird Told Me	1958	20.00	40.00	80.00
RCA VICTOR					
❏ 47-5175	(Now and Then There's) A Fool Such As I/My Heart's the Biggest Fool	1953	125.00	250.00	500.00
❏ 47-5271	Oh Why/All Night Baby	1953	100.00	200.00	400.00
❏ 47-5434	How Would You Know/Let's Go to the Dance	1953	100.00	200.00	400.00
❏ 47-5486	My Baby Done Told Me/I'll Do It	1953	75.00	150.00	300.00
❏ 47-5489	Ten Days in Jail/Empty Bottles	1953	50.00	100.00	200.00
❏ 47-5564	Get It Off Your Mind/Don't Stop Now	1953	50.00	100.00	200.00
SPARK					
❏ 103	Riot in Cell Block #9/Wrap It Up	1954	75.00	150.00	300.00
—Copies on yellow labels are bootlegs					
❏ 107	Loop De Loop Mambo/Framed	1954	25.00	50.00	100.00
—Red label					
❏ 107	Loop De Loop Mambo/Framed	1954	75.00	150.00	300.00
—Silver top label					
❏ 110	If Teardrops Were Kisses/Whadaya Want	1955	25.00	50.00	100.00
—Blue label					
❏ 110	If Teardrops Were Kisses/Whadaya Want	1955	75.00	150.00	300.00
—Red label					
❏ 113	One Kiss/I Love Paris	1955	75.00	150.00	300.00
❏ 116	I Must Be Dreamin'/The Hatchet Man	1955	12.50	25.00	50.00
—Yellow label					
❏ 116	I Must Be Dreamin'/The Hatchet Man	1955	50.00	100.00	200.00
—Red label					
❏ 122	Smokey Joe's Cafe/Just Like a Fool	1955	87.50	175.00	350.00
WHIPPET					
❏ 200	Cherry Lips/Out of the Picture	1956	20.00	40.00	80.00
❏ 201	Hurt Me/Merry-Go-Rock	1956	17.50	35.00	70.00
❏ 203	That Old Black Magic/Since I First Met You	1956	17.50	35.00	70.00
❏ 206	A Fool in Love/All of a Sudden My Heart Sings	1957	17.50	35.00	70.00
❏ 208	Every Night/Where's the Fire	1957	17.50	35.00	70.00
❏ 211	In My Dreams/Keep Your Mind on Me	1957	17.50	35.00	70.00
❏ 212	Snowball/You Wanted Fun	1958	17.50	35.00	70.00
Albums					
GNP CRESCENDO					
❏ GNPS-9034	The Best of the Robins	1975	3.75	7.50	15.00
WHIPPET					
❏ WLP-703 [M]	Rock 'n' Roll with the Robins	1958	200.00	400.00	800.00
ROBINS, THE (2)					
45s					
ARDENT					
❏ 106	Batman/Batarang	1966	7.50	15.00	30.00
ROBINS, THE (3)					
45s					
LAVENDER					
❏ 001	The White Cliffs of Dover/How Many More Times	1961	10.00	20.00	40.00
❏ 002	Magic of a Dream/Mary Lou Loves to Hootchy Kootchy Koo	1961	10.00	20.00	40.00
ROBINS, THE (4)					
45s					
NEW HIT					
❏ 3010	Johnny/Doing the Popeye	1963	3.75	7.50	15.00
SWEET TAFFY					
❏ 400	Johnny/Doing the Popeye	1963	7.50	15.00	30.00
ROBINS, THE (U) These could be by any of the above, or none of the above.					
45s					
ARVEE					
❏ 5001	Just Like That/Whole Lot of Imagination	1960	6.25	12.50	25.00
❏ 5013	Live Wire Suzie/Oh No	1960	6.25	12.50	25.00

Number	Title (A Side/B Side)	Yr	VG	VG+	NM
DOT					
❏ 16519	Blue Grass Blues/Top 40 Blues	1963	3.00	6.00	12.00
GONE					
❏ 5101	Baby Love/We Loved	1961	7.50	15.00	30.00
MUSICOR					
❏ 1050	Cry Over You/Lucy Watusi	1964	3.75	7.50	15.00

ROBINSON, BILL, AND THE QUAILS
45s

Number	Title (A Side/B Side)	Yr	VG	VG+	NM
DATE					
❏ 1620	Do I Love You/Lay My Head on Your Shoulder	1969	2.50	5.00	10.00
DELUXE					
❏ 6030	Lonely Star/Quit Pushin'	1954	50.00	100.00	200.00
❏ 6047	I Know She's Gone/ Baby Don't Want Me No More	1954	75.00	150.00	300.00
❏ 6057	A Little Bit of Love/ Somewhere Somebody Cares	1954	50.00	100.00	200.00
❏ 6059	Why Do I Wait/Heaven Is the Place	1954	50.00	100.00	200.00
❏ 6074	Love of My Life/Oh Sugar	1955	37.50	75.00	150.00
❏ 6085	The Things She Used to Do/Pretty Huggin' Baby	1955	17.50	35.00	70.00
—As "The Quails"					

ROBINSON, FLOYD
45s

Number	Title (A Side/B Side)	Yr	VG	VG+	NM
DOT					
❏ 16290	The Art of Making Love/Don't Let Me Fall	1961	3.00	6.00	12.00
❏ 16352	I Need You/Show Boat	1961	3.00	6.00	12.00
GROOVE					
❏ 58-0040	My Little Martian/Surprise	1964	20.00	40.00	80.00
JAMIE					
❏ 1186	Mother Nature/ Is There Something I Ought to Know?	1961	3.75	7.50	15.00
RCA VICTOR					
❏ 47-7529	Makin' Love/My Girl	1959	5.00	10.00	20.00
❏ 47-7637	Tonight You Belong to Me/Let It Be Me	1959	3.75	7.50	15.00
❏ 47-7685	Little Sir Echo/Alphabet Song	1960	3.75	7.50	15.00
❏ 47-7693	Tattletale/I Believe in Love	1960	6.25	12.50	25.00
❏ 47-7736	Boys and Girls/Sonja	1960	3.75	7.50	15.00
❏ 47-7789	A Girl Like You/Why Can't It Go On	1960	3.75	7.50	15.00
❏ 47-7827	Out of Gas/Magic Lamp	1960	7.50	15.00	30.00
UNITED ARTISTS					
❏ 534	Heartaches/I've Got a Sweetheart	1963	3.00	6.00	12.00
❏ 986	Sidewalk Surfer/Motorcycle Man	1966	3.75	7.50	15.00
7-Inch Extended Plays					
RCA VICTOR					
❏ EPA-4350	(contents unknown)	1959	12.50	25.00	50.00
❏ EPA-4350 [PS]	Makin' Love	1959	12.50	25.00	50.00
Albums					
RCA VICTOR					
❏ LPM-2162 [M]	Floyd Robinson	1960	20.00	40.00	80.00
❏ LSP-2162 [S]	Floyd Robinson	1960	30.00	60.00	120.00

ROBINSON, FREDDY
45s

Number	Title (A Side/B Side)	Yr	VG	VG+	NM
CHECKER					
❏ 1143	The Creeper/Go Go Girl	1966	2.50	5.00	10.00
LIBERTY					
❏ 56214	Carmalita/Stone Stallion	1970	—	3.00	6.00
LIMELIGHT					
❏ 3005	Not Like Now/Five Feet of Lovin'	1963	3.00	6.00	12.00
MERCURY					
❏ 71270	Be Mine/You and Me	1958	3.00	6.00	12.00
PACIFIC JAZZ					
❏ 88152	Before Six/The Coming Atlantis	1969	—	3.00	6.00
❏ 88155	Black Fox/The Oogue Boogum Song	1970	—	3.00	6.00
QUEEN					
❏ 24005	The Buzzard/The Hawk	196?	2.50	5.00	10.00
Albums					
ENTERPRISE					
❏ ENS-1025	Freddy Robinson at the Drive-In	1972	3.00	6.00	12.00
PACIFIC JAZZ					
❏ ST-20162	The Coming Atlantis	1970	3.75	7.50	15.00
❏ ST-20176	Hot Fun in the Summertime	1971	3.75	7.50	15.00

ROBINSON, JOHNNY
45s

Number	Title (A Side/B Side)	Yr	VG	VG+	NM
EPIC					
❏ 10578	God Is Love/Kansas City	1970	2.50	5.00	10.00
❏ 10607	Person to Person/Lady Doctor	1970	2.50	5.00	10.00
MERCURY					
❏ 72434	I Gotta Kick the Habit (Part 1)/ I Gotta Kick the Habit (Part 2)	1965	5.00	10.00	20.00
OKEH					
❏ 7307	Gone But Not Forgotten/ I Need Your Love So Bad	1968	25.00	50.00	100.00
❏ 7317	Poor Man/When a Man Cries	1968	5.00	10.00	20.00
❏ 7328	Green Green Grass of Home/ You've Been With Him	1969	5.00	10.00	20.00
Albums					
EPIC					
❏ BN 26528	Memphis High	1970	5.00	10.00	20.00

ROBINSON, MARK
45s

Number	Title (A Side/B Side)	Yr	VG	VG+	NM
JAMIE					
❏ 1103	Pretty Jane/Want Me	1958	6.25	12.50	25.00
TEE GEE					
❏ 104	Pretty Jane/Want Me	1958	10.00	20.00	40.00

ROBINSON, SMOKEY Also see THE MIRACLES; RON AND BILL.
12-Inch Singles

Number	Title (A Side/B Side)	Yr	VG	VG+	NM
MOTOWN					
❏ M00004D1	Vitamin U/Chalk It Up	1977	5.00	10.00	20.00
—B-side by Jerry Butler					
❏ 00027	Get Ready/(Instrumental)	1979	3.00	6.00	12.00

Number	Title (A Side/B Side)	Yr	VG	VG+	NM
❏ PR-92 [DJ]	Tell Me Tomorrow/Right in the Middle (vocal) (instrumental)	1982	2.50	5.00	10.00
—B-side by Bettye Lavette					
❏ L33-17828 [DJ]	(It's the) Same Old Love (3 versions)	1990	—	3.00	6.00
❏ L33-18141 [DJ]	Everything You Touch (3 versions)/ It's the Same Old Feeling	1990	—	3.00	6.00
❏ 50109	Everything You Touch (3 versions)/ It's the Same Old Feeling	1990	—	3.50	7.00
TAMLA					
❏ 145 [DJ]	And I Don't Love You (7:10)/ And I Don't Love You (Dub)	1984	2.00	4.00	8.00
45s					
COLUMBIA					
❏ 07727	I Know You by Heart/ Could I Have Your Autograph	1988	—	—	3.00
—With Dolly Parton					
MOTOWN					
❏ 914	(It's the) Same Old Love/(Instrumental)	1990	—	2.00	4.00
❏ 1877	Just to See Her/I'm Gonna Love You Like There's No Tomorrow	1987	—	—	3.00
❏ 1877 [PS]	Just to See Her/I'm Gonna Love You Like There's No Tomorrow	1987	2.00	4.00	8.00
❏ 1897	One Heartbeat/Love Will Set You Free (Theme from Solarbabies)	1987	—	—	3.00
❏ 1897 [PS]	One Heartbeat/Love Will Set You Free (Theme from Solarbabies)	1987	—	3.00	6.00
❏ 1911	What's Too Much/ I've Made Love to You a Thousand Times	1987	—	—	3.00
❏ 1911 [PS]	What's Too Much/ I've Made Love to You a Thousand Times	1987	—	2.50	5.00
❏ 1925	Love Don't Give No Reason/ Hanging On by a Thread	1988	—	—	3.00
❏ 1925 [PS]	Love Don't Give No Reason/ Hanging On by a Thread	1988	—	2.50	5.00
SBK					
❏ 07379	Double Good Everything/ Guess What I Got for You	1991	—	2.00	4.00
TAMLA					
❏ 1601	Tell Me Tomorrow (Part 1)/ Tell Me Tomorrow (Part 2)	1982	—	2.00	4.00
❏ 1615	Old Fashioned Love/Destiny	1982	—	2.00	4.00
❏ 1630	Are You Still Here?/Yes It's You Lady	1982	—	2.00	4.00
❏ 1655	I've Made Love to You a Thousand Times/Into Each Rain Some Life Must Fall	1983	—	2.00	4.00
❏ 1678	Touch the Sky/All My Life's a Lie	1983	—	2.00	4.00
❏ 1684	Blame It on Love/Even Tho'	1983	—	2.00	4.00
—With Barbara Mitchell					
❏ 1700	Don't Play Another Love Song/ Wouldn't You Like to Know	1983	—	2.00	4.00
❏ 1735	And I Don't Love You/Dynamite	1984	—	2.00	4.00
❏ 1756	I Can't Find/Gimme What You Want	1984	—	2.00	4.00
❏ 1786	First Time on a Ferris Wheel/Train of Thought	1985	—	2.00	4.00
❏ 1828	Hold On to Your Love/Train of Thought	1985	—	2.00	4.00
❏ 1828 [PS]	Hold On to Your Love/Train of Thought	1985	—	3.00	6.00
❏ 1839	Sleepless Nights/ Close Encounters of the First Kind	1986	—	2.00	4.00
❏ 1839 [PS]	Sleepless Nights/ Close Encounters of the First Kind	1986	—	2.50	5.00
❏ 1855	Girl I'm Standing There/Because of You (It's the Best It's Ever Been)	1986	—	2.00	4.00
❏ 1868	Love Will Set You Free (Theme from Solarbabies) (Parts 1 & 2)	1986	—	2.00	4.00
❏ 54233	Sweet Harmony/Want to Know My Mind	1973	—	2.50	5.00
❏ 54239	Baby Come Close/A Silent Partner in a Three- Way Love Affair	1973	—	2.50	5.00
❏ 54246	It's Her Turn to Live/Just My Soul Responding	1974	—	2.50	5.00
❏ 54250	Virgin Man/Fulfill Your Need	1974	—	2.50	5.00
❏ 54251	I Am, I Am/The Family Song	1974	—	2.50	5.00
❏ 54258	Baby That's Backatcha/Just Passing Through	1975	—	2.50	5.00
❏ 54261	The Agony and the Ecstasy/Wedding Song	1975	—	2.50	5.00
❏ 54265	Quiet Storm/Asleep on My Love	1975	—	2.50	5.00
❏ 54267	Open/Coincidentally	1976	—	2.50	5.00
❏ 54272	An Old Fashioned Man/(B-side unassigned)	1976	—	—	—
—Unreleased					
❏ 54276	An Old Fashioned Man/Just Passing Through	1976	—	2.50	5.00
❏ 54279	There Will Come a Day (I'm Gonna Happen to You)/Humming Song	1977	—	2.50	5.00
❏ 54284	Vitamin U/Holly	1977	—	2.50	5.00
❏ 54288	Theme from Big Time (Part 1)/ Theme from Big Time (Part 2)	1977	—	2.50	5.00
❏ 54293	Daylight and Darkness/ Why You Wanna See My Bad Side	1978	—	2.50	5.00
❏ 54296	I'm Loving You Softly/Shoe Soul	1978	—	2.50	5.00
❏ 54301	Get Ready/Ever Had a Dream	1979	—	2.00	4.00
❏ 54306	Cruisin'/Ever Had a Dream	1979	—	2.00	4.00
❏ 54311	Let Me Be the Clock/Travelin' Through	1980	—	2.00	4.00
❏ 54313	Heavy on Pride/I Love the Nearness of You	1980	—	2.00	4.00
❏ 54318	I Want to Be Your Love/Wine, Women and Song	1980	—	2.00	4.00
❏ 54321	Being with You/What's In Your Life for Me	1981	—	2.00	4.00
❏ 54325	Aquicontigo/Being with You (Aquicontigo)	1981	—	2.00	4.00
❏ 54327	You Are Forever/I Hear the Children Singing	1981	—	2.00	4.00
❏ 54332	Who's Sad/Food for Thought	1981	—	2.00	4.00
Albums					
MOTOWN					
❏ M5-118V1	Motown Superstar Series, Vol. 18	1981	2.50	5.00	10.00
❏ M5-134V1	Smokey	1981	2.00	4.00	8.00
—Reissue of Tamla 328					
❏ M5-154V1	Deep in My Soul	1981	2.00	4.00	8.00
—Reissue of Tamla 350					
❏ M5-168V1	Pure Smokey	1981	2.00	4.00	8.00
—Reissue of Tamla 331					
❏ M5-197V1	A Quiet Storm	1981	2.00	4.00	8.00
—Reissue of Tamla 337					
❏ 5267ML	Where There;s Smoke	1982	2.00	4.00	8.00
—Reissue of Tamla 366					

R

Number	Title (A Side/B Side)	Yr	VG	VG+	NM
❑ 5349ML	Being with You	1983	2.00	4.00	8.00
—Reissue of Tamla 375					
❑ MOT-6226	One Heartbeat	1987	2.50	5.00	10.00
❑ MOT-6268	Love, Smokey	1990	3.00	6.00	12.00
TAMLA					
❑ T 328	Smokey	1973	3.00	6.00	12.00
❑ T6-331	Pure Smokey	1974	3.00	6.00	12.00
❑ T6-337	A Quiet Storm	1975	3.00	6.00	12.00
❑ T6-341	Smokey's Family Robinson	1976	3.00	6.00	12.00
❑ T6-350	Deep in My Soul	1977	3.00	6.00	12.00
❑ T7-359	Love Breeze	1978	3.00	6.00	12.00
❑ T9-363 [(2)]	Smokin'	1979	3.75	7.50	15.00
❑ T7-366	Where There's Smoke	1979	2.50	5.00	10.00
❑ T8-367	Warm Thoughts	1980	2.50	5.00	10.00
❑ T8-375	Being with You	1981	2.50	5.00	10.00
❑ 6001TL	Yes It's You Lady	1982	2.50	5.00	10.00
❑ 6030TL	Touch the Sky	1983	2.50	5.00	10.00
❑ 6064TL	Blame It on Love & All the Great Hits	1983	2.50	5.00	10.00
❑ 6098TL	Essar	1984	2.50	5.00	10.00
❑ 6156TL	Smoke Signals	1986	2.50	5.00	10.00

ROBINSON, SMOKEY, AND THE MIRACLES See THE MIRACLES.

ROBINSON, SUGAR CHILE
45s
CAPITOL

Number	Title (A Side/B Side)	Yr	VG	VG+	NM
❑ F1386	Broken Down Piano/I'll Get My Spinach	1951	6.25	12.50	25.00
❑ F1526	Baby Blues/The Donkey Song	1951	6.25	12.50	25.00
❑ F1719	The Hunkie Man/				
	The Green Grass Grows All Around	1951	6.25	12.50	25.00

ROBINSON, VICKI SUE
12-Inch Singles
PRELUDE

Number	Title (A Side/B Side)	Yr	VG	VG+	NM
❑ 532	Hot Summer Night/(Version)	1981	3.00	6.00	12.00
PROFILE					
❑ 7025	To Sir with Love/(Instrumental)	1983	2.00	4.00	8.00
❑ 7039	Everlasting Love/(Instrumental)	1983	2.00	4.00	8.00
RCA					
❑ PD-11029	Hold Tight/Falling in Love	1977	3.75	7.50	15.00
❑ PD-11228	Trust in Me (7:03)/				
	Don't Try to Win Me Back Again (6:06)	1978	3.00	6.00	12.00
❑ PD-11442	Nighttime Fantasy (8:15)/				
	Feels So Good It Must Be Wrong	1979	3.00	6.00	12.00
❑ PC-11507	Turn the Beat Around/Hold Tight	1979	3.00	6.00	12.00
❑ PC-11520	Nighttime Fantasy (8:15)/				
	Feels So Good It Must Be Wrong	1980	2.00	4.00	8.00
❑ PD-11721	What's Happening in My Life (5:42)/Movin' On	1979	3.00	6.00	12.00
45s					
PRELUDE					
❑ 8038	Hot Summer Nights/(Version)	1981	—	2.00	4.00
PROFILE					
❑ 5025	To Sir with Love/(Instrumental)	1983	—	2.00	4.00
❑ 5039	Everlasting Love/(Instrumental)	1983	—	2.00	4.00
RCA					
❑ PB-10775	Daylight/Never Gonna Let You Go	1976	—	2.00	4.00
❑ PB-10863	Should I Stay-I Won't Let You Go/When You're				
	Loving Me	1976	—	2.00	4.00
❑ GB-10944	Turn the Beat Around/Daylight	1977	—	—	3.00
—Gold Standard Series					
❑ PB-11028	Falling in Love/Hold Tight	1977	—	2.00	4.00
❑ PB-11227	Trust in Me/Don't Try to Win Me Back Again	1978	—	2.00	4.00
❑ PB-11280	Freeway Song/Half and Half	1978	—	2.00	4.00
❑ PB-11384	Jealousy/We Found Each Other	1978	—	2.00	4.00
❑ PB-11441	Nighttime Fantasy/				
	Feel So Good It Must Be Wrong	1978	—	2.00	4.00
❑ PB-11720	What's Happening in My Life/Movin' On	1979	—	2.00	4.00
RCA VICTOR					
❑ PB-10282	Baby, Now That I've Found You/Thanks a Million	1975	—	2.00	4.00
❑ PB-10435	Never Gonna Let You Go (Part 1)/Never Gonna				
	Let You Go (Part 2)	1975	—	2.00	4.00
❑ PB-10562	Turn the Beat Around/Lack of Respect	1976	—	2.50	5.00
Albums					
RCA VICTOR					
❑ APL1-1256	Never Gonna Let You Go	1976	3.00	6.00	12.00
❑ APL1-1829	Vicki Sue Robinson	1977	3.00	6.00	12.00
❑ AFL1-2294	Half and Half	1978	3.00	6.00	12.00
❑ AYL1-3949	Turn the Beat Around	1981	2.00	4.00	8.00

ROBINSON, WANDA
45s
PERCEPTION

Number	Title (A Side/B Side)	Yr	VG	VG+	NM
❑ 505	John Harvey's Blues/Final Hour	1971	2.00	4.00	8.00
Albums					
PERCEPTION					
❑ 18	Black Ivory	1971	3.00	6.00	12.00

ROCCO, LENNY
45s
DELSEY

Number	Title (A Side/B Side)	Yr	VG	VG+	NM
❑ 301	Sugar Girl/Rochelle	1961	75.00	150.00	300.00

ROCHELL AND THE CANDLES
45s
CHALLENGE

Number	Title (A Side/B Side)	Yr	VG	VG+	NM
❑ 9158	Turn Her Down/Each Night	1962	10.00	20.00	40.00
❑ 9191	Annie's Not an Orphan Anymore/				
	Let's Run Away and Get Married	1963	5.00	10.00	20.00
SWINGIN'					
❑ 623	Once Upon a Time/When My Baby Is Gone	1960	5.00	10.00	20.00
❑ 634	So Far Away/Hey, Pretty Baby	1961	5.00	10.00	20.00
❑ 640	Peg of My Heart/Squat with Me, Baby	1962	5.00	10.00	20.00
❑ 652	Big Boy Pete/A Long Time Ago	1963	5.00	10.00	20.00

ROCK BROTHERS, THE
45s
KING

Number	Title (A Side/B Side)	Yr	VG	VG+	NM
❑ 4851	Dungaree Doll/Livin' It Up	1955	7.50	15.00	30.00
❑ 4882	Oh, Didn't I Ramble/I Gotta Get Back	1956	6.25	12.50	25.00

ROCK GARDEN, THE
45s
B.T. PUPPY

Number	Title (A Side/B Side)	Yr	VG	VG+	NM
❑ 536	Sweet Pajamas/Perhaps the Joy of Giving	1967	2.50	5.00	10.00

ROCK ISLAND
45s
PROJECT 3

Number	Title (A Side/B Side)	Yr	VG	VG+	NM
❑ 1382	Babe I'm Gonna Leave You/				
	Hard and Never Easy	1970	2.50	5.00	10.00
Albums					
PROJECT 3					
❑ PR-4005 SD	Rock Island	1970	7.50	15.00	30.00

ROCK-A-FELLAS, THE
45s
ABC-PARAMOUNT

Number	Title (A Side/B Side)	Yr	VG	VG+	NM
❑ 9923	Don't Torment Me/Red Lips	1958	5.00	10.00	20.00
DEVERE					
❑ 313	Don't Torment Me/Red Lips	1958	12.50	25.00	50.00

ROCK-A-TEENS, THE
45s
DORAN

Number	Title (A Side/B Side)	Yr	VG	VG+	NM
❑ 3515	Woo Hoo/Untrue	1959	37.50	75.00	150.00
ROULETTE					
❑ 4192	Woo Hoo/Untrue	1959	7.50	15.00	30.00
❑ 4217	Twangy/Doggone It, Baby	1959	6.25	12.50	25.00
Albums					
ROULETTE					
❑ R-25109 [M]	Woo-Hoo	1960	37.50	75.00	150.00
❑ SR-25109 [S]	Woo-Hoo	1960	62.50	125.00	250.00

ROCKA, BILLY
45s
BRUNSWICK

Number	Title (A Side/B Side)	Yr	VG	VG+	NM
❑ 55049	Listen Pretty Baby/				
	I'm Gonna Sit Right Down and Cry	1958	15.00	30.00	60.00

ROCKAWAYS, THE
45s
RED BIRD

Number	Title (A Side/B Side)	Yr	VG	VG+	NM
❑ 10-005	Top Down Time/Don't Cry	1964	6.25	12.50	25.00

ROCKERS, THE
45s
CARTER

Number	Title (A Side/B Side)	Yr	VG	VG+	NM
❑ 3029	Tell Me Why/Count Every Star	1955	200.00	400.00	800.00
FEDERAL					
❑ 12267	What Am I to Do/I'll Die in Love with You	1956	50.00	100.00	200.00
❑ 12273	Down in the Bottom/Why Don't You Believe Me	1956	25.00	50.00	100.00

ROCKETEERS, THE (1)
45s
GLAD HAMP

Number	Title (A Side/B Side)	Yr	VG	VG+	NM
❑ 2017	Drag Strip/Summertime	1963	10.00	20.00	40.00

ROCKETEERS, THE (2)
45s
HERALD

Number	Title (A Side/B Side)	Yr	VG	VG+	NM
❑ 415	Foolish One/Gonna Feed My Baby Poison	1953	175.00	350.00	700.00
—Black vinyl					
❑ 415	Foolish One/Gonna Feed My Baby Poison	1953	500.00	1000.	2000.
—Red vinyl					

ROCKETEERS, THE (3)
45s
MODERN

Number	Title (A Side/B Side)	Yr	VG	VG+	NM
❑ 999	Talk It Over Baby/Hey Rube	1956	12.50	25.00	50.00

ROCKETEERS, THE (4)
45s
M.J.C.

Number	Title (A Side/B Side)	Yr	VG	VG+	NM
❑ 501	My Reckless Heart/They Turned the Party Out				
	Down at Bessie's House	1958	500.00	1000.	2000.

ROCKETEERS, THE (U)
45s
VAL-UE

Number	Title (A Side/B Side)	Yr	VG	VG+	NM
❑ 102	Rippin' and Rockin'/Downtown	1960	7.50	15.00	30.00

ROCKETONES, THE
45s
MELBA

Number	Title (A Side/B Side)	Yr	VG	VG+	NM
❑ 113	Mexico/Dee I	1957	12.50	25.00	50.00
❑ 113	Mexico/I Do	1957	15.00	30.00	60.00

ROCKETS, THE (2)
45s
ATLANTIC

Number	Title (A Side/B Side)	Yr	VG	VG+	NM
❑ 988	Open the Door/Big Leg Mama	1953	25.00	50.00	100.00

ROCKETS, THE (3)
45s
COLUMBIA

Number	Title (A Side/B Side)	Yr	VG	VG+	NM
❑ 41512	Gibraltar Rock/Walkin' Home	1959	6.25	12.50	25.00

ROCKETS, THE (4)
45s
MODERN

Number	Title (A Side/B Side)	Yr	VG	VG+	NM
❑ 992	You Are the First One/Be Lovey Dovey	1956	10.00	20.00	40.00

Number	Title (A Side/B Side)	Yr	VG	VG+	NM
Albums					
WHITE WHALE					
❏ WWS-7116	The Rockets	1968	6.25	12.50	25.00
ROCKETS, THE (5) Features three future members of CRAZY HORSE.					
45s					
WHITE WHALE					
❏ 270	Hole in My Pocket/Let Me Go	1968	3.75	7.50	15.00
ROCKETTES, THE					
45s					
PARROT					
❏ 789	I Can't Forget/Love Nobody	1954	1000.	2000.	3000.
ROCKIN' BERRIES, THE					
45s					
REPRISE					
❏ 0329	He's in Town/Flashbook	1964	3.00	6.00	12.00
❏ 0355	What in the World's Come Over You/You Don't Know What to Do	1965	2.50	5.00	10.00
❏ 0377	Poor Man's Son/Follow Me	1965	2.50	5.00	10.00
❏ 0400	You're My Girl/Brother Bill (Last Clean Shirt)	1965	2.50	5.00	10.00
❏ 0442	Doesn't Time Fly/The Water Is Over My Head	1965	2.50	5.00	10.00
ROCKIN' CHAIRS, THE					
45s					
RECORTE					
❏ 402	Rockin' Chair Boogie/A Kiss Is a Kiss	1958	25.00	50.00	100.00
❏ 404	Please Mary/Come On Baby	1958	12.50	25.00	50.00
❏ 412	Memories of Love/Girl of Mine	1959	12.50	25.00	50.00
ROCKIN' DUKES, THE					
45s					
O.J.					
❏ 1007	Angel and a Rose/My Baby Left Me	1957	75.00	150.00	300.00
ROCKIN' KIDS, THE					
45s					
DOT					
❏ 15749	Black Stockings/Yea Yea (I'm in the Mood)	1958	7.50	15.00	30.00
ROCKIN' R'S, THE					
45s					
STEPHENY					
❏ 1842	Walkin' You to School/Bewitched (Bothered and Bewildered)	1960	6.25	12.50	25.00
TEMPUS					
❏ 1507	Nameless/Heat	1959	7.50	15.00	30.00
❏ 1515	Mustang/I'm Still in Love with You	1959	7.50	15.00	30.00
❏ 7541	Crazy Baby/The Beat	1959	10.00	20.00	40.00
VEE JAY					
❏ 334	Mustang/I'm Still in Love with You	1959	5.00	10.00	20.00
❏ 346	Hum Bug/The Mix	1960	5.00	10.00	20.00
ROCKIN' RAMRODS, THE					
45s					
BON-BON					
❏ 1315	She Lies/The Girl Can't Help It	1964	10.00	20.00	40.00
CLARIDGE					
❏ 301	Don't Fool with Fu Manchu/Tears	1965	5.00	10.00	20.00
❏ 317	Play It/Got My Mojo Workin'	1966	7.50	15.00	30.00
PLYMOUTH					
❏ 2961	I Wanna Be Your Man/I'll Be On My Way	1964	7.50	15.00	30.00
❏ 2963	Mister Wind/Bright Lit Blue Skies	1966	6.25	12.50	25.00
—As "The Ramrods"					
❏ 2965	Flowers in My Mind/Mary, Mary	1967	7.50	15.00	30.00
—As "The Ramrods"					
ROCKIN' REBELS, THE Includes records by "The Hot-Toddys" and "The Rebels."					
45s					
CORSICAN					
❏ 0056	Rockin' Crickets/Shakin' and Stompin'	1959	10.00	20.00	40.00
—As "The Hot-Toddys"					
ITZY					
❏ 8	Wild Weekend/Wild Weekend Cha Cha	1963	5.00	10.00	20.00
LOST-NITE					
❏ 239	Wild Weekend/Donkey Twine	196?	—	2.50	5.00
—Reissue					
MAR-LEE					
❏ 0094	Wild Weekend/Wild Weekend Cha Cha	1960	25.00	50.00	100.00
—As "The Rebels"					
❏ 0095	Buffalo Blues/Donkey Walk	1961	7.50	15.00	30.00
—As "The Buffalo Rebels"					
❏ 0096	Theme from Rebel/Any Way You Want Me	1961	7.50	15.00	30.00
—As "The Buffalo Rebels"					
SHAN-TODD					
❏ 0056	Rockin' Crickets/Shakin' and Stompin'	1959	20.00	40.00	80.00
—As "The Hot-Toddys"					
STORK					
❏ STK-3	Bongo Blue Beat/Burn Baby Burn	1964	6.25	12.50	25.00
SWAN					
❏ 4125	Wild Weekend/Wild Weekend Cha Cha	1962	7.50	15.00	30.00
—Second pressings credit "Rockin' Rebels" and do not have "Don't Drop Out" on the label					
❏ 4125	Wild Weekend/Wild Weekend Cha Cha	1962	10.00	20.00	40.00
—First pressings credit "The Rebels"					
❏ 4125	Wild Weekend/Wild Weekend Cha Cha	1963	5.00	10.00	20.00
—Later pressings credit "Rockin' Rebels" and have "Don't Drop Out" on the label					
❏ 4140	Rockin' Crickets/Hully Gully Rock	1963	6.25	12.50	25.00
—A-side is the same recording as on Corsican and Shan-Todd					
❏ 4150	Another Wild Weekend/Happy Popcorn	1963	6.25	12.50	25.00
❏ 4161	Monday Morning/Flibbity Jibbit	1963	6.25	12.50	25.00
❏ 4248	Wild Weekend/Donkey Twine	1966	5.00	10.00	20.00
Albums					
SWAN					
❏ SLP-509 [M]	Wild Weekend	1963	50.00	100.00	200.00
ROCKIN' SAINTS, THE					
45s					
DECCA					
❏ 30990	Saints Rock/Alright Baby	1959	7.50	15.00	30.00
❏ 31144	Cheat on Me, Baby/Half and Half	1960	20.00	40.00	80.00
ROCKIN' SIDNEY					
45s					
EPIC					
❏ 34-05430	My Toot Toot/Jalapeno Lena	1985	—	2.00	4.00
GOLDBAND					
❏ 1158	Actions Speak Louder Than Words/Lais Per La Patate	196?	3.00	6.00	12.00
❏ 1159	My Poor Heart/Something Working Baby	196?	3.00	6.00	12.00
❏ 1163	Deedle Didie Da/Life Without Love	196?	2.50	5.00	10.00
❏ 1170	Gonna Be Looking/Shed So Many Tears	196?	2.50	5.00	10.00
❏ 1177	Corpus Christi/(B-side unknown)	196?	3.00	6.00	12.00
❏ 1178	Trust/Put On It	196?	2.50	5.00	10.00
❏ 1183	Soul Christmas (Part 1)/Soul Christmas (Part 2)	1966	3.00	6.00	12.00
❏ 1186	The Grandpa/Feel Delicious	1967	2.50	5.00	10.00
JIN					
❏ 110	My Little Girl/Don't Say Goodbye	1959	12.50	25.00	50.00
❏ 141	Walking Out on You/Rocky	1960	7.50	15.00	30.00
❏ 156	No Good Woman/You Ain't Nothin' But Fine	1960	7.50	15.00	30.00
❏ 164	Send Me Some Lovin'/Past Bedtime	196?	7.50	15.00	30.00
❏ 168	No Good Man/If I Could, I Win	196?	7.50	15.00	30.00
❏ 170	Don't Let Me Cross Over/You Don't Have to Go	196?	7.50	15.00	30.00
❏ 174	Something's Wrong/It Really Is a Hurtin' Thing	196?	7.50	15.00	30.00
❏ 177	Ya Ya/Wasted Days and Wasted Nights	196?	7.50	15.00	30.00
MAISON DE SOUL					
❏ 1017	Good Time Woman/You Ain't Nothin' But Fine	198?	—	3.00	6.00
❏ 1020	Dance and Show Off/Relax and Go Slow	198?	—	3.00	6.00
❏ 1021	Boogie for Me/Sweet Li'l Woman	198?	—	3.00	6.00
❏ 1024	My Toot Toot/Zydeco Shoes	1984	2.00	4.00	8.00
❏ 1025	Party This Christmas/Christmas Without You	1984	—	3.00	6.00
Albums					
EPIC					
❏ 5E 40153 [EP]	My Toot Toot	1985	2.00	4.00	8.00
ZBC					
❏ LP-100	A Holiday Celebration with Rockin' Sidney	1983	3.75	7.50	15.00
ROCKIN' STOCKIN', THE					
45s					
SUN					
❏ 350	Rockin' Lang Syne/Yuleville U.S.A.	1960	7.50	15.00	30.00
❏ 1960	Rockin' Lang Syne/Yuleville U.S.A.	197?	3.75	7.50	15.00
—Reissue with green and red print on a white label with original Sun logo					
ROCKIN' VICKERS					
45s					
COLUMBIA					
❏ 43818	Dandy/I Don't Need Your Love	1966	3.00	6.00	12.00
ROCKING BROTHERS, THE					
45s					
IMPERIAL					
❏ 5333	Rock It/Behind the Sun	1955	7.50	15.00	30.00
❏ 5341	Blow Torch/Evening Shadows	1955	7.50	15.00	30.00
SAVOY					
❏ 1144	Play Boy Hop/The Grinder	1955	12.50	25.00	50.00
WHIPPET					
❏ 207	Yeah! Yeah!/Little Mike	1957	5.00	10.00	20.00
ROCKY AND HIS FRIENDS					
45s					
TOWER					
❏ 178	Riot City/You're Not Wrong	1965	3.00	6.00	12.00
ROCKY FELLERS, THE					
45s					
DONNA					
❏ 1383	Don't Sit Down/The Beachcomber Song	1963	3.00	6.00	12.00
PARKWAY					
❏ 836	Long Tall Sally/South Pacific Twist	1962	3.00	6.00	12.00
SCEPTER					
❏ 1245 [DJ]	Santa Santa (same on both sides)	196?	2.00	4.00	8.00
—Promo reissue; white label with mid-1960s Scepter Records logo (black oval)					
❏ 1245	Santa Santa/Great Big World	1962	5.00	10.00	20.00
—A-side is a very early Neil Diamond composition					
❏ 1245 [DJ]	Santa Santa/Santa's Grove	1963	3.00	6.00	12.00
—Promo reissue with new B-side. All-white label (no black oval)					
❏ 1246	Killer Joe/Lonely Teardrops	1963	3.75	7.50	15.00
❏ 1254	Like the Big Guys Do/Great Big World	1963	3.00	6.00	12.00
❏ 1254 [PS]	Like the Big Guys Do/Great Big World	1963	5.00	10.00	20.00
❏ 1258	Ching-a-Ling Baby/Hey Little Donkey	1963	3.00	6.00	12.00
❏ 1263	Bye Bye Baby/She Makes Me Wanna Dance	1963	3.00	6.00	12.00
❏ 1271	My Prayer/Two Guys from Trinidad	1964	3.00	6.00	12.00
VALMOR					
❏ 2004	Opus/Orange Peel	1962	3.75	7.50	15.00
WARNER BROS.					
❏ 5440	(Everybody Wants to Be a) Tiger/Jeannie Memsoh	1964	2.50	5.00	10.00
❏ 5459	Better Let Her Go/Nina	1964	2.50	5.00	10.00
❏ 5497	Man with the Blue Guitar/Don't Throw My Toys Away	1965	2.50	5.00	10.00
❏ 5613	Rented Tuxedo/Two Steps Downstairs in the Basement	1965	2.50	5.00	10.00
Albums					
SCEPTER					
❏ SP-512 [M]	Killer Joe	1964	7.50	15.00	30.00
❏ SPS-512 [S]	Killer Joe	1964	10.00	20.00	40.00
ROD AND CAROLYN					
45s					
PARKWAY					
❏ 918	Young Love/Talk to Me	1964	2.50	5.00	10.00
❏ 934	Love Is Where You Are/I've Got You on My Mind	1964	2.50	5.00	10.00

R

Number	Title (A Side/B Side)	Yr	VG	VG+	NM

RODGERS, JIMMIE (1) Legendary country & western singer known as "The Singing Brakeman."

45s

RCA VICTOR

Number	Title (A Side/B Side)	Yr	VG	VG+	NM
❏ 27-0098	Blue Yodel (T for Texas)/				
	Away Out on the Mountain	1950	5.00	10.00	20.00
❏ 27-0099	Never No Mo' Blues/Daddy and Home	1950	5.00	10.00	20.00
❏ 27-0100	Frankie and Johnny/The Brakeman's Blues	1950	5.00	10.00	20.00
—The above three comprise box set WPT 21					
❏ 27-0101	Blue Yodel No. 4/Waiting for a Train	1950	5.00	10.00	20.00
❏ 27-0102	My Old Pal/Desert Blues	1950	5.00	.10.00	20.00
❏ 27-0103	Blue Yodel No. 3/I'm Sorry We Met	1950	5.00	10.00	20.00
—The above three comprise box set WPT 22					
❏ 27-0104	Sleep, Baby, Sleep/My Carolina Sunshine Girl	1950	5.00	10.00	20.00
❏ 27-0105	Blue Yodel No. 2/				
	Tuck Away My Lonesome Blues	1950	5.00	10.00	20.00
❏ 27-0106	Blue Yodel No. 6/				
	Dear Old Sunny South by the Sea	1950	5.00	10.00	20.00
—The above three comprise box set WPT 23					
❏ 47-6092	In the Jailhouse Now No. 2/Peach Pickin' Time				
	Down in Georgia	1955	5.00	10.00	20.00
❏ 47-6205	Mule Skinner Blues/				
	Mother, the Queen of My Heart	1955	5.00	10.00	20.00
❏ 47-6408	Never No Mo' Blues/Daddy and Home	1955	5.00	10.00	20.00
❏ WPT 21 [PS]	Yodelingly Yours, Jimmie Rodgers, Volume 1	1950	5.00	10.00	20.00
—Box for 27-0098, 27-0099 and 27-0100					
❏ WPT 22 [PS]	Yodelingly Yours, Jimmie Rodgers, Volume 2	1950	5.00	10.00	20.00
—Box for 27-0101, 27-0102 and 27-0103					
❏ WPT 23 [PS]	Yodelingly Yours, Jimmie Rodgers, Volume 3	1950	5.00	10.00	20.00
—Box for 27-0104, 27-0105 and 27-0106					
❏ AMAO-0130	Mule Skinner Blues/Waiting for a Train	1973	2.00	4.00	8.00
—Gold Standard Series reissue					

7-Inch Extended Plays

RCA VICTOR

Number	Title (A Side/B Side)	Yr	VG	VG+	NM
❏ EPAT 23	*My Carolina Sunshine Girl/Sleep, Baby, Sleep/				
	Blue Yodel No. 2/				
	Tuck Away My Lonesome Blues	1952	5.00	10.00	20.00
❏ EPAT 23 [PS]	Yodelingly Yours, Jimmie Rodgers, Volume 3	1952	5.00	10.00	20.00
❏ EPAT 409	Never No Mo' Blues/Daddy and Home//Waiting				
	for a Train/Blue Yodel No. 4 (California Blues)	1953	5.00	10.00	20.00
❏ EPAT 409 [PS]	Yodelingly Yours, Jimmie Rodgers, Volume 4	1953	5.00	10.00	20.00
❏ EPAT 410	(contents unknown)	195?	5.00	10.00	20.00
❏ EPAT 410 [PS]	Yodelingly Yours, Jimmie Rodgers, Volume 5	195?	5.00	10.00	20.00
❏ EPAT 411	*You and My Old Guitar/Prairie Lullaby/Old Pal				
	of My Heart/My Little Lady	195?	5.00	10.00	20.00
❏ EPAT 411 [PS]	Yodelingly Yours, Jimmie Rodgers, Volume 6	195?	5.00	10.00	20.00
❏ 547-0901	Never No Mo' Blues/Daddy and Home//Jimmie's				
	Mean Mama Blues/Old Pal of My Heart	1955	5.00	10.00	20.00
—"Side 1" and "Side 4" of EPB-1232					
❏ 547-0902	Blue Yodel No. 4/Waiting for a Train//Prairie				
	Lullaby/Blue Yodel No. 6	1955	5.00	10.00	20.00
—"Side 2" and "Side 3" of EPB-1232					
❏ EPB-1232 [PS]	Never No Mo' Blues — Jimmie Rodgers				
	Memorial Album	1955	5.00	10.00	20.00
—Gatefold cover for 547-0901 and 547-0902					

Albums

RCA VICTOR

Number	Title (A Side/B Side)	Yr	VG	VG+	NM
❏ DPL2-0075 [(2)]	The Legendary Jimmie Rodgers, Vol. 1	1974	10.00	20.00	40.00
—Special-products issue for Country Music Magazine					
❏ ANL1-1209	My Rough and Rowdy Ways	1976	2.50	5.00	10.00
❏ LPM-1232 [M]	Never No Mo' Blues — A Memorial Album	1955	37.50	75.00	150.00
❏ LPM-1640 [M]	Train Whistle Blues	1957	37.50	75.00	150.00
❏ LPM-2112 [M]	My Rough and Rowdy Ways	1960	20.00	40.00	80.00
❏ LPM-2213 [M]	Jimmie the Kid	1961	20.00	40.00	80.00
❏ CPL1-2504	A Legendary Performer	1977	2.50	5.00	10.00
❏ LPM-2531 [M]	Country Music Hall of Fame	1962	20.00	40.00	80.00
❏ LPM-2634 [M]	The Short But Brilliant Life of Jimmie Rodgers	1963	20.00	40.00	80.00
❏ LPM-2865 [M]	My Time Ain't Long	1964	12.50	25.00	50.00
❏ LPT-3037 [10]	Yodelingly Yours Jimmie Rodgers, Volume 1	1953	100.00	200.00	400.00
❏ LPT-3038 [10]	Yodelingly Yours Jimmie Rodgers, Volume 2	1953	100.00	200.00	400.00
❏ LPT-3039 [10]	Yodelingly Yours Jimmie Rodgers, Volume 3	1953	100.00	200.00	400.00
❏ LPM-3073 [10]	Travelin' Blues	1952	100.00	200.00	400.00
❏ AHL1-3315	The Best of the Legendary Jimmie Rodgers	197?	2.00	4.00	8.00
—Reissue with new prefix					
❏ LPM-3315 [M]	The Best of the Legendary Jimmie Rodgers	1965	10.00	20.00	40.00
❏ LSP-3315 [R]	The Best of the Legendary Jimmie Rodgers	1965	5.00	10.00	20.00
❏ VPS-6091(e) [(2)]	This Is Jimmie Rodgers	1971	5.00	10.00	20.00

ROUNDER

Number	Title (A Side/B Side)	Yr	VG	VG+	NM
❏ 1056	First Sessions 1927-1928	1990	3.00	6.00	12.00
❏ 1057	The Early Years 1928-1929	1990	3.00	6.00	12.00

RODGERS, JIMMIE (2) Pop-country vocalist, no relation to the above.

45s

A&M

Number	Title (A Side/B Side)	Yr	VG	VG+	NM
❏ 842	I'll Say Goodbye/Shadows	1967	—	3.00	6.00
❏ 871	Child of Clay/Turnaround	1967	—	3.00	6.00
❏ 898	If I Were the Man/What a Strange Town	1967	—	3.00	6.00
❏ 902	I Believe It All/You Pass Me By	1968	—	3.00	6.00
❏ 930	How Do You Say Goodbye/I Wanna Be Free	1968	—	3.00	6.00
❏ 976	Today/The Lovers	1968	—	3.00	6.00
❏ 1055	The Windmills of Your Mind/L.A. Break Down				
	(And Take Me Back In)	1969	—	3.00	6.00
❏ 1120	Father Paul/Me About You	1969	—	3.00	6.00
❏ 1152	Cycles/Tomorrow My Dreams	1969	—	3.00	6.00
❏ 1213	Troubled Times/The Dum Dum Song	1970	—	2.50	5.00

DOT

Number	Title (A Side/B Side)	Yr	VG	VG+	NM
❏ 16378	No One Will Ever Know/Because	1962	2.50	5.00	10.00
❏ 16378 [PS]	No One Will Ever Know/Because	1962	3.75	7.50	15.00
❏ 16407	Rainbow at Midnight/Rhumba Boogie	1962	2.50	5.00	10.00
❏ 16428	I'll Never Stand in Your Way/Afraid	1963	2.50	5.00	10.00
❏ 16450	Lonely Tears/A Face in the Crowd	1963	2.50	5.00	10.00
❏ 16467	(I Don't Know Why) I Just Do/Load 'Em Up (And				
	Keep a Steppin')	1963	2.50	5.00	10.00
❏ 16490	Poor Little Raggedy Ann/				
	I'm Gonna Be the Winner	1963	2.50	5.00	10.00
❏ 16527	Two-Ten Six-Eighteen (Doesn't Anybody Know				
	My Name)/The Banana Boat Song	1963	2.50	5.00	10.00

Number	Title (A Side/B Side)	Yr	VG	VG+	NM
❏ 16561	Together/Mama Was a Cotton Picker	1963	2.50	5.00	10.00
❏ 16595	The World I Used to Know/I Forgot More Than				
	You'll Ever Know	1964	2.50	5.00	10.00
❏ 16653	Water Boy/Someplace Green	1964	2.50	5.00	10.00
❏ 16673	Two Tickets/				
	I Forgot More Than You'll Ever Know	1964	2.50	5.00	10.00
❏ 16694	(All My Friends Are Gonna Be) Strangers/Bon				
	Soir Mademoiselle	1965	2.00	4.00	8.00
❏ 16720	Careless Love/				
	When I'm Right You Don't Remember	1965	2.00	4.00	8.00
❏ 16749	Are You Going My Way (Little Beachcomber)/				
	Little Schoolgirl	1965	2.00	4.00	8.00
❏ 16781	Bye Bye Love/Hollow Words	1965	2.00	4.00	8.00
❏ 16795	The Chipmunk Song (Christmas Don't Be Late)/				
	In the Snow	1965	2.00	4.00	8.00
❏ 16826	A Falen Star/Brother, Where Are You	1966	2.00	4.00	8.00
❏ 16861	It's Over/Anita, You're Dreaming	1966	2.50	5.00	10.00
❏ 16916	Morning Means Tomorrow/New Ideas	1966	2.00	4.00	8.00
❏ 16973	Love Me, Please Love Me/Wonderful You	1966	2.00	4.00	8.00
❏ 17040	Time/Yours and Mine	1967	2.00	4.00	8.00

EPIC

Number	Title (A Side/B Side)	Yr	VG	VG+	NM
❏ 10828	Froggy's Fable/Daylight Lights the Dawning	1972	—	2.50	5.00
❏ 10857	Kick the Can/Go On By	1972	—	2.50	5.00

MGM

Number	Title (A Side/B Side)	Yr	VG	VG+	NM
❏ 11732	Mama, Don't Cry at My Wedding/				
	You Don't Live Here No More	1954	6.25	12.50	25.00

ROULETTE

Number	Title (A Side/B Side)	Yr	VG	VG+	NM
❏ 4015	Honeycomb/Their Hearts Were Full of Spring	1957	5.00	10.00	20.00
❏ 4031	Kisses Sweeter Than Wine/				
	Better Loved You'll Never Be	1957	5.00	10.00	20.00
❏ 4045	Oh-Oh, I'm Falling in Love Again/				
	The Long Hot Summer	1958	3.75	7.50	15.00
—White label with colored spokes					
❏ 4045	Oh-Oh, I'm Falling in Love Again/				
	The Long Hot Summer	1958	5.00	10.00	20.00
—Red label					
❏ 4070	Secretly/Make Me a Miracle	1958	5.00	10.00	20.00
❏ 4070 [PS]	Secretly/Make Me a Miracle	1958	10.00	20.00	40.00
❏ 4090	Are You Really Mine/The Wizard	1958	3.75	7.50	15.00
❏ 4090 [PS]	Are You Really Mine/The Wizard	1958	10.00	20.00	40.00
❏ 4116	Bimbombey/You Understand Me	1958	3.75	7.50	15.00
❏ 4129	I'm Never Gonna Tell/Because You're Young	1959	3.75	7.50	15.00
❏ 4158 [M]	Ring-a-Ling-a-Lario/Wonderful You	1959	3.75	7.50	15.00
❏ 4158 [PS]	Ring-a-Ling-a-Lario/Wonderful You	1959	6.25	12.50	25.00
❏ SSR-4158 [S]	Ring-a-Ling-a-Lario/Wonderful You	1959	7.50	15.00	30.00
❏ 4191	Tucumcari/That Night You Became Seventeen	1959	3.75	7.50	15.00
❏ 4205	It's Christmas Once Again/Wistful Willie	1959	5.00	10.00	20.00
❏ 4218 [M]	T.L.C. Tender Love and Care/Waltzing Matilda	1960	3.00	6.00	12.00
❏ SSR-4218 [S]	T.L.C. Tender Love and Care/Waltzing Matilda	1960	7.50	15.00	30.00
❏ 4234	Just a Closer Walk with Thee/Joshua Fit the				
	Battle of Jericho	1960	3.00	6.00	12.00
❏ 4260	The Wreck of the John B/				
	Four Little Girls in Boston	1960	3.00	6.00	12.00
❏ 4293	Woman from Liberia/Come Along Julie	1960	3.00	6.00	12.00
❏ 4293 [PS]	Woman from Liberia/Come Along Julie	1960	5.00	10.00	20.00
❏ 4318	When Love Is Young/				
	The Little Shepherd of Kingdom Come	1960	3.00	6.00	12.00
❏ 4349	Everytime My Heart Sings/I'm On My Way	1961	3.00	6.00	12.00
❏ 4371	John Brown's Baby/I'm Going Home	1961	3.00	6.00	12.00
❏ 4384	A Little Dog Cried/Englidh Country Garden	1961	3.00	6.00	12.00
❏ 4439	You Are Everything to Me/Wanderin' Eyes	1962	3.00	6.00	12.00
❏ SSR-8001 [S]	Bo Diddley/Soldier Won't You Marry Me	1959	7.50	15.00	30.00
❏ SSR-8007 [S]	Froggy Went a-Courtin'/Lisa	1959	7.50	15.00	30.00
❏ SSR-8010 [S]	St. James Infirmary/Just a Wearyin' for You	1959	7.50	15.00	30.00

SCRIMSHAW

Number	Title (A Side/B Side)	Yr	VG	VG+	NM
❏ 1313	A Good Woman Likes to Drink with the Boys/				
	Dancing on the Moon	1977	—	2.00	4.00
❏ 1314	Everytime I Sing a Love Song/Just a Little Time	1978	—	2.00	4.00
❏ 1316	When Our Love Began (Cowboys and Indians)/				
	(B-side unknown)	1978	—	2.00	4.00
❏ 1318	Secretly/Shovelin' Coal	1978	—	2.00	4.00
❏ 1319/20	Easy to Love/Easy	1979	—	2.00	4.00
—With Michele					

7-Inch Extended Plays

ROULETTE

Number	Title (A Side/B Side)	Yr	VG	VG+	NM
❏ EPR-1-303	Woman from Liberia/The Mating Call//Hey Little				
	Baby/Water Boy	1957	12.50	25.00	50.00
❏ EPR-1-303 [PS]	Jimmie Rodgers	1957	12.50	25.00	50.00
❏ EPR-1-312	*Honeycomb/Oh-Oh, I'm Falling in Love Again/				
	The Preacher/Better Loved You'll Never Be	195?	12.50	25.00	50.00
❏ EPR-1-312 [PS]	Jimmie Rodgers Sings	195?	12.50	25.00	50.00
❏ EPR-1-313	Tammy/The Song from Moulin Rouge//Love				
	Letters in the Sand/Hey There	195?	12.50	25.00	50.00
❏ EPR-1-313 [PS]	The Number One Ballads, Part 1	195?	12.50	25.00	50.00
❏ EPR-1-315	Bo Diddley/Riddle Song//The Fox and the				
	Goose/Black Is the Color	1960	12.50	25.00	50.00
❏ EPR-1-315 [PS]	Jimmie Rodgers Sings Folk Songs, Part I	1960	12.50	25.00	50.00
❏ EPR-1-316	Waltzing Matilda/The Crocodile//Lord Randal/				
	Gotta Lotta Tunes in My Guitar	195?	12.50	25.00	50.00
❏ EPR-1-316 [PS]	Jimmie Rodgers Sings Folk Songs, Part II	195?	12.50	25.00	50.00
❏ EPR-1-317	Soldier, Won't You Marry Me?/Lassie O'Mine//				
	Liza/Froggy Went a-Courtin'	1960	12.50	25.00	50.00
❏ EPR-1-317 [PS]	Jimmie Rodgers Sings Folk Songs, Part III	1960	12.50	25.00	50.00

Albums

A&M

Number	Title (A Side/B Side)	Yr	VG	VG+	NM
❏ SP-130 [M]	Child of Clay	1967	6.25	12.50	25.00
❏ SP-4130 [S]	Child of Clay	1967	3.75	7.50	15.00
❏ SP-4187	Windmills of Your Mind	1969	3.75	7.50	15.00
❏ SP-4242	Troubled Times	1970	3.75	7.50	15.00

ACCORD

Number	Title (A Side/B Side)	Yr	VG	VG+	NM
❏ SN-7198	Honeycomb & Other Hits	198?	2.50	5.00	10.00

DOT

Number	Title (A Side/B Side)	Yr	VG	VG+	NM
❏ DLP-3453 [M]	No One Will Ever Know	1962	3.75	7.50	15.00
❏ DLP-3496 [M]	Jimmie Rodgers Folk Concert	1963	3.75	7.50	15.00
❏ DLP-3502 [M]	My Favorite Hymns	1963	3.75	7.50	15.00
❏ DLP-3525 [M]	Honeycomb & Kisses Sweeter Than Wine	1963	3.75	7.50	15.00

Number	Title (A Side/B Side)	Yr	VG	VG+	NM
❑ DLP-3556 [M]	The World I Used to Know	1964	3.75	7.50	15.00
—Retitled version of above					
❑ DLP-3556 [M]	Town and Country	1964	5.00	10.00	20.00
❑ DLP-3579 [M]	12 Great Hits	1964	3.75	7.50	15.00
❑ DLP-3614 [M]	Deep Purple	1965	3.75	7.50	15.00
❑ DLP 3657 [M]	Christmas with Jimmie	1965	3.00	6.00	12.00
❑ DLP-3687 [M]	The Nashville Sound	1966	3.75	7.50	15.00
❑ DLP-3710 [M]	Country Music 1966	1966	3.75	7.50	15.00
❑ DLP-3717 [M]	It's Over	1966	3.75	7.50	15.00
❑ DLP-3780 [M]	Love Me, Please Love Me	1967	3.75	7.50	15.00
❑ DLP-3815 [M]	Golden Hits/15 Hits of Jimmie Rodgers	1967	5.00	10.00	20.00
❑ DLP-25453 [S]	No One Will Ever Know	1962	5.00	10.00	20.00
❑ DLP-25496 [S]	Jimmie Rodgers Folk Concert	1963	5.00	10.00	20.00
❑ DLP-25502 [S]	My Favorite Hymns	1963	5.00	10.00	20.00
❑ DLP-25525 [S]	Honeycomb & Kisses Sweeter Than Wine	1963	5.00	10.00	20.00
❑ DLP-25556 [S]	The World I Used to Know	1964	5.00	10.00	20.00
—Retitled version of above					
❑ DLP-25556 [S]	Town and Country	1964	6.25	12.50	25.00
❑ DLP-25579 [S]	12 Great Hits	1964	5.00	10.00	20.00
❑ DLP-25614 [S]	Deep Purple	1965	5.00	10.00	20.00
❑ DLP-25657 [S]	Christmas with Jimmie	1965	3.75	7.50	15.00
❑ DLP-25687 [S]	The Nashville Sound	1966	5.00	10.00	20.00
❑ DLP-25710 [S]	Country Music 1966	1966	5.00	10.00	20.00
❑ DLP-25717 [S]	It's Over	1966	5.00	10.00	20.00
❑ DLP-25780 [S]	Love Me, Please Love Me	1967	5.00	10.00	20.00
❑ DLP-25815 [S]	Golden Hits/15 Hits of Jimmie Rodgers	1967	3.75	7.50	15.00
FORUM					
❑ F-9025 [M]	At Home with Jimmie Rodgers: An Evening of Folk Songs	196?	3.00	6.00	12.00
❑ SF-9025 [S]	At Home with Jimmie Rodgers: An Evening of Folk Songs	196?	3.00	6.00	12.00
❑ F-9049 [M]	Just for You	196?	3.00	6.00	12.00
❑ SF-9049 [S]	Just for You	196?	3.00	6.00	12.00
❑ F-9059 [M]	Jimmie Rodgers Sings Folk Songs	196?	3.00	6.00	12.00
❑ SF-9059 [S]	Jimmie Rodgers Sings Folk Songs	196?	3.00	6.00	12.00
HAMILTON					
❑ HL-114 [M]	6 Favorite Hymns and 6 Favorite Folk Ballads	1964	3.00	6.00	12.00
❑ HL-148 [M]	12 Immortal Songs	196?	3.00	6.00	12.00
❑ HS-12114 [S]	6 Favorite Hymns and 6 Favorite Folk Ballads	1964	3.00	6.00	12.00
❑ HS-12148 [S]	12 Immortal Songs	196?	3.00	6.00	12.00
PARAMOUNT					
❑ PAS-2-1042 [(2)]	Honeycomb	1974	3.75	7.50	15.00
PICKWICK					
❑ PC-3040 [M]	Jimmie Rodgers	196?	3.00	6.00	12.00
❑ SPC-3040 [S]	Jimmie Rodgers	196?	3.00	6.00	12.00
❑ SPC-3106	Am I That Easy to Forget	196?	3.00	6.00	12.00
❑ SPC-3599	Big Hits	197?	2.50	5.00	10.00
ROULETTE					
❑ R-25020 [M]	Jimmie Rodgers	1957	12.50	25.00	50.00
—Black label					
❑ R-25020 [M]	Jimmie Rodgers	1959	6.25	12.50	25.00
—White label with colored spokes					
❑ R-25033 [M]	Number One Ballads	1958	12.50	25.00	50.00
—Black label					
❑ R-25033 [M]	Number One Ballads	1959	6.25	12.50	25.00
—White label with colored spokes					
❑ R-25042 [M]	Jimmie Rodgers Sings Folk Songs	1958	12.50	25.00	50.00
—Black label					
❑ R-25042 [M]	Jimmie Rodgers Sings Folk Songs	1959	6.25	12.50	25.00
—White label with colored spokes					
❑ R-25057 [M]	His Golden Year	1959	6.25	12.50	25.00
❑ R-25071 [M]	TV Favorites	1959	7.50	15.00	30.00
❑ SR-25071 [S]	TV Favorites	1959	12.50	25.00	50.00
❑ R-25081 [M]	Twilight on the Trail	1959	7.50	15.00	30.00
❑ SR-25081 [S]	Twilight on the Trail	1959	12.50	25.00	50.00
❑ R 25095 [M]	It's Christmas Once Again	1959	7.50	15.00	30.00
❑ SR 25095 [S]	It's Christmas Once Again	1959	12.50	25.00	50.00
❑ R-25103 [M]	When the Spirit Moves You	1960	7.50	15.00	30.00
❑ SR-25103 [S]	When the Spirit Moves You	1960	10.00	20.00	40.00
❑ R-25128 [M]	At Home with Jimmie Rodgers: An Evening of Folk Songs	1960	7.50	15.00	30.00
❑ SR-25128 [S]	At Home with Jimmie Rodgers: An Evening of Folk Songs	1960	10.00	20.00	40.00
❑ R-25150 [M]	The Folk Song World of Jimmie Rodgers	1961	7.50	15.00	30.00
❑ SR-25150 [S]	The Folk Song World of Jimmie Rodgers	1961	10.00	20.00	40.00
❑ R-25160 [M]	The Best of Jimmie Rodgers' Folk Tunes	1961	7.50	15.00	30.00
❑ SR-25160 [S]	The Best of Jimmie Rodgers' Folk Tunes	1961	10.00	20.00	40.00
—Black vinyl					
❑ SR-25160 [S]	The Best of Jimmie Rodgers' Folk Tunes	1961	62.50	125.00	250.00
—Red vinyl					
❑ R-25179 [M]	15 Million Sellers	1962	6.25	12.50	25.00
❑ SR-25179 [P]	15 Million Sellers	1962	5.00	10.00	20.00
—Orange and yellow label					
❑ SR-25179 [P]	15 Million Sellers	1962	7.50	15.00	30.00
—White label with colored spokes					
❑ R-25199 [M]	Folk Songs	1963	5.00	10.00	20.00
❑ SR-25199 [S]	Folk Songs	1963	6.25	12.50	25.00
❑ SR-42006	Yours Truly	1968	3.75	7.50	15.00

RODRIGUEZ, JOHNNY
45s
CAPITOL

Number	Title (A Side/B Side)	Yr	VG	VG+	NM
❑ B-44071	I Didn't (Every Chance I Had)/ I'm Not That Good at Goodbye	1987	—	2.00	4.00
❑ B-44204	I Wanta Wake Up with You/ Someday I'm Gonna Finish Leaving You	1988	—	2.00	4.00
❑ B-44245	You Might Want to Use Me Again/ She Loves Austin	1988	—	2.00	4.00
❑ B-44325	No Chance to Dance/Back to Stay	1989	—	2.00	4.00
❑ B-44403	Back to Stay/ Someday I'm Gonna Finish Leaving You	1989	—	2.00	4.00

COLUMBIA

Number	Title (A Side/B Side)	Yr	VG	VG+	NM
❑ 02987	The Most Beautiful Girl/Too Far Gone	1982	—	2.00	4.00
—With Ray Conniff; B-side by Zella Lehr with Ray Conniff					
EPIC					
❑ 01033	I Want You Tonight/ Your Love Isn't Mine Anymore	1981	—	—	3.00

Number	Title (A Side/B Side)	Yr	VG	VG+	NM
❑ 02411	Trying Not to Love You/Mexico Rain	1981	—	—	3.00
❑ 02638	It's Not the Same Old You/Born with the Blues	1981	—	—	3.00
❑ 03275	He's Not Entitled to Your Love/ Starting All Over Again	1982	—	—	3.00
❑ 03598	Foolin'/Because of You	1983	—	—	3.00
❑ 03972	How Could I Love Her So Much/ Somethin' About a Jukebox	1983	—	—	3.00
❑ 04206	Back on Her Mind Again/Eleven Roses	1983	—	—	3.00
❑ 04336	Too Late to Go Home/ No Memories Hangin' 'Round	1984	—	—	3.00
❑ 04460	Let's Leave the Lights On Tonight/ What a Movie You'd Make	1984	—	—	3.00
❑ 04562	First Time Burned/Hand Me Another of Those	1984	—	—	3.00
❑ 04628	Rose of My Heart/Down in the Boondocks	1984	—	—	3.00
❑ 04838	Here I Am Again/Full Circle	1985	—	—	3.00
❑ 05732	She Don't Cry Like She Used To/ Back on Her Mind Again	1985	—	—	3.00
❑ 05863	Maxine/Full Circle	1986	—	—	3.00
❑ 50671	Down on the Rio Grande/Mexico Holiday	1979	—	2.00	4.00
❑ 50735	Fools for Each Other/Street Walker	1979	—	2.00	4.00
❑ 50791	I Hate the Way I Love It/Almost Persuaded	1979	—	2.00	4.00
—With Charly McClain					
❑ 50808	What'll I Tell Virginia/Whatever Gets Me Through the Night	1979	—	2.00	4.00
❑ 50859	Love, Look At Us Now/Where Did It Go	1980	—	2.00	4.00
❑ 50932	North of the Border/ When She Gets Around to Me	1980	—	2.00	4.00
MERCURY					
❑ 55004	Eres Tu/You Put a Hold on Me	1977	—	2.00	4.00
❑ 55012	Savin' This Love Song for You/Que Te Quiero	1977	—	2.00	4.00
❑ 55020	We Believe in Happy Endings/The Immigrant	1978	—	2.00	4.00
❑ 55029	Love Me with All Your Heart (Cuando Caliente El Sol)	1978	—	2.00	4.00
❑ 55050	Alibis/Rest Your Love on Me	1978	—	2.00	4.00
❑ 73334	Pass Me By (If You're Only Passing Through)/ Jealous Heart	1972	—	2.50	5.00
❑ 73368	You Always Come Back (To Hurting Me)/I Wonder Where You Are Tonight	1973	—	2.50	5.00
❑ 73416	Ridin' My Thumb to Mexico/Release Me	1973	—	2.50	5.00
❑ 73446	That's the Way Love Goes/ I Really Don't Want to Know	1973	—	2.50	5.00
❑ 73471	Something/Born to Lose	1974	—	2.50	5.00
❑ 73493	Dance with Me (Just One More Time)/ Faded Love	1974	—	2.00	4.00
—Chicago skyline label					
❑ 73493	Dance with Me (Just One More Time)/ Faded Love	1974	—	2.50	5.00
—Red label					
❑ 73621	We're Over/Oh I Miss You	1974	—	2.00	4.00
❑ 73659	I Just Can't Get Her Out of My Mind/ Have I Told You Lately	1975	—	2.00	4.00
❑ 73682	Just Get Up and Close the Door/ Am I That Easy to Forget	1975	—	2.00	4.00
❑ 73715	Love Put a Song in My Heart/Steppin' Out on You	1975	—	2.00	4.00
❑ 73769	I Couldn't Be Me Without You/ Sometimes I Wish I Were You	1976	—	2.00	4.00
❑ 73815	I Wonder If I Ever Said Goodbye/Louisiana	1976	—	2.00	4.00
❑ 73855	Hillbilly Heart/Commonly Known As the Blues	1976	—	2.00	4.00
❑ 73878	Desperado/There'll Always Be Honky-Tonks in Texas	1976	—	2.00	4.00
❑ 73914	If Practice Makes Perfect/Hard Times	1977	—	2.00	4.00

Albums
CAPITOL

Number	Title	Yr	VG	VG+	NM
❑ C1-90040	Gracias	1988	2.50	5.00	10.00
EPIC					
❑ JE 36014	Rodriguez	1979	2.50	5.00	10.00
❑ JE 36274	Through My Eyes	1980	2.50	5.00	10.00
❑ JE 36587	Gypsy	1980	2.50	5.00	10.00
❑ FE 37103	After the Rain	1981	2.50	5.00	10.00
❑ FE 38321	Biggest Hits	1982	2.50	5.00	10.00
❑ FE 38806	For Every Rose	1983	2.50	5.00	10.00
❑ FE 39172	Foolin' with Fire	1984	2.50	5.00	10.00
❑ FE 39583	Full Circle	1985	2.50	5.00	10.00
MERCURY					
❑ SRM-1-686	All I Ever Meant to Do Was Sing	1973	3.75	7.50	15.00
❑ SRM-1-699	My Third Album	1974	3.75	7.50	15.00
❑ SRM-1-1012	Songs About Ladies and Love	1974	3.75	7.50	15.00
❑ SRM-1-1032	Just Get Up and Close the Door	1975	3.75	7.50	15.00
❑ SRM-1-1057	Love Put a Song in My Heart	1975	3.75	7.50	15.00
❑ SRM-1-1078	The Greatest Hits of Johnny Rodriguez	1976	3.75	7.50	15.00
❑ SRM-1-1110	Reflecting	1976	3.00	6.00	12.00
❑ SRM-1-1144	Practice Makes Perfect	1977	3.00	6.00	12.00
❑ SRM-1-5003	Just for You	1977	3.00	6.00	12.00
❑ SRM-1-5011	Love Me with All You Heart	1978	3.00	6.00	12.00
❑ SRM-1-5015	Johnny Rodriguez Was Here	1979	3.00	6.00	12.00
❑ SRM-1-5022	Sketches	1980	3.00	6.00	12.00
❑ SR-61378	Introducing Johnny Rodriguez	1973	3.75	7.50	15.00
❑ 826271-1	The Greatest Hits of Johnny Rodriguez	1985	2.00	4.00	8.00
—Reissue					

ROE, TOMMY
45s
ABC

Number	Title (A Side/B Side)	Yr	VG	VG+	NM
❑ 10762	Sweet Pea/Much More Love	1966	2.50	5.00	10.00
—Reissue; this was the common version when this song was a hit; earliest copies have "ABC Records" standing alone (not in a circle)					
❑ 10852	Hooray for Hazel/Need Your Love	1966	2.50	5.00	10.00
❑ 10888	It's Now Winters Day/Kick Me Charlie	1966	2.00	4.00	8.00
❑ 10888 [PS]	It's Now Winters Day/Kick Me Charlie	1966	3.75	7.50	15.00
❑ 10908	Sing Along with Me/Night Time	1967	2.00	4.00	8.00
❑ 10933	Moon Talk/Sweet Sounds	1967	2.00	4.00	8.00
❑ 10945	Little Miss Sunshine/You I Need	1967	2.00	4.00	8.00
❑ 10989	Melancholy Mood/Paisley Dreams	1967	2.00	4.00	8.00
❑ 11039	Dottie I Like It/Soft Words	1968	2.00	4.00	8.00
❑ 11076	An Oldie But a Goodie/Sugar Cane	1968	2.00	4.00	8.00
❑ 11140	It's Gonna Hurt Me/Gotta Keep Rolling Along	1968	2.00	4.00	8.00
❑ 11164	Dizzy/The You I Need	1969	2.50	5.00	10.00

R

Number	Title (A Side/B Side)	Yr	VG	VG+	NM
❑ 11211	Heather Honey/Money Is My Pay	1969	—	3.00	6.00
❑ 11229	Jack and Jill/Tip Toe Tina	1969	—	3.00	6.00
❑ 11247	Jam Up Jelly Tight/Moontalk	1969	2.00	4.00	8.00
❑ 11247 [PS]	Jam Up Jelly Tight/Moontalk	1969	3.00	6.00	12.00
❑ 11258	Stir It Up and Serve It/Fire Fly	1970	—	3.00	6.00
❑ 11266	Pearl/A Dollar's Worth of Pennies	1970	—	3.00	6.00
❑ 11273	We Can Make Music/Gotta Keep Rolling Along	1970	—	3.00	6.00
❑ 11273 [PS]	We Can Make Music/Gotta Keep Rolling Along	1970	—	3.00	6.00
❑ 11281	King of Fools/Brush a Little Sunshine	1970	—	3.00	6.00
❑ 11287	Little Miss Goodie Two Shoes/Traffic Jam	1971	—	3.00	6.00
❑ 11293	King of Fools/Pistol-Legged Mama	1971	—	3.00	6.00
❑ 11307	Stagger Lee/Back Streets and Alleys	1971	—	3.00	6.00
ABC-PARAMOUNT					
❑ 10329	Sheila/Save Your Kisses	1962	3.75	7.50	15.00
❑ 10362	Susie Darlin'/Piddle De Pat	1962	3.00	6.00	12.00
❑ 10362 [PS]	Susie Darlin'/Piddle De Pat	1962	6.25	12.50	25.00
❑ 10379	Town Crier/Rainbow	1962	3.00	6.00	12.00
❑ 10379 [PS]	Town Crier/Rainbow	1962	7.50	15.00	30.00
❑ 10389	Don't Cry Donna/Gonna Take a Chance	1962	3.00	6.00	12.00
❑ 10423	The Folk Singer/Count on Me	1963	2.50	5.00	10.00
❑ 10454	Kiss and Run/What Makes the Blues	1963	2.50	5.00	10.00
❑ 10478	Everybody/Sorry I'm Late, Lisa	1963	3.75	7.50	15.00
❑ 10515	Come On/There Will Be Better Years	1964	2.50	5.00	10.00
❑ 10543	Carol/Be a Good Little Girl	1964	2.50	5.00	10.00
❑ 10555	Dance with Henry/Wild Water Skiing Weekend	1964	5.00	10.00	20.00
❑ 10579	Oh So Right/I Think I Love You	1964	3.00	6.00	12.00
❑ 10604	Party Girl/Oh How I Could Love You	1964	2.50	5.00	10.00
❑ 10623	Love Me, Love Me/				
	Diane from Manchester Square	1965	3.00	6.00	12.00
❑ 10665	Fourteen Pair of Shoes/Combo Music	1965	2.50	5.00	10.00
❑ 10696	The Gunfighter/I'm a Rambler, I'm a Gambler	1965	5.00	10.00	20.00
❑ 10706	I Keep Remembering (Things I Forgot)/				
	Wish You Didn't Have to Go	1965	2.50	5.00	10.00
❑ 10738	Doesn't Anybody Know My Name/				
	Everytime a Bluebird Cries	1965	2.50	5.00	10.00
❑ 10762	Sweet Pea/Much More Love	1966	6.25	12.50	25.00
AWESOME					
❑ 104	First Things First/(B-side unknown)	1984	—	3.00	6.00
❑ 108	Sittin' on a Mood/(B-side unknown)	1984	—	3.00	6.00
BGO					
❑ 1003	She Do Run Run/(B-side unknown)	1982	2.50	5.00	10.00
JUDD					
❑ 1018	Caveman/I Gotta Girl	1960	12.50	25.00	50.00
❑ 1022	Sheila/Pretty Girl	1960	37.50	75.00	150.00
MARK IV					
❑ 001	Caveman/I Gotta Girl	1960	25.00	50.00	100.00
MCA CURB					
❑ 52711	Some Such Foolishness/Barbara Lou	1985	—	2.00	4.00
❑ 52778	Radio Romance/Barbara Lou	1986	—	2.00	4.00
MERCURY					
❑ 888206-7	Let's Be Fools Like That Again/Barbara Lou	1986	—	—	3.00
❑ 888497-7	Back When It Really Mattered/Radio Romance	1987	—	—	3.00
MGM SOUTH					
❑ 7001	Mean Little Woman, Rosalie/Skyline	1972	—	2.50	5.00
❑ 7008	Sarah My Love/Chewing on Sugar Cane	1972	—	2.50	5.00
❑ 7013	Working Class Hero/Sun in My Eyes	1973	—	2.50	5.00
❑ 7025	Silver Eyes/Memphis Me	1973	—	3.00	6.00
MONUMENT					
❑ 45-205	Early in the Morning/Bad News	1976	—	2.50	5.00
❑ 45-228	Your Love Will See Me Through/				
	Working Class Hero	1977	—	2.50	5.00
❑ 8644	Glitter and Gleam/Bad News	1975	—	2.50	5.00
❑ 8662	Snowing Me Under/Rita and Her Band	1975	—	2.50	5.00
❑ 8684	Slow Dancing/Burn On Love Light	1976	—	2.50	5.00
❑ 8705	Everybody/Energy	1976	—	2.50	5.00
TRUMPET					
❑ 1401	Caveman/I Gotta Girl	1960	50.00	100.00	200.00
WARNER BROS.					
❑ 8660	Dreamin' Again/Love the Way You Love Me Up	1978	—	2.00	4.00
❑ 8720	Just Look at Me/Love the Way You Love Me Up	1978	—	2.50	5.00
❑ 8800	Massachusetts/Just Look at Me	1979	—	2.50	5.00
❑ 49085	You Better Move On/Just Look at Me	1979	—	2.00	4.00
❑ 49235	Charlie, I Love Your Wife/There Is No Sun on				
	Sunset Boulevard	1980	—	2.00	4.00
Albums					
ABC					
❑ S-467 [R]	Something for Everybody	1968	12.50	25.00	50.00
—Issued in rechanneled stereo four years after its original release					
❑ 594 [M]	It's Now Winters Day	1967	5.00	10.00	20.00
❑ S-594 [S]	It's Now Winters Day	1967	6.25	12.50	25.00
❑ 610 [M]	Phantasy	1967	10.00	20.00	40.00
❑ S-610 [S]	Phantasy	1967	10.00	20.00	40.00
❑ S-683	Dizzy	1969	5.00	10.00	20.00
❑ S-700	12 in a Roe/A Collection of Tommy Roe's				
	Greatest Hits	1969	5.00	10.00	20.00
❑ S-714	We Can Make Music	1970	3.75	7.50	15.00
❑ S-732	Beginnings	1971	3.75	7.50	15.00
❑ X-762	16 Greatest Hits	1972	3.75	7.50	15.00
❑ ST-90883 [S]	Sweet Pea	1966	10.00	20.00	40.00
—Capitol Record Club issue					
❑ T-90883 [M]	Sweet Pea	1966	10.00	20.00	40.00
—Capitol Record Club issue					
ABC-PARAMOUNT					
❑ 432 [M]	Sheila	1962	10.00	20.00	40.00
❑ S-432 [S]	Sheila	1962	12.50	25.00	50.00
❑ 467 [M]	Something for Everybody	1964	7.50	15.00	30.00
❑ 575 [M]	Sweet Pea	1966	7.50	51.00	30.00
❑ S-575 [S]	Sweet Pea	1966	10.00	20.00	40.00
ACCORD					
❑ SN-7155	Sheila	1981	2.50	5.00	10.00
MCA					
❑ 1519	Collectibles — Greatest Hits	1982	2.00	4.00	8.00
MONUMENT					
❑ 7604	Energy	1977	2.50	5.00	10.00
—Reissue of 34182					
❑ 7614	Full Bloom	1977	2.50	5.00	10.00
❑ PZ 34182	Energy	1976	3.00	6.00	12.00

Number	Title (A Side/B Side)	Yr	VG	VG+	NM
ROECKER, SHERRILL					
45s					
SWAN					
❑ 4173	Don't Say Nothin' (If You Can't Say Anything				
	Nice)/It's All Over	1964	2.50	5.00	10.00
ROEMANS, THE TOMMY ROE's backing group.					
45s					
ABC					
❑ 10814	When the Sun Shines in the Mornin'/Love (That's				
	All I Want)	1966	3.75	7.50	15.00
❑ 10871	All the Good Things/Pleasing You Pleases Me	1966	3.75	7.50	15.00
ABC-PARAMOUNT					
❑ 10583	Give Me a Chance/Your Friend	1964	5.00	10.00	20.00
❑ 10671	Miserlou/Don't	1965	5.00	10.00	20.00
❑ 10723	Universal Soldier/Lost Little Girl	1965	5.00	10.00	20.00
❑ 10757	Listen to Me/You Make Me Feel Good	1965	5.00	10.00	20.00
ROGER AND THE TRAVELERS					
45s					
EMBER					
❑ 1079	You're Daddy's Little Girl/				
	Just Gonna Be That Way	1961	25.00	50.00	100.00
LOST-NITE					
❑ 421	You're Daddy's Little Girl/				
	Just Gonna Be That Way	197?	—	3.00	6.00
—Reissue					
ROGERS, CHARLIE					
45s					
HIT					
❑ 155	The Spirit of This Land/Ringo	1964	2.00	4.00	8.00
—B-side by John Preston					
ROGERS, JIMMY					
45s					
CHESS					
❑ 1506	I Used to Love a Woman/Back Door Friend	1952	50.00	100.00	200.00
—Earlier Jimmy Rogers 45s on Chess are not known to exist					
❑ 1519	The Last Time/Out on the Road	1952	50.00	100.00	200.00
❑ 1543	Left Me with a Broken Heart/				
	Act Like You Love Me	1953	50.00	100.00	200.00
❑ 1574	Chicago Bound/Sloppy Drunk	1954	75.00	150.00	300.00
❑ 1616	You're the One/Blues All Day Long	1956	12.50	25.00	50.00
❑ 1643	Walking By Myself/If It Ain't Me	1956	12.50	25.00	50.00
❑ 1659	One Kiss/I Can't Believe	1957	12.50	25.00	50.00
❑ 1687	What Have I Done/Trace of You	1958	10.00	20.00	40.00
❑ 1721	Rock This House/My Last Meal	1959	7.50	15.00	30.00
ROGERS, JULIE					
45s					
MEGA					
❑ 0075	Almost Close to You/Where Do You Go	1972	—	2.50	5.00
MERCURY					
❑ 72332	The Wedding/Without Your Love	1964	2.00	4.00	8.00
—Red label					
❑ 72332	The Wedding/Without Your Love	1964	2.50	5.00	10.00
—Black label					
❑ 72380	Like a Child/The Love of a Boy	1965	2.00	4.00	8.00
❑ 72380 [PS]	Like a Child/The Love of a Boy	1965	3.00	6.00	12.00
❑ 72426	Hawaiian Wedding Song/				
	Turn Around, Look at Me	1965	2.00	4.00	8.00
❑ 72535	Another Year, Another Love, Another				
	Heartache/				
	Don't Waste Your Young Years on Him	1966	2.00	4.00	8.00
❑ 72646	Climb Ev'ry Mountain/				
	While the Angelus Was Ringing	1966	2.00	4.00	8.00
Albums					
MERCURY					
❑ MG-20981 [M]	Julie Rogers	1965	3.75	7.50	15.00
❑ SR-60981 [S]	Julie Rogers	1965	5.00	10.00	20.00
ROGERS, KENNY Also see THE BOBBY DOYLE THREE; THE FIRST EDITION; THE NEW CHRISTY MINSTRELS; THE SCHOLARS (1).					
45s					
CARLTON					
❑ 454	That Crazy Feeling/				
	We'll Always Have Each Other	1958	25.00	50.00	100.00
—As "Kenneth Rogers"					
❑ 454	That Crazy Feeling/				
	We'll Always Have Each Other	1958	25.00	50.00	100.00
—As "Kenny Rogers"					
❑ 468	For You Alone/I've Got a Lot to Learn	1958	15.00	30.00	60.00
KEN-LEE					
❑ 102	Jole Blon/Lonely	195?	25.00	50.00	100.00
LIBERTY					
❑ 1380	Lady/Sweet Music Man	1980	—	2.00	4.00
❑ 1380 [PS]	Lady/Sweet Music Man	1980	—	2.50	5.00
❑ 1391	Long Arm of the Law/You Were a Good Friend	1980	—	2.00	4.00
❑ 1415	I Don't Need You/Without You in My Life	1981	—	—	3.00
❑ 1415 [PS]	I Don't Need You/Without You in My Life	1981	—	2.00	4.00
❑ 1430	Share Your Love with Me/Greybeard	1981	—	—	3.00
❑ 1430 [PS]	Share Your Love with Me/Greybeard	1981	—	2.00	4.00
❑ 1438	Kentucky Homemade Christmas/				
	Carol of the Bells	1981	—	2.50	5.00
❑ 1438 [PS]	Kentucky Homemade Christmas/				
	Carol of the Bells	1981	—	3.00	6.00
❑ 1441	Blaze of Glory/The Good Life	1981	—	—	3.00
❑ 1444	Through the Years/So In Love with You	1981	—	—	3.00
❑ 1471	Love Will Turn You Around/I Want a Son	1982	—	—	3.00
❑ 1471 [PS]	Love Will Turn You Around/I Want a Son	1982	—	2.50	5.00
❑ 1485	A Love Song/Fool in Me	1982	—	—	3.00
❑ 1492	We've Got Tonight/You Are So Beautiful	1983	—	2.00	4.00
—A-side with Sheena Easton					
❑ 1492 [PS]	We've Got Tonight/You Are So Beautiful	1983	—	2.50	5.00
❑ 1495	All My Life/The Farther I Go	1983	—	—	3.00
❑ 1495 [PS]	All My Life/The Farther I Go	1983	—	2.00	4.00
❑ 1503	Scarlet Fever/What I Learned from Loving You	1983	—	—	3.00

Number	Title (A Side/B Side)	Yr	VG	VG+	NM
❏ 1511	Sweet Music Man/You Were a Good Friend	1983	—	—	3.00
❏ 1524	A Stranger in My Place/Love Is What We Make It	1985	—	—	3.00
❏ 1525	Twentieth Century Fool/It Turns Me Inside Out	1985	—	—	3.00
❏ 1526	Abraham, Martin and John/Goodbye Marie	1985	—	—	3.00
❏ 4065 [DJ]	Christmas Everyday//Kentucky Homemade Christmas/Carol Of The Bells	198?	—	3.00	6.00
MERCURY					
❏ 72545	Here's That Rainy Day/Take Life in Stride	1966	6.25	12.50	25.00
RCA					
❏ 5016-7-R	They Don't Make Them Like They Used To/ Just the Thought of Losing You	1986	—	—	3.00
❏ 5016-7-R [PS]	They Don't Make Them Like They Used To/ Just the Thought of Losing You	1986	—	—	3.00
❏ 5078-7-R	Twenty Years Ago/The Heart of the Matter	1986	—	—	3.00
❏ 5209-7-R	Make No Mistake, She's Mine/You're My Love	1987	—	—	3.00
—With Ronnie Milsap					
❏ 5258-7-R	I Prefer the Moonlight/We're Doin' Alright	1987	—	—	3.00
❏ 6832-7-R	The Factory/One More Day	1987	—	—	3.00
❏ 8381-7-R	I Prefer the Moonlight/ Make No Mistake, She's Mine	1988	—	—	3.00
—Gold Standard Series; B-side with Ronnie Milsap					
❏ 8390-7-R	I Don't Call Him Daddy/We're Doin' Alright	1988	—	—	3.00
❏ PB-13710	This Woman/Buried Treasure	1984	—	—	3.00
❏ PB-13710 [PS]	This Woman/Buried Treasure	1984	—	2.00	4.00
❏ JK-13713 [DJ]	Buried Treasure (same on both sides)	1984	—	2.50	5.00
❏ PB-13774	Eyes That See in the Dark/Hold Me	1984	—	—	3.00
❏ PB-13832	Evening Star/Midsummer Nights	1984	—	—	3.00
❏ PB-13899	What About Me/The Rest of Last Night	1984	—	—	3.00
—With Kim Carnes and James Ingram					
❏ PB-13899 [PS]	What About Me/The Rest of Last Night	1984	—	2.00	4.00
❏ PB-13944	The Christmas Song/Medley: Winter Wonderland-Sleigh Ride	1984	—	2.00	4.00
—B-side by Dolly Parton					
❏ PB-13975	Crazy/The Stranger	1984	—	—	3.00
❏ PB-13975 [PS]	Crazy/The Stranger	1984	—	2.00	4.00
❏ GB-14074	This Woman/What About Me	1985	—	—	3.00
—Gold Standard Series; B-side by Kenny Rogers, Kim Carnes and James Ingram					
❏ PB-14194	Morning Desire/People in Love	1985	—	—	3.00
❏ PB-14194 [PS]	Morning Desire/People in Love	1985	—	2.00	4.00
—Fold-out poster sleeve					
❏ PB-14298	Tomb of the Unknown Love/Our Perfect Song	1986	—	—	3.00
❏ PB-14298 [PS]	Tomb of the Unknown Love/Our Perfect Song	1986	—	2.00	4.00
❏ GB-14353	Crazy/Morning Desire	1986	—	—	3.00
—Gold Standard Series					
❏ PB-14384	The Pride Is Back/Didn't We?	1986	—	2.00	4.00
—A-side: With Nickie Ryder					
❏ PB-14384 [PS]	The Pride Is Back/Didn't We?	1986	—	2.00	4.00
REPRISE					
❏ PRO-S-3904 [DJ]	Maybe (same on both sides)	1990	—	3.00	6.00
—With Holly Dunn					
❏ 18835	Bed of Roses/I'll Be There for You	1992	—	—	3.00
❏ 18967	Someone Must Feel Like a Fool Tonight/ Sunshine	1992	—	—	3.00
❏ 19080	If You Want to Find Love/Sunshine	1991	—	—	3.00
❏ 19324	Walk Away/What I Did for Love	1991	—	—	3.00
❏ 19504	Lay My Body Down/Crazy in Love	1991	—	—	3.00
❏ 19972	Maybe/If I Knew Then What I Know Now	1990	—	—	3.00
—A-side with Holly Dunn; B-side with Gladys Knight					
❏ 22750	Christmas in America/Joy to the World	1989	—	—	3.00
❏ 22750 [PS]	Christmas in America/Joy to the World	1989	—	—	3.00
❏ 22828	The Vows Go Unbroken (Always True to You)/ One Night	1989	—	—	3.00
❏ 22853	(Something Inside) So Strong/When You Put Your Heart In It	1989	—	—	3.00
❏ 27690	Planet Texas/When You Put Your Heart in It	1988	—	—	3.00
❏ 27690 [PS]	Planet Texas/When You Put Your Heart in It	1988	—	—	3.00
❏ 27812	When You Put Your Heart In It/(Instrumental)	1988	—	—	3.00
❏ 27812 [PS]	When You Put Your Heart In It/(Instrumental)	1988	—	—	3.00
UNITED ARTISTS					
❏ XW746	Love Lifted Me/Home-Made Love	1975	—	2.00	4.00
❏ XW798	There's an Old Man in Our Town/Home-Made Love	1976	—	2.00	4.00
❏ XW812	I Would Like to See You Again/While the Feeling's Good	1976	—	2.00	4.00
❏ XW868	Laura (What's He Got That I Ain't Got)/ I Wasn't Mad Enough	1976	—	2.00	4.00
❏ XW929	Lucille/Till I Get It Right	1976	—	2.00	4.00
❏ XW1027	Daytime Friends/We Don't Make Love Anymore	1977	—	2.00	4.00
❏ XW1095	Sweet Music Man/Lying Again	1977	—	2.00	4.00
❏ XW1151	Love Lifted Me/Reuben James	1978	—	2.00	4.00
❏ XW1152	Today I Started Loving You Again/ Just Dropped In (To See What Condition My Condition Was In)	1978	—	2.00	4.00
❏ XW1153	Daytime Friends/But You Know I Love You	1978	—	2.00	4.00
❏ XW1154	Lucille/Something's Burning	1978	—	2.00	4.00
❏ XW1155	Sweet Music Man/ Ruby, Don't Take Your Love to Town	1978	—	2.00	4.00
—B-sides of the above five singles are re-recordings of First Edition hits paired with early United Artists country hits					
❏ XW1210	Love Or Something Like It/Starting Again	1978	—	2.00	4.00
❏ XW1250	The Gambler/Momma's Waiting	1978	—	2.00	4.00
❏ XW1273	She Believes in Me/Morgana Jones	1979	—	2.00	4.00
❏ XW1273 [PS]	She Believes in Me/Morgana Jones	1979	—	2.50	5.00
❏ 1315	You Decorated My Life/One Man's Woman	1979	—	2.00	4.00
❏ 1315 [PS]	You Decorated My Life/One Man's Woman	1979	—	2.50	5.00
❏ 1327	Coward of the County/I Wanna Make You Smile	1979	—	2.00	4.00
❏ 1345	Don't Fall in Love with a Dreamer/Intro: Goin' Home to the Rock-Gideon Tanner	1980	—	2.00	4.00
—A-side: With Kim Carnes					
❏ 1345 [PS]	Don't Fall in Love with a Dreamer/Intro: Goin' Home to the Rock-Gideon Tanner	1980	—	2.50	5.00
❏ 1359	Love the World Away/Sayin' Goodbye-Requiem	1980	—	2.00	4.00
Albums					
LIBERTY					
❏ LO-607	Love Lifted Me	1981	2.00	4.00	8.00
—Reissue of United Artists 607					

Number	Title (A Side/B Side)	Yr	VG	VG+	NM
❏ LO-689	Kenny Rogers	1981	2.00	4.00	8.00
—Reissue of United Artists 689					
❏ LO-754	Daytime Friends	1981	2.00	4.00	8.00
—Reissue of United Artists 754					
❏ LO-835	Ten Years of Gold	1981	2.00	4.00	8.00
—Reissue of United Artists 835					
❏ LO-903	Love Or Something Like It	1981	2.00	4.00	8.00
—Reissue of United Artists 903					
❏ LO-934	The Gambler	1981	2.00	4.00	8.00
—Reissue of United Artists 934					
❏ LOO-979	Kenny	1981	2.00	4.00	8.00
—Reissue of United Artists 979					
❏ LOO-1035	Gideon	1981	2.00	4.00	8.00
—Reissue of United Artists 1035					
❏ LOO-1072	Kenny Rogers' Greatest Hits	1980	2.00	4.00	8.00
❏ LOO-1108	Share Your Love	1981	2.00	4.00	8.00
❏ LN-10207	Love Lifted Me	1984	—	3.00	6.00
❏ LN-10208	Kenny Rogers	1983	—	3.00	6.00
—Budget-line reissue					
❏ LN-10240	Christmas	198?	2.00	4.00	8.00
—Reissue of LOO 51115					
❏ LN-10243	Gideon	1984	—	3.00	6.00
—Budget-line reissue					
❏ LN-10245	We've Got Tonight	1984	—	3.00	6.00
—Budget-line reissue					
❏ LN-10246	Love Will Turn You Around	1984	—	3.00	6.00
—Budget-line reissue					
❏ LN-10247	The Gambler	1984	—	3.00	6.00
—Budget-line reissue					
❏ LN-10248	Kenny	1984	—	3.00	6.00
—Budget-line reissue					
❏ LN-10249	Daytime Friends	1984	—	3.00	6.00
—Budget-line reissue					
❏ LN-10250	Love Or Something Like It	1984	—	3.00	6.00
—Budget-line reissue					
❏ LN-10254	Ten Years of Gold	1984	—	3.00	6.00
—Budget-line reissue					
❏ LOO-51115	Christmas	1981	2.50	5.00	10.00
❏ LO-51124	Love Will Turn You Around	1982	2.00	4.00	8.00
❏ LO-51143	We've Got Tonight	1983	2.00	4.00	8.00
❏ LV-51152	Twenty Greatest Hits	1983	2.00	4.00	8.00
❏ LO-51154	Duets	1984	2.00	4.00	8.00
❏ LO-51157	Love Is What We Make It	1985	2.00	4.00	8.00
MOBILE FIDELITY					
❏ 1-044	The Gambler	1981	5.00	10.00	20.00
—Audiophile vinyl					
❏ 1-049	Kenny Rogers' Greatest Hits	1981	5.00	10.00	20.00
—Audiophile vinyl					
RCA					
❏ 5833-1-R	They Don't Make Them Like They Used To	1986	2.00	4.00	8.00
❏ 6484-1-R	I Prefer the Moonlight	1987	2.00	4.00	8.00
❏ 8371-1-R	Greatest Hits	1988	2.00	4.00	8.00
RCA VICTOR					
❏ AFL1-4697	Eyes That See in the Dark	1983	2.00	4.00	8.00
❏ AFL1-4697	Eyes That See in the Dark	1983	50.00	100.00	200.00
—Picture disc on one side, regular RCA label on other; possibly an in-house demo at the RCA Indianapolis pressing plant					
❏ AJL1-5335	What About Me	1984	2.00	4.00	8.00
❏ AJL1-7023	The Heart of the Matter	1985	2.00	4.00	8.00
REPRISE					
❏ 25792	Something Inside So Strong	1989	2.50	5.00	10.00
❏ 25973	Christmas in America	1989	3.00	6.00	12.00
❏ R 144593	Love Is Strange	1990	5.00	10.00	20.00
—Only available on vinyl from BMG Direct Marketing					
UNITED ARTISTS					
❏ UA-LA607-G	Love Lifted Me	1976	3.75	7.50	15.00
❏ UA-LA689-G	Kenny Rogers	1976	2.50	5.00	10.00
❏ UA-LA754-G	Daytime Friends	1977	2.50	5.00	10.00
❏ UA-LA835-H	Ten Years of Gold	1978	2.50	5.00	10.00
❏ UA-LA903-H	Love Or Something Like It	1978	2.50	5.00	10.00
❏ UA-LA934-H	The Gambler	1978	2.50	5.00	10.00
❏ LWAK-979	Kenny	1979	2.50	5.00	10.00
❏ LOO-1035	Gideon	1980	2.50	5.00	10.00

ROGERS, KENNY, AND DOLLY PARTON Also see each artist's individual listings.
12-Inch Singles
RCA

Number	Title (A Side/B Side)	Yr	VG	VG+	NM
❏ JR-13662 [DJ]	Islands in the Stream (same on both sides)	1983	2.00	4.00	8.00
45s					
RCA					
❏ 5352-7-R	Christmas Without You/I Believe in Santa Claus	1987	—	—	3.00
—B-side by Dolly Parton					
❏ 9070-7-R	Christmas Without You/Medley: Winter Wonderland-Sleigh Ride	1989	—	—	3.00
—B-side by Dolly Parton					
❏ PB-13615	Islands in the Stream/I Will Always Love You	1983	—	—	3.00
❏ PB-13615 [PS]	Islands in the Stream/I Will Always Love You	1983	—	2.00	4.00
—Version 2: With Dolly Parton's name the same size as Kenny Rogers'					
❏ PB-13615 [PS]	Islands in the Stream/I Will Always Love You	1983	—	2.50	5.00
—Version 1: With "(Duet with Dolly Parton)" in small letters					
❏ PB-13945	The Greatest Gift of All/White Christmas	1984	—	2.00	4.00
❏ PB-14058	Real Love/I Can't Be True	1985	—	—	3.00
❏ GB-14073	Islands in the Stream/Eyes That See in the Dark	1985	—	—	3.00
—Gold Standard Series; B-side by Kenny Rogers					
❏ PB-14261	Christmas Without You/A Christmas to Remember	1985	—	—	3.00
❏ PB-14261 [PS]	Christmas Without You/A Christmas to Remember	1985	—	2.00	4.00
REPRISE					
❏ 19760	Love Is Strange/Walk Away	1990	—	—	3.00
Albums					
RCA VICTOR					
❏ ASL1-5307	Once Upon a Christmas	1984	2.50	5.00	10.00

R

Number	Title (A Side/B Side)	Yr	VG	VG+	NM

ROGERS, KENNY, AND THE FIRST EDITION See THE FIRST EDITION.

ROGERS, KENNY, AND DOTTIE WEST Also see each artist's individual listings.
45s
LIBERTY

Number	Title (A Side/B Side)	Yr	VG	VG+	NM
❏ 1516	Baby I'm-a Want You/Together Again	1984	—	—	3.00
UNITED ARTISTS					
❏ XW1137	Every Time Two Fools Collide/We Love Each Other	1978	—	2.00	4.00
❏ XW1234	Anyone Who Isn't Me Tonight/You and Me	1978	—	2.00	4.00
❏ XW1276	All I Ever Need Is You/Another Somebody Done Somebody Wrong Song	1979	—	2.00	4.00
❏ XW1299	Till I Can Make It on My Own/Midnight Flyer	1979	—	2.00	4.00

Albums
UNITED ARTISTS

Number	Title	Yr	VG	VG+	NM
❏ UA-LA864-G	Every Time Two Fools Collide	1978	2.50	5.00	10.00
❏ UA-LA946-H	Classics	1979	2.50	5.00	10.00

ROGERS, MORRIS, AND THE CONTINENTALS
45s
DELTA

Number	Title (A Side/B Side)	Yr	VG	VG+	NM
❏ 601/2	The Leg/Wonders of Love	1963	50.00	100.00	200.00

ROGERS, TIMMIE
45s
CADET

Number	Title (A Side/B Side)	Yr	VG	VG+	NM
❏ 5685	Super Soul Brothers/It Rolls Through Everything	1971	—	2.50	5.00
CAMEO					
❏ 116	Back to School Again/I've Got a Dog Who Loves Me	1957	7.50	15.00	30.00
❏ 131	Take Me to Your Leader/Fla-Ga-La-Pa	1958	6.25	12.50	25.00
CAPITOL					
❏ F2406	Saturday Night/If I Were You, Baby	1953	6.25	12.50	25.00
❏ F2509	Oh Yeah/Nothin' Wrong with Nothin'	1953	6.25	12.50	25.00
EPIC					
❏ 9813	If You Can't Smile and Say Yes (Please Don't Cry and Say No)/Chum Goy Tum Toy Fricasee (Soy Soy Soo)	1965	2.00	4.00	8.00
❏ 9899	Everybody Wants to Go to Heaven, But Nobody Wants to Die/Too Young to Go Steady	1966	2.00	4.00	8.00
MERCURY					
❏ 70451	If I Give My Heart to You/Teedle-Dee Teedle-Dum	1954	10.00	20.00	40.00
PAR-TEE					
❏ 1303	Watergate/Snake Hips	1973	—	2.50	5.00
PARKWAY					
❏ 814	I Love Ya, I Love Ya, I Love Ya/Tee-Hee	1960	3.75	7.50	15.00
PHILIPS					
❏ 40074	Oh Yeah/Fla-Ga-La-Pa	1962	2.50	5.00	10.00
SIGNATURE					
❏ 12037	First Proposal/Underwater Cha Cha Cha	1960	3.75	7.50	15.00

Albums
PHILIPS

Number	Title	Yr	VG	VG+	NM
❏ PHM 200088 [M]	If I Were President	1963	5.00	10.00	20.00
❏ PHS 600088 [S]	If I Were President	1963	6.25	12.50	25.00

ROGERS, WELDON
45s
IMPERIAL

Number	Title (A Side/B Side)	Yr	VG	VG+	NM
❏ 5451	So Long, Good Luck and Goodbye/Trying to Get to You	1957	50.00	100.00	200.00

—B-side is actually The Teen Kings' version rather than Rogers'; by mistake, the wrong recording left Norman Petty's studio for Imperial.

JE-WEL

Number	Title (A Side/B Side)	Yr	VG	VG+	NM
❏ 103	Everybody Wants You/This Song's Just for You	1956	250.00	500.00	1000.

ROKES, THE
45s
RCA VICTOR

Number	Title (A Side/B Side)	Yr	VG	VG+	NM
❏ 47-9199	Let's Live for Today/Change of Papers	1967	3.00	6.00	12.00
❏ 47-9546	When the Wind Arises/The Works of Bartholomew	1968	3.00	6.00	12.00

Albums
RCA VICTOR INTERNATIONAL

Number	Title	Yr	VG	VG+	NM
❏ FPM-185 [M]	Che Mondo Strano	1967	20.00	40.00	80.00

ROLLERS, THE
45s
LIBERTY

Number	Title (A Side/B Side)	Yr	VG	VG+	NM
❏ 55303	Bonneville/Got My Eye on You	1961	5.00	10.00	20.00
❏ 55320	The Continental Walk/I Want You So	1961	5.00	10.00	20.00
❏ 55357	The Bounce/Teenager's Waltz	1961	5.00	10.00	20.00

ROLLETTES, THE
45s
CLASS

Number	Title (A Side/B Side)	Yr	VG	VG+	NM
❏ 201	Sad Fool/Wham Bam	1957	10.00	20.00	40.00
❏ 203	Kiss Me Benny/More Than You Realize	1957	10.00	20.00	40.00
MELKER					
❏ 103	An Understanding/I'm Trying (To Make You Love Me)	1960	500.00	1000.	2000.

ROLLING STONES, THE Also see BRIAN JONES; RONNIE WOOD; MICK TAYLOR.
12-Inch Singles
ROLLING STONES

Number	Title (A Side/B Side)	Yr	VG	VG+	NM
❏ PR 70 [DJ]	Hot Stuff/Crazy Mama	1976	20.00	40.00	80.00

—Black and blue "splash" vinyl (counterfeits have black spots in blue vinyl)

Number	Title (A Side/B Side)	Yr	VG	VG+	NM
❏ DSKO 119 [DJ]	Miss You (8:36) (same on both sides)	1978	12.50	25.00	50.00
❏ DSKO 174 [DJ]	Miss You (8:34)/Hot Stuff (5:21)	1979	10.00	20.00	40.00
❏ DMD 253 [DJ]	If I Was a Dancer (Dance Pt. II)/Dance (Instrumental)	1981	7.50	15.00	30.00
❏ PR 367 [DJ]	Emotional Rescue (4:18) (5:38)	1980	10.00	20.00	40.00
❏ PR 397 [DJ]	Start Me Up (same on both sides)	1981	7.50	15.00	30.00
❏ PR 574 [DJ]	She Was Hot/Think I'm Going Mad	1983	10.00	20.00	40.00
❏ DMD 685 [DJ]	Undercover of the Night (6:22) (Album Version 4:31)	1983	3.75	7.50	15.00

—Yellow label promo

Number	Title (A Side/B Side)	Yr	VG	VG+	NM
❏ PR 692 [DJ]	Too Much Blood (12:33)/(Dub 8:00) (Album 6:25)	1983	5.00	10.00	20.00
❏ CAS 1765 [DJ]	Mixed Emotions (Chris Kimsey's 12" Mix 6:12)/(LP Version 4:00)	1989	10.00	20.00	40.00
❏ CAS 2275 [DJ]	Harlem Shuffle (same on both sides)	1986	3.75	7.50	15.00
❏ CAS 2340 [DJ]	One Hit (To the Body) (London Mix 7:00) (Edit) (LP Version)	1986	5.00	10.00	20.00
❏ CAS 4051 [DJ]	Sexdrive (Club Version 6:00)/(Edited Club Version 4:32) (Single Edit 4:26)	1991	15.00	30.00	60.00
❏ DK 4609	Miss You (8:36)/Far Away Eyes (4:24)	1978	2.50	5.00	10.00

—With "Atlantic/Atco Disco" sleeve

Number	Title (A Side/B Side)	Yr	VG	VG+	NM
❏ DK 4609	Miss You (8:36)/Far Away Eyes (4:24)	1978	3.00	6.00	12.00

—With "The Rolling Stones Miss You" die-cut sleeve

Number	Title (A Side/B Side)	Yr	VG	VG+	NM
❏ DK 4616	Miss You (8:34)/Hot Stuff (5:21)	1979	7.50	15.00	30.00
❏ 44-05365	Harlem Shuffle (NY Mix 6:25)/(London Mix 6:19)	1986	2.50	5.00	10.00
❏ 44-05388	One Hit (To the Body) (London Mix 7:00)//One Hit (To the Body) (Edit)/Fight	1986	2.00	4.00	8.00
❏ 44-73133	Rock and a Hard Place (Dance Mix 6:54) (Oh-Oh Hard Dub Mix 6:50)/(Michael Brauer Mix 6:57) (Bonus Beats 4:02)	1989	3.75	7.50	15.00
❏ 96902	Too Much Blood (12:33)/(Dub 8:00) (Album 6:25)	1984	3.75	7.50	15.00
❏ 96978	Undercover of the Night (6:22)/Feel On Baby (Instrumental 6:27)	1983	2.50	5.00	10.00
VIRGIN					
❏ SPRO-12746 [DJ]	Anybody Seen My Baby? (Armand van Helden Rolling Steelo Mix 4:08) (Soul Solution Vocal Dub 3:44) (Casanova New Vocal Mix 4:00)	1997	10.00	20.00	40.00
❏ SPRO-12788 [(2)DJ]	Saint of Me (Deep Dish Club Mix 7:35) (Deep Dish Grunge Garage Dub 7:23) (Deep Dish Rolling Dub 7:16)//(Todd Terry Extended Remix 6:00) (Todd Terry Fade 3:35)/(Todd Terry's Freeze Dub 7:45) (Todd Terry Dub #2 7:45)	1998	17.50	35.00	70.00
❏ Y-38446	Love Is Strong (Teddy Riley Extended Remix 5:02) (Teddy Riley Extended Rock Remix 4:47) (Teddy Riley Dub Remix 4:05)/(Joe the Butcher Club Mix 5:26) (Album Version 3:46) (Teddy Riley Instrumental 4:47)	1994	2.00	4.00	8.00
❏ Y-38468	You Got Me Rocking (Perfecto Mix 5:00) (Sexy Dub Mix 6:16)//(Trance Mix 4:58) (Album Version 3:34)/Jump on Top of Me	1995	2.00	4.00	8.00
❏ Y-38626	Saint of Me (Deep Dish Club Mix 7:35) (Deep Dish Grunge Dub 7:23)//(Todd Terry Extended Remix 6:00)/Anyway You Look at It	1998	2.00	4.00	8.00

45s
ABKCO

Number	Title (A Side/B Side)	Yr	VG	VG+	NM
❏ 4701	I Don't Know Why/Try a Little Harder	1975	—	2.50	5.00

—With A-side writing credits of "Wonder, Riser, Hunter, Hardaway"

Number	Title (A Side/B Side)	Yr	VG	VG+	NM
❏ 4701	I Don't Know Why/Try a Little Harder	1975	2.50	5.00	10.00

—With A-side writing credits of "Jagger, Richards, Taylor"

Number	Title (A Side/B Side)	Yr	VG	VG+	NM
❏ 4701 [DJ]	I Don't Know Why (same on both sides)	1975	5.00	10.00	25.00
❏ 4702	Out of Time/Jiving Sister Fanny	1975	—	3.00	6.00
❏ 4702 [DJ]	Out of Time/Jiving Sister Fanny	1975	5.00	10.00	25.00
LONDON					
❏ 901	Paint It, Black/Stupid Girl	1966	3.75	7.50	15.00
❏ 901 [DJ]	Paint It, Black/Stupid Girl	1966	25.00	50.00	75.00

—Orange swirl label

Number	Title (A Side/B Side)	Yr	VG	VG+	NM
❏ 901 [PS]	Paint It, Black/Stupid Girl	1966	15.00	30.00	60.00
❏ 902	Mothers Little Helper/Lady Jane	1966	3.75	7.50	15.00
❏ 902 [DJ]	Mothers Little Helper/Lady Jane	1966	25.00	50.00	75.00

—Orange swirl label

Number	Title (A Side/B Side)	Yr	VG	VG+	NM
❏ 902 [PS]	Mothers Little Helper/Lady Jane	1966	15.00	30.00	60.00
❏ 903	Have You Seen Your Mother, Baby, Standing in the Shadow?/Who's Driving My Plane	1966	3.75	7.50	15.00
❏ 903 [DJ]	Have You Seen Your Mother, Baby, Standing in the Shadow?/Who's Driving My Plane	1966	25.00	50.00	75.00

—Orange swirl label

Number	Title (A Side/B Side)	Yr	VG	VG+	NM
❏ 903 [PS]	Have You Seen Your Mother, Baby, Standing in the Shadow?/Who's Driving My Plane	1966	15.00	30.00	60.00
❏ 904	Ruby Tuesday/Let's Spend the Night Together	1967	3.75	7.50	15.00
❏ 904 [DJ]	Ruby Tuesday/Let's Spend the Night Together	1967	25.00	50.00	75.00

—Orange swirl label

Number	Title (A Side/B Side)	Yr	VG	VG+	NM
❏ 904 [PS]	Let's Spend the Night Together/Ruby Tuesday	1967	15.00	30.00	60.00
❏ 905	Dandelion/We Love You	1967	5.00	10.00	20.00
❏ 905 [DJ]	Dandelion/We Love You	1967	25.00	50.00	75.00

—With full-length version of "We Love You"; orange swirl label

Number	Title (A Side/B Side)	Yr	VG	VG+	NM
❏ 905 [DJ]	Dandelion/We Love You	1967	50.00	100.00	150.00

—With 3:10 edited version of "We Love You"; orange swirl label

Number	Title (A Side/B Side)	Yr	VG	VG+	NM
❏ 905 [PS]	We Love You/Dandelion	1967	100.00	300.00	600.00
❏ 906	She's a Rainbow/2000 Light Years from Home	1967	5.00	10.00	20.00
❏ 906 [DJ]	She's a Rainbow/2000 Light Years from Home	1967	25.00	50.00	75.00

—Orange swirl label

Number	Title (A Side/B Side)	Yr	VG	VG+	NM
❏ 906 [PS]	She's a Rainbow/2000 Light Years from Home	1967	12.50	25.00	50.00
❏ 907	In Another Land/The Lantern	1967	6.25	12.50	25.00

—A-side credited to Bill Wyman, though taken from "Their Satanic Majesties Request"

Number	Title (A Side/B Side)	Yr	VG	VG+	NM
❏ 907 [DJ]	In Another Land/The Lantern	1967	25.00	50.00	75.00

—A-side credited to Bill Wyman; orange swirl label

Number	Title (A Side/B Side)	Yr	VG	VG+	NM
❏ 907 [PS]	In Another Land/The Lantern	1967	12.00	30.00	75.00
❏ 908	Jumpin' Jack Flash/Child of the Moon	1968	3.75	7.50	15.00
❏ 908 [DJ]	Jumpin' Jack Flash/Child of the Moon	1968	25.00	50.00	75.00

—Orange swirl label

Number	Title (A Side/B Side)	Yr	VG	VG+	NM
❏ 908 [PS]	Jumpin' Jack Flash/Child of the Moon	1968	10.00	20.00	40.00
❏ 909	Street Fighting Man/No Expectations	1968	5.00	10.00	20.00
❏ 909 [DJ]	Street Fighting Man/No Expectations	1968	25.00	50.00	75.00

—Orange swirl label

Number	Title (A Side/B Side)	Yr	VG	VG+	NM
❏ 909 [PS]	Street Fighting Man/No Expectations	1968	4000.	8000.	10000.
❏ 910	Honky Tonk Women/You Can't Always Get What You Want	1969	3.75	7.50	15.00
❏ 910 [PS]	Honky Tonk Women/You Can't Always Get What You Want	1969	7.50	15.00	30.00
❏ 9641	I Wanna Be Your Man/Stoned	1964	3000.	6000.	9000.

The Rolling Stones, "(I Can't Get No) Satisfaction," London 45-9766, picture sleeve, $200-$500.

The Rolling Stones, *Out of Our Heads*, London LL 3429, mono LP, maroon label with "London" unboxed at top, $20-$40.

The Rolling Stones, "Paint It, Black," London 45-901, picture sleeve, $30-$60.

The Rolling Stones and others, *Jamming with Edward*, Rolling Stones COC 39100, stereo LP, $7.50-$15.

The Rolling Stones, *Some Girls*, Rolling Stones COC 39108, stereo LP, with all faces visible and no "cover under reconstruction" patchwork, $7.50-$15.

The Rolling Stones, "Beast of Burden," Rolling Stones RS 19309, picture sleeve, $1,500-$2,000 (beware of counterfeits).

Number	Title (A Side/B Side)	Yr	VG	VG+	NM
9641 [DJ]	I Wanna Be Your Man/Stoned	1964	300.00	600.00	1000.

—With similar label to stock copy, except in white, black and gray

Number	Title (A Side/B Side)	Yr	VG	VG+	NM
9641 [DJ]	I Wanna Be Your Man/Stoned	1964	200.00	500.00	1500.

—White label, black print, script "London" at top

9657	Not Fade Away/I Wanna Be Your Man	1964	2.00	4.00	8.00

—Blue swirl label

9657	Not Fade Away/I Wanna Be Your Man	1964	10.00	20.00	40.00

—White, purple and blue label

9657 [DJ]	Not Fade Away/I Wanna Be Your Man	1964	200.00	400.00	900.00

—With similar label to original stock copy, except in white, black and gray

9657 [DJ]	Not Fade Away/I Wanna Be Your Man	1964	300.00	600.00	1000.

—White label, black print, script "London" at top

| 9657 [PS] | Not Fade Away/I Wanna Be Your Man | 1964 | 75.00 | 300.00 | 450.00 |
| 9682 | Tell Me (You're Coming Back)/I Just Want to Make Love to You | 1964 | 2.50 | 5.00 | 10.00 |

—Blue swirl label

9682	Tell Me (You're Coming Back)/I Just Want to Make Love to You	1964	10.00	20.00	40.00

—White, purple and blue label

9682 [DJ]	Tell Me (You're Coming Back)/I Just Want to Make Love to You	1964	25.00	50.00	75.00

—Orange swirl label

9682 [PS]	Tell Me (You're Coming Back)/I Just Want to Make Love to You	1964	50.00	125.00	175.00
5N 9682	Tell Me (You're Coming Back)/I Just Want to Make Love to You	1977	3.00	6.00	12.00

—Sunrise label; this version plays the LP version rather than the single edit, even though the label says "Time: 2:35"; number in trail-off wax is "5N-9682-A"

9687	It's All Over Now/Good Times Bad Times	1964	2.50	5.00	10.00

—Blue swirl label

9687	It's All Over Now/Good Times, Bad Times	1964	10.00	20.00	40.00

—White, purple and blue label

9687 [DJ]	It's All Over Now/Good Times, Bad Times	1964	25.00	50.00	75.00

—Orange swirl label

9687 [PS]	It's All Over Now/Good Times, Bad Times	1964	50.00	85.00	125.00
9708	Time Is On My Side/Congratulations	1964	2.50	5.00	10.00

—Blue swirl label

9708	Time Is On My Side/Congratulations	1964	7.50	15.00	30.00

—White, purple and blue label

9708 [DJ]	Time Is On My Side/Congratulations	1964	25.00	50.00	75.00

—Orange swirl label

9708 [PS]	Time Is On My Side/Congratulations	1964	25.00	50.00	100.00
9725	Heart of Stone/What a Shame	1964	2.50	5.00	10.00

—Blue swirl label

9725	Heart of Stone/What a Shame	1964	7.50	15.00	30.00

—White, purple and blue label

9725 [DJ]	Heart of Stone/What a Shame	1964	25.00	50.00	75.00

—Orange swirl label

9725 [PS]	Heart of Stone/What a Shame	1964	200.00	400.00	800.00
9741	The Last Time/Play with Fire	1965	2.50	5.00	10.00

—Blue swirl label, "London" in black letters

9741	The Last Time/Play with Fire	1965	3.75	7.50	15.00

—Blue swirl label, "London" in white letters

9741	The Last Time/Play with Fire	1965	6.25	12.50	25.00

—White, purple and blue label

9741 [DJ]	The Last Time/Play with Fire	1965	25.00	50.00	75.00

—Orange swirl label

9741 [PS]	The Last Time/Play with Fire	1965	37.50	75.00	150.00
9766	(I Can't Get No) Satisfaction/The Under Assistant West Coast Promotion Man	1965	5.00	10.00	20.00
9766 [DJ]	(I Can't Get No) Satisfaction/The Under Assistant West Coast Promotion Man	1965	25.00	50.00	75.00

—Orange swirl label

9766 [PS]	(I Can't Get No) Satisfaction/The Under Assistant West Coast Promotion Man	1965	100.00	200.00	500.00
5N-9766 [DJ]	(I Can't Get No) Satisfaction/The Under Assistant West Coast Promotion Man	1975	20.00	40.00	60.00

—Promo reissue; orange swirl label

9792	Get Off of My Cloud/I'm Free	1965	5.00	10.00	20.00
9792 [DJ]	Get Off of My Cloud/I'm Free	1965	25.00	50.00	75.00

—Orange swirl label

9792 [PS]	Get Off of My Cloud/I'm Free	1965	15.00	30.00	60.00
9808	As Tears Go By/Gotta Get Away	1965	3.75	7.50	15.00
9808 [DJ]	As Tears Go By/Gotta Get Away	1965	25.00	50.00	75.00

—Orange swirl label

9808 [PS]	As Tears Go By/Gotta Get Away	1965	15.00	30.00	60.00
9823	19th Nervous Breakdown/Sad Day	1966	3.75	7.50	15.00
9823 [DJ]	19th Nervous Breakdown/Sad Day	1966	25.00	50.00	75.00

—Orange swirl label

9823 [PS]	19th Nervous Breakdown/Sad Day	1966	15.00	30.00	60.00

ROLLING STONES

(no #)	Tongue Sleeve	1972	2.00	4.00	8.00

—Sleeve used on some copies of "Tumbling Dice" and "Hang Fire," and possibly some other Rolling Stones Records 45s

PR 228 [DJ]	Time Waits for No One (mono/stereo)	1974	15.00	50.00	75.00
PR 228 [PS]	Time Waits for No One (mono/stereo)	1974	75.00	125.00	175.00
PR 316 [DJ]	Before They Make Me Run (mono/stereo)	1978	6.25	12.50	25.00
PR 316 [PS]	Before They Make Me Run (mono/stereo)	1978	10.00	20.00	50.00
38-05802	Harlem Shuffle/Had It with You	1986	—	—	3.00
38-05802 [DJ]	Harlem Shuffle (same on both sides)	1986	5.00	10.00	20.00
38-05802 [DJ]	Harlem Shuffle/Had It with You	1986	—	—	3.00
38-05802 [PS]	Harlem Shuffle	1986	5.00	10.00	20.00

—"Demonstration Not for Sale" on sleeve, and no B-side listed

38-05906	One Hit (To the Body)/Fight	1986	—	—	3.00
38-05906 [DJ]	One Hit (To the Body) (same on both sides)	1986	5.00	10.00	20.00
38-05906 [DJ]	One Hit (To the Body)/Fight	1986	—	—	3.00
38-05906 [PS]	One Hit (To the Body)	1986	5.00	10.00	20.00

—"Demonstration Not for Sale" on sleeve, and no B-side listed

19100	Brown Sugar/Bitch	1971	—	2.50	5.00
19100 [DJ]	Brown Sugar (mono/stereo)	1971	10.00	20.00	30.00
19101	Wild Horses/Sway	1971	—	2.50	5.00
19101 [DJ]	Wild Horses (mono/stereo, both full length)	1971	10.00	20.00	30.00
19101 [DJ]	Wild Horses (long version/short version)	1971	20.00	30.00	50.00
19103	Tumbling Dice/Sweet Black Angel	1972	—	2.50	5.00
19103 [DJ]	Tumbling Dice (mono/stereo)	1972	10.00	20.00	30.00
19104	Happy/All Down the Line	1972	—	2.50	5.00
19104 [DJ]	Happy/All Down the Line	1972	10.00	20.00	30.00

Number	Title (A Side/B Side)	Yr	VG	VG+	NM
19105	Angie/Silver Train	1973	—	2.50	5.00

—With "Angie" listed as "Side One" and "Silver Train" listed as "Side Two," or with no reference at all to "Side One" and "Side Two"

19105	Silver Train/Angie	1973	3.00	6.00	12.00

—With "Silver Train" listed as "Side One" and "Angie" listed as "Side Two"

19105 [DJ]	Angie (mono/stereo)	1973	10.00	20.00	30.00
19109	Doo Doo Doo Doo Doo (Heartbreaker)/Dancing with Mr. D.	1973	—	2.50	5.00
19109 [DJ]	Doo Doo Doo Doo Doo (Heartbreaker) (mono/stereo)	1973	10.00	20.00	30.00
19301	It's Only Rock 'N' Roll (But I Like It)/Through the Lonely Nights	1974	—	2.50	5.00
19301 [DJ]	It's Only Rock 'N' Roll (But I Like It) (Edit/Long Version)	1974	10.00	20.00	30.00
19302	Ain't Too Proud to Beg/Dance Little Sister	1974	—	2.50	5.00
19302 [DJ]	Ain't Too Proud to Beg (mono/stereo)	1974	10.00	20.00	30.00
19304	Fool to Cry/Crazy Mama	1976	—	—	—

—Promotional 12-inch singles exist with this coupling, but do U.S. 45s? Please advise.

19304	Fool to Cry/Hot Stuff	1976	—	2.00	4.00
19304 [DJ]	Fool to Cry (same on both sides)	1976	10.00	20.00	30.00
19304 [DJ]	Hot Stuff (same on both sides)	1976	10.00	20.00	30.00
19304 [DJ]	Fool to Cry (long/short versions)	1976	15.00	25.00	35.00
19304 [DJ]	Hot Stuff (long/short versions)	1976	15.00	25.00	35.00
19304 [DJ]	Fool to Cry/Hot Stuff	1976	50.00	100.00	200.00
19307	Miss You/Far Away Eyes	1978	—	2.00	4.00
19307 [DJ]	Miss You (same on both sides)	1978	10.00	20.00	30.00
19307 [DJ]	Far Away Eyes (same on both sides)	1978	50.00	100.00	250.00
19307 [PS]	Miss You/Far Away Eyes	1978	—	2.00	4.00
19309	Beast of Burden/When the Whip Comes Down	1978	—	2.00	4.00
19309 [DJ]	Beast of Burden (long/short versions)	1978	10.00	20.00	30.00
19309 [PS]	Beast of Burden/When the Whip Comes Down	1978	1000.	1500.	2000.

—Beware of counterfeits! Original copies have a 1/2-inch inner fold on the inside of the picture sleeve (counterfeits have a much smaller fold). Also, the originals are a light lavender, almost pink, color (counterfeits are a grape or purple color).

19310	Shattered/Everything Is Turning to Gold	1978	—	2.00	4.00
19310 [DJ]	Shattered (same on both sides)	1978	5.00	10.00	20.00
19310 [PS]	Shattered/Everything Is Turning to Gold	1978	—	3.00	6.00
20001	Emotional Rescue/Down in the Hole	1980	—	2.00	4.00
20001 [DJ]	Emotional Rescue (edit/LP versions)	1980	5.00	10.00	20.00
20001 [PS]	Emotional Rescue/Down in the Hole	1980	—	2.00	4.00
21001	She's So Cold/Send It to Me	1980	—	2.00	4.00
21001 [DJ]	She's So Cold (edit/LP versions)	1980	5.00	10.00	20.00
21001 [PS]	She's So Cold/Send It to Me	1980	—	3.00	6.00
21003	Start Me Up/No Use in Crying	1981	—	2.00	4.00
21003 [DJ]	Start Me Up (same on both sides)	1981	5.00	10.00	20.00
21003 [PS]	Start Me Up/No Use in Crying	1981	—	2.00	4.00
21004	Waiting on a Friend/Little T & A	1981	—	2.00	4.00
21004 [DJ]	Waiting on a Friend (same on both sides)	1981	5.00	10.00	20.00
21004 [PS]	Waiting on a Friend/Little T & A	1981	—	2.00	4.00
21300	Hang Fire/Neighbours	1982	—	2.00	4.00
21300 [DJ]	Hang Fire (same on both sides)	1982	5.00	10.00	20.00
21301	Going to A-Go-Go/Beast of Burden	1982	—	2.00	4.00
21301 [DJ]	Going to A-Go-Go/Beast of Burden	1982	5.00	10.00	20.00
21301 [PS]	Going to A-Go-Go/Beast of Burden	1982	—	2.00	4.00
38-69008	Mixed Emotions/Fancy Man Blues	1989	—	—	3.00
38-69008 [DJ]	Mixed Emotions (same on both sides)	1989	10.00	20.00	45.00
38-73057	Rock and a Hard Place/Cook Cook Blues	1989	—	—	3.00
38-73093	Almost Hear You Sigh/Break the Spell	1989	—	—	3.00
38-73742	Highwire/2000 Light Years from Home	1991	—	2.50	5.00
38-73789	Sexdrive/Undercover of the Night	1991	2.00	4.00	8.00
99724	Too Tough/Miss You	1984	10.00	20.00	40.00
99724 [DJ]	Miss You (same on both sides)	1984	10.00	20.00	30.00
99788	She Was Hot/Think I'm Going Mad	1984	—	—	3.00
99788 [DJ]	She Was Hot (long/short versions)	1984	10.00	20.00	30.00
99788 [PS]	She Was Hot/Think I'm Going Mad	1984	—	—	3.00
99813	Undercover of the Night/All the Way Down	1983	—	—	3.00
99813 [DJ]	Undercover of the Night (same on both sides)	1983	5.00	10.00	20.00
99813 [PS]	Undercover of the Night/All the Way Down	1983	—	—	3.00
99978	Time Is On My Side (Live)/Twenty Flight Rock	1982	—	2.50	5.00
99978 [DJ]	Time Is On My Side (Live) (same on both sides)	1982	5.00	10.00	20.00
99978 [PS]	Time Is On My Side (Live)/Twenty Flight Rock	1982	—	2.50	5.00

VIRGIN

NR-38446	Love Is Strong/The Storm/Love Is Strong (Teddy Riley Remix)	1994	—	2.50	5.00
NR-38446 [PS]	Love Is Strong//The Storm/Love Is Strong (Teddy Riley Remix)	1994	—	2.50	5.00
NR-38459	Out of Tears//Out of Tears (Bob Clearmountain Remix Edit)/I'm Gonna Drive	1994	—	2.50	5.00
NR-38459 [PS]	Out of Tears//Out of Tears (Bob Clearmountain Remix Edit)/I'm Gonna Drive	1994	—	2.50	5.00
NR-38626	Saint of Me/Anyway You Look At It	1998	—	—	2.00
NR-38626 [PS]	Saint of Me/Anyway You Look At It	1998	—	—	2.00

7-Inch Extended Plays

LONDON

SBG 23	Around and Around/2120 South Michigan Avenue/Confessin' the Blues//Time Is On My Side/Grown Up Wrong/It's All Over Now	1964	50.00	100.00	200.00

—Jukebox issue; small hole, plays at 33 1/3 rpm

SBG 23 [PS]	12x5	1964	50.00	100.00	200.00
SBG 34	Down the Road Apiece/Off the Hook/Oh Baby (We Got a Good Thing Goin')//Everybody Needs Somebody to Love/Heart of Stone/Surprise, Surprise	1965	50.00	100.00	200.00

—Jukebox issue; small hole, plays at 33 1/3 rpm

SBG 34 [PS]	The Rolling Stones, Now!	1965	50.00	100.00	200.00
SBG 37	The Spider and the Fly/One More Try/Hitch Hike//The Last Time/Good Times/Mercy Mercy	1965	50.00	100.00	200.00

—Jukebox issue; small hole, plays at 33 1/3 rpm

SBG 37 [PS]	Out of Our Heads	1965	50.00	100.00	200.00
SBG 43	Talkin' 'Bout You/Look What You've Done/Get Off of My Cloud//I'm Free/Gotta Get Away/As Tears Go By	1965	50.00	100.00	200.00

—Jukebox issue; small hole, plays at 33 1/3 rpm

SBG 43 [PS]	December's Children (and Everybody's)	1965	50.00	100.00	200.00
SBG 54	She's a Rainbow/2,000 Light Years from Home//In Another Land/Citadel/2000 Man	1967	62.50	125.00	250.00

—Jukebox issue; small hole, plays at 33 1/3 rpm

Number	Title (A Side/B Side)	Yr	VG	VG+	NM
❑ SBG 54 [PS]	Their Satanic Majesties Request	1967	62.50	125.00	250.00

ROLLING STONES

Number	Title (A Side/B Side)	Yr	VG	VG+	NM
❑ PR 287 [DJ]	If You Can't Rock Me/Get Off of My Cloud/Brown Sugar//Jumpin' Jack Flash/Hot Stuff	1977	7.50	15.00	30.00

—Large hole; promo-only sampler from "Love You Live"

❑ PR 287 [PS]	Love You Live	1977	12.50	25.00	50.00
❑ COC 7-22900	Rip This Joint/Hip Shake/Tumbling Dice//Rocks Off/Sweet Virginia	1972	20.00	40.00	80.00

—Jukebox issue; small hole, plays at 33 1/3 rpm

❑ COC 7-22900 [PS]	Exile on Main St.	1972	20.00	40.00	80.00

—Part of "Little LP" series (LLP #199)

❑ CO7-59101	Star Star/Hide Your Love//Can You Hear the Music/100 Years Ago	1973	20.00	40.00	80.00

—Jukebox issue; small hole, plays at 33 1/3 rpm

❑ CO7-59101 [PS]	Goats Head Soup	1973	20.00	40.00	80.00

Albums

ABKCO

Number	Title (A Side/B Side)	Yr	VG	VG+	NM
❑ ANA 1 [P]	Metamorphosis	1975	3.00	6.00	12.00
❑ MPD-1 [DJ]	Songs of the Rolling Stones	1975	175.00	350.00	700.00

—"Band in field" cover

❑ MPD-1 [DJ]	Songs of the Rolling Stones	1975	1000.	2000.	3000.

—"Rock and Roll Circus" cover

❑ DVL2-0268 [(2)P]	The Rolling Stones' Greatest Hits	1977	5.00	10.00	20.00

—RCA Special Products mail-order offer

❑ 1218-1 [(4)]	Singles Collection: The London Years	1989	12.50	25.00	50.00
❑ AB-4224	Necrophilia	1973	2000.	4000.	8000.

—Canceled; covers exist. Value is for complete tri-fold cover.

LONDON

Number	Title (A Side/B Side)	Yr	VG	VG+	NM
❑ NP 1 [M]	Big Hits (High Tide and Green Grass)	1966	10.00	20.00	40.00

—With five lines of type on the front cover, all in capital letters

❑ NP 1 [M]	Big Hits (High Tide and Green Grass)	1966	2000.	4000.	8000.

—With two lines of type on the front cover, all in small letters

❑ NPS 1 [R]	Big Hits (High Tide and Green Grass)	1966	2.50	5.00	10.00
❑ RSD-1 [DJ]	The Rolling Stones — The Promotional Album	1969	1000.	2000.	3000.

—Not to be confused with imports of this rare promo

❑ NP 2 [M]	Their Satanic Majesties Request	1967	62.50	125.00	250.00
❑ NPS 2 [S]	Their Satanic Majesties Request	1967	10.00	20.00	40.00

—With 3-D cover

❑ NPS 2 [S]	Their Satanic Majesties Request	197?	2.00	4.00	8.00

—Without 3-D cover

❑ NPS 3 [P]	Through the Past, Darkly (Big Hits Vol. 2)	1969	2.50	5.00	10.00

—With hexagonal cover

❑ NPS 3 [PD]	Through the Past, Darkly (Big Hits Vol. 2)	1969	3000.	4500.	6000.

—Prototype picture discs that used the cover art from "Big Hits (High Tide and Green Grass)" either on one or both sides.

❑ NPS 3 [P]	Through the Past, Darkly (Big Hits Vol. 2)	197?	5.00	10.00	20.00

—Reissue with regular square cover

❑ NPS 4 [S]	Let It Bleed	1969	2.50	5.00	10.00

—Without poster

❑ NPS 4 [S]	Let It Bleed	1969	3.75	7.50	15.00

—With poster

❑ NPS-4	Let It Bleed	1970	5000.	7500.	10000.

—One-of-a-kind red/yellow/blue/green vinyl (all on the same record!)

❑ NPS 5 [S]	Get Yer Ya-Ya's Out!	1970	2.50	5.00	10.00
❑ PS 375 [R]	England's Newest Hit Makers — The Rolling Stones	1964	75.00	150.00	300.00

—Dark blue label; lower left-hand corner of cover advertises a bonus photo

❑ PS 375 [R]	England's Newest Hit Makers — The Rolling Stones	1965	6.25	12.50	25.00

—Dark blue label with "London" unboxed at top

❑ PS 375 [R]	England's Newest Hit Makers — The Rolling Stones	1966	2.50	5.00	10.00

—Dark blue label with "London" boxed at top

❑ PS 402 [R]	12 x 5	1964	6.25	12.50	25.00

—Dark blue label with "London" unboxed at top

❑ PS 402 [R]	12 x 5	1965	2.50	5.00	10.00

—Dark blue label with "London" boxed at top

❑ PS 420 [R]	The Rolling Stones, Now!	1965	6.25	12.50	25.00

—Dark blue label with "London" unboxed at top. Add 20% for complete liner notes (or sticker) on back cover (both columns of type about equal in length).

❑ PS 420 [R]	The Rolling Stones, Now!	1966	2.50	5.00	10.00

—Dark blue label with "London" boxed at top. Add 20% for censored liner notes (or sticker) on back cover (second column an inch shorter than the first column; "offensive" notes were quietly restored in the 1970s).

❑ PS 429 [R]	Out of Our Heads	1965	2.50	5.00	10.00

—Dark blue label with "London" boxed at top

❑ PS 429 [R]	Out of Our Heads	1965	6.25	12.50	25.00

—Dark blue label with "London" unboxed at top

❑ PS 429 [R]	Out of Our Heads	1965	25.00	50.00	100.00

—Dark blue label with "London/ffrr" in a box at top and "Made in England by the Decca Record Co. Ltd." at top edge

❑ PS 451 [P]	December's Children (and Everybody's)	1965	6.25	12.50	25.00

—Dark blue label with "London" boxed at top

❑ PS 451 [P]	December's Children (and Everybody's)	1966	2.50	5.00	10.00

—Dark blue label with "London" boxed at top. "Look What You've Done" is in true stereo; all other tracks are rechanneled.

❑ PS 476 [S]	Aftermath	1966	2.50	5.00	10.00
❑ PS 493 [P]	Got Live If You Want It!	1966	2.50	5.00	10.00

—"Fortune Teller" is rechanneled (it's actually an early studio recording with overdubbed crowd noise)

❑ PS 499 [S]	Between the Buttons	1967	2.50	5.00	10.00
❑ PS 509	Back Behind and In Front	1967	1250.	2500.	5000.

—Prototype cover slick for an unreleased LP; the same number was used for "Flowers"

❑ PS 509 [P]	Flowers	1967	2.50	5.00	10.00

—"Have You Seen Your Mother, Baby, Standing in the Shadow?" and "Mother's Little Helper" are rechanneled; all others are true stereo

❑ PS 509 [M]	Flowers	197?	2.00	4.00	8.00

—Some later "stereo" copies of this LP are actually entirely in mono

❑ PS 539	Beggars Banquet	1968	2500.	5000.	10000.

—Original "toilet graffiti" cover slick (not on a cover)

❑ PS 539 [S]	Beggars Banquet	1968	2.50	5.00	10.00

—With "Rev. Wilkins: credited as composer of "Prodigal Son"

❑ PS 539 [S]	Beggars Banquet	1968	6.25	12.50	25.00

—With all songs credited to "Jagger-Richard"

Number	Title (A Side/B Side)	Yr	VG	VG+	NM
❑ 2PS 606/7 [(2)P]	Hot Rocks 1964-1971	1971	5.00	10.00	20.00

—With regular versions of all tracks. All of Side 1 and "Mothers Little Helper" and "19th Nervous Breakdown" on Side 2 are rechanneled. All of Side 3 and 4 are stereo.

❑ 2PS 606/7 [(2)P]	Hot Rocks 1964-1971	1971	250.00	500.00	1000.

—With alternate versions of "Brown Sugar" and "Wild Horses" unavailable elsewhere. The date "11-5-71" or "11-18-71" is in the Side 4 trail-off area.

❑ 2PS 626/7 [(2)P]	More Hot Rocks (Big Hits and Fazed Cookies)	1972	5.00	10.00	20.00

—All of Sides 1 and 4 are rechanneled; Side 2 and 3, except "Have You Seen Your Mother, Baby, Standing in the Shadow?" are in true stereo

❑ LL 3375	England's Newest Hit Makers — The Rolling Stones Bonus Photo	1964	50.00	100.00	200.00
❑ LL 3375 [DJ]	England's Newest Hit Makers — The Rolling Stones	1964	750.00	1500.	3000.

—White label promo

❑ LL 3375 [M]	England's Newest Hit Makers — The Rolling Stones	1964	75.00	150.00	300.00

—Maroon label with "Full Frequency Range Recording" inside horizontal lines that go through the center hole; lower left-hand corner of cover advertises a bonus photo

❑ LL 3375 [M]	England's Newest Hit Makers — The Rolling Stones	1965	15.00	30.00	60.00

—Maroon label with "London" unboxed at top

❑ LL 3375 [M]	England's Newest Hit Makers — The Rolling Stones	1966	10.00	20.00	40.00

—Red or maroon label with "London" boxed at top

❑ LL 3402 [M]	12 x 5	1964	15.00	30.00	60.00

—Maroon label with "London" unboxed at top

❑ LL 3402 [M]	12 x 5	1964	50.00	100.00	200.00

—Maroon label with "London/ffrr" in a box at top

❑ LL 3402 [M]	12 x 5	1964	5000.	7500.	10000.

—Maroon label with "London" unboxed at top; possibly unique blue vinyl pressing

❑ LL 3402 [M]	12 x 5	1965	10.00	20.00	40.00

—Red or maroon label with "London" boxed at top

❑ LL 3420 [M]	The Rolling Stones, Now!	1965	15.00	30.00	60.00

—Maroon label with "London" unboxed at top and no lines on label. Add 20% for complete liner notes (or sticker) on back cover (both columns of type about equal in length).

❑ LL 3420 [M]	The Rolling Stones, Now!	1965	50.00	100.00	200.00

—Maroon label with "London/ffrr" in a box at top. Add 20% for complete liner notes (or sticker) on back cover (both columns of type about equal in length).

❑ LL 3420 [M]	The Rolling Stones, Now!	1965	100.00	200.00	400.00

—Maroon label with "London" unboxed, but with "ffrr" ear above "London" and "Full Frequency Range Recording" inside horizontal lines that go through the center hole

❑ LL 3420 [M]	The Rolling Stones, Now!	1965	100.00	200.00	400.00

—Maroon label with "London" unboxed, with horizontal lines that go through the center hole, but with NO "ffrr" ear at the top and NO "Full Frequency Range Recording" between the horizontal lines

❑ LL 3420 [M]	The Rolling Stones, Now!	1966	10.00	20.00	40.00

—Red or maroon label with "London" boxed at top and censored liner notes (second column an inch shorter than the first column)

❑ LL 3429 [M]	Out of Our Heads	1965	10.00	20.00	40.00

—Maroon label with "London" unboxed at top

❑ LL 3429 [M]	Out of Our Heads	1965	50.00	100.00	200.00

—Maroon label with "London/ffrr" in a box at top

❑ LL 3429 [M]	Out of Our Heads	1966	6.25	12.50	25.00

—Red or maroon label with "London" boxed at top

❑ LL 3451 [M]	December's Children (and Everybody's)	1965	10.00	20.00	40.00

—Maroon label with "London" unboxed at top

❑ LL 3451 [M]	December's Children (and Everybody's)	1966	6.25	12.50	25.00

—Maroon label with "London" boxed at top

❑ LL 3476 [M]	Aftermath	1966	10.00	20.00	40.00
❑ LL 3493 [M]	Got Live If You Want It!	1966	10.00	20.00	40.00
❑ LL 3499 [M]	Between the Buttons	1967	10.00	20.00	40.00
❑ LL 3509 [M]	Flowers	1967	12.50	25.00	50.00

LONDON/ABKCO

Number	Title (A Side/B Side)	Yr	VG	VG+	NM
❑ 62671 [(2)P]	Hot Rocks 1964-1971	1986	3.75	7.50	15.00

—"Digitally Remastered from Original Master Recording" on cover; red label; same stereo content as original

❑ 62671 [(2)P]	More Hot Rocks (Big Hits and Fazed Cookies)	1986	3.75	7.50	15.00

—"Digitally Remastered from Original Master Recording" on cover; red label

❑ 73751 [M]	England's Newest Hit Makers — The Rolling Stones	1986	2.00	4.00	8.00

—"Digitally Remastered from Original Master Recording" on cover; red label

❑ 74021 [M]	12 x 5	1986	2.00	4.00	8.00

—"Digitally Remastered from Original Master Recording" on cover; red label

❑ 74201 [P]	The Rolling Stones, Now!	1986	2.00	4.00	8.00

—"Digitally Remastered from Original Master Recording" on cover; red label; four tracks are in true stereo

❑ 74291 [P]	Out of Our Heads	1986	2.00	4.00	8.00

—"Digitally Remastered from Original Master Recording" on cover; red label

❑ 74511 [P]	December's Children (and Everybody's)	1986	2.00	4.00	8.00

—"Digitally Remastered from Original Master Recording" on cover; red label

❑ 74761 [S]	Aftermath	1986	2.00	4.00	8.00

—"Digitally Remastered from Original Master Recording" on cover; red label

❑ 74931 [S]	Got Live If You Want It!	1986	2.00	4.00	8.00

—"Digitally Remastered from Original Master Recording" on cover; red label

❑ 74991 [S]	Between the Buttons	1986	2.00	4.00	8.00

—"Digitally Remastered from Original Master Recording" on cover; red label

❑ 75091 [S]	Flowers	1986	2.00	4.00	8.00

—"Digitally Remastered from Original Master Recording" on cover; red label

❑ 75391 [S]	Beggars Banquet	1986	3.00	6.00	12.00

—"Digitally Remastered from Original Master Recording" on cover; red label; original banned "toilet cover" released for the first time on this reissue

❑ 80011 [M]	Big Hits (High Tide and Green Grass)	1986	2.00	4.00	8.00

—"Digitally Remastered from Original Master Recording" on cover; red label

❑ 80021 [S]	Their Satanic Majesties Request	1986	2.00	4.00	8.00

—"Digitally Remastered from Original Master Recording" on cover; red label

❑ 80031 [S]	Through the Past, Darkly (Big Hits Vol. 2)	1986	2.00	4.00	8.00

—"Digitally Remastered from Original Master Recording" on cover; red label

❑ 80041	Let It Bleed	1986	2.00	4.00	8.00

—"Digitally Remastered from Original Master Recording" on cover; red label

❑ 80051	Get Yer Ya-Ya's Out!	1986	2.00	4.00	8.00

—"Digitally Remastered from Original Master Recording" on cover; red label

MOBILE FIDELITY

Number	Title (A Side/B Side)	Yr	VG	VG+	NM
❑ RC-1 [(11)]	The Rolling Stones	1984	125.00	250.00	500.00

—London LPs pressed on audiophile vinyl in box

❑ 1-060	Sticky Fingers	1980	12.50	25.00	50.00

—Audiophile vinyl

❑ 1-087	Some Girls	1982	12.50	25.00	50.00

—Audiophile vinyl

R

Number	Title (A Side/B Side)	Yr	VG	VG+	NM

RADIO PULSEBEAT NEWS

❑ 4	It's Here Luv!!	1965	45.00	90.00	180.00

—*Ed Rudy interview album; this has been counterfeited, but originals can be identified thus: Charlie Watts' jacket should be completely black with no white marks; the label is very clear; the vinyl is all black*

ROLLING STONES

❑ PR 164 [DJ]	Interview with Mick Jagger by Tom Donahue	1971	50.00	100.00	200.00

—*Yellow label*

❑ COC 2-2900 [(2)]	Exile on Main St.	1972	3.75	7.50	15.00

—*Original covers have Unipak design -- cover has to be opened to remove the records. Add 33% for sheet of postcards.*

❑ COC 2-2900 [(2)]	Exile on Main St.	1973	3.00	6.00	12.00

—*Reissue covers have two pockets, one for each record*

❑ COC 2-9001 [(2)]	Love You Live	1977	3.00	6.00	12.00
❑ COC 16015	Emotional Rescue	1980	2.50	5.00	10.00

—*Without poster*

❑ COC 16015	Emotional Rescue	1980	3.75	7.50	15.00

—*Originally released with a large poster wrapped around the outside of the record jacket*

❑ COC 16028	Sucking in the Seventies	1981	2.50	5.00	10.00
❑ COC 16052	Tattoo You	1981	2.50	5.00	10.00
❑ COC 39100	Jamming with Edward	1972	3.75	7.50	15.00

—*Not an official Stones album, this includes Jagger, Watts and Wyman with Ry Cooder and Nicky Hopkins*

❑ COC 39100 [DJ]	Jamming with Edward	1972	43.75	87.50	175.00

—*White label stereo promo*

❑ COC 39100 [M]	Jamming with Edward	1972	62.50	125.00	250.00

—*White label mono promo*

❑ COC 39105	Sticky Fingers	1977	2.00	4.00	8.00

—*Reissue on Atlantic with photo of zipper only*

❑ COC 39105	Sticky Fingers	1977	2.50	5.00	10.00

—*Reissue on Atlantic with working zipper*

❑ COC 39106	Goats Head Soup	1977	2.00	4.00	8.00

—*Reissue on Atlantic*

❑ COC 39107	Made in the Shade	1977	2.00	4.00	8.00

—*Reissue on Atlantic*

❑ COC 39108	Some Girls	1978	2.50	5.00	10.00

—*With "cover under reconstruction." Nine different color schemes exist for the front cover.*

❑ COC 39108	Some Girls	1978	3.75	7.50	15.00

—*With all women's faces visible. Nine different color schemes exist for the front cover.*

❑ COC 39113	Still Life (American Concert 1981)	1982	2.50	5.00	10.00
❑ COC 39114 [PD]	Still Life (American Concert 1981)	1982	10.00	20.00	40.00
❑ OC 40250	Dirty Work	1986	2.00	4.00	8.00

—*Originals came with red shrink wrap; add 50% if it is still with the package*

❑ FC 40488	Sticky Fingers	1986	2.00	4.00	8.00

—*Reissue on CBS with photo of zipper only*

❑ CG2 40489 [(2)]	Exile on Main St.	1986	2.50	5.00	10.00

—*Reissue on CBS*

❑ FC 40492	Goats Head Soup	1986	2.00	4.00	8.00

—*Reissue on CBS*

❑ FC 40493	It's Only Rock 'n' Roll	1986	2.00	4.00	8.00

—*Reissue on CBS*

❑ FC 40494	Made in the Shade	1986	2.00	4.00	8.00

—*Reissue on CBS*

❑ FC 40495	Black and Blue	1986	2.00	4.00	8.00

—*Reissue on CBS*

❑ CG2 40496 [(2)]	Love You Live	1986	2.50	5.00	10.00

—*Reissue on CBS*

❑ FC 40499	Some Girls	1986	2.00	4.00	8.00

—*Reissue on CBS*

❑ FC 40500	Emotional Rescue	1986	2.00	4.00	8.00

—*Reissue on CBS*

❑ FC 40501	Sucking in the Seventies	1986	2.00	4.00	8.00

—*Reissue on CBS*

❑ FC 40502	Tattoo You	1986	2.00	4.00	8.00

—*Reissue on CBS*

❑ FC 40503	Still Life (American Concert 1981)	1986	2.00	4.00	8.00

—*Reissue on CBS*

❑ FC 40504	Undercover	1986	2.00	4.00	8.00

—*Reissue on CBS has no stickers on cover*

❑ FC 40505	Rewind (1971-1984)	1986	2.00	4.00	8.00

—*Reissue on CBS*

❑ OC 45333	Steel Wheels	1989	2.50	5.00	10.00
❑ C 47456	Flashpoint	1991	5.00	10.00	20.00
❑ COC 59100	Sticky Fingers	1971	3.00	6.00	12.00

—*With working zipper*

❑ COC 59100 [DJ]	Sticky Fingers	1971	75.00	150.00	300.00

—*White label stereo promo*

❑ COC 59100 [M]	Sticky Fingers	1971	125.00	250.00	500.00

—*White label mono promo*

❑ COC 59101	Goats Head Soup	1973	2.50	5.00	10.00

—*Without bonus photo*

❑ COC 59101	Goats Head Soup	1973	3.75	7.50	15.00

—*With bonus photo*

❑ COC 79101	It's Only Rock 'n' Roll	1974	2.50	5.00	10.00
❑ COC 79102	Made in the Shade	1975	2.50	5.00	10.00
❑ COC 79104	Black and Blue	1976	2.50	5.00	10.00
❑ 90120	Undercover	1983	2.00	4.00	8.00

—*With stickers peeled off*

❑ 90120	Undercover	1983	3.00	6.00	12.00

—*With stickers intact*

❑ 90176	Rewind (1971-1984)	1984	6.25	12.50	25.00

VIRGIN

❑ V 2750 (8 39782 1) [(2)]	Voodoo Lounge	1994	5.00	10.00	20.00

—*U.S. versions pressed in U.K., but have UPC code paste-over and blue sticker "Marketed by Caroline"*

❑ V 2801 (8 41040 1) [(2)]	Stripped	1995	3.75	7.50	15.00

—*U.S. versions pressed in U.K., but have UPC code paste-over with "Marketed and Distributed by Caroline Records"*

❑ 8 44712 1 [(2)]	Bridges to Babylon	1997	3.75	7.50	15.00

—*U.S. versions pressed in U.K., but have "Virgin Records America Inc." on back cover*

❑ 8 46740 1 [(2)]	No Security	1998	3.75	7.50	15.00

—*U.S. versions pressed in U.K., but have "Virgin Records America Inc." on back cover*

❑ 47863	Sticky Fingers	1999	6.25	12.50	25.00

—*Limited-edition reissue with 180-gram vinyl and original working zipper cover*

❑ 47864 [(2)]	Exile on Main St.	1999	12.50	25.00	50.00

—*Limited-edition reissue with 180-gram vinyl and all original inserts*

❑ 47867	Some Girls	1999	6.25	12.50	25.00

—*Limited-edition reissue with 180-gram vinyl and original inserts (except it has the "cover under reconstruction" inner sleeve)*

ROMAN NUMERALS, THE
45s
COLUMBIA

❑ 44314	The Come-On/Matchstick in a Whirlpool	1967	5.00	10.00	20.00
❑ 44314 [PS]	The Come-On/Matchstick in a Whirlpool	1967	7.50	15.00	30.00

ROME, RICHARD
45s
PARKWAY

❑ 978	Happiness Is/Back in Sixty Seconds	1966	2.50	5.00	10.00

SWAN

❑ 4021	Bluebird of Happiness/Leaf in the Wind	1959	3.00	6.00	12.00

ROMEOS, THE (1) Featuring Philly Soul producers KENNY GAMBLE and Leon Huff.
45s
MARK II

❑ 101	Precious Memories/Juicy Lucy	1967	3.75	7.50	15.00
❑ 103	A Tear and a Smile/Seaching	1967	3.75	7.50	15.00

Albums
MARK II

❑ 1001	Precious Memories	1967	6.25	12.50	25.00

ROMEOS, THE (2)
45s
AMY

❑ 840	The Tiger's Wide Awake (The Lion Sleeps Tonight)/Hitch-Hikin'	1962	3.75	7.50	15.00

ROMEOS, THE (3)
45s
APOLLO

❑ 461	Love Me/I Beg You Please	1954	150.00	300.00	600.00

ROMEOS, THE (4)
45s
ATCO

❑ 6107	Moments to Remember You By/Fine, Fine Baby	1958	15.00	30.00	60.00

FOX

❑ 749	Gone, Gone, Get Away/Let's Be Partners	1957	30.00	60.00	120.00

—*Yellow label*

❑ 749	Gone, Gone, Get Away/Let's Be Partners	1957	75.00	150.00	300.00

—*Cream label*

❑ 846	Moments to Remember You By/Fine, Fine Baby	1957	30.00	60.00	120.00

—*Yellow label*

❑ 846	Moments to Remember You By/Fine, Fine Baby	1957	125.00	250.00	500.00

—*Cream label*

ROMEOS, THE (5)
45s
COLUMBIA

❑ 43074	Baby Stay in Line/Two of the Chosen Few	1964	2.50	5.00	10.00

ROMEOS, THE (U) If these are any of the above groups, the most likely contenders are groups (1), (2) or (5).
45s
FELSTED

❑ 8528	Two Innocent Loves/Love-Mobile	1958	7.50	15.00	30.00
❑ 8672	Julie/I'm Gonna Rebuild This World	1963	5.00	10.00	20.00

LOMA

❑ 2028	Mucho Soul/Are You Ready for That	1966	3.00	6.00	12.00
❑ 2041	Calypso Chili/Mon Petite Chow	1966	3.00	6.00	12.00

ROMERO, CHAN
45s
CHALLENGE

❑ 59285	The Funniest Things/It's Not Fine	1965	3.75	7.50	15.00

DEL-FI

❑ 4119	The Hippy Hippy Shake/If I Had My Way	1959	25.00	50.00	100.00
❑ 4126	I Don't Care Now/My Little Rudy	1959	15.00	30.00	60.00

PHILIPS

❑ 40391	Humpy Bumpy/Man Can't Dog a Woman	1966	2.50	5.00	10.00

RON AND BILL Ron White and Bill "SMOKEY" ROBINSON.
45s
ARGO

❑ 5350	It/Don't Say Bye Bye	1959	12.50	25.00	50.00

TAMLA

❑ 54025	It/Don't Say Bye Bye	1960	30.00	60.00	120.00

RON-DELLS, THE
45s
ARLEN

❑ 723	I'll Be Gone/Slow Down	1963	3.75	7.50	15.00

RON-DELS, THE Delbert McClinton was in this group.
45s
BROWNFIELD

❑ 18	If You Really Want Me To, I'll Go/Walk About	1965	6.25	12.50	25.00

DOT

❑ 16593	Far Horizons/On the Run	1964	6.25	12.50	25.00
❑ 17323	Matilda/Tina	1970	2.50	5.00	10.00

SHALIMAR

❑ 104	Matilda/Tina	1963	3.75	7.50	15.00

SMASH

❑ 1986	If You Really Want Me To, I'll Go/Walk About	1965	2.50	5.00	10.00
❑ 2002	She's My Girl/Over	1965	2.00	4.00	8.00
❑ 2014	A Picture of You/Lose Your Money	1965	2.00	4.00	8.00

RONDELLS, THE More than one group.
45s
ABC-PARAMOUNT

❑ 10690	Don't Say That You Love Me/Parking in the Ko Ko Mo	1965	3.75	7.50	15.00

CARLTON

❑ 467	Good Good/Dreamy	1958	5.00	10.00	20.00

Number	Title (A Side/B Side)	Yr	VG	VG+	NM

RONDELS, THE
45s
AMY
❏ 825	Back Beat #1/Shades of Green	1961	6.25	12.50	25.00
❏ 830	My Prayer/Satan's Theme	1961	6.25	12.50	25.00
❏ 839	Caldonia/110 Lbs. of Drums	1962	6.25	12.50	25.00
❏ 844	Red Peppers/Flute Salad	1962	6.25	12.50	25.00
❏ 857	Meet Us at the Peppermint Lounge/ Cover Charge	1962	6.25	12.50	25.00

RONDO, DON
45s
ATLANTIC
| ❏ 2194 | Malibu/So Did I | 1963 | 2.00 | 4.00 | 8.00 |
CARLTON
❏ 531	Friends/Hoot an' a Holler	1960	2.00	4.00	8.00
❏ 536	Wanderlust/The King of Holiday Island	1960	2.00	4.00	8.00
❏ 551	You'll Never Walk Alone/They Were You	1961	2.00	4.00	8.00
DECCA
❏ 29738	Evening Star/Beyond the Mighty River	1955	3.00	6.00	12.00
❏ 30248	I Offer You My Heart/Evening Star	1957	3.00	6.00	12.00
❏ 32561	Statue of a Fool/I'll Be True	1969	—	2.50	5.00
JUBILEE
❏ 5256	Two Different Worlds/He Made You Mine	1956	3.00	6.00	12.00
❏ 5270	Don't/The Love I Never Had	1957	3.00	6.00	12.00
❏ 5282	To Belong/On Forgotten Street	1957	3.00	6.00	12.00
❏ 5288	White Silver Sands/Stars Fell on Alabama	1957	3.00	6.00	12.00
❏ 5297	Forsaking All Others/There's Only You	1957	3.00	6.00	12.00
❏ 5305	Wanderin' Heart/In Chi-Chi-Chihuahua	1957	2.50	5.00	10.00
❏ 5313	Made for Each Other/What a Shame	1958	2.50	5.00	10.00
❏ 5319	There Goes My Heart Again/Blonde Bombshell	1958	2.50	5.00	10.00
❏ 5320	School Dance/I've Got Bells in My Heart	1958	2.50	5.00	10.00
❏ 5325	Dormi, Dormi, Dormi/Her Hair Was Yellow	1958	2.50	5.00	10.00
❏ 5334	City Lights/As Long As I Have You	1958	2.50	5.00	10.00
❏ 5341	I Could Be a Mountain/Great Adventure	1958	2.50	5.00	10.00
❏ 5354	Song from "Geisha Boy"/Gretna Green	1958	2.50	5.00	10.00
❏ 5364	My Foolish Heart/Leave Your Trouble on My Lips	1959	2.50	5.00	10.00
❏ 5372	You're On My Mind Again/Cuckoo Girl	1959	2.50	5.00	10.00
❏ 5381	Because of You/Alone in the World	1960	2.00	4.00	8.00
❏ 5421	Two Different Worlds/Blonde Bombshell	1962	2.00	4.00	8.00
❏ 5522	Love Me Back/Play the Other Side	1966	—	3.00	6.00
ROULETTE
❏ 4202	Batch of Love/Quiet Girl	1959	2.50	5.00	10.00
❏ 4216	Wall to Wall Tears/The Golden Rule	1959	2.50	5.00	10.00
❏ 4236	That's My Girl/Even the Heavens Cried	1960	2.50	5.00	10.00
UNITED ARTISTS
| ❏ 50111 | Till the World Knows You're Mine/Is There Room in Your Tomorrow | 1967 | — | 3.00 | 6.00 |
| ❏ 50191 | Let's Live for Today/Oh Why My Love | 1967 | — | 3.00 | 6.00 |
Albums
JUBILEE
| ❏ JLP-1052 [M] | Rondo | 195? | 5.00 | 10.00 | 20.00 |
| ❏ JLP-1081 [M] | Have You Met Don Rondo | 195? | 5.00 | 10.00 | 20.00 |
VOCALION
| ❏ VL 73897 | Two Different Worlds | 1970 | 3.00 | 6.00 | 12.00 |

RONETTES, THE　Also see RONNIE SPECTOR.
45s
A&M
| ❏ 1040 | You Came, You Saw, You Conquered/ Oh, I Love You | 1969 | 4.00 | 8.00 | 16.00 |
BUDDAH
| ❏ 384 | Go Out and Get It/Lover, Lover | 1973 | 5.00 | 10.00 | 20.00 |
—As "Ronnie Spector and the Ronettes"
| ❏ 408 | I Wish I Never Saw the Sunshine/ I Wonder What He's Doing | 1974 | 5.00 | 10.00 | 20.00 |
COLPIX
| ❏ 601 | I Want a Boy/Sweet Sixteen | 1961 | 25.00 | 50.00 | 100.00 |
—As "Ronnie and the Relatives"
| ❏ 646 | I'm Gonna Quit While I'm Ahead/ I'm On the Wagon | 1962 | 15.00 | 30.00 | 60.00 |
DIMENSION
| ❏ 1046 | He Did It/Recipe for Love | 1965 | 12.50 | 25.00 | 50.00 |
MAY
| ❏ 111 | My Darling Angel/ I'm Gonna Quit While I'm Ahead | 1961 | 37.50 | 75.00 | 150.00 |
—As "Ronnie and the Relatives"
| ❏ 114 | Silhouettes/You Bet I Would | 1962 | 12.50 | 25.00 | 50.00 |
| ❏ 138 | Memory/Good Girls | 1963 | 12.50 | 25.00 | 50.00 |
PAVILLION
| ❏ 03333 | I Saw Mommy Kissing Santa Claus/Rudolph the Red-Nosed Reindeer | 1982 | — | 2.50 | 5.00 |
—B-side by The Crystals
PHILLES
❏ 116	Be My Baby/Tedesco and Pittman	1963	7.50	15.00	30.00
❏ 118	Baby I Love You/Miss Joan and Mr. Sam	1963	7.50	15.00	30.00
❏ 120	(The Best Part of) Breakin' Up/Big Red	1964	7.50	15.00	30.00
❏ 121	Do I Love You?/Bebe and Susu	1964	7.50	15.00	30.00
❏ 123	Walkin' in the Rain/How Does It Feel	1964	10.00	20.00	40.00
❏ 123 [PS]	Walkin' in the Rain/How Does It Feel	1964	37.50	75.00	150.00
❏ 126	Born to Be Together/Blues for Baby	1965	6.25	12.50	25.00
❏ 126 [PS]	Born to Be Together/Blues for Baby	1965	37.50	75.00	150.00
❏ 128	Is This What I Get for Loving You?/ Oh, I Love You	1965	6.25	12.50	25.00
❏ 128 [PS]	Is This What I Get for Loving You?/ Oh, I Love You	1965	37.50	75.00	150.00
❏ 133	I Can Hear Music/When I Saw You	1966	7.50	15.00	30.00
Albums
COLPIX
| ❏ CP-486 [M] | The Ronettes Featuring Veronica | 1965 | 25.00 | 50.00 | 100.00 |
—Blue label
| ❏ CP-486 [M] | The Ronettes Featuring Veronica | 1965 | 50.00 | 100.00 | 200.00 |
—Gold label
| ❏ SCP-486 [S] | The Ronettes Featuring Veronica | 1965 | 37.50 | 75.00 | 150.00 |
—Blue label

| ❏ SCP-486 [S] | The Ronettes Featuring Veronica | 1965 | 75.00 | 150.00 | 300.00 |
—Gold label
PHILLES
| ❏ PHLP-4006 [M] | Presenting the Fabulous Ronettes Featuring Veronica | 1964 | 100.00 | 200.00 | 400.00 |
—Yellow and red label
| ❏ PHLP-4006 [M] | Presenting the Fabulous Ronettes Featuring Veronica | 1964 | 200.00 | 400.00 | 800.00 |
—Blue and black label
| ❏ PHLP-ST-4006 [S] | Presenting the Fabulous Ronettes Featuring Veronica | 1965 | 150.00 | 300.00 | 600.00 |
| ❏ ST-90721 [S] | Presenting the Fabulous Ronettes Featuring Veronica | 1965 | 100.00 | 200.00 | 400.00 |
—Capitol Record Club edition
| ❏ T-90721 [M] | Presenting the Fabulous Ronettes Featuring Veronica | 1965 | 62.50 | 125.00 | 250.00 |
—Capitol Record Club edition

RONNIE AND THE DEL-AIRES　See THE DEL-AIRES.

RONNIE AND THE HI-LITES
45s
ABC-PARAMOUNT
| ❏ 10685 | High School Romance/Too Young | 1965 | 5.00 | 10.00 | 20.00 |
JOY
| ❏ 260 | I Wish That We Were Married/ Twistin' and Kissin' | 1962 | 6.25 | 12.50 | 25.00 |
| ❏ 265 | Be Kind/Send My Love (Special Delivery) | 1962 | 5.00 | 10.00 | 20.00 |
RAVEN
| ❏ 8000 | Valerie/The Fact of the Matter | 1963 | 5.00 | 10.00 | 20.00 |
WIN
❏ 250	A Slow Dance/What the Next Day May Bring	1963	5.00	10.00	20.00
❏ 251	The Fact of the Matter/You Keep Me Guessin'	1963	5.00	10.00	20.00
❏ 252	High School Romance/Uptown-Downtown	1963	6.25	12.50	25.00

RONNIE AND THE POMONA CASUALS
45s
DONNA
| ❏ 1400 | Swimming at the Rainbow/Casual Blues | 1964 | 3.00 | 6.00 | 12.00 |
| ❏ 1402 | I Wanna Do the Jerk/Sloopy | 1965 | 3.00 | 6.00 | 12.00 |
Albums
DONNA
| ❏ 2113 [M] | Everybody Jerk | 1965 | 7.50 | 15.00 | 30.00 |

RONNIE AND THE RED CAPS　The first released record by RONNIE DIO.
45s
REB
| ❏ 45-105 | Conquest/Lover | 1958 | 62.50 | 125.00 | 250.00 |

RONNIE AND THE RELATIVES— See THE RONETTES.

RONNIE AND THE ROCKIN' KINGS
45s
RCA VICTOR
| ❏ 47-7248 | Rock and Roll Sal/You Know | 1958 | 10.00 | 20.00 | 40.00 |

RONNY AND THE DAYTONAS
45s
MALA
❏ 481	G.T.O./Hot Rod Baby	1964	6.25	12.50	25.00
❏ 490	California Bound/Hey Little Girl	1964	5.00	10.00	20.00
❏ 492	Bucket "T"/Little Rail Job	1964	5.00	10.00	20.00
❏ 497	Little Scrambler/Teenage Years	1965	5.00	10.00	20.00
❏ 503	Beach Boy/No Wheels	1965	6.25	12.50	25.00
❏ 513	Sandy/(Instrumental)	1965	5.00	10.00	20.00
❏ 525	Goodbye Baby/Somebody to Love Me	1966	5.00	10.00	20.00
❏ 531	Antique '32 Studebaker Dictator Coupe/Then the Rains Came	1966	5.00	10.00	20.00
❏ 542	I'll Think of Summer/Little Scrambler	1966	3.75	7.50	15.00
RCA VICTOR
❏ 47-8896	All American Girl/Dianne, Dianne	1966	3.00	6.00	12.00
❏ 47-8896 [PS]	All American Girl/Dianne, Dianne	1966	6.25	12.50	25.00
❏ 47-9022	Winter Weather/Young	1966	3.00	6.00	12.00
❏ 47-9107	Walk with the Sun/The Last Letter	1967	3.00	6.00	12.00
❏ 47-9253	Brave New World/Hold Onto Your Heart	1968	3.00	6.00	12.00
❏ 47-9435	The Girls and the Boys/Alfie	1968	3.00	6.00	12.00
SHOW BIZ
| ❏ 21207 [DJ] | 4-Cast She'll Love Me Again | 1968 | 5.00 | 10.00 | 20.00 |
—One-sided promo
Albums
BEAT ROCKET
| ❏ BR 119 | G.T.O. | 199? | 3.00 | 6.00 | 12.00 |
—Reissue of Mala 4001 with four bonus tracks
| ❏ BR 120 | Sandy | 199? | 3.00 | 6.00 | 12.00 |
—Reissue of Mala 4002 with three bonus tracks
MALA
❏ 4001 [M]	G.T.O.	1964	30.00	60.00	120.00
❏ 4002 [M]	Sandy	1966	20.00	40.00	80.00
❏ 4002S [S]	Sandy	1966	25.00	50.00	100.00
SUNDAZED
| ❏ LP 5050 | G.T.O. — Best of the Mala Recordings | 1997 | 2.50 | 5.00 | 10.00 |

RONSON, MICK
45s
RCA VICTOR
❏ APBO-0212	Love Me Tender/Only After Dark	1974	—	3.00	6.00
❏ APBO-0291	Slaughter on Tenth Avenue/ Leave My Heart Alone	1974	—	3.00	6.00
❏ PB-10237	Easy Days/Billy Porter	1975	—	3.00	6.00
7-Inch Extended Plays
RCA VICTOR
| ❏ DJEO-0259 [DJ] | Slaughter on 10th Avenue/Growing Up and I'm Fine//All Cut Up on You/Andy Warhol | 1974 | 3.00 | 6.00 | 12.00 |
—Promo-only EP with B-side by Dana Gillespie
Albums
RCA VICTOR
| ❏ APL1-0353 | Slaughter on 10th Avenue | 1974 | 3.00 | 6.00 | 12.00 |
| ❏ APL1-0681 | Play Don't Worry | 1975 | 3.00 | 6.00 | 12.00 |

R

RONSTADT, LINDA

Number	Title (A Side/B Side)	Yr	VG	VG+	NM

12-Inch Singles

ASYLUM

Number	Title (A Side/B Side)	Yr	VG	VG+	NM
❏ ED 4935 [DJ]	What's New (same on both sides)	1983	2.50	5.00	10.00
❏ AS 11431 [DJ]	Blue Bayou/Lago Azul	1977	7.50	15.00	30.00
—Blue vinyl					
❏ 67973 [DJ]	Get Closer (same on both sides)	1982	5.00	10.00	20.00

CAPITOL

Number	Title (A Side/B Side)	Yr	VG	VG+	NM
❏ ST-1003 [DJ]	Living Like a Fool (same on both sides)	1977	7.50	15.00	30.00
—Red vinyl; yellow label, "Capitol" in red at bottom					
❏ ST-1003 [DJ]	Living Like a Fool (same on both sides)	1977	10.00	20.00	40.00
—Red vinyl; yellow "SM" label with Capitol tower					

45s

ASYLUM

Number	Title (A Side/B Side)	Yr	VG	VG+	NM
❏ 11026	Love Has No Pride/I Can Almost See It	1973	—	2.50	5.00
❏ 11032	Silver Threads and Golden Needles/Don't Cry Now	1974	—	2.50	5.00
❏ 11039	Desperado/Colorado	1974	—	2.50	5.00
❏ 45271	Love Is a Rose/Silver Blue	1975	—	3.00	6.00
❏ 45282	Heat Wave/Love Is a Rose	1975	—	2.00	4.00
❏ 45295	Tracks of My Tears/The Sweetest Gift	1975	—	2.00	4.00
—B-side with Emmylou Harris					
❏ 45340	That'll Be the Day/Try Me Again	1976	—	2.00	4.00
—Clouds label					
❏ 45340	That'll Be the Day/Try Me Again	1976	—	2.50	5.00
—All-blue label					
❏ 45361	Someone to Lay Down Beside Me/Crazy	1976	—	2.00	4.00
❏ 45402	Lose Again/Lo Siento Mi Vida	1977	2.00	4.00	8.00
❏ 45431	Blue Bayou/Old Paint	1977	—	2.00	4.00
❏ 45438	It's So Easy/Lo Siento Mi Vida	1977	—	2.00	4.00
❏ 45462	Poor Poor Pitiful Me/Simple Man, Simple Dream	1978	—	2.00	4.00
❏ 45464	Lago Azul/Lo Siento Mi Vida	1978	3.00	6.00	12.00
❏ 45479	Tumbling Dice/I Never Will Marry	1978	—	2.00	4.00
❏ 45519	Back in the U.S.A./White Rhythm and Blues	1978	—	2.00	4.00
❏ 45519 [PS]	Back in the U.S.A./White Rhythm and Blues	1978	—	3.00	6.00
❏ 45546	Ooh Baby Baby/Blowing Away	1978	—	2.00	4.00
❏ 46011	Just One Look/Love Me Tender	1979	—	2.00	4.00
❏ 46034	Alison/Mohammed's Radio	1979	—	2.00	4.00
❏ 46602	How Do I Make You/Rambler Gambler	1980	—	2.00	4.00
❏ 46602 [PS]	How Do I Make You/Rambler Gambler	1980	—	2.50	5.00
❏ 46624	Hurt So Bad/Justine	1980	—	2.00	4.00
❏ 46654	I Can't Let Go/Look Out for My Love	1980	—	2.00	4.00
❏ 69476	(I Love You) For Sentimental Reasons/Straighten Up and Fly Right	1987	—	2.00	4.00
❏ 69507	When You Wish Upon a Star/Little Girl Blue	1986	—	2.00	4.00
❏ 69507 [PS]	When You Wish Upon a Star/Little Girl Blue	1986	—	2.00	4.00
❏ 69653	When I Fall in Love/It Never Entered My Mind	1985	—	2.00	4.00
❏ 69671	Lush Life/Skylark	1985	—	2.00	4.00
❏ 69725	Someone to Watch Over Me/What'll I Do	1984	—	2.00	4.00
❏ 69752	I've Got a Crush on You/Lover Man	1984	—	2.00	4.00
❏ 69780	What's New/Crazy He Calls Me	1983	—	2.00	4.00
❏ 69838	Easy for You to Say/Mr. Radio	1983	—	2.00	4.00
❏ 69853	I Knew You When/Talk to Me of Mendocino	1982	—	2.00	4.00
❏ 69853 [PS]	I Knew You When/Talk to Me of Mendocino	1982	—	2.50	5.00
❏ 69948	Get Closer/Sometimes You Just Can't Win	1982	—	2.00	4.00
❏ 69948 [PS]	Get Closer/Sometimes You Just Can't Win	1982	—	2.50	5.00

CAPITOL

Number	Title (A Side/B Side)	Yr	VG	VG+	NM
❏ 2438	Dolphins/The Long Way Around	1969	3.00	6.00	12.00
❏ 2767	Lovesick Blues/Will You Love Me Tomorrow	1970	2.00	4.00	8.00
❏ 2846	Long Long Time/Nobody's	1970	2.00	4.00	8.00
❏ 3021	The Long Way Around/(She's a) Very Lovely Woman	1971	—	3.00	6.00
❏ 3210	I Fall to Pieces/Can It Be True	1971	—	3.00	6.00
❏ 3273	Rock Me on the Water/Crazy Arms	1972	—	3.00	6.00
❏ 3990	You're No Good/I Can't Help It (If I'm Still in Love with You)	1974	—	2.00	4.00
❏ 4050	When Will I Be Loved/It Doesn't Matter Anymore	1975	—	2.00	4.00

ELEKTRA

Number	Title (A Side/B Side)	Yr	VG	VG+	NM
❏ 64427	The Waiting/Walk On	1995	—	—	3.00
❏ 64987	All My Life/Shattered	1990	—	—	3.00
—With Aaron Neville					
❏ 69261	Don't Know Much/Cry Like a Rainstorm	1989	—	—	3.00
—With Aaron Neville					

ELEKTRA SPUN GOLD

Number	Title (A Side/B Side)	Yr	VG	VG+	NM
❏ 45073	Love Has No Pride/Silver Threads and Golden Needles	1975	—	2.00	4.00
—Reissue					
❏ 45081	Heat Wave/Tracks of My Tears	1977	—	—	3.00
—Reissue					
❏ 45089	Blue Bayou/It's So Easy	1979	—	—	3.00
—Reissue					
❏ 45092	Poor, Poor, Pitiful Me/Tumbling Dice	1979	—	—	3.00
—Reissue					
❏ 45102	Back in the U.S.A./Ooh, Baby, Baby	1980	—	—	3.00
—Reissue					
❏ 45116	Hurt So Bad/How Do I Make You	1981	—	—	3.00
—Reissue					
❏ 65934	Don't Know Much/When Something Is Wrong with My Baby	1993	2.00	4.00	8.00
—With Aaron Neville; B-side's only appearance on U.S. 45					
❏ 65965	When You Wish Upon a Star/(I Love You) For Sentimental Reasons	1988	—	—	3.00
—Reissue					
❏ 65988	What's New/I've Got a Crush on You	1985	—	—	3.00
—Reissue					
❏ 65989	I Knew You When/Get Closer	1985	—	—	3.00
—Reissue					

MCA

Number	Title (A Side/B Side)	Yr	VG	VG+	NM
❏ 52973	Somewhere Out There/(Instrumental)	1986	—	—	3.00
—With James Ingram					
❏ 52973 [PS]	Somewhere Out There/(Instrumental)	1986	—	2.00	4.00

Albums

ASYLUM

Number	Title (A Side/B Side)	Yr	VG	VG+	NM
❏ 6E-104	Simple Dreams	1977	2.50	5.00	10.00
❏ 6E-106	Greatest Hits	1977	2.50	5.00	10.00
❏ 6E-155	Living in the U.S.A.	1978	2.50	5.00	10.00
❏ DP-401 [PD]	Living in the U.S.A.	1978	4.50	9.00	18.00
❏ 5E-510	Mad Love	1980	2.50	5.00	10.00
❏ 5E-516	Greatest Hits, Volume 2	1980	2.50	5.00	10.00
❏ 5E-540	Keeping Out of Mischief	1981	—	—	—
—Canceled					
❏ 7E-1045	Prisoner in Disguise	1975	2.50	5.00	10.00
❏ 7E-1072	Hasten Down the Wind	1976	2.50	5.00	10.00
—"Clouds" label					
❏ 7E-1072	Hasten Down the Wind	1976	3.75	7.50	15.00
—Solid blue label with white stylized "a" at top					
❏ 7E-1092	Greatest Hits	1976	3.00	6.00	12.00
❏ SD 5064	Don't Cry Now	1973	2.50	5.00	10.00
❏ 60185	Get Closer	1982	2.50	5.00	10.00
❏ 60260	What's New	1983	2.50	5.00	10.00
❏ 60387	Lush Life	1984	2.50	5.00	10.00
❏ 60474	For Sentimental Reasons	1987	2.50	5.00	10.00
❏ 60489 [(3)]	'Round Midnight: The Nelson Riddle Sessions	1987	6.25	12.50	25.00
❏ 60765	Canciones De Mi Padre	1988	3.00	6.00	12.00

CAPITOL

Number	Title (A Side/B Side)	Yr	VG	VG+	NM
❏ ST-208	Hand Sown…Home Grown	1969	5.00	10.00	20.00
—Black label with colorband					
❏ ST-208	Hand Sown…Home Grown	1970	3.75	7.50	15.00
—Green label					
❏ ST-208	Hand Sown…Home Grown	1971	3.00	6.00	12.00
—Red label					
❏ ST-407	Silk Purse	1970	3.75	7.50	15.00
—Green label					
❏ ST-407	Silk Purse	1971	3.00	6.00	12.00
—Red label					
❏ ST-8-0407	Silk Purse	1970	5.00	10.00	20.00
—Capitol Record Club edition					
❏ SMAS-635	Linda Ronstadt	1972	3.00	6.00	12.00
❏ ST-11269	Different Drum	1974	3.00	6.00	12.00
—Also includes Stone Poneys tracks					
❏ ST-11358	Heart Like a Wheel	1974	3.00	6.00	12.00
❏ SW-11358	Heart Like a Wheel	1975	2.50	5.00	10.00
❏ SKBB-11629 [(2)]	A Retrospective	1977	3.75	7.50	15.00
—Also includes Stone Poneys tracks					
❏ SN-16130	Hand Sown…Home Grown	1980	2.00	4.00	8.00
❏ SN-16131	Silk Purse	1980	2.00	4.00	8.00
❏ SN-16132	Linda Ronstadt	1980	2.00	4.00	8.00
❏ SN-16133	Beginnings	1980	2.00	4.00	8.00
❏ SN-16299	Different Drum	198?	2.00	4.00	8.00
—Budget-line reissue					

DCC COMPACT CLASSICS

Number	Title (A Side/B Side)	Yr	VG	VG+	NM
❏ LPZ-2048	Greatest Hits	1997	20.00	40.00	80.00
—Audiophile vinyl					
❏ LPZ-2065	Greatest Hits, Volume Two	1998	10.00	20.00	40.00
—Audiophile vinyl					

ELEKTRA

Number	Title (A Side/B Side)	Yr	VG	VG+	NM
❏ 60872	Cry Like a Rainstorm, Howl Like the Wind	1989	3.00	6.00	12.00

MOBILE FIDELITY

Number	Title (A Side/B Side)	Yr	VG	VG+	NM
❏ 1-158	What's New	1984	12.50	25.00	50.00
—Audiophile vinyl					

NAUTILUS

Number	Title (A Side/B Side)	Yr	VG	VG+	NM
❏ NR-26	Simple Dreams	1982	12.50	25.00	50.00
—Audiophile vinyl					

PAIR

Number	Title (A Side/B Side)	Yr	VG	VG+	NM
❏ PDL2-1070 [(2)]	Prime of Life	1986	3.00	6.00	12.00
❏ PDL2-1125 [(2)]	Rockfile	1986	3.00	6.00	12.00

RONSTADT, LINDA, AND THE STONE PONEYS See STONE PONEYS.

ROOFTOP SINGERS, THE

45s

ATCO

Number	Title (A Side/B Side)	Yr	VG	VG+	NM
❏ 6526	My Life Is My Own/Kites	1967	—	3.00	6.00

PHILCO-FORD

Number	Title (A Side/B Side)	Yr	VG	VG+	NM
❏ HP-37	Walk Right In/Tom Cat	1969	3.75	7.50	15.00
—4-inch plastic "Hip Pocket Record" with color sleeve					

VANGUARD

Number	Title (A Side/B Side)	Yr	VG	VG+	NM
❏ 35017	Walk Right In/Cool Water	1962	2.50	5.00	10.00
❏ 35019	Tom Cat/Shoes	1963	2.00	4.00	8.00
❏ 35019 [PS]	Tom Cat/Shoes	1963	3.00	6.00	12.00
❏ 35020	Mama Don't Allow/It Don't Mean a Thing	1963	2.00	4.00	8.00
❏ 35020 [PS]	Mama Don't Allow/It Don't Mean a Thing	1963	3.00	6.00	12.00
❏ 35024	Sail Away Ladies/Twelve String	1964	2.00	4.00	8.00
❏ 35029	Rainy Day/Buddy Won't You Roll Down the Line	1964	2.00	4.00	8.00
❏ 35034	Ham and Eggs/Somebody Came Home	1965	2.00	4.00	8.00

Albums

VANGUARD

Number	Title (A Side/B Side)	Yr	VG	VG+	NM
❏ VSD-2136 [S]	Walk Right In	1963	5.00	10.00	20.00
❏ VRS-9123 [M]	Walk Right In	1963	3.75	7.50	15.00
❏ VRS-9134 [M]	Good Time	1964	3.75	7.50	15.00
❏ VRS-9190 [M]	Rainy River	1965	3.75	7.50	15.00
❏ VSD-79134 [S]	Good Time	1964	5.00	10.00	20.00
❏ VSD-79190 [S]	Rainy River	1965	5.00	10.00	20.00

ROOMATES, THE Also see CATHY JEAN AND THE ROOMATES.

45s

BAN

Number	Title (A Side/B Side)	Yr	VG	VG+	NM
❏ 691	A Place Called Love/Knowing You	1985	—	2.50	5.00

CAMEO

Number	Title (A Side/B Side)	Yr	VG	VG+	NM
❏ 233	Sunday Kind of Love/A Lovely Way to Spend An Evening	1962	7.50	15.00	30.00

CANADIAN AMERICAN

Number	Title (A Side/B Side)	Yr	VG	VG+	NM
❏ 166	My Heart/Just for Tonight	1964	10.00	20.00	40.00

PHILIPS

Number	Title (A Side/B Side)	Yr	VG	VG+	NM
❏ 40105	Gee/Answer Me, My Love	1963	6.25	12.50	25.00
❏ 40153	The Nearness of You/Don't Cheat on Me	1963	6.25	12.50	25.00

PROMO

Number	Title (A Side/B Side)	Yr	VG	VG+	NM
❏ 2211	I Want a Little Girl/Making Believe	196?	5.00	10.00	20.00
—Sources conflict as to date (1960 or 1964)					

VALMOR

Number	Title (A Side/B Side)	Yr	VG	VG+	NM
❏ 008	Glory of Love/Never Know	1961	5.00	10.00	20.00
❏ 010	Band of Gold/O Baby Love	1961	5.00	10.00	20.00
❏ 013	My Foolish Heart/My Kisses for Your Thoughts	1962	5.00	10.00	20.00

Number	Title (A Side/B Side)	Yr	VG	VG+	NM
ROONEY, TEDDY					
45s					
IMPERIAL					
❑ 5644	Bite Your Tongue/After the Dance	1960	10.00	20.00	40.00
ROOSTERS, THE More than one group.					
45s					
A&M					
❑ 746	Shake a Tail Feather/Rooster Walk	1964	3.00	6.00	12.00
EPIC					
❑ 9487	Let's Try Again/Pretty Girl	1962	3.75	7.50	15.00
FELSTED					
❑ 8642	Chicken Hop/Fun House	1962	3.75	7.50	15.00
PHILIPS					
❑ 40504	Love Machine/I'm Suspectin'	1968	2.50	5.00	10.00
❑ 40559	Good Good Lovin'/Home Down Right	1968	2.00	4.00	8.00
SHAR-DEE					
❑ 704	Chicken Hop/Fun House	1959	5.00	10.00	20.00
ROSE, BIFF					
45s					
BUDDAH					
❑ 218	The Captain/I Forgot to Tell You	1971	—	2.50	5.00
TETRAGRAMMATON					
❑ 1506	What's Gnawing at Me/Molly	1969	—	3.00	6.00
❑ 1510	Buzz the Fuzz/Gentle People	1969	—	3.00	6.00
❑ 1543	Take Care of My Brother/Myrtle's Files	1970	—	3.00	6.00
Albums					
BUDDAH					
❑ BDS-5069	Ride On!	1970	3.00	6.00	12.00
❑ BDS-5075	The Thorn in Mrs. Rose's Side	1971	3.00	6.00	12.00
—Reissue of Tetragrammaton 103					
❑ BDS-5076	Children of Light	1971	3.00	6.00	12.00
—Reissue of Tetragrammaton 116					
❑ BDS-5078	Half Live at the Bitter End	1971	3.00	6.00	12.00
TETRAGRAMMATON					
❑ T-103	The Thorn in Mrs. Rose's Side	1968	3.75	7.50	15.00
❑ T-116	Children of Light	1969	3.75	7.50	15.00
UNITED ARTISTS					
❑ UAS-5594	Uncle Jesus Auntie Christ	1972	3.00	6.00	12.00
ROSE, TIM					
45s					
CAPITOL					
❑ 3001	I've Gotta Get a Message to You/Janie Sue	1970	—	3.00	6.00
COLUMBIA					
❑ 43563	I'm Bringing It Home/				
	Mother, Father, Where Are You	1966	2.00	4.00	8.00
❑ 43648	Hey Joe/The Lonely Blue King	1966	2.00	4.00	8.00
❑ 43722	Where Was I/I Gotta Do Things My Way	1966	2.00	4.00	8.00
❑ 43958	I'm Gonna Be Strong/I Got a Loneliness	1967	2.00	4.00	8.00
❑ 44031	Morning Dew/You're Slipping Away from Me	1967	2.00	4.00	8.00
❑ 44387	Long Time Man/Come Away Melinda	1967	2.00	4.00	8.00
❑ 44603	Long-Haired Boy/Looking at a Baby	1968	—	3.00	6.00
❑ 44792	Angela/Whatcha Gonna Do	1969	—	3.00	6.00
❑ 44849	Babe Do You Turn Me On/Roanoke	1969	—	3.00	6.00
PLAYBOY					
❑ 50005	It Takes a Little Longer/Ride Your Love Away	1972	—	2.50	5.00
❑ 50012	Goin' Down in Hollywood/(B-side unknown)	1972	—	2.50	5.00
Albums					
CAPITOL					
❑ ST-673	Love, A Kind of Hate Story	1970	3.00	6.00	12.00
COLUMBIA					
❑ CS 9577	Tim Rose	1968	3.00	6.00	12.00
❑ CS 9772	Thru Rose Colored Glasses	1969	3.00	6.00	12.00
PLAYBOY					
❑ P-101	Tim Rose	1972	3.00	6.00	12.00
ROSE GARDEN, THE					
45s					
ATCO					
❑ 6510	Next Plane to London/Flower Town	1967	3.00	6.00	12.00
❑ 6564	Here's Today/If My World Falls Through	1968	2.50	5.00	10.00
7-Inch Extended Plays					
ATCO					
❑ EP-C-4522 [DJ]	Rider/Long Time//				
	February Sunshine/I'm Only Second	1967	5.00	10.00	20.00
—White label, red print					
❑ EP-C-4522 [PS]	The Rose Garden	1967	7.50	15.00	30.00
Albums					
ATCO					
❑ 33-225 [M]	The Rose Garden	1968	15.00	30.00	60.00
❑ SD 33-225 [S]	The Rose Garden	1968	6.25	12.50	25.00
ROSEBUDS, THE (1)					
45s					
GEE					
❑ 1033	Dearest Darling/Unconditional Surrender	1957	12.50	25.00	50.00
LANCER					
❑ 102	Kiss Me Goodnight/Joey	1959	15.00	30.00	60.00
ROSEBUDS, THE (2)					
45s					
TOWER					
❑ 104	Say You'll Be Mine/Mama Said	1964	3.00	6.00	12.00
ROSELLA, CARMELA					
45s					
NANCY					
❑ 1004	Oh, It Was Elvis/Where?	1961	10.00	20.00	40.00
ROSELLI, JIMMY					
45s					
LENOX					
❑ 5571	Mala Femmina/Her Eyes Shone Like Diamonds	1963	2.00	4.00	8.00
❑ 5576	Passione/Satte Vincino A Me	1963	2.00	4.00	8.00

Number	Title (A Side/B Side)	Yr	VG	VG+	NM
RIC					
❑ 138	Yellow and Green Make Blue/Anema E Core	1964	2.00	4.00	8.00
❑ 148	Don't Cry Little Girl, Don't Cry/				
	Just Say I Love Her	1965	2.00	4.00	8.00
UNITED ARTISTS					
❑ 866	Laugh It Off/Why Don't We Do This More Often	1965	—	3.00	6.00
❑ 928	Have You Ever Been Lonely/Rage to Live	1965	—	3.00	6.00
❑ 957	New York: My Port of Call/This Is My Kind of Love	1965	—	3.00	6.00
❑ 996	I'll Never Let You Cry/				
	I'm Gonna Change Everything	1966	—	3.00	6.00
❑ 1659	Buon Natale				
	(Means Merry Christmas To You)/Christmas	1966	—	3.00	6.00
—"Silver Spotlight Series"					
❑ 50059	Love Me Love/Lusingame	1966	—	3.00	6.00
❑ 50064	This Planet Earth/Who Can Say (Africa Addio)	1966	—	3.00	6.00
❑ 50179	There Must Be a Way/I'm Yours to Command	1967	—	3.00	6.00
❑ 50217	Walkin' My Baby Back Home/All the Time	1967	—	3.00	6.00
❑ 50234	I Don't Want to Walk Without You/				
	Please Believe Me	1967	—	3.00	6.00
❑ 50273	Bella/O Surdato 'Enammurato	1968	—	3.00	6.00
❑ 50287	Get Out of My Heart/Oh What It Seemed to Be	1968	—	3.00	6.00
❑ 50480	My Heart Cries for You/Why Did You Leave Me	1969	—	2.50	5.00
❑ 50490	Buona Sera, Mrs. Campbell/I'll Take Care of You	1969	—	2.50	5.00
❑ 50496	Buona Sera, Mrs. Campbell (Italian)/Te Purtavo				
	Na Rosa	1969	2.00	4.00	8.00
❑ 50546	E Rose Parlano/Senza Mamma E Inamurata	1969	—	2.50	5.00
❑ 50624	I'm Coming Home, Los Angeles/Angelina	1970	—	2.50	5.00
Albums					
UNITED ARTISTS					
❑ UXS-83 [(2)]	Jimmy Roselli Superpak	1972	3.75	7.50	15.00
❑ UAL-3429 [M]	Life & Love Italian Style	1965	3.00	6.00	12.00
❑ UAL-3430 [M]	Mala Femmina	1965	3.00	6.00	12.00
❑ UAL-3438 [M]	The Great Ones!	1965	3.00	6.00	12.00
❑ UAL-3451 [M]	Saloon Songs	1966	3.00	6.00	12.00
❑ UAL-3467 [M]	New York: My Port of Call	1966	3.00	6.00	12.00
❑ UAL 3539 [M]	The Christmas Album	1966	3.00	6.00	12.00
❑ UAL-3544 [M]	The Italian Album	1966	3.00	6.00	12.00
❑ UAL-3564 [M]	Sold Out	1967	3.00	6.00	12.00
❑ UAL-3585 [M]	Saloon Songs, Vol. 2	1967	3.00	6.00	12.00
❑ UAL-3611 [M]	There Must Be a Way	1967	3.75	7.50	15.00
❑ UAS-5641	Simmo 'e Napule	1972	3.00	6.00	12.00
❑ UAS-6429 [S]	Life & Love Italian Style	1965	3.75	7.50	15.00
❑ UAS-6430 [S]	Mala Femmina	1965	3.75	7.50	15.00
❑ UAS-6438 [S]	The Great Ones!	1965	3.75	7.50	15.00
❑ UAS-6451 [S]	Saloon Songs	1966	3.75	7.50	15.00
❑ UAS-6467 [S]	New York: My Port of Call	1966	3.75	7.50	15.00
❑ UAS 6539 [S]	The Christmas Album	1966	3.75	7.50	15.00
❑ UAS-6544 [S]	The Italian Album	1966	3.75	7.50	15.00
❑ UAS-6564 [S]	Sold Out	1967	3.75	7.50	15.00
❑ UAS-6585 [S]	Saloon Songs, Vol. 2	1967	3.75	7.50	15.00
❑ UAS-6611 [S]	There Must Be a Way	1967	3.75	7.50	15.00
❑ UAS-6635	Core Napulitano	1968	3.75	7.50	15.00
❑ UAS-6645	The Best of Jimmy Roselli	1968	3.75	7.50	15.00
❑ UAS-6665	3 A.M.	1968	3.00	6.00	12.00
❑ UAS-6698	Core Spezzato	1969	3.75	7.50	15.00
❑ UAS-6724	Let Me Sing	1969	3.00	6.00	12.00
❑ UAS-6747	It's Been Swell	1970	3.00	6.00	12.00
❑ UAS-6775	I'te Voglio Bene Assale	1970	3.00	6.00	12.00
ROSES, THE					
45s					
DOT					
❑ 15816	Almost Paradise/I Kissed An Angel	1958	6.25	12.50	25.00
ROSIE AND THE ORIGINALS					
45s					
BRUNSWICK					
❑ 55205	Lonely Blue Nights/We'll Have a Chance	1961	6.25	12.50	25.00
—By "Rosie, formerly with the Originals"					
❑ 55212	My Darling Forever/The Time Is Near	1961	6.25	12.50	25.00
—By "Rosie, formerly with the Originals"					
ERA BACK TO BACK HITS					
❑ 038	Angel Baby/Bumble Boogie	197?	—	3.00	6.00
—B-side by B. Bumble and the Stingers					
HIGHLAND					
❑ 1011	Angel Baby/Give Me Love	1960	6.25	12.50	25.00
❑ 1032	Lonely Blue Nights/We'll Have a Chance	196?	6.25	12.50	25.00
—Actually a reissue of Brunswick 55205, but harder to find					
Albums					
BRUNSWICK					
❑ BL 54102 [M]	Lonely Blue Nights with Rosie	1961	37.50	75.00	150.00
❑ BL 754102 [S]	Lonely Blue Nights with Rosie	1961	50.00	100.00	200.00
ROSS, DIANA Also see THE SUPREMES.					
12-Inch Singles					
MCA					
❑ L33-1801 [DJ]	Ease On Down the Road (6:02)				
	(same on both sides)	1978	15.00	30.00	60.00
—With Michael Jackson					
MOTOWN					
❑ M 00010D1	Your Love Is So Good for Me (6:32)/I Can't Go				
	On Living Without Your Love (4:32)	1978	6.25	12.50	25.00
—B-side by Thelma Houston					
❑ M 00011D1	What You Gave Me (6:06)/Free Me from My				
	Freedom-Tie Me to a Tree (Handcuff Me)				
	(8:25)	1978	5.00	10.00	20.00
—B-side by Bonnie Pointer					
❑ PR-16 [DJ]	Love Hangover (7:49)/I Want You				
	(Vocal 4:33) (Instrumental 4:36)	1976	50.00	100.00	200.00
—B-side by Marvin Gaye on Tamla label					
❑ M 00026D1	The Boss (Remix 7:23)/				
	Lovin', Livin' and Givin' (5:11)	1979	3.75	7.50	15.00
❑ PR 42 [DJ]	What You Gave Me (6:06) (same on both sides)	1979	3.75	7.50	15.00
❑ PR 54 [DJ]	It's My House//No One Gets the Prize/The Boss	1979	5.00	10.00	20.00
—No label name on label					
❑ PR 72 [DJ]	Upside Down (4:05)/Big Time (6:27)	1980	12.50	25.00	50.00
—No label name on label; B-side by Rick James					

R

Number	Title (A Side/B Side)	Yr	VG	VG+	NM
❏ PR-75 [DJ]	I'm Coming Out (5:23)//Rock and Roll Me (3:38)/ Shake It Lady (3:09)	1980	12.50	25.00	50.00

—No label name on label; first song on B-side by Mira Waters; second song on B-side by Legend

Number	Title (A Side/B Side)	Yr	VG	VG+	NM
❏ P12-1008 [DJ]	You're Gonna Love It (6 versions)	1991	2.00	4.00	8.00
❏ 37463 1011 1	Waiting in the Wings (LP Version) (Remix Edit) (Extended)	1992	5.00	10.00	20.00
❏ P12-1014 [DJ]	You're Gonna Love It (E-Smoove's Groovy Radio Edit 4:51) (E-Smoove's Groovy Remix 6:20) (E-Smoove's Groovy Instrumental 6:20)/ (Underground Mix 7:29) (The Reel House Mix 6:59) (Mo's Flutestrumental 7:10)	1991	2.00	4.00	8.00
❏ 37463 1212 1	The Boss (EP Version) (Radio Edit) (BYC Mix)/ I'm Coming Out (EP Version Radio Edit) (Monstrumental)	1994	5.00	10.00	20.00
❏ 37463 1322 1	Take Me Higher (6 versions)	1995	3.00	6.00	12.00
❏ 37463 1379 1	If You're Not Gonna Love Me Right (4 versions)	1996	3.00	6.00	12.00
❏ 37463 1392 1	Voice of the Heart/ If You're Not Gonna Love Me Right	1996	2.50	5.00	10.00
❏ U8P-1519 [DJ]	Until We Meet Again (4 versions)	1999	3.00	6.00	12.00
❏ L33-1643 [DJ]	When You Tell Me That You Love Me (same on both sides)	1991	3.00	6.00	12.00
❏ 37463 3001 1	I Will Survive (12" Vocal Mix) (LP Version) (7" Vocal Mix) (12" Instrumental) (7" Acapella)	1997	3.75	7.50	15.00
❏ MOT-4632	Love Hangover '89 (12" Version) (Urban Remix) (Dance Mix)	1989	2.00	4.00	8.00
❏ MOT-4639	Workin' Overtime (3 versions)	1989	2.50	5.00	10.00
❏ MOT-4678	Bottom Line (3 versions)	1989	2.00	4.00	8.00
❏ 37463 4812 1	You're Gonna Love It (4 versions)	1991	—	3.00	6.00
❏ L33-17770 [DJ]	Love Hangover '89 (5 versions)	1989	2.00	4.00	8.00
❏ L33-17827 [DJ]	Workin' Overtime (6 versions)	1989	2.00	4.00	8.00
❏ L33-17909 [DJ]	Paradise (Club Mix 7:45) (Dub Mix 8:08) (7" Version 3:58)	1989	2.50	5.00	10.00
❏ L33-17963 [DJ]	This House (4:20) (5:34)	1989	2.00	4.00	8.00
❏ L33-18048 [DJ]	Bottom Line (7" Remix) (Extended Remix) (LP Version) (Instrumental)	1989	2.00	4.00	8.00
❏ 56266	Until We Meet Again (4 versions)	1999	2.00	4.00	8.00

RCA

Number	Title (A Side/B Side)	Yr	VG	VG+	NM
❏ 6416-1-RD	Dirty Looks (Remix Version 7:43) (Bonus Beats) (Instrumental Version 5:51)	1987	2.50	5.00	10.00
❏ PD-13022	Mirror, Mirror (6:06)/Sweet Nothings	1981	3.75	7.50	15.00
❏ PD-13202	Work That Body (6:32)/Two Can Make It	1982	3.00	6.00	12.00
❏ PD-13382	Muscles (6:38)/I Am Me	1982	2.50	5.00	10.00
❏ PD-13568	Pieces of Ice (7:19)/(Instrumental)	1983	2.50	5.00	10.00
❏ PD-13625	Up Front (Special Club Remix 6:56)/Love or Loneliness	1983	3.75	7.50	15.00
❏ PD-13672	Let's Go Up/Girls	1983	2.50	5.00	10.00
❏ JD-13865 [DJ]	Swept Away (Long Version 7:37)/ (Shorter Version 5:20)	1984	3.75	7.50	15.00
❏ PD-13865	Swept Away (Long Version 7:37)/ (Instrumental 7:14)	1984	2.50	5.00	10.00
❏ JR-14033 [DJ]	Telephone (4:08) (same on both sides)	1985	3.00	6.00	12.00
❏ JD-14183 [DJ]	Eaten Alive (Extended Version 5:51)/ (Instrumental 5:51)	1985	2.50	5.00	10.00

—White label, different prefix from stock copy

Number	Title (A Side/B Side)	Yr	VG	VG+	NM
❏ PD-14183	Eaten Alive (Extended Version 5:51)/ (Instrumental 5:51)	1985	2.50	5.00	10.00
❏ JD-14245 [DJ]	Chain Reaction (3:47) (same on both sides)	1985	2.50	5.00	10.00
❏ JR-14267 [DJ]	Chain Reaction (6:52) (same on both sides)	1985	2.00	4.00	8.00
❏ PD-14267	Chain Reaction (6:52)/More and More	1985	2.50	5.00	10.00

45s

MCA

Number	Title (A Side/B Side)	Yr	VG	VG+	NM
❏ 40947	Ease On Down the Road/Poppy Girls	1978	—	2.50	5.00

—With Michael Jackson; B-side by Quincy Jones

Number	Title (A Side/B Side)	Yr	VG	VG+	NM
❏ 40947 [PS]	Ease On Down the Road/Poppy Girls	1978	—	2.50	5.00

—With Michael Jackson

Number	Title (A Side/B Side)	Yr	VG	VG+	NM
❏ 53448	If We Hold On Together/(Instrumental)	1988	—	—	3.00
❏ 53448 [PS]	If We Hold On Together/(Instrumental)	1988	—	—	3.00

MOTOWN

Number	Title (A Side/B Side)	Yr	VG	VG+	NM
❏ (no #) [PS]	Diana Ross TV Special 4/8/71	1971	2.00	4.00	8.00

—Special sleeve issued with some Motown (usually Diana Ross) 45s in March and April 1971

Number	Title (A Side/B Side)	Yr	VG	VG+	NM
❏ 1165	Reach Out and Touch (Somebody's Hand)/ Dark Side of the World	1970	—	2.50	5.00
❏ 1165 [PS]	Reach Out and Touch (Somebody's Hand)/ Dark Side of the World	1970	3.00	6.00	12.00
❏ 1169	Ain't No Mountain High Enough/ Can't It Wait Until Tomorrow	1970	—	2.50	5.00
❏ 1169 [PS]	Ain't No Mountain High Enough/ Can't It Wait Until Tomorrow	1970	3.00	6.00	12.00
❏ 1176	Remember Me/What About You	1971	—	2.50	5.00
❏ 1176 [PS]	Remember Me/What About You	1971	3.00	6.00	12.00
❏ 1184	Reach Out I'll Be There/Close to You	1971	—	2.50	5.00
❏ 1188	Surrender/I'm a Winner	1971	—	2.50	5.00
❏ 1192	I'm Still Waiting/A Simple Thing Like Cry	1971	—	2.50	5.00
❏ 1211	Good Morning Heartache/God Bless the Child	1972	—	2.50	5.00
❏ 1211 [PS]	Good Morning Heartache/God Bless the Child	1972	2.50	5.00	10.00
❏ 1239	Touch Me in the Morning/I Won't Last a Day Without You	1973	—	2.50	5.00
❏ 1278	Last Time I Saw Him/Save the Children	1973	—	2.50	5.00
❏ 1295	Sleepin'/You	1974	—	2.50	5.00
❏ 1335	Sorry Doesn't Always Make It Right/Together	1975	—	2.50	5.00
❏ 1335 [PS]	Sorry Doesn't Always Make It Right/Together	1975	3.00	6.00	12.00
❏ 1377	Theme from Mahogany (Do You Know Where You're Going To)/ No One's Gonna Be a Fool Forever	1975	—	2.50	5.00
❏ 1377	Do You Know Where You're Going To/No One's Gonna Be a Fool Forever	1975	3.00	6.00	12.00

—Possibly Canadian release only, with different A-side title

Number	Title (A Side/B Side)	Yr	VG	VG+	NM
❏ 1377 [PS]	Theme from Mahogany (Do You Know Where You're Going To)/ No One's Gonna Be a Fool Forever	1975	5.00	10.00	20.00
❏ 1387	I Thought It Took a Little Time (But Today I Fell in Love)/After You	1976	—	2.50	5.00
❏ 1387 [PS]	I Thought It Took a Little Time (But Today I Fell in Love)/After You	1976	2.50	5.00	10.00
❏ 1392	Love Hangover/Kiss Me Now	1976	—	2.50	5.00
❏ 1398	One Love in My Lifetime/Smile	1976	—	2.50	5.00
❏ 1427	Gettin' Ready for Love/Confide in Me	1977	—	2.50	5.00

Number	Title (A Side/B Side)	Yr	VG	VG+	NM
❏ 1436	Your Love Is So Good for Me/Baby It's Me	1978	—	2.50	5.00
❏ 1442	You Got It/Too Shy to Say	1978	—	2.50	5.00
❏ 1449 [DJ]	Top of the World (same on both sides)	1978	12.50	25.00	50.00

—Promo only; withdrawn before stock copies were pressed

Number	Title (A Side/B Side)	Yr	VG	VG+	NM
❏ 1450	Lovin' Livin' and Givin'/Baby It's Me	1978			

—Unreleased

Number	Title (A Side/B Side)	Yr	VG	VG+	NM
❏ 1456	What You Gave Me/Together	1979	—	2.00	4.00
❏ 1462	The Boss/I'm in the World	1979	—	2.00	4.00
❏ 1471	It's My House/Sparkle	1979	—	2.00	4.00
❏ 1491	I'm Coming Out/Give Up	1980	—	2.00	4.00
❏ 1494	Upside Down/Friend to Friend	1980	—	2.00	4.00
❏ 1496	It's My Turn/Together	1980	—	2.00	4.00
❏ 1496 [PS]	It's My Turn/Together	1980	3.00	6.00	12.00
❏ 1508	One More Chance/After You	1981	—	2.00	4.00
❏ 1513	To Love Again/Crying My Heart Out for You	1981	—	2.00	4.00
❏ 1519	Endless Love/(Instrumental)	1981	—	2.00	4.00

—With Lionel Richie

Number	Title (A Side/B Side)	Yr	VG	VG+	NM
❏ 1531	My Old Piano/Now That You're Gone	1981	—	2.00	4.00
❏ 1626	We Can Never Light That Old Flame Again/ Old Funky Rolls	1982	—	2.00	4.00
❏ 1964	Workin' Overtime/(Instrumental)	1989	—	—	3.00
❏ 1964 [PS]	Workin' Overtime/(Instrumental)	1989	—	—	3.00
❏ 1998	This House/Paradise	1989	—	—	3.00
❏ 2003	Bottom Line/(Instrumental)	1989	—	—	3.00
❏ 2139	When You Tell Me That You Love Me/You and I	1991	—	2.00	4.00
❏ S45-17886 [DJ]	Workin' Overtime (4:18) (same on both sides)	1989	2.50	5.00	10.00

RCA

Number	Title (A Side/B Side)	Yr	VG	VG+	NM
❏ 5172-7-R	Dirty Looks/So Close	1987	—	—	3.00
❏ 5172-7-R [PS]	Dirty Looks/So Close	1987	—	—	3.00
❏ 5297-7-R	Tell Me Again/I Am Me	1987	—	—	3.00
❏ 5297-7-R [PS]	Tell Me Again/I Am Me	1987	—	—	3.00
❏ PB-12349	Why Do Fools Fall in Love/Think I'm in Love	1981	—	2.00	4.00
❏ JB-13013 [DJ]	Endless Love (Long)/(Short)	1981	3.00	6.00	12.00

—Promo only

Number	Title (A Side/B Side)	Yr	VG	VG+	NM
❏ PB-13021	Mirror, Mirror/Sweet Nothings	1981	—	2.00	4.00
❏ PB-13201	Work That Body/You Can Make It	1982	—	2.00	4.00
❏ PB-13348	Muscles/I Am Me	1982	—	2.00	4.00
❏ PB-13348 [PS]	Muscles/I Am Me	1982	—	2.00	4.00
❏ PB-13424	So Close/Fool for Your Love	1983	—	2.00	4.00
❏ GB-13479	Why Do Fools Fall in Love/Mirror, Mirror	1983	—	—	3.00

—Gold Standard Series

Number	Title (A Side/B Side)	Yr	VG	VG+	NM
❏ PB-13549	Pieces of Ice/Still in Love	1983	—	2.00	4.00
❏ PB-13549 [PS]	Pieces of Ice/Still in Love	1983	—	2.00	4.00
❏ PB-13624	Up Front/Love or Loneliness	1983	—	2.00	4.00
❏ PB-13671	Let's Go Up/Girls	1983	—	2.00	4.00
❏ GB-13798	Muscles/Pieces of Ice	1984	—	—	3.00

—Gold Standard Series

Number	Title (A Side/B Side)	Yr	VG	VG+	NM
❏ PB-13864	Swept Away/Fight for It	1984	—	—	3.00
❏ PB-13864 [PS]	Swept Away/Fight for It	1984	—	—	3.00
❏ PB-13966	Missing You/We Are the Children of the World	1984	—	—	3.00
❏ PB-13966 [PS]	Missing You/We Are the Children of the World	1984	—	—	3.00
❏ PB-14032	Telephone/Fool for Your Love	1985	—	—	3.00
❏ PB-14032 [PS]	Telephone/Fool for Your Love	1985	—	—	3.00
❏ PB-14181	Eaten Alive/(Instrumental)	1985	—	—	3.00
❏ PB-14181 [PS]	Eaten Alive/(Instrumental)	1985	—	—	3.00
❏ PB-14244	Chain Reaction/More and More	1985	—	2.00	4.00
❏ PB-14244 [PS]	Chain Reaction/More and More	1985	—	—	3.00
❏ PB-14244	Chain Reaction (Special New Mix)/ More and More	1986	—	—	3.00
❏ GB-14342	Missing You/Swept Away	1986	—	—	3.00

—Gold Standard Series

7-Inch Extended Plays

MOTOWN

Number	Title (A Side/B Side)	Yr	VG	VG+	NM
❏ M 60724	My Place//Baby It's Love/The Long and Winding Road//How About You/I'm Still Waiting/ Everything Is Everything	1970	3.00	6.00	12.00

—Jukebox issue; small hole, plays at 33 1/3 rpm

Number	Title (A Side/B Side)	Yr	VG	VG+	NM
❏ M 60724 [PS]	Everything Is Everything	1970	3.00	6.00	12.00

—Part of "Little LP" series (LLP #133)

Albums

MOTOWN

Number	Title (A Side/B Side)	Yr	VG	VG+	NM
❏ M5-135V1	Diana Ross	1981	2.00	4.00	8.00

—Reissue of 711

Number	Title (A Side/B Side)	Yr	VG	VG+	NM
❏ M5-155V1	Diana!	1981	2.00	4.00	8.00

—Reissue of 719

Number	Title (A Side/B Side)	Yr	VG	VG+	NM
❏ M5-163V1	Touch Me in the Morning	1981	2.00	4.00	8.00

—Reissue of 772

Number	Title (A Side/B Side)	Yr	VG	VG+	NM
❏ M5-169V1	Diana Ross Live at Caesars Palace	1981	2.00	4.00	8.00

—Reissue of 801

Number	Title (A Side/B Side)	Yr	VG	VG+	NM
❏ M5-198V1	The Boss	1981	2.00	4.00	8.00

—Reissue of 923

Number	Title (A Side/B Side)	Yr	VG	VG+	NM
❏ M5-214V1	Duets with Diana	1981	2.50	5.00	10.00
❏ MS-711	Diana Ross	1970	3.75	7.50	15.00
❏ MS-719	Diana!	1971	3.75	7.50	15.00
❏ MS-723	Surrender	1971	3.75	7.50	15.00
❏ MS-724	Everything Is Everything	1970	3.75	7.50	15.00
❏ M-758D [(2)]	Lady Sings the Blues	1972	3.75	7.50	15.00

—With booklet; all but four tracks are by Diana Ross

Number	Title (A Side/B Side)	Yr	VG	VG+	NM
❏ M-772L	Touch Me in the Morning	1973	3.75	7.50	15.00
❏ M6-801S1	Diana Ross Live at Caesars Palace	1974	3.00	6.00	12.00
❏ M7-812V1	Last Time I Saw Him	1974	3.00	6.00	12.00
❏ M6-861S1	Diana Ross	1976	3.00	6.00	12.00
❏ M6-869S1	Diana Ross' Greatest Hits	1976	3.00	6.00	12.00
❏ M7-877R2 [(2)]	An Evening with Diana Ross	1977	3.75	7.50	15.00
❏ M7-890R1	Baby It's Me	1977	3.00	6.00	12.00
❏ M7-907R1	Ross	1978	3.00	6.00	12.00
❏ M8-923M1	The Boss	1979	2.50	5.00	10.00
❏ M8-936	Diana	1980	2.50	5.00	10.00
❏ M8-951M1	To Love Again	1981	2.50	5.00	10.00
❏ M13-960C2 [(2)]	All the Great Hits	1981	2.00	4.00	8.00
❏ 5294 ML	Diana Ross	1983	2.00	4.00	8.00

—Reissue of 861

Number	Title (A Side/B Side)	Yr	VG	VG+	NM
❏ 6049 ML2 [(2)]	Diana Ross Anthology	1983	3.75	7.50	15.00
❏ MOT-6274	Workin' Overtime	1989	2.50	5.00	10.00
❏ 37463-6377-1	The Remixes	1994	3.00	6.00	12.00

Number	Title (A Side/B Side)	Yr	VG	VG+	NM
NAUTILUS					
❏ NR-37	Diana	1981	10.00	20.00	40.00
—Audiophile vinyl					
RCA VICTOR					
❏ AFL1-4153	Why Do Fools Fall in Love	1981	2.50	5.00	10.00
❏ AFL1-4384	Silk Electric	1982	2.50	5.00	10.00
❏ AFL1-4677	Ross	1983	2.00	4.00	8.00
❏ AFL1-5009	Swept Away	1984	2.00	4.00	8.00
❏ AYL1-5162	Why Do Fools Fall in Love	1985	—	3.00	6.00
—"Best Buy Series" reissue					
❏ AFL1-5422	Eaten Alive	1985	2.00	4.00	8.00
❏ 6388-1-R	Red Hot Rhythm and Blues	1987	2.00	4.00	8.00

ROSS, DIANA, AND MARVIN GAYE Also see each artist's individual listings.
45s

Number	Title (A Side/B Side)	Yr	VG	VG+	NM
MOTOWN					
❏ 1269	My Mistake (Was to Love You)/ Include Me in Your Life	1973	—	2.50	5.00
❏ 1280	You're a Special Part of Me/ I'm Falling in Love with You	1973	—	2.50	5.00
❏ 1296	Don't Knock My Love/Just Say Just Say	1974	—	2.50	5.00
Albums					
MOTOWN					
❏ M5-124V1	Diana & Marvin	1981	2.00	4.00	8.00
—Reissue					
❏ M7-803	Diana & Marvin	1973	3.75	7.50	15.00

ROSS, DIANA; MARVIN GAYE; SMOKEY ROBINSON; AND STEVIE WONDER
Also see each artist's individual listings.
12-Inch Singles

Number	Title (A Side/B Side)	Yr	VG	VG+	NM
MOTOWN					
❏ M00015 D1	Pops, We Love You (6:32) (same on both sides)	1979	3.00	6.00	12.00
45s					
MOTOWN					
❏ 1455	Pops, We Love You/(Instrumental)	1979	—	2.00	4.00
—Later version is 3:30 and has no monologue					
❏ 1455	Pops, We Love You/(Instrumental)	1979	2.00	4.00	8.00
—Original version is 3:59 and has a monologue by Diana Ross					
❏ 1455 [DJ]	Pops, We Love You (same on both sides)	1979	2.50	5.00	10.00
—Original version is 3:59 and has a monologue by Diana Ross					
❏ M9-1455	Pops, We Love You/(Instrumental)	1979	3.75	7.50	15.00
—Heart-shaped red vinyl record in plastic sleeve					

ROSS, DIANA, AND THE SUPREMES See THE SUPREMES.

ROSS, JACKIE
45s

Number	Title (A Side/B Side)	Yr	VG	VG+	NM
BRUNSWICK					
❏ 55325	Keep Your Chin Up/Love Is Easy to Lose	1967	2.00	4.00	8.00
❏ 55361	Mr. Sunshine/Walk on My Side	1968	2.00	4.00	8.00
CAPITOL					
❏ 4308	I Can't Stand to See You Go/Ain't No Fun to Me	1976	—	2.00	4.00
CHESS					
❏ 1903	Selfish One/Everything But Love	1964	2.00	4.00	8.00
❏ 1913	I've Got the Skill/Change Your Ways	1964	2.00	4.00	8.00
❏ 1915	Haste Makes Waste/Wasting Time	1964	2.00	4.00	8.00
❏ 1920	Jerk and Twine/New Lover	1965	2.00	4.00	8.00
❏ 1929	You Really Know How to Hurt a Girl/ Dynamite Lovin'	1965	2.00	4.00	8.00
❏ 1938	Take Me for a Little While/Honey Dear	1965	2.00	4.00	8.00
❏ 1940	We Can Do It/Honey Dear	1965	2.00	4.00	8.00
GSF					
❏ 6886	Woman Get Nothing from Love/Do I	1972	—	2.50	5.00
❏ 6895	A One Woman Man/Take the Weight Off Me	1973	—	2.50	5.00
MERCURY					
❏ 73041	Angel of the Morning/Showcase	1970	—	3.00	6.00
❏ 73185	Glory Be/I Must Give You Time	1971	—	3.00	6.00
SAR					
❏ 129	Hard Times/Hold Me	1962	3.75	7.50	15.00
—As "Jacki Ross"					
SCEPTER					
❏ 12345	The World's in a Hell of a Shape/What Would You Give	1972	—	2.50	5.00
Albums					
CHESS					
❏ LP-1489 [M]	In Full Bloom	1966	7.50	15.00	30.00
❏ LPS-1489 [S]	In Full Bloom	1966	10.00	20.00	40.00

ROSSINI, TONI
45s

Number	Title (A Side/B Side)	Yr	VG	VG+	NM
SUN					
❏ 349	I Gotta Know/Is It Too Late	1960	5.00	10.00	20.00
❏ 366	Well I Ask Ya/Darlena	1961	5.00	10.00	20.00
❏ 378	Meet Me After School/Just Around the Corner	1962	5.00	10.00	20.00
❏ 380	New Girl in Town/You Made It Sound So Easy	1962	5.00	10.00	20.00
❏ 387	Nobody/Moved to Kansas City	1964	5.00	10.00	20.00

ROTARY CONNECTION Also see MINNIE RIPERTON.
45s

Number	Title (A Side/B Side)	Yr	VG	VG+	NM
CADET CONCEPT					
❏ DJ-1 [DJ]	Lady Jane/Amen	1968	3.75	7.50	15.00
❏ 7000	Like a Rollin' Stone/Turn Me On	1967	2.50	5.00	10.00
❏ 7002	Ruby Tuesday/Soul Man	1968	2.50	5.00	10.00
❏ 7007	Paper Castle/Teach Me How to Fly	1968	2.50	5.00	10.00
❏ 7008	Aladdin/Magical World	1968	2.50	5.00	10.00
❏ 7009	Silent Night Chant/Peace At Least	1968	3.00	6.00	12.00
❏ 7014	The Weight/Respect	1969	2.50	5.00	10.00
❏ 7018	Want You to Know/Memory Band	1969	2.50	5.00	10.00
❏ 7021	Love Me Now/May Our Amens Be True	1970	2.50	5.00	10.00
❏ 7027	Stormy Monday Blues/Teach Me How to Fly	1970	2.50	5.00	10.00
❏ 7028	Hey Love/If I Sing My Song	1971	2.50	5.00	10.00
—As "New Rotary Connection"					
JANUS					
❏ 249	Living Alone/Magical World	1975	—	2.50	5.00
—As "Minnie Riperton and Rotary Connection"					

Number	Title (A Side/B Side)	Yr	VG	VG+	NM
Albums					
CADET					
❏ CS-50006	Hey Love	1971	5.00	10.00	20.00
CADET CONCEPT					
❏ LP-312 [M]	Rotary Connection	1968	15.00	30.00	60.00
—Mono appears to be promo only					
❏ LPS-312 [S]	Rotary Connection	1968	6.25	12.50	25.00
❏ LPS-317	Aladdin	1968	6.25	12.50	25.00
❏ LPS 318	Peace	1969	5.00	10.00	20.00
❏ LPS-322	Songs	1969	6.25	12.50	25.00
❏ LSP-328	Dinner Music	1970	6.25	12.50	25.00

ROTATIONS, THE (1)
45s

Number	Title (A Side/B Side)	Yr	VG	VG+	NM
FRANTIC					
❏ 200	Put a Nickel on D-9 (Pt. 1)/ Put a Nickel on D-9 (Pt. 2)	1965	37.50	75.00	150.00
❏ 202	Changed Man/Heartaches	1967	25.00	50.00	100.00
MALA					
❏ 576	Misty Roses/Trying to Make You My Own	1967	7.50	15.00	30.00

ROTATIONS, THE (2)
45s

Number	Title (A Side/B Side)	Yr	VG	VG+	NM
ORIGINAL SOUND					
❏ 41	The Crusher/Heavies	1964	25.00	50.00	100.00
—Produced by FRANK ZAPPA					

ROULETTES, THE More than one group.
45s

Number	Title (A Side/B Side)	Yr	VG	VG+	NM
ANGLE					
❏ 1001	Surfer's Charge/Archibald II (Duke of Nothing)	1963	12.50	25.00	50.00
CHAMP					
❏ 102	I See a Star/Come On, Baby	1958	20.00	40.00	80.00
EBB					
❏ 124	The Way You Carry On/You Don't Care Anymore	1957	7.50	15.00	30.00
LOST-NITE					
❏ 233	I See a Star/Come On, Baby	196?	—	2.50	5.00
—Reissue					
SCEPTER					
❏ 1204	Hasten Jason/Wouldn't It Be Goin' Steady	1959	150.00	300.00	600.00
UNITED ARTISTS					
❏ 718	Can You Go/Soon You'll Be Leaving Me	1964	2.50	5.00	10.00
❏ 990	Long Cigarette/Junk	1966	2.50	5.00	10.00

ROUND, JONATHAN
45s

Number	Title (A Side/B Side)	Yr	VG	VG+	NM
WESTBOUND					
❏ 186	Don't It Make You Want to Go Home/ Train a-Comin'	1971	2.00	4.00	8.00
❏ 199	Sympathy for the Devil/Travelin' Mama Blues	1972	2.50	5.00	10.00
Albums					
WESTBOUND					
❏ 2009	Jonathan Round	1971	7.50	15.00	30.00
—Round cover					
❏ 2009	Jonathan Round	1972	3.75	7.50	15.00
—Square cover					

ROUND ROBIN
45s

Number	Title (A Side/B Side)	Yr	VG	VG+	NM
CAPITOL					
❏ 5962	Ton of Joy/Vulture	1967	3.00	6.00	12.00
DOMAIN					
❏ 1019	Do the Slauson/Slauson Shuffle Time	1963	3.75	7.50	15.00
❏ 1400	Do the Slauson/Slauson Shuffle Time	1963	3.75	7.50	15.00
❏ 1402	Slauson Town/Malloy, The Engineer	1963	3.75	7.50	15.00
❏ 1405	The Roundest of Them All/8069 Vineland	1964	3.75	7.50	15.00
❏ 1406	I Know/Giddyap Kick	1964	3.75	7.50	15.00
❏ 1407	Don't Let Go/Up and Down	1964	3.75	7.50	15.00
❏ 1420	Land of 1000 Dances/Yea Yea	1965	3.00	6.00	12.00
❏ 1422	Sit and Dance/Little People	1965	3.00	6.00	12.00
❏ 1424	I'm the Wolfman/Sit and Dance	1965	3.00	6.00	12.00

ROUTERS, THE
45s

Number	Title (A Side/B Side)	Yr	VG	VG+	NM
MERCURY					
❏ 73418	Superbird/Sack of Woe	1973	—	3.00	6.00
WARNER BROS.					
❏ 5283	Let's Go (pony)/Mashy	1962	3.75	7.50	15.00
❏ 5332	Half Time/Make It Snappy	1963	3.00	6.00	12.00
❏ 5349	Sting Ray/Snap Happy	1963	3.00	6.00	12.00
❏ 5379	A-Ooga/Big Band	1963	3.00	6.00	12.00
❏ 5403	Snap, Crackle and Pop/Amoeba	1963	3.00	6.00	12.00
❏ 5444	Crack Up/Let's Dance	1964	3.00	6.00	12.00
❏ 5467	Stamp and Shake/Ah-Ya	1964	3.00	6.00	12.00
❏ 7117	Let's Go (pony)/Mashy	1967	2.50	5.00	10.00
Albums					
WARNER BROS.					
❏ W 1490 [M]	Let's Go! with the Routers	1963	6.25	12.50	25.00
❏ WS 1490 [S]	Let's Go! with the Routers	1963	7.50	15.00	30.00
❏ W 1524 [M]	1963's Great Instrumental Hits	1964	7.50	15.00	30.00
❏ WS 1524 [S]	1963's Great Instrumental Hits	1964	10.00	20.00	40.00
❏ W 1559 [M]	Charge!	1964	6.25	12.50	25.00
❏ WS 1559 [S]	Charge!	1964	7.50	15.00	30.00
❏ W 1595 [M]	Go Go Go with the Chuck Berry Songbook	1965	5.00	10.00	20.00
❏ WS 1595 [S]	Go Go Go with the Chuck Berry Songbook	1965	6.25	12.50	25.00

ROUZAN SISTERS, THE
45s

Number	Title (A Side/B Side)	Yr	VG	VG+	NM
FRISCO					
❏ 113	Men of War/Dance Every Dance	1965	2.50	5.00	10.00

ROVER BOYS, THE
45s

Number	Title (A Side/B Side)	Yr	VG	VG+	NM
ABC-PARAMOUNT					
❏ 9659	Come to Me/Love Me Again	1955	3.75	7.50	15.00
❏ 9678	My Queen/Sixteen Teens	1956	3.75	7.50	15.00

R

Number	Title (A Side/B Side)	Yr	VG	VG+	NM
❑ 9700	Graduation Day/I Hear Music	1956	3.75	7.50	15.00
❑ 9732	From a School Ring to a Wedding Ring/ Young Love	1956	3.75	7.50	15.00
❑ 9760	The Piano Tuner/Whoop Doodly Baby	1956	3.75	7.50	15.00
❑ 9779	Little Did I Know/Again and Again	1957	3.75	7.50	15.00
CORAL					
❑ 61271	Show Me/You've Got It	1954	5.00	10.00	20.00
DECCA					
❑ 31485	Shalom/I Hear Havana	1963	2.00	4.00	8.00
RCA VICTOR					
❑ 47-7432	Magic Lamp/Little Darlin'	1959	3.00	6.00	12.00
❑ 47-7482	Sweet Violets/Julia	1959	3.00	6.00	12.00
UNITED ARTISTS					
❑ 288	Is It Me/Marry Young	1961	2.50	5.00	10.00
❑ 331	For Every Boy or Girl/If You Plant a Little Kiss	1961	2.50	5.00	10.00
VIK					
❑ 0283	Soft Sands/My Baby's Steppin' Out	1957	5.00	10.00	20.00
❑ 0302	What Can I Do for a Heartache/I Got to You	1957	5.00	10.00	20.00
❑ 0313	Blue Willow/You're My Everything	1958	5.00	10.00	20.00
❑ 0317	Blind Date/Make Room for Me	1958	5.00	10.00	20.00
❑ 0338	S'Agapo/Ask Me Who Loves You	1958	5.00	10.00	20.00

ROVERS, THE (1)
45s
CAPITOL

❑ F3078	Why Oh-h/Ichi-Bon Tami Dachi	1955	12.50	25.00	50.00
MUSIC CITY					
❑ 750	Why Oh-h/Ichi-Bon Tami Dachi	1954	20.00	40.00	80.00
—Black vinyl					
❑ 750	Why Oh-h/Ichi-Bon Tami Dachi	1954	62.50	125.00	250.00
—Red vinyl					
❑ 780	Salute to Johnny Ace/Jadda	1955	20.00	40.00	80.00
—Black vinyl					
❑ 780	Salute to Johnny Ace/Jadda	1955	62.50	125.00	250.00
—Red vinyl					

ROVERS, THE (2)
45s
CHATTAHOOCHIE

❑ 653	The Web/Can't Be the First	1964	2.50	5.00	10.00

ROVERS, THE (3)
45s
KAPP

❑ 278	Delia's Gone/I Know Where I'm Goin'	1959	3.00	6.00	12.00

ROVIN' KIND, THE
45s
DUNWICH

❑ 146	My Generation/Girl	1967	5.00	10.00	20.00
❑ 154	She/Didn't Want to Have to Do It	1967	5.00	10.00	20.00
ROULETTE					
❑ 4687	Right on Time/Night People	1966	3.75	7.50	15.00

ROWLES, JOHN
Albums
KAPP

❑ KS-3597	Exciting	1969	3.75	7.50	15.00
❑ KS-3637	Cheryl Moana Marie	1971	3.75	7.50	15.00
MCA					
❑ 549	John Rowles	197?	2.50	5.00	10.00

ROXY MUSIC Also see BRYAN FERRY.
12-Inch Singles
WARNER BROS.

❑ PRO-A-1056 [DJ]Take a Chance with Me (2 versions)/ More Than This/Avalon	1982	3.00	6.00	12.00
❑ PRO-A-2033 [DJ]More Than This/Avalon	1982	2.50	5.00	10.00

45s
ATCO

❑ 7018	The Thrill of It All/The Application Failed	1975	—	2.00	4.00
❑ 7042	Love Is the Drug/Both Ends Burning	1975	—	2.00	4.00
❑ 7100	Dance Away/Trash 2	1979	—	2.00	4.00
❑ 7204	Angel Eyes/My Little Girl	1979	—	2.00	4.00
❑ 7301	Over You/My Only Love	1980	—	2.00	4.00
❑ 7310	Oh Yeah (On the Radio)/Rain, Rain, Rain	1980	—	2.00	4.00
❑ 7315	In the Midnight Hour/(B-side unknown)	1980	—	2.00	4.00
❑ 7329	Jealous Guy/To Turn You On	1981	—	2.00	4.00
❑ 7329 [PS]	Jealous Guy/To Turn You On	1981	—	2.00	4.00
ATLANTIC OLDIES SERIES					
❑ 13269	Love Is the Drug/Dance Away	198?	—	—	3.00
—Reissue					
REPRISE					
❑ 1124	Virginia Plan/The Numberer	1972	—	2.50	5.00
WARNER BROS.					
❑ GWB 0316	Do the Strand/Virginia Plain	197?	—	—	3.00
—"Back to Back Hits" series					
❑ 7719	Do the Strand/Editions of You	1973	—	2.50	5.00
❑ 29912	More Than This/Always Unknowing	1982	—	—	3.00
❑ 29978	Take a Chance with Me/India	1982	—	—	3.00
❑ 29978 [PS]	Take a Chance with Me/India	1982	—	—	3.00

Albums
ATCO

❑ SD 32-102	Flesh + Blood	1980	2.50	5.00	10.00
❑ SD 38-103	Greatest Hits	1977	2.50	5.00	10.00
❑ SD 36-106	Country Life	1975	6.25	12.50	25.00
—Original cover shows two semi-naked women on a grassy background					
❑ SD 36-106A	Country Life	1975	2.50	5.00	10.00
—Revised cover deletes women, leaves only the grassy background					
❑ SD 38-114	Manifesto	1979	2.50	5.00	10.00
❑ SD 38-114 [PD]Manifesto	1979	7.50	15.00	30.00
—Picture disc					
❑ SD 36-127	Siren	1975	2.50	5.00	10.00
—Originals have yellow labels					
❑ SD 36-133	The First Roxy Music Album	1975	3.00	6.00	12.00
—Reissue of Reprise MS 2114; originals have yellow labels					

Number	Title (A Side/B Side)	Yr	VG	VG+	NM
❑ SD 36-134	For Your Pleasure	1975	3.00	6.00	12.00
—Reissue of Warner Bros. BS 2696; originals have yellow labels					
❑ SD 36-139	Viva! Roxy Music (Live)	1976	2.50	5.00	10.00
—Originals have yellow labels					
❑ SD 7045	Stranded	1974	3.00	6.00	12.00
❑ 90122	The Atlantic Years (1973-80)	1983	2.50	5.00	10.00
REPRISE					
❑ MS 2114	Roxy Music	1972	7.50	15.00	30.00
❑ 25857 [(2)]	Street Life: 20 Greatest Hits	1989	3.75	7.50	15.00
—By "Bryan Ferry & Roxy Music"					
WARNER BROS.					
❑ BS 2696	For Your Pleasure	1973	6.25	12.50	25.00
❑ 23686	Avalon	1982	2.50	5.00	10.00
❑ 23808 [EP]	Musique — The High Road	1983	2.00	4.00	8.00

ROY C
45s
ALAGA

❑ 1000	In Divorce Court/I Don't Want to Worry	1970	2.50	5.00	10.00
❑ 1003	Falling in Love/I Found a Man in My Bed	1970	2.50	5.00	10.00
❑ 1005	A Merry Black Christmas/I Don't Want To Worry	1970	2.50	5.00	10.00
❑ 1006	Got to Get Enough (Of Your Sweet Love Stuff)/ An Open Letter to the President	1971	2.50	5.00	10.00
❑ 1007	I Wasn't There/Those Days Are Gone	1971	2.50	5.00	10.00
❑ 1008	I'll Never Leave You Lonely/I'm Gonna Love (Somebody Else's Woman)	1972	2.50	5.00	10.00
❑ 1009	Since I Met You Baby/Lonely I Was	1972	2.50	5.00	10.00
—With Linda Caver					
❑ 1013	I Caught You in the Act/Back Into My Arms	1973	2.50	5.00	10.00
❑ 1014	Since God Made a Woman/ We're On the Road to Hell	1973	2.50	5.00	10.00
BLACK HAWK					
❑ 12101	Shotgun Wedding/I'm Gonna Make It	1965	3.00	6.00	12.00
MERCURY					
❑ 73391	Don't Blame the Man/I'm Bustin' My Rocks	1973	—	3.00	6.00
❑ 73445	She Kept On Walkin'/Back Into My Arms	1973	—	3.00	6.00
❑ 73605	Loneliness Has Got a Hold on Me/ If I Could Love You Forever	1974	—	2.50	5.00
❑ 73672	Love Me Till Tomorrow Comes/Virgin Girl	1975	—	2.50	5.00
❑ 73735	My Girl (Reggae)/The Second Time Around	1975	—	2.50	5.00
❑ 73780	Every Woman Has a Right/ Don't Stop Short of Satisfaction	1976	—	2.50	5.00
❑ 73848	You Can't Judge a Man (By the Color of His Skin)/I Wanna Do It Again	1976	—	2.50	5.00
❑ 73981	From the Outside Looking In (He Used to Be My Friend)/After Loving You	1977	—	2.50	5.00
SHOUT					
❑ 206	Gone Gone/Stop What You're Doing	1966	2.50	5.00	10.00
UPTOWN					
❑ 731	Shotgun Wedding/High School Dropout	1966	2.50	5.00	10.00

Albums
MERCURY

❑ SRM-1-678	Sex and Soul	1974	3.75	7.50	15.00
❑ SRM-1-1056	Nice	1976	3.75	7.50	15.00
❑ SRM-1-1192	More	1978	3.75	7.50	15.00

ROYAL, BILLY JOE
45s
ALL WOOD

❑ 401	Wait for Me Baby/If It Wasn't for a Woman	1962	5.00	10.00	20.00
ATLANTIC					
❑ 2328	Never in a Hundred Years/ We Haven't a Moment to Lose	1966	2.50	5.00	10.00
❑ 87770	If the Jukebox Took Teardrops/How Could You	1991	—	2.00	4.00
❑ 87867	Ring Where a Ring Used to Be/We Need to Walk	1990	—	2.00	4.00
❑ 87933	Searchin' for Some Kind of Clue/ This Too Shall Pass	1990	—	2.00	4.00
❑ 88815	Till I Can't Take It Anymore/He Don't Know	1990	—	2.00	4.00
ATLANTIC AMERICA					
❑ 99217	Love Has No Right/ Cross My Heart and Hope to Try	1989	—	—	3.00
❑ 99217 [PS]	Love Has No Right/ Cross My Heart and Hope to Try	1989	—	2.00	4.00
❑ 99242	Tell It Like It Is/Losing You	1989	—	—	3.00
❑ 99242 [PS]	Tell It Like It Is/Losing You	1989	—	2.00	4.00
❑ 99295	It Keeps Right On Hurtin'/Let It Rain	1988	—	—	3.00
❑ 99295 [PS]	It Keeps Right On Hurtin'/Let It Rain	1988	—	—	3.00
❑ 99364	Out of Sight and On My Mind/ She Don't Cry Like She Used To	1988	—	—	3.00
❑ 99364 [PS]	Out of Sight and On My Mind/ She Don't Cry Like She Used To	1988	—	—	3.00
❑ 99404	I'll Pin a Note on Your Pillow/ A Place for a Heartache	1987	—	—	3.00
❑ 99404 [PS]	I'll Pin a Note on Your Pillow/ A Place for a Heartache	1987	—	—	3.00
❑ 99485	Old Bridges Burn Slow/ We've Both Got a Lot to Learn	1987	—	—	3.00
❑ 99485 [PS]	Old Bridges Burn Slow/ We've Both Got a Lot to Learn	1987	—	—	3.00
❑ 99519	I Miss You Already/Another Endless Night	1986	—	—	3.00
❑ 99555	Boardwalk Angel/Out of Sight and On My Mind	1986	—	—	3.00
❑ 99599	Burned Like a Rocket/Lonely Loving You	1985	—	—	3.00
COLUMBIA					
❑ 43305	Down in the Boondocks/Oh, What a Night	1965	2.50	5.00	10.00
❑ 43305 [DJ]	Down in the Boondocks (same on both sides)	1965	10.00	20.00	40.00
—Red vinyl promo					
❑ 43390	I Knew You When/Steal Away	1965	2.50	5.00	10.00
❑ 43390 [DJ]	I Knew You When (same on both sides)	1965	10.00	20.00	40.00
—Red vinyl promo					
❑ 43465	I've Got to Be Somebody/ You Make Me Feel Like a Man	1965	2.00	4.00	8.00
❑ 43465 [DJ]	I've Got to Be Somebody (same on both sides)	1965	7.50	15.00	30.00
—Red vinyl promo					
❑ 43538	It's a Good Time/Don't Wait Up for Me Mama	1966	2.00	4.00	8.00
❑ 43622	Heart's Desire/Keep Inside Me	1966	2.00	4.00	8.00
❑ 43740	Campfire Girls/Should I Come Back	1966	2.00	4.00	8.00
❑ 43883	Yo-Yo/We Tried	1966	2.00	4.00	8.00

Number	Title (A Side/B Side)	Yr	VG	VG+	NM
❑ 44003	Wisdom of a Fool/Everything Turned Blue	1967	2.00	4.00	8.00
❑ 44103	These Are Not My People/The Greatest Love	1967	2.00	4.00	8.00
❑ 44277	Hush/Watching from the Bandstand	1967	2.00	4.00	8.00
❑ 44468	Don't You Be Ashamed (To Call My Name)/				
	Don't You Think It's Time	1968	2.00	4.00	8.00
❑ 44574	Storybook Children/Just Between You and Me	1968	2.00	4.00	8.00
❑ 44677	Movies in My Mind/Gabriel	1968	—	3.00	6.00
❑ 44743	Bed of Roses/The Greatest Love	1969	—	3.00	6.00
❑ 44814	Nobody Loves You But Me/				
	Baby I'm Thinking of You	1969	—	2.50	5.00
❑ 44902	Cherry Hill Park/Helping Hand	1969	2.00	4.00	8.00
❑ 45085	Mama's Song/Me Without You	1970	—	2.50	5.00
❑ 45220	Burning a Hole/Every Night	1970	—	2.50	5.00
❑ 45289	Tulsa/Pick Up the Pieces	1970	—	2.50	5.00
❑ 45406	Poor Little Pearl/Lady Lives to Love	1971	—	2.50	5.00
❑ 45495	Colorado Rain/We Go Back	1971	—	2.50	5.00
❑ 45557	Later/The Family	1972	—	3.00	6.00
❑ 45620	Child of Mine/Natchez Trace	1972	—	3.00	6.00
FAIRLANE					
❑ 21009	Never in a Hundred Years/				
	We Haven't a Moment to Lose	1961	7.50	15.00	30.00
❑ 21013	Dark Glasses/Perhaps	1962	7.50	15.00	30.00
KAT FAMILY					
❑ 01044	(Who is Like You) Sweet America/				
	No Love Like a First Love	1981	—	2.00	4.00
❑ 02074	You Really Got a Hold on Me/				
	No Love Like a First Love	1981	—	2.00	4.00
❑ 02297	Wasted Time/Outrun the Sun	1981	—	2.00	4.00
MERCURY					
❑ 76069	Mr. Kool/Let's Talk It Over	1980	—	2.00	4.00
MGM SOUTH					
❑ 7011	This Magic Moment/Mountain Woman	1973	—	2.50	5.00
❑ 7018	Summertime Skies/Look What I Found	1973	—	2.50	5.00
❑ 7022	If This Is the Last Time/Perfect Harmony	1973	—	2.50	5.00
❑ 7032	Star Again/Sugar Blue	1974	—	2.50	5.00
PLAYER'S					
❑ 1	I'm Specialized/Really You	1965	5.00	10.00	20.00
PRIVATE STOCK					
❑ 45,192	Under the Boardwalk/Precious Time	1978	—	2.50	5.00
❑ 45,212 [DJ]	Anchors Aweigh (mono/stereo)	1979	—	2.50	5.00
SCEPTER					
❑ 12419	All Night Rain/Time Don't Pass By Here	1976	—	2.00	4.00
TOLLIE					
❑ 9011	Mama Didn't Raise No Fools/Get Behind Me,				
	Devil	1964	3.75	7.50	15.00
Albums					
ATLANTIC AMERICA					
❑ 90508	Looking Ahead	1986	2.50	5.00	10.00
❑ 90658	The Royal Treatment	1987	2.50	5.00	10.00
❑ 91064	Tell It Like It Is	1989	2.50	5.00	10.00
COLUMBIA					
❑ CL 2403 [M]	Down in the Boondocks	1965	5.00	10.00	20.00
❑ CL 2781 [M]	Billy Joe Royal	1967	6.25	12.50	25.00
❑ CS 9203 [S]	Down in the Boondocks	1965	6.25	12.50	25.00
❑ CS 9581 [S]	Billy Joe Royal	1967	6.25	12.50	25.00
❑ CS 9974	Cherry Hill Park	1969	6.25	-12.50	25.00
KAT FAMILY					
❑ JW 37342	Billy Joe Royal	1982	2.50	5.00	10.00
MERCURY					
❑ SRM-1-3837	Billy Joe Royal	1980	2.50	5.00	10.00

ROYAL DEBS, THE
45s
TIFCO

Number	Title (A Side/B Side)	Yr	VG	VG+	NM
❑ 826	I Do/Jerry	1962	6.25	12.50	25.00

ROYAL DRIFTERS, THE
45s
TEEN

| ❑ 506 | S'Why Hard/Little Linda | 1959 | 25.00 | 50.00 | 100.00 |
| ❑ 508 | To Each His Own/Da Kind | 1959 | 37.50 | 75.00 | 150.00 |

ROYAL GUARDSMEN, THE
45s
LAURIE

❑ 112	Snoopy's Christmas/The Smallest Astronaut	197?	—	2.00	4.00
—B-side by Barry Winslow; reissue					
❑ 3359	Baby Let's Wait/Leaving Me	1966	2.50	5.00	10.00
❑ 3366	Snoopy vs. the Red Baron/I Needed You	1966	3.00	6.00	12.00
—Regular red, black and white label					
❑ 3366	Snoopy vs. the Red Baron/I Needed You	1966	3.75	7.50	15.00
—Light blue label					
❑ 3379	The Return of the Red Baron/Sweetmeats Slide	1967	2.50	5.00	10.00
❑ 3391	Airplane Song (My Airplane)/Om	1967	2.00	4.00	8.00
❑ 3397	Wednesday/So Right (To Be in Love)	1967	2.00	4.00	8.00
❑ 3416	Snoopy's Christmas/				
	It Kinda Looks Like Christmas	1967	2.50	5.00	10.00
❑ 3416 [PS]	Snoopy's Christmas/				
	It Kinda Looks Like Christmas	1967	5.00	10.00	20.00
❑ 3428	I Say Love/I'm Not Gonna Stay	1968	2.00	4.00	8.00
❑ 3451	Snoopy for President/Down Behind the Lines	1968	2.00	4.00	8.00
❑ 3461	Baby Let's Wait/Biplane "Evermore"	1968	2.00	4.00	8.00
❑ 3461	Baby Let's Wait/So Right (To Be in Love)	1968	2.00	4.00	8.00
❑ 3494	Magic Window/Mother, Where's Your Daughter	1969	2.50	5.00	8.00
❑ 3590	Snoopy for President/Down Behind the Lines	1972	—	3.00	6.00
❑ 3646	Snoopy for President/Sweetmeats Slide	1976	—	2.50	5.00
Albums					
HOLIDAY					
❑ HDY 1913	Merry Snoopy's Christmas	1980	2.50	5.00	10.00
—Reissue of Laurie 2042					
LAURIE					
❑ LLP-2038 [M]	Snoopy vs. the Red Baron	1967	5.00	10.00	20.00
❑ SLP-2038 [S]	Snoopy vs. the Red Baron	1967	6.25	12.50	25.00
❑ LLP-2039 [M]	The Return of the Red Baron	1967	5.00	10.00	20.00
❑ SLP-2039 [S]	The Return of the Red Baron	1967	6.25	12.50	25.00

Number	Title (A Side/B Side)	Yr	VG	VG+	NM
❑ LLP 2042 [M]	Snoopy and His Friends	1967	3.75	7.50	15.00
—With "Merry Snoopy's Christmas" poster missing					
❑ LLP 2042 [M]	Snoopy and His Friends	1967	6.25	12.50	25.00
—With "Merry Snoopy's Christmas" poster still attached to back cover					
❑ SLP 2042 [S]	Snoopy and His Friends	1967	5.00	10.00	20.00
—With "Merry Snoopy's Christmas" poster missing					
❑ SLP 2042 [S]	Snoopy and His Friends	1967	7.50	15.00	30.00
—With "Merry Snoopy's Christmas" poster still attached to back cover					
❑ SLP-2046	Snoopy for President	1968	6.25	12.50	25.00

ROYAL HALOS, THE
45s
ALADDIN

| ❑ 3460 | My Love Is True/Nobody But Me and My Girl | 1959 | 10.00 | 20.00 | 40.00 |

ROYAL HOLIDAYS, THE
45s
CARLTON

❑ 472	Margaret/I'm Sorry	1958	6.25	12.50	25.00
HERALD					
❑ 536	Rockin' at the Bandstand/Down in Cuba	1959	37.50	75.00	150.00
—Most, and perhaps all, copies were labeled "Chip Chip"/"Running to You" by the Mello-Kings					
PENTHOUSE					
❑ 9357	Margaret/I'm Sorry	1958	37.50	75.00	150.00

ROYAL PLAYBOYS, THE
Albums
WALDORF

| ❑ 33-136 [10] | Rock and Roll/New Orleans Blues | 195? | 125.00 | 250.00 | 500.00 |

ROYAL ROBINS, THE
45s
ABC-PARAMOUNT

❑ 10504	Turn Me Loose/Country Fool	1963	7.50	15.00	30.00
❑ 10542	How High the Moon/				
	Something You've Got, Baby	1964	7.50	15.00	30.00

ROYAL TEENS, THE Bob Gaudio, later of THE FOUR SEASONS, was in this group.
45s
ABC-PARAMOUNT

❑ 9882	Short Shorts/Planet Rock	1958	7.50	15.00	30.00
❑ 9918	Big Name Button/Sham Rock	1958	6.25	12.50	25.00
❑ 9945	Harvey's Got a Girl Friend/Hangin' Around	1958	6.25	12.50	25.00
❑ 9955	Open the Door/My Kind of Dream	1958	6.25	12.50	25.00
ALLNEW					
❑ 1415	Short Short Twist/Royal Twist	1962	5.00	10.00	20.00
ASTRA					
❑ 1012	Mad Gass/Sittin' with My Baby	196?	3.75	7.50	15.00
CAPITOL					
❑ F4261	Believe Me/Little Cricket	1959	7.50	15.00	30.00
❑ 4335	The Moon's Not Meant for Lovers/				
	Was It a Dream	1960	7.50	15.00	30.00
❑ 4402	With You/It's the Talk of the Town	1960	7.50	15.00	30.00
JUBILEE					
❑ 5418	Short Short Twist/Royal Twist	1962	3.75	7.50	15.00
MIGHTY					
❑ 111	Leotards/Royal Blues	1959	6.25	12.50	25.00
❑ 112	Cave Man/Wounded Heart	1959	7.50	15.00	30.00
❑ 200	My Memories of You/Little Trixie	1961	10.00	20.00	40.00
MUSICOR					
❑ 1398	Smile a Little Smile for Me/Hey Jude	1969	2.50	5.00	10.00
POWER					
❑ 113	Mad Gass/Sittin' with My Baby	1959	10.00	20.00	40.00
❑ 215	Short Shorts/Planet Rock	1957	37.50	75.00	150.00
SWAN					
❑ 4200	I'll Love You ('Til the End of Time)/(Instrumental)	1965	25.00	50.00	100.00
TCF HALL					
❑ 117	Bad Girl/Do the Montoona	1965	3.75	7.50	15.00
Albums					
COLLECTABLES					
❑ COL-5094	Short Shorts: Golden Classics	198?	2.50	5.00	10.00
MUSICOR					
❑ MS-3186	Newies But Oldies	1970	5.00	10.00	20.00
TRU-GEMS					
❑ 1001	Short Shorts & Others	1975	5.00	10.00	20.00

ROYAL TONES, THE
45s
TITANIC

| ❑ 5014 | Black Lightnin'/Surfer's Junction | 1964 | 15.00 | 30.00 | 60.00 |

ROYALETTES, THE
45s
CHANCELLOR

❑ 1133	No Big Thing/Yesterday's Lovers	1963	5.00	10.00	20.00
❑ 1140	Willie the Wolf/Blue Summer	1963	3.75	7.50	15.00
MGM					
❑ 13283	He's Gone/Don't You Cry	1964	3.00	6.00	12.00
❑ 13327	Poor Boy/Watch What Happens	1965	3.00	6.00	12.00
❑ 13366	It's Gonna Take a Miracle/				
	Out of Sight, Out of Mind	1965	3.75	7.50	15.00
❑ 13405	I Want to Meet Him/Never Again	1965	3.00	6.00	12.00
❑ 13451	You Bring Me Down/Only When You're Lonely	1966	3.00	6.00	12.00
❑ 13507	It's a Big Mistake/It's Better Not to Know	1966	3.00	6.00	12.00
❑ 13544	I Don't Want to Be the One/				
	An Affair to Remember	1966	3.00	6.00	12.00
❑ 13588	Love Without An End/When Summer's Gone	1966	3.00	6.00	12.00
❑ 13627	My Man/Take My Love	1966	3.00	6.00	12.00
ROULETTE					
❑ 4768	River of Ters/Something Wonderful	1967	2.50	5.00	10.00
WARNER BROS.					
❑ 5439	There He Goes/Come to Me	1964	3.75	7.50	15.00
Albums					
MGM					
❑ E-4332 [M]	It's Gonna Take a Miracle	1965	5.00	10.00	20.00
❑ SE-4332 [S]	It's Gonna Take a Miracle	1965	6.25	12.50	25.00

R

Number	Title (A Side/B Side)	Yr	VG	VG+	NM
❏ E-4366 [M]	The Elegant Sound of the Royalettes	1966	5.00	10.00	20.00
❏ SE-4366 [S]	The Elegant Sound of the Royalettes	1966	6.25	12.50	25.00

ROYALS, THE (1) Later known as THE MIDNIGHTERS. Also see HANK BALLARD AND THE MIDNIGHTERS.
45s
FEDERAL

Number	Title (A Side/B Side)	Yr	VG	VG+	NM
❏ 12064	Every Beat of My Heart/All Night Long	1952	375.00	750.00	1500.
❏ 12064AA	Every Beat of My Heart/All Night Long	1952	1000.	2000.	3000.
—Blue vinyl					
❏ 12077	I Know I Love You So/Starting From Tonight	1952	625.00	1250.	2500.
❏ 12088	Moonrise/Fifth Street Blues	1952	500.00	1000.	2000.
❏ 12088	Moonrise/Fifth Street Blues	1952	1000.	2000.	3000.
—Blue vinyl					
❏ 12098	A Love in My Heart/I'll Never Let You Go	1952	250.00	500.00	1000.
❏ 12113	Are You Forgetting?/What Did I Do	1952	150.00	300.00	600.00
❏ 12121	The Shrine of St. Cecelia/I Feel So Blue	1953	200.00	400.00	800.00
❏ 12133	Get It/No It Ain't	1953	50.00	100.00	200.00
❏ 12150	Hello Miss Fine/I Feel That-A-Way	1953	50.00	100.00	200.00
❏ 12160	That's It/Someone Like You	1953	62.50	125.00	250.00
❏ 12169	Work With Me Annie/Until I Die	1954	62.50	125.00	250.00
—Original pressing; for reissues, see "Midnighters, The"					
❏ 12177 [DJ]	Give It Up/That Woman	1954	75.00	150.00	300.00
—Evidently, some promos exist crediting The Royals					

ROYALS, THE (2) Also see CHUCK WILLIS.
45s
OKEH

Number	Title (A Side/B Side)	Yr	VG	VG+	NM
❏ 6832	If You Love Me/Dreams of You	1951	250.00	500.00	1000.

ROYALS, THE (3)
45s
PENGUIN

Number	Title (A Side/B Side)	Yr	VG	VG+	NM
❏ 1008	Thunder Wagon/Teen Beat	1959	7.50	15.00	30.00

ROYALS, THE (4)
45s
VAGABOND

Number	Title (A Side/B Side)	Yr	VG	VG+	NM
❏ 134	Surfin' Lagoon/Wild Safari	1962	12.50	25.00	50.00
❏ 444	Christmas Party/White Christmas	1963	12.50	25.00	50.00
—Black vinyl					
❏ 444	Christmas Party/White Christmas	1963	25.00	50.00	100.00
—Red vinyl					

ROYALS, THE (5) This Royals later became The Scooters.
45s
VENUS

Number	Title (A Side/B Side)	Yr	VG	VG+	NM
❏ 103	Someday We'll Meet Again/I Want You to Be My Mambo Baby	1954	100.00	200.00	400.00

ROYALTONES, THE
45s
GOLDISC

Number	Title (A Side/B Side)	Yr	VG	VG+	NM
❏ 3004	Short Line/Big Wheel	1960	2.50	5.00	10.00
❏ 3011	Flamingo Express/Secret Love	1960	2.50	5.00	10.00
❏ 3011	Flamingo Express/Tacos	1960	2.50	5.00	10.00
❏ 3016	Butterscotch/Dixie Cup	1961	2.00	4.00	8.00
❏ 3017	Royal Whirl/Dixie Rock	1961	2.00	4.00	8.00
❏ 3026	Peppermint Twist/Scotch and Soda	1962	2.00	4.00	8.00
❏ 3028	Do the Early Bird/Scotch and Soda	1962	2.00	4.00	8.00
JUBILEE					
❏ 5338	Poor Boy/Wail!	1958	3.75	7.50	15.00
—Black label with rainbow					
❏ 5338	Poor Boy/Wail!	1958	6.25	12.50	25.00
—Dark blue label, silver print					
❏ 5362	Seesaw/Little Bo	1959	3.00	6.00	12.00
MALA					
❏ 473	Holy Smokes/Our Faded Love	1964	2.00	4.00	8.00
❏ 482	El Toro/Lonely World	1964	2.00	4.00	8.00
❏ 487	The Yea Yea Song/Misty Sea	1964	2.00	4.00	8.00
OLD TOWN					
❏ 1018	Crazy Love/Never Let Me Go	1956	25.00	50.00	100.00
PORT					
❏ 70037	Poor Boy/See Saw	1963	3.00	6.00	12.00

ROYCE, EARL, AND THE OLYMPICS British group; no relation to other Olympics groups.
45s
TOWER

Number	Title (A Side/B Side)	Yr	VG	VG+	NM
❏ 137	Que Sera Sera Sera/I Really Do	1965	2.00	4.00	8.00

ROZZI, LITTLE SAMMY
45s
PELHAM

Number	Title (A Side/B Side)	Yr	VG	VG+	NM
❏ 722	Christine/Over the Rainbow	1961	50.00	100.00	200.00

RUBBER BAND, THE (1)
45s
ABC

Number	Title (A Side/B Side)	Yr	VG	VG+	NM
❏ 10849	Plastic Soul/Let's Sail Away	1966	2.50	5.00	10.00
COLUMBIA					
❏ 44013	In and Out of My Life/Bring Your Love	1967	2.50	5.00	10.00
REPRISE					
❏ 0637	I'm Gonna Make It/Messin' Up the Mind of a Young Girl	1967	2.50	5.00	10.00

RUBBER BAND, THE (2)
45s
GRT

Number	Title (A Side/B Side)	Yr	VG	VG+	NM
❏ 1	Sunshine of Your Love/Deserted Cities of the Heart	1969	—	3.00	6.00

Albums
GRT

Number	Title (A Side/B Side)	Yr	VG	VG+	NM
❏ 10000	Cream Songbook	1969	6.25	12.50	25.00
❏ 10007	Hendrix Songbook	1969	6.25	12.50	25.00
❏ 10015	Beatles Songbook	1969	6.25	12.50	25.00

RUBBER MEMORY
Albums
R.P.C.

Number	Title (A Side/B Side)	Yr	VG	VG+	NM
❏ 69401	Welcome	196?	250.00	500.00	1000.

RUBEN AND THE JETS Also see FRANK ZAPPA.
45s
MERCURY

Number	Title (A Side/B Side)	Yr	VG	VG+	NM
❏ 73381	If I Could Be Your Love Again/Wedding Bells	1973	—	3.00	6.00
❏ 73411	Charlena/Mah Man Flash	1973	—	3.00	6.00

Albums
MERCURY

Number	Title (A Side/B Side)	Yr	VG	VG+	NM
❏ SRM-1-659	For Real	1973	3.75	7.50	15.00
❏ SRM-1-694	Con Safos	1974	3.00	6.00	12.00

RUBETTES
45s
POLYDOR

Number	Title (A Side/B Side)	Yr	VG	VG+	NM
❏ 15089	Sugar Baby Love/You Could Have Told Me	1974	—	2.50	5.00
❏ 15092	Tonight/Silent Movie Queen	1974	—	2.00	4.00
❏ 15102	I Can Do It/If You've Got the Time	1975	—	2.00	4.00
STATE/MCA					
❏ 40549	Juke Box Jive/Put a Back Beat to That Music	1976	—	2.00	4.00
❏ 40632	Rock Is Dead/Dark Side of the World	1976	—	2.00	4.00

Albums
STATE

Number	Title (A Side/B Side)	Yr	VG	VG+	NM
❏ MCA-2193	Rubettes	1976	3.00	6.00	12.00

RUBIN
45s
KAPP

Number	Title (A Side/B Side)	Yr	VG	VG+	NM
❏ 869	You've Been Away/Baby, You're My Everything	1967	15.00	30.00	60.00

RUBY AND THE ROMANTICS
45s
A&M

Number	Title (A Side/B Side)	Yr	VG	VG+	NM
❏ 1042	Hurting Each Other/Baby, I Could Be So Good at Loving You	1969	2.00	4.00	8.00
ABC					
❏ 10911	Twilight Time/Una Bella Brazilian Melody	1967	2.50	5.00	10.00
❏ 10941	Only Heaven Knows/This Is No Laughing Matter	1967	2.50	5.00	10.00
❏ 11065	On a Clear Day You Can See Forever/More Than Yesterday, Less Than Tomorrow	1968	2.50	5.00	10.00
KAPP					
❏ 501	Our Day Will Come/Moonlight and Music	1963	3.75	7.50	15.00
❏ 525	My Summer Love/Sweet Love and Sweet Forgiveness	1963	3.00	6.00	12.00
❏ 544	Hey There Lonely Boy/Not a Moment Too Soon	1963	3.00	6.00	12.00
❏ 544 [PS]	Hey There Lonely Boy/Not a Moment Too Soon	1963	3.75	7.50	15.00
❏ 557	Young Wings Can Fly (Higher Than You Know)/Day Dreaming	1963	3.00	6.00	12.00
❏ 557 [PS]	Young Wings Can Fly (Higher Than You Know)/Day Dreaming	1963	3.75	7.50	15.00
❏ 578	Our Everlasting Love/Much Better Off Than I've Ever Been	1964	3.00	6.00	12.00
❏ 601	Baby Come Home/Every Day's a Holiday	1964	3.00	6.00	12.00
❏ 615	When You're Young and In Love/I Cry Alone	1964	3.00	6.00	12.00
❏ 646	Does He Really Care for Me/Nevertheless (I'm in Love with You)	1965	3.00	6.00	12.00
❏ 665	We'll Meet Again/Your Baby Doesn't Love You Anymore	1965	3.00	6.00	12.00
❏ 702	Nobody But My Baby/Imagination	1965	3.00	6.00	12.00
❏ 759	We Can Make It/Remember Me	1966	2.50	5.00	10.00
❏ 773	Hey There Lonely Boy/Think	1966	2.50	5.00	10.00
❏ 839	I Know/We'll Love Again	1967	2.50	5.00	10.00

Albums
ABC

Number	Title (A Side/B Side)	Yr	VG	VG+	NM
❏ S-638	More Than Yesterday	1968	5.00	10.00	20.00
KAPP					
❏ KL-1323 [M]	Our Day Will Come	1963	7.50	15.00	30.00
❏ KL-1341 [M]	Till Then	1963	6.25	12.50	25.00
❏ KL-1458 [M]	The Greatest Hits Album	1966	5.00	10.00	20.00
❏ KL-1526 [M]	Ruby and the Romantics	1967	6.25	12.50	25.00
❏ KS-3323 [S]	Our Day Will Come	1963	10.00	20.00	40.00
❏ KS-3341 [S]	Till Then	1963	7.50	15.00	30.00
❏ KS-3458 [S]	The Greatest Hits Album	1966	6.25	12.50	25.00
❏ KS-3526 [S]	Ruby and the Romantics	1967	6.25	12.50	25.00
MCA					
❏ 541	The Greatest Hits Album	197?	2.50	5.00	10.00
PICKWICK					
❏ SPC-3519	Makin' Out	197?	2.50	5.00	10.00

RUFFIN, DAVID Also see DARYL HALL AND JOHN OATES; JIMMY AND DAVID RUFFIN; THE TEMPTATIONS; THE VOICE MASTERS.
45s
ANNA

Number	Title (A Side/B Side)	Yr	VG	VG+	NM
❏ 1127	I'm in Love/One of These Days	1961	15.00	30.00	60.00
CHECK MATE					
❏ 1003	You Can Get What I Got/Action Speaks Louder Than Words	1961	15.00	30.00	60.00
❏ 1010	Mr. Bus Driver — Hurry!/Knock You Out (With Love)	1962	15.00	30.00	60.00
MOTOWN					
❏ 1140	My Whole World Ended (The Moment You Left Me)/I've Got to Find Myself a Brand New Baby	1968	—	3.00	6.00
❏ 1149	I've Lost Everything I've Ever Loved/We'll Have a Good Thing Going On	1969	—	3.00	6.00
❏ 1158	I'm So Glad I Fell for You/I Pray Every Day You Won't Regret Loving Me	1969	—	3.00	6.00
❏ 1178	Each Day Is a Lifetime/Don't Stop Loving Me	1971	—	3.00	6.00
❏ 1187	You Can Come Right Back to Me/Dinah	1971	—	3.00	6.00
❏ 1204	A Day in the Life of a Working Man/A Little More Trust	1972	—	3.00	6.00
❏ 1223	Blood Donors Needed/Go On with Your Bad Self	1973	—	3.00	6.00
❏ 1259	Common Man/I'm Just a Mortal Man	1973	—	3.00	6.00

Number	Title (A Side/B Side)	Yr	VG	VG+	NM
❏ 1327	Me and Rock and Roll (Are Here to Stay)/ Smiling Faces Sometimes	1974	—	3.00	6.00
❏ 1332	Take Me Clear from Here/ I Just Want to Celebrate	1975	—	—	—
—Unreleased					
❏ 1336	Superstar/No Matter Where	1975	—	2.50	5.00
❏ 1376	Walk Away from Love/ Love Can Be Hazardous to Your Health	1975	—	2.50	5.00
❏ 1388	Heavy Love/ Love Can Be Hazardous To Your Health	1976	—	2.50	5.00
❏ 1393	Everything's Coming Up Love/No Matter Where	1976	—	2.50	5.00
❏ 1405	On and Off/Statue of a Fool	1976	—	2.50	5.00
❏ 1420	Just Let Me Hold You for a Night/Rode by the Place (Where We Used to Stay)	1977	—	2.50	5.00
❏ 1435	You're My Peace of Mind/Rose By the Place (Where We Used to Stay)	1978	—	2.50	5.00
WARNER BROS.					
❏ 49030	Sexy Dancer/Break My Heart	1979	—	2.00	4.00
❏ 49123	I Get Excited/Chain on the Brain	1979	—	2.00	4.00
❏ 49277	Slow Dance/Don't You Go Home	1980	—	2.00	4.00
❏ 49577	Still in Love with You/I Wanna Be with You	1980	—	2.00	4.00
Albums					
MOTOWN					
❏ M5-146V1	My Whole World Ended	1981	2.00	4.00	8.00
—Reissue					
❏ M5-211V1	At His Best	1981	2.00	4.00	8.00
—Reissue					
❏ MS-685	My Whole World Ended	1969	5.00	10.00	20.00
❏ MS-696	Feelin' Good	1969	3.75	7.50	15.00
❏ M 733	David Ruffin	1971	—	—	—
—Canceled					
❏ M-762	David Ruffin	1973	3.00	6.00	12.00
❏ M6-818	Me 'N' Rock 'N' Roll Are Here to Stay	1974	3.00	6.00	12.00
❏ M6-849	Who I Am	1975	3.00	6.00	12.00
❏ M6-866	Everything's Coming Up Love	1976	3.00	6.00	12.00
❏ M6-885	In My Stride	1977	3.00	6.00	12.00
❏ M7-895	At His Best	1978	3.00	6.00	12.00
WARNER BROS.					
❏ BSK 3306	So Soon We Change	1979	2.50	5.00	10.00
❏ BSK 3416	Gentleman Ruffin	1980	2.50	5.00	10.00

RUFFIN, DAVID, AND EDDIE KENDRICK Also see each artist's individual listings; DARYL HALL AND JOHN OATES; THE TEMPTATIONS.
45s
RCA

Number	Title (A Side/B Side)	Yr	VG	VG+	NM
❏ 5313-7-R	I Couldn't Believe It/Don't Know Why You're Dreamin'	1987	—	—	3.00
❏ 6925-7-R	One More for the Lonely Hearts Club/Don't Know Why You're Dreaming	1988	—	—	3.00

RUFFIN, JIMMY
45s
ATCO

Number	Title (A Side/B Side)	Yr	VG	VG+	NM
❏ 6926	Tears of Joy/Goin' Home	1973	2.00	4.00	8.00
CHESS					
❏ 2160	Tell Me What You Want/Do You Know Me	1974	—	2.50	5.00
❏ 2168	What You See (Ain't Always What You Get)/Boy from Mississippi	1975	—	2.50	5.00
EPIC					
❏ 50339	Fallin' in Love with You/Fallin' in Love with You	1977	—	2.50	5.00
❏ 50384	Fallin' in Love with You/Fallin' in Love with You	1977	—	2.50	5.00
MIRACLE					
❏ 1	Don't Feel Sorry for Me/Heart	1961	50.00	100.00	200.00
RSO					
❏ 1021	Hold On to My Love/(Instrumental)	1980	—	2.50	5.00
❏ 1042	Night of Love/Searchin'	1980	—	2.50	5.00
SOUL					
❏ 35002	Since I've Lost You/I Want Her Love	1964	10.00	20.00	40.00
❏ 35016	As Long As There Is L-O-V-E/ How Can I Say I'm Sorry	1965	2.50	5.00	10.00
❏ 35022	What Becomes of the Brokenhearted/ Baby I've Got It	1966	3.75	7.50	15.00
❏ 35027	I've Passed This Way Before/Tomorrow's Tears	1966	2.50	5.00	10.00
❏ 35032	Gonna Give Her All the Love I've Got/World So Wide (Nowhere to Hide from Your Heart)	1967	2.00	4.00	8.00
❏ 35035	Don't You Miss Me A Little Bit Baby /I Want Her Love	1967	2.00	4.00	8.00
❏ 35043	I'll Say Forever My Love/Everybody Needs Love	1968	2.00	4.00	8.00
❏ 35046	Don't Let Him Take Your Love from Me/ Lonely, Lonely Man I	1968	2.00	4.00	8.00
❏ 35053	Sad and Lonesome Feeling/Gonna Keep On Trying Till I Win Your Love	1968	2.00	4.00	8.00
❏ 35060	Farewell Is a Lonely Sound/ If You Will Let Me, I Know I Can	1969	2.00	4.00	8.00
❏ 35077	Maria (You Were the Only One)/ Living in a World I Created For Myself	1970	2.00	4.00	8.00
❏ 35092	Our Favorite Melody/You Gave Me Love	1972	—	3.00	6.00
Albums					
RSO					
❏ RS-1-3078	Sunrise	1980	2.50	5.00	10.00
SOUL					
❏ 704 [M]	Top Ten	1967	6.25	12.50	25.00
—Full-color cover					
❏ 704 [M]	Top Ten	1967	12.50	25.00	50.00
—One-color cover					
❏ S-704 [S]	Top Ten	1967	6.25	12.50	25.00
❏ S-708	Ruff'n Ready	1969	6.25	12.50	25.00
❏ SS-727	The Groove Governor	1970	5.00	10.00	20.00

RUFFIN, JIMMY AND DAVID Also see DAVID RUFFIN; JIMMY RUFFIN.
45s
SOUL

Number	Title (A Side/B Side)	Yr	VG	VG+	NM
❏ 35076	Stand By Me/Your Love Was Worth Waiting For	1970	—	2.50	5.00
❏ 35082	When My Love Hand Comes Down/ Steppin' On a Dream	1971	—	2.50	5.00
❏ 35086	Lo and Behold/The Things We Have to Do	1971	—	2.50	5.00

Number	Title (A Side/B Side)	Yr	VG	VG+	NM
Albums					
MOTOWN					
❏ M5-108V1	Motown Superstar Series, Vol. 8	1981	2.50	5.00	10.00
SOUL					
❏ SS-728	I Am My Brother's Keeper	1970	5.00	10.00	20.00

RUFUS Includes records as "Rufus Featuring Chaka Khan" and "Rufus and Chaka." Also see THE AMERICAN BREED.
45s
ABC

Number	Title (A Side/B Side)	Yr	VG	VG+	NM
❏ 11356	Slip 'N Slide/I Finally Found You	1973	2.00	4.00	8.00
❏ 11376	Whoever's Thrilling You (Is Killing Me)/I Finally Found You	1973	—	3.00	6.00
❏ 11394	Feel Good/Keep It Coming	1973	—	3.00	6.00
❏ 11427	Tell Me Something Good/Smokin' Room	1974	—	3.00	6.00
❏ 12010	Tell Me Something Good/Smokin' Room	1974	—	2.50	5.00
❏ 12032	You Got the Love/Rags to Rufus	1974	—	2.50	5.00
❏ 12066	Once You Get Started/Rufusized	1975	—	2.50	5.00
❏ 12099	Please Pardon Me (You Remind Me of a Friend)/ Somebody's Watching You	1975	—	2.50	5.00
❏ 12149	Sweet Thing/Circles	1975	—	2.50	5.00
❏ 12179	Dance Wit' Me/Everybody's Got an Aura	1976	—	2.50	5.00
❏ 12197	Jive Talkin'/On Time	1976	—	2.50	5.00
❏ 12239	At Midnight (My Love Will Lift You Up)/ Better Days	1976	—	2.50	5.00
❏ 12269	Holywood/Earth Song	1977	—	2.50	5.00
❏ 12296	Everlasting Love/Close the Door	1977	—	2.50	5.00
❏ 12349	Stay/My Ship Will Sail	1978	—	2.50	5.00
❏ 12390	Blue Love/Turn	1978	—	2.50	5.00
❏ 12444	Keep It Together (Declaration of Love)/ Red Hot Poker	1979	—	2.50	5.00
EPIC					
❏ 10691	Read All About It/Brand New Day	1971	3.00	6.00	12.00
❏ 10691 [PS]	Read All About It/Brand New Day	1971	5.00	10.00	20.00
❏ 10726	Follow the Lamb/Fire One, Fire Two, Fire Three	1971	3.00	6.00	12.00
MCA					
❏ 41025	Ain't Nobody Like You/You're to Blame	1979	—	2.00	4.00
❏ 41131	Do You Love What You Feel/Dancin' Mood	1979	—	2.00	4.00
❏ 41191	What Am I Missing/Any Love	1980	—	2.00	4.00
❏ 41230	I'm Dancing for Your Love/Walk the Rockway	1980	—	2.00	4.00
❏ 51070	Tonight We Love/Afterwards	1981	—	2.00	4.00
❏ 51125	Party 'Til You're Broke/Hold On to a Friend	1981	—	2.00	4.00
❏ 51203	Sharing the Love/We Got the Way	1981	—	2.00	4.00
❏ 52002	True Love/Better Together	1982	—	2.00	4.00
WARNER BROS.					
❏ 29406	One Million Kisses/Stay	1983	—	2.00	4.00
❏ 29555	Ain't Nobody/Sweet Thing	1983	—	2.00	4.00
❏ 29675	Blinded by the Boogie/You're Really Out of Line	1983	—	2.00	4.00
❏ 29790	Take It to the Hop/Distant Lover	1983	—	2.00	4.00
Albums					
ABC					
❏ X-783	Rufus	1973	2.50	5.00	10.00
❏ X-809	Rags to Rufus	1974	2.50	5.00	10.00
❏ D-837	Rufusized	1974	2.50	5.00	10.00
❏ D-909	Rufus Featuring Chaka Khan	1975	2.50	5.00	10.00
❏ D-975	Ask Rufus	1977	2.50	5.00	10.00
❏ AA-1049	Street Player	1978	2.50	5.00	10.00
❏ AA-1049 [PD]	Street Player	1978	6.25	12.50	25.00
—Promo-only picture disc					
❏ AA-1098	Numbers	1979	2.50	5.00	10.00
❏ AA-1098 [PD]	Numbers	1979	5.00	10.00	20.00
—Promo-only picture disc					
COMMAND					
❏ CQD-40023 [Q]	Rufusized	1974	5.00	10.00	20.00
❏ CQD-40024 [Q]	Rags to Rufus	1974	5.00	10.00	20.00
MCA					
❏ 642	Rufus	1980	—	3.00	6.00
—Reissue of ABC 783					
❏ 5103	Masterjam	1979	2.50	5.00	10.00
❏ 5159	Party 'Til You're Broke	1981	2.50	5.00	10.00
❏ 5270	Camouflage	1982	2.50	5.00	10.00
❏ 5339	The Very Best of Rufus	1983	2.50	5.00	10.00
❏ 37034	Rags to Rufus	1980	—	3.00	6.00
—Reissue of ABC 809					
❏ 37035	Rufusized	1980	—	3.00	6.00
—Reissue of ABC 837					
❏ 37036	Rufus Featuring Chaka Khan	1980	—	3.00	6.00
—Reissue of ABC 909					
❏ 37037	Ask Rufus	1980	—	3.00	6.00
—Reissue of ABC 975					
❏ 37038	Street Player	1980	—	3.00	6.00
—Reissue of ABC 1049					
❏ 37039	Numbers	1980	—	3.00	6.00
—Reissue of ABC 1098					
❏ 37157	Masterjam	198?	—	3.00	6.00
—Reissue of 5103					
WARNER BROS.					
❏ 23679 [(2)]	Live: Stompin' at the Savoy	1983	3.00	6.00	12.00
❏ 23753	Seal in Red	1984	2.50	5.00	10.00

RUFUS AND CARLA Also see CARLA THOMAS; RUFUS THOMAS.
45s
ATCO

Number	Title (A Side/B Side)	Yr	VG	VG+	NM
❏ 6177	Cause I Love You/Deep Down Inside	1960	6.25	12.50	25.00
—As "Carla and Rufus"					
❏ 6199	I Didn't Believe/Yeah, Yea-Ah	1961	6.25	12.50	25.00
—As "Rufus and Friend"					
SATELLITE					
❏ 102	Cause I Love You/Deep Down Inside	1960	10.00	20.00	40.00
STAX					
❏ 151	That's Really Some Good/ Night Time Is the Right Time	1964	3.00	6.00	12.00
❏ 176	When You Move You Lose/We're Tight	1965	3.00	6.00	12.00
❏ 184	Birds and Bees/Never Let You Go	1966	3.00	6.00	12.00

R

Number	Title (A Side/B Side)	Yr	VG	VG+	NM
Albums					
STAX					
❏ STX-4124	Chronicle	1979	3.75	7.50	15.00
RUGBYS, THE					
45s					
AMAZON					
❏ 1	You, I/Stay with Me	1969	2.00	4.00	8.00
—Black vinyl					
❏ 1 [DJ]	You, I/Stay with Me	1969	5.00	10.00	20.00
—Colored vinyl					
❏ 4	The Light/Wendegahl Warlock	1970	2.00	4.00	8.00
❏ 6	Rockin' All Over/Juditha Gina	1970	2.00	4.00	8.00
SMASH					
❏ 1997	James Is the Name/Til the Day I Die	1965	3.00	6.00	12.00
Albums					
AMAZON					
❏ 1000	Hot Cargo	1970	5.00	10.00	20.00
RUMBLERS, THE					
45s					
DOT					
❏ 16421	Boss/I Don't Need You No More	1963	3.75	7.50	15.00
❏ 16455	Boss Strikes Back/Sorry	1963	3.75	7.50	15.00
❏ 16480	Angry Sea (Walmea)/Bugged	1963	3.75	7.50	15.00
❏ 16521	It's a Gas/Tootananny	1963	3.75	7.50	15.00
DOWNEY					
❏ 103	Boss/I Don't Need You No More	1962	7.50	15.00	30.00
❏ 106	Boss Strikes Back/Sorry	1963	7.50	15.00	30.00
❏ 107	Angry Sea (Walmea)/Bugged	1963	7.50	15.00	30.00
❏ 111	It's a Gas/Tootananny	1963	7.50	15.00	30.00
❏ 114	High Octane/Night Scene	1964	6.25	12.50	25.00
❏ 119	The Hustler/Riot in Cell Block #9	1964	6.25	12.50	25.00
❏ 127	Soulful Jerk/Hey-Did-a-Da-Do	1964	6.25	12.50	25.00
❏ 133	Boss Soul/Till Always	1965	6.25	12.50	25.00
HIGHLAND					
❏ 1026	Intersection/Stomping Theme	1962	12.50	25.00	50.00
Albums					
DOT					
❏ DLP-3509 [M]	Boss!	1963	12.50	25.00	50.00
❏ DLP-25509 [S]	Boss!	1963	15.00	30.00	60.00
DOWNEY					
❏ DLP-1001 [M]	Boss!	1963	45.00	90.00	180.00
❏ DLPS-1001 [S]	Boss!	1963	62.50	125.00	250.00
RUNAROUNDS, THE Probably more than one group.					
45s					
CAPITOL					
❏ 5644	Perfect Woman/You're a Drag	1966	6.25	12.50	25.00
COUSINS					
❏ 1004	Mashed Potato Mary/I'm All Alone	1964	5.00	10.00	20.00
FELSTED					
❏ 8704	Send Her Back/Carrie, You're An Angel	1964	7.50	15.00	30.00
KC					
❏ 116	Unbelievable/Hurray for Love	1963	6.25	12.50	25.00
❏ 116	Unbelievable/Hurray for Love	1963	10.00	20.00	40.00
—Brown vinyl					
MGM					
❏ 13763	My Little Girl/You Lied	1967	3.75	7.50	15.00
PIO					
❏ 107	The Nearest Thing to Heaven/Lover's Lane	1961	37.50	75.00	150.00
TARHEEL					
❏ 065	Are You Looking for a Sweetheart/Let Them Talk	1963	5.00	10.00	20.00
RUNDGREN, TODD Also see NAZZ (1); UTOPIA.					
12-Inch Singles					
FORWARD					
❏ 7008 [DJ]	Day Job (LP Version) (Radio Version) (Dub)	1993	3.75	7.50	15.00
WARNER BROS.					
❏ PRO-A-2371 [DJ]	Something to Fall Back On (same on both sides)	1985	2.50	5.00	10.00
45s					
AMPEX					
❏ 31001	We Gotta Get You a Woman/Medley	1970	2.50	5.00	10.00
—As "Runt"					
BEARSVILLE					
❏ 0003	I Saw the Light/Marlene	1972	3.00	6.00	12.00
❏ 0003	I Saw the Light/Marlene	1972	3.00	6.00	12.00
—Blue vinyl					
❏ 0007	Couldn't I Just Tell You/Wolfman Jack	1972	—	3.00	6.00
❏ 0009	Hello It's Me/Cold Morning Light	1973	—	3.00	6.00
❏ 0020	A Dream Goes On Forever/Heavy Metal Kids	1974	—	3.00	6.00
❏ 0030	We Gotta Get You a Woman/I Saw the Light	1973	—	2.00	4.00
—"Back to Back Hits" series					
❏ 0301	Breathless/Wolfman Jack	1974	—	3.00	6.00
❏ 0304	Real Man/Prana	1975	—	2.50	5.00
❏ 0309	Good Vibrations/When I Pray	1976	—	2.50	5.00
❏ 0310	Love of the Common Man/Black and White	1976	—	2.50	5.00
❏ 0324	Can We Still Be Friends/Determination	1978	—	2.50	5.00
❏ 0324	Can We Still Be Friends/Out of Control	1978	—	2.50	5.00
❏ 0330	You Cried Wolf/Onomatopoeia	1978	—	2.50	5.00
❏ 0335	It Wouldn't Have Made Any Difference/Did You Ever Learn	1979	—	2.50	5.00
❏ 29686	Bang the Drum All Day/Chant	1983	—	3.00	6.00
❏ 29759	Emperor of the Highway/Hideaway	1983	—	2.00	4.00
❏ 31002	Be Nice to Me/Broke Down and Busted	1971	2.00	4.00	8.00
—As "Runt-Todd Rundgren"					
❏ 31004	A Long Time, A Long Way to Go/Parole	1971	2.00	4.00	8.00
—As "Runt-Todd Rundgren"					
❏ 49696	Time Heals/Tiny Demons	1981	—	2.00	4.00
❏ 49771	Compassion/Pulse	1981	—	2.50	5.00
COLUMBIA					
❏ 06151	Loving You's a Dirty Job (But Somebody's Gotta Do It)/Before This Night Is Through	1986	—	2.00	4.00
—With Bonnie Tyler					

Number	Title (A Side/B Side)	Yr	VG	VG+	NM
GUARDIAN					
❏ S7-19726	Can We Still Be Friends/I Saw the Light	1997	—	—	3.00
RHINO					
❏ 74426	Bang the Drum All Day/Can We Still Be Friends	1987	—	2.00	4.00
WARNER BROS.					
❏ 22868	I Love My Life/Parallel Lines	1989	—	—	3.00
❏ 28821	Something to Fall Back On/Lockjaw	1986	—	2.00	4.00
7-Inch Extended Plays					
BEARSVILLE					
❏ SB 2066	I Saw the Light/You Left Me Sore/Hello It's Me//Piss Aaron/It Takes Two to Tango/Sweeter Memories	1972	3.00	6.00	12.00
—Jukebox issue; small hole, plays at 33 1/3 rpm					
❏ SB 2066 [PS]	Something/Anything?	1972	3.00	6.00	12.00
—Part of "Little LP" series (LLP #236)					
❏ BHS 3522-EP	Time Heals/Tiny Demons	1981		2.50	5.00
—33 1/3 rpm, small hole; bonus record included with the LP "Healing"					
Albums					
AMPEX					
❏ A-10105	Runt	1970	12.50	25.00	50.00
—LP jacket and label list 10 tracks and album actually has 10					
❏ A-10105	Runt	1970	25.00	50.00	100.00
—LP jacket and label list 10 tracks, but the album has 11					
❏ A-10105	Runt	1970	37.50	75.00	150.00
—LP jacket and label list 10 tracks, but the album has 12					
BEARSVILLE					
❏ PRO 524 [DJ]	The Todd Rundgren Radio Show	1972	37.50	75.00	150.00
❏ PRO 597 [DJ]	Ikon/Todd Rundgren Interview	1974	30.00	60.00	120.00
❏ PRO-A-788 [DJ]	Todd Rundgren Radio Sampler	1978	12.50	25.00	50.00
—Highlights of "Back to the Bars" plus interview of Todd by Patti Smith					
❏ BR 2046	Runt	1972	3.75	7.50	15.00
—Another reissue, after switch from Ampex to Warner Bros. distribution					
❏ BR 2047	The Ballad of Todd Rundgren	1972	3.75	7.50	15.00
—Reissue of 10116					
❏ 2BX 2066 [(2)]	Something/Anything?	1972	6.25	12.50	25.00
—Regular copy with black vinyl					
❏ 2BX 2066 [(2)]	Something/Anything?	1972	100.00	200.00	400.00
—White label with one record on red vinyl and the other on blue vinyl					
❏ BR 2133	A Wizard/A True Star	1973	3.00	6.00	12.00
❏ BHS 3522	Healing	1981	2.50	5.00	10.00
—Add $5 if bonus 7-inch 33 1/3 single (Time Heals/Tiny Demons) is included					
❏ 2BR 6952 [(2)]	Todd	1974	3.75	7.50	15.00
❏ BR 6957	Initiation	1975	2.50	5.00	10.00
❏ BR 6963	Faithful	1976	2.50	5.00	10.00
❏ BRK 6981	Hermit of Mink Hollow	1978	2.50	5.00	10.00
❏ 2BRX 6986 [(2)]	Back to the Bars	1978	3.00	6.00	12.00
❏ A-10105	Runt	1971	6.25	12.50	25.00
—Reissue with new label					
❏ A-10116	The Ballad of Todd Rundgren	1971	20.00	40.00	80.00
❏ 23732	The Ever Popular Tortured Artist Effect	1983	2.50	5.00	10.00
MOBILE FIDELITY					
❏ 2-225	Something/Anything?	1995	10.00	20.00	40.00
—Audiophile vinyl					
RHINO					
❏ RNLP 70862	Runt	1987	2.50	5.00	10.00
❏ RNLP 70863	The Ballad of Todd Rundgren	1987	2.50	5.00	10.00
❏ RNLP 70864	A Wizard/A True Star	1987	2.50	5.00	10.00
❏ RNLP 70866	Initiation	1987	2.50	5.00	10.00
❏ RNLP 70868	Faithful	1987	2.50	5.00	10.00
❏ RNLP 70871	Hermit of Mink Hollow	1988	2.50	5.00	10.00
❏ RNLP 70874	Healing	1987	2.50	5.00	10.00
❏ RNLP 70876	The Ever Popular Tortured Artist Effect	1988	2.50	5.00	10.00
❏ RNDA 71107	Something/Anything?	1987	3.00	6.00	12.00
❏ RNDA 71108	Todd	1987	3.00	6.00	12.00
❏ RNDA 71109	Back to the Bars	1987	3.00	6.00	12.00
❏ R1-71491	Anthology (1968-1985)	1989	5.00	10.00	20.00
WARNER BROS.					
❏ 25128	A Cappella	1985	2.50	5.00	10.00
❏ 25881	Nearly Human	1989	3.75	7.50	15.00
RUSH					
12-Inch Singles					
MERCURY					
❏ MK-75 [DJ]	The Trees//Prelude/Circumstances	1978	10.00	20.00	40.00
❏ MK-125 [DJ]	The Spirit of Radio/The Trees/Working Man	1980	15.00	30.00	60.00
❏ MK-137 [DJ]	Entre Nous (4:37) (3:45)	1980	15.00	30.00	60.00
❏ MK-188 [DJ]	A Passage to Bangkok (Live)/Freewill (Live)	1981	6.25	12.50	25.00
❏ MK-216 [DJ]	New World Man/Vital Signs (Live)	1981	6.25	12.50	25.00
—Clear vinyl					
❏ PRO 276-1 [DJ]	Distant Early Warning/Between the Wheels	1984	3.75	7.50	15.00
❏ PRO 290-1 [DJ]	The Body Electric (same on both sides)	1984	5.00	10.00	20.00
❏ PRO 320-1 [DJ]	Red Sector A/The Enemy Within	1984	7.50	15.00	30.00
—Red vinyl					
❏ PRO 382-1 [DJ]	The Big Money (same on both sides)	1985	3.00	6.00	12.00
❏ PRO 400-1 [DJ]	Mystic Rhythms (6:08) (same on both sides)	1985	6.25	12.50	25.00
❏ PRO 532-1 [DJ]	Force Ten (same on both sides)	1987	3.75	7.50	15.00
❏ PRO 689-1 [DJ]	Marathon (Live) (same on both sides)	1988	5.00	10.00	20.00
45s					
MERCURY					
❏ PRO 319-7 [DJ]	Red Sector A (same on both sides)	1984	5.00	10.00	20.00
❏ PRO 383-7 [DJ]	The Big Money (5:35)/(4:32)	1985	5.00	10.00	20.00
❏ DJ-407 (73623) [DJ]	Finding My Way (mono/stereo)	1974	15.00	30.00	60.00
❏ DJ-417 (73647) [DJ]	In the Mood (mono/stereo)	1974	15.00	30.00	60.00
❏ DJ-553 (73681) [DJ]	Fly by Night/Anthem	1975	15.00	30.00	60.00
❏ 73623	Finding My Way/Need Some Love	1974	20.00	40.00	80.00
❏ 73647	In the Mood/What You're Doing	1974	20.00	40.00	80.00
❏ 73681	Fly by Night/Anthem	1975	20.00	40.00	80.00
❏ 73728	Return of the Prince/I Think I'm Going Bald	1975	20.00	40.00	80.00
❏ 73728 [DJ]	Return of the Prince (3:01)/(2:54)	1975	15.00	30.00	60.00
❏ 73737	Lakeside Park/Bastille Day	1975	20.00	40.00	80.00
❏ 73737 [DJ]	Lakeside Park (3:16) (mono/stereo)	1975	15.00	30.00	60.00
❏ 73803	The Twilight Zone/Lessons	1976	20.00	40.00	80.00
❏ 73803 [DJ]	The Twilight Zone (mono/stereo)	1976	15.00	30.00	60.00
❏ 73873	Fly by Night-In the Mood/Something for Nothing	1976	2.50	5.00	10.00
❏ 73912	Making Memories/The Temples of Syrinx	1977	2.50	5.00	10.00
❏ 73958	Closer to the Heart/Madrigal	1977	2.50	5.00	10.00

Number	Title (A Side/B Side)	Yr	VG	VG+	NM
❏ 73990	Fly by Night/Anthem	1978	2.50	5.00	10.00
❏ 74051	The Trees/Circumstances	1979	2.50	5.00	10.00
❏ 76044	The Spirit of Radio/Circumstances	1980	2.50	5.00	10.00
❏ 76060	Entre Nous/Different Strings	1980	2.50	5.00	10.00
❏ 76095	Limelight/XYZ	1981	2.50	5.00	10.00
❏ 76109	Tom Sawyer/Witch Hunt	1981	2.50	5.00	10.00
❏ 76109 [PS]	Tom Sawyer/Witch Hunt	1981	6.25	12.50	25.00
❏ 76124	Closer to the Heart/Freewill	1981	2.00	4.00	8.00
❏ 76179	New World Man/Vital Signs	1982	2.00	4.00	8.00
❏ 76179 [PS]	New World Man/Vital Signs	1982	3.75	7.50	15.00
❏ 76196	Subdivisions/Countdown	1982	2.50	5.00	10.00
❏ 880050-7	The Body Electric/Between the Wheels	1984	2.50	5.00	10.00
❏ 884191-7	The Big Money/Red Sector A	1985	2.00	4.00	8.00
❏ 884191-7 [PS]	The Big Money/Red Sector A	1985	2.50	5.00	10.00
❏ 888891-7	Time Stand Still/High Water	1987	—	3.00	6.00
❏ 888891-7 [PS]	Time Stand Still/High Water	1987	2.50	5.00	10.00

Albums

ATLANTIC

Number	Title	Yr	VG	VG+	NM
❏ 82040	Presto	1989	5.00	10.00	20.00
❏ 83531 [(2)]	Vapor Trails	2002	3.75	7.50	15.00

MERCURY

Number	Title	Yr	VG	VG+	NM
❏ MK-32 [DJ]	Everything Your Listener Ever Wanted to Hear by Rush ... But You Were Afraid to Play	1977	37.50	75.00	150.00
❏ MK-185 [DJ]	Rush 'N' Roulette	1981	30.00	60.00	120.00

—Promo-only six-track EP that has six grooves cut in it; the song it plays is based on where you place the stylus

❏ SRM-1-1011	Rush	1974	2.50	5.00	10.00

—Based on the LP's release date, original copies theoretically have red labels, rather than the common "Chicago skyline" labels; those would be worth at least twice this price

❏ SRM-1-1011	Rush	1983	2.00	4.00	8.00
—Black label					
❏ SRM-1-1023	Fly by Night	1975	2.50	5.00	10.00
—"Chicago skyline" label					
❏ SRM-1-1023	Fly by Night	1983	2.00	4.00	8.00
—Black label					
❏ SRM-1-1046	Caress of Steel	1975	2.50	5.00	10.00
—"Chicago skyline" label					
❏ SRM-1-1046	Caress of Steel	1983	2.00	4.00	8.00
—Black label					
❏ SRM-1-1079	2112	1976	2.50	5.00	10.00
—"Chicago skyline" label					
❏ SRM-1-1079	2112	1983	2.00	4.00	8.00
—Black label					
❏ SRM-1-1184	A Farewell to Kings	1977	2.50	5.00	10.00
—"Chicago skyline" label					
❏ SRM-1-1184	A Farewell to Kings	1983	2.00	4.00	8.00
—Black label					
❏ SRP-1-1300 [PD]	Hemispheres	1979	10.00	20.00	40.00
❏ SRM-1-3743	Hemispheres	1978	2.50	5.00	10.00
—"Chicago skyline" label; with poster					
❏ SRM-1-3743	Hemispheres	1983	2.00	4.00	8.00
—Black label					
❏ SRM-1-4001	Permanent Waves	1980	2.50	5.00	10.00
—Custom label					
❏ SRM-1-4013	Moving Pictures	1981	2.50	5.00	10.00
—Custom label					
❏ SRM-1-4063	Signals	1982	2.50	5.00	10.00
❏ SRM-2-7001 [(2)]	Exit... Stage Left	1981	3.00	6.00	12.00
❏ SRM-2-7508 [(2)]	All the World's a Stage	1976	3.00	6.00	12.00
—"Chicago skyline" labels					
❏ SRM-2-7508 [(2)]	All the World's a Stage	1983	2.50	5.00	10.00
—Black labels					
❏ SRM-3-9200 [(3)]	Archives	1978	5.00	10.00	20.00
—"Chicago skyline" labels					
❏ SRM-3-9200 [(3)]	Archives	1983	3.75	7.50	15.00
—Black labels					
❏ 818476-1	Grace Under Pressure	1984	2.50	5.00	10.00
❏ 822541-1	Rush	1985	2.00	4.00	8.00
—Reissue with new number					
❏ 822542-1	Fly by Night	1985	2.00	4.00	8.00
—Reissue with new number					
❏ 822543-1	Caress of Steel	1985	2.00	4.00	8.00
—Reissue with new number					
❏ 822545-1	2112	1985	2.00	4.00	8.00
—Reissue with new number					
❏ 822546-1	A Farewell to Kings	1985	2.00	4.00	8.00
—Reissue with new number					
❏ 822547-1	Hemispheres	1985	2.00	4.00	8.00
—Reissue with new number					
❏ 822548-1	Permanent Waves	1985	2.00	4.00	8.00
—Reissue with new number					
❏ 822549-1	Moving Pictures	1985	2.00	4.00	8.00
—Reissue with new number					
❏ 822550-1	Signals	1985	2.00	4.00	8.00
—Reissue with new number					
❏ 822551-1 [(2)]	Exit...Stage Left	1985	2.50	5.00	10.00
—Reissue with new number					
❏ 822552-1 [(2)]	All the World's a Stage	1985	2.50	5.00	10.00
—Reissue with new number					
❏ 822553-1 [(3)]	Archives	1985	3.75	7.50	15.00
—Reissue with new number					
❏ 826098-1	Power Windows	1985	2.50	5.00	10.00
❏ 832464-1	Hold Your Fire	1987	2.50	5.00	10.00
❏ 836346-1 [(2)]	A Show of Hands	1988	3.00	6.00	12.00

RUSH, MERRILEE

45s

AGP

Number	Title	Yr	VG	VG+	NM
❏ 107	Reach Out/Love Street	1969	—	3.00	6.00
❏ 112	Your Loving Eyes Are Blind/ Everyday Livin' Days	1969	—	3.00	6.00
❏ 121	Sign On for the Good Times/Robin McCarver	1969	—	3.00	6.00
❏ 126	Angel of the Morning/It's Worth It All	1970	—	3.00	6.00

BELL

❏ 705	Angel of the Morning/Reap What You Sow	1968	2.00	4.00	8.00
❏ 738	Sunshine and Roses/That Kind of Woman	1968	2.00	4.00	8.00

SCEPTER

❏ 12329	Child of Mine/Everything Has Got to Be Free	1971	—	3.00	6.00

UNITED ARTISTS

❏ XW930	Could It Be Love I Found Tonight/Be True to You	1976	—	2.00	4.00
❏ XW993	Save Me/Easy, Soft and Slow	1977	—	2.00	4.00
❏ XW1103	Mama/Rainstorm	1977	—	2.00	4.00
❏ XW1181	Angel of the Morning/Save	1978	—	2.00	4.00

Albums

BELL

❏ 6020	Angel of the Morning	1968	5.00	10.00	20.00

LIBERTY

❏ LN-10166	Merilee Rush	1981	2.00	4.00	8.00
—Budget-line reissue					

UNITED ARTISTS

❏ UA-LA735-G	Merilee Rush	1977	2.50	5.00	10.00

RUSH, RAY

45s

PARKWAY

❏ 846	So What/Can This Be Love	1962	3.75	7.50	15.00

RUSH, TOM

45s

COLUMBIA

Number	Title	Yr	VG	VG+	NM
❏ 10021	Ladies Love Outlaws/Maggie	1974	—	2.00	4.00
❏ 10087	No Regrets/Maggie	1975	—	2.00	4.00
❏ 4S-45149	Drop Down Mama/Child's Song	1970	—	3.00	6.00
❏ 45185	Old Man's Song/Lost My Drivin' Wheel	1970	—	2.50	5.00
❏ 45364	Wrong End of the Rainbow/Merrimac County	1971	—	2.50	5.00
❏ 45584	Wind on the Water/Mother Earth	1972	—	2.50	5.00
❏ 45669	Kids These Days/Seems the Songs	1972	—	2.50	5.00

ELEKTRA

❏ 45604	Who Do You Love/On the Road Again	1966	2.00	4.00	8.00
❏ 45607	Sugar Babe/Urge for Going	1967	2.00	4.00	8.00
❏ 45630	No Regrets/Shadow Dream Song	1968	—	3.00	6.00
❏ 45718	Something in the Way She Moves/ Who Do You Love	1971	—	3.00	6.00

PRESTIGE

❏ 289	Diamond Joe/Every Day in the Week	1964	3.00	6.00	12.00

Albums

COLUMBIA

Number	Title	Yr	VG	VG+	NM
❏ CS 9972	Tom Rush	1970	3.00	6.00	12.00
—Orange label					
❏ CS 9972	Tom Rush	1970	3.75	7.50	15.00
—Red "360 Sound" label					
❏ C 30402	Wrong End of the Rainbow	1970	3.00	6.00	12.00
❏ KC 31306	Merrimack County	1972	3.00	6.00	12.00
❏ KC 33054	Ladies Love Outlaws	1974	3.00	6.00	12.00
❏ PC 33907	The Best of Tom Rush	1976	3.00	6.00	12.00

ELEKTRA

❏ EKL-288 [M]	Tom Rush	1965	3.75	7.50	15.00
❏ EKL-308 [M]	Take a Little Walk with Me	1966	3.75	7.50	15.00
❏ EKS-7288 [S]	Tom Rush	1965	3.75	7.50	15.00
❏ EKS-7308 [S]	Take a Little Walk with Me	1966	3.75	7.50	15.00
❏ EKS-74018	The Circle Game	1968	3.75	7.50	15.00
❏ EKS-74062	Classic Rush	1971	3.75	7.50	15.00

FANTASY

❏ 24709 [(2)]	Tom Rush	1973	3.75	7.50	15.00
—Reissue of Prestige/Folklore recordings					

FOLKLORE

❏ FRLP-14003 [M]	Got a Mind to Ramble	1964	5.00	10.00	20.00
❏ FRST-14003 [S]	Got a Mind to Ramble	1964	6.25	12.50	25.00

LY CORNU

❏ SA-70-2	Tom Rush at the Unicorn	1962	25.00	50.00	100.00

PRESTIGE

❏ PR-7374 [M]	Blues — Songs — Ballads	1965	5.00	10.00	20.00
❏ PRST-7374 [S]	Blues — Songs — Ballads	1965	6.25	12.50	25.00
❏ PRST-7536	Got a Mind to Ramble	1968	3.75	7.50	15.00
—Reissue of Folklore LP					

RUSS, LONNIE

45s

4J

Number	Title	Yr	VG	VG+	NM
❏ 501	My Wife Can't Cook/ Something Old, Something New	1962	3.75	7.50	15.00
❏ 504	Flip Flop/Tell Me Now	1963	6.25	12.50	25.00
❏ 507	We Belong Together (same on both sides)	1963	5.00	10.00	20.00
❏ 510	Lil' Evett/Them Greens	1963	5.00	10.00	20.00

RUSSELL, BOBBY

45s

BUENA VISTA

Number	Title	Yr	VG	VG+	NM
❏ 473	The Ballad of Smith & Gabriel Jimmy Boy/ Summer Sweet	1969	2.50	5.00	10.00
❏ 474	The Ballad of Smith & Gabriel Billyboy/ Summer Sweet	1969	2.50	5.00	10.00

COLUMBIA

❏ 45901	Mid American Manufacturing Tycoon/ Ships in the Night	1973	—	2.00	4.00
❏ 46045	The Night the Lights Went Out in Georgia/ Go Chase Your Rainbow	1974	—	2.00	4.00

D

❏ 1115	Not Even Friends/Shackled	1960	3.00	6.00	12.00
—With Sadie Russell					

ELF

❏ 90014	Dusty/I Made You This Way	1968	—	3.00	6.00
❏ 90020	1432 Franklin Pike Circle Hero/ Let's Talk About It	1968	—	3.00	6.00
❏ 90023	Carlie/Ain't Society Great	1969	—	3.00	6.00
❏ 90027	Then She's a Lover/He Wrote a Song	1969	—	3.00	6.00
❏ 90031	Better Homes and Gardens/Summer Sweet	1969	—	3.00	6.00

F&L

❏ 518	Camp Getcha 'Losa Ya/Arm Chair Quarterback	1982	—	3.00	6.00

FELSTED

❏ 8520	The Raven/She's Gonna Be Sorry	1958	3.75	7.50	15.00

R

Number	Title (A Side/B Side)	Yr	VG	VG+	NM
HIT					
❏ 63	The Reverend Mr. Black/Little Band of Gold	1963	2.50	5.00	10.00
—With the Tennessee Three					
❏ 66	Still/Losing You	1963	2.50	5.00	10.00
—B-side by Katy Richards					
IMAGE					
❏ 1014	Goin' Steady Dream/ To the Ones with Broken Hearts	1961	3.00	6.00	12.00
MONUMENT					
❏ 899	Once a Day/You Were Mine	1965	2.00	4.00	8.00
❏ 929	Friends and Memories/Wish I'd Say That	1966	2.00	4.00	8.00
NATIONAL GENERAL					
❏ 006	As Far As I'm Concerned/Traveling with a Star	1970	2.00	4.00	8.00
PRIVATE STOCK					
❏ 45,046	Little Boxes/(B-side unknown)	1975	—	2.50	5.00
RISING SONS					
❏ 700	Bluebird/Tears Tell	1967	2.00	4.00	8.00
UNITED ARTISTS					
❏ 50788	Saturday Morning Confusion/ Little Ole Song About Love	1971	—	2.50	5.00
❏ 50853	Goodbye/It Hurts	1971	—	2.50	5.00
❏ 50888	Easy Made for Lovin'/The Bell	1972	—	2.50	5.00
❏ 50904	You Babe/Back to Sausalito	1972	—	2.50	5.00
❏ 50959	Welcome to the U.S. Army/This Is the Life	1972	—	2.50	5.00
Albums					
ELF					
❏ 9500	Words, Music, Laughter & Tears	1969	5.00	10.00	20.00
❏ 9501	Unlimited	1970	3.75	7.50	15.00
UNITED ARTISTS					
❏ UAS-5548	Saturday Morning Confusion	1971	3.00	6.00	12.00

RUSSELL, KURT
45s

Number	Title (A Side/B Side)	Yr	VG	VG+	NM
CAPITOL					
❏ 2823	I Believe in Love/It Ain't Gonna Rain Anymore	1970	2.50	5.00	10.00
Albums					
CAPITOL					
❏ SKAO-492	Kurt Russell	1970	7.50	15.00	30.00

RUSSELL, LEE See LEON RUSSELL.

RUSSELL, LEON Includes records by his country-western alter ego, "Hank Wilson" and "Hank and Mary Wilson." Also see WILLIE NELSON.
45s

Number	Title (A Side/B Side)	Yr	VG	VG+	NM
A&M					
❏ 734	Cindy/Misty	1964	5.00	10.00	20.00
ARK 21					
❏ S7-58714	Daddy Sang Bass/ He Stopped Loving Her Today	1998	—	—	3.00
DOT					
❏ 16771	Everybody's Talkin' 'Bout the Young/ It's Alright with Me	1965	3.75	7.50	15.00
PARADISE					
❏ 628	Good Time Charlie's Got the Blues/ Ain't No Love in the City	1984	—	2.00	4.00
❏ 629	Wabash Cannonball/Tennessee Waltz	1984	—	2.00	4.00
—As "Hank Wilson"; A-side with Willie Nelson					
❏ 631	Rescue My Heart/Lost Love	1985	—	2.00	4.00
❏ 631 [PS]	Rescue My Heart/Lost Love	1985	2.50	5.00	10.00
❏ 8208	Rainbow in Your Eyes/ Love's Supposed to Be That Way	1976	—	2.00	4.00
—As "Leon and Mary Russell"					
❏ 8274	Satisfy You/Windsong	1976	—	2.00	4.00
—As "Leon and Mary Russell"					
❏ 8369	Love Crazy/Say You Will	1977	—	2.00	4.00
—As "Leon and Mary Russell"					
❏ 8438	Easy Love/Hold On to This Feeling	1977	—	2.00	4.00
—As "Leon and Mary Russell"					
❏ 8667	Elvis and Marilyn/Anita Bryant	1978	—	2.50	5.00
❏ 8667 [PS]	Elvis and Marilyn/Anita Bryant	1978	—	2.50	5.00
❏ 8719	Midnight Lover/From Maine to Mexico	1978	—	2.50	5.00
❏ 49662	Over the Rainbow/I've Just Seen a Face	1981	—	2.00	4.00
RCA VICTOR					
❏ 47-6884	(I Tasted) Tears on Your Lips/A Catchy Tune	1957	7.50	15.00	30.00
—As "Lee Russell"					
ROULETTE					
❏ 4049	Honky Tonk Woman/Rainbow at Midnight	1958	6.25	12.50	25.00
—As "Lee Russell"					
SHELTER					
❏ 301	Roll Away the Stone/Hummingbird	1970	—	3.00	6.00
❏ 7302	It Takes a Lot to Laugh, It Takes a Train to Cry/ Home Sweet Oklahoma	1970	—	3.00	6.00
❏ 7305	A Hard Rain's A-Gonna Fall/Me and Baby Jane	1971	—	3.00	6.00
❏ 7316	A Song for You/A Hard Rain's A-Gonna Fall	1971	—	3.00	6.00
❏ 7325	Tight Rope/This Masquerade	1972	—	2.50	5.00
❏ 7328	Slipping Into Christmas/Christmas in Chicago	1972	—	2.50	5.00
❏ 7328 [PS]	Slipping Into Christmas/Christmas in Chicago	1972	6.25	12.50	25.00
❏ 7336	Roll in My Sweet Baby's Arms/ I'm So Lonesome I Could Cry	1973	—	2.50	5.00
—As "Hank Wilson"					
❏ 7337	Queen of the Roller Derby/Roll Away the Stone	1973	—	2.50	5.00
❏ 7338	A Six Pack to Go/Uncle Pen	1973	—	2.50	5.00
—As "Hank Wilson"					
❏ 40210	If I Were a Carpenter/Wild Horses	1974	—	2.00	4.00
❏ 40210 [PS]	If I Were a Carpenter/Wild Horses	1974	2.00	4.00	8.00
❏ 40277	Time for Love/Leaving Whipporwhill	1974	—	2.00	4.00
❏ 40378	Lady Blue/Laying Right Here in Heaven	1975	—	2.00	4.00
❏ 40483	Back to the Island/Little Hideaway	1975	—	2.00	4.00
❏ 62004	Bluebird/Back to the Island	1976	—	2.00	4.00
❏ 65033	Slipping Into Christmas/Christmas in Chicago	1975	—	2.50	5.00
—Reissue of 7328					
Albums					
MCA					
❏ 682	Leon Russell	1979	2.00	4.00	8.00
—Reissue of Shelter 52007					

Number	Title (A Side/B Side)	Yr	VG	VG+	NM
❏ 683	Leon Russell and the Shelter People	1979	2.00	4.00	8.00
—Reissue of Shelter 52008					
❏ 685	Carney	1979	2.00	4.00	8.00
—Reissue of Shelter 52011					
❏ 686	Will O' the Wisp	1979	2.00	4.00	8.00
—Reissue of Shelter 52020					
❏ 37114	Best of Leon	1980	2.00	4.00	8.00
—Reissue of Shelter 52004					
PARADISE					
❏ 0002	Hank Wilson Vol. II	1984	3.00	6.00	12.00
❏ PR 2943	Wedding Album	1976	3.00	6.00	12.00
—As "Leon and Mary Russell"					
❏ BSK 3066	Make Love to the Music	1977	3.00	6.00	12.00
—As "Leon and Mary Russell"					
❏ BSK 3172	Americana	1978	3.00	6.00	12.00
❏ BSK 3341	Life and Love	1979	3.00	6.00	12.00
❏ BSK 3532	The Live Album	1981	2.50	5.00	10.00
SHELTER					
❏ SHE-1001	Leon Russell	1968	5.00	10.00	20.00
❏ SR 2108	Stop All That Jazz	1974	3.75	7.50	15.00
❏ SR 2118	Leon Russell	1974	3.00	6.00	12.00
—Reissue of 8901					
❏ SR 2119	Leon Russell and the Shelter People	1974	3.00	6.00	12.00
—Reissue of 8903					
❏ SR 2121	Carney	1974	3.00	6.00	12.00
—Reissue of 8911					
❏ SR 2138	Will O' the Wisp	1975	3.75	7.50	15.00
❏ SW-8901	Leon Russell	1970	3.75	7.50	15.00
—Early reissue of 1001					
❏ SW-8903	Leon Russell and the Shelter People	1971	3.75	7.50	15.00
❏ SW-8911	Carney	1972	3.75	7.50	15.00
❏ STCO-8917 [(3)]	Leon Live	1973	5.00	10.00	20.00
❏ SW-8923	Hank Wilson's Back, Vol. 1	1973	3.75	7.50	15.00
—As "Hank Wilson"					
❏ 52004	Best of Leon	1976	2.50	5.00	10.00
❏ 52007	Leon Russell	1977	2.50	5.00	10.00
—Reissue of 2118					
❏ 52008	Leon Russell and the Shelter People	1977	2.50	5.00	10.00
—Reissue of 2119					
❏ 52011	Carney	1977	2.50	5.00	10.00
—Reissue of 2121					
❏ 52014	Hank Wilson's Back, Vol. 1	1977	2.50	5.00	10.00
—Reissue of 8923					
❏ 52016	Stop All That Jazz	1977	2.50	5.00	10.00
—Reissue of 2108					
❏ 52020	Will O' the Wisp	1977	2.50	5.00	10.00
—Reissue of 2138					

RUSSELL, LEON, AND MARC BENNO See ASYLUM CHOIR.

RUSTIX
45s

Number	Title (A Side/B Side)	Yr	VG	VG+	NM
RARE EARTH					
❏ 5011	Can't You Hear the Music Play/ I Guess This Is Goodbye	1969	—	3.00	6.00
❏ 5014	Come On People/Free Again	1970	—	3.00	6.00
❏ 5034	My Peace of Heaven/Down, Down	1971	—	—	—
—Canceled					
❏ 5037	We All End Up in Boxes/Down, Down	1971	—	3.00	6.00
Albums					
RARE EARTH					
❏ RS-508	Bedlam	1969	3.75	7.50	15.00
—Regular cover					
❏ RS-508	Bedlam	1969	7.50	15.00	30.00
—Rounded-top cover					
❏ RS-513	Come On, People	1970	3.00	6.00	12.00

RUSTY AND DOUG See RUSTY AND DOUG KERSHAW.

RYAN, BARRY Also see PAUL AND BARRY RYAN.
45s

Number	Title (A Side/B Side)	Yr	VG	VG+	NM
MGM					
❏ 14010	Eloise/Love, I Almost Found You	1968	2.00	4.00	8.00
POLYDOR					
❏ 14014	Look to the Right, Look to the Left/ Oh For the Love of Me	1970	—	3.00	6.00
❏ 14035	Give Me a Sign/Kitsch	1970	—	3.00	6.00
❏ 14065	It Is Written/Annabelle	1970	—	—	—
—Canceled					
❏ 14108	Can't Let You Go/When I Was a Child	1971	—	3.00	6.00
PRIDE					
❏ 1012	Alimony Money Blues/From My Head to My Toe	1972	—	2.50	5.00
❏ 1032	Can't Let You Go/L.A. Woman	1973	—	2.50	5.00

RYAN, CATHY
45s

Number	Title (A Side/B Side)	Yr	VG	VG+	NM
KING					
❏ 4848	Come Home/The Cricket, the Dove, and the Goldfish	1955	7.50	15.00	30.00
❏ 4890	Only a Dream/High Falutin' Heart	1956	7.50	15.00	30.00
❏ 4916	Lazy River/Love You with All My Might	1956	7.50	15.00	30.00

RYAN, PAUL AND BARRY Also see BARRY RYAN.
45s

Number	Title (A Side/B Side)	Yr	VG	VG+	NM
MGM					
❏ 13442	Don't Bring Me Your Heartaches/ To Remind You of Our Love	1966	2.50	5.00	10.00
❏ 13472	Have Pity on the Boy/There You Go	1966	2.50	5.00	10.00
❏ 13546	Silent Street/'Twas on a Night Like This	1966	2.50	5.00	10.00
❏ 13609	Have You Ever Loved Somebody/ I'll Tell You Later	1966	2.50	5.00	10.00
❏ 13719	Keep It Out of Sight/Who Told You	1967	2.00	4.00	8.00
❏ 13911	Madrigal/Pictures of Today	1968	2.00	4.00	8.00

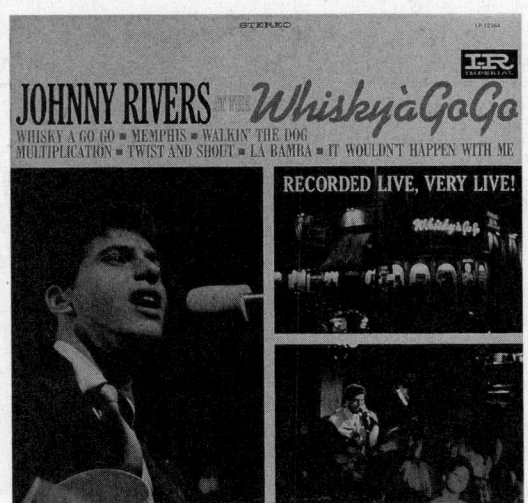

Johnny Rivers, *Johnny Rivers at the Whiskey A Go Go,* Imperial LP 12264, stereo LP, black, pink and white label, $12.50-$25.

Jimmie Rodgers, "Secretly," Roulette 4070, picture sleeve, $20-$40.

Tommy Roe, "Jam Up Jelly Tight," ABC 11247, picture sleeve, $6-$12.

Linda Ronstadt, *Silk Purse,* Capitol ST-407, stereo LP, lime green label, $7.50-$15.

Rush, *2112,* Mercury SRM-1-1079, stereo LP, "Chicago skyline" label, $5-$10.

Bobby Rydell, "I've Got Bonnie," Cameo 209, picture sleeve, $10-$20.

Number	Title (A Side/B Side)	Yr	VG	VG+	NM

RYDELL, BOBBY
45s
CAMEO

Number	Title (A Side/B Side)	Yr	VG	VG+	NM
❑ (no #) [DJ]	Steel Pier	1963	6.25	12.50	25.00
—One-sided "Steel Pier Promotion"					
❑ 160	Please Don't Be Mad/Makin' Time	1959	12.50	25.00	50.00
❑ 164	All I Want Is You/For You, For You	1959	5.00	10.00	20.00
❑ 167	Kissin' Time/You'll Never Tame Me	1959	3.75	7.50	15.00
❑ 167 [PS]	Kissin' Time/You'll Never Tame Me	1959	6.25	12.50	25.00
❑ 169	We Got Love/I Dig Girls	1959	3.75	7.50	15.00
❑ 169 [PS]	We Got Love/I Dig Girls	1959	6.25	12.50	25.00
❑ 171	Wild One/Little Bitty Girl	1960	3.75	7.50	15.00
❑ 171 [PS]	Wild One/Little Bitty Girl	1960	6.25	12.50	25.00
❑ 175	Swingin' School/Ding-a-Ling	1960	3.75	7.50	15.00
❑ 175 [PS]	Swingin' School/Ding-a-Ling	1960	6.25	12.50	25.00
❑ 179	Volare/I'd Do It Again	1960	3.75	7.50	15.00
❑ 179 [PS]	Volare/I'd Do It Again	1960	6.25	12.50	25.00
❑ 182	Sway/Groovy Tonight	1961	3.75	7.50	15.00
❑ 182 [PS]	Sway/Groovy Tonight	1961	6.25	12.50	25.00
❑ 186	Good Time Baby/Cherie	1961	3.75	7.50	15.00
❑ 186 [PS]	Good Time Baby/Cherie	1961	6.25	12.50	25.00
❑ 190	That Old Black Magic/Don't Be Afraid (To Fall in Love)	1961	3.75	7.50	15.00
❑ 190 [PS]	That Old Black Magic/Don't Be Afraid (To Fall in Love)	1961	6.25	12.50	25.00
❑ 192	The Fish/The Third House	1961	3.75	7.50	15.00
❑ 192 [PS]	The Fish/The Third House	1961	6.25	12.50	25.00
❑ 201	I Wanna Thank You/The Door to Paradise	1961	3.75	7.50	15.00
❑ 201 [PS]	I Wanna Thank You/The Door to Paradise	1961	6.25	12.50	25.00
❑ 209	I've Got Bonnie/Lose Her	1962	3.00	6.00	12.00
❑ 209 [PS]	I've Got Bonnie/Lose Her	1962	5.00	10.00	20.00
❑ 217	I'll Never Dance Again/Gee It's Wonderful	1962	3.00	6.00	12.00
❑ 217 [PS]	I'll Never Dance Again/Gee It's Wonderful	1962	5.00	10.00	20.00
❑ 228	The Cha-Cha-Cha/The Best Man Cried	1962	3.75	7.50	15.00
❑ 228 [PS]	The Cha-Cha-Cha/The Best Man Cried	1962	6.25	12.50	25.00
❑ 242	Butterfly Baby/Love Is Blind	1963	3.75	7.50	15.00
❑ 242 [PS]	Butterfly Baby/Love Is Blind	1963	6.25	12.50	25.00
❑ 252	Wildwood Days/Will You Be My Baby	1963	3.00	6.00	12.00
❑ 252 [PS]	Wildwood Days/Will You Be My Baby	1963	5.00	10.00	20.00
❑ 265	Little Queenie/The Woodpecker Song	1963	3.75	7.50	15.00
❑ 265 [PS]	Little Queenie/The Woodpecker Song	1963	6.25	12.50	25.00
❑ 272	Let's Make Love Tonight/Childhood Sweetheart	1963	3.00	6.00	12.00
❑ 272 [PS]	Let's Make Love Tonight/Childhood Sweetheart	1963	5.00	10.00	20.00
❑ 280	Forget Him/Love, Love Go Away	1963	3.00	6.00	12.00
❑ 280 [PS]	Forget Him/Love, Love Go Away	1963	5.00	10.00	20.00
❑ 309	Make Me Forget/Little Girl, You've Had a Busy Day	1964	3.00	6.00	12.00
❑ 309 [PS]	Make Me Forget/Little Girl, You've Had a Busy Day	1964	5.00	10.00	20.00
❑ 320	A World Without Love/Our Faded Love	1964	3.75	7.50	15.00
❑ 320 [PS]	A World Without Love/Our Faded Love	1964	6.25	12.50	25.00
❑ 361	Ciao, Ciao Bambino/Voce de la Notte	1965	3.75	7.50	15.00
❑ 1070	Forget Him/A Message from Bobby	1963	5.00	10.00	20.00
—Bonus single with Cameo LP C-1070, "Top Hits of 1963"					

CAPITOL

Number	Title (A Side/B Side)	Yr	VG	VG+	NM
❑ 5305	I Just Can't Say Goodbye/Two Is the Loneliest Number	1964	2.50	5.00	10.00
❑ 5305 [PS]	I Just Can't Say Goodbye/Two Is the Loneliest Number	1964	3.75	7.50	15.00
❑ 5352	Diana/Stranger in the World	1965	2.50	5.00	10.00
❑ 5436	The Joker/Side Show	1965	2.50	5.00	10.00
❑ 5513	When I See That Girl of Mine/It Takes Two	1965	2.50	5.00	10.00
❑ 5556	Roses in the Snow/A Word for Today	1965	2.50	5.00	10.00
❑ 5696	She Was the Girl/Not You	1966	2.50	5.00	10.00
❑ 5780	Open for Business As Usual/You Gotta Enjoy Joy	1966	2.50	5.00	10.00

P.I.P.

Number	Title (A Side/B Side)	Yr	VG	VG+	NM
❑ 6515	Sway/Feels Good	1976	—	2.50	5.00
❑ 6521	You're Not the Only Girl for Me/Give Me Your Answer	1976	—	2.00	4.00
❑ 6531	It's Getting Better/The Singles Scene	1976	—	2.00	4.00

PERCEPTION

Number	Title (A Side/B Side)	Yr	VG	VG+	NM
❑ 519	California Sunshine/Honey Buns	1973	—	2.50	5.00
❑ 552	Everything Seemed Better (When I Was Younger)/Sunday Son	1974	—	2.50	5.00

RCA VICTOR

Number	Title (A Side/B Side)	Yr	VG	VG+	NM
❑ 47-9892	Chapel on the Hill/It Must Be Love	1970	—	3.00	6.00

REPRISE

Number	Title (A Side/B Side)	Yr	VG	VG+	NM
❑ 0656	The Lovin' Thing/It's Getting Better	1968	2.00	4.00	8.00
❑ 0684	The River Is Wide/Absence Makes the Heart Grow Fonder	1968	2.00	4.00	8.00
❑ 0751	Every Little Bit Hurts/Time and Changes	1968	2.00	4.00	8.00

VEKO

Number	Title (A Side/B Side)	Yr	VG	VG+	NM
❑ 730/1	Dream Age/Fatty Fatty	1958	30.00	60.00	120.00

VENISE

Number	Title (A Side/B Side)	Yr	VG	VG+	NM
❑ 201	Fatty, Fatty/Happy Happy	1961	7.50	15.00	30.00

7-Inch Extended Plays
CAPITOL

Number	Title (A Side/B Side)	Yr	VG	VG+	NM
❑ SXA-2281	You're Nobody Till Somebody Loves You/Stranger in the World/Bellazza//Time Out for Tears/Dansero/It's a Sin to Tell a Lie	1965	2.50	5.00	10.00
—Jukebox issue; small hole, plays at 33 1/3 rpm					
❑ SXA-2281 [PS]	Somebody Loves You	1965	2.50	5.00	10.00

Albums
CAMEO

Number	Title (A Side/B Side)	Yr	VG	VG+	NM
❑ C-1006 [M]	We Got Love	1959	15.00	30.00	60.00
❑ C-1007 [M]	Bobby Sings	1960	12.50	25.00	50.00
❑ C-1009 [M]	Bobby's Biggest Hits	1961	6.25	12.50	25.00
—Standard cover					
❑ C-1009 [M]	Bobby's Biggest Hits	1961	20.00	40.00	80.00
—Original with die-cut cover and textured inner sleeve					
❑ C-1010 [M]	Bobby Rydell Salutes "The Great Ones"	1961	6.25	12.50	25.00
❑ SC-1010 [S]	Bobby Rydell Salutes "The Great Ones"	1961	10.00	20.00	40.00
❑ C-1011 [M]	Rydell at the Copa	1961	6.25	12.50	25.00
❑ SC-1011 [S]	Rydell at the Copa	1961	10.00	20.00	40.00

Number	Title (A Side/B Side)	Yr	VG	VG+	NM
❑ C-1019 [M]	All the Hits	1962	6.25	12.50	25.00
—Black vinyl					
❑ C-1019 [M]	All the Hits	1962	37.50	75.00	150.00
—Red vinyl					
❑ C-1028 [M]	Bobby Rydell's Biggest Hits, Volume 2	1962	6.25	12.50	25.00
❑ C-1040 [M]	All the Hits, Volume 2	1963	6.25	12.50	25.00
❑ SC-1040 [P]	All the Hits, Volume 2	1963	10.00	20.00	40.00
❑ C-1043 [M]	Bye Bye Birdie	1963	6.25	12.50	25.00
❑ C-1055 [M]	Wild (Wood) Days	1963	5.00	10.00	20.00
❑ SC-1055 [S]	Wild (Wood) Days	1963	7.50	15.00	30.00
❑ C-1070 [M]	The Top Hits of 1963	1963	5.00	10.00	20.00
—Came with bonus single, also numbered 1070					
❑ SC-1070 [S]	The Top Hits of 1963	1963	7.50	15.00	30.00
—Came with bonus single, also numbered 1070					
❑ C-1080 [M]	Forget Him	1964	5.00	10.00	20.00
❑ SC-1080 [R]	Forget Him	1964	5.00	10.00	20.00
❑ C-2001 [M]	16 Golden Hits	1965	5.00	10.00	20.00
❑ SC-2001 [R]	16 Golden Hits	1965	5.00	10.00	20.00

CAPITOL

Number	Title (A Side/B Side)	Yr	VG	VG+	NM
❑ ST 2281 [S]	Somebody Loves You	1965	5.00	10.00	20.00
❑ T 2281 [M]	Somebody Loves You	1965	3.75	7.50	15.00

P.I.P.

Number	Title (A Side/B Side)	Yr	VG	VG+	NM
❑ 6818	Born with a Smile	1976	2.50	5.00	10.00

SPIN-O-RAMA

Number	Title (A Side/B Side)	Yr	VG	VG+	NM
❑ 143 [M]	Starring Bobby Rydell	196?	3.00	6.00	12.00
❑ S-143 [S]	Starring Bobby Rydell	196?	3.00	6.00	12.00

STRAND

Number	Title (A Side/B Side)	Yr	VG	VG+	NM
❑ SL-1120 [M]	Bobby Rydell Sings	196?	6.25	12.50	25.00
❑ SLS-1120 [R]	Bobby Rydell Sings	196?	5.00	10.00	20.00

VENISE

Number	Title (A Side/B Side)	Yr	VG	VG+	NM
❑ 10035 [M]	Twistin'	1962	6.25	12.50	25.00
—Also includes tracks by Barry Norman and Stephen Garrick					

RYDELL, BOBBY/CHUBBY CHECKER Also see each artist's individual listings.
45s
CAMEO

Number	Title (A Side/B Side)	Yr	VG	VG+	NM
❑ 12E [DJ]	Chubby Sings Bobby-Bobby Sings Chubby	1962	10.00	20.00	40.00
—B-side blank, promo only					
❑ 13E [DJ]	What Are You Doing New Year's Eve?	1962	10.00	20.00	40.00
—B-side blank, promo only					
❑ 205	Jingle Bell Rock/Jingle Bell Imitations	1961	3.75	7.50	15.00
❑ 205 [PS]	Jingle Bell Rock/Jingle Bell Imitations	1961	6.25	12.50	25.00
❑ 214	Teach Me to Twist/Swingin' Together	1962	3.75	7.50	15.00
❑ 214 [PS]	Teach Me to Twist/Swingin' Together	1962	6.25	12.50	25.00

Albums
CAMEO

Number	Title (A Side/B Side)	Yr	VG	VG+	NM
❑ C 1013 [M]	Bobby Rydell/Chubby Checker	1961	7.50	15.00	30.00
❑ C-1063 [M]	Chubby Checker and Bobby Rydell	1963	5.00	10.00	20.00

RYDER, MITCH Also see DETROIT; MITCH RYDER AND THE DETROIT WHEELS.
12-Inch Singles
RIVA

Number	Title (A Side/B Side)	Yr	VG	VG+	NM
❑ MK 244 [DJ]	When You Were Mine (same on both sides)	1983	2.50	5.00	10.00

45s
AVCO EMBASSY

Number	Title (A Side/B Side)	Yr	VG	VG+	NM
❑ 4550	Jenny Take a Ride/I Never Had It Better	1970	2.50	5.00	10.00

DOT

Number	Title (A Side/B Side)	Yr	VG	VG+	NM
❑ 17290	I Believe (There Must Be Someone)/Sugar Bee (We Three)	1970	—	3.00	6.00
❑ 17325	It's Been a Long, Long, Long Time/Direct Me	1970	—	3.00	6.00

DYNOVOICE

Number	Title (A Side/B Side)	Yr	VG	VG+	NM
❑ 901	What Now My Love/Blessing in Disguise	1967	2.00	4.00	8.00
❑ 905	Personality-Chantilly Lace/I Make a Fool of Myself	1968	2.00	4.00	8.00
❑ 916	Lights of the Night/I Need Loving You	1968	2.00	4.00	8.00
❑ 934	Baby I Need Your Loving/Ring Your Bell	1969	2.00	4.00	8.00

NEW VOICE

Number	Title (A Side/B Side)	Yr	VG	VG+	NM
❑ 824	Joy/I'd Rather Go to Jail	1967	2.00	4.00	8.00
❑ 826	You Are My Sunshine/Wild Child	1967	2.00	4.00	8.00
❑ 828	Come See About Me/A Face in the Crowd	1968	2.00	4.00	8.00
❑ 830	Ruby Baby/You Get Your Kicks	1968	2.00	4.00	8.00

RIVA

Number	Title (A Side/B Side)	Yr	VG	VG+	NM
❑ 213	When You Were Mine/Stand	1983	—	2.50	5.00

Albums
DYNO VOICE

Number	Title (A Side/B Side)	Yr	VG	VG+	NM
❑ 1901 [M]	What Now My Love	1967	5.00	10.00	20.00
❑ 31901 [S]	What Now My Love	1967	5.00	10.00	20.00

RIVA

Number	Title (A Side/B Side)	Yr	VG	VG+	NM
❑ RV 7503	Never Kick a Sleeping Dog	1983	2.50	5.00	10.00

SEEDS & STEMS

Number	Title (A Side/B Side)	Yr	VG	VG+	NM
❑ 7801	How I Spent My Summer Vacation	1978	3.00	6.00	12.00
❑ 7804	Naked But Not Dead	1980	3.00	6.00	12.00

RYDER, MITCH, AND THE DETROIT WHEELS Also see DETROIT; THE DETROIT WHEELS; BILLY LEE AND THE RIVIERAS; MITCH RYDER.
45s
NEW VOICE

Number	Title (A Side/B Side)	Yr	VG	VG+	NM
❑ 801	I Need Help/I Hope	1965	2.50	5.00	10.00
❑ 806	Jenny Take a Ride!/Baby Jane (Mo-Mo Jane)	1965	3.00	6.00	12.00
—Actual A-side title					
❑ 806	Jenny Takes a Ride!/Baby Jane (Mo-Mo Jane)	1965	6.25	12.50	25.00
—Note slightly different A-side title					
❑ 808	Little Latin Lupe Lu/I Hope	1966	2.50	5.00	10.00
❑ 811	Break Out/I Need Help	1966	2.50	5.00	10.00
❑ 814	Takin' All I Can Get/You Get Your Kicks	1966	2.50	5.00	10.00
❑ 817	Devil with a Blue Dress On & Good Golly Miss Molly/I Had It Made	1966	3.00	6.00	12.00
❑ 820	Sock It To Me — Baby!/I Never Had It Better	1967	2.50	5.00	10.00
—Version 2: With lyric "Hits me like a PUNCH!" with no doubt about the last word. The copies of this we've seen have a blue label, both "painted on" and not "painted on," but we can't say yet that ALL copies with that label have this version.					
❑ 820	Sock It To Me — Baby!/I Never Had It Better	1967	6.25	12.50	25.00
—Version 1: With lyric "Feels like a punch," mumbled to the point that it sounds obscene. The copy of this we've seen has a multicolor, concentric circle label, but we can't yet say that ALL copies with this label are this version.					

Number	Title (A Side/B Side)	Yr	VG	VG+	NM
❏ 820 [PS]	Sock It To Me — Baby!/I Never Had It Better	1967	5.00	10.00	20.00
—Black strip at the top with white and red print					
❏ 820 [PS]	Sock It To Me — Baby!/I Never Had It Better	1967	7.50	15.00	30.00
—White strip at the top with black print					
❏ 822	Too Many Fish in the Sea & Three Little Fishes/				
	One Grain of Sand	1967	2.50	5.00	10.00
❏ 822 [PS]	Too Many Fish in the Sea & Three Little Fishes/				
	One Grain of Sand	1967	5.00	10.00	20.00
PHILCO-FORD					
❏ HP-4	Jenny Take a Ride/Sock It To Me Baby	1967	3.75	7.50	15.00
—4-inch plastic "Hip Pocket Record" with color sleeve					
Albums					
CREWE					
❏ CR-1335	All Mitch Ryder Hits!	1969	3.75	7.50	15.00
—Reissue of New Voice 2004					
NEW VOICE					
❏ 2000 [M]	Take a Ride	1966	6.25	12.50	25.00
❏ S-2000 [S]	Take a Ride	1966	7.50	15.00	30.00
❏ 2002 [M]	Breakout…!!!	1966	5.00	10.00	20.00
—With "Devil with a Blue Dress On/Good Golly Miss Molly"					
❏ 2002 [M]	Breakout…!!!	1966	6.25	12.50	25.00
—Without "Devil with a Blue Dress On/Good Golly Miss Molly"					
❏ S-2002 [S]	Breakout…!!!	1966	6.25	12.50	25.00
—With "Devil with a Blue Dress On/Good Golly Miss Molly"					
❏ S-2002 [S]	Breakout…!!!	1966	7.50	15.00	30.00
—Without "Devil with a Blue Dress On/Good Golly Miss Molly"					
❏ 2003 [M]	Sock It To Me!	1967	6.25	12.50	25.00
❏ S-2003 [S]	Sock It To Me!	1967	7.50	15.00	30.00
❏ 2004 [M]	All Mitch Ryder Hits!	1967	7.50	15.00	30.00
❏ NVS-2004 [S]	All Mitch Ryder Hits!	1967	5.00	10.00	20.00
❏ S-2005	Mitch Ryder Sings the Hits	1968	5.00	10.00	20.00
RHINO					
❏ R1-70941	Rev Up: The Best of Mitch Ryder				
	and the Detroit Wheels	1989	3.00	6.00	12.00
SUNDAZED					
❏ LP 5083	Breakout ... !!!	2001	3.00	6.00	12.00
—Reissue on 180-gram vinyl					
VIRGO					
❏ 12001	The Best of Mitch Ryder and the Detroit Wheels	1972	3.00	6.00	12.00

S

Number	Title (A Side/B Side)	Yr	VG	VG+	NM
SA-SHAYS, THE					
45s					
ALFI					
❏ 1	Boo Hoo Hoo/You Got Love	1961	6.25	12.50	25.00
ZEN					
❏ 110	Boo Hoo Hoo/You Got Love	1961	3.00	6.00	12.00
SABERS, THE					
45s					
BULLSEYE					
❏ 101	You Can Depend on Me/Calypso Baby	1955	62.50	125.00	250.00
CAL-WEST					
❏ 847	Cool, Cool Christmas/Always and Forever	1955	100.00	200.00	400.00
SABRE, JOHNNY, AND THE PASSIONS					
45s					
ADONIS					
❏ 103	Wish It Could Be Me/Dolly in a Toy Shop	1959	50.00	100.00	200.00
SACCO See LOU CHRISTIE.					
SACRED MUSHROOM, THE Members of this group were later in POCO and PURE PRAIRIE LEAGUE.					
Albums					
PARALLAX					
❏ P-4001	The Sacred Mushroom	1969	37.50	75.00	150.00
SAD SACKS, THE					
45s					
IMPERIAL					
❏ 5517	Sack Dresses/Guard Your Heart	1958	3.75	7.50	15.00
SADLER, SSGT. BARRY					
45s					
RCA VICTOR					
❏ 47-8739	The Ballad of the Green Berets/				
	Letter from Vietnam	1966	—	3.00	6.00
❏ 47-8739 [PS]	The Ballad of the Green Berets/				
	Letter from Vietnam	1966	2.00	4.00	8.00
❏ 47-8804	The "A" Team/An Empty Glass	1966	—	3.00	6.00
❏ 47-8804 [PS]	The "A" Team/An Empty Glass	1966	2.00	4.00	8.00
❏ 47-8966	Not Just Lonely/One Day Nearer Home	1966	—	3.00	6.00
❏ 47-9008	I Won't Be Home This Christmas/				
	A Woman Is a Weepin' Willow Tree	1966	2.00	4.00	8.00
7-Inch Extended Plays					
RCA VICTOR					
❏ VLP 3547	The Ballad of the Green Berets/I'm a Lucky One/				
	Letter from Vietnam//I'm Watching the				
	Raindrops Fall/Saigon/Garet Trooper	1966	2.50	5.00	10.00
—Jukebox issue; small hole, plays at 33 1/3 rpm					
❏ VLP 3547 [PS]	Ballads of the Green Berets	1966	2.50	5.00	10.00
Albums					
RCA VICTOR					
❏ LPM-3547 [M]	Ballads of the Green Berets	1966	3.75	7.50	15.00
❏ LSP-3547 [S]	Ballads of the Green Berets	1966	5.00	10.00	20.00
❏ LPM-3605 [M]	"A" Team, The	1966	3.75	7.50	15.00
❏ LSP-3605 [S]	"A" Team, The	1966	5.00	10.00	20.00
❏ LPM-3691 [M]	Back Home	1967	5.00	10.00	20.00
❏ LSP-3691 [S]	Back Home	1967	3.75	7.50	15.00
SAFARIS, THE					
45s					
DEE JAY					
❏ 203	My Image of a Girl (Is You)/C'mon Everybody	1989	—	2.00	4.00
—Red vinyl					
❏ 203 [PS]	My Image of a Girl (Is You)/C'mon Everybody	1989	—	2.00	4.00
ELDO					
❏ 101	Image of a Girl/Four Steps to Love	1960	6.25	12.50	25.00
❏ 105	The Girl with the Story in Her Eyes/				
	Summer Nights	1960	6.25	12.50	25.00
❏ 110	In the Still of the Night/Shadows	1960	7.50	15.00	30.00
❏ 113	Garden of Love/Soldier of Fortune	1961	7.50	15.00	30.00
VALIANT					
❏ 6036	Kick Out/Lonely Surf Guitar	1963	7.50	15.00	30.00
SAGES, THE					
45s					
RCA VICTOR					
❏ 47-8760	In the Beginning/I'm Not Going to Cry	1965	6.25	12.50	25.00
SAGITTARIUS					
45s					
COLUMBIA					
❏ 44163	My World Fell Down/Libra	1967	2.50	5.00	10.00
❏ 44289	Hotel Indiscreeet/Virgo	1967	2.50	5.00	10.00
❏ 44398	Another Time/Pisces	1967	2.50	5.00	10.00
❏ 44503	The Truth Is Not Real/				
	You Know I've Found a Way	1968	2.50	5.00	10.00
❏ 44613	Keeper of the Games/I'm Not Living Here	1968	2.50	5.00	10.00
TOGETHER					
❏ 105	In My Room/Navajo Girl	1969	2.50	5.00	10.00
❏ 122	I Can Still See Your Face/I Guess the Lord Must				
	Be in New York City	1969	2.50	5.00	10.00
Albums					
COLUMBIA					
❏ CS 9644	Present Tense	1968	7.50	15.00	30.00
TOGETHER					
❏ STT-1002	The Blue Marble	1969	12.50	25.00	50.00
—With two bonus photos; deduct 25 percent if missing					

S

Number	Title (A Side/B Side)	Yr	VG	VG+	NM
SAHL, MORT					
45s					
GNP CRESCENDO					
❏ 467	Nixon's Odyssey/Watergate	1973	—	2.50	5.00
REPRISE					
❏ 20038	About Women (Part 1)/About Women (Part 2)	1961	2.50	5.00	10.00
Albums					
FANTASY					
❏ 7005 [M]	Mort Sahl at Sunset	196?	7.50	15.00	30.00
—Black vinyl					
❏ 7005 [M]	Mort Sahl at Sunset	196?	10.00	20.00	40.00
—Red vinyl					
GNP CRESCENDO					
❏ GNPS-2070	Sing a Song of Watergate	1973	3.75	7.50	15.00
MERCURY					
❏ MG-21112 [M]	Anyway…Onward	1967	5.00	10.00	20.00
❏ SR-61112 [S]	Anyway…Onward	1967	5.00	10.00	20.00
REPRISE					
❏ R-5002 [M]	The New Frontier	1961	5.00	10.00	20.00
❏ R9-5002 [S]	The New Frontier	1961	6.25	12.50	25.00
❏ R-5003 [M]	Mort Sahl On Relationships	1961	10.00	20.00	40.00
❏ R9-5003 [S]	Mort Sahl On Relationships	1961	12.50	25.00	50.00
—Joan Collins appears on the cover					
VERVE					
❏ MGV-15002 [M]	The Future Lies Ahead	1959	5.00	10.00	20.00
❏ MGV-15004 [M]	1960: Look Forward in Anger	1959	5.00	10.00	20.00
❏ MGV-15006 [M]	A Way of Life	1960	5.00	10.00	20.00
❏ MGV-15012 [M]	Mort Sahl at the Hungry I	1960	5.00	10.00	20.00
❏ MGVS-15012 [S]	Mort Sahl at the Hungry I	1960	6.25	12.50	25.00
❏ V-15021 [M]	The Next President	1961	5.00	10.00	20.00
❏ V6-15021 [S]	The Next President	1961	6.25	12.50	25.00
❏ V-15049 [M]	Great Moments of Comedy	1965	3.75	7.50	15.00
SAHM, DOUG Also see SIR DOUGLAS QUINTET.					
45s					
ABC DOT					
❏ 17656	Cowboy Peyton Place/I Love the Way You Love (The Way I Love You)	1976	—	3.00	6.00
❏ 17674	Crying Inside Sometimes/I'm Missing You	1976	—	3.00	6.00
ATLANTIC					
❏ 2946	Is Anybody Going to San Antone/ Don't Turn Around	1973	2.00	4.00	8.00
COBRA					
❏ 116	Just a Moment/Sapphire	1961	12.50	25.00	50.00
CRAZY CAJUN					
❏ 2004	If You Really Want/Not Tomato Man	1974	—	2.50	5.00
HARLEM					
❏ 108	Baby Tell Me/Sapphire	1960	12.50	25.00	50.00
❏ 108 [DJ]	Baby Tell Me/Sapphire	1960	25.00	50.00	100.00
—Gold vinyl promo					
❏ 113	More and More/Slow Down	1960	12.50	25.00	50.00
MERCURY					
❏ 73098	Be Real/I Don't Want to Go Home	1970	5.00	10.00	20.00
—As "Wayne Douglas"					
PERSONALITY					
❏ 260	Baby, What's On Your Mind/ Crazy, Crazy Feeling	1962	12.50	25.00	50.00
RENNER					
❏ 212	Big Hat/Makes No Difference	1961	10.00	20.00	40.00
❏ 212 [DJ]	Big Hat/Makes No Difference	1961	25.00	50.00	100.00
—Red vinyl promo					
❏ 215	Baby, What's On Your Mind/ Crazy, Crazy Feeling	1961	10.00	20.00	40.00
❏ 215 [DJ]	Baby, What's On Your Mind/ Crazy, Crazy Feeling	1961	25.00	50.00	100.00
—Red vinyl promo					
❏ 226	Two Hearts in Love/Just Because	1962	10.00	20.00	40.00
❏ 232	Little Angel/Cry	1963	10.00	20.00	40.00
❏ 240	Lucky Me/A Year Ago Tonight	1963	10.00	20.00	40.00
❏ 247	Mr. Kool/Bill Beatty	1964	12.50	25.00	50.00
SARG					
❏ 113	A Real American Joe/Rolling Rolling	1958	25.00	50.00	100.00
—As "Little Doug"					
SATIN					
❏ 100	Crazy Daisy/I Can't Believe You Wanna Leave	1959	12.50	25.00	50.00
SOFT					
❏ 1031	Cry/Down the Pike	1965	7.50	15.00	30.00
SWINGIN'					
❏ 625	Why, Why, Why/If You Ever Need Me	1960	6.25	12.50	25.00
TEAR DROP					
❏ 3074	It's a Man Down There/4 A.M.	1966	6.25	12.50	25.00
—As "Him"					
TEARDROP					
❏ 3479	Who Were You Thinking Of/Velma	1982	—	2.00	4.00
—With Augie Myers					
❏ 3481	I'm Not a Fool Anymore/Don't Fight It	1982	—	2.00	4.00
—With Augie Myers					
WARNER BROS.					
❏ 7819	Girls Today/Groover's Paradise	1974	—	2.50	5.00
WARRIOR					
❏ 507	Crazy Daisy/If I Ever Need You	1958	20.00	40.00	80.00
Albums					
ABC DOT					
❏ DO-2057	Texas Rock for Country Rollers	1976	3.75	7.50	15.00
ANTONE'S					
❏ ANT-0008	Juke Box Music	1989	3.00	6.00	12.00
ATLANTIC					
❏ SD 7254	Doug Sahm and Band	1973	3.75	7.50	15.00
MERCURY					
❏ SRM-1-655	Rough Edges	1972	7.50	15.00	30.00
TAKOMA					
❏ TAK-7075	Hell of a Spell	1980	3.00	6.00	12.00
TEARDROP					
❏ TD-5000	The West Side Sound Rolls Again	1982	3.00	6.00	12.00

Number	Title (A Side/B Side)	Yr	VG	VG+	NM
WARNER BROS.					
❏ BS 2810	Groovers Paradise	1974	5.00	10.00	20.00
SAIGONS, THE					
45s					
DOOTONE					
❏ 375	You're Heavenly/Honey Gee	1955	100.00	200.00	400.00
SAILCAT					
45s					
ELEKTRA					
❏ 45782	Motorcycle Mama/Rainbow Road	1972	—	2.50	5.00
❏ 45817	Bee Bee Gunn/Baby Ruth	1972	—	2.50	5.00
❏ 45844	She Showed Me/Sweet Little Jenny	1973	—	2.50	5.00
Albums					
ELEKTRA					
❏ EKS-75029	Sailcat	1972	3.75	7.50	15.00
45s					
DAISY					
❏ 501	Big Bad World/Mr. Heartbreak	1963	12.50	25.00	50.00
ST. ANDREW'S FAIRWAY					
45s					
TMI					
❏ 75-0101	Pocketful of Pennies/Cross Over	1972	—	3.00	6.00
❏ ZS7 9009	Pocketful of Pennies/Cross Over	1972	—	3.50	7.00
ST. ANTHONY'S FIRE					
Albums					
ZONK					
❏ (# unknown)	St. Anthony's Fire	1968	100.00	200.00	400.00
ST. CLOUD, ENDLE					
45s					
INTERNATIONAL ARTISTS					
❏ 129	Tell Me One More Time/(B-side unknown)	1969	5.00	10.00	20.00
❏ 139	She Wears It Like a Badge/Laughter	1970	5.00	10.00	20.00
Albums					
INTERNATIONAL ARTISTS					
❏ IA-12	Thank You All Very Much	1970	15.00	30.00	60.00
ST. JAMES, HOLLY					
45s					
ABC					
❏ 10996	That's Not Love/Two Good Reasons	1967	15.00	30.00	60.00
❏ 11042	Waiting for My Friend/Magic Moments	1968	5.00	10.00	20.00
ST. JOHN, BARRY					
45s					
GRT					
❏ 2	Cry Like a Baby/Long and Lonely Nights	1969	—	3.00	6.00
ST. JOHN, DICK Also see DICK AND DEEDEE; SANDY AND DICK.					
45s					
DOT					
❏ 17080	Childhood/Lady of the Burning Green-Jade	1968	2.00	4.00	8.00
—Of Dick and Deedee					
❏ 17140	Leaving on a Jet Plane/Brand New Season	1968	2.00	4.00	8.00
LIBERTY					
❏ 55380	Gonna Stick By You/Sha-Ta	1961	3.00	6.00	12.00
PHILIPS					
❏ 40256	Love's a Funny Little Game/Believe Me Baby	1965	2.50	5.00	10.00
❏ 40325	Swanee River/You Know What I Mean	1965	2.50	5.00	10.00
POM POM					
❏ 4156	Gonna Stick By You/Sha-Ta	1961	6.25	12.50	25.00
ROMA					
❏ 1001	Hey, Little Gal/Boogie Man (I Ain't Afraid of You)	1961	3.75	7.50	15.00
ST. JOHN, TAMMY					
45s					
CONGRESS					
❏ 236	He's the One for Me/I'm Tired Just Lookin' at You	1965	2.50	5.00	10.00
❏ 258	Dark Shadows and Empty Hallways/I Mustn't Cry	1965	2.50	5.00	10.00
ST. LOUIS JIMMY					
45s					
DUKE					
❏ 110	Drinkin' Woman/Why Work	1953	30.00	60.00	120.00
HERALD					
❏ 407	Hard Luck Boogie/Good Book Blues	1953	50.00	100.00	200.00
❏ 408	Your Evil Ways/Whiskey Drinkin' Woman	1953	50.00	100.00	200.00
PARROT					
❏ 823	Going Down Slow/Murder in the First Degree	1955	50.00	100.00	200.00
Albums					
BLUESVILLE					
❏ BVLP-1028 [M]	Goin' Down Blues	1961	30.00	60.00	120.00
—Blue label, silver print					
❏ BVLP-1028 [M]	Goin' Down Blues	1964	6.25	12.50	25.00
—Blue label, trident logo at right					
ST. LOUIS UNION					
45s					
PARROT					
❏ 9812	Girl/Respect	1966	2.00	4.00	8.00
ST. PETERS, CRISPIAN					
45s					
JAMIE					
❏ 1302	At This Moment/You'll Forget Me, Goodbye	1965	3.75	7.50	15.00
❏ 1309	At This Moment/No No	1966	2.50	5.00	10.00
❏ 1310	You Were On My Mind/What I'm Gonna Be	1966	2.50	5.00	10.00
❏ 1320	The Pied Piper/Sweet Dawn My True Love	1966	3.00	6.00	12.00
❏ 1324	Changes/My Little Brown Eyes	1966	2.50	5.00	10.00
❏ 1328	Your Ever Changin' Mind/But She's Untrue	1966	2.50	5.00	10.00
❏ 1334	Almost Persuaded/You Are Gone	1967	2.50	5.00	10.00
❏ 1344	Free Spirit/I'm Always Crying	1967	2.50	5.00	10.00
❏ 1359	Please Take Me Back/Look Into My Teardrops	1968	2.00	4.00	8.00

Number	Title (A Side/B Side)	Yr	VG	VG+	NM

Albums

JAMIE

Number	Title (A Side/B Side)	Yr	VG	VG+	NM
❏ JLPM-3027 [M]	The Pied Piper	1966	12.50	25.00	50.00
❏ JLPS-3027 [R]	The Pied Piper	1966	8.75	17.50	35.00

ST. ROMAIN, KIRBY

45s

IMCO

❏ 2103	Baby Doll/Summertime Fun	1964	2.50	5.00	10.00

INETTE

❏ 103	Summer's Comin'/Miss You So	1963	3.00	6.00	12.00
❏ 104	Butterflies/Walk On Mr. Blue	1963	3.00	6.00	12.00
❏ 106	Love Is Magic/I Don't Wanna Fall in Love	1964	3.00	6.00	12.00

TEARDROP

❏ 3036	Oh Baby Doll/Summertime Fun	1964	2.50	5.00	10.00

ST. SHAW, MIKE

45s

REPRISE

❏ 0273	Take This Hammer/What's That I Hear	1964	2.50	5.00	10.00
❏ 0282	Mike's Mid-Nite Special/Summer Skies and Golden Sands	1964	2.50	5.00	10.00
❏ 0325	From the Bottom of My Heart/Send Me Some Lovin'	1964	3.00	6.00	12.00

Albums

REPRISE

❏ R-6128 [M]	The Mike St. Shaw Trio	1964	5.00	10.00	20.00
❏ RS-6128 [S]	The Mike St. Shaw Trio	1964	6.25	12.50	25.00

SAINT STEVEN

45s

PROBE

❏ 463	Louisiana Home/Aye Aye Poe Day	1969	5.00	10.00	20.00

Albums

PROBE

❏ CPLP-4506	Over the Hills	1969	15.00	30.00	60.00

SAINTE-MARIE, BUFFY

45s

ABC

❏ 12183	Starwalker/Free the Lady	1976	—	2.50	5.00
❏ 12203	Look at the Facts/(B-side unknown)	1976	—	2.50	5.00

MCA

❏ 40193	Can't Believe the Feeling When You're Gone/Waves	1974	—	2.50	5.00
❏ 40216	Sweet Little Vera/Waves	1974	—	2.50	5.00
❏ 40286	I Can't Take It No More/Native North American Child: An Odyssey	1974	—	2.50	5.00
❏ 40347	Sweet, Fast Hooker Blues/Generation	1975	—	2.50	5.00
❏ 40368	Love's Got to Breathe and Fly/Nobody Will Ever Know It's Real But You	1975	—	2.50	5.00

VANGUARD

❏ 35028	Until It's Time for You to Go/The Flower and the Apple Tree	1963	2.50	5.00	10.00
❏ 35050	Until It's Time for You to Go/Jusqu'au Jour Ou Tu Partiras	1967	2.00	4.00	8.00
❏ 35053	Circle Game/Until It's Time for You to Go	1967	2.00	4.00	8.00
❏ 35064	Soulful Shade of Blue/Piney Wood Hills	1968	2.00	4.00	8.00
❏ 35072	Better to Find Out for Yourself/Sometimes When I Get to Thinkin'	1968	2.00	4.00	8.00
❏ 35075	From the Bottom of My Heart/I'm Gonna Be a Country Girl Again	1969	2.00	4.00	8.00
❏ 35091	He's a Keeper of the Fire/Better to Find Out for Yourself	1970	—	3.00	6.00
❏ 35108	The Circle Game/Better to Find Out for Yourself	1970	—	3.00	6.00
❏ 35116	Soldier Blue/Until It's Time for You to Go	1970	—	3.00	6.00
❏ 35127	She Used to Wanna Be a Ballerina/Moratorium	1971	—	3.00	6.00
❏ 35135	Helpless/Now You've Been Gone a Long Time	1971	—	3.00	6.00
❏ 35143	I'm Gonna Be a Country Girl Again/Piney Wood Hills	1971	—	2.50	5.00
❏ 35151	Mister Can't You See/Moonshot	1972	—	2.50	5.00
❏ 35156	He's an Indian Cowboy in the Rodeo/Not the Lovin' Kind	1972	—	2.50	5.00
❏ 35172	I Wanna Hold Your Hand Forever/Jeremiah	1972	—	2.50	5.00
❏ 35180	Soldier Blue/(B-side unknown)	1973	—	2.50	5.00

Albums

ABC

❏ D-929	Sweet America	1976	3.00	6.00	12.00

MCA

❏ 405	Buffy	1974	3.00	6.00	12.00
❏ 451	Changing Woman	1975	3.00	6.00	12.00

VANGUARD

❏ VSD 3/4 [(2)]	The Best of Buffy Sainte-Marie	1970	5.00	10.00	20.00
❏ VSD 33/34 [(2)]	The Best of Buffy Sainte-Marie, Vol. 2	1974	3.75	7.50	15.00
❏ VRS 9142 [M]	It's My Way	1964	3.75	7.50	15.00
❏ VRS 9171 [M]	Many a Mile	1965	3.75	7.50	15.00
❏ VRS 9211 [M]	Little Wheel Spin and Spin	1966	3.75	7.50	15.00
❏ VRS 9250 [M]	Fire & Fire & Candlelight	1967	3.75	7.50	15.00
❏ VSQ 40003 [Q]	Moon Shot	1972	6.25	12.50	25.00
❏ VSQ 40020 [Q]	Quiet Places	1973	6.25	12.50	25.00
❏ VMS 73113	The Best of Buffy Sainte-Marie	1985	2.50	5.00	10.00
❏ VSD 79142 [S]	It's My Way	1964	5.00	10.00	20.00
❏ VSD 79171 [S]	Many a Mile	1965	5.00	10.00	20.00
❏ VSD 79211 [S]	Little Wheel Spin and Spin	1966	5.00	10.00	20.00
❏ VSD 79250 [S]	Fire & Fire & Candlelight	1967	5.00	10.00	20.00
❏ VSD 79280	I'm Gonna Be a Country Girl Again	1968	3.75	7.50	15.00
❏ VSD 79300	Illuminations	1969	3.75	7.50	15.00
❏ VSD 79311	She Used to Wanna Be a Ballerina	1971	3.75	7.50	15.00
❏ VSD 79312	Moon Shot	1972	3.75	7.50	15.00
❏ VSD 79330	Quiet Places	1973	3.00	6.00	12.00
❏ VSD 79340	Native Child: Odyssey	1974	3.00	6.00	12.00

SAKAMOTO, KYU

45s

CAPITOL

❏ 4945	Sukiyaki/Anoko No Namaewa Nantenkana	1963	2.00	4.00	8.00

—Third pressing: A-side spelled correctly with no subtitle

❏ 4945	Sukiyaki/Anoko No Namaewa Nantenkana	1963	2.50	5.00	10.00

—Second pressing: A-side spelled correctly, subtittled "Music of 'Ue O Muite Aruko' "

❏ 4945	Sukiyaki/Anoko No Namaewa Nantenkana	1963	3.75	7.50	15.00

—First pressing: Misspelled A-side

❏ 5016	China Nights (Shina No Yoru)/Benkyo No Cha Cha Cha	1963	2.00	4.00	8.00
❏ 5080	The Olympics Song/Tankobushi	1963	2.00	4.00	8.00
❏ 5262	Sayonara Tokyo/I Like You	1964	2.00	4.00	8.00

EMI

❏ 4150	Why/Elimo	1975	—	2.50	5.00

Albums

CAPITOL

❏ DT 10349 [R]	Sukiyaki and Other Japanese Hits	1963	3.75	7.50	15.00
❏ T 10349 [M]	Sukiyaki and Other Japanese Hits	1963	6.25	12.50	25.00

SALAS BROTHERS, THE

45s

FARO

❏ 614	Leaving You/Darling, Please Bring Your Love	1964	2.50	5.00	10.00
❏ 619	The Return of Farmer John/Love Is Strange	1965	2.50	5.00	10.00
❏ 625	Donde Este Santa Claus/One Like Mine	1966	2.00	4.00	8.00

SALEM MASS

Albums

SALEM MASS

❏ SM-101	Witch Burning	1972	62.50	125.00	250.00

SALEMS, THE

45s

EPIC

❏ 9480	Ol' Man River/Maria	1961	3.75	7.50	15.00

MERCURY

❏ 71754	My Precious Love/I'll Still Go On Loving You	1961	3.75	7.50	15.00

SALES, SOUPY

45s

ABC-PARAMOUNT

❏ 10646	The Mouse/Pachalafaka	1965	3.00	6.00	12.00
❏ 10681	Speedy Gonzales/Hey, Pearl	1965	2.50	5.00	10.00
❏ 10747	I'm a Bird Watching Man/Where the Blue Folks Go	1965	2.50	5.00	10.00

BRUNSWICK

❏ 55472	Break Your Back/Tom Jones (Push and Pull)	1972	2.50	5.00	10.00

CAPITOL

❏ 5752	Spanish Flea/That Wasn't No Girl	1966	2.50	5.00	10.00
❏ 5766	Backwards Alphabet/Use Your Noggin	1966	2.50	5.00	10.00

MOTOWN

❏ 1141	Muck-Arty Park/Green Grow the Lilacs	1968	10.00	20.00	40.00

REPRISE

❏ 244	Santa Claus Is Surfin' to Town/Santa Claus Is Comin' to Town	1963	7.50	15.00	30.00
❏ 0368	Pie in the Face/Soupy Sez	1965	3.75	7.50	15.00
❏ 20041	Hippy's Cha Cha Hips/White Fang	1961	3.75	7.50	15.00
❏ 20064	Because of Black Tooth/Soupy's Theme	1962	3.75	7.50	15.00
❏ 20108	My Baby's Got a Crush on Frankenstein/Doggone Doggie	1962	3.75	7.50	15.00
❏ 20189	And That's a Shame/Hilly Billy Ding Dong Choo Choo	1963	3.75	7.50	15.00

Albums

ABC-PARAMOUNT

❏ 503 [M]	Spy with a Pie	1965	6.25	12.50	25.00
❏ S-503 [S]	Spy with a Pie	1965	7.50	15.00	30.00
❏ 517 [M]	Soupy Sales Sez Do the Mouse and Other Teen Hits	1965	6.25	12.50	25.00
❏ S-517 [S]	Soupy Sales Sez Do the Mouse and Other Teen Hits	1965	7.50	15.00	30.00

MCA

❏ 5274	Still Soupy After All These Years	1981	3.00	6.00	12.00

MOTOWN

❏ MS 686	A Bag of Soup	1969	6.25	12.50	25.00

REPRISE

❏ R 6010 [M]	The Soupy Sales Show	1961	7.50	15.00	30.00
❏ R9 6010 [S]	The Soupy Sales Show	1961	10.00	20.00	40.00
❏ R 6052 [M]	Up in the Air	1962	7.50	15.00	30.00
❏ R9 6052 [S]	Up in the Air	1962	10.00	20.00	40.00

SALLEE, VICKIE

45s

DOT

❏ 16651	Jimmy Darling/Wild Angel	1964	2.50	5.00	10.00
❏ 16710	Little Wishing Star/Oh My Love	1965	2.50	5.00	10.00

REPRISE

❏ 20118	There Goes the Lucky One/Your Favorite Lie	1962	3.75	7.50	15.00

SALLYANGIE Also see MIKE OLDFIELD.

Albums

WARNER BROS.

❏ WS 1783	Children of the Sun	1969	3.75	7.50	15.00

SALSOUL ORCHESTRA, THE

12-Inch Singles

SALSOUL

❏ 358 [DJ]	Deck the Halls (7:29)/The Salsoul Christmas Suite (7:59)	1981	3.00	6.00	12.00

45s

SALSOUL

❏ 2002	Salsoul Hustle/Salsoul Hustle (Part 2)	1975	—	2.50	5.00
❏ 2004	Tangerine/Salsoul Hustle	1975	—	2.50	5.00
❏ 2007	You're Just the Right Size/Chicago Bus Stop (Ooh I Like It)	1976	—	2.50	5.00
❏ 2011	Nice 'n' Naasty/Nightcrawler	1976	—	2.50	5.00

S

Number	Title (A Side/B Side)	Yr	VG	VG+	NM
❏ 2016	My Love Is Free/(B-side unknown)	1976	—	2.50	5.00
❏ 2018	Ritzy Mambo/Salsoul: 3001	1977	—	2.50	5.00
❏ 2037	Short Shorts/It's a New Day	1977	—	2.50	5.00
❏ 2038	Getaway/Magic Bird of Fire	1977	—	2.50	5.00
❏ 2052	We Wish You a Merry Christmas/ Merry Christmas All	1976	—	2.50	5.00
❏ 2052 [PS]	We Wish You a Merry Christmas/ Merry Christmas All	1976	—	3.00	6.00
❏ 2064	West Side Encounter — West Side Story (Medley)/Evergreen	1978	—	2.00	4.00
❏ 2072	Sgt. Pepper's Lonely Hearts Club Band/ Ease On Down the Road	1978	—	2.00	4.00
❏ 2077	The Little Drummer Boy/Christmas Time	1978	—	2.50	5.00
❏ 2086	Somebody to Love/(B-side unknown)	1979	—	2.00	4.00
❏ 2093	Street Sense/Sun After the Rain	1979	—	2.00	4.00
❏ 2096	How High/Nothing Can Change This Love	1979	—	2.00	4.00
❏ 2155	Deck The Halls/The Salsoul Christmas Suite	1981	—	2.00	4.00
❏ 7026	Take Some Time Out (For Love)/ (B-side unknown)	1982	—	—	3.00
❏ 7050	How I Love It So/(B-side unknown)	1983	—	—	3.00

Albums
SALSOUL

❏ CA-1001	Christmas Jollies	198?	2.00	4.00	8.00
—Reissue					
❏ CA-1004	Christmas Jollies II	198?	2.00	4.00	8.00
—Reissue					
❏ SZS 5501	The Salsoul Orchestra	1975	2.50	5.00	10.00
❏ SZS 5502	Nice 'n' Naasty	1976	2.50	5.00	10.00
❏ SZS 5507	Christmas Jollies	1976	3.00	6.00	12.00
❏ SZS 5515	Magic Journey	1977	2.50	5.00	10.00
❏ SA-8500	Up the Yellow Brick Road	1978	2.50	5.00	10.00
❏ SA-8508	Greatest Disco Hits/Music for Non-Stop Dancing	1978	2.50	5.00	10.00
❏ SA-8516	Street Sense	1979	2.50	5.00	10.00
❏ SA-8528	How High	1980	2.50	5.00	10.00
❏ SA 8547	Christmas Jollies II	1981	3.00	6.00	12.00
❏ SA-8552	Heat It Up	1982	2.50	5.00	10.00

SALT WATER TAFFY
45s
BUDDAH

❏ 37	Finders Keepers/He'll Pay	1968	2.00	4.00	8.00
❏ 57	Sticks and Stones/Suddenly I See	1968	2.00	4.00	8.00

METROMEDIA

❏ 220	Summertime Girl/Spend the Sunshine	1971	2.00	4.00	8.00

UNITED ARTISTS

❏ 50691	Summertime Girl/One Hand Washes the Other	1970	2.50	5.00	10.00

Albums
BUDDAH

❏ BDS-5021	Finders Keepers	1968	5.00	10.00	20.00

SALVATION
45s
ABC

❏ 11025	Love Comes in Funny Packages/Think Twice	1967	2.00	4.00	8.00

UNITED ARTISTS

❏ 50695	Tomorrow Is the First Day of the Rest of Your Life/Someday the Gray Will Come	1970	2.00	4.00	8.00

Albums
ABC

❏ S-623	Salvation	1968	5.00	10.00	20.00
❏ S-653	Gypsy Carnival Caravan	1968	5.00	10.00	20.00

SAM AND DAVE Also see SAM MOORE.
45s
ALSTON

❏ 777	Never, Never/Lotta Lovin'	1964	5.00	10.00	20.00

ATLANTIC

❏ 2517	You Don't Know What You Mean to Me/ This Is Your World	1968	—	3.00	6.00
❏ 2540	Can't You Find Another Way (Of Doing It)/ Still Is the Night	1968	—	3.00	6.00
❏ 2568	Everybody Got to Believe in Somebody/ If I Didn't Have a Girl Like You	1968	—	3.00	6.00
❏ 2590	Soul Sister, Brown Sugar/Come On In	1968	—	3.00	6.00
❏ 2608	Born Again/Get It	1969	—	3.00	6.00
❏ 2668	Holdin' On/Ooh Ooh Ooh	1969	—	3.00	6.00
❏ 2714	I'm Not an Indian Giver/ Baby-Baby Don't Stop Now	1970	—	3.00	6.00
❏ 2728	One Part Love, Two Parts Pain/ When You Steal from Me	1970	—	3.00	6.00
❏ 2733	When You Steal from Me (You're Only Hurting Yourself)/You Easily Excite Me	1970	—	3.00	6.00
❏ 2839	Don't Pull Your Love/Jody Ryder Got Killed	1971	—	3.00	6.00

CONTEMPO

❏ 7004	We Can Work It Out/Why Did You Do It	1977	—	2.50	5.00

MARLIN

❏ 6100	I Need Love/Keep a-Walkin'	1961	10.00	20.00	40.00
❏ 6104	No More Pain/My Love Belongs to You	1961	10.00	20.00	40.00

ROULETTE

❏ 4419	I Need Love/Keep a-Walkin'	1962	3.00	6.00	12.00
❏ 4445	No More Pain/My Love Belongs to You	1962	3.00	6.00	12.00
❏ 4461	She's Alright/It Feels So Nice	1962	3.00	6.00	12.00
❏ 4480	It Was So Nice While It Lasted/You Ain't No Big Thing, Baby	1963	3.00	6.00	12.00
❏ 4508	If She'll Still Have Me/Listening for My Name	1963	3.00	6.00	12.00
❏ 4533	I Found Out/I Got a Thing Going On	1963	3.00	6.00	12.00
❏ 4671	It Feels So Nice/It Was So Nice While It Lasted	1966	2.00	4.00	8.00

STAX

❏ 168	Goodnight Baby/A Place Nobody Can Find	1965	3.75	7.50	15.00
❏ 175	I Take What I Want/Sweet Home	1965	3.00	6.00	12.00
❏ 180	You Don't Know Like I Know/Blame Me (Don't Blame My Heart)	1965	3.00	6.00	12.00
❏ 189	Hold On! I'm a-Comin'/I Got Everything I Need	1966	3.75	7.50	15.00
❏ 198	Said I Wasn't Gonna Tell Nobody/ If You Got the Loving	1966	2.50	5.00	10.00
❏ 204	You Got Me Hummin'/Sleep Good Tonight	1967	2.50	5.00	10.00

Number	Title (A Side/B Side)	Yr	VG	VG+	NM
❏ 210	When Something Is Wrong with My Baby/Small Portion of Your Love	1967	2.50	5.00	10.00
❏ 218	Soothe Me/I Can't Stand Up for Falling Down	1967	2.50	5.00	10.00
❏ 231	Soul Man/May I Baby	1967	3.00	6.00	12.00
❏ 242	I Thank You/Wrap It Up	1968	3.00	6.00	12.00

UNITED ARTISTS

❏ XW438	A Little Bit of Good (Cures a Whole Lot of Bad)/ Blinded by Love	1974	—	3.00	6.00
❏ XW531	Under the Boardwalk/Give It What You Can	1974	—	3.00	6.00

Albums
ATLANTIC

❏ SD 8205	I Thank You	1968	6.25	12.50	25.00
❏ SD 8218	The Best of Sam and Dave	1969	5.00	10.00	20.00
❏ 81279	The Best of Sam and Dave	1985	2.50	5.00	10.00
❏ 81718	Soul Men	1987	2.50	5.00	10.00
—Reissue of Stax 725					

GUSTO

❏ 0045	Sweet and Funky Gold	197?	2.50	5.00	10.00

ROULETTE

❏ R-25323 [M]	Sam and Dave	1966	7.50	15.00	30.00
❏ SR-25323 [S]	Sam and Dave	1966	10.00	20.00	40.00

STAX

❏ ST-708 [M]	Hold On, I'm Comin'	1966	10.00	20.00	40.00
❏ STS-708 [S]	Hold On, I'm Comin'	1966	12.50	25.00	50.00
❏ ST-712 [M]	Double Dynamite	1966	7.50	15.00	30.00
❏ STS-712 [S]	Double Dynamite	1966	10.00	20.00	40.00
❏ ST-725 [M]	Soul Men	1967	7.50	15.00	30.00
❏ STS-725 [S]	Soul Men	1967	10.00	20.00	40.00

UNITED ARTISTS

❏ UA-LA524-G	Back At 'Cha!	1975	3.00	6.00	12.00

SAM THE SHAM AND THE PHARAOHS
45s
ATLANTIC

❏ 2767	Me and Bobby McGee/Key to the Highway	1970	—	2.50	5.00
—As "Sam Samudio"					

DINGO

❏ 001	Haunted House/ How Does a Cheating Woman Feel	1964	50.00	100.00	200.00

FRETONE

❏ 048	Wookie (Part 1)/Wookie (Part 2)	1977	2.50	5.00	10.00
—As "Sam the Sham"					
❏ 049	Ain't No Lie/Baby You Got It	1977	2.50	5.00	10.00
—As "Sam the Sham"					

MGM

❏ 13322	Wooly Bully/Ain't Gonna Move	1965	3.75	7.50	15.00
❏ 13364	Ju Ju Hand/Big City Lights	1965	3.00	6.00	12.00
❏ 13364 [PS]	Ju Ju Hand/Big City Lights	1965	5.00	10.00	20.00
❏ 13397	Ring Dang Doo/Don't Try It Again	1965	3.00	6.00	12.00
❏ 13397 [PS]	Ring Dang Doo/Don't Try It Again	1965	5.00	10.00	20.00
❏ 13452	Red Hot/Long Long Way	1966	3.00	6.00	12.00
❏ 13506	Lil' Red Riding Hood/Love Me Like Before	1966	3.75	7.50	15.00
❏ 13581	The Hair on My Chinny Chin Chin/ (I'm In with the) Out Crowd	1966	3.00	6.00	12.00
❏ 13581 [PS]	The Hair on My Chinny Chin Chin/ (I'm In with the) Out Crowd	1966	5.00	10.00	20.00
❏ 13649	How Do You Catch a Girl/Love You Left Behind	1966	3.00	6.00	12.00
❏ 13649 [PS]	How Do You Catch a Girl/Love You Left Behind	1966	5.00	10.00	20.00
❏ 13713	Oh That's Good, No That's Bad/ Take What You Can Get	1967	2.50	5.00	10.00
❏ 13747	Black Sheep/My Day's Gonna Come	1967	2.50	5.00	10.00
❏ 13803	Banned in Boston/Money's My Problem	1967	2.50	5.00	10.00
—As "The Sam the Sham Revue"					
❏ 13863	Yakety Yak/Let Our Love Light Shine	1967	2.50	5.00	10.00
—As "The Sam the Sham Revue"					
❏ 13920	Old Mac Donald Has a Boogaloo Farm/I Never Was No One	1968	2.50	5.00	10.00
❏ 13972	I Couldn't Spell !!@!/Down Home Strut	1968	3.75	7.50	15.00
❏ 14021	Wolly Bully/Ain't Gonna Move	1968	2.50	5.00	10.00
❏ 14642	Fate/Oh Lo	1973	2.50	5.00	10.00

PHILCO-FORD

❏ HP-3	Ju Ju Hand/Wooly Bully	1967	7.50	15.00	30.00
—4-inch plastic "Hip Pocket Record" with color sleeve					

TUPELO

❏ 2982	Betty and Dupree/Manchild	1963	15.00	30.00	60.00

XL

❏ 905	The Signifyin' Monkey/Juimonos	1964	12.50	25.00	50.00
❏ 906	Wooly Bully/Ain't Gonna Move	1965	75.00	150.00	300.00

Albums
ATLANTIC

❏ SD 8271	Hard and Heavy	1971	3.75	7.50	15.00
—As "Sam Samudio"					

MGM

❏ E-4297 [M]	Wooly Bully	1965	7.50	15.00	30.00
❏ SE-4297 [S]	Wooly Bully	1965	10.00	20.00	40.00
❏ E-4317 [M]	Their Second Album	1965	6.25	12.50	25.00
❏ SE-4317 [S]	Their Second Album	1965	7.50	15.00	30.00
❏ E-4347 [M]	On Tour	1966	6.25	12.50	25.00
❏ SE-4347 [S]	On Tour	1966	7.50	15.00	30.00
❏ E-4407 [M]	Lil' Red Riding Hood	1966	6.25	12.50	25.00
❏ SE-4407 [S]	Lil' Red Riding Hood	1966	7.50	15.00	30.00
❏ E-4422 [M]	The Best of Sam the Sham and the Pharaohs	1967	5.00	10.00	20.00
❏ SE-4422 [S]	The Best of Sam the Sham and the Pharaohs	1967	6.25	12.50	25.00
❏ E-4477 [M]	Nefertiti	1967	6.25	12.50	25.00
❏ SE-4477 [S]	Nefertiti	1967	6.25	12.50	25.00
❏ SE-4477	The Sam The Sham Revue	1968	5.00	10.00	20.00
—Retitled reissue					
❏ SE-4526	Ten of Pentacles	1968	5.00	10.00	20.00
❏ ST 90422 [S]	Wooly Bully	1965	12.50	25.00	50.00
—Capitol Record Club edition					
❏ T 90422 [M]	Wooly Bully	1965	10.00	20.00	40.00
—Capitol Record Club edition					

POLYDOR

❏ 827917-1	The Best of Sam the Sham and the Pharaohs	1985	2.50	5.00	10.00

Number	Title (A Side/B Side)	Yr	VG	VG+	NM

RHINO
- ❏ RNLP-122 — Pharoahization: The Best of Sam the Sham and the Pharoahs (1965-1967) — 1986 — 2.50 — 5.00 — 10.00

SAMMY AND THE DEL-LARKS
45s
EA-JAY
- ❏ 100 — Baby Come On/I Never Will Forget — 1961 — 50.00 — 100.00 — 200.00

SAMMY AND THEODORE
45s
HIT
- ❏ 235 — Sounds of Silence/Flowers on the Wall — 1966 — 2.00 — 4.00 — 8.00
—B-side by the Sheridan Brothers
- ❏ 246 — Homeward Bound/Woman — 1966 — 2.00 — 4.00 — 8.00
—B-side by Bobby and Buddy
- ❏ 259 — I Am a Rock/Did You Ever Have to Make Up Your Mind — 1966 — 2.00 — 4.00 — 8.00
—B-side by the Jalopy Five
- ❏ 323 — Scarborough Fair (/Canticle)/(Theme from) Valley of the Dolls — 1968 — 2.00 — 4.00 — 8.00
—B-side by Kathy Shannon

SAMUDIO, SAM   See SAM THE SHAM AND THE PHAROAHS.

SAN REMO GOLDEN STRINGS
45s
GORDY
- ❏ 7060 — Festival Time/Joy Road — 1967 — 6.25 — 12.50 — 25.00
RIC-TIC
- ❏ 104 — Hungry for Love/All Turned On — 1965 — 3.00 — 6.00 — 12.00
- ❏ 108 — I'm Satisfied/Blueberry Hill — 1965 — 3.00 — 6.00 — 12.00
- ❏ 112 — Festival Time/Joy Road — 1966 — 3.00 — 6.00 — 12.00
- ❏ 116 — International Love Theme/Quanto Si Bella — 1966 — 3.00 — 6.00 — 12.00
Albums
GORDY
- ❏ G-923 [M] — Hungry for Love — 1967 — 6.25 — 12.50 — 25.00
- ❏ GS-923 [S] — Hungry for Love — 1967 — 7.50 — 15.00 — 30.00
- ❏ GS-928 — Swing — 1968 — 5.00 — 10.00 — 20.00
RIC-TIC
- ❏ 901 [M] — Hungry for Love — 1966 — 12.50 — 25.00 — 50.00
- ❏ S-901 [S] — Hungry for Love — 1966 — 15.00 — 30.00 — 60.00

SAN SEBASTIAN STRINGS, THE
45s
WARNER BROS.
- ❏ 7012 — Days of the Dancing/Pushing the Clouds Away — 1967 — — — 2.50 — 5.00
- ❏ 7084 — Mud Kids/Tender Earth — 1967 — — — 2.50 — 5.00
- ❏ 7754 — And Every Day Was Christmas/Sunset Colors — 1973 — — — 2.50 — 5.00
Albums
STANYAN
- ❏ 10043 — La Mer — 1972 — 2.50 — 5.00 — 10.00
WARNER BROS.
- ❏ W 1670 [M] — The Sea — 1967 — 3.75 — 7.50 — 15.00
- ❏ WS 1670 [S] — The Sea — 1967 — 3.00 — 6.00 — 12.00
- ❏ W 1705 [M] — The Earth — 1967 — 3.75 — 7.50 — 15.00
- ❏ WS 1705 [S] — The Earth — 1967 — 3.00 — 6.00 — 12.00
- ❏ WS 1720 — The Sky — 1968 — 3.00 — 6.00 — 12.00
- ❏ 3WS 1730 [(3)] — The Sea, The Earth, The Sky — 1968 — 5.00 — 10.00 — 20.00
- ❏ WS 1764 — Home to the Sea — 1968 — 3.00 — 6.00 — 12.00
- ❏ WS 1795 — For Lovers — 1969 — 3.00 — 6.00 — 12.00
- ❏ 3WS 1827 [(3)] — The Complete Sea — 1969 — 5.00 — 10.00 — 20.00
- ❏ WS 1839 — The Soft Sea — 1970 — 3.00 — 6.00 — 12.00
- ❏ BS 2622 — Winter — 1972 — 2.50 — 5.00 — 10.00
- ❏ BS 2707 — Summer — 1973 — 2.50 — 5.00 — 10.00
- ❏ BS4-2707 [Q] — Summer — 1973 — 3.75 — 7.50 — 15.00
- ❏ 4WS 2754 [(4)] — Seasons — 1973 — 5.00 — 10.00 — 20.00
- ❏ BS 2768 — Bouquet — The Best of the San Sebastian Strings — 1974 — 2.50 — 5.00 — 10.00
- ❏ BS 2837 — With Love — 1975 — 2.50 — 5.00 — 10.00
- ❏ ST-91618 — Home to the Sea — 1968 — 3.75 — 7.50 — 15.00
—Capitol Record Club edition

SANCHEZ, JOE
45s
IMPERIAL
- ❏ 66190 — Unlucky Me/Our Love Baby Is Running Down — 1966 — 5.00 — 10.00 — 20.00

SANDALS, THE
45s
AURA
- ❏ 4501 — School's Out/Wild As the Sea — 1964 — 6.25 — 12.50 — 25.00
—As "The Sandells"
WORLD PACIFIC
- ❏ 405 — Scrambler/Out Front — 1964 — 6.25 — 12.50 — 25.00
—As "The Sandells"
- ❏ 415 — Endless Summer/6-Pak — 1964 — 6.25 — 12.50 — 25.00
- ❏ 421 — All Over Again/Always — 1965 — 3.75 — 7.50 — 15.00
- ❏ 77840 — Theme from Endless Summer/6-Pak — 1966 — 3.75 — 7.50 — 15.00
- ❏ 77852 — Tell Us Dylan/Why Should I Cry — 1966 — 3.75 — 7.50 — 15.00
- ❏ 77867 — Cloudy/House of Painted Glass — 1967 — 3.75 — 7.50 — 15.00
Albums
WORLD PACIFIC
- ❏ ST-1818 [S] — Scrambler — 1964 — 25.00 — 50.00 — 100.00
—As "The Sandells"; black vinyl
- ❏ ST-1818 [S] — Scrambler — 1964 — 62.50 — 125.00 — 250.00
—As "The Sandells"; red vinyl
- ❏ WP-1818 [M] — Scrambler — 1964 — 20.00 — 40.00 — 80.00
- ❏ ST-1832 [S] — The Endless Summer — 1966 — 7.50 — 15.00 — 30.00
- ❏ WP-1832 [M] — The Endless Summer — 1966 — 6.25 — 12.50 — 25.00
- ❏ ST-21884 — The Last of the Ski Bums — 1969 — 6.25 — 12.50 — 25.00
—With skiers' silhouettes on cover
- ❏ ST-21884 — The Last of the Ski Bums — 1969 — 6.25 — 12.50 — 25.00
—With Volkswagon bus on cover

SANDERS, BOBBY
45s
KAYBO
- ❏ 618 — It Was You/I'm On My Way — 1961 — 25.00 — 50.00 — 100.00
KENT
- ❏ 382 — Maybe I'm Wrong/You've Forgotten Me — 1962 — 75.00 — 150.00 — 300.00
PICK-A-HIT
- ❏ 100 — Lover/The Way I Feel — 196? — 2.50 — 5.00 — 10.00

SANDERS, ED
Albums
REPRISE
- ❏ MS 2105 — Beer Cans on the Moon — 1972 — 6.25 — 12.50 — 25.00
- ❏ RS-6374 — Sanders' Truckstop — 1969 — 6.25 — 12.50 — 25.00

SANDFORD, CHRIS
45s
FONTANA
- ❏ 1534 — (I Wish They Wouldn't Always Say) I Sound Like the Guy from USA Blues/Little Man-Nobody Cares — 1965 — 3.00 — 6.00 — 12.00

SANDLER AND YOUNG   Also known as "Tony Sandler and Ralph Young."
45s
CAPITOL
- ❏ 2083 — In the Sunshine Days/Seven Lonely Days — 1968 — — — 3.00 — 6.00
- ❏ 2157 — Cotton Fields/Can I Trust You — 1968 — — — 3.00 — 6.00
- ❏ 2333 — I Sing Noel/Santa Claus Is Coming to Town — 1968 — — — 3.00 — 6.00
- ❏ 2362 — Life Is/Something Is Happening — 1968 — — — 3.00 — 6.00
- ❏ 2423 — Cuando Sali De Cuba/Viva El Amor — 1969 — — — 3.00 — 6.00
- ❏ 2578 — Heather/Pretty Things Come in Twos — 1969 — — — 2.50 — 5.00
- ❏ 2636 — Brazilian Love Song/On Days Like This — 1969 — — — 2.50 — 5.00
- ❏ 5590 — Let It Be Now/When Summer Is Gone — 1966 — — — 3.00 — 6.00
- ❏ 5795 — Chicago/Dominique — 1966 — — — 3.00 — 6.00
- ❏ 5873 — C'est Si Bon/Walk an Autumn Day with Me — 1967 — — — 3.00 — 6.00
- ❏ 5928 — More and More/Imagine Me — 1967 — — — 3.00 — 6.00
P.I.P.
- ❏ 6514 — Medley: I Believe-Ave Maria/(B-side unknown) — 1975 — — — 2.00 — 4.00
Albums
CAPITOL
- ❏ ST-159 — Together — 1968 — 3.00 — 6.00 — 12.00
- ❏ ST-241 — Pretty Things Come in Twos — 1969 — 3.00 — 6.00 — 12.00
- ❏ ST-449 — Honey Come Back — 1970 — 3.00 — 6.00 — 12.00
- ❏ ST 2598 [S] — Side by Side — 1966 — 3.75 — 7.50 — 15.00
- ❏ T 2598 [M] — Side by Side — 1966 — 3.00 — 6.00 — 12.00
—also known as "Tony Sandler and Ralph Young"
- ❏ ST 2686 [S] — On the Move — 1967 — 3.75 — 7.50 — 15.00
- ❏ T 2686 [M] — On the Move — 1967 — 3.00 — 6.00 — 12.00
- ❏ ST 2802 [S] — More and More — 1967 — 3.00 — 6.00 — 12.00
- ❏ T 2802 [M] — More and More — 1967 — 3.75 — 7.50 — 15.00
- ❏ ST 2967 — The Christmas World of Sandler and Young — 1968 — 3.00 — 6.00 — 12.00
HOLIDAY
- ❏ HDY 1942 — Happy Holidays! — 1981 — 2.00 — 4.00 — 8.00
—Reissue of True Value 2 (almost identical front cover, different back cover)
RALTON
- ❏ SY 200 — Re-Discover Christmas — 19?? — 3.75 — 7.50 — 15.00
—Has same contents as "Happy Holidays, Volume 11"; is this the original?
TRUE VALUE
- ❏ 1 — Happy Holidays, Album Eleven — 1975 — 2.50 — 5.00 — 10.00
—Sold only at True Value Hardware stores
- ❏ 2 — Happy Holidays! Album Twelve — 1976 — 2.50 — 5.00 — 10.00
—Sold only at True Value Hardware stores

SANDMEN, THE (1)
45s
BLUE JAY
- ❏ 5002 — If You Want Me/Searching for a New Love — 1965 — 6.25 — 12.50 — 25.00

SANDMEN, THE (2)   BROOK BENTON was in this group.
45s
OKEH
- ❏ 7052 — When I Grow Too Old to Dream/Somebody to Love — 1955 — 12.50 — 25.00 — 50.00

SANDPIPERS, THE
45s
A&M
- ❏ 806 — Guantanamera/What Makes You Dream, Pretty Girl — 1966 — — — 3.00 — 6.00
- ❏ 819 — Louie Louie/Things We Said Today — 1966 — 2.00 — 4.00 — 8.00
- ❏ 835 — La Bamba/For Baby — 1967 — — — 3.00 — 6.00
- ❏ 851 — It's Over/Glass — 1967 — — — 3.00 — 6.00
- ❏ 861 — Woman/Bon Soir Dame — 1967 — — — 3.00 — 6.00
- ❏ 880 — Softly, As I Leave You/Cuando Sali De Cuba — 1967 — — — 3.00 — 6.00
- ❏ 939 — Wooden Heart/Quando M'annamoro — 1968 — — — 3.00 — 6.00
- ❏ 968 — Softly/Cancion de Amor — 1968 — — — 3.00 — 6.00
- ❏ 997 — Suzanne/Let Go! — 1968 — — — 3.00 — 6.00
- ❏ 1085 — Temptations/Wave — 1969 — — — 3.00 — 6.00
- ❏ 1116 — Kum-Ba-Ya/Yellow Days — 1969 — — — 3.00 — 6.00
- ❏ 1134 — Come Saturday Morning/Pretty Flamingo — 1969 — — — 3.00 — 6.00
- ❏ 1185 — Come Saturday Morning/To Put Up with You — 1970 — — — 2.50 — 5.00
- ❏ 1208 — Beyond the Valley of the Dolls/Santo Domingo — 1970 — — — 2.50 — 5.00
- ❏ 1227 — Free to Carry On/The Whole World in His Hands — 1970 — — — 2.50 — 5.00
- ❏ 1249 — Drifter/Sound of Love — 1971 — — — 2.50 — 5.00
- ❏ 1280 — Chotta Matte Kudasel/Free to Carry On — 1971 — — — 2.50 — 5.00
- ❏ 1306 — Never My Love/Leland Loftis — 1971 — — — 2.50 — 5.00
- ❏ 1314 — A Gift of Song/Never My Love — 1971 — — — 2.50 — 5.00
- ❏ 1372 — Old Fashioned Love Song/Never Can Say Goodbye — 1972 — — — 2.50 — 5.00
- ❏ 1388 — The World Is a Circle/(Baby I Could Be) So Good at Lovin' You — 1972 — — — 2.50 — 5.00
Albums
A&M
- ❏ LP-117 [M] — Guantanamera — 1966 — 3.00 — 6.00 — 12.00
- ❏ LP-125 [M] — The Sandpipers — 1967 — 3.75 — 7.50 — 15.00
- ❏ SP-3525 [(2)] — Foursider — 1973 — 3.00 — 6.00 — 12.00
- ❏ SP-4117 [S] — Guantanamera — 1966 — 3.75 — 7.50 — 15.00

S

Number	Title (A Side/B Side)	Yr	VG	VG+	NM
❏ SP-4125 [S]	The Sandpipers	1967	3.00	6.00	12.00
❏ SP-4135	Misty Roses	1967	3.00	6.00	12.00
❏ SP-4147	Softly	1968	3.00	6.00	12.00
❏ SP-4159	The Spanish Album	1969	3.00	6.00	12.00
❏ SP-4180	The Wonder of You	1969	3.00	6.00	12.00
❏ SP-4246	Greatest Hits	1970	3.00	6.00	12.00
❏ SP-4262	Come Saturday Morning	1970	3.00	6.00	12.00
❏ SP-4328	A Gift of Song	1972	3.00	6.00	12.00
❏ SP-6014 [(2)]	Foursider	198?	2.50	5.00	10.00
—Reissue of 3525					

SANDS, JODIE
45s
ABC-PARAMOUNT

Number	Title (A Side/B Side)	Yr	VG	VG+	NM
❏ 10337	We Had Words/Uno Momento	1962	3.00	6.00	12.00
❏ 10376	Hello, Heartache/This Little Fool	1962	3.00	6.00	12.00
❏ 10451	Time to Love/Charming Little Barefoot	1963	3.00	6.00	12.00
BERNLO					
❏ 1003	Love Me Always/Everybody Needs Somebody	1957	6.25	12.50	25.00
CHANCELLOR					
❏ 1003	With All My Heart/More Than Only Friends	1957	6.25	12.50	25.00
❏ 1005	If You're Not Completely Satisfied/Sayonara	1957	5.00	10.00	20.00
❏ 1009	The Way I Love You/Tantalizin' Love	1957	5.00	10.00	20.00
❏ 1015	Love Me Again/All I Ask of You	1958	5.00	10.00	20.00
❏ 1023	Someday/Always in My Heart	1958	5.00	10.00	20.00
PARIS					
❏ 543	I'd Cry No Tears/Kiss By Kiss	1960	3.75	7.50	15.00
❏ 551	Love Me Forever/Give Me a Break	1960	3.75	7.50	15.00
SIGNATURE					
❏ 12015	Turnabout Heart/Solo A Te Mio Amor	1959	3.75	7.50	15.00
TEEN					
❏ 109	Love Me Always/Everybody Needs Somebody	1955	10.00	20.00	40.00
THOR					
❏ 101	Hold Me/What Does It Mean	1959	5.00	10.00	20.00

SANDS, TOMMY
45s
(NO LABEL)

Number	Title (A Side/B Side)	Yr	VG	VG+	NM
❏ T 929 [DJ]	People in Love/That's All I Want from You	1957	12.50	25.00	50.00
—"Promotion Record" with no label name; used to promote the movie "Sing Boy Sing"; T 929 is catalog number of LP and the most prominent number on label					
ABC-PARAMOUNT					
❏ 10466	Connie/Young Man's Fancy	1963	2.50	5.00	10.00
❏ 10480	Cinderella/Only 'Cause I'm Lonely	1963	2.50	5.00	10.00
❏ 10539	Won't You Be My Girl/Ten Dollars and a Clean White Shirt	1964	2.50	5.00	10.00
❏ 10591	Something More/Kisses (Love Theme)	1964	2.50	5.00	10.00
CAPITOL					
❏ F3639	Teen-Age Crush/Hep Dee Hootie	1957	6.25	12.50	25.00
❏ F3690	Ring-A-Ding-A-Ding/My Love Song	1957	6.25	12.50	25.00
❏ F3723	Goin' Steady/Ring My Phone	1957	6.25	12.50	25.00
❏ F3743	Let Me Be Loved/Fantastically Foolish	1957	5.00	10.00	20.00
❏ F3810	A Swingin' Romance/Man, Like Wow!	1957	5.00	10.00	20.00
❏ F3867	Sing, Boy, Sing/Crazy 'Cause I Love You	1957	5.00	10.00	20.00
❏ F3953	Teenage Doll/Hawaiian Rock	1958	5.00	10.00	20.00
❏ F3985	Big Date/After the Senior Prom	1958	5.00	10.00	20.00
❏ F4036	Blue Ribbon Baby/I Love You Because	1958	5.00	10.00	20.00
❏ F4082	Bigger Than Texas/The Worryin' Kind	1958	5.00	10.00	20.00
❏ F4160	Is It Ever Gonna Happen/I Ain't Gittin' Rid of You	1959	3.75	7.50	15.00
❏ F4231	Sinner Man/Bring Me Your Love	1959	3.75	7.50	15.00
❏ F4259	I'll Be Seeing You/That's the Way I Am	1959	3.75	7.50	15.00
❏ F4259 [PS]	I'll Be Seeing You/That's the Way I Am	1959	7.50	15.00	30.00
❏ 4316	You Hold the Future/I Gotta Have You	1959	3.75	7.50	15.00
❏ 4366	That's Love/Crossroads	1960	3.75	7.50	15.00
❏ 4405	The Old Oaken Bucket/These Are the Things You Are	1960	3.75	7.50	15.00
❏ 4470	Doctor Heartache/On and On	1960	3.75	7.50	15.00
❏ 4580	Love in a Goldfish Bowl/I Love My Baby	1961	3.00	6.00	12.00
❏ 4611	Rainbow/Remember Me to Jennie	1961	3.00	6.00	12.00
❏ 4660	Wrong Side of Love/Jimmy's Song	1961	3.00	6.00	12.00
IMPERIAL					
❏ 66174	As Long As I'm Travelin'/It's the Only One I've Got	1966	2.00	4.00	8.00
❏ 66229	Second Star to the Left/Candy Store Prophet	1967	2.00	4.00	8.00
LIBERTY					
❏ 55807	Love's Funny/One Rose Today, One Rose Tomorrow	1965	2.00	4.00	8.00
❏ 55842	The Statue/Little Rosita	1965	2.00	4.00	8.00
❏ 55864	Waitin' in Your Welfare Line/Don't Do It Darlin'	1966	—	—	—
—Unreleased					
RCA VICTOR					
❏ 47-5435	Love Pains/Transfer	1953	7.50	15.00	30.00
❏ 47-5510	Roses Speak Louder Than Words/Spanish Coquita	1953	7.50	15.00	30.00
❏ 47-5628	A Dime and a Dollar/Life Is So Lonesome	1954	7.50	15.00	30.00
❏ 47-5697	Never Let Me Go/I Know About the Bees	1954	7.50	15.00	30.00
❏ 47-5800	Don't Drop It/A Place for Girls Like You	1954	7.50	15.00	30.00
❏ 47-6007	Kissin' Ain't No Fun/Something's Bound to Go Wrong	1955	7.50	15.00	30.00
❏ 47-6868	Don't Drop It/Love Pains	1957	5.00	10.00	20.00
SUPERSCOPE					
❏ 007	Seasons in the Sun/Ain't No Big Thing	1969	—	3.00	6.00

7-Inch Extended Plays
CAPITOL

Number	Title (A Side/B Side)	Yr	VG	VG+	NM
❏ PRO 351 [DJ]	Goin' Steady/I Don't Know Why (I Just Do)//Graduation Day/A-You're Adorable (The Alphabet Song)	1957	10.00	20.00	40.00
—Promotional sampler from "Steady Date" album					
❏ EAP 1-848	*Goin' Steady/Teach Me Tonight/Gonna Get a Girl/Somewhere Along the Way	1957	7.50	15.00	30.00
❏ EAP 1-848 [PS]	Steady Date with Tommy Sands, Part 1	1957	7.50	15.00	30.00
❏ EAP 2-848	Walkin' My Baby Back Home/Too Young to Go Steady/A-You're Adorable (The Alphabet Song)/Graduation Day	1957	7.50	15.00	30.00
❏ EAP 2-848 [PS]	Steady Date with Tommy Sands, Part 2	1957	7.50	15.00	30.00

Number	Title (A Side/B Side)	Yr	VG	VG+	NM
❏ EAP 3-848	Ring My Phone/I Don't Know Why//Too Young/I Don't Care Who Knows It	1957	7.50	15.00	30.00
❏ EAP 3-848 [PS]	Steady Date with Tommy Sands, Part 3	1957	7.50	15.00	30.00
❏ EAP 1-851	*Teen-Age Crush/My Love Song/Hep Dee Hootie (Cutie Wootie)/Ring-a-Ding-a-Ding	1957	7.50	15.00	30.00
❏ EAP 1-851 [PS]	Teen-Age Crush	1957	7.50	15.00	30.00
❏ EAP 1-929	*I'm Gonna Walk and Talk with My Lord/Who Baby/Rock of Ages/Sing Boy Sing	1958	7.50	15.00	30.00
❏ EAP 1-929 [PS]	Sing Boy Sing, Part 1	1958	7.50	15.00	30.00
❏ EAP 2-929	*A Bundle of Dreams/Just a Little Bit More/Soda-Pop Pop/Would I Love You	1958	7.50	15.00	30.00
❏ EAP 2-929 [PS]	Sing Boy Sing, Part 2	1958	7.50	15.00	30.00
❏ EAP 3-929	People in Love/Crazy Cause I Love You//Your Daddy Wants to Do Right/That's All I Want from You	1958	7.50	15.00	30.00
❏ EAP 3-929 [PS]	Sing Boy Sing, Part 3	1958	7.50	15.00	30.00

Albums
CAPITOL

Number	Title (A Side/B Side)	Yr	VG	VG+	NM
❏ T 848 [M]	Steady Date with Tommy Sands	1957	15.00	30.00	60.00
❏ T 929 [M]	Sing Boy Sing	1958	15.00	30.00	60.00
❏ T 1081 [M]	Sands Storm	1959	12.50	25.00	50.00
❏ ST 1123 [S]	This Thing Called Love	1959	10.00	20.00	40.00
❏ T 1123 [M]	This Thing Called Love	1959	7.50	15.00	30.00
❏ ST 1239 [S]	When I'm Thinking of You	1960	10.00	20.00	40.00
❏ T 1239 [M]	When I'm Thinking of You	1960	7.50	15.00	30.00
❏ ST 1364 [S]	Sands at the Sands	1960	10.00	20.00	40.00
❏ T 1364 [M]	Sands at the Sands	1960	7.50	15.00	30.00
❏ ST 1426 [S]	Dream with Me	1961	10.00	20.00	40.00
❏ T 1426 [M]	Dream with Me	1961	7.50	15.00	30.00
GREEN LINNET					
❏ SIF-3044	Singing of the Times	1989	3.00	6.00	12.00

SANDY, FRANK
45s
MARK

Number	Title (A Side/B Side)	Yr	VG	VG+	NM
❏ 138	Shamrock/Here She Comes	1959	10.00	20.00	40.00
MGM					
❏ 12626	Somebody Loves Me/Tarantella Rock	1958	12.50	25.00	50.00
❏ 12678	Let's Go Rock 'N' Roll/Midnight Stomp	1958	25.00	50.00	100.00

SANDY AND DICK   Also see DICK ST. JOHN.
45s
CONGRESS

Number	Title (A Side/B Side)	Yr	VG	VG+	NM
❏ 6015	Groove With What You Got/Sing Along with Groove With What You Got	1970	2.00	4.00	8.00
❏ 6021	Sweet Sweet Lovin'/Quick Like a Bunny	1970	2.00	4.00	8.00

SANETTES, THE
45s
OHN-J

Number	Title (A Side/B Side)	Yr	VG	VG+	NM
❏ 1001	Merry Christmas/Blessings From Above	1964	2.50	5.00	10.00

SANG, SAMANTHA
45s
ATCO

Number	Title (A Side/B Side)	Yr	VG	VG+	NM
❏ 6705	Don't Let It Happen Again/Love of a Woman	1969	—	3.00	6.00
❏ 6875	Nothing in the World Like Love/Mia Bamba	1972	—	2.50	5.00
PRIVATE STOCK					
❏ 45,178	Emotion/When Love Is Gone	1977	—	2.00	4.00
—Originals have brown labels					
❏ 45,178	Emotion/When Love Is Gone	1978	—	—	3.00
—Second pressings have skyline labels					
❏ 45,188	You Keep Me Dancing/Change of Heart	1978	—	—	3.00
UNITED ARTISTS					
❏ XW1297	I'll Never Get Enough of You/From Dance to Love	1979	—	—	3.00
❏ 1313	In the Midnight Hour/Now	1979	—	—	3.00
Albums					
LIBERTY					
❏ LN-10017	From Dance to Love	1980	2.00	4.00	8.00
—Budget-line reissue					
PRIVATE STOCK					
❏ PS-7009	Emotion	1978	2.50	5.00	10.00
UNITED ARTISTS					
❏ UA-LA965-H	From Dance to Love	1979	2.50	5.00	10.00

SANS, PEGGY
45s
TOLLIE

Number	Title (A Side/B Side)	Yr	VG	VG+	NM
❏ 9018	Give Your Love/Snow Man	1964	2.50	5.00	10.00

SANTANA   Also see JOURNEY; CARLOS SANTANA.
12-Inch Singles
COLUMBIA

Number	Title (A Side/B Side)	Yr	VG	VG+	NM
❏ AS 383 [DJ]	She's Not There (4:08) (2:58) (stereo/mono)	1977	3.75	7.50	15.00
❏ AS 517 [DJ]	Well All Right (short) (long)	1978	3.00	6.00	12.00
❏ AS 585 [DJ]	One Chain (Don't Make No Prison) (Long) (Short) (both on each side)	1978	2.00	4.00	8.00
❏ AS 842 [DJ]	Love Theme from Spartacus/Song for My Brother/Swapan Tari	1980	3.00	6.00	12.00
❏ AS 937 [DJ]	Winning/E Papa Ne	1981	2.00	4.00	8.00
❏ AS 1266 [DJ]	Sensitive Kind/Sensitive Kind (Live)	1981	2.50	5.00	10.00
❏ AS 1998 [DJ]	Say It Again (same on both sides)	1985	—	3.00	6.00
❏ CAS 2068 [DJ]	I'm the One Who Loves You (same on both sides)	1985	—	3.00	6.00
❏ CAS 2630 [DJ]	Veracruz (same on both sides)	1987	—	3.00	6.00
❏ 06762	Vera Cruz (Cool Mix)/Vera Cruz (Cool Whip Mix)	1987	—	3.00	6.00
❏ 10957	One Chain (Don't Make No Prison)/Life Is a Lady Holiday	1978	2.50	5.00	10.00

45s
ARISTA

Number	Title (A Side/B Side)	Yr	VG	VG+	NM
❏ 13773	Maria Maria (featuring The Product G&B)/Smooth (featuring Rob Thomas)	2000	—	2.50	5.00
❏ 50980	The Game of Love/Nothing at All	2003	—	2.00	4.00
—A-side featuring Michelle Branch; B-side featuring Musiq					
COLUMBIA					
❏ 01050	Winning/The Brightest Star	1981	—	2.00	4.00

Number	Title (A Side/B Side)	Yr	VG	VG+	NM
❏ AE7 1064 [DJ]	All the Love of the Universe/Just in Time to See the Sun	1972	2.50	5.00	10.00
❏ 02178	The Sensitive Kind/American Gypsy	1981	—	2.00	4.00
❏ 02178 [PS]	The Sensitive Kind/American Gypsy	1981	—	2.50	5.00
❏ 02519	Searchin'/Tales of Kilimanjaro	1981	—	2.00	4.00
❏ 03160	Hold On/Oxun	1982	—	2.00	4.00
❏ 03268	Hold On	1982	—	3.00	6.00
—One-sided budget release					
❏ 03376	Nowhere to Run/Nueva York	1982	—	2.00	4.00
❏ 04034	Havana Moon/Lightnin'	1983	—	2.00	4.00
❏ 04758	Say It Again/Touchdown Raiders	1985	—	—	3.00
❏ 04758 [PS]	Say It Again/Touchdown Raiders	1985	—	2.00	4.00
❏ 04912	I'm the One Who Loves You/Right Now	1985	—	—	3.00
❏ 05677	They All Went to Mexico/Slow Movin' Outlaw	1985	—	—	3.00
—A-side: Willie Nelson and Carlos Santana; B-side: Willie and Lacy J. Dalton					
❏ 06654	Vera Cruz/Manuela	1987	—	2.00	4.00
❏ 07038	Vera Cruz (Remix)/Manuela	1987	—	—	3.00
❏ 07140	Praise/Love Is You	1987	—	—	3.00
❏ 10073	Mirage/Flor de Canela	1974	—	2.50	5.00
❏ 10088	Give and Take/Love Is Anew	1975	—	2.50	5.00
❏ 10336	Let It Shine/Tell Me Are You Tired	1976	—	2.50	5.00
❏ 10353	Dance Sister Dance (Baila Mi Hermana)/Let Me	1976	—	2.50	5.00
❏ 10421	Take Me with You/Europa (Earth's Cry Heaven's Smile)	1976	—	2.50	5.00
❏ 10481	Let the Children Play/Carnival	1977	—	2.50	5.00
❏ 10524	Give Me Love/Revelations	1977	—	2.50	5.00
❏ 10616	She's Not There/Zulu	1977	—	2.50	5.00
❏ 10677	Black Magic Woman/I'll Be Waiting	1978	—	2.50	5.00
❏ 10839	Well, All Right/Jericho	1978	—	2.50	5.00
❏ 10873	Stormy/Move On	1978	—	2.50	5.00
❏ 10938	One Chain (Don't Make a Prison)/Life Is a Lady-Holiday	1979	—	2.00	4.00
❏ 11144	You Know That I Love You/Aqua Marine	1979	—	2.00	4.00
❏ 11218	All I Ever Wanted/Lightning in the Sky	1980	—	2.00	4.00
❏ 45010	Jin-Go-Lo-Ba/Persuasion	1969	—	3.00	6.00
—Same song, different A-side title					
❏ 45010	Jingo/Persuasion	1969	—	3.00	6.00
❏ 45069	Evil Ways/Waiting	1970	—	3.00	6.00
❏ 45270	Black Magic Woman/Hope You're Feeling Better	1970	—	3.00	6.00
❏ 45270 [PS]	Black Magic Woman/Hope You're Feeling Better	1970	3.00	6.00	12.00
❏ 45330	Oye Como Va/Samba Pa Ti	1971	—	2.50	5.00
❏ 45330 [PS]	Oye Como Va/Samba Pa Ti	1971	2.00	4.00	8.00
❏ 45472	Everybody's Everything/Guajira	1971	—	2.50	5.00
❏ 45552	No One to Depend On/Taboo	1972	—	2.50	5.00
—Gray label					
❏ 45552 [PS]	No One to Depend On/Taboo	1972	2.00	4.00	8.00
❏ 45552	No One to Depend On/Taboo	1973	—	2.00	4.00
—Orange label					
❏ 45753	Look Up/All the Love of the Universe	1973	—	2.50	5.00
❏ 45999	When I Look Into Your Eyes/Samba De Sausalito	1974	—	2.50	5.00
❏ 46067	Incident at Neshabur/Samba Pa Ti	1974	—	2.50	5.00
7-Inch Extended Plays					
COLUMBIA					
❏ 7-30595	Taboo/Everything's Coming Our Way//Jungle Strut/Batuka	1971	2.50	5.00	10.00
—Jukebox issue; small hole, plays at 33 1/3 rpm					
❏ 7-30595 [PS]	The New Santana Album	1971	2.50	5.00	10.00
Albums					
ARISTA					
❏ 19080 [(2)]	Supernatural	2000	10.00	20.00	40.00
—Classic Records audiophile vinyl issue in gatefold cover with booklet					
CICADELIC					
❏ 1004	Santana '68	1988	3.00	6.00	12.00
COLUMBIA					
❏ CS 9781	Santana	1969	3.75	7.50	15.00
—"360 Sound" on label					
❏ CS 9781	Santana	1970	2.50	5.00	10.00
—Orange label					
❏ PC 9781	Santana	198?	2.00	4.00	8.00
❏ CQ 30130 [Q]	Abraxas	1972	5.00	10.00	20.00
❏ JC 30130	Abraxas	1977	2.00	4.00	8.00
❏ KC 30130	Abraxas	197?	2.50	5.00	10.00
—With no poster					
❏ KC 30130	Abraxas	1970	3.75	7.50	15.00
—Original copies have a poster					
❏ PC 30130	Abraxas	1985	2.00	4.00	8.00
❏ CQ 30595 [Q]	Santana	1972	5.00	10.00	20.00
❏ KC 30595	Santana	1971	3.00	6.00	12.00
—Not the same album as CS 9781; this is often called "Santana III"					
❏ PC 30595	Santana	197?	2.00	4.00	8.00
❏ KC 31610	Caravanserai	1972	3.00	6.00	12.00
❏ PC 31610	Caravanserai	197?	2.00	4.00	8.00
❏ PCQ 31610 [Q]	Caravanserai	1974	5.00	10.00	20.00
❏ PC 32455	Welcome	1973	3.00	6.00	12.00
—No bar code on cover					
❏ PC 32455	Welcome	1979	2.00	4.00	8.00
—With bar code on cover					
❏ PCQ 32455 [Q]	Welcome	1974	5.00	10.00	20.00
❏ PCQ 32964 [Q]	Santana	1974	5.00	10.00	20.00
—Quadraphonic issue of their debut album (9781)					
❏ JC 33050	Santana's Greatest Hits	1977	2.00	4.00	8.00
❏ PC 33050	Santana's Greatest Hits	1974	3.00	6.00	12.00
—No bar code on cover					
❏ PCQ 33050 [Q]	Santana's Greatest Hits	1974	5.00	10.00	20.00
❏ PC 33135	Borboletta	1974	3.00	6.00	12.00
—No bar code on cover					
❏ PC 33135	Borboletta	1979	2.00	4.00	8.00
—With bar code on cover					
❏ PCQ 33135 [Q]	Borboletta	1974	5.00	10.00	20.00
❏ PC 33576	Amigos	1976	3.00	6.00	12.00
—No bar code on cover					
❏ PC 33576	Amigos	1979	2.00	4.00	8.00
—With bar code on cover					
❏ PCQ 33576 [Q]	Amigos	1976	5.00	10.00	20.00
❏ JC 34423	Festival	1977	3.00	6.00	12.00
❏ JCQ 34423 [Q]	Festival	1977	5.00	10.00	20.00

Number	Title (A Side/B Side)	Yr	VG	VG+	NM
❏ PC 34423	Festival	198?	2.00	4.00	8.00
❏ C2 34914 [(2)]	Moonflower	1977	3.75	7.50	15.00
❏ FC 35600	Inner Secrets	1978	3.00	6.00	12.00
❏ PC 35600	Inner Secrets	198?	2.00	4.00	8.00
—Budget-line reissue					
❏ FC 36154	Marathon	1979	3.00	6.00	12.00
❏ PC 36154	Marathon	198?	2.00	4.00	8.00
—Budget-line reissue					
❏ C2 36590 [(2)]	Swing of Delight	1980	3.75	7.50	15.00
❏ FC 37158	Zebop!	1981	3.00	6.00	12.00
❏ PC 37158	Zebop!	198?	2.00	4.00	8.00
—Budget-line reissue					
❏ FC 38122	Shango	1982	3.00	6.00	12.00
❏ PC 38122	Shango	198?	2.00	4.00	8.00
—Budget-line reissue					
❏ FC 39527	Beyond Appearances	1985	2.50	5.00	10.00
❏ PC 39527	Beyond Appearances	198?	2.00	4.00	8.00
—Budget-line reissue					
❏ HC 40130	Abraxas	1981	20.00	40.00	80.00
—Half-speed mastered edition					
❏ FC 40272	Freedom	1987	2.50	5.00	10.00
❏ C3X 44344 [(3)]	Viva Santana	1988	5.00	10.00	20.00
❏ HC 47158	Zebop!	1981	10.00	20.00	40.00
—Half-speed mastered edition					

SANTANA, CARLOS Also see SANTANA.
45s
COLUMBIA

❏ 03925	Tales of Kilimanjaro/Watch Your Step	1983	—	2.00	4.00

Albums
COLUMBIA

❏ AS 573 [DJ]	The Solo Guitar of Devadip Carlos Santana	1979	3.75	7.50	15.00
❏ JC 35686	Oneness/Silver Dreams-Golden Reality	1979	2.50	5.00	10.00
❏ C2 36590 [(2)]	The Swing of Delight	1980	3.00	6.00	12.00
❏ FC 38642	Havana Moon	1983	2.50	5.00	10.00
❏ FC 40875	Blues for Salvador	1987	2.50	5.00	10.00

SANTANA, CARLOS, AND MAHAVISHNU JOHN MCLAUGHLIN
Albums
COLUMBIA

❏ KC 32034	Love Devotion Surrender	1973	2.50	5.00	10.00
❏ PC 32034	Love Devotion Surrender	197?	2.00	4.00	8.00
—Reissue with new prefix					

SANTANA, CARLOS, AND BUDDY MILES Also see each artist's individual listings.
45s
COLUMBIA

❏ 45666	Them Changes/Evil Ways	1972	—	2.50	5.00

Albums
COLUMBIA

❏ KC 31308	Carlos Santana and Buddy Miles! Live!	1972	3.00	6.00	12.00
❏ PC 31308	Carlos Santana and Buddy Miles! Live!	197?	2.00	4.00	8.00
—Reissue with new prefix					

SANTO AND JOHNNY
45s
CANADIAN AMERICAN

❏ 103	Sleep Walk/All Night Diner	1959	6.25	12.50	25.00
❏ 107	Tear Drop/The Long Walk Home	1959	3.75	7.50	15.00
❏ 111	Caravan/Summertime	1960	3.75	7.50	15.00
❏ 115	The Breeze and I/Lazy Day	1960	3.75	7.50	15.00
❏ 118	Love Lost/Annie	1960	3.75	7.50	15.00
❏ 118 [PS]	Love Lost/Annie	1960	12.50	25.00	50.00
❏ 120	Twistin' Bells/Bullseye!	1960	4.00	8.00	16.00
❏ 120 [PS]	Twistin' Bells/Bullseye!	1960	10.00	20.00	40.00
❏ 124	Hop Scotch/Sea Shells	1961	3.75	7.50	15.00
❏ 128	Theme from Come September/The Long Walk Home	1961	3.75	7.50	15.00
❏ 131	The Mouse/Birmingham	1961	3.75	7.50	15.00
❏ 132	Twistin' Bells/Christmas Day	1961	5.00	10.00	20.00
—B-side by Linda Scott					
❏ 137	Spanish Harlem/Stage to Cimarron	1962	3.00	6.00	12.00
❏ 141	Three Caballeros/Step Aside	1962	3.00	6.00	12.00
❏ 144	Misirlou/Tokyo Twilight	1962	3.00	6.00	12.00
❏ 148	Twistin' Bells/Manhattan	1962	3.00	6.00	12.00
❏ 151	On Your Mark/Manhattan	1963	3.00	6.00	12.00
❏ 155	The Wandering Sea/Manhattan Spiritual	1963	3.00	6.00	12.00
❏ 161	Love Letters in the Sand/Lido Beach	1963	3.00	6.00	12.00
❏ 164	I'll Remember (In the Still of the Night)/Song for Rosemary	1964	3.00	6.00	12.00
❏ 164 [PS]	I'll Remember (In the Still of the Night)/Song for Rosemary	1964	6.25	12.50	25.00
❏ 167	A Thousand Miles Away/Road Block	1964	3.00	6.00	12.00
❏ 167 [PS]	A Thousand Miles Away/Road Block	1964	6.25	12.50	25.00
❏ 174	Sugar Stroll/Rattler	1964	3.00	6.00	12.00
❏ 177	A Hard Day's Night/And I Love Her	1964	3.75	7.50	15.00
❏ 182	Goldfinger/Sleep Walk	1964	3.00	6.00	12.00
❏ 182 [PS]	Goldfinger/Sleep Walk	1964	6.25	12.50	25.00
❏ 189	Brazilian Summer/Off Tempo	1965	3.00	6.00	12.00
❏ 194	Watermelon Man/Return to Naples	1965	3.00	6.00	12.00
❏ 204	Come with Me/The Young World	1967	2.50	5.00	10.00
IMPERIAL					
❏ 66269	Live for Life/See You in September	1968	2.50	5.00	10.00
❏ 66292	Sleep Walk '68/It Must Be Him	1968	2.50	5.00	10.00
PAUSA					
❏ 703	Come Back Soldier/Flamingo	1976	—	2.50	5.00
UNITED ARTISTS					
❏ 970	Thunderball/Mister Kiss Kiss Bang Bang	1966	2.50	5.00	10.00

7-Inch Extended Plays
CANADIAN AMERICAN

❏ 1001	(contents unknown)	1959	20.00	40.00	80.00
❏ 1001 [PS]	Santo and Johnny	1959	20.00	40.00	80.00

Albums
CANADIAN AMERICAN

❏ CALP-1001 [M]	Santo & Johnny	1959	15.00	30.00	60.00
❏ SCALP-1001 [S]	Santo & Johnny	1959	20.00	40.00	80.00

S

Number	Title (A Side/B Side)	Yr	VG	VG+	NM
❑ CALP-1002 [M]	Encore	1960	10.00	20.00	40.00
❑ SCALP-1002 [S]	Encore	1960	12.50	25.00	50.00
❑ CALP-1004 [M]	Hawaii	1961	10.00	20.00	40.00
❑ SCALP-1004 [S]	Hawaii	1961	12.50	25.00	50.00
❑ CALP-1006 [M]	Come On In	1962	7.50	15.00	30.00
❑ SCALP-1006 [S]	Come On In	1962	10.00	20.00	40.00
❑ CALP-1008 [M]	Around the World with Santo and Johnny	1962	7.50	15.00	30.00
❑ SCALP-1008 [S]	Around the World with Santo and Johnny	1962	10.00	20.00	40.00
❑ CALP-1011 [M]	Off Shore	1963	7.50	15.00	30.00
❑ SCALP-1011 [S]	Off Shore	1963	10.00	20.00	40.00
❑ CALP-1014 [M]	In the Still of the Night	1963	7.50	15.00	30.00
❑ SCALP-1014 [S]	In the Still of the Night	1963	10.00	20.00	40.00
❑ CALP-1016 [M]	Wish You Love	1964	7.50	15.00	30.00
❑ SCALP-1016 [S]	Wish You Love	1964	10.00	20.00	40.00
❑ CALP-1017 [M]	The Beatles' Greatest Hits	1965	10.00	20.00	40.00
❑ SCALP-1017 [S]	The Beatles' Greatest Hits	1965	12.50	25.00	50.00
❑ CALP-1018 [M]	Mucho	1965	7.50	15.00	30.00
❑ SCALP-1018 [S]	Mucho	1965	10.00	20.00	40.00
IMPERIAL					
❑ LP-9363 [M]	Brilliant Guitar Sounds	1967	3.75	7.50	15.00
❑ LP-12363 [S]	Brilliant Guitar Sounds	1967	5.00	10.00	20.00
❑ LP-12366	Golden Guitars	1968	3.75	7.50	15.00
❑ LP-12418	On the Road Again	1968	3.75	7.50	15.00

SANTOS, LARRY
45s
ATLANTIC

Number	Title (A Side/B Side)	Yr	VG	VG+	NM
❑ 2250	Someday (When I'm Gone)/True	1964	5.00	10.00	20.00

—With the Four Seasons on backup

BIG TREE

| ❑ 136 | Life Is Beautiful/Touchin' You | 1972 | — | 2.50 | 5.00 |

CASABLANCA

| ❑ 844 | Can't Get You Off My Mind/ We Can't Hide It Anymore | 1975 | — | 3.00 | 6.00 |

—With "Can't Get You Off My Mind" listed as "Side A"

| ❑ 844 | We Can't Hide It Anymore/ Can't Get You Off My Mind | 1976 | — | 2.00 | 4.00 |

—With "We Can't Hide It Anymore" listed as "Side A"

| ❑ 869 | You Are Everything I Need/Long, Long Time | 1976 | — | 2.00 | 4.00 |
| ❑ 881 | Magic Mountain/Don't Let the Music Stop | 1977 | — | 2.00 | 4.00 |

EVOLUTION

❑ 1007	Tomorrow Without Love/ You Got Me Where You Want Me	1969	—	3.00	6.00
❑ 1010	Subway Man/Woman-Child	1969	—	3.00	6.00
❑ 1018	Great Divide/Paper Chase	1970	—	3.00	6.00
❑ 1024	Mornin' Sun/Wandering Man	1970	—	3.00	6.00
❑ 1029	Now That I Have Found You/Wandering Man	1970	—	3.00	6.00
❑ 1039	Let It End/Little Bit of You	1971	—	3.00	6.00
❑ 1043	I Love You More Than Everything/Let It End	1971	—	3.00	6.00

Albums
CASABLANCA

| ❑ NBLP 7030 | You Are Everything I Need | 1976 | 3.00 | 6.00 | 12.00 |
| ❑ NBLP 7061 | Don't Let the Music Stop | 1977 | 3.00 | 6.00 | 12.00 |

EVOLUTION

| ❑ 2002 | Just a Man | 1969 | 5.00 | 10.00 | 20.00 |
| ❑ 2015 | Morning Sun | 1971 | 3.75 | 7.50 | 15.00 |

SAPODILLA PUNCH
Albums
PHILIPS

| ❑ PHS 600312 | Sapodilla Punch | 1969 | 5.00 | 10.00 | 20.00 |

SAPPHIRES, THE (1)
45s
ABC-PARAMOUNT

❑ 10559	Hearts Are Made to Be Broken/Let's Break Up for Awhile	1964	3.75	7.50	15.00
❑ 10590	Thank You for Loving Me/ Our Love Is Everywhere	1964	3.75	7.50	15.00
❑ 10639	Gee I'm Sorry, Baby/Gotta Have Your Love	1965	3.75	7.50	15.00
❑ 10693	Evil One/How Could I Say Goodbye	1965	3.75	7.50	15.00
❑ 10753	You'll Never Stop Me from Loving You/ Gonna Be a Big Thing	1965	3.75	7.50	15.00
❑ 10778	Our Love Is Everywhere/Slow Fizz	1966	3.75	7.50	15.00

ITZY

| ❑ 8 | Who Do You Love/Oh So Soon | 1963 | 10.00 | 20.00 | 40.00 |

LOST-NITE

| ❑ 260 | Gee I'm Sorry, Baby/Gotta Have Your Love | 196? | — | 2.50 | 5.00 |

—Reissue

SWAN

❑ 4143	Your True Love/Where Is Johnny Now	1963	3.75	7.50	15.00
❑ 4162	Who Do You Love/Oh So Soon	1963	3.75	7.50	15.00
❑ 4177	I Found Out Too Late/ I've Got Mine, You Better Get Yours	1964	3.75	7.50	15.00
❑ 4184	Gotta Be More Than Friends/Moulin Rouge	1964	3.75	7.50	15.00

Albums
COLLECTABLES

| ❑ COL-5007 | Who Do You Love | 198? | 2.50 | 5.00 | 10.00 |

SWAN

| ❑ LP-513 [M] | Who Do You Love | 1964 | 75.00 | 150.00 | 300.00 |

SAPPHIRES, THE (2)
45s
RCA VICTOR

| ❑ 47-7357 | Everyone Knows/So Glad | 1958 | 5.00 | 10.00 | 20.00 |

SARATOGAS, THE
45s
IMPERIAL

| ❑ 5738 | I'll Be Loving You/Get It in a Minute | 1961 | 7.50 | 15.00 | 30.00 |

SARDO, FRANKIE
45s
ABC-PARAMOUNT

| ❑ 9963 | Class Room/Fake Out | 1958 | 5.00 | 10.00 | 20.00 |
| ❑ 10003 | No Love Like Mine/Oh Linda | 1959 | 5.00 | 10.00 | 20.00 |

Number	Title (A Side/B Side)	Yr	VG	VG+	NM
LIDO					
❑ 602	Kiss and Make Up/ The Girl I'm Gonna Dream About	1959	5.00	10.00	20.00
MGM					
❑ 12621	May I/My Story of Love	1958	5.00	10.00	20.00
NEWTOWN					
❑ 5005	I Got You Where I Want You/Mr. Make Believe	1962	6.25	12.50	25.00
RAYNA					
❑ 5005	Ring of Love/She Taught Me How to Cry	1962	3.75	7.50	15.00
STUDIO					
❑ 9910	Just You Watch Me/I'm Sittin' at Home	1961	12.50	25.00	50.00
20TH FOX					
❑ 208	I Know Why and So Do You/ When the Bells Stop Ringing	1960	5.00	10.00	20.00
❑ 221	Dream Lover/Bonnie, Bonnie	1960	6.25	12.50	25.00

SARDO, JOHNNY
45s
CHOCK FULL-O-HITS

| ❑ 104 | (Hip Hop) Take a Ride with Me/Hollywood Sign | 1958 | 25.00 | 50.00 | 100.00 |

WARNER BROS.

| ❑ 5014 | I Wanna Rock/Used Heart | 1958 | 6.25 | 12.50 | 25.00 |
| ❑ 5044 | Late, Late, Late to School/New Kid in Town | 1959 | 6.25 | 12.50 | 25.00 |

SARNE, MIKE
45s
ASCOT

| ❑ 2213 | An Englishman Sings "America Swings"/ Can't Wait for Spring | 1966 | 2.50 | 5.00 | 10.00 |

CAMEO

| ❑ 220 | Come On Outside/Fountain of Love | 1962 | 3.00 | 6.00 | 12.00 |

STELLAR

| ❑ 1506 | Come Outside/Fountain of Love | 1962 | 3.00 | 6.00 | 12.00 |

SARSTEDT, PETER
45s
SIRE

| ❑ 1028 | Beirut/The Hollywood Sign | 1978 | — | 2.00 | 4.00 |

UNITED ARTISTS

| ❑ 50923 | You're a Lady/What Makes One Man Feel | 1972 | — | 2.50 | 5.00 |

WORLD PACIFIC

❑ 77906	I Am a Cathedral/Blagged	1969	—	3.00	6.00
❑ 77911	Where Do You Go To (My Lovely)/Morning Mountain	1969	2.00	4.00	8.00
❑ 77919	Frozen Orange Juice/Aretuza Loser	1969	—	3.00	6.00
❑ 77919 [PS]	Frozen Orange Juice/Aretuza Loser	1969	2.50	5.00	10.00
❑ 77933	Step Into the Battlefield/I Thought It Was	1970	—	3.00	6.00

Albums
UNITED ARTISTS

| ❑ UAS-5558 | Every Word You Say Is Written Down | 1971 | 2.50 | 5.00 | 10.00 |

WORLD PACIFIC

| ❑ WPS-21895 | Where Do You Go To, My Lovely | 1969 | 3.75 | 7.50 | 15.00 |
| ❑ WPS-21899 | As Though It Were a Movie | 1969 | 3.75 | 7.50 | 15.00 |

SATAN AND THE DISCIPLES Allegedly, this is FREDDY FENDER.
45s
GOLDBAND

| ❑ 1188 | Mummies Curse/Cat's Meow | 1969 | 6.25 | 12.50 | 25.00 |

Albums
GOLDBAND

| ❑ 7750 | Underground | 1969 | 10.00 | 20.00 | 40.00 |

SATANS, THE
Albums
(NO LABEL)

| ❑ (no #) [M] | Raisin' Hell | 1962 | 75.00 | 150.00 | 300.00 |

SATAN'S FOUR
45s
B.T. PUPPY

| ❑ 515 | I Can't Find the Girl on My Mind/Oh Cathy | 1966 | 3.75 | 7.50 | 15.00 |

Albums
B.T. PUPPY

| ❑ BTS-1010 | Mixed Soul | 1970 | 37.50 | 75.00 | 150.00 |

—With the Cinnamon Angels

SATELLITES, THE More than one group.
45s
ABC-PARAMOUNT

| ❑ 10038 | Linda Jean/Rockateen | 1959 | 10.00 | 20.00 | 40.00 |

CLASS

| ❑ 234 | Heavenly Angel/You Ain't Sayin' Nothin' | 1958 | 7.50 | 15.00 | 30.00 |

CUPID

| ❑ (no #) | Linda Jean/Rockateen | 1959 | 20.00 | 40.00 | 80.00 |

D-M-G

| ❑ 4001 | Each Night/Darktown Strutters Ball | 1960 | 7.50 | 15.00 | 30.00 |

MALYNN

| ❑ 231 | Heavenly Angel/You Ain't Sayin' Nothin' | 1958 | 6.25 | 12.50 | 25.00 |

PALACE

| ❑ 102 | Buzz Buzz/We Like Birdland | 1960 | 5.00 | 10.00 | 20.00 |

PARROT

| ❑ 313 | Bodacious/El San Juan | 1966 | 6.25 | 12.50 | 25.00 |

UNITED ARTISTS

| ❑ 141 | I Found a Girl/My Piggie's Gotta Dance | 1958 | 10.00 | 20.00 | 40.00 |

SATINTONES, THE
45s
MOTOWN

| ❑ 1000 | Sugar Daddy/My Beloved | 1960 | 100.00 | 200.00 | 400.00 |

—With strings. Matrix number of A-side is "1000 G-3"

| ❑ 1000 | Sugar Daddy/My Beloved | 1960 | 100.00 | 200.00 | 400.00 |

—Without strings. Matrix number of A-side is "MNT 12345"

| ❑ 1006 | Tomorrow and Always/A Love That Can Never Be | 1961 | 62.50 | 125.00 | 250.00 |

—With strings

Number	Title (A Side/B Side)	Yr	VG	VG+	NM
❏ 1006	Tomorrow and Always/A Love That Can Never Be	1961	62.50	125.00	250.00
—Without strings					
❏ 1006	Angel/A Love That Can Never Be	1961	375.00	750.00	1500.
❏ 1010	I Know How It Feels/My Kind of Love	1961	50.00	100.00	200.00
❏ 1020	Zing Went the Strings of My Heart/Faded Letter	1962	50.00	100.00	200.00
TAMLA					
❏ 54026	Motor City/Going to the Hop	1960	200.00	400.00	800.00

SATISFACTIONS, THE (1)
45s
LIONEL

Number	Title (A Side/B Side)	Yr	VG	VG+	NM
❏ 3201	This Bitter Earth/Ol' Man River	1970	3.00	6.00	12.00
❏ 3205	One Light Two Lights/Turn Back the Tears	1970	3.00	6.00	12.00
❏ 3214	God I'm Losing My Baby/O-o-o La La	1971	3.75	7.50	15.00

SATISFACTIONS, THE (2)
45s
CHESAPEKE

Number	Title (A Side/B Side)	Yr	VG	VG+	NM
❏ 610	We Will Walk Together/Oh Why	1962	7.50	15.00	30.00

SATISFACTIONS, THE (3)
45s
IMPERIAL

Number	Title (A Side/B Side)	Yr	VG	VG+	NM
❏ 66170	Bring It All Down/ Daddy, You Just Gotta Let Him In	1966	5.00	10.00	20.00
SMASH					
❏ 2059	Give Me Your Love/Stop Following Me	1966	3.75	7.50	15.00
❏ 2098	Take It or Leave It/You Got to Share	1967	7.50	15.00	30.00

SATISFACTIONS, THE (U) These could be group (1) or (3).
45s
1-2-3

Number	Title (A Side/B Side)	Yr	VG	VG+	NM
❏ 1716	Gonna Get Right Tonight/Living on a Prayer, a Hope and a Hand-Me-Down	1969	3.00	6.00	12.00
TWIN TOWN					
❏ 714	Bad Times/Don't Tell Me	1966	6.25	12.50	25.00

SATISFIERS, THE
45s
CORAL

Number	Title (A Side/B Side)	Yr	VG	VG+	NM
❏ 61727	Come Away, Love/Where'll I Be Tomorrow Night	1956	3.75	7.50	15.00
❏ 61788	Over the Rainbow/Solitude	1957	3.75	7.50	15.00
❏ 61945	Will o' the Wisp/ Remember That Crazy Rock and Roll	1958	3.75	7.50	15.00
JUBILEE					
❏ 5205	All or Nothing at All/Lies, Nothing But Lies	1955	5.00	10.00	20.00
VEGAS					
❏ 626	Ghost of a Chance/Fair Exchange	1960	3.00	6.00	12.00

SATURDAY, PATTY
45s
SWAN

Number	Title (A Side/B Side)	Yr	VG	VG+	NM
❏ 4022	Ladies Choice/Love Is a Beautiful Thing	1959	6.25	12.50	25.00

SATURDAY KNIGHTS, THE
45s
NOCTURNE

Number	Title (A Side/B Side)	Yr	VG	VG+	NM
❏ 1030	Sea Mist/Queen of the Nile	1963	12.50	25.00	50.00
SWAN					
❏ 4075	Ticonderoga/Tiger Lily	1961	5.00	10.00	20.00
—As "The Saturday Knights"					
❏ 4075	Ticonderoga/Tiger Lily	1961	7.50	15.00	30.00
—As "The Saturday Nights"					
❏ 4081	Hawaiian Tears/Texas Tommy	1961	5.00	10.00	20.00

SATURDAY'S CHILDREN
45s
ABC-PARAMOUNT

Number	Title (A Side/B Side)	Yr	VG	VG+	NM
❏ 10505	Raindrops/Cry Wind	1963	2.50	5.00	10.00
DUNWICH					
❏ 139	Born on Saturday/You Don't Know Better	1966	3.75	7.50	15.00
❏ 144	The Christmas Song/Deck Five	1967	3.75	7.50	15.00
❏ 156	Leave That Baby Alone/I Hardly Know Her	1967	3.75	7.50	15.00

SAUNDERS, LITTLE BUTCHIE
45s
HERALD

Number	Title (A Side/B Side)	Yr	VG	VG+	NM
❏ 485	Lindy Lou/Rock 'N' Roll Indian Dance	1956	12.50	25.00	50.00
❏ 491	Great Big Heart/I Wanna Holler	1956	12.50	25.00	50.00

SAUNDERS, MERL
45s
FANTASY

Number	Title (A Side/B Side)	Yr	VG	VG+	NM
❏ 600	High Heel Sneakers//(B-side unknown)	1964	2.50	5.00	10.00
❏ 620	Five More/Julia	1969	2.00	4.00	8.00
❏ 668	Save Mother Earth (Part 1)/ Save Mother Earth (Part 2)	1971	—	3.00	6.00
❏ 678	My Problems Got Problems/ Welcome to the Basement	1972	—	3.00	6.00
GALAXY					
❏ 747	I Pity the Fool/Tighten Up	1966	2.00	4.00	8.00
❏ 755	Soul Grooving/Up-Up and Away	1967	2.00	4.00	8.00
❏ 776	Iron Horse/A Little Bit of Righteousness	1970	2.00	4.00	8.00
Albums					
CRYSTAL CLEAR					
❏ 5006	Do I Move You	1980	5.00	10.00	20.00
—Direct-to-disc recording					
FANTASY					
❏ MPF-4533	Keystone Encores, Vol. 1	1988	3.00	6.00	12.00
❏ MPF-4534	Keystone Encores, Vol. 2	1988	3.00	6.00	12.00
❏ MPF-4535	Live at the Keystone, Vol. 1	1988	3.00	6.00	12.00
❏ MPF-4536	Live at the Keystone, Vol. 2	1988	3.00	6.00	12.00
❏ 8421	Heavy Turbulence	1972	3.75	7.50	15.00
❏ 9421	Fire Up	1973	5.00	10.00	20.00
—With Jerry Garcia and Tom Fogerty					
❏ 9460	Saunders	1974	3.75	7.50	15.00
❏ 9503	Leave Your Hat On	1976	3.00	6.00	12.00
❏ 79002 [(2)]	Live at the Keystone	198?	5.00	10.00	20.00

GALAXY

Number	Title (A Side/B Side)	Yr	VG	VG+	NM
❏ 8209	Soul Grooving	197?	3.75	7.50	15.00

SAVAGE, BOB
45s
ABC-PARAMOUNT

Number	Title (A Side/B Side)	Yr	VG	VG+	NM
❏ 9915	Rock Around the World/Butterfingers	1958	5.00	10.00	20.00

SAVAGE, DUKE, AND THE ARRIBINS
45s
ARGO

Number	Title (A Side/B Side)	Yr	VG	VG+	NM
❏ 5346	Your Love/Hey Baby	1959	10.00	20.00	40.00

SAVAGE GRACE
45s
REPRISE

Number	Title (A Side/B Side)	Yr	VG	VG+	NM
❏ 0924	Hymn to Freedom/Come On Down	1970	—	3.00	6.00
❏ 0952	Watchtower (All Alone)/Come On Down	1970	—	3.00	6.00
❏ 0988	Ivy/Save It for Me	1971	—	3.00	6.00
❏ 1022	Friends/Yonder	1971	—	3.00	6.00
Albums					
REPRISE					
❏ RS 6399	Savage Grace	1970	3.75	7.50	15.00
❏ RS 6484	Savage Grace 2	1971	3.75	7.50	15.00

SAVAGE RESURRECTION
45s
MERCURY

Number	Title (A Side/B Side)	Yr	VG	VG+	NM
❏ 72778	Thing in "E"/The Fox Is Sick	1968	3.00	6.00	12.00
Albums					
MERCURY					
❏ MG-21156 [M]	Savage Resurrection	1968	50.00	100.00	200.00
❏ SR-61156 [S]	Savage Resurrection	1968	25.00	50.00	100.00

SAVALAS, TELLY
45s
MCA

Number	Title (A Side/B Side)	Yr	VG	VG+	NM
❏ 40301	If/Rubber Bands and Bits of String	1974	—	2.00	4.00
❏ 40363	Help Me Make It Through the Night/ You've Lost That Lovin' Feelin'	1975	—	2.00	4.00
❏ 40468	Who Loves Ya Baby/Nevertheless (I'm in Love with You)	1975	—	2.00	4.00
Albums					
AUDIO FIDELITY					
❏ AFSD-6271	Telly Savalas	1975	3.75	7.50	15.00
MCA					
❏ 436	Telly	1974	3.75	7.50	15.00
❏ 2160	Who Loves Ya Baby	1976	3.75	7.50	15.00

SAVITT, BUDDY
45s
PARKWAY

Number	Title (A Side/B Side)	Yr	VG	VG+	NM
❏ 857	Smoke Gets in Your Eyes/Come Blow Your Horn	1962	3.00	6.00	12.00

SAVOY, RONNIE
45s
EPIC

Number	Title (A Side/B Side)	Yr	VG	VG+	NM
❏ 9619	I Hear Violins/The Marriage	1963	2.00	4.00	8.00
❏ 9708	Little Rascals/Sally Blue	1964	2.00	4.00	8.00
GONE					
❏ 5079	Ooh, What a Girl/Love Me As I Love You	1959	3.00	6.00	12.00
MGM					
❏ 12950	And the Heavens Cried/Big Chain	1960	5.00	10.00	20.00
❏ 13001	Bewitched/It's Gotta Be Love	1961	3.75	7.50	15.00
❏ 13042	Jungle Love Call/Your Cheatin' Heart	1961	3.75	7.50	15.00
PHILIPS					
❏ 40032	A Fool, A Loser, A Clown/Big Hand, Little Hand	1962	2.00	4.00	8.00
❏ 40071	Moonlight to Sunlight/21,000 Happiness Street	1962	2.00	4.00	8.00
WINGATE					
❏ 001	Memories Linger/Loving You	1965	6.25	12.50	25.00

SAVOY BROWN
45s
LONDON

Number	Title (A Side/B Side)	Yr	VG	VG+	NM
❏ 206	Everybody Loves a Drinkin' Man/Ride On Babe	1974	—	2.50	5.00
❏ 234	Walkin' 'n' Talkin'/Stranger Blues	1976	—	2.50	5.00
PARROT					
❏ 40034	Shake 'Em On Down/(B-side unknown)	1968	3.75	7.50	15.00
❏ 40037	Grits Ain't Groceries/She's Got a Ring in His Nose and a Ring on Her Hand	1969	2.00	4.00	8.00
❏ 40039	Train to Nowhere/Made Up My Mind	1969	2.00	4.00	8.00
❏ 40042	I'm Tired/Stay with Me Baby	1969	2.00	4.00	8.00
❏ 40046	Hard Way to Go/ The Incredible Gnome Meets Jaxman	1970	—	3.00	6.00
❏ 40057	Poor Girl/Mr. Hare	1970	—	3.00	6.00
❏ 40060	Sitting and Thinking/(B-side unknown)	1971	—	3.00	6.00
❏ 40066	Tell Mama/Rock and Roll on the Radio	1971	—	3.00	6.00
❏ 40075	Coming Down Your Way/Can't Find You	1973	—	3.00	6.00
TOWN HOUSE					
❏ 1054	Lay Back in the Arms of Someone/ Don't Tell Me I Told You	1981	—	2.00	4.00
❏ 1054 [PS]	Lay Back in the Arms of Someone/ Don't Tell Me I Told You	1981	—	2.00	4.00
❏ 1055	Run to Me/Georgie	1981	—	2.00	4.00
Albums					
GNP CRESCENDO					
❏ GNPS-2193	Make Me Sweat	1988	2.50	5.00	10.00
❏ GNPS-2196	Kings of Boogie	1989	2.50	5.00	10.00
LONDON					
❏ APS 638	Boogie Brothers	1974	2.50	5.00	10.00
❏ PS 659	Wire Fire	1975	2.50	5.00	10.00
❏ PS 670	Skin 'n' Bone	1976	2.50	5.00	10.00
❏ PS 718	Savage Return	1978	2.50	5.00	10.00
❏ LC-50000	The Best of Savoy Brown	1977	2.50	5.00	10.00
PARROT					
❏ PAS 71024	Getting to the Point	1968	6.25	12.50	25.00

S

Number	Title (A Side/B Side)	Yr	VG	VG+	NM
❑ PAS 71027	Blue Matter	1969	6.25	12.50	25.00
❑ PAS 71029	A Step Further	1969	3.75	7.50	15.00
❑ PAS 71036	Raw Sienna	1970	3.75	7.50	15.00
❑ PAS 71042	Looking In	1970	3.75	7.50	15.00
❑ PAS 71047	Street Corner Talking	1971	3.75	7.50	15.00
❑ XPAS 71052	Hellbound Train	1972	3.75	7.50	15.00
❑ XPAS 71057	Lion's Share	1972	3.75	7.50	15.00
❑ XPAS 71059	Jack the Toad	1973	3.75	7.50	15.00

TOWN HOUSE

Number	Title (A Side/B Side)	Yr	VG	VG+	NM
❑ ST-7002	Rock 'n' Roll Warriors	1981	3.00	6.00	12.00
❑ SKBK-7003	[(2)]Greatest Hits Live in Concert	1982	3.75	7.50	15.00

SAWBUCK
45s
FILLMORE

Number	Title (A Side/B Side)	Yr	VG	VG+	NM
❑ ZS7 7007	There Will Be Love/Bible Burning	1972	2.00	4.00	8.00

Albums
FILLMORE

Number	Title (A Side/B Side)	Yr	VG	VG+	NM
❑ Z 31248	Sawbuck	1972	5.00	10.00	20.00

SAWYER, RAY Also see DR. HOOK.
45s
CAPITOL

Number	Title (A Side/B Side)	Yr	VG	VG+	NM
❑ 4344	(One More Year of) Daddy's Little Girl/I Need That High (But I Can't Stand the Taste)	1976	—	2.00	4.00
❑ 4386	Red-Winged Blackbird/The One I'm Holding Now	1977	—	—	4.00
❑ 4416	Walls and Doors/I Need That HIgh (But I Can't Stand the Taste)	1977	—	2.00	4.00
❑ 4592	Dancing Fool/Rhythm Guitar	1978	—	2.00	4.00
❑ 4747	What I'm Holding/I Want Johnny's Job	1979	—	2.00	4.00
❑ 4820	Drinking Wine Alone/I Don't Feel Like Smilin'	1980	—	2.00	4.00

SANDY

Number	Title (A Side/B Side)	Yr	VG	VG+	NM
❑ 1030	Rockin' Satellite/Bells in My Heart	1961	10.00	20.00	40.00
❑ 1037	I'm Gonna Leave/You Gave Me the Right	1961	6.25	12.50	25.00

Albums
CAPITOL

Number	Title (A Side/B Side)	Yr	VG	VG+	NM
❑ ST-11591	Ray Sawyer	1976	2.50	5.00	10.00

SAXON, EDDIE, AND THE PARAMOUNTS
45s
EMPRESS

Number	Title (A Side/B Side)	Yr	VG	VG+	NM
❑ 106	Blues No More/If It's Meant to Be	1962	37.50	75.00	150.00
❑ 106 [DJ]	Blues No More	1962	50.00	100.00	200.00

—Single-sided promo

SAXON, SKY Later recorded with THE SEEDS. Also see RITCHIE MARSH.
45s
CONQUEST

Number	Title (A Side/B Side)	Yr	VG	VG+	NM
❑ 777	They Say/Go Ahead and Cry	1964	7.50	15.00	30.00

Albums
GNP CRESCENDO

Number	Title (A Side/B Side)	Yr	VG	VG+	NM
❑ GNP-2040 [M]	A Full Spoon of Seedy Blues	1967	10.00	20.00	40.00
❑ GNPS-2040 [S]	A Full Spoon of Seedy Blues	1967	7.50	15.00	30.00

SAYER, LEO
12-Inch Singles
WARNER BROS.

Number	Title (A Side/B Side)	Yr	VG	VG+	NM
❑ PRO-A-699 [DJ]	Thunder in My Heart (Disco Version) (same on both sides)	1977	2.00	4.00	8.00

45s
WARNER BROS.

Number	Title (A Side/B Side)	Yr	VG	VG+	NM
❑ 7768	The Show Must Go On/Innocent Bystander	1974	2.00	4.00	8.00
❑ 7824	One Man Band/Drop Back	1974	—	3.00	6.00
❑ 8043	Long Tall Glasses/In My Life	1974	—	3.00	6.00

—First pressings have no A-side subtitle

Number	Title (A Side/B Side)	Yr	VG	VG+	NM
❑ 8043	Long Tall Glasses (I Can Dance)/In My Life	1975	—	2.50	5.00

—Later pressings add subtitle to A-side

Number	Title (A Side/B Side)	Yr	VG	VG+	NM
❑ 8097	One Man Band/Telepath	1975	—	2.50	5.00
❑ 8153	Moonlighting/Streets of Your Town	1975	—	2.50	5.00
❑ 8283	You Make Me Feel Like Dancing/Magdalena	1976	—	2.50	5.00
❑ 8319	How Much Love/I Hear the Laughter	1977	—	2.50	5.00
❑ 8332	When I Need You/I Think We Fell in Love Too Fast	1977	—	2.50	5.00
❑ 8465	Thunder in My Heart/Get the Girl	1977	—	2.50	5.00
❑ 8502	Easy to Love/Haunting Me	1977	—	2.50	5.00
❑ 8682	Raining in My Heart/No Looking Back	1978	—	2.00	4.00
❑ 8738	Don't Look Back/No Looking Back	1979	—	2.00	4.00
❑ 29904	Paris Dies in the Morning/We've Got Ourselves in Love	1982	—	2.00	4.00
❑ 29960	End of the Game/Heart	1982	—	2.00	4.00
❑ 49134	Oh Girl/Englishman in the U.S.A.	1979	—	2.00	4.00
❑ 49565	More Than I Can Say/Millionaire	1980	—	2.00	4.00
❑ 49657	Living in a Fantasy/Only Foolin'	1981	—	2.00	4.00
❑ 49714	Where Did We Go Wrong/She's Not Coming Back	1981	—	2.00	4.00
❑ 50060	Have You Ever Been in Love/I Don't Need Dreaming Anymore	1982	—	2.00	4.00

Albums
CHRYSALIS

Number	Title (A Side/B Side)	Yr	VG	VG+	NM
❑ PV 41087	Another Year	1985	2.00	4.00	8.00

—Reissue of Warner Bros. 2885

Number	Title (A Side/B Side)	Yr	VG	VG+	NM
❑ PV 41125	Endless Flight	1985	2.00	4.00	8.00

—Reissue of Warner Bros. 3101

Number	Title (A Side/B Side)	Yr	VG	VG+	NM
❑ PV 41154	Thunder in My Heart	1985	2.00	4.00	8.00

—Reissue of Warner Bros. 3089

Number	Title (A Side/B Side)	Yr	VG	VG+	NM
❑ PV 41198	Leo Sayer	1985	2.00	4.00	8.00

—Reissue of Warner Bros. 3200

Number	Title (A Side/B Side)	Yr	VG	VG+	NM
❑ PV 41240	Here	1985	2.00	4.00	8.00

—Reissue of Warner Bros. 3374

WARNER BROS.

Number	Title (A Side/B Side)	Yr	VG	VG+	NM
❑ BS 2738	Silverbird	1973	3.00	6.00	12.00
❑ BS 2836	Just a Boy	1974	2.50	5.00	10.00
❑ BS 2885	Another Year	1975	2.50	5.00	10.00
❑ BS 2962	Endless Flight	1976	2.50	5.00	10.00
❑ BSK 3089	Thunder in My Heart	1977	2.50	5.00	10.00
❑ BSK 3101	Endless Flight	1977	2.00	4.00	8.00

—Reissue of 2962

Number	Title (A Side/B Side)	Yr	VG	VG+	NM
❑ BSK 3200	Leo Sayer	1978	2.50	5.00	10.00
❑ BSK 3374	Here	1979	2.50	5.00	10.00
❑ BSK 3483	Living in a Fantasy	1980	2.50	5.00	10.00
❑ 23560	World Radio	1982	2.50	5.00	10.00

SCAFFOLD, THE With Mike McGear, Paul McCartney's brother.
45s
BELL

Number	Title (A Side/B Side)	Yr	VG	VG+	NM
❑ 701	Thank U Very Much/Ide B the First	1968	4.00	8.00	16.00
❑ 724	Do You Remember/Carry On Krow	1968	4.00	8.00	16.00
❑ 747	Lily the Pink/Buttons of Your Mind	1968	4.00	8.00	16.00
❑ 821	Charity Bubbles/Goose	1969	4.00	8.00	16.00
❑ 849	Jelly Covered Cloud/Liver Birds	1969	3.00	6.00	12.00

WARNER BROS.

Number	Title (A Side/B Side)	Yr	VG	VG+	NM
❑ 8001	Liverpool Lou/Ten Years After on Strawberry Jam	1974	—	3.00	6.00

Albums
BELL

Number	Title (A Side/B Side)	Yr	VG	VG+	NM
❑ 6018 [M]	Thank U Very Much	1968	12.50	25.00	50.00

—Mono copies are promo only

Number	Title (A Side/B Side)	Yr	VG	VG+	NM
❑ 6018 [S]	Thank U Very Much	1968	12.50	25.00	50.00

SCAGGS, BOZ
12-Inch Singles
COLUMBIA

Number	Title (A Side/B Side)	Yr	VG	VG+	NM
❑ AS 380 [DJ]	Hard Times (same on both sides)	1977	2.00	4.00	8.00
❑ 11350	Look What You've Done to Me/Jojo	1980	2.50	5.00	10.00

45s
ATLANTIC

Number	Title (A Side/B Side)	Yr	VG	VG+	NM
❑ 2692	I'm Easy/I'll Be Long Gone	1969	2.50	5.00	10.00

COLUMBIA

Number	Title (A Side/B Side)	Yr	VG	VG+	NM
❑ 01023	You Can Have Me Anytime/Georgia	1981	—	2.00	4.00
❑ 02423	Jojo/Miss Sun	1981	—	—	3.00

—Reissue

Number	Title (A Side/B Side)	Yr	VG	VG+	NM
❑ 02424	Breakdown Dead Ahead/Look What You've Done to Me	1981	—	—	3.00

—Reissue

Number	Title (A Side/B Side)	Yr	VG	VG+	NM
❑ 07780	Heart of Mine/You'll Never Know	1988	—	—	3.00
❑ 07780 [PS]	Heart of Mine/You'll Never Know	1988	—	2.00	4.00
❑ 07981	Cool Running/You'll Never Know	1988	—	—	3.00
❑ 08068	What's Number 1/Claudia	1988	—	—	3.00
❑ 10027	Slow Dancer/Pain of Love	1974	—	3.00	6.00
❑ 10124	You Make It So Hard (To Say Goodbye)/There Is Something Else	1975	—	2.50	5.00
❑ 10319	It's Over/Harbor Lights	1976	—	2.50	5.00
❑ 10367	Lowdown/Harbor Lights	1976	—	2.50	5.00
❑ 10440	What Can I Say/We're All Alone	1976	—	2.50	5.00
❑ 10491	Lido Shuffle/We're All Alone	1977	—	2.50	5.00
❑ 10606	Hard Times/We're Waiting	1977	—	2.50	5.00
❑ 10606 [PS]	Hard Times/We're Waiting	1977	2.50	5.00	10.00
❑ 10679	Hollywood/A Clue	1978	—	2.50	5.00
❑ 11241	Breakdown Dead Ahead/Isn't It Time	1980	—	2.00	4.00
❑ 11281	Jojo/Do Like You Do in New York	1980	—	2.00	4.00
❑ 11349	Look What You've Done to Me/Simone	1980	—	2.00	4.00
❑ 11406	Miss Sun/Dinah Flo	1980	—	2.00	4.00
❑ 45353	We Were Always Sweethearts/Painted Bells	1971	—	3.00	6.00
❑ 45408	Near You/Downright Woman	1971	—	3.00	6.00
❑ 45540	Here to Stay/Runnin' Blue	1972	—	3.00	6.00
❑ 45670	Dinah Flo/He's a Fool for You	1972	—	3.00	6.00
❑ 46025	You Make It So Hard (To Say Goodbye)/There Is Someone Else	1974	—	3.00	6.00

FULL MOON

Number	Title (A Side/B Side)	Yr	VG	VG+	NM
❑ 49676	You Make It So Hard (To Say Goodbye)/Something's Missing in My Life	1981	—	2.00	4.00

—B-side by Lady Sylvia

VIRGIN

Number	Title (A Side/B Side)	Yr	VG	VG+	NM
❑ S7-18048	I'll Be the One/Time Change	1994	—	2.00	4.00
❑ S7-19529	It All Went Down the Drain/I've Got Your Love	1997	—	—	3.00
❑ S7-19651	Fly Like a Bird/Sick and Tired	1997	—	—	3.00

Albums
ATLANTIC

Number	Title (A Side/B Side)	Yr	VG	VG+	NM
❑ SD 8239	Boz Scaggs	1969	3.00	6.00	12.00
❑ SD 19166	Boz Scaggs	1977	2.00	4.00	8.00

COLUMBIA

Number	Title (A Side/B Side)	Yr	VG	VG+	NM
❑ A2S 71 [(2)DJ]	KSAN Live Concert	1974	12.50	25.00	50.00

—Promo-only set released in plain cardboard jacket

Number	Title (A Side/B Side)	Yr	VG	VG+	NM
❑ AS 203 [DJ]	The Boz Scaggs Sampler	1976	5.00	10.00	20.00
❑ KC 30454	Moments	1971	2.50	5.00	10.00
❑ PC 30454	Moments	197?	2.00	4.00	8.00
❑ KC 30976	Boz Scaggs & Band	1971	2.50	5.00	10.00
❑ PC 30976	Boz Scaggs & Band	197?	2.00	4.00	8.00
❑ KC 31384	My Time	1972	2.50	5.00	10.00
❑ PC 31384	My Time	197?	2.00	4.00	8.00
❑ KC 32760	Slow Dancer	1974	2.50	5.00	10.00

—Second cover has a male dancer who is not Boz Scaggs

Number	Title (A Side/B Side)	Yr	VG	VG+	NM
❑ KC 32760	Slow Dancer	1974	3.00	6.00	12.00

—Original cover has Boz Scaggs on a beach in only a bathing suit

Number	Title (A Side/B Side)	Yr	VG	VG+	NM
❑ PC 32760	Slow Dancer	197?	2.00	4.00	8.00
❑ JC 33920	Silk Degrees	1977	2.50	5.00	10.00

—Early reissue with new prefix

Number	Title (A Side/B Side)	Yr	VG	VG+	NM
❑ PC 33920	Silk Degrees	1976	3.00	6.00	12.00

—Original edition with "PC" prefix and no bar code on back cover

Number	Title (A Side/B Side)	Yr	VG	VG+	NM
❑ PC 33920	Silk Degrees	1985	2.00	4.00	8.00

—Budget-line reissue; bar code on back cover

Number	Title (A Side/B Side)	Yr	VG	VG+	NM
❑ FC 36106	Middle Man	1980	2.50	5.00	10.00
❑ PC 36106	Middle Man	198?	2.00	4.00	8.00

—Budget-line reissue

Number	Title (A Side/B Side)	Yr	VG	VG+	NM
❑ FC 36841	Hits!	1980	2.50	5.00	10.00
❑ PC 36841	Hits!	198?	2.00	4.00	8.00

—Budget-line reissue

Number	Title (A Side/B Side)	Yr	VG	VG+	NM
❑ PC 37249	Down Two Then Left	198?	2.00	4.00	8.00

—Budget-line reissue

Number	Title (A Side/B Side)	Yr	VG	VG+	NM
❑ JC 37429	Down Two Then Left	1977	2.50	5.00	10.00
❑ FC 40463	Other Roads	1988	2.50	5.00	10.00
❑ HC 43920	Silk Degrees	1981	7.50	15.00	30.00

—Half-speed mastered edition

Number	Title (A Side/B Side)	Yr	VG	VG+	NM
SCARLETS, THE (1)					
45s					
DOT					
❏ 16004	Stampede/Park Avenue	1959	6.25	12.50	25.00
PRINCE					
❏ 1207	Stampede/Park Avenue	1959	12.50	25.00	50.00
SCARLETS, THE (2)					
45s					
EVENT					
❏ 4287	Dear One/I've Lost	1958	10.00	20.00	40.00
LOST-NITE					
❏ 189	True Love/Cry Baby	196?	—	3.00	6.00
—Reissue					
❏ 338	Dear One/I've Lost	197?	—	2.50	5.00
—Reissue					
❏ 343	Darling, I'm Yours/Love Doll	197?	—	2.50	5.00
—Reissue					
❏ 347	Kiss Me/Indian Fever	197?	—	2.50	5.00
—Reissue					
RED ROBIN					
❏ 128	Dear One/I've Lost	1954	125.00	250.00	500.00
❏ 133	Darling, I'm Yours/Love Doll	1954	125.00	250.00	500.00
❏ 135	True Love/Cry Baby	1955	125.00	250.00	500.00
❏ 138	Kiss Me/Indian Fever	1955	150.00	300.00	600.00
SCARLETS, THE (3)					
45s					
TOWER					
❏ 144	I've Had It/You Don't Love Me	1965	2.50	5.00	10.00
SCARLETS, THE (U) Could be group (1).					
45s					
FURY					
❏ 1036	Truly Yours/East of the Sun	1960	7.50	15.00	30.00
SCAVENGERS, THE					
45s					
FENTON					
❏ 987	Curfew/Oasis	1964	12.50	25.00	50.00
MOBILE FIDELITY					
❏ 1005	The Angels Listened In/My Love Waits for Me	1963	7.50	15.00	30.00
❏ 1212	Devil's Reef/Little Annie	1963	7.50	15.00	30.00
STARS OF HOLLYWOOD					
❏ 1210	Shot Gun/Cream Puff	1963	12.50	25.00	50.00
❏ 1211	Shot Gun/Zip Code	1963	12.50	25.00	50.00
—"Cream Puff" and "Zip Code" are different titles for the same recording					
❏ 1212	Devil's Reef/Little Annie	1963	12.50	25.00	50.00
SUEMI					
❏ 4552	Bogus/Ghost Riders '65	1965	6.25	12.50	25.00
SCENE, THE					
45s					
B.T. PUPPY					
❏ 533	Scenes (From Another World)/You're in a Bad Way	1967	2.50	5.00	10.00
SCHAFF, MURRAY, AND THE ARISTOCRATS					
45s					
JOSIE					
❏ 788	The Unfinished Rock/Ooh How I Love Ya	1956	7.50	15.00	30.00
KING					
❏ 4977	How Many Miles/Tombstone Number 9	1956	7.50	15.00	30.00
SCHIFRIN, LALO Listings include many of his soundtrack LPs.					
12-Inch Singles					
CTI					
❏ OJ-2	Flamingo/Quiet Village/Jaws	1976	3.75	7.50	15.00
PABLO					
❏ RD-11004	Unicorn/Free Ride	1977	3.00	6.00	12.00
—With Dizzy Gillespie					
TABU					
❏ 5520	No One Home/(Instrumental)	1979	3.00	6.00	12.00
45s					
A&M					
❏ 1756	Theme from "The Master Gunfighter"/Theme from "The Trial of Billy Jack"	1975	—	2.50	5.00
AUDIO FIDELITY					
❏ 084	The Ugly Duckling/(B-side unknown)	196?	2.50	5.00	10.00
CTI					
❏ 29	Turning Point/Flamingo	1976	—	2.00	4.00
❏ 36	Roller Coaster (From the Universal Film)/Love Theme from "The Eagle Has Landed"	1977	—	3.00	6.00
DOT					
❏ 17059	Mission Impossible/Jim on the Move	1967	2.50	5.00	10.00
MCA					
❏ 40748	Magic Carousel/Merry-Go-Round	1977	—	2.00	4.00
❏ 52175	Heliotrope Bouquet/The Entertainer	1983	—	2.00	4.00
—B-side by Marvin Hamlisch					
MGM					
❏ 13139	Broken Date/Good Life	1963	2.50	5.00	10.00
❏ 13151	Hud/Jive Orbit	1963	2.50	5.00	10.00
❏ 13163	Haunting/Theme from "Dime with a Halo"	1963	2.50	5.00	10.00
❏ 13224	Seven Faces of Dr. Lao/The Wave	1964	2.50	5.00	10.00
❏ 13251	Theme from "Rhino"/Rhino Bomp	1964	2.50	5.00	10.00
❏ 13425	The Cincinnati Kid/So Many Times	1965	2.00	4.00	8.00
❏ 13670	Venice After Dark/Our Venetian Affair	1967	2.00	4.00	8.00
❏ 14153	Burning Bridges/Kelly's Heroes	1970	—	3.00	6.00
❏ 14180	Theme from "Medical Center"/(B-side unknown)	1970	—	3.00	6.00
PABLO					
❏ RB-11003	Unicorn/Free Ride	1977	—	2.00	4.00
—With Dizzy Gillespie					
PARAMOUNT					
❏ 0001	Self Destruct/The Getaway	1969	2.00	4.00	8.00
❏ 0002	Mannix/End Game	1969	2.00	4.00	8.00

Number	Title (A Side/B Side)	Yr	VG	VG+	NM
TABU					
❏ 5509	Moonlight Gypsies/Prophecy of Love	1978	—	2.00	4.00
❏ 5519	No One Home/Middle of the Night	1979	—	2.00	4.00
TETRAGRAMMATON					
❏ 1533	Theme from "Che"/Embo Scada	1969	2.00	4.00	8.00
20TH CENTURY					
❏ 2150	Ape Shuffle/Escape from Tomorrow	1974	—	2.50	5.00
❏ 2205	Bolero/Dona Donna	1975	—	2.50	5.00
UNITED ARTISTS					
❏ 50649	What's New Pussycat/Pussycat, Pussycat, I Love You	1970	—	2.50	5.00
VERVE					
❏ 10290	Broken Date/Good Life	1963	2.00	4.00	8.00
❏ 10331	New Fantasy/Bachianas Brasilerias #5	1964	2.00	4.00	8.00
❏ 10365	Man from Thrush/Blues-A-Go-Go	1965	2.50	5.00	10.00
❏ 10434	The Wig/Beneath a Weeping Willow Shade	1966	2.00	4.00	8.00
❏ 10663	Agnus Dei/Sanctus Benedictus	1971	—	3.00	6.00
❏ 10663	Theme from "Medical Center"/All for the Love of Sunshine	1971	2.00	4.00	8.00
WARNER BROS.					
❏ 7173	Foxtail/That Night	1968	—	3.00	6.00
❏ 7263	Bullitt/That Night	1969	—	3.00	6.00
Albums					
AMERICAN INT'L.					
❏ AILP 3003	The Amityville Horror	1979	2.50	5.00	10.00
AUDIO FIDELITY					
❏ AFLP-1981 [M]	Bossa Nova — New Brazilian Jazz	1962	5.00	10.00	20.00
❏ AFLP-2117 [M]	Eso Es Latino Jazz	1963	5.00	10.00	20.00
❏ AFSD-5981 [S]	Bossa Nova — New Brazilian Jazz	1962	6.25	12.50	25.00
❏ AFSD-6117 [S]	Eso Es Latino Jazz	1963	6.25	12.50	25.00
❏ AFSD-6195	The Other Side of Lalo Schifrin	1968	3.75	7.50	15.00
COLGEMS					
❏ COMO-5003 [M]	Murderer's Row	1967	12.50	25.00	50.00
❏ COSO-5003 [S]	Murderer's Row	1967	25.00	50.00	100.00
CTI					
❏ 5000	Black Widow	1976	3.00	6.00	12.00
❏ 5003	Towering Toccata	1977	3.00	6.00	12.00
DOT					
❏ DLP-3831 [M]	Music from Mission: Impossible	1967	7.50	15.00	30.00
❏ DLP-3833 [M]	Cool Hand Luke	1968	12.50	25.00	50.00
❏ DLP-25831 [S]	Music from Mission: Impossible	1967	10.00	20.00	40.00
❏ DLP-25833 [S]	Cool Hand Luke	1968	12.50	25.00	50.00
❏ DLP-25852	There's a Whole Lot of Schifrin Goin' On	1968	5.00	10.00	20.00
DRG					
❏ SBL-12591	The Fourth Protocol	1987	3.75	7.50	15.00
ENTR'ACTE					
❏ ERS-6508	Voyage of the Damned	1977	6.25	12.50	25.00
❏ ERS-6510	The Eagle Has Landed/The Four Musketeers	1980	3.00	6.00	12.00
MCA					
❏ 2284	Rollercoaster	1977	3.75	7.50	15.00
❏ 2374	Nunzio	1978	3.00	6.00	12.00
❏ 5185	The Competition	1980	2.50	5.00	10.00
❏ 25012	The Cincinnati Kid	1986	2.00	4.00	8.00
❏ 25137	Liquidator	1966	2.00	4.00	8.00
MGM					
❏ E-4110 [M]	Piano, Strings and Bossa Nova	1963	3.75	7.50	15.00
❏ SE-4110 [S]	Piano, Strings and Bossa Nova	1963	5.00	10.00	20.00
❏ E-4156 [M]	Between Broadway and Hollywood	1963	3.75	7.50	15.00
❏ SE-4156 [S]	Between Broadway and Hollywood	1963	5.00	10.00	20.00
❏ E-4313 [M]	The Cincinnati Kid	1965	5.00	10.00	20.00
❏ SE-4313 [S]	The Cincinnati Kid	1965	6.25	12.50	25.00
❏ E-4413 ST [M]	Liquidator	1966	5.00	10.00	20.00
❏ SE-4413 ST [S]	Liquidator	1966	6.25	12.50	25.00
❏ SE-4742	Medical Center and Other Great Themes	1971	5.00	10.00	20.00
NAUTILUS					
❏ NR-51	Ins and Outs	198?	10.00	20.00	40.00
—Audiophile vinyl					
PALO ALTO					
❏ 8055	Ins and Outs	1983	3.00	6.00	12.00
PARAMOUNT					
❏ PAS-5002	More Music from Mission: Impossible	1969	10.00	20.00	40.00
❏ PAS-5004	Mannix	1969	7.50	15.00	30.00
ROULETTE					
❏ SR-42013	"Lalole" — The Latin Sound	1968	3.75	7.50	15.00
❏ R 52088 [M]	Lalo Brilliance	1962	5.00	10.00	20.00
❏ SR 52088 [S]	Lalo Brilliance	1962	6.25	12.50	25.00
TABU					
❏ JZ 35436	Gypsies	1978	3.00	6.00	12.00
❏ JZ 36091	No One Home	1979	3.00	6.00	12.00
TETRAGRAMMATON					
❏ T-5006	Che!	1969	7.50	15.00	30.00
TICO					
❏ LP-1070 [M]	Piano Espanol	1960	6.25	12.50	25.00
❏ LPS-1070 [S]	Piano Espanol	1960	7.50	15.00	30.00
VARESE SARABANDE					
❏ STV-81198	The Osterman Weekend	1983	2.50	5.00	10.00
VERVE					
❏ V-8543 [M]	Samba Paros Dos	1963	3.75	7.50	15.00
—With Bob Brookmeyer					
❏ V6-8543 [S]	Samba Paros Dos	1963	5.00	10.00	20.00
—With Bob Brookmeyer					
❏ V-8601 [M]	New Fantasy	1964	3.75	7.50	15.00
❏ V6-8601 [S]	New Fantasy	1964	5.00	10.00	20.00
❏ V-8624 [M]	Once a Thief and Other Themes	1965	3.75	7.50	15.00
❏ V6-8624 [S]	Once a Thief and Other Themes	1965	5.00	10.00	20.00
❏ V-8654 [M]	The Dissection and Reconstruction of Music from the Past	1966	3.75	7.50	15.00
❏ V6-8654 [S]	The Dissection and Reconstruction of Music from the Past	1966	5.00	10.00	20.00
❏ V6-8785	Insensatez	1968	3.75	7.50	15.00
❏ V6-8801	Rock Requiem	1971	3.00	6.00	12.00
WARNER BROS.					
❏ WS 1777	Bullitt	1968	12.50	25.00	50.00
❏ BS 2727	Enter the Dragon	1973	12.50	25.00	50.00
❏ BSK 3328	Boulevard Nights	1979	2.50	5.00	10.00

S

Number	Title (A Side/B Side)	Yr	VG	VG+	NM
SCHILLER, LAWRENCE					
Albums					
CAPITOL					
❑ TAO 2574 [M]	LSD	1966	25.00	50.00	100.00
❑ KAO 2630 [M]	Why Did Lenny Bruce Die?	1967	7.50	15.00	30.00
❑ KAO 2652 [M]	Homosexuality in the American Male	1967	7.50	15.00	30.00
SCHILLING, JOHNNY, AND THE SHERWOODS					
45s					
C&A					
❑ 507	King of the World/Marcelle	1963	25.00	50.00	100.00
SCHOLARS, THE Featuring a young KENNY ROGERS.					
45s					
CUE					
❑ 7927/8	The Poor Little Doggie/What Did I Do Wrong	1956	10.00	20.00	40.00
DOT					
❑ 15498	Rock Road/Spin the Wheel	1956	5.00	10.00	20.00
❑ 15519	If You Listen with Your Heart/Poor Little Doggie	1956	5.00	10.00	20.00
IMPERIAL					
❑ 5449	I Didn't Want to Do It/Beloved	1957	6.25	12.50	25.00
❑ 5459	Eternally Yours/Kan-Gu-Wa	1957	6.25	12.50	25.00
SCHOOLBOYS, THE					
45s					
JUANITA					
❑ 103	Angel of Love/The Slide	1958	37.50	75.00	150.00
OKEH					
❑ 7076	Shirley/Please Say You Want Me	1957	7.50	15.00	30.00
—"Shirley" was the hit, but "Please Say You Want Me" is the side that has lived on					
❑ 7085	I Am Old Enough/Mary	1957	6.25	12.50	25.00
❑ 7090	Pearl/Carol	1957	6.25	12.50	25.00
SCHORY, DICK					
Albums					
CONCERT DISC					
❑ SC-21 [M]	Re-Percussion	1957	15.00	30.00	60.00
RCA VICTOR					
❑ LPM-1866 [M]	Music for Bang, Barroom and Harp	1958	15.00	30.00	60.00
❑ LSP-1866 [S]	Music for Bang, Barroom and Harp	1958	50.00	100.00	200.00
❑ LPM-2125 [M]	Music to Break Any Mood	1960	7.50	15.00	30.00
❑ LSP-2125 [S]	Music to Break Any Mood	1960	25.00	50.00	100.00
❑ LPM-2289 [M]	Wild Percussion and Horns A-Plenty	1960	7.50	15.00	30.00
❑ LSP-2289 [S]	Wild Percussion and Horns A-Plenty	1960	15.00	30.00	60.00
❑ LSA-2306 [S]	Runnin' Wild	1960	10.00	20.00	40.00
❑ LSA-2382 [S]	Stereo Action Goes Broadway	1961	10.00	20.00	40.00
❑ LPM-2485 [M]	Holiday for Percussion	1962	7.50	15.00	30.00
❑ LSA-2485 [S]	Holiday for Percussion	1962	10.00	20.00	40.00
❑ LSP-2613 [S]	Supercussion	1963	10.00	20.00	40.00
❑ LPM-2738 [M]	Politely Percussive	1963	7.50	15.00	30.00
❑ LSP-2738 [S]	Politely Percussive	1963	10.00	20.00	40.00
❑ LPM-2806 [M]	Dick Schory on Tour	1964	5.00	10.00	20.00
❑ LSP-2806 [S]	Dick Schory on Tour	1964	6.25	12.50	25.00
❑ LPM-2926 [M]	The Happy Hits	1964	5.00	10.00	20.00
❑ LSP-2926 [S]	The Happy Hits	1964	6.25	12.50	25.00
SCHUMACHER, CHRISTINE, SINGS WITH THE SUPREMES Also see THE SUPREMES.					
45s					
MOTOWN					
❑ L-294-MO5 [DJ]	Mother You, Smother You (same on both sides)	1968	75.00	150.00	300.00
—Schumacher won a "Record a Record with the Supremes" contest on WKNR of Detroit. This is the rare result.					
SCOOBY DOO					
45s					
ZEPHYR					
❑ 006	Moonglow/Ernie's Journey	195?	5.00	10.00	20.00
Albums					
ZEPHYR					
❑ ZMP-12002 [M]	Jerry Leiber Presents Scooby Doo	1959	12.50	25.00	50.00
SCORPION					
Albums					
TOWER					
❑ ST 5171	Scorpion	1969	12.50	25.00	50.00
SCORPIONS					
12-Inch Singles					
MERCURY					
❑ MK 212 [DJ]	You Give Me All I Need (same on both sides)	1982	2.00	4.00	8.00
❑ 265 [DJ]	Rock You Like a Hurricane (same on both sides)	1984	2.50	5.00	10.00
❑ 359 [DJ]	Big City Nights (Edit) (LP)/No One Like You (Live)	1985	2.00	4.00	8.00
❑ 378 [DJ]	Loving You Sunday Morning/No One Like You	1985	2.00	4.00	8.00
❑ 833 [DJ]	I'm Leaving You (Long) (Short)	1984	2.00	4.00	8.00
45s					
MERCURY					
❑ 76008	Coast to Coast/Loving You Sunday Morning	1979	—	2.00	4.00
❑ 76070	Make It Real/(B-side unknown)	1980	—	2.00	4.00
❑ 76084	Lady Starlight/(B-side unknown)	1980	—	2.00	4.00
❑ 76153	No One Like You/Now	1982	—	2.00	4.00
❑ 818440-7	Rock You Like a Hurricane/Coming Home	1984	—	—	3.00
❑ 818440-7 [PS]	Rock You Like a Hurricane/Coming Home	1984	—	2.50	5.00
❑ 866236-7	Send Me an Angel/Wind of Change (Russian Version)	1991	—	2.00	4.00
❑ 868180-7	Wind of Change/Money and Fame	1991	—	2.00	4.00
❑ 870323-7	Rhythm of Love/We Let It Rock…We Let It Roll	1988	—	—	3.00
❑ 870323-7 [PS]	Rhythm of Love/We Let It Rock…We Let It Roll	1988	—	—	3.00
❑ 870559-7	Believe in Love/Love on the Run	1988	—	—	3.00
❑ 872372-7	Passion Rules the Game/Media Overkill	1988	—	—	3.00
❑ 880082-7	Still Loving You/Bad Boys Running Wild	1984	—	—	3.00
❑ 880319-7	I'm Leaving You/Same Thrill	1984	—	—	3.00
RCA VICTOR					
❑ PB-10574	Speedy's Gone/They Need a Million	1976	—	3.00	6.00
❑ PB-10691	In Trance/Night Lights	1976	—	3.00	6.00

Number	Title (A Side/B Side)	Yr	VG	VG+	NM
Albums					
BILLINGSGATE					
❑ 1004	Lonesome Crow	1974	7.50	15.00	30.00
MERCURY					
❑ SRM-1-3795	Lovedrive	1979	2.50	5.00	10.00
❑ SRM-1-3825	Animal Magnetism	1980	2.50	5.00	10.00
❑ SRM-1-4039	Blackout	1982	2.50	5.00	10.00
❑ 814981-1	Love at First Sting	1984	2.50	5.00	10.00
—With man and woman on cover					
❑ 818885-1	Blackout	198?	2.00	4.00	8.00
—Reissue of 4039					
❑ 822038-1	Love at First Sting	1984	3.00	6.00	12.00
—Reissue with band on cover					
❑ 822555-1	Lovedrive	198?	2.00	4.00	8.00
—Reissue of 3795					
❑ 822556-1	Animal Magnetism	198?	2.00	4.00	8.00
—Reissue of 3825					
❑ 824344-1 [(2)]	World Wide Live	1985	3.00	6.00	12.00
❑ 832963-1	Savage Amusement	1988	2.50	5.00	10.00
❑ 842002-1	Best of Rockers 'N' Ballads	1989	2.50	5.00	10.00
❑ 846908-1	Crazy World	1990	3.75	7.50	15.00
RCA VICTOR					
❑ AFL1-2628	Taken by Force	1978	3.00	6.00	12.00
❑ CPL2-3039 [(2)]	Toyko Tapes	1978	3.75	7.50	15.00
❑ AFL1-3516	Best of Scorpions	1979	2.50	5.00	10.00
❑ AYL1-3659	Virgin Killer	1980	2.00	4.00	8.00
—"Best Buy Series" reissue					
❑ AFL1-4025	Fly to the Rainbow	1977	2.50	5.00	10.00
—Reissue with new prefix					
❑ PPL1-4025	Fly to the Rainbow	1975	3.00	6.00	12.00
❑ AFL1-4128	In Trance	1977	2.50	5.00	10.00
—Reissue with new prefix					
❑ PPL1-4128	In Trance	1976	3.00	6.00	12.00
❑ PPL1-4225	Virgin Killer	1977	3.00	6.00	12.00
❑ AYL1-4657	In Trance	1983	2.00	4.00	8.00
—"Best Buy Series" reissue					
❑ AYL1-5057	Fly to the Rainbow	1984	2.00	4.00	8.00
—"Best Buy Series" reissue					
❑ AFL1-5085	Best of Scorpions, Vol. 2	1984	2.50	5.00	10.00
SCOTT, BETTY					
45s					
HIT					
❑ 78	My Whole World Is Falling Down/Twist It Up	1963	2.00	4.00	8.00
—B-side by Herbert Hunter					
SCOTT, BILLY					
45s					
CAMEO					
❑ 121	You're the Greatest/That's Why I Was Born	1957	6.25	12.50	25.00
❑ 143	A Million Boys/The Town of Never Worry	1958	5.00	10.00	20.00
EVEREST					
❑ 19315	Carole/Stairway to the Stars	1959	3.75	7.50	15.00
LAMON					
❑ 10114	Merry Christmas/A Night to Remember	1983	—	2.00	4.00
SCOTT, BUDDY					
45s					
HIT					
❑ 230	May the Bird of Paradise Fly Up Your Nose/Turn! Turn! Turn!	1965	2.50	5.00	10.00
—B-side by Jackie and the Giants					
SCOTT, CALVIN					
45s					
ATCO					
❑ 6696	I'm Taking You Home to Mama/Sonny Boy (Be a Man)	1969	3.00	6.00	12.00
❑ 6729	Cry Like a Baby/More Than You'll Ever Know	1970	3.00	6.00	12.00
STAX					
❑ 0094	Shame on the Family Name/I've Made a Reservation	1971	2.50	5.00	10.00
❑ 0110	Goin' Back to Eden/The Sadness for Things	1971	2.50	5.00	10.00
Albums					
STAX					
❑ STS-2046	I'm Not Blind… I Just Can't See	1972	20.00	40.00	80.00
SCOTT, CHRISTOPHER					
Albums					
DECCA					
❑ DL 75141	Switched-On Bacharach	1969	3.75	7.50	15.00
❑ DL 75243	More Switched-On Bacharach	1970	3.75	7.50	15.00
MCA					
❑ 282	Switched-On Bacharach	1973	3.00	6.00	12.00
—Reissue of Decca 75141					
SCOTT, FREDDIE Also see THE SYMPHONICS (2).					
45s					
COLPIX					
❑ 692	Hey Girl/The Slide	1963	3.00	6.00	12.00
❑ 709	I Got a Woman/Brand New World	1963	2.50	5.00	10.00
❑ 724	Where Does Love Go/Where Have All the Flowers Gone	1964	2.50	5.00	10.00
❑ 752	On Broadway/If I Had a Hammer	1964	2.50	5.00	10.00
COLUMBIA					
❑ 43112	Mr. Heartache/One Heartache Too Many	1964	2.50	5.00	10.00
❑ 43199	Lonely Man/I'll Try Again	1964	2.50	5.00	10.00
❑ 43316	Don't Let It End/Come Up Singing	1965	2.50	5.00	10.00
❑ 43623	One Iddy Biddy Needle/Forget Me If You Can	1966	2.50	5.00	10.00
JOY					
❑ 250	Baby, You're a Long Time Dead/Lost the Right	1961	3.00	6.00	12.00
❑ 255	I Gotta Stand Tall/When the Wind Changes	1961	3.00	6.00	12.00
❑ 280	I Gotta Stand Tall/When the Wind Changes	1963	2.50	5.00	10.00
P.I.P.					
❑ 8932	Deep Is the Night/The Great If	1972	—	2.50	5.00

Number	Title (A Side/B Side)	Yr	VG	VG+	NM
PROBE					
❏ 481	I Shall Be Released/Girl I Love You	1970	—	3.00	6.00
SHOUT					
❏ 207	Are You Lonely for Me/Where Were You	1966	2.00	4.00	8.00
❏ 211	Cry to Me/No One Could Ever Love You	1967	2.00	4.00	8.00
❏ 212	Am I Grooving You/Never You Mind	1967	2.00	4.00	8.00
❏ 216	He Will Break Your Heart/I'll Be Gone	1967	2.00	4.00	8.00
❏ 220	He Ain't Give You None/Run Joy	1967	2.00	4.00	8.00
❏ 227	Just Like a Flower/Spanish Harlem	1968	2.00	4.00	8.00
❏ 233	(You) Got What I Need/Powerful Love	1968	2.50	5.00	10.00
❏ 238	Loving You Is Killing Me/Eileen	1968	2.00	4.00	8.00
❏ 245	Forever My Darling/(You) Got What I Need	1969	2.50	5.00	10.00
VANGUARD					
❏ 35137	I Guess God Wants It This Way/Please Listen	1971	—	2.50	5.00
Albums					
COLPIX					
❏ CP-461 [M]	Freddie Scott Sings and Sings and Sings	1964	15.00	30.00	60.00
—Gold label					
❏ CP-461 [M]	Freddie Scott Sings and Sings and Sings	1965	10.00	20.00	40.00
—Blue label					
❏ SCP-461 [S]	Freddie Scott Sings and Sings and Sings	1964	30.00	60.00	120.00
—Gold label					
❏ SCP-461 [R]	Freddie Scott Sings and Sings and Sings	1965	7.50	15.00	30.00
—Blue label					
COLUMBIA					
❏ CL 2258 [M]	Everything I Have Is Yours	1964	5.00	10.00	20.00
❏ CL 2660 [M]	Lonely Man	1967	5.00	10.00	20.00
❏ CS 9058 [S]	Everything I Have Is Yours	1964	6.25	12.50	25.00
❏ CS 9460 [S]	Lonely Man	1967	6.25	12.50	25.00
PROBE					
❏ CPLP-4517	I Shall Be Released	1970	6.25	12.50	25.00
SHOUT					
❏ SLP-501 [M]	Are You Lonely for Me	1967	5.00	10.00	20.00
❏ SLPS-501 [S]	Are You Lonely for Me	1967	6.25	12.50	25.00

SCOTT, FREDDIE, AND THE CHIMES
45s

Number	Title (A Side/B Side)	Yr	VG	VG+	NM
ARROW					
❏ 724	Please Call/A Letter Came This Morning	1958	10.00	20.00	40.00
❏ 726	Lovin' Baby/A Faded Memory	1958	10.00	20.00	40.00

SCOTT, JACK
45s

Number	Title (A Side/B Side)	Yr	VG	VG+	NM
ABC					
❏ 10843	Before the Bird Flies/Insane	1966	5.00	10.00	20.00
ABC-PARAMOUNT					
❏ 9818	Baby She's Gone/You Can Bet Your Bottom Dollar	1957	37.50	75.00	150.00
❏ 9860	Two Timin' Woman/I Need Your Love	1957	37.50	75.00	150.00
CAPITOL					
❏ 4554	A Little Feeling (Called Love)/Now That I	1961	6.25	12.50	25.00
❏ 4554 [PS]	A Little Feeling (Called Love)/Now That I	1961	12.50	25.00	50.00
❏ 4597	My Dream Came True/Strange Desire	1961	5.00	10.00	20.00
❏ 4597 [PS]	My Dream Came True/Strange Desire	1961	12.50	25.00	50.00
❏ 4637	Steps 1 and 2/One of These Days	1961	5.00	10.00	20.00
❏ 4637 [PS]	Steps 1 and 2/One of These Days	1961	12.50	25.00	50.00
❏ 4689	Cry, Cry, Cry/Grizzly Bear	1962	5.00	10.00	20.00
❏ 4689 [PS]	Cry, Cry, Cry/Grizzly Bear	1962	12.50	25.00	50.00
❏ 4738	The Part Where I Cry/You Only See What You Wanna See	1962	5.00	10.00	20.00
❏ 4796	Sad Story/I Can't Hold Your Letters	1962	5.00	10.00	20.00
❏ 4855	If Only/Green, Green Valley	1962	5.00	10.00	20.00
❏ 4903	Strangers/Laugh and the World Laughs With You	1963	5.00	10.00	20.00
❏ 4955	All I See Is Blue/Meo Myo	1963	5.00	10.00	20.00
CARLTON					
❏ 462	My True Love/Leroy	1958	7.50	15.00	30.00
❏ 483	With Your Love/Geraldine	1958	7.50	15.00	30.00
❏ 483 [PS]	With Your Love/Geraldine	1958	15.00	30.00	60.00
❏ 493	Goodbye Baby/Save My Soul	1959	7.50	15.00	30.00
❏ 493 [PS]	Goodbye Baby/Save My Soul	1959	15.00	30.00	60.00
❏ 504	I Never Felt Like This/Bella	1959	7.50	15.00	30.00
❏ 514	The Way I Walk/Midgie	1959	7.50	15.00	30.00
❏ 519 [M]	There Comes a Time/Baby Marie	1959	5.00	10.00	20.00
❏ ST-519 [S]	There Comes a Time/Baby Marie	1959	10.00	20.00	40.00
DOT					
❏ 17475	May You Never Be Alone/Face to the Wall	1973	—	2.50	5.00
❏ 17504	You're Just Getting Better/Walk Through My Mind	1974	—	2.50	5.00
GROOVE					
❏ 58-0027	There's Trouble Brewin'/Jingle Bell Slide	1963	5.00	10.00	20.00
❏ 58-0031	Blue Skies (Moving In on Me)/I Knew You First	1964	3.75	7.50	15.00
❏ 58-0037	Wiggle On Out/What a Wonderful Night Out	1964	5.00	10.00	20.00
❏ 58-0042	Thou Shalt Not Steal/I Prayed for an Angel	1964	3.75	7.50	15.00
❏ 58-0049	Flakey John/Tall Tales	1964	5.00	10.00	20.00
GRT					
❏ 35	Billy Jack/Mary, Marry Me	1971	—	2.50	5.00
GUARANTEED					
❏ 209	What Am I Living For/Indiana Waltz	1960	7.50	15.00	30.00
❏ 211	No One Will Ever Know/Go Wild Little Sadie	1960	7.50	15.00	30.00
JUBILEE					
❏ 5606	My Special Angel/I Keep Changin' My Mind	1967	5.00	10.00	20.00
PONIE					
❏ 7021-10	Geraldine/Midgie	197?	—	2.00	4.00
❏ 7021-11	There's Trouble Brewin'/Jingle Bell Slide	197?	—	2.00	4.00
❏ 7021-12	Flakey John/Wiggle On Out	197?	—	2.00	4.00
❏ 5121-15	Baby She's Gone/Two Timin' Woman	197?	—	2.00	4.00
❏ 6063-20	Leroy/Go Wild Little Sadie	197?	—	2.00	4.00
❏ 6083-20	Country Witch/Blues, Stay Away from Me-Stones	197?	—	2.00	4.00
❏ 4104-30	Spirit of '76/(Instrumental)	1976	—	2.00	4.00
RCA VICTOR					
❏ 47-8505	Separation's Now Granted/I Don't Believe in Tea Leaves	1965	3.75	7.50	15.00
❏ 47-8685	Looking for Linda/I Hope I Think I Wish	1965	3.75	7.50	15.00

Number	Title (A Side/B Side)	Yr	VG	VG+	NM
❏ 47-8724	Don't Hush the Laughter/Let's Learn to Live and Love Again	1965	3.75	7.50	15.00
TOP RANK					
❏ 2028 [M]	What in the World's Come Over You/Baby Baby	1959	7.50	15.00	30.00
❏ 2028 [S]	What in the World's Come Over You/Baby Baby	1959	10.00	20.00	40.00
❏ 2041 [M]	Burning Bridges/Oh Little One	1960	6.25	12.50	25.00
❏ 2041 [PS]	Burning Bridges/Oh Little One	1960	15.00	30.00	60.00
❏ 2041 [S]	Burning Bridges/Oh Little One	1960	15.00	30.00	60.00
❏ 2055	It Only Happened Yesterday/Cool Water	1960	5.00	10.00	20.00
❏ 2075	Patsy/Old Time Religion	1960	5.00	10.00	20.00
❏ 2093	Is There Something on Your Mind/Found a Woman	1960	5.00	10.00	20.00
❏ 2093 [PS]	Is There Something on Your Mind/Found a Woman	1960	15.00	30.00	60.00

7-Inch Extended Plays

Number	Title (A Side/B Side)	Yr	VG	VG+	NM
CARLTON					
❏ EP 7/1070	Save My Soul/I Can't Help It//Geraldine/With Your Love	1959	50.00	100.00	200.00
❏ EP 7/1070 [PS]	Presenting Jack Scott (Volume 1)	1959	50.00	100.00	200.00
❏ EP 7/1071	Indiana Waltz/Midgie//My True Love/Leroy	1959	50.00	100.00	200.00
❏ EP 7/1071 [PS]	Presenting Jack Scott (Volume 2)	1959	50.00	100.00	200.00
❏ EP 7/1072	No One Will Ever Know/Goodbye Baby//I'm Dreaming Of You/The Way I Walk	1959	50.00	100.00	200.00
❏ EP 7/1072 [PS]	Jack Scott Sings	1959	50.00	100.00	200.00
TOP RANK					
❏ 1001	What in the World's Come Over You/My King//Burning Bridges/Oh, Little One	1960	50.00	100.00	200.00
❏ 1001 [PS]	What in the World's Come Over You	1960	50.00	100.00	200.00
Albums					
CAPITOL					
❏ ST 2035 [S]	Burning Bridges	1964	37.50	75.00	150.00
❏ ST-8-2035	Burning Bridges	196?	50.00	100.00	200.00
—Capitol Record Club edition					
❏ T 2035 [M]	Burning Bridges	1964	20.00	40.00	80.00
CARLTON					
❏ LP-12-107 [M]	Jack Scott	1959	37.50	75.00	150.00
❏ STLP-12-107 [S]	Jack Scott	1959	50.00	100.00	200.00
—With "Stereo" printed across the top					
❏ STLP-12-107 [S]	Jack Scott	1959	75.00	150.00	300.00
—With "Stereo" in felt letters horizontally along the top of cover					
❏ STLP-12-107 [S]	Jack Scott	1959	100.00	200.00	400.00
—With "Stereo" in felt letters vertically along the left of cover					
❏ LP-12-122 [M]	What Am I Living For	1959	30.00	60.00	120.00
❏ STLP-12-122 [S]	What Am I Living For	1959	80.00	160.00	320.00
JADE					
❏ J33-113	Jack Is Back	198?	3.75	7.50	15.00
❏ J33-114	The Way I Rock	198?	3.75	7.50	15.00
PONIE					
❏ 563	Jack Scott	1974	3.75	7.50	15.00
❏ 7055	Jack Scott	1977	3.75	7.50	15.00
TOP RANK					
❏ RM-319 [M]	I Remember Hank Williams	1960	37.50	75.00	150.00
❏ RM-326 [M]	What in the World's Come Over You	1960	37.50	75.00	150.00
❏ RM-348 [M]	The Spirit Moves Me	1961	37.50	75.00	150.00
❏ SM-619 [S]	I Remember Hank Williams	1960	62.50	125.00	250.00
❏ SM-626 [S]	What in the World's Come Over You	1960	62.50	125.00	250.00
❏ SM-648 [S]	The Spirit Moves Me	1961	62.50	125.00	250.00

SCOTT, JOEL
45s

Number	Title (A Side/B Side)	Yr	VG	VG+	NM
PHILLES					
❏ 101	Here I Stand/You're My Only Love	1962	6.25	12.50	25.00

SCOTT, LINDA
45s

Number	Title (A Side/B Side)	Yr	VG	VG+	NM
CANADIAN AMERICAN					
❏ 123	I've Told Every Little Star/Three Guesses	1961	5.00	10.00	20.00
❏ 127	Don't Bet Money Honey/Starlight, Starbright	1961	5.00	10.00	20.00
❏ 129	I Don't Know Why/It's All Because	1961	5.00	10.00	20.00
❏ 132	Christmas Day/Twistin' Bells	1961	5.00	10.00	20.00
—B-side by Santo and Johnny					
❏ 133	Count Every Star/Land of Stars	1962	3.75	7.50	15.00
❏ 134	Bermuda/Lonely for You	1962	3.75	7.50	15.00
CONGRESS					
❏ 101	Yessiree/Town Crier	1962	3.75	7.50	15.00
❏ 103	Never in a Million Years/Through the Summer	1962	3.75	7.50	15.00
❏ 106	I Left My Heart in the Balcony/Lopsided Love Affair	1962	3.75	7.50	15.00
❏ 108	I'm So Afraid of Losing You/The Loneliest Girl in Town	1962	3.75	7.50	15.00
❏ 110	I'm Gonna Sit Right Down and Write Myself a Letter/Ain't That Fun	1963	3.75	7.50	15.00
❏ 200	Let's Fall in Love/I Know It, You Know It	1963	3.75	7.50	15.00
❏ 204	Who's Been Sleeping in My Bed/My Baby	1963	3.75	7.50	15.00
❏ 206	Let's Fall in Love/I Know It, You Know It	1964	3.75	7.50	15.00
❏ 209	I Envy You/Everybody Stopped Laughing at Jane	1964	3.75	7.50	15.00
KAPP					
❏ 610	That Old Feeling/This Is My Prayer	1964	2.50	5.00	10.00
❏ 641	If I Love Again/Patch It Up	1965	2.50	5.00	10.00
❏ 677	Don't Lose Your Head/I'll See You in My Dreams	1965	2.50	5.00	10.00
❏ 713	You Baby/I Can't Get Through to You	1965	2.50	5.00	10.00
❏ 762	Toys/Take a Walk Bobby	1966	2.50	5.00	10.00
RCA VICTOR					
❏ 47-9424	They Don't Know You/Three Miles High	1967	2.50	5.00	10.00

7-Inch Extended Plays

Number	Title (A Side/B Side)	Yr	VG	VG+	NM
CANADIAN AMERICAN					
❏ CAEP 1005	Count Every Star/Catch a Falling Star//Stars Fell on Alabama/Blue Star	196?	12.50	25.00	50.00
❏ CAEP 1005 [PS]	(title unknown)	196?	12.50	25.00	50.00
Albums					
CANADIAN AMERICAN					
❏ CALP-1005 [M]	Starlight, Starbright	1961	25.00	50.00	100.00
❏ SCALP-1005 [S]	Starlight, Starbright	1961	37.50	75.00	150.00
❏ CALP-1007 [M]	Great Scott!! Her Greatest Hits	1962	25.00	50.00	100.00
❏ SCALP-1007 [S]	Great Scott!! Her Greatest Hits	1962	37.50	75.00	150.00

S

Number	Title (A Side/B Side)	Yr	VG	VG+	NM
CONGRESS					
❏ CGL-3001 [M]	Linda	1962	10.00	20.00	40.00
❏ CGS-3001 [S]	Linda	1962	12.50	25.00	50.00
KAPP					
❏ KL-1424 [M]	Hey, Look at Me Now	1965	10.00	20.00	40.00
❏ KS-3424 [S]	Hey, Look at Me Now	1965	12.50	25.00	50.00

SCOTT, PEGGY, AND JO JO BENSON

45s

Number	Title (A Side/B Side)	Yr	VG	VG+	NM
SSS INTERNATIONAL					
❏ 736	Lover's Holiday/Here with Me	1968	2.00	4.00	8.00
❏ 748	Pickin' Wild Mountain Berries/Pure Love and Pleasure	1968	2.00	4.00	8.00
❏ 761	Soulshake/We Were Made for Each Other	1969	2.00	4.00	8.00
❏ 769	I Want to Love You Baby/We Got Our Bag	1969	2.00	4.00	8.00
❏ 781	Sugarmaker/Lover's Heaven	1969	2.00	4.00	8.00
❏ 805	Let's Spend a Day Out in the Country/Little Things That Count	1970	—	3.00	6.00
Albums					
SSS INTERNATIONAL					
❏ 1	Soulshake	1968	6.25	12.50	25.00
❏ 2	Lover's Heaven	1969	6.25	12.50	25.00

SCOTT, RICKY

45s

Number	Title (A Side/B Side)	Yr	VG	VG+	NM
CUB					
❏ 9079	I Didn't Mean It/Darlin' Darlin'	1960	5.00	10.00	20.00
X-CLUSIVE					
❏ 1001	I Didn't Mean It/Darlin' Darlin'	1960	20.00	40.00	80.00

SCOTT, RODNEY

45s

Number	Title (A Side/B Side)	Yr	VG	VG+	NM
CANON					
❏ 225	Granny Went Rockin'/Bitter Tears	1961	50.00	100.00	200.00
❏ 231	You're So Square (Baby I Don't Care)/He'll Be There	1961	50.00	100.00	200.00
MR. PEEKE					
❏ 119	You're So Square (Baby I Don't Care)/He'll Be There	1962	20.00	40.00	80.00
❏ 126	That's the Way It Goes/Bitter Tears	1963	7.50	15.00	30.00

SCOTT, SHERREE

45s

Number	Title (A Side/B Side)	Yr	VG	VG+	NM
ROBBINS					
❏ 105	Twinkle Toes (The Littlest Reindeer)/Our Christmas Day	1959	10.00	20.00	40.00
❏ 1036	Fascinating Baby/You and I	1957	37.50	75.00	150.00
ROCKET					
❏ 101	Whole Lotta Shakin' Goin' On/Unhappy Birthday	1958	37.50	75.00	150.00
❏ 101 [PS]	Whole Lotta Shakin' Goin' On/Unhappy Birthday	1958	50.00	100.00	200.00

SCOTT, SIMON

45s

Number	Title (A Side/B Side)	Yr	VG	VG+	NM
IMPERIAL					
❏ 66089	My Baby's Got Soul/Midnight	1965	3.75	7.50	15.00

SCOTT, TERRY

45s

Number	Title (A Side/B Side)	Yr	VG	VG+	NM
VALIANT					
❏ 6016	Little Angel/Love Only Me	1962	3.00	6.00	12.00

SCOTT, WALTER Lead singer with BOB KUBAN AND THE IN-MEN.

45s

Number	Title (A Side/B Side)	Yr	VG	VG+	NM
MUSICLAND U.S.A.					
❏ 111	Just You Wait/Silly Girl	1967	5.00	10.00	20.00
❏ 20009	Watch Out/My Shadow Is Gone	1966	3.75	7.50	15.00
❏ 20014	It's Been a Long Time/Proud	1966	3.75	7.50	15.00
PZAZZ					
❏ 026	Soul Stew Recipe/Feeling Something New Inside	1969	2.50	5.00	10.00
WHITE WHALE					
❏ 259	Just You Wait/Silly Girl	1967	5.00	10.00	20.00
Albums					
MUSICLAND U.S.A.					
❏ LP-3502 [M]	Great Scott	1967	5.00	10.00	20.00
❏ SLP-3502 [S]	Great Scott	1967	6.25	12.50	25.00
WHITE WHALE					
❏ WWS-7131	Walter Scott	1970	5.00	10.00	20.00

SCOTT BROTHERS, THE

45s

Number	Title (A Side/B Side)	Yr	VG	VG+	NM
COMET					
❏ 2153	Welcome Me/Letter from My Baby	1963	3.75	7.50	15.00
❏ 2161	Love Me Tenderly/It's Gonna Happen Soon	1963	3.75	7.50	15.00
FTP					
❏ 409	Mama's Little Baby/Cindy, Oh Cindy	1960	3.75	7.50	15.00
❏ 415	Kingdom of Love/Lonely Bluebird	1961	3.75	7.50	15.00
❏ 418	On Again, Off Again/Sometimes I Wonder	1961	3.75	7.50	15.00
RIBBON					
❏ 6905	Keep Laughin'/Stolen Angel	1960	6.25	12.50	25.00
❏ 6911	Lost Love/Only Then	1960	6.25	12.50	25.00
SMASH					
❏ 2139	Got to Get a Groove/My Day Has Come	1967	3.75	7.50	15.00
TODDLIN' TOWN					
❏ 125	A Hunk o' Funk/They All Came Back	1969	3.75	7.50	15.00
❏ 131	I Don't Wanna Lose You/(B-side unknown)	1969	3.75	7.50	15.00
❏ 134	Top of the Mountain/(B-side unknown)	1969	3.75	7.50	15.00
ZACHRON					
❏ 602	Magic Wand/We Like Girls	196?	3.75	7.50	15.00

SCOTT RICHARD CASE See SRC.

SCOTT-HERON, GIL Includes records with Brian Jackson.

12-Inch Singles

Number	Title (A Side/B Side)	Yr	VG	VG+	NM
ARISTA					
❏ 9216	Re-Ron/Re-Ron (Special Mix)	1984	2.50	5.00	10.00

45s

Number	Title (A Side/B Side)	Yr	VG	VG+	NM
ARISTA					
❏ 0117	Superman/We Beg Your Pardon America	1975	—	2.50	5.00
❏ 0152	Johannesburg/Fell Together	1975	—	2.50	5.00
❏ 0225	The Bottle Part 1/The Bottle Part 2	1976	—	2.50	5.00
❏ 0285	Hello Sunday! Hello Road!/Song of the Wind	1977	—	2.50	5.00
❏ 0317	Under the Hammer/Backtrack in France	1978	—	2.50	5.00
❏ 0366	Angel Dust/Third World Revolution	1978	—	2.00	4.00
❏ 0390	Show Bizness/Better Days Ahead	1979	—	2.00	4.00
❏ 0488	Shut 'Um Down/Baltimore	1980	—	2.00	4.00
❏ 0583	Legend in His Own Mind/(B-side unknown)	1980	—	2.00	4.00
❏ 0647	"B" Movie/(B-side unknown)	1981	—	2.00	4.00
❏ 1011	Blue Collar/Fast Lane	1982	—	2.00	4.00
❏ 9253	Re-Ron/Re-Ron (Special Mix)	1984	—	2.00	4.00
Albums					
ARISTA					
❏ AL 4030	The First Minute of a New Day	1975	2.50	5.00	10.00
❏ AL 4044	From South Africa to South Carolina	1975	2.50	5.00	10.00
❏ AL 4147	Bridges	1977	2.50	5.00	10.00
❏ AB 4189	Secrets	1978	2.50	5.00	10.00
❏ A2L 5001 [(2)]	It's Your World	1976	3.00	6.00	12.00
❏ AL 8248	The Best of Gil Scott-Heron	1984	2.50	5.00	10.00
❏ AL 8301	The Mind of Gil Scott-Heron	1980	3.75	7.50	15.00
❏ ALB6-8306	The Best of Gil Scott-Heron	1985	2.00	4.00	8.00
—Reissue of 8248					
❏ AL 9514	1980	1980	2.50	5.00	10.00
❏ AL 9540	Real Eyes	1980	2.50	5.00	10.00
❏ AL 9566	Reflections	1981	2.50	5.00	10.00
❏ AL 9606	Moving Target	1982	2.50	5.00	10.00
BLUEBIRD					
❏ 6994-1-RB	The Revolution Will Not Be Televised	1988	3.00	6.00	12.00
FLYING DUTCHMAN					
❏ BLD1-0613	The Revolution Will Not Be Televised	1974	5.00	10.00	20.00
❏ BXL1-0613	The Revolution Will Not Be Televised	1978	3.00	6.00	12.00
—Reissue with new prefix					
❏ BXL1-2834	Pieces of a Man	1978	3.00	6.00	12.00
—Reissue of 10143					
❏ AYL1-3818	The Revolution Will Not Be Televised	1980	2.00	4.00	8.00
—"Best Buy Series" reissue					
❏ AYL1-3819	Pieces of a Man	1980	2.00	4.00	8.00
—"Best Buy Series" reissue					
❏ FD-10143	Pieces of a Man	1971	5.00	10.00	20.00
❏ FD-10153	Free Will	1972	5.00	10.00	20.00
STRATA-EAST					
❏ SES-19742	Winter in America	1974	6.25	12.50	25.00

SCOTTIES, THE

45s

Number	Title (A Side/B Side)	Yr	VG	VG+	NM
HIT					
❏ 95	Popsicles and Icicles/Louie Louie	1963	2.00	4.00	8.00
—B-side by I Kadez					

SCOTTSVILLE SQUIRREL BARKERS, THE Chris Hillman, later of THE BYRDS, makes his first appearance on record here.

Albums

Number	Title (A Side/B Side)	Yr	VG	VG+	NM
CROWN					
❏ CST-346 [S]	Bluegrass Favorites	1963	15.00	30.00	60.00
❏ CLP-5346 [M]	Bluegrass Favorites	1963	12.50	25.00	50.00

SCRAMBLERS, THE

45s

Number	Title (A Side/B Side)	Yr	VG	VG+	NM
ARVEE					
❏ 6502	Super Surfer U.S.A./Go Getera Go	1963	6.25	12.50	25.00
DEL-FI					
❏ 4237	The Beatle Walk/The Beatle Blues	1964	6.25	12.50	25.00
Albums					
CROWN					
❏ CST-384 [S]	Cycle Psychos	1964	6.25	12.50	25.00
❏ CLP-5384 [M]	Cycle Psychos	1964	5.00	10.00	20.00
DIPLOMAT					
❏ D-2316 [M]	Motorcycle Scramble	1964	5.00	10.00	20.00
❏ DS-2316 [S]	Motorcycle Scramble	1964	6.25	12.50	25.00
WYNCOTE					
❏ SW-9048 [S]	Little Honda	1964	6.25	12.50	25.00
❏ W-9048 [M]	Little Honda	1964	5.00	10.00	20.00

SCREAMING GYPSY BANDITS

Albums

Number	Title (A Side/B Side)	Yr	VG	VG+	NM
BAR-B-Q					
❏ 004	The Dancer Inside You	1974	20.00	40.00	80.00
❏ 22185	In the Eye	1973	20.00	40.00	80.00

SEA, JOHNNY Some of these were as "Johnny Seay."

45s

Number	Title (A Side/B Side)	Yr	VG	VG+	NM
CAPITOL					
❏ 4585	The Torch and the Flame/No Tears Tonight	1961	2.50	5.00	10.00
❏ 4646	Livin' Is Lovin'/The Wayward Wind	1961	2.50	5.00	10.00
COLUMBIA					
❏ 4-44268	If/Behind My Baby's Bedroom Door	1967	—	3.00	6.00
❏ 4-44423	Going Out to Tulsa/There's a Shadow Bar	1968	—	2.50	5.00
❏ 4-44542	Mama When I'm Gone Don't Cry for Me/Song Number 9 1/2 on the Album	1968	—	2.50	5.00
❏ 4-44634	Three Six-Packs, Two Arms and a Juke Box/I Loved Her Fine for a Time	1968	—	2.50	5.00
—As "Johnny Seay"					
❏ 4-44717	I've Learned a Lot Today/A Poor Boy Just Trying to Get Along	1968	—	2.50	5.00
❏ 4-44805	Cryin' Gray Tombstone/Everybody's Friend	1969	—	2.50	5.00
NRC					
❏ 006	It Won't Be Easy to Forget/I Love You	1958	3.00	6.00	12.00
❏ 019	Frankie's Man, Johnny/Loneliness	1959	3.00	6.00	12.00
❏ 026	Stranger/Judy and Johnny	1959	3.00	6.00	12.00
❏ 049	Nobody's Darling But Mine/My Time to Cry	1959	3.00	6.00	12.00
❏ 060	Ghost Riders in the Sky/Mr. and Mrs. Sippi	1960	3.00	6.00	12.00
—As "Johnny Seay"					

Number	Title (A Side/B Side)	Yr	VG	VG+	NM
PHILIPS					
☐ 40164	My Baby Walks All Over Me/				
	There's Another Man	1964	2.00	4.00	8.00
☐ 40214	All Mixed Up/Standing Room Only	1964	2.00	4.00	8.00
☐ 40267	My Old Faded Rose/It's a Shame	1965	2.00	4.00	8.00
☐ 40307	If It Wasn't for Hard Luck/Hitchin' and Hikin'	1965	2.00	4.00	8.00
SOUND FACTORY					
☐ 411	Bobby's Got a Thing About Trains/				
	(B-side unknown)	1980	—	3.00	6.00
VIKING					
☐ 1011	Fort Worth Girl/Willie's Drunk and Willie's Dying	1970	—	2.50	5.00
☐ 1017	Annie's Going to Sing Her Song/				
	Stormy Weather Girl	1971	—	3.00	6.00
WARNER BROS.					
☐ PRO 233 [DJ]	Day for Decision/Listen to the Message	1966	3.00	6.00	12.00
—Promo-only edition with different B-side					
☐ 5820	Day for Decision/Mary Rocks Him to Sleep	1966	—	3.00	6.00
☐ 5861	Things You Gave Me/Wheels on the Highway	1966	—	3.00	6.00
☐ 5889	Nothin's Bad As Bein' Lonely/Ain't That Right	1967	—	3.00	6.00
Albums					
HILLTOP					
☐ JM-6018	Everybody's Favorite	196?	3.00	6.00	12.00
PHILIPS					
☐ PHM 200139 [M]	World of a Country Boy	1964	5.00	10.00	20.00
☐ PHM 200194 [M]	Live at the Bitter End	1965	5.00	10.00	20.00
☐ PHS 600139 [S]	World of a Country Boy	1964	6.25	12.50	25.00
☐ PHS 600194 [S]	Live at the Bitter End	1965	6.25	12.50	25.00
WARNER BROS.					
☐ W 1659 [M]	Day for Decision	1966	3.75	7.50	15.00
☐ WS 1659 [S]	Day for Decision	1966	5.00	10.00	20.00
SEA SHELLS, THE					
45s					
GOLIATH					
☐ 1357	Love Those Beach Boys/Close to Jimmy	1964	10.00	20.00	40.00
JUBILEE					
☐ 5587	Hit the Surf/Barefoot in the Sand	1967	5.00	10.00	20.00
SEALS, JIMMY Also see THE CHAMPS; SEALS AND CROFTS.					
45s					
CARLTON					
☐ 470	Sneaky Pete/Benguela	1958	7.50	15.00	30.00
CHALLENGE					
☐ 9153	Wish for You, Want for You, Wait for You/				
	Runaway Heart	1962	7.50	15.00	30.00
☐ 9200	Lady Heartbreak/Grounded	1963	7.50	15.00	30.00
☐ 59270	Everybody's Doing the Jerk/Wa-Hoo	1965	5.00	10.00	20.00
☐ 59299	She's Not a Bad Girl/The Yesterday of Our Love	1965	5.00	10.00	20.00
WINSTON					
☐ 1021	Sneaky Pete/Benguela	1958	10.00	20.00	50.00
☐ 1027	Biscayne Bay/Juarez	1958	10.00	20.00	50.00
SEALS AND CROFTS Also see THE CHAMPS; JIMMY SEALS.					
12-Inch Singles					
WARNER BROS.					
☐ PRO-A-722 [DJ]	You're the Love (5:22) (stereo/mono)	1978	3.75	7.50	15.00
45s					
T-A					
☐ 188	In Tune/Seldom's Sister	1969	2.00	4.00	8.00
☐ 191	See My Life/(B-side unknown)	1969	2.00	4.00	8.00
☐ 206	See My Life/In Tune//Hollow Reed/Leave	1970	2.50	5.00	10.00
☐ 208	Ridin' Thumb/Leave	1970	2.00	4.00	8.00
☐ 210	Gabriel Go On Home/Robin	1971	2.00	4.00	8.00
WARNER BROS.					
☐ 7536	When I Meet Them/Irish Linen	1971	—	3.00	6.00
☐ 7565	Sudan Village/High on a Mountain	1972	—	3.00	6.00
☐ 7606	Summer Breeze/East of Ginger Trees	1972	—	2.50	5.00
☐ 7671	Hummingbird/Say	1972	—	2.50	5.00
☐ 7697	We May Never Pass This Way (Again)/Intone				
	My Servant	1973	—	—	—
—Unreleased?					
☐ 7708	Diamond Girl/Wisdom	1973	—	2.50	5.00
☐ 7740	We May Never Pass This Way (Again)/Jessica	1973	—	2.50	5.00
☐ 7771	Unborn Child/Ledges	1974	—	2.00	4.00
☐ 7810	King of Nothing/Follow Me	1974	—	2.00	4.00
☐ 8075	I'll Play for You/Truth Is But a Woman	1975	—	2.00	4.00
☐ 8130	Castles in the Sand/Golden Rainbow	1975	—	2.00	4.00
☐ 8190	Get Closer/Don't Fail	1976	—	2.00	4.00
☐ 8190 [PS]	Get Closer/Don't Fail	1976	5.00	10.00	20.00
☐ 8277	Baby, I'll Give It to You/Advance Guards	1976	—	2.00	4.00
☐ 8405	My Fair Share/East of Ginger Trees	1977	—	2.00	4.00
☐ 8405 [PS]	My Fair Share/East of Ginger Trees	1977	—	3.00	6.00
☐ 8551	You're the Love/Midnight Blue	1978	—	2.00	4.00
☐ 8639	Magnolia Moon/Takin' It Easy	1978	—	2.00	4.00
☐ 49522	First Love/Kite Dreams	1980	—	2.00	4.00
7-Inch Extended Plays					
WARNER BROS.					
☐ S 2761 [DJ]	Rachel/King of Nothing/Desert People//				
	The Story of Her Love/Dance				
	by the Light of the Moon	1974	2.00	4.00	8.00
—33 1/3 rpm, small hole jukebox edition					
☐ S 2761 [PS]	Unborn Child	1974	2.50	5.00	10.00
Albums					
K-TEL					
☐ NU 9610	Collection: 16 of Their Greatest Hits	1979	3.00	6.00	12.00
NAUTILUS					
☐ NR-10	Summer Breeze	1980	7.50	15.00	30.00
—Audiophile vinyl					
T-A					
☐ 5001	Seals and Crofts	1969	6.25	12.50	25.00
☐ 5004	Down Home	1970	6.25	12.50	25.00
WARNER BROS.					
☐ BS 2568	Year of Sunday	1971	3.00	6.00	12.00
—Green "WB" label					
☐ BS 2568	Year of Sunday	1973	2.50	5.00	10.00
—"Burbank" palm-tree label					

Number	Title (A Side/B Side)	Yr	VG	VG+	NM
☐ BS 2629	Summer Breeze	1972	3.00	6.00	12.00
—Green "WB" label					
☐ BS 2629	Summer Breeze	1973	2.50	5.00	10.00
—"Burbank" palm-tree label					
☐ BS 2629	Summer Breeze	1979	2.00	4.00	8.00
—White or tan label					
☐ BS4 2629 [Q]	Summer Breeze	1974	5.00	10.00	20.00
☐ BS 2699	Diamond Girl	1973	3.00	6.00	12.00
—"Burbank" palm-tree label					
☐ BS 2699	Diamond Girl	1979	2.00	4.00	8.00
—White or tan label					
☐ BS4 2699 [Q]	Diamond Girl	1974	5.00	10.00	20.00
☐ BS 2761	Unborn Child	1974	3.00	6.00	12.00
☐ BS4 2761 [Q]	Unborn Child	1974	5.00	10.00	20.00
☐ 2WS 2809 [(2)]	Seals & Crofts I and II	1974	3.75	7.50	15.00
—Reissue of the two T-A LPs in one package					
☐ BS 2848	I'll Play for You	1975	2.50	5.00	10.00
☐ BS4 2848 [Q]	I'll Play for You	1975	5.00	10.00	20.00
☐ BS 2886	Greatest Hits	1975	2.50	5.00	10.00
☐ BS 2907	Get Closer	1976	2.50	5.00	10.00
☐ BS 2976	Sudan Village	1976	2.50	5.00	10.00
☐ BSK 3109	Greatest Hits	1977	2.00	4.00	8.00
—Reissue; any label variation					
☐ BSK 3165	Takin' It Easy	1978	2.50	5.00	10.00
☐ BSK 3365	The Longest Road	1980	2.50	5.00	10.00
SEAN AND THE BRANDYWINES					
45s					
DECCA					
☐ 31910	She Ain't No Good/Cod'ine	1966	5.00	10.00	20.00
—Produced by Gary Usher					
SEARCH PARTY, THE					
Albums					
CENTURY CUSTOM					
☐ 32013	Montgomery Chapel	1969	500.00	1000.	2000.
SEARCHERS, THE					
45s					
KAPP					
☐ KJB-22	Needles and Pins/Ain't That Just Like Me	1964	2.00	4.00	8.00
—Orange label "Winners Circle Series"					
☐ KJB-27	Love Potion Number Nine/Hi-Heel Sneakers	1964	2.50	5.00	10.00
—Orange label "Winners Circle Series"; no black label counterpart					
☐ KJB-29	Bumble Bee/Everything You Do	1964	2.50	5.00	10.00
—Orange label "Winners Circle Series"; no black label counterpart					
☐ KJB-49	Bumble Bee/Everything You Do	1964	3.00	6.00	12.00
—Orange label "Winners Circle Series"; no black label counterpart					
☐ KJB-49	Bumble Bee/A Tear Fell	1965	2.50	5.00	10.00
—Orange label "Winners Circle Series"; no black label counterpart					
☐ 577	Needles and Pins/Saturday Night Out	1964	2.50	5.00	10.00
☐ 577	Needles and Pins/Ain't That Just Like Me	1964	3.00	6.00	12.00
☐ 577 [PS]	Needles and Pins/Ain't That Just Like Me	1964	12.50	25.00	50.00
—Promo-only version with red print					
☐ 577 [PS]	Needles and Pins/Ain't That Just Like Me	1964	25.00	50.00	100.00
—Promo-only "Rush Release" version with black print					
☐ 577 [PS]	Needles and Pins/Saturday Night Out	1964	7.50	15.00	30.00
—Photo sleeve with blue background					
☐ 584	Ain't That Just Like Me/Ain't Gonna Kiss You	1964	2.50	5.00	10.00
☐ 584 [PS]	Ain't That Just Like Me (special promo sleeve)	1964	12.50	25.00	50.00
☐ 593	Don't Throw Your Love Away/				
	I Pretend I'm with You	1964	2.50	5.00	10.00
☐ 609	Someday We're Gonna Love Again/				
	No One Else Could Love Me	1964	2.50	5.00	10.00
☐ 609 [PS]	Someday We're Gonna Love Again/				
	No One Else Could Love Me	1964	7.50	15.00	30.00
☐ 618	When You Walk in the Room/I'll Be Missing You	1964	2.50	5.00	10.00
☐ 644	What Have They Done to the Rain/				
	This Feeling Inside	1965	2.50	5.00	10.00
☐ 658	Goodbye My Lover Goodbye/'Til I Met You	1965	2.50	5.00	10.00
☐ 686	He's Got No Love/So Far Away	1965	2.50	5.00	10.00
☐ 706	Don't You Know Why/You Can't Lie to a Liar	1965	2.50	5.00	10.00
☐ 729	Take Me for What I'm Worth/Too Many Miles	1966	2.50	5.00	10.00
☐ 783	Have You Ever Loved Somebody/				
	It's Just the Way	1966	2.50	5.00	10.00
☐ 811	Lovers/Popcorn Double Feature	1966	2.50	5.00	10.00
LIBERTY					
☐ 55646	Sugar and Spice/Saints and Sinners	1963	6.25	12.50	25.00
☐ 55689	Sugar and Spice/Saints and Sinners	1964	3.75	7.50	15.00
MERCURY					
☐ 72172	Sweets for My Sweet/It's All Been a Dream	1963	6.25	12.50	25.00
☐ 72390	(Ain't That) Just Like Me/I Can Tell	1964	3.75	7.50	15.00
RCA VICTOR					
☐ 74-0484	Desdemona/The World Is Waiting for Tomorrow	1971	—	3.00	6.00
☐ 74-0652	Love Is Everywhere/And the Button	1972	—	3.00	6.00
SIRE					
☐ 49175	It's Too Late/Don't Hang On	1980	—	2.00	4.00
☐ 49665	Love's Melody/Little Bit of Heaven	1981	—	2.00	4.00
WORLD PACIFIC					
☐ 77908	Umbrella Man/Over the Weekend	1969	2.00	4.00	8.00
Albums					
KAPP					
☐ KL-1363 [M]	Meet the Searchers	1964	6.25	12.50	25.00
—With black label					
☐ KL-1363 [M]	Meet the Searchers	1964	10.00	20.00	40.00
—With black and blue label					
☐ KL-1409 [M]	This Is Us	1964	6.25	12.50	25.00
—Version 2: With sticker on front cover referring to "Love Potion No. 9"					
☐ KL-1409 [M]	This Is Us	1964	6.25	12.50	25.00
—Version 1: No sticker on front cover					
☐ KL-1412 [M]	The New Searchers LP	1965	6.25	12.50	25.00
☐ KL-1449 [M]	The Searchers No. 4	1965	6.25	12.50	25.00
☐ KL-1477 [M]	Take Me for What I'm Worth	1966	6.25	12.50	25.00
☐ KS-3363 [S]	Meet the Searchers	1964	7.50	15.00	30.00
—With black label					
☐ KS-3363 [S]	Meet the Searchers	1964	12.50	25.00	50.00
—With black and blue label					

S

Number	Title (A Side/B Side)	Yr	VG	VG+	NM
❑ KS-3409 [S]	This Is Us	1964	7.50	15.00	30.00
—Version 2: With sticker on front cover referring to "Love Potion No. 9"					
❑ KS-3409 [S]	This Is Us	1964	7.50	15.00	30.00
—Version 1: No sticker on front cover					
❑ KS-3412 [S]	The New Searchers LP	1965	7.50	15.00	30.00
❑ KS-3419 [S]	The Searchers No. 4	1965	7.50	15.00	30.00
❑ KS-3477 [S]	Take Me for What I'm Worth	1966	7.50	15.00	30.00
MERCURY					
❑ MG-20914 [M]	Hear! Hear!	1964	7.50	15.00	30.00
—Version 3: With "Live from the Star Club" imprinted on cover					
❑ MG-20914 [M]	Hear! Hear!	1964	10.00	20.00	40.00
—Version 2: With sticker "Live from the Star Club" on cover					
❑ MG-20914 [M]	Hear! Hear!	1964	12.50	25.00	50.00
—White label promo					
❑ MG-20914 [M]	Hear! Hear!	1964	12.50	25.00	50.00
—Version 1: With only the title on the front cover					
❑ MG-20994 [M]	The Searchers Meet the Rattles	1965	18.75	37.50	75.00
❑ SR-60914 [S]	Hear! Hear!	1964	6.25	12.50	25.00
—Version 3: With "Live from the Star Club" imprinted on cover					
❑ SR-60914 [S]	Hear! Hear!	1964	7.50	15.00	30.00
—Version 2: With sticker "Live from the Star Club" on cover					
❑ SR-60914 [S]	Hear! Hear!	1964	10.00	20.00	40.00
—Version 1: With only the title on the front cover					
❑ SR-60994 [S]	The Searchers Meet the Rattles	1965	12.50	25.00	50.00
PYE					
❑ 501	The Searchers	197?	3.75	7.50	15.00
—Reissue of Kapp hits					
❑ 508	The Searchers, Vol. 2	1976	3.75	7.50	15.00
RHINO					
❑ RNLP 162	Greatest Hits	1985	2.50	5.00	10.00
❑ R1-70162	Greatest Hits	1988	2.00	4.00	8.00
—Reissue of RNLP 162					
SIRE					
❑ SRK 3523	Love's Melodies	1981	2.50	5.00	10.00
❑ SRK 6082	The Searchers	1980	2.50	5.00	10.00

SEARS, RICKY
45s
MUSICOR

Number	Title (A Side/B Side)	Yr	VG	VG+	NM
❑ 1193	Borrowed Love/Bring Me Some Water	1966	2.00	4.00	8.00
❑ 1231	I'm Gonna Roast Your Duck/Where's My Love	1967	2.00	4.00	8.00
❑ 1255	Make Him Go/No One Will Know	1967	2.00	4.00	8.00
❑ 1281	Change of Heart/Faded Memory	1967	2.00	4.00	8.00

SEATRAIN
45s
A&M

Number	Title (A Side/B Side)	Yr	VG	VG+	NM
❑ 994	As I Lay Losing/Let the Duchess Know	1968	2.00	4.00	8.00
—As "Sea Train"					
❑ 994 [PS]	As I Lay Losing/Let the Duchess Know	1968	3.75	7.50	15.00
—As "Sea Train"					
CAPITOL					
❑ 3067	13 Questions/Oh My Love-Sally Goodin	1971	—	3.00	6.00
❑ 3140	Song of Job/Waiting for Elijah	1971	—	3.00	6.00
❑ 3201	Marblehead Messenger/Despair Tire	1971	—	3.00	6.00
❑ 3275	Gramercy/How Sweet Thy Song	1972	—	3.00	6.00
WARNER BROS.					
❑ 7696	Flute Thing/Freedom Is the Reason	1973	—	2.50	5.00
Albums					
A&M					
❑ SP-4171	Sea Train	1969	3.75	7.50	15.00
CAPITOL					
❑ SMAS-650	Seatrain	1970	3.75	7.50	15.00
❑ SMAS-829	Marblehead Messenger	1971	3.75	7.50	15.00
❑ SN-16102	Seatrain	1980	2.00	4.00	8.00
—Budget-line reissue					
❑ SN-16103	Marblehead Messenger	1980	2.00	4.00	8.00
—Budget-line reissue					
WARNER BROS.					
❑ BS 2692	Watch	1973	3.00	6.00	12.00

SEAY, JOHNNY See JOHNNY SEA.

SEBASTIAN, JOHN Also see THE LOVIN' SPOONFUL.
45s
KAMA SUTRA

Number	Title (A Side/B Side)	Yr	VG	VG+	NM
❑ 254	She's a Lady/The Room Nobody Lives In	1968	2.50	5.00	10.00
❑ 254 [PS]	She's a Lady/The Room Nobody Lives In	1968	3.75	7.50	15.00
❑ 505	Younger Generation/Boredom	1970	2.00	4.00	8.00
MGM					
❑ 14122	Rainbows All Over Your Blues/ You're a Big Boy Now	1970	—	3.00	6.00
REPRISE					
❑ 0902	Fa-Fana-Fa/Magical Connection	1970	—	3.00	6.00
❑ 0918	What She Thinks About/Red-Eye Express	1970	—	3.00	6.00
❑ 1026	I Don't Want Nobody Else/Sweet Muse	1971	—	3.00	6.00
❑ 1050	We'll See/Well, Well, Well	1971	—	3.00	6.00
❑ 1074	Give Us a Break/Music for People Who Don't Speak English	1972	—	3.00	6.00
❑ 1349	Welcome Back/Warm Baby	1976	—	2.00	4.00
—Revised A-side title					
❑ 1349	Welcome Back Kotter/Warm Baby	1976	2.00	4.00	8.00
—Original A-side title					
❑ 1355	Hideaway/One Step Forward, Two Steps Back	1976	—	2.00	4.00
Albums					
MGM					
❑ SE-4654	John B. Sebastian	1969	3.75	7.50	15.00
❑ SE-4720	John Sebastian Live	1970	3.75	7.50	15.00
REPRISE					
❑ MS 2036	Cheapo-Cheapo Productions Presents Real Live John Sebastian	1971	3.00	6.00	12.00
❑ MS 2041	The Four of Us	1971	3.00	6.00	12.00
❑ MS 2187	Tarzana Kid	1974	3.00	6.00	12.00
❑ MS 2249	Welcome Back	1976	3.00	6.00	12.00
❑ RS 6379	John B. Sebastian	1969	5.00	10.00	20.00
—Same album as MGM 4654, but a different mix					
RHINO					
❑ R1-70170	The Best of John Sebastian (1969-1976)	1989	3.00	6.00	12.00

SECOND TIME, THE
45s
TOWER

Number	Title (A Side/B Side)	Yr	VG	VG+	NM
❑ 432	Listen to the Music/Psychedelic Senate	1968	2.50	5.00	10.00
Albums					
TOWER					
❑ ST 5146	Listen to the Music	1968	5.00	10.00	20.00

SECRET OYSTER
Albums
PETERS INT'L.

Number	Title (A Side/B Side)	Yr	VG	VG+	NM
❑ 9003	Furtive Pearl	1973	7.50	15.00	30.00
❑ 9009	Sea Son	1974	6.25	12.50	25.00

SECRETS, THE (1) Girl group.
45s
OMEN

Number	Title (A Side/B Side)	Yr	VG	VG+	NM
❑ 15	Here I Am/I Feel a Thrill Coming On	1966	3.00	6.00	12.00
PHILIPS					
❑ 40146	The Boy Next Door/Learnin' to Forget	1963	3.75	7.50	15.00
❑ 40173	Hey Big Boy/The Other Side of Town	1964	3.00	6.00	12.00
❑ 40173 [PS]	Hey Big Boy/The Other Side of Town	1964	5.00	10.00	20.00
❑ 40196	Here He Comes Now!/Oh Donnie	1964	3.00	6.00	12.00
❑ 40222	He's the Boy/He Doesn't Want You	1964	3.00	6.00	12.00

SECRETS, THE (2)
45s
SWAN

Number	Title (A Side/B Side)	Yr	VG	VG+	NM
❑ 4097	Hot Toddy/Twin Exhaust	1962	6.25	12.50	25.00
❑ 4097 [PS]	Hot Toddy/Twin Exhaust	1962	12.50	25.00	50.00

SECRETS, THE (U) Could be group (1).
45s
RED BIRD

Number	Title (A Side/B Side)	Yr	VG	VG+	NM
❑ 10-076	Every Day/A Smile Upside Down	1966	2.50	5.00	10.00

SEDAKA, NEIL Also see THE TOKENS.
12-Inch Singles
ELEKTRA

Number	Title (A Side/B Side)	Yr	VG	VG+	NM
❑ AS-11396-C [DJ]	All You Need Is the Music (5:30) (same on both sides)	1978	5.00	10.00	20.00
MCA CURB					
❑ L33-1196 [DJ]	New Orleans (With Gary U.S. Bonds 5:00) (Instrumental 3:18)/Come See About Me (With Mary Wilson 4:33)	1984	3.00	6.00	12.00

45s
COLLECTABLES

Number	Title (A Side/B Side)	Yr	VG	VG+	NM
❑ 4945	Laughter in the Rain/The Immigrant	1994	—	—	3.00
❑ 4946	Bad Blood/Breaking Up Is Hard to Do	1994	—	—	3.00
DECCA					
❑ 30520	Laura Lee/Snowtime	1957	15.00	30.00	60.00
ELEKTRA					
❑ 45406	Amarillo/The Leaving Game	1977	—	2.00	4.00
❑ 45421	Alone at Last/Sleazy Love	1977	—	2.00	4.00
❑ 45525	Candy Kisses/All You Need Is the Music	1978	—	2.00	4.00
❑ 46017	Sad, Sad Story/Tillie the Twirler	1979	—	2.00	4.00
❑ 46615	Should've Never Let You Go/ You're So Good for Me	1980	—	2.00	4.00
—With Dara Sedaka					
❑ 47017	Letting Go/It's Good to Be Alive Again	1980	—	3.00	6.00
❑ 47184	My World Keeps Slipping Away/Love Is Spreading Over the World	1981	—	2.00	4.00
GUYDEN					
❑ 2004	Ring-a-Rockin'/Fly, Don't Fly on Me	1958	12.50	25.00	50.00
KIRSHNER					
❑ SP-45-291 [DJ]	I'm a Song (Sing Me)/Silent Movies	1971	2.00	4.00	8.00
—Promo only number (mono versions)					
❑ SP-45-370 [DJ]	Beautiful You (Long)/Beautiful You (Short)	1972	2.00	4.00	8.00
—Promo only number					
❑ 63-5017	I'm a Song (Sing Me)/Silent Movies	1971	—	2.50	5.00
—As "Sedaka"					
❑ 63-5020	Superbird/Rosemary Blue	1972	—	2.50	5.00
❑ 63-5024	Beautiful You/Anywhere You're Gonna Be (Leba's Song)	1972	—	3.00	6.00
LEGION					
❑ 133	Ring-a-Rockin'/Fly, Don't Fly on Me	1958	25.00	50.00	100.00
MCA					
❑ 60189	Laughter in the Rain/The Immigrant	197?	—	—	3.00
—Reissue					
MCA CURB					
❑ 52307	Your Precious Love/Searchin'	1983	—	2.00	4.00
—With Dara Sedaka					
❑ 52400	New Orleans/Rhythm of the Rain	1984	—	2.00	4.00
—With Gary U.S. Bonds					
MGM					
❑ 14564	Standing on the Inside/Let Daddy Know	1973	—	2.50	5.00
❑ 14661	Alone in New York in the Rain/Suspicions	1973	—	2.50	5.00
PYRAMID					
❑ 623	Oh Delilah/Neil's Twist	1962	7.50	15.00	30.00
—B-side is an instrumental version of the A-side credited to The Marvels					
RCA VICTOR					
❑ 37-7829	Calendar Girl/The Same Old Fool	1960	12.50	25.00	50.00
—"Compact Single 33" (small hole, plays at LP speed)					
❑ 37-7874	Little Devil/I Must Be Dreaming	1961	12.50	25.00	50.00
—"Compact Single 33" (small hole, plays at LP speed)					
❑ 37-7922	Sweet Little You/I Found My World in You	1961	12.50	25.00	50.00
—"Compact Single 33" (small hole, plays at LP speed)					
❑ 37-7957	Happy Birthday Sweet Sixteen/ Don't Lead Me On	1961	12.50	25.00	50.00
—"Compact Single 33" (small hole, plays at LP speed)					
❑ 47-7408	The Diary/No Vacancy	1958	5.00	10.00	20.00
❑ 47-7408 [DJ]	The Diary/No Vacancy	1958	10.00	20.00	40.00
—White label promo with Sedaka's photo on label					
❑ 47-7473	I Go Ape/Moon of Gold	1959	5.00	10.00	20.00
❑ 47-7530	You Gotta Learn Your Rhythm and Blues/ Crying My Heart Out for You	1959	6.25	12.50	25.00

Number	Title (A Side/B Side)	Yr	VG	VG+	NM
47-7595	Oh! Carol/One Way Ticket (To the Blues)	1959	5.00	10.00	20.00
47-7709	Stairway to Heaven/Forty Winks Away	1960	3.75	7.50	15.00
47-7781	You Mean Everything to Me/Run Samson Run	1960	3.75	7.50	15.00
47-7781 [PS]	You Mean Everything to Me/Run Samson Run	1960	6.25	12.50	25.00
47-7829	Calendar Girl/The Same Old Fool	1960	3.75	7.50	15.00
47-7829 [PS]	Calendar Girl/The Same Old Fool	1960	6.25	12.50	25.00
47-7874	Little Devil/I Must Be Dreaming	1961	3.75	7.50	15.00
47-7874 [PS]	Little Devil/I Must Be Dreaming	1961	6.25	12.50	25.00
47-7922	Sweet Little You/I Found My World in You	1961	3.75	7.50	15.00
47-7922 [PS]	Sweet Little You/I Found My World in You	1961	6.25	12.50	25.00
47-7957	Happy Birthday Sweet Sixteen/Don't Lead Me On	1961	3.75	7.50	15.00
47-8007	King of Clowns/Walk with Me	1962	3.75	7.50	15.00
47-8007 [PS]	King of Clowns/Walk with Me	1962	6.25	12.50	25.00
47-8046	Breaking Up Is Hard to Do/As Long As I Live	1962	3.75	7.50	15.00
47-8046 [PS]	Breaking Up Is Hard to Do/As Long As I Live	1962	6.25	12.50	25.00
47-8086	Next Door to An Angel/I Belong to You	1962	3.75	7.50	15.00
47-8086 [PS]	Next Door to An Angel/I Belong to You	1962	6.25	12.50	25.00
47-8137	Alice in Wonderland/Circulate	1963	3.00	6.00	12.00
47-8137 [PS]	Alice in Wonderland/Circulate	1963	6.25	12.50	25.00
47-8169	Let's Go Steady Again/Waiting for Never	1963	3.00	6.00	12.00
47-8169 [PS]	Let's Go Steady Again/Waiting for Never	1963	6.25	12.50	25.00
47-8209	The Dreamer/Look Inside Your Heart	1963	3.00	6.00	12.00
47-8209 [PS]	The Dreamer/Look Inside Your Heart	1963	6.25	12.50	25.00
47-8254	Bad Girl/Wait 'Til You See My Baby	1963	3.00	6.00	12.00
47-8341	The Closest Thing to Heaven/Without a Song	1964	2.50	5.00	10.00
47-8341 [PS]	The Closest Thing to Heaven/Without a Song	1964	5.00	10.00	20.00
47-8382	Sunny/She'll Never Be You	1964	2.50	5.00	10.00
47-8453	I Hope He Breaks Your Heart/Too Late	1964	2.50	5.00	10.00
47-8511	Let the People Talk/In the Chapel with You	1965	2.50	5.00	10.00
47-8511 [PS]	Let the People Talk/In the Chapel with You	1965	5.00	10.00	20.00
47-8637	The World Through a Tear/High On a Mountain	1965	2.50	5.00	10.00
47-8637 [PS]	The World Through a Tear/High On a Mountain	1965	5.00	10.00	20.00
47-8737	The Answer to My Prayer/Blue Boy	1965	2.50	5.00	10.00
47-8844	The Answer Lies Within/Grown-Up Games	1966	2.50	5.00	10.00
47-9004	We Can Make It If We Try/Too Late	1966	2.50	5.00	10.00
61-7595 [S]	Oh! Carol/One Way Ticket (To the Blues)	1959	12.50	25.00	50.00

—"Living Stereo" (large hole, plays at 45 rpm)

Number	Title (A Side/B Side)	Yr	VG	VG+	NM
61-7709 [S]	Stairway to Heaven/Forty Winks Away	1960	12.50	25.00	50.00

—"Living Stereo" (large hole, plays at 45 rpm)

Number	Title (A Side/B Side)	Yr	VG	VG+	NM
61-7781 [S]	You Mean Everything to Me/Run Samson Run	1960	12.50	25.00	50.00

—"Living Stereo" (large hole, plays at 45 rpm)

Number	Title (A Side/B Side)	Yr	VG	VG+	NM
61-7829 [S]	Calendar Girl/The Same Old Fool	1960	12.50	25.00	50.00

—"Living Stereo" (large hole, plays at 45 rpm)

Number	Title (A Side/B Side)	Yr	VG	VG+	NM
447-0575	Oh! Carol/Calendar Girl	196?	—	3.00	6.00

—Gold Standard Series; black label

Number	Title (A Side/B Side)	Yr	VG	VG+	NM
447-0575	Oh! Carol/Calendar Girl	197?	—	2.00	4.00

—Gold Standard Series; red label

Number	Title (A Side/B Side)	Yr	VG	VG+	NM
447-0597	The Diary/Happy Birthday Sweet Sixteen	196?	—	3.00	6.00

—Gold Standard Series; black label

Number	Title (A Side/B Side)	Yr	VG	VG+	NM
447-0597	The Diary/Happy Birthday Sweet Sixteen	197?	—	2.00	4.00

—Gold Standard Series; red label

Number	Title (A Side/B Side)	Yr	VG	VG+	NM
447-0701	Breaking Up Is Hard to Do/Next Door to An Angel	196?	—	3.00	6.00

—Gold Standard Series; black label

Number	Title (A Side/B Side)	Yr	VG	VG+	NM
447-0701	Breaking Up Is Hard to Do/Next Door to An Angel	197?	—	2.00	4.00

—Gold Standard Series; red label

Number	Title (A Side/B Side)	Yr	VG	VG+	NM
447-0939	Little Devil/Stairway to Heaven	196?	—	3.00	6.00

—Gold Standard Series; black label

Number	Title (A Side/B Side)	Yr	VG	VG+	NM
SP-45-96 [DJ]	RCA Victor Special DJ Spots	1960	12.50	25.00	50.00

—White label promo only; Sedaka introduces six songs and promotes his current release

ROCKET

Number	Title (A Side/B Side)	Yr	VG	VG+	NM
40313	Laughter in the Rain/Endlessly	1974	—	2.00	4.00
40370	The Immigrant/Hey Mister Sunshine	1975	—	2.00	4.00

—No mention of John Lennon on label

Number	Title (A Side/B Side)	Yr	VG	VG+	NM
40370	The Immigrant/Hey Mister Sunshine	1975	2.50	5.00	10.00

—With "Dedicated to John Lennon" under title in bold

Number	Title (A Side/B Side)	Yr	VG	VG+	NM
40426	That's When the Music Takes Me/Standing on the Inside	1975	—	2.00	4.00
40460	Bad Blood/Your Favorite Entertainer	1975	—	2.00	4.00
40500	Breaking Up Is Hard to Do/Nana's Song	1975	—	2.00	4.00
40543	Love in the Shadows/Baby Don't Let It Mess Your Mind	1976	—	2.00	4.00
40582	Steppin' Out/I Let You Walk Away	1976	—	2.00	4.00
40614	You Gotta Make Your Own Sunshine/Perfect Strangers	1976	—	2.00	4.00

SGC

Number	Title (A Side/B Side)	Yr	VG	VG+	NM
005	Star-Crossed Lovers/We Had a Good Thing Going	1969	—	3.00	6.00
008	Rainy Jane/Jeannine	1970	—	3.00	6.00

7-Inch Extended Plays

RCA VICTOR

Number	Title (A Side/B Side)	Yr	VG	VG+	NM
LPC-105	Oh! Carol/Stairway to Heaven//The Diary/Run Samson Run	1961	12.50	25.00	50.00

—"Compact Double 33" with small hole

Number	Title (A Side/B Side)	Yr	VG	VG+	NM
LPC-105 [PS]	Neil's Best	1961	12.50	25.00	50.00
LPC-135	Little Devil/Circulate//Calendar Girl/We Kiss in a Shadow	1961	12.50	25.00	50.00

—"Compact Double 33" with small hole

Number	Title (A Side/B Side)	Yr	VG	VG+	NM
LPC-135 [PS]	Little Devil	1961	12.50	25.00	50.00
EPA-4334	I Go Ape/All I Need Is You//Stop! You're Knocking Me Out/I Belong to You	1959	15.00	30.00	60.00
EPA-4334 [PS]	I Go Ape	1959	15.00	30.00	60.00
EPA-4353	Oh! Carol/Going Home to Mary Lou//The Girl for Me/I Ain't Hurtin' No More	1959	15.00	30.00	60.00
EPA-4353 [PS]	Oh! Carol	1959	15.00	30.00	60.00

Albums

ACCORD

Number	Title (A Side/B Side)	Yr	VG	VG+	NM
SN-7152	Singer, Songwriter, Melody Maker	1981	2.50	5.00	10.00

ELEKTRA

Number	Title (A Side/B Side)	Yr	VG	VG+	NM
6E-102	A Song	1977	2.50	5.00	10.00
6E-161	All You Need Is Music	1978	2.50	5.00	10.00
6E-259	In the Pocket	1980	2.50	5.00	10.00
6E-348	Neil Sedaka Now	1981	2.50	5.00	10.00

51 WEST

Number	Title (A Side/B Side)	Yr	VG	VG+	NM
Q 16003	I'm a Song	1979	3.00	6.00	12.00

INTERMEDIA

Number	Title (A Side/B Side)	Yr	VG	VG+	NM
QS 5015	Superbird	1982	2.50	5.00	10.00

KIRSHNER

Number	Title (A Side/B Side)	Yr	VG	VG+	NM
KES-111	Emergence	1971	3.75	7.50	15.00
KES-117	Solitaire	1972	3.75	7.50	15.00

MCA

Number	Title (A Side/B Side)	Yr	VG	VG+	NM
2357	Sedaka's Back	1978	2.50	5.00	10.00

—Reissue of Rocket 463

Number	Title (A Side/B Side)	Yr	VG	VG+	NM
5466	Come See About Me	1984	2.50	5.00	10.00

ORBIT

Number	Title (A Side/B Side)	Yr	VG	VG+	NM
RB-17196	Bravo!	1983	2.50	5.00	10.00

PICKWICK

Number	Title (A Side/B Side)	Yr	VG	VG+	NM
ACL1-7006	Breaking Up Is Hard to Do	197?	2.00	4.00	8.00

POLYDOR

Number	Title (A Side/B Side)	Yr	VG	VG+	NM
831235-1	My Friend	1986	2.50	5.00	10.00

RCA CAMDEN

Number	Title (A Side/B Side)	Yr	VG	VG+	NM
ACL-7006	Breaking Up Is Hard to Do	197?	2.50	5.00	10.00

RCA SPECIAL PRODUCTS

Number	Title (A Side/B Side)	Yr	VG	VG+	NM
DPL2-0149 [(2)]	Original Hits	1975	5.00	10.00	20.00

RCA VICTOR

Number	Title (A Side/B Side)	Yr	VG	VG+	NM
ANL1-0879	Oh! Carol	1975	2.50	5.00	10.00
AFL1-0928	Neil Sedaka Sings His Greatest Hits	1977	2.50	5.00	10.00

—Reissue with new prefix

Number	Title (A Side/B Side)	Yr	VG	VG+	NM
APL1-0928	Neil Sedaka Sings His Greatest Hits	1975	3.00	6.00	12.00

—Reissue of LSP-2627

Number	Title (A Side/B Side)	Yr	VG	VG+	NM
ANL1-1314	Pure Gold	1976	2.50	5.00	10.00
VPL1-1540	Live in Australia	1976	3.00	6.00	12.00
APL1-1789	Emergence	1976	3.00	6.00	12.00

—Reissue of Kirshner 111

Number	Title (A Side/B Side)	Yr	VG	VG+	NM
APL1-1790	Solitaire	1976	3.00	6.00	12.00

—Reissue of Kirshner 117

Number	Title (A Side/B Side)	Yr	VG	VG+	NM
LPM-2035 [M]	Neil Sedaka	1959	15.00	30.00	60.00
LSP-2035 [S]	Neil Sedaka	1959	25.00	50.00	100.00
AFL1-2254	Sedaka — The '50s and '60s	1977	2.50	5.00	10.00
LPM-2317 [M]	Circulate	1960	12.50	25.00	50.00
LSP-2317 [S]	Circulate	1960	15.00	30.00	60.00
LPM-2421 [M]	"Little Devil" and His Other Hits	1961	12.50	25.00	50.00
LSP-2421 [S]	"Little Devil" and His Other Hits	1961	15.00	30.00	60.00
AFL1-2524	The Many Sides of Neil Sedaka	1978	2.50	5.00	10.00
LPM-2627 [M]	Neil Sedaka Sings His Greatest Hits	1962	10.00	20.00	40.00
LSP-2627 [S]	Neil Sedaka Sings His Greatest Hits	1962	12.50	25.00	50.00

—Black label, dog on top, "Living Stereo" at bottom

Number	Title (A Side/B Side)	Yr	VG	VG+	NM
LSP-2627 [S]	Neil Sedaka Sings His Greatest Hits	1969	5.00	10.00	20.00

—Reissue; orange label

Number	Title (A Side/B Side)	Yr	VG	VG+	NM
ANL1-3465	Neil Sedaka Sings His Greatest Hits	1979	2.00	4.00	8.00

—Reissue of AFL1-0928

Number	Title (A Side/B Side)	Yr	VG	VG+	NM
R 133511	Let's Go Steady Again	1976	3.75	7.50	15.00

—RCA Record Club edition

ROCKET

Number	Title (A Side/B Side)	Yr	VG	VG+	NM
MCA-463	Sedaka's Back	1974	3.00	6.00	12.00
PIG-2157	The Hungry Years	1975	3.00	6.00	12.00
PIG-2195	Steppin' Out	1976	3.00	6.00	12.00
PIG-2297	Neil Sedaka's Greatest Hits	1977	3.00	6.00	12.00

ROLLER SKATE

Number	Title (A Side/B Side)	Yr	VG	VG+	NM
TLA-50172	Is Anybody Gonna Miss You	1982	3.75	7.50	15.00

SEDAKA, NEIL, AND THE TOKENS WITH THE COINS Also see each artist's individual listings.

Albums

CROWN

Number	Title (A Side/B Side)	Yr	VG	VG+	NM
CST-366 [R]	Neil Sedaka and the Tokens and the Coins	1963	5.00	10.00	20.00
CLP-5366 [M]	Neil Sedaka and the Tokens and the Coins	1963	7.50	15.00	30.00

SEEDS, THE Also see RITCHIE MARSH; SKY SAXON.

45s

GNP CRESCENDO

Number	Title (A Side/B Side)	Yr	VG	VG+	NM
354	Can't Seem to Make You Mine/Daisy Mae	1965	3.75	7.50	15.00
354	Can't Seem to Make You Mine/I Tell Myself	1967	2.50	5.00	10.00
354 [PS]	Can't Seem to Make You Mine/I Tell Myself	1967	12.50	25.00	50.00
364	You're Pushing Too Hard/Out of the Question	1965	3.75	7.50	15.00
370	The Other Place/Try to Understand	1966	3.75	7.50	15.00
372	Pushin' Too Hard/Try to Understand	1966	3.00	6.00	12.00

—With "GNP Crescendo" in box at top of label

Number	Title (A Side/B Side)	Yr	VG	VG+	NM
372	Pushin' Too Hard/Try to Understand	1966	3.75	7.50	15.00

—With "GNP Crescendo" standing alone at top of label (no box)

Number	Title (A Side/B Side)	Yr	VG	VG+	NM
383	Mr. Farmer/No Escape	1967	2.00	4.00	8.00
383	Mr. Farmer/Up in Her Room	1967	2.00	4.00	8.00
383 [PS]	Mr. Farmer/Up in Her Room	1967	12.50	25.00	50.00
394	A Thousand Shadows/March of the Flower Children	1967	2.00	4.00	8.00
394 [PS]	A Thousand Shadows/March of the Flower Children	1967	5.00	10.00	20.00
398	The Wind Blows Your Hair/Six Dreams	1967	2.00	4.00	8.00
408	Satisfy You/900 Million People Daily	1968	2.00	4.00	8.00
422	Fallin' Off the Edge of My Mind/Wild Blood	1969	2.50	5.00	10.00

MGM

Number	Title (A Side/B Side)	Yr	VG	VG+	NM
14163	Wish Me Up/Bad Part of Town	1970	5.00	10.00	20.00
14190	Did He Die/Love in a Summer Blanket	1970	5.00	10.00	20.00

PHILCO-FORD

Number	Title (A Side/B Side)	Yr	VG	VG+	NM
HP-26	Pushin' Too Hard/Can't Seem to Make You Mine	1968	6.25	12.50	25.00

—4-inch plastic "Hip Pocket Record" with color sleeve

Albums

GNP CRESCENDO

Number	Title (A Side/B Side)	Yr	VG	VG+	NM
GNP-2023 [M]	The Seeds	1966	15.00	30.00	60.00
GNPS-2023 [S]	The Seeds	1966	10.00	20.00	40.00
GNP-2033 [M]	A Web of Sound	1967	15.00	30.00	60.00
GNPS-2033 [S]	A Web of Sound	1967	10.00	20.00	40.00
GNP-2038 [M]	Future	1967	10.00	20.00	40.00

—Deduct 25% if two inserts are missing

Number	Title (A Side/B Side)	Yr	VG	VG+	NM
GNPS-2038 [S]	Future	1967	7.50	15.00	30.00

—Deduct 25% if two inserts are missing

Number	Title (A Side/B Side)	Yr	VG	VG+	NM
GNP-2040 [M]	A Full Spoon of Seedy Blues	1968	15.00	30.00	60.00
GNPS-2040 [S]	A Full Spoon of Seedy Blues	1968	6.25	12.50	25.00
GNPS-2043	Raw and Alive	1968	6.25	12.50	25.00
GNPS-2107	Fallin' Off the Edge	1977	2.50	5.00	10.00
ST-91224	A Web of Sound	1968	7.50	15.00	30.00

—Capitol Record Club edition

S

Number	Title (A Side/B Side)	Yr	VG	VG+	NM

SEEGER, PETE Also see THE WEAVERS.

45s

COLUMBIA

Number	Title (A Side/B Side)	Yr	VG	VG+	NM
☐ 42940	Little Boxes/Mail Myself to You	1963	2.00	4.00	8.00
☐ 43349	Healing River/Johnny Give Me	1965	2.00	4.00	8.00
☐ 43699	Draft Dodger Rag/Guantanamera	1966	2.00	4.00	8.00
☐ 44273	Waist Deep in the Big Muddy/Down by the Riverside	1967	2.00	4.00	8.00

FOLKWAYS

Number	Title (A Side/B Side)	Yr	VG	VG+	NM
☐ 45-201	The Battle of New Orleans/My Home's Across the Smokey Mountains	1959	3.00	6.00	12.00

Albums

ARAVEL

Number	Title (A Side/B Side)	Yr	VG	VG+	NM
☐ AB 1006 [M]	Live Hootenanny	1963	3.75	7.50	15.00

BROADSIDE

| ☐ 502 [(2)] | Pete Seeger Sings and Answers Questions | 1970 | 3.75 | 7.50 | 15.00 |

BULLDOG

| ☐ BDL-2011 | 20 Golden Pieces of Pete Seeger | 198? | 2.50 | 5.00 | 10.00 |

CAPITOL

☐ DW 2172 [R]	Folk Songs	1964	3.00	6.00	12.00
☐ W 2172 [M]	Folk Songs	1964	5.00	10.00	20.00
☐ DT 2718 [R]	Freight Train	1967	3.00	6.00	12.00
☐ T 2718 [M]	Freight Train	1967	5.00	10.00	20.00

COLUMBIA

☐ CL 1668 [M]	Pete Seeger Story Songs	1961	6.25	12.50	25.00
☐ CL 1916 [M]	The Bitter and the Sweet	1962	6.25	12.50	25.00
☐ CL 1947 [M]	Children's Concert at Town Hall	1963	6.25	12.50	25.00
☐ CL 2101 [M]	We Shall Overcome	1963	3.75	7.50	15.00
☐ CL 2257 [M]	I Can See a New Day	1965	3.75	7.50	15.00
☐ CL 2334 [M]	Strangers and Cousins	1964	3.75	7.50	15.00
☐ CL 2432 [M]	God Bless the Grass	1966	3.75	7.50	15.00
☐ CL 2503 [M]	Dangerous Songs?	1966	3.75	7.50	15.00
☐ CL 2616 [M]	Pete Seeger's Greatest Hits	1967	5.00	10.00	20.00
☐ CL 2705 [M]	Waist Deep in the Big Muddy	1967	5.00	10.00	20.00
☐ CS 8468 [S]	Pete Seeger Story Songs	1961	7.50	15.00	30.00
☐ CS 8716 [S]	The Bitter and the Sweet	1962	7.50	15.00	30.00
☐ CS 8747 [S]	Children's Concert at Town Hall	1963	7.50	15.00	30.00
☐ CS 8901 [S]	We Shall Overcome	1963	5.00	10.00	20.00
☐ CS 9057 [S]	I Can See a New Day	1965	5.00	10.00	20.00
☐ CS 9134 [S]	Strangers and Cousins	1964	5.00	10.00	20.00
☐ CS 9232 [S]	God Bless the Grass	1966	5.00	10.00	20.00
☐ CS 9303 [S]	Dangerous Songs?	1966	5.00	10.00	20.00
☐ CS 9416 [S]	Pete Seeger's Greatest Hits	1967	3.75	7.50	15.00
☐ PC 9416	Pete Seeger's Greatest Hits	198?	2.00	4.00	8.00
—Reissue with new prefix					
☐ CS 9505 [S]	Waist Deep in the Big Muddy	1967	3.75	7.50	15.00
☐ CS 9717	Pete Seeger Now	1968	3.75	7.50	15.00
☐ CS 9873	Young vs. Old	1969	3.75	7.50	15.00
☐ C 30739	Rainbow Race	1971	3.00	6.00	12.00
☐ KG 31949 [(2)]	The World of Pete Seeger	1972	3.75	7.50	15.00

DISC

| ☐ D-101 [M] | Sing with Seeger | 1964 | 5.00 | 10.00 | 20.00 |

EVEREST ARCHIVE OF FOLK & JAZZ

| ☐ 201 | Pete Seeger | 1966 | 3.00 | 6.00 | 12.00 |

FOLKWAYS

☐ FP-3 [10]	Darling Corey	1950	25.00	50.00	100.00
☐ FP-10 [10]	Lonesome Valley	195?	25.00	50.00	100.00
☐ FP-43 [10]	A Pete Seeger Sampler	195?	25.00	50.00	100.00
☐ FP-45 [10]	Goofing Off Suite	195?	25.00	50.00	100.00
☐ FP-701 [10]	American Folk Songs for Children	195?	25.00	50.00	100.00
☐ FP-710 [10]	Birds, Beasts, Bugs and Little Fishes	1954	25.00	50.00	100.00
☐ FP-911 [10]	Folk Songs of Four Continents	195?	25.00	50.00	100.00
☐ FA-2003 [10]	Darling Corey	1950	20.00	40.00	80.00
☐ FA-2010 [10]	Lonesome Valley	195?	20.00	40.00	80.00
☐ FA-2043 [10]	A Pete Seeger Sampler	1954	20.00	40.00	80.00
☐ FA-2045 [10]	Goofing Off Suite	1954	20.00	40.00	80.00
☐ FA-2175 [10]	Frontier Ballads, Volume 1	1954	20.00	40.00	80.00
☐ FA-2176 [10]	Frontier Ballads, Volume 2	1954	20.00	40.00	80.00
☐ FA-2311 [M]	Traditional Christmas Carols	1956	7.50	15.00	30.00
☐ FA-2319 [M]	American Ballads	1957	7.50	15.00	30.00
☐ FA-2320 [M]	American Favorite Ballads, Vol. 1	1957	7.50	15.00	30.00
☐ FA-2321 [M]	American Favorite Ballads, Vol. 2	1958	7.50	15.00	30.00
☐ FA-2322 [M]	American Favorite Ballads, Vol. 3	1958	7.50	15.00	30.00
☐ FA-2323 [M]	American Favorite Ballads, Vol. 4	1961	5.00	10.00	20.00
☐ FA-2412 [M]	Pete Seeger and Sonny Terry	1958	7.50	15.00	30.00
☐ FA-2439 [M]	Nonesuch	196?	5.00	10.00	20.00
☐ FA-2445 [M]	American Favorite Ballads, Vol. 5: Tunes and Songs As Sung by Pete Seeger	1962	5.00	10.00	20.00
☐ FA-2450 [M]	Highlights of Pete Seeger at the Village Gate with Memphis Slim and Willie Dixon	1960	7.50	15.00	30.00
☐ FA-2451 [M]	Pete Seeger at the Village Gate — Vol. 2	1960	7.50	15.00	30.00
☐ FA-2452 [M]	With Voices Together We Sing	1956	6.25	12.50	25.00
☐ FA-2453 [M]	Love Songs for Friends and Foes	1956	6.25	12.50	25.00
☐ FA-2454 [M]	Rainbow Quest	1960	6.25	12.50	25.00
☐ FA-2455 [M]	Sing Out with Pete!	1961	5.00	10.00	20.00
☐ FA-2456 [M]	Broadsides	1964	5.00	10.00	20.00
☐ FA-2501 [M]	Gazette, Vol. 1	1958	6.25	12.50	25.00
☐ FA-2502 [M]	Gazette, Vol. 2	1962	5.00	10.00	20.00
☐ FN-2511 [M]	Hootenanny Tonight!	195?	6.25	12.50	25.00
☐ FN-2513 [M]	Sing Out! Hootenanny	1963	5.00	10.00	20.00
☐ FS-3851 [M]	Indian Summer	1960	6.25	12.50	25.00
—With Michael Seeger					
☐ 5003 [(2)]	Frontier Ballads	1954	25.00	50.00	100.00
☐ FH-5210 [M]	Champlain Valley Songs	1960	6.25	12.50	25.00
☐ FH-5233 [M]	Songs of Struggle and Protest 1930-50	1959	6.25	12.50	25.00
☐ FH-5251 [M]	American Industrial Ballads	1956	7.50	15.00	30.00
☐ FH-5257	Fifty Sail On Newburgh Bay	1976	3.00	6.00	12.00
☐ FH-5302 [M]	Broadside Ballads, Vol. 2	1963	5.00	10.00	20.00
☐ FH-5436 [M]	Songs of the Spanish Civil War, Vol. 1	1961	5.00	10.00	20.00
☐ FH-5485 [M]	Ballads of Sacco and Vanzetti	1963	5.00	10.00	20.00
☐ FH-5595 [M]	WNEW's Story of Selma	1965	5.00	10.00	20.00
☐ FH-5702 [(2)]	Pete Seeger Sings and Answers Questions	1968	6.25	12.50	25.00
☐ FW-6843 [10]	German Folk Songs	1954	20.00	40.00	80.00
☐ FW-6911 [10]	Folk Songs of Four Continents	1955	20.00	40.00	80.00
☐ FW-6912 [10]	Bantu Choral Folk Songs	1955	20.00	40.00	80.00
☐ FC-7020 [10]	Songs to Grow On — Vol. 2	1951	20.00	40.00	80.00

Number	Title (A Side/B Side)	Yr	VG	VG+	NM
☐ FC-7027 [10]	Songs to Grow On — Vol. 3	1951	20.00	40.00	80.00
☐ FC-7526 [M]	Song and Play Time	195?	12.50	25.00	50.00
☐ 7527	Zhitkov's How I Hunted the Little Fellows	1980	3.00	6.00	12.00
☐ FC-7601 [10]	American Folk Songs for Children	1953	20.00	40.00	80.00
☐ FC-7610 [10]	Birds, Beasts, Bugs and Little Fishes	1954	20.00	40.00	80.00
☐ FC-7611 [10]	Birds, Beasts, Bugs and Bigger Fishes	1954	12.50	25.00	50.00
☐ FC-7674 [M]	American Game and Activity Songs for Children	1962	5.00	10.00	20.00
☐ FI-8303 [M]	How to Play the Five String Banjo	195?	6.25	12.50	25.00
☐ FI-8354 [M]	Folksinger's Guitar Guide Vol. 1: An Instruction Record	1955	7.50	15.00	30.00
☐ FQ-8354 [M]	The Folksinger's Guitar Gude	1955	6.25	12.50	25.00
☐ FI-8371 [M]	12-String Guitar As Played by Leadbelly	1962	5.00	10.00	20.00
☐ FTS-31002 [R]	Pete Seeger Sings Woody Guthrie	1968	3.00	6.00	12.00
☐ FTS-31017 [R]	American Favorite Ballads	1968	3.00	6.00	12.00
☐ FTS-31018 [R]	Wimoweh and Other Songs of Freedom and Protest	1968	3.00	6.00	12.00
☐ FTS-31022 [R]	Pete Seeger Sings Leadbelly	1968	3.00	6.00	12.00
☐ FTS-31040 [R]	Banks of Marble and Other Songs	1974	3.00	6.00	12.00
☐ FTS-32311 [R]	Traditional Christmas Carols	1967	3.75	7.50	15.00
☐ FT-35001 [(2)]	The Nativity: By Sholem Asch	1963	3.75	7.50	15.00
☐ FXM-36055 [(2)]	Sing Along	1980	3.75	7.50	15.00
☐ 37232	God Bless the Grass	1982	3.00	6.00	12.00

HARMONY

| ☐ HS 11337 | John Henry and Other Folk Favorites | 1969 | 3.00 | 6.00 | 12.00 |

ODYSSEY

| ☐ 32160266 | 3 Saints, 4 Sinners and 6 Other People | 1968 | 3.75 | 7.50 | 15.00 |

OLYMPIC

| ☐ 7102 | America's Balladeer | 1973 | 3.00 | 6.00 | 12.00 |

PAIR

| ☐ PDL2-1076 [(2)] | Clearwater Classics | 1986 | 3.00 | 6.00 | 12.00 |

PHILIPS

| ☐ PHM 2-300 [(2)M] | The Story of the Nativity | 1963 | 5.00 | 10.00 | 20.00 |
| ☐ PHS 2-300 [(2)S] | The Story of the Nativity | 1963 | 6.25 | 12.50 | 25.00 |

SMITHSONIAN FOLKWAYS

| ☐ SF-40024 | Traditional Christmas Carols | 1989 | 3.00 | 6.00 | 12.00 |

STINSON

☐ SLP-52 [10]	Lincoln Brigade	1953	25.00	50.00	100.00
☐ SLP-57 [10]	A Pete Seeger Concert	1953	25.00	50.00	100.00
☐ SLP-90 [M]	Pete	1963	6.25	12.50	25.00

TRADITION

| ☐ 2107 | Folk Music of the World | 1973 | 3.00 | 6.00 | 12.00 |

VANGUARD

☐ VSD-97/98 [(2)]	The Essential Pete Seeger	1978	3.75	7.50	15.00
☐ VSD-73111	The Essential Pete Seeger, Vol. 1	198?	2.00	4.00	8.00
☐ VSD-73112	The Essential Pete Seeger, Vol. 2	198?	2.00	4.00	8.00

VERVE FOLKWAYS

☐ FV-9008 [M]	Pete Seeger and Big Bill Broonzy in Concert	1965	5.00	10.00	20.00
☐ FVS-9008 [S]	Pete Seeger and Big Bill Broonzy in Concert	1965	6.25	12.50	25.00
☐ FV-9009 [M]	Pete Seeger On Campus	1965	5.00	10.00	20.00
☐ FVS-9009 [S]	Pete Seeger On Campus	1965	6.25	12.50	25.00
☐ FV-9013 [M]	Folk Music Live at the Village Gate	1965	5.00	10.00	20.00
☐ FVS-9013 [S]	Folk Music Live at the Village Gate	1965	6.25	12.50	25.00
☐ FV-9020 [M]	Little Boxes and Other Broadsides	1965	5.00	10.00	20.00
☐ FVS-9020 [S]	Little Boxes and Other Broadsides	1965	6.25	12.50	25.00

WARNER BROS.

| ☐ BSK 3329 | Circles and Seasons | 1979 | 3.00 | 6.00 | 12.00 |

SEEKERS, THE

45s

ATMOS

| ☐ 711 | Myra/Wild Rover | 1965 | 3.75 | 7.50 | 15.00 |

CAPITOL

☐ 2013	When the Good Apples Fall/Myra (Shake Up the Party)	1967	2.50	5.00	10.00
☐ 2122	Love Is Kind, Love Is Wine/All I Can Remember	1968	2.50	5.00	10.00
☐ 5383	I'll Never Find Another You/ Open Up Them Pearly Gates	1965	3.00	6.00	12.00
☐ 5430	A World of Our Own/Sinner Man	1965	3.00	6.00	12.00
☐ 5430 [PS]	A World of Our Own/Sinner Man	1965	5.00	10.00	20.00
☐ 5531	The Carnival Is Over/We Shall Not Be Moved	1965	2.50	5.00	10.00
☐ 5622	Some Day, One Day/Nobody Knows the Trouble I've Seen	1966	2.50	5.00	10.00
☐ 5756	Georgy Girl/When the Stars Begin to Fall	1966	3.00	6.00	12.00
☐ 5787	Morningtown Ride/Walk with Me	1967	2.50	5.00	10.00
☐ 5974	I Wish You Could Be Here/On the Other Side	1967	2.50	5.00	10.00

CAPITOL CREATIVE PRODUCTS

☐ 50 [DJ]	Island of Dreams/Breaking My Back — Instead of Using My Mind	1966	3.75	7.50	15.00
—B-side by Lou Rawls					
☐ 50 [PS]	Island of Dreams/Breaking My Back — Instead of Using My Mind	1966	5.00	10.00	20.00
—Custom sleeve; no titles or artist, but "#50" is at right and "Capitol has specially produced this record for Frito-Lay" is under the center hole					

MARVEL

| ☐ 1060 | Chilly Winds/The Light from the Lighthouse | 1965 | 3.75 | 7.50 | 15.00 |

Albums

CAPITOL

☐ ST-135 [S]	The Seekers Live	1969	3.00	6.00	12.00
☐ ST 2319 [S]	The New Seekers	1965	3.75	7.50	15.00
☐ T 2319 [M]	The New Seekers	1965	3.00	6.00	12.00
☐ DT 2369 [R]	A World of Our Own	1965	3.00	6.00	12.00
☐ T 2369 [M]	A World of Our Own	1965	3.00	6.00	12.00
☐ ST 2431 [S]	Georgy Girl	1966	3.75	7.50	15.00
☐ T 2431 [M]	Georgy Girl	1966	3.00	6.00	12.00
☐ SM-2746 [P]	The Best of the Seekers	197?	2.50	5.00	10.00
☐ ST 2746 [P]	The Best of the Seekers	196?	2.50	5.00	10.00
—Red and white "star" Starline label					
☐ ST 2746 [P]	The Best of the Seekers	1967	3.00	6.00	12.00
—Red and white "target" Starline label; though the cover has an "ST" prefix, the record and trail-off wax have a "DT" prefix; "Morningtown Ride," "Turn, Turn, Turn," and "We're Moving On" are in stereo					
☐ T 2746 [M]	The Best of the Seekers	1967	3.00	6.00	12.00
☐ KAO 2821 [M]	The Seekers Seen in Green	1968	10.00	20.00	40.00
☐ SKAO 2821 [S]	The Seekers Seen in Green	1968	3.75	7.50	15.00
☐ SN-16104 [P]	The Best of the Seekers	1980	2.00	4.00	8.00

MARVEL

| ☐ 2060 [M] | The Seekers | 1965 | 3.00 | 6.00 | 12.00 |
| ☐ 3060 [R] | The Seekers | 1965 | 2.50 | 5.00 | 10.00 |

Sam the Sham and the Pharaohs, "Wooly Bully," XL 906, 45 rpm record, $150-$300.

Jack Scott, "Burning Bridges," Top Rank 2041, picture sleeve, $30-$60.

Neil Sedaka, *Oh! Carol*, RCA Victor EPA-4353, 7-inch EP, $60-$120 (cover and record together).

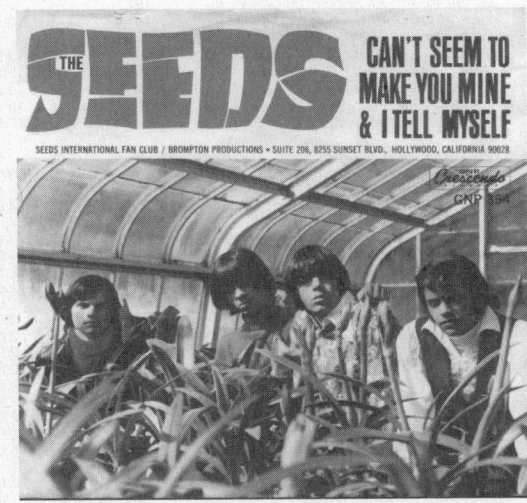

The Seeds, "Can't Seem to Make You Mine," GNP Crescendo 354, picture sleeve, $25-$50.

The Searchers, *Meet the Searchers*, Kapp KL-1363, mono LP, black and blueish label, $20-$40.

The Seekers, *The Best of the Seekers*, Capitol ST 2746, stereo LP, red and white target "Starline" label, $6-$12.

S

Number	Title (A Side/B Side)	Yr	VG	VG+	NM

SEGAL, GEORGE
45s
PHILIPS
| ❏ 40468 | The Yama-Yama Man/Yes Sir, That's My Baby | 1967 | 2.00 | 4.00 | 8.00 |

SIGNATURE
| ❏ SB-10099 | If You Like-a Me/What You Goin' to Do When the Rent Comes Around | 1974 | — | 3.00 | 6.00 |

Albums
PHILIPS
| ❏ PHM 200242 [M]The Yama-Yama Man | | 1967 | 5.00 | 10.00 | 20.00 |
| ❏ PHS 600242 [S]The Yama-Yama Man | | 1967 | 5.00 | 10.00 | 20.00 |

SIGNATURE
| ❏ BSL1-0654 | A Touch of Ragtime | 1976 | 3.75 | 7.50 | 15.00 |

SEGER, BOB Includes records with The Last Heard, The Bob Seger System and The Silver Bullet Band. Also see THE BEACH BUMS.
12-Inch Singles
CAPITOL
❏ SPRO-8987 [DJ]We've Got Tonite (single)/We've Got Tonite (LP)		1978	3.00	6.00	12.00
❏ SPRO-9085/6 [DJ]Old Time Rock and Roll/Sunspot Baby		1979	3.75	7.50	15.00
❏ SPRO-9641/2 [DJ]American Storm (Edit)/American Storm (LP)		1986	—	3.00	6.00
❏ SPRO-9687/8 [DJ]Tryin' to Live My Life Without You (3:00)/(3:46)		1981	2.50	5.00	10.00
❏ SPRO-9705 [DJ]Like a Rock (Edit)/Like a Rock (LP)		1986	2.00	4.00	8.00
❏ SPRO-9736 [DJ]The Aftermath (remix)/The Aftermath (LP)		1986	—	3.00	6.00
❏ SPRO-9778 [DJ]It's You (45 remix)/The Aftermath (remix)		1986	—	3.00	6.00
❏ SPRO-9866/74 [DJ]Miami (Extended)/Miami (LP)		1986	—	3.00	6.00

45s
ABKCO
❏ 4015	East Side Story/East Side Sound	1973	—	3.00	6.00
❏ 4016	Chain Smokin'/Persecution Smith	1973	—	3.00	6.00
❏ 4017	Heavy Music - Pt. I/Heavy Music - Pt. II	1973	—	3.00	6.00
❏ 4031	Heavy Music - Pt. I/Heavy Music - Pt. II	1973	—	2.50	5.00

CAMEO
❏ 438	East Side Story/East Side Sound	1966	6.25	12.50	25.00
❏ 444	Sock It To Me, Santa/Florida Time	1966	7.50	15.00	30.00
❏ 465	Chain Smokin'/Persecution Smith	1967	6.25	12.50	25.00
❏ 473	Vagrant Winter/Very Few	1967	6.25	12.50	25.00
❏ 494	Heavy Music/Heavy Music (Part 2)	1967	5.00	10.00	20.00

CAPITOL
❏ 2143	2 + 2 = ?/Death Row	1968	3.75	7.50	15.00
❏ 2297	Ramblin' Gamblin' Man/Tales of Lucy Blue	1968	3.00	6.00	12.00
❏ 2480	Ivory/The Lost Song (Love Needs to Be Loved)	1969	2.00	4.00	8.00
❏ 2576	Noah/Lennie Johnson	1969	2.00	4.00	8.00
❏ 2640	Lonely Man/Innervenus Eyes	1970	2.00	4.00	8.00
❏ 2748	Lucifer/Big River	1970	2.00	4.00	8.00
❏ 3187	Lookin' Back/Highway Child	1971	2.00	4.00	8.00
❏ 4062	Beautiful Loser/Fine Memory	1975	—	2.50	5.00
❏ 4116	Katmandu/Black Night	1975	—	2.50	5.00
❏ 4183	Nutbush City Limits/Travelin' Man	1975	—	2.50	5.00
❏ 4269	Nutbush City Limits/Lookin' Back	1976	—	2.50	5.00
❏ 4300	Beautiful Loser/Travelin' Man	1976	—	2.50	5.00
❏ 4369	Night Moves/Ship of Fools	1976	—	2.00	4.00
❏ 4422	Mainstreet/Jody Girl	1977	—	2.00	4.00
❏ 4449	Rock and Roll Never Forgets/Fire Down Below	1977	—	2.00	4.00
❏ 4581	Still the Same/Feel Like a Number	1978	—	2.00	4.00
❏ 4618	Hollywood Nights/Brave Strangers	1978	—	2.00	4.00
❏ 4653	We've Got Tonite/Ain't Got No Money	1978	—	2.00	4.00
❏ 4653 [DJ]	We've Got Tonite (mono/stereo)	1978	2.50	5.00	10.00
—Silver vinyl					
❏ 4653 [PS]	We've Got Tonite/Ain't Got No Money	1978	—	3.00	6.00
❏ 4702	Old Time Rock and Roll/Sunspot Baby	1979	—	2.00	4.00
❏ 4702 [PS]	Old Time Rock and Roll/Sunspot Baby	1979	—	3.00	6.00
❏ 4836	Fire Lake/Long Twin Silver Line	1980	—	2.00	4.00
❏ 4836 [PS]	Fire Lake/Long Twin Silver Line	1980	—	3.00	6.00
❏ 4863	Against the Wind/No Man's Land	1980	—	2.00	4.00
❏ 4863 [PS]	Against the Wind/No Man's Land	1980	—	3.00	6.00
❏ 4904	You'll Accomp'ny Me/Betty Lou's Gettin' Out Tonight	1980	—	2.50	5.00
❏ 4904 [PS]	You'll Accomp'ny Me/Betty Lou's Gettin' Out Tonight	1980	—	3.00	6.00
❏ 4951	The Horizontal Bop/Her Strut	1980	—	2.50	5.00
❏ 4951 [PS]	The Horizontal Bop/Her Strut	1980	25.00	50.00	100.00
❏ A-5042	Tryin' to Live My Life Without You/Brave Strangers	1981	—	—	3.00
❏ A-5042 [PS]	Tryin' to Live My Life Without You/Brave Strangers	1981	—	2.00	4.00
❏ A-5077	Feel Like a Number/Hollywood Nights	1981	—	2.00	4.00
❏ A-5077 [PS]	Feel Like a Number/Hollywood Nights	1981	—	2.50	5.00
❏ B-5187	Shame on the Moon/House Behind a House	1982	—	—	3.00
❏ B-5187 [PS]	Shame on the Moon/House Behind a House	1982	—	2.00	4.00
❏ B-5213	Even Now/Little Victories	1983	—	—	3.00
❏ B-5213 [PS]	Even Now/Little Victories	1983	—	2.00	4.00
❏ B-5235	Roll Me Away/Boomtown Blues	1983	—	—	3.00
❏ B-5235 [PS]	Roll Me Away/Boomtown Blues	1983	—	2.00	4.00
❏ B-5276	Old Time Rock and Roll/Till It Shines	1983	—	—	3.00
❏ B-5276 [PS]	Old Time Rock and Roll/Till It Shines	1983	—	2.50	4.00
❏ B-5413	Understanding/East L.A.	1984	—	—	3.00
❏ B-5413 [PS]	Understanding/East L.A.	1984	—	2.00	4.00
❏ B-5532	American Storm/Fortunate Son	1986	—	—	3.00
❏ B-5532 [PS]	American Storm/Fortunate Son	1986	—	—	3.00
❏ B-5592	Like a Rock/Livin' Inside My Heart	1986	—	—	3.00
❏ B-5592 [PS]	Like a Rock/Livin' Inside My Heart	1986	—	—	3.00
❏ B-5623	It's You/The Aftermath (12" Remix)	1986	—	—	3.00
❏ B-5623 [PS]	It's You/The Aftermath (12" Remix)	1986	—	—	3.00
❏ B-5658	Miami/Somewhere Tonight	1986	—	—	3.00
❏ B-5658 [PS]	Miami/Somewhere Tonight	1986	6.25	12.50	25.00
—May only have been released in the New York metro area, as it quotes reviewers from four different New York newspapers					
❏ SPRO 8433 [DJ]Travelin' Man/Beautiful Loser		1976	2.50	5.00	10.00
❏ S7-18298	C'est La Vie/Night Moves	1995	—	2.00	4.00
❏ NR-44761	The Real Love/Roll Me Away	1991	—	2.00	4.00
❏ NR-44793	The Fire Inside/New Coat of Paint	1991	—	2.00	4.00
❏ S7-56784	Like a Rock/Sunspot Baby	1992	—	2.00	4.00
❏ S7-57732	New Coat of Paint/Blind Love	1992	—	2.00	4.00
❏ S7-57742	Night Moves/Her Strut	1992	—	2.00	4.00
❏ S7-57797	Old Time Rock and Roll/Turn the Page	1992	—	2.00	4.00

HIDEOUT
| ❏ 1013 | East Side Story/East Side Sound | 1966 | 12.50 | 25.00 | 50.00 |
| ❏ 1014 | Chain Smokin'/Persecution Smith | 1966 | 12.50 | 25.00 | 50.00 |

MCA
❏ 53094	Shakedown/The Aftermath	1987	—	—	3.00
❏ 53094 [PS]	Shakedown/The Aftermath	1987	—	2.00	4.00
—Picture of Bob Seger on front cover					
❏ 53094 [PS]	Shakedown/The Aftermath	1987	3.75	7.50	15.00
—Picture of Eddie Murphy as Axel Foley on front cover					

PALLADIUM
❏ 1079	If I Were a Carpenter/Jesse James	1972	2.50	5.00	10.00
❏ 1117	Turn On Your Love Light/Who Do You Love?	1972	2.50	5.00	10.00
❏ 1143	Rosalie/Neon Sky	1972	2.50	5.00	10.00
❏ 1171	Need Ya/Seen a Lot of Floors	1973	2.50	5.00	10.00
❏ 1205	Get Out of Denver/Long Song Comin'	1974	2.50	5.00	10.00
❏ 1316	This Ole House/U.M.C.	1974	3.75	7.50	15.00

REPRISE
| ❏ PRO 571 [DJ] | Midnight Rider (same on both sides) | 1972 | 3.75 | 7.50 | 15.00 |

Albums
CAPITOL
❏ (no #) [PD]	Night Moves	1977	10.00	20.00	40.00
—Promo-only picture disc					
❏ SM-172	Ramblin' Gamblin' Man	1977	2.00	4.00	8.00
❏ ST-172	Ramblin' Gamblin' Man	1969	7.50	15.00	30.00
—Black label with colorband					
❏ ST-236	Noah	1969	20.00	40.00	80.00
❏ SKAO-499	Mongrel	1970	6.25	12.50	25.00
❏ SM-499	Mongrel	1977	2.00	4.00	8.00
❏ ST-731	Brand New Morning	1971	25.00	50.00	100.00
❏ SPRO-8433 [DJ]Consensus Cuts Edited for Airplay from "Live Bullet"		1976	6.25	12.50	25.00
❏ ST-11378	Beautiful Loser	1975	2.50	5.00	10.00
—Originals have orange labels					
❏ ST-11378	Beautiful Loser	1978	2.00	4.00	8.00
—Purple label with large Capitol logo					
❏ SKBB-11523 [(2)]Live Bullet		1976	3.75	7.50	15.00
—Originals have orange labels					
❏ SKBB-11523 [(2)]Live Bullet		1978	3.00	6.00	12.00
—Purple label with large Capitol logo					
❏ SKBB-11523 [(2)]Live Bullet		1983	3.00	6.00	12.00
—Black label, print in colorband					
❏ STBK-11523 [(2)]Live Bullet		1988	3.00	6.00	12.00
—Purple label with smaller Capitol logo					
❏ ST-11557	Night Moves	1976	2.50	5.00	10.00
❏ SW-11698	Stranger in Town	1978	2.50	5.00	10.00
❏ ST-11746	Smokin' O.P.'s	1978	2.50	5.00	10.00
❏ ST-11748	Seven	1978	2.50	5.00	10.00
❏ SEAX-11904 [PD]Stranger in Town		1978	6.25	12.50	25.00
❏ SOO-12041	Against the Wind	1980	2.50	5.00	10.00
❏ STBK-12182 [(2)]Nine Tonight		1981	3.75	7.50	15.00
❏ ST-12254	The Distance	1983	2.50	5.00	10.00
❏ PT-12398	Like a Rock	1986	2.50	5.00	10.00
❏ SN-16105	Ramblin' Gamblin' Man	1980	2.00	4.00	8.00
❏ SN-16106	Mongrel	1980	2.00	4.00	8.00
❏ SN-16107	Smokin' O.P.'s	1980	2.00	4.00	8.00
❏ SN-16108	Seven	1980	2.00	4.00	8.00
❏ SN-16315	Beautiful Loser	1984	2.00	4.00	8.00
❏ C1-30334	Greatest Hits	1994	3.75	7.50	15.00
❏ C1-91134	The Fire Inside	1991	3.00	6.00	12.00
❏ C1-99774	It's a Mystery	1995	—	—	—
—Canceled					

MOBILE FIDELITY
❏ 1-034	Night Moves	1980	10.00	20.00	40.00
—Audiophile vinyl					
❏ 1-127	Against the Wind	1983	10.00	20.00	40.00
—Audiophile vinyl					

PALLADIUM
| ❏ P-1006 | Smokin' O.P.'s | 1972 | 6.25 | 12.50 | 25.00 |

REPRISE
❏ MS 2109	Smokin' O.P.'s	1972	3.75	7.50	15.00
❏ MS 2126	Back in '72	1973	15.00	30.00	60.00
❏ MS 2184	Seven	1974	5.00	10.00	20.00

SELECTIONS, THE
45s
ANTONE
| ❏ 101 | Guardian Angel/Soft and Sweet | 1958 | 62.50 | 125.00 | 250.00 |

MONA LEE
| ❏ 129 | Guardian Angel/Soft and Sweet | 1959 | 15.00 | 30.00 | 60.00 |

SPECIALTY
| ❏ 751 | Guardian Angel/Soft and Sweet | 197? | 2.50 | 5.00 | 10.00 |

SELF, MACK
45s
PHILLIPS INT'L.
| ❏ 3548 | Mad at You/Willie Brown | 1959 | 6.25 | 12.50 | 25.00 |

SUN
| ❏ 273 | Easy to Love/Every Day | 1957 | 7.50 | 15.00 | 30.00 |

SELF, RONNIE
45s
ABC-PARAMOUNT
| ❏ 9714 | Pretty Bad Blues/Three Hearts Later | 1956 | 25.00 | 50.00 | 100.00 |
| ❏ 9768 | Alone/Sweet Love | 1956 | 25.00 | 50.00 | 100.00 |

AMY
| ❏ 11009 | High on Life/The Road Keeps Winding | 1968 | 2.50 | 5.00 | 10.00 |

COLUMBIA
❏ 40875	Big Fool/Flame of Love	1957	10.00	20.00	40.00
❏ 40989	Ain't I'm a Dog/Rocky Road Blues	1957	10.00	20.00	40.00
❏ 41101	Bop-A-Lena/I Ain't Going Nowhere	1958	7.50	15.00	30.00
❏ 41166	Big Blon' Baby/Date Bait	1958	7.50	15.00	30.00
❏ 41241	Petrified/You're So Right for Me	1958	20.00	40.00	80.00

DECCA
❏ 30958	Big Town/This Must Be the Place	1959	6.25	12.50	25.00
❏ 31131	I've Been There/So High	1960	6.25	12.50	25.00
❏ 31351	Instant Man/Some Things You Can't Change	1962	6.25	12.50	25.00
❏ 31431	Oh Me, Oh My/Past, Present and Future	1962	6.25	12.50	25.00

KAPP
| ❏ 546 | Houdini/Bless My Broken Heart | 1963 | 5.00 | 10.00 | 20.00 |

Number	Title (A Side/B Side)	Yr	VG	VG+	NM

7-Inch Extended Plays
COLUMBIA

Number	Title (A Side/B Side)	Yr	VG	VG+	NM
❏ B-2149	(contents unknown)	1957	50.00	100.00	200.00
❏ B-2149 [PS]	Ain't I'm a Dog	1957	50.00	100.00	200.00

SELLERS, PETER
45s
CAPITOL

❏ F4159	I'm So Ashamed/A Drop of the Hard Stuff	1959	3.00	6.00	12.00
❏ 5580	A Hard Day's Night/Help	1966	3.75	7.50	15.00

UNITED ARTISTS

❏ X1221	Thank Heaven for Little Girls/Singin' in the Rain	1978	2.50	5.00	10.00

—As "Inspector Clouseau"
Albums
ACAPELLA

❏ 1	Fool Brittania	1963	6.25	12.50	25.00

—With Joan Collins and Anthony Newley
ANGEL

❏ 35884 [M]	The Best of Sellers	1960	7.50	15.00	30.00
❏ S 35884 [S]	The Best of Sellers	1960	10.00	20.00	40.00

EMI AMERICA

❏ SN-16396	Songs for Swingin' Sellers	1986	5.00	10.00	20.00

—First American issue of 1959 U.K. LP.

SELLERS, PETER, AND SOPHIA LOREN
45s
CAPITOL

❏ 4505	Bangers and Mash/Goodness Gracious Me	1961	3.00	6.00	12.00

Albums
ANGEL

❏ 35910 [M]	Peter Sellers and Sophia Loren	1961	7.50	15.00	30.00
❏ S 35910 [S]	Peter Sellers and Sophia Loren	1961	10.00	20.00	40.00

SENATOR BOBBY
45s
PARKWAY

❏ 127	Wild Thing/Wild Thing	1966	3.00	6.00	12.00

—B-side by "Senator McKinley"

❏ 137	Mellow Yellow/White Christmas	1967	2.50	5.00	10.00

—A-side by "Senator Bobby & Senator McKinley"; B-side by "Bobby the Poet" (Dylan impersonation)

❏ 150	The Congressional Record/The Hardly Worthit Melody	1967	2.50	5.00	10.00

—By The Hardly Worthit Players
RCA VICTOR

❏ 47-9522	Sock It To Me, Bobby/Sock It To Me, Baby	1968	2.50	5.00	10.00

—B-side by the Bobby Sockers
Albums
PARKWAY

❏ P 7057 [M]	Boston Soul with the Hardly-Worthit Players	1967	5.00	10.00	20.00
❏ SP 7057 [S]	Boston Soul with the Hardly-Worthit Players	1967	5.00	10.00	20.00

SENATORS, THE (1)
45s
ABC-PARAMOUNT

❏ 10178	There's a New Man in the White House/A Sing-Along Song	1961	3.75	7.50	15.00

SENATORS, THE (2)
45s
ABNER

❏ 1031	Julie/It Doesn't Matter	1959	30.00	60.00	120.00

GOLDEN CREST

❏ 514	Loretta/Poor Little Puppet	1958	37.50	75.00	150.00

SENATORS, THE (3)
45s
BRISTOL

❏ 1916	Scheming/Tafu	1959	100.00	200.00	400.00

WINN

❏ 1917	Wedding Bells/I Shouldn't Care	1962	62.50	125.00	250.00

SENIORS, THE (1)
45s
ABC-PARAMOUNT

❏ 10736	No Surfin' 'Round Here/Cindy	1965	7.50	15.00	30.00

SENIORS, THE (2)
45s
DECCA

❏ 31112	I've Lived Before/Hello Mr. Robin	1960	5.00	10.00	20.00
❏ 31244	When I Fall in Love/Baby, Say the Word	1961	5.00	10.00	20.00

SENIORS, THE (3)
45s
EXCELLO

❏ 2130	Why Did You Leave Me/Sloo Foot Soo	1958	10.00	20.00	40.00

LOST-NITE

❏ 194	Evening Shadows Falling (I Think of You)/I've Got Plenty of Love	196?	—	3.00	6.00

—Reissue
TETRA

❏ 4446	Evening Shadows Falling (I Think of You)/I've Got Plenty of Love	1956	50.00	100.00	200.00

SENIORS, THE (U)
45s
ESV

❏ 1016	Ah Sweet Mystery of Love/Rock and Rolly	1960	6.25	12.50	25.00

KENT

❏ 342	Hully Gully Fever/Pitter Patter Heart	1960	5.00	10.00	20.00

TAMPA

❏ 163	Who's Gonna Know/It's Been a Long Time	1959	10.00	20.00	40.00

SENORS, THE Allegedly THE ISLEY BROTHERS in disguise.
45s
SUE

❏ 756	May I Have This Dance/Searching for Olive Oil	1962	12.50	25.00	50.00

SENSATIONS, THE Also see YVONNE BAKER.
45s
ARGO

Number	Title (A Side/B Side)	Yr	VG	VG+	NM
❏ 5391	Music, Music, Music/A Part of Me	1961	2.50	5.00	10.00
❏ 5405	Let Me In/Oh Yes I'll Be True	1961	3.00	6.00	12.00

—Brown label

❏ 5405	Let Me In/Oh Yes I'll Be True	1961	5.00	10.00	20.00

—Black label

❏ 5412	That's My Desire/Eyes	1962	2.50	5.00	10.00

—By "Yvonne Baker and the Sensations"

❏ 5420	Party Across the Hall/No Changes	1962	2.50	5.00	10.00

—By "Yvonne Baker and the Sensations"

❏ 5446	When My Lover Comes Home/Father Dear	1963	2.50	5.00	10.00

—By "Yvonne Baker and the Sensations"
ATCO

❏ 6056	Yes Sir, That's My Baby/Sympathy	1955	10.00	20.00	40.00
❏ 6067	Please Mr. Disc Jockey/Ain't He Sweet	1956	10.00	20.00	40.00
❏ 6075	Cry Baby Cry/My Heart Cries for You	1956	10.00	20.00	40.00
❏ 6083	Little Wallflower/Such a Love	1957	10.00	20.00	40.00
❏ 6090	My Debut to Love/You Made Me Love You	1957	10.00	20.00	40.00
❏ 6115	Kiddy Car Love/Romance in the Dark	1958	10.00	20.00	40.00

JUNIOR

❏ 1002	We Were Meant to Be/It's Good Enough for Me	1963	3.00	6.00	12.00
❏ 1005	You Made a Fool of Me/That's What You've Gotta Do	1963	5.00	10.00	20.00
❏ 1010	I Can't Change/Mend the Torn Pieces	1964	3.00	6.00	12.00
❏ 1021	We Were Meant to Be/It's Good Enough for Me	1964	3.00	6.00	12.00

LOST-NITE

❏ 255	Let Me In/Oh Yes I'll Be True	196?	—	2.50	5.00

—Reissue
TOLLIE

❏ 9009	You Made a Fool of Me/That's What You've Gotta Do	1964	2.50	5.00	10.00

Albums
ARGO

❏ LP-4022 [M]	Let Me In/Music, Music, Music	1963	125.00	250.00	500.00

SENSATIONS OF LONDON, THE
45s
YORK

❏ 406	Look at My Baby/What a Wonderful Feeling	1966	3.75	7.50	15.00

SENTIMENTALS, THE
45s
CHECKER

❏ 875	I Want to Love You/Teenie Teenager	1957	10.00	20.00	40.00

CORAL

❏ 62100	We Three/Understanding Love	1959	6.25	12.50	25.00
❏ 62172	Deep Down in My Heart/Two Different Worlds	1960	6.25	12.50	25.00

MINT

❏ 801	I Want to Love You/Tommie Teenager	1957	12.50	25.00	50.00
❏ 802	Sunday Kind of Love/Wedding Bells	1957	10.00	20.00	40.00
❏ 803	I'm Your Fool, Always/Rock Me, Mama	1958	10.00	20.00	40.00
❏ 805	You're Mine/Danny Boy	1958	10.00	20.00	40.00
❏ 807	Found a New Baby/I'll Miss These Things	196?	3.00	6.00	12.00
❏ 808	This Time/I Want to Love You	196?	3.00	6.00	12.00

VANITY

❏ 589	Love Is a Gamble/If It Isn't for You	1959	6.25	12.50	25.00

SENTINALS, THE
45s
ADMIRAL

❏ 900	Roughshod/Copy Cat Walk	1961	12.50	25.00	50.00

DEL-FI

❏ 4197	Big Surf/Sunset Beach	1963	7.50	15.00	30.00

ERA

❏ 3082	Torchula/Latin'ia	1962	7.50	15.00	30.00
❏ 3097	Christmas Eve/Latin Soul	1962	7.50	15.00	30.00
❏ 3117	Infinity/Encinada	1963	7.50	15.00	30.00

—As "The Sentinal Six"
POINT

❏ 5100	The Bee/Over You	1963	12.50	25.00	50.00
❏ 5101	Blue Booze/Bony Moronie	1962	12.50	25.00	50.00

WCEB

❏ 23	Torchula/Latin'ia	1962	12.50	25.00	50.00

WESTCO

❏ 12	I've Been Blue/Hit the Road	1964	7.50	15.00	30.00
❏ 14	Tell Me/Hit the Road	1964	7.50	15.00	30.00

Albums
DEL-FI

❏ DFLP-1232 [M]	Big Surf!	1963	25.00	50.00	100.00
❏ DFST-1232 [S]	Big Surf!	1963	37.50	75.00	150.00
❏ DLF 1232	Big Surf!	1997	3.00	6.00	12.00
❏ DFLP-1241 [M]	Surfer Girl	1963	17.50	35.00	70.00
❏ DFST-1241 [S]	Surfer Girl	1963	25.00	50.00	100.00
❏ DLF 1241	Surfer Girl	1997	3.00	6.00	12.00

SUTTON

❏ SSU-338 [S]	Vegas Go-Go	1964	12.50	25.00	50.00
❏ SU-338 [M]	Vegas Go-Go	1964	10.00	20.00	40.00

SEQUINS, THE More than one group.
45s
A&M

❏ 761	I'll Be Satisfied/Who Says You Can't Jerk to the Old Time Music	1965	3.00	6.00	12.00

ASCOT

❏ 2140	You Can't Sit Still/Mr. Leader of the Band	1963	3.75	7.50	15.00

CAMEO

❏ 161	To Be Young/The Mountains	1959	5.00	10.00	20.00

GOLD STAR

❏ 101	Hey Romeo/I've Got to Overcome	1970	—	3.00	6.00

LOST-NITE

❏ 344	Why Can't You Treat Me Right/Don't Fall in Love	197?	—	2.50	5.00

—Reissue

S

Number	Title (A Side/B Side)	Yr	VG	VG+	NM
RED ROBIN					
❏ 140	Why Can't You Treat Me Right/Don't Fall in Love	1956	100.00	200.00	400.00
TERRACE					
❏ 7511	Love Me Forever/You're Dancing Now	1962	3.75	7.50	15.00
❏ 7515	Hideaway/I Ain't Gonna Cry (No More)	1963	3.75	7.50	15.00

SERENADERS, THE (1)
45s
Number	Title (A Side/B Side)	Yr	VG	VG+	NM
CHOCK FULL O' HITS					
❏ 101	I Wrote a Letter/Never Let Me Go	1957	75.00	150.00	300.00
❏ 102	Dance Darling, Dance/Give Me a Girl	1957	50.00	100.00	200.00
MGM					
❏ 12623	I Wrote a Letter/Never Let Me Go	1958	25.00	50.00	100.00
❏ 12666	Dance Darling, Dance/Give Me a Girl	1958	30.00	60.00	120.00
MOTOWN					
❏ 1046	If Your Heart Says Yes/I'll Cry Tomorrow	1963	1000.	1500.	2000.
RAE COX					
❏ 101	Gotta Go to School/My Girl Flip-Flop	1959	15.00	30.00	60.00
RIVERSIDE					
❏ 4549	Adios, My Love/Two Lovers Make One Fool	1963	25.00	50.00	100.00
V.I.P.					
❏ 25002	If Your Heart Says Yes/I'll Cry Tomorrow	1964	25.00	50.00	100.00

SERENADERS, THE (2)
45s
Number	Title (A Side/B Side)	Yr	VG	VG+	NM
CORAL					
❏ 60720	It's Funny/Confession Is Good for the Soul	1952	75.00	150.00	300.00
❏ 65093	Misery/But I Forgive You	1952	75.00	150.00	300.00
DELUXE					
❏ 6022	Please, Please Forgive Me/Baby	1953	125.00	250.00	500.00
JVB					
❏ 2001	Tomorrow Night/Why Don't You Do Right	1952	100.00	200.00	400.00
LOST-NITE					
❏ 334	Will She Know?/I Want to Love You Baby	197?	—	2.50	5.00
—Reissue					
RED ROBIN					
❏ 115	Will She Know?/I Want to Love You Baby	1953	375.00	750.00	1500.
SWING TIME					
❏ 347	M-A-Y-B-E-L-L/Ain't Gonna Cry No More	1954	300.00	600.00	1200.

SERENADERS, THE (3)
45s
Number	Title (A Side/B Side)	Yr	VG	VG+	NM
HANOVER					
❏ 4507	Honolulu/Summer Job	1959	3.75	7.50	15.00
❏ 4514	Alaska/Where Did You Go	1959	3.75	7.50	15.00

SERENADERS, THE (U) Could be group (1) or (2).
45s
Number	Title (A Side/B Side)	Yr	VG	VG+	NM
STARFIRE					
❏ 115	Nite Owl/I'm Gonna Love You	1980	—	3.00	6.00
TEEN LIFE					
❏ 9	Love Me Now/Gates of Gold	1958	175.00	350.00	700.00

SERENADETTS, THE
45s
Number	Title (A Side/B Side)	Yr	VG	VG+	NM
ENRICA					
❏ 1008	Boyfriend/The Big Night	1961	3.00	6.00	12.00

SERENDIPITY SINGERS, THE
45s
Number	Title (A Side/B Side)	Yr	VG	VG+	NM
PHILIPS					
❏ 40175	Don't Let the Rain Come Down (Crooked Little Man)/Freedom's Star	1964	2.50	5.00	10.00
❏ 40175	Crooked Little Man/Freedom's Star	1964	3.00	6.00	12.00
❏ 40198	Beans in My Ears/Sailin' Away	1964	2.00	4.00	8.00
❏ 40215	The New Frankie and Johnny Song/Down Where the Winds Blow	1964	2.00	4.00	8.00
❏ 40236	Autumn Wind/Same Old Reason	1964	2.00	4.00	8.00
❏ 40246	Little Brown Jug/High North Star	1964	2.00	4.00	8.00
❏ 40273	My Heart Keeps Following You/Rider	1965	2.00	4.00	8.00
❏ 40292	Run, Run, Chicken, Run/We Belong Together	1965	2.00	4.00	8.00
❏ 40309	The Bells of Rhymney/Oh Brother	1965	2.00	4.00	8.00
❏ 40331	When Peaches Grow on Lilac Trees/Plastic	1965	2.00	4.00	8.00
❏ 40356	Phoenix Love Theme (Sinza Fina)/If You Come Back in Summer	1966	2.00	4.00	8.00
❏ 40410	Born Free/Autumn Bound	1966	2.00	4.00	8.00
UNITED ARTISTS					
❏ 50137	Hawaii/Wishing Doll	1967	—	3.00	6.00
❏ 50166	The Way West/Love to Love	1967	—	3.00	6.00
❏ 50168	Signs of Love/The Boat That I Row	1967	—	3.00	6.00
❏ 50317	Rain Doll/Love Is a State of Mind	1968	—	3.00	6.00
❏ 50457	What Will We Do with the Child/Illusions	1968	—	3.00	6.00
❏ 50532	Come Softly to Me/Cotton Mouth River	1969	—	3.00	6.00
Albums					
PHILIPS					
❏ PHM 200115 [M]	The Serendipity Singers	1964	3.75	7.50	15.00
❏ PHM 200134 [M]	The Many Sides of the Serendipity Singers	1964	3.75	7.50	15.00
❏ PHM 200151 [M]	Take Your Shoes Off with the Serendipity Singers	1964	3.75	7.50	15.00
❏ PHM 200180 [M]	We Belong Together	1965	3.75	7.50	15.00
❏ PHM 200190 [M]	Love, Lies and Flying Festoons	1965	3.75	7.50	15.00
❏ PHS 600115 [S]	The Serendipity Singers	1964	5.00	10.00	20.00
❏ PHS 600134 [S]	The Many Sides of the Serendipity Singers	1964	5.00	10.00	20.00
❏ PHS 600151 [S]	Take Your Shoes Off with the Serendipity Singers	1964	5.00	10.00	20.00
❏ PHS 600180 [S]	We Belong Together	1965	5.00	10.00	20.00
❏ PHS 600190 [S]	Love, Lies and Flying Festoons	1965	5.00	10.00	20.00

SERPENT POWER
Albums
Number	Title (A Side/B Side)	Yr	VG	VG+	NM
VANGUARD					
❏ VRS-9252 [M]	Serpent Power	1967	30.00	60.00	120.00
❏ VSD-79252 [S]	Serpent Power	1967	15.00	30.00	60.00

SERRATT, HOWARD
45s
Number	Title (A Side/B Side)	Yr	VG	VG+	NM
SUN					
❏ 198	I Must Be Saved/Troublesome Waters	1954	500.00	1000.	2000.

SEVEN BLENDS, THE
Albums
Number	Title (A Side/B Side)	Yr	VG	VG+	NM
ROULETTE					
❏ R-25172 [M]	Twistin' at the Miami Beach Peppermint Lounge	1962	5.00	10.00	20.00
❏ SR-25172 [S]	Twistin' at the Miami Beach Peppermint Lounge	1962	6.25	12.50	25.00

SEVEN OF US
45s
Number	Title (A Side/B Side)	Yr	VG	VG+	NM
RED BIRD					
❏ 10-069	The Way to Your Heart/How Could You	1966	7.50	15.00	30.00
❏ 10-080	Jamboree/It's Not Easy to Forget	1966	7.50	15.00	30.00

7TH AVENUE AVIATORS, THE See FRANKIE KARL.

SEVENTH SONS, THE
Albums
Number	Title (A Side/B Side)	Yr	VG	VG+	NM
ESP-DISK'					
❏ 1078	The Seventh Sons	1967	7.50	15.00	30.00

SEVENTH WAVE, THE
Albums
Number	Title (A Side/B Side)	Yr	VG	VG+	NM
JANUS					
❏ 7008	Things to Come	1974	5.00	10.00	20.00
❏ 7021	Psi-Fi	1975	5.00	10.00	20.00

SEVERINSON, DOC
45s
Number	Title (A Side/B Side)	Yr	VG	VG+	NM
AMHERST					
❏ 110	Tonight Show Theme/Skyliner	1986	—	2.50	5.00
COMMAND					
❏ 4039	Cry Me a River/This Is All I Ask	1963	2.50	5.00	10.00
❏ 4065	It Ain't Necessarily So/Manha de Carnival	1965	2.00	4.00	8.00
❏ 4071	Phantom Trumpet/You Are My Sunshine	1965	2.00	4.00	8.00
❏ 4080	In a Little Spanish Town/Tennessee Waltz	1966	2.00	4.00	8.00
❏ 4084	If He Walked Into My Life/Mothers and Daughters	1966	2.00	4.00	8.00
❏ 4087	Sunday Morning/When the Saints Go Marching In	1967	2.00	4.00	8.00
❏ 4091	Is Paris Burning/Walk On By	1967	2.00	4.00	8.00
❏ 4098	Monday, Monday/Music to Think By	1967	2.00	4.00	8.00
❏ 4101	Canadian Sunset/One Step Above	1968	—	3.00	6.00
❏ 4117	Trumpets and Crumpets/Free Again	1968	—	3.00	6.00
❏ 4122	Lullaby from "Rosemary's Baby"/That's What Love's About	1968	—	3.00	6.00
❏ 4124	Summer's Coming Back/That's What Love's About	1969	—	3.00	6.00
❏ 4125	Barbarella/Knowing When to Leave	1969	—	3.00	6.00
❏ 4133	Come Together/Carry That Weight	1970	—	3.00	6.00
❏ 4137	Power to the People/Bottleneck	1971	—	3.00	6.00
EPIC					
❏ 9311	Do You Know a Story/Oh, Mr. Dillon	1959	3.00	6.00	12.00
❏ 50220	I Wanna Be with You/The World's Gone Home	1976	—	2.00	4.00
❏ 50318	Little Tiny Feets/Melody (Aria)	1976	—	2.00	4.00
RCA VICTOR					
❏ 74-0904	Last Tango in Paris/Alone Again	1973	—	2.00	4.00
Albums					
ABC					
❏ S-737	16 Great Performances	1971	2.50	5.00	10.00
❏ X-771	Trumpets, Crumpets	1973	2.50	5.00	10.00
AMHERST					
❏ AMH-3311	The Tonight Show Band with Doc Severinson	1986	2.50	5.00	10.00
❏ AMH-3312	The Tonight Show Band with Doc Severinson, Vol. II	1987	2.50	5.00	10.00
❏ AMH-3319	Facets	1988	2.50	5.00	10.00
COMMAND					
❏ RS 819 SD [S]	Tempestuous Trumpet	1961	5.00	10.00	20.00
❏ RS 819 [M]	Tempestuous Trumpet	1961	3.75	7.50	15.00
❏ RS 837 SD [S]	The Big Band's Back in Town	1962	5.00	10.00	20.00
❏ RS 33-837 [M]	The Big Band's Back in Town	1962	3.75	7.50	15.00
❏ RS 859 SD [S]	Torch Songs for Trumpet	1963	5.00	10.00	20.00
❏ RS 33-859 [M]	Torch Songs for Trumpet	1963	3.75	7.50	15.00
❏ RS 883 SD [S]	High, Wide and Wonderful	1965	5.00	10.00	20.00
❏ RS 33-883 [M]	High, Wide and Wonderful	1965	3.75	7.50	15.00
❏ RS 893 SD [S]	Fever!	1966	3.75	7.50	15.00
❏ RS 33-893 [M]	Fever!	1966	3.00	6.00	12.00
❏ RS 901 SD [S]	Live!	1966	3.75	7.50	15.00
❏ RS 33-901 [M]	Live!	1966	3.00	6.00	12.00
❏ RS 904 SD [S]	Command Performances	1966	3.75	7.50	15.00
❏ RS 33-904 [M]	Command Performances	1966	3.00	6.00	12.00
❏ RS 909 SD [S]	Swinging and Singing	1967	3.00	6.00	12.00
❏ RS 33-909 [M]	Swinging and Singing	1967	3.75	7.50	15.00
❏ RS 917 SD [S]	The New Sound	1967	3.00	6.00	12.00
❏ RS 33-917 [M]	The New Sound	1967	3.75	7.50	15.00
❏ RS 927 SD	The Great Arrival	1968	3.00	6.00	12.00
❏ RS 937 SD	Doc Severinson with Strings	1969	3.00	6.00	12.00
❏ RS 950 SD	The Closet	1970	3.00	6.00	12.00
❏ RS 952 SD	The Best of Doc Severinson	1970	3.00	6.00	12.00
❏ QD-40003 [Q]	Fever!	1972	3.75	7.50	15.00
EPIC					
❏ PE 34078	Night Journey	1976	2.50	5.00	10.00
❏ PE 34925	A Brand New Thing	1977	2.50	5.00	10.00
EVEREST ARCHIVE OF FOLK & JAZZ					
❏ 334	Doc Severinson and Friends	1978	2.50	5.00	10.00
FIRSTLINE					
❏ FDLP 5001	London Sessions	1980	3.00	6.00	12.00
JUNO					
❏ 1001	I Feel Good	1970	3.00	6.00	12.00
MCA					
❏ 4168 [(2)]	The Best of Doc Severinson	198?	2.50	5.00	10.00
PICKWICK					
❏ SPC-3608	Torch Songs for Trumpet	1978	2.00	4.00	8.00
❏ SPC 3627	Tempestuous Trumpet	1978	2.00	4.00	8.00

Number	Title (A Side/B Side)	Yr	VG	VG+	NM
RCA VICTOR					
❏ APL1-0273	Rhapsody for Now!	1973	3.00	6.00	12.00
❏ LSP-4522	Brass Roots	1971	3.00	6.00	12.00
❏ AFL1-4669	Doc	1977	2.50	5.00	10.00
—Reissue with new prefix					
❏ LSP-4669	Doc	1972	3.00	6.00	12.00

SEVILLE, DAVID Also see ROSS BAGDASARIAN; THE CHIPMUNKS.
45s

Number	Title (A Side/B Side)	Yr	VG	VG+	NM
LIBERTY					
❏ 55041	Armen's Theme/Carousel in Rome	1956	6.25	12.50	25.00
❏ 55055	The Donkey and the Schoolboy/The Gift	1957	6.25	12.50	25.00
❏ 55079	Camel Rock/Gotta Get to Your House	1957	6.25	12.50	25.00
❏ 55079 [PS]	Camel Rock/Gotta Get to Your House	1957	12.50	25.00	50.00
❏ 55105	Pretty Dark Eyes/Cecelia	1957	6.25	12.50	25.00
❏ 55113	Bagdad Express/Starlight, Starbright	1957	6.25	12.50	25.00
❏ 55124	Bonjour Tristesse/Dance from Bonjour Tristesse	1958	6.25	12.50	25.00
❏ 55132	Witch Doctor/Don't Whistle at Me Baby	1958	7.50	15.00	30.00
❏ 55140	The Bird on My Head/Hey There Moon	1958	6.25	12.50	25.00
❏ 55153	Little Brass Band/Take Five	1958	6.25	12.50	25.00
❏ 55163	The Mountain/Mr. Grape	1958	6.25	12.50	25.00
❏ 55272	Witch Doctor/Swanee River	1960	5.00	10.00	20.00
❏ 55314	Oh Judge, Your Honor, Dear Sir, Sweetheart/Freddy, Freddy	1961	6.25	12.50	25.00
UNITED ARTISTS					
❏ 0063	Witch Doctor/The Bird on My Head	1973	—	2.00	4.00
—"Silver Spotlight Series" reissue					
7-Inch Extended Plays					
LIBERTY					
❏ LSX-1003	(contents unknown)	1958	10.00	20.00	40.00
❏ LSX-1003 [PS]	Witch Doctor	1958	10.00	20.00	40.00
Albums					
LIBERTY					
❏ LRP-3073 [M]	The Music of David Seville	1957	20.00	40.00	80.00
❏ LRP-3092 [M]	The Witch Doctor	1958	25.00	50.00	100.00

SEVILLE, DAVID, AND THE CHIPMUNKS See THE CHIPMUNKS.

SEVILLES, THE
45s

Number	Title (A Side/B Side)	Yr	VG	VG+	NM
CAL-GOLD					
❏ 172	Don't You Know I Care/(B-side unknown)	1962	5.00	10.00	20.00
GALAXY					
❏ 717	Treat You Right/Hey, Hey, Hey	1963	3.75	7.50	15.00
❏ 721	Charlena/Loving You	1963	3.75	7.50	15.00
❏ 727	Creation/Baby	1964	3.75	7.50	15.00
JC					
❏ 116	Charlena/Loving You (Is My Desire)	1960	7.50	15.00	30.00
❏ 118	Louella/Salt Mine	1961	6.25	12.50	25.00
❏ 120	Fat Sally/Working Hard	1961	5.00	10.00	20.00

SEWARD, ALEC
Albums

Number	Title (A Side/B Side)	Yr	VG	VG+	NM
BLUESVILLE					
❏ BVLP-1076 [M]	Creepin' Blues	1963	20.00	40.00	80.00
—Blue label, silver print					
❏ BVLP-1076 [M]	Creepin' Blues	1964	6.25	12.50	25.00
—Blue label, trident logo at right					

SH-BOOMS, THE See THE CHORDS.

SHA NA NA
45s

Number	Title (A Side/B Side)	Yr	VG	VG+	NM
KAMA SUTRA					
❏ 503	Lovers Never Say Goodbye/Remember Then	1970	—	3.00	6.00
❏ 507	Pay Day/Rock and Roll Is Here to Stay	1970	—	3.00	6.00
❏ 522	Only One Song/Yakety Yak	1971	—	3.00	6.00
❏ 528	Top Forty of the Lord/I Wonder Why	1971	—	3.00	6.00
❏ 528 [PS]	Top Forty of the Lord/I Wonder Why	1971	2.50	5.00	10.00
❏ 555	Bounce in Your Buggy/Bless My Soul	1972	—	3.00	6.00
❏ 555 [PS]	Bounce in Your Buggy/Bless My Soul	1972	2.50	5.00	10.00
❏ 560	In the Still of the Night/Sea Cruise	1972	—	2.50	5.00
❏ 578 [DJ]	In the Still of the Night (mono/stereo)	1973	3.75	7.50	15.00
—As "Eddie and the Evergreens"; may be promo only					
❏ 592	Maybe I'm Old Fashioned/Stroll All Night	1974	—	2.50	5.00
❏ 592 [PS]	Maybe I'm Old Fashioned/Stroll All Night	1974	2.50	5.00	10.00
❏ 596	Too Chubby to Boogie/(B-side unknown)	1974	—	2.50	5.00
❏ 602	Just Like Romeo and Juliet/Circles of Love	1975	—	2.50	5.00
❏ 603	You're the Only Light on My Horizon Now	1975	—	2.50	5.00
❏ 604	Shanghied/Chills in My Spine	1975	—	2.50	5.00
RSO					
❏ 909	Rock and Roll Is Here to Stay/Greased Lightnin'	1978	—	2.00	4.00
—B-side by John Travolta					
❏ 930	Blue Moon/Sandy	1979	—	2.00	4.00
—B-side by John Travolta					
Albums					
ACCORD					
❏ SN-7115	Remember Then	1981	2.50	5.00	10.00
❏ SN-7146	Sh-Boom	1981	2.50	5.00	10.00
BUDDAH					
❏ BDM-5692	Rock & Roll Is Here to Stay!	1978	2.50	5.00	10.00
❏ BDM-5703	The Best of Sha Na Na	1978	2.50	5.00	10.00
EMUS					
❏ ES-12037	On Stage	1978	2.50	5.00	10.00
KAMA SUTRA					
❏ KSBS-2010	Rock & Roll Is Here to Stay!	1969	3.75	7.50	15.00
❏ KSBS-2034	Sha Na Na	1971	3.75	7.50	15.00
❏ KSBS-2050	The Night Is Still Young	1972	3.75	7.50	15.00
❏ KSBS-2073 [(2)]	The Golden Age of Rock 'n' Roll	1973	5.00	10.00	20.00
❏ KSBS-2075	From the Streets of New York	1973	3.75	7.50	15.00
❏ KSBS-2077	Rock & Roll Is Here to Stay!	1974	3.75	7.50	15.00
❏ KSBS-2600	Hot Sox	1974	3.75	7.50	15.00
❏ KSBS-2605	Sha Na Now	1975	3.75	7.50	15.00
❏ KSBS-2609 [(2)]	The Best…Sha Na Na	1976	3.75	7.50	15.00
NASHVILLE					
❏ NR-12348-122 [(2)]	Rockin' in the 80's	1980	3.00	6.00	12.00

Number	Title (A Side/B Side)	Yr	VG	VG+	NM
REALM					
❏ 2V 8058 [(2)]	All-Time Greatest Rock 'n' Roll Hits	1977	3.75	7.50	15.00
❏ 1V 8059	Rock 'n' Roll Dance Party	1977	3.00	6.00	12.00

SHA-WEES, THE
45s

Number	Title (A Side/B Side)	Yr	VG	VG+	NM
ALADDIN					
❏ 3170	No One to Love Me/Early Sunday Morning	1953	1000.	2000.	4000.

SHADES, THE More than one group.
45s

Number	Title (A Side/B Side)	Yr	VG	VG+	NM
ALADDIN					
❏ 3453	Dear Lori/One Touch of Heaven	1959	75.00	150.00	300.00
AOK					
❏ 1028	Ginger Bread Man/The Hip	1967	7.50	15.00	30.00
BIG TOP					
❏ 3003	Sun Glasses/Undivided Attention	1958	25.00	50.00	100.00
—B-side by The Knott Sisters					

SHADES OF BLUE
45s

Number	Title (A Side/B Side)	Yr	VG	VG+	NM
IMPACT					
❏ 1007	Oh, How Happy/Little Orphan Boy	1966	5.00	10.00	20.00
❏ 1014	Lonely Summer/With This Ring	1966	5.00	10.00	20.00
❏ 1015	Happiness/The Night	1966	5.00	10.00	20.00
❏ 1026	All I Want Is Love/How Do You Save a Dying Love	1967	5.00	10.00	20.00
❏ 1028	Penny Arcade/Funny Kind of Love	1967	5.00	10.00	20.00
Albums					
IMPACT					
❏ IM-101 [M]	Happiness Is the Shades of Blue	1966	12.50	25.00	50.00
❏ IM-1001 [S]	Happiness Is the Shades of Blue	1966	15.00	30.00	60.00

SHADES OF JOY
45s

Number	Title (A Side/B Side)	Yr	VG	VG+	NM
FONTANA					
❏ 1659	Soul Truth/I Do Like Rock	1969	2.50	5.00	10.00
Albums					
FONTANA					
❏ SRF-67592	Shades of Joy	1969	5.00	10.00	20.00

SHADOWS, THE (1) Backing group for CLIFF RICHARD. Includes early records as "The Drifters" and "The Four Jets." Also see JET HARRIS AND TONY MEEHAN.
45s

Number	Title (A Side/B Side)	Yr	VG	VG+	NM
ABC-PARAMOUNT					
❏ 10073	Saturday Dance/Lonesome Fella	1960	7.50	15.00	30.00
❏ 10138	Apache/Quartermaster's Stores	1960	7.50	15.00	30.00
ATLANTIC					
❏ 2111	FBI/The Frightened City	1961	5.00	10.00	20.00
❏ 2135	Kon-Tiki/Man of Mystery	1962	5.00	10.00	20.00
❏ 2146	Wonderful Land/Stars Fell on Stockton	1962	5.00	10.00	20.00
❏ 2166	Guitar Tango/What a Lovely Thing	1962	5.00	10.00	20.00
❏ 2177	Dance On/The Rumble	1963	5.00	10.00	20.00
❏ 2235	Theme for Young Lovers/The Rise and Fall of Flingel Bunt	1964	5.00	10.00	20.00
❏ 2257	Rhythm and Greens/The Miracle	1964	5.00	10.00	20.00
CAPITOL					
❏ F-4220	Feelin' Fine/Don't Be a Fool	1959	10.00	20.00	40.00
—As "The Drifters"					
❏ F-4270	Driftin'/Jet Black	1959	10.00	20.00	40.00
—As "The Four Jets"					
EPIC					
❏ 9793	Mary Anne/Chu Chi	1965	5.00	10.00	20.00
❏ 9826	Stingray/Alice in Sunderland	1965	5.00	10.00	20.00
❏ 9848	Don't Make My Baby Blue/My Grandfather's Clock	1965	5.00	10.00	20.00
❏ 10020	I Met a Girl/Last Night Set	1966	5.00	10.00	20.00
Albums					
ATLANTIC					
❏ 8084 [M]	Out of the Shadows	1962	50.00	100.00	200.00
—Canada-only release?					
❏ 8089 [M]	Surfing with the Shadows	1963	37.50	75.00	150.00
❏ SD 8089 [S]	Surfing with the Shadows	1963	75.00	150.00	300.00
❏ 8097 [M]	The Shadows Know	1964	25.00	50.00	100.00
❏ SD 8097 [S]	The Shadows Know	1964	50.00	100.00	200.00

SHADOWS, THE (2)
45s

Number	Title (A Side/B Side)	Yr	VG	VG+	NM
DECCA					
❏ 28765	No Use/Stay	1953	62.50	125.00	250.00
❏ 48307	Tell Her/Don't Be Bashful	1954	75.00	150.00	300.00
❏ 48322	Big Mouth Mama/Better Than Gold	1954	75.00	150.00	300.00

SHADOWS, THE (3)
45s

Number	Title (A Side/B Side)	Yr	VG	VG+	NM
DEL-FI					
❏ 4109	Under the Stars of Love/Jungle Fever	1958	15.00	30.00	60.00

SHADOWS, THE (4)
45s

Number	Title (A Side/B Side)	Yr	VG	VG+	NM
DOTTIE					
❏ 1006	I Wonder Why/Tell This Lonely Heart Goodbye	1961	5.00	10.00	20.00

SHADOWS, THE (U) Could be group (3) or an entirely different group.
45s

Number	Title (A Side/B Side)	Yr	VG	VG+	NM
DELTA					
❏ 1509	Bop-A-Lena/There Stands the Glass	1958	50.00	100.00	200.00

SHADOWS OF KNIGHT, THE
45s

Number	Title (A Side/B Side)	Yr	VG	VG+	NM
ATCO					
❏ 6634	Gloria '69/A Spaniard at My Door	1968	4.00	8.00	16.00
❏ 6776	I Am the Hunter/Warwick County Affair	1970	4.00	8.00	16.00
AURAVISION					
❏ (no #)	Potato Chip	196?	15.00	30.00	60.00
—One-sided cardboard disc, 5 inches wide with small hole					

S

Number	Title (A Side/B Side)	Yr	VG	VG+	NM

DUNWICH
❑ 116	Gloria/Dark Side	1966	3.75	7.50	15.00
—Dark pink and yellow label; other label variations may exist					
❑ 116	Gloria/Dark Side	1966	5.00	10.00	20.00
—Yellow label, "Distributed by Atco Record Sales Co."					
❑ 116	Gloria/Dark Side	1966	6.25	12.50	25.00
—Gold label, no mention of Atco Records					
❑ 122	Oh Yeah/Light Bulb Blues	1966	5.00	10.00	20.00
❑ 122 [PS]	Oh Yeah/Light Bulb Blues	1966	7.50	15.00	30.00
❑ 128	Bad Little Woman/Gospel Zone	1966	3.75	7.50	15.00
❑ 128 [PS]	Bad Little Woman/Gospel Zone	1966	50.00	100.00	200.00
❑ 141	I'm Gonna Make You Mine/I'll Make You Sorry	1966	6.25	12.50	25.00
❑ 151	The Behemoth/Willie Jean	1967	5.00	10.00	20.00
❑ 167	Someone Like Me/There for Love	1967	5.00	10.00	20.00

PHONOGRAPH
| ❑ 1002/2001 | Sweetness in Motion/Nikki-Hoki (No One Else Will Ever Do) | 1986 | 2.00 | 4.00 | 8.00 |

SUPER K
| ❑ 108 | Taurus/My Fire Department Needs a Fireman | 1969 | 2.50 | 5.00 | 10.00 |
| ❑ 110 | Run, Run, Billy Porter/My Fire Department Needs a Fireman | 1969 | 2.50 | 5.00 | 10.00 |

TEAM
| ❑ 520 | Shake/From Way Out to Way In | 1968 | 4.00 | 8.00 | 16.00 |
Albums
DUNWICH
❑ 666 [M]	Gloria	1966	12.50	25.00	50.00
❑ S-666 [S]	Gloria	1966	20.00	40.00	80.00
❑ 667 [M]	Back Door Men	1966	12.50	25.00	50.00
❑ S-667 [S]	Back Door Men	1966	20.00	40.00	80.00
SUNDAZED
❑ LP 5006	Raw and Live at the Cellar 1966	1992	2.50	5.00	10.00
❑ LP 5034	Gloria	1999	3.00	6.00	12.00
—Reissue on 180-gram vinyl					
❑ LP 5035	Back Door Men	1999	3.00	6.00	12.00
—Reissue on 180-gram vinyl					
SUPER K
| ❑ SKS-6002 | The Shadows of Knight | 1969 | 12.50 | 25.00 | 50.00 |

SHADRACK
Albums
IGL
| ❑ 132 | Chameleon | 1971 | 75.00 | 150.00 | 300.00 |

SHAFTO, BOBBY
45s
RUST
❑ 5082	She's My Girl/Wonderful You	1964	2.50	5.00	10.00
❑ 5092	I'll Never Get Over You/ Who Wouldn't Love a Girl Like That	1964	2.50	5.00	10.00
❑ 5096	Baby Then/ How Could You Do a Thing Like That to Me	1965	2.50	5.00	10.00
❑ 5108	Lonely Is As Lonely Does/The Same Old Room	1966	3.00	6.00	12.00
❑ 5110	See Me Cry/A Little Like You	1966	2.50	5.00	10.00

SHAG, THE
45s
CAPITOL
| ❑ 5995 | Stop and Listen/Melissa | 1967 | 5.00 | 10.00 | 20.00 |

SHAGGS, THE (1)
45s
CAPITOL
| ❑ 2511 | Mean Woman Blues/She Makes Me Happy | 1969 | 2.50 | 5.00 | 10.00 |

SHAGGS, THE (2) This all-male band comprised students at the University of Notre Dame.
Albums
MCM
| ❑ 1295 | Wink | 1967 | 62.50 | 125.00 | 250.00 |
| —No number on label -- this number is found in the trail-off wax on each side | | | | | |

SHAGGS, THE (3) This band comprised three sisters from New Hampshire attempting to sing and play.
45s
FLEETWOOD
| ❑ 4584 | My Pal Foot-Foot/Things I Wonder | 1969 | — | — | — |
| —Listed on a Fleetwood Records discography, but was it ever released? | | | | | |
Albums
ROUNDER
| ❑ 3032 | Philosophy of the World | 1980 | 6.25 | 12.50 | 25.00 |
| ❑ 3056 | Shaggs' Own Thing | 1982 | 6.25 | 12.50 | 25.00 |
THIRD WORLD
| ❑ 3001 | Philosophy of the World | 1969 | 500.00 | 1000. | 2000. |

SHAGGY BOYS, THE
45s
RED BIRD
| ❑ 10-074 | Stop the Clock/In the Morning | 1966 | 3.75 | 7.50 | 15.00 |
UNITED ARTISTS
| ❑ 50100 | You and Me/Joy in the Morning | 1966 | 3.75 | 7.50 | 15.00 |
| ❑ 50135 | That's the Only Way/Behind These Stained Glass Windows | 1967 | 3.75 | 7.50 | 15.00 |

SHAKERS, THE
45s
ABC
| ❑ 10960 | Love, Love, Love/One Wonderful Moment | 1967 | 2.00 | 4.00 | 8.00 |
AUDIO FIDELITY
| ❑ 119 | Break It All/Ticket to Ride | 1966 | 2.50 | 5.00 | 10.00 |
Albums
AUDIO FIDELITY
| ❑ AFLP-2155 [M] | The Shakers Break It All | 1966 | 10.00 | 20.00 | 40.00 |
| ❑ AFSD-6155 [S] | The Shakers Break It All | 1966 | 12.50 | 25.00 | 50.00 |

SHAKEY JAKE
45s
BLUESVILLE
| ❑ 807 | My Foolish Heart/Jake's Blues | 1960 | 5.00 | 10.00 | 20.00 |

Albums
BLUESVILLE
❑ BVLP-1008 [M] Good Times		1960	30.00	60.00	120.00
—Blue label, silver print					
❑ BVLP-1008 [M] Good Times		1964	7.50	15.00	30.00
—Blue label, trident logo at right					
❑ BVLP-1027 [M] Mouth Harp Blues		1961	30.00	60.00	120.00
—Blue label, silver print					
❑ BVLP-1027 [M] Mouth Harp Blues		1964	7.50	15.00	30.00
—Blue label, trident logo at right					
WORLD PACIFIC
| ❑ WPS-21886 | Blues Makers | 196? | 7.50 | 15.00 | 30.00 |

SHAKEY VICK
Albums
JANUS
| ❑ JLS-3000 | Little Woman, You're So Sweet | 1970 | 5.00 | 10.00 | 20.00 |

SHAM-ETTES, THE
45s
MGM
| ❑ 13618 | Big Bad Wolf (Hey There)/I'd Rather Have You | 1966 | 3.75 | 7.50 | 15.00 |
| ❑ 13798 | He'll Come Back/You're Welcome Back | 1967 | 3.00 | 6.00 | 12.00 |

SHANE, BOB Also see THE KINGSTON TRIO.
45s
DECCA
| ❑ 32239 | Simple Gifts/Weeping Annaleah | 1967 | 2.50 | 5.00 | 10.00 |
| ❑ 32275 | Honey/I Don't Think of You Anymore | 1968 | 2.50 | 5.00 | 10.00 |

SHANGRI-LAS, THE
45s
LANA
| ❑ 143 | Leader of the Pack/What Is Love | 196? | 2.50 | 5.00 | 10.00 |
| —Oldies reissue | | | | | |
MERCURY
| ❑ 72645 | I'll Never Learn/Sweet Sounds of Summer | 1966 | 5.00 | 10.00 | 20.00 |
| ❑ 72670 | Footsteps on the Roof/Take the Time | 1967 | 5.00 | 10.00 | 20.00 |
RED BIRD
❑ 10-008	Remember (Walkin' in the Sand)/ It's Easier to Cry	1964	6.25	12.50	25.00
❑ 10-014	Leader of the Pack/What Is Love	1964	6.25	12.50	25.00
❑ 10-018	Give Him a Great Big Kiss/Twist and Shout	1964	6.25	12.50	25.00
❑ 10-019	Maybe/Shout	1964	5.00	10.00	20.00
❑ 10-025	Out in the Streets/The Boy	1965	5.00	10.00	20.00
❑ 10-030	Give Us Your Blessings/Heaven Only Knows	1965	5.00	10.00	20.00
❑ 10-036	Right Now and Not Later/ The Train from Kansas City	1965	5.00	10.00	20.00
❑ 10-043	I Can Never Go Home Anymore/Bull Dog	1965	5.00	10.00	20.00
❑ 10-043	I Can Never Go Home Anymore/ Sophisticated Boom Boom	1965	7.50	15.00	30.00
❑ 10-048	Long Live Our Love/Bull Dog	1966	5.00	10.00	20.00
❑ 10-048	Long Live Our Love/Sophisticated Boom Boom	1966	5.00	10.00	20.00
❑ 10-053	He Cried/Dressed in Black	1966	5.00	10.00	20.00
❑ 10-068	Past, Present and Future/ Love You More Than Yesterday	1966	5.00	10.00	20.00
❑ 10-068	Past, Present and Future/Paradise	1966	5.00	10.00	20.00
SCEPTER
| ❑ 1291 | Wishing Well/Hate to Say I Told You So | 1964 | 5.00 | 10.00 | 20.00 |
SMASH
| ❑ 1866 | Simon Says/Simon Speaks | 1963 | 10.00 | 20.00 | 40.00 |
SPOKANE
| ❑ 4006 | Wishing Well/Hate to Say I Told You So | 1964 | 7.50 | 15.00 | 30.00 |
Albums
COLLECTABLES
| ❑ COL-5011 | Remember…Their Greatest Hits | 198? | 2.50 | 5.00 | 10.00 |
MERCURY
| ❑ MG-21099 [M] | The Shangri-Las' Golden Hits | 1966 | 10.00 | 20.00 | 40.00 |
| ❑ SR-61099 [S] | The Shangri-Las' Golden Hits | 1966 | 12.50 | 25.00 | 50.00 |
POLYDOR
| ❑ 824807-1 | Golden Hits of the Shangri-Las | 1985 | 2.50 | 5.00 | 10.00 |
POST
| ❑ 4000 | The Shangri-Las Sing | 196? | 5.00 | 10.00 | 20.00 |
RED BIRD
❑ 20101 [M]	Leader of the Pack	1965	37.50	75.00	150.00
❑ 20104 [M]	Shangri-Las '65	1965	37.50	75.00	150.00
❑ 20104 [M]	I Can Never Go Home Anymore	1966	25.00	50.00	100.00
—Retitled version with title song added and "Sophisticated Boom Boom" dropped					

SHANK AND MAYDIEA
45s
FLIP
| ❑ 361 | Why Don't You Tell Me/Bye Bye Baby (My Pride) | 1962 | 2.50 | 5.00 | 10.00 |

SHANKAR, ANANDA
Albums
REPRISE
| ❑ RS-6398 | Ananda Shankar | 1970 | 5.00 | 10.00 | 20.00 |

SHANKAR, RAVI Also see GEORGE HARRISON AND FRIENDS.
45s
APPLE
❑ 1838	Joi Bangla-Oh Bhaugowan/ Raga Mishra-Jhinjhoti	1971	2.00	4.00	8.00
—By Ravi Shankar & Ali Akbar with Alla Rakah					
❑ 1838 [PS]	Joi Bangla-Oh Bhaugowan/ Raga Mishra-Jhinjhoti	1971	5.00	10.00	20.00
DARK HORSE
| ❑ 10001 | I Am Missing You/Lost | 1974 | — | 2.50 | 5.00 |
SPARK
| ❑ SP-07 | Transmigration/(B-side unknown) | 1973 | — | 3.00 | 6.00 |
| —As "R. Shankar" | | | | | |
WORLD PACIFIC
| ❑ 77871 | Pather Panchali/Gat Kirawani | 1967 | 2.00 | 4.00 | 8.00 |
| ❑ 77898 | Charly Theme/Love Montage | 1968 | 2.00 | 4.00 | 8.00 |

Number	Title (A Side/B Side)	Yr	VG	VG+	NM

Albums

ANGEL

❏ 35468 [M]	Music of India	196?	6.25	12.50	25.00
❏ S 36026 [S]	West Meets East, Vol. 2	1968	3.75	7.50	15.00
❏ 36418 [M]	West Meets East	1967	6.25	12.50	25.00
—With Yahudi Menuhin					
❏ S 36418 [S]	West Meets East	1967	5.00	10.00	20.00
—With Yahudi Menuhin					
❏ S 36806	Concerto for Sitar and Orchestra	1972	3.00	6.00	12.00
❏ DS-37920	Raga Mishra Piloo	1982	2.50	5.00	10.00
❏ DS-37935	Raga-Mala (Sitar Concert No. 2)	1983	2.50	5.00	10.00

APPLE

❏ SWAO-3384	Raga	1971	6.25	12.50	25.00
❏ SVBB-3396 [(2)]	Ravi Shankar In Concert	1973	10.00	20.00	40.00

BLUESVILLE

❏ BVLP-1078 [M]	The Master Musician of India	1964	6.25	12.50	25.00

CAPITOL

❏ DT 2720 [R]	Three Ragas	1967	3.75	7.50	15.00
❏ T 2720 [M]	Three Ragas	1967	5.00	10.00	20.00
❏ ST 10482 [S]	Two Raga Moods	196?	6.25	12.50	25.00
❏ T 10482 [M]	Two Raga Moods	196?	5.00	10.00	20.00
❏ ST 10497 [S]	Exotic Sitar and Sarod	196?	6.25	12.50	25.00
❏ T 10497 [M]	Exotic Sitar and Sarod	196?	5.00	10.00	20.00
❏ ST 10504	Ravi	196?	3.75	7.50	15.00
❏ SP-10561	Raga Parameshwari	1972	3.00	6.00	12.00

COLUMBIA

❏ WL 119 [M]	The Sounds of India	196?	6.25	12.50	25.00
❏ CL 2496 [M]	Sounds of India	1966	3.75	7.50	15.00
❏ CL 2760 [M]	The Genius of Ravi Shankar	1967	5.00	10.00	20.00
❏ OS 3230	Chappaqua	1968	3.75	7.50	15.00
❏ CS 9296 [S]	Sounds of India	1966	5.00	10.00	20.00
❏ CS 9560 [S]	The Genius of Ravi Shankar	1967	3.75	7.50	15.00

DARK HORSE

❏ SP 22002	Shankar Family and Friends	1974	3.00	6.00	12.00
❏ SP 22007	Music Festival from India	1975	3.00	6.00	12.00

DEUTCHE GRAMMOPHON

❏ 2531 216	Ragas Hameer & Gara	198?	2.50	5.00	10.00
❏ 2531 280	Raga Jogeshwari	198?	2.50	5.00	10.00
❏ 2531 356	Homage to Mahatma Gandhi; Homage to Baba Allauddin	198?	2.50	5.00	10.00
❏ 2531 381	Pad Hasapa, for Koto; etc.	198?	2.50	5.00	10.00

FANTASY

❏ 24714 [(2)]	Ragas	1973	3.75	7.50	15.00

ORIENTAL

❏ BGRP-108	Raga Sanjh Kalyan	198?	2.50	5.00	10.00

PRIVATE MUSIC

❏ 2016-1-P	The Shankar Project: Tana Mana	1988	2.50	5.00	10.00
❏ 2044-1-P	Inside the Kremlin	1989	2.50	5.00	10.00

SPARK

❏ 06	Transmigration Macabre	1973	3.00	6.00	12.00

WORLD PACIFIC

❏ WP-1421 [M]	Ravi Shankar In Concert	1965	3.75	7.50	15.00
❏ WP-1422 [M]	India's Master Musician	1965	3.75	7.50	15.00
❏ WP-1430 [M]	Ravi Shankar In London	1966	3.75	7.50	15.00
❏ WP-1431 [M]	Ragas and Talas	1966	3.75	7.50	15.00
❏ WP-1432 [M]	Portrait of Genius	1966	3.75	7.50	15.00
❏ WP-1434 [M]	Sound of the Sitar	1967	3.75	7.50	15.00
❏ WP-1438 [M]	Three Ragas	1967	3.75	7.50	15.00
❏ WP-1441 [M]	Ravi Shankar in New York	1967	3.75	7.50	15.00
❏ WP-1442 [M]	Ravi Shankar at the Monterey International Pop Festival	1967	5.00	10.00	20.00
❏ ST-21421 [S]	Ravi Shankar In Concert	1965	5.00	10.00	20.00
❏ ST-21422 [S]	India's Master Musician	1965	5.00	10.00	20.00
❏ ST-21430 [S]	Ravi Shankar In London	1966	5.00	10.00	20.00
❏ ST-21431 [S]	Ragas and Talas	1966	5.00	10.00	20.00
❏ ST-21432 [S]	Portrait of Genius	1966	5.00	10.00	20.00
❏ ST-21434 [S]	Sound of the Sitar	1967	5.00	10.00	20.00
❏ ST-21438 [S]	Three Ragas	1967	5.00	10.00	20.00
❏ ST-21441 [S]	Ravi Shankar in New York	1967	5.00	10.00	20.00
❏ ST-21442 [S]	Ravi Shankar at the Monterey International Pop Festival	1967	5.00	10.00	20.00
❏ ST-21449	Ravi Shankar in San Francisco	1968	5.00	10.00	20.00
❏ ST-21454	Charly	1969	3.75	7.50	15.00
❏ ST-21464	Morning Raga/Evening Raga	1970	3.75	7.50	15.00
❏ ST-21467	Ravi Shankar at Woodstock	1970	3.75	7.50	15.00
❏ WPS-26201 [(2)]	His Festival from India	1968	5.00	10.00	20.00

SHANNON　See MARTY WILDE.

SHANNON, DEL
45s

ABC DUNHILL

❏ 4193	Sweet Mary Lou/Comin' Back to me	1969	3.75	7.50	15.00
❏ 4224	Sister Isabelle/Colorado Rain	1970	3.75	7.50	15.00

AMY

❏ 897	Mary Jane/Stains on My Letter	1964	6.25	12.50	25.00
❏ 905	Handy Man/Give Her Lots of Lovin'	1964	3.75	7.50	15.00
❏ 911	Do You Want to Dance/This Is All I Have to Give	1964	3.75	7.50	15.00
❏ 915	Keep Searchin' (We'll Follow the Sun)/ Broken Promises	1964	4.00	8.00	16.00
❏ 919	Stranger in Town/Over You	1965	4.00	8.00	16.00
❏ 925	Why Don't You Tell Him/Break Up	1965	3.75	7.50	15.00
❏ 937	Move It On Over/She Still Remembers Tony	1965	3.75	7.50	15.00
❏ 947	I Can't Believe My Ears/ I Wish I Wasn't Me Tonight	1966	10.00	20.00	40.00
—Withdrawn shortly after release; promos worth about half these values					

BERLEE

❏ 501	Sue's Gotta Be Mine/Now She's Gone	1963	3.75	7.50	15.00
❏ 502	That's the Way Love Is/Time of the Day	1964	3.75	7.50	15.00

BIG TOP

❏ 3067	Runaway/Jody	1961	7.50	15.00	30.00
❏ 3075	Hats Off to Larry/Don't Gild the Lily, Lily	1961	6.25	12.50	25.00
❏ 3083	So Long Baby/The Answer to Everything	1961	6.25	12.50	25.00
❏ 3091	Hey! Little Girl/I Don't Care Anymore	1961	6.25	12.50	25.00
❏ 3098	Ginny in the Mirror/I Won't Be There	1962	6.25	12.50	25.00
❏ 3112	Cry Myself to Sleep/I'm Gonna Move On	1962	6.25	12.50	25.00

Number	Title (A Side/B Side)	Yr	VG	VG+	NM
❏ 3117	The Swiss Maid/You Never Talked About Me	1962	6.25	12.50	25.00
❏ 3131	Little Town Flirt/The Wamboo	1962	6.25	12.50	25.00
❏ 3143	Two Kinds of Teardrops/Kelly	1963	6.25	12.50	25.00
❏ 3152	From Me to You/Two Silhouettes	1963	15.00	30.00	60.00
—A-side is the first American version of a Beatles song					

ERIC

❏ 189 [S]	Runaway/Hats Off to Larry	1972	—	3.00	6.00
—Both sides of this reissue are the original recordings in true stereo!					

ISLAND

❏ 021	Tell Her No/Restless	1975	3.75	7.50	15.00
❏ 038	Cry Baby Cry/In My Arms Again	1975	3.75	7.50	15.00

LANA

❏ 141	Runaway/Jody	196?	2.00	4.00	8.00
—Oldies reissue					
❏ 142	Hats Off to Larry/Don't Gild the Lily, Lily	196?	2.00	4.00	8.00
—Oldies reissue					

LIBERTY

❏ 55866	The Big Hurt/I Got It Bad	1966	3.00	6.00	12.00
❏ 55889	Hey Little Star/For a Little While	1966	3.00	6.00	12.00
❏ 55894	Show Me/Never Thought I Could	1966	3.00	6.00	12.00
❏ 55904	Under My Thumb/She Was Mine	1966	3.00	6.00	12.00
❏ 55939	She/What Makes You Run	1967	3.00	6.00	12.00
❏ 55961	Led Along/I Can't Be True	1967	3.00	6.00	12.00
❏ 55993	Runaway '67/He Cheated	1967	3.75	7.50	15.00
❏ 56018	Runnin' On Back/Thinkin' It Over	1968	2.50	5.00	10.00
❏ 56018 [PS]	Runnin' On Back/Thinkin' It Over	1968	7.50	15.00	30.00
❏ 56036	Magical Musical Box/Gemini	1968	2.50	5.00	10.00
❏ 56070	Raindrops/You Don't Love Me	1968	2.50	5.00	10.00

LOST-NITE

❏ 220	Runaway/Hey Little Girl	196?	—	2.50	5.00
—Reissue					
❏ 222	Hats Off to Larry/Little Town Flirt	196?	—	2.50	5.00
—Reissue					

NETWORK

❏ 47951	Sea of Love/Midnight Train	1981	—	2.50	5.00
❏ 48006	To Love Someone/Liar	1982	—	2.50	5.00

TWIRL

❏ 4001	Runaway/Hey Little Girl	196?	—	3.00	6.00
❏ 4002	Hats Off to Larry/Little Town Flirt	196?	—	3.00	6.00

WARNER BROS.

❏ 28853	Stranger on the Run/ What You Gonna Do with That	1985	—	2.50	5.00
❏ 29029	In My Arms Again/You Can't Forgive Me	1985	—	2.50	5.00

Albums

AMY

❏ 8003 [M]	Handy Man	1964	12.50	25.00	50.00
❏ S-8003 [S]	Handy Man	1964	20.00	40.00	80.00
❏ 8004 [M]	Del Shannon Sings Hank Williams	1965	12.50	25.00	50.00
❏ S-8004 [S]	Del Shannon Sings Hank Williams	1965	20.00	40.00	80.00
❏ 8006 [M]	1,661 Seconds with Del Shannon	1965	12.50	25.00	50.00
❏ S-8006 [S]	1,661 Seconds with Del Shannon	1965	20.00	40.00	80.00

BIG TOP

❏ 12-1303 [M]	Runaway	1961	75.00	150.00	300.00
❏ 12-1303 [S]	Runaway	1961	400.00	800.00	1600.
❏ 12-1308 [B]	Little Town Flirt	1963	250.00	500.00	1000.
—One side is mono, one side is stereo; should be played to identify					
❏ 12-1308 [M]	Little Town Flirt	1963	37.50	75.00	150.00
❏ 12-1308 [S]	Little Town Flirt	1963	375.00	750.00	1500.
—Stereo copies are not identified as such on either cover or label; some, but not all, copies have an "S" in the dead wax. Playing is the best way to identify.					

DOT

❏ DLP 3824 [M]	The Best of Del Shannon	1967	12.50	25.00	50.00
❏ DLP 25824 [R]	The Best of Del Shannon	1967	10.00	20.00	40.00

ELEKTRA

❏ 5E-568	Drop Down and Get Me	1981	2.50	5.00	10.00

LIBERTY

❏ LRP-3453 [M]	This Is My Bag	1966	7.50	15.00	30.00
❏ LRP-3479 [M]	Total Commitment	1966	7.50	15.00	30.00
❏ LRP-3539 [M]	The Further Adventures of Charles Westover	1967	12.50	25.00	50.00
❏ LST-7453 [S]	This Is My Bag	1966	10.00	20.00	40.00
❏ LST-7479 [S]	Total Commitment	1966	10.00	20.00	40.00
❏ LST-7539 [S]	The Further Adventures of Charles Westover	1967	20.00	40.00	80.00

PICKWICK

❏ SPC-3595 [R]	The Best of Del Shannon	197?	2.50	5.00	10.00

POST

❏ 9000 [R]	Del Shannon Sings	196?	10.00	20.00	40.00

RHINO

❏ RNLP-71056 [M]	Runaway Hits	1986	2.50	5.00	10.00

SIRE

❏ SASH-3708 [(2)P]	The Vintage Years	1975	6.25	12.50	25.00

TWIRL

❏ 5001 [M]	Del Shannon's Greatest Hits	196?	50.00	100.00	200.00
—LP was never issued; price is for front cover slick, which is known to exist					

UNITED ARTISTS

❏ UA-LA151-E	Del Shannon Live in England	1973	6.25	12.50	25.00

SHANNON, JACKIE　See JACKIE DeSHANNON.

SHANNON, KATHY
45s

HIT

❏ 290	Love Eyes/This Is My Song	1967	2.00	4.00	8.00
❏ 296	Don't Sleep in the Subway/Jackson	1967	2.00	4.00	8.00
—B-side by Jack and Sherry Young					
❏ 298	I Take It Back/Little Bit o' Soul	1967	2.00	4.00	8.00
—B-side by the Chellows					
❏ 303	Ode to Billie Joe/White Rabbit	1967	2.00	4.00	8.00
—B-side by the Chords (2)					
❏ 310	It Must Be Him/ The Rain, the Park, and Other Things	1967	2.00	4.00	8.00
—B-side by the Flowers					
❏ 311	To Sir with Love/Even the Bad Times Are Good	1967	2.00	4.00	8.00
—B-side by the Jalopy Five					
❏ 323	(Theme from) Valley of the Dolls/ Scarborough Fair (/Canticle)	1968	2.00	4.00	8.00
—B-side by Sammy and Theodore					

S

Number	Title (A Side/B Side)	Yr	VG	VG+	NM
❑ 327	Do You Know the Way to San Jose/				
	Cry Like a Baby	1968	2.00	4.00	8.00
—B-side by the Jalopy Five					
❑ 334	Angel of the Morning/Jumpin' Jack Flash	1968	2.00	4.00	8.00
—B-side by the Jalopy Five					
❑ 340	The House That Jack Built/1-2-3, Red Light	1968	2.00	4.00	8.00
—B-side by the Fantastics					
❑ 343	Harper Valley P.T.A./Hey Jude	1968	2.00	4.00	8.00
—B-side by the Jalopy Five					
❑ 346	Those Were the Days/Girl Watcher	1968	2.00	4.00	8.00
—B-side by the Chords (2)					
❑ 353	Son-of-a-Preacher-Man/Worst That Could				
	Happen	1969	2.00	4.00	8.00
—B-side by the Chords (2)					

SHANNON, PAT
45s
AMOS

Number	Title (A Side/B Side)	Yr	VG	VG+	NM
❑ 152	I Ain't Got Time Anymore/(B-side unknown)	1970	—	2.50	5.00
❑ 163	Liar/Something's Coming My Way	1971	—	2.50	5.00
CAPITOL					
❑ 3802	Eleanor Jones/102 Times a Day	1973	—	2.00	4.00
DECCA					
❑ 30545	Maybelle/Knock, Knock, Who's There	1958	3.00	6.00	12.00
❑ 30666	You're So Wild/Awaiting Love	1958	7.50	15.00	30.00
❑ 30751	Summer's Over/We Found Love	1958	3.00	6.00	12.00
❑ 30905	Summertime's Comin'/				
	The Snake and the Bookworm	1959	3.00	6.00	12.00
❑ 31072	Everything But You/So Happy Now	1960	3.00	6.00	12.00
UNI					
❑ 55191	Back to Dreamin' Again/Moody	1969	—	2.50	5.00
❑ 55229	It's So Easy/102 Times a Day	1970	—	2.50	5.00
❑ 55229	It's So Easy/The Story of Your Life	1970	—	2.50	5.00
WARNER BROS.					
❑ 7210	Candy Apple, Cotton Candy/She Sleeps Alone	1968	—	3.00	6.00
❑ 7237	Here They Come Again/Run to Home	1968	—	3.00	6.00

SHANTONS, THE
45s
JAY-MAR

Number	Title (A Side/B Side)	Yr	VG	VG+	NM
❑ (# unknown)	Triangle Love/Lover's March	1959	100.00	200.00	400.00
❑ 241	To Be in Love with You/Lucille	1959	200.00	400.00	800.00
❑ 1292	The Christmas Song/				
	Santa Claus Is Coming to Town	1960	50.00	100.00	200.00

SHANTY BOYS, THE
Albums
ELEKTRA

Number	Title (A Side/B Side)	Yr	VG	VG+	NM
❑ EKL-142 [M]	Off-Beat Folk Songs	1958	7.50	15.00	30.00

SHAPIRO, HELEN
45s
CAPITOL

Number	Title (A Side/B Side)	Yr	VG	VG+	NM
❑ 4561	Don't Treat Me Like a Child/When I'm With You	1961	3.00	6.00	12.00
❑ 4627	You Don't Know/A Marvelous Lie	1961	3.00	6.00	12.00
❑ 4662	Walkin' Back to Happiness/Kiss 'N' Run	1961	3.00	6.00	12.00
❑ 4735	Tell Me What He Said/I Apologize	1962	3.00	6.00	12.00
EPIC					
❑ 9549	Little Miss Lonely/Keep Away from Other Girls	1962	3.00	6.00	12.00
❑ 9599	Woe Is Me/No Trespassing	1963	3.00	6.00	12.00
JANUS					
❑ 120	A Glass of Wine/				
	Waiting on the Shores of Nowhere	1970	—	3.00	6.00
MUSICOR					
❑ 1075	It Might As Well Rain Until September/				
	Shop Around	1965	2.50	5.00	10.00
TOWER					
❑ 346	Make Me Belong to You/The Way of the World	1967	2.00	4.00	8.00
Albums					
EPIC					
❑ LN 24075 [M]	A Teenager in Love	1962	6.25	12.50	25.00
❑ BN 26075 [S]	A Teenager in Love	1962	7.50	15.00	30.00

SHARKS
45s
MCA

Number	Title (A Side/B Side)	Yr	VG	VG+	NM
❑ 40120	Follow Me/Ole Jelly Roll	1973	—	2.50	5.00
❑ 40246	Kung Fu/Elevator Dancing	1974	—	2.50	5.00
Albums					
MCA					
❑ 351	First Water	1973	3.00	6.00	12.00
❑ 415	Jab It in Your Eye	1974	3.00	6.00	12.00

SHARMEERS, THE
45s
RED TOP

Number	Title (A Side/B Side)	Yr	VG	VG+	NM
❑ 109	A School Girl in Love/You're My Love	1958	37.50	75.00	150.00

SHARMETTES, THE
45s
KING

Number	Title (A Side/B Side)	Yr	VG	VG+	NM
❑ 5648	Answer Me/My Dream	1962	3.75	7.50	15.00
❑ 5686	I Want to Be Loved/Tell Me	1962	3.75	7.50	15.00

SHARON MARIE
45s
CAPITOL

Number	Title (A Side/B Side)	Yr	VG	VG+	NM
❑ 5064	Run-Around Lover/Summertime	1963	62.50	125.00	250.00
❑ 5195	The Story of My Life/Thinkin' 'Bout You Baby	1964	50.00	100.00	200.00
—Both these records were produced by Brian Wilson					

SHARP, DEE DEE Includes records as "Dee Dee Sharp Gamble."
45s
ATCO

Number	Title (A Side/B Side)	Yr	VG	VG+	NM
❑ 6445	Bye Bye Baby/My Best Friend's Man	1966	2.50	5.00	10.00
❑ 6502	Baby I Love You/What Am I Gonna Do	1967	2.00	4.00	8.00

Number	Title (A Side/B Side)	Yr	VG	VG+	NM
❑ 6557	We Got a Thing Goin' On/				
	What 'Cha Gonna Do About It	1968	2.00	4.00	8.00
—With Ben E. King					
❑ 6576	Woman Will Do Wrong/				
	You're Just a Fool in Love	1968	2.00	4.00	8.00
❑ 6587	This Love Won't Run Out/Help Me Find My Glove	1968	2.00	4.00	8.00
CAMEO					
❑ 212	Mashed Potato Time/Set My Heart at Ease	1962	5.00	10.00	20.00
❑ 219	Gravy (For My Mashed Potatoes)/Baby Cakes	1962	3.75	7.50	15.00
❑ 219 [PS]	Gravy (For My Mashed Potatoes)/Baby Cakes	1962	6.25	12.50	25.00
❑ 230	Ride!/The Night	1962	3.75	7.50	15.00
❑ 230 [PS]	Ride!/The Night	1962	6.25	12.50	25.00
❑ 244	Do the Bird/Lover Boy	1963	3.75	7.50	15.00
❑ 244 [PS]	Do the Bird/Lover Boy	1963	6.25	12.50	25.00
❑ 260	Rock Me in the Cradle of Love/				
	You'll Never Be Mine	1963	3.75	7.50	15.00
❑ 260 [PS]	Rock Me in the Cradle of Love/				
	You'll Never Be Mine	1963	6.25	12.50	25.00
❑ 274	Wild!/Why Doncha Ask Me	1963	3.75	7.50	15.00
❑ 274 [PS]	Wild!/Why Doncha Ask Me	1963	6.25	12.50	25.00
❑ 296	Where Did I Go Wrong/Willyam, Willyam	1964	3.00	6.00	12.00
❑ 296 [PS]	Where Did I Go Wrong/Willyam, Willyam	1964	5.00	10.00	20.00
❑ 329	Never Pick a Pretty Boy/He's No Ordinary Guy	1964	3.00	6.00	12.00
❑ 335	Deep Dark Secret/Good	1964	3.00	6.00	12.00
❑ 347	To Know Him Is to Love Him/There Ain't Nothin'				
	I Wouldn't Do for You	1965	2.50	5.00	10.00
❑ 357	Let's Twine/That's What My Mama Said	1965	2.50	5.00	10.00
❑ 375	I Really Love You/Standing in the Need of Love	1965	2.50	5.00	10.00
❑ 375 [PS]	I Really Love You/Standing in the Need of Love	1965	3.75	7.50	15.00
❑ 382	It's a Funny Situation/There Ain't Nothin' I				
	Wouldn't Do for You	1965	2.50	5.00	10.00
FAIRMOUNT					
❑ 1004	(It's Wonderful) The Love I Feel for You/				
	Willyam, Wilyam	1966	2.50	5.00	10.00
GAMBLE					
❑ 219	What Kind of Lady/You're Gonna Miss Me				
	(When I'm Gone)	1968	5.00	10.00	20.00
❑ 4005	The Bottle or Me/You're Gonna Miss Me				
	(When I'm Gone)	1969	3.75	7.50	15.00
PHILADELPHIA INT'L.					
❑ 02041	Breaking and Entering/I Love You Anyway	1981	—	2.00	4.00
❑ 3512	Conquer the World Together/				
	We Gotta Good Thing Goin'	1971	—	3.00	6.00
—With Bunny Sigler					
❑ 3625	Flashback/Nobody Can Take Your Place	1977	—	2.50	5.00
❑ 3636	I'd Really Love to See You Tonight/				
	What Color Is Love	1977	—	2.50	5.00
❑ 3638	I Believe in Love/				
	Just As Long As I Know You're Mine	1978	—	2.50	5.00
❑ 3644	Tryin' to Get the Feeling Again/				
	I Wanna Be Your Woman	1978	—	2.50	5.00
❑ 70058	I Love You Anyway/Easy Money	1981	—	2.00	4.00
—Philadelphia International records as "Dee Dee Sharp Gamble"					
TSOP					
❑ 4776	Happy 'Bout the Whole Thing/Touch My Life	1976	—	2.50	5.00
❑ 4778	I'm Not in Love/Make It Till Tomorrow	1976	—	2.50	5.00
Albums					
CAMEO					
❑ C-1018 [M]	It's Mashed Potato Time	1962	15.00	30.00	60.00
❑ C-1022 [M]	Songs of Faith	1962	10.00	20.00	40.00
❑ SC-1022 [S]	Songs of Faith	1962	12.50	25.00	50.00
❑ C-1027 [M]	All the Hits	1962	10.00	20.00	40.00
❑ SC-1027 [S]	All the Hits	1962	12.50	25.00	50.00
❑ C-1032 [M]	All the Hits, Vol. 2	1963	10.00	20.00	40.00
❑ SC-1032 [S]	All the Hits, Vol. 2	1963	12.50	25.00	50.00
❑ C-1050 [M]	Do the Bird	1963	10.00	20.00	40.00
❑ SC-1050 [S]	Do the Bird	1963	12.50	25.00	50.00
❑ C-1062 [M]	Biggest Hits	1963	10.00	20.00	40.00
❑ C-1074 [M]	Down Memory Lane	1963	10.00	20.00	40.00
❑ C-2002 [M]	18 Golden Hits	1964	10.00	20.00	40.00
❑ SC-2002 [S]	18 Golden Hits	1964	12.50	25.00	50.00
PHILADELPHIA INT'L.					
❑ PZ 33839	Happy 'Bout the Whole Thing	1976	2.50	5.00	10.00
❑ PZ 34437	What Color Is Love	1977	2.50	5.00	10.00
❑ JZ 36370	Dee Dee	1980	2.50	5.00	10.00

SHARP, DEE DEE, AND CHUBBY CHECKER Also see each artist's individual listings.
45s
CAMEO

Number	Title (A Side/B Side)	Yr	VG	VG+	NM
❑ 103 [DJ]	Do You Love Me?/One More Time	1962	10.00	20.00	40.00
—Yellow label, black print, promo only					
Albums					
CAMEO					
❑ C-1029 [M]	Down to Earth	1962	10.00	20.00	40.00
❑ SC-1029 [S]	Down to Earth	1962	12.50	25.00	50.00

SHARPE, RAY
45s
A&M

Number	Title (A Side/B Side)	Yr	VG	VG+	NM
❑ 1297	Dream On, Donna/Another Piece of the Puzzle	1971	—	2.50	5.00
ATCO					
❑ 6402	Help Me (Get the Feeling) Part 1/Help Me (Get				
	the Feeling) Part 2	1966	2.50	5.00	10.00
❑ 6437	I Can't Take It/Mary Jane	1966	2.50	5.00	10.00
DOT					
❑ 15788	Oh, My Baby's Gone/That's the Way I Feel	1958	3.75	7.50	15.00
❑ 15974	Oh, My Baby's Gone/That's the Way I Feel	1959	3.00	6.00	12.00
GREGMARK					
❑ 14	(The New) Linda Lu/The Bus Song	1963	3.00	6.00	12.00
HAMILTON					
❑ 50002	Oh, My Baby's Gone/That's the Way I Feel	1959	2.50	5.00	10.00
JAMIE					
❑ 1128	Linda Lu/Red Sails in the Sunset	1959	3.75	7.50	15.00
❑ 1128	Linda Lu/Monkey's Uncle	1959	6.25	12.50	25.00
❑ 1138	Long John/T.A. Blues	1959	3.75	7.50	15.00
❑ 1149	Bermuda/Gonna Let It Go This Time	1960	3.75	7.50	15.00

Number	Title (A Side/B Side)	Yr	VG	VG+	NM
❑ 1155	For You My Love/Red Sails in the Sunset	1960	3.75	7.50	15.00
❑ 1164	Give'n Up/Kewpie Doll	1960	3.75	7.50	15.00
LHI					
❑ 1215	Linda Lu/Monkey's Uncle	1967	2.00	4.00	8.00
MONUMENT					
❑ 874	Let's Go, Let's Go, Let's Go/It's Too Cold	1965	2.50	5.00	10.00
PARK AVE.					
❑ 4904	Do the Thaxton/Baby Ora	196?	2.50	5.00	10.00
❑ 4906	Almost Grown//(B-side unknown)	196?	2.50	5.00	10.00
TREY					
❑ 3011	Justine/On the Street Where You Live	1961	3.00	6.00	12.00
Albums					
AWARD					
❑ LMP-711 [M]	Welcome Back, Linda Lu	1964	30.00	60.00	120.00

SHARPS, THE Possibly more than one group.
45s
ALADDIN

Number	Title (A Side/B Side)	Yr	VG	VG+	NM
❑ 3401	What Will I Gain/Shufflin'	1957	12.50	25.00	50.00
❑ 3401	What Will I Gain/Shufflin'	1957	100.00	200.00	400.00
—Purple vinyl					
CHESS					
❑ 1690	6 Months, 3 Weeks, 2 Days/Cha-Cho Bop	1958	7.50	15.00	30.00
—B-side by Jack McVea					
COMBO					
❑ 146	All My Love/Look What You've Done to Me	1958	12.50	25.00	50.00
DOT					
❑ 15806	All My Love/Look What You've Done to Me	1958	3.75	7.50	15.00
JAMIE					
❑ 1040	Sweet Sweetheart/Come On	1957	10.00	20.00	40.00
❑ 1108	Have Love, Will Travel/Look at Me	1958	12.50	25.00	50.00
❑ 1114	Here's My Heart/Gig-A-Lene	1958	7.50	15.00	30.00
LAMP					
❑ 2007	Our Love Is Here to Stay/Lock My Heart	1957	7.50	15.00	30.00
STAR-HI					
❑ 10406	Double Clutch/If Love Is What You Want	1960	7.50	15.00	30.00
TAG					
❑ 2200	6 Months, 3 Weeks, 2 Days/Cha-Cho Bop	1957	25.00	50.00	100.00
—B-side by Jack McVea					
VIK					
❑ 0264	Sweet Sweetheart/Come On	1957	6.25	12.50	25.00
WIN					
❑ 702	Teenage Girl/We Three	1958	12.50	25.00	50.00

SHARPTONES, THE
45s
POST

Number	Title (A Side/B Side)	Yr	VG	VG+	NM
❑ 2009	Since I Fell for You/Made to Love	1955	100.00	200.00	400.00

SHATNER, WILLIAM
45s
DECCA

Number	Title (A Side/B Side)	Yr	VG	VG+	NM
❑ 32399	How Insensitive/Transformed Man	1969	5.00	10.00	20.00
Albums					
DECCA					
❑ DL 5043 [M]	The Transformed Man	1969	37.50	75.00	150.00
—Mono is white label promo only; in stereo cover with "Monaural" sticker					
❑ DL 75043 [S]	The Transformed Man	1969	15.00	30.00	60.00
K-TEL					
❑ NC 494 [(2)]	Captain of the Starship	1978	12.50	25.00	50.00
—Reissue of Lemli album					
LEMLI					
❑ 9400 [(2)]	William Shatner — Live!	1977	7.50	15.00	30.00

SHAW, ARTIE
Albums
RCA VICTOR

Number	Title (A Side/B Side)	Yr	VG	VG+	NM
❑ VPM-6062 [(2)]	This Is Artie Shaw, Volume 2	1976	3.00	6.00	12.00
—Black labels, dog near top					

SHAW, JIMMY
45s
IMPERIAL

Number	Title (A Side/B Side)	Yr	VG	VG+	NM
❑ 5603	Take a Chance on Me/Big Chief Hug-Um An' Kiss-Um	1959	5.00	10.00	20.00

SHAW, JOHN, AND THE DELL-OS
45s
U-C

Number	Title (A Side/B Side)	Yr	VG	VG+	NM
❑ 5002	Why Did You Leave Me/Why Does It Have to Be Her	1957	2000.	3000.	4000.

SHAW, MARLENA
12-Inch Singles
COLUMBIA

Number	Title (A Side/B Side)	Yr	VG	VG+	NM
❑ 11025	Love Dancin'/No One Yet	1979	—	2.50	5.00
POLYDOR					
❑ PRO 628 [DJ]	I Want to Know (same on both sides)	1988	2.00	4.00	8.00
SOUTH BAY					
❑ 1004	More Room at the Top/At Last	1982	2.50	5.00	10.00
❑ 22004	Never Give Up on You/(B-side unknown)	1983	2.00	4.00	8.00
45s					
BLUE NOTE					
❑ XW209	Last Tango in Paris/(B-side unknown)	1973	—	2.50	5.00
❑ XW366	Easy Evil/Just Don't Want to Be Lonely	1973	—	2.50	5.00
❑ XW550	The Feeling's Good/But For Now	1974	—	2.50	5.00
❑ XW649	You/Loving You Is Like a Party	1975	—	2.50	5.00
❑ XW691	Feel Like Makin' Love/You Taught Me How to Speak in Love	1975	—	2.50	5.00
❑ XW790	It's Better Than Walkin' Out/Be for Real	1976	—	2.50	5.00
❑ XW844	Love Has Gone Away/This Time I'll Be Sweeter	1976	—	2.50	5.00
❑ 1981	Somewhere/You Must Believe	1972	—	3.00	6.00
CADET					
❑ 5549	Let's Wade in the Water/Show Time	1966	2.00	4.00	8.00
❑ 5557	Mercy, Mercy, Mercy/Go Away Little Boy	1967	2.00	4.00	8.00

Number	Title (A Side/B Side)	Yr	VG	VG+	NM
❑ 5571	Brother Where Are You/Waiting for Charlie to Come Home	1967	2.00	4.00	8.00
❑ 5592	Matchmaker, Matchmaker/A Couple of Losers	1968	—	3.00	6.00
❑ 5618	Looking Through the Eyes of Love/Anyone Can Move a Mountain	1968	—	3.00	6.00
❑ 5638	California Soul/The House That Jack Built	1969	—	3.00	6.00
❑ 5650	Woman of the Ghetto/I'm Satisfied	1969	—	3.00	6.00
❑ 5656	Looking Through the Eyes of Love/California Soul	1969	—	3.00	6.00
COLUMBIA					
❑ 10542	Yu-Ma/Go Away Little Boy//No Deposit, No Return	1977	—	2.50	5.00
❑ 10589	Johnny/Pictures and Memories	1977	—	2.50	5.00
❑ 10661	Don't Ask to Stay Until Tomorrow/No Deposit, No Return	1978	—	2.50	5.00
❑ 10746	Dreamin'/Places	1978	—	2.50	5.00
❑ 11034	Love Dancin'/No One Yet	1979	3.00	6.00	12.00
POLYDOR					
❑ 887776-7	I Want to Know/Love Is In Flight	1988	—	2.00	4.00
Albums					
BLUE NOTE					
❑ BN-LA143-F	From the Depths of My Soul	1974	3.75	7.50	15.00
❑ BN-LA397-G	Who Is This Bitch, Anyway?	1975	3.75	7.50	15.00
❑ BN-LA606-G	Just a Matter	1976	3.75	7.50	15.00
❑ BST-84422	Marlena	1972	3.75	7.50	15.00
CADET					
❑ LPS-803	Different Bags	1968	5.00	10.00	20.00
❑ LPS-833	Spice of Life	1969	5.00	10.00	20.00
COLUMBIA					
❑ PC 34458	Sweet Beginnings	1977	3.00	6.00	12.00
❑ JC 35073	Acting Up	1978	3.00	6.00	12.00
❑ JC 35632	Take a Bite	1979	3.00	6.00	12.00
❑ JC 36367	The Best of Marlena Shaw	1980	2.50	5.00	10.00
VERVE					
❑ 831438-1	It Is Love	1987	2.50	5.00	10.00
❑ 837312-1	Love Is In Flight	1988	2.50	5.00	10.00

SHAW, SANDIE
45s
MERCURY

Number	Title (A Side/B Side)	Yr	VG	VG+	NM
❑ 72315	Ya, Ya, Da, Da/As Long As You're Happy	1964	3.75	7.50	15.00
RCA VICTOR					
❑ 47-9594	Together/One More Lie	1968	2.00	4.00	8.00
❑ 74-0118	Voice in the Crowd/Monsieur Dupont	1969	2.00	4.00	8.00
❑ 74-0370	Love Is For the Two of Us/Wight Is Wight	1970	2.00	4.00	8.00
REPRISE					
❑ 0320	(There's) Always Something There to Remind Me/Don't You Know	1964	3.00	6.00	12.00
❑ 0342	Girl Don't Come/I'd Be Far Better Off Without You	1965	2.50	5.00	10.00
❑ 0365	I'll Stop at Nothing/You Can't Blame Him	1965	2.50	5.00	10.00
❑ 0375	Long Live Love/I've Heard About Him	1965	2.50	5.00	10.00
❑ 0394	Stop Feeling Sorry for Yourself/I'll Stop at Nothing	1965	2.50	5.00	10.00
❑ 0427	If Ever You Need Me/How Can You Tell	1965	2.50	5.00	10.00
❑ 0449	Tomorrow/Hurting You	1966	2.50	5.00	10.00
❑ 0488	Nothing Comes Easy/Stop Before You Start	1966	2.50	5.00	10.00
❑ 0546	Think Sometime About Me/Hide All Emotion	1967	2.50	5.00	10.00
❑ 0575	Puppet on a String/I Had a Dream Last Night	1967	2.50	5.00	10.00
❑ 20191	Me/Now	1963	3.75	7.50	15.00
—B-side by Bob Candee					
Albums					
REPRISE					
❑ R-6166 [M]	Sandie Shaw	1965	10.00	20.00	40.00
❑ RS-6166 [R]	Sandie Shaw	1965	12.50	25.00	50.00
❑ R-6191 [M]	Me	1966	7.50	15.00	30.00
❑ RS-6191 [S]	Me	1966	10.00	20.00	40.00

SHAW, SERENA
Albums
RAMA

Number	Title (A Side/B Side)	Yr	VG	VG+	NM
❑ RLP-5001 [M]	Cry My Love	1956	100.00	200.00	400.00

SHEAN AND JENKYNS
45s
GNP CRESCENDO

Number	Title (A Side/B Side)	Yr	VG	VG+	NM
❑ 198	Goofy-Footer Ho-Dad/Do the Commercial	1963	6.25	12.50	25.00

SHEARING, GEORGE
45s
CAPITOL

Number	Title (A Side/B Side)	Yr	VG	VG+	NM
❑ 4418	Blue Malibu/Honeysuckle Rose	1960	2.00	4.00	8.00
❑ 4922	The Stripper/Fairy Tales	1963	2.00	4.00	8.00
❑ 5850	On a Clear Day You Can See Forever/Call Me	1967	—	3.00	6.00
MGM					
❑ 10647	In a Chinese Garden//(B-side unknown)	1950	5.00	10.00	20.00
—Note: Earlier George Shearing 45s on MGM may exist					
❑ 10687	I'll Remember April/Jumping with Symphony Sid	1950	5.00	10.00	20.00
❑ 10720	I Didn't Know What Time It Was/How's Trix	1950	5.00	10.00	20.00
❑ 10763	When Your Lover Has Gone/Carnegie Horizons	1950	5.00	10.00	20.00
❑ 10859	Roses of Picardy/Pick Yourself Up	1950	5.00	10.00	20.00
❑ 10907	For You/Little White Lies	1951	3.75	7.50	15.00
❑ 10956	I'll Be Around/Quintessence	1951	3.75	7.50	15.00
❑ 10986	The Breeze and I/I Remember You	1951	3.75	7.50	15.00
❑ 11046	Don't Blame Me/Brain Waves	1951	3.75	7.50	15.00
❑ 11153	Thine Alone/Geneva's Move	1952	3.75	7.50	15.00
❑ 11199	To a Wild Rose/Swedish Pastry	1952	3.75	7.50	15.00
❑ 11282	Simplicity/5 O'Clock Whistle	1952	3.75	7.50	15.00
❑ 11354	Lullaby of Birdland/When Lights Are Low	1952	3.75	7.50	15.00
❑ 11425	There's a Lull in My Life/Midnight Belongs to You	1953	3.75	7.50	15.00
❑ 11493	Body and Soul/I Hear a Rhapsody	1953	3.75	7.50	15.00
❑ 11545	Indian Summer/Appreciation	1953	3.75	7.50	15.00
❑ 11600	Easy to Love/Wrap Your Troubles in Dreams	1953	3.75	7.50	15.00
❑ 11639	Tiempo de Concerro (Part 1)/Tiempo de Concerro (Part 2)	1953	3.75	7.50	15.00
❑ 11677	A Sinner Kissed an Angel/Mood for Milt	1954	3.00	6.00	12.00
❑ 11754	I've Never Been in Love Before/Mambo Inn	1954	3.00	6.00	12.00

S

Number	Title (A Side/B Side)	Yr	VG	VG+	NM
❏ 11833	Lullaby of Birdland/Love Is Here to Stay	1954	3.00	6.00	12.00
❏ 11876	Adieu/Undecided	1954	3.00	6.00	12.00
❏ 11943	The Lady Is a Tramp/Cool Mambo	1955	3.00	6.00	12.00
❏ 12038	Ill Wind/Drune Negrita	1955	3.00	6.00	12.00
❏ 12079	Get Off My Back/Love Is Just Around the Corner	1955	3.00	6.00	12.00
❏ 12132	Stranger in Paradise/Point and Counterpoint	1955	3.00	6.00	12.00
❏ 12182	Hallelujah/Basso Profundo	1956	3.00	6.00	12.00
❏ 12227	Spring Is Here/Minor Trouble	1956	3.00	6.00	12.00
❏ 12309	Over the Rainbow/Lonely Moments	1956	3.00	6.00	12.00
❏ 12349	My Silent Love/As Long As There's Music	1956	3.00	6.00	12.00

7-Inch Extended Plays
CAPITOL

Number	Title (A Side/B Side)	Yr	VG	VG+	NM
❏ EAP 1-648	Autumn in New York/The Man I Love	195?	3.00	6.00	12.00
❏ EAP 1-648 [PS]	The Shearing Spell, Part 1	195?	3.00	6.00	12.00
❏ EAP 1-858	The Folks Who Live on the Hill//Moon Song/ Medley: As Long As I Live-Let's Live Again	195?	3.00	6.00	12.00
❏ EAP 1-858 [PS]	Black Satin, Part 1	195?	3.00	6.00	12.00
❏ EAP 2-858	If I Should Lose You/Starlight Souvenirs// Nothing Ever Changes My Love for You	195?	3.00	6.00	12.00
❏ EAP 2-858 [PS]	Black Satin, Part 2	195?	3.00	6.00	12.00

MGM

Number	Title (A Side/B Side)	Yr	VG	VG+	NM
❏ X1006	For You/I Remember You//Thine Alone/ I'll Be Around	1953	3.75	7.50	15.00
❏ X1006 [PS]	For You	1953	3.75	7.50	15.00
❏ X1017	(contents unknown)	1953	3.75	7.50	15.00
❏ X1017 [PS]	In a Chinese Garden	1953	3.75	7.50	15.00

Albums
BASF

Number	Title (A Side/B Side)	Yr	VG	VG+	NM
❏ 25340	Light, Airy and Swinging	1973	3.00	6.00	12.00
❏ 25351	The Way We Are	1974	3.00	6.00	12.00
❏ MC-25612	Continental Experience	1975	3.00	6.00	12.00

CAPITOL

Number	Title (A Side/B Side)	Yr	VG	VG+	NM
❏ SKAO-139	The Best of George Shearing, Vol. 2	1969	3.00	6.00	12.00
❏ ST-181	Fool on the Hill	1969	3.00	6.00	12.00
❏ T 648 [M]	The Shearing Spell	1956	7.50	15.00	30.00
—Turquoise label					
❏ T 648 [M]	The Shearing Spell	1959	5.00	10.00	20.00
—Black label with colorband, logo on left					
❏ DT 720 [R]	Velvet Carpet	196?	3.00	6.00	12.00
❏ T 720 [M]	Velvet Carpet	1956	7.50	15.00	30.00
—Turquoise label					
❏ T 720 [M]	Velvet Carpet	1959	5.00	10.00	20.00
—Black label with colorband, logo on left					
❏ T 720 [M]	Velvet Carpet	1962	3.75	7.50	15.00
—Black label with colorband, logo on top					
❏ DT 737 [R]	Latin Escapade	196?	3.00	6.00	12.00
❏ T 737 [M]	Latin Escapade	1957	7.50	15.00	30.00
—Turquoise label					
❏ T 737 [M]	Latin Escapade	1959	5.00	10.00	20.00
—Black label with colorband, logo on left					
❏ T 737 [M]	Latin Escapade	1962	3.75	7.50	15.00
—Black label with colorband, logo on top					
❏ ST 858 [S]	Black Satin	1959	5.00	10.00	20.00
—Black label with colorband, logo on top					
❏ ST 858 [S]	Black Satin	1962	3.75	7.50	15.00
—Black label with colorband, logo on top					
❏ T 858 [M]	Black Satin	1957	7.50	15.00	30.00
—Turquoise label					
❏ T 858 [M]	Black Satin	1959	5.00	10.00	20.00
—Black label with colorband, logo on left					
❏ T 858 [M]	Black Satin	1962	3.75	7.50	15.00
—Black label with colorband, logo on top					
❏ T 909 [M]	Shearing Piano	1957	7.50	15.00	30.00
—Turquoise label					
❏ T 909 [M]	Shearing Piano	1959	5.00	10.00	20.00
—Black label with colorband, logo on left					
❏ T 943 [M]	Night Mist	1957	7.50	15.00	30.00
—Turquoise label					
❏ ST 1038 [S]	Burnished Brass	1959	6.25	12.50	25.00
—Black label with colorband, logo on left					
❏ ST 1038 [S]	Burnished Brass	1962	5.00	10.00	20.00
—Black label with colorband, logo on top					
❏ T 1038 [M]	Burnished Brass	1958	5.00	10.00	20.00
—Black label with colorband, logo on left					
❏ T 1038 [M]	Burnished Brass	1962	3.75	7.50	15.00
—Black label with colorband, logo on top					
❏ ST 1082 [S]	Latin Lace	1958	6.25	12.50	25.00
—Black label with colorband, logo on left					
❏ ST 1082 [S]	Latin Lace	1962	5.00	10.00	20.00
—Black label with colorband, logo on top					
❏ T 1082 [M]	Latin Lace	1958	5.00	10.00	20.00
—Black label with colorband, logo on left					
❏ T 1082 [M]	Latin Lace	1962	3.75	7.50	15.00
—Black label with colorband, logo on top					
❏ ST 1124 [S]	Blue Chiffon	1959	6.25	12.50	25.00
—Black label with colorband, logo on left					
❏ ST 1124 [S]	Blue Chiffon	1962	5.00	10.00	20.00
—Black label with colorband, logo on top					
❏ T 1124 [M]	Blue Chiffon	1959	5.00	10.00	20.00
—Black label with colorband, logo on left					
❏ T 1124 [M]	Blue Chiffon	1962	3.75	7.50	15.00
—Black label with colorband, logo on top					
❏ ST 1187 [S]	George Shearing On Stage	1959	6.25	12.50	25.00
—Black label with colorband, logo on top					
❏ ST 1187 [S]	George Shearing On Stage	1962	5.00	10.00	20.00
—Black label with colorband, logo on top					
❏ T 1187 [M]	George Shearing On Stage	1959	5.00	10.00	20.00
—Black label with colorband, logo on left					
❏ T 1187 [M]	George Shearing On Stage	1962	3.75	7.50	15.00
—Black label with colorband, logo on top					
❏ ST 1275 [S]	Latin Affair	1960	6.25	12.50	25.00
—Black label with colorband, logo on top					
❏ ST 1275 [S]	Latin Affair	1962	5.00	10.00	20.00
—Black label with colorband, logo on top					
❏ T 1275 [M]	Latin Affair	1960	5.00	10.00	20.00
—Black label with colorband, logo on left					

Number	Title (A Side/B Side)	Yr	VG	VG+	NM
❏ T 1275 [M]	Latin Affair	1962	3.75	7.50	15.00
—Black label with colorband, logo on top					
❏ ST 1334 [S]	White Satin	1960	6.25	12.50	25.00
—Black label with colorband, logo on left					
❏ ST 1334 [S]	White Satin	1962	5.00	10.00	20.00
—Black label with colorband, logo on top					
❏ T 1334 [M]	White Satin	1960	5.00	10.00	20.00
—Black label with colorband, logo on left					
❏ T 1334 [M]	White Satin	1962	3.75	7.50	15.00
—Black label with colorband, logo on top					
❏ ST 1416 [S]	On the Sunny Side of the Strip	1960	6.25	12.50	25.00
—Black label with colorband, logo on left					
❏ ST 1416 [S]	On the Sunny Side of the Strip	1962	5.00	10.00	20.00
—Black label with colorband, logo on top					
❏ T 1416 [M]	On the Sunny Side of the Strip	1960	5.00	10.00	20.00
—Black label with colorband, logo on left					
❏ T 1416 [M]	On the Sunny Side of the Strip	1962	3.75	7.50	15.00
—Black label with colorband, logo on top					
❏ SM-1472	The Shearing Touch	1977	2.50	5.00	10.00
—Reissue with new prefix					
❏ ST 1472 [S]	The Shearing Touch	1961	6.25	12.50	25.00
—Black label with colorband, logo on left					
❏ ST 1472 [S]	The Shearing Touch	1962	5.00	10.00	20.00
—Black label with colorband, logo on top					
❏ T 1472 [M]	The Shearing Touch	1961	5.00	10.00	20.00
—Black label with colorband, logo on left					
❏ T 1472 [M]	The Shearing Touch	1962	3.75	7.50	15.00
—Black label with colorband, logo on top					
❏ ST 1567 [S]	Mood Latino	1961	6.25	12.50	25.00
—Black label with colorband, logo on left					
❏ ST 1567 [S]	Mood Latino	1962	5.00	10.00	20.00
—Black label with colorband, logo on top					
❏ T 1567 [M]	Mood Latino	1961	5.00	10.00	20.00
—Black label with colorband, logo on left					
❏ T 1567 [M]	Mood Latino	1962	3.75	7.50	15.00
—Black label with colorband, logo on top					
❏ ST 1628 [S]	Satin Affair	1961	6.25	12.50	25.00
—Black label with colorband, logo on left					
❏ ST 1628 [S]	Satin Affair	1962	5.00	10.00	20.00
—Black label with colorband, logo on top					
❏ T 1628 [M]	Satin Affair	1961	5.00	10.00	20.00
—Black label with colorband, logo on left					
❏ T 1628 [M]	Satin Affair	1962	3.75	7.50	15.00
—Black label with colorband, logo on top					
❏ ST 1715 [S]	San Francisco Scene	1962	5.00	10.00	20.00
❏ T 1715 [M]	San Francisco Scene	1962	3.75	7.50	15.00
❏ ST 1755 [S]	Concerto for My Love	1962	5.00	10.00	20.00
❏ T 1755 [M]	Concerto for My Love	1962	3.75	7.50	15.00
❏ ST 1827 [S]	Jazz Moments	1963	5.00	10.00	20.00
❏ T 1827 [M]	Jazz Moments	1963	3.75	7.50	15.00
❏ ST 1873 [S]	Bossa Nova	1963	5.00	10.00	20.00
❏ T 1873 [M]	Bossa Nova	1963	3.75	7.50	15.00
❏ ST 1874 [S]	Touch Me Softly	1963	5.00	10.00	20.00
❏ T 1874 [M]	Touch Me Softly	1963	3.75	7.50	15.00
❏ ST 1992 [S]	Jazz Concert	1963	5.00	10.00	20.00
❏ T 1992 [M]	Jazz Concert	1963	3.75	7.50	15.00
❏ ST 2048 [S]	Old Gold and Ivory	1964	3.75	7.50	15.00
❏ T 2048 [M]	Old Gold and Ivory	1964	3.00	6.00	12.00
❏ SM-2104	The Best of George Shearing	1977	2.50	5.00	10.00
—Reissue with new prefix					
❏ ST 2104 [S]	The Best of George Shearing	1964	3.75	7.50	15.00
❏ T 2104 [M]	The Best of George Shearing	1964	3.00	6.00	12.00
❏ ST 2143 [S]	Deep Velvet	1964	3.75	7.50	15.00
❏ T 2143 [M]	Deep Velvet	1964	3.00	6.00	12.00
❏ ST 2272 [S]	Out of the Woods	1965	3.75	7.50	15.00
❏ T 2272 [M]	Out of the Woods	1965	3.00	6.00	12.00
❏ ST 2326 [S]	Latin Rendezvous	1965	3.75	7.50	15.00
❏ T 2326 [M]	Latin Rendezvous	1965	3.00	6.00	12.00
❏ ST 2372 [S]	Here and Now	1965	3.75	7.50	15.00
❏ T 2372 [M]	Here and Now	1965	3.00	6.00	12.00
❏ ST 2447 [S]	Rare Form	1965	3.75	7.50	15.00
❏ T 2447 [M]	Rare Form	1965	3.00	6.00	12.00
❏ ST 2567 [S]	That Fresh Feeling	1966	3.75	7.50	15.00
❏ T 2567 [M]	That Fresh Feeling	1966	3.00	6.00	12.00
❏ ST 2699 [S]	George Shearing Today	1967	3.00	6.00	12.00
❏ T 2699 [M]	George Shearing Today	1967	3.75	7.50	15.00
❏ SM-11454	Latin Escapade	197?	2.50	5.00	10.00
❏ SM-11800	Black Satin	1978	2.50	5.00	10.00

CONCORD CONCERTO

Number	Title (A Side/B Side)	Yr	VG	VG+	NM
❏ CC-2010	George Shearing and Barry Tuckwell Play the Music of Cole Porter	1986	2.50	5.00	10.00

CONCORD JAZZ

Number	Title (A Side/B Side)	Yr	VG	VG+	NM
❏ CJ-110	Blues Alley Jazz	1980	2.50	5.00	10.00
❏ CJ-132	On a Clear Day	1981	2.50	5.00	10.00
—With Brian Torff					
❏ CJ-171	Alone Together	1981	2.50	5.00	10.00
❏ CJ-177	First Edition	1982	2.50	5.00	10.00
❏ CJ-246	Live at the Café Carlyle	1984	2.50	5.00	10.00
❏ CJ-281	Grand Piano	1985	2.50	5.00	10.00
❏ CJ-318	More Grand Piano	1987	2.50	5.00	10.00
❏ CJ-335	Breakin' Out	1988	2.50	5.00	10.00
❏ CJ-346	Dexterity	1988	2.50	5.00	10.00
❏ CJ-357	A Perfect Match	1988	2.50	5.00	10.00
—With Ernestine Anderson					
❏ CJ-371	The Spirit of 176	1989	3.00	6.00	12.00
—With Hank Jones					
❏ CJ-388	George Shearing in Dixieland	1989	3.00	6.00	12.00
❏ CJ-400	Piano	1989	3.00	6.00	12.00

DISCOVERY

Number	Title (A Side/B Side)	Yr	VG	VG+	NM
❏ DL-3002 [10]	George Shearing Quintet	1950	15.00	30.00	60.00

EVEREST ARCHIVE OF FOLK & JAZZ

Number	Title (A Side/B Side)	Yr	VG	VG+	NM
❏ 223	Young George Shearing	1968	2.50	5.00	10.00
❏ 236	The Early Years, Vol. 2	1969	2.50	5.00	10.00

LONDON

Number	Title (A Side/B Side)	Yr	VG	VG+	NM
❏ LL 295 [10]	Souvenirs	1951	15.00	30.00	60.00
❏ LL 1343 [M]	By Request	1956	7.50	15.00	30.00

Number	Title (A Side/B Side)	Yr	VG	VG+	NM
MGM					
❏ E-90 [10]	A Touch of Genius	1951	12.50	25.00	50.00
❏ GAS-143	You're Hearing George Shearing	1970	3.00	6.00	12.00
❏ E-155 [10]	I Hear Music	1952	12.50	25.00	50.00
❏ E-226 [10]	When Lights Are Low	1953	12.50	25.00	50.00
❏ E-252 [10]	An Evening with George Shearing	1954	12.50	25.00	50.00
❏ E-518 [10]	You're Hearing the George Shearing Quartet	1950	15.00	30.00	60.00
❏ E-3122 [M]	An Evening with Shearing	1955	7.50	15.00	30.00
❏ E-3175 [M]	Shearing Caravan	1955	7.50	15.00	30.00
❏ E-3216 [M]	You're Hearing George Shearing	1955	7.50	15.00	30.00
❏ E-3264 [M]	When Lights Are Low	1955	7.50	15.00	30.00
❏ E-3265 [M]	Touch of Genius	1955	7.50	15.00	30.00
❏ E-3266 [M]	I Hear Music	1955	7.50	15.00	30.00
❏ E-3293 [M]	Shearing in Hi-Fi	1955	7.50	15.00	30.00
❏ E-3796 [M]	You're Hearing the Best of George Shearing	1960	3.75	7.50	15.00
❏ E-4041 [M]	Satin Latin	1962	3.75	7.50	15.00
❏ SE-4041 [R]	Satin Latin	1962	3.00	6.00	12.00
❏ E-4042 [M]	Soft and Silky	1962	3.75	7.50	15.00
❏ SE-4042 [R]	Soft and Silky	1962	3.00	6.00	12.00
❏ E-4043 [M]	Smooth and Swinging	1962	3.75	7.50	15.00
❏ SE-4043 [R]	Smooth and Swinging	1962	3.00	6.00	12.00
❏ E-4169 [M]	The Very Best of George Shearing	1963	3.75	7.50	15.00
❏ SE-4169 [R]	The Very Best of George Shearing	1963	3.00	6.00	12.00
MOSAIC					
❏ MQ7-157 [(7)]	The Complete Capitol Live Recordings of George Shearing	199?	30.00	60.00	120.00
PAUSA					
❏ 7035	Light, Airy and Swinging	1977	2.50	5.00	10.00
❏ PR 7049	The Reunion	1977	2.50	5.00	10.00
—With Stephane Grappelli					
❏ 7072	500 Miles High	1979	2.50	5.00	10.00
❏ 7088	Getting in the Swing of Things	1981	2.50	5.00	10.00
❏ 7116	On Target	198?	2.50	5.00	10.00
❏ 9030	The Shearing Touch	198?	2.50	5.00	10.00
❏ 9036	Jazz Moments	1985	2.50	5.00	10.00
❏ 9065	Latin Affair	1986	2.50	5.00	10.00
PICKWICK					
❏ SPC-3039	Lullaby of Birdland	197?	2.50	5.00	10.00
❏ SPC-3100	You Stepped Out of a Dream	197?	2.50	5.00	10.00
SAVOY					
❏ MG-15003 [10]	Piano Solo	1951	15.00	30.00	60.00
SAVOY JAZZ					
❏ SJL-1117	So Rare	198?	2.50	5.00	10.00
SHEBA					
❏ 101	Out of This World	197?	3.00	6.00	12.00
❏ 103	George Shearing Trio	197?	3.00	6.00	12.00
❏ 104	George Shearing Quartet	197?	3.00	6.00	12.00
❏ 105	As Requested	197?	3.00	6.00	12.00
❏ 106	Music to Hear	197?	3.00	6.00	12.00
❏ 107	GAS	197?	3.00	6.00	12.00
VERVE					
❏ VSP-9 [M]	Classic Shearing	1966	3.75	7.50	15.00
❏ VSPS-9 [R]	Classic Shearing	1966	3.00	6.00	12.00
❏ 821664-1	My Ship	198?	2.50	5.00	10.00
❏ 827977-1 [(2)]	Lullaby of Birdland	1986	3.00	6.00	12.00

SHEARING, GEORGE, AND THE MONTGOMERY BROTHERS
Albums

FANTASY					
❏ OJC-040	George Shearing and the Montgomery Brothers	198?	2.50	5.00	10.00
JAZZLAND					
❏ JLP-55 [M]	Love Walked In	1961	7.50	15.00	30.00
—Cover has Shearing and the brothers					
❏ JLP-55 [M]	Love Walked In	1962	6.25	12.50	25.00
—Cover has a woman					
❏ JLP-955 [S]	Love Walked In	1961	10.00	20.00	40.00
—Cover has Shearing and the brothers					
❏ JLP-955 [S]	Love Walked In	1962	7.50	15.00	30.00
—Cover has a woman					
RIVERSIDE					
❏ 6087	George Shearing and the Montgomery Brothers	197?	2.50	5.00	10.00
—Reissue of Jazzland LP					

SHEARING, GEORGE, AND MEL TORME Also see each artist's individual listings.
Albums

CONCORD JAZZ					
❏ CJ-190	An Evening with George Shearing and Mel Torme	1982	2.50	5.00	10.00
❏ CJ-219	Top Drawer	1983	2.50	5.00	10.00
❏ CJ-248	An Evening at Charlie's	1984	2.50	5.00	10.00
❏ CJ-294	An Elegant Evening	1985	2.50	5.00	10.00
❏ CJ-341	A Vintage Year	1988	2.50	5.00	10.00

SHEARS, BILLY, AND THE ALL AMERICANS
45s

SILVER FOX					
❏ 12+1	Brother Paul/Message to Seymour	1969	3.00	6.00	12.00

SHEEP, THE By the same people who gave us THE STRANGELOVES.
45s

BOOM					
❏ 60000	Hide and Seek/Twelve Months Later	1966	5.00	10.00	20.00
❏ 60007	Dynamite/I Feel Good	1966	5.00	10.00	20.00

SHEFFIELDS, THE
45s

DESTINATION					
❏ 613	My Loving Days Are Through/Please Come Back	1966	3.00	6.00	12.00
❏ 621	Do You Still Love Me/Nothing I Can Do	1966	3.00	6.00	12.00
DOT					
❏ 16722	Plenty of Love/Bags Groove	1965	3.75	7.50	15.00

SHEIKS, THE More than one group. Some of these were labeled "The Shieks."
45s

AMY					
❏ 807	Come On Back/Please Don't Take Away the Girl I Love	1960	50.00	100.00	200.00
CAT					
❏ 116	Walk That Walk/The Kissing Song (Sweetie Lover)	1955	10.00	20.00	40.00
EF-N-DE					
❏ 1000	Give Me Another Chance/Baby Don't You Cry	1955	200.00	400.00	600.00
FEDERAL					
❏ 12237	So Fine/Sentimental Heart	1955	37.50	75.00	150.00
JAMIE					
❏ 1147	Candlelight Cafe/The Song of Old Paree	1959	5.00	10.00	20.00
LEGRAND					
❏ 1013	What I'd Do for Your Love/Why Should I Dance	1961	25.00	50.00	100.00
❏ 1016	Cocoanut Woman/Twist That Twist	1962	6.25	12.50	25.00
MGM					
❏ 12876	Baghdad Rock (Part 1)/Baghdad Rock (Part 2)	1960	5.00	10.00	20.00

SHELDON, DOUG
45s

CONGRESS					
❏ 266	How Can I Tell Her/It's Because of You	1966	2.50	5.00	10.00
MGM					
❏ 13261	Lonely Boy/Hello There Lonely Baby	1964	3.00	6.00	12.00

SHELLS, THE
45s

END					
❏ 1022	Pretty Little Girl/Sippin' Soda	1958	37.50	75.00	150.00
❏ 1050	Whispering Wings/Shooma Dom Dom	1959	12.50	25.00	50.00
GONE					
❏ 5103	Pretty Little Girl/Sippin' Soda	1961	6.25	12.50	25.00
JOHNSON					
❏ 099	My Cherie/Explain It to Me	1972	—	3.00	6.00
❏ 104	Baby Oh Baby/Angel Eyes	1957	10.00	20.00	40.00
❏ 104	Baby Oh Baby/What's in An Angel's Eyes	1960	3.75	7.50	15.00
—Note lengthened B-side title					
❏ 106	Don't Say Goodbye/Pleading	1958	25.00	50.00	100.00
❏ 107	Explain It to Me/An Island Unknown	1961	6.25	12.50	25.00
❏ 109	Better Forget Him/Can't Take It	1961	6.25	12.50	25.00
❏ 110	In the Dim Light of the Dark/O-Mi Yum-Mi Yum-Mi	1961	6.25	12.50	25.00
❏ 112	Sweetest One/Baby Walk On In	1961	7.50	15.00	30.00
❏ 119	Deep in My Heart/(It's a) Happy Holiday	1962	7.50	15.00	30.00
❏ 120	The Drive/A Toast to Your Birthday	1962	7.50	15.00	30.00
❏ 127	On My Honor/My Royal Love	1963	12.50	25.00	50.00
❏ 332	Explain It to Me/An Island Unknown	1961	3.75	7.50	15.00
JOSIE					
❏ 912	Deep in My Heart/Our Wedding Day	1963	5.00	10.00	20.00
ROULETTE					
❏ 4156	The Thief/She Wasn't Meant for Me	1959	7.50	15.00	30.00
Albums					
CANDELITE					
❏ 1000	Accapella	197?	3.75	7.50	15.00
COLLECTABLES					
❏ COL-5077	Golden Classics	198?	2.50	5.00	10.00

SHELTON, GARY
45s

ALPINE					
❏ 56	Honey Bee/Till the End of the Line	1960	7.50	15.00	30.00
MARK					
❏ 145	Goodbye Little Darlin' Goodbye/Stop the World	1960	50.00	100.00	200.00
MERCURY					
❏ 71310	Kissin' at the Drive-In/Yours Till I Die	1958	7.50	15.00	30.00

SHEP AND THE LIMELITES Also see THE HEARTBEATS; SHANE SHEPPARD.
45s

HULL					
❏ 740	Daddy's Home/This I Know	1961	5.00	10.00	20.00
—Tan label. Note: Any colored vinyl version is a counterfeit.					
❏ 740	Daddy's Home/This I Know	1961	6.25	12.50	25.00
—Red label					
❏ 740	Daddy's Home/This I Know	1961	10.00	20.00	40.00
—Pink label					
❏ 742	Ready for Your Love/You'll Be Sorry	1961	5.00	10.00	20.00
❏ 747	Three Steps from the Altar/Oh What a Feeling	1961	5.00	10.00	20.00
❏ 748	Our Anniversary/Who Told the Sandman	1962	5.00	10.00	20.00
❏ 751	What Did Daddy Do/Teach Me, Teach Me How to Twist	1962	5.00	10.00	20.00
❏ 753	Gee Baby, What About You/Everything Is Going to Be Alright	1962	5.00	10.00	20.00
❏ 756	Remember Baby/The Monkey	1963	5.00	10.00	20.00
❏ 757	Stick By Me (And I'll Stick By You)/It's All Over Now	1963	5.00	10.00	20.00
❏ 759	Steal Away (With Your Baby)/For All My Love	1963	5.00	10.00	20.00
❏ 761	Easy to Remember (When You Want to Forget)/Why, Why Won't You Believe Me	1964	5.00	10.00	20.00
❏ 767	I'm All Alone/Why Did You Fall for Me	1964	5.00	10.00	20.00
❏ 770	Party for Two/You Better Believe	1965	7.50	15.00	30.00
❏ 772	In Case I Forget/I'm a-Hurting Inside	1965	5.00	10.00	20.00
Albums					
HULL					
❏ 1001 [M]	Our Anniversary	1962	300.00	600.00	1200.
ROULETTE					
❏ R-25350 [M]	Our Anniversary	1967	20.00	40.00	80.00
❏ SR-25350 [R]	Our Anniversary	1967	12.50	25.00	50.00

SHEPARDS, THE
45s

ABC-PARAMOUNT					
❏ 10758	Little Girl Lost/Let Yourself Go	1965	6.25	12.50	25.00

S

Number	Title (A Side/B Side)	Yr	VG	VG+	NM

SHEPHERD, CYBILL
45s
PARAMOUNT
| ❏ 0299 | My Heart Belongs to Daddy/Anything Goes | 1974 | 2.50 | 5.00 | 10.00 |

Albums
PARAMOUNT
| ❏ PAS-1018 | Cybill Does It...to Cole Porter | 1974 | 5.00 | 10.00 | 20.00 |
—With poster

SHEPHERD SISTERS
Some of these spelled the name "Shepard," others "Sheppard," but they are all the same group.
45s
ATLANTIC
| ❏ 2176 | What Makes Little Girls Cry/Don't Mention My Name | 1963 | 2.50 | 5.00 | 10.00 |
| ❏ 2195 | Talk Is Cheap/The Greatest Lover | 1963 | 2.50 | 5.00 | 10.00 |
BIG TOP
| ❏ 3066 | Hapsburg Serenade/Schoen-A, Schoen-A | 1961 | 3.75 | 7.50 | 15.00 |
LANCE
| ❏ 125 | Alone (Why Must I Be Alone)/Congratulations to Someone | 1957 | 6.25 | 12.50 | 25.00 |
MELBA
| ❏ 100 | Gone with the Wind/Rock and Roll, Cha Cha | 1956 | 6.25 | 12.50 | 25.00 |
| ❏ 108 | Remember That Crazy Rock and Roll Turf/I Walked Beside the Sea | 1957 | 6.25 | 12.50 | 25.00 |
MERCURY
❏ 71244	Gettin' Ready for Freddie/The Best Thing There Is	1957	6.25	12.50	25.00
❏ 71306	Eatin' Pizza/A Boy and a Girl	1958	5.00	10.00	20.00
❏ 71350	Dancing Baby/Is It a Crime	1958	5.00	10.00	20.00
MGM
❏ 12766	Heart and Soul/(It's No) Sin	1959	5.00	10.00	20.00
PRIVATE STOCK
❏ 45,063	Our Town/(B-side unknown)	1975	—	3.00	6.00
20TH CENTURY FOX
❏ 468	I've Got a Secret/Finders Keepers	1964	2.50	5.00	10.00
UNITED ARTISTS
❏ 350	Deeply/I'm Still Dancin'	1961	3.00	6.00	12.00
❏ 456	Lolita Ya Ya/Marvin	1962	3.00	6.00	12.00
WARWICK
❏ 511	Here Comes Heaven Again/I Think It's Time	1959	3.75	7.50	15.00
❏ 530	Alone/Rocky	1960	3.75	7.50	15.00
❏ 548	Yea Yea Dixie/How Softly a Heart Breaks	1960	3.75	7.50	15.00
YORK
❏ 50002	Alone (New Version)/Alone (Original Version)	1965	2.50	5.00	10.00

SHEPPARD, BUDDY, AND THE HOLIDAYS
THE BELMONTS in disguise.
45s
SABINA
| ❏ 506 | My Love Is Real/Brahms' Lullaby (Time to Dream) | 1962 | 12.50 | 25.00 | 50.00 |
| ❏ 510 | Now It's All Over/That Background Sound | 1963 | 12.50 | 25.00 | 50.00 |

SHEPPARD, NEIL
45s
ALMONT
| ❏ 314 | You Can't Go Far Without a Guitar (Unless You're Ringo Starr)/Betty Is the Girl for You | 1964 | 7.50 | 15.00 | 30.00 |

SHEPPARD, SHANE
Also see SHEP AND THE LIMELITES.
45s
APT
| ❏ 25039 | Too Young to Wed/Two Loving Hearts | 1960 | 12.50 | 25.00 | 50.00 |
| ❏ 25046 | One Week from Today/I'm So Lonely (What Can I Do) | 1960 | 10.00 | 20.00 | 40.00 |

SHEPPARDS, THE
More than one group?
45s
ABNER
| ❏ 7006 | Elevator Operator/Loving You | 1961 | 3.00 | 6.00 | 12.00 |
APEX
❏ 7750	Loving You/Island of Love	1959	10.00	20.00	40.00
❏ 7752	Just Like You/Feel Like Lovin'	1959	6.25	12.50	25.00
❏ 7755	It's Crazy/Meant to Be	1960	6.25	12.50	25.00
❏ 7759	Just When I Need You Most/Society Gal	1960	6.25	12.50	25.00
❏ 7760	Come Home, Come Home/Just Like You	1960	6.25	12.50	25.00
❏ 7762	Tragic/Feel Like Lovin'	1961	6.25	12.50	25.00
BUNKY
❏ 7764	Island of Love/Steal Away	1969	—	3.00	6.00
❏ 7766	I'm Not Wanted/Your Love (Has a Hole in It)	1969	—	3.00	6.00
CONSTELLATION
❏ 123	Island of Love/Give a Hug to Me	1964	2.50	5.00	10.00
❏ 176	Island of Love/Give a Hug to Me	1966	2.00	4.00	8.00
IMPACT
❏ 1018	Poor Man's Thing/When Johnny Comes Marching Home	1967	7.50	15.00	30.00
LOST-NITE
❏ 223	Island of Love/Never Felt This Way Before	196?	—	2.50	5.00
—Reissue
OKEH
| ❏ 7173 | Walkin'/Pretend You're Still Mine | 1963 | 2.50 | 5.00 | 10.00 |
PAM
| ❏ 1001 | Never Let Me Go/Give a Hug to Me | 1961 | 3.00 | 6.00 | 12.00 |
SHARP
| ❏ 6039 | What's the Name of the Game/Glitter in Your Eyes | 1961 | 3.00 | 6.00 | 12.00 |
UNITED
| ❏ 198 | Sherry/Mozelle | 1957 | 62.50 | 125.00 | 250.00 |
VEE JAY
| ❏ 406 | Every Now and Then/Glitter in Your Eyes | 1961 | 3.00 | 6.00 | 12.00 |
| ❏ 441 | Tragic/Come to Me | 1962 | 5.00 | 10.00 | 20.00 |
Albums
COLLECTABLES
| ❏ COL-5078 | Golden Classics | 198? | 2.50 | 5.00 | 10.00 |

CONSTELLATION
| ❏ C-4 [M] | Collectors Showcase: The Sheppards | 1964 | 20.00 | 40.00 | 80.00 |
| ❏ CS-4 [R] | Collectors Showcase: The Sheppards | 1964 | 10.00 | 20.00 | 40.00 |
SOLID SMOKE
| ❏ SS-8004 | The Sheppards | 1980 | 2.50 | 5.00 | 10.00 |
| ❏ SS-8028 | 18 Dusty Diamonds | 1984 | 2.50 | 5.00 | 10.00 |

SHERIDAN, BOBBY
45s
SUN
| ❏ 354 | Red Man/Sad News | 1961 | 7.50 | 15.00 | 30.00 |

SHERIDAN, MIKE, AND THE NIGHTRIDERS
45s
LIVERPOOL SOUND
| ❏ 902 | Please Mr. Postman/In Love | 1964 | 30.00 | 60.00 | 120.00 |

SHERIDAN, TONY, AND THE BEAT BROTHERS
See THE BEATLES.

SHERIDAN BROTHERS, THE
45s
HIT
| ❏ 235 | Flowers on the Wall/Sounds of Silence | 1966 | 2.00 | 4.00 | 8.00 |
—B-side by Sammy and Theodore

SHERIFF AND THE RAVELS
45s
VEE JAY
| ❏ 306 | Shombalor/Lonely One | 1959 | 10.00 | 20.00 | 40.00 |

SHERLOCKS, THE
45s
DOT
| ❏ 16890 | Skin of My Teeth/Turn Her Down | 1966 | 5.00 | 10.00 | 20.00 |
| ❏ 16953 | Shades of Blue/Too Good to Be True | 1966 | 3.00 | 6.00 | 12.00 |

SHERMAN, ALLAN
45s
RCA VICTOR
❏ 47-8412	The End of a Symphony (Part 1)/The End of a Symphony (Part 2)	1964	2.50	5.00	10.00
❏ 47-8412 [PS]	The End of a Symphony (Part 1)/The End of a Symphony (Part 2)	1964	7.50	15.00	30.00
❏ 47-9693	Fig Leaves Are Falling/Juggling	1968	—	3.00	6.00
WARNER BROS.
❏ 5378	Hello Mudduh! Hello Fadduh! (A Letter from Camp)/Rat Fink	1963	3.00	6.00	12.00
❏ 5378	Hello Mudduh! Hello Fadduh! (A Letter from Camp)/Here's to the Crabgrass	1963	3.75	7.50	15.00
❏ 5378 [PS]	Hello Mudduh! Hello Fadduh! (A Letter from Camp)/Rat Fink	1963	5.00	10.00	20.00
❏ 5406	The Twelve Gifts of Christmas/You Went the Wrong Way, Old King Louie	1963	6.25	12.50	25.00
❏ 5419	My Son the Vampire/I Can't Dance	1964	3.00	6.00	12.00
❏ 5435	Skin (Heart)/The Drop-Outs March	1964	2.50	5.00	10.00
❏ 5449	Hello Mudduh! Hello Fadduh! New 1964 Version/Hello Mudduh! Hello Fadduh! Original Version	1964	3.00	6.00	12.00
❏ 5449 [PS]	Hello Mudduh! Hello Fadduh! New 1964 Version/Hello Mudduh! Hello Fadduh! Original Version	1964	5.00	10.00	20.00
❏ 5490	Pop Hates the Beatles/Grow Mrs. Goldfarb	1964	3.75	7.50	15.00
❏ 5614	Crazy Downtown/The Drop-Outs March	1965	2.50	5.00	10.00
❏ 5672	The Drinking Man's Diet/The Laarge Daark Aardvark Song	1965	2.50	5.00	10.00
❏ 5806	His Own Little Island/Odd Ball	1966	2.50	5.00	10.00
❏ 5896	Westchester Hadassah/Strange Things in My Soup	1967	2.50	5.00	10.00
❏ 7112	Hello Mudduh! Hello Fadduh! (A Letter from Camp)/Sarah Jackman	1968	—	3.00	6.00
—"Back to Back Hits" series -- originals have green "W7" labels
7-Inch Extended Plays
WARNER BROS.
| ❏ PRO 145 [DJ] | Sarah Jackman/Oh Boy//Jump Down, Spin Around/Shake Hands with Your Uncle Max | 196? | 5.00 | 10.00 | 20.00 |
—Promo-only EP from "My Son, the Folk Singer"; probably not issued with picture sleeve
| ❏ S 1487 | Won't You Come Home Disraeli?/Medley/The Let's All Call Up AT&T†March//Mexican Hat Dance/When I Was A Lad/Me | 196? | 3.75 | 7.50 | 15.00 |
—Jukebox issue; small hole, plays at 33 1/3 rpm
| ❏ S 1487 [PS] | My Son, the Celebrity | 196? | 3.75 | 7.50 | 15.00 |
Albums
JUBLIEE
| ❏ JGM 5019 [M] | More Folk Songs by Allan Sherman | 1963 | 5.00 | 10.00 | 20.00 |
—Two early Allan Sherman sides plus comedy bits by others
RCA RED SEAL
| ❏ LM-2773 [M] | Peter and the Commissar | 1964 | 5.00 | 10.00 | 20.00 |
| ❏ LSC-2773 [S] | Peter and the Commissar | 1964 | 6.25 | 12.50 | 25.00 |
—With Arthur Fiedler and the Boston Pops Orchestra
RHINO
| ❏ RNLP-005 | The Best of Allan Sherman | 198? | 2.50 | 5.00 | 10.00 |
| ❏ RNLP 70818 | A Gift of Laughter | 1986 | 2.50 | 5.00 | 10.00 |
WARNER BROS.
| ❏ W 1475 [M] | My Son, the Folk Singer | 1962 | 3.75 | 7.50 | 15.00 |
| ❏ WS 1475 [S] | My Son, the Folk Singer | 1962 | 5.00 | 10.00 | 20.00 |
—Gold label
| ❏ W 1487 [M] | My Son, the Celebrity | 1963 | 3.75 | 7.50 | 15.00 |
| ❏ WS 1487 [S] | My Son, the Celebrity | 1963 | 5.00 | 10.00 | 20.00 |
—Gold label
| ❏ W 1501 [M] | My Son, the Nut | 1963 | 3.75 | 7.50 | 15.00 |
| ❏ WS 1501 [S] | My Son, the Nut | 1963 | 5.00 | 10.00 | 20.00 |
—Gold label
| ❏ W 1539 [M] | Allan in Wonderland | 1964 | 3.00 | 6.00 | 12.00 |
| ❏ WS 1539 [S] | Allan in Wonderland | 1964 | 3.75 | 7.50 | 15.00 |
—Gold label
| ❏ W 1569 [M] | For Swingin' Livers Only! | 1964 | 3.00 | 6.00 | 12.00 |
| ❏ WS 1569 [S] | For Swingin' Livers Only! | 1964 | 3.75 | 7.50 | 15.00 |

Number	Title (A Side/B Side)	Yr	VG	VG+	NM
❏ W 1604 [M]	My Name Is Allan	1965	3.00	6.00	12.00
❏ WS 1604 [S]	My Name Is Allan	1965	3.75	7.50	15.00
—Gold label					
❏ W 1649 [M]	Allan Sherman — Live	1966	3.00	6.00	12.00
❏ WS 1649 [S]	Allan Sherman — Live	1966	3.75	7.50	15.00
—Gold label					
❏ W 1684 [M]	Togetherness	1967	3.75	7.50	15.00
❏ WS 1684 [S]	Togetherness	1967	5.00	10.00	20.00
—Gold label					

SHERMAN, BOBBY
45s
CAMEO

Number	Title (A Side/B Side)	Yr	VG	VG+	NM
❏ 403	Happiness Is/Can't Get Used to Loving You	1966	2.50	5.00	10.00
❏ 403 [DJ]	Happiness Is	1966	5.00	10.00	20.00
—One-sided promo					
CONDOR					
❏ 1002	I'll Never Tell You/Telegram	1969	2.50	5.00	10.00
DECCA					
❏ 31672	Man Overboard/You Make Me Happy	1964	3.75	7.50	15.00
❏ 31741	It Hurts Me/Give Me Your Word	1965	3.75	7.50	15.00
❏ 31741 [PS]	It Hurts Me/Give Me Your Word	1965	12.50	25.00	50.00
❏ 31779	Hey Little Girl/Well All Right	1965	3.75	7.50	15.00
DOT					
❏ 16566	I Want to Hear It From Her/Nobody's Sweetheart	1963	3.75	7.50	15.00
EPIC					
❏ 10181	Cold Girl/Think of Rain	1967	2.50	5.00	10.00
❏ 10181 [PS]	Cold Girl/Think of Rain	1967	5.00	10.00	20.00
JANUS					
❏ 246	Runaway/Mr. Success	1975	—	2.00	4.00
❏ 254	Our Last Song Together/Sunshine Rose	1975	—	2.00	4.00
METROMEDIA					
❏ 68-0100	Early in the Morning/Unborn Lullaby	1973	—	2.50	5.00
❏ 121	Little Woman/One Too Many Mornings	1969	—	2.50	5.00
❏ 121 [PS]	Little Woman/One Too Many Mornings	1969	—	2.50	5.00
❏ 150	La La La (If I Had You)/Time	1969	—	2.50	5.00
❏ 150 [PS]	La La La (If I Had You)/Time	1969	—	2.50	5.00
❏ 177	Easy Come, Easy Go/July Seventeen	1970	—	2.50	5.00
❏ 177	Easy Come, Easy Go/Sounds Along the Way	1970	—	2.50	5.00
❏ 177 [PS]	Easy Come, Easy Go/July Seventeen	1970	—	2.50	5.00
❏ 188	Hey, Mister Sun/Two Blind Mice	1970	—	2.50	5.00
❏ 188 [PS]	Hey, Mister Sun/Two Blind Mice	1970	—	2.50	5.00
❏ 194	Julie, Do Ya Love Me/Spend Some Time Lovin' Me	1970	—	2.50	5.00
❏ 194 [PS]	Julie, Do Ya Love Me/Spend Some Time Lovin' Me	1970	—	2.50	5.00
❏ 204	Goin' Home (Sing a Song of Christmas Cheer)/Love's What You're Gettin' for Christmas	1970	—	3.00	6.00
❏ 204 [PS]	Goin' Home (Sing a Song of Christmas Cheer)/Love's What You're Gettin' for Christmas	1970	2.00	4.00	8.00
❏ 206	Cried Like a Baby/Is Anybody There	1971	—	2.50	5.00
❏ 206 [PS]	Cried Like a Baby/Is Anybody There	1971	—	2.50	5.00
❏ 217	The Drum/Free Now to Roam	1971	—	2.50	5.00
❏ 217 [PS]	The Drum/Free Now to Roam	1971	—	2.50	5.00
❏ 222	Waiting at the Bus Stop/Run Away	1971	—	2.50	5.00
❏ 222 [PS]	Waiting at the Bus Stop/Run Away	1971	—	2.50	5.00
❏ 227	Jennifer/Getting Together	1971	—	2.50	5.00
❏ 227 [PS]	Jennifer/Getting Together	1971	—	2.50	5.00
❏ 240	Together Again/Picture a Little Girl	1972	—	2.50	5.00
❏ 240 [PS]	Together Again/Picture a Little Girl	1972	—	2.50	5.00
❏ 249	I Don't Believe in Magic/Just a Little While Longer	1972		2.50	5.00
PARKWAY					
❏ 967	Goody Galumshus/Anything Your Little Heart Desires	1966	2.50	5.00	10.00
STARCREST					
❏ 100	Judy, You'll Never Know/Telegram	1962	5.00	10.00	20.00

Albums
METROMEDIA

Number	Title	Yr	VG	VG+	NM
❏ MD 1014	Bobby Sherman	1969	3.75	7.50	15.00
❏ MD 1028	Here Comes Bobby	1970	3.75	7.50	15.00
❏ MD 1032	With Love, Bobby	1970	3.75	7.50	15.00
❏ MD 1038	Bobby Sherman Christmas Album	1970	3.75	7.50	15.00
❏ MD 1040	Portrait of Bobby	1971	3.75	7.50	15.00
❏ MD 1045	Getting Together	1971	3.75	7.50	15.00
❏ KMD 1048	Bobby Sherman's Greatest Hits	1972	3.00	6.00	12.00
❏ MD 1060	Just for You	1973	3.75	7.50	15.00

SHERRYS, THE
45s
GUYDEN

Number	Title	Yr	VG	VG+	NM
❏ 2068	Pop-Pop-Pop-Eye/Your Hand in Mine	1962	3.75	7.50	15.00
❏ 2077	Slop Time/Let's Stomp Again	1963	3.75	7.50	15.00
❏ 2084	Saturday Night/I've Got No One	1963	3.75	7.50	15.00
❏ 2094	Monk, Monk, Monkey/That Boy of Mine	1963	3.75	7.50	15.00
MERCURY					
❏ 72256	No No Baby/That Guy of Mine	1964	3.00	6.00	12.00
ROBERTS					
❏ 701	Slow Jerk/Confusion	1965	3.00	6.00	12.00

Albums
GUYDEN

Number	Title	Yr	VG	VG+	NM
❏ GLP 503 [M]	At the Hop with the Sherrys	1963	62.50	125.00	250.00

SHEVELLES, THE
45s
WORLD ARTISTS

Number	Title	Yr	VG	VG+	NM
❏ 1023	Oo Poo Pa Doo/Like I Love You	1964	3.00	6.00	12.00
❏ 1025	How Would You Like Me to Love You/I Could Conquer the World	1964	3.00	6.00	12.00

SHEVETON, TONY
45s
PARROT

Number	Title	Yr	VG	VG+	NM
❏ 10616	Dance with Me/A Million Drums	1964	3.75	7.50	15.00

SHIEKS, THE See THE SHEIKS.

SHIELDS, BILLY Pseudonym of TONY ORLANDO.
45s
HARBOUR

Number	Title	Yr	VG	VG+	NM
❏ 304	I Was a Boy/Moments from Now	1969	6.25	12.50	25.00

SHIELDS, BOBBY
45s
MELBA

Number	Title (A Side/B Side)	Yr	VG	VG+	NM
❏ 105	Land of Rock and Roll/I Wouldn't Change You for the World	1956	15.00	30.00	60.00

SHIELDS, THE
45s
ATCO

Number	Title	Yr	VG	VG+	NM
❏ 7071	The Way I Feel Tonight/All Right by Me	1977	—	2.50	5.00
CONTINENTAL					
❏ 4072	You Told Another Lie/Barnyard Dance	1961	100.00	200.00	400.00
DOT					
❏ 136	You Cheated/Nature Boy	196?	2.50	5.00	10.00
—Reissue; black label					
❏ 15805	You Cheated/That's the Way It's Gonna Be	1958	6.25	12.50	25.00
❏ 15856	I'm Sorry Now/Nature Boy	1958	7.50	15.00	30.00
❏ 15940	Fare Thee Well/Play the Game Fair	1959	6.25	12.50	25.00
TENDER					
❏ 513	You Cheated/That's the Way It's Gonna Be	1958	10.00	20.00	40.00
—With reference to Dot Records on label					
❏ 513	You Cheated/That's the Way It's Gonna Be	1958	37.50	75.00	150.00
—No reference to Dot Records on label					
❏ 518	I'm Sorry Now/Nature Boy	1958	15.00	30.00	60.00
❏ 521	Fare Thee Well/Play the Game Fair	1959	15.00	30.00	60.00
TRANSCONTINENTAL					
❏ 1013	The Girl Around the Corner/Fare Thee Well, My Love	1960	25.00	50.00	100.00

SHILOH Don Henley, later of EAGLES, was in this group. The album was produced by KENNY ROGERS.
45s
AMOS

Number	Title	Yr	VG	VG+	NM
❏ 140	Jennifer/Tell Her to Get Out of Your Life	1970	3.00	6.00	12.00
❏ 162	Down on the Farm/Simple Little Down Home Rock & Roll Love Song for Rosie	1971	3.00	6.00	12.00

Albums
AMOS

Number	Title	Yr	VG	VG+	NM
❏ AAS-7015	Shiloh	1971	20.00	40.00	80.00

SHINDIGS, THE Also known as THE BOBBY FULLER FOUR.
45s
MUSTANG

Number	Title	Yr	VG	VG+	NM
❏ 3003	Thunder Reef/Wolfman	1965	10.00	20.00	40.00

SHIP, THE
Albums
ELEKTRA

Number	Title	Yr	VG	VG+	NM
❏ EKS-75036	The Ship	1972	5.00	10.00	20.00

SHIRELLES, THE
45s
BELL

Number	Title	Yr	VG	VG+	NM
❏ 760	A Most Unusual Boy/Look What You've Done to My Heart	1969	2.50	5.00	10.00
❏ 787	Looking Glass/Playthings	1969	2.50	5.00	10.00
❏ 815	Never Give You Up/Go Away and Find Yourself	1969	2.50	5.00	10.00
BLUE ROCK					
❏ 4051	Don't Mess with Cupid/Sweet Sweet Lovin'	1968	2.50	5.00	10.00
❏ 4066	Call Me/There's a Storm Goin' Home in My Heart	1968	2.50	5.00	10.00
DECCA					
❏ 25506	I Met Him on a Sunday/My Love Is a Charm	196?	3.75	7.50	15.00
—Early reissue					
❏ 30588	I Met Him on a Sunday/I Want You to Be My Boyfriend	1958	6.25	12.50	25.00
❏ 30669	My Love Is a Charm/Slop Time	1958	10.00	20.00	40.00
❏ 30761	Stop Me/I Got the Message	1958	10.00	20.00	40.00
PHILCO-FORD					
❏ HP-30	Soldier Boy/My Heart Belongs to You	1968	5.00	10.00	20.00
—4-inch plastic "Hip Pocket Record" with color sleeve					
RCA VICTOR					
❏ 47-0902	Let's Give Each Other Love/Deep in the Night	1973	2.00	4.00	8.00
❏ 48-1019	No Sugar Tonight/Strange, I Still Love You	1971	2.50	5.00	10.00
❏ 48-1032	Brother, Brother/Sunday Dreaming	1972	2.50	5.00	10.00
❏ APBO-0192	Touch the Wind (Eres Tu)/Do What You've a Mind To	1973	2.00	4.00	8.00
SCEPTER					
❏ 1203	Dedicated to the One I Love/Look A Here Baby	1958	5.00	10.00	20.00
—Red label					
❏ 1203	Dedicated to the One I Love/Look A Here Baby	1958	10.00	20.00	40.00
—White label					
❏ 1205	A Teardrop and a Lollipop/Doin' the Ronde	1959	5.00	10.00	20.00
—Red label					
❏ 1205	A Teardrop and a Lollipop/Doin' the Ronde	1959	7.50	15.00	30.00
—White label					
❏ 1207	Please Be My Boyfriend/I Saw a Tear	1960	5.00	10.00	20.00
—Red label					
❏ 1207	Please Be My Boyfriend/I Saw a Tear	1960	7.50	15.00	30.00
—White label					
❏ 1208	Tonight's the Night/The Dance Is Over	1960	5.00	10.00	20.00
—Red label					
❏ 1208	Tonight's the Night/The Dance Is Over	1960	6.25	12.50	25.00
—Pink label					
❏ 1208	Tonight's the Night/The Dance Is Over	1960	7.50	15.00	30.00
—White label					
❏ 1211	Will You Love Me Tomorrow/Boys	1960	7.50	15.00	30.00
—Revised A-side title					
❏ 1211	Tomorrow/Boys	1960	10.00	20.00	40.00
—Original A-side title					
❏ 1217	Mama Said/Blue Holiday	1961	5.00	10.00	20.00
❏ 1220	A Thing of the Past/What a Sweet Thing That Was	1961	5.00	10.00	20.00
❏ 1223	Big John/Twenty-One	1961	5.00	10.00	20.00
❏ 1227	Baby It's You/Things I Want to Hear (Pretty Words)	1961	5.00	10.00	20.00
❏ 1228	Soldier Boy/Love Is a Swingin' Thing	1962	3.75	7.50	15.00

S

Number	Title (A Side/B Side)	Yr	VG	VG+	NM
❑ 1234	Welcome Home Baby/Mama, Here Comes the Bride	1962	3.75	7.50	15.00
❑ 1237	Stop the Music/It's Love That Really Counts	1962	3.75	7.50	15.00
❑ 1243	Everybody Loves a Lover/I Don't Think So	1962	3.75	7.50	15.00
❑ 1248	Foolish Little Girl/Not for All the Money in the World	1963	3.75	7.50	15.00
❑ 1248 [PS]	Foolish Little Girl/Not for All the Money in the World	1963	10.00	20.00	40.00
❑ 1255	Don't Say Goodnight and Mean Goodbye/I Didn't Mean to Hurt You	1963	3.00	6.00	12.00
❑ 1255 [PS]	Don't Say Goodnight and Mean Goodbye/I Didn't Mean to Hurt You	1963	10.00	20.00	40.00
❑ 1259	What Does a Girl Do?/Don't Let It Happen to You	1963	3.00	6.00	12.00
❑ 1260	It's a Mad, Mad, Mad/31 Flavors	1963	3.00	6.00	12.00
❑ 1264	Tonight You're Gonna Fall in Love with Me/20th Century Rock and Roll	1963	3.00	6.00	12.00
❑ 1267	Sha-La-La/His Lips Get In the Way	1964	3.00	6.00	12.00
❑ 1278	Thank You Baby/Doomsday	1964	3.00	6.00	12.00
❑ 1284	Maybe Tonight/Lost Love	1964	3.00	6.00	12.00
❑ 1292	Are You Still My Baby/I Saw a Tear	1964	3.00	6.00	12.00
❑ 1296	Shh, I'm Watching the Movies/A Plus B	1965	3.00	6.00	12.00
❑ 12101	March (You'll Be Sorry)/Everybody's Goin' Mad	1965	2.50	5.00	10.00
❑ 12114	My Heart Belongs to You/Love That Man	1965	2.50	5.00	10.00
❑ 12123	(Mama) My Soldier Boy Is Coming Home/Soldier Boy	1965	2.50	5.00	10.00
❑ 12132	I Met Him on a Sunday — '66/Love That Man	1966	2.50	5.00	10.00
❑ 12150	Till My Baby Comes Home/Que Sera, Sera	1966	2.50	5.00	10.00
❑ 12162	Shades of Blue/After Midnight	1966	2.50	5.00	10.00
❑ 12162	Shades of Blue/Looking Around	1966	2.50	5.00	10.00
❑ 12178	Teasin' Me/Look Away	1966	2.50	5.00	10.00
❑ 12185	Don't Go Home (My Little Baby)/Nobody Baby After You	1967	2.50	5.00	10.00
❑ 12192	Too Much of a Good Thing/Bright Shiny Colors	1967	2.50	5.00	10.00
❑ 12198	Last Minute Miracle/No Doubt About It	1967	2.50	5.00	10.00
❑ 12209	Wild and Sweet/Wait Till I Give the Signal	1968	2.50	5.00	10.00
❑ 12217	Hippie Walk (Part 1)/Hippie Walk (Part 2)	1968	2.50	5.00	10.00

TIARA

Number	Title (A Side/B Side)	Yr	VG	VG+	NM
❑ 6112	I Met Him on a Sunday/I Want You to Be My Boyfriend	1958	200.00	400.00	800.00

—Note: Copies with any catalog number except 6112 are reproductions with little collector value

UNITED ARTISTS

Number	Title (A Side/B Side)	Yr	VG	VG+	NM
❑ 50648	There Goes My Baby-Be My Baby/Strange, I Still Love You	1970	2.00	4.00	8.00
❑ 50693	It's Gonna Take a Miracle/Lost	1970	2.00	4.00	8.00
❑ 50740	Take Me for a Little While/Dedicated to the One I Love	1971	2.00	4.00	8.00

Albums

RCA VICTOR

Number	Title (A Side/B Side)	Yr	VG	VG+	NM
❑ LSP-4581	Happy and In Love	1971	3.75	7.50	15.00
❑ LSP-4698	The Shirelles	1972	3.75	7.50	15.00

RHINO

Number	Title (A Side/B Side)	Yr	VG	VG+	NM
❑ RNDA-1101 [(2)]	Anthology (1959-1967)	1984	3.00	6.00	12.00

SCEPTER

Number	Title (A Side/B Side)	Yr	VG	VG+	NM
❑ S-501 [M]	Tonight's the Night	1961	50.00	100.00	200.00
—"Scepter" in scroll at top of label					
❑ SPM-501 [M]	Tonight's the Night	1962	15.00	30.00	60.00
—"Scepter Records" at left of label					
❑ SPS-501 [S]	Tonight's the Night	1965	25.00	50.00	100.00
❑ S-502 [M]	The Shirelles Sing to Trumpets and Strings	1961	50.00	100.00	200.00
—"Scepter" in scroll at top of label					
❑ SPM-502 [M]	The Shirelles Sing to Trumpets and Strings	1962	15.00	30.00	60.00
—"Scepter Records" at left of label					
❑ SPS-502 [S]	The Shirelles Sing to Trumpets and Strings	1965	25.00	50.00	100.00
❑ SPM-504 [M]	Baby It's You	1962	25.00	50.00	100.00
❑ SPS-504 [S]	Baby It's You	1965	25.00	50.00	100.00
❑ SPM-505 [M]	A Twist Party	1962	20.00	40.00	80.00
❑ SPS-505 [S]	A Twist Party	1965	25.00	50.00	100.00
❑ SPM-507 [M]	The Shirelles' Greatest Hits	1962	10.00	20.00	40.00
❑ SPS-507 [S]	The Shirelles' Greatest Hits	1965	12.50	25.00	50.00
❑ SPM-511 [M]	Foolish Little Girl	1963	12.50	25.00	50.00
❑ SPS-511 [S]	Foolish Little Girl	1965	20.00	40.00	80.00
❑ SPM-514 [M]	It's a Mad, Mad, Mad, Mad World	1963	10.00	20.00	40.00
❑ SPS-514 [S]	It's a Mad, Mad, Mad, Mad World	1965	12.50	25.00	50.00
❑ SPM-516 [M]	The Shirelles Sing the Golden Oldies	1964	10.00	20.00	40.00
❑ SPS-516 [S]	The Shirelles Sing the Golden Oldies	1964	12.50	25.00	50.00
❑ SPM-560 [M]	The Shirelles' Greatest Hits, Volume 2	1967	5.00	10.00	20.00
❑ SPS-560 [S]	The Shirelles' Greatest Hits, Volume 2	1967	6.25	12.50	25.00
❑ SPM-562 [M]	Spontaneous Combustion	1967	10.00	20.00	40.00
❑ SPS-562 [S]	Spontaneous Combustion	1967	12.50	25.00	50.00
❑ SPS-569	Eternally Soul	1968	7.50	15.00	30.00
❑ SPS-2-599 [(2)]	Remember When	1972	5.00	10.00	20.00

SPRINGBOARD

Number	Title (A Side/B Side)	Yr	VG	VG+	NM
❑ 4006	The Shirelles Sing Their Very Best	1973	2.00	4.00	8.00

UNITED ARTISTS

Number	Title (A Side/B Side)	Yr	VG	VG+	NM
❑ UA-LA340-E	The Very Best of the Shirelles	1974	2.50	5.00	10.00

SHIRLEY (AND COMPANY) Shirley Goodman, earlier of SHIRLEY AND LEE.
45s

VIBRATION

Number	Title (A Side/B Side)	Yr	VG	VG+	NM
❑ 532	Shame, Shame, Shame/(Instrumental)	1974	—	2.50	5.00
❑ 535	Cry, Cry, Cry/(Instrumental)	1975	—	2.50	5.00
❑ 539	Disco Shirley/Keep On Rolling On	1975	—	2.50	5.00
❑ 542	I Like to Dance/Jim Doc C'ain	1976	—	2.50	5.00
❑ 579	Revelations True/(Instrumental)	1978	—	2.50	5.00

Albums

VIBRATION

Number	Title (A Side/B Side)	Yr	VG	VG+	NM
❑ 128	Shame Shame Shame	1975	2.50	5.00	10.00

SHIRLEY AND LEE Also see SHIRLEY (AND COMPANY).
45s

ALADDIN

Number	Title (A Side/B Side)	Yr	VG	VG+	NM
❑ 3153	I'm Gone/Sweethearts	1952	25.00	50.00	100.00
❑ 3173	Baby/Shirley Come Back to Me	1953	30.00	60.00	120.00
❑ 3192	Shirley's Back/So In Love	1953	15.00	30.00	60.00
❑ 3205	Two Happy People/The Proposal	1953	12.50	25.00	50.00
❑ 3222	Why Did I/Lee Goofed	1954	12.50	25.00	50.00
❑ 3244	Confessin'/Keep On	1954	12.50	25.00	50.00

Number	Title (A Side/B Side)	Yr	VG	VG+	NM
❑ 3258	Comin' Over/Takes Money	1954	12.50	25.00	50.00
❑ 3289	Feel So Good/You'd Be Thinking of Me	1955	10.00	20.00	40.00
❑ 3302	Let's Dream/I'll Do It	1955	10.00	20.00	40.00
❑ 3325	Let the Good Times Roll/Do You Mean to Hurt Me So	1956	15.00	30.00	60.00
❑ 3338	I Feel Good/Now That It's Over	1956	6.25	12.50	25.00
❑ 3362	When I Saw You/That's What I Want to Do	1957	5.00	10.00	20.00
❑ 3369	I Want to Dance/Marry Me	1957	5.00	10.00	20.00
❑ 3380	Rock All Night/Don't You Know I Love You	1957	5.00	10.00	20.00
❑ 3390	Rockin' with the Clock/The Flirt	1957	5.00	10.00	20.00
❑ 3405	Love No One But You (I Love You So)/I'll Thrill You	1958	5.00	10.00	20.00
❑ 3418	Everybody's Rocking/Don't Leave Me Here to Cry	1958	5.00	10.00	20.00
❑ 3432	Come On and Have Your Fun/All I Want to Do Is Cry	1958	5.00	10.00	20.00
❑ 3455	True Love/When Day Is Done	1959	5.00	10.00	20.00

IMPERIAL

Number	Title (A Side/B Side)	Yr	VG	VG+	NM
❑ 013	Let the Good Times Roll/Feel So Good	196?	2.50	5.00	10.00
—"The Golden Series" reissue; gold label, Imperial logo at top					
❑ 5818	Together We Stand (Divided We Fall)/The Joker	1962	2.50	5.00	10.00
❑ 5854	My Last Letter/I'm Early Enough	1962	2.50	5.00	10.00
❑ 5868	Don't Stop Now/A Little Thing	1962	2.50	5.00	10.00
❑ 5922	The Golden Rule/Hey Little Boy	1963	2.50	5.00	10.00
❑ 5970	Dancing World/I'm Gone	1963	2.50	5.00	10.00
❑ 5979	Paper Doll/The Brink of Disaster	1963	2.50	5.00	10.00
❑ 66000	Somebody Put a Jukebox in the Study Hall/Never Let Me Go	1963	2.50	5.00	10.00

UNITED ARTISTS

Number	Title (A Side/B Side)	Yr	VG	VG+	NM
❑ 0087	Let the Good Times Roll/Feel So Good	1973	—	2.00	4.00
—"Silver Spotlight Series" reissue					
❑ XW274	Let the Good Times Roll/That's What I Wanna Do	1973	—	2.50	5.00

WARWICK

Number	Title (A Side/B Side)	Yr	VG	VG+	NM
❑ 581	Let the Good Times Roll/Keep Loving Me	1960	3.00	6.00	12.00
❑ 609	Two Peas in a Pod/Your Love Makes the Difference	1961	3.00	6.00	12.00
❑ 664	Well-a, Well-a/Our Kids	1961	3.00	6.00	12.00
❑ 679	Let's Live It Up/Girl, You're Married Now	1962	3.00	6.00	12.00

Albums

ALADDIN

Number	Title (A Side/B Side)	Yr	VG	VG+	NM
❑ 807 [M]	Let the Good Times Roll	1956	375.00	750.00	1500.

IMPERIAL

Number	Title (A Side/B Side)	Yr	VG	VG+	NM
❑ LP-9179 [M]	Let the Good Times Roll	1962	75.00	150.00	300.00
—Reissue of Aladdin LP					

SCORE

Number	Title (A Side/B Side)	Yr	VG	VG+	NM
❑ SLP-4023 [M]	Let the Good Times Roll	1957	200.00	400.00	800.00
—Reissue of Aladdin LP					

WARWICK

Number	Title (A Side/B Side)	Yr	VG	VG+	NM
❑ W-2028 [M]	Let the Good Times Roll	1961	37.50	75.00	150.00
❑ W-2028ST [S]	Let the Good Times Roll	1961	75.00	150.00	300.00

SHOCKING BLUE, THE
45s

BUDDAH

Number	Title (A Side/B Side)	Yr	VG	VG+	NM
❑ 258	Sleepless at Midnight/Serenade	1971	—	3.00	6.00

COLOSSUS

Number	Title (A Side/B Side)	Yr	VG	VG+	NM
❑ 108	Venus/Hot Sand	1969	2.50	5.00	10.00
❑ 108 [PS]	Venus/Hot Sand	1969	3.75	7.50	15.00
❑ 111	Mighty Joe/I'm a Woman	1970	2.00	4.00	8.00
❑ 111 [PS]	Mighty Joe/I'm a Woman	1970	3.00	6.00	12.00
❑ 116	Long and Lonesome Road/Ackaragh	1970	2.00	4.00	8.00
❑ 123	Never Love a Railroad Man/Never Marry	1970	2.00	4.00	8.00
❑ 141	Boll Weevil/Long and Lonesome Road	1971	—	3.00	6.00

MGM

Number	Title (A Side/B Side)	Yr	VG	VG+	NM
❑ 14481	When I Was a Girl/Eve and the Apple	1973	—	3.00	6.00
❑ 14543	Oh Love/Inkpot	1973	—	3.00	6.00

21 RECORDS

Number	Title (A Side/B Side)	Yr	VG	VG+	NM
❑ 99517	Venus/Mighty Joe	1986	—	2.00	4.00

Albums

COLOSSUS

Number	Title (A Side/B Side)	Yr	VG	VG+	NM
❑ CS-1000	The Shocking Blue	1970	6.25	12.50	25.00

SHONDELL, TROY
45s

AVM

Number	Title (A Side/B Side)	Yr	VG	VG+	NM
❑ 14	(I'm Looking for Some) New Blue Jeans/(B-side unknown)	1988	—	3.50	7.00

BEAR

Number	Title (A Side/B Side)	Yr	VG	VG+	NM
❑ 2002	No One Knows/Sweet Enough	1989	—	3.00	6.00

BRITE STAR

Number	Title (A Side/B Side)	Yr	VG	VG+	NM
❑ 2453	This Time/You're Nobody's Child	1973	2.00	4.00	8.00
❑ 2459	Still Loving You/Rip It Up	1973	2.00	4.00	8.00
❑ 4691	Deeper and Deeper in Love/Love Stuff	1974	2.00	4.00	8.00

DECCA

Number	Title (A Side/B Side)	Yr	VG	VG+	NM
❑ 31742	You Can't Catch Me/Walkin' in a Memory	1964	2.50	5.00	10.00

EVEREST

Number	Title (A Side/B Side)	Yr	VG	VG+	NM
❑ 2015	Gone/Some People Never Learn	1963	2.50	5.00	10.00
❑ 2018	I've Got a Woman/No Fool Like an Old Fool	1963	2.50	5.00	10.00
❑ 2041	Trouble/Little Miss Tease	1964	2.50	5.00	10.00

GAYE

Number	Title (A Side/B Side)	Yr	VG	VG+	NM
❑ 2010	This Time/I Catch Myself Crying	1961	20.00	40.00	80.00

GOLDCREST

Number	Title (A Side/B Side)	Yr	VG	VG+	NM
❑ 161-A	This Time/Girl After Girl	1961	6.25	12.50	25.00
—With "Distributed by Liberty Record Sales" on label					
❑ 161-A	This Time/Girl After Girl	1961	7.50	15.00	30.00
—With no "Distributed by Liberty" on label					

ITCO

Number	Title (A Side/B Side)	Yr	VG	VG+	NM
❑ 105	And We Made Love/Imitation Woman	198?	—	2.50	5.00

LIBERTY

Number	Title (A Side/B Side)	Yr	VG	VG+	NM
❑ 55353	This Time/Girl After Girl	1961	5.00	10.00	20.00
❑ 55398	Tears from an Angel/Island in the Sky	1961	4.00	8.00	16.00
❑ 55445	Just Because/Na-Ne-No	1962	4.00	8.00	16.00

RIC

Number	Title (A Side/B Side)	Yr	VG	VG+	NM
❑ 174	Just a Dream/Just Like Me	1965	2.50	5.00	10.00
❑ 184	Big Windy City/I Thought That You Were Mine	1966	2.50	5.00	10.00

Number	Title (A Side/B Side)	Yr	VG	VG+	NM
STAR-FOX					
❏ 77	Still Loving You/Doctor Love	1979	2.00	4.00	8.00
TELESONIC					
❏ 804	(Sittin' Here) Lovin' You/(Here I Am) Single Again	1980	2.00	4.00	8.00
TRX					
❏ 5001	A Rose and a Baby Ruth/Here It Comes Again	1967	2.00	4.00	8.00
❏ 5003	Head Man/She's Got Everything She Needs	1967	2.00	4.00	8.00
❏ 5015	Let's Go All the Way/Let Me Love You	1968	2.00	4.00	8.00
❏ 5019	Something's Wrong in Indiana/A Rose and a Baby Ruth	1969	2.00	4.00	8.00
Albums					
EVEREST					
❏ 1206 [S]	The Many Sides of Troy Shondell	1963	20.00	40.00	80.00
❏ 5206 [M]	The Many Sides of Troy Shondell	1963	12.50	25.00	50.00
SUNSET					
❏ SUM-1174 [M]	This Time	1967	3.75	7.50	15.00
❏ SUS-5174 [S]	This Time	1967	3.75	7.50	15.00

SHONDELLES, THE
45s

Number	Title (A Side/B Side)	Yr	VG	VG+	NM
KING					
❏ 5597	Don't Cry My Soldier Boy/My Love	1962	5.00	10.00	20.00
❏ 5656	Wonderful One/I Gotta Tell It	1962	5.00	10.00	20.00
❏ 5705	Muscle Bound/Special Delivery	1963	5.00	10.00	20.00
❏ 5755	Watusi, One More/Ooo, Sometimes	1963	5.00	10.00	20.00

SHONDELLS, THE　See TOMMY JAMES AND THE SHONDELLS.

SHOOTERS, THE　With OTIS REDDING.
45s

Number	Title (A Side/B Side)	Yr	VG	VG+	NM
TRANS WORLD					
❏ 6908	Tuff Enuff/She's All Right	1960	25.00	50.00	100.00

SHORE, DINAH
45s

Number	Title (A Side/B Side)	Yr	VG	VG+	NM
CAPITOL					
❏ 4344	So Many Things to Do Today/When the Sparrows Learn to Fly	1960	2.00	4.00	8.00
❏ 4476	I Ain't Down Yet/I Gotta Love You	1960	2.00	4.00	8.00
❏ 4618	Mississippi Mud/This Is a Changing World	1961	2.00	4.00	8.00
❏ 4774	That'll Show Him/Just a Brief Encounter	1962	2.00	4.00	8.00
COLUMBIA					
❏ 1-111	So in Love/Always True to You in My Fashion	1949	7.50	15.00	30.00
—Microgroove 33 1/3 rpm 7-inch single					
❏ 1-134	Forever and Ever/I've Been Hit	1949	7.50	15.00	30.00
—Microgroove 33 1/3 rpm 7-inch single					
❏ 1-155	Having Wonderful Time/The Story of My Life	1949	7.50	15.00	30.00
—Microgroove 33 1/3 rpm 7-inch single					
❏ 1-197	A Wonderful Guy/Younger Than Springtime	1949	7.50	15.00	30.00
—Microgroove 33 1/3 rpm 7-inch single					
❏ 1-200	Baby, It's Cold Outside/My One and Only Highland Fling	1949	7.50	15.00	30.00
—With Buddy Clark; Microgroove 33 1/3 rpm 7-inch single					
❏ 1-220 (?)	I'm Gonna Wash That Man Right Out of My Hair/Kiss Me, Sweet	1949	7.50	15.00	30.00
—Microgroove 33 1/3 rpm 7-inch single					
❏ 1-250 (?)	Till My Ship Comes In/Lovers Gold	1949	7.50	15.00	30.00
—Microgroove 33 1/3 rpm 7-inch single					
❏ 1-260 (?)	Homework/You Can Have Him	1949	7.50	15.00	30.00
—With Doris Day; Microgroove 33 1/3 rpm 7-inch single					
❏ 1-290 (?)	Through a Long and Sleepless Night/I'm Yours	1949	7.50	15.00	30.00
—Microgroove 33 1/3 rpm 7-inch single					
❏ 1-330 (?)	The Story of Annie Laurie/A Thousand Violins	1949	7.50	15.00	30.00
—Microgroove 33 1/3 rpm 7-inch single					
❏ 1-368	Dear Hearts and Gentle People/Speak a Word of Love	1949	7.50	15.00	30.00
—Microgroove 33 1/3 rpm 7-inch single					
❏ 1-369	Star of Bethlehem/Merry Christmas	1949	10.00	20.00	40.00
—Microgroove 33 1/3 rpm 7-inch single					
❏ 1-437	Bibbidi-Bobbidi-Boo (The Magic Song)/Happy Time	1950	7.50	15.00	30.00
❏ 1-440 (?)	The Shoe Is On the Other Foot Now/Wedding Dolls	1950	7.50	15.00	30.00
—With George Morgan; Microgroove 33 1/3 rpm 7-inch single					
❏ 1-445 (?)	Lucky Us/Nobody Home at My House	1950	7.50	15.00	30.00
—Microgroove 33 1/3 rpm 7-inch single					
❏ 1-450 (?)	Scarlet Ribbons (For Her Hair)/Sitting by the Window	1950	7.50	15.00	30.00
—Microgroove 33 1/3 rpm 7-inch single					
❏ 1-469	It's So Nice to Have a Man Around the House/More Than Anything Else	1950	7.50	15.00	30.00
—Microgroove 33 1/3 rpm 7-inch single					
❏ 1-580 (?)	You've Been Playing Checkers/Ask Me No Questions	1950	7.50	15.00	30.00
—With Dusty Walker; Microgroove 33 1/3 rpm 7-inch single					
❏ 1-599	Scottish Samba/Never Had a Worry	1950	7.50	15.00	30.00
—Microgroove 33 1/3 rpm 7-inch single					
❏ 1-630 (?)	A Simple Melody/I Still Get a Thrill	1950	7.50	15.00	30.00
—Microgroove 33 1/3 rpm 7-inch single					
❏ 1-660 (?)	I Didn't Know What Time It Was/I'll Always Love You	1950	7.50	15.00	30.00
—Microgroove 33 1/3 rpm 7-inch single					
❏ 1-690 (?)	Cotton Candy and a Toy Balloon/1812	1950	7.50	15.00	30.00
—Microgroove 33 1/3 rpm 7-inch single					
❏ 1-719	Tunnel of Love/With the Wind and the Rain in Your Hair	1950	7.50	15.00	30.00
—Microgroove 33 1/3 rpm 7-inch single					
❏ 1-759	Can Anyone Explain? (No! No! No!)/Dream a Little Dream of Me	1950	7.50	15.00	30.00
—Microgroove 33 1/3 rpm 7-inch single					
❏ 6-759	Can Anyone Explain? (No! No! No!)/Dream a Little Dream of Me	1950	6.25	12.50	25.00
❏ 1-770 (?)	It's Easy to Remember/Don't Rock the Boat, Dear	1950	7.50	15.00	30.00
—Microgroove 33 1/3 rpm 7-inch single					
❏ 6-770 (?)	It's Easy to Remember/Don't Rock the Boat, Dear	1950	6.25	12.50	25.00

Number	Title (A Side/B Side)	Yr	VG	VG+	NM
DECCA					
❏ 32468	Crying Time/Rocky Top	1969	—	2.50	5.00
MERCURY					
❏ 73465	Me and Ole Crazy Bill/Wait a Little Longer	1974	—	2.00	4.00
PROJECT 3					
❏ 1313	All at Once It's Love/Loneliness Is My Lover	1967	—	3.00	6.00
❏ 1328	Trains and Boats and Planes/Faces and Voices	1968	—	3.00	6.00
RCA VICTOR					
❏ 19-0001	You're Just in Love/(B-side unknown)	1951	6.25	12.50	25.00
—With Russell Nype; "Green Label Series" issue					
❏ 47-3978	My Heart Cries for You/Nobody's Chasing Me	1950	5.00	10.00	20.00
❏ 47-4015	Wait for Me/Down in Nashville, Tennessee	1951	5.00	10.00	20.00
❏ 47-4019	A Penny a Kiss/In Your Arms	1951	5.00	10.00	20.00
—With Tony Martin					
❏ 47-4045	I'm Through with Love/Makin' Whoopee	1951	3.75	7.50	15.00
❏ 47-4046	Orchids in the Moonlight/Around the Corner	1951	3.75	7.50	15.00
❏ 47-4047	My Isle of Golden Dreams/Wonder Where My Baby Is Tonight	1951	3.75	7.50	15.00
—The above three comprise a box set					
❏ 47-4060	Lonesome Gal/Too Late Now	1951	5.00	10.00	20.00
❏ 47-4107	Cause I Love You/Three Cornered Tune	1951	5.00	10.00	20.00
❏ 47-4136	I Wish, I Wish/The Kissing Song	1951	3.75	7.50	15.00
—With Tony Martin					
❏ 47-4174	Sweet Violets/If You Turn Me Down	1951	5.00	10.00	20.00
❏ 47-4175	Ten Thousand Miles/How Many Times	1951	3.75	7.50	15.00
❏ 47-4233	It's All in the Game/Stay Awhile	1951	3.75	7.50	15.00
❏ 47-4286	Getting to Know You/End of a Love Affair	1951	3.75	7.50	15.00
❏ 47-4317	The Lie-De-Lie Song/Oh How I Needed You Joe	1951	3.75	7.50	15.00
❏ 47-4345	Manhattan/If You Catch a Little Cold	1951	3.75	7.50	15.00
—With Tony Martin					
❏ 47-4421	Life Is a Beautiful Thing/Why Should I Believe in Love	1951	3.75	7.50	15.00
❏ 47-4434	Saturday Night in Punkin' Crick/Life Is a Beautiful Thing	1951	3.00	6.00	12.00
❏ 47-4436	Cheres/Pure Night	1951	3.00	6.00	12.00
—B-side by Alan Young					
❏ 47-4437	Marshmallow Moon/Why Should I Believe in Love	1951	3.00	6.00	12.00
—The above three are 75% of a box set					
❏ 47-4478	Until/Take Me Home	1952	3.00	6.00	12.00
❏ 47-4493	Marshmallow Moon/Warm Hearted Woman	1952	3.00	6.00	12.00
❏ 47-4561	Double Shuffle/Senator from Tennessee	1952	5.00	10.00	20.00
—With Tex Williams					
❏ 47-4666	I Am a Heart/To Be Loved by You	1952	3.00	6.00	12.00
❏ 47-4718	No Other Girl for Me/If Someone Had Told Me	1952	3.00	6.00	12.00
—With Tony Martin					
❏ 47-4719	Delicado/The World Has a Promise	1952	3.00	6.00	12.00
❏ 47-4768	West of the Mountains/From the Time You Say Goodbye	1952	3.00	6.00	12.00
❏ 47-4926	Blues in Advance/Bella Musica	1952	3.00	6.00	12.00
❏ 47-4992	Keep It a Secret/Hi-Lili, Hi-Lo	1952	3.00	6.00	12.00
❏ 47-5176	Let Me Know/Salomay	1953	3.00	6.00	12.00
❏ 47-5247	Sweet Thing/Why Come Crying to Me	1953	3.00	6.00	12.00
❏ 47-5335	I'm Your Girl/Marriage-Type Love	1953	3.00	6.00	12.00
❏ 47-5390	Blue Canary/Eternally	1953	3.00	6.00	12.00
❏ 47-5438	Choo Choo Train/Reflections on the Water	1953	3.00	6.00	12.00
❏ 47-5515	Changing Partners/Think	1953	3.00	6.00	12.00
❏ 47-5622	I'll Hate Myself in the Morning/Pass the Jam, Sam	1954	3.00	6.00	12.00
❏ 47-5725	Come Back to My Arms/This Must Be the Place	1954	3.00	6.00	12.00
❏ 47-5755	Three Coins in the Fountain/Pakistan	1954	3.00	6.00	12.00
❏ 47-5825	Tempting/Anyplace I Hang My Hat Is Home	1954	3.00	6.00	12.00
❏ 47-5838	If I Give My Heart to You/Tempting	1954	3.00	6.00	12.00
❏ 47-5863	I Have to Tell You/Never Underestimate Melody of Love	1954	3.00	6.00	12.00
❏ 47-5975	You're Getting to Be a Habit with Me	1955	2.50	5.00	10.00
—With Tony Martin					
❏ 47-6010	Then I'll Be Happy/The Stow-Away	1955	2.50	5.00	10.00
❏ 47-6077	Whatever Lola Wants (Lola Gets)/Church Twice on Sundays	1955	2.50	5.00	10.00
❏ 47-6266	Love and Marriage/Compare	1955	2.50	5.00	10.00
❏ 47-6360	Stolen Love/That's All There Is to That	1955	2.50	5.00	10.00
❏ 47-6469	I Could Have Danced All Night/What a Heavenly Lover	1956	2.50	5.00	10.00
❏ 47-6683	High Heels/The Whistling Tree	1956	2.50	5.00	10.00
❏ 47-6733	A New-Fangled Tango/I'll Come Back	1956	2.50	5.00	10.00
❏ 47-6792	Chantez-Chantez (Shan-Tay, "Sing")/Honkytonk Heart	1957	2.50	5.00	10.00
❏ 47-6897	The Cattle Call/Promises, Promises	1957	2.50	5.00	10.00
❏ 47-6980	Fascination/Till	1957	2.50	5.00	10.00
❏ 47-7056	I'll Never Say "Never Again" Again/The Kiss That Rocked the Cradle	1957	2.50	5.00	10.00
❏ 47-7138	I Never Left Your Arms/Thirteen Men	1958	2.50	5.00	10.00
❏ 47-7211	The Secret of Happiness/It's the Second Time You Meet That Matters	1958	2.50	5.00	10.00
❏ 47-7349	I'm Sitting on Top of the World/Scene of the Crime	1958	2.50	5.00	10.00
❏ 47-6077 [PS]	Whatever Lola Wants (Lola Gets)/Church Twice on Sundays	1955	6.25	12.50	25.00
—Special "This Is Her Life" promotional sleeve					

7-Inch Extended Plays

Number	Title (A Side/B Side)	Yr	VG	VG+	NM
CHEVROLET					
❏ 2886/7	You Meet The Nicest People/Jingle Bells//Silent Night/The Coventry Carol	1960	2.50	5.00	10.00
—7-inch 33 1/3 rpm, small hole record from Capitol Custom Services					
❏ 2886/7 [PS]	Season's Best	1960	2.50	5.00	10.00
COLUMBIA					
❏ B-2539	Buttons and Bows/Better Luck Next Time//Little White Lies/I'll Be Seeing You	195?	3.00	6.00	12.00
❏ B-2539	Dinah Shore (Hall of Fame Series)	195?	3.00	6.00	12.00
RCA VICTOR					
❏ DJ-56 [DJ]	Chantez-Chantez/Honkytonk Heart//Too Much/Playing for Keeps	1956	50.00	100.00	200.00
—B-side tracks by Elvis Presley; white label; each side is labeled with the corresponding nuimber for the regular 45 rpm issue					

S

Number	Title (A Side/B Side)	Yr	VG	VG+	NM
☐ EPA-405	Blues in the Night/Wabash Blues//I Got It Bad and That Ain't Good/The Birth of the Blues	1952	3.75	7.50	15.00
☐ EPA-405 [PS]	Dinah Shore Sings the Blues, Vol. 1	1952	3.75	7.50	15.00
☐ EPA-411	Hello, Young Lovers/Getting to Know You//I Whistle a Merry Tune/Shall We Dance	195?	3.00	6.00	12.00
☐ EPA-411 [PS]	Hits from "The King and I"	195?	3.00	6.00	12.00
☐ EPA-4119	Opening/You Meet the Nicest People/Have Yourself a Merry Little Christmas//Christmas Party/Happy Christmas Little Friend/Closing	1957	3.00	6.00	12.00
☐ EPA-4119 [PS]	You Meet the Nicest People at Christmas	1957	3.00	6.00	12.00
Albums					
BAINBRIDGE					
☐ 6232	Once Upon a Summertime	198?	2.50	5.00	10.00
CAPITOL					
☐ ST 1247 [S]	Dinah, Yes Indeed	1959	6.25	12.50	25.00
☐ T 1247 [M]	Dinah, Yes Indeed	1959	5.00	10.00	20.00
☐ ST 1296 [S]	Somebody Loves Me	1959	6.25	12.50	25.00
☐ T 1296 [M]	Somebody Loves Me	1959	5.00	10.00	20.00
☐ ST 1354 [S]	Dinah Sings Some Blues with Red	1960	7.50	15.00	30.00
☐ T 1354 [M]	Dinah Sings Some Blues with Red	1960	6.25	12.50	25.00
☐ ST 1422 [S]	Dinah Sings/Previn Plays	1960	6.25	12.50	25.00
☐ T 1422 [M]	Dinah Sings/Previn Plays	1960	5.00	10.00	20.00
☐ ST 1655 [S]	Dinah Down Home	1962	6.25	12.50	25.00
☐ T 1655 [M]	Dinah Down Home	1962	5.00	10.00	20.00
☐ ST 1704 [S]	The Fabulous Hits of Dinah Shore	1962	3.75	7.50	15.00
—Black label with colorband, logo at top					
☐ ST 1704 [S]	The Fabulous Hits of Dinah Shore	1962	6.25	12.50	25.00
—Black label with colorband, logo at left					
☐ T 1704 [M]	The Fabulous Hits of Dinah Shore	1962	3.00	6.00	12.00
—Black label with colorband, logo at top					
☐ T 1704 [M]	The Fabulous Hits of Dinah Shore	1962	5.00	10.00	20.00
—Black label with colorband, logo at left					
COLUMBIA					
☐ CL 6004 [10]	Dinah Shore Sings	1949	12.50	25.00	50.00
☐ CL 6069 [10]	Reminiscing	1949	12.50	25.00	50.00
☐ C 34395	The Best of Dinah Shore	1977	2.50	5.00	10.00
HARMONY					
☐ HL 7010 [M]	Dinah Shore Sings Cole Porter and Richard Rodgers	195?	5.00	10.00	20.00
☐ HL 7188 [M]	Buttons and Bows	195?	3.75	7.50	15.00
☐ HL 7239 [M]	Lavender Blue	1959	3.75	7.50	15.00
PICKWICK					
☐ SPC-3524	It's So Nice to Have a Man Around the House	197?	2.00	4.00	8.00
PROJECT 3					
☐ PR-5018 SD	Songs for Sometime Losers	1968	3.75	7.50	15.00
RCA VICTOR					
☐ LPM-1154 [M]	Holding Hands at Midnight	1955	7.50	15.00	30.00
☐ ANL1-1158	The Best of Dinah Shore	1976	2.50	5.00	10.00
☐ LPM-1214 [M]	Bouquet of Blues	1956	7.50	15.00	30.00
☐ LPM-1719 [M]	Moments Like These	1958	6.25	12.50	25.00
☐ LPM-3103 [10]	Dinah Shore Sings the Blues	1953	10.00	20.00	40.00
☐ LPM-3214 [10]	The Dinah Shore TV Show	1954	10.00	20.00	40.00
REPRISE					
☐ R-6150 [M]	The Lower East Side Revisited	1965	3.00	6.00	12.00
☐ RS-6150 [S]	The Lower East Side Revisited	1965	3.75	7.50	15.00
SEAGULL					
☐ LG-8203	Oh Lonesome Me	198?	2.50	5.00	10.00
STANYAN					
☐ 10071	Dinah Sings the Blues	197?	2.50	5.00	10.00
☐ 10125	Once Upon a Summertime	197?	2.50	5.00	10.00
☐ 10139	For Always	1977	2.50	5.00	10.00

SHORT CROSS
Albums
GRIZZLY

Number	Title (A Side/B Side)	Yr	VG	VG+	NM
☐ S-16013	Arising	1970	62.50	125.00	250.00

SHOTGUN EXPRESS With ROD STEWART.
45s
UPTOWN

Number	Title (A Side/B Side)	Yr	VG	VG+	NM
☐ 747	I Could Feel the Whole World Turn/Curtains	1967	7.50	15.00	30.00

SHOTGUN LTD.
45s
PROPHESY

Number	Title (A Side/B Side)	Yr	VG	VG+	NM
☐ 55004	River of Hope/(B-side unknown)	1971	2.00	4.00	8.00
Albums					
PROPHESY					
☐ 6050	Shotgun Ltd.	1971	5.00	10.00	20.00

SHOWMEN, THE With General Johnson, later of CHAIRMEN OF THE BOARD.
45s
AMY

Number	Title (A Side/B Side)	Yr	VG	VG+	NM
☐ 11036	Action/What Would It Take	1968	2.00	4.00	8.00
IMPERIAL					
☐ 66033	It Will Stand/Country Fool	1964	3.00	6.00	12.00
☐ 66071	Country Fool/Somebody Help Me	1964	3.00	6.00	12.00
LIBERTY					
☐ 56166	It Will Stand/Country Fool	1970	—	3.00	6.00
MINIT					
☐ 632	It Will Stand/Country Fool	1961	5.00	10.00	20.00
—Black label					
☐ 632	It Will Stand/Country Fool	1961	7.50	15.00	30.00
—Orange label					
☐ 643	The Wrong Girl/Fate Planned It This Way	1962	12.50	25.00	50.00
☐ 647	Com'n Home/I Love You, Can't You See	1962	6.25	12.50	25.00
☐ 654	True Fine Mama/The Owl Sees You	1962	6.25	12.50	25.00
☐ 662	39-21-46/Swish Fish	1963	6.25	12.50	25.00
☐ 32007	39-21-46/Swish Fish	1966	2.50	5.00	10.00
SWAN					
☐ 4213	In Paradise/Take It Baby	1965	2.50	5.00	10.00
☐ 4219	Our Love Will Grow/You're Everything	1965	2.50	5.00	10.00
☐ 4241	Please Try and Understand/Honey House	1966	2.50	5.00	10.00
UNITED ARTISTS					
☐ 0100	It Will Stand/I'm a Happy Man	1973	—	2.50	5.00
—"Silver Spotlight Series" reissue; B-side by the Jive Five					

Number	Title (A Side/B Side)	Yr	VG	VG+	NM
Albums					
COLLECTABLES					
☐ COL-5162	Golden Classics	198?	2.50	5.00	10.00

SHUFFLES, THE
45s
RAYCO

Number	Title (A Side/B Side)	Yr	VG	VG+	NM
☐ 508	Do You Remember My Darling/Dancin' Little Girl	1963	50.00	100.00	200.00

SHUT DOWNS, THE
45s
DIMENSION

Number	Title (A Side/B Side)	Yr	VG	VG+	NM
☐ 1016	Four on the Floor/Beach Buggy	1963	6.25	12.50	25.00
KARSONG					
☐ 501	Four on the Floor/Straightaway	1963	12.50	25.00	50.00

SICKNICKS, THE
45s
AMY

Number	Title (A Side/B Side)	Yr	VG	VG+	NM
☐ 824	The Presidential Press Conference (Part 1)/The Presidential Press Conference (Part 2)	1961	3.75	7.50	15.00
☐ 824 [PS]	The Presidential Press Conference (Part 1)/The Presidential Press Conference (Part 2)	1961	6.25	12.50	25.00
☐ 831	Wadja Say Mr. K (Part 1)/Wadja Say Mr. K (Part 2)	1961	3.75	7.50	15.00
Albums					
AMY					
☐ 2 [M]	Sick #2	1961	7.50	15.00	30.00

SIDEKICKS, THE
45s
RCA VICTOR

Number	Title (A Side/B Side)	Yr	VG	VG+	NM
☐ 47-8864	Suspicions/Up on the Roof	1966	2.50	5.00	10.00
☐ 47-8969	Fifi the Flea/Not Now	1966	2.50	5.00	10.00
☐ 47-9079	He's My Friend/Miss Charlotte	1967	2.50	5.00	10.00
☐ 47-9174	Sight and Sound/You Gave Me Somebody to Love	1967	2.50	5.00	10.00
Albums					
RCA VICTOR					
☐ LPM-3712 [M]	Fifi the Flea	1966	5.00	10.00	20.00
☐ LSP-3712 [S]	Fifi the Flea	1966	6.25	12.50	25.00

SIDEWALK SURFERS, THE
45s
JUBILEE

Number	Title (A Side/B Side)	Yr	VG	VG+	NM
☐ 5496	Skate Board/Fun Last Summer	1965	12.50	25.00	50.00

SIDEWINDERS, THE
45s
RCA VICTOR

Number	Title (A Side/B Side)	Yr	VG	VG+	NM
☐ 48-1033	Rendezvous/O Miss Mary	1972	2.00	4.00	8.00
Albums					
RCA VICTOR					
☐ LSP-4694	The Sidewinders	1972	5.00	10.00	20.00

SIERRAS, THE
45s
DOT

Number	Title (A Side/B Side)	Yr	VG	VG+	NM
☐ 16569	Plan for Love/Then I'll Still Love You	1963	3.00	6.00	12.00
GOLDISC					
☐ G-4	I Should Have Loved You/I'll Believe It When I See It	1963	7.50	15.00	30.00
KNOX					
☐ 102	So Many Sleepless Nights/Nearer My Heart	1962	25.00	50.00	100.00
MAIL CALL					
☐ 2333/4	Stormy Weather/Chance	1963	50.00	100.00	200.00

SIGLER, BUNNY
12-Inch Singles
GOLD MIND

Number	Title (A Side/B Side)	Yr	VG	VG+	NM
☐ 501	Glad to Be Your Lover (8:48)/I'm Funkin' You Tonight (5:30)	1979	3.00	6.00	12.00
45s					
CRAIG					
☐ 501	I Won't Cry/Come On Home	1961	7.50	15.00	30.00
—As Bunny "Mr. Emotions" Sigler					
DECCA					
☐ 31880	Everything's Gonna Be All Right/For Cryin' Out Loud	1965	6.25	12.50	25.00
☐ 31947	Will You Love Me Tomorrow/Comparatively Speaking	1966	3.00	6.00	12.00
☐ 32183	Will You Love Me Tomorrow/Let Them Talk	1967	2.50	5.00	10.00
GOLD MIND					
☐ 4008	Let Me Party with You (Part 1) (Party, Party, Party)/Let Me Party with You (Part 2) (Party, Party, Party)	1977	—	2.50	5.00
☐ 4010	I Got What You Need/It's Time to Twist	1978	—	2.50	5.00
☐ 4012	Only You/Good Good Feeling	1978	—	3.00	6.00
—A-side with Loleatta Holloway; B-side is Holloway solo					
☐ 4014	Don't Even Try (Give It Up)/I'm a Fool	1978	—	2.50	5.00
☐ 4018	By the Way You Dance (I Knew It Was You)/Glad to Be Your Lover	1979	—	2.50	5.00
☐ 4020	I'm Funking You Tonight with My Music/Glad to Be Your Lover	1979	—	2.50	5.00
NEPTUNE					
☐ 14	Where Do the Lonely Go/Great Big Liar	1969	2.00	4.00	8.00
☐ 15	We're Only Human/Sure Didn't Take Long	1969	2.00	4.00	8.00
—With Cindy Scott					
☐ 24	Conquer the World Together/We're Only Human	1970	2.00	4.00	8.00
—With Cindy Scott					
☐ 25	Don't Stop Doing What You're Doing/Where Do the Lonely Go	1970	2.00	4.00	8.00
PARKWAY					
☐ 123	Girl Don't Make Me Wait/Always in the Wrong Place (At the Wrong Time)	1966	2.50	5.00	10.00

Number	Title (A Side/B Side)	Yr	VG	VG+	NM
❏ 153	Let the Good Times Roll & Feel So Good/There's No Love Left (In This Old Heart of Mine)	1967	3.00	6.00	12.00
❏ 6000	Lovey Dovey & You're So Fine/Sunny Sunday	1967	2.50	5.00	10.00
❏ 6001	Follow Your Heart/Can You Dig It	1967	2.50	5.00	10.00

PHILADELPHIA INT'L.

Number	Title	Yr	VG	VG+	NM
❏ 3505	Everybody Needs Good Lovin' (Part 1)/Everybody Needs Good Lovin' (Part 2)	1971	—	3.00	6.00
❏ 3512	Conquer the World Together/We Gotta Good Thing Goin'	1971	—	3.00	6.00

—With Dee Dee Sharp

❏ 3519	Heaven Knows I've Changed/Regina	1972	—	3.00	6.00
❏ 3523	Tossin' and Turnin'/Picture Us	1972	—	3.00	6.00
❏ 3532	Theme from "Five Fingers of Death"/Regina	1973	—	3.00	6.00
❏ 3536	That's How Long I'll Be Loving You/Heaven Knows I've Changed	1973	—	3.00	6.00
❏ 3545	Love Train (Part 1)/Love Train (Part 2)	1974	—	3.00	6.00
❏ 3554	Keep Smilin'/Somebody Free	1974	—	3.00	6.00
❏ 3560	Shake Your Booty/Your Love Is Good	1975	—	3.00	6.00
❏ 3575	Somebody Free/That's How Long I'll Be Loving You	1975	—	3.00	6.00
❏ 3582	Jingle Bells (Part 1)/Jingle Bells (Part 2)	1975	—	2.50	5.00
❏ 3597	My Music/Can't Believe That You Love Me	1976	—	3.00	6.00
❏ 3608	Somebody Loves You/Woman, Woman	1976	—	3.00	6.00

SALSOUL

❏ 2114	How Can I Tell Her (It's Over)/Since the Day I First Saw You	1980	—	2.00	4.00
❏ 2125	Super Duper Duper Superman/Kool Aid	1980	—	2.00	4.00

V-TONE

❏ 500	Family Dance/Hold On	196?	5.00	10.00	20.00

Albums

GOLD MIND

❏ 7502	Let Me Party with You	1978	3.00	6.00	12.00
❏ 9503	I've Always Wanted to Sing...Not Just Write Songs	1979	3.00	6.00	12.00

PARKWAY

❏ P-50000 [M]	Let the Good Times Roll	1967	10.00	20.00	40.00
❏ PS-50000 [S]	Let the Good Times Roll	1967	10.00	20.00	40.00

PHILADELPHIA INT'L.

❏ KZ 32589	That's How Long I'll Be Loving You	1974	3.75	7.50	15.00
❏ KZ 33249	Keep Smilin'	1974	3.75	7.50	15.00
❏ PZ 34267	My Music	1976	3.75	7.50	15.00

SALSOUL

❏ SA-8531	Let It Snow	1980	3.00	6.00	12.00

SIGNATURES, THE
45s
NORMAN

❏ 210	Julie Is Her Name/Someone in Love	1957	75.00	150.00	300.00

WHIPPET

❏ 210	Julie Is Her Name/Someone in Love	1957	12.50	25.00	50.00

Albums

WARNER BROS.

❏ W 1250 [M]	The Signatures Sing In	1958	7.50	15.00	30.00
❏ WS 1250 [S]	The Signatures Sing In	1958	10.00	20.00	40.00
❏ W 1353 [M]	Prepare to Flip!	1959	7.50	15.00	30.00
❏ WS 1353 [S]	Prepare to Flip!	1959	10.00	20.00	40.00

WHIPPET

❏ WLP-702 [M]	The Signatures — Their Voices and Instruments	1957	15.00	30.00	60.00

SILBERMAN, BENEDICT, ORCHESTRA AND CHORUS
45s
PALETTE

❏ 5037	The Chipmunk Song/Lovers of Paris	1959	2.50	5.00	10.00

SILHOUETTES, THE
45s
ACE

❏ 552	I Sold My Heart to the Junkman/What Would You Do	1958	5.00	10.00	20.00
❏ 562	Evelyn/Never Will Part	1959	5.00	10.00	20.00

—As "Bill Horton and the Silhouettes"

EMBER

❏ 1029	Get a Job/I Am Lonely	1958	7.50	15.00	30.00

—Red label

❏ 1029	Get a Job/I Am Lonely	1958	10.00	20.00	40.00

—Orange label

❏ 1029	Get a Job/I Am Lonely	1960	5.00	10.00	20.00

—Black label

❏ 1032	Headin' for the Poorhouse/Miss Thing	1958	5.00	10.00	20.00
❏ 1037	Bing Bong/Voodoo Eyes	1958	5.00	10.00	20.00

GOODWAY

❏ 101	Not Me Baby/Gaucho Serenade	1966	50.00	100.00	200.00

—As "The New Silhouettes"

GRAND

❏ 142	Wish I Could Be There/Move On Over	1956	50.00	100.00	200.00

IMPERIAL

❏ 5899	The Push/Which Way Did She Go	1962	3.00	6.00	12.00

JUNIOR

❏ 391	Get a Job/I Am Lonely	1957	150.00	300.00	600.00

—Blue label (second press)

❏ 391	Get a Job/I Am Lonely	1957	200.00	400.00	800.00

—Brown label (first press)

❏ 396	I Sold My Heart to the Junkman/What Would You Do	1958	25.00	50.00	100.00
❏ 400	Evelyn/Never Will Part	1959	50.00	100.00	200.00
❏ 993	Your Love/Rent Man	1963	7.50	15.00	30.00

LANA

❏ 108	Get a Job/I Am Lonely	196?	2.00	4.00	8.00

—Oldies reissue

LOST-NITE

❏ 254	Get a Job/I Am Lonely	196?	—	2.50	5.00

—Reissue

❏ 418	Bing Bong/Voodoo Eyes	197?	—	2.50	5.00

—Reissue

UNITED ARTISTS

❏ 147	I Sold My Heart to the Junkman/What Would You Do	1958	—	—	—

—Canceled

Albums

GOODWAY

❏ GLP-100	The Silhouettes 1958-1968/Get a Job	1968	75.00	150.00	300.00

SILK   Also see MICHAEL STANLEY BAND.
45s
DECCA

❏ 32829	Come Over Here/Falling in Love Isn't Easy	1971	2.00	4.00	8.00

Albums

ABC

❏ S-694	Smooth As Raw Silk	1969	6.25	12.50	25.00

SILKIE, THE
45s
FONTANA

❏ 1525	You've Got to Hide Your Love Away/City Winds	1965	3.75	7.50	15.00

—Light blue label; A-side was produced by John Lennon and Paul McCartney, with the two and George Harrison playing along

❏ 1525	You've Got to Hide Your Love Away/City Wind	1965	5.00	10.00	20.00

—Dark blue label

❏ 1536	The Keys to My Soul/Leave Me to Cry	1965	2.50	5.00	10.00
❏ 1551	Born to Be With You/I'm So Sorry	1966	2.50	5.00	10.00

Albums

FONTANA

❏ MGF 27548 [M]	You've Got to Hide Your Love Away	1965	10.00	20.00	40.00

—With purplish, black and white cover

❏ MGF 27548 [M]	You've Got to Hide Your Love Away	1965	12.50	25.00	50.00

—With full-color cover

❏ SRF 67548 [R]	You've Got to Hide Your Love Away	1965	7.50	15.00	30.00

—With purplish, black and white cover

❏ SRF 67548 [R]	You've Got to Hide Your Love Away	1965	10.00	20.00	40.00

—With full-color cover

SILLY SURFERS, THE
Albums
MERCURY

❏ MG-20977 [M]	The Sounds of the Silly Surfers	1965	20.00	40.00	80.00
❏ SR-60977 [S]	The Sounds of the Silly Surfers	1965	25.00	50.00	100.00

SILLY SURFERS, THE / THE WEIRD-OHS
Albums
HAIRY

❏ 101 [M]	The Sounds of the Silly Surfers/The Sounds of the Weird-Ohs	1964	37.50	75.00	150.00

SILVA TONES, THE
45s
ARGO

❏ 5281	Chi-Wa-Wa (That's All I Want from You)/Roses Are Blooming	1957	6.25	12.50	25.00
❏ 5281	That's All I Want from You/Roses Are Blooming	1957	7.50	15.00	30.00

MONARCH

❏ 615	That's All I Want from You/Roses Are Blooming	1957	7.50	15.00	30.00

—Black label

❏ 615	That's All I Want from You/Weepin' and a-Wailin'	1957	12.50	25.00	50.00

—Yellow label

SILVER APPLES
45s
KAPP

❏ 923	Whirly Bird/Oscillations	1968	2.00	4.00	8.00

Albums

KAPP

❏ KS-3562	Silver Apples	1968	7.50	15.00	30.00

—Add 1/3 if poster is enclosed

❏ KS-3584	Contact	1969	7.50	15.00	30.00

SILVER CONVENTION
12-Inch Singles
MIDSONG INT'L.

❏ L33-1977 [DJ]	Spend the Night with Me (9:27)/Mission to Venus (8:45)	1978	3.75	7.50	15.00
❏ JD-11027 [DJ]	Hollywood Music/(B-side unknown)	1976	3.75	7.50	15.00
❏ 13906	Spend the Night with Me (9:27)/Mission to Venus (8:45)	1978	3.00	6.00	12.00

45s
MIDLAND INT'L.

❏ MB-10212	Save Me/Save Me Again	1975	—	2.00	4.00
❏ MB-10339	Fly, Robin, Fly/Chains of Love	1975	—	2.00	4.00

—Second pressing: "Fly, Robin, Fly" is 3:05, matrix number is 10339-Z

❏ MB-10339	Fly, Robin, Fly/Chains of Love	1975	—	3.00	6.00

—First pressing: "Fly, Robin, Fly" is 3:45, matrix number is 10339-A

❏ MB-10571	Get Up and Boogie (That's Right)/Son of a Gun	1976	—	2.00	4.00

—Second pressing: "Get Up and Boogie" is under three minutes long

❏ MB-10571	Get Up and Boogie (That's Right)/Son of a Gun	1976	—	3.00	6.00

—First pressing: "Get Up and Boogie" is 4:05, matrix number is 10571-A

❏ MB-10571 [PS]	Get Up and Boogie (That's Right)/Son of a Gun	1976	—	3.00	6.00
❏ MB-10723	No, No Joe/Another Girl	1976	—	2.00	4.00
❏ MB-10849	Thank You Mr. D.J./Dancing in the Aisles (Take Me Higher)	1976	—	2.00	4.00

MIDSONG INT'L.

❏ GB-10939	Fly, Robin, Fly/Get Up and Boogie (That's Right)	1977	—	—	3.00

—Gold Standard Series

❏ MB-10972	Telegram/(B-side unknown)	1977	—	2.00	4.00
❏ MB-11062	Save Me '77/Hotshot	1977	—	2.00	4.00
❏ 40896	Breakfast in Bed/Spend the Night with Me	1978	—	2.00	4.00

Albums

MIDLAND INT'L.

❏ BKL1-1129	Save Me	1975	2.50	5.00	10.00
❏ BKL1-1369	Silver Convention	1976	2.50	5.00	10.00
❏ BKL1-1824	Madhouse	1976	2.50	5.00	10.00

S

Number	Title (A Side/B Side)	Yr	VG	VG+	NM

MIDSONG INT'L.

Number	Title (A Side/B Side)	Yr	VG	VG+	NM
❏ BXL1-1129	Save Me	1978	2.00	4.00	8.00

—*Reissue with new prefix*

❏ BXL1-1369	Silver Convention	1978	2.00	4.00	8.00

—*Reissue with new prefix*

❏ BXL1-1824	Madhouse	1978	2.00	4.00	8.00

—*Reissue with new prefix*

❏ BKL1-2296	Golden Girls	1977	2.50	5.00	10.00
❏ BXL1-2296	Golden Girls	1978	2.00	4.00	8.00

—*Reissue with new prefix*

SILVER DUST
45s
SUN

❏ 1124	Father and Son/Castle in the Sun	1971	—	2.50	5.00

SILVER FLEET A precursor to 10CC.
45s
UNI

❏ 55271	Look Out World/C'mon Plane	1971	6.25	12.50	25.00

SILVERSTEIN, SHEL
45s
COLUMBIA

❏ 10053	Everybody's Makin' It Big But Me/The Man Who Got No Sign	1974	—	2.50	5.00
❏ 10153	Sahra Cynthia Sylvia Stout Would Not Take the Garbage Out/The Man Who Got No Sign	1975	—	2.50	5.00
❏ 45450	A Front Row Seat to Hear Ole Johnny Sing/26 Second Song	1971	—	3.00	6.00
❏ 45772	Sahra Cynthia Sylvia Stout Would Not Take the Garbage Out/Stacey Brown Got Two	1973	—	3.00	6.00
❏ 45885	All About You/Peace Proposal	1973	—	3.00	6.00

RCA VICTOR

❏ 47-9844	Policeman, Woman, Taxicab/Three Legged Man	1970	2.00	4.00	8.00
❏ 74-0158	A Boy Named Sue/Somebody Stole My Rig	1969	2.00	4.00	8.00

Albums
ATLANTIC

❏ 8072 [M]	Inside Folk Songs	1962	7.50	15.00	30.00
❏ SD 8072 [S]	Inside Folk Songs	1962	10.00	20.00	40.00

CADET

❏ LP 4052 [M]	I'm So Good I Don't Have to Brag!	1965	6.25	12.50	25.00
❏ LPS 4052 [S]	I'm So Good I Don't Have to Brag!	1965	7.50	15.00	30.00
❏ LP 4054 [M]	Drain My Brain	1966	6.25	12.50	25.00
❏ LPS 4054 [S]	Drain My Brain	1966	7.50	15.00	30.00

COLUMBIA

❏ KC 31119	Freakin' at the Freakers' Ball	1972	3.75	7.50	15.00
❏ PC 31119	Freakin' at the Freakers' Ball	1979	2.00	4.00	8.00

—*Budget-line reissue*

❏ FC 39412	Where the Sidewalk Ends	1984	2.50	5.00	10.00
❏ 9C9 39611 [PD]	Where the Sidewalk Ends	1984	6.25	12.50	25.00

—*Picture disc*

❏ FC 40219	A Light in the Attic	1985	2.50	5.00	10.00

CRESTVIEW

❏ CRV 804 [M]	Stag Party	1963	6.25	12.50	25.00
❏ CRS 7804 [S]	Stag Party	1963	7.50	15.00	30.00

ELEKTRA

❏ EKL-176 [M]	Hairy Jazz	1961	25.00	50.00	100.00
❏ EKS-7176 [S]	Hairy Jazz	1961	37.50	75.00	150.00

FLYING FISH

❏ FF-211	Conch Train Robbery	1980	3.00	6.00	12.00

JANUS

❏ 2JLS 3052 [(2)]	Crouching on the Outside	1973	3.75	7.50	15.00

PARACHUTE

❏ RRLP-9007	Songs and Stories	1978	3.00	6.00	12.00
❏ 20512 [DJ]	Selected Cuts from Songs and Stories	1978	5.00	10.00	20.00

—*Promo-only EP*
RCA VICTOR

❏ LSP-4192	A Boy Named Sue (And His Other Country Songs)	1969	5.00	10.00	20.00

SIMMONS, "JUMPIN'" GENE
45s
AGP

❏ 119	Back Home Again/Don't Worry About Me	1969	2.00	4.00	8.00

CHECKER

❏ 948	Bad Boy Willie/Goin' Back to Memphis	1960	3.00	6.00	12.00

DELTUNE

❏ 1201	Why Didn't I Think of That/Tennessee Party Time	1977	2.00	4.00	8.00

—*As "Gene Simmons"*
EPIC

❏ 10601	She's There When I Come Home/Magnolia Street	1970	—	3.00	6.00

HI

❏ 2034	Teddy Bear/Your True Love	1961	2.50	5.00	10.00
❏ 2050	Caldonia/Be Her Number One	1962	2.50	5.00	10.00
❏ 2076	Haunted House/Hey, Hey Little Girl	1964	3.75	7.50	15.00

—*As "Gene Simmons"*

❏ 2076	Haunted House/Hey, Hey Little Girl	1964	3.75	7.50	15.00

—*As "Jumpin' Gene Simmons"*

❏ 2080	The Dodo/The Jump	1964	2.50	5.00	10.00
❏ 2086	Skinnie Minnie/I'm a Ramblin' Man	1965	2.50	5.00	10.00
❏ 2092	Mattie Rae/Folsom Prison Blues	1965	2.50	5.00	10.00
❏ 2102	The Batman/Bossy Boss	1966	3.75	7.50	15.00
❏ 2113	Go On Shoes/Keep That Meat in the Pan	1966	2.50	5.00	10.00

MALA

❏ 12012	I'm Just a Loser/Lila	1968	2.50	5.00	10.00

SANDY

❏ 1027	The Waiting Game/Shenandoah Waltz	1959	5.00	10.00	20.00

—*As "Morris Gene Simmons"*

SUN

❏ 299	Drinkin' Wine/I Done Told You	1958	37.50	75.00	150.00

—*As "Gene Simmons"*
Albums
HI

❏ HL 2018 [M]	Jumpin' Gene Simmons	1964	12.50	25.00	50.00
❏ SHL 32018 [S]	Jumpin' Gene Simmons	1964	17.50	35.00	70.00

SIMON, CARLY Also see THE SIMON SISTERS.
12-Inch Singles
ELEKTRA

❏ 11399 [DJ]	Tranquillo (same on both sides)	1978	2.50	5.00	10.00

EPIC

❏ 05277	My New Boyfriend (3 versions)	1985	—	3.00	6.00

45s
ARISTA

❏ 2083	Better Not Tell Her/Happy Birthday	1990	—	—	3.00
❏ 2164	Life Is Eternal/We Just Got Here	1990	—	—	3.00
❏ 9525	Coming Around Again/Itsy Bitsy Spider	1986	—	—	3.00
❏ 9525 [PS]	Coming Around Again/Itsy Bitsy Spider	1986	—	2.00	4.00

—*Black and white photo of Carly Simon*

❏ 9525 [PS]	Coming Around Again/Itsy Bitsy Spider	1986	—	2.00	4.00

—*Color photo of Carly Simon*

❏ 9525 [PS]	Coming Around Again/Itsy Bitsy Spider	1986	2.00	4.00	8.00

—*With "Heartburn" movie scenes*

❏ 9587	Give Me All Night/Sleight of Hand	1987	—	—	3.00
❏ 9587 [PS]	Give Me All Night/Sleight of Hand	1987	—	—	3.00
❏ 9619	The Stuff That Dreams Are Made Of/As Time Goes By	1987	—	—	3.00
❏ 9619 [PS]	The Stuff That Dreams Are Made Of/As Time Goes By	1987	—	—	3.00
❏ 9653	All I Want Is You/On a Hot Summer Night	1987	—	—	3.00
❏ 9653 [PS]	All I Want Is You/On a Hot Summer Night	1987	—	—	3.00
❏ 9732 [DJ]	Do the Walls Come Down (same on both sides)	1988	—	2.50	5.00

—*Not released as stock copy on this number*

❏ 9732 [PS]	Do the Walls Come Down (same on both sides)	1988	—	2.50	5.00

—*Promo-only picture sleeve*

❏ 9754	You're So Vain/Do the Walls Come Down	1988	—	—	3.00
❏ 9754 [PS]	You're So Vain/Do the Walls Come Down	1988	—	—	3.00
❏ 9793	Let the River Run/The Turn of the Tide	1988	—	—	3.00
❏ 9793 [PS]	Let the River Run/The Turn of the Tide	1988	—	—	3.00

ELEKTRA

❏ 45246	Attitude Dancing/Are You Ticklish	1975	—	2.50	5.00
❏ 45248	Slave/Look Me in the Eyes	1975	—	—	—

—*Unreleased?*

❏ 45263	Waterfall/After the Storm	1975	—	2.50	5.00
❏ 45278	More and More/Love Out in the Street	1975	—	2.50	5.00
❏ 45325	It Keeps You Runnin'/Look Me in the Eyes	1976	—	2.00	4.00
❏ 45341	Half a Chance/Libby	1976	—	2.00	4.00

—*Butterfly label*

❏ 45341	Half a Chance/Libby	1976	—	2.50	5.00

—*Red label*

❏ 45413	Nobody Does It Better/After the Storm	1977	—	2.00	4.00
❏ 45477	You Belong to Me/In a Small Moment	1978	—	2.00	4.00
❏ 45477 [PS]	You Belong to Me/In a Small Moment	1978	—	3.00	6.00
❏ 45506	Devoted to You/Boys in the Trees	1978	—	2.00	4.00

—*A-side with James Taylor*

❏ 45544	Tranquillo (Melt My Heart)/Back Down to Earth	1978	—	2.00	4.00
❏ 45724	That's the Way I've Always Heard It Should Be/Alone	1971	—	3.00	6.00
❏ 45748	Our First Day Together/Share the Land	1971	—	—	—

—*Unreleased*

❏ 45759	Anticipation/The Garden	1971	—	3.00	6.00
❏ 45774	Legend in Your Own Time/Julie Through the Glass	1972	—	3.00	6.00
❏ 45796	The Girl You Think You Are/Share the Land	1972	—	3.00	6.00
❏ 45824	You're So Vain/His Friends Are More Than Fond of Robin	1972	—	3.00	6.00
❏ 45843	The Right Thing to Do/We Have No Secrets	1973	—	2.50	5.00
❏ 45880	Mockingbird/Grownup	1974	—	2.50	5.00

—*A-side with James Taylor*

❏ 45887	Haven't Got Time for the Pain/Mind on My Man	1974	—	2.50	5.00
❏ 46051	Vengeance/Love You by Heart	1979	—	2.00	4.00
❏ 46051 [PS]	Vengeance/Love You by Heart	1979	—	2.50	5.00
❏ 46514	Spy/Pure Sin	1979	—	2.00	4.00
❏ 69953	Hidin' Away/Fight for It	1982	—	2.00	4.00

—*With Jesse Colin Young*

❏ 69953 [PS]	Hidin' Away/Fight for It	1982	—	3.00	6.00

—*With Jesse Colin Young*
EPIC

❏ 05419	Tired of Being Blonde/Black Honeymoon	1985	—	—	3.00
❏ 05419 [PS]	Tired of Being Blonde/Black Honeymoon	1985	—	2.00	4.00
❏ 05596	My New Boyfriend/The Wives Are in Connecticut	1985	—	—	3.00

MIRAGE

❏ 4051	Why/Why	1982	—	2.00	4.00

—*B-side by Chic*

❏ 4051 [PS]	Why/Why	1982	—	3.00	6.00
❏ 99963	Why/(Instrumental)	1982	—	2.00	4.00

PLANET

❏ YB-13779	Someone Waits for You/(B-side unknown)	1984	—	2.00	4.00

WARNER BROS.

❏ 29428	Hello Big Man/Dawn You Get to Me	1983	—	2.00	4.00
❏ 29484	You Know What to Do/Orpheus	1983	—	2.00	4.00
❏ 29484 [PS]	You Know What to Do/Orpheus	1983	—	2.50	5.00
❏ 49518	Jesse/Stardust	1980	—	2.00	4.00
❏ 49518 [PS]	Jesse/Stardust	1980	—	2.50	5.00
❏ 49630	Take Me As I Am/James	1981	—	2.00	4.00
❏ 49689	Come Upstairs/Them	1981	—	2.00	4.00
❏ 49880	From the Heart/Hurt	1981	—	2.00	4.00
❏ 50027	Body and Soul/Get Along Without You Very Well	1982	—	2.00	4.00

Albums
ARISTA

❏ AL-8443	Coming Around Again	1987	2.00	4.00	8.00
❏ AL-8526	Greatest Hits Live	1988	2.00	4.00	8.00

Number	Title (A Side/B Side)	Yr	VG	VG+	NM
❏ AL-8582	My Romance	1990	3.00	6.00	12.00
❏ AL-8650	Have You Seen Me Lately?	1990	3.00	6.00	12.00
DIRECT DISK					
❏ SD-16608	Boys in the Trees	1980	12.50	25.00	50.00
—Audiophile vinyl					
ELEKTRA					
❏ 6E-109	The Best of Carly Simon	1977	2.00	4.00	8.00
—Reissue of 7E-1048					
❏ 6E-128	Boys in the Trees	1978	2.50	5.00	10.00
❏ 5E-506	Spy	1979	2.50	5.00	10.00
❏ 7E-1002	Hotcakes	1974	2.50	5.00	10.00
❏ EQ-1002 [Q]	Hotcakes	1974	5.00	10.00	20.00
❏ 7E-1033	Playing Possum	1975	2.50	5.00	10.00
❏ EQ-1033 [Q]	Playing Possum	1975	5.00	10.00	20.00
❏ 7E-1048	The Best of Carly Simon	1975	2.50	5.00	10.00
❏ EQ-1048 [Q]	The Best of Carly Simon	1975	5.00	10.00	20.00
❏ 7E-1064	Another Passenger	1976	2.50	5.00	10.00
❏ EQ-1064 [Q]	Another Passenger	1976	—	—	—
—Not released					
❏ EQ-4082 [Q]	Carly Simon	1974	5.00	10.00	20.00
❏ EQ-5049 [Q]	No Secrets	1974	5.00	10.00	20.00
❏ EKS-74082	Carly Simon	1971	3.00	6.00	12.00
❏ EKS-75016	Anticipation	1971	3.00	6.00	12.00
❏ EKS-75049	No Secrets	1972	3.00	6.00	12.00
—With lyrics on innersleeve					
❏ EKS-75049	No Secrets	1973	2.50	5.00	10.00
—Without lyrics on innersleeve					
EPIC					
❏ FE 39970	Spoiled Girl	1985	2.50	5.00	10.00
WARNER BROS.					
❏ BSK 3443	Come Upstairs	1980	2.50	5.00	10.00
❏ BSK 3592	Torch	1981	2.50	5.00	10.00
❏ 23886	Hello Big Man	1983	2.50	5.00	10.00

SIMON, JOE

12-Inch Singles

SPRING

Number	Title (A Side/B Side)	Yr	VG	VG+	NM
❏ 025 [DJ]	One Step at a Time (5:33) (3:39)	1977	3.75	7.50	15.00
❏ 057 [DJ]	Love Vibration (same on both sides)	1978	3.00	6.00	12.00

45s

COMPLEAT

Number	Title (A Side/B Side)	Yr	VG	VG+	NM
❏ 140	It Turns Me Inside Out/Morning, Noon and Night	1985	—	2.00	4.00
❏ 146	Mr. Right or Mr. Right Now/ Let Me Have My Way with You	1985	—	2.00	4.00
DOT					
❏ 16570	Just Like Yesterday/Only a Dream	1964	2.00	4.00	8.00
HUSH					
❏ 103	It's a Miracle/Land of Love	1960	3.00	6.00	12.00
❏ 104	Call My Name/Everybody Needs Somebody	1961	3.00	6.00	12.00
❏ 106	Pledge of Love/It's All Over	1961	3.00	6.00	12.00
❏ 107	I See Your Face/Troubles	1961	3.00	6.00	12.00
❏ 108	Land of Love/I Keep Remembering	1962	3.00	6.00	12.00
POSSE					
❏ 5001	Baby, When Love Is In Your Heart (It's In Your Eyes)/Are We Breaking Up	1980	—	2.50	5.00
❏ 5005	Glad You Came My Way/ I Don't Wanna Make Love	1980	—	2.50	5.00
❏ 5010	Are We Breaking Up/We're Together	1981	—	2.50	5.00
❏ 5014	Fallin' in Love with You/Magnolia	1981	—	2.50	5.00
❏ 5018	You Give Life to Me/(Instrumental)	1982	—	2.50	5.00
—With Clare Bathe					
❏ 5019	Go Sam/(Instrumental)	1982	—	2.50	5.00
❏ 5021	Get Down, Get Down "82"/ It Be's That Way Sometime	1982	—	2.50	5.00
❏ 5038	Deeper Than Love/Step by Step	198?	—	2.50	5.00
SOUND STAGE 7					
❏ 1508	Misty Blue/That's the Way I Want Our Love	1972	—	2.50	5.00
❏ 1512	Who's Julie/The Girl's Alright with Me	1973	—	2.50	5.00
❏ 1514	Someone to Lean On/I Got a Whole Lotta Lovin'	1974	—	2.50	5.00
❏ 1521	Funny How Time Slips Away/ Message from Maria	1976	—	2.50	5.00
❏ 2564	Teenager's Prayer/Long Hot Summer	1966	2.00	4.00	8.00
❏ 2569	Too Many Teardrops/ What Makes a Man Feel Good	1966	2.00	4.00	8.00
❏ 2577	My Special Prayer/Travelin' Man	1966	2.00	4.00	8.00
❏ 2583	Put Your Trust in Me (Depend on Me)/ Just a Dream	1967	2.00	4.00	8.00
❏ 2589	Nine Pound Steel/The Girl's Alright with Me	1967	2.00	4.00	8.00
❏ 2602	No Sad Songs/Come On and Get It	1967	2.00	4.00	8.00
❏ 2608	(You Keep Me) Hangin' On/Long Hot Summer	1968	2.00	4.00	8.00
❏ 2617	Message from Maria/I Worry About You	1968	2.00	4.00	8.00
❏ 2622	Looking Back/Standing in the Safety Zone	1968	2.00	4.00	8.00
❏ 2628	The Chokin' Kind/Come On and Get It	1969	—	3.00	6.00
❏ 2634	Baby, Don't Be Looking in My Mind/Don't Let Me Lose the Feeling	1969	—	3.00	6.00
❏ 2637	Oon-Guela (Part 1)/Oon-Guela (Part 2)	1969	2.00	4.00	8.00
❏ 2641	It's Hard to Get Along/ San Francisco Is a Lonely Town	1969	—	3.00	6.00
❏ 2651	Moon Walk Part 1/Moon Walk Part 2	1969	—	3.00	6.00
❏ 2656	Farther On Down the Road/Wounded Man	1970	—	3.00	6.00
❏ 2664	Yours Love/I Got a Whole Lotta Lovin'	1970	—	3.00	6.00
❏ 2667	That's the Way I Want Our Love/When	1970	—	3.00	6.00
SPRING					
❏ 108	Your Time to Cry/I Love You More (Than Anything)	1970	—	2.50	5.00
❏ 113	Help Me Make It Through the Night/ To Lay Down Beside You	1971	—	2.50	5.00
❏ 113 [PS]	Help Me Make It Through the Night/ To Lay Down Beside You	1971	—	3.00	6.00
❏ 115	You're the One for Me/I Ain't Givin' Up	1971	—	2.50	5.00
❏ 118	Georgia Blues/All My Hard Times	1971	—	2.50	5.00
❏ 120	Drowning in the Sea of Love/Let Me Be the One	1971	—	2.50	5.00
❏ 124	Pool of Bad Luck/Glad to Be Your Lover	1972	—	2.50	5.00
❏ 128	Power of Love/The Mirror Don't Lie	1972	—	2.50	5.00
❏ 130	Trouble in My Home/I Found My Dad	1972	—	2.50	5.00
❏ 133	Step by Step/Talk Don't Bother Me	1973	—	2.50	5.00

Number	Title (A Side/B Side)	Yr	VG	VG+	NM
❏ 138	Theme from Cleopatra Jones/Who Is That Lady	1973	—	2.50	5.00
❏ 138 [PS]	Theme from Cleopatra Jones/Who Is That Lady	1973	—	3.00	6.00
❏ 141	River/Love Never Hurt Nobody	1973	—	2.50	5.00
❏ 145	Carry Me/Do You Know What It's Like to Be Lonesome	1974	—	2.50	5.00
❏ 149	The Best Time of My Life/What We Gonna Do Now	1974	—	2.50	5.00
❏ 156	Get Down, Get Down (Get On the Floor)/ In My Baby's Arms	1975	—	2.50	5.00
❏ 159	Music in My Bones/Fire Burning	1975	—	2.50	5.00
❏ 163	I Need You, You Need Me/I'll Take Care (Of You)	1975	—	2.50	5.00
❏ 166	Come Get to This/Let the Good Times Roll	1976	—	2.50	5.00
❏ 169	Easy to Love/Can't Stand the Pain	1976	—	2.50	5.00
❏ 172	You Didn't Have to Play No Games/ What's Left to Do	1977	—	2.50	5.00
❏ 176	One Step at a Time/Track of Your Love	1977	—	2.50	5.00
❏ 178	For Your Love, Love, Love/ I've Got a Jones on You Baby	1977	—	2.50	5.00
❏ 184	I.O.U./It Must Be Love	1978	—	2.50	5.00
❏ 190	Love Vibration/(Instrumental)	1978	—	2.50	5.00
❏ 194	Going Through These Changes/I Can't Stand a Liar	1979	—	2.50	5.00
❏ 3003	I Wanna Taste Your Love/ Make Every Moment Count	1979	—	2.50	5.00
❏ 3006	Hooked on Disco Music/I Still Love You	1980	—	2.50	5.00
VEE JAY					
❏ 609	My Adorable One/Say (That My Love Is True)	1964	2.00	4.00	8.00
❏ 663	When You're Near/When I'm Gone	1965	2.00	4.00	8.00
❏ 694	Let's Do It Over/The Whoo Pee	1965	2.00	4.00	8.00

Albums

BUDDAH

Number	Title (A Side/B Side)	Yr	VG	VG+	NM
❏ BDS-7512	Joe Simon	1969	6.25	12.50	25.00
COMPLEAT					
❏ 671015-1	Mr. Right	1985	3.00	6.00	12.00
POSSE					
❏ 10002	Glad You Came My Way	1981	3.00	6.00	12.00
❏ 10003	By Popular Demand	1982	3.00	6.00	12.00
SOUND STAGE 7					
❏ 5000 [(2)]	The World of Joe Simon	197?	3.00	6.00	12.00
—Reissue of 32536					
❏ SSM-5003 [M]	Pure Soul	1967	7.50	15.00	30.00
❏ SSS-15003 [S]	Pure Soul	1967	10.00	20.00	40.00
❏ SSS-15004	No Sad Songs	1968	10.00	20.00	40.00
❏ SSS-15005	Simon Sings	1968	10.00	20.00	40.00
❏ SSS-15006	The Chokin' Kind	1969	7.50	15.00	30.00
❏ SSS-15008	Joe Simon…Better Than Ever	1969	7.50	15.00	30.00
❏ SSS-15009	The Best of Joe Simon	1972	3.75	7.50	15.00
❏ KZ 31916	Greatest Hits	1972	3.00	6.00	12.00
❏ ZG 32536 [(2)]	The World of Joe Simon	1974	3.75	7.50	15.00
❏ ZG 33879 [(2)]	The Chokin' Kind/Joe Simon…Better Than Ever	1975	3.75	7.50	15.00
SPRING					
❏ SPR-4701	The Sounds of Simon	1971	6.25	12.50	25.00
❏ SPR-5702	Drowning in the Sea of Love	1972	6.25	12.50	25.00
❏ SPR-5704	The Power of Joe Simon	1973	6.25	12.50	25.00
❏ SPR-5705	Simon Country	1973	3.75	7.50	15.00
❏ SPR-6702	Mood, Heart and Soul	1974	3.75	7.50	15.00
❏ SPR-6706	Get Down	1975	3.75	7.50	15.00
❏ SPR-6710	Today	1975	3.75	7.50	15.00
❏ SPR-6713	Easy to Love	1976	3.75	7.50	15.00
❏ SPR-6716	Bad Case of Love	1977	3.75	7.50	15.00
❏ SPR-6720	Love Vibrations	1979	3.75	7.50	15.00

SIMON, PAUL

SIMON, PAUL Includes records under various pseudonyms, such as "Paul Kane," "Jerry Landis" and "True Taylor." Also see SIMON AND GARFUNKEL; TICO AND THE TRIUMPHS; TOM AND JERRY (1).

12-Inch Singles

WARNER BROS.

Number	Title (A Side/B Side)	Yr	VG	VG+	NM
❏ PRO-A-889 [DJ]	Late in the Evening/ How the Heart Approaches What It Yearns	1980	2.50	5.00	10.00
❏ PRO-A-2100 [DJ]	Allergies (LP) (7" Version)	1983	2.00	4.00	8.00
❏ PRO-A-2610 [DJ]	Graceland (LP Version) (Edit)	1986	—	3.00	6.00
❏ PRO-A-2652 [DJ]	The Boy in the Bubble (LP Version) (Extended)	1987	—	3.00	6.00
❏ PRO-A-4480 [DJ]	The Obvious Child (The Single) (same on both sides)	1990	2.00	4.00	8.00

45s

AMY

Number	Title (A Side/B Side)	Yr	VG	VG+	NM
❏ 875	The Lone Teen Ranger/Lisa	1962	15.00	30.00	60.00
—As "Jerry Landis"					
BIG					
❏ 614	True or False/Teenage Fool	1958	25.00	50.00	100.00
—As "True Taylor"					
CANADIAN AMERICAN					
❏ 130	I'm Lonely/I Wish I Weren't in Love	1961	25.00	50.00	100.00
—As "Jerry Landis"; the rarest of his pre-Columbia solo singles					
COLUMBIA					
❏ 10197	Gone at Last/Take Me to the Mardi Gras	1975	—	2.50	5.00
—A-side with Phoebe Snow and the Jesse Dixon Singers					
❏ 10270	50 Ways to Leave Your Lover/ Some Folks Lives Roll Easy	1975	—	2.50	5.00
❏ 10332	Still Crazy After All These Years/ I Do It for Your Love (Live)	1976	—	2.50	5.00
❏ 10630	Slip Slidin' Away/Something So Right	1977	—	2.50	5.00
—Later pressings correct the LP title to "Greatest Hits, Etc." The Oak Ridge Boys are credited in the fine print.					
❏ 10630	Slip Slidin' Away/Something So Right	1977	—	3.00	6.00
—First pressings claim the A-side came from the LP "Blatant Greatest Hits." The Oak Ridge Boys are not mentioned.					
❏ 10711	Stranded in a Limousine/Have a Good Time	1978	—	3.00	6.00
❏ 45547	Mother and Child Reunion/Paranoia Blues	1972	—	2.00	4.00
—Gray label					
❏ 45547	Mother and Child Reunion/Paranoia Blues	1972	—	2.50	5.00
—Orange label					
❏ 45585	Me and Julio Down by the Schoolyard/ Congratulations	1972	—	2.00	4.00
—Gray label					

Number	Title (A Side/B Side)	Yr	VG	VG+	NM
❑ 45585	Me and Julio Down by the Schoolyard/ Congratulations	1972	—	2.50	5.00

—Orange label

Number	Title (A Side/B Side)	Yr	VG	VG+	NM
❑ 45638	Duncan/Run That Body Down	1972	—	2.50	5.00
❑ 45859	Kodachrome/Tenderness	1973	—	2.50	5.00

—With printing on label: "Kodachrome is a registered trademark for color film."

❑ 45859	Kodachrome/Tenderness	1973	—	3.00	6.00

—With sticker on label: "Kodachrome is a registered trademark for color film."

❑ 45859	Kodachrome/Tenderness	1973	—	3.00	6.00

—With no trademark disclaimer on label

❑ 45900	American Tune/One Man's Ceiling Is Another Man's Floor	1973	—	2.50	5.00
❑ 45900 [PS]	American Tune/One Man's Ceiling Is Another Man's Floor	1973	2.50	5.00	10.00
❑ 45907	Loves Me Like a Rock/Learn How to Fall	1973	—	2.50	5.00

—With the Dixie Hummingbirds

❑ 46038	The Sound of Silence/Mother and Child Reunion	1974	2.00	4.00	8.00

MGM

❑ 12822	Anna Belle/Loneliness	1959	12.50	25.00	50.00

—As "Jerry Landis"

TRIBUTE

❑ 128	Carlos Dominguez/He Was My Brother	1963	15.00	30.00	60.00

—As "Paul Kane"; authentic copies make no mention of Paul Simon on the label

WARNER BROS.

❑ 19464	Proof/The Coast	1991	—	—	3.00
❑ 27903	Graceland/Hearts and Bones	1988	—	2.50	5.00
❑ 28221	Under African Skies/I Know What I Know	1987	—	—	3.00

—A-side with Linda Ronstadt

❑ 28221 [PS]	Under African Skies/I Know What I Know	1987	—	—	3.00
❑ 28389	Diamonds on the Soles of Her Shoes/All Around the World Or the Myth of Fingerprints	1987	—	—	3.00
❑ 28389 [PS]	Diamonds on the Soles of Her Shoes/All Around the World Or the Myth of Fingerprints	1987	—	—	3.00
❑ 28460	The Boy in the Bubble/Crazy Love, Part 2	1987	—	—	3.00
❑ 28460 [PS]	The Boy in the Bubble/Crazy Love, Part 2	1987	—	—	3.00
❑ 28522	Graceland/Hearts and Bones	1986	—	—	3.00
❑ 28522 [PS]	Graceland/Hearts and Bones	1986	—	—	3.00
❑ 28667	You Can Call Me Al/Gumboots	1986	—	—	3.00
❑ 28667 [PS]	You Can Call Me Al/Gumboots	1986	—	—	3.00
❑ 29333	Think Too Much/Song About the Moon	1984	—	2.00	4.00
❑ 29453	Allergies/Think Too Much (ii)	1983	—	2.00	4.00
❑ 29453 [PS]	Allergies/Think Too Much (ii)	1983	—	2.00	4.00
❑ 49511	Late in the Evening/How the Heart Approaches What It Yearns	1980	—	2.00	4.00
❑ 49511 [PS]	Late in the Evening/How the Heart Approaches What It Yearns	1980	—	2.50	5.00
❑ 49601	One-Trick Pony/Long, Long Day	1980	—	2.00	4.00
❑ 49675	Oh, Marion/God Bless the Absentee	1981	—	2.00	4.00

WARWICK

❑ 522	Swanee/Toot, Toot, Tootsie Goodbye	1960	12.50	25.00	50.00

—As "Jerry Landis"

❑ 552	Shy/Just a Boy	1960	12.50	25.00	50.00

—As "Jerry Landis"

❑ 588	I'd Like to Be/Just a Boy	1960	12.50	25.00	50.00

—As "Jerry Landis"

❑ 619	Play Me a Sad Song/It Means a Lot to Them	1961	12.50	25.00	50.00

—As "Jerry Landis"

Albums

COLUMBIA

❑ CQ 30750 [Q]	Paul Simon	1974	5.00	10.00	20.00
❑ KC 30750	Paul Simon	1972	2.50	5.00	10.00
❑ CQ 32280 [Q]	There Goes Rhymin' Simon	1974	5.00	10.00	20.00
❑ KC 32280	There Goes Rhymin' Simon	1973	2.50	5.00	10.00
❑ PC 32280	There Goes Rhymin' Simon	1980	2.00	4.00	8.00
❑ PC 32855	Paul Simon in Concert — Live Rhymin'	1974	2.50	5.00	10.00
❑ PC 33540	Still Crazy After All These Years	1975	2.50	5.00	10.00

—Original release has no bar code on cover

❑ PC 33540	Still Crazy After All These Years	1980	2.00	4.00	8.00

—With bar code on cover

❑ PCQ 33540 [Q]	Still Crazy After All These Years	1975	5.00	10.00	20.00
❑ JC 35032	Greatest Hits, Etc.	1977	2.50	5.00	10.00
❑ C5X 37581 [(5)]	Collected Works	1981	10.00	20.00	40.00

—Contains his first four post-S&G solo albums plus the elusive "Paul Simon Songbook," otherwise unavailable in U.S.

❑ HC 43540	Still Crazy After All These Years	1981	10.00	20.00	40.00

—Half-speed mastered edition

❑ HC 45032	Greatest Hits, Etc.	1981	10.00	20.00	40.00

—Half-speed mastered edition

DCC COMPACT CLASSICS

❑ LPZ-2060	Paul Simon	1998	7.50	15.00	30.00

—Audiophile vinyl

❑ LPZ-2062	There Goes Rhymin' Simon	1998	7.50	15.00	30.00

—Audiophile vinyl

WARNER BROS.

❑ WBMS-140 [(2)DJ]	The Paul Simon Interview Show	1986	12.50	25.00	50.00

—Promo-only "Graceland"-era program in the "Warner Bros. Music Show" series

❑ HS 3472	One-Trick Pony	1980	2.50	5.00	10.00
❑ 23942	Hearts and Bones	1983	2.50	5.00	10.00
❑ 23942 [DJ]	Hearts and Bones	1983	5.00	10.00	20.00

—Promo only on Quiex II vinyl

❑ 25447	Graceland	1986	2.50	5.00	10.00
❑ 25588	Paul Simon	1988	3.00	6.00	12.00
❑ 25589	There Goes Rhymin' Simon	1988	3.00	6.00	12.00
❑ 25590	Paul Simon in Concert — Live Rhymin'	1988	3.00	6.00	12.00
❑ 25591	Still Crazy After All These Years	1988	3.00	6.00	12.00
❑ 25789 [(2)]	Negotiations and Love Songs	1988	3.75	7.50	15.00
❑ 26098	The Rhythm of the Saints	1990	3.75	7.50	15.00
❑ 46814	Songs from The Capeman	1997	3.75	7.50	15.00

SIMON AND GARFUNKEL Also see ART GARFUNKEL; PAUL SIMON; TOM AND JERRY (1).

45s

ABC-PARAMOUNT

❑ 10788	That's My Story/Tia-Juana Blues	1966	5.00	10.00	20.00

—Outtakes from Tom and Jerry days

COLUMBIA

Number	Title (A Side/B Side)	Yr	VG	VG+	NM
❑ AE 43 [DJ]	Keep the Customer Satisfied/America	1971	3.00	6.00	12.00

—Both sides are stereo

❑ 10230	My Little Town//Art Garfunkel: Rag Doll/Paul Simon: You're Kind	1975	—	2.50	5.00
❑ 10230 [PS]	My Little Town//Art Garfunkel: Rag Doll/Paul Simon: You're Kind	1975	—	2.50	5.00
❑ 43396	The Sounds of Silence/ We've Got a Groovey Thing Goin'	1965	2.50	5.00	10.00

—With the "folk-rock" hit version of the A-side

❑ 43396	The Sounds of Silence/ We've Got a Groovey Thing Goin'	1965	12.50	25.00	50.00

—With the original acoustic version of the A-side; a known stock copy is pressed on vinyl rather than styrene and has the number "ZSP 111384-1G" in the dead wax

❑ 43396 [DJ]	The Sounds of Silence (Acoustic)/(Electric)	1965	12.50	25.00	50.00

—Red vinyl promo containing, possibly in error, the acoustic version on one side and the electric version on the other; the acoustic version has ZSP-111384-1D in the trail-off wax and the electric version has ZSP-111384-1C in the trail-off

❑ 43511	Homeward Bound/Leaves That Are Green	1966	2.50	5.00	10.00
❑ 43511 [DJ]	Homeward Bound (same on both sides)	1966	12.50	25.00	50.00

—Red vinyl promo

❑ 43617	I Am a Rock/Flowers Never Bend with the Rainfall	1966	2.50	5.00	10.00
❑ 43617 [DJ]	I Am a Rock (same on both sides)	1966	12.50	25.00	50.00

—Red vinyl promo

❑ 43728	The Dangling Conversation/ The Big Bright Green Pleasure Machine	1966	2.50	5.00	10.00
❑ 43728 [DJ]	The Dangling Conversation (same on both sides)	1966	12.50	25.00	50.00

—Red vinyl promo

❑ 43728 [PS]	The Dangling Conversation/The Big Bright Green Pleasure Machine	1966	5.00	10.00	20.00
❑ 43873	A Hazy Shade of Winter/For Emily, Wherever I May Find Her	1966	2.50	5.00	10.00
❑ 44046	At the Zoo/The 59th Street Bridge Song (Feelin' Groovy)	1967	2.50	5.00	10.00
❑ 44046 [PS]	At the Zoo/The 59th Street Bridge Song (Feelin' Groovy)	1967	10.00	20.00	40.00
❑ 44232	Fakin' It/You Don't Know Where Your Interest Lies	1967	2.50	5.00	10.00

—As far as we can tell, all copies have the A-side listed with a time of "2:74"

❑ 44465	Scarborough Fair (/Canticle)/ April Come She Will	1968	2.50	5.00	10.00
❑ 44511	Mrs. Robinson/Old Friends-Bookends	1968	2.00	4.00	8.00

—Label says "From the Columbia Lp BOOKENDS," etc. with no reference to "The Graduate"

❑ 44511	Mrs. Robinson/Old Friends-Bookends	1968	2.50	5.00	10.00

—Label says "From the Motion Picture 'The Graduate'"

❑ 44785	The Boxer/Baby Driver	1969	—	3.00	6.00

—B-side mix (mono) is different than stereo LP version, especially near the end of the song

❑ 44785 [DJ]	Baby Driver (mono/stereo)	1969	3.75	7.50	15.00

—Promo 45s exist promoting this song as the "hit"!

❑ 44785 [PS]	The Boxer/Baby Driver	1969	2.00	4.00	8.00
❑ 45079	Bridge Over Troubled Water/ Keep the Customer Satisfied	1970	—	3.00	6.00
❑ 45079 [PS]	Bridge Over Troubled Water/ Keep the Customer Satisfied	1970	2.00	4.00	8.00
❑ 45133	Cecilia/The Only Living Boy in New York	1970	—	3.00	6.00

—Red label, "Columbia" in black at top

❑ 45133	Cecilia/The Only Living Boy in New York	1970	2.50	5.00	10.00

—Red label, continuous "Columbia Records" in white along outer edge

❑ 45133 [PS]	Cecilia/The Only Living Boy in New York	1970	2.00	4.00	8.00
❑ 45237	El Condor Pasa/Why Don't You Write Me	1970	—	3.00	6.00
❑ 45663	America/For Emily, Whenever I May Find Her	1972	—	3.00	6.00
❑ JZSP 116469 [DJ]	7 O'Clock News-Silent Night (same on both sides)	1966	6.25	12.50	25.00

—Promo-only Christmas release for radio stations

WARNER BROS.

❑ 50053	Wake Up Little Susie/ Me and Julio Down by the Schoolyard	1982	—	2.00	4.00

7-Inch Extended Plays

COLUMBIA

❑ 7-9529	A Hazy Shade of Winter/Mrs. Robinson/ Bookends Theme//At the Zoo/Old Friends/ Fakin' It	1968	3.75	7.50	15.00

—Jukebox issue; small hole, plays at 33 1/3 rpm

❑ 7-9529 [PS]	Bookends	1968	3.75	7.50	15.00
❑ 7-9914	Song for the Asking/So Long, Frank Lloyd Wright/El Condor Pasa//Keep the Customer Satisfied/Why Don't You Write Me/ Bye Bye Love	1970	3.75	7.50	15.00

—Jukebox issue; small hole, plays at 33 1/3 rpm

❑ 7-9914 [PS]	Bridge Over Troubled Water	1970	3.75	7.50	15.00

Albums

CBS

❑ KCS 9914	Bridge Over Troubled Water	1970	3.75	7.50	15.00

—"360 Sound Stereo" on label; pressed in U.S. for export

COLUMBIA

❑ CL 2249 [M]	Wednesday Morning, 3 A.M.	1964	6.25	12.50	25.00

—"Guaranteed High Fidelity" on label

❑ CL 2249 [M]	Wednesday Morning, 3 A.M.	1965	3.75	7.50	15.00

—"Mono" on label

❑ CL 2469 [M]	Sounds of Silence	1966	3.75	7.50	15.00

—With "Simon and Garfunkel" and "Sounds of Silence" in large upper and lowercase letters on front cover with all song titles listed; "Tiger Beat" magazines on back cover are airbrushed out

❑ CL 2469 [M]	Sounds of Silence	1966			

—With "Simon and Garfunkel" and "Sounds of Silence" in large upper and lowercase letters on front cover with all song titles listed; "Tiger Beat" magazine is pictured twice on back cover

❑ CL 2469 [M]	Sounds of Silence	1966	7.50	15.00	30.00

—With "Simon and Garfunkel" and "Sounds of Silence" in all capital letters on front cover with no list of songs

❑ CL 2563 [M]	Parsley, Sage, Rosemary and Thyme	1966	5.00	10.00	20.00
❑ KCL 2729 [M]	Bookends	1968	25.00	50.00	100.00

—Red label, "Mono" at bottom

❑ CS 9049 [S]	Wednesday Morning, 3 A.M.	1964	6.25	12.50	25.00

—"360 Sound Stereo" in black on label

Number	Title (A Side/B Side)	Yr	VG	VG+	NM
❏ CS 9049 [S]	Wednesday Morning, 3 A.M.	1965	3.75	7.50	15.00
—"360 Sound Stereo" in white on label					
❏ CS 9049 [S]	Wednesday Morning, 3 A.M.	1970	2.50	5.00	10.00
—Orange label					
❏ PC 9049 [S]	Wednesday Morning, 3 A.M.	197?	2.00	4.00	8.00
—Budget-line reissue					
❏ CS 9269 [S]	Sounds of Silence	1966	3.00	6.00	12.00
—With "Simon and Garfunkel" and "Sounds of Silence" in large upper and lowercase letters on front cover with all song titles listed; "Tiger Beat" magazines on back cover are airbrushed out					
❏ CS 9269 [S]	Sounds of Silence	1966	5.00	10.00	20.00
—With "Simon and Garfunkel" and "Sounds of Silence" in large upper and lowercase letters on front cover with all song titles listed; "Tiger Beat" magazine is pictured twice on back cover					
❏ CS 9269 [S]	Sounds of Silence	1966	7.50	15.00	30.00
—With "Simon and Garfunkel" and "Sounds of Silence" in all capital letters on front cover with no list of songs					
❏ CS 9269 [S]	Sounds of Silence	1970	2.50	5.00	10.00
—Orange label					
❏ JC 9269	Sounds of Silence	197?	2.00	4.00	8.00
—Reissue with new prefix					
❏ PC 9269 [S]	Sounds of Silence	198?	2.00	4.00	8.00
—Budget-line reissue					
❏ CS 9363 [S]	Parsley, Sage, Rosemary and Thyme	1966	3.75	7.50	15.00
—"360 Sound Stereo" on label					
❏ CS 9363 [S]	Parsley, Sage, Rosemary and Thyme	1970	2.50	5.00	10.00
—Orange label					
❏ PC 9363 [S]	Parsley, Sage, Rosemary and Thyme	197?	2.00	4.00	8.00
—Budget-line reissue					
❏ KCS 9529 [M]	Bookends	1968	7.50	15.00	30.00
—White label "Special Mono Radio Station Copy"					
❏ KCS 9529 [S]	Bookends	1968	3.00	6.00	12.00
—"360 Sound Stereo" on label; add 25% for poster					
❏ KCS 9529 [S]	Bookends	1970	2.50	5.00	10.00
—Orange label					
❏ PC 9529 [S]	Bookends	197?	2.00	4.00	8.00
—Budget-line reissue					
❏ JC 9914	Bridge Over Troubled Water	197?	2.00	4.00	8.00
—Reissue with new prefix					
❏ KCS 9914	Bridge Over Troubled Water	1970	2.50	5.00	10.00
—Orange label					
❏ KCS 9914	Bridge Over Troubled Water	1970	3.00	6.00	12.00
—"360 Sound Stereo" on label					
❏ KCS 9914	Bridge Over Troubled Water	2000	6.25	12.50	25.00
—Classic Records reissue on audiophile vinyl					
❏ PC 9914	Bridge Over Troubled Water	198?	2.00	4.00	8.00
—Budget-line reissue					
❏ CQ 30995 [Q]	Bridge Over Troubled Water	1971	6.25	12.50	25.00
❏ PCQ 30995 [Q]	Bridge Over Troubled Water	1974	5.00	10.00	20.00
—Reissue with new prefix; possibly the only difference between this and the original is a sticker on the cover with the new number					
❏ JC 31350	Simon and Garfunkel's Greatest Hits	197?	2.00	4.00	8.00
—Reissue with new prefix					
❏ KC 31350	Simon and Garfunkel's Greatest Hits	1972	3.00	6.00	12.00
—Original covers are slightly oversized					
❏ C5X 37587 [(5)]	Collected Works	1981	10.00	20.00	40.00
❏ HC 41350	Simon and Garfunkel's Greatest Hits	1982	7.50	15.00	30.00
—Half-speed mastered edition					
❏ HC 49914	Bridge Over Troubled Water	1982	7.50	15.00	30.00
—Half-speed mastered edition					
MOBILE FIDELITY					
❏ 1-173	Bridge Over Troubled Water	198?	10.00	20.00	40.00
—Audiophile vinyl					
PICKWICK					
❏ PC-3059 [M]	The Hit Sounds of Simon and Garfunkel	1966	15.00	30.00	60.00
❏ SPC-3059 [R]	The Hit Sounds of Simon and Garfunkel	1966	7.50	15.00	30.00
SEARS					
❏ SPS-435	Simon and Garfunkel	196?	7.50	15.00	30.00
WARNER BROS.					
❏ 2BSK 3654 [(2)]	The Concert in Central Park	1982	3.00	6.00	12.00

SIMON SISTERS, THE CARLY SIMON and her sister Lucy.
45s

Number	Title (A Side/B Side)	Yr	VG	VG+	NM
CHILDREN'S RECORDS OF AMERICA					
❏ 100	My Love Is Like a Red, Red Rose/The Lamb	1968	5.00	10.00	20.00
COLUMBIA					
❏ 02675	Maryanne/(B-side unknown)	1982	—	2.00	4.00
—As "Carly and Lucy Simon"					
❏ 45840	Red, Red Rose/Lobster Quadrille	1973	—	3.00	6.00
—As "Carly and Lucy Simon"					
KAPP					
❏ 586	Winkin', Blinkin' and Nod/So Glad I'm Here	1964	3.75	7.50	15.00
❏ 624	Cuddlebug/No One to Talk My Troubles To	1964	3.75	7.50	15.00
Albums					
COLUMBIA					
❏ CR 21525	The Lobster Quadrille	1969	3.75	7.50	15.00
❏ CR 21539	The Simon Sisters Sing for Children	1972	3.75	7.50	15.00
❏ CC 24506	The Lobster Quadrille	1969	5.00	10.00	20.00
—Special edition with booklet					
KAPP					
❏ KL-1359 [M]	Winkin', Blinkin' and Nod	1964	7.50	15.00	30.00
❏ KL-1397 [M]	Cuddlebug	1964	10.00	20.00	40.00
❏ KS-3359 [S]	Winkin', Blinkin' and Nod	1964	10.00	20.00	40.00
❏ KS-3397 [S]	Cuddlebug	1964	12.50	25.00	50.00

SIMONE, NINA
45s

Number	Title (A Side/B Side)	Yr	VG	VG+	NM
BETHLEHEM					
❏ 3031	My Baby Just Cares for Me/He Needs Me	1962	2.00	4.00	8.00
❏ 3099	I Loves You Porgy/My Baby Just Cares for Me	1970	—	2.50	5.00
❏ 11021	I Loves You, Porgy/Love Me or Leave Me	1959	3.00	6.00	12.00
❏ 11052	Little Girl Blue/He Needs Me	1960	2.50	5.00	10.00
❏ 11055	Don't Smoke in Bed/African Mailman	1960	2.50	5.00	10.00
❏ 11057	Mood Indigo/Central Park Blues	1960	2.50	5.00	10.00
❏ 11087	For All We Know/Good Bait	1960	2.50	5.00	10.00
❏ 11088	You'll Never Walk Alone/Plain Gold Ring	1960	2.50	5.00	10.00
❏ 11089	He's Got the Whole World in His Hands/ Central Park Blues	1960	2.50	5.00	10.00

Number	Title (A Side/B Side)	Yr	VG	VG+	NM
COLPIX					
❏ 116	Solitaire/Chilly Winds	1959	2.50	5.00	10.00
❏ 124	Children Go Where I Send Thee/ Willow Weep for Me	1959	2.50	5.00	10.00
❏ 135	It Might As Well Be Spring/The Other Woman	1959	2.50	5.00	10.00
❏ 143	Summertime/Fine and Mellow	1960	2.50	5.00	10.00
❏ 151	Since My Love Has Gone/Tomorrow (We Shall Meet Once More)	1960	2.50	5.00	10.00
❏ 156	If Only for Tonight/(B-side unknown)	1960	2.50	5.00	10.00
❏ 158	Nobody Knows You When You're Down and Out/Black Is the Color of My True Love's Hair	1960	2.50	5.00	10.00
❏ 175	Trouble in Mind/Cotton-Eyed Joe	1960	2.50	5.00	10.00
❏ 197	The Work Song/Memphis in June	1961	2.50	5.00	10.00
❏ 608	You Can Have Him/Gin House Blues	1961	2.50	5.00	10.00
❏ 614	Come On Back, Jack/ You've Been Gone Too Long	1961	2.50	5.00	10.00
❏ 635	In the Evening by the Moonlight/ Chilly Winds Don't Blow	1962	2.00	4.00	8.00
❏ 647	I Got It Bad/I Want a Little Sugar in My Bowl	1962	2.00	4.00	8.00
❏ 703	Blackbird/Little Liza Jane	1963	2.00	4.00	8.00
CTI					
❏ 44	Baltimore/The Family	1978	—	2.50	5.00
❏ 46	Forget/Baltimore	1978	—	2.50	5.00
❏ 49	The Family/That's All I Want from You	1978	—	2.50	5.00
PHILIPS					
❏ 40194	I Loves You Porgy/Old Jim Crow	1964	2.00	4.00	8.00
❏ 40216	Mississippi Goddam/Sea Lion Woman	1964	2.00	4.00	8.00
❏ 40232	Don't Let Me Be Misunderstood/A Monster	1964	2.00	4.00	8.00
❏ 40254	I Am Blessed/How Can I	1965	2.00	4.00	8.00
❏ 40286	I Put a Spell on You/Gimme Some	1965	2.00	4.00	8.00
❏ 40337	Either Way I Lose/Break Down and Let It All Out	1965	2.00	4.00	8.00
❏ 40359	Why Keep On Breaking My Heart/ I Love Your Lovin' Ways	1966	—	3.00	6.00
❏ 40376	See-Line Woman/I Love Your Lovin' Ways	1966	—	3.00	6.00
❏ 40404	What More Can I Say/Four Women	1966	—	3.00	6.00
❏ 40418	Don't Pay Them No Mind/(B-side unknown)	1966	—	3.00	6.00
RCA VICTOR					
❏ 47-9120	Do I Move You/Day and Night	1967	—	3.00	6.00
❏ 47-9286	It Be's That Way Sometime/You'll Go to Hell	1967	—	3.00	6.00
❏ 47-9375	Cherish/I Wish I Knew How It Would Feel to Be Free	1967	—	3.00	6.00
❏ 47-9447	To Love Somebody/I Can't See Nobody	1968	—	3.00	6.00
❏ 47-9286	Why (Part 1)/Why (Part 2)	1968	—	3.00	6.00
❏ 47-9602	Do What You Gotta Do/Peace of Mind	1968	—	3.00	6.00
❏ 47-9686	Ain't Got No; I Got Life/Real, Real	1968	—	3.00	6.00
❏ 47-9730	Revolution (Part 1)/Revolution (Part 2)	1969	—	3.00	6.00
❏ 47-9749	Suzanne/Turn, Turn, Turn (To Everything There Is a Season)	1969	—	3.00	6.00
❏ 74-0269	To Be Young, Gifted and Black/Save Me	1969	—	3.00	6.00
❏ 74-0311	Who Knows Where the Time Goes/The Assignment Song	1970	—	3.00	6.00
❏ 74-0467	Here Comes the Sun/New World Coming	1971	—	—	—
—Canceled					
❏ 74-0471	New World Coming/O-o-h Child	1971	—	3.00	6.00
❏ 74-0514	Here Comes the Sun/Angel of the Morning	1971	—	3.00	6.00
❏ 74-0871	My Sweet Lord-Today Is a Killer/Poppies	1973	—	3.00	6.00
Albums					
ACCORD					
❏ SN-7108	In Concert	1981	2.50	5.00	10.00
BETHLEHEM					
❏ BCP-6003	Nina Simone's Finest	197?	3.00	6.00	12.00
❏ BCP-6028 [M]	Jazz As Played in an Exclusive Side Street Club	1959	20.00	40.00	80.00
❏ BCP-6028 [M]	The Original Nina Simone	1961	7.50	15.00	30.00
—Retitled reissue					
❏ SBCP-6028 [S]	Jazz As Played in an Exclusive Side Street Club	1959	25.00	50.00	100.00
❏ SBCP-6028 [S]	The Original Nina Simone	1961	10.00	20.00	40.00
—Retitled reissue					
❏ BCP-6041 [M]	Nina Simone and Her Friends	1960	10.00	20.00	40.00
❏ SBCP-6041 [S]	Nina Simone and Her Friends	1960	12.50	25.00	50.00
—With Carmen McRae and Chris Connor					
CANYON					
❏ 7705	Gifted and Black	1971	3.75	7.50	15.00
COLPIX					
❏ CP-407 [M]	The Amazing Nina Simone	1959	6.25	12.50	25.00
❏ SCP-407 [S]	The Amazing Nina Simone	1959	7.50	15.00	30.00
❏ CP-409 [M]	Nina at Town Hall	1960	6.25	12.50	25.00
❏ SCP-409 [S]	Nina at Town Hall	1960	7.50	15.00	30.00
❏ CP-412 [M]	Nina at Newport	1960	6.25	12.50	25.00
❏ SCP-412 [S]	Nina at Newport	1960	7.50	15.00	30.00
❏ CP-419 [M]	Forbidden Fruit	1961	6.25	12.50	25.00
❏ SCP-419 [S]	Forbidden Fruit	1961	7.50	15.00	30.00
❏ CP-421 [M]	Nina Simone at the Village Gate	1961	6.25	12.50	25.00
❏ SCP-421 [S]	Nina Simone at the Village Gate	1961	7.50	15.00	30.00
❏ CP-425 [M]	Nina Sings Ellington	1962	6.25	12.50	25.00
❏ SCP-425 [S]	Nina Sings Ellington	1962	7.50	15.00	30.00
❏ CP-443 [M]	Nina's Choice	1963	6.25	12.50	25.00
❏ SCP-443 [S]	Nina's Choice	1963	7.50	15.00	30.00
❏ CP-455 [M]	Nina Simone at Carnegie Hall	1963	6.25	12.50	25.00
❏ SCP-455 [S]	Nina Simone at Carnegie Hall	1963	7.50	15.00	30.00
❏ CP-465 [M]	Folksy Nina	1964	6.25	12.50	25.00
❏ SCP-465 [S]	Folksy Nina	1964	7.50	15.00	30.00
❏ CP-496 [M]	Nina with Strings	1966	6.25	12.50	25.00
❏ SCP-496 [S]	Nina with Strings	1966	7.50	15.00	30.00
CTI					
❏ 7084	Baltimore	1978	3.00	6.00	12.00
PHILIPS					
❏ PHM 200135 [M]	Nina Simone In Concert	1964	3.75	7.50	15.00
❏ PHM 200148 [M]	Broadway...Blues...Ballads	1964	3.75	7.50	15.00
❏ PHM 200172 [M]	I Put a Spell on You	1965	3.75	7.50	15.00
❏ PHM 200187 [M]	Pastel Blues	1965	3.75	7.50	15.00
❏ PHM 200202 [M]	Let It All Out	1966	3.75	7.50	15.00
❏ PHM 200207 [M]	Wild Is the Wind	1966	3.75	7.50	15.00
❏ PHM 200219 [M]	The High Priestess of Soul	1967	3.75	7.50	15.00
❏ PHS 600135 [S]	Nina Simone In Concert	1964	5.00	10.00	20.00
❏ PHS 600148 [S]	Broadway...Blues...Ballads	1964	5.00	10.00	20.00
❏ PHS 600172 [S]	I Put a Spell on You	1965	5.00	10.00	20.00

S

Number	Title (A Side/B Side)	Yr	VG	VG+	NM
❏ PHS 600187 [S]	Pastel Blues	1965	5.00	10.00	20.00
❏ PHS 600202 [S]	Let It All Out	1966	5.00	10.00	20.00
❏ PHS 600207 [S]	Wild Is the Wind	1966	5.00	10.00	20.00
❏ PHS 600219 [S]	The High Priestess of Soul	1967	5.00	10.00	20.00
❏ PHS 600298	The Best of Nina Simone	1969	5.00	10.00	20.00
❏ 822846-1	The Best of Nina Simone	198?	2.50	5.00	10.00
PM					
❏ 018	A Very Rare Evening	1979	3.00	6.00	12.00
QUINTESSENCE					
❏ 25421	Silk and Soul	1979	2.50	5.00	10.00
RCA VICTOR					
❏ AFL1-0241	It Is Finished — Nina 1974	1977	2.50	5.00	10.00
—Reissue with new prefix					
❏ APL1-0241	It Is Finished — Nina 1974	1974	3.00	6.00	12.00
❏ AFL1-1788	Poets	1977	2.50	5.00	10.00
—Reissue with new prefix					
❏ APL1-1788	Poets	1976	3.00	6.00	12.00
❏ LPM-3789 [M]	Nina Simone Sings the Blues	1967	6.25	12.50	25.00
❏ LSP-3789 [S]	Nina Simone Sings the Blues	1967	3.75	7.50	15.00
❏ LPM-3837 [M]	Silk and Soul	1967	6.25	12.50	25.00
❏ LSP-3837 [S]	Silk and Soul	1967	3.75	7.50	15.00
❏ LSP-4065	'Nuff Said	1968	3.75	7.50	15.00
❏ LSP-4102	Nina Simone and Piano	1968	3.75	7.50	15.00
❏ LSP-4152	To Love Somebody	1969	3.75	7.50	15.00
❏ LSP-4248	Black Gold	1970	3.75	7.50	15.00
❏ AFL1-4374	The Best of Nina Simone	1977	2.50	5.00	10.00
—Reissue with new prefix					
❏ LSP-4374	The Best of Nina Simone	1970	3.75	7.50	15.00
❏ AFL1-4536	Here Comes the Sun	1977	2.50	5.00	10.00
—Reissue with new prefix					
❏ LSP-4536	Here Comes the Sun	1971	3.75	7.50	15.00
❏ LSP-4757	Emergency Ward!	1972	3.75	7.50	15.00
SALSOUL					
❏ SA-8546	Little Girl Blue	1982	2.50	5.00	10.00
TRIP					
❏ 8020 [(2)]	Live in Europe	1973	3.00	6.00	12.00
❏ 8021 [(2)]	Black Is the Color	1973	3.00	6.00	12.00
❏ 9521	Portrait	197?	2.50	5.00	10.00
VERVE					
❏ 831437-1	Let It Be Me	1987	2.50	5.00	10.00

SIMPSON, VALERIE Also see ASHFORD AND SIMPSON.
45s

Number	Title (A Side/B Side)	Yr	VG	VG+	NM
TAMLA					
❏ 54204	Back to Nowhere/Can't It Wait Until Tomorrow	1971	—	2.50	5.00
❏ 54224	Silly Wasn't I/I Believe I'm Gonna Take This Ride	1972	—	2.50	5.00
❏ 54231	Genius/One More Baby Child Born	1973	—	2.50	5.00
Albums					
TAMLA					
❏ T 311	Valerie Simpson Exposed	1971	3.75	7.50	15.00
❏ T 317	Valerie Simpson	1972	3.75	7.50	15.00
❏ T6-351	Keep It Comin'	1977	3.00	6.00	12.00

SIMS, BOBBY
45s

Number	Title (A Side/B Side)	Yr	VG	VG+	NM
HIT					
❏ 269	Poor Side of Town/If I Were a Carpenter	1966	2.00	4.00	8.00
—B-side by Bobby Brooks					
❏ 272	That's Life/Snoopy vs. the Red Baron	1966	2.00	4.00	8.00
—B-side by the Chords (2)					
❏ 276	Wild Thing/Music to Watch Girls By	1967	2.00	4.00	8.00
—B-side by the Jalopy Five					
❏ 287	I Think We're Alone Now/Penny Lane	1967	2.50	5.00	10.00
—B-side by the Jalopy Five					
❏ 297	San Francisco (Be Sure to Wear Flowers in Your Hair)/A Whiter Shade of Pale	1967	2.00	4.00	8.00
—B-side by the Fantastics					
❏ 309	Please Love Me Forever/People Are Strange	1967	2.00	4.00	8.00
—B-side by the Fantastics					
❏ 312	An Open Letter to My Teenage Son/Keep the Ball Rollin'	1967	2.00	4.00	8.00
—B-side by Jimmy Lewis and the Elfs					
❏ 320	Honey/The Ballad of Bonnie and Clyde	1968	2.00	4.00	8.00
—B-side by Ed Hardin					
❏ 339	Dreams of the Everyday Housewife/Hello, I Love You	1968	2.00	4.00	8.00
—B-side by the Chords (2)					
❏ 348	Who's Making Love/White Room	1968	2.00	4.00	8.00
—B-side by the Fantastics					

SIMS, FRANKIE LEE
45s

Number	Title (A Side/B Side)	Yr	VG	VG+	NM
ACE					
❏ 524	What Will Lucy Do/Misery Blues	1957	10.00	20.00	40.00
❏ 527	Hey Little Girl/Walking with Frankie	1957	10.00	20.00	40.00
❏ 539	I Warned You Baby/My Talk Didn't Do No Good	1957	10.00	20.00	40.00
SPECIALTY					
❏ 459	Lucky Man Blues/Don't Take It Out on Me	1953	12.50	25.00	50.00
❏ 478	I'm Long, Long Gone/Yeh Baby	1953	10.00	20.00	40.00
❏ 487	I'll Get Along Somehow/Rhumba My Boogie	1954	10.00	20.00	40.00
VIN					
❏ 1006	She Likes to Boogie Low/Well Goodbye Baby	1958	7.50	15.00	30.00

SIMS TWINS, THE
45s

Number	Title (A Side/B Side)	Yr	VG	VG+	NM
KENT					
❏ 4556	Bring It On Home Where You Belong/Under the Double Eagle	1971	—	3.00	6.00
PARKWAY					
❏ 6002	Together/Baby It's Real	1968	2.50	5.00	10.00
SAR					
❏ 117	Soothe Me/I'll Never Come Running Back to You	1961	3.75	7.50	15.00
❏ 125	The Smile/Right to Love	1962	3.00	6.00	12.00
❏ 130	Double Portion of Love/You're Pickin' in the Right Cotton Patch	1962	3.00	6.00	12.00
❏ 136	I Gopher You/Good Good Lovin'	1963	3.00	6.00	12.00
❏ 138	That's Where It's At/Movin' and a Groovin'	1963	3.00	6.00	12.00
SPECIALTY					
❏ 731	Make It On Up/Something Hanging on Your Mind	197?	—	3.00	6.00

SINATRA, FRANK Also see TOMMY DORSEY.
12-Inch Singles

Number	Title (A Side/B Side)	Yr	VG	VG+	NM
QWEST					
❏ PRO-A-2216 [DJ]	Mack the Knife (Remix 4:50) (same on both sides)	1984	3.00	6.00	12.00
REPRISE					
❏ PRO-A-674 [DJ]	Night and Day/Everybody Ought to Be in Love	1977	20.00	40.00	80.00
❏ PRO-A-865 [DJ]	Theme from New York, New York (same on both sides)	1980	12.50	25.00	50.00

45s

Number	Title (A Side/B Side)	Yr	VG	VG+	NM
(NO LABEL)					
❏ KB-2077/8	High Hopes with Jack Kennedy/Jack Kennedy All the Way	1960	75.00	150.00	300.00
—No artist or label shown, but Sinatra does sing the A-side					
CAPITOL					
❏ X1-1069 [S]	titles unknown	196?	5.00	10.00	20.00
—Stereo jukebox single, 33 1/3 rpm, small hole					
❏ X2-1069 [S]	titles unknown	196?	5.00	10.00	20.00
—Stereo jukebox single, 33 1/3 rpm, small hole					
❏ X3-1069 [S]	Day In — Day Out/Saturday Night	196?	5.00	10.00	20.00
—Stereo jukebox single, 33 1/3 rpm, small hole					
❏ X1-1417 [S]	That Old Feeling/How Deep Is the Ocean	1960	5.00	10.00	20.00
—Stereo jukebox single, 33 1/3 rpm, small hole					
❏ X2-1417 [S]	Fools Rush In/I've Got a Crush on You	1960	5.00	10.00	20.00
—Stereo jukebox single, 33 1/3 rpm, small hole					
❏ X1-1491 [S]	When You're Smiling/It All Depends on You	1961	5.00	10.00	20.00
—Stereo jukebox single, 33 1/3 rpm, small hole					
❏ X2-1491 [S]	S'posin'/Blue Moon	1961	5.00	10.00	20.00
—Stereo jukebox single, 33 1/3 rpm, small hole					
❏ X3-1491 [S]	titles unknown	1961	5.00	10.00	20.00
—Stereo jukebox single, 33 1/3 rpm, small hole					
❏ X4-1491 [S]	I Concentrate on You/Should I	1961	5.00	10.00	20.00
—Stereo jukebox single, 33 1/3 rpm, small hole					
❏ X5-1491 [S]	September in the Rain/You Do Something to Me	1961	5.00	10.00	20.00
—Stereo jukebox single, 33 1/3 rpm, small hole					
❏ X1-1594 [S]	titles unknown	1961	5.00	10.00	20.00
—Stereo jukebox single, 33 1/3 rpm, small hole					
❏ X2-1594 [S]	Five Minutes More/Almost Like Being in Love	1961	5.00	10.00	20.00
—Stereo jukebox single, 33 1/3 rpm, small hole					
❏ X3-1594 [S]	Yes Indeed/American Beauty Rose	1961	5.00	10.00	20.00
—Stereo jukebox single, 33 1/3 rpm, small hole					
❏ F1699	Young at Heart/I've Got the World on a String	1955	25.00	50.00	100.00
—Early reissue					
❏ PRO 1707/8 [DJ]	Mistletoe and Holly (with spoken intro)/Mistletoe and Holly	1960	25.00	50.00	100.00
—Christmas Seals record for 1960, with Sinatra introducing the song					
❏ XE-1729 [S]	They Came to Cordura/I Gotta Right to Sing the Blues	1962	5.00	10.00	20.00
—Stereo jukebox single, 33 1/3 rpm, small hole					
❏ F2450	I'm Walking Behind You/Lean Baby	1953	6.25	12.50	25.00
—Add 50% for intact center					
❏ F2505	My One and Only Love/I've Got the World on a String	1953	5.00	10.00	20.00
—Add 50% for intact center					
❏ F2560	Anytime, Anywhere/From Here to Eternity	1953	5.00	10.00	20.00
❏ F2638	I Love You/South of the Border	1953	5.00	10.00	20.00
❏ F2703	Young at Heart/Take a Chance	1953	5.00	10.00	20.00
❏ F2787	Don't Worry 'Bout Me/I Could Have Told You	1954	5.00	10.00	20.00
❏ F2816	Three Coins in the Fountain/Rain	1954	5.00	10.00	20.00
❏ F2864	The Girl That Got Away/Half as Lovely	1954	5.00	10.00	20.00
❏ F2922	It Worries Me/When I Stop Loving You	1954	5.00	10.00	20.00
❏ 2954	White Christmas/The Christmas Waltz	1962	2.50	5.00	10.00
—Reissue without the "F" prefix on orange and yellow swirl label					
❏ F2954	White Christmas/The Christmas Waltz	1954	5.00	10.00	20.00
❏ F2993	You My Love/Someone to Watch Over Me	1954	5.00	10.00	20.00
❏ F3018	Melody of Love/I'm Gonna Live Till I Die	1954	5.00	10.00	20.00
❏ F3050	Why Should I Cry Over You?/Don't Change Your Mind About Me	1954	5.00	10.00	20.00
❏ F3084	Two Hearts, Two Kisses/From the Bottom to the Top	1955	3.75	7.50	15.00
❏ F3102	Learnin' the Blues/If I Had Three Wishes	1955	3.75	7.50	15.00
❏ F3130	Not as a Stranger/How Could You Do a Thing Like That to Me?	1955	3.75	7.50	15.00
❏ F3218	Same Old Saturday Night/Fairy Tale	1955	3.75	7.50	15.00
❏ F3260	Love and Marriage/The Impatient Years	1955	5.00	10.00	20.00
❏ F3290	(Love Is) The Tender Trap/Weep They Will	1955	3.75	7.50	15.00
❏ F3350	Flowers Mean Forgiveness/You'll Get Yours	1956	3.75	7.50	15.00
❏ F3423	(How Little It Maters) How Little We Know/Five Hundred Guys	1956	3.75	7.50	15.00
❏ F3469	You're Sensational/Johnny Concho Theme (Wait for Me)	1956	3.75	7.50	15.00
❏ F3507	Well, Did You Evah?/True Love	1956	3.75	7.50	15.00
—A-side by Bing Crosby and Frank Sinatra; b-side by Bing Crosby and Grace Kelly					
❏ F3508	Who Wants to Be a Millionaire/Mind If I Make Love to You?	1956	3.75	7.50	15.00
❏ F3552	Hey! Jealous Lover/You Forgot All the Words	1956	3.75	7.50	15.00
❏ F3552	Jealous Lover/You Forgot All the Words	1956	6.25	12.50	25.00
—Original pressings contain this title					
❏ F3608	Can I Steal a Little Love/Your Love for Me	1956	3.75	7.50	15.00
❏ F3703	Crazy Love/So Long, My Love	1957	3.00	6.00	12.00
❏ F3744	You're Cheatin' Yourself (If You're Cheatin' On Me)/Something Wonderful Happens in Summer	1957	3.00	6.00	12.00
❏ F3793	All the Way/Chicago	1957	3.00	6.00	12.00
❏ F3859	Witchcraft/Tell Her You Love Her	1957	3.00	6.00	12.00
❏ F3900	Mistletoe and Holly/The Christmas Waltz	1957	3.75	7.50	15.00
—"The Christmas Waltz" here is a different version than that on Capitol 2954.					
❏ F3952	How Are Ya' Fixed for Love?/Nothin' in Common	1958	3.00	6.00	12.00
—By Frank Sinatra and Keely Smith					
❏ F4003	Same Old Song and Dance/Monique (Song from Kings Go Forth)	1958	3.00	6.00	12.00
❏ F4070	Mr. Success/Sleep Warm	1958	3.00	6.00	12.00
❏ F4103	Song from "Some Came Running"/No One Ever Tells You	1958	3.00	6.00	12.00
❏ F4103	To Love and Be Loved/No One Ever Tells You	1958	3.00	6.00	12.00

Number	Title (A Side/B Side)	Yr	VG	VG+	NM
❑ F4103 [PS]	To Love and Be Loved/No One Ever Tells You	1958	25.00	50.00	100.00
—Promo-only sleeve					
❑ F4155	French Foreign Legion/Time After Time	1959	3.00	6.00	12.00
❑ F4214	High Hopes/All My Tomorrows	1959	3.75	7.50	15.00
❑ F4214 [PS]	High Hopes/All My Tomorrows	1959	50.00	100.00	200.00
❑ F4284	Talk to Me/They Came to Cordura	1959	3.00	6.00	12.00
❑ 4376	River, Stay 'Way from My Door/It's Over, It's Over, It's Over	1960	3.00	6.00	12.00
❑ 4408	Nice 'N' Easy/This Was My Love	1960	3.00	6.00	12.00
❑ 4466	Ol' MacDonald/You'll Always Be the One I Love	1960	3.00	6.00	12.00
❑ 4546	My Blue Heaven/Sentimental Baby	1960	3.00	6.00	12.00
❑ 4615	American Beauty Rose/Sentimental Journey	1961	3.00	6.00	12.00
❑ 4677	The Moon Was Yellow/ I've Heard That Song Before	1962	3.00	6.00	12.00
❑ 4729	Five Minutes More/I'll Remember April	1962	3.00	6.00	12.00
❑ 4815	I Love Paris/Hidden Persuasion	1962	3.00	6.00	12.00
❑ 6019	Young at Heart/Learnin' the Blues	196?	—	3.00	6.00
—Starline reissue label					
❑ 6027	All the Way/High Hopes	196?	—	3.00	6.00
—Starline reissue label					
❑ 6078	Witchcraft/Chicago	1966	—	3.00	6.00
—Starline reissue label					
❑ 6193	One for My Baby/I've Got You Under My Skin	197?	—	3.00	6.00
❑ 6195	In the Wee Small Hours of the Morning/ Night and Day	197?	—	3.00	6.00
❑ S7-17704	I've Got You Under My Skin/ Come Rain or Come Shine	1994	—	—	—
—A-side with Bono, B-side with Gloria Estefan; canceled					
❑ S7-18204	Jingle Bells/I'll Be Home for Christmas	1994	—	2.50	5.00
—Red vinyl					
❑ 58741	Mistletoe and Holly/The Christmas Waltz	1998	—	—	3.00
❑ 77683	Witchcraft/When You're Smiling	2001	—	—	3.00
—B-side by Dean Martin					
COLUMBIA					
❑ 1-106	Sunflower/Once in Love with Amy	1948	15.00	30.00	60.00
—All records with a "1-" prefix are Microgroove 33 1/3 rpm 7-inch singles					
❑ 1-112	Why Can't You Behave/No Orchids for My Lady	1948	15.00	30.00	60.00
❑ B-112 [(4)]	The Voice of Frank Sinatra	1950	37.50	75.00	150.00
—Includes records 36918, 36919, 36920 and 36921 plus box					
❑ 1-130	Comme Ci, Comme Ca/ While the Angelus Was Ringing	1948	15.00	30.00	60.00
❑ 1-144	When Is Sometime/ If You Stub Your Toe on the Moon	1949	15.00	30.00	60.00
❑ 1-154	Where Is the One/Bop Goes My Heart	1949	15.00	30.00	60.00
❑ B-167 [(4)]	Christmas Songs by Sinatra	1950	37.50	75.00	150.00
—Includes records 38256, 38257, 38258 and 38259 plus box					
❑ 1-174	Bali Ha'i/Some Enchanted Evening	1949	15.00	30.00	60.00
❑ 1-191	The Right Girl for Me/Night After Night	1949	15.00	30.00	60.00
❑ B-197 [(4)]	Dedicated to You	1950	37.50	75.00	150.00
—Includes records 38683, 38684, 38685 and 38686 plus box					
❑ B-218 [(4)]	Sing and Dance with Frank Sinatra	1950	37.50	75.00	150.00
—Includes records 38996, 38997, 38998 and 38999 plus box					
❑ 1-222	It Happens Every Spring/The Hucklebuck	1949	15.00	30.00	60.00
❑ 1-260	Let's Take an Old-Fashioned Walk/Just One Way to Say I Love You	1949	15.00	30.00	60.00
—With Doris Day					
❑ 1-307	I Only Have Eyes for You/It All Depends on You	1949	15.00	30.00	60.00
❑ 1-315	Don't Cry Joe/The Wedding of Lili Marlene	1949	15.00	30.00	60.00
❑ 1-316	Just a Kiss Apart/Bye Bye Baby	1949	15.00	30.00	60.00
❑ 1-326	If I Ever Love Again/Every Man Should Marry	1949	15.00	30.00	60.00
❑ 1-372	Could'ja/That Lucky Old Sun	1949	15.00	30.00	60.00
❑ 1-380	On the Island of Stromboli/Mad About You	1949	15.00	30.00	60.00
❑ 1-427	The Old Master Painter/Lost in the Stars	1949	15.00	30.00	60.00
❑ 1-440	Sorry/Why Remind Me	1949	15.00	30.00	60.00
❑ 1-491	Sunshine Cake/We've Got a Sure Thing	1949	15.00	30.00	60.00
❑ 1-496	Chattanoogie Shoe Shine Boy/God's Country	1950	15.00	30.00	60.00
❑ 1-508	You'll Never Walk Alone/Begin the Beguine	1950	15.00	30.00	60.00
❑ 1-511	Among My Souvenirs/September Song	1950	15.00	30.00	60.00
❑ 1-611	Kisses and Tears/When the Sun Goes Down	1950	15.00	30.00	60.00
❑ 1-624	American Beauty Rose/ Just an Old Stone House	1950	15.00	30.00	60.00
❑ 1-650	Poinciana/ There's No Business Like Show Business	1950	15.00	30.00	60.00
❑ 1-669	Peachtree Street/This Is the Night	1950	15.00	30.00	60.00
❑ 1-718	Goodnight Irene/My Blue Heaven	1950	15.00	30.00	60.00
❑ 6-718	Goodnight Irene/My Blue Heaven	1950	7.50	15.00	30.00
❑ 1-780	Life Is So Peculiar/Dear Little Boy of Mine	1950	15.00	30.00	60.00
❑ 1-845	One Finger Melody/Accidents Will Happen	1950	15.00	30.00	60.00
❑ 1-888	Nevertheless/ I Guess I'll Have to Dream the Rest	1950	15.00	30.00	60.00
❑ 6-888	Nevertheless/ I Guess I'll Have to Dream the Rest	1950	7.50	15.00	30.00
❑ 1-924	Remember Me in Your Dreams/Let It Snow, Let It Snow, Let It Snow	1950	15.00	30.00	60.00
❑ 6-924	Remember Me in Your Dreams/Let It Snow, Let It Snow, Let It Snow	1950	7.50	15.00	30.00
❑ 1-936	I Am Loved/You Don't Remind Me	1950	15.00	30.00	60.00
❑ 6-936	I Am Loved/You Don't Remind Me	1950	7.50	15.00	30.00
❑ 13-33011	Nancy/Ol' Man River	1975	—	3.00	6.00
—Hall of Fame series; new prefix					
❑ 3-33011	Nancy/Ol' Man River	1961	12.50	25.00	50.00
—Hall of Fame series; Compact Single 33					
❑ 4-33011	Nancy/Ol' Man River	1960	2.50	5.00	10.00
❑ 33306	I've Got a Crush on You/The Birth of the Blues	1977	—	3.00	6.00
—Hall of Fame series					
❑ 33319	Among My Souvenirs/September Song	1977	—	3.00	6.00
—Hall of Fame series					
❑ 36814	If You Are But a Dream/Put Your Dreams Away	1950	5.00	10.00	20.00
—Most Columbia 45s from 36000-39000 are reissues of titles that first appeared on 78s					
❑ 36825	You'll Never Walk Alone/If I Loved You	1950	5.00	10.00	20.00
❑ 36918	You Go to My Head/I Don't Know Why	1950	5.00	10.00	20.00
❑ 36919	These Foolish Things/A Ghost of a Chance	1950	5.00	10.00	20.00
❑ 36920	Why Shouldn't I?/Try a Little Tenderness	1950	5.00	10.00	20.00
❑ 36921	Paradise/Someone to Watch Over Me	1950	5.00	10.00	20.00
—The above four comprise the box set The Voice of Frank Sinatra, B-112					
❑ 37161	Among My Souvenirs/September Song	1950	5.00	10.00	20.00
❑ 37257	That Old Black Magic/How Deep Is the Ocean?	1950	5.00	10.00	20.00

Number	Title (A Side/B Side)	Yr	VG	VG+	NM
❑ 37259	She's Funny That Way/Embraceable You	1950	5.00	10.00	20.00
❑ 38151	I've Got a Crush on You/Ever Homeward	1950	5.00	10.00	20.00
❑ 38163	All of Me/I Went Down to Virginia	1950	5.00	10.00	20.00
❑ 38256	Silent Night/Adeste Fideles	1950	5.00	10.00	20.00
❑ 38257	Jingle Bells/White Christmas	1950	5.00	10.00	20.00
❑ 38258	O Little Town Of Bethlehem/ It Came Upon A Midnight Clear	1950	5.00	10.00	20.00
❑ 38259	Have Yourself a Merry Little Christmas/Santa Claus Is Comin' to Town	1950	5.00	10.00	20.00
—The above four comprise the box set Christmas Songs by Sinatra, B-167					
❑ 38446	Bali Ha'i/Some Enchanted Evening	1950	5.00	10.00	20.00
❑ 38683	The Moon Was Yellow/The Music Stopped	1950	5.00	10.00	20.00
❑ 38684	Strange Music/I Love You	1950	5.00	10.00	20.00
❑ 38685	Where or When/None But the Lonely Heart	1950	5.00	10.00	20.00
❑ 38686	Always/Why Was I Born?	1950	5.00	10.00	20.00
—The above four comprise the box set Dedicated to You, B-197					
❑ 38829	Poinciana/There's No Business Like Show Business	1950	5.00	10.00	20.00
❑ 38892	Goodnight Irene/My Blue Heaven	1950	3.75	7.50	15.00
—Reissue of Columbia 6-718					
❑ 38996	Lover/When You're Smiling	1950	5.00	10.00	20.00
❑ 38997	The Continental/It's Only a Paper Moon	1950	5.00	10.00	20.00
❑ 38998	Should I?/My Blue Heaven	1950	5.00	10.00	20.00
❑ 38999	It All Depends on You/You Do Something to Me	1950	5.00	10.00	20.00
—The above four comprise the box set Sing and Dance with Frank Sinatra, B-218					
❑ 39044	Nevertheless/ I Guess I'll Have to Dream the Rest	1950	3.75	7.50	15.00
—Reissue of Columbia 6-888					
❑ 39069	Remember Me in Your Dreams/Let It Snow, Let It Snow, Let It Snow	1950	3.75	7.50	15.00
—Reissue of Columbia 6-924					
❑ 39079	I Am Loved/You Don't Remind Me	1950	3.75	7.50	15.00
—Reissue of Columbia 6-936					
❑ 39118	Take My Love/Come Back to Sorrento	1950	3.75	7.50	15.00
❑ 3-39118	Take My Love/Come Back to Sorrento	1950	50.00	100.00	150.00
—Microgroove 33 1/3 rpm, 7-inch single					
❑ 39141	Love Means Love/Cherry Pies Ought to Be You	1951	6.25	12.50	25.00
❑ 3-39141	Love Means Love/Cherry Pies Ought to Be You	1951	200.00	400.00	600.00
—Microgroove 33 1/3 rpm, 7-inch single					
❑ 39213	Faithful/You're the One	1951	5.00	10.00	20.00
❑ 3-39213	Faithful/You're the One	1951	50.00	100.00	150.00
—Microgroove 33 1/3 rpm, 7-inch single					
❑ 39294	Hello, Young Lovers/We Kissed in a Shadow	1951	3.75	7.50	15.00
❑ 39346	I Whistle a Happy Tune/un One	1951	3.75	7.50	15.00
❑ 39425	Mama Will Bark/I'm a Fool to Want You	1951	10.00	20.00	40.00
—"Frank Sinatra & Dagmar"; the record Ol' Blue Eyes called his worst					
❑ 39493	I Fall in Love with You Everyday/It's a Long Way from Your House	1951	5.00	10.00	20.00
❑ 39498	It Never Entered My Mind/ Try a Little Tenderness	1951	3.75	7.50	15.00
❑ 39527	Castle Rock/Deep Night	1951	5.00	10.00	20.00
❑ 39592	April in Paris/London by Night	1951	3.75	7.50	15.00
❑ 39652	I Hear a Rhapsody/I Could Write a Book	1952	3.75	7.50	15.00
❑ 39687	Feet of Clay/Don't Ever Be Afraid to Go Home	1952	5.00	10.00	20.00
❑ 39726	My Girl/Walkin' in the Sunshine	1952	5.00	10.00	20.00
❑ 39787	Luna Rosa/Tennessee Newsboy	1952	5.00	10.00	20.00
❑ 39819	Azure-Te/Bim Bam Baby	1952	3.75	7.50	15.00
❑ 39882	The Birth of the Blues/ Why Try to Change Me Now?	1952	3.75	7.50	15.00
❑ 40229	I'm Glad There Is You/ You Can Take My Word For It Baby	1954	5.00	10.00	20.00
❑ 40522	Dream/American Beauty Rose	1955	3.75	7.50	15.00
❑ 40565	Sheila/Day by Day	1955	7.50	15.00	30.00
❑ 41133	I'm a Fool to Want You/If I Forget You	1958	3.75	7.50	15.00
❑ 50003	Among My Souvenirs/September Song	1954	2.50	5.00	10.00
—Hall of Fame series					
❑ 50028	I've Got a Crush on You/The Birth of the Blues	1954	2.50	5.00	10.00
—Hall of Fame series					
❑ 50053	Nancy/The Girl That I Marry	1955	2.50	5.00	10.00
—Hall of Fame series					
❑ 50066	You'll Never Walk Alone/If I Loved You	1955	2.50	5.00	10.00
—Hall of Fame series					
❑ 50069	Saturday Night/Five Minutes More	1955	2.50	5.00	10.00
—Hall of Fame series					
❑ 50079	Silent Night/Adeste Fideles	1955	2.50	5.00	10.00
—Hall of Fame series					
❑ JZSP 116427/8 [DJ]	White Christmas/Have Yourself A Merry Little Christmas	1966	12.50	25.00	50.00
ISLAND/CAPITOL					
❑ 858076-7	I've Got You Under My Skin/Stay (Faraway, So Close!)	1994	—	2.00	4.00
—A-side: Frank Sinatra and Bono; B-side: U2					
❑ 858076-7 [PS]	I've Got You Under My Skin/Stay (Faraway, So Close!)	1994	—	2.00	4.00
—A-side: Frank Sinatra and Bono; B-side: U2					
MCA					
❑ 55127	Fly Me to the Moon/Check Yes or No	1995	—	2.00	4.00
—A-side with George Strait; B-side is George Strait solo					
QWEST					
❑ 28844	The Best of Everything/Teach Me Tonight	1985	—	2.00	4.00
❑ 29139	Mack the Knife/It's All Right with Me	1984	—	2.50	5.00
❑ 29223	L.A. Is My Lady/ Until the Real Thing Comes Along	1984	—	2.50	5.00
❑ 29223 [PS]	L.A. Is My Lady/ Until the Real Thing Comes Along	1984	3.75	7.50	15.00
RCA VICTOR					
❑ 27-0012	Night and Day/The Lamplighter's Serenade	1948	3.75	7.50	15.00
—All RCA and 45s are reissues of material first issued on 78s. Part of WPT-5					
❑ 27-0076	Stardust/(B-side unknown)	1949	3.75	7.50	15.00
—From WDT 15					
❑ 27-0077	I'll Never Smile Again/(B-side unknown)	1949	3.75	7.50	15.00
—From WDT 15					
❑ 27-0095	Somewhere A Voice Is Calling/ (B-side unknown)	1949	3.75	7.50	15.00
—From WDT 20					
❑ 27-0151	Daybreak/There Are Such Things	1948	3.75	7.50	15.00
❑ 447-0116	I'll Never Smile Again/I'll Be Seeing You	1950	3.00	6.00	12.00
❑ 447-0123	Stardust/There Are Such Things	1950	3.00	6.00	12.00

S

Number	Title (A Side/B Side)	Yr	VG	VG+	NM
447-0408	Night and Day/The Lamplighter's Serenade	1952	3.00	6.00	12.00
447-0445	Street of Dreams/East of the Sun	1952	3.00	6.00	12.00
447-0928	Night and Day/The Night We Called It a Day	1972	—	3.00	6.00
447-0929	The Song Is You/The Lamplighter's Serenade	1972	—	3.00	6.00
DTAO-3001	Street of Dreams/Whispering	1973	3.00	6.00	12.00
DTBO-3012	The One I Love/This Love of Mine	1973	3.00	6.00	12.00

REPRISE

Number	Title (A Side/B Side)	Yr	VG	VG+	NM
0053	I'll Be Seeing You/Without a Song	1962	50.00	100.00	200.00

—Released in Great Britain as 20,053; pressed in the United States later

Number	Title (A Side/B Side)	Yr	VG	VG+	NM
GRE 0113	Bad, Bad Leroy Brown/Let Me Try Again	1975	5.00	10.00	20.00

—"Back to Back Hits" series

Number	Title (A Side/B Side)	Yr	VG	VG+	NM
GRE 0122	Theme from New York, New York/ You and Me (We Wanted It All)	1981	—	2.00	4.00

—"Back to Back Hits" series

Number	Title (A Side/B Side)	Yr	VG	VG+	NM
S 168 [S]	Moon River/Days of Wine and Roses	1964	5.00	10.00	20.00
S 169 [S]	Three Coins in the Fountain/ The Way You Look Tonight	1964	5.00	10.00	20.00
S 170 [S]	Secret Love/ In the Cool, Cool, Cool of the Evening	1964	5.00	10.00	20.00
S 171 [S]	It Might As Well Be Spring/Swinging on a Star	1964	5.00	10.00	20.00
S 172 [S]	All the Way/The Continental	1964	5.00	10.00	20.00

—The above five are 33 1/3 rpm, small hole jukebox singles

Number	Title (A Side/B Side)	Yr	VG	VG+	NM
243	Have Yourself a Merry Little Christmas/How Shall I Send Thee?	1963	5.00	10.00	20.00

—B-side by Les Baxter

Number	Title (A Side/B Side)	Yr	VG	VG+	NM
0249	Stay with Me/Talk to Me Baby	1963	2.50	5.00	10.00
0279	My Kind of Town/I Like to Lead When I Dance	1964	2.50	5.00	10.00
0279 [PS]	My Kind of Town/I Like to Lead When I Dance	1964	37.50	75.00	150.00

—Sleeve issued with promo copies only

Number	Title (A Side/B Side)	Yr	VG	VG+	NM
0301	Softly, As I Leave You/Then Suddenly Love	1964	2.50	5.00	10.00
0314	I Heard the Bells on Christmas Day/ The Little Drummer Boy	1964	5.00	10.00	20.00
0314 [PS]	I Heard the Bells on Christmas Day/ The Little Drummer Boy	1964	12.50	25.00	50.00
0317	We Wish You the Merriest/ Go Tell It on the Mountain	1964	10.00	20.00	40.00

—By Frank Sinatra/Bing Crosby/Fred Waring

Number	Title (A Side/B Side)	Yr	VG	VG+	NM
0317 [PS]	We Wish You the Merriest/ Go Tell It on the Mountain	1964	15.00	30.00	60.00

—By Frank Sinatra/Bing Crosby/Fred Waring

Number	Title (A Side/B Side)	Yr	VG	VG+	NM
0332	Somewhere in Your Heart/Emily	1964	2.00	4.00	8.00

—From here through 0677, originals on dark brown & orange label

Number	Title (A Side/B Side)	Yr	VG	VG+	NM
0350	Anytime at All/Available	1964	2.00	4.00	8.00
0373	Tell Her (You Love Her Each Day)/ Here's to the Losers	1965	2.00	4.00	8.00
0380	Forget Domani/I Can't Believe I'm Losing You	1965	2.00	4.00	8.00
0398	When Somebody Loves You/When I'm Not Near the Girl I Love	1965	2.00	4.00	8.00
0410	Everybody Has the Right to Be Wrong/I'll Only Miss Her When I Think of Her	1965	2.00	4.00	8.00
0429	It Was a Very Good Year/Moment to Moment	1965	2.00	4.00	8.00
0429 [PS]	It Was a Very Good Year/Moment to Moment	1965	6.25	12.50	25.00
0470	Strangers in the Night/Oh, You Crazy Moon	1966	2.50	5.00	10.00
0493	Frank Sinatra Reads from Gunga Din	1966	125.00	250.00	500.00

—300 pressed and given away to friends; no stock copies

Number	Title (A Side/B Side)	Yr	VG	VG+	NM
0509	Summer Wind/You Make Me Feel So Young	1966	2.50	5.00	10.00
0531	That's Life/The September of My Years	1966	2.50	5.00	10.00
0531 [PS]	That's Life/The September of My Years	1966	6.25	12.50	25.00
0561	Somethin' Stupid/I Will Wait for You	1967	2.00	4.00	8.00

—A-side: Nancy Sinatra and Frank Sinatra

Number	Title (A Side/B Side)	Yr	VG	VG+	NM
0561	Somethin' Stupid/Give Her Love	1967	2.50	5.00	10.00

—A-side: Nancy Sinatra and Frank Sinatra

Number	Title (A Side/B Side)	Yr	VG	VG+	NM
0610	The World We Knew (Over and Over)/You Are There	1967	2.00	4.00	8.00
0631	This Town/This Is My Love	1967	2.00	4.00	8.00
0677	I Can't Believe I'm Losing You/How Old Am I?	1967	2.00	4.00	8.00
0702	My Kind of Town/That's Life	1968	—	2.50	5.00

—"Back to Back Hits" series

Number	Title (A Side/B Side)	Yr	VG	VG+	NM
0706	September of My Years/Softly, As I Leave You	1968	—	2.50	5.00

—"Back to Back Hits" series

Number	Title (A Side/B Side)	Yr	VG	VG+	NM
0710	Strangers in the Night/Summer Wind	1968	—	2.50	5.00

—"Back to Back Hits" series

Number	Title (A Side/B Side)	Yr	VG	VG+	NM
0713	It Was a Very Good Year/Stay with Me	1968	—	2.50	5.00

—"Back to Back Hits" series

Number	Title (A Side/B Side)	Yr	VG	VG+	NM
0727	Somethin' Stupid/The World We Knew (Over and Over)	1968	—	2.50	5.00

—"Back to Back Hits" series; A-side with Nancy Sinatra

Number	Title (A Side/B Side)	Yr	VG	VG+	NM
0734	My Way/Cycles	1970	—	2.50	5.00

—"Back to Back Hits" series

Number	Title (A Side/B Side)	Yr	VG	VG+	NM
0764	Cycles/My Way of Life	1968	—	3.00	6.00

—From here though 0865, orange/tan label with "W7/:r" logo

Number	Title (A Side/B Side)	Yr	VG	VG+	NM
0790	Whatever Happened to Christmas?/I Wouldn't Trade Christmas	1968	3.00	6.00	12.00

—B-side by The Sinatra Family

Number	Title (A Side/B Side)	Yr	VG	VG+	NM
0798	Rain in My Heart/Star	1968	—	3.00	6.00
0817	My Way/Blue Lace	1969	2.50	5.00	10.00
0852	Love's Been Good to Me/A Man Alone	1969	2.00	4.00	8.00
0865	Goin' Out of My Head/Forget to Remember	1969	2.00	4.00	8.00
0895	I Would Be in Love (Anyway)/Watertown	1970	2.00	4.00	8.00

—From here through 29903, orange (or tan) label with ":r" logo in square

Number	Title (A Side/B Side)	Yr	VG	VG+	NM
0920	The Train/What's Now Is Now	1969	2.00	4.00	8.00
0970	Lady Day/Song of the Sabia	1969	2.00	4.00	8.00
0980	Feelin' Kinda Sunday/Kids	1970	2.00	4.00	8.00

—A-side by Nancy Sinatra and Frank Sinatra; B-side by Nancy Sinatra

Number	Title (A Side/B Side)	Yr	VG	VG+	NM
0981	Something/Bein' Green	1970	2.00	4.00	8.00
PRO-S-1007	To Love a Child (mono/stereo)	1982	75.00	150.00	300.00

—Special pressing of 500 with small hole, given to Nancy Reagan for distribuiton at a White House function.

Number	Title (A Side/B Side)	Yr	VG	VG+	NM
1010	Witchcraft/Young at Heart	1971	2.00	4.00	8.00
1011	Life's a Trippy Thing/I'm Not Afraid	1971	2.00	4.00	8.00

—A-side by Nancy Sinatra and Frank Sinatra

Number	Title (A Side/B Side)	Yr	VG	VG+	NM
1181	Let Me Try Again/Send In the Clowns	1973	2.00	4.00	8.00
1190	You Will Be My Music/Winners	1973	2.00	4.00	8.00
1196	Bad, Bad Leroy Brown/ I'm Gonna Make It All the Way	1974	2.00	4.00	8.00
1208	You Turned My World Around/ Satisfy Me One More Time	1974	2.00	4.00	8.00

Number	Title (A Side/B Side)	Yr	VG	VG+	NM
1327	Anytime (I'll Be There)/ The Hurt Doesn't Go Away	1975	2.00	4.00	8.00
1335	I Believe I'm Gonna Love You/ The Only Couple on the Floor	1975	2.00	4.00	8.00
1335 [PS]	I Believe I'm Gonna Love You	1975	10.00	20.00	40.00

—Issued with promo copies only

Number	Title (A Side/B Side)	Yr	VG	VG+	NM
1342	A Baby Just Like You/Christmas Mem'ries	1975	2.50	5.00	10.00
1342 [PS]	A Baby Just Like You/Christmas Mem'ries	1975	5.00	10.00	20.00

—Red and black printing, released with stock copies

Number	Title (A Side/B Side)	Yr	VG	VG+	NM
1342 [PS]	A Baby Just Like You/Christmas Mem'ries	1975	10.00	20.00	40.00

—Blue printing, released with promo copies only

Number	Title (A Side/B Side)	Yr	VG	VG+	NM
1343	Empty Tables/The Saddest Thing of All	1976	2.00	4.00	8.00
1347	I Sing the Songs (I Write the Songs)/ Empty Tables	1976	2.50	5.00	10.00
1364	Stargazer/The Best I Ever Had	1976	2.00	4.00	8.00
1364 [PS]	Stargazer/The Best I Ever Had	1976	3.75	7.50	15.00

—Special sleeve: "New Sinatra Single"

Number	Title (A Side/B Side)	Yr	VG	VG+	NM
1377	Dry Your Eyes/Like a Sad Song	1976	2.00	4.00	8.00
1382	I Love My Wife/Send In the Clowns	1976	2.50	5.00	10.00
1386	Night and Day/Everybody Ought to Be in Love	1977	2.00	4.00	8.00
15999	My Way/Cycles	199?	—	—	3.00

—"Back to Back Hits" series

Number	Title (A Side/B Side)	Yr	VG	VG+	NM
19355	Fly Me to the Moon/The Last Dance	1991	—	2.00	4.00
20001	The Second Time Around/Tina	1961	6.25	12.50	25.00

—Originals on light blue label

Number	Title (A Side/B Side)	Yr	VG	VG+	NM
20010	Granada/The Curse of an Aching Heart	1961	3.75	7.50	15.00

—From here through 0317, originals on peach label

Number	Title (A Side/B Side)	Yr	VG	VG+	NM
20010 [PS]	Granada/The Curse of an Aching Heart	1961	6.25	12.50	25.00
20023	I'll Be Seeing You/The One I Love	1961	3.75	7.50	15.00
20024	Imagination/It's Always You	1961	3.75	7.50	15.00
20025	I'm Getting Sentimental Over You/East of the Sun (And West of the Moon)	1961	3.75	7.50	15.00
20026	There Are Such Things/ Polkadots and Moonbeams	1961	3.75	7.50	15.00
20027	Without a Song/It Started All Over Again	1961	3.75	7.50	15.00
20028	Take Me/Daybreak	1961	3.75	7.50	15.00
20040	Pocketful of Miracles/Name It and It's Yours	1961	3.75	7.50	15.00
20040 [PS]	Pocketful of Miracles/Name It and It's Yours	1961	15.00	30.00	60.00
20059	Stardust/Come Rain or Come Shine	1962	3.75	7.50	15.00
20063	Everybody's Twistin'/Nothin' But the Best	1962	3.75	7.50	15.00
20063 [PS]	Everybody's Twistin'/Nothin' But the Best	1962	7.50	15.00	30.00
20092	Goody, Goody/Love Is Just Around the Corner	1962	3.00	6.00	12.00
20107	The Look of Love/ I Left My Heart in San Francisco	1962	12.50	25.00	50.00
20107	The Look of Love/Indiscreet	1962	12.50	25.00	50.00
20128	Me and My Shadow/Sam's Song	1962	3.75	7.50	15.00

—A-side by Frank Sinatra and Sammy Davis, Jr.; B-side by Sammy Davis Jr. and Dean Martin

Number	Title (A Side/B Side)	Yr	VG	VG+	NM
20128 [PS]	Me and My Shadow/Sam's Song	1962	12.50	25.00	50.00

—A-side by Frank Sinatra and Sammy Davis, Jr.; B-side by Sammy Davis Jr. and Dean Martin

Number	Title (A Side/B Side)	Yr	VG	VG+	NM
20151	Call Me Irresponsible/Tina	1963	2.50	5.00	10.00

—B-side changed for commercial release

Number	Title (A Side/B Side)	Yr	VG	VG+	NM
20151	Call Me Irresponsible/Come Blow Your Horn	1963	125.00	250.00	500.00

—One stock copy is known to exist!

Number	Title (A Side/B Side)	Yr	VG	VG+	NM
20151 [DJ]	Call Me Irresponsible/Come Blow Your Horn	1963	25.00	50.00	100.00
20151 [PS]	Call Me Irresponsible/Come Blow Your Horn	1963	50.00	100.00	200.00

—Sleeve accompanies promo copies only

Number	Title (A Side/B Side)	Yr	VG	VG+	NM
20157	California/America the Beautiful	1963	62.50	125.00	250.00

—No stock copies isssued

Number	Title (A Side/B Side)	Yr	VG	VG+	NM
20157 [PS]	California/America the Beautiful	1963	187.50	375.00	750.00

—No stock copies isssued

Number	Title (A Side/B Side)	Yr	VG	VG+	NM
20157 [DJ]	California/America the Beautiful	1978	50.00	100.00	200.00

—Private pressing of 1,000 for Sinatra's personal use

Number	Title (A Side/B Side)	Yr	VG	VG+	NM
20184	I Have Dreamed/Come Blow Your Horn	1963	2.50	5.00	10.00
20209	Love Isn't Just for the Young/You Brought a New Kind of Love to Me	1963	3.00	6.00	12.00
20209 [PS]	Love Isn't Just for the Young/You Brought a New Kind of Love to Me	1963	12.50	25.00	50.00
20217	Fugue for Tinhorns/The Oldest Established (Permanent Floating Crap Game in New York)	1963	3.75	7.50	15.00

—By Frank Sinatra/Bing Crosby/Dean Martin

Number	Title (A Side/B Side)	Yr	VG	VG+	NM
20217 [PS]	Fugue for Tinhorns/The Oldest Established (Permanent Floating Crap Game in New York)	1963	18.75	37.50	75.00

—By Frank Sinatra/Bing Crosby/Dean Martin

Number	Title (A Side/B Side)	Yr	VG	VG+	NM
20235	Tangerine/A New Kind of Love	1963	—	—	—

—Unreleased

Number	Title (A Side/B Side)	Yr	VG	VG+	NM
29677	Here's to the Band/It's Sunday	1983	2.00	4.00	8.00
29903	To Love a Child/ That's What God Looks Like to Me	1982	2.00	4.00	8.00
29903 [PS]	To Love a Child/ That's What God Looks Like to Me	1982	3.75	7.50	15.00
40003	I Never Knew/Don't Be That Way	196?	5.00	10.00	20.00

—Jukebox 33 1/3 rpm, small hole single

Number	Title (A Side/B Side)	Yr	VG	VG+	NM
40006	Imagination/It's Always You	196?	5.00	10.00	20.00

—Jukebox record; small hole, plays at 33 1/3 rpm

Number	Title (A Side/B Side)	Yr	VG	VG+	NM
40009	It Started All Over Again/Without a Song	196?	5.00	10.00	20.00

—Jukebox 33 1/3 rpm, small hole single

Number	Title (A Side/B Side)	Yr	VG	VG+	NM
40013	Come Rain or Come Shine/ It Might As Well Be Spring	196?	5.00	10.00	20.00

—Jukebox 33 1/3 rpm, small hole single

Number	Title (A Side/B Side)	Yr	VG	VG+	NM
40036	Pennies from Heaven/Please Be Kind	196?	5.00	10.00	20.00

—Jukebox 33 1/3 rpm, small hole single

Number	Title (A Side/B Side)	Yr	VG	VG+	NM
40037	The Tender Trap/Looking at the World Thru Rose Colored Glasses	1963	5.00	10.00	20.00

—Jukebox 33 1/3 rpm, small hole single

Number	Title (A Side/B Side)	Yr	VG	VG+	NM
40038	My Kind of Girl/I Only Have Eyes for You	1963	5.00	10.00	20.00

—Jukebox 33 1/3 rpm, small hole single

Number	Title (A Side/B Side)	Yr	VG	VG+	NM
40039	Nice Work If You Can Get It/Learnin' the Blues	1963	5.00	10.00	20.00

—Jukebox 33 1/3 rpm, small hole single

Number	Title (A Side/B Side)	Yr	VG	VG+	NM
40040	I'm Gonna Sit Right Down and Write Myself a Letter/I Won't Dance	1963	5.00	10.00	20.00

—Jukebox 33 1/3 rpm, small hole single

Number	Title (A Side/B Side)	Yr	VG	VG+	NM
40050	Please Be Kind/My Kind of Girl	1963	5.00	10.00	20.00

—Jukebox 33 1/3 rpm, small hole single

Number	Title (A Side/B Side)	Yr	VG	VG+	NM
49233	Theme from New York, New York/ That's What God Looks Like to Me	1980	2.50	5.00	10.00
49233 [PS]	Theme from New York, New York/That's What God Looks Like to Me	1980	3.75	7.50	15.00

Number	Title (A Side/B Side)	Yr	VG	VG+	NM
❏ 49517	You and Me (We Wanted It All)/I've Been There	1980	2.00	4.00	8.00
❏ 49827	Say Hello/Good Thing Going	1981	2.00	4.00	8.00
—B-side listed on label as "RE-2"					
❏ 49827	Say Hello/Good Thing Going	1981	2.00	4.00	8.00
—B-side listed on label as "RE-1"					

7-Inch Extended Plays

CAPITOL

Number	Title (A Side/B Side)	Yr	VG	VG+	NM
❏ EAP 1-488	My Funny Valentine/The Girl Next Door//They Can't Take That Away from Me/Violets for Your Furs	1954	5.00	10.00	20.00
❏ EAP 1-488 [PS]	Songs for Young Lovers, Vol. 1	1954	5.00	10.00	20.00
❏ EAP 2-488	A Foggy Day/Like Someone I Love//I Get a Kick Out of You/Little Girl Blue	1954	5.00	10.00	20.00
❏ EAP 2-488 [PS]	Songs for Young Lovers, Vol. 2	1954	5.00	10.00	20.00
❏ EBF 488 [PS]	Songs for Young Lovers	1954	12.50	25.00	50.00
—Both of above EPs in gatefold sleeve					
❏ EAP 1-510	Young at Heart/I've Got the World on a String//From Here to Eternity/South of the Border	1954	6.25	12.50	25.00
❏ EAP 1-510 [PS]	Young at Heart	1954	6.25	12.50	25.00
❏ EAP 1-528	Just One of Those Things/I'm Gonna Sit Right Down and Write Myself a Letter//Sunday/Wrap Your Troubles in Dreams	1954	5.00	10.00	20.00
❏ EAP 1-528 [PS]	Swing Easy, Part I	1954	5.00	10.00	20.00
❏ EAP 2-528	Taking a Chance on Love/Jeepers Creepers//Get Happy/All of Me	1954	5.00	10.00	20.00
❏ EAP 2-528 [PS]	Swing Easy, Part II	1954	5.00	10.00	20.00
❏ EBF 528 [PS]	Swing Easy	1954	12.50	25.00	50.00
—Both 1-528 and 2-528 EPs in gatefold sleeve					
❏ EAP 1-542	Three Coins in the Fountain/My One and Only Love//Don't Worry 'Bout Me/I Love You	1954	6.25	12.50	25.00
❏ EAP 1-542 [PS]	3 Coins in the Fountain	1954	6.25	12.50	25.00
❏ EAP 1-571	Young at Heart/Someone to Watch Over Me//Just One of Those Things/You, My Love	1954	6.25	12.50	25.00
❏ EAP 1-571 [PS]	Frank Sinatra Sings Songs from His Warner Bros. Picture "Young at Heart"	1954	6.25	12.50	25.00
❏ EAP 1-581	In the Wee Small Hours of the Morning/I See Your Face Before Me//I'll Never Be the Same/This Love of Mine	1954	5.00	10.00	20.00
❏ EAP 1-581 [PS]	In the Wee Small Hours, Part 1	1955	5.00	10.00	20.00
❏ EAP 2-581	I'll Be Around/I Get Along Without You Very Well/It Never Entered My Mind//Dancing on the Ceiling	1955	5.00	10.00	20.00
❏ EAP 2-581 [PS]	In the Wee Small Hours, Part 2	1955	5.00	10.00	20.00
❏ EAP 3-581	Deep in a Dream/Mood Indigo//Glad to Be Unhappy/Ill Wind	1955	5.00	10.00	20.00
❏ EAP 3-581 [PS]	In the Wee Small Hours, Part 3	1955	5.00	10.00	20.00
❏ EAP 4-581	Can't We Be Friends/When Your Lover Has Gone//What Is This Thing Called Love/Last Night When We Were Young	1955	5.00	10.00	20.00
❏ EAP 4-581 [PS]	In the Wee Small Hours, Part 4	1955	5.00	10.00	20.00
❏ EBF 1-581 [PS]	In the Wee Small Hours, Parts 1 and 2	1955	12.50	25.00	50.00
—Gatefold sleeve for some editions of EAP 1-581 and 2-581					
❏ EBF 2-581 [PS]	In the Wee Small Hours, Parts 3 and 4	1955	12.50	25.00	50.00
—Gatefold sleeve for some editions of EAP 3-581 and 4-581					
❏ EAP 1-590	I'm Gonna Live Till I Die/Day In — Day Out//Melody of Love/Ever Since You Went Away	1955	6.25	12.50	25.00
—Second song on B-side by The Skyliners with Ray Anthony (no Sinatra involvement)					
❏ EAP 1-590 [PS]	Melody of Love	1955	6.25	12.50	25.00
❏ EAP 1-629	Two Hearts, Two Kisses (Make One Love)/Don't Change Your Mind About Me//Learnin' the Blues/Why Should I Cry Over You?	1955	6.25	12.50	25.00
❏ EAP 1-629 [PS]	Session with Sinatra	1955	6.25	12.50	25.00
❏ DU-653	It Happened in Monterey/Too Marvelous for Words/Anything Goes//You Make Me Feel So Young/I've Got You Under My Skin	196?	6.25	12.50	25.00
—Jukebox EP, plays at 33 1/3 rpm, small hole					
❏ DU-653 [PS]	Songs for Swingin' Lovers	196?	6.25	12.50	25.00
❏ EAP 1-653	You Make Me Feel So Young/It Happened in Monterey//Anything Goes/How About You	1956	6.25	12.50	25.00
❏ EAP 1-653 [PS]	Songs for Swingin' Lovers, Part 1	1956	5.00	10.00	20.00
—With Sinatra facing away from the embracing couple					
❏ EAP 1-653 [PS]	Songs for Swingin' Lovers, Part 1	1957	5.00	10.00	20.00
—With Sinatra facing toward the embracing couple					
❏ EAP 2-653	You're Getting to Be a Habit with Me/You Brought a New Kind of Love to Me//Makin' Whoopee/Swingin' Down the Lane	1956	5.00	10.00	20.00
❏ EAP 2-653 [PS]	Songs for Swingin' Lovers, Part 2	1956	6.25	12.50	25.00
—With Sinatra facing away from the embracing couple					
❏ EAP 2-653 [PS]	Songs for Swingin' Lovers, Part 2	1957	5.00	10.00	20.00
—With Sinatra facing toward the embracing couple					
❏ EAP 3-653	Too Marvelous for Words/Old Devil Moon//We'll Be Together Again	1956	5.00	10.00	20.00
❏ EAP 3-653 [PS]	Songs for Swingin' Lovers, Part 3	1956	6.25	12.50	25.00
—With Sinatra facing away from the embracing couple					
❏ EAP 3-653 [PS]	Songs for Swingin' Lovers, Part 3	1957	5.00	10.00	20.00
—With Sinatra facing toward the embracing couple					
❏ EAP 4-653	Pennies from Heaven/I've Got You Under My Skin/I Thought About You	1956	5.00	10.00	20.00
❏ EAP 4-653 [PS]	Songs for Swingin' Lovers, Part 4	1956	6.25	12.50	25.00
—With Sinatra facing away from the embracing couple					
❏ EAP 4-653 [PS]	Songs for Swingin' Lovers, Part 4	1957	5.00	10.00	20.00
—With Sinatra facing toward the embracing couple					
❏ EBF 1-653 [PS]	Songs for Swingin' Lovers, Parts 1 and 2	1956	15.00	30.00	60.00
—Gatefold sleeve for some editions of EAP 1-653 and 2-653; with Sinatra facing away from the embracing couple					
❏ EBF 1-653 [PS]	Songs for Swingin' Lovers, Parts 1 and 2	1957	12.50	25.00	50.00
—Gatefold sleeve for some editions of EAP 1-653 and 2-653; with Sinatra facing toward the embracing couple					
❏ EBF 2-653 [PS]	Songs for Swingin' Lovers, Parts 3 and 4	1956	15.00	30.00	60.00
—Gatefold sleeve for some editions of EAP 3-653 and 4-653; with Sinatra facing away from the embracing couple					
❏ EBF 2-653 [PS]	Songs for Swingin' Lovers, Parts 3 and 4	1957	12.50	25.00	50.00
—Gatefold sleeve for some editions of EAP 3-653 and 4-653; with Sinatra facing toward the embracing couple					
❏ EAP 1-673	Our Town/The Impatient Years//Love and Marriage/Look to Your Heart	1956	12.50	25.00	50.00
❏ EAP 1-673 [PS]	Our Town	1956	12.50	25.00	50.00
❏ DU-768	I've Got the World on a String/Three Coins in the Fountain/Love and Marriage//South of the Border/Young at Heart/The Tender Trap	196?	6.25	12.50	25.00
—Jukebox EP, plays at 33 1/3 rpm, small hole					
❏ DU-768 [PS]	This Is Sinatra	196?	6.25	12.50	25.00
❏ EAP 1-789	Close to You/Love Locked Out//The End of a Love Affair	1956	5.00	10.00	20.00
❏ EAP 1-789 [PS]	Close to You, Part 1	1956	5.00	10.00	20.00
❏ EAP 2-789	P.S. I Love You//With Every Breath I Take/I Couldn't Sleep a Wink Last Night	1956	5.00	10.00	20.00
❏ EAP 2-789 [PS]	Close to You, Part 2	1956	5.00	10.00	20.00
❏ EAP 3-789	Everything Happens to Me/It Could Happen to You//I've Had My Moments	1956	5.00	10.00	20.00
❏ EAP 3-789 [PS]	Close to You, Part 3	1956	5.00	10.00	20.00
❏ EAP 4-789	Don't Like Goodbyes//It's Easy to Remember/Blame It on My Youth	1956	5.00	10.00	20.00
❏ EAP 4-789 [PS]	Close to You, Part 4	1956	5.00	10.00	20.00
❏ EBF 1-789 [PS]	Close to You, Parts 1 and 2	1956	12.50	25.00	50.00
—Gatefold sleeve for some editions of EAP 1-789 and 2-789					
❏ EBF 2-789 [PS]	Close to You, Parts 3 and 4	1956	12.50	25.00	50.00
—Gatefold sleeve for some editions of EAP 3-789 and 4-789					
❏ EAP 1-800	How Little We Know/Flowers Mean Forgiveness//You Forgot All the Words/Hey! Jealous Lover	1956	7.50	15.00	30.00
❏ EAP 1-800 [PS]	Hey! Jealous Lover	1956	7.50	15.00	30.00
❏ EAP 1-803	The Lonesome Road/You'd Be So Nice to Come Home To//From This Moment On/Nice Work If You Can Get It	1957	5.00	10.00	20.00
❏ EAP 1-803 [PS]	A Swingin' Affair, Part 1	1957	5.00	10.00	20.00
❏ EAP 2-803	I Won't Dance/At Long Last Love//I Got It Bad and That Ain't Good/I Guess I'll Have to Change My Plan	1957	5.00	10.00	20.00
❏ EAP 2-803 [PS]	A Swingin' Affair, Part 2	1957	5.00	10.00	20.00
❏ EAP 3-803	No One Ever Tells You/If I Had You//I Wish I Were in Love Again/I Got Plenty o' Nuttin'	1957	5.00	10.00	20.00
❏ EAP 3-803 [PS]	A Swingin' Affair, Part 3	1957	5.00	10.00	20.00
❏ EAP 4-803	Oh! Look at Me Now/Stars Fell on Alabama//Night and Day	1957	5.00	10.00	20.00
❏ EAP 4-803 [PS]	A Swingin' Affair, Part 4	1957	5.00	10.00	20.00
❏ EBF 1-803 [PS]	A Swingin' Affair, Parts 1 and 2	1957	12.50	25.00	50.00
—Gatefold sleeve for some editions of EAP 1-803 and 2-803					
❏ EBF 2-803 [PS]	A Swingin' Affair, Parts 3 and 4	1957	12.50	25.00	50.00
—Gatefold sleeve for some editions of EAP 3-803 and 4-803					
❏ EAP 1-855	Where Are You?/Where Is the One//Baby Won't You Please Come Home	1957	5.00	10.00	20.00
❏ EAP 1-855 [PS]	Where Are You? Part 1	1957	5.00	10.00	20.00
❏ EAP 2-855	I'm a Fool to Want You//I Cover the Waterfront/Laura	1957	5.00	10.00	20.00
❏ EAP 2-855 [PS]	Where Are You? Part 2	1957	5.00	10.00	20.00
❏ EAP 3-855	Lonely Town//The Night We Called It a Day/Autumn Leaves	1957	5.00	10.00	20.00
❏ EAP 3-855 [PS]	Where Are You? Part 3	1957	5.00	10.00	20.00
❏ EAP 4-855	There's No You//I Think of You/Maybe You'll Be There	1957	5.00	10.00	20.00
❏ EAP 4-855 [PS]	Where Are You? Part 4	1957	5.00	10.00	20.00
❏ EBF 1-855 [PS]	Where Are You? Parts 1 and 2	1957	12.50	25.00	50.00
—Gatefold sleeve for some editions of EAP 1-855 and 2-855					
❏ EBF 2-855 [PS]	Where Are You? Parts 3 and 4	1957	12.50	25.00	50.00
—Gatefold sleeve for some editions of EAP 3-855 and 4-855					
❏ EAP 1-894	Jingle Bells/The Christmas Song//Mistletoe and Holly/I'll Be Home for Christmas	1957	3.00	6.00	12.00
❏ EAP 1-894 [PS]	A Jolly Christmas from Frank Sinatra, Part 1	1957	3.00	6.00	12.00
❏ EAP 2-894	The Christmas Waltz/Have Yourself a Merry Little Christmas//The First Noel/Hark the Herald Angels Sing	1957	3.00	6.00	12.00
❏ EAP 2-894 [PS]	A Jolly Christmas from Frank Sinatra, Part 2	1957	3.00	6.00	12.00
❏ EAP 3-894	O Little Town of Bethlehem/Adeste Fideles//It Came Upon a Midnight Clear/Silent Night	1957	3.00	6.00	12.00
❏ EAP 3-894 [PS]	A Jolly Christmas from Frank Sinatra, Part 3	1957	3.00	6.00	12.00
❏ EAP 1-920	Come Fly with Me/Isle of Capri//It's Nice to Go Trav'ling	1958	3.75	7.50	15.00
❏ EAP 1-920 [PS]	Come Fly with Me, Part 1	1958	3.75	7.50	15.00
❏ EAP 2-920	Autumn in New York//April in Paris/Around the World	1958	3.75	7.50	15.00
❏ EAP 2-920 [PS]	Come Fly with Me, Part 2	1958	3.75	7.50	15.00
❏ EAP 3-920	Moonlight in Vermont//London by Night/Let's Get Away from It All	1958	3.75	7.50	15.00
❏ EAP 3-920 [PS]	Come Fly with Me, Part 3	1958	3.75	7.50	15.00
❏ EAP 4-920	On the Road to Mandalay//Blue Hawaii/Brazil	1958	3.75	7.50	15.00
❏ EAP 4-920 [PS]	Come Fly with Me, Part 4	1958	3.75	7.50	15.00
❏ SU-920	Come Fly with Me/Moonlight in Vermont//April in Paris/On the Road to Mandalay	196?	6.25	12.50	25.00
—Jukebox EP, plays at 33 1/3 rpm, small hole					
❏ SU-920 [PS]	Come Fly with Me	196?	6.25	12.50	25.00
❏ EAP 1-982	Hey! Jealous Lover/Everybody Loves Somebody//I Believe/Put Your Dreams Away	1958	5.00	10.00	20.00
❏ EAP 1-982 [PS]	This Is Sinatra, Volume Two, Part 1	1958	5.00	10.00	20.00
❏ EAP 2-982	Something Wonderful Happens in Summer/Half As Lovely//So Long My Love/It's the Same Old Dreams	1958	5.00	10.00	20.00
❏ EAP 2-982 [PS]	This Is Sinatra, Volume Two, Part 2	1958	5.00	10.00	20.00
❏ EAP 3-982	You're Cheatin' Yourself/You'll Always Be the One I Love//Johnny Concho Theme (Wait for Me)/If You Are But a Dream	1958	5.00	10.00	20.00
❏ EAP 3-982 [PS]	This Is Sinatra, Volume Two, Part 3	1958	5.00	10.00	20.00
❏ EAP 4-982	You Forgot All the Words/How Little We Know//Time After Time/Crazy Love	1958	5.00	10.00	20.00
❏ EAP 4-982 [PS]	This Is Sinatra, Volume 2, Part 4	1958	5.00	10.00	20.00
❏ EAP 1-1013	The Lady Is a Tramp/Witchcraft//Come Fly with Me/Tell Her You Love Her	1958	7.50	15.00	30.00
❏ EAP 1-1013 [PS]	Frank Sinatra!	1958	7.50	15.00	30.00
❏ EAP 1-1053	Only the Lonely/Blues in the Night	1958	5.00	10.00	20.00
❏ EAP 1-1053 [PS]	Frank Sinatra Sings for Only the Lonely	1958	5.00	10.00	20.00
❏ EAP 1-1069	Come Dance with Me/Something's Gotta Give//The Song Is You/The Last Dance	1958	3.75	7.50	15.00
❏ EAP 1-1069 [PS]	Come Dance with Me, Part 1	1958	3.75	7.50	15.00

S

Number	Title (A Side/B Side)	Yr	VG	VG+	NM
❑ EAP 2-1069	Just in Time/Dancing in the Dark//Cheek to Cheek/Baubles, Bangles and Beads	1958	3.75	7.50	15.00
❑ EAP 2-1069 [PS]	Come Dance with Me, Part 2	1958	3.75	7.50	15.00
❑ EAP 3-1069	Saturday Night/Day In — Day Out/Too Close for Comfort/I Could Have Danced All Night	1958	3.75	7.50	15.00
❑ EAP 3-1069 [PS]	Come Dance with Me, Part 3	1958	3.75	7.50	15.00
❑ EAP 1-1159	Angel Eyes/Willow Weep for Me	1958	7.50	15.00	30.00
❑ EAP 1-1159 [PS]	Frank Sinatra Sings Angel Eyes	1958	7.50	15.00	30.00
❑ EAP 1-1221	When No One Cares/I'll Never Smile Again//A Cottage for Sale/None But the Lonely Heart	1959	3.75	7.50	15.00
❑ EAP 1-1221 [PS]	No One Cares, Part 1	1959	3.75	7.50	15.00
❑ EAP 2-1221	I Don't Stand a Ghost of a Chance with You/Here's That Rainy Day//I Can't Get Started	1959	3.75	7.50	15.00
❑ EAP 2-1221 [PS]	No One Cares, Part 2	1959	3.75	7.50	15.00
❑ EAP 3-1221	*Stormy Weather/Where Do You Go/Why Try to Change Me Now/Just Friends	1959	3.75	7.50	15.00
❑ EAP 3-1221 [PS]	No One Cares, Part 3	1959	3.75	7.50	15.00
❑ EAP 1-1224	High Hopes/All My Tomorrows//French Foreign Legion/Mr. Success	1959	7.50	15.00	30.00
❑ EAP 1-1224 [PS]	High Hopes	1959	7.50	15.00	30.00
❑ SEP 1-1233 [S]	French Foreign Legion	1959	12.50	25.00	50.00
❑ SEP 1-1233 [S]	French Foreign Legion/Mr. Success//Come Dance with Me/The Last Dance	1959	12.50	25.00	50.00
❑ EAP 1-1348	Talk to Me/They Came to Cordura//When No One Cares/Where Do You Go?	1959	7.50	15.00	30.00
❑ EAP 1-1348 [PS]	Talk to Me	1959	7.50	15.00	30.00
❑ EAP 1-1417	*Nice 'n' Easy/That Old Feeling/She's Funny That Way/Dream	1960	5.00	10.00	20.00
❑ EAP 1-1417 [PS]	Nice 'n' Easy, Part 1	1960	5.00	10.00	20.00
❑ EAP 2-1417	How Deep Is the Ocean/Mam'selle//Try a Little Tenderness/Embraceable You	1960	5.00	10.00	20.00
❑ EAP 2-1417 [PS]	Nice 'n' Easy, Part 2	1960	5.00	10.00	20.00
❑ EAP 3-1417	You Go to My Head/I've Got a Crush on You//Fools Rush In/Nevertheless	1960	5.00	10.00	20.00
❑ EAP 3-1417 [PS]	Nice 'n' Easy, Part 3	1960	5.00	10.00	20.00
❑ EAP 1-1491	When You're Smiling (The Whole World Smiles With You)/Blue Moon//S'posin/It All Depends on You	1961	6.25	12.50	25.00
❑ EAP 1-1491 [PS]	Sinatra's Swingin' Session, Part 1	1961	6.25	12.50	25.00
❑ EAP 2-1491	Always/I Can't Believe You're in Love with Me//It's Only a Paper Moon/My Blue Heaven	1961	6.25	12.50	25.00
❑ EAP 2-1491 [PS]	Sinatra's Swingin' Session, Part 2	1961	6.25	12.50	25.00
❑ EAP 3-1491	Should I/September in the Rain//I Concentrate on You/You Do Something to Me	1961	6.25	12.50	25.00
❑ EAP 3-1491 [PS]	Sinatra's Swingin' Session, Part 3	1961	6.25	12.50	25.00
❑ EAP 1-1594	(contents unknown)	1961	6.25	12.50	25.00
❑ EAP 1-1594 [PS]	Come Swing with Me, Part 1	1961	6.25	12.50	25.00
❑ EAP 2-1594	(contents unknown)	1961	6.25	12.50	25.00
❑ EAP 2-1594 [PS]	Come Swing with Me, Part 2	1961	6.25	12.50	25.00
❑ EAP 3-1594	(contents unknown)	1961	6.25	12.50	25.00
❑ EAP 3-1594 [PS]	Come Swing with Me, Part 3	1961	6.25	12.50	25.00
❑ SU-1762	All the Way/Hey Jealous Lover/Lean Baby//Witchcraft/One for My Baby	196?		12.50	25.00
—Jukebox EP, plays at 33 1/3 rpm, small hole					
❑ SU-1762 [PS]	All the Way/Hey Jealous Lover/Lean Baby//Witchcraft/One for My Baby	196?	6.25	12.50	25.00
❑ SXA-1762	(Love Is) The Tender Trap/It's Over, It's Over, It's Over/The Nearness of You//The Gal That Got Away/When Your Lover Has Gone/The Last Dance	196?	6.25	12.50	25.00
—Jukebox EP, plays at 33 1/3 rpm, small hole					
❑ SXA-1762 [PS]	The Great Years	196?	6.25	12.50	25.00
COLUMBIA					
❑ B-112 [PS]	The Voice of Frank Sinatra	1950	12.50	25.00	50.00
—Gatefold cover for 2-EP set (1115 and 1116)					
❑ B-167 [PS]	Christmas Songs by Sinatra	1952	12.50	25.00	50.00
—Gatefold cover for 2-EP set (1322 and 1323)					
❑ B-218 [PS]	Sing and Dance with Frank Sinatra	1950	12.50	25.00	50.00
—Gatefold sleeve for 2-EP set (1129 and 1130)					
❑ B-337 [PS]	Requested By You	1953	6.25	12.50	25.00
—Gatefold cover for 2-EP set (1559 and 1560)					
❑ B-419 [PS]	I've Got a Crush on You	1952	12.50	25.00	50.00
—Gatefold cover for 2-EP set (1907 and 1908)					
❑ 5-1115	You Go to My Head/Someone to Watch Over Me//A Ghost of a Chance/Paradise	1952	6.25	12.50	25.00
—One record of 2-EP version of B-112					
❑ 5-1116	These Foolish Things/Why Shouldn't I//I Don't Know Why/Try a Little Tenderness	1952	6.25	12.50	25.00
—One record of 2-EP version of B-112					
❑ 5-1129	Lover/It's Only a Paper Moon//The Continental/When You're Smiling	1952	6.25	12.50	25.00
—One record of 2-EP version of B-218					
❑ 5-1130	My Blue Heaven/It All Depends on You//You Do Something to Me/Should I	1952	6.25	12.50	25.00
—One record of 2-EP version of B-218					
❑ 5-1193	Always/Blue Skies//How Deep Is the Ocean/They Say It's Wonderful	1952	6.25	12.50	25.00
—Record that goes with cover B-1524					
❑ 5-1322	White Christmas/Jingle Bells//Have Yourself a Merry Little Christmas/Have Yourself a Merry Little Christmas	1952	6.25	12.50	25.00
—One record of 2-EP version of B-167					
❑ 5-1323	Silent Night, Holy Night/Adeste Fideles//O Little Town of Bethlehem/It Came Upon a Midnight Clear	1952	6.25	12.50	25.00
—One record of 2-EP version of B-167					
❑ 5-1355	Some Enchanted Evening/Bali Ha'i//People Will Say We're in Love/Oh, What a Beautiful Morning	1952	7.50	15.00	30.00
—Record that goes with cover B-1608					
❑ 5-1389	Soliloquy//If I Loved You/You'll Never Walk Alone	1952	7.50	15.00	30.00
—Record that goes with cover B-1673					
❑ B-1524 [PS]	Frank Sinatra Sings Irving Berlin	1952	6.25	12.50	25.00
❑ 5-1555	Embraceable You/I've Got a Crush on You//Someone to Watch Over Me/Where Is My Bess?	1953	6.25	12.50	25.00
—Record that goes with cover B-1673					
❑ 5-1559	(contents unknown)	1953	6.25	12.50	25.00
—Side 1 and Side 4 of B-337					
❑ 5-1560	Deep Purple/Body and Soul//Begin the Beguine/Laura	1953	6.25	12.50	25.00
—Side 2 and Side 3 of B-337					
❑ B-1608 [PS]	Frank Sinatra Sings Hits from South Pacific and Oklahoma	1952	7.50	15.00	30.00
❑ B-1620 [PS]	Carousel Sung by Frank Sinatra	1952	7.50	15.00	30.00
❑ B-1673 [PS]	Frank Sinatra Sings George Gershwin	1953	6.25	12.50	25.00
❑ B-1702	Ol' Man River/All the Things You Are//Why Was I Born/The Song Is You	1953	6.25	12.50	25.00
❑ B-1702 [PS]	Frank Sinatra Sings Jerome Kern	1953	6.25	12.50	25.00
❑ B-1815	I Concentrate on You/Why Can't You Behave//Why Shouldn't I/You Do Something to Me	1954	6.25	12.50	25.00
❑ B-1815 [PS]	Frank Sinatra Sings Cole Porter	1954	6.25	12.50	25.00
❑ B-1872	(contents unknown)	1954	6.25	12.50	25.00
❑ B-1872 [PS]	Frank Sinatra Sings Rodgers and Hart	1954	6.25	12.50	25.00
❑ 5-1907	I've Got a Crush on You/They Say It's Wonderful//If I Loved You/You Do Something to Me	1952	6.25	12.50	25.00
—One record of 2-EP set B-419					
❑ 5-1908	I Only Have Eyes for You/The Girl That I Marry//I Hear a Rhapsody/April in Paris	1952	6.25	12.50	25.00
—One record of 2-EP set B-419					
❑ B-1984	Hello Young Lovers/I Only Have Eyes for You//Falling in Love with Love/You'll Never Know	1955	6.25	12.50	25.00
❑ B-1984 [PS]	Frankie, Vol. 1	1955	6.25	12.50	25.00
❑ B-1985	It All Depends on You/S'posin//All of Me/Time After Time	1955	6.25	12.50	25.00
❑ B-1985 [PS]	Frankie, Vol. 2	1955	6.25	12.50	25.00
❑ B-1986	How Cute Can You Be/Almost Like Being in Love//Nancy/Oh! What It Seemed to Be	1955	6.25	12.50	25.00
❑ B-1986 [PS]	Frankie, Vol. 3	1955	6.25	12.50	25.00
❑ B-2515	I Couldn't Sleep a Wink Last Night/A Lovely Way to Spend an Evening//People Will Say We're in Love/Oh, What a Beautiful Mornin'	1957	6.25	12.50	25.00
❑ B-2515 [PS]	Nancy (With the Laughing Face)/Day by Day//They Say It's Wonderful/The Girl That I Marry	1957	6.25	12.50	25.00
❑ B-2516 [PS]	Frank Sinatra (Hall of Fame Series)	1957	6.25	12.50	25.00
❑ B-2517	The Birth of the Blues/I've Got a Crush on You//Five Minutes More/Someone to Watch Over Me	1957	6.25	12.50	25.00
❑ B-2517 [PS]	Frank Sinatra (Hall of Fame Series)	1957	6.25	12.50	25.00
❑ B-2542	Castle Rock/Farewell, Farewell to Love//A Little Learnin' Is a Dangerous Thing	1957	12.50	25.00	50.00
❑ B-2542 [PS]	Frank Sinatra with Harry James and Pearl Bailey	1957	12.50	25.00	50.00
❑ B-2559	I Could Write a Book/If You Are But a Dream//I'm a Fool to Want You/I Should Care	1958	6.25	12.50	25.00
❑ B-2559 [PS]	Frank Sinatra (Hall of Fame Series)	1958	6.25	12.50	25.00
❑ B-2564	Ol' Man River/You'll Never Walk Alone//Soliloquy	1958	6.25	12.50	25.00
❑ B-2564 [PS]	Frank Sinatra (Hall of Fame Series)	1958	6.25	12.50	25.00
❑ B-2589	September Song/Among My Souvenirs//The Things We Did Last Summer/Oh! What It Seemed to Be	1958	6.25	12.50	25.00
❑ B-2589 [PS]	Frank Sinatra (Hall of Fame Series)	1958	6.25	12.50	25.00
❑ B-2614	One for My Baby/If I Loved You//Put Your Dreams Away/You'll Never Know	1958	6.25	12.50	25.00
❑ B-2614 [PS]	Frank Sinatra (Hall of Fame Series)	1958	6.25	12.50	25.00
❑ B-2626	Close to You/Embraceable You//The Charm of You/I Dream of You	1958	6.25	12.50	25.00
❑ B-2626 [PS]	Frank Sinatra (Hall of Fame Series)	1958	6.25	12.50	25.00
❑ B-2638	Stormy Weather/Why Was I Born//The House I Live In/How Deep is the Ocean	1958	6.25	12.50	25.00
❑ B-2638 [PS]	Frank Sinatra (Hall of Fame Series)	1958	6.25	12.50	25.00
❑ B-2641	All or Nothing at All/You Go to My Head//Why Try to Change Me Now/I Concentrate on You	1958	6.25	12.50	25.00
❑ B-2641 [PS]	Frank Sinatra (Hall of Fame Series)	1958	6.25	12.50	25.00
❑ B-7431	I Don't Know Why (I Just Do)/Try a Little Tenderness//(I Don't Stand) A Ghost of a Chance/Paradise	1955	6.25	12.50	25.00
❑ B-7431 [PS]	The Voice, Vol. I	1955	6.25	12.50	25.00
❑ B-7432	(contents unknown)	1955	6.25	12.50	25.00
❑ B-7432 [PS]	The Voice, Vol. II	1955	6.25	12.50	25.00
❑ B-7433	Over the Rainbow/That Old Black Magic//Spring Is Here/Lover	1955	6.25	12.50	25.00
❑ B-7433 [PS]	The Voice, Vol. III	1955	6.25	12.50	25.00
❑ B-9021	That Old Feeling/Blue Skies//Autumn in New York/Don't Cry Joe	1956	6.25	12.50	25.00
❑ B-9021 [PS]	That Old Feeling	1956	6.25	12.50	25.00
❑ B-9022	The Nearness of You/That Lucky Old Sun//Full Moon and Empty Arms/Once in Love with Amy	1956	6.25	12.50	25.00
❑ B-9022 [PS]	The Nearness of You	1956	6.25	12.50	25.00
❑ B-9023	A Fellow Needs a Girl/Poinciana (Song of the Tree)//For Every Man There's a Woman/Mean to Me	1956	6.25	12.50	25.00
❑ B-9023 [PS]	A Fellow Needs a Girl	1956	6.25	12.50	25.00
❑ B-9531	I Guess I'll Have to Dream the Rest/If Only She'd Look My Way//Love Me/Nevertheless	1957	6.25	12.50	25.00
❑ B-9531 [PS]	Adventures of the Heart, Vol. I	1957	6.25	12.50	25.00
❑ B-9532	We Kiss in a Shadow/I Am Loved//Take My Love/I Could Write a Book	1957	6.25	12.50	25.00
❑ B-9532 [PS]	Adventures of the Heart, Vol. II	1957	6.25	12.50	25.00
❑ B-9533	Mad About You/Sorry//On the Island of Stromboli/It's Only a Paper Moon	1957	6.25	12.50	25.00
❑ B-9533 [PS]	Adventures of the Heart, Vol. III	1957	6.25	12.50	25.00
❑ B-10321	White Christmas/Jingle Bells//Have Yourself a Merry Little Christmas//Santa Claus Is Coming to Town	1957	7.50	15.00	30.00
❑ B-10321 [PS]	Christmas Dreaming, Vol. 1	1957	10.00	20.00	40.00
❑ B-10322	Silent Night, Holy Night/Adeste Fideles//O Little Town of Bethlehem/It Came Upon the Midnight Clear	1957	7.50	15.00	30.00
❑ B-10322 [PS]	Christmas Dreaming, Vol. 2	1957	10.00	20.00	40.00
❑ ZTEP 28595/6 [DJ]	Nancy/I'm a Fool to Want You/Full Moon and Empty Arms/The Birth of the Blues	1958	12.50	25.00	50.00
❑ ZTEP 28595/6 [PS]	Nancy	1958	12.50	25.00	50.00
—Limited edition EP for the B.T. Babbit Soap Co.					

Number	Title (A Side/B Side)	Yr	VG	VG+	NM
RCA VICTOR					
❑ 947-0176	Night and Day/East of the Sun//Fools Rush In/ The Lamplighter's Serenade	1954	7.50	15.00	30.00
—Part 1 of EPBT 3063					
❑ 947-0177	Everything Happens to Me/I'll Be Seeing You// This Is the Beginning of the End/ Street of Dreams	1954	7.50	15.00	30.00
—Part 2 of EPBT 3063					
❑ EPBT-3063 [PS]	Fabulous Frankie	1954	10.00	20.00	40.00
—Cover for 947-0176 and 947-0177					
❑ EPA-5014	Oh! Look at Me Now/This Love of Mine/I Guess I'll Have to Dream the Rest/How Do You Do Without Me	1958	5.00	10.00	20.00
❑ EPA-5014 [PS]	Frankie and Tommy	1958	5.00	10.00	20.00
❑ EPA-5147	The Lamplighter's Serenade/The Night We Called It a Day//The Song Is You/ Night and Day	1960	6.25	12.50	25.00
❑ EPA-5147 [PS]	Frank Sinatra	1960	6.25	12.50	25.00
REPRISE					
❑ SR 1012	Fly Me to the Moon/I Wanna Be Around/More// I Can't Stop Loving You/The Good Life/ I Wish You Love	1965	5.00	10.00	20.00
—33 1/3 rpm, small hole, "Promotion"					
❑ SR 1012 [PS]	It Might As Well Be Swing	1965	5.00	10.00	20.00
❑ SR 1013	Dear Heart/Pass Me By/I Can't Believe I'm Losing You//Come Blow Your Horn/Softly As I Leave You/Then Suddenly Love	1965	5.00	10.00	20.00
—Jukebox issue; small hole, plays at 33 1/3 rpm					
❑ SR 1013 [PS]	Softly As I Leave You	1965	5.00	10.00	20.00
❑ SR 1018	Moon Love/Moonlight Serenade//Moonlight Becomes You/The Moon Got in My Eyes/I Wished on the Moon	1966	5.00	10.00	20.00
—Jukebox issue; 33 1/3 rpm, small hole					
❑ SR 1018 [PS]	Moonlight Sinatra	1966	5.00	10.00	20.00
❑ SR 1024	Follow Me/Sunny//Yellow Days/Indian Summer	1968	5.00	10.00	20.00
—As "Francis A. Sinatra & Edward K. Ellington"; jukebox issue; 33 1/3 rpm, small hole					
❑ SR 1024 [PS]	Francis A. and Edward K.	1968	5.00	10.00	20.00
❑ PRO-S-2115 [DJ]	You'd Be So Easy to Love/ Theme from New York, New York// Come Fly with Me/Summer Wind	1984	5.00	10.00	20.00
—Small hole, plays at 33 1/3 rpm					
❑ PRO-S-2115 [PS]	Stereo Review Salutes Frank Sinatra	1984	5.00	10.00	20.00
—Special promo available from "Stereo Review" magazine					
❑ SR 2155	Let Me Try Again/You Will Be My Music// Winners/You're So Right (For What's Wrong in My Life)	1973	5.00	10.00	20.00
—Jukebox issue; small hole, plays at 33 1/3 rpm					
❑ SR 2155 [PS]	Ol' Blue Eyes Is Back	1973	5.00	10.00	20.00
—Part of Little LP series (# LLP 233)					
Albums					
ARTANIS					
❑ ARZ 101 [(2)]	Sinatra '57 In Concert	1999	—	—	—
—Canceled					
BOOK-OF-THE-MONTH					
❑ (# unknown) [(6)]	Tommy Dorsey/Frank Sinatra: The Complete Sessions	1983	25.00	50.00	100.00
CAPITOL					
❑ DWBB-254 [(2)R]	Close-Up	1969	5.00	10.00	20.00
—Reissue in one package of "This Is Sinatra" and "This Is Sinatra, Volume Two"					
❑ DKAO-374 [R]	Frank Sinatra's Greatest Hits	1969	3.00	6.00	12.00
❑ H 488 [10]	Songs for Young Lovers	1954	15.00	30.00	60.00
❑ H 528 [10]	Swing Easy	1954	15.00	30.00	60.00
❑ STBB-529 [(2)]	What Is This Thing Called Love?/ The Night We Called It a Day	1970	3.75	7.50	15.00
❑ DW 581 [R]	In the Wee Small Hours	196?	3.00	6.00	12.00
❑ H1-581 [10]	In the Wee Small Hours, Part 1	1955	25.00	50.00	100.00
❑ H2-581 [10]	In the Wee Small Hours, Part 2	1955	25.00	50.00	100.00
❑ SM-581	In the Wee Small Hours	197?	2.00	4.00	8.00
❑ W 581 [M]	In the Wee Small Hours	1955	10.00	20.00	40.00
—Gray label original					
❑ W 581 [M]	In the Wee Small Hours	1959	6.25	12.50	25.00
—Black label with colorband					
❑ W 587 [M]	Swing Easy/Songs for Young Lovers	1955	10.00	20.00	40.00
—Gray label original; 12-inch version of two 10-inch LPs					
❑ W 587 [M]	Swing Easy/Songs for Young Lovers	1959	6.25	12.50	25.00
—Black label with colorband					
❑ DW 653 [R]	Songs for Swingin' Lovers!	196?	3.00	6.00	12.00
❑ SM-653	Songs for Swingin' Lovers!	197?	2.00	4.00	8.00
❑ W 653 [M]	Songs for Swingin' Lovers!	1956	10.00	20.00	40.00
—Gray label; cover has Sinatra facing toward the embracing couple					
❑ W 653 [M]	Songs for Swingin' Lovers!	1956	12.50	25.00	50.00
—Gray label; cover has Sinatra facing away from the embracing couple					
❑ W 653 [M]	Songs for Swingin' Lovers!	1959	6.25	12.50	25.00
—Black label with colorband					
❑ STBB-724 [(2)]	My One and Only Love/Sentimental Journey	1971	3.75	7.50	15.00
❑ T 735 [M]	Frank Sinatra Conducts Tone Poems of Color	1956	15.00	30.00	60.00
—Turquoise label					
❑ T 735 [M]	Frank Sinatra Conducts Tone Poems of Color	1959	10.00	20.00	40.00
—Black label with colorband					
❑ DT 768 [R]	This Is Sinatra!	196?	3.00	6.00	12.00
❑ T 768 [M]	This Is Sinatra!	1956	7.50	15.00	30.00
—Turquoise label					
❑ T 768 [M]	This Is Sinatra!	196?	3.75	7.50	15.00
—Gold "Starline" label					
❑ T 768 [M]	This Is Sinatra!	196?	5.00	10.00	20.00
—Black "Starline" label					
❑ DW 789 [R]	Close to You	196?	3.00	6.00	12.00
❑ W 789 [M]	Close to You	1957	7.50	15.00	30.00
—Gray label					
❑ W 789 [M]	Close to You	1959	5.00	10.00	20.00
—Black label with colorband					
❑ DW 803 [R]	A Swingin' Affair!	196?	3.00	6.00	12.00
❑ W 803 [M]	A Swingin' Affair!	1957	5.00	10.00	20.00
—Black label with colorband					
❑ W 803 [M]	A Swingin' Affair!	1957	7.50	15.00	30.00
—Gray label					

Number	Title (A Side/B Side)	Yr	VG	VG+	NM
❑ SW 855 [S]	Where Are You?	1959	10.00	20.00	40.00
—Originals do not include "I Cover the Waterfront"					
❑ SW 855 [S]	Where Are You?	196?	7.50	15.00	30.00
—Later releases restore "I Cover the Waterfront"					
❑ W 855 [M]	Where Are You?	1957	7.50	15.00	30.00
—Gray label					
❑ W 855 [M]	Where Are You?	1959	5.00	10.00	20.00
—Black label with colorband					
❑ DT 894 [R]	The Sinatra Christmas Album	196?	2.50	5.00	10.00
—Rechanneled reissue of A Jolly Christmas with Frank Sinatra with same contents; some copies have this cover and "A Jolly Christmas" labels					
❑ SM-894 [R]	The Sinatra Christmas Album	197?	2.00	4.00	8.00
—Reissue in rechanneled stereo; any color label					
❑ T 894 [M]	The Sinatra Christmas Album	196?	5.00	10.00	20.00
—Reissue of A Jolly Christmas with Frank Sinatra with same contents; some copies have this cover and "A Jolly Christmas" labels					
❑ W 894 [M]	A Jolly Christmas from Frank Sinatra	1957	10.00	20.00	40.00
—Original mono with gray label					
❑ W 894 [M]	A Jolly Christmas from Frank Sinatra	1958	7.50	15.00	30.00
—Black colorband label, logo at left					
❑ SM-920	Come Fly with Me	197?	2.00	4.00	8.00
❑ SW 920 [S]	Come Fly with Me	1959	7.50	15.00	30.00
❑ W 920 [M]	Come Fly with Me	1958	10.00	20.00	40.00
—Gray label					
❑ W 920 [M]	Come Fly with Me	1959	5.00	10.00	20.00
—Black label with colorband					
❑ DW 982 [R]	This Is Sinatra, Volume Two	196?	3.00	6.00	12.00
❑ W 982 [M]	This Is Sinatra, Volume Two	1958	10.00	20.00	40.00
—Gray label					
❑ W 982 [M]	This Is Sinatra, Volume Two	1959	5.00	10.00	20.00
—Black label with colorband, logo at left					
❑ W 982 [M]	This Is Sinatra, Volume Two	1963	3.75	7.50	15.00
—Black label with colorband, logo at top					
❑ SW 1053 [S]	Frank Sinatra Sings for Only the Lonely	1959	7.50	15.00	30.00
—Originals do not include "It's a Lonesome Old Town" and "Spring Is Here"					
❑ SW 1053 [S]	Frank Sinatra Sings for Only the Lonely	196?	6.25	12.50	25.00
—Later releases restore "It's a Lonesome Old Town" and "Spring Is Here"					
❑ W 1053 [M]	Frank Sinatra Sings for Only the Lonely	1958	10.00	20.00	40.00
—Gray label					
❑ W 1053 [M]	Frank Sinatra Sings for Only the Lonely	1959	5.00	10.00	20.00
—Black label with colorband					
❑ SW 1069 [S]	Come Dance with Me!	1959	7.50	15.00	30.00
❑ W 1069 [M]	Come Dance with Me!	1959	5.00	10.00	20.00
❑ DW 1164 [R]	Look to Your Heart	196?	3.00	6.00	12.00
❑ W 1164 [M]	Look to Your Heart	1959	7.50	15.00	30.00
❑ SM-1221	No One Cares	197?	2.00	4.00	8.00
❑ SW 1221 [S]	No One Cares	1959	7.50	15.00	30.00
❑ W 1221 [M]	No One Cares	1959	5.00	10.00	20.00
❑ SW 1417 [S]	Nice 'N' Easy	1960	6.25	12.50	25.00
❑ W 1417 [M]	Nice 'N' Easy	1960	5.00	10.00	20.00
❑ DW 1429 [R]	Swing Easy	1960	3.00	6.00	12.00
❑ W 1429 [M]	Swing Easy	1960	5.00	10.00	20.00
❑ DW 1432 [R]	Songs for Young Lovers	1960	3.00	6.00	12.00
❑ W 1432 [M]	Songs for Young Lovers	1960	5.00	10.00	20.00
❑ SM-1491	Sinatra's Swingin' Session!!!	197?	2.00	4.00	8.00
❑ SW 1491 [S]	Sinatra's Swingin' Session!!!	1961	6.25	12.50	25.00
❑ W 1491 [M]	Sinatra's Swingin' Session!!!	1961	5.00	10.00	20.00
❑ SW 1538 [S]	All the Way	1961	6.25	12.50	25.00
❑ W 1538 [M]	All the Way	1961	5.00	10.00	20.00
❑ SW 1594 [S]	Come Swing with Me!	1961	6.25	12.50	25.00
❑ W 1594 [M]	Come Swing with Me!	1961	5.00	10.00	20.00
❑ SM-1676	Point of No Return	197?	2.00	4.00	8.00
❑ SW 1676 [S]	Point of No Return	1962	6.25	12.50	25.00
❑ W 1676 [M]	Point of No Return	1962	5.00	10.00	20.00
❑ SW 1729 [P]	Sinatra Sings…Of Love and Things	1962	5.00	10.00	20.00
❑ W 1729 [M]	Sinatra Sings…Of Love and Things	1962	5.00	10.00	20.00
❑ SWCO 1762 [(3)P]	Sinatra, The Great Years	1962	10.00	20.00	40.00
❑ WCO 1762 [(3)M]	Sinatra, The Great Years	1962	7.50	15.00	30.00
❑ DW 1825 [R]	Sinatra Sings Rodgers and Hart	1963	3.00	6.00	12.00
❑ W 1825 [M]	Sinatra Sings Rodgers and Hart	1963	5.00	10.00	20.00
❑ DT 1919 [R]	Tell Her You Love Her	1963	3.00	6.00	12.00
❑ T 1919 [M]	Tell Her You Love Her	1963	5.00	10.00	20.00
❑ DW 1994 [R]	Sinatra Sings the Select Johnny Mercer	1963	3.00	6.00	12.00
❑ W 1994 [M]	Sinatra Sings the Select Johnny Mercer	1963	5.00	10.00	20.00
❑ DT 2036 [R]	The Greatest Hits of Frank Sinatra	1964	3.00	6.00	12.00
❑ T 2036 [M]	The Greatest Hits of Frank Sinatra	1964	5.00	10.00	20.00
❑ PRO-2163/4/5/6 [(2)DJ]	Selections from Sinatra, The Great Years	1962	10.00	20.00	40.00
❑ DW 2301 [R]	Sinatra Sings the Select Cole Porter	1965	3.00	6.00	12.00
❑ W 2301 [M]	Sinatra Sings the Select Cole Porter	1965	5.00	10.00	20.00
❑ DT 2602 [R]	Forever Frank	1966	3.00	6.00	12.00
❑ T 2602 [M]	Forever Frank	1966	5.00	10.00	20.00
❑ DT 2700 [R]	The Movie Songs	1967	3.00	6.00	12.00
❑ T 2700 [M]	The Movie Songs	1967	5.00	10.00	20.00
❑ STFL 2814 [(6)P]	The Frank Sinatra Deluxe Set	1968	15.00	30.00	60.00
❑ TFL 2814 [(6)M]	The Frank Sinatra Deluxe Set	1968	25.00	50.00	100.00
❑ DKAO 2900 [R]	The Best of Frank Sinatra	1968	3.75	7.50	15.00
❑ PRO-2974/5 [DJ]	Frank Sinatra Minute Masters	1965	10.00	20.00	40.00
—Edited version of 20 songs					
❑ DNFR 7630 [(6)P]	The Sinatra Touch	19??	15.00	30.00	60.00
❑ ST-11309	One More for the Road	1973	2.50	5.00	10.00
❑ SABB-11367 [(2)P]	Round #1	1974	3.75	7.50	15.00
❑ SM-11502	A Swingin' Affair!	1976	2.50	5.00	10.00
❑ SM-11801	Come Swing with Me	1978	2.50	5.00	10.00
❑ M-11883	This Is Sinatra	1979	2.50	5.00	10.00
❑ SN-16109	The Best of Frank Sinatra	198?	2.00	4.00	8.00
—Budget-line reissue					
❑ DN-16110	What Is This Thing Called Love	198?	2.00	4.00	8.00
—Budget-line reissue					
❑ SN-16111	The Night We Called It a Day	198?	2.00	4.00	8.00
—Budget-line reissue					
❑ N-16112	My One and Only Love	198?	2.00	4.00	8.00
—Budget-line reissue					
❑ SN-16113	Sentimental Journey	198?	2.00	4.00	8.00
—Budget-line reissue					
❑ N-16148	Look to Your Heart	198?	2.00	4.00	8.00
—Budget-line reissue					

S

Number	Title (A Side/B Side)	Yr	VG	VG+	NM
SN-16149	Sinatra Sings…Of Love and Things	198?	2.00	4.00	8.00
—Budget-line reissue					
SN-16202	Frank Sinatra Sings for Only the Lonely	198?	2.00	4.00	8.00
—Budget-line reissue					
SN-16203	Come Dance with Me!	198?	2.00	4.00	8.00
—Budget-line reissue					
SN-16204	Nice 'N' Easy	198?	2.00	4.00	8.00
—Budget-line reissue					
SN-16205	All the Way	198?	2.00	4.00	8.00
—Budget-line reissue					
SN-16267	Where Are You	198?	2.00	4.00	8.00
—Budget-line reissue					
DN-16268	This Is Sinatra, Volume Two	198?	2.00	4.00	8.00
—Budget-line reissue					
C1-89611	Duets	1993	5.00	10.00	20.00
DW 90986 [R]	Sentimental Journey	1966	3.75	7.50	15.00
—Capitol Record Club issue					
W 90986 [M]	Sentimental Journey	1966	6.25	12.50	25.00
—Capitol Record Club issue					
DQBO 91261 [(2)R]Songs for the Young at Heart		196?	7.50	15.00	30.00
—Capitol Record Club issue					
C1-94777 [(5)] The Capitol Years		1990	25.00	50.00	100.00
—With book and wraparound banner. Only 5,000 were pressed					
STBB-95191 [(2)]Sinatra Sings the Great Ones		1973	5.00	10.00	20.00
—Longines Symphonette (formerly Capitol) Record Club issue					
CAPITOL PICKWICK SERIES					
PC-3450 [M]	The Nearness of You	196?	3.00	6.00	12.00
SPC-3450 [R]	The Nearness of You	196?	2.50	5.00	10.00
PC-3452 [M]	Try a Little Tenderness	196?	3.00	6.00	12.00
SPC-3452 [R]	Try a Little Tenderness	196?	2.50	5.00	10.00
PC-3456 [M]	Nevertheless	196?	3.00	6.00	12.00
SPC-3456 [R]	Nevertheless	196?	2.50	5.00	10.00
PC-3457 [M]	Just One of Those Things	196?	3.00	6.00	12.00
SPC-3457 [R]	Just One of Those Things	196?	2.50	5.00	10.00
PC-3458 [M]	This Love of Mine	196?	3.00	6.00	12.00
SPC-3458 [R]	This Love of Mine	196?	2.50	5.00	10.00
PC-3463 [M]	My Cole Porter	196?	3.00	6.00	12.00
SPC-3463 [R]	My Cole Porter	196?	2.50	5.00	10.00
COLUMBIA					
C2L 6 [(2)M]	The Frank Sinatra Story	1958	7.50	15.00	30.00
S3L 42 [(3)M]	The Essential Frank Sinatra	1966	25.00	50.00	100.00
S3S 42 [(3)R]	The Essential Frank Sinatra	1966	12.50	25.00	50.00
CL 606 [M]	Frankie	1955	6.25	12.50	25.00
—Cover has Frank with Debbie Reynolds					
CL 606 [M]	Frankie	1955	7.50	15.00	30.00
—Cover has drawing of Frank Sinatra wearing a hat					
CL 743 [M]	The Voice	1956	6.25	12.50	25.00
CL 743 [M]	The Voice	1999	6.25	12.50	25.00
—Classic Records reissue on audiophile vinyl					
CL 884 [M]	Frank Sinatra Conducts Music of Alec Wilder	1956	10.00	20.00	40.00
—Reissue of Columbia Masterworks ML 4271					
CL 902 [M]	That Old Feeling	1956	6.25	12.50	25.00
CL 953 [M]	Adventures of the Heart	1957	6.25	12.50	25.00
CL 1032 [M]	Christmas Dreaming	1957	20.00	40.00	80.00
CL 1136 [M]	Put Your Dreams Away	1958	6.25	12.50	25.00
CL 1241 [M]	Love Is a Kick	1958	6.25	12.50	25.00
CL 1297 [M]	The Broadway Kick	1958	6.25	12.50	25.00
CL 1359 [M]	Come Back to Sorrento	1959	6.25	12.50	25.00
CL 1448 [M]	Reflections	1959	15.00	30.00	60.00
CL 2474 [M]	Greatest Hits, The Early Years, Vol. 1	1966	3.75	7.50	15.00
CAS 2475 [DJ]	The Voice: The Columbia Years Sampler	1986	10.00	20.00	40.00
CL 2521 [10]	Get Happy	1955	15.00	30.00	60.00
—"House Party Series" release					
CL 2539 [10]	I've Got a Crush on You	1955	15.00	30.00	60.00
—"House Party Series" release; different contents from CL 6290					
CL 2542 [10]	Christmas with Sinatra	1955	15.00	30.00	60.00
—"House Party Series" release					
CL 2572 [M]	Greatest Hits, The Early Years, Vol. 2	1966	3.75	7.50	15.00
CL 2739 [M]	The Essential Frank Sinatra, Volume 1	1967	6.25	12.50	25.00
CL 2740 [M]	The Essential Frank Sinatra, Volume 2	1967	6.25	12.50	25.00
CL 2741 [M]	The Essential Frank Sinatra, Volume 3	1967	6.25	12.50	25.00
CL 2913 [M]	Frank Sinatra in Hollywood	1968	20.00	40.00	80.00
CL 6001 [10]	The Voice of Frank Sinatra	1949	17.50	35.00	70.00
—Original in pink paper cover					
CL 6001 [10]	The Voice of Frank Sinatra	1950	15.00	30.00	60.00
—Blue cardboard cover					
CL 6019 [10]	Christmas Songs by Sinatra	1948	25.00	50.00	100.00
—With "gingerbread man" cover					
CL 6019 [10]	Christmas Songs by Sinatra	1949	20.00	40.00	80.00
—With green vinylite cover					
CL 6059 [10]	Frankly Sentimental	1951	15.00	30.00	60.00
CL 6087 [10]	Songs by Sinatra, Volume 1	1952	15.00	30.00	60.00
CL 6096 [10]	Dedicated to You	1952	25.00	50.00	100.00
—Three of the tracks on this LP are alternate takes unavailable on vinyl anywhere else					
CL 6143 [10]	Sing and Dance with Frank Sinatra	1953	15.00	30.00	60.00
CL 6290 [10]	I've Got a Crush on You	1954	15.00	30.00	60.00
CS 9274 [R]	Greatest Hits, The Early Years, Vol. 1	1966	2.50	5.00	10.00
PC 9274	Greatest Hits, The Early Years, Vol. 1	197?	2.00	4.00	8.00
CS 9372 [R]	Greatest Hits, The Early Years, Vol. 2	1966	2.50	5.00	10.00
PC 9372	Greatest Hits, The Early Years, Vol. 2	197?	2.00	4.00	8.00
CS 9539 [R]	The Essential Frank Sinatra, Volume 1	1967	3.00	6.00	12.00
CS 9540 [R]	The Essential Frank Sinatra, Volume 2	1967	3.00	6.00	12.00
CS 9541 [R]	The Essential Frank Sinatra, Volume 3	1967	3.00	6.00	12.00
CS 9713 [R]	Frank Sinatra in Hollywood	1968	3.00	6.00	12.00
KG 31358 [(2)]	In the Beginning	1971	10.00	20.00	40.00
—Original edition; titles of songs at left on front cover					
PG 31358 [(2)]	In the Beginning	197?	3.00	6.00	12.00
—Revised version; titles of songs at right on front cover					
C6X 40343 [(6)]The Voice: The Columbia Years 1943-1952		1986	20.00	40.00	80.00
PC 40707	Christmas Dreaming	1987	7.50	15.00	30.00
—Reissue of CL 1032 with an extra track					
C2X 40897 [(2)]Hello Young Lovers		1988	7.50	15.00	30.00
PC 44238 [M]	Sinatra Rarities	1989	10.00	20.00	40.00
COLUMBIA MASTERWORKS					
ML 4271 [M]	Frank Sinatra Conducts Music of Alec Wilder	1955	25.00	50.00	100.00
HARMONY					
HL 7400 [M]	Have Yourself a Merry Little Christmas	1967	7.50	15.00	30.00
HL 7405 [M]	Romantic Scenes from the Early Years	1967	7.50	15.00	30.00
HS 11200 [R]	Have Yourself a Merry Little Christmas	1967	5.00	10.00	20.00
—At least two different cover designs exist					
HS 11205 [R]	Romantic Scenes from the Early Years	1967	3.00	6.00	12.00
HS 11277 [R]	Someone to Watch Over Me	1968	3.75	7.50	15.00
HS 11390 [R]	Frank Sinatra	1969	3.75	7.50	15.00
KH 30318 [R]	Greatest Hits, Early Years	1971	3.75	7.50	15.00
LONGINES SYMPHONETTE					
LS-308A [(10)]	Sinatra: The Works	1972	18.75	37.50	75.00
LS-309A [(6)]	Sinatra: The Works	1973	10.00	20.00	40.00
—Abridged version of LS-308A					
SYS-5637	Sinatra Like Never Before	1972	6.25	12.50	25.00
—Bonus LP with purchase of LS-308A					
MOBILE FIDELITY					
SC-1 [(16)]	Sinatra	1983	150.00	300.00	600.00
—Audiophile vinyl; only two of the 16 records in this box were released individually					
1-086	Nice 'N' Easy	1981	10.00	20.00	40.00
—Audiophile vinyl					
1-135	A Jolly Christmas from Frank Sinatra	1984	10.00	20.00	40.00
—Audiophile vinyl using the original title					
PAIR					
PDL2-1027 [(2)]All-Time Classics		1986	3.00	6.00	12.00
PDL2-1028 [(2)]Timeless		1986	3.00	6.00	12.00
PDL2-1122 [(2)]Classic Performances		1986	3.00	6.00	12.00
QWEST					
25145	L.A. Is My Lady	1984	3.00	6.00	12.00
RCA VICTOR					
APL1-0497 [R]	What'll I Do	1974	3.00	6.00	12.00
LPV-583 [M]	This Love of Mine	1971	10.00	20.00	40.00
ANL1-1050 [R]	What'll I Do	1976	2.50	5.00	10.00
LPM-1569 [M]	Tommy Plays, Frankie Sings	1957	10.00	20.00	40.00
—Second issue with new title					
LPM-1569 [M]	Frankie and Tommy	1957	15.00	30.00	60.00
—First issue of this LP					
LPM-1632 [M]	We Three	1958	10.00	20.00	40.00
—Second issue, "RE" on cover					
LPM-1632 [M]	We Three	1958	15.00	30.00	60.00
—First issue					
LPT-3063 [10]	Fabulous Frankie	1953	15.00	30.00	60.00
CPL2-4334 [(2)]The Sinatra/Dorsey Sessions, Vol. 1		1982	6.25	12.50	25.00
CPL2-4335 [(2)]The Sinatra/Dorsey Sessions, Vol. 2		1982	6.25	12.50	25.00
CPL2-4336 [(2)]The Sinatra/Dorsey Sessions, Vol. 3		1982	6.25	12.50	25.00
AFL1-4741 [R]	Radio Years (Sinatra/Dorsey/Stordahl)	1983	3.75	7.50	15.00
REPRISE					
F 1001 [M]	Ring-a-Ding-Ding!	1961	5.00	10.00	20.00
R9 1001 [M]	Ring-a-Ding-Ding!	1961	6.25	12.50	25.00
F 1002 [M]	Sinatra Swings	1961	5.00	10.00	20.00
—Retitled version of "Swing Along with Me"; Capitol threatened legal action because of its "Come Swing With Me!" collection					
F 1002 [M]	Swing Along with Me	1961	10.00	20.00	40.00
—Original title					
R9 1002 [S]	Sinatra Swings	1961	6.25	12.50	25.00
—Retitled version of "Swing Along with Me"; Capitol threatened legal action because of its "Come Swing With Me!" collection					
R9 1002 [S]	Swing Along with Me	1961	12.50	25.00	50.00
—Original title					
F 1003 [M]	I Remember Tommy	1961	5.00	10.00	20.00
R9 1003 [M]	I Remember Tommy	1961	6.25	12.50	25.00
F 1004 [M]	Sinatra & Strings	1962	3.75	7.50	15.00
R9 1004 [S]	Sinatra & Strings	1962	5.00	10.00	20.00
F 1005 [M]	Sinatra and Swingin' Brass	1962	3.75	7.50	15.00
R9 1005 [S]	Sinatra and Swingin' Brass	1962	5.00	10.00	20.00
F 1006 [M]	Great Songs from Great Britain	1962	20.00	40.00	80.00
—Only released in the UK					
R9 1006 [S]	Great Songs from Great Britain	1962	25.00	50.00	100.00
—Only released in the UK					
F 1007 [M]	All Alone	1962	3.75	7.50	15.00
R9 1007 [M]	All Alone	1962	5.00	10.00	20.00
F 1008 [M]	Sinatra-Basie	1963	3.75	7.50	15.00
R9 1008 [S]	Sinatra-Basie	1963	5.00	10.00	20.00
F 1009 [M]	The Concert Sinatra	1963	3.75	7.50	15.00
R9 1009 [S]	The Concert Sinatra	196?	5.00	10.00	20.00
—Without cover reference to "35mm Stereo"					
R9 1009 [S]	The Concert Sinatra	1963	6.25	12.50	25.00
—Original pressings declare this was recorded in "35mm Stereo"					
R-1010 [M]	Sinatra's Sinatra	1963	3.75	7.50	15.00
—Gatefold jacket; some copies have eight photos of previous Frank Sinatra Reprise LPs at the right side of the inside gatefold; we don't yet know the relative rarity of these variations, or which came first, or whether they also exist on stereo copies					
R-1010 [M]	Sinatra's Sinatra	1963	3.75	7.50	15.00
—Gatefold jacket; some copies have a large photo of Sinatra holding a pack of Lucky Strikes at the right side of the inside gatefold; we don't yet know the relative rarity of these variations, or which came first, or whether they also exist on stereo copies					
R9 1010 [S]	Sinatra's Sinatra	1963	5.00	10.00	20.00
F 1011 [M]	Days of Wine and Roses, Moon River, and Other Academy Award Winners	1964	3.75	7.50	15.00
FS 1011 [S]	Days of Wine and Roses, Moon River, and Other Academy Award Winners	1964	5.00	10.00	20.00
F 1012 [M]	It Might As Well Be Swing	1964	3.75	7.50	15.00
FS 1012 [S]	It Might As Well Be Swing	1964	5.00	10.00	20.00
F 1013 [M]	Softly, As I Leave You	1964	3.75	7.50	15.00
FS 1013 [S]	Softly, As I Leave You	1964	5.00	10.00	20.00
F 1014 [M]	September of My Years	1965	3.75	7.50	15.00
FS 1014 [S]	September of My Years	1965	5.00	10.00	20.00
F 1015 [M]	My Kind of Broadway	1965	3.75	7.50	15.00
FS 1015 [S]	My Kind of Broadway	1965	5.00	10.00	20.00
2F 1016 [(2)M]	A Man and His Music	1965	5.00	10.00	20.00
2F/2FS 1016	A Man and His Music Special Box	1965	50.00	100.00	200.00
—Blue slipcase with embossed silver front, raised letters, plus 4-page booklet and a signed card (deduct 50% if card missing). Add this to LP value.					
2FS 1016 [(2)S]A Man and His Music		1965	6.25	12.50	25.00
F 1017 [M]	Strangers in the Night	1966	3.00	6.00	12.00
FS 1017 [S]	Strangers in the Night	1966	3.75	7.50	15.00
F 1018 [M]	Moonlight Sinatra	1966	3.75	7.50	15.00
FS 1018 [S]	Moonlight Sinatra	1966	5.00	10.00	20.00
2F 1019 [(2)]	Sinatra at the Sands	1966	5.00	10.00	20.00
2FS 1019 [(2)S]Sinatra at the Sands		1966	6.25	12.50	25.00
F 1020 [M]	That's Life	1966	3.00	6.00	12.00

The Shadows of Knight, "Oh Yeah," Dunwich 122, picture sleeve, $15-$30.

Del Shannon, *Del Shannon's Greatest Hits,* Twirl 5001, unreleased LP, but cover slick exists, $100-$200 or more for the cover slick.

The Shocking Blue, "Venus," Colossus 108, picture sleeve, $7.50-$15.

Simon and Garfunkel, *Sounds of Silence*, Columbia CS 9269, stereo LP, original cover as shown, $15-$30.

Frank Sinatra, *Swing Easy/Songs for Young Lovers,* Capitol W 587, mono LP, gray label, $20-$40.

Nancy Sinatra, *Boots*, Reprise R 6202, mono LP, $12.50-$25.

Number	Title (A Side/B Side)	Yr	VG	VG+	NM
❏ FS 1020 [S]	That's Life	1966	3.75	7.50	15.00
❏ F 1021 [M]	Francis Albert Sinatra & Antonio Carlos Jobim	1967	3.00	6.00	12.00
❏ FS 1021 [S]	Francis Albert Sinatra & Antonio Carlos Jobim	1967	3.75	7.50	15.00
❏ F 1022 [M]	Frank Sinatra (The World We Knew)	1967	3.75	7.50	15.00
❏ FS 1022 [S]	Frank Sinatra (The World We Knew)	1967	3.75	7.50	15.00
❏ FS 1023	The Sinatra Christmas Album	1967	25.00	50.00	100.00

—Album never released; value is for cover slick

❏ FS 1024	Francis A. and Edward K.	1968	5.00	10.00	20.00
❏ FS 1025	Frank Sinatra's Greatest Hits	1968	3.75	7.50	15.00
❏ FS 1027	Cycles	1969	3.75	7.50	15.00
❏ FS 1028	SinatraJobim	1969	2000.	3000.	4000.

—Unreleased; test pressings exist (value is for one of these). 8-track tapes also exist and are 10% of this value

❏ FS 1029	My Way	1969	3.75	7.50	15.00
❏ FS4 1029 [Q]	My Way	1974	6.25	12.50	25.00
❏ FS 1030	A Man Alone & Other Songs of Rod McKuen	1969	3.75	7.50	15.00
❏ FS 1030	A Man Alone & Other Songs of Rod McKuen	1969	100.00	200.00	400.00

—Signed copies with gatefold cover and hardbound book; 400 made

| ❏ FS 1031 | Watertown | 1970 | 6.25 | 12.50 | 25.00 |

—With gatefold and poster

| ❏ FS 1032 | Frank Sinatra's Greatest Hits, Vol. 2 | 1970 | — | — | — |

—Canceled?

❏ FS 1033	Sinatra and Company	1971	3.75	7.50	15.00
❏ FS 1034	Frank Sinatra's Greatest Hits, Vol. 2	1972	3.75	7.50	15.00
❏ FS4-1034 [Q]	Frank Sinatra's Greatest Hits, Vol. 2	1974	6.25	12.50	25.00
❏ FS 2155	Ol' Blue Eyes Is Back	1973	3.00	6.00	12.00
❏ FS4 2155 [Q]	Ol' Blue Eyes Is Back	1974	6.25	12.50	25.00
❏ FS4 2194 [Q]	Some Nice Things I've Missed	1974	6.25	12.50	25.00
❏ FS 2195	Some Nice Things I've Missed	1974	3.00	6.00	12.00
❏ FS 2207	Sinatra — The Main Event Live	1974	3.00	6.00	12.00
❏ 3FS 2300 [(3)]	Trilogy: Past, Present, Future	1980	5.00	10.00	20.00
❏ FS 2305	She Shot Me Down	1981	3.00	6.00	12.00
❏ 5004 [DJ]	A Man and His Music, Part II	1966	75.00	150.00	300.00

—Promotional album for use by Budweiser

❏ 5230 [DJ]	Songbook, Vol. 1	1971	12.50	25.00	50.00
❏ 5267 [(2)DJ]	Songbook, Vol. 2	1972	25.00	50.00	100.00
❏ 5409 [DJ]	I Sing the Songs	1976	12.50	25.00	50.00
❏ F 6045 [M]	Sinatra Conducts Music from Pictures and Plays	1962	7.50	15.00	30.00
❏ R9 6045 [S]	Sinatra Conducts Music from Pictures and Plays	1962	10.00	2.00	40.00
❏ R 6167 [M]	Sinatra '65	1965	3.75	7.50	15.00
❏ RS 6167 [S]	Sinatra '65	1965	5.00	10.00	20.00
❏ R1 73798 [S]	Francis Albert Sinatra & Antonio Carlos Jobim	2004	3.75	7.50	15.00

—180-gram reissue

| ❏ R1 73799 [S] | September of My Years | 2004 | 3.75 | 7.50 | 15.00 |

—180-gram reissue

| ❏ SMAS-92081 | A Man Alone & Other Songs of Rod McKuen | 1969 | 5.00 | 10.00 | 20.00 |

—Capitol Record Club edition

| ❏ SMAS-93119 | Watertown | 1970 | 6.25 | 12.50 | 25.00 |

—Capitol Record Club edition; does not contain poster

TIME-LIFE

| ❏ SLGD-02 [(2)] | Legendary Singers: Frank Sinatra | 1985 | 6.25 | 12.50 | 25.00 |

SINATRA, FRANK; DEAN MARTIN; SAMMY DAVIS, JR.
Albums
ARTANIS

| ❏ ARZ 102 [(2)] | The Summit | 1999 | — | — | — |

—Canceled

SINATRA, NANCY Includes duets with Lee Hazlewood. Also see MEL TILLIS.
45s
ELEKTRA

| ❏ 46659 | Let's Keep It That Way/One Jump Ahead of the Storm | 1979 | — | 2.50 | 5.00 |

PRIVATE STOCK

❏ 45,022	Annabel of Mobile/(B-side unknown)	1975	—	2.50	5.00
❏ 45,075	Kinky Love/She Played the Piano and He Beat the Drum	1976	—	2.50	5.00
❏ 45,108	Indian Summer/Holly and Hawkeye	1976	—	2.50	5.00

—With Lee Hazlewood

| ❏ 45,158 | It's For My Dad/A Gentle Man Like You | 1977 | — | 2.50 | 5.00 |

RCA VICTOR

| ❏ 47-0864 | It's the Love/Kind of a Woman | 1973 | 2.00 | 4.00 | 8.00 |
| ❏ 74-0614 | Paris Summer/Down from Dover | 1971 | 2.00 | 4.00 | 8.00 |

—With Lee Hazlewood

| ❏ APBO-0029 | Ain't No Sunshine/Sugar Me | 1973 | — | 2.50 | 5.00 |

REPRISE

❏ 0238	Tammy/Thanks to You	1963	5.00	10.00	20.00
❏ 0263	Where Do the Lonely Go/Just Think About the Good Times	1964	5.00	10.00	20.00
❏ 0292	This Love of Mine/There Goes the Bride	1964	5.00	10.00	20.00
❏ 0335	The Answer to Everything/True Love	1965	3.75	7.50	15.00
❏ 0407	So Long Babe/If He'd Love Me	1965	3.75	7.50	15.00
❏ 0432	These Boots Are Made for Walkin'/The City Never Sleeps at Night	1965	3.00	6.00	12.00
❏ 0461	How Does That Grab You, Darlin'?/The Last of the Secret Agents	1966	2.50	5.00	10.00
❏ 0491	Friday's Child/Hutchinson Jail	1966	2.50	5.00	10.00
❏ 0514	In Our Time/Leave My Dog Alone	1966	2.50	5.00	10.00
❏ 0527	Sugar Town/Summer Wine	1966	3.00	6.00	12.00
❏ 0559	Love Eyes/Coastin'	1967	2.50	5.00	10.00
❏ 0561	Somethin' Stupid/I Will Wait for You	1967	2.00	4.00	8.00

—A-side: Nancy Sinatra and Frank Sinatra; B-side: Frank Sinatra

| ❏ 0561 | Somethin' Stupid/Give Her Love | 1967 | 2.50 | 5.00 | 10.00 |

—A-side: Nancy Sinatra and Frank Sinatra; B-side: Frank Sinatra

| ❏ 0595 | Jackson/You Only Live Twice | 1967 | 2.50 | 5.00 | 10.00 |

—A-side: With Lee Hazlewood

❏ 0620	Lightning's Girl/Until It's Time for You to Go	1967	2.50	5.00	10.00
❏ 0620 [PS]	Lightning's Girl/Until It's Time for You to Go	1967	5.00	10.00	20.00
❏ 0629	Lady Bird/Sand	1967	2.00	4.00	8.00

—With Lee Hazlewood

| ❏ 0636 | Tony Rome/This Town | 1967 | 2.00 | 4.00 | 8.00 |
| ❏ 0651 | Some Velvet Morning/Oh Lonesome Me | 1967 | 2.00 | 4.00 | 8.00 |

—With Lee Hazlewood

| ❏ 0670 | 100 Years/See the Little Children | 1968 | 2.00 | 4.00 | 8.00 |
| ❏ 0701 | These Boots Are Made for Walkin'/Love Eyes | 1968 | — | 2.50 | 5.00 |

—"Back to Back Hits" series

Number	Title (A Side/B Side)	Yr	VG	VG+	NM
❏ 0721	Sugar Town/Summer Wine	1968	—	2.50	5.00

—"Back to Back Hits" series

| ❏ 0726 | Jackson/Summer Wine | 1968 | — | 2.50 | 5.00 |

—With Lee Hazlewood; "Back to Back Hits" series

| ❏ 0729 | Lightning's Girl/One Velvet Morning | 1968 | — | 2.50 | 5.00 |

—B-side with Lee Hazlewood; "Back to Back Hits" series

❏ 0756	Happy/Nice 'N' Easy	1968	2.00	4.00	8.00
❏ 0789	Good Time Girl/Old Devil Moon	1968	2.00	4.00	8.00
❏ 0813	God Knows I Love You/Just Plain Old Me	1969	2.00	4.00	8.00
❏ 0821	Here We Go Again/Memories	1969	2.00	4.00	8.00
❏ 0851	Drummer Man/Home	1969	2.00	4.00	8.00
❏ 0880	It's Such a Lonely Time of the Year/Kids	1969	2.50	5.00	10.00
❏ 0890	I Love Them All/Home	1970	2.00	4.00	8.00
❏ 0932	Hello L.A., Bye Bye Birmingham/White Tattoo	1970	2.00	4.00	8.00
❏ 0968	I'm Not a Girl Anymore/How Are Things in California	1970	2.00	4.00	8.00
❏ 0980	Feelin' Kinda Sunday/Kids	1970	2.00	4.00	8.00

—A-side by Nancy Sinatra and Frank Sinatra

❏ 0991	Is Anybody Goin' to San Antone/Hook and Ladder	1971	2.00	4.00	8.00
❏ 0991 [PS]	Is Anybody Goin' to San Antone/Hook and Ladder	1971	3.75	7.50	15.00
❏ 1011	Life's a Trippy Thing/I'm Not Afraid	1971	2.00	4.00	8.00

—A-side by Nancy Sinatra and Frank Sinatra; B-side by Frank Sinatra solo

| ❏ 1021 | Did You Ever/Back on the Road | 1971 | 2.00 | 4.00 | 8.00 |

—As "Nancy and Lee"

❏ 1034	Glory Road/Is Anybody Goin' to San Antone	1971	2.00	4.00	8.00
❏ 20017	Not Just Your Friend/Cuff Links and a Tie Clip	1961	5.00	10.00	20.00
❏ 20017 [PS]	Not Just Your Friend/Cuff Links and a Tie Clip	1961	15.00	30.00	60.00
❏ 20045	To Know Him Is to Love Him/Like I Do	1962	5.00	10.00	20.00
❏ 20097	June, July and August/Think of Me	1962	5.00	10.00	20.00
❏ 20127	Tonight You Belong to Me/You Can Have Any Boy	1962	5.00	10.00	20.00
❏ 20144	Put Your Head on My Shoulder/I See the Moon	1963	5.00	10.00	20.00
❏ 20188	The Cruel War/One Way	1963	5.00	10.00	20.00

7-Inch Extended Plays
REPRISE

| ❏ SR 6251 | It's Such a Pretty World/Jackson/When It's Over/Oh Lonesome Me/End of the World/Lay Some Happiness on Me | 1967 | 3.75 | 7.50 | 15.00 |

—Jukebox issue; small hole, plays at 33 1/3 rpm

| ❏ SR 6251 [PS] | Country My Way | 1967 | 3.75 | 7.50 | 15.00 |

Albums
RCA VICTOR

| ❏ LSP-4645 | Nancy and Lee Again | 1972 | 7.50 | 15.00 | 30.00 |

—With Lee Hazlewood

| ❏ LSP-4774 | Woman | 1973 | 6.25 | 12.50 | 25.00 |
| ❏ VPS-6078 [(2)] | This Is Nancy Sinatra | 1972 | 12.50 | 25.00 | 50.00 |

REPRISE

❏ R-6202 [M]	Boots	1966	6.25	12.50	25.00
❏ RS-6202 [S]	Boots	1966	7.50	15.00	30.00
❏ R-6207 [M]	How Does That Grab You?	1966	5.00	10.00	20.00
❏ RS-6207 [S]	How Does That Grab You?	1966	6.25	12.50	25.00
❏ R-6221 [M]	Nancy in London	1966	5.00	10.00	20.00
❏ RS-6221 [S]	Nancy in London	1966	6.25	12.50	25.00
❏ R-6239 [M]	Sugar	1967	6.25	12.50	25.00
❏ RS-6239 [S]	Sugar	1967	5.00	10.00	20.00
❏ R-6251 [M]	Country, My Way	1967	6.25	12.50	25.00
❏ RS-6251 [S]	Country, My Way	1967	5.00	10.00	20.00
❏ RS-6273	Nancy and Lee	1968	5.00	10.00	20.00

—With Lee Hazlewood

❏ R-6277 [M]	Movin' with Nancy	1967	6.25	12.50	25.00
❏ RS-6277 [S]	Movin' with Nancy	1967	5.00	10.00	20.00
❏ RS-6333	Nancy	1969	5.00	10.00	20.00
❏ RS-6409	Nancy's Greatest Hits	1970	5.00	10.00	20.00
❏ ST-91341 [S]	Boots	1967	10.00	20.00	40.00

—Capitol Record Club edition

| ❏ ST-91349 [S] | Movin' with Nancy | 1967 | 7.50 | 15.00 | 30.00 |

—Capitol Record Club edition

RHINO

| ❏ R1-70166 | Fairy Tales and Fantasies: The Best of Nancy and Lee | 1989 | 2.50 | 5.00 | 10.00 |

—With Lee Hazlewood

| ❏ RNLP-70227 | Boots: Nancy Sinatra's All-Time Hits (1966-1970) | 1987 | 2.50 | 5.00 | 10.00 |

SINATRA FAMILY, THE See VARIOUS ARTISTS COMPILATIONS in back.

SINCERES, THE (1)
45s
COLUMBIA

| ❏ 43110 | Sincerely/Snap Your Fingers | 1964 | 3.75 | 7.50 | 15.00 |

EPIC

| ❏ 9583 | Kookie Ookie/Our Winter Love | 1963 | 3.75 | 7.50 | 15.00 |

TAURUS

| ❏ 377 | The Magic of Love/Tell Her | 1966 | 7.50 | 15.00 | 30.00 |

SINCERES, THE (2)
45s
JORDAN

| ❏ 117 | You're Too Young/Forbidden Love | 1960 | 62.50 | 125.00 | 250.00 |

RICHIE

| ❏ 545 | Please Don't Cheat on Me/If You Should Leave Me | 1961 | 25.00 | 50.00 | 100.00 |

—With Roulette Records distribution mentioned on label

| ❏ 545 | Please Don't Cheat on Me/If You Should Leave Me | 1961 | 175.00 | 350.00 | 700.00 |

—No mention of Roulette Records on label

SIGMA

| ❏ 1003/4 | Darling/Do You Remember | 1960 | 100.00 | 200.00 | 400.00 |

SINFIELD, PETE
Albums
MANTICORE

| ❏ MC 66667 | Still | 1973 | 2.50 | 5.00 | 10.00 |

Number	Title (A Side/B Side)	Yr	VG	VG+	NM
SING A SONG WITH THE BEATLES					
Albums					
TOWER					
❑ DKAO 5000 [R]	Sing a Song with the Beatles	1965	50.00	100.00	200.00
❑ KAO 5000 [M]	Sing a Song with the Beatles	1965	37.50	75.00	150.00
—No artist listed on label					
SINGER, JOHNNY					
45s					
HIT					
❑ 178	Ode to the Little Brown Shack Out Back/ Do-Wacka-Do	1965	2.00	4.00	8.00
—B-side by Charlie Bare					
❑ 233	Make the World Go Away/Fever	1965	2.00	4.00	8.00
—B-side by the Chords (2)					
SINGING DOGS, THE, DON CHARLES PRESENTS					
45s					
RCA					
❑ PA-10129	Jingle Bells/Oh! Susanna	1976	—	2.00	4.00
—Black label, dog near top					
RCA VICTOR					
❑ 47-6344	Oh! Susannah//Pat-a-Cake/Three Blind Mice/ Jingle Bells	1955	3.75	7.50	15.00
—"Jingle Bells" is part of a medley and lasts 1:15					
❑ 47-6344 [PS]	Oh! Susannah//Pat-a-Cake/Three Blind Mice/ Jingle Bells	1955	6.25	12.50	25.00
❑ 47-6432	Hot Dog Rock and Roll/Hot Dog Boogie	1956	3.00	6.00	12.00
❑ 48-1020	Jingle Bells/Oh! Susannah	1971	—	2.50	5.00
—First reissue; "Jingle Bells" lengthened to 1:47 on this and future issues					
❑ 48-1021	Hot Dog Rock and Roll/Hot Dog Boogie	1971	—	2.50	5.00
❑ F2NW-7846/7 [DJ]	Pearl's Jingle Bells/Caesar's Pat-A-Cake/ King's Three Blind Mice//Dolly's Oh! Susanna (Fast)/ Dolly's Oh! Susanna (Slow)	1955	10.00	20.00	40.00
—Banded version for radio use ("Jingle Bells" is 1:15)					
❑ PA-10129	Jingle Bells/Oh! Susannah	1974	2.00	4.00	8.00
—First issue of PA-10129 has tan or brown (also possibly orange) labels					
SINGING MCENTIRES, THE (PAKE, REBA AND SUSIE)					
45s					
BOSS					
❑ SPS-194	The Ballad of John McEntire/Interview by the Grandchildren	1969	125.00	250.00	500.00
—Supposedly only 25 copies were pressed					
SINGING NUN, THE					
45s					
PHILIPS					
❑ 40152	Dominique/Entres Les Etoiles (Among the Stars)	1963	—	3.00	6.00
❑ 40152 [PS]	Dominique/Entres Les Etoiles (Among the Stars)	1963	3.00	6.00	12.00
❑ 40163	Dominique/Les Pieds de Missionaires	1963	—	3.00	6.00
❑ 40163 [PS]	Dominique/Les Pieds de Missionaires	1963	3.75	7.50	15.00
—Almost identical to the 40152 sleeve					
❑ 40165	Tous Les Chemins/Frere "Tout Le" Monde	1964	—	2.50	5.00
❑ 40165 [PS]	Tous Les Chemins/Frere "Tout Le" Monde	1964	3.00	6.00	12.00
❑ 40195	Une Fleur (A Flower)/Avec Toi (With You)	1964	—	2.50	5.00
Albums					
PHILIPS					
❑ PCC 203 [M]	Soeur Sourire: The Singing Nun	1963	3.75	7.50	15.00
❑ PCC 209 [M]	Her Joy, Her Songs	1964	3.75	7.50	15.00
❑ PCC 603 [S]	Soeur Sourire: The Singing Nun	1963	3.75	7.50	15.00
❑ PCC 609 [S]	Her Joy, Her Songs	1964	3.75	7.50	15.00
SINGING REINDEER, THE See DANCER, PRANCER, AND NERVOUS.					
SINGLETON, MARGIE Also see LEON ASHLEY; GEORGE JONES.					
45s					
ASHLEY					
❑ 200	The Little Girl I Didn't Have the Courage to Keep/ Seemed You'd Never Been Good	197?	2.00	4.00	8.00
❑ 2000	Sooner or Later/Angel Hands	1967	2.50	5.00	10.00
❑ 2011	Ode to Billie Joe/Big Boys Don't Need Mamas	1967	2.50	5.00	10.00
❑ 2050	Wandering Mind/Your Conscience Sends Me Flowers	1968	2.50	5.00	10.00
❑ 2090	Chill Winds/Little Darlin'	1968	2.50	5.00	10.00
❑ 5000	Harper Valley P.T.A./(B-side unknown)	1968	2.50	5.00	10.00
❑ 7500	Jesus Is My Pusher/Lord Take Me Right Now	1969	2.50	5.00	10.00
❑ 35002	All That Love Is Gone/Blindness of the Wife	197?	—	3.00	6.00
❑ 35006	Enough of a Woman/Dreaming Bigger Than You	197?	—	3.00	6.00
❑ 35012	I Guess I've Just Loved You Too Long/ The Well's Not Dry	197?	—	3.00	6.00
D					
❑ 1007	I Want to Be Where You're Gonna Be/ Shattered Kingdom	1958	7.50	15.00	30.00
MERCURY					
❑ 71359	Oo-Wee, You're the One for Me/Teddy	1958	5.00	10.00	20.00
❑ 71672	Destination Love/Toss a Pebble	1960	3.75	7.50	15.00
❑ 71733	She Will Break Your Heart/Voices of Love	1960	3.75	7.50	15.00
❑ 71814	Your Old Love Letters/Are You Ever Too Young	1961	3.00	6.00	12.00
❑ 71928	I'll Just Walk On By/ Her Image Keeps Getting in the Way	1962	3.00	6.00	12.00
❑ 72002	Chained to a Promise/Living in the Danger Zone	1962	3.00	6.00	12.00
❑ 72079	Magic Star (Telstar)/Only Your Shadow Knows	1963	3.00	6.00	12.00
❑ 72124	I Don't Have to Look Pretty/ Walkin' Back to Happiness	1963	3.00	6.00	12.00
❑ 72213	Old Records/How Do You Say Goodbye	1963	3.00	6.00	12.00
❑ 72268	Forget Me Not/I Don't Want You This Way	1964	3.00	6.00	12.00
❑ 72363	Don't Be Good to Me/It's Too Much	1964	3.00	6.00	12.00
STARDAY					
❑ 287	One Step Nearer to You/Not What He's Got	1957	6.25	12.50	25.00
❑ 309	My Picture of You/Love Is a Treasure	1957	6.25	12.50	25.00
❑ 323	Beautiful Dawn/Take Time Out for Love	1957	6.25	12.50	25.00
❑ 443	Nothin' But True Love/It's Better to Know	1959	5.00	10.00	20.00
❑ 472	The Eyes of Love/Angel Hands	1959	5.00	10.00	20.00
❑ 502	For the Love of Jim/My Special Dream	1960	5.00	10.00	20.00
UNITED ARTISTS					
❑ 896	What Could I Do/You Shake My Hand and Kiss Me on the Cheek	1965	2.50	5.00	10.00
❑ 939	I'm Guilty This Time/You Took the Easy Way Out	1965	2.50	5.00	10.00
Albums					
ASHLEY					
❑ 3003	Margie Singleton Sings Country Music with Soul	1968	3.75	7.50	15.00
PICKWICK					
❑ SPC-3133	Harper Valley P.T.A.	197?	2.50	5.00	10.00
UNITED ARTISTS					
❑ UAL-3459 [M]	Crying Time	1965	3.75	7.50	15.00
❑ UAS-6459 [S]	Crying Time	1965	5.00	10.00	20.00
SINGLETON, MARGIE, AND FARON YOUNG Also see each artist's individual listings.					
45s					
MERCURY					
❑ 72237	Keeping Up with the Joneses/ No Thanks, I Just Had One	1964	3.00	6.00	12.00
❑ 72237 [PS]	Keeping Up with the Joneses/ No Thanks, I Just Had One	1964	5.00	10.00	20.00
❑ 72312	Another Woman's Man — Another Man's Woman/Honky Tonk Happy	1964	3.00	6.00	12.00
SIR DOUGLAS QUINTET Also see THE DEVONS; DOUG SAHM.					
45s					
ATLANTIC					
❑ 2965	The Nitty Gritty/I'm Just Tired of Getting Burned	1973	2.00	4.00	8.00
❑ 2985	Texas Tornado/Blue Horizon	1973	2.00	4.00	8.00
—As "Sir Douglas Band"					
CASABLANCA					
❑ 828	Roll With the Punches/I'm Not That Kat Anymore	1975	6.25	12.50	25.00
MERCURY					
❑ 73181	Michoacan/Westside Blues Again	1971	—	3.00	6.00
PACEMAKER					
❑ 280	Sugar Bee/Blue Norther	1964	5.00	10.00	20.00
PHILIPS					
❑ 40676	What About Tomorrow/A Nice Song	1970	2.00	4.00	8.00
❑ 40676 [PS]	What About Tomorrow/A Nice Song	1970	3.75	7.50	15.00
❑ 40687	Pretty Flower/Catch the Man on the Fly	1970	2.00	4.00	8.00
❑ 40708	Wasted Days, Wasted Nights/ Me and My Destiny	1971	2.00	4.00	8.00
SMASH					
❑ 2169	Are Inlaws Really Outlaws/Sell a Song	1968	2.00	4.00	8.00
❑ 2191	Mendocino/I Wanna Be Your Mama Again	1968	2.00	4.00	8.00
❑ 2222	Lawd, I'm Just a Country Boy in This Great Big Freaky City/It Didn't Even Bring Me Down	1969	2.00	4.00	8.00
❑ 2233	Dynamite Woman/Too Many Dociled Minds	1969	2.00	4.00	8.00
❑ 2253	At the Crossroads/Texas Me	1969	2.00	4.00	8.00
❑ 2259	Nuevo Laredo/I Don't Wanna Go Home	1970	2.00	4.00	8.00
TRIBE					
❑ 8308	She's About a Mover/ We'll Take Our Last Walk Tonight	1965	3.00	6.00	12.00
—Gray label with Indian head					
❑ 8308	She's About a Mover/ We'll Take Our Last Walk Tonight	1965	3.75	7.50	15.00
—White label (not marked as a promo)					
❑ 8310	The Tracker/Blue Brother	1965	2.50	5.00	10.00
—Gray label with Indian head					
❑ 8310	The Tracker/Blue Brother	1965	3.00	6.00	12.00
—White label (not marked as a promo)					
❑ 8312	In Time/The Story of John Hardy	1965	2.50	5.00	10.00
❑ 8314	The Rains Came/Bacon Fat	1966	2.50	5.00	10.00
❑ 8317	She's Gotta Be Boss/Quarter to Three	1966	2.50	5.00	10.00
❑ 8318	Beginning of the End/Love Don't Treat Me Fair	1966	2.50	5.00	10.00
❑ 8321	She Digs My Love/When I Sing the Blues	1966	2.50	5.00	10.00
❑ 8323	Hang Loose/I'm Sorry	1967	2.50	5.00	10.00
Albums					
ABC DOT					
❑ DO-2057	Texas Rock for Country Rollers	1976	3.75	7.50	15.00
—As "Sir Doug and the Texas Tornadoes"					
ATLANTIC					
❑ SD 7287	Texas Tornado	1974	3.75	7.50	15.00
—As "Sir Douglas Band"					
BEAT ROCKET					
❑ BR 123	The Best of the Sir Douglas Quintet	2000	3.00	6.00	12.00
—Reissue of Tribe LP on 180-gram vinyl					
❑ BR 124	The Sir Douglas Quintet Is Back!	2000	3.00	6.00	12.00
—New compilation of Tribe material on 180-gram vinyl					
PHILIPS					
❑ PHS 600344	1 + 1 + 1 = 4	1970	6.25	12.50	25.00
❑ PHS 600353	The Return of Doug Saldana	1971	6.25	12.50	25.00
R&M					
❑ UDL-2343	The Tracker	1981	5.00	10.00	20.00
SMASH					
❑ SRS-67108	Sir Douglas Quintet + 2 = Honkey Blues	1968	7.50	15.00	30.00
❑ SRS-67115	Mendocino	1969	6.25	12.50	25.00
❑ SRS-67130	Together After Five	1970	6.25	12.50	25.00
TAKOMA					
❑ TAK-7086	The Best of the Sir Douglas Quintet	1980	3.00	6.00	12.00
❑ TAK-7088	Border Wave	1981	3.00	6.00	12.00
❑ TAK-7095	Sir Douglas Quintet Live	1985	3.00	6.00	12.00
TRIBE					
❑ TR 37001 [M]	The Best of the Sir Douglas Quintet	1966	17.50	35.00	70.00
❑ TRS 47001 [R]	The Best of the Sir Douglas Quintet	1966	12.50	25.00	50.00
VARRICK					
❑ 004	Quintessence	1983	3.00	6.00	12.00
SIR LORD BALTIMORE					
45s					
MERCURY					
❑ 73181	I Got a Woman/Master Headache	1970	2.00	4.00	8.00
Albums					
MERCURY					
❑ SRM-1-613	Sir Lord Baltimore	1971	6.25	12.50	25.00
❑ SR-61328	Kingdom Come	1970	6.25	12.50	25.00

S

Number	Title (A Side/B Side)	Yr	VG	VG+	NM
SIR WALTER RALEIGH AND THE COUPONS					
45s					
A&M					
❏ 757	White Cliffs of Dover/Something or Other	1965	2.50	5.00	10.00
❏ 764	While I Wait/Somethin'	1965	2.50	5.00	10.00
JERDEN					
❏ 760	Tomorrow's Gonna Be Another Day/Whitcomb St.	1965	3.00	6.00	12.00
—As "Sir Raleigh and the Coupons"					
TOWER					
❏ 156	Tell Her Tonight/If You Need Me	1965	2.50	5.00	10.00
❏ 220	I Don't Want to Cry/Always	1966	2.50	5.00	10.00
SISK, SHIRLEY					
45s					
SUN					
❏ 365	I Forgot to Remember to Forget/The Other Side	1961	6.25	12.50	25.00
SISTER SLEDGE					
12-Inch Singles					
ATLANTIC					
❏ DSKO 97 [DJ]	As (same on both sides)	1977	3.75	7.50	15.00
❏ 850 [DJ]	Frankie (Club Mix) (Dub Mix)/Hold Out Poppy	1985	—	3.00	6.00
❏ 868 [DJ]	Dancing on the Jagged Edge/(Dub)	1985	—	3.00	6.00
❏ 979 [DJ]	Here to Stay (2 mixes)/Make a Wish	1986	—	3.00	6.00
—B-side by Joe Cruz					
❏ 86862	Dancing on the Jagged Edge/(Dub)	1985	—	3.00	6.00
COTILLION					
❏ 229 [DJ]	Reach Your Peak (5:26) (same on both sides)	1980	2.00	4.00	8.00
❏ 277 [DJ]	He's Just a Runaway (6:05) (3:57)	1981	2.00	4.00	8.00
❏ 645 [DJ]	B.Y.O.B. (Bring Your Own Body) (6:43) (3:50)	1983	—	3.00	6.00
RHINO					
❏ 76019	We Are Family (2 mixes)/Lost in Music (2 mixes)	1993	2.00	4.00	8.00
45s					
ATCO					
❏ 6924	The Weatherman/Have You Met My Friend	1973	—	3.00	6.00
❏ 6940	Mama Never Told Me/Neither One of Us	1973	—	3.00	6.00
❏ 7008	Love Don't You Go Through No Changes on Me/Don't You Miss Him	1974	—	2.50	5.00
❏ 7020	Circle of Love (Caught in the Middle)/Cross My Heart	1975	—	2.50	5.00
❏ 7035	Love Ain't Easy/Love Has Found Me	1975	—	2.50	5.00
ATLANTIC					
❏ 89357	Here to Stay/Make a Wish	1986	—	—	3.00
—B-side by Joe Cruz					
❏ 89466	You're Fine/(B-side unknown)	1985	—	—	3.00
❏ 89520	You Need Me/Dancing on the Jagged Edge	1985	—	—	3.00
❏ 89547	Frankie/Hold Out Poppy	1985	—	—	3.00
❏ 89547 [PS]	Frankie/Hold Out Poppy	1985	—	2.00	4.00
COTILLION					
❏ 44202	Thank You for Today/Have Love Will Travel	1976	—	2.50	5.00
❏ 44208	Cream of the Crop/Love Ain't Easy	1976	—	2.50	5.00
❏ 44220	Blockbuster Boy/Moondance	1977	—	2.50	5.00
❏ 44226	Baby, It's the Rain/Hold Onto This Feeling	1977	—	2.50	5.00
❏ 44234	Do It to the Max/I've Seen Better Days	1978	—	2.50	5.00
❏ 44245	He's the Greatest Dancer/Somebody Loves Me	1978	—	2.00	4.00
❏ 44251	We Are Family/Easier to Love	1979	—	2.00	4.00
❏ 45001	Lost in Music/Thinking of You	1979	—	2.00	4.00
❏ 45007	Got to Love Somebody/Good Girl Now	1979	—	2.00	4.00
❏ 45013	Reach Your Peak/You Fooled Around	1980	—	2.00	4.00
❏ 45020	Let's Go on Vacation/Easy Street	1980	—	2.00	4.00
❏ 46007	All American Girls/Happy Feelings	1981	—	2.00	4.00
❏ 46012	Next Time You'll Know/If You Really Want Me	1981	—	2.00	4.00
❏ 46017	He's Just a Runaway/He's Just a Runaway (Long Version)	1981	—	2.00	4.00
❏ 47000	My Guy/Il Macquillace Lady	1982	—	2.00	4.00
❏ 47007	All the Man That I Need/Light Footin'	1982	—	2.00	4.00
❏ 99834	Gotta Get Back to Love/Lifetime Lover	1983	—	2.00	4.00
❏ 99885	B.Y.O.B. (Bring Your Own Baby)/(B-side unknown)	1983	—	2.00	4.00
Albums					
ATCO					
❏ SD 36-105	Circle of Love	1975	5.00	10.00	20.00
ATLANTIC					
❏ 81255	When the Boys Meet the Girls	1985	2.50	5.00	10.00
COTILLION					
❏ SD 5209	We Are Family	1979	2.50	5.00	10.00
❏ SD 5231	The Sisters	1982	2.50	5.00	10.00
❏ SD 9919	Together	1976	3.00	6.00	12.00
❏ SD 16012	Love Somebody Today	1980	2.50	5.00	10.00
❏ SD 16027	All American Girls	1981	2.50	5.00	10.00
❏ 90069	Bet Cha Say That to All the Girls	1983	2.50	5.00	10.00
SIX PENTZ, THE					
45s					
BRENT					
❏ 7062	Imitation Situation/Please Come Home	1967	5.00	10.00	20.00
❏ 7064	Don't Say You're Sorry/Tinkle Talk	1967	5.00	10.00	20.00
SIX TEENS, THE					
45s					
FLIP					
❏ 315	A Casual Look/Teenage Promise	1956	5.00	10.00	20.00
❏ 317	Send Me Flowers/Afar Into the Night	1956	3.75	7.50	15.00
❏ 320	My Special Guy/Only Jim	1956	3.75	7.50	15.00
❏ 322	Arrow of Love/Was It a Dream of Mine	1957	3.75	7.50	15.00
❏ 326	Baby You're Dynamite/My Surprise	1957	3.75	7.50	15.00
❏ 329	My Secret/Stop Playing Ping Pong	1958	3.75	7.50	15.00
❏ 333	Danny/Love's Funny That Way	1958	3.75	7.50	15.00
❏ 338	Baby-O/Oh, It's Crazy	1958	5.00	10.00	20.00
❏ 346	Why Do I Go to School/Heaven Knows I Love You	1959	6.25	12.50	25.00
❏ 350	So Happy/That Wonderful Secret of Love	1960	3.75	7.50	15.00
❏ 351	A Little Prayer/Suddenly in Love	1960	3.75	7.50	15.00

Number	Title (A Side/B Side)	Yr	VG	VG+	NM
SIXPENCE, THE					
45s					
ALL AMERICAN					
❏ 313	Fortune Teller/My Flash on You	1966	10.00	20.00	40.00
❏ 333	Hey Joe/(B-side unknown)	1967	7.50	15.00	30.00
❏ 353	Fortune Teller/My Flash on You	1967	7.50	15.00	30.00
DOT					
❏ 16959	Fortune Teller/My Flash on You	1966	6.25	12.50	25.00
IMPACT					
❏ 1025	What to Do/You're the Love	1967	6.25	12.50	25.00
SKA KINGS, THE					
45s					
ATLANTIC					
❏ 2232	Jamaica Ska/Oil in My Lamp	1964	2.50	5.00	10.00
❏ 2236	Last Night Ska/Watermelon Man Ska	1964	2.50	5.00	10.00
SKARLETTONES, THE					
45s					
EMBER					
❏ 1053	Do You Remember/Will You Dream	1959	30.00	60.00	120.00
SKEE BROTHERS, THE					
45s					
EPIC					
❏ 9275	Big Deal/While I'm Away	1958	25.00	50.00	100.00
OKEH					
❏ 7108	That's All She Wrote/Four Aces	1959	12.50	25.00	50.00
ROULETTE					
❏ 4164	Romeo Joe/Lu Ann	1959	5.00	10.00	20.00
SKELLERN, PETER					
45s					
LONDON					
❏ 20075	You're a Lady/Manifesto	1972	—	2.50	5.00
PRIVATE STOCK					
❏ 45,028	Hold On to Love/(B-side unknown)	1975	—	2.00	4.00
❏ 45,054	Hard Times/And Then You'll Fall	1975	—	2.00	4.00
SKELTON, EDDIE					
45s					
DIXIE					
❏ 2011	Keep It Swinging/Without You	1958	500.00	1000.	1500.
STARDAY					
❏ 294	My Heart Gets Lonely/Let Me Be With You Forever	1957	37.50	75.00	150.00
SKID ROW					
Albums					
EPIC					
❏ E 30404	Skid Row	1971	5.00	10.00	20.00
❏ E 30913	34 Hours	1971	6.25	12.50	25.00
SKIP AND FLIP Also see GARY PAXTON.					
45s					
BRENT					
❏ 7002	It Was I/Lunch Hour	1959	6.25	12.50	25.00
❏ 7005	Fancy Nancy/It Could Be	1959	6.25	12.50	25.00
❏ 7010	Cherry Pie/I'll Quit Cryin' Over You	1960	6.25	12.50	25.00
❏ 7013	Teenage Honeymoon/Hully Gully Cha Cha Cha	1960	5.00	10.00	20.00
❏ 7017	The Green Door/Willow Tree	1960	5.00	10.00	20.00
❏ 7028	Over the Mountain/One More Drink for Julie	1962	5.00	10.00	20.00
CALIFORNIA					
❏ 2325	Tossin' and Turnin'/Everyday I Have to Cry	1963	3.75	7.50	15.00
REV					
❏ 3523	Why Not Confess/Johnny Risk	1959	6.25	12.50	25.00
—As "Gary and Clyde"					
TIME					
❏ 1007	Why Not Confess/Johnny Risk	1959	—	—	—
—May not exist; we know of a different record using the number 1007 on Time					
❏ 1031	Betty Jean/Doubt	1961	5.00	10.00	20.00
SKIP AND THE CREATIONS					
Albums					
JUSTICE					
❏ (# unknown)	Mobam	196?	100.00	200.00	400.00
SKY Doug Fieger, later of The Knack, was in this group.					
45s					
RCA VICTOR					
❏ 74-0419	Goodie Two Shoes/Make It in Time	1971	—	3.00	6.00
❏ 74-0611	Let It Lie Low/Taking the Long Way Home	1971	—	3.00	6.00
Albums					
RCA VICTOR					
❏ LSP-4457	Sky	1970	3.75	7.50	15.00
❏ LSP-4514	Sailor's Delight	1971	3.75	7.50	15.00
SKYLARK					
45s					
CAPITOL					
❏ 3378	What Would I Do Without You/Suites for My Lady	1972	—	2.00	4.00
❏ 3511	Wildflower/The Writings on the Wall	1973	—	2.50	5.00
❏ 3661	I'll Have to Go Away/Twenty-Six Years	1973	—	2.00	4.00
❏ 3773	Virgin Green/If That's the Way You Want It	1973	—	2.00	4.00
Albums					
CAPITOL					
❏ ST-11048	Skylark	1972	3.75	7.50	15.00
❏ ST-11256	Skylark 2	1973	3.00	6.00	12.00
SKYLARKS, THE (1)					
45s					
ADMIRAL					
❏ 500	I'll Surf Around the World/How Many Times	1963	7.50	15.00	30.00

Number	Title (A Side/B Side)	Yr	VG	VG+	NM
SKYLARKS, THE (2)					
45s					
DECCA					
❏ 48241	The Glory of Love/You and I	1951	125.00	250.00	500.00
SKYLARKS, THE (3)					
45s					
EVERLAST					
❏ 5022	Everybody's Got Somebody/Jeannie	1963	7.50	15.00	30.00
SKYLARKS, THE (4)					
45s					
RCA VICTOR					
❏ 47-5257	Home in Pasadena/I Had the Craziest Dream	1953	6.25	12.50	25.00
SKYLARKS, THE (5)					
45s					
VERVE					
❏ 10082	Ol' Man River/There's a Boat Dat's Leavin' for New York	1957	5.00	10.00	20.00
SKYLARKS, THE (U)					
45s					
THUNDERBIRD					
❏ 102	Do You Know?/Here Comes the Fool	196?	3.00	6.00	12.00
SKYLINERS, THE					
45s					
ATCO					
❏ 6270	Since I Fell for You/I'd Die	1963	10.00	20.00	40.00
CALICO					
❏ 103/4	Since I Don't Have You/One Night, One Night	1959	12.50	25.00	50.00
❏ 106	This I Swear/Tomorrow	1959	7.50	15.00	30.00
❏ 109	It Happened Today/Lonely Way	1959	7.50	15.00	30.00
❏ 114	How Much/Lorraine from Spain	1960	6.25	12.50	25.00
❏ 117	Pennies from Heaven/I'll Be Seeing You	1960	6.25	12.50	25.00
❏ 120	Believe Me/Happy Time	1960	6.25	12.50	25.00
CAMEO					
❏ 215	Three Coins in the Fountain/Everyone But You	1962	10.00	20.00	40.00
CAPITOL					
❏ 3979	Where Have They Gone/I Could Have Loved You So Well	1974	6.25	12.50	25.00
—As "Jimmy Beaumont and the Skyliners"					
CLASSIC ARTISTS					
❏ 123	You're My Christmas Present/Another Lonely New Year's Eve	1990	—	2.50	5.00
COLPIX					
❏ 188	I'll Close My Eyes/The Door Is Still Open	1961	10.00	20.00	40.00
❏ 607	Ba'ion Rhythms/The End of a Story	196?	10.00	20.00	40.00
—As "Jimmy Beaumont and the Skyliners"					
❏ 613	Close Your Eyes/Our Love Will Last	1961	10.00	20.00	40.00
DRIVE					
❏ 6250	Our Day Is Here/The Day the Clown Cried	1976	2.00	4.00	8.00
JUBILEE					
❏ 5506	The Loser/Everything Is Fine	1965	3.75	7.50	15.00
❏ 5512	Who Do You Love/Get Yourself a Baby	1965	3.75	7.50	15.00
❏ 5520	I Run to You/Don't Hurt Me Baby	1965	3.75	7.50	15.00
MOTOWN					
❏ 1046 [DJ]	Since I Fell for You/I'd Die	1963	1000.	1500.	2000.
—Record never got beyond the test pressing stage (2 known copies)					
ORIGINAL SOUND					
❏ 35	Since I Don't Have You/One Night, One Night	1963	3.75	7.50	15.00
❏ 36	Pennies from Heaven/I'll Be Seeing You	1963	3.75	7.50	15.00
❏ 37	This I Swear/It Happened Today	1963	3.75	7.50	15.00
TORTOISE INT'L.					
❏ PB-11243	Oh How Happy/We've Got Love on Our Side	1978	2.00	4.00	8.00
❏ PB-11312	Smile On Me/Love Bug (Done Bit Me Again)	1978	2.00	4.00	8.00
VISCOUNT					
❏ 104	Comes Love/Tell Me	1962	5.00	10.00	20.00
Albums					
CALICO					
❏ LP-3000 [M]	The Skyliners	1959	200.00	400.00	600.00
—Yellow and blue label					
❏ LP-3000 [M]	The Skyliners	196?	50.00	100.00	200.00
—Blue label					
KAMA SUTRA					
❏ KSBS-2026	Once Upon a Time	1971	6.25	12.50	25.00
ORIGINAL SOUND					
❏ OS-5010 [M]	Since I Don't Have You	1963	12.50	25.00	50.00
❏ OSS-8873 [S]	Since I Don't Have You	1963	17.50	35.00	70.00
❏ OSS-8873 [S]	Since I Don't Have You	197?	3.75	7.50	15.00
—Reissue on thinner vinyl					
SLADE Includes early releases as "Ambrose Slade." Also see THE IN-BE-TWEENS.					
45s					
CBS ASSOCIATED					
❏ 04398	Run Runaway/Can't Tame a Hurricane	1984	—	2.00	4.00
❏ 04528	My Oh My/High and Dry	1984	—	2.00	4.00
❏ 04865	Little Sheila/Lock Up Your Daughters	1985	—	2.00	4.00
COTILLION					
❏ 44128	Get Down and Get With It/The Gospel According to Rasputin	1971	6.25	12.50	25.00
❏ 44139	Cos I Love You/Gotta Keep a-Rockin'	1971	6.25	12.50	25.00
❏ 44150	Look Wot You Dun/Candidate	1972	6.25	12.50	25.00
POLYDOR					
❏ 15041	Look Wot You Dun/Candidate	1972	2.50	5.00	10.00
❏ 15044	Cuz I Love You/My Life Is Natural	1972	2.50	5.00	10.00
❏ 15046	Take Me Back 'Ome/Wondering Why	1972	2.50	5.00	10.00
❏ 15053	Mama Weer All Crazee Now/Man Who Speeks Evil	1972	2.50	5.00	10.00
❏ 15060	Gudbuy T' Jane/I Won't Let It 'Appen Again	1973	2.50	5.00	10.00
❏ 15069	Cum On Feel the Noize/I'm Mee, I'm Now, An' That's Orl	1973	3.75	7.50	15.00
❏ 15080	Let the Good Times Roll/Feel So Fine-I Don' Mind	1973	2.50	5.00	10.00
REPRISE					
❏ 1182	Skweeze Me Pleeze Me/My Town	1973	2.00	4.00	8.00
WARNER BROS.					
❏ 7759	Merry Christmas Everybody/Don't Blame Me	1973	2.50	5.00	10.00
❏ 7777	Good Time Gals/We're Really Gonna Raise the Roof	1974	2.00	4.00	8.00
❏ 7808	How Can It Be/When the Lights Are Out	1974	2.00	4.00	8.00
❏ 8134	How Does It Feel/OK, Yesterday Was Yesterday	1975	2.00	4.00	8.00
❏ 8185	Nobody's Fool/When the Chips Are Down	1976	2.00	4.00	8.00
Albums					
CBS ASSOCIATED					
❏ FZ 39336	Keep Your Hands Off My Power Supply	1984	2.50	5.00	10.00
❏ PZ 39336	Keep Your Hands Off My Power Supply	1985	2.00	4.00	8.00
—Budget-line reissue					
❏ FZ 39976	Rogues Gallery	1985	2.50	5.00	10.00
COTILLION					
❏ SD 9035	Play It Loud	1970	5.00	10.00	20.00
FONTANA					
❏ SRF-67598	Ballzy	1969	20.00	40.00	80.00
❏ SRF-67598 [DJ]	Ballzy	1969	12.50	25.00	50.00
—White label promo					
POLYDOR					
❏ PD-5508	Slade Alive!	1972	3.75	7.50	15.00
❏ PD-5524	Slayed?	1973	3.75	7.50	15.00
REPRISE					
❏ MS 2173	Sladest	1973	3.00	6.00	12.00
WARNER BROS.					
❏ BS 2770	Stomp Your Hands, Clap Your Feet	1974	3.00	6.00	12.00
❏ BS 2865	Slade in Flame	1975	3.00	6.00	12.00
❏ BS 2936	Nobody's Fools	1976	3.00	6.00	12.00
SLADES, THE					
45s					
DOMINO					
❏ 500	You Cheated/The Waddle	1958	10.00	20.00	40.00
❏ 800	You Gambled/No Time	1959	10.00	20.00	40.00
❏ 901	Just You/It's Better to Love	1959	7.50	15.00	30.00
❏ 906	It's Your Turn/Take My Heart	1961	10.00	20.00	40.00
❏ 1000	Summertime/You Must Try	1961	7.50	15.00	30.00
LIBERTY					
❏ 55118	Baby/You Mean Everything to Me	1957	6.25	12.50	25.00
❏ 55118	Baby/You Mean Everything to Me	1957	12.50	25.00	50.00
—As "The Spades," in error					
SLATKIN, FELIX					
45s					
LIBERTY					
❏ 55282	Theme from The Sundowners/Gaythers Gone	1960	2.50	5.00	10.00
❏ 55299	My Own True Love/It's Not Forever	1961	2.50	5.00	10.00
❏ 55326	Streets of Laredo/(B-side unknown)	1961	2.50	5.00	10.00
❏ 55329	Theme from The Pleasure of Your Company/Street Scene	1961	2.50	5.00	10.00
❏ 55372	King of Kings/Mandolin	1961	2.50	5.00	10.00
❏ 55487	A Theme Searching for a Picture/Theme from "My Geisha"	1962	2.00	4.00	8.00
❏ 55523	Orange Blossom Special/Maiden's Prayer	1962	2.00	4.00	8.00
Albums					
LIBERTY					
❏ LRP-3150 [M]	Fantastic Percussion	1960	3.75	7.50	15.00
❏ LRP-3287 [M]	Our Winter Love	1963	3.00	6.00	12.00
❏ LST-7150 [S]	Fantastic Percussion	1960	5.00	10.00	20.00
❏ LST-7287 [S]	Our Winter Love	1963	3.75	7.50	15.00
❏ LMM-13001 [M]	Paradise Found	1960	3.75	7.50	15.00
❏ LMM-13008 [M]	Street Scene	1961	3.75	7.50	15.00
❏ LMM-13011 [M]	Many Splendored Themes	1962	3.75	7.50	15.00
❏ LMM-13019 [M]	Inspired Themes from the Inspired Films	1962	3.75	7.50	15.00
❏ LMM-13021 [M]	Fantastic Strings Play Fantastic Themes	1962	3.75	7.50	15.00
❏ LMM-13024 [M]	Hoedown	1963	3.75	7.50	15.00
❏ LMM-13027 [M]	The Ballad of New Orleans	1963	3.75	7.50	15.00
❏ LSS-14001 [S]	Paradise Found	1960	4.50	9.00	18.00
❏ LSS-14008 [S]	Street Scene	1961	4.50	9.00	18.00
❏ LSS-14011 [S]	Many Splendored Themes	1962	4.50	9.00	18.00
❏ LSS-14019 [S]	Inspired Themes from the Inspired Films	1962	4.50	9.00	18.00
❏ LSS-14021 [S]	Fantastic Strings Play Fantastic Themes	1962	4.50	9.00	18.00
❏ LSS-14024 [S]	Hoedown	1963	4.50	9.00	18.00
❏ LSS-14027 [S]	The Ballad of New Orleans	1963	4.50	9.00	18.00
SUNSET					
❏ SUM-1106 [M]	Love Strings	196?	3.00	6.00	12.00
❏ SUM-1141 [M]	Seasons Greetings	196?	3.00	6.00	12.00
❏ SUM-1170 [M]	Tender Strings	196?	3.00	6.00	12.00
❏ SUS-5106 [S]	Love Strings	196?	3.00	6.00	12.00
❏ SUS-5141 [S]	Seasons Greetings	196?	3.00	6.00	12.00
❏ SUS-5170 [S]	Tender Strings	196?	3.00	6.00	12.00
UNITED ARTISTS					
❏ UAS-6818	Classic Country	1971	2.50	5.00	10.00
SLAVIN, SLICK					
45s					
IMPERIAL					
❏ 5540	Speed Crazy/She Says She's Mine	1958	7.50	15.00	30.00
SLED, BOB, AND THE TOBOGGANS					
45s					
CAMEO					
❏ 400	Here We Go (Surfer Boys Are Going Skiing)/Sea and Ski	1966	12.50	25.00	50.00
SLEDGE, PERCY					
12-Inch Singles					
CAPRICORN					
❏ PRO 672 [DJ]	When She's Touching Me (same on both sides)	1977	3.00	6.00	12.00
45s					
ATLANTIC					
❏ 2326	When a Man Loves a Woman/Love Me Like You Mean It	1966	5.00	10.00	20.00
❏ 2342	Warm and Tender Love/Sugar Puddin'	1966	2.50	5.00	10.00

S

Number	Title (A Side/B Side)	Yr	VG	VG+	NM
❏ 2358	It Tears Me Up/Heart of a Child	1966	2.50	5.00	10.00
❏ 2383	Baby, Help Me/You Got That Something Wonderful	1967	2.50	5.00	10.00
❏ 2396	Out of Left Field/It Can't Be Stopped	1967	2.50	5.00	10.00
❏ 2414	Love Me Tender/What Am I Living For	1967	2.50	5.00	10.00
❏ 2434	Just Out of Reach (Of My Two Empty Arms)/Hard to Believe	1967	2.50	5.00	10.00
❏ 2453	Cover Me/Behind Every Great Man There Is a Woman	1967	2.50	5.00	10.00
❏ 2490	Take Time to Know Her/It's All Wrong But It's Alright	1968	3.00	6.00	12.00
❏ 2539	Sudden Stop/Between These Arms	1968	2.50	5.00	10.00
❏ 2563	You're All Around Me/Self-Preservation	1968	2.50	5.00	10.00
❏ 2594	My Special Prayer/Bless Your Little Sweet Soul	1969	2.00	4.00	8.00
❏ 2616	Any Day Now/The Angels Listened In	1969	2.50	5.00	10.00
❏ 2646	Woman of the Night/Kind Woman	1969	2.00	4.00	8.00
❏ 2679	Faithful and True/True Love Travels on a Gravel Road	1969	2.00	4.00	8.00
❏ 2719	Too Many Rivers to Cross/Push Mr. Pride Aside	1970	2.00	4.00	8.00
❏ 2754	Help Me Make It Through the Night/Thief in the Night	1970	2.00	4.00	8.00
❏ 2826	Stop the World Tonight/That's the Way I Want to Live	1971	—	3.00	6.00
❏ 2848	Rainbow Road/Standing on the Mountain	1971	—	3.00	6.00
❏ 2886	Sunday Brother/Everything You'll Ever Need	1972	—	3.00	6.00
❏ 2963	Sunshine/Unchanging Love	1973	—	3.00	6.00
❏ 89262	When a Man Loves a Woman/Cover Me	1987	—	—	3.00
❏ 89262 [PS]	When a Man Loves a Woman/Cover Me	1987	—	2.00	4.00

CAPRICORN

Number	Title (A Side/B Side)	Yr	VG	VG+	NM
❏ 0209	I'll Be Your Everything/Blue Water	1974	—	2.50	5.00
❏ 0220	If This Is the Last Time/Behind Closed Doors	1975	—	2.50	5.00
❏ 0273	When a Boy Becomes a Man/When She Touches Me	1977	—	2.50	5.00

MONUMENT

Number	Title (A Side/B Side)	Yr	VG	VG+	NM
❏ 03612	You Had to Be There/Hard Lovin' Woman	1983	—	2.00	4.00
❏ 03878	She's Too Pretty to Cry/Home Type Thing	1983	—	2.00	4.00

PHILCO-FORD

Number	Title (A Side/B Side)	Yr	VG	VG+	NM
❏ HP-12	When a Man Loves a Woman/Baby Help Me	1967	6.25	12.50	25.00

—4-inch plastic "Hip Pocket Record" with color sleeve

Albums

ATLANTIC

Number	Title (A Side/B Side)	Yr	VG	VG+	NM
❏ 8125 [M]	When a Man Loves a Woman	1966	12.50	25.00	50.00
❏ SD 8125 [R]	When a Man Loves a Woman	1966	7.50	15.00	30.00
❏ 8132 [M]	Warm and Tender Soul	1966	12.50	25.00	50.00
❏ SD 8132 [R]	Warm and Tender Soul	1966	7.50	15.00	30.00
❏ 8146 [M]	The Percy Sledge Way	1967	12.50	25.00	50.00
❏ SD 8146 [S]	The Percy Sledge Way	1967	12.50	25.00	50.00
❏ SD 8180	Take Time to Know Her	1968	12.50	25.00	50.00
❏ SD 8210	The Best of Percy Sledge	1969	6.25	12.50	25.00

CAPRICORN

Number	Title (A Side/B Side)	Yr	VG	VG+	NM
❏ CP 0147	I'll Be Your Everything	1974	3.75	7.50	15.00

MONUMENT

Number	Title (A Side/B Side)	Yr	VG	VG+	NM
❏ FW 38532	Percy	1983	3.00	6.00	12.00

SLICK, GRACE Also see THE GREAT SOCIETY; JEFFERSON AIRPLANE; JEFFERSON STARSHIP; PAUL KANTNER AND GRACE SLICK.

12-Inch Singles

RCA

Number	Title (A Side/B Side)	Yr	VG	VG+	NM
❏ JD-13708 [DJ]	All the Machines (Long)/All the Machines (Short)	1984	—	3.00	6.00

45s

GRUNT

Number	Title (A Side/B Side)	Yr	VG	VG+	NM
❏ BFBO-0183	Theme from "Manhole"/Come Again, Toucan	1973	—	3.00	6.00

RCA

Number	Title (A Side/B Side)	Yr	VG	VG+	NM
❏ PB-11939	Seasons/Angel of Night	1980	—	2.00	4.00
❏ PB-11939 [PS]	Seasons/Angel of Night	1980	—	2.50	5.00
❏ PB-12041	Dreams/Do It the Hard Way	1980	—	2.00	4.00
❏ PB-12171	Sea of Love/Full Moon Man	1981	—	2.00	4.00
❏ PB-12172	Mistreater/Full Moon Man	1981	—	—	—

—Canceled

Number	Title (A Side/B Side)	Yr	VG	VG+	NM
❏ PB-12186	Round and Round/Full Moon Man	1981	—	—	—

—Canceled

Number	Title (A Side/B Side)	Yr	VG	VG+	NM
❏ PB-13764	Through the Window/Habits	1984	—	2.00	4.00

Albums

GRUNT

Number	Title (A Side/B Side)	Yr	VG	VG+	NM
❏ BFL1-0347	Manhole	1974	3.00	6.00	12.00
❏ AYL1-3736	Manhole	1981	2.00	4.00	8.00

—"Best Buy Series" reissue

RCA VICTOR

Number	Title (A Side/B Side)	Yr	VG	VG+	NM
❏ AFL1-3544	Dreams	1980	2.50	5.00	10.00
❏ AQL1-3851	Welcome to the Wrecking Ball	1981	2.50	5.00	10.00
❏ DJL1-3922 [DJ]	Welcome to the Wrecking Ball Interview	1981	5.00	10.00	20.00
❏ DJL1-3923 [DJ]	RCA Special Radio Series	1981	5.00	10.00	20.00

SLLEDNATS, THE See THE STANDELLS.

SLOAN, P.F. Cohort of STEVE BARRI. Also see THE FANTASTIC BAGGYS; THE GRASS ROOTS; THE IMAGINATIONS (2); THE INNER CIRCLE; THE LIFEGUARDS (2); PHILIP AND STEPHAN; THE RALLY PACKS; THE RINCON SURFSIDE BAND; THE STREET CLEANERS; THEMES INC.; WILLIE AND THE WHEELS.

45s

ALADDIN

Number	Title (A Side/B Side)	Yr	VG	VG+	NM
❏ 3461	All I Want Is Lovin'/Little Girl in the Cabin	1959	6.25	12.50	25.00

—As "Flip Sloan"

ATCO

Number	Title (A Side/B Side)	Yr	VG	VG+	NM
❏ 6663	Star Gazin'/New Design	1969	5.00	10.00	20.00

DUNHILL

Number	Title (A Side/B Side)	Yr	VG	VG+	NM
❏ 4007	Sins of the Family/This Mornin'	1965	3.75	7.50	15.00
❏ 4016	Halloween Mary/I'd Have to Be Out of My Mind	1965	3.75	7.50	15.00
❏ 4016 [PS]	Halloween Mary/I'd Have to Be Out of My Mind	1965	6.25	12.50	25.00

—Sleeve is promo only

Number	Title (A Side/B Side)	Yr	VG	VG+	NM
❏ 4024	From a Distance/Patterns	1966	6.25	12.50	25.00
❏ 4037	City Women/Top of a Fence	1966	3.75	7.50	15.00
❏ 4054	I Found a Girl/A Melody for You	1966	3.75	7.50	15.00
❏ 4064	Sunflower, Sunflower/The Man Behind the Red Balloon	1967	6.25	12.50	25.00
❏ 4064 [PS]	Sunflower, Sunflower/The Man Behind the Red Balloon	1967	7.50	15.00	30.00

Number	Title (A Side/B Side)	Yr	VG	VG+	NM
❏ 4106	Karma (Study of Divination)/I Can't Help But Wonder, Elizabeth	1967	6.25	12.50	25.00

—As "Philip Sloan"

MART

Number	Title (A Side/B Side)	Yr	VG	VG+	NM
❏ 802	She's My Girl/If You Believe in Me	1960	20.00	40.00	80.00

MUMS

Number	Title (A Side/B Side)	Yr	VG	VG+	NM
❏ 6010	Let Me Be/Springtime	1972	5.00	10.00	20.00

Albums

ATCO

Number	Title (A Side/B Side)	Yr	VG	VG+	NM
❏ SD 33-268	Measure of Pleasure	1968	6.25	12.50	25.00

DUNHILL

Number	Title (A Side/B Side)	Yr	VG	VG+	NM
❏ D-50004 [M]	Songs of Our Times	1965	6.25	12.50	25.00
❏ DS-50004 [S]	Songs of Our Times	1965	7.50	15.00	30.00
❏ D-50007 [M]	Twelve More Times	1966	6.25	12.50	25.00
❏ DS-50007 [S]	Twelve More Times	1966	7.50	15.00	30.00

MUMS

Number	Title (A Side/B Side)	Yr	VG	VG+	NM
❏ KZ 31260	Raised on Records	1972	5.00	10.00	20.00

RHINO

Number	Title (A Side/B Side)	Yr	VG	VG+	NM
❏ RNLP-70133	Precious Times: The Best of P.F. Sloan	1986	2.50	5.00	10.00

SLY See SLY STEWART.

SLY AND THE FAMILY STONE Also see GRAHAM CENTRAL STATION; SLY STEWART.

45s

EPIC

Number	Title (A Side/B Side)	Yr	VG	VG+	NM
❏ 10229	Higher/Underdog	1967	2.50	5.00	10.00
❏ 10256	Dance to the Music/Let Me Hear It from You	1967	2.50	5.00	10.00
❏ 10353	Life/M'Lady	1968	2.00	4.00	8.00
❏ 10407	Everyday People/Sing a Simple Song	1968	2.50	5.00	10.00
❏ 10407 [PS]	Everyday People/Sing a Simple Song	1968	3.00	6.00	12.00
❏ 10450	Stand!/I Want to Take You Higher	1969	2.50	5.00	10.00
❏ 10450 [PS]	Stand!/I Want to Take You Higher	1969	3.00	6.00	12.00
❏ 10497	Hot Fun in the Summertime/Fun	1969	2.50	5.00	10.00
❏ 10555	Thank You Falettinme Be Mice Elf Agin/Everybody Is a Star	1969	—	3.00	6.00
❏ 10555 [PS]	Thank You Falettinme Be Mice Elf Agin/Everybody Is a Star	1969	2.50	5.00	10.00
❏ 10805	Family Affair/Luv N' Haight	1971	—	3.00	6.00
❏ 10829	Runnin' Away/Brave & Strong	1972	—	3.00	6.00
❏ 10850	Smilin'/Luv N' Haight	1972	—	3.00	6.00
❏ 11017	If You Want Me to Stay/Babies Makin' Babies	1973	—	3.00	6.00
❏ 11017	If You Want Me to Stay/Thankful N' Thoughtful	1973	—	3.00	6.00
❏ 11060	Frisky/If It Were Left Up to Me	1973	—	3.00	6.00
❏ 11140	Time for Livin'/Small Talk	1974	—	3.00	6.00
❏ 8-50033	Loose Booty/Can't Strain My Brain	1974	—	3.00	6.00
❏ 50119	Hot Fun in the Summertime/Fun	1975	2.00	4.00	8.00
❏ 50135	I Get High on You/That's Lovin' You	1975	—	2.50	5.00
❏ 50175	Li Lo Li/Who Do You Love	1975	—	2.50	5.00
❏ 50201	Greed/Crossword Puzzle	1976	—	2.50	5.00
❏ 50331	Family Again/Nothing Less Than Happiness	1977	—	2.50	5.00

LOADSTONE

Number	Title (A Side/B Side)	Yr	VG	VG+	NM
❏ 3951	I Ain't Got Nobody/I Can't Turn You Loose	1967	5.00	10.00	20.00

WARNER BROS.

Number	Title (A Side/B Side)	Yr	VG	VG+	NM
❏ 29682	High Y'All/Ha Ha He He	1983	—	2.00	4.00
❏ 49062	Sheer Energy/Remember Who You Are	1979	—	2.00	4.00
❏ 49132	Who's to Say/Same Thing	1979	—	2.00	4.00

7-Inch Extended Plays

EPIC

Number	Title (A Side/B Side)	Yr	VG	VG+	NM
❏ 7-30986	You Caught Me Smilin'/Runnin' Away/Space Cowboy/Just Like a Baby/P.O.E.T.	1971	3.75	7.50	15.00

—Jukebox issue; small hole, plays at 33 1/3 rpm

Number	Title (A Side/B Side)	Yr	VG	VG+	NM
❏ 7-30986 [PS]	There's a Riot Goin' On	1971	3.75	7.50	15.00

Albums

EPIC

Number	Title (A Side/B Side)	Yr	VG	VG+	NM
❏ AS 264 [DJ]	Everything You Always Wanted to Hear by Sly and the Family Stone But Were Afraid to Ask For	1976	6.25	12.50	25.00

—Promo-only compilation

Number	Title (A Side/B Side)	Yr	VG	VG+	NM
❏ LN 24324 [M]	A Whole New Thing	1967	5.00	10.00	20.00
❏ LN 24371 [M]	Dance to the Music	1968	10.00	20.00	40.00
❏ BN 26324 [S]	A Whole New Thing	1967	5.00	10.00	20.00
❏ BN 26371 [S]	Dance to the Music	1968	3.75	7.50	15.00
❏ BN 26397	Life	1968	3.75	7.50	15.00
❏ BN 26456	Stand!	1969	3.75	7.50	15.00
❏ PE 26456	Stand!	1986	2.00	4.00	8.00

—Budget-line reissue

Number	Title (A Side/B Side)	Yr	VG	VG+	NM
❏ EQ 30325 [Q]	Sly and the Family Stone's Greatest Hits	1971	25.00	50.00	100.00

—Has alternate mixes of "Hot Fun in the Summertime," "Thank You" and "Everybody Is a Star," which are not rechanneled stereo as they are on other LPs

Number	Title (A Side/B Side)	Yr	VG	VG+	NM
❏ KE 30325	Sly and the Family Stone's Greatest Hits	1970	3.00	6.00	12.00

—Yellow label, gatefold cover

Number	Title (A Side/B Side)	Yr	VG	VG+	NM
❏ PE 30325	Sly and the Family Stone's Greatest Hits	1979	2.00	4.00	8.00

—Budget-line reissue

Number	Title (A Side/B Side)	Yr	VG	VG+	NM
❏ E 30333	Life	1971	3.00	6.00	12.00

—Reissue of 26397

Number	Title (A Side/B Side)	Yr	VG	VG+	NM
❏ E 30334	Dance to the Music	1971	3.00	6.00	12.00

—Reissue of 26371

Number	Title (A Side/B Side)	Yr	VG	VG+	NM
❏ E 30335	A Whole New Thing	1971	3.00	6.00	12.00

—Reissue of 26324

Number	Title (A Side/B Side)	Yr	VG	VG+	NM
❏ KE 30986	There's a Riot Goin' On	1971	3.00	6.00	12.00

—Yellow label, gatefold cover

Number	Title (A Side/B Side)	Yr	VG	VG+	NM
❏ KE 32134	Fresh	1973	2.50	5.00	10.00

—Orange label

Number	Title (A Side/B Side)	Yr	VG	VG+	NM
❏ PE 32930	Small Talk	1974	2.50	5.00	10.00

—Orange label

Number	Title (A Side/B Side)	Yr	VG	VG+	NM
❏ PEQ 32930 [Q]	Small Talk	1974	6.25	12.50	25.00
❏ PE 33835	High on You	1975	2.50	5.00	10.00

—Orange label

Number	Title (A Side/B Side)	Yr	VG	VG+	NM
❏ PEQ 33835 [Q]	High on You	1975	6.25	12.50	25.00
❏ PE 34348	Heard Ya Missed Me, Well I'm Back	1976	2.50	5.00	10.00

—Orange label

Number	Title (A Side/B Side)	Yr	VG	VG+	NM
❏ JE 35974	Ten Years Too Soon	1979	2.50	5.00	10.00
❏ E2 37071 [(2)]	Anthology	1981	3.75	7.50	15.00

WARNER BROS.

Number	Title (A Side/B Side)	Yr	VG	VG+	NM
❏ BSK 3303	Back on the Right Track	1979	2.50	5.00	10.00
❏ 23700	Ain't But the Right Way	1983	2.50	5.00	10.00

Number	Title (A Side/B Side)	Yr	VG	VG+	NM

SMACK, THE
Albums
AUDIO HOUSE

❏ (# unknown)	The Smack	1968	500.00	1000.	2000.

SMALL, MILLIE
45s
ATCO

❏ 6384	Tongue Tied/Blood Shot Eyes	1965	2.50	5.00	10.00

ATLANTIC

❏ 2266	Bring It On Home to Me/ I've Fallen in Love with a Snowman	1965	2.50	5.00	10.00

BRIT

❏ 7002	My Street/Mixed-Up, Lonely, Self-Centered, Spoiled Kind of Boy	1965	3.00	6.00	12.00

SMASH

❏ 1893	My Boy Lollipop/Something's Gotta Be Done	1964	3.75	7.50	15.00
❏ 1920	Sweet William/What Am I Living For	1964	3.00	6.00	12.00
❏ 1940	I Love the Way You Love/Bring It On Home to Me	1964	3.00	6.00	12.00
❏ 1946	Don't You Know/Tom Hark	1964	3.00	6.00	12.00

Albums
SMASH

❏ MGS-27055 [M]	My Boy Lollipop	1964	12.50	25.00	50.00
❏ SRS-67055 [R]	My Boy Lollipop	1964	10.00	20.00	40.00

SMALL FACES Also see FACES.
45s
IMMEDIATE

❏ 501	Itchykoo Park/I'm Only Dreaming	1967	3.00	6.00	12.00
❏ 1902	Here Come the Nice/Talk to You	1967	2.50	5.00	10.00
❏ 5003	Tin Soldier/I Feel Much Better	1968	2.50	5.00	10.00
❏ 5003 [PS]	Tin Soldier/I Feel Much Better	1968	6.25	12.50	25.00
❏ 5007	Lazy Sunday/Rollin' Over	1968	2.50	5.00	10.00
❏ 5009	The Universal/Donkey Rides A Penny A Glass	1968	3.75	7.50	15.00
❏ 5012	Mad John/The Journey	1969	3.75	7.50	15.00
❏ 5014	Afterglow of Your Love/ Wham, Bam, Thank You Ma'am	1969	3.75	7.50	15.00

PRESS

❏ 5007	Almost Grown/Hey Girl	1969	5.00	10.00	20.00
❏ 9794	What 'Cha Gonna Do About It/What's a Matter	1965	6.25	12.50	25.00
❏ 9826	Sha-La-La-La-Lee/Grow Your Own	1966	3.75	7.50	15.00

PRIDE

❏ 1006	Runaway/Shake	1972	3.00	6.00	12.00

RCA VICTOR

❏ 47-8949	Understanding/All or Nothing	1966	5.00	10.00	20.00
❏ 47-8949 [PS]	Understanding/All or Nothing	1966	7.50	15.00	30.00
❏ 47-9055	My Mind's Eye/I Can't Dance with You	1966	5.00	10.00	20.00

Albums
ACCORD

❏ AN-7157	By Appointment	1982	2.50	5.00	10.00

ATLANTIC

❏ SD 19113	Playmates	1977	2.50	5.00	10.00
❏ SD 19171	78 in the Shade	1978	2.50	5.00	10.00

COMPLEAT

❏ 67-2004 [(2)]	Big Music	1985	3.00	6.00	12.00
❏ 67-5003	Ogden's Nut Gone Flake	1985	2.50	5.00	10.00

—Reissue

IMMEDIATE

❏ 4225	Ogden's Nut Gone Flake	1973	3.75	7.50	15.00

—Reissue has a standard square cover

❏ Z12 52002 [S]	There Are But Four Small Faces	1967	12.50	25.00	50.00

—Color cover (counterfeits have either black and white or black and green covers)

❏ Z12 52008 [S]	Ogden's Nut Gone Flake	1968	12.50	25.00	50.00

—Originals have a round cover

MGM

❏ M3F-4955	Archetypes	1974	3.00	6.00	12.00

PRIDE

❏ PRD 0001 [R]	Early Faces	1972	3.75	7.50	15.00
❏ PRD 0014 [P]	The History of the Small Faces	1973	3.00	6.00	12.00

SIRE

❏ SASH-3709 [(2)]	The Vintage Years	1976	3.75	7.50	15.00

SMART TONES, THE
45s
HERALD

❏ 529	Bob-O-Link/Ginny	1958	25.00	50.00	100.00

SMILE (1) Brian May and Roger Taylor, later of QUEEN, were in this group.
45s
MERCURY

❏ 72977	Earth/Step on Me	1968	50.00	100.00	200.00

SMILE (2)
45s
UNI

❏ 55313	A Year Every Night/Southbound	1972	—	3.00	6.00
❏ 55336	Tonight/One Night Stand	1972	—	3.00	6.00

SMITH Also see GAYLE McCORMACK.
45s
ABC DUNHILL

❏ 4206	Baby It's You/I Don't Believe (I Believe)	1969	2.00	4.00	8.00
❏ 4206 [PS]	Baby It's You/I Don't Believe (I Believe)	1969	3.00	6.00	12.00
❏ 4228	Take a Look Around/Mojalesky Ridge	1970	—	3.00	6.00
❏ 4238	What Am I Gonna Do/Born in Boston	1970	—	3.00	6.00
❏ 4238 [PS]	What Am I Gonna Do/Born in Boston	1970	2.50	5.00	10.00
❏ 4246	Comin' Back to Me (Ooh Baby)/Minus-Plus	1970	—	3.00	6.00

Albums
ABC DUNHILL

❏ DS-50056	A Group Called Smith	1969	3.75	7.50	15.00
❏ DS-50081	Minus-Plus	1970	3.75	7.50	15.00

SMITH, ARLENE Also see THE CHANTELS.
45s
BIG TOP

❏ 3073	Love, Love, Love/ He Knows I Love Him Too Much	1961	7.50	15.00	30.00

SPECTORIOUS

❏ 150	Good Girls/Everything	196?	25.00	50.00	100.00

SMITH, BETTY, GROUP
45s
LONDON

❏ 1763	Virginia/Double Shuffle	1958	3.00	6.00	12.00
❏ 1787	Bewitched/Hand Jive	1958	3.00	6.00	12.00
❏ 1819	My Foolsih Heart/Betty's Blues	1958	3.00	6.00	12.00

SMITH, BOB
Albums
KENT

❏ KST-551 [(2)]	The Visit	1970	25.00	50.00	100.00

—Deduct 25 percent if poster is missing

SMITH, BOBBIE, AND THE DREAM GIRLS See THE DREAM GIRLS.

SMITH, CAL
45s
DECCA

❏ 32768	That's What It's Like to Be Lonesome/The Only Girl in the Game	1971	—	3.00	6.00
❏ 32815	Free Streets/Goin' Home to Do My Time	1971	—	3.00	6.00
❏ 32878	Woman on the Inside/To Save, My Wife	1971	—	3.00	6.00
❏ 32959	I've Found Someone of My Own/ Lights of the Living	1972	—	3.00	6.00
❏ 33003	For My Baby/Handful of Stars	1972	—	3.00	6.00
❏ 33040	The Lord Knows I'm Drinking/Sweet Things I Remember About You	1972	—	3.00	6.00

KAPP

❏ 748	I'll Just Go On Home/ Silver Dew on the Blue Grass Tonight	1966	2.50	5.00	10.00
❏ 788	The Only Thing I Want/Stranger in the House	1966	2.00	4.00	8.00
❏ 834	I'll Never Be Lonesome with You/If I Had My Life to Live Over	1967	2.00	4.00	8.00
❏ 851	I'll Sail My Ship Alone/ You're Not Drowning Your Heartache	1967	2.00	4.00	8.00
❏ 884	Destination Atlanta G.A./Did She Ask About Me	1968	2.00	4.00	8.00
❏ 913	Jacksonville/I Love You a Thousand Ways	1968	2.00	4.00	8.00
❏ 938	Drinking Champagne/Honky Tonk Blues	1968	2.00	4.00	8.00
❏ 960	Empty Arms/So Much to Do	1969	2.00	4.00	8.00
❏ 994	It Takes All Night Long/Daddy's Arms	1969	2.00	4.00	8.00
❏ 2037	You Can't Housebreak a Tomcat/ At the Sight of You	1969	—	3.00	6.00
❏ 2059	Heaven Is Just a Touch Away/ I Overlooked an Orchid	1969	—	3.00	6.00
❏ 2076	The Difference Between Going and Really Gone/My Happiness Goes Off	1970	—	3.00	6.00

MCA

❏ 40061	I Can Feel the Leavin' Comin' On/I've Loved You All Over the World	1973	—	2.50	5.00
❏ 40136	Bleep You/An Hour and a Six-Pack	1973	—	2.50	5.00
❏ 40191	Country Bumpkin/It's Not the Miles You Traveled	1974	—	2.50	5.00
❏ 40265	Between Lust and Watching TV/ Some Kind of a Woman	1974	—	2.50	5.00
❏ 40335	It's Time to Pay the Fiddler/ Love Is the Foundation	1974	—	2.50	5.00
❏ 40394	She Talked a Lot About Texas/Baby's Gone	1975	—	2.50	5.00
❏ 40467	Jason's Farm/You Slip Into My Mind	1975	—	2.50	5.00
❏ 40517	Thunderstorms/19 Years and 1800 Miles	1976	—	2.00	4.00
❏ 40563	MacArthur's Hand/Sunday Morning Christian	1976	—	2.00	4.00
❏ 40618	Woman Don't Try to Sing My Song/I Play a Man	1976	—	2.00	4.00
❏ 40671	I Just Came Home to Count the Memories/ Feelin' the Weight of My Chains	1976	—	2.00	4.00
❏ 40714	Come See About Me/The In Crowd	1977	—	2.00	4.00
❏ 40789	Helen/I'm Forty Now	1977	—	2.00	4.00
❏ 40839	Throwin' Memories on the Fire/Tabernacle Tom	1977	—	2.00	4.00
❏ 40864	I'm Just a Farmer/The Ghost of Jim Bob Wilson	1978	—	2.00	4.00
❏ 40911	Bits and Pieces of Life/Leona	1978	—	2.00	4.00
❏ 40982	The Rise and Fall of the Roman Empire/ Oklahoma Sunshine	1978	—	2.00	4.00
❏ 41001	One Little Skinny Rib/I Fed Her Love	1979	—	2.00	4.00
❏ 41128	The Room at the Top of the Stairs/Happy Anniversary	1979	—	2.00	4.00
❏ 60053	Drinking Champagne/It Takes All Night Long	1973	—	2.00	4.00

—Reissue; black label with rainbow

❏ 60171	The Lord Knows I'm Drinking/I've Found Someone of My Own	1974	—	2.00	4.00

—Reissue; black label with rainbow

❏ 60187	Country Bumpkin/Thunderstorms	1977	—	2.00	4.00

—Reissue; black label with rainbow

PLAID

❏ 1003	Eleven Long Years/Tear Stained Pillow	1961	5.00	10.00	20.00

STEP ONE

❏ 353	Bein' Gone/I Know It's Not Over	1986	—	2.00	4.00
❏ 358	King Lear/Country Bumpkin	1986	—	2.00	4.00

SUN RIZE

❏ 130	Take the Time to Love Somebody/Baby Can You Love Me Like She Used To	198?	—	3.00	6.00

Albums
DECCA

❏ DL 75369	I've Found Someone of My Own	1972	3.75	7.50	15.00

KAPP

❏ KL-1504 [M]	All the World Is Lonely Now	1966	6.25	12.50	25.00
❏ KL-1537 [M]	Goin' to Cal's Place	1967	6.25	12.50	25.00
❏ KL-1544 [M]	Travelin' Man	1968	10.00	20.00	40.00

—White label promo only; in stereo cover with "Mono" sticker

❏ KS-3504 [S]	All the World Is Lonely Now	1966	5.00	10.00	20.00
❏ KS-3537 [S]	Goin' to Cal's Place	1967	5.00	10.00	20.00
❏ KS-3544 [S]	Travelin' Man	1968	5.00	10.00	20.00
❏ KS-3585	Drinking Champagne	1968	5.00	10.00	20.00

S

Number	Title (A Side/B Side)	Yr	VG	VG+	NM
❏ KS-3608	Cal Smith Sings It Takes Me All Night Long	1969	5.00	10.00	20.00
❏ KS-3642	The Best of Cal Smith	1969	3.75	7.50	15.00
MCA					
❏ 70	The Best of Cal Smith	1973	2.50	5.00	10.00
—Reissue of Kapp 3642					
❏ 344	Cal Smith	1973	2.50	5.00	10.00
—Reissue of Decca LP					
❏ 424	Country Bumpkin	1974	2.50	5.00	10.00
❏ 467	It's Time to Pay the Fiddler	1975	2.50	5.00	10.00
❏ 485	My Kind of Country	1975	2.50	5.00	10.00
❏ 2172	Jason's Farm	1976	2.50	5.00	10.00
❏ 2266	I Just Came Home to Count the Memories	1977	2.50	5.00	10.00

SMITH, CARL
45s

Number	Title (A Side/B Side)	Yr	VG	VG+	NM
ABC HICKORY					
❏ 54004	A Way with Words/Till I Stop Meeting You	1976	—	2.50	5.00
❏ 54009	Show Me a Brick Wall/It's Teardrop Time	1977	—	2.50	5.00
❏ 54016	This Kinda Love Ain't Meant for Sunday School/There Stands the Glass	1977	—	2.50	5.00
❏ 54022	This Lady Loving Me/Loose Talk	1978	—	2.50	5.00
❏ 54030	Remembered by Someone (Remembered by Me)/It Takes Four Feet to Make a Yard	1978		2.50	5.00
❏ 54037	I Can't Get the Last Memory Down/Silver Tongued Cowboy	1978		2.50	5.00
COLUMBIA					
❏ 4-20712	Guilty Conscience/Washing My Dreams in Tears	1950	7.50	15.00	30.00
❏ 4-20741	I Overlooked an Orchid/I Betcha My Heart I Love You	1950	7.50	15.00	30.00
❏ 4-20765	This Side of Heaven/I Won't Be at Home	1950	7.50	15.00	30.00
❏ 4-20796	Let's Live a Little/There's Nothing As Sweet As My Baby	1951	6.25	12.50	25.00
❏ 4-20825	Mr. Moon/If Teardrops Were Pennies	1951	6.25	12.50	25.00
❏ 4-20862	Let Old Mother Nature Have Her Way/Me and My Broken Heart	1951	6.25	12.50	25.00
❏ 4-20893	(When You Feel Like You're in Love) Don't Just Stand There/The Little Girl in My Home Town	1952	6.25	12.50	25.00
❏ 4-20922	Are You Teasing Me?/It's a Lovely, Lovely World	1952	6.25	12.50	25.00
❏ 4-20942	It's a Lovely, Lovely World/(When You Feel Like You're in Love) Don't Just Stand There	1952	6.25	12.50	25.00
❏ 4-21008	Our Honeymoon/Sing Her a Love Song	1952	6.25	12.50	25.00
❏ 4-21040	The Blood That Stained the Old Rugged Cross/Gethsemane	1951	7.50	15.00	30.00
—With the Carters					
❏ 4-21051	That's the Kind of Love I'm Looking For/My Lonely Heart's Runnin' Wild	1952	5.00	10.00	20.00
❏ 4-21087	Orchids Mean Goodbye/Just Wait 'Til I Get You Alone	1953	5.00	10.00	20.00
❏ 4-21110	Nail Scarred Hand/We Shall Meet Someday	1953	6.25	12.50	25.00
❏ 4-21119	Trademark/Do I Like It?	1953	5.00	10.00	20.00
❏ 4-21129	Hey Joe!/Darling Am I the One	1953	5.00	10.00	20.00
❏ 4-21166	Satisfaction Guaranteed/Who'll Buy My Heartaches	1953	5.00	10.00	20.00
❏ 4-21192	How About You/I'll Be Listening	1953	5.00	10.00	20.00
❏ 4-21197	Dog-Gone It, Baby, I'm in Love/What Am I Going to Do	1954	5.00	10.00	20.00
❏ 4-21226	Back Up Buddy/If You Tried As Hard to Love Me	1954	5.00	10.00	20.00
❏ 4-21266	Go, Boy, Go/If You Saw Her Through My Eyes	1954	5.00	10.00	20.00
❏ 4-21317	Loose Talk/More Than Anything Else in the World	1954	5.00	10.00	20.00
❏ 4-21340	Kisses Don't Lie/No, I Don't Believe I Will	1955	5.00	10.00	20.00
❏ 4-21368	Wait a Little Longer Please, Jesus/Works of the Lord	1955	6.25	12.50	25.00
❏ 4-21382	There She Goes/Old Lonesome Times	1955	5.00	10.00	20.00
❏ 4-21411	Baby I'm Ready/I Just Don't Care Anymore	1955	5.00	10.00	20.00
❏ 4-21429	Don't Tease Me/I Just Dropped In to Say Goodbye	1955	5.00	10.00	20.00
❏ 4-21462	You're Free to Go/I Feel Like Cryin'	1955	5.00	10.00	20.00
❏ 4-21493	I've Changed/If You Do Dear	1956	5.00	10.00	20.00
❏ 4-21507	Answers/My Dream of the Old Rugged Cross	1956	6.25	12.50	25.00
❏ 4-21552	You Are the One/Doorstep to Heaven	1956	5.00	10.00	20.00
❏ 4-21552	Before I Met You/Wicked Lies	1956	5.00	10.00	20.00
❏ 30848 [S]	(titles unknown)	1960	3.75	7.50	15.00
❏ 30849 [S]	(titles unknown)	1960	3.75	7.50	15.00
❏ 30850 [S]	(titles unknown)	1960	3.75	7.50	15.00
❏ 30851 [S]	(titles unknown)	1960	3.75	7.50	15.00
❏ 31473 [S]	(titles unknown)	1962	3.75	7.50	15.00
❏ 31474 [S]	(titles unknown)	1962	3.75	7.50	15.00
❏ 31475 [S]	(titles unknown)	1962	3.75	7.50	15.00
❏ 31476 [S]	(titles unknown)	1962	3.75	7.50	15.00
❏ 31477 [S]	(titles unknown)	1962	3.75	7.50	15.00
—The above 10 are "Stereo Seven" 7-inch 33 1/3 rpm singles with small holes					
❏ 4-40823	You Can't Hurt Me Anymore/That's the Way I Like You the Best	1957	3.75	7.50	15.00
❏ 4-40918	Mr. Lost/Try to Take It Like a Man	1957	3.75	7.50	15.00
❏ 4-40970	No Trespassing/Happy Street	1957	—	—	—
—Canceled					
❏ 4-40984	Why, Why/Emotions	1957	3.75	7.50	15.00
❏ 4-41092	Your Name Is Beautiful/You're So Easy to Love	1958	3.75	7.50	15.00
❏ 4-41170	Guess I've Been Around Too Long/Goodnight Mr. Sun	1958	3.75	7.50	15.00
❏ 4-41243	Walking the Slow Walk/A Love Was Born	1958	3.75	7.50	15.00
❏ 4-41290	The Best Years of Your Life/Mr. Moon	1958	3.75	7.50	15.00
❏ 4-41344	It's All My Heartache/I'll Kiss the Past Goodbye	1959	3.00	6.00	12.00
❏ 4-41417	Ten Thousand Drums/The Tall, Tall Gentleman	1959	3.00	6.00	12.00
❏ 4-41417 [PS]	Ten Thousand Drums/The Tall, Tall Gentleman	1959	6.25	12.50	25.00
❏ 4-41489	Tomorrow Night/I'll Walk with You	1959	3.00	6.00	12.00
❏ 4-41557	Make the Waterwheel Roll/Past	1960	3.00	6.00	12.00
❏ 4-41610	A Pain a Pill Can't Locate/If I Had You (I'd Live for You Only)	1962	3.00	6.00	12.00
❏ 4-41642	Cut Across Shorty/Why Did You Come My Way	1960	3.00	6.00	12.00
❏ 4-41729	If the World Don't End Tomorrow/Lonely Old Room	1960	3.00	6.00	12.00
❏ 4-41819	You Make Me Live Again/I Don't Know How	1960	3.00	6.00	12.00
❏ 4-41948	Are You True to Me/More Habit Than Desire	1961	3.00	6.00	12.00

Number	Title (A Side/B Side)	Yr	VG	VG+	NM
❏ 4-42042	Kisses Never Lie/Why Can't You Be Satisfied with Me	1961	3.00	6.00	12.00
❏ 4-42222	Air Mail to Heaven/Things That Mean the Most	1961	3.00	6.00	12.00
❏ 4-42349	The Best Dressed Beggar (In Town)/I Used to Be	1962	3.00	6.00	12.00
❏ 4-42490	Gettin' Even/I Volunteer	1962	3.00	6.00	12.00
❏ 4-42610	A Pain a Pill Can't Locate/If I Had You (I'd Live for You Only)	1962	3.00	6.00	12.00
❏ 4-42686	Live for Tomorrow/Let's Talk This Thing Over	1963	3.00	6.00	12.00
❏ 4-42768	In the Back Room Tonight/Take My Love with You, Too	1963	3.00	6.00	12.00
❏ 4-42858	Triangle/I Almost Forgot Her Today	1963	3.00	6.00	12.00
❏ 4-42949	The Pillow That Whispers/Sweet Little Country Girl	1964	3.00	6.00	12.00
❏ 4-43033	Take My Ring Off Your Finger/The Ballad of Hershel Lawson	1964	3.00	6.00	12.00
❏ 4-43124	Lonely Girl/When It's Over	1964	3.00	6.00	12.00
❏ 4-43200	She Called Me Baby/My Friends Are Gonna Be Strangers	1965	2.50	5.00	10.00
❏ 4-43266	Be Good to Her/Keep Me Fooled	1965	2.50	5.00	10.00
❏ 4-43361	Let's Walk Away Strangers/Ain't Love a Hurting Thing	1965	2.50	5.00	10.00
❏ 4-43485	Why Do I Keep Doing This to Us/Why Can't You Feel Sorry for Me	1966	2.50	5.00	10.00
❏ 4-43599	Sweet Temptation/(Is My) Ring on Your Finger	1966	2.50	5.00	10.00
❏ 4-43753	Man with a Plan/You Mean Ol' Moon	1966	2.50	5.00	10.00
❏ 4-43866	You Better Be Better to Me/It's Only a Matter of Time	1966	2.50	5.00	10.00
❏ 4-44034	I Should Get Away for Awhile (From You)/Mighty Day	1967	2.00	4.00	8.00
❏ 4-44233	Deep Water/I Really Don't Want to Know	1967	2.00	4.00	8.00
❏ 4-44396	Foggy River/When Will the Rainbow Follow the Rain	1967	2.00	4.00	8.00
❏ 4-44486	You Ought to Hear Me Cry/I Used Up My Last Chance Last Night	1968	2.00	4.00	8.00
❏ 4-44620	There's No More Love/Remember Me (I'm the One Who Loves You)	1968	2.00	4.00	8.00
❏ 4-44702	Faded Love and Winter Roses/Until I Looked at You	1968	2.00	4.00	8.00
❏ 4-44816	Good Deal, Lucille/Never Gonna Cry No More	1969	2.00	4.00	8.00
❏ 4-44939	I Love You Because/Mister, Come and Get Your Wife	1969	2.00	4.00	8.00
❏ 4-45031	Heartbreak Avenue/It's Nice to See You Once Again	1969	2.00	4.00	8.00
❏ 4-45086	Pull My String and Wind Me Up/It's All Right	1970	2.00	4.00	8.00
❏ 4-45177	Pick Me Up on Your Way Down/Bonaparte's Retreat	1970	2.00	4.00	8.00
❏ 4-45225	How I Love Them Old Songs/Little Crop of Cotton Tops	1970	2.00	4.00	8.00
❏ 4-45262	Big Murph/My Mother's Eyes	1970	2.00	4.00	8.00
❏ 4-45293	Don't Worry 'Bout the Mule (Just Load the Wagon)/Darling Days	1970	2.00	4.00	8.00
❏ 4-45382	Lost It on the Road/I'm Wound Up Tight	1971	2.00	4.00	8.00
❏ 4-45436	Red Door/You Walked in My Sleep Last Night	1971	2.00	4.00	8.00
❏ 4-45497	Don't Say You're Mine/Country Soul Man	1971	2.00	4.00	8.00
❏ 4-45558	Mama Bear/Before My Time	1972	2.00	4.00	8.00
❏ 4-45648	If This Is Goodbye/If You Saw Her	1972	2.00	4.00	8.00
❏ 4-45832	What a Difference Your Love Would Make/When You're Gone (There Will Be Nothing Left)	1973	2.00	4.00	8.00
❏ 4-45923	I Need Help/Yesterday Is Gone	1973	2.00	4.00	8.00
HICKORY/MGM					
❏ 329	Dreaming Again/I Ain't Getting Nowhere with You	1974	—	3.00	6.00
❏ 337	The Way I Lose My Mind/Happy Birthday My Darlin'	1975	—	2.50	5.00
❏ 347	Everything I Touch Turns to Sugar/Lost Highway	1975	—	2.50	5.00
❏ 352	The Girl I Love/Me and My Broken Heart	1975	—	2.50	5.00
❏ 357	Roly Poly/Remembered by Someone (Remembered by Me)	1975	—	2.50	5.00
❏ 363	She Is/I Can't Go On Like This	1976	—	2.50	5.00
❏ 371	If You Don't, Somebody Else Will/It's Gonna Be One of Those Days	1976	—	2.50	5.00

7-Inch Extended Plays

Number	Title (A Side/B Side)	Yr	VG	VG+	NM
COLUMBIA					
❏ B-2131	*You Are the One/You Can't Hurt Me Anymore/That's the Way I Like You Best/Before I Met You	1957	6.25	12.50	25.00
❏ B-2131 [PS]	Four Hits by Carl Smith	1957	6.25	12.50	25.00
❏ B-2801	*Let Old Mother Nature Have Her Way/Me and My Broken Heart/If Teardrops Were Pennies/I Overlooked an Orchid	1959	5.00	10.00	20.00
❏ B-2801 [PS]	Carl Smith (Hall of Fame Series)	1959	5.00	10.00	20.00
❏ B-10221	San Antonio Rose/Time Changes Everything//Lovin' Is Livin'/Oh, No!	1957	5.00	10.00	20.00
❏ B-10221 [PS]	Smith's the Name, Vol. I	1957	5.00	10.00	20.00
❏ B-10222	If I Could Hold Back the Dawn/That's What You Think//Live and Let Live/If You Want It, I've Got It	1957	5.00	10.00	20.00
❏ B-10222 [PS]	Smith's the Name, Vol. II	1957	5.00	10.00	20.00
❏ B-10223	Please Come Back Home/Look What Thoughts Done to Me/The House That Love Built/Come Back to Me	1957	5.00	10.00	20.00
❏ B-10223 [PS]	Smith's the Name, Vol. III	1957	5.00	10.00	20.00

Albums

Number	Title (A Side/B Side)	Yr	VG	VG+	NM
ABC HICKORY					
❏ HB-44005	This Lady Loves Me	1977	3.00	6.00	12.00
❏ HB-44015	The Silver-Tongued Cowboy	1978	3.00	6.00	12.00
COLUMBIA					
❏ GP 31 [(2)]	The Carl Smith Anniversary Album/20 Years of Hits	1970	6.25	12.50	25.00
❏ CL 959 [M]	Sunday Down South	1957	12.50	25.00	50.00
❏ CL 1022 [M]	Smith's the Name	1957	12.50	25.00	50.00
❏ CL 1172 [M]	Let's Live a Little	1958	12.50	25.00	50.00
❏ CL 1532 [M]	The Carl Smith Touch	1960	6.25	12.50	25.00
❏ CL 1740 [M]	Easy to Please	1961	6.25	12.50	25.00
❏ CL 1937 [M]	Carl Smith's Greatest Hits	1962	5.00	10.00	20.00
❏ CL 2091 [M]	The Tall, Tall Gentleman	1963	5.00	10.00	20.00
❏ CL 2173 [M]	There Stands the Glass	1964	5.00	10.00	20.00

Number	Title (A Side/B Side)	Yr	VG	VG+	NM
❏ CL 2293 [M]	I Want to Live and Love	1965	5.00	10.00	20.00
❏ CL 2358 [M]	Kisses Don't Lie	1965	5.00	10.00	20.00
❏ CL 2501 [M]	Man with a Plan	1966	5.00	10.00	20.00
❏ CL 2579 [10]	Carl Smith	1955	25.00	50.00	100.00
❏ CL 2610 [M]	The Country Gentleman	1967	5.00	10.00	20.00
❏ CL 2687 [M]	The Country Gentleman Sings His Favorites	1967	6.25	12.50	25.00
❏ CL 2822 [M]	Deep Water	1968	7.50	15.00	30.00
❏ CL 2888 [M]	Country on My Mind	1968	12.50	25.00	50.00
❏ CS 8352 [S]	The Carl Smith Touch	1960	7.50	15.00	30.00
❏ CS 8540 [S]	Easy to Please	1961	7.50	15.00	30.00
❏ CS 8737 [S]	Carl Smith's Greatest Hits	1962	6.25	12.50	25.00
❏ CS 8891 [S]	The Tall, Tall Gentleman	1963	6.25	12.50	25.00
❏ CS 8973 [S]	There Stands the Glass	1964	6.25	12.50	25.00
❏ CL 9023 [10]	Sentimental Songs	195?	25.00	50.00	100.00
❏ CL 9026 [10]	Softly and Tenderly	195?	20.00	40.00	80.00
❏ CS 9093 [S]	I Want to Live and Love	1965	6.25	12.50	25.00
❏ CS 9158 [S]	Kisses Don't Lie	1965	6.25	12.50	25.00
❏ CS 9301 [S]	Man with a Plan	1966	6.25	12.50	25.00
❏ CS 9410 [S]	The Country Gentleman	1967	6.25	12.50	25.00
❏ CS 9487 [S]	The Country Gentleman Sings His Favorites	1967	5.00	10.00	20.00
❏ CS 9622 [S]	Deep Water	1968	5.00	10.00	20.00
❏ CS 9688 [S]	Country on My Mind	1968	5.00	10.00	20.00
❏ CS 9786	Faded Love and Winter Roses	1969	5.00	10.00	20.00
❏ CS 9807	Carl Smith's Greatest Hits, Vol. 2	1969	5.00	10.00	20.00
❏ CS 9870	Carl Smith Sings a Tribute to Roy Acuff	1969	5.00	10.00	20.00
❏ CS 9898	I Love You Because	1970	5.00	10.00	20.00
❏ C 30215	Carl Smith with the Tunesmiths	1970	5.00	10.00	20.00
❏ C 30548	Bluegrass	1971	5.00	10.00	20.00
❏ C 31277	Don't Say You're Mine	1972	5.00	10.00	20.00
❏ KC 31606	If This Is Goodbye	1972	5.00	10.00	20.00
❏ FC 38906	Carl Smith	198?	2.50	5.00	10.00

HICKORY/MGM

Number	Title (A Side/B Side)	Yr	VG	VG+	NM
❏ H3G 4518	The Way I Lose My Mind	1975	3.00	6.00	12.00
❏ H3G 4522	The Girl I Love	1975	3.00	6.00	12.00

ROUNDER

Number	Title (A Side/B Side)	Yr	VG	VG+	NM
❏ SS-25	Old Lonesome Times	1988	2.50	5.00	10.00

SMITH, CARL; LEFTY FRIZZELL; MARTY ROBBINS
Albums

COLUMBIA

Number	Title (A Side/B Side)	Yr	VG	VG+	NM
❏ CL 2544 [10]	Carl, Lefty and Marty	1955	100.00	200.00	400.00

SMITH, CONNIE
45s

COLUMBIA

Number	Title (A Side/B Side)	Yr	VG	VG+	NM
❏ 10051	I've Got My Baby on My Mind/ Why Don't You Love Me	1974	—	2.00	4.00
❏ 10086	I Got a Lot of Hurtin' Done Today/ Back in the Country	1975	—	2.00	4.00
❏ 10135	Why Don't You Love Me/Loving You (Has Changed My Whole Life)	1975	—	2.00	4.00
❏ 10210	The Song We Fell in Love To/One Little Reason	1975	—	2.00	4.00
❏ 10277	('Til) I Kissed You/Ridin' on a Rainbow	1975	—	2.00	4.00
❏ 10345	So Sad (To Watch Good Love Go Bad)/ Constantly	1976	—	2.00	4.00
❏ 10393	I Don't Wanna Talk It Over Anymore/You Crossed My Mind a Thousand Times	1976	—	2.00	4.00
❏ 10501	The Latest Shade of Blue/ I'm All Wrapped Up in You	1977	—	2.00	4.00
❏ 45816	You've Got Me (Right Where You Want Me)/ A Picture of Me	1973	—	2.50	5.00
❏ 45954	Ain't Love a Good Thing/I Still Feel the Same About You	1973	—	2.50	5.00
❏ 46008	Dallas/That's the Way Love Goes	1974	—	2.50	5.00
❏ 46058	I Never Knew (What That Song Meant Before)/ Did We Have to Come This Far	1974	—	2.50	5.00

EPIC

Number	Title (A Side/B Side)	Yr	VG	VG+	NM
❏ 05414	A Far Cry from You/Don't Touch (The Pain's Not Dry)	1986	—	—	3.00
❏ 06250	Hold Me Back/Walk Me to the Door	1986	—	—	3.00

MONUMENT

Number	Title (A Side/B Side)	Yr	VG	VG+	NM
❏ 45-219	Coming Around/You and Love and I	1977	—	2.00	4.00
❏ 45-231	I Just Want to Be Your Everything/Scrapbook	1977	—	2.00	4.00
❏ 45-241	Lovin' You Baby/All of a Sudden	1978	—	2.00	4.00
❏ 45-252	There'll Never Be Another for Me/ The Wayward Wind	1978	—	2.00	4.00
❏ 45-266	Smooth Sailin'/ Loving You Has Sure Been Good to Me	1978	—	2.00	4.00
❏ 45-281	Lovin' You, Lovin' Me/Ten Thousand and One	1979	—	2.00	4.00
❏ 45-284	Don't Say Love/I Don't Want to Be Free	1979	—	2.00	4.00
❏ 03857	Rough at the Edges/Don't Make Me Dream	1983	—	2.00	4.00

RCA VICTOR

Number	Title (A Side/B Side)	Yr	VG	VG+	NM
❏ 47-8416	Once a Day/The Threshold	1964	2.50	5.00	10.00
❏ 47-8489	Then and Only Then/Tiny Blue Transistor Radio	1964	2.00	4.00	8.00
❏ 47-8551	I Can't Remember/Senses	1965	2.00	4.00	8.00
❏ 47-8663	If I Talk to Him/I Don't Have Anyplace to Go	1965	2.00	4.00	8.00
❏ 47-8746	Nobody But a Fool (Would Love Him)/I'll Never Get Over Loving You	1965	2.00	4.00	8.00
❏ 47-8842	Ain't Had No Lovin'/Five Fingers to Spare	1966	2.00	4.00	8.00
❏ 47-8964	The Hurtin's All Over/Invisible Tears	1966	2.00	4.00	8.00
❏ 47-9108	I'll Come Runnin'/It's Now or Never	1967	2.00	4.00	8.00
❏ 47-9214	Cincinnati, Ohio/Don't Feel Sorry for Me	1967	2.00	4.00	8.00
❏ 47-9335	Burning a Hole in My Mind/Only for Me	1967	2.00	4.00	8.00
❏ 47-9413	Baby's Back Again/It Only Hurts for a Little While	1967	2.00	4.00	8.00
❏ 47-9513	Run Away Little Tears/ Let Me Help You Work It Out	1968	2.00	4.00	8.00
❏ 47-9624	Cry, Cry, Cry/The Hurt Goes On	1968	2.00	4.00	8.00
❏ 47-9832	I Never Once Stopped Loving You/The Sun Shines Down on Me	1970	—	3.00	6.00
❏ 47-9887	Louisiana Man/Alone with You	1970	—	3.00	6.00
❏ 47-9938	Where Is My Castle/Clinging to a Saving Hand	1970	—	3.00	6.00
❏ 47-9981	Just One Time/I Don't Walk Away	1971	—	3.00	6.00
❏ 74-0101	Ribbon of Darkness/A Lonely Woman	1969	2.00	4.00	8.00
❏ 74-0258	You and Your Sweet Love/ I Can't Get Used to Being Lonely	1969	2.00	4.00	8.00
❏ 74-0535	I'm Sorry If My Love Got In Your Way/ Plenty of Time	1971	—	3.00	6.00

Number	Title (A Side/B Side)	Yr	VG	VG+	NM
❏ 74-0655	Just for What I Am/ I'd Still Want to Serve Him Today	1972	—	3.00	6.00
❏ 74-0752	If It Ain't Love (Let's Leave It Alone)/ Living Without You	1972	—	3.00	6.00
❏ 74-0860	Love Is the Look You're Looking For/My Ecstasy	1972	—	3.00	6.00
❏ 74-0971	Dream Painter/Once a Day	1973	—	3.00	6.00
❏ APBO-0156	Everybody Loves Somebody/ I Don't Want Your Memories	1973	—	2.50	5.00
❏ PB-10051	Someone to Give My Love To/ I'm Sorry If My Love Got In Your Way	1974	—	2.50	5.00

Albums

COLUMBIA

Number	Title (A Side/B Side)	Yr	VG	VG+	NM
❏ KC 32185	A Lady Named Smith	1973	3.00	6.00	12.00
❏ KC 32492	God Is Abundant	1973	3.00	6.00	12.00
❏ KC 32581	That's the Way Love Goes	1974	3.00	6.00	12.00
❏ KC 33055	I Never Knew (What That Song Meant Before)	1974	3.00	6.00	12.00
❏ KC 33375	I Got a Lot of Hurtin' Done Today/I've Got My Baby on My Mind	1975	3.00	6.00	12.00
❏ KC 33414	Connie Smith Sings Hank Williams Gospel	1975	3.00	6.00	12.00
❏ KC 33918	The Song We Fell in Love To	1976	3.00	6.00	12.00
❏ KC 34270	I Don't Want to Talk It Over Anymore	1976	3.00	6.00	12.00
❏ KC 34877	The Best of Connie Smith	1977	3.00	6.00	12.00

MONUMENT

Number	Title (A Side/B Side)	Yr	VG	VG+	NM
❏ 7609	Pure Connie Smith	1977	3.00	6.00	12.00
❏ 7624	New Horizons	1978	3.00	6.00	12.00

RCA CAMDEN

Number	Title (A Side/B Side)	Yr	VG	VG+	NM
❏ ACL1-0250	Even the Bad Times Are Good	1973	2.50	5.00	10.00
—With Nat Stuckey					
❏ CAL-2120 [M]	Connie in the Country	1967	3.75	7.50	15.00
❏ CAS-2120 [S]	Connie in the Country	1967	3.00	6.00	12.00
❏ CAS-2495	My Heart Has a Mind of Its Own	1971	2.50	5.00	10.00
❏ CAS-2550	City Lights — Country Favorites	1972	2.50	5.00	10.00

RCA VICTOR

Number	Title (A Side/B Side)	Yr	VG	VG+	NM
❏ APL1-0188	Dream Painter	1973	3.00	6.00	12.00
❏ APL1-0275	Connie Smith's Greatest Hits, Volume 1	1973	3.00	6.00	12.00
❏ APL1-0607	Now	1974	3.00	6.00	12.00
❏ LPM-3341 [M]	Connie Smith	1965	5.00	10.00	20.00
❏ LSP-3341 [S]	Connie Smith	1965	6.25	12.50	25.00
❏ LPM-3444 [M]	Cute 'n' Country	1965	5.00	10.00	20.00
❏ LSP-3444 [S]	Cute 'n' Country	1965	6.25	12.50	25.00
❏ LPM-3520 [M]	Miss Smith Goes to Nashville	1966	5.00	10.00	20.00
❏ LSP-3520 [S]	Miss Smith Goes to Nashville	1966	6.25	12.50	25.00
❏ LPM-3589 [M]	Connie Smith Sings Great Sacred Songs	1966	5.00	10.00	20.00
❏ LSP-3589 [S]	Connie Smith Sings Great Sacred Songs	1966	6.25	12.50	25.00
❏ LPM-3628 [M]	Born to Sing	1966	5.00	10.00	20.00
❏ LSP-3628 [S]	Born to Sing	1966	6.25	12.50	25.00
❏ LPM-3725 [M]	Downtown Country	1967	6.25	12.50	25.00
❏ LSP-3725 [S]	Downtown Country	1967	5.00	10.00	20.00
❏ LPM-3768 [M]	Connie Smith Sings Bill Anderson	1967	6.25	12.50	25.00
❏ LSP-3768 [S]	Connie Smith Sings Bill Anderson	1967	5.00	10.00	20.00
❏ LPM-3848 [M]	The Best of Connie Smith	1967	6.25	12.50	25.00
❏ LSP-3848 [S]	The Best of Connie Smith	1967	5.00	10.00	20.00
❏ LPM-3889 [M]	Soul of Country Music	1968	12.50	25.00	50.00
❏ LSP-3889 [S]	Soul of Country Music	1968	5.00	10.00	20.00
❏ LPM-4002 [M]	I Love Charley Brown	1968	20.00	40.00	80.00
❏ LSP-4002 [S]	I Love Charley Brown	1968	5.00	10.00	20.00
❏ LSP-4077	Sunshine and Rain	1968	5.00	10.00	20.00
❏ LSP-4132	Connie's Country	1969	5.00	10.00	20.00
❏ LSP-4229	Back in Baby's Arms	1969	5.00	10.00	20.00
❏ LSP-4324	The Best of Connie Smith Volume II	1970	5.00	10.00	20.00
❏ LSP-4394	I Never Once Stopped Loving You	1970	5.00	10.00	20.00
❏ LSP-4474	Where's My Castle	1971	3.75	7.50	15.00
❏ LSP-4537	Just One Time	1971	3.75	7.50	15.00
❏ LSP-4598	Come Along and Walk with Me	1971	5.00	10.00	20.00
❏ LSP-4694	Ain't We Having a Good Time	1972	3.75	7.50	15.00
❏ LSP-4748	"If It Ain't Love" And Other Great Dallas Frazier Songs	1972	3.75	7.50	15.00
❏ LSP-4840	Love Is the Look You're Looking For	1973	3.75	7.50	15.00

SMITH, CONNIE, AND NAT STUCKEY
45s

RCA VICTOR

Number	Title (A Side/B Side)	Yr	VG	VG+	NM
❏ 47-9805	If God Is Dead (Who's That Living in My Soul)/ His Love Takes Care of Me	1970	2.00	4.00	8.00
❏ 74-0181	Young Love/Something Pretty	1969	2.00	4.00	8.00

Albums

RCA VICTOR

Number	Title (A Side/B Side)	Yr	VG	VG+	NM
❏ LSP-4190	Young Love	1969	5.00	10.00	20.00
❏ LSP-4300	Sunday Morning	1970	3.75	7.50	15.00

SMITH, HUEY "PIANO"
45s

ACE

Number	Title (A Side/B Side)	Yr	VG	VG+	NM
❏ 521	Everybody's Wailin'/Little Liza Jane	1956	6.25	12.50	25.00
❏ 530	Rockin' Pneumonia and the Boogie Woogie Flu (Part 1/Part 2)	1957	7.50	15.00	30.00
❏ 538	Free, Single and Disengaged/ Just a Lonely Clown	1957	6.25	12.50	25.00
❏ 545	Don't You Just Know It/High Blood Pressure	1958	6.25	12.50	25.00
❏ 548	Havin' a Good Time/We Like Birdland	1958	6.25	12.50	25.00
❏ 553	Don't You Know Yockomo/ Well, I'll Be John Brown	1958	6.25	12.50	25.00
❏ 562	Would You Believe It (I Have a Cold)/Genevieve	1959	5.00	10.00	20.00
❏ 571	Tu-Ber-Cu-Lucas and the Sinus Blues/ Dearest Darling	1959	5.00	10.00	20.00
❏ 584	Beatnik Blues/For Cryin' Out Loud	1960	3.75	7.50	15.00
❏ 638	She Got Low Down/Mean, Mean, Mean	1961	3.75	7.50	15.00
❏ 639	She Got Low Down/Mean, Mean, Mean//Little Liza Jane/Rockin' Pnuemonia	1961	6.25	12.50	25.00
❏ 649	Pop-Eye/Scald Dog	1962	3.75	7.50	15.00
❏ 672	Every Once in a While/Somebody Told It	1962	3.00	6.00	12.00
❏ 8002	Talk to Me Baby/If It Ain't One Thing, It's Another	1962	3.00	6.00	12.00
❏ 8008	Let's Bring 'Em Back Again/Quiet as It's Kept	1963	3.75	7.50	15.00

CONSTELLATION

Number	Title (A Side/B Side)	Yr	VG	VG+	NM
❏ 102	He's Back Again/Quiet As It's Kept	1963	2.50	5.00	10.00

S

Number	Title (A Side/B Side)	Yr	VG	VG+	NM

COTILLION

| ❏ 44142 | Rockin' Pneumonia and the Boogie Woogie Flu (Part 1/Part 2) | 1971 | — | 3.00 | 6.00 |

IMPERIAL

❏ 5721	The Little Moron/Someone to Love	1961	3.00	6.00	12.00
❏ 5747	Behind the Wheel — Part 1/Behind the Wheel — Part 2	1961	3.00	6.00	12.00
❏ 5772	More Girls/Sassy Sara	1961	3.00	6.00	12.00
❏ 5789	Don't Knock It/Shag-a-Tooth	1961	3.00	6.00	12.00

INSTANT

❏ 3287	I'll Never Forget/Bury Me Dead	1967	2.00	4.00	8.00
❏ 3297	Two Way Pockaway (Part 1)/Two Way Pockaway (Part 2)	1969	2.00	4.00	8.00
❏ 3301	Epitaph of Uncle Tom/Eight Bars of Amen	1969	2.00	4.00	8.00
❏ 3303	You Got Too (Part 1)/You Got Too (Part 2)	1969	2.00	4.00	8.00
❏ 3305	Ballad of a Black Man/The Whatcha Call 'Em	1970	2.00	4.00	8.00

SAVOY

| ❏ 1113 | You Made Me Cry/You're Down with Me | 1953 | 25.00 | 50.00 | 100.00 |

VIN

| ❏ 1024 | I Didn't Do It/They Kept On | 1960 | 3.75 | 7.50 | 15.00 |

Albums

ACE

❏ LP-1004 [M]	Having a Good Time	1959	100.00	200.00	400.00
❏ LP-1015 [M]	For Dancing	1961	62.50	125.00	250.00
❏ LP-1027 [M]	'Twas the Night Before Christmas	1962	62.50	125.00	250.00
❏ LP-1027 [M]	'Twas the Night Before Christmas	198?	3.75	7.50	15.00
—Reissue with "Dr. John Band" credited on front cover and label					
❏ LP-2021	Rock 'N' Roll Revival	197?	7.50	15.00	30.00
❏ 2038	Good Old Rock & Roll	198?	3.75	7.50	15.00

GRAND PRIX

| ❏ K-418 [M] | Huey "Piano" Smith | 196? | 5.00 | 10.00 | 20.00 |
| ❏ KS-418 [R] | Huey "Piano" Smith | 196? | 3.00 | 6.00 | 12.00 |

RHINO

| ❏ RNLP-70222 | Serious Clownin': The History of Huey "Piano" Smith and the Clowns | 1986 | 3.00 | 6.00 | 12.00 |

SMITH, HURRICANE

45s

CAPITOL

❏ 3148	Don't Let It Die/The Writer Sings His Song	1971	—	2.50	5.00
❏ 3383	Oh Babe, What Would You Say?/Getting to Know You	1972	—	2.00	4.00
—Orange label with "Capitol" at bottom					
❏ 3383	Oh Babe, What Would You Say?/Getting to Know You	1972	—	3.00	6.00
—Red and orange "target" label					
❏ 3455	Who Was It?/Take Suki Home	1972	—	2.00	4.00

EMI

| ❏ 3809 | Beautiful Day-Beautiful Night/Sam | 1973 | — | 2.00 | 4.00 |

Albums

CAPITOL

| ❏ ST-11139 | Hurricane Smith | 1972 | 2.50 | 5.00 | 10.00 |

SMITH, KEELY   Also see LOUIS PRIMA AND KEELY SMITH.

45s

ATLANTIC

| ❏ 2429 | One Less Bell to Answer/Begin the Beguine | 1967 | — | 3.00 | 6.00 |
| ❏ 2457 | Open Your Heart/All Fall Down | 1967 | — | 3.00 | 6.00 |

CAPITOL

❏ F3445	I Wish You Love/Shy	1956	3.75	7.50	15.00
❏ F3545	High School Affair/Hurt Me	1956	3.00	6.00	12.00
❏ F3663	Sentimental Journey/Baby, Won't You Please Come Home	1957	3.00	6.00	12.00
❏ F3698	Young and In Love/You Better Go Now	1957	3.00	6.00	12.00
❏ F3740	You'll Never Know/Good Behavior	1957	3.00	6.00	12.00
❏ F3820	Autumn Leaves/I Keep Forgetting	1957	3.00	6.00	12.00
❏ F3952	How Are Ya' Fixed for Love?/Nothin' in Common	1958	3.00	6.00	12.00
—By Frank Sinatra and Keely Smith					
❏ F3975	The Whippoorwill/Sometimes	1958	3.00	6.00	12.00

DOT

❏ 15989	Don't Let the Stars Get In Your Eyes/I'd Climb the Highest Mountain	1959	3.00	6.00	12.00
❏ 16089	Close/Tea Leaves	1960	3.00	6.00	12.00
❏ 16146	Here in My Heart/Clearance Sale	1960	3.00	6.00	12.00
❏ 16147	Christmas Island/Silent Night	1960	3.75	7.50	15.00
❏ 16182	La-Bou-Lay-A/Young in Years	1961	2.50	5.00	10.00
❏ 16228	I Keep Coming Back for More/Little Lover Boy	1961	2.50	5.00	10.00
❏ 16257	Prisoner of Love/The Loveliest Night of the Year	1961	2.50	5.00	10.00
❏ 16298	Can't Help Falling in Love/You'll Never Walk Alone	1961	2.50	5.00	10.00
❏ 16338	Confidential/How Deep Is the Ocean	1962	2.50	5.00	10.00
❏ 16386	What Kind of Fool Am I/If I Should Lose You	1962	2.50	5.00	10.00

RCA VICTOR

| ❏ 74-0543 | Your Love/Loving Gift | 1971 | — | 2.50 | 5.00 |

REPRISE

❏ 0294	Let Me Call You Sweetheart/Sunday Mornin'	1964	2.00	4.00	8.00
❏ 0303	I'll Always Love You/I Can't Get You Out of My Heart	1964	2.00	4.00	8.00
❏ 0313	Turn Around, Look at Me/The Wedding	1964	2.00	4.00	8.00
❏ 0346	You're Breaking My Heart/Crazy	1965	—	3.00	6.00
❏ 0374	Have You Ever Been Lonely/Something Wonderful Happened	1965	—	3.00	6.00
❏ 0396	Someday (You'll Want Me to Love You)/Standing in the Ruins	1965	—	3.00	6.00
❏ 0402	That Old Black Magic/Standing in the Ruins	1965	—	3.00	6.00
❏ 0428	It's All in the Way You Look at Life/I'll Bring You Water	1965	—	3.00	6.00
❏ 0452	Good-Bye My Love/Where Are You	1966	—	3.00	6.00
❏ 0482	The Wonder of You/Who's Afraid	1966	—	3.00	6.00
❏ 20149	Going Through the Motions/When You Cry	1963	2.00	4.00	8.00
❏ 20211	Love Again/No One Ever Tells You	1963	2.00	4.00	8.00

Albums

CAPITOL

❏ SW 914 [S]	I Wish You Love	1959	7.50	15.00	30.00
—Black label with colorband, Capitol logo at left					
❏ SW 914 [S]	I Wish You Love	1962	3.75	7.50	15.00
❏ W 914 [M]	I Wish You Love	1957	12.50	25.00	50.00
—Turquoise label					
❏ W 914 [M]	I Wish You Love	1959	7.50	15.00	30.00
—Black label with colorband, Capitol logo at left					
❏ W 914 [M]	I Wish You Love	1962	3.75	7.50	15.00
—Black label with colorband, Capitol logo at top					
❏ ST 1073 [S]	Politely!	1959	12.50	25.00	50.00
—Black label with colorband, Capitol logo at left					
❏ ST 1073 [S]	Politely!	1962	5.00	10.00	20.00
—Black label with colorband, Capitol logo at top					
❏ T 1073 [M]	Politely!	1958	10.00	20.00	40.00
—Black label with colorband, Capitol logo at left					
❏ T 1073 [M]	Politely!	1962	3.75	7.50	15.00
—Black label with colorband, Capitol logo at top					
❏ ST 1145 [S]	Swingin' Pretty	1959	12.50	25.00	50.00
—Black label with colorband, Capitol logo at left					
❏ ST 1145 [S]	Swingin' Pretty	1962	5.00	10.00	20.00
—Black label with colorband, Capitol logo at top					
❏ T 1145 [M]	Swingin' Pretty	1959	10.00	20.00	40.00
—Black label with colorband, Capitol logo at left					
❏ T 1145 [M]	Swingin' Pretty	1962	3.75	7.50	15.00
—Black label with colorband, Capitol logo at top					

DOT

❏ DLP-3241 [M]	Be My Love	1959	6.25	12.50	25.00
❏ DLP-3265 [M]	Swing, You Lovers	1960	6.25	12.50	25.00
❏ DLP-3287 [M]	Dearly Beloved	1961	6.25	12.50	25.00
❏ DLP-3345 [M]	A Keely Christmas	1961	6.25	12.50	25.00
❏ DLP-3415 [M]	Because You're Mine	1962	6.25	12.50	25.00
❏ DLP-3423 [M]	Twist with Keely Smith	1962	6.25	12.50	25.00
❏ DLP-3460 [M]	Cherokeely Swings	1962	6.25	12.50	25.00
❏ DLP-3461 [M]	What Kind of Fool Am I	1962	6.25	12.50	25.00
❏ DLP-25241 [S]	Be My Love	1959	7.50	15.00	30.00
❏ DLP-25265 [S]	Swing, You Lovers	1960	7.50	15.00	30.00
❏ DLP-25287 [S]	Dearly Beloved	1961	7.50	15.00	30.00
❏ DLP-25345 [S]	A Keely Christmas	1961	7.50	15.00	30.00
❏ DLP-25415 [S]	Because You're Mine	1962	7.50	15.00	30.00
❏ DLP-25423 [S]	Twist with Keely Smith	1962	7.50	15.00	30.00
❏ DLP-25460 [S]	Cherokeely Swings	1962	7.50	15.00	30.00
❏ DLP-25461 [S]	What Kind of Fool Am I	1962	7.50	15.00	30.00

HARMONY

| ❏ HS 11333 | That Old Black Magic | 1968 | 3.00 | 6.00 | 12.00 |

REPRISE

❏ R-6086 [M]	Little Girl Blue, Little Girl New	1963	5.00	10.00	20.00
❏ R9-6086 [S]	Little Girl Blue, Little Girl New	1963	6.25	12.50	25.00
❏ R-6132 [M]	The Intimate Keely Smith	1964	5.00	10.00	20.00
❏ RS-6132 [S]	The Intimate Keely Smith	1964	6.25	12.50	25.00
❏ R-6142 [M]	Keely Smith Sings the John Lennon/Paul McCartney Songbook	1964	6.25	12.50	25.00
❏ RS-6142 [S]	Keely Smith Sings the John Lennon/Paul McCartney Songbook	1964	7.50	15.00	30.00
❏ R-6175 [M]	That Old Black Magic	1965	5.00	10.00	20.00
❏ RS-6175 [S]	That Old Black Magic	1965	6.25	12.50	25.00

SMITH, LENDON, AND THE JESTERS

45s

METEOR

| ❏ 5030 | Women/Lost Love | 1956 | 37.50 | 75.00 | 150.00 |

SMITH, LEON

45s

EPIC

| ❏ 9326 | Little 40 Ford/Cry All the Time | 1959 | 10.00 | 20.00 | 40.00 |

LAVENDER

| ❏ 1851 | Basic Surf/Jailer, Bring Me Water | 196? | 7.50 | 15.00 | 30.00 |

WILLIAMETTE

❏ 101	Little 40 Ford/Once I Had a Heart	1959	30.00	60.00	120.00
❏ 105	Honey Honey/That's the Way	1959	7.50	15.00	30.00
❏ 109	Flip, Flop and Fly/Sweet Love	1960	7.50	15.00	30.00

SMITH, O.C.

45s

BIG TOP

| ❏ 3039 | You Are My Sunshine/Well I'm Dancin' | 1960 | 3.00 | 6.00 | 12.00 |
| —As "Ocie Smith" | | | | | |

CADENCE

❏ 1304	Slow Walk/Forbidden Fruit	1956	3.75	7.50	15.00
—As "Ocie Smith"					
❏ 1312	If You Don't Love Me/Bad Man of Missouri	1957	3.75	7.50	15.00
—As "Ocie Smith"					
❏ 1329	Lighthouse/Too Many	1957	3.75	7.50	15.00
—As "Ocie Smith"					

CARIBOU

| ❏ 9017 | Together/Just Couldn't Help Myself | 1976 | — | 2.50 | 5.00 |
| ❏ 9021 | Simple Wife/Come with Me | 1977 | — | 2.50 | 5.00 |

COLUMBIA

❏ 10031	La La Peace Song/When Morning Comes	1974	—	2.50	5.00
❏ 43525	That's Life/I'm Your Man	1966	2.00	4.00	8.00
❏ 43809	Beyond the Next Hill/On Easy Street	1966	2.00	4.00	8.00
❏ 44151	Double Life/The Season	1967	2.00	4.00	8.00
❏ 44425	The Son of Hickory Holler's Tramp/The Best Man	1968	2.00	4.00	8.00
❏ 44555	Main Street Mission/Gas Food Lodging	1968	2.00	4.00	8.00
❏ 44616	Little Green Apples/Long Black Limousine	1968	2.00	4.00	8.00
❏ 44705	Isn't It Lonely Together/I Ain't the Worryin' Kind	1968	—	3.00	6.00
❏ 44751	Honey (I Miss You)/Keep On Keepin' On	1969	—	3.00	6.00
❏ 44859	Friend, Lover, Woman, Wife/I Taught Her Everything She Knows	1969	—	3.00	6.00
❏ 44948	Daddy's Little Man/If I Leave You Now	1969	—	3.00	6.00
❏ 44948 [PS]	Daddy's Little Man/If I Leave You Now	1969	2.00	4.00	8.00
❏ 45038	Me and You/Can't Take My Eyes Off You	1969	—	3.00	6.00
❏ 45098	Isn't Life Beautiful/Moody	1970	—	3.00	6.00
❏ 45160	Primrose Lane/Melodee	1970	—	3.00	6.00
❏ 45206	Baby I Need Your Loving/San Francisco Is a Lonely Town	1970	—	3.00	6.00
❏ 45301	Downtown U.S.A./That's What Life Is All About	1971	—	3.00	6.00

Number	Title (A Side/B Side)	Yr	VG	VG+	NM
❑ 45343	Clean Up Your Own Back Yard/I've Been There	1971	—	3.00	6.00
❑ 45435	Help Me Make It Through the Night/Diamond in the Rough	1971	—	3.00	6.00
❑ 45655	Don't Misunderstand/If You Touch Me	1972	—	3.00	6.00
❑ 45863	La La Peace Song/When Morning Comes	1973	—	3.00	6.00
FAMILY					
❑ 5000	Dreams Come True/(B-side unknown)	1980	—	2.50	5.00
MGM					
❑ 12321	Just Kiss Me/At Last My Baby's Coming Home	1956	3.75	7.50	15.00
—As "Ocie Smith"					
MOTOWN					
❑ 1623	Love Changes/Got to Know	1982	—	2.50	5.00
❑ 1636	I Betcha/That's One for Love	1982	—	2.50	5.00
RENDEZVOUS					
❑ 101	What'cha Gonna Do/(B-side unknown)	1986	—	2.00	4.00
❑ 102	You're the First, the Last, My Everything/(B-side unknown)	1986	—	2.00	4.00
❑ 103	Brenda/(B-side unknown)	1986	—	2.00	4.00
SHADY BROOK					
❑ 1045	Love to Burn/Give Me Time	1978	—	2.50	5.00
❑ 1049	Living Without Your Love/Can't Be the One to Say It's Over	1978	—	2.50	5.00
❑ 45012	Love Is Forever/(B-side unknown)	197?	—	2.50	5.00
SOUTH BAY					
❑ 1003	Love Changes/Got to Know	1982	—	3.00	6.00
7-Inch Extended Plays					
COLUMBIA					
❑ 7-9680	The Son of Hickory Holler's Tramp/Little Green Apples//By the Time I Get to Phoenix/Sitting on the Dock of the Bay	1968	3.00	6.00	12.00
—Jukebox issue; small hole, plays at 33 1/3 rpm					
❑ 7-9680 [PS]	Hickory Holler Revisited	1968	3.00	6.00	12.00
Albums					
CARIBOU					
❑ PZ 34471	Together	1977	2.50	5.00	10.00
COLUMBIA					
❑ CL 2714 [M]	The Dynamic O.C. Smith	1967	5.00	10.00	20.00
❑ CS 9514 [S]	The Dynamic O.C. Smith	1967	3.75	7.50	15.00
❑ CS 9680 [M]	Hickory Holler Revisited	1968	6.25	12.50	25.00
—White label promo "Special Mono Radio Station Copy" with stereo number					
❑ CS 9680 [S]	Hickory Holler Revisited	1968	3.00	6.00	12.00
❑ CS 9756	For Once in My Life	1969	3.00	6.00	12.00
❑ CS 9908	O.C. Smith at Home	1969	3.00	6.00	12.00
❑ C 30227	O.C. Smith's Greatest Hits	1970	3.00	6.00	12.00
❑ C 30664	Help Me Make It Through the Night	1971	3.00	6.00	12.00
❑ KC 33247	La La Peace Song	1974	2.50	5.00	10.00
HARMONY					
❑ KH 30317	O.C. Smith	1971	2.50	5.00	10.00
MOTOWN					
❑ 6019 ML	Love Changes	1982	2.50	5.00	10.00
SHADYBROOK					
❑ SB-012	Love Is Forever	1978	2.50	5.00	10.00

SMITH, OCIE See O.C. SMITH.

SMITH, PATTI, GROUP

12-Inch Singles

Number	Title (A Side/B Side)	Yr	VG	VG+	NM
ARISTA					
❑ SP-62 [DJ]	Frederick (Studio)/Frederick (Live)	1977	3.75	7.50	15.00
❑ 9688	People Have the Power/Where Duty Calls/Wild Leaves	1988	—	3.00	6.00
45s					
ARISTA					
❑ SP-2 [DJ]	Pissing in the River (mono/stereo)	1976	6.25	12.50	25.00
❑ SP-4 [DJ]	Ask the Angels (mono/stereo)	1977	6.25	12.50	25.00
—With lyric insert (deduct 20% if missing)					
❑ 0171	Gloria/My Generation	1976	2.50	5.00	10.00
❑ 0171 [PS]	Gloria/My Generation	1976	2.50	5.00	10.00
❑ 0318	Because the Night/God Speed	1978	—	2.00	4.00
—A-side co-written by Bruce Springsteen					
❑ 0318 [PS]	Because the Night/God Speed	1978	2.00	4.00	8.00
❑ 0427	Frederick/Frederick (Live)	1979	—	2.00	4.00
❑ 0427 [PS]	Frederick/Frederick (Live)	1979	2.00	4.00	8.00
❑ 0453	So You Want to Be a Rock and Roll Star//5-4-3-2-1/A Fire of Unknown Origin	1979	—	2.00	4.00
❑ 0453 [PS]	So You Want to Be a Rock and Roll Star//5-4-3-2-1/A Fire of Unknown Origin	1979	5.00	10.00	20.00
❑ 9173	Because the Night/So You Want to Be a Rock 'n' Roll Star	198?	—	—	3.00
—"Flashback" reissue					
❑ 9689	People Have the Power/Wild Leaves	1988	—	—	3.00
❑ 9689 [PS]	People Have the Power/Wild Leaves	1988	—	—	3.00
❑ 9762	I Was (Looking for You)/Up There Down There	1988	—	—	3.00
MER					
❑ 601	Hey Joe/Piss Factory	1974	20.00	40.00	80.00
SIRE					
❑ 1009	Hey Joe/Piss Factory	1977	2.00	4.00	8.00
Albums					
ARISTA					
❑ AL 4066	Horses	1975	3.00	6.00	12.00
—With the word "Horses" in white letters on the front cover					
❑ AL 4066	Horses	1975	3.75	7.50	15.00
—With the word "Horses" in black letters on the front cover					
❑ AL 4097	Radio Ethiopia	1977	3.00	6.00	12.00
❑ AB 4171	Easter	1978	3.00	6.00	12.00
❑ AB 4221	Wave	1979	2.50	5.00	10.00
❑ ALB6-8349	Easter	198?	2.00	4.00	8.00
—Reissue					
❑ ALB6-8362	Horses	198?	2.00	4.00	8.00
—Reissue					
❑ ALB6-8379	Radio Ethiopia	198?	2.00	4.00	8.00
—Reissue					
❑ AL 8453	Dreams of Life	1988	2.50	5.00	10.00
❑ AL 8546	Wave	1990	2.00	4.00	8.00
—Reissue					
❑ R 100469	Dreams of Life	1988	3.00	6.00	12.00
—BMG Music Service edition					

SMITH, RAY

45s

Number	Title (A Side/B Side)	Yr	VG	VG+	NM
CELEBRITY CIRCLE					
❑ 6901	I Walk the Line/Fool #1	1964	3.75	7.50	15.00
CINNAMON					
❑ 755	Tiilted Cup of Love/I'd Traded Better for Worse	1973	—	2.50	5.00
❑ 760	It Wasn't Easy/It's Just Not the Same	1973	—	2.50	5.00
❑ 773	The First Lonely Weekend/A Handful of Friends	1973	—	2.50	5.00
❑ 795	Ten Steps Out in Front/Because of Losing You	1974	—	2.50	5.00
COLUMBIA					
❑ 2-225 (?)	Rainbow/Waltz of the Alamo	1949	10.00	20.00	40.00
—Microgroove 33 1/3 rpm single, small hole					
❑ 2-290 (?)	Snowdeer/Roll Along Kentucky Moon	1949	10.00	20.00	40.00
—Microgroove 33 1/3 rpm single, small hole					
❑ 2-300 (?)	An Old Christmas Card/Jolly Old St. Nicholas	1949	10.00	20.00	40.00
—Microgroove 33 1/3 rpm single, small hole					
❑ 2-305 (?)	Wedding Bells/I'm Throwing Rice (At the Girl I Love)	1949	10.00	20.00	40.00
—Microgroove 33 1/3 rpm single, small hole					
❑ 2-310 (?)	Pretty Little Eyes of Blue/Tennessee Polka	1949	10.00	20.00	40.00
—Microgroove 33 1/3 rpm single, small hole					
❑ 2-531	Unfaithful One/Daddy's Little Girl	1950	10.00	20.00	40.00
—Microgroove 33 1/3 rpm single, small hole					
❑ 2-534 (?)	I'm Saving Mother's Wedding Ring for You/Mommy Can I Take My Doll	1950	10.00	20.00	40.00
—Microgroove 33 1/3 rpm single, small hole					
❑ 2-590 (?)	No Trespassing/The Sun Has Gone Down	1950	10.00	20.00	40.00
—Microgroove 33 1/3 rpm single, small hole					
DIAMOND					
❑ 193	Everybody's Goin' Somewhere/Au-Go-Go-Go	1965	3.75	7.50	15.00
ERA BACK TO BACK HITS					
❑ 048	Rockin' Little Angel/Robbin' the Cradle	197?	—	2.50	5.00
—B-side by Tony Bellus					
HEART					
❑ 250	Gone, Baby, Gone/(B-side unknown)	195?	1000.	1500.	2000.
INFINITY					
❑ 003	After This Night Is Through/Turn On the Moonlight	1961	3.75	7.50	15.00
❑ 007	Let Yourself Go/Johnny the Hummer	1961	3.75	7.50	15.00
JUDD					
❑ 1016	Rockin' Little Angel/That's All Right	1959	7.50	15.00	30.00
❑ 1017	Maria Elena/Put Your Arms Around Me Honey	1960	7.50	15.00	30.00
❑ 1019	One Wonderful Love/Makes Me Feel Good	1960	7.50	15.00	30.00
❑ 1021	Blonde Hair, Blue Eyes/You Don't Want Me	1960	7.50	15.00	30.00
NU-TONE					
❑ 1182	Deep in My Heart/She's Mine	1964	3.75	7.50	15.00
SHI-RAY					
❑ 101	Sleepy Eyed Woman/Pretty Juke Box	197?	—	3.00	6.00
SMASH					
❑ 1787	Room 503/These Four Precious Years	1962	3.75	7.50	15.00
SUN					
❑ 298	So Right/Right Behind You Baby	1958	7.50	15.00	30.00
❑ 308	Why, Why, Why/You Made a Hit	1958	7.50	15.00	30.00
❑ 319	Rockin' Bandit/Sail Away	1959	7.50	15.00	30.00
❑ 372	Travelin' Salesman/I Won't Miss You ('Til You're Gone)	1961	7.50	15.00	30.00
❑ 375	Hey Boss Man/Candy Doll	1962	7.50	15.00	30.00
TOLLIE					
❑ 9029	Here Comes My Baby Back Again/Did We Have a Party	1964	5.00	10.00	20.00
TOPPA					
❑ 1071	Almost Alone/A Place Within My Heart	1962	5.00	10.00	20.00
VEE JAY					
❑ 579	Rockin' Robin/Robbin' the Cradle	1964	3.75	7.50	15.00
WARNER BROS.					
❑ 5371	I'm Snowed/Turn Over a New Leaf	1963	3.75	7.50	15.00
ZIRKON					
❑ 1055	After This Night Is Through/Turn On the Moonlight	1961	5.00	10.00	20.00
Albums					
COLUMBIA					
❑ CL 1937 [M]	Ray Smith's Greatest Hits	1963	6.25	12.50	25.00
❑ CS 8737 [S]	Ray Smith's Greatest Hits	1963	7.50	15.00	30.00
JUDD					
❑ JLPA-701 [M]	Travelin' with Ray	1960	175.00	350.00	700.00
STOMP OFF					
❑ SOS-1012	Jungle Blues	198?	3.00	6.00	12.00
"T"					
❑ 56062 [M]	The Best of Ray Smith	196?	25.00	50.00	100.00
WIX					
❑ 1000	I'm Gonna Rock Some More	197?	3.75	7.50	15.00

SMITH, ROBERT CURTIS

45s

Number	Title (A Side/B Side)	Yr	VG	VG+	NM
ARHOOLIE					
❑ 502	Love Each Other/Please Don't Drive Me Away	1961	5.00	10.00	20.00
Albums					
BLUESVILLE					
❑ BVLP-1064 [M]	Clarksdale Blues	1963	20.00	40.00	80.00
—Blue label, silver print					
❑ BVLP-1064 [M]	Clarksdale Blues	1964	6.25	12.50	25.00
—Blue label, trident logo at right					

SMITH, RONNIE

45s

Number	Title (A Side/B Side)	Yr	VG	VG+	NM
BRUNSWICK					
❑ 55137	Lookie, Lookie, Lookie/Tiny Kisses	1959	10.00	20.00	40.00
HAMILTON					
❑ 50003	My Babe/I've Got a Love	1959	6.25	12.50	25.00
IMPERIAL					
❑ 5667	It Hurts Me So/Long Time No Love	1960	7.50	15.00	30.00
❑ 5679	I Hear You Knocking/I Started Out Walkin'	1960	7.50	15.00	30.00

S

Number	Title (A Side/B Side)	Yr	VG	VG+	NM
SMITH, SAMMI					
45s					
COLUMBIA					
❏ 44212	He Went a Little Bit Farther/Foxy Dan	1967	2.50	5.00	10.00
❏ 44370	So Long, Charlie Brown, Don't Look for Me Around/Turn Around	1967	2.00	4.00	8.00
❏ 44523	Why Do You Do Me Like You Do/22 Road Markers to a Mile	1968	2.00	4.00	8.00
❏ 4-44663	Sand Covered Angels/It's Not Time Now	1968	2.00	4.00	8.00
❏ 44905	Brownsville Lumberyard/Shadows of Your Mind	1969	2.00	4.00	8.00
CYCLONE					
❏ 100	What a Lie/It's Not My Way	1979	—	2.00	4.00
❏ 104	The Letter/It's a Day for Sad Songs	1979	—	2.00	4.00
ELEKTRA					
❏ 45292	Huckleberry Pie/ I Won't Sing No Love Songs Anymore	1975	—	2.50	5.00
—With Even Stevens					
❏ 45300	As Long As There's a Sunday/Children	1976	—	2.00	4.00
❏ 45320	Rabbit Tracks/I'll Get Better	1976	—	2.00	4.00
❏ 45334	Sunday School to Broadway/Goodmornin', Sunshine, Goodbye	1976	—	2.00	4.00
❏ 45374	Loving Arms/I Just Wanted to Sing	1977	—	2.00	4.00
❏ 45398	I Can't Stop Loving You/De Grazia's Song	1977	—	2.00	4.00
❏ 45429	Days That End in "Y"/Hallelujah for Beer	1977	—	2.00	4.00
❏ 45476	It Just Won't Feel Like Cheating (With You)/I Ain't Got Time to Rock No Babies	1978	—	2.00	4.00
❏ 45504	Norma Jean/Lookin' for Lovin'	1978	—	2.00	4.00
MEGA					
❏ 0001	He's Everywhere/This Room for Rent	1970	—	2.50	5.00
❏ 0015	Help Me Make It Through the Night/ When Michael Calls	1970	—	3.00	6.00
❏ 0026	Then You Walk In/Willie	1971	—	2.50	5.00
❏ 0039	For the Kids/Saunder's Ferry Lane	1971	—	2.50	5.00
❏ 0056	Kentucky/The Marionette	1971	—	2.50	5.00
❏ 0068	Girl in New Orleans/Isn't It Sad	1972	—	2.50	5.00
❏ 0079	I've Got to Have You/Jimmy's in Georgia	1972	—	2.50	5.00
❏ 0097	The Toast of '45/Tony	1972	—	2.50	5.00
❏ 0109	I Miss You Most When You're Here/Billy Jacks	1973	—	2.50	5.00
❏ 0118	City of New Orleans/ Don't Blow No Smoke on Me	1973	—	2.50	5.00
❏ 204	The Rainbow in Daddy's Eyes/ Birmingham Mistake	1974	—	2.50	5.00
❏ 210	Never Been to Spain/It's Not Easy	1974	—	2.50	5.00
❏ 212	Help Me Make It Through the Night/ When Michael Calls	1974	—	2.00	4.00
—Reissue of 0015					
❏ 1214	Long Black Veil/Paste Me On Some Feathers	1974	—	2.50	5.00
❏ 1222	Cover Me/He Makes It Hard to Say Goodbye	1975	—	2.50	5.00
❏ 1233	She's in Love with a Rodeo Man/ Fool for Something Years	1975	—	2.50	5.00
❏ 1236	Today I Started Loving You Again/Fine As Wine	1975	—	2.50	5.00
❏ 1246	My Window Faces the South/ Before the Next Teardrop Falls	1976	—	2.50	5.00
PLAYBACK					
❏ 1340	Gonna Lay Me Down Beside My Memories/ I'd Do It All Over Again	1989	—	2.50	5.00
❏ 1354	Cloudy Days/(B-side unknown)	1989	—	2.50	5.00
SOUND FACTORY					
❏ 425	I Just Want to Be with You/I've Never Loved You More Than I Do Now	1980	—	2.00	4.00
❏ 427	Cheatin's a Two-Way Street/ The Legend of Wooley Swamp	1981	—	2.00	4.00
❏ 432	Waltz Across Texas/ I Need Thatr Shoulder After All	1981	—	3.00	6.00
—With Ernest Tubb					
❏ 433	Gypsy and Joe/(B-side unknown)	1982	—	2.00	4.00
❏ 446	Sometimes I Cry When I'm Alone/Once or Twice	1981	—	2.00	4.00
STEP ONE					
❏ 342	You Just Hurt My Last Feeling/Lying in My Arms	1985	—	2.00	4.00
❏ 347	An Offer I Couldn't Refuse/ One Away from One Too Many	1985	—	2.00	4.00
❏ 351	Love Me All Over/Don't Let It Happen Again	1986	—	2.00	4.00
ZODIAC					
❏ 1000	Help Me Make It Through the Night/ Saunder's Ferry Drive	1976	—	2.00	4.00
❏ 1005	Just You 'n' Me/Walking in the Sunshine	1976	—	2.00	4.00
❏ 1013	Rings for Sale/You Don't Want My Love	1976	—	2.00	4.00
Albums					
ELEKTRA					
❏ 7E-1058	As Long As There's a Sunday	1976	2.50	5.00	10.00
❏ 7E-1108	Mixed Emotions	1977	2.50	5.00	10.00
HARMONY					
❏ H 30616	The World of Sammi Smith	1971	2.50	5.00	10.00
MEGA					
❏ MLPS-601	Rainbow in Daddy's Eyes	1974	3.00	6.00	12.00
❏ MLPS-604	Sammi's Greatest Hits	1974	3.00	6.00	12.00
❏ MLPS-612	Today I Started Loving You Again	1975	3.00	6.00	12.00
❏ 31-1000	Help Me Make It Through the Night	1971	3.00	6.00	12.00
❏ 31-1007	Lonesome	1971	3.00	6.00	12.00
❏ 31-1011	Something Old, Something New, Something Blue	1972	3.00	6.00	12.00
❏ 31-1019	The Best of Sammi Smith	1973	3.00	6.00	12.00
❏ 31-1021	The Toast of '45	1973	3.00	6.00	12.00
PICKWICK					
❏ 6167	Help Me Make It Through the Night	197?	2.50	5.00	10.00
ZODIAC					
❏ 5004	Her Way	1976	2.50	5.00	10.00
SMITH, SHELBY					
45s					
REBEL					
❏ 728	Rockin' Mama/Since My Baby Said Goodbye	1962	100.00	200.00	400.00
SMITH, SOMETHIN', AND THE REDHEADS					
45s					
EPIC					
❏ 5-9025	Gee/Just in Case You Change Your Mind	1954	3.00	6.00	12.00
—As "Somethin' Smith and the Skylarks"					
❏ 5-9048	If I Could Be with You/Oh Jane	1954	2.50	5.00	10.00
❏ 5-9093	It's a Sin to Tell a Lie/My Baby Just Cares for Me	1955	2.50	5.00	10.00
❏ 5-9106	The Ace in the Hole/Charley, My Boy	1955	2.50	5.00	10.00
❏ 5-9119	When All the Streets Are Dark/Pretty Baby	1955	2.50	5.00	10.00
❏ 5-9140	Red Head/Pinch Me (I Must Be Dreamin')	1956	2.50	5.00	10.00
❏ 5-9168	In a Shanty in Old Shanty Town/ Coal Dust on the Fiddle	1956	2.50	5.00	10.00
❏ 5-9179	Heartaches/Cecelia	1956	2.50	5.00	10.00
❏ 5-9188	When I Grow Too Old to Dream/ We'll Build a Bungalow	1956	2.50	5.00	10.00
❏ 5-9197	Sweet Stuff/I Hope You Know What You're Doin'	1957	2.50	5.00	10.00
❏ 5-9208	Ma (She's Makin' Eyes at Me)/Mambo, Tango, Samba, Chalypso Rhumba Blues	1957	2.50	5.00	10.00
❏ 5-9221	You Always Hurt the One You Love/My Melancholy Baby	1957	2.50	5.00	10.00
❏ 5-9247	Ev'ry Night at 9 O'Clock/I'm Gonna Wrap Up All My Heartaches	1957	2.50	5.00	10.00
❏ 5-9264	School Bus Rock/I Thank You, Mr. Moon	1958	3.00	6.00	12.00
❏ 5-9269	My Secret Inspiration/The Brush Off	1958	2.50	5.00	10.00
❏ 5-9280	I Don't Want to Set the World on Fire/You Made Me Love You	1958	2.50	5.00	10.00
❏ 5-9313	Mr. D.J. (Please Play a Song for Me)/That's Togetherness	1959	2.50	5.00	10.00
❏ 5-9340	Poor Butterfly/Ten Chaperones	1959	2.50	5.00	10.00
❏ 5-9389	Ballin' the Jack/It's a Sin to Tell a Lie	1960	2.00	4.00	8.00
MGM					
❏ 13023	Ain't We Got Fun/We'll Meet Again	1961	2.00	4.00	8.00
7-Inch Extended Plays					
EPIC					
❏ EG 7117	There's a Little Bit of Corn Born in All of Us-California Here I Come/It's a Sin to Tell a Lie/ Pretty Baby/Back in Your Own Back Yard	195?	5.00	10.00	20.00
❏ EG 7117 [PS]	It's a Sin to Tell a Lie	195?	5.00	10.00	20.00
Albums					
EPIC					
❏ LN 3138 [M]	Somethin' Smith and the Redheads	1959	7.50	15.00	30.00
❏ LN 3373 [M]	Put the Blame on Mame	196?	6.25	12.50	25.00
MGM					
❏ E-3941 [M]	Ain't We Got Fun Kinda Songs	1961	5.00	10.00	20.00
❏ SE-3941 [S]	Ain't We Got Fun Kinda Songs	1961	6.25	12.50	25.00
SMITH, WARREN					
45s					
LIBERTY					
❏ 55248	I Don't Believe I'll Fall in Love Today/Cave-In	1960	5.00	10.00	20.00
❏ 55302	Odds and Ends (Bits and Pieces)/ A Whole Lot of Nothin'	1961	5.00	10.00	20.00
❏ 55336	Call of the Wild/Old Lonesome Feeling	1961	5.00	10.00	20.00
❏ 55361	Why Baby Why/Why I'm Walking	1961	5.00	10.00	20.00
—With Shirley Collie					
❏ 55409	Bad News Gets Around/Five Minutes of the Latest Blues	1962	5.00	10.00	20.00
❏ 55475	Book of Broken Hearts/160 Pounds of Hurt	1962	5.00	10.00	20.00
❏ 55615	Big City Ways/That's Why I Sing in a Honky Tonk	1963	3.75	7.50	15.00
❏ 55699	Blue Smoke/Judge and Jury	1964	3.75	7.50	15.00
MERCURY					
❏ 72825	Lie to Me/When the Heartaches Get to Me	1968	2.50	5.00	10.00
SUN					
❏ 239	Rock and Roll Ruby/ I'd Rather Be Safe Than Sorry	1956	20.00	40.00	80.00
❏ 250	Ubangi Stomp/Black Jack David	1956	15.00	30.00	60.00
❏ 268	Miss Froggie/So Long, I'm Gone	1957	10.00	20.00	40.00
❏ 286	I Fell in Love/I've Got Love If You Want It	1958	7.50	15.00	30.00
❏ 314	Goodbye Mr. Love/Sweet Sweet Girl	1959	10.00	20.00	40.00
WARNER BROS.					
❏ 5125	Dear Santa/The Meaning of Christmas	1959	6.25	12.50	25.00
Albums					
LIBERTY					
❏ LRP-3199 [M]	The First Country Collection of Warren Smith	1961	12.50	25.00	50.00
❏ LST-7199 [S]	The First Country Collection of Warren Smith	1961	17.50	35.00	70.00
SMITH, WHISTLING JACK					
45s					
DERAM					
❏ 85005	I Was Kaiser Bill's Batman/ The British Grin 'N' Bear	1967	2.00	4.00	8.00
❏ 85041	Only When I Laff/Early One Morning	1969	—	3.00	6.00
Albums					
DERAM					
❏ DE 16006 [M]	I Was Kaiser Bill's Batman	1967	6.25	12.50	25.00
❏ DES 18006 [S]	I Was Kaiser Bill's Batman	1967	5.00	10.00	20.00
SMOKE, THE (1) California group. Jimmy Greenspoon, later a member of THREE DOG NIGHT, appears on the LP cover, but not on the record itself.					
Albums					
SIDEWALK					
❏ ST 5912	The Smoke	1968	10.00	20.00	40.00
SMOKE, THE (2) Houston-based group.					
45s					
ORBIT					
❏ 1126	Mainstream/Church House Blues	1968	12.50	25.00	50.00
UNI					
❏ 55154	Choose It (Part 1)/Choose It (Part 2)	1969	2.50	5.00	10.00
Albums					
UNI					
❏ 73052	The Smoke	1969	6.25	12.50	25.00
❏ 73065	The Smoke at George's Coffee Shop	1970	6.25	12.50	25.00

Number	Title (A Side/B Side)	Yr	VG	VG+	NM
SMOKE RINGS, THE					
45s					
DOT					
❏ 16975	Love's the Thing/She Gives Me Love	1966	5.00	10.00	20.00
PROSPECT					
❏ 101	Love's the Thing/She Gives Me Love	1966	10.00	20.00	40.00
SMOKE RISE, THE					
45s					
PARAMOUNT					
❏ 0113	I'm Here (Love Me)/Survival	1971	2.00	4.00	8.00
Albums					
PARAMOUNT					
❏ PAS-9000 [(2)]	The Survival of St. Joan	1971	5.00	10.00	20.00
—With booklet					
SMOKESTACK LIGHTNIN'					
45s					
BELL					
❏ 755	Light in My Window/Long Stemmed Eyes	1968	—	3.00	6.00
❏ 777	I Idolize You/Something's Got a Hold on You	1969	—	3.00	6.00
❏ 836	Baby Don't Get Crazy/The Blue Albino Shuffle	1969	—	3.00	6.00
❏ 861	Hello L.A., Bye-Bye Birmingham/Well Tuesday	1970	—	3.00	6.00
WHITE WHALE					
❏ 243	Nadine/Crossroadds Blues	1967	2.00	4.00	8.00
❏ 256	Look What You've Done/Got a Good Love	1967	2.00	4.00	8.00
Albums					
BELL					
❏ 6026	Off the Wall	1969	5.00	10.00	20.00
SMOKEY JOE					
45s					
FLIP					
❏ 228	The Signifying Monkey/Listen to Me Baby	1955	125.00	250.00	500.00
SUN					
❏ 228	The Signifying Monkey/Listen to Me Baby	1956	75.00	150.00	300.00
❏ 393	The Signifying Monkey/Listen to Me Baby	1964	50.00	100.00	200.00
SMOKIE					
45s					
MCA					
❏ 40429	If You Think You Know How to Love Me/'Tis Me	1975	—	2.50	5.00
—As "Smokey"					
❏ 40471	Don't Play Your Rock 'N' Roll to Me/ Talking Her 'Round	1975	—	2.50	5.00
—As "Smokey"					
RSO					
❏ 860	Living Next Door to Alice/ When My Back Was Against the Wall	1976	—	2.50	5.00
❏ 874	If You Think You Know How to Love Me/ Make Ya Boogie	1977	—	2.00	4.00
❏ 881	Needles and Pins/ No One Could Ever Love You More	1977	—	2.00	4.00
❏ 900	For a Few Dollars More/ I Can't Stay Here Tonight	1978	—	2.00	4.00
❏ 934	No More Letters/Oh Carol	1979	—	2.00	4.00
Albums					
MCA					
❏ 2152	Smokey	1975	3.00	6.00	12.00
—As "Smokey"					
RSO					
❏ RS-1-3005	Midnight Café	1976	2.50	5.00	10.00
❏ RS-1-3029	Bright Lights and Back Alleys	1978	2.50	5.00	10.00
SMOOTHIES, THE With JOHN PHILLIPS and SCOTT McKENZIE.					
45s					
DECCA					
❏ 31105	Softly/Joanie	1960	5.00	10.00	20.00
❏ 31159	Ride, Ride, Ride/Lonely Boy and Pretty Girl	1960	5.00	10.00	20.00
SMOTHERS, DICK Also see THE SMOTHERS BROTHERS.					
45s					
MERCURY					
❏ 72717	Saturday Night at the World/They Are Gone	1967	5.00	10.00	20.00
❏ 72717 [PS]	Saturday Night at the World/They Are Gone	1967	6.25	12.50	25.00
SMOTHERS BROTHERS, THE Also see DICK SMOTHERS.					
45s					
MERCURY					
❏ 72027	Fly Ezekiel/They Call the Wind Maria	1962	2.50	5.00	10.00
❏ 72182	Jenny Brown/You Go This-a-Way	1963	2.50	5.00	10.00
❏ 72323	Coo Coo/Slithery Dee	1964	2.50	5.00	10.00
❏ 72483	The Three Song/The World I Used to Know	1965	2.00	4.00	8.00
❏ 72483 [PS]	The Three Song/The World I Used to Know	1965	3.75	7.50	15.00
❏ 72519	The Toy Song/Little Sacha Sugar	1966	2.00	4.00	8.00
❏ 72519 [PS]	The Toy Song/Little Sacha Sugar	1966	3.75	7.50	15.00
❏ 72573	Writer of Songs/Lark Day	1966	2.00	4.00	8.00
SMOTHERS INC.					
❏ 79151	The Christmas Bunny Part 1/ The Christmas Bunny Part 2	1969	6.25	12.50	25.00
❏ 79151 [PS]	The Christmas Bunny Part 1/ The Christmas Bunny Part 2	1969	12.50	25.00	50.00
Albums					
MERCURY					
❏ MGDJ-20 [DJ]	Best of the Smothers Brothers	1964	10.00	20.00	40.00
❏ MGDJ-25 [DJ]	It's Brothers Smothers Month	1964	10.00	20.00	40.00
❏ MG-20611 [M]	The Songs and Comedy of the Smothers Brothers!	1962	3.75	7.50	15.00
❏ MG-20675 [M]	The Two Sides of the Smothers Brothers	1962	3.75	7.50	15.00
❏ MG-20777 [M]	(Think Ethnic!)	1963	3.75	7.50	15.00
❏ MG-20862 [M]	Curb Your Tongue, Knave!	1963	3.75	7.50	15.00
❏ MG-20904 [M]	It Must Have Been Something I Said!	1964	3.75	7.50	15.00
❏ MG-20948 [M]	Tour De Farce American History and Other Unrelated Subjects	1964	3.75	7.50	15.00
❏ MG-20989 [M]	Aesop's Fables the Smothers Brothers Way	1965	3.75	7.50	15.00
❏ MG-21051 [M]	Mom Always Liked You Best!	1965	3.75	7.50	15.00
❏ MG-21064 [M]	The Smothers Brothers Play It Straight	1966	3.75	7.50	15.00
❏ MG-21089 [M]	Golden Hits of the Smothers Brothers, Vol. 2	1966	3.75	7.50	15.00
❏ SR-60611 [S]	The Songs and Comedy of the Smothers Brothers!	1962	5.00	10.00	20.00
❏ SR-60675 [S]	The Two Sides of the Smothers Brothers	1962	5.00	10.00	20.00
❏ SR-60777 [S]	(Think Ethnic!)	1963	5.00	10.00	20.00
❏ SR-60862 [S]	Curb Your Tongue, Knave!	1963	5.00	10.00	20.00
❏ SR-60904 [S]	It Must Have Been Something I Said!	1964	5.00	10.00	20.00
❏ SR-60948 [S]	Tour De Farce American History and Other Unrelated Subjects	1964	5.00	10.00	20.00
❏ SR-60989 [S]	Aesop's Fables the Smothers Brothers Way	1965	5.00	10.00	20.00
❏ SR-61051 [S]	Mom Always Liked You Best!	1965	5.00	10.00	20.00
❏ SR-61064 [S]	The Smothers Brothers Play It Straight	1966	5.00	10.00	20.00
❏ SR-61089 [S]	Golden Hits of the Smothers Brothers, Vol. 2	1966	5.00	10.00	20.00
❏ SR-61193	Smothers Comedy Brothers Hour	1968	5.00	10.00	20.00
RHINO					
❏ R1-70188	Sibling Revelry: The Best of the Smothers Brothers	1988	2.50	5.00	10.00
SNOW, EDDIE					
45s					
SUN					
❏ 226	Ain't That Right/Bring Your Love Back Home	1955	50.00	100.00	200.00
SNOW, HANK					
45s					
RCA					
❏ 2721-7-R	I've Been Everywhere/Ancient History	1990	—	—	3.00
—"Gold Standard Series" reissue					
❏ PB-10804	You're Wondering Why/Somewhere Someone Is Waiting for You	1976	—	2.50	5.00
❏ PB-11021	Trouble in Mind/ Trying to Get My Baby Off My Mind	1977	—	2.50	5.00
❏ PB-11080	I'm Still Movin' On/ I'm Gonna Bid My Blues Goodbye	1977	—	2.50	5.00
❏ PB-11153	Breakfast with the Blues/ I've Done At Least One Thing	1977	—	2.50	5.00
❏ PB-11192	That Heart Belongs to Me/Love Is So Elusive	1978	—	2.50	5.00
❏ PB-11276	Nevertheless/Don't Rock the Boat	1978	—	2.50	5.00
❏ PB-11377	Ramblin' Rose/Red Roses	1978	—	2.50	5.00
❏ PB-11487	The Mysterious Lady from St. Martinique/Get On My Love Train	1979	—	2.50	5.00
❏ PB-11622	A Good Gal Is Hard to Find/ I Wish My Heart Could Talk	1979	—	2.50	5.00
❏ PB-11734	It Takes Too Long/6 String Tennessee Flattop	1979	—	2.50	5.00
RCA VICTOR					
❏ 37-7869	Beggar to a King/Poor Little Jimmie	1961	6.25	12.50	25.00
—"Compact Single 33" with small hole					
❏ 47-4095	Hobo Bill's Last Ride/Wreck of the Old 97	1951	5.00	10.00	20.00
❏ 47-4096	Ben Dewberry's Final Run/Engineer's Child	1951	5.00	10.00	20.00
❏ 47-4097	The Mystery of Number Five/One More Ride	1951	5.00	10.00	20.00
—The above three comprise a box set					
❏ 47-4346	Music Makin' Mama from Memphis/❏ The Highest Bidder	1951	6.25	12.50	25.00
❏ 47-4398	Pray/These Things Shall Pass	1951	6.25	12.50	25.00
❏ 47-4522	The Gold Rush Is Over/Why Do You Promise Me	1952	6.25	12.50	25.00
❏ 47-4593	I'm Movin' On/Marriage Vow	1952	5.00	10.00	20.00
❏ 47-4594	Music Makin' Mama from Memphis/Down the Trail of Aching Hearts	1952	5.00	10.00	20.00
❏ 47-4595	Unwanted Sign Upon Your Heart/ The Rhumba Boogie	1952	5.00	10.00	20.00
❏ 47-4596	The Golden Rocket/Bluebird Island	1952	5.00	10.00	20.00
—The above four comprise a box set					
❏ 47-4632	My Mother/I Just Telephone Upstairs	1952	6.25	12.50	25.00
❏ 47-4733	Lady's Man/Married by the Bible, Divorced by the Law	1952	6.25	12.50	25.00
❏ 47-4856	Jesus Wept/I'm in the Mood for Love	1952	6.25	12.50	25.00
❏ 47-4909	I Went to Your Wedding/ Boogie Woogie Flying Cloud	1952	6.25	12.50	25.00
❏ 47-4973	Zeb Turney's Gal/Golden River	1952	5.00	10.00	20.00
❏ 47-4974	Moanin'/I Knew That We'd Meet Again	1952	5.00	10.00	20.00
❏ 47-4975	My Little Golden Horseshoe/ The Yodeling Cowboy	1952	5.00	10.00	20.00
❏ 47-4976	Confused with the Blues/ On That Old Hawaiian Shore	1952	5.00	10.00	20.00
—The above four comprise a box set					
❏ 47-5006	Broken Hearted/ I Wonder Where You Are Tonight	1952	5.00	10.00	20.00
❏ 47-5026	Love Entered the Iron Door/ I Cried But My Tears Were Too Late	1952	5.00	10.00	20.00
❏ 47-5034	(Now and Then, There's) A Fool Such As I/ The Gal Who Invented Kissin'	1952	5.00	10.00	20.00
❏ 47-5155	Honeymoon on a Rocket Ship/ There Wasn't an Organ at Our Wedding	1953	5.00	10.00	20.00
❏ 47-5220	Jimmie the Kid/My Blue Eyed Jane	1953	3.75	7.50	15.00
❏ 47-5221	When Jimmie Rodgers Said Goodbye/ Treasure Untold	1953	3.75	7.50	15.00
❏ 47-5222	Southern Cannonball/Anniversary Blue Yodel	1953	3.75	7.50	15.00
❏ 47-5223	Why Did You Give Me Your Love/ Mississippi River Blues	1953	3.75	7.50	15.00
—The above four comprise a box set					
❏ 47-5249	Glory Land March/In Daddy's Footsteps	1953	5.00	10.00	20.00
❏ 47-5296	Spanish Fire Ball/Between Fire and Water	1953	5.00	10.00	20.00
❏ 47-5340	Christmas Roses/Reindeer Boogie	1953	6.25	12.50	25.00
❏ 47-5380	For Now and Always/ A Message from the Tradewinds	1953	5.00	10.00	20.00
❏ 47-5490	When Mexican Joe Met Jole Blon/ No Longer a Prisoner	1953	5.00	10.00	20.00
❏ 47-5548	I'm Glad I'm On the Inside/Invisible Hands	1953	5.00	10.00	20.00
❏ 47-5592	Panamara/Act 1, Act 2, Act 3	1954	5.00	10.00	20.00
❏ 47-5648	My Religion's Not Old Fashioned/Old Rattler	1954	6.25	12.50	25.00
—With Grandpa Jones					
❏ 47-5698	I Don't Hurt Anymore/My Arabian Baby	1954	5.00	10.00	20.00
❏ 47-5794	The Alphabet/My Religion's Not Old Fashioned	1954	5.00	10.00	20.00
❏ 47-5912	That Crazy Mambo Thing/ The Next Voice You Hear	1954	5.00	10.00	20.00
❏ 47-5960	Let Me Go, Lover!/I've Forgotten You	1954	5.00	10.00	20.00

S

Number	Title (A Side/B Side)	Yr	VG	VG+	NM
47-6057	Yellow Roses/Would You Mind	1955	3.75	7.50	15.00
47-6154	Cryin', Prayin', Waitin', Hopin'/I'm Glad I Got to See You Once Again	1955	3.75	7.50	15.00
47-6269	Born to Be Happy/Mainliner (The Hawk with Silver Wings)	1955	3.75	7.50	15.00
47-6326	In an Eighteenth Century Drawing Room/La Cucaracha	1955	3.75	7.50	15.00
47-6379	These Hands/I'm Moving In	1956	3.75	7.50	15.00
47-6578	Conscience I'm Guilty/Hula Rock	1956	6.25	12.50	25.00
47-6715	Stolen Moments/Two Won't Care	1956	3.75	7.50	15.00
47-6772	Oh, Wonderful World/Carnival of Venice	1957	3.75	7.50	15.00
47-6831	Calypso Sweethearts/Marriage and Divorce	1957	3.75	7.50	15.00
47-6955	Tangled Mind/My Arms Are a House	1957	3.75	7.50	15.00
47-7060	Unfaithful/Intro to Listeners-Squid Giggin' Ground	1957	3.75	7.50	15.00
47-7121	The Blue Danube Waltz/Under the Double Eagle	1957	3.75	7.50	15.00
47-7154	Whispering Rain/I Wish I Was the Moon	1958	3.75	7.50	15.00
47-7233	Big Wheels/I'm Hurting All Over	1958	3.75	7.50	15.00
47-7325	A Woman Captured Me/My Lucky Friend	1958	3.75	7.50	15.00
47-7448	Doggone That Train/Father Time and Mother Love	1959	3.75	7.50	15.00
47-7524	Chasin' a Rainbow/I Heard My Heart Break Last Night	1959	3.75	7.50	15.00
47-7586	The Last Ride/The Party of the Second Part	1959	3.75	7.50	15.00
47-7702	Rockin', Rollin' Ocean/Walkin' and Talkin'	1960	3.75	7.50	15.00
47-7748	Miller's Cave/The Change of the Tide	1960	3.75	7.50	15.00
47-7803	The Man Behind the Gun/I'm Asking for a Friend	1960	3.75	7.50	15.00
47-7869	Beggar to a King/Poor Little Jimmie	1961	3.00	6.00	12.00
47-7933	The Restless One/I Know	1961	3.00	6.00	12.00
47-8009	You Take the Future (And I'll Take the Past)/Dog Bone	1962	3.00	6.00	12.00
47-8072	I've Been Everywhere/Ancient History	1962	3.00	6.00	12.00
47-8151	The Man Who Robbed the Bank at Santa Fe/You're Losing Your Baby	1963	3.00	6.00	12.00
47-8151 [PS]	The Man Who Robbed the Bank at Santa Fe/You're Losing Your Baby	1963	6.25	12.50	25.00
47-8239	Ninety Miles an Hour (Down a Dead End Street)/Blue Roses	1963	3.00	6.00	12.00
47-8334	Breakfast with the Blues/I Stepped Over the Line	1964	3.00	6.00	12.00
47-8437	My Memories of You/Ninety Days	1964	3.00	6.00	12.00
47-8488	The Wishing Well (Down in the Well)/Human	1964	3.00	6.00	12.00
47-8548	Trouble in Mind/In the Misty Moonlight	1965	2.50	5.00	10.00
47-8655	The Queen of Draw Poker Town/Tears in the Trade Winds	1965	2.50	5.00	10.00
47-8713	I've Cried a Mile/Crazy Little Train (Of Love)	1965	2.50	5.00	10.00
47-8808	The Count Down/Isle of Sicily	1966	2.50	5.00	10.00
47-9012	Hula Love/Letter from Vietnam	1966	2.50	5.00	10.00
47-9030	Christmas Cannonball/God Is My Santa Claus	1966	3.00	6.00	12.00
47-9188	Down at the Pawn Shop/Listen	1967	2.50	5.00	10.00
47-9300	Learnin' a New Way of Life/Wild Flower	1967	2.50	5.00	10.00
47-9433	Who Will Answer? (Aleluya No. 1)/I Just Wanted to Know (How the Wind Was Blowing)	1968	2.50	5.00	10.00
47-9523	The Late and Great Love (Of My Life)/Born for You	1968	2.50	5.00	10.00
47-9685	The Name of the Game Was Love/The Gypsy and Me	1968	2.00	4.00	8.00
47-9856	Vanishing Breed/What More Can I Say	1970	2.00	4.00	8.00
47-9907	Come the Morning/Francesca	1970	2.00	4.00	8.00
47-9964	Duquesne, Pennsylvania/So Goes My Heart	1971	2.00	4.00	8.00
48-0056	Marriage Vow/The Star Spangled Waltz	1949	10.00	20.00	40.00
—Originals on green vinyl					
48-0056	Marriage Vow/The Star Spangled Waltz	195?	6.25	12.50	25.00
—Reissues on black vinyl					
48-0088	The Blind Boy's Dog/Anniversary of My Broken Heart	1949	10.00	20.00	40.00
—Originals on green vinyl					
48-0104	My Filipino Rose/The Law of Love	1949	10.00	20.00	40.00
—Originals on green vinyl					
48-0147	Nobody's Child/The Only Rose	1950	10.00	20.00	40.00
—Originals on green vinyl					
48-0214	Blue Ranger/Only a Rose from My Mother's Grave	1950	7.50	15.00	30.00
—Originals on green vinyl					
48-0224	Brand on My Heart/I'll Not Forget My Mother's Prayers	1950	7.50	15.00	30.00
—Originals on green vinyl					
48-0303	The Drunkard's Son/I Wonder Where You Are Tonight	1950	7.50	15.00	30.00
—Originals on green vinyl					
48-0328	I'm Movin' On/With This Ring I Thee Wed	1950	5.00	10.00	20.00
—Reissues on black vinyl					
48-0328	I'm Movin' On/With This Ring I Thee Wed	1950	10.00	20.00	40.00
—Originals on green vinyl					
48-0356	The Night I Stole Sammy Morgan's Gin/I Cried But My Tears Were Too Late	1950	7.50	15.00	30.00
—Originals on green vinyl					
48-0362	No Golden Tomorrow Ahead/You Broke the Chain That Held Our Hearts	1950	6.25	12.50	25.00
—Originals on green vinyl					
48-0363	Wasted Love/My Two Timin' Woman	1950	6.25	12.50	25.00
—Originals on green vinyl					
48-0364	Somewhere Along Life's Highway/Within This Broken Heart of Mine	1950	6.25	12.50	25.00
—Originals on green vinyl					
48-0400	The Golden Rocket/Paving the Highway with Tears	1950	7.50	15.00	30.00
—Originals on green vinyl					
48-0431	The Rhumba Boogie/You Pass Me By	1951	6.25	12.50	25.00
48-0498	Unwanted Sign Upon Your Heart/Your Locket Is My Broken Heart	1951	6.25	12.50	25.00
74-0151	Rome Wasn't Built in a Day/I Saw a Bird	1969	2.00	4.00	8.00
74-0251	That's When the Hurtin' Sets In/I'm Movin'	1969	2.00	4.00	8.00
74-0459	Blue Christmas/Nestor, The Long Eared Christmas Donkey	1971	—	—	—
—Unreleased					
74-0544	No One Will Ever Know/Seashores of Old Mexico	1971	2.00	4.00	8.00
74-0676	Canadian Pacific/My Way	1972	—	3.50	7.00
74-0818	The Governor's Hand/Rolling Thunder in My Mind	1972	—	3.50	7.00
74-0915	North to Chicago/Friend	1973	—	3.50	7.00
APBO-0215	Hello Love/Until the End of Time	1974	—	3.50	7.00
APBO-0307	That's You and Me/Brand on My Heart	1974	—	3.50	7.00
PB-10108	Easy to Love/Just a Faded Petal from a Beautiful Bouquet	1974	—	3.00	6.00
PB-10136	A Letter to Santa Claus/Christmas Roses	1974	—	3.50	7.00
PB-10225	Merry-Go-Round of Love/My Filipino Love	1975	—	3.00	6.00
PB-10338	Hijack/The Last Ride	1975	—	3.00	6.00
PB-10439	Colorado Country Morning/I Keep Dreaming of You All the Time	1975	—	3.00	6.00
PB-10459	Blue Christmas/Nestor, The Long Eared Christmas Donkey	1975	—	3.50	7.00
GB-10513	Hello Love/Until the End of Time	1976	—	2.00	4.00
—"Gold Standard Series" reissue					
PB-10681	Who's Been Here Since I've Been Gone/That's When He Dropped the World in My Hands	1976	—	3.00	6.00

7-Inch Extended Plays

RCA VICTOR

Number	Title (A Side/B Side)	Yr	VG	VG+	NM
547-0097	I'm Movin' On/Down the Trail of Achin' Hearts//The Rhumba Boogie/Bluebird Island	195?	5.00	10.00	20.00
—One record of 2-EP set EPB 3026					
547-0098	The Golden Rocket/Unwanted Sign Upon Your Heart/Music Makin' Mama from Memphis/Marriage Vow	195?	5.00	10.00	20.00
—One record of 2-EP set EPB 3026					
EPA 295	You Broke the Chain That Held Our Hearts/Wasted Love//No Golden Tomorrows Ahead/My Two Timin' Woman	195?	5.00	10.00	20.00
EPA 295 [PS]	Hank Snow Favorites	195?	5.00	10.00	20.00
EPA 310	*The Wreck of the Old '97/One More Ride/The Mystery of Number Five/Hobo Bill's Last Ride	195?	5.00	10.00	20.00
EPA 310 [PS]	Hank Snow Sings Famous Railroading Songs	195?	5.00	10.00	20.00
EPA 472	Frosty the Snowman/Silent Night//Christmas Roses/The Reindeer Boogie	1953	5.00	10.00	20.00
EPA 472 [PS]	A Country Christmas with Hank Snow	1953	5.00	10.00	20.00
EPA 503	These Things Shall Pass/He'll Understand and Say "Well Done"//Jesus Wept/The Glory Land March	195?	5.00	10.00	20.00
EPA 503 [PS]	These Things Shall Pass	195?	5.00	10.00	20.00
EPA 582	Twelfth Street Rag/Rainbow Boogie//Vaya Con Dios (May God Be with You)/Madison Madness	1954	5.00	10.00	20.00
EPA 582 [PS]	Hank Snow's Country Guitar	1954	5.00	10.00	20.00
547-0606	Just Keep a-Movin'/The Bill Is Falling Due//Caribbean/Blue Sea Blues	1955	5.00	10.00	20.00
—One record of 2-EP set EPB-1113					
547-0607	Can't Have You Blues/A Scale to Measure Love//Cuba Rhumba/Blossoms in the Springtime	1955	5.00	10.00	20.00
—One record of 2-EP set EPB-1113					
EPA 794	Country Classics	1956	5.00	10.00	20.00
EPA 794	I'm Movin' On/The Rhumba Boogie//The Golden Rocket/Music Making Mama from Memphis	1956	5.00	10.00	20.00
EPB-1113 [PS]	Just Keep a-Movin'	1955	5.00	10.00	20.00
—Gatefold cover for 547-0606 and 547-0607					
VLP-2812	Stolen Moments/Miller's Cave/Just a Faded Petal from a Beautiful Bouquet//Let Me Go Lover/The Gal Who Invented Kissing/Tangled Mind	196?	3.75	7.50	15.00
VLP-2812 [PS]	More Hank Snow Souvenirs	196?	3.75	7.50	15.00
EPB 3026 [PS]	Country Classics	195?	5.00	10.00	20.00
—Gatefold cover for 547-0097 and 547-0098					
EPA-5062	I'm Moving On/Marriage Vow//The Rhumba Boogie/With This Ring I Thee Wed	1958	3.75	7.50	15.00
EPA-5062 [PS]	Hank Snow (Gold Standard Series)	1958	3.75	7.50	15.00
EPA-5086	(Now and Then, There's) A Fool Such As I/The Golden Rocket//I Don't Hurt Anymore/The Star Spangled Waltz	195?	3.75	7.50	15.00
EPA-5086 [PS]	The Golden Rocket (Gold Standard Series)	195?	3.75	7.50	15.00

Albums

PAIR

Number	Title (A Side/B Side)	Yr	VG	VG+	NM
PDL2-1004 [(2)]	I'm Movin' On	1986	3.00	6.00	12.00

RCA CAMDEN

Number	Title (A Side/B Side)	Yr	VG	VG+	NM
ACL1-0124	Snowbird	1973	2.50	5.00	10.00
ACL2-0337 [(2)]	When My Blue Moon Turns to Gold Again	197?	3.75	7.50	15.00
CAL-514 [M]	The Singing Ranger	1959	5.00	10.00	20.00
CAS-514 [R]	The Singing Ranger	196?	3.00	6.00	12.00
ACL1-0540	I'm Movin' On	1974	2.50	5.00	10.00
CAL-680 [M]	The Southern Cannonball	1961	5.00	10.00	20.00
CAS-680 [R]	The Southern Cannonball	196?	3.00	6.00	12.00
CAL-722 [M]	The One and Only Hank Snow	1962	5.00	10.00	20.00
CAS-722 [R]	The One and Only Hank Snow	1962	3.00	6.00	12.00
CAL-782 [M]	The Last Ride	1963	5.00	10.00	20.00
CAS-782 [R]	The Last Ride	1963	3.00	6.00	12.00
CAL-836 [M]	Old and Great Songs	1964	3.75	7.50	15.00
CAS-836 [S]	Old and Great Songs	1964	3.00	6.00	12.00
CAL-910 [M]	The Highest Bidder	1965	3.00	6.00	12.00
CAS-910 [S]	The Highest Bidder	1965	3.75	7.50	15.00
CAL-964 [M]	Travelin' Blues	1966	3.00	6.00	12.00
CAS-964 [S]	Travelin' Blues	1966	3.75	7.50	15.00
CAL-2160 [M]	My Early Favorites	1967	3.75	7.50	15.00
CAS-2160 [S]	My Early Favorites	1967	3.00	6.00	12.00
CAS-2257	My Nova Scotia Home	1968	3.00	6.00	12.00
CAS-2348	I Went to Your Wedding	1969	3.00	6.00	12.00
CAS-2443	Memories Are Made of This	1970	3.00	6.00	12.00
CAS-2513	Lonesome Whistle	1972	3.00	6.00	12.00
CAS-2560	The Legend of Old Doc Brown	1972	3.00	6.00	12.00
CXS-9009 [(2)]	The Wreck of the 97	197?	3.75	7.50	15.00

RCA VICTOR

Number	Title (A Side/B Side)	Yr	VG	VG+	NM
DPL2-0134 [(2)]	The Living Legend	197?	25.00	50.00	100.00
—RCA Special Products release					
APL1-0162	Grand Ole Opry Favorites	1973	3.75	7.50	15.00
APL1-0441	Hello Love	1974	3.75	7.50	15.00
APL1-0608	That's You and Me	1974	3.75	7.50	15.00
APL1-0908	You're Easy to Love	1975	3.75	7.50	15.00

Number	Title (A Side/B Side)	Yr	VG	VG+	NM
❑ LPM-1113 [M]	Just Keep a-Movin'	1955	25.00	50.00	100.00
❑ LPM-1156 [M]	Old Doc Brown and Other Narrations	1955	25.00	50.00	100.00
❑ ANL1-1207	Grand Ole Opry Favorites	1975	2.50	5.00	10.00
—Reissue of APL1-0162					
❑ LPM-1233 [M]	Country Classics	1956	20.00	40.00	80.00
❑ APL1-1361	Live from Evangel Temple	1976	3.00	6.00	12.00
—With Jimmy Snow					
❑ LPM-1419 [M]	Country and Western Jamboree	1957	20.00	40.00	80.00
❑ LPM-1435 [M]	Hank Snow's Country Guitar	1957	20.00	40.00	80.00
❑ LPM-1638 [M]	Hank Snow Sings Sacred Songs	1958	15.00	30.00	60.00
❑ LPM-2043 [M]	Hank Snow Sings Jimmie Rodgers Songs	1959	12.50	25.00	50.00
❑ LSP-2043 [S]	Hank Snow Sings Jimmie Rodgers Songs	1959	20.00	40.00	80.00
❑ ANL1-2194	The Jimmie Rodgers Story	1977	2.50	5.00	10.00
—Reissue of 4708					
❑ LPM-2285 [M]	Hank Snow Souvenirs	1961	7.50	15.00	30.00
❑ LSP-2285 [S]	Hank Snow Souvenirs	1961	10.00	20.00	40.00
❑ APL1-2400	#104 — Still Movin' On	1977	3.00	6.00	12.00
❑ LPM-2458 [M]	Big Country Hits	1961	7.50	15.00	30.00
❑ LSP-2458 [S]	Big Country Hits	1961	10.00	20.00	40.00
❑ LPM-2675 [M]	I've Been Everywhere	1963	7.50	15.00	30.00
❑ LSP-2675 [S]	I've Been Everywhere	1963	10.00	20.00	40.00
❑ LPM-2705 [M]	Railroad Man	1963	7.50	15.00	30.00
❑ LSP-2705 [S]	Railroad Man	1963	10.00	20.00	40.00
❑ LPM-2812 [M]	More Hank Snow Souvenirs	1964	6.25	12.50	25.00
❑ LSP-2812 [S]	More Hank Snow Souvenirs	1964	7.50	15.00	30.00
❑ LPM-2901 [M]	Songs of Tragedy	1964	6.25	12.50	25.00
❑ LSP-2901 [S]	Songs of Tragedy	1964	7.50	15.00	30.00
❑ LPM-3026 [10]	Country Classics	1952	50.00	100.00	200.00
❑ LPM-3070 [10]	Hank Snow Sings	1952	45.00	90.00	180.00
❑ LPM-3131 [10]	Hank Snow Salutes Jimmie Rodgers	1953	45.00	90.00	180.00
❑ AHL1-3208	Mysterious Lady	1979	3.00	6.00	12.00
❑ LPM-3267 [10]	Hank Snow's Country Guitar	1954	45.00	90.00	180.00
❑ LPM-3317 [M]	Your Favorite Country Hits	1965	6.25	12.50	25.00
❑ LSP-3317 [S]	Your Favorite Country Hits	1965	7.50	15.00	30.00
❑ LPM-3378 [M]	Gloryland March	1965	6.25	12.50	25.00
❑ LSP-3378 [S]	Gloryland March	1965	7.50	15.00	30.00
❑ ANL1-3470	The Best of Hank Snow	1980	2.00	4.00	8.00
❑ LPM-3471 [M]	Heartbreak Trail -				
	A Tribute to the Sons of the Pioneers	1966	6.25	12.50	25.00
❑ LSP-3471 [S]	Heartbreak Trail -				
	A Tribute to the Sons of the Pioneers	1966	7.50	15.00	30.00
❑ LPM-3478 [M]	The Best of Hank Snow	1966	5.00	10.00	20.00
❑ LSP-3478 [S]	The Best of Hank Snow	1966	6.25	12.50	25.00
❑ AHL1-3511	Instrumentally Yours	1980	3.00	6.00	12.00
❑ LPM-3548 [M]	Guitar Stylings of Hank Snow	1966	6.25	12.50	25.00
❑ LSP-3548 [S]	Guitar Stylings of Hank Snow	1966	7.50	15.00	30.00
❑ LPM-3595 [M]	Gospel Train	1966	7.50	15.00	30.00
❑ LSP-3595 [S]	Gospel Train	1966	10.00	20.00	40.00
❑ LPM-3737 [M]	Snow in Hawaii	1967	7.50	15.00	30.00
❑ LSP-3737 [S]	Snow in Hawaii	1967	6.25	12.50	25.00
❑ LPM-3826 [M]	Christmas with Hank Snow	1967	7.50	15.00	30.00
❑ LSP-3826 [S]	Christmas with Hank Snow	1967	6.25	12.50	25.00
❑ LPM-3857 [M]	Spanish Fire Ball and Other				
	Great Hank Snow Stylings	1967	7.50	15.00	30.00
❑ LSP-3857 [S]	Spanish Fire Ball and Other				
	Great Hank Snow Stylings	1967	6.25	12.50	25.00
❑ LPM-3965 [M]	Hits, Hits and More Hits	1968	25.00	50.00	100.00
❑ LSP-3965 [S]	Hits, Hits and More Hits	1968	6.25	12.50	25.00
❑ LSP-4032	Tales of the Yukon	1968	6.25	12.50	25.00
❑ LSP-4122	Snow in All Seasons	1969	6.25	12.50	25.00
❑ LSP-4306	Hank Snow Sings in Memory of Jimmie Rodgers	1970	5.00	10.00	20.00
❑ LSP-4379	Cure for the Blues	1970	5.00	10.00	20.00
❑ LSP-4501	Tracks and Trains	1971	5.00	10.00	20.00
❑ LSP-4601	Award Winners	1971	5.00	10.00	20.00
❑ LSP-4708	The Jimmie Rodgers Story	1972	3.75	7.50	15.00
❑ LSP-4798	The Best of Hank Snow, Vol. 2	1972	3.75	7.50	15.00
❑ AHL1-5497	Collector's Series	1986	2.50	5.00	10.00
❑ LPM-6014 [(2)M]	This Is My Story	1966	10.00	20.00	40.00
❑ LSP-6014 [(2)S]	This Is My Story	1966	12.50	25.00	50.00
READER'S DIGEST					
❑ RDA-216 [(6)]	I'm Movin' On	197?	30.00	60.00	120.00
SCHOOL OF MUSIC					
❑ 1149 [M]	The Guitar	1958	62.50	125.00	250.00
—Deduct 20 percent if instruction book is missing					

SNOW, HANK, AND CHET ATKINS
Albums
RCA VICTOR

Number	Title (A Side/B Side)	Yr	VG	VG+	NM
❑ LPM-2952 [M]	Reminiscing	1964	6.25	12.50	25.00
❑ LSP-2952 [S]	Reminiscing	1964	7.50	15.00	30.00
❑ LSP-4254	By Special Request - C.B. Atkins and C.E. Snow	1970	5.00	10.00	20.00

SNOW, HANK, AND ANITA CARTER
45s
RCA VICTOR

Number	Title (A Side/B Side)	Yr	VG	VG+	NM
❑ 47-6500	Keep Your Promise, Willie Thomas/It's You, Only You, That I Love	1956	3.75	7.50	15.00
❑ 48-0441	Down the Trail of Achin' Hearts/Bluebird Island	1951	6.25	12.50	25.00

Albums
RCA VICTOR

Number	Title (A Side/B Side)	Yr	VG	VG+	NM
❑ LPM-2580 [M]	Together Again	1962	7.50	15.00	30.00
❑ LSP-2580 [S]	Together Again	1962	10.00	20.00	40.00

SNOW, HANK, AND KELLY FOXTON
45s
RCA

Number	Title (A Side/B Side)	Yr	VG	VG+	NM
❑ PB-11891	Hasn't It Been Good Together/It Was Love	1980	—	2.50	5.00
❑ PB-11967	There's Something About You/ All I Want to Do Is Touch You	1980	—	2.50	5.00
❑ PB-12102	Pain Didn't Shout/Check	1980	—	2.50	5.00
❑ PB-12235	Things/Forbidden Lovers	1981	—	2.50	5.00

Albums
RCA VICTOR

Number	Title (A Side/B Side)	Yr	VG	VG+	NM
❑ AHL1-3496	Lovingly Yours	1980	2.50	5.00	10.00
❑ AYL1-3987	Win Some, Lose Some, Lonesome	1981	2.50	5.00	10.00

SNOW, HANK; PORTER WAGONER; HANK LOCKLIN
Albums
RCA VICTOR

Number	Title (A Side/B Side)	Yr	VG	VG+	NM
❑ LPM-2723 [M]	Three Country Gentlemen	1963	7.50	15.00	30.00
❑ LSP-2723 [S]	Three Country Gentlemen	1963	10.00	20.00	40.00

SNOW, PHOEBE
12-Inch Singles
ELEKTRA

Number	Title (A Side/B Side)	Yr	VG	VG+	NM
❑ ED 5370 [DJ]	If I Can Just Get Through the Night (same on both sides)	1989	—	3.00	6.00
❑ ED 5383 [DJ]	Something Real (same on both sides)	1989	—	3.00	6.00

COLUMBIA

Number	Title (A Side/B Side)	Yr	VG	VG+	NM
❑ 10315	Two Fisted Love/Inspired Insanity	1976	—	2.50	5.00
❑ 10351	All Over/No Regrets	1976	—	2.50	5.00
❑ 10463	Shakey Ground/Don't Sleep with Your Eyes Closed	1976	—	2.50	5.00
❑ 10504	Teach Me Tonight/Autobiography (Shine, Shine, Shine)	1977	—	2.50	5.00
❑ 10626	Never Letting Go/The Middle of the Night	1977	—	2.50	5.00
❑ 10654	Love Makes a Woman/Electra	1977	—	2.50	5.00
❑ 10856	Every Night/Random Time	1978	—	2.50	5.00

ELEKTRA

Number	Title (A Side/B Side)	Yr	VG	VG+	NM
❑ 69290	Something Real/Best of My Love	1989	—	—	3.00
❑ 69305	If I Can Just Get Through the Night/Soothin'	1989	—	—	3.00

MIRAGE

Number	Title (A Side/B Side)	Yr	VG	VG+	NM
❑ 3800	Games/Down in the Basement	1981	—	2.00	4.00
❑ 3818	Mercy, Mercy, Mercy/Something Good	1981	—	2.00	4.00
❑ 3843	Rock Away/Baby Please	1981	—	2.00	4.00

SHELTER

Number	Title (A Side/B Side)	Yr	VG	VG+	NM
❑ 40278	Harpo's Blues/Let the Good Times Roll	1974	—	2.50	5.00
❑ 40353	Poetry Man/Either or Both	1974	—	3.00	6.00
❑ 40400	Easy Street/Harpo's Blues	1975	—	2.50	5.00

Albums
COLUMBIA

Number	Title (A Side/B Side)	Yr	VG	VG+	NM
❑ PC 33952	Second Childhood	1976	2.50	5.00	10.00
—Original with no bar code					
❑ PC 33952	Second Childhood	198?	2.00	4.00	8.00
—Budget-line reissue with bar code					
❑ PCQ 33952 [Q]	Second Childhood	1976	3.75	7.50	15.00
❑ PC 34387	It Looks Like Snow	1976	2.50	5.00	10.00
—Original with no bar code					
❑ PC 34387	It Looks Like Snow	198?	2.00	4.00	8.00
—Budget-line reissue with bar code					
❑ JC 34875	Never Letting Go	1977	2.50	5.00	10.00
❑ JC 35456	Against the Grain	1978	2.50	5.00	10.00
❑ JC 37091	The Best of Phoebe Snow	1981	2.50	5.00	10.00
❑ PC 37091	The Best of Phoebe Snow	1981	2.00	4.00	8.00
—Budget-line reissue					

DCC COMPACT CLASSICS

Number	Title (A Side/B Side)	Yr	VG	VG+	NM
❑ LPZ-2027	Phoebe Snow	1996	7.50	15.00	30.00
—Audiophile vinyl					

ELEKTRA

Number	Title (A Side/B Side)	Yr	VG	VG+	NM
❑ 60852	Something Real	1989	2.50	5.00	10.00

MCA

Number	Title (A Side/B Side)	Yr	VG	VG+	NM
❑ 37119	Phoebe Snow	198?	2.00	4.00	8.00
—Budget-line reissue of Shelter LP					

MIRAGE

Number	Title (A Side/B Side)	Yr	VG	VG+	NM
❑ SD 19297	Rock Away	1981	2.50	5.00	10.00

SHELTER

Number	Title (A Side/B Side)	Yr	VG	VG+	NM
❑ 2109	Phoebe Snow	1974	2.50	5.00	10.00
❑ 52017	Phoebe Snow	1977	2.00	4.00	8.00
—Reissue with ABC distribution					

SNOW MEN, THE Early version of THE SUNRAYS.
45s
CHALLENGE

Number	Title (A Side/B Side)	Yr	VG	VG+	NM
❑ 59227	Ski Storm (Part 1)/Ski Storm (Part 2)	1964	7.50	15.00	30.00

SNYDER, TERRY, AND THE ALL-STARS See ENOCH LIGHT.

SOCIALITES, THE
45s
ARRAWAK

Number	Title (A Side/B Side)	Yr	VG	VG+	NM
❑ 1004	Jimmy/The Click	1962	5.00	10.00	20.00

WARNER BROS.

Number	Title (A Side/B Side)	Yr	VG	VG+	NM
❑ 5476	You're Losing Your Touch/Jive Jimmy	1964	3.00	6.00	12.00

SOCIETY'S CHILDREN
45s
ATCO

Number	Title (A Side/B Side)	Yr	VG	VG+	NM
❑ 6538	White Christmas/I'll Let You Know	1967	3.00	6.00	12.00
❑ 6553	Count the Ways/Golden Child	1968	2.50	5.00	10.00
❑ 6597	Live for Today/I'll Let You Know	1968	2.50	5.00	10.00
❑ 6618	A Tribute to the Four Seasons/Golden Child	1968	5.00	10.00	20.00

SOF-TONES, THE
45s
CEE BEE

Number	Title (A Side/B Side)	Yr	VG	VG+	NM
❑ 1062	Oh Why!/(B-side unknown)	195?	4000.	6000.	8000.

SOFT MACHINE, THE
45s
PROBE

Number	Title (A Side/B Side)	Yr	VG	VG+	NM
❑ 452	Joy of a Toy/Why Are We Sleeping	1969	2.50	5.00	10.00

Albums
ACCORD

Number	Title (A Side/B Side)	Yr	VG	VG+	NM
❑ SN-7178	Memories	1981	2.50	5.00	10.00

COLUMBIA

Number	Title (A Side/B Side)	Yr	VG	VG+	NM
❑ G 30339 [(2)]	Third	1970	3.75	7.50	15.00
❑ C 30754	Fourth	1971	3.00	6.00	12.00
❑ KC 31604	5	1972	3.00	6.00	12.00
❑ KG 32260 [(2)]	Six	1973	3.75	7.50	15.00
❑ KC 32716	Seven	1974	3.00	6.00	12.00

Number	Title (A Side/B Side)	Yr	VG	VG+	NM
COMMAND					
❏ 964 SD [(2)]	Soft Machine	1973	3.75	7.50	15.00
—Reissue of Probe LPs in one package					
PROBE					
❏ CPLP-4500	The Soft Machine	1968	10.00	20.00	40.00
—Cover with moving parts					
❏ CPLP-4500	The Soft Machine	1969	5.00	10.00	20.00
—Regular cover					
❏ CPLP-4505	The Soft Machine, Vol. 2	1969	6.25	12.50	25.00

SOLDIER BOYS, THE Also see DON COVAY.
45s
Number	Title (A Side/B Side)	Yr	VG	VG+	NM
SCEPTER					
❏ 1230	I'm Your Soldier Boy/You Picked Me	1962	15.00	30.00	60.00

SOLITAIRES, THE
45s
Number	Title (A Side/B Side)	Yr	VG	VG+	NM
ARGO					
❏ 5316	Walking Along/Please Kiss This Letter	1958	7.50	15.00	30.00
MGM					
❏ 13221	Fool That I Am/Fair Weather Lover	1964	7.50	15.00	30.00
OLD TOWN					
❏ 1000	Blue Valentine/Wonder Boy	1954	100.00	200.00	400.00
—Black vinyl					
❏ 1000	Blue Valentine/Wonder Boy	1954	375.00	750.00	1500.
—Red vinyl					
❏ 1003	Chapel of St. Clair/If I Loved You	1954	—	—	—
—Unreleased?					
❏ 1006/7	Please Remember My Heart/South of the Border	1954	175.00	350.00	700.00
—Black vinyl					
❏ 1006/7	Please Remember My Heart/South of the Border	1954	1000.	2000.	3000.
—Red vinyl					
❏ 1006/8	Please Remember My Heart/Chances I've Taken	1954	37.50	75.00	150.00
❏ 1008	Chances I've Taken/Lonely	1954	175.00	350.00	700.00
❏ 1008	Please Remember My Heart/Chances I've Taken	196?	6.25	12.50	25.00
—Blue label					
❏ 1010	I Don't Stand a Ghost of a Chance/Girl of Mine	1955	125.00	250.00	500.00
❏ 1012	My Dear/What Did She Say	1955	100.00	200.00	400.00
—Logo in Old English style					
❏ 1012	My Dear/What Did She Say	1956	18.75	37.50	75.00
—Logo in block letters					
❏ 1014	The Wedding/Don't Fall in Love	1955	25.00	50.00	100.00
❏ 1015	Magic Rose/Later for You Baby	1955	25.00	50.00	100.00
❏ 1019	The Honeymoon/Fine Little Girl	1956	25.00	50.00	100.00
❏ 1026	You've Sinned/The Angels Sang	1956	25.00	50.00	100.00
❏ 1026	You've Sinned/You're Back with Me	1956	75.00	150.00	300.00
❏ 1032	Give Me One More Chance/Nothing Like a Little Love	1956	50.00	100.00	200.00
❏ 1034	Walking Along/Please Kiss This Letter	1957	18.75	37.50	75.00
—Yellow label					
❏ 1034	Walking Along/Please Kiss This Letter	196?	6.25	12.50	25.00
—Blue label					
❏ 1044	I Really Love You So/Thrill of Love	1957	100.00	200.00	400.00
❏ 1049	Walkin' and Talkin'/No More Sorrows	1958	25.00	50.00	100.00
❏ 1059	Please Remember My Heart/Big Mary's House	1958	10.00	20.00	40.00
❏ 1066	Embraceable You/Round Goes My Heart	1959	10.00	20.00	40.00
❏ 1071	Light a Candle in the Chapel/Helpless	1959	10.00	20.00	40.00
❏ 1096	Lonesome Lover/Pretty Thing	1961	10.00	20.00	40.00
❏ 1139	The Time Is Here/Honey Babe	1963	7.50	15.00	30.00

SOME OF CHET'S FRIENDS Also see CHET ATKINS.
45s
Number	Title (A Side/B Side)	Yr	VG	VG+	NM
RCA VICTOR					
❏ 47-9229	Chet's Tune/Country Gentleman	1967	2.50	5.00	10.00
❏ 47-9229 [PS]	Chet's Tune/Country Gentleman	1967	3.75	7.50	15.00
❏ 74-0799	Chet's Tune (Part 1)/Chet's Tune (Part 2)	1972	—	3.00	6.00

SOMETHING WILD
45s
Number	Title (A Side/B Side)	Yr	VG	VG+	NM
PSYCHEDELIC					
❏ 1691	Trippin' Out/She's Kinda Weird	1966	12.50	25.00	50.00

SOMETHING YOUNG
45s
Number	Title (A Side/B Side)	Yr	VG	VG+	NM
FONTANA					
❏ 1556	Oh, Don't Come Crying/The Words I'm Seeking	1966	6.25	12.50	25.00

SOMMERS, JOANIE
45s
Number	Title (A Side/B Side)	Yr	VG	VG+	NM
ABC					
❏ 12323	Peppermint Choo Choo/Peppermint Engineer	1978	—	2.50	5.00
CAPITOL					
❏ 5936	Trains and Boats and Planes/Yesterday's Morning	1967	2.00	4.00	8.00
COLUMBIA					
❏ 43567	You've Got Possibilities/Never Throw Your Dreams	1966	2.00	4.00	8.00
❏ 43731	Alfie/You Take What Comes Along	1966	2.00	4.00	8.00
❏ 43950	It Doesn't Matter Anymore/Take a Broken Heart	1966	2.00	4.00	8.00
HAPPY TIGER					
❏ 522	Step Inside Love/Little Girl from Greenwood, Ga.	1970	—	3.00	6.00
❏ 537	Sunshine After the Rain/Tell Him	1970	—	3.00	6.00
WARNER BROS.					
❏ 5157	One Boy/I'll Never Be Free	1960	3.75	7.50	15.00
❏ 5157 [DJ]	One Boy/I'll Never Be Free	1960	12.50	25.00	50.00
—Promo only on gold vinyl					
❏ 5177	Be My Love/Why Don't You Do Right	1960	3.75	7.50	15.00
❏ 5183	Ruby Duby Du/Bob White	1960	3.75	7.50	15.00
❏ 5201	I Don't Want to Walk Without You/Seems Like Long, Long Ago	1961	3.75	7.50	15.00
❏ 5201 [DJ]	I Don't Want to Walk Without You/Seems Like Long, Long Ago	1961	12.50	25.00	50.00
—Promo only on gold vinyl					

Number	Title (A Side/B Side)	Yr	VG	VG+	NM
❏ 5201 [PS]	I Don't Want to Walk Without You/Seems Like Long, Long Ago	1961	12.50	25.00	50.00
—Sleeve is promo only					
❏ 5226	Piano Boy/Serenade of the Bells	1961	3.75	7.50	15.00
❏ 5241	Makin' Whoopee/What's Wrong with Me	1961	3.75	7.50	15.00
❏ 5275	Johnny Get Angry/(Theme from) A Summer Place	1962	5.00	10.00	20.00
❏ 5308	When the Boys Get Together/Passing Strangers	1962	3.00	6.00	12.00
❏ 5324	Goodbye Joey/Bobby's Hobbies	1962	3.00	6.00	12.00
❏ 5339	Memories, Memories/Since Randy Moved Away	1963	3.00	6.00	12.00
❏ 5350	Little Bit of Everything/Henny Penny	1963	3.00	6.00	12.00
❏ 5361	One Boy/June Is Bustin' Out All Over	1963	3.00	6.00	12.00
❏ 5374	Little Girl Bad/Wishing Well	1963	3.00	6.00	12.00
❏ 5390	Goodbye Summer/Big Man	1963	3.00	6.00	12.00
❏ 5437	I'd Be So Good for You/I'm Gonna Know He's Mine	1964	2.50	5.00	10.00
❏ 5454	If You Love Him/I Think I'm Gonna Cry Now	1964	2.50	5.00	10.00
❏ 5507	Makin' Whoopee/What's Wrong with Me + 2	1961	6.25	12.50	25.00
—Part of Warner Bros. "+2" series, with two new songs and excerpts of two prior hits					
❏ 5507 [PS]	Makin' Whoopee/What's Wrong with Me + 2	1961	7.50	15.00	30.00
❏ 5629	Don't Pity Me/My Block	1965	2.50	5.00	10.00
❏ 7129	Johnny Get Angry/One Boy	1968	—	3.00	6.00
—"Back to Back Hits" series -- originals have green labels with "W7" logo					
❏ 7251	Great Divide/Talk Until Midnight	1968	2.00	4.00	8.00
Albums					
COLUMBIA					
❏ CL 2495 [M]	Come Alive	1966	5.00	10.00	20.00
❏ CS 9295 [S]	Come Alive	1966	6.25	12.50	25.00
DISCOVERY					
❏ DS-883	Dream	1983	3.00	6.00	12.00
—With Bob Florence					
WARNER BROS.					
❏ W 1346 [M]	Positively the Most	1960	7.50	15.00	30.00
❏ WS 1346 [S]	Positively the Most	1960	10.00	20.00	40.00
❏ B 1348 [M]	Behind Closed Doors at a Recording Session	1960	37.50	75.00	150.00
—Record comes in a box with a booklet included					
❏ W 1412 [M]	Joanie Sommers	1961	7.50	15.00	30.00
❏ WS 1412 [S]	Joanie Sommers	1961	10.00	20.00	40.00
❏ W 1436 [M]	For Those Who Think Young	1962	7.50	15.00	30.00
❏ WS 1436 [S]	For Those Who Think Young	1962	10.00	20.00	40.00
❏ W 1470 [M]	Johnny Get Angry	1962	10.00	20.00	40.00
❏ WS 1470 [S]	Johnny Get Angry	1962	12.50	25.00	50.00
❏ W 1474 [M]	Let's Talk About Love	1962	7.50	15.00	30.00
❏ WS 1474 [S]	Let's Talk About Love	1962	10.00	20.00	40.00
❏ W 1504 [M]	Sommers' Seasons	1963	6.25	12.50	25.00
❏ WS 1504 [S]	Sommers' Seasons	1963	7.50	15.00	30.00
❏ W 1575 [M]	Softly, The Brazilian Sound	1964	6.25	12.50	25.00
❏ WS 1575 [S]	Softly, The Brazilian Sound	1964	7.50	15.00	30.00

SOMMERS, RONNY See SONNY.

SONICS, THE (1) Male vocal group.
45s
Number	Title (A Side/B Side)	Yr	VG	VG+	NM
AMCO					
❏ 001	It's You/Preacher Man	1962	50.00	100.00	200.00
CHECKER					
❏ 922	This Broken Heart/You Made Me Cry	1959	6.25	12.50	25.00
HARVARD					
❏ 801	This Broken Heart/You Made Me Cry	1959	100.00	200.00	400.00
❏ 922	This Broken Heart/You Made Me Cry	1959	12.50	25.00	50.00
JAMIE					
❏ 1235	Sugaree/Beautiful Brown Eyes	1962	5.00	10.00	20.00
X-TRA					
❏ 107	Once in a Lifetime/It Ain't True	1958	500.00	1000.	2000.

SONICS, THE (2) Rock band from the Pacific Northwest.
45s
Number	Title (A Side/B Side)	Yr	VG	VG+	NM
BURDETTE					
❏ 106	Dirty Old Man/Bama Lama Bama Loo	1975	2.00	4.00	8.00
ETIQUETTE					
❏ 11	Keep a-Knockin'/The Witch	1965	7.50	15.00	30.00
❏ 16	The Hustler/Boss Hoss	1965	7.50	15.00	30.00
❏ 18	Don't Be Afraid of the Dark/Shot Down	1965	7.50	15.00	30.00
❏ 22	Don't Believe in Christmas/Christmas Spirit	1965	7.50	15.00	30.00
—B-side by the Wailers					
❏ 23	Louie Louie/Cinderella	1966	7.50	15.00	30.00
GREAT NORTHWEST					
❏ 702	The Witch/Bama Lama Bama Loo	1979	—	2.50	5.00
JERDEN					
❏ 809	Love Lights/You Got Your Head On Backwards	1966	3.75	7.50	15.00
❏ 810	The Witch/Like No Other	1966	3.75	7.50	15.00
❏ 811	Psycho/Maintaining My Cool	1966	3.75	7.50	15.00
NORTON					
❏ 45-066	Don't Believe in Christmas/Santa Claus	1997	—	—	2.00
—A-side is reissue of Etiquette 22					
❏ 45-066 [PS]	Don't Believe in Christmas/Santa Claus	1997	—	—	2.00
PICCADILLY					
❏ 244	Anyway the Wind Blows/Lost Love	1967	5.00	10.00	20.00
—A-side written by Frank Zappa					
UNI					
❏ 55039	Anyway the Wind Blows/Lost Love	1967	3.75	7.50	15.00
—A-side written by Frank Zappa					
Albums					
BEAT ROCKET					
❏ BR 114	Introducing the Sonics	199?	3.00	6.00	12.00
BOMP!					
❏ 4011	Sinderella	1980	3.75	7.50	15.00
BUCKSHOT					
❏ 001	Explosives	1973	50.00	100.00	200.00
ETIQUETTE					
❏ ETALB-024 [M]	Here Are the Sonics!!!	1965	50.00	100.00	200.00
—Purple label					
❏ ETALB-024 [M]	Here Are the Sonics!!!	1965	62.50	125.00	250.00
—Red label					
❏ ETLPS-024 [S]	Here Are the Sonics!!!	1965	75.00	150.00	300.00
—Purple label					

Number	Title (A Side/B Side)	Yr	VG	VG+	NM
❏ ETLPS-024 [S] Here Are the Sonics!!!		1965	100.00	200.00	400.00
—Red label					
❏ ETLPS-024	Here Are the Sonics!!!	1984	2.50	5.00	10.00
—Purple label, flimsier vinyl, with date on back cover					
❏ ETALB-027 [M] The Sonics Boom		1966	75.00	150.00	300.00
❏ ETLPS-027 [R] The Sonics Boom		1966	50.00	100.00	200.00
❏ ETLPS-027	The Sonics Boom	1984	2.50	5.00	10.00
—Flimsier vinyl, with date on back cover					
FIRST AMERICAN					
❏ FA-7715	Original Northwest Punk	1978	5.00	10.00	20.00
❏ FA-7719	Unreleased	1980	5.00	10.00	20.00
❏ FA-7779	Fire and Ice	1983	5.00	10.00	20.00
JERDEN					
❏ JRL-7007 [M] Introducing the Sonics		1967	50.00	100.00	200.00
❏ JRS-7007 [R] Introducing the Sonics		1967	37.50	75.00	150.00

SONICS, THE (2); THE WAILERS; THE GALAXIES
Albums

Number	Title (A Side/B Side)	Yr	VG	VG+	NM
ETIQUETTE					
❏ ETALB-025 [M] Merry Christmas		1965	125.00	250.00	500.00
❏ ETALB-025	Merry Christmas	1984	2.50	5.00	10.00
—Flimsier vinyl, with date on back cover					

SONICS, THE (U) Some of these could be group (1); none of these are group (2).
45s

Number	Title (A Side/B Side)	Yr	VG	VG+	NM
ARMONIA					
❏ 102	Funny/I Get That Feeling	1962	37.50	75.00	150.00
GAITY					
❏ 114	Marlene/(B-side unknown)	1959	1000.	1500.	2000.
GROOVE					
❏ 0112	Bumble Bee/As I Live On	1955	50.00	100.00	200.00
NOCTURNE					
❏ 110	Triangle Love/Evil Eye	1959	20.00	40.00	80.00
RKO UNIQUE					
❏ 411	Triangle Love/Evil Eye	1957	15.00	30.00	60.00

SONNETS, THE
45s

Number	Title (A Side/B Side)	Yr	VG	VG+	NM
GUYDEN					
❏ 2112	I Can't Get Sentimental/Forever for You	1964	3.75	7.50	15.00
HERALD					
❏ 477	Please Won't You Call Me/ Why Should We Break Up	1956	15.00	30.00	60.00

SONNY Contains many records he made under aliases. Also see SONNY AND CHER.
45s

Number	Title (A Side/B Side)	Yr	VG	VG+	NM
ATCO					
❏ 6369	Laugh at Me/Tony	1965	3.00	6.00	12.00
—B-side credited to "Sonny's Group"					
❏ 6386	The Revolution Kind/Georgia and John Quetzal	1965	3.00	6.00	12.00
❏ 6505	Misty Roses/I Told My Girl to Go Away	1967	2.50	5.00	10.00
❏ 6531	Pammie's on a Bummer/My Best Friend's Girl Is Out of Sight	1967	2.50	5.00	10.00
FIDELITY					
❏ 3020	Wearing Black/Don't Have to Tell Me	1960	6.25	12.50	25.00
—As "Don Christy"					
GO					
❏ 1001	As Long As You Love Me/I'll Always Be Grateful	1960	6.25	12.50	25.00
—As "Don Christy"					
HIGHLAND					
❏ 1160	I'll Change/Try It Out on Me	1963	7.50	15.00	30.00
—As "Sonny Bono"					
MCA					
❏ 40139	Rub Your Nose/Laugh at Me	1973	—	2.00	4.00
—As "Sonny Bono"					
❏ 40271	Our Last Show/Classified 1A	1974	—	2.00	4.00
—As "Sonny Bono"					
NAME					
❏ 3	As Long As You Love Me/I'll Always Be Grateful	1960	6.25	12.50	25.00
—As "Don Christy"					
SPECIALTY					
❏ 672	Wearing Black/One Little Answer	1959	6.25	12.50	25.00
—As "Don Christy"					
❏ 733	One Little Answer/Comin' Down the Chimney	1974	—	3.00	6.00
—As "Sonny Bono and Little Tootsie"					
SWAMI					
❏ 1001	Don't Shake My Tree/(Mama) Come Get Your Baby Boy	1961	6.25	12.50	25.00
—As "Ronny Sommers"					
VEE JAY					
❏ 710	Midnight Surf/Ride the Wild Quetzal	1966	6.25	12.50	25.00
—As "Sonny Bono"					
Albums					
ATCO					
❏ 33-229 [M] Inner Views		1967	5.00	10.00	20.00
❏ SD 33-229 [S] Inner Views		1967	5.00	10.00	20.00

SONNY AND CHER Includes early records as "Caesar and Cleo." Also see CHER; SONNY.
45s

Number	Title (A Side/B Side)	Yr	VG	VG+	NM
ATCO					
❏ 6345	Just You/Sing C'est La Vie	1965	2.50	5.00	10.00
❏ 6359	I Got You Babe/It's Gonna Rain	1965	3.00	6.00	12.00
❏ 6381	But You're Mine/Hello	1965	3.00	6.00	12.00
❏ 6395	What Now My Love/I Look for You	1965	3.00	6.00	12.00
❏ 6420	Have I Stayed Too Long/Leave Me Be	1966	2.50	5.00	10.00
❏ 6440	Little Man/Monday	1966	2.50	5.00	10.00
❏ 6449	Living for You/Love Don't Come	1966	2.50	5.00	10.00
❏ 6461	The Beat Goes On/Love Don't Come	1967	3.00	6.00	12.00
❏ 6480	A Beautiful Story/Podunk	1967	2.50	5.00	10.00
❏ 6486	Plastic Man/It's the Little Things	1967	2.50	5.00	10.00
❏ 6507	It's the Little Things/Don't Talk to Strangers	1967	2.50	5.00	10.00
❏ 6541	Good Combination/You and Me	1968	2.50	5.00	10.00
❏ 6555	Circus/I Would Marry You Today	1968	2.50	5.00	10.00
❏ 6605	You Gotta Have a Thing of Your Own/ I Got You Babe	1968	2.50	5.00	10.00

Number	Title (A Side/B Side)	Yr	VG	VG+	NM
❏ 6684	You're a Friend of Mine/ I Would Marry You Today	1969	2.50	5.00	10.00
❏ 6758	Get It Together/Hold Me Tighter	1970	2.00	4.00	8.00
KAPP					
❏ 2141	Real People/Somebody	1971	—	2.00	4.00
❏ 2151	All I Ever Need Is You/I Got You Babe	1971	—	2.50	5.00
❏ 2163	A Cowboy's Work Is Never Done/Somebody	1972	—	2.50	5.00
❏ 2176	When You Say Love/Crystal Clear and Muddy Waters	1972	—	2.00	4.00
MCA					
❏ 40026	Mama Was a Rock and Roll Singer, Papa Used to Write All Her Songs (Parts 1 & 2)	1973	—	2.00	4.00
❏ 40083	The Greatest Show on Earth/ You Know Darn Well	1973	—	2.00	4.00
PHILCO-FORD					
❏ HP-8	I Got You Babe/The Beat Goes On	1967	6.25	12.50	25.00
—4-inch plastic "Hip Pocket Record" with color sleeve					
REPRISE					
❏ 0308	Love Is Strange/Do You Want to Dance	1964	5.00	10.00	20.00
—As "Caesar and Cleo"					
❏ 0309	Baby Don't Go/Walkin' the Quetzal	1964	5.00	10.00	20.00
❏ 0392	Baby Don't Go/Walkin' the Quetzal	1965	3.75	7.50	15.00
❏ 0419	Love Is Strange/Let the Good Times Roll	1965	5.00	10.00	20.00
❏ 0419 [PS]	Love Is Strange/Let the Good Times Roll	1965	10.00	20.00	40.00
—As "Caesar and Cleo"					
❏ 0723	Baby Don't Go/Love Is Strange	1968	—	2.50	5.00
—"Back to Back Hits" series -- originals have both "r:" and "W7" logos					
VAULT					
❏ 909	The Letter/Spring Fever	1964	7.50	15.00	30.00
—As "Caesar and Cleo"					
❏ 916	The Letter/Spring Fever	1965	3.00	6.00	12.00
❏ 916 [PS]	The Letter/Spring Fever	1965	12.50	25.00	50.00
WARNER BROS.					
❏ 8341	You're Not Right for Me/Wrong Number	1977	—	2.50	5.00

7-Inch Extended Plays

Number	Title (A Side/B Side)	Yr	VG	VG+	NM
ATCO					
❏ LSD 33-177	It's Gonna Rain/You've Really Got a Hold on Me/ /I Got You Babe/The Letter/Why Don't They Let Us Fall in Love	1965	6.25	12.50	25.00
—Jukebox issue; small hole, plays at 33 1/3 rpm					
❏ LSD 33-177 [PS] Look At Us		1965	6.25	12.50	25.00
KAPP					
❏ 34875	More Today Than Yesterday/I Love What You Did With The Love I Gave You/Here Comes That Rainy Day Feeling//Crystal Clear-Muddy Waters/United We Stand/ All I Ever Need Is You	1972	2.50	5.00	10.00
—Jukebox issue; small hole, plays at 33 1/3 rpm					
❏ 34875 [PS]	All I Ever Need Is You	1972	2.50	5.00	10.00
—Part of "Little LP" series (LLP #184)					

Albums

Number	Title (A Side/B Side)	Yr	VG	VG+	NM
ATCO					
❏ 33-177 [M]	Look At Us	1965	3.75	7.50	15.00
—With white box that says "Includes Their Big Hit 'I Got You Babe'" (second edition)					
❏ 33-177 [M]	Look At Us	1965	5.00	10.00	20.00
—Without white box that says "Includes Their Big Hit 'I Got You Babe'" (original)					
❏ SD 33-177 [S]	Look At Us	1965	3.75	7.50	15.00
—With white box that says "Includes Their Big Hit 'I Got You Babe'" (second edition)					
❏ SD 33-177 [S]	Look At Us	1965	6.25	12.50	25.00
—Without white box that says "Includes Their Big Hit 'I Got You Babe'" (original)					
❏ 33-183 [M]	The Wondrous World of Sonny and Cher	1966	3.75	7.50	15.00
❏ SD 33-183 [S]	The Wondrous World of Sonny and Cher	1966	5.00	10.00	20.00
❏ 33-203 [M]	In Case You're in Love	1967	3.75	7.50	15.00
❏ SD 33-203 [S]	In Case You're in Love	1967	5.00	10.00	20.00
❏ 33-214 [M]	Good Times	1967	3.75	7.50	15.00
❏ SD 33-214 [S]	Good Times	1967	5.00	10.00	20.00
❏ 33-219 [M]	The Best of Sonny and Cher	1967	3.75	7.50	15.00
❏ SD 33-219 [P]	The Best of Sonny and Cher	1967	5.00	10.00	20.00
—"What Now My Love," "A Beautiful Story," "But You're Mine" and "Laugh at Me" are rechanneled					
❏ SD 2-804 [(2)]	The Two of Us	1972	5.00	10.00	20.00
—Combines "Look at Us" and "In Case You're in Love"					
❏ A2M 5177 [(2)M] Sonny & Cher's Greatest Hits		1967	7.50	15.00	30.00
—Columbia Record Club exclusive					
❏ A2S 5178 [(2)S] Sonny & Cher's Greatest Hits		1967	7.50	15.00	30.00
—Columbia Record Club exclusive					
❏ SD 11000	The Beat Goes On	1975	3.75	7.50	15.00
KAPP					
❏ KS-3654	Sonny & Cher Live	1971	3.75	7.50	15.00
❏ KS-3660	All I Ever Need Is You	1972	3.75	7.50	15.00
—Orange and red swirl label					
❏ KS-3660	All I Ever Need Is You	1972	5.00	10.00	20.00
—Black label with red "Kapp" cap at top					
❏ KS-3660	All I Ever Need Is You	1972	7.50	15.00	30.00
—Red label with red "Kapp" cap at top					
❏ KRS-5560	All I Ever Need Is You	1972	3.00	6.00	12.00
—Reissue; orange and red swirl label; some of these have a sticker on the front cover with the new number with no difference in value					
❏ ST-94312	All I Ever Need Is You	1972	5.00	10.00	20.00
—Capitol Record Club edition					
MCA					
❏ 2009	Sonny & Cher Live	1973	3.00	6.00	12.00
—Reissue of Kapp 3654					
❏ 2021	All I Ever Need Is You	1973	3.00	6.00	12.00
—Reissue of Kapp 3660					
❏ 2101	Mama Was a Rock & Roll Singer Papa Used to Write All Her Songs	1973	3.00	6.00	12.00
❏ 2117	Greatest Hits	1974	3.00	6.00	12.00
❏ 2-8004 [(2)]	Sonny & Cher Live in Las Vegas, Vol. 2	1973	3.75	7.50	15.00
PAIR					
❏ PDL2-1140 [(2)] Sonny & Cher At Their Best		1986	3.00	6.00	12.00
REPRISE					
❏ R 6177 [M]	Baby Don't Go	1965	7.50	15.00	30.00
❏ RS 6177 [P]	Baby Don't Go	1965	7.50	15.00	30.00
—By "Sonny & Cher & Friends" (also includes The Lettermen, Bill Medley and The Blendells)					
TVP					
❏ TVP-1021	The Hits of Sonny & Cher	1977	3.00	6.00	12.00

S

Number	Title (A Side/B Side)	Yr	VG	VG+	NM

SONNY AND THE DEMONS
Albums
UNITED ARTISTS

Number	Title (A Side/B Side)	Yr	VG	VG+	NM
❏ UAL-3316 [M]	Drag Kings	1964	12.50	25.00	50.00
❏ UAS-6316 [S]	Drag Kings	1964	15.00	30.00	60.00

SONS OF CHAMPLIN, THE With Bill Champlin, later of CHICAGO.
45s
ARIOLA AMERICA

Number	Title (A Side/B Side)	Yr	VG	VG+	NM
❏ 7606	Look Out/Queen of the Rain	1975	—	2.00	4.00
❏ 7627	Hold On/Still in Love with You	1976	—	2.00	4.00
❏ 7633	You/Imagination's Sake	1976	—	2.00	4.00
❏ 7653	Follow Your Heart/Here Is Where Your Love Belongs	1976	—	2.00	4.00
❏ 7664	Saved by the Grace of Your Love/West End	1977	—	2.00	4.00

CAPITOL

Number	Title (A Side/B Side)	Yr	VG	VG+	NM
❏ 2437	1982-A/Black and Blue Rainbow	1969	2.00	4.00	8.00
❏ 2534	Freedom/Hello Sunlight	1969	2.00	4.00	8.00
❏ 2663	It's Time/Why Do People Run	1969	2.00	4.00	8.00
❏ 2786	You Can Fly/Terry's Tune	1970	—	3.00	6.00

COLUMBIA

Number	Title (A Side/B Side)	Yr	VG	VG+	NM
❏ 45872	Welcome to the Dance/Swim	1973	—	2.50	5.00

GOLDMINE

Number	Title (A Side/B Side)	Yr	VG	VG+	NM
❏ 101	Look Out/Queen of the Rain	1975	—	2.50	5.00

VERVE

Number	Title (A Side/B Side)	Yr	VG	VG+	NM
❏ 10500	Sing Me a Lullaby/Fat City	1967	2.50	5.00	10.00

Albums
ARIOLA AMERICA

Number	Title (A Side/B Side)	Yr	VG	VG+	NM
❏ SW-50002	The Sons of Champlin	1975	2.50	5.00	10.00
❏ ST-50007	A Circle Filled with Love	1976	2.50	5.00	10.00
❏ SW-50017	Loving Is Why	1977	2.50	5.00	10.00

CAPITOL

Number	Title (A Side/B Side)	Yr	VG	VG+	NM
❏ SWBB-200 [(2)]	Loosen Up Naturally	1969	5.00	10.00	20.00
—With the F-word airbrushed off the cover artwork					
❏ SWBB-200 [(2)]	Loosen Up Naturally	1969	6.25	12.50	25.00
—With the F-word scratched off the cover artwork					
❏ SWBB-200 [(2)]	Loosen Up Naturally	1969	12.50	25.00	50.00
—With the F-word clearly visible as part of the cover artwork					
❏ SKAO-322	The Sons	1969	6.25	12.50	25.00
❏ ST-675	Follow Your Heart	1971	5.00	10.00	20.00

COLUMBIA

Number	Title (A Side/B Side)	Yr	VG	VG+	NM
❏ KC 32341	Welcome to the Dance	1973	3.75	7.50	15.00

GOLDMINE

Number	Title (A Side/B Side)	Yr	VG	VG+	NM
❏ GM 94930	The Sons of Champlin	1975	5.00	10.00	20.00

SONS OF CHAMPLIN

Number	Title (A Side/B Side)	Yr	VG	VG+	NM
❏ (no #)	Minus Seeds and Stems	1969	125.00	250.00	500.00

SONS OF THE PIONEERS
45s
CORAL

Number	Title (A Side/B Side)	Yr	VG	VG+	NM
❏ 9-61186	River of No Return/The Lilies Grow High	1954	5.00	10.00	20.00
❏ 9-61316	Montana/Lonely Little Room	1954	5.00	10.00	20.00
❏ 9-64172	Sierra Nevada/If You Would Only Be Mine	1954	5.00	10.00	20.00

DECCA

Number	Title (A Side/B Side)	Yr	VG	VG+	NM
❏ 9-29814	Cool Water/Tumbling Tumbleweeds	1956	3.75	7.50	15.00

GRANITE

Number	Title (A Side/B Side)	Yr	VG	VG+	NM
❏ 550	Cool Water/Pretty Painted Ladies	1976	—	3.00	6.00
❏ 551	Indian Woman/(B-side unknown)	1977	—	3.00	6.00

RCA VICTOR

Number	Title (A Side/B Side)	Yr	VG	VG+	NM
❏ 47-2836	Cool Water/Chant of the Wanderer	1949	7.50	15.00	30.00
❏ 47-2837	Tumbling Tumbleweeds/The Everlasting Hills of Oklahoma	1949	7.50	15.00	30.00
❏ 47-2838	Trees/The Timber Trail	1949	7.50	15.00	30.00
—The above three comprise a box set; quickly reissued as 48-0004, 0005 and 0006					
❏ 47-3983	America Forever/Little White Cross	1950	6.25	12.50	25.00
❏ 47-4071	Roses/Mexicali Rose	1951	5.00	10.00	20.00
❏ 47-4072	Moonlight and Roses/Bring Your Roses to Her Now	1951	5.00	10.00	20.00
❏ 47-4073	San Antonio Rose/Room Full of Roses	1951	5.00	10.00	20.00
—The above three comprise a box set					
❏ 47-4131	Daddy's Little Cowboy/Baby I Ain't Gonna Cry No More	1951	5.00	10.00	20.00
❏ 47-4264	Heart Break Hill/The Wind	1951	5.00	10.00	20.00
❏ 47-4347	The Lord's Prayer/Resurectus	1951	5.00	10.00	20.00
❏ 47-4431	Outlaws/I Still Do	1951	5.00	10.00	20.00
❏ 47-4459	I Told Them All About You/Ho-Le-O	1952	5.00	10.00	20.00
❏ 47-4571	Land Beyond the Sun/Waltz of the Roses	1952	5.00	10.00	20.00
❏ 47-4639	Diesel Smoke/Almost	1952	5.00	10.00	20.00
❏ 47-4937	Let's Pretend/The Everlasting Hills of Oklahoma	1952	5.00	10.00	20.00
❏ 47-6055	The Ballad of Davy Crockett/Graveyard Filler of the West	1955	6.25	12.50	25.00
❏ 47-6109	I Wonder When We'll Ever Know/The King's Highway	1955	3.75	7.50	15.00
❏ 47-6123	The Tennessee Rock 'n' Roll/The Three of Us	1955	6.25	12.50	25.00
❏ 47-6184	Be What You Want to Be/Epidemic	1955	3.75	7.50	15.00
❏ 47-6276	Yaller Yaller Gold/King of the River	1955	5.00	10.00	20.00
❏ 47-6376	How Great Thou Art/The Last Frontier	1956	3.75	7.50	15.00
❏ 47-6507	The Searchers/Song of the Prodigal Son	1956	3.75	7.50	15.00
❏ 47-6655	For the Love of You/Timmy's Tune	1956	3.75	7.50	15.00
❏ 47-6890	One More Time/Hasta La Vista	1957	3.75	7.50	15.00
❏ 47-7024	Ballad of the Cowboy Sailor/The Piney Woods	1957	3.75	7.50	15.00
❏ 47-7079	High Ridin' Woman/God Has His Arms Around Me	1957	3.75	7.50	15.00
❏ 47-7392	A Fiddle, a Rifle, an Ax and a Bible/My Last Goodbye	1958	3.00	6.00	12.00
❏ 47-8310	Crazy Arms/Cattle Call Rondolet	1963	2.50	5.00	10.00
❏ 47-8575	Destiny/Green Ice and Mountain Men	1965	2.50	5.00	10.00
❏ 47-9509	Gringo's Guitar/Margretta	1968	2.00	4.00	8.00
❏ 48-0004	Cool Water/Chant of the Wanderer	1949	7.50	15.00	30.00
—Green vinyl original					
❏ 48-0004	Cool Water/Chant of the Wanderer	1951	5.00	10.00	20.00
—Black vinyl reissue					
❏ 48-0005	Tumbling Tumbleweeds/Everlasting Hills of Oklahoma	1949	5.00	10.00	20.00
—Black vinyl reissue					

Number	Title (A Side/B Side)	Yr	VG	VG+	NM
❏ 48-0005	Tumbling Tumbleweeds/Everlasting Hills of Oklahoma	1949	7.50	15.00	30.00
—Green vinyl					
❏ 48-0006	Trees/The Timber Trail	1949	5.00	10.00	20.00
—Black vinyl reissue					
❏ 48-0006	Trees/The Timber Trail	1949	7.50	15.00	30.00
—Green vinyl original					
❏ 48-0007	Blue Prairie/Cowboy Camp Meetin'	1949	5.00	10.00	20.00
—Black vinyl reissue					
❏ 48-0007	Blue Prairie/Cowboy Camp Meetin'	1949	7.50	15.00	30.00
—Green vinyl original					
❏ 48-0060	Room Full of Roses/Riders in the Sky	1949	7.50	15.00	30.00
—Green vinyl original					
❏ 48-0094	Rounded Up in Glory/Too High, Too Wide, Too Low	1949	7.50	15.00	30.00
—Green vinyl original					
❏ 48-0095	Lead Me Gently Home Father/Power in the Blood	1949	7.50	15.00	30.00
—Green vinyl original					
❏ 48-0096	The Old Rugged Cross/Read the Bible Every Day	1949	7.50	15.00	30.00
—Green vinyl original					
❏ 48-0101	Lie Low Little Doggies/Bar None Ranch	1949	7.50	15.00	30.00
—Green vinyl original					
❏ 48-0141	Red River Valley/Santa Fe, New Mexico	1950	7.50	15.00	30.00
—Green vinyl original					
❏ 48-0171	Wedding Bells/Love at the County Fair	1950	7.50	15.00	30.00
—With Dale Evans; green vinyl original					
❏ 48-0183	Cigareets, Whusky and Wild, Wild Women/My Best to You	1950	7.50	15.00	30.00
—Green vinyl; reissue of hit 78 rpm from 1947					
❏ 48-0184	Let's Go West Again/Let Me Share Your Name	1950	7.50	15.00	30.00
—Green vinyl original					
❏ 48-0220	Teardrops in My Heart/You Don't Know What Lonesome Is	1950	7.50	15.00	30.00
—Green vinyl; reissue of hit 78 from 1947					
❏ 48-0221	The Sea Walker/The Touch of God's Hand	1950	7.50	15.00	30.00
—Green vinyl original					
❏ 48-0306	Roses/The Eagle's Heart	1950	6.25	12.50	25.00
—Green vinyl original					
❏ 48-0315	Rollin' Dust/Wagons West	1950	6.25	12.50	25.00
—Green vinyl original					
❏ 48-0345	Song of the Wagonmaster/Chuckawalla Swing	1950	6.25	12.50	25.00
—Green vinyl original					
❏ 48-0366	Land Beyond the Sun/I Told Them All About You	1950	6.25	12.50	25.00
—Green vinyl original					
❏ 48-0368	Old Man Atom/What This Country Needs	1950	6.25	12.50	25.00
—Green vinyl original					
❏ 48-0388	Where Are You/What This Country Needs	1950	6.25	12.50	25.00
—Green vinyl original					
❏ 48-0486	Lonesome/The Wondrous Word	1951	5.00	10.00	20.00
❏ 74-0199	Talli Wind/Hawaiian Lullaby	1969	2.00	4.00	8.00
❏ WBY-25	The Ballad of Davy Crockett/The Graveyard Filler of the West	1955	7.50	15.00	30.00
❏ WBY-25 [PS]	The Ballad of Davy Crockett/The Graveyard Filler of the West	1955	12.50	25.00	50.00
❏ WBY-27	A Whale of a Tale/Old Betsy	1955	6.25	12.50	25.00
❏ WBY-46	Home on the Range/Cheyenne	1957	5.00	10.00	20.00
❏ WBY-46 [PS]	Home on the Range/Cheyenne	1957	7.50	15.00	30.00
❏ WBY-68	Wagon Train/Lie Low Little Doggies	195?	5.00	10.00	20.00
❏ WBY-71	The Restless Gun/Bunkhouse Bugle Boy	1957	5.00	10.00	20.00
❏ WBY-71 [PS]	The Restless Gun/Bunkhouse Bugle Boy	1957	7.50	15.00	30.00
❏ VP-3-2668 [S]	El Paso/Your Cheatin' Heart	196?	3.75	7.50	15.00
—B-side by Skeeter Davis; jukebox issue; small hole, plays at 33 1/3 rpm					

7-Inch Extended Plays
RCA VICTOR

Number	Title (A Side/B Side)	Yr	VG	VG+	NM
❏ 547-0029	Cool Water/Chant of the Wanderer//Tumbling Tumbleweeds/The Everlasting Hills of Oklahoma	195?	5.00	10.00	20.00
—One record of 2-EP set EPB 3032					
❏ 547-0030	Cowboy Camp Meetin'/Blue Prairie//The Timber Trail/Trees	195?	5.00	10.00	20.00
—One record of 2-EP set EPB 3032					
❏ EPA 422	Empty Saddles/There's a Gold Mine in the Sky//Home on the Range/Old Pioneer	1952	6.25	12.50	25.00
❏ EPA 422 [PS]	Sons of the Pioneers Sing Western Favorites	1952	6.25	12.50	25.00
❏ EPA 650	Tumbling Tumbleweeds/Press Along to the Big Corral/Wind/Bunkhouse Bugle Boy//Home on the Range/La Borachita/Timber Trail/Happy Cowboy	1955	5.00	10.00	20.00
❏ EPA 650 [PS]	Favorite Cowboy Songs Vol. I	1955	5.00	10.00	20.00
❏ EPB 3032 [PS]	Cowboy Classics	195?	5.00	10.00	20.00
—Gatefold cover for 547-0029 and 547-0030					

Albums
COLUMBIA

Number	Title (A Side/B Side)	Yr	VG	VG+	NM
❏ FC 37439	The Sons of the Pioneers: Columbia Historical Edition	1981	2.50	5.00	10.00

MCA

Number	Title (A Side/B Side)	Yr	VG	VG+	NM
❏ 730	Tumbleweed Trails	198?	2.50	5.00	10.00

RCA CAMDEN

Number	Title (A Side/B Side)	Yr	VG	VG+	NM
❏ CAL-413 [M]	Wagons West	1958	5.00	10.00	20.00
❏ CAS-413 [R]	Wagons West	1963	3.00	6.00	12.00
❏ CAL-587 [M]	Room Full of Roses	1960	5.00	10.00	20.00

RCA VICTOR

Number	Title (A Side/B Side)	Yr	VG	VG+	NM
❏ PRM-104 [M]	Westward Ho!	1961	6.25	12.50	25.00
—Special-products issue					
❏ LPM-1130 [M]	Favorite Cowboy Songs	1955	12.50	25.00	50.00
❏ LPM-1431 [M]	How Great Thou Art	1957	12.50	25.00	50.00
❏ LPM-1483 [M]	One Man's Songs	1957	12.50	25.00	50.00
❏ LPM-2118 [M]	Cool Water	1960	6.25	12.50	25.00
❏ LSP-2118 [S]	Cool Water	1960	7.50	15.00	30.00
❏ ANL1-2332	A Country-Western Songbook	1977	3.75	7.50	15.00
❏ LPM-2356 [M]	Lure of the West	1961	6.25	12.50	25.00
❏ LSP-2356 [S]	Lure of the West	1961	7.50	15.00	30.00
❏ LPM-2456 [M]	Tumbleweed Trails	1962	6.25	12.50	25.00
❏ LSP-2456 [S]	Tumbleweed Trails	1962	7.50	15.00	30.00

Number	Title (A Side/B Side)	Yr	VG	VG+	NM
❏ LPM-2603 [M]	Our Men Out West	1963	5.00	10.00	20.00
❏ LSP-2603 [S]	Our Men Out West	1963	6.25	12.50	25.00
❏ LPM-2652 [M]	Hymns of the Cowboy	1963	5.00	10.00	20.00
❏ LSP-2652 [S]	Hymns of the Cowboy	1963	6.25	12.50	25.00
❏ LPM-2737 [M]	Trail Dust	1963	5.00	10.00	20.00
❏ LSP-2737 [S]	Trail Dust	1963	6.25	12.50	25.00
❏ LPM-2855 [M]	Country Fare	1964	5.00	10.00	20.00
❏ LSP-2855 [S]	Country Fare	1964	6.25	12.50	25.00
❏ LPM-2957 [M]	Down Memory Trail	1964	5.00	10.00	20.00
❏ LSP-2957 [S]	Down Memory Trail	1964	6.25	12.50	25.00
❏ LPM-3032 [10]	Cowboy Classics	1952	25.00	50.00	100.00
❏ LPM-3095 [10]	Cowboy Hymns and Spirituals	1952	25.00	50.00	100.00
❏ LPM-3162 [10]	Western Classics	1953	25.00	50.00	100.00
❏ LPM-3351 [M]	Legends of the West	1965	3.75	7.50	15.00
❏ LSP-3351 [S]	Legends of the West	1965	5.00	10.00	20.00
❏ ANL1-3468	The Best of the Sons of the Pioneers	1980	2.50	5.00	10.00
❏ LPM-3476 [M]	The Best of Sons of the Pioneers	1966	3.75	7.50	15.00
❏ LSP-3476 [S]	The Best of Sons of the Pioneers	1966	5.00	10.00	20.00
❏ LPM-3554 [M]	The Songs of Bob Nolan	1966	3.75	7.50	15.00
❏ LSP-3554 [S]	The Songs of Bob Nolan	1966	5.00	10.00	20.00
❏ AYL1-3679	Cool Water	1980	2.50	5.00	10.00
❏ LPM-3714 [M]	Campfire Favorites	1967	6.25	12.50	25.00
❏ LSP-3714 [S]	Campfire Favorites	1967	5.00	10.00	20.00
❏ LPM-3964 [M]	South of the Border	1968	20.00	40.00	80.00
❏ LSP-3964 [S]	South of the Border	1968	5.00	10.00	20.00
❏ AYM1-4092	Let's Go West Again	1981	2.50	5.00	10.00
READER'S DIGEST					
❏ RBA-135-A [(7)]	Down Memory Trail with the Sons of the Pioneers	1981	15.00	30.00	60.00

SOOTZ, MANNY
45s
PIRATE

Number	Title (A Side/B Side)	Yr	VG	VG+	NM
❏ 841	Cape Canaveral (Part 1)/ Cape Canaveral (Part 2)	1957	6.25	12.50	25.00

SOPHISTICATES, THE
45s
VIVA

Number	Title (A Side/B Side)	Yr	VG	VG+	NM
❏ 61	When Elvis Comes Marching Home/Woody's Place	1960	12.50	25.00	50.00

SOPHOMORES, THE (1)
45s
CHORD

Number	Title (A Side/B Side)	Yr	VG	VG+	NM
❏ 1302	Charades/What Can I Do	1957	10.00	20.00	40.00
DAWN					
❏ 216	Cool, Cool Baby/Every Night About This Time	1956	6.25	12.50	25.00
❏ 218	Linda/I Get a Thrill	1956	6.25	12.50	25.00
❏ 223	Ocean Blue/I Left My Sugar	1956	6.25	12.50	25.00
❏ 225	Is There Someone for Me/Everybody Loves Me	1957	6.25	12.50	25.00
❏ 228	I Just Can't Keep the Tears from Tumblin' Down/ If I Should Lose Your Love	1957	6.25	12.50	25.00
❏ 237	Checkers/Each Time I Hold You	1958	6.25	12.50	25.00
EPIC					
❏ 9259	Charades/What Can I Do	1957	5.00	10.00	20.00

SOPHOMORES, THE (2)
45s
SOUND STAGE 7

Number	Title (A Side/B Side)	Yr	VG	VG+	NM
❏ 2533	Summer of '64/I Know I Should (Every Night)	1964	2.50	5.00	10.00

SOPWITH "CAMEL," THE
45s
KAMA SUTRA

Number	Title (A Side/B Side)	Yr	VG	VG+	NM
❏ 217	Hello Hello/Treadin'	1966	3.00	6.00	12.00
❏ 224	Postcard from Jamaica/Little Orphan Annie	1967	3.00	6.00	12.00
❏ 224 [PS]	Postcard from Jamaica/Little Orphan Annie	1967	5.00	10.00	20.00
❏ 236	Great Morpheum/ Saga of the Lowdown Letdown	1967	3.00	6.00	12.00
REPRISE					
❏ 1179	Sleazy Love/Fazon	1973	2.00	4.00	8.00
Albums					
KAMA SUTRA					
❏ KSBS-2063	Hello Hello	1973	5.00	10.00	20.00
❏ KLP-8060 [M]	The Sopwith Camel	1967	7.50	15.00	30.00
❏ KLPS-8060 [S]	The Sopwith Camel	1967	7.50	15.00	30.00
REPRISE					
❏ MS 2108	The Miraculous Hump Returns	1973	6.25	12.50	25.00

SORENSON BROTHERS, THE
45s
MARLINDA

Number	Title (A Side/B Side)	Yr	VG	VG+	NM
❏ 7507/8	They've Landed/Stowaway	196?	12.50	25.00	50.00

SORROWS, THE
45s
WARNER BROS.

Number	Title (A Side/B Side)	Yr	VG	VG+	NM
❏ 5662	Take a Heart/We Should Get Along Fine	1965	3.00	6.00	12.00

SOUL, DAVID
45s
MGM

Number	Title (A Side/B Side)	Yr	VG	VG+	NM
❏ 13510	The Covered Man/I Will Warm Your Heart	1966	2.50	5.00	10.00
❏ 13589	Was I Ever So Wrong/Before	1966	2.50	5.00	10.00
❏ 13842	No One's Gonna Cry/Quiet Kind of Hate	1967	2.50	5.00	10.00
PRIVATE STOCK					
❏ 45,129	Don't Give Up on Us/Black Bean Soup	1976	—	2.00	4.00
❏ 45,150	Going in with My Eyes Open/Topanga	1977	—	2.00	4.00
❏ 45,163	Silver Lady/The Rider	1977	—	2.00	4.00
Albums					
PRIVATE STOCK					
❏ PS-2019	David Soul	1977	2.50	5.00	10.00
❏ PS-7001	Playing to an Audience of One	1977	2.50	5.00	10.00

SOUL, JIMMY
45s
SPQR

Number	Title (A Side/B Side)	Yr	VG	VG+	NM
❏ 3221	My Little Room/Ella Is Yella	1964	2.50	5.00	10.00
❏ 3300	Twistin' Matilda/I Can't Hold Out Any Longer	1962	3.00	6.00	12.00
❏ 3302	When Matilda Comes Back/Some Kinda Nut	1962	3.00	6.00	12.00
❏ 3304	Guess Things Happen That Way/ My Baby Loves to Bowl	1963	3.00	6.00	12.00
❏ 3305	If You Wanna Be Happy/Don't Release Me	1963	3.75	7.50	15.00
❏ 3305 [PS]	If You Wanna Be Happy/Don't Release Me	1963	7.50	15.00	30.00
❏ 3310	Treat 'Em Tough/ Church Street in the Summertime	1963	3.00	6.00	12.00
❏ 3312	Go 'Way Christina/Everybody's Gone Ape	1963	3.00	6.00	12.00
❏ 3314	Change Partners/I Hate You Baby	1963	3.00	6.00	12.00
❏ 3315	My Girl-She Sure Can Cook/A Woman Is Smarter in Every Kinda Way	1964	2.50	5.00	10.00
❏ 3318	You Can't Have Your Cake/ Take Me to Los Angeles	1964	2.50	5.00	10.00
❏ 3319	Twistin' Matilda/Treat 'Em Tough	1964	2.50	5.00	10.00
20TH FOX					
❏ 413	Respectable/I Wish I Could Dance	1963	2.50	5.00	10.00
Albums					
SPQR					
❏ E 16001	If You Wanna Be Happy	1963	37.50	75.00	150.00

SOUL AGENTS, THE
45s
CAMEO

Number	Title (A Side/B Side)	Yr	VG	VG+	NM
❏ 350	Let's Make It Pretty Baby/The Seventh Son	1965	5.00	10.00	20.00
INTERPHON					
❏ 7702	I Just Want to Make Love to You/ Mean Woman Blues	1964	5.00	10.00	20.00

SOUL BROTHERS SIX
45s
ATLANTIC

Number	Title (A Side/B Side)	Yr	VG	VG+	NM
❏ 2406	Some Kind of Wonderful/I'll Be Loving You	1967	3.75	7.50	15.00
❏ 2456	You Better Check Yourself/ What Can You Do When You Ain't Got Nobody	1967	3.00	6.00	12.00
❏ 2535	Your Love Is Such a Wonderful Love/ I Can't Live Without You	1968	3.00	6.00	12.00
❏ 2592	Somebody Else Is Loving My Baby/ Thank You Baby for Loving Me	1969	3.00	6.00	12.00
❏ 2645	What You Got (Is So Good for Me)/Drive	1969	3.00	6.00	12.00
PHIL-L.A. OF SOUL					
❏ 355	Funky Funky Way of Making Love/Let Me Be the One	1972	—	3.00	6.00
❏ 360	You're My World/You Gotta Come a Little Closer	1973	—	3.00	6.00
❏ 365	Let Me Do What We Ain't Doin'/Lost the Will to Live	1974	—	3.00	6.00

SOUL CHILDREN, THE
45s
EPIC

Number	Title (A Side/B Side)	Yr	VG	VG+	NM
❏ 50178	Finders Keepers/Midnight Sunshine	1976	—	2.50	5.00
❏ 50236	If You Move I'll Fall/Little Understanding	1976	—	2.50	5.00
❏ 50345	Where Is Your Woman Tonight?/ Merry-Go-Round	1977	—	2.50	5.00
❏ 50405	There Always/You Don't Need a Ring	1977	—	2.50	5.00
STAX					
❏ 0008	Give 'Em Love/Move Over	1968	2.00	4.00	8.00
❏ 0018	I'll Understand/Doin' Our Thing	1969	2.00	4.00	8.00
❏ 0030	Tighten Up My Thang/Take Up the Slack	1969	2.00	4.00	8.00
❏ 0050	The Sweeter He Is — Part 1/ The Sweeter He Is — Part 2	1969	2.00	4.00	8.00
❏ 0062	Hold On, I'm Coming/Make It Good	1970	—	3.50	7.00
❏ 0075	Give Me One Good Reason Why/Finish Me Off	1970	—	3.50	7.00
❏ 0086	Let's Make a Sweet Thing Sweeter/Finish Me Off	1971	—	3.50	7.00
❏ 0119	Hearsay/Don't Take My Sunshine	1972	—	3.50	7.00
❏ 0132	Don't Take My Kindness for Weakness/ Just the One	1972	—	3.50	7.00
❏ 0152	It Ain't Always What You Do (It's Who You Let See You Do It)/All That Shines Ain't Gold	1973	—	3.50	7.00
❏ 0170	Love Is a Hurtin' Thing/Poem on the School House Door	1973	—	3.50	7.00
❏ 0182	I'll Be the Other Woman/Come Back Kind of Love	1973	—	3.00	6.00
❏ 0218	Love Makes It Right/ Love Makes It Right — Part 2	1974	—	3.00	6.00
❏ 0230	What's Happening Baby/What's Happening Baby — Part 2	1974	—	3.00	6.00
❏ 3206	Can't Give Up a Good Thing/Signed, Sealed and Delivered	1978	—	2.50	5.00
❏ 3211	Summer in the Shade/Hard Living with a Woman	1978	—	2.50	5.00
❏ 3214	Who You Used to Be/Believing	1978	—	2.50	5.00
Albums					
EPIC					
❏ PE 33902	Finders Keepers	1976	3.75	7.50	15.00
❏ PE 34455	Where Is Your Woman Tonight	1977	3.75	7.50	15.00
STAX					
❏ STS-2018	Soul Children	1969	7.50	15.00	30.00
❏ STS-2043	The Best of Two Worlds	1971	7.50	15.00	30.00
❏ STS-3003	Genesis	1972	7.50	15.00	30.00
❏ STX-4105	Open Door Policy	1978	3.75	7.50	15.00
❏ STX-4120	Chronicle	1979	3.00	6.00	12.00
❏ STS-5507	Friction	1974	7.50	15.00	30.00

SOUL CLAN, THE SOLOMON BURKE, ARTHUR CONLEY, DON COVAY, BEN E. KING and JOE TEX.
45s
ATLANTIC

Number	Title (A Side/B Side)	Yr	VG	VG+	NM
❏ 2530	Soul Meeting/That's How It Feels	1968	2.50	5.00	10.00
❏ 2530 [PS]	Soul Meeting/That's How It Feels	1968	3.75	7.50	15.00

SOUL COMFORTERS, THE
45s
HOLLYWOOD

Number	Title (A Side/B Side)	Yr	VG	VG+	NM
❏ 1042	White Christmas/Silent Night	1955	7.50	15.00	30.00

S

Number	Title (A Side/B Side)	Yr	VG	VG+	NM
SOUL FINDERS, THE					
Albums					
RCA CAMDEN					
❏ CAL-2170 [M]	Sweet Soul Music	1967	7.50	15.00	30.00
❏ CAS-2170 [S]	Sweet Soul Music	1967	7.50	15.00	30.00
❏ CAL-2239 [M]	An Explosive Album of Soul	1968	7.50	15.00	30.00
❏ CAS-2239 [S]	An Explosive Album of Soul	1968	7.50	15.00	30.00
SOUL GENERATION, THE					
45s					
EBONY SOUNDS					
❏ 175	That's the Way It's Got to Be (Body and Soul)/ Mandingo Woman	1972	2.50	5.00	10.00
❏ 176	Million Dollars/Super Fine	1973	2.50	5.00	10.00
❏ 177	A Ray of Hope/Young Bird	1973	2.50	5.00	10.00
❏ 181	I Wonder What She's Doin'/Key to Your Heart	1973	3.00	6.00	12.00
❏ 181	Praying for a Miracle/In Your Way	1974	3.75	7.50	15.00
Albums					
EBONY SOUNDS					
❏ 2000	Beyond Body and Soul	1972	5.00	10.00	20.00
SOUL SISTERS, THE					
45s					
GUYDEN					
❏ 2066	The Warm-Up/Because I Love You	1962	6.25	12.50	25.00
KAYO					
❏ 5101	I Can't Let Him Go/(B-side unknown)	1963	6.25	12.50	25.00
SUE					
❏ 10-005	Good Time Tonight/Foolish Dreamer	1964	3.75	7.50	15.00
❏ 107	Loop de Loop/Long Gone	1964	3.75	7.50	15.00
❏ 111	Just a Moment Ago/ I Won't Be Your Fool Anymore	1964	3.75	7.50	15.00
❏ 130	Think About the Good Times/The Right Time	1965	3.75	7.50	15.00
❏ 140	Flashback/Give Me Some Satisfaction	1966	3.75	7.50	15.00
❏ 799	I Can't Stand It/Blueberry Hill	1964	3.75	7.50	15.00
VEEP					
❏ 1291	A Thousand Mountains/You Got 'Em Beat	1968	3.00	6.00	12.00
Albums					
SUE					
❏ LP-1022 [M]	I Can't Stand It	1964	50.00	100.00	200.00
❏ STLP-1022 [S]	I Can't Stand It	1964	100.00	200.00	400.00
SOUL SOCIETY, THE					
45s					
DOT					
❏ 17136	Sidewinder/Afro-Desia	1968	2.50	5.00	10.00
Albums					
DOT					
❏ DLP-25842	Satisfaction	1969	6.25	12.50	25.00
SOUL SURFERS, THE					
45s					
CHALLENGE					
❏ 9209	Cannonball/Home from Camp	1963	10.00	20.00	40.00
❏ 59249	Cannonball/In the Misty Moonlight	1964	3.75	7.50	15.00
—*B-side by Jerry Wallace*					
SOUL SURVIVORS					
45s					
ATCO					
❏ 6627	Turn Out the Fire/Go Out Walking	1968	2.00	4.00	8.00
❏ 6650	Tell Daddy/Mama Soul	1969	2.00	4.00	8.00
❏ 6735	Still Got My Head/Tempting 'Bout to Get Me	1970	2.00	4.00	8.00
CRIMSON					
❏ 1010	Expressway to Your Heart/Hey Gyp	1967	3.00	6.00	12.00
❏ 1012	Explosion (In Your Soul)/Dathon's Theme	1967	2.50	5.00	10.00
❏ 1016	Poor Man's Dream/Impossible Mission	1968	2.50	5.00	10.00
DECCA					
❏ 32080	Devil with a Blue Dress On/Shakin' with Linda	1967	3.75	7.50	15.00
DOT					
❏ 16793	Look at Me/Can't Stand to Be in Love with You	1965	5.00	10.00	20.00
❏ 16830	Hung Up on Losin'/Snow Man	1966	3.00	6.00	12.00
LOST-NITE					
❏ 331	Expressway to Your Heart/Hey Gyp	197?	—	2.50	5.00
—*Reissue*					
PHILADELPHIA INT'L.					
❏ 3595	Happy Birthday America (Part 1)/ Happy Birthday America (Part 2)	1976	—	2.50	5.00
❏ 3595 [PS]	Happy Birthday America (Part 1)/ Happy Birthday America (Part 2)	1976	2.00	4.00	8.00
TSOP					
❏ 4756	City of Brotherly Love/ The Best Time Was the Last Time	1974	—	3.00	6.00
❏ 4760	What It Takes/Virgin Girl	1974	—	3.00	6.00
❏ 4768	Your Love/Lover to Me	1975	—	3.00	6.00
Albums					
ATCO					
❏ SD 33-277	Take Another Look	1969	6.25	12.50	25.00
CRIMSON					
❏ CR-502 [M]	When the Whistle Blows Anything Goes	1967	12.50	25.00	50.00
❏ CR-502 S [S]	When the Whistle Blows Anything Goes	1967	7.50	15.00	30.00
TSOP					
❏ KZ 33186	The Soul Survivors	1975	3.00	6.00	12.00
SOULFUL STRINGS, THE					
45s					
CADET					
❏ 5559	Paint It Black/Love Is a Hurtin' Thing	1967	—	3.00	6.00
❏ 5576	Burning Spear/Within You Without You	1968	—	3.00	6.00
❏ 5607	(Sittin' On) The Dock of the Bay/The Stripper	1968	—	3.00	6.00
❏ 5617	The Who Who Song/Jericho	1968	—	3.00	6.00
❏ 5633	I Wish It Would Rain/Listen Here	1969	—	3.00	6.00
❏ 5654	A Love Song/Zabezi	1969	—	3.00	6.00
Albums					
CADET					
❏ LP-776 [M]	Paint It Black	1967	3.75	7.50	15.00
❏ LPS-776 [S]	Paint It Black	1967	3.00	6.00	12.00
❏ LPS-796	Groovin' with the Soulful Strings	1967	3.00	6.00	12.00
❏ LPS-805	Another Exposure	1968	3.00	6.00	12.00
❏ LPS-814	The Magic of Christmas	1968	3.00	6.00	12.00
❏ LPS-820	In Concert/Back by Demand	1969	3.00	6.00	12.00
❏ LPS-834	String Fever	1969	3.00	6.00	12.00
❏ LPS-846	Gamble-Huff	1971	2.50	5.00	10.00
❏ 50022 [(2)]	Best of the Soulful Strings	1973	3.00	6.00	12.00
SOUND SYMPOSIUM, THE					
45s					
DOT					
❏ 17296	The Mighty Quinn/I'll Be Your Baby Tonight	1969	2.50	5.00	10.00
Albums					
DOT					
❏ DLP-3871 [M]	Paul Simon Interpreted	1968	7.50	15.00	30.00
—*Stereo cover with white "Monaural" sticker; label is regular stock copy*					
❏ DLP-25871 [S]	Paul Simon Interpreted	1968	5.00	10.00	20.00
❏ DLP-25952	Bob Dylan Interpreted	1969	5.00	10.00	20.00
SOUNDS, INC.					
45s					
LIBERTY					
❏ 55709	The Spartans/Detroit	1964	2.00	4.00	8.00
❏ 55729	Rinky Dink/Spanish Harlem	1964	2.00	4.00	8.00
❏ 55789	In the Hall of the Mountain King/Time for You	1965	2.00	4.00	8.00
❏ 55844	On the Brink/I Am Comin' Thru	1965	2.00	4.00	8.00
SOUNDS LIKE US					
45s					
FONTANA					
❏ 1570	Outside Chance/Clock on the Wall	1967	6.25	12.50	25.00
JILL ANN					
❏ 101	Outside Chance/Clock on the Wall	1966	12.50	25.00	50.00
SOMA					
❏ 8108	It Was a Very Good Year/ The Other Side of the Record	1967	5.00	10.00	20.00
SOUNDS OF OUR TIMES, THE					
45s					
CAPITOL					
❏ 2109	The Look of Love/A Whiter Shade of Pale	1968	2.00	4.00	8.00
❏ 2291	Hey Jude/Harper Valley P.T.A.	1968	3.75	7.50	15.00
—*Collectible for its inexplicable error in composer's credit on "Hey Jude," claiming the song was written by "Paul Lennon" and "John McCartney"!*					
Albums					
CAPITOL					
❏ ST-117	Hey Jude	1969	3.00	6.00	12.00
❏ ST-8-0117	Hey Jude	1969	3.75	7.50	15.00
—*Capitol Record Club edition*					
❏ ST-182	Galveston	1969	3.00	6.00	12.00
❏ ST 2817 [S]	Music of the Flower Children	1968	3.00	6.00	12.00
❏ T 2817 [M]	Music of the Flower Children	1968	5.00	10.00	20.00
❏ ST 2892 [S]	The Sounds of Our Time Play "Love Is Blue"	1968	3.00	6.00	12.00
❏ T 2892 [M]	The Sounds of Our Time Play "Love Is Blue"	1968	6.25	12.50	25.00
SOUNDS OF SUNSHINE					
45s					
P.I.P.					
❏ 6527	Nadia's Theme (Vocal)/Nadia's Theme (Instrumental)	1976	—	2.00	4.00
RANWOOD					
❏ 896	Love Means (You Never Have to Say You're Sorry)/Linda, the Untouchable	1971	—	2.50	5.00
❏ 912	It's Hard to Say Goodbye Forever/ I Do All My Crying in the Rain	1971	—	2.00	4.00
❏ 913	Yesterday Keeps Getting in the Way/ Anything Can Happen	1971	—	2.00	4.00
❏ 921	Make It Happy/Nature Boy	1972	—	2.00	4.00
❏ 925	Today Is the First Day (Of the Rest of Your Life)/ Make Believe Saturday Night	1972	—	2.00	4.00
❏ 932	The End of the World/Over and Over	1972	—	2.00	4.00
❏ 940	Sea Gull/She Takes Care of Me	1973	—	2.00	4.00
Albums					
P.I.P.					
❏ 6823	Nadia's Theme	1976	2.50	5.00	10.00
RANWOOD					
❏ 8089	Love Means You Never Have to Say You're Sorry	1971	2.50	5.00	10.00
❏ 8095	Today Is the First Day (Of the Rest of Your Life)	1972	2.50	5.00	10.00
SOUNDS ORCHESTRAL					
45s					
JANUS					
❏ 124	Love in the Shadows/Louie, Louie	1970	—	3.00	6.00
PARKWAY					
❏ 120	Pretty Flamingo/Sounds Like Jacques	1966	2.00	4.00	8.00
❏ 155	A Man and a Woman/West of Carnaby	1967	2.00	4.00	8.00
❏ 942	Cast Your Fate to the Wind/To Wendy With Love	1965	2.50	5.00	10.00
❏ 958	Canadian Sunset/Have Faith in Your Love	1965	2.00	4.00	8.00
❏ 968	A Boy and a Girl/Go Home Girl	1966	2.00	4.00	8.00
❏ 973	Thunderball/Mr. Kiss Kiss Bang Bang	1966	2.00	4.00	8.00
Albums					
JANUS					
❏ JLS-3014	One More Time	197?	3.75	7.50	15.00
PARKWAY					
❏ P 7046 [M]	Cast Your Fate to the Wind	1965	3.75	7.50	15.00
❏ SP 7046 [S]	Cast Your Fate to the Wind	1965	5.00	10.00	20.00
❏ P 7047 [M]	The Soul of Sounds Orchestral	1965	3.75	7.50	15.00
❏ SP 7047 [S]	The Soul of Sounds Orchestral	1965	5.00	10.00	20.00
❏ P 7050 [M]	Impressions of James Bond	1966	5.00	10.00	20.00
❏ SP 7050 [S]	Impressions of James Bond	1966	7.50	15.00	30.00

Number	Title (A Side/B Side)	Yr	VG	VG+	NM
SOUNDS UNLIMITED					
45s					
ABC					
❑ 10803	Nobody But Me/Why Doesn't She Believe Me	1966	5.00	10.00	20.00
DUNWICH					
❑ 157	A Girl As Sweet As You/Little Brother	1967	6.25	12.50	25.00
SOUP					
Albums					
ARF ARM					
❑ 1	Soup	1970	30.00	60.00	120.00
BIG TREE					
❑ BTS 2007	The Album Soup	1971	6.25	12.50	25.00
SOUTH, JOE					
45s					
ALLWOOD					
❑ 402	Just Remember You're Mine/Silly Me	1962	3.00	6.00	12.00
APT					
❑ 25084	Deep Inside Me/I Want to Be Somebody	1965	2.50	5.00	10.00
CAPITOL					
❑ 2060	Birds of a Feather/It Got Away	1967	2.00	4.00	8.00
❑ 2169	How Can I Unlove You/She's Almost You	1968	2.00	4.00	8.00
❑ 2248	Games People Play/Mirror of Your Mind	1968	2.00	4.00	8.00
❑ 2284	Redneck/Don't Throw Your Love to the Wind	1968	2.00	4.00	8.00
❑ 2491	Leanin' On You/Don't You Be Ashamed	1969	—	3.00	6.00
❑ 2532	Birds of a Feather/These Are Not My People	1969	—	3.00	6.00
❑ 2592	Don't It Make You Want to Go Home/ Heart's Desire	1969	—	3.00	6.00
❑ 2704	Walk a Mile in My Shoes/Sheltered	1969	—	3.00	6.00
❑ 2755	Children/The Clock Up On the Wall	1970	—	2.50	5.00
❑ 2916	Why Does a Man Do What He Has to Do/ Be a Believer	1970	—	2.50	5.00
❑ 3008	Rose Garden/Mirror of Your Mind	1971	—	3.00	6.00
❑ 3053	United We Stand/So the Seeds Are Growing	1971	—	2.50	5.00
❑ 3204	Fool Me/Devil May Care	1971	—	2.50	5.00
❑ 3450	One Man Band/Coming Down All Alone	1972	—	2.50	5.00
❑ 3487	I'm a Star/Misunderstanding	1972	—	2.50	5.00
❑ 3554	Real Thing/Save Your Best	1973	—	2.50	5.00
❑ 3717	Riverdog/It Hurts Me Too	1973	—	2.50	5.00
COLUMBIA					
❑ 43983	Backfield in Motion/I'll Come Back to You	1967	3.00	6.00	12.00
❑ 44218	A Fool in Love/Great Day	1967	3.00	6.00	12.00
FAIRLANE					
❑ 21006	You're the Reason/Jukebox	1961	5.00	10.00	20.00
❑ 21010	Masquerade/I'm Sorry for You	1961	3.75	7.50	15.00
❑ 21015	Slippin' Around/Just to Be with You Again	1962	3.75	7.50	15.00
ISLAND					
❑ 034	To Have, to Hold and Let Go/Midnight Rainbows	1975	—	2.00	4.00
MGM					
❑ 13145	Same Old Song/Standing Invitation	1963	2.50	5.00	10.00
❑ 13196	Concrete Jungle/The Last One to Know	1963	2.50	5.00	10.00
❑ 13276	Naughty Claudie/Little Queenie	1964	2.50	5.00	10.00
NRC					
❑ 002	I'm Snowed/It's Only You	1958	10.00	20.00	40.00
❑ 022	Chills/What a Night	1959	3.75	7.50	15.00
❑ 041	Little Bluebird/Play It Cool	1959	3.75	7.50	15.00
❑ 053	Tell the Truth/If You Only Knew Her	1960	3.75	7.50	15.00
❑ 065	Let's Talk It Over/Formality	1961	3.75	7.50	15.00
❑ 5000	The Purple People Eater Meets the Witch Doctor/My Fondest Memories	1958	3.75	7.50	15.00
❑ 5001	One Fool to Another/ Texas Ain't the Biggest Anymore	1958	3.75	7.50	15.00
Albums					
ACCORD					
❑ SN-7119	Party People	1981	2.50	5.00	10.00
CAPITOL					
❑ ST-108	Introspect	1968	5.00	10.00	20.00
❑ ST-235	Games People Play	1969	3.75	7.50	15.00
❑ ST-392	Don't It Make You Want to Go Home	1969	3.75	7.50	15.00
❑ SM-450	Joe South's Greatest Hits	1977	2.00	4.00	8.00
—Reissue with new prefix					
❑ ST-450	Joe South's Greatest Hits	1970	3.75	7.50	15.00
❑ ST-637	So the Seeds Are Growing	1971	3.00	6.00	12.00
❑ ST-845	Joe South	1972	3.00	6.00	12.00
❑ ST-11074	A Look Inside	1972	3.00	6.00	12.00
ISLAND					
❑ ILPS-9328	Midnight Rainbows	1975	2.50	5.00	10.00
MINE					
❑ MSG-1100	Walkin' Shoes	1971	3.00	6.00	12.00
—Reissue with new title					
❑ MSG-1100	The Joe South Story	1971	3.75	7.50	15.00
NASHVILLE					
❑ 2092	You're the Reason	1970	3.00	6.00	12.00
PICKWICK					
❑ SPC-3314	Games People Play	197?	2.50	5.00	10.00
SOUTH 40					
45s					
METROBEAT					
❑ 4450	The Penny Song/Good Lovin'	1967	3.00	6.00	12.00
❑ 4457	I Want Sunshine/Goin' Someplace Else	1968	3.00	6.00	12.00
Albums					
METROBEAT					
❑ MBS-1000	Live at the Someplace Else	1968	6.25	12.50	25.00
SOUTHER, J.D. Includes records as "John David Souther." Also see THE SOUTHER, HILLMAN, FURAY BAND.					
12-Inch Singles					
WARNER BROS.					
❑ PRO-A-2140 [DJ]	Bad News/Homeby Down/Go Ahead	1984	—	3.00	6.00
45s					
ASYLUM					
❑ 11009	How Long/The Fast One	1972	—	2.50	5.00
❑ 45332	Silver Blue/Black Rose	1976	—	2.00	4.00
—As "John David Souther"					

Number	Title (A Side/B Side)	Yr	VG	VG+	NM
❑ 45364	Faithless Love/Midnight Prowl	1976	—	2.00	4.00
—As "John David Souther"					
COLUMBIA					
❑ 02422	You're Only Lonely/If You Don't Want My Love	1981	—	—	3.00
—Reissue					
❑ 11079	You're Only Lonely/Songs of Love	1979	—	2.00	4.00
❑ 11196	White Rhythm and Blues/The Last in Love	1980	—	2.00	4.00
❑ 11302	'Til the Bar Burns Down/ If You Don't Want My Love	1980	—	2.00	4.00
—With Johnny Duncan					
FULL MOON					
❑ 49612	You're Only Lonely/Once in a Lifetime	1980	—	2.00	4.00
—B-side by Bonnie Raitt					
WARNER BROS.					
❑ 29289	Go Ahead and Rain/All I Want	1984	—	—	3.00
Albums					
ASYLUM					
❑ 7E-1059	Black Rose	1976	2.50	5.00	10.00
❑ SD 5055	John David Souther	1972	3.00	6.00	12.00
COLUMBIA					
❑ JC 36093	You're Only Lonely	1979	2.50	5.00	10.00
❑ PC 36093	You're Only Lonely	198?	2.00	4.00	8.00
—Budget-line reissue					
WARNER BROS.					
❑ 25081	Home By Dawn	1985	2.50	5.00	10.00
SOUTHER, HILLMAN, FURAY BAND, THE Also see J.D. SOUTHER.					
45s					
ASYLUM					
❑ 45201	Fallin' in Love/Heavenly Fire	1974	—	2.00	4.00
❑ 45217	Border Town/Safe at Home	1974	—	2.00	4.00
❑ 45251	Mexico/Move Me Real Slow	1975	—	2.00	4.00
❑ 45267	Trouble in Paradise/On the Line	1975	—	2.00	4.00
❑ 45280	For Someone I Love/Move Me Real Slow	1975	—	2.00	4.00
Albums					
ASYLUM					
❑ 7E-1006	The Souther, Hillman, Furay Band	1974	2.50	5.00	10.00
❑ 7E-1036	Trouble in Paradise	1975	2.50	5.00	10.00
❑ EQ-1036 [Q]	Trouble in Paradise	1975	4.50	9.00	18.00
SOUTHWEST F.O.B. ENGLAND DAN AND JOHN FORD COLEY were in this group.					
45s					
GPC					
❑ 1945	Smell of Incense/Green Skies	1968	3.75	7.50	15.00
HIP					
❑ 8002	Smell of Incense/Green Skies	1968	2.00	4.00	8.00
❑ 8009	Nadine/All One Big Game	1969	2.00	4.00	8.00
❑ 8015	Independent Me/As I Look at You	1969	2.00	4.00	8.00
❑ 8022	Feelin' Groovy/Beggar Man	1969	2.00	4.00	8.00
Albums					
HIP					
❑ 7001	Smell of Incense	1969	7.50	15.00	30.00
SOUVENIRS, THE May be three different groups.					
45s					
DOOTO					
❑ 412	So Long Daddy/ Arlene, Sweet Little Texas Queen	1957	12.50	25.00	50.00
INFERNO					
❑ 2001	I Could Have Danced All Night/It's Too Bad	1967	12.50	25.00	50.00
REPRISE					
❑ 20065	The Worm/The Bump	1962	3.75	7.50	15.00
❑ 20066	The Real McCoy/The Watusi	1962	3.75	7.50	15.00
SOVINE, RED Also see JOHNNY BOND.					
45s					
CHART					
❑ 5142	Old Pine Tree/Two Hearts on a Post Card	1971	—	2.50	5.00
❑ 5152	Six Broken Hearts/The Greatest Grand Ol' Opry	1972	—	2.50	5.00
❑ 5161	Down Through the Years/Petunia	1972	—	2.50	5.00
❑ 5176	The Guilty One/The Day the Preacher Came	1973	—	2.50	5.00
❑ 5207	Midnight Rider/Why the Grass Is Green	1974	—	2.50	5.00
❑ 5216	From Champagne to Beer/Mama's Birthday	1974	—	2.50	5.00
❑ 5220	It'll Come Back/Down Through the Years	1974	—	2.50	5.00
❑ 5230	Can I Keep Him Daddy/Red's So Fine	1974	—	2.50	5.00
❑ 5231	Santa Claus Is a Texas Cowboy/ The Legend of the Christmas Rose	1974	—	2.50	5.00
❑ 7507	Daddy's Girl/(B-side unknown)	1975	—	2.50	5.00
DECCA					
❑ 29068	My New Love Affair/How Do You Think I Feel	1954	3.75	7.50	15.00
❑ 29211	Don't Drop It/Don't Be the One	1954	3.75	7.50	15.00
❑ 29335	Outlaw/Which One Should I Choose	1954	3.75	7.50	15.00
❑ 29529	I Hope You Don't Care/ I'm Glad You Found a Place for Me	1955	3.75	7.50	15.00
❑ 29739	Why Baby Why/Sixteen Tons	1955	5.00	10.00	20.00
—A-side with Webb Pierce					
❑ 29755	Why Baby Why/Missing You	1955	3.75	7.50	15.00
—A-side with Webb Pierce					
❑ 29825	If Jesus Came to Your House/I Got Religion	1956	3.75	7.50	15.00
❑ 29876	Little Rosa/Hold Everything (Till I Get Home)	1956	3.75	7.50	15.00
—A-side with Webb Pierce					
❑ 30018	The Best Years of Your Life/My Little Rat	1956	3.00	6.00	12.00
❑ 30162	A Poor Man's Riches/ Down on the Corner of Love	1956	3.00	6.00	12.00
❑ 30239	Juke Joint Johnny/No Thanks, Bartender	1957	7.50	15.00	30.00
❑ 30458	Wrong/Who Knows Better Than You and I	1957	3.00	6.00	12.00
❑ 30595	Once More/For Arms	1958	3.00	6.00	12.00
❑ 30715	Courtin' Time in Tennessee/ Where Will Mommie Go	1958	3.00	6.00	12.00
❑ 30814	You Used to Be My Baby/Leave Me Alone	1959	2.50	5.00	10.00
❑ 30920	Cold Hands of Fate/One Sided Love Affair	1959	2.50	5.00	10.00
❑ 31028	A Lot Like You/Ooooh How I Love You	1959	2.50	5.00	10.00
❑ 31903	You Used to Be My Baby/Leave Me Alone	1966	2.00	4.00	8.00
GUSTO					
❑ 169	Woman Behind the Man Behind the Wheel/ Jealous Heart	1977	—	2.00	4.00

S

Number	Title (A Side/B Side)	Yr	VG	VG+	NM
❏ 175	Lay Down Sally/The Farmers and the Miners	1978	—	2.00	4.00
❏ 180	Lay Down Sally/The King's Last Concert	1978	—	3.00	6.00
❏ 188	The Days of Me and You/I'd Love to Make Love	1978	—	2.00	4.00
❏ 9005	A Place for Mama's Roses/Does Steppin' Out Mean Daddy Took a Walk	1978		2.00	4.00
❏ 9015	Christmas Is For Kids/ What Does Christmas Look Like	1978	—	2.00	4.00
❏ 9016	The Waylon and Willie Machine/ Colorado Cool-Aid	1979	—	2.50	5.00
❏ 9017	Mr. F.C.C./Flesh and Blood	1979	—	2.00	4.00
❏ 9019	The Prettiest Dress/Flesh and Blood	1979	—	2.00	4.00
❏ 9021	The Hero/Flesh and Blood	1979	—	2.00	4.00
❏ 9026	The First Time I Saw Her/18 Wheels a-Hummin' Home Sweet Home	1980		2.00	4.00
❏ 9028	The Little Family Soldier/ She Was Loving Me Goodbye	1980	—	2.00	4.00
❏ 9030	It'll Come Back/Love Is	1980	—	2.00	4.00
MGM					
❏ 10717	When I Get Rich/ You're Barking Up the Wrong Tree	1950	6.25	12.50	25.00
❏ 10782	Christmas Alone/Dear Mister Santa Claus	1950	6.25	12.50	25.00
❏ 10887	Billy Goat Boogie/Big Dipper	1951	5.00	10.00	20.00
❏ 10981	Four Flusher/Farewell, So Long	1951	5.00	10.00	20.00
❏ 11090	Don't Worry/Sundown Sue	1951	5.00	10.00	20.00
❏ 11214	It'd Surprise You/Loveless Marriage	1952	5.00	10.00	20.00
❏ 11323	Okey Dokey/Till Today	1952	5.00	10.00	20.00
❏ 11402	A Quarter's Worth of Heartaches/ I'm Gonna Lock My Heart	1953	5.00	10.00	20.00
❏ 11567	You Taught Me How/If You'll Be a Baby	1953	5.00	10.00	20.00
RCA VICTOR					
❏ 47-7981	The Cajun Queen/Big Dreams	1962	3.00	6.00	12.00
RIC					
❏ 131	Big Ol' Ugly Fool/Hiding Out	1964	2.00	4.00	8.00
❏ 154	Losing My Grip/Star of the Show	1965	2.00	4.00	8.00
❏ 168	I Wish I Had Seen Sunshine/Salt on My Eggs	1965	2.00	4.00	8.00
STARDAY					
❏ 101	Phantom 309/(B-side unknown)	1975	—	2.00	4.00
❏ 137	Giddyup Go/Tonight My Lady Learns to Love	1976	—	2.00	4.00
❏ 142	Teddy Bear/Daddy	1976	—	2.50	5.00
❏ 144	Little Joe/Cold Love to Go	1976	—	2.00	4.00
❏ 147	Last Goodbye/Lonely Arms of Mine	1976	—	2.00	4.00
❏ 148	Just Gettin' By/I'm Gonna Move	1977	—	2.00	4.00
❏ 152	I'm Only Seventeen/No One's Too Big to Cry	1977	—	2.00	4.00
❏ 158	Daddy's Girl/Love Is All She Ever Wants from Me	1977	—	2.00	4.00
❏ 510	Burn the School/One Is a Lonely Number	1960	2.50	5.00	10.00
❏ 521	No Money in This Deal/If I Could Come Back	1960	2.50	5.00	10.00
❏ 540	Why Baby Why/Little Rosa	1961	2.50	5.00	10.00
❏ 553	Heart of a Man/Brand New Low	1961	2.50	5.00	10.00
❏ 567	Color of the Blues/Hold Everything	1961	2.50	5.00	10.00
❏ 579	East of West Berlin/Thanks for Nothing	1962	2.50	5.00	10.00
❏ 598	Rose of Love/She Can't Read My Writing	1962	2.50	5.00	10.00
❏ 616	Sittin' and Thinkin'/A Million to One	1962	2.50	5.00	10.00
❏ 632	Waltzing with Sin/I Forgot to Keep Her with Me	1963	2.50	5.00	10.00
❏ 650	Dream House for Sale/King of the Open Road	1963	2.50	5.00	10.00
❏ 672	Old Pipeliner/Peace of Mind	1964	2.50	5.00	10.00
❏ 737	Giddyup Go/A Kiss and the Keys	1965	2.00	4.00	8.00
❏ 757	Long Night/Too Much	1966	2.00	4.00	8.00
❏ 766	I'm the Man/I Think I Can Sleep Tonight	1966	2.00	4.00	8.00
❏ 774	Alabam/Nobody's Business	1966	2.00	4.00	8.00
—With Minnie Pearl					
❏ 779	Class of '49/I Hope My Wife Don't Find Out	1966	2.00	4.00	8.00
❏ 794	I Didn't Jump the Fence/ Don't Let My Glass Run Dry	1967	2.00	4.00	8.00
❏ 811	Phantom 309/In Your Heart	1967	2.50	5.00	10.00
❏ 823	Tell Maude I Slipped/Not Like It Was with You	1967	2.00	4.00	8.00
❏ 831	Twenty-One/Sparkling Wine	1968	2.00	4.00	8.00
❏ 842	Loser Making Good/Good Enough for Nothing	1968	2.00	4.00	8.00
❏ 852	Normally, Norma Loves Me/ Live and Let Live and Be Happy	1968	2.00	4.00	8.00
❏ 857	Between Closing Time and Dawn/ The Father of Judy Ann	1968	2.00	4.00	8.00
❏ 864	Blues Stay Away from Me/ Whiskey Flavored Kisses	1969	—	3.00	6.00
❏ 872	Who Am I/Three Hearts in a Tangle	1969	—	3.00	6.00
❏ 882	Truck Drivers Prayer/Chairman of the Board	1969	2.00	4.00	8.00
❏ 885	Castle of Shame/ Why Don't You Haul Off and Love Me	1969	—	3.00	6.00
—With Lois Williams					
❏ 889	I Know You're Married But I Love You Still/ Money, Marbles and Chalk	1970	—	3.00	6.00
❏ 896	Freightliner Fever/Mr. Sunday Sun	1970	—	3.00	6.00
❏ 915	Enough to Take the Me Out of Men/ I'm Waiting Just for You	1970	—	3.00	6.00
❏ 918	Unfinished Letter/The Thought of Losing You	1970	—	3.00	6.00
❏ 926	Get in Touch/Violets Blue	1971	—	3.00	6.00
❏ 933	Happy Birthday, My Darlin'/I'll Sail My Ship Alone	1971	—	3.00	6.00
❏ 934	I Am a Pilgrim/Beautiful Life	1971	—	3.00	6.00
❏ 960	Go Hide John/Tear Stained Guitar	1973	—	2.50	5.00
❏ 977	Take Time to Remember/(B-side unknown)	1973	—	2.50	5.00
❏ 7004	Why Baby Why/Little Rosa	197?	—	2.00	4.00
—Reissue of 540					
❏ 7022	Six Days on the Road/Truck Drivin' Man	197?	—	2.00	4.00
❏ 7037	He'll Have to Go/I'll Step Aside	197?	—	2.00	4.00
❏ 8000	Giddyup Go/Phantom 309	197?	—	2.00	4.00
❏ 8023	Little Rosa/Ruby, Don't Take Your Love to Town	197?	—	2.00	4.00
❏ 8033	Truck Driving Son-of-a-Gun/Radar Blues	197?	—	2.00	4.00
—B-side by Coleman Wilson					
Albums					
CHART					
❏ 1052	The Greatest Grand Ol' Opry	1972	3.75	7.50	15.00
❏ 2056	It'll Come Back	1974	3.75	7.50	15.00
DECCA					
❏ DL 4445 [M]	Red Sovine	1963	7.50	15.00	30.00
❏ DL 4736 [M]	Country Music Time	1966	7.50	15.00	30.00
❏ DL 74445 [R]	Red Sovine	1963	5.00	10.00	20.00
❏ DL 74736 [R]	Country Music Time	1966	5.00	10.00	20.00

Number	Title (A Side/B Side)	Yr	VG	VG+	NM
GUSTO					
❏ 3010	16 All-Time Favorites	1978	3.00	6.00	12.00
❏ E-3465 [M]	Red Sovine	1957	15.00	30.00	60.00
NASHVILLE					
❏ 2033	Giddy-Up Go	196?	3.00	6.00	12.00
❏ 2044	A Dear John Letter	196?	3.00	6.00	12.00
❏ 2056	Anytime	196?	3.00	6.00	12.00
❏ 2083	Don't Take Your Love to Town	1969	3.00	6.00	12.00
POWER PAK					
❏ 270	Phantom 309	197?	2.50	5.00	10.00
STARDAY					
❏ SLP-132 [M]	The One and Only Red Sovine	1961	10.00	20.00	40.00
❏ SLP-197 [M]	Golden Country Ballads of the 1960s	1962	10.00	20.00	40.00
❏ SLP-341 [M]	Little Rosa	1965	6.25	12.50	25.00
❏ SLP-357	That's Truckdrivin'	196?	5.00	10.00	20.00
❏ SLP-363 [M]	Giddy-Up Go	1966	5.00	10.00	20.00
❏ SLP-383 [M]	Town and Country Action	1966	5.00	10.00	20.00
❏ SLP-396 [M]	The Nashville Sound of Red Sovine	1967	5.00	10.00	20.00
❏ SLP-405 [M]	I Didn't Jump the Fence	1967	5.00	10.00	20.00
❏ SLP-414 [M]	Phantom 309	1967	5.00	10.00	20.00
❏ SLP-420	Tell Maude I Slipped	1968	5.00	10.00	20.00
❏ SLP-427	Sunday with Sovine	1968	5.00	10.00	20.00
❏ SLP-436	Classic Narrations	1968	5.00	10.00	20.00
❏ SLP-441	Closing Time 'Til Dawn	1969	5.00	10.00	20.00
❏ SLP-445	Who Am I	1969	5.00	10.00	20.00
❏ SLP-459	I Know You're Married But I Love You Still	1970	5.00	10.00	20.00
❏ 952	The Best of Red Sovine	197?	3.75	7.50	15.00
❏ 968	Teddy Bear	1976	3.75	7.50	15.00
❏ 970	Woodrow Wilson Sovine	1977	3.75	7.50	15.00
❏ 991	Red Sovine's 16 Greatest Hits	1977	3.75	7.50	15.00
❏ ST-90712 [S]	Giddy-Up Go	1966	7.50	15.00	30.00
—Capitol Record Club edition					
❏ T-90712 [M]	Giddy-Up Go	1966	6.25	12.50	25.00
—Capitol Record Club edition					
VOCALION					
❏ VL 3829 [M]	The Country Way	196?	3.75	7.50	15.00
❏ VL 73829 [R]	The Country Way	196?	3.00	6.00	12.00

SOVINE, RED, AND GOLDIE HILL
45s

Number	Title (A Side/B Side)	Yr	VG	VG+	NM
DECCA					
❏ 9-29411	Are You Mine/Ko Ko Mo	1955	3.75	7.50	15.00

SPACEMEN, THE
45s

Number	Title (A Side/B Side)	Yr	VG	VG+	NM
ALTON					
❏ 254	The Clouds/The Lonely Jet Pilot	1959	5.00	10.00	20.00

SPADES, THE (1) Nashville studio group.
45s

Number	Title (A Side/B Side)	Yr	VG	VG+	NM
HIT					
❏ 226	You've Got Your Troubles/ Everybody Loves a Clown	1965	2.00	4.00	8.00
—B-side by Jason Allen					

SPADES, THE (2) For records on Liberty, see THE SLADES.

SPADES, THE (3)
45s

Number	Title (A Side/B Side)	Yr	VG	VG+	NM
MAJOR					
❏ 1007	Close to You/I'm on Fire	1959	15.00	30.00	60.00

SPADES, THE (4) Evolved into THE THIRTEENTH FLOOR ELEVATORS. Zero 10001 was recorded before Roky Erickson joined the group.
45s

Number	Title (A Side/B Side)	Yr	VG	VG+	NM
ZERO					
❏ 10001	I Need a Girl/Do You Want to Dance	1965	15.00	30.00	60.00
❏ 10002	You're Gonna Miss Me/We Sell Soul	1966	100.00	200.00	400.00

SPANIELS, THE Also see POOKIE HUDSON.
45s

Number	Title (A Side/B Side)	Yr	VG	VG+	NM
BUDDAH					
❏ 153	Goodnight Sweetheart/Maybe	1969	2.00	4.00	8.00
CALLA					
❏ 172	Fairy Tales/Jealous Heart	1970	—	3.00	6.00
CANTERBURY					
❏ 101	Peace of Mind/She Sang to Me/Danny Boy	1974	—	2.50	5.00
CHANCE					
❏ 1141	Baby It's You/Bounce	1953	125.00	250.00	500.00
❏ 1141	Baby It's You/Bounce	1953	500.00	1000.	2000.
—Red vinyl					
LOST-NITE					
❏ 262	Baby It's You/Bounce	197?	—	2.00	4.00
❏ 265	The Bells Ring Out/House Cleaning	197?	—	2.00	4.00
❏ 268	Goodnite, Sweetheart, Goodnite/You Don't Move Me	197?	—	2.00	4.00
❏ 271	Do-Wah/Don'cha Go	197?	—	2.00	4.00
❏ 274	Play It Cool/Let's Make Up	197?	—	2.00	4.00
❏ 277	False Love/Do You Really	197?	—	2.00	4.00
❏ 280	You Painted Pictures/Hey, Sister Lizzie	197?	—	2.00	4.00
❏ 283	Dear Heart/Why Won't You Dance	197?	—	2.00	4.00
❏ 286	Everyone's Laughing/I.O.U.	197?	—	2.00	4.00
❏ 289	I Lost You/Crazy Baby	197?	—	2.00	4.00
❏ 292	You Gave Me Peace of Mind/ Please Don't Tease	197?	—	2.00	4.00
❏ 295	You're Gonna Cry/I Like It Like That	197?	—	2.00	4.00
❏ 298	Stormy Weather/Here Is Why I Love You	197?	—	2.00	4.00
❏ 301	Tina/Great Googley Moo	197?	—	2.00	4.00
❏ 304	Since I Fell for You/Baby Come Along with Me	197?	—	2.00	4.00
❏ 307	This Is a Lovely Way to Spend an Evening/Red Sails in the Sunset	197?	—	2.00	4.00
❏ 446	I Know/Bus Fare Home	197?	—	2.00	4.00
NEPTUNE					
❏ 124	I Love You For Sentimental Reasons/Meek Man	1961	5.00	10.00	20.00
—As "Pookie Hudson and the Spaniels"					

Number	Title (A Side/B Side)	Yr	VG	VG+	NM
NORTH AMERICAN					
❑ 001	Fairy Tales/Jealous Heart	1970	—	2.50	5.00
❑ 002	Stand in Line/Lonely Man	1970	—	2.50	5.00
❑ 1114	Come Back to These Arms/Money Blues	1970	—	2.50	5.00
OWL					
❑ 328	Little Goe/The Posse	1973	—	2.50	5.00
VEE JAY					
❑ 101	Baby It's You/Bounce	1953	200.00	400.00	800.00
—Black vinyl, maroon label					
❑ 101	Baby It's You/Bounce	1953	1125.	2250.	4500.
—Red vinyl					
❑ 101	Baby It's You/Bounce	1961	10.00	20.00	40.00
—Black vinyl, black label					
❑ 103	The Bells Ring Out/House Cleaning	1953	75.00	150.00	300.00
❑ 103	The Bells Ring Out/House Cleaning	1953	150.00	300.00	600.00
—Red vinyl					
❑ 107	Goodnite, Sweetheart, Goodnite/You Don't Move Me	1953	50.00	100.00	200.00
—Black vinyl, correct spelling					
❑ 107	Goodnite, Sweetheart, Goodnite/You Don't Move Me	1953	75.00	150.00	300.00
—Black vinyl; as "Spanials"					
❑ 107	Goodnite, Sweetheart, Goodnite/You Don't Move Me	1953	200.00	400.00	800.00
—Red vinyl; no "Trade Mark Reg" on label					
❑ 107	Goodnite, Sweetheart, Goodnite/You Don't Move Me	1993	2.00	4.00	8.00
—Red vinyl; "Trade Mark Reg" on label; included in Vee-Jay CD box set					
❑ 116	Play It Cool/Let's Make Up	1954	25.00	50.00	100.00
❑ 116	Play It Cool/Let's Make Up	1954	125.00	250.00	500.00
—Red vinyl					
❑ 131	Do-Wah/Don'cha Go	1955	20.00	40.00	80.00
❑ 131	Do-Wah/Don'cha Go	1955	125.00	250.00	500.00
—Red vinyl					
❑ 154	You Painted Pictures/Hey, Sister Lizzie	1955	12.50	25.00	50.00
—As "Spanials"					
❑ 154	You Painted Pictures/Hey, Sister Lizzie	1955	15.00	30.00	60.00
❑ 178	False Love/Do You Really	1956	37.50	75.00	150.00
❑ 189	Dear Heart/Why Won't You Dance	1956	37.50	75.00	150.00
❑ 202	Since I Fell for You/Baby Come Along with Me	1956	37.50	75.00	150.00
❑ 229	Please Don't Tease/You Gave Me Peace of Mind	1956	15.00	30.00	60.00
❑ 246	Everyone's Laughing/I.O.U.	1957	15.00	30.00	60.00
❑ 257	You're Gonna Cry/I Need Your Kisses	1957	15.00	30.00	60.00
❑ 264	I Love You/Crazee Babee	1958	15.00	30.00	60.00
❑ 278	Tina/Great Googly Moo	1958	15.00	30.00	60.00
❑ 290	Stormy Weather/Here Is Why I Love You	1958	15.00	30.00	60.00
❑ 301	Baby It's You/Heart and Soul	1958	15.00	30.00	60.00
❑ 310	Trees/I Like It Like That	1959	15.00	30.00	60.00
❑ 328	These Three Words/100 Years from Today	1959	15.00	30.00	60.00
❑ 342	People Will Say We're in Love/The Bells Ring Out	1960	25.00	50.00	100.00
❑ 350	I Know/Bus Fare Home	1960	10.00	20.00	40.00
Albums					
LOST-NITE					
❑ LLP-19 [10]	The Spaniels	1981	3.00	6.00	12.00
—Red vinyl					
VEE JAY					
❑ LP-1002 [M]	Goodnite, It's Time to Go	1958	150.00	300.00	600.00
—Maroon label; group pictured on cover					
❑ LP-1002 [M]	Goodnite, It's Time to Go	1961	50.00	100.00	200.00
—Black label; dogs on cover					
❑ VJLP-1002 [M]	Goodnite, It's Time to Go	198?	3.00	6.00	12.00
—Legitimate reissue on flimsier vinyl than originals					
❑ LP-1024 [M]	The Spaniels	1960	75.00	150.00	300.00
SPANKY AND OUR GANG					
45s					
EPIC					
❑ 50170	When I Wanna/I Won't Brand You	1975	—	2.50	5.00
❑ 50206	L.A. Freeway/Standing Room Only	1976	—	2.50	5.00
MERCURY					
❑ DJ-101 [DJ]	Give a Damn (mono/stereo)	1968	3.00	6.00	12.00
—Special promo for the New York Urban Coalition					
❑ DJ-101 [PS]	Give a Damn (mono/stereo)	1968	5.00	10.00	20.00
—Fold-open sleeve with insert letter					
❑ 72598	And Your Bird Can Sing/Sealed with a Kiss	1966	5.00	10.00	20.00
❑ 72679	Sunday Will Never Be the Same/Distance	1967	2.00	4.00	8.00
❑ 72714	Making Every Minute Count/If You Could Only Be Me	1967	2.00	4.00	8.00
❑ 72714 [PS]	Making Every Minute Count/If You Could Only Be Me	1967	2.50	5.00	10.00
❑ 72732	Lazy Day/(It Ain't Necessarily) Byrd Avenue	1967	2.00	4.00	8.00
❑ 72732 [PS]	Lazy Day/(It Ain't Necessarily) Byrd Avenue	1967	2.50	5.00	10.00
❑ 72765	Sunday Morning/Echoes	1968	2.00	4.00	8.00
❑ 72765 [PS]	Sunday Morning/Echoes	1968	2.50	5.00	10.00
❑ 72795	Like to Get to Know You/Three Ways from Tomorrow	1968	2.00	4.00	8.00
—Orange and tan swirl label					
❑ 72795	Like to Get to Know You/Three Ways from Tomorrow	1968	2.50	5.00	10.00
—Red label with white "Mercury" in all caps across top of label					
❑ 72795 [PS]	Like to Get to Know You/Three Ways from Tomorrow	1968	2.50	5.00	10.00
❑ 72831	Give a Damn/Swinging Gate	1968	2.00	4.00	8.00
❑ 72871	Yesterday's Rain/Without Rhyme or Reason	1968	2.00	4.00	8.00
❑ 72890	Anything You Choose/Mecca Flat Blues	1969	2.00	4.00	8.00
❑ 72926	And She's Mine/Leopard Skinned Phones	1969	2.00	4.00	8.00
❑ 72982	Everybody's Talkin'/(B-side unknown)	1969	2.00	4.00	8.00
PHILCO-FORD					
❑ HP-19	Making Every Minute Count/Byrd Avenue	1968	3.75	7.50	15.00
—4-inch plastic "Hip Pocket Record" with color sleeve					
Albums					
EPIC					
❑ PE 33580	Change	1975	3.00	6.00	12.00

Number	Title (A Side/B Side)	Yr	VG	VG+	NM
MERCURY					
❑ MG-21124 [M]	Spanky and Our Gang	1967	7.50	15.00	30.00
❑ SR-61124 [S]	Spanky and Our Gang	1967	5.00	10.00	20.00
❑ SR-61161	Like to Get to Know You	1968	5.00	10.00	20.00
❑ SR-61183	Anything You Choose/Without Rhyme or Reason	1969	5.00	10.00	20.00
❑ SR-61227	Spanky's Greatest Hit(s)	1969	5.00	10.00	20.00
❑ SR-61326	Live	1971	3.75	7.50	15.00
RHINO					
❑ RNLP-70131	The Best of Spanky and Our Gang (1967-1969)	1986	3.00	6.00	12.00
SPARKLETONES, THE (1) Also see JOE BENNETT AND THE SPARKLETONES.					
45s					
ABC-PARAMOUNT					
❑ 10659	Run Rabbit Run/Well Dressed Man	1965	3.75	7.50	15.00
SPARKLETONES, THE (2)					
45s					
PAGEANT					
❑ 604	Just One Chance/Dear Little Boy	196?	12.50	25.00	50.00
SPARKS Includes records as "Halfnelson." This group did not use the article "The" before its name.					
Albums					
ANTILLES					
❑ ANT-7044	Kimono My House	198?	2.50	5.00	10.00
—Reissue of Island 9272					
ATLANTIC					
❑ SD 19347	Angst in My Pants	1982	2.50	5.00	10.00
❑ 80055	Sparks in Outer Space	1983	2.50	5.00	10.00
❑ 80160	Pulling Rabbits Out of a Hat	1984	2.50	5.00	10.00
BEARSVILLE					
❑ BV 2048	Halfnelson	1971	6.25	12.50	25.00
—Original issue of "Sparks" as "Halfnelson"					
❑ BV 2048	Sparks	1972	3.00	6.00	12.00
—Reissue under the group's new name					
❑ BR 2110	A Woofer in Tweeter's Clothing	1973	3.00	6.00	12.00
COLUMBIA					
❑ PC 34359	Big Beat	1976	2.50	5.00	10.00
—Originals have no bar code					
❑ PC 34901	Introducing Sparks	1977	2.50	5.00	10.00
—Originals have no bar code					
ELEKTRA					
❑ 6E-186	No. 1 in Heaven	1979	2.50	5.00	10.00
ISLAND					
❑ ILPS-9272	Kimono My House	1974	3.00	6.00	12.00
—Originals have multicolor island-scene label					
❑ ILPS-9312	Propaganda	1975	3.00	6.00	12.00
—Originals have multicolor island-scene label					
❑ ILPS-9345	Indiscreet	1975	3.00	6.00	12.00
—Originals have black label and no Warner Bros. distribution					
MCA CURB					
❑ 5780	Music That You Can Dance To	1986	2.50	5.00	10.00
RCA VICTOR					
❑ AFL1-4091	Whomp That Sucker	1981	2.50	5.00	10.00
RHINO					
❑ R1-70841	Interior Design	1988	2.50	5.00	10.00
SPARKS, THE Possibly more than one group.					
45s					
ARWIN					
❑ 114	Something's Happened/Robin Redbreast	1958	5.00	10.00	20.00
CARLTON					
❑ 522	The Genie/Gee, That's Bad	1959	5.00	10.00	20.00
CUB					
❑ 9151	Woe, Woe/Cool It	1967	2.50	5.00	10.00
DECCA					
❑ 30378	Ol' Man River/Merry, Merry Lou	1957	3.00	6.00	12.00
❑ 30509	Roamin' Candle/A Cuddle and a Kiss	1957	3.00	6.00	12.00
❑ 30974	Why Did You Leave/La Macerena	1959	2.50	5.00	10.00
HULL					
❑ 723	Danny Boy/Run Run Run	1957	100.00	200.00	400.00
❑ 724	Adreann/Finger	1957	37.50	75.00	150.00
SPARKS OF RHYTHM, THE					
45s					
APOLLO					
❑ 479	Women, Women, Women/Don't Love You Anymore	1955	75.00	150.00	300.00
❑ 481	Hurry Home/Stars Are in the Sky	1955	75.00	150.00	300.00
❑ 541	Handy Man/Everybody Rock and Roll	1959	12.50	25.00	50.00
SPARROW, THE Evolved into STEPPENWOLF. Also see MARS BONFIRE.					
45s					
COLUMBIA					
❑ 10234	Eli's Coming/Oh Doctor	1975	2.50	5.00	10.00
❑ 43755	Tomorrow's Ship/Isn't It Strange	1966	6.25	12.50	25.00
—As "The Sparrows"					
❑ 43755 [PS]	Tomorrow's Ship/Isn't It Strange	1966	25.00	50.00	100.00
—As "The Sparrows"					
❑ 43960	Green Bottle Lover/Down Goes Your Love Life	1967	6.25	12.50	25.00
—As "The Sparrows"					
Albums					
COLUMBIA					
❑ CS 9758	John Kay and Sparrow	1969	10.00	20.00	40.00
—Red "360 Sound" label					
SPARROWS, THE Probably three different groups.					
45s					
DAVIS					
❑ 456	Love Me Tender/Come Back to Me	1957	75.00	150.00	300.00
JAY DEE					
❑ 783	Tell Me Baby/Why Did You Leave Me	1953	125.00	250.00	500.00
❑ 790	I'll Be Loving You/Hey!	1954	125.00	250.00	500.00
Albums					
ELKAY					
❑ 3009 [M]	That Mersey Sound	1964	10.00	20.00	40.00

S

Number	Title (A Side/B Side)	Yr	VG	VG+	NM

SPARTAS, THE
45s
HIT
| ❏ 137 | House of the Rising Sun/Bread and Butter | 1964 | 3.75 | 7.50 | 15.00 |

—*B-side by Danny and Deanie*

| ❏ 154 | I'm Crying/Have I the Right | 1964 | 3.75 | 7.50 | 15.00 |
| ❏ 158 | Dance, Dance, Dance/Everything's Alright | 1964 | 3.00 | 6.00 | 12.00 |

—*B-side by the Roamers*

| ❏ 181 | Sha La La/Midnight Special | 1965 | 3.00 | 6.00 | 12.00 |

—*B-side by Harvey Frolic*

| ❏ 251 | Good Lovin'/Soul and Inspiration | 1966 | 3.00 | 6.00 | 12.00 |

—*B-side by John Brooks*

SPATS, THE
45s
ABC-PARAMOUNT
❏ 10585	Gator Tails and Monkey Ribs/The Roach	1964	2.50	5.00	10.00
❏ 10600	She Kissed Me Last Night/				
	There's a Party in the Pad Down Below	1964	2.50	5.00	10.00
❏ 10640	Billy, the Blue Grasshoper/				
	Gotta Tell Ya All About It, Baby	1965	2.50	5.00	10.00
❏ 10711	Go Go Yamaha/Have You Ever Seen Me Crying	1965	2.50	5.00	10.00
❏ 10790	Scoobee Doo/She Done Moved	1966	2.50	5.00	10.00

ENITH
| ❏ 1268 | Gator Tails and Monkey Ribs/The Roach | 1964 | 6.25 | 12.50 | 25.00 |

Albums
ABC-PARAMOUNT
| ❏ 502 [M] | Cookin' with the Spats | 1965 | 5.00 | 10.00 | 20.00 |
| ❏ S-502 [S] | Cookin' with the Spats | 1965 | 7.50 | 15.00 | 30.00 |

SPECTOR, PHIL Also see THE TEDDY BEARS; THE RIGHTEOUS BROTHERS.
45s
PAVILLION
| ❏ AE7 1354 [DJ] | Phil Spector's Christmas Medley | | | | |
| | (same on both sides) | 1981 | 3.75 | 7.50 | 15.00 |

—*Promo-only sampler from the Pavillion reissue of Phil Spector's Christmas Album*
PHILLES
| ❏ (no #) [DJ] | Thanks for Giving Me the Right Time! | | | | |
| | (same on both sides) | 1965 | 250.00 | 500.00 | 1000. |

—*Has Phil's picture on label; actually plays "Ebb Tide" by the Righteous Brothers*

SPECTOR, RONNIE Also see THE RONETTES; VERONICA.
12-Inch Singles
COLUMBIA
| ❏ CAS 2701 [DJ] | Who Can Sleep (same on both sides) | 1987 | 2.00 | 4.00 | 8.00 |
EPIC
| ❏ ASF 350 [DJ] | Say Goodbye to Hollywood/ | | | | |
| | Baby Please Don't Go | 1977 | 10.00 | 20.00 | 40.00 |
TOM CAT
| ❏ JD-10380 [DJ] | You'd Be Good for Me (same on both sides) | 197? | 7.50 | 15.00 | 30.00 |

—*Promo only on red vinyl*
45s
ALSTON
| ❏ 3738 | It's a Heartache/I Wanna Come Over | 1978 | 2.00 | 4.00 | 8.00 |
APPLE
| ❏ 1832 | Try Some, Buy Some/Tandoori Chicken | 1971 | — | 3.50 | 7.00 |
| ❏ 1832 | Try Some, Buy Some/Tandoori Chicken | 1971 | 2.00 | 4.00 | 8.00 |

—*With star on A-side label*

| ❏ 1832 [PS] | Try Some, Buy Some/Tandoori Chicken | 1971 | 2.50 | 5.00 | 10.00 |
COLUMBIA
❏ 07082	Who Can Sleep/When We Danced	1987	—	2.00	4.00
❏ 07082 [PS]	Who Can Sleep/When We Danced	1987	—	2.00	4.00
❏ 07300	Love on a Rooftop/Good Love Is Hard to Find	1987	—	2.00	4.00
EPIC
❏ 50374	Say Goodbye to Hollywood/				
	Baby Please Don't Go	1977	2.50	5.00	10.00
❏ 50374 [PS]	Say Goodbye to Hollywood/				
	Baby Please Don't Go	1977	6.25	12.50	25.00
POLISH
| ❏ 202 | Darlin'/Tonight | 1980 | — | 2.50 | 5.00 |
TOM CAT
| ❏ JB-10380 [DJ] | You'd Be Good for Me/Something Tells Me | 1975 | 2.50 | 5.00 | 10.00 |

—*Promo only on blue vinyl*

| ❏ PB-10380 | You'd Be Good for Me/Something Tells Me | 1975 | — | 2.50 | 5.00 |
WARNER/SPECTOR
| ❏ 0409 | Paradise/When I Saw You | 1976 | 2.50 | 5.00 | 10.00 |

Albums
COLUMBIA
| ❏ C 40620 | Unfinished Business | 1987 | 2.50 | 5.00 | 10.00 |
POLISH
| ❏ PRG-808 | Siren | 1980 | 3.00 | 6.00 | 12.00 |

SPECTORS THREE, THE
45s
TREY
| ❏ 3001 | I Really Do/I Know Why | 1959 | 6.25 | 12.50 | 25.00 |
| ❏ 3005 | My Heart Stood Still/Mr. Robin | 1960 | 6.25 | 12.50 | 25.00 |

SPEEDO AND THE IMPALAS See THE IMPALAS.

SPEEDY AND THE REVERBS
45s
REVERB
| ❏ 51 | 100 Proof/Gas Chamber | 196? | 12.50 | 25.00 | 50.00 |

SPELLMAN, BENNY
45s
ACE
| ❏ 630 | That's All I Ask of You/Roll On Big Wheel | 1961 | 5.00 | 10.00 | 20.00 |
ALON
❏ 9018	Tain't the Truth/No Don't Stop	1965	2.50	5.00	10.00
❏ 9024	The Word Game/I Feel Good	1965	5.00	10.00	20.00
❏ 9027	It Must Be Love/Spirit of Loneliness	1965	2.50	5.00	10.00
❏ 9031	It's for You/This Is My Love	1966	2.50	5.00	10.00
ATLANTIC
| ❏ 2291 | The Word Game/I Feel Good | 1965 | 2.50 | 5.00 | 10.00 |

MINIT
❏ 606	Life Is Too Short/Ammerette	1960	3.75	7.50	15.00
❏ 613	Darling No Matter Where/I Didn't Know	1960	3.75	7.50	15.00
❏ 644	Lipstick Traces (On a Cigarette)/Fortune Teller	1962	3.00	6.00	12.00
❏ 652	Every Now and Then/I'm in Love	1962	3.00	6.00	12.00
❏ 659	Stickin' Whicha' Baby/You Got to Get It	1963	3.00	6.00	12.00
❏ 664	Ammerette/Talk About Love	1963	3.00	6.00	12.00
SANSU
| ❏ 462 | But If You Love Her/Sinner Girl | 1967 | 2.00 | 4.00 | 8.00 |
WATCH
| ❏ 6336 | Slow Down Baby (You Drive Too Fast)/ | | | | |
| | Someday They'll Understand | 1964 | 2.50 | 5.00 | 10.00 |

SPELLMAN, JIMMY
45s
DOT
| ❏ 15564 | Here I Am/Make Up Your Mind | 1957 | 7.50 | 15.00 | 30.00 |
| ❏ 15607 | Doggonit/I'll Never Smile Again | 1957 | 7.50 | 15.00 | 30.00 |

SPENCE, ALEXANDER "SKIP" Also see MOBY GRAPE.
Albums
COLUMBIA
| ❏ CS 9831 | Oar | 1969 | 15.00 | 30.00 | 60.00 |
SUNDAZED
| ❏ LP 5030 | Oar | 2000 | 3.00 | 6.00 | 12.00 |

—*Reissue on 180-gram vinyl*

SPENCER, JEREMY Also see FLEETWOOD MAC.
45s
ATLANTIC
❏ 3588	Cool Breeze/You Got the Right	1979	—	2.50	5.00
❏ 3601	Cool Breeze/You Got the Right	1979	—	2.50	5.00
❏ 3624 [DJ]	Travelin' (same on both sides)	1979	—	2.50	5.00

—*May be promo-only*
COLUMBIA
| ❏ 45854 | Can You Hear the Song/The World in Her Heart | 1973 | — | 2.50 | 5.00 |
Albums
ATLANTIC
| ❏ SD 19236 | Flee | 1979 | 2.50 | 5.00 | 10.00 |
COLUMBIA
| ❏ KC 31990 | Jeremy Spencer and the Children of God | 1972 | 3.75 | 7.50 | 15.00 |

SPENCER AND SPENCER DICKIE GOODMAN and Mickey Shorr.
45s
ARGO
| ❏ 5331 | Russian Bandstand/Brass Wail | 1959 | 6.25 | 12.50 | 25.00 |
GONE
| ❏ 5053 | Stagger Lawrence/Strogonoff Cha Cha | 1959 | 6.25 | 12.50 | 25.00 |

SPHEERIS, JIMMY
45s
COLUMBIA
| ❏ 45646 | I Am the Mercury/The Nest | 1972 | — | 2.50 | 5.00 |
| ❏ 45875 | The Original Tap Dancing Kid/Beautiful News | 1973 | — | 2.50 | 5.00 |
EPIC
| ❏ 50159 | Tequila Moonlight/Sunken Skies | 1975 | — | 2.00 | 4.00 |
| ❏ 50286 | It's All in the Game/The Captain Comes Cold | 1976 | — | 2.00 | 4.00 |
Albums
COLUMBIA
| ❏ C 30988 | The Isle of View | 1972 | 3.75 | 7.50 | 15.00 |
| ❏ KC 32157 | The Original Tap Dancing Kid | 1973 | 3.75 | 7.50 | 15.00 |
EPIC
| ❏ PE 33565 | The Dragon Is Dancing | 1975 | 3.00 | 6.00 | 12.00 |
| ❏ PE 34276 | Ports of the Heart | 1976 | 3.00 | 6.00 | 12.00 |

SPICES, THE
45s
CARLTON
| ❏ 480 | Tell Me Little Girl/Money, Fortune and Fame | 1958 | 75.00 | 150.00 | 300.00 |

SPIDELLS, THE
45s
CORAL
❏ 62508	Pushed Out of the Picture/With You in Mind	1966	12.50	25.00	50.00
❏ 62531	Don't You Forget That You're My Baby/If It Ain't				
	One Thing (It's Another)	1967	5.00	10.00	20.00

SPIDERS, THE (1)
45s
IMPERIAL
❏ 5265	I Didn't Want to Do It/You're the One	1954	25.00	50.00	100.00
❏ 5280	Tears Begin to Flow/I'll Stop Cryin'	1954	25.00	50.00	100.00
❏ 5291	I'm Searching/I'm Slippin' In	1954	62.50	125.00	250.00
❏ 5305	The Real Thing/Mm Mm Baby	1954	25.00	50.00	100.00
❏ 5318	She Keeps Me Wondering/(3 x 7) = "21"	1954	25.00	50.00	100.00
❏ 5331	That's Enough/Lost and Bewildered	1955	18.75	37.50	75.00
❏ 5344	Am I the One/Sukey, Sukey, Sukey	1955	18.75	37.50	75.00
❏ 5354	Bells in My Heart/For a Thrill	1955	25.00	50.00	100.00

—*Red label*

| ❏ 5354 | Bells in My Heart/For a Thrill | 1957 | 7.50 | 15.00 | 30.00 |

—*Black label*

| ❏ 5366 | Is It True/Witchcraft | 1955 | 10.00 | 20.00 | 40.00 |

—*Red label*

| ❏ 5366 | Is It True/Witchcraft | 1955 | 25.00 | 50.00 | 100.00 |

—*Blue label*

| ❏ 5376 | Don't Pity Me/How I Feel | 1956 | 10.00 | 20.00 | 40.00 |

—*Featuring Chuck Carbo*

| ❏ 5393 | A-1 in My Heart/Dear Mary | 1956 | 7.50 | 15.00 | 30.00 |

—*As "The Spiders with Chuck Carbo"*

❏ 5618	I Didn't Want to Do It/You're the One	1959	7.50	15.00	30.00
❏ 5714	You're the One/Tennessee Slim	1960	7.50	15.00	30.00
❏ 5739	Witchcraft/(True) You Don't Love Me	1961	7.50	15.00	30.00

Albums
IMPERIAL
| ❏ LP-9142 [M] | I Didn't Wanna Do It | 1961 | 150.00 | 300.00 | 600.00 |

Number	Title (A Side/B Side)	Yr	VG	VG+	NM

SPIDERS, THE (2) Early ALICE COOPER.
45s
MASCOT
| □ 112 | Why Don't You Love Me/Hitch Hike | 1965 | 375.00 | 750.00 | 1500. |

SANTA CRUZ
| □ 003 | Don't Blow Your Mind/No Price Tag | 1966 | 250.00 | 500.00 | 1000. |

SPIDERS, THE (U) Definitely not group (2); could be group (1).
45s
LAWN
| □ 234 | Run Boy Run/Baby Doll | 1964 | 3.00 | 6.00 | 12.00 |

PHILIPS
| □ 40363 | No No Boy/How Could I Fall in Love | 1966 | 2.00 | 4.00 | 8.00 |

SPIKE DRIVERS, THE
45s
OM 1000
| □ 1676 | High Time/Baby Won't You Let Me Tell You How I Lost My Mind | 1966 | 7.50 | 15.00 | 30.00 |

REPRISE
| □ 0535 | High Time/Baby Won't You Let Me Tell You How I Lost My Mind | 1966 | 5.00 | 10.00 | 20.00 |
| □ 0558 | Strange Mysterious Sounds/Break Out the Wine | 1967 | 5.00 | 10.00 | 20.00 |

SPINDLES, THE
45s
ABC
| □ 10802 | To Make You Mine/And the Band Played On | 1966 | 5.00 | 10.00 | 20.00 |
| □ 10850 | No One Loves You (The Way I Do)/Ten Shades of Blue | 1966 | 6.25 | 12.50 | 25.00 |

SPINDRIFTS, THE
45s
ABC-PARAMOUNT
| □ 9904 | Belinda/Cha Cha Doo | 1958 | 6.25 | 12.50 | 25.00 |

SPINNERS Many, though not all, of these did not use the article "The" before the name. These are all by the group known as "The Detroit Spinners" in the U.K.
45s
ATLANTIC
□ 2904	I'll Be Around/How Could I Let You Get Away	1972	—	2.50	5.00
□ 2927	Could It Be I'm Falling in Love/Just You and Me Baby	1972	—	2.50	5.00
□ 2962	One of a Kind (Love Affair)/Don't Let the Green Grass Fool You	1973	—	2.50	5.00
□ 2973	Ghetto Child/We Belong Together	1973	—	2.50	5.00
□ 3006	Mighty Love — Pt. 1/Mighty Love — Pt. 2	1974	—	2.50	5.00
□ 3027	I'm Coming Home/He'll Never Love You Like I Do	1974	—	2.50	5.00
□ 3029	Then Came You/Just As Long As We Have Love	1974	—	3.00	6.00
—With Dionne Warwicke
| □ 3202 | Then Came You/Just As Long As We Have Love | 1974 | — | 2.50 | 5.00 |
—With Dionne Warwicke
□ 3206	Love Don't Love Nobody (Part 1)/Love Don't Love Nobody (Part 2)	1974	—	2.50	5.00
□ 3252	Living a Little, Loving a Little/Smile, We Have Each Other	1975	—	2.50	5.00
□ 3268	Sadie/Lazy Susan	1975	—	2.50	5.00
□ 3284	They Just Can't Stop it the (Games People Play)/I Don't Want to Lose You	1975	—	2.50	5.00
—Same A-side, altered title
□ 3284	Games People Play/I Don't Want to Lose You	1975	2.50	5.00	10.00
□ 3309	Love Or Leave/You Made a Promise to Me	1975	—	2.50	5.00
□ 3341	Wake Up Susan/If You Can't Be in Love	1976	—	2.50	5.00
□ 3355	The Rubberband Man/Now That We're Together	1976	—	2.50	5.00
□ 3382	You're Throwing a Good Love Away/You're All I Need in Life	1977	—	2.50	5.00
□ 3400	Me and My Music/I'm Riding Your Shadow	1977	—	2.50	5.00
□ 3425	Heaven on Earth (So Fine)/I'm Tired of Giving	1977	—	2.50	5.00
□ 3462	Easy Come, Easy Go/Love Is One Step Away	1978	—	2.50	5.00
□ 3483	If You Wanna Do a Dance/One in a Life Proposal	1978	—	2.50	5.00
□ 3546	Are You Ready for Love/Once You Fall in Love	1979	—	2.50	5.00
□ 3590	Don't Let the Man Get You/I Love the Music	1979	—	2.50	5.00
□ 3619	Body Language/With My Eyes	1979	—	2.50	5.00
□ 3637	Working My Way Back to You-Forgive Me, Girl/Disco Ride	1979	—	2.00	4.00
□ 3637	Working My Way Back to You/Disco Ride	1979	2.00	4.00	8.00
—Original pressings mention only one song on the A-side
□ 3664	Cupid-I've Loved You for a Long Time/Pipedreams	1980	—	2.00	4.00
□ 3757	Love Trippin'/Now That You're Mine Again	1980	—	2.00	4.00
□ 3765	I Just Want to Fall in Love/Heavy on the Sunshine	1980	—	2.00	4.00
□ 3798	Yesterday Once More-Nothing Remains the Same/Be My Love	1981	—	2.00	4.00
□ 3814	Long Live Soul Music/Give Your Lady What She Wants	1981	—	2.00	4.00
□ 3827	Winter of Our Love/The Deacon	1981	—	2.00	4.00
□ 3848	What You Feel Is Real/Street Talk	1981	—	2.00	4.00
—With Gino Soccio
| □ 3865 | You Go Your Way (I'll Go Mine)/Got to Be Love | 1981 | — | 2.00 | 4.00 |
| □ 3882 [DJ] | Love Connection (same on both sides) | 1981 | — | 2.50 | 5.00 |
—May be promo only
□ 4007	Never Thought I'd Fall in Love/Send a Little Love	1982	—	2.00	4.00
□ 89226	Spaceballs/Spaceballs (Dub Version)	1987	—	—	3.00
□ 89648	(We Have Come Into) Our Time for All/All Your Love	1984	—	2.00	4.00
□ 89689	Right or Wrong/Love Is In Season	1984	—	2.00	4.00
□ 89862	City Full of Memories/No Other Love	1983	—	2.00	4.00
□ 89922	Funny How Time Slips Away/I'm Calling You Now	1982	—	2.00	4.00
□ 89962	Magic in the Moonlight/So Far Away	1982	—	2.00	4.00
MIRAGE
□ 99580	She Does/(B-side unknown)	1986	—	—	3.00
□ 99604	Put Us Together Again/Show Us Your Magic	1985	—	—	3.00
MOTOWN
□ 1067	Sweet Thing/How Can I	1964	3.75	7.50	15.00
□ 1078	I'll Always Love You/Tomorrow May Never Come	1965	3.75	7.50	15.00
□ 1093	Truly Yours/Where Is That Girl	1966	3.75	7.50	15.00
□ 1109	For All We Know/Cross My Heart	1967	3.75	7.50	15.00
□ 1136	I Just Can't Help But Feel the Pain/Bad, Bad Weather	1968	3.75	7.50	15.00
□ 1155	In My Diary/(She's Gonna Love Me) At Sundown	1969	375.00	750.00	1500.
□ 1235	Together We Can Make Such Sweet Music/Bad, Bad Weather	1973	2.00	4.00	8.00
TRI-PHI
□ 1001	That's What Girls Are Made For/Heebie-Jeebies	1961	6.25	12.50	25.00
□ 1004	Love (I'm So Glad I Found You)/Sudbuster	1961	6.25	12.50	25.00
□ 1007	What Did She Use/Itching for My Baby, I Know Where to Scratch	1962	6.25	12.50	25.00
□ 1010	She Loves Me So/Whistling About You	1962	6.25	12.50	25.00
□ 1013	I've Been Hurt/I Got Your Water Boiling Baby (I'm Gonna Cook Your Goose)	1962	6.25	12.50	25.00
□ 1018	She Don't Love Me/Too Young, Too Much, Too Soon	1962	7.50	15.00	30.00
V.I.P.
□ 25050	In My Diary/(She's Gonna Love Me) At Sundown	1969	6.25	12.50	25.00
□ 25054	Message from a Black Man/(She's Gonna Love Me) At Sundown	1970	3.00	6.00	12.00
□ 25057	It's a Shame/Together We Can Make Such Sweet Music	1970	3.00	6.00	12.00
□ 25060	We'll Have It Made/My Whole World Ended (The Moment You Left Me)	1971	3.00	6.00	12.00

7-Inch Extended Plays
ATLANTIC
| □ SD 7-7256 | One Of A Kind (Love Affair)/Just You and Me Baby/ I'll Be Around//Just Can't Get You Out of My Mind/Could It Be I'm Falling in Love | 1973 | 3.00 | 6.00 | 12.00 |
—Jukebox issue; small hole, plays at 33 1/3 rpm
| □ SD 7-7256 | Spinners | 1973 | 3.00 | 6.00 | 12.00 |
—Part of "Little LP" series (LLP #216)
| □ SD 7-7296 | Since I Been Gone/Love Has Gone Away//Ain't No Price on Happiness/I'm Glad You Walked Into My Life | 1974 | 2.50 | 5.00 | 10.00 |
—Jukebox issue; small hole, plays at 33 1/3 rpm
| □ SD 7-7296 [PS] | Mighty Love | 1974 | 2.50 | 5.00 | 10.00 |

Albums
ATLANTIC
□ SD 2-910 [(2)]	Spinners Live!	1975	3.75	7.50	15.00
□ QD 7256 [Q]	Spinners	1974	5.00	10.00	20.00
□ SD 7256	Spinners	1973	3.00	6.00	12.00
□ SD 7296	Mighty Love	1974	3.00	6.00	12.00
□ SD 16032	Labor of Love	1981	2.50	5.00	10.00
□ QD 18118 [Q]	New and Improved	1974	5.00	10.00	20.00
□ SD 18118	New and Improved	1974	3.00	6.00	12.00
□ QD 18141 [Q]	Pick of the Litter	1975	5.00	10.00	20.00
□ SD 18141	Pick of the Litter	1975	3.00	6.00	12.00
□ SD 18181	Happiness is Being with the Spinners	1976	3.00	6.00	12.00
□ SD 19100	Yesterday, Today & Tomorrow	1977	3.00	6.00	12.00
□ SD 19146	Spinners/8	1977	3.00	6.00	12.00
□ SD 19179	The Best of the Spinners	1978	3.00	6.00	12.00
□ SD 19219	From Here to Eternally	1979	3.00	6.00	12.00
□ SD 19256	Dancin' and Lovin'	1980	2.50	5.00	10.00
□ SD 19270	Love Trippin'	1980	2.50	5.00	10.00
□ SD 19318	Can't Shake This Feelin'	1981	2.50	5.00	10.00
□ 80020	Grand Slam	1982	2.50	5.00	10.00
MIRAGE
□ 90456	Lovin' Feelings	1985	2.50	5.00	10.00
MOTOWN
□ M5-109V1	Motown Superstar Series, Vol. 9	1982	2.00	4.00	8.00
□ M5-132V1	The Original Spinners	1981	3.00	6.00	12.00
—Reissue of Motown 639
| □ M5-199V1 | The Best of the Spinners | 1981 | 3.00 | 6.00 | 12.00 |
—Reissue of Motown 769
□ M 639 [M]	The Original Spinners	1967	6.25	12.50	25.00
□ MS 639 [P]	The Original Spinners	1967	7.50	15.00	30.00
□ M 769	The Best of the Spinners	1973	3.75	7.50	15.00
V.I.P.
□ 405	2nd Time Around	1970	10.00	20.00	40.00
VOLT
□ V-3403	Down to Business	1989	3.00	6.00	12.00

SPINNERS, THE None of these are the popular soul group. Also see THE LIVERPOOL SPINNERS.
45s
CAPITOL
| □ F3955 | Love's Prayer/Goofin' | 1958 | 10.00 | 20.00 | 40.00 |
CRYSTALETTE
| □ 736 | Boomerang/Slave Chain | 1960 | 12.50 | 25.00 | 50.00 |
—Reissued under different titles and on different labels credited to the Crestriders and Duke Mitchell
END
| □ 1045 | Bird Watcher/Richard Pry, Private Eye | 1959 | 10.00 | 20.00 | 40.00 |
—Multicolor label
| □ 1045 | Bird Watcher/Richard Pry, Private Eye | 1959 | 25.00 | 50.00 | 100.00 |
—Gray label
LAWSON
| □ 324 | Surfing Monkey/Beatle Mania | 1964 | 7.50 | 15.00 | 30.00 |
LIBERTY
| □ 55339 | Till the End of Time/Dream | 1961 | 2.50 | 5.00 | 10.00 |
RCA VICTOR
| □ 47-8427 | All I Want/It Must Be Love | 1964 | 2.50 | 5.00 | 10.00 |
RHYTHM
| □ 125 | Marvella/My Love and Your Love | 1958 | 100.00 | 200.00 | 400.00 |
SMASH
| □ 1845 | Happy Hootenanny/Nothin' | 1963 | 2.50 | 5.00 | 10.00 |
WARNER BROS.
| □ 5084 | Little Otis/Rag Mop | 1959 | 3.00 | 6.00 | 12.00 |
Albums
TIME
| □ S-2092 [S] | Party — My Pad After Surfin' | 1963 | 7.50 | 15.00 | 30.00 |
| □ 52092 [M] | Party — My Pad After Surfin' | 1963 | 6.25 | 12.50 | 25.00 |

Number	Title (A Side/B Side)	Yr	VG	VG+	NM

SPINNEY, CARROLL
45s
COLUMBIA

Number	Title (A Side/B Side)	Yr	VG	VG+	NM
❏ 4-45247	I Love Trash/Up and Down	1970	2.00	4.00	8.00

—As "Oscar (Carroll Spinney)"; B-side by Jim Henson and Frank Oz as "Two Monsters"

SPIRAL STARECASE
45s
COLUMBIA

Number	Title (A Side/B Side)	Yr	VG	VG+	NM
❏ 44442	Makin' My Mind Up/Baby What I Mean	1968	—	3.00	6.00
❏ 44566	Inside, Outside, Upside Down/I'll Run	1968	—	3.00	6.00
❏ 44741	More Today Than Yesterday/Broken Hearted Man	1969	2.00	4.00	8.00
❏ 44924	Sweet Little Thing/No One for Me to Turn To	1969	—	2.50	5.00
❏ 45048	She's Ready/Judas to the Love We Know	1969	—	2.50	5.00

Albums
COLUMBIA

Number	Title (A Side/B Side)	Yr	VG	VG+	NM
❏ CS 9852	More Today Than Yesterday	1969	6.25	12.50	25.00

—"360 Sound" label

SPIRALS, THE
45s
CAPITOL

Number	Title (A Side/B Side)	Yr	VG	VG+	NM
❏ F4084	Rockin' Cow/Everybody Knows	1958	12.50	25.00	50.00

SMASH

Number	Title (A Side/B Side)	Yr	VG	VG+	NM
❏ 1719	Please Be My Love/Forever and a Day	1961	25.00	50.00	100.00

SPIRES, BIG BOY
45s
CHANCE

Number	Title (A Side/B Side)	Yr	VG	VG+	NM
❏ 1137	About to Lose My Mind/Which One Do I Love	1953	625.00	1250.	2500.

SPIRIT Also see RANDY CALIFORNIA.
12-Inch Singles
MERCURY

Number	Title (A Side/B Side)	Yr	VG	VG+	NM
❏ 301 [DJ]	I Got a Line on You (Edit)/Black Satin Nights	1984	—	3.00	6.00

45s
EPIC

Number	Title (A Side/B Side)	Yr	VG	VG+	NM
❏ 10648	Animal Zoo/Red Light Roll On	1970	—	3.00	6.00
❏ 10685	Soldier/Mr. Skin	1970	—	3.00	6.00
❏ 10701	Mr. Skin/Nature's Way	1971	—	2.50	5.00
❏ 10849	Darkness/Cadillac Cowboys	1972	—	2.50	5.00
❏ 11020	Mr. Skin/Nature's Way	1973	—	2.00	4.00

MERCURY

Number	Title (A Side/B Side)	Yr	VG	VG+	NM
❏ 73697	America the Beautiful-The Times They Are a-Changin'/Lady of the Lakes	1975	—	2.50	5.00
❏ 73722	Holy Man/Looking Into Darkness	1975	—	2.50	5.00
❏ 73837	Atomic Boogie/Farther Along	1976	—	2.00	4.00

ODE

Number	Title (A Side/B Side)	Yr	VG	VG+	NM
❏ 108	Mechanical World/Uncle Jack	1967	2.50	5.00	10.00
❏ 115	I Got a Line on You/She Smiles	1968	2.50	5.00	10.00
❏ 122	Dark Eyed Woman/New Dope in Town	1969	2.00	4.00	8.00
❏ 128	1984/Sweet Stella Baby	1969	2.00	4.00	8.00

POTATO

Number	Title (A Side/B Side)	Yr	VG	VG+	NM
❏ 1722	Nature's Way/Rock and Roll Planet	1978	—	2.50	5.00
❏ 1722 [PS]	Nature's Way/Rock and Roll Planet	1978	—	2.50	5.00

RHINO

Number	Title (A Side/B Side)	Yr	VG	VG+	NM
❏ 008	Turn to the Right/Potato Land Theme Song	1980	—	2.50	5.00

Albums
EPIC

Number	Title (A Side/B Side)	Yr	VG	VG+	NM
❏ E 30267	Twelve Dreams of Dr. Sardonicus	1970	5.00	10.00	20.00

—Yellow label

| ❏ KE 30267 | Twelve Dreams of Dr. Sardonicus | 1973 | 2.50 | 5.00 | 10.00 |

—Orange label

| ❏ PE 30267 | Twelve Dreams of Dr. Sardonicus | 197? | 2.00 | 4.00 | 8.00 |

—Orange or dark blue label, with or without bar code

| ❏ KE 31175 | Feedback | 1972 | 5.00 | 10.00 | 20.00 |

—Yellow label

| ❏ KE 31175 | Feedback | 1973 | 2.50 | 5.00 | 10.00 |

—Orange label

| ❏ KEG 31457 [(2)] | Spirit | 1972 | 3.75 | 7.50 | 15.00 |

—Reissue of Ode 44004 and 44016 in one package; yellow labels

| ❏ PEG 31457 [(2)] | Spirit | 197? | 3.00 | 6.00 | 12.00 |

—Reissue with new prefix and orange labels

| ❏ KE 31461 | The Family That Plays Together | 1972 | 3.00 | 6.00 | 12.00 |

—Reissue of Ode 44014 with slightly different cover; yellow label

| ❏ KE 31461 | The Family That Plays Together | 1973 | 2.50 | 5.00 | 10.00 |

—Orange label

| ❏ KE 32271 | The Best of Spirit | 1973 | 3.00 | 6.00 | 12.00 |
| ❏ PE 32271 | The Best of Spirit | 1979 | 2.00 | 4.00 | 8.00 |

—Dark blue label; bar code on cover

| ❏ BG 33761 [(2)] | The Family That Plays Together/Feedback | 1976 | 3.00 | 6.00 | 12.00 |

I.R.S.

| ❏ 82007 | Rapture in the Chambers | 1989 | 3.00 | 6.00 | 12.00 |

MERCURY

❏ SRM-2-804 [(2)]	Spirit of '76	1975	3.75	7.50	15.00
❏ SRM-1-1053	Son of Spirit	1975	3.00	6.00	12.00
❏ SRM-1-1094	Farther Along	1976	3.00	6.00	12.00
❏ SRM-1-1122	Future Games	1977	3.00	6.00	12.00
❏ 818514-1	Spirit of '84	1984	2.50	5.00	10.00

ODE

❏ Z12 44003 [M]	Spirit	1968	10.00	20.00	40.00
❏ Z12 44004 [S]	Spirit	1968	6.25	12.50	25.00
❏ Z12 44014	The Family That Plays Together	1968	6.25	12.50	25.00
❏ Z12 44016	Clear Spirit	1969	6.25	12.50	25.00

POTATO

| ❏ 2001 | Live | 1978 | 2.50 | 5.00 | 10.00 |

RHINO

| ❏ RNSP-303 | Potatoland | 1981 | 2.50 | 5.00 | 10.00 |

SUNDAZED

❏ LP 5067	Now or Anywhere	2000	3.00	6.00	12.00
❏ LP 5068	Eventide	2000	3.00	6.00	12.00
❏ LP 5082	Clear	2001	3.00	6.00	12.00
❏ LP 5085	The Family That Plays Together	2001	3.00	6.00	12.00

SPIRITS AND WORM
45s
A&M

Number	Title (A Side/B Side)	Yr	VG	VG+	NM
❏ 1104	Fanny Firecracker/You and I Together	1969	10.00	20.00	40.00

Albums
A&M

| ❏ SP-4229 | Spirits and Worm | 1969 | 200.00 | 400.00 | 800.00 |

SPLINTER Also see BILL ELLIOTT AND THE ELASTIC OZ BAND.
45s
DARK HORSE

Number	Title (A Side/B Side)	Yr	VG	VG+	NM
❏ 8439	Round and Round/I'll Bend for You	1977	—	2.00	4.00
❏ 8523	I Need Your Love/Motions of Love	1978	—	2.00	4.00
❏ 10002	Costafine Town/Elly-Mae	1974	—	3.00	6.00
❏ 10002 [PS]	Costafine Town/Elly-Mae	1974	2.00	4.00	8.00
❏ 10003	China Light/Haven't Got Time	1975	—	3.00	6.00
❏ 10007	Which Way Will I Get Home/What Is It (If You Never Tried It Yourself)	1975	—	3.00	6.00
❏ 10010	After Five Years/Halfway There	1976	—	2.50	5.00

Albums
DARK HORSE

❏ DH 3073	Two Man Band	1977	2.50	5.00	10.00
❏ SP-22001	The Place I Love	1974	2.50	5.00	10.00
❏ SP-22006	Harder to Live	1975	2.50	5.00	10.00

SPOKESMEN, THE
45s
DECCA

Number	Title (A Side/B Side)	Yr	VG	VG+	NM
❏ 31844	The Dawn of Correction/For You Babe	1965	3.00	6.00	12.00
❏ 31874	It Ain't Fair/Have Courage, Be Careful	1965	2.50	5.00	10.00
❏ 31895	Michelle/Better Days Are Yet to Come	1966	2.50	5.00	10.00
❏ 31949	Today's the Day/Enchante	1966	2.50	5.00	10.00
❏ 32049	I Love How You Love Me/Beautiful Girl	1966	2.50	5.00	10.00

WINCHESTER

| ❏ 1001 | Mary Jane/Flashback | 1967 | 3.00 | 6.00 | 12.00 |

Albums
DECCA

| ❏ DL 4712 [M] | The Dawn of Correction | 1965 | 6.25 | 12.50 | 25.00 |
| ❏ DL 74712 [S] | The Dawn of Correction | 1965 | 7.50 | 15.00 | 30.00 |

SPOOKY TOOTH Also see PATTO; GARY WRIGHT.
45s
A&M

Number	Title (A Side/B Side)	Yr	VG	VG+	NM
❏ 1144	That Was Only Yesterday/Waitin' for the Wind	1969	2.00	4.00	8.00

ISLAND

| ❏ 004 | The Mirror/Hell or High Water | 1974 | — | 2.50 | 5.00 |
| ❏ 1219 | All Sewn Up/Things Change | 1973 | — | 3.00 | 6.00 |

MALA

| ❏ 12013 | Love Really Changed Me/Spooky Blow | 1968 | 2.50 | 5.00 | 10.00 |
| ❏ 12022 | The Weight/Do Right People | 1968 | 2.50 | 5.00 | 10.00 |

Albums
A&M

| ❏ SP-3124 | Spooky Two | 198? | 2.00 | 4.00 | 8.00 |

—Budget-line reissue

❏ SP-4194	Spooky Two	1969	3.75	7.50	15.00
❏ SP-4225	Ceremony	1970	3.75	7.50	15.00
❏ SP-4266	The Last Puff	1970	3.75	7.50	15.00
❏ SP-4300	Tobacco Road	1971	3.75	7.50	15.00

—Reissue of Bell LP

| ❏ SP-4385 | You Broke My Heart So I Busted Your Jaw | 1973 | 3.75 | 7.50 | 15.00 |

ACCORD

| ❏ SN-7168 | Hell or High Water | 1982 | 2.50 | 5.00 | 10.00 |

BELL

| ❏ 6019 [M] | Spooky Tooth | 1968 | 15.00 | 30.00 | 60.00 |

—Mono is white label promo only; record in stereo cover

| ❏ 6019 [S] | Spooky Tooth | 1968 | 6.25 | 12.50 | 25.00 |

ISLAND

❏ SW-9255	Witness	1973	3.00	6.00	12.00
❏ SW-9292	The Mirror	1974	3.00	6.00	12.00
❏ ILPS-9337	Witness	1974	2.50	5.00	10.00

SPORTONES, THE
45s
MUNICH

Number	Title (A Side/B Side)	Yr	VG	VG+	NM
❏ 101	In My Dreams/So Sincere	1959	125.00	250.00	500.00

SPOTLIGHTERS, THE Two different groups?
45s
ALADDIN

Number	Title (A Side/B Side)	Yr	VG	VG+	NM
❏ 3436	Please Be My Girlfriend/Whisper	1958	25.00	50.00	100.00
❏ 3441	This Is My Story/Preaching	1959	25.00	50.00	100.00

IMPERIAL

| ❏ 5342 | It's Cold/Bam Jingle Jingle | 1955 | 31.25 | 62.50 | 125.00 |
| ❏ 5342 | It's Cold/Bam Jingle Jingle | 1955 | 62.50 | 125.00 | 250.00 |

—Red vinyl

SPOTNICKS, THE
45s
ATCO

Number	Title (A Side/B Side)	Yr	VG	VG+	NM
❏ 6261	Orange Blossom Special/Hava Nagila	1963	3.00	6.00	12.00

FELSTED

| ❏ 8649 | Spotnick/Old Spinning Wheel | 1962 | 3.00 | 6.00 | 12.00 |

LAURIE

❏ 3241	I'm Goin' Home/Orange Blossom Special	1964	2.50	5.00	10.00
❏ 3260	Summer in Sweden/Endless Sleep	1964	2.50	5.00	10.00
❏ 3297	Just Listen to My Heart/Pony Express	1965	2.50	5.00	10.00
❏ 3333	Drum Didley/Orange Blossom Special	1966	2.50	5.00	10.00

SPOTSWOOD, KENDRA
45s
TUFF

Number	Title (A Side/B Side)	Yr	VG	VG+	NM
❏ 407	Stickin' with My Baby/Jive Guy	1965	2.50	5.00	10.00

Number	Title (A Side/B Side)	Yr	VG	VG+	NM

SPRING Also see AMERICAN SPRING.
45s
UNITED ARTISTS

Number	Title (A Side/B Side)	Yr	VG	VG+	NM
❑ 50848	Now Everything's Been Said/Awake	1971	7.50	15.00	30.00
❑ 50907	Good Times/Sweet Mountain	1972	20.00	40.00	80.00

Albums
UNITED ARTISTS

Number	Title (A Side/B Side)	Yr	VG	VG+	NM
❑ UAS-5571	Spring	1972	6.25	12.50	25.00
❑ UAS-5571 [DJ]	Spring	1972	25.00	50.00	100.00

—*Special promo package in 12x12 folder; includes LP, press kit and a packet of seeds*

SPRINGERS, THE
45s
WALES

Number	Title (A Side/B Side)	Yr	VG	VG+	NM
❑ 428	Nothing's Too Good for My Baby/(B-side unknown)	196?	375.00	750.00	1500.

SPRINGFIELD, DUSTY Also see THE SPRINGFIELDS.
12-Inch Singles
CASABLANCA

Number	Title (A Side/B Side)	Yr	VG	VG+	NM
❑ 20245 [DJ]	Donnez-Moi/I Am Curious + 1	1982	3.75	7.50	15.00

UNITED ARTISTS

Number	Title (A Side/B Side)	Yr	VG	VG+	NM
❑ SP-178 [DJ]	That's the Kind of Love I've Got for You (7:06) (same on both sides)	1978	5.00	10.00	20.00

45s
ABC DUNHILL

Number	Title (A Side/B Side)	Yr	VG	VG+	NM
❑ 4341	Who Gets Your Love/Of All the Things	1973	—	3.00	6.00
❑ 4344	Mama's Little Girl/Learn to Say Goodbye	1973	—	3.00	6.00
❑ 4357	Mama's Little Girl/Learn to Say Goodbye	1973	2.00	4.00	8.00

ATLANTIC

Number	Title (A Side/B Side)	Yr	VG	VG+	NM
❑ 2580	Son-of-a-Preacher-Man/Just a Little Lovin'	1968	2.50	5.00	10.00
❑ 2580 [PS]	Son-of-a-Preacher-Man/Just a Little Lovin'	1968	3.75	7.50	15.00
❑ 2606	Breakfast in Bed/Don't Forget About Me	1969	2.00	4.00	8.00
❑ 2623	The Windmills of Your Mind/I Don't Want to Hear It Anymore	1969	2.00	4.00	8.00
❑ 2647	Willie & Laura May Jones/That Old Sweet Roll	1969	—	3.00	6.00
❑ 2673	In the Land of Make Believe/So Much Love	1969	—	3.00	6.00
❑ 2685	A Brand New Me/Bad Case of the Blues	1969	—	3.00	6.00
❑ 2705	Silly, Silly, Fool/Joe	1970	—	3.00	6.00
❑ 2729	I Wanna Be a Free Girl/Let Me In Your Way	1970	—	3.00	6.00
❑ 2739	Never Love Again/Lost	1970	—	3.00	6.00
❑ 2771	What Good Is I Love You/What Do You Do When Love Dies	1970	—	3.00	6.00
❑ 2825	Nothing Is Forever/Haunted	1971	—	3.00	6.00
❑ 2841	I Believe in You/Someone Who Cared	1971	—	3.00	6.00

CASABLANCA

Number	Title (A Side/B Side)	Yr	VG	VG+	NM
❑ 2356	I Am Curious/Donnez-Moi	1981	—	2.00	4.00

ENIGMA

Number	Title (A Side/B Side)	Yr	VG	VG+	NM
❑ 75042	Nothing Has Been Proved/(Instrumental)	1989	—	2.50	5.00

PHILIPS

Number	Title (A Side/B Side)	Yr	VG	VG+	NM
❑ 40162	I Only Want to Be with You/Once Upon a Time	1963	3.00	6.00	12.00
❑ 40180	Stay Awhile/Something Special	1964	2.50	5.00	10.00
❑ 40180 [PS]	Stay Awhile/Something Special	1964	5.00	10.00	20.00
❑ 40207	Wishin' and Hopin'/Do Re Mi (Forget About the Do and Think About Me)	1964	3.00	6.00	12.00
❑ 40229	All Cried Out/I Wish I'd Never Loved You	1964	2.50	5.00	10.00
❑ 40229 [PS]	All Cried Out/I Wish I'd Never Loved You	1964	5.00	10.00	20.00
❑ 40245	Guess Who/Live It Up	1964	2.50	5.00	10.00
❑ 40245 [PS]	Guess Who/Live It Up	1964	5.00	10.00	20.00
❑ 40270	Losing You/Here She Comes	1965	2.50	5.00	10.00
❑ 40270 [PS]	Losing You/Here She Comes	1965	5.00	10.00	20.00
❑ 40303	In the Middle of Nowhere/Baby, Don't You Know	1965	2.50	5.00	10.00
❑ 40303 [PS]	In the Middle of Nowhere/Baby, Don't You Know	1965	5.00	10.00	20.00
❑ 40319	I Just Don't Know What to Do with Myself/Some of Your Lovin'	1965	2.50	5.00	10.00
❑ 40319 [PS]	I Just Don't Know What to Do with Myself/Some of Your Lovin'	1965	5.00	10.00	20.00
❑ 40371	You Don't Have to Say You Love Me/Little by Little	1966	2.50	5.00	10.00
❑ 40371 [PS]	You Don't Have to Say You Love Me/Little by Little	1966	5.00	10.00	20.00
❑ 40396	All I See Is You/I'm Gonna Leave You	1966	2.50	5.00	10.00
❑ 40396 [PS]	All I See Is You/I'm Gonna Leave You	1966	5.00	10.00	20.00
❑ 40439	I'll Try Anything/The Corrupt Ones	1967	2.50	5.00	10.00
❑ 40439 [PS]	I'll Try Anything/The Corrupt Ones	1967	5.00	10.00	20.00
❑ 40465	The Look of Love/Give Me Time	1967	2.50	5.00	10.00
❑ 40498	What's It Gonna Be/Small Town Girl	1967	2.50	5.00	10.00
❑ 40498 [PS]	What's It Gonna Be/Small Town Girl	1967	4.00	8.00	16.00
❑ 40547	Sweet Ride/No Stranger Am I	1968	2.50	5.00	10.00
❑ 40553	La Bamba/I Close My Eyes and Count to Ten	1968	2.50	5.00	10.00

20TH CENTURY

Number	Title (A Side/B Side)	Yr	VG	VG+	NM
❑ 2457	It Goes Like It Goes/I Wish That Love Would Last	1980	—	2.50	5.00

UNITED ARTISTS

Number	Title (A Side/B Side)	Yr	VG	VG+	NM
❑ XW1006	Let Me Love You Once Before You Go/I'm Your Child	1977	—	2.50	5.00
❑ XW1205	Checkmate/Sandra	1978	—	2.50	5.00
❑ XW1225	Give Me the Night/Checkmate	1978	—	2.50	5.00
❑ XW1255	Living Without Your Love/Get Yourself a Lover	1978	—	2.50	5.00

7-Inch Extended Plays
PHILIPS

Number	Title (A Side/B Side)	Yr	VG	VG+	NM
❑ PL-2700 [PS]	The Look of Love	196?	5.00	10.00	20.00
❑ PL-2700 [S]	The Look of Love/Give Me Time/Chained to a Memory//Sunny/What's It Gonna Be/If You Go Away	196?	5.00	10.00	20.00

—*Jukebox issue; small hole, plays at 33 1/3 rpm*

Albums
ABC DUNHILL

Number	Title (A Side/B Side)	Yr	VG	VG+	NM
❑ DSX-50128	Cameo	1973	3.75	7.50	15.00
❑ DSX-50186	Longings	1974	—	—	—

—*Unreleased*
ATLANTIC

Number	Title (A Side/B Side)	Yr	VG	VG+	NM
❑ SD 8214	Dusty in Memphis	1969	3.75	7.50	15.00

—*Second pressings have green and red labels*

Number	Title (A Side/B Side)	Yr	VG	VG+	NM
❑ SD 8214	Dusty in Memphis	1969	7.50	15.00	30.00

—*Originals have purple and brown labels*

Number	Title (A Side/B Side)	Yr	VG	VG+	NM
❑ 8249 [DJ]	A Brand New Me	1970	10.00	20.00	40.00

—*Mono white label promo*

Number	Title (A Side/B Side)	Yr	VG	VG+	NM
❑ SD 8249	A Brand New Me	1970	3.75	7.50	15.00

CASABLANCA

Number	Title (A Side/B Side)	Yr	VG	VG+	NM
❑ NBLP-7271	White Heat	1982	3.00	6.00	12.00

LIBERTY

Number	Title (A Side/B Side)	Yr	VG	VG+	NM
❑ LN-10024	It Begins Again	1980	2.00	4.00	8.00

—*Budget-line reissue of United Artists LP of same name*

Number	Title (A Side/B Side)	Yr	VG	VG+	NM
❑ LN-10026	Living Without Your Love	1980	2.00	4.00	8.00

—*Budget-line reissue of United Artists LP of same name*
PHILIPS

Number	Title (A Side/B Side)	Yr	VG	VG+	NM
❑ PHM-200133 [M]	Stay Awhile	1964	7.50	15.00	30.00
❑ PHM-200156 [M]	Dusty	1964	7.50	15.00	30.00
❑ PHM-200174 [M]	Ooooo Weeeee!	1965	10.00	20.00	40.00
❑ PHM-200210 [M]	You Don't Have to Say You Love Me	1966	7.50	15.00	30.00
❑ PHM-200220 [M]	Dusty Springfield's Golden Hits	1966	6.25	12.50	25.00

—*With "Goin' Back"*

Number	Title (A Side/B Side)	Yr	VG	VG+	NM
❑ PHM-200220 [M]	Dusty Springfield's Golden Hits	1967	5.00	10.00	20.00

—*Without "Goin' Back"*

Number	Title (A Side/B Side)	Yr	VG	VG+	NM
❑ PHM-200256 [M]	The Look of Love	1967	6.25	12.50	25.00
❑ PHM-200303 [M]	Everything's Coming Up Dusty	1967	6.25	12.50	25.00
❑ PHS-600133 [P]	Stay Awhile	1964	10.00	20.00	40.00
❑ PHS-600156 [P]	Dusty	1964	10.00	20.00	40.00
❑ PHS-600174 [S]	Ooooo Weeeee!	1965	12.50	25.00	50.00
❑ PHS-600210 [S]	You Don't Have to Say You Love Me	1966	10.00	20.00	40.00
❑ PHS-600220 [P]	Dusty Springfield's Golden Hits	1966	8.75	17.50	35.00

—*With "Goin' Back"*

Number	Title (A Side/B Side)	Yr	VG	VG+	NM
❑ PHS-600220 [P]	Dusty Springfield's Golden Hits	1967	6.25	12.50	25.00

—*Without "Goin' Back"*

Number	Title (A Side/B Side)	Yr	VG	VG+	NM
❑ PHS-600256 [S]	The Look of Love	1967	7.50	15.00	30.00
❑ PHS-600303 [S]	Everything's Coming Up Dusty	1967	7.50	15.00	30.00

POLYDOR

Number	Title (A Side/B Side)	Yr	VG	VG+	NM
❑ 824467-1	Dusty Springfield's Golden Hits	1985	2.50	5.00	10.00

UNITED ARTISTS

Number	Title (A Side/B Side)	Yr	VG	VG+	NM
❑ UA-LA791	It Begins Again	1978	3.75	7.50	15.00
❑ UA-LA936	Living Without Your Love	1979	3.75	7.50	15.00

WING

Number	Title (A Side/B Side)	Yr	VG	VG+	NM
❑ PKW-2-120 [(2)]	Something Special	196?	5.00	10.00	20.00
❑ SRW-16380	Just Dusty	196?	3.00	6.00	12.00

SPRINGFIELD, RICK
12-Inch Singles
RCA

Number	Title (A Side/B Side)	Yr	VG	VG+	NM
❑ 8393-1-R	Honeymoon in Beirut/Tear It All Down	1988	—	3.00	6.00
❑ PD-12273	I've Done Everything for You/Love Is Alright Tonite	1981	2.00	4.00	8.00
❑ PD-13009	Love Is Alright Tonite/Everybody's Girl	1981	2.00	4.00	8.00
❑ PD-13075	Don't Talk to Strangers/Calling All Girls	1982	2.00	4.00	8.00
❑ JD-13509 [DJ]	Affair of the Heart (Long) (Short)	1983	2.00	4.00	8.00
❑ JR-13577 [DJ]	Human Touch (same on both sides)	1983	2.00	4.00	8.00
❑ PD-13617	Human Touch (Vocal)/(Instrumental)	1983	2.50	5.00	10.00
❑ PD-13651	Souls/Souls (Live)	1983	2.00	4.00	8.00
❑ JR-13747 [DJ]	Love Somebody (same on both sides)	1984	2.00	4.00	8.00
❑ JD-13815 [DJ]	Don't Walk Away (3:38) (4:00)	1984	2.00	4.00	8.00
❑ PD-13868	Bop 'Til You Drop/Taxi Dancing	1984	2.00	4.00	8.00
❑ JR-13882 [DJ]	Bop 'Til You Drop (same on both sides)	1984	2.00	4.00	8.00
❑ JR-14051 [DJ]	Celebrate Youth (same on both sides)	1985	—	3.00	6.00
❑ PD-14052	Celebrate Youth (Long) (Short)	1985	—	3.00	6.00
❑ JR-14119 [DJ]	State of the Heart (Special Rock Radio Edited Version) (same on both sides)	1985	2.00	4.00	8.00

45s
CAPITOL

Number	Title (A Side/B Side)	Yr	VG	VG+	NM
❑ 3340	Speak to the Sky/Why	1972	2.00	4.00	8.00
❑ 3340 [PS]	Speak to the Sky/Why	1972	3.75	7.50	15.00
❑ 3466	What Would the Children Think/Come On Everybody	1972	2.00	4.00	8.00
❑ 3466 [PS]	What Would the Children Think/Come On Everybody	1972	3.75	7.50	15.00
❑ 3637	I'm Your Superman/Why Are You Waiting	1973	2.00	4.00	8.00
❑ 3713	Believe in Me/The Liar	1973	3.00	6.00	12.00

CHELSEA

Number	Title (A Side/B Side)	Yr	VG	VG+	NM
❑ 3051	Take a Hand/Archangel	1976	—	2.50	5.00
❑ 3055	Million Dollar Face/(B-side unknown)	1976	—	2.50	5.00
❑ 3056	Jessica/Archangel	1976	—	2.50	5.00

COLUMBIA

Number	Title (A Side/B Side)	Yr	VG	VG+	NM
❑ 45935	Believe in Me/The Liar	1973	—	3.00	6.00
❑ 46032	Streakin' Across the U.S.A./Music to Streak By	1974	—	3.00	6.00
❑ 46057	American Girls/Weep No More	1974	—	2.50	5.00

MERCURY

Number	Title (A Side/B Side)	Yr	VG	VG+	NM
❑ 880405-7	Bruce/Guenevere	1984	—	2.00	4.00
❑ 880405-7 [PS]	Bruce/Guenevere	1984	—	2.50	5.00

RCA

Number	Title (A Side/B Side)	Yr	VG	VG+	NM
❑ 6853-7-R	Rock of Life/The Language of Love	1988	—	—	3.00
❑ 6853-7-R [PS]	Rock of Life/The Language of Love	1988	—	—	3.00
❑ 8391-7-R	Honeymoon in Beirut/My Father's Chair	1988	—	—	3.00
❑ 8391-7-R [PS]	Honeymoon in Beirut/My Father's Chair	1988	—	—	3.00
❑ PB-12166	I've Done Everything for You/Red Hot and Blue Love	1981	—	2.00	4.00
❑ PB-12166 [PS]	I've Done Everything for You/Red Hot and Blue Love	1981	—	2.00	4.00
❑ PB-12201	Jessie's Girl/Carry Me Away	1981	—	2.00	4.00
❑ PB-12201 [PS]	Jessie's Girl/Carry Me Away	1981	—	2.50	5.00
❑ PB-13008	Love Is Alright Tonite/Everybody's Girl	1981	—	2.00	4.00
❑ PB-13008 [PS]	Love Is Alright Tonite/Everybody's Girl	1981	—	2.00	4.00
❑ PB-13070	Don't Talk to Strangers/Tonight	1982	—	2.00	4.00
❑ PB-13070 [PS]	Don't Talk to Strangers/Tonight	1982	—	2.00	4.00
❑ PB-13245	What Kind of Fool Am I/How Do You Talk to Girls	1982	—	2.00	4.00
❑ PB-13303	I Get Excited/Kristina	1982	—	2.00	4.00
❑ PB-13303 [PS]	I Get Excited/Kristina	1982	—	2.00	4.00
❑ GB-13482	Jessie's Girl/I've Done Everything for You	1983	—	—	3.00

—*Gold Standard Series*

Number	Title (A Side/B Side)	Yr	VG	VG+	NM
❑ GB-13483	Don't Talk to Strangers/What Kind of Fool Am I	1983	—	—	3.00

—*Gold Standard Series*

Number	Title (A Side/B Side)	Yr	VG	VG+	NM
❑ PB-13497	Affair of the Heart/Like Father, Like Son	1983	—	—	3.00
❑ PB-13497 [PS]	Affair of the Heart/Like Father, Like Son	1983	—	2.00	4.00
❑ PB-13576	Human Touch/Alyson	1983	—	—	3.00

S

Number	Title (A Side/B Side)	Yr	VG	VG+	NM
PB-13650	Souls/Souls (Live)	1983	—	—	3.00
PB-13650 [PS]	Souls/Souls (Live)	1983	—	2.00	4.00
PB-13738	Love Somebody/The Great Lost Art of Conversation	1984	—	—	3.00
PB-13738 [PS]	Love Somebody/The Great Lost Art of Conversation	1984	—	—	3.00

—*Without sticker on sleeve*

Number	Title (A Side/B Side)	Yr	VG	VG+	NM
PB-13738 [PS]	Love Somebody/The Great Lost Art of Conversation	1984	—	3.00	6.00

—*With "Special Dollar Refund Offer" sticker on sleeve and $1 off coupon for the purchase of the LP "Hard to Hold" inside*

Number	Title (A Side/B Side)	Yr	VG	VG+	NM
GB-13794	Affair of the Heart/Human Touch	1984	—	—	3.00

—*Gold Standard Series*

Number	Title (A Side/B Side)	Yr	VG	VG+	NM
PB-13813	Don't Walk Away/S.F.O.	1984	—	—	3.00
PB-13813 [PS]	Don't Walk Away/S.F.O.	1984	—	—	3.00
PB-13861	Bop 'Til You Drop/Taxi Dancing	1984	—	—	3.00

—*B-side: With Randy Crawford*

Number	Title (A Side/B Side)	Yr	VG	VG+	NM
PB-13861 [PS]	Bop 'Til You Drop/Taxi Dancing	1984	—	—	3.00
PB-14047	Celebrate Youth/Stranger in the House	1985	—	—	3.00
PB-14047 [PS]	Celebrate Youth/Stranger in the House	1985	—	—	3.00
PB-14120	State of the Heart/The Power of Love (The Tao of Love)	1985	—	—	3.00
PB-14120 [PS]	State of the Heart/The Power of Love (The Tao of Love)	1985	—	—	3.00

Albums
CAPITOL

Number	Title (A Side/B Side)	Yr	VG	VG+	NM
SMAS-11047	Beginnings	1972	5.00	10.00	20.00
SMAS-11206	Comic Book Heroes	1973	10.00	20.00	40.00

—*Withdrawn and reissued on Columbia*

Number	Title (A Side/B Side)	Yr	VG	VG+	NM
SN-16251	Beginnings	1981	2.00	4.00	8.00

—*Budget-line reissue*

CHELSEA

Number	Title (A Side/B Side)	Yr	VG	VG+	NM
515	Wait for Night	1976	3.75	7.50	15.00

COLUMBIA

Number	Title (A Side/B Side)	Yr	VG	VG+	NM
KC 32704	Comic Book Heroes	1973	3.75	7.50	15.00
PC 32704	Comic Book Heroes	1981	2.00	4.00	8.00

—*Budget-line reissue*

MERCURY

Number	Title (A Side/B Side)	Yr	VG	VG+	NM
824107-1	Beautiful Feelings	1984	2.50	5.00	10.00

RCA

Number	Title (A Side/B Side)	Yr	VG	VG+	NM
6620-1-R	Rock of Life	1988	2.00	4.00	8.00
9817-1-R	Rick Springfield's Greatest Hits	1989	3.00	6.00	12.00

RCA VICTOR

Number	Title (A Side/B Side)	Yr	VG	VG+	NM
ARL1-3697	Working Class Dog	1981	2.50	5.00	10.00
AFL1-4125	Success Hasn't Spoiled Me Yet	1982	2.50	5.00	10.00
AFL1-4235	Wait for Night	1982	2.50	5.00	10.00

—*Reissue of Chelsea LP*

Number	Title (A Side/B Side)	Yr	VG	VG+	NM
AFL1-4660	Living in Oz	1983	2.50	5.00	10.00
AYL1-4766	Working Class Dog	1983	2.00	4.00	8.00

—*"Best Buy Series" reissue*

Number	Title (A Side/B Side)	Yr	VG	VG+	NM
AYL1-4767	Success Hasn't Spoiled Me Yet	1983	2.00	4.00	8.00

—*"Best Buy Series" reissue*

Number	Title (A Side/B Side)	Yr	VG	VG+	NM
ABL1-4935	Hard to Hold	1984	2.50	5.00	10.00
AJL1-5370	Tao	1985	2.50	5.00	10.00

SPRINGFIELD RIFLE, THE
45s
ABC

Number	Title (A Side/B Side)	Yr	VG	VG+	NM
10878	The Bears/There Is Life on Mars	1966	2.50	5.00	10.00

JERDEN

Number	Title (A Side/B Side)	Yr	VG	VG+	NM
812	Stop and Take a Look Around/100 or Two	1967	3.00	6.00	12.00
815	All She Said/It Ain't Happened	1967	3.00	6.00	12.00
901	I'll Be Standing There/Will You Love Me Tomorrow	196?	3.00	6.00	12.00
902	Left of Nowhere/I Must Go for a Walk	196?	3.00	6.00	12.00
905	I Love You/That's All I Really Need	196?	3.00	6.00	12.00

TOWER

Number	Title (A Side/B Side)	Yr	VG	VG+	NM
455	I Love Her/That's All I Really Need	1968	2.50	5.00	10.00

Albums
BURDETTE

Number	Title (A Side/B Side)	Yr	VG	VG+	NM
ST-5159	The Springfield Rifle	1969	6.25	12.50	25.00

SPRINGFIELDS, THE   Also see DUSTY SPRINGFIELD.
45s
PHILIPS

Number	Title (A Side/B Side)	Yr	VG	VG+	NM
40038	Silver Threads and Golden Needles/Aunt Rhody	1962	3.75	7.50	15.00
40072	Dear Hearts and Gentle People/Gotta Travel On	1962	3.00	6.00	12.00
40092	Little By Little/Waf-Woof	1963	3.00	6.00	12.00
40099	Foggy Mountain Top/Island of Dreams	1963	3.00	6.00	12.00
40121	Say I Won't Be There/Little Boat	1963	3.00	6.00	12.00

Albums
PHILIPS

Number	Title (A Side/B Side)	Yr	VG	VG+	NM
PHM 200052 [M]	Silver Threads and Golden Needles	1962	7.50	15.00	30.00
PHM 200076 [M]	Folksongs from the Hills	1963	7.50	15.00	30.00
PHS 600052 [S]	Silver Threads and Golden Needles	1962	10.00	20.00	40.00
PHS 600076 [S]	Folksongs from the Hills	1963	10.00	20.00	40.00

SPRINGSTEEN, BRUCE
12-Inch Singles
ASYLUM

Number	Title (A Side/B Side)	Yr	VG	VG+	NM
11442 [DJ]	Devil with a Blue Dress Medley/Before the Deluge	1979	10.00	20.00	40.00

—*B-side by Jackson Browne*

COLUMBIA

Number	Title (A Side/B Side)	Yr	VG	VG+	NM
AS 928 [DJ]	Fade Away/Be True/Held Up Without a Gun	1981	12.50	25.00	50.00
AS 1329 [DJ]	Santa Claus Is Comin' to Town (same on both sides)	1981	10.00	20.00	40.00

—*White label promo*

Number	Title (A Side/B Side)	Yr	VG	VG+	NM
AS 1862 [DJ]	Dancing in the Dark (same on both sides)	1984	5.00	10.00	20.00

—*Red label, black and white cover*

Number	Title (A Side/B Side)	Yr	VG	VG+	NM
AS 1959 [DJ]	Born in the U.S.A. (same on both sides)	1984	5.00	10.00	20.00

—*Red label, black and white cover*

Number	Title (A Side/B Side)	Yr	VG	VG+	NM
AS 2007 [DJ]	I'm on Fire (same on both sides)	1985	5.00	10.00	20.00

—*Red label, black and white cover*

Number	Title (A Side/B Side)	Yr	VG	VG+	NM
AS 2082 [DJ]	Glory Days (same on both sides)	1985	5.00	10.00	20.00

—*Red label, black and white cover*

Number	Title (A Side/B Side)	Yr	VG	VG+	NM
CAS 2147 [DJ]	I'm Goin' Down (same on both sides)	1985	5.00	10.00	20.00

—*Red label, black and white cover*

Number	Title (A Side/B Side)	Yr	VG	VG+	NM
CAS 2223 [DJ]	My Hometown (same on both sides)	1985	5.00	10.00	20.00

—*Red label, black and white cover*

Number	Title (A Side/B Side)	Yr	VG	VG+	NM
CAS 2636 [DJ]	Fire/Because the Night/Seeds	1986	6.25	12.50	25.00
CAS 2806 [DJ]	Brilliant Disguise (same on both sides)	1987	3.75	7.50	15.00
05028	Dancing in the Dark (Blaster Mix)/(Radio) (Dub)	1984	3.00	6.00	12.00
05087	Cover Me (Undercover Mix) (Dub 1)/(Dub 2) (Radio)	1984	3.00	6.00	12.00
05147	Born in the U.S.A. (Freedom Mix)/(Dub) (Radio)	1984	3.00	6.00	12.00
74416	57 Channels (And Nothin' On) (Little Steven Remix 1 & 2)//There's a Riot Goin' On/Part Man Part Monkey	1992	3.75	7.50	15.00

45s
COLUMBIA

Number	Title (A Side/B Side)	Yr	VG	VG+	NM
AE7 1088 [DJ]	Rosalita (Come Out Tonight)//Spirit in the Night/Growin' Up	1974	75.00	150.00	300.00

—*Small hole, plays at 33 1/3 RPM*

Number	Title (A Side/B Side)	Yr	VG	VG+	NM
AE7 1332 [DJ]	Santa Claus Is Coming to Town (same on both sides)	1981	5.00	10.00	20.00
AE7 1332 [PS]	Santa Claus Is Coming to Town (same on both sides)	1981	6.25	12.50	25.00
03243	Hungry Heart/Fade Away	198?	—	—	3.00

—*"Columbia Hall of Fame" series; gray label*

Number	Title (A Side/B Side)	Yr	VG	VG+	NM
03243	Hungry Heart/Fade Away	1983	—	2.00	4.00

—*"Columbia Hall of Fame" series; red label*

Number	Title (A Side/B Side)	Yr	VG	VG+	NM
04463	Dancing in the Dark/Pink Cadillac	1984	—	2.00	4.00
04463 [PS]	Dancing in the Dark/Pink Cadillac	1984	—	2.50	5.00
04561	Cover Me/Jersey Girl	1984	—	2.00	4.00

—*Spoken intro to "Jersey Girl" is deleted. Dead wax has matrix number followed by "-2" and a letter.*

Number	Title (A Side/B Side)	Yr	VG	VG+	NM
04561	Cover Me/Jersey Girl	1984	2.50	5.00	10.00

—*First pressings have a spoken intro to "Jersey Girl." Dead wax has matrix number followed by "-1" and a letter.*

Number	Title (A Side/B Side)	Yr	VG	VG+	NM
04561 [PS]	Cover Me/Jersey Girl	1984	—	2.50	5.00
04680	Born in the U.S.A./Shut Out the Light	1984	—	2.50	5.00
04680 [PS]	Born in the U.S.A./Shut Out the Light	1984	—	2.50	5.00
04772	I'm on Fire/Johnny Bye Bye	1985	—	2.00	4.00
04772 [PS]	I'm on Fire/Johnny Bye Bye	1985	—	2.50	5.00
04924	Glory Days/Stand On It	1985	—	2.00	4.00
04924 [PS]	Glory Days/Stand On It	1985	—	2.50	5.00
05603	I'm Goin' Down/Janey, Don't You Lose Heart	1985	—	2.00	4.00
05603 [PS]	I'm Goin' Down/Janey, Don't You Lose Heart	1985	—	2.50	5.00
05728	My Hometown/Santa Claus Is Coming to Town	1985	—	2.00	4.00
05728 [PS]	My Hometown/Santa Claus Is Coming to Town	1985	—	2.00	4.00
06432	War/Merry Christmas Baby	1986	—	2.00	4.00
06432 [PS]	War/Merry Christmas Baby	1986	—	2.00	4.00
06657	Fire/Incident on 57th Street	1987	—	2.50	5.00
06657 [PS]	Fire/Incident on 57th Street	1987	—	2.50	5.00
07595	Brilliant Disguise/Lucky Man	1987	—	2.00	4.00
07595 [PS]	Brilliant Disguise/Lucky Man	1987	—	2.00	4.00
07663	Tunnel of Love/Two for the Road	1987	—	2.00	4.00
07663 [PS]	Tunnel of Love/Two for the Road	1987	—	2.00	4.00
07726	One Step Up/Roulette	1988	—	2.00	4.00
07726 [PS]	One Step Up/Roulette	1988	—	2.00	4.00
08408	Dancing in the Dark/Pink Cadillac	1984	—	—	3.00

—*Gray label reissue*

Number	Title (A Side/B Side)	Yr	VG	VG+	NM
08409	Cover Me/Jersey Girl	1984	—	—	3.00

—*Gray label reissue*

Number	Title (A Side/B Side)	Yr	VG	VG+	NM
08410	Born in the U.S.A./Shut Out the Light	1984	—	—	3.00

—*Gray label reissue*

Number	Title (A Side/B Side)	Yr	VG	VG+	NM
08411	I'm on Fire/Johnny Bye Bye	1985	—	—	3.00

—*Gray label reissue*

Number	Title (A Side/B Side)	Yr	VG	VG+	NM
08412	Glory Days/Stand On It	1985	—	—	3.00

—*Gray label reissue*

Number	Title (A Side/B Side)	Yr	VG	VG+	NM
08413	I'm Goin' Down/Janey, Don't You Lose Heart	1985	—	—	3.00

—*Gray label reissue*

Number	Title (A Side/B Side)	Yr	VG	VG+	NM
08414	My Hometown/Santa Claus Is Coming to Town	1985	—	—	3.00

—*Gray label reissue; many copies of this were issued with Columbia 05728 picture sleeves*

Number	Title (A Side/B Side)	Yr	VG	VG+	NM
10209	Born to Run/Meeting Across the River	1975	5.00	10.00	20.00
10274	Tenth Avenue Freeze-Out/She's the One	1976	3.75	7.50	15.00
10763	Prove It All Night/Factory	1978	3.00	6.00	12.00
10801	Badlands/Streets of Fire	1978	3.00	6.00	12.00
11391	Hungry Heart/Held Up Without a Gun	1980	—	2.00	4.00
11391 [PS]	Hungry Heart/Held Up Without a Gun	1980	—	3.00	6.00
11431	Fade Away/Be True	1981	—	2.00	4.00

—*Corrected second pressing*

Number	Title (A Side/B Side)	Yr	VG	VG+	NM
11431	Fade Away/To Be True	1981	6.25	12.50	25.00

—*Erroneous first pressing*

Number	Title (A Side/B Side)	Yr	VG	VG+	NM
11431 [PS]	Fade Away/Be True	1981	—	3.00	6.00
33323	Born to Run/Spirit in the Night	1976	—	2.00	4.00

—*"Columbia Hall of Fame" series; red label*

Number	Title (A Side/B Side)	Yr	VG	VG+	NM
33323	Born to Run/Spirit in the Night	198?	—	—	3.00

—*"Columbia Hall of Fame" series; gray label*

Number	Title (A Side/B Side)	Yr	VG	VG+	NM
45805	Blinded by the Light/The Angel	1972	125.00	250.00	500.00
45805 [DJ]	Blinded by the Light (mono/stereo)	1972	12.50	25.00	50.00
45805 [PS]	Blinded by the Light/The Angel	1972	100.00	200.00	400.00
45864	Spirit in the Night/For You	1973	375.00	750.00	1500.
45864 [DJ]	Spirit in the Night (mono/stereo)	1973	12.50	25.00	50.00
73796	Tunnel of Love/Two for the Road	1991	—	—	3.00

—*Reissue*

Number	Title (A Side/B Side)	Yr	VG	VG+	NM
73943	One Step Up/Roulette	1991	—	—	3.00

—*Reissue*

Number	Title (A Side/B Side)	Yr	VG	VG+	NM
74273	Human Touch/Better Days	1992	—	2.00	4.00
74354	57 Channels (And Nothin' On)/Part Man Part Monkey	1992	—	2.00	4.00
77384	Streets of Philadelphia/If I Should Fall Behind	1994	—	2.00	4.00
77847	Secret Garden/Thunder Road (Live)	1995	—	—	3.00
77847 [PS]	Secret Garden/Thunder Road (Live)	1995	—	—	3.00

Albums
COLUMBIA

Number	Title (A Side/B Side)	Yr	VG	VG+	NM
(# unknown) [PD]	Darkness on the Edge of Town	1978	37.50	75.00	150.00

—*Promo-only picture disc*

Number	Title (A Side/B Side)	Yr	VG	VG+	NM
AS 978 [DJ]	As Requested Around the World	1981	12.50	25.00	50.00
AS 1957 [DJ]	Bruce Springsteen	1985	7.50	15.00	30.00

—*Five-song mini-LP with five B-sides of singles from Born in the U.S.A.*

Number	Title (A Side/B Side)	Yr	VG	VG+	NM
❑ AS 1957 [DJ]	Bruce Springsteen	1987	5.00	10.00	20.00

—Five-song mini-LP with five B-sides of singles from Born in the U.S.A.; second pressings say so on the label

Number	Title (A Side/B Side)	Yr	VG	VG+	NM
❑ AS 2543 [DJ]	Bruce Springsteen and the E Street Band: Live 1975-1985.	1986	7.50	15.00	30.00

—Sampler from 5-LP live set

Number	Title (A Side/B Side)	Yr	VG	VG+	NM
❑ JC 31903	Greetings from Asbury Park, N.J.	1977	2.00	4.00	8.00

—Reissue of the first PC-prefix version

Number	Title (A Side/B Side)	Yr	VG	VG+	NM
❑ KC 31903	Greetings from Asbury Park, N.J.	1973	5.00	10.00	20.00
❑ KC 31903 [DJ]	Greetings from Asbury Park, N.J.	1973	50.00	100.00	200.00

—Promotional copy with timing strip and "Bruce Springsteen Fact Sheet" attached to back cover. Authentic fact sheets are on glossy stock

Number	Title (A Side/B Side)	Yr	VG	VG+	NM
❑ PC 31903	Greetings from Asbury Park, N.J.	1975	2.50	5.00	10.00

—Without bar code on cover

Number	Title (A Side/B Side)	Yr	VG	VG+	NM
❑ PC 31903	Greetings from Asbury Park, N.J.	1979	2.00	4.00	8.00

—With bar code on cover

Number	Title (A Side/B Side)	Yr	VG	VG+	NM
❑ JC 32432	The Wild, the Innocent & the E Street Shuffle.	1977	2.00	4.00	8.00

—Reissue of the first PC-prefix version

Number	Title (A Side/B Side)	Yr	VG	VG+	NM
❑ KC 32432	The Wild, the Innocent & the E Street Shuffle.	1973	5.00	10.00	20.00
❑ PC 32432	The Wild, the Innocent & the E Street Shuffle.	1975	2.50	5.00	10.00

—Without bar code on cover

Number	Title (A Side/B Side)	Yr	VG	VG+	NM
❑ PC 32432	The Wild, the Innocent & the E Street Shuffle.	1979	2.00	4.00	8.00

—With bar code on cover

Number	Title (A Side/B Side)	Yr	VG	VG+	NM
❑ HC 33795	Born to Run.	1981	12.50	25.00	50.00

—Half-speed mastered edition (original)

Number	Title (A Side/B Side)	Yr	VG	VG+	NM
❑ JC 33795	Born to Run.	1977	2.00	4.00	8.00
❑ PC 33795	Born to Run.	1975	2.50	5.00	10.00

—Jon Landau's name is correct on the back cover

Number	Title (A Side/B Side)	Yr	VG	VG+	NM
❑ PC 33795	Born to Run.	1975	3.75	7.50	15.00

—Sticker with the correct spelling of Jon Landau is on the back cover

Number	Title (A Side/B Side)	Yr	VG	VG+	NM
❑ PC 33795	Born to Run.	1975	6.25	12.50	25.00

—Jon Landau's name is misspelled "John" on the back cover

Number	Title (A Side/B Side)	Yr	VG	VG+	NM
❑ PC 33795 [DJ]	Born to Run.	1975	25.00	50.00	100.00

—White label promo

Number	Title (A Side/B Side)	Yr	VG	VG+	NM
❑ PC 33795 [DJ]	Born to Run.	1975	400.00	800.00	1200.

—Test pressing with "Bruce Springsteen -- Born to Run" in script print. Also includes mailing envelope, letter from CBS and orange patch

Number	Title (A Side/B Side)	Yr	VG	VG+	NM
❑ PC 33795	Born to Run.	1999	6.25	12.50	25.00

—Classic Records reissue, identified as such on back cover; corrected pressing with gatefold

Number	Title (A Side/B Side)	Yr	VG	VG+	NM
❑ PC 33795	Born to Run.	1999	10.00	20.00	40.00

—Classic Records reissue, identified as such on back cover; "error" first pressing with no gatefold

Number	Title (A Side/B Side)	Yr	VG	VG+	NM
❑ JC 35318	Darkness on the Edge of Town.	1978	2.50	5.00	10.00

—Original pressings have thick paper innersleeves and small titles on back cover

Number	Title (A Side/B Side)	Yr	VG	VG+	NM
❑ JC 35318 [DJ]	Darkness on the Edge of Town.	1978	25.00	50.00	100.00

—White label promo

Number	Title (A Side/B Side)	Yr	VG	VG+	NM
❑ JC 35318	Darkness on the Edge of Town.	198?	2.00	4.00	8.00

—Later pressings have thin paper innersleeves and larger titles on back cover

Number	Title (A Side/B Side)	Yr	VG	VG+	NM
❑ PC2 36854 [(2)]	The River.	1980	3.00	6.00	12.00
❑ PC2 36854 [(2)DJ]	The River.	1980	10.00	20.00	40.00

—White label promo, without letter

Number	Title (A Side/B Side)	Yr	VG	VG+	NM
❑ PC2 36854 [(2)DJ]	The River.	1980	18.75	37.50	75.00

—White label promo, with photocopied letter from CBS

Number	Title (A Side/B Side)	Yr	VG	VG+	NM
❑ TC 38358	Nebraska.	1982	2.50	5.00	10.00
❑ QC 38653	Born in the U.S.A.	1984	2.50	5.00	10.00
❑ C5X 40558 [(5)]	Bruce Springsteen and the E Street Band: Live 1975-1985.	1986	10.00	20.00	40.00
❑ OC 40999	Tunnel of Love.	1987	2.50	5.00	10.00
❑ HC 43795	Born to Run.	1982	10.00	20.00	40.00

—Half-speed mastered edition (reissue)

Number	Title (A Side/B Side)	Yr	VG	VG+	NM
❑ 3C 44445 [EP]	Chimes of Freedom.	1988	2.50	5.00	10.00
❑ HC 45318	Darkness on the Edge of Town.	1981	10.00	20.00	40.00

—Half-speed mastered edition

Number	Title (A Side/B Side)	Yr	VG	VG+	NM
❑ C 53000	Human Touch.	1992	3.00	6.00	12.00
❑ C 53001	Lucky Town.	1992	3.00	6.00	12.00
❑ C2 67060 [(2)]	Greatest Hits.	1995	3.75	7.50	15.00
❑ C 67484	The Ghost of Tom Joad.	1995	3.00	6.00	12.00
❑ C2 69746 [(2)]	18 Tracks.	1999	3.75	7.50	15.00
❑ C3 85490 [(3)]	Live in New York City.	2001	5.00	10.00	20.00

—As of press date, all known copies contain "Born to Run," but the song is not listed on either the record jacket or label

Number	Title (A Side/B Side)	Yr	VG	VG+	NM
❑ C2 86600 [(2)]	The Rising.	2002	3.75	7.50	15.00

SPUR
Albums
CINEMA

Number	Title (A Side/B Side)	Yr	VG	VG+	NM
❑ CSLP-1500	Spur of the Moment	196?	20.00	40.00	80.00

SPUTNIKS, THE
45s
CLASS

Number	Title (A Side/B Side)	Yr	VG	VG+	NM
❑ 217	My Love Is Gone/Hey Maryann	1958	12.50	25.00	50.00
❑ 222	Wait a Little While/Johnny's Little Lamb	1958	10.00	20.00	40.00

PAM MAR

Number	Title (A Side/B Side)	Yr	VG	VG+	NM
❑ 601	My Love Is Gone/Hey Maryann	1957	62.50	125.00	250.00

SQUIRES, THE (1)
45s
ALADDIN

Number	Title (A Side/B Side)	Yr	VG	VG+	NM
❑ 3360	Dreamy Eyes/Danglin' with My Heart	1957	25.00	50.00	100.00

KICKS

Number	Title (A Side/B Side)	Yr	VG	VG+	NM
❑ 1	Dream Come True/Lucy Lou	1954	200.00	400.00	800.00

MAMBO

Number	Title (A Side/B Side)	Yr	VG	VG+	NM
❑ 105	Sindy/Do-Be-Do-Be-Wop-Wop	1955	37.50	75.00	150.00

VITA

Number	Title (A Side/B Side)	Yr	VG	VG+	NM
❑ 105	Sindy/Do-Be-Do-Be-Wop-Wop	1960	25.00	50.00	100.00
❑ 113	Sweet Girl/Me and My Deal	1955	25.00	50.00	100.00
❑ 116	Heavenly Angel/Sweet Girl	1955	25.00	50.00	100.00

SQUIRES, THE (2)
45s
ATCO

Number	Title (A Side/B Side)	Yr	VG	VG+	NM
❑ 6442	Go Ahead/Going All the Way	1966	10.00	20.00	40.00

SQUIRES, THE (3)
45s
CHAN

Number	Title (A Side/B Side)	Yr	VG	VG+	NM
❑ 102	Movin' Out/Our Theme	1961	7.50	15.00	30.00
❑ 105	Mean Misery/Chattanooga Choo Choo	1962	7.50	15.00	30.00

MGM

Number	Title (A Side/B Side)	Yr	VG	VG+	NM
❑ 13044	Movin' Out/Our Theme	1961	3.75	7.50	15.00

SQUIRES, THE (4)
45s
COMBO

Number	Title (A Side/B Side)	Yr	VG	VG+	NM
❑ 35	Let's Give Love a Try/Whop	1952	125.00	250.00	500.00
❑ 42	Oh Darling/My Little Girl	1953	150.00	300.00	600.00

SQUIRES, THE (U) We can't conclusively place any of these with the above groups. Of course, they may not be any of the above groups.
45s
CONGRESS

Number	Title (A Side/B Side)	Yr	VG	VG+	NM
❑ 223	Joyce/Can't Believe That You've Grown Up	1964	15.00	30.00	60.00

FLAIR

Number	Title (A Side/B Side)	Yr	VG	VG+	NM
❑ 1030	Sayonara/Mia Bella Donna	1954	7.50	15.00	30.00

GEE

Number	Title (A Side/B Side)	Yr	VG	VG+	NM
❑ 1082	Don't Accuse Me/So Many Tears Ago	1962	12.50	25.00	50.00

HERALD

Number	Title (A Side/B Side)	Yr	VG	VG+	NM
❑ 580	Why Should I Suffer/Walkin'	1963	7.50	15.00	30.00

STARLITE

Number	Title (A Side/B Side)	Yr	VG	VG+	NM
❑ 1/2	Movin'/Night Road	1964	12.50	25.00	50.00

V

Number	Title (A Side/B Side)	Yr	VG	VG+	NM
❑ 109	The Sultan/Aurora	1961	250.00	500.00	1000.

—Canadian release only; with a very early Neil Young

SQUIRRELS, THE
45s
CAMEO

Number	Title (A Side/B Side)	Yr	VG	VG+	NM
❑ 284	Grandma's House/The Girl That I'll Adore	1963	2.50	5.00	10.00

—B-side by the Philadelphia Minstrels

SRC
45s
A-SQUARE

Number	Title (A Side/B Side)	Yr	VG	VG+	NM
❑ 301	I'm So Glad/Who Is That Girl	1967	6.25	12.50	25.00

—As "Scott Richard Case"

Number	Title (A Side/B Side)	Yr	VG	VG+	NM
❑ 402	Get the Picture/I Need You	1967	6.25	12.50	25.00

—B-side by the Rationals

CAPITOL

Number	Title (A Side/B Side)	Yr	VG	VG+	NM
❑ 2327	Black Sheep/Morning Hood	1968	2.50	5.00	10.00
❑ 2457	Turn Into Love/Up All Night	1969	2.50	5.00	10.00
❑ 2726	Never Before Now/My Fortune's Coming True	1970	2.50	5.00	10.00

Albums
CAPITOL

Number	Title (A Side/B Side)	Yr	VG	VG+	NM
❑ ST-134	Milestones	1969	10.00	20.00	40.00
❑ SKAO-273	Travellers Tale	1970	10.00	20.00	40.00
❑ ST 2991	SRC	1968	15.00	30.00	60.00

STACKRIDGE
45s
DECCA

Number	Title (A Side/B Side)	Yr	VG	VG+	NM
❑ 32923	Dora the Female Explorer/(B-side unknown)	1972	2.50	5.00	10.00

SIRE

Number	Title (A Side/B Side)	Yr	VG	VG+	NM
❑ 717	The Last Plimsoul/Spin Around the Room	1974	—	2.50	5.00

Albums
DECCA

Number	Title (A Side/B Side)	Yr	VG	VG+	NM
❑ DL 75317	Stackridge	1971	6.25	12.50	25.00

MCA

Number	Title (A Side/B Side)	Yr	VG	VG+	NM
❑ 308	Friendliness	1973	2.50	5.00	10.00

SIRE

Number	Title (A Side/B Side)	Yr	VG	VG+	NM
❑ SASD-7503	Pinafore Days	1974	2.50	5.00	10.00
❑ SASD-7509	Extravaganza	1975	2.50	5.00	10.00

STAFFORD, JIM
45s
COLUMBIA

Number	Title (A Side/B Side)	Yr	VG	VG+	NM
❑ 04339	Little Bits and Pieces/Banjo Billy	1984	—	—	3.00

ELEKTRA

Number	Title (A Side/B Side)	Yr	VG	VG+	NM
❑ 47013	Don't Fool Around (When There's a Fool Around)/I Took Your Love Lightly	1980	—	2.00	4.00
❑ 47226	Isabel and Samantha/Yeller Dog Blues	1981	—	2.00	4.00

MGM

Number	Title (A Side/B Side)	Yr	VG	VG+	NM
❑ 14496	Swamp Witch/Nifty Fifties Blues	1973	—	2.00	4.00
❑ 14648	Spiders and Snakes/Undecided	1973	—	2.00	4.00
❑ 14718	My Girl Bill/L.A. Mama	1974	—	2.00	4.00
❑ 14737	Wildwood Weed/The Last Chant	1974	—	2.00	4.00
❑ 14775	Your Bulldog Drinks Champagne/Real Good Time	1974	—	2.00	4.00
❑ 14819	I Got Stoned and I Missed It/I Ain't Workin'	1975	—	2.00	4.00

POLYDOR

Number	Title (A Side/B Side)	Yr	VG	VG+	NM
❑ 14309	Jasper/I Can't Find Nobody Home	1976	—	2.00	4.00

TOWN HOUSE

Number	Title (A Side/B Side)	Yr	VG	VG+	NM
❑ 1062	What Mama Don't Know/That's What Little Kids Do	1982	—	2.00	4.00

WARNER BROS.
Albums
MGM

Number	Title (A Side/B Side)	Yr	VG	VG+	NM
❑ M3G-4947	Jim Stafford	1974	2.50	5.00	10.00
❑ M3G-4984	Not Just Another Pretty Foot	1975	2.50	5.00	10.00

POLYDOR

Number	Title (A Side/B Side)	Yr	VG	VG+	NM
❑ PD-1-6072	Jim Stafford	1976	2.00	4.00	8.00

—Reissue of MGM 4947

STAFFORD, JO Also see JONATHAN AND DARLENE EDWARDS.
45s
CAPITOL

Number	Title (A Side/B Side)	Yr	VG	VG+	NM
❑ 54-785	Scarlet Ribbons (For Her Hair)/Happy Times	1949	6.25	12.50	25.00
❑ F808	Fools Rush In/Just One of Those Things	1950	5.00	10.00	20.00
❑ F824	Diamonds Are a Girl's Best Friend/Open Door, Open Arms	1950	5.00	10.00	20.00
❑ F868	Near Me/Beyond the Sunset	1950	5.00	10.00	20.00
❑ F914	Day by Day/When April Comes Again	1950	5.00	10.00	20.00
❑ F927	Tumbling Tumbleweeds/Someone to Love	1950	5.00	10.00	20.00
❑ F946	Ask Me No Questions/On the Outgoing Tide	1950	5.00	10.00	20.00
❑ F989	Begin the Beguine/In the Still of the Night	1950	3.75	7.50	15.00
❑ F990	September Song/Yesterdays	1950	3.75	7.50	15.00
❑ F991	The Best Things in Life Are Free/The Gentleman Is a Dope	1950	3.75	7.50	15.00

S

Number	Title (A Side/B Side)	Yr	VG	VG+	NM
❏ F992	Here I'll Stay/Almost Like Being in Love	1950	3.75	7.50	15.00
❏ F993	Sometimes I'm Happy/				
	Why Can't You Believe Me	1950	3.75	7.50	15.00
❏ F994	Barbara Allen/He's Gone Away	1950	3.75	7.50	15.00
❏ F995	Walkin' My Baby Back Home/Over the Rainbow	1950	3.75	7.50	15.00
❏ F996	On the Alamo/Roses of Picardy	1950	3.75	7.50	15.00
❏ F997	Baby Won't You Please Come Home/I'll Be With				
	You in Apple Blossom Time	1950	3.75	7.50	15.00
❏ F998	Ave Maria/Shinin' Through	1950	3.75	7.50	15.00
❏ F999	Where Are You Gonna Be/Driftin' Down the				
	Dreamy Old Ohio	1950	3.75	7.50	15.00

—Whether the above 11 (F989-F999) were released individually, as a box set, or as several box sets, we don't know.

Number	Title (A Side/B Side)	Yr	VG	VG+	NM
❏ F1039	Play a Simple Melody/Pagan Love Song	1950	5.00	10.00	20.00
❏ F1053	No Other Love/Sometime	1950	5.00	10.00	20.00
❏ F1061	The Rosary/Perfect Day	1950	5.00	10.00	20.00
❏ F1142	Goodnight Irene/Our Very Own	1950	5.00	10.00	20.00
❏ F1153	La Vie En Rose/La Vie En Rose	1950	5.00	10.00	20.00

—B-side by Paul Weston

Number	Title (A Side/B Side)	Yr	VG	VG+	NM
❏ F1195	In the Middle of a Riddle/Tea for Two	1950	5.00	10.00	20.00
❏ F1248	Autumn Leaves/Autumn in New York	1950	5.00	10.00	20.00
❏ F1262	White Christmas/Silent Night	1950	3.75	7.50	15.00
❏ F1312	Love Is a Masquerade/It Was So Beautiful	1950	5.00	10.00	20.00
❏ F1651	Tumbling Tumbleweeds/				
	On the Sunny Side of the Street	1951	3.75	7.50	15.00

—Reissue

Number	Title (A Side/B Side)	Yr	VG	VG+	NM
❏ F1685	Sometime/No Other Love	1951	3.75	7.50	15.00

—Reissue

Number	Title (A Side/B Side)	Yr	VG	VG+	NM
❏ PRO 2756 [DJ]	Christmas Is The Season/Merry Christmas	1964	2.50	5.00	10.00
❏ 54-90042	Silent Night/White Christmas	1949	3.75	7.50	15.00

COLPIX

Number	Title (A Side/B Side)	Yr	VG	VG+	NM
❏ 623	Misty/Adios My Love	1962	2.50	5.00	10.00
❏ 633	My Heart Had a Window/Symphony	1962	2.50	5.00	10.00

COLUMBIA

Number	Title (A Side/B Side)	Yr	VG	VG+	NM
❏ 1-900 (?)	Where or When/Use Your Imagination	1950	7.50	15.00	30.00

—Microgroove 33 1/3 rpm 7-inch single

Number	Title (A Side/B Side)	Yr	VG	VG+	NM
❏ 6-900 (?)	Where or When/Use Your Imagination	1950	6.25	12.50	25.00

—First edition of 45

Number	Title (A Side/B Side)	Yr	VG	VG+	NM
❏ 1-905 (?)	Stardust/You Don't Remind Me	1950	7.50	15.00	30.00

—Microgroove 33 1/3 rpm 7-inch single

Number	Title (A Side/B Side)	Yr	VG	VG+	NM
❏ 6-905 (?)	Stardust/You Don't Remind Me	1950	6.25	12.50	25.00

—First edition of 45

Number	Title (A Side/B Side)	Yr	VG	VG+	NM
❏ 1-910 (?)	Tennessee Waltz/If You've Got the Money, I've				
	Got the Time	1950	7.50	15.00	30.00

—Microgroove 33 1/3 rpm 7-inch single

Number	Title (A Side/B Side)	Yr	VG	VG+	NM
❏ 6-910 (?)	Tennessee Waltz/If You've Got the Money, I've				
	Got the Time	1950	6.25	12.50	25.00

—First edition of 45

Number	Title (A Side/B Side)	Yr	VG	VG+	NM
❏ 39049	Where or When/Use Your Imagination	1950	5.00	10.00	20.00

—Second edition of this 45

Number	Title (A Side/B Side)	Yr	VG	VG+	NM
❏ 39056	Stardust/You Don't Remind Me	1950	5.00	10.00	20.00

—Second edition of this 45

Number	Title (A Side/B Side)	Yr	VG	VG+	NM
❏ 39065	Tennessee Waltz/				
	If You've Got the Money, I've Got the Time	1950	5.00	10.00	20.00

—Second edition of this 45

Number	Title (A Side/B Side)	Yr	VG	VG+	NM
❏ 39082	If/It Is No Secret (What God Can Do)	1950	5.00	10.00	20.00
❏ 3-39082	If/It Is No Secret (What God Can Do)	1950	7.50	15.00	30.00

—Microgroove 33 1/3 rpm 7-inch single

Number	Title (A Side/B Side)	Yr	VG	VG+	NM
❏ 39129	Tennessee Waltz/Goodnight Pillow	1950	5.00	10.00	20.00
❏ 39130	If You've Got the Money, I've Got the Time/				
	Handsome Stranger	1950	5.00	10.00	20.00
❏ 39206	San Antonio Rose/Lovely Is the Evening	1951	5.00	10.00	20.00
❏ 39301	Make Man Love Me/Along the Colorado Trail	1951	5.00	10.00	20.00
❏ 39389	Somebody/Allentown Jail	1951	5.00	10.00	20.00
❏ 39448	Star of Hope/He Bought My Soul	1951	5.00	10.00	20.00
❏ 39529	Kissin' Bug Boogie/Hawaiian War Chant	1951	5.00	10.00	20.00
❏ 39581	Shrimp Boats/Love Mystery	1951	5.00	10.00	20.00
❏ 39653	Ay-Round the Corner (Bee-Hind the Bush)/				
	Heaven Drops the Curtain	1952	3.75	7.50	15.00
❏ 39720	Don't Worry 'Bout Me/As You Desire Me	1952	3.00	6.00	12.00
❏ 39721	Something to Remember You By/Spring Is Here	1952	3.00	6.00	12.00
❏ 39722	September in the Rain/Easy Come, Easy Go	1952	3.00	6.00	12.00
❏ 39723	Blue Moon/I'm In the Mood for Love	1952	3.00	6.00	12.00

—The above four comprise a box set

Number	Title (A Side/B Side)	Yr	VG	VG+	NM
❏ 39725	Raminay/With You in My Arms	1952	3.75	7.50	15.00
❏ 39811	You Belong to Me/Pretty Boy	1952	3.75	7.50	15.00
❏ 39838	Jambalaya/Early Autumn	1952	3.75	7.50	15.00
❏ 39891	Keep It a Secret/Once to Every Heart	1952	3.75	7.50	15.00
❏ 39893	Christmas Roses/Chow, Willy	1952	3.75	7.50	15.00

—With Frankie Laine

Number	Title (A Side/B Side)	Yr	VG	VG+	NM
❏ 39930	(Now and Then, There's) A Fool Such As I/Just				
	Because You're You	1953	3.75	7.50	15.00
❏ 39951	Smoking My Sad Cigarette/Without My Lover	1953	3.75	7.50	15.00
❏ 40000	My Dearest, My Darling/Just Another Polka	1953	3.75	7.50	15.00
❏ 40021	Someone's Been Readin' My Mail/I'm Your Girl	1953	3.75	7.50	15.00
❏ 40034	Till We Meet Again/With These Hands	1953	3.75	7.50	15.00

—With Nelson Eddy

Number	Title (A Side/B Side)	Yr	VG	VG+	NM
❏ 40059	Living for Only You/Cups of Joy	1953	3.75	7.50	15.00
❏ 40103	The Christmas Blues/				
	What Good Am I Without You	1953	3.75	7.50	15.00
❏ 40143	Make Love to Me!/Adi-Adios, Amigo	1953	3.00	6.00	12.00
❏ 40170	April and You/Indiscretion	1954	3.00	6.00	12.00

—With Liberace

Number	Title (A Side/B Side)	Yr	VG	VG+	NM
❏ 40190	It Is No Secret (What God Can Do)/Beautiful				
	Garden of Prayer	1954	2.50	5.00	10.00
❏ 40191	Star of Hope/Peace in the Valley (For Me)	1954	2.50	5.00	10.00
❏ 40192	You Bought My Soul at Calvary/Invisible Hands	1954	2.50	5.00	10.00
❏ 40193	I Found a Friend/Beautiful Isle of Somewhere	1954	2.50	5.00	10.00

—The above four comprise a box set

Number	Title (A Side/B Side)	Yr	VG	VG+	NM
❏ 40230	The Temple of an Understanding Heart/Don't				
	Get Around Much Anymore	1954	—	—	—

—Canceled

Number	Title (A Side/B Side)	Yr	VG	VG+	NM
❏ 40250	Thank You for Calling/Where Are You	1954	3.00	6.00	12.00
❏ 40291	Nearer My Love to Me/The Temple of an				
	Understanding Heart	1954	3.00	6.00	12.00
❏ 40351	Teach Me Tonight/Suddenly	1954	3.00	6.00	12.00

Number	Title (A Side/B Side)	Yr	VG	VG+	NM
❏ 40406	Don't Get Around Much Anymore/Darling!				
	Darling! Darling!	1955	3.00	6.00	12.00
❏ 40451	Please Don't Go So Soon/I Got a Sweetie	1955	3.00	6.00	12.00
❏ 40495	Be Sure, Beloved/Young and Foolish	1955	3.00	6.00	12.00
❏ 40538	Ain'tcha Comin' Out T-Tonight/St. Louis Blues	1955	3.00	6.00	12.00
❏ 40559	Suddenly There's a Valley/The Night Watch	1955	3.00	6.00	12.00
❏ 40595	It's Almost Tomorrow/If You Want to Love Me,				
	You Have to Cry	1955	3.00	6.00	12.00
❏ 40640	All Night Long/As I Love You	1956	2.50	5.00	10.00
❏ 40697	Warm All Over/Big D	1956	2.50	5.00	10.00
❏ 40718	With a Little Bit of Luck/One Little Kiss	1956	2.50	5.00	10.00
❏ 40745	Love Me Good/A Perfect Love	1956	2.50	5.00	10.00
❏ 40782	On London Bridge/Bells Are Ringing	1956	2.50	5.00	10.00
❏ 40832	Wind in the Willow/King of Paris	1957	2.50	5.00	10.00
❏ 40926	I'll Be There (When We Get Lonely)/Underneath				
	the Overpass	1957	2.50	5.00	10.00
❏ 41006	Star of Love/What's Botherin' You Baby	1957	2.50	5.00	10.00
❏ 41007	Echoes in the Night/Beyond the Stars	1957	2.50	5.00	10.00
❏ 41078	Sweet Little Darlin'/I'll Buy It	1957	2.50	5.00	10.00
❏ 41129	Sweet Little Darlin'/It's Never Quite the Same	1958	2.50	5.00	10.00
❏ 41160	I May Never Pass This Way Again/				
	It Won't Be Easy	1958	2.50	5.00	10.00
❏ 41281	Lazy Moon/Hibiscus	1958	2.50	5.00	10.00
❏ 41321	How Can We Say Goodbye/				
	My Heart Is From Missouri	1959	2.50	5.00	10.00
❏ 41413	All Yours/Pine Top's Boogie	1959	2.50	5.00	10.00
❏ 41517	It's Been So Long/Just Tell 'Em You Love Me	1959	2.50	5.00	10.00
❏ 41535	You're Starting to Get to Me/				
	Every Night When the Sun Goes In	1959	2.50	5.00	10.00
❏ 41640	Happy Is the Word/What a Feeling	1960	2.50	5.00	10.00
❏ 41690	Candy/Indoor Sport	1960	2.50	5.00	10.00

DECCA

Number	Title (A Side/B Side)	Yr	VG	VG+	NM
❏ 25734	You Belong to Me/St. Louis Blues	1968	—	3.00	6.00
❏ 25740	Make Love to Me/I'll Be Seeing You	1968	—	3.00	6.00

DOT

Number	Title (A Side/B Side)	Yr	VG	VG+	NM
❏ 16791	Do I Hear a Waltz/Down in the Valley	1965	2.00	4.00	8.00
❏ 16904	Falling in Love Again/Cry, Cry Darling	1966	2.00	4.00	8.00

REPRISE

Number	Title (A Side/B Side)	Yr	VG	VG+	NM
❏ 20205	Country Bumpkin/Writing on the Wall	1963	2.00	4.00	8.00

7-Inch Extended Plays

COLUMBIA

Number	Title (A Side/B Side)	Yr	VG	VG+	NM
❏ 5-1796	My Heart's in the Highlands/John Anderson, My				
	Jo//My Jean/The Bonnie Lad That's Far Away	195?	3.00	6.00	12.00

—Alternate numbers are "B-362-1" and "B-362-4"

Number	Title (A Side/B Side)	Yr	VG	VG+	NM
❏ B-2526	You Belong to Me/Shrimp Boats//Keep It a				
	Secret/Jambalaya	1957	3.75	7.50	15.00
❏ B-2526 [PS]	Jo Stafford (Hall of Fame Series)	1957	3.75	7.50	15.00
❏ B-2527	*Make Love to Me!/Early Autumn/Stardust/				
	Teach Me Tonight	1957	3.75	7.50	15.00
❏ B-2527 [PS]	Jo Stafford (Hall of Fame Series)	1957	3.75	7.50	15.00
❏ B-9101	Baby It's Cold Outside/Moonlight in Vermont//				
	Let It Snow! Let It Snow! Let It Snow!/				
	By the Fireside	1956	3.00	6.00	12.00
❏ B-9101 [PS]	Ski Trails, Vol. 1	1956	3.00	6.00	12.00
❏ B-9102	*Winter Song/It Happened in Sun Valley/				
	I've Got My Love to Keep Me Warm/				
	The Nearness of You	1956	3.00	6.00	12.00
❏ B-9102 [PS]	Ski Trails, Vol. 2	1956	3.00	6.00	12.00
❏ B-9103	Winter Wonderland/June in January//				
	The Whiffenpoof Song/Sleigh Ride	1956	3.00	6.00	12.00
❏ B-9103 [PS]	Ski Trails, Vol. 3	1956	3.00	6.00	12.00

Albums

BAINBRIDGE

Number	Title (A Side/B Side)	Yr	VG	VG+	NM
❏ 6234	Look at Me Now	1982	2.50	5.00	10.00

CAPITOL

Number	Title (A Side/B Side)	Yr	VG	VG+	NM
❏ H 75 [10]	American Folk Songs	1950	15.00	30.00	60.00
❏ H 197 [10]	Autumn in New York	195?	15.00	30.00	60.00
❏ T 197 [M]	Autumn in New York	1955	12.50	25.00	50.00

—Turquoise or gray label

Number	Title (A Side/B Side)	Yr	VG	VG+	NM
❏ T 197 [M]	Autumn in New York	1959	7.50	15.00	30.00

—Black colorband label, Capitol logo at left

Number	Title (A Side/B Side)	Yr	VG	VG+	NM
❏ H 247 [10]	Songs for Sunday Evening	195?	15.00	30.00	60.00
❏ T 423 [M]	Memory Songs	1955	12.50	25.00	50.00

—Turquoise or gray label

Number	Title (A Side/B Side)	Yr	VG	VG+	NM
❏ T 423 [M]	Memory Songs	1959	7.50	15.00	30.00

—Black colorband label, Capitol logo at left

Number	Title (A Side/B Side)	Yr	VG	VG+	NM
❏ H 435 [10]	Starring Jo Stafford	1953	15.00	30.00	60.00
❏ T 435 [M]	Starring Jo Stafford	1955	12.50	25.00	50.00

—Turquoise or gray label

Number	Title (A Side/B Side)	Yr	VG	VG+	NM
❏ T 435 [M]	Starring Jo Stafford	1959	7.50	15.00	30.00

—Black colorband label, Capitol logo at left

Number	Title (A Side/B Side)	Yr	VG	VG+	NM
❏ ST 1653 [S]	American Folk Songs	1962	6.25	12.50	25.00
❏ T 1653 [M]	American Folk Songs	1962	5.00	10.00	20.00
❏ SM-1696	Whispering Hope	1977	2.50	5.00	10.00

—Reissue with new prefix

Number	Title (A Side/B Side)	Yr	VG	VG+	NM
❏ ST 1921 [S]	The Hits of Jo Stafford	1963	6.25	12.50	25.00
❏ T 1921 [M]	The Hits of Jo Stafford	1963	5.00	10.00	20.00
❏ ST 2069 [S]	Sweet Hour of Prayer	1964	6.25	12.50	25.00
❏ T 2069 [M]	Sweet Hour of Prayer	1964	5.00	10.00	20.00
❏ ST 2166 [S]	The Joyful Season	1964	6.25	12.50	25.00
❏ T 2166 [M]	The Joyful Season	1964	5.00	10.00	20.00
❏ H 9014 [10]	Songs of Faith	1950	15.00	30.00	60.00
❏ SM-11889	The Hits of Jo Stafford	1979	2.50	5.00	10.00

COLUMBIA

Number	Title (A Side/B Side)	Yr	VG	VG+	NM
❏ CL 578 [M]	New Orleans	1954	10.00	20.00	40.00

—Maroon label, gold print

Number	Title (A Side/B Side)	Yr	VG	VG+	NM
❏ CL 578 [M]	New Orleans	1955	7.50	15.00	30.00

—Red and black label with six "eye" logos

Number	Title (A Side/B Side)	Yr	VG	VG+	NM
❏ CL 584 [M]	Jo Stafford Sings Broadway's Best	1954	10.00	20.00	40.00

—Maroon label, gold print

Number	Title (A Side/B Side)	Yr	VG	VG+	NM
❏ CL 584 [M]	Jo Stafford Sings Broadway's Best	1955	7.50	15.00	30.00

—Red and black label with six "eye" logos

Number	Title (A Side/B Side)	Yr	VG	VG+	NM
❏ CL 691 [M]	Happy Holiday	1955	15.00	30.00	60.00
❏ CL 910 [M]	Ski Trails	1956	10.00	20.00	40.00
❏ CL 968 [M]	Once Over Lightly	1957	10.00	20.00	40.00
❏ CL 1043 [M]	Songs of Scotland	1957	10.00	20.00	40.00

Number	Title (A Side/B Side)	Yr	VG	VG+	NM
❑ CL 1124 [M]	Swingin' Down Broadway	1958	10.00	20.00	40.00
❑ CL 1228 [M]	Jo Stafford's Greatest Hits	1958	10.00	20.00	40.00
—Red and black label with six "eye" logos					
❑ CL 1228 [M]	Jo Stafford's Greatest Hits	1963	5.00	10.00	20.00
—Red label with "Guaranteed High Fidelity" in black					
❑ CL 1228 [M]	Jo Stafford's Greatest Hits	1965	3.75	7.50	15.00
—Red label with "360 Sound Mono" in white					
❑ CL 1262 [M]	I'll Be Seeing You	1959	7.50	15.00	30.00
❑ CL 1339 [M]	Ballad of the Blues	1959	7.50	15.00	30.00
❑ CL 1561 [M]	Jo + Jazz	1960	10.00	20.00	40.00
❑ CL 2501 [10]	Soft and Sentimental	1955	10.00	20.00	40.00
❑ CL 2591 [10]	A Gal Named Jo	1955	10.00	20.00	40.00
❑ CL 6210 [10]	As You Desire Me	1952	12.50	25.00	50.00
❑ CL 6238 [10]	Jo Stafford Sings Broadway's Best	1953	12.50	25.00	50.00
❑ CL 6268 [10]	New Orleans	1954	12.50	25.00	50.00
❑ CL 6274 [10]	My Heart's in the Highland	1954	12.50	25.00	50.00
❑ CL 6286 [10]	Garden of Prayer	1954	12.50	25.00	50.00
❑ CS 8080 [S]	I'll Be Seeing You	1959	10.00	20.00	40.00
❑ CS 8139 [S]	Ballad of the Blues	1959	10.00	20.00	40.00
❑ CS 8361 [S]	Jo + Jazz	1960	15.00	30.00	60.00
CORINTHIAN					
❑ COR-105	G.I. Jo	1977	2.50	5.00	10.00
❑ COR-106	Greatest Hits	1977	2.50	5.00	10.00
❑ COR-108	Jo + Jazz	197?	2.50	5.00	10.00
❑ COR-110	Jo Stafford Sings American Folk Songs	197?	2.50	5.00	10.00
❑ COR-111	Songs of Faith, Hope and Love	197?	2.50	5.00	10.00
❑ COR-112	Jo + Broadway	197?	2.50	5.00	10.00
❑ COR-113	Ski Trails	197?	2.50	5.00	10.00
❑ COR-114	Jo + Blues	197?	2.50	5.00	10.00
❑ COR-115	International Hits	197?	2.50	5.00	10.00
❑ COR-118	Broadway Revisited	198?	2.50	5.00	10.00
❑ COR-119	By Request	198?	2.50	5.00	10.00
❑ COR-123	Music of My Life	1986	2.50	5.00	10.00
DECCA					
❑ DL 74973	Jo Stafford's Greatest Hits	1968	3.75	7.50	15.00
DOT					
❑ DLP-3673 [M]	Do I Hear a Waltz?	1966	3.75	7.50	15.00
❑ DLP-3745 [M]	This Is Jo Stafford	1967	3.75	7.50	15.00
❑ DLP-25673 [S]	Do I Hear a Waltz?	1966	5.00	10.00	20.00
❑ DLP-25745 [S]	This Is Jo Stafford	1967	5.00	10.00	20.00
REPRISE					
❑ R-6090 [M]	Getting Sentimental Over Tommy Dorsey	1963	5.00	10.00	20.00
❑ R9-6090 [S]	Getting Sentimental Over Tommy Dorsey	1963	6.25	12.50	25.00
STANYAN					
❑ 10073	Look at Me Now	197?	3.00	6.00	12.00
TIME-LIFE					
❑ SLGD-14 [(2)]	Legendary Singers: Jo Stafford	1986	3.75	7.50	15.00
VOCALION					
❑ VL 73856 [R]	Happy Holidays	1968	3.00	6.00	12.00
❑ VL 73866 [R]	Sweet Singer of Songs	1969	3.00	6.00	12.00
❑ VL 73892	In the Mood for Love	1970	3.00	6.00	12.00

STAFFORD, JO, AND VIC DAMONE Also see each artist's individual listings.
45s

Number	Title (A Side/B Side)	Yr	VG	VG+	NM
COLUMBIA					
❑ 40968	Silence Is Golden/Good Nite	1957	2.50	5.00	10.00

STAFFORD, JO, AND GORDON MACRAE Also see each artist's individual listings.
45s

Number	Title (A Side/B Side)	Yr	VG	VG+	NM
CAPITOL					
❑ 54-690	Whispering Hope/Thought in the Heart	1949	6.25	12.50	25.00
❑ 54-782	Bibbidi-Bobbidi-Boo (The Magic Song)/Echoes	1949	6.25	12.50	25.00
❑ F858	Dearie/Monday, Tuesday, Wednesday	1950	5.00	10.00	20.00
❑ F969	Down the Lane/You Are My Love	1950	5.00	10.00	20.00
❑ F1235	Yesterday/I'll See You After Church	1950	5.00	10.00	20.00
❑ F1307	To Think You've Chosen Me/Hold Me, Hold Me	1950	5.00	10.00	20.00
❑ F1523	When It's Springtime...You Tell Me/Nights of Splendor	1951	5.00	10.00	20.00
❑ F1642	Whispering Hope/I'll String Along with You	1951	3.75	7.50	15.00
—Reissue of 1949 hit					
❑ F1659	Wunderbar/Beyond the Sunset	1951	3.75	7.50	15.00
—Reissue					
7-Inch Extended Plays					
CAPITOL					
❑ EAP 1-428	*Wunderbar/Need You/Beyond the Sunset/ Whispering Hope	195?	3.00	6.00	12.00
❑ EAP 1-428 [PS]	Memory Songs	195?	3.00	6.00	12.00
❑ EAP 1-9021	Songs Of Christmas Part 1/Songs Of Christmas Part 2	195?	2.50	5.00	10.00
❑ EAP 1-9021 [PS]	Songs of Christmas	195?	2.50	5.00	10.00
Albums					
CAPITOL					
❑ H 247 [10]	Sunday Evening Songs	1952	15.00	30.00	60.00
❑ T 423 [M]	Memory Songs	1955	12.50	25.00	50.00
❑ ST 1696 [S]	Whispering Hope	1962	6.25	12.50	25.00
❑ T 1696 [M]	Whispering Hope	1962	5.00	10.00	20.00
❑ ST 1916 [S]	There's Peace in the Valley	1963	6.25	12.50	25.00
❑ T 1916 [M]	There's Peace in the Valley	1963	5.00	10.00	20.00
❑ SM-11890	There's Peace in the Valley	1978	2.50	5.00	10.00
—Reissue					

STAFFORD, TERRY
45s

Number	Title (A Side/B Side)	Yr	VG	VG+	NM
A&M					
❑ 707	Heartaches on the Way/You Left Me Here to Cry	1963	3.00	6.00	12.00
ATLANTIC					
❑ CY-4006	Amarillo by Morning/Say, Has Anybody Seen My Sweet Gypsy Rose	1973	2.00	4.00	8.00
❑ 4015	Captured/It Sure Is Bad to Love Her	1974	—	3.00	6.00
❑ 4026	Stop If You Love Me/We've Grown Close	1974	—	3.00	6.00
CASINO					
❑ 113	It Sure Is Bad to Love Her/(B-side unknown)	1977	—	3.00	6.00
CRUSADER					
❑ 101	Suspicion/Judy	1964	3.75	7.50	15.00
❑ 105	I'll Touch a Star/Playing with Fire	1964	3.00	6.00	12.00
❑ 109	Follow the Rainbow/Are You a Fool Like Me	1964	3.00	6.00	12.00

Number	Title (A Side/B Side)	Yr	VG	VG+	NM
❑ 110	A Little Bit Better/Hoping	1964	3.00	6.00	12.00
EASTLAND					
❑ 101	Back Together/Life's Railway to Heaven	198?	—	2.50	5.00
LANA					
❑ 139	Suspicion/Judy	196?	2.00	4.00	8.00
—Oldies reissue					
MELODYLAND					
❑ 6009	Darling, Think It Over/I Can't Find It	1975	—	2.50	5.00
MERCURY					
❑ 72538	Out of the Picture/Forbidden	1966	2.50	5.00	10.00
MGM					
❑ 14232	Mean Woman Blues-Candy Man/Chilly Chicago	1971	—	3.00	6.00
❑ 14271	California Dancer/The Walk	1971	—	3.00	6.00
PLAYER					
❑ 134	Lonestar Lonesome/(B-side unknown)	1989	—	3.00	6.00
SIDEWALK					
❑ 902	Soldier Boy/When Sin Stops, Love Begins	1966	2.50	5.00	10.00
❑ 914	A Step or Two Behind You/The Joke's on Me	1967	2.50	5.00	10.00
WARNER BROS.					
❑ 7286	Big in Dallas/Will a Man Ever Learn	1969	—	3.00	6.00
Albums					
ATLANTIC					
❑ SD 7282	Say, Has Anybody Seen My Sweet Gypsy Rose	1974	3.00	6.00	12.00
CRUSADER					
❑ CLP-1001 [M]	Suspicion!	1964	10.00	20.00	40.00
❑ CLP-1001S [S]	Suspicion!	1964	15.00	30.00	60.00

STAIRSTEPS, THE See THE FIVE STAIRSTEPS.

STALK-FORREST GROUP, THE Early version of BLUE OYSTER CULT.
45s

Number	Title (A Side/B Side)	Yr	VG	VG+	NM
ELEKTRA					
❑ 45693	What Is Quicksand/Arthur Comics	1970	12.50	25.00	50.00

STAMPEDERS
45s

Number	Title (A Side/B Side)	Yr	VG	VG+	NM
BELL					
❑ 45120	Sweet City Woman/Gator Road	1971	—	3.00	6.00
❑ 45154	Devil You/Giant in the Streets	1971	—	2.50	5.00
❑ 45188	Monday Morning Choo-Choo/Then Came the White Man	1972	—	3.00	6.00
❑ 45226	Wild Eyes/Carryin' On	1972	—	3.00	6.00
❑ 45331	Oh My Lady/No Destination	1973	—	3.00	6.00
CAPITOL					
❑ 3868	Goodbye Goodbye/Me and My Stone	1974	—	2.00	4.00
❑ 3964	Running Out of Time/Ramona	1974	—	2.00	4.00
MGM					
❑ 13970	Be a Woman/I Don't Believe	1968	3.00	6.00	12.00
POLYDOR					
❑ 14060	Carry Me/I Didn't Need You Anyhow	1970	2.50	5.00	10.00
QUALITY					
❑ 501	Hard Lovin' Woman/Hit the Road Jack	1976	—	2.00	4.00
❑ 505	Sweet Love Bandit/Let It Begin	1976	—	2.00	4.00
Albums					
BELL					
❑ 6068	Sweet City Woman	1971	3.75	7.50	15.00
CAPITOL					
❑ ST-11288	From the Fire	1973	3.00	6.00	12.00
❑ ST-11328	New Day	1974	3.00	6.00	12.00
QUALITY					
❑ 1001	Hit the Road	1976	3.00	6.00	12.00

STANDARDS, THE The record on Amos may be by a different group than the others.
45s

Number	Title (A Side/B Side)	Yr	VG	VG+	NM
AMOS					
❑ 134	When You Wish Upon a Star/(Instrumental)	1969	2.50	5.00	10.00
CHESS					
❑ 1869	My Heart Belongs to You/Hello Love	1963	10.00	20.00	40.00
DEBRO					
❑ 3178	Tears Bring Heartaches/No, No, No	1963	50.00	100.00	200.00
GLENDEN					
❑ 1315	It Isn't Fair/Everybody Knows	1964	5.00	10.00	20.00
MAGNA					
❑ 1314	My Heart Belongs to You/Hello Love	1963	20.00	40.00	80.00
❑ 1315	It Isn't Fair/Everybody Knows	1963	12.50	25.00	50.00
ROULETTE					
❑ 4487	Tears Bring Heartaches/No, No, No	1963	7.50	15.00	30.00

STANDELLS, THE Also see DICK DODD.
45s

Number	Title (A Side/B Side)	Yr	VG	VG+	NM
LIBERTY					
❑ 55680	The Peppermint Beatle/The Shake	1964	6.25	12.50	25.00
❑ 55722	Help Yourself/I'll Go Crazy	1964	5.00	10.00	20.00
❑ 55743	So Fine/Linda Lou	1964	5.00	10.00	20.00
MGM					
❑ 13350	Someday You'll Cry/Zebra in the Kitchen	1965	7.50	15.00	30.00
SUNSET					
❑ 61000	Ooh Poo Pah Doo/Help Yourself	1966	5.00	10.00	20.00
TOWER					
❑ 185	Dirty Water/Rari	1966	5.00	10.00	20.00
❑ 257	Sometimes Good Guys Don't Wear White/Why Did You Hurt Me	1966	3.75	7.50	15.00
❑ 282	Why Pick on Me/Mr. Nobody	1966	3.75	7.50	15.00
❑ 310	Try It/Poor Shell of a Man	1967	3.75	7.50	15.00
❑ 310 [PS]	Try It/Poor Shell of a Man	1967	12.50	25.00	50.00
❑ 312	Don't Tell Me What to Do/When I Was a Cowboy	1967	20.00	40.00	80.00
—By "The Sllednats" (Standells backwards)					
❑ 314	Riot on Sunset Strip/Black Hearted Woman	1967	3.75	7.50	15.00
❑ 314 [PS]	Riot on Sunset Strip/Black Hearted Woman	1967	20.00	40.00	80.00
❑ 348	Can't Help But Love You/ Ninety-Nine and One Half	1967	3.75	7.50	15.00
❑ 398	Animal Girl/Soul Drippin'	1968	3.75	7.50	15.00
VEE JAY					
❑ 643	The Boy Next Door/B.J. Quetzal	1965	5.00	10.00	20.00
❑ 643 [PS]	The Boy Next Door/B.J. Quetzal	1965	50.00	100.00	200.00
❑ 679	Big Boss Man/Don't Say Goodbye	1965	5.00	10.00	20.00

S

Number	Title (A Side/B Side)	Yr	VG	VG+	NM
Albums					
LIBERTY					
❏ LRP-3384 [M]	The Standells In Person at P.J.'s	1964	20.00	40.00	80.00
❏ LST-7384 [S]	The Standells In Person at P.J.'s	1964	25.00	50.00	100.00
RHINO					
❏ RNLP-107	The Best of the Standells	1983	2.50	5.00	10.00
❏ RNLP-115	Rarities	1983	2.50	5.00	10.00
❏ RNLP-70176	The Best of the Standells (Golden Archive Series)	1987	2.50	5.00	10.00
SUNSET					
❏ SUM-1136 [M]	Live and Out of Sight	1966	6.25	12.50	25.00
❏ SUS-5136 [S]	Live and Out of Sight	1966	7.50	15.00	30.00
TOWER					
❏ ST 5027 [R]	Dirty Water	1966	12.50	25.00	50.00
❏ T 5027 [M]	Dirty Water	1966	15.00	30.00	60.00
❏ ST 5044 [S]	Why Pick on Me	1966	15.00	30.00	60.00
❏ T 5044 [M]	Why Pick on Me	1966	12.50	25.00	50.00
❏ ST 5049 [S]	The Hot Ones	1966	15.00	30.00	60.00
❏ T 5049 [M]	The Hot Ones	1966	12.50	25.00	50.00
❏ ST-5098 [S]	Try It	1967	15.00	30.00	60.00
❏ T 5098 [M]	Try It	1967	12.50	25.00	50.00

STANLEY, MICHAEL, BAND

Number	Title (A Side/B Side)	Yr	VG	VG+	NM
45s					
ARISTA					
❏ 0348	Why Should Love Be This Way/Late Show	1978	—	2.00	4.00
❏ 0368	Baby If You Wanna Dance/Fool's Parade	1978	—	2.00	4.00
❏ 0436	Last Night/Down to the Wire	1979	—	2.00	4.00
EMI AMERICA					
❏ 8063	He Can't Love You/Carolyn	1980	—	—	3.00
❏ 8064	Lover/Save a Little Piece for Me	1981	—	—	3.00
❏ 8090	Falling in Love Again/Does It Hurt	1981	—	—	3.00
❏ 8097	Victim of Circumstance/When Your Heart Says It's Right	1981	—	—	3.00
❏ 8130	When I'm Holding You Tight/In Between the Lines	1982	—	—	3.00
❏ 8146	Take the Time/Just a Little Bit Longer	1982	—	—	3.00
❏ 8178	My Town/Just How Good	1983	—	—	3.00
❏ 8189	Someone Like You/Highlife	1983	—	—	3.00
EPIC					
❏ 50116	I'm Gonna Love You/Step the Way	1975	—	2.00	4.00
❏ 50151	Face the Music/Song for My Children	1975	—	2.00	4.00
❏ 50242	Ladies' Choice/Sweet Refrain	1976	—	2.00	4.00
❏ 50416	Love Hasn't Been Here/Nothing's Gonna Change My Mind	1977	—	2.00	4.00
MCA					
❏ 40177	Roll On/Yours for a Song	1974	—	2.50	5.00
TUMBLEWEED					
❏ TWA-1010	Rock and Roll Man/Denver Rain	1972	2.50	5.00	10.00
—As "Michael Stanley"					
Albums					
ARISTA					
❏ AL 4182	Cabin Fever	1978	2.50	5.00	10.00
❏ AL 4236	Greatest Hints	1979	2.50	5.00	10.00
EMI AMERICA					
❏ SN-16352	Heartland	1985	2.00	4.00	8.00
—Budget-line reissue					
❏ SN-16353	You Can't Fight Fashion	1985	2.00	4.00	8.00
—Budget-line reissue					
❏ SN-16392	MSB	1986	2.00	4.00	8.00
—Budget-line reissue					
❏ SW-17040	Heartland	1980	2.50	5.00	10.00
❏ SW-17056	North Coast	1981	2.50	5.00	10.00
❏ ST-17071	MSB	1982	2.50	5.00	10.00
❏ ST-17100	You Can't Fight Fashion	1983	2.50	5.00	10.00
EPIC					
❏ PE 33492	You Break It...You Bought It!	1975	3.00	6.00	12.00
—Original with orange label and no bar code					
❏ PE 33492	You Break It...You Bought It!	198?	2.00	4.00	8.00
—Reissue with dark blue label and bar code					
❏ PE 33917	Ladies' Choice	1976	3.00	6.00	12.00
—Original with orange label and no bar code					
❏ PE 33917	Ladies' Choice	198?	2.00	4.00	8.00
—Reissue with dark blue label and bar code					
❏ PEG 34661 [(2)]	Stagepass	1977	3.75	7.50	15.00
MCA					
❏ 372	Friends and Legends	1973	3.00	6.00	12.00
TUMBLEWEED					
❏ TWS 106	Michael Stanley	1972	5.00	10.00	20.00
—Blue textured cover					

STANSHALL, VIVIAN　Also see THE BONZO DOG BAND.

Number	Title (A Side/B Side)	Yr	VG	VG+	NM
45s					
LIBERTY					
❏ 56171	Labio-Dental Fricative/Paper-Round	1970	5.00	10.00	20.00

STAPLE SINGERS, THE　Also see MAVIS STAPLES.

Number	Title (A Side/B Side)	Yr	VG	VG+	NM
12-Inch Singles					
PRIVATE I					
❏ 05078	Slippery People (5:30)/(Instrumental)	1984	—	2.50	5.00
❏ 05266	Are You Ready? (Extended) (Dub)	1985	—	2.50	5.00
45s					
CURTOM					
❏ 0109	Let's Do It Again/After Sex	1975	—	2.00	4.00
❏ 0113	New Orleans/A Whole Lot of Love	1976	—	2.00	4.00
EPIC					
❏ 9748	Be Careful of Stones That You Throw/More Than a Hammer and Nail	1964	2.50	5.00	10.00
❏ 9776	Do Something for Yourself/Samson and Delilah	1965	2.50	5.00	10.00
❏ 9825	Freedom Highway/The Funeral	1965	2.50	5.00	10.00
❏ 9880	Why/What Are They Doing	1965	2.50	5.00	10.00
❏ 10054	King of Kings/Step Aside	1966	2.50	5.00	10.00
❏ 10104	Pray On/It's Been a Change	1966	2.50	5.00	10.00
❏ 10158	Why (Am I Treated So Bad)/What Are They Doing (In Heaven Today)	1967	2.00	4.00	8.00
❏ 10220	For What It's Worth/Are You Sure	1967	2.00	4.00	8.00

Number	Title (A Side/B Side)	Yr	VG	VG+	NM
❏ 10264	Deliver Me/He	1967	2.00	4.00	8.00
❏ 10294	Let's Get Together/Power of Love	1968	2.00	4.00	8.00
❏ 10339	Crying in the Chapel/Nothing Lasts Forever	1968	2.00	4.00	8.00
❏ 10742	For What It's Worth/Why	1971	—	3.00	6.00
PRIVATE I					
❏ 04384	H-A-T-E (Don't Live Here Anymore)/Can You Hang	1984	—	2.00	4.00
❏ 04583	Slippery People/On My Own Again	1984	—	2.00	4.00
❏ 04711	This Is Our Night/Turning Point	1984	—	2.00	4.00
❏ 05565	Are You Ready/Love Wowks in Strange Ways	1985	—	2.00	4.00
❏ 05565 [PS]	Are You Ready/Love Wowks in Strange Ways	1985	—	3.00	6.00
❏ 05727	Nobody Can Make It on Their Own/Reasons to Love	1985	—	2.00	4.00
RIVERSIDE					
❏ 4518	Gloryland/Hammer and Nails	1962	3.00	6.00	12.00
❏ 4531	Gambling Man/Use What You Got	1962	3.00	6.00	12.00
❏ 4540	There Was a Star/The Virgin Mary Had One Son	1962	3.00	6.00	12.00
❏ 4553	I Can't Help from Cryin'/Let That Liar Again	1963	3.00	6.00	12.00
❏ 4563	Cotton Fields/This Land	1963	3.00	6.00	12.00
❏ 4568	Blowing in the Wind/Wish I Had Answered	1963	3.00	6.00	12.00
SHARP					
❏ 603	This May Be the Last Time/This Same Jesus	1960	3.75	7.50	15.00
STAX					
❏ 0007	Long Walk to D.C./Stay with Us	1968	—	3.00	6.00
❏ 0019	The Ghetto/Got to Be Some Changes Made	1968	—	3.00	6.00
❏ 0031	(Sittin' On) The Dock of the Bay/Top of the Mountain	1969	—	3.00	6.00
❏ 0039	The Gardener/The Challenge	1969	—	3.00	6.00
❏ 0052	When Will We Be Paid/Tend to Your Own Business	1969	—	3.00	6.00
❏ 0066	Give a Damn/God Bless the Children	1970	—	3.00	6.00
❏ 0074	Brand New Day/God Bless the Children	1970	—	3.00	6.00
❏ 0083	Heavy Makes You Happy (Sha-Na-Boom-Boom)/Love Is Plentiful	1970	—	3.00	6.00
❏ 0084	Who Took the Merry Out of Christmas/(Instrumental)	1970	2.00	4.00	8.00
❏ 0093	You've Got to Earn It/I'm a Lover	1971	—	2.50	5.00
❏ 0104	Respect Yourself/You're Gonna Make Me Cry	1971	—	2.50	5.00
❏ 0125	I'll Take You There/I'm Just Another Soldier	1972	—	2.50	5.00
❏ 0137	This World/Are You Sure	1972	—	2.50	5.00
❏ 0156	Oh La De Da/We the People	1973	—	2.50	5.00
❏ 0164	Be What You Are/I Like the Things About Me	1973	—	2.50	5.00
—B-side by Cal Starr					
❏ 0179	If You're Ready (Come Go with Me)/Love Comes in All Colors	1973	—	2.50	5.00
❏ 0196	Touch a Hand, Make a Friend/Tellin' Lies	1974	—	2.50	5.00
❏ 0213	What's Your Thing/Whicha Way Did It Go	1974	—	2.50	5.00
—B-side by Pops Staples					
❏ 0215	City in the Sky/That's What Friends Are For	1974	—	2.50	5.00
❏ 0227	My Main Man/Who Made the Man	1974	—	2.50	5.00
❏ 0248	Back Road Into Town/My Main Man	1975	—	2.50	5.00
20TH CENTURY					
❏ 2508	Hold On to Your Dreams/Cold and Windy Night	1981	—	2.00	4.00
UNITED					
❏ 165	It Rained Children/Won't You Sit Down	1955	100.00	200.00	400.00
VEE JAY					
❏ 169	God's Wonderful Love/If I Could Hear My Mother	1956	5.00	10.00	20.00
❏ 224	Uncloudy Day/I Know I Got Religion	1956	5.00	10.00	20.00
❏ 846	Let Me Ride/I'm Coming Home	1957	5.00	10.00	20.00
❏ 856	I Had a Dream/Help Me Jesus	1958	3.75	7.50	15.00
❏ 866	Love Is the Way/On My Way to Heaven	1959	3.75	7.50	15.00
❏ 870	I'm Leaving/Going Away	1959	3.75	7.50	15.00
❏ 881	Downward Road/So Soon	1959	3.75	7.50	15.00
❏ 893	Pray On/Too Close	1960	3.00	6.00	12.00
❏ 902	I've Been Scorned/Don't Knock	1961	3.00	6.00	12.00
❏ 912	Sit Down Servant/Swing Low	1962	3.00	6.00	12.00
❏ 930	Swing Low Sweet Chariot/I'm So Glad	1963	3.00	6.00	12.00
WARNER BROS.					
❏ 8279	Love Me, Love Me, Love Me/Pass It On	1976	—	2.00	4.00
❏ 8317	Sweeter Than the Sweet/Making Love	1977	—	2.00	4.00
❏ 8460	See a Little Further (Than My Bed)/Let's Go to the Disco	1977	—	2.00	4.00
❏ 8510	I Honestly Love You/Family Tree	1978	—	2.00	4.00
❏ 8669	Unlock Your Mind/Mystery Train	1978	—	2.00	4.00
❏ 8748	Chica Boom/Handwriting on the Wall	1979	—	2.00	4.00
❏ 49598	God Can/Unlock Your Mind	1980	—	2.00	4.00
—Warner Bros. titles as "The Staples"					
Albums					
ARCHIVE OF GOSPEL MUSIC					
❏ 62	The Staple Singers	1968	3.00	6.00	12.00
❏ 72	The Staple Singers, Vol. 2	1969	3.00	6.00	12.00
BUDDAH					
❏ BDS-2009	The Best of the Staple Singers	1969	5.00	10.00	20.00
❏ BDS-7508	Will the Circle Be Unbroken	1969	5.00	10.00	20.00
CURTOM					
❏ CU 5005	Let's Do It Again	1975	3.00	6.00	12.00
EPIC					
❏ LN 24132 [M]	Amen	1965	5.00	10.00	20.00
❏ LN 24163 [M]	Freedom Highway	1965	5.00	10.00	20.00
❏ LN 24196 [M]	Why	1966	5.00	10.00	20.00
❏ LN 24237 [M]	Pray On	1967	6.25	12.50	25.00
❏ LN 24332 [M]	For What It's Worth	1967	6.25	12.50	25.00
❏ BN 26132 [S]	Amen	1965	6.25	12.50	25.00
❏ BN 26163 [S]	Freedom Highway	1965	6.25	12.50	25.00
❏ BN 26196 [S]	Why	1966	6.25	12.50	25.00
❏ BN 26237 [S]	Pray On	1967	5.00	10.00	20.00
❏ BN 26332 [S]	For What It's Worth	1967	5.00	10.00	20.00
❏ BN 26373	What the World Needs Now Is Love	1968	5.00	10.00	20.00
❏ EG 30635 [(2)]	The Staple Singers Make You Happy	1971	5.00	10.00	20.00
FANTASY					
❏ 9423	Use What You Got	1973	3.75	7.50	15.00
❏ 9442	The 25th Day of December	1973	3.75	7.50	15.00
HARMONY					
❏ KH 31775	Tell It Like It Is	1972	3.00	6.00	12.00
MILESTONE					
❏ 47028 [(2)]	A Great Day	197?	3.75	7.50	15.00

Number	Title (A Side/B Side)	Yr	VG	VG+	NM
PICKWICK					
❑ 7001	The Staple Singers	197?	2.50	5.00	10.00
PRIVATE I					
❑ FZ 39460	The Turning Point	1984	2.50	5.00	10.00
❑ BFZ 40109	The Staple Singers	1985	2.50	5.00	10.00
STAX					
❑ STS-2004	Soul Folk in Action	1968	6.25	12.50	25.00
❑ STS-2016	We'll Get Over	1969	5.00	10.00	20.00
❑ STS-2034	The Staple Swingers	1971	5.00	10.00	20.00
❑ STS-3002	Be Altitude: Respect Yourself	1972	3.75	7.50	15.00
❑ STS-3015	Be What You Are	1973	3.75	7.50	15.00
❑ STX-4116	Be Altitude: Respect Yourself	198?	2.50	5.00	10.00
—Reissue of 3002					
❑ STX-4119	Chronicle	198?	2.50	5.00	10.00
❑ STS-5515	City in the Sky	1974	3.75	7.50	15.00
❑ STS-5523	The Best of the Staple Singers	1975	3.75	7.50	15.00
❑ MPS-8511	This Time Around	198?	2.50	5.00	10.00
❑ MPS-8532	We'll Get Over	198?	2.50	5.00	10.00
—Reissue of 2016					
❑ MPS-8553	Be What You Are	1990	3.00	6.00	12.00
—Reissue of 3015					
TRIP					
❑ 7000	Uncloudy Day	197?	2.50	5.00	10.00
❑ 7014	Swing Low	197?	2.50	5.00	10.00
❑ 7019	The Best of the Staple Singers	197?	2.50	5.00	10.00
❑ 8014	The Other Side of the Staple Singers	1972	2.50	5.00	10.00
20TH CENTURY					
❑ T-636	Hold On to Your Dream	1981	2.50	5.00	10.00
VEE JAY					
❑ LP-5000 [M]	Uncloudy Day	1959	7.50	15.00	30.00
❑ LP-5008 [M]	Will the Circle Be Unbroken	1960	7.50	15.00	30.00
❑ LP-5014 [M]	Swing Low	1961	7.50	15.00	30.00
❑ LP-5019 [M]	Best of the Staple Singers	1962	7.50	15.00	30.00
❑ LP-5030 [M]	Swing Low Sweet Chariot	1963	7.50	15.00	30.00
VEE JAY/CHAMELEON					
❑ D1-74782 [(2)]	The Best of the Staple Singers	1988	3.75	7.50	15.00
WARNER BROS.					
❑ BS 2945	Pass It On	1976	3.00	6.00	12.00
—As "The Staples"					
❑ BS 3084	Family Tree	1977	3.00	6.00	12.00
—As "The Staples"					
❑ BSK 3192	Unlock Your Mind	1978	3.00	6.00	12.00
—As "The Staples"					

STAPLES, GORDON, AND THE MOTOWN STRINGS
45s

Number	Title (A Side/B Side)	Yr	VG	VG+	NM
MOTOWN					
❑ 1180	Strung Out/Sounds of the Zodiac	1971	7.50	15.00	30.00
❑ 1180 [DJ]	Strung Out (same on both sides)	1971	7.50	15.00	30.00
—Red vinyl promo					

STAPLES, MAVIS Also see THE STAPLE SINGERS.
12-Inch Singles

Number	Title (A Side/B Side)	Yr	VG	VG+	NM
PAISLEY PARK					
❑ PRO-A-4397 [DJ]	Melody Cool (Edit) (LP)	1990	2.00	4.00	8.00
❑ PRO-A-5991 [DJ]	The Voice (same on both sides)	1993	2.50	5.00	10.00
❑ 21287	Jaguar (4 versions)	1989	2.00	4.00	8.00
❑ 21748	Melody Cool (4 versions)/				
	Time Waits for No One (Edit)	1990	2.00	4.00	8.00
WARNER BROS.					
❑ PRO-A-2444 [DJ]	Show Me How It Works (same on both sides)	1986	—	3.00	6.00
❑ 8837	Tonight I Feel Like Dancing/If I Can't Have You	1979	3.00	6.00	12.00
45s					
CURTOM					
❑ 0132	A Piece of the Action/Till Blossoms Bloom	1977	—	2.00	4.00
PAISLEY PARK					
❑ 22968	20th Century Express/				
	All the Discomforts of Home	1989	—	—	3.00
PHONO					
❑ 1051	Love Gone Bad/(B-side unknown)	1984	—	2.50	5.00
VOLT					
❑ 4044	I Have Learned to Do Without You/				
	Since I Fell for You	1970	—	2.50	5.00
❑ 4086	Endlessly/Don't Change Me Now	1972	—	2.50	5.00
WARNER BROS.					
❑ PRO-S-3878 [DJ]	Christmas Vacation (same on both sides)	1989	—	2.50	5.00
❑ 8838	Tonight I Feel Like Dancing/If I Can't Have You	1979	—	2.00	4.00
❑ 28765	Show Me How It Works/Half Time	1986	—	—	3.00
❑ 49054	Oh What a Feeling/If I Can't Have You	1979	—	2.00	4.00
Albums					
CURTOM					
❑ CU 5019	A Piece of the Action	1977	3.00	6.00	12.00
PAISLEY PARK					
❑ 25798	Time Waits for No One	1989	3.00	6.00	12.00
STAX					
❑ STX-4118	Mavis Staples	198?	2.50	5.00	10.00
—Reissue of Volt 6007					
❑ MPS-8539	Only for the Lonely	1987	2.50	5.00	10.00
—Reissue of Volt 6010					
VOLT					
❑ VOS-6007	Mavis Staples	1969	5.00	10.00	20.00
❑ VOS-6010	Only for the Lonely	1970	5.00	10.00	20.00
WARNER BROS.					
❑ BSK 3319	Oh What a Feeling	1979	3.00	6.00	12.00

STAR FIRES, THE
45s

Number	Title (A Side/B Side)	Yr	VG	VG+	NM
HARAL					
❑ 777	Each Night at Nine/What Good Is Money	1962	25.00	50.00	100.00
LAURIE					
❑ 3332	You Done Me Wrong/Like Socks and Shoes	1966	5.00	10.00	20.00

STARFIRES, THE (1)
45s

Number	Title (A Side/B Side)	Yr	VG	VG+	NM
APT					
❑ 25030	Fender Bender/Camel Walk	1959	5.00	10.00	20.00
PACE					
❑ 101	Fender Bender/Camel Walk	1959	10.00	20.00	40.00

STARFIRES, THE (2)
45s

Number	Title (A Side/B Side)	Yr	VG	VG+	NM
BARGAIN					
❑ 5001	You're the One/So Much	1961	15.00	30.00	60.00
❑ 5003	Love Will Break Your Heart/The Dances	1961	15.00	30.00	60.00
D&H					
❑ 200	These Foolish Things/Let's Do the Pony	1961	30.00	60.00	120.00

STARFIRES, THE (3)
45s

Number	Title (A Side/B Side)	Yr	VG	VG+	NM
BERNICE					
❑ 201	Yearning for You/Do-Ko-Icki-No	1958	37.50	75.00	150.00
DECCA					
❑ 30730	Three Roses/I Have Someone	1958	10.00	20.00	40.00
❑ 30916	Love Is Here to Stay/Tomorrow	1959	12.50	25.00	50.00

STARFIRES, THE (4)
45s

Number	Title (A Side/B Side)	Yr	VG	VG+	NM
DUEL					
❑ 518	Fools Fall in Love/Under the Stars	1962	12.50	25.00	50.00
TRIUMPH					
❑ 61	Fink/Work Out Fine	1965	5.00	10.00	20.00
Albums					
OHIO RECORDING SERVICE					
❑ 34 [M]	The Starfires Play	1964	12.50	25.00	50.00

STARFIRES, THE (5)
45s

Number	Title (A Side/B Side)	Yr	VG	VG+	NM
G.I.					
❑ 4001	I Never Loved Her/Linda	1965	625.00	1250.	2500.
❑ 4002	Rockin' Dixie/(B-side unknown)	1965	25.00	50.00	100.00
❑ 4004	Cry for Freedom/(B-side unknown)	1965	25.00	50.00	100.00
Albums					
LABREA					
❑ LS-8018 [M]	Teenbeat A-Go-Go	1965	12.50	25.00	50.00

STARFIRES, THE (6) Early version of THE OUTSIDERS.
45s

Number	Title (A Side/B Side)	Yr	VG	VG+	NM
PAMA					
❑ 115	Ring of Love/Cheating Game	196?	10.00	20.00	40.00
❑ 117	Chartreuse Caboose/Billy's Blues	196?	10.00	20.00	40.00

STARFIRES, THE (7)
45s

Number	Title (A Side/B Side)	Yr	VG	VG+	NM
ROUND					
❑ 1016	Space Needle/The Jordan Stomp	1962	10.00	20.00	40.00
❑ 1016 [PS]	Space Needle/The Jordan Stomp	1962	15.00	30.00	60.00

STARFIRES, THE (8)
45s

Number	Title (A Side/B Side)	Yr	VG	VG+	NM
SONIC					
❑ 7163	Re-Entry/Hand Full of Blood	1963	7.50	15.00	30.00

STARLETS, THE (1) Later recorded as THE ANGELS (1).
45s

Number	Title (A Side/B Side)	Yr	VG	VG+	NM
ASTRO					
❑ 202/3	P.S. I Love You/Where Is My Love Tonight	1960	7.50	15.00	30.00
❑ 204	Romeo and Juliet/Listen for a Lonely				
	Tambourine	1960	6.25	12.50	25.00

STARLETS, THE (2)
45s

Number	Title (A Side/B Side)	Yr	VG	VG+	NM
CHESS					
❑ 1997	My Baby's Real/Loving You Is Something New	1967	6.25	12.50	25.00
❑ 2038	I Wanna Be Good to You/Watered Down	1968	5.00	10.00	20.00

STARLETS, THE (3) This is the same group that, as THE BLUE-BELLES, recorded "I Sold My Heart to the Junkman."
45s

Number	Title (A Side/B Side)	Yr	VG	VG+	NM
LUTE					
❑ 5909	I'm So Young/He's Got It	1960	6.25	12.50	25.00
PAM					
❑ 1003	Better Tell Him No/You Are the One	1961	5.00	10.00	20.00
❑ 1004	My Last Cry/Money Hungry	1961	5.00	10.00	20.00

STARLETTES, THE
45s

Number	Title (A Side/B Side)	Yr	VG	VG+	NM
CHECKER					
❑ 895	Please Ring My Phone/Jungle Love	1958	37.50	75.00	150.00

STARLIGHTERS, THE
45s

Number	Title (A Side/B Side)	Yr	VG	VG+	NM
CAPITOL					
❑ F844	Rag Mop/It's Not Bad	1950	7.50	15.00	30.00
CRYSTALETTE					
❑ 661	Sweetheart of Sigma Chi/Don't Call Me Coach,				
	Call Me George	1952	6.25	12.50	25.00
❑ 662	Christmas Won't Be the Same (With You Away)/				
	La Pinata (Mexican Christmas Song)	1952	7.50	15.00	30.00
END					
❑ 1031	It's Twelve O'Clock/The Birdland	1958	125.00	250.00	500.00
❑ 1049	I Cried/You're the One to Blame	1959	20.00	40.00	80.00
❑ 1072	A Story of Love/Let's Take a Stroll	1960	30.00	60.00	120.00
IRMA					
❑ 101	Love Cry/Last Night	1956	100.00	200.00	400.00
LAMP					
❑ 2014	Slipping Out/Rocking Too Much	1958	12.50	25.00	50.00
SUN COAST					
❑ 1001	Until You Return/Whomp, Whomp	1956	62.50	125.00	250.00

S

Number	Title (A Side/B Side)	Yr	VG	VG+	NM
WHEEL					
❑ 1004	Hot Licks/Creepin'	1960	3.75	7.50	15.00

STARLINGS, THE (1)
45s
DAWN

Number	Title (A Side/B Side)	Yr	VG	VG+	NM
❑ 212	I'm Just a Crying Fool/Hokey-Smokey Mama	1955	150.00	300.00	600.00
❑ 213	A-Loo, A-Loo/I Gotta Go Now	1955	100.00	200.00	400.00
JOSIE					
❑ 760	My Plea for Love/Music, Maestro, Please	1954	125.00	250.00	500.00

STARLINGS, THE (2)
45s
WORLD PACIFIC

Number	Title (A Side/B Side)	Yr	VG	VG+	NM
❑ 809	All I Want/That's Me	1959	10.00	20.00	40.00

STARLITES, THE (2) For records on Everlast, Fury and Sphere Sound, see JACKIE AND THE STARLITES.

STARR, ANDY
45s
KAPP

Number	Title (A Side/B Side)	Yr	VG	VG+	NM
❑ 190	Do It Right Now/I Waited for You to Remember	1957	6.25	12.50	25.00
MGM					
❑ 12263	Rockin' Rollin' Stone/I Wanna Go South	1956	37.50	75.00	150.00
❑ 12315	She's a-Going, Jessie/Old Deacon Jones	1956	37.50	75.00	150.00
❑ 12364	Round and Round/Give Me a Woman	1957	37.50	75.00	150.00
❑ 12421	No Room for Your Kind/One More Time	1957	37.50	75.00	150.00

STARR, EDWIN
12-Inch Singles
A.S.K.

Number	Title (A Side/B Side)	Yr	VG	VG+	NM
❑ S-29116	Hit Me with Your Love/Over and Over	198?	2.00	4.00	8.00
20TH CENTURY					
❑ TCD-62	I Just Wanna Do My Thing/ Mr. Davenport and Mr. James	1977	3.75	7.50	15.00
❑ TCD-107 [DJ]	Tell a Star (same on both sides)	1980	2.50	5.00	10.00
❑ TCD-128 [DJ]	Real Live #10 (stereo/mono)	1981	2.50	5.00	10.00
45s					
GORDY					
❑ 7066	Gonna Keep On Tryin' Til I Win Your Love/ I Want My Baby Back	1967	—	3.00	6.00
❑ 7071	I Am the Man for You Baby/My Weakness Is You	1968	—	3.00	6.00
❑ 7078	Way Over There/If My Heart Could Tell the Story	1968	—	3.00	6.00
❑ 7083	Twenty-Five Miles/Love Is the Destination	1969	—	3.00	6.00
❑ 7087	I'm Still a Struggling Man/Pretty Little Angel	1969	—	3.00	6.00
❑ 7090	Oh How Happy/Ooh Baby Baby	1969	—	3.00	6.00
—With Blinky					
❑ 7097	Time/Running Back and Forth	1970	—	3.00	6.00
❑ 7101	War/He Who Picks a Rose	1970	—	3.00	6.00
❑ 7104	Stop the War Now/Gonna Keep On Tryin' Til I Win Your Love	1970	—	3.00	6.00
❑ 7107	Funky Music Sho Nuff Turns Me On/Cloud Nine	1971	—	3.00	6.00
GRANITE					
❑ 522	Pain/I'll Never Forget You	1975	—	2.50	5.00
❑ 528	Stay with Me/Party	1975	—	2.50	5.00
❑ 532	Abyssinia Jones/Beginning	1975	—	2.50	5.00
MONTAGE					
❑ 1216	Tired of It/(B-side unknown)	1982	—	2.00	4.00
MOTOWN					
❑ 1276	You've Got My Soul on Fire/ Love (The Lonely People's Prayer)	1973	—	2.50	5.00
❑ 1284	Ain't It Hell Up in Harlem/ Don't It Feel Good to Be Free	1973	—	2.50	5.00
❑ 1300	Big Papa/Like We Used to Do	1974	—	2.50	5.00
❑ 1326	Who's Right or Wrong/ Lonely Rainy Days in San Diego	1974	—	2.50	5.00
RIC-TIC					
❑ 103	Agent Double-O-Soul/(Instrumental)	1965	3.75	7.50	15.00
❑ 107	Back Street/(Instrumental)	1965	3.75	7.50	15.00
❑ 109	Stop Her on Sight (S.O.S.)/I Have Faith in You	1966	3.75	7.50	15.00
❑ 109X [DJ]	Scott's On Swingers (S.O.S.)/I Have Faith in You	1966	12.50	25.00	50.00
❑ 114	Headline News/Harlem	1966	3.75	7.50	15.00
❑ 118	It's My Turn Now/Girls Are Getting Prettier	1967	3.75	7.50	15.00
❑ 120	You're My Mellow/My Kind of Woman	1967	15.00	30.00	60.00
SOUL					
❑ 35096	Take Me Clear from Here/Ball of Confusion	1972	—	3.00	6.00
❑ 35100	Who Is the Leader of the People/ Don't Tell Me I'm Crazy	1972	—	3.00	6.00
❑ 35103	There You Go/(Instrumental)	1973	—	3.00	6.00
20TH CENTURY					
❑ 2338	I Just Wanna Do My Thing/ Mr. Davenport and Mr. James	1977	—	2.00	4.00
❑ 2389	I'm So Into You/Don't Waste Your Time	1978	—	2.00	4.00
❑ 2396	Contact/Don't Waste Your Time	1978	—	2.00	4.00
❑ 2408	H.A.P.P.Y. Radio/My Friend	1979	—	2.00	4.00
❑ 2420	It's Called the Rock/Patiently	1979	—	2.00	4.00
❑ 2423	It's Called the Rock/H.A.P.P.Y. Radio	1979	—	2.00	4.00
❑ 2441	It's Called the Rock/H.A.P.P.Y. Radio	1980	—	2.00	4.00
❑ 2445	Stronger Than You Think I Am/(Instrumental)	1980	—	2.00	4.00
❑ 2450	Tell-A-Star/Boop Boop Song	1980	—	2.00	4.00
❑ 2455	Get Up-Whirlpool/Better and Better	1980	—	2.00	4.00
❑ 2477	Twenty-Five Miles/Never Turn My Back on You	1980	—	2.00	4.00
❑ 2496	Real Live #10/Sweat	1981	—	2.00	4.00
Albums					
GORDY					
❑ GS-931	Soul Master	1968	6.25	12.50	25.00
❑ GS-940	25 Miles	1969	6.25	12.50	25.00
❑ GS-945	Just We Two	1969	5.00	10.00	20.00
—With Blinky					
❑ GS-948	War & Peace	1970	5.00	10.00	20.00
❑ GS-956	Involved	1971	5.00	10.00	20.00
GRANITE					
❑ 1005	Free to Be Myself	1975	3.00	6.00	12.00
MOTOWN					
❑ M5-103V1	Superstar Series, Vol. 3	1981	2.50	5.00	10.00
❑ M5-170V1	War & Peace	1981	2.50	5.00	10.00

Number	Title (A Side/B Side)	Yr	VG	VG+	NM
PICKWICK					
❑ SPC-3387	25 Miles	197?	2.50	5.00	10.00
20TH CENTURY					
❑ T-538	Edwin Starr	1977	2.50	5.00	10.00
❑ T-559	Clean	1978	2.50	5.00	10.00
❑ T-591	Happy Radio	1979	2.50	5.00	10.00
❑ T-615	Stronger Than You	1980	2.50	5.00	10.00
❑ T-634	The Best of Edwin Starr	1981	2.50	5.00	10.00

STARR, KAY
45s
ABC

Number	Title (A Side/B Side)	Yr	VG	VG+	NM
❑ 11013	When the Lights Go On Again (All Over the World)/Only When You're Lonely	1967	—	2.50	5.00
❑ 11049	My Melancholy Baby/Some Sweet Tomorrow	1968	—	2.50	5.00
CAPITOL					
❑ 54-681	I Wish I Had a Wishbone/ There's Yes! Yes! In Your Eyes	1949	7.50	15.00	30.00
❑ F811	Stormy Weather/You're the One I Care For	1950	6.25	12.50	25.00
❑ F936	Bonaparte's Retreat/Someday Sweetheart	1950	5.00	10.00	20.00
❑ F980	Hoop-Dee-Doo/A Woman Likes to Be Told	1950	5.00	10.00	20.00
❑ F1072	Mississippi/He's a Good Man to Have Around	1950	5.00	10.00	20.00
❑ F1124	I'll Never Be Free/ Ain't Nobody's Business But My Own	1950	6.25	12.50	25.00
—With Tennessee Ernie Ford					
❑ F1152	When You're a Long Way from Home/Is There Anything Wrong with Texas (The Texas Song)	1950	3.75	7.50	15.00
❑ F1194	Nobody's Sweetheart/The Honeymoon	1950	3.75	7.50	15.00
❑ F1205	Mama Goes Everywhere Papa Goes/ Please Love Me	1950	3.75	7.50	15.00
—With Tennessee Ernie Ford					
❑ F1256	Christopher Robin/The Man with the Bag	1950	3.75	7.50	15.00
❑ F1278	Oh Babe/Everybody's Somebody's Fool	1950	3.75	7.50	15.00
❑ F1357	Lovesick Blues/Evenin'	1951	3.75	7.50	15.00
❑ F1492	Come Back Darling/ Then You've Never Been Blue	1951	3.75	7.50	15.00
❑ F1567	Oceans of Tears/You're My Sugar	1951	3.75	7.50	15.00
—With Tennessee Ernie Ford					
❑ F1615	You Were Only Fooling (While I Was Falling in Love)/If I Could Be with You	1951	3.00	6.00	12.00
—Reissue of 78 from 1948					
❑ F1649	I'm the Lonesomest Gal in Town/You've Got to See Mama Every Night	1951	3.00	6.00	12.00
—Reissue					
❑ F1652	Bonaparte's Retreat/The Honeymoon	1951	3.00	6.00	12.00
—Reissue					
❑ F1660	So Tired/Wabash Cannon Ball	195?	3.00	6.00	12.00
—Reissue					
❑ F1677	Wheel of Fortune/Angry	195?	2.50	5.00	10.00
—Reissue					
❑ F1688	Side by Side/Breeze	1954	2.50	5.00	10.00
❑ F1710	Come On-a My House/Hold Me, Hold Me	1951	3.75	7.50	15.00
❑ F1796	Don't Tell Him What's Happened to Me/Angry	1951	3.75	7.50	15.00
❑ F1856	Two Brothers/On Honky Tonk Hardwood Floor	1951	3.75	7.50	15.00
❑ F1902	So Help Me/Hold Me, Hold Me	1951	3.75	7.50	15.00
❑ F1964	Wheel of Fortune/I Wanna Love You	1952	3.75	7.50	15.00
❑ F2062	I Waited a Little Too Long/Me Too	1952	3.00	6.00	12.00
❑ F2151	Fool, Fool, Fool/Kay's Lament	1952	3.00	6.00	12.00
❑ F2213	Comes A-Long A-Love/Three Letters	1952	3.00	6.00	12.00
❑ F2334	Side by Side/Noah	1953	3.00	6.00	12.00
❑ F2464	Half a Photograph/Allez-Vous-En	1953	3.00	6.00	12.00
❑ F2595	When My Dreamboat Comes Home/Swamp Fire	1953	3.75	7.50	15.00
❑ F2657	Changing Partners/ I'll Always Be in Love with You	1953	3.00	6.00	12.00
❑ F2769	If You Love Me (Really Love Me)/ The Man Upstairs	1954	3.00	6.00	12.00
❑ F2887	Fortune in Dreams/Am I a Toy or Treasure	1954	3.00	6.00	12.00
❑ F4295	Riders in the Sky/Night Train	1959	2.00	4.00	8.00
❑ 4339	You Always Hurt the One You Love/ Gonna Get a Guy	1960	2.00	4.00	8.00
❑ 4419	Out in the Cold Again/Just for a Thrill	1960	2.00	4.00	8.00
❑ 4542	Foolin' Around/Kay's Lament	1961	2.00	4.00	8.00
❑ 4583	I'll Never Be Free/Nobody	1961	2.00	4.00	8.00
❑ 4620	Well I Ask Ya/Rough Riders	1961	2.00	4.00	8.00
❑ 4835	Four Walls/Oh Lonesome Me	1962	2.00	4.00	8.00
❑ 4835 [PS]	Four Walls/Oh Lonesome Me	1962	3.00	6.00	12.00
❑ 4894	Bossa Nova Casanova/ Swingin' at the Hungry-O	1962	2.00	4.00	8.00
❑ 4983	No Regrets/Cherche La Rose	1963	2.00	4.00	8.00
❑ 5046	To Each His Own/Make a Circle	1963	2.00	4.00	8.00
❑ 5194	It's Happening All Over Again/ Dancing on My Tears	1964	—	3.00	6.00
❑ 5259	Together Again/Friends	1964	—	3.00	6.00
❑ 5328	Look on the Brighter Side/Lorna's Here	1965	—	3.00	6.00
❑ 5386	Happy/I Forgot to Forget	1965	—	3.00	6.00
❑ 5492	I Never Dreamed I Could Love You/ I Know That You Know That We…	1965	—	3.00	6.00
❑ 5601	Old Records/Tears and Photographs	1966	—	3.00	6.00
DOT					
❑ 17183	Something Happened to Me/12th Street Marching Band	1968	—	2.50	5.00
GNP CRESCENDO					
❑ 468	The Ranger's Waltz/Saturday Night	1973	—	2.00	4.00
❑ 476	The New Frankie and Johnny/(B-side unknown)	1974	—	2.00	4.00
❑ 488	Tie a Yellow Ribbon Round the Ole Oak Tree/ Something's Missing	1974	—	2.00	4.00
❑ 493	What Can I Say After I Say I'm Sorry/What Is This Thing Called Love	1975	—	2.00	4.00
HAPPY TIGER					
❑ 553	Knock, Knock (Who's There)/Sweet Blindness	1970	—	2.50	5.00
RCA VICTOR					
❑ 47-5999	Turn Right/If Anyone Finds This, I Love You	1955	2.50	5.00	10.00
❑ 47-6079	For Better or Worse/Foolishly Yours	1955	2.50	5.00	10.00
❑ 47-6146	Good and Lonesome/Where, What or When	1955	2.50	5.00	10.00
❑ 47-6247	Home Sweet Home on the Range/ Without a Song	1955	2.50	5.00	10.00

The Skyliners, *The Skyliners,* Calico LP-3000, mono LP, yellow and blue label, $300-$600.

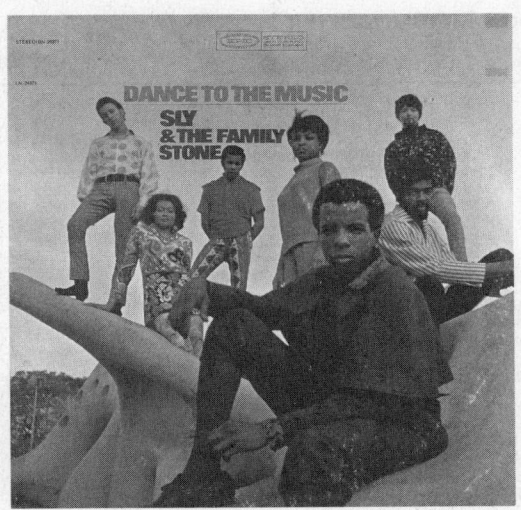

Sly and the Family Stone, *Dance to the Music,* Epic BN 26371, stereo LP, yellow label, $7.50-$15.

Spanky and Our Gang, "Like to Get to Know You," Mercury 72795, picture sleeve, $5-$10.

Dusty Springfield, *Stay Awhile/I Only Want to Be with You,* Philips PHS 600-133, stereo LP, $20-$40.

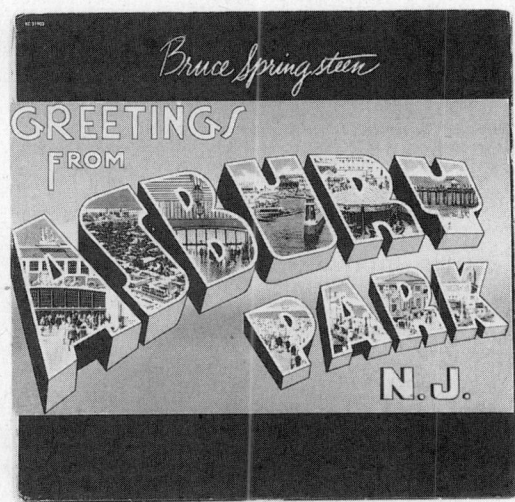

Bruce Springsteen, *Greetings from Asbury Park, N.J.,* Columbia KC 31903, stereo LP with original prefix, $10-$20.

Ringo Starr, "La De Da," Mercury MELP-195, promotional only, picture sleeve, $7.50-$15.

Number	Title (A Side/B Side)	Yr	VG	VG+	NM
❏ 47-6359	Rock and Roll Waltz/I've Changed My Mind a Thousand Times	1955	2.50	5.00	10.00
❏ 47-6541	Second Fiddle/Love Ain't Right	1956	2.50	5.00	10.00
❏ 47-6617	The Good Book/The Things I Never Had	1956	2.50	5.00	10.00
❏ 47-6748	The Brass Ring/Touch and Go	1956	2.50	5.00	10.00
❏ 47-6864	Jamie Boy/A Little Loneliness	1957	2.50	5.00	10.00
❏ 47-6981	My Heart Reminds Me/Flim Flam Floo	1957	2.50	5.00	10.00
❏ 47-7114	The Last Song and Dance/Help Me	1957	2.50	5.00	10.00
❏ 47-7218	Stroll Me/Rockin' Chair	1958	2.50	5.00	10.00
❏ 47-7338	Voodoo Man/Bridge of Sighs	1958	2.50	5.00	10.00
❏ 47-7414	He Cha-Cha'd Me/Oh How I Miss You Tonight	1958	2.50	5.00	10.00
❏ 47-7521	I Couldn't Care Less/Only Love Me	1959	2.50	5.00	10.00
❏ AMBO-0131	Rock and Roll Waltz/Down by the Riverside	1973	—	2.00	4.00

—"Gold Standard Series" reissue

7-Inch Extended Plays

CAPITOL

Number	Title (A Side/B Side)	Yr	VG	VG+	NM
❏ EBF 1-363	Side by Side/It's the Talk of the Town//Too Busy!/What Can I Say After I Say I'm Sorry	195?	3.00	6.00	12.00
❏ EBF 2-363	Waiting at the End of the Road/I Just Couldn't Take It Baby//The Breeze (That's Bringin' My Honey Back to Me)/To-Night You Belong to Me	195?	3.00	6.00	12.00
❏ EBF-363 [PS]	The Kay Starr Style	195?	3.00	6.00	12.00
❏ EAP 1-415	(contents unknown)	195?	3.00	6.00	12.00
❏ EAP 1-415 [PS]	The Hits of Kay Starr	195?	3.00	6.00	12.00
❏ EAP 1-580	(contents unknown)	195?	3.00	6.00	12.00
❏ EAP 1-580 [PS]	Kay Starr in a Blue Mood, Part 1	195?	3.00	6.00	12.00
❏ EAP 2-580	He's Funny That Way/I Got the Spring Fever Blues//I Got It Bad and That Ain't Good/It Will Have to Do Until the Real Thing Comes Along	195?	3.00	6.00	12.00
❏ EAP 2-580 [PS]	Kay Starr in a Blue Mood, Part 2	195?	3.00	6.00	12.00

RCA VICTOR

Number	Title (A Side/B Side)	Yr	VG	VG+	NM
❏ 547-0719	Wrap Your Troubles in Dreams/Fit as a Fiddle//Georgia on My Mind/Jump for Joy	1955	3.00	6.00	12.00

—One record of 2-EP set EPB-1149

| ❏ 547-0720 | You Can Depend on Me/I'll Never Say "Never Again" Again//The Prisoner's Song/Once More | 1955 | 3.00 | 6.00 | 12.00 |

—One record of 2-EP set EPB-1149

| ❏ EPB-1149 [PS] | The One and Only Kay Starr | 1955 | 3.75 | 7.50 | 15.00 |

—Cover for 2-EP set (547-0719, 547-0720)

Albums

ABC

Number	Title	Yr	VG	VG+	NM
❏ S-631	When the Lights Go On Again	1968	3.00	6.00	12.00

CAPITOL

Number	Title	Yr	VG	VG+	NM
❏ H 211 [10]	Songs by Starr	1950	17.50	35.00	70.00
❏ T 211 [M]	Songs by Starr	1955	12.50	25.00	50.00
❏ H 363 [10]	The Kay Starr Style	1953	17.50	35.00	70.00
❏ T 363 [M]	The Kay Starr Style	1955	12.50	25.00	50.00
❏ DT 415 [R]	The Hits of Kay Starr	196?	3.00	6.00	12.00
❏ H 415 [10]	The Hits of Kay Starr	1953	17.50	35.00	70.00
❏ T 415 [M]	The Hits of Kay Starr	1955	12.50	25.00	50.00

—Turquoise or gray label

| ❏ T 415 [M] | The Hits of Kay Starr | 1958 | 7.50 | 15.00 | 30.00 |

—Black label with colorband, Capitol logo at left

| ❏ T 415 [M] | The Hits of Kay Starr | 1962 | 5.00 | 10.00 | 20.00 |

—Black label with colorband, Capitol logo at top

❏ T 580 [M]	In a Blue Mood	1955	12.50	25.00	50.00
❏ ST 1254 [S]	Movin'	1959	7.50	15.00	30.00
❏ T 1254 [M]	Movin'	1959	6.25	12.50	25.00
❏ ST 1303 [S]	Losers Weepers	1960	7.50	15.00	30.00
❏ T 1303 [M]	Losers Weepers	1960	6.25	12.50	25.00
❏ ST 1358 [S]	One More Time	1960	7.50	15.00	30.00
❏ T 1358 [M]	One More Time	1960	6.25	12.50	25.00
❏ ST 1374 [S]	Movin' on Broadway	1960	7.50	15.00	30.00
❏ T 1374 [M]	Movin' on Broadway	1960	6.25	12.50	25.00
❏ ST 1438 [S]	Kay Starr, Jazz Singer	1960	10.00	20.00	40.00
❏ T 1438 [M]	Kay Starr, Jazz Singer	1960	7.50	15.00	30.00
❏ ST 1468 [S]	All Starr Hits	1961	7.50	15.00	30.00
❏ T 1468 [M]	All Starr Hits	1961	6.25	12.50	25.00
❏ ST 1681 [S]	I Cry by Night	1962	6.25	12.50	25.00
❏ T 1681 [M]	I Cry by Night	1962	5.00	10.00	20.00
❏ ST 1795 [S]	Just Plain Country	1962	6.25	12.50	25.00
❏ ST-8-1795 [S]	Just Plain Country	196?	7.50	15.00	30.00

—Capitol Record Club edition

❏ T 1795 [M]	Just Plain Country	1962	5.00	10.00	20.00
❏ ST 2106 [S]	The Fabulous Favorites	1964	3.75	7.50	15.00
❏ T 2106 [M]	The Fabulous Favorites	1964	3.00	6.00	12.00
❏ ST 2550 [S]	Tears and Heartaches/Old Records	1966	3.75	7.50	15.00
❏ T 2550 [M]	Tears and Heartaches/Old Records	1966	3.00	6.00	12.00
❏ SM-11323	Kay Starrs Again	1977	2.00	4.00	8.00

—Reissue with new prefix

| ❏ ST-11323 | Kay Starrs Again | 1974 | 2.50 | 5.00 | 10.00 |
| ❏ SM-11880 | Movin' | 1979 | 2.50 | 5.00 | 10.00 |

CORONET

Number	Title	Yr	VG	VG+	NM
❏ CX-106 [M]	Kay Starr Sings	196?	3.00	6.00	12.00
❏ CXS-106 [S]	Kay Starr Sings	196?	3.00	6.00	12.00

GNP CRESCENDO

Number	Title	Yr	VG	VG+	NM
❏ GNPS-2083	Country	1974	2.50	5.00	10.00
❏ GNPS-2090	Back to the Roots	1975	2.50	5.00	10.00

HINDSIGHT

Number	Title	Yr	VG	VG+	NM
❏ HSR-214	Kay Starr 1947	1985	2.50	5.00	10.00

LIBERTY

Number	Title	Yr	VG	VG+	NM
❏ LRP-3280 [M]	Swingin' with the Starr	1963	6.25	12.50	25.00

—Reissue of 9001

| ❏ LRP-9001 [M] | Swingin' with the Starr | 1956 | 12.50 | 25.00 | 50.00 |

PARAMOUNT

Number	Title	Yr	VG	VG+	NM
❏ PAS-5001	How About This	1969	3.00	6.00	12.00

RCA CAMDEN

Number	Title	Yr	VG	VG+	NM
❏ CAL-567 [M]	Kay Starr	196?	3.00	6.00	12.00

RCA VICTOR

Number	Title	Yr	VG	VG+	NM
❏ LPM-1149 [M]	The One and Only Kay Starr	1955	7.50	15.00	30.00
❏ ANL1-1311	Pure Gold	1976	2.00	4.00	8.00
❏ LPM-1549 [M]	Blue Starr	1957	7.50	15.00	30.00
❏ LPM-1720 [M]	Rockin' with Kay	1958	12.50	25.00	50.00
❏ LPM-2055 [M]	I Hear the Word	1959	6.25	12.50	25.00
❏ LSP-2055 [S]	I Hear the Word	1959	7.50	15.00	30.00

RONDO-LETTE

Number	Title	Yr	VG	VG+	NM
❏ A-3 [M]	Them There Eyes	1958	6.25	12.50	25.00

SUNSET

Number	Title	Yr	VG	VG+	NM
❏ SUM-1126 [M]	Portrait of a Starr	196?	3.75	7.50	15.00
❏ SUS-5126 [R]	Portrait of a Starr	196?	2.50	5.00	10.00

STARR, KAY/ERROLL GARNER Also see each artist's individual listings.

Albums

CROWN

Number	Title	Yr	VG	VG+	NM
❏ CLP-5003 [M]	Singin' Kay Starr, Swingin' Erroll Garner	1957	7.50	15.00	30.00

MODERN

Number	Title	Yr	VG	VG+	NM
❏ MLP-1203 [M]	Singin' Kay Starr, Swingin' Erroll Garner	1956	20.00	40.00	80.00

STARR, RAY

45s

KING

Number	Title (A Side/B Side)	Yr	VG	VG+	NM
❏ 5652	I Have to Laugh to Keep from Crying/In the Middle of Two Hearts	1962	2.50	5.00	10.00

STARR, RINGO Also see THE BEATLES; GEORGE HARRISON AND FRIENDS.

12-Inch Singles

ATLANTIC

Number	Title (A Side/B Side)	Yr	VG	VG+	NM
❏ DSKO 93 [DJ]	Drowning in the Sea of Love (5:08) (same on both sides)	1977	7.50	15.00	30.00

45s

APPLE

Number	Title (A Side/B Side)	Yr	VG	VG+	NM
❏ 1826 [PS]	Beaucoups of Blues/Coochy-Coochy	1970	10.00	20.00	40.00

—Sleeve with wrong catalog number (actually 2969)

| ❏ 1831 | It Don't Come Easy/Early 1970 | 1971 | 2.00 | 4.00 | 8.00 |
| ❏ 1831 | It Don't Come Easy/Early 1970 | 1971 | 3.00 | 6.00 | 12.00 |

—With star on A-side label

| ❏ 1831 [PS] | It Don't Come Easy/Early 1970 | 1971 | 7.50 | 15.00 | 30.00 |
| ❏ 1831 | It Don't Come Easy/Early 1970 | 1975 | 7.50 | 15.00 | 30.00 |

—With "All rights reserved" on label

| ❏ 1849 | Back Off Boogaloo/Blindman | 1972 | 2.00 | 4.00 | 8.00 |

—Green-background label

| ❏ 1849 | Back Off Boogaloo/Blindman | 1972 | 18.75 | 37.50 | 75.00 |

—Blue-background label

| ❏ 1849 [DJ] | Back Off Boogaloo/Blindman | 1972 | 37.50 | 75.00 | 150.00 |

—White label

| ❏ 1849 [PS] | Back Off Boogaloo/Blindman | 1972 | 3.75 | 7.50 | 15.00 |

—Black paper with flat finish

| ❏ 1849 [PS] | Back Off Boogaloo/Blindman | 1972 | 10.00 | 20.00 | 40.00 |

—Glossy black on one side, gray on the other

| ❏ 1849 [PS] | Back Off Boogaloo/Blindman | 1972 | 10.00 | 20.00 | 40.00 |

—Glossy black paper on both sides

| ❏ 1865 | Photograph/Down and Out | 1973 | — | 3.00 | 6.00 |

—Custom star label

❏ 1865 [PS]	Photograph/Down and Out	1973	5.00	10.00	20.00
❏ P-1865 [DJ]	Photograph (mono/stereo)	1973	12.50	25.00	50.00
❏ 1870	You're Sixteen/Devil Woman	1973	—	3.00	6.00

—Custom star label

| ❏ 1870 | You're Sixteen/Devil Woman | 1973 | 6.25 | 12.50 | 25.00 |

—Regular Apple label

❏ 1870 [PS]	You're Sixteen/Devil Woman	1973	6.25	12.50	25.00
❏ P-1870 [DJ]	You're Sixteen (mono/stereo)	1973	12.50	25.00	50.00
❏ 1872	Oh My My/Step Lightly	1974	—	3.00	6.00

—Custom star label

| ❏ 1872 | Oh My My/Step Lightly | 1974 | 2.00 | 4.00 | 8.00 |

—Regular Apple label

| ❏ P-1872 [DJ] | Oh My My (Edited Mono)/Oh My My (Long Stereo) | 1974 | 12.50 | 25.00 | 50.00 |
| ❏ 1876 | Only You/Call Me | 1974 | — | 3.00 | 6.00 |

—Custom nebula label

| ❏ 1876 | Only You/Call Me | 1974 | 2.00 | 4.00 | 8.00 |

—Regular Apple label

❏ 1876 [PS]	Only You/Call Me	1974	5.00	10.00	20.00
❏ P-1876 [DJ]	Only You (mono/stereo)	1974	10.00	20.00	40.00
❏ 1880	No No Song/Snookeroo	1975	—	3.00	6.00

—Custom nebula label

❏ P-1880 [DJ]	No No Song/Snookeroo (both mono)	1975	10.00	20.00	40.00
❏ P-1880 [DJ]	No No Song/Snookeroo (both stereo)	1975	10.00	20.00	40.00
❏ 1882	It's All Down to Goodnight Vienna/Oo-Wee	1975	—	3.00	6.00

—Custom nebula label

❏ 1882 [PS]	It's All Down to Goodnight Vienna/Oo-Wee	1975	5.00	10.00	20.00
❏ P-1882 [DJ]	It's All Down to Goodnight Vienna (mono/stereo)	1975	10.00	20.00	40.00
❏ P-1882 [DJ]	Oo-Wee/Oo-Wee	1975	17.50	35.00	70.00
❏ 2969	Beaucoups of Blues/Coochy-Coochy	1970	2.00	4.00	8.00

—With "Mfd. by Apple" on label and no star on A-side label

| ❏ 2969 | Beaucoups of Blues/Coochy-Coochy | 1970 | 6.25 | 12.50 | 25.00 |

—With small Capitol logo on bottom of B-side label and star on A-side label

| ❏ 2969 | Beaucoups of Blues/Coochy-Coochy | 1970 | 10.00 | 20.00 | 40.00 |

—With "Mfd. by Apple" on label and star on A-side label

| ❏ 2969 [PS] | Beaucoups of Blues/Coochy-Coochy | 1970 | 12.50 | 25.00 | 50.00 |

—Sleeve with correct catalog number

ATLANTIC

Number	Title (A Side/B Side)	Yr	VG	VG+	NM
❏ 3361	A Dose of Rock 'N' Roll/Cryin'	1976	2.50	5.00	10.00
❏ 3361 [DJ]	A Dose of Rock 'N' Roll (With Intro)/(Without Intro)	1976	3.75	7.50	15.00

—Light blue label with Atlantic logo at top

| ❏ 3361 [DJ] | A Dose of Rock 'N' Roll (With Intro)/(Without Intro) | 1976 | 25.00 | 50.00 | 100.00 |

—All-white label with no Atlantic logo at top

| ❏ 3371 | Hey Baby/Lady Gaye | 1976 | 7.50 | 15.00 | 30.00 |
| ❏ 3371 [DJ] | Hey Baby (mono/stereo) | 1976 | 3.75 | 7.50 | 15.00 |

—Red and white label on mono side, light blue label on stereo side

| ❏ 3371 [DJ] | Hey Baby (mono/stereo) | 1976 | 25.00 | 50.00 | 100.00 |

—All-white label with no Atlantic logo at top

| ❏ 3371 [DJ] | Hey Baby/(B-side blank) | 1976 | 75.00 | 150.00 | 300.00 |

—Light blue label

❏ 3412	Drowning in the Sea of Love/Just a Dream	1977	30.00	60.00	120.00
❏ 3412 [DJ]	Drowning in the Sea of Love (mono/stereo)	1977	6.25	12.50	25.00
❏ 3429	Wings/Just a Dream	1977	7.50	15.00	30.00
❏ 3429 [DJ]	Wings (mono/stereo)	1977	3.75	7.50	15.00

—Red and white label on mono side, light blue label on stereo side

| ❏ 3429 [DJ] | Wings (mono/stereo) | 1977 | 25.00 | 50.00 | 100.00 |

—All-white label with no Atlantic logo at top

Number	Title (A Side/B Side)	Yr	VG	VG+	NM
BOARDWALK					
NB7-11-130	Wrack My Brain/Drumming Is My Madness	1981	—	2.50	5.00
NB7-11-130 [DJ]	Wrack My Brain (mono/stereo)	1981	3.75	7.50	15.00
NB7-11-130 [PS]	Wrack My Brain/Drumming Is My Madness	1981	—	2.50	5.00
NB7-11-134	Private Property/Stop and Take the Time to Smell the Roses	1982	3.00	6.00	12.00
NB7-11-134 [DJ]	Private Property (same on both sides)	1982	3.75	7.50	15.00
CAPITOL					
1831	It Don't Come Easy/Early 1970	1976	6.25	12.50	25.00
—Orange label					
1831	It Don't Come Easy/Early 1970	1978	—	3.00	6.00
—Purple late-1970s label					
1831	It Don't Come Easy/Early 1970	1983	—	3.00	6.00
—Black colorband label					
1831	It Don't Come Easy/Early 1970	1988	—	2.50	5.00
—Purple late-1980s label (wider)					
1849	Back Off Boogaloo/Blindman	1976	7.50	15.00	30.00
—Orange label					
1849	Back Off Boogaloo/Blindman	1978	2.00	4.00	8.00
—Purple late-1970s label					
1865	Photograph/Down and Out	1978	2.00	4.00	8.00
—Purple late-1970s label					
1865	Photograph/Down and Out	1983	2.00	4.00	8.00
—Black colorband label					
1865	Photograph/Down and Out	1988	—	3.00	6.00
—Purple late-1980s label (wider)					
1870	You're Sixteen/Devil Woman	1976	15.00	30.00	60.00
—Orange label					
1870	You're Sixteen/Devil Woman	1978	2.00	4.00	8.00
—Purple late-1970s label					
1870	You're Sixteen/Devil Woman	1983	2.00	4.00	8.00
—Black colorband label					
1870	You're Sixteen/Devil Woman	1988	—	2.50	5.00
—Purple late-1980s label (wider)					
1876	Only You/Call Me	1978	2.00	4.00	8.00
—Purple late-1970s label					
1876	Only You/Call Me	1983	25.00	50.00	100.00
—Black colorband label					
1880	No No Song/Snookeroo	1978	2.00	4.00	8.00
—Purple late-1970s label					
1880	No No Song/Snookeroo	1983	2.00	4.00	8.00
—Black colorband label					
1880	No No Song/Snookeroo	1988	7.50	15.00	30.00
—Purple late-1980s label (wider)					
1882	It's All Down to Goodnight Vienna/Oo-Wee	1978	2.00	4.00	8.00
—Purple late-1970s label					
2969	Beaucoups of Blues/Coochy-Coochy	1976	10.00	20.00	40.00
—Orange label					
B-44409	Act Naturally/Key's in the Mailbox	1989	3.75	7.50	15.00
—A-side with Buck Owens; B-side is Owens solo					
P-B-44409 [DJ]	Act Naturally (same on both sides)	1989	7.50	15.00	30.00
—With Buck Owens					
MERCURY					
MELP-195 [DJ]	La De Da/Everyday	1998	3.75	7.50	15.00
—Number only in the dead wax					
MELP-195 [PS]	La De Da/Everyday	1998	3.75	7.50	15.00
—The above record and sleeve were a giveaway from Beatlefest and J&R's Music World with advance purchase of the CD "Vertical Man" and later from Beatlefest with any Ringo Starr Mercury CD.					
PORTRAIT					
6-70015	Lipstick Traces (On a Cigarette)/Old Time Relovin'	1978	3.75	7.50	15.00
6-70015 [DJ]	Lipstick Traces (On a Cigarette) (mono/stereo)	1978	5.00	10.00	20.00
6-70018	Heart on My Sleeve/Who Needs a Heart	1978	3.75	7.50	15.00
6-70018 [DJ]	Heart on My Sleeve (mono/stereo)	1978	5.00	10.00	20.00
THE RIGHT STUFF					
S7-18178	In My Car/She's About a Mover	1994	2.00	4.00	8.00
—Gold/orange vinyl					
S7-18179	Wrack My Brain/Private Property	1994	2.00	4.00	8.00
—Red vinyl					
Albums					
APPLE					
SW-3365	Sentimental Journey	1970	5.00	10.00	20.00
SMAS-3368	Beaucoups of Blues	1970	5.00	10.00	20.00
SWAL-3413	Ringo	1973	5.00	10.00	20.00
—Standard issue with booklet; Side 1, Song 2 identified on cover as "Hold On"					
SWAL-3413	Ringo	1973	100.00	200.00	400.00
—With a 5:26 version of "Six O'Clock." On later copies, the song is shortened to 4:05 though the label still says 5:26. All known copies have a promo punch-hole in top corner of jacket; on Side 2 record, "Six O'Clock" will be the widest track.					
SWAL-3413	Ringo	1974	6.25	12.50	25.00
—Later issue with booklet; Side 1, Song 2 identified on cover as "Have You Seen My Baby"					
SW-3417	Goodnight Vienna	1974	3.00	6.00	12.00
SW-3422	Blast from Your Past	1975	3.75	7.50	15.00
ATLANTIC					
SD 18193	Ringo's Rotogravure	1976	3.75	7.50	15.00
—Deduct 2/3 for cut-outs					
SD 18193 [DJ]	Ringo's Rotogravure	1976	7.50	15.00	30.00
—With "DJ Only" scrawled into trail-off area					
SD 19108	Ringo the 4th	1977	3.75	7.50	15.00
—Deduct 1/2 for cut-outs					
SD 19108 [DJ]	Ringo the 4th	1977	7.50	15.00	30.00
—With "DJ Only" scrawled into trail-off area					
BOARDWALK					
NB1-33246	Stop and Smell the Roses	1981	2.50	5.00	10.00
—Deduct 1/2 for cut-outs					
CAPITOL					
SW-3365	Sentimental Journey	197?	10.00	20.00	40.00
—Purple label, large Capitol logo					
SN-16114	Ringo	198?	3.75	7.50	15.00
—Green label budget-line reissue with all errors corrected					
SN-16218	Sentimental Journey	198?	6.25	12.50	25.00
—Green label budget-line reissue					
SN-16219	Goodnight Vienna	198?	6.25	12.50	25.00
—Green label budget-line reissue					
SN-16235	Beaucoups of Blues	198?	5.00	10.00	20.00
—Green label budget-line reissue					
SN-16236	Blast from Your Past	198?	3.75	7.50	15.00
—Green label budget-line reissue					
PORTRAIT					
JR 35378	Bad Boy	1978	3.75	7.50	15.00
—Deduct 1/3 for cut-outs					
JR 35378 [DJ]	Bad Boy	1978	7.50	15.00	30.00
—Regular white-label promo in standard jacket					
JR 35378 [DJ]	Bad Boy	1978	25.00	50.00	100.00
—White label promo with "Advance Promotion" on label; in plain white cover					
RHINO					
R1 70199	Starr Struck: Ringo's Best 1976-1983	1989	6.25	12.50	25.00
RYKODISC					
RALP 0190	Ringo Starr and His All-Starr Band	1990	7.50	15.00	30.00
—With limited, numbered obi (deduct $5 if missing)					

STARR, SALLY Philadelphia TV star backed by members of BILL HALEY AND HIS COMETS.

Number	Title (A Side/B Side)	Yr	VG	VG+	NM
45s					
ARCADE					
157	Rocky the Rockin' Rabbit/Sing a Song of Happiness	1960	7.50	15.00	30.00
CLYMAX					
301	Rockin' in the Nursery/Little Pedro	1959	10.00	20.00	40.00
7-Inch Extended Plays					
CLYMAX					
EP-1001	Cuckoo in the Clock/Sing a Song of Happiness//TV Pal/A.B.C. Rock	1959	7.50	15.00	30.00
—Second record of 3-EP set; master numbers are JB 142/JB 143					
EP-1001	Rockin' in the Nursery/Little Pedro//Rockin' Horse Cowgirl/Good Night Dear Lord	1959	7.50	15.00	30.00
—Third record of 3-EP set; master numbers are JB-144/JB-145					
EP-1001	Toy Shop in the Town/Happy Birthday//Candy Red/Blue Ranger	1959	7.50	15.00	30.00
—First record of 3-EP set; master numbers are JB-140/JB-141					
EP-1001/2/3 [PS]	Our Gal Sal	1959	10.00	20.00	40.00
—Triple gatefold cover for all three EP-1001 records (despite what the cover says, the records are each numbered 1001)					
Albums					
ARCADE					
1001 [M]	Our Gal Sal	1960	20.00	40.00	80.00
CLYMAX					
1001 [M]	Our Gal Sal	1959	50.00	100.00	200.00

STARSHIP (2) No relation to the 1980s Starship, this features MICKEY DOLENZ.

Number	Title (A Side/B Side)	Yr	VG	VG+	NM
45s					
LION					
132	Johnny B. Goode/It's Amazing to Me	1973	6.25	12.50	25.00

STATENS, THE

Number	Title (A Side/B Side)	Yr	VG	VG+	NM
45s					
MARK-X					
8011	Summertime Is the Time for Love/That Certain Kind	1961	20.00	40.00	80.00

STATLER BROTHERS, THE

Number	Title (A Side/B Side)	Yr	VG	VG+	NM
45s					
COLUMBIA					
43069	The Wreck of the Old 97/Hammer and Nails	1964	3.00	6.00	12.00
43146	I Still Miss Someone/You're a Foolish Game	1964	3.00	6.00	12.00
43315	Flowers on the Wall/Billy Christian	1965	2.50	5.00	10.00
43315 [DJ]	Flowers on the Wall (same on both sides)	1965	5.00	10.00	20.00
—Promo only on red vinyl					
43526	The Doodlin' Song/My Darling Hildegarde	1966	2.00	4.00	8.00
43624	The Right One/Is That What You'd Have Me Do	1966	2.00	4.00	8.00
43868	That'll Be the Day/Makin' Rounds	1966	2.00	4.00	8.00
44070	Ruthless/Do You Love Me Tonight	1967	2.00	4.00	8.00
44245	You Can't Have Your Kate and Edith, Too/Walking in the Sunshine	1967	2.00	4.00	8.00
44480	Jump for Joy/Take a Bow, Rufus Humfry	1968	2.00	4.00	8.00
44608	Sissy/I Am the Boy	1968	2.00	4.00	8.00
44899	Oh Happy Day/How Great Thou Art	1969	2.00	4.00	8.00
MERCURY					
DJ 557 [DJ]	Star Spangled Banner (With Spoken Intro)/Star Spangled Banner (Without Spoken Intro)	197?	2.00	4.00	8.00
PRO 790-7 [DJ]	Don't Wait on Me (Live Edited Version/Live with Intro)	1989	2.00	4.00	8.00
—"US 99 10-In-a-Row Country Commemorative Edition" at top (other similar pressings may exist)					
55000	Silver Medals and Sweet Memories/The Regular Saturday Night Setback Card Game	1977	—	2.00	4.00
55013	Some I Wrote/Carried Away	1977	—	2.00	4.00
55022	Do You Know You Are My Sunshine/You're the First	1978	—	2.00	4.00
55037	Who Am I to Say/I Dreamed About You	1978	—	2.00	4.00
55046	I Believe in Santa's Cause/Who Do You Think	1978	—	2.00	4.00
55048	The Official Historian on Shirley Jean Berrell/The Best That I Can Do	1978	—	2.00	4.00
55057	How to Be a Country Star/A Little Farther Down the Road	1979	—	2.00	4.00
55066	Here We Are Again/Mr. Autry	1979	—	2.00	4.00
57007	Nothing As Original As You/Counting My Memories	1979	—	2.00	4.00
57012	(I'll Even Love You) Better Than I Did Then/Almost in Love	1980	—	2.00	4.00
57031	Charlotte's Web/One Less Day to Go	1980	—	2.00	4.00
57037	Don't Forget Yourself/We Got Paid by Cash	1980	—	2.00	4.00
57048	In the Garden/How Are Things in Clay, Kentucky	1981	—	2.00	4.00
57051	Don't Wait on Me/Chet Atkins' Band	1981	—	2.00	4.00
57059	Years Ago/Dad	1981	—	2.00	4.00
73071	Bed of Rose's/The Last Goodbye	1970	—	2.50	5.00
73194	New York City/This Part of the World	1971	—	2.50	5.00
73229	Pictures/Making Memories	1971	—	2.50	5.00
73253	You Can't Go Home/Second Thoughts	1971	—	2.50	5.00
73275	Do You Remember These/Since Then	1972	—	2.50	5.00
73315	The Class of '57/Every Time I Trust a Gal	1972	—	2.50	5.00
73360	Monday Morning Secretary/Special Song for Wanda	1973	—	2.50	5.00

S

Number	Title (A Side/B Side)	Yr	VG	VG+	NM
❏ 73392	Woman Without a Home/				
	I'll Be Your Baby Tonight	1973	—	2.50	5.00
❏ 73415	Carry Me Back/I Wish I Could Be	1973	—	2.50	5.00
❏ 73448	Whatever Happened to Randolph Scott/				
	The Strand	1974	—	2.50	5.00
❏ 73485	Thank You World/The Blackwood Brothers by				
	the Statler Brothers	1974	—	2.50	5.00
❏ 73625	Susan When She Tried/She's Too Good	1974	—	2.50	5.00
❏ 73665	All American Girl/A Few Old Memories	1975	—	2.50	5.00
❏ 73687	I'll Go to My Grave Loving You/You've Been Like				
	a Mother to Me	1975	—	2.50	5.00
❏ 73732	How Great Thou Art/Noah Found Grace in the				
	Eyes of the Lord	1975	—	2.50	5.00
❏ 73785	Your Picture in the Paper/All the Times	1976	—	2.50	5.00
❏ 73846	Thank God I've Got You/Hat and Boots	1976	—	2.50	5.00
❏ 73877	The Movies/You Could Be Coming to Me	1976	—	2.50	5.00
❏ 73906	I Was There/				
	Somebody New Will Be Coming Along	1977	—	2.50	5.00
❏ 76130	I Never Spend A Christmas That I Don't Think				
	Of You/Who Do You Think?	1981	—	2.00	4.00
❏ 76142	You'll Be Back (Every Night in My Dreams)/We				
	Ain't Even Started Yet	1982	—	—	3.00
❏ 76162	Whatever/Do You Know You Are My Sunshine	1982	—	—	3.00
❏ 76184	A Child of the Fifties/I'll Love You All Over Again	1982	—	—	3.00
❏ 811488-7	Oh Baby Mine (I Get So Lonely)/I'm Dyin' a Little				
	Each Day	1983	—	—	3.00
❏ 812988-7	Guilty/I Never Want to Kiss You Goodbye	1983	—	—	3.00
❏ 814881-7	Elizabeth/Class of '57	1983	—	—	3.00
❏ 818700-7	Atlanta Blue/If It Makes Any Difference	1984	—	—	3.00
❏ 818700-7 [PS]	Atlanta Blue/If It Makes Any Difference	1984	—	2.00	4.00
❏ 866302-7	Atlanta Blue/Put It on the Card	1991	—	2.00	4.00
❏ 868140-7	Remember Me/				
	My Music, My Memories and You	1991	—	—	3.00
❏ 868484-7	You've Been Like a Mother to Me/Jesus Is the				
	Answer	1991	—	2.00	4.00
❏ 868892-7	There's Still Times/Elizabeth	1991	—	—	3.00
❏ 870164-7	The Best I Know How/I Lost My Heart to You	1988	—	—	3.00
❏ 870442-7	Am I Crazy?/Beyond Romance	1988	—	—	3.00
❏ 870681-7	Let's Get Started If We're Gonna Break My				
	Heart/Guilty	1988	—	—	3.00
❏ 872604-7	Moon Pretty Moon/I'll Be the One	1989	—	—	3.00
❏ 874196-7	More Than a Name on the Wall/Atlanta Blue	1989	—	—	3.00
❏ 875498-7	Small Small World/My Music, My Memories and				
	You	1990	—	—	3.00
❏ 876112-7	Don't Wait on Me/A Hurt I Can't Handle	1989	—	—	3.00
❏ 876876-7	Walkin' Heartache in Disguise/The Official				
	Historian on Shirley Jean Berrell	1990	—	—	3.00
❏ 878386-7	He Is There/Nobody Else	1991	—	2.00	4.00
❏ 880130-7	One Takes the Blame/Give It Your Best	1984	—	—	3.00
❏ 880411-7	My Only Love/Let's Just Take One Night at a				
	Time	1984	—	—	3.00
❏ 880685-7	Hello Mary Lou/Remembering You	1985	—	—	3.00
❏ 884016-7	Too Much on My Heart/Her Heart or Mine	1985	—	—	3.00
❏ 884317-7	Sweeter and Sweeter/Amazing Grace	1985	—	—	3.00
❏ 884320-7	Christmas Eve (Kodia's Theme)/Mary's Sweet				
	Smile	1985	—	—	3.00
❏ 884721-7	Count On Me/Will You Be There?	1986	—	—	3.00
❏ 888042-7	Only You/We Got the Mem'ries	1986	—	—	3.00
❏ 888219-7	Forever/More Like Daddy Than Me	1986	—	—	3.00
❏ 888650-7	I'll Be the One/Deja Vu	1987	—	—	3.00
❏ 888920-7	Maple Street Mem'ries/Jesus Showed Me So	1987	—	—	3.00

7-Inch Extended Plays
MERCURY

Number	Title (A Side/B Side)	Yr	VG	VG+	NM
❏ DJ 577 [DJ]	I Never Spend a Christmas That I Don't Think of				
	You/Jingle Bells//Away in a Manger/The				
	Carols Those Kids Used to Sing	1978	—	3.00	6.00
❏ DJ 577 [PS]	A Very Merry Christmas from the Statler				
	Brothers	1978	2.00	4.00	8.00

Albums
COLUMBIA

Number	Title (A Side/B Side)	Yr	VG	VG+	NM
❏ CL 2449 [M]	Flowers on the Wall	1966	6.25	12.50	25.00
❏ CL 2719 [M]	The Big Hits	1967	7.50	15.00	30.00
❏ CS 9249 [S]	Flowers on the Wall	1966	7.50	15.00	30.00
❏ PC 9249	Flowers on the Wall	198?	2.00	4.00	8.00
—Reissue with new prefix					
❏ CS 9519 [S]	The Big Hits	1967	6.25	12.50	25.00
❏ PC 9519	The Big Hits	198?	2.00	4.00	8.00
—Reissue with new prefix					
❏ CS 9878	Oh Happy Day	1969	6.25	12.50	25.00
❏ PC 9878	Oh Happy Day	198?	2.00	4.00	8.00
—Reissue with new prefix					
❏ CG 31557 [(2)]	The World of the Statler Brothers	198?	3.00	6.00	12.00
—Reissue with new prefix					
❏ KG 31557 [(2)]	The World of the Statler Brothers	1972	5.00	10.00	20.00
❏ C 31560	How Great Thou Art	197?	2.50	5.00	10.00
—Reissue of Harmony 31560					

HARMONY

Number	Title (A Side/B Side)	Yr	VG	VG+	NM
❏ H 30610	Big Country Hits	1971	3.00	6.00	12.00
❏ KH 31560	How Great Thou Art	1972	3.00	6.00	12.00
❏ KH 32256	Do You Love Me Tonight	1973	3.00	6.00	12.00

MERCURY

Number	Title (A Side/B Side)	Yr	VG	VG+	NM
❏ SRM-2-101 [(2)]	Holy Bible/The Old and New Testaments	1978	5.00	10.00	20.00
—Reissue of 1051 and 1052 in one package					
❏ SRM-1-676	Carry Me Back	1973	3.75	7.50	15.00
❏ SRM-1-707	Thank You World	1974	3.75	7.50	15.00
❏ SRM-1-1019	Sons of the Motherland	1975	3.75	7.50	15.00
❏ SRM-1-1037	The Best of the Statler Brothers	1975	3.00	6.00	12.00
❏ SRM-1-1051	Holy Bible: Old Testament	1975	3.75	7.50	15.00
❏ SRM-1-1052	Holy Bible: New Testament	1975	3.75	7.50	15.00
❏ SRM-1-1077	Harold, Lew, Phil & Don	1976	3.75	7.50	15.00
❏ SRM-1-1125	The Country America Loves	1977	3.75	7.50	15.00
❏ SRM-1-4048	The Legend Goes On	1982	3.00	6.00	12.00
❏ SRM-1-5001	Short Stories	1977	3.00	6.00	12.00
❏ SRM-1-5007	Entertainers...On and Off the Record	1978	3.00	6.00	12.00
❏ SRM-1-5012	Christmas Card	1978	2.50	5.00	10.00
❏ SRM-1-5016	The Originals	1979	3.00	6.00	12.00

Number	Title (A Side/B Side)	Yr	VG	VG+	NM
❏ SRM-1-5024	The Best of the Statler Brothers Rides Again,				
	Volume II	1980	3.00	6.00	12.00
❏ SRM-1-5027	10th Anniversary	1980	3.00	6.00	12.00
❏ SRM-1-6002	Years Ago	1981	3.00	6.00	12.00
❏ SR-61317	Bed of Rose's	1970	3.75	7.50	15.00
❏ SR-61349	Pictures of Moments to Remember	1971	3.75	7.50	15.00
❏ SR-61358	Innerview	1972	3.75	7.50	15.00
❏ SR-61367	Country Music "Then and Now"	1972	3.75	7.50	15.00
❏ SR-61374	The Statler Brothers Sing Country				
	Symphonies in E Major	1973	3.75	7.50	15.00
❏ 812184-1	Today	1983	2.50	5.00	10.00
❏ 812282-1	10th Anniversary	1983	2.00	4.00	8.00
❏ 812283-1	Entertainers...On and Off the Record	1983	2.00	4.00	8.00
❏ 812284-1	Carry Me Back	1983	2.00	4.00	8.00
❏ 818652-1	Atlanta Blue	1984	2.50	5.00	10.00
❏ 822524-1	The Best of the Statler Brothers	1984	2.00	4.00	8.00
❏ 822525-1	The Best of the Statler Brothers Rides Again,				
	Volume II	1984	2.00	4.00	8.00
❏ 822743-1	Christmas Card	1985	2.00	4.00	8.00
❏ 824420-1	Pardners in Rhyme	1985	2.50	5.00	10.00
❏ 824785-1	Christmas Present	1985	2.50	5.00	10.00
❏ 826247-1	Bed of Rose's	1986	2.00	4.00	8.00
❏ 826259-1	Innerview	1986	2.00	4.00	8.00
❏ 826260-1	Country Music "Then and Now"	1986	2.00	4.00	8.00
❏ 826264-1 [(2)]	Holy Bible/The Old and New Testaments	1986	2.50	5.00	10.00
❏ 826267-1	Holy Bible: Old Testament	1986	2.00	4.00	8.00
❏ 826268-1	Holy Bible: New Testament	1986	2.00	4.00	8.00
❏ 826269-1	Harold, Lew, Phil & Don	1986	2.00	4.00	8.00
❏ 826275-1	The Country America Loves	1986	2.00	4.00	8.00
❏ 826278-1	The Legend Goes On	1986	2.00	4.00	8.00
❏ 826280-1	Short Stories	1986	2.00	4.00	8.00
❏ 826281-1	The Originals	1986	2.00	4.00	8.00
❏ 826710-1	Radio Gospel Favorites	1986	2.50	5.00	10.00
❏ 826782-1	Four for the Show	1986	2.50	5.00	10.00
❏ 832404-1	Maple Street Memories	1987	2.50	5.00	10.00
❏ 834626-1	The Statlers Greatest Hits	1988	2.50	5.00	10.00
❏ 838231-1	Statler Brothers Live — Sold Out	1989	3.75	7.50	15.00

PRIORITY

Number	Title (A Side/B Side)	Yr	VG	VG+	NM
❏ PU 37709	Country Gospel	1982	2.50	5.00	10.00

TIME-LIFE

Number	Title (A Side/B Side)	Yr	VG	VG+	NM
❏ STW-105	Country Music	1981	2.50	5.00	10.00

STATLERS, THE
45s
LITTLE STAR

Number	Title (A Side/B Side)	Yr	VG	VG+	NM
❏ 108	Vicky/Gone	1962	37.50	75.00	150.00

STATON, CANDI
12-Inch Singles
LA

Number	Title (A Side/B Side)	Yr	VG	VG+	NM
❏ 8012	Without You I Cry (4:47)/(B-side unknown)	1981	2.50	5.00	10.00

SUGAR HILL

Number	Title (A Side/B Side)	Yr	VG	VG+	NM
❏ 568	Count On Me/(Instrumental)	1981	2.50	5.00	10.00
❏ 571	Suspicious Minds/Love and Be Free	1982	2.50	5.00	10.00

WARNER BROS.

Number	Title (A Side/B Side)	Yr	VG	VG+	NM
❏ PRO-A-772 [DJ]	Honest I Do Love You (6:31) (same on both				
	sides)	1978	3.00	6.00	12.00
❏ PRO-A-827 [DJ]	Chance (5:34)/Rock (7:16)	1979	3.00	6.00	12.00
❏ PRO-A-867 [DJ]	Looking for Love (same on both sides)	1980	3.00	6.00	12.00
❏ 8820	When You Wake Up Tomorrow/Rough Times	1979	3.00	6.00	12.00

45s
FAME

Number	Title (A Side/B Side)	Yr	VG	VG+	NM
❏ XW256	Something's Burning/It's Not Love	1973	—	2.50	5.00
❏ XW328	Love Chain/I'm Gonna Hold On	1973	—	2.50	5.00
❏ 1456	I'd Rather Be an Old Man's Sweetheart (Than a				
	Young Man's Fool)/For You	1969	—	3.00	6.00
❏ 1459	Never in Public/You Don't Love Me No More	1969	—	3.00	6.00
❏ 1460	I'm Just a Prisoner (Of Your Good Lovin')/Heart				
	on a String	1969	—	3.00	6.00
❏ 1466	Sweet Feeling/Evidence	1970	—	3.00	6.00
❏ 1472	Stand By Your Man/How Can I Put Out the Flame				
	(When You Keep the Fire Burning)	1970	—	3.00	6.00
❏ 1476	He Called Me Baby/What Would Become of Me	1970	—	3.00	6.00
❏ 1478	Mr. and Mrs. Untrue/Too Hurt to Cry	1971	—	3.00	6.00
❏ 91000	In the Ghetto/Sure As Sin	1972	—	2.50	5.00
❏ 91005	Lovin' You, Lovin' Me/You Don't Love Me No				
	More	1972	—	2.50	5.00
❏ 91009	Do It in the Name of Love/The Thanks I Get for				
	Loving You	1972	—	2.50	5.00

LA

Number	Title (A Side/B Side)	Yr	VG	VG+	NM
❏ 0080	Without You I Cry/(B-side unknown)	1981	—	2.50	5.00

SUGAR HILL

Number	Title (A Side/B Side)	Yr	VG	VG+	NM
❏ 770	Count on Me/(B-side unknown)	1981	—	2.50	5.00
❏ 776	Suspicious Minds/(B-side unknown)	1982	—	2.50	5.00
❏ 784	Hurry Sundown/Count on Me	1982	—	2.50	5.00

UNITY

Number	Title (A Side/B Side)	Yr	VG	VG+	NM
❏ 711	Now That You Have the Upper Hand/(B-side				
	unknown)	196?	37.50	75.00	150.00

WARNER BROS.

Number	Title (A Side/B Side)	Yr	VG	VG+	NM
❏ 8038	As Long As He Takes Care of Business/Little				
	Taste of Love	1974	—	2.00	4.00
❏ 8078	Here I Am Again/Your Opening Night	1975	—	2.00	4.00
❏ 8112	Six Nights and a Day/We Can Work It Out	1975	—	2.00	4.00
❏ 8181	Young Hearts Run Free/I Know	1976	—	2.00	4.00
❏ 8249	Run to Me/What a Feeling	1976	—	2.00	4.00
❏ 8320	A Dreamer of a Dream/When You Want Love	1977	—	2.00	4.00
❏ 8387	Nights on Broadway/You Are	1977	—	2.00	4.00
❏ 8461	Music Speaks Louder Than Words/Cotton Candi	1977	—	2.00	4.00
❏ 8477	Listen to the Music/				
	Music Speaks Louder Than Words	1977	—	2.00	4.00
❏ 8582	Victim/So Blue	1978	—	2.00	4.00
❏ 8691	Honest I Do Love You/❏ I'm Gonna Make Me				
	Love You	1978	—	2.00	4.00
❏ 8821	When You Wake Up Tomorrow/				
	Rough Times	1979	—	2.00	4.00
❏ 49061	Chance/I Live	1979	—	2.00	4.00
❏ 49240	Looking for Love/It's Real	1980	—	2.00	4.00

Number	Title (A Side/B Side)	Yr	VG	VG+	NM
❏ 49240 [PS]	Looking for Love/It's Real	1980	—	3.00	6.00
❏ 49536	The Hunter Gets Captured by the Game/If You Feel the Need	1980	—	2.00	4.00

Albums
FAME

❏ 1800	Candi Staton	1972	5.00	10.00	20.00
❏ ST-4201	I'm a Prisoner	1970	5.00	10.00	20.00
❏ ST-4202	Stand By Your Man	1971	5.00	10.00	20.00

WARNER BROS.

❏ BS 2830	Candi	1974	3.00	6.00	12.00
❏ BS 2948	Young Hearts Run Free	1976	3.00	6.00	12.00
❏ BS 3040	Music Speaks Louder Than Words	1977	3.00	6.00	12.00
❏ BSK 3207	House of Love	1978	3.00	6.00	12.00
❏ BSK 3333	Chance	1979	3.00	6.00	12.00
❏ BSK 3428	Candi Staton	1980	3.00	6.00	12.00

STATON, DAKOTA
45s
CAPITOL

❏ PRO 408/9 [DJ]	Trust in Me/The Late, Late Show	1957	5.00	10.00	20.00
—White label "Special DJ Album Highlights"					
❏ F3010	My Heart's Delight/What Do You Know About Love	1955	3.00	6.00	12.00
❏ F3059	For the Rest of My Life/No Mama, No Papa	1955	3.00	6.00	12.00
❏ F3128	Don't Leave Me Now/Little You	1955	3.00	6.00	12.00
❏ F3181	Abracadabra/I Never Dreamt	1955	3.00	6.00	12.00
❏ F3293	It Feels So Nice/Dangerous Age	1955	3.00	6.00	12.00
❏ F3361	How High the Moon/Weak for the Man	1956	3.00	6.00	12.00
❏ F3489	My Friend/Don't Mean Maybe	1956	3.00	6.00	12.00
❏ F3546	You Know I Do/I Told You So	1956	3.00	6.00	12.00
❏ F3876	The Late Late Show/Trust in Me	1958	2.50	5.00	10.00
❏ F3958	Invitation/The Party's Over	1958	2.50	5.00	10.00
❏ F4012	Confessin' the Blues/Blues in My Heart	1958	2.50	5.00	10.00
❏ F4299	Where Did You Go?/Avalon	1959	2.50	5.00	10.00
❏ 4372	My Babe/Romance in the Dark	1960	2.50	5.00	10.00
❏ 4465	First Things First/I Don't Worry	1960	2.50	5.00	10.00
❏ 4512	All in My Mind/Hey Lawdy Mama	1961	2.50	5.00	10.00
❏ 4673	When I Grow Too Old to Dream/Mean and Evil Blues	1961	2.50	5.00	10.00
❏ 4790	Porgy/On Chapel Hill	1962	2.50	5.00	10.00
❏ 4910	Once There Lived a Fool/You'd Better Go Now	1963	2.50	5.00	10.00

GROOVE MERCHANT

❏ 1011	Let It Be Me/Losing Battle	1972	—	2.50	5.00
❏ 1017	(I Want a) Country Man/I Love You More Than You'll Ever Know	1973	—	2.50	5.00
❏ 1019	How Did He Look/Girl Talk	1973	—	2.50	5.00

UNITED ARTISTS

❏ 611	When It's Sleepy Time Down South/Massachusetts	1963	2.00	4.00	8.00

7-Inch Extended Plays
CAPITOL

❏ EAP 1-876	*Broadway/Trust in Me/Moonray/Ain't No Use	1958	3.75	7.50	15.00
❏ EAP 1-876 [PS]	The Late, Late Show, Part 1	1958	3.75	7.50	15.00
❏ EAP 2-876	Summertime/Misty//Give Me the Simple Life/You Showed Me the Way	1958	3.75	7.50	15.00
❏ EAP 2-876 [PS]	The Late, Late Show, Part 2	1958	3.75	7.50	15.00
❏ EAP 1-1170	*Crazy He Calls Me/Idaho/How Does It Feel?/How High the Moon	1959	3.75	7.50	15.00
❏ EAP 1-1170 [PS]	Crazy He Calls Me, Part 1	1959	3.75	7.50	15.00
❏ EAP 2-1170	(contents unknown)	1959	3.75	7.50	15.00
❏ EAP 2-1170 [PS]	Crazy He Calls Me, Part 2	1959	3.75	7.50	15.00

Albums
CAPITOL

❏ DT 876 [R]	The Late, Late Show	196?	3.00	6.00	12.00
❏ SM-876	The Late, Late Show	1977	2.50	5.00	10.00
—Reissue with new prefix					
❏ T 876 [M]	The Late, Late Show	1957	12.50	25.00	50.00
—Turquoise or gray label					
❏ T 876 [M]	The Late, Late Show	1959	7.50	15.00	30.00
—Black label with colorband, Capitol logo at left					
❏ T 876 [M]	The Late, Late Show	1962	3.75	7.50	15.00
—Black label with colorband, Capitol logo at top					
❏ M-1003	In the Night	1976	2.50	5.00	10.00
—Reissue with new prefix					
❏ T 1003 [M]	In the Night	1958	12.50	25.00	50.00
—Turquoise or gray label					
❏ T 1003 [M]	In the Night	1959	7.50	15.00	30.00
—Black label with colorband, Capitol logo at left					
❏ ST 1054 [S]	Dynamic!	1959	10.00	20.00	40.00
—Black label with colorband, Capitol logo at left					
❏ ST 1054 [S]	Dynamic!	1962	5.00	10.00	20.00
—Black label with colorband, Capitol logo at top					
❏ T 1054 [M]	Dynamic!	1958	7.50	15.00	30.00
—Black label with colorband, Capitol logo at left					
❏ T 1054 [M]	Dynamic!	1962	3.75	7.50	15.00
—Black label with colorband, Capitol logo at top					
❏ ST 1170 [S]	Crazy He Calls Me	1959	10.00	20.00	40.00
—Black label with colorband, Capitol logo at left					
❏ ST 1170 [S]	Crazy He Calls Me	1962	5.00	10.00	20.00
—Black label with colorband, Capitol logo at top					
❏ T 1170 [M]	Crazy He Calls Me	1959	7.50	15.00	30.00
—Black label with colorband, Capitol logo at left					
❏ T 1170 [M]	Crazy He Calls Me	1962	3.75	7.50	15.00
—Black label with colorband, Capitol logo at top					
❏ ST 1241 [S]	Time to Swing	1959	10.00	20.00	40.00
—Black label with colorband, Capitol logo at left					
❏ ST 1241 [S]	Time to Swing	1962	5.00	10.00	20.00
—Black label with colorband, Capitol logo at top					
❏ T 1241 [M]	Time to Swing	1959	7.50	15.00	30.00
—Black label with colorband, Capitol logo at left					
❏ T 1241 [M]	Time to Swing	1962	3.75	7.50	15.00
—Black label with colorband, Capitol logo at top					
❏ ST 1325 [S]	More Than the Most	1960	10.00	20.00	40.00
—Black label with colorband, Capitol logo at left					
❏ ST 1325 [S]	More Than the Most	1962	5.00	10.00	20.00
—Black label with colorband, Capitol logo at top					

Number	Title (A Side/B Side)	Yr	VG	VG+	NM
❏ T 1325 [M]	More Than the Most	1960	7.50	15.00	30.00
—Black label with colorband, Capitol logo at left					
❏ T 1325 [M]	More Than the Most	1962	3.75	7.50	15.00
—Black label with colorband, Capitol logo at top					
❏ ST 1387 [S]	Ballads and the Blues	1960	10.00	20.00	40.00
—Black label with colorband, Capitol logo at left					
❏ ST 1387 [S]	Ballads and the Blues	1962	5.00	10.00	20.00
—Black label with colorband, Capitol logo at top					
❏ T 1387 [M]	Ballads and the Blues	1960	7.50	15.00	30.00
—Black label with colorband, Capitol logo at left					
❏ T 1387 [M]	Ballads and the Blues	1962	3.75	7.50	15.00
—Black label with colorband, Capitol logo at top					
❏ ST 1427 [S]	Softly	1961	10.00	20.00	40.00
—Black label with colorband, Capitol logo at left					
❏ ST 1427 [S]	Softly	1962	5.00	10.00	20.00
—Black label with colorband, Capitol logo at top					
❏ T 1427 [M]	Softly	1961	7.50	15.00	30.00
—Black label with colorband, Capitol logo at left					
❏ T 1427 [M]	Softly	1962	3.75	7.50	15.00
—Black label with colorband, Capitol logo at top					
❏ ST 1490 [S]	Dakota	1961	10.00	20.00	40.00
—Black label with colorband, Capitol logo at left					
❏ ST 1490 [S]	Dakota	1962	5.00	10.00	20.00
—Black label with colorband, Capitol logo at top					
❏ T 1490 [M]	Dakota	1961	7.50	15.00	30.00
—Black label with colorband, Capitol logo at left					
❏ T 1490 [M]	Dakota	1962	3.75	7.50	15.00
—Black label with colorband, Capitol logo at top					
❏ ST 1597 [S]	'Round Midnight	1961	10.00	20.00	40.00
—Black label with colorband, Capitol logo at left					
❏ ST 1597 [S]	'Round Midnight	1962	5.00	10.00	20.00
—Black label with colorband, Capitol logo at top					
❏ T 1597 [M]	'Round Midnight	1961	7.50	15.00	30.00
—Black label with colorband, Capitol logo at left					
❏ T 1597 [M]	'Round Midnight	1962	3.75	7.50	15.00
—Black label with colorband, Capitol logo at top					
❏ ST 1649 [S]	Dakota at Storyville	1962	6.25	12.50	25.00
❏ T 1649 [M]	Dakota at Storyville	1962	5.00	10.00	20.00

GROOVE MERCHANT

❏ 510	Madame Foo-Foo	1972	3.00	6.00	12.00
❏ 521	I Want a Country Man	1973	3.00	6.00	12.00
❏ 532	Ms. Soul	1974	3.00	6.00	12.00
❏ 4410 [(2)]	Confessin'	197?	3.75	7.50	15.00

LONDON

❏ PS 495 [S]	Dakota '67	1967	3.75	7.50	15.00
❏ LL 3495 [M]	Dakota '67	1967	5.00	10.00	20.00

MUSE

❏ MR-5401	Dakota Staton	1991	3.75	7.50	15.00

UNITED ARTISTS

❏ UAL-3292 [M]	From Dakota with Love	1963	5.00	10.00	20.00
❏ UAL-3312 [M]	Live and Swinging	1963	5.00	10.00	20.00
❏ UAL-3355 [M]	Dakota Staton with Strings	1964	5.00	10.00	20.00
❏ UAS-6292 [S]	From Dakota with Love	1963	6.25	12.50	25.00
❏ UAS-6316 [S]	Live and Swinging	1963	6.25	12.50	25.00
❏ UAS-6355 [S]	Dakota Staton with Strings	1964	6.25	12.50	25.00

VERVE

❏ V6-8799	I've Been There	1971	3.75	7.50	15.00

STATUES, THE
45s
HOLIDAY

❏ 1026 [DJ]	White Christmas/Get Off My Roof	197?	3.00	6.00	12.00
—B-side by Jerry and the Landsliders					

LIBERTY

❏ 55245	Blue Velvet/Keep the Hall Light Burning	1959	5.00	10.00	20.00
❏ 55292	White Christmas/Jeannie with the Light Brown Hair	1960	6.25	12.50	25.00
❏ 55363	Ten Commandments of Love/Love at First Sight	1961	5.00	10.00	20.00

STATUS CYMBAL, THE
45s
RCA VICTOR

❏ 47-9344	Blang-Dang (Yesterday and Tomorrow)/Takin' My Time	1967	2.50	5.00	10.00
❏ 47-9419	In the Morning/Having Fun Again	1967	2.50	5.00	10.00
❏ 47-9598	From My Swing/With a Little Love	1968	2.50	5.00	10.00

Albums
RCA VICTOR

❏ LPM-3993 [M]	In the Morning	1968	10.00	20.00	40.00
❏ LSP-3993 [S]	In the Morning	1968	5.00	10.00	20.00

STATUS QUO
45s
A&M

❏ 1425	Don't Waste My Time/All the Reasons	1973	—	2.50	5.00
❏ 1445	Paper Plane/All the Reasons	1973	—	2.50	5.00
❏ 1510	Carolina/Softer Ride	1974	—	2.50	5.00

BELL

❏ 45417	Gerdundula/(B-side unknown)	1973	—	2.50	5.00

CADET CONCEPT

❏ 7001	Pictures of Matchstick Men/Gentleman Joe's Sidewalk Café	1968	2.50	5.00	10.00
❏ 7006	Ice in the Sun/When My Mind Is Not Live	1968	2.00	4.00	8.00
❏ 7010	Technicolor Dreams/Spicks and Specks	1969	2.00	4.00	8.00
❏ 7015	Black Veils of Melancholy/To Be Free	1969	2.00	4.00	8.00
❏ 7017	The Price of Love/Little Miss Nothing	1969	2.00	4.00	8.00

CAPITOL

❏ 4039	Nightride/Down Down	1975	—	2.00	4.00
❏ 4125	Bye Bye Johnny/Down Down	1975	—	2.00	4.00
❏ 4407	Wild Side of Life/All Through the Night	1977	—	2.00	4.00

JANUS

❏ 127	Down the Dustpipe/Face Without a Soul	1970	—	3.00	6.00
❏ 141	Gerdundula/In My Chair	1970	—	3.00	6.00

PYE

❏ 65000	Good Thinking/Tuned to the Music	1971	—	3.00	6.00
❏ 65017	Mean Girl/Everything	1971	—	3.00	6.00

S

Number	Title (A Side/B Side)	Yr	VG	VG+	NM
RIVA					
❏ 206	Living on an Island/(B-side unknown)	1980	—	2.50	5.00
Albums					
A&M					
❏ SP-3615	Hello!	1974	3.00	6.00	12.00
❏ SP-3649	Quo	1974	3.00	6.00	12.00
❏ SP-4381	Piledriver	1973	3.00	6.00	12.00
CADET CONCEPT					
❏ LPS-315	Messages from the Status Quo	1968	12.50	25.00	50.00
CAPITOL					
❏ ST-11381	On the Level	1975	2.50	5.00	10.00
❏ ST-11509	Status Quo	1976	2.50	5.00	10.00
❏ SKBB-11623 [(2)]	Status Quo Live	1977	3.00	6.00	12.00
❏ ST-11749	Rockin' All Over the World	1978	2.50	5.00	10.00
JANUS					
❏ JLS-3018	Ma Kelly's Greasy Spoon	1970	3.75	7.50	15.00
MERCURY					
❏ 836651-1	Status Quo	1989	3.00	6.00	12.00
PYE					
❏ 3301	Dog of Two Head	1971	3.75	7.50	15.00
RIVA					
❏ 7402	Now Here This	1980	2.50	5.00	10.00

STEALERS WHEEL   Also see GERRY RAFFERTY.

45s

Number	Title (A Side/B Side)	Yr	VG	VG+	NM
A&M					
❏ 1416	Stuck in the Middle with You/Jose	1973	—	2.50	5.00
❏ 1450	Everyone's Agreed That Everything Will Turn Out Fine/Next to Me	1973	—	2.00	4.00
❏ 1483	Star/What More Could You Want	1973	—	2.00	4.00
❏ 1483 [PS]	Star/What More Could You Want	1973	—	3.00	6.00
❏ 1529	You Put Something Better Inside of Me/Wheelin'	1974	—	2.00	4.00
❏ 1675	This Morning/Found My Way to You	1975	—	2.00	4.00
❏ 2075	(Everyone's Agreed That) Everything Will Turn Out Fine/Who Cares	1978	—	2.50	5.00
Albums					
A&M					
❏ SP-4377	Stealers Wheel	1973	3.00	6.00	12.00
❏ SP-4419	Ferguslie Park	1974	3.00	6.00	12.00
❏ SP-4517	Right or Wrong	1974	3.00	6.00	12.00
❏ SP-4708	Stuck in the Middle with You — The Best of Stealers Wheel	1978	2.50	5.00	10.00

STEAM

45s

Number	Title (A Side/B Side)	Yr	VG	VG+	NM
FONTANA					
❏ 1667	Na Na Hey Hey Kiss Him Goodbye/ It's the Magic in You Girl	1969	2.00	4.00	8.00
MERCURY					
❏ 30160	Na Na Hey Hey Kiss Him Goodbye/ Don't Stop Lovin' Me	1976	—	2.00	4.00
—Reissue					
❏ 30160 [PS]	Na Na Hey Hey Kiss Him Goodbye/ Don't Stop Lovin' Me	1976	5.00	10.00	20.00
—Special Chicago White Sox sleeve, available only in that area					
❏ 73020	I've Gotta Make You Love Me/ One Good Woman	1970	—	3.00	6.00
❏ 73053	What I'm Saying Is True/ I'm the One Who Loves You	1970	—	3.00	6.00
❏ 73117	Don't Stop Lovin' Me/Do Unto Others	1970	—	3.00	6.00
Albums					
MERCURY					
❏ SR 61254	Steam	1969	5.00	10.00	20.00

STEAMHAMMER

Albums

Number	Title (A Side/B Side)	Yr	VG	VG+	NM
EPIC					
❏ BN 26490	Reflection	1969	7.50	15.00	30.00
❏ BN 26552	Steamhammer	1970	7.50	15.00	30.00

STEEL

45s

Number	Title (A Side/B Side)	Yr	VG	VG+	NM
EPIC					
❏ 5-10753	Never on a Monday/Rosie Lee	1971	2.00	4.00	8.00
Albums					
EPIC					
❏ E 30875	Steel	1971	5.00	10.00	20.00

STEELE, TOMMY

45s

Number	Title (A Side/B Side)	Yr	VG	VG+	NM
BUENA VISTA					
❏ 457	Fortuosity/I'm a Brass Band Today	1967	2.00	4.00	8.00
LONDON					
❏ 1706	Doomsday Rock/Elevator Rock	1957	3.75	7.50	15.00
❏ 1735	Butterfingers/Teenage Party	1957	3.75	7.50	15.00
❏ 1760	Water, Water/A Handful of Songs	1958	3.75	7.50	15.00
❏ 1795	Nairobi/Neon Sign	1958	3.75	7.50	15.00
❏ 1824	Swaller Tail Coat/The Only Man Across the Way	1959	3.75	7.50	15.00
❏ 1838	Hey You/Number 22 Across the Way	1959	3.75	7.50	15.00
❏ 1878	The Trail/Give, Give, Give	1959	3.75	7.50	15.00
❏ 1950	She's My Baby/Happy-Go-Lucky Blues	1960	3.75	7.50	15.00
RCA VICTOR					
❏ 47-8602	Half a Sixpence/If the Rain's Got to Fall	1965	2.50	5.00	10.00
❏ 47-9458	Half a Sixpence/If the Rain's Got to Fall	1968	2.00	4.00	8.00
WAM					
❏ 45-1	Doomsday Rock/Elevator Rock	1956	7.50	15.00	30.00
Albums					
LIBERTY					
❏ LRP-3426 [M]	Everything's Coming Up Broadway	1965	5.00	10.00	20.00
❏ LRP-3566 [M]	Sixpenny Millionaire	1968	7.50	15.00	30.00
—Stereo cover with "Audition Mono LP Not for Sale" sticker attached; label is stock					
❏ LST-7426 [S]	Everything's Coming Up Broadway	1965	6.25	12.50	25.00
❏ LST-7566 [S]	Sixpenny Millionaire	1968	3.75	7.50	15.00
LONDON					
❏ LL 1770 [M]	Rock Around the World	195?	12.50	25.00	50.00

STEELEYE SPAN

45s

Number	Title (A Side/B Side)	Yr	VG	VG+	NM
CHRYSALIS					
❏ 2008	Gaudete/Royal Forester	1972	—	3.00	6.00
❏ 2102	Gaudete/Royal Forester	1974	—	2.50	5.00
❏ 2262	Rag Doll/Hunting the Wren	1978	—	2.00	4.00
Albums					
BIG TREE					
❏ BTS 2004	Please to See the King	1971	7.50	15.00	30.00
CHRYSALIS					
❏ CHR 1008	Below the Salt	1972	3.75	7.50	15.00
—Green label, "3300 Warner Blvd." address					
❏ CHR 1008	Below the Salt	1977	3.00	6.00	12.00
—Blue label, New York address					
❏ CHR 1046	Parcel of Rogues	1973	3.75	7.50	15.00
—Green label, "3300 Warner Blvd." address					
❏ CHR 1046	Parcel of Rogues	1977	3.00	6.00	12.00
—Blue label, New York address					
❏ CHR 1053	Now We Are Six	1974	3.75	7.50	15.00
—Green label, "3300 Warner Blvd." address					
❏ CHR 1053	Now We Are Six	1977	3.00	6.00	12.00
—Blue label, New York address					
❏ CHR 1071	Commoners Crown	1975	3.75	7.50	15.00
—Green label, "3300 Warner Blvd." address					
❏ CHR 1071	Commoners Crown	1977	3.00	6.00	12.00
—Blue label, New York address					
❏ CHR 1091	All Around My Hat	1975	3.75	7.50	15.00
—Green label, "3300 Warner Blvd." address					
❏ CHR 1091	All Around My Hat	1977	3.00	6.00	12.00
—Blue label, New York address					
❏ CHR 1119	Please to See the King	1976	3.75	7.50	15.00
—Reissue of Big Tree LP; green label, "3300 Warner Blvd." address					
❏ CHR 1119	Please to See the King	1977	3.00	6.00	12.00
—Blue label, New York address					
❏ CHR 1120	Hark the Village Wait	1976	3.75	7.50	15.00
—First US issue of debut LP; green label, "3300 Warner Blvd." address					
❏ CHR 1120	Hark the Village Wait	1977	3.00	6.00	12.00
—Blue label, New York address					
❏ CHR 1121	Ten Man Mop	1976	3.75	7.50	15.00
—First US issue of third UK LP; green label, "3300 Warner Blvd." address					
❏ CHR 1121	Ten Man Mop	1977	3.00	6.00	12.00
—Blue label, New York address					
❏ CHR 1123	Rocket Cottage	1976	3.75	7.50	15.00
—Green label, "3300 Warner Blvd." address					
❏ CHR 1123	Rocket Cottage	1977	3.00	6.00	12.00
—Blue label, New York address					
❏ CHR2 1136 [(2)]	The Steeleye Span Story: Original Masters	1977	3.75	7.50	15.00
❏ CHR 1151	Storm Force Ten	1978	3.00	6.00	12.00
❏ CHR 1199	Live at Last	1978	3.00	6.00	12.00
❏ V2X 41136 [(2)]	The Steeleye Span Story: Original Masters	1984	3.00	6.00	12.00
—Reissue of 1136					
MOBILE FIDELITY					
❏ 1-027	All Around My Hat	1980	6.25	12.50	25.00
—Audiophile vinyl					
PAIR					
❏ CRPDL-2-1021 [(2)]	Dogs and Ferrets	1983	3.75	7.50	15.00
SHANACHIE					
❏ 64020	Tempted and Tried	1989	3.00	6.00	12.00
❏ 79039	Below the Salt	1989	3.00	6.00	12.00
❏ 79045	Parcel of Rogues	1989	3.00	6.00	12.00
❏ 79049	Ten Man Mop	1989	3.00	6.00	12.00
❏ 79052	Hark the Village Wait	1989	3.00	6.00	12.00
❏ 79059	All Around My Hat	1989	3.00	6.00	12.00
❏ 79060	Now We Are Six	1989	3.00	6.00	12.00
❏ 79063	Back in Line	1989	3.00	6.00	12.00
❏ 79071/2 [(2)]	Portfolio	1990	5.00	10.00	20.00
TAKOMA					
❏ TAK-7097	Sails of Silver	1981	2.50	5.00	10.00

STEELY DAN

12-Inch Singles

Number	Title (A Side/B Side)	Yr	VG	VG+	NM
ABC					
❏ SPDJ-26 [DJ]	Aja (same on both sides)	1977	5.00	10.00	20.00
❏ SPDJ-32 [DJ]	Deacon Blues (same on both sides)	1978	5.00	10.00	20.00
❏ SPDJ-36 [DJ]	Josie (same on both sides)	1978	5.00	10.00	20.00
❏ SPDJ-47 [DJ]	Here at the Western World (same on both sides)	1978	3.75	7.50	15.00

45s

Number	Title (A Side/B Side)	Yr	VG	VG+	NM
ABC					
❏ 11323	Dallas/Sail the Waterway	1972	7.50	15.00	30.00
—Neither of these songs has appeared on a U.S. Steely Dan album -- not even the "complete" CD box set!					
❏ 11338	Do It Again/Fire in the Hole	1972	—	2.00	4.00
❏ 11352	Reeling In the Years/Only a Fool Would Say That	1973	—	2.00	4.00
—Later pressings have "abc" in a rainbow box					
❏ 11352	Reeling In the Years/Only a Fool Would Say That	1973	—	2.50	5.00
—Original pressings have "abc" children's blocks in a white triangle					
❏ 11382	Show Biz Kids/Razor Boy	1973	—	2.00	4.00
❏ 11396	My Old School/Pearl of the Quarter	1973	—	2.00	4.00
❏ 11439	Rikki Don't Lose That Number/Any Major Dude Will Tell You	1974	—	2.00	4.00
❏ 12014	Rikki Don't Lose That Number/Any Major Dude Will Tell You	1974	—	3.00	6.00
❏ 12033	Pretzel Logic/Through with Buzz	1974	—	2.00	4.00
❏ 12101	Black Friday/Throw Back the Little Ones	1975	—	2.00	4.00
❏ 12128	Chain Lightning/Bad Sneakers	1975	—	2.00	4.00
❏ 12195	Kid Charlemagne/Green Earrings	1976	—	2.00	4.00
❏ 12222	The Fez/Sign In Stranger	1976	—	2.00	4.00
❏ 12320	Peg/I Got the News	1977	—	2.00	4.00
❏ 12355	Deacon Blues/Home at Last	1978	—	2.00	4.00
❏ 12404	Josie/Black Cow	1978	—	2.00	4.00
MCA					
❏ 40894	FM (No Static at All)/(Instrumental)	1978	—	2.00	4.00
❏ 51036	Hey Nineteen/Bodhisattva	1980	—	2.00	4.00
❏ 51082	Time Out of Mind/Bodhisattva	1981	—	2.00	4.00

Number	Title (A Side/B Side)	Yr	VG	VG+	NM
Albums					
ABC					
❏ 758	Can't Buy a Thrill	1972	3.00	6.00	12.00
—*Black label*					
❏ 758	Can't Buy a Thrill	1974	2.50	5.00	10.00
—*Multicolor label*					
❏ 779	Countdown to Ecstasy	1973	3.00	6.00	12.00
—*Black label*					
❏ 779	Countdown to Ecstasy	1974	2.50	5.00	10.00
—*Multicolor label*					
❏ 806	Pretzel Logic	1974	2.50	5.00	10.00
—*Multicolor label*					
❏ 806	Pretzel Logic	1974	3.00	6.00	12.00
—*Black label*					
❏ 846	Katy Lied	1975	3.00	6.00	12.00
❏ 931	The Royal Scam	1976	3.00	6.00	12.00
❏ AA-1006	Aja	1977	3.00	6.00	12.00
❏ AK-1107 [(2)]	Greatest Hits	1978	3.75	7.50	15.00
ABC DUNHILL					
❏ SMAS-94976	Can't Buy a Thrill	1973	6.25	12.50	25.00
—*Capitol Record Club edition pressed on the wrong label*					
COMMAND					
❏ QD-40009 [Q]	Can't Buy a Thrill	1974	5.00	10.00	20.00
—*Second issue with no border around the cover*					
❏ QD-40009 [Q]	Can't Buy a Thrill	1974	6.25	12.50	25.00
—*First issue with wide border around outside of cover*					
❏ QD-40010 [Q]	Countdown to Ecstasy	1974	5.00	10.00	20.00
❏ QD-40015 [Q]	Pretzel Logic	1974	5.00	10.00	20.00
MCA					
❏ AA-1006	Aja	1980	2.50	5.00	10.00
❏ 1591	Can't Buy a Thrill	1987	—	3.00	6.00
❏ 1592	Countdown to Ecstasy	1987	—	3.00	6.00
❏ 1593	Pretzel Logic	1987	—	3.00	6.00
❏ 1594	Katy Lied	1987	—	3.00	6.00
❏ 1595	The Royal Scam	1987	—	3.00	6.00
❏ 1688	Aja	1987	—	3.00	6.00
❏ 1693	Gaucho	1987	—	3.00	6.00
—*Many in the 1500 and 1600 series have a gold stamp with the new number on the cover*					
❏ 5324	Gold	1982	2.50	5.00	10.00
❏ 2-6008 [(2)]	Greatest Hits	1980	3.00	6.00	12.00
❏ 6102	Gaucho	1980	2.50	5.00	10.00
❏ 16009	Gaucho	1981	12.50	25.00	50.00
—*Audiophile pressing*					
❏ 16016	Gold	1982	12.50	25.00	50.00
—*Audiophile pressing*					
❏ 37040	Can't Buy a Thrill	1980	2.00	4.00	8.00
❏ 37041	Countdown to Ecstasy	1980	2.00	4.00	8.00
❏ 37042	Pretzel Logic	1980	2.00	4.00	8.00
❏ 37043	Katy Lied	1980	2.00	4.00	8.00
❏ 37044	The Royal Scam	1980	2.00	4.00	8.00
❏ 37243	Gold	1984	2.00	4.00	8.00
MOBILE FIDELITY					
❏ 1-007	Katy Lied	1979	20.00	40.00	80.00
—*Audiophile vinyl*					
❏ 1-033	Aja	1980	12.50	25.00	50.00
—*Audiophile vinyl*					

STEIN, FRANK N., AND THE TOMBSTONES

45s
MARCO

| ❏ 003 | Mess Around/Graveyard Giggle | 1962 | 10.00 | 20.00 | 40.00 |

STEIN, FRANKIE, AND THE GHOULS

45s
KING

| ❏ 6414 | Franken Boogie/All She Wants to Do Is Boogie | 1972 | 2.50 | 5.00 | 10.00 |

POWER

| ❏ 338 | Goon River/Weerdo the Wolf | 1964 | 6.25 | 12.50 | 25.00 |
| ❏ 338 [PS] | Goon River/Weerdo the Wolf | 1964 | 7.50 | 15.00 | 30.00 |

STEINBERG, DAVID

45s
COLUMBIA

| ❏ 46075 | The Nixon Tapes/The Exam | 1974 | — | 2.50 | 5.00 |

Albums
COLUMBIA

| ❏ KC 32563 | Booga Booga | 1974 | 2.50 | 5.00 | 10.00 |
| ❏ PC 33390 | Goodbye to the Seventies | 1975 | 2.50 | 5.00 | 10.00 |

ELEKTRA

| ❏ EKS-74063 | Disguised as a Normal Person | 1970 | 3.00 | 6.00 | 12.00 |

UNI

| ❏ 73013 | The Incredible Shrinking God | 1968 | 3.75 | 7.50 | 15.00 |

STEPHENS, LEIGH

45s
PHILIPS

| ❏ 40628 | Red Weather/Saki Swadoo | 1969 | 3.00 | 6.00 | 12.00 |

Albums
PHILIPS

| ❏ PHS 600294 | Red Weather | 1969 | 20.00 | 40.00 | 80.00 |

STEPPENWOLF   Also see SPARROW.

45s
ABC

❏ 1436	The Pusher/Born to Be Wild	1970	—	2.00	4.00
—*"Goldies 45" series*					
❏ 1436 [PS]	The Pusher/Born to Be Wild	1970	—	3.00	6.00

ABC DUNHILL

❏ 4138	Born to Be Wild/Everybody's Next One	1968	2.00	4.00	8.00
❏ 4161	Magic Carpet Ride/Sookie Sookie	1968	2.00	4.00	8.00
❏ 4182	Rock Me/Jupiter Child	1969	2.00	4.00	8.00
❏ 4192	It's Never Too Late/Happy Birthday	1969	—	3.00	6.00
❏ 4205	Move Over/Power Play	1969	—	3.00	6.00
❏ 4221	Monster/Berry Rides Again	1969	—	3.00	6.00
❏ 4234	Hey Lawdy Mama/Twisted	1970	—	3.00	6.00
❏ 4248	Screaming Night Hog/Spiritual Fantasy	1970	—	3.00	6.00

Number	Title (A Side/B Side)	Yr	VG	VG+	NM
❏ 4261	Who Needs Ya/Earschplittenloudenboomer	1970	—	3.00	6.00
❏ 4269	Snow Blind Friend/Hippo Stomp	1971	—	2.50	5.00
❏ 4283	Ride with Me/For Madmen Only	1971	—	2.50	5.00
❏ 4283	Ride with Me/Black Pit	1971	10.00	20.00	40.00
—*This is much rarer than the version with the other flip side*					
❏ 4283 [PS]	Ride with Me/For Madmen Only	1971	—	3.00	6.00
❏ 4292	For Ladies Only/Sparkle Eyes	1971	—	2.50	5.00
ALLEGIANCE					
❏ 3909	Hot Night in a Cold Town/Every Man for Himself	1983	—	2.00	4.00
—*As "John Kay and Steppenwolf"*					
DUNHILL					
❏ 4109	The Ostrich/A Girl I Know	1967	2.50	5.00	10.00
❏ 4123	Sookie Sookie/Take What You Need	1968	2.50	5.00	10.00
MUMS					
❏ 6031	Straight Shootin' Woman/Justice, Don't Be Slow	1974	—	2.00	4.00
❏ 6031 [PS]	Straight Shootin' Woman/Justice, Don't Be Slow	1974	—	3.00	6.00
❏ 6034	Get Into the Wind/Morning Blue	1974	—	2.00	4.00
❏ 6036	Fool's Fantasy/Smokey Factory Blues	1975	—	2.00	4.00
❏ 6040	Caroline (Are You Ready for the Outlaw)/Angel Drawers	1975	—	2.00	4.00
Albums					
ABC					
❏ AC-30008	The ABC Collection	1976	3.75	7.50	15.00
ABC DUNHILL					
❏ DS-50029 [S]	Steppenwolf	1968	5.00	10.00	20.00
❏ DS-50037	The Second	1968	6.25	12.50	25.00
—*With chrome border on cover*					
❏ DS-50037	The Second	1968	7.50	15.00	30.00
—*With white border on cover*					
❏ DSX-50053	At Your Birthday Party	1969	5.00	10.00	20.00
❏ DS-50060	Early Steppenwolf	1969	5.00	10.00	20.00
—*Actually a 1967 concert by Sparrow (pre-Steppenwolf)*					
❏ DS-50066	Monster	1969	5.00	10.00	20.00
❏ DSD-50075 [(2)]	Steppenwolf 'Live'	1970	6.25	12.50	25.00
❏ DSX-50090	Steppenwolf 7	1970	5.00	10.00	20.00
❏ DSX-50099	Steppenwolf Gold/Their Great Hits	1971	5.00	10.00	20.00
❏ DSX-50110	For Ladies Only	1971	5.00	10.00	20.00
❏ DSX-50124	Rest in Peace	1972	5.00	10.00	20.00
❏ DSX-50135	16 Greatest Hits	1973	5.00	10.00	20.00
DUNHILL					
❏ D-50029 [M]	Steppenwolf	1968	37.50	75.00	150.00
❏ DS-50029 [S]	Steppenwolf	1968	10.00	20.00	40.00
❏ ST-91487	Steppenwolf	1968	6.25	12.50	25.00
—*Capitol Record Club edition*					
❏ SKAO-93083	Monster	1969	6.25	12.50	25.00
—*Capitol Record Club edition on old-style Dunhill label*					
EPIC					
❏ PE 33583	Hour of the Wolf	1975	3.00	6.00	12.00
❏ PE 34120	Skullduggery	1976	3.00	6.00	12.00
❏ JE 34382	Reborn to Be Wild	1977	3.00	6.00	12.00
MCA					
❏ 1599	16 Greatest Hits	198?	2.00	4.00	8.00
—*Reissue of 37049*					
❏ 2-6013 [(2)]	Steppenwolf 'Live'	198?	2.50	5.00	10.00
❏ 37045	Steppenwolf	1979	2.00	4.00	8.00
❏ 37046	The Second	1979	2.00	4.00	8.00
❏ 37047	Steppenwolf 7	1979	2.00	4.00	8.00
❏ 37049	16 Greatest Hits	1979	2.00	4.00	8.00
❏ DSX-50099	Steppenwolf Gold/Their Great Hits	1980	3.00	6.00	12.00
—*Columbia House edition on blue rainbow label, but retaining the original ABC Dunhill catalog number*					
MUMS					
❏ PZ 33093	Slow Flux	1974	3.75	7.50	15.00
NAUTILUS					
❏ NR-53	Wolftracks	198?	12.50	25.00	50.00
—*As "John Kay and Steppenwolf"; audiophile vinyl*					
PICKWICK					
❏ SPC-3603	Best of Steppenwolf	1978	2.50	5.00	10.00

STEVE & EYDIE   See STEVE LAWRENCE AND EYDIE GORME.

STEVENS, APRIL   Also see NINO TEMPO AND APRIL STEVENS.

45s
A&M

| ❏ 1636 | Marry Me Again/Gotta Leave You Baby | 1974 | — | 2.00 | 4.00 |

ATCO

| ❏ 6346 | Teach Me Tiger 1965/Morning Till Midnight | 1965 | 2.00 | 4.00 | 8.00 |
| ❏ 6380 | Lovin' Valentine/No Hair Say | 1965 | 2.00 | 4.00 | 8.00 |

CONTRACT

| ❏ 429 | You and Only You/Love Kitten | 1961 | 3.75 | 7.50 | 15.00 |

IMPERIAL

❏ 5626	Teach Me, Tiger/That Warm Afternoon	1959	5.00	10.00	20.00
❏ 5666	In Other Words/Jonny	1960	3.75	7.50	15.00
❏ 5761	You and Only You/Love Kitten	1961	3.75	7.50	15.00
❏ 5907	Fly Me to the Moon/That's My Name	1963	3.75	7.50	15.00

KING

| ❏ 5826 | Soft Warm Lips/How Could Red Riding Hood | 1963 | 2.50 | 5.00 | 10.00 |

RCA VICTOR

❏ 47-4148	I'm in Love Again/Roller Coaster	1951	5.00	10.00	20.00
—*With Henri Rene*					
❏ 47-4208	Gimme a Little Kiss, Will Ya, Huh?/Dreamy Melody	1951	5.00	10.00	20.00
—*With Henri Rene*					
❏ 47-4283	And So to Sleep Again/Aw, C'mon	1951	5.00	10.00	20.00
❏ 47-4381	Put Me in Your Pocket/The Tricks of the Trade	1951	5.00	10.00	20.00
❏ 47-4567	I Love the Way You're Breaking My Heart/Meant to Tell You	1952	5.00	10.00	20.00
❏ 47-4876	I Like to Talk to Myself/That Naughty Waltz	1952	5.00	10.00	20.00

Albums
AUDIO LAB

| ❏ AL-1534 [M] | Torrid Tunes | 1959 | 50.00 | 100.00 | 200.00 |

IMPERIAL

| ❏ LP-9118 [M] | Teach Me Tiger | 1960 | 15.00 | 30.00 | 60.00 |
| ❏ LP-12055 [S] | Teach Me Tiger | 1960 | 25.00 | 50.00 | 100.00 |

S

Number	Title (A Side/B Side)	Yr	VG	VG+	NM

STEVENS, CAT
12-Inch Singles
A&M

❏ 8440 [DJ]	Was Dog a Doughnut (Remix) (same on both sides)	1977	3.75	7.50	15.00

45s
A&M

❏ 1211	Lady D'Arbanville/Time — Fill My Eyes	1970	—	2.50	5.00
❏ 1231	Wild World/Miles from Nowhere	1970	—	2.50	5.00
❏ 1265	Moon Shadow/I Think I See the Light	1971	—	2.00	4.00
❏ 1265 [PS]	Moon Shadow/I Think I See the Light	1971	—	3.00	6.00
❏ 1291	Peace Train/Where Do the Children Play	1971	—	2.00	4.00
❏ 1291 [PS]	Peace Train/Where Do the Children Play	1971	—	3.00	6.00
❏ 1335	Morning Has Broken/I Want to Live in a Wigwam	1972	—	2.00	4.00
❏ 1335 [PS]	Morning Has Broken/I Want to Live in a Wigwam	1972	—	3.00	6.00
❏ 1396	Sitting/Crab Dance	1972	—	2.00	4.00
❏ 1396 [PS]	Sitting/Crab Dance	1972	—	3.00	6.00
❏ 1418	The Hurt/Silent Sunlight	1973	—	2.00	4.00
❏ 1418 [PS]	The Hurt/Silent Sunlight	1973	—	3.00	6.00
❏ 1503	Oh Very Young/100 I Dream	1974	—	2.00	4.00
❏ 1503 [PS]	Oh Very Young/100 I Dream	1974	—	3.00	6.00
❏ 1549	Another Saturday Night/Home in the Sky	1974	—	—	—
—Unreleased?					
❏ 1602	Another Saturday Night/Home in the Sky	1974	—	2.00	4.00
❏ 1602 [PS]	Another Saturday Night/Home in the Sky	1974	—	3.00	6.00
❏ 1645	Ready/I Think I See the Light	1974	—	2.00	4.00
❏ 1700	Two Fine People/Bad Penny	1975	—	2.00	4.00
❏ 1785	Banapple Gas/Ghost Town	1976	—	2.00	4.00
❏ 1785 [PS]	Banapple Gas/Ghost Town	1976	3.00	6.00	12.00
❏ 1924	(I Never Wanted) To Be a Star/Land O' Freelove and Goodbye	1977	—	2.00	4.00
❏ 1948	(Remember the Days of the) Old School Yard/ Land O' Freelove and Goodbye	1977	—	2.00	4.00
❏ 1948 [PS]	(Remember the Days of the) Old School Yard/ Land O' Freelove and Goodbye	1977	—	3.00	6.00
❏ 1971	Was Dog a Doughnut/Sweet Jamaica	1977	—	2.00	4.00
❏ 2109	Bad Brakes/Nascimento	1979	—	2.00	4.00
❏ 2126	Randy/Nascimento	1979	—	2.00	4.00
❏ 2683	If You Want to Sing Out, Sing Out/I Want to Live in a Wigwam	1984	—	2.00	4.00
❏ 2711 [DJ]	Father and Son (same on both sides)	1985	2.50	5.00	10.00
—No stock copies issued					

DERAM

❏ 7501	I Love My Dog/Portobello Road	1966	2.50	5.00	10.00
❏ 7505	Matthew and Son/Granny	1967	2.50	5.00	10.00
❏ 7518	Kitty/The Blackness of the Night	1968	2.00	4.00	8.00
❏ 85006	I'm Gonna Get Me a Gun/School Is Out	1967	2.50	5.00	10.00
❏ 85015	Laughing Apple/Bad Night	1967	2.50	5.00	10.00
❏ 85079	Kitty/Where Are You	1972	—	3.00	6.00

7-Inch Extended Plays
A&M

❏ LLP-4391	Foreigner Suite (Part 1)/(Part 2)	1973	2.00	4.00	8.00
—Jukebox issue; small hole, plays at 33 1/3 rpm					
❏ LLP-4391 [PS]	Foreigner	1973	2.00	4.00	8.00
—Part of "Little LP" series (LLP #227)					

Albums
A&M

❏ SP-3160	Mona Bone Jakon	198?	2.00	4.00	8.00
—Reissue of 4260					
❏ SP-3285	Footsteps in the Dark — Greatest Hits, Volume Two	1986	2.00	4.00	8.00
—Reissue of 3736					
❏ SP-3623	Buddha and the Chocolate Box	1974	3.00	6.00	12.00
❏ SP-3736	Footsteps in the Dark — Greatest Hits, Volume Two	1984	2.50	5.00	10.00
❏ SP-4260	Mona Bone Jakon	1970	3.00	6.00	12.00
—Brown label					
❏ SP-4260	Mona Bone Jakon	1974	2.50	5.00	10.00
—Mostly silver label with gradually fading "A&M"					
❏ SP-4280	Tea for the Tillerman	1971	3.00	6.00	12.00
—Brown label					
❏ SP-4280	Tea for the Tillerman	1974	2.50	5.00	10.00
—Mostly silver label with gradually fading "A&M"					
❏ SP-4313	Teaser and the Firecat	1971	3.00	6.00	12.00
—Brown label					
❏ SP-4313	Teaser and the Firecat	1974	2.50	5.00	10.00
—Mostly silver label with gradually fading "A&M"					
❏ SP-4365	Catch Bull at Four	1972	3.00	6.00	12.00
❏ SP-4391	Foreigner	1973	3.00	6.00	12.00
❏ SP-4519	Greatest Hits	1975	3.00	6.00	12.00
❏ SP-4555	Numbers	1975	3.00	6.00	12.00
❏ SP-4702	Izitso	1977	3.00	6.00	12.00
❏ SP-4735	Back to Earth	1978	3.00	6.00	12.00
❏ QU-53623 [Q]	Buddha and the Chocolate Box	1974	5.00	10.00	20.00
❏ QU-54280 [Q]	Tea for the Tillerman	1974	—	—	—
—Not released					
❏ QU-54313 [Q]	Teaser and the Firecat	1974	—	—	—
—Not released					
❏ QU-54365 [Q]	Catch Bull at Four	1974	—	—	—
—Not released					
❏ QU-54391 [Q]	Foreigner	1974	5.00	10.00	20.00
❏ QU-54519 [Q]	Greatest Hits	1975	5.00	10.00	20.00

DERAM

❏ DE 16005 [M]	Matthew and Son	1967	5.00	10.00	20.00
❏ DES 18005 [P]	Matthew and Son	1967	3.75	7.50	15.00
❏ DES 18005/10 [(2)P]	Matthew and Son/New Masters	1971	3.75	7.50	15.00
❏ DES 18010 [S]	New Masters	1968	3.75	7.50	15.00
❏ DES 18061 [P]	Very Young and Early Songs	1972	3.00	6.00	12.00

LONDON

❏ LC-50010	Cat's Cradle	1977	3.00	6.00	12.00
❏ 820321-1	Cat's Cradle	1985	2.00	4.00	8.00

MOBILE FIDELITY

❏ 1-035	Tea for the Tillerman	1979	10.00	20.00	40.00
—Audiophile vinyl					
❏ MFQR-035	Tea for the Tillerman	1984	30.00	60.00	120.00
—Ultra High Quality Recording in a box					

❏ 1-244	Teaser and the Firecat	1996	10.00	20.00	40.00
—Audiophile vinyl					
❏ 1-254	Izitso	1996	6.25	12.50	25.00
—Audiophile vinyl					

STEVENS, CONNIE   Also see EDD BYRNES.
45s
BELL

❏ 866	She'll Never Understand Him/5:30 Plane	1970	—	2.50	5.00
❏ 922	Keep Growing Strong/Tick-Tock	1970	—	2.50	5.00
❏ 992	Keep Growing Strong/(B-side unknown)	1971	—	2.50	5.00
❏ 45234	Simple Girl/(B-side unknown)	1972	—	2.50	5.00

MGM

❏ 13906	Cinderella Could Have Saved Us All/Wouldn't It Be Nice (To Have Wings and Fly)	1968	—	3.00	6.00

WARNER BROS.

❏ 5092	Apollo/Why Do I Cry for Joey	1959	5.00	10.00	20.00
❏ 5137	Sixteen Reasons/Little Sister	1960	3.00	6.00	12.00
—Second pressing has red label with arrows					
❏ 5137	Sixteen Reasons/Little Sister	1960	3.75	7.50	15.00
—First pressing has pink labels					
❏ 5159	Too Young to Go Steady/ A Little Kiss Is a Kiss Is a Kiss	1960	3.00	6.00	12.00
❏ 5159 [PS]	Too Young to Go Steady/ A Little Kiss Is a Kiss Is a Kiss	1960	7.50	15.00	30.00
❏ 5217	Make Believe Lover/And This Is Mine	1961	3.00	6.00	12.00
❏ 5232	If You Don't, Somebody Else Will/ Greenwood Tree	1961	3.00	6.00	12.00
❏ 5265	Why'd You Wanna Make Me Cry/Just One Kiss	1962	3.00	6.00	12.00
❏ 5289	Mr. Songwriter/I Couldn't Say No	1962	3.00	6.00	12.00
❏ 5318	Hey, Good Lookin'/Nobody's Lonesome for Me	1962	3.00	6.00	12.00
❏ 5380	Little Miss Understood/There Goes Your Guy	1963	2.50	5.00	10.00
❏ 5425	A Girl Never Knows/They're Jealous of Me	1964	2.50	5.00	10.00
❏ 5610	Now That You've Gone/Lost in Wonderland	1965	3.00	6.00	12.00
❏ 5656	In the Deep of Night/Something Beautiful	1965	2.50	5.00	10.00
❏ 5691	Don't You Want to Love Me/In My Room (El Amor)	1966	2.50	5.00	10.00
❏ 5804	All of My Life/That's All I Want from You	1966	2.50	5.00	10.00
❏ 5834	How Bitter the Taste of Love/Most of All	1966	2.50	5.00	10.00
❏ 5872	It'll Never Happen Again/What Will I Tell Him	1966	2.50	5.00	10.00
❏ 7128	Sixteen Reasons/Make Believe Lover	1968	—	2.50	5.00
—"Back to Back Hits" series -- originals have green labels with "W7" logo					

Albums
HARMONY

❏ HS 11312	The Hank Williams Songbook	1969	3.75	7.50	15.00

WARNER BROS.

❏ W 1208 [M]	Conchetta	1958	12.50	25.00	50.00
❏ WS 1208 [S]	Conchetta	1958	15.00	30.00	60.00
❏ W 1382 [M]	Connie Stevens from "Hawaiian Eye"	1960	7.50	15.00	30.00
❏ WS 1382 [S]	Connie Stevens from "Hawaiian Eye"	1960	10.00	20.00	40.00
❏ W 1431 [M]	From Me to You	1962	7.50	15.00	30.00
❏ WS 1431 [S]	From Me to You	1962	10.00	20.00	40.00
❏ W 1432 [M]	Connie	1962	7.50	15.00	30.00
❏ WS 1432 [S]	Connie	1962	10.00	20.00	40.00
❏ W 1460 [M]	The Hank Williams Songbook	1962	7.50	15.00	30.00
❏ WS 1460 [S]	The Hank Williams Songbook	1962	10.00	20.00	40.00

STEVENS, DEBBIE
45s
ABC-PARAMOUNT

❏ 10034	Billy Boy's Theme/I Sit and Cry	1959	3.75	7.50	15.00

APT

❏ 25027	If You Can't Rock Me/What Will I Tell My Heart	1959	6.25	12.50	25.00

STEVENS, DODIE
45s
CRYSTALETTE

❏ 724	Pink Shoe Laces/Coming of Age	1959	5.00	10.00	20.00
❏ 728	Yes-Sir-Ee/The Five Pennies	1959	5.00	10.00	20.00

DOLTON

❏ 83	You Don't Have to Prove a Thing to Me/ I Wore Out Our Record	1963	3.00	6.00	12.00
❏ 88	Sailor Boy/Does Goodnight Mean Goodbye	1964	3.00	6.00	12.00

DOT

❏ 15975	Miss Lonely Heart/Poor Butterfly	1959	5.00	10.00	20.00
❏ 16002	Steady Date/Mairzy Doats	1959	5.00	10.00	20.00
❏ 16067	Candy Store Blues/Gringo's Guitar	1960	3.75	7.50	15.00
❏ 16103	No/A Tasket, A Tasket	1960	3.75	7.50	15.00
❏ 16139	Am I Too Young/So Let's Dance	1960	3.75	7.50	15.00
❏ 16166	Merry Christmas Baby/Jingle Bells	1960	5.00	10.00	20.00
❏ 16167	Yes, I'm Lonesome Tonight/Too Young	1960	5.00	10.00	20.00
❏ 16200	I Fall to Pieces/Turn Around	1961	3.75	7.50	15.00
❏ 16259	Let Me Tell You About Johnny/ You Are the Only One	1961	3.75	7.50	15.00
❏ 16279	The In-Between Years/Trade Winds	1961	3.75	7.50	15.00
❏ 16339	I Cried/Dancing on My Ceiling	1962	3.75	7.50	15.00
❏ 16389	Pink Shoelaces/Yes-Sir-Ee	1962	3.75	7.50	15.00

IMPERIAL

❏ 5908	Don't Send Me No Roses/Daddy Could Get Me One of These	1963	3.75	7.50	15.00
❏ 5930	Hello Stranger/For a Little While	1963	3.75	7.50	15.00

Albums
DOT

❏ DLP-3212 [M]	Dodie Stevens	1960	7.50	15.00	30.00
❏ DLP-3323 [M]	Over the Rainbow	1960	7.50	15.00	30.00
❏ DLP-3371 [M]	Pink Shoelaces	1961	7.50	15.00	30.00
❏ DLP-25212 [S]	Dodie Stevens	1960	10.00	20.00	40.00
❏ DLP-25323 [S]	Over the Rainbow	1960	10.00	20.00	40.00
❏ DLP-25371 [S]	Pink Shoelaces	1961	10.00	20.00	40.00

STEVENS, JOHNNY
45s
FORD

❏ 123	Oh Yeah/Last Chicken in the Shack	1963	7.50	15.00	30.00

PARKWAY

❏ 805	Apple Taffy/Mm, Baby, Mm	1959	6.25	12.50	25.00

STEVENS, MARK, AND THE CHARMERS

45s

ALLISON

Number	Title (A Side/B Side)	Yr	VG	VG+	NM
❏ 921	Magic Rose/Come Back to My Heart	1962	15.00	30.00	60.00

STEVENS, NEIL

45s

BRUNSWICK

Number	Title (A Side/B Side)	Yr	VG	VG+	NM
❏ 55095	More and More/What Could Be Better	1958	7.50	15.00	30.00

—With the Dee-Vines

GOLDISC

Number	Title (A Side/B Side)	Yr	VG	VG+	NM
❏ 3019	Ballad of Love/Tonight My Heart She Is Crying	1961	5.00	10.00	20.00

—With the Temptations

GONE

Number	Title (A Side/B Side)	Yr	VG	VG+	NM
❏ 5067	Ballad of Love/Gambler's Game	1959	12.50	25.00	50.00

STEVENS, RAY

45s

BARNABY

Number	Title (A Side/B Side)	Yr	VG	VG+	NM
❏ 514	Gitarzan/Unwind	197?	—	2.00	4.00
❏ 515	Everything Is Beautiful/Turn Your Radio On	197?	—	2.00	4.00
❏ 516	Mr. Businessman/Sunday Morning Comin' Down	197?	—	2.00	4.00
❏ 517	Ahab the Arab/Along Came Jones	197?	—	2.00	4.00
❏ 518	Freddie Feelgood (And His Funky Little Five Piece Band)/Isn't It Lonely Together	197?	—	2.00	4.00
❏ 519	Have a Little Talk with Myself/Bridget the Midget (The Queen of the Blues)	197?	—	2.00	4.00

—Barnaby releases in the 500 series are reissues; some may be re-recordings

Number	Title (A Side/B Side)	Yr	VG	VG+	NM
❏ 600	The Streak/You've Got the Music Inside	1974	—	2.00	4.00

—Multicolor label

Number	Title (A Side/B Side)	Yr	VG	VG+	NM
❏ 600	The Streak/You've Got the Music Inside	1974	—	2.50	5.00

—White label (not a promo)

Number	Title (A Side/B Side)	Yr	VG	VG+	NM
❏ 604	Moonlight Special/Just So Proud to Be Here	1974	—	2.00	4.00
❏ 610	Everybody Needs a Rainbow/Inside	1974	—	2.00	4.00
❏ 614	Misty/Sunshine	1975	—	2.00	4.00
❏ 616	Indian Love Call/Piece of Paradise	1975	—	2.00	4.00
❏ 618	Young Love/Deep Purple	1975	—	2.00	4.00
❏ 619	Lady of Spain/Mockingbird Hill	1976	—	2.00	4.00
❏ 2011	Everything Is Beautiful/A Brighter Day	1970	—	3.00	6.00
❏ 2016	America, Communicate with Me/Monkey See, Monkey Do	1970	—	2.50	5.00
❏ 2021	Sunset Strip/Islands	1970	—	2.50	5.00
❏ 2024	Bridget the Midget (The Queen of the Blues)/Night People	1970	—	2.50	5.00
❏ 2024 [PS]	Bridget the Midget (The Queen of the Blues)/Night People	1970	2.50	5.00	10.00
❏ 2029	A Mama and a Papa/Melt	1971	—	2.50	5.00
❏ 2039	All My Trials/Have a Little Talk with Myself	1971	—	2.50	5.00
❏ 2048	Turn Your Radio On/Loving You on Paper	1971	—	2.50	5.00
❏ 2058	Love Lifted Me/Glory Special	1972	—	2.50	5.00
❏ 2058	Love Lifted Me/Monkey See, Monkey Do	1972	—	2.50	5.00
❏ 2065	Losing Streak/Inside	1972	—	2.50	5.00
❏ 5020	Golden Age/Nashville	1973	—	2.00	4.00
❏ 5028	Love Me Longer/Float	1973	—	2.00	4.00

CAPITOL

Number	Title (A Side/B Side)	Yr	VG	VG+	NM
❏ F3967	Chickie Chickie Wah Wah/Crying Goodbye	1958	6.25	12.50	25.00
❏ F4030	Cat Pants/Love Goes On Forever	1958	7.50	15.00	30.00
❏ F4101	The School/The Clown	1958	6.25	12.50	25.00
❏ 7PRO-79430 [DJ]	Help Me Make It Through the Night (same on both sides)	1991	—	2.50	5.00

—Vinyl is promo only

MCA

Number	Title (A Side/B Side)	Yr	VG	VG+	NM
❏ 52451	Joggin'/I'm Kissin' You Goodbye	1984	—	2.00	4.00
❏ 52492	Mississippi Squirrel Revival/Ned Nostril	1984	—	2.00	4.00
❏ 52548	It's Me Again, Margaret/Joggin'	1985	—	—	3.00
❏ 52657	The Haircut Song/Punk Country Love	1985	—	—	3.00
❏ 52738	Santa Claus Is Watching You/Armchair Quarterback	1985	—	2.00	4.00
❏ 52738 [PS]	Santa Claus Is Watching You/Armchair Quarterback	1985	—	2.00	4.00
❏ 52771	Vacation Bible School/The Ballad of the Blue Cyclone	1986	—	—	3.00
❏ 52906	The Camping Trip/Southern Air	1986	—	—	3.00
❏ 52924	People's Court/Dudley Doright (Of the Highway Patrol)	1986	—	—	3.00
❏ 53007	Can He Love You Half As Much As I Do/Dudley Doright (Of the Highway Patrol)	1987	—	—	3.00
❏ 53007 [DJ]	Can He Love You Half As Much As I Do (same on both sides)	1987	2.50	5.00	10.00

—Blue vinyl promo

Number	Title (A Side/B Side)	Yr	VG	VG+	NM
❏ 53101	Would Jesus Wear a Rolex?/Cool Down Willard	1987	—	2.00	4.00
❏ 53178	Three-Legged Man/Doctor, Doctor (Have Mercy on Me)	1987	—	—	3.00
❏ 53232	Sex Symbols/The Ballad of Cactus Pete and Lefty	1987	—	—	3.00
❏ 53372	Surfin' U.S.S.R./Language, Nudity, Violence & Sex	1988	—	—	3.00
❏ 53423	The Day I Tried to Teach Charlene MacKenzie How to Drive/I Don't Need None of That	1988	—	—	3.00
❏ 53661	I Saw Elvis in a U.F.O./I Used to Be Crazy	1989	2.50	5.00	10.00

MERCURY

Number	Title (A Side/B Side)	Yr	VG	VG+	NM
❏ 71843	Jeremiah Peabody's Poly Unsaturated Quick Dissolving Fast Acting Pleasant Tasting Green and Purple Pills/Teen Years	1961	3.75	7.50	15.00
❏ 71843 [PS]	Jeremiah Peabody's Poly Unsaturated Quick Dissolving Fast Acting Pleasant Tasting Green and Purple Pills/Teen Years	1961	6.25	12.50	25.00
❏ 71888	Scratch My Back/When You Wish Upon a Star	1961	3.75	7.50	15.00
❏ 71966	Ahab, the Arab/It's Been So Long	1962	3.75	7.50	15.00
❏ 71966 [PS]	Ahab, the Arab/It's Been So Long	1962	7.50	15.00	30.00
❏ 72039	Further More/Saturday Night at the Movies	1962	3.75	7.50	15.00
❏ 72058	Santa Claus Is Watching You/Loved and Lost	1962	3.75	7.50	15.00
❏ 72058 [PS]	Santa Claus Is Watching You/Loved and Lost	1962	6.25	12.50	25.00
❏ 72098	Funny Man/Just One of Life's Little Tragedies	1963	3.75	7.50	15.00
❏ 72125	Harry the Hairy Ape/Little Stone Statue	1963	3.75	7.50	15.00
❏ 72125 [PS]	Harry the Hairy Ape/Little Stone Statue	1963	6.25	12.50	25.00

Number	Title (A Side/B Side)	Yr	VG	VG+	NM
❏ 72189	Speed Ball/It's Party Time	1963	3.75	7.50	15.00
❏ 72255	Butch Barbarian (Sure Footed Mountain Climber World Famous Yodeling Champion)/Don't Say Anything	1963	3.75	7.50	15.00
❏ 72307	Bubble Gum the Bubble Dancer/Laughing Over My Grave	1964	3.75	7.50	15.00
❏ 72382	Rockin' Teenage Mummies/It Only Hurts When I Love	1965	5.00	10.00	20.00
❏ 72430	Mr. Baker the Undertaker/Old English Surfer	1965	5.00	10.00	20.00
❏ 72816	Funny Man/Just One of Life's Little Tragedies	1968	3.00	6.00	12.00
❏ 812496-7	Pice of Paradise Called Tennessee/Mary Lou Nights	1983	—	2.00	4.00
❏ 812906-7	My Dad/Game Show Love	1983	—	2.50	5.00
❏ 814196-7	Love Will Beat Your Brains Out/Game Show Love	1983	—	2.00	4.00
❏ 818057-7	My Dad/Me	1984	—	2.00	4.00

MONUMENT

Number	Title (A Side/B Side)	Yr	VG	VG+	NM
❏ 911	A-B-C/Party People	1966	2.50	5.00	10.00
❏ 927	Devil-May-Care/Make a Few Memories	1966	2.50	5.00	10.00
❏ 946	Freddy Feelgood (And His Funky Little Five Piece Band)/There's One in Every Crowd	1966	2.50	5.00	10.00
❏ 1001	Mary, My Secretary/Answer Me, My Love	1967	2.00	4.00	8.00
❏ 1048	Unwind/For He's a Jolly Good Fellow	1968	2.00	4.00	8.00
❏ 1083	Mr. Businessman/Face the Music	1968	2.00	4.00	8.00
❏ 1099	Isn't It Lonely Together/The Great Escape	1968	2.00	4.00	8.00
❏ 1131	Gitarzan/Bagpipes-That's My Bag	1969	2.00	4.00	8.00
❏ 1150	Along Came Jones/Yakety Yak	1969	2.00	4.00	8.00
❏ 1163	Sunday Mornin' Comin' Down/The Minority	1969	—	3.00	6.00
❏ 1171	Have a Little Talk with Myself/Little Woman	1969	—	3.00	6.00
❏ 1187	I'll Be Your Baby Tonight/Fool on the Hill	1970	—	3.00	6.00

NRC

Number	Title (A Side/B Side)	Yr	VG	VG+	NM
❏ 031	High School Yearbook (Deck of Cards)/Truly True	1959	6.25	12.50	25.00
❏ 042	What Would I Do Without You/My Heart Cries for You	1959	6.25	12.50	25.00
❏ 057	Sergeant Preston of the Yukon/Who Do You Love	1960	6.25	12.50	25.00
❏ 063	Happy Blue Year/White Christmas	1960	6.25	12.50	25.00

PREP

Number	Title (A Side/B Side)	Yr	VG	VG+	NM
❏ 108	Rang Tang Ding Dong (I'm the Japanese Sandman)/Silver Bracelet	1957	6.25	12.50	25.00
❏ 122	Five More Steps/Tingle	1957	6.25	12.50	25.00

RCA

Number	Title (A Side/B Side)	Yr	VG	VG+	NM
❏ PB-11911	Shriner's Convention/You're Never Goin' to Tampa With Me	1980	—	2.00	4.00
❏ PB-12069	Night Games/Let's Do It Right This Time	1980	—	2.00	4.00
❏ PB-12170	One More Last Chance/I Believe You Love Me	1981	—	2.00	4.00
❏ PB-12185	The Streak/Misty	1981	—	2.00	4.00
❏ GB-12368	Everything Is Beautiful/Gitarzan	1981	—	—	3.00

—Gold Standard Series

Number	Title (A Side/B Side)	Yr	VG	VG+	NM
❏ GB-12370	Shriner's Convention/You're Never Goin' to Tampa With Me	1981	—	—	3.00

—Gold Standard Series

Number	Title (A Side/B Side)	Yr	VG	VG+	NM
❏ PB-13038	Written Down in My Heart/Country Boy, Country Club Girl	1981	—	2.00	4.00
❏ PB-13207	Where the Sun Don't Shine/Why Don't We Go Somewhere and Love	1982	—	2.00	4.00

WARNER BROS.

Number	Title (A Side/B Side)	Yr	VG	VG+	NM
❏ 8198	You Are So Beautiful/One Man Band	1976	—	2.00	4.00
❏ 8237	Honky Tonk Waltz/Om	1976	—	2.00	4.00
❏ 8301	In the Mood/Classical Cluck	1976	—	3.00	6.00

—As "Henhouse Five Plus Too"

Number	Title (A Side/B Side)	Yr	VG	VG+	NM
❏ 8318	Get Crazy with Me/Dixie Hummingbird	1977	—	2.00	4.00
❏ 8393	Dixie Hummingbird/Feel the Music	1977	—	2.00	4.00
❏ 8603	Be Your Own Best Friend/With a Smile	1978	—	2.00	4.00
❏ 8785	I Need Your Help Barry Manilow/Daydream Romance	1979	—	2.00	4.00
❏ 8785 [PS]	I Need Your Help Barry Manilow/Daydream Romance	1979	—	3.00	6.00
❏ 8849	The Feeling's Not Right Again/Get Crazy with Me	1979	—	2.00	4.00

Albums

BARNABY

Number	Title	Yr	VG	VG+	NM
❏ 5004	Ray Stevens' Greatest Hits	1974	2.50	5.00	10.00

—Reissue of 30770

Number	Title	Yr	VG	VG+	NM
❏ 5005	Nashville	1974	2.50	5.00	10.00

—Reissue of 15007

Number	Title	Yr	VG	VG+	NM
❏ 6003	Boogity Boogity	1974	3.00	6.00	12.00
❏ 6012	Misty	1975	3.00	6.00	12.00
❏ 6018	The Very Best of Ray Stevens	1975	3.00	6.00	12.00
❏ BR 15007	Nashville	1973	3.00	6.00	12.00
❏ Z 30092	Ray Stevens…Unreal!!!	1970	3.00	6.00	12.00
❏ Z 30770	Ray Stevens' Greatest Hits	1971	3.00	6.00	12.00
❏ ZQ 30770 [Q]	Ray Stevens' Greatest Hits	1971	5.00	10.00	20.00
❏ Z 30809	Turn Your Radio On	1972	3.00	6.00	12.00
❏ ZQ 30809 [Q]	Turn Your Radio On	1972	5.00	10.00	20.00
❏ KZ 32139	Losin' Streak	1972	3.00	6.00	12.00
❏ Z12 35005	Everything Is Beautiful	1970	3.75	7.50	15.00

MCA

Number	Title	Yr	VG	VG+	NM
❏ 5517	He Thinks He's Ray Stevens	1984	2.50	5.00	10.00
❏ 5635	I Have Returned	1985	2.50	5.00	10.00
❏ 5795	Surely You Joust	1986	2.50	5.00	10.00
❏ 5918	Greatest Hits	1987	2.50	5.00	10.00
❏ 42020	Crackin' Up!	1987	2.50	5.00	10.00
❏ 42062	Greatest Hits, Volume 2	1987	2.50	5.00	10.00
❏ 42172	I Never Made a Record I Didn't Like	1988	2.50	5.00	10.00
❏ 42303	Beside Myself	1989	2.50	5.00	10.00

MERCURY

Number	Title	Yr	VG	VG+	NM
❏ MG-20732 [M]	1,837 Seconds of Humor	1962	10.00	20.00	40.00
❏ MG-20828 [M]	This Is Ray Stevens	1963	6.25	12.50	25.00
❏ SR-60732 [S]	1,837 Seconds of Humor	1962	12.50	25.00	50.00
❏ SR-60828 [S]	This Is Ray Stevens	1963	7.50	15.00	30.00
❏ SR-61272	The Best of Ray Stevens	1968	3.75	7.50	15.00
❏ 812780-1	Me	1984	2.50	5.00	10.00

MONUMENT

Number	Title	Yr	VG	VG+	NM
❏ SLP-18102	Even Stevens	1968	3.75	7.50	15.00

S

Number	Title (A Side/B Side)	Yr	VG	VG+	NM
❑ SLP-18115	Gitarzan	1969	3.75	7.50	15.00
❑ SLP-18134	Have a Little Talk with Myself	1970	3.75	7.50	15.00
PICKWICK					
❑ SPC-3266	Rock and Roll Show	1971	2.50	5.00	10.00
PRIORITY					
❑ PU 38075	Turn Your Radio On	1982	2.50	5.00	10.00
—Reissue of Barnaby 30809					
RCA VICTOR					
❑ AHL1-3574	Shriner's Convention	1980	2.50	5.00	10.00
❑ AHL1-3841	One More Last Chance	1981	2.50	5.00	10.00
❑ AYL1-4253	Shriner's Convention	1982	2.00	4.00	8.00
—"Best Buy Series" reissue					
❑ AHL1-4288	Don't Laugh Now	1982	2.50	5.00	10.00
❑ AHL1-4727	Greatest Hits	1983	2.50	5.00	10.00
❑ AYL1-5153	Greatest Hits	1985	2.00	4.00	8.00
—"Best Buy Series" reissue					
❑ CPL1-7161	Collector's Series	1986	2.50	5.00	10.00
WARNER BROS.					
❑ BS 2914	Just for the Record	1976	2.50	5.00	10.00
❑ BS 2997	Feel the Music	1977	2.50	5.00	10.00
❑ BS 3098	There Is Something...	1977	2.50	5.00	10.00
❑ BS 3195	Be Your Own Best Friend	1978	2.50	5.00	10.00
❑ BSK 3332	The Feeling's Not Right Again	1979	2.50	5.00	10.00

STEVENS, TERRI
45s
RCA VICTOR

Number	Title (A Side/B Side)	Yr	VG	VG+	NM
❑ 47-6165	Why Am I to Blame/What Am I Trying to Forget	1955	5.00	10.00	20.00
❑ 47-6300	All I Want Is You/I've Always Loved You	1955	5.00	10.00	20.00
❑ 47-6393	Dood-ly Dood-ly/I'll Come When You Call	1956	5.00	10.00	20.00
❑ 47-6633	Sweet World/That's How I Cried Over You	1956	5.00	10.00	20.00
❑ 47-7014	Pick-Up Girl/Untouched Heart	1957	5.00	10.00	20.00

STEVENSON, B.W.
45s
MCA

Number	Title (A Side/B Side)	Yr	VG	VG+	NM
❑ 41151	A Special Wish/Holding a Special Place for You	1979	—	2.00	4.00
❑ 41166	Headin' Home/Holding a Special Place for You	1980	—	2.00	4.00
PRIVATE STOCK					
❑ 45,208	Holdin' On for Dear Love/I'm a Better Man for Lovin' You	1979	—	2.00	4.00
RCA VICTOR					
❑ 47-0728	Say What I Feel/Lonesome Song	1972	—	2.50	5.00
❑ 47-0778	On My Own/Highway One	1972	—	2.50	5.00
❑ 47-0840	Minuet for My Lady/Don't Go to Mexico	1972	—	2.50	5.00
❑ 47-0952	Shambala/My Feet Are So Weary	1973	—	3.00	6.00
❑ APBO-0030	My Maria/August Evening Lady	1973	—	3.00	6.00
❑ APBO-0171	River of Love/Lucky Touch	1973	—	2.50	5.00
❑ APBO-0242	Song for Katy/Look for the Light	1974	—	2.00	4.00
❑ APBO-0279	Remember Me/Roll On	1974	—	2.00	4.00
❑ PB-10012	Here We Go Again/Little Bit of Understanding	1974	—	2.00	4.00
❑ GB-10158	My Maria/Shambala	1975	—	—	3.00
—Gold Standard Series					
WARNER BROS.					
❑ 8184	Jerrry's Bar and Grill/Way Down by the Ocean	1976	—	2.00	4.00
❑ 8247	Dream Baby/Wastin' Time	1976	—	2.00	4.00
❑ 8343	Down to the Station/May You Find Yourself in Heaven	1977	—	2.00	4.00

Albums
MCA

Number	Title (A Side/B Side)	Yr	VG	VG+	NM
❑ 3215	Lifeline	1980	2.50	5.00	10.00
RCA VICTOR					
❑ APL1-0088	My Maria	1973	3.00	6.00	12.00
❑ APD1-0410 [Q]	Calabasas	1974	5.00	10.00	20.00
❑ APL1-0410	Calabasas	1974	3.00	6.00	12.00
❑ APL1-2394	The Best of B.W. Stevenson	1977	2.50	5.00	10.00
❑ LSP-4685	B.W. Stevenson	1972	3.75	7.50	15.00
❑ LSP-4794	Lead Free	1972	3.75	7.50	15.00
WARNER BROS.					
❑ BS 2901	We Be Sailin'	1976	2.50	5.00	10.00
❑ BS 3012	Lost	1977	2.50	5.00	10.00

STEWART, AL
45s
ARISTA

Number	Title (A Side/B Side)	Yr	VG	VG+	NM
❑ 0362	Time Passages/Almost Lucy	1978	—	2.00	4.00
❑ 0389	Song on the Radio/A Man for All Seasons	1979	—	2.00	4.00
❑ 0552	Midnight Rocks/Constantinople	1980	—	2.00	4.00
❑ 0576	Paint by Numbers/Optical Illusion	1980	—	2.00	4.00
❑ 0585	Running Man/Merlin's Theme	1981	—	2.00	4.00
❑ 0639	Indian Summer/Soko (Needless to Say)	1981	—	2.00	4.00
JANUS					
❑ 243	Nostradamus/Terminal Eyes	1974	—	2.50	5.00
❑ 250	Carol/Sirens of Titan	1975	—	2.50	5.00
❑ 266	Year of the Cat/Broadway Hotel	1976	—	2.50	5.00
❑ 267	On the Border/Flying Sorcery	1977	—	2.50	5.00

Albums
ARISTA

Number	Title (A Side/B Side)	Yr	VG	VG+	NM
❑ AL 4190	Time Passages	1978	2.50	5.00	10.00
❑ AL6-8326	Year of the Cat	198?	2.00	4.00	8.00
—Reissue of Arista 9503					
❑ AL6-8342	Time Passages	198?	2.00	4.00	8.00
—Reissue of 4190					
❑ AL6-8359	Past, Present and Future	198?	2.00	4.00	8.00
—Reissue of Arista 9524					
❑ A2L 8607 [(2)]	Live/Indian Summer	1981	3.00	6.00	12.00
❑ AL 9503	Year of the Cat	1979	2.50	5.00	10.00
—Reissue of Janus 7022					
❑ AL 9520	24 Carrots	1980	2.50	5.00	10.00
❑ AL 9524	Past, Present and Future	1980	2.50	5.00	10.00
—Reissue of Janus 3063					
❑ AL 9525	Modern Times	1980	2.50	5.00	10.00
—Reissue of Janus 7012					
ENIGMA					
❑ D1-73316	Last Days of the Century	1988	3.00	6.00	12.00

Number	Title (A Side/B Side)	Yr	VG	VG+	NM
EPIC					
❑ BN 26564	Love Chronicles	1970	5.00	10.00	20.00
JANUS					
❑ 3063	Past, Present and Future	1974	3.75	7.50	15.00
❑ 7012	Modern Times	1975	3.00	6.00	12.00
❑ 7022	Year of the Cat	1976	3.00	6.00	12.00
❑ 7026 [(2)]	The Early Years	1977	3.75	7.50	15.00
❑ 7026 [DJ]	The Early Years	1977	7.50	15.00	30.00
—Promo-only condensation of 2-LP set with rubber-stamp cover					
MOBILE FIDELITY					
❑ 1-009	Year of the Cat	1979	10.00	20.00	40.00
—Audiophile vinyl					
❑ 1-082	Time Passages	1981	7.50	15.00	30.00
—Audiophile vinyl					
NAUTILUS					
❑ NR-34	24 Carrots	198?	7.50	15.00	30.00
—Audiophile vinyl					
PASSPORT					
❑ PB-6042	Russians and Americans	1986	3.00	6.00	12.00

STEWART, ANDY
45s
CAPITOL

Number	Title (A Side/B Side)	Yr	VG	VG+	NM
❑ 4809	The Road and the Miles to Dundee/Take Me Back	1962	2.50	5.00	10.00
WARWICK					
❑ 627	The Scottish Soldier/The Muckin' O' Georgie's Brye	1961	3.00	6.00	12.00
❑ 665	Donald Where's Your Troosers?/The Battle's Over	1961	3.00	6.00	12.00
❑ 676	The Road and the Miles to Dundee/Take Me Back	1962	3.00	6.00	12.00

Albums
CAPITOL

Number	Title (A Side/B Side)	Yr	VG	VG+	NM
❑ ST 10320 [S]	Andy Stewart's Scotland	196?	5.00	10.00	20.00
❑ T 10320 [M]	Andy Stewart's Scotland	196?	3.75	7.50	15.00
EPIC					
❑ LF 18027 [M]	A Scottish Soldier	196?	3.00	6.00	12.00
❑ LF 18031 [M]	Tunes of Glory	196?	3.00	6.00	12.00
❑ LF 18048 [M]	I'm Off to Bonnie Scotland	196?	3.00	6.00	12.00
❑ BF 19027 [S]	A Scottish Soldier	196?	3.75	7.50	15.00
❑ BF 19031 [S]	Tunes of Glory	196?	3.75	7.50	15.00
❑ BF 19048 [S]	I'm Off to Bonnie Scotland	196?	3.75	7.50	15.00
WARWICK					
❑ W 3043 [M]	A Scottish Soldier	1961	5.00	10.00	20.00
❑ WST 3043 [S]	A Scottish Soldier	1961	7.50	15.00	30.00

STEWART, BILLY
45s
ARGO

Number	Title (A Side/B Side)	Yr	VG	VG+	NM
❑ 5256	Billy's Blues (Part 1)/Billy's Blues (Part 2)	1956	10.00	20.00	40.00
CHESS					
❑ 1625	Billy's Blues (Part 1)/Billy's Blues (Part 2)	1956	15.00	30.00	60.00
❑ 1820	Reap What You Sow/Fat Boy	1962	3.00	6.00	12.00
❑ 1835	True Fine Lovin'/Wedding Bells	1962	3.00	6.00	12.00
❑ 1852	Scramble/Oh What Can the Matter Be	1963	3.00	6.00	12.00
❑ 1868	Strange Feeling/Sugar and Spice	1963	3.00	6.00	12.00
❑ 1888	Count Me Out/A Fat Boy Can Cry	1964	2.50	5.00	10.00
❑ 1905	Tell It Like It Is/My Sweet Senorita	1964	2.50	5.00	10.00
❑ 1922	I Do Love You/Keep Loving	1965	2.50	5.00	10.00
❑ 1932	Sitting in the Park/Once Again	1965	2.50	5.00	10.00
❑ 1941	How Nice It Is/No Girl	1965	2.50	5.00	10.00
❑ 1948	Because I Love You/Mountain of Love	1965	2.50	5.00	10.00
❑ 1960	Love Me/Why Am I Lonely	1966	2.50	5.00	10.00
❑ 1966	Summertime/To Love, To Love	1966	3.00	6.00	12.00
—Blueish label					
❑ 1966	Summertime/To Love, To Love	1966	3.75	7.50	15.00
—Black label					
❑ 1978	Secret Love/Look Back and Smile	1966	2.50	5.00	10.00
❑ 1991	Every Day I Have the Blues/Ol' Man River	1967	2.50	5.00	10.00
❑ 2002	Cross My Heart/Why (Do I Love You So)	1967	2.50	5.00	10.00
❑ 2053	Tell Me the Truth/What Have I Done	1968	2.50	5.00	10.00
❑ 2063	I'm in Love (Oh Yes I Am)/Crazy 'Bout You Baby	1969	2.50	5.00	10.00
❑ 2080	By the Time I Get to Phoenix/We'll Always Be Together	1969	2.50	5.00	10.00
OKEH					
❑ 7095	Baby, You're My Only Love/Billy's Heartache	1957	75.00	150.00	300.00
UNITED ARTISTS					
❑ 340	This Is a Fine Time/Young in Years	1961	3.75	7.50	15.00

Albums
CHESS

Number	Title (A Side/B Side)	Yr	VG	VG+	NM
❑ LP-1496 [M]	I Do Love You	196?	7.50	15.00	30.00
—Green "woman" cover					
❑ LP-1496 [M]	I Do Love You	1965	20.00	40.00	80.00
—Red cover, black "wheel"					
❑ LPS-1496 [S]	I Do Love You	196?	10.00	20.00	40.00
—Green "woman" cover					
❑ LPS-1496 [S]	I Do Love You	1965	25.00	50.00	100.00
—Red cover, black "wheel"					
❑ LP-1499 [M]	Unbelievable	1966	7.50	15.00	30.00
❑ LPS-1499 [S]	Unbelievable	1966	10.00	20.00	40.00
❑ LP-1513 [M]	Billy Stewart Teaches Old Standards New Tricks	1967	7.50	15.00	30.00
❑ LPS-1513 [S]	Billy Stewart Teaches Old Standards New Tricks	1967	10.00	20.00	40.00
❑ LPS-1547	Billy Stewart Remembered	1970	6.25	12.50	25.00
❑ CH-9104	The Greatest Sides	198?	2.50	5.00	10.00
❑ CH-50059	Cross My Heart	1974	3.75	7.50	15.00

STEWART, DANNY See SLY STEWART.

STEWART, JOHN Also see THE KINGSTON TRIO.
45s
ALLEGIANCE

Number	Title (A Side/B Side)	Yr	VG	VG+	NM
❑ 3900	The Queen of Hollywood High/Judy in G Major	198?	—	2.00	4.00
CAPITOL					
❑ 2469	Mother Country/Shackles and Chains	1969	—	3.00	6.00
❑ 2538	July, You're a Woman/She Believes in Me	1969	—	3.00	6.00

Number	Title (A Side/B Side)	Yr	VG	VG+	NM
❏ 2605	Armstrong/Anna on a Memory	1969	—	3.00	6.00
❏ 2711	Earth Rider/The Lady and the Outlaw	1969	—	3.00	6.00
❏ 2712	World of No Return/Wild Is Love	1969	2.00	4.00	8.00
—B-side by Patti Drew					
❏ 2842	Clack Clack/Marshall Wind	1970	—	3.00	6.00
RCA VICTOR					
❏ 74-0970	Chilly Winds/Durango	1973	—	2.50	5.00
❏ APBO-0109	Anna on a Memory/Wheatfield	1973	—	2.50	5.00
❏ PB-10003	July, You're a Woman/Runaway Fool of Love	1974	—	2.50	5.00
❏ PB-10227	Survivors/Josie	1975	—	2.50	5.00
❏ PB-10268	Survivors/Josie	1975	—	2.50	5.00
RSO					
❏ 894	Promise the Wind/Morning Thunder	1978	—	2.00	4.00
❏ 931	Gold/Comin' Out of Nowhere	1979	—	2.00	4.00
❏ 1000	Midnight Wind/Somewhere Down the Line	1979	—	2.00	4.00
❏ 1016	Lost Her in the Sun/Heart of the Dream	1979	—	2.00	4.00
❏ 1031	(Odin) Spirit of the Water/Love Has Tied My Wings	1980	—	2.00	4.00
VITA					
❏ 169	Rockin' Anna/Lorraine	1958	62.50	125.00	250.00
—As "Johnny Stewart"					
WARNER BROS.					
❏ 7525	Daydream Believer/Sweet Lizard	1971	—	2.50	5.00
❏ 7552	Light Come Shine/A Little Road and a Stone to Roll	1972	—	2.50	5.00
❏ 7592	An Accent of Halley's Comet/Arkansas Breakout	1972	—	2.50	5.00
Albums					
AFFORDABLE DREAMS					
❏ AD-01	Trancas	1984	2.50	5.00	10.00
ALLEGIANCE					
❏ AV-431	Blondes	1982	2.50	5.00	10.00
CAPITOL					
❏ ST-203	California Bloodlines	1969	3.75	7.50	15.00
❏ ST-540	Willard	1970	3.75	7.50	15.00
❏ SM-2975	Signals Through the Glass	1977	2.50	5.00	10.00
—Reissue with new prefix					
❏ ST 2975	Signals Through the Glass	1968	5.00	10.00	20.00
❏ SN-16150	California Bloodlines	198?	2.00	4.00	8.00
—Budget-line reissue					
❏ SN-16151	Willard	198?	2.00	4.00	8.00
—Budget-line reissue					
CYPRESS					
❏ 661117-1	Punch the Big Guy	1987	2.50	5.00	10.00
HOMECOMING					
❏ HC-0200	Centennial	1984	2.50	5.00	10.00
❏ HC-0300	The Last Campaign	1985	2.50	5.00	10.00
❏ HC-0500	The Trio Years	1986	2.50	5.00	10.00
RCA VICTOR					
❏ CPL2-0265 [(2)]	The Phoenix Concerts — Live	1974	3.75	7.50	15.00
❏ APL1-0816	Wingless Angels	1975	3.00	6.00	12.00
❏ AFL1-3513	John Stewart in Concert	1980	2.50	5.00	10.00
❏ AYL1-3731	Cannons in the Rain	1981	2.00	4.00	8.00
—"Best Buy Series" reissue					
❏ LSP-4827	Cannons in the Rain	1973	3.00	6.00	12.00
RSO					
❏ RS-1-3027	Fire in the Wind	1977	2.50	5.00	10.00
❏ RS-1-3051	Bombs Away Dream Babies	1979	2.50	5.00	10.00
❏ RS-1-3074	Dream Babies Go Hollywood	1980	2.50	5.00	10.00
WARNER BROS.					
❏ WS 1948	The Lonesome Picker Rides Again	1971	3.00	6.00	12.00
❏ BS 2611	Sunstorm	1972	3.00	6.00	12.00

STEWART, ROD Also see JEFF BECK; FACES; PYTHON LEE JACKSON; SHOTGUN EXPRESS.

12-Inch Singles

Number	Title (A Side/B Side)	Yr	VG	VG+	NM
GEFFEN					
❏ PRO-A-2787 [DJ]	Twistin' the Night Away (same on both sides)	1987	2.00	4.00	8.00
WARNER BROS.					
❏ PRO 680 [DJ]	The Killing of Georgie (6:31) (same on both sides)	1977	6.25	12.50	25.00
—Promo only on blue vinyl					
❏ PRO 680 [DJ]	The Killing of Georgie (6:31) (same on both sides)	1977	25.00	50.00	100.00
—Promo only on red vinyl					
❏ PRO-A-921 [DJ]	Passion (Long Version 7:30) (LP Version 5:35)	1980	3.00	6.00	12.00
❏ PRO-A-989 [DJ]	Young Turks (Edit) (LP Version)	1981	3.00	6.00	12.00
❏ PRO-A-1078 [DJ]	Guess I'll Always Love You (same on both sides)	1982	2.50	5.00	10.00
❏ PRO-A-2032 [DJ]	Baby Jane (same on both sides?)	1983	2.50	5.00	10.00
❏ PRO-A-2063 [DJ]	Dancin' Alone/Ghetto Blaster/What Am I Gonna Do	1983	2.00	4.00	8.00
❏ PRO-A-2148 [DJ]	Infatuation (Edit 4:03) (LP Version 5:12)	1984	2.00	4.00	8.00
❏ PRO-A-2184 [DJ]	Some Guys Have All the Luck (Edit)/Bad for You	1984	2.00	4.00	8.00
❏ PRO-A-2505 [DJ]	Love Touch (Edit) (LP Version)	1986	2.00	4.00	8.00
❏ PRO-A-2538 [DJ]	A Night Like This (same on both sides)	1986	2.00	4.00	8.00
❏ PRO-A-2559 [DJ]	Another Heartache (Another Heartache) (Edit)	1986	2.50	5.00	10.00
❏ PRO-A-2618 [DJ]	Every Beat of My Heart (English Edit) (LP Version)	1986	2.00	4.00	8.00
❏ PRO-A-3837 [DJ]	This Old Heart of Mine (2 versions?)	1990	2.50	5.00	10.00
❏ WBSD 8727	Da Ya Think I'm Sexy?/Scarred and Scared	1978	3.00	6.00	12.00
❏ 21268	Crazy About Her (4 versions)/Dynamite	1989	—	—	3.00
45s					
COLLECTABLES					
❏ 4947	Your Song/Twisting the Night Away	199?	—	—	3.00
—This is the first appearance of "Your Song" on a U.S. 45					
GEFFEN					
❏ 28303	Twistin' the Night Away/Let's Get Small	1987	—	2.00	4.00
—B-side by Steve Martin					
❏ 28303 [PS]	Twistin' the Night Away/Let's Get Small	1987	—	2.00	4.00
J					
❏ 21249	These Foolish Things/It Had to Be You	2002	—	—	3.00
MERCURY					
❏ 73009	Handbags and Gladrags/An Old Raincoat Won't Ever Let You Down	1970	2.50	5.00	10.00
❏ 73031	Handbags and Gladrags/Man of Constant Sorrow	1970	2.00	4.00	8.00
❏ 73095	It's All Over Now/Joe's Lament	1970	2.50	5.00	10.00
❏ 73115	Only a Hero/Gasoline Alley	1970	2.50	5.00	10.00
❏ 73156	Cut Across Shorty/Gasoline Alley	1970	2.50	5.00	10.00
❏ 73175	My Way of Giving/Lady Day	1971	—	3.00	6.00
❏ 73196	Country Comfort/Gasoline Alley	1971	—	3.00	6.00
❏ 73224	Maggie May/Reason to Believe	1971	—	3.00	6.00
❏ 73244	(I Know) I'm Losing You/Mandolin Wind	1971	—	2.50	5.00
❏ 73330	You Wear It Well/True Blue	1972	—	2.50	5.00
❏ 73330 [PS]	You Wear It Well/True Blue	1972	3.75	7.50	15.00
❏ 73344	Angel/Lost Paraguayos	1972	—	2.50	5.00
❏ 73412	Twistin' the Night Away//True Blue-Lady Day	1973	—	2.50	5.00
❏ 73412 [PS]	Twistin' the Night Away//True Blue-Lady Day	1973	—	3.00	6.00
❏ 73426	Oh No Not My Baby/Jodie	1973	—	2.50	5.00
❏ 73426 [PS]	Oh No Not My Baby/Jodie	1973	—	3.00	6.00
❏ 73636	Mine for Me/Farewell	1974	—	2.50	5.00
❏ 73660	Let Me Be Your Car/Sailor	1974	—	3.00	6.00
❏ 73802	Every Picture Tells a Story/What's Made Milwaukee Famous (Has Made a Loser Out of Me)	1976	—	2.50	5.00
PRESS					
❏ 9722	Good Morning Little Schoolgirl/I'm Gonna Move to the Outskirts of Town	1965	10.00	20.00	40.00
PRIVATE STOCK					
❏ 45,130	Shake/Bright Lights, Big City	1976	—	3.00	6.00
WARNER BROS.					
❏ 8066	As Long As You Tell Him/You Can Make Me Dance, Sing or Anything	1975	—	2.50	5.00
—As "Rod Stewart and Faces"					
❏ 8102	As Long As You Tell Him/You Can Make Me Dance, Sing or Anything	1975	—	2.00	4.00
—As "Rod Stewart and Faces"					
❏ 8146	Sailing/All in the Name of Rock and Roll	1975	—	2.00	4.00
❏ 8170	This Old Heart of Mine/Still Love Again	1975	—	2.50	5.00
❏ 8262	Tonight's the Night (Gonna Be Alright)/Fool for You	1976	—	2.00	4.00
❏ 8321	The First Cut Is the Deepest/Ball Trap	1977	—	2.00	4.00
❏ 8396	The Killing of Georgie (Part 1 and 2)/Rosie	1977	—	2.00	4.00
❏ 8475	You're In My Heart (The Final Acclaim)/You Got a Nerve	1977	—	2.00	4.00
❏ 8535	Hot Legs/You're Insane	1978	—	2.00	4.00
❏ 8535 [PS]	Hot Legs/You're Insane	1978	—	2.50	5.00
❏ 8568	I Was Only Joking/Born Loose	1978	—	2.00	4.00
❏ 8568 [PS]	I Was Only Joking/Born Loose	1978	—	2.50	5.00
❏ 8724	Da Ya Think I'm Sexy?/Scarred and Scared	1978	—	2.00	4.00
❏ 8724 [DJ]	Da Ya Think I'm Sexy? (Edited Version 4:16)/(Full Version 5:21)	1978	—	3.00	6.00
❏ 8724 [PS]	Da Ya Think I'm Sexy?/Scarred and Scared	1978	—	2.50	5.00
❏ 8810	Ain't Love a Bitch/Last Summer	1979	—	2.00	4.00
❏ 8810 [PS]	Ain't Love a Bitch/Last Summer	1979	—	2.50	5.00
❏ 15995	Broken Arrow/Downtown Train	1993	—	—	3.00
—"Back to Back Hits" series; only U.S. 45 release of A-side					
❏ 17195	Ooh La La/A Night Like This	1998	—	—	3.00
❏ 17459	If We Fall in Love Tonight/Tom Traubert's Blues (Waltzing Matilda)	1996	—	—	3.00
❏ 17847	Leave Virginia Alone/Shock to the System	1995	—	—	3.00
❏ 17854	This/The Groom's Still Waiting at the Altar	1995	—	—	3.00
❏ 18424	Having a Party/Sweet Little Rock and Roller	1993	—	—	3.00
❏ 18427	Reason to Believe/It's All Over Now	1993	—	—	3.00
❏ 18511	Have I Told You Lately/Gasoline Alley	1993	—	2.00	4.00
❏ 19322	The Motown Song/Sweet Soul Marie	1991	—	—	3.00
❏ 19366	Rhythm of My Heart/Moment of Glory	1991	—	—	3.00
❏ 19983	This Old Heart of Mine/You're In My Heart	1990	—	—	3.00
❏ 22685	Downtown Train/The Killing of Georgie (Part 1 and 2)	1989	—	—	3.00
❏ 22685 [PS]	Downtown Train/The Killing of Georgie (Part 1 and 2)	1989	2.00	4.00	8.00
❏ 27657	Crazy About Her/Dynamite	1989	—	—	3.00
❏ 27729	My Heart Can't Tell You No/The Wild Horse	1988	—	—	3.00
❏ 27729 [PS]	My Heart Can't Tell You No/The Wild Horse	1988	—	—	3.00
❏ 27796	Forever Young/Days of Rage	1988	—	—	3.00
❏ 27796 [PS]	Forever Young/Days of Rage	1988	—	—	3.00
❏ 27927	Lost in You/Almost Illegal	1988	—	—	3.00
❏ 27927 [PS]	Lost in You/Almost Illegal	1988	—	—	3.00
❏ 28625	Every Beat of My Heart/Trouble	1986	—	—	3.00
❏ 28625 [PS]	Every Beat of My Heart/Trouble	1986	—	—	3.00
❏ 28631	Another Heartache/You're In My Heart (The Final Acclaim)	1986	—	—	3.00
❏ 28631 [PS]	Another Heartache/You're In My Heart (The Final Acclaim)	1986	—	—	3.00
❏ 28668	Love Touch (Love Theme from Legal Eagles)/Heart Is on the Line	1986	—	—	3.00
❏ 28668 [PS]	Love Touch (Love Theme from Legal Eagles)/Heart Is on the Line	1986	—	—	3.00
❏ 29122	All Right Now/Dancin' Alone	1984	—	2.00	4.00
❏ 29215	Some Guys Have All the Luck/I Was Only Joking	1984	—	2.00	4.00
❏ 29215 [PS]	Some Guys Have All the Luck/I Was Only Joking	1984	—	2.00	4.00
❏ 29256	Infatuation/She Won't Dance with Me	1984	—	2.00	4.00
❏ 29256 [PS]	Infatuation/She Won't Dance with Me	1984	—	2.00	4.00
❏ 29564	What Am I Gonna Do (I'm So in Love with You)/Dancin' Alone	1983	—	2.00	4.00
❏ 29564 [PS]	What Am I Gonna Do (I'm So in Love with You)/Dancin' Alone	1983	—	2.00	4.00
❏ 29608	Baby Jane/Ready Now	1983	—	2.00	4.00
❏ 29874	Guess I'll Always Love You/Rock My Plimsoul	1982	—	2.00	4.00
❏ 29874 [PS]	Guess I'll Always Love You/Rock My Plimsoul	1982	—	2.50	5.00
❏ 49138	I Don't Want to Talk About It/Best Days of My Life	1979	—	2.00	4.00
❏ 49138 [PS]	I Don't Want to Talk About It/Best Days of My Life	1979	—	2.50	5.00
❏ 49617	Passion/Better Off Dead	1980	—	2.00	4.00
❏ 49617 [DJ]	Passion (Edit 4:45) (Full Version 5:29)	1980	—	3.00	6.00
❏ 49617 [PS]	Passion/Better Off Dead	1980	—	2.50	5.00
❏ 49686	Somebody Special/She Won't Dance with Me	1981	—	2.00	4.00
❏ 49843	Young Turks/Sonny	1981	—	2.00	4.00
❏ 49843 [PS]	Young Turks/Sonny	1981	—	2.50	5.00
❏ 49886	Tonight I'm Yours (Don't Hurt Me)/Tora, Tora, Tora	1981	—	2.00	4.00
❏ 49886 [PS]	Tonight I'm Yours (Don't Hurt Me)/Tora, Tora, Tora	1981	—	2.50	5.00

S

Number	Title (A Side/B Side)	Yr	VG	VG+	NM
❏ 50051	How Long/Jealous	1982	—	2.00	4.00
❏ 50051 [PS]	How Long/Jealous	1982	—	2.50	5.00

7-Inch Extended Plays
MERCURY

Number	Title (A Side/B Side)	Yr	VG	VG+	NM
❏ MEPL-28 [DJ]	I'd Rather Go Blind/What's Made Milwaukee Famous//Italian Girls/Twistin' the Night Away	1972	2.50	5.00	10.00
❏ MEPL-28 [PS]	A Rod Stewart Promotion Special	1972	2.50	5.00	10.00

Albums
ACCORD

Number	Title (A Side/B Side)	Yr	VG	VG+	NM
❏ SN-7142	Rod the Mod	1981	3.00	6.00	12.00

DCC COMPACT CLASSICS

Number	Title (A Side/B Side)	Yr	VG	VG+	NM
❏ LPZ-2010	Never a Dull Moment	1995	7.50	15.00	30.00
—Audiophile vinyl					

MERCURY

Number	Title (A Side/B Side)	Yr	VG	VG+	NM
❏ SRM-1-609	Every Picture Tells a Story	1971	2.50	5.00	10.00
—With poster missing; red label					
❏ SRM-1-609	Every Picture Tells a Story	1971	3.75	7.50	15.00
—Original cover has an attached, perforated poster					
❏ SRM-1-646	Never a Dull Moment	1972	3.00	6.00	12.00
—Red label					
❏ SRM-1-680	Sing It Again Rod	1973	3.00	6.00	12.00
—Red label					
❏ SRM-1-697	Rod Stewart/Faces Live: Coast to Coast Overtures and Beginners	1973	3.75	7.50	15.00
—By "Rod Stewart/Faces"					
❏ SRM-1-1017	Smiler	1974	3.00	6.00	12.00
—Chicago skyline label					
❏ SRM-2-7507 [(2)]	The Best of Rod Stewart	1976	3.75	7.50	15.00
❏ SRM-2-7509 [(2)]	The Best of Rod Stewart, Volume 2	1977	3.75	7.50	15.00
❏ SR-61237	The Rod Stewart Album	1969	6.25	12.50	25.00
—Cover is yellow with no black border					
❏ SR-61237	The Rod Stewart Album	1971	3.75	7.50	15.00
—Cover is yellow with black border; red label					
❏ SR-61264	Gasoline Alley	1970	5.00	10.00	20.00
—Cover is textured, most noticeably on the pebbles					
❏ SR-61264	Gasoline Alley	1971	3.75	7.50	15.00
—Cover is not textured; red label					
❏ 822385-1	Every Picture Tells a Story	1984	2.00	4.00	8.00
❏ 822791-1 [(2)]	The Best of Rod Stewart, Volume 2	1985	3.00	6.00	12.00
❏ 824881-1	Gasoline Alley	1985	2.00	4.00	8.00
❏ 824882-1	Sing It Again Rod	1985	2.00	4.00	8.00
❏ 826287-1 [(2)]	The Best of Rod Stewart	1985	3.00	6.00	12.00

MOBILE FIDELITY

Number	Title (A Side/B Side)	Yr	VG	VG+	NM
❏ 1-054	Blondes Have More Fun	1980	6.25	12.50	25.00
—Audiophile vinyl					

PRIVATE STOCK

Number	Title (A Side/B Side)	Yr	VG	VG+	NM
❏ PS-2021	A Shot of Rhythm and Blues	1976	3.75	7.50	15.00

SPRINGBOARD

Number	Title (A Side/B Side)	Yr	VG	VG+	NM
❏ SPB-4030	Rod Stewart and The Faces	197?	3.00	6.00	12.00
❏ SPB-4063	Rod Stewart and Steampacket	197?	3.00	6.00	12.00

TRIP

Number	Title (A Side/B Side)	Yr	VG	VG+	NM
❏ TOP-16-31	Looking Back/16 Early Hits	1974	3.00	6.00	12.00

UNITED DISTRIBUTORS

Number	Title (A Side/B Side)	Yr	VG	VG+	NM
❏ UDL-2391	The Day Will Come	1981	5.00	10.00	20.00

WARNER BROS.

Number	Title (A Side/B Side)	Yr	VG	VG+	NM
❏ BS 2875	Atlantic Crossing	1975	2.50	5.00	10.00
❏ BS 2938	A Night on the Town	1976	2.50	5.00	10.00
❏ BSK 3092	Foot Loose and Fancy Free	1977	2.50	5.00	10.00
❏ BSK 3108	Atlantic Crossing	1977	2.00	4.00	8.00
—Reissue of 2875					
❏ BSK 3116	A Night on the Town	1977	2.00	4.00	8.00
—Reissue of 2938					
❏ BSK 3261	Blondes Have More Fun	1978	2.50	5.00	10.00
❏ BSP 3276 [PD]	Blondes Have More Fun	1978	5.00	10.00	20.00
❏ HS 3373	Rod Stewart Greatest Hits	1979	2.50	5.00	10.00
❏ HS 3485	Foolish Behaviour	1980	2.50	5.00	10.00
❏ BSK 3602	Tonight I'm Yours	1981	2.50	5.00	10.00
❏ 23743 [(2)]	Absolutely Live	1982	3.00	6.00	12.00
❏ 23743 [(2)DJ]	Absolutely Live	1982	6.25	12.50	25.00
—Promo only on Quiex II vinyl					
❏ 23877	Body Wishes	1983	2.00	4.00	8.00
❏ 23877 [DJ]	Body Wishes	1983	3.75	7.50	15.00
—Promo only on Quiex II vinyl					
❏ 25095	Camouflage	1984	2.00	4.00	8.00
—Issued with 16 different back covers, all of equal value, that, when assembled, form a giant poster					
❏ 25446	Rod Stewart	1986	2.00	4.00	8.00
❏ 25884	Out of Order	1988	2.00	4.00	8.00
❏ 26158	Downtown Train: Selections from the Storyteller Anthology	1990	3.00	6.00	12.00

STEWART, SANDY

45s
ATCO

Number	Title (A Side/B Side)	Yr	VG	VG+	NM
❏ 6137	Playmates/Heavenly Father	1959	2.50	5.00	10.00

COLPIX

Number	Title (A Side/B Side)	Yr	VG	VG+	NM
❏ 669	My Coloring Book/I Heard You Cried Last Night	1962	2.00	4.00	8.00
❏ 669 [PS]	My Coloring Book/I Heard You Cried Last Night	1962	3.75	7.50	15.00
❏ 681	My Favorite Song/Promise of Love	1963	2.00	4.00	8.00
❏ 704	I Know He Needs Her/ Please Don't Fall in Love with Me Again	1963	2.00	4.00	8.00

DCP

Number	Title (A Side/B Side)	Yr	VG	VG+	NM
❏ 1004	Draw Me a Circle/Little Child (Mommy Dear)	1964	2.00	4.00	8.00
❏ 1122	Yellow and Green Make Me Blue/I'll Never Go There Anymore	1964	2.00	4.00	8.00

EASTWEST

Number	Title (A Side/B Side)	Yr	VG	VG+	NM
❏ 122	To My Love/Music, Music, Music	1958	2.50	5.00	10.00

EPIC

Number	Title (A Side/B Side)	Yr	VG	VG+	NM
❏ 9070	No One Came to My Party/Mama, Mama	1954	3.00	6.00	12.00

OKEH

Number	Title (A Side/B Side)	Yr	VG	VG+	NM
❏ 6941	Since You Went Away from Me/Before	1953	3.00	6.00	12.00
❏ 6967	If My Heart Had a Window/Punch Brother Punch	1953	3.00	6.00	12.00
❏ 6991	Loved and Lost/Please Come Home	1953	3.00	6.00	12.00

20TH CENTURY

Number	Title (A Side/B Side)	Yr	VG	VG+	NM
❏ 5007	The Game of Love/Do Ya Do Ya	1954	3.00	6.00	12.00
❏ 5014	I'm Goin' Home/Saturday Night	1954	3.00	6.00	12.00

UNITED ARTISTS

Number	Title (A Side/B Side)	Yr	VG	VG+	NM
❏ 232	Indoor Sports/Time Waits for No One	1960	2.50	5.00	10.00
❏ 287	Past the Age of Innocence/Richest Girl in the World	1961	2.50	5.00	10.00
❏ 332	Nice Guy/Lord and Master	1961	2.50	5.00	10.00

"X"

Number	Title (A Side/B Side)	Yr	VG	VG+	NM
❏ 0126	Johnny Darling/No More Love	1955	3.00	6.00	12.00
❏ 0156	Puddin' 'n' Pie/In Nuevo Laredo	1955	3.00	6.00	12.00
❏ 0176	Could It Be?/I'll Take Care of You	1955	3.00	6.00	12.00

Albums
AUDIOPHILE

Number	Title (A Side/B Side)	Yr	VG	VG+	NM
❏ AP-205	Sandy Stewart Sings Songs of Jerome Kern	1985	2.50	5.00	10.00
—Accompanied by Dick Hyman on piano					

COLPIX

Number	Title (A Side/B Side)	Yr	VG	VG+	NM
❏ CP-441 [M]	My Coloring Book	1963	6.25	12.50	25.00
❏ SCP-441 [S]	My Coloring Book	1963	7.50	15.00	30.00

STEWART, SLY
Sylvester Stewart, later "Sly" of SLY AND THE FAMILY STONE.

12-Inch Singles
EPIC

Number	Title (A Side/B Side)	Yr	VG	VG+	NM
❏ 50794	Dance to the Music/Sing a Simple Song	1979	3.75	7.50	15.00
—As "Sly Stone"					

45s
A&M

Number	Title (A Side/B Side)	Yr	VG	VG+	NM
❏ 2890	Eek-Ah-Bo-Static Automatic/Black Girls	1986	—	—	3.00
—B-side by Rae Dawn Chong					
❏ 2896	Love and Affection/Black Girls	1986	—	—	3.00
—A-side as "Sly Stone and Martha Davis"; B-side by Rae Dawn Chong					

AUTUMN

Number	Title (A Side/B Side)	Yr	VG	VG+	NM
❏ 3	I Just Learned How to Swim/Scat Swim	1964	5.00	10.00	20.00
—Sylvester Stewart, later "Sly" of The Family Stone					
❏ 14	Buttermilk — Part 1/Buttermilk — Part 2	1965	5.00	10.00	20.00
—As "Sly"					
❏ 26	Temptation Walk/Temptation Walk — Part 2	1966	5.00	10.00	20.00

EPIC

Number	Title (A Side/B Side)	Yr	VG	VG+	NM
❏ 50795	Dance to the Music/Sing a Simple Song	1979	—	2.50	5.00
—As "Sly Stone"					

G&P

Number	Title (A Side/B Side)	Yr	VG	VG+	NM
❏ 901	Help Me With My Heart/A Long Time Away	1962	62.50	125.00	250.00
—As "Sylvester Stewart"					

LUKE

Number	Title (A Side/B Side)	Yr	VG	VG+	NM
❏ 1008	A Long Time Alone/I'm Just a Fool	1961	62.50	125.00	250.00
—As "Danny Stewart"					

Albums
SCULPTURE

Number	Title (A Side/B Side)	Yr	VG	VG+	NM
❏ SCP-2001	San Francisco Recordings 1964-1967	197?	5.00	10.00	20.00

STEWART, WYNN

45s
ATLANTIC

Number	Title (A Side/B Side)	Yr	VG	VG+	NM
❏ 4025	When/Why Don't You Come to Me	1974	—	2.50	5.00

CAPITOL

Number	Title (A Side/B Side)	Yr	VG	VG+	NM
❏ 2012	Love's Gonna Happen to Me/Waltz of the Angels	1967	2.00	4.00	8.00
❏ 2012 [PS]	Love's Gonna Happen to Me/Waltz of the Angels	1967	3.00	6.00	12.00
❏ 2137	Something Pretty/Built in Love	1968	—	3.50	7.00
❏ 2137 [PS]	Something Pretty/Built in Love	1968	3.00	6.00	12.00
❏ 2240	In Love/My Own Little World	1968	—	3.50	7.00
❏ 2240 [PS]	In Love/My Own Little World	1968	3.00	6.00	12.00
❏ 2341	Strings/Happy Blues	1968	—	3.50	7.00
❏ 2421	Let the Whole World Sing It with Me/ Who Are You	1969	—	3.50	7.00
❏ 2549	World-Wide Travelin' Man/Cry Baby	1969	—	3.50	7.00
❏ 2657	Yours Forever/Goin' Steady	1969	—	3.50	7.00
❏ 2751	You Don't Care What Happens to Me/ Young As Spring	1970	—	3.00	6.00
❏ 2888	It's a Beautiful Day/Prisoner on the Run	1970	—	3.00	6.00
❏ 3000	Heavenly/You're No Secret of Mine	1970	—	3.00	6.00
❏ 3080	Baby, It's Yours/I Was the First One to Know	1971	—	3.00	6.00
❏ 3157	Hello Little Rock/You Can't Take It With You	1971	—	3.00	6.00
❏ F3408	The Waltz of the Angels/Why Do I Love You So	1956	5.00	10.00	20.00
❏ F3515	The Keeper of the Keys/Slowly But Surely	1956	5.00	10.00	20.00
❏ F3594	That Just Kills Me/You Took Her Off My Hands	1956	5.00	10.00	20.00
❏ F3651	Hold Back Tomorrow/New Love	1957	5.00	10.00	20.00
❏ F3803	A Night to Remember/ I Wish I Could Say the Same	1957	5.00	10.00	20.00
❏ 5271	Half of This, Half of That	1964	2.00	4.00	8.00
❏ 5271 [PS]	Half of This, Half of That	1964	3.75	7.50	15.00
❏ 5397	Sha Marie/Does He Love You Like I Do	1965	2.00	4.00	8.00
❏ 5485	I Keep Forgettin' That I Forgot About You/ My Rosalie	1965	2.00	4.00	8.00
❏ 5593	Angels Don't Lie/The Tourist	1966	2.00	4.00	8.00
❏ 5831	It's Such a Pretty World Today/ Ol' What's Her Name	1967	2.00	4.00	8.00
❏ 5937	'Cause I Love You/That's the Only Way to Cry	1967	2.00	4.00	8.00
❏ 5937 [PS]	'Cause I Love You/That's the Only Way to Cry	1967	3.00	6.00	12.00

CHALLENGE

Number	Title (A Side/B Side)	Yr	VG	VG+	NM
❏ 9121	Big Big Love/One More Memory	1961	3.75	7.50	15.00
❏ 9142	I Done Done It/I Don't Feel at Home	1962	—	—	—
❏ 9155	Don't Look Back/Loversville	1962	3.75	7.50	15.00
❏ 9164	Another Day, Another Dollar/Donna on My Mind	1962	3.75	7.50	15.00
❏ 9192	Slightly Used/I'm Not the Man I Used to Be	1963	3.75	7.50	15.00
❏ 59061	Wishful Thinking/Uncle Tom Got Caught	1958	15.00	30.00	60.00
—The B-side is sought after by rockabilly collectors					
❏ 59084	Heartaches for a Dime/Playboy	1960	3.75	7.50	15.00
❏ 59095	If You See My Baby/I'd Rather Have America	1960	3.75	7.50	15.00
❏ 59216	Big City/One Way to Go	1963	3.75	7.50	15.00
❏ 59379	Girl in White/Fallin' for You	1967	2.00	4.00	8.00

FOUR STAR

Number	Title (A Side/B Side)	Yr	VG	VG+	NM
❏ 8001	Inflation Blues/Heartbreak Mountain	1980	—	3.00	6.00

JACKPOT

Number	Title (A Side/B Side)	Yr	VG	VG+	NM
❏ 48005	Come On/School Bus Love Affair	1959	75.00	150.00	300.00
❏ 48019	Open Up My Heart/Above and Beyond	1960	5.00	10.00	20.00

PLAYBOY

Number	Title (A Side/B Side)	Yr	VG	VG+	NM
❏ 6035	Lonely Rain/Just Now Thought of You	1975	—	2.50	5.00
❏ 6060	I'm Gonna Kill You/Seasons of My Heart	1976	—	3.00	6.00

Number	Title (A Side/B Side)	Yr	VG	VG+	NM
❑ 6080	After the Storm/Don't Monkey with My Widow	1976	—	2.50	5.00
❑ 6091	Sing a Sad Song/It's Such a Pretty World Today	1976	—	2.50	5.00
PRETTY WORLD					
❑ 001	Wait Till I Get My Hands on You/Would You Want the World to End	1985	2.00	4.00	8.00
RCA VICTOR					
❑ 74-0819	Paint Me a Rainbow/I Know They'll Make Room for You	1972	—	2.50	5.00
❑ 74-0891	Everything Needs a Little Woman's Touch/Search Through the Ashes	1973	—	2.50	5.00
❑ APBO-0004	Love Ain't Worth a Dime Unless It's Free/Me and My Jesus Would Know	1973	—	2.50	5.00
❑ APBO-0114	It's Raining in Seattle/If I Were You	1973	—	2.50	5.00
WIN					
❑ 126	Eyes Big as Dallas/Such a Perfect Day for Making Love	1978	—	3.00	6.00
❑ 127	Could I Talk You Into Loving Me Again/I Was Raised Down on the Farm	1979	—	3.00	6.00
Albums					
CAPITOL					
❑ ST-113	In Love	1969	5.00	10.00	20.00
❑ ST-214	Let the Whole World Sing It with Me	1969	5.00	10.00	20.00
❑ ST-324	Yours Forever	1969	5.00	10.00	20.00
❑ ST 2332 [S]	The Songs of Wynn Stewart	1965	6.25	12.50	25.00
❑ T 2332 [M]	The Songs of Wynn Stewart	1965	5.00	10.00	20.00
❑ ST 2737 [S]	It's Such a Pretty World Today	1967	6.25	12.50	25.00
❑ T 2737 [M]	It's Such a Pretty World Today	1967	5.00	10.00	20.00
❑ ST 2849 [S]	Love's Gonna Happen to Me	1968	5.00	10.00	20.00
❑ T 2849 [M]	Love's Gonna Happen to Me	1968	7.50	15.00	30.00
❑ ST 2921	Something Pretty	1968	5.00	10.00	20.00
HILLTOP					
❑ JM-6050 [M]	Above and Beyond the Call of Love	1967	3.75	7.50	15.00
❑ JS-6050 [S]	Above and Beyond the Call of Love	1967	3.00	6.00	12.00
PLAYBOY					
❑ PB 416	After the Storm	1976	2.50	5.00	10.00
WRANGLER					
❑ W-1006 [M]	Wynn Stewart	1962	7.50	15.00	30.00
❑ W-31006 [S]	Wynn Stewart	1962	10.00	20.00	40.00

STEWART, WYNN, AND JAN HOWARD
45s

Number	Title (A Side/B Side)	Yr	VG	VG+	NM
CHALLENGE					
❑ 59071	Wrong Company/We'll Never Love Again	1960	3.75	7.50	15.00
❑ 59264	How the Other Half Lives/We'll Never Love Again	1964	3.00	6.00	12.00
JACKPOT					
❑ 48014	How the Other Half Lives/Yankee Go Home	1960	5.00	10.00	20.00
Albums					
CHALLENGE					
❑ CHL-611 [M]	Sweethearts of Country Music	1961	12.50	25.00	50.00
STARDAY					
❑ SLP-421	Wynn Stewart and Jan Howard Sing Their Hits	1968	6.25	12.50	25.00

STEWART, WYNN, AND WEBB PIERCE
Albums

Number	Title (A Side/B Side)	Yr	VG	VG+	NM
DESIGN					
❑ DLP-604 [M]	Country and Western Stars	196?	3.00	6.00	12.00

STEWART BROTHERS, THE With Sylvester "SLY" STEWART, later of SLY AND THE FAMILY STONE.
45s

Number	Title (A Side/B Side)	Yr	VG	VG+	NM
ENSIGN					
❑ 4032	The Rat/Ra Ra Roo	1959	25.00	50.00	100.00
KEEN					
❑ 2113	Sleep on the Porch/Yum Yum	1960	25.00	50.00	100.00

STILLROVEN, THE
45s

Number	Title (A Side/B Side)	Yr	VG	VG+	NM
AUGUST					
❑ 101	Little Picture Playhouse/Cast Thy Burden Upon the Stone	1968	6.25	12.50	25.00
❑ 102	Necessary Person/Have You Ever Seen Me	1968	6.25	12.50	25.00
❑ 102	Necessary Person/Come in the Morning	1968	25.00	50.00	100.00
FALCON					
❑ 69	Hey Joe/Sunny Day	1967	12.50	25.00	50.00
❑ 7296	She's Your Woman/I'm Not Your Steppin' Stone	1966	50.00	100.00	200.00
ROULETTE					
❑ 4748	Hey Joe/Sunny Day	1967	3.75	7.50	15.00

STILLS, STEPHEN Also see BUFFALO SPRINGFIELD; CROSBY, STILLS AND NASH; CROSBY, STILLS, NASH AND YOUNG; THE STILLS-YOUNG BAND.
12-Inch Singles

Number	Title (A Side/B Side)	Yr	VG	VG+	NM
ATLANTIC					
❑ PR 623 [DJ]	Stranger (same on both sides)	1984	—	3.00	6.00
❑ PR 650 [DJ]	Can't Let Go (same on both sides)	1984	—	3.00	6.00
45s					
ATLANTIC					
❑ 2778	Love the One You're With/To a Flame	1970	—	3.00	6.00
❑ 2790	Sit Yourself Down/We Are Not Helpless	1971	—	2.50	5.00
❑ 2806	Change Partners/Relaxing Town	1971	—	2.50	5.00
❑ 2806 [PS]	Change Partners/Relaxing Town	1971	—	3.00	6.00
❑ 2820	Marianne/Nothin' to Do But Today	1971	—	2.50	5.00
❑ 2876	It Doesn't Matter/Rock & Roll's Crazy Medley	1972	—	2.50	5.00
❑ 2888	Rock and Roll Crazies/Colorado	1972	—	2.50	5.00
—With Manassas					
❑ 2917	Down the Road/Guaguanco De Vero	1972	—	2.50	5.00
—With Manassas					
❑ 2959	So Many Times/Isn't It About Time	1973	—	2.50	5.00
❑ 89597	Only Love Can Break Your Heart/Love Again	1984	—	2.00	4.00
❑ 89611	Can't Let Go/Grey to Green	1984	—	2.00	4.00
—With Walter Finnegan					
❑ 89633	Stranger/No Hiding Place	1984	—	2.00	4.00
❑ 89633 [PS]	Stranger/No Hiding Place	1984	—	2.00	4.00
COLUMBIA					
❑ 10179	Turn Back the Pages/Shuffle Just as Bad	1975	—	2.50	5.00
❑ 10369	Buyin' Time/Soldier	1976	—	2.50	5.00

Number	Title (A Side/B Side)	Yr	VG	VG+	NM
❑ 10804	Lowdown/Can't Get No Booty	1978	—	2.50	5.00
❑ 10872	Thoroughfare Gap/Lowdown	1978	—	2.50	5.00
7-Inch Extended Plays					
ATLANTIC					
❑ SD 7-7206	Bluebird Revisited/Ecology Song//Sugar Babe/Marianne/Relaxing Town	1971	3.00	6.00	12.00
—Jukebox issue; small hole, plays at 33 1/3 rpm					
❑ SD 7-7206 [PS]	Stephen Stills 2	1971	3.00	6.00	12.00
—Part of "Little LP" series (LLP #157)					
Albums					
ATLANTIC					
❑ SD 2-903 [(2)]	Manassas	1972	3.75	7.50	15.00
❑ SD 7202	Stephen Stills	1970	3.00	6.00	12.00
❑ SD 7206	Stephen Stills 2	1971	3.00	6.00	12.00
❑ SD 7250	Down the Road	1973	3.00	6.00	12.00
❑ SD 18156	Stephen Stills Live	1975	3.00	6.00	12.00
❑ SD 18201	Still Stills — The Best of Stephen Stills	1976	2.50	5.00	10.00
❑ 80177	Right By You	1984	2.00	4.00	8.00
COLUMBIA					
❑ PC 33575	Stills	1975	2.50	5.00	10.00
—No bar code on cover					
❑ PC 33575	Stills	198?	2.00	4.00	8.00
—Bar code on cover					
❑ PCQ 33575 [Q]	Stills	1975	5.00	10.00	20.00
❑ PC 34348	Illegal Stills	1976	2.50	5.00	10.00
❑ JC 35380	Thoroughfare Gap	1978	2.50	5.00	10.00

STILLS-YOUNG BAND, THE STEPHEN STILLS and NEIL YOUNG.
45s

Number	Title (A Side/B Side)	Yr	VG	VG+	NM
REPRISE					
❑ 1365	Long May You Run//12/8 Blues (All the Same)	1976	—	3.00	6.00
❑ 1378	Midnight on the Bay/Black Coral	1976	—	2.50	5.00
Albums					
REPRISE					
❑ MS 2253	Long May You Run	1976	2.50	5.00	10.00

STINGERS, THE
Albums

Number	Title (A Side/B Side)	Yr	VG	VG+	NM
CROWN					
❑ CST-476 [S]	Guitars A Go Go	196?	10.00	20.00	40.00
❑ CLP-5476 [M]	Guitars A Go Go	196?	7.50	15.00	30.00

STINIT, DANE
45s

Number	Title (A Side/B Side)	Yr	VG	VG+	NM
SUN					
❑ 402	Always on the Go/Don't Knock What You Don't Understand	1966	3.75	7.50	15.00
❑ 405	Sweet Country Girl/That Muddy Ole River	1967	3.75	7.50	15.00

STITES, GARY
45s

Number	Title (A Side/B Side)	Yr	VG	VG+	NM
CARLTON					
❑ 508	Lonely for You/Shine That Ring	1959	5.00	10.00	20.00
❑ 516	A Girl Like You/Hey Little Girl	1959	5.00	10.00	20.00
❑ 521	Starry Eyed/Without Your Love	1959	5.00	10.00	20.00
❑ 525	Lawdy Miss Clawdy/Don't Wanna Say Goodbye	1960	5.00	10.00	20.00
❑ 529	Gloria Lee/Hey, Hey	1960	5.00	10.00	20.00
EPIC					
❑ 10064	Hurting/Thinking of You	1966	3.00	6.00	12.00
MADISON					
❑ 138	Young Love/Little Tear	1960	3.75	7.50	15.00
❑ 155	Honey Girl/Little Lonely One	1961	3.75	7.50	15.00
MR. PEEKE					
❑ 122	You Doubted Me/Only a Fool Would Say	1962	3.75	7.50	15.00
Albums					
CARLTON					
❑ LP-120 [M]	Lonely for You	1960	20.00	40.00	80.00
❑ STLP-120 [S]	Lonely for You	1960	30.00	60.00	120.00

STOECKLEIN, VAL
45s

Number	Title (A Side/B Side)	Yr	VG	VG+	NM
DOT					
❑ 17200	Sounds of Yesterday/Say It's Not Over	1969	3.75	7.50	15.00
❑ 17234	All the Way Home/I Wonder Who I'll Be Tomorrow	1969	3.75	7.50	15.00
Albums					
DOT					
❑ DLP-3904 [M]	Grey Life	1968	25.00	50.00	100.00
—Label is black, as if stock copy, but record is found inside stereo (25904) cover with "Monaural Promotion Not for Sale" sticker on front					
❑ DLP-25904 [S]	Grey Life	1968	10.00	20.00	40.00

STOMPERS, THE
45s

Number	Title (A Side/B Side)	Yr	VG	VG+	NM
GONE					
❑ 5120	Stompin' Round the Christmas Tree/Forgive Me	1961	37.50	75.00	150.00
LANDA					
❑ 684	Foolish One/Quarter to Four Stomp	1962	6.25	12.50	25.00
❑ 684	Foolish One/Surf Stompin'	1962	6.25	12.50	25.00
MERCURY					
❑ 72111	Frump/Blacksmith Blues	1963	3.75	7.50	15.00
—As "The Ski Stompers"					
SOUVENIR					
❑ 1003	I Miss You So/Blue Moon of Kentucky	1960	25.00	50.00	100.00

STONE, JIMMY
45s

Number	Title (A Side/B Side)	Yr	VG	VG+	NM
CROSS COUNTRY					
❑ 523	Found/Mine	1956	75.00	150.00	300.00
GONE					
❑ 5001	Found/Mine	1957	50.00	100.00	200.00

S

Number	Title (A Side/B Side)	Yr	VG	VG+	NM

STONE, SLY See SLY STEWART.

STONE CIRCUS, THE
45s
MAINSTREAM

Number	Title (A Side/B Side)	Yr	VG	VG+	NM
❏ 694	Mister Grey//(B-side unknown)	1969	5.00	10.00	20.00

Albums
MAINSTREAM

❏ S-6119	The Stone Circus	1969	20.00	40.00	80.00

STONE COUNTRY
45s
RCA VICTOR

❏ 47-9534	Wheels on Fire/Million Dollar Bash	1968	2.00	4.00	8.00

Albums
RCA VICTOR

❏ LSP-3958	Stone Country	1968	5.00	10.00	20.00

STONE PONEYS Also see LINDA RONSTADT.
45s
CAPITOL

❏ 2004	Different Drum/I've Got to Know	1967	3.75	7.50	15.00
❏ 2110	Up to My Neck in High Muddy Water/ Carnival Bear	1968	2.50	5.00	10.00
❏ 2110 [PS]	Up to My Neck in High Muddy Water/ Carnival Bear	1968	10.00	20.00	40.00
—By "Linda Ronstadt and the Stone Poneys"					
❏ 2195	Hobo (Mornin' Glory)/Some of Shelly's Blues	1968	2.50	5.00	10.00
❏ 5838	All the Beautiful Things/ Sweet Summer Blue and Gold	1967	2.50	5.00	10.00
❏ 5910	One for One/Evergreen	1967	2.50	5.00	10.00
SIDEWALK					
❏ 937	So Fine/Everyone Has Their Own Ideas	1968	50.00	100.00	200.00

Albums
CAPITOL

❏ ST 2666 [S]	The Stone Poneys	1967	7.50	15.00	30.00
❏ T 2666 [M]	The Stone Poneys	1967	6.25	12.50	25.00
❏ ST 2763 [S]	Evergreen, Vol. 2	1967	7.50	15.00	30.00
❏ T 2763 [M]	Evergreen, Vol. 2	1967	10.00	20.00	40.00
❏ ST 2863	Linda Ronstadt/ Stone Poneys and Friends Vol. III	1968	12.50	25.00	50.00
❏ ST-11383	The Stone Poneys Featuring Linda Ronstadt	1974	2.50	5.00	10.00
PICKWICK					
❏ SPC-3298	Stoney End	1976	3.00	6.00	12.00

STONE THE CROWS
45s
POLYDOR

❏ 14033	Fool on the Hill/Raining in My Heart	1969	—	—	—
—Canceled					

Albums
POLYDOR

❏ 24-4019	Stone the Crows	1970	5.00	10.00	20.00
❏ PD-5020	Teenage Licks	1972	5.00	10.00	20.00
❏ PD-5037	Continuous Performance	1972	5.00	10.00	20.00

STONES, THE
45s
SOLLY

❏ 928	She Said Yeah/Watch Me	1966	6.25	12.50	25.00
—Reissued with group renamed "The Tracers"					

STONEY AND MEATLOAF Also see MEAT LOAF.
45s
RARE EARTH

❏ 5027	What You See Is What You Get/Lady Be Mine	1971	—	3.00	6.00
❏ 5033	The Way You Do the Things You Do/It Takes All Kinds of People	1971	—	3.00	6.00

Albums
PRODIGAL

❏ 10	Stoney and Meatloaf	1978	3.00	6.00	12.00
RARE EARTH					
❏ R 528	Stoney and Meatloaf	1971	5.00	10.00	20.00

STOOGES, THE See IGGY AND THE STOOGES.

STOOKEY, PAUL Also see PETER, PAUL AND MARY.
45s
BENSON

❏ 5616 [DJ]	For Christmas (same on both sides)	198?	—	2.00	4.00
—As "Noel Paul Stookey and the Bodyworks Band"					
❏ 5616 [PS]	For Christmas (same on both sides)	198?	—	2.00	4.00
WARNER BROS.					
❏ 7511	Wedding Song (There Is Love)/Give a Damn	1971	—	3.00	6.00
❏ 7602	Hey, Sad Sack/Sebastian	1972	—	2.50	5.00
❏ 7683	Funky Monkey (Part 1)/Blessed	1973	—	2.50	5.00
—As "Noel Paul Stookey"					

Albums
WARNER BROS.

❏ WS 1912	Paul and...	1971	2.50	5.00	10.00
❏ BS 2674	One Night Stand	1973	2.50	5.00	10.00
—As "Noel Paul Stookey"					

STORIES
45s
KAMA SUTRA

❏ 545	I'm Coming Home/You Told Me	1972	—	2.00	4.00
❏ 558	Top of the City/Stepback	1972	—	2.00	4.00
❏ 566	Darling/Take Cover	1972	—	2.00	4.00
❏ 574	Love in Motion/Changes Have Begun	1973	—	2.00	4.00
❏ 577	Brother Louie/What Comes After	1973	—	2.50	5.00
❏ 577	Brother Louie/Changes Have Begun	1973	—	3.00	6.00
❏ 584	Mammy Blue/Travelling Underground	1973	—	2.00	4.00
❏ 588	Circles/If It Feels Good	1974	—	2.00	4.00
❏ 594	Another Love/Love Is In Motion	1974	—	2.00	4.00

Albums
KAMA SUTRA

❏ KSBS-2051	Stories	1972	3.00	6.00	12.00
❏ KSBS-2068	About Us	1973	3.00	6.00	12.00
—Regular cover; "Brother Louie" added as the last song on side 2					
❏ KSBS-2068	About Us	1973	3.75	7.50	15.00
—Gatefold cover; "Brother Louie" added as the last song on side 2					
❏ KSBS-2068	About Us	1973	7.50	15.00	30.00
—Gatefold; does NOT contain "Brother Louie"					
❏ KSBS-2078	Traveling Underground	1974	3.00	6.00	12.00

STORM, BILLY
45s
ATLANTIC

❏ 2076	In the Chapel in the Moonlight/Sure As You're Born	1960	3.00	6.00	12.00
❏ 2098	When You Dance/Dear One	1961	3.00	6.00	12.00
❏ 2112	Honey Love/A Kiss from Your Lips	1961	3.00	6.00	12.00
BUENA VISTA					
❏ 403	Puppy Love Is Here to Stay/Push Over	1962	3.75	7.50	15.00
❏ 413	Love Theme from El Cid/Cee Cee Rider	1962	3.75	7.50	15.00
❏ 415	Double Date/Good Girl	1963	3.75	7.50	15.00
❏ 418	'Deed I Do/Lonely People Do Foolish Things	1963	3.75	7.50	15.00
❏ 424	He Knows How Much We Can Bear/ Motherless Child	1963	5.00	10.00	20.00
❏ 429	Since I Fell for You/Body and Soul	1964	5.00	10.00	20.00
COLUMBIA					
❏ 4-41356	This Is Always/I've Come of Age	1959	3.75	7.50	15.00
❏ 41431	Easy Chair/You Just Can't Plan These Things	1959	3.75	7.50	15.00
❏ 41494	I Can't Stop Crying for You/Emotion	1959	3.75	7.50	15.00
❏ 41545	Enchanted/When the Whole World Smiles Again	1959	3.75	7.50	15.00
GREGMARK					
❏ 9	3000 Tears/Who'll Keep an Eye on Jane	1961	3.00	6.00	12.00
HANNA-BARBERA					
❏ 474	Please Don't Mention Her Name/ The Warmest Love	1966	5.00	10.00	20.00
❏ 474 [PS]	Please Don't Mention Her Name/ The Warmest Love	1966	6.25	12.50	25.00
INFINITY					
❏ 013	Love Theme from El Cid/Don't Let Go	1962	3.00	6.00	12.00
❏ 018	Since I Fell for You/A Million Miles from Nowhere	1963	3.00	6.00	12.00
❏ 023	I Can't Help It/Educated Fool	1963	3.00	6.00	12.00
LOMA					
❏ 2001	Baby, Don't Look Down/ I Never Want to Dream Again	1964	2.50	5.00	10.00
❏ 2009	Goldfinger Theme/Debbie and Mitch	1965	2.50	5.00	10.00
ODE					
❏ 120	Coal Mine/Tonight I'll Be Staying Here with You	1968	2.00	4.00	8.00

Albums
BUENA VISTA

❏ BV-3315 [M]	Billy Storm	1963	25.00	50.00	100.00
❏ STER-3315 [S]	Billy Storm	1963	30.00	60.00	120.00
FAMOUS					
❏ F-504	This Is the Night	1969	25.00	50.00	100.00

STORM, GALE
45s
DOT

❏ 15412	I Hear You Knocking/Never Leave Me	1955	5.00	10.00	20.00
❏ 15436	Teen-Age Prayer/Memories Are Made of This	1955	3.75	7.50	15.00
❏ 15448	Why Do Fools Fall in Love/I Walk Alone	1956	3.75	7.50	15.00
❏ 15458	Ivory Tower/I Ain't Gonna Worry	1956	3.75	7.50	15.00
❏ 15474	Tell Me Why/Don't Be That Way	1956	3.75	7.50	15.00
❏ 15492	Now Is the Hour/A Heart Without a Sweetheart	1956	2.50	5.00	10.00
—Second pressings have black labels					
❏ 15492	Now Is the Hour/A Heart Without a Sweetheart	1956	3.75	7.50	15.00
—Originals have maroon labels					
❏ 15515	My Heart Belongs to You/Orange Blossoms	1956	2.50	5.00	10.00
❏ 15528	I Need You So/On Treasure Island	1957	2.50	5.00	10.00
❏ 15539	On Treasure Island/Lucky Lips	1957	2.50	5.00	10.00
❏ 15558	Dark Moon/A Little Too Late	1957	2.50	5.00	10.00
❏ 15606	On My Mind Again/Love by the Jukebox Light	1957	2.50	5.00	10.00
❏ 15666	Go 'Way from My Window/Winter Warm	1957	2.50	5.00	10.00
❏ 15691	A Farewell to Arms/I Get That Feeling	1958	2.50	5.00	10.00
❏ 15734	Angry/You	1958	2.50	5.00	10.00
❏ 15783	South of the Border/Soon I'll Wed My Love	1958	2.50	5.00	10.00
❏ 15861	Oh, Lonely Crowd/Happiness Left Yesterday	1958	2.50	5.00	10.00
❏ 16031	I Hear You Knocking/Ivory Tower	1960	2.00	4.00	8.00
❏ 16032	Dark Moon/Memories Are Made of This	1960	2.00	4.00	8.00
❏ 16057	On Treasure Island/I Need You So	1960	2.00	4.00	8.00
❏ 16111	Please Help Me, I'm Falling/He's There	1960	2.00	4.00	8.00

Albums
DOT

❏ DLP-3011 [M]	Gale Storm	1956	12.50	25.00	50.00
❏ DLP-3017 [M]	Sentimental Me	1956	12.50	25.00	50.00
❏ DLP-3098 [M]	Gale Storm Hits	1958	10.00	20.00	40.00
❏ DLP-3197 [M]	Softly and Tenderly	1959	7.50	15.00	30.00
❏ DLP-3209 [M]	Gale Storm Sings	1959	7.50	15.00	30.00
❏ DLP-25197 [S]	Softly and Tenderly	1959	10.00	20.00	40.00
❏ DLP-25209 [S]	Gale Storm Sings	1959	10.00	20.00	40.00
HAMILTON					
❏ HLP-171 [M]	I Don't Want to Walk	1966	3.00	6.00	12.00
❏ HLP-12171 [S]	I Don't Want to Walk	1966	3.75	7.50	15.00
MCA					
❏ 1504	Gale Storm	198?	2.50	5.00	10.00

STORM, RORY, AND THE HURRICANES The group that Ringo Starr drummed for before joining the Beatles. He is not on this record.
45s
COLUMBIA

❏ 43018	I Can Tell/Let's Stomp	1964	6.25	12.50	25.00
—B-side by Faron's Flamingos					

Number	Title (A Side/B Side)	Yr	VG	VG+	NM

STORM, TOM, AND THE PEPS
45s
GE GE
❏ 501	I Love You/That's the Way Love Is	1965	7.50	15.00	30.00

STORME, ROBB
45s
AURORA
❏ 162	Here Today/Don't Cry	1966	3.00	6.00	12.00
CAPITOL
❏ 5452	Love Is Strange/Shy Guy	1965	2.50	5.00	10.00

STORMS, THE   Also see JODY REYNOLDS.
45s
SUNDOWN
❏ 114	Thunder/Tarantula	1959	12.50	25.00	50.00
—This was re-recorded on Indigo 127

STORYTELLERS, THE
45s
CAPITOL
❏ 5042	I Don't Want an Angel/Down in the Valley	1964	6.25	12.50	25.00
CLASSIC ARTISTS
❏ 137	Christmas Time Is Coming/White Christmas	1990	—	2.50	5.00
—B-side by The Storytellers and Vicky Tafoya
DIMENSION
❏ 1014	When Two People/Time Will Tell	1963	5.00	10.00	20.00
RAMARCA
❏ 501	When Two People/Time Will Tell	1963	7.50	15.00	30.00
STACK
❏ 500	Hey Baby/You Played Me for a Fool	1959	50.00	100.00	200.00

STOWAWAYS, THE
Albums
JUSTICE
❏ JLP-148	The Stowaways	1968	125.00	250.00	500.00

STRANGE, BILLY
45s
BUENA VISTA
❏ 406	I'll Remember April/The Mooncussors	1962	2.50	5.00	10.00
❏ 417	Johnny Shiloh/Day by Day	1963	2.50	5.00	10.00
COLISEUM
❏ 605	A Lotta Limbo (Part 1)/A Lotta Limbo (Part 2)	1963	3.00	6.00	12.00
GNP CRESCENDO
❏ 308	Wildwood Flower/Wabash Cannonball	1964	2.00	4.00	8.00
❏ 309	Charade/Where's Baby Gone	1964	2.00	4.00	8.00
❏ 320	The James Bond Theme/007 Theme	1964	2.00	4.00	8.00
❏ 334	Goldfinger/(Theme from) The Munsters	1965	2.00	4.00	8.00
❏ 341	The Man with the Golden Arm/Raunchy	1965	2.00	4.00	8.00
❏ 360	Remember Me (I'm the One Who Loves You)/Trains and Boats and Planes	1965	2.00	4.00	8.00
❏ 367	Our Man Flint/Run, Spy, Run	1966	2.00	4.00	8.00
❏ 374	Caliente/Have Tequila	1966	2.00	4.00	8.00
❏ 390	Go Ahead and Cry/Yours Is a World I Can't Live In	1967	—	3.00	6.00
❏ 395	You Only Live Twice/For a Few Dollars More	1967	—	3.00	6.00
❏ 413	Hang 'Em High/Five Card Stud	1968	—	3.00	6.00
❏ 417	The High Chaparral/Gunsmoke	1968	—	3.00	6.00
❏ 477	Chattanooga Choo Choo/Track Walkin'	1974	—	2.00	4.00
❏ 800	Star Trek/Theme from "Jaws"	1975	—	2.50	5.00
LIBERTY
❏ 55362	Long Steel Road/Soft Chains of Love	1961	2.50	5.00	10.00
❏ 55414	A Life of Pretend/I'm Still Crying	1962	2.50	5.00	10.00
TOWER
❏ 515	De Sade/Nocturne Permission	1969	2.00	4.00	8.00
Albums
CHESS
❏ CH2-6027 [(2)]	One More Time	1988	3.00	6.00	12.00
COLISEUM
❏ CM-1001 [M]	Limbo Rock	1962	10.00	20.00	40.00
GNP CRESCENDO
❏ GNP-94 [M]	Twelve String Guitar	1963	3.00	6.00	12.00
❏ GNPS-94 [S]	Twelve String Guitar	1963	3.75	7.50	15.00
❏ GNP-97 [M]	Mr. Guitar	1963	3.00	6.00	12.00
❏ GNPS-97 [S]	Mr. Guitar	1963	3.75	7.50	15.00
❏ GNP-98 [M]	Five String Banjo	1964	3.00	6.00	12.00
❏ GNPS-98 [S]	Five String Banjo	1964	3.75	7.50	15.00
❏ GNP-2004 [M]	The James Bond Theme	1964	3.00	6.00	12.00
❏ GNPS-2004 [S]	The James Bond Theme	1964	3.75	7.50	15.00
❏ GNP-2006 [M]	Goldfinger	1965	3.00	6.00	12.00
❏ GNPS-2006 [S]	Goldfinger	1965	3.75	7.50	15.00
❏ GNP-2009 [M]	English Hits of '65	1965	3.00	6.00	12.00
❏ GNPS-2009 [S]	English Hits of '65	1965	3.75	7.50	15.00
❏ GNP-2012 [M]	Billy Strange Plays the Hits	1965	3.00	6.00	12.00
❏ GNPS-2012 [S]	Billy Strange Plays the Hits	1965	3.75	7.50	15.00
❏ GNP-2016 [M]	Folk Rock Hits	1965	3.00	6.00	12.00
❏ GNPS-2016 [S]	Folk Rock Hits	1965	3.75	7.50	15.00
❏ GNP-2019 [M]	Secret Agent File	1966	3.00	6.00	12.00
❏ GNPS-2019 [S]	Secret Agent File	1966	3.75	7.50	15.00
❏ GNP-2022 [M]	In the Mexican Bag	1966	3.00	6.00	12.00
❏ GNPS-2022 [S]	In the Mexican Bag	1966	3.75	7.50	15.00
❏ GNP-2024 [M]	Billy Strange Plays Roger Miller Hits	1966	3.00	6.00	12.00
❏ GNPS-2024 [S]	Billy Strange Plays Roger Miller Hits	1966	3.75	7.50	15.00
❏ GNP-2030 [M]	Billy Strange with the Challengers	1966	3.75	7.50	15.00
❏ GNPS-2030 [S]	Billy Strange with the Challengers	1966	5.00	10.00	20.00
❏ GNP-2037 [M]	The Best of Billy Strange	1967	3.00	6.00	12.00
❏ GNPS-2037 [S]	The Best of Billy Strange	1967	3.00	6.00	12.00
❏ GNPS-2039	A James Bond Double Feature	1967	3.00	6.00	12.00
❏ GNPS-2041	Railroad Man	1968	3.00	6.00	12.00
❏ GNPS-2046	Great Western Themes	1969	3.00	6.00	12.00
❏ GNPS-2094	Dyn-o-mite Guitar	197?	2.50	5.00	10.00
SUNSET
❏ SUS-5209	Mr. Guitar	1968	2.50	5.00	10.00
SURREY
❏ SS-1002	The Best of Billy Strange	1965	3.75	7.50	15.00
TRADITION
❏ 2080	Strange Country	1969	2.50	5.00	10.00

STRANGE, TOMMY
45s
ERA
❏ 3157	Don't Bug Me Baby/Two Steps Forward	1965	2.00	4.00	8.00
RAMCO
❏ 1986	Piano Man from Louisiana/My Mind Just Don't Fit My Head	1967	2.00	4.00	8.00
❏ 1995	She Was Never Mine to Lose/One More Time	1967	2.00	4.00	8.00
ROCKO
❏ 504	Nervous and Shakin' All Over/What Am I to Do	1958	50.00	100.00	200.00

STRANGEBREW
45s
ABC
❏ 11217	Union Man/I Can Hardly Wait to Live	1969	3.00	6.00	12.00
Albums
ABC
❏ ABCS-672	Very Strangebrew	1969	5.00	10.00	20.00

STRANGELOVES, THE   Also see THE SHEEP.
45s
BANG
❏ 501	I Want Candy/It's About My Baby	1965	3.75	7.50	15.00
❏ 508	Cara-Lin/(Roll On) Mississippi	1965	3.00	6.00	12.00
❏ 514	Night Time/Rhythm of Love	1965	3.00	6.00	12.00
❏ 524	Hand Jive/I Gotta Dance	1966	3.00	6.00	12.00
❏ 544	Just the Way You Are/Quarter to Three	1967	3.00	6.00	12.00
SIRE
❏ 4102	I Wanna Do It/Honey Do	1968	2.50	5.00	10.00
SWAN
❏ 4192	Love Love (That's All I Want from You)/I'm on Fire	1964	5.00	10.00	20.00
Albums
BANG
❏ BLP-211 [M]	I Want Candy	1965	20.00	40.00	80.00
❏ BLPS-211 [S]	I Want Candy	1965	25.00	50.00	100.00

STRANGERS, THE
45s
CAPITOL
❏ 3144	Song from Sleepwalk/Slow 'n Easy	1971	2.00	4.00	8.00
—By "Merle Haggard's Strangers"
❏ 3376	I'm a Light Boy/Shoulder to Cry On	1972	2.50	5.00	10.00

STRANGERS, THE (1)   Instrumental group; the only Strangers that made the charts.
45s
TITAN
❏ 1701	The Caterpillar Crawl/Rockin' Rebel	1959	7.50	15.00	30.00
❏ 1702	Hill Stomp/A Lost Soul	1959	6.25	12.50	25.00
❏ 1704	Boogie Man/Young Maggie	1960	6.25	12.50	25.00
❏ 1711	Navajo/Dance of the Ants	1960	6.25	12.50	25.00

STRANGERS, THE (2)
45s
CHATTAHOOCHIE
❏ 710	Like a Stranger/Can't Get the Water from My Eye	1966	3.00	6.00	12.00
JUBILEE
❏ 5514	Plan On Someone New/What's the Matter Baby	1965	3.00	6.00	12.00

STRANGERS, THE (3)
45s
CHECKER
❏ 1010	Darlin'/Pa and Billie	1962	3.75	7.50	15.00

STRANGERS, THE (4)
45s
CHOICE
❏ 5	"Bart" Maverick/"Bret" Maverick	1960	5.00	10.00	20.00

STRANGERS, THE (5)
45s
CHRISTY
❏ 107	We're in Love, We're in Love, We're in Love/Crab Louie	1959	7.50	15.00	30.00
❏ 108	J-U-D-Y/The Lord Will Welcome You	1959	6.25	12.50	25.00

STRANGERS, THE (6)   Group that backed BOBBY VEE on some of his later records, most notably "Come Back When You Grow Up."
45s
CUCA
❏ 1172	Runaway/John Henry	1960	50.00	100.00	200.00
LIBERTY
❏ 55481	Toy Soldier/Loco	1962	5.00	10.00	20.00
❏ 55550	Card Shark/Mindreader	1963	5.00	10.00	20.00

STRANGERS, THE (7)
45s
KING
❏ 4697	My Friends/I've Got Eyes	1954	100.00	200.00	400.00
❏ 4709	Blue Flowers/Beg and Steal	1954	125.00	250.00	500.00
❏ 4728	Hoping You'll Understand/Just Don't Care	1954	100.00	200.00	400.00
❏ 4745	Drop Down to My Place/Get It One More Time	1954	75.00	150.00	300.00
❏ 4766	How Long Must I Wait/Dreams Came True	1955	62.50	125.00	250.00
❏ 4821	Without a Friend/Think Again	1955	15.00	30.00	60.00
—With "High Fidelity" on label
❏ 4821	Without a Friend/Think Again	1955	62.50	125.00	250.00
—Without "High Fidelity" on label (original)

STRANGERS, THE (8)
45s
LINDA
❏ 118	Easy Livin'/Tell Me	1965	7.50	15.00	30.00
WARNER BROS.
❏ 5438	Night Winds/These Are the Things I Love	1964	5.00	10.00	20.00

S

Number	Title (A Side/B Side)	Yr	VG	VG+	NM

STRANGERS, THE (9)
45s
MGM
| ❑ 11980 | Strange Lady in Town/North Dakota | 1955 | 10.00 | 20.00 | 40.00 |

STRASSMAN, MARCIA
45s
UNI
❑ 55006	The Flower Children/Out of the Picture	1967	2.50	5.00	10.00
❑ 55023	The Groovy World of Jack and Jill/ The Flower Shop	1967	2.50	5.00	10.00
❑ 55023 [PS]	The Groovy World of Jack and Jill/ The Flower Shop	1967	3.75	7.50	15.00
❑ 55056	Star Gazer/Self-Analysis	1968	2.50	5.00	10.00

STRAWBERRY ALARM CLOCK
45s
ALL AMERICAN
| ❑ 373 | Incense and Peppermints/
The Birdman of Alcatrash | 1967 | 50.00 | 100.00 | 200.00 |
UNI
❑ 55018	Incense and Peppermints/ The Birdman of Alcatrash	1967	3.00	6.00	12.00
❑ 55046	Tomorrow/Birds in My Tree	1967	2.50	5.00	10.00
❑ 55055	Pretty Song from Psych-Out/Sit with the Guru	1968	2.50	5.00	10.00
❑ 55076	Barefoot in Baltimore/Angry Young Man	1968	2.50	5.00	10.00
❑ 55093	Paxton's Back Street Carnival/Sea Shell	1968	2.50	5.00	10.00
❑ 55113	Stand By/Miss Attraction	1969	2.00	4.00	8.00
❑ 55125	Good Morning Starshine/Me and the Township	1969	2.00	4.00	8.00
❑ 55158	Desiree/Changes	1969	2.00	4.00	8.00
❑ 55185	Small Package/Starting Out the Day	1969	2.00	4.00	8.00
❑ 55190	I Climbed the Mountain/Three	1969	2.00	4.00	8.00
❑ 55218	California Day/Three	1970	5.00	10.00	20.00
❑ 55241	Girl from the City/Three	1970	5.00	10.00	20.00
Albums
UNI
❑ 3014 [M]	Incense and Peppermints	1967	12.50	25.00	50.00
❑ 73014 [S]	Incense and Peppermints	1967	10.00	20.00	40.00
❑ 73025	Wake Up It's Tomorrow	1968	10.00	20.00	40.00
❑ 73035	The World in a Sea Shell	1968	10.00	20.00	40.00
❑ 73054	Good Morning Starshine	1969	10.00	20.00	40.00
❑ 73074	The Best of the Strawberry Alarm Clock	1970	10.00	20.00	40.00
VOCALION
❑ VL 73915	Changes	1971	12.50	25.00	50.00

STRAWBS, THE
45s
A&M
❑ 944	Oh How She Changed/Or Am I Dreaming	1968	—	2.50	5.00
❑ 998	Poor Jimmy Wilson/The Man Who Called Himself Jesus	1968	—	2.50	5.00
❑ 1242 [DJ]	Where Is This Dream of Your Youth (mono/ stereo)	1971	—	3.00	6.00
—No stock copies known
❑ 1364	Heavy Disguise/Benedictus	1972	—	2.50	5.00
❑ 1419	Part of the Union/Tomorrow	1973	—	2.50	5.00
❑ 1451	Lay Down/The Winter and the Summer	1973	—	2.50	5.00
❑ 1476	Shine On Silver Sun/And Wherefore	1973	—	2.50	5.00
❑ 1519	Round and Round/The Heroine's Theme	1974	—	2.50	5.00
❑ 1687	Where Do You Go/Lemon Pie	1975	—	2.00	4.00
❑ 1747	Little Sleepy/Golden Salamander	1975	—	2.00	4.00
ARISTA
❑ 0327	I Don't Want to Talk About It/Words of Wisdom	1978	—	2.00	4.00
OYSTER
❑ 702	I Only Want My Love to Grow on You/(Wasting My Time) Thinking of You	1976	—	2.00	4.00
❑ 704	So Close and Yet So Far Away/ (B-side unknown)	1977	—	2.00	4.00
❑ 705	Burning for Me/Heartbreaker	1977	—	2.00	4.00
Albums
A&M
❑ SP-3607	Hero and Heroine	1974	3.75	7.50	15.00
❑ SP-4288	Just a Collection of Antiques and Curios	1971	3.75	7.50	15.00
❑ SP-4304	From the Witchwood	1971	3.75	7.50	15.00
❑ SP-4344	Grave New World	1972	3.75	7.50	15.00
❑ SP-4383	Bursting at the Seams	1973	3.75	7.50	15.00
❑ SP-4506	Ghosts	1975	3.75	7.50	15.00
❑ SP-4544	Nomadness	1975	3.75	7.50	15.00
❑ SP-6005 [(2)]	Best of the Strawbs	1978	3.00	6.00	12.00
ARISTA
❑ AB 4172	Deadlines	1978	2.50	5.00	10.00
OYSTER
❑ OY-1603	Deep Cuts	1976	3.00	6.00	12.00
❑ OY-1604	Burning for You	1977	3.00	6.00	12.00

STREAMERS, THE
45s
DOT
| ❑ 16648 | Slip-Stream/Blue Mountain | 1964 | 7.50 | 15.00 | 30.00 |

STREET CLEANERS, THE Yet another incarnation of P.F. SLOAN and STEVE BARRI.
45s
AMY
| ❑ 914 | Garbage City/That's Cool, That's Trash | 1964 | 7.50 | 15.00 | 30.00 |

STREET CORNERS, THE
45s
PARKWAY
| ❑ 997 | My Generation/I Don't Care | 1966 | 2.50 | 5.00 | 10.00 |

STREET NOISE
45s
EVOLUTION
| ❑ 1014 | Run or Die/Six Days on the Road | 1969 | 2.00 | 4.00 | 8.00 |
Albums
EVOLUTION
| ❑ 2010 | Street Noise | 1970 | 5.00 | 10.00 | 20.00 |

STREISAND, BARBRA Also see BARBRA AND NEIL.
12-Inch Singles
CASABLANCA
| ❑ NBD 20199 | No More Tears (Enough Is Enough) (11:40)/
(B-side blank) | 1979 | 2.50 | 5.00 | 10.00 |
—With Donna Summer
COLUMBIA
❑ AS 217 [DJ]	Shake Me, Wake Me, When It's Over (same on both sides)	1975	25.00	50.00	100.00
❑ AS 625 [DJ]	The Main Event/Fight (11:42) (same on both sides)	1979	6.25	12.50	25.00
❑ AS 1610 [DJ]	Memory (same on both sides)	1981	10.00	20.00	40.00
❑ AS99 1791 [DJ]	The Way He Makes Me Feel (same on both sides?)	1983	12.50	25.00	50.00
—Promo-only picture disc in plastic sleeve with sticker
| ❑ 43-02089 | Promises (5:55)/Make It Like a Memory | 1981 | 6.25 | 12.50 | 25.00 |
| ❑ 44-05167 | Emotion (Vocal Dance Version 6:34)
(Instrumental 4:44) | 1985 | 5.00 | 10.00 | 20.00 |
45s
ARISTA
| ❑ 0123 | How Lucky Can You Get/More Than You Know | 1975 | — | 3.00 | 6.00 |
COLUMBIA
❑ 11-02065	Promises/Make It Like a Memory	1981	—	2.00	4.00
❑ 18-02621	Comin' In and Out of Your Life/Lost Inside of You	1981	—	2.00	4.00
❑ 18-02717	Memory/Evergreen (Love Theme from "A Star Is Born")	1982	—	2.00	4.00
❑ 38-04177	The Way He Makes Me Feel (Studio)/(Film Version)	1983	—	—	3.00
❑ 38-04177 [PS]	The Way He Makes Me Feel (Studio)/(Film Version)	1983	—	2.00	4.00
❑ 38-04357	Papa Can You Hear Me?/ Will Someone Ever Look at Me That Way	1984	—	—	3.00
❑ 38-04357 [PS]	Papa Can You Hear Me?/ Will Someone Ever Look at Me That Way	1984	—	2.00	4.00
❑ 38-04605	Left in the Dark/Here We Are at Last	1984	—	—	3.00
❑ 38-04605 [PS]	Left in the Dark/Here We Are at Last	1984	—	2.00	4.00
❑ 38-04695	Make No Mistake, He's Mine/Clear Sailing	1984	—	—	3.00
—A-side with Kim Carnes
❑ 38-04695 [PS]	Make No Mistake, He's Mine/Clear Sailing	1984	—	2.00	4.00
❑ 38-04707	Emotion/Here We Are at Last	1984	—	—	3.00
❑ 38-04707 [PS]	Emotion/Here We Are at Last	1984	—	2.00	4.00
❑ 38-05680	Somewhere/Not While I'm Around	1985	—	—	3.00
❑ 38-05680 [PS]	Somewhere/Not While I'm Around	1985	—	2.00	4.00
❑ 38-05837	Send In the Clowns/Being Alive	1986	—	2.00	4.00
❑ 38-05837 [PS]	Send In the Clowns/Being Alive	1986	2.00	4.00	8.00
❑ 38-08026	All I Ask of You/On My Way to You	1988	—	2.00	4.00
❑ 38-08026 [PS]	All I Ask of You/On My Way to You	1988	—	2.00	4.00
❑ 38-08062	Till I Loved You/Two People	1988	—	—	3.00
—A-side with Don Johnson
❑ 38-08062 [PS]	Till I Loved You/Two People	1988	—	2.00	4.00
❑ 10075	Love in the Afternoon/Guava Jelly	1974	—	2.50	5.00
❑ 10130	Let the Good Times Roll/Jubilation	1975	—	2.50	5.00
❑ 10198	My Father's Song/By the Way	1975	—	2.50	5.00
❑ 10272	Shake Me, Wake Me, When It's Over/ Widescreen	1975	—	2.50	5.00
❑ 3-10450	Love Theme from "A Star Is Born" (Evergreen)/ I Believe in Love	1976	—	2.50	5.00
❑ 3-10450 [PS]	Love Theme from "A Star Is Born" (Evergreen)/ I Believe in Love	1976	—	3.00	6.00
❑ 3-10555	My Heart Belongs to Me/Answer Me	1977	—	2.50	5.00
❑ 3-10756	Songbird/Honey Can I Put On Your Clothes	1978	—	2.00	4.00
❑ 3-10777	Love Theme from "Eyes of Laura Mars" (Prisoner)/Laura and Nevil	1978	—	2.00	4.00
❑ 3-10931	Superman/A Man I Loved	1979	—	2.00	4.00
❑ 3-11008	The Main Event/Fight//(Instrumental)	1979	—	2.00	4.00
❑ 1-11125	No More Tears (Enough Is Enough)/Wet	1979	—	2.00	4.00
—A-side with Donna Summer
❑ 1-11125 [PS]	No More Tears (Enough Is Enough)/Wet	1979	—	2.50	5.00
❑ 1-11179	Kiss Me in the Rain/I Ain't Gonna Cry Tonight	1980	—	2.00	4.00
❑ 1-11364	Woman in Love/Run Wild	1980	—	2.00	4.00
❑ 11-11390	Guilty/Life Story	1980	—	2.00	4.00
—A-side with Barry Gibb
| ❑ 11-11430 | What Kind of Fool/The Love Inside | 1981 | — | 2.00 | 4.00 |
—A-side with Barry Gibb
❑ 42631	Happy Days Are Here Again/ When the Sun Comes Out	1962	5.00	10.00	20.00
❑ 42648	My Coloring Book/Lover Come Back to Me	1962	3.75	7.50	15.00
❑ 42937	Gotta Move/Make Believe	1964	3.75	7.50	15.00
❑ 42965	People/I Am Woman	1964	2.50	5.00	10.00
❑ 43127	Funny Girl/Absent Minded Me	1964	2.50	5.00	10.00
❑ 43248	Why Did I Choose You/My Love	1965	2.00	4.00	8.00
❑ 43323	My Man/Where Is the Wonder	1965	2.00	4.00	8.00
❑ 43403	He Touched Me/I Like Him	1965	2.00	4.00	8.00
❑ 43469	Second Hand Rose/ The Kind of Man a Woman Needs	1965	2.00	4.00	8.00
❑ 43518	Where Am I Going?/You Wanna Bet	1966	—	3.00	6.00
❑ 43612	Sam, You Made the Pants Too Long/ The Minute Waltz	1966	—	3.00	6.00
❑ 43739	La Mer/C'est Rien	1966	2.00	4.00	8.00
❑ 43808	Free Again/I've Been Here	1966	—	3.00	6.00
❑ 43896	Sleep in Heavenly Peace (Silent Night)/ Gounod's Ave Maria	1966	2.50	5.00	10.00
❑ 43896 [PS]	Sleep in Heavenly Peace (Silent Night)/ Gounod's Ave Maria	1966	5.00	10.00	20.00
❑ 44225	Stout-Hearted Men/Look	1967	—	3.00	6.00
❑ 44331	Lover Man (Oh, Where Can You Be)/ My Funny Valentine	1967	—	3.00	6.00
❑ 44350	Jingle Bells?/White Christmas	1967	7.50	15.00	30.00
❑ 44350 [PS]	Jingle Bells?/White Christmas	1967	10.00	20.00	40.00
❑ 44351	Have Yourself a Merry Little Christmas/ The Best Gift	1967	2.50	5.00	10.00
❑ 44351 [PS]	Have Yourself a Merry Little Christmas/ The Best Gift	1967	5.00	10.00	20.00
❑ 44352	My Favorite Things/The Christmas Song	1967	7.50	15.00	30.00
❑ 44352 [PS]	My Favorite Things/The Christmas Song	1967	10.00	20.00	40.00
❑ 44354	I Wonder As I Wander/The Lord's Prayer	1967	7.50	15.00	30.00
❑ 44476	Our Corner of the Night/He Could Show Me	1968	—	2.50	5.00

Number	Title (A Side/B Side)	Yr	VG	VG+	NM
❏ 44532	Morning After/Where Is the Wonder	1968	—	2.50	5.00
❏ 44622	Funny Girl/I'd Rather Be Blue Over You	1968	—	2.50	5.00
❏ 44704	Don't Rain on My Parade/My Man	1968	—	3.00	6.00
❏ 44775	Punky's Dilemma/Frank Mills	1969	—	2.50	5.00
❏ 44921	Honey Pie/Little Tin Soldier	1969	—	2.50	5.00
❏ 45040	What About Today/What Are You Doing the Rest of Your Life	1969	—	2.50	5.00
❏ 45072	Love Is Only Love/Before the Parade Passes By	1970	—	2.50	5.00
❏ 45147	The Best Thing You've Ever Done/Summer Me, Winter Me	1970	—	2.50	5.00
❏ 45236	Stoney End/I'll Be Home	1970	—	2.50	5.00
❏ 45341	Time and Love/No Easy Way Down	1971	—	2.50	5.00
❏ 45384	Flim Flam Man/Maybe	1971	—	2.50	5.00
❏ 45414	Where You Lead/Since I Fell for You	1971	—	2.50	5.00
❏ 45471	Mother/The Summer Knows	1971	—	2.50	5.00
❏ 45511	One Less Bell to Answer-A House Is Not a Home/Space Captain	1971	—	2.50	5.00
❏ 45626	Sweet Inspiration-Where You Lead/Didn't We	1972	—	2.50	5.00
❏ 45686	Sing a Song-Make Your Own Kind of Music/ Starting Here-Starting Now	1972	—	2.50	5.00
❏ 45739	Didn't We/On a Clear Day	1972	—	2.50	5.00
❏ 45780	If I Close My Eyes/(Instrumental)	1973	—	2.50	5.00
❏ 45944	The Way We Were/What Are You Doing the Rest of Your Life	1973	—	2.50	5.00
—A-side contains a different vocal than most of the album versions					
❏ 46024	All in Love Is Fair/My Buddy-How About Me	1974	—	2.50	5.00
❏ 68691	What Were We Thinking Of/Why Let It Go	1989	—	—	3.00
❏ 73016	We're Not Makin' Love Anymore/Here We Are at Last	1989	—	—	3.00
❏ 73794	Till I Loved You/Two People	1991	—	—	3.00
—Reissue					
❏ 38-73944	All I Ask of You/On My Way to You	1991	—	—	3.00
—Reissue					
❏ 38-77533	Ordinary Miracles/(Live)	1994	—	2.00	4.00
❏ JZSP 79183/4 [DJ]	I'm All Smiles/Autumn	1964	7.50	15.00	30.00
—White label promo only					

7-Inch Extended Plays

COLUMBIA MASTERWORKS
Number	Title (A Side/B Side)	Yr	VG	VG+	NM
❏ 7-3220	Funny Girl/My Man/People//Roller Skate Rag/I'd Rather Be Blue Over You/Don't Rain on My Parade	1964	3.75	7.50	15.00
—Jukebox issue; small hole, plays at 33 1/3 rpm					
❏ 7-3220 [PS]	Funny Girl	1964	3.75	7.50	15.00

Albums

COLUMBIA
Number	Title (A Side/B Side)	Yr	VG	VG+	NM
❏ A2S 1779 [(2)DJ]	The Legend of Barbra Streisand	1983	20.00	40.00	80.00
—Promo-only interview LP for "Yentl"					
❏ CL 2007 [M]	The Barbra Streisand Album	1963	5.00	10.00	20.00
—"Guaranteed High Fidelity" on label					
❏ CL 2007 [M]	The Barbra Streisand Album	1966	3.00	6.00	12.00
—"360 Sound Mono" on label					
❏ CL 2054 [M]	The Second Barbra Streisand Album	1963	5.00	10.00	20.00
—"Guaranteed High Fidelity" on label					
❏ CL 2054 [M]	The Second Barbra Streisand Album	1963	50.00	100.00	200.00
—Promo only on blue vinyl (white label)					
❏ CL 2054 [M]	The Second Barbra Streisand Album	1966	3.00	6.00	12.00
—"360 Sound Mono" on label					
❏ CL 2154 [M]	The Third Album	1964	5.00	10.00	20.00
—"Guaranteed High Fidelity" on label					
❏ CL 2154 [M]	The Third Album	1966	3.00	6.00	12.00
—"360 Sound Mono" on label					
❏ CL 2215 [M]	People	1964	5.00	10.00	20.00
—"Guaranteed High Fidelity" on label					
❏ CL 2215 [M]	People	1966	3.00	6.00	12.00
—"360 Sound Mono" on label					
❏ CL 2336 [M]	My Name Is Barbra	1965	5.00	10.00	20.00
—"Guaranteed High Fidelity" on label					
❏ CL 2336 [M]	My Name Is Barbra	1966	3.00	6.00	12.00
—"360 Sound Mono" on label					
❏ CL 2409 [M]	My Name Is Barbra, Two	1965	3.75	7.50	15.00
❏ CL 2478 [M]	Color Me Barbra	1966	3.75	7.50	15.00
❏ CL 2478 [M]	Color Me Barbra	1966	50.00	100.00	200.00
—Promo only on red vinyl (white label)					
❏ CL 2547 [M]	Je M'Appelle Barbra	1966	3.75	7.50	15.00
❏ CL 2682 [M]	Simply Streisand	1967	7.50	15.00	30.00
❏ CL 2757 [M]	A Christmas Album	1967	6.25	12.50	25.00
❏ CS 8807 [S]	The Barbra Streisand Album	1963	6.25	12.50	25.00
—"360 Sound Stereo" in black on label					
❏ CS 8807 [S]	The Barbra Streisand Album	1966	3.75	7.50	15.00
—"360 Sound Stereo" in white on label					
❏ CS 8807 [S]	The Barbra Streisand Album	1970	2.50	5.00	10.00
—Orange label					
❏ PC 8807	The Barbra Streisand Album	197?	2.00	4.00	8.00
—Reissue with new prefix					
❏ CS 8854 [S]	The Second Barbra Streisand Album	1963	6.25	12.50	25.00
—"360 Sound Stereo" in black on label					
❏ CS 8854 [S]	The Second Barbra Streisand Album	1963	50.00	100.00	200.00
—Promo only on blue vinyl (white label)					
❏ CS 8854 [S]	The Second Barbra Streisand Album	1966	3.75	7.50	15.00
—"360 Sound Stereo" in white on label					
❏ CS 8854 [S]	The Second Barbra Streisand Album	1970	2.50	5.00	10.00
—Orange label					
❏ PC 8854	The Second Barbra Streisand Album	197?	2.00	4.00	8.00
—Reissue with new prefix					
❏ CS 8954 [S]	The Third Album	1964	6.25	12.50	25.00
—"360 Sound Stereo" in black on label					
❏ CS 8954 [S]	The Third Album	1966	3.75	7.50	15.00
—"360 Sound Stereo" in white on label					
❏ CS 8954 [S]	The Third Album	1970	2.50	5.00	10.00
—Orange label					
❏ PC 8954	The Third Album	197?	2.00	4.00	8.00
—Reissue with new prefix					
❏ CS 9015 [S]	People	1964	6.25	12.50	25.00
—"360 Sound Stereo" in black on label					
❏ CS 9015 [S]	People	1966	3.75	7.50	15.00
—"360 Sound Stereo" in white on label					

Number	Title (A Side/B Side)	Yr	VG	VG+	NM
❏ CS 9015 [S]	People	1970	2.50	5.00	10.00
—Orange label					
❏ PC 9015	People	197?	2.00	4.00	8.00
—Reissue with new prefix					
❏ CS 9136 [S]	My Name Is Barbra	1965	6.25	12.50	25.00
—"360 Sound Stereo" in black on label					
❏ CS 9136 [S]	My Name Is Barbra	1966	3.75	7.50	15.00
—"360 Sound Stereo" in white on label					
❏ CS 9136 [S]	My Name Is Barbra	1970	2.50	5.00	10.00
—Orange label					
❏ PC 9136	My Name Is Barbra	197?	2.00	4.00	8.00
—Reissue with new prefix					
❏ CS 9209 [S]	My Name Is Barbra, Two	1965	5.00	10.00	20.00
—Red "360 Sound Stereo" label					
❏ CS 9209 [S]	My Name Is Barbra, Two	1970	2.50	5.00	10.00
—Orange label					
❏ PC 9209	My Name Is Barbra, Two	197?	2.00	4.00	8.00
—Reissue with new prefix					
❏ CS 9278 [S]	Color Me Barbra	1966	5.00	10.00	20.00
—Red "360 Sound Stereo" label					
❏ CS 9278 [S]	Color Me Barbra	1966	50.00	100.00	200.00
—Promo only on red vinyl (white label)					
❏ CS 9278 [S]	Color Me Barbra	1970	2.50	5.00	10.00
—Orange label					
❏ PC 9278	Color Me Barbra	197?	2.00	4.00	8.00
—Reissue with new prefix					
❏ CS 9347 [S]	Je M'Appelle Barbra	1966	5.00	10.00	20.00
—Red "360 Sound Stereo" label					
❏ CS 9347 [S]	Je M'Appelle Barbra	1970	2.50	5.00	10.00
—Orange label					
❏ PC 9347	Je M'Appelle Barbra	197?	2.00	4.00	8.00
—Reissue with new prefix					
❏ CS 9482 [S]	Simply Streisand	1967	5.00	10.00	20.00
—Red "360 Sound Stereo" label					
❏ CS 9482 [S]	Simply Streisand	1970	2.50	5.00	10.00
—Orange label					
❏ PC 9482	Simply Streisand	197?	2.00	4.00	8.00
—Reissue with new prefix					
❏ CS 9557 [S]	A Christmas Album	1967	5.00	10.00	20.00
—Red "360 Sound Stereo" label					
❏ CS 9557 [S]	A Christmas Album	1970	2.00	4.00	8.00
—Orange label					
❏ PC 9557	A Christmas Album	198?	—	3.00	6.00
—Reissue with new prefix and bar code					
❏ CS 9710	A Happening in Central Park	1968	3.75	7.50	15.00
—Red "360 Sound Stereo" label					
❏ CS 9710	A Happening in Central Park	1970	2.50	5.00	10.00
—Orange label					
❏ PC 9710	A Happening in Central Park	197?	2.00	4.00	8.00
—Reissue with new prefix					
❏ CS 9816	What About Today?	1969	3.75	7.50	15.00
—Red "360 Sound Stereo" label					
❏ CS 9816	What About Today?	1970	2.50	5.00	10.00
—Orange label					
❏ PC 9816	What About Today?	197?	2.00	4.00	8.00
—Reissue with new prefix					
❏ JC 9968	Barbra Streisand's Greatest Hits	197?	—	3.00	6.00
—Another reissue with a new prefix (postdates PC)					
❏ KCS 9968	Barbra Streisand's Greatest Hits	1970	2.50	5.00	10.00
—Orange label					
❏ KCS 9968	Barbra Streisand's Greatest Hits	1970	3.75	7.50	15.00
—Red "360 Sound Stereo" label					
❏ PC 9968	Barbra Streisand's Greatest Hits	197?	2.00	4.00	8.00
—Reissue with new prefix					
❏ CQ 30378 [Q]	Stoney End	1972	6.25	12.50	25.00
❏ KC 30378	Stoney End	1971	3.75	7.50	15.00
❏ PC 30378	Stoney End	197?	2.00	4.00	8.00
—Reissue with new prefix					
❏ CQ 30792 [Q]	Barbra Joan Streisand	1972	6.25	12.50	25.00
❏ KC 30792	Barbra Joan Streisand	1971	3.75	7.50	15.00
❏ PC 30792	Barbra Joan Streisand	197?	2.00	4.00	8.00
—Reissue with new prefix					
❏ CQ 31760 [Q]	Live Concert at the Forum	1972	6.25	12.50	25.00
❏ KC 31760	Live Concert at the Forum	1972	3.75	7.50	15.00
❏ PC 31760	Live Concert at the Forum	197?	2.00	4.00	8.00
—Reissue with new prefix					
❏ KC 32655	Barbra Streisand…And Other Musical Instruments	1973	3.00	6.00	12.00
❏ PC 32655	Barbra Streisand…And Other Musical Instruments	197?	2.00	4.00	8.00
—Reissue with new prefix					
❏ JC 32801	The Way We Were	197?	2.00	4.00	8.00
—Reissue with new prefix					
❏ PC 32801	The Way We Were	1974	3.00	6.00	12.00
—Revised version; has this title on spine, label and front cover					
❏ PC 32801	Barbra Streisand Featuring The Way We Were and All In Love Is Fair	1974	5.00	10.00	20.00
—Original version with this title on spine and label, and no title on front cover					
❏ PCQ 32801 [Q]	The Way We Were	1974	6.25	12.50	25.00
❏ PC 33095	Butterfly	1974	3.00	6.00	12.00
—Original with no bar code					
❏ PC 33095	Butterfly	198?	2.00	4.00	8.00
—Reissue with bar code					
❏ PCQ 33095 [Q]	Butterfly	1974	5.00	10.00	20.00
❏ PC 33815	Lazy Afternoon	1975	3.00	6.00	12.00
—Original with no bar code					
❏ PC 33815	Lazy Afternoon	198?	2.00	4.00	8.00
—Reissue with bar code					
❏ PCQ 33815 [Q]	Lazy Afternoon	1975	6.25	12.50	25.00
❏ JS 34403	A Star Is Born	1976	3.00	6.00	12.00
—With Kris Kristofferson					
❏ JC 34830	Streisand Superman	1977	3.00	6.00	12.00
❏ PC 34830	Streisand Superman	198?	2.00	4.00	8.00
—Budget-line reissue					
❏ PC 35275	Songbird	198?	2.00	4.00	8.00
—Budget-line reissue					
❏ JC 35375	Songbird	1978	3.00	6.00	12.00

S

Number	Title (A Side/B Side)	Yr	VG	VG+	NM
❏ FC 35679	Barbra Streisand's Greatest Hits, Volume 2	1978	3.00	6.00	12.00
❏ FC 36258	Wet	1979	2.50	5.00	10.00
❏ FC 36750	Guilty	1980	2.50	5.00	10.00
❏ TC 37678	Memories	1981	2.50	5.00	10.00
❏ JS 39152	Yentl	1983	2.50	5.00	10.00
❏ QC 39480	Emotion	1984	2.50	5.00	10.00
❏ OC 40092	The Broadway Album	1985	2.50	5.00	10.00
❏ OC 40788	One Voice	1987	2.50	5.00	10.00
❏ OC 40880	Till I Loved You	1988	2.50	5.00	10.00
❏ HC 42801	The Way We Were	1982	7.50	5.00	30.00
—Half-speed mastered edition					
❏ OC 45369	A Collection: Greatest Hits.. And More	1989	3.75	7.50	15.00
❏ HC 45679	Barbra Streisand's Greatest Hits, Volume 2	1980	7.50	15.00	30.00
—Half-speed mastered edition					
❏ HC 46750	Guilty	1982	7.50	15.00	30.00
—Half-speed mastered edition					
❏ HC 47647	Memories	1982	7.50	15.00	30.00
—Half-speed mastered edition					
COLUMBIA MASTERWORKS					
❏ M 33452	Classical Barbra	1976	3.00	6.00	12.00

STRENGTH, "TEXAS" BILL
45s
SUN

Number	Title (A Side/B Side)	Yr	VG	VG+	NM
❏ 346	Guess I'd Better Go/Senorita	1960	6.25	12.50	25.00
—As "Bill Strength"					

STRIDER
Albums
WARNER BROS.

Number	Title (A Side/B Side)	Yr	VG	VG+	NM
❏ BS 2722	Exposed	1973	5.00	10.00	20.00

STRIDERS, THE (1)
45s
APOLLO

Number	Title (A Side/B Side)	Yr	VG	VG+	NM
❏ 480	I Wonder/Hesitating Fool	1955	75.00	150.00	300.00

DERBY

Number	Title (A Side/B Side)	Yr	VG	VG+	NM
❏ 857	Come Back to Me Tomorrow/Rollin'	1954	50.00	100.00	200.00

STRIDERS, THE (2)
45s
COLUMBIA

Number	Title (A Side/B Side)	Yr	VG	VG+	NM
❏ 43738	Sorrow/Say You Love Me	1966	5.00	10.00	20.00
❏ 43948	Am I On Your Mind/There's a Storm Comin'	1966	5.00	10.00	20.00
❏ 44143	When You Walk In the Room/Do It Now	1967	3.75	7.50	15.00

STRIKES, THE
45s
IMPERIAL

Number	Title (A Side/B Side)	Yr	VG	VG+	NM
❏ 5433	Baby I'm Sorry/If You Can't Rock Me	1957	12.50	25.00	50.00
❏ 5446	Rockin'/I Don't Want to Cry Over You	1957	12.50	25.00	50.00

LIN

Number	Title (A Side/B Side)	Yr	VG	VG+	NM
❏ 5006	Baby I'm Sorry/If You Can't Rock Me	1957	18.75	37.50	75.00

STRING CHEESE
Albums
WOODEN NICKEL

Number	Title (A Side/B Side)	Yr	VG	VG+	NM
❏ WNS-1001	String Cheese	1971	5.00	10.00	20.00

STRING-A-LONGS, THE
45s
ATCO

Number	Title (A Side/B Side)	Yr	VG	VG+	NM
❏ 6694	Popi/Places I Remember	1969	2.00	4.00	8.00

DOT

Number	Title (A Side/B Side)	Yr	VG	VG+	NM
❏ 16331	Twistwatch/Sunday	1962	2.50	5.00	10.00
❏ 16379	Spinnin' My Wheels/My Blue Heaven	1962	2.50	5.00	10.00
❏ 16393	Matilda/Replica	1962	2.50	5.00	10.00
❏ 16448	Heartaches/Happy Melody	1963	2.50	5.00	10.00
❏ 16575	Myna Bird/My Babe	1964	2.50	5.00	10.00
❏ 16592	Beatles, You Bug Me/Bloomin' Bird	1964	4.00	8.00	16.00
—As "The Bug Men"					
❏ 16708	Caravan/Mathilda	1965	2.50	5.00	10.00

7 ARTS

Number	Title (A Side/B Side)	Yr	VG	VG+	NM
❏ 700	Tell the World/For My Angel	1961	3.75	7.50	15.00
—As "Mickey Boyd and the Plain Viewers"					

WARWICK

Number	Title (A Side/B Side)	Yr	VG	VG+	NM
❏ 603	Wheels/Am I Asking Too Much	1960	3.75	7.50	15.00
❏ 603	Wheels/Tell the World	1960	5.00	10.00	20.00
—Red label					
❏ 603	Wheels/Tell the World	1960	6.25	12.50	25.00
—White label (not marked as a promo)					
❏ 606	Tell the World/For an Angel	1960	3.75	7.50	15.00
❏ 625	Brass Buttons/Panic Button	1961	3.75	7.50	15.00
❏ 654	Take a Minute/Should I	1961	3.75	7.50	15.00
❏ 668	Myna Bird/Scottie	1961	3.75	7.50	15.00
❏ 675	Theme for Twisters/Nearly Sunrise	1962	3.75	7.50	15.00

Albums
ATCO

Number	Title (A Side/B Side)	Yr	VG	VG+	NM
❏ SD 33-241	Wide World Hits	1969	6.25	12.50	25.00

DOT

Number	Title (A Side/B Side)	Yr	VG	VG+	NM
❏ DLP-3463 [M]	Matilda	1962	6.25	12.50	25.00
❏ DLP-3723 [M]	Great Instrumental Hits	1966	5.00	10.00	20.00
❏ DLP-25463 [S]	Matilda	1962	7.50	15.00	30.00
❏ DLP-25723 [S]	Great Instrumental Hits	1966	6.25	12.50	25.00

WARWICK

Number	Title (A Side/B Side)	Yr	VG	VG+	NM
❏ W-2036 [M]	Pick-A-Hit Featuring "Wheels"	1961	12.50	25.00	50.00
❏ W-2036ST [S]	Pick-A-Hit Featuring "Wheels"	1961	20.00	40.00	80.00

STRONG, BARRETT
45s
ANNA

Number	Title (A Side/B Side)	Yr	VG	VG+	NM
❏ 1111	Money (That's What I Want)/Oh I Apologize	1960	7.50	15.00	30.00
❏ 1116	You Know What to Do/Yes, No, Maybe So	1960	6.25	12.50	25.00

ATCO

Number	Title (A Side/B Side)	Yr	VG	VG+	NM
❏ 6225	Seven Sins/What Went Wrong	1962	10.00	20.00	40.00

CAPITOL

Number	Title (A Side/B Side)	Yr	VG	VG+	NM
❏ 4052	Is It True/Anywhere	1975	—	2.50	5.00
❏ 4120	Surrender/There's Something About You	1975	—	2.50	5.00
❏ 4223	Gonna Make It Right/The Man Up in the Sky	1976	—	2.50	5.00

EPIC

Number	Title (A Side/B Side)	Yr	VG	VG+	NM
❏ 11011	Stand Up and Cheer for the Preacher (Part 1)/ Stand Up and Cheer for the Preacher (Part 2)	1973	—	2.50	5.00

PHASE II

Number	Title (A Side/B Side)	Yr	VG	VG+	NM
❏ 02048	Rock It Easy/Love Will Make It Right	1981	—	2.00	4.00

TAMLA

Number	Title (A Side/B Side)	Yr	VG	VG+	NM
❏ 54022	Let's Rock/Do the Very Best You Can	1960	1000.	1500.	2000.
❏ 54027	Money (That's What I Want)/Oh I Apologize	1960	12.50	25.00	50.00
—Globe label					
❏ 54027	Money (That's What I Want)/Oh I Apologize	1960	30.00	60.00	120.00
—Horizontal lines label					
❏ 54029	You Know What to Do/Yes, No, Maybe So	1960	12.50	25.00	50.00
❏ 54033	I'm Gonna Cry/Whirl Wind	1960	12.50	25.00	50.00
❏ 54035	You Got What It Takes/Money and Me	1961	12.50	25.00	50.00
❏ 54043	Two Wrongs Don't Make a Right/Misery	1961	12.50	25.00	50.00

TOLLIE

Number	Title (A Side/B Side)	Yr	VG	VG+	NM
❏ 9023	Make Up Your Mind/I Better Run	1964	7.50	15.00	30.00

Albums
CAPITOL

Number	Title (A Side/B Side)	Yr	VG	VG+	NM
❏ ST-11376	Stronghold	1975	3.00	6.00	12.00

STRONG, NOLAN, AND THE DIABLOS
Some of these refer only to "The Diablos," others only to "Nolan Strong."
45s
FORTUNE

Number	Title (A Side/B Side)	Yr	VG	VG+	NM
❏ 509/10	Adios, My Desert Love/(I Want) An Old Fashioned Girl	1954	25.00	50.00	100.00
❏ 511	The Wind/Baby, Be Mine	1954	25.00	50.00	100.00
❏ 511	The Wind/Baby, Be Mine	196?	5.00	10.00	20.00
—Later pressing adds reference to LP on which it appears					
❏ 514	Hold Me Until Eternity/Route 16	1955	25.00	50.00	100.00
❏ 516	Daddy Rockin' Strong/Do You Remember What You Did Last Night	1955	25.00	50.00	100.00
❏ 518	The Way You Dog Me Around/Jump, Shake and Move	1955	25.00	50.00	100.00
❏ 519	You're the Only Girl, Dolores/You Are	1956	20.00	40.00	80.00
❏ 522	Teardrop from Heaven/Try Me One More Time	1956	20.00	40.00	80.00
❏ 525	Can't We Talk This Over/The Mambo of Love	1957	20.00	40.00	80.00
❏ 529	For Old Times' Sake/My Heart Will Always Belong to You	1959	10.00	20.00	40.00
❏ 531	I Am With You/Goodbye Matilda	1959	10.00	20.00	40.00
❏ 532	If I Could Be with You Tonite/I Wanna Know	1959	10.00	20.00	40.00
❏ 536	Since You're Gone/What You Gonna Do	1960	7.50	15.00	30.00
❏ 544	Blue Moon/I Don't Care	1962	5.00	10.00	20.00
❏ 546	Mind Over Matter (I'm Gonna Make You Mine)/ Beside You	1962	5.00	10.00	20.00
❏ 553	I Really Love You/You're My Love	1963	5.00	10.00	20.00
❏ 556	(Yeah, Baby) It's Because of You/You're Every Beat of My Heart	1963	5.00	10.00	20.00
❏ 564	Are You Making a Fool Out of Me/You're My Happiness	1964	3.75	7.50	15.00
❏ 569	(What Did That Genie Mean When He Said) Ali-Coochie/(You're Not Good Looking But) You're Presentable	1964	3.75	7.50	15.00
❏ 574	The Way You Dog Me Around/Jump with Me	1980	3.75	7.50	15.00

PYRAMID

Number	Title (A Side/B Side)	Yr	VG	VG+	NM
❏ 159	White Christmas/Danny Boy	19??	3.75	7.50	15.00

Albums
FORTUNE

Number	Title (A Side/B Side)	Yr	VG	VG+	NM
❏ LP-8010 [M]	Fortune of Hits	196?	12.50	25.00	50.00
—Yellow label					
❏ LP-8010 [M]	Fortune of Hits	1961	55.00	110.00	220.00
—Purple label, thick vinyl					
❏ LP-8010 [M]	Fortune of Hits	197?	3.75	7.50	15.00
—Purple label, thinner, more flexible vinyl					
❏ LP-8012 [M]	Fortune of Hits, Vol. 2	196?	12.50	25.00	50.00
—Yellow label					
❏ LP-8012 [M]	Fortune of Hits, Vol. 2	1962	55.00	110.00	220.00
—Purple label, thick vinyl					
❏ LP-8012 [M]	Fortune of Hits, Vol. 2	197?	3.75	7.50	15.00
—Purple label, thinner, more flexible vinyl					
❏ LP-8015 [M]	Mind Over Matter	196?	15.00	30.00	60.00
—Yellow label					
❏ LP-8015 [M]	Mind Over Matter	1963	62.50	125.00	250.00
—Purple label, thick vinyl					
❏ LP-8015 [M]	Mind Over Matter	197?	5.00	10.00	20.00
—Purple label, thinner, more flexible vinyl					

STRUNK, JUD
45s
AD-MEDIA

Number	Title (A Side/B Side)	Yr	VG	VG+	NM
❏ 6416	The Santa Song/A Special Christmas Tree	1969	2.50	5.00	10.00
❏ 6416 [PS]	The Santa Song/A Special Christmas Tree	1969	3.75	7.50	15.00

CAPITOL

Number	Title (A Side/B Side)	Yr	VG	VG+	NM
❏ 3960	My Country/The Will	1974	—	3.00	6.00

COLUMBIA

Number	Title (A Side/B Side)	Yr	VG	VG+	NM
❏ 4-45121	David's Place/Lion in the Park	1970	2.00	4.00	8.00
❏ 4-45189	Self-Eating Watermelon/Children at Play	1970	2.00	4.00	8.00

MCA

Number	Title (A Side/B Side)	Yr	VG	VG+	NM
❏ 40872	Tell Me Where I Am Tonight/ Fool on My Shoulder	1978	—	2.00	4.00

MELODYLAND

Number	Title (A Side/B Side)	Yr	VG	VG+	NM
❏ 6015	The Biggest Parakeets in Town/ I Wasn't Wrong About You	1975	—	2.50	5.00
❏ 6027	Pamela Brown/They're Tearing Down a Town	1975	—	2.50	5.00

MGM

Number	Title (A Side/B Side)	Yr	VG	VG+	NM
❏ 14388	Jacob Brown/Long Ride Home	1972	—	3.00	6.00
❏ 14463	Daisy a Day/The Searchers	1972	—	3.50	7.00
❏ 14572	Next Door Neighbor's Kid/ I'd Prefer to Do It All Again	1973	—	3.00	6.00

Albums
COLUMBIA

Number	Title (A Side/B Side)	Yr	VG	VG+	NM
❏ CS 9990	Downeast Viewpoint	1970	3.75	7.50	15.00

Number	Title (A Side/B Side)	Yr	VG	VG+	NM
HARMONY					
❏ KH 32344	Mr. Bojangles and Other Favorites	1973	2.50	5.00	10.00
MCA					
❏ 2309	A Semi-Reformed Tequila Crazed Gypsy	1977	2.50	5.00	10.00
MGM					
❏ SE-4790	Jones General Store	1972	3.00	6.00	12.00
❏ SE-4898	Daisy a Day	1973	3.00	6.00	12.00

STUART, CHAD Also see CHAD AND JEREMY.
45s

Number	Title (A Side/B Side)	Yr	VG	VG+	NM
SIDEWALK					
❏ 944	Good Morning Sunrise/Paxton's Song	1968	2.00	4.00	8.00
❏ 944 [PS]	Good Morning Sunrise/Paxton's Song	1968	3.75	7.50	15.00

STUART, CHAD AND JILL Also see CHAD STUART.
45s

Number	Title (A Side/B Side)	Yr	VG	VG+	NM
COLUMBIA					
❏ 43467	The Cruel War/I Can't Talk to You	1965	2.00	4.00	8.00
❏ 43467 [PS]	The Cruel War/I Can't Talk to You	1965	3.75	7.50	15.00

STUART, CHAD, AND JEREMY CLYDE See CHAD AND JEREMY.

STUBBS, JOE
45s

Number	Title (A Side/B Side)	Yr	VG	VG+	NM
LU-PINE					
❏ 120	Keep On Loving Me/What's My Destiny	1964	50.00	100.00	200.00

STUDENT NURSES, THE
45s

Number	Title (A Side/B Side)	Yr	VG	VG+	NM
RCA VICTOR					
❏ 47-8482	Kiss Me Goodnight/Simply	1964	6.25	12.50	25.00

STUDENTS, THE
45s

Number	Title (A Side/B Side)	Yr	VG	VG+	NM
ARGO					
❏ 5386	I'm So Young/Every Day of the Week	1961	5.00	10.00	20.00
CHECKER					
❏ 902	I'm So Young/Every Day of the Week	1958	10.00	20.00	40.00
❏ 1004	My Vow to You/That's How I Feel	1962	3.75	7.50	15.00
NOTE					
❏ 10012	I'm So Young/Every Day of the Week	1958	125.00	250.00	500.00
❏ 10019	My Vow to You/That's How I Feel	1959	100.00	200.00	400.00
RED TOP					
❏ 100	My Heart Is an Open Door/Mommy and Daddy	1958	10.00	20.00	40.00
—Red label					
❏ 100	My Heart Is an Open Door/Mommy and Daddy	1958	50.00	100.00	200.00
—Blue label					

STUFFY AND HIS FROZEN PARACHUTE BAND
Albums

Number	Title (A Side/B Side)	Yr	VG	VG+	NM
PARAMOUNT					
❏ PAS-6070	Stuffy and His Frozen Parachute Band	1974	6.25	12.50	25.00
—Reissue of Water Street 1002					
WATER STREET					
❏ WST 1002	Stuffy and His Frozen Parachute Band	1974	12.50	25.00	50.00

STYLERS, THE (1)
45s

Number	Title (A Side/B Side)	Yr	VG	VG+	NM
GOLDEN CREST					
❏ 117	You Tell Me/Blues in the Night	1957	10.00	20.00	40.00
❏ 117 [PS]	You Tell Me/Blues in the Night	1957	25.00	50.00	100.00
❏ 129	Kiss and Run Lover/Girlie, Girlie, Girlie	1957	10.00	20.00	40.00
JUBILEE					
❏ 5168	Believe It or Not/The World Is Yours	1954	10.00	20.00	40.00
❏ 5188	Shoo Shoo Sha La La/I Love Ya Like Crazy	1955	10.00	20.00	40.00
❏ 5246	Lost John/Huffin' and Puffin'	1956	10.00	20.00	40.00
❏ 5253	Confession of a Sinner/Gonna Tell 'Em	1956	10.00	20.00	40.00
❏ 5279	Breaker of Hearts/Miracle in Milan	1957	7.50	15.00	30.00

STYLERS, THE (U) These could both be by group (1), or they may be different groups.
45s

Number	Title (A Side/B Side)	Yr	VG	VG+	NM
GORDY					
❏ 7018	Going Steady Anniversary/Pushing Up Daisies	1963	15.00	30.00	60.00
KICKS					
❏ 2	Gentle as a Teardrop/There Were Others	1954	125.00	250.00	500.00

STYLES, THE (1)
45s

Number	Title (A Side/B Side)	Yr	VG	VG+	NM
JOSIE					
❏ 920	I Love You for Sentimental Reasons/School Bells to Chapel Bells	1964	15.00	30.00	60.00
SERENE					
❏ 1501	Scarlet Angel/Gotta Go, Go, Go	1961	37.50	75.00	150.00

STYLES, THE (2)
45s

Number	Title (A Side/B Side)	Yr	VG	VG+	NM
MODERN					
❏ 1048	I Know You Know That I Know/Baby You're Alive	1967	3.00	6.00	12.00
SWAN					
❏ 4258	I Do Love You/Hush Little Girl	1966	3.00	6.00	12.00

STYLISTICS, THE
12-Inch Singles

Number	Title (A Side/B Side)	Yr	VG	VG+	NM
H&L					
❏ 2008	The Lion Sleeps Tonight (5:29)/Fly! (6:09)	1977	3.75	7.50	15.00
STREETWISE					
❏ 2236	Give a Little Love/Give a Little Love (Sing Along Version)	1984	2.00	4.00	8.00
❏ 2237	Some Things Never Change/Row Your Love	1985	2.00	4.00	8.00
❏ 2238	Special/(B-side unknown)	1985	2.00	4.00	8.00
❏ 2241	Let's Go Rockin' (Tonight)/(B-side unknown)	1986	2.00	4.00	8.00

45s

Number	Title (A Side/B Side)	Yr	VG	VG+	NM
AMHERST					
❏ 301	Because I Love You Girl/My Love, Come Live With Me	1985	—	2.00	4.00
AVCO					
❏ 4581	You Are Everything/Country Living	1971	—	2.50	5.00
❏ 4591	Betcha by Golly, Wow/Ebony Eyes	1972	—	2.50	5.00
❏ 4595	People Make the World Go Round/Point of No Return	1972	—	2.50	5.00
❏ 4603	I'm Stone in Love with You/Make It Last	1972	—	2.50	5.00
❏ 4611	Break Up to Make Up/You and Me	1973	—	2.50	5.00
❏ 4618	You'll Never Get to Heaven (If You Break My Heart)/If You Don't Watch Out	1973	—	2.50	5.00
❏ 4625	Rockin' Roll Baby/Pieces	1973	—	2.50	5.00
❏ 4634	You Make Me Feel Brand New/Only for the Children	1974	—	2.50	5.00
❏ 4640	Let's Put It All Together/I Take It Out on You	1974	—	2.50	5.00
❏ 4647	Heavy Fallin' Out/Go Now	1974	—	2.50	5.00
❏ 4649	Star on a TV Show/Hey Girl, Come and Get It	1975	—	2.50	5.00
❏ 4652	Thank You Baby/Sing, Baby, Sing	1975	—	2.50	5.00
❏ 4656	Can't Give You Anything (But My Love)/I'd Rather Be Hurt by You	1975	—	2.50	5.00
❏ 4661	Funky Weekend/If You Are There	1975	—	2.50	5.00
❏ 4664	You Are Beautiful/Michael and Me	1976	—	2.50	5.00
❏ 4664 [PS]	You Are Beautiful/Michael and Me	1976	2.50	5.00	10.00
AVCO EMBASSY					
❏ 4555	You're a Big Girl Now/Let the Junkie Beat the Pusher	1970	—	3.00	6.00
❏ 4572	Stop, Look, Listen (To Your Heart)/If I Love You	1971	—	3.00	6.00
H&L					
❏ 4669	Can't Help Falling in Love/Jenny	1976	—	2.00	4.00
❏ 4674	Because I Love You, Girl/You Are	1976	—	2.00	4.00
❏ 4676	Only You/What Goes Around Comes Around	1976	—	2.00	4.00
❏ 4678	I Got a Letter/Satin Doll	1977	—	2.00	4.00
❏ 4681	Shame and Scandal in the Family/That Don't Shake Me	1977	—	2.00	4.00
❏ 4686	I'm Coming Home/I Run to You	1977	—	2.00	4.00
❏ 4695	Fool of the Year/Good Thing Goin'	1978	—	2.00	4.00
MERCURY					
❏ 74005	First Impressions/Your Love's Too Good to Be Forgotten	1978	—	2.00	4.00
❏ 74022	I Can't Stop Livin'/You're the Best Thing in My Life	1978	—	2.00	4.00
❏ 74042	Love at First Sight/Broken Wing	1979	—	2.00	4.00
❏ 74057	Don't Know Where I'm Going/You Make Me Feel So Doggone Good	1979	—	2.00	4.00
PHILADELPHIA INT'L.					
❏ 02901	Callin' You/Don't Come Telling Me Lies	1982	—	2.00	4.00
❏ 03085	Lighten Up/We Should Be Lovers	1982	—	2.00	4.00
SEBRING					
❏ 8370	You're a Big Girl Now/Let the Junkie Beat the Pusher	1970	7.50	15.00	30.00
STREETWISE					
❏ 1136	Give a Little Love/Give a Little Love (Sing Along Version)	1984	—	2.00	4.00
❏ 1137	Some Things Never Change/Row Your Love	1985	—	2.00	4.00
❏ 1138	Special/(B-side unknown)	1985	—	2.00	4.00
TSOP					
❏ 02195	What's Your Name/Almost There	1981	—	2.00	4.00
❏ 02588	Mine All Mine/Closer Than Close	1981	—	2.00	4.00
❏ 02702	Habit/I've Got This Feeling	1982	—	2.00	4.00
❏ 4789	Hurry Up This Way Again/It Started Out	1980	—	2.00	4.00
❏ 4798	And I'll See You No More/Driving Me Wild	1980	—	2.00	4.00

Albums

Number	Title (A Side/B Side)	Yr	VG	VG+	NM
AMHERST					
❏ AMH-743	The Best of the Stylistics	1986	2.50	5.00	10.00
❏ AMH-744	All-Time Classics	1986	2.50	5.00	10.00
❏ AMH-745	The Best of the Stylistics, Vol. 2	1986	2.50	5.00	10.00
❏ AMH-746	Greatest Love Hits	1986	2.50	5.00	10.00
AVCO					
❏ 11006	Round 2: The Stylistics	1972	5.00	10.00	20.00
❏ 11010	Rockin' Roll Baby	1973	5.00	10.00	20.00
❏ AV-33023	The Stylistics	1971	5.00	10.00	20.00
❏ AV-69001	Let's Put It All Together	1974	3.75	7.50	15.00
❏ AV-69004	Heavy	1974	3.75	7.50	15.00
❏ AV-69005	The Best of the Stylistics	1975	3.75	7.50	15.00
❏ 69008	Thank You Baby	1975	3.75	7.50	15.00
❏ 69010	You Are Beautiful	1975	3.75	7.50	15.00
H&L					
❏ 69013	Fabulous	1976	3.00	6.00	12.00
❏ 69032	Wonder Woman	1978	3.00	6.00	12.00
MERCURY					
❏ SRM-1-3727	In Fashion	1978	3.00	6.00	12.00
❏ SRM-1-3753	Love Spell	1979	3.00	6.00	12.00
PHILADELPHIA INT'L.					
❏ FZ 37955	1982	1982	2.50	5.00	10.00
TSOP					
❏ JZ 36470	Hurry Up This Way Again	1980	2.50	5.00	10.00
❏ FZ 37458	Closer Than Close	1981	2.50	5.00	10.00

STYLISTS, THE
45s

Number	Title (A Side/B Side)	Yr	VG	VG+	NM
V.I.P.					
❏ 25066	What Is Love/Where Did the Children Go	1970	6.25	12.50	25.00

STYX
12-Inch Singles

Number	Title (A Side/B Side)	Yr	VG	VG+	NM
A&M					
❏ SP-17021 [DJ]	The Grand Illusion (same on both sides)	1977	3.75	7.50	15.00

45s

Number	Title (A Side/B Side)	Yr	VG	VG+	NM
A&M					
❏ 1786	Lorelei/Midnight Ride	1976	—	2.00	4.00
❏ 1818	Born for Adventure/Light Up	1976	—	2.50	5.00
❏ 1877	Mademoiselle/Light Up	1976	—	2.50	5.00
❏ 1900	Jennifer/Shooz	1976	—	2.50	5.00
❏ 1931	Crystal Ball/Put Me On	1977	—	2.50	5.00
❏ 1977	Come Sail Away/Put Me On	1977	—	2.00	4.00
❏ 1977 [PS]	Come Sail Away/Put Me On	1977	—	3.00	6.00
❏ 2007	Fooling Yourself (The Angry Young Man)/The Grand Finale	1978	—	2.00	4.00
❏ 2007 [PS]	Fooling Yourself (The Angry Young Man)/The Grand Finale	1978	—	3.00	6.00

S

Number	Title (A Side/B Side)	Yr	VG	VG+	NM
❏ 2087	Blue Collar Man (Long Nights)/Superstars	1978	—	2.00	4.00
❏ 2087 [PS]	Blue Collar Man (Long Nights)/Superstars	1978	—	3.00	6.00
❏ 2110	Renegade/Sing for the Day	1979	—	2.00	4.00
❏ 2110	Sing for the Day/Queen of Spades	1979	—	2.50	5.00
❏ 2110 [PS]	Renegade/Sing for the Day	1979	—	2.50	5.00
❏ 2188	Babe/I'm O.K.	1979	—	2.00	4.00
❏ 2206	Why Me/Lights	1979	—	2.00	4.00
❏ 2228	Borrowed Time/Eddie	1980	—	2.00	4.00
❏ 2294	The Best of Times/Lights	1980	—	—	—
—Unreleased?					
❏ 2300	The Best of Times/Lights	1981	—	2.00	4.00
❏ 2300 [PS]	The Best of Times/Lights	1981	—	2.00	4.00
❏ 2323	Too Much Time on My Hands/Queen of Spades	1981	—	2.00	4.00
❏ 2348	Nothing Ever Goes As Planned/				
	Never Say Never	1981	—	2.00	4.00
❏ 2525	Mr. Roboto/Snowblind	1983	—	—	3.00
❏ 2525 [PS]	Mr. Roboto/Snowblind	1983	—	—	3.00
❏ 2543	Don't Let It End/Rockin' the Paradise	1983	—	—	3.00
❏ 2543 [PS]	Don't Let It End/Rockin' the Paradise	1983	—	—	3.00
❏ 2560	Double Life/Haven't We Been Here Before	1983	—	—	3.00
❏ 2568	High Time/Double Life	1983	—	—	3.00
❏ 2625	Music Time/Heavy Metal Poisoning	1984	—	—	3.00
❏ 2625 [PS]	Music Time/Heavy Metal Poisoning	1984	—	—	3.00
❏ 8696	Show Me the Way/Love at First Sight	1993	—	2.00	4.00
—Reissue series; both songs were unreleased on 45 until this record					
WOODEN NICKEL					
❏ BWBO-0065	You Need Love/Winner Take All	1973	—	2.50	5.00
❏ 65-0106	Best Thing/What Has Come Between	1972	—	2.50	5.00
❏ 65-0111	I'm Gonna Make You Feel It/Quick Is the Beat				
	of My Heart	1972	—	2.50	5.00
❏ 65-0116	Lady/You Better Ask	1973	2.50	5.00	10.00
❏ BWBO-0252	Young Man/Unfinished Song	1974	—	2.50	5.00
❏ WB-10027	Lies/22 Years	1974	—	2.50	5.00
❏ WB-10102	Lady/Children of the Land	1974	—	2.50	5.00
❏ WB-10272	You Need Love/You Better Ask	1975	—	2.50	5.00
❏ WB-10329	Best Thing/Havin' a Ball	1975	—	2.50	5.00
❏ GB-10492	Lady/Children of the Land	1975	—	2.00	4.00
—Gold Standard Series					
❏ WB-11205	Winner Take All/Best Thing	1978	—	2.50	5.00
Albums					
A&M					
❏ SP-3217	Equinox	1984	2.00	4.00	8.00
❏ SP-3218	Crystal Ball	1984	2.00	4.00	8.00
❏ SP-3223	The Grand Illusion	1984	2.00	4.00	8.00
❏ SP-3224	Pieces of Eight	1984	2.00	4.00	8.00
❏ SP-3239	Cornerstone	1984	2.00	4.00	8.00
❏ SP-3240	Paradise Theater	1984	2.00	4.00	8.00
—3200 series LPs are reissues					
❏ SP-3711	Cornerstone	1979	2.50	5.00	10.00
❏ SP-3711	Cornerstone	1979	7.50	15.00	30.00
—Silver vinyl pressing, reportedly for fan club members					
❏ SP-3719	Paradise Theater	1981	2.50	5.00	10.00
❏ SP-3734	Kilroy Was Here	1983	2.50	5.00	10.00
❏ SP-4559	Equinox	1975	2.50	5.00	10.00
❏ SP-4604	Crystal Ball	1976	2.50	5.00	10.00
❏ SP-4637	The Grand Illusion	1977	2.50	5.00	10.00
❏ PR-4724 [PD]	Pieces of Eight	1978	6.25	12.50	25.00
❏ SP-4724	Pieces of Eight	1978	2.50	5.00	10.00
❏ 75021 5327 1	Edge of the Century	1990	3.75	7.50	15.00
❏ SP-6514 [(2)]	Caught in the Act	1984	3.00	6.00	12.00
❏ SP-8431 [(2)DJ]	The Styx Radio Special	1977	6.25	12.50	25.00
—Promo only; green cover					
❏ SP-17053 [(3)DJ]	Styx Radio Special	1978	10.00	20.00	40.00
—Promo-only box set					
❏ SP-17222 [(2)DJ]	Radio Sampler and Interview Album	1983	6.25	12.50	25.00
—Promo only; with "Kilroy Was Here" album graphic on cover					
MOBILE FIDELITY					
❏ 1-026	The Grand Illusion	1979	7.50	15.00	30.00
—Audiophile vinyl					
NAUTILUS					
❏ NR-15	Pieces of Eight	1981	6.25	12.50	25.00
—Audiophile vinyl					
❏ NR-27	Cornerstone	1982	5.00	10.00	20.00
—Audiophile vinyl					
❏ NR-45	Paradise Theater	198?	7.50	15.00	30.00
—Audiophile vinyl					
RCA VICTOR					
❏ AFL1-3593	Styx	1979	2.50	5.00	10.00
❏ AFL1-3594	Lady	1979	2.50	5.00	10.00
—Retitled version of "Styx II"					
❏ AFL1-3595	Serpent	1979	2.50	5.00	10.00
—Retitled version of "The Serpent Is Rising"					
❏ AFL1-3596	Miracles	1979	2.50	5.00	10.00
—Retitled version of "Man of Miracles"					
❏ AFL1-3597	Best of Styx	1979	2.50	5.00	10.00
❏ AYL1-3888	Styx	1980	2.00	4.00	8.00
❏ AYL1-4233	Lady	1981	2.00	4.00	8.00
—Retitled version of "Styx II"					
❏ AYL1-4756	Best of Styx	1982	2.00	4.00	8.00
WOODEN NICKEL					
❏ BWL1-0287	The Serpent Is Rising	1974	5.00	10.00	20.00
❏ BWL1-0638	Man of Miracles	1974	5.00	10.00	20.00
—Second version contains "Best Thing"					
❏ BWL1-0638	Man of Miracles	1974	7.50	15.00	30.00
—Original version contains "Lies"					
❏ BWL1-1008	Styx	1975	3.75	7.50	15.00
❏ WNS-1008	Styx	1972	5.00	10.00	20.00
❏ BWL1-1012	Styx II	1975	3.75	7.50	15.00
❏ WNS-1012	Styx II	1973	5.00	10.00	20.00
—With die-cut cover					
❏ BWL1-2250	Best of Styx	1977	3.00	6.00	12.00

STYX (2)
45s
ABC

Number	Title (A Side/B Side)	Yr	VG	VG+	NM
❏ 10848	Don't Bring Me Down/MacDougal Street	1966	3.00	6.00	12.00

STYX (U) Definitely not the more famous Styx; could be group (2), though.
45s
ONYX

Number	Title (A Side/B Side)	Yr	VG	VG+	NM
❏ 2200	Puppetmaster/Hey, I'm Lost	1966	6.25	12.50	25.00
PARAMOUNT					
❏ 0104	Promised Land/Soul Flow	1971	—	3.00	6.00

SUDDENS, THE Also recorded as THE SAFARIS.
45s
SUDDEN

❏ 103	Garden of Love/Childish Ways	1961	25.00	50.00	100.00

SUGAR BEARS, THE KIM CARNES was in this group.
45s
BIG TREE

❏ 122	Someone Like You/You Are the One	1971	—	3.00	6.00
❏ 143	Right On/Happiness Train	1972	—	3.00	6.00
❏ 151	Some Kind of a Summer/Put Some Love Into It	1972	—	3.00	6.00
Albums					
BIG TREE					
❏ BTS-2009	Introducing the Sugar Bears	1972	5.00	10.00	20.00

SUGAR CANES, THE
45s
KING

❏ 5157	Poor Boy/Sioux Rock	1958	6.25	12.50	25.00

SUGAR CREEK
Albums
METROMEDIA

❏ MD 1020	Please Tell a Friend	1969	15.00	30.00	60.00

SUGARLOAF
45s
BRUT

❏ 805	Round and Round/Colorado Jones	1973	—	2.50	5.00
❏ 815	I Got a Song/Myra, Myra	1973	—	2.50	5.00
❏ 815 [PS]	I Got a Song/Myra, Myra	1973	—	3.00	6.00
CLARIDGE					
❏ 402	Don't Call Us, We'll Call You/Texas Two-Lane	1974	—	2.50	5.00
❏ 405	Stars in My Eyes/Myra, Myra	1975	—	2.50	5.00
❏ 408	Boogie Man/I Got a Song	1975	—	2.50	5.00
❏ 415	Have a Good Time/You Set My Dreams to Music	1976	—	2.50	5.00
❏ 422	Last Dance, Take a Chance/				
	Satisfaction Guaranteed	1976	—	2.50	5.00
LIBERTY					
❏ 56183	Green-Eyed Lady/West of Tomorrow	1970	—	3.00	6.00
❏ 56218	Tongue in Cheek/Woman	1970	—	2.50	5.00
❏ 56218 [PS]	Tongue in Cheek/Woman	1970	2.50	5.00	10.00
UNITED ARTISTS					
❏ 0062	Green-Eyed Lady/Tongue in Cheek	1973	—	2.00	4.00
—"Silver Spotlight Series" reissue					
❏ 50757	Woman/Tongue in Cheek	1971	—	—	—
—Unreleased					
❏ 50784	Chest Fever/Mother Nature's Wine	1971	—	2.50	5.00
Albums					
BRUT					
❏ 6006	I Got a Song	1973	3.75	7.50	15.00
CLARIDGE					
❏ 1000	Don't Call Us, We'll Call You	1975	3.00	6.00	12.00
LIBERTY					
❏ LST-7640	Sugarloaf	1970	5.00	10.00	20.00
❏ LST-11010	Spaceship Earth	1971	5.00	10.00	20.00

SUGGS, BRAD
45s
METEOR

❏ 5034	Charcoal Suit/Bop Baby Bop	1956	100.00	200.00	400.00
PHILLIPS INT'L.					
❏ 3545	Low Outside/706 Union	1959	6.25	12.50	25.00
❏ 3549	I Walk the Line/Ooh-Wee	1959	6.25	12.50	25.00
❏ 3554	Cloudy/Partly Cloudy	1960	6.25	12.50	25.00
❏ 3563	My Gypsy/Sam's Tune	1960	6.25	12.50	25.00
❏ 3571	Elephant Walk/Catching Up	1961	6.25	12.50	25.00

SULLIVAN, JIM
45s
LONDON

❏ 9585	Back and Forth/Toad Stool	1963	3.00	6.00	12.00

SULLIVAN, NIKI Also see THE CRICKETS (1).
45s
DOT

❏ 15751	Three Steps to Heaven/It's All Over	1958	25.00	50.00	100.00
JOLI					
❏ 073	Do the Dive/My Lost Dream	196?	15.00	30.00	60.00
❏ 075	It Really Doesn't Matter/				
	You Better Get a Move On	196?	18.75	37.50	75.00

SULTANS, THE (1)
45s
ASCOT

❏ 2228	I Wanna Know/Gloria	1967	5.00	10.00	20.00

SULTANS, THE (2)
45s
DUKE

❏ 125	Good Thing Baby/How Deep Is the Ocean	1954	25.00	50.00	100.00
❏ 133	I Cried My Heart Out/Baby Don't Put Me Down	1954	25.00	50.00	100.00
❏ 135	Boppin' with the Mambo/What Makes Me Feel				
	This Way	1954	25.00	50.00	100.00
❏ 178	My Love Is So High/If I Could Tell	1957	12.50	25.00	50.00

SULTANS, THE (3)
45s
GUYDEN

❏ 2079	Someone You Can Trust/Christina	1963	3.75	7.50	15.00

Number	Title (A Side/B Side)	Yr	VG	VG+	NM
JAM					
❑ 103	Toss in My Sleep/I Feel Your Love Growing Cold	1962	7.50	15.00	30.00
❑ 107	Mary, Mary/How Far Does a Friendship Go	1963	7.50	15.00	30.00
❑ 113	Poor Boy/Don't Tie Me Down	1964	7.50	15.00	30.00
TILT					
❑ 782	It'll Be Easy/You Got Me Goin'	1961	10.00	20.00	40.00
—Black label					
❑ 782	It'll Be Easy/You Got Me Goin'	1961	25.00	50.00	100.00
—Yellow label					

SULTANS, THE (4)
45s

Number	Title (A Side/B Side)	Yr	VG	VG+	NM
JUBILEE					
❑ 5054	Lemon Squeezing Daddy/You Captured My Heart	1951	62.50	125.00	250.00
❑ 5077	Blues at Dawn/Don't Be Angry	1952	200.00	400.00	800.00

SUMAC, YMA
45s

Number	Title (A Side/B Side)	Yr	VG	VG+	NM
CAPITOL					
❑ CDF 244 [PS]	Voice of the Xtabay	195?	3.75	7.50	15.00
—Box for 15647, 15648, 15649 and 19650 (listed separately)					
❑ F1717	Virgin of the Sun God/Lure of the Unknown Love	1951	5.00	10.00	20.00
❑ F1819	Birds/Najalas Lament	1951	5.00	10.00	20.00
❑ F1819 [PS]	Birds/Najalas Lament	1951	10.00	20.00	40.00
❑ F2079	Babalu/Wimoweh	1952	5.00	10.00	20.00
❑ F15647	Virgin of the Sun God/Lure of the Unknown Love	195?	3.75	7.50	15.00
❑ F15648	Monkeys/High Andes	195?	3.75	7.50	15.00
❑ F15649	Dance of the Winds/Chant of the Chosen Maidens	195?	3.75	7.50	15.00
❑ F15650	Dance of the Moon Festival/Earthquake	195?	3.75	7.50	15.00
—The above four comprise box set CDF-244, "Voice of the Xtabay"					
CORAL					
❑ 60741	The Sun Maidens/Beautiful Eyes	1952	5.00	10.00	20.00
❑ 60742	Cholitas Punenas/The Hummingbird	1952	5.00	10.00	20.00
❑ 60743	One Love/Indian Love	1952	5.00	10.00	20.00
❑ 60744	La Benita/I Love Only You	1952	5.00	10.00	20.00
—The above four comprise a box set					

7-Inch Extended Plays

Number	Title (A Side/B Side)	Yr	VG	VG+	NM
CAPITOL					
❑ EAP 1-299	(contents unknown)	1955	6.25	12.50	25.00
❑ EAP 1-299 [PS]	Legend of the Sun Virgin, Part 1	1955	6.25	12.50	25.00
❑ EAP 2-299	(contents unknown)	1955	6.25	12.50	25.00
❑ EAP 2-299 [PS]	Legend of the Sun Virgin, Part 2	1955	6.25	12.50	25.00
❑ EAP 1-564	(contents unknown)	1955	6.25	12.50	25.00
❑ EAP 1-564 [PS]	Mambo!	1955	6.25	12.50	25.00
❑ EAP 2-564	(contents unknown)	1955	6.25	12.50	25.00
❑ EAP 2-564 [PS]	Mambo!	1955	6.25	12.50	25.00
❑ EAP 1-770	(contents unknown)	1956	5.00	10.00	20.00
❑ EAP 1-770 [PS]	Legend of the Jivaro, Part 1	1956	5.00	10.00	20.00
❑ EAP 2-770	(contents unknown)	1956	5.00	10.00	20.00
❑ EAP 2-770 [PS]	Legend of the Jivaro, Part 2	1956	5.00	10.00	20.00
❑ EAP 3-770	(contents unknown)	1956	5.00	10.00	20.00
❑ EAP 3-770 [PS]	Legend of the Jivaro, Part 3	1956	5.00	10.00	20.00
CORAL					
❑ EC 81050	(contents unknown)	1954	12.50	25.00	50.00
❑ EC 81050 [PS]	Presenting Yma Sumac	1954	12.50	25.00	50.00
❑ EC 81051	(contents unknown)	1954	12.50	25.00	50.00
❑ EC 81051 [PS]	Presenting Yma Sumac	1954	12.50	25.00	50.00

Albums

Number	Title (A Side/B Side)	Yr	VG	VG+	NM
CAPITOL					
❑ H 244 [10]	Voice of the Xtabay	1952	25.00	50.00	100.00
❑ L 299 [10]	Legend of the Sun Virgin	1952	30.00	60.00	120.00
❑ SM-299 [M]	Legend of the Sun Virgin	197?	3.00	6.00	12.00
❑ T 299 [M]	Legend of the Sun Virgin	1955	12.50	25.00	50.00
❑ L 423 [10]	Inca Taqui	1953	25.00	50.00	100.00
❑ H 564 [10]	Mambo!	1954	25.00	50.00	100.00
❑ T 564 [M]	Mambo!	1955	12.50	25.00	50.00
❑ DW 684 [R]	Voice of the Xtabay and Inca Taqui	1963	3.75	7.50	15.00
❑ SM-684	Voice of the Xtabay and Inca Taqui	197?	3.00	6.00	12.00
—On this reissue, Side 1 is in mono					
❑ W 684 [M]	Voice of the Xtabay and Inca Taqui	1955	12.50	25.00	50.00
—Gray label					
❑ W 684 [M]	Voice of the Xtabay and Inca Taqui	1963	5.00	10.00	20.00
—Black colorband label, "Capitol" at top					
❑ T 770 [M]	Legend of the Jivaro	1956	12.50	25.00	50.00
—Turquoise label					
❑ T 770 [M]	Legend of the Jivaro	1963	5.00	10.00	20.00
—Black colorband label, "Capitol" at top					
❑ ST 1169 [S]	Fuego del Andes	1959	12.50	25.00	50.00
❑ T 1169 [M]	Fuego del Andes	1959	10.00	20.00	40.00
❑ M-11892	Mambo!	1979	3.00	6.00	12.00
CORAL					
❑ CRL 56058 [10]	Presenting Yma Sumac	1952	30.00	60.00	120.00
LONDON					
❑ XPS 608	Miracles	1972	5.00	10.00	20.00

SUMMER, DONNA
12-Inch Singles

Number	Title (A Side/B Side)	Yr	VG	VG+	NM
ATLANTIC					
❑ DMD 1333 [DJ]	This Time I Know It's for Real (Extended Remix 7:21) (Instrumental 3:34)/If It Makes You Feel Good	1989	3.75	7.50	15.00
❑ DMD 1382 [DJ]	Love's About to Change My Heart (PWL 12" Mix) (PWL 7" Mix) (Clivilles & Cole 12" Mix) (Dub 2) (Clivilles & Cole 7" Mix)	1989	2.50	5.00	10.00
❑ DMD 1431 [DJ]	Breakaway (Extended Mix 6:08) (Power Radio Mix 4:02)/I Don't Wanna Get Hurt (12" Mix)	1989	3.75	7.50	15.00
❑ DMD 1709 [DJ]	When Love Cries (Vocal Club Dub) (Radio Mix) (Club Mix) (Instrumental)	1991	2.50	5.00	10.00
❑ DMD 1758 [DJ]	Work That Magic (4:34) (6:20) (5:00)/Let There Be Peace	1991	3.00	6.00	12.00
❑ DMD 2574 [(2)DJ]	The Power of One (Johnathan Peters Club Mix) (Johnathan Peters Radio Mix) (Tommy Musto Vocal Mix) (Musto Beats) (Gel Dub) (JP Sound Factory Dub) (Sound Factory Club Mix) (Drum-a-Pella)	2000	7.50	15.00	30.00
❑ 85021	The Power of One (4 versions)	2000	3.00	6.00	12.00
❑ 85961	When Love Cries (4 versions)	1991	2.00	4.00	8.00
❑ 86255	Breakaway (Extended Mix) (Power Radio Mix)/I Don't Wanna Get Hurt (12" Mix)	1989	2.50	5.00	10.00
❑ 86309	Love's About to Change My Heart (5 versions)	1989	2.50	5.00	10.00
❑ 86415	This Time I Know It's for Real (Extended) (Instrumental) (LP Version)	1989	2.50	5.00	10.00
CASABLANCA					
❑ NBD 100	Winter Melody/Spring Affair	1977	3.75	7.50	15.00
❑ PRO 1148 [DJ]	Love to Love You Baby (16:49)/Flash Light (10:43)	1994	5.00	10.00	20.00
—B-side by Parliament; promo-only reissue					
❑ NBLP 7041	Love to Love You Baby (16:50)/Try Me, I Know We Can Make It (17:55)	1976	5.00	10.00	20.00
—One song on each side, yet it has an LP catalog number					
❑ NBD 20104	I Feel Love (8:15)/Theme from "The Deep" (Down, Deep Inside) (6:06)//(B-side blank)	1977	5.00	10.00	20.00
❑ NBD 20112 [DJ]	Rumour Has It/I Love You//(B-side blank)	1978	3.75	7.50	15.00
❑ NBD 20148 [DJ]	Mac Arthur Park Suite (17:33)//(B-side blank)	1978	3.75	7.50	15.00
❑ NBD 20159 [DJ]	Hot Stuff (Long Version)//(B-side blank)	1979	3.00	6.00	12.00
❑ NBD 20167	Hot Stuff/Bad Girls//(B-side blank)	1979	3.75	7.50	15.00
❑ NBD 20193 [DJ]	Dim All the Lights (7:10)/(B-side blank)	1979	6.25	12.50	25.00
❑ NBD 20199	No More Tears (Enough Is Enough) (11:40)/(B-side blank)	1979	2.50	5.00	10.00
—With Barbra Streisand					
❑ NBD 20226 [DJ]	Walk Away (Disco Mix 7:15)/(B-side blank)	1979	3.75	7.50	15.00
❑ 856357-1	Melody of Love (Classic Club Mix) (Boss Mix) (Epris Mix) (Mijango's Powertools Trip #1)	1994	2.50	5.00	10.00
EPIC					
❑ EAS 42153 [DJ]	I Will Go with You (Con Te Partiro) (Club 69 Future Mix) (Rosabel Dark Dub) (Rosabel Main Vox 12") (Hex Hector Extended Vocal Mix)	1999	2.50	5.00	10.00
❑ EAS 42547 [DJ]	I Will Go with You (Con Te Partiro) (Club 69 Underground Anthem) (Welcome Summertime Fun Extended Mix) (Warren Rigg Summer Dub) (Club 69 Underground Dub)	1999	3.00	6.00	12.00
❑ EAS 42676 [DJ]	I Will Go with You (Con Te Partiro) (Skill Masters Remix 5:08) (Messy Boys Jazz Dub 6:37) (Welcome Downtempo Extended Remix 4:46) (Trouser Enthusiasts Twisted Kiss Mix 10:18) (Johnny Newman Drifting Mix 5:59)	1999	3.75	7.50	15.00
❑ EAS 42892 [DJ]	Love Is the Healer (Thunderpuss 2000 Club Mix 8:58) (Eric Kupper's I Feel Healed 7" Mix) (JP's Sound Factory Mix 9:27) (Thunderpuss 2000 Radio Mix 3:19)	1999	3.00	6.00	12.00
❑ EAS 46473 [DJ]	Love Is the Healer (4 versions)	1999	3.75	7.50	15.00
❑ 49-79202	I Will Go with You (Con Te Partiro) (4 versions)	1999	2.50	5.00	10.00
❑ 49-79226	I Will Go with You (Con Te Partiro) (Club 69 Underground Anthem) (Rosabel Dark Dub) (Warren Rigg Summer Dub) (Club 69 Trippy Dub)	1999	2.00	4.00	8.00
GEFFEN					
❑ PRO-A-910 [DJ]	The Wanderer (stereo/mono)	1980	3.75	7.50	15.00
❑ PRO-A-925 [DJ]	Cold Love/Looking Up/Who Do You Think You're Foolin'	1980	2.50	5.00	10.00
❑ PRO-A-1041 [DJ]	Love Is In Control (Edit) (LP)	1982	2.50	5.00	10.00
❑ PRO-A-2180 [DJ]	There Goes My Baby (same on both sides)	1984	2.50	5.00	10.00
❑ PRO-A-2802 [DJ]	Dinner with Gershwin (7:43) (same on both sides)	1987	2.50	5.00	10.00
❑ PRO-A-3036 [DJ]	All Systems Go (Dance Mix)/Fascination	1987	2.50	5.00	10.00
❑ 20273	Supernatural Love (Extended Dance Remix 6:12)/Face the Music (4:14)	1984	2.00	4.00	8.00
❑ 20635	Dinner with Gershwin (Extended) (Instrumental)	1987	2.00	4.00	8.00
❑ 29938	Love Is In Control (Dance Remix 7:03)/(Instrumental)	1982	2.00	4.00	8.00
INTERHIT					
❑ 10164	Carry On (Outta Control Mix) (Hot Tracks Mix) (Slammin' Cox Mix) (Hysteria Mix)	1997	2.50	5.00	10.00
—With Giorgio Moroder					
MERCURY					
❑ PRO 226-1 [DJ]	Unconditional Love (Club Mix 5:20)/(Instrumental 4:40)	1983	3.00	6.00	12.00
❑ 812370-1	She Works Hard for the Money (Special Long Version) (Instrumental)	1983	2.50	5.00	10.00
❑ 814592-1	Unconditional Love (Remix)/She Works Hard for the Money (Remix)	1983	2.50	5.00	10.00
UNIVERSAL					
❑ U8P-1130 [DJ]	Whenever There Is Love (Club Mix) (Club Dub) (Riff Dub) (Tribal Beats) (Instrumental) (7" Mix)	1998	10.00	20.00	40.00

45s

Number	Title (A Side/B Side)	Yr	VG	VG+	NM
ATLANTIC					
❑ 88792	Breakaway/Thinkin' Bout My Baby	1989	—	2.00	4.00
❑ 88840	Love's About to Change My Heart (PWL 7" Mix)/(Clivilles & Cole 7" Mix)	1989	—	—	3.00
❑ 88899	This Time I Know It's for Real/If It Makes You Feel Good	1989	—	—	3.00
❑ 88899 [PS]	This Time I Know It's for Real/If It Makes You Feel Good	1989	—	2.00	4.00
CASABLANCA					
❑ 872	Spring Affair/Come with Me	1976	—	2.50	5.00
❑ 874	Winter Melody/Spring Affair	1977	—	2.50	5.00
❑ 884	I Feel Love/Can't We Just Sit Down (And Talk It Over)	1977	—	2.50	5.00
—Second pressings have "I Feel Love" listed as "Side A"					
❑ 884	Can't We Just Sit Down (And Talk It Over)/I Feel Love	1977	—	3.00	6.00
—Original copies have "Can't We Just Sit Down" labeled as "Side A"					
❑ 884 [DJ]	I Feel Love (stereo/mono)	1977	2.00	4.00	8.00
—Both sides are shorter than the version on the stock 45					
❑ 884 [DJ]	Can't We Just Sit Down (And Talk It Over) (stereo/mono)	1977	2.50	5.00	10.00
❑ 907	I Love You/Once Upon a Time	1977	—	2.50	5.00
❑ 916	Rumour Has It/Once Upon a Time	1978	—	2.50	5.00
❑ 926	Last Dance/With Your Love	1978	—	2.00	4.00
❑ 939	Mac Arthur Park/Once Upon a Time	1978	—	2.00	4.00

S

Number	Title (A Side/B Side)	Yr	VG	VG+	NM
❏ 959	Heaven Knows/Only One Love	1979	—	2.00	4.00
—A-side with Brooklyn Dreams					
❏ 978	Hot Stuff/Journey to the Center of Your Heart	1979	—	2.00	4.00
❏ 988	Bad Girls/On My Honor	1979	—	2.00	4.00
❏ 2201	Dim All the Lights/There Will Always Be a You	1979	—	2.00	4.00
❏ 2236	On the Radio/There Will Always Be a You	1980	—	2.00	4.00
❏ 2273	Our Love/Sunset People	1980	—	2.50	5.00
❏ 2300	Walk Away/Could It Be Magic	1980	—	2.00	4.00
❏ 858366-7	Melody of Love/The Christmas Song	1994	—	—	3.00
❏ 858366-7 [PS]	Melody of Love/The Christmas Song	1994	—	—	3.00
EPIC					
❏ 38-79201	I Will Go with You (Con Te Partiro)/Love On & On	1999	—	—	3.00
GEFFEN					
❏ 27939	Fascination/All Systems Go	1988	—	2.00	4.00
❏ 28165	Only the Fool Survives/Love Shock	1987	—	2.00	4.00
—A-side with Mickey Thomas					
❏ 28165 [PS]	Only the Fool Survives/Love Shock	1987	—	2.00	4.00
—A-side with Mickey Thomas					
❏ 28418	Dinner with Gershwin/(Instrumental)	1987	—	2.00	4.00
❏ 28418 [PS]	Dinner with Gershwin/(Instrumental)	1987	—	2.00	4.00
❏ 29142	Supernatural Love/Face the Music	1984	—	2.00	4.00
❏ 29142 [PS]	Supernatural Love/Face the Music	1984	—	2.00	4.00
❏ 29291	There Goes My Baby/Maybe It's Over	1984	—	2.00	4.00
❏ 29291 [PS]	There Goes My Baby/Maybe It's Over	1984	—	2.00	4.00
❏ 29805	The Woman in Me/Livin' in America	1982	—	2.00	4.00
❏ 29805 [PS]	The Woman in Me/Livin' in America	1982	—	2.00	4.00
❏ 29895	State of Independence/Love Is Just a Breath Away	1982	—	2.00	4.00
❏ 29895 [PS]	State of Independence/Love Is Just a Breath Away	1982	—	2.00	4.00
❏ 29982	Love Is In Control (Finger on the Trigger)/Sometimes Like Butterflies	1982	—	2.00	4.00
❏ 29982 [PS]	Love Is In Control (Finger on the Trigger)/Sometimes Like Butterflies	1982	—	2.50	5.00
❏ 49563	The Wanderer/Stop Me	1980	—	2.00	4.00
—Second pressings have WB logo replaced by Geffen logo					
❏ 49563 [PS]	The Wanderer/Stop Me	1980	—	2.50	5.00
❏ 49634	Cold Love/Grand Illusion	1980	—	2.00	4.00
❏ 49634 [PS]	Cold Love/Grand Illusion	1980	—	2.50	5.00
❏ 49664	Who Do You Think You're Foolin'/Runnin' for Cover	1981	—	2.00	4.00
MERCURY					
❏ 812370-7	She Works Hard for the Money/I Do Believe (I'll Fall in Love)	1983	—	2.00	4.00
❏ 812370-7 [PS]	She Works Hard for the Money/I Do Believe (I'll Fall in Love)	1983	—	2.50	5.00
❏ 814088-7	Unconditional Love/Woman	1983	—	2.00	4.00
❏ 814088-7 [PS]	Unconditional Love/Woman	1983	—	2.50	5.00
❏ 814922-7	Love Has a Mind of Its Own/Stop, Look and Listen	1983	—	2.00	4.00
—A-side with Matthew Ward					
OASIS					
❏ 401 A /B	Love to Love You Baby/Need-A-Man Blues	1975	3.00	6.00	12.00
—"Love to Love You Baby" has a radically different mix on the above first pressing					
❏ 401 AA/BB	Love to Love You Baby (4:55)/Love to Love You Baby (3:24)	1975	—	3.00	6.00
—Both sides are remixed compared to the original 45 mix					
❏ 405	Could It Be Magic/Whispering Waves	1976	—	3.00	6.00
❏ 406	Try Me, I Know We Can Make It/Wasted	1976	—	3.00	6.00
❏ 406 [PS]	Try Me, I Know We Can Make It/Wasted	1976	2.00	4.00	8.00
WARNER BROS./GEFFEN					
❏ 49563	The Wanderer/Stop Me	1980	—	3.00	6.00
—Original pressings have a WB logo on the left side and "Geffen Records" in a box at the top of the label					
Albums					
ATLANTIC					
❏ 81987	Another Place and Time	1989	3.00	6.00	12.00
CASABLANCA					
❏ NBLP 7038	Four Seasons of Love	1976	2.50	5.00	10.00
❏ NBLP 7056	I Remember Yesterday	1977	2.50	5.00	10.00
❏ NBLP 7078 [(2)]	Once Upon a Time...	1977	3.00	6.00	12.00
❏ NBLP 7119 [(2)]	Live and More	1978	3.00	6.00	12.00
❏ NBPIX 7119 [PD]	The Best of Live and More	1979	5.00	10.00	20.00
❏ NBLP 7150 [(2)]	Bad Girls	1979	3.00	6.00	12.00
❏ NBLP 7191 [(2)]	On the Radio — Greatest Hits Vols. 1 and 2	1979	3.00	6.00	12.00
❏ NBLP 7201	Greatest Hits, Vol. 1	1979	2.00	4.00	8.00
❏ NBLP 7202	Greatest Hits, Vol. 2	1979	2.00	4.00	8.00
❏ NBLP 7244	Walk Away — Collector's Edition (The Best of 1977-1980)	1980	2.50	5.00	10.00
❏ 811123-1 [(2)]	Live and More	1985	2.50	5.00	10.00
❏ 822557-1 [(2)]	Bad Girls	1984	2.50	5.00	10.00
❏ 822558-1 [(2)]	On the Radio — Greatest Hits Vols. 1 and 2	1984	2.50	5.00	10.00
❏ 822559-1	Greatest Hits, Vol. 2	1984	2.00	4.00	8.00
❏ 822560-1	Walk Away	1984	2.00	4.00	8.00
EPIC					
❏ E2 69910 [(2)]	Live and More Encore	1999	3.75	7.50	15.00
GEFFEN					
❏ GHS 2000	The Wanderer	1980	2.50	5.00	10.00
❏ GHS 2005	Donna Summer	1982	2.50	5.00	10.00
❏ GHS 24040	Cats Without Claws	1984	2.50	5.00	10.00
❏ GHS 24040 [DJ]	Cats Without Claws	1984	3.75	7.50	15.00
—Promo only on Quiex II vinyl					
❏ GHS 24102	All Systems Go	1987	2.50	5.00	10.00
MERCURY					
❏ 812265-1	She Works Hard for the Money	1983	2.50	5.00	10.00
❏ 826144-1	The Summer Collection	1985	2.50	5.00	10.00
OASIS					
❏ OCLP 5003	Love to Love You Baby	1975	3.00	6.00	12.00
—Add 50% if poster is included					
❏ OCLP 5004	A Love Trilogy	1976	3.00	6.00	12.00
❏ 822792-1	Love to Love You Baby	1985	2.00	4.00	8.00

SUMMER SOUNDS, THE
Albums

Number	Title (A Side/B Side)	Yr	VG	VG+	NM
LAUREL					
❏ 90973	Up Down	196?	250.00	500.00	1000.

Number	Title (A Side/B Side)	Yr	VG	VG+	NM
SUMMERHILL					
45s					
TETRAGRAMMATON					
❏ 1528	Soft Voice/The Last Day	1969	2.50	5.00	10.00
Albums					
TETRAGRAMMATON					
❏ T-114	Summerhill	1969	7.50	15.00	30.00

SUMMERS, DAVEY, AND THE SINGING ANTS
45s

Number	Title (A Side/B Side)	Yr	VG	VG+	NM
DORE					
❏ 684	Gonna Climb That Big Ole Hill/Doin' the Davey Drag	1963	10.00	20.00	40.00

SUMMERS, GENE
45s

Number	Title (A Side/B Side)	Yr	VG	VG+	NM
CAPRI					
❏ 502	Blue Diamond/You Said You Loved Me	196?	5.00	10.00	20.00
❏ 507	Alabama Shake/Just Because	1964	15.00	30.00	60.00
JAMIE					
❏ 1273	Blue Diamond/You Said You Loved Me	1964	3.75	7.50	15.00
JAN					
❏ 100	School of Rock 'N' Roll/Straight Skirt	1958	15.00	30.00	60.00
❏ 102	Nervous/Gotta Love That	1959	15.00	30.00	60.00
❏ 106	Twixteen/I'll Never Be Lonely	1959	15.00	30.00	60.00
MERCURY					
❏ 72606	Green-Eyed Monster/The Clown	1966	3.75	7.50	15.00
TEARDROP					
❏ 3405	Goodbye Priscilla (Bye Bye Baby Blue)/Down on the Farm	1977	2.00	4.00	8.00
❏ 3405 [DJ]	Goodbye Priscilla (Bye Bye Blue Baby)	1977	3.00	6.00	12.00
—Single-sided promo copies have erroneous subtitle					

SUMMERS, JOHNNY
45s

Number	Title (A Side/B Side)	Yr	VG	VG+	NM
YORKTOWN					
❏ 1007	Prove It to Me/(B-side unknown)	196?	125.00	250.00	500.00
❏ 1009	I Can't Let Go/(B-side unknown)	196?	300.00	600.00	1200.

SUN-RAYS, THE
45s

Number	Title (A Side/B Side)	Yr	VG	VG+	NM
SUN					
❏ 293	Love Is a Stranger/The Lonely Hours	1958	10.00	20.00	40.00

SUNBEAMS, THE (1)
45s

Number	Title (A Side/B Side)	Yr	VG	VG+	NM
ACME					
❏ 109	Please Say You'll Be Mine/You've Got to Rock and Roll	1957	750.00	1500.	3000.
HERALD					
❏ 451	Tell Me Why/Come Back Baby	1955	75.00	150.00	300.00
LOST-NITE					
❏ 427	Tell Me Why/Come Back Baby	197?	—	2.50	5.00
—Reissue					

SUNBEAMS, THE (2)
45s

Number	Title (A Side/B Side)	Yr	VG	VG+	NM
DOT					
❏ 1271	I'm Gonna Go Home to Mama/Blue Mountain Waltz	1955	7.50	15.00	30.00
❏ 1280	How About It/Wrap It Up and Save It	1956	7.50	15.00	30.00

SUNBEAMS, THE (3)
45s

Number	Title (A Side/B Side)	Yr	VG	VG+	NM
TOLLIE					
❏ 9022	Sing a Song/Good Old Days	1964	3.00	6.00	12.00

SUNDAY FUNNIES, THE
45s

Number	Title (A Side/B Side)	Yr	VG	VG+	NM
CAPITOL					
❏ 5614	Another Time, Another Place/Headlines	1966	3.00	6.00	12.00
HIDEOUT					
❏ 1070	Heavy Music/Path of Freedom	196?	7.50	15.00	30.00
MERCURY					
❏ 72571	Wonder Woman/She's Not at All Like You	1966	3.00	6.00	12.00
RARE EARTH					
❏ 5035	Walk Down the Path of Freedom/It's Just a Dream	1971	2.00	4.00	8.00
UNI					
❏ 55157	Baby, I Could Be So Good at Loving You/See Things My Way	1969	2.50	5.00	10.00
Albums					
RARE EARTH					
❏ RS-526	The Sunday Funnies	1971	3.00	6.00	12.00
❏ RS-538	Benediction	1972	3.00	6.00	12.00

SUNDIALS, THE
45s

Number	Title (A Side/B Side)	Yr	VG	VG+	NM
GUYDEN					
❏ 2065	Chapel of Love/Whether to Resist	1962	50.00	100.00	200.00

SUNDOWN PLAYBOYS, THE
45s

Number	Title (A Side/B Side)	Yr	VG	VG+	NM
APPLE					
❏ 1852	Saturday Night Special/Valse De Soleil Coucher	1972	3.75	7.50	15.00
GOLDBAND					
❏ 1073	Sundown Waltz/River Two Step	195?	7.50	15.00	30.00

SUNDOWNERS, THE
45s

Number	Title (A Side/B Side)	Yr	VG	VG+	NM
JAMIE					
❏ 1271	A Shot of Rhythm 'N' Blues/Come On In	1964	3.00	6.00	12.00
Albums					
LIBERTY					
❏ LRP-3269 [M]	Folk Songs for the Rich	1962	5.00	10.00	20.00
❏ LST-7269 [S]	Folk Songs for the Rich	1962	6.25	12.50	25.00

Number	Title (A Side/B Side)	Yr	VG	VG+	NM

SUNGLOWS, THE See SUNNY AND THE SUNLINERS.

SUNLINERS, THE
45s
GOLDEN WORLD
❏ 31	The Swingin' Kind/All Alone	1965	7.50	15.00	30.00

MGM
| ❏ 13809 | Land of Nod/Well One | 1967 | 6.25 | 12.50 | 25.00 |

SUNNY AND THE HORIZONS
45s
LUXOR
| ❏ 1013 | Nature's Creation/Because They Tell Me | 1962 | 18.75 | 37.50 | 75.00 |

—*Red label*
| ❏ 1013 | Nature's Creation/Because They Tell Me | 1962 | 50.00 | 100.00 | 200.00 |

—*Yellow label*

SUNNY AND THE SUNGLOWS See SUNNY AND THE SUNLINERS.

SUNNY AND THE SUNLINERS
45s
DISCO GRANDE
| ❏ 1021 | Peanuts (La Cacahuata)/Fallaste Corazon | 1965 | 5.00 | 10.00 | 20.00 |

—*A later issue than first pressings of Sunglow 107*
KEY-LOC
| ❏ 1010 | I Want To Come Home For Christmas/ (B-side unknown) | 1966 | 2.00 | 4.00 | 8.00 |

OKEH
| ❏ 7143 | Golly Gee/Touring | 1962 | 3.00 | 6.00 | 12.00 |

—*As "Sunny and the Sunglows"*
SUNGLOW
❏ 102	Sylvia/(B-side unknown)	1961	3.75	7.50	15.00
❏ 103	A Dream/The Lasso	1961	3.75	7.50	15.00
❏ 104	Golly Gee/Touring	1961	3.75	7.50	15.00
❏ 105	Once in a While/Ho Ho Ha Ha	1962	3.75	7.50	15.00
❏ 106	Won't You Tell Me/(B-side unknown)	1962	3.75	7.50	15.00
❏ 107	Peanuts (La Cacahuata)/Fallaste Corazon	1962	5.00	10.00	20.00
❏ 107	La Cacahuata/Fallaste Corazon	1962	7.50	15.00	30.00

—*Original issue of this record; no mention of "Peanuts" on label; composer listed as "Desconocido" (Spanish for "Unknown")*
❏ 107	Peanuts (La Cacahuata)/Happy Hippo	1963	3.75	7.50	15.00
❏ 107	Peanuts (La Cacahuata)/Love Me (All My Love Belongs to You)	1965	3.00	6.00	12.00
❏ 109	Close Your Eyes/Ooo Poo Pa Doo	1963	3.75	7.50	15.00
❏ 110	Talk to Me/Pony Time	1963	5.00	10.00	20.00
❏ 111	Rags to Riches/It Won't Be Me	1963	4.50	9.00	18.00
❏ 112	The Dog/You Can Make It If You Try	1963	3.75	7.50	15.00
❏ 115	Till the End of Time/La Bamba	1964	3.75	7.50	15.00
❏ 116	Guess Who/Just as I Thought	1964	3.75	7.50	15.00
❏ 117	Love Me/Honey Child	1964	3.75	7.50	15.00
❏ 118	Popcorn/The Circus	1964	3.75	7.50	15.00
❏ 118	Popcorn/All Night Worker	1965	3.75	7.50	15.00
❏ 119	Baby I Apologize/Cut Across Shorty	1965	3.75	7.50	15.00
❏ 120	Oh Heart/Latin Trumpet	1965	3.75	7.50	15.00
❏ 122	Fly Me to the Moon/La Macarena	1966	3.75	7.50	15.00
❏ 123	If You Don't Love Me/(B-side unknown)	1966	3.75	7.50	15.00
❏ 124	Just a Game/Maria Elena	1966	3.75	7.50	15.00
❏ 125	Again/Roly Poly	1967	3.75	7.50	15.00
❏ 127	It's Okay/99 + 1	1968	3.75	7.50	15.00

—*All Sunglow releases as "The Sunglows"*
TEAR DROP
| ❏ 3014 | Talk to Me/Every Week, Every Month, Every Year | 1963 | 2.50 | 5.00 | 10.00 |

—*A-side as "Sunny and the Sunglows"*
❏ 3016	Carino Nuevo/(B-side unknown)	1963	3.00	6.00	12.00
❏ 3022	Rags to Riches/Not Even Judgment Day	1963	2.50	5.00	10.00
❏ 3025	Cuando El Destino/(B-side unknown)	1963	3.00	6.00	12.00
❏ 3027	Out of Sight, Out of Mind/No One Else Will Do	1964	2.50	5.00	10.00
❏ 3031	Pa Que Sientas, Lo Que Sientex Que Tal Te Sientes/De Mi Nada Mas, Usted	1964	3.00	6.00	12.00

—*As "Sunny Ozuna"*
❏ 3035	It's Too Late/You Gave Me a True Love	1964	2.50	5.00	10.00
❏ 3037	Tu Nueva Viva/Dime Como Le Haces	1964	3.00	6.00	12.00
❏ 3040	You Send Me/His Greatest Creation	1964	2.50	5.00	10.00
❏ 3045	Something's Got a Hold on Me/Teenage Promise-I'm Not a Fool Anymore	1964	2.50	5.00	10.00
❏ 3056	Token of Love/Little Dancing Girl	1965	2.50	5.00	10.00

—*As "Sunny Ozuna"*
❏ 3066	El Ta Conazo/La Diudades	1965	3.00	6.00	12.00
❏ 3067	Hitch Hike/That Night in San Antonio	1965	2.50	5.00	10.00
❏ 3071	Too Young/The Very Thought of You	1965	2.50	5.00	10.00
❏ 3079	Trick Bag/Cheatin' Traces	1965	2.50	5.00	10.00
❏ 3094	Fly Me to the Moon/Short Short Shorty	1966	2.00	4.00	8.00
❏ 3096	Tristie Y Lastimado/(B-side unknown)	1966	3.00	6.00	12.00
❏ 3123	No One Else Will Do/Cheatin' Traces	1966	2.00	4.00	8.00
❏ 3183	Wonderful Girl/Talk That Trash	1966	2.00	4.00	8.00

WHITE WHALE
| ❏ 324 | It's Okay/99 + 1 | 1969 | 2.00 | 4.00 | 8.00 |

—*As "The Sunglows"*
Albums
KEY-LOC
❏ 3001 [M]	Smile Now, Cry Later	196?	6.25	12.50	25.00
❏ 3002 [M]	No Te Chifles	196?	6.25	12.50	25.00
❏ 3003 [M]	Sunny and the Sunliners Live in Hollywood	196?	6.25	12.50	25.00
❏ 3004 [M]	Canta Sunny	196?	6.25	12.50	25.00
❏ 3005 [M]	A Little Brown-Eyed Soul	196?	6.25	12.50	25.00
❏ 3006 [M]	This Is My Band	196?	6.25	12.50	25.00
❏ 3007 [M]	Versatile	196?	6.25	12.50	25.00
❏ 3008 [M]	Adelante	196?	6.25	12.50	25.00
❏ 3009 [M]	Sky High	196?	6.25	12.50	25.00
❏ 3010 [M]	The Missing Link	196?	6.25	12.50	25.00

SUNGLOW
| ❏ SLP-101 [M] | Sunny Ozuna and the Sunglows | 1963 | 25.00 | 50.00 | 100.00 |

—*As "The Sunglows"*
| ❏ SLP-102 [M] | The Fabulous Sunglows | 1964 | 25.00 | 50.00 | 100.00 |

—*As "The Sunglows"*

| ❏ SLP-103 [M] | The Original Peanuts | 1965 | 20.00 | 40.00 | 80.00 |

—*As "The Sunglows"*
| ❏ SLP-103S [S] | The Original Peanuts | 1965 | 25.00 | 50.00 | 100.00 |

—*As "The Sunglows"*
TEAR DROP
❏ LPM-2000 [M]	Talk to Me	1963	25.00	50.00	100.00
❏ LPM-2001 [M]	Las Vegas Welcomes Sunny and the Sunliners	1964	10.00	20.00	40.00
❏ LPM-2008 [M]	Teardrop Presents Sunny and the Sunliners	196?	10.00	20.00	40.00

SUNRAYS, THE Also see THE SNOW MEN.
45s
TOWER
❏ 101	Outta Gas/Car Party	1964	5.00	10.00	20.00
❏ 148	I Live for the Sun/Bye Baby Bye	1965	3.00	6.00	12.00
❏ 191	Andrea/You Don't Phase Me	1966	3.00	6.00	12.00
❏ 224	Still/When You're Not There	1966	3.00	6.00	12.00
❏ 256	Don't Take Yourself Too Seriously/I Look Baby, I Can't See	1966	3.00	6.00	12.00
❏ 256 [PS]	Don't Take Yourself Too Seriously/I Look Baby, I Can't See	1966	6.25	12.50	25.00
❏ 290	Hi, How Are You/Just 'Round the River Bend	1966	3.75	7.50	15.00
❏ 340	Loaded with Love/Time (A Special Thing)	1967	3.75	7.50	15.00

WARNER BROS.
| ❏ 5253 | Talk to Him/Gideon | 1962 | 3.75 | 7.50 | 15.00 |

Albums
TOWER
| ❏ ST 5017 [S] | Andrea | 1966 | 15.00 | 30.00 | 60.00 |
| ❏ T 5017 [M] | Andrea | 1966 | 12.50 | 25.00 | 50.00 |

SUNSET DRAGSTERS, THE
Albums
PALACE
| ❏ M-775 [M] | Hot Rod Rally | 196? | 15.00 | 30.00 | 60.00 |
| ❏ PST-775 [S] | Hot Rod Rally | 196? | 20.00 | 40.00 | 80.00 |

SUNSETS, THE (1)
45s
CHALLENGE
❏ 9186	C.C. Rider/The Chug-a-Lug	1963	10.00	20.00	40.00
❏ 9198	Lonely Surfer Boy/Playmate of the Year	1963	10.00	20.00	40.00
❏ 9208	My Little Beach Bunny/My Little Surfin' Woody	1963	12.50	25.00	50.00

PETAL
| ❏ 1040 | Lydia/Only You, Only Me | 1963 | 12.50 | 25.00 | 50.00 |

Albums
PALACE
| ❏ M-752 [M] | Surfing with the Sunsets | 1963 | 10.00 | 20.00 | 40.00 |
| ❏ PST-752 [S] | Surfing with the Sunsets | 1963 | 12.50 | 25.00 | 50.00 |

SUNSETS, THE (2)
45s
RAE COX
| ❏ 102 | How Will I Remember/Sittin' and Cryin' | 1959 | 10.00 | 20.00 | 40.00 |

SUNSHINE COMPANY, THE
45s
IMPERIAL
| ❏ 66241 | Up Up and Away/Blue May | 1967 | — | — | — |

—*Unreleased*
❏ 66247	Happy/Blue May	1967	2.50	5.00	10.00
❏ 66260	Back on the Street Again/I Just Want to Be Your Friend	1967	2.50	5.00	10.00
❏ 66278	Reflections on an Angel/It's Sunday	1968	—	—	—

—*Unreleased*
❏ 66280	Look, Here Comes the Sun/It's Sunday	1968	2.50	5.00	10.00
❏ 66298	Let's Get Together/Sunday Brought the Rain	1968	2.50	5.00	10.00
❏ 66308	On a Beautiful Day/Darcy Farrow	1968	2.50	5.00	10.00
❏ 66324	Love Poem/Willie Jean	1968	2.50	5.00	10.00
❏ 66399	The Only Thing That Matters/Bolaro	1969	2.50	5.00	10.00

UNITED ARTISTS
| ❏ 0132 | Happy/Back on the Street Again | 1973 | — | 2.00 | 4.00 |

—*"Silver Spotlight Series" reissue*
Albums
IMPERIAL
| ❏ LP-9359 [M] | Happy Is the Sunshine Company | 1967 | 5.00 | 10.00 | 20.00 |
| ❏ LP-9368 [M] | The Sunshine Company | 1968 | 6.25 | 12.50 | 25.00 |

—*Mono copies are promo only*
❏ LP-12359 [S]	Happy Is the Sunshine Company	1967	5.00	10.00	20.00
❏ LP-12368 [S]	The Sunshine Company	1968	5.00	10.00	20.00
❏ LP-12399	Sunshine and Shadows	1969	5.00	10.00	20.00

SUPER K GENERATION, THE
45s
LAURIE
| ❏ 3413 | Heartful O'Soul (Part 1)/Heartful O'Soul (Part 2) | 1967 | 2.50 | 5.00 | 10.00 |

SUPER STOCKS, THE
45s
CAPITOL
| ❏ 5153 | Thunder Road/Wheel Stands | 1964 | 6.25 | 12.50 | 25.00 |

Albums
CAPITOL
❏ ST 1997 [S]	Hot Rod Rally	1963	17.50	35.00	70.00
❏ T 1997 [M]	Hot Rod Rally	1963	12.50	25.00	50.00
❏ (S)T 2060	Thunder Road Bonus Poster	1964	12.50	25.00	50.00
❏ ST 2060 [S]	Thunder Road	1964	31.25	62.50	125.00
❏ T 2060 [M]	Thunder Road	1964	25.00	50.00	100.00
❏ ST 2113 [S]	Surf Route 101	1964	31.25	62.50	125.00

—*Without bonus single*
| ❏ ST 2113 [S] | Surf Route 101 | 1964 | 37.50 | 75.00 | 150.00 |

—*With bonus single, "Doin' the Surfink"/"Finksville, U.S.A." by Mr. Gasser and the Weirdos, in special pocket on front cover*
| ❏ T 2113 [M] | Surf Route 101 | 1964 | 25.00 | 50.00 | 100.00 |

—*Without bonus single*
| ❏ T 2113 [M] | Surf Route 101 | 1964 | 31.25 | 62.50 | 125.00 |

—*With bonus single, "Doin' the Surfink"/"Finksville, U.S.A." by Mr. Gasser and the Weirdos, in special pocket on front cover*
| ❏ ST 2190 [S] | School Is a Drag | 1964 | 30.00 | 60.00 | 120.00 |
| ❏ T 2190 [M] | School Is a Drag | 1964 | 25.00 | 50.00 | 100.00 |

S

Number	Title (A Side/B Side)	Yr	VG	VG+	NM

SUPERFINE DANDELION, THE
45s
MAINSTREAM

Number	Title (A Side/B Side)	Yr	VG	VG+	NM
❑ 672	People in the Street/(B-side unknown)	1967	3.00	6.00	12.00
❑ 673	Crazy Town/Janie's Tomb	1967	3.00	6.00	12.00

Albums
MAINSTREAM

Number	Title (A Side/B Side)	Yr	VG	VG+	NM
❑ S-6102 [S]	The Superfine Dandelion	1967	10.00	20.00	40.00
❑ 56102 [M]	The Superfine Dandelion	1967	10.00	20.00	40.00

SUPERIORS, THE (1)
45s
ATCO

Number	Title (A Side/B Side)	Yr	VG	VG+	NM
❑ 6106	Lost Love/Don't Say Goodbye	1957	17.50	35.00	70.00

LOST-NITE

Number	Title (A Side/B Side)	Yr	VG	VG+	NM
❑ 177	Lost Love/Don't Say Goodbye	196?	—	3.00	6.00

—*Reissue*
MAIN LINE

Number	Title (A Side/B Side)	Yr	VG	VG+	NM
❑ 104	Lost Love/Don't Say Goodbye	1958	150.00	300.00	600.00

—*With Fairmount Ave., Philadelphia street address on label*

Number	Title (A Side/B Side)	Yr	VG	VG+	NM
❑ 104	Lost Love/Don't Say Goodbye	1962	10.00	20.00	40.00

—*No address on label or only "Philadelphia, Pennsylvania" address on label*

SUPERIORS, THE (2)
45s
FAL

Number	Title (A Side/B Side)	Yr	VG	VG+	NM
❑ 301	What Is Love/Flee the Scene	1961	20.00	40.00	80.00

FEDERAL

Number	Title (A Side/B Side)	Yr	VG	VG+	NM
❑ 12436	I'm Sorry Baby (I Didn't Mean to Do You Wrong)/ Dance of Love	1961	7.50	15.00	30.00

SUPERIORS, THE (3)
45s
MGM

Number	Title (A Side/B Side)	Yr	VG	VG+	NM
❑ 13503	Can't Make It Without You/Let Me Make You Happy	1966	3.00	6.00	12.00

SUE

Number	Title (A Side/B Side)	Yr	VG	VG+	NM
❑ 12	Heavenly Angel/I'd Rather Die	1969	2.00	4.00	8.00

VERVE

Number	Title (A Side/B Side)	Yr	VG	VG+	NM
❑ 10370	Tell Me to Go/What Would I Do	1965	5.00	10.00	20.00

SUPERSAX
Albums
CAPITOL

Number	Title (A Side/B Side)	Yr	VG	VG+	NM
❑ ST-11177	Supersax Plays Bird	1973	2.50	5.00	10.00
❑ ST-11271	Supersax Plays Bird, Volume 2/Salt Peanuts	1974	2.50	5.00	10.00
❑ ST-11371	Supersax Plays Bird with Strings	1975	2.50	5.00	10.00

COLUMBIA

Number	Title (A Side/B Side)	Yr	VG	VG+	NM
❑ FC 39140	Supersax and L.A. Voices	1984	2.50	5.00	10.00
❑ FC 39925	Supersax and L.A. Voices, Vol. 2	1985	2.50	5.00	10.00
❑ FC 40547	Supersax and L.A. Voices Volume 3: Straighten Up and Fly Right	1986	2.50	5.00	10.00
❑ FC 44436	Stone Bird	1989	3.00	6.00	12.00

MOBILE FIDELITY

Number	Title (A Side/B Side)	Yr	VG	VG+	NM
❑ 1-511	Supersax Plays Bird	1981	10.00	20.00	40.00

—*Audiophile vinyl*
PAUSA

Number	Title (A Side/B Side)	Yr	VG	VG+	NM
❑ 7038	Chasin' the Bird	1977	2.50	5.00	10.00
❑ 7082	Dynamite!	1979	2.50	5.00	10.00
❑ 9028	Supersax Plays Bird, Volume 2/Salt Peanuts	198?	2.00	4.00	8.00

SUPERSISTER
Albums
DWARF

Number	Title (A Side/B Side)	Yr	VG	VG+	NM
❑ PDLP-2001	Supersister	197?	7.50	15.00	30.00

SUPERTRAMP
12-Inch Singles
A&M

Number	Title (A Side/B Side)	Yr	VG	VG+	NM
❑ SP-12254	I'm Beggin' You (3 remixes)	1987	2.00	4.00	8.00
❑ SP-17320 [DJ]	Cannonball (Edit) (Single Version) (Direct-to-Disc Version)	1985	2.50	5.00	10.00

45s
A&M

Number	Title (A Side/B Side)	Yr	VG	VG+	NM
❑ 1305	Forever/Your Poppa Don't Mind	1971	—	3.00	6.00
❑ 1660	Bloody Well Right/Dreamer	1975	—	2.50	5.00
❑ 1766	Lady/You Started Laughing When I Held You in My Arms	1975	—	—	—

—*Unreleased?*

Number	Title (A Side/B Side)	Yr	VG	VG+	NM
❑ 1793	Lady/You Started Laughing When I Held You in My Arms	1976	—	2.50	5.00
❑ 1814	Sister Moonshine/Ain't Nobody But Me	1976	—	2.50	5.00
❑ 1938	Give a Little Bit/Downstream	1977	—	2.00	4.00
❑ 1938 [PS]	Give a Little Bit/Downstream	1977	—	3.00	6.00
❑ 1981	Dreamer/From Now On	1977	—	2.50	5.00
❑ 1981 [PS]	Dreamer/From Now On	1977	—	3.00	6.00
❑ 2128	The Logical Song/Just Another Nervous Wreck	1979	—	2.00	4.00
❑ 2128 [PS]	The Logical Song/Just Another Nervous Wreck	1979	—	2.50	5.00
❑ 2162	Goodbye Stranger/ Even in the Quietest Moments	1979	—	2.00	4.00
❑ 2162 [PS]	Goodbye Stranger/ Even in the Quietest Moments	1979	—	2.50	5.00
❑ 2193	Take the Long Way Home/Ruby	1979	—	2.00	4.00
❑ 2193 [PS]	Take the Long Way Home/Ruby	1979	—	2.00	4.00

—*With yellow maze*

Number	Title (A Side/B Side)	Yr	VG	VG+	NM
❑ 2193 [PS]	Take the Long Way Home/Ruby	1979	—	2.50	5.00

—*With green maze*

Number	Title (A Side/B Side)	Yr	VG	VG+	NM
❑ 2193 [PS]	Take the Long Way Home/Ruby	1979	—	2.50	5.00

—*With red maze. Other colors may exist as well.*

Number	Title (A Side/B Side)	Yr	VG	VG+	NM
❑ 2269	Dreamer/From Now On	1980	—	2.00	4.00
❑ 2269 [PS]	Dreamer/From Now On	1980	—	2.50	5.00
❑ 2292	Breakfast in America/You Started Laughing	1980	—	2.00	4.00
❑ 2502	It's Raining Again/Bonnie	1982	—	2.00	4.00
❑ 2502 [PS]	It's Raining Again/Bonnie	1982	—	2.00	4.00
❑ 2517	My Kind of Lady/Know Who You Are	1983	—	2.00	4.00
❑ 2517 [PS]	My Kind of Lady/Know Who You Are	1983	—	2.00	4.00

Number	Title (A Side/B Side)	Yr	VG	VG+	NM
❑ 2720 [DJ]	Still in Love with You (same on both sides)	1985	—	—	—

—*Unreleased?*

Number	Title (A Side/B Side)	Yr	VG	VG+	NM
❑ 2731	Cannonball/Every Open Door	1985	—	—	3.00
❑ 2731 [PS]	Cannonball/Every Open Door	1985	—	—	3.00
❑ 2760	Better Days/No In-Between	1985	—	—	3.00
❑ 2985	I'm Beggin' You/No Inbetween	1987	—	—	3.00
❑ 2985 [PS]	I'm Beggin' You/No Inbetween	1987	—	—	3.00
❑ 2996	Free as a Bird/Thing for You	1987	—	—	3.00

Albums
A&M

Number	Title (A Side/B Side)	Yr	VG	VG+	NM
❑ SP-3129	Indelibly Stamped	198?	2.00	4.00	8.00

—*Budget-line reissue*

Number	Title (A Side/B Side)	Yr	VG	VG+	NM
❑ SP-3149	Supertramp	198?	2.00	4.00	8.00

—*Budget-line reissue*

Number	Title (A Side/B Side)	Yr	VG	VG+	NM
❑ SP-3214	Crisis? What Crisis?	1982	2.00	4.00	8.00

—*Budget-line reissue*

Number	Title (A Side/B Side)	Yr	VG	VG+	NM
❑ SP-3215	Even in the Quietest Moments	1982	2.00	4.00	8.00

—*Budget-line reissue*

Number	Title (A Side/B Side)	Yr	VG	VG+	NM
❑ SP-3284	…Famous Last Words…	1986	2.00	4.00	8.00

—*Budget-line reissue*

Number	Title (A Side/B Side)	Yr	VG	VG+	NM
❑ SP-3647	Crime of the Century	1974	3.00	6.00	12.00
❑ SP-3708	Breakfast in America	1979	2.50	5.00	10.00
❑ SP-3730 [PD]	Breakfast in America	1979	125.00	250.00	500.00

—*In-house picture discs featuring A&M staff members posing with the cover model*

Number	Title (A Side/B Side)	Yr	VG	VG+	NM
❑ SP-3732	…Famous Last Words…	1982	2.50	5.00	10.00
❑ SP-4274	Supertramp	197?	2.50	5.00	10.00

—*Second edition with silverish label*

Number	Title (A Side/B Side)	Yr	VG	VG+	NM
❑ SP-4274	Supertramp	1970	5.00	10.00	20.00

—*First edition with brown label*

Number	Title (A Side/B Side)	Yr	VG	VG+	NM
❑ SP-4311	Indelibly Stamped	197?	2.50	5.00	10.00

—*Second edition with silverish label*

Number	Title (A Side/B Side)	Yr	VG	VG+	NM
❑ SP-4311	Indelibly Stamped	1971	5.00	10.00	20.00

—*First edition with brown label*

Number	Title (A Side/B Side)	Yr	VG	VG+	NM
❑ SP-4560	Crisis? What Crisis?	1975	3.00	6.00	12.00
❑ SP-4634	Even in the Quietest Moments…	1977	3.00	6.00	12.00
❑ SP-4665	Supertramp	1978	3.00	6.00	12.00

—*Reissue of 4274*

Number	Title (A Side/B Side)	Yr	VG	VG+	NM
❑ SP-5013	Brother Where You Bound	1985	2.50	5.00	10.00
❑ SP-5181	Free as a Bird	1987	2.50	5.00	10.00
❑ SP-6702 [(2)]	Paris	1980	3.00	6.00	12.00

MOBILE FIDELITY

Number	Title (A Side/B Side)	Yr	VG	VG+	NM
❑ 1-005	Crime of the Century	1979	10.00	20.00	40.00

—*Audiophile vinyl*

Number	Title (A Side/B Side)	Yr	VG	VG+	NM
❑ MFQR-005	Crime of the Century	1983	30.00	60.00	120.00

—*Ultra High Quality Recording; in box*

Number	Title (A Side/B Side)	Yr	VG	VG+	NM
❑ 1-045	Breakfast in America	1980	12.50	25.00	50.00

—*Audiophile vinyl*
SWEET THUNDER

Number	Title (A Side/B Side)	Yr	VG	VG+	NM
❑ 5	Even in the Quietest Moments…	198?	10.00	20.00	40.00

—*Audiophile vinyl*

SUPREMES, THE
Motown girl group. Also see FLORENCE BALLARD; THE PRIMETTES; DIANA ROSS.
12-Inch Singles
MOTOWN

Number	Title (A Side/B Side)	Yr	VG	VG+	NM
❑ 37463 1157 1 [DJ]	Someday We'll Be Together (Sound Factory Mix 6:57) (Def Mix 8:42) (Radio Edit Mix 3:03)	1994	3.75	7.50	15.00

—*As "Diana Ross and the Supremes"; remixes of the 1969 hit*
45s
EEOC

Number	Title (A Side/B Side)	Yr	VG	VG+	NM
❑ SL4M-3114 [DJ]	Things Are Changing (same on both sides)	1965	37.50	75.00	150.00
❑ SL4M-3114 [PS]	Things Are Changing (same on both sides)	1965	37.50	75.00	150.00

—*Promotional item for the Equal Employment Opportunity Commission (number not on sleeve)*
GEORGE ALEXANDER INC.

Number	Title (A Side/B Side)	Yr	VG	VG+	NM
❑ 1079 [DJ]	The Only Time I'm Happy/Supremes Interview	1965	15.00	30.00	60.00

MOTOWN

Number	Title (A Side/B Side)	Yr	VG	VG+	NM
❑ 1008	I Want a Guy/Never Again	1961	75.00	150.00	300.00
❑ 1027	Your Heart Belongs to Me/(He's) Seventeen	1962	6.25	12.50	25.00
❑ 1027 [PS]	Your Heart Belongs to Me/(He's) Seventeen	1962	100.00	200.00	400.00
❑ 1034	Let Me Go the Right Way/Time Changes Things	1962	12.50	25.00	50.00
❑ 1040	My Heart Can't Take It No More/You Bring Back Memories	1963	10.00	20.00	40.00
❑ 1044	A Breath Taking Guy/Rock and Roll Banjo Band	1963	6.25	12.50	25.00
❑ 1044	A Breath Taking, First Sight Love Making, One Night Love Making, Next Day Heart Breaking Guy/Rock and Roll Banjo Band	1963	25.00	50.00	100.00

—*Original pressing with long title. This does exist on stock copies as well as on promos.*

Number	Title (A Side/B Side)	Yr	VG	VG+	NM
❑ 1051	When the Lovelight Starts Shining Through His Eyes/Standing at the Crossroads of Love	1963	5.00	10.00	20.00
❑ 1054	Run, Run, Run/I'm Giving You Your Freedom	1964	6.25	12.50	25.00
❑ 1060	Where Did Our Love Go/He Means the World to Me	1964	5.00	10.00	20.00
❑ 1060 [PS]	Where Did Our Love Go/He Means the World to Me	1964	7.50	15.00	30.00
❑ 1066	Baby Love/Ask Any Girl	1964	5.00	10.00	20.00
❑ 1066 [PS]	Baby Love/Ask Any Girl	1964	7.50	15.00	30.00
❑ 1068	Come See About Me/Always in My Heart	1964	5.00	10.00	20.00
❑ 1074	Stop! In the Name of Love/I'm in Love Again	1965	3.75	7.50	15.00
❑ 1074 [PS]	Stop! In the Name of Love/I'm in Love Again	1965	7.50	15.00	30.00
❑ 1075	Back in My Arms Again/Whisper You Love Me Boy	1965	3.75	7.50	15.00
❑ 1075 [PS]	Back in My Arms Again/Whisper You Love Me Boy	1965	7.50	15.00	30.00
❑ 1080	Nothing But Heartaches/He Holds His Own	1965	3.75	7.50	15.00
❑ 1080 [PS]	Nothing But Heartaches/He Holds His Own	1965	7.50	15.00	30.00
❑ 1083	I Hear a Symphony/ Who Could Ever Doubt My Love	1965	3.75	7.50	15.00
❑ 1085	Children's Christmas Song/ Twinkle, Twinkle Little Me	1965	5.00	10.00	20.00
❑ 1085 [DJ]	Children's Christmas Song/ Twinkle, Twinkle Little Me	1965	6.25	12.50	25.00

—*Promo only on red vinyl*

Number	Title (A Side/B Side)	Yr	VG	VG+	NM
❑ 1085 [PS]	Children's Christmas Song/ Twinkle, Twinkle Little Me	1965	8.75	17.50	35.00
❑ 1089	My World Is Empty Without You/Everything Is Good About You	1966	3.75	7.50	15.00
❑ 1094	Love Is Like an Itching in My Heart/He's All I Got	1966	3.75	7.50	15.00
❑ 1097	You Can't Hurry Love/Put Yourself in My Place	1966	3.75	7.50	15.00
❑ 1097 [PS]	You Can't Hurry Love/Put Yourself in My Place	1966	7.50	15.00	30.00
❑ 1101	You Keep Me Hangin' On/Remove This Doubt	1966	3.75	7.50	15.00
❑ 1101 [PS]	You Keep Me Hangin' On/Remove This Doubt	1966	7.50	15.00	30.00

Steely Dan, "Dallas," ABC 11323, 45 rpm single, possibly promo only, $15-$30.

Cat Stevens, "Moon Shadow," A&M 1265, picture sleeve, $3-$6.

Rod Stewart, "You Wear It Well," Mercury 73330, picture sleeve, $7.50-$15.

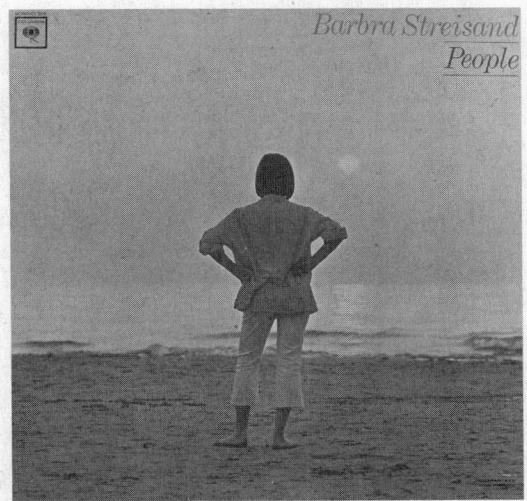

Barbra Streisand, *People*, Columbia CL 2215, mono LP, with "Guaranteed High Fidelity" on label, $10-$20.

Styx, *Man of Miracles*, Wooden Nickel BWL1-0638, stereo LP, with "Lies" on album, $15-$30.

The Supremes, *Where Did Our Love Go*, Motown MS-621, stereo LP, $20-$40.

Number	Title (A Side/B Side)	Yr	VG	VG+	NM
❏ 1103	Love Is Here and Now You're Gone/There's No Stopping Us Now	1967	3.00	6.00	12.00
❏ 1107	The Happening/All I Know About You	1967	3.00	6.00	12.00
❏ 1111	Reflections/Going Down for the Third Time	1967	2.00	4.00	8.00
—Starting here, through 1156, as "Diana Ross and the Supremes"					
❏ 1116	In and Out of Love/I Guess I'll Always Love You	1967	2.00	4.00	8.00
❏ 1122	Forever Came Today/Time Changes Things	1968	2.00	4.00	8.00
❏ 1125	What the World Needs Now/Your Kiss of Fire	1968	—	—	—
—Unreleased					
❏ 1126	Some Things You Never Get Used To/You've Been So Wonderful to Me	1968	2.00	4.00	8.00
❏ 1135	Love Child/Will This Be the Day	1968	2.00	4.00	8.00
❏ 1139	I'm Livin' in Shame/I'm So Glad I Got Somebody	1969	2.00	4.00	8.00
❏ 1146	The Composer/The Beginning of the End	1969	2.00	4.00	8.00
❏ 1148	No Matter What Sign You Are/The Young Folks	1969	2.00	4.00	8.00
❏ 1156	Someday We'll Be Together/He's My Sunny Boy	1969	2.00	4.00	8.00
❏ 1162	Up the Ladder to the Roof/Bill, When Are You Coming Home	1970	—	3.00	6.00
—Starting here, name reverts to "The Supremes" (unless noted)					
❏ 1167	Everybody's Got the Right to Love/But I Love You More	1970	—	3.00	6.00
❏ 1172	Stoned Love/Shine on Me	1970	—	3.00	6.00
❏ 1182	Nathan Jones/Happy (Is a Bumpy Road)	1971	—	3.00	6.00
❏ 1190	Touch/It's So Hard for Me to Say Goodbye	1971	—	3.00	6.00
❏ 1195	Floy Joy/This Is the Story	1972	—	2.50	5.00
❏ 1200	Automatically Sunshine/Precious Little Things	1972	—	2.50	5.00
❏ 1206	Your Wonderful, Sweet Sweet Love/The Wisdom of Time	1972	—	2.50	5.00
❏ 1213	I Guess I'll Miss the Man/Over and Over	1972	—	2.50	5.00
❏ 1225	Bad Weather/Oh Be My Love	1973	—	2.50	5.00
❏ 1350	It's All Been Said Before/(B-side unassigned)	1975	—	—	—
—Unreleased					
❏ 1357	He's My Man/Give Out But Don't Give Up	1975	—	2.50	5.00
❏ 1374	Where Do I Go from Here/Give Out But Don't Give Up	1975	—	2.50	5.00
❏ 1391	I'm Gonna Let My Heart Do the Walking/Early Morning Love	1976	—	2.50	5.00
❏ 1407	You're My Driving Wheel/You're What's Missing in My Life	1976	—	2.50	5.00
❏ 1415	Let Yourself Go/You Are the Heart of Me	1977	—	2.50	5.00
❏ 1488	Medley of Hits/Where Did We Go Wrong	1980	—	2.00	4.00
—As "Diana Ross and the Supremes"					
❏ 1523	Medley of Hits/Where Did We Go Wrong	1981	—	2.00	4.00
—As "Diana Ross and the Supremes"					

TAMLA

Number	Title (A Side/B Side)	Yr	VG	VG+	NM
❏ 54038	I Want a Guy/Never Again	1961	15.00	30.00	60.00
—Globes label					
❏ 54038	I Want a Guy/Never Again	1961	31.25	62.50	125.00
—Lines label					
❏ 54045	Buttered Popcorn/Who's Lovin' You	1961	15.00	30.00	60.00
—Globes label					
❏ 54045	Buttered Popcorn/Who's Lovin' You	1961	31.25	62.50	125.00
—Lines label					

TOPPS/MOTOWN

Number	Title (A Side/B Side)	Yr	VG	VG+	NM
❏ 1	Baby Love	1967	18.75	37.50	75.00
—Cardboard record					
❏ 2	Stop in the Name of Love	1967	18.75	37.50	75.00
—Cardboard record					
❏ 3	Where Did Our Love Go	1967	18.75	37.50	75.00
—Cardboard record					
❏ 15	Come See About Me	1967	18.75	37.50	75.00
—Cardboard record					
❏ 16	My World Is Empty Without You	1967	18.75	37.50	75.00
—Cardboard record					

7-Inch Extended Plays

MOTOWN

Number	Title (A Side/B Side)	Yr	VG	VG+	NM
❏ S 621 [PS]	Where Did Our Love Go	1965	6.25	12.50	25.00
❏ S 621 [S]	He Means the World to Me/Baby Love/Ask Any Girl//Where Did Our Love Go/Come See About Me/Run, Run, Run	1965	6.25	12.50	25.00
—33 1/3 rpm, small hole					

Albums

DORAL

Number	Title (A Side/B Side)	Yr	VG	VG+	NM
❏ DRL 104	Doral Presents Diana Ross and the Supremes	1971	12.50	25.00	50.00
—Available through Doral cigarettes					

MOTOWN

Number	Title (A Side/B Side)	Yr	VG	VG+	NM
❏ M5-101V1	Superstar Series, Vol. 1	1981	3.00	6.00	12.00
—By "Diana Ross and the Supremes"					
❏ PR-102 [DJ]	Touch Interview	1971	6.25	12.50	25.00
❏ M5-138V1	The Supremes A' Go-Go	1981	3.00	6.00	12.00
—Reissue of Motown 649					
❏ M5-147V1	I Hear a Symphony	1981	3.00	6.00	12.00
—Reissue of Motown 643					
❏ M5-158V1	The Supremes Sing Country Western and Pop	1981	2.00	4.00	8.00
—Reissue of Motown 625					
❏ M5-162V1	The Supremes at the Copa	1981	3.00	6.00	12.00
—Reissue of Motown 636					
❏ M5-182V1	The Supremes Sing Holland-Dozier-Holland	1981	3.00	6.00	12.00
—Reissue of Motown 650					
❏ M5-203V1	Diana Ross and the Supremes Greatest Hits, Volume 3	1981	3.00	6.00	12.00
—Reissue of Motown 702					
❏ M5-223V1	Meet the Supremes	1982	2.00	4.00	8.00
—Reissue of Motown 606					
❏ M5-237V1	Greatest Hits	1982	2.50	5.00	10.00
—Reissue (unknown if it's the complete 2-record set or an edited version)					
❏ M 606 [M]	Meet the Supremes	1963	7.50	15.00	30.00
—With close-up of group's faces					
❏ M 606 [M]	Meet the Supremes	1963	225.00	450.00	900.00
—With group sitting on stools					
❏ MS 606 [S]	Meet the Supremes	1964	10.00	20.00	40.00
—With close-up of group's faces					
❏ MT/MS 610	The Supremes Sing Ballads and Blues	1963	—	—	—
—Unreleased					
❏ M 621 [M]	Where Did Our Love Go	1964	7.50	15.00	30.00
❏ MS 621 [S]	Where Did Our Love Go	1964	10.00	20.00	40.00

Number	Title (A Side/B Side)	Yr	VG	VG+	NM
❏ M 623 [M]	A Bit of Liverpool	1964	10.00	20.00	40.00
❏ MS 623 [S]	A Bit of Liverpool	1964	12.50	25.00	50.00
❏ M 625 [M]	The Supremes Sing Country, Western & Pop	1965	7.50	15.00	30.00
❏ MT-625 [M]	The Supremes Sing Country, Western & Pop	1965	6.25	12.50	25.00
❏ MT/MS 626	The Supremes Live! Live! Live!	1965	—	—	25.00
—Unreleased					
❏ M 627 [M]	More Hits by the Supremes	1965	6.25	12.50	25.00
❏ MS 627 [S]	More Hits by the Supremes	1965	7.50	15.00	30.00
❏ MT/MS 628	There's a Place for Us	1965	—	—	—
—Unreleased					
❏ M 629 [M]	We Remember Sam Cooke	1965	6.25	12.50	25.00
❏ MS 629 [S]	We Remember Sam Cooke	1965	7.50	15.00	30.00
—The above LP came out before Motown 627					
❏ M 636 [M]	The Supremes at the Copa	1965	6.25	12.50	25.00
❏ MS 636 [S]	The Supremes at the Copa	1965	7.50	15.00	30.00
❏ MT/MS 637	A Tribute to the Girls	1965	—	—	—
—Unreleased					
❏ MS 638 [S]	Merry Christmas	1965	10.00	20.00	40.00
—Same as above, but in stereo					
❏ MT 638 [M]	Merry Christmas	1965	7.50	15.00	30.00
❏ M 643 [M]	I Hear a Symphony	1966	6.25	12.50	25.00
❏ MS 643 [S]	I Hear a Symphony	1966	7.50	15.00	30.00
❏ MTMS 648	Pure Gold	1966	—	—	—
—Unreleased					
❏ M 649 [M]	The Supremes A' Go-Go	1966	6.25	12.50	25.00
❏ MS 649 [S]	The Supremes A' Go-Go	1966	7.50	15.00	30.00
❏ M 650 [M]	The Supremes Sing Holland-Dozier-Holland	1967	6.25	12.50	25.00
❏ MS 650 [S]	The Supremes Sing Holland-Dozier-Holland	1967	7.50	15.00	30.00
❏ M 659 [M]	The Supremes Sing Rodgers & Hart	1967	6.25	12.50	25.00
❏ MS 659 [S]	The Supremes Sing Rodgers & Hart	1967	7.50	15.00	30.00
❏ M 663 [(2)M]	Diana Ross and the Supremes Greatest Hits	1967	7.50	15.00	30.00
❏ MS 663 [(2)S]	Diana Ross and the Supremes Greatest Hits	1967	10.00	20.00	40.00
❏ MT/MS 663	Diana Ross and the Supremes Greatest Hits Poster	1967	2.50	5.00	10.00
❏ M 665 [M]	Reflections	1968	7.50	15.00	30.00
❏ MS 665 [S]	Reflections	1968	5.00	10.00	20.00
❏ MS 670	Love Child	1968	5.00	10.00	20.00
❏ M 672 [M]	Funny Girl	1968	7.50	15.00	30.00
—Mono appears to be promo only					
❏ MS 672 [S]	Funny Girl	1968	5.00	10.00	20.00
—The above LP came out before Motown 670					
❏ M 676 [M]	Live at London's Talk of the Town	1968	7.50	51.00	30.00
—Mono is promo only					
❏ MS 676 [S]	Live at London's Talk of the Town	1968	5.00	10.00	20.00
—The above LP came out before Motown 670 and 672					
❏ MS 689	Let the Sunshine In	1969	5.00	10.00	20.00
❏ MS 694	Cream of the Crop	1969	5.00	10.00	20.00
❏ MS 702	Diana Ross and the Supremes Greatest Hits, Volume 3	1970	5.00	10.00	20.00
❏ MS 705	Right On	1970	3.75	7.50	15.00
—By "The Supremes"; the first LP after Diana Ross left					
❏ MS 708 [(2)]	Farewell	1970	6.25	12.50	25.00
—By "Diana Ross and the Supremes"					
❏ MS 720	New Ways But Love Stays	1970	3.75	7.50	15.00
❏ MS 737	Touch	1971	3.75	7.50	15.00
❏ MS 746	Promises Kept	1972	—	—	—
—Unreleased					
❏ M 751L	Floy Joy	1972	3.75	7.50	15.00
❏ M 756L	The Supremes	1972	3.75	7.50	15.00
❏ M9-794L3 [(3)]	Anthology (1962-1969)	1974	6.25	12.50	25.00
—By "Diana Ross and the Supremes"					
❏ M6-828	The Supremes	1975	3.75	7.50	15.00
❏ M6-863S1	High Energy	1976	3.75	7.50	15.00
❏ M6-873S1	Mary, Scherrie and Susaye	1976	3.75	7.50	15.00
❏ M7-904R1	The Supremes at Their Best	1978	3.75	7.50	15.00
❏ 5245 ML	Love Child	1982	2.00	4.00	8.00
—Reissue of MS 670					
❏ 5252 ML	Merry Christmas	1982	2.50	5.00	10.00
—Reissue of MS 638					
❏ 5270 ML	Where Did Our Love Go	1982	2.00	4.00	8.00
—Reissue of MS 621					
❏ 5278 ML	Captured Live on Stage	1982	2.00	4.00	8.00
—Reissue?					
❏ 5305 ML	Let the Sunshine In	1983	2.00	4.00	8.00
—Reissue of MS 689					
❏ 5313 ML	Great Songs and Performances That Inspired the Motown 25th Anniversary TV Special	1983	2.50	5.00	10.00
❏ 5361 ML	Motown Legends	1985	2.50	5.00	10.00
❏ 5371 ML	Diana Ross and the Supremes Sing Motown	1985	2.50	5.00	10.00
❏ 5381 ML3 [(3)]	25th Anniversary	1986	5.00	10.00	20.00
—By "Diana Ross and the Supremes"					

NATURAL RESOURCES

Number	Title (A Side/B Side)	Yr	VG	VG+	NM
❏ NR 4006T1	Where Did Our Love Go	1978	3.00	6.00	12.00
—Reissue of Motown 621					
❏ NR 4010	Merry Christmas	1978	3.00	6.00	12.00
—Reissue of Motown 638					

PICKWICK

Number	Title (A Side/B Side)	Yr	VG	VG+	NM
❏ SPC-3383	Baby Love	197?	3.00	6.00	12.00
—Edited reissue of Motown 621					

SUPREMES, THE (2)

45s

ACE

Number	Title (A Side/B Side)	Yr	VG	VG+	NM
❏ 534	Just for You and I/Don't Leave Me Here to Cry	1957	20.00	40.00	80.00

SUPREMES, THE (3)

45s

APT

Number	Title (A Side/B Side)	Yr	VG	VG+	NM
❏ 25055	Another Chance to Love/Fidgety	1961	10.00	20.00	40.00

SUPREMES, THE (4)

45s

KITTEN

Number	Title (A Side/B Side)	Yr	VG	VG+	NM
❏ 6969	Could This Be You/Margie	1956	125.00	250.00	500.00

Number	Title (A Side/B Side)	Yr	VG	VG+	NM

SUPREMES, THE (5)
45s
MARK
| ☐ 129 | Nobody Can Love You/Snap, Crackle and Pop | 1958 | 200.00 | 400.00 | 800.00 |

SUPREMES, THE (6)
45s
MASCOT
| ☐ 126 | Little Sally Walker/Just Yell | 1960 | 25.00 | 50.00 | 100.00 |

SUPREMES, THE (7)
45s
OLD TOWN
| ☐ 1024 | Tonight/My Babe | 1956 | 25.00 | 50.00 | 100.00 |
| ☐ 1024 | Tonight/She Don't Want Me No More | 1956 | 37.50 | 75.00 | 150.00 |

SUPREMES, THE, AND THE FOUR TOPS Also see each artist's individual listings.
45s
MOTOWN
| ☐ 1173 | River Deep-Mountain High/Together We Can Make Such Sweet Music | 1970 | — | 3.00 | 6.00 |
| ☐ 1181 | You Gotta Have Love in Your Heart/I'm Glad About It | 1971 | — | 3.00 | 6.00 |
Albums
MOTOWN
| ☐ M5-123V1A | The Magnificent Seven | 1981 | 3.00 | 6.00 | 12.00 |
—Reissue of Motown 717
☐ MS 717	The Magnificent Seven	1970	3.75	7.50	15.00
☐ MS 736	The Return of the Magnificent Seven	1971	3.75	7.50	15.00
☐ MS 745	Dynamite	1971	3.75	7.50	15.00

SUPREMES, THE, DIANA ROSS AND, AND THE TEMPTATIONS Also see each artist's individual listings.
45s
MOTOWN
☐ 1137	I'm Gonna Make You Love Me/A Place in the Sun	1968	—	3.50	7.00
☐ 1137 [PS]	I'm Gonna Make You Love Me/A Place in the Sun	1968	5.00	10.00	20.00
☐ 1142	I'll Try Something New/The Way You Do the Things You Do	1969	—	3.50	7.00
☐ 1150	Stubborn Kind of Fellow/Try It Baby	1969	—	3.50	7.00
☐ 1153	The Weight/For Better or Worse	1969	—	3.50	7.00
Albums
MOTOWN
☐ M5-139V1	Diana Ross and the Supremes Join the Temptations	1981	3.00	6.00	12.00
—Reissue of Motown 679
| ☐ M5-171V1 | TCB | 1981 | 3.00 | 6.00 | 12.00 |
—Reissue of Motown 682
☐ M 679 [M]	Diana Ross and the Supremes Join the Temptations	1968	7.50	15.00	30.00
☐ MS 679 [S]	Diana Ross and the Supremes Join the Temptations	1968	5.00	10.00	20.00
☐ MS 682	TCB	1968	5.00	10.00	20.00
☐ MS 692	Together	1969	5.00	10.00	20.00
☐ MS 699	On Broadway	1969	5.00	10.00	20.00

SUPREMES FOUR, THE
45s
SARA
| ☐ 1032 | I Lost My Job/I Love You Patricia | 1958 | 500.00 | 1000. | 2000. |

SURE CURE, THE
45s
PARKWAY
| ☐ 145 | Anything You Want/I Wanna Do It | 1967 | 2.50 | 5.00 | 10.00 |

SURF BOYS, THE
45s
KARATE
| ☐ 526 | Da Doo Ron Ron/Hurt | 1966 | 6.25 | 12.50 | 25.00 |
SCEPTER
| ☐ 12180 | Stuck in the Chimney/I Told Santa Claus I Want You | 1966 | 6.25 | 12.50 | 25.00 |

SURF BREAKERS, THE
45s
MERCURY
| ☐ 72174 | Hang Ten/Ridin' In #9 | 1963 | 12.50 | 25.00 | 50.00 |

SURF BUNNIES, THE
45s
DOT
| ☐ 16523 | Our Surfer Boys/Surf Bunny Beach | 1963 | 7.50 | 15.00 | 30.00 |
GOLIATH
| ☐ 1352 | Our Surfer Boys/Surf Bunny Beach | 1963 | 12.50 | 25.00 | 50.00 |
| ☐ 1353 | Surf City High/Met the Boy I Adore | 1963 | 12.50 | 25.00 | 50.00 |

SURF RIDERS, THE
45s
DECCA
| ☐ 31477 | The Birds/Blues for the Birds | 1963 | 7.50 | 15.00 | 30.00 |
NASCO
| ☐ 6008 | I'm Out/Rocko Socko | 1958 | 15.00 | 30.00 | 60.00 |

SURF STOMPERS, THE Also see BRUCE JOHNSTON.
Albums
DEL-FI
☐ DFLP-1236 [M]	The Original Surfer Stomp	1963	15.00	30.00	60.00
☐ DFST-1236 [S]	The Original Surfer Stomp	1963	20.00	40.00	80.00
☐ DLF-1236	The Original Surfer Stomp	1997	3.00	6.00	12.00

SURF TEENS, THE
Albums
SUTTON
| ☐ SSU-339 [S] | Surf Mania | 1963 | 15.00 | 30.00 | 60.00 |
| ☐ SU-339 [M] | Surf Mania | 1963 | 12.50 | 25.00 | 50.00 |

SURFARIS, THE (1)
45s
DECCA
☐ 31538	Point Panic/Waikiki Run	1963	3.75	7.50	15.00
☐ 31561	A Surfer's Christmas List/Santa's Speed Shop	1963	7.50	15.00	30.00
☐ 31581	I Wanna Take a trip to the Islands/Scatter Shield	1964	5.00	10.00	20.00
☐ 31605	Murphy the Surfie/Go Go Go For Louie's Place	1964	3.75	7.50	15.00
☐ 31641	Bossa Barracuda/Dune Buggy	1964	3.75	7.50	15.00
☐ 31682	Hot Rod High/Karen	1964	3.75	7.50	15.00
☐ 31731	Beat '65/Black Denim	1965	5.00	10.00	20.00
☐ 31784	Theme of the Battle Maiden/Somethin' Else	1965	5.00	10.00	20.00
☐ 31835	Catch a Little Ride with Me/Don't Hurt My Little Sister	1965	5.00	10.00	20.00
☐ 31954	Hey Joe Where Are You Going/So Get Out	1966	5.00	10.00	20.00
☐ 32003	Wipe Out/I'm a Hog for You	1966	2.50	5.00	10.00
DFS
☐ 11/12	Wipe Out/Surfer Joe	1963	1500.	2250.	3000.
DOT
☐ 144	Wipe Out/Surfer Joe	1966	2.50	5.00	10.00
—Black label, script "Dot" in multicolor letters
| ☐ 144 [DJ] | Wipe Out (same on both sides) | 1966 | 25.00 | 50.00 | 100.00 |
—Red vinyl
| ☐ 144 [DJ] | Wipe Out (same on both sides) | 1966 | 37.50 | 75.00 | 150.00 |
—Red vinyl; error pressing with "Surfer Joe" on both sides
| ☐ 144 | Wipe Out/Surfer Joe | 1969 | — | 3.00 | 6.00 |
—Multicolor label, "DOT" in all capital letters in box at top
| ☐ 16479 | Wipe Out/Surfer Joe | 1963 | 3.75 | 7.50 | 15.00 |
| ☐ 16757 | Surfer Joe/Can't Sit Down | 1965 | 7.50 | 15.00 | 30.00 |
—B-side by the Challengers, but credited to the Surfaris
| ☐ 16757 | Surfer Joe/Can't Sit Down | 1965 | 12.50 | 25.00 | 50.00 |
—B-side by the Challengers, and credited correctly
| ☐ 16966 | Show Biz/Chicago Green | 1966 | 2.50 | 5.00 | 10.00 |
| ☐ 17008 | Shake/The Search | 1967 | 2.50 | 5.00 | 10.00 |
PRINCESS
| ☐ 50 | Wipe Out/Surfer Joe | 1963 | 37.50 | 75.00 | 150.00 |
—With short versions of both songs. "RE-1" is in the trail-off area.
| ☐ 50 | Wipe Out/Surfer Joe | 1963 | 100.00 | 200.00 | 400.00 |
—With long versions of both songs. No "RE-1" is in the trail-off area.
| ☐ 52 | Spanish Moon/She's Got the Blues | 1963 | 25.00 | 50.00 | 100.00 |
—Reissued on Vault 911 credited to THE TRAVELERS; we don't know if Princess 52 exists credited to the Travelers, but we know this version exists
Albums
DECCA
☐ DL 4470 [M]	The Surfaris Play Wipe Out	1963	6.25	12.50	25.00
☐ DL 4487 [M]	Hit City '64	1964	10.00	20.00	40.00
☐ DL 4560 [M]	Fun City, U.S.A.	1964	10.00	20.00	40.00
☐ DL 4614 [M]	Hit City '65	1965	10.00	20.00	40.00
☐ DL 4663 [M]	It Ain't Me, Babe	1965	10.00	20.00	40.00
☐ DL 74470 [S]	The Surfaris Play Wipe Out	1963	7.50	15.00	30.00
☐ DL 74487 [S]	Hit City '64	1964	12.50	25.00	50.00
☐ DL 74560 [S]	Fun City, U.S.A.	1964	12.50	25.00	50.00
☐ DL 74614 [S]	Hit City '65	1965	12.50	25.00	50.00
☐ DL 74663 [S]	It Ain't Me, Babe	1965	12.50	25.00	50.00
DOT
☐ DLP-3535 [M]	Wipe Out	1963	7.50	15.00	30.00
—With no back cover photo of the Surfaris
| ☐ DLP-3535 [M] | Wipe Out | 1963 | 10.00 | 20.00 | 40.00 |
—With back cover photo featuring four Surfaris
| ☐ DLP-3535 [M] | Wipe Out | 1963 | 12.50 | 25.00 | 50.00 |
—With back cover photo featuring five Surfaris
| ☐ DLP-25535 [S] | Wipe Out | 1963 | 10.00 | 20.00 | 40.00 |
—With no back cover photo of the Surfaris
| ☐ DLP-25535 [S] | Wipe Out | 1963 | 12.50 | 25.00 | 50.00 |
—With back cover photo featuring four Surfaris
| ☐ DLP-25535 [S] | Wipe Out | 1963 | 20.00 | 40.00 | 80.00 |
—With back cover photo featuring five Surfaris
PICKWICK
| ☐ SPC-3636 | Wipe Out and Surfer Joe | 1978 | 3.75 | 7.50 | 15.00 |

SURFARIS, THE (2) This group was forced to change its name to "The Original Surfaris."
45s
CHANCELLOR
| ☐ 1142 | The Midnight Surf/Psyche-Out | 1963 | 12.50 | 25.00 | 50.00 |
DEL-FI
| ☐ 4219 | Surfari/Bombora | 1963 | 25.00 | 50.00 | 100.00 |
FELSTED
| ☐ 8688 | Tor-Chula/Psyche-Out | 1964 | 12.50 | 25.00 | 50.00 |
NORTHRIDGE
| ☐ 1001 | Moment of Truth/Church Key | 1963 | 15.00 | 30.00 | 60.00 |
—B-side by the Biscaynes
REGANO
| ☐ 1062 | Surfin' '63/Boss Beat | 1963 | 12.50 | 25.00 | 50.00 |
—As "The Original Surfaris"
REPRISE
| ☐ 20180 | Moment of Truth/Church Key | 1963 | 7.50 | 15.00 | 30.00 |
—B-side by the Biscaynes
SURFARI
| ☐ 301 | Gum Dipped Slicks/High Time | 1964 | 25.00 | 50.00 | 100.00 |
—As "The Original Surfaris"
Albums
DIPLOMAT
| ☐ D-2309 [M] | Wheels-Shorts-Hot Rods | 1963 | 6.25 | 12.50 | 25.00 |
—As "The Original Surfaris"
| ☐ DS-2309 [S] | Wheels-Shorts-Hot Rods | 1963 | 7.50 | 15.00 | 30.00 |
—As "The Original Surfaris"
SUNDAZED
| ☐ LP-5014 | Bombora! | 199? | 2.50 | 5.00 | 10.00 |
—As "The Original Surfaris"

SURFRIDERS, THE
Albums
VAULT
| ☐ LP-105 [M] | Surfbeat, Volume 2 | 1963 | 7.50 | 15.00 | 30.00 |
| ☐ VS-105 [S] | Surfbeat, Volume 2 | 1963 | 10.00 | 20.00 | 40.00 |

S

Number	Title (A Side/B Side)	Yr	VG	VG+	NM

SURFSIDERS, THE
Albums
DESIGN
| ❑ DLP-208 [M] | The Beach Boys Songbook | 1965 | 3.75 | 7.50 | 15.00 |
| ❑ DLPS-208 [S] | The Beach Boys Songbook | 1965 | 5.00 | 10.00 | 20.00 |

SURVIVORS, THE Dave Nowlen, Bob Norberg and friends with help from BRIAN WILSON. This record is NOT by the Beach Boys.
45s
CAPITOL
| ❑ 5102 | Pamela Jean/After the Game | 1963 | 250.00 | 500.00 | 1000. |

SUSIE AND THE FOUR TRUMPETS
45s
UNITED ARTISTS
| ❑ 471 | Starry Eyes/Blue Little Girl | 1962 | 15.00 | 30.00 | 60.00 |

SUTCH, SCREAMING LORD
45s
CAMEO
| ❑ 341 | She's Fallen in Love with the Monster Man/Bye Bye Baby | 1964 | 3.75 | 7.50 | 15.00 |
COTILLION
| ❑ 44149 | Gotta Keep a-Rocking/Country Club | 1972 | 2.50 | 5.00 | 10.00 |
—As "Lord Sutch"
Albums
COTILLION
| ❑ SD 9015 | Lord Sutch and Heavy Friends | 1970 | 7.50 | 15.00 | 30.00 |
—With Jimmy Page, John Bonham and Jeff Beck
| ❑ SD 9049 | Hands of Jack the Ripper | 1972 | 7.50 | 15.00 | 30.00 |

SUTHERLAND BROTHERS Also see SUTHERLAND BROTHERS AND QUIVER.
45s
COLUMBIA
| ❑ 10758 | One More Night with You/When I Say I Love You (The Pie) | 1978 | — | 2.00 | 4.00 |
| ❑ 11003 | On the Rocks/As Long As I've Got You | 1979 | — | 2.00 | 4.00 |
ISLAND
| ❑ 1203 | Long Long Day/The Pie | 1972 | — | 2.50 | 5.00 |
| ❑ 1209 | Sailing/Hallelujah | 1972 | — | 2.50 | 5.00 |
Albums
COLUMBIA
| ❑ JC 35293 | Down to Earth | 1978 | 2.50 | 5.00 | 10.00 |
| ❑ JC 35703 | When the Night Comes Down | 1979 | 2.50 | 5.00 | 10.00 |
ISLAND
| ❑ SW-9315 | The Sutherland Brothers Band | 1972 | 3.00 | 6.00 | 12.00 |

SUTHERLAND BROTHERS AND QUIVER Also see each artist's individual listings.
45s
COLUMBIA
❑ 10284	Arms of Mary/Love on the Moon	1976	—	2.50	5.00
❑ 10362	When the Train Comes/Mad Trail	1976	—	2.50	5.00
❑ 10460	Secrets/Something's Burning	1976	—	2.50	5.00
ISLAND
❑ 1217	(I Don't Want to Love You But) You Got Me Anyway/Rock and Roll Show	1973	—	2.00	4.00
❑ 1220	Dream Kid/Silver Sister	1974	—	2.00	4.00
Albums
COLUMBIA
| ❑ PC 33982 | Reach for the Sky | 1976 | 2.50 | 5.00 | 10.00 |
| ❑ PC 34376 | Slipstream | 1977 | 2.50 | 5.00 | 10.00 |
ISLAND
| ❑ SW-9326 | Lifeboat | 1973 | 2.50 | 5.00 | 10.00 |
| ❑ SW-9341 | Dream Kid | 1974 | 2.50 | 5.00 | 10.00 |

SUZY AND THE RED STRIPES Actually Linda McCartney with Wings. Also see PAUL McCARTNEY.
12-Inch Singles
CAPITOL
| ❑ V-15244 | Seaside Woman/B-Side to Seaside | 1986 | 10.00 | 20.00 | 40.00 |
EPIC
| ❑ ASF 361 [DJ] | Seaside Woman (same on both sides) | 1977 | 7.50 | 15.00 | 30.00 |
45s
CAPITOL
| ❑ B-5608 | Seaside Woman/B-Side to Seaside | 1986 | 7.50 | 15.00 | 30.00 |
EPIC
| ❑ 50403 | Seaside Woman/B-Side to Seaside | 1977 | 2.50 | 5.00 | 10.00 |
| ❑ 50403 [DJ] | Seaside Woman (mono/stereo) | 1977 | 6.25 | 12.50 | 25.00 |
—Red vinyl, orange label on one side, white on the other
| ❑ 50403 [DJ] | Seaside Woman (mono/stereo) | 1977 | 25.00 | 50.00 | 100.00 |
—"Advance Promotion" label, black vinyl
| ❑ 50403 [DJ] | Seaside Woman (mono/stereo) | 1977 | 25.00 | 50.00 | 100.00 |
—Black vinyl, orange label on one side, white on the other

SWAGMEN, THE
45s
PARKWAY
| ❑ 854 | By the Yonder Tree/East Virginia | 1962 | 3.00 | 6.00 | 12.00 |
Albums
PARKWAY
| ❑ SP-7015 [S] | Meet the Swagmen | 1962 | 12.50 | 25.00 | 50.00 |

SWALLOWS, THE
45s
AFTER HOURS
| ❑ 104 | My Baby/Good Time Girls | 1954 | 800.00 | 1600. | 2400. |
FEDERAL
❑ 12319	Oh Lonesome Me/Angel Baby	1958	10.00	20.00	40.00
❑ 12328	We Want to Rock/Rock-a-Bye-Baby Rock	1958	10.00	20.00	40.00
❑ 12329	Beside You/Laughing Boy	1958	10.00	20.00	40.00
❑ 12333	Itchy Twitchy Feeling/Who Knows, Do You?	1958	10.00	20.00	40.00
KING
❑ 4458	Will You Be Mine/Dearest	1951	500.00	1000.	1500.
❑ 4466	Since You've Been Away/Wishing for You	1951	—	—	—
—Unconfirmed on 45 rpm

| ❑ 4501 | Eternally/It Ain't the Meat | 1952 | 200.00 | 400.00 | 800.00 |
—Black vinyl
| ❑ 4501 | Eternally/It Ain't the Meat | 1952 | 625.00 | 1250. | 2500. |
—Blue vinyl
| ❑ 4501 | Eternally/It Ain't the Meat | 1952 | 625.00 | 1250. | 2500. |
—Green vinyl
❑ 4515	Tell Me Why/Roll, Roll, Pretty Baby	1952	1000.00	1500.	2000.
❑ 4525	Beside You/You Left Me	1952	100.00	200.00	400.00
❑ 4533	You Walked In/I Only Have Eyes for You	1952	200.00	400.00	800.00
❑ 4579	Where Do I Go from Here/Please, Baby, Please	1952	200.00	400.00	800.00
❑ 4612	Laugh (Though You Want to Cry)/Our Love Is Dying	1953	125.00	250.00	500.00
❑ 4632	Nobody's Lovin' Me/Bicycle Tillie	1953	125.00	250.00	500.00
❑ 4656	Trust Me/Pleading Blues	1953	100.00	200.00	400.00
❑ 4676	I'll Be Waiting/It Feels So Good	1953	100.00	200.00	400.00

SWALLOWS, THE (2)
45s
GUYDEN
| ❑ 2023 | How Long Must a Fool Go On/You Must Try | 1959 | 12.50 | 25.00 | 50.00 |
—Reissued credited to "The Guides"

SWAMP RATS, THE
45s
CO & CE
| ❑ 245 | In the Midnight Hour/It's Not Easy | 1967 | 5.00 | 10.00 | 20.00 |
ST. CLAIR
❑ 69	Louie Louie/Hey Joe	1966	12.50	25.00	50.00
❑ 2222	Psycho/Here, There and Everywhere	1966	50.00	100.00	200.00
❑ 3333	Two Tymes Two/(B-side unknown)	1966	12.50	25.00	50.00
❑ 711711	It's Not Easy/No Friend of Mine	1966	12.50	25.00	50.00

SWAN, BILLY
45s
A&M
| ❑ 2046 | Hello! Remember Me/Never Go Lookin' Again | 1978 | — | 2.00 | 4.00 |
| ❑ 2103 | No Way Around It (It's Love)/Forever in Your Love | 1978 | — | 2.00 | 4.00 |
COLUMBIA
| ❑ 10443 | Shake, Rattle and Roll/I Got It for You | 1976 | — | 2.00 | 4.00 |
| ❑ 10486 | Swept Away/California Song (For Malibu) | 1977 | — | 2.00 | 4.00 |
EPIC
❑ 02196	I'm Into Lovin' You/Not Far from Forty	1981	—	—	3.00
❑ 02601	Stuck Right in the Middle of Your Love/Soft Touch	1981	—	—	3.00
❑ 02841	With Their Kind of Money and Our Kind of Love/Lay Down and Love Me Tonight	1982	—	—	3.00
❑ 03226	Your Picture Still Loves Me (And I Still Love You)/Give Your Lovin' to Me	1982	—	—	3.00
❑ 03505	Rainbows and Butterflies/Only Be You	1982	—	—	3.00
❑ 03917	Yes/I Can't Stop Writing Love Songs	1983	—	—	3.00
❑ 51000	Do I Have to Draw a Picture/I Want to Change Your Life	1981	—	—	3.00
MERCURY
❑ 884668-7	You Must Be Lookin' for Me/Three Chord Rock & Roll	1986	—	—	3.00
❑ 888320-7	I'm Gonna Get You/Three Chord Rock & Roll	1987	—	—	3.00
MGM
❑ 14008	El Paso/The Sweet Sound of Your Name	1968	2.50	5.00	10.00
MONUMENT
❑ 45-275	Don't Be Cruel/Vanessa	1979	—	2.00	4.00
❑ 940	Breakin' Up/Out of Her System	1966	3.00	6.00	12.00
❑ 988	I've Got to Have You/Below Average Everyday Girl	1966	3.00	6.00	12.00
❑ 8597	Wedding Bells/P.M.S.	1974	—	2.50	5.00
❑ 8621	I Can Help/The Ways of a Woman in Love	1974	—	2.50	5.00
❑ 8641	I'm Her Fool/I'd Like to Work for You	1975	—	2.00	4.00
❑ 8651	Come By/Woman Handled My Mind	1975	—	2.00	4.00
❑ 8661	Everything's the Same (Ain't Nothing Changed)/Overnite Thing (Usually)	1975	—	2.00	4.00
❑ 8682	Just Want to Taste Your Wine/Love You Baby to the Bone	1976	—	2.00	4.00
❑ 8697	Vanessa/Number 1	1976	—	2.00	4.00
❑ 8706	You're the One/Mr. Misery	1976	—	2.00	4.00
RISING SONS
❑ 702	Friendship/You Got Me Laughing	1967	2.50	5.00	10.00
Albums
A&M
| ❑ SP-4686 | You're OK, I'm OK | 1978 | 2.50 | 5.00 | 10.00 |
COLUMBIA
| ❑ PZ 33279 | I Can Help | 1977 | 2.00 | 4.00 | 8.00 |
—Reissue of Monument 33279
| ❑ PZ 33805 | Rock 'n' Roll Moon | 1977 | 2.00 | 4.00 | 8.00 |
—Reissue of Monument 33805
| ❑ PZ 34183 | Billy Swan | 1977 | 2.00 | 4.00 | 8.00 |
—Reissue of Monument 34183
| ❑ PC 34473 | Four | 1977 | 2.50 | 5.00 | 10.00 |
EPIC
| ❑ FE 37079 | I'm Into Lovin' You | 1981 | 2.50 | 5.00 | 10.00 |
MONUMENT
❑ 7629	Billy Swan At His Best	1978	2.50	5.00	10.00
❑ KZ 33279	I Can Help	1974	2.50	5.00	10.00
❑ PZ 33805	Rock 'n' Roll Moon	1975	2.50	5.00	10.00
❑ PZ 34183	Billy Swan	1976	2.50	5.00	10.00

SWANS, THE (1)
45s
BALLAD
| ❑ 1003/6 | It's a Must/Night Train | 1954 | 150.00 | 300.00 | 600.00 |
| ❑ 1007 | Happy/The Santa Claus Boogie | 1955 | 150.00 | 300.00 | 600.00 |
FORTUNE
| ❑ 822 | I'll Forever Love You/Mister Cool Breeze | 1955 | 200.00 | 400.00 | 800.00 |
LOST-NITE
| ❑ 134 | No More/My True Love | 196? | 2.00 | 4.00 | 8.00 |
—Reissue

Number	Title (A Side/B Side)	Yr	VG	VG+	NM
RAINBOW					
❏ 233	No More/My True Love	1954	375.00	750.00	1500.
—Red vinyl					
STEAMBOAT					
❏ 101	Believe in Me/In the Morning	1956	625.00	1250.	2500.
SWANS, THE (2)					
45s					
CAMEO					
❏ 302	The Boy with the Beatle Hair/Please Hurry Home	1964	10.00	20.00	40.00
PARKWAY					
❏ 881	Daydreamin' of You/The Promise	1963	7.50	15.00	30.00
SWAN					
❏ 4151	He's Mine/You Better Be a Good Girl Now	1963	7.50	15.00	30.00
SWANS, THE (3)					
45s					
ROULETTE					
❏ 4213	He Wasn't On the Air Again Today/If I Could Stop Every Clock	1959	6.25	12.50	25.00
SWANSON, BOBBY					
45s					
DONNA					
❏ 1326	Tom and Susie/China Doll	1960	6.25	12.50	25.00
❏ 1336	Janie's Face/Peggy's Last Birthday	1961	6.25	12.50	25.00
❏ 1356	Twisting at the Top/Hello There Lover Doll	1962	6.25	12.50	25.00
IGLOO					
❏ 1003	Rockin' Little Eskimo/Ballad of an Angel	1959	100.00	200.00	400.00
SWATLEY, HANK					
45s					
AARON					
❏ 101	Oakie Boogie/I Can't Help It	1957	125.00	250.00	500.00
SWEATHOG					
45s					
COLUMBIA					
❏ 45416	Things Yet to Come/Runneth Over	1971	—	2.50	5.00
❏ 45492	Hallelujah/Still on the Road	1971	—	2.50	5.00
❏ 45575	Things Yet to Come/Rejoice, Rejoice, Rejoice	1972	—	2.50	5.00
❏ 45609	Rock and Roll Revival/Ride Louise Ride	1972	—	2.50	5.00
Albums					
COLUMBIA					
❏ C 30601	Sweathog	1971	3.00	6.00	12.00
❏ KC 31144	Hallelujah	1972	3.00	6.00	12.00
SWEET, THE (1) British pop-rock band.					
45s					
BELL					
❏ 45106	Funny, Funny/You're Not Wrong for Loving Me	1971	2.00	4.00	8.00
❏ 45126	Co-Co/You're Not Wrong for Loving Me	1971	—	3.00	6.00
❏ 45184	Poppa Joe/Jeanie	1972	—	3.00	6.00
❏ 45251	Little Willy/Man from Mecca	1972	—	3.00	6.00
❏ 45361	Blockbuster/Need a Lot of Lovin'	1973	—	2.50	5.00
❏ 45408	Wig-Wam Bam/New York Connection	1973	—	2.50	5.00
CAPITOL					
❏ 4055	Ballroom Blitz/Restless	1975	—	2.50	5.00
❏ 4157	Fox on the Run/Burn On the Flame	1975	—	2.50	5.00
❏ 4220	Action/Medussa	1976	—	2.50	5.00
❏ 4429	Fever of Love/Heartbreak Today	1977	—	2.50	5.00
❏ 4454	Funk It Up (David's Song)/Stairway to the Stars	1977	—	2.50	5.00
❏ 4549	Love Is Like Oxygen/Cover Girl	1978	—	2.50	5.00
❏ 4610	California Nights/Dream On	1978	—	2.50	5.00
❏ 4730	Mother Earth/Why Don't You	1979	—	2.00	4.00
❏ 4908	Sixties Man/Water's Edge	1980	—	2.00	4.00
PARAMOUNT					
❏ 0044	All You'll Ever Get from Me/The Juicer	1970	5.00	10.00	20.00
20TH CENTURY					
❏ 2033	It's Lonely Out There/I'm On My Way	1973	2.50	5.00	10.00
—U.S. issue of 1968 material that was on Fontana in the U.K.					
Albums					
BEAT ROCKET					
❏ BR 125	Hell Raisers!	2000	3.00	6.00	12.00
BELL					
❏ 1125	The Sweet	1973	6.25	12.50	25.00
CAPITOL					
❏ SPRO-8371/2 [DJ]	For A.O.R. Radio Only	1976	6.25	12.50	25.00
❏ SPRO-8849 [DJ]	Short and Sweet	1978	7.50	15.00	30.00
❏ ST-11395	Desolation Boulevard	1975	3.00	6.00	12.00
❏ ST-11496	Give Us a Wink	1976	3.00	6.00	12.00
❏ STAO-11636	Off the Record	1977	3.00	6.00	12.00
❏ SKAO-11744	Level Headed	1978	3.00	6.00	12.00
❏ PRO-11929 [DJ]	Cut Above the Rest	1979	12.50	25.00	50.00
—Special promo box contains record, cassette, 8-track, photo, bio					
❏ ST-11929	Cut Above the Rest	1979	3.00	6.00	12.00
❏ ST-12106	Sweet VI	1980	3.00	6.00	12.00
❏ SN-16115	Give Us a Wink	1980	2.00	4.00	8.00
—Budget-line reissue					
❏ SN-16116	Off the Record	1980	2.00	4.00	8.00
—Budget-line reissue					
❏ SN-16117	Level Headed	1980	2.00	4.00	8.00
—Budget-line reissue					
❏ SN-16118	Cut Above the Rest	1980	2.00	4.00	8.00
—Budget-line reissue					
❏ SN-16287	Desolation Boulevard	1981	2.00	4.00	8.00
—Budget-line reissue					
KORY					
❏ 3009	The Sweet	1977	2.50	5.00	10.00
—Reissue of Bell LP					
SWEET, THE (2)					
45s					
SMASH					
❏ 2116	Got to Have More Love/You Can't Win at Love	1967	3.75	7.50	15.00
❏ 2136	Broken Heart Attack/Don't Do It	1967	3.75	7.50	15.00

Number	Title (A Side/B Side)	Yr	VG	VG+	NM
SWEET INSPIRATIONS, THE Also see CISSY HOUSTON.					
12-Inch Singles					
CARIBOU					
❏ ASD 333 [DJ]	Black Sunday Parts 1 and 2 (same on both sides)	1977	3.75	7.50	15.00
RSO					
❏ 304 [DJ]	Love Is On the Way (6:10)/(Instrumental)	1979	3.00	6.00	12.00
45s					
ATLANTIC					
❏ 2410	Why (Am I Treated So Bad)/I Don't Want to Go On Without You	1967	2.00	4.00	8.00
❏ 2418	Let It Be Me/When Something Is Wrong with My Baby	1967	2.00	4.00	8.00
❏ 2436	I've Been Loving You Too Long (To Stop Now)/That's How Strong My Love Is	1967	2.00	4.00	8.00
❏ 2449	O' What a Fool I've Been/Don't Fight It	1967	2.00	4.00	8.00
❏ 2465	Reach Out for Me/Do Right Woman — Do Right Man	1967	2.00	4.00	8.00
❏ 2476	Sweet Inspiration/I'm Blue	1968	2.00	4.00	8.00
❏ 2529	To Love Somebody/Where Did It Go	1968	2.00	4.00	8.00
❏ 2551	Unchained Melody/Am I Ever Gonna See My Baby Again	1968	2.00	4.00	8.00
❏ 2571	What the World Needs Now Is Love/You Really Didn't Mean It	1968	2.00	4.00	8.00
❏ 2620	Crying in the Rain/Everyday Will Be Like a Holiday	1969	2.00	4.00	8.00
❏ 2638	Sweets for My Sweet/Get a Little Order	1969	2.00	4.00	8.00
❏ 2653	Don't Go/Chained	1969	2.00	4.00	8.00
❏ 2686	(Gotta Find) A Brand New Lover — Part I/(Gotta Find) A Brand New Lover — Part II	1969	2.00	4.00	8.00
❏ 2720	At Last I Found a Love/That's the Way My Baby Is	1970	—	3.00	6.00
❏ 2732	Them Boys/Flash in the Pan	1970	—	3.00	6.00
❏ 2750	This World/A Light Sings	1970	—	3.00	6.00
❏ 2779	Evidence/Change Me Not	1970	—	3.00	6.00
CARIBOU					
❏ 9022	Black Sunday/(Instrumental)	1977	—	2.00	4.00
RSO					
❏ 932	Love Is On the Way/(Instrumental)	1979	—	2.50	5.00
❏ 1013	Love Is On the Way/(Instrumental)	1979	—	2.00	4.00
STAX					
❏ 0178	Emercury/Slipped and Tripped	1973	—	2.50	5.00
❏ 0203	Try a Little Tenderness/Dirty Tricks	1974	—	2.50	5.00
Albums					
ATLANTIC					
❏ SD 8155	The Sweet Inspirations	1968	5.00	10.00	20.00
❏ SD 8182	Songs of Faith and Inspiration	1968	5.00	10.00	20.00
❏ 8201 [M]	What the World Needs Now Is Love	1969	12.50	25.00	50.00
—Mono is white label promo only; "dj copy monaural" sticker on stereo cover					
❏ SD 8201 [S]	What the World Needs Now Is Love	1969	5.00	10.00	20.00
❏ SD 8225	Sweets for My Sweet	1969	5.00	10.00	20.00
❏ SD 8253	Sweet, Sweet Soul	1970	5.00	10.00	20.00
RSO					
❏ RS-1-3058	Hot Butterfly	1979	2.50	5.00	10.00
STAX					
❏ STS-3017	Estelle, Myrna and Sylvia	1973	5.00	10.00	20.00
SWEET MARQUEES, THE					
45s					
APACHE					
❏ 1516	You Lied/I Love My Baby	1961	75.00	150.00	300.00
SWEET PANTS					
Albums					
BARKLEY					
❏ 1141	Fat Peter Presents Sweet Pants	1969	50.00	100.00	200.00
SWEET SENSATION					
45s					
PYE					
❏ 71002	Sad Sweet Dreamer/Surething, Yes I Do	1974	—	2.00	4.00
❏ 71026	Ride Away from the Sun/(B-side unknown)	1975	—	2.00	4.00
❏ 71049	Mr. Cool/(B-side unknown)	1975	—	2.00	4.00
Albums					
PYE					
❏ 12110	Sweet Sensation	1975	2.50	5.00	10.00
SWEET SICK TEENS, THE					
45s					
RCA VICTOR					
❏ 37-7940	The Pretzel/Agnes, the Teenage Russian Spy	1961	20.00	40.00	80.00
—"Compact Single 33" (small hole, plays at LP speed)					
❏ 47-7940	The Pretzel/Agnes, the Teenage Russian Spy	1961	10.00	20.00	40.00
SWEET TEENS, THE					
45s					
FLIP					
❏ 311	Forever More/Don't Worry About a Thing	1955	15.00	30.00	60.00
GEE					
❏ 1030	My Valentine/With This Ring	1957	15.00	30.00	60.00
SWEET TOOTHE					
Albums					
DOMINION					
❏ NR-7360	Testing	1974	75.00	150.00	300.00
SWEETIES, THE					
45s					
END					
❏ 1110	After You/Paul's Love	1962	5.00	10.00	20.00
SWEETWATER					
45s					
REPRISE					
❏ 0787	My Crystal Spiker/What's Wrong	1968	2.00	4.00	8.00
❏ 0816	Motherless Child/Why Oh Why	1969	2.00	4.00	8.00
❏ 0835	For Pete's Sake/Bondeau	1969	2.00	4.00	8.00

S

Number	Title (A Side/B Side)	Yr	VG	VG+	NM
❏ 0987	Just for You/Look Out	1971	—	3.00	6.00
❏ 1002	Day Song/Without Me	1971	—	3.00	6.00
❏ 1076	Join the Band (Part 1)/Join the Band (Part 2)	1972	—	3.00	6.00
Albums					
REPRISE					
❏ RS 6313	Sweetwater	1968	3.75	7.50	15.00
❏ RS 6417	Just for You	1970	3.75	7.50	15.00
❏ RS 6473	Melon	1971	3.75	7.50	15.00

SWENSONS, THE
45s
X-TRA

Number	Title (A Side/B Side)	Yr	VG	VG+	NM
❏ 100	Remember Me to My Darling/Golly Boo	1957	50.00	100.00	200.00

SWIFT, BASIL, AND THE SEEGRAMS Also see DANNY HUTTON.
45s
MERCURY

Number	Title (A Side/B Side)	Yr	VG	VG+	NM
❏ 72386	Farmer's Daughter/Shambles	1965	50.00	100.00	200.00

SWIFT, DICK
45s
HIT

Number	Title (A Side/B Side)	Yr	VG	VG+	NM
❏ 21	Sealed with a Kiss/Breaking Up Is Hard to Do	1962	2.00	4.00	8.00

—B-side by Bill Arndt

SWIFT RAIN
Albums
HI

Number	Title (A Side/B Side)	Yr	VG	VG+	NM
❏ SHL-32064	Coming Down	1971	6.25	12.50	25.00

SWINGIN' MEDALLIONS
45s
CAPITOL

Number	Title (A Side/B Side)	Yr	VG	VG+	NM
❏ 2338	Sun, Sand and Sea/Hey, Hey Baby	1968	2.00	4.00	8.00
DOT					
❏ 16721	Bye Bye, Silly Girl/I Want to Be Your Guy	1965	3.00	6.00	12.00
4 SALE					
❏ 002	Double Shot (Of My Baby's Love)/ Here It Comes Again	1966	25.00	50.00	100.00
1-2-3					
❏ 1723	We're Gonna Hate Ourselves in the Morning/ It's Alright	1970	2.00	4.00	8.00
❏ 1732	Rollin' Rovin' River/ Don't Let Your Feet Touch the Ground	1971	2.00	4.00	8.00
SMASH					
❏ 2033	Double Shot (Of My Baby's Love)/ Here It Comes Again	1966	3.75	7.50	15.00
❏ 2050	She Drives Me Out of My Mind/ You Gotta Have Faith	1966	3.00	6.00	12.00
❏ 2075	I Don't Want to Lose It for You Baby/Night Owl	1966	3.00	6.00	12.00
❏ 2084	Don't Cry No More/I Found a Rainbow	1967	2.50	5.00	10.00
❏ 2107	Turn On the Music/ Summer's Not the Same This Year	1967	2.50	5.00	10.00
❏ 2129	Bow and Arrow/Where Can I Go to Get Soul	1967	2.50	5.00	10.00
Albums					
SMASH					
❏ MGS-27083 [M]Double Shot (Of My Baby's Love)		1966	7.50	15.00	30.00

—Later pressings contain a "censored" version of the title song

Number	Title (A Side/B Side)	Yr	VG	VG+	NM
❏ MGS-27083 [M]Double Shot (Of My Baby's Love)		1966	10.00	20.00	40.00

—First pressing contains the original 45 version of the title song

Number	Title (A Side/B Side)	Yr	VG	VG+	NM
❏ SRS-67083 [S] Double Shot (Of My Baby's Love)		1966	10.00	20.00	40.00

—Later pressings contain a "censored" version of the title song

Number	Title (A Side/B Side)	Yr	VG	VG+	NM
❏ SRS-67083 [S] Double Shot (Of My Baby's Love)		1966	12.50	25.00	50.00

—First pressing contains the original 45 version of the title song

SWINGING BLUE JEANS, THE Also see TERRY SYLVESTER.
45s
IMPERIAL

Number	Title (A Side/B Side)	Yr	VG	VG+	NM
❏ 66021	Hippy Hippy Shake/Now I Must Go	1964	3.75	7.50	15.00
❏ 66030	Good Golly Miss Molly/Shaking Feeling	1964	3.00	6.00	12.00
❏ 66049	Shake, Rattle and Roll/You're No Good	1964	3.00	6.00	12.00
❏ 66059	Tutti Frutti/Promise You'll Tell Her	1964	3.00	6.00	12.00
❏ 66090	It Isn't There/One of These Days	1965	3.00	6.00	12.00
❏ 66154	Don't Make Me Over/What Can I Do Today	1966	3.00	6.00	12.00
❏ 66225	Now the Summer's Gone/ Rumors, Gossip, Words Untrue	1967	2.50	5.00	10.00
❏ 66255	Something's Coming Along/Tremblin'	1967	2.50	5.00	10.00
Albums					
IMPERIAL					
❏ LP-9261 [M]	Hippy Hippy Shake	1964	20.00	40.00	80.00
❏ LP-12261 [R]	Hippy Hippy Shake	1964	20.00	40.00	80.00

SWINGING TIGERS
45s
TAMLA

Number	Title (A Side/B Side)	Yr	VG	VG+	NM
❏ 54024	Snake Walk (Part 1)/Snake Walk (Part 2)	1960	75.00	150.00	300.00

SWINGLE SINGERS, THE
45s
PHILIPS

Number	Title (A Side/B Side)	Yr	VG	VG+	NM
❏ 40157	Fugue in D Minor/Prelude in F Minor	1963	—	3.00	6.00
Albums					
COLUMBIA					
❏ PC 34194	Rags and All That Jazz	1976	2.50	5.00	10.00
COLUMBIA MASTERWORKS					
❏ M 33013	Love Songs for Madrigals and Madriguys	1976	2.50	5.00	10.00
MMG					
❏ 1115	Swingle Skyliner	198?	2.00	4.00	8.00
❏ 1125	Folio	198?	2.00	4.00	8.00
PHILIPS					
❏ PHS 2-5400 [(2)]Bachanalia		1972	3.00	6.00	12.00

—Reissue of 600-197 and 600-126 in same package

Number	Title (A Side/B Side)	Yr	VG	VG+	NM
❏ PHM 200097 [M]Bach's Greatest Hits		1963	2.50	5.00	10.00
❏ PHM 200126 [M]Going Baroque		1964	2.50	5.00	10.00
❏ PHM 200149 [M]Anyone for Mozart?		1965	2.50	5.00	10.00
❏ PHM 200191 [M]Getting Romantic		1965	2.50	5.00	10.00
❏ PHM 200214 [M]Rococo A-Go-Go		1966	2.50	5.00	10.00
❏ PHM 200225 [M]Encounter		1966	3.00	6.00	12.00

—With the Modern Jazz Quartet

Number	Title (A Side/B Side)	Yr	VG	VG+	NM
❏ PHM 200261 [M]Spanish Masters		1967	2.50	5.00	10.00
❏ PHS 600097 [S]Bach's Greatest Hits		1963	3.00	6.00	12.00
❏ PHS 600126 [S]Going Baroque		1964	3.00	6.00	12.00
❏ PHS 600149 [S]Anyone for Mozart?		1965	3.00	6.00	12.00
❏ PHS 600191 [S]Getting Romantic		1965	3.00	6.00	12.00
❏ PHS 600214 [S]Rococo A-Go-Go		1966	3.00	6.00	12.00
❏ PHS 600225 [S]Encounter		1966	3.75	7.50	15.00

—With the Modern Jazz Quartet

Number	Title (A Side/B Side)	Yr	VG	VG+	NM
❏ PHS 600261 [S]Spanish Masters		1967	3.00	6.00	12.00
❏ PHS 600288	Back to Bach	1968	2.50	5.00	10.00
❏ PHS 700004	The Joy of Singing	1973	2.50	5.00	10.00
❏ 824544-1	Jazz Sebastian Bach	1985	2.00	4.00	8.00
❏ 824545-1	Place Vendome	1985	2.00	4.00	8.00

—With the Modern Jazz Quartet; reissue of 600-225

SWISHER, DEBRA
45s
BOOM

Number	Title (A Side/B Side)	Yr	VG	VG+	NM
❏ 60001	You're So Good to Me/Thank You and Goodnight	1966	3.00	6.00	12.00

SYCAMORES, THE
45s
GROOVE

Number	Title (A Side/B Side)	Yr	VG	VG+	NM
❏ 0121	I'll Be Waiting/Darling, Is It True	1955	50.00	100.00	200.00

SYDELLS, THE
45s
BELTONE

Number	Title (A Side/B Side)	Yr	VG	VG+	NM
❏ 2032	In the Night/The Hokey Pokey	1963	3.75	7.50	15.00

SYLVERS, FOSTER Also see THE SYLVERS.
45s
A&M

Number	Title (A Side/B Side)	Yr	VG	VG+	NM
❏ 1480	I'll Do It/Pretty Baby	1990	—	2.50	5.00

—As "Foster Sylvers & Hy-Tech"

Number	Title (A Side/B Side)	Yr	VG	VG+	NM
CAPITOL					
❏ 4553	Don't Let Me Go for Someone Else/Super Scoop	1978	—	2.00	4.00
MGM					
❏ 14580	Misdemeanor/So Close	1973	—	2.50	5.00
❏ 14630	Hey Little Girl/I'll Get You in the End	1973	—	2.50	5.00
PRIDE					
❏ 1031	Misdemeanor/So Close	1973	2.50	5.00	10.00
Albums					
PRIDE					
❏ 0027	Foster Sylvers	1973	3.00	6.00	12.00

SYLVERS, THE Also see FOSTER SYLVERS.
12-Inch Singles
GEFFEN

Number	Title (A Side/B Side)	Yr	VG	VG+	NM
❏ 20258	In One Love and Out the Other (Extended)/ (Instrumental)	1984	—	3.00	6.00
45s					
CAPITOL					
❏ 4179	Boogie Fever/Free Style	1975	—	2.00	4.00
❏ 4255	Cotton Candy/I Can Be for Real	1976	—	2.00	4.00
❏ 4336	Hot Line/That's What Love Is Made Of	1976	—	2.00	4.00
❏ 4405	High School Dance/ Lovin' You Is Like Lovin' the Wind	1977	—	2.00	4.00
❏ 4493	Any Way You Want Me/Lovin' Me Back	1977	—	2.00	4.00
❏ 4532	New Horizon/Charisma	1978	—	2.00	4.00
CASABLANCA					
❏ 938	Don't Stop, Get Off/Love Won't Let Me Go	1978	—	2.00	4.00
❏ 953	Forever Yours/Diamonds Are Rare	1978	—	2.00	4.00
❏ 992	I Feel So Good Tonight/ Hoochie Coochie Dancin'	1979	—	2.00	4.00
❏ 2207	I Feels So Good Tonight/Mahogany	1979	—	2.00	4.00
GEFFEN					
❏ 29061	Falling for Your Love/(Instrumental)	1985	—	—	3.00
❏ 29293	In One Love and Out the Other/ Falling for Your Love	1984	—	—	3.00
❏ 29293 [PS]	In One Love and Out the Other/ Falling for Your Love	1984	—	—	3.00
MGM					
❏ 14352	You Got What It Takes/Time to Ride	1972	—	3.00	6.00
❏ 14579	Stay Away from Me/I'll Never Be Ashamed	1973	—	3.00	6.00
❏ 14678	Through the Love in My Heart/Cry of a Dreamer	1973	—	2.00	4.00
❏ 14698	Hang On Sloopy/Na Na Hey Hey Kiss Him Goodbye	1974	—	2.00	4.00

—As "Foster, Pat & Angie Sylivers"

Number	Title (A Side/B Side)	Yr	VG	VG+	NM
❏ 14721	I Aim to Please/Wish You Were Here	1974	—	2.00	4.00
PRIDE					
❏ 1001	Fool's Paradise/I'm Truly Happy	1972	—	2.50	5.00
❏ 1019	Wish That I Could Talk to You/How Love Hurts	1972	—	2.50	5.00
❏ 1029	Stay Away from Me/I'll Never Be Ashamed	1973	—	2.50	5.00
❏ 1029 [PS]	Stay Away from Me/I'll Never Be Ashamed	1973	—	3.00	6.00
SOLAR					
❏ 47949	Come Back, Lover, Come Back/There's a Place	1981	—	2.00	4.00
❏ 48002	Take It to the Top/I'm Getting Over	1982	—	2.00	4.00
VERVE					
❏ 10664	Come On Give Me a Chance/ I'm Just a Lonely Soul	1971	2.50	5.00	10.00
Albums					
CAPITOL					
❏ ST-11465	Showcase	1976	2.50	5.00	10.00
❏ ST-11580	Something Special	1976	2.50	5.00	10.00
❏ ST-11705	New Horizons	1977	2.50	5.00	10.00
❏ ST-11868	Best of the Sylvers	1978	2.50	5.00	10.00
CASABLANCA					
❏ NBLP 7103	Forever Yours	1978	2.50	5.00	10.00
❏ NBLP 7151	Disco Fever	1979	2.50	5.00	10.00
GEFFEN					
❏ GHS 24039	Bizarre	1984	2.50	5.00	10.00

Number	Title (A Side/B Side)	Yr	VG	VG+	NM
MGM					
❏ SE-4930	The Sylvers III	1974	2.50	5.00	10.00
PRIDE					
❏ 0007	The Sylvers	1972	3.00	6.00	12.00
❏ 0026	The Sylvers II	1973	3.00	6.00	12.00
SOLAR					
❏ 22	Concept	1981	2.50	5.00	10.00

SYLVESTER, TERRY Also see THE HOLLIES; THE SWINGING BLUE JEANS.
45s

Number	Title (A Side/B Side)	Yr	VG	VG+	NM
EPIC					
❏ 20002	It's Better Off This Way/				
	For the Peace of All Mankind	1974	—	2.00	4.00
❏ 20002 [PS]	It's Better Off This Way/				
	For the Peace of All Mankind	1974	—	2.50	5.00
❏ 50017	It's Better Off This Way/				
	For the Peace of All Mankind	1974	—	2.00	4.00
❏ 50532	Silver and Gold/Realistic Situation	1978	—	2.00	4.00
Albums					
EPIC					
❏ KE 33076	Terry Sylvester	1974	3.00	6.00	12.00

SYLVESTER, TONY, AND THE NEW INGREDIENT See THE MAIN INGREDIENT.

SYLVIA, MARGO See TUNE WEAVERS.

SYLVIA (1) R&B singer and record company mogul (All Platinum/Stang/Vibration, Sugar Hill). Also see MICKEY AND SYLVIA.
45s

Number	Title (A Side/B Side)	Yr	VG	VG+	NM
ALL PLATINUM					
❏ 2303	I Can't Help It/It's a Good Life	1969	2.00	4.00	8.00
❏ 2350	Sho Nuff Boogie (Part 1)/Sho Nuff Boogie (Part 2)	1974	—	2.50	5.00
—With the Moments					
JUBILEE					
❏ 5093	Drive, Daddy, Drive/I Found Somebody to Love	1952	12.50	25.00	50.00
—As "Little Sylvia"					
STANG					
❏ 5015	Have You Had Any Lately/Anytime	1970	—	3.00	6.00
SUGAR HILL					
❏ 781	It's Good to Be the Queen/(B-side unknown)	1982	—	2.00	4.00
VIBRATION					
❏ 512	Next Time I See You/Gimme a Little Action	1972	—	3.00	6.00
❏ 521	Pillow Talk/My Thing	1973	—	3.00	6.00
❏ 524	Didn't I/Had Any Lately	1973	—	2.50	5.00
❏ 525	Soul Je T'Aime/Sunday	1973	—	2.50	5.00
—With Ralfi Pagan					
❏ 527	Alfredo/Lay It On Me	1973	—	2.50	5.00
❏ 528	Private Performance/If You Get the Notion	1974	—	2.50	5.00
❏ 529	Sweet Stuff/Had Any Lately	1974	—	2.50	5.00
❏ 530	Easy Evil/Give It Up in Vain	1974	—	2.50	5.00
❏ 536	Pussy Cat (Part 1)/Pussy Cat (Part 2)	1975	—	2.50	5.00
❏ 567	L.A. Sunshine/Taxi	1976	—	2.50	5.00
❏ 570	Lay It On Me (Vocal)/(Instrumental)	1977	—	2.50	5.00
❏ 572	Lollipop Man/Lay It On Me	1977	—	2.50	5.00
❏ 576	Automatic Lover/Stop Boy	1978	—	2.50	5.00
Albums					
STANG					
❏ 1010	Sylvia	197?	5.00	10.00	20.00
SUGAR HILL					
❏ 258	Sylvia I	1981	2.50	5.00	10.00
VIBRATION					
❏ 126	Pillow Talk	1973	3.75	7.50	15.00
❏ 131	Lay It On Me	1977	3.00	6.00	12.00
❏ 143	Brand New Funk	197?	3.00	6.00	12.00

SYMBOLS, THE (1)
45s

Number	Title (A Side/B Side)	Yr	VG	VG+	NM
DORE					
❏ 666	Last Year About This Time/Better Get Your Own One Buddy	1963	3.75	7.50	15.00

SYMBOLS, THE (2)
45s

Number	Title (A Side/B Side)	Yr	VG	VG+	NM
IMPERIAL					
❏ 66382	I Will Still Be There/The Wrong Girl	1969	2.00	4.00	8.00

SYMBOLS, THE (3)
45s

Number	Title (A Side/B Side)	Yr	VG	VG+	NM
MGM					
❏ 13348	One Fine Girl/Don't Go	1965	2.50	5.00	10.00
❏ 13463	Don't Go/Oo Wee Baby	1966	2.50	5.00	10.00

SYMBOLS, THE (4)
45s

Number	Title (A Side/B Side)	Yr	VG	VG+	NM
VINTAGE					
❏ 1007	Bye Bye/I Love You	1973	—	2.50	5.00

SYMBOLS, THE (U)
45s

Number	Title (A Side/B Side)	Yr	VG	VG+	NM
LAURIE					
❏ 3401	Bye Bye Baby/The Things You Do to Me	1967	2.50	5.00	10.00
❏ 3435	The Best Part of Breaking Up/Again	1968	2.50	5.00	10.00
PRESIDENT					
❏ 102	Canadian Sunset/The Gentle Art of Loving	1966	2.50	5.00	10.00

SYMPHONICS, THE (1)
45s

Number	Title (A Side/B Side)	Yr	VG	VG+	NM
ABC					
❏ 11068	Boy (Please Help Me)/It's Gonna Be Real Hard	1968	2.00	4.00	8.00
BRUNSWICK					
❏ 55303	Don't Fail Me Now/Silent Kind of Guy	1966	2.50	5.00	10.00
❏ 55313	No More/(She's Just a) Sad Girl	1967	2.50	5.00	10.00

SYMPHONICS, THE (2) This Symphonics features FREDDIE SCOTT.
45s

Number	Title (A Side/B Side)	Yr	VG	VG+	NM
ENRICA					
❏ 1002	Come On Honey/A Blessing to You	1959	5.00	10.00	20.00

SYNDICATE, THE
45s

Number	Title (A Side/B Side)	Yr	VG	VG+	NM
DORE					
❏ 743	My Baby Is Barefoot/Love Will Take Away	1965	50.00	100.00	200.00
DOT					
❏ 16807	Egyptian Thing/She Haunts You	1965	10.00	20.00	40.00

SYNDICATE OF SOUND
45s

Number	Title (A Side/B Side)	Yr	VG	VG+	NM
BELL					
❏ 640	Little Girl/You	1966	5.00	10.00	20.00
❏ 646	Rumors/Upper Hand	1966	3.75	7.50	15.00
❏ 655	Goodtime Music/Keep It Up	1966	3.75	7.50	15.00
❏ 666	Mary/That Kind of Man	1967	3.75	7.50	15.00
BUDDAH					
❏ 156	Brown Paper Bag/Reverb Beat	1970	2.50	5.00	10.00
❏ 183	Mexico/First to Love You	1970	2.50	5.00	10.00
CAPITOL					
❏ 2426	You're Looking Fine/Change the World	1969	2.50	5.00	10.00
DEL-FI					
❏ 4304	Prepare for Love/Tell the World	1965	5.00	10.00	20.00
HUSH					
❏ 228	Little Girl/You	1966	12.50	25.00	50.00
PHILCO-FORD					
❏ HP-29	Little Girl/Rumors	1968	5.00	10.00	20.00
—4-inch plastic "Hip Pocket Record" with color sleeve					
SCARLET					
❏ 503	Prepare for Love/Tell the World	1965	7.50	15.00	30.00
Albums					
BELL					
❏ 6001 [M]	Little Girl	1966	12.50	25.00	50.00
❏ S-6001 [S]	Little Girl	1966	20.00	40.00	80.00
SUNDAZED					
❏ LP 5051	Little Girl	2001	3.00	6.00	12.00
—Reissue on 180-gram vinyl					

SYNERGY
12-Inch Singles

Number	Title (A Side/B Side)	Yr	VG	VG+	NM
AUDION					
❏ 12204 [DJ]	Redstone/Metropolitan Theme	1987	3.00	6.00	12.00
PASSPORT					
❏ SP-30 [DJ]	Phobos and Deimos Go to Mars (Edit) (LP)	1978	3.75	7.50	15.00
45s					
PASSPORT					
❏ 7907	Classical Gas/Cybersports	1976	2.00	4.00	8.00
Albums					
AUDION					
❏ SYN 204	Metropolitan Suite	1987	2.50	5.00	10.00
PASSPORT					
❏ PG-1	Computer Experiments Volume One	1981	3.75	7.50	15.00
❏ PB 6000	Cords	1978	2.50	5.00	10.00
—Later pressings on black vinyl					
❏ PB 6000	Cords	1978	3.75	7.50	15.00
—First pressing on clear vinyl					
❏ PB 6001	Electronic Realizations for Rock Orchestra	1979	2.50	5.00	10.00
—Reissue of 98009					
❏ PB 6002	Sequencer	1979	2.50	5.00	10.00
—Reissue of 98014					
❏ PB 6003	Games	1979	2.50	5.00	10.00
❏ PB 6005	Audion	1981	2.50	5.00	10.00
❏ P2B 11002 [(2)]	Semi-Conductor	1984	3.00	6.00	12.00
❏ PPSD-98009	Electronic Realizations for Rock Orchestra	1975	3.00	6.00	12.00
❏ PPSD-98014	Sequencer	1976	3.00	6.00	12.00

SYREETA Also see BILLY PRESTON AND SYREETA.
12-Inch Singles

Number	Title (A Side/B Side)	Yr	VG	VG+	NM
MOTOWN					
❏ PR 90 [DJ]	Quick Slick/Out of the Box	1981	2.50	5.00	10.00
45s					
MOTOWN					
❏ 1297	Come and Get This Stuff/Black Maybe	1974	—	2.50	5.00
❏ 1317	I'm Goin' Left/Heavy day	1974	—	2.50	5.00
❏ 1328	Your Kiss Is Sweeter/Spinnin' and Spinnin'	1975	—	2.50	5.00
❏ 1353	Harmour Love/Cause We've Ended As Lovers	1975	—	2.50	5.00
❏ 1353 [DJ]	Harmour Love (same on both sides?)	1975	2.50	5.00	10.00
—Promo only on red vinyl					
MOWEST					
❏ 5016	I Love Every Little Thing About You/Black Maybe	1972	—	3.00	6.00
❏ 5021	Happiness/To Know You Is to Love You	1972	—	3.00	6.00
TAMLA					
❏ 1610	I Must Be in Love/Wish Upon a Star	1982	—	2.00	4.00
❏ 1675	Forever Is Not Enough/She's Leaving Home	1983	—	2.00	4.00
❏ 54333	Quick Slick/I Don't Know	1981	—	2.00	4.00
Albums					
MOTOWN					
❏ M6-808	Stevie Wonder Presents Syreeta	1974	2.50	5.00	10.00
❏ M6-891	Rich Love, Poor Love	1977	2.50	5.00	10.00
—With G.C. Cameron					
MOWEST					
❏ 113	Syreeta	1972	3.00	6.00	12.00
TAMLA					
❏ T6-349	One	1977	2.50	5.00	10.00
❏ T7-372	Syreeta	1980	2.50	5.00	10.00
❏ T8-376	Set My Love in Motion	1981	2.50	5.00	10.00
❏ 6039 TF	The Spell	1983	2.50	5.00	10.00

SZIGETI, SANDY
45s

Number	Title (A Side/B Side)	Yr	VG	VG+	NM
DECCA					
❏ 32862	America's Sweetheart/My Steady Diet	1971	2.50	5.00	10.00
—Produced by Rick Nelson					

S

Number	Title (A Side/B Side)	Yr	VG	VG+	NM

T

T.C. ATLANTIC
45s
AESOP'S LABEL

❏ 6044	Once Upon a Melody/I Love You So, Little Girl	1965	10.00	20.00	40.00

B. SHARP

❏ 272	Mona/My Babe	1966	7.50	15.00	30.00

CANDY FLOSS

❏ 101	I'm So Glad/Twenty Years Ago	1968	10.00	20.00	40.00

PARAMOUNT

❏ 0098	Judgment Train/Shine the Light	1971	3.75	7.50	15.00

PARROT

❏ 330	I'm So Glad/Twenty Years Ago	1968	5.00	10.00	20.00
❏ 338	Love Is Just/Faces	1969	5.00	10.00	20.00

TURTLE

❏ 1103	Faces/Baby, Please Don't Go	1966	25.00	50.00	100.00
❏ 1105	Shake/Spanish Harlem	1967	10.00	20.00	40.00

Albums
DOVE

❏ LP-4459	T.C. Atlantic	1966	25.00	50.00	100.00

T.I.M.E.
45s
LIBERTY

❏ 56020	Take Me Along/Make It Right	1968	2.50	5.00	10.00
❏ 56020 [PS]	Take Me Along/Make It Right	1968	3.75	7.50	15.00
❏ 56060	Tripping Into Sunshine/				
	What Would Life Be Without You	1968	2.50	5.00	10.00

Albums
LIBERTY

❏ LST-7558	T.I.M.E.	1968	6.25	12.50	25.00
❏ LST-7605	Smooth Ball	1969	6.25	12.50	25.00

T. REX
45s
A&M

❏ 955	Child Star/Debora	1968	3.00	6.00	12.00

—As "Tyrannosaurus Rex"
BLUE THUMB

❏ 212	By the Light of the Magical Moon/				
	Find a Little Wood	1971	—	3.00	6.00
❏ SP-6115/6 [DJ]	Ride a White Swan/Is It Love	1970	3.00	6.00	12.00

—As "Tyrannosaurus Rex"

❏ 7121	Ride a White Swan/Summertime Blues	1970	2.00	4.00	8.00

—As "Tyrannosaurus Rex"
CASABLANCA

❏ 810	Precious Star/(B-side unknown)	1974		3.00	6.00

REPRISE

❏ 1006	Hot Love//One Inch Rock/Seagull Woman	1971	—	3.00	6.00
❏ 1032	Bang a Gong (Get It On)/Raw Ramp	1971	2.00	4.00	8.00
❏ 1056	Jeepster/Rip Off	1971	—	3.00	6.00
❏ 1078	Telegram Sam/Cadillac	1972	—	3.00	6.00
❏ 1095	Metal Guru/Lady	1972	—	3.00	6.00
❏ 1122	The Slider/Rock On	1972	—	3.00	6.00
❏ 1150	Bang a Gong (Get It On)/Telegram Sam	1972	—	2.00	4.00

—"Back to Back Hits" series

❏ 1151	Jeepster/Metal Guru	1972	—	2.00	4.00

—"Back to Back Hits" series

❏ 1161	Born to Boogie/The Groover	1973	—	2.50	5.00
❏ 1161 [PS]	Born to Boogie/The Groover	1973	6.25	12.50	25.00
❏ 1170	Hot Love/Rip Off	1973	—	2.50	5.00

Albums
A&M

❏ SP-3514 [(2)]	Tyrannosaurus Rex (A Beginning)	1972	3.75	7.50	15.00

—Compilation of early LPs Prophets, Seers & Sages and My People Were Fair and Had Sky in Their Hair But Now They're Content to Wear Stars on Their Brows
BLUE THUMB

❏ BTS 7	Unicorn	1969	5.00	10.00	20.00
❏ BTS 18	A Beard of Stars	1970	5.00	10.00	20.00

—Add $5 for bonus single SP-6115/6, "Ride a White Swan"/"Is It Love." For reasons unknown, the single seems to be much more readily available than the LP.
CASABLANCA

❏ NBLP 7005	Light of Love	1974	3.00	6.00	12.00

—Reissue of 9006

❏ NB 9006	Light of Love	1974	3.75	7.50	15.00

—Original, distributed by Warner Bros.
MARC ON WAX/RELATIVITY

❏ 8249	Bolan's Zip Gun	198?	2.50	5.00	10.00
❏ 8250	Zinc Alloy & The Hidden Riders of Tomorrow	198?	2.50	5.00	10.00
❏ 8251	Dandy in the Underworld	198?	2.50	5.00	10.00
❏ 8252	Futuristic Dragon	198?	2.50	5.00	10.00
❏ 8253	The Slider	198?	2.50	5.00	10.00
❏ 8254	Tanx	198?	2.50	5.00	10.00

REPRISE

❏ PRO 511 [DJ]	An Interview with Marc Bolan	1971	25.00	50.00	100.00
❏ MS 2095	The Slider	1972	3.00	6.00	12.00
❏ MS 2132	Tanx	1973	3.00	6.00	12.00
❏ RS 6440	T. Rex	1971	3.00	6.00	12.00
❏ RS 6466	Electric Warrior	1971	3.00	6.00	12.00

RHINO

❏ R1-76111	Electric Warrior	2003	3.75	7.50	15.00

—Reissue on 180-gram vinyl
WARNER BROS.

❏ 25333	T. Rextasy: The Best of T. Rex, 1970-1973	1985	2.50	5.00	10.00

T.S.U. TORONADOES, THE
45s
ATLANTIC

❏ 2579	Getting the Corners/What Good Am I!	1968	2.00	4.00	8.00
❏ 2614	Got to Get Through to You/The Goose	1969	2.00	4.00	8.00

VOLT

❏ 4030	My Thing Is a Moving Thing/Still Love You	1969	—	3.00	6.00
❏ 4038	One Flight Too Many/				
	Play the Music Toronadoes	1970	—	3.00	6.00

T2
Albums
LONDON

❏ PS 583	It'll All Work Out in Boomland	1971	20.00	40.00	80.00

T.V. AND THE TRIBESMEN
Albums
HANNA-BARBERA

❏ HLP-9507 [S]	Barefootin'	1966	6.25	12.50	25.00

T-BIRDS, THE
45s
CHESS

❏ 1778	Green Stamps/Come On Dance with Me	1961	6.25	12.50	25.00
❏ 1792	Hog Wild/Taco Harry	1961	6.25	12.50	25.00

GONE

❏ 5141	Wild Stomp/Soft Smoke	1962	5.00	10.00	20.00

T-BIRD

❏ 101	Green Stamps/Come On Dance with Me	1961	10.00	20.00	40.00

VEGAS

❏ 720	Nobody But You/				
	Have You Ever Been in Love Before	1968	15.00	30.00	60.00

T-BONES, THE
Members of this group later formed HAMILTON, JOE FRANK AND REYNOLDS.
45s
LIBERTY

❏ 55677	Draggin'/Rail-Vette	1964	5.00	10.00	20.00
❏ 55814	That's Where It's At/Pearlin'	1965	3.75	7.50	15.00
❏ 55836	No Matter What Shape (Your Stomach's In)/				
	Feelin' Fine	1965	3.00	6.00	12.00
❏ 55867	Sippin' & Chippin'/Moment of Softness	1966	2.50	5.00	10.00
❏ 55885	Wherever You Look, Wherever You Go/				
	Underwater	1966	2.50	5.00	10.00
❏ 55906	Let's Go Get Stoned/Farre Thee Well	1966	2.50	5.00	10.00
❏ 55925	Balboa Blues/Walkin' My Cat Named Dog	1966	2.50	5.00	10.00
❏ 55951	Tee Hee Hee (My Life Seems Different Now)/				
	Proper Thing to Do	1967	2.50	5.00	10.00

UNITED ARTISTS

❏ 0068	No Matter What Shape (Your Stomach's In)/				
	Sippin' N Chippin'	1973	—	2.50	5.00

—"Silver Spotlight Series" reissue
7-Inch Extended Plays
LIBERTY

❏ LST-4-7439	*Hole in the Wall/Let's Hang On/Lies/Fever/				
	Don't Think Twice, It's Alright	1966	5.00	10.00	20.00

—Jukebox issue; small hole, plays at 33 1/3 rpm

❏ LST-4-7439 [PS]	No Matter What Shape (Your Stomach's In)	1966	5.00	10.00	20.00

Albums
LIBERTY

❏ LRP-3346 [M]	Boss Drag	1963	15.00	30.00	60.00
❏ LRP-3363 [M]	Boss Drag at the Beach	1964	15.00	30.00	60.00
❏ LRP-3404 [M]	Doin' the Jerk	1965	10.00	20.00	40.00
❏ LRP-3439 [M]	No Matter What Shape (Your Stomach's In)	1966	5.00	10.00	20.00
❏ LRP-3446 [M]	Sippin' and Chippin'	1966	5.00	10.00	20.00
❏ LRP-3471 [M]	Everyone's Gone to the Moon	1966	5.00	10.00	20.00
❏ LST-7346 [S]	Boss Drag	1963	25.00	50.00	100.00
❏ LST-7363 [S]	Boss Drag at the Beach	1964	25.00	50.00	100.00
❏ LST-7404 [S]	Doin' the Jerk	1965	15.00	30.00	60.00
❏ LST-7439 [S]	No Matter What Shape (Your Stomach's In)	1966	6.25	12.50	25.00
❏ LST-7446 [S]	Sippin' and Chippin'	1966	6.25	12.50	25.00
❏ LST-7471 [S]	Everyone's Gone to the Moon	1966	6.25	12.50	25.00

SUNSET

❏ SUM-1119 [M]	Shapin' Things Up	196?	3.00	6.00	12.00
❏ SUS-5119 [S]	Shapin' Things Up	196?	3.75	7.50	15.00

TABBYS, THE
45s
TIME

❏ 1008	Yes I Do/My Darling	1959	6.25	12.50	25.00

—Red label

❏ 1008	Yes I Do/My Darling	1959	12.50	25.00	50.00

—Blue label

TABS, THE
45s
DOT

❏ 15887	Avenue of Tears/The First Star	1959	7.50	15.00	30.00

GARDENA

❏ 110	Never Forget/Rock and Roll Holiday	1960	12.50	25.00	50.00

NASCO

❏ 6016	Will We Meet Again/Still Love You Baby	1958	7.50	15.00	30.00

NOBLE

❏ 719	Never Forget/Rock and Roll Holiday	1959	37.50	75.00	150.00
❏ 720	Oops/My Girl Is Gone	1959	100.00	200.00	400.00

VEE JAY

❏ 418	Dance All By Myself/Dance Party	1961	5.00	10.00	20.00
❏ 446	Mash Dem Taters/But You're My Baby	1962	5.00	10.00	20.00

WAND

❏ 130	Two Stupid Feet/Footsteps	1962	3.75	7.50	15.00
❏ 139	I'm with You/Take My Love Along with You	1963	3.75	7.50	15.00

TADS, THE
45s
DOT

❏ 15518	Your Reason/The Pink Panther	1956	6.25	12.50	25.00

LIBERTY BELL

❏ 9010	Your Reason/The Pink Panther	1956	12.50	25.00	50.00

REV

❏ 3513	Wolf Call/She Is My Dream	1958	12.50	25.00	50.00

TAFFYS, THE
45s
AMY

❏ 933	Bongo Man/The Game Called Love	1965	3.75	7.50	15.00

FAIRMOUNT

❏ 610	Everybody South Street/Key to My Heart	1963	2.50	5.00	10.00

Number	Title (A Side/B Side)	Yr	VG	VG+	NM
PAGEANT					
❑ 608	Can't We Just Be Friends/Peter Cottontail	1963	2.50	5.00	10.00
PARKWAY					
❑ 872	Everybody South Street/				
	Can't We Just Be Friends	1963	3.75	7.50	15.00

TAGES, THE With PETER FRAMPTON.
45s
VERVE

Number	Title (A Side/B Side)	Yr	VG	VG+	NM
❑ 10626	Halcyon Days/I Read You Like an Open Book	1968	5.00	10.00	20.00

TAKERS, THE
45s
INTERPHON

Number	Title (A Side/B Side)	Yr	VG	VG+	NM
❑ 7709	Think/If You Don't Come Back	1964	2.50	5.00	10.00

TALLEY, JOHNNY T.
45s
MERCURY

Number	Title (A Side/B Side)	Yr	VG	VG+	NM
❑ 70902	Lonesome Train/(I've Changed My) Wild Mind	1956	75.00	150.00	300.00

TALLYSMEN, THE
45s
TALLY

Number	Title (A Side/B Side)	Yr	VG	VG+	NM
❑ 200688	Little By Little/You Don't Care About Me	1966	15.00	30.00	60.00

TAMANEERS, THE
45s
BRAMLEY

Number	Title (A Side/B Side)	Yr	VG	VG+	NM
❑ 102	Searching/Be Anything (But Be Mine)	1960	100.00	200.00	400.00

TAMBLYN, LARRY
45s
FARO

Number	Title (A Side/B Side)	Yr	VG	VG+	NM
❑ 601	Patty Ann/Dearest	1960	5.00	10.00	20.00
❑ 603	The Lie/My Bride-to-Be	1960	5.00	10.00	20.00
❑ 612	This Is the Night/Destiny	1961	6.25	12.50	25.00
LINDA					
❑ 112	You'll Be Mine Someday/The Girl in My Heart	1963	5.00	10.00	20.00
—With the Standells					

TAMMI AND THE BACHELORS
45s
BANGAR

Number	Title (A Side/B Side)	Yr	VG	VG+	NM
❑ 00610	My Summer Love/My Love	1964	6.25	12.50	25.00

TAMMYS, THE
45s
UNITED ARTISTS

Number	Title (A Side/B Side)	Yr	VG	VG+	NM
❑ 632	Take Back Your Ring/Part of Growing Up	1963	3.00	6.00	12.00
❑ 678	Egyptian Shamba/What's So Sweet About				
	Sweet Sixteen	1963	3.00	6.00	12.00
VEEP					
❑ 1210	Gypsy/Hold Back the Light of Dawn	1965	3.00	6.00	12.00
❑ 1220	His Actions Speak Louder Than Words/				
	Blues Sixteen	1965	3.00	6.00	12.00

TAMPA RED
45s
RCA VICTOR

Number	Title (A Side/B Side)	Yr	VG	VG+	NM
❑ 47-4275	Boogie Woogie Women/I Won't Let Her Do It	1951	12.50	25.00	50.00
❑ 47-4399	She's a Cool Operator/Green and Lucky Blues	1951	12.50	25.00	50.00
❑ 47-4722	But I Forgive You/I'm Gonna Put You Down	1952	12.50	25.00	50.00
❑ 47-4898	True Love/Look-a There, Look-a There	1952	12.50	25.00	50.00
❑ 47-5134	All Mixed Up Over You/Too Late Too Long	1953	10.00	20.00	40.00
❑ 47-5273	I'll Never Let You Go/				
	Got a Mind to Leave This Town	1953	10.00	20.00	40.00
❑ 47-5523	So Craazy About You Baby/So Much Trouble	1953	10.00	20.00	40.00
❑ 47-5594	If She Don't Come Back/Big Stars Falling	1954	10.00	20.00	40.00
❑ 50-0002	If You Ever Change Your Ways/				
	Chicago Breakdown	1949	30.00	60.00	120.00
—Gray label, orange vinyl; With Big Maceo					
❑ 50-0019	Come On If You're Coming/				
	When Things Go Wrong with You	1950	30.00	60.00	120.00
—Gray label, orange vinyl					
❑ 50-0027	It's a Brand New Boogie/				
	Put Your Money Where Your Mouth Is	1950	30.00	60.00	120.00
—Gray label, orange vinyl					
❑ 50-0041	I'll Find My Way/That's Her Own Business	1950	30.00	60.00	120.00
—Gray label, orange vinyl					
❑ 50-0071	It's Too Late Now/Please Try to See It My Way	1950	25.00	50.00	100.00
—Gray label, orange vinyl					
❑ 50-0084	1950 Blues/Love Her with a Feelin'	1950	25.00	50.00	100.00
—Gray label, orange vinyl					
❑ 50-0094	It's Good Like That/New Deal Blues	1950	25.00	50.00	100.00
—Gray label, orange vinyl					
❑ 50-0107	Sweet Little Angel/Don't Blame Shorty for That	1951	20.00	40.00	80.00
❑ 50-0112	Midnight Boogie/I Miss My Lovin' Blues	1951	20.00	40.00	80.00
❑ 50-0123	She's Dynamite/Early in the Morning	1951	20.00	40.00	80.00
❑ 50-0136	Pretty Baby Blues/Since My Baby's Been Gone	1951	20.00	40.00	80.00
Albums					
BLUEBIRD					
❑ AXM2-5501 [(2)]Guitar Wizard		1975	3.75	7.50	15.00
BLUES CLASSICS					
❑ 25	Guitar Wizard (1935-53)	197?	3.00	6.00	12.00
BLUESVILLE					
❑ BVLP-1030 [M] Don't Tampa with the Blues		1961	30.00	60.00	120.00
—Blue label, silver print					
❑ BVLP-1030 [M] Don't Tampa with the Blues		1963	7.50	15.00	30.00
—Blue label, trident logo at right					
❑ BVLP-1043 [M] Don't Jive Me		1962	30.00	60.00	120.00
—Blue label, silver print					
❑ BVLP-1043 [M] Don't Jive Me		1963	7.50	15.00	30.00
—Blue label, trident logo at right					
FANTASY					
❑ OBC-516	Don't Tampa with the Blues	198?	2.50	5.00	10.00
YAZOO					
❑ 1039	Bottleneck Guitar	197?	3.00	6.00	12.00

TAMS, THE
45s
ABC

Number	Title (A Side/B Side)	Yr	VG	VG+	NM
❑ 10825	Holding On/Is It Better to Have Loved a Little	1966	2.00	4.00	8.00
❑ 10885	Shelter/Get Away (Leave Me Alone)	1966	2.00	4.00	8.00
❑ 10929	Breaking Up/How 'Bout It	1967	2.00	4.00	8.00
❑ 10956	Everything Else Is Gone/				
	Mary, Mary, Row Your Boat	1967	2.00	4.00	8.00
❑ 11019	All My Heard Times/A Little More Soul	1967	2.00	4.00	8.00
❑ 11066	Be Young, Be Foolish, Be Happy/				
	That Same Old Song	1968	2.00	4.00	8.00
❑ 11128	Laugh at the World/Trouble Maker	1968	2.00	4.00	8.00
❑ 11183	Sunshine, Rainbow, Blue Sky, Brown Eyed Girl/				
	There's a Great Big Change in Me	1969	2.00	4.00	8.00
❑ 11228	Be Young, Be Foolish, Be Happy/				
	Love, Love, Love	1969	2.00	4.00	8.00
❑ 11358	Don't You Just Know It/Making Music	1973	—	2.50	5.00
ABC DUNHILL					
❑ 4290	Hey Girl Don't Bother Me/Weep Little Girl	1971	—	3.00	6.00
❑ 4290 [PS]	Hey Girl Don't Bother Me/Weep Little Girl	1971	2.50	5.00	10.00
—Title sleeve with "#1 in England"					
ABC-PARAMOUNT					
❑ 10502	What Kind of Fool (Do You Think I Am)/				
	Laugh It Off	1963	3.75	7.50	15.00
❑ 10533	It's All Right (You're Just in Love)/				
	You Lied to Your Daddy	1964	3.00	6.00	12.00
❑ 10573	Hey Girl Don't Bother Me/Take Away	1964	3.00	6.00	12.00
❑ 10601	Silly Little Girl/Weep Little Girl	1964	3.00	6.00	12.00
❑ 10614	The Truth Hurts/Why Did My Little Girl Cry	1965	2.50	5.00	10.00
❑ 10635	What Do You Do/Unlove You	1965	2.50	5.00	10.00
❑ 10702	Concrete Jungle/Till the End of Time	1965	2.50	5.00	10.00
❑ 10741	Carryin' On/I've Been Hurt	1965	2.50	5.00	10.00
❑ 10779	Got to Get Used to a Broken Heart/				
	Riding for a Fall	1966	2.50	5.00	10.00
APT					
❑ 26010	Long Distance Operator/Numbers	1970	—	3.00	6.00
ARLEN					
❑ 711	Untie Me/Disillusioned	1962	3.00	6.00	12.00
❑ 717	Deep Inside Me/If You're So Smart				
	(Why Do You Have a Broken Heart)	1962	3.00	6.00	12.00
❑ 720	You'll Never Know/Blue Shadows	1963	3.00	6.00	12.00
❑ 729	Don't Ever Go/Find Another Love	1963	3.00	6.00	12.00
CAPITOL					
❑ 3050	The Tams Medley/Wire Help	1971	—	3.00	6.00
COMPLEAT					
❑ 109	My Baby Sure Can Shag/Making True Love	1983	—	2.00	4.00
GENERAL AMERICAN					
❑ 714	My Baby Loves Me/Find Another Love	1962	3.75	7.50	15.00
HERITAGE					
❑ 101	Vacation Time/If Love Were Like Rivers	1961	75.00	150.00	300.00
KING					
❑ 6012	Untie Me/Find Another Love	1965	2.50	5.00	10.00
1-2-3					
❑ 1726	How Long Love/Too Much Foolin' Around	1970	—	3.00	6.00
SWAN					
❑ 4055	Sorry/Valley of Love	1960	3.75	7.50	15.00
Albums					
ABC					
❑ ABCS-481 [R] Presenting the Tams		1968	5.00	10.00	20.00
—Reissue of ABC-Paramount 481					
❑ ABCS-499 [S] Hey Girl, Don't Bother Me		1964	5.00	10.00	20.00
—Reissue of ABC-Paramount 499					
❑ ABC-596 [M] Time for the Tams		1967	7.50	15.00	30.00
❑ ABCS-596 [S] Time for the Tams		1967	7.50	15.00	30.00
❑ ABCS-627	A Little More Soul	1968	6.25	12.50	25.00
❑ ABCS-673	A Portrait of the Tams	1969	6.25	12.50	25.00
ABC-PARAMOUNT					
❑ ABC-481 [M] Presenting the Tams		1964	12.50	25.00	50.00
❑ ABCS-481 [R] Presenting the Tams		1964	7.50	15.00	30.00
❑ ABC-499 [M] Hey Girl, Don't Bother Me		1964	7.50	15.00	30.00
❑ ABCS-499 [S] Hey Girl, Don't Bother Me		1964	10.00	20.00	40.00
CAPITOL					
❑ SM-11839	The Best of the Tams	1979	3.00	6.00	12.00
COMPLEAT					
❑ CMLP-5001 [EP]Beach Music from the Tams		198?	2.00	4.00	8.00
1-2-3					
❑ ST-567	The Best of the Tams	1970	5.00	10.00	20.00
SOUNDS SOUTH					
❑ SO-16010	The Mighty, Mighty Tams	1977	3.75	7.50	15.00

TAMS, THE (2)
45s
MINK

Number	Title (A Side/B Side)	Yr	VG	VG+	NM
❑ 22	Memory Lane/Teenage Kids	1959	10.00	20.00	40.00
—Originally issued as "The Stereos"					
PARKWAY					
❑ 863	Memory Lane/A Lovely Piano	1963	5.00	10.00	20.00
—The same record was reissued as "The Hippies"					

TANEGA, NORMA
45s
NEW VOICE

Number	Title (A Side/B Side)	Yr	VG	VG+	NM
❑ 807	Walkin' My Cat Named Dog/I'm the Sky	1966	3.00	6.00	12.00
❑ 810	A Street That Rhymes at 6 A.M./Treat Me Right	1966	2.50	5.00	10.00
❑ 815	Bread/Waves	1966	2.50	5.00	10.00
❑ 821	No Stranger Am I/Run on the Run	1967	2.50	5.00	10.00
Albums					
NEW VOICE					
❑ NV-2001 [M]	Walkin' My Cat Named Dog	1966	10.00	20.00	40.00
❑ NVS-2001 [S]	Walkin' My Cat Named Dog	1966	20.00	40.00	80.00

T

Number	Title (A Side/B Side)	Yr	VG	VG+	NM

TANGEERS, THE
45s
OKEH

❑ 7319	Let My Heart and Soul Be Free/				
	What's the Use of Me Trying	1968	10.00	20.00	40.00

TANGERINE DREAM
12-Inch Singles
RELATIVITY

❑ EMC 8044	Streethawk (2 versions)/Tiergarten	1985	5.00	10.00	20.00
45s					
MCA					
❑ 40740	Betrayal (Sorcerer's Theme)/Grind	1977	2.50	5.00	10.00
VIRGIN					
❑ 9516	Moonlight (Part 2)/Coldwater Canyon (Part 2)	1977	2.50	5.00	10.00
❑ 9516 [DJ]	Moonlight (Part 2) (mono/stereo)	1977	2.50	5.00	10.00
❑ 9516 [DJ]	Moonlight/Cherokee Lane	1977	2.50	5.00	10.00
❑ 9516 [DJ]	Moonlight/Desert Dream	1977	2.50	5.00	10.00
Albums					
CAROLINE					
❑ CAROL 1349	Livemiles	1988	3.00	6.00	12.00
ELEKTRA					
❑ 5E-521	Thief	1981	2.50	5.00	10.00
❑ 5E-557	Exit	1981	2.50	5.00	10.00
EMI AMERICA					
❑ ST-17141	Flashpoint	1984	2.50	5.00	10.00
MCA					
❑ 2277	Sorcerer	1977	3.00	6.00	12.00
❑ 6165	Legend	1986	2.00	4.00	8.00
PRIVATE MUSIC					
❑ 2042-1-P	Optical Race	1988	3.75	7.50	15.00
❑ 2047-1-P	Miracle Mile	1989	3.75	7.50	15.00
❑ 2057-1-P	Lily on the Beach	1989	3.75	7.50	15.00
RELATIVITY					
❑ EMC 8043	Le Parc	198?	3.00	6.00	12.00
❑ EMC 8045 [(2)]	Poland	198?	3.75	7.50	15.00
❑ 86561 8068	Electronic Meditation	1986	3.00	6.00	12.00
❑ 86561 8069	Alpha Centauri	1986	3.00	6.00	12.00
❑ 86561 8070 [(2)]	Zeit	1986	3.75	7.50	15.00
❑ 86561 8071	Atam	1986	3.00	6.00	12.00
❑ 86561 8072	Green Desert	1986	3.00	6.00	12.00
❑ 86561 8113	Underwater Sunlight	1986	3.00	6.00	12.00
VIRGIN					
❑ VR 13-108	Phaedra	1974	3.75	7.50	15.00
❑ VR 13-116	Rubycon	1975	3.75	7.50	15.00
❑ PZ 34427	Stratosfear	1976	3.75	7.50	15.00
❑ PZG 35014 [(2)]	Encore	1977	5.00	10.00	20.00
VIRGIN INTERNATIONAL					
❑ VI 2010	Phaedra	1979	2.50	5.00	10.00
—Reissue					
❑ VI 2025	Rubycon	1979	2.50	5.00	10.00
—Reissue					
❑ VI 2044	Ricochet	1975	3.75	7.50	15.00
❑ VI 2068	Stratosfear	1979	3.00	6.00	12.00
—Reissue of 34427					
❑ VI 2097	Cyclone	1979	2.50	5.00	10.00
—Reissue					
❑ VI 2111	Force Majeure	1979	3.00	6.00	12.00

TANGERINE ZOO, THE
45s
MAINSTREAM

❑ 682	A Trip to the Zoo/One More Heartache	1968	5.00	10.00	20.00
❑ 690	Like People/(B-side unknown)	1968	5.00	10.00	20.00
Albums					
MAINSTREAM					
❑ S-6107	Tangerine Zoo	1968	12.50	25.00	50.00
❑ S-6118	Outside Looking In	1969	17.50	35.00	70.00

TANGIERS, THE Possibly more than one group. Also see THE HOLLYWOOD FLAMES.
45s
A-J

❑ 905	The Plea/The Waddle	1962	6.25	12.50	25.00
CLASS					
❑ 224	School Days Will Be Over/Don't Try	1958	7.50	15.00	30.00
DECCA					
❑ 29603	I Won't Be Around/Tabarin	1955	37.50	75.00	150.00
❑ 29971	Remember Me/Oh, Baby!	1956	37.50	75.00	150.00
STRAND					
❑ 25039	Ping Pong/Don't Stop the Music	1961	7.50	15.00	30.00

TANTONES, THE
45s
LAMP

❑ 2002	No Matter/I Love You, Really I Do	1957	37.50	75.00	150.00
❑ 2008	So Afraid/Tell Me	1957	37.50	75.00	150.00

TARANTULA
45s
A&M

❑ 1156	Billy the Birdman/Love Is for Peace	1969	2.00	4.00	8.00
Albums					
A&M					
❑ SP-4202	Tarantula	1969	5.00	10.00	20.00

TARANTULAS, THE
45s
ATLANTIC

❑ 2102	Tarantula/Black Widow	1961	6.25	12.50	25.00
STOP					
❑ 102	Herky Jerky/Vera Brown	1964	2.50	5.00	10.00

TARGETS, THE
45s
KING

❑ 5538	It Doesn't Matter/Girls, Girls, Girls	1961	10.00	20.00	40.00

TARRIERS, THE Also see VINCE MARTIN.
45s
DECCA

❑ 31387	Last Night I Had the Strangest Dream/				
	Lonesome Traveler	1962	2.50	5.00	10.00
❑ 31470	Casey Jones/Mary Ann	1963	2.50	5.00	10.00
❑ 31524	Lonesome Traveller/Seven Daffodils	1963	2.50	5.00	10.00
❑ 31631	San Francisco Bay Blues/Guantanamera	1964	2.50	5.00	10.00
GLORY					
❑ 246	Wishing Well Song/East Virginia	1956	3.75	7.50	15.00
❑ 249	The Banana Boat Song/No Hidin' Place	1956	5.00	10.00	20.00
❑ 254	Those Brown Eyes/Chaucon	1957	3.75	7.50	15.00
❑ 255	I Know Where I'm Going/Pretty Boy	1957	3.75	7.50	15.00
❑ 264	Dunya/Quinto	1957	3.75	7.50	15.00
❑ 271	Lonesome Traveler/East Virginia	1958	3.75	7.50	15.00
❑ 286	Tom Dooley/Everybody Loves Saturday Night	1958	3.75	7.50	15.00
UNITED ARTISTS					
❑ 168	Hard Travelin'/Times Are Getting Hard	1959	3.00	6.00	12.00
Albums					
ATLANTIC					
❑ 8042 [M]	Tell the World	1960	7.50	15.00	30.00
❑ SD 8042 [S]	Tell the World	1960	10.00	20.00	40.00
DECCA					
❑ DL 4342 [M]	The Tarriers	1962	6.25	12.50	25.00
❑ DL 4538 [M]	Gather 'Round	1964	6.25	12.50	25.00
❑ DL 74342 [S]	The Tarriers	1962	7.50	15.00	30.00
❑ DL 74538 [S]	Gather 'Round	1964	7.50	15.00	30.00
GLORY					
❑ PG-1200 [M]	The Tarriers	1958	15.00	30.00	60.00
KAPP					
❑ KL 1349 [M]	The Original Tarriers	1963	6.25	12.50	25.00
❑ KS 3349 [S]	The Original Tarriers	1963	7.50	15.00	30.00
UNITED ARTISTS					
❑ UAL-4033 [M]	Hard Travelin'	1959	7.50	15.00	30.00
❑ UAS-5033 [S]	Hard Travelin'	1959	10.00	20.00	40.00

TARRYTONS, THE
45s
DOT

❑ 16537	Rough Surfin'/Mansion on the Hill	1963	6.25	12.50	25.00
EXCLUSIVE					
❑ 2270	Rough Surfin'/Mansion on the Hill	1963	10.00	20.00	40.00

TASSELS, THE
45s
AMY

❑ 946	To a Soldier Boy/The Boy for Me	1966	2.50	5.00	10.00
MADISON					
❑ 117	To a Soldier Boy/The Boy for Me	1959	6.25	12.50	25.00
❑ 121	To a Young Lover/My Guy and I	1959	5.00	10.00	20.00

TASTE RORY GALLAGHER was in this group.
Albums
ATCO

❑ SD 33-296	Taste	1969	6.25	12.50	25.00
❑ SD 33-322	On the Boards	1970	6.25	12.50	25.00

TATE, BILLY
45s
IMPERIAL

❑ 5337	Single Life/You Told Me	1955	50.00	100.00	200.00
—Script logo					
PEACOCK					
❑ 1671	Don't Call My Name/Right from Wrong	1957	7.50	15.00	30.00

TATE, HOWARD
45s
ATLANTIC

❑ 2836	Keep Cool (Don't Be a Fool)/Strugglin'	1971	—	3.00	6.00
❑ 2860	She's a Burglar/				
	You Don't Know Nothing About Love	1972	—	3.00	6.00
❑ 2894	Eight Days on the Road/Girl of the North Country	1972	—	3.00	6.00
EPIC					
❑ 11118	Can You Top This/Ain't Got Nobody to Give It To	1974	—	2.50	5.00
TURNTABLE					
❑ 505	These Are the Things That Make Me Know				
	You're Gone/That's What Happens	1969	2.00	4.00	8.00
❑ 1018	My Soul's Got a Hole In It/It's Too Late	1970	2.00	4.00	8.00
UTOPIA					
❑ 510	Half a Man/(B-side unknown)	1966	6.25	12.50	25.00
VERVE					
❑ 10420	Ain't Nobody Home/				
	How Come My Bull Dog Don't Bark	1966	2.00	4.00	8.00
❑ 10464	Look at Granny Run, Run/Half a Man	1966	2.00	4.00	8.00
❑ 10496	Get It While You Can/Glad I Knew Better	1967	2.00	4.00	8.00
❑ 10525	Baby I Love You/How Blue Can You Get	1967	2.00	4.00	8.00
❑ 10547	I Learned It All the Hard Way/Part-Time Love	1967	2.00	4.00	8.00
❑ 10573	Stop/Shoot 'Em All Down	1967	2.00	4.00	8.00
❑ 10604	Night Owl/Everyday I Have the Blues	1968	2.00	4.00	8.00
❑ 10625	I'm Your Servant/Sweet Love Child	1968	2.00	4.00	8.00
Albums					
ATLANTIC					
❑ SD 8303	Howard Tate	1971	5.00	10.00	20.00
TURNTABLE					
❑ 5002	Reaction	1969	5.00	10.00	20.00
VERVE					
❑ V-5022 [M]	Get It While You Can	1967	5.00	10.00	20.00
❑ V6-5022 [S]	Get It While You Can	1967	6.25	12.50	25.00

TATE, LAURIE
45s
ATLANTIC

❑ 965	Rock Me Daddy/You Can't Stop My Crying	1952	25.00	50.00	100.00

Number	Title (A Side/B Side)	Yr	VG	VG+	NM

TATE, TOMMY
45s
ABC-PARAMOUNT

❏ 10626	What's the Matter/Ordinarily	1965	6.25	12.50	25.00

KOKO

❏ 722	Hardtimes S.O.S./Always	1976	—	3.00	6.00
❏ 723	If You Ain't Man Enough/Revelations	1976	—	3.00	6.00
❏ 727	I'm So Satisfied/If You Ain't Man Enough	1977	—	3.00	6.00
❏ 2109	I Remember/Help Me Love	1971	—	3.00	6.00
❏ 2112	School of Life/I Remember	1972	—	3.00	6.00
❏ 2114	I Ain't Gonna Worry/More Power To You	1972	—	3.00	6.00

OKEH

❏ 7242	Are You From Heaven/I'm Taking On Pain	1966	5.00	10.00	20.00
❏ 7253	Big Blue Diamonds/Lover's Reward	1967	5.00	10.00	20.00

TAUPIN, BERNIE ELTON JOHN's songwriting partner.
45s
RCA

❏ 5162-7-R	Friend of the Flag/Backbone	1987	—	—	3.00
❏ 5162-7-R [PS]	Friend of the Flag/Backbone	1987	—	—	3.00
❏ 5216-7-R	Citizen Jane/White Boys in Chains	1987	—	—	3.00
❏ 5216-7-R [PS]	Citizen Jane/White Boys in Chains	1987	—	—	3.00

Albums
ASYLUM

❏ 6E-263	He Who Rides the Tiger	1980	3.00	6.00	12.00

ELEKTRA

❏ EKS-75020	Bernie Taupin	1972	3.75	7.50	15.00

RCA

❏ 5922-1-R	Tribe	1987	2.50	5.00	10.00
❏ 6420-1-RAB	[(2)DJ]Interview Album	1987	5.00	10.00	20.00

TAVARES Also see CHUBBY AND THE TURNPIKES.
12-Inch Singles
CAPITOL

❏ SPRO-9087	[DJ]Straight from the Heart (7:23) (same on both sides)	1979	3.00	6.00	12.00

JDC

❏ 002	C'est La Vie/Good 'n' Plenty/On My Mind Tonight	198?	—	3.00	6.00
❏ 003	She Freaks Out on the Floor (4 versions)	198?	—	3.00	6.00

RCA

❏ PD-13434	Got to Find My Way Back to You/I Hope You Will Be Very Unhappy Without Me	1983	2.00	4.00	8.00
❏ PD-13612	Deeper in Love/I Really Miss You Baby	1983	2.00	4.00	8.00

45s
CAPITOL

❏ 3674	Check It Out/The Judgment Day	1973	—	2.50	5.00
❏ 3794	That's the Sound That Lonely Makes/Little Girl	1973	—	2.50	5.00
❏ 3882	Too Late/Leave It Up to the Lady	1974	—	2.50	5.00
❏ 3957	She's Gone/To Love You	1974	—	2.50	5.00
❏ 4010	Remember What I Told You to Forget/My Ship	1974	—	2.50	5.00
❏ 4111	It Only Takes a Minute/I Hope She Chooses Me	1975	—	2.50	5.00
❏ 4184	Free Ride/In the Eyes of Love	1975	—	2.50	5.00
❏ 4221	The Love I Never Had/In the City	1976	—	2.50	5.00
❏ 4270	Heaven Must Be Missing An Angel (Part 1)/ Heaven Must Be Missing An Angel (Part 2)	1976	—	2.50	5.00
❏ 4348	Don't Take Away the Music/Guiding Star	1976	—	2.50	5.00
❏ 4398	Whodunit/Fool of the Year	1977	—	2.50	5.00
❏ 4453	Goodnight My Love/ Watchin' the Woman's Movement	1977	—	2.50	5.00
❏ 4500	More Than a Woman/Keep in Touch	1977	—	2.00	4.00
❏ 4544	The Ghost of Love (Part 1)/ The Ghost of Love (Part 2)	1978	—	2.00	4.00
❏ 4583	Timber/Feel So Good	1978	—	2.00	4.00
❏ 4658	Never Had a Love Like This Before/ Positive Forces	1978	—	2.00	4.00
❏ 4703	Straight from the Heart/I'm Back for Me	1979	—	2.00	4.00
❏ 4738	One Telephone Call Away/ Let Me Heal the Bruises	1979	—	2.00	4.00
❏ 4781	Hard Core Poetry/Stabilize	1979	—	2.00	4.00
❏ 4811	Bad Times/Got to Have Your Love	1979	—	2.00	4.00
❏ 4846	I Can't Go On Living Without You/ Why Can't We Fall in Love	1980	—	2.00	4.00
❏ 4880	I Don't Want You Anymore/Paradise	1980	—	2.00	4.00
❏ 4933	Love Uprising/Not Love	1980	—	2.00	4.00
❏ 4969	Loneliness/Break Down for Love	1981	—	2.00	4.00
❏ A-5019	Turn Out the Nightlight/House of Music	1981	—	2.00	4.00
❏ A-5043	Loveline/Right On Time	1981	—	2.00	4.00

RCA

❏ PB-13292	A Penny for Your Thoughts/The Skin You're In	1982	—	2.00	4.00
❏ PB-13433	Got to Find My Way Back to You/I Hope You Will Be Very Unhappy Without Me	1983	—	2.00	4.00
❏ PB-13530	Abra-Ca-Dabra Love You Too/Mystery Lady	1983	—	2.00	4.00
❏ PB-13611	Deeper in Love/I Really Miss You Baby	1983	—	2.00	4.00
❏ PB-13684	Words and Music/ I'll Send Love (We Go Together)	1983	—	2.00	4.00
❏ GB-13799	A Penny for Your Thoughts/Got to Find My Way Back to You	1984	—	—	3.00

—Gold Standard Series

Albums
CAPITOL

❏ ST-11258	Check It Out	1973	2.50	5.00	10.00
❏ ST-11316	Hard Core Poetry	1974	2.50	5.00	10.00
❏ ST-11519	In the City	1975	2.50	5.00	10.00
❏ ST-11533	Sky-High!	1976	2.50	5.00	10.00
❏ ST-11628	Love Storm	1977	2.50	5.00	10.00
❏ ST-11701	The Best of Tavares	1977	2.50	5.00	10.00
❏ SW-11719	Future Bound	1978	2.50	5.00	10.00
❏ SW-11874	Madam Butterfly	1979	2.50	5.00	10.00
❏ ST-12026	Supercharged	1980	2.50	5.00	10.00
❏ ST-12117	Love Uprising	1981	2.50	5.00	10.00
❏ ST-12167	Loveline	1982	2.50	5.00	10.00
❏ SN-16206	Love Storm	1981	2.00	4.00	8.00

—Budget-line reissue

Number	Title (A Side/B Side)	Yr	VG	VG+	NM
❏ SN-16207	Future Bound	1981	2.00	4.00	8.00

—Budget-line reissue

RCA VICTOR

❏ AFL1-4357	New Directions	1982	2.50	5.00	10.00
❏ AFL1-4700	Words and Music	1983	2.50	5.00	10.00

TAVARES, ERNIE, TRIO
45s
DOOTONE

❏ 325	I'm Alone Tonight/It's Christmas	1953	37.50	75.00	150.00

—B-side by the Bonairs

TAVENER, JOHN
Albums
APPLE

❏ SMAS-3369	The Whale	1972	5.00	10.00	20.00

TAX FREE
Albums
POLYDOR

❏ 24-4053	Tax Free	1971	5.00	10.00	20.00

TAYLOR, ALEX
45s
BANG

❏ 739	Don't Look at Me That Way/Sunny Day to Rain	1978	—	2.00	4.00

CAPRICORN

❏ 0004	Comin' Back to You/Who Will the Next Fool Be	1972	—	2.50	5.00
❏ 0018	Lizzie and the Rainman/ Change Your Sexy Ways	1973	—	2.50	5.00
❏ 8013	Highway Song/C Song	1971	—	2.50	5.00
❏ 8016	Baby Ruth/All in Line	1971	—	2.50	5.00
❏ 8019	Night Owl/Southern Kids	1971	—	2.50	5.00

Albums
CAPRICORN

❏ CP 0101	Dinnertime	1972	2.50	5.00	10.00
❏ 860	With Friends and Neighbors	1971	2.50	5.00	10.00

TAYLOR, ANDREW
45s
GONE

❏ 5109	That's How I Feel About You/Never Bite Off More Than You Could Chew	1961	50.00	100.00	200.00

TAYLOR, BILL, AND SMOKEY JO
45s
FLIP

❏ 502	Split Personality/Lonely Sweetheart	1955	375.00	750.00	1500.

TAYLOR, BILLY
45s
CITATION

❏ 5002	Income Taxes and You/Lullaby to Carolyn	1962	3.75	7.50	15.00

FAME

❏ 502	Little Jewel/Study Hall Romance	196?	75.00	150.00	300.00

FELCO

❏ 101	Wombie Zombie/I'm Young	1959	5.00	10.00	20.00

FELSTED

❏ 8564	Bandstand Baby/Cat with No Future	1959	5.00	10.00	20.00

TOWER

❏ 421	Sunny/ I Wish I Knew How I Would Feel to Be Free	1968	2.00	4.00	8.00

Albums
ABC IMPULSE!

❏ AS-71 [S]	My Fair Lady Loves Jazz	1968	3.75	7.50	15.00

ABC-PARAMOUNT

❏ ABC-112 [M]	Evergreens	1956	12.50	25.00	50.00
❏ ABC-134 [M]	Billy Taylor At the London House	1956	12.50	25.00	50.00
❏ ABC-162 [M]	Billy Taylor Introduces Ira Sullivan	1957	12.50	25.00	50.00
❏ ABC-177 [M]	My Fair Lady Loves Jazz	1957	12.50	25.00	50.00
❏ ABC-226 [M]	The New Trio	1958	12.50	25.00	50.00
❏ ABCS-226 [S]	The New Trio	1958	10.00	20.00	40.00

ARGO

❏ LP-650 [M]	Taylor Made Flute	1959	12.50	25.00	50.00
❏ LPS-650 [S]	Taylor Made Flute	1959	10.00	20.00	40.00

ATLANTIC

❏ ALR-113 [10]	Piano Panorama	1951	37.50	75.00	150.00
❏ 1277 [M]	The Billy Taylor Touch	1958	12.50	25.00	50.00
—Black label					
❏ 1277 [M]	The Billy Taylor Touch	1961	6.25	12.50	25.00
—Multicolor label, white "fan" logo at right					
❏ 1329 [M]	One for Fun	1960	12.50	25.00	50.00
—Black label					
❏ SD 1329 [S]	One for Fun	1960	12.50	25.00	50.00
—Green label					

BELL

❏ S-6049	OK Billy!	1970	3.75	7.50	15.00

CAPITOL

❏ ST 2039 [S]	Right Here, Right Now	1963	6.25	12.50	25.00
❏ T 2039 [M]	Right Here, Right Now	1963	5.00	10.00	20.00
❏ ST 2302 [S]	Midnight Piano	1965	6.25	12.50	25.00
❏ T 2302 [M]	Midnight Piano	1965	5.00	10.00	20.00

CONCORD JAZZ

❏ CJ-145	Where've You Been	1981	2.50	5.00	10.00

FANTASY

❏ OJC-015	The Billy Taylor Trio with Candido	1982	2.50	5.00	10.00
❏ OJC-1730	Cross Section	198?	2.50	5.00	10.00

IMPULSE!

❏ A-71 [M]	My Fair Lady Loves Jazz	1965	5.00	10.00	20.00
❏ AS-71 [S]	My Fair Lady Loves Jazz	1965	6.25	12.50	25.00

MERCURY

❏ MG-20722 [M]	Impromptu	1962	5.00	10.00	20.00
❏ SR-60722 [S]	Impromptu	1962	6.25	12.50	25.00

MONMOUTH-EVERGREEN

❏ 7089	Jazz Alive	1978	3.00	6.00	12.00

Number	Title (A Side/B Side)	Yr	VG	VG+	NM
MOODSVILLE					
❑ MVLP-16 [M]	Interlude	1961	12.50	25.00	50.00
—Green label					
❑ MVLP-16 [M]	Interlude	1965	6.25	12.50	25.00
—Blue label, trident logo at right					
NEW JAZZ					
❑ NJLP-8313 [M]	Live! At Town Hall	1963	—	—	—
—Canceled; reassigned to Status					
PAUSA					
❑ 7096	Sleeping Bee	198?	2.50	5.00	10.00
PRESTIGE					
❑ PRLP-139 [10]	Billy Taylor Trio, Volume 1	1953	55.00	110.00	220.00
❑ PRLP-165 [10]	Billy Taylor Trio, Volume 2	1953	55.00	110.00	220.00
❑ PRLP-168 [10]	Billy Taylor Trio, Volume 3	1953	55.00	110.00	220.00
❑ PRLP-184 [10]	Billy Taylor Trio	1954	50.00	100.00	200.00
❑ PRLP-188 [10]	Billy Taylor Trio	1954	50.00	100.00	200.00
❑ PRLP-194 [10]	Billy Taylor Trio In Concert at Town Hall, December 17, 1954	1955	50.00	100.00	200.00
❑ PRLP-7001 [M]	A Touch of Taylor	1955	20.00	40.00	80.00
❑ PRLP-7015 [M]	Billy Taylor Trio, Volume 1	1956	20.00	40.00	80.00
❑ PRLP-7016 [M]	Billy Taylor Trio, Volume 2	1956	20.00	40.00	80.00
❑ PRLP-7051 [M]	The Billy Taylor Trio with Candido	1956	20.00	40.00	80.00
❑ PRLP-7071 [M]	Cross Section	1956	20.00	40.00	80.00
❑ PRLP-7093 [M]	Billy Taylor Trio at Town Hall	1957	20.00	40.00	80.00
❑ PRST-7664 [R]	A Touch of Taylor	1969	3.75	7.50	15.00
❑ PRST-7762	Today!	1970	3.75	7.50	15.00
RIVERSIDE					
❑ RLP 12-306 [M]	Billy Taylor with Four Flutes	1959	12.50	25.00	50.00
❑ RLP 12-319 [M]	Billy Taylor Trio Uptown	1960	12.50	25.00	50.00
❑ RLP 12-339 [M]	Warming Up	1960	12.50	25.00	50.00
❑ RLP-1151 [S]	Billy Taylor with Four Flutes	1959	10.00	20.00	40.00
❑ RLP-1168 [S]	Billy Taylor Trio Uptown	1960	10.00	20.00	40.00
❑ RLP-1195 [S]	Warming Up	1960	10.00	20.00	40.00
ROOST					
❑ R-406 [10]	Jazz at Storyville	1952	30.00	60.00	120.00
❑ R-409 [10]	Taylor Made Jazz	1952	30.00	60.00	120.00
SAVOY					
❑ MG-9035 [10]	Billy Taylor Piano	1953	30.00	60.00	120.00
SESAC					
❑ N-3001 [M]	Custom Taylored	1959	15.00	30.00	60.00
❑ SN-3001 [S]	Custom Taylored	1959	12.50	25.00	50.00
STATUS					
❑ ST-8313 [M]	Live! At Town Hall	1965	10.00	20.00	40.00
SURREY					
❑ S-1033 [M]	Easy Life	1966	6.25	12.50	25.00
❑ SS-1033 [S]	Easy Life	1966	7.50	15.00	30.00
TOWER					
❑ ST-5111 [S]	I Wish I Knew	1968	6.25	12.50	25.00
WEST 54					
❑ 8008	Live at Storyville	198?	3.00	6.00	12.00

TAYLOR, BOBBY, AND THE VANCOUVERS
45s

Number	Title (A Side/B Side)	Yr	VG	VG+	NM
GORDY					
❑ 7069	Does Your Mama Know About Me/Fading Away	1968	5.00	10.00	20.00
❑ 7073	I Am Your Man/If You Love Her	1968	5.00	10.00	20.00
❑ 7079	Malinda/It's Growing	1968	5.00	10.00	20.00
❑ 7088	Oh I've Been Blessed/ It Should Have Been Me Loving Her	1969	150.00	300.00	600.00
❑ 7092	My Girl Is Gone/ It Should Have Been Me Loving Her	1969	5.00	10.00	20.00
INTEGRA					
❑ 103	This Is My Woman/(B-side unknown)	1968	25.00	50.00	100.00
MOWEST					
❑ 5006	Hey Lordy/Just a Little Bit Closer	1971	3.75	7.50	15.00
PLAYBOY					
❑ 6046	Why Play Games/Don't Wonder Why	1975	—	2.50	5.00
SUNFLOWER					
❑ 126	There Are Roses Somewhere in the World/ It Was a Good Time	1972	6.25	12.50	25.00
V.I.P.					
❑ 25053	Oh I've Been Blessed/Blackmail	1969	6.25	12.50	25.00
Albums					
GORDY					
❑ G-930 [M]	Bobby Taylor and the Vancouvers	1968	20.00	40.00	80.00
—Mono is promo only					
❑ GS-930 [S]	Bobby Taylor and the Vancouvers	1968	15.00	30.00	60.00
❑ GS-942	Taylor Made Soul	1969	15.00	30.00	60.00

TAYLOR, CARMEN
45s

Number	Title (A Side/B Side)	Yr	VG	VG+	NM
APOLLO					
❑ 489	Oh Please/Teen Age Ball	1956	15.00	30.00	60.00
ATLANTIC					
❑ 1002	Lovin' Daddy/Ding Dong	1953	12.50	25.00	50.00
❑ 1015	Big Mamou Daddy/Mamma Me and Johnny Free	1953	12.50	25.00	50.00
❑ 1041	Freddie/Ooh I	1954	30.00	60.00	120.00
GUYDEN					
❑ 100	Let Me Go Lover/No More, No Less	1954	10.00	20.00	40.00
KAMA SUTRA					
❑ 206	My Son/You're Puttin' Me On	1966	3.00	6.00	12.00
KING					
❑ 5085	So What/Why Did You Leave Me Alone	1957	12.50	25.00	50.00

TAYLOR, CHIP
45s

Number	Title (A Side/B Side)	Yr	VG	VG+	NM
BUDDAH					
❑ 325	Angel of the Morning/(B-side unknown)	1972	—	3.00	6.00
❑ 344	Londonderry Company/(B-side unknown)	1973	—	3.00	6.00
CAPITOL					
❑ 4692	Saint Sebastian/One Night Out with the Boys	1979	—	2.00	4.00
❑ 4840	Stealin' Each Other Blind/ He Ain't Makin' Music Anymore	1980	—	2.00	4.00
COLUMBIA					
❑ 10446	Hello Atlanta/Farmer's Daughter	1976	—	2.00	4.00

Number	Title (A Side/B Side)	Yr	VG	VG+	NM
❑ 10520	Three Younger Bandits/Nothing Like You Girl	1977	—	2.00	4.00
❑ 44736	It's Such a Lonely Time of Year/(Instrumental)	1968	3.00	6.00	12.00
EPIC					
❑ 10567	It's Such a Lonely Time of Year/(Instrumental)	1969	2.50	5.00	10.00
MALA					
❑ 476	On My World/Joanie's Blues	1964	3.00	6.00	12.00
❑ 489	Suzannah (Comin' Home to Louisiana)/ (B-side unknown)	1964	3.00	6.00	12.00
❑ 507	Young Love/Betty Ann	1965	2.50	5.00	10.00
MGM					
❑ 12993	Foolin' Around/Innocent Eyes	1961	5.00	10.00	20.00
❑ 13040	If You Don't Want Me Now/Sad Songs	1961	5.00	10.00	20.00
WARNER BROS.					
❑ 5314	Here I Am/I Love You But I Know	1962	3.75	7.50	15.00
❑ 5333	Lucky Star/A Guy Don't Need a Lot of Time	1963	3.75	7.50	15.00
❑ 8050	Me As I Am/Comin' From Behind	1974	—	2.00	4.00
❑ 8090	Early Sunday Morning/Shickshinny	1975	—	2.00	4.00
❑ 8128	Big River/John Tucker's On the Wagon Again	1975	—	2.00	4.00
❑ 8159	Circle of Tears/You're Alright, Charlie	1975	—	2.00	4.00
Albums					
BUDDAH					
❑ BDS-5118	Gasoline	1972	3.00	6.00	12.00
CAPITOL					
❑ ST-11909	Saint Sebastian	1979	2.50	5.00	10.00
COLUMBIA					
❑ KC 34345	Somebody Shoot Out the Jukebox	1977	2.50	5.00	10.00
WARNER BROS.					
❑ BS 2718	Last Chance	1973	3.00	6.00	12.00
❑ BS 2824	Some of Us	1974	3.00	6.00	12.00

TAYLOR, DEBBIE
45s

Number	Title (A Side/B Side)	Yr	VG	VG+	NM
ARISTA					
❑ 0144	I Don't Wanna Leave You/Just Don't Pay	1975	2.50	5.00	10.00
DECCA					
❑ 32259	Check Yourself/Wait Until I'm Gone	1968	3.75	7.50	15.00
GWP					
❑ 501	Never Gonna Let Him Know/ Let's Prove Them Wrong	1969	3.75	7.50	15.00
❑ 510	Don't let It End/How Long Can This Last	1969	3.75	7.50	15.00
❑ 512	Momma Look Sharp/No Brag, Just Fact	1969	3.75	7.50	15.00
GWP'S GRAPEVINE					
❑ 202	Don't Nobody Mess with My Baby/Stop	1970	3.75	7.50	15.00
POLYDOR					
❑ 14219	I Have Learned to Do Without You/ Cheaper in the Long Run	1974	7.50	15.00	30.00
❑ 14252	Superstar/A Good Woman Don't Grow on Trees	1974	—	—	—
—Canceled					
TODAY					
❑ TLP-1007	Comin' Down on You	1972	10.00	20.00	40.00
❑ 1510	No Deposit, No Return/Too Sad to Tell	1972	3.00	6.00	12.00

TAYLOR, EDDIE
45s

Number	Title (A Side/B Side)	Yr	VG	VG+	NM
VEE JAY					
❑ 149	Bad Boy/E.T. Blues	1955	30.00	60.00	120.00
❑ 185	Big Town Playboy/Ride 'Em On Down	1956	20.00	40.00	80.00
❑ 206	You'll Always Have a Home/ Don't Knock at My Door	1956	15.00	30.00	60.00
❑ 267	I'm Gonna Love You/Looking for Trouble	1958	10.00	20.00	40.00
VIVID					
❑ 104	I'm Sitting Here/Do You Want Me to Cry	1964	5.00	10.00	20.00

TAYLOR, FAITH, AND THE SWEET TEENS
45s

Number	Title (A Side/B Side)	Yr	VG	VG+	NM
BEA & BABY					
❑ 104	I Need Him to Love Me/I Love You Darling	1959	12.50	25.00	50.00
FEDERAL					
❑ 12334	Your Candy Kisses/ Won't Someone Tell Me Why?	1958	12.50	25.00	50.00

TAYLOR, FELICE
45s

Number	Title (A Side/B Side)	Yr	VG	VG+	NM
KENT					
❑ 483	Good Luck/I Can Feel Your Love	1967	3.75	7.50	15.00
❑ 488	Captured by Your Love/New Love	1968	3.75	7.50	15.00
MUSTANG					
❑ 3024	It May Be Winter Outside (But In My Heart It's Spring)/Winter Again	1966	3.75	7.50	15.00
❑ 3026	I'm Under the Influence of Love/Love Theme	1967	5.00	10.00	20.00

TAYLOR, FRANK
45s

Number	Title (A Side/B Side)	Yr	VG	VG+	NM
BRACK					
❑ 106	When Two Worlds Collide/ Talk Back Trembling Lips	196?	2.50	5.00	10.00
❑ 118	Oh Lonesome Me/Somewhere in Kentucky	196?	2.50	5.00	10.00
❑ 124	Lovesick Blues/Indifferent Bartenders	196?	2.50	5.00	10.00
❑ 129	Bayou Pon Pon/Talk Back Trembling Lips	196?	2.50	5.00	10.00
CHART					
❑ 502	Bubbles in the Glass/A Part of You	1963	3.75	7.50	15.00
❑ 1055	From Brown to Blue/You Didn't Leave Me Much to Live For	1964	3.00	6.00	12.00
❑ 1095	Lost, Strayed or Stolen/She Used to Be My Girl	1964	3.00	6.00	12.00
❑ 1150	Blue Part of the Blues/Tears and Tears to Pay	1964	3.00	6.00	12.00
❑ 1235	Forty Winks/I Can't Stand This Living Alone	1965	3.00	6.00	12.00
❑ 1495	Judas Feet/Life of Reilly	1967	2.50	5.00	10.00
CHART ACTION					
❑ 113	If You Were on Trial for Loving Me/ Nobody's Darlin' But Mine	196?	5.00	10.00	20.00
❑ 117	Countryfied/Most of All	196?	5.00	10.00	20.00
❑ 801	Diesel on My Tail/Live and Let Live	196?	3.75	7.50	15.00

Number	Title (A Side/B Side)	Yr	VG	VG+	NM

TAYLOR, GLORIA
45s
COLUMBIA

Number	Title (A Side/B Side)	Yr	VG	VG+	NM
❏ 4-45986	Deep Inside You/World That's Not Real	1974	3.00	6.00	12.00

GLO-WHIZ

❏ 1	You Got to Pay the Price/ Loving You and Being Loved By You	1969	6.25	12.50	25.00

KING SOUL

❏ 493	Poor Unfortunate Me/ You Might Need Me Another Day	1968	15.00	30.00	60.00
❏ 865	Do Your Duty/Born a Woman	196?	10.00	20.00	40.00

MERCURY

❏ 73137	Yesterday Will Never Come Again/Unyielding	1970	5.00	10.00	20.00
❏ 73186	Don't Want to Be a Girl That Cries/Total Disaster	1970	15.00	30.00	60.00

SELECTOR SOUND

❏ 1976	Had It All the Time/What's Your World	197?	10.00	20.00	40.00

SILVER FOX

❏ 14	You Got to Pay the Price/Loving You and Being Loved By You	1969	3.00	6.00	12.00
❏ 19	Grounded Part 1/Part 2	1970	3.75	7.50	15.00

TAYLOR, JAMES
12-Inch Singles
COLUMBIA

❏ ASF 358 [DJ]	Handy Man (mono/stereo)	1977	3.75	7.50	15.00
❏ AS 1240 [DJ]	Summer's Here/Hard Times	1981	2.00	4.00	8.00

45s
APPLE

❏ 1805	Carolina in My Mind/Taking It In	1969	75.00	150.00	300.00
❏ 1805	Carolina in My Mind/Something's Wrong	1970	2.00	4.00	8.00
—Without star on A-side label					
❏ 1805	Carolina in My Mind/Something's Wrong	1970	2.50	5.00	10.00
—With star on A-side label					
❏ 1805 [DJ]	Carolina on My Mind/Something's Wrong	1970	7.50	15.00	30.00
—Promo with error in title on A-side					

COLUMBIA

❏ 02093	Hard Times/Summer's Here	1981	—	—	3.00
❏ 02093 [PS]	Hard Times/Summer's Here	1981	—	2.00	4.00
❏ 05681	Everyday/Limousine Driver	1985	—	—	3.00
❏ 05681 [PS]	Everyday/Limousine Driver	1985	—	2.00	4.00
❏ 05785	Only One/Mona	1986	—	—	3.00
❏ 05785 [PS]	Only One/Mona	1986	—	—	3.00
❏ 05884	That's Why I'm Here/ Going Around One More Time	1986	—	—	3.00
❏ 06278	Only a Dream in Rio/Turn Away	1986	—	—	3.00
❏ 07616	Never Die Young/Valentine's Day	1987	—	—	3.00
❏ 07616 [PS]	Never Die Young/Valentine's Day	1987	—	2.00	4.00
❏ 07948	Baby Boom Baby/Letter in the Mail	1988	—	—	3.00
❏ 08493	Sweet Potato Pie/First of May	1988	—	—	3.00
❏ 10557	Handy Man/Bartender's Blues	1977	—	2.00	4.00
❏ 10602	Your Smiling Face/ If I Keep My Heart Out of Sight	1977	—	2.00	4.00
❏ 10676	(What a) Wonderful World/Wooden Planes	1978	—	3.00	6.00
—By Art Garfunkel with Paul Simon and James Taylor; B-side is Garfunkel solo					
❏ 10689	Honey Don't Leave L.A./Another Grey Morning	1978	—	2.00	4.00
❏ 11005	Up on the Roof/Chanson Francaise	1979	—	2.00	4.00
❏ 60514	Her Town Too/Believe It or Not	1981	—	2.00	4.00
—A-side: James Taylor and J.D. Souther					

WARNER BROS.

❏ 7387	Sweet Baby James/Suite for 20G	1970	2.00	4.00	8.00
❏ 7423	Fire and Rain/Anywhere Like Heaven	1970	2.00	4.00	8.00
❏ 7460	Country Road/Sunny Skies	1970	—	3.00	6.00
❏ 7498	You've Got a Friend/You Can Close Your Eyes	1971	—	3.00	6.00
❏ 7521	Long Ago and Far Away/Let Me Ride	1971	—	2.50	5.00
❏ 7655	Don't Let Me Be Lonely Tonight/ Wow, Don't You Know	1972	—	2.50	5.00
❏ 7682	One Man Parade/Nobody But You	1973	—	2.50	5.00
❏ 7695	Hymn/Fanfare	1973	—	2.50	5.00
❏ 8015	Let It All Fall Down/Daddy's Baby	1974	—	2.50	5.00
❏ 8028	Walking Man/Daddy's Baby	1974	—	2.50	5.00
❏ 8109	How Sweet It Is (To Be Loved By You)/ Sarah Maria	1975	—	2.50	5.00
❏ 8137	Mexico/Gorilla	1975	—	2.50	5.00
❏ 8222	Shower the People/I Can Dream of You	1976	—	2.50	5.00
❏ 8278	Woman's Gotta Have It/You Make It Easy	1976	—	2.50	5.00

7-Inch Extended Plays
WARNER BROS.

❏ S 2561	Places in My Past/Love Has Brought Me Around/ Hey Mister, That's Me Up on the Jukebox//Mud Slide Slim/Isn't It Nice to Be Home Again/ Riding on a Railroad	1971	2.50	5.00	10.00
—Jukebox issue; small hole, plays at 33 1/3 rpm					
❏ S 2561 [PS]	Mud Slide Slim	1971	2.50	5.00	10.00
—Part of "Little LP" series (LLP #150)					

Albums
APPLE

❏ SKAO 3352	James Taylor	1969	6.25	12.50	25.00
—With title in black print					
❏ SKAO 3352	James Taylor	1970	5.00	10.00	20.00
—With title in orange print					

COLUMBIA

❏ JC 34811	JT	1977	2.50	5.00	10.00
❏ PC 34811	JT	198?	2.00	4.00	8.00
❏ FC 36058	Flag	1979	2.50	5.00	10.00
❏ PC 36058	Flag	198?	2.00	4.00	8.00
❏ PC 37009	Dad Loves His Work	198?	2.00	4.00	8.00
❏ TC 37009	Dad Loves His Work	1981	2.50	5.00	10.00
❏ FC 40052	That's Why I'm Here	1985	2.50	5.00	10.00
❏ FC 40851	Never Die Young	1988	2.50	5.00	10.00
❏ HC 47009	Dad Loves His Work	1983	10.00	20.00	40.00
—Half-speed mastered edition					

EUPHORIA

❏ EST-2	James Taylor and the Original Flying Machine 1967	1971	3.00	6.00	12.00

NAUTILUS

❏ NR-29	Gorilla	1981	10.00	20.00	40.00
—Audiophile pressing					

TRIP

❏ TLP-9513	Rainy Day Man	197?	2.50	5.00	10.00
—Reissue of Euphoria album					

WARNER BROS.

❏ WS 1843	Sweet Baby James	1970	2.50	5.00	10.00
—Green "WB" label with "Contains Fire and Rain and Country Road" added to front cover					
❏ WS 1843	Sweet Baby James	1970	3.75	7.50	15.00
—Green "WB" label with no reference to other songs on front cover					
❏ WS 1843	Sweet Baby James	1970	6.25	12.50	25.00
—Very early pressings have green label with "W7" logo					
❏ WS 1843	Sweet Baby James	1973	2.00	4.00	8.00
—"Burbank" label or cream label					
❏ BS 2561	Mud Slide Slim and the Blue Horizon	1971	2.50	5.00	10.00
—Green "WB" label					
❏ BS 2561	Mud Slide Slim and the Blue Horizon	1973	2.00	4.00	8.00
—"Burbank" label or cream label					
❏ BS 2660	One Man Dog	1972	2.50	5.00	10.00
—Green "WB" label					
❏ BS 2660	One Man Dog	1973	2.00	4.00	8.00
—"Burbank" label or cream label					
❏ BS4 2660 [Q]	One Man Dog	1975	3.75	7.50	15.00
❏ BS 2794	Walking Man	1973	2.50	5.00	10.00
—"Burbank" label					
❏ BS 2794	Walking Man	1979	2.00	4.00	8.00
—Cream label					
❏ BS 2866	Gorilla	1975	2.50	5.00	10.00
—"Burbank" label					
❏ BS 2866	Gorilla	1979	2.00	4.00	8.00
—Cream label					
❏ BS4 2866 [Q]	Gorilla	1975	3.75	7.50	15.00
❏ BS 2912	In the Pocket	1976	2.50	5.00	10.00
—"Burbank" label					
❏ BS 2912	In the Pocket	1979	2.00	4.00	8.00
—Cream label					
❏ BS 2979	Greatest Hits	1976	3.00	6.00	12.00
—This and other variations of this title have re-recorded versions of "Carolina in My Mind" and "Something in the Way She Moves."					
❏ BSK 3113	Greatest Hits	1977	2.50	5.00	10.00
—"Burbank" label					
❏ BSK 3113	Greatest Hits	1979	2.00	4.00	8.00
—Cream label					
❏ ST-93138	Sweet Baby James	1970	5.00	10.00	20.00
—Capitol Record Club edition					

TAYLOR, JOHNNIE
12-Inch Singles
BEVERLY GLEN

❏ BG 2002	What About My Love/Reaganomics	1982	2.50	5.00	10.00

45s
BEVERLY GLEN

❏ 2003	What About My Love/Reaganomics	1982	—	2.00	4.00
❏ 2004	I'm So Proud/I Need a Freak	1982	—	2.00	4.00
❏ 2007	Just Ain't Good Enough/Don't Wait	1983	—	2.00	4.00
❏ 2016	Seconds of Your Love/Shoot for the Stars	1983	—	2.00	4.00

COLUMBIA

❏ AE7 1153 [DJ]	God Is Standing By/God Is Amazing	1977	2.00	4.00	8.00
—B-side by Deniece Williams; promo with "Suggested Christmas Programming" on label					
❏ 10281	Disco Lady/You're the Best in the World	1976	—	2.50	5.00
❏ 10334	Somebody's Gettin' It/Please Don't Stop (That Song from Playing)	1976	—	2.50	5.00
❏ 10478	Love Is Better in the A.M. (Part 1)/Love Is Better in the A.M. (Part 2)	1977	—	2.50	5.00
❏ 10541	Your Love Is Rated X/Here I Go (Through These Chains Again)	1977	—	2.50	5.00
❏ 10610	Disco 9000/Right Now	1977	—	2.00	4.00
❏ 10709	Keep On Dancing/ I Love to Make Love When It's Raining	1978	—	2.00	4.00
❏ 10776	Give Me My Baby/Ever Ready	1978	—	2.00	4.00
❏ 11084	(Ooh-Wee) She's Killing Me/ Play Something Pretty	1979	—	2.00	4.00
❏ 11315	I Got This Thing for Your Love/ Signing Off with Love	1980	—	2.00	4.00
❏ 11373	I Wanna Get Into You/Baby Don't Hesitate	1980	—	2.00	4.00

DERBY

❏ 101	Shine, Shine, Shine/Dance What You Wanna	1963	3.75	7.50	15.00
❏ 1006	Baby, We've Got Love/In Love with You	1963	3.75	7.50	15.00
❏ 1010	I Need Lots of Love/Getting Married Soon	1964	3.75	7.50	15.00

MALACO

❏ 2107	Lady, My Whole World Is You/L-O-V-E	1984	—	—	3.00
❏ 2111	Good with My Hips/This Is Your Night	1985	—	—	3.00
❏ 2118	Still Called the Blues/She's Cheatin' on Me	1985	—	—	3.00
❏ 2125	Wall to Wall/(B-side unknown)	1986	—	—	3.00
❏ 2128	Can I Love You/There's Nothing I Wouldn't Do	1986	—	—	3.00
❏ 2132	Just Because/When She Stops Asking	1987	—	—	3.00
❏ 2135	Don't Make Me Late/Happy Time	1987	—	—	3.00
❏ 2140	If I Lose Your Love/Something Is Going Wrong	1987	—	—	3.00
❏ 2143	Everything's Out in the Open/ Got to Leave This Woman	1988	—	—	3.00
❏ 2153	In Control/I Found a Love	1989	—	—	3.00
❏ 2159	Still Crazy for You/(B-side unknown)	1989	—	—	3.00

RCA

❏ PB-11137	I Want You Back Again/ Heaven Bless This Home	1977	—	2.50	5.00

SAR

❏ 114	A Whole Lotta Woman/Why Oh Why	1961	5.00	10.00	20.00
❏ 131	Never Never/Rome (Wasn't Built in a Day)	1962	10.00	20.00	40.00
❏ 156	Oh, How I Love You/Run, But You Can't Hide	1964	3.75	7.50	15.00

STAX

❏ 0009	Who's Making Love/I'm Trying	1968	2.00	4.00	8.00
❏ 0023	Take Care of Your Homework/ Hold On This Time	1969	2.00	4.00	8.00
❏ 0033	Testify (I Wanna)/I Had a Fight with Love	1969	2.00	4.00	8.00

T

Number	Title (A Side/B Side)	Yr	VG	VG+	NM
❏ 0042	Just Keep On Loving Me/My Life	1969	2.00	4.00	8.00
—With Carla Thomas					
❏ 0046	I Could Never Be President/It's Amazing	1969	2.00	4.00	8.00
❏ 0055	Love Bones/Mr. Nobody Is Somebody	1969	2.00	4.00	8.00
❏ 0068	Steal Away/Friday Night	1970	—	3.00	6.00
❏ 0078	I Am Somebody (Part 1)/I Am Somebody (Part 2)	1970	—	3.00	6.00
❏ 0085	Jody's Got Your Girl and Gone/A Fool Like Me	1970	—	3.00	6.00
❏ 0089	I Don't Wanna Lose You/Party Life	1971	—	3.00	6.00
❏ 0096	Hijackin' Love/Love in the Streets	1971	—	3.00	6.00
❏ 0114	Standing In for Jody/Shackin' Up	1972	—	3.00	6.00
❏ 0122	Doing My Own Thing (Part 1)/				
	Doing My Own Thing (Part 2)	1972	—	3.00	6.00
❏ 0142	Stop Doggin' Me/Stop Teasin' Me	1972	—	3.00	6.00
❏ 0155	Don't You Fool with My Soul (Part 1)/				
	Don't You Fool with My Soul (Part 2)	1973	—	3.00	6.00
❏ 0161	I Believe in You (You Believe in Me)/				
	Love Depression	1973		3.00	6.00
—With A-side time listed at 4:37					
❏ 0161	I Believe in You (You Believe in Me)/				
	Love Depression	1973	—	3.00	6.00
—With A-side time listed at 3:58					
❏ 0176	Cheaper to Keep Her/				
	I Can Read Between the Lines	1973	—	3.00	6.00
❏ 186	I Had a Dream/Changes	1966	2.50	5.00	10.00
❏ 193	I Got to Love Somebody's Baby/				
	Just the One I've Been Looking For	1966	2.50	5.00	10.00
❏ 0193	We're Getting Careless with Our Love/				
	Poor Make Believer	1974	—	3.00	6.00
❏ 202	Little Bluebird/Toe Hold	1967	2.50	5.00	10.00
❏ 0208	I've Been Born Again/At Night Time	1974	—	3.00	6.00
❏ 209	Ain't That Loving You/Outside Love	1967	2.50	5.00	10.00
❏ 226	If I Had It to Do Over/You Can't Get Away from It	1967	2.50	5.00	10.00
❏ 0226	It's September/Just One Moment	1974	—	3.00	6.00
❏ 235	Somebody's Sleeping in My Bed/Strange Thing	1967	2.50	5.00	10.00
❏ 0241	Try Me Tonight/Free	1975	—	3.00	6.00
❏ 247	Next Time/Sundown	1968	2.50	5.00	10.00
❏ 253	I Ain't Particular/				
	Where There's Smoke There's Fire	1968	2.50	5.00	10.00
❏ 3201	It Don't Pay to Get Up in the Mornin'/				
	Just Keep On Loving Me	1977	—	2.50	5.00

Albums

BEVERLY GLEN

❏ 10001	Just Ain't Good Enough	1982	3.00	6.00	12.00

COLUMBIA

❏ PC 33951	Eargasm	1976	3.00	6.00	12.00
—Originals have no bar code					
❏ PC 33951	Eargasm	1986	2.00	4.00	8.00
—Budget-line reissue with bar code					
❏ PCQ 33951 [Q]	Eargasm	1976	5.00	10.00	20.00
❏ PC 34401	Rated Extraordinaire	1977	3.00	6.00	12.00
❏ PCQ 34401 [Q]	Rated Extraordinaire	1977	5.00	10.00	20.00
❏ JC 35340	Ever Ready	1978	3.00	6.00	12.00
❏ JC 36061	She's Killing Me	1979	3.00	6.00	12.00
❏ JC 36548	A New Day	1980	3.00	6.00	12.00
❏ JC 37127	The Best of Johnnie Taylor	1981	3.00	6.00	12.00

ICHIBAN

❏ ICH-1022	Stuck in the Mud	198?	2.50	5.00	10.00
❏ ICH-1042	Ugly Man	198?	2.50	5.00	10.00

MALACO

❏ MAL-7421	This Is Your Night	198?	2.50	5.00	10.00
❏ MAL-7431	Wall to Wall	198?	2.50	5.00	10.00
❏ MAL-7440	Lover Boy	198?	2.50	5.00	10.00
❏ MAL-7446	In Control	198?	2.50	5.00	10.00
❏ MAL-7452	Crazy 'Bout You	1989	2.50	5.00	10.00
❏ MAL-7460	Just Can't Do Right	1991	2.50	5.00	10.00
❏ MAL-7463	The Best of Johnnie Taylor on Malaco, Vol. 1	1992	2.50	5.00	10.00

STAX

❏ ST-715 [M]	Wanted: One Soul Singer	1967	12.50	25.00	50.00
❏ STS-715 [S]	Wanted: One Soul Singer	1967	15.00	30.00	60.00
❏ STS-2005	Who's Making Love	1968	10.00	20.00	40.00
❏ STS-2008	Raw Blues	1969	6.25	12.50	25.00
❏ STS-2012	Rare Stamps	1969	6.25	12.50	25.00
❏ STS-2023	The Johnnie Taylor Philosophy Continues	1969	6.25	12.50	25.00
❏ STS-2030	One Step Beyond	1971	6.25	12.50	25.00
❏ STS-2032	Johnnie Taylor's Greatest Hits	1970	6.25	12.50	25.00
❏ STS-3014	Taylored in Silk	1973	5.00	10.00	20.00
❏ STX-4115	Who's Making Love	198?	2.50	5.00	10.00
—Reissue of 2005					
❏ STS-5509	Super Taylor	1974	5.00	10.00	20.00
❏ STS-5521	The Best of Johnnie Taylor	1975	5.00	10.00	20.00
❏ MPS-8508	Raw Blues	1982	2.50	5.00	10.00
❏ MPS-8520	Super Hits	1983	2.50	5.00	10.00
❏ MPS-8537	Taylored in Silk	1987	2.50	5.00	10.00
—Reissue of 3014					
❏ MPS-8558	Little Bluebird	1988	2.50	5.00	10.00
❏ 88001 [(2)]	Chronicle	1977	5.00	10.00	20.00

TAYLOR, KATE

45s

COLUMBIA

Number	Title (A Side/B Side)	Yr	VG	VG+	NM
❏ 10596	It's In His Kiss (The Shoop Shoop Song)/				
	Jason and Ida	1977	—	2.00	4.00
❏ 10787	It's Growin'/Slow and Steady	1978	—	2.00	4.00
❏ 11017	It's the Same Old Song/Champagne and Wine	1979	—	2.00	4.00

COTILLION

❏ 44112	Handbags and Gladrags/				
	You Can Close Your Eyes	1971	—	2.50	5.00
❏ 44124	Lo and Behold-Jesus Is Just Alright/Home Again	1971	—	2.50	5.00

Albums

COLUMBIA

❏ JC 35089	Kate Taylor	1978	2.50	5.00	10.00
❏ JC 36034	It's In There and It's Got to Come Out	1979	2.50	5.00	10.00

COTILLION

❏ SD 9045	Sister Kate	1971	2.50	5.00	10.00

TAYLOR, KATHY

45s

HIT

Number	Title (A Side/B Side)	Yr	VG	VG+	NM
❏ 55	The End of the World/Our Day Will Come	1963	2.00	4.00	8.00
—B-side by Clara and the Cleftones					
❏ 86	I Can't Stay Mad at You/Wonderful! Wonderful!	1963	2.00	4.00	8.00
—B-side by Wayne Harris					

TAYLOR, KINGSIZE, AND THE DOMINOES

Albums

MIDNIGHT

❏ HLP-2101 [M]	Real Gonk Man	1965	12.50	25.00	50.00
❏ HST-2101 [S]	Real Gonk Man	1965	25.00	50.00	100.00

TAYLOR, KOKO

45s

CHECKER

❏ 1092	I Got What It Takes/What Kind of Man Is This	1964	3.75	7.50	15.00
❏ 1106	Don't Mess with the Messer/				
	Whatever I Am You Made Me	1965	3.75	7.50	15.00
❏ 1135	Wang Dang Doodle/Blues Heaven	1966	3.75	7.50	15.00
❏ 1140	Good Advice/When I Think of My Baby	1966	3.75	7.50	15.00
❏ 1148	Good Advice/Tell Me the Truth	1966	3.75	7.50	15.00
❏ 1166	Just Love Me/Egg on the Run	1967	3.75	7.50	15.00
❏ 1174	(I Got) All You Need/All Money Spent				
	(On Feeling Good)	1967	3.75	7.50	15.00
❏ 1191	Fire/Insane Asylum	1968	3.75	7.50	15.00
❏ 1230	Separate or Integrate/I Don't Care	1968	3.75	7.50	15.00

U.S.A.

❏ 745	Like Heaven to Me/Honky Tonky	1963	6.25	12.50	25.00

YAMBO

❏ 107/108	A Mighty Love/Instant Everything	197?	5.00	10.00	20.00

Albums

ALLIGATOR

❏ AL 4711	The Earthshaker	1978	3.00	6.00	12.00
❏ AL 4724	From the Heart of a Woman	1981	2.50	5.00	10.00
❏ AL 4740	Queen of the Blues	1985	2.50	5.00	10.00
❏ AL 4754	An Audience with the Queen	1987	2.50	5.00	10.00
❏ AL 4784	Jump for Joy	1990	3.75	7.50	15.00

CHESS

❏ CH-9263	Koko Taylor	1987	3.00	6.00	12.00
—Reissue of 1532					

TAYLOR, LEROY

45s

BRUNSWICK

❏ 55345	Oh Linda/Nobody Can Love You	1967	15.00	30.00	60.00

COLPIX

❏ 739	Dr. Fix-It/Time (Brings About a Change)	1964	6.25	12.50	25.00

COLUMBIA

❏ 4-42258	Dooley Walk/Hey, I Like It	1962	5.00	10.00	20.00

SHRINE

❏ 0101	Takin' My Time/I'll Understand	1965	75.00	150.00	300.00
—As "Leroy Taylor and the Four Kays"					

TAYLOR, LITTLE JOHNNY

45s

GALAXY

❏ 718	You'll Need Another Favor/				
	What You Need Is a Ball	1963	3.00	6.00	12.00
❏ 722	Part Time Love/Somewhere Down the Line	1963	5.00	10.00	20.00
❏ 725	Since I Found a New Love/My Heart Is Filled				
	with Pain	1963	3.00	6.00	12.00
❏ 729	First Class Love/If You Love Me	1964	2.50	5.00	10.00
❏ 731	You Win, I Lose/Nightingale Melody	1964	2.50	5.00	10.00
❏ 733	True Love/I Smell Trouble	1964	2.50	5.00	10.00
❏ 735	For Your Precious Love/I've Never Had a				
	Woman Like You Before	1965	2.00	4.00	8.00
❏ 736	Help Yourself/Somebody's Got to Pay	1965	2.00	4.00	8.00
❏ 739	One More Chance/Looking at the Future	1965	2.00	4.00	8.00
❏ 743	Please Come Home For Christmas/				
	Miracle Maker	1965	2.00	4.00	8.00
❏ 745	My Love Is Real/All I Want Is You	1966	2.00	4.00	8.00
❏ 748	Zig Zag Lightning/The Things I Used to Do	1966	2.00	4.00	8.00
❏ 752	I Know You Hear Me Calling/Big Blue Diamonds	1967	2.00	4.00	8.00
❏ 756	Driving Wheel/Darling Believe in Me	1967	2.00	4.00	8.00
❏ 764	Double or Nothing/Sometimey Woman	1968	2.00	4.00	8.00

ICHIBAN

❏ 169	Christmas Is Here Again/Ugly Man	1988	—	3.00	6.00
❏ 174	Christmas Is Here Again/I Enjoy You	1989	—	3.00	6.00

RONN

❏ 43	Make Love to Me Baby/Sweet Soul Woman	1970	—	3.00	6.00
❏ 48	How Can a Broke Man Survive/				
	Make Love to Me Baby	1970	—	3.00	6.00
❏ 51	How Are You Fixed for Love/				
	Keep On Keepin' On	1971	—	3.00	6.00
❏ 55	Everybody Knows About My Good Thing Pt. 1/				
	Pt. 2	1971	—	3.00	6.00
❏ 59	It's My Fault Darling/				
	There Is Something On Your Mind	1972	—	3.00	6.00
❏ 64	Open House at My House (Part 1)/				
	Open House at My House (Part 2)	1972	—	3.00	6.00
❏ 66	As Long As I Don't See You/				
	Strange Bed with a Bad Head	1972	—	3.00	6.00
❏ 69	I'll Make It Worth Your While/				
	You're Not the Only One	1973	—	3.00	6.00
❏ 73	My Special Rose/A Thousand Miles Away	1973	—	3.00	6.00
❏ 78	You're Savin' Your Best Lovin' for Me/What				
	Would I Do Without You	1974	—	3.00	6.00
❏ 83	I Don't Want It All/				
	I Can't See Myself As a One-Woman Man	1974	—	3.00	6.00
❏ 85	Found a New Love/Oh, How I Love My Baby	1975	—	3.00	6.00
❏ 87	True Love/When Are You Coming Home	1975	—	3.00	6.00
❏ 88	A Hard Head Makes a Sore Behind/The Future	1976	—	3.00	6.00
❏ 92	L.J.T./I Should Have Known	197?	—	3.00	6.00
❏ 98	Just One More Chance/New Song	197?	—	3.00	6.00

Number	Title (A Side/B Side)	Yr	VG	VG+	NM
Albums					
FANTASY					
❑ MPF-4510	Little Johnny Taylor's Greatest Hits	1982	2.50	5.00	10.00
GALAXY					
❑ 203 [M]	Little Johnny Taylor	1963	25.00	50.00	100.00
❑ 207 [M]	Little Johnny Taylor	1964	25.00	50.00	100.00
❑ 8203 [S]	Little Johnny Taylor	1963	37.50	75.00	150.00
❑ 8207 [S]	Little Johnny Taylor's Greatest Hits	1964	37.50	75.00	150.00
RONN					
❑ LPS-7530	Everybody Knows About My Good Thing	1972	6.25	12.50	25.00
❑ LSP-7532	Open House at My House	1973	6.25	12.50	25.00
❑ LSP-7535	L.J.T.	1975	5.00	10.00	20.00

TAYLOR, LITTLE JOHNNY, AND TED TAYLOR
45s

Number	Title (A Side/B Side)	Yr	VG	VG+	NM
RONN					
❑ 75	Walking the Floor/Cry It Out Baby	1973	—	3.00	6.00
❑ 89	Pretending Love/Funky Ghetto	1976	—	3.00	6.00
Albums					
RONN					
❑ LSP-7533	The Super Taylors	1973	5.00	10.00	20.00

TAYLOR, LIVINGSTON
45s

Number	Title (A Side/B Side)	Yr	VG	VG+	NM
CAPRICORN					
❑ 0032	Somewhere Over the Rainbow/Lady Tomorrow	1973	—	2.00	4.00
❑ 0045	I Can Dream of You/Loving Be My New Horizon	1974	—	2.00	4.00
❑ 8012	Carolina Day/Sit On Back	1971	—	2.50	5.00
❑ 8025	Get Out of Bed/Mom, Dad	1971	—	2.50	5.00
CRITIQUE					
❑ 99255	City Lights/Louie	1989	—	—	3.00
EPIC					
❑ 50604	I Will Be in Love with You/How Much Your Sweet Love Means to Me	1978	—	2.00	4.00
❑ 50667	I'll Come Running/No Thank You Skycap	1979	—	2.00	4.00
❑ 50894	First Time Love/Pajamas	1980	—	2.00	4.00
Albums					
ATCO					
❑ SD 33-334	Livingston Taylor	1970	3.00	6.00	12.00
CAPRICORN					
❑ CP 0114	Over the Rainbow	1973	2.50	5.00	10.00
❑ 863	Liv	1971	2.50	5.00	10.00
EPIC					
❑ JE 36153	Man's Best Friend	1979	2.50	5.00	10.00

TAYLOR, MAD MAN
45s

Number	Title (A Side/B Side)	Yr	VG	VG+	NM
EASTWEST					
❑ 117	Rumble Tumble/Rock and Roll Espanola	1958	18.75	37.50	75.00

TAYLOR, R. DEAN
45s

Number	Title (A Side/B Side)	Yr	VG	VG+	NM
AUDIO MASTER					
❑ 1	At the High School Dance/How Wrong Can You Be?	1960	50.00	100.00	200.00
FARR					
❑ 001	We'll Show Them All/Magdalena	1976	—	2.50	5.00
MALA					
❑ 444	I'll Remember/It's a Long Way to St. Louis	1962	25.00	50.00	100.00
RARE EARTH					
❑ 5013	Indiana Wants Me/Love's Your Name	1970	—	3.00	6.00
❑ 5023	Ain't It a Sad Thing/Back Street	1970	—	2.50	5.00
❑ 5023 [PS]	Ain't It a Sad Thing/Back Street	1970	2.50	5.00	10.00
❑ 5026	Gotta See Jane/Back Street	1971	—	2.50	5.00
❑ 5030	Candy Apple Red/Woman Alive	1971	—	2.50	5.00
❑ 5041	Taos New Mexico/Shadow	1972	—	2.50	5.00
STRUMMER					
❑ 3748	Let's Talk It Over/(B-side unknown)	1982	—	3.00	6.00
20TH CENTURY					
❑ 2510	Let's Talk It Over/Add Up the Score	1981	—	2.00	4.00
V.I.P.					
❑ 25042	Don't Fool Around/There's a Ghost in My House	1966	6.25	12.50	25.00
❑ 25045	Gotta See Jane/Don't Fool Around	1967	6.25	12.50	25.00
Albums					
RARE EARTH					
❑ RS-522	I Think, Therefore I Am	1971	3.75	7.50	15.00

TAYLOR, RENEE
45s

Number	Title (A Side/B Side)	Yr	VG	VG+	NM
FELSTED					
❑ 8620	His Pigs/I'm in Love with Jack	1961	3.00	6.00	12.00

TAYLOR, SHEILA
45s

Number	Title (A Side/B Side)	Yr	VG	VG+	NM
MELODYLAND					
❑ 6013	How Important Can It Be/She Satisfies	1975	—	2.50	5.00

TAYLOR, SHERRI
45s

Number	Title (A Side/B Side)	Yr	VG	VG+	NM
GLORECO					
❑ 1002	I've Got a Crush/(B-side unknown)	196?	15.00	30.00	60.00
MOTOWN					
❑ 1004	Lover/That's Why I Love You So Much	1960	10.00	20.00	40.00
—With Singin' Sammy Ward					

TAYLOR, TED
12-Inch Singles

Number	Title (A Side/B Side)	Yr	VG	VG+	NM
MCA					
❑ L33-1985 [DJ]	Keepin' My Head Above Water (6:58) (3:17)	1978	3.75	7.50	15.00
T.K. DISCO					
❑ TKD 31	Ghetto Disco (7:03)/(Part 2)	1977	6.25	12.50	25.00

45s

Number	Title (A Side/B Side)	Yr	VG	VG+	NM
ALARM					
❑ 110	Everybody's Stealing/Caught Up in a Good Woman's Love	1975	2.00	4.00	8.00
❑ 112	Steal Away/Somebody's Gettin' It	1976	2.00	4.00	8.00
❑ 114	Gonna Hate Myself/Stick By Me	1976	2.00	4.00	8.00
❑ 117	Ghetto Disco/You Can Make It If You Try	1977	2.00	4.00	8.00
❑ 2119	Paying for My Love Mistakes/Two Minute Warning	1977	2.00	4.00	8.00
❑ 2123	Talk to Me/You Made Loving You Easy	1978	2.00	4.00	8.00
❑ 2124	Spanish Harlem/Paying for My Love Mistakes	1978	2.00	4.00	8.00
APT					
❑ 25063	Little Things Mean a Lot/My Days and Nights	1962	6.25	12.50	25.00
ATCO					
❑ 6388	Dancing Annie/Try Me Again	1965	3.75	7.50	15.00
❑ 6408	Long Distance Love/River's Invitation	1966	2.50	5.00	10.00
❑ 6434	Help the Bear/Thank You for Helping Me See the Light	1966	3.75	7.50	15.00
❑ 6481	Baby Come Back to Me/Feed the Flame	1967	3.75	7.50	15.00
DADE					
❑ 5000	I Lost the Best Thing I Ever Had/Darling If You Must Leave	1963	10.00	20.00	40.00
DUKE					
❑ 304	Be Ever Wonderful/Since You're Home	1959	6.25	12.50	25.00
❑ 308	Count the Stars/Hold Me Tight	1959	6.25	12.50	25.00
EBB					
❑ 113	Days Are Dark/Everywhere I Go	1957	7.50	15.00	30.00
❑ 132	If I Don't See You Again/Keep Walking On	1958	7.50	15.00	30.00
❑ 151	Very Truly Yours/Wrapped Up in a Dream	1958	10.00	20.00	40.00
GOLD EAGLE					
❑ 1805	My Darling/She's a Winner	196?	5.00	10.00	20.00
❑ 1808	Bandstand Drag/Rockin' Hoss	196?	3.75	7.50	15.00
—As "Ted Taylor Combo"; these are instrumentals					
❑ 1810	That Happy Day/I Don't Care	196?	5.00	10.00	20.00
❑ 1812	No Matter What You Do/Never in My Life	196?	5.00	10.00	20.00
JEWEL					
❑ 748	Days Are Dark/Very Truly Yours	1965	2.50	5.00	10.00
❑ 759	You've Been Crying/Close Your Eyes	1966	2.50	5.00	10.00
❑ 774	Keep Walking On/Everywhere I Go	1966	2.50	5.00	10.00
LAURIE					
❑ 3067	Push Push/A Heart That's True	1960	3.75	7.50	15.00
—As "Austin Taylor"					
❑ 3076	You've Been Crying/Little Boy How Old Are You	1960	3.75	7.50	15.00
❑ 3082	I Don't Want to Love You/Lovin' Hands	1961	3.75	7.50	15.00
—As "Austin Taylor"					
❑ 3095	I Love Being Loved by You/Together Forever	1961	3.75	7.50	15.00
—As "Austin Taylor"					
MCA					
❑ 40937	Keepin' My Head Above Water/I Can't Fake It Anymore	1978	2.50	5.00	10.00
❑ 40977	Chase the World Away/Double My Money Bag	1978	3.75	7.50	15.00
OKEH					
❑ 4-7154	Don't Lie/Pretending Love	1962	5.00	10.00	20.00
❑ 4-7159	You Must Have Been Meant for Me/Time Has a Way	1962	3.75	7.50	15.00
❑ 4-7165	I'll Release You/Can't Take No More	1962	3.75	7.50	15.00
❑ 4-7171	Be Ever Wonderful/That's Life I Guess	1963	5.00	10.00	20.00
❑ 4-7176	You Give Me Nothing to Go On/Him Instead of Me	1963	5.00	10.00	20.00
❑ 4-7179	It Ain't Like That No More/I'll Make It Up to You	1963	5.00	10.00	20.00
❑ 4-7190	So Hard/Need You Home	1964	3.75	7.50	15.00
❑ 4-7198	Somebody's Always Trying/Top of the World	1964	15.00	30.00	60.00
❑ 4-7206	Don't Deceive Me (Please Don't Go)/If It Wasn't for You	1964	5.00	10.00	20.00
❑ 4-7214	So Long, Bye Bye/I Love You, Yes I Do	1965	5.00	10.00	20.00
❑ 4-7222	(Love Is Like a) Ramblin' Rose/I'm So Satisfied	1965	5.00	10.00	20.00
❑ 4-7231	Stay Away from My Baby/Walking Out of Your Life	1965	3.75	7.50	15.00
❑ 4-7240	Daddy's Baby/Mercy Have Pity	1966	3.75	7.50	15.00
❑ 4-7252	Big Wheel/No One But You	1966	3.75	7.50	15.00
RONN					
❑ 15	Miss You So/I'm Gonna Get Tough	1967	2.50	5.00	10.00
❑ 21	Ollie Mae/I Need Your Love So Bad	1968	2.50	5.00	10.00
❑ 25	Honey Lou/Without a Woman	1968	2.50	5.00	10.00
❑ 29	Strangest Feeling/You Got to Feel It	1969	2.50	5.00	10.00
❑ 33	Long Ago/I'm Gonna Send You Back to Oklahoma	1969	2.50	5.00	10.00
❑ 34	It's Too Late/The Road of Love	1969	2.50	5.00	10.00
❑ 37	I'm Lonely Tonight/If I Thought You Needed Me	1969	2.50	5.00	10.00
❑ 40	Loving Physician/I Feel a Chill	1970	2.50	5.00	10.00
❑ 44	Something Strange Is Goin' On in My House/Funky Thing	1970	2.50	5.00	10.00
❑ 46	It's a Funky Situation/I'm Glad You're Home	1970	2.50	5.00	10.00
❑ 49	Can't Take No More/Singing Man	1971	2.50	5.00	10.00
❑ 52	How's Your Love Life Baby/(This Is a) Troubled World	1971	2.50	5.00	10.00
❑ 57	How Do You Walk Away from Fear/Only the Lonely Knows	1971	2.50	5.00	10.00
❑ 63	Houston Town/I'm Just a Crumb in Your Breadbox	1972	2.50	5.00	10.00
❑ 65	I Want to Be Part of You Girl/Going in the Hole	1972	2.50	5.00	10.00
❑ 72	What a Fool/Make Up for Lost Time	1973	2.00	4.00	8.00
❑ 74	Break of Day/Fair Weather Woman	1973	2.00	4.00	8.00
❑ 77	She Loves to Do It As Well As You/Ready for the Heartbreak	1974	2.00	4.00	8.00
❑ 82	For All the Days in My Life/I've Got to Find Somebody New	1974	2.00	4.00	8.00
❑ 106	Cummin's Prison Farm/Houston Town	1984	—	3.00	6.00
❑ 112	Be Ever Wonderfiul/I Love You Just the Same	198?	—	3.00	6.00
❑ 114	Little Red Rooster/Stay Away from My Baby	198?	—	3.00	6.00
❑ 116	Steal Away/My Key Jump Back in My Hand	198?	—	3.00	6.00
SOLPUGIDS					
❑ 101	I Let You Hurt Me Too Long/Pleading for Love	198?	2.00	4.00	8.00
❑ 102	You're Tippin', She's Rippin'/Little Red Rooster	198?	2.00	4.00	8.00
TOP RANK					
❑ 2011	I'm Saving My Love/Chanta-Lula	1959	6.25	12.50	25.00
❑ 2048	I Need You So/Has My Love Grown Cold	1960	6.25	12.50	25.00
❑ 2076	Darling Take Me Back/Look Out	1960	7.50	15.00	30.00
❑ 3001	You Know I Do/Someday (I Know, I Know)	1961	7.50	15.00	30.00
WARWICK					
❑ 628	You Know I Do/Someday (I Know, I Know)	1961	5.00	10.00	20.00

Number	Title (A Side/B Side)	Yr	VG	VG+	NM

Albums
ALARM

| ❑ 1000 | 1976 | 1976 | 7.50 | 15.00 | 30.00 |

MCA

| ❑ 3059 | Keepin' My Head Above Water | 1978 | 3.00 | 6.00 | 12.00 |

OKEH

❑ OKM-12104 [M]	Be Ever Wonderful	1963	7.50	15.00	30.00
❑ OKM-12109 [M]	Blues and Soul	1965	7.50	15.00	30.00
❑ OKM-12113 [M]	Ted Taylor's Greatest Hits	1966	6.25	12.50	25.00
❑ OKS-14104 [S]	Be Ever Wonderful	1963	10.00	20.00	40.00
❑ OKS-14109 [S]	Blues and Soul	1965	10.00	20.00	40.00
❑ OKS-14113 [S]	Ted Taylor's Greatest Hits	1966	7.50	15.00	30.00

RONN

❑ LPS-7528	Shades of Blue	1969	3.00	6.00	12.00
❑ LPS-7529	You Can Dig It!	197?	3.00	6.00	12.00
❑ LPS-7531	Taylor Made	1972	3.00	6.00	12.00
❑ LP-8003	Be Ever Wonderful	198?	2.50	5.00	10.00
❑ LP-8004	Steal Away	198?	2.50	5.00	10.00

SOLPUGIDS

| ❑ 1001 | Be Ever Wonderful | 198? | 3.75 | 7.50 | 15.00 |
| ❑ 1002 | Taylor Made for You | 198? | 3.75 | 7.50 | 15.00 |

TAYLOR, TRUE See PAUL SIMON.

TAYLOR, VERNON
45s
DOT

| ❑ 15632 | I've Got the Blues/The Losing Game | 1957 | 25.00 | 50.00 | 100.00 |
| ❑ 15697 | Satisfaction Guaranteed/
Why Must You Leave Me | 1958 | 12.50 | 25.00 | 50.00 |

SUN

| ❑ 310 | Breeze/Today Is a Blue Day | 1958 | 6.25 | 12.50 | 25.00 |
| ❑ 325 | Sweet and Easy to Love/Mystery Train | 1959 | 8.75 | 17.50 | 35.00 |

TAYLOR, VINCE
45s
PALETTE

| ❑ 5065 | I'll Be Your Hero/Jet Black Machine | 1960 | 3.00 | 6.00 | 12.00 |
| ❑ 5084 | Move Over Tiger/What Cha Gonna Do | 1961 | 3.00 | 6.00 | 12.00 |

TAYLOR, ZOLA
45s
RPM

| ❑ 405 | Make Love to Me/Oh My Dear | 1954 | 75.00 | 150.00 | 300.00 |

TAZMEN, THE
45s
ABC-PARAMOUNT

| ❑ 9812 | Easy Pickin'/The Chicken | 1957 | 3.75 | 7.50 | 15.00 |

TEA COMPANY, THE
45s
SMASH

| ❑ 2176 | Come and Have Some Tea with Me/Flowers | 1968 | 3.75 | 7.50 | 15.00 |

Albums
SMASH

| ❑ SRS-67105 | Come and Have Some Tea | 1968 | 12.50 | 25.00 | 50.00 |

TEAM MATES, THE
45s
ABC-PARAMOUNT

| ❑ 10760 | If Only I Had Known/You Must Pay | 1965 | 3.00 | 6.00 | 12.00 |

LE CAM

❑ 701	I Just Might/Sooner or Later	196?	6.25	12.50	25.00
❑ 706	If Only I Had Known/You Must Pay	196?	6.25	12.50	25.00
❑ 707	Once There Was a Time/Come On Baby	1962	6.25	12.50	25.00

PAULA

| ❑ 220 | Most of All/Please Believe Me | 1965 | 7.50 | 15.00 | 30.00 |

PHILIPS

| ❑ 40029 | Once There Was a Time/Never Believed in Love | 1962 | 3.00 | 6.00 | 12.00 |

TEARDROPS, THE (1)
45s
DORE

| ❑ 679 | Little Orphan Boy/(Instrumental) | 1963 | 3.00 | 6.00 | 12.00 |

TEARDROPS, THE (2)
45s
DOT

| ❑ 15669 | Bridge of Love/Jellyfish | 1957 | 6.25 | 12.50 | 25.00 |

RENDEZVOUS

| ❑ 102 | Catch Me, I'm Falling Again/Sugar Baby | 1958 | 7.50 | 15.00 | 30.00 |

TEARDROPS, THE (3)
45s
JOSIE

| ❑ 766 | The Stars Are Out Tonight/Oh Stop It | 1954 | 75.00 | 150.00 | 300.00 |
| ❑ 771 | My Heart/Ooh Baby | 1954 | 125.00 | 250.00 | 500.00 |

PORT

| ❑ 70019 | The Stars Are Out Tonight/Oh Stop It | 1960 | 6.25 | 12.50 | 25.00 |

TEARDROPS, THE (4) Even though on the same label as group (3), this is a different group.
45s
JOSIE

❑ 856	We Won't Tell/Al Chiar Di Luna (Porto Fortuna)	1959	6.25	12.50	25.00
❑ 862	Cry No More/You're My Hollywood Star	1959	6.25	12.50	25.00
❑ 873	Daddy's Little Girl/Always You	1960	6.25	12.50	25.00

TEARDROPS, THE (5)
45s
KING

| ❑ 5004 | My Inspiration/I Prayed for Love | 1956 | 6.25 | 12.50 | 25.00 |
| ❑ 5037 | After School/Don't Be Afraid to Love | 1957 | 6.25 | 12.50 | 25.00 |

TEARDROPS, THE (6) Girl group.
45s
MUSICOR

| ❑ 1139 | Tears Come Tumbling/You Won't Be There | 1965 | 3.75 | 7.50 | 15.00 |
| ❑ 1218 | I Will Love You Dear Forever/Bubblegummers | 1966 | 3.75 | 7.50 | 15.00 |

Number	Title (A Side/B Side)	Yr	VG	VG+	NM

SAXONY

❑ 1007	Tonight I'm Gonna Fall in Love Again/ That's Why I'll Get By	1964	20.00	40.00	80.00
❑ 1008	I'm Gonna Steal Your Boyfriend/ Call Me and I'll Be Happy	1965	6.25	12.50	25.00
❑ 1009	Tears Come Tumbling/You Won't Be There	1965	5.00	10.00	20.00

TEARDROPS, THE (7)
45s
SAMPSON

| ❑ 634 | Come Back to Me/Sweet Lovin' Daddy-O | 1952 | 100.00 | 200.00 | 400.00 |

TEARDROPS, THE (U)
Albums
20TH CENTURY FOX

| ❑ FXG-5011 [M] | The Teardrops at Trinchi's | 1963 | 6.25 | 12.50 | 25.00 |

TEASERS, THE
45s
CHECKER

| ❑ 800 | I Was a Fool to Love You/
How Could You Hurt One So | 1954 | 150.00 | 300.00 | 600.00 |
| ❑ 800 | I Was a Fool to Love You/
How Could You Hurt One So | 1954 | 300.00 | 600.00 | 1200. |

—Red vinyl

TECHNICS, THE
45s
CHEX

| ❑ 1010 | Has He Told You/Workout With a Pretty Girl | 1963 | 7.50 | 15.00 | 30.00 |

—As "Tony and the Technics"

| ❑ 1012 | Because I Really Love You/A Man's Confusion | 1963 | 7.50 | 15.00 | 30.00 |
| ❑ 1013 | Hey Girl Don't Leave Me/I Met Her on the First
of September | 1963 | 10.00 | 20.00 | 40.00 |

TECHNIQUES, THE (1)
45s
ROULETTE

❑ 4030	Hey! Little Girl/In a Round-About Way	1957	6.25	12.50	25.00
❑ 4048	(Why Did I Ever) Let Her Go/Marindy	1958	6.25	12.50	25.00
❑ 4097	The Wisest Man You Know/Moon Tan	1958	6.25	12.50	25.00

STARS

| ❑ 551 | Hey Little Girl/In a Round-About Way | 1957 | 10.00 | 20.00 | 40.00 |

TECHNIQUES, THE (2) Unrelated to the above, this group evidently is from the Lubbock, Texas area.
45s
VENUS

| ❑ RK4M-8540/1 | Dream Theme/Autumn Rain | 1964 | 5.00 | 10.00 | 20.00 |

TEDDY AND HIS PATCHES
45s
CHANCE

❑ 100	Suzy Creamcheese/From Day to Day	1967	25.00	50.00	100.00
❑ 668	Suzy Creamcheese/It Ain't Nothin'	1967	25.00	50.00	100.00
❑ 669	Haight Ashbury/It Ain't Nothin'	1967	25.00	50.00	100.00

TEDDY AND THE CONTINENTALS
45s
PIK

| ❑ 235 | Tick Tick Tock/Everybody Pony | 1961 | 6.25 | 12.50 | 25.00 |

RAGO

| ❑ 201 | Tick Tick Tock/Wild Christening Party | 1962 | 6.25 | 12.50 | 25.00 |

—B-side by the Teen Kings

RICHIE

| ❑ 445 | Do You/Tighten Up | 1961 | 10.00 | 20.00 | 40.00 |

—With Roulette Records distribution mentioned on label

| ❑ 445 | Do You/Tighten Up | 1961 | 25.00 | 50.00 | 100.00 |

—With no mention of Roulette distribution on label

| ❑ 453 | Crying Over You/Crossfire With Me Baby | 1963 | 12.50 | 25.00 | 50.00 |
| ❑ 1001 | Tick Tick Tock/Everybody Pony | 1961 | 15.00 | 30.00 | 60.00 |

TEDDY AND THE TWILIGHTS
45s
SWAN

❑ 4102	Woman Is a Man's Best Friend/Goodbye to Love	1962	6.25	12.50	25.00
❑ 4115	You Gotta Be Alone to Cry/Running Around	1962	5.00	10.00	20.00
❑ 4126	I'm Just Your Clown/Bimini Bimbo	1962	5.00	10.00	20.00

TEDDY BEARS, THE With PHIL SPECTOR and Annette Kleinbard (a.k.a. Carol Connors).
45s
DORE

| ❑ 503 | To Know Him, Is to Love Him/Don't You Worry
My Little Pet | 1958 | 7.50 | 15.00 | 30.00 |
| ❑ 520 | Wonderful Loveable You/Till You'll Be Mine | 1959 | 5.00 | 10.00 | 20.00 |

IMPERIAL

❑ 5562	Oh Why/I Don't Need You Anymore	1959	7.50	15.00	30.00
❑ 5581	You Said Goodbye/If You Only Knew	1959	7.50	15.00	30.00
❑ 5594	Seven Lonely Days/Don't Go Away	1959	7.50	15.00	30.00

Albums
IMPERIAL

| ❑ LP-9067 [M] | The Teddy Bears Sing! | 1959 | 75.00 | 150.00 | 300.00 |
| ❑ LP-12010 [S] | The Teddy Bears Sing! | 1959 | 300.00 | 600.00 | 1200. |

TEDDY BOYS, THE
45s
CAMEO

| ❑ 433 | Where Have All the Good Times Gone/La La | 1966 | 5.00 | 10.00 | 20.00 |
| ❑ 448 | Mona/Good Morning Blues | 1966 | 5.00 | 10.00 | 20.00 |

MGM

| ❑ 13515 | Jezebel/It's You | 1966 | 5.00 | 10.00 | 20.00 |

TEE, WILLIE
45s
A.F.O.

| ❑ 307 | All for One/Always Accused | 1962 | 3.75 | 7.50 | 15.00 |
| ❑ 311 | Why Lie/I Found Out You Are My Cousin | 1963 | 3.75 | 7.50 | 15.00 |

Number	Title (A Side/B Side)	Yr	VG	VG+	NM
ATLANTIC					
❑ 2273	Teasin' You/Walkin' Up a One-Way Street	1965	2.50	5.00	10.00
❑ 2287	Thank You John/Dedicated to You	1965	2.50	5.00	10.00
❑ 2302	I Want Somebody/You Better Say Yes	1965	2.50	5.00	10.00
CAPITOL					
❑ 2369	Walk Tall (Baby, That's What I Need)/ I'm Only a Man	1968	2.00	4.00	8.00
❑ 2892	Reach Out for Me/The Love of a Married Man	1970	2.00	4.00	8.00
CINDERELLA					
❑ 1202	Foolish Girl/(B-side unknown)	196?	10.00	20.00	40.00
GATOR					
❑ 701	She Really Did Surprise Me/(B-side unknown)	196?	7.50	15.00	30.00
HOT LINE					
❑ 910	Close Your Eyes/I Heard Everything You Said	196?	2.00	4.00	8.00
NOLA					
❑ 708	Teasin' You/Walkin' Up a One-Way Street	1964	62.50	125.00	250.00
UNITED ARTISTS					
❑ XW910	I'd Give It to You/Look Out World	1976	—	2.50	5.00
Albums					
CAPITOL					
❑ ST-199	I'm Only a Man	1969	3.75	7.50	15.00
UNITED ARTISTS					
❑ UA-LA655-G	Anticipation	1976	3.00	6.00	12.00

TEE SET, THE
45s

Number	Title (A Side/B Side)	Yr	VG	VG+	NM
COLOSSUS					
❑ 107	Ma Belle Amie/Angels Coming in the Holy Night	1969	—	2.50	5.00
❑ 107 [PS]	Ma Belle Amie/Angels Coming in the Holy Night	1969	—	3.00	6.00
❑ 114	If You Do Believe in Love/Charmaine	1970	—	2.00	4.00
❑ 139	She Likes Weeds/(B-side unknown)	1971	—	2.00	4.00
Albums					
COLOSSUS					
❑ CCS-1001	Ma Belle Amie	1970	3.75	7.50	15.00

TEEGARDEN AND VAN WINKLE
45s

Number	Title (A Side/B Side)	Yr	VG	VG+	NM
PLUMM					
❑ 68102	God, Love, and Rock & Roll (We Believe)/ Work Me Tomorrow	1970	3.75	7.50	15.00
WESTBOUND					
❑ 170	God, Love and Rock & Roll/Work Me Tomorrow	1970	—	2.50	5.00
❑ 170 [PS]	God, Love and Rock & Roll/Work Me Tomorrow	1970	—	3.00	6.00
❑ 171	Everything Is Going to Be All Right/You Do	1970	—	2.50	5.00
❑ 187	Stoned on the Love for Jesus/I Need You	1971	—	2.50	5.00
❑ 200	Passing Gas/Ride Away with Me	1971	—	2.50	5.00
❑ 210	Carry On/Ride Away with Me	1972	—	2.50	5.00
Albums					
ATCO					
❑ 33-272 [M]	An Evening at Home with Teegarden and Van Winkle	1968	10.00	20.00	40.00
—Mono is white label promo only					
❑ SD 33-272 [S]	An Evening at Home with Teegarden and Van Winkle	1968	3.75	7.50	15.00
WESTBOUND					
❑ 2003	But Anyhow	1969	3.75	7.50	15.00
❑ 2010	On Our Way	1971	3.75	7.50	15.00

TEEMATES, THE
45s

Number	Title (A Side/B Side)	Yr	VG	VG+	NM
AUDIO FIDELITY					
❑ 104	Dream On Little Girl/Moving Out	1964	3.75	7.50	15.00
❑ 105	Night Fall/No More Tomorrows	1964	3.75	7.50	15.00
Albums					
AUDIO FIDELITY					
❑ AFLP-3042 [M]	Jet Set Dance Discotheque	1964	10.00	20.00	40.00
❑ AFSD-7042 [S]	Jet Set Dance Discotheque	1964	12.50	25.00	50.00

TEEN ANGELS, THE
45s

Number	Title (A Side/B Side)	Yr	VG	VG+	NM
SUN					
❑ 388	Ain't Gonna Let You (Break My Heart)/ Tell Me My Love	1964	7.50	15.00	30.00

TEEN CLEFS, THE
45s

Number	Title (A Side/B Side)	Yr	VG	VG+	NM
DICE					
❑ 98/99	Sputnik/Hiding My Tears with a Smile	1959	37.50	75.00	150.00

TEEN KINGS, THE See ROY ORBISON.

TEEN-KINGS, THE
45s

Number	Title (A Side/B Side)	Yr	VG	VG+	NM
BEE					
❑ 1114/5	That's a Teen-Age Love/Tell Me If You Know	1959	500.00	1000.	1500.
—Legitimate original copies are on black vinyl					
WILLETT					
❑ 118	Don't Just Stand There/My Greatest Wish	1959	62.50	125.00	250.00

TEEN QUEENS, THE
45s

Number	Title (A Side/B Side)	Yr	VG	VG+	NM
ANTLER					
❑ 4014	There's Nothing on My Mind (Part 1)/ There's Nothing on My Mind (Part 2)	1959	3.75	7.50	15.00
❑ 4015	Politician/I'm a Fool	1959	3.75	7.50	15.00
❑ 4016	Donny (Part 1)/Donny (Part 2)	1960	3.75	7.50	15.00
❑ 4017	I Hear Violins/Magoo Can See	1960	3.75	7.50	15.00
KENT					
❑ 359	Eddie My Love/Just Goofed	1961	3.00	6.00	12.00
RCA VICTOR					
❑ 47-7206	Dear Tommy/You Good Boy-You Get Cookie	1958	4.00	8.00	16.00
❑ 47-7396	Movie Star/First Crush	1958	4.00	8.00	16.00
RPM					
❑ 453	Eddie My Love/Just Goofed	1956	7.50	15.00	30.00
—Black label					

Number	Title (A Side/B Side)	Yr	VG	VG+	NM
❑ 453	Eddie My Love/Just Goofed	1956	30.00	60.00	120.00
—Red label					
❑ 460	So All Alone/Baby Mine	1956	6.25	12.50	25.00
❑ 464	Billy Boy/Until the Day I Die	1956	6.25	12.50	25.00
❑ 470	Red Top/Love Sweet Love	1956	6.25	12.50	25.00
❑ 480	My First Love/(B-side unknown)	1956	6.25	12.50	25.00
❑ 484	Rock Everybody/My Heart's Desire	1957	5.00	10.00	20.00
❑ 500	I Miss You/Two Loves and Two Lives	1957	5.00	10.00	20.00
Albums					
CROWN					
❑ CST-373 [R]	The Teen Queens	1963	7.50	15.00	30.00
❑ CLP-5022 [M]	Eddie My Love	1956	62.50	125.00	250.00
—Black label, all silver print					
❑ CLP-5022 [M]	Eddie My Love	196?	25.00	50.00	100.00
—Black label, "CROWN" in alternating colored letters					
❑ CLP-5373 [M]	The Teen Queens	1963	12.50	25.00	50.00
RPM					
❑ LRP-3007 [M]	Eddie My Love	1956	—	—	—
—Canceled					

TEEN TONES, THE More than one group. Some may be listed as "Teen-Tones."
45s

Number	Title (A Side/B Side)	Yr	VG	VG+	NM
DANDY DAN					
❑ 2	Darling I Love You/My Sweet	1958	20.00	40.00	80.00
DECCA					
❑ 30895	Don't Call Me Baby, I'll Call You/Yes You May	1959	7.50	15.00	30.00
GONE					
❑ 5061	The Rockin' Rumble/Latino Part 2	1959	7.50	15.00	30.00
SWAN					
❑ 4040	My Little Baby/Head Strong Baby	1959	7.50	15.00	30.00
TRI-DISC					
❑ 102	I'm So Happy/Shoutin' Twist	1961	3.75	7.50	15.00
WYNNE					
❑ 107	Faded Love/Gypsy Boogie	1958	6.25	12.50	25.00

TEENAGE MOONLIGHTERS
45s

Number	Title (A Side/B Side)	Yr	VG	VG+	NM
MARK					
❑ 134	Sorry Sorry/I Want to Cry	1960	1000.	1500.	2000.

TEENAGERS, THE These are records by the original group without FRANKIE LYMON. Also see FRANKIE LYMON AND THE TEENAGERS.
45s

Number	Title (A Side/B Side)	Yr	VG	VG+	NM
END					
❑ 1071	Crying/Tonight's the Night	1960	15.00	30.00	60.00
❑ 1076	Can You Tell Me/A Little Wiser Now	1960	10.00	20.00	40.00
GEE					
❑ 1046	Flip Flop/Everything to Me	1957	7.50	15.00	30.00
ROULETTE					
❑ 4086	My Broken Heart/Momma Wanna Rock	1958	20.00	40.00	80.00

TEENBEATS, THE
45s

Number	Title (A Side/B Side)	Yr	VG	VG+	NM
TEENBEAT					
❑ (No #)	Surfbound/Mr. Moto	1963	20.00	40.00	80.00

TEENETTES, THE
45s

Number	Title (A Side/B Side)	Yr	VG	VG+	NM
BRUNSWICK					
❑ 55125	I Want a Boy with a Hi-Fi Supersonic Stereophonic Bloop Bleep/From the Word Go	1959	6.25	12.50	25.00
JOSIE					
❑ 830	My Lucky Star/Too Young to Fall in Love	1958	15.00	30.00	60.00

TELSTARS, THE
45s

Number	Title (A Side/B Side)	Yr	VG	VG+	NM
COLUMBIA					
❑ 44141	Keep On Running/Hold Tight	1967	5.00	10.00	20.00
IMPERIAL					
❑ 5903	Continental Mash/Stomp Happy	1962	6.25	12.50	25.00
TEEN					
❑ 510	Continental Mash/Stomp Happy	1962	10.00	20.00	40.00
❑ 513	Pow Wow/Lovina	1963	8.75	17.50	35.00
❑ 516	Topless/Spaghetti Strap	1964	8.75	17.50	35.00
❑ 517	Tough George/'Cause I Really Do	1964	8.75	17.50	35.00

TEMPEST
Albums

Number	Title (A Side/B Side)	Yr	VG	VG+	NM
WARNER BROS.					
❑ BS 2682	Tempest	1973	6.25	12.50	25.00

TEMPLE, BOB
45s

Number	Title (A Side/B Side)	Yr	VG	VG+	NM
KING					
❑ 4958	Come Back, Come Back/Vam Vam Vamoose	1956	7.50	15.00	30.00

TEMPO, NINO Also see NINO TEMPO AND APRIL STEVENS.
45s

Number	Title (A Side/B Side)	Yr	VG	VG+	NM
A&M					
❑ 1461	Sister James/Clair De Lune (In Jazz)	1973	—	2.00	4.00
❑ 1499	Roll It/Hawkeye	1974	—	2.00	4.00
❑ 1532	High on the Music/ Come See Me 'Round Midnight	1974		2.00	4.00
❑ 1625	Gettin' Off/Don't Stop Now	1974	—	2.00	4.00
❑ 2131	Hooked on Young Stuff/Ronan's Road	1979	—	2.00	4.00
RCA VICTOR					
❑ 47-7424	15 Girl Friends/Loonie 'Bout Junie	1958	3.00	6.00	12.00
❑ 47-7647	Ding-a-Ling/When You Were Sweet Sixteen	1959	3.00	6.00	12.00
❑ 47-7694	Jack the Ripper/ Main Theme from "Jack the Ripper"	1960	2.50	5.00	10.00
—B-side by Pete Rugolo					
TOWER					
❑ 369	Boys Town/Boys Town (Sing Along)	1967	—	3.00	6.00
UNITED ARTISTS					
❑ 256	What Is Love to a Teenager/Lipstick on Your Lips	1960	2.50	5.00	10.00

T

Number	Title (A Side/B Side)	Yr	VG	VG+	NM
Albums					
A&M					
❏ SP-3629	Come See Me 'Round Midnight	1974	2.50	5.00	10.00
LIBERTY					
❏ LRP-3023 [M]	Rock 'n' Roll Beach Party	1958	30.00	60.00	120.00

TEMPO, NINO, AND APRIL STEVENS Also see each artist's individual listings.

Number	Title (A Side/B Side)	Yr	VG	VG+	NM
45s					
A&M					
❏ 1394	Love Story/Hoochy Coochy — Wing Dang Doo	1972	—	2.00	4.00
❏ 1443	Put It Where You Want It/				
	I Can't Get Over You Baby	1973	—	2.00	4.00
❏ 1674	Never Had a Lover/You Turn Me On	1975	—	2.00	4.00
ATCO					
❏ 6224	Sweet and Lovely/True Love	1962	2.50	5.00	10.00
❏ 6248	Indian Love Call/Paradise	1962	2.50	5.00	10.00
❏ 6263	(We'll Always Be) Together/Baby Weemus	1963	2.50	5.00	10.00
❏ 6273	Deep Purple/I've Been Carrying a Torch for You				
	So Long That I Burned a Great Big Hole				
	in My Heart	1963	3.00	6.00	12.00
❏ 6281	Whispering/Tweedlee Dee	1963	2.50	5.00	10.00
❏ 6286	Stardust/I-45	1964	2.00	4.00	8.00
❏ 6294	Tea for Two/I'm Confessin' (That I Love You)	1964	2.00	4.00	8.00
❏ 6306	I Surrender Dear/Who	1964	2.00	4.00	8.00
❏ 6314	Melancholy Baby/Ooh La La	1964	2.00	4.00	8.00
❏ 6325	Our Love/Honeywell Rose	1964	2.00	4.00	8.00
❏ 6337	These Arms of Mine/				
	The Coldest Night of the Year	1965	2.00	4.00	8.00
❏ 6350	Swing Me/Tomorrow Is Soon a Memory	1965	2.00	4.00	8.00
❏ 6360	Think of You/I'm Sweet on You	1965	2.00	4.00	8.00
❏ 6368	That's My Desire/King Kong	1965	2.00	4.00	8.00
❏ 6375	I Love How You Love Me/Tears of Sorrow	1965	2.00	4.00	8.00
❏ 6391	Hey Baby/The Poison of Your Kisses	1965	2.00	4.00	8.00
❏ 6410	Bye Bye Blues/King Kong	1966	2.00	4.00	8.00
❏ 6897	She's My Baby/Tomorrow Is Soon a Memory	1972	—	3.00	6.00
BELL					
❏ 769	Did I or Didn't I/Yesterday I Heard the Rain	1969	2.00	4.00	8.00
❏ 823	Seas of Love-Dock of the Bay/Twilight	1969	2.00	4.00	8.00
CHELSEA					
❏ 3052	What Kind of Fool Am I/(B-side unknown)	1976	—	2.00	4.00
MGM					
❏ 13825	Falling in Love Again/Wanting You	1967	2.00	4.00	8.00
❏ 14266	How About Me/Makin' Love to Rainbow Colors	1971	—	3.00	6.00
UNITED ARTISTS					
❏ 272	Ooeah (That's What You Do to Me)/				
	High School Sweetheart	1960	2.50	5.00	10.00
WHITE WHALE					
❏ 236	All Strung Out/I Can't Go On Living				
	Baby Without You	1966	2.00	4.00	8.00
❏ 241	You'll Be Needing Me Baby/				
	Habit of Lovin' You Baby	1966	2.00	4.00	8.00
❏ 246	Wings of Love/My Old Flame	1967	2.00	4.00	8.00
❏ 252	I Can't Go On Living				
	Baby Without You/Little Child	1967	2.00	4.00	8.00
❏ 252	I Can't Go On Living				
	Without You Baby/Little Child	1967	3.00	6.00	12.00
—Some copies have the above erroneous A-side title					
❏ 268	Let It Be Me/Words of Love	1968	2.00	4.00	8.00
❏ 271	Ooh Poo Pa Doo/Let It Be Me	1968	2.00	4.00	8.00
Albums					
ATCO					
❏ 33-156 [M]	Deep Purple	1963	10.00	20.00	40.00
❏ SD 33-156 [S]	Deep Purple	1963	12.50	25.00	50.00
❏ 33-162 [M]	Nino and April Sing the Great Songs	1964	7.50	15.00	30.00
❏ SD 33-162 [S]	Nino and April Sing the Great Songs	1964	10.00	20.00	40.00
❏ 33-180 [M]	Hey Baby	1966	7.50	15.00	30.00
❏ SD 33-180 [S]	Hey Baby	1966	10.00	20.00	40.00
RCA CAMDEN					
❏ CAL-824 [M]	A Nino Tempo/April Stevens Program	1966	3.00	6.00	12.00
—Actually contains solo recordings by each, packaged together to capitalize on the success of "Deep Purple"					
WHITE WHALE					
❏ WW-113 [M]	All Strung Out	1967	5.00	10.00	20.00
❏ WWS-7113 [S]	All Strung Out	1967	6.25	12.50	25.00

TEMPO-TONES, THE

Number	Title (A Side/B Side)	Yr	VG	VG+	NM
45s					
ACME					
❏ 713	Get Yourself Another Fool/Ride Along	1957	37.50	75.00	150.00
❏ 715	In My Dreams/My Boy Sleep Pete	1957	125.00	250.00	500.00
❏ 718	Come Into My Heart/				
	Somewhere There Is Sunshine	1957	125.00	250.00	500.00
❏ 722	The Day I Met You/Wishing All the Time	1957	100.00	200.00	400.00

TEMPOS, THE Probably more than one group.

Number	Title (A Side/B Side)	Yr	VG	VG+	NM
45s					
ASCOT					
❏ 2167	When You Loved Me/My Barbara Ann	1965	6.25	12.50	25.00
❏ 2173	I Wish It Were Summer/My Barbara Ann	1965	6.25	12.50	25.00
CANTERBURY					
❏ 504	Here I Come (Countdown) Part 1/Here I Come				
	(Countdown) Part 2	1967	3.75	7.50	15.00
CLIMAX					
❏ 102	See You in September/Bless You My Love	1959	5.00	10.00	20.00
❏ 105	The Crossroads of Love/Whatever Happens	1959	5.00	10.00	20.00
FAIRMOUNT					
❏ 611	Oh Play That Thing/Monkey Doo	1963	3.00	6.00	12.00
HI-Q					
❏ 100	It's Tough/Sham-Rock	1959	10.00	20.00	40.00
KAPP					
❏ 178	Kingdom of Love/That's What You Do to Me	1957	6.25	12.50	25.00
❏ 199	Prettiest Girl in School/Never You Mind	1957	6.25	12.50	25.00
❏ 213	I Got a Job/Strollin' with My Baby	1958	6.25	12.50	25.00
MONTEL					
❏ 955	I Gotta Make a Move/It Was You	1966	3.75	7.50	15.00

Number	Title (A Side/B Side)	Yr	VG	VG+	NM
PARIS					
❏ 550	Look Homeward, Angel/Under Ten Flags	1960	5.00	10.00	20.00
RHYTHM					
❏ 121	Promise Me/Never Let Me Go	1958	125.00	250.00	500.00
RILEY'S					
❏ 8781	Don't Leave Me/I Need You	1966	7.50	15.00	30.00
U.S.A.					
❏ 810	Why Don't You Write Me/A Thief in the Night	1965	6.25	12.50	25.00
Albums					
JUSTICE					
❏ JLP-104	Speaking of the Tempos	1966	125.00	250.00	500.00

TEMPREES

Number	Title (A Side/B Side)	Yr	VG	VG+	NM
45s					
EPIC					
❏ 50192	I Found Love on a Disco Floor/				
	There Ain't a Dream Been Dreamed	1976	—	2.50	5.00
WE PRODUCE					
❏ 1801	I'm for You, You for Me/Rules and Regulations	1971	2.00	4.00	8.00
❏ 1803	(Girl) I Love You/I Love You, You Love Me	1971	2.00	4.00	8.00
❏ 1805	My Baby Love/If I Could Say What's On My Mind	1972	2.00	4.00	8.00
❏ 1807	Explain It to Her Mama/				
	Love Can Be So Wonderful	1972	2.00	4.00	8.00
❏ 1808	Dedicated to the One I Love/				
	I Love You, You Love Me	1972	2.00	4.00	8.00
❏ 1810	A Thousand Miles Away/Chalk It Up to				
	Experience	1973	2.00	4.00	8.00
❏ 1811	Love's Maze/Wrap Me in Love	1973	2.00	4.00	8.00
❏ 1812	At Last/Love Can Be So Wonderful	1974	—	3.50	7.00
❏ 1813	You Make Me Love You/You Make the Sunshine	1974	—	3.50	7.00
❏ 1814	Mr. Cool That Ain't Cool/Lovin' You Is So Easy	1974	—	3.50	7.00
❏ 1815	I Love, I Love/Your Love	1975	—	3.50	7.00
❏ 1816	Come and Get Your Love/I'll Live Her Life	1975	—	3.50	7.00
Albums					
WE PRODUCE					
❏ 1901	Love Men	1972	15.00	30.00	60.00
❏ 1903	Love Maze	1973	15.00	30.00	60.00
❏ 1905	Temprees 3	1974	15.00	30.00	60.00

TEMPTATIONS, THE The famous Detroit/Motown male vocal group. Also see EDDIE KENDRICKS; DAVID RUFFIN; THE SUPREMES AND THE TEMPTATIONS.

Number	Title (A Side/B Side)	Yr	VG	VG+	NM
12-Inch Singles					
GORDY					
❏ PR-68 [DJ]	Power (6:06)/Behind the Groove (6:04)	1980	6.25	12.50	25.00
—B-side by Teena Marie					
❏ PR-131 [DJ]	Miss Busy Body (Get Your Body Busy) (5:28)				
	(Instrumental Part 2 5:32)	1983	2.50	5.00	10.00
—No label name mentioned; listed here as the 45 was on Gordy					
❏ PR-163 [DJ]	Treat Her Like a Lady (Club Mix 6:10) (Dub				
	Reprise 3:45)/Let It All Blow (Club Mix 6:10)				
	(Blowy's Reprise Instrumental 4:48) (Radio				
	Edit of Club Mix 3:40)	1984	7.50	15.00	30.00
—B-side by Dazz Band; it also may have a "Motown" promo label					
❏ 4550GG	Do You Really Love Your Baby (Club Mix 6:36)				
	(Radio Edit of Club Mix 4:17) (Dub Mix 5:04)/				
	I'll Keep My Light in Your Window	1985	2.00	4.00	8.00
MOTOWN					
❏ PR-180 [DJ]	A Fine Mess (same on both sides)	1986	2.00	4.00	8.00
❏ 37463 1025 1 [DJ]	Hoops on Fire (3 versions)	1992	2.00	4.00	8.00
❏ 1132 [DJ]	Get Ready 1990 (4 versions)	1990	2.50	5.00	10.00
❏ 1604 [DJ]	The Jones' (4 versions)	1991	2.50	5.00	10.00
❏ 4590MG	Papa Was a Rollin' Stone (Vocal 8:57)				
	(Instrumental 7:15)	1987	—	—	—
—Canceled					
❏ 4598MG	Look What You Started (12-Inch Vocal 7:00)				
	(Radio Edit 4:40)//(12-Inch Piano Dub 7:03)				
	(12-Inch Beat Acapella 4:35)/				
	More Love, Your Love	1987	2.50	5.00	10.00
❏ MOT-4649	All I Want from You/(Instrumental)	1989	2.00	4.00	8.00
❏ MOT-4679	Special/O.A.O. Lover	1989	2.00	4.00	8.00
❏ MOT-4698	Soul to Soul (unknown versions)	1990	2.00	4.00	8.00
❏ L33-17880 [DJ]	All I Want from You (Club Mix)/				
	(Debbie Favorite Mix)	1989	2.00	4.00	8.00
❏ L33-18149 [DJ]	Soul to Soul (3 versions)	1990	2.50	5.00	10.00
❏ L33-18206 [DJ]	One Step at a Time (3 versions)	1990	2.50	5.00	10.00
❏ 20073 [DJ]	I'm Here (Radio Edit) (Instrumental)				
	(LP Version) (Acappella)	2000	3.75	7.50	15.00
❏ 53954	Get Ready 1990 (4 versions)	1990	2.50	5.00	10.00
45s					
ATLANTIC					
❏ 3436	In a Lifetime/I Could Never Stop Loving You	1977	—	2.00	4.00
❏ 3461	Think for Yourself/Let's Live in Place	1978	—	2.00	4.00
❏ 3517	Bare Back/I See My Child	1978	—	2.00	4.00
❏ 3538	Ever Ready Love/Touch Me Again	1978	—	2.00	4.00
❏ 3567	Mystic Woman/				
	I Just Don't Know How to Let You Go	1979	—	2.00	4.00
GORDY					
❏ 1616	Standing on the Top-Part 1/Part 2	1982	—	2.00	4.00
—With Rick James					
❏ 1631	More on the Inside/Money's Hard to Get	1982	—	2.00	4.00
❏ 1654	Silent Night/Everything for Christmas	1982	—	3.00	6.00
❏ 1666	Love on My Mind Tonight/Bring Your Body Here	1983	—	2.00	4.00
❏ 1683	Made in America/Surface Thrills	1983	—	2.00	4.00
❏ 1707	Miss Busy Body (Get Your Body Busy)/				
	(Instrumental)	1983	—	2.00	4.00
❏ 1713	Silent Night/Everything for Christmas	1983	—	2.50	5.00
❏ 1720	Sail Away/Isn't the Night Fantastic	1984	—	2.00	4.00
❏ 1765	Treat Her Like a Lady/Isn't the Night Fantastic	1984	—	2.00	4.00
❏ 1781	My Love Is True (Truly for You)/				
	Set Your Love Right	1985	—	2.00	4.00
❏ 1789	How Can You Say That It's Over/				
	I'll Keep My Light in My Window	1985	—	2.00	4.00
❏ 1818	Do You Really Love Your Baby/				
	I'll Keep My Light in My Window	1985	—	2.00	4.00
❏ 1834	Touch Me/Set Your Love Right	1986	—	2.00	4.00
❏ 1856	Lady Soul/Put Us Together Again	1986	—	2.00	4.00

Number	Title (A Side/B Side)	Yr	VG	VG+	NM
1871	To Be Continued/You're the One	1986	—	2.00	4.00
1871 [PS]	To Be Continued/You're the One	1986	—	3.00	6.00
1881	Someone/Love Me Right	1987	—	2.00	4.00
7001	Dream Come True/Isn't She Pretty	1962	10.00	20.00	40.00
7010	Paradise/Slow Down Heart	1962	7.50	15.00	30.00
7015	I Want a Love I Can See/The Further You Look, The Less You See	1963	6.25	12.50	25.00
7020	May I Have This Dance?/Farewell, My Love	1963	6.25	12.50	25.00
7028	The Way You Do the Things You Do/Just Let Me Know	1964	3.75	7.50	15.00
7032	I'll Be in Trouble/The Girl's Alright with Me	1964	3.75	7.50	15.00
7035	Girl (Why You Wanna Make Me Blue)/Baby, Baby I Need You	1964	3.75	7.50	15.00
7038	My Girl/Nobody But My Baby	1965	3.75	7.50	15.00
7038 [PS]	My Girl/Nobody But My Baby	1965	30.00	60.00	120.00
7040	It's Growing/What Love Has Joined Together	1965	3.75	7.50	15.00
7043	Since I Lost My Baby/You've Got to Earn It	1965	3.75	7.50	15.00
7047	My Baby/Don't Look Back	1965	3.75	7.50	15.00
7049	Get Ready/Fading Away	1966	3.75	7.50	15.00
7054	Ain't Too Proud to Beg/You'll Lose a Precious Love	1966	3.75	7.50	15.00
7055	Beauty Is Only Skin Deep/You're Not an Ordinary Girl	1966	3.75	7.50	15.00
7055 [PS]	Beauty Is Only Skin Deep/You're Not an Ordinary Girl	1966	10.00	20.00	40.00
7057	(I Know) I'm Losing You/I Couldn't Cry If I Wanted To	1966	3.75	7.50	15.00
7061	All I Need/Sorry Is a Sorry Word	1967	2.50	5.00	10.00
7063	You're My Everything/I've Been Good to You	1967	2.50	5.00	10.00

—"Gordy" on left

| 7063 | You're My Everything/I've Been Good to You | 1967 | 3.75 | 7.50 | 15.00 |

—"Gordy" on top

7065	(Loneliness Made Me Realize) It's You That I Need/Don't Send Me Away	1967	2.50	5.00	10.00
7068	I Wish It Would Rain/I Truly, Truly Believe	1967	2.50	5.00	10.00
7072	I Could Never Love Another (After Loving You)/Gonna Give Her All the Love I've Got	1968	2.50	5.00	10.00
7074	Please Return Your Love to Me/How Can I Forget	1968	2.50	5.00	10.00
7081	Cloud Nine/Why Did She Have to Leave Me	1968	2.00	4.00	8.00
7082	Silent Night/Rudolph, the Red-Nosed Reindeer	1968	3.00	6.00	12.00
7084	Run Away Child, Running Wild/I Need Your Love	1969	2.00	4.00	8.00
7086	Don't Let the Joneses Get You Down/Since I've Lost You	1969	2.00	4.00	8.00
7093	I Can't Get Next to You/Running Away (Ain't Gonna Help You)	1969	2.00	4.00	8.00
7096	Psychedelic Shack/That's the Way Love Is	1970	—	3.00	6.00
7099	Ball of Confusion (That's What the World Is Today)/It's Summer	1970	—	3.00	6.00
7099 [PS]	Ball of Confusion (That's What the World Is Today)/It's Summer	1970	5.00	10.00	20.00
7102	Ungena Za Ulimwengu (Unite the World)/Hum Along and Dance	1970	—	3.00	6.00
7105	Just My Imagination (Running Away with Me)/You Make Your Own Heaven and Hell Right Here on Earth	1971	—	3.00	6.00
7109	It's Summer/I'm the Exception to the Rule	1971	—	3.00	6.00
7111	Superstar (Remember How You Got Where You Are)/Gonna Keep On Tryin' Till I Win Your Love	1971	—	3.00	6.00
7115	Take a Look Around/Smooth Sailing (From Now On)	1972	—	3.00	6.00
7119	Mother Nature/Funky Music Sho Nuff Turns Me On	1972	—	3.00	6.00
7121	Papa Was a Rollin' Stone/(Instrumental)	1972	—	3.00	6.00
7126	Masterpiece/(Instrumental)	1973	—	3.00	6.00
7129	Plastic Man/Hurry Tomorrow	1973	—	3.00	6.00
7131	Hey Girl (I Like Your Style)/Ma	1973	—	3.00	6.00
7133	Let Your Hair Down/Ain't No Justice	1973	—	3.00	6.00
7135	Heavenly/Zoom	1974	—	3.00	6.00
7136	You've Got My Soul on Fire/I Need You	1974	—	3.00	6.00
7138	Happy People/(Instrumental)	1974	—	3.00	6.00
7142	Shakey Ground/I'm a Bachelor	1975	—	3.00	6.00
7144	Glasshouse/The Prophet	1975	—	3.00	6.00
7146	Keep Holding On/What You Need Most (I Do Best of All)	1975	—	3.00	6.00
7150	Up the Creek (Without a Paddle)/Darling Stand By Me (Song for a Woman)	1976	—	3.00	6.00
7151	Who Are You (And What Are You Doing the Rest of Your Life)/Darling Stand By Me (Song for a Woman)	1976	—	—	—

—Unreleased

7152	Let Me Count the Ways (I Love You)/Who Are You (And What Are You Doing the Rest of Your Life)	1976	—	3.00	6.00
7183	Power/Power (Part 2)	1980	—	2.00	4.00
7183 [DJ]	Power (same on both sides)	1980	5.00	10.00	20.00

—Promo only on red vinyl

7188	Struck by Lightning Twice/I'm Coming Home	1980	—	2.00	4.00
7208	Aiming at Your Heart/Life of a Cowboy	1981	—	2.00	4.00
7213	Oh What a Night/Isn't the Night Fantastic	1981	—	2.00	4.00

MIRACLE

Number	Title (A Side/B Side)	Yr	VG	VG+	NM
5	Oh, Mother of Mine/Romance Without Finance	1961	25.00	50.00	100.00
12	Check Yourself/Your Wonderful Love	1961	25.00	50.00	100.00

MOTOWN

Number	Title (A Side/B Side)	Yr	VG	VG+	NM
903	One Step at a Time/(Instrumental)	1990	—	2.00	4.00
1501	Take Me Away/There's More Where That Came From	1980	—	2.00	4.00
1837	A Fine Mess/Wishful Thinking	1986	—	2.00	4.00
1837 [PS]	A Fine Mess/Wishful Thinking	1986	—	3.00	6.00
1908	I Wonder Who She's Seeing Now/Girls (They Like It)	1987	—	—	3.00
1908 [PS]	I Wonder Who She's Seeing Now/Girls (They Like It)	1987	—	2.00	4.00
1920	Look What You Started/More Love, Your Love	1987	—	—	3.00
1933	Do You Wanna Go with Me/Put Your Foot Down	1988	—	—	3.00
1974	All I Want from You/(Instrumental)	1989	—	—	3.00
2004	Special/O.A.O. Lover	1989	—	2.00	4.00
2023	Soul to Soul (same on both sides?)	1990	—	2.00	4.00
860862-7	Stay/My Girl	1998	—	—	3.00

MOTOWN YESTERYEAR

Number	Title (A Side/B Side)	Yr	VG	VG+	NM
690	Silent Night/Everything for Christmas	198?	—	2.00	4.00

TOPPS/MOTOWN

Number	Title (A Side/B Side)	Yr	VG	VG+	NM
4	My Girl	1967	18.75	37.50	75.00

—Cardboard record

| 13 | The Way You Do the Things You Do | 1967 | 18.75 | 37.50 | 75.00 |

—Cardboard record

Albums

ATLANTIC

Number	Title	Yr	VG	VG+	NM
SD 19143	Hear to Tempt You	1977	3.00	6.00	12.00
SD 19188	Bare Back	1978	3.00	6.00	12.00

GORDY

Number	Title	Yr	VG	VG+	NM
G 911 [M]	Meet the Temptations	1964	7.50	15.00	30.00
GS 911 [S]	Meet the Temptations	1964	10.00	20.00	40.00

—Script "Gordy" at top of label

| GS 911 [S] | Meet the Temptations | 1967 | 5.00 | 10.00 | 20.00 |

—Block "GORDY" inside "G" on left of label

| G 912 [M] | The Temptations Sing Smokey | 1965 | 7.50 | 15.00 | 30.00 |
| GS 912 [S] | The Temptations Sing Smokey | 1965 | 10.00 | 20.00 | 40.00 |

—Script "Gordy" at top of label

| GS 912 [S] | The Temptations Sing Smokey | 1967 | 5.00 | 10.00 | 20.00 |

—Block "GORDY" inside "G" on left of label

| G 914 [M] | Temptin' Temptations | 1965 | 6.25 | 12.50 | 25.00 |
| GS 914 [S] | Temptin' Temptations | 1965 | 7.50 | 15.00 | 30.00 |

—Script "Gordy" at top of label

| GS 914 [S] | Temptin' Temptations | 1967 | 5.00 | 10.00 | 20.00 |

—Block "GORDY" inside "G" on left of label

| G 918 [M] | Gettin' Ready | 1966 | 6.25 | 12.50 | 25.00 |
| GS 918 [S] | Gettin' Ready | 1966 | 7.50 | 15.00 | 30.00 |

—Script "Gordy" at top of label

| GS 918 [S] | Gettin' Ready | 1967 | 5.00 | 10.00 | 20.00 |

—Block "GORDY" inside "G" on left of label

| G 919 [M] | The Temptations' Greatest Hits | 1966 | 6.25 | 12.50 | 25.00 |
| GS 919 [S] | The Temptations' Greatest Hits | 1966 | 7.50 | 15.00 | 30.00 |

—Script "Gordy" at top of label

| GS 919 [S] | The Temptations' Greatest Hits | 1967 | 5.00 | 10.00 | 20.00 |

—Block "GORDY" inside "G" on left of label

| G 921 [M] | Temptations Live! | 1967 | 6.25 | 12.50 | 25.00 |
| GS 921 [S] | Temptations Live! | 1967 | 5.00 | 10.00 | 20.00 |

—Block "GORDY" inside "G" on left of label

| GS 921 [S] | Temptations Live! | 1967 | 7.50 | 15.00 | 30.00 |

—Script "Gordy" at top of label

| G 922 [M] | With a Lot o' Soul | 1967 | 6.25 | 12.50 | 25.00 |
| GS 922 [S] | With a Lot o' Soul | 1967 | 5.00 | 10.00 | 20.00 |

—Block "GORDY" inside "G" on left of label

| GS 922 [S] | With a Lot o' Soul | 1967 | 6.25 | 12.50 | 25.00 |

—Script "Gordy" at top of label

G 924 [M]	The Temptations in a Mellow Mood	1967	6.25	12.50	25.00
GS 924 [S]	The Temptations in a Mellow Mood	1967	6.25	12.50	25.00
G 927 [M]	The Temptations Wish It Would Rain	1968	10.00	20.00	40.00

—Mono is white-label promo only

GS 927 [S]	The Temptations Wish It Would Rain	1968	5.00	10.00	20.00
GS 933	The Temptations Show	1969	5.00	10.00	20.00
GS 938	Live at the Copa	1968	5.00	10.00	20.00
GS 939	Cloud Nine	1969	5.00	10.00	20.00
GS 947	Psychedelic Shack	1970	5.00	10.00	20.00
GS 949	Puzzle People	1969	5.00	10.00	20.00
GS 951	The Temptations' Christmas Card	1969	6.25	12.50	25.00
GS 953	Live at London's Talk of the Town	1970	5.00	10.00	20.00
GS 954	Temptations Greatest Hits II	1970	5.00	10.00	20.00
GS 957	Sky's the Limit	1971	5.00	10.00	20.00
G 961L	Solid Rock	1972	5.00	10.00	20.00
G 962L	All Directions	1972	5.00	10.00	20.00
G 965L	Masterpiece	1973	5.00	10.00	20.00
G 966V1	1990	1973	3.75	7.50	15.00
G6-969S1	A Song for You	1975	3.75	7.50	15.00
G6-971S1	Wings of Love	1976	3.75	7.50	15.00
G6-973S1	House Party	1975	3.75	7.50	15.00
G7-975S1	The Temptations Do the Temptations	1976	3.75	7.50	15.00
G8-994M1	Power	1980	3.00	6.00	12.00
G8-998M1	Give Love at Christmas	1980	3.75	7.50	15.00
G8-1006M1	The Temptations	1981	3.00	6.00	12.00
6008 GL	Reunion	1982	3.00	6.00	12.00
6032 GL	Surface Thrills	1983	3.00	6.00	12.00
6085 GL	Back to Basics	1984	3.00	6.00	12.00
6119 GL	Truly for You	1984	3.00	6.00	12.00
6164 GL	Touch Me	1986	3.00	6.00	12.00
6207 GL	To Be Continued	1986	3.00	6.00	12.00

MOTOWN

Number	Title	Yr	VG	VG+	NM
M5-140V1	Meet the Temptations	1981	3.00	6.00	12.00

—Reissue of Gordy 911

| M5-144V1 | Masterpiece | 1981 | 3.00 | 6.00 | 12.00 |

—Reissue of Gordy 965

| M5-159V1 | Cloud Nine | 1981 | 3.00 | 6.00 | 12.00 |

—Reissue of Gordy 939

| M5-164V1 | Psychedelic Shack | 1981 | 3.00 | 6.00 | 12.00 |

—Reissue of Gordy 947

| M5-172V1 | Puzzle People | 1981 | 3.00 | 6.00 | 12.00 |

—Reissue of Gordy 949

| M5-205V1 | The Temptations Sing Smokey | 1981 | 3.00 | 6.00 | 12.00 |

—Reissue of Gordy 912

M5-212V1	All the Million Sellers	1982	3.00	6.00	12.00
M 782 [(3)]	Anthology	1973	6.25	12.50	25.00
5251 ML	The Temptations Christmas Card	1982	2.50	5.00	10.00

—Reissue of Gordy 951

| 5279 ML | Give Love at Christmas | 1983 | 2.50 | 5.00 | 10.00 |

—Reissue of Gordy 998

5389 ML [(2)]	25th Anniversary	1986	3.75	7.50	15.00
6246 ML	Together Again	1987	3.00	6.00	12.00
MOT-6275	Special	1989	3.00	6.00	12.00

NATURAL RESOURCES

Number	Title	Yr	VG	VG+	NM
NR 4005T1	The Temptations in a Mellow Mood	1978	3.00	6.00	12.00

—Reissue of Gordy 924

Number	Title (A Side/B Side)	Yr	VG	VG+	NM
PICKWICK					
❑ SPC-3540	Psychedelic Shack	197?	3.00	6.00	12.00
—*Reissue of Gordy 947*					
TEMPTATIONS, THE (2) *White doo-wop group.*					
45s					
GOLDISC					
❑ 3001	Barbara/Someday	1960	5.00	10.00	20.00
—*Multicolor (black, red, gold) label*					
❑ 3001	Barbara/Someday	1960	7.50	15.00	30.00
—*All-black label*					
❑ 3007	Letter of Devotion/Fickle Little Girl	1960	6.25	12.50	25.00
TEMPTATIONS, THE (3)					
45s					
KING					
❑ 5118	Standing Alone/Roaches Rock	1958	75.00	150.00	300.00
TEMPTATIONS, THE (4)					
45s					
PARKWAY					
❑ 803	Temptations/Birds N' Bees	1959	7.50	15.00	30.00
TEMPTATIONS, THE (5)					
45s					
P&L					
❑ 1001	Blue Surf/Egyptian Surf	1963	15.00	30.00	60.00
TEMPTATIONS, THE (6)					
45s					
SAVOY					
❑ 1532	Mister Juke Box/Mad at Love	1958	5.00	10.00	20.00
❑ 1550	I Love You/Don't You Know	1958	5.00	10.00	20.00
TEMPTONES, THE *DARYL HALL was in this group.*					
45s					
ARCTIC					
❑ 130	Girl, I Love You/Good-Bye	1967	10.00	20.00	40.00
❑ 136	Say These Words of Love/This Could Be the Start of Something Good	1967	10.00	20.00	40.00
TEN BROKEN HEARTS *Allegedly, NEIL DIAMOND appears on this record.*					
45s					
DIAMOND					
❑ 123	Ten Lonely Guys/Shining Star	1962	10.00	20.00	40.00
10CC *Also see GRAHAM GOULDMAN; HOTLEGS.*					
45s					
MERCURY					
❑ 73678	I'm Not in Love/Channel Swimmer	1975	—	2.50	5.00
❑ 73725	Art for Art's Sake/Get It While You Can	1975	—	2.50	5.00
❑ 73725 [PS]	Art for Art's Sake/Get It While You Can	1975	2.00	4.00	8.00
❑ 73779	I'm Mandy Fly Me/How Dare You	1976	—	2.50	5.00
❑ 73875	The Things We Do for Love/Hot to Trot	1976	—	2.50	5.00
❑ 73917	People in Love/Don't Squeeze Me Like Toothpaste	1977	—	2.50	5.00
❑ 73943	Good Morning Judge/I'm So Laid Back I'm Laid Out	1977	—	2.50	5.00
❑ 73980	You've Got a Cold/The Wall Street Shuffle	1977	—	2.50	5.00
POLYDOR					
❑ 14511	Dreadlock Holiday/Nothing Can Move Me	1978	—	2.50	5.00
❑ 14528	For You and I/Take These Chains	1978	—	2.50	5.00
UK					
❑ 49005	Donna/Hot Sun Rock	1972	—	3.00	6.00
❑ 49015	Ruber Bullets/Waterfall	1973	—	3.00	6.00
❑ 49019	Headline Hustler/Speed Kills	1973	—	3.00	6.00
❑ 49023	The Wall Street Shuffle/Gismo My Way	1974	—	3.00	6.00
WARNER BROS.					
❑ 29973	Power of Love/Action Man in Motown Suit	1982	—	2.50	5.00
❑ 49266	It Doesn't Matter Anymore/Strange Lover	1980	—	2.50	5.00
Albums					
MERCURY					
❑ SRM-1-1029	The Original Soundtrack	1975	3.00	6.00	12.00
❑ SRM-1-1061	How Dare You!	1976	3.00	6.00	12.00
❑ SRM-1-3702	Deceptive Bends	1977	3.00	6.00	12.00
❑ SRM-2-8600 [(2)]	Live and Let Live	1977	3.75	7.50	15.00
POLYDOR					
❑ PD-1-6161	Bloody Tourists	1978	2.50	5.00	10.00
❑ PD-1-6244	Greatest Hits 1972-1978	1979	2.50	5.00	10.00
U.K.					
❑ 53105	10cc	1973	3.75	7.50	15.00
❑ AUKS 53107	Sheet Music	1974	3.75	7.50	15.00
❑ 53110	100cc	1975	3.75	7.50	15.00
WARNER BROS.					
❑ BSK 3442	Look Hear?	1980	2.50	5.00	10.00
❑ BSK 3575	Ten Out of Ten	1981	2.50	5.00	10.00
TEN WHEEL DRIVE					
45s					
CAPITOL					
❑ 3700	Monsoon Rain/Close Up the Cheese	1973	—	2.50	5.00
POLYDOR					
❑ 14015	Tightrope/Lapidary	1969	—	2.50	5.00
❑ 14024	Eye of the Needle/I Am a Want Ad	1970	—	2.50	5.00
❑ 14037	Morning Much Better/Stay with Me	1970	—	2.50	5.00
❑ 14052	Don't Blame Me/20 Miles from Home	1971	—	2.50	5.00
Albums					
CAPITOL					
❑ ST-11199	Ten Wheel Drive	1973	2.50	5.00	10.00
POLYDOR					
❑ 24-4008	Construction #1	1969	3.00	6.00	12.00
❑ 24-4024	Brief Replies	1970	3.00	6.00	12.00
❑ 24-4062	Peculiar Friends	1971	3.00	6.00	12.00

Number	Title (A Side/B Side)	Yr	VG	VG+	NM
TEN YEARS AFTER					
45s					
COLUMBIA					
❑ 45457	I'd Love to Change the World/Let the Sky Fall	1971	—	2.50	5.00
❑ 45530	Baby Won't You Let Me Rock 'N' Roll You/Once There Was a Time	1972	—	2.50	5.00
❑ 45736	You Can't Win Them All/Choo Choo Mama	1972	—	2.50	5.00
❑ 45787	Tomorrow, I'll Be Out of Town/Convention Prevention	1973	—	2.50	5.00
❑ 45915	I'm Going Home/You Give Me Loving	1973	—	2.50	5.00
❑ 46061	It's Getting Harder/I Wanted to Boogie	1974	—	2.50	5.00
DERAM					
❑ 7529	If You Should Love Me/Love Like a Man	1970	2.00	4.00	8.00
❑ 85027	Portable People/The Sounds	1968	2.00	4.00	8.00
❑ 85035	Hear Me Calling/I'm Going Home	1968	2.00	4.00	8.00
Albums					
CHRYSALIS					
❑ CHS 1083	Ssssh	1975	2.50	5.00	10.00
❑ CHS 1084	Cricklewood Green	1975	2.50	5.00	10.00
❑ CHS 1085	Watt	1975	2.50	5.00	10.00
❑ F1-21001	A Space in Time	1989	2.00	4.00	8.00
❑ F1-21009	Rock and Roll Music to the World	1989	2.00	4.00	8.00
❑ F1-21083	Ssssh	1989	2.00	4.00	8.00
❑ F1-21084	Cricklewood Green	1989	2.00	4.00	8.00
❑ F1-21085	Watt	1989	2.00	4.00	8.00
❑ F1-21573	Positive Vibrations	1989	2.00	4.00	8.00
❑ F1-21580	Universal	1989	2.00	4.00	8.00
❑ F1-21722	About Time	1989	3.00	6.00	12.00
❑ PV 41001	A Space in Time	1987	2.00	4.00	8.00
❑ PV 41009	Rock and Roll Music to the World	1987	2.00	4.00	8.00
❑ FV 41049 [(2)]	Recorded Live	1987	2.50	5.00	10.00
❑ PV 41083	Ssssh	1983	2.00	4.00	8.00
❑ PV 41084	Cricklewood Green	1983	2.00	4.00	8.00
❑ PV 41085	Watt	1983	2.00	4.00	8.00
❑ PV 41573	Positive Vibrations	1987	2.00	4.00	8.00
❑ FV 41580	Universal	1988	2.50	5.00	10.00
COLUMBIA					
❑ CQ 30801 [Q]	A Space in Time	1973	4.00	8.00	16.00
❑ KC 30801	A Space in Time	1971	3.00	6.00	12.00
❑ PC 30801	A Space in Time	1979	2.00	4.00	8.00
❑ C 31779	Rock and Roll Music to the World	197?	2.50	5.00	10.00
—*Reissue with new prefix*					
❑ KC 31779	Rock and Roll Music to the World	1972	3.00	6.00	12.00
❑ C2X 32288 [(2)]	Recorded Live	1973	3.75	7.50	15.00
❑ PC 32851	Positive Vibrations	1974	2.50	5.00	10.00
❑ PC 34366	Classic Performances of Ten Years After	1976	2.50	5.00	10.00
DERAM					
❑ DE 16009 [M]	Ten Years After	1968	12.50	25.00	50.00
❑ DES 18009 [S]	Ten Years After	1968	5.00	10.00	20.00
❑ DES 18016	Undead	1968	3.75	7.50	15.00
❑ DES 18021	Stonedhenge	1969	3.75	7.50	15.00
❑ DES 18029	Ssssh	1969	3.75	7.50	15.00
❑ DES 18038	Cricklewood Green	1970	3.75	7.50	15.00
❑ XDES 18050	Watt	1970	3.75	7.50	15.00
—*With large "DERAM" on top half of label*					
❑ XDES 18050	Watt	1970	6.25	12.50	25.00
—*With "LONDON" under smaller "DERAM" at top of label*					
❑ XDES 18064	Alvin Lee and Company	1972	3.00	6.00	12.00
❑ DES 18072	Goin' Home! Their Greatest Hits	1975	3.00	6.00	12.00
❑ SMAS-93428	Watt	1970	5.00	10.00	20.00
—*Capitol Record Club edition*					
LONDON					
❑ LC 50008	Greatest Hits	1977	2.50	5.00	10.00
❑ 820324-1	Greatest Hits	1986	2.00	4.00	8.00
TENDER SLIM					
45s					
GREY CLIFF					
❑ 723	Teenage Hayride/Hey Joe!	1959	3.75	7.50	15.00
HERALD					
❑ 571	Don't Cut Out on Me/I'm Checkin' Up	1962	3.75	7.50	15.00
TENDER TONES, THE					
45s					
DUCKY					
❑ 713	I Love You So/Just for a Little While	1959	200.00	400.00	800.00
TENDERFOOTS, THE					
45s					
FEDERAL					
❑ 12214	Kissing Bug/Watussi Wussi Wo	1955	15.00	30.00	60.00
❑ 12219	My Confession/Save Me Some Kisses	1955	15.00	30.00	60.00
❑ 12225	Those Golden Bells/I'm Yours Anyhow	1955	20.00	40.00	80.00
❑ 12228	Sindy/Sugar Ways	1955	30.00	60.00	120.00
TENNESSEE DRIFTERS, THE					
45s					
DOT					
❑ 1166	Boogie Woogie Baby/Drive Those Blues Away	1953	7.50	15.00	30.00
❑ 1187	Corrine, Corrina/Somebody Loves You	1954	7.50	15.00	30.00
TENNESSEE ERNIE *See TENNESSEE ERNIE FORD.*					
TENNESSEE GUITARS, THE					
45s					
SUN					
❑ 1102	Tennessee Toddy/Trophy Run	1969	—	3.00	6.00
TENNESSEE SIX AND FOUR MORE, THE					
45s					
HIT					
❑ 89	Down at Papa Joe's/I'm Leaving It Up to You	1963	2.00	4.00	8.00
—*B-side by Dotty and Dan*					

Number	Title (A Side/B Side)	Yr	VG	VG+	NM

TERMITES, THE
45s
BEE

| ❏ 1825 | Give Me Your Heart/Carrie Lou | 1964 | 12.50 | 25.00 | 50.00 |

TERRACETONES, THE
45s
APT

| ❏ 25016 | Words of Wisdom/Ride of Paul Revere | 1958 | 25.00 | 50.00 | 100.00 |

TERRELL, ERNIE
45s
ARGO

| ❏ 5511 | Dear Abbie/I Can't Wait | 1965 | 3.00 | 6.00 | 12.00 |

TERRELL, TAMMI Also see MARVIN GAYE AND TAMMI TERRELL; TAMMY MONTGOMERY.
45s
MOTOWN

❏ 1086	I Can't Believe You Love Me/Hold Me Oh My Darling	1965	2.50	5.00	10.00
❏ 1095	Come On and See Me/Baby Don'tcha Worry	1966	2.50	5.00	10.00
❏ 1115	What a Good Man He Is/There Are Things	1967	2.50	5.00	10.00
❏ 1138	This Old Heart of Mine (Is Weak for You)/Just Too Much to Hope For	1968	2.50	5.00	10.00

Albums
MOTOWN

| ❏ M5-231V1 | Irresistible Tammi | 1982 | 2.50 | 5.00 | 10.00 |
| ❏ MS-652 | Irresistible Tammi | 1969 | 12.50 | 25.00 | 50.00 |

TERRI AND THE KITTENS
45s
IMPERIAL

| ❏ 5728 | Wedding Bells/You Cheated | 1961 | 5.00 | 10.00 | 20.00 |

TERRI AND THE VELVETEENS
45s
KERWOOD

| ❏ 711 | Bells of Love/You've Broken My Heart | 1962 | 10.00 | 20.00 | 40.00 |

TERRI-TONES, THE
45s
CORTLAND

| ❏ 105 | Go/The Sinner | 1962 | 12.50 | 25.00 | 50.00 |

REGENCY

| ❏ 929 | Go/The Sinner | 1962 | 7.50 | 15.00 | 30.00 |

TERRY, DON
45s
LIN

| ❏ 5018 | Knees Shakin'/She Giggles | 1959 | 37.50 | 75.00 | 150.00 |

TERRY, DOSSIE
45s
KING

| ❏ 5072 | Thunderbird/I Got a Watch Dog | 1957 | 12.50 | 25.00 | 50.00 |
| ❏ 5890 | Thunderbird/Be-Bop Wino | 1964 | 3.75 | 7.50 | 15.00 |

—B-side by the Lamplighters
RCA VICTOR

❏ 47-4474	Didn't Satisfy You/24 Years	1952	15.00	30.00	60.00
❏ 47-4648	When I Hit the Number/My Love Is Gone	1952	15.00	30.00	60.00
❏ 47-4864	Lost My Head/Sad, Sad Affair	1952	15.00	30.00	60.00

TERRY, GENE
45s
GOLDBAND

❏ 1066	Cindy Lou/Teardrops in My Eyes	1958	30.00	60.00	120.00
❏ 1081	Never Let Her Go/No Mail Today	1958	10.00	20.00	40.00
❏ 1088	Cinderella, Cinderella/Guy with a Million Dreams	1959	7.50	15.00	30.00

SAVOY

| ❏ 1559 | This Should Go On Forever/Fine, Fine, Fine | 1959 | 5.00 | 10.00 | 20.00 |

TERRY, LARRY
45s
TESTA

| ❏ 006 | Hep Cat/Why Did She Go | 1960 | 300.00 | 600.00 | 1200. |

TERRY, NAT
45s
IMPERIAL

| ❏ 5150 | Take It Easy/I Don't Know Why | 1951 | 25.00 | 50.00 | 100.00 |

TERRY, SONNY
45s
CAPITOL

| ❏ F931 | Telephone Blues/Dirty Mistreater Don't You Know | 1950 | 30.00 | 60.00 | 120.00 |

CHESS

| ❏ 1860 | Dangerous Woman/Hootenanny Blues | 1963 | 5.00 | 10.00 | 20.00 |

CHOICE

| ❏ 15 | Hootin'/Dupre | 1961 | 5.00 | 10.00 | 20.00 |

GOTHAM

| ❏ 517 | Baby Let's Have Some Fun/Four O'Clock Blues | 1951 | 10.00 | 20.00 | 40.00 |
| ❏ 518 | Harmonica Rhumba/Lonesome Room | 1951 | 10.00 | 20.00 | 40.00 |

GRAMERCY

| ❏ 1004 | Hootin' Blues/(B-side unknown) | 1952 | 12.50 | 25.00 | 50.00 |

—Black vinyl

| ❏ 1004 | Hootin' Blues/(B-side unknown) | 1952 | 25.00 | 50.00 | 100.00 |

—Colored vinyl
GROOVE

| ❏ 0015 | Lost Jawbone/Louise | 1954 | 7.50 | 15.00 | 30.00 |
| ❏ 0135 | Ride and Roll/Hootin' Blues #2 | 1956 | 7.50 | 15.00 | 30.00 |

HARLEM

| ❏ 2327 | Dangerous Woman/I Love You Baby | 1954 | 75.00 | 150.00 | 300.00 |

JAX

| ❏ 305 | I Don't Worry (Sittin' on Top of the World)/Man Ain't Nothin' But a Fool | 195? | 100.00 | 200.00 | 400.00 |

—Colored vinyl

OLD TOWN

| ❏ 1023 | Uncle Bud/Climbing on Top of the Hill | 1956 | 6.25 | 12.50 | 25.00 |

RCA VICTOR

| ❏ 47-5492 | Hootin' and Jumpin'/Hooray, Hooray | 1953 | 25.00 | 50.00 | 100.00 |
| ❏ 47-5577 | Sonny Is Drinking/I'm Gonna Rock My Wig | 1954 | 25.00 | 50.00 | 100.00 |

RED ROBIN

| ❏ 110 | Harmonica Hop/Doggin' My Heart Around | 1952 | 75.00 | 150.00 | 300.00 |

Albums
ALLIGATOR

| ❏ AL-4734 | Whoopin' | 198? | 3.00 | 6.00 | 12.00 |

—With Johnny Winter, Willie Dixon and others
BLUE LABOR

| ❏ 101 | Robbin' the Grave | 197? | 3.00 | 6.00 | 12.00 |

BLUESVILLE

| ❏ BVLP-1025 [M] | Sonny's Story | 1961 | 20.00 | 40.00 | 80.00 |

—Bright blue label, no trident logo

| ❏ BVLP-1025 [M] | Sonny's Story | 1964 | 6.25 | 12.50 | 25.00 |

—Blue label with trident logo on right

| ❏ BVLP-1069 [M] | Sonny Is King | 1963 | 20.00 | 40.00 | 80.00 |

—Bright blue label, no trident logo

| ❏ BVLP-1069 [M] | Sonny Is King | 1964 | 6.25 | 12.50 | 25.00 |

—Blue label with trident logo on right
COLLECTABLES

| ❏ COL-5195 | Chain Gang Blues | 198? | 2.50 | 5.00 | 10.00 |
| ❏ COL-5307 | Sonny Terry | 198? | 2.50 | 5.00 | 10.00 |

ELEKTRA

| ❏ EKL-14 [10] | Folk Blues | 1954 | 37.50 | 75.00 | 150.00 |
| ❏ EKL-15 [10] | City Blues | 1954 | 37.50 | 75.00 | 150.00 |

—With Alec Stewart
FANTASY

| ❏ OBC-521 | Sonny Is King | 198? | 2.50 | 5.00 | 10.00 |

FOLKWAYS

| ❏ FP-35 [10] | Harmonica and Vocal Solos | 1952 | 37.50 | 75.00 | 150.00 |
| ❏ FA-2006 [10] | Sonny Terry's Washboard Band | 195? | 25.00 | 50.00 | 100.00 |

—Black and white cover (reissue)

| ❏ FP-2006 [10] | Sonny Terry's Washboard Band | 1950 | 37.50 | 75.00 | 150.00 |

—Blue and white cover

❏ FA-2035 [10]	Harmonica and Vocal Solos	1952	25.00	50.00	100.00
❏ FS-2369	On the Road	196?	3.75	7.50	15.00
❏ 3821	A New Sound	198?	3.00	6.00	12.00

PRESTIGE

| ❏ PRST-7802 | Sonny Is King | 1970 | 3.75 | 7.50 | 15.00 |

RIVERSIDE

| ❏ RLP-644 [M] | Sonny Terry and His Mouth Harp | 195? | 20.00 | 40.00 | 80.00 |

STINSON

| ❏ 55 | Sonny Terry and His Mouth Harp | 197? | 3.00 | 6.00 | 12.00 |

—Reissue of 10-inch LP

| ❏ SLP-55 [10] | Sonny Terry and His Mouth Harp | 1950 | 37.50 | 75.00 | 150.00 |

TERRY, SONNY, AND BROWNIE MCGHEE Also see each artist's individual listings.
45s
BLUESVILLE

❏ 802	Let Me Be Your Big Dig/Stranger Here	196?	5.00	10.00	20.00
❏ 809	Pawnshop/Too Nicey Mama	196?	5.00	10.00	20.00
❏ 818	Freight Train/Beggin' and Tryin'	196?	5.00	10.00	20.00

CHOICE

| ❏ 1 | John Henry/Oh Lawdy Pick a Bale of Cotton | 196? | 5.00 | 10.00 | 20.00 |

—As "Brownie & Sonny"

| ❏ 7 | Study War No More/I'm Gonna Tell God | 196? | 5.00 | 10.00 | 20.00 |

—As "Brownie & Sonny"
Albums
A&M

| ❏ SP-4379 | Sonny & Brownie | 1973 | 3.00 | 6.00 | 12.00 |

ARCHIVE OF FOLK MUSIC

| ❏ 242 | Brownie & Sonny | 198? | 3.00 | 6.00 | 12.00 |

BLUESVILLE

| ❏ BVLP-1002 [M] | Down Home Blues | 1960 | 20.00 | 40.00 | 80.00 |

—Bright blue label, no trident logo

| ❏ BVLP-1002 [M] | Down Home Blues | 1964 | 6.25 | 12.50 | 25.00 |

—Blue label with trident logo on right

| ❏ BVLP-1005 [M] | Blues and Folk | 1960 | 20.00 | 40.00 | 80.00 |

—Bright blue label, no trident logo

| ❏ BVLP-1005 [M] | Blues and Folk | 1964 | 6.25 | 12.50 | 25.00 |

—Blue label with trident logo on right

| ❏ BVLP-1020 [M] | Blues All Around My Head | 1961 | 20.00 | 40.00 | 80.00 |

—Bright blue label, no trident logo

| ❏ BVLP-1020 [M] | Blues All Around My Head | 1964 | 6.25 | 12.50 | 25.00 |

—Blue label with trident logo on right

| ❏ BVLP-1033 [M] | Blues in My Soul | 1961 | 20.00 | 40.00 | 80.00 |

—Bright blue label, no trident logo

| ❏ BVLP-1033 [M] | Blues in My Soul | 1964 | 6.25 | 12.50 | 25.00 |

—Blue label with trident logo on right

| ❏ BVLP-1058 [M] | Live at the Second Fret | 1962 | 20.00 | 40.00 | 80.00 |

—Bright blue label, no trident logo

| ❏ BVLP-1058 [M] | Live at the Second Fret | 1964 | 6.25 | 12.50 | 25.00 |

—Blue label with trident logo on right
BLUESWAY

| ❏ BLS-6028 | Long Way from Home | 1969 | 3.75 | 7.50 | 15.00 |
| ❏ BLS-6059 | Couldn't Believe My Eyes | 1970 | 3.75 | 7.50 | 15.00 |

COLLECTABLES

| ❏ COL-5198 | Golden Classics: Blowin' the Fuses | 198? | 2.50 | 5.00 | 10.00 |

EVEREST

| ❏ 206 | Sonny Terry | 1968 | 6.25 | 12.50 | 25.00 |
| ❏ 242 | Brownie McGhee and Sonny Terry | 1969 | 6.25 | 12.50 | 25.00 |

FANTASY

❏ OBC-503	Sonny's Story	1984	2.50	5.00	10.00
❏ OBC-505	Brownie's Blues	1984	2.50	5.00	10.00
❏ F-3254 [M]	Sonny Terry & Brownie McGhee	1961	10.00	20.00	40.00

—Black vinyl

| ❏ F-3254 [M] | Sonny Terry & Brownie McGhee | 1961 | 37.50 | 75.00 | 150.00 |

—Red vinyl

| ❏ F-3296 [M] | Just a Closer Walk with Thee | 1962 | 10.00 | 20.00 | 40.00 |

—Black vinyl

| ❏ F-3296 [M] | Just a Closer Walk with Thee | 1962 | 37.50 | 75.00 | 150.00 |

—Red vinyl

T

Number	Title (A Side/B Side)	Yr	VG	VG+	NM
❑ F-3317 [M]	Blues and Shouts	1962	10.00	20.00	40.00
—Black vinyl					
❑ F-3317 [M]	Blues and Shouts	1962	37.50	75.00	150.00
—Red vinyl					
❑ F-3340 [M]	Sonny and Brownie at Sugar Hill	1962	10.00	20.00	40.00
—Black vinyl					
❑ F-3340 [M]	Sonny and Brownie at Sugar Hill	1962	37.50	75.00	150.00
—Red vinyl					
❑ FS-8091 [S]	Sonny and Brownie at Sugar Hill	1962	10.00	20.00	40.00
—Black vinyl					
❑ FS-8091 [S]	Sonny and Brownie at Sugar Hill	1962	37.50	75.00	150.00
—Blue vinyl					
❑ 24708 [(2)]	Back to New Orleans	1972	3.75	7.50	15.00
❑ 24721 [(2)]	Midnight Special	1977	3.75	7.50	15.00
❑ 24723 [(2)]	California Blues	1981	3.75	7.50	15.00
FOLKLORE					
❑ FRLP-14013 [M]	Down Home Blues	1964	10.00	20.00	40.00
❑ FRST-14013 [S]	Down Home Blues	1964	12.50	25.00	50.00
FOLKWAYS					
❑ FA-2327 [M]	Blues and Folk Songs	1960	7.50	15.00	30.00
❑ F-2421 [M]	Traditional Blues, Volume 1	1961	7.50	15.00	30.00
❑ FS-2421 [S]	Traditional Blues, Volume 1	1961	10.00	20.00	40.00
❑ F-2422 [M]	Traditional Blues, Volume 2	1961	7.50	15.00	30.00
❑ FS-2422 [S]	Traditional Blues, Volume 2	1961	10.00	20.00	40.00
FONTANA					
❑ SGF-67599	Where the Blues Begin	1969	6.25	12.50	25.00
KIMBERLEY					
❑ 2017 [M]	Southern Meetin'	1963	5.00	10.00	20.00
❑ 11017 [S]	Southern Meetin'	1963	6.25	12.50	25.00
MAINSTREAM					
❑ M-6049 [M]	Hometown Blues	1966	5.00	10.00	20.00
❑ MS-6049 [S]	Hometown Blues	1966	6.25	12.50	25.00
MOBILE FIDELITY					
❑ 1-233	Sonny and Brownie	1996	5.00	10.00	20.00
—Audiophile vinyl					
MUSE					
❑ 5117	Hootin'	198?	3.00	6.00	12.00
❑ 5131	You Hear Me Talkin'	198?	3.00	6.00	12.00
OLYMPIC					
❑ 7108	Hootin' & Hollerin'	1972	3.00	6.00	12.00
PRESTIGE					
❑ PRLP-7715	Best of Sonny Terry and Brownie McGhee	1969	3.75	7.50	15.00
❑ PRLP-7803	Live at the Second Fret	1970	3.75	7.50	15.00
ROULETTE					
❑ R-25074 [M]	The Folk Songs of Sonny & Brownie	1959	12.50	25.00	50.00
❑ RS-25074 [S]	The Folk Songs of Sonny & Brownie	1959	20.00	40.00	80.00
SAVOY					
❑ SJL-1137	Climbin' Up	1984	2.50	5.00	10.00
❑ 12218	Down Home Blues	1973	3.00	6.00	12.00
SHARP					
❑ 2003 [M]	Down Home Blues	195?	37.50	75.00	150.00
SMASH					
❑ MGS-27067 [M]	Brownie McGhee at the Bunkhouse	1965	7.50	15.00	30.00
❑ SRS-67067 [S]	Brownie McGhee at the Bunkhouse	1965	10.00	20.00	40.00
SMITHSONIAN/FOLKWAYS					
❑ SF-40011	Sing	198?	2.50	5.00	10.00
STORYVILLE					
❑ 4007	Brownie & Sonny	1972	3.00	6.00	12.00
TOPIC					
❑ T-29 [M]	Songs	1958	12.50	25.00	50.00
VEE JAY					
❑ VJLP-1138	Coffee House Blues	198?	2.50	5.00	10.00
—With Lightnin' Hopkins					
VERVE					
❑ MGV 3008 [M]	Blues Is My Companion	1961	20.00	40.00	80.00
VERVE FOLKWAYS					
❑ FV 9010 [M]	Get Together	1965	6.25	12.50	25.00
❑ FVS 9010 [S]	Get Together	1965	7.50	15.00	30.00
❑ FV 9019 [M]	Guitar Highway	1965	6.25	12.50	25.00
❑ FVS 9019 [S]	Guitar Highway	1965	7.50	15.00	30.00
WASHINGTON					
❑ W-702 [M]	Talkin' 'Bout the Blues	1961	12.50	25.00	50.00
WORLD PACIFIC					
❑ ST-1294 [S]	Blues Is a Story	1960	20.00	40.00	80.00
❑ WP-1294 [M]	Blues Is a Story	1960	12.50	25.00	50.00
❑ ST-1296 [S]	Down South Summit Meetin'	1960	20.00	40.00	80.00
❑ WP-1296 [M]	Down South Summit Meetin'	1960	12.50	25.00	50.00

TERRY AND THE MACS
45s

ABC-PARAMOUNT

Number	Title (A Side/B Side)	Yr	VG	VG+	NM
❑ 9668	Baby-O-Mine/Love Is a Beautiful Thing	1956	5.00	10.00	20.00
❑ 9721	You Don't Have to Explain/Spinning, Spinning, Spinning	1956	5.00	10.00	20.00
❑ 9753	Please Don't Tease/The Mystery of Love	1956	5.00	10.00	20.00

TERRY AND THE PIRATES
45s

CHESS

Number	Title (A Side/B Side)	Yr	VG	VG+	NM
❑ 1696	Talk About the Girl/What Did He Say	1958	10.00	20.00	40.00

TERRY AND THE TAGS
45s

SYLVESTER

Number	Title (A Side/B Side)	Yr	VG	VG+	NM
❑ 100	Rampage/The Twomp	1962	12.50	25.00	50.00

TEX, JOE
12-Inch Singles

EPIC

Number	Title (A Side/B Side)	Yr	VG	VG+	NM
❑ 50352	Ain't Gonna Bump No More (With No Big Fat Woman)/Be Cool (Willie Is Dancing with a Sissy)	1977	5.00	10.00	20.00

45s

ACE

Number	Title (A Side/B Side)	Yr	VG	VG+	NM
❑ 544	Cut It Out/Just for You and Me	1958	15.00	30.00	60.00
❑ 550	Mother's Advice/You Little Baby Face Thing	1958	20.00	40.00	80.00

Number	Title (A Side/B Side)	Yr	VG	VG+	NM
❑ 559	Charlie Brown Got Expelled/Blessed Are These Tears	1959	15.00	30.00	60.00
❑ 572	Don't Hold It Against Me/Yum, Yum, Yum	1959	15.00	30.00	60.00
❑ 591	Boys Will Be Boys/Grannie Stole the Show	1960	10.00	20.00	40.00
❑ 674	Boys Will Be Boys/Baby You're Right	1963	3.75	7.50	15.00
ANNA					
❑ 1119	All I Could Do Was Cry (Part 1)/All I Could Do Was Cry (Part 2)	1960	10.00	20.00	40.00
❑ 1124	I'll Never Break Your Heart (Part 1)/I'll Never Break Your Heart (Part 2)	1960	10.00	20.00	40.00
❑ 1128	Baby, You're Right/Ain't It a Mess	1961	10.00	20.00	40.00
ATLANTIC					
❑ 2874	I'll Never Fall in Love Again (Part 1)/I'll Never Fall in Love Again (Part 2)	1972	—	3.00	6.00
CHECKER					
❑ 1104	Baby, You're Right/All I Could Do Was Cry (Part 2)	1965	3.00	6.00	12.00
DIAL					
❑ 1001	Bad Feet/I Know Him	1971	—	3.00	6.00
❑ 1003	Papa's Dream/I'm Comin' Home	1971	—	3.00	6.00
❑ 1006 [DJ]	King Thaddeus (mono/stereo)	1971	—	3.50	7.00
—May be promo only					
❑ 1008	Give the Baby Anything the Baby Wants/Takin' a Chance	1971	—	3.00	6.00
❑ 1010	I Gotcha/A Mother's Prayer	1972	—	3.00	6.00
❑ 1012	You Said a Bad Word/It Ain't Gonna Work Baby	1972	—	3.00	6.00
❑ 1018	Rain Go Away/King Thaddeus	1973	—	3.00	6.00
❑ 1020	Woman Stealer/Cat's Got Her Tongue	1973	—	3.00	6.00
❑ 1020 [PS]	Woman Stealer/Cat's Got Her Tongue	1973	2.00	4.00	8.00
❑ 1021	All the Heaven a Man Really Needs/Let's Go Somewhere and Talk	1973	—	3.00	6.00
❑ 1024	Trying to Win Your Love/I've Seen Enough	1973	—	3.00	6.00
❑ 1154	Sassy Sexy Wiggle/Under Your Powerful Love	1975	—	3.00	6.00
❑ 1155	I'm Goin' Back Again/My Body Wants You	1975	—	3.00	6.00
❑ 1156	Baby, It's Rainin'/Have You Ever	1975	—	3.00	6.00
❑ 1157	Mama Red/Love Shortage	1975	—	3.00	6.00
❑ 2800	Loose Caboose/Music Ain't Got No Color	1979	—	2.50	5.00
❑ 2801	Who Gave Birth to the Funk/If You Don't Want the Man	1979	—	2.50	5.00
❑ 2802	Discomania/Fat People	1979	—	2.50	5.00
❑ 3000	What Should I Do/The Only Girl I've Ever Loved	1961	3.00	6.00	12.00
❑ 3002	One Giant Step/The Rib	1961	3.00	6.00	12.00
❑ 3003	Popeye Johnny/Hand Shakin', Love Makin', Girl Talkin', Son-of-a-Gun From Next Door	1962	3.00	6.00	12.00
❑ 3007	Meet Me in Church/Be Your Own Judge	1962	3.00	6.00	12.00
❑ 3009	I Let Her Get Away/The Peck	1963	3.00	6.00	12.00
❑ 3013	Someone to Take Your Place/I Should Have Kissed You More	1963	3.00	6.00	12.00
❑ 3016	I Wanna Be Free/Blood's Thicker Than Water	1963	3.00	6.00	12.00
❑ 3019	Looking for My Pig/Say Thank You	1964	3.00	6.00	12.00
❑ 3020	I'd Rather Have You/Old Time Lover	1964	3.00	6.00	12.00
❑ 3023	I Had a Good Thing But I Left (Part 1)/I Had a Good Thing But I Left (Part 2)	1964	3.00	6.00	12.00
❑ 4001	Hold What You've Got/Fresh Out of Tears	1964	3.75	7.50	15.00
❑ 4003	You Better Get It/You Got What It Takes	1965	2.50	5.00	10.00
❑ 4006	A Woman Can Change a Man/Don't Let Your Left Hand Know	1965	2.50	5.00	10.00
❑ 4011	One Monkey Don't Stop No Show/Build Your Love on a Solid Foundation	1965	2.50	5.00	10.00
❑ 4016	I Want To (Do Everything For You)/Funny Bone	1965	2.50	5.00	10.00
❑ 4022	A Sweet Woman Like You/Close the Door	1965	2.50	5.00	10.00
❑ 4026	The Love You Save (May Be Your Own)/If Sugar Was As Sweet As You	1966	2.50	5.00	10.00
❑ 4028	S.Y.S.L.J.F.M. (Letter Song)/I'm a Man	1966	2.50	5.00	10.00
❑ 4033	I Believe I'm Gonna Make It/Better Believe It, Baby	1966	2.50	5.00	10.00
❑ 4045	I've Got to Do a Little Bit Better/What in the World	1966	2.50	5.00	10.00
❑ 4051	Papa Was Too/Truest Woman in the World	1966	2.50	5.00	10.00
❑ 4055	Show Me/A Woman Sees a Hard Time (When Her Man Is Gone)	1967	2.00	4.00	8.00
❑ 4059	Woman Like That, Yeah/I'm Going and Get It	1967	2.00	4.00	8.00
❑ 4061	A Woman's Hands/See See Rider	1967	2.00	4.00	8.00
❑ 4063	Skinny Legs and All/Watch the One	1967	2.50	5.00	10.00
❑ 4068	I'll Make Every Day Christmas (For My Woman)/Don't Give Up	1967	3.00	6.00	12.00
❑ 4069	Men Are Gettin' Scarce/You're Gonna Thank Me, Woman	1968	2.00	4.00	8.00
❑ 4076	I'll Never Do You Wrong/Wooden Spoon	1968	2.00	4.00	8.00
❑ 4079	Chocolate Cherry/Betwixt and Between	1968	2.00	4.00	8.00
❑ 4083	Keep the One You Got/Go Home and Do It	1968	2.00	4.00	8.00
❑ 4086	You Need Me, Baby/Baby, Be Good	1968	2.00	4.00	8.00
❑ 4089	That's Your Baby/Sweet, Sweet Woman	1968	2.00	4.00	8.00
❑ 4090	Buying a Book/Chicken Crazy	1969	2.00	4.00	8.00
❑ 4093	That's the Way/Anything You Wanna Know	1969	2.00	4.00	8.00
❑ 4094	We Can't Sit Down Now/It Ain't Sanitary	1969	2.00	4.00	8.00
❑ 4095	I Can't See You No More (When Johnny Comes Marching Home Again)/Sure Is Good	1969	2.00	4.00	8.00
❑ 4096	Everything Happens on Time/You're Right, Ray Charles	1970	2.00	4.00	8.00
❑ 4098	I'll Never Fall in Love Again/The Only Way I Know to Love You	1970	2.00	4.00	8.00
EPIC					
❑ 50313	Ain't Gonna Bump No More (With No Big Fat Woman)/I Mess Up Everything I Get My Hands On	1976	—	2.50	5.00
❑ 50426	Hungry for Your Love/I Almost Got to Heaven Once	1977	—	2.50	5.00
❑ 50494	Rub Down/Be Kind to Old People	1977	—	2.50	5.00
❑ 50530	Get Back, Leroy/You Can Be My Star	1978	—	2.50	5.00
HANDSHAKE					
❑ 02565	Don't Do Da Do/Here Comes No. 34 (Do the Earl Campbell)	1981	—	2.00	4.00
KING					
❑ 4840	Come In This House/Davy, You Upset My Home	1955	15.00	30.00	60.00
❑ 4884	My Biggest Mistake/Right Back to My Arms	1956	12.50	25.00	50.00
❑ 4911	She's Mine/I Had to Come Back to You	1956	12.50	25.00	50.00
❑ 4980	Get Way Back/Pneumonia	1956	12.50	25.00	50.00

Number	Title (A Side/B Side)	Yr	VG	VG+	NM
❏ 5064	I Want to Have a Talk with You/ Ain't Nobody's Business	1957	12.50	25.00	50.00
❏ 5981	Come In This House/ I Want to Have a Talk with You	1965	2.50	5.00	10.00

Albums
ACCORD

❏ SN-7174	J.T.'s Funk	1982	2.50	5.00	10.00

ATLANTIC

❏ 8106 [M]	Hold What You've Got	1965	10.00	20.00	40.00
❏ SD 8106 [P]	Hold What You've Got	1965	12.50	25.00	50.00
❏ 8115 [M]	The New Boss	1965	10.00	20.00	40.00
❏ SD 8115 [S]	The New Boss	1965	12.50	25.00	50.00
❏ 8124 [M]	The Love You Save	1966	10.00	20.00	40.00
❏ SD 8124 [S]	The Love You Save	1966	12.50	25.00	50.00
❏ 8133 [M]	I've Got to Do a Little Better	1966	10.00	20.00	40.00
❏ SD 8133 [S]	I've Got to Do a Little Better	1966	12.50	25.00	50.00
❏ 8144 [M]	The Best of Joe Tex	1967	5.00	10.00	20.00
❏ SD 8144 [P]	The Best of Joe Tex	1967	6.25	12.50	25.00
❏ SD 8156	Live and Lively	1968	5.00	10.00	20.00
❏ 8187 [M]	Soul Country	1968	10.00	20.00	40.00

—Mono is white label promo only; "d/j copy monaural" sticker on cover

❏ 8187 [S]	Soul Country	1968	5.00	10.00	20.00
❏ SD 8211	Happy Soul	1969	5.00	10.00	20.00
❏ SD 8231	Buying a Book	1969	5.00	10.00	20.00
❏ SD 8254	Joe Tex Sings with Strings and Things	1970	3.75	7.50	15.00
❏ SD 8292	From the Roots Came the Rapper	1972	3.75	7.50	15.00
❏ 81278	The Best of Joe Tex	1985	2.50	5.00	10.00

CHECKER

❏ LP-2993 [M]	Hold On	1965	37.50	75.00	150.00

DIAL

❏ DL 6002	I Gotcha	1972	3.75	7.50	15.00
❏ DL 6004	Joe Tex Spills the Beans	1973	3.75	7.50	15.00
❏ DL 6100	He Who Is Without Funk Cast the First Stone	1979	2.50	5.00	10.00

EPIC

❏ PE 34666	Bumps and Bruises	1977	3.00	6.00	12.00

KING

❏ 935 [M]	The Best of Joe Tex	1965	25.00	50.00	100.00
❏ KS-935 [R]	The Best of Joe Tex	1965	18.75	37.50	75.00

LONDON

❏ LC-50017	Super Soul	1977	2.50	5.00	10.00

PARROT

❏ PA 61002 [M]	The Best of Joe Tex	1965	12.50	25.00	50.00
❏ PAS 71002 [R]	The Best of Joe Tex	1965	7.50	15.00	30.00

PRIDE

❏ PRD-0020	The History of Joe Tex	1973	2.50	5.00	10.00

RHINO

❏ RNLP-70191	I Believe I'm Gonna Make It: The Best of Joe Tex 1964-1972	1988	2.50	5.00	10.00

TEX AND THE CHEX
45s
ATLANTIC

❏ 2116	I Do Love You/My Love	1961	15.00	30.00	60.00

NEWTOWN

❏ 5010	Watching Willie Wobble/ Be on the Lookout for My Girl	1963	5.00	10.00	20.00

20TH FOX

❏ 411	Beach Party/Now (Love Me)	1963	7.50	15.00	30.00

TEXANS, THE Also see JOHNNY AND DORSEY BURNETTE.
45s
GOTHIC

❏ 001	Old Reb/Rockin' Johnny Home	1961	7.50	15.00	30.00

INFINITY

❏ 001	Green Grass of Texas/Bloody River	1961	7.50	15.00	30.00

JOX

❏ 001	Old Reb/Rockin' Johnny Home	1965	7.50	15.00	30.00

VEE JAY

❏ 658	Green Grass of Texas/Bloody River	1965	5.00	10.00	20.00

THARP, CHUCK, AND THE FIREBALLS See THE FIREBALLS.

THEE MIDNITERS
45s
CHATTAHOOCHIE

❏ 666	Land of a Thousand Dances (Part 1)/ Land of a Thousand Dances (Part 2)	1965	3.75	7.50	15.00
❏ 666-2	Land of a Thousand Dances (Part 1)/ Ball O' Twine	1965	3.75	7.50	15.00
❏ 674	Sad Girl/Heat Wave	1965	4.00	8.00	16.00
❏ 675	Sad Girl/Heat Wave	1965	3.75	7.50	15.00
❏ 684	Whittier Blvd./Evil Love	1965	3.75	7.50	15.00
❏ 693	I Need Someone/Empty Heart	1965	5.00	10.00	20.00
❏ 695	Brother, Where Are You/Heat Wave	1966	3.75	7.50	15.00
❏ 706	Are You Angry/I Found a Peanut	1966	3.75	7.50	15.00

UNI

❏ 55170	She Only Wants What She Can't Get/ I've Come Alive	1969	2.50	5.00	10.00

WHITTIER

❏ 201	That's All/To Be with You	196?	3.00	6.00	12.00
❏ 500	Love, Special Delivery/Don't Go Away	1966	5.00	10.00	20.00
❏ 501	The Midnite Feeling/It'll Never Be Over for Me	1966	5.00	10.00	20.00
❏ 503	Dragon Fly/The Big Ranch	1966	5.00	10.00	20.00
❏ 504	Never Knew I Had It So Bad/The Walking Song	1967	5.00	10.00	20.00
❏ 504	Never Knew I Had It So Bad/ Everybody Needs Somebody	1967	7.50	15.00	30.00
❏ 507	Jump Five and Harmonize/ Looking Out a Window	1967	5.00	10.00	20.00
❏ 508	Chile Con Soul/Tu Despedida	1967	5.00	10.00	20.00
❏ 509	Breakfast on the Grass/Dreaming Casually	1967	5.00	10.00	20.00
❏ 511	You're Gonna Make Me Cry/Make Ends Meet	1968	50.00	100.00	200.00
❏ 512	The Ballad of Cesar Chavez/The Ballad of Cesar Chavez (Spanish)	1968	5.00	10.00	20.00
❏ 513	Chicano Power/Never Goin' to Give You Up	1968	5.00	10.00	20.00
❏ 674	Sad Girl/Heat Wave	1968	3.00	6.00	12.00
❏ 694	It's Not Unusual/It's Not Unusual	1969	3.00	6.00	12.00

Albums
CHATTAHOOCHIE

❏ C-1001 [M]	Thee Midniters	1965	15.00	30.00	60.00
❏ CS-1001 [S]	Thee Midniters	1965	20.00	40.00	80.00

WHITTIER

❏ W-5000 [M]	Bring You Love Special Delivery	1966	10.00	20.00	40.00
❏ WS-5000 [S]	Bring You Love Special Delivery	1966	12.50	25.00	50.00
❏ W-5001 [M]	Unlimited	1966	10.00	20.00	40.00
❏ WS-5001 [S]	Unlimited	1966	12.50	25.00	50.00
❏ W-5002 [M]	Giants	1967	10.00	20.00	40.00
❏ WS-5002 [S]	Giants	1967	12.50	25.00	50.00

ZYANYA/RHINO

❏ RNLP-063	The Best of Thee Midniters	1983	3.00	6.00	12.00

THEE MUFFINS
Albums
(NO LABEL)

❏ (no #)	Thee Muffins Pop Up!	1967	50.00	100.00	200.00

THEE PROPHETS
45s
KAPP

❏ 962	Playgirl/Patricia Ann	1969	2.50	5.00	10.00
❏ 997	Some Kind of Wonderful/They Call Her Sorrow	1969	2.50	5.00	10.00
❏ 2038	Rag Doll Boy/It Isn't So Easy	1969	2.50	5.00	10.00
❏ 2087	Little Bit of Love/Come to Me Girl	1970	2.50	5.00	10.00

Albums
KAPP

❏ KS-3596	Playgirl	1969	5.00	10.00	20.00

THEM Also see BELFAST GYPSIES; VAN MORRISON.
45s
A&M

❏ 1201	Baby Please Don't Go/ Danger Heartbreak Dead Ahead	1988	—	2.00	4.00

—B-side by the Marvelettes

❏ 1201 [PS]	Danger Heartbreak Dead Ahead/ Baby Please Don't Go	1988	—	2.00	4.00

—"Good Morning Vietnam" sleeve

HAPPY TIGER

❏ 525	Lonely Weekends/I Am Waiting	1969	3.75	7.50	15.00
❏ 534	Memphis Lady/Nobody Cares	1970	3.00	6.00	12.00

PARROT

❏ 365	Gloria/Bring 'Em On In	1971	2.50	5.00	10.00
❏ 3003	Richard Cory/Don't You Know	1966	3.75	7.50	15.00
❏ 3006	Don't Start Crying Now/ I Can Only Give You Everything	1966	3.75	7.50	15.00
❏ 9702	Don't Start Crying Now/One, Two Brown Eyes	1964	5.00	10.00	20.00
❏ 9727	Gloria/Baby, Please Don't Go	1965	4.00	8.00	16.00
❏ 9749	Here Comes the Night/All By Myself	1965	3.75	7.50	15.00
❏ 9784	Gonna Dress in Black/Half As Much	1965	3.75	7.50	15.00
❏ 9796	Mystic Eyes/If You and I Could Be As Two	1965	3.75	7.50	15.00
❏ 9819	Call My Name/Bring 'Em On In	1966	3.75	7.50	15.00

RUFF

❏ 1088	Walking in the Queen's Garden/ I Happen to Love You	1967	6.25	12.50	25.00

TOWER

❏ 384	Walking in the Queen's Garden/ I Happen to Love You	1967	3.00	6.00	12.00
❏ 384 [PS]	Walking in the Queen's Garden/ I Happen to Love You	1967	7.50	15.00	30.00
❏ 407	But It's Alright/Square Room	1968	3.00	6.00	12.00
❏ 461	Waltz of the Flies/We All Agreed to Help	1969	3.00	6.00	12.00
❏ 493	Corina/Dark Are the Shadows	1969	3.00	6.00	12.00

Albums
HAPPY TIGER

❏ HT-1004	Them	1969	12.50	25.00	50.00
❏ HT-1012	Them In Reality	1971	30.00	60.00	120.00

LONDON

❏ PS 639 [P]	Backtrackin'	1974	2.50	5.00	10.00
❏ LC-50001 [R]	The Story of Them	1977	2.50	5.00	10.00
❏ 820326-1	Them Featuring Van Morrison	1985	2.50	5.00	10.00

PARROT

❏ PA 61005 [M]	Them Featuring "Here Comes the Night"	1965	20.00	40.00	80.00
❏ PA 61005 [M]	Them Featuring "Gloria"	1966	12.50	25.00	50.00

—Same album as above, but with slightly different title

❏ PA 61008 [M]	Them Again	1966	20.00	40.00	80.00
❏ PAS 71005 [R]	Them Featuring "Here Comes the Night"	1965	17.50	35.00	70.00
❏ PAS 71005 [R]	Them Featuring "Gloria"	1966	10.00	20.00	40.00

—Same album as above, but with slightly different title

❏ PAS 71008 [R]	Them Again	1966	12.50	25.00	50.00
❏ BP 71053 [(2)P]	Them Featuring Van Morrison	1972	3.00	6.00	12.00

—"Gloria," "Here Comes the Night," "If You and I Could Be as Two," "One More Time" and "One Two Brown Eyes" are true stereo.

TOWER

❏ ST 5104 [S]	Now and Them	1967	20.00	40.00	80.00
❏ T 5104 [M]	Now and Them	1967	12.50	25.00	50.00
❏ ST 5116 [S]	Time Out! Time In for Them	1968	25.00	50.00	100.00

THEM (2)
45s
KING

❏ 5967	Don't Look Now/A Girl Like You	1964	3.75	7.50	15.00

THEMES, INC. Yet another creation of STEVE BARRI and P.F. SLOAN.
45s
VEE JAY

❏ 635	Theme from Petyon Place/Paula's Percussion	1964	3.75	7.50	15.00

THERRIEN, JOE, JR.
45s
BRUNSWICK

❏ 9-55005	Hey Babe, Let's Go Downtown/ Come Back to Me Darling	1957	10.00	20.00	40.00
❏ 9-55017	Wheels/You're Long Gone	1957	20.00	40.00	80.00

T

Number	Title (A Side/B Side)	Yr	VG	VG+	NM
JAT					
❑ 101	I Ain't Gonna Be Around/Play Me a Blue Song	1958	20.00	40.00	80.00
LIDO					
❑ 505	Hey Babe, Let's Go Downtown/				
	Come Back to Me Darling	1957	30.00	60.00	120.00
THESE TRAILS					
Albums					
SINERGIA					
❑ (# unknown)	These Trails	1973	30.00	60.00	120.00
THIN LIZZY					
12-Inch Singles					
WARNER BROS.					
❑ PRO-A-754 [DJ]	Cowboy Song/				
	The Boys Are Back in Town/Rosalie	1978	5.00	10.00	20.00
45s					
LONDON					
❑ 20076	Whiskey in the Jar/Black Boys on the Corner	1972	2.00	4.00	8.00
❑ 20078	Broken Dreams/Randolph's Tango	1973	2.00	4.00	8.00
❑ 20082	Little Darling/The Rocket	1973	2.00	4.00	8.00
MERCURY					
❑ 73786	The Boys Are Back in Town/Jailbreak	1976	—	2.50	5.00
❑ 73841	Cowboy Song/Angel from the Coast	1976	—	2.50	5.00
❑ 73867	Rocky/Half-Caste	1976	—	2.50	5.00
❑ 73882	Old Flame/Johnny the Fox Meets Jimmy the Weed	1977		2.50	5.00
❑ 73892	Don't Believe a Word/Boogie Woogie Dance	1977	—	2.50	5.00
❑ 73945	Bad Reputation/Dancing in the Moonlight (It's Caught Me in the Spotlight)	1977	—	2.50	5.00
VERTIGO					
❑ 202	Night Life/Showdown	1974	—	3.00	6.00
❑ 205	Wild One/Freedom Song	1975	—	3.00	6.00
WARNER BROS.					
❑ 8648	Cowboy Song/Johnny the Fox Meets Jimmy the Weed	1978		2.50	5.00
❑ 49019	S & M/Do Anything You Want To	1979	—	2.50	5.00
❑ 49078	Got to Give It Up/With Love	1979	—	2.50	5.00
❑ 49643	Killer on the Loose/Sugar Blues	1980	—	2.00	4.00
❑ 49679	We Will Be Strong/Sweetheart	1981	—	2.00	4.00
❑ 50056	Hollywood/Pressure Will Blow	1982	—	2.00	4.00
Albums					
LONDON					
❑ PS 594	Thin Lizzy	1971	10.00	20.00	40.00
❑ PS 636	Vagabonds of the Western World	1973	7.50	15.00	30.00
❑ LC-50004	The Rocker (1971-1974)	1977	3.00	6.00	12.00
MERCURY					
❑ SRM-1-1081	Jailbreak	1976	3.00	6.00	12.00
❑ SRM-1-1107	Night Life	1976	3.00	6.00	12.00
—Reissue of Vertigo 2002					
❑ SRM-1-1108	Fighting	1976	3.00	6.00	12.00
—Reissue of Vertigo 2005					
❑ SRM-1-1119	Johnny the Fox	1976	3.00	6.00	12.00
❑ SRM-1-1186	Bad Reputation	1977	3.00	6.00	12.00
VERTIGO					
❑ VEL-2002	Night Life	1974	3.75	7.50	15.00
❑ VEL-2005	Fighting	1975	3.75	7.50	15.00
WARNER BROS.					
❑ BS2 3213 [(2)]	Live and Dangerous	1978	3.00	6.00	12.00
❑ BSK 3338	Black Rose/A Rock Legend	1979	2.50	5.00	10.00
❑ BSK 3496	Chinatown	1980	2.50	5.00	10.00
❑ BSK 3622	Renegade	1982	2.50	5.00	10.00
❑ 23831	Thunder and Lightning	1983	2.50	5.00	10.00
❑ 23986 [(2)]	"Life" — Live	1984	3.00	6.00	12.00
THIN MEN, THE					
45s					
PARKWAY					
❑ 916	Indian Love Call/Guitar Blues	1964	3.75	7.50	15.00
THINGS TO COME					
45s					
DUNWICH					
❑ 124	I'm Not Talkin'/'Til the End	1966	12.50	25.00	50.00
STARFIRE					
❑ 103	Sweet Gina/(B-side unknown)	1966	10.00	20.00	40.00
WARNER BROS.					
❑ 7164	Come Alive/Dancer	1968	3.75	7.50	15.00
❑ 7228	Cool Day/Hello	1968	3.75	7.50	15.00
THINK					
45s					
BIG TREE					
❑ 15000	Once You Understand/Gather	1974	—	2.00	4.00
COLUMBIA					
❑ 44627	Faster Faster/Stop Runnin' Away	1968	—	3.00	6.00
❑ 44848	California (Is Getting So Heavy)/ It's a Good Thing	1969	—	3.00	6.00
LAURIE					
❑ 3583	Once You Understand/Gather	1972	—	2.50	5.00
❑ 3594	It's Not the World — It's the People/ Who Are You to Tell Me What to Do?	1972	—	2.50	5.00
Albums					
LAURIE					
❑ SLLP-2052	Encounter	1972	3.00	6.00	12.00
THIRD POWER					
Albums					
VANGUARD					
❑ VSD-6554	Believe	1970	7.50	15.00	30.00
THIRD RAIL, THE					
45s					
CAMEO					
❑ 445	The Subway Train That Came to Life/ Train Rush Hour Stomp	1966	3.75	7.50	15.00

Number	Title (A Side/B Side)	Yr	VG	VG+	NM
EPIC					
❑ 10191	Run, Run, Run/No Return	1967	2.50	5.00	10.00
❑ 10240	Boppa Do Down Down/Invisible Man	1967	2.00	4.00	8.00
❑ 10285	Overdose of Love/It's Time to Say Goodbye	1968	2.00	4.00	8.00
❑ 10323	Shape of Things to Come/She Ain't No Choir Girl	1968	2.00	4.00	8.00
❑ 10457	The Ballad of General Humpty/ Beggin' Me to Stay	1969	2.00	4.00	8.00
Albums					
EPIC					
❑ LN 24327 [M]	Id Music	1967	7.50	15.00	30.00
❑ BN 26327 [S]	Id Music	1967	10.00	20.00	40.00
THIRTEENTH FLOOR ELEVATORS, THE					
45s					
CONTACT					
❑ 5269	You're Gonna Miss Me/Tried to Hide	1966	25.00	50.00	100.00
HANNA-BARBERA					
❑ 492	You're Gonna Miss Me/Tried to Hide	1966	50.00	100.00	200.00
INTERNATIONAL ARTISTS					
❑ 107	You're Gonna Miss Me/Tried to Hide	1967	5.00	10.00	20.00
—Yellow label					
❑ 107	You're Gonna Miss Me/Tried to Hide	1967	7.50	15.00	30.00
—Blue label					
❑ 111	Reverberation (Doubt)/Fire Engine	1967	5.00	10.00	20.00
❑ 113	Before You Accuse Me/Levitation	1968	5.00	10.00	20.00
❑ 121	Baby Blue/She Lives	1968	5.00	10.00	20.00
❑ 122	Slip Inside This House/Splash 1	1968	5.00	10.00	20.00
❑ 126	May the Circle Remain Unbroken/I'm Gonna Love You Too	1968	5.00	10.00	20.00
❑ 130	Livin' On/Scarlet and Gold	1969	10.00	20.00	40.00
Albums					
INTERNATIONAL ARTISTS					
❑ 1 [M]	Psychedelic Sounds	1967	62.50	125.00	250.00
—Green and yellow label					
❑ 1 [M]	Psychedelic Sounds	1968	37.50	75.00	150.00
—All-yellow label					
❑ 1 [S]	Psychedelic Sounds	1968	37.50	75.00	150.00
—All-yellow label					
❑ 1 [S]	Psychedelic Sounds	1968	50.00	100.00	200.00
—Aqua-blue label					
❑ 1 [S]	Psychedelic Sounds	1979	7.50	15.00	30.00
—Repressing with "Masterfonics" in dead wax					
❑ 5 [M]	Easter Everywhere	1968	100.00	200.00	400.00
—Mono is promo only					
❑ 5 [S]	Easter Everywhere	1968	37.50	75.00	150.00
—With custom inner sleeve					
❑ 5 [S]	Easter Everywhere	1968	37.50	75.00	150.00
—Without custom inner sleeve					
❑ 5 [S]	Easter Everywhere	1979	7.50	15.00	30.00
—Repressing with "Masterfonics" in dead wax					
❑ 8	13th Floor Elevators Live	1968	25.00	50.00	100.00
❑ 8	13th Floor Elevators Live	1979	6.25	12.50	25.00
—Repressing with "Masterfonics" in dead wax					
❑ 9	Bull of the Woods	1968	20.00	40.00	80.00
❑ 9	Bull of the Woods	1979	6.25	12.50	25.00
—Repressing with "Masterfonics" in dead wax					
31ST OF FEBRUARY, THE					
45s					
VANGUARD					
❑ 35066	Sandcastles/Pick a Gripe	1968	2.50	5.00	10.00
❑ 35087	In the Morning When I'm Real/Porcelain Mirrors	1969	2.50	5.00	10.00
Albums					
VANGUARD					
❑ VSD-6503	The 31st of February	1969	10.00	20.00	40.00
31 FLAVORS, THE					
Albums					
CROWN					
❑ CST-592	Hair	1968	12.50	25.00	50.00
THOMAS, B.J.					
45s					
ABC					
❑ 12054	(Hey, Won't You Play) Another Somebody Done Somebody Wrong Song/City Blues	1974	—	2.00	4.00
❑ 12121	We Are Happy Together/Help Me Make It (To My Rockin' Chair)	1975	—	2.00	4.00
BRAGG					
❑ 103	Billy and Sue/Never Tell	1964	5.00	10.00	20.00
CLEVELAND INT'L.					
❑ 03492	Whatever Happened to Old Fashioned Love/ I Just Sing	1983	—	2.00	4.00
❑ 04608	From This Moment On/The Girl Most Likely To	1984	—	2.00	4.00
COLUMBIA					
❑ 03985	New Looks from an Old Lover/ You Keep the Man in Me Happy	1983	—	2.00	4.00
❑ 04237	Two Car Garage/Beautiful World	1983	—	2.00	4.00
❑ 04431	The Whole World's in Love When You're Lonely/ We're Here to Love	1984	—	—	3.00
❑ 04531	Rock and Roll Shoes/Then I'll Be Over You	1984	—	—	3.00
—Ray Charles and B.J. Thomas					
❑ 05647	A Part of Me That Needs You Most/ Northern Lights	1985	—	—	3.00
❑ 05771	America Is/Broken Toys	1986	—	—	3.00
❑ 05771 [PS]	America Is/Broken Toys	1986	—	2.00	4.00
❑ 06314	Night Life/Make the World Go Away	1986	—	—	3.00
HICKORY					
❑ 1395	Billy and Sue/Never Tell	1966	2.50	5.00	10.00
LORI					
❑ 9547	I've Got a Feeling/Hey Judy	1963	6.25	12.50	25.00
❑ 9561	For Your Precious Love/Here I Am Again	1964	6.25	12.50	25.00
MCA					
❑ 40735	Don't Worry Baby/My Love	1977	—	2.00	4.00
❑ 40812	Still the Lovin' Is Fun/ Play Me a Little Traveling Music	1977	—	2.00	4.00

Number	Title (A Side/B Side)	Yr	VG	VG+	NM
❑ 40854	Everybody Loves a Rain Song/Dusty Roads	1978	—	2.00	4.00
❑ 40914	Sweet Young America/Aloha	1978	—	2.00	4.00
❑ 40986	We Could Have Been the Closest of Friends/ In My Heart	1979	—	2.00	4.00
❑ 41134	God Bless the Children/On This Christmas Night	1979	—	2.00	4.00
❑ 41134 [PS]	God Bless the Children/On This Christmas Night	1979	—	2.50	5.00
❑ 41207	Nothin' Could Be Better/Walkin' on a Cloud	1980	—	2.00	4.00
❑ 41281	Everything Always Works Out for the Best/ No Limit	1980	—	2.00	4.00
❑ 51087	Some Love Songs Never Die/ There Ain't No Love	1981	—	2.00	4.00
❑ 51151	The Lovin' Kind/I Recall a Gypsy Woman	1981	—	2.00	4.00
❑ 52053	I Really Got the Feeling/But Love Me	1982	—	2.00	4.00
MYRRH					
❑ 166	Home Where I Belong/Hallelujah	1977	—	2.50	5.00
❑ 176	Without a Doubt/(B-side unknown)	1977	—	2.50	5.00
❑ 234	Uncloudy Day/(B-side unknown)	1981	—	2.50	5.00
PACEMAKER					
❑ 227	I'm So Lonesome I Could Cry/Candy Baby	1964	5.00	10.00	20.00
❑ 231	Mama/Wendy	1965	3.75	7.50	15.00
❑ 234	Bring Back the Time/ I Don't Have a Mind of My Own	1965	3.75	7.50	15.00
❑ 239	Tomorrow Never Comes/Your Tears Leave Me Cold	1965	3.75	7.50	15.00
❑ 247	Plain Jane/My Home Town	1965	3.75	7.50	15.00
❑ 253	I'm Not a Fool Anymore/Baby Cried	1965	3.75	7.50	15.00
❑ 256	I Can't Help It (If I'm Still in Love with You)/ Baby Cried	1965	3.75	7.50	15.00
❑ 259	Pretty Country Girl/Houston Town	1965	3.75	7.50	15.00
PARAMOUNT					
❑ 0218	Songs/Goodbye's a Long, Long Time	1973	—	2.50	5.00
❑ 0218 [PS]	Songs/Goodbye's a Long, Long Time	1973	—	3.00	6.00
❑ 0239	Sunday Sunrise/Early Morning Rush	1973	—	2.50	5.00
❑ 0239	Sunday Sunrise/Talkin' Confidentially	1973	—	2.50	5.00
❑ 0277	Play Something Sweet (Brickyard Blues)/ Talkin' Confidentially	1974	—	2.50	5.00
REPRISE					
❑ 22837	Don't Leave Love (Out There All Alone)/ One Woman	1989	—	—	3.00
SCEPTER					
❑ 12129	I'm So Lonesome I Could Cry/Candy Baby	1966	2.50	5.00	10.00
❑ 12139	Mama/Wendy	1966	2.00	4.00	8.00
❑ 12154	Bring Back the Time/ I Don't Have a Mind of My Own	1966	2.00	4.00	8.00
❑ 12165	Tomorrow Never Comes/ Your Tears Leave Me Cold	1966	2.00	4.00	8.00
❑ 12179	Plain Jane/My Home Town	1966	2.00	4.00	8.00
❑ 12194	I Can't Help It (If I'm Still in Love with You)/ Baby Cried	1967	2.00	4.00	8.00
❑ 12200	Just the Wisdom of a Fool/Treasure of Love	1967	2.00	4.00	8.00
❑ 12201	Wisdom of a Fool/Human	1967	2.00	4.00	8.00
❑ 12205	The Girl Can't Help It/Walkin' Back	1967	2.00	4.00	8.00
❑ 12219	The Eyes of a New York Woman/ I May Never Get to Heaven	1968	2.00	4.00	8.00
❑ 12230	Hooked on a Feeling/ I've Been Down This Road Before	1968	2.00	4.00	8.00
❑ 12244	It's Only Love/You Don't Love Me Anymore	1969	—	3.00	6.00
❑ 12255	Pass the Apple Eve/Fairy Tale of Time	1969	—	3.00	6.00
❑ 12259	You Don't Love Me Anymore/Skip a Rope	1969	—	3.00	6.00
❑ 12265	Raindrops Keep Fallin' on My Head/ Never Had It So Good	1969	—	3.50	7.00
❑ 12277	Everybody's Out of Town/Living Again	1970	—	3.00	6.00
❑ 12283	I Just Can't Help Believing/ Send My Picture to Scranton, Pa.	1970	—	3.00	6.00
❑ 12299	Most of All/The Mask	1970	—	2.50	5.00
❑ 12307	No Love at All/Have a Heart	1971	—	2.50	5.00
❑ 12320	Mighty Clouds of Joy/Life	1971	—	2.50	5.00
❑ 12335	Long Ago Tomorrow/Burnin' a Hole in My Mind	1971	—	2.50	5.00
❑ 12344	Rock and Roll Lullaby/Are We Losing Touch	1972	—	3.00	6.00
❑ 12354	That's What Friends Are For/I Get Enthused	1972	—	2.50	5.00
❑ 12364	Happier Than the Morning Sun/We Have Got to Get Out Ship Together	1972	—	2.50	5.00
❑ 12379	Sweet Cherry Wine/Roads	1973	—	2.50	5.00
VALERIE					
❑ 226	I've Got a Feeling/Hey Judy	1963	5.00	10.00	20.00
WARNER BROS.					
❑ 5491	Billy and Sue/Never Tell	1964	5.00	10.00	20.00
Albums					
ABC					
❑ ABDP-858	Reunion	1975	2.50	5.00	10.00
❑ ABCD-912	Help Me Make It to My Rockin' Chair	1976	2.50	5.00	10.00
ACCORD					
❑ SN-7106	Lovin' You	198?	2.50	5.00	10.00
BUCKBOARD					
❑ 1023	B.J. Thomas Sings Hank Williams and Other Favorites	198?	2.50	5.00	10.00
CLEVELAND INT'L.					
❑ FC 38561	New Looks	1983	2.50	5.00	10.00
❑ PC 38561	New Looks	1984	2.00	4.00	8.00
—Budget-line reissue					
❑ FC 39111	The Great American Dream	1983	2.50	5.00	10.00
❑ PC 39111	The Great American Dream	1984	2.00	4.00	8.00
—Budget-line reissue					
❑ FC 39337	Shining	1984	2.50	5.00	10.00
❑ FC 40157	Throwing Rocks at the Moon	1985	2.50	5.00	10.00
COLUMBIA					
❑ PC 38400	Love Shines	1984	2.00	4.00	8.00
—Reissue of Priority 38400					
❑ PC 40148	All Is Calm, All Is Bright...	1985	2.50	5.00	10.00
❑ FC 40496	Night Life	1986	2.50	5.00	10.00
DORAL					
❑ (# unknown)	Doral Presents B.J. Thomas	1971	5.00	10.00	20.00
—Mail-order promotion from Doral cigarettes					
EVEREST					
❑ 4104	Golden Greats	1981	2.50	5.00	10.00

Number	Title (A Side/B Side)	Yr	VG	VG+	NM
HICKORY					
❑ LPM-133 [M]	The Very Best of B.J. Thomas	1966	5.00	10.00	20.00
❑ LPS-133 [S]	The Very Best of B.J. Thomas	1966	6.25	12.50	25.00
❑ ST 90956 [S]	The Very Best of B.J. Thomas	1966	7.50	15.00	30.00
—Capitol Record Club edition					
❑ T 90956 [M]	The Very Best of B.J. Thomas	1966	6.25	12.50	25.00
—Capitol Record Club edition					
MCA					
❑ 746	Everybody Loves a Rain Song	1980	2.00	4.00	8.00
—Budget-line reissue					
❑ 2286	B.J. Thomas	1977	2.50	5.00	10.00
❑ 3035	Everybody Loves a Rain Song	1978	2.50	5.00	10.00
❑ 3231	For the Best	1979	2.50	5.00	10.00
❑ 5155	In Concert	1980	2.50	5.00	10.00
❑ 5195	Some Love Songs Never Die	1980	2.50	5.00	10.00
❑ 5296	As We Know Him	1982	2.50	5.00	10.00
❑ 27032	In Concert	198?	2.00	4.00	8.00
—Reissue of MCA 5155					
MYRRH					
❑ MSB-6574	Home Where I Belong	1978	2.50	5.00	10.00
❑ MSB-6593	A Happy Man	1979	2.50	5.00	10.00
❑ MSB-6633	You Gave Me Love	1979	2.50	5.00	10.00
❑ MSB-6653	The Best of B.J. Thomas	1980	2.50	5.00	10.00
❑ MSB-6675	Amazing Grace	1981	2.50	5.00	10.00
❑ MSB-6705	Miracle	1983	2.50	5.00	10.00
❑ MSB-6710	Peace in the Valley	1983	2.50	5.00	10.00
❑ MSB-6725	The Best of B.J. Thomas, Volume 2	1984	2.50	5.00	10.00
❑ WR-8153	Peace in the Valley	1985	2.50	5.00	10.00
—Reissue of 6710					
❑ WR-8200	Amazing Grace	1985	2.00	4.00	8.00
—Reissue of 6675					
PACEMAKER					
❑ PLP-3001 [M]	B.J. Thomas and the Triumphs	1965	50.00	100.00	200.00
PAIR					
❑ PDL2-1099 [(2)]	Greatest Hits	1986	3.00	6.00	12.00
PARAMOUNT					
❑ PAS 1020	Longhorns & Londonbridges	1974	3.00	6.00	12.00
❑ PAS-6052	B.J. Thomas Songs	1973	3.00	6.00	12.00
PICKWICK					
❑ SPC-3623	The Best of B.J. Thomas	197?	2.50	5.00	10.00
PRIORITY					
❑ JU 38400	Love Shines	1982	2.50	5.00	10.00
REPRISE					
❑ 25898	Midnight Minute	1989	3.00	6.00	12.00
SCEPTER					
❑ SPS-535 [S]	I'm So Lonesome I Could Cry	1966	6.25	12.50	25.00
❑ SRM-535 [M]	I'm So Lonesome I Could Cry	1966	5.00	10.00	20.00
❑ SPS-556 [S]	Tomorrow Never Comes	1966	5.00	10.00	20.00
❑ SRM-556 [M]	Tomorrow Never Comes	1966	3.75	7.50	15.00
❑ SPS-561 [S]	For Lovers and Losers	1967	3.75	7.50	15.00
❑ SRM-561 [M]	For Lovers and Losers	1967	5.00	10.00	20.00
❑ SPS-570 [S]	On My Way	1968	3.75	7.50	15.00
❑ SRM-570 [M]	On My Way	1968	7.50	15.00	30.00
—Mono appears to be white label promo only; in stereo cover with "Promotional DJ Copy Monaural Not for Sale" sticker on front					
❑ SPS-576	Young and In Love	1969	3.75	7.50	15.00
❑ SPS-578	Greatest Hits, Volume 1	1969	3.00	6.00	12.00
❑ SPS-580	Raindrops Keep Fallin' on My Head	1970	3.00	6.00	12.00
—Remixed version; trail-off wax number on Side 1 is "SPS-580-A-1C" or "SPS-580-A-1D" and on Side 2 is "SPS-580-B-1C"					
❑ SPS-580	Raindrops Keep Fallin' on My Head	1970	3.75	7.50	15.00
—Original "muddy mix"; trail-off wax number on Side 1 is "SPS-580-A-1B" and on Side 2 is "SPS-580-B-1A"					
❑ SPS-582	Everybody's Out of Town	1970	3.00	6.00	12.00
❑ SPS-586	Most of All	1970	3.00	6.00	12.00
❑ SPS-597	Greatest Hits, Volume Two	1971	3.00	6.00	12.00
❑ 5101	Billy Joe Thomas	1972	3.00	6.00	12.00
❑ 5108	B.J. Thomas Country	1972	3.00	6.00	12.00
❑ 5112 [(2)]	Greatest All-Time Hits	1973	3.75	7.50	15.00
STARDAY					
❑ 992	The Best of B.J. Thomas	197?	2.50	5.00	10.00
UNITED ARTISTS					
❑ UA-LA389-E	The Very Best of B.J. Thomas	1974	3.00	6.00	12.00

THOMAS, BUELL

45s

Number	Title (A Side/B Side)	Yr	VG	VG+	NM
DALTON					
❑ 102	Shepherds & Kings/My Christmas Star	19??	—	2.00	4.00
—B-side by Jean Doran					
DOOTONE					
❑ 316	Santa Claus Walks Just Like Daddy/ You're My Christmas	1953	7.50	15.00	30.00
—B-side by Gerri Goodley					
❑ 318	Green Christmas/ For My Bride At Christmas Time	1953	7.50	15.00	30.00

THOMAS, CARLA Also see OTIS AND CARLA; RUFUS AND CARLA.

45s

Number	Title (A Side/B Side)	Yr	VG	VG+	NM
ATLANTIC					
❑ 2086	Gee Whiz (Look at His Eyes)/For You	1960	3.75	7.50	15.00
❑ 2101	A Love of My Own/Promises	1961	3.00	6.00	12.00
❑ 2113	Wish Me Good Luck/In Your Spare Time	1961	3.00	6.00	12.00
❑ 2132	The Masquerade Is Over/I Kinda Think He Does	1962	3.00	6.00	12.00
❑ 2163	I'll Bring It On Home to You/I Can't Take It	1962	3.00	6.00	12.00
❑ 2189	What a Fool I've Been/The Life I Live	1963	3.00	6.00	12.00
❑ 2212	Gee Whiz, It's Christmas/ All I Want for Christmas Is You	1963	3.75	7.50	15.00
❑ 2238	I've Got No Time to Lose/A Boy Named Tom	1964	3.00	6.00	12.00
❑ 2258	A Woman's Love/Don't Let the Love Light Leave	1964	3.00	6.00	12.00
❑ 2272	How Do You Quit (Someone You Love)/ The Puppet	1965	3.00	6.00	12.00
GUSTO					
❑ 816	All I Want for Christmas Is You/ Gee Whiz, It's Christmas	1979	2.50	5.00	10.00
—A Canadian import ($5) from 1986 exists on King					

T

Number	Title (A Side/B Side)	Yr	VG	VG+	NM
SATELLITE					
❑ 104	Gee Whiz (Look at His Eyes)/For You	1960	125.00	250.00	500.00
STAX					
❑ 0011	I've Fallen in Love/Where Do I Go	1968	2.00	4.00	8.00
❑ 0024	I Like What You're Doing (To Me)/Strung Out	1969	2.00	4.00	8.00
❑ 0042	Just Keep On Loving My Love	1969	2.00	4.00	8.00
—With Johnnie Taylor					
❑ 0044	I Can't Stop/I Need You Woman	1969	—	2.50	5.00
—With William Bell					
❑ 0056	Guide Me Well/Some Other Man (Is Beating Your Time)	1970	2.00	4.00	8.00
❑ 0061	The Time for Love Is Anytime/Living in the City	1970	—	3.00	6.00
❑ 0067	All I Have to Do Is Dream/Leave the Girl Alone	1970	—	2.50	5.00
—With William Bell					
❑ 0080	Hi De Ho (That Old Sweet Roll)/I Loved You Like I Love My Very Life	1970	—	3.00	6.00
❑ 0113	You've Got a Cushion to Fall On/Love Means (You Never Have to Say You're Sorry)	1972	—	3.00	6.00
❑ 0133	Sugar/You've Got a Cushion to Fall On	1972	—	3.00	6.00
❑ 0149	I May Not Be All You Want/Sugar	1972	—	3.00	6.00
❑ 172	Stop! Look What You're Doing/Every Ounce of Strength	1965	3.00	6.00	12.00
❑ 0173	I Have a God Who Loves/Love Among People	1973	—	3.00	6.00
❑ 183	Comfort Me/I'm for You	1966	3.00	6.00	12.00
❑ 188	Let Me Be Good to You/Another Night Without My Man	1966	3.00	6.00	12.00
❑ 188 [PS]	Let Me Be Good to You/Another Night Without My Man	1966	25.00	50.00	100.00
❑ 195	B-A-B-Y/What Have You Got to Offer Me	1966	3.75	7.50	15.00
❑ 206	All I Want for Christmas Is You/Winter Snow	1966	3.00	6.00	12.00
❑ 207	Something Good (Is Going to Happen to You)/It's Starting to Grow	1967	2.50	5.00	10.00
❑ 214	Unchanging Love/When Tomorrow Comes	1967	2.50	5.00	10.00
❑ 222	I'll Always Have Faith in You/Stop Thief	1967	2.50	5.00	10.00
❑ 239	Pick Up the Pieces/Separation	1967	2.50	5.00	10.00
❑ 251	A Dime a Dozen/I Want You Back	1968	2.50	5.00	10.00
Albums					
ATLANTIC					
❑ 8057 [M]	Gee Whiz	1961	25.00	50.00	100.00
—With white "fan" logo					
❑ 8057 [M]	Gee Whiz	1963	10.00	20.00	40.00
—With black "fan" logo					
❑ SD 8057 [S]	Gee Whiz	1961	37.50	75.00	150.00
—With white "fan" logo					
❑ SD 8057 [S]	Gee Whiz	1963	12.50	25.00	50.00
—With black "fan" logo					
❑ SD 8232	The Best of Carla Thomas	1969	6.25	12.50	25.00
STAX					
❑ 706 [M]	Comfort Me	1966	8.75	17.50	35.00
❑ 706 [P]	Comfort Me	1966	12.50	25.00	50.00
❑ 709 [M]	Carla	1966	8.75	17.50	35.00
❑ 709 [S]	Carla	1966	12.50	25.00	50.00
❑ 718 [M]	The Queen Alone	1967	8.75	17.50	35.00
❑ 718 [S]	The Queen Alone	1967	12.50	25.00	50.00
❑ STS-2019	Memphis Queen	1969	8.75	17.50	35.00
❑ STS-2044	Love Means Carla Thomas	1971	8.75	17.50	35.00
❑ MPS-8538	Memphis Queen	1987	2.50	5.00	10.00
—Budget-line reissue					

THOMAS, CARLA, AND RUFUS THOMAS See RUFUS AND CARLA.

THOMAS, DANNY
45s

Number	Title (A Side/B Side)	Yr	VG	VG+	NM
DECCA					
❑ 9-29641	Bring Back Our Beale Street/It's Wonderful When	1955	3.00	6.00	12.00
❑ 9-29842	Nobody Knows But the Lord/Little Miss Tippy Toes	1956	3.00	6.00	12.00
MYRRH					
❑ 120	People We've Grown to Love/Little Boy Tracks	1973	—	3.50	7.00
❑ 131	I'll Still Be Loving You/Jesus Is My Kind of People	197?	—	3.50	7.00
❑ 134	I'll Still Be Loving You/(B-side unknown)	1974	—	3.50	7.00
RCA VICTOR					
❑ 47-5142	Oh Moon/Hush-a-Bye	1952	3.75	7.50	15.00

THOMAS, GENE Also see GENE AND DEBBE.
45s

Number	Title (A Side/B Side)	Yr	VG	VG+	NM
CIMARRON					
❑ 103	First Times/Goldrush Can Do the Waltz and Rhumba Too	197?	—	3.50	7.00
❑ 104	Minnowhauling Man/I Taught You So Many Things	197?	—	3.50	7.00
HICKORY					
❑ 1592	Babe, I Wish You Well/Listen Buddy	1971	—	3.50	7.00
❑ 1608	Lay It Down/Remembered by Someone	1971	—	3.50	7.00
❑ 1631	Touch Something Good/Watching It Go	1972	—	3.50	7.00
PICTURE					
❑ 6971	Only Me/What Will My Mary Say	196?	7.50	15.00	30.00
SAN					
❑ 1516	It Hurts/My Baby's in Love with Another Guy	196?	5.00	10.00	20.00
❑ 1517	Long Black Limousine/Play That Lonely Record	196?	5.00	10.00	20.00
❑ 1518	I Took You for Granted Too Long/Blame It on the Moon	196?	5.00	10.00	20.00
TRX					
❑ 5023	Destiny's Children/The More I Think	1969	—	3.50	7.00
❑ 5025	The Nature of a Man/Reasons	1969	—	3.50	7.00
UNITED ARTISTS					
❑ 338	Sometime/Everyday	1961	3.00	6.00	12.00
❑ 501	It's Make Believe/So Wrong	1962	3.00	6.00	12.00
❑ 583	Peace of Mind/The Puppet	1963	3.00	6.00	12.00
❑ 584	Baby's Gone/Stand By Love	1963	—	—	—
—Canceled					
❑ 640	Baby's Gone/Stand By Love	1963	3.00	6.00	12.00
❑ 725	The Last Song/Bobby and the Boys	1964	2.50	5.00	10.00
❑ 771	Playing Those Old Records/Together Again	1964	2.50	5.00	10.00
❑ 799	Half the Time/I'd Rather Not Talk About It	1964	2.50	5.00	10.00
❑ 871	Down the Road/It's a Sad World	1965	2.50	5.00	10.00

Number	Title (A Side/B Side)	Yr	VG	VG+	NM
VENUS					
❑ 1439	Sometime/Every Night	1961	7.50	15.00	30.00
❑ 1441	Lamp of Love/Two Lips	1961	5.00	10.00	20.00
❑ 1443	Mysteries of Love/That's What You Are to Me	1962	5.00	10.00	20.00
❑ 1444	Down the Road/(B-side unknown)	1962	20.00	40.00	80.00
❑ 1445	It's Make Believe/So Wrong	1962	15.00	30.00	60.00

THOMAS, IAN
12-Inch Singles

Number	Title (A Side/B Side)	Yr	VG	VG+	NM
CHRYSALIS					
❑ CHS-2-PDJ [DJ]	Goodnight Mrs. Calabash (same on both sides?)	1976	2.50	5.00	10.00
MERCURY					
❑ PRO 300-1 [DJ]	Do You Right (same on both sides)	1984	2.50	5.00	10.00
❑ PRO 402-1 [DJ]	Harmony (same on both sides)	1985	2.50	5.00	10.00
45s					
ATLANTIC					
❑ 3470	Coming Home/Clear Sailing	1978	—	2.50	5.00
❑ 3505	Sally/(B-side unknown)	1978	—	2.50	5.00
CHRYSALIS					
❑ 2116	Liars/(B-side unknown)	1976	—	3.00	6.00
JANUS					
❑ 224	Painted Ladies/Will You Still Love Me	1973	—	3.00	6.00
❑ 242	Long Long Way/Count Your Blessings	1974	—	3.50	7.00
Albums					
ATLANTIC					
❑ SD 19167	Still Here	1978	2.50	5.00	10.00
CHRYSALIS					
❑ CHR 1126	Goodnight Mrs. Calabash	1976	3.00	6.00	12.00
JANUS					
❑ JLS-3058	Ian Thomas	1973	3.00	6.00	12.00
❑ JXS-7005	Long Long Way	1974	3.00	6.00	12.00
MERCURY					
❑ 822319-1	Riders on Dark Horses	1984	2.50	5.00	10.00
❑ 826030-1	Add Water	1985	3.00	6.00	12.00

THOMAS, IRMA
45s

Number	Title (A Side/B Side)	Yr	VG	VG+	NM
CANYON					
❑ 21	Save a Little Bit for Me/That's How I Feel About You	1970	—	3.00	6.00
❑ 31	I'll Do It All Over You/We Won't Be In Your Way Anymore	1970	—	3.00	6.00
CHESS					
❑ 2010	Cheater Man/Somewhere Crying	1967	2.00	4.00	8.00
❑ 2017	A Woman Will Do Wrong/I Gave You Everything	1967	2.00	4.00	8.00
❑ 2036	Good to Me/We Got Something Good	1968	2.00	4.00	8.00
COTILLION					
❑ 44144	Full Time Woman/She's Taken My Part	1972	—	3.00	6.00
IMPERIAL					
❑ 66013	Wish Someone Would Care/Break-A-Way	1964	3.00	6.00	12.00
❑ 66041	Time Is On My Side/Anyone Who Knows What Love Is (Will Understand)	1964	3.00	6.00	12.00
❑ 66069	Times Have Changed/Moments to Remember	1964	2.50	5.00	10.00
❑ 66080	He's My Guy/(I Want a) True, True Love	1964	2.50	5.00	10.00
❑ 66095	Some Things You Better Get Used To/You Don't Miss a Good Thing	1965	2.50	5.00	10.00
❑ 66106	Nobody Wants to Hear Nobody's Troubles/I'm Gonna Cry Till My Tears Run Dry	1965	2.50	5.00	10.00
❑ 66120	Hurts All Over/It's Starting to Get Me Now	1965	2.50	5.00	10.00
❑ 66137	Take a Look/What Are You Trying to Do	1965	2.50	5.00	10.00
❑ 66178	It's a Man-Woman's World (Part 1)/It's a Man-Woman's World (Part 2)	1966	2.50	5.00	10.00
MINIT					
❑ 625	Cry On/Girl Needs Boy	1961	3.00	6.00	12.00
❑ 633	It's Too Soon to Know/That's All I Ask	1961	3.00	6.00	12.00
❑ 642	Gone/Done Got Over It	1962	3.00	6.00	12.00
❑ 653	It's Raining/I Did My Part	1962	3.00	6.00	12.00
❑ 660	Somebody Told Me/Two Winters Long	1963	3.00	6.00	12.00
❑ 666	Ruler of My Heart/Hitting on Nothing	1963	3.00	6.00	12.00
RON					
❑ 328	Don't Mess with My Man/Set Me Free	1960	3.75	7.50	15.00
❑ 330	Good Man/I May Be Wrong	1960	3.75	7.50	15.00
UNITED ARTISTS					
❑ 0088	Wish Someone Would Care/Take a Look	1973	—	2.00	4.00
—"Silver Spotlight Series" reissue					
Albums					
BANDY					
❑ 70003	Irma Thomas Sings	197?	7.50	15.00	30.00
FUNGUS					
❑ FB-25150	In Between Tears	1973	10.00	20.00	40.00
IMPERIAL					
❑ LP-9266 [M]	Wish Someone Would Care	1964	12.50	25.00	50.00
❑ LP-9302 [M]	Take a Look	1966	12.50	25.00	50.00
❑ LP-12266 [S]	Wish Someone Would Care	1964	15.00	30.00	60.00
❑ LP-12302 [S]	Take a Look	1966	15.00	30.00	60.00
RCS					
❑ 1004	Safe with Me	1980	7.50	15.00	30.00

THOMAS, JAMO
45s

Number	Title (A Side/B Side)	Yr	VG	VG+	NM
CHESS					
❑ 1971	Must I Holler/I'll Be Your Fool	1966	3.75	7.50	15.00
DECCA					
❑ 32293	Education Is Where It's At (Part 1)/(Part 2)	1968	3.75	7.50	15.00
❑ 32406	Bahama Mama (Part I)/(Part II)	1968	3.75	7.50	15.00
SOUND STAGE 7					
❑ 2584	Nassau Daddy/Jive Mother-in-Law	1967	5.00	10.00	20.00
❑ 2596	Bahama Mama (Part I)/(Part II)	1967	3.75	7.50	15.00
THOMAS					
❑ 303	I Spy (For the FBI)/Snake Hip Mama	1966	3.75	7.50	15.00
❑ 303 [PS]	I Spy (For the FBI)/Snake Hip Mama	1966	7.50	15.00	30.00
❑ 304	Arrest Me/Jamo's Soul	1966	6.25	12.50	25.00
❑ 304 [PS]	Arrest Me/Jamo's Soul	1966	12.50	25.00	50.00

Number	Title (A Side/B Side)	Yr	VG	VG+	NM

THOMAS, JON
45s
ABC-PARAMOUNT

Number	Title (A Side/B Side)	Yr	VG	VG+	NM
❏ 10122	Heartbreak (It's Hurtin' Me)/Tearin'	1960	3.75	7.50	15.00
❏ 10140	Hey Hey Baby/Buffalo Blues	1960	3.75	7.50	15.00
❏ 10190	The Snake/Story Telling	1961	3.00	6.00	12.00
❏ 10238	Boss Hoss/Flip, Flop, Fly	1961	3.00	6.00	12.00
❏ 10274	The Thomas Twist/So Good	1961	3.00	6.00	12.00

CHECKER

❏ 809	Rib Tips/Hi-Fi	1955	7.50	15.00	30.00

MERCURY

❏ 71078	Hard Head (Part 1)/Hard Head (Part 2)	1957	7.50	15.00	30.00
❏ 71151	St. Louis Blues/Fat Back	1957	6.25	12.50	25.00

NOTE

❏ 10001	Rib Tips/Hi-Fi	1954	10.00	20.00	40.00

Albums
ABC-PARAMOUNT

❏ 351 [M]	Heartbreak	1960	7.50	15.00	30.00
❏ S-351 [S]	Heartbreak	1960	10.00	20.00	40.00

WING

❏ MGW-12258 [M]	The Big Beat on the Organ	1963	5.00	10.00	20.00
❏ SRW-16258 [R]	The Big Beat on the Organ	1963	3.00	6.00	12.00

THOMAS, PAT
45s
MGM

❏ K13102	Desafinado (Slightly Out of Tune)/One Note Samba	1962	2.00	4.00	8.00
❏ K13102 [PS]	Desafinado (Slightly Out of Tune)/One Note Samba	1962	3.00	6.00	12.00
❏ K13124	Home in the Meadow/Where There's Love, There's Hope	1963	5.00	10.00	20.00
❏ K13171	I'm in the Mood for Love/Just Say Auf Wiederseh'n	1963	2.50	5.00	10.00

VERVE

❏ 10269	Desafinado (Slightly Out of Tune)/One Note Samba	1962	2.50	5.00	10.00
❏ 10269 [PS]	Desafinado (Slightly Out of Tune)/One Note Samba	1962	3.00	6.00	12.00
❏ 10333	Long Long Night/I Can't Wait Until I See My Baby's Face	1964	2.50	5.00	10.00

Albums
MGM

❏ E-4103 [M]	Desafinado	1962	3.75	7.50	15.00
❏ SE-4103 [S]	Desafinado	1962	5.00	10.00	20.00
❏ E-4206 [M]	Moody's Mood	1964	5.00	10.00	20.00
❏ SE-4206 [S]	Moody's Mood	1964	6.25	12.50	25.00

STRAND

❏ SL-1015 [M]	Jazz Patterns	1961	10.00	20.00	40.00
❏ SLS-1015 [S]	Jazz Patterns	1961	12.50	25.00	50.00

THOMAS, RAY Also see THE MOODY BLUES.
45s
THRESHOLD

❏ 67020	High Above My Head/Love Is the Key	1975	—	2.50	5.00
❏ 67023	One Night Stand/Carousel	1975	—	2.50	5.00

Albums
THRESHOLD

❏ THS 16	From Mighty Oaks	1975	3.75	7.50	15.00
❏ THS 17	Hopes Wishes & Dreams	1976	3.75	7.50	15.00
❏ THSX-102 [DJ]	Ray Thomas Discusses The Recording of His First Solo Album From Mighty Oaks	1975	12.50	25.00	50.00

THOMAS, RUFUS Also see RUFUS AND CARLA.
12-Inch Singles
ICHIBAN

❏ 12-103	Rappin' Rufus (3 versions)	1985	2.00	4.00	8.00

45s
ARTISTS OF AMERICA

❏ 126	If There Were No Music/Blues in the Basement	1976	—	2.50	5.00

AVI

❏ 149	Who's Makin' Love to Your Old Lady/Hot Grits	1977	—	2.00	4.00
❏ 178	I Ain't Gettin' Older, I'm Gettin' Better (Part 1)/I Ain't Gettin' Older, I'm Gettin' Better (Part 2)	1977	—	2.00	4.00

HI

❏ 78520	Fried Chicken/I Ain't Got Time	1978	—	2.00	4.00

HIGH STACKS

❏ 9801	Hey Rufus!/Body Fine	1999	—	—	3.00

—B-side by the Barkays

ICHIBAN

❏ 85-103	Rappin' Rufus/(Instrumental)	1985	—	2.00	4.00

METEOR

❏ 5039	I'm Steady Holdin' On/The Easy Livin' Plan	1956	37.50	75.00	150.00

STAX

❏ 0010	Funky Mississippi/So Hard to Get Along With	1968	—	3.00	6.00
❏ 0022	Funky Way/I Want to Hold You	1969	—	3.00	6.00
❏ 0059	Do the Funky Chicken/Turn Your Damper Down	1969	—	3.00	6.00
❏ 0071	Sixty Minute Man/The Preacher and the Bear	1970	—	3.00	6.00
❏ 0079	(Do the) Push and Pull Part I/(Do the) Push and Pull Part II	1970	—	3.00	6.00
❏ 0090	The World Is Round/(I Love You) For Sentimental Reasons	1971	—	3.00	6.00
❏ 0098	The Breakdown (Part 1)/The Breakdown (Part 2)	1971	—	3.00	6.00
❏ 0112	Do the Funky Penguin (Part 1)/Do the Funky Penguin (Part 2)	1971	—	3.00	6.00
❏ 126	It's Aw-Rite/Can't Ever Let You Go	1962	3.75	7.50	15.00
❏ 0129	Love Trap/6-3-8	1972	—	3.00	6.00
❏ 130	The Dog/Did You Ever Love a Woman	1963	3.75	7.50	15.00
❏ 140	Walking the Dog/You Said	1963	3.00	6.00	12.00
❏ 140	Walking the Dog/Fine and Mellow	1963	7.50	15.00	30.00
❏ 0140	Itch and Scratch (Part 1)/Itch and Scratch (Part 2)	1972	—	3.00	6.00
❏ 144	Can Your Monkey Do the Dog/I Want to Get Married	1964	3.00	6.00	12.00
❏ 149	Somebody Stole My Dog/I Want to Be Loved	1964	3.00	6.00	12.00

Number	Title (A Side/B Side)	Yr	VG	VG+	NM
❏ 0153	Funky Robot (Part 1)/Funky Robot (Part 2)	1973	—	3.00	6.00
❏ 157	Jump Back/All Night Worker	1964	3.00	6.00	12.00
❏ 167	Baby Walk/Little Sally Walker	1965	2.00	4.00	8.00
❏ 173	Willy Nilly/Sho' Gonna Mess Him Up	1965	2.00	4.00	8.00
❏ 0177	I Know You Don't Want Me No More/I'm Still in Love with You	1973	—	3.00	6.00
❏ 178	Chicken Scratch/The World Is Round	1965	2.00	4.00	8.00
❏ 0187	I'll Be Your Santa Baby/That Makes Christmas Day	1973	—	3.00	6.00
❏ 0192	The Funky Bird/Steal a Little	1974	—	3.00	6.00
❏ 200	Talkin' 'Bout True Love/Sister's Got a Boyfriend	1967	2.00	4.00	8.00
❏ 0219	Boogie Ain't Nothin' (But Gettin' Down) (Part 1)/Boogie Ain't Nothin' (But Gettin' Down) (Part 2)	1974	—	3.00	6.00
❏ 221	Sophisticated Sissy/Grasy Spoon	1967	2.00	4.00	8.00
❏ 0236	Do the Double Bump/Do the Double Bump	1975	—	3.00	6.00
❏ 240	Down Ta My House/Steady Holding On	1968	2.00	4.00	8.00
❏ 250	The Memphis Train/I Think I Made a Boo-Boo	1968	2.00	4.00	8.00
❏ 0254	Jump Back '75 (Part 1)/Jump Back '75 (Part 2)	1975	—	3.00	6.00
❏ 1073	I'll Be Your Santa Claus/Christmas Comes Once A Year	197?	—	2.50	5.00

—B-side by Albert King; reissue

SUN

❏ 181	Bear Cat/Walking in the Rain	1953	50.00	100.00	200.00

—No subtitle on A-side

❏ 181	Bear Cat (The Answer to Hound Dog)/Walking in the Rain	1953	87.50	175.00	350.00

—With subtitle on A-side

❏ 188	Tiger Man (King of the Jungle)/Save Your Money	1953	125.00	250.00	500.00

Albums
A.V.I.

❏ 6015	If There Were No Music	1977	3.75	7.50	15.00
❏ 6046	I Ain't Gettin' Older, I'm Gettin' Better	1978	3.75	7.50	15.00

ALLIGATOR

❏ AV-4769	That Woman Is Poison	1988	2.50	5.00	10.00

GUSTO

❏ 0064	Rufus Thomas	1980	2.50	5.00	10.00

STAX

❏ ST-704 [M]	Walking the Dog	1963	37.50	75.00	150.00
❏ STS-2028	Do the Funky Chicken	1970	6.25	12.50	25.00
❏ STS-2039	Rufus Thomas Live! Doing the Push and Pull at P.J.'s	1971	6.25	12.50	25.00
❏ STS-3004	Did You Hear Me	1972	6.25	12.50	25.00
❏ STS-3008	Crown Prince of Dance	1973	6.25	12.50	25.00

THOMAS, TIMMY
12-Inch Singles
GOLD MOUNTAIN

❏ 81203	Gotta Give a Little Love/Gotta Give a Little Love (Dub)	1984	—	3.00	6.00
❏ 81203 [DJ]	Gotta Give a Little Love (5:26) (4:35)	1984	2.00	4.00	8.00

45s
GLADES

❏ 1703	Why Can't We Live Together/Funky Me	1972	—	3.00	6.00
❏ 1709	People Are Changin'/Rainbow Power	1973	—	3.00	6.00
❏ 1712	Let Me Be Your Eyes/Cold Cold People	1973	—	3.00	6.00
❏ 1717	What Can I Tell Her/Opportunity	1973	—	3.00	6.00
❏ 1719	One Brief Moment/Rio Girl	1974	—	3.00	6.00
❏ 1721	Deep in You/Spread Us Around	1974	—	2.50	5.00
❏ 1723	I've Got to See You Tonight/You're the Song (I've Always Wanted to Sing)	1974	—	2.50	5.00
❏ 1727	Sexy Woman/Sweet Brown Sugar	1975	—	2.50	5.00
❏ 1730	Ebony Affair/It's What They Can't See	1975	—	2.50	5.00
❏ 1735	Love Shine/Running Out of Time	1976	—	2.50	5.00
❏ 1740	Stone to the Bone/Watch It! Watch It!	1977	—	2.50	5.00
❏ 1748	Touch to Touch/When a House Got Music	1978	—	2.50	5.00
❏ 1749	Freak In, Freak Out/Say Love, Can You Chase	1978	—	2.50	5.00
❏ 1758	Drown in My Own Tears (Part 1)/Drown in My Own Tears (Part 2)	1980	—	2.50	5.00

GOLD MOUNTAIN

❏ 82004	Gotta Give a Little Love (Ten Years After)/Same Old Song	1984	—	2.00	4.00
❏ 82008	Love Is Never Too Late/Let It Flow	1984	—	2.00	4.00

GOLDWAX

❏ 320	Have Some Boogaloo/Liquid Mood	1967	3.75	7.50	15.00
❏ 327	It's My Life/Whole Lotta Shakin' Goin' On	1967	3.75	7.50	15.00

MARLIN

❏ 3348	Are You Crazy??? (Pt. 1)/Are You Crazy??? (Pt. 2)	1981	—	2.00	4.00

Albums
GLADES

❏ 33-6501	Why Can't We Live Together	1973	3.75	7.50	15.00

GOLD MOUNTAIN

❏ GM-80006	Gotta Give a Little Love	1984	2.50	5.00	10.00

THOMAS, VIC
45s
PHILIPS

❏ 40183	Napoleon Bonaparte/Marianne	1964	18.75	37.50	75.00
❏ 40228	Village of Love/There Stands An Empty Man	1964	18.75	37.50	75.00

THOMPSON, BILLY
45s
COLUMBUS

❏ 1043	Black Eyed Girl/Kiss Tomorrow Goodbye	1965	50.00	100.00	200.00

WAND

❏ 1108	Black Eyed Girl/Kiss Tomorrow Goodbye	1966	15.00	30.00	60.00

THOMPSON, HANK
45s
ABC

❏ 12409	I'm Just Gettin' By/I Hear the South Callin' Me	1978	—	2.50	5.00
❏ 12447	Dance with Me Molly/Point of No Return	1979	—	2.50	5.00

ABC DOT

❏ 17535	Mama Don't 'Low/Wait a Little Longer Baby	1974	—	3.00	6.00
❏ 17556	That's Just My Truckin' Luck/After You Have Made Me Over	1975	—	3.00	6.00

Number	Title (A Side/B Side)	Yr	VG	VG+	NM
❏ 17583	Mona Lisa/Too Young	1975	—	3.00	6.00
❏ 17612	Asphalt Cowboy/Fifteen Miles to Clarksville	1976	—	3.00	6.00
❏ 17649	Big Band Days/Forgive Me	1976	—	3.00	6.00
❏ 17673	Honky Tonk Girl/Another Shot of Today	1976	—	3.00	6.00
❏ 17695	Just an Old Flame/				
	Don't Get Around Much Anymore	1977	—	3.00	6.00
CAPITOL					
❏ F876	All That Goes Up Must Come Down/Standing on				
	the Outside	1950	7.50	15.00	30.00
❏ F1016	Take a Look at This Broken Heart/She's a Girl				
	Without a Sweetheart	1950	7.50	15.00	30.00
❏ F1113	Humpty Dumpty Heart/California Women	1950	6.25	12.50	25.00
❏ F1114	Soft Lips/Give a Little, Take a Little	1950	6.25	12.50	25.00
❏ F1115	Whoa Sailor/Today	1950	6.25	12.50	25.00
❏ F1116	Swing Wide/Tomorrow Night	1950	6.25	12.50	25.00
❏ F1117	Second Hand Gal/Don't Flirt with Me	1950	6.25	12.50	25.00
❏ F1118	Green Light/Mary Had a Little Lamb	1950	6.25	12.50	25.00
❏ F1119	The Grass Looks Greener/Rock in the Ocean	1950	6.25	12.50	25.00
❏ F1120	My Front Door Is Open/A Cat Has Nine Lives	1950	6.25	12.50	25.00
❏ F1121	I Find You Cheatin' on Me/You Remembered Me	1950	6.25	12.50	25.00
❏ F1163	When God Calls His Children Home/I Can't Feel				
	at Home	1950	7.50	15.00	30.00
❏ F1198	Humpty Dumpty Boogie/Daddy Blues	1950	7.50	15.00	30.00
❏ F1327	A Broken Heart and a Glass of Beer/If I Cry	1950	7.50	15.00	30.00
❏ F1379	New Roving Gambler/Playin' Possum	1951	6.25	12.50	25.00
❏ F1444	Where Is Your Heart Tonight/Those Things				
	Money Can't Buy	1951	6.25	12.50	25.00
❏ F1528	I Ain't Crying Over You/Hangover Heart	1951	6.25	12.50	25.00
❏ F1632	Humpty Dumpty Heart/Green Light	1951	5.00	10.00	20.00
—Reissue of hit A-sides from 1948					
❏ F1745	Love Thief/How Do You Feel	1951	6.25	12.50	25.00
❏ F1870	Teardrops on the Tea Leaves/I'll Be Your				
	Sweetheart	1951	6.25	12.50	25.00
❏ F1942	The Wild Side of Life/Cryin' in the Deep Blue Sea	1952	6.25	12.50	25.00
❏ F2063	Waiting in the Lobby of Your Heart/Don't Make				
	Me Cry Again	1952	6.25	12.50	25.00
❏ F2169	How Cold Hearted Can You Get/It's Better to				
	Have Loved a Little	1952	6.25	12.50	25.00
❏ F2178	Whoa Sailor/Mary Had a Little Lamb	1952	5.00	10.00	20.00
❏ F2269	The New Wears Off Too Fast/You're Walking on				
	My Heart	1952	6.25	12.50	25.00
❏ F2377	No Help Wanted/I'd Have Never Found				
	Somebody New	1953	6.25	12.50	25.00
❏ F2445	Rub-a-Dub-Dub/I'll Sign My Heart Away	1953	6.25	12.50	25.00
❏ F2553	Yesterday's Girl/John Henry	1953	6.25	12.50	25.00
❏ F2646	Wake Up, Irene/Go Cry Your Heart Out	1953	6.25	12.50	25.00
❏ F2758	A Fooler, a Faker/Breakin' the Rules	1954	5.00	10.00	20.00
❏ F2792	Jersey Bounce/Sunrise Serenade	1954	6.25	12.50	25.00
❏ F2823	Honky-Tonk Girl/We've Gone Too Far	1954	5.00	10.00	20.00
❏ F2920	The New Green Light/A Lonely Heart Knows	1954	5.00	10.00	20.00
❏ F2998	Dardanelle/Johnson Rag	1954	5.00	10.00	20.00
❏ F3030	If Lovin' You Is Wrong/Annie Over	1955	5.00	10.00	20.00
❏ F3106	Wildwood Flower/Breakin' In Another Heart	1955	5.00	10.00	20.00
—A-side with Merle Travis					
❏ F3188	Most of All/Simple Simon	1955	5.00	10.00	20.00
❏ F3235	Westphalia Waltz/Red Skin Gal	1955	5.00	10.00	20.00
❏ F3275	Don't Take It Out on Me/Honey, Honey Bee Ball	1955	5.00	10.00	20.00
❏ F3347	The Blackboard of My Heart/				
	I'm Not Mad, Just Hurt	1956	5.00	10.00	20.00
❏ F3440	Weeping Willow/				
	You Can Give Me Back My Heart	1956	5.00	10.00	20.00
❏ F3536	It Makes No Difference Now/Taking My Chances	1956	5.00	10.00	20.00
❏ F3623	Rockin' in the Congo/I Was the First One	1957	10.00	20.00	40.00
❏ F3709	Girl in the Night/Quicksand	1957	5.00	10.00	20.00
❏ F3781	Tears Are Only Rain/Under the Double Eagle	1957	5.00	10.00	20.00
❏ F3850	Just an Old Flame/If I'm Not Too Late	1957	5.00	10.00	20.00
❏ F3950	How Do You Hold a Memory/Li'l Liza Jane	1958	5.00	10.00	20.00
❏ F4017	Squaws Along the Yukon/Gathering Flowers	1958	5.00	10.00	20.00
❏ F4085	I've Run Out of Tomorrows/You're Going Back				
	to Your Old Ways Again	1958	5.00	10.00	20.00
❏ F4138	Tuxedo Junction/The Cocoanut Grove	1959	5.00	10.00	20.00
❏ F4182	Anybody's Girl/Total Strangers	1959	5.00	10.00	20.00
❏ F4269	I Didn't Mean to Fall in Love/I Guess I'm Gettin'				
	Over You	1959	5.00	10.00	20.00
❏ 4334	A Six Pack to Go/What Made Her Change	1960	5.00	10.00	20.00
❏ 4386	She's Just a Whole Lot Like You/There My				
	Future Goes	1960	5.00	10.00	20.00
❏ 4454	It's Got to Be a Habit/				
	Will We Start It All Over Again	1960	5.00	10.00	20.00
❏ 4502	Just One Step Away/				
	Two Hearts Deep in the Blues	1961	5.00	10.00	20.00
❏ 4556	Oklahoma Hills/Teach Me to Lie	1961	5.00	10.00	20.00
❏ 4605	Hangover Tavern/Give the World a Smile	1961	5.00	10.00	20.00
❏ 4649	Lost John/I've Convinced Everyone But Myself	1961	5.00	10.00	20.00
❏ 4649 [PS]	Lost John/I've Convinced Everyone But Myself	1961	7.50	15.00	30.00
❏ 4694	That's the Recipe for a Heartache/				
	Drop Me Gently	1962	3.75	7.50	15.00
❏ 4722	Blue Skirt Waltz/Westphalia Waltz	1962	3.75	7.50	15.00
❏ 4786	How Many Teardrops Will It Take/I Cast a				
	Lonesome Shadow	1962	3.75	7.50	15.00
❏ 4871	Honky Tonk Town/I				
	'd Look Forward to Tomorrow	1963	3.75	7.50	15.00
❏ 4912	Yesterday's Girl/The Wild Side of Life	1963	3.75	7.50	15.00
❏ 4968	I Wasn't Even in the Running/The More in Love				
	Your Heart Is	1963	3.75	7.50	15.00
❏ 5008	Too in Love/Blackboard of My Heart	1963	3.75	7.50	15.00
❏ 5071	Twice As Much/Reaching for the Moon	1964	3.75	7.50	15.00
❏ 5123	Just to Ease the Pain/Stirring Up the Ashes	1964	3.75	7.50	15.00
❏ 5217	Whatever Happened to Mary/Luckiest				
	Heartache in Town	1964	3.75	7.50	15.00
❏ 5310	Mr. and Mrs. Snowman/I'd Like to Have an				
	Elephant for Christmas	1964	3.75	7.50	15.00
❏ 5344	I'm Gonna Practice Freedom/				
	Life's Sweetest Moment	1965	3.75	7.50	15.00
❏ 5422	Then I'll Start Believing in You/				
	In the Back of Your Mind	1965	3.75	7.50	15.00
❏ 5507	Paper Doll/You Only Hurt the One You Love	1965	3.75	7.50	15.00

Number	Title (A Side/B Side)	Yr	VG	VG+	NM
❏ 5535	Little Christmas/				
	Gonna Wrap My Heart in Angel Ribbons	1965	3.75	7.50	15.00
❏ 5599	Pick Me Up on Your Way Down/				
	You Nearly Lose Your Mind	1966	3.00	6.00	12.00
❏ F40264	Give a Little, Take a Little/A Cat Has Nine Lives	1949	7.50	15.00	30.00
CHURCHILL					
❏ 7779	Rockin' in the Congo/The Convict and the Rose	1981	2.00	4.00	8.00
❏ 7779 [PS]	Rockin' in the Congo/The Convict and the Rose	1981	2.50	5.00	10.00
❏ 94003	Cocaine Blues/Drop Me Gently	1982	—	2.50	5.00
❏ 94009	Driving Nails in My Coffin/				
	What Ever Happened to Mary	1982	—	2.50	5.00
❏ 94026	Once in a Blue Moon/				
	Let's Stop What We Started	1983	—	2.50	5.00
❏ 94026 [PS]	Once in a Blue Moon/				
	Let's Stop What We Started	1983	—	3.00	6.00
CURB					
❏ D7-73035	Gotta Sell Them Chickens/Total Stranger	1997	—	2.00	4.00
—A-side with Junior Brown; B-side with Lyle Lovett					
DOT					
❏ 17108	On Tap, In the Can, or In the Bottle	1968	2.00	4.00	8.00
❏ 17163	Smoky the Bar/				
	Clubs, Spades, Diamonds and Hearts	1968	2.00	4.00	8.00
❏ 17207	I See Them Everywhere/Today	1969	2.00	4.00	8.00
❏ 17262	The Pathway of My Life/At Certain Times	1969	2.00	4.00	8.00
❏ 17307	Oklahoma Home Brew/				
	Let's Get Drunk and Be Somebody	1969	2.00	4.00	8.00
❏ 17347	But That's All Right/Take It All Away	1970	2.00	4.00	8.00
❏ 17354	One of the Fortunate Few/I'm Afraid I Lied	1970	2.00	4.00	8.00
❏ 17365	Next Time I Fall in Love (I Won't)/Big Boat Across				
	Oklahoma	1971	—	3.50	7.00
❏ 17385	The Mark of a Heel/Promise Her Anything	1971	—	3.50	7.00
❏ 17390	Oklahoma Stomp/Maiden's Prayer	1971	—	3.50	7.00
❏ 17399	I've Come Awful Close/Teardrops on the Rocks	1971	—	3.50	7.00
❏ 17410	Cab Driver/Gloria	1972	—	3.50	7.00
❏ 17430	Glow Worm/You're Nobody Till				
	Somebody Loves You	1972	—	3.50	7.00
❏ 17447	Roses in the Wine/That's Why I Sing	1973	—	3.50	7.00
❏ 17470	Kindly Keep It Country/Jill's Jack in the Box	1973	—	3.50	7.00
❏ 17490	The Older the Violin, the Sweeter the Music/				
	A Six Pack to Go	1974	—	3.50	7.00
❏ 17512	Who Left the Door to Heaven Open/When My				
	Blue Moon Turns to Gold Again	1974	—	3.50	7.00
MCA					
❏ 41079	I Hear the South Callin' Me/				
	Through the Bottom of the Glass	1979	—	2.00	4.00
❏ 41176	Tony's Tank-Up, Drive-In Cafe/				
	Point of No Return	1980	—	2.00	4.00
❏ 41274	You're Poppin' Tops/				
	Rollin' in Your Sweet Sunshine	1980	—	2.00	4.00
❏ 51030	King of Western Swing/Take Me Back to Tulsa	1980	—	2.00	4.00
STEP ONE					
❏ 382	Here's to Country Music/				
	The Hand I'm Holding Now	1988	—	2.00	4.00
❏ 394	If I Were You I'd Fall in Love with Me/				
	(B-side unknown)	1988	—	2.00	4.00
WARNER BROS.					
❏ 5858	Where Is the Circus/Love Walked Out				
	Long Before She Did	1966	2.50	5.00	10.00
❏ 5886	He's Got a Way with Women/				
	Let the Four Winds Choose	1967	2.50	5.00	10.00
7-Inch Extended Plays					
CAPITOL					
❏ EAP 1-418	Yesterday's Girl/When You're Lovin', You're				
	Livin'//John Henry/I Saw My Mother's Name	195?	5.00	10.00	20.00
❏ EAP 1-418 [PS]	Songs of the Brazos Valley, Part 1	195?	5.00	10.00	20.00
❏ EAP 2-418	You Don't Have the Nerve/At the Rainbow's End/				
	/The Letter Edged in Black/				
	Mother, Queen of My Heart	195?	5.00	10.00	20.00
❏ EAP 2-418 [PS]	Songs of the Brazos Valley, Part 2	195?	5.00	10.00	20.00
❏ EAP 3-418	(contents unknown)	195?	5.00	10.00	20.00
❏ EAP 3-418 [PS]	Songs of the Brazos Valley, Part 3	195?	5.00	10.00	20.00
❏ EAP 1-601	(contents unknown)	195?	6.25	12.50	25.00
❏ EAP 1-601 [PS]	Hank Thompson	195?	6.25	12.50	25.00
❏ EAP 1-618	(contents unknown)	195?	5.00	10.00	20.00
❏ EAP 1-618 [PS]	North of the Rio Grande, Part 1	195?	5.00	10.00	20.00
❏ EAP 2-618	(contents unknown)	195?	5.00	10.00	20.00
❏ EAP 2-618 [PS]	North of the Rio Grande, Part 2	195?	5.00	10.00	20.00
❏ EAP 3-618	(contents unknown)	195?	5.00	10.00	20.00
❏ EAP 3-618 [PS]	North of the Rio Grande, Part 3	195?	5.00	10.00	20.00
❏ EAP 1-705	(contents unknown)	195?	6.25	12.50	25.00
❏ EAP 1-705 [PS]	Dancing Western Style	195?	6.25	12.50	25.00
❏ EAP 1-729	Humpty Dumpty Heart/Today//				
	You Remembered Me/				
	I'll Be Your Sweetheart for a Day	1957	3.75	7.50	15.00
❏ EAP 1-729 [PS]	New Recordings of Hank Thompson's				
	All-Time Hits, Part 1	1957	3.75	7.50	15.00
❏ EAP 2-729	Don't Flirt with Me/The Grass Looks Greener//				
	Swing Wide Your Gate of Love/I Find You				
	Cheatin' on Me	1957	3.75	7.50	15.00
❏ EAP 2-729 [PS]	New Recordings of Hank Thompson's				
	All-Time Hits, Part 2	1957	3.75	7.50	15.00
❏ EAP 3-729	My Front Door Is Open/Standing on the Outside/				
	/Whoa Sailor/Tomorrow Night	1957	3.75	7.50	15.00
❏ EAP 3-729 [PS]	New Recordings of Hank Thompson's				
	All-Time Hits, Part 3	1957	3.75	7.50	15.00
❏ EAP 1-826	(contents unknown)	1957	3.75	7.50	15.00
❏ EAP 1-826 [PS]	Hank! Part 1	1957	3.75	7.50	15.00
❏ EAP 2-826	(contents unknown)	1957	3.75	7.50	15.00
❏ EAP 2-826 [PS]	Hank! Part 2	1957	3.75	7.50	15.00
❏ EAP 3-826	Ole Napoleon/Across the Alley from the Alamo/				
	/Don't Get Around Much Anymore/Prosperity				
	Special	1957	3.75	7.50	15.00
❏ EAP 3-826 [PS]	Hank! Part 3	1957	3.75	7.50	15.00
❏ EAP 1-975	(contents unknown)	1958	3.75	7.50	15.00
❏ EAP 1-975 [PS]	Dance Ranch, Part 1	1958	3.75	7.50	15.00
❏ EAP 2-975	(contents unknown)	1958	3.75	7.50	15.00
❏ EAP 2-975 [PS]	Dance Ranch, Part 2	1958	3.75	7.50	15.00

Number	Title (A Side/B Side)	Yr	VG	VG+	NM
❏ EAP 3-975	(contents unknown)	1958	3.75	7.50	15.00
❏ EAP 3-975 [PS]	Dance Ranch, Part 3	1958	3.75	7.50	15.00
❏ EAP 1-1111	Shenandoah Waltz/Wednesday Night Waltz//In the Valley of the Moon/Fifty Year Ago Waltz	1959	3.75	7.50	15.00
❏ EAP 1-1111 [PS]	Favorite Waltzes by Hank Thompson, Part 1	1959	3.75	7.50	15.00
❏ EAP 2-1111		1959	3.75	7.50	15.00
❏ EAP 2-1111 [PS]	Favorite Waltzes by Hank Thompson, Part 2	1959	3.75	7.50	15.00
❏ EAP 3-1111		1959	3.75	7.50	15.00
❏ EAP 3-1111 [PS]	Favorite Waltzes by Hank Thompson, Part 3	1959	3.75	7.50	15.00
❏ EAP 1-1246	(contents unknown)	1960	3.75	7.50	15.00
❏ EAP 1-1246 [PS]	Songs for Rounders, Part 1	1960	3.75	7.50	15.00
❏ EAP 2-1246	(contents unknown)	1960	3.75	7.50	15.00
❏ EAP 2-1246 [PS]	Songs for Rounders, Part 2	1960	3.75	7.50	15.00
❏ EAP 3-1246	(contents unknown)	1960	3.75	7.50	15.00
❏ EAP 3-1246 [PS]	Songs for Rounders, Part 3	1960	3.75	7.50	15.00

Albums
ABC

Number	Title (A Side/B Side)	Yr	VG	VG+	NM
❏ AB-1095	Brand New Hank	1978	3.00	6.00	12.00

ABC DOT

❏ DOSD-2003	Moving On	1974	3.00	6.00	12.00
❏ DOSD-2032	Hank Thompson Sings Nat King Cole	1975	3.00	6.00	12.00
❏ DOSD-2060	Back in the Swing of Things	1976	3.00	6.00	12.00
❏ DOSD-2069	The Thompson Touch	1977	3.00	6.00	12.00
❏ DO-2091	Doin' My Thing	1977	3.00	6.00	12.00

CAPITOL

❏ H 418 [10]	Songs of the Brazos Valley	1953	30.00	60.00	120.00
❏ T 418 [M]	Songs of the Brazos Valley	1956	20.00	40.00	80.00
—Turquoise or gray label					
❏ T 418 [M]	Songs of the Brazos Valley	1959	7.50	15.00	30.00
—Black colorband label, logo at left					
❏ T 418 [M]	Songs of the Brazos Valley	1962	5.00	10.00	20.00
—Black colorband label, logo at top					
❏ H 618 [10]	North of the Rio Grande	1953	30.00	60.00	120.00
❏ T 618 [M]	North of the Rio Grande	1956	20.00	40.00	80.00
—Turquoise or gray label					
❏ H 729 [10]	New Recordings of Hank's All-Time Hits	195?	30.00	60.00	120.00
❏ T 729 [M]	New Recordings of Hank's All-Time Hits	1956	20.00	40.00	80.00
—Turquoise or gray label					
❏ T 729 [M]	New Recordings of Hank's All-Time Hits	1959	7.50	15.00	30.00
—Black colorband label, logo at left					
❏ T 729 [M]	New Recordings of Hank's All-Time Hits	1962	5.00	10.00	20.00
—Black colorband label, logo at top					
❏ T 826 [M]	Hank!	1957	20.00	40.00	80.00
—Turquoise or gray label					
❏ T 826 [M]	Hank!	1959	7.50	15.00	30.00
—Black colorband label, logo at left					
❏ T 826 [M]	Hank!	1962	5.00	10.00	20.00
—Black colorband label, logo at top					
❏ T 911 [M]	Hank Thompson Favorites	1957	20.00	40.00	80.00
—Turquoise or gray label					
❏ T 975 [M]	Hank Thompson's Dance Ranch	1958	20.00	40.00	80.00
—Turquoise or gray label					
❏ T 975 [M]	Hank Thompson's Dance Ranch	1959	7.50	15.00	30.00
—Black colorband label, logo at left					
❏ T 975 [M]	Hank Thompson's Dance Ranch	1962	5.00	10.00	20.00
—Black colorband label, logo at top					
❏ T 1111 [M]	Favorite Waltzes	1959	20.00	40.00	80.00
—Black colorband label, logo at left					
❏ T 1111 [M]	Favorite Waltzes	1962	5.00	10.00	20.00
—Black colorband label, logo at top					
❏ ST 1246 [S]	Songs for Rounders	1959	10.00	20.00	40.00
❏ T 1246 [M]	Songs for Rounders	1959	7.50	15.00	30.00
❏ ST 1360 [S]	Most of All	1960	10.00	20.00	40.00
—Black colorband label, logo at left					
❏ ST 1360 [S]	Most of All	1962	6.25	12.50	25.00
—Black colorband label, logo at top					
❏ T 1360 [M]	Most of All	1960	7.50	15.00	30.00
—Black colorband label, logo at left					
❏ T 1360 [M]	Most of All	1962	5.00	10.00	20.00
—Black colorband label, logo at top					
❏ ST 1469 [S]	This Broken Heart of Mine	1960	10.00	20.00	40.00
—Black colorband label, logo at left					
❏ ST 1469 [S]	This Broken Heart of Mine	1962	6.25	12.50	25.00
—Black colorband label, logo at top					
❏ T 1469 [M]	This Broken Heart of Mine	1960	7.50	15.00	30.00
—Black colorband label, logo at left					
❏ T 1469 [M]	This Broken Heart of Mine	1962	5.00	10.00	20.00
—Black colorband label, logo at top					
❏ ST 1544 [S]	An Old Love Affair	1961	7.50	15.00	30.00
—Black colorband label, logo at left					
❏ ST 1544 [S]	An Old Love Affair	1962	5.00	10.00	20.00
—Black colorband label, logo at top					
❏ T 1544 [M]	An Old Love Affair	1961	6.25	12.50	25.00
—Black colorband label, logo at left					
❏ T 1544 [M]	An Old Love Affair	1962	3.75	7.50	15.00
—Black colorband label, logo at top					
❏ ST 1632 [S]	Hank Thompson at the Golden Nugget	1961	7.50	15.00	30.00
—Black colorband label, logo at left					
❏ ST 1632 [S]	Hank Thompson at the Golden Nugget	1962	5.00	10.00	20.00
—Black colorband label, logo at top					
❏ T 1632 [M]	Hank Thompson at the Golden Nugget	1961	6.25	12.50	25.00
—Black colorband label, logo at left					
❏ T 1632 [M]	Hank Thompson at the Golden Nugget	1962	3.75	7.50	15.00
—Black colorband label, logo at top					
❏ DT 1741 [R]	The #1 Country and Western Band	1962	3.00	6.00	12.00
—Black colorband label, logo at top					
❏ DT 1741 [R]	The #1 Country and Western Band	1962	5.00	10.00	20.00
—Black colorband label, logo at top					
❏ T 1741 [M]	The #1 Country and Western Band	1962	5.00	10.00	20.00
—Black colorband label, logo at left					
❏ T 1741 [M]	The #1 Country and Western Band	1962	7.50	15.00	30.00
—Black colorband label, logo at top					
❏ ST 1775 [S]	Cheyenne Frontier Days	1962	6.25	12.50	25.00
❏ T 1775 [M]	Cheyenne Frontier Days	1962	5.00	10.00	20.00
❏ ST 1878 [S]	The Best of Hank Thompson	1963	6.25	12.50	25.00
❏ T 1878 [M]	The Best of Hank Thompson	1963	5.00	10.00	20.00
❏ ST 1955 [S]	Hank Thompson at the State Fair of Texas	1963	6.25	12.50	25.00

Number	Title (A Side/B Side)	Yr	VG	VG+	NM
❏ T 1955 [M]	Hank Thompson at the State Fair of Texas	1963	5.00	10.00	20.00
❏ ST 2089 [S]	Golden Country Hits	1964	6.25	12.50	25.00
❏ T 2089 [M]	Golden Country Hits	1964	5.00	10.00	20.00
❏ ST 2154 [S]	It's Christmas Time	1963	6.25	12.50	25.00
❏ T 2154 [M]	It's Christmas Time	1963	5.00	10.00	20.00
❏ ST 2274 [S]	Breakin' In Another Heart	1965	6.25	12.50	25.00
❏ T 2274 [M]	Breakin' In Another Heart	1965	5.00	10.00	20.00
❏ ST 2342 [S]	Luckiest Heartache in Town	1965	6.25	12.50	25.00
❏ T 2342 [M]	Luckiest Heartache in Town	1965	5.00	10.00	20.00
❏ ST 2460 [S]	A Six Pack to Go	1966	6.25	12.50	25.00
❏ T 2460 [M]	A Six Pack to Go	1966	5.00	10.00	20.00
❏ ST 2575 [S]	Breakin' the Rules	1966	6.25	12.50	25.00
❏ T 2575 [M]	Breakin' the Rules	1966	5.00	10.00	20.00
❏ ST 2661 [S]	The Best of Hank Thompson Vol. 2	1967	5.00	10.00	20.00
❏ T 2661 [M]	The Best of Hank Thompson Vol. 2	1967	6.25	12.50	25.00
❏ ST 2826 [S]	Just an Old Flame	1967	5.00	10.00	20.00
❏ T 2826 [M]	Just an Old Flame	1967	6.25	12.50	25.00

DOT

❏ DOS 2-2000 [(2)]	Hank Thompson's 25th Anniversary Album	1971	5.00	10.00	20.00
❏ DLP-25864	Hank Thompson Sings the Gold Standards	1968	3.75	7.50	15.00
❏ DLP-25894	On Tap, In the Can, or In the Bottle	1968	3.75	7.50	15.00
❏ DLP-25932	Smoky the Bar	1969	3.75	7.50	15.00
❏ DLP-25971	Hank Thompson Salutes Oklahoma	1969	3.75	7.50	15.00
❏ DLP-25991	Next Time I Fall in Love (I Won't)	1971	3.75	7.50	15.00
❏ DOS-25996	Cab Driver (A Salute to the Mills Brothers)	1972	3.75	7.50	15.00
❏ DOS-26004	Hank Thompson's Greatest Hits Vol. 1	1972	3.75	7.50	15.00
❏ DOS-26015	Kindly Keep It Country	1973	3.75	7.50	15.00

HILLTOP

❏ JS-6085 [S]	You Always Hurt the One You Love	196?	3.00	6.00	12.00
—Five tracks are rechanneled, five are true stereo					

MCA

❏ 689	Brand New Hank	198?	2.00	4.00	8.00
❏ 3250	Take Me Back to Tulsa	1980	2.50	5.00	10.00

WARNER BROS.

❏ W 1664 [M]	Where Is the Circus and Other Heart Breakin' Hits	1966	3.75	7.50	15.00
❏ WS 1664 [S]	Where Is the Circus and Other Heart Breakin' Hits	1966	5.00	10.00	20.00
❏ W 1679 [M]	The Countrypolitan Sound of Hank Thompson	1967	3.75	7.50	15.00
❏ WS 1679 [S]	The Countrypolitan Sound of Hank Thompson	1967	5.00	10.00	20.00
❏ W 1686 [M]	The Gold Standard Collection of Hank Thompson	1967	3.75	7.50	15.00
❏ WS 1686 [S]	The Gold Standard Collection of Hank Thompson	1967	5.00	10.00	20.00

THOMPSON, JUNIOR

45s
ATCO

❏ 6500	You're the One/Jungle Girl	1967	3.00	6.00	12.00

METEOR

❏ 5029	Mama's Little Baby/Raw Deal	1956	100.00	200.00	400.00

THOMPSON, KAY

45s
CADENCE

❏ CCS 3	Eloise/Just One of Those Things	1956	3.00	6.00	12.00
❏ CCS 3 [PS]	Eloise/Just One of Those Things	1956	5.00	10.00	20.00
❏ 1286	Eloise/Just One of Those Things	1956	—	—	—
—Evidently not released on this number					

MGM

❏ K11888	It's All Right with Me/I Hadn't Anyone Till You	1954	3.00	6.00	12.00
❏ K12075	Moonglow/How Deep Is the Ocean	1955	3.00	6.00	12.00

VERVE

❏ 10052	Bazazz/Light Up the Candle on the Birthday Cake	1957	3.00	6.00	12.00

THOMPSON, LORETTA

45s
SKOOP

❏ 1050	Buddy-Big Bopper-Ritchie/Square from Nowhere	1959	12.50	25.00	50.00

UNITED

❏ 214	He Do Ho Rock 'N' Roll/Let's Change the Alphabet	1958	10.00	20.00	40.00

THOMPSON, PEGGY

45s
HIT

❏ 04	Love Letters/Soldier Boy	1962	2.00	4.00	8.00
❏ 07	Mashed Potato Time/(B-side unknown)	1962	2.00	4.00	8.00
❏ 15	I Sold My Heart to the Junkman/Snap Your Fingers	1962	2.00	4.00	8.00
—B-side by Benny Lattimore					

THOMPSON, RICHARD Also see FAIRPORT CONVENTION; RICHARD AND LINDA THOMPSON.

45s
CAPITOL

❏ S7-18043	I Can't Wake Up to Save My Life/Easy There	1994	—	2.50	5.00
❏ 58810	Crawl Back (Under My Stone)/Bathsheba Smiles	1999	—	—	3.00

Albums
BONG LOAD

❏ BL 44 [(2)]	Mock Tudor	1999	3.75	7.50	15.00
❏ BL 52 [(2)]	Action Packed	2001	3.75	7.50	15.00
—1,000 copies pressed on "Coke-bottle green" vinyl					

CAPITOL

❏ C1-48845	Amnesia	1988	2.00	4.00	8.00
❏ C1-95713	Rumor & Sigh	1991	3.00	6.00	12.00

CARTHAGE

❏ CGLP-4405	Henry the Human Fly	1983	2.00	4.00	8.00
—Reissue of Reprise LP					
❏ CGLP-4409	Strict Tempo	1983	2.00	4.00	8.00
❏ CGLP-4413 [(2)]	Richard Thompson (Guitar/Vocal)	1983	2.50	5.00	10.00
—Reissue of Island 9421 with original UK title					

HANNIBAL

❏ HNLP-1313	Heart of Kindness	1983	2.50	5.00	10.00

T

Number	Title (A Side/B Side)	Yr	VG	VG+	NM
❏ HNLP-1316	Small Town Romance	1984	2.50	5.00	10.00
POLYDOR					
❏ 825421-1	Across a Crowded Room	1985	2.00	4.00	8.00
❏ 829728-1	Daring Adventures	1986	2.00	4.00	8.00
REPRISE					
❏ MS 2112	Henry the Human Fly	1972	5.00	10.00	20.00

THOMPSON, RICHARD AND LINDA
Albums
CARTHAGE

Number	Title (A Side/B Side)	Yr	VG	VG+	NM
❏ CGLP-4403	Sunnyvista	1983	2.50	5.00	10.00
—First U.S. issue of this LP					
❏ CGLP-4404	Pour Down Like Silver	1983	2.00	4.00	8.00
—Reissue of Island 9348					
❏ CGLP-4407	I Want to See the Bright Lights Tonight	1983	2.50	5.00	10.00
—Reissue of Island 9266 (UK)					
❏ CGLP-4408	Hokey Pokey	1983	2.00	4.00	8.00
—Reissue of Island 9305					
❏ CGLP-4412	First Light	1983	2.00	4.00	8.00
—Reissue of Chrysalis 1177					
CHRYSALIS					
❏ CHR 1177	First Light	1978	3.75	7.50	15.00
❏ CHR 1247	Sunnyvista	1979	—	—	—
—Unreleased in U.S.					
HANNIBAL					
❏ HNBL 1303	Shoot Out the Lights	1982	2.50	5.00	10.00
ISLAND					
❏ ILPS 9266	I Want to See the Bright Lights Tonight	1974	—	—	—
—Unreleased in U.S. on this number					
❏ ILPS 9305	Hokey Pokey	1974	3.75	7.50	15.00
❏ ILPS 9348	Pour Down Like Silver	1975	3.75	7.50	15.00
❏ ISLA 9421 [(2)]	Bright Lights and Live! More or Less	1977	5.00	10.00	20.00
—First U.S. issue of "I Want to See the Bright Lights Tonight" plus an LP of unreleased material					

THOMPSON, SUE Also see DON GIBSON AND SUE THOMPSON.
45s
DECCA

Number	Title (A Side/B Side)	Yr	VG	VG+	NM
❏ 29314	Walkin' in the Snow/Come a Little Bit Closer	1954	6.25	12.50	25.00
—With Hank Penny					
❏ 29545	Day Dreaming/Your Mommie and Your Daddy	1955	6.25	12.50	25.00
❏ 30435	Walkin' to Missouri/Red Hot Honey Brown	1957	6.25	12.50	25.00
HICKORY					
❏ 1144	Throwin' Kisses/Angel, Angel	1961	5.00	10.00	20.00
❏ 1153	Sad Movies (Make Me Cry)/Nine Little Teardrops	1961	5.00	10.00	20.00
❏ 1159	Norman/Never Love Again	1961	5.00	10.00	20.00
❏ 1166	Two of a Kind/It Has to Be	1962	3.75	7.50	15.00
❏ 1174	Have a Good Time/The Boy Only Knew	1962	3.75	7.50	15.00
❏ 1183	James (Hold the Ladder Steady)/My Hero	1962	3.75	7.50	15.00
❏ 1196	Willie Can/Too Much in Love	1962	3.75	7.50	15.00
❏ 1204	What's Wrong Bill/I Need a Harbor	1963	3.75	7.50	15.00
❏ 1204 [PS]	What's Wrong Bill/I Need a Harbor	1963	5.00	10.00	20.00
❏ 1217	True Confession/Suzie	1963	3.75	7.50	15.00
❏ 1217 [PS]	True Confession/Suzie	1963	5.00	10.00	20.00
❏ 1221	Too Hot to Dance/I Like Your Kind of Love	1963	3.00	6.00	12.00
—With Bob Luman					
❏ 1234	'Cause I Ask You To/It's Twelve Thirty-Five	1963	3.00	6.00	12.00
❏ 1240	Big Daddy/I'd Like to Know You Better	1964	3.00	6.00	12.00
❏ 1255	Bad Boy/Toys	1964	3.00	6.00	12.00
❏ 1270	Big Hearted Me/Looking for a Good Boy	1964	3.00	6.00	12.00
❏ 1284	Paper Tiger/Mama, Don't Cry at My Wedding	1964	3.75	7.50	15.00
❏ 1308	Stop Th' Music/What I'm Needin' Is You	1965	3.00	6.00	12.00
❏ 1328	Afraid/It's Break-Up Time	1965	3.00	6.00	12.00
❏ 1340	Just Kiss Me/Sweet Hunk of Misery	1965	3.00	6.00	12.00
❏ 1359	Walkin' My Baby/I'm Lookin' (For a World)	1965	3.00	6.00	12.00
❏ 1381	What Should I Do/After the Heartache	1966	2.50	5.00	10.00
❏ 1403	I Can't Help It/Put It Back	1966	2.50	5.00	10.00
❏ 1423	Someone/From My Balcony	1966	2.50	5.00	10.00
❏ 1431	Language of Love/Let Me Down Hard	1967	2.50	5.00	10.00
❏ 1457	Don't Forget to Cry/Ferris Wheel	1967	2.50	5.00	10.00
❏ 1469	That's Just Too Much/Straight to Helen	1967	2.50	5.00	10.00
❏ 1488	Dear Boy/Love Has Come My Way	1967	2.50	5.00	10.00
❏ 1493	How Do You Start Over/Why Not	1968	2.00	4.00	8.00
❏ 1512	You Deserve Each Other/Doin' Nothing	1968	2.00	4.00	8.00
❏ 1524	Don't Try to Change Me/The Real Me	1968	2.00	4.00	8.00
❏ 1534	Tennessee Waltz/Who's Gonna Mow Your Grass	1969	2.00	4.00	8.00
❏ 1547	Pair of Broken Hearts/You Two-Timed Me One Time Too Often	1969	2.00	4.00	8.00
❏ 1560	I Just Keep Hangin' On/Lost Highway	1970	—	3.00	6.00
❏ 1577	Whole Lot of Walkin'/Guess Who's Coming to Dinner Tonight	1970	—	3.00	6.00
❏ 1587	Because You Love Me/Take a Little Time	1971	—	3.00	6.00
❏ 1596	Here's To Forever/What You See Is What You Get	1971	—	3.00	6.00
❏ 1612	Swiss Cottage Place/Thanks to Rumors	1971	—	3.00	6.00
❏ 1622	Let Your Thoughts Be Sweet/What a Woman in Love Won't Do	1972	—	3.00	6.00
❏ 1641	Sweet Memories/Take Me As I Am	1972	—	3.00	6.00
❏ 1652	Candy and Roses/Full Time Job	1972	—	3.00	6.00
❏ 1669	How I Love Them Old Songs/Just Two Young People	1973	—	2.50	5.00
HICKORY/MGM					
❏ 308	Just Plain Country/Oh Johnny, Oh Johnny, Oh	1973	—	2.50	5.00
❏ 313	Find Out/Stay Another Day	1974	—	2.50	5.00
❏ 320	Making Love to You Is Just Like Eating Peanuts/Sweet Memories	1974	—	2.50	5.00
❏ 330	Trains/And Love Me	1974	—	2.50	5.00
❏ 339	The Thought of Losing You/Tennessee Waltz	1975	—	2.00	4.00
❏ 346	I Can't Stop Loving You/Any Other Morning	1975	—	2.00	4.00
❏ 354	Big Mabel Murphy/Big Daddy	1975	—	2.00	4.00
❏ 364	Never Naughty Rosie/He Cheats on Me	1976	—	2.00	4.00
❏ 370	Baby's Not Home/I Want It All	1976	—	2.00	4.00
MERCURY					
❏ 6325	You're Getting a Good Girl (When You Get Me)/What've You Got (That Makes Me Love You So)	1951	10.00	20.00	40.00

Number	Title (A Side/B Side)	Yr	VG	VG+	NM
❏ 6377	Just Walking Out the Door/I'll Hate Myself in the Morning	1952	7.50	15.00	30.00
❏ 6390	Junior's a Big Boy Now/Tadpole	1952	7.50	15.00	30.00
❏ 6407	You Belong to Me/You're an Angel on the Outside	1952	7.50	15.00	30.00
❏ 6416	Red Hot Henrietta Brown/Last Night I Heard Somebody Cry	1952	7.50	15.00	30.00
❏ 70066	How Many Tears/If You Should Change	1953	6.25	12.50	25.00
❏ 70084	Take Care My Love/Things I Might Have Been	1953	6.25	12.50	25.00
❏ 70089	You and Me/Say It with Your Heart	1953	6.25	12.50	25.00
❏ 70152	I'm Not That Kind of Girl/I Long to Tell You	1953	6.25	12.50	25.00
❏ 70309	Donna Wanna/Gee But I Hate to Go Home Alone	1954	6.25	12.50	25.00

Albums
HICKORY

Number	Title (A Side/B Side)	Yr	VG	VG+	NM
❏ LPM-104 [M]	Meet Sue Thompson	1962	12.50	25.00	50.00
❏ LPS-104 [S]	Meet Sue Thompson	1962	20.00	40.00	80.00
❏ LPM-107 [M]	Two of a Kind	1962	7.50	15.00	30.00
❏ LPS-107 [S]	Two of a Kind	1962	10.00	20.00	40.00
❏ LPM-111 [M]	Sue Thompson's Golden Hits	1963	7.50	15.00	30.00
❏ LPS-111 [S]	Sue Thompson's Golden Hits	1963	10.00	20.00	40.00
❏ LPM-121 [M]	Paper Tiger	1965	7.50	15.00	30.00
❏ LPS-121 [S]	Paper Tiger	1965	10.00	20.00	40.00
❏ LPM-130 [M]	Sue Thompson with Strings Attached	1966	7.50	15.00	30.00
❏ LPS-130 [S]	Sue Thompson with Strings Attached	1966	10.00	20.00	40.00
❏ LPS-148	This Is Sue Thompson Country	1969	5.00	10.00	20.00
❏ H3F-4511	Sweet Memories	1974	3.75	7.50	15.00
❏ H3G-4515	…And Love Me	1974	3.75	7.50	15.00
WING					
❏ MGW-12317 [M]	The Country Side of Sue Thompson	1965	5.00	10.00	20.00
❏ SRW-16317 [R]	The Country Side of Sue Thompson	1965	3.75	7.50	15.00

THOR-ABLES, THE
45s
TITANIC

Number	Title (A Side/B Side)	Yr	VG	VG+	NM
❏ 1001	Our Love Song/Get That Bread	1962	75.00	150.00	300.00
❏ 1002	My Reckless Heart/Batman and Robin	1962	75.00	150.00	300.00

THORINSHIELD
45s
PHILIPS

Number	Title (A Side/B Side)	Yr	VG	VG+	NM
❏ 40492	The Best of All/Life Is a Dream	1967	2.00	4.00	8.00
❏ 40521	Family of Man/Lonely Mountain Again	1968	2.00	4.00	8.00

Albums
PHILIPS

Number	Title (A Side/B Side)	Yr	VG	VG+	NM
❏ PHS 600251	Thorinshield	1968	5.00	10.00	20.00

THORNE, DAVID
45s
ADMIRAL

Number	Title (A Side/B Side)	Yr	VG	VG+	NM
❏ 750	Time Out for Tears/Since You Went Away	1964	3.75	7.50	15.00
❏ 756	I Love You, Yes I Do/Send a Little My Way	1964	3.75	7.50	15.00
❏ 761	You're Next/Talkin' to Myself	1965	3.75	7.50	15.00
❏ 768	If You Were Mine Again/Where'll I Be Tomorrow Night	1965	3.75	7.50	15.00
❏ 772	Dearest/Turning Point	1965	3.75	7.50	15.00
CHOICE					
❏ 10	Night-Time Baby/Annie Doesn't Live Here Any More	1960	5.00	10.00	20.00
—As "David Throne"					
RIVERSIDE					
❏ 4520	I'll Be There/If You Should Ever Need Me	1962	3.00	6.00	12.00
❏ 4530	The Alley Cat Song/The Moon Was Yellow	1962	3.00	6.00	12.00
❏ 4552	Don't Let It Get Away/One More Fool, One More Broken Heart	1963	3.00	6.00	12.00
SAVOY					
❏ 1577	You Can't Do Me This Way/These Are the Things	1959	5.00	10.00	20.00

THORNTON, BIG MAMA
45s
ARHOOLIE

Number	Title (A Side/B Side)	Yr	VG	VG+	NM
❏ 512	Swing It On Home/My Heavy Load	1968	2.00	4.00	8.00
❏ 520	Ball and Chain/Wade in the Water	1968	2.00	4.00	8.00
BAYTONE					
❏ 107	You Did Me Wrong/Big Mama's Blues	1961	3.75	7.50	15.00
GALAXY					
❏ 749	Life Goes On/Because It's Love	1966	2.50	5.00	10.00
KENT					
❏ 424	Before Day/Me and My Chauffeur	1965	2.50	5.00	10.00
MERCURY					
❏ 72981	Hound Dog/Let's Go Get Started	1969	2.00	4.00	8.00
PEACOCK					
❏ 1603	Everytime I Think of You/Mischievous Boogie	1952	25.00	50.00	100.00
❏ 1612	Hound Dog/Nightmare	1953	45.00	90.00	180.00
❏ 1612	Hound Dog/Rock-a-Bye Baby	1953	50.00	100.00	200.00
❏ 1621	They Call Me Big Mama/Cotton Pickin' Blues	1953	25.00	50.00	100.00
❏ 1626	Big Change/I Ain't No Fool Either	1953	25.00	50.00	100.00
❏ 1632	I've Searched the Whole World/I Smell a Rat	1954	15.00	30.00	60.00
❏ 1642	Stop Hoppin' on Me/Story of My Blues	1954	15.00	30.00	60.00
❏ 1647	Walking Blues/Rock-a-Bye Baby	1955	15.00	30.00	60.00
❏ 1650	The Fish/Laugh, Laugh, Laugh	1955	15.00	30.00	60.00
❏ 1681	Just Like a Dog/My Man Called Me	1957	10.00	20.00	40.00
SOTOPLAY					
❏ SO-0033/34	Summer Time/The Truth'll Come to the Light	1965	3.75	7.50	15.00

Albums
ARHOOLIE

Number	Title (A Side/B Side)	Yr	VG	VG+	NM
❏ F-1028 [M]	Big Mama Thornton in Europe	1966	7.50	15.00	30.00
❏ F-1032 [M]	Chicago Blues: The Queen at Monterey	1967	7.50	15.00	30.00
❏ F-1039 [M]	Ball and Chain	1968	7.50	15.00	30.00
BACK BEAT					
❏ BLP-68	She's Back	1970	6.25	12.50	25.00
MERCURY					
❏ SR-61225	Stronger Than Dirt	1969	6.25	12.50	25.00
❏ SR-61249	The Way It Is	1970	6.25	12.50	25.00
PENTAGRAM					
❏ PE-10005	Saved	1971	5.00	10.00	20.00

T. Rex (as "Tyrannosaurus Rex"), *A Beard of Stars,* Blue Thumb BTS 18, stereo LP, with bonus 45 of "Ride a White Swan" included, $12.50-$25.

James Taylor, *James Taylor,* Apple SKAO 3352, stereo LP with title in orange letters, $10-$20.

Johnnie Taylor, *Johnnie Taylor's Greatest Hits,* Stax STS-2032, stereo LP, $12.50-$25.

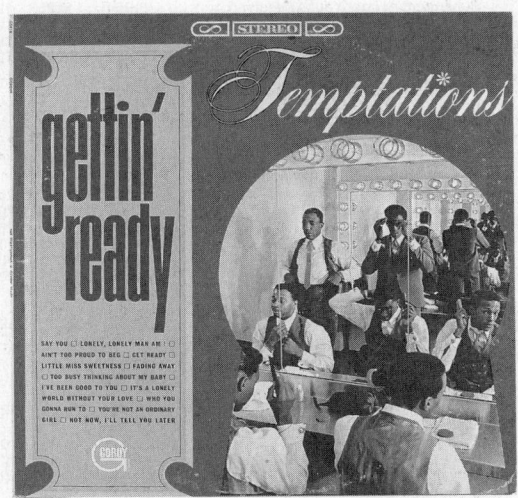

The Temptations, *Gettin' Ready*, Gordy GS 918, stereo LP with "Gordy" in script at top of label, $15-$30.

10CC, "Art for Art's Sake," Mercury 73725, picture sleeve, $4-$8.

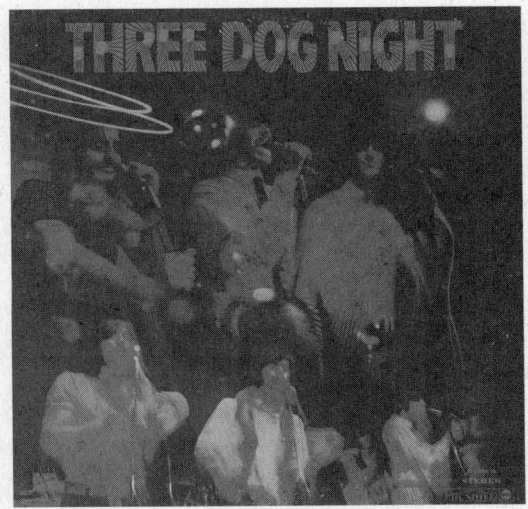

Three Dog Night, *Three Dog Night,* ABC-Dunhill DS-50048, without the word "One" on cover, $7.50-$15.

Number	Title (A Side/B Side)	Yr	VG	VG+	NM
VANGUARD					
❏ VSD-79351	Jail	1974	3.75	7.50	15.00
❏ VSD-79354	Sassy Mama	1975	3.75	7.50	15.00

THORNTON, FRADKIN AND UNGER
45s
ESP-DISK

Number	Title (A Side/B Side)	Yr	VG	VG+	NM
❏ 63019	God Bless California/Sometimes	1972	3.75	7.50	15.00

—*Paul McCartney appears on this record*

THREE BELLS, THE
45s
LAWN

Number	Title (A Side/B Side)	Yr	VG	VG+	NM
❏ 251	He Doesn't Love Me/Softly in the Night	1965	3.00	6.00	12.00

THREE BLONDE MICE
45s
ATCO

Number	Title (A Side/B Side)	Yr	VG	VG+	NM
❏ 6324	Ringo Bells/The 12 Days of Christmas	1964	7.50	15.00	30.00
❏ 6353	Alley Cat/What Did I Say	1965	2.50	5.00	10.00

THREE CHUCKLES, THE Also see TEDDY RANDAZZO.
45s
BOULEVARD

Number	Title (A Side/B Side)	Yr	VG	VG+	NM
❏ 100	Runaround/At Last You Understand	1954	20.00	40.00	80.00
VIK					
❏ 0186	Anyway/The Funny Little Things We Used to Do	1956	5.00	10.00	20.00
❏ 0194	Tell Me/And the Angels Sing	1956	5.00	10.00	20.00
❏ 0216	Gypsy in My Soul/We're Still Holding Hands	1956	5.00	10.00	20.00
❏ 0232	Fallen Out of Love/Midnight 'Til Dawn	1956	5.00	10.00	20.00
❏ 0244	Won't You Give Me a Chance/We're Gonna Rock Tonight	1956	5.00	10.00	20.00
"X"					
❏ 0066	Runaround/At Last You Understand	1954	6.25	12.50	25.00
❏ 0095	Foolishly/If I Should Love Again	1955	6.25	12.50	25.00
❏ 0134	So Long/You Should Have Told Me	1955	6.25	12.50	25.00
❏ 0150	Blue Lover/Realize	1955	6.25	12.50	25.00
❏ 0162	Times Two, I Love You/Still Thinking of You	1955	6.25	12.50	25.00
❏ 0186	Anyway/The Funny Little Things We Used to Do	1956	6.25	12.50	25.00
❏ 0194	Tell Me/And the Angels Sing	1956	6.25	12.50	25.00
❏ 0216	Gypsy in My Soul/We're Still Holding Hands	1956	6.25	12.50	25.00

7-Inch Extended Plays
"X"

Number	Title (A Side/B Side)	Yr	VG	VG+	NM
❏ EXA-192	To Each His Own/Solitude//In the Still of the Night/It's Been a Long, Long Time	1955	10.00	20.00	40.00
❏ EXA-192 [PS]	The Three Chuckles (Vol. 1)	1955	10.00	20.00	40.00
❏ EXA-193	(contents unknown)	1955	10.00	20.00	40.00
❏ EXA-193 [PS]	The Three Chuckles (Vol. 2)	1955	10.00	20.00	40.00
❏ EXA-194	(contents unknown)	1955	10.00	20.00	40.00
❏ EXA-194 [PS]	The Three Chuckles (Vol. 3)	1955	10.00	20.00	40.00

Albums
VIK

Number	Title (A Side/B Side)	Yr	VG	VG+	NM
❏ LX-1067 [M]	The Three Chuckles	1956	62.50	125.00	250.00

THREE D'S, THE (1)
45s
BRUNSWICK

Number	Title (A Side/B Side)	Yr	VG	VG+	NM
❏ 55152	Nothing to Wear/The Happiest Boy and Girl	1959	6.25	12.50	25.00
PARIS					
❏ 503	Little Billy Boy/Let Me Know	1957	5.00	10.00	20.00
❏ 508	Never Let You Go/Birth of An Angel	1957	5.00	10.00	20.00
❏ 511	Baby Doll/Crazy Little Woman	1958	5.00	10.00	20.00
❏ 514	Jumpin' Jack/I Never Saw My Pretty Little Baby Alone	1958	5.00	10.00	20.00
PILGRIM					
❏ 719	Broken Dreams/Tell Me That You Love Me	1956	6.25	12.50	25.00
SQUARE					
❏ 502	Squeeze/Graveyard Cha-Cha	1959	20.00	40.00	80.00

THREE D'S, THE (2)
45s
CAPITOL

Number	Title (A Side/B Side)	Yr	VG	VG+	NM
❏ 5188	Sinner Man/Give, Said the Little Stream	1964	2.50	5.00	10.00
❏ 5249	Chim Chim Cheree/Crayon Box	1964	2.50	5.00	10.00

Albums
CAPITOL

Number	Title (A Side/B Side)	Yr	VG	VG+	NM
❏ ST 2171 [S]	New Dimensions in Folk Songs	1964	6.25	12.50	25.00
❏ T 2171 [M]	New Dimensions in Folk Songs	1964	5.00	10.00	20.00
❏ ST 2314 [S]	I Won't Be Worried Long	1965	6.25	12.50	25.00
❏ T 2314 [M]	I Won't Be Worried Long	1965	5.00	10.00	20.00

THREE D'S, THE (U)
45s
DEAN

Number	Title (A Side/B Side)	Yr	VG	VG+	NM
❏ 521	Broken Hearted/I Love You So	1961	5.00	10.00	20.00

THREE DEGREES, THE
45s
ARIOLA AMERICA

Number	Title (A Side/B Side)	Yr	VG	VG+	NM
❏ 801	My Simple Heart/Hot Summer Night	1980	—	2.00	4.00
❏ 7721	Giving Up, Giving In/Woman in Love	1978	—	2.00	4.00
❏ 7742	Woman in Love/Out of Love Again	1979	—	2.00	4.00
❏ 7746	The Runner/Out of Love Again	1979	—	2.00	4.00
EPIC					
❏ 50283	What I Did for Love/Macaronie Man	1976	—	2.00	4.00
❏ 50330	In Love We Grow/Standing Up for Love	1977	—	2.00	4.00
ICHIBAN					
❏ 89-167	Tie U Up//(B-side unknown)	1989	—	2.50	5.00
METROMEDIA					
❏ 109	Down in the Boondocks/Warm Weather Music	1969	2.00	4.00	8.00
❏ 128	Feeling of Love/Warm Weather Music	1969	2.00	4.00	8.00
NEPTUNE					
❏ 23	Reflections of Yesterday/What I See	1970	—	3.00	6.00
PHILADELPHIA INT'L.					
❏ 3534	Dirty Ol Man/Can't You See What You're Doing to Me	1973	—	3.00	6.00
❏ 3539	Year of Decision/A Woman Needs a Good Man	1974	—	2.50	5.00
❏ 3550	When Will I See You Again/Year of Decision	1974	—	2.50	5.00
❏ 3561	I Didn't Know/Dirty Ol Man	1975	—	2.50	5.00
❏ 3568	Take Good Care of Yourself/Here I Am	1975	—	2.50	5.00
❏ 3585	Free Ride/Loving Cup	1976	—	2.50	5.00
ROULETTE					
❏ 7072	Melting Pot/The Grass Will Sing for You	1970	—	3.00	6.00
❏ 7079	Maybe/Collage	1970	—	3.00	6.00
❏ 7079	Maybe/Sugar on Sunday	1970	—	3.00	6.00
❏ 7088	I Do Take You/You're the Fool	1970	—	3.00	6.00
❏ 7097	You're the One/Stardust	1971	—	3.00	6.00
❏ 7102	There's So Much Love All Around/Yours	1971	—	3.00	6.00
❏ 7105	Ebb Tide/Low Down	1971	—	3.00	6.00
❏ 7117	Trade Winds/I Turn to You	1972	—	3.00	6.00
❏ 7125	Find My Way/I Wanna Be Your Baby	1972	—	3.00	6.00
❏ 7137	I Won't Let You Go/Through Misty Eyes	1972	—	3.00	6.00
SWAN					
❏ 4197	Gee Baby (I'm Sorry)/Do What You're Supposed to Do	1965	3.00	6.00	12.00
❏ 4214	I'm Gonna Need You/Just Right for Love	1965	3.00	6.00	12.00
❏ 4224	Close Your Eyes/Gotta Draw the Line	1965	3.00	6.00	12.00
❏ 4235	Look in My Eyes/Drivin' Me Mad	1965	3.00	6.00	12.00
❏ 4245	Maybe/Yours	1966	3.00	6.00	12.00
❏ 4253	I Wanna Be Your Baby/Tales Are True	1966	3.00	6.00	12.00
❏ 4267	Love of My Life/Are You Satisfied	1967	3.00	6.00	12.00
WARNER BROS.					
❏ 7198	Contact/Oh No Not Again	1968	2.50	5.00	10.00

Albums
ARIOLA AMERICA

Number	Title (A Side/B Side)	Yr	VG	VG+	NM
❏ OL 1501	Three D	1980	2.50	5.00	10.00
❏ SW-50044	New Dimensions	1978	2.50	5.00	10.00
EPIC					
❏ PE 34385	Standing Up for Love	1977	3.00	6.00	12.00
ICHIBAN					
❏ ICH-1041	Three Degrees...And Holding	198?	2.50	5.00	10.00
PHILADELPHIA INT'L.					
❏ KZ 32406	The Three Degrees	1974	3.00	6.00	12.00
❏ KZ 33162	International	1975	3.00	6.00	12.00
❏ PZ 33840	The Three Degrees Live	1975	3.00	6.00	12.00
ROULETTE					
❏ 3015	So Much Love	1975	2.50	5.00	10.00
❏ SR-42050	Maybe	1970	10.00	20.00	40.00

THREE DOG NIGHT Also see DANNY HUTTON; CORY WELLS AND THE ENEMYS.
45s
ABC

Number	Title (A Side/B Side)	Yr	VG	VG+	NM
❏ 12114	'Til the World Ends/Yo Te Quiero Hablo (Take You Down)	1975	—	2.00	4.00
❏ 12192	Everybody Is a Masterpiece/Drive On, Ride On	1976	—	2.00	4.00
ABC DUNHILL					
❏ 4168	Nobody/It's for You	1968	3.00	6.00	12.00
❏ 4168 [PS]	Nobody/It's for You	1968	7.50	15.00	30.00
—*Sleeve is promo only*					
❏ 4177	Try a Little Tenderness/That No One Ever Hurt So Bad	1969	2.00	4.00	8.00
❏ 4191	One/Chest Fever	1969	2.00	4.00	8.00
❏ 4203	Easy to Be Hard/Dreaming Isn't Good for You	1969	2.00	4.00	8.00
❏ 4215	Eli's Coming/Circle for a Landing	1969	2.00	4.00	8.00
❏ 4229	Celebrate/Feeling Alright	1970	—	3.00	6.00
❏ 4239	Mama Told Me (Not to Come)/Rock and Roll Widow	1970	—	3.00	6.00
❏ 4239 [PS]	Mama Told Me (Not to Come)/Rock and Roll Widow	1970	3.00	6.00	12.00
❏ 4250	Out in the Country/Good Time Living	1970	—	3.00	6.00
❏ 4262	One Man Band/It Ain't Easy	1970	—	3.00	6.00
❏ 4272	Joy to the World/I Can Hear You Calling	1971	—	2.50	5.00
❏ 4282	Liar/Can't Get Enough of It	1971	—	2.50	5.00
❏ 4294	An Old Fashioned Love Song/Jam	1971	—	2.50	5.00
❏ 4299	Never Been to Spain/Peace of Mind	1972	—	2.50	5.00
❏ 4299	Never Been to Spain//Intro Poem: Mistakes and Illusions/Peace of Mind	1972	—	3.00	6.00
❏ 4306	The Family of Man/Going in Circles	1972	—	2.50	5.00
❏ 4317	Black and White/Freedom for the Stallion	1972	—	2.50	5.00
❏ 4331	Pieces of April/The Writings on the Wall	1972	—	2.50	5.00
❏ 4352	Shambala/Our "B" Side	1973	—	2.00	4.00
—*Later pressings have "Dunhill" in a box on both labels (1968-72 style)*					
❏ 4352	Shambala/Our "B" Side	1973	—	2.50	5.00
—*Transitional pressings have "Dunhill" in children's blocks on one label and "Dunhill" in a box on the other label*					
❏ 4352	Shambala/Our "B" Side	1973	—	2.50	5.00
—*First pressings have "Dunhill" spelled out in children's blocks*					
❏ 4370	Let Me Serenade You/Storybook Feeling	1973	—	2.00	4.00
❏ 4382	The Show Must Go On/On the Way Back Home	1974	—	2.00	4.00
❏ 15001	Sure As I'm Sittin' Here/Anytime Babe	1974	—	2.00	4.00
❏ 15010	The Show Must Go On/On the Way Back Home	1974	2.00	4.00	8.00
❏ 15013	Play Something Sweet (Brickyard Blues)/I'd Be So Happy	1974	—	2.00	4.00
PASSPORT					
❏ 7921	It's a Jungle Out There/Somebody's Gonna Get Hurt	1983	—	2.50	5.00

7-Inch Extended Plays
ABC DUNHILL

Number	Title (A Side/B Side)	Yr	VG	VG+	NM
❏ LLP-231	Happy Song/Play Children Play//Storybook Feeling/Ridin' Thumb	1973	3.00	6.00	12.00
—*Jukebox issue; small hole, plays at 33 1/3 rpm*					
❏ LLP-231 [PS]	Cyan	1973	3.00	6.00	12.00
❏ PRO-50108	My Impersonal Life/An Old Fashioned Love Song//Never Dreamed You'd Leave in Summer/Jam	1971	3.00	6.00	12.00
—*Jukebox issue; small hole, plays at 33 1/3 rpm*					
❏ PRO-50108 [PS]	Harmony	1971	3.00	6.00	12.00

Albums
ABC

Number	Title (A Side/B Side)	Yr	VG	VG+	NM
❏ 888	Coming Down Your Way	1975	2.50	5.00	10.00
❏ 928	American Pastime	1976	2.50	5.00	10.00
ABC DUNHILL					
❏ DS-50048	Three Dog Night	1968	3.75	7.50	15.00

Number	Title (A Side/B Side)	Yr	VG	VG+	NM
❑ DS-50048	Three Dog Night "One"	1969	3.00	6.00	12.00
—Same album as above, but with revised title on cover					
❑ DS-50058	Suitable for Framing	1969	3.00	6.00	12.00
❑ DS-50068	Three Dog Night Was Captured Live at the Forum	1969	3.00	6.00	12.00
❑ DS-50078	It Ain't Easy	1970	3.00	6.00	12.00
—Regular front cover with gatefold					
❑ DS-50078	It Ain't Easy	1970	25.00	50.00	100.00
—Original cover with band members in the nude					
❑ DSX-50088	Naturally	1970	3.00	6.00	12.00
—With detachable cardboard poster intact					
❑ DSX-50098	Golden Bisquits	1971	3.00	6.00	12.00
—With detachable cardboard poster intact; interestingly, the label spells the LP title "Golden Biscuits"					
❑ DSX-50108	Harmony	1971	3.00	6.00	12.00
❑ DSD-50118	Seven Separate Fools	1972	3.00	6.00	12.00
—With seven oversize playing cards included					
❑ DSY-50138 [(2)]	Around the World with Three Dog Night	1973	3.75	7.50	15.00
❑ DSX-50158	Cyan	1973	3.00	6.00	12.00
❑ DSD-50168	Hard Labor	1974	2.50	5.00	10.00
—With huge Band-Aid as part of the LP artwork					
❑ DSD-50168	Hard Labor	1974	3.75	7.50	15.00
—With huge Band-Aid attached to jacket, covering the "childbirth"					
❑ DSD-50168	Hard Labor	1974	7.50	15.00	30.00
—With uncensored "childbirth" front cover					
❑ DSD-50178	Joy to the World: Their Greatest Hits	1974	3.00	6.00	12.00
—With gatefold cover					
❑ DSD-50178	Joy to the World: Their Greatest Hits	1975	2.50	5.00	10.00
—With standard cover					
AT EASE					
❑ MD 11109	Three Dog Night: Their Greatest Recordings	1978	5.00	10.00	20.00
—"This Album Compiled Exclusively for Military Personnel" by ABC					
COMMAND					
❑ QD-40014 [Q]	Hard Labor	1974	5.00	10.00	20.00
❑ QD-40018 [Q]	Coming Down Your Way	1975	5.00	10.00	20.00
MCA					
❑ 6018 [(2)]	The Best of Three Dog Night	1982	3.00	6.00	12.00
❑ 37120	Joy to the World: Their Greatest Hits	1980	2.00	4.00	8.00
PASSPORT					
❑ PB 5001 [EP]	It's a Jungle	1983	2.00	4.00	8.00

THREE DOTS AND A DASH With JESSE BELVIN.
45s
IMPERIAL

❑ 5164	I'll Never Love Again/Let's Do It	1951	125.00	250.00	500.00

THREE FRIENDS, THE (1)
45s
CAL-GOLD

❑ 169	Walkin' Shoes/Blue Ribbon Baby	1961	50.00	100.00	200.00
IMPERIAL					
❑ 5763	Dedicated (To the Songs I Love)/ Happy as a Man Can Be	1961	7.50	15.00	30.00
❑ 5773	You're a Square/Go On to School	1961	5.00	10.00	20.00

THREE FRIENDS, THE (2)
45s
BRUNSWICK

❑ 55032	Jinx/Chinese Tearoom	1957	7.50	15.00	30.00
LIDO					
❑ 500	Baby I'll Cry/Blanche	1956	10.00	20.00	40.00
—Blue label					
❑ 500	Baby I'll Cry/Blanche	1956	15.00	30.00	60.00
—Gray label					
❑ 502	I'm Only a Boy/Jinx	1957	12.50	25.00	50.00
❑ 504	Now That You've Gone/Chinese Tea Room	1957	12.50	25.00	50.00
LOST-NITE					
❑ 398	Baby I'll Cry/Blanche	197?	—	2.50	5.00
—Reissue					

THREE G'S, THE
45s
COLUMBIA

❑ 4-41175	Let's Go Steady for the Summer/Wild Man	1958	5.00	10.00	20.00
❑ 4-41256	I'll Wait Forever/Sweet Thing	1958	3.75	7.50	15.00
❑ 4-41292	These Are the Little Things/Wonder	1958	3.75	7.50	15.00
❑ 4-41383	When It's Summer Again/Oh, Suzette	1959	3.75	7.50	15.00
❑ 4-41513	Barbara/Don't Cry Kathy	1959	3.75	7.50	15.00
❑ 4-41584	Eeny-Meeny-Miny-Moe/Take That Step	1960	3.75	7.50	15.00
❑ 4-41678	Let's Go Steady for the Summer/Love Call	1960	3.75	7.50	15.00
❑ 4-41868	She's Mine/Take My Love	1960	3.75	7.50	15.00
❑ 4-41955	Foolish Tears/Blueberry Hill	1961	3.75	7.50	15.00
RIP					
❑ 138	Toy Telephone/Going Steady	1958	7.50	15.00	30.00

THREE MAN ARMY, THE
Albums
KAMA SUTRA

❑ KSBS-2044	A Third of a Lifetime	1971	7.50	15.00	30.00
—Pink label, gatefold cover					
REPRISE					
❑ MS 2150	Three Man Army	1973	5.00	10.00	20.00
❑ MS 2182	Three Man Army Two	1974	5.00	10.00	20.00

THREE PENNIES, THE
45s
B.T. PUPPY

❑ 501	A Penny for Your Thoughts/Why Am I So Shy	1964	3.00	6.00	12.00

THREE PLAYMATES, THE
45s
SAVOY

❑ 1523	Giddy-Up-a-Ding-Dong/It Must Be Love	1957	6.25	12.50	25.00
❑ 1528	Sugah Wooga/Lovey Dovey Pair	1958	6.25	12.50	25.00
❑ 1537	(Do-oo, Do-oo) I Dreamer/Give Your Love to Me	1958	6.25	12.50	25.00

THREE SOULS, THE
45s
ARGO

Number	Title (A Side/B Side)	Yr	VG	VG+	NM
❑ 5369	The Horse/Madisonville	1960	5.00	10.00	20.00
❑ 5472	Hi-Heel Sneakers/Dangerous Dan Express	1964	3.75	7.50	15.00
❑ 5514	You're No Good/Chitterlins Con Carne	1965	3.00	6.00	12.00
NOTE					
❑ 10015	Night Time/Smorgasbord	1959	5.00	10.00	20.00
Albums					
ARGO					
❑ LP-4005 [M]	Almost Like Being In Love	1960	—	—	—
—Canceled					
❑ LPS-4005 [S]	Almost Like Being In Love	1960	—	—	—
—Canceled					
❑ LP-4036 [M]	Dangerous Dan Express	1964	5.00	10.00	20.00
❑ LPS-4036 [S]	Dangerous Dan Express	1964	6.25	12.50	25.00
❑ LP-4044 [M]	Soul Sounds	1965	5.00	10.00	20.00
❑ LPS-4044 [S]	Soul Sounds	1965	6.25	12.50	25.00

THREE SUNS, THE
45s
RCA VICTOR

❑ 47-2756	Dancing Tambourine/Stumbling	1949	2.50	5.00	10.00
❑ 47-2757	Dizzy Fingers/Eccentric	1949	2.50	5.00	10.00
❑ 47-2758	Nola/The Doll Dance	1949	2.50	5.00	10.00
❑ 47-2759	Canadian Capers/ The Wedding of the Painted Doll	1949	2.50	5.00	10.00
—The above four comprise a box set					
❑ 47-2839	Twilight Time/Hindustan	1949	2.50	5.00	10.00
❑ 47-2840	Deep Purple/Dardanella	1949	2.50	5.00	10.00
❑ 47-2841	Sunrise Serenade/When Day Is Done	1949	2.50	5.00	10.00
❑ 47-2842	I'll Never Wish for More Than This/ The Breeze and I	1949	2.50	5.00	10.00
—The above four comprise a box set					
❑ 47-2898	Hurry! Hurry! Hurry!/Ballin' the Jack	1949	3.00	6.00	12.00
❑ 47-2924	Ting-a-Ling/Everybody Kiss the Bride	1949	3.00	6.00	12.00
❑ 47-2964	Lover's Gold/ In a Shady Nook by a Babbling Brook	1949	3.00	6.00	12.00
❑ 47-2996	Hop Scotch Polka/The Windmill's Turning	1949	3.00	6.00	12.00
❑ 47-3025	Soft Lips/Give Me Some Sugar, Sugar Baby	1949	3.00	6.00	12.00
❑ 47-3057	Adeste Fideles/Santa Claus Is Coming to Town	1949	2.50	5.00	10.00
❑ 47-3058	Winter Wonderland/White Christmas	1949	2.50	5.00	10.00
❑ 47-3059	Jingle Bells/Silent Night	1949	2.50	5.00	10.00
—The above three comprise box set WP 250, "The Three Suns Present Your Christmas Favorites"					
❑ 47-3079	Close Your Eyes and Dream/ Merry Maiden Polka	1949	3.00	6.00	12.00
❑ 47-3094	The Donkey Serenade/Serenade	1949	2.50	5.00	10.00
❑ 47-3095	Penthouse Serenade/Frasquita Serenade	1949	2.50	5.00	10.00
❑ 47-3096	Serenade from the Student Prince/ Serenade in the Night	1949	2.50	5.00	10.00
—The above three comprise a box set					
❑ 47-3105	Beyond the Sunset/The Game of Broken Hearts	1949	7.50	15.00	30.00
—With Rosalie Allen and Elton Britt					
❑ 47-3202	Sugar Blues/The French Can-Can Song	1949	3.00	6.00	12.00
❑ 47-3230	Goofus/Ragging the Scale	1949	2.50	5.00	10.00
❑ 47-3231	Josephine/Parade of the Wooden Soldiers	1949	2.50	5.00	10.00
❑ 47-3232	The Darktown Strutters' Ball/The Glow-Worm	1949	2.50	5.00	10.00
—The above three comprise a box set					
❑ 47-3272	Cruising Down the River/Allah's Holiday	1949	3.00	6.00	12.00
❑ 47-3722	Blue Prelude/I May Hate Myself in the Morning	1950	3.00	6.00	12.00
❑ 47-3768	The Flying Red Horse Polka/ Leicester Square Rag	1950	3.00	6.00	12.00
❑ 47-3786	Abide with Me/Ave Maria	1950	2.50	5.00	10.00
❑ 47-3787	Lead Kindly Light/Whispering Hope	1950	2.50	5.00	10.00
❑ 47-3788	Beautiful Isle of Somewhere/In the Garden	1950	2.50	5.00	10.00
—The above three comprise a box set					
❑ 47-3817	Miaianne/When the Saints Go Marching In	1950	3.00	6.00	12.00
❑ 47-3824	Gone Fishin'/So Tall a Tree	1950	3.00	6.00	12.00
❑ 47-3843	Jalousie (Jealousy)/Fiddle Faddle	1950	3.00	6.00	12.00
❑ 47-3844	Ritual Fire Dance/Malaguena	1950	3.00	6.00	12.00
❑ 47-3924	Sleigh Ride/I'll Find You	1949	3.75	7.50	15.00
❑ 47-3976	It Is No Secret (What God Can Do)/ To Think You've Chosen Me	1950	3.00	6.00	12.00
❑ 47-4010	After You've Gone/ Remember Me in Your Dreams	1950	3.00	6.00	12.00
❑ 47-4090	The Syncopated Clock/March of Cards	1951	3.00	6.00	12.00
❑ 47-4122	What Will I Tell My Heart/I Whistle a Happy Tune	1951	3.00	6.00	12.00
❑ 47-4150	Tom's Tune/These Things I Offer You	1951	3.00	6.00	12.00
❑ 47-4199	Come On-a My House/Hula Blues	1951	2.50	5.00	10.00
❑ 47-4200	Auf Wiedersehn/Hands Across the Table	1951	2.50	5.00	10.00
❑ 47-4201	Autumn Leaves/La Vie En Rose	1951	2.50	5.00	10.00
❑ 47-4202	You and the Night and the Music/ Yours Is My Heart Alone	1951	2.50	5.00	10.00
—The above four comprise a box set					
❑ 47-4221	The Bird of Happiness/At the End of Day	1951	3.00	6.00	12.00
❑ 47-4258	Kol Nidre/Eili Eili	1951	3.00	6.00	12.00
❑ 47-4287	Little Jumping Jack/Painting Clouds with Sunshine	1951	3.00	6.00	12.00
❑ 47-4323	Sleigh Ride/Uncle Mistletoe	1951	3.75	7.50	15.00
❑ 47-4385	Sunshower/Sleepy Serenade	1951	3.00	6.00	12.00
❑ 47-4463	Laura/My Reverie	1952	2.50	5.00	10.00
❑ 47-4464	April in Paris/Moonglow	1952	2.50	5.00	10.00
❑ 47-4465	Intermezzo/Moonlight Sonata	1952	2.50	5.00	10.00
❑ 47-4466	My Silent Love/Smoke Rings	1952	2.50	5.00	10.00
—The above four comprise a box set					
❑ 47-4510	Cool, Cool Kisses/Stolen Love	1952	3.00	6.00	12.00
❑ 47-4562	You're Not Worth My Tears/Two Wrongs Never Make a Right	1952	3.00	6.00	12.00
❑ 47-4677	Delicado/Plink, Plank, Plunk	1952	3.00	6.00	12.00
❑ 47-4790	Birds 'n' Bees/Sky-High	1952	3.00	6.00	12.00
❑ 47-5082	Twilight Boogie/Junga-Junga	1952	3.00	6.00	12.00
❑ 47-5185	Waggashoe/Ecstacy Tango	1953	3.00	6.00	12.00
❑ 47-5246	Anna/Little Red Monkey	1953	3.00	6.00	12.00
❑ 47-5347	Under Paris Skies/Don't Take Love from Me	1953	3.00	6.00	12.00
❑ 47-5417	Invisible Hands/One Step	1953	3.00	6.00	12.00
❑ 47-5463	Peg o' My Heart/Jealous	1953	3.00	6.00	12.00
❑ 47-5553	The Creep/Just One More Chance	1953	3.00	6.00	12.00

T

Number	Title (A Side/B Side)	Yr	VG	VG+	NM
❏ 47-5711	Under a Blanket of Blue/Gimme a Little Kiss	1954	3.00	6.00	12.00
❏ 47-5768	Moonlight and Roses (Bring Mem'ries of You)/ Crazy Legs	1954	3.00	6.00	12.00
❏ 47-5874	Touch/Southern Star	1954	3.00	6.00	12.00
❏ 47-5961	For You/Perdido	1954	3.00	6.00	12.00
❏ 47-6084	I Wonder, I Wonder, I Wonder/Dancing with Tears in My Eyes	1955	2.50	5.00	10.00
❏ 47-6202	Satan Takes a Holiday/You and You Alone	1955	2.50	5.00	10.00
❏ 47-6273	Arrivederci Roma/Cha Cha Joe	1955	2.50	5.00	10.00
❏ 47-6461	The Beautiful Girls of Vienna/Petite Papillon	1956	2.50	5.00	10.00
❏ 47-6574	Theme from The Proud Ones/Haunted Guitar	1956	2.50	5.00	10.00
❏ 47-6713	Postmark: Vienna/Wind River Valley	1956	2.50	5.00	10.00
❏ 47-6881	The Lovers/Wailin' Guitar	1957	2.50	5.00	10.00
❏ 47-7072	Tumbling Tumbleweeds/Sentimental Journey	1957	2.50	5.00	10.00
❏ 47-7187	Rainbow/Tweety	1958	2.50	5.00	10.00
❏ 47-7416	Volcano/Cha Cha Charleston	1958	2.50	5.00	10.00
❏ 47-7970	Honey Bee/Fun in the Sun	1961	2.00	4.00	8.00
❏ 47-8373	My Man/Happy Wedding Song	1964	2.00	4.00	8.00
❏ WP 250 [(3)]	Your Christmas Favorites	1949	10.00	20.00	40.00
—Three records (47-3057, 47-3058, 47-3059) plus box					

7-Inch Extended Plays
RCA VICTOR

Number	Title (A Side/B Side)	Yr	VG	VG+	NM
❏ 547-0032	Sunrise Serenade/I'll Never Wish for More Than This//Deep Purple/Hindustan	1952	3.00	6.00	12.00
—One record of 2-EP set EPB 3034					
❏ 547-0087	My Reverie/Moon Glow//Intermezzo/Smoke Rings	1952	3.00	6.00	12.00
—One record of 2-EP set EPB 3012					
❏ 547-0088	My Silent Love/Moonlight Sonata//April in Paris/ Laura	1952	3.00	6.00	12.00
—One record of 2-EP set EPB 3012					
❏ LPC-110	(contents unknown)	1961	2.50	5.00	10.00
—"Compact 33 Double"; small hole, plays at 33 1/3 rpm					
❏ LPC-110 [PS]	Twilight Time	1961	2.50	5.00	10.00
❏ 547-0208	Sweet & Low/Out of Nowhere//Someone to Watch Over Me/My Prayer	195?	3.00	6.00	12.00
—One record of 2-EP set EPB 3075					
❏ 547-0209	Because/Yesterdays//Lullaby of the Leaves/ Deep Night	195?	3.00	6.00	12.00
—One record of 2-EP set EPB 3075					
❏ EPA 250	White Christmas/Winter Wonderland//Silent Night/Jingle Bells	195?	3.00	6.00	12.00
❏ EPA 250 [PS]	The Three Suns Present Your Christmas Favorites	195?	3.00	6.00	12.00
❏ EPA 330	Hands Across the Table/Auf Wiedersehen// You and the Night and the Music/ Yours Is My Heart Alone	195?	3.00	6.00	12.00
❏ EPA 330 [PS]	Hands Across the Table	195?	3.00	6.00	12.00
❏ EPA-618	Autumn Leaves/Waltz Serenade// La Vie En Rose/Waltz in A Flat	1955	3.00	6.00	12.00
❏ EPA-618 [PS]	Autumn Leaves	1955	3.00	6.00	12.00
❏ EPA 655	White Christmas/Santa Claus Is Coming to Town/Der Tannenbaum//It Came Upon a Midnight Clear/Greensleeves/ God Rest Ye Merry Gentlemen	1955	3.00	6.00	12.00
❏ EPA 655 [PS]	White Christmas	1955	3.00	6.00	12.00
❏ EPA 736	My Reverie/Intermezzo//Tenderly/Laura	1956	2.50	5.00	10.00
❏ EPA 736 [PS]	(title unknown)	1956	2.50	5.00	10.00
❏ 547-1040	There Is No Greater Love/A Sinner Kissed an Angel//Autumn Nocturne/Blue Orchids	1954	2.50	5.00	10.00
—One record of 2-EP set EPB 1041					
❏ 547-1041	Stars Fell on Alabama/The Touch of Your Lips/ /Moonlight in Vermont/Flamingo	1954	2.50	5.00	10.00
—One record of 2-EP set EPB 1041					
❏ EPB 1041 [PS]	Soft and Sweet	1954	2.50	5.00	10.00
❏ EPB 3012 [PS]	Twilight Moods	1952	3.00	6.00	12.00
—Two-pocket jacket for two-EP set					
❏ EPB 3034 [PS]	The Three Suns Present	1952	3.00	6.00	12.00
—Two-pocket jacket for two-EP set					
❏ EPB 3075 [PS]	Slumber Time	195?	3.00	6.00	12.00
❏ EPA-5021	Twilight Time/Hindustan//Peg o' My Heart/ Canadian Capers	1958	2.50	5.00	10.00
❏ EPA-5021 [PS]	The Three Suns (Gold Standard Series)	1958	2.50	5.00	10.00

ROYALE

Number	Title (A Side/B Side)	Yr	VG	VG+	NM
❏ EP 121	Twilight Time/It's Dawn Again// Star Dust/Barcarolle	195?	2.50	5.00	10.00
❏ EP 121 [PS]	The Three Suns	195?	2.50	5.00	10.00

Albums
GOLDEN TONE

Number	Title (A Side/B Side)	Yr	VG	VG+	NM
❏ 14094	In Orbit	195?	3.00	6.00	12.00

PICKWICK

| ❏ SPC-3037 | Twilight Time | 197? | 2.50 | 5.00 | 10.00 |

RCA CAMDEN

| ❏ CAL-633 [M] | The Sound of Christmas | 1964 | 3.00 | 6.00 | 12.00 |
| ❏ CAS-633(e) [R] | The Sound of Christmas | 1964 | 3.00 | 6.00 | 12.00 |

RCA VICTOR

❏ LPM-3 [10]	Three-Quarter Time	1951	12.50	25.00	50.00
❏ LPM-28 [10]	Hands Across the Table	1951	12.50	25.00	50.00
❏ LPM-52 [10]	Christmas Favorites	1951	12.50	25.00	50.00
❏ LPM-1041 [M]	Soft and Sweet	1955	7.50	15.00	30.00
❏ LPM-1132 [M]	Sounds of Christmas	1955	7.50	15.00	30.00
❏ LPM-1171 [M]	Twilight Time	1956	7.50	15.00	30.00
❏ LPM-1173 [M]	My Reverie	1956	7.50	15.00	30.00
❏ LPM-1219 [M]	Slumber Time	1956	7.50	15.00	30.00
❏ LPM-1220 [M]	Malaguena	1956	7.50	15.00	30.00
❏ LPM-1249 [M]	High Fi and Wide	1956	7.50	15.00	30.00
❏ LPM-1316 [M]	Easy Listening	1956	7.50	15.00	30.00
❏ LPM-1333 [M]	Midnight for Two	1957	7.50	15.00	30.00
❏ LPM-1543 [M]	The Things in Love in Hi-Fi	1958	5.00	10.00	20.00
❏ LSP-1543 [S]	The Things in Love in Hi-Fi	1958	7.50	15.00	30.00
❏ LPM-1578 [M]	Let's Dance with the Three Suns	1958	5.00	10.00	20.00
❏ LSP-1578 [S]	Let's Dance with the Three Suns	1958	7.50	15.00	30.00
❏ LPM-1669 [M]	Love in the Afternoon	1959	5.00	10.00	20.00
❏ LSP-1669 [S]	Love in the Afternoon	1959	7.50	15.00	30.00
❏ LPM-1734 [M]	Having a Ball with the Three Suns	1959	5.00	10.00	20.00
❏ LSP-1734 [S]	Having a Ball with the Three Suns	1959	7.50	15.00	30.00

Number	Title (A Side/B Side)	Yr	VG	VG+	NM
❏ ANL1-1779(e)	Pure Gold	1974	2.50	5.00	10.00
❏ LPM-1964 [M]	Swingin' on a Star	1959	5.00	10.00	20.00
❏ LSP-1964 [S]	Swingin' on a Star	1959	7.50	15.00	30.00
❏ LPM-2054 [M]	A Ding Dong Dandy Christmas!	1959	5.00	10.00	20.00
❏ LSP-2054 [S]	A Ding Dong Dandy Christmas!	1959	7.50	15.00	30.00
❏ LPM-2120 [M]	Twilight Memories	1960	5.00	10.00	20.00
❏ LSP-2120 [S]	Twilight Memories	1960	6.25	12.50	25.00
❏ LPM-2235 [M]	On a Magic Carpet	1960	5.00	10.00	20.00
❏ LSP-2235 [S]	On a Magic Carpet	1960	6.25	12.50	25.00
❏ LPM-2307 [M]	Dancing on a Cloud	1961	5.00	10.00	20.00
❏ LSP-2307 [S]	Dancing on a Cloud	1961	6.25	12.50	25.00
❏ LPM-2310 [M]	Fever and Smoke	1961	5.00	10.00	20.00
❏ LSP-2310 [S]	Fever and Smoke	1961	6.25	12.50	25.00
❏ LPM-2437 [M]	Fun in the Sun	1961	5.00	10.00	20.00
❏ LSP-2437 [S]	Fun in the Sun	1961	6.25	12.50	25.00
❏ LPM-2532 [M]	Movin' 'N' Groovin'	1962	5.00	10.00	20.00
❏ LSP-2532 [S]	Movin' 'N' Groovin'	1962	6.25	12.50	25.00
❏ LPM-2617 [M]	Warm and Tender	1962	5.00	10.00	20.00
❏ LSP-2617 [S]	Warm and Tender	1962	6.25	12.50	25.00
❏ LPM-2715 [M]	Everything Under the Sun	1963	3.75	7.50	15.00
❏ LSP-2715 [S]	Everything Under the Sun	1963	5.00	10.00	20.00
❏ LPM-2904 [M]	One Enchanted Evening	1964	3.75	7.50	15.00
❏ LSP-2904 [S]	One Enchanted Evening	1964	5.00	10.00	20.00
❏ LPM-2963 [M]	A Swingin' Thing	1964	3.75	7.50	15.00
❏ LSP-2963 [S]	A Swingin' Thing	1964	5.00	10.00	20.00
❏ LPM-3012 [10]	Twilight Moods	1952	12.50	25.00	50.00
❏ LPM-3034 [10]	The Three Suns Present	1952	12.50	25.00	50.00
❏ LPM-3040 [10]	Busy Fingers	1952	12.50	25.00	50.00
❏ LPM-3056 [10]	Christmas Party	1952	12.50	25.00	50.00
❏ LPM-3075 [10]	Slumbertime	1953	12.50	25.00	50.00
❏ LPM-3113 [10]	Pops Concert Favorites	1953	12.50	25.00	50.00
❏ LPM-3125 [10]	Mods	1953	12.50	25.00	50.00
❏ LPM-3130 [10]	Top Pops	1953	12.50	25.00	50.00
❏ LPM-3146 [10]	Polka Time	1954	12.50	25.00	50.00
❏ LPM-3174 [10]	Sacred Hymns	1954	12.50	25.00	50.00
❏ LPM-3354 [M]	Country Music Shindig	1965	3.75	7.50	15.00
❏ LSP-3354 [S]	Country Music Shindig	1965	5.00	10.00	20.00
❏ LPM-3447 [M]	The Best of the Three Suns	1965	3.75	7.50	15.00
❏ LSP-3447 [S]	The Best of the Three Suns	1965	5.00	10.00	20.00
❏ VPS-6075 [(2)]	This Is the Three Suns	1972	3.75	7.50	15.00

ROYALE

| ❏ 1 [10] | Twilight Time | 1951 | 12.50 | 25.00 | 50.00 |
| ❏ 29 [10] | Midnight Time | 1951 | 12.50 | 25.00 | 50.00 |

SEARS

| ❏ SPS-437 | Twilight Time | 1969 | 3.00 | 6.00 | 12.00 |

VARSITY

| ❏ VLP-6001 [10] | Twilight Time | 1950 | 12.50 | 25.00 | 50.00 |
| ❏ VLP-6048 [10] | Midnight Time | 1950 | 12.50 | 25.00 | 50.00 |

THREE VALES, THE
45s
CINDY

| ❏ 3007 | Blue Lights/Ay, Ay, Ay | 1957 | 30.00 | 60.00 | 120.00 |

THREETEENS, THE
45s
REV

| ❏ 3516 | Dear 53310761/Doowaddie | 1958 | 10.00 | 20.00 | 40.00 |
| ❏ 3522 | X + Y = Z/For the Love of Mike | 1959 | 6.25 | 12.50 | 25.00 |

TODD

| ❏ 1021 | X + Y = Z/For the Love of Mike | 1959 | 5.00 | 10.00 | 20.00 |

THRILLERS, THE (1)
45s
BIG TOWN

| ❏ 109 | The Drunkard/Mattie, Leave Me Alone | 1953 | 100.00 | 200.00 | 400.00 |

HERALD

| ❏ 432 | Lizabeth/Please Talk to Me | 1954 | 100.00 | 200.00 | 400.00 |

THRILLER

| ❏ 3530 | Lessie Mae/I'm Going to Live My Life Alone | 1953 | 250.00 | 500.00 | 1000. |

THRILLERS, THE (2)
45s
UPTOWN

| ❏ 715 | Come What May/This I Know Little Girl | 1965 | 3.00 | 6.00 | 12.00 |

THRILLINGTON, PERCY "THRILLS" See PAUL McCARTNEY.

THRILLS, THE
45s
CAPITOL

❏ 5631	What Can Go Wrong/No One	1966	5.00	10.00	20.00
❏ 5719	Here's a Heart/Bring It On Home to Me	1966	5.00	10.00	20.00
❏ 5871	Show the World Where It's At/Underneath My Make-Up	1967	5.00	10.00	20.00

THUNDER, JOHNNY
45s
CALLA

| ❏ 161 | I'm Alive/Verbal Expressions of T.V. | 1969 | — | 3.00 | 6.00 |

DIAMOND

❏ 129	Loop De Loop/Don't Be Ashamed	1962	3.75	7.50	15.00
❏ 132	Rock-a-Bye My Darling/The Rosy Dance	1963	2.50	5.00	10.00
❏ 132 [PS]	Rock-a-Bye My Darling/The Rosy Dance	1963	5.00	10.00	20.00
❏ 137	The Outlaw/Jailer, Bring Me Water	1963	2.50	5.00	10.00
❏ 148	Hey Child/Darling Je Vous Aime Beaucoup	1963	2.50	5.00	10.00
❏ 152	Constitution of Love/Good Morning Sadness	1964	2.00	4.00	8.00
❏ 155	Everybody Likes to Dance with Johnny/ Zoo-Lee-Oh	1964	2.00	4.00	8.00
❏ 169	More, More More Love, Love, Love/ Shout It to the World	1964	2.00	4.00	8.00
❏ 175	Send Her to Me/Shout It to the World	1964	2.00	4.00	8.00
❏ 185	Suzie-Q/Dear John, I'm Going to Leave You	1965	2.00	4.00	8.00
❏ 192	Everybody Do the Sloopy/Beautiful	1965	2.00	4.00	8.00
❏ 196	My Prayer/A Broken Heart	1966	2.00	4.00	8.00
❏ 206	Bewildered/Just Me and You	1966	2.00	4.00	8.00
❏ 218	Make Love to Me/Teach Me Tonight	1967	2.00	4.00	8.00
—With Ruby Winters					

Number	Title (A Side/B Side)	Yr	VG	VG+	NM
❏ 222	Am I Right or Am I Wrong/You Send Me	1967	2.00	4.00	8.00
❏ 238	We Only Have One Life (Let's Live It Together)/ Teach Me Tonight	1968	2.00	4.00	8.00
—With Ruby Winters					
❏ 246	Put It in Motion/Groovy Two Shoes	1968	2.00	4.00	8.00
EPIC					
❏ 9329	Ever Your Man/Horror Show	1959	3.75	7.50	15.00
UNITED ARTISTS					
❏ 50736	Power to the People/Love Trip	1971	—	3.00	6.00
Albums					
DIAMOND					
❏ D-5001 [M]	Loop De Loop	1963	25.00	50.00	100.00
❏ DS-5001 [S]	Loop De Loop	1963	37.50	75.00	150.00
REAL					
❏ RR-1	So Alone	196?	3.75	7.50	15.00

THUNDER AND ROSES
45s
UNITED ARTISTS

Number	Title (A Side/B Side)	Yr	VG	VG+	NM
❏ 50536	Country Life/I Love a Woman	1969	3.00	6.00	12.00
Albums					
UNITED ARTISTS					
❏ UAS-6709	King of the Black Sunrise	1969	7.50	15.00	30.00

THUNDER BOLTS, THE
45s
RONDACK

Number	Title (A Side/B Side)	Yr	VG	VG+	NM
❏ 7546	Thunder Head/Blending	196?	12.50	25.00	50.00

THUNDER HEADS, THE
45s
CARTWHEEL

Number	Title (A Side/B Side)	Yr	VG	VG+	NM
❏ 100	Thunder Head/Unemployment	1966	7.50	15.00	30.00

THUNDERBOLTS, THE
45s
DOT

Number	Title (A Side/B Side)	Yr	VG	VG+	NM
❏ 16496	Lost Planets/March of the Spacemen	1963	5.00	10.00	20.00

THUNDERCLAP NEWMAN Jimmy McCulloch, later of WINGS, was in this group.
45s
TRACK

Number	Title (A Side/B Side)	Yr	VG	VG+	NM
❏ 2656	Something in the Air/Wilhelmina	1969	2.50	5.00	10.00
❏ 2769	Something in the Air/Wilhelmina	1970	—	3.00	6.00
Albums					
MCA					
❏ 354	Hollywood Dream	1974	2.50	5.00	10.00
—Reissue of Track 354					
TRACK					
❏ 354	Hollywood Dream	1973	3.00	6.00	12.00
—Reissue of Track 8264					
❏ SD 8264	Hollywood Dream	1970	6.25	12.50	25.00

THUNDERGRIN
45s
EPIC

Number	Title (A Side/B Side)	Yr	VG	VG+	NM
❏ 10215	Women in the Street/Mr. Simms	1967	2.50	5.00	10.00

THUNDERKLOUD, BILLY, AND THE CHIEFTONES
45s
POLYDOR

Number	Title (A Side/B Side)	Yr	VG	VG+	NM
❏ 14321	Indian Nation (The Lament of the Cherokee Reservation Indian)/I'm Going Right to Where I Do Wrong	1976	—	2.50	5.00
❏ 14338	Try a Little Tenderness/A Natural Feelin' for You	1976	—	2.50	5.00
❏ 14362	It's Alright/The Wanderer	1976	—	2.50	5.00
❏ 14383	Let Me Be Your Man/A Hundred Years from Now	1977	—	2.50	5.00
❏ 14412	Oklahoma Wind/The Trouble with Angels	1977	—	2.50	5.00
❏ 14449	Let Me Love You/My Lady	1977	—	2.50	5.00
20TH CENTURY					
❏ 2116	You Touched My Life/When Love Is Right	1974	—	3.00	6.00
❏ 2164	Kick the Can/I'm Havin' a Party	1975	—	2.50	5.00
❏ 2181	What Time of Day/When Love Is Right	1975	—	2.50	5.00
❏ 2239	Pledging My Love/I Will Love You Until I Die	1975	—	2.50	5.00
Albums					
SUPERIOR					
❏ SR-103	All Through the Night	197?	3.75	7.50	15.00
❏ S-2010	Where Do I Begin to Tell the Story	1975	3.75	7.50	15.00
20TH CENTURY					
❏ T-452	Off the Reservation	1974	3.00	6.00	12.00
❏ T-471	What Time of Day	1975	3.00	6.00	12.00

THUNDERPUSSY
Albums
M.R.T.

Number	Title (A Side/B Side)	Yr	VG	VG+	NM
❏ 31748	Documents of Captivity	1973	37.50	75.00	150.00

THUNDERTONES, THE
45s
DONNA

Number	Title (A Side/B Side)	Yr	VG	VG+	NM
❏ 1343	Thunder Rhythm/Pay Day	1961	7.50	15.00	30.00
DOT					
❏ 16137	Jungle Fever/Hot Ice	1960	7.50	15.00	30.00
❏ 16177	The Street Beat/Happy Little Jug	1961	7.50	15.00	30.00
—As "Lenny and the Thundertones"					

THUNDERTREE
Albums
ROULETTE

Number	Title (A Side/B Side)	Yr	VG	VG+	NM
❏ SR-42038	Thundertree	1970	7.50	15.00	30.00

THURSDAY'S CHILDREN
45s
INTERNATIONAL ARTISTS

Number	Title (A Side/B Side)	Yr	VG	VG+	NM
❏ 110	Air Conditioned Man/Sominoes	1967	37.50	75.00	150.00
❏ 115	Help, Murder, Police/ You Can't Forget About That	1967	37.50	75.00	150.00

Number	Title (A Side/B Side)	Yr	VG	VG+	NM
N-JOY					
❏ 1019	Running Around on Me/I Don't Need Your Love	1967	3.75	7.50	15.00
PARADISE					
❏ 1022	You'll Never Be My Girl/Try, Girl	1966	250.00	500.00	1000.

THYME
45s
A-SQUARE

Number	Title (A Side/B Side)	Yr	VG	VG+	NM
❏ 201	Somehow/Shame, Shame	1969	10.00	20.00	40.00
❏ 202	Time of the Season/I Found a Love	1969	10.00	20.00	40.00
BANG					
❏ 546	Love to Love/Very Last Day	1967	5.00	10.00	20.00

TIATT, LYNN, AND THE COMETS
45s
PUSSYCAT

Number	Title (A Side/B Side)	Yr	VG	VG+	NM
❏ 1	Dad Is Home/Vilma's Jump-Up	195?	75.00	150.00	300.00

TICO AND THE TRIUMPHS PAUL SIMON was a member.
45s
AMY

Number	Title (A Side/B Side)	Yr	VG	VG+	NM
❏ 835	Motorcycle/I Don't Believe Them	1961	25.00	50.00	100.00
❏ 845	Wildflower/Express Train	1962	25.00	50.00	100.00
❏ 860	Cry, Lil' Boy, Cry/Get Up and Do the Wobble	1962	25.00	50.00	100.00
❏ 876	Cards of Love/Noise	1963	50.00	100.00	200.00
MADISON					
❏ 169	Motorcycle/I Don't Believe Them	1961	50.00	100.00	200.00

TIDES, THE
45s
HIT

Number	Title (A Side/B Side)	Yr	VG	VG+	NM
❏ 42	Telstar/The Lonely Bull	1962	2.50	5.00	10.00
—B-side by the Dan Rubin Orchestra					

TIEKEN, FREDDIE, AND THE ROCKERS
Albums
I.T.

Number	Title (A Side/B Side)	Yr	VG	VG+	NM
❏ 2301 [M]	By Popular Demand	1957	12.50	25.00	50.00
❏ 2304 [M]	Freddie Tieken and the Rockers	1958	12.50	25.00	50.00

TIFFANY SHADE, THE
45s
MAINSTREAM

Number	Title (A Side/B Side)	Yr	VG	VG+	NM
❏ 677	One Good Reason/ Would You Take My Mind Out for a Walk	1968	3.75	7.50	15.00
❏ 680	An Older Man/Sam	1968	3.75	7.50	15.00
Albums					
MAINSTREAM					
❏ S-6105	The Tiffany Shade	1968	25.00	50.00	100.00

TIFFANYS, THE Probably not all the same group.
45s
ARCTIC

Number	Title (A Side/B Side)	Yr	VG	VG+	NM
❏ 101	Love Me/Happiest Girl in the World	1964	5.00	10.00	20.00
ATLANTIC					
❏ 2240	Please Tell Me/Gossip	1964	5.00	10.00	20.00
JOSIE					
❏ 942	I Feel the Same Way Too/I Just Wanna Be a Girl	1965	3.00	6.00	12.00
❏ 952	Heaven on Earth/Take Another Look at Me	1966	3.00	6.00	12.00
KR					
❏ 120	He's Good for Me/It's Got to Be a Great Song	1967	5.00	10.00	20.00
—As "The Tiffanies"					
MRS					
❏ 777	Please Tell Me/Gossip	1964	20.00	40.00	80.00
RKO					
❏ 120	He's Good for Me/It's Got to Be a Great Song	1967	2.50	5.00	10.00
—Are the KR and RKO releases one and the same? We don't know					
ROCKIN' ROBIN					
❏ 1	I've Got a Girl/I Don't Dig Western Movies	1963	75.00	150.00	300.00
SWAN					
❏ 4104	Atlanta/The Pleasure of Love	1962	5.00	10.00	20.00

TIGERS, THE
45s
COLPIX

Number	Title (A Side/B Side)	Yr	VG	VG+	NM
❏ 773	GeeTO Tiger/The Prowl	1965	12.50	25.00	50.00
❏ SPEC-773	GeeTO Tiger/The Big Sounds of the GeeTO Tiger	1965	20.00	40.00	80.00
—Special promotional issue					
❏ SPEC-773 [PS]	GeeTO Tiger/The Big Sounds of the GeeTO Tiger	1965	50.00	100.00	200.00
—Sleeve appears to have been available only with the promotional B-side					

TIKIS, THE
45s
ASCOT

Number	Title (A Side/B Side)	Yr	VG	VG+	NM
❏ 2186	Stop-Look-Listen/Cream in My Coffee	1965	2.50	5.00	10.00
❏ 2204	High School Dropout Blues/Whole Lotta Soul	1966	2.50	5.00	10.00
AUTUMN					
❏ 18	If I've Been Dreaming/Pay Attention to Me	1965	2.50	5.00	10.00
—As "The Other Tikis"					
❏ 28	Bye Bye Bye/Lost My Love Today	1966	2.50	5.00	10.00
—As "The Other Tikis"					
DIAL					
❏ 4048	Somebody's Sun/Little Miss Lovelight	1966	2.50	5.00	10.00
MINARET					
❏ 115	Big Feet/One More Chance	196?	3.00	6.00	12.00
❏ 116	Popsicle/All That Talk	196?	3.00	6.00	12.00
❏ 118	Traveling Shoes/Valley of Tears	196?	3.00	6.00	12.00
WARNER BROS.					
❏ 5818	Bye Bye Bye/Lost My Love Today	1966	2.50	5.00	10.00
Albums					
MINARET					
❏ TLP-7001 [M]	The Tikis	196?	25.00	50.00	100.00
PHILIPS					
❏ PHM 200043 [M]	The Tikis	1962	6.25	12.50	25.00
❏ PHS 600043 [S]	The Tikis	1962	7.50	15.00	30.00

T

TIKIS, THE, AND THE FABULONS

45s

PANORAMA

Number	Title (A Side/B Side)	Yr	VG	VG+	NM
❑ 13	Take a Look/For Your Love	1965	5.00	10.00	20.00

TOWER

Number	Title (A Side/B Side)	Yr	VG	VG+	NM
❑ 181	Take a Look/Cherry Pie	1965	3.00	6.00	12.00

TIL, SONNY Also see THE ORIOLES.

45s

JUBILEE

Number	Title (A Side/B Side)	Yr	VG	VG+	NM
❑ 5060	I Never Knew (I Could Love Anybody)/My Prayer	1951	75.00	150.00	300.00
❑ 5066	Fool's World/For All We Know	1951	75.00	150.00	300.00
—Black vinyl					
❑ 5066	Fool's World/For All We Know	1951	200.00	400.00	800.00
—Red vinyl					
❑ 5090	Once in Awhile/I Only Have Eyes for You	1952	12.50	25.00	50.00
—With Edna McGriff					
❑ 5099	Good/Picadilly	1952	20.00	40.00	80.00
—With Edna McGriff					
❑ 5112	Have You Heard/Lonely Wine	1953	50.00	100.00	200.00
❑ 5118	(Danger) Soft Shoulders/Congratulations to Someone	1953	50.00	100.00	200.00
❑ 5394	Night and Day/Shimmy Time	1960	5.00	10.00	20.00

RCA VICTOR

Number	Title (A Side/B Side)	Yr	VG	VG+	NM
❑ 47-9733	You're All I Need/After You	1969	2.00	4.00	8.00
❑ 47-9759	Tears and Misery/I Better Leave Love Alone	1969	2.00	4.00	8.00
❑ 74-0390	Don't Feel No Pain/One Big Happy Family	1970	2.00	4.00	8.00
❑ 74-0432	Colours/Love Is What It's All About	1971	2.00	4.00	8.00
❑ 74-0529	'Til Then/Love or Desire	1971	2.00	4.00	8.00
❑ 74-0606	Crying in the Chapel/What Are You Doing New Year's Eve	1971	2.00	4.00	8.00

ROULETTE

Number	Title (A Side/B Side)	Yr	VG	VG+	NM
❑ 4079	Shy/First Blush	1958	5.00	10.00	20.00

Albums

DOBRE

Number	Title (A Side/B Side)	Yr	VG	VG+	NM
❑ 1026	Back to the Chapel	1978	3.00	6.00	12.00

RCA VICTOR

Number	Title (A Side/B Side)	Yr	VG	VG+	NM
❑ LSP-4451	Sonny Til Returns	1970	5.00	10.00	20.00
❑ LSP-4538	Old Gold/New Gold	1971	3.75	7.50	15.00

TILLER, FLOYD

45s

HIT

Number	Title (A Side/B Side)	Yr	VG	VG+	NM
❑ 275	Born Free/Winchester Cathedral	1966	2.00	4.00	8.00
—B-side by the New Orleans Band					

TILLIS, MEL

45s

COLUMBIA

Number	Title (A Side/B Side)	Yr	VG	VG+	NM
❑ 4-40845	It Takes a Worried Man to Sing a Worried Song/Honky Tonk Song	1957	5.00	10.00	20.00
❑ 4-40904	Case of the Blues/It's My Life	1957	5.00	10.00	20.00
❑ 4-40944	Juke Box Man/If You'll Be My Love	1957	6.25	12.50	25.00
❑ 4-41038	This Heart/Take My Hand	1957	5.00	10.00	20.00
❑ 4-41115	Teen Age Wedding/Lonely Street	1958	7.50	15.00	30.00
❑ 4-41189	The Violet and a Rose/No Song to Sing	1958	3.75	7.50	15.00
❑ 4-41277	Finally/The Brooklyn Bridge	1958	3.75	7.50	15.00
❑ 4-41632	It's So Easy/Loco Weed	1960	3.75	7.50	15.00
❑ 4-41863	Say/Walk On, Boy	1960	3.75	7.50	15.00
❑ 4-41986	Hearts of Stone/That's Where the Hurt Comes In	1961	5.00	10.00	20.00
❑ 4-42262	Party Girl/If I Lost Your Love	1962	5.00	10.00	20.00

DECCA

Number	Title (A Side/B Side)	Yr	VG	VG+	NM
❑ 31474	Don't Tell Mama/Half Laughing, Half Crying	1963	2.50	5.00	10.00
❑ 31528	Couldn't See the Forest for the Trees/It's No Surprise	1963	2.50	5.00	10.00
❑ 31623	It'll Be Easy/I'm Gonna Act Right	1964	2.50	5.00	10.00

ELEKTRA

Number	Title (A Side/B Side)	Yr	VG	VG+	NM
❑ 46536	Blind in Love/Blackjack, Water Back	1979	—	2.00	4.00
❑ 46583	Lying Time Again/Fooled Around and Fell in Love	1980	—	2.00	4.00
❑ 46628	Your Body Is an Outlaw/Rain on My Parade	1980	—	2.00	4.00
❑ 47015	Steppin' Out/Whiskey Chasin'	1980	—	2.00	4.00
❑ 47082	Southern Rains/Forgive Me for Giving You the Blues	1980	—	2.00	4.00
❑ 47116	A Million Old Goodbyes/Louisiana Lonely	1981	—	2.00	4.00
❑ 47178	One-Night Fever/Time Has Treated You Well	1981	—	2.00	4.00
❑ 47233 [DJ]	White Christmas/Blue Christmas	1981	—	3.00	6.00
—B-side by Eddy Raven					
❑ 47412	It's a Long Way to Daytona/Always You, Always Me	1982	—	2.00	4.00
❑ 47453	The One That Got Away/Why Ain't Life the Way It's S'posed to Be	1982	—	2.00	4.00
❑ 69963	Stay a Little Longer/Dream of Me	1982	—	2.00	4.00

KAPP

Number	Title (A Side/B Side)	Yr	VG	VG+	NM
❑ 764	Mental Revenge/Guide Me Home My Georgia Moon	1966	2.50	5.00	10.00
❑ 772	Stateside/Home Is Where the Hurt Is	1966	2.00	4.00	8.00
❑ 804	Life Turned Her That Way/If I Could Only Start Over	1967	2.00	4.00	8.00
❑ 804 [PS]	Life Turned Her That Way/If I Could Only Start Over	1967	3.75	7.50	15.00
❑ 837	Goodbye Wheeling/At the Sight of You	1967	2.00	4.00	8.00
❑ 867	Survival of the Fittest/The Old Gang's Gone	1967	2.00	4.00	8.00
❑ 881	All Right (I'll Sign the Papers)/Helpless, Hopeless Fool	1968	2.00	4.00	8.00
❑ 905	Something Special/You Name It	1968	2.00	4.00	8.00
❑ 941	Destroyed by Man/I Haven't Seen Mary in Years	1968	2.00	4.00	8.00
❑ 959	Who's Julie/Give Me One More Day	1968	2.00	4.00	8.00
❑ 986	Old Faithful/Sorrow Overtakes the Wine	1969	2.00	4.00	8.00
❑ 2031	These Lonely Hands of Mine/Cover Mama's Flowers	1969	—	3.50	7.00
❑ 2072	She'll Be Hanging 'Round Somewhere/Where Love Has Died	1970	—	3.50	7.00
❑ 2086	Heart Over Mind/Lingering Memories	1970	—	3.50	7.00
❑ 2103	Too Lonely, Too Long/Memories Made This House	1970	—	3.50	7.00

Number	Title (A Side/B Side)	Yr	VG	VG+	NM
❑ 2121	One More Drink/I Could Never Be Ashamed of You	1971	—	3.50	7.00

MCA

Number	Title (A Side/B Side)	Yr	VG	VG+	NM
❑ KFC-001 [DJ]	There's No Turning Back/A Brandy Alexander	1977	3.00	6.00	12.00
—Promo only; "America's Country Good Music from Kentucky Fried Chicken" on label					
❑ 40559	Love Revival/Gator Bar	1976	—	2.50	5.00
❑ 40627	Good Woman Blues/You Can't Trust a Crazy Man	1976	—	2.50	5.00
❑ 40667	Heart Healer/It's Just Not That Easy to Say	1976	—	2.50	5.00
❑ 40710	Burning Memories/Golden Nugget Gambling Casino	1977	—	2.50	5.00
❑ 40764	I Got the Hoss/It's Been a Long Time	1977	—	2.50	5.00
❑ 40836	What Did I Promise Her Last Night/Woman, You Should Be in the Movies	1977	—	2.50	5.00
❑ 40900	I Believe in You/She Don't Trust You Daddy	1978	—	2.50	5.00
❑ 40946	Ain't No California/What Comes Natural to a Fool	1978	—	2.50	5.00
❑ 40983	Send Me Down to Tucson/Charlie's Angel	1978	—	2.50	5.00
❑ 41041	Coca Cola Cowboy/Cottonmouth	1979	—	2.50	5.00
❑ 52182	In the Middle of the Night/Even at Her Worst (She's Still the Best)	1983	—	—	3.00
❑ 52247	A Cowboy's Dream/After All This Time	1983	—	—	3.00
❑ 52285	She Meant Forever When She Said Goodbye/Try It Again	1983	—	—	3.00
❑ 52373	New Patches/Almost Like You Never Went Away	1984	—	—	3.00

MERCURY

Number	Title (A Side/B Side)	Yr	VG	VG+	NM
❑ 870192-7	You'll Come Back (You Always Do)/Try It Again	1988	—	—	3.00

MGM

Number	Title (A Side/B Side)	Yr	VG	VG+	NM
❑ 14148	Heaven Everyday/How You Drink the Wine	1970	—	3.00	6.00
❑ 14176	Commercial Affection/I Thought About You	1970	—	3.00	6.00
❑ 14211	The Arms of a Fool/Veil of White Lace	1971	—	3.00	6.00
❑ 14275	Brand New Mister Me/Brand New Wrapper	1971	—	3.00	6.00
❑ 14329	Untouched/I Went a Ramblin'	1971	—	3.00	6.00
❑ 14372	Would You Want the World to End/Things Have Changed a Lot	1972	—	3.00	6.00
❑ 14418	I Ain't Never/Burden of Love	1972	—	3.00	6.00
❑ 14454	Neon Rose/It's My Love	1972	—	3.00	6.00
❑ 14522	Thank You for Being You/Over the Hill	1973	—	3.00	6.00
❑ 14585	Sawmill/Mama's Gonna Pray	1973	—	3.00	6.00
❑ 14689	Midnight, Me and the Blues/Modern Home Magazine	1974	—	3.00	6.00
❑ 14720	Stomp Them Grapes/Hang My Pictures in Your Heart	1974	—	3.00	6.00
❑ 14744	Memory Maker/Second Best	1974	—	3.00	6.00
❑ 14782	Best Way I Know How/Honey Dew Melon	1975	—	3.00	6.00
❑ 14804	Woman in the Back of My Mind/Kissing Your Picture (Is So Cold)	1975	—	3.00	6.00
❑ 14835	Lookin' for Tomorrow (And Findin' Yesterdays)/Tennessee Banjo Man	1975	—	3.00	6.00
❑ 14846	Mental Revenge/My Bad Girl Treats Me Good	1976	—	3.00	6.00
❑ 14850	Always Just a Memory Away/Come On Home	1976	—	3.00	6.00

RADIO

Number	Title (A Side/B Side)	Yr	VG	VG+	NM
❑ 001	City Lights/Who's Julie	1989	—	—	3.00

RCA

Number	Title (A Side/B Side)	Yr	VG	VG+	NM
❑ PB-14061	You Done Me Wrong/Another Heart Down	1985	—	—	3.00
❑ PB-14175	California Road/One More Time	1985	—	—	3.00

RIC

Number	Title (A Side/B Side)	Yr	VG	VG+	NM
❑ 150	Ode to the Little Brown Shack Out Back/Not in Front of the Kids	1965	3.00	6.00	12.00
❑ 158	Wine/Buried Alive	1965	3.00	6.00	12.00
❑ 178	Bring On the Blues/Mr. Dropout	1965	3.00	6.00	12.00

STARDAY

Number	Title (A Side/B Side)	Yr	VG	VG+	NM
❑ 8036	Wine/Stateside	197?	—	2.50	5.00

Albums

COLUMBIA

Number	Title (A Side/B Side)	Yr	VG	VG+	NM
❑ CL 1724 [M]	Heart Over Mind and Other Big Country Hits	1962	7.50	15.00	30.00
❑ CS 8524 [S]	Heart Over Mind and Other Big Country Hits	1962	10.00	20.00	40.00
❑ C 30253	Heart Over Mind	1970	3.00	6.00	12.00

ELEKTRA

Number	Title (A Side/B Side)	Yr	VG	VG+	NM
❑ 6E-236	Me and Pepper	1979	2.50	5.00	10.00
❑ 6E-271	Your Body Is an Outlaw	1980	2.50	5.00	10.00
❑ 6E-310	Southern Rain	1980	2.50	5.00	10.00
❑ 60016	It's a Long Way to Daytona	1982	2.50	5.00	10.00
❑ 60192	Mel Tillis' Greatest Hits	1982	2.50	5.00	10.00

HARMONY

Number	Title (A Side/B Side)	Yr	VG	VG+	NM
❑ HL 7370 [M]	The Great Mel Tillis Sings Walk On, Boy and Other Great Country Hits	196?	3.75	7.50	15.00
❑ HS 11170 [S]	The Great Mel Tillis Sings Walk On, Boy and Other Great Country Hits	196?	3.00	6.00	12.00
❑ KH 31952	Mel	1972	3.00	6.00	12.00

HILLTOP

Number	Title (A Side/B Side)	Yr	VG	VG+	NM
❑ JS-6153	Detroit City	197?	2.50	5.00	10.00

KAPP

Number	Title (A Side/B Side)	Yr	VG	VG+	NM
❑ KL-1493 [M]	Stateside	1966	3.75	7.50	15.00
❑ KL-1514 [M]	Life Turned Her That Way	1967	3.75	7.50	15.00
❑ KL-1535 [M]	Mr. Mel	1967	5.00	10.00	20.00
❑ KS-3493 [S]	Stateside	1966	5.00	10.00	20.00
❑ KS-3514 [S]	Life Turned Her That Way	1967	5.00	10.00	20.00
❑ KS-3535 [S]	Mr. Mel	1967	3.75	7.50	15.00
❑ KS-3543	Let Me Talk to You	1968	3.75	7.50	15.00
❑ KS-3570	Something Special	1968	3.75	7.50	15.00
❑ KS-3589	Mel Tillis' Greatest Hits	1969	3.75	7.50	15.00
❑ KS-3594	Who's Julie	1969	3.75	7.50	15.00
❑ KS-3609	Mel Tillis Sings Old Faithful	1969	3.75	7.50	15.00
❑ KS-3630	She'll Be Hanging 'Round Somewhere	1970	3.75	7.50	15.00
❑ KS-3639	Mel Tillis In Person	1970	3.75	7.50	15.00

MCA

Number	Title (A Side/B Side)	Yr	VG	VG+	NM
❑ 66	Mel Tillis' Greatest Hits	1973	3.00	6.00	12.00
—Reissue of Kapp 3589					
❑ 550	Mel Tillis In Person	197?	2.50	5.00	10.00
—Reissue of Kapp 3639					
❑ 649	Love Revival	198?	2.00	4.00	8.00
—Reissue of 2204					
❑ 650	Heart Healer	198?	2.00	4.00	8.00
—Reissue of 2252					

Number	Title (A Side/B Side)	Yr	VG	VG+	NM
❏ 651	Love's Troubled Waters	198?	2.00	4.00	8.00
—Reissue of 2288					
❏ 652	I Believe in You	198?	2.00	4.00	8.00
—Reissue of 2364					
❏ 653	Are You Sincere	198?	2.00	4.00	8.00
—Reissue of 3077					
❏ 789	M-M-Mel Live	198?	2.00	4.00	8.00
—Reissue of 3208					
❏ 2204	Love Revival	1976	3.00	6.00	12.00
❏ 2252	Heart Healer	1977	3.00	6.00	12.00
❏ 2288	Love's Troubled Waters	1977	3.00	6.00	12.00
❏ 2364	I Believe in You	1978	3.00	6.00	12.00
❏ 3077	Are You Sincere	1979	3.00	6.00	12.00
❏ 3167	Mr. Entertainer	1979	3.00	6.00	12.00
❏ 3208	M-M-Mel Live	1980	3.00	6.00	12.00
❏ 3274	The Very Best of Mel Tillis	1980	2.50	5.00	10.00
❏ 4091 [(2)]	The Best of Mel Tillis	1975	3.75	7.50	15.00
❏ 5378	After All This Time	1983	2.00	4.00	8.00
❏ 5472	New Patches	1984	2.00	4.00	8.00
❏ 37121	Mr. Entertainer	198?	2.00	4.00	8.00
—Reissue of 3167					
MERCURY					
❏ 835310-1	Brand New Mister Me	1988	2.00	4.00	8.00
MGM					
❏ SE-4681	One More Time	1970	3.75	7.50	15.00
❏ SE-4757	The Arms of a Fool/Commercial Affection	1971	3.75	7.50	15.00
❏ SE-4788	Recorded Live at the Sam Houston Coliseum, Houston, Texas	1971	3.75	7.50	15.00
❏ SE-4806	The Very Best of Mel Tillis and the Statesiders	1972	3.75	7.50	15.00
❏ SE-4841	Would You Want Your World to End	1972	3.75	7.50	15.00
❏ SE-4870	I Ain't Never/Neon Rose	1972	3.75	7.50	15.00
❏ SE-4889	Mel Tillis and the Statesiders On Stage at the Birmingham Municipal Auditorium	1973	3.75	7.50	15.00
❏ SE-4907	Sawmill	1973	3.75	7.50	15.00
❏ M3F-4960	Stomp Them Grapes	1974	3.00	6.00	12.00
❏ M3G-4970	Mel Tillis' Greatest Hits	1974	3.00	6.00	12.00
❏ M3G-4981	Mel Tillis Time	1975	—	—	—
—Canceled					
❏ M3G-4987	Mel Tillis and the Statesiders	1975	3.00	6.00	12.00
❏ MG-1-5002	M-M-Mel	1975	3.00	6.00	12.00
❏ MG-1-5021	The Best of Mel Tillis and the Statesiders	1976	3.00	6.00	12.00
❏ MG-1-5022	Welcome to Mel Tillis Country	1976	3.00	6.00	12.00
❏ MG-2-5402 [(2)]	24 Great Hits	1977	3.75	7.50	15.00
❏ MG-2-5404 [(2)]	Live at the Sam Houston Coliseum & Birmingham Municipal Auditorium	1978	3.75	7.50	15.00
—Combines 4788 and 4889 in one package					
POWER PAK					
❏ PO-295	Mel Tillis & Friends	197?	2.50	5.00	10.00
RCA VICTOR					
❏ AHL1-5483	California Road	1985	2.00	4.00	8.00
STARDAY					
❏ SLP-471	Stateside	1972	3.00	6.00	12.00
TIME-LIFE					
❏ STW-111	Country Music	1981	2.50	5.00	10.00
VOCALION					
❏ VL 73914	Big 'n' Country	1970	3.00	6.00	12.00

TILLIS, MEL, AND SHERRY BRYCE
45s

Number	Title (A Side/B Side)	Yr	VG	VG+	NM
MGM					
❏ 14255	Take My Hand/Life's Little Surprises	1971	—	3.00	6.00
❏ 14303	Living and Learning/Tangled Vines	1971	—	3.00	6.00
❏ 14365	Anything's Better Than Nothing/ Then It Will Be All Over	1972	—	3.00	6.00
❏ 14472	Back to Life/Happyville	1972	—	3.00	6.00
❏ 14660	Let's Go All the Way Tonight/In the Vine	1973	—	3.00	6.00
❏ 14714	Don't Let Go/Why Not Do the Things (They Think We've Done)	1974	—	3.00	6.00
❏ 14776	You Are the One/I Saw Heaven in You	1974	—	3.00	6.00
❏ 14803	Mr. Right and Mrs. Wrong/Just Two Strangers Passing in the Night	1975	—	3.00	6.00

Albums

Number	Title (A Side/B Side)	Yr	VG	VG+	NM
MGM					
❏ SE-4800	Living and Learning/Take My Hand	1971	3.75	7.50	15.00
❏ SE-4937	Let's Go All the Way Tonight	1974	3.75	7.50	15.00

TILLIS, MEL, WITH GLEN CAMPBELL Also see each artist's individual listings.
45s

Number	Title (A Side/B Side)	Yr	VG	VG+	NM
MCA					
❏ 52474	Slow Nights/Midnight Love	1984	—	—	3.00

TILLIS, MEL, AND BILL PHILLIPS
45s

Number	Title (A Side/B Side)	Yr	VG	VG+	NM
COLUMBIA					
❏ 4-41416	Sawmill/You Are the Reason	1959	3.75	7.50	15.00
❏ 4-41530	Georgia Town Blues/ Till I Get Enough of These Blues	1959	3.75	7.50	15.00

TILLIS, MEL, AND WEBB PIERCE Also see each artist's individual listings.
45s

Number	Title (A Side/B Side)	Yr	VG	VG+	NM
DECCA					
❏ 31445	How Come Your Dog Don't Bite Nobody But Me/ So Soon	1962	2.50	5.00	10.00

TILLIS, MEL, AND NANCY SINATRA Also see each artist's individual listings.
45s

Number	Title (A Side/B Side)	Yr	VG	VG+	NM
ELEKTRA					
❏ 47157	Texas Cowboy Night/After the Lovin'	1981	—	2.50	5.00
❏ 47234 [DJ]	Rudolph the Red-Nosed Reindeer/Winter Wonderland	1981	2.00	4.00	8.00
—As "Mel and Nancy"; B-side by Dave Rowland and Sugar					
❏ 47247	Play Me or Trade Me/Where Would I Be	1981	—	2.50	5.00

Albums

Number	Title (A Side/B Side)	Yr	VG	VG+	NM
ELEKTRA					
❏ 5E-549	Mel and Nancy	1981	3.00	6.00	12.00

TILLMAN, BERTHA
45s

Number	Title (A Side/B Side)	Yr	VG	VG+	NM
BRENT					
❏ 7029	Oh My Angel/Lovin' Time	1962	7.50	15.00	30.00
❏ 7032	I Wish/(I Believe) Something Funny Is Going On	1962	10.00	20.00	40.00
JOCKO					
❏ 599	What Am I Trying to Prove?/(B-side unknown)	196?	5.00	10.00	20.00

TILLOTSON, JOHNNY
45s

Number	Title (A Side/B Side)	Yr	VG	VG+	NM
AMOS					
❏ 117	Tears on My Pillow/Remember When	1969	—	3.00	6.00
❏ 125	What Am I Living For/Joy to the World	1969	—	3.00	6.00
❏ 128	Raining in My Heart/ Today I Started Loving You Again	1969	—	3.00	6.00
❏ 136	Susan/Love Waits for Me	1970	—	3.00	6.00
❏ 146	I Don't Believe In It Anymore/ Kansas City, Kansas	1970	—	3.00	6.00
ATLANTIC					
❏ 87978	Bim Bam Boom/(B-side unknown)	1990	—	2.00	4.00
BUDDAH					
❏ 232	Star Spangled Bus/Apple Bend	1971	—	2.50	5.00
❏ 256	Welfare Hero/The Flower Kissed the Shoes That Jesus Wore	1971	—	2.50	5.00
❏ 279	Make Me Believe/The Flower Kissed the Shoes That Jesus Wore	1972	—	2.50	5.00
❏ 311	Your Love's Been a Long Time Comin'/ Apple Bend	1972	—	2.50	5.00
CADENCE					
❏ 1353	Dreamy Eyes/Well, I'm Your Man	1958	5.00	10.00	20.00
❏ 1354	I'm Never Gonna Kiss You/Cherie, Cherie	1958	6.25	12.50	25.00
—With Genevieve					
❏ 1365	True True Happiness/Love Is Blind	1959	5.00	10.00	20.00
❏ 1372	Why Do I Love You So/Never Let Me Go	1959	5.00	10.00	20.00
❏ 1377	Earth Angel/Pledging My Love	1960	5.00	10.00	20.00
❏ 1377 [PS]	Earth Angel/Pledging My Love	1960	7.50	15.00	30.00
❏ 1384	Poetry in Motion/Princess, Princess	1960	5.00	10.00	20.00
❏ 1391	Jimmy's Girl/His True Love Said Godbye	1960	3.75	7.50	15.00
❏ 1391 [PS]	Jimmy's Girl/His True Love Said Godbye	1960	7.50	15.00	30.00
❏ 1404	Without You/Cutie Pie	1961	3.75	7.50	15.00
❏ 1409	Dreamy Eyes/Well, I'm Your Man	1961	3.75	7.50	15.00
❏ 1418	It Keeps Right On a-Hurtin'/ She Gave Sweet Love to Me	1962	3.75	7.50	15.00
❏ 1424	Send Me the Pillow You Dream On/What'll I Do	1962	3.75	7.50	15.00
❏ 1432	I Can't Help It (If I'm Still in Love with You)/I'm So Lonesome I Could Cry	1962	3.75	7.50	15.00
❏ 1434	Out of My Mind/Empty Feelin'	1963	3.75	7.50	15.00
❏ 1437	You Can Never Stop Me Loving You/ Judy, Judy, Judy	1963	3.75	7.50	15.00
❏ 1441	Funny How Time Slips Away/ A Very Good Year for Girls	1963	3.75	7.50	15.00
COLUMBIA					
❏ 10125	Big Ole Jean/Mississippi Lady	1975	—	2.50	5.00
❏ 10199	Right Here in Your Arms/ Willow County Request Live	1975	—	2.50	5.00
❏ 45842	Sunshine of My Life/If You Wouldn't Be My Lady	1973	—	2.50	5.00
❏ 45984	So Much of My Life/I Love How She Needs Me	1973	—	2.50	5.00
❏ 46065	Till I Can't Take It Anymore/ Sunday Kind of Woman	1974	—	2.50	5.00
MGM					
❏ 13181	Talk Back Trembling Lips/Another You	1963	3.00	6.00	12.00
❏ 13181 [PS]	Talk Back Trembling Lips/Another You	1963	5.00	10.00	20.00
❏ 13193	Worried Guy/Please Don't Go Away	1963	2.50	5.00	10.00
❏ 13193 [PS]	Worried Guy/Please Don't Go Away	1963	5.00	10.00	20.00
❏ 13232	I Rise, I Fall/I'm Watching My Watch	1964	2.50	5.00	10.00
❏ 13232 [PS]	I Rise, I Fall/I'm Watching My Watch	1964	5.00	10.00	20.00
❏ 13255	Worry/Sufferin' from a Heartache	1964	2.50	5.00	10.00
❏ 13255 [PS]	Worry/Sufferin' from a Heartache	1964	5.00	10.00	20.00
❏ 13284	She Understands Me/Tomorrow	1964	2.50	5.00	10.00
❏ 13284 [PS]	She Understands Me/Tomorrow	1964	5.00	10.00	20.00
❏ 13316	Angel/Little Boy	1965	2.50	5.00	10.00
❏ 13316 [PS]	Angel/Little Boy	1965	5.00	10.00	20.00
❏ 13344	Then I'll Count Again/One's Yours, One's Mine	1965	2.50	5.00	10.00
❏ 13344 [PS]	Then I'll Count Again/One's Yours, One's Mine	1965	5.00	10.00	20.00
❏ 13376	Heartaches by the Number/ Your Mem'ry Comes Along	1965	2.50	5.00	10.00
❏ 13376 [PS]	Heartaches by the Number/ Your Mem'ry Comes Along	1965	5.00	10.00	20.00
❏ 13408	Our World/(Wait 'Till You See) My Gidget	1965	2.50	5.00	10.00
❏ 13445	Hello Enemy/I Never Loved You Anyway	1966	2.50	5.00	10.00
❏ 13499	Me, Myself and I/Country Boy, Country Boy	1966	2.50	5.00	10.00
❏ 13519	No Love at All/What Am I Gonna Do	1966	2.50	5.00	10.00
❏ 13598	More Than Before/Baby's Gone	1966	2.50	5.00	10.00
❏ 13598	More Than Before/Open Up Your Heart	1966	2.50	5.00	10.00
❏ 13633	Christmas Country Style/ Christmas Is the Best of All	1966	2.50	5.00	10.00
❏ 13684	Strange Things Happen/Tommy Jones	1967	2.50	5.00	10.00
❏ 13738	Don't Tell Me It's Raining/Takin' It Easy	1967	2.50	5.00	10.00
❏ 13829	You're the Reason/Countin' My Teardrops	1967	2.50	5.00	10.00
❏ 13888	I Can Spot a Cheater/It Keeps Right On a-Hurtin'	1968	2.00	4.00	8.00
❏ 13924	I Haven't Begun to Love You Yet/Why So Lonely	1968	2.00	4.00	8.00
❏ 13977	Letter to Emily/Your Mem'ry Comes Along	1968	2.00	4.00	8.00
REWARD					
❏ 03327	Baby You Do It for Me (And I'll Do It for You)/ She's Not As Married As She Used to Be	1982	—	2.00	4.00
❏ 03901	Crying/You're a Beautiful Place to Be	1983	—	2.00	4.00
❏ 04123	Burnin'/What's Another Year	1983	—	2.00	4.00
❏ 04346	Lay Back (In the Arms of Somebody)/ What's Another Year	1984	—	2.00	4.00
SCEPTER					
❏ 12389	Song for Hank Williams (mono/stereo)	1973	2.00	4.00	8.00
—With John Edward Beland; may be promo-only					
UNITED ARTISTS					
❏ XW860	It Could've Been Nashville/Summertime Lovin'	1976	—	2.50	5.00
❏ XW986	Toy Hearts/Just An Ordinary Man	1977	—	2.50	5.00

T

Number	Title (A Side/B Side)	Yr	VG	VG+	NM
7-Inch Extended Plays					
CADENCE					
❏ CLLP 33-1	Poetry in Motion/Jimmy's Girl/True, True Happiness//Earth Angel/Why Do I Love You So/Pledging My Love	1961	5.00	10.00	20.00
—Jukebox issue; small hole, plays at 33 1/3 rpm					
❏ CLLP 33-1 [PS]	This Is Johnny Tillotson	1961	7.50	15.00	30.00
—Cardboard insert in heavy vinyl envelope					
❏ CLLP 33-2	Without You/Much Beyond Compare/Well I'm Your Man//Princess Princess/Dreamy Eyes/Cutie Pie	1961	5.00	10.00	20.00
—Jukebox issue; small hole, plays at 33 1/3 rpm					
❏ CLLP 33-2 [PS]	Words and Music by Johnny Tillotson	1961	7.50	15.00	30.00
—Cardboard insert in heavy vinyl envelope					
❏ CEP-114	True True Happiness/Love Is Blind//Dreamy Eyes/Well I'm Your Man	1960	6.25	12.50	25.00
❏ CEP-114 [PS]	Johnny Tillotson	1960	6.25	12.50	25.00
Albums					
ACCORD					
❏ SN-7194	Scrapbook	1982	2.50	5.00	10.00
AMOS					
❏ AAS 7006	Tears on My Pillow	1969	5.00	10.00	20.00
BARNABY					
❏ BR-4007	Johnny Tillotson's Greatest	1977	3.00	6.00	12.00
BUDDAH					
❏ BDS-5112	Johnny Tillotson	1972	3.75	7.50	15.00
CADENCE					
❏ CLP-3052 [M]	Johnny Tillotson's Best	1961	10.00	20.00	40.00
—Maroon and silver label					
❏ CLP-3052 [M]	Johnny Tillotson's Best	1962	6.25	12.50	25.00
—Red and black label					
❏ CLP-3058 [M]	It Keeps Right On a-Hurtin'	1962	7.50	15.00	30.00
❏ CLP-3067 [M]	You Can Never Stop Me Loving You	1963	7.50	15.00	30.00
❏ CLP-25052 [P]	Johnny Tillotson's Best	1961	12.50	25.00	50.00
—Maroon and silver label					
❏ CLP-25052 [P]	Johnny Tillotson's Best	1962	7.50	15.00	30.00
—Red and black label					
❏ CLP-25058 [S]	It Keeps Right On a-Hurtin'	1962	10.00	20.00	40.00
❏ CLP-25067 [P]	You Can Never Stop Me Loving You	1963	10.00	20.00	40.00
EVEREST					
❏ 4113	Johnny Tillotson's Greatest Hits	1982	2.50	5.00	10.00
METRO					
❏ M-561 [M]	Johnny Tillotson Sings Tillotson	1967	3.75	7.50	15.00
❏ MS-561 [S]	Johnny Tillotson Sings Tillotson	1967	5.00	10.00	20.00
MGM					
❏ E-4188 [M]	Talk Back Trembling Lips	1964	5.00	10.00	20.00
❏ SE-4188 [S]	Talk Back Trembling Lips	1964	6.25	12.50	25.00
❏ E-4224 [M]	The Tillotson Touch	1964	5.00	10.00	20.00
❏ SE-4224 [S]	The Tillotson Touch	1964	6.25	12.50	25.00
❏ E-4270 [M]	She Understands Me	1965	5.00	10.00	20.00
❏ SE-4270 [S]	She Understands Me	1965	6.25	12.50	25.00
❏ E-4302 [M]	That's My Style	1965	5.00	10.00	20.00
❏ SE-4302 [S]	That's My Style	1965	6.25	12.50	25.00
❏ E-4328 [M]	Our World	1965	5.00	10.00	20.00
❏ SE-4328 [S]	Our World	1965	6.25	12.50	25.00
❏ E-4395 [M]	No Love at All	1966	5.00	10.00	20.00
❏ SE-4395 [S]	No Love at All	1966	6.25	12.50	25.00
❏ E-4402 [M]	The Christmas Touch	1966	5.00	10.00	20.00
❏ SE-4402 [S]	The Christmas Touch	1966	6.25	12.50	25.00
❏ E-4452 [M]	Here I Am	1967	5.00	10.00	20.00
❏ SE-4452 [S]	Here I Am	1967	6.25	12.50	25.00
❏ E-4532 [M]	The Best of Johnny Tillotson	1968	7.50	15.00	30.00
—May be promo only (yellow label)					
❏ SE-4532 [S]	The Best of Johnny Tillotson	1968	5.00	10.00	20.00
❏ SE-4814	The Very Best of Johnny Tillotson	1971	3.00	6.00	12.00
❏ ST 90410 [S]	The Tillotson Touch	1965	7.50	15.00	30.00
—Capitol Record Club edition					
❏ T 90410 [M]	The Tillotson Touch	1965	7.50	15.00	30.00
—Capitol Record Club edition					
UNITED ARTISTS					
❏ UA-LA759-G	Johnny Tillotson	1977	2.50	5.00	10.00

TIM TAM AND THE TURN-ONS

Number	Title (A Side/B Side)	Yr	VG	VG+	NM
45s					
PALMER					
❏ 5002	Wait a Minute/Ophelia	1965	6.25	12.50	25.00
❏ 5003	Cheryl Ann/Sealed with a Kiss	1966	7.50	15.00	30.00
❏ 5006	Kimberly/I Leave You in Tears	1966	10.00	20.00	40.00
❏ 5014	Don't Say Hi/(Instrumental)	1967	6.25	12.50	25.00

TIMBER CREEK

Number	Title (A Side/B Side)	Yr	VG	VG+	NM
Albums					
RENEGADE					
❏ 95014	Hellbound Highway	1975	37.50	75.00	150.00

TIMERS, THE With GARY USHER and BRIAN WILSON.

Number	Title (A Side/B Side)	Yr	VG	VG+	NM
45s					
REPRISE					
❏ 20231	No-Go Showboat/Competition Coupe	1963	25.00	50.00	100.00

TIMMOTHY

Number	Title (A Side/B Side)	Yr	VG	VG+	NM
Albums					
PEAR					
❏ (# unknown)	Strange But True	1972	50.00	100.00	200.00

TIN HOUSE

Number	Title (A Side/B Side)	Yr	VG	VG+	NM
45s					
EPIC					
❏ 10739	I Want Your Baby/Be Good and Be Kind	1971	2.00	4.00	8.00
Albums					
EPIC					
❏ E 30511	Tin House	1971	5.00	10.00	20.00

TIN TIN

Number	Title (A Side/B Side)	Yr	VG	VG+	NM
45s					
ATCO					
❏ 6794	Toast and Marmalade for Tea/Manhattan Woman	1971	2.00	4.00	8.00
❏ 6821	Is That the Way/Swans on the Canal	1971	—	3.00	6.00
❏ 6853	Set Sail for England/The Cavalry Is Coming	1971	—	3.00	6.00
POLYDOR					
❏ 15055	Talking Turkey/The Cavalry Is Coming	1972	—	3.00	6.00
SIRE					
❏ 29750	Kiss Me/Kiss Me	1983	—	2.50	5.00
Albums					
ATCO					
❏ SD 33-350	Tin Tin	1970	3.75	7.50	15.00
❏ SD 33-370	Astral Taxi	1971	3.75	7.50	15.00

TINA WITH DADDY AND MOMMY "Mommy and Daddy" are TAMMY WYNETTE and GEORGE JONES; Tina is their stepdaughter.

Number	Title (A Side/B Side)	Yr	VG	VG+	NM
45s					
EPIC					
❏ 11099	Telephone Call/No Charge	1974	—	2.50	5.00

TINDLEY, GEORGE

Number	Title (A Side/B Side)	Yr	VG	VG+	NM
45s					
EMBER					
❏ 1058	The Gypsy/I Wish	1960	3.75	7.50	15.00
❏ 1060	Wedding Bells/No Lonely Nights	1960	3.75	7.50	15.00
HERALD					
❏ 558	Close Your Eyes/Heart of Gold	1961	3.00	6.00	12.00
PARKWAY					
❏ 834	Fairy Tales/Just For You	1962	3.00	6.00	12.00
WAND					
❏ 11205	Ain't That Peculiar/It's All Over But the Shouting	1969	2.00	4.00	8.00
❏ 11208	Honky Tonk Women/So Help Me Woman	1969	2.00	4.00	8.00
❏ 11215	Wan-Tu-Wah-Zuree/Pity the Poor Man	1970	2.00	4.00	8.00

TINGLING MOTHER'S CIRCUS

Number	Title (A Side/B Side)	Yr	VG	VG+	NM
45s					
MUSICOR					
❏ 1335	Positively Negative/Sunday Kind of Feeling	1968	2.50	5.00	10.00
❏ 1359	I Found a New Love/Happy Bubble	1969	2.50	5.00	10.00
ROULETTE					
❏ 4758	Face in My Mind/Isn't It Strange	1967	3.75	7.50	15.00
Albums					
MUSICOR					
❏ MS-3167	Circus of the Mind	1968	6.25	12.50	25.00

TINY TIM

Number	Title (A Side/B Side)	Yr	VG	VG+	NM
45s					
BLUE CAT					
❏ 127	April Showers/Little Girl	1966	3.00	6.00	12.00
CLOUDS					
❏ 17	Tip Toe to the Gas Pumps/Hickey on Your Neck	1979	2.50	5.00	10.00
REPRISE					
❏ 0679	Tip-Toe Thru' the Tulips with Me/Fill Your Heart	1968	2.00	4.00	8.00
❏ 0740	Tip-Toe Thru' the Tulips with Me/Don't Bite the Hand That's Feeding You	1971	—	2.00	4.00
—"Back to Back Hits" series					
❏ 0760	Bring Back Those Rock-A-Bye Baby Days/Hello, Hello	1968	—	3.00	6.00
❏ 0760	Bring Back Those Rock-A-Bye Baby Days/This Is All I Ask	1968	—	3.00	6.00
❏ 0769	Be My Love/This Is All I Ask	1968	—	3.00	6.00
❏ 0802	Great Balls of Fire/As Time Goes By	1969	—	3.00	6.00
❏ 0837	On the Good Ship Lollipop/America I Love You	1969	—	3.00	6.00
❏ 0855	Mickey the Monkey/Neighborhood Children	1969	—	3.00	6.00
❏ 0867	I'm a Lonesome Little Raindrop/What the World Needs Now Is Love	1969	—	3.00	6.00
❏ 0939	Don't Bite the Hand That's Feeding You/What Kind of American Are You	1970	—	3.00	6.00
❏ 0985	Why/Spaceship Song	1971	—	3.00	6.00
—With Miss Vicky					
❏ 20174	Bring Back Rockabye Baby Days/Just Say I Love Her	1963	3.00	6.00	12.00
—B-side by Johnny Prophet					
SCEPTER					
❏ 12351	Am I Just Another Pretty Face/The Movies	1972	—	3.00	6.00
VICTIM					
❏ 1001	Rudolph The Red-Nosed Reindeer/White Christmas	198?	3.00	6.00	12.00
Albums					
BOUQUET					
❏ SLP-711	Love and Kisses from Tiny Tim	1968	3.00	6.00	12.00
REPRISE					
❏ R 6292 [M]	God Bless Tiny Tim	1968	10.00	20.00	40.00
—Mono copies may all be white label promos					
❏ RS 6292 [S]	God Bless Tiny Tim	1968	3.75	7.50	15.00
❏ RS 6323	Tiny Tim's Second Album	1969	3.75	7.50	15.00
❏ RS 6351	For All My Little Friends	1969	3.75	7.50	15.00

TINY TIM AND THE HITS

Number	Title (A Side/B Side)	Yr	VG	VG+	NM
45s					
ROULETTE					
❏ 4123	Wedding Bells/Doll Baby	1958	12.50	25.00	50.00

TIP TOPS, THE

Number	Title (A Side/B Side)	Yr	VG	VG+	NM
45s					
PARKWAY					
❏ 868	Oo-Kook-a-Boo/He's a Braggin'	1963	3.00	6.00	12.00
ROULETTE					
❏ 4684	Meetcha at the Cheetah/A Little Bit More	1966	30.00	60.00	120.00

Number	Title (A Side/B Side)	Yr	VG	VG+	NM

TIPTON, JOHN
45s
DATE
| ❏ 2-1641 | Spring/Two Lonely Lips | 1969 | 2.00 | 4.00 | 8.00 |
| ❏ 2-1663 | Game of Promise/Sleepy Eyes | 1969 | 2.00 | 4.00 | 8.00 |

TIPTON, LESTER
45s
LA BEAT
| ❏ P 6607 | This Won't Change/Go On | 196? | 1000. | 2000. | 4000. |

TITANS, THE More than one group.
45s
BANGAR
| ❏ 00611 | Surfer's Lullaby/Motivation | 1964 | 6.25 | 12.50 | 25.00 |
CLASS
| ❏ 244 | No Time/The Tootin' Tutor | 1959 | 6.25 | 12.50 | 25.00 |
DUFF'S
| ❏ 111 | Little Girl/Pretty Young Thing | 1969 | 3.00 | 6.00 | 12.00 |
| ❏ 112 | Ode to Billy Martin/Please Don't Be Angry | 1970 | 3.00 | 6.00 | 12.00 |
FIDELITY
| ❏ 3016 | What Have I Done/Everybody Happy? | 1960 | 7.50 | 15.00 | 30.00 |
METROBEAT
| ❏ 4452 | To Covet the Turf/Mountain of Love | 196? | 5.00 | 10.00 | 20.00 |
MGM
| ❏ 13207 | Yojimbo/Midnight in Tokyo | 1964 | 3.00 | 6.00 | 12.00 |
—B-side by the Tokyo Boys
NOLTA
| ❏ 351 | A-Rab/Marquette | 1961 | 6.25 | 12.50 | 25.00 |
SOMA
| ❏ 1402 | A Summer Place/Tchaikovsky Rides Again | 1963 | 5.00 | 10.00 | 20.00 |
| ❏ 1411 | The No Place Special/Reveille Rock | 1964 | 5.00 | 10.00 | 20.00 |
SOUND OF MUSIC
| ❏ 12186 | Need You/Fun Seekers | 196? | 3.00 | 6.00 | 12.00 |
| ❏ 12186 [PS] | Need You/Fun Seekers | 196? | 12.50 | 25.00 | 50.00 |
SPECIALTY
❏ 614	Sweet Peach/Free and Easy	1957	6.25	12.50	25.00
❏ 625	Don't You Just Know It/Can It Be	1958	6.25	12.50	25.00
❏ 632	Arlene/Love Is a Wonderful Thing	1958	6.25	12.50	25.00
STUDIO CITY
❏ 1008	The No Place Special/Reveille Rock	1964	10.00	20.00	40.00
VITA
❏ 148	Rhythm and Blues/❏ So Hard to Laugh, So Easy to Cry	1957	18.75	37.50	75.00
❏ 158	G'Wan Home Calypso/Look What You're Doing Baby	1957	15.00	30.00	60.00
Albums
MGM
❏ E-3992 [M]	Today's Teen Beat	1961	7.50	15.00	30.00
❏ SE-3992 [S]	Today's Teen Beat	1961	10.00	20.00	40.00

TITONES, THE
45s
SCEPTER
| ❏ 1206 | Symbol of Love/The Movies | 1960 | 6.25 | 12.50 | 25.00 |
—Red label
| ❏ 1206 | Symbol of Love/The Movies | 1960 | 12.50 | 25.00 | 50.00 |
—White label
WAND
| ❏ 105 | Symbol of Love/My Movie Queen | 1960 | 5.00 | 10.00 | 20.00 |

TITUS GROAN
Albums
JANUS
| ❏ JLS-3024 | Titus Groan | 1971 | 7.50 | 15.00 | 30.00 |

TITUS OATES
Albums
LIPS
| ❏ (no #) | Jungle Lady | 1974 | 50.00 | 100.00 | 200.00 |

TOAD HALL
45s
BARNABY
| ❏ ZS7 2052 | Hallelujah! I'm a Bum/I'm Leaving You Louisiana | 1971 | 2.00 | 4.00 | 8.00 |
Albums
LIBERTY
| ❏ LST-7580 | Toad Hall | 1968 | 6.25 | 12.50 | 25.00 |

TODAY AND TOMORROW
45s
NOOSE
| ❏ 812 | Dooley Swings (Part 1)/Dooley Swings (Part 2) | 1959 | 10.00 | 20.00 | 40.00 |

TODAY'S PEOPLE
45s
20TH CENTURY
| ❏ 2032 | He/I Didn't Know | 1973 | — | 3.00 | 6.00 |
| ❏ 2079 | I Belong/Come Back to Save Us | 1974 | — | 3.00 | 6.00 |

TODD, ART AND DOTTY
45s
ABBOTT
| ❏ 3006 | Busy Signal/Oh Honey Why Don't Cha | 1955 | 5.00 | 10.00 | 20.00 |
CAPITOL
| ❏ 4778 | Sweet Someone/Ring-a-Ding | 1962 | 2.00 | 4.00 | 8.00 |
DART
❏ 404	Wait for Me/Joie de Vivre	1956	3.00	6.00	12.00
❏ 405	Chop Chop/Say You	1956	3.00	6.00	12.00
❏ 51986	Blueberry Hill/Wonderful, Loveable You	1959	2.50	5.00	10.00
DECCA
❏ 31261	Ca C'est La Vie/Drifting and Dreaming	1961	2.50	5.00	10.00
❏ 31329	Your Cheatin' Heart/Sweet Cha Cha Chariot	1961	2.50	5.00	10.00
DOT
❏ 16939	I'll Take Care of Your Cares/Bodie Tree	1966	—	3.00	6.00

ERA
❏ 1064	Chanson D'Amour (Song of Love)/Along the Trail with You	1957	3.00	6.00	12.00
❏ 1076	Au Revoir Amour/Der Glockenspiel	1958	2.50	5.00	10.00
❏ 1087	Pray/Don't You Worry My Little Pet	1958	2.50	5.00	10.00
❏ 1088	Straight as an Arrow/Stand There Mountain	1959	2.50	5.00	10.00
❏ 3001	Paradise/Ayuh Ayuh	1959	2.50	5.00	10.00
RCA VICTOR
❏ 47-5029	Heavenly-Heavenly/Broken Wings	1952	3.75	7.50	15.00
SIGNET
❏ 2020	Bernadette Soubirous/Bodie Tree	1965	2.00	4.00	8.00
Albums
DART
❏ D-444 [M]	Black Velvet Eyes	1959	10.00	20.00	40.00
DOT
❏ DLP-3742 [M]	Chanson d'Amour (Song of Love)	1966	6.25	12.50	25.00
❏ DLP-25742 [S]	Chanson d'Amour (Song of Love)	1966	7.50	15.00	30.00

TODD, DYLAN
45s
RCA VICTOR
❏ 47-6463	The Ballad of James Dean/More Precious Than Gold	1956	7.50	15.00	30.00
❏ 47-6463 [PS]	The Ballad of James Dean/More Precious Than Gold	1956	12.50	25.00	50.00
❏ 47-6711	Timber/Golden Spurs and a Silver Saddle	1956	5.00	10.00	20.00

TODD, FULLER
45s
KING
❏ 5048	Old Fashioned/Proud Lady Heart Stealer	1957	6.25	12.50	25.00
❏ 5075	Real True Love/Young Hearts Are True	1957	6.25	12.50	25.00
❏ 5111	Top Ten Rock/Jeannie Marie	1958	6.25	12.50	25.00

TODD, JOHNNY
45s
MODERN
| ❏ 1003 | Pink Cadillac/What's Up | 1956 | 30.00 | 60.00 | 120.00 |

TODD, NICK
45s
DOT
❏ 15643	Plaything/The Honey Song	1957	5.00	10.00	20.00
❏ 15675	At the Hop/I Do	1957	5.00	10.00	20.00
❏ 15688	Teen-Age Cutie/Ever Since I Met Lucy	1958	5.00	10.00	20.00
❏ 15772	Forever and a Day/Too Much Rosita	1958	5.00	10.00	20.00
❏ 15860	My Little Girl/Does Your Heart Beat for Me?	1958	5.00	10.00	20.00
❏ 15893	Red Roses for a Blue Lady/Little Rosey Red	1959	3.75	7.50	15.00
❏ 15951	Tiger/Twice As Nice	1959	3.75	7.50	15.00
❏ 15981	Invisible Man/Sayin' Something	1959	3.75	7.50	15.00
❏ 16109	Each Moment/Your Love's Gotta Grip on Me	1960	3.75	7.50	15.00

TOE FAT
45s
RARE EARTH
| ❏ 5019 | Bad Side of the Moon/Just Like Me | 1970 | — | 3.00 | 6.00 |
Albums
RARE EARTH
| ❏ RS-511 | Toe Fat | 1970 | 6.25 | 12.50 | 25.00 |
| ❏ RS-525 | Toe Fat Two | 1971 | 6.25 | 12.50 | 25.00 |

TOGGERY FIVE, THE Also see FREDDIE AND THE DREAMERS.
45s
TOWER
| ❏ 119 | I'm Gonna Jump/Bye Bye Bird | 1965 | 3.75 | 7.50 | 15.00 |

TOKAYS, THE
45s
BONNIE
| ❏ 102 | Lost and Found/Fatty-Boom Bi Laddy | 1962 | 25.00 | 50.00 | 100.00 |
BRUTE
| ❏ 001 | Hey Senorita/Baby Baby Baby | 1967 | 30.00 | 60.00 | 120.00 |
SCORPIO
| ❏ 403 | Now/Ask Me No Questions | 1966 | 5.00 | 10.00 | 20.00 |

TOKENS, THE NEIL SEDAKA was (very) briefly a member. Also see THE COEDS; CROSS COUNTRY; THE FOUR WINDS (1); JOHNNY AND THE TOKENS; UNITED STATES DOUBLE QUARTET.
45s
ATCO
| ❏ 7009 | The Lord Can't Sing a Solo/Penny Whistle Band | 1974 | — | 3.00 | 6.00 |
B.T. PUPPY
❏ 500	A Girl Named Arlene/Swing	1964	3.00	6.00	12.00
❏ 502	He's in Town/Oh Cathy	1964	3.00	6.00	12.00
❏ 504	You're My Girl/Havin' Fun	1964	3.00	6.00	12.00
❏ 505	Nobody But You/Mr. Cupid	1965	2.50	5.00	10.00
❏ 507	A Message to the World/Sylvie Sleepin'	1965	2.50	5.00	10.00
❏ 512	Only My Friend/Cattle Call	1965	2.50	5.00	10.00
❏ 513	The Bells of St. Mary/Just One Smile	1966	2.50	5.00	10.00
❏ 515	The Three Bells/Message to the World	1966	2.50	5.00	10.00
❏ 518	I Hear Trumpets Blow/Don't Cry, Sing Along with the Music	1966	2.50	5.00	10.00
❏ 519	Breezy/Greatest Moments of a Girl's Life	1966	2.50	5.00	10.00
❏ 519 [PS]	Breezy/Greatest Moments of a Girl's Life	1966	6.25	12.50	25.00
❏ 525	Green Plant/Saloogy	1967	2.50	5.00	10.00
❏ 552	Please Say You Want Me/Get a Job	1969	2.50	5.00	10.00
BELL
❏ 45190	You and Me/I Like to Throw My Head Back and Sing	1972	—	3.00	6.00
BUDDAH
❏ 151	She Lets Her Hair Down (Early in the Morning)/Oh to Get Away	1970	—	3.00	6.00
❏ 159	Don't Worry Baby/If the Shoe Fits Ya Baby	1970	—	2.50	5.00
❏ 159	Don't Worry Baby/Some People Sleep	1970	—	2.50	5.00
❏ 174	Both Sides Now/I Could See Me (Dancin' with You)	1970	—	2.50	5.00
❏ 187	Listen to the Words (Listen to the Music)/Groovin' On the Sunshine	1970	—	2.50	5.00

T

Number	Title (A Side/B Side)	Yr	VG	VG+	NM
DATE					
❏ 2737	Oh What a Night/(Hey Hey) Juanita	1961	12.50	25.00	50.00
GARY					
❏ 1006	Doom-Lang/Come Dance with Me	1961	25.00	50.00	100.00
LAURIE					
❏ 3180	I'll Always Love You/Please Write	1963	5.00	10.00	20.00
MELBA					
❏ 104	While I Dream/I Love My Baby	1956	12.50	25.00	50.00
RCA					
❏ 8749-7-R	Re-Doo-Wopp/I'm Through with You	1988	—	2.00	4.00
❏ 8836-7-R	Re-Doo-Wopp (Edit)/I'm Through with You	1988	—	2.00	4.00
RCA VICTOR					
❏ 37-7896	When I Go to Sleep at Night/Dry Your Eyes	1961	10.00	20.00	40.00
—"Compact Single 33" (small hole, plays at LP speed)					
❏ 37-7925	Sincerely/When the Summer Is Through	1961	10.00	20.00	40.00
—"Compact Single 33" (small hole, plays at LP speed)					
❏ 37-7954	The Lion Sleeps Tonight/Tina	1961	12.50	25.00	50.00
—"Compact Single 33" (small hole, plays at LP speed)					
❏ 37-7991	B'wa Nina/Weeping River	1962	10.00	20.00	40.00
—"Compact Single 33" (small hole, plays at LP speed)					
❏ 37-8018	The Riddle/Big Boat	1962	10.00	20.00	40.00
—"Compact Single 33" (small hole, plays at LP speed)					
❏ 47-7896	When I Go to Sleep at Night/Dry Your Eyes	1961	5.00	10.00	20.00
❏ 47-7896 [PS]	When I Go to Sleep at Night/Dry Your Eyes	1961	10.00	20.00	40.00
❏ 47-7925	Sincerely/When the Summer Is Through	1961	5.00	10.00	20.00
❏ 47-7954	The Lion Sleeps Tonight/Tina	1961	6.25	12.50	25.00
❏ 47-7991	B'wa Nina/Weeping River	1962	5.00	10.00	20.00
❏ 47-7991 [PS]	B'wa Nina/Weeping River	1962	7.50	15.00	30.00
—"The Lion Sleeps Tonight" LP mentioned on sleeve					
❏ 47-7991 [PS]	B'wa Nina/Weeping River	1962	12.50	25.00	50.00
—No mention of "The Lion Sleeps Tonight" LP on sleeve					
❏ 47-8018	The Riddle/Big Boat	1962	5.00	10.00	20.00
❏ 47-8018 [PS]	The Riddle/Big Boat	1962	10.00	20.00	40.00
❏ 47-8052	La Bomba/A Token of Love	1962	5.00	10.00	20.00
❏ 47-8052 [PS]	La Bomba/A Token of Love	1962	10.00	20.00	40.00
❏ 47-8089	I'll Do My Crying Tomorrow/Dream Angel Goodnight	1962	5.00	10.00	20.00
❏ 47-8089 [PS]	I'll Do My Crying Tomorrow/Dream Angel Goodnight	1962	10.00	20.00	40.00
❏ 47-8114	A Bird Flies Out of Sight/Wishing	1962	5.00	10.00	20.00
❏ 47-8114 [PS]	A Bird Flies Out of Sight/Wishing	1962	10.00	20.00	40.00
❏ 47-8148	Tonight I Met An Angel/Hindi Lullabye	1963	3.75	7.50	15.00
❏ 47-8148 [PS]	Tonight I Met An Angel/Hindi Lullabye	1963	7.50	15.00	30.00
❏ 47-8210	Hear the Bells/ABC 1-2-3	1963	3.75	7.50	15.00
❏ 47-8210 [PS]	Hear the Bells/ABC 1-2-3	1963	7.50	15.00	30.00
❏ 47-8309	Two Cars/Let's Go to the Drag Strip	1963	3.75	7.50	15.00
❏ 47-8309 [PS]	Two Cars/Let's Go to the Drag Strip	1963	20.00	40.00	80.00
ROULETTE					
❏ 4174	Roses Are Red/Pictures in My Wallet	1959	7.50	15.00	30.00
—As "Darrell and the Oxfords"					
❏ 4230	Can't You Tell/Your Mother Said So	1960	7.50	15.00	30.00
—As "Darrell and the Oxfords"					
RUST					
❏ 5094	Arlene/Rumble in the Park	1965	2.50	5.00	10.00
WARNER BROS.					
❏ 5900	Portrait of My Love/She Comes and Goes	1967	2.00	4.00	8.00
❏ 5900 [PS]	Portrait of My Love/She Comes and Goes	1967	5.00	10.00	20.00
❏ 7056	It's a Happening World/How Nice	1967	—	3.00	6.00
❏ 7099	Ain't That Peculiar/Bye, Bye, Bye	1967	—	3.00	6.00
❏ 7118	Portrait of My Love/It's a Happening World	1968	—	2.50	5.00
—"Back to Back Hits" series -- originals have green labels with "W7" logo					
❏ 7169	Till/Poor Man	1968	—	3.00	6.00
❏ 7183	Mister Swail/Needles of Evergreen	1968	2.50	5.00	10.00
—As "Margo, Margo, Medress and Siegel"					
❏ 7202	Animal/Bathroom Wall	1968	—	3.00	6.00
❏ 7233	Grandfather/The Banana Boat Song	1968	—	3.00	6.00
❏ 7255	The World Is Full of Wonderful Things/Some People Sleep	1968	—	3.00	6.00
❏ 7280	Go Away Little Girl-Young Girl/I Want to Make Love to You	1969	—	3.00	6.00
❏ 7323	I Could Be/End of the World	1969	—	3.00	6.00
WARWICK					
❏ 615	Tonight I Fell in Love/I'll Always Love You	1961	7.50	15.00	30.00
Albums					
B.T. PUPPY					
❏ BTP-1000 [M]	I Hear Trumpets Blow	1966	5.00	10.00	20.00
❏ BTPS-1000 [P]	I Hear Trumpets Blow	1966	6.25	12.50	25.00
❏ BTPS-1006	Tokens of Gold	1969	6.25	12.50	25.00
❏ BTPS-1012	Greatest Moments	1970	6.25	12.50	25.00
❏ BTPS-1014	December 5th	1971	50.00	100.00	200.00
❏ BTPS-1027	Intercourse	1971	150.00	300.00	600.00
BUDDAH					
❏ BDS-5059	Both Sides Now	1971	3.75	7.50	15.00
DIPLOMAT					
❏ D-2308 [M]	Kings of the Hot Rods	196?	6.25	12.50	25.00
❏ DS-2308 [S]	Kings of the Hot Rods	196?	7.50	15.00	30.00
RCA					
❏ 8534-1-R	Re-Doo-Wopp	1988	2.50	5.00	10.00
RCA VICTOR					
❏ LPM-2514 [M]	The Lion Sleeps Tonight	1961	20.00	40.00	80.00
❏ LSP-2514 [S]	The Lion Sleeps Tonight	1961	37.50	75.00	150.00
❏ LPM-2631 [M]	We, The Tokens, Sing Folk	1962	10.00	20.00	40.00
❏ LSP-2631 [S]	We, The Tokens, Sing Folk	1962	12.50	25.00	50.00
❏ LPM-2886 [M]	Wheels	1964	20.00	40.00	80.00
❏ LSP-2886 [S]	Wheels	1964	25.00	50.00	100.00
❏ LPM-3685 [M]	The Tokens Again	1966	10.00	20.00	40.00
❏ LSP-3685 [S]	The Tokens Again	1966	12.50	25.00	50.00
WARNER BROS.					
❏ W 1685 [M]	It's a Happening World	1967	6.25	12.50	25.00
❏ WS 1685 [S]	It's a Happening World	1967	5.00	10.00	20.00

TOKENS, THE AND THE HAPPENINGS Also see each artist's individual listings.

Albums

Number	Title (A Side/B Side)	Yr	VG	VG+	NM
B.T. PUPPY					
❏ BTP-1002 [M]	Back to Back	1967	6.00	10.00	20.00
—Half this LP is by the Tokens, the other half by the Happenings					
❏ BTPS-1002 [S]	Back to Back	1967	6.25	12.50	25.00

Number	Title (A Side/B Side)	Yr	VG	VG+	NM
TOLBERT, ISRAEL					
45s					
WARREN/STAX					
❏ 106	Big Leg Woman (With a Short Short Mini Skirt)/I Got Love	1970	2.00	4.00	8.00
❏ 107	Shake Your Big Hips/Lost Love	1971	2.50	5.00	10.00
TOLLIVER, MICKEY, AND THE CAPITOLS					
45s					
CINDY					
❏ 3002	Rose Marie/Millie	1957	50.00	100.00	200.00
TOM AND JERRIO					
45s					
ABC-PARAMOUNT					
❏ 10638	Boo-Ga-Loo/Boomerang	1965	3.00	6.00	12.00
❏ 10704	Great Goo-Ga Moo-Ga/Come On and Love Me	1965	3.00	6.00	12.00
❏ 10787	Oolya-Coo/Bacardi	1966	3.00	6.00	12.00
LOST-NITE					
❏ 248	Boo-Ga-Loo/Boomerang	196?	—	2.50	5.00
—Reissue					

TOM AND JERRY (1) "Tommy Graph" and "Jerry Landis," i.e., ART GARFUNKEL and PAUL SIMON. Also see SIMON AND GARFUNKEL.

45s

Number	Title (A Side/B Side)	Yr	VG	VG+	NM
ABC-PARAMOUNT					
❏ 10363	Surrender, Please Surrender/Fightin' Mad	1962	10.00	20.00	40.00
❏ 10788	That's My Story/Tia-Juana Blues	1966	5.00	10.00	20.00
—As "Simon and Garfunkel" (may have been reissued as "Tom and Jerry", but we don't know)					
BELL					
❏ 120	Baby Talk/I'm Gonna Get Married	1959	12.50	25.00	50.00
—B-side by Ronnie Lawrence					
❏ 120 [PS]	Baby Talk/I'm Gonna Get Married	1959	25.00	50.00	100.00
BIG					
❏ 613	Hey, Schoolgirl/Dancin' Wild	1957	12.50	25.00	50.00
—With songwriting credits as "Paul Simon-Art Garfunkel"					
❏ 613	Hey, Schoolgirl/Dancin' Wild	1957	12.50	25.00	50.00
—With songwriting credits as "Tommy Graph-Jerry Landis"					
❏ 616	Our Song/Two Teen Agers	1958	12.50	25.00	50.00
❏ 618	That's My Story/Don't Say Goodbye	1958	12.50	25.00	50.00
❏ 621	Baby Talk/Two Teen Agers	1959	—	—	—
—Unreleased?					
EMBER					
❏ 1094	I'm Lonesome/Looking at You	1959	12.50	25.00	50.00
HUNT					
❏ 319	That's My Story/Don't Say Goodbye	1959	12.50	25.00	50.00
KING					
❏ 5167	Hey, Schoolgirl/Dancin' Wild	1958	20.00	40.00	80.00

TOM AND JERRY (2) Tommy Tomlinson and Jerry Kennedy, a country instrumental duo.

45s

Number	Title (A Side/B Side)	Yr	VG	VG+	NM
MERCURY					
❏ 71753	Golden Wildwood Flower/South	1961	5.00	10.00	20.00
❏ 71827	Swing Low/Sugarfoot Rag	1961	5.00	10.00	20.00
❏ 71930	I'll Drown in My Tears/French Twist	1961	5.00	10.00	20.00
Albums					
MERCURY					
❏ MG-20626 [M]	Guitar's Greatest Hits	1961	7.50	15.00	30.00
❏ MG-20671 [M]	Guitars Play the Sound of Ray Charles	1962	7.50	15.00	30.00
❏ MG-20756 [M]	Guitar's Greatest Hits, Vol. 2	1962	7.50	15.00	30.00
❏ MG-20842 [M]	Surfin' Hootenanny	1963	10.00	20.00	40.00
❏ SR-60626 [S]	Guitar's Greatest Hits	1961	10.00	20.00	40.00
❏ SR-60671 [S]	Guitars Play the Sound of Ray Charles	1962	10.00	20.00	40.00
❏ SR-60756 [S]	Guitar's Greatest Hits, Vol. 2	1962	10.00	20.00	40.00
❏ SR-60842 [S]	Surfin' Hootenanny	1963	12.50	25.00	50.00
TOMBOYS, THE					
45s					
SWAN					
❏ 4181	I'd Rather Fight Than Switch/Mary Had a Little Kiss	1964	2.50	5.00	10.00
TOMBSTONES, THE					
45s					
CAPITOL					
❏ 5997	Times Will Be Hard/Mary Jane	1967	2.50	5.00	10.00
TOMITA					
45s					
RCA					
❏ PB-10819	Planet Mars/Planet Venus	1976	—	2.00	4.00
RCA VICTOR					
❏ APBO-0308	Golliwog's Cakewalk/Clair de Lune	1974	—	2.50	5.00
❏ APBO-0308 [PS]	Golliwog's Cakewalk/Clair de Lune	1974	2.00	4.00	8.00
❏ PB-10296	The Great Gate of Kiev/Baba Yaya	1975	—	2.50	5.00
❏ PB-10683	Firebird Suite: Infernal Dance/Firebird Suite: Finale	1976			5.00
Albums					
RCA RED SEAL					
❏ ARD1-0488 [Q]	Snowflakes Are Dancing	1974	3.75	7.50	15.00
❏ ARL1-0488	Snowflakes Are Dancing	1974	2.50	5.00	10.00
❏ ARD1-0838 [Q]	Moussorgsky: Pictures at an Exhibition	1975	3.75	7.50	15.00
❏ ARL1-0838	Moussorgsky: Pictures at an Exhibition	1975	2.50	5.00	10.00
❏ ARD1-1312 [Q]	Firebird	1976	3.75	7.50	15.00
❏ ARL1-1312	Firebird	1976	2.50	5.00	10.00
❏ ARL1-1919	Holst: The Planets	1976	2.50	5.00	10.00
❏ ARL1-2616	Kosmos	1978	2.50	5.00	10.00
❏ ARL1-2885	The Bermuda Triangle	1979	2.50	5.00	10.00
❏ ARL1-3412	Ravel: Bolero	1980	2.50	5.00	10.00
❏ ARL1-3439	Greatest Hits	1980	2.50	5.00	10.00
❏ ARL1-4019	A Voyage Through His Greatest Hits, Vol. 2	1981	2.50	5.00	10.00
❏ ARL1-4317	Grand Canyon Suite	1982	2.50	5.00	10.00
❏ ATL1-4332	Snowflakes Are Dancing	1982	3.00	6.00	12.00
—Reissue with die-cut cover and custom innersleeve					
❏ ARL1-5037	Spacewalk — Impressions of an Astronaut	1984	2.50	5.00	10.00
❏ ARL1-5184	Canon of the 3 Stars	1984	2.50	5.00	10.00
❏ ARL1-5461	Live at Linz, 1984 — The Mind of the Universe	1985	2.50	5.00	10.00

Number	Title (A Side/B Side)	Yr	VG	VG+	NM
TOMLIN, LILY					
45s					
POLYDOR					
❑ 14180	20th Century Blues/Blues	1973	—	2.50	5.00
❑ 14283	Edith Ann/Detroit City	1975	—	2.50	5.00
Albums					
ARISTA					
❑ AB 4142	Lily Tomlin On Stage	1977	3.00	6.00	12.00
POLYDOR					
❑ 24-4055	This Is a Recording	1971	2.50	5.00	10.00
❑ PD 5023	And That's the Truth	1972	2.50	5.00	10.00
❑ PD 6051	Modern Scream	1976	3.00	6.00	12.00
TOMMY AND THE HUSTLERS					
45s					
FANTASY					
❑ 573	Diggin' Out/The Right Size	1963	6.25	12.50	25.00
❑ 573	Diggin' Out/The Right Size	1963	10.00	20.00	40.00
—Green vinyl					
TOMMY AND THE TWISTERS					
45s					
REGENT					
❑ 205	Mr. Twist/Hucklebuck Twist	1962	3.00	6.00	12.00
Albums					
REGENT					
❑ MG-6104 [M]	Let's All Do the Twist	1961	10.00	20.00	40.00
TOMPALL AND THE GLASER BROTHERS					
45s					
DECCA					
❑ 9-30805	Oh Little Mary/Lay Down the Gun	1959	3.75	7.50	15.00
❑ 9-30900	Ooie-Gooie/She Loves the Love I Give Her	1959	3.00	6.00	12.00
❑ 31011	I'll Never Tell/21 Miles from Home	1959	3.00	6.00	12.00
❑ 31051	Careless Love, Goodbye/Alibi	1960	3.00	6.00	12.00
❑ 31180	Same Old Memories/Sweet Love, Goodbye	1960	3.00	6.00	12.00
❑ 31258	Judy's Growin' Up/Words Come Easy	1961	3.00	6.00	12.00
❑ 31322	Tired of Crying Over You/Let Me Down Easy	1961	3.00	6.00	12.00
❑ 31398	I Can't Remember/I'm Losing Again	1962	3.00	6.00	12.00
❑ 31447	False Hearted Lover/Odds and Ends (Bits and Pieces)	1962	3.00	6.00	12.00
❑ 31494	Stand Beside Me/Trackin' Me Down	1963	2.50	5.00	10.00
❑ 31551	Blow Out the Candles/Mr. Lonesome	1963	2.50	5.00	10.00
❑ 31632	A Girl Like You/I've Got Troubles	1964	2.50	5.00	10.00
❑ 31736	Baby, They're Playing Our Song/Winner Take All	1965	2.50	5.00	10.00
❑ 31809	Back in Each Other's Arms Again/ Teardrops 'Til Dawn	1965	2.50	5.00	10.00
ELEKTRA					
❑ 46595	Weight of My Chains/The Ballad of Lucy Jordan	1980	—	2.00	4.00
❑ 47056	Sweet City Woman/Tryin' to Outrun the Wind	1980	—	2.00	4.00
❑ 47134	Lovin' Her Was Easier (Than Anything I'll Ever Do Again)/United We Fall	1981	—	2.00	4.00
❑ 47193	Just One Time/Feelin' the Weight of My Chains	1981	—	2.00	4.00
❑ 47230 [DJ]	Silver Bells/Please Come Home for Christmas	1981	—	3.00	6.00
—B-side by Johnny Lee					
❑ 47405	It'll Be Her/A Mansion on the Hill	1982	—	2.00	4.00
❑ 47461	I Still Love You (After All These Years)/Feelin' the Weight of My Chains	1982	—	2.00	4.00
❑ 69947	Maria Consuela/I Can Never Live Alone Again	1982	—	2.00	4.00
MGM					
❑ 13531	The Last Thing on My Mind/More or Less	1966	2.50	5.00	10.00
❑ 13611	Gone, On the Other Hand/Streets of Baltimore	1966	2.00	4.00	8.00
❑ 13754	Through the Eyes of Love/ She Loved the Wrong Man	1967	2.00	4.00	8.00
❑ 13880	The Moods of Mary/No End of Love	1967	2.00	4.00	8.00
❑ 13954	One of These Days/ Where Has All the Love Gone	1968	2.00	4.00	8.00
❑ 14036	California Girl (And the Tennessee Square)/ All That Keeps Ya Goin'	1969	—	3.50	7.00
❑ 14064	Wicked California/This Eve of Parting	1969	—	3.50	7.00
❑ 14113	All That Keeps Ya Goin'/Theme from "...tick ...tick ...tick"	1970	—	3.50	7.00
❑ 14169	Gone Girl/I'll Say My Words	1970	—	3.50	7.00
❑ 14249	Faded Love/Pretty Eyes	1971	—	3.00	6.00
—With Leon McAuliffe and the Cimarron Boys					
❑ 14291	Rings/That's When I Love You the Most	1971	—	3.00	6.00
❑ 14349	Sweet, Love Me Good Woman/Stand Beside Me	1971	—	3.00	6.00
❑ 14390	Ain't It All Worth Living For/Blue Ridge Mountain	1972	—	3.00	6.00
❑ 14462	A Girl Like You/Delta Lost	1972	—	3.00	6.00
❑ 14516	Charlie/Lovin' You Again	1973	—	3.00	6.00
RICH					
❑ 1004	The Cry of the Wild Goose/Yakety Yak	196?	3.75	7.50	15.00
ROBBINS					
❑ 1006	Sweet Lies/Yakety Yak	1958	7.50	15.00	30.00
Albums					
DECCA					
❑ DL 4041 [M]	This Land Folk Songs	1960	7.50	15.00	30.00
❑ DL 74041 [S]	This Land Folk Songs	1960	10.00	20.00	40.00
ELEKTRA					
❑ 5E-542	Lovin' Her Was Easier	1981	2.50	5.00	10.00
❑ 60148	After All These Years	1982	2.50	5.00	10.00
MGM					
❑ E-4465 [M]	Tompall & the Glaser Brothers	1967	6.25	12.50	25.00
❑ SE-4465 [S]	Tompall & the Glaser Brothers	1967	5.00	10.00	20.00
❑ SE-4510	Through the Eyes of Love	1968	3.75	7.50	15.00
❑ SE-4620	Now Country	1969	3.75	7.50	15.00
❑ SE-4775	Award Winners	1971	3.75	7.50	15.00
❑ SE-4812	Rings and Things	1972	3.75	7.50	15.00
❑ SE-4888	Great Hits from Two Decades	1973	3.75	7.50	15.00
❑ SE-4976	Vocal Group of the Decade	1974	3.75	7.50	15.00
TOMS, GARY, EMPIRE					
45s					
MCA					
❑ 40770	Turn It Out (Tear This Building Down)/Hurricane	1977	—	2.00	4.00
MERCURY					
❑ 74012	1-2-3-4/Feelin' Good Again	1978	—	2.00	4.00
❑ 74023	Welcome to Harlem/(B-side unknown)	1978	—	2.00	4.00
P.I.P.					
❑ 6504	7-6-5-4-3-2-1 (Blow Your Whistle)/7-6-5-4-3-2-1 (Blow Your Whistle) (Long Version)	1975	—	2.50	5.00
❑ 6509	Drive My Car/The New Empire	1975	—	2.50	5.00
❑ 6517	Love Me Right (Short Version)/Love Me Right (Long Version)	1976	—	2.50	5.00
❑ 6524	Stand Up and Shout/Party Hardy	1976	—	2.50	5.00
Albums					
MCA					
❑ 2289	Turn It Out	1977	2.50	5.00	10.00
MERCURY					
❑ SRM-1-3731	Do It Again	1978	2.50	5.00	10.00
P.I.P.					
❑ 6814	7-6-5-4-3-2-1 Blow Your Whistle	1975	2.50	5.00	10.00
TONETTES, THE Two different groups?					
45s					
ABC-PARAMOUNT					
❑ 9905	Oh What a Baby/Howie	1958	5.00	10.00	20.00
DOE					
❑ 101	Oh What a Baby/Howie	1958	20.00	40.00	80.00
❑ 103	Uh Oh/He Loves Me, He Loves Me Not	1958	15.00	30.00	60.00
MODERN					
❑ 997	Tonight You Belong to Me/ Don't Fall in Love Too Soon	1956	6.25	12.50	25.00
VOLT					
❑ 101	Please Don't Go/No Tears	1962	5.00	10.00	20.00
❑ 104	Stolen Angel/Teardrop Sea	1963	5.00	10.00	20.00
TONEY, OSCAR, JR.					
45s					
BELL					
❑ 672	For Your Precious Love/Ain't That True Love	1967	2.50	5.00	10.00
❑ 681	Turn On Your Love Light/Any Day Now	1967	2.50	5.00	10.00
❑ 688	Unlucky Guy/ You Can Lead Your Woman to the Altar	1967	2.50	5.00	10.00
❑ 699	Without Love (There Is Nothing)/Love That Never Grows Old	1968	2.50	5.00	10.00
❑ 714	Never Get Enough of Your Love/ Love That Never Grows Old	1968	2.50	5.00	10.00
CAPRICORN					
❑ 0005	I Do What You Wish/Thank You, Honey Chile	1972	—	3.00	6.00
❑ 8005	Down on My Knees/Seven Days Tomorrow	1970	2.00	4.00	8.00
❑ 8010	I Wouldn't Be a Poor Boy/Person to Person	1970	2.00	4.00	8.00
❑ 8018	Workin' Together/Baby Is Mine	1971	2.00	4.00	8.00
KING					
❑ 5906	Can It All Be Love/You Are Going to Need Me	1964	5.00	10.00	20.00
❑ 6108	Keep On Loving Me/I've Found a True Love	1967	3.00	6.00	12.00
Albums					
BELL					
❑ 6006 [M]	For Your Precious Love	1967	6.25	12.50	25.00
❑ S-6006 [S]	For Your Precious Love	1967	7.50	15.00	30.00
TONGUE AND GROOVE					
45s					
FONTANA					
❑ 1640	Cherry Ball/Devil	1969	2.00	4.00	8.00
❑ 1653	Come On in My Kitchen/Mailman's Sack	1969	2.00	4.00	8.00
Albums					
FONTANA					
❑ SRF-67593	Tongue and Groove	1968	5.00	10.00	20.00
TONTO'S EXPANDING HEAD BAND					
Albums					
EMBRYO					
❑ SD 732	Zero Time	1971	5.00	10.00	20.00
TONY AND JOE					
45s					
DORE					
❑ 619	Twist and Freeze/Long Black Stockings	1961	3.75	7.50	15.00
❑ 688	The Freeze/Gonna Get a Little Kissin' Tonight	1963	3.75	7.50	15.00
ERA					
❑ 1075	The Freeze/Gonna Get a Little Kissin' Tonight	1958	5.00	10.00	20.00
❑ 1083	Play Something Sentimental Mr. D.J./Where Can You Be?	1958	6.25	12.50	25.00
FLYTE					
❑ 106	Fairytale Love/(B-side unknown)	1959	3.75	7.50	15.00
GARDENA					
❑ 103	Instant Love/The Duck Walk	1960	3.75	7.50	15.00
TONY AND THE DAYDREAMS					
45s					
PLANET					
❑ 1008	Why Don't You Be Nice/I'll Never Tell	1958	25.00	50.00	100.00
❑ 1054	Christmas Lullaby/Handin' Hand	1961	50.00	100.00	200.00
TONY AND THE HOLIDAYS					
45s					
ABC-PARAMOUNT					
❑ 10295	There Goes My Heart Again/My Love Is Real	1962	50.00	100.00	200.00
TONY AND THE MASQUINS					
45s					
RUTHIE					
❑ 1000	My Angel Eyes/Fugi Womma	1961	25.00	50.00	100.00
TONY AND THE RAINDROPS					
45s					
CHESAPEKE					
❑ 609	While Walking/Our Love Is Over	1961	15.00	30.00	60.00
CROSLEY					
❑ 340	Tina/My Heart Cried	1962	50.00	100.00	200.00

T

Number	Title (A Side/B Side)	Yr	VG	VG+	NM

TONY AND THE TECHNICS See THE TECHNICS.

TONY AND THE TWILIGHTERS Early version of ANTHONY AND THE SOPHOMORES.
45s
JALYNNE
| ❏ 106 | Be My Girl/Did You Make Up Your Mind | 1960 | 20.00 | 40.00 | 80.00 |

RED TOP
| ❏ 127 | Key to My Heart/Yes or No | 1960 | 50.00 | 100.00 | 200.00 |

TONY AND TYRONE
45s
ATLANTIC
| ❏ 2458 | Please Operator/Apple of My Eye | 1967 | 7.50 | 15.00 | 30.00 |

COLUMBIA
| ❏ 43432 | Turn It On/Talkin' About the People | 1965 | 3.75 | 7.50 | 15.00 |

TOOMORROW OLIVIA NEWTON-JOHN was in this group.
45s
KIRSHNER
| ❏ 63-5005 | Goin' Back/You're My Baby Now | 1970 | 15.00 | 30.00 | 60.00 |

TOONE, GENE
45s
ANNETTE
| ❏ 1001 | You're My Baby/Jose | 1964 | 50.00 | 100.00 | 200.00 |
| —Produced by Phil Spector | | | | | |

SIMCO
❏ 30000	What More Do You Want/(B-side unknown)	196?	300.00	600.00	1200.
❏ 30002	A Love Triangle/Turn to Be	196?	25.00	50.00	100.00
❏ 30003	So Glad Trouble Don't Last/Every Now and Then	196?	25.00	50.00	100.00

WAND
| ❏ 11293 | Baby Boy (Part 1)/Baby Boy (Part 2) | 1975 | — | 3.00 | 6.00 |

TOOTIE AND THE BOUQUETS
45s
PARKWAY
| ❏ 887 | The Conqueror/You Done Me Wrong | 1963 | 6.25 | 12.50 | 25.00 |

TOOTS AND THE MAYTALS
Albums
ISLAND
| ❏ ILPS 9330 | Funky Kingston | 1975 | 3.00 | 6.00 | 12.00 |

MANGO
❏ MLPS 9330	Funky Kingston	197?	2.50	5.00	10.00
—Reissue of Island 9330					
❏ MLPS 9374	Reggae Got Soul	1976	3.00	6.00	12.00
❏ MLPS 9534	Pass the Pipe	198?	2.50	5.00	10.00
❏ MLPS 9590	Just Like That	1980	2.50	5.00	10.00
❏ MLPS 9647	Live	1980	3.00	6.00	12.00
❏ MLPS 9670	Knock Out	1982	2.50	5.00	10.00
❏ 9781	Reggae Greats	198?	2.50	5.00	10.00

TOP DRAWER
Albums
WISH BONE
| ❏ 721207 | Solid Oak | 1969 | 100.00 | 200.00 | 400.00 |

TOP HITS, THE
45s
NORMAN
| ❏ 504 | Love No One/Thum-A-Lum-A | 1961 | 50.00 | 100.00 | 200.00 |

TOP NOTES, THE
45s
ABC-PARAMOUNT
| ❏ 10399 | I Love You So Much/It's Alright | 1963 | 2.50 | 5.00 | 10.00 |

ATLANTIC
❏ 2066	A Wonderful Time/Walkin' with Love	1960	3.75	7.50	15.00
❏ 2080	Say Man/Warm Your Heart	1960	3.75	7.50	15.00
❏ 2097	Hearts of Stone/The Basic Things	1961	3.75	7.50	15.00
❏ 2115	Twist and Shout/Always Late (Why Lead Me On)	1961	6.25	12.50	25.00

TOPICS, THE Also see THE FOUR SEASONS.
45s
DREAM
| ❏ 1 | Have Your Fun/(B-side unknown) | 196? | 300.00 | 600.00 | 1200. |

PERRI
| ❏ 1007 | The Girl in My Dreams/(B-side blank) | 1961 | 37.50 | 75.00 | 150.00 |
| —One-sided record | | | | | |

TOPPERS, THE More than one group.
45s
ABC-PARAMOUNT
❏ 9667	George Washington/Honey, Honey	1956	5.00	10.00	20.00
❏ 9699	God Bless Kids and Little Animals/Tornado	1956	5.00	10.00	20.00
❏ 9759	Three Roads/Lonely	1956	5.00	10.00	20.00

AVALON
| ❏ 63707 | I Love You, I Love You/Bow-Legged Boy | 1954 | 10.00 | 20.00 | 40.00 |

DECCA
| ❏ 30209 | The Purple Hills/Stashu Pandowski | 1957 | 3.75 | 7.50 | 15.00 |
| ❏ 30297 | Pots and Pans/It Was Twice As Big As I Thought It Was | 1957 | 3.75 | 7.50 | 15.00 |

JUBILEE
| ❏ 5136 | Let Me Bang Your Box/You're Laughing 'Cause I'm Crying | 1954 | 37.50 | 75.00 | 150.00 |

STACY
| ❏ 927 | Tell Me Why/All Around | 1962 | 3.00 | 6.00 | 12.00 |

TOPPS, THE
45s
RED ROBIN
| ❏ 126 | What Do You Do (To Make You Love You So)/Tippin' | 1954 | 75.00 | 150.00 | 300.00 |
| ❏ 131 | I've Got a Feeling/Won't You Come Home Baby | 1954 | 75.00 | 150.00 | 300.00 |

TOPS, THE
45s
SINGULAR
| ❏ 712 | An Innocent Kiss/Walkin' with My Baby | 1957 | 30.00 | 60.00 | 120.00 |

TOPSIDERS, THE
45s
JOSIE
| ❏ 907 | Heartbreak Hotel/Let the Good Times Roll | 1963 | 3.00 | 6.00 | 12.00 |

Albums
JOSIE
| ❏ JOZ-4000 [M] | Rock Goes Folk | 1963 | 6.25 | 12.50 | 25.00 |

TORME, MEL
45s
ATLANTIC
❏ 2165	Comin' Home Baby/Right Now	1962	2.50	5.00	10.00
❏ 2183	Cast Your Fate to the Wind/The Gift	1963	2.50	5.00	10.00
❏ 2187	Gravy Waltz/My Gal's Back in Town	1963	2.50	5.00	10.00
❏ 2202	You Belong to Me/You Can't Love 'Em All	1963	2.50	5.00	10.00
❏ 2219	42nd Street/Sunday in New York	1964	2.50	5.00	10.00

BETHLEHEM
| ❏ 11008 | Lulu's Back in Town/Keeping Myself for You | 1958 | 3.00 | 6.00 | 12.00 |

CAPITOL
❏ F1000	Bewitched/Piccolino	1950	5.00	10.00	20.00
❏ F1177	Recipe for Romance/Do Do Do	1950	5.00	10.00	20.00
❏ F1237	I Owe a Kiss/Say No More	1950	5.00	10.00	20.00
❏ F1291	Skylark/Lullaby of the Leaves	1950	5.00	10.00	20.00
❏ F1383	Around the World/Sidewalk Shufflers	1951	5.00	10.00	20.00
❏ F1402	You're Getting to Be a Habit with Me/Sailin' Away on Henry Clay	1951	5.00	10.00	20.00
❏ F1524	The World Is Yours/Bundle of Love	1951	5.00	10.00	20.00
❏ F1598	You Locked My Heart/Qho Sends You Orchids	1951	5.00	10.00	20.00
❏ F1662	Bewitched/Blue Moon	1951	3.75	7.50	15.00
—Reissue					
❏ F1712	One for Me/Love Is Such a Cheat	1951	5.00	10.00	20.00
❏ F1761	My Buddy/Take My Heart	1951	5.00	10.00	20.00
❏ F1864	Foolish Rumors/You're a Heavenly Thing	1951	5.00	10.00	20.00
❏ F2131	Don't Leave Me/Black Moonlight	1952	5.00	10.00	20.00
❏ F2263	Casually/Anywhere I Wander	1952	5.00	10.00	20.00
❏ 2613	Games People Play/Willie and Laura Mae Jones	1969	—	3.00	6.00
❏ 2743	Requiem: 820 Latham/Spinning Wheel	1970	—	3.00	6.00

COLUMBIA
❏ 43022	I Know Your Heart/You Better Love Me	1964	2.00	4.00	8.00
❏ 43087	Once in a Lifetime/I See It Now	1964	2.00	4.00	8.00
❏ 43167	Every Day's a Holiday/One Little Snowflake	1964	3.00	6.00	12.00
❏ 43167 [DJ]	Every Day's a Holiday/One Little Snowflake	1964	3.75	7.50	15.00
—Promo only on green vinyl					
❏ 43230	Do I Love You Because You're Beautiful/That's All	1965	2.00	4.00	8.00
❏ 43383	Ho-Ba-La-Ba/My Romance	1965	2.00	4.00	8.00
❏ 43550	The Power of Love/Dominique's Discotheque	1966	2.00	4.00	8.00
❏ 43677	All That Jazz/Hang On to Me	1966	2.00	4.00	8.00
❏ 44180	Lover's Roulette/I Remember Suzanne	1967	2.00	4.00	8.00
❏ 44399	Wait Until Dark/Lima Lady	1967	2.00	4.00	8.00
❏ 45283	The Christmas Song/(B-side unknown)	1970	—	3.00	6.00

CORAL
❏ 61136	Anything Can Happen Mambo/Just One More Chance	1954	3.75	7.50	15.00
❏ 61295	All of You/Spellbound	1954	3.75	7.50	15.00
❏ 61452	It Don't Mean a Thing/Rose O'Day	1955	3.75	7.50	15.00
❏ 61507	Goody Goody/Jeepers Creepers	1955	3.75	7.50	15.00

LIBERTY
| ❏ 56022 | A Day in the Life of Bonnie and Clyde/Brother Can You Spare a Dime | 1968 | 2.50 | 5.00 | 10.00 |
| ❏ 56066 | Didn't We/Five-Four | 1968 | 2.00 | 4.00 | 8.00 |

LONDON
| ❏ 171 | Whose Garden Was This?/Morning Star | 1971 | — | 3.00 | 6.00 |
| ❏ 180 | A Phone Call to the Past/I Cried for You | 1972 | — | 3.00 | 6.00 |

VERVE
❏ 10174	The Crossroads/Frenesi	1959	3.00	6.00	12.00
❏ 10211	Wayfaring Stranger/Walk Like a Dragon	1960	3.00	6.00	12.00
❏ 10232	Her Face/Yes Indeed	1961	3.00	6.00	12.00

Albums
ALLEGRO ELITE
| ❏ 4117 [10] | Mel Torme Sings | 195? | 7.50 | 15.00 | 30.00 |

ATLANTIC
❏ 8066 [M]	Mel Torme at the Red Hill Inn	1962	7.50	15.00	30.00
❏ SD 8066 [S]	Mel Torme at the Red Hill Inn	1962	10.00	20.00	40.00
❏ 8069 [M]	Comin' Home Baby	1962	7.50	15.00	30.00
❏ SD 8069 [S]	Comin' Home Baby	1962	10.00	20.00	40.00
❏ 8091 [M]	Sunday in New York	1963	7.50	15.00	30.00
❏ SD 8091 [S]	Sunday in New York	1963	10.00	20.00	40.00
❏ SD 18129	Live at the Maisonette	1975	3.00	6.00	12.00
❏ 80078	Songs of New York	1982	2.50	5.00	10.00

AUDIOPHILE
| ❏ 67 | Mel Torme Sings About Love | 198? | 5.00 | 10.00 | 20.00 |

BETHLEHEM
❏ BCP-34 [M]	It's a Blue World	1956	12.50	25.00	50.00
❏ BCP-52 [M]	Mel Torme and the Marty Paich Dektette	1956	12.50	25.00	50.00
❏ BCP 6013 [M]	Mel Torme Sings Fred Astaire	1957	12.50	25.00	50.00
❏ BCP 6016 [M]	California Suite	1957	12.50	25.00	50.00
❏ BCP 6020 [M]	Mel Torme Live at the Crescendo	1958	12.50	25.00	50.00
❏ BCP 6031 [M]	Songs for Any Taste	1959	12.50	25.00	50.00
❏ BCP 6042	The Torme Touch	1978	3.00	6.00	12.00
—Reissue of BCP 52					

CAPITOL
❏ P 200 [M]	California Suite	1950	25.00	50.00	100.00
❏ ST-313	A Time for Us	1969	3.00	6.00	12.00
❏ ST-430	Raindrops Keep Falling on My Head	1970	3.00	6.00	12.00

COLUMBIA
❏ CL 2318 [M]	That's All — A Lush Romantic Album	1965	3.75	7.50	15.00
❏ CL 2535 [M]	Mel Torme Right Now	1966	3.00	6.00	12.00
❏ CS 9118 [S]	That's All — A Lush Romantic Album	1965	5.00	10.00	20.00
❏ CS 9335 [S]	Mel Torme Right Now	1966	3.75	7.50	15.00

Number	Title (A Side/B Side)	Yr	VG	VG+	NM
COLUMBIA SPECIAL PRODUCTS					
❑ P 13090	That's All	1976	3.00	6.00	12.00
CONCORD JAZZ					
❑ CJ-306	Mel Torme with Rob McConnell and the Boss Brass	1986	2.50	5.00	10.00
❑ CJ-360	Reunion	1988	2.50	5.00	10.00
❑ CJ-382	In Concert Tokyo	1989	2.50	5.00	10.00
—Above two with the Marty Paich Dek-Tette					
CORAL					
❑ CRL 57012 [M]	Gene Norman Presents Mel Torme "Live" at the Crescendo	1955	12.50	25.00	50.00
❑ CRL 57044 [M]	Musical Sounds Are the Best Songs	1956	12.50	25.00	50.00
DISCOVERY					
❑ 910	Sings His California Suite	1986	2.50	5.00	10.00
—Reissue of Capitol 200					
EVEREST ARCHIVE OF FOLK & JAZZ					
❑ 324	The Velvet Fog	1976	2.50	5.00	10.00
FINESSE					
❑ W2X 37484 [(2)]	Mel Torme & Friends Recorded at Marty's, New York City	1981	3.00	6.00	12.00
GLENDALE					
❑ 6007	Mel Torme	1978	2.50	5.00	10.00
❑ 6018	Easy to Remember	1979	2.50	5.00	10.00
GRYPHON					
❑ G-916	A New Album	1980	2.50	5.00	10.00
LIBERTY					
❑ LRP-3560 [M]	A Day in the Life of Bonnie and Clyde	1968	10.00	20.00	40.00
—Stock copy mono inside stereo cover with "Audition Mono LP Not for Sale" sticker					
❑ LST-7560 [S]	A Day in the Life of Bonnie and Clyde	1968	5.00	10.00	20.00
METRO					
❑ M-532 [M]	I Wished on the Moon	1965	3.00	6.00	12.00
❑ MS-532 [S]	I Wished on the Moon	1965	3.75	7.50	15.00
MGM					
❑ E 552 [10]	Mel Torme Sings	1952	25.00	50.00	100.00
MUSICRAFT					
❑ 508	Mel Torme, Volume 1	1983	2.50	5.00	10.00
❑ 510	It Happened in Monterey	1983	2.50	5.00	10.00
❑ 2005	Gone with the Wind	1986	2.50	5.00	10.00
STASH					
❑ ST-252	'Round Midnight	1985	2.50	5.00	10.00
STRAND					
❑ SL-1076 [M]	Mel Torme Sings	1960	5.00	10.00	20.00
❑ SLS-1076 [S]	Mel Torme Sings	1960	6.25	12.50	25.00
TIME-LIFE					
❑ SLGD-13 [(2)]	Legendary Singers: Mel Torme	1986	3.75	7.50	15.00
TOPS					
❑ L-1615 [M]	Prelude to a Kiss	1958	6.25	12.50	25.00
VENISE					
❑ 10021 [M]	The Touch of Your Lips	196?	5.00	10.00	20.00
—Yellow vinyl; reissue of Tops L-1615 without patter in between songs					
VERVE					
❑ MGV 2105 [M]	Torme	1958	12.50	25.00	50.00
❑ V-2105 [M]	Torme	1961	5.00	10.00	20.00
—Reissue					
❑ V6-2105 [S]	Torme	1961	6.25	12.50	25.00
—Reissue					
❑ MGV 2117 [M]	Ole Torme! Mel Torme Goes South of the Border with Billy May	1959	12.50	25.00	50.00
❑ V-2117 [M]	Ole Torme! Mel Torme Goes South of the Border with Billy May	1961	5.00	10.00	20.00
—Reissue					
❑ V6-2117 [S]	Ole Torme! Mel Torme Goes South of the Border with Billy May	1961	6.25	12.50	25.00
—Reissue					
❑ MGV 2120 [M]	Back in Town	1959	12.50	25.00	50.00
❑ V-2120 [M]	Back in Town	1961	5.00	10.00	20.00
—Reissue					
❑ V6-2120 [S]	Back in Town	1961	6.25	12.50	25.00
—Reissue					
❑ MGV 2132 [M]	Mel Torme Swings Schubert Alley	1960	12.50	25.00	50.00
❑ V-2132 [M]	Mel Torme Swings Shubert Alley	1961	5.00	10.00	20.00
—Reissue					
❑ V6-2132 [S]	Mel Torme Swings Shubert Alley	196?	6.25	12.50	25.00
—Reissue of 62132					
❑ MGV 2144 [M]	Swingin' on the Moon	1960	12.50	25.00	50.00
❑ V-2144 [M]	Swingin' on the Moon	1961	5.00	10.00	20.00
—Reissue					
❑ V6-2144 [S]	Swingin' on the Moon	1961	6.25	12.50	25.00
—Reissue of 62144					
❑ MGV 2146 [M]	Broadway, Right Now	1961	12.50	25.00	50.00
❑ V-2146 [M]	Broadway, Right Now	1961	5.00	10.00	20.00
—Reissue					
❑ V6-2146 [S]	Broadway, Right Now	1961	6.25	12.50	25.00
❑ MGV 2153 [M]	I Dig the Duke! I Dig the Count!	1961	—	—	—
—Canceled; moved to 8491					
❑ UMV-2521	Mel Torme Swings Shubert Alley	1981	2.50	5.00	10.00
❑ UMV-2675	Back in Town	1982	2.50	5.00	10.00
❑ MGVS 6015 [S]	Torme	1960	12.50	25.00	50.00
❑ MGVS 6058 [S]	Ole Torme! Mel Torme Goes South of the Border with Billy May	1960	12.50	25.00	50.00
❑ MGVS 6063 [S]	Back in Town	1960	12.50	25.00	50.00
❑ MGVS 6146 [S]	Mel Torme Swings Shubert Alley	1960	12.50	25.00	50.00
❑ V-8440 [M]	My Kind of Music	1962	6.25	12.50	25.00
❑ V6-8440 [S]	My Kind of Music	1962	7.50	15.00	30.00
❑ V-8491 [M]	I Dig the Duke! I Dig the Count!	1962	6.25	12.50	25.00
❑ V6-8491 [S]	I Dig the Duke! I Dig the Count!	1962	7.50	15.00	30.00
❑ V-8593 [M]	Verve's Choice — The Best of Mel Torme	1964	3.00	6.00	12.00
❑ V6-8593 [S]	Verve's Choice — The Best of Mel Torme	1964	3.75	7.50	15.00
❑ MGVS 62132 [S]	Mel Torme Swings Shubert Alley	196?	10.00	20.00	40.00
—Early reissue of 6146					
❑ MGVS 62144 [S]	Swingin' on the Moon	1960	15.00	30.00	60.00
❑ 823248-1	The Duke Ellington and Count Basie Songbooks	1984	2.50	5.00	10.00
—Reissue of Verve 8491					
VOCALION					
❑ VL 73905	The Velvet Fog	197?	2.50	5.00	10.00

Number	Title (A Side/B Side)	Yr	VG	VG+	NM
TORME, MEL, AND BUDDY RICH					
Albums					
CENTURY					
❑ 1100	Together Again — For the First Time	1978	6.25	12.50	25.00
—Direct-to-disc recording					
GRYPHON					
❑ G-903	Together Again — For the First Time	1978	2.50	5.00	10.00
TORNADOES, THE (1) British band.					
45s					
DATE					
❑ 1519	Hey Baby!/Next Stop Kansas City	1966	3.00	6.00	12.00
LONDON					
❑ 9561	Telstar/Jungle Fever	1962	6.25	12.50	25.00
❑ 9579	Globetrottin'/Like Locomotion	1963	5.00	10.00	20.00
❑ 9581	Ridin' the Wind/The Breeze and I	1963	5.00	10.00	20.00
❑ 9599	Life on Venus (Telstar II)/Robot	1963	5.00	10.00	20.00
❑ 9614	Theme from "The Scales of Justice"/The Ice Cream Man	1963	5.00	10.00	20.00
❑ 11003	Telestar/Jungle Fever	1964	5.00	10.00	20.00
—Gold label "Demand Performance" with misspelled A-side					
TOWER					
❑ 152	Stompin' Through the Rye/Early Bird	1965	3.75	7.50	15.00
❑ 171	Stingray/Aqua Marina	1965	3.75	7.50	15.00
Albums					
LONDON					
❑ LL 3279 [M]	Telstar	1963	50.00	100.00	200.00
❑ LL 3293 [M]	The Sounds of the Tornadoes	1963	50.00	100.00	200.00
—Basically the same album as above, but with a new cover, one different track and the song order shuffled.					
TORNADOES, THE (2) California surf band, also called "Hollywood Tornadoes."					
45s					
AERTAUN					
❑ 100	Bustin' Surfboards/Beyond the Surf	*1962	10.00	20.00	40.00
❑ 101	The Gremmie (Part 1)/The Gremmie (Part 2)	1963	6.25	12.50	25.00
—As "The Hollywood Tornadoes"					
❑ 102	Inebriated Surfer/Moon Dawg	1963	7.50	15.00	30.00
—As "The Hollywood Tornadoes"					
❑ 103	Phantom Surfer/Shootin' Beavers	1963	7.50	15.00	30.00
❑ 103	Phantom Surfer/Lightnin'	1964	6.25	12.50	25.00
—B-side is same recording as "Shootin' Beavers" but retitled					
Albums					
JOSIE					
❑ J-4005 [M]	Bustin' Surfboards	1963	50.00	100.00	200.00
❑ JS-4005 [S]	Bustin' Surfboards	1963	75.00	150.00	300.00
SUNDAZED					
❑ LP-5024	Bustin' Surfboards	1996	2.50	5.00	10.00
TORNADOES, THE (3)					
45s					
ABC-PARAMOUNT					
❑ 10174	Cora/Like a Frog	1960	5.00	10.00	20.00
TORNADOES, THE (4)					
45s					
CUCA					
❑ 1092	Scalping Party/7-0-7	1962	10.00	20.00	40.00
❑ 1099	Loneliest Guy in the World /It Always Makes Me Cry	1962	7.50	15.00	30.00
❑ 1104	Hey There/Standing Watch	1963	7.50	15.00	30.00
TOROK, MITCHELL					
45s					
ABBOTT					
❑ 136	Little Hoo-Wee/Judalina	1953	6.25	12.50	25.00
❑ 140	Carribean/Weep Away	1953	7.50	15.00	30.00
—All copies we've seen misspell the A-side title as above					
❑ 150	Hootchy Kootchy Henry (From Hawaii)/Gigolo	1953	6.25	12.50	25.00
❑ 156	Edgar the Eager Easter Bunny/Living on Love	1954	6.25	12.50	25.00
❑ 162	Dancerette/Haunting Waterfall	1954	6.25	12.50	25.00
CAPITOL					
❑ 4846	Rio Grande/Fools Disguise	1962	2.00	4.00	8.00
❑ 4946	Mighty Mighty Man/For Someone Who's Supposed to Be Hurtin'	1963	2.00	4.00	8.00
DECCA					
❑ 29326	Roulette/Havana Huddle	1954	5.00	10.00	20.00
❑ 29408	Peasant's Guitar/The World Keeps Turning Around	1955	3.75	7.50	15.00
❑ 29576	Too Late Now/Smooth Talk	1955	3.75	7.50	15.00
❑ 29661	Marching My Blues Away/Country and Western	1955	3.75	7.50	15.00
❑ 29863	No Money Down/Red Light, Green Light	1956	3.75	7.50	15.00
❑ 9-29986	When Mexico Gave Up the Rhumba (To Do the Rock and Roll)/I Wish I Was a Little Bit Younger (And Knew What I Know Now)	1956	3.75	7.50	15.00
❑ 30134	Take This Heart/Drink Up and Go Home	1956	3.75	7.50	15.00
❑ 30230	Pledge of Love/ What's Behind That Strange Door	1957	3.75	7.50	15.00
❑ 30424	Two Words/You're Tempting Me	1957	3.75	7.50	15.00
❑ 30599	Be Kind to Me/How Much Do I Love You	1958	3.00	6.00	12.00
❑ 30661	Sweet Revenge/Love Me Like You Mean It	1958	3.00	6.00	12.00
❑ 30742	Date with a Teardrop/These Things I Hold Dear	1958	3.00	6.00	12.00
❑ 30859	Go Ahead and Be a Fool/Memories of You Haunting Me Night and Day	1959	3.00	6.00	12.00
❑ 30901	PTA Rock and Roll/Teenie Weenie Bikini	1959	5.00	10.00	20.00
GUYDEN					
❑ 2018	Caribbean/Hootchy Kootchy Henry (From Hawaii)	1959	3.00	6.00	12.00
❑ 2028	You Are the One/Mexican Joe	1959	2.50	5.00	10.00
❑ 2032	Guardian Angel/I Want to Know Everything	1960	2.50	5.00	10.00
❑ 2034	Pink Chiffon/What You Don't Know	1960	2.50	5.00	10.00
❑ 2034 [PS]	Pink Chiffon/What You Don't Know	1960	5.00	10.00	20.00
❑ 2040	Happy Street/Little Boy in Love	1960	2.50	5.00	10.00
INETTE					
❑ 105	Are You Trying to Tell Me Something/ Love Is Magic	1963	2.50	5.00	10.00

T

Number	Title (A Side/B Side)	Yr	VG	VG+	NM
MERCURY					
❏ 71816	El Tigre/Eating My Heart Out	1961	2.50	5.00	10.00
PARJO					
❏ 1003	Acupuncture/Pledge of Love	1972	2.00	4.00	8.00
—As "Mitch Torok"; B-side with Ramona Redd					
RCA VICTOR					
❏ 47-8646	I Needed All the Help I Can Get/				
	Man with a Golden Hand	1965	2.00	4.00	8.00
❏ 47-8703	Caribbean/Witch Woman	1965	2.00	4.00	8.00
REPRISE					
❏ 0541	Instant Love/Put Me in the Driver's Seat	1966	—	3.00	6.00
❏ 0568	Falling in Love Again/Baby, Baby, Baby	1967	—	3.00	6.00
Albums					
GUYDEN					
❏ GLP-502 [M]	Caribbean	1960	10.00	20.00	40.00
❏ ST-502 [S]	Caribbean	1960	12.50	25.00	50.00
REPRISE					
❏ R 6223 [M]	Guitar Course	1966	5.00	10.00	20.00
❏ RS 6223 [S]	Guitar Course	1966	6.25	12.50	25.00

TORQUAYS, THE
45s

Number	Title (A Side/B Side)	Yr	VG	VG+	NM
AERTAUN					
❏ 1020	Turmoil/Crying in the Chapel	1964	7.50	15.00	30.00
COLPIX					
❏ 782	Image of a Girl/Stolen Moments	1965	5.00	10.00	20.00
GEE CEE					
❏ 8163	Escondido/Surfer's City	1963	12.50	25.00	50.00
GYPSY					
❏ 265	Busting Point/The Other Side	1965	12.50	25.00	50.00
ORIGINAL SOUND					
❏ 66	Harmonica Man/Our Teenage Love	1967	5.00	10.00	20.00
PUNCH					
❏ 1007	Shake a Tail Feather/Temptation	196?	5.00	10.00	20.00
ROCK-IT					
❏ 1004	Image of a Girl/Stolen Moments	1965	7.50	15.00	30.00
❏ 1005	Hooked on Her/Harmonica Man	1965	7.50	15.00	30.00

TORQUES, THE
45s

Number	Title (A Side/B Side)	Yr	VG	VG+	NM
DIAL					
❏ 4060	Merry Maker/You Make Me Feel So Good	1967	5.00	10.00	20.00
LEMCO					
❏ 880	Tidal Wave/Harlem Nocturne	1965	7.50	15.00	30.00
❏ 890	Mercy Mercy/Bumpin'	1966	7.50	15.00	30.00
❏ 1001	Linden Walk/Deep Blue, At Dusk	196?	7.50	15.00	30.00
❏ 1007	I've Been Hurt/Bumpin'	1966	6.25	12.50	25.00
Albums					
LEMCO					
❏ 604	The Torques Live	1966	50.00	100.00	200.00
WIGGINS					
❏ 64010	Zoom!	1967	50.00	100.00	200.00

TORQUETTS, THE
45s

Number	Title (A Side/B Side)	Yr	VG	VG+	NM
SANTA CRUZ					
❏ 10002	Any More/(Who's Got The) Tortillas	196?	12.50	25.00	50.00
TORQUETT					
❏ 005/6	Feedback/Bacardi	196?	12.50	25.00	50.00
❏ 007/8	Side Swiped/Blue Corral	196?	6.25	12.50	25.00

TORRANCE, RICHARD
45s

Number	Title (A Side/B Side)	Yr	VG	VG+	NM
CAPITOL					
❏ 4417	Leave My Love Behind/Rio De Janeiro Blue	1977	—	2.00	4.00
❏ 4554	Long Lonely Nights/I Can't Ask for Anymore				
	Than You	1978	—	2.00	4.00
❏ 4644	Be Bop 'n Holla/Let's Call It a Night	1978	—	2.00	4.00
SHELTER					
❏ 40374	Don't Let Me Down Again/Hard Heavy Road	1975	—	2.00	4.00
❏ 40419	Lady/Southern Belles	1975	—	2.00	4.00
Albums					
CAPITOL					
❏ SW-11610	Bareback	1977	2.50	5.00	10.00
❏ SW-11660	Anything's Possible	1978	2.50	5.00	10.00
❏ SW-11699	Double Take	1978	2.50	5.00	10.00
SHELTER					
❏ 2112	Eureka	1974	3.00	6.00	12.00
❏ 2134	Belle of the Ball	1975	2.50	5.00	10.00

TORRENCE, GEORGE
45s

Number	Title (A Side/B Side)	Yr	VG	VG+	NM
DUO DISC					
❏ 117	Together at Last/Fine Foxy Frame	1965	5.00	10.00	20.00
EPIC					
❏ 5-9453	Such a Fool Was I/Way Over Yonder	1961	5.00	10.00	20.00
KING					
❏ 5376	Go Away/So Good to Me	1960	5.00	10.00	20.00
SHOUT					
❏ 224	(Mama Come Quick and Bring Your) Licking				
	Stick/So Long Goodbye	1968	3.00	6.00	12.00

TORRENCE, JOHNNY
45s

Number	Title (A Side/B Side)	Yr	VG	VG+	NM
IMPERIAL					
❏ 5230	Sad Day/Bad Habit	1953	30.00	60.00	120.00
❏ 5897	Rat Race/Your Lover Man	1962	3.75	7.50	15.00
R&B					
❏ 1306	Rosalie/Living from Day to Day	1954	50.00	100.00	200.00
—With the Jewels					

TOUCH
Albums

Number	Title (A Side/B Side)	Yr	VG	VG+	NM
GEAR FAB					
❏ GF 105 [(2)]	Street Suite	1999	6.25	12.50	25.00
—Reissue of rare album plus bonus tracks					

Number	Title (A Side/B Side)	Yr	VG	VG+	NM
MAINLINE					
❏ 2001	Street Suite	1969	1000.	1500.	2000.

TOUCHSTONE
Albums

Number	Title (A Side/B Side)	Yr	VG	VG+	NM
UNITED ARTISTS					
❏ UAS-5563	Tarot	1972	7.50	15.00	30.00

TOUSAN, AL   See ALLEN TOUSSAINT.

TOUSSAINT, ALLEN
45s

Number	Title (A Side/B Side)	Yr	VG	VG+	NM
ALON					
❏ 9021	Go Back Home/Poor Boy, Got to Move	1965	2.50	5.00	10.00
BELL					
❏ 732	Get Out of My Life, Woman/Gotta Travel On	1968	2.00	4.00	8.00
❏ 748	Hans Christian Anderson/				
	I've Got That Feeling Now	1968	2.00	4.00	8.00
❏ 782	Tequila/We the People	1969	2.00	4.00	8.00
RCA VICTOR					
❏ 47-7192	Whirlaway/Happy Times	1958	6.25	12.50	25.00
—As "Al Tousan"					
REPRISE					
❏ 1109	Soul Sister/She Once Belonged to Me	1972	—	2.50	5.00
❏ 1132	Am I Expecting Too Much/Out of the City	1972	—	2.50	5.00
❏ 1334	Country John/When the Party's Over	1975	—	2.00	4.00
SCEPTER					
❏ 12317	From a Whisper to a Scream/Secret Touch of				
	Love	1971	—	3.00	6.00
❏ 12334	Working in a Coal Mine/What Is Success	1971	—	3.00	6.00
SEVILLE					
❏ 103	Chico/Sweetie-Pie	1960	3.75	7.50	15.00
—All Seville releases as "Al Tousan"					
❏ 110	Back Home in Indiana/Naomi	1960	3.75	7.50	15.00
❏ 113	A Blue Mood/Moo Moo	1961	3.75	7.50	15.00
❏ 124	Twenty Years Later/Real Churchy	1962	3.75	7.50	15.00
WARNER BROS.					
❏ 8561	Night People/Optimism Blues	1978	—	2.00	4.00
❏ 8609	Happiness/Lover of Love	1978	—	2.00	4.00
Albums					
RCA VICTOR					
❏ LPM-1767 [M]	The Wild Sounds of New Orleans	1958	75.00	150.00	300.00
—As "Al Tousan"					
REPRISE					
❏ MS 2062	Life, Love and Faith	1972	6.25	12.50	25.00
SCEPTER					
❏ 24003	Toussaint	1971	6.25	12.50	25.00
WARNER BROS.					
❏ BSK 3142	Motion	1978	3.00	6.00	12.00

TOWER OF POWER
12-Inch Singles

Number	Title (A Side/B Side)	Yr	VG	VG+	NM
COLUMBIA					
❏ 10738	Lovin' You Is Gonna See Me Through/Yin-Yang				
	Thang	1978	2.50	5.00	10.00

45s

Number	Title (A Side/B Side)	Yr	VG	VG+	NM
COLUMBIA					
❏ 10409	You Ought to Be Havin' Fun/While We Went to				
	the Moon	1976	—	2.50	5.00
❏ 10461	Ain't Nothin' Stoppin' Us Now/Because I Think				
	the World of You	1976	—	2.50	5.00
❏ 10718	Lovin' You Is Gonna See Me Through/I Am a				
	Fool	1978	—	2.00	4.00
❏ 10780	Love Bug/We Came to Play	1978	—	2.00	4.00
❏ 11012	Rock Baby/Heaven Must Have Made You	1979	—	2.00	4.00
❏ 11157	In Due Time/And You Know It	1979	—	2.00	4.00
WARNER BROS.					
❏ 7612	You're Still a Young Man/Skating on Thin Ice	1972	—	3.00	6.00
❏ 7635	Down to the Nightclub/What Happened to the				
	World That Day	1972	—	3.00	6.00
❏ 7687	So Very Hard to Go/Clean Slate	1973	—	3.00	6.00
❏ 7733	This Time It's Real/Soul Vaccination	1973	—	3.00	6.00
❏ 7748	What is Hip?/Clever Girl	1973	—	3.00	6.00
❏ 7796	Time Will Tell/Oakland Stroke	1974	—	3.00	6.00
❏ 7828	Don't Change Horses (In the Middle of a				
	Stream)/I Got the Chop	1974	—	3.00	6.00
❏ 8055	Only So Much Oil in the Ground/Give Me the				
	Proof	1974	—	3.00	6.00
❏ 8083	Willing to Learn/Walkin' Up Hip Street	1975	—	2.50	5.00
❏ 8121	You're So Wonderful, So Marvelous/Stroke '75	1975	—	2.50	5.00
❏ 8151	Soul of a Child/Treat Me Like Your Man	1975	—	2.50	5.00
Albums					
COLUMBIA					
❏ PC 34302	Ain't Nothin' Stoppin' Us Now	1976	2.50	5.00	10.00
—No bar code on cover					
❏ PC 34302	Ain't Nothin' Stoppin' Us Now	198?	2.00	4.00	8.00
—Budget-line reissue with bar code					
❏ PCQ 34302 [Q]	Ain't Nothin' Stoppin' Us Now	1976	3.75	7.50	15.00
❏ JC 34906	We Came to Play!	1978	2.50	5.00	10.00
❏ JC 35784	Back on the Streets	1979	2.50	5.00	10.00
DIRECT DISC					
❏ SD 16601	Back to Oakland	1980	6.25	12.50	25.00
—Audiophile vinyl					
SAN FRANCISCO					
❏ SD 204	East Bay Grease	1971	12.50	25.00	50.00
SHEFFIELD LABS					
❏ 17	Direct	1982	6.25	12.50	25.00
—Direct-to-disc recording					
WARNER BROS.					
❏ BS 2616	Bump City	1972	3.75	7.50	15.00
—Green "WB" label					
❏ BS 2681	Tower of Power	1973	3.00	6.00	12.00
—"Burbank" palm trees label					
❏ BS 2681	Tower of Power	1973	3.75	7.50	15.00
—Green "WB" label					

Number	Title (A Side/B Side)	Yr	VG	VG+	NM
BS 2681	Tower of Power	1979	2.00	4.00	8.00

—White or tan label

| BS 2749 | Back to Oakland | 1974 | 3.75 | 7.50 | 15.00 |

—"Burbank" palm trees label

| BS 2749 | Back to Oakland | 1979 | 2.00 | 4.00 | 8.00 |

—White or tan label

| BS 2834 | Urban Renewal | 1975 | 3.75 | 7.50 | 15.00 |

—"Burbank" palm trees label

| BS 2880 | In the Slot | 1975 | 3.75 | 7.50 | 15.00 |

—"Burbank" palm trees label

| BS 2924 | Live and In Living Color | 1976 | 3.75 | 7.50 | 15.00 |

—"Burbank" palm trees label

| BS 2924 | Live and In Living Color | 1979 | 2.00 | 4.00 | 8.00 |

—White or tan label

TOWNSEND, BOB
45s
MINARET

| 106 | Christmas Message From Space/The Night Before New Year's | 1962 | 2.50 | 5.00 | 10.00 |

TOWNSEND, ED
45s
ALADDIN

| 3373 | Every Night/Love Never Dies | 1957 | 6.25 | 12.50 | 25.00 |

CAPITOL

F3926	For Your Love/Over and Over Again	1958	3.75	7.50	15.00
F3994	What Shall I Do/Please Never Change	1958	3.00	6.00	12.00
F4048	When I Grow Too Old to Dream/You Are My Everything	1958	3.00	6.00	12.00
F4104	Richer Than I/Getting By Without You	1958	3.00	6.00	12.00
F4171	Don't Ever Leave Me/Lover Come Back to Me	1959	3.00	6.00	12.00
F4240	This Little Love of Mine/Hold On	1959	3.00	6.00	12.00
4314	Be My Love/With No One to Love	1959	3.00	6.00	12.00

CHALLENGE

9118	Ed Townsend's Boogie Woogie (Part 1)/Ed Townsend's Boogie Woogie (Part 2)	1961	3.00	6.00	12.00
9129	And Then Came Love/Little Bitty Dave	1961	3.00	6.00	12.00
9144	You Walked In/I Love to Hear That Best	1962	3.00	6.00	12.00

DOT

| 15596 | Tall Grows the Sycamore/My Need for You | 1957 | 5.00 | 10.00 | 20.00 |

LIBERTY

55516	Tell Her/Down Home	1962	3.00	6.00	12.00
55516	Tell Her/Hard Way to Go	1962	3.00	6.00	12.00
55542	That's What I Get for Loving You/There's No End	1963	3.00	6.00	12.00

MAXX

| 325 | I Love You/I Might Like It | 1964 | 2.50 | 5.00 | 10.00 |

MGM

| 13784 | Mommy's Never Comin' Back Again/Who Would Deny Me | 1967 | 2.50 | 5.00 | 10.00 |

POLYDOR

| 14021 | No/Color Me Human | 1970 | — | 3.00 | 6.00 |

WARNER BROS.

| 5174 | Stay with Me/I Love Everything About You | 1960 | 3.00 | 6.00 | 12.00 |
| 5200 | Cherrigale/Dream World | 1961 | 3.00 | 6.00 | 12.00 |

Albums
CAPITOL

ST 1140 [S]	New in Town	1959	7.50	15.00	30.00
T 1140 [M]	New in Town	1959	6.25	12.50	25.00
ST 1214 [S]	Glad to Be Here	1959	7.50	15.00	30.00
T 1214 [M]	Glad to Be Here	1959	6.25	12.50	25.00

CURTOM

| 5006 | Ed Townsend Now | 1976 | 3.00 | 6.00 | 12.00 |

TOWNSEND, HENRY
Albums
BLUESVILLE

| BVLP-1041 [M] | Tired Bein' Mistreated | 1962 | 30.00 | 60.00 | 120.00 |

—Blue label, silver print

| BVLP-1041 [M] | Tired Bein' Mistreated | 1964 | 7.50 | 15.00 | 30.00 |

—Blue label, trident logo at side

TOWNSEND, SHERRELL
45s
GONE

| 5135 | He Thinks I Still Care/Glass of Tears | 1962 | 5.00 | 10.00 | 20.00 |

LITTLE STAR

| 115 | I Love You Alone/Summer Days Are Here | 1962 | 10.00 | 20.00 | 40.00 |

LUTE

| 6015 | I Love You Alone/Summer Days Are Here | 1961 | 7.50 | 15.00 | 30.00 |

TOWNSHEND, PETE Also see THE WHO.
12-Inch Singles
ATCO

PR 804 [DJ]	Face the Face (long and short)/Hiding Out	1985	3.75	7.50	15.00
PR 863 [DJ]	Secondhand Love (same on both sides)	1985	2.00	4.00	8.00
PR 1009 [DJ]	Ask Yourself/Brooklyn Kids	1987	2.00	4.00	8.00
96833	Face the Face (6:08)/Won't Get Fooled Again (Live)	1985	—	3.50	7.00

45s
ATCO

7217	Let My Love Open the Door/And I Moved	1980	—	2.00	4.00
7312	A Little Is Enough/Cat's in a Cupboard	1980	—	2.00	4.00
7318	Rough Boys/Jools and Jim	1980	—	2.00	4.00
99499	Barefootin'/Behind Blue Eyes	1986	—	—	3.00
99499 [PS]	Barefootin'/Behind Blue Eyes	1986	—	2.00	4.00
99553	Secondhand Love/White City Fighting	1986	—	—	3.00
99577	Give Blood/Magic Bus	1986	—	—	3.00
99577 [PS]	Give Blood/Magic Bus	1986	—	—	3.00
99590	Face the Face/Hiding Out	1985	—	—	3.00
99590 [PS]	Face the Face/Hiding Out	1985	—	—	3.00
99884	Bargain/Dirty Water	1983	—	2.00	4.00
99884 [PS]	Bargain/Dirty Water	1983	—	2.00	4.00
99973	Slit Skirts/Uniforms	1982	—	2.00	4.00
99989	Face Dances Part Two/Man Watching	1982	—	2.00	4.00
99989 [PS]	Face Dances Part Two/Man Watching	1982	—	2.00	4.00

ATLANTIC

| 88875 | A Friend Is a Friend/Man Machines | 1989 | — | — | 3.00 |
| 88875 [PS] | A Friend Is a Friend/Man Machines | 1989 | — | — | 3.00 |

Albums
ATCO

SD 32-100	Empty Glass	1980	2.50	5.00	10.00
SD 38-149	All the Best Cowboys Have Chinese Eyes	1982	2.50	5.00	10.00
PR 940 [EP]	Deep End Sampler	1986	5.00	10.00	20.00

—Promo-only sampler from Deep End Live

90063 [(2)]	Scoop	1983	3.00	6.00	12.00
90473	White City — A Novel	1985	2.50	5.00	10.00
90539 [(2)]	Another Scoop	1987	3.00	6.00	12.00
90553	Pete Townshend's Deep End Live!	1986	2.50	5.00	10.00

ATLANTIC

| 81996 | The Iron Man: The Musical by Pete Townshend | 1989 | 2.50 | 5.00 | 10.00 |

—Also includes tracks by John Lee Hooker, Simon Townshend, Nina Simone, The Who

DECCA

| 79189 | Who Came First | 1972 | 5.00 | 10.00 | 20.00 |

—With poster (deduct 50% if missing). Evidently a near-simultaneous release with Track 79189

EEL PIE

| EPR-0007 [(2)] | Another Scoop | 2002 | 10.00 | 20.00 | 40.00 |

—Classic Records edition on "Quiex SV" vinyl

| EPR-0013 [(3)] | Scoop 3 | 2001 | 12.50 | 25.00 | 50.00 |

—Classic Records edition on "Quiex SV" vinyl

MCA

| 2026 | Who Came First | 1973 | 3.00 | 6.00 | 12.00 |

—Reissue of 79189

TRACK

| PR-A-160 [DJ] | Pete Townshend Talks To and About Thunderclap Newman | 1970 | 25.00 | 50.00 | 100.00 |

—One-sided promo-only interview record

| 79189 | Who Came First | 1972 | 5.00 | 10.00 | 20.00 |

—With poster (deduct 50% if missing)

TOWNSHEND, PETE, AND RONNIE LANE Also see each artist's individual listings.
45s
MCA

| 40818 | My Baby Gives It Away/April Fool | 1977 | — | 2.00 | 4.00 |
| 40878 | Nowhere to Run/Keep Me Turning | 1978 | — | 2.00 | 4.00 |

Albums
ATCO

| 90097 | Rough Mix | 1983 | 2.00 | 4.00 | 8.00 |

—Reissue of MCA LP

MCA

| 2295 | Rough Mix | 1977 | 2.50 | 5.00 | 10.00 |

TOWNSMEN, THE
45s
CARDINAL

| 1022 | Pretty Patricia/My Memories | 195? | 3.75 | 7.50 | 15.00 |

COLUMBIA

| 43207 | Please Don't Say Goodbye/Gotta Get Moving | 1965 | 2.50 | 5.00 | 10.00 |

EVENT

| 503 | (Gloria's Theme) From "Burrerfield 8"/(B-side unknown) | 196? | 5.00 | 10.00 | 20.00 |

HERALD

| 585 | Is It All Over/Just a Little Bit | 1963 | 3.75 | 7.50 | 15.00 |

JOEY

| 6202 | Moonlight Was Made for Lovers/I'm in the Mood for Love | 1963 | 6.25 | 12.50 | 25.00 |

PJ

| 1341 | That's All I'll Ever Need/I Can't Let Go | 1963 | 50.00 | 100.00 | 200.00 |

VANITY

| 579/80 | It's Time/Little Jeanie | 1960 | 5.00 | 10.00 | 20.00 |

WARNER BROS.

| 5190 | You're Having the Last Dance with Me/Gloria's Theme from "Butterfield-8" | 1960 | 3.00 | 6.00 | 12.00 |

TOY DOLLS, THE
45s
ERA

| 3093 | Little Tin Soldier/Fly Away | 1962 | 3.75 | 7.50 | 15.00 |

TOYS, THE
45s
DYNO VOICE

209	A Lover's Concerto/This Night	1965	3.00	6.00	12.00
214	Attack/See How They Run	1965	2.50	5.00	10.00
218	My My Heart Be Cast Into Stone/On Backstreet	1966	2.50	5.00	10.00
219	Can't Get Enough of You Baby/Silver Spoon	1966	2.50	5.00	10.00
222	Baby Toys/Happy Birthday Broken Heart	1966	2.50	5.00	10.00

DYNO VOX

| 209 | A Lover's Concerto/This Night | 1965 | 6.25 | 12.50 | 25.00 |

MUSICOR

| 1300 | You Got It Baby/You've Got to Give Her Love | 1968 | 2.00 | 4.00 | 8.00 |
| 1319 | Sealed with a Kiss/I Got My Heart Set on You | 1968 | 2.00 | 4.00 | 8.00 |

PHILIPS

| 40432 | Ciao Baby/I Got Carried Away | 1967 | 2.50 | 5.00 | 10.00 |
| 40456 | My Love Sonata/I Close My Eyes | 1967 | 2.50 | 5.00 | 10.00 |

Albums
DYNOVOICE

| 9002 [M] | The Toys Sing "A Lover's Concerto" and "Attack!" | 1966 | 10.00 | 20.00 | 40.00 |
| S-9002 [P] | The Toys Sing "A Lover's Concerto" and "Attack!" | 1966 | 12.50 | 25.00 | 50.00 |

TRACERS, THE
45s
SULLY

| 928 | She Said Yeah/Watch Me | 1966 | 6.25 | 12.50 | 25.00 |

—Originally released under the name "The Stones"

TRACEY, WREG
45s
ANNA

| 1105 | All I Want Is You/Take Me Back | 1959 | 10.00 | 20.00 | 40.00 |
| 1126 | All I Want for Christmas (Is Your Love)/Take Me Back | 1960 | 10.00 | 20.00 | 40.00 |

Number	Title (A Side/B Side)	Yr	VG	VG+	NM
TRACEY TWINS, THE					
45s					
EASTWEST					
❏ 108	Heartbreak Hill/Don't Mean Maybe Baby	1958	5.00	10.00	20.00
EPIC					
❏ 9230	Kissin' Diploma/Because We Are Young	1957	5.00	10.00	20.00
RESERVE					
❏ 110	Tonight You Belong to Me/(B-side unknown)	1956	6.25	12.50	25.00
❏ 114	Do You Ever Think of Me/(B-side unknown)	195?	6.25	12.50	25.00
TRACY, BILL					
45s					
DEL-FI					
❏ 4124	You're My Girl/Tops to Summer	1959	5.00	10.00	20.00
❏ 4132	I'm So Happy/January Love	1959	5.00	10.00	20.00
DOT					
❏ 15797	One Chance/Hold Me, Thrill Me, Kiss Me	1958	15.00	30.00	60.00
❏ 15868	Flame Out/Disappointed	1958	10.00	20.00	40.00
RADIANT					
❏ 1504	High School Hero/Lost Love	1961	3.75	7.50	15.00
RPM					
❏ 489	Kiss at Daybreak/No One But You	1957	10.00	20.00	40.00
TRADE WINDS, THE					
45s					
KAMA SUTRA					
❏ 212	Mind Excursion/Little Susan's Dreamin'	1966	3.00	6.00	12.00
❏ 218	I Believe in Her/Catch Me in the Meadow	1966	3.00	6.00	12.00
❏ 234	Mind Excursion/Only When I'm Dreamin'	1967	3.00	6.00	12.00
RED BIRD					
❏ 10-020	New York's a Lonely Town/Club Seventeen	1965	5.00	10.00	20.00
❏ 10-028	Girl from Greenwich Village/				
	There's a Rock and Roll Show in Town	1965	5.00	10.00	20.00
❏ 10-033	Summertime Girl/The Party Starts at Nine	1965	10.00	20.00	40.00
Albums					
KAMA SUTRA					
❏ KLP-8057 [M]	Excursions	1967	6.25	12.50	25.00
❏ KSLP-8057 [S]	Excursions	1967	7.50	15.00	30.00
TRADER HORNE					
Albums					
JANUS					
❏ JLS-3012	Morning Way	1970	7.50	15.00	30.00
TRADEWINDS, THE					
45s					
DAWN CORY					
❏ 1005	Surfin' Thunder/Gotcha	196?	20.00	40.00	80.00
RCA VICTOR					
❏ 47-7511	Toni/Twins	1959	5.00	10.00	20.00
❏ 47-7553	Furry Murray/Crossroads	1959	5.00	10.00	20.00
TRADITIONS, THE					
45s					
A-BET					
❏ 9435	Ruby Tuesday/Twinkle Little Star	1969	50.00	100.00	200.00
ARTCO					
❏ 45-102	On Fire/My Heart	1966	500.00	1000.	2000.
BAR CLAY					
❏ 19671	Oh My Love/Girls	1967	15.00	30.00	60.00
❏ 19678	My Life with You/Something Gone Wrong	1967	17.50	35.00	70.00
TRAFFIC Also see JIM CAPALDI; DAVE MASON; STEVE WINWOOD.					
45s					
ASYLUM					
❏ 45207	Walking in the Wind/(Instrumental)	1974	—	2.50	5.00
ISLAND					
❏ 1201	Rock and Roll Stew (Part 1)/Rock and Roll Stew (Part 2)	1972	—	2.50	5.00
UNITED ARTISTS					
❏ 0129	Paper Sun/Empty Pages	1973	—	2.00	4.00
—"Silver Spotlight Series" reissue					
❏ 1694	Feelin' Alright?/You Can All Join In	197?	—	2.50	5.00
—"Silver Spotlight Series" reissue					
❏ 50195	Paper Sun/Giving to You	1967	2.50	5.00	10.00
❏ 50218	Hole in My Shoe/Smiling Phases	1967	2.50	5.00	10.00
❏ 50232	Here We Go 'Round the Mulberry Bush/Coloured Rain	1967	2.50	5.00	10.00
❏ 50261	Heaven Is In Your Mind/No Face, No Name and No Number	1968	2.00	4.00	8.00
❏ 50460	Feelin' Alright?/Withering Tree	1968	2.00	4.00	8.00
❏ 50500	Medicated Goo/Pearly Queen	1969	—	3.00	6.00
❏ 50692	Empty Pages/Stranger to Himself	1970	—	3.00	6.00
❏ 50841	Gimme Some Lovin' (Part 1)/Gimme Some Lovin' (Part 2)	1971	—	3.00	6.00
—By "Traffic, Etc."					
❏ 50883	Glad (Part 1)/Glad (Part 2)	1972	—	3.00	6.00
VIRGIN					
❏ S7-17971	Here Comes a Man (Rock Mix)/Glad (Live)	1994	—	2.00	4.00
❏ S7-18134	Some Kinda Woman/Forty Thousand Headmen (Live)	1994	—	2.00	4.00
Albums					
ASYLUM					
❏ 7E-1020	When the Eagle Flies	1974	3.00	6.00	12.00
ISLAND					
❏ ILSD 2 [(2)]	Traffic — On the Road	197?	3.75	7.50	15.00
—Reissue					
❏ ILPS 9180	The Low Spark of High Heeled Boys	197?	3.00	6.00	12.00
—Reissue					
❏ ILPS 9224	Shoot Out at the Fantasy Factory	197?	3.00	6.00	12.00
—Reissue					
❏ SW-9306	The Low Spark of High Heeled Boys	1971	3.75	7.50	15.00
❏ SW-9323	Shoot Out at the Fantasy Factory	1973	3.75	7.50	15.00
❏ SMAS-9336 [(2)]	Traffic — On the Road	1973	5.00	10.00	20.00
❏ 90026	The Low Spark of High Heeled Boys	1983	2.00	4.00	8.00
—Reissue					
❏ 90027	Shoot Out at the Fantasy Factory	1983	2.00	4.00	8.00
—Reissue					
❏ 90028 [(2)]	Traffic — On the Road	1983	3.00	6.00	12.00
—Reissue					
❏ 90058	John Barleycorn Must Die	1983	2.00	4.00	8.00
—Reissue					
❏ 90059	Traffic	1983	2.00	4.00	8.00
—Reissue					
❏ 90060	Mr. Fantasy	1983	2.00	4.00	8.00
—Reissue					
MOBILE FIDELITY					
❏ 1-209	The Low Spark of High Heeled Boys	1994	6.25	12.50	25.00
—Audiophile vinyl					
UNITED ARTISTS					
❏ UA-LA421-G	Heavy Traffic	1975	3.75	7.50	15.00
❏ UA-LA526-G	More Heavy Traffic	1975	3.75	7.50	15.00
❏ UAL-3651 [M]	Heaven Is In Your Mind	1967	15.00	30.00	60.00
❏ UAS-5500	Best of Traffic	1969	5.00	10.00	20.00
—Originals have pink and orange labels					
❏ UAS-5504	John Barleycorn Must Die	1970	5.00	10.00	20.00
—Originals have black and orange labels					
❏ UAS-5550	Welcome to the Canteen	1971	3.75	7.50	15.00
❏ UAS-6651 [S]	Heaven Is In Your Mind	1967	12.50	25.00	50.00
❏ UAS-6651 [S]	Mr. Fantasy	1968	6.25	12.50	25.00
—Retitled version of "Heaven Is In Your Mind" with green strip across top of back with song titles					
❏ UAS-6651 [S]	Mr. Fantasy	1968	8.75	17.50	35.00
—Retitled version of "Heaven Is In Your Mind" with old title still on back cover					
❏ UAS-6676	Traffic	1968	5.00	10.00	20.00
—Originals have purple and orange labels					
❏ UAS-6702	Last Exit	1969	5.00	10.00	20.00
—Originals have purple and orange labels					
❏ ST-92018	Last Exit	1969	7.50	15.00	30.00
—Capitol Record Club edition; label is the old-style black with circles at the top!					
TRAILER, REX, AND THE PLAYBOYS					
Albums					
CROWN					
❏ CLP-5158 [M]	Country & Western	1958	6.25	12.50	25.00
TRAITS, THE Also see ROY HEAD.					
45s					
ASCOT					
❏ 2108	Linda Lou/Little Mama	1962	7.50	15.00	30.00
PACEMAKER					
❏ 254	Too Good to Be True/Gotta Keep Cool	1967	5.00	10.00	20.00
RENNER					
❏ 221	Linda Lou/Little Mama	1962	10.00	20.00	40.00
❏ 229	Got My Mojo Working/Woe Woe	1962	6.25	12.50	25.00
—Black vinyl					
❏ 229 [DJ]	Got My Mojo Working/Woe Woe	1962	10.00	20.00	40.00
—Promo only on colored vinyl					
SCEPTER					
❏ 12169	Harlem Shuffle/Strange Lips Start Old Memories	1966	2.00	4.00	8.00
❏ 12169	Harlem Shuffle/Somewhere	1966	2.50	5.00	10.00
TNT					
❏ 164	One More Time/Don't Be Blue	1959	5.00	10.00	20.00
—Later reissued on TNT 194 credited to "Roy Head"					
❏ 175	Live It Up/Yes I Do	1960	5.00	10.00	20.00
❏ 177	My Baby's Fine/Here I Am in Love Again	1960	5.00	10.00	20.00
❏ 181	Summer Time Love/Your Turn to Cry	1960	5.00	10.00	20.00
❏ 185	Night Time Blues/Walking All Day	1961	5.00	10.00	20.00
UNIVERSAL					
❏ 30494	Harlem Shuffle/Somewhere	1966	7.50	15.00	30.00
TRAMLINE					
Albums					
A&M					
❏ SP-4208	Somewhere Down the Line	1969	5.00	10.00	20.00
TRAMMELL, BOBBY LEE					
45s					
ABC-PARAMOUNT					
❏ 9890	Shirley Lee/I Sure Do Love You Baby	1958	20.00	40.00	80.00
ALLEY					
❏ 1001	It's All Your Fault/Arkansas Twist	1962	6.25	12.50	25.00
❏ 1004	Come On Baby/I Tried Not to Cry	1963	6.25	12.50	25.00
ATLANTA					
❏ 1101	Just Let Me Love You One More Time/Tator	196?	6.25	12.50	25.00
❏ 1501	Carolyn/Sally Twist	196?	6.25	12.50	25.00
❏ 1502	Come On/I Love 'Em All	196?	6.25	12.50	25.00
❏ 1503	Give Me That Good Lovin'/New Dance in France	196?	6.25	12.50	25.00
❏ 3001	I'll Step Aside/Mary Ann	196?	6.25	12.50	25.00
ATLANTIC					
❏ 2332	Shimmy Loo/You Make Me Feel So Fine	1966	3.00	6.00	12.00
CAPITOL					
❏ 3718	Love Don't Let Me Down/I Couldn't Believe My Eyes	1973	2.00	4.00	8.00
❏ 3801	You Mostest Girl/You Stand a Chance of Losing What You've Got	1973	2.00	4.00	8.00
CINNAMON					
❏ 797	The Warmth of Your Love/Marion County Tradition	1974	—	3.00	6.00
CONFEDERATE					
❏ 125	Shake Me Baby/Run Fool Run	195?	250.00	500.00	1000.
FABOR					
❏ 127	You Mostest Girl/Uh Oh	1964	3.00	6.00	12.00
❏ 4038	Shirley Lee/I Sure Do Love You Baby	1957	37.50	75.00	150.00
HOT					
❏ 101	Shimmy Lou/(B-side unknown)	1959	10.00	20.00	40.00
❏ 102	Betty Jean/(B-side unknown)	1959	10.00	20.00	40.00
RADIO					
❏ 102	You Mostest Girl/Uh Oh	1958	12.50	25.00	50.00
❏ 114	My Susie Jane/Should I Make Amends	1958	10.00	20.00	40.00

Number	Title (A Side/B Side)	Yr	VG	VG+	NM
SANTO					
❏ 9052	Hi-O Silver/Don't You Know I Love You	196?	5.00	10.00	20.00
SIMS					
❏ 183	Good Lovin'/New Dance in France	1964	3.00	6.00	12.00
❏ 195	Come On and Love Me/				
	If You Don't Wanna, You Don't Have To	1964	3.00	6.00	12.00
❏ 225	Twenty-Four Hours/				
	Just Let Me Move You One More Time	1965	3.00	6.00	12.00
❏ 241	I Tried/Am I Satisfying You	1965	3.00	6.00	12.00
❏ 254	Long Tall Sally/The Saints Go Marchin' In	1965	3.00	6.00	12.00
SKYLA					
❏ 1307	You Mostest Girl/Uh Oh	1961	3.75	7.50	15.00
SOUNCOT					
❏ 1100	I Dare America to Be Great/A Gift from God	1970	—	3.00	6.00
❏ 1104	24 Hours a Day/I Lost the Girl I Love Tonight	1970	—	3.00	6.00
❏ 1113	You Mostest Girl/Whole Lotta Shakin' Goin' On	1971	—	3.00	6.00
❏ 1119	My Shoes Keep Walkin' Back to You/Let's Wash				
	the World and Make It Clean	1971	—	3.00	6.00
❏ 1128	Don't Let the Stars Get In Your Eyes/Sheila	1971	—	3.00	6.00
❏ 1130	You Were Worth the Wait/Wadin' in the Water	1972	—	3.00	6.00
❏ 1135	Love Isn't Love (Till You Give It Away)/				
	Tell Me That You Want Me	1972	—	3.00	6.00
❏ 1143	I Believe in You/My Love Keeps Growing	1972	—	3.00	6.00
❏ 1145	You Put Love Back in My Heart/I Lost the Girl I				
	Love Tonight	1972	—	3.00	6.00
SUN					
❏ 1135	Jenny Lee/It's All Your Fault	1977	—	3.00	6.00
WARRIOR					
❏ 1554	Woe Is Me/Open Up Your Heart	1959	20.00	40.00	80.00
Albums					
ATLANTA					
❏ 1503 [M]	Arkansas Twist	1962	250.00	500.00	1000.
SOUNCOT					
❏ SC-1102	I Dare America to Be Great	1971	5.00	10.00	20.00
❏ SC-1141	Love Isn't Love Till You Give It Away	1972	3.75	7.50	15.00

TRAMMPS, THE Also see THE VOLCANOS.

12-Inch Singles

Number	Title (A Side/B Side)	Yr	VG	VG+	NM
ATLANTIC					
❏ PR 102 [DJ]	The Night the Lights Went Out (same on both				
	sides)	1977	3.00	6.00	12.00
❏ PR 139 [DJ]	Soul Bones/Love Magnet	1978	3.00	6.00	12.00
❏ PR 170 [DJ]	Teaser/Life Insurance Policy	1979	3.00	6.00	12.00
❏ DSKO 173	The Night the Lights Went Out (7:06)/Hooked				
	for Life (4:40)	1977	3.75	7.50	15.00
❏ PR 224 [DJ]	Hard Rock and Disco (same on both sides)	1980	3.00	6.00	12.00
❏ PR 251 [DJ]	Looking for You/Mellow Out	1980	3.00	6.00	12.00
VENTURE					
❏ 5024	Up on the Hill (Mt. U)	1983	—	3.50	7.00
45s					
ATLANTIC					
❏ 3286	Hooked for Life/I'm Alright	1975	—	2.50	5.00
❏ 3306	That's Where the Happy People Go (Short)/				
	That's Where the Happy People Go (Long)	1975	—	2.50	5.00
❏ 3345	Soul Searchin' Time/Love Is a Funky Thing	1976	—	2.50	5.00
❏ 3365	Ninety-Nine and a Half (Won't Do)/Can We				
	Come Together	1976	—	2.50	5.00
❏ 3389	Disco Inferno/You Touch My Hot Line	1977	—	3.00	6.00
❏ 3389 [PS]	Disco Inferno/You Touch My Hot Line	1977	2.00	4.00	8.00
❏ 3389	Disco Inferno/				
	That's Where the Happy People Go	1978	—	2.50	5.00
	—Reissue in conjunction with the success of "Saturday Night Fever"				
❏ 3403	I Feel Like I've Been Livin' (On the Dark Side of				
	the Moon)/Don't Burn Bridges	1977	—	2.50	5.00
❏ 3442	The Night the Lights Went Out/				
	I'm So Glad You Came Along	1977	—	2.50	5.00
❏ 3460	Seasons for Girls/Body Contact Contract	1978	—	2.50	5.00
❏ 3460	Seasons for Girls/Love Ain't Been Easy	1978	—	2.50	5.00
❏ 3537	Soul Bones/Love Magnet	1978	—	2.50	5.00
❏ 3573	More Good Times to Remember/Teaser	1979	—	2.50	5.00
❏ 3654	Dance Contest/Hard Rock and Disco	1980	—	2.00	4.00
❏ 3669	Music Freek/V.I.P.	1980	—	2.00	4.00
❏ 3777	Mellow Out/Looking for You	1980	—	2.00	4.00
❏ 3797	I Don't Want to Ever Lose Your Love/				
	Breathtaking View	1981	—	2.00	4.00
BUDDAH					
❏ 306	Zing Went the Strings of My Heart/				
	Penguin at the Big Apple	1972	—	3.00	6.00
	—As "Trammps"				
❏ 306	Zing Went the Strings of My Heart/				
	Penguin at the Big Apple	1972	2.50	5.00	10.00
	—As "Tramps"				
❏ 321	Sixty Minute Man/Scrub Board	1972	—	3.00	6.00
❏ 339	Rubber Band/Pray All You Sinners	1973	—	3.00	6.00
❏ 507	Hold Back the Night/Tom's Song	1975	—	2.50	5.00
GOLDEN FLEECE					
❏ 3251	Love Epidemic/I Know That Feeling	1973	—	3.00	6.00
❏ 3253	Where Do We Go from Here/Shout	1974	—	3.00	6.00
❏ 3255	Trusting Heart/Down These Dark Streets	1974	—	3.00	6.00
Albums					
ATLANTIC					
❏ SD 18172	Where the Happy People Go	1976	2.50	5.00	10.00
❏ SD 18211	Disco Inferno	1977	2.50	5.00	10.00
❏ SD 19148	The Trammps III	1977	2.50	5.00	10.00
❏ SD 19194	The Best of the Trammps	1978	2.50	5.00	10.00
❏ SD 19210	The Whole World's Dancing	1979	2.50	5.00	10.00
❏ SD 19267	Mixin' It Up	1980	2.50	5.00	10.00
❏ SD 19290	Slipping Out	1981	2.50	5.00	10.00
BUDDAH					
❏ BDS-5641	The Legendary Zing Album				
	Featuring the Fabulous Trammps	1975	3.00	6.00	12.00
GOLDEN FLEECE					
❏ KZ 33163	Trammps	1975	2.50	5.00	10.00
PHILADELPHIA INT'L.					
❏ PZ 33163	Disco Champs	1977	2.00	4.00	8.00
	—Reissue of Golden Fleece LP				

Number	Title (A Side/B Side)	Yr	VG	VG+	NM
TRANQUILS, THE					
45s					
HAMILTON					
❏ 50005	You're Such a Much/One Billion,				
	Seven Million and Thirty-Three	1959	7.50	15.00	30.00
TRANSIENTS, THE					
Albums					
HORIZON					
❏ WP-1633 [M]	The Funky 12 String Guitar	1963	5.00	10.00	20.00
❏ WPS-1633 [S]	The Funky 12 String Guitar	1963	6.25	12.50	25.00
TRAPEZE					
45s					
THRESHOLD					
❏ 67001	Send Me No More Letters/Another Day	1970	2.00	4.00	8.00
❏ 67005 [DJ]	Black Cloud (mono/stereo)	1971	2.50	5.00	10.00
❏ 67011	Coast to Coast/Your Love Is Alright	1972	2.00	4.00	8.00
Albums					
PAID					
❏ 2003	Hold On	1981	2.50	5.00	10.00
THRESHOLD					
❏ THS 2	Trapeze	1970	10.00	20.00	40.00
❏ THS 4	Medusa	1971	20.00	40.00	80.00
❏ THS 8	You Are the Music, We're Just the Band	1972	10.00	20.00	40.00
❏ THS 11	The Final Swing	1974	10.00	20.00	40.00
WARNER BROS.					
❏ BS 2828	Hot Wire	1974	3.00	6.00	12.00
❏ BS 2887	Trapeze	1975	3.00	6.00	12.00
TRAPP, SANDY					
45s					
PARKWAY					
❏ 840	Love Sickness/I Don't Know	1962	2.50	5.00	10.00
TRASH					
45s					
APPLE					
❏ 1804	Road to Nowhere/Illusions	1969	12.50	25.00	50.00
	—Without star on A-side label				
❏ 1804	Road to Nowhere/Illusions	1969	25.00	50.00	100.00
	—With star on A-side label				
❏ 1811	Golden Slumbers-Carry That Weight/Trash Can	1969	3.75	7.50	15.00
	—A-side listed as "Golden Slumbers/Carry That Weight"				
❏ 1811	Golden Slumbers-Carry That Weight/Trash Can	1969	5.00	10.00	20.00
	—A-side listed as "Golden Slumbers and Carry That Weight"				
❏ 1811	Golden Slumbers-Carry That Weight/Trash Can	1969	5.00	10.00	20.00
	—A-side listed as "Golden Slumbers Carry That Weight"				
❏ PRO-4671/2	Road to Nowhere (Edit)/Road to Nowhere	1969	20.00	40.00	80.00
TRASHMEN, THE					
45s					
ARGO					
❏ 5516	Bird '65/Ubangi Stomp	1965	12.50	25.00	50.00
BEAR					
❏ 1966	Keep Your Hands Off My Baby/Lost Angel	1965	5.00	10.00	20.00
ERA BACK TO BACK HITS					
❏ 016	Liar, Liar/Surfin' Bird	197?	—	2.50	5.00
	—B-side by the Castaways				
ERIC					
❏ 247	Surfin' Bird/Liar, Liar	197?	—	2.50	5.00
	—B-side by the Castaways; reissue				
GARRETT					
❏ 4002	Surfin' Bird/King of the Surf	1963	7.50	15.00	30.00
❏ 4003	Bird Dance Beat/A-Bone	1964	5.00	10.00	20.00
❏ 4005	Bad News/On the Move	1964	5.00	10.00	20.00
❏ 4010	Peppermint Man/New Generation	1964	5.00	10.00	20.00
❏ 4012	Whoa Dad/Walkin' My Baby	1964	5.00	10.00	20.00
❏ 4012 [PS]	Whoa Dad/Walkin' My Baby	1964	62.50	125.00	250.00
❏ 4013	Dancing with Santa/Real Live Doll	1964	6.25	12.50	25.00
❏ 4013 [PS]	Dancing with Santa/Real Live Doll	1964	62.50	125.00	250.00
GET HIP					
❏ 2	Well All Right/That's What They Say	1994	—	2.50	4.00
LANA					
❏ 136	Surfin' Bird/King of the Surf	196?	2.50	5.00	10.00
	—Oldies reissue				
METROBEAT					
❏ 7927	Green, Green Backs of Home/Address				
	Enclosed	1968	3.75	7.50	15.00
OLDIES 45					
❏ 301	Surfin' Bird/King of the Surf	1965	3.00	6.00	12.00
	—Early reissue				
SOMA					
❏ 1469	Surfin' Bird/Liar, Liar	1966	3.00	6.00	12.00
	—B-side by the Castaways				
SUNDAZED					
❏ 102	Henrietta/Rumble	1995	—	—	2.00
❏ 102 [PS]	Henrietta/Rumble	1995	—	—	2.00
❏ 103	Lucille/Green Onions	1995	—	—	2.00
❏ 103 [PS]	Lucille/Green Onions	1995	—	—	2.00
❏ 104	Roll Over Beethoven/Betty Jean	1995	—	—	2.00
❏ 104 [PS]	Roll Over Beethoven/Betty Jean	1995	—	—	2.00
❏ 112	Dancing with Santa/Real Live Doll	1996	—	—	2.00
	—Red vinyl				
❏ 112 [PS]	Dancing with Santa/Real Live Doll	1996	—	—	2.00
TERRIFIC					
❏ 5003	Surfin' Bird/Bird Dance Beat	196?	2.50	5.00	10.00
	—Early reissue				
TRIBE					
❏ 8315	Hanging On Me/Some Lies	1966	6.25	12.50	25.00
Albums					
BEAT ROCKET					
❏ BR 107	Surfin' Bird	1999	3.00	6.00	12.00
	—Reissue on 180-gram vinyl				
GARRETT					
❏ GA-200 [M]	Surfin' Bird	1964	55.00	110.00	220.00
❏ GAS-200 [R]	Surfin' Bird	1964	87.50	175.00	350.00

T

Number	Title (A Side/B Side)	Yr	VG	VG+	NM
SUNDAZED					
❑ LP 5002	Live Bird '65-'67	1991	2.50	5.00	10.00
❑ LP 5003	Great Lost Album	1991	2.50	5.00	10.00
TRAVELERS, THE Probably more than one group.					
45s					
ABC-PARAMOUNT					
❑ 10119	June, July, August and September/				
	What a Weekend	1960	5.00	10.00	20.00
ANDEX					
❑ 2011	I'll Be Home for Christmas/Katie the Kangaroo	1958	7.50	15.00	30.00
❑ 4033	I Go for You/I'll Always Be in Love with You	1959	7.50	15.00	30.00
❑ 34006	Why/Teenage Machine Age	1957	7.50	15.00	30.00
❑ 34012	He's Got the Whole World in His Hands/				
	Green Town Girl	1957	7.50	15.00	30.00
DECCA					
❑ 31215	Ivy on the Old School Wall/Cadwallader 0002	1961	10.00	20.00	40.00
❑ 31282	White Rose/Oh My Love (Love Me)	1961	10.00	20.00	40.00
DON RAY					
❑ 5965	Traveler/Seven Minutes Till Four	1963	12.50	25.00	50.00
MAGIC LAMP					
❑ 516	Big House/Goin' Home	1964	3.00	6.00	12.00
VAULT					
❑ 911	Spanish Moon/She's Got the Blues	1964	3.75	7.50	15.00
YELLOW SAND					
❑ 2	Windy and Warm/Last Date	1963	12.50	25.00	50.00
❑ 451	Groovy/(B-side unknown)	1965	7.50	15.00	30.00
❑ 452	Malibu Sunset/Hang On	1965	7.50	15.00	30.00
TRAVELING SALESMEN					
45s					
RCA VICTOR					
❑ 47-9167	I'm Alive/Days of My Years	1967	5.00	10.00	20.00
TRAVELLERS, THE					
45s					
GASS					
❑ 1000	Tie Me Surfer Board Down, Sport/In the Pines	1963	10.00	20.00	40.00
TRAVERS, MARY Also see PETER, PAUL AND MARY.					
45s					
CHRYSALIS					
❑ 2202	The Air That I Breathe/You Turn Me Around	1977	—	2.50	5.00
❑ 2367	Freedom/(B-side unknown)	1979	—	2.00	4.00
WARNER BROS.					
❑ 7481	Follow Me/I Guess He'd Rather Be in Colorado	1971	—	2.50	5.00
❑ 7517	The Song Is Love/				
	Ericka with the Windy Yellow Hair	1971	—	2.50	5.00
❑ 7588	Morning Glory/That's Enough for Me	1972	—	2.50	5.00
❑ 7675	Too Many Mondays/				
	That Year There Was No Winter	1972	—	2.50	5.00
❑ 7731	Five Hundred Miles/Oh, What a Feeling	1973	—	2.50	5.00
❑ 7790	Circles/I'll Have to Say I Love You in a Song	1974	—	2.50	5.00
Albums					
CHRYSALIS					
❑ CHR 1168	It's In Everyone of Us	1978	2.50	5.00	10.00
WARNER BROS.					
❑ WS 1907	Mary	1971	3.00	6.00	12.00
—Green "WB" label					
❑ BS 2609	Morning Glory	1972	3.00	6.00	12.00
—Green "WB" label					
❑ BS 2677	All My Choices	1973	3.00	6.00	12.00
—Green "WB" label					
❑ BS 2795	Circles	1974	3.00	6.00	12.00
—"Burbank" palm-trees label					
TRAVIS AND BOB					
45s					
BIG TOP					
❑ 3054	Pocahontas/Day Dreams	1960	3.75	7.50	15.00
MERCURY					
❑ 71797	Give Your Love to Me/Stay Close to Me	1961	3.75	7.50	15.00
❑ 71866	The Spider and the Fly/What a Change	1961	3.75	7.50	15.00
SANDY					
❑ 1017	Tell Him No/We're Too Young	1959	5.00	10.00	20.00
—With Dot Records distribution mentioned on label					
❑ 1017	Tell Him No/We're Too Young	1959	6.25	12.50	25.00
—With no mention of Dot Records on label					
❑ 1019	Teenage Vision/Little Bitty Johnny	1959	5.00	10.00	20.00
❑ 1024	Lover's Rendezvous/Oh Yeah	1959	5.00	10.00	20.00
❑ 1029	That's How Long/Wake Up and Cry	1960	5.00	10.00	20.00
TRAYNOR, JAY Also see JAY AND THE AMERICANS.					
45s					
ABC					
❑ 10809	Come On/The Merry-Go-Round Is Slowing You				
	Down	1966	3.75	7.50	15.00
❑ 10845	Up and Over/Don't Let the End Begin	1966	7.50	15.00	30.00
CORAL					
❑ 62396	How Sweet It Is/I Rise, I Fall	1964	3.00	6.00	12.00
—As "JAY, formerly of Jay & the Americans"					
❑ 62420	I've Known You All My Life/Little Sister	1964	3.00	6.00	12.00
TREADWELL, IRENE					
45s					
JAY DEE					
❑ 782	Church Bells Are Ringing on Christmas Morning/				
	Dear Santa Bring Back My Daddy to Me	1953	5.00	10.00	20.00
TREASURERS, THE					
45s					
CROWN					
❑ 005	Story of Love/I Walk with An Angel	1961	75.00	150.00	300.00

Number	Title (A Side/B Side)	Yr	VG	VG+	NM
TREASURES, THE					
45s					
SHIRLEY					
❑ 500	Hold Me Tight/Pete Meets Vinnie	1964	7.50	15.00	30.00
VALOR					
❑ (# unknown)	Minor Chaos/Valley of the Broken Hearts	1964	25.00	50.00	100.00
—Sources differ as to what the number of this record is, and we've never seen a copy, so we haven't listed one.					
❑ (# unknown)	Minor Chaos/Valley of the Broken Hearts	1964	50.00	100.00	200.00
—Green vinyl					
❑ (# unknown)	Minor Chaos/Valley of the Broken Hearts	1964	100.00	200.00	400.00
—Marbled vinyl					
TREBELAIRES, THE					
45s					
NESTOR					
❑ 16	There Goes That Train/I Gotta	1954	25.00	50.00	100.00
TREBLE CHORDS, THE					
45s					
DECCA					
❑ 31015	Teresa/My Little Girl	1959	25.00	50.00	100.00
TREE					
Albums					
GOAT FARM					
❑ 580	Tree	1970	17.50	35.00	70.00
TREE SWINGERS, THE					
45s					
BIG TOP					
❑ 3058	Only Forever/Kissin' and Cookin'	1960	3.75	7.50	15.00
GUYDEN					
❑ 2036	Kookie Little Paradise/				
	Teaching the Natives to Sing	1960	3.75	7.50	15.00
TREMAINES, THE					
45s					
CASH					
❑ 100/1	Jingle, Jingle/Moon Shining Bright	1958	100.00	200.00	400.00
KANE					
❑ 008	Heavenly/Wonderful, Marvelous	1959	12.50	25.00	50.00
OLD TOWN					
❑ 1051	Jingle, Jingle/Moon Shining Bright	1958	12.50	25.00	50.00
V-TONE					
❑ 507	Heavenly/Wonderful, Marvelous	1959	6.25	12.50	25.00
VAL					
❑ 100/1	Jingle, Jingle/Moon Shining Bright	1958	62.50	125.00	250.00
TREMELOES, THE Also see BRIAN POOLE AND THE TREMELOES.					
45s					
DJM					
❑ 1008	Hard Woman/My Friend Delaney	1976	—	2.50	5.00
❑ 1016	September, November, December/				
	(B-side unknown)	1976	—	2.50	5.00
EPIC					
❑ 10075	Good Day Sunshine/What a State I'm In	1966	3.00	6.00	12.00
❑ 10139	Here Comes My Baby/Gentlemen of Pleasure	1967	2.50	5.00	10.00
❑ 10184	Silence Is Golden/Let Your Hair Hang Down	1967	2.50	5.00	10.00
❑ 10184 [PS]	Silence Is Golden/Let Your Hair Hang Down	1967	3.75	7.50	15.00
❑ 10233	Even the Bad Times Are Good/Jenny's All Right	1967	2.00	4.00	8.00
❑ 10233 [PS]	Even the Bad Times Are Good/Jenny's All Right	1967	3.75	7.50	15.00
❑ 10293	Suddenly You Love Me/Suddenly Winter	1968	2.00	4.00	8.00
❑ 10328	Girl from Nowhere/Helule, Helule	1968	2.00	4.00	8.00
❑ 10376	My Little Lady/All the World to Me	1968	2.00	4.00	8.00
❑ 10437	I Shall Be Released/I Miss My Baby	1969	2.00	4.00	8.00
❑ 10467	Up, Down, All Around/Hello World	1969	2.00	4.00	8.00
❑ 10548	(Call Me) Number One/Instant Whip	1969	2.00	4.00	8.00
❑ 10621	Breakheart Motel/By the Way	1970	2.50	5.00	10.00
❑ 10682	Me and My Life/Try Me	1970	2.00	4.00	8.00
❑ 10807	My Woman/Hello Buddy	1971	—	3.00	6.00
❑ 10996	Yodelay/Blue Suede Tie	1973	—	3.00	6.00
7-Inch Extended Plays					
EPIC					
❑ 5-26388	Peggy Sue/The Lion Sleeps Tonight/Willy and				
	the Hand Jive//Everyday/Rag Doll/Ain't				
	Nothing But a House Party	1968	3.75	7.50	15.00
—Jukebox issue; small hole, plays at 33 1/3 rpm					
❑ 5-26388 [PS]	World Explosion	1968	3.75	7.50	15.00
Albums					
DJM					
❑ 2	Shiner	1974	3.00	6.00	12.00
EPIC					
❑ LN 24310 [M]	Here Comes My Baby	1967	7.50	15.00	30.00
❑ LN 24326 [M]	Even the Bad Times Are Good	1967	6.25	12.50	25.00
❑ LN 24363 [M]	Suddenly You Love Me	1968	7.50	15.00	30.00
❑ LN 24388 [M]	World Explosion '58/'68	1968	15.00	30.00	60.00
—White label promo only					
❑ BN 26310 [R]	Here Comes My Baby	1967	5.00	10.00	20.00
❑ BN 26326 [P]	Even the Bad Times Are Good	1967	7.50	15.00	30.00
❑ BN 26363 [R]	Suddenly You Love Me	1968	5.00	10.00	20.00
❑ BN 26388 [S]	World Explosion '58/'68	1968	7.50	15.00	30.00
TREMELOES, THE/THE HOLLIES					
45s					
EPIC					
❑ 10184/0 [DJ]	Silence Is Golden/Carrie-Anne	1967	25.00	50.00	100.00
—Promo only on red vinyl					
❑ 10184/0 [PS]	Silence Is Golden/Carrie-Anne	1967	75.00	150.00	300.00
—"There's Room for Two at the Top!" across top of sleeve; has photos of both bands; all the print is in red					
TREMELOS, THE					
45s					
ROCKLAND					
❑ 102	Jaguar/Fly	196?	12.50	25.00	50.00

Number	Title (A Side/B Side)	Yr	VG	VG+	NM
TREMONTS, THE					
45s					
BRUNSWICK					
❑ 55217	Believe My Heart/Legend of Love	1961	7.50	15.00	30.00
PAT RICCIO					
❑ 101	Believe My Heart/Legend of Love	1961	25.00	50.00	100.00
TREN-DELLS, THE					
45s					
CAPITOL					
❑ 4852	Nite Owl/Hully Gully Jones	1962	3.00	6.00	12.00
JAM					
❑ 101	Nite Owl/Hully Gully Jones	1962	6.25	12.50	25.00
❑ 111	Hey Da-Da Dow/Tough Little Buggy	1962	6.25	12.50	25.00
SOUND STAGE 7					
❑ 2508	Mr. Doughnut Man/Ain't That Funny	1963	3.00	6.00	12.00
TILT					
❑ 779	I'm So Young/Don't You Hear Me Calling Baby	1961	7.50	15.00	30.00
—As "The Trend-Els"					
❑ 788	Moments Like This/I Miss You So	1962	7.50	15.00	30.00
TREN-TEENS, THE					
45s					
CARNIVAL					
❑ 501	My Baby's Gone/Your Yah Yah Is Gone	1964	25.00	50.00	100.00
TRENDS, THE (1)					
45s					
ABC					
❑ 10817	A Night for Love/Gonna Have to Show You	1966	6.25	12.50	25.00
❑ 10881	No One There/That's How I Like It	1966	6.25	12.50	25.00
❑ 10944	Check My Tears/Don't Drop Out of School	1967	5.00	10.00	20.00
❑ 10993	Thanks for a Little Lovin'/I Never Knew How Good I Had It	1967	5.00	10.00	20.00
❑ 11091	Soul Clap/Big Parade	1968	5.00	10.00	20.00
❑ 11150	Not Another Day/ You Sure Know How to Hurt a Guy	1968	10.00	20.00	40.00
ABC-PARAMOUNT					
❑ 10731	Not Too Old to Cry/If You Don't Dig the Blues	1965	10.00	20.00	40.00
SMASH					
❑ 1914	Dance with My Baby/To Be Happy Enough	1964	6.25	12.50	25.00
❑ 1933	Get Something Going/ That's the Way the Story Goes	1964	6.25	12.50	25.00
TRENDS, THE (2)					
45s					
ARGO					
❑ 5341	I'll Be True/Class Ring	1959	7.50	15.00	30.00
SCOPE					
❑ 102	Gone Again/Silly Grin	1959	20.00	40.00	80.00
TRENDS, THE (U) Definitely not group (1), but it may not be group (2), either.					
45s					
RCA VICTOR					
❑ 47-7733	The Beard/Chug-a-Lug	1960	3.75	7.50	15.00
TRENIERS, THE					
45s					
BRUNSWICK					
❑ 55014	Holy Mackerel Andy/Rock Calypso Joe	1957	5.00	10.00	20.00
❑ 55033	Pennies from Heaven/Ooh-La-La	1957	5.00	10.00	20.00
❑ 55047	Goodnight Irene/ Rubbing Noses in the Midnight Sun	1958	5.00	10.00	20.00
DOM					
❑ 410	Gotta Travel On/Let It All Hang Out	1968	2.00	4.00	8.00
DOT					
❑ 15882	Never Never/ When Your Hair Has Turned to Silver	1958	5.00	10.00	20.00
EPIC					
❑ 9127	Go! Go! Go!/Doin' 'Em Up	1955	6.25	12.50	25.00
❑ 9144	Rock'n Roll Call/ Day-Old Bread and Canned Beans	1956	6.25	12.50	25.00
❑ 9162	Boodie Green/Good Rockin' Tonight	1956	6.25	12.50	25.00
OKEH					
❑ 6804	Go! Go! Go!/Plenty of Money	1951	12.50	25.00	50.00
❑ 6826	Hey, Little Girl/Old Woman Blues	1951	10.00	20.00	40.00
❑ 6853	It Rocks, It Rolls, It Swings/Taxi Blues	1952	10.00	20.00	40.00
❑ 6876	Hadacol, That's All/Long Distance Blues	1952	10.00	20.00	40.00
❑ 6904	Rockin' on Sunday Night/Cheatin' On Me	1952	10.00	20.00	40.00
❑ 6932	Hi-Yo Silver/Poon-Tang!	1953	10.00	20.00	40.00
❑ 6937	The Moondog/Poon-Tang!	1953	12.50	25.00	50.00
❑ 6960	Rockin' Is Our Bizness/Sugar Doo	1953	10.00	20.00	40.00
❑ 6984	I'd Do Nothin' But Grieve/This Is It	1953	10.00	20.00	40.00
❑ 7012	You Know, Yeah! Tiger/Bug Dance	1953	10.00	20.00	40.00
❑ 7023	Rock-a-Beatin' Boogie/Trapped	1954	10.00	20.00	40.00
❑ 7035	Bald Head/Come On Let's Face It	1954	10.00	20.00	40.00
❑ 7050	Who Put the "Ungh" in the Mambo/ Get Out of the Car	1955	7.50	15.00	30.00
❑ 7057	Devil's Mambo/Do, Do, Do (Do-Be-Oo-Be-Oo)	1955	7.50	15.00	30.00
VIK					
❑ 0214	Lover Come Back to Me/Sorrento	1956	6.25	12.50	25.00
❑ 0227	Rock and Roll President/Cool It Baby	1956	6.25	12.50	25.00
7-Inch Extended Plays					
EPIC					
❑ EG-7014	(contents unknown)	1955	12.50	25.00	50.00
❑ EG-7014 [PS]	Go! Go! Go!	1955	12.50	25.00	50.00
❑ EG-7114	(contents unknown)	195?	12.50	25.00	50.00
❑ EG-7114 [PS]	Those Crazy Treniers	195?	12.50	25.00	50.00
Albums					
DOT					
❑ DLP-3257 [M]	Souvenir Album	1960	25.00	50.00	100.00
EPIC					
❑ LG 3125 [M]	The Treniers on TV	1955	50.00	100.00	200.00

Number	Title (A Side/B Side)	Yr	VG	VG+	NM
TRENT, JACKIE The record on Nasco may be by a different singer than the others.					
45s					
A&M					
❑ 1022	Hollywood/Don't Send Me Away	1969	—	3.00	6.00
KAPP					
❑ 583	Only One Such As You/ If You Love Me, Really Love Me	1964	3.00	6.00	12.00
❑ 630	Somewhere in the World/I Heard Someone Say	1964	3.00	6.00	12.00
NASCO					
❑ 6012	Little Andy/What's He Got	1958	6.25	12.50	25.00
PARKWAY					
❑ 941	Don't Stand in My Way/How Soon	1965	3.00	6.00	12.00
❑ 955	Where Are You Now My Love/ On the Other Side of the Tracks	1965	3.00	6.00	12.00
❑ 963	To Show I Love Him/When Summertime Is Over	1965	3.00	6.00	12.00
WARNER BROS.					
❑ 5683	It's All in the Way You Look at Life/ Time After Time	1965	2.50	5.00	10.00
❑ 5865	If You Ever Leave Me/Take Me Away	1966	2.50	5.00	10.00
❑ 7022	Hummingbird/I'll Be with You	1967	2.00	4.00	8.00
❑ 7070	It's Not Easy Loving You/ Your Love Is Everywhere	1967	2.00	4.00	8.00
❑ 7178	7:10 to Suburbia/Stop Me and Buy One	1968	2.00	4.00	8.00
❑ 7189	I'll Be With You/Two of Us	1968	2.00	4.00	8.00
TRENTONS, THE					
45s					
SHEPHERD					
❑ 2204	All Alone/Star Bright	1962	20.00	40.00	80.00
TREVOR, VAN					
45s					
ATLANTIC					
❑ 2175	Tuesday Girl/I Want to Cry	1963	2.50	5.00	10.00
BAND BOX					
❑ 367	Born to Be in Love with You/ It's So Good to Be Loved	1966	2.00	4.00	8.00
❑ 371	Our Side/When You've Lost Your Baby	1966	2.00	4.00	8.00
❑ 373 [DJ]	Christmas In The Country/Holiday Driving (PSA Announcements)	1966	2.50	5.00	10.00
❑ 374	He's Losing His Mind/A Fool Called Me	1967	2.00	4.00	8.00
CANADIAN AMERICAN					
❑ 181	Louisiana Hot Sauce/Satisfaction Is Guaranteed	1964	5.00	10.00	20.00
❑ 188	The Girl from the Main Street Diner/For This Girl	1965	3.75	7.50	15.00
CLARIDGE					
❑ 305	Christmas in Washington Square/Melting Snow	1965	3.75	7.50	15.00
DATE					
❑ 1565	You've Been So Good to Me/Sunday Morning	1967	2.00	4.00	8.00
❑ 1594	Take Me Along with You/Guitar	1968	2.00	4.00	8.00
ROYAL AMERICAN					
❑ 3	Mercy Hospital/Something Missing in Me	1970	—	2.50	5.00
❑ 9	Luziana River/Sweet Diana	1970	—	2.50	5.00
❑ 23	Wish I Was Home Instead/ Did I Have a Good Time	1970	—	2.50	5.00
❑ 31	Lonely Looking Woman/Johnnie and Annie	1971	—	2.50	5.00
❑ 67	Shiny New Penny/You and Only You	1972	—	2.50	5.00
❑ 280	The Things That Matter/Band of Gold	1969	—	3.00	6.00
❑ 283	A Man Away from Home/ I've Got Today to Live For	1969	—	3.00	6.00
❑ 289	Funny Familiar Forgotten Feelings/ Daddy's Little Man	1969	—	3.00	6.00
VIVID					
❑ 1004	C'mon Now Baby/A Fling of the Past	1963	7.50	15.00	30.00
—Backing group is The Four Seasons					
Albums					
BAND BOX					
❑ (# unknown)	Come On Over to Our Side	1967	5.00	10.00	20.00
DATE					
❑ DES-4008	You've Been So Good to Me	1967	3.75	7.50	15.00
ROYAL AMERICAN					
❑ 2800	Funny Familiar Forgotten Feelings	1969	3.75	7.50	15.00
TREXLER, GARY					
45s					
RCA VICTOR					
❑ 47-7258	I Flipped/Turn About	1958	3.75	7.50	15.00
❑ 47-7420	The Look/You Made Up for Everything	1958	3.75	7.50	15.00
REV					
❑ 3507	Teen Baby/Cloud Full of Tears	1957	5.00	10.00	20.00
TRIANGLE, THE					
45s					
AMARET					
❑ 108	Music, Music, Music/Magic Touch	1969	2.50	5.00	10.00
❑ 113	Ninety Nine and a Half/Lucille	1969	2.50	5.00	10.00
Albums					
AMARET					
❑ 5000	How Now Brown Cow	1969	6.25	12.50	25.00
TRIANGLES, THE					
45s					
FARGO					
❑ 1023	Dance the Magoo/Step-Up-and-Go	1962	3.75	7.50	15.00
FIFO					
❑ 107	My Oh My/Really I Do	1964	50.00	100.00	200.00
HERALD					
❑ 549	Savin' My Love/'Tis a Pity	1960	10.00	20.00	40.00
TRIBULATIONS, THE					
45s					
IMPERIAL					
❑ 66416	Mama's Love/You Gave Me Up for Promises	1969	7.50	15.00	30.00

T

Number	Title (A Side/B Side)	Yr	VG	VG+	NM

TRICKELS, THE
45s
GONE
| ❏ 5078 | With Each Step a Tear/Outside the Chapel Door | 1959 | 25.00 | 50.00 | 100.00 |

POWER
| ❏ 250 | With Each Step a Tear/When I Fall in Love | 1958 | 50.00 | 100.00 | 200.00 |

TRICYCLE
Albums
ABC
| ❏ S-674 | Tricycle | 1969 | 5.00 | 10.00 | 20.00 |

TRIDELS, THE
45s
SAN-DEE
| ❏ 1009 | Land of Love/Image of My Love | 1963 | 12.50 | 25.00 | 50.00 |

TRINA, MARGUERITE
45s
BELLA
| ❏ 19 | The Rocking Tree/The Brat | 1959 | 3.00 | 6.00 | 12.00 |

TRINIDADS, THE
45s
FORMAL
| ❏ 1005 | Don't Say Goodbye/On My Happy Way | 1959 | 50.00 | 100.00 | 200.00 |
| ❏ 1006 | One Lonely Night/When We're Together | 1959 | 50.00 | 100.00 | 200.00 |

TRIOLO, FRANK
45s
FLAGSHIP
| ❏ 106 | Ice Cream Baby/Pretty Little Woman | 1958 | 100.00 | 200.00 | 400.00 |

TRIPP, PAUL
45s
MUSICOR
| ❏ 1125 | An Old-Fashioned Christmas/I've Got a Date with Santa | 1965 | 3.00 | 6.00 | 12.00 |

TRIPP, TOM
45s
HIT
| ❏ 93 | Since I Fell for You/Dominique | 1963 | 2.00 | 4.00 | 8.00 |
—B-side by Betty Coleson

TRIPSICHORD MUSIC BOX, THE
Albums
JANUS
| ❏ JLS-3016 | The Tripsichord Music Box | 1971 | 50.00 | 100.00 | 200.00 |

TRIUMVIRAT
45s
CAPITOL
| ❏ 4700 | Waterfall/Jo Ann Walker | 1979 | — | 2.50 | 5.00 |
Albums
CAPITOL
❏ ST-11392	Spartacus	1975	3.00	6.00	12.00
❏ ST-11551	Old Loves Die Hard	1976	3.00	6.00	12.00
❏ ST-11697	Pompeii	1977	3.00	6.00	12.00
❏ ST-11862	A La Carte	1978	3.00	6.00	12.00
❏ SN-16119	Illusions on a Double Dimple	1980	2.00	4.00	8.00
—Budget-line reissue
| ❏ SN-16120 | Pompeii | 1980 | 2.00 | 4.00 | 8.00 |
—Budget-line reissue
| ❏ SN-16121 | Spartacus | 1980 | 2.00 | 4.00 | 8.00 |
—Budget-line reissue
| ❏ SN-16122 | Old Loves Die Hard | 1980 | 2.00 | 4.00 | 8.00 |
—Budget-line reissue
| ❏ SN-16123 | A La Carte | 1980 | 2.00 | 4.00 | 8.00 |
—Budget-line reissue
HARVEST
| ❏ ST-11311 | Illusions on a Double Dimple | 1974 | 3.75 | 7.50 | 15.00 |

TROGGS, THE
45s
ATCO
| ❏ 6415 | Wild Thing/I Want You | 1966 | 5.00 | 10.00 | 20.00 |
| ❏ 6415 | Wild Thing/With a Girl Like You | 1966 | 5.00 | 10.00 | 20.00 |
—"Wild Thing" writer is correctly credited as "Taylor."
| ❏ 6415 | Wild Thing/With a Girl Like You | 1966 | 6.25 | 12.50 | 25.00 |
—"Wild Thing" writer is incorrectly credited as "Presley."
| ❏ 6444 | I Can't Control Myself/Gonna Make You | 1966 | 3.75 | 7.50 | 15.00 |
BELL
| ❏ 45405 | Listen to the Man/Queen of Sorrow | 1973 | 2.00 | 4.00 | 8.00 |
| ❏ 45426 | Strange Movies/I'm on Fire | 1973 | 2.00 | 4.00 | 8.00 |
FONTANA
❏ 1548	Wild Thing/From Home	1966	2.50	5.00	10.00
❏ 1552	With a Girl Like You/I Want You	1966	2.50	5.00	10.00
❏ 1557	I Can't Control Myself/Gonna Make You	1966	2.50	5.00	10.00
❏ 1576	You're Lying/Give It To Me	1967	2.00	4.00	8.00
❏ 1585	6-5-4-3-2-1/Anyway That You Want Me	1967	2.00	4.00	8.00
❏ 1593	Night of the Long Grass/Girl in Black	1967	2.00	4.00	8.00
❏ 1607	Love Is All Around/When Will the Rain Come	1967	2.50	5.00	10.00
❏ 1622	You Can Cry If You Want To/There's Something About You	1968	2.00	4.00	8.00
❏ 1630	Surprise, Surprise/Cousin Jane	1968	2.00	4.00	8.00
❏ 1634	Hip Hip Hooray/Say Darlin'	1968	2.00	4.00	8.00
PAGE ONE
❏ 21026	Evil Woman/Heads Or Tails	1969	—	3.00	6.00
❏ 21030	Easy Lovin'/Give Me Something	1970	—	3.00	6.00
❏ 21032	Come Now/Lover	1970	—	3.00	6.00
❏ 21035	The Raver/You	1970	—	3.00	6.00
PRIVATE STOCK
❏ 45,102	Rolling Stone/(B-side unknown)	1976	—	2.50	5.00
PYE
❏ 65011	Feels Like a Woman/Everything's Funny	1972	2.00	4.00	8.00
❏ 71015	Good Vibrations/Push It Up to Me	1975	—	2.50	5.00

| ❏ 71035 | Summertime/Jerry Come Down | 1975 | — | 2.50 | 5.00 |
| ❏ 71054 | Satisfaction/(B-side unknown) | 1975 | — | 2.50 | 5.00 |
Albums
ATCO
| ❏ 33-193 [M] | Wild Thing | 1966 | 12.50 | 25.00 | 50.00 |
| ❏ SD 33-193 [R] | Wild Thing | 1966 | 10.00 | 20.00 | 40.00 |
FONTANA
| ❏ MGF 27556 [M] | Wild Thing/With a Girl Like You | 1966 | 10.00 | 20.00 | 40.00 |
—Contents identical to the Atco LP; two slightly different cover variations are known; record has mono number and plays mono; number "27556" in trail-off
| ❏ MGF 27556 [R] | Wild Thing/With a Girl Like You | 1966 | 7.50 | 15.00 | 30.00 |
—Contents identical to the Atco LP; two slightly different cover variations are known; record has mono number but plays in rechanneled stereo; number "2/67556" in trail-off
| ❏ SRF 67556 [R] | Wild Thing/With a Girl Like You | 1966 | 7.50 | 15.00 | 30.00 |
—Contents identical to the Atco LP; two slightly different cover variations are known
| ❏ SRF 67576 [R] | Love Is All Around | 1968 | 7.50 | 15.00 | 30.00 |
MKC
| ❏ 214 | Live at Max's Kansas City | 1980 | 3.00 | 6.00 | 12.00 |
PRIVATE STOCK
| ❏ PS-2008 | The Troggs Tapes | 1976 | 3.00 | 6.00 | 12.00 |
PYE
| ❏ 12112 | The Troggs | 1975 | 3.00 | 6.00 | 12.00 |
RHINO
| ❏ RNLP-118 | The Best of the Troggs | 1985 | 2.50 | 5.00 | 10.00 |
| ❏ R1 70118 | The Best of the Troggs | 1988 | 2.00 | 4.00 | 8.00 |
SIRE
| ❏ SASH-3714 [(2)] | The Vintage Years | 1976 | 3.75 | 7.50 | 15.00 |

TROLL, THE
45s
SMASH
| ❏ 2208 | Satin City News/Professor Potts' Pornographic Projector | 1969 | 3.00 | 6.00 | 12.00 |
Albums
SMASH
| ❏ SRS-67114 | Animated Music | 1969 | 12.50 | 25.00 | 50.00 |

TROLLS, THE
45s
ABC
❏ 10823	Every Day and Every Night/Are You the One	1966	3.00	6.00	12.00
❏ 10884	Laughing All the Way/Someone Here Inside	1966	2.50	5.00	10.00
❏ 10916	They Don't Know/There Was a Time	1967	2.50	5.00	10.00
❏ 10952	Baby. What You Ain't Got (I Ain't in Need)/Who Was That Boy	1967	2.50	5.00	10.00
RUFF
❏ 1010	Into My Arms/That's the Way My Love Is	1966	10.00	20.00	40.00
U.S.A.
❏ 905	I Got to Have You/Don't Come Around	1968	6.25	12.50	25.00
WARRIOR
❏ 173	Stupid Girl/I Don't Recall	1967	3.00	6.00	12.00
❏ 173 [PS]	Stupid Girl/I Don't Recall	1967	5.00	10.00	20.00

TROMBONES UNLIMITED
45s
LIBERTY
❏ 55874	The Phoenix Love Theme/Daydream	1966	2.00	4.00	8.00
❏ 55908	You're Gonna Hear from Me/Modesty	1966	2.00	4.00	8.00
❏ 55980	A Night in Israel (Or, We Spent a Week There One Monday Night)/Holiday for Trombones	1967	2.00	4.00	8.00
Albums
LIBERTY
❏ LRP-3449 [M]	These Bones are Made for Walking	1966	3.75	7.50	15.00
❏ LRP-3472 [M]	You're Gonna Hear From Me	1966	3.75	7.50	15.00
❏ LRP-3494 [M]	Big Boss Bones	1967	5.00	10.00	20.00
❏ LRP-3527 [M]	Holiday for Trombones	1967	5.00	10.00	20.00
❏ LRP-3549 [M]	One of Those Songs	1968	6.25	12.50	25.00
❏ LST-7449 [S]	These Bones are Made for Walking	1966	5.00	10.00	20.00
❏ LST-7472 [S]	You're Gonna Hear From Me	1966	5.00	10.00	20.00
❏ LST-7494 [S]	Big Boss Bones	1967	3.75	7.50	15.00
❏ LST-7527 [S]	Holiday for Trombones	1967	3.75	7.50	15.00
❏ LST-7549 [S]	One of Those Songs	1968	3.75	7.50	15.00
❏ LST-7592 [S]	Grazing in the Grass	1968	3.75	7.50	15.00

TROPHIES, THE More than one group?
45s
CHALLENGE
❏ 9133	Desire/Doggone It	1962	15.00	30.00	60.00
❏ 9149	Peg O' My Heart/I Laughed So Hard I Cried	1962	3.75	7.50	15.00
❏ 9170	That's All I Want from You/Felicia	1962	3.75	7.50	15.00
KAPP
❏ 714	Everywhere I Go/Baby Don't Live Here Anymore	1965	3.75	7.50	15.00
❏ 750	Leave My Girl Alone/You're the Queen	1966	3.75	7.50	15.00
NORK
❏ 79907	Walkin' the Dog/Somethin' Blue	196?	5.00	10.00	20.00

TROUBADOURS DE ROI BAUDOUIN
Albums
PHILIPS
| ❏ PCC 206 [M] | Missa Luba | 1963 | 3.75 | 7.50 | 15.00 |
| ❏ PCC 606 [S] | Missa Luba | 1963 | 3.75 | 7.50 | 15.00 |
—Released in '63, this didn't chart until 1969

TROWER, ROBIN Also see JACK BRUCE/ROBIN TROWER; PROCOL HARUM.
12-Inch Singles
ATLANTIC
| ❏ PR 2251 [DJ] | Shattered (LP version)/Shattered (Live Version) | 1988 | 2.00 | 4.00 | 8.00 |
| ❏ PR 2374 [DJ] | Love Won't Wait Forever (same on both sides) | 1988 | — | 3.00 | 6.00 |
GNP CRESCENDO
❏ PRO-1 [DJ]	Secret Doors (same on both sides)	1986	2.00	4.00	8.00
❏ PRO-2 [DJ]	No Time (same on both sides)	1987	2.00	4.00	8.00
❏ PRO-3 [DJ]	Caroline (same on both sides)	1987	2.00	4.00	8.00
45s
CHRYSALIS
| ❏ 2009 | Man of the World/Take a Fast Train | 1973 | — | 3.00 | 6.00 |
| ❏ 2113 | Too Rolling Stoned (Part 1)/Too Rolling Stoned (Part 2) | 1976 | — | 3.00 | 6.00 |

Number	Title (A Side/B Side)	Yr	VG	VG+	NM
❏ 2122	Caledonia/Messin' the Blues	1976	—	3.00	6.00
❏ 2172	Sweet Wine of Love/In City Dreams	1977	—	2.50	5.00
❏ 2206	Somebody Calling/Bluebird	1978	—	2.50	5.00
❏ 2238	My Love (Burning Love)/(B-side unknown)	1978	—	2.50	5.00
❏ 2272	It's for You/Birthday Boy	1979	—	2.50	5.00

Albums
ATLANTIC

Number	Title (A Side/B Side)	Yr	VG	VG+	NM
❏ 81838	Take What You Need	1988	2.50	5.00	10.00
❏ 82080	In the Line of Fire	1990	3.00	6.00	12.00

CHRYSALIS

Number	Title (A Side/B Side)	Yr	VG	VG+	NM
❏ CHR 1039	Twice Removed from Yesterday	1973	3.00	6.00	12.00
—Green label, "3300 Warner Blvd." address					
❏ CHR 1039	Twice Removed from Yesterday	1977	2.50	5.00	10.00
—Blue label, New York address					
❏ CHR 1057	Bridge of Sighs	1974	3.00	6.00	12.00
—Green label, "3300 Warner Blvd." address					
❏ CHR 1057	Bridge of Sighs	1977	2.50	5.00	10.00
—Blue label, New York address					
❏ CHR 1073	For Earth Below	1975	3.00	6.00	12.00
—Green label, "3300 Warner Blvd." address					
❏ CHR 1073	For Earth Below	1977	2.50	5.00	10.00
—Blue label, New York address					
❏ CHR 1089	Robin Trower Live!	1976	3.00	6.00	12.00
—Green label, "3300 Warner Blvd." address					
❏ CHR 1089	Robin Trower Live!	1977	2.50	5.00	10.00
—Blue label, New York address					
❏ CHR 1107	Long Misty Days	1976	3.00	6.00	12.00
—Green label, "3300 Warner Blvd." address					
❏ CHR 1107	Long Misty Days	1977	2.50	5.00	10.00
—Blue label, New York address					
❏ CHR 1148	In City Dreams	1977	3.00	6.00	12.00
❏ CHR 1189	Caravan to Midnight	1978	3.00	6.00	12.00
❏ CHR 1215	Victims of the Fury	1980	3.00	6.00	12.00
❏ CHR 1324	B.L.T.	1981	2.50	5.00	10.00
❏ PV 41039	Twice Removed from Yesterday	1983	2.00	4.00	8.00
—Reissue					
❏ FV 41057	Bridge of Sighs	1984	2.00	4.00	8.00
—Reissue					
❏ PV 41057	Bridge of Sighs	1986	2.00	4.00	8.00
—Reissue					
❏ PV 41073	For Earth Below	1984	2.00	4.00	8.00
—Reissue					
❏ PV 41089	Robin Trower Live!	1983	2.00	4.00	8.00
—Reissue					
❏ PV 41107	Long Misty Days	1983	2.00	4.00	8.00
—Reissue					
❏ PV 41148	In City Dreams	1984	2.00	4.00	8.00
—Reissue					
❏ PV 41189	Caravan to Midnight	1984	2.00	4.00	8.00
—Reissue					
❏ PV 41215	Victims of the Fury	1983	2.00	4.00	8.00
—Reissue					
❏ PV 41324	B.L.T.	1984	2.00	4.00	8.00
—Reissue					
❏ FV 41420	Back It Up	1983	2.50	5.00	10.00
❏ PV 41420	Back It Up	1986	2.00	4.00	8.00
—Reissue					

GNP CRESCENDO

Number	Title (A Side/B Side)	Yr	VG	VG+	NM
❏ 2187	Passion	1986	2.50	5.00	10.00

PASSPORT

Number	Title (A Side/B Side)	Yr	VG	VG+	NM
❏ PB-6049	Beyond the Mist	1985	2.50	5.00	10.00

TROY, BILLY
45s
BARNABY

Number	Title (A Side/B Side)	Yr	VG	VG+	NM
❏ ZS7 2035	Longer Than Awhile/My Nancy's Love	1971	2.00	4.00	8.00
❏ ZS7 2054	Isn't It Lonely Together/Sally's Sayin' Somethin'	1971	2.00	4.00	8.00

TROY, DORIS
45s
APPLE

Number	Title (A Side/B Side)	Yr	VG	VG+	NM
❏ 1820	Ain't That Cute/Vaya Con Dios	1970	2.00	4.00	8.00
❏ 1824	Jacob's Ladder/Get Back	1970	2.00	4.00	8.00

ATLANTIC

Number	Title (A Side/B Side)	Yr	VG	VG+	NM
❏ 2188	Just One Look/Bossa Nova Blues	1963	5.00	10.00	20.00
❏ 2206	Tomorrow Is Another Day/What'cha Gonna Do About It	1963	3.00	6.00	12.00
❏ 2222	One More Chance/Please Little Angel	1964	3.00	6.00	12.00
❏ 2269	Hurry/He Don't Belong to Me	1965	3.00	6.00	12.00

CALLA

Number	Title (A Side/B Side)	Yr	VG	VG+	NM
❏ 114	Heartaches/I'll Do Anything	1966	5.00	10.00	20.00

CAPITOL

Number	Title (A Side/B Side)	Yr	VG	VG+	NM
❏ 2043	Face Up to the Truth/He's Qualified	1967	2.00	4.00	8.00

MIDLAND INT'L.

Number	Title (A Side/B Side)	Yr	VG	VG+	NM
❏ MB-10806	Lyin' Eyes/Give God Glory	1976	—	2.50	5.00
❏ MB-11082	Can't Hold On/Another Look	1977	—	2.50	5.00

Albums
APPLE

Number	Title (A Side/B Side)	Yr	VG	VG+	NM
❏ ST-3371	Doris Troy	1970	6.25	12.50	25.00

ATLANTIC

Number	Title (A Side/B Side)	Yr	VG	VG+	NM
❏ 8088 [M]	Just One Look	1964	7.50	15.00	30.00
❏ SD 8088 [P]	Just One Look	1964	12.50	25.00	50.00
—The title song is rechanneled					

TROYKA
Albums
COTILLION

Number	Title (A Side/B Side)	Yr	VG	VG+	NM
❏ SD 9020	Troyka	1970	7.50	15.00	30.00

TRU-TONES, THE
45s
CHART

Number	Title (A Side/B Side)	Yr	VG	VG+	NM
❏ 634	Tears in My Eyes/Magic	1957	200.00	400.00	800.00

DEN RIC

Number	Title (A Side/B Side)	Yr	VG	VG+	NM
❏ 4527	I'm the Guy/(B-side unknown)	196?	10.00	20.00	40.00

KEB

Number	Title (A Side/B Side)	Yr	VG	VG+	NM
❏ 6037	Soldier's Last Letter/(B-side unknown)	196?	10.00	20.00	40.00

TRUELEERS, THE
45s
CHECKER

Number	Title (A Side/B Side)	Yr	VG	VG+	NM
❏ 1026	Forget About Him/Waiting for You	1962	3.00	6.00	12.00

TRUMPETEERS, THE (1) Gospel group. Also known as "The CBS Trumpeteers."
45s
IMPERIAL

Number	Title (A Side/B Side)	Yr	VG	VG+	NM
❏ 5972	Milky White Way/Leave That Lie Alone	1963	3.75	7.50	15.00
❏ 5994	Seven Angels/Just a Little Walk with Jesus	1963	3.75	7.50	15.00

JUBILEE

Number	Title (A Side/B Side)	Yr	VG	VG+	NM
❏ 5654	Milky White Way/Prayer for Today	1969	2.50	5.00	10.00
—As "The CBS Trumpeteers"					

NASHBORO

Number	Title (A Side/B Side)	Yr	VG	VG+	NM
❏ 788	God Is Coming/One Day I Was Walking	1963	3.75	7.50	15.00
—As "The CBS Trumpeteers"					
❏ 805	Everything Moves/My Heart Bubbles Over	1964	3.75	7.50	15.00
—As "The CBS Trumpeteers"					
❏ 887	Little Wooden Church/Lord, Ease My Weary Mind	1966	3.75	7.50	15.00
—As "The CBS Trumpeteers"					

OKEH

Number	Title (A Side/B Side)	Yr	VG	VG+	NM
❏ 6871	Don't Miss That Train/Home Don't Seem Like Home	1952	25.00	50.00	100.00
❏ 6890	I'll Fly Away/Leave It in His Hands	1953	25.00	50.00	100.00

TRUMPETEERS, THE (2) For records on Splash, see BILLY MURE.

TRYTHALL, GIL
45s
ATHENA

Number	Title (A Side/B Side)	Yr	VG	VG+	NM
❏ 5013	Yakety Moog/Foggy Mountain Breakdown	1970	—	3.00	6.00

Albums
ATHENA

Number	Title (A Side/B Side)	Yr	VG	VG+	NM
❏ 6003	Switched On Nashville/Country Moog	1970	3.00	6.00	12.00
❏ 6004	Nashville Gold	1970	3.00	6.00	12.00

TUBB, ERNEST
45s
CACHET

Number	Title (A Side/B Side)	Yr	VG	VG+	NM
❏ 4501	Waltz Across Texas/Jealous Loving Heart	1979	—	3.00	6.00
❏ 4507	Walking the Floor Over You/Let's Say Goodbye Like We Said Hello	1979	—	3.00	6.00
—A-side with Merle Haggard					

COLLECTABLES

Number	Title (A Side/B Side)	Yr	VG	VG+	NM
❏ 90214	Waltz Across Texas/Walking the Floor Over You	199?	—	—	3.00
—Reissue					

DECCA

Number	Title (A Side/B Side)	Yr	VG	VG+	NM
❏ 25758	Blue Christmas/White Christmas	196?	2.00	4.00	8.00
—Reissue					
❏ 9-28067	Somebody's Stolen My Honey/My Mother Must Have Been a Girl Like You	1952	5.00	10.00	20.00
❏ 9-28310	Fortunes in Memories/So Many Times	1952	5.00	10.00	20.00
❏ 9-28448	Somebody Loves You/Don't Trifle on Your Sweetheart	1952	5.00	10.00	20.00
❏ 9-28453	Merry Texas Christmas, You All/Blue Snowflakes	1952	6.25	12.50	25.00
❏ 9-28550	Dear Judge/I Will Miss You When You Go	1953	5.00	10.00	20.00
❏ 9-28630	Hank It Will Never Be the Same Without You/Beyond the Sunset	1953	7.50	15.00	30.00
❏ 9-28696	Jimmie Rodgers' Last Thoughts/When Jimmie Said Goodbye	1953	6.25	12.50	25.00
❏ 9-28777	Don't Brush Them on Me/My Wasted Past	1953	5.00	10.00	20.00
❏ 9-28837	A Dear John Letter/The Mean Age, In Between Age Blues	1953	5.00	10.00	20.00
—As "Bill and Ernest Tubb"					
❏ 9-28869	Divorce Granted/Counterfeit Kisses	1953	5.00	10.00	20.00
❏ 9-28946	I'm Trimming My Christmas Tree with Teardrops/We Need God for Christmas	1953	5.00	10.00	20.00
❏ 9-29011	Honky Tonk Heart/I'm Not Looking for an Angel	1954	5.00	10.00	20.00
❏ 9-29020	Jealous Loving Heart/Till We Two Are One	1954	5.00	10.00	20.00
❏ 9-29103	Baby Your Mother (Like She Babies You)/Your Mother, Your Darling, Your Friend	1954	6.25	12.50	25.00
❏ 9-29220	Two Glasses, Joe/Journey's End	1954	5.00	10.00	20.00
❏ 9-29350	I'll Be Walkin' the Floor This Christmas/Lonely Christmas Eve	1954	5.00	10.00	20.00
❏ 9-29415	Kansas City Blues/The Woman's Touch	1955	3.75	7.50	15.00
❏ 9-29520	It's a Lonely World/Have You Seen My Boogie Woogie Baby	1955	3.75	7.50	15.00
❏ 9-29624	I Met a Friend/When Jesus Calls	1955	3.75	7.50	15.00
❏ 9-29633	The Yellow Rose of Texas/A Million Miles from Here	1955	3.75	7.50	15.00
❏ 9-29731	Thirty Days (To Come Back Home)/Answer the Phone	1955	5.00	10.00	20.00
❏ 9-29836	So Doggone Lonesome/If I Never Have Anything Else	1956	3.75	7.50	15.00
❏ 9-29934	Jimmie Rodgers' Last Blue Yodel/Will You Be Satisfied That Way	1956	3.75	7.50	15.00
❏ 9-30098	Treat Her Right/Loving You Is My Weakness	1956	3.75	7.50	15.00
❏ 9-30219	Don't Forbid Me/God's Eye	1957	3.75	7.50	15.00
❏ 9-30305	Mister Love/Leave Me	1957	3.75	7.50	15.00
❏ 9-30422	My Treasure/Go Home	1957	3.75	7.50	15.00
❏ 9-30526	Geisha Girl/I Found My Girl in the U.S.A.	1957	3.75	7.50	15.00
❏ 9-30549	House of Glass/Heaven Help Me	1958	3.75	7.50	15.00
❏ 9-30610	Hey, Mr. Bluebird/How Do We Know	1958	3.75	7.50	15.00
❏ 9-30685	Half a Mind/The Blues	1958	3.75	7.50	15.00
❏ 9-30759	What Am I Living For/Goodbye Sunshine, Hello Blues	1958	3.75	7.50	15.00
❏ 9-30872	I Cried a Tear/I'd Rather Be	1959	3.75	7.50	15.00
❏ 9-30952	Next Time/What I Know About Her	1959	3.75	7.50	15.00
❏ 9-31082	Live It Up/Accidentally on Purpose	1960	3.00	6.00	12.00
❏ 9-31119	Ev'rybody's Somebody's Fool/Let the Little Girl Dance	1960	3.00	6.00	12.00
❏ 31161	White Silver Sands/A Guy Named Joe	1960	3.00	6.00	12.00
❏ 31196	Girl from Abilene/Little Old Band of Gold	1961	3.00	6.00	12.00
❏ 31241	Thoughts of a Fool/Don't Just Stand There	1961	3.00	6.00	12.00
❏ 31300	Through That Door/What Will You Tell Them	1961	3.00	6.00	12.00

T

Number	Title (A Side/B Side)	Yr	VG	VG+	NM
❑ 31334	Christmas Is Just Another Day for Me/				
	Rudolph the Red-Nosed Reindeer	1961	3.00	6.00	12.00
❑ 31357	Go to Sleep Conscience (Don't Hurt Me This				
	Time)/I Could Never Say No	1962	3.00	6.00	12.00
❑ 31399	I'm Looking High and Low for My Baby/				
	Show Her Lots of Gold	1962	3.00	6.00	12.00
❑ 31428	House of Sorrow/No Letter Today	1962	3.00	6.00	12.00
❑ 31476	Mr. Juke Box/Walking the Floor Over You	1963	3.00	6.00	12.00
❑ 31526	Thanks a Lot/The Way That You're Living	1963	3.00	6.00	12.00
❑ 31614	Be Better to Your Baby/				
	Think of Me, Thinking of You	1964	2.50	5.00	10.00
❑ 31706	Pass the Booze/(A Memory)				
	That's All You'll Ever Be to Me	1964	2.50	5.00	10.00
❑ 31742	Do What You Do Well/Turn Around, Walk Away	1965	2.50	5.00	10.00
❑ 31824	Waltz Across Texas/Lots of Luck	1965	2.50	5.00	10.00
❑ 31861	It's for God, and Country, and You Mom (That's				
	Why I'm Fighting in Viet Nam)/				
	After the Boy Gets the Girl	1965	2.50	5.00	10.00
❑ 31866	Who's Gonna Be Your Santa Claus This Year/				
	Blue Christmas Tree	1965	2.50	5.00	10.00
❑ 31908	Till Me Getup Has Gotup and Gone/				
	Just One More	1966	2.50	5.00	10.00
❑ 32022	Another Story/There's No Room in My Heart				
	(For the Blues)	1966	2.50	5.00	10.00
❑ 32131	In the Jailhouse Now/				
	Yesterday's Winner Is a Loser Today	1967	2.50	5.00	10.00
❑ 32237	Too Much of Not Enough/				
	Nothing Is Better Than You	1968	2.00	4.00	8.00
❑ 32315	I'm Gonna Make Like a Snake/				
	Mama, Who Was That Man	1968	2.00	4.00	8.00
❑ 32377	Just Pack Up and Go/It Sure Helps a Lot	1968	2.00	4.00	8.00
❑ 32448	Saturday Satan Sunday Saint/Tommy's Doll	1969	2.00	4.00	8.00
❑ 32532	Just a Drink Away/One More Memory	1969	2.00	4.00	8.00
❑ 32632	It's America/Somebody Better Than Me	1970	2.00	4.00	8.00
❑ 32690	Dear Judge/A Good Year for the Wine	1970	2.00	4.00	8.00
❑ 32800	One Sweet Hello/Once Ole Going Gets a-Goin'	1971	2.00	4.00	8.00
❑ 32849	Don't Back a Man Up in a Corner/				
	Shenandoah Waltz	1971	2.00	4.00	8.00
❑ 32943	Say Something Nice to Sarah/				
	Teach My Daddy How to Pray	1972	2.00	4.00	8.00
❑ 33014	Baby, It's So Hard to Be Good/In This Corner	1972	2.00	4.00	8.00
❑ 7-34271 [S]	Rudolph the Red-Nosed Reindeer/				
	(B-side unknown)	1963	5.00	10.00	20.00
❑ 7-34272 [S]	White Christmas/Christmas Island	1963	5.00	10.00	20.00
❑ 7-34273 [S]	Blue Christmas/Merry Texas Christmas, You All	1963	5.00	10.00	20.00
❑ 7-34274 [S]	I'll Be Walking the Floor This Christmas/				
	Lonely Christmas	1963	5.00	10.00	20.00
❑ 7-34275 [S]	C-H-R-I-S-T-M-A-S/I'm Trimming the Christmas				
	Tree with Teardrops	1963	5.00	10.00	20.00

—The above five were a set issued to jukebox operators; each has a small hole and plays at 33 1/3 rpm

Number	Title (A Side/B Side)	Yr	VG	VG+	NM
❑ 38181 [S]	You Win Again/Do It Now	196?	5.00	10.00	20.00
❑ 38182 [S]	White Silver Sands/A Guy Named Joe	196?	5.00	10.00	20.00
❑ 38183 [S]	Mister Blues/Pick Me Up on Your Way Down	196?	5.00	10.00	20.00
❑ 38184 [S]	(titles unknown)	196?	5.00	10.00	20.00
❑ 38185 [S]	The Kind of Love She Gave to Me/				
	Why I'm Walkin'	196?	5.00	10.00	20.00

—The above five were a set issued to jukebox operators; each has a small hole and plays at 33 1/3 rpm

Number	Title (A Side/B Side)	Yr	VG	VG+	NM
❑ 38253 [S]	Candy Kisses/(B-side unknown)	196?	5.00	10.00	20.00

—Jukebox issue; small hole, plays at 33 1/3 rpm

Number	Title (A Side/B Side)	Yr	VG	VG+	NM
❑ 38303 [S]	Slipping Around/(B-side unknown)	196?	5.00	10.00	20.00
❑ 38304 [S]	Filipino Baby//(B-side unknown)	196?	5.00	10.00	20.00
❑ 38305 [S]	(titles unknown)	196?	5.00	10.00	20.00
❑ 38306 [S]	(titles unknown)	196?	5.00	10.00	20.00
❑ 38307 [S]	Rainbow at Midnight/(B-side unknown)	196?	5.00	10.00	20.00

—The above five were a set issued to jukebox operators; each has a small hole and plays at 33 1/3 rpm

Number	Title (A Side/B Side)	Yr	VG	VG+	NM
❑ 9-46006	Walking the Floor Over You/I'll Always Be Glad				
	to Take You Back	1950	10.00	20.00	40.00

—One of three discs included in "Album No. 9-146"; 78 first issued with this number in 1946; black label with lines on either side of "Decca"

Number	Title (A Side/B Side)	Yr	VG	VG+	NM
❑ 9-46018	Rainbow at Midnight/I Don't Blame You	1950	10.00	20.00	40.00

—78 first issued in 1946

Number	Title (A Side/B Side)	Yr	VG	VG+	NM
❑ 9-46186	White Christmas/Blue Christmas	1950	7.50	15.00	30.00

—78 first issued in 1949; black label, lines on either side of "Decca"

Number	Title (A Side/B Side)	Yr	VG	VG+	NM
❑ 9-46243	Throw Your Love My Way/Give Me an Old				
	Fashioned Love	1950	10.00	20.00	40.00
❑ 9-46257	You Don't Have to Be a Baby to Cry/G-I-R-L				
	Spells Trouble	1950	7.50	15.00	30.00
❑ 9-46268	Christmas Island/Christmas	1950	7.50	15.00	30.00

—Black label, lines on either side of "Decca"

Number	Title (A Side/B Side)	Yr	VG	VG+	NM
❑ 9-46269	(Remember Me) I'm the One Who Loves You/I				
	Need Attention Bad	1950	7.50	15.00	30.00
❑ 9-46289	Tomorrow Never Comes/				
	Are You Waiting Just for Me	1951	6.25	12.50	25.00
❑ 9-46295	When It's Prayer Meetin' Time in the Hollow/May				
	the Good Lord Bless and Keep You	1951	6.25	12.50	25.00
❑ 9-46296	Don't Stay Too Long/If You Want Some Lovin'	1951	6.25	12.50	25.00
❑ 9-46306	Mother, Queen of My Heart/I'm Lonely and Blue	1951	5.00	10.00	20.00
❑ 9-46307	Why Did You Give Me Your Love/I'm Free from				
	the Blues	1951	5.00	10.00	20.00
❑ 9-46308	Hobo's Meditation/Why Should I Be Lonely	1951	5.00	10.00	20.00
❑ 9-46309	Any Old Time/A Drunkard's Child	1951	5.00	10.00	20.00

—The above four comprise a box set

Number	Title (A Side/B Side)	Yr	VG	VG+	NM
❑ 9-46338	Hey La La/Precious Little Baby	1951	6.25	12.50	25.00
❑ 9-46343	Rose of the Mountain/I'm With the Crowd, But				
	So Alone	1951	6.25	12.50	25.00
❑ 9-46377	Driftwood on the River/				
	I'm Stepping Out of the Picture	1951	6.25	12.50	25.00
❑ 9-46389	Missing in Action/				
	A Heartsick Soldier on Heartbreak Ridge	1952	6.25	12.50	25.00

DECCA FAITH SERIES

Number	Title (A Side/B Side)	Yr	VG	VG+	NM
❑ 9-14506	Stand By Me/				
	When I Take My Vacation in Heaven	1950	10.00	20.00	40.00
❑ 9-14515	What a Friend We Have in Jesus/				
	The Wonderful City	1950	10.00	20.00	40.00
❑ 9-14532	Farther Along/The Old Rugged Cross	1951	7.50	15.00	30.00
❑ 9-14561	When It's Prayer Meetin' Time in the Hollow/May				
	the Good Lord Bless and Keep You	1951	7.50	15.00	30.00

FIRST GENERATION

Number	Title (A Side/B Side)	Yr	VG	VG+	NM
❑ 001	Sometimes I Do/Half My Heart's in Texas	1977	—	3.50	7.00
❑ 002	Journey's End/A Month of Sundays	1977	—	3.50	7.00
❑ 006	Thanks a Lot/Half a Mind	1978	—	3.50	7.00

MCA

Number	Title (A Side/B Side)	Yr	VG	VG+	NM
❑ 40056	I've Got All the Heartaches I Can Handle/				
	The Texas Troubadour	1973	—	3.00	6.00
❑ 40222	Anything But This/				
	Don't Water Down the Bad News	1974	—	3.00	6.00
❑ 40436	If You Don't Quit Checkin' on Me (I'm Checkin'				
	Out on You)/I'd Like to Live It Again	1975	—	3.00	6.00
❑ 60078	Waltz Across Texas/Walking the Floor Over You	1973	—	2.50	5.00

—Reissue

Number	Title (A Side/B Side)	Yr	VG	VG+	NM
❑ 65024	White Christmas/Blue Christmas	1973	—	2.00	4.00

—Black label with rainbow

Number	Title (A Side/B Side)	Yr	VG	VG+	NM
❑ 65024	White Christmas/Blue Christmas	1980	—	—	3.00

—Blue label with rainbow

RHINO

Number	Title (A Side/B Side)	Yr	VG	VG+	NM
❑ 74415	Walking the Floor Over You/Thanks a Lot	1991	—	3.00	6.00

—Red vinyl

Number	Title (A Side/B Side)	Yr	VG	VG+	NM
❑ 74415	Walking the Floor Over You/Thanks a Lot	1991	—	3.50	7.00

—Blue vinyl

Number	Title (A Side/B Side)	Yr	VG	VG+	NM
❑ 74415	Walking the Floor Over You/Thanks a Lot	1991	3.00	6.00	12.00

—Black vinyl

Number	Title (A Side/B Side)	Yr	VG	VG+	NM
❑ 74415 [PS]	Walking the Floor Over You/Thanks a Lot	1991	—	3.00	6.00

7-Inch Extended Plays

DECCA

Number	Title (A Side/B Side)	Yr	VG	VG+	NM
❑ ED 2026	Filipino Baby/Till the End of the World//				
	Seaman's Blues/Slipping Around	195?	6.25	12.50	25.00
❑ ED 2026 [PS]	Ernest Tubb Sings	195?	6.25	12.50	25.00
❑ ED 2089	(contents unknown)	195?	6.25	12.50	25.00
❑ ED 2089 [PS]	White Christmas	195?	6.25	12.50	25.00
❑ ED 2356	Walking the Floor Over You/I'll Always Be Glad				
	to Take You Back//Rainbow at Midnight/				
	I Don't Blame You	1956	5.00	10.00	20.00
❑ ED 2356 [PS]	Ernest Tubb Favorites, Vol. 1	1956	5.00	10.00	20.00
❑ ED 2357	*Have You Ever Been Lonely/Let's Say				
	Goodbye Like We Said Hello/				
	Try Me One More Time/Soldier's Last Letter	1956	5.00	10.00	20.00
❑ ED 2357 [PS]	Ernest Tubb Favorites, Vol. 2	1956	5.00	10.00	20.00
❑ ED 2521	You're Breaking My Heart/I Know My Baby				
	Loves Me in Her Own Peculiar Way//I've Got				
	the Blues for Mammy				
	This Troubled Mind o' Mine	1957	5.00	10.00	20.00
❑ ED 2521 [PS]	The Daddy of 'Em All	1957	5.00	10.00	20.00
❑ ED 2522	I Dreamed of an Old Love Affair/Mississippi Gal/				
	/When a Soldier Knocks and Finds Nobody				
	Home/Daisy May	1957	5.00	10.00	20.00
❑ ED 2522 [PS]	Encores	1957	5.00	10.00	20.00
❑ ED 2523	I Knew the Moment I Lost You/You're the Only				
	Good Thing (That's Happened to Me)//				
	My Hillbilly Baby/				
	There's No Fool Like a Young Fool	1957	5.00	10.00	20.00
❑ ED 2523 [PS]	My Hillbilly Baby	1957	5.00	10.00	20.00
❑ ED 2563	Geisha Girl/I Found My Girl in the U.S.A.//Home				
	of the Blues/Tangled Mind	1958	5.00	10.00	20.00
❑ ED 2563 [PS]	Ernest Tubb Sings the Hits	1958	5.00	10.00	20.00
❑ ED 2626	House of Glass/My Treasure//Treat Her Right/				
	Don't Forbid Me	1959	5.00	10.00	20.00
❑ ED 2626 [PS]	Ernest Tubb	1959	5.00	10.00	20.00
❑ ED 2627	*Mister Love/Leave Me/				
	Hey Mr. Bluebird/How Do I Know	1959	5.00	10.00	20.00
❑ ED 2627 [PS]	Ernest Tubb and the Wilburn Brothers	1959	5.00	10.00	20.00
❑ ED 2643	*I'm a Long Gone Daddy/San Antonio Rose//				
	Your Cheatin' Heart/				
	It Makes No Difference Now	1959	5.00	10.00	20.00
❑ ED 2643	The Importance of Being Ernest	1959	5.00	10.00	20.00
❑ ED 2655 [M]	Have You Ever Been Lonely (Have You Ever				
	Been Blue)/Rainbow at Midnight//Careless				
	Darlin'/You Nearly Lose Your Mind	1959	5.00	10.00	20.00
❑ ED 2655 [PS]	More Ernest Tubb	1959	5.00	10.00	20.00
❑ ED 7-2655 [PS]	The Ernest Tubb Story	1959	7.50	15.00	30.00
❑ ED 7-2655 [S]	*Have You Ever Been Lonely/Rainbow at				
	Midnight/Careless Darlin'/				
	You Nearly Lost Your Mind	1959	7.50	15.00	30.00
❑ ED 2680	*He'll Have to Go/White Silver Sands/Am I That				
	Easy to Forget/Guy Named Joe	1960	5.00	10.00	20.00
❑ ED 2680 [PS]	The Ernest Tubb Record Shop	1960	5.00	10.00	20.00
❑ ED 2691	*Ev'rybody's Somebody's Fool/Let the Little Girl				
	Dance/Live It Up/Accidentally on Purpose	1960	5.00	10.00	20.00
❑ ED 2691 [PS]	Ernest Tubb	1960	5.00	10.00	20.00
❑ ED 2706	(contents unknown)	1962	5.00	10.00	20.00
❑ ED 2706 [PS]	(contents unknown)	1962	5.00	10.00	20.00
❑ ED 2718	*What Will You Tell Them/Thoughts of a Fool/				
	Go to Sleep Conscience/I Never Could Say No	1961	5.00	10.00	20.00
❑ ED 2718 [PS]	Ernest Tubb	1961	5.00	10.00	20.00
❑ ED 2728	*Show Her Lots of Gold/I'm Looking High and				
	Low for My Baby/I Walk the Line/Crazy Arms	1962	6.25	12.50	25.00
❑ ED 2728 [PS]	Show Her Lots of Gold	1962	6.25	12.50	25.00
❑ ED 2739	*No Letter Today/Women Make a Fool Out of				
	Me/House of Sorrow/Go On Home	1963	6.25	12.50	25.00
❑ ED 2739 [PS]	Ernest Tubb	1963	6.25	12.50	25.00
❑ ED 2769	(contents unknown)	1964	6.25	12.50	25.00
❑ ED 2769 [PS]	Ernest Tubb	1964	6.25	12.50	25.00
❑ ED 2774	*Thanks a Lot/Mr. Juke Box/Last Letter/Just Call				
	Me Lonesome	1964	6.25	12.50	25.00
❑ ED 2774 [PS]	Thanks a Lot	1964	6.25	12.50	25.00
❑ ED 2787	(contents unknown)	1965	7.50	15.00	30.00
❑ ED 2787 [PS]	Be Better to Your Baby	1965	7.50	15.00	30.00
❑ ED 2797	(contents unknown)	1965	7.50	15.00	30.00
❑ ED 2797 [PS]	Pass the Booze	1965	7.50	15.00	30.00
❑ 7-4518 [PS]	Blue Christmas	1964	3.75	7.50	15.00
❑ 7-4518 [S]	(contents unknown)	1964	3.75	7.50	15.00

—33 1/3 rpm, small hole jukebox edition

Number	Title (A Side/B Side)	Yr	VG	VG+	NM
Albums					
CACHET					
❏ 33001	Ernest Tubb: The Legend and the Legacy, Volume One	1979	3.00	6.00	12.00
DECCA					
❏ DXA 159 [(2)M]	The Ernest Tubb Story	1959	20.00	40.00	80.00
—Deduct 25 percent if book is missing					
❏ DL 4046 [M]	All Time Hits	1961	7.50	15.00	30.00
❏ DL 4064 [M]	The Ernest Tubb Record Shop	1960	10.00	20.00	40.00
❏ DL 4118 [M]	Ernest Tubb's Golden Favorites	1961	7.50	15.00	30.00
❏ DL 4321 [M]	On Tour	1962	6.25	12.50	25.00
❏ DL 4385 [M]	Just Call Me Lonesome	1962	6.25	12.50	25.00
❏ DL 4397 [M]	The Family Bible	1963	6.25	12.50	25.00
❏ DL 4514 [M]	Thanks a Lot	1964	6.25	12.50	25.00
❏ DL 4518 [M]	Blue Christmas	1963	6.25	12.50	25.00
❏ DL 4640 [M]	My Pick of the Hits	1965	6.25	12.50	25.00
❏ DL 4681 [M]	Hittin' the Road	1965	6.25	12.50	25.00
❏ DL 4746 [M]	By Request	1966	6.25	12.50	25.00
❏ DL 4772 [M]	Ernest Tubb Sings Country Hits Old & New	1966	6.25	12.50	25.00
❏ DL 4867 [M]	Another Story	1967	7.50	15.00	30.00
❏ DL 4957 [M]	Ernest Tubb Sings Hank Williams	1968	12.50	25.00	50.00
❏ DL 5006 [M]	Ernest Tubb's Greatest Hits	1968	20.00	40.00	80.00
—White label promo only					
❏ DL 5301 [10]	Ernest Tubb Favorites	1951	37.50	75.00	150.00
❏ DL 5334 [10]	The Old Rugged Cross	1951	37.50	75.00	150.00
❏ DL 5336 [10]	Jimmie Rodgers Songs Sung by Ernest Tubb	1951	37.50	75.00	150.00
❏ DL 5497 [10]	Sing a Song of Christmas	1951	37.50	75.00	150.00
❏ DXSA 7159 [(2)R]	The Ernest Tubb Story	196?	7.50	15.00	30.00
—Deduct 25 percent if book is missing					
❏ DL 8291 [M]	Ernest Tubb Favorites	1955	17.50	35.00	70.00
❏ DL 8553 [M]	The Daddy of 'Em All	1956	17.50	35.00	70.00
❏ DL 8834 [M]	The Importance of Being Ernest	1959	12.50	25.00	50.00
❏ DL 74046 [S]	All Time Hits	1961	10.00	20.00	40.00
❏ DL 74064 [S]	The Ernest Tubb Record Shop	1960	12.50	25.00	50.00
❏ DL 74118 [S]	Ernest Tubb's Golden Favorites	1961	10.00	2.00	40.00
❏ DL 74321 [S]	On Tour	1962	7.50	15.00	30.00
❏ DL 74385 [S]	Just Call Me Lonesome	1962	7.50	15.00	30.00
❏ DL 74397 [S]	The Family Bible	1963	7.50	15.00	30.00
❏ DL 74514 [S]	Thanks a Lot	1964	7.50	15.00	30.00
❏ DL 74518 [S]	Blue Christmas	1963	7.50	15.00	30.00
❏ DL 74640 [S]	My Pick of the Hits	1965	7.50	15.00	30.00
❏ DL 74681 [S]	Hittin' the Road	1965	7.50	15.00	30.00
❏ DL 74746 [S]	By Request	1966	7.50	15.00	30.00
❏ DL 74772 [S]	Ernest Tubb Sings Country Hits Old & New	1966	7.50	15.00	30.00
❏ DL 74867 [S]	Another Story	1967	6.25	12.50	25.00
❏ DL 74957 [S]	Ernest Tubb Sings Hank Williams	1968	6.25	12.50	25.00
❏ DL 75006 [S]	Ernest Tubb's Greatest Hits	1968	6.25	12.50	25.00
❏ DL 75072	Country Hit Time	1968	5.00	10.00	20.00
❏ DL 75114	Let's Turn Back the Years	1969	3.75	7.50	15.00
❏ DL 75122	Saturday Satan, Sunday Saint	1969	5.00	10.00	20.00
❏ DL 75222	A Great Year for the Wine	1970	5.00	10.00	20.00
❏ DL 75252	Ernest Tubb's Greatest Hits, Vol. 2	1970	5.00	10.00	20.00
❏ DL 75301	One Sweet Hello	1971	5.00	10.00	20.00
❏ DL 75345	Say Something Nice to Sarah	1972	5.00	10.00	20.00
❏ DL 75388	Baby, It's So Hard to Be Good	1972	5.00	10.00	20.00
❏ DL 78834 [S]	The Importance of Being Ernest	1959	15.00	30.00	60.00
FIRST GENERATION					
❏ LP-0002 [(2)]	The Legend and the Legacy	1979	10.00	20.00	40.00
—With ad for Ernest Tubb Record Shop on back cover					
❏ LP-0002 [(2)]	The Legend and the Legacy	1979	12.50	25.00	50.00
—No ads on back cover					
❏ TV-1033 [(2)]	The Legend and the Legacy	1979	6.25	12.50	25.00
—Mail-order version					
MCA					
❏ 16	Ernest Tubb's Greatest Hits	1973	3.00	6.00	12.00
—Reissue of Decca 75006					
❏ 24	Ernest Tubb's Greatest Hits, Vol. 2	1973	3.00	6.00	12.00
—Reissue of Decca 75252					
❏ 84	Ernest Tubb's Golden Favorites	1973	3.00	6.00	12.00
—Reissue of Decca 74118					
❏ 341	I've Got All the Heartaches I Can Handle	1973	3.00	6.00	12.00
❏ 496	Ernest Tubb	1975	3.00	6.00	12.00
❏ 512	Baby, It's So Hard to Be Good	197?	3.00	6.00	12.00
—Reissue of Decca 75388					
❏ 4040 [(2)]	The Ernest Tubb Story	197?	3.75	7.50	15.00
—Reissue of Decca DXSA 7159					

TUBB, ERNEST, AND RED FOLEY See RED FOLEY AND ERNEST TUBB.

TUBB, ERNEST, AND LORETTA LYNN Also see each artist's individual listings.

45s

Number	Title (A Side/B Side)	Yr	VG	VG+	NM
DECCA					
❏ 31643	Mr. and Mrs. Used to Be/Love Was Right Here All the Time	1964	2.50	5.00	10.00
❏ 31793	Our Hearts Are Holding Hands/We're Not Kids Anymore	1965	2.50	5.00	10.00
❏ 32091	Sweet Thang/Beautiful, Unhappy Home	1967	2.50	5.00	10.00
❏ 32496	Who's Gonna Take the Garbage Out/Somewhere Between	1969	2.00	4.00	8.00
❏ 32570	I Chased You Till You Caught Me/If We Put Our Heads Together	1969	2.00	4.00	8.00
MCA					
❏ 60155	Sweet Thang/Beautiful, Unhappy Home	197?	—	2.50	5.00
—Reissue					
Albums					
DECCA					
❏ DL 4639 [M]	Mr. and Mrs. Used to Be	1965	7.50	15.00	30.00
❏ DL 4872 [M]	Singin' Again	1967	7.50	15.00	30.00
❏ DL 74639 [S]	Mr. and Mrs. Used to Be	1965	10.00	20.00	40.00
❏ DL 74872 [S]	Singin' Again	1967	6.25	12.50	25.00
❏ DL 75115	If We Put Our Heads Together	1969	6.25	12.50	25.00
MCA					
❏ 4000	The Ernest Tubb/Loretta Lynn Story	1973	3.75	7.50	15.00

Number	Title (A Side/B Side)	Yr	VG	VG+	NM
TUBES, THE					
12-Inch Singles					
A&M					
❏ SP-17068 [DJ]	Prime Time/No Way Out	1979	2.50	5.00	10.00
CAPITOL					
❏ SPRO 9012 [DJ]	The Monkey Time (same on both sides)	1983	2.50	5.00	10.00
❏ SPRO 9332 [DJ]	Piece by Piece (same on both sides)	1985	—	3.00	6.00
❏ SPRO 9728 [DJ]	Gonna Get It Next Time (same on both sides)	1982	2.00	4.00	8.00
45s					
A&M					
❏ 1733	White Punks on Dope (Part 1)/White Punks on Dope (Part 2)	1975	2.00	4.00	8.00
❏ 1733 [PS]	White Punks on Dope (Part 1)/White Punks on Dope (Part 2)	1975	3.00	6.00	12.00
❏ 1755	What Do You Want from Life/Space Baby	1975	—	3.50	7.00
❏ 1826	Don't Touch Me There/Proud to Be an American	1976	—	3.00	6.00
❏ 1956	This Town/I'm Just a Mess	1977	—	3.00	6.00
❏ 2037	Show Me a Reason/I Saw Her Standing There	1978	—	3.00	6.00
❏ 2120	Prime Time/No Way Out	1979	—	3.00	6.00
❏ 2149	Love's a Mystery (I Don't Understand)/Telecide	1979	—	3.00	6.00
❏ 8591	White Punks on Dope/What Do You Want from Life?	198?	—	—	3.00
—Reissue					
CAPITOL					
❏ A-5007	Don't Want to Wait Anymore/Think About Me	1981	—	—	3.00
❏ A-5007 [PS]	Don't Want to Wait Anymore/Think About Me	1981	—	—	3.00
❏ A-5016	Talk To Ya Later/Power Tools	1981	—	3.00	6.00
❏ B-5091	Gonna Get It Next Time/Sports Fans	1982	—	3.00	6.00
❏ B-5217	She's a Beauty/When You're Ready to Come	1983	—	—	3.00
—Second pressing has a black label with colorband					
❏ B-5217	She's a Beauty/When You're Ready to Come	1983	—	2.00	4.00
—First pressing has a purple label					
❏ B-5217 [PS]	She's a Beauty/When You're Ready to Come	1983	2.00	4.00	8.00
❏ B-5254	The Monkey Time/Sports Fans	1983	—	—	3.00
❏ B-5254 [PS]	The Monkey Time/Sports Fans	1983	—	—	3.00
❏ B-5258	Tip of My Tongue/Keyboard Kids	1983	—	2.00	4.00
❏ B-5443	Piece by Piece/Night People	1985	—	—	3.00
❏ B-5443 [PS]	Piece by Piece/Night People	1985	—	2.00	4.00
❏ SPRO-9740 [DJ]	Sports Fans (same on both sides)	1982	—	2.50	5.00
❏ SPRO-9909 [DJ]	She's a Beauty (same on both sides)	1983	3.00	6.00	12.00
CAPITOL STARLINE					
❏ X-6328	Don't Want to Wait Anymore/Talk To Ya Later	198?	—	—	3.00
TUBES					
❏ 12682XS	Tubular Holiday	1982	12.50	25.00	50.00
—Fan club flexidisc					
❏ 833502XS	Happy Holidaze	1983	12.50	25.00	50.00
—Fan club flexidisc					
Albums					
A&M					
❏ SP-3161	The Tubes	198?	2.00	4.00	8.00
—Reissue of SP-4534					
❏ SP-3222	Young and Rich	198?	2.00	4.00	8.00
—Reissue of SP-4580					
❏ SP-3242	Remote Control	198?	2.00	4.00	8.00
—Reissue of SP-4751					
❏ SP-3243	Now	198?	2.50	5.00	10.00
—Reissue of SP-4632					
❏ SP-3244	T.R.A.S.H. (Tubes Rarities And Smash Hits)	198?	2.00	4.00	8.00
—Reissue of SP-4870					
❏ SP-4534	The Tubes	1975	3.00	6.00	12.00
❏ SP-4580	Young and Rich	1976	3.00	6.00	12.00
❏ SP-4632	Now	1977	3.00	6.00	12.00
❏ SP-4751	Remote Control	1979	3.00	6.00	12.00
❏ SP-4870	T.R.A.S.H. (Tubes Rarities And Smash Hits)	1981	2.50	5.00	10.00
❏ SP-6003 [(2)]	What Do You Want From Live!	1978	3.75	7.50	15.00
❏ SP-17012 [DJ]	Tubes Live/Edited for Trouble-Free Airplay (The First "Clean" Tubes Album)	1978	5.00	10.00	20.00
—Generic cover with sticker; promo only					
CAPITOL					
❏ SOO-12151	The Completion Backward Principle	1981	2.50	5.00	10.00
❏ ST-12260	Outside/Inside	1983	2.50	5.00	10.00
❏ ST-12381	Love Bomb	1985	2.50	5.00	10.00
❏ SN-16360	Outside/Inside	1985	2.00	4.00	8.00
—Reissue of ST-12260					
❏ SN-16378	The Completion Backward Principle	1986	2.00	4.00	8.00
—Reissue of SOO-12151					
❏ SN-16446	Love Bomb	1987	2.00	4.00	8.00
—Reissue of ST-12381					
TUCKER, BILLY JOE					
45s					
DOT					
❏ 16240	Boogie Woogie Bill/Mail Train	1961	25.00	50.00	100.00
MAHA					
❏ 103	Boogie Woogie Bill/Mail Train	1961	75.00	150.00	300.00
TUCKER, RICK					
45s					
COLUMBIA					
❏ 4-41041	Patty Baby/Don't Do Me This Way	1957	25.00	50.00	100.00
HITSVILLE					
❏ 6035	I Heard a Song/Plans That We Made	1976	—	3.00	6.00
OAK					
❏ 1066	Honey I'm Just Walking Out the Door/(B-side unknown)	1989	—	2.50	5.00
TUCKER, TANYA					
45s					
ARISTA					
❏ 0677	Feel Right/Cry	1982	—	2.00	4.00
❏ 1053	Changes/Too Long	1983	—	2.00	4.00
❏ 9006	Changes/Too Long	1983	—	—	3.00
❏ 9046	Baby I'm Yours/I Don't Want You to Go	1983	—	—	3.00

Number	Title (A Side/B Side)	Yr	VG	VG+	NM
CAPITOL					
❑ 4986	Why Don't We Just Sleep on It Tonight/				
	It's Your World	1981	—	2.00	4.00
—With Glen Campbell					
❑ B-5533	One Love at a Time/Fool Fool Heart	1985	—	—	3.00
❑ B-5533 [PS]	One Love at a Time/Fool Fool Heart	1985	—	—	3.00
❑ B-5604	Just Another Love/You Could Change My Mind	1986	—	—	3.00
❑ B-5604 [PS]	Just Another Love/You Could Change My Mind	1986	—	—	3.00
❑ B-5652	I'll Come Back As Another Woman/Somebody				
	to Care	1986	—	—	3.00
❑ B-5694	It's Only Over for You/Girls Like Me	1987	—	—	3.00
❑ B-5694	It's Only for You/Girls Like Me	1987	—	2.50	5.00
—First pressing had erroneous A-side title					
❑ B-44036	Love Me Like You Used To/If I Didn't Love You	1987	—	—	3.00
❑ B-44036 [PS]	Love Me Like You Used To/If I Didn't Love You	1987	—	—	3.00
❑ B-44100	I Won't Take Less Than Your Love/Heartbreaker	1987	—	—	3.00
—With Paul Davis and Paul Overstreet					
❑ B-44142	If It Don't Come Easy/				
	I'll Tennessee You in My Dreams	1988	—	—	3.00
❑ B-44188	Strong Enough to Bend/Back on My Feet	1988	—	—	3.00
❑ B-44271	Highway Robbery/Lonesome Town	1989	—	—	3.00
❑ B-44348	Call on Me/Daddy and Home	1989	—	—	3.00
❑ B-44401	Daddy and Home/Playing for Keeps	1989	—	—	3.00
❑ B-44469	My Arms Stay Open All Night/				
	Love Me Like You Used To	1989	—	—	3.00
❑ NR-44520	Walking Shoes/This Heart of Mine	1990	—	2.00	4.00
❑ NR-44586	Don't Go Out/(B-side unknown)	1990	—	2.50	5.00
—With T. Graham Brown; may only have been released on cassette single					
❑ 7PRO-79810	My Arms Stay Open All Night (same on both				
	sides)	1989	—	2.50	5.00
—Originally promo only; stock copy on 44469					
CAPITOL NASHVILLE					
❑ S7-19515	Little Things/You Don't Do It	1997	—	—	3.00
❑ S7-19628	Ridin' Out the Heartache/				
	I Don't Believe That's How You Feel	1997	—	—	3.00
❑ NR-44774	(Without You)				
	What Do I Do with Me/Oh What It Did to Me	1991	—	2.50	5.00
❑ 7PRO-79149	Don't Go Out (same on both sides)	1990	—	2.50	5.00
—With T. Graham Brown; vinyl may be promo only					
❑ 7PRO-79338	It Won't Be Me (same on both sides)	1990	—	3.00	6.00
—Vinyl is promo only					
❑ 7PRO-79535	Oh What It Did to Me (same on both sides)	1991	—	3.00	6.00
—Vinyl is promo only					
❑ 7PRO-79711	Down to My Last Teardrop (same on both sides)	1991	—	3.00	6.00
—Vinyl is promo only					
COLLECTABLES					
❑ 6109	Down to My Last Teardrop/In San Antone	199?	—	—	3.00
—B-side by Dan Seals					
❑ 6202	Don't Go Out/Hopelessly Yours	199?	—	—	3.00
—B-side with Lee Greenwood; reissue					
❑ 6349	Two Sparrows in a Hurricane/It's a Little Too Late	199?	—	—	3.00
—Reissue					
❑ 90254	Lizzie and the Rainman/San Antonio Stroll	199?	—	—	3.00
—Reissue					
COLUMBIA					
❑ 10069	I Believe the South Is Gonna Rise Again/				
	Old Dan Tucker's Daughter	1974	—	2.50	5.00
❑ 10127	Spring/Bed of Roses	1975	—	2.50	5.00
❑ 10236	Greener Than the Grass (We Laid On)/Guess				
	I'll Have to Love Him More	1975	—	2.50	5.00
❑ 10577	You Are So Beautiful/Almost Persuaded	1977	—	2.00	4.00
❑ 33237	Delta Dawn/Love's the Answer	197?	—	2.00	4.00
—"Hall of Fame" series; red and black label					
❑ 33237	Delta Dawn/Love's the Answer	198?	—	—	3.00
—"Hall of Fame" series; grayish label					
❑ 33245	Blood Red and Goin' Down/				
	What's Your Mama's Name	197?	—	2.00	4.00
—"Hall of Fame" series; red and black label					
❑ 33245	Blood Red and Goin' Down/				
	What's Your Mama's Name	198?	—	—	3.00
—"Hall of Fame" series; grayish label					
❑ 33275	Would You Lay with Me (In a Field of Stone)/The				
	Man That Turned My Mama On	197?	—	2.00	4.00
—"Hall of Fame" series; red and black label					
❑ 33275	Would You Lay with Me (In a Field of Stone)/The				
	Man That Turned My Mama On	198?	—	—	3.00
—"Hall of Fame" series; grayish label					
❑ 33321	Spring/Greener Than the Grass We Laid On	197?	—	2.00	4.00
—"Hall of Fame" series; red and black label					
❑ 33321	Spring/Greener Than the Grass We Laid On	198?	—	—	3.00
—"Hall of Fame" series; grayish label					
❑ 45588	Delta Dawn/I Love the Way He Loves Me	1972	—	2.50	5.00
❑ 45588 [PS]	Delta Dawn/I Love the Way He Loves Me	1972	2.50	5.00	10.00
❑ 45721	Love's the Answer/The Jamestown Ferry	1972	—	2.50	5.00
❑ 45799	What's Your Mama's Name/Rainy Girl	1973	—	2.50	5.00
❑ 45892	Blood Red and Goin' Down/The Missing Piece				
	of the Puzzle	1973	—	2.50	5.00
❑ 45991	Would You Lay with Me (In a Field of Stone)/				
	No Man's Land	1974	—	2.50	5.00
❑ 46047	The Man That Turned My Mama On/				
	Satisfied with Missing You	1974	—	2.50	5.00
LIBERTY					
❑ S7-17594	Soon/Sneaky Moon	1993	—	2.00	4.00
❑ S7-17803	We Don't Have to Do This/Silence Is King	1994	—	2.00	4.00
❑ S7-17908	Hangin' In/Let the Good Times Roll	1994	—	2.00	4.00
❑ S7-18135	You Just Watch Me/I Love You Anyway	1994	—	2.00	4.00
❑ S7-18485	Between the Two of Them/Love Will	1995	—	2.00	4.00
❑ S7-18583	Something/All My Loving	1995	—	2.00	4.00
—B-side by Suzy Bogguss and Chet Atkins					
❑ S7-56825	Two Sparrows in a Hurricane/Danger Ahead	1992	—	2.00	4.00
❑ S7-56953	It's a Little Too Late/Rainbow Rider	1993	—	2.00	4.00
❑ S7-56985	Tell Me About It/What Do They Know	1993	—	2.00	4.00
—A-side with Delbert McClinton					
❑ S7-57703	Some Kind of Trouble/Oh What It Did to Me	1992	—	2.50	5.00
❑ S7-57768	If Your Heart Ain't Busy Tonight/				
	Down to My Last Teardrop	1992	—	2.50	5.00
❑ S7-57895	Winter Wonderland/What Child Is This	1992	—	2.00	4.00

Number	Title (A Side/B Side)	Yr	VG	VG+	NM
MCA					
❑ 40402	Lizzie and the Rainman/Traveling Salesman	1975	—	2.00	4.00
❑ 40444	San Antonio Stroll/The Serenade That We				
	Played	1975	—	2.00	4.00
❑ 40497	Don't Believe My Heart Can Stand Another You/				
	Depend on You	1975	—	2.00	4.00
❑ 40540	You've Got Me to Hold On To/Ain't That a Shame	1976	—	2.00	4.00
❑ 40598	Here's Some Love/The Pride of Franklin County	1976	—	2.00	4.00
❑ 40650	Ridin' Rainbows/Short Cut	1976	—	2.00	4.00
❑ 40708	It's a Cowboy Lovin' Night/Morning Comes	1977	—	2.00	4.00
❑ 40755	Dancing the Night Away/Let's Keep It That Way	1977	—	2.00	4.00
❑ 40902	Save Me/Slippin' Away	1978	—	2.00	4.00
❑ 40902 [PS]	Save Me/Slippin' Away	1978	—	3.00	6.00
❑ 40976	Texas (When I Die)/Not Fade Away	1978	—	2.00	4.00
❑ 40976 [PS]	Texas (When I Die)/Not Fade Away	1978	—	3.00	6.00
❑ 41005	I'm the Singer, You're the Song/Lover Goodbye	1979	—	2.00	4.00
❑ 41144	Lay Back in the Arms of Someone/				
	By Day By Day	1979	—	2.00	4.00
❑ 41194	Tear Me Apart/Better Late Than Never	1980	—	2.00	4.00
❑ 41305	Pecos Promenade/King of Country Music	1980	—	2.00	4.00
❑ 41323	Dream Lover/Bronco	1980	—	2.00	4.00
—A-side with Glen Campbell					
❑ 51037	Can I See You Tonight/Let Me Count the Ways	1980	—	2.00	4.00
❑ 51096	Love Knows We Tried/				
	Somebody (Trying to Tell You Something)	1981	—	2.00	4.00
❑ 51131	Should I Do It/Lucky Enough for Two	1981	—	2.00	4.00
❑ 51184	Rodeo Girls/Halfway to Heaven	1981	—	2.00	4.00
❑ 52017	Somebody Buy This Cowgirl a Beer/Delta Dawn	1982	—	2.00	4.00
❑ 53588	Texas (When I Die)/Pecos Promenade	198?	—	—	3.00
—"Double Play" reissue					
❑ 53605	Can I See You Tonight/Dream Lover	198?	—	—	3.00
—"Double Play" reissue					
❑ 60188	Lizzie and the Rainman/San Antonio Stroll	197?	—	2.00	4.00
—Reissue					
Albums					
ARISTA					
❑ AL 8381	Changes	1984	2.00	4.00	8.00
—Reissue of 9596					
❑ AL 9596	Changes	1982	2.50	5.00	10.00
CAPITOL					
❑ ST-12474	Girls Like Me	1986	2.50	5.00	10.00
❑ CLT-46870	Love Me Like You Used To	1987	2.50	5.00	10.00
❑ C1-48865	Strong Enough to Bend	1988	2.50	5.00	10.00
❑ C1-91814	Greatest Hits	1989	3.00	6.00	12.00
CAPITOL NASHVILLE					
❑ 1P 8140	What Do I Do with Me	1991	5.00	10.00	20.00
—Only available on vinyl through Columbia House					
COLUMBIA					
❑ KC 31742	Delta Dawn	1972	3.75	7.50	15.00
❑ PC 31742	Delta Dawn	198?	2.00	4.00	8.00
❑ KC 32272	What's Your Mama's Name	1973	3.75	7.50	15.00
❑ KC 32744	Would You Lay with Me (In a Field of Stone)	1974	3.00	6.00	12.00
❑ PC 32744	Would You Lay with Me (In a Field of Stone)	197?	2.00	4.00	8.00
❑ KC 33355	Greatest Hits	1975	3.00	6.00	12.00
—No bar code on cover					
❑ PC 33355	Greatest Hits	197?	2.00	4.00	8.00
—With bar code on cover					
❑ PC 34733	You Are So Beautiful	197?	2.00	4.00	8.00
—With bar code on cover					
❑ PC 34733	You Are So Beautiful	1977	3.00	6.00	12.00
—No bar code on cover					
COLUMBIA SPECIAL PRODUCTS					
❑ P 15770	The Best of Tanya Tucker	1981	3.00	6.00	12.00
MCA					
❑ 654	Tanya Tucker	1980	2.00	4.00	8.00
—Reissue of 2141					
❑ 655	Lovin' and Learnin'	1980	2.00	4.00	8.00
—Reissue of 2167					
❑ 656	Here's Some Love	1980	2.00	4.00	8.00
—Reissue of 2213					
❑ 657	Ridin' Rainbows	1980	2.00	4.00	8.00
—Reissue of 2253					
❑ 2141	Tanya Tucker	1975	3.00	6.00	12.00
❑ 2167	Lovin' and Learnin'	1976	3.00	6.00	12.00
❑ 2213	Here's Some Love	1976	3.00	6.00	12.00
❑ 2253	Ridin' Rainbows	1977	3.00	6.00	12.00
❑ 3032	Tanya Tucker's Greatest Hits	1978	3.00	6.00	12.00
❑ 3066	TNT	1978	3.00	6.00	12.00
—Original gatefold cover					
❑ 5106	Tear Me Apart	1979	2.50	5.00	10.00
❑ 5140	Dreamlovers	1980	2.50	5.00	10.00
❑ 5228	Should I Do It	1981	2.50	5.00	10.00
❑ 5299	Tanya Tucker Live	1982	2.50	5.00	10.00
❑ 5357	The Best of Tanya Tucker	1983	2.50	5.00	10.00
❑ 27030	Dreamlovers	198?	2.00	4.00	8.00
—Reissue of 5140					
❑ 37075	TNT	1981	2.00	4.00	8.00
—Reissue of 3066; gatefold removed					
❑ 37158	Tear Me Apart	1981	2.00	4.00	8.00
—Reissue of 5106					
❑ 37225	Greatest Hits	1984	2.00	4.00	8.00
—Reissue of 3032					
❑ 37242	Tanya Tucker Live	1984	2.00	4.00	8.00
—Reissue of 5299					

TUCKER, TOMMY May be two different performers.

45s

Number	Title (A Side/B Side)	Yr	VG	VG+	NM
CHECKER					
❑ 1067	Hi-Heel Sneakers/I Don't Want 'Cha	1964	6.25	12.50	25.00
❑ 1075	Long Tall Shorty/Mo' Shorty	1964	3.75	7.50	15.00
❑ 1112	Alimony/All About Melanie	1965	3.75	7.50	15.00
❑ 1133	Chewing Gum/I've Been a Fool	1966	2.50	5.00	10.00
❑ 1178	I'm Shorty/Sitting Home Alone	1967	2.00	4.00	8.00
❑ 1186	A Whole Lot of Fun Before the Weekend Is Done/				
	Real True Love	1967	2.00	4.00	8.00

Number	Title (A Side/B Side)	Yr	VG	VG+	NM
HI					
❏ 2014	Loving Lil/A Man in Love	1959	7.50	15.00	30.00
❏ 2020	Miller's Cave/The Strangers	1960	6.25	12.50	25.00
MGM					
❏ 10854	Christmas In Killarney/Jing-A-Ling	1950	3.75	7.50	15.00
RCA VICTOR					
❏ 37-7838	The Return of the Teenage Queen/ Since You Have Gone	1961	6.25	12.50	25.00
—"Compact Single 33" (small hole, plays at LP speed)					
❏ 47-7838	The Return of the Teenage Queen/ Since You Have Gone	1961	3.75	7.50	15.00
❏ 68-7838	The Return of the Teenage Queen/ Since You Have Gone	1961	7.50	15.00	30.00
—"Compact Single 33" in "Living Stereo"					
SUNBEAM					
❏ 128	My Blue Heaven/That Man Comes Around	1959	3.75	7.50	15.00
Albums					
CHECKER					
❏ LP-2990 [M]	Hi-Heel Sneakers	1964	62.50	125.00	250.00
—Black label					
❏ LP-2990 [M]	Hi-Heel Sneakers	1965	30.00	60.00	120.00
—Blue label with checkers					
TUCKY BUZZARD					
45s					
CAPITOL					
❏ 3171	Pisces Apple Lady/Time Will Be Your Doctor	1971	—	3.00	6.00
PASSPORT					
❏ 7901	Gold Medallions/Fast Bluesy Woman	1974	—	2.50	5.00
Albums					
CAPITOL					
❏ ST-787	Tucky Buzzard	1971	3.75	7.50	15.00
❏ ST-864	Warm Slash	1972	3.75	7.50	15.00
PASSPORT					
❏ 97001	Alright in the Night	1973	3.75	7.50	15.00
❏ 98002	Tucky Buzzard	1974	3.75	7.50	15.00
TUDOR MINSTRELS, THE					
45s					
LONDON					
❏ 1012	Love in the Open Air/ A Theme from "The Family Way"	1966	12.50	25.00	50.00
TUFFS, THE					
45s					
DORE					
❏ 757	I Only Cry Once a Day Now/The Moon Out There	1966	6.25	12.50	25.00
DOT					
❏ 16304	Surfer Stomp (Part 1)/Surfer Stomp (Part 2)	1962	6.25	12.50	25.00
TULLY, LEE, AND MILT MOSS					
45s					
FLAIR-X					
❏ 3007	Around the World with Elwood Pretzel (Part 1)/ Around the World with Elwood Pretzel (Part 2)	1956	12.50	25.00	50.00
TUNE ROCKERS, THE					
45s					
UNITED ARTISTS					
❏ 139	The Green Mosquito/Warm Up	1958	5.00	10.00	20.00
❏ 0145	The Green Mosquito/Bust Out	1973	—	2.00	4.00
—"Silver Spotlight Series" reissue; B-side by the Busters					
TUNE WEAVERS, THE					
45s					
CASA GRANDE					
❏ 101	Little Boy/Look Down That Lonesome Road	1959	10.00	20.00	40.00
❏ 3038	My Congratulations Baby/This Can't Be Love	1960	7.50	15.00	30.00
❏ 4037	Happy, Happy Birthday Baby/Ol' Man River	1957	37.50	75.00	150.00
❏ 4038	I Remember Dear/Pamela Jean	1957	7.50	15.00	30.00
❏ 4040	There Stands My Love/I'm Cold	1958	10.00	20.00	40.00
CHECKER					
❏ 872	Happy, Happy Birthday Baby/Ol' Man River	1957	6.25	12.50	25.00
❏ 872	Happy, Happy Birthday Baby/Yo Yo Walk	1957	6.25	12.50	25.00
—B-side by Paul Gayten					
❏ 880	Ol' Man River/Tough Enough	1957	6.25	12.50	25.00
—B-side by Paul Gayten					
❏ 1007	Congratulations on Your Wedding/Your Skies of Blue	1962	6.25	12.50	25.00
CLASSIC ARTISTS					
❏ 104	Come Back to Me/I've Tried	1988	—	2.00	4.00
—As "Margo Sylvia and Tune Weavers"					
❏ 107	Merry, Merry Christmas Baby/What Are You Doing New Year's Eve	1988	—	2.00	4.00
—As "Margo Sylvia and Tune Weavers"					
TUNEDROPS, THE					
45s					
GONE					
❏ 5003	Rosie Lee/Speak for Yourself	1957	10.00	20.00	40.00
❏ 5072	Smoothie/Jumpin' Jellybeans	1959	6.25	12.50	25.00
METRO					
❏ 20028	Smoothie/Jumpin' Jelly Beans	1959	10.00	20.00	40.00
TUNEMASTERS, THE					
45s					
MARK					
❏ 7002	Sending This Letter/It's All Over	1957	75.00	150.00	300.00
TURBANS, THE Also see THE TURKS/THE TURBANS.					
45s					
HERALD					
❏ 458	When You Dance/ Let Me Show You (Around My Heart)	195?	5.00	10.00	20.00
—Yellow label, block print inside flag					

Number	Title (A Side/B Side)	Yr	VG	VG+	NM
❏ 458	When You Dance/Let Me Show You (Around My Heart)	1955	12.50	25.00	50.00
—Yellow label, script print inside flag					
❏ 469	Sister Sookey/I'll Always Watch Over You	1956	7.50	15.00	30.00
❏ 478	B-I-N-G-O (Bingo)/I'm Nobody's	1956	7.50	15.00	30.00
❏ 486	It Was a Nite Like This/All of My Love	1956	7.50	15.00	30.00
❏ 495	Valley of Love/Bye and Bye	1957	7.50	15.00	30.00
❏ 510	Congratulations/The Wadda-Do	1957	6.25	12.50	25.00
IMPERIAL					
❏ 5807	Six Questions/The Lament of Silver Gulch	1962	10.00	20.00	40.00
❏ 5828	This Is My Story/Clicky Clicky Clack	1962	6.25	12.50	25.00
❏ 5847	I Wonder (I Wanna Know)/The Damage Is Done	1962	5.00	10.00	20.00
LOST-NITE					
❏ 414	When You Dance/Let Me Show You (Around My Heart)	197?	—	2.50	5.00
—Reissue					
❏ 432	Congratulations/The Wadda-Do	197?	—	2.50	5.00
—Reissue					
❏ 433	Sister Sookey/I'll Always Watch Over You	197?	—	2.50	5.00
—Reissue					
MONEY					
❏ 209	Tick Tock Awoo/Nest Is Warm	1955	50.00	100.00	200.00
❏ 209	Tick Tock Awoo/No No Cherry	1955	50.00	100.00	200.00
PARKWAY					
❏ 820	When You Dance/Golden Rings	1961	6.25	12.50	25.00
RED TOP					
❏ 115	I Promise You Love/Curfew Time	1959	12.50	25.00	50.00
ROULETTE					
❏ 4281	Diamonds and Pearls/Bad Man	1960	5.00	10.00	20.00
❏ 4326	Three Friends (Two Lovers)/I'm Not Your Fool Anymore	1961	5.00	10.00	20.00
Albums					
HERALD					
❏ 5009	Presenting the Turbans	197?	5.00	10.00	20.00
—No such album was released in the 1950s; this is a bootleg that has some collector value.					
LOST-NITE					
❏ LLP-25 [10]	The Turbans	1981	2.50	5.00	10.00
—Red vinyl					
RELIC					
❏ 5009	The Turbans' Greatest Hits	198?	3.00	6.00	12.00
TURBINES, THE					
45s					
CENCO					
❏ 116	We Got to Start Over/(B-side unknown)	196?	300.00	600.00	1200.
TURKS, THE More than one group.					
45s					
BALLY					
❏ 1017	This Heart of Mine/Why Did You	1956	7.50	15.00	30.00
CASH					
❏ 1042	It Can't Be True/Wagon Wheels	1956	7.50	15.00	30.00
—As "The Original Turks"					
CLASS					
❏ 256	Hully Gully/Rockville U.S.A.	1959	5.00	10.00	20.00
IMPERIAL					
❏ 5783	I'm a Fool/It Can't Be True	1961	3.00	6.00	12.00
KEEN					
❏ 3-4016	Father Time/Okay	1958	5.00	10.00	20.00
KNIGHT					
❏ 2005	I'm a Fool/It Can't Be True	1958	5.00	10.00	20.00
MONEY					
❏ 215	I'm a Fool/I've Been Accused	1956	10.00	20.00	40.00
P.B.D.					
❏ 112	Baja/Dianne	196?	7.50	15.00	30.00
❏ 113	Wipeout/Hideaway	196?	7.50	15.00	30.00
TURKS, THE / THE TURBANS Also see each artist's individual listings.					
45s					
MONEY					
❏ 211	Emily/When I Return	1955	15.00	30.00	60.00
TURLEY, RICHARD					
45s					
DOT					
❏ 16231	I Wanna Dance/Since I Met You	1961	10.00	20.00	40.00
FRATERNITY					
❏ 845	Makin' Love with My Baby/All About Ann	1959	10.00	20.00	40.00
TURNER, IKE Also see IKE AND TINA TURNER.					
45s					
ARTISTIC					
❏ 1504	(I Know) You Don't Love Me/Down and Out	1958	7.50	15.00	30.00
COBRA					
❏ 5033	Box Top/Walking Down the Aisle	1959	7.50	15.00	30.00
FEDERAL					
❏ 12297	Do You Mean It/She Made My Blood Run Cold	1957	25.00	50.00	100.00
❏ 12304	Rock a Bucket/The Big Question	1957	12.50	25.00	50.00
❏ 12307	You've Changed My Love/Trail Blazer	1957	10.00	20.00	40.00
FLAIR					
❏ 1040	Cubano Jump/Loosely	1954	15.00	30.00	60.00
❏ 1059	Cuban Getaway/Go To It	1955	15.00	30.00	60.00
KING					
❏ 5553	The Big Question/She Made My Blood Run Cold	1961	3.75	7.50	15.00
LIBERTY					
❏ 56194	Takin' Back My Name/Love Is a Game	1970	—	2.50	5.00
RPM					
❏ 356	You're Driving Me Insane/Trouble and Heartaches	1952	100.00	200.00	400.00
❏ 362	My Heart Belongs to You/Lookin' for My Baby	1952	15.00	30.00	60.00
—As "Bonnie and Ike Turner"					
❏ 446	As Long As I Have You/ I Wanna Make Love to You	1955	10.00	20.00	40.00
SUE					
❏ 722	My Love/That's All I Need	1959	5.00	10.00	20.00

T

Number	Title (A Side/B Side)	Yr	VG	VG+	NM
UNITED ARTISTS					
XW460	Take My Hand, Precious Lord/Father Alone	1974	—	2.50	5.00
50865	River Deep Mountain High/Na Na	1971	—	2.50	5.00
50900	Right On/Tacks in My Shoes	1972	—	2.50	5.00
50930	Lawdy Miss Clawdy/Tacks in My Shoes	1972	—	2.50	5.00
51102	Dust My Broom/You Won't Let Me Go	1973	—	2.50	5.00
Albums					
CROWN					
CST-367 [R]	Ike Turner Rocks the Blues	1963	25.00	50.00	100.00
CLP-5367 [M]	Ike Turner Rocks the Blues	1963	50.00	100.00	200.00
FANTASY					
F-9597	The Edge	1980	2.50	5.00	10.00
POMPEII					
SD 6003	A Black Man's Soul	1969	3.75	7.50	15.00
UNITED ARTISTS					
UA-LA087-F	Bad Dreams	1973	3.75	7.50	15.00
UAS-5576	Blues Roots	1972	3.75	7.50	15.00

TURNER, IKE AND TINA Also see IKE TURNER; TINA TURNER.

12-Inch Singles

Number	Title (A Side/B Side)	Yr	VG	VG+	NM
STRIPED HORSE					
1201	Living for the City (5:02)/Bootsy Whitelaw (4:01)	1985	3.75	7.50	15.00
45s					
A&M					
1118	River Deep, Mountain High/I'll Keep You Happy	1969	2.50	5.00	10.00
1170	A Love Like Yours/Save the Last Dance for Me	1970	2.50	5.00	10.00
BLUE THUMB					
101	I've Been Loving You Too Long/Grumbling	1969	—	3.00	6.00
102	The Hunter/Crazy 'Bout You Baby	1969	—	3.00	6.00
104	Bold Soul Sister/I Know	1969	—	3.00	6.00
202	I've Been Loving You Too Long/Crazy 'Bout You Baby	1971	—	2.50	5.00
CENCO					
112	Get It-Get It/You Weren't Ready (For My Love)	1967	3.75	7.50	15.00
INNIS					
6666	Betcha Can't Kiss Me/Don't Lie to Me	1968	2.50	5.00	10.00
6667	So Fine/So Blue Over You	1968	2.50	5.00	10.00
KENT					
402	I Can't Believe What You Say (For Seeing What You Do)/My Baby Now	1964	2.50	5.00	10.00
409	Am I a Fool in Love/Please, Please, Please	1964	2.50	5.00	10.00
418	Chicken Shack/He's the One	1965	2.50	5.00	10.00
4514	Plaese, Please, Please (Part 1)/Please, Please, Please (Part 2)	1970	—	3.00	6.00
LIBERTY					
56177	I Want to Take You Higher/Contact High	1970	—	3.00	6.00
56207	Workin' Together/The Way You Love Me	1970	—	3.00	6.00
56216	Proud Mary/Funkier Than a Mosquito's Tweeter	1970	—	3.00	6.00
LOMA					
2011	I'm Thru with Love/Tell Her I'm Not Home	1965	2.50	5.00	10.00
2015	Somebody Needs You/Just to Be with You	1965	2.50	5.00	10.00
MINIT					
32060	I'm Gonna Do All I Can (To Do Right By My Man)/You've Got Too Many Ties That Bind	1969	—	3.00	6.00
32068	I Wish It Would Rain/With a Little Help from My Friends	1969	—	3.00	6.00
32077	I Wanna Jump/Treating Us Funky	1969	—	3.00	6.00
32087	Come Together/Honky Tonk Women	1970	—	3.00	6.00
MODERN					
1007	Good Bye, So Long/Hurt Is All You Gave Me	1965	2.50	5.00	10.00
1012	I Don't Need/Gonna Have Fun	1965	2.50	5.00	10.00
PHILLES					
131	River Deep — Mountain High/I'll Keep You Happy	1966	5.00	10.00	20.00
134	Two to Tango/A Man Is a Man Is a Man	1966	3.75	7.50	15.00
135	I'll Never Need More Love Than This/The Cash Box Blues Or (Oops We Printed the Wrong Story Again)	1967	3.75	7.50	15.00
136	I Idolize You/A Love Like Yours	1967	3.75	7.50	15.00
POMPEII					
7003	Betcha Can't Kiss Me/Cussin', Cryin', and Carryin' On	1969	2.00	4.00	8.00
66675	It Sho' Ain't Me/We Need An Understanding	1968	2.00	4.00	8.00
66700	Shake a Tail Feather/Cussin', Cryin', and Carryin' On	1969	2.00	4.00	8.00
SONJA					
2001	If I Can't Be First/I'm Going Back Home	1968	3.00	6.00	12.00
2005	You Can't Miss Nothing That You Never Had/God Gave Me You	1968	3.00	6.00	12.00
SUE					
135	Two Is a Couple/Tin Top House	1965	3.75	7.50	15.00
138	The New Breed (Part 1)/The New Breed (Part 2)	1965	3.75	7.50	15.00
139	Stagger Lee and Billy/Can't Chance a Breakup	1965	3.75	7.50	15.00
146	Dear John/I Made a Promise Up Above	1966	3.00	6.00	12.00
730	A Fool in Love/The Way You Love Me	1960	7.50	15.00	30.00
734	You're My Baby/A Fool Too Long	1960	6.25	12.50	25.00
735	I Idolize You/Letter from Tina	1960	6.25	12.50	25.00
740	I'm Jealous/You're My Baby	1961	6.25	12.50	25.00
749	It's Gonna Work Out Fine/Won't You Forgive Me	1961	7.50	15.00	30.00
—With correct A-side title					
749	Gonna Work Out Fine/Won't You Forgive Me	1961	12.50	25.00	50.00
—With erroneous A-side title					
753	Poor Fool/You Can't Blame Me	1961	5.00	10.00	20.00
757	Tra La La La La/Puppy Love	1962	3.75	7.50	15.00
760	Prancing/It's Gonna Work Out Fine	1962	3.75	7.50	15.00
765	You Shoulda Treated Me Right/Sleepless	1962	3.75	7.50	15.00
768	Tina's Dilemma/I Idolize You	1962	3.75	7.50	15.00
772	The Argument/Mind in a Whirl	1962	3.75	7.50	15.00
774	Please Don't Hurt Me/Worried and Hurtin' Inside	1962	3.75	7.50	15.00
784	Don't Play Me Cheap/Wake Up	1963	3.75	7.50	15.00
TANGERINE					
963	Beauty Is Only Skin Deep/Anything You Wasn't Born With	1966	2.50	5.00	10.00
967	Dust My Broom/I'm Hooked	1966	2.50	5.00	10.00

Number	Title (A Side/B Side)	Yr	VG	VG+	NM
UNITED ARTISTS					
SP-48 [DJ]	I Want to Take You Higher/Ooh Poo Pah Doo	1971	2.50	5.00	10.00
0119	A Fool in Love/I Idolize You	1973	—	2.00	4.00
0120	It's Gonna Work Out Fine/Poor Fool	1973	—	2.00	4.00
0121	I Want to Take You Higher/Come Together	1973	—	2.00	4.00
0122	Proud Mary/Tra La La La La	1973	—	2.00	4.00
—0119 through 0122 are "Silver Spotlight Series" reissues					
XW174	With a Little Help from My Friends/Early One Morning	1973	—	2.50	5.00
XW257	Work On Me/Born Free	1973	—	2.50	5.00
XW298	Nutbosh City Limits/Help Him	1973	—	3.00	6.00
XW409	Get it Out of Your Mind/Sweet Rhode Island Red	1974	—	2.50	5.00
XW524	Nutbush City Limits/Ooh Poo Pah Doo	1974	—	2.00	4.00
—Reissue					
XW528	Sexy Ida (Part 1)/Sexy Ida (Part 2)	1974	—	2.50	5.00
XW598X	Baby, Get It On/Baby, Get It On (Disco Version)	1975	—	2.50	5.00
50782	Ooh Poo Pah Doo/I Wanna Jump	1971	—	2.50	5.00
50837	I'm Yours/Doin' It	1971	—	2.50	5.00
50881	Do Wah Ditty (Got to Get Ya)/Up in Heah	1972	—	2.50	5.00
50913	Outrageous/Feel Good	1972	—	2.50	5.00
50939	Games People Play/Pick Me Up	1972	—	2.50	5.00
50955	Let Me Touch Your Mind/Chopper	1972	—	2.50	5.00
WARNER BROS.					
5433	A Fool for a Fool/No Tears to Cry	1964	3.00	6.00	12.00
5433 [PS]	A Fool for a Fool/No Tears to Cry	1964	10.00	20.00	40.00
5461	It's All Over/Finger Poppin'	1964	3.00	6.00	12.00
5493	Ooh Poop A Doo/Merry Christmas Baby	1964	3.00	6.00	12.00
Albums					
A&M					
SP-3179	River Deep — Mountain High	1982	2.50	5.00	10.00
—Budget-line reissue					
SP-4178	River Deep — Mountain High	1969	6.25	12.50	25.00
—Official release of Philles 4011					
ABC					
4014	16 Great Performances	1975	3.00	6.00	12.00
ACCORD					
SN-7147	Hot and Sassy	1981	2.50	5.00	10.00
BLUE THUMB					
BTS 5	Outta Season	1968	3.75	7.50	15.00
BTS 11	The Hunter	1969	3.75	7.50	15.00
BTS 49	The Best of Ike & Tina Turner	1973	3.00	6.00	12.00
BTS-8805	Outta Season	1971	3.00	6.00	12.00
—Early reissue of Blue Thumb 5					
CAPITOL					
ST-571	Her Man, His Woman	1971	3.75	7.50	15.00
COLLECTABLES					
COL-5107	Golden Classics	198?	2.50	5.00	10.00
COL-5137	It's Gonna Work Out Fine	198?	2.50	5.00	10.00
EMI AMERICA					
ST-17212	It's Gonna Work Out Fine	1986	2.50	5.00	10.00
SQ-17216	Workin' Together	1986	2.50	5.00	10.00
HARMONY					
HS 11360	Ooh Poo Pah Doo	1969	3.75	7.50	15.00
H 30567	Something's Got a Hold on Me	1971	3.75	7.50	15.00
KENT					
KST-514 [S]	The Ike and Tina Turner Revue Live	1964	10.00	20.00	40.00
KST-519 [S]	The Soul of Ike and Tina	1966	10.00	20.00	40.00
KST-538	Festival of Live Performances	1969	7.50	15.00	30.00
KST-550	Please Please Please	1971	7.50	15.00	30.00
K-5014 [M]	The Ike and Tina Turner Revue Live	1964	7.50	15.00	30.00
K-5019 [M]	The Soul of Ike and Tina	1966	7.50	15.00	30.00
LIBERTY					
LT-917	Airwaves	1981	2.00	4.00	8.00
LST-7637	Come Together	1970	3.75	7.50	15.00
LST-7650	Workin' Together	1970	3.75	7.50	15.00
LO-51156	Get Back!	1985	2.50	5.00	10.00
LOMA					
L 5904 [M]	Live! The Ike & Tina Turner Show Vol. 2	1966	6.25	12.50	25.00
LS 5904 [S]	Live! The Ike & Tina Turner Show, Vol. 2	1966	7.50	15.00	30.00
—Reissue of Warner Bros. 1579?					
MINIT					
24018	In Person	1969	5.00	10.00	20.00
PHILLES					
PHLP 4011 [M]	River Deep — Mountain High	1967	2000.	4000.	8000.
—Value is for record alone; covers were not printed					
PICKWICK					
SPC-3284	Too Hot to Hold	197?	2.50	5.00	10.00
POMPEII					
SD 6000	So Fine	1968	6.25	12.50	25.00
SD 6004	Cussin', Cryin' and Carryin' On	1969	6.25	12.50	25.00
SD 6006	Get It Together	1969	6.25	12.50	25.00
STRIPED HORSE					
SHL-2001	Golden Empire	1986	2.50	5.00	10.00
SUE					
LP 1038 [M]	The Greatest Hits of Ike and Tina Turner	1965	75.00	150.00	300.00
LP 2001 [M]	The Soul of Ike and Tina Turner	1961	100.00	200.00	400.00
LP 2003 [M]	Ike and Tina Turner's Kings of Rhythm Dance	1962	100.00	200.00	400.00
—Despite the title, this is an all-instrumental album (Tina's vocals do not appear)					
LP 2004 [M]	Dynamite	1963	100.00	200.00	400.00
LP 2005 [M]	Don't Play Me Cheap	1963	100.00	200.00	400.00
LP 2007 [M]	It's Gonna Work Out Fine	1963	100.00	200.00	400.00
SUNSET					
SUS-5265	The Fantastic Ike & Tina Turner	1969	3.75	7.50	15.00
SUS-5286	Ike & Tima Turner's Greatest Hits	1969	3.75	7.50	15.00
UNART					
S 21021	Greatest Hits	197?	2.50	5.00	10.00
UNITED ARTISTS					
UA-LA064-G [(2)]	The World of Ike & Tina Live	1973	3.75	7.50	15.00
UA-LA180-F	Nutbush City Limits	1973	3.00	6.00	12.00
UA-LA203-G	The Gospel According to Ike & Tina Turner	1974	3.00	6.00	12.00
UA-LA312-G	Sweet Rhode Island Red	1974	3.00	6.00	12.00
UA-LA592-G	Greatest Hits	1976	3.00	6.00	12.00
UA-LA707-H	Delilah's Power	1977	3.00	6.00	12.00
UA-LA917-H	Airwaves	1978	3.00	6.00	12.00
UAS-5530	'Nuff Said	1971	3.00	6.00	12.00

Number	Title (A Side/B Side)	Yr	VG	VG+	NM
❏ UAS-5598	Feel Good	1972	3.00	6.00	12.00
❏ UAS-5660	Let Me Touch Your Mind	1972	3.00	6.00	12.00
❏ UAS-5667	Ike & Tina Turner's Greatest Hits	1972	3.00	6.00	12.00
❏ UAS-9953 [(2)]	Live at Carnegie Hall/ What You Hear Is What You Get	1971	3.75	7.50	15.00
WARNER BROS.					
❏ W 1579 [M]	Live! The Ike & Tina Turner Show	1965	7.50	15.00	30.00
❏ WS 1579 [S]	Live! The Ike & Tina Turner Show	1965	10.00	20.00	40.00
❏ WS 1810	Ike & Tina Turner's Greatest Hits	1969	6.25	12.50	25.00

TURNER, JESSE LEE
45s

Number	Title (A Side/B Side)	Yr	VG	VG+	NM
CARLTON					
❏ 496	The Little Space Girl/Shake, Baby, Shake	1959	5.00	10.00	20.00
❏ 509	Baby Please Don't Tease/Thinkin'	1959	5.00	10.00	20.00
❏ 509 [PS]	Baby Please Don't Tease/Thinkin'	1959	10.00	20.00	40.00
FRATERNITY					
❏ 855	Teen-Age Misery/That's My Girl	1959	5.00	10.00	20.00
❏ 855 [PS]	Teen-Age Misery/That's My Girl	1959	10.00	20.00	40.00
GNP CRESCENDO					
❏ 184	All You Gotta Do (Is Ask Me To)/ Voice Changing Song	1962	3.00	6.00	12.00
❏ 188	Shotgun Boogie/Ballad of Billy Sol Estes	1962	15.00	30.00	60.00
IMPERIAL					
❏ 5635	Slippin' Around/Early in the Morning	1960	3.75	7.50	15.00
❏ 5649	I'm the Little Space Girl's Father/ Valley of Lost Soldiers	1960	5.00	10.00	20.00
TOP RANK					
❏ 2064	Do I Worry/All Right, Be That Way	1960	5.00	10.00	20.00

TURNER, JOE
45s

Number	Title (A Side/B Side)	Yr	VG	VG+	NM
ATLANTIC					
❏ 939	Chains of Love/After My Laughter Came Tears	1951	125.00	250.00	500.00
❏ 949	The Chill Is On/Bump Miss Suzie	1951	200.00	400.00	800.00
❏ 960	Sweet Sixteen/I'll Never Stop Loving You	1952	30.00	60.00	120.00
❏ 970	Don't You Cry/Poor Lover's Blues	1952	25.00	50.00	100.00
❏ 982	Still in Love/Baby I Still Want You	1953	25.00	50.00	100.00
❏ 1001	Honey Hush/Crawdad Hole	1953	50.00	100.00	200.00
❏ 1016	TV Mama/Oke-She-Moke-She-Pop	1954	30.00	60.00	120.00
❏ 1026	Shake, Rattle, and Roll/You Know I Love You	1954	20.00	40.00	80.00
❏ 1040	Well All Right/Married Woman	1954	17.50	35.00	70.00
❏ 1053	Flip, Flop, and Fly/Ti-Ri-Lee	1955	12.50	25.00	50.00
❏ 1069	Hide and Seek/Midnight Cannonball	1955	12.50	25.00	50.00
❏ 1080	Morning, Noon and Night/The Chicken and the Hawk	1956	12.50	25.00	50.00
❏ 1088	Corinne, Corrina/Boogie Woogie Country Girl	1956	7.50	15.00	30.00
❏ 1100	Rock a While/Lipstick, Powder, and Paint	1956	7.50	15.00	30.00
❏ 1122	Midnight Special Train/Feeling Happy	1957	7.50	15.00	30.00
❏ 1131	Red Sails in the Sunset/After a While	1957	7.50	15.00	30.00
❏ 1146	Love Roller Coaster/A World of Trouble	1957	7.50	15.00	30.00
❏ 1155	I Need a Girl/Trouble in Mind	1957	7.50	15.00	30.00
❏ 1167	Teen-Age Letter/Wee Baby Blues	1957	7.50	15.00	30.00
❏ 1184	Blues in the Night/Jump for Joy	1958	7.50	15.00	30.00
❏ 2034	Got You On My Mind/Love, Oh Careless Love	1959	5.00	10.00	20.00
❏ 2044	Tomorrow Night/Honey Hush	1959	5.00	10.00	20.00
❏ 2054	Chains of Love/My Little Honey Dripper	1960	5.00	10.00	20.00
❏ 2072	My Reason for Living/Sweet Sue	1960	5.00	10.00	20.00
BAYOU					
❏ 015	The Blues Jumped the Rabbit/ The Sun Is Shining	1951	75.00	150.00	300.00
BLUESTIME					
❏ 45001	Two Loves Have I/Shake, Rattle and Roll	195?	10.00	20.00	40.00
BLUESWAY					
❏ 61009	Big Wheel/Bluer Than Blue	1967	2.00	4.00	8.00
CORAL					
❏ 62408	I Walk a Lonely Mile/I'm Packin' Up	1964	3.75	7.50	15.00
❏ 62429	Shake, Rattle and Roll/ There'll Be Some Tears Falling	1964	3.75	7.50	15.00
DECCA					
❏ 29711	Piney Brown Blues/I Got a Gal for Every Day of the Week	1955	10.00	20.00	40.00
❏ 29924	Corrine, Corrina/It's the Same Old Story	1956	10.00	20.00	40.00
KENT					
❏ 512	Love Ain't Nothin'/10-20-25-30	1969	—	3.00	6.00
❏ 4561	Chains of Love/Battle Hymn of the Republic	1971	—	3.00	6.00
❏ 4569	One Hour in Your Garden/ You've Been Squeezin' My Lemons	1972	—	3.00	6.00
MGM					
❏ 10719	Moody Baby/Feeling So Sad	1951	75.00	150.00	300.00
OKEH					
❏ 6829	Cherry Red/Joe Turner Blues	1951	50.00	100.00	200.00
RONN					
❏ 28	Up on the Mountain/I Love You Baby	1969	—	3.00	6.00
❏ 35	Morning Glory/Night-Time Is the Right Time	1969	—	3.00	6.00
RPM					
❏ 345	Riding Blues/Playful Baby	1952	50.00	100.00	200.00
—With Pete Johnson					

7-Inch Extended Plays

Number	Title (A Side/B Side)	Yr	VG	VG+	NM
ATLANTIC					
❏ EP 536	(contents unknown)	1955	37.50	75.00	150.00
❏ EP 536 [PS]	Joe Turner Sings	1955	37.50	75.00	150.00
❏ EP 565	(contents unknown)	1956	37.50	75.00	150.00
❏ EP 565 [PS]	Joe Turner	1956	37.50	75.00	150.00
❏ EP 586	*Corrine Corrina/The Chicken and the Hawk/ Feeling Happy/Hide and Seek	195?	37.50	75.00	150.00
❏ EP 586 [PS]	Joe Turner	195?	37.50	75.00	150.00
❏ EP 606	*Crawdad Hole/The Chicken and the Hawk/ Boogie Woogie Country Girl/ Midnight Special Train	195?	30.00	60.00	120.00
❏ EP 606 [PS]	Rock with Joe Turner	195?	30.00	60.00	120.00
EMARCY					
❏ EP-1-6132	(contents unknown)	195?	25.00	50.00	100.00
❏ EP-1-6132 [PS]	Joe Turner	195?	25.00	50.00	100.00

Number	Title (A Side/B Side)	Yr	VG	VG+	NM
Albums					
ARHOOLIE					
❏ 2004 [M]	Jumpin' the Blues	1962	5.00	10.00	20.00
ATCO					
❏ SD 33-376	Joe Turner — His Greatest Recordings	1971	3.75	7.50	15.00
ATLANTIC					
❏ 1234 [M]	The Boss of the Blues	1956	30.00	60.00	120.00
—Black label					
❏ 1234 [M]	The Boss of the Blues	1960	25.00	50.00	100.00
—White "bullseye" label					
❏ 1234 [M]	The Boss of the Blues	1961	10.00	20.00	40.00
—White "fan" logo on label					
❏ 1234 [M]	The Boss of the Blues	1963	3.75	7.50	15.00
—Black "fan" logo on label					
❏ SD 1234 [S]	The Boss of the Blues	1959	45.00	90.00	180.00
—Green label					
❏ SD 1234 [S]	The Boss of the Blues	1960	37.50	75.00	150.00
—White "bullseye" label					
❏ SD 1234 [S]	The Boss of the Blues	1961	12.50	25.00	50.00
—White "fan" logo on label					
❏ SD 1234 [S]	The Boss of the Blues	1963	5.00	10.00	20.00
—Black "fan" logo on label					
❏ 1332 [M]	Big Joe Rides Again	1959	37.50	75.00	150.00
—Black label					
❏ 1332 [M]	Big Joe Rides Again	1960	10.00	20.00	40.00
—White "fan" logo on label					
❏ 1332 [M]	Big Joe Rides Again	1963	3.75	7.50	15.00
—Black "fan" logo on label					
❏ SD 1332 [S]	Big Joe Rides Again	1959	50.00	100.00	200.00
—Green label					
❏ SD 1332 [S]	Big Joe Rides Again	1960	12.50	25.00	50.00
—White "fan" logo on label					
❏ SD 1332 [S]	Big Joe Rides Again	1963	5.00	10.00	20.00
—Black "fan" logo on label					
❏ 8005 [M]	Joe Turner	1957	37.50	75.00	150.00
—Black label					
❏ 8005 [M]	Joe Turner	1961	10.00	20.00	40.00
—White "fan" logo on label					
❏ 8005 [M]	Joe Turner	1963	3.75	7.50	15.00
—Black "fan" logo on label					
❏ 8023 [M]	Rockin' the Blues	1958	30.00	60.00	120.00
—Black label					
❏ 8023 [M]	Rockin' the Blues	1960	10.00	20.00	40.00
—White "fan" logo on label					
❏ 8023 [M]	Rockin' the Blues	1963	3.75	7.50	15.00
—Black "fan" logo on label					
❏ 8033 [M]	Big Joe Is Here	1959	30.00	60.00	120.00
—Black label					
❏ 8033 [M]	Big Joe Is Here	1960	10.00	20.00	40.00
—White "fan" logo on label					
❏ 8033 [M]	Big Joe Is Here	1960	25.00	50.00	100.00
—White "bullseye" label					
❏ 8033 [M]	Big Joe Is Here	1963	3.75	7.50	15.00
—Black "fan" logo on label					
❏ 8081 [M]	The Best of Joe Turner	1963	12.50	25.00	50.00
❏ SD 8812	Boss of the Blues	1981	2.50	5.00	10.00
—Reissue of 1234					
❏ 81752	Greatest Hits	1987	2.50	5.00	10.00
BLUES SPECTRUM					
❏ BS-104	Great Rhythm and Blues Oldies Vol. 4	197?	3.75	7.50	15.00
BLUESTIME					
❏ 9002 [M]	The Real Boss of the Blues	196?	10.00	20.00	40.00
❏ 29002 [S]	The Real Boss of the Blues	196?	7.50	15.00	30.00
BLUESWAY					
❏ BL 6006 [M]	Singing the Blues	1967	5.00	10.00	20.00
❏ BLS-6006 [S]	Singing the Blues	1967	6.25	12.50	25.00
❏ S-6060	Roll 'Em	1973	3.75	7.50	15.00
DECCA					
❏ DL 8044 [M]	Joe Turner Sings Kansas City Jazz	1953	62.50	125.00	250.00
FANTASY					
❏ OJC-497	Trumpet Kings Meet Joe Turner	1991	3.00	6.00	12.00
INTERMEDIA					
❏ QS-5008	Rock This Joint	198?	2.50	5.00	10.00
❏ QS-5026	The Very Best of Joe Turner — Live	198?	2.50	5.00	10.00
❏ QS-5030	The Blues Boss — Live	198?	2.50	5.00	10.00
❏ QS-5036	Everyday I Have the Blues	198?	2.50	5.00	10.00
❏ QS-5043	Roll Me Baby	198?	2.50	5.00	10.00
KENT					
❏ KST-542	Joe Turner Turns On the Blues	1973	3.75	7.50	15.00
MCA					
❏ 1325	Early Big Joe	198?	2.50	5.00	10.00
MUSE					
❏ MR-5293	Blues Train	198?	2.50	5.00	10.00
—With Roomful of Blues and Dr. John					
PABLO					
❏ 2310717	Trumpet Kings Meet Joe Turner	197?	3.00	6.00	12.00
❏ 2310760	Nobody in Mind	197?	3.00	6.00	12.00
❏ 2310776	In the Evening	197?	3.00	6.00	12.00
❏ 2310800	Things That I Used to Do	197?	3.00	6.00	12.00
❏ 2310818	Every Day I Have the Blues	198?	3.00	6.00	12.00
❏ 2310848	The Best of Joe Turner	1980	3.00	6.00	12.00
❏ 2310863	Have No Fear, Joe Turner Is Here	1983	3.00	6.00	12.00
❏ 2310883	Singing the Same, Sad, Happy, Forever Blues	1983	3.00	6.00	12.00
❏ 2310913	Patcha, Patcha, All Night Long	198?	3.00	6.00	12.00
❏ 2310937	Flip, Flop and Fly	1989	3.00	6.00	12.00
❏ 2405404	The Best of "Big" Joe Turner	198?	3.00	6.00	12.00
SAVOY					
❏ MG-14012 [M]	Blues'll Make You Happy	1958	37.50	75.00	150.00
❏ MG-14106 [M]	Careless Love	1963	20.00	40.00	80.00
SAVOY JAZZ					
❏ SJC-406	Blues'll Make You Happy	1985	2.50	5.00	10.00
—Reissue of Savoy 14012					
❏ SJL-2223 [(2)]	Have No Fear	197?	3.75	7.50	15.00

T

Number	Title (A Side/B Side)	Yr	VG	VG+	NM
TURNER, JOE (2)					
Albums					
CHIAROSCURO					
❏ 147	King of Stride	1976	3.75	7.50	15.00
CLASSIC JAZZ					
❏ 138	Effervescent	1976	3.75	7.50	15.00
PABLO					
❏ 2310763	Another Epoch Stride Piano	197?	3.00	6.00	12.00
TURNER, JOE, AND PETE JOHNSON					
Albums					
EMARCY					
❏ MG-36014 [M]	Joe Turner and Pete Johnson	1955	50.00	100.00	200.00
TURNER, ODELLE					
45s					
ATLANTIC					
❏ 964	Alarm Clock Boogie/Draggin' Hours	1952	37.50	75.00	150.00
TURNER, SAMMY					
45s					
BIG TOP					
❏ 3007	Thunderbolt/Sweet Annie Laurie	1959	6.25	12.50	25.00
❏ 3016 [M]	Lavender-Blue/Wrapped Up in a Dream	1959	5.00	10.00	20.00
❏ 3016 [S]	Lavender-Blue/Wrapped Up in a Dream	1959	15.00	30.00	60.00
❏ 3029 [M]	Always/Symphony	1959	5.00	10.00	20.00
❏ 3029 [S]	Always/Symphony	1959	12.50	25.00	50.00
❏ 3032	Paradise/I'd Be a Fool Again	1960	5.00	10.00	20.00
❏ 3038	Goodnight Irene/I Want to Be Loved	1960	5.00	10.00	20.00
❏ 3049	Fools Fall in Love/Stay My Love	1960	5.00	10.00	20.00
❏ 3061	Falling/The Things I Love	1961	3.75	7.50	15.00
❏ 3065	Little Sir Echo/Love Keeps Calling	1961	3.75	7.50	15.00
❏ 3070	Starlight, Starbright/Let's Donkey On Down	1961	3.75	7.50	15.00
❏ 3082	Pour It On/The Fool of the Year	1961	3.75	7.50	15.00
❏ 3089	Falling/Raincoat in the River	1961	6.25	12.50	25.00
—B-side produced by Phil Spector					
MILLENNIUM					
❏ 616	Do You Know (What Life Is All About)/Nothing Can Separate Me (From Your Love)	1978	—	2.50	5.00
MOTOWN					
❏ 1055	Only You/Right Now	1964	7.50	15.00	30.00
PACIFIC					
❏ 3016	Lavender-Blue/Wrapped Up in a Dream	1959	10.00	20.00	40.00
—Despite label name, Pacific Records was in North Carolina!					
20TH FOX					
❏ 6610	For Your Love I'll Die/The House I Live In	1965	2.50	5.00	10.00
VERVE					
❏ 10465	A Child Was Born/Come to Me Comf'tably	1966	7.50	15.00	30.00
Albums					
BIG TOP					
❏ 12-1301 [M]	Lavender Blue Moods	1959	75.00	150.00	300.00
—May not exist in stereo					
TURNER, SPYDER					
45s					
KWANZA					
❏ 7688	Since I Don't Have You/Happy Days	1973	—	3.00	6.00
MGM					
❏ 13617	Stand By Me/You're Good Enough for Me	1966	2.50	5.00	10.00
❏ 13692	Don't Hold Back/I Can't Take It Anymore	1967	2.00	4.00	8.00
❏ 13739	For Your Precious Love/I Can't Wait to See My Baby's Face	1967	2.00	4.00	8.00
❏ 14263	I Can't Make It Anymore/I'm Alive with a Lovin' Feeling	1971	—	3.00	6.00
WHITFIELD					
❏ 8526	I've Been Waiting/Tomorrow's Only Yesterday	1978	—	2.00	4.00
❏ 8596	Get Down/Is It Love You're After	1978	—	2.00	4.00
❏ 49190	You're So Fine/Only Love	1980	—	2.00	4.00
Albums					
MGM					
❏ E-4450 [M]	Stand By Me	1967	6.25	12.50	25.00
❏ SE-4450 [S]	Stand By Me	1967	7.50	15.00	30.00
WHITFIELD					
❏ BSK 3124	Music Web	1978	2.50	5.00	10.00
❏ BSK 3397	Only Love	1979	2.50	5.00	10.00
TURNER, TINA Also see IKE AND TINA TURNER.					
12-Inch Singles					
CAPITOL					
❏ V-8579	Let's Stay Together (5:14)/I Wrote a Letter	1983	2.00	4.00	8.00
❏ V-8597	What's Love Got to Do with It/Rock 'N' Roll Widow	1984	2.00	4.00	8.00
❏ V-8609	Better Be Good to Me (7:40)/When I Was Young	1984	2.00	4.00	8.00
❏ V-8620	Private Dancer/Nutbush City Limits	1985	2.50	5.00	10.00
❏ V-8635	Show Some Respect (Remix 5:42)/Let's Pretend We're Married	1985	2.00	4.00	8.00
❏ V-8655	We Don't Need Another Hero/(Instrumental)	1985	2.00	4.00	8.00
❏ SPRO-9140 [DJ]	I Might Have Been Queen/Better Be Good to Me//Steel Claw/Private Dancer	1984	3.75	7.50	15.00
—With "legs" cover					
❏ SPRO-9146 [DJ]	What's Love Got to Do with It (LP Version 3:49) (same on both sides)	1984	3.00	6.00	12.00
❏ SPRO-9196 [DJ]	What's Love Got to Do with It (Extended) (same on both sides)	1984	3.00	6.00	12.00
❏ SPRO-9224/34 [DJ]	Better Be Good to Me (LP Version) (Single Version)	1985	2.50	5.00	10.00
❏ SPRO-9238 [DJ]	Better Be Good to Me (3 versions)	1985	2.50	5.00	10.00
❏ SPRO-9264 [DJ]	Better Be Good to Me (Live) (same on both sides)	1984	2.50	5.00	10.00
❏ SPRO-9425/6 [DJ]	We Don't Need Another Hero (Remix) (Instrumental)	1985	—	3.00	6.00
❏ SPRO-9493/4 [DJ]	One of the Living (Club Version) (Single Version)	1985	2.50	5.00	10.00
❏ SPRO-9826 [DJ]	Back Where You Started (same on both sides)	1986	2.00	4.00	8.00
❏ SPRO-9867 [DJ]	Overnight Sensation (same on both sides)	1987	2.50	5.00	10.00

Number	Title (A Side/B Side)	Yr	VG	VG+	NM
❏ V-15205	One of the Living (Special Club Version) (Dub) (Instrumental)	1985	2.00	4.00	8.00
❏ V-15249	Typical Male (Dance Mix) (Single Version) (Dub Mix)/Don't Turn Around	1986	2.00	4.00	8.00
❏ V-15261	Two People (Dance Mix) (Dub Mix) (Single Mix)/Havin' a Party	1986	2.00	4.00	8.00
❏ V-15273	What You Get Is What You See (4 versions)	1987	2.00	4.00	8.00
❏ V-15296	Break Every Rule (3 versions)/Take Me to the River	1987	2.00	4.00	8.00
❏ V-15349	Afterglow (12" Vocal Dance Mix) (7" Mix) (Glowing Dub) (Tina's House Mix)	1987	—	3.50	7.00
❏ V-15543	Steamy Windows (Vocal Mix) (House Mix) (12" Mix) (12" House Dub Mix)	1989	—	3.50	7.00
❏ SPRO-79168/92 [DJ]	Afterglow (4 versions)	1987	2.00	4.00	8.00
FANTASY					
❏ D-161	Party Vibes (8:11)/Shame, Shame, Shame (5:06)	1980	3.00	6.00	12.00
VIRGIN					
❏ SPRO 11056 [DJ]	Goldeneye (Morales Club Mix 10:00) (LP Version 4:47)/(Morales 007 Dub 9:37) (Morales Dub of Bond 5:36)	1995	—	3.50	7.00
❏ SPRO-12716 [DJ]	On Silent Wings (Soul Solutions' Club Mix) (Instrumental) (Percappella) (Radio Edit)	1996	3.75	7.50	15.00
❏ SPRO 14918 [DJ]	When the Heartache Is Over (Hex Hector 12" Vocal Mix 8:45) (Hex Hector 7" Vocal Mix 3:30) (Hex Hector 12" Just Drums Mix 5:01)	1999	3.00	6.00	12.00
❏ SPRO 14951 [(2)DJ]	When the Heartache Is Over (Hex Hector 12" Vocal Mix 8:45) (Hex Hector 7" Vocal Mix 3:30) (Hex Hector 12" Instrumental 8:45) (Hex Hector Acapella 4:02) (Metro Mix 5:45) (7th District Mix 5:11) (Hex Hector 12" Just Drums Mix 5:01) (LP Version 3:46)	1999	5.00	10.00	20.00
❏ SPRO 14964 [DJ]	When the Heartache Is Over (Superchumbo Mix) (same on both sides)	1999	10.00	20.00	40.00
❏ Y-38578	In Your Wildest Dreams (Pink Noise Club Mix) (Deep Dish Paradise Mix) (Pleasant Instrumental) (Joe Extended Remix) (Antonio Banderas Crossover Mix) (Crossover Dub)	1996	2.50	5.00	10.00
—With Barry White					
❏ Y-38691	When the Heartache Is Over (Hex Hector 12" Vocal Mix 8:45) (Hex Hector 7" Vocal Mix 3:30) (Hex Hector 12" Instrumental 8:45) (Metro Mix 5:45) (7th District Mix 5:11) (Hex Hector Acapella 4:02)	1999	2.00	4.00	8.00
45s					
CAPITOL					
❏ B-5322	Let's Stay Together/I Wrote a Letter	1984	—	—	3.00
❏ B-5322 [PS]	Let's Stay Together/I Wrote a Letter	1984	—	2.50	5.00
❏ B-5354	What's Love Got to Do with It/Rock 'N' Roll Widow	1984	—	—	3.00
❏ B-5354 [PS]	What's Love Got to Do with It/Rock 'N' Roll Widow	1984	—	2.00	4.00
❏ B-5387	Better Be Good to Me/When I Was Young	1984	—	—	3.00
❏ B-5387 [PS]	Better Be Good to Me/When I Was Young	1984	—	2.00	4.00
❏ B-5433	Private Dancer/Nutbush City Limits	1984	—	—	3.00
❏ B-5433 [PS]	Private Dancer/Nutbush City Limits	1984	—	2.00	4.00
❏ B-5461	Show Some Respect/Let's Pretend We're Married	1985	—	—	3.00
❏ B-5461 [PS]	Show Some Respect/Let's Pretend We're Married	1985	—	2.00	4.00
❏ B-5491	We Don't Need Another Hero (Thunderdome)/(Instrumental)	1985	—	—	3.00
❏ B-5491 [PS]	We Don't Need Another Hero (Thunderdome)/(Instrumental)	1985	—	2.00	4.00
❏ B-5518	One of the Living/One of the Living (Dub)	1985	—	—	3.00
❏ B-5518 [PS]	One of the Living/One of the Living (Dub)	1985	—	2.00	4.00
❏ B-5615	Typical Male/Don't Turn Around	1986	—	—	3.00
❏ B-5615 [PS]	Typical Male/Don't Turn Around	1986	—	—	3.00
❏ B-5644	Two People/Havin' a Party	1986	—	—	3.00
❏ B-5644 [PS]	Two People/Havin' a Party	1986	—	—	3.00
❏ B-5668	What You Get Is What You See/What You Get Is What You See (Live)	1987	—	—	3.00
❏ B-5668 [PS]	What You Get Is What You See/What You Get Is What You See (Live)	1987	—	—	3.00
❏ B-44003	Break Every Rule/Take Me to the River	1987	—	—	3.00
❏ B-44003 [PS]	Break Every Rule/Take Me to the River	1987	—	—	3.00
❏ B-44111	Afterglow/(B-side unknown)	1987	—	2.00	4.00
❏ B-44442	The Best/Undercover Agent for the Blues	1989	—	—	3.00
❏ B-44442 [PS]	The Best/Undercover Agent for the Blues	1989	—	—	3.00
❏ B-44473	Steamy Windows/The Best	1989	—	—	3.00
❏ B-44473 [PS]	Steamy Windows/The Best	1989	—	—	3.00
❏ NR-44510	Look Me in the Heart/Stronger Than the Wind	1990	—	—	3.00
❏ S7-57702	Way of the World/You Know Who	1992	—	—	3.00
FANTASY					
❏ 948	Lean On Me/Shame, Shame, Shame	1984	—	2.00	4.00
POLYDOR					
❏ PRO-002 [DJ]	Acid Queen/Pinball Wizard	1975	10.00	20.00	40.00
—B-side by Elton John; promo-only					
POMPEII					
❏ 66682	Too Hot to Hold/You Got What You Wanted	1968	2.50	5.00	10.00
UNITED ARTISTS					
❏ XW 724	Whole Lotta Love/Rockin' 'N' Rollin'	1975	—	3.00	6.00
❏ XW 730	Delilah's Power/That's My Power	1975	—	3.00	6.00
❏ XW 920	Come Together/I Want to Take You Higher	1977	—	3.00	6.00
❏ XW 1265	Fire Down Below/Viva La Money	1979	—	2.50	5.00
VIRGIN					
❏ S7-17401	I Don't Wanna Fight/Tina's Wish	1993	—	—	3.00
❏ S7-17498	Why Must We Wait Until Tonight/Shake a Tail Feather	1993	—	—	3.00
❏ S7-18047	Proud Mary (Edit Live Version)/The Best (Live)	1994	—	2.50	5.00
—Red vinyl					
❏ S7-19217	Missing You/Do Something	1996	—	—	3.00
❏ 38691	When the Heartache Is Over/On Silent Wings	2000	—	—	3.00

Number	Title (A Side/B Side)	Yr	VG	VG+	NM
Albums					
CAPITOL					
❏ 1P 8192 [(2)]	Simply the Best	1991	5.00	10.00	20.00
—Columbia House edition (only US vinyl version)					
❏ ST-12330	Private Dancer	1984	2.00	4.00	8.00
❏ PJ-12530	Break Every Rule	1986	2.00	4.00	8.00
❏ C1-90126 [(2)]	Tina Live in Europe	1988	3.00	6.00	12.00
❏ C1-91873	Foreign Affair	1989	2.00	4.00	8.00
FANTASY					
❏ MFP-4520 [EP]	Mini	1984	2.00	4.00	8.00
SPRINGBOARD					
❏ SPB-4033	The Queen	1972	2.50	5.00	10.00
UNITED ARTISTS					
❏ UA-LA200-F	Tina Turns the Country On	1973	3.75	7.50	15.00
❏ UA-LA495-G	Acid Queen	1975	3.00	6.00	12.00
❏ UA-LA919-G	Rough	1978	3.00	6.00	12.00
WAGNER					
❏ 14108	Good Hearted Woman	1979	3.00	6.00	12.00

TURNER, TITUS
45s

Number	Title (A Side/B Side)	Yr	VG	VG+	NM
ATCO					
❏ 6310	Baby Girl (Part 1)/Baby Girl (Part 2)	1964	2.00	4.00	8.00
ATLANTIC					
❏ 1127	A-Knockin' at My Baby's Door/Hungry Man	1957	5.00	10.00	20.00
COLUMBIA					
❏ 42873	Young Wings Can Fly/Goodbye Rose	1963	2.50	5.00	10.00
❏ 42947	Make Someone Love You/ I'm a Fool About My Mama	1964	2.50	5.00	10.00
ENJOY					
❏ 1005	People Sure Act Funny/My Darkest Hour	1962	2.50	5.00	10.00
❏ 1015	Soulville/My Darkest Hour	1963	2.50	5.00	10.00
❏ 2010	Bow Wow/I Love You Baby	1963	2.50	5.00	10.00
GLOVER					
❏ 201	We Told You Not to Marry/ Taking Care of Business	1959	6.25	12.50	25.00
❏ 202	When the Sergeant Comes Marching Home/ (B-side unknown)	1960	6.25	12.50	25.00
JAMIE					
❏ 1174	Sound-Off/Me and My Lonely Telephone	1960	3.75	7.50	15.00
❏ 1177	Pony Train/Bla, Bla, Cha Cha Cha	1961	3.00	6.00	12.00
❏ 1184	Hey Doll Baby/I Want a Steady Girl	1961	3.00	6.00	12.00
❏ 1189	Horsin' Around/Chances Go Around	1961	3.00	6.00	12.00
❏ 1202	Shake the Hand of a Fool/Beautiful Stranger	1961	3.00	6.00	12.00
❏ 1213	Walk on the Wild Twist/Twistin' Train	1962	2.50	5.00	10.00
JOSIE					
❏ 990	I Just Can't Keep It to Myself/ People Sure Are Funny	1968	—	3.00	6.00
❏ 1012	His Funeral, My Trial/Do You Dig It	1969	—	3.00	6.00
KING					
❏ 5067	Have Mercy Baby/You Turned Lamps Too	1957	3.00	6.00	12.00
❏ 5095	Hold Your Loving/Stop the Rain	1957	3.00	6.00	12.00
❏ 5129	Follow Me/Way Down Yonder	1958	3.00	6.00	12.00
❏ 5140	Coralee/Tears of Joy Fill My Eyes	1958	3.00	6.00	12.00
❏ 5186	The Return of Staggolee/Answer Me	1959	3.00	6.00	12.00
❏ 5213 [M]	Tarzan/Fall Guy	1959	3.00	6.00	12.00
❏ S-5213 [S]	Tarzan/Fall Guy	1959	7.50	15.00	30.00
❏ 5243	Bonnie Baby/Miss Rubberneck Jones	1959	3.00	6.00	12.00
❏ 5465	Way Down Yonder/Miss Rubberneck Jones	1961	2.50	5.00	10.00
MURBO					
❏ 1001	Huckle Buckle Beanstalk/ Hoop Hoop Hoop a Hoopa Doo	1965	2.00	4.00	8.00
OKEH					
❏ 6844	Same Old Feeling/ Don't Take Everybody to Be Your Friend	1951	7.50	15.00	30.00
❏ 6883	What'cha Gonna Do for Me/ Got So Much Trouble	1952	6.25	12.50	25.00
❏ 6907	Jambalaya/Please Baby	1952	6.25	12.50	25.00
❏ 6929	Christmas Morning/Be Sure You Know	1952	7.50	15.00	30.00
❏ 6938	My Plea/It's Too Late Now	1953	6.25	12.50	25.00
❏ 6961	Big Mary's/Living in Misery	1953	6.25	12.50	25.00
❏ 7027	Over the Rainbow/My Lonely Room	1954	6.25	12.50	25.00
❏ 7038	Hello Stranger/Devilish Woman	1954	6.25	12.50	25.00
❏ 7244	Eye to Eye/What Kinda Deal Is This	1966	2.00	4.00	8.00
PHILIPS					
❏ 40445	(I'm Afraid the) Masquerade Is Over/Mary Mack	1967	2.00	4.00	8.00
WING					
❏ 90006	All Around the World/Do You Know	1955	5.00	10.00	20.00
❏ 90033	Sweet and Low/Big John	1955	5.00	10.00	20.00
❏ 90058	Get on the Right Track, Baby/I'll Wait Forever	1956	5.00	10.00	20.00
Albums					
JAMIE					
❏ JLP-3018 [M]	Sound Off	1961	5.00	10.00	20.00
❏ JLPS-3018 [S]	Sound Off	1961	7.50	15.00	30.00

TURNER, VELVERT, GROUP
Albums

Number	Title (A Side/B Side)	Yr	VG	VG+	NM
FAMILY PRODUCTIONS					
❏ FPS-2704	Velvert Turner Group	1972	12.50	25.00	50.00

TURNER, ZEB
Albums

Number	Title (A Side/B Side)	Yr	VG	VG+	NM
AUDIO LAB					
❏ AL-1537 [M]	Country Music in the Turner Style	1959	37.50	75.00	150.00

TURNPIKES, THE
45s

Number	Title (A Side/B Side)	Yr	VG	VG+	NM
CAPITOL					
❏ 2234	Cast a Spell/Nothing But Promises	1968	6.25	12.50	25.00

TURNQUIST REMEDY
Albums

Number	Title (A Side/B Side)	Yr	VG	VG+	NM
PENTAGRAM					
❏ PE-10004	Turnquist Remedy	1970	6.25	12.50	25.00

TURTLES, THE   Also see FLO AND EDDIE.
45s

Number	Title (A Side/B Side)	Yr	VG	VG+	NM
LOST-NITE					
❏ 435	Elenore/Is It Any Wonder	197?	—	2.50	5.00
❏ 436	Happy Together/The Walking Song	197?	—	2.50	5.00

Number	Title (A Side/B Side)	Yr	VG	VG+	NM
❏ 437	It Ain't Me, Babe/Almost There	197?	—	2.50	5.00
—Reissue					
❏ 438	Let Me Be/Your Maw Said You Cried	197?	—	2.50	5.00
—Reissue					
❏ 439	She'd Rather Be with Me/ Rugs of Woods & Flowers	197?	—	2.50	5.00
❏ 440	She's My Girl/Chicken Little Was Right	197?	—	2.50	5.00
—Reissue					
❏ 441	You Baby/Wanderin' Kind	197?	—	2.50	5.00
—Reissue					
❏ 442	You Showed Me/Buzz Saw	197?	—	2.50	5.00
—Reissue					
RHINO					
❏ RNOR 4504	You Know What I Mean/She's My Girl	1984	—	2.00	4.00
WHITE WHALE					
❏ 222	It Ain't Me, Babe/Almost There	1965	3.00	6.00	12.00
❏ 224	Let Me Be/Your Maw Said You Cried	1965	2.50	5.00	10.00
❏ 227	You Baby/Wanderin' Kind	1966	2.50	5.00	10.00
❏ 231	Grim Reaper of Love/Come Back	1966	5.00	10.00	20.00
❏ 234	We'll Meet Again/Outside Chance	1966	3.75	7.50	15.00
❏ 237	Outside Chance/Making My Mind Up	1966	2.50	5.00	10.00
❏ 238	Can I Get to Know You Better?/Like the Seasons	1966	2.50	5.00	10.00
❏ 244	Happy Together/Like the Seasons	1967	2.00	4.00	8.00
❏ 244 [PS]	Happy Together/Like the Seasons	1967	10.00	20.00	40.00
❏ 249	She'd Rather Be with Me/The Walking Song	1967	2.00	4.00	8.00
❏ 249 [PS]	She'd Rather Be with Me/The Walking Song	1967	6.25	12.50	25.00
❏ 251	Guide for the Married Man/Think I'll Run Away	1967	10.00	20.00	40.00
—Withdrawn shortly after release					
❏ 254	You Know What I Mean/ Rugs of Woods and Flowers	1967	2.00	4.00	8.00
❏ 254 [PS]	You Know What I Mean/ Rugs of Woods and Flowers	1967	3.75	7.50	15.00
❏ 260	She's My Girl/Chicken Little Was Right	1967	2.00	4.00	8.00
—White concentric circles on mostly blue label					
❏ 260	She's My Girl/Chicken Little Was Right	1967	2.50	5.00	10.00
—All-blue label					
❏ 260 [PS]	She's My Girl/Chicken Little Was Right	1967	5.00	10.00	20.00
❏ 264	Sound Asleep/Umbassa the Dragon	1968	2.00	4.00	8.00
❏ 264 [PS]	Sound Asleep/Umbassa the Dragon	1968	3.75	7.50	15.00
❏ 273	The Story of Rock and Roll/ Can't You Hear the Cows	1968	2.00	4.00	8.00
❏ 273 [PS]	The Story of Rock and Roll/ Can't You Hear the Cows	1968	12.50	25.00	50.00
❏ 276	Elenore/Surfer Dan	1968	2.00	4.00	8.00
❏ 276 [PS]	Elenore/Surfer Dan	1968	3.00	6.00	12.00
❏ 292	You Showed Me/Buzz Saw	1969	2.00	4.00	8.00
❏ 292 [PS]	You Showed Me/Buzz Saw	1969	3.00	6.00	12.00
❏ 306	House on the Hill/Come Over	1969	5.00	10.00	20.00
❏ 308	You Don't Have to Walk in the Rain/Come Over	1969	2.00	4.00	8.00
❏ 308 [PS]	You Don't Have to Walk in the Rain/Come Over	1969	2.50	5.00	10.00
❏ 326	Love in the City/Bachelor Mother	1969	2.00	4.00	8.00
❏ 326 [PS]	Love in the City/Bachelor Mother	1969	2.50	5.00	10.00
❏ 334	Lady-O/Somewhere Friday Nite	1969	2.00	4.00	8.00
❏ 341	Who Would Ever Think That I Would Marry Margaret?/We Ain't Gonna Party No More	1970	3.75	7.50	15.00
❏ 350	Is It Any Wonder?/Wanderin' Kind	1970	2.00	4.00	8.00
❏ 355	Eve of Destruction/Wanderin' Kind	1970	2.00	4.00	8.00
❏ 364	Me About You/Think I'll Run Away	1970	2.00	4.00	8.00
Albums					
RHINO					
❏ RNLP 151	It Ain't Me Babe	1983	2.50	5.00	10.00
❏ RNLP 152	Happy Together	1983	2.50	5.00	10.00
❏ RNLP 153	You Baby	1983	2.50	5.00	10.00
❏ RNLP 154	Wooden Head	1983	2.50	5.00	10.00
❏ RNLP 160	Greatest Hits	1983	2.50	5.00	10.00
❏ RNDF 280 [EP]	Turtle-Sized	1984	3.00	6.00	12.00
—Green vinyl turtle-shaped EP					
❏ RNPD 900	1968	1984	2.00	4.00	8.00
❏ RNPD 901 [PD]	1968	1984	3.00	6.00	12.00
❏ RNLP 70155	Chalon Road	1986	2.50	5.00	10.00
❏ RNLP 70156	The Turtles Present the Battle of the Bands	1986	2.50	5.00	10.00
❏ RNLP 70157	Turtle Soup	1986	2.50	5.00	10.00
❏ RNLP 70158	Shell Shock	1986	2.50	5.00	10.00
❏ RNLP 70159	Turtle Wax: The Best of the Turtles, Vol. 2	1988	2.50	5.00	10.00
❏ RNLP 70177	The Best of the Turtles (Golden Archives Series)	1987	2.50	5.00	10.00
SIRE					
❏ SASH-3703 [(2)]	The Turtles' Greatest Hits/ Happy Together Again	1974	5.00	10.00	20.00
WHITE WHALE					
❏ WW 111 [M]	It Ain't Me Babe	1965	7.50	15.00	30.00
❏ WW 112 [M]	You Baby	1966	7.50	15.00	30.00
❏ WW 114 [M]	Happy Together	1967	5.00	10.00	20.00
❏ WW 115 [M]	The Turtles! Golden Hits	1967	6.25	12.50	25.00
❏ WWS 7111 [S]	It Ain't Me Babe	1965	10.00	20.00	40.00
❏ WWS 7112 [S]	You Baby	1966	10.00	20.00	40.00
❏ WWS 7114 [S]	Happy Together	1967	6.25	12.50	25.00
❏ WWS 7115 [S]	The Turtles! Golden Hits	1967	5.00	10.00	20.00
❏ WWS 7118	The Turtles Present the Battle of the Bands	1968	6.25	12.50	25.00
❏ WW 7124	Turtle Soup	1969	6.25	12.50	25.00
❏ WW 7127	The Turtles! More Golden Hits	1970	5.00	10.00	20.00
❏ WW 7133	Wooden Head	1970	5.00	10.00	20.00

TURTLES, THE (2)
45s

Number	Title (A Side/B Side)	Yr	VG	VG+	NM
RCA VICTOR					
❏ 47-6356	Mystery Train/Say You Care	1955	6.25	12.50	25.00

TWEETERS, THE
45s

Number	Title (A Side/B Side)	Yr	VG	VG+	NM
DECCA					
❏ 30725	Mascara Mama/The Campus Rock	1958	7.50	15.00	30.00

TWENTIETH CENTURY ZOO, THE
45s

Number	Title (A Side/B Side)	Yr	VG	VG+	NM
CAZ					
❏ 103	You Don't Remember/Love in Your Face	1967	6.25	12.50	25.00
VAULT					
❏ 948	Rainbow/Bullfrog	1969	3.00	6.00	12.00

Number	Title (A Side/B Side)	Yr	VG	VG+	NM
7-Inch Extended Plays					
SUNDAZED					
❑ SEP 145	You Don't Remember//Love in Your Face/				
	Tossin' and Turnin'	1999	—	—	2.00
❑ SEP 145 [PS]	You Don't Remember	1999	—	—	2.00
Albums					
VAULT					
❑ LPS-122	Thunder on a Clear Day	1968	15.00	30.00	60.00
21ST CENTURY, THE					
45s					
GOSPEL TRUTH					
❑ 1209	Who's Supposed to Be Raising Who/				
	If the Shoe Fits, Wear It	1973	3.75	7.50	15.00
RCA VICTOR					
❑ PB-10201	Remember the Rain/You're My Only World	1975	2.00	4.00	8.00
❑ PB-10364	Child/See My Love Growin' Old	1975	—	3.00	6.00
Albums					
RCA VICTOR					
❑ APL1-1189	Ahead of Our Time	1975	7.50	15.00	30.00
23 SKIDOO					
45s					
MERCURY					
❑ 72874	The New Year's Song/Courtesy	1968	2.50	5.00	10.00
TWICE AS MUCH					
45s					
MGM					
❑ 13530	Sittin' on a Fence/Baby I Want You	1966	3.75	7.50	15.00
—A-side is a Mick Jagger-Keith Richards song that only later was released by the Rolling Stones.					
❑ 13530 [PS]	Sittin' on a Fence/Baby I Want You	1966	7.50	15.00	30.00
❑ 13600	Step Out of Line/Simplified	1966	2.50	5.00	10.00
TWIGGY					
45s					
CAPITOL					
❑ 5903	Over and Over/When I Think of You	1967	2.50	5.00	10.00
❑ 5903 [PS]	Over and Over/When I Think of You	1967	7.50	15.00	30.00
MERCURY					
❑ 73863	Rain on the Roof/Vanilla Olay	1976	—	3.00	6.00
❑ 73923	I Lie Awake and Dream of You/Woman in Love	1977	—	3.00	6.00
Albums					
MERCURY					
❑ SRM-1-1093	Twiggy	1976	3.00	6.00	12.00
❑ SRM-1-1138	Please Get My Name Right	1977	3.00	6.00	12.00
TWILIGHTERS, THE (1)					
45s					
BELL					
❑ 624	Be Faithful/Thumper	1965	5.00	10.00	20.00
TWILIGHTERS, THE (2)					
45s					
BUBBLE					
❑ 1334	My Silent Prayer/Little Bitty Bed Bug	1962	10.00	20.00	40.00
CHESS					
❑ 1803	Scratchin'/Tears	1961	6.25	12.50	25.00
CHOLLY					
❑ 712	Let There Be Love/Eternally	1957	250.00	500.00	1000.
DOT					
❑ 15526	Eternally/I Believe	1957	10.00	20.00	40.00
EBB					
❑ 117	Pride and Joy/Live Like a King	1957	10.00	20.00	40.00
ELDO					
❑ 115	Nothin'/Do You Believe	1961	6.25	12.50	25.00
IMPERIAL					
❑ 66201	Shake a Tail Feather/Road to Fortune	1966	3.00	6.00	12.00
❑ 66238	I Still Love You/Meat Ball	1967	3.00	6.00	12.00
JVB					
❑ 83	How Many Times/Water-Water	1957	200.00	400.00	800.00
MGM					
❑ 55011	Little Did I Dream/Gotta Get On the Train	1955	75.00	150.00	300.00
❑ 55014	Lovely Lady/Half Angel	1955	100.00	200.00	400.00
PICO					
❑ 2801	Eternally/I Believe	1957	20.00	40.00	80.00
TWILIGHTERS, THE (3)					
45s					
CADDY					
❑ 103	Eternally/I Believe	1955	62.50	125.00	250.00
TWILIGHTERS, THE (4)					
45s					
FRATERNITY					
❑ 889	To Love in Vain/The Beginning of Love	1961	6.25	12.50	25.00
—As "The Twi-Lighters"					
TWILIGHTERS, THE (5)					
45s					
MARSHALL					
❑ 702	Please Tell Me You're Mine/Wondering	1953	50.00	100.00	200.00
—Black vinyl					
❑ 702	Please Tell Me You're Mine/Wondering	1953	250.00	500.00	1000.
—Red vinyl					
TWILIGHTERS, THE (6)					
45s					
SPECIALTY					
❑ 548	It's True/Wha-Bop-Sh-Wah	1955	15.00	30.00	60.00
TWILIGHTERS, THE (7)					
45s					
SPIN					
❑ 0001	Yes You Are/A Possibility	1960	50.00	100.00	200.00

Number	Title (A Side/B Side)	Yr	VG	VG+	NM
TWILIGHTERS, THE (U)					
45s					
GROOVE					
❑ 0154	Sittin' in a Corner/It's a Cold, Cold, Rainy Day	1956	15.00	30.00	60.00
—As "The Twi-Lighters"					
RICKI					
❑ 907	Help Me/Rockin' Mule	1961	10.00	20.00	40.00
SARA					
❑ 1048	Restless Love/Can't You Stay a Little Longer	1961	15.00	30.00	60.00
VANCO					
❑ 204	Out of My Mind/I Need Your Lovin'	1968	2.50	5.00	10.00
TWILLEY, DWIGHT					
12-Inch Singles					
ARISTA					
❑ SP-79 [DJ]	Somebody to Love/Money	1979	3.00	6.00	12.00
CBS ASSOCIATED					
❑ ZAS 2360 [DJ]	Sexual (same on both sides)	1986	2.50	5.00	10.00
EMI AMERICA					
❑ SPRO-9104 [DJ]	Little Bit of Love (Edit)/Little Bit of Love (LP)	1984	2.00	4.00	8.00
45s					
ARISTA					
❑ 0278	Rock and Roll 47/Twilley Don't Mind	1977	—	2.50	5.00
❑ 0299	Trying to Find My Baby/Here She Comes	1977	—	2.50	5.00
❑ 0311	Looking for the Magic/Invasion	1978	—	2.50	5.00
❑ 0415	Out of My Hands/				
	Nothing's Ever Gonna Change So Fast	1979	—	2.00	4.00
❑ 0433	Runaway/Burnin' Sand	1979	—	2.00	4.00
❑ 0478	Somebody to Love/Money (That's What I Want)	1979	—	2.00	4.00
CBS ASSOCIATED					
❑ 06050	Sexual/Wild Dogs	1986	—	—	3.00
EMI AMERICA					
❑ 8109	Later That Night/Somebody to Love	1982	—	2.00	4.00
❑ 8115	I Found the Magic/I'm Back Again	1982	—	2.00	4.00
❑ 8196	Girls/To Get to You	1984	—	—	3.00
❑ 8196 [PS]	Girls/To Get to You	1984	—	2.00	4.00
❑ 8206	Little Bit of Love/Mad Dog	1984	—	—	3.00
❑ 8206 [PS]	Little Bit of Love/Mad Dog	1984	—	2.00	4.00
❑ 8235	Why You Wanna Break My Heart/				
	Chilly D's Theme	1984	—	—	3.00
❑ 8235 [PS]	Why You Wanna Break My Heart/				
	Chilly D's Theme	1984	—	—	3.00
PRIVATE I					
❑ 04820	Keep On Working/(Instrumental)	1985	—	—	3.00
SHELTER					
❑ 40380	I'm on Fire/Did You See What Happened	1975	—	2.50	5.00
❑ 40380 [PS]	I'm on Fire/Did You See What Happened	1975	2.50	5.00	10.00
❑ 40450	Sincerely/You Were So Warm	1975	—	2.50	5.00
❑ 62003	Could Be Love/Feeling in the Dark	1976	—	2.50	5.00
❑ 62003 [PS]	Could Be Love/Feeling in the Dark	1976	2.00	4.00	8.00
THE RIGHT STUFF					
❑ S7-19563	I'm on Fire/Looking for the Magic	1997	—	—	3.00
Albums					
ARISTA					
❑ AB 4140	Twilley Don't Mind	1977	2.50	5.00	10.00
❑ AB 4214	Twilley	1979	2.50	5.00	10.00
❑ AB 4251	Blueprint	1980	—	—	—
—Unreleased					
CBS ASSOCIATED					
❑ BFZ 40266	Wild Dogs	1986	2.00	4.00	8.00
EMI AMERICA					
❑ ST-17064	Scuba Divers	1982	2.50	5.00	10.00
❑ ST-17107	Jungle	1984	2.50	5.00	10.00
MCA					
❑ 688	Sincerely	1981	2.00	4.00	8.00
—Reissue of Shelter LP					
SHELTER					
❑ SA-52001	Sincerely	1976	2.50	5.00	10.00
TWIN-TONES, THE See THE TWINS.					
TWINK					
Albums					
SIRE					
❑ SES-97022	Think Pink	1970	25.00	50.00	100.00
TWINKLE					
45s					
AURORA					
❑ 163	The End of the World/				
	What Am I Doing Here with You	1966	2.50	5.00	10.00
TOLLIE					
❑ 9040	The Boy of My Dreams/Terry	1965	3.00	6.00	12.00
❑ 9047	Ain't Nobody Home But Me/Golden Lights	1965	3.00	6.00	12.00
TWINS, THE					
45s					
LANCER					
❑ 106	Heart of Gold/Buttercup	1959	3.75	7.50	15.00
❑ 106 [PS]	Heart of Gold/Buttercup	1959	7.50	15.00	30.00
—Number not on sleeve					
RCA VICTOR					
❑ 47-7148	My Dear/The Flip Skip	1958	5.00	10.00	20.00
—As "The Twin-Tones"					
❑ 47-7235	Jo-Ann's Sister/Who Knows the Secret	1958	5.00	10.00	20.00
❑ 47-7382	Classroom Rock/Gee Whiz	1958	5.00	10.00	20.00
7-Inch Extended Plays					
RCA VICTOR					
❑ EPA-4107	Jo-Ann/Before You Go//My Dancing Lady/				
	One Mail a Day	1957	5.00	10.00	20.00
—As "The Twin-Tones"					
❑ EPA-4107 [PS]	Jim and John The Twin-Tones	1957	5.00	10.00	20.00
❑ EPA-4237	My Dear/The Flip Skip//I Want a Girl/				
	Together Forever	1958	5.00	10.00	20.00
❑ EPA-4237 [PS]	Teenagers Love the Twins	1958	5.00	10.00	20.00

Number	Title (A Side/B Side)	Yr	VG	VG+	NM
Albums					
RCA VICTOR					
❏ LPM-1708 [M]	Teenagers Love the Twins	1958	12.50	25.00	50.00
TWISTERS, THE					
45s					
APT					
❏ 25045	Come Go with Me/Pretty Little Girl Next Door	1960	5.00	10.00	20.00
CAMPUS					
❏ 125	Elvis Leaves Sorrento/Street Dance	1961	7.50	15.00	30.00
CAPITOL					
❏ 4451	Turn the Page/Dancing Little Clown	1960	5.00	10.00	20.00
DUAL					
❏ 502	Silly Chilli/Peppermint Twist Time	1962	3.00	6.00	12.00
FELCO					
❏ 103	Count Down 1-2-3/Speed Limit	1959	6.25	12.50	25.00
SUN-SET					
❏ 501	Please Come Back/This Is the End	1961	150.00	300.00	600.00
Albums					
TREASURE					
❏ TLP-890 [M]	Doin' the Twist	1962	7.50	15.00	30.00
TWISTIN' KINGS					
45s					
MOTOWN					
❏ 1022	Xmas Twist/White House Twist	1961	10.00	20.00	40.00
❏ 1023	Congo (Part 1)/Congo (Part 2)	1962	10.00	20.00	40.00
Albums					
MOTOWN					
❏ M-601 [M]	Twistin' the World Around	1961	75.00	150.00	300.00
TWITTY, CONWAY Also see CONWAY TWITTY AND LORETTA LYNN.					
45s					
ABC-PARAMOUNT					
❏ 10507	Go On and Cry/She Loves Me	1963	3.75	7.50	15.00
❏ 10550	Such a Night/My Baby Left Me	1964	6.25	12.50	25.00
COLLECTABLES					
❏ 90063	Hello Darlin'/Don't Take It Away	199?	—	—	3.00
—Reissue					
❏ 90112	Tight Fittin' Jeans/Red Neckin' Love Makin' Night	199?	—	—	3.00
—Reissue					
DECCA					
❏ 31833	Together Forever/That Kind of Girl	1965	2.50	5.00	10.00
❏ 31897	Guess My Eyes Were Bigger Than Her Heart/Honky Tonk Man	1966	2.00	4.00	8.00
❏ 31983	Look Into My Teardrops/If You Were Mine to Lose	1966	2.00	4.00	8.00
❏ 32081	I Don't Want to Be with Me/Before I'll Set Her Free	1967	2.00	4.00	8.00
❏ 32147	Don't Put Your Hurt in My Heart/Walk Me to the Door	1967	2.00	4.00	8.00
❏ 32208	Funny (But I'm Not Laughing)/Working Girl	1967	2.00	4.00	8.00
❏ 32272	The Image of Me/Dim Lights, Thick Smoke (And Loud, Loud Music)	1968	2.00	4.00	8.00
❏ 32361	Next in Line/I'm Checking Out	1968	2.00	4.00	8.00
❏ 32424	Darling, You Know I Wouldn't Lie/Table in the Corner	1968	2.00	4.00	8.00
❏ 32481	I Love You More Today/Bad Girl	1969	2.00	4.00	8.00
❏ 32546	To See My Angel Cry/I Did the Best I Could	1969	2.00	4.00	8.00
❏ 32599	That's When She Started to Stop Loving You/I'll Get Over Losing You	1969	2.00	4.00	8.00
❏ 32661	Hello Darlin'/Girl at the Bar	1970	—	3.50	7.00
❏ 32742	Fifteen Years Ago/Up Comes the Bottle	1970	—	3.50	7.00
❏ 32801	How Much More Can She Stand/Just Like a Stranger	1971	—	3.50	7.00
❏ 32842	I Wonder What She'll Think About Me Leaving/A Heartache Just Walked In	1971	—	3.50	7.00
❏ 32895	I Can't See Me Without You/I Didn't Lose Her	1971	—	3.50	7.00
❏ 32945	(Lost Her Love) On Our Last Date/I'll Never Make It Home Tonight	1972	—	3.50	7.00
❏ 32988	I Can't Stop Loving You/She Needs Someone to Hold Her (When She Cries)	1972	—	3.50	7.00
❏ 32988	I Can't Stop Loving You/Since She's Not with the One She Loves	1972	—	3.50	7.00
❏ 33033	She Needs Someone to Hold Her (When She Cries)/This Road That I Walk	1972	—	3.50	7.00
ELEKTRA					
❏ 47302	The Clown/The Boy Next Door	1982	—	2.00	4.00
❏ 47302 [PS]	The Clown/The Boy Next Door	1982	—	2.50	5.00
❏ 47443	Slow Hand/When Love Was Something Else	1982	—	2.00	4.00
❏ 69854	The Rose/It's Only Make Believe	1982	—	2.00	4.00
❏ 69854 [PS]	The Rose/It's Only Make Believe	1982	—	2.50	5.00
❏ 69964	We Did But Now You Don't/A Good Love Died Tonight	1982	—	2.00	4.00
MCA					
❏ 40027	Baby's Gone/Dim Lonely Places	1973	—	2.50	5.00
❏ 40094	You've Never Been This Far Before/You Make It Hard	1973	—	2.50	5.00
❏ 40173	There's a Honky Tonk Angel (Who'll Take Me Back In)/Don't Let It Go to Your Heart	1973	—	2.50	5.00
❏ 40224	I'm Not Through Loving You Yet/Before Your Time	1974	—	2.50	5.00
❏ 40282	I See the Want To in Your Eyes/Girl from Tupelo	1974	—	2.50	5.00
❏ 40339	Linda on My Mind/She's Just Not Over You Yet	1974	—	2.50	5.00
❏ 40407	Touch the Hand/Don't Cry Joni	1975	—	2.50	5.00
❏ 40492	This Time I've Hurt Her More Than She Loves Me/She Did, It Did, I Didn't	1975	—	2.50	5.00
❏ 40534	After All the Good Is Gone/I Got a Good Thing Going	1976	—	2.50	5.00
❏ 40601	The Games That Daddies Play/There's More Love in the Arms You're Leaving	1976	—	2.50	5.00
❏ 40649	I Can't Believe She Gives It All to Me/I Can't Help It If She Can't Stop Loving Me	1976	—	2.50	5.00
❏ 40682	Play, Guitar, Play/One in a Million	1977	—	2.50	5.00
❏ 40754	I've Already Loved You in My Mind/I Changed My Mind	1977	—	2.50	5.00
❏ 40805	Talkin' 'Bout You/Georgia Keeps Pulling on My Ring	1977	—	2.50	5.00
❏ 40857	I'm Used to Losing You/The Grandest Lady of Them All	1978	—	2.50	5.00
❏ 40929	That's All She Wrote/Boogie Grass Band	1978	—	2.50	5.00
❏ 40963	Your Love Had Taken Me That High/My Woman Knows	1978	—	2.50	5.00
❏ 41002	Don't Take It Away/Draggin' Chains	1979	—	2.00	4.00
❏ 41059	I May Never Get to Heaven/Grand Ole Blues	1979	—	2.00	4.00
❏ 41135	Happy Birthday Darlin'/Heavy Tears	1979	—	2.00	4.00
❏ 41174	I'd Just Love to Lay You Down/She Thinks I Still Care	1980	—	2.00	4.00
❏ 41174	I'd Love to Lay You Down/She Thinks I Still Care	1980	—	2.50	5.00
—Note slightly different A-side title					
❏ 41271	I've Never Seen the Likes of You/Soulful Woman	1980	—	2.00	4.00
❏ 51011	A Bridge That Just Won't Burn/You'll Be Back	1980	—	2.00	4.00
❏ 51059	Rest Your Love on Me/I Am the Dreamer (You Are the Dream)	1981	—	2.00	4.00
❏ 51137	Tight Fittin' Jeans/I Made You a Woman	1981	—	2.00	4.00
❏ 51199	Red Neckin' Love Makin' Night/Hearts	1981	—	2.00	4.00
❏ 52032	Over Thirty (Not Over the Hill)/Love Salvation	1982	—	2.00	4.00
❏ 52154	We Had It All/Cheatin' Fire	1983	—	2.00	4.00
❏ 53034	Julia/Everybody Needs a Hero	1987	—	2.00	4.00
❏ 53134	I Want to Know You Before We Make Love/Snake Boots	1987	—	2.00	4.00
❏ 53200	That's My Job/Lonely Town	1987	—	2.00	4.00
❏ 53276	Goodbye Time/Your Loving Side	1988	—	2.00	4.00
❏ 53373	Saturday Night Special/If You Were Mine to Lose	1988	—	2.00	4.00
❏ 53456	I Wish I Was Still in Your Dreams/If You Were Mine to Lose	1988	—	2.00	4.00
❏ 53558	After All the Good Is Gone/I Can't Believe She Gives It All to Me	198?	—	—	3.00
—"Double Play" reissue					
❏ 53559	I May Never Get to Heaven/Happy Birthday Darlin'	198?	—	—	3.00
—"Double Play" reissue					
❏ 53560	Boogie Grass Band/Your Love Had Taken Me That High	198?	—	—	3.00
—"Double Play" reissue					
❏ 53561	I've Already Loved You in My Mind/Georgia Keeps Pulling on My Ring	198?	—	—	3.00
—"Double Play" reissue					
❏ 53562	Tight Fittin' Jeans/Red Neckin' Love Makin' Night	198?	—	—	3.00
—"Double Play" reissue					
❏ 53563	Linda on My Mind/Touch the Hand	198?	—	—	3.00
—"Double Play" reissue					
❏ 53564	There's a Honky Tonk Angel (Who'll Take Me Back In)/I See the Want To in Your Eyes	198?	—	—	3.00
—"Double Play" reissue					
❏ 53565	I Can't Stop Loving You/You've Never Been This Far Before	198?	—	—	3.00
—"Double Play" reissue					
❏ 53566	Hello Darlin'/Don't Take It Away	198?	—	—	3.00
—"Double Play" reissue					
❏ 53567	Fifteen Years Ago/This Time I've Hurt Her More Than She Loves Me	198?	—	—	3.00
—"Double Play" reissue					
❏ 53602	She Needs Someone to Hold Her (When She Cries)/(Lost Her Love) On Our Last Date	198?	—	—	3.00
—"Double Play" reissue					
❏ 53633	She's Got a Single Thing in Mind/Too White to Sing the Blues	1989	—	2.00	4.00
❏ 53688	The House on Old Lonesome Road/Nobody Can Fill Your Shoes	1989	—	2.00	4.00
❏ 53759	Who's Gonna Know/Private Part of My Heart	1989	—	2.00	4.00
❏ 53983	I Couldn't See You Leavin'/Just the Thought of Losing You	1991	—	2.00	4.00
❏ 54077	One Bridge I Didn't Burn/I'm Tired of Being Something	1991	—	2.00	4.00
❏ 54186	She's Got a Man on Her Mind/You Put It There	1991	—	2.00	4.00
❏ 54281	Who Did They Think He Was/Let the Pretty Lady Dance	1991	—	2.00	4.00
❏ 54716	I'm the Only Thing (I'll Hold Against You)/Final Touches	1993	—	2.00	4.00
❏ 54766	Don't It Make You Lonely/I Don't Love You	1993	—	2.00	4.00
❏ 60079	Look Into My Teardrops/The Image of Me	197?	—	2.00	4.00
—Reissue series; black label with rainbow					
❏ 60080	Hello Darlin'/Fifteen Years Ago	197?	—	2.00	4.00
—Reissue series; black label with rainbow					
❏ 60158	She Needs Someone to Hold Her (When She Cries)/This Road That I Walk	197?	—	2.00	4.00
—Reissue series; black label with rainbow					
❏ 60175	You've Never Been This Far Before/You Make It Hard	197?	—	2.00	4.00
—Reissue series; black label with rainbow					
❏ 60180	Hello Darlin' (English Version)/(Russian Version)	1975	2.50	5.00	10.00
—Reissue series; only 45 rpm issue of the version played in space during the joint U.S.-Soviet Apollo-Soyuz mission in 1975					
❏ 60182	Touch the Hand/Don't Cry Joni	1976	—	2.00	4.00
—Reissue series; black label with rainbow					
❏ 60184	Linda on My Mind/I See the Want To in Your Eyes	1976	—	2.00	4.00
—Reissue series; black label with rainbow					
❏ 60185	There's a Honky Tonk Angel (Who'll Take Me Back In)/I'm Not Through Loving You Yet	1976	—	2.00	4.00
—Reissue series; black label with rainbow					
❏ 79000	Fit to Be Tied Down/When You're Cool (The Sun Shines All the Time)	1990	—	2.00	4.00
❏ 79067	Crazy in Love/Hearts Breakin' All Over Town	1990	—	2.00	4.00
MERCURY					
❏ 71086	I Need Your Lovin'/Born to Sing the Blues	1957	10.00	20.00	40.00
❏ 71148	Maybe Baby/Shake It Up	1957	10.00	20.00	40.00
❏ 71384	Why Can't I Get Through to You/Double Talk Baby	1958	10.00	20.00	40.00
MGM					
❏ 12677 [M]	It's Only Make Believe/I'll Try	1958	6.25	12.50	25.00
❏ 12748	The Story of My Love/Make Me Know You're Mine	1959	6.25	12.50	25.00
❏ 12785	Hey Little Lucy! (Don'tcha Put No Lipstick On)/When I'm Not with You	1959	6.25	12.50	25.00
❏ 12804	Mona Lisa/Heavenly	1959	6.25	12.50	25.00

T

Number	Title (A Side/B Side)	Yr	VG	VG+	NM
❏ 12826 [M]	Danny Boy/Halfway to Heaven	1959	5.00	10.00	20.00
—Second pressings on black labels					
❏ 12826 [M]	Danny Boy/Halfway to Heaven	1959	6.25	12.50	25.00
—First pressings on yellow labels					
❏ 12857	Lonely Blue Boy/Star Spangled Heaven	1959	5.00	10.00	20.00
—Black label					
❏ 12857	Lonely Blue Boy/Star Spangled Heaven	1959	7.50	15.00	30.00
—Yellow label					
❏ 12886	What Am I Living For/The Hurt in My Heart	1960	5.00	10.00	20.00
❏ 12886 [PS]	What Am I Living For/The Hurt in My Heart	1960	12.50	25.00	50.00
❏ 12911	Is a Blue Bird Blue/She's Mine	1960	5.00	10.00	20.00
❏ 12911 [PS]	Is a Blue Bird Blue/She's Mine	1960	12.50	25.00	50.00
❏ 12918	What a Dream/Tell Me One More Time	1960	3.75	7.50	15.00
❏ 12943	Teasin'/I Need You So	1960	3.75	7.50	15.00
❏ 12962	Whole Lot of Shakin' Going On/The Flame	1960	3.75	7.50	15.00
❏ 12969	C'est Si Bon (It's So Good)/ Don't You Dare Let Me Down	1960	3.75	7.50	15.00
❏ 12969 [PS]	C'est Si Bon (It's So Good)/ Don't You Dare Let Me Down	1960	12.50	25.00	50.00
❏ 12998	The Next Kiss (Is the Last Goodbye)/ A Man Alone	1961	3.75	7.50	15.00
❏ 12998 [PS]	The Next Kiss (Is the Last Goodbye)/ A Man Alone	1961	12.50	25.00	50.00
❏ 13011	I'm in a Blue, Blue Mood/A Million Teardrops	1961	3.75	7.50	15.00
❏ 13034	It's Drivin' Me Wild/Sweet Sorrow	1961	3.75	7.50	15.00
❏ 13034 [PS]	It's Drivin' Me Wild/Sweet Sorrow	1961	10.00	20.00	40.00
❏ 13050	Portrait of a Fool/Tower of Tears	1961	3.75	7.50	15.00
❏ 13072	Little Piece of My Heart/Comfy N' Cozy	1962	3.75	7.50	15.00
❏ 13089	There's Something on Your Mind/ Unchained Melody	1962	3.75	7.50	15.00
❏ 13112	I Hope, I Think, I Wish/The Pickup	1962	3.75	7.50	15.00
❏ 13149	I Got My Mojo Working/She Ain't No Angel	1963	3.75	7.50	15.00
❏ 14172	It's Only Make Believe/Lonely Blue Boy	1970	—	2.50	5.00
❏ 14205	What Am I Living For/I'll Try	1970	—	2.50	5.00
❏ 14274	What a Dream/Long Black Train	1971	—	2.50	5.00
❏ 14355	It's Too Late/I Hope, I Think, I Wish	1972	—	2.50	5.00
❏ 14408	Walk On By/Hey Miss Ruby	1972	—	2.50	5.00
❏ 14447	Boss Man/Fever	1972	—	2.50	5.00
❏ 14582	Danny Boy/The Pickup	1973	—	2.50	5.00
❏ SK-50107 [S]	It's Only Make Believe/I'll Try	1958	25.00	50.00	100.00
❏ SK-50130 [S]	Danny Boy/Halfway to Heaven	1959	25.00	50.00	100.00
WARNER BROS.					
❏ 28577	Fallin' for You for Years/I'll Try	1986	—	2.00	4.00
❏ 28692	Desperado Love/I Can't See Me Without You	1986	—	2.00	4.00
❏ 28772	You'll Never Know How Much I Needed You Today/Fifteen Years Ago	1986	—	2.00	4.00
❏ 28866	The Legend and the Man/(I Can't Believe) She Gives It All to Me	1985	—	2.00	4.00
❏ 28966	Between Blue Eyes and Jeans/Baby's Gone	1985	—	2.00	4.00
❏ 29057	Don't Call Him a Cowboy/ After All the Good Is Gone	1985	—	2.00	4.00
❏ 29129	White Christmas/Happy the Christmas Clown	1984	—	2.50	5.00
❏ 29129 [PS]	White Christmas/Happy the Christmas Clown	1984	—	2.50	5.00
❏ 29137	Ain't She Somethin' Else/ The Games That Daddies Play	1984	—	2.00	4.00
❏ 29227	I Don't Know a Thing About Love (The Moon Song)/Don't Cry Joni	1984	—	2.00	4.00
❏ 29308	Somebody's Needin' Somebody/ (Lying Here with) Linda on My Mind	1984	—	2.00	4.00
❏ 29395	Three Times a Lady/I Think I'm in Love	1983	—	2.00	4.00
❏ 29505	Heartache Tonight/Hello Darlin'	1983	—	2.00	4.00
❏ 29636	Lost in the Feeling/ You've Never Been This Far Before	1983	—	2.00	4.00
❏ 69854	The Rose/It's Only Make Believe	1982	—	—	3.00
—Reissue of Elektra 69854					
7-Inch Extended Plays					
DECCA					
❏ DL 734732	Be Proud of Your Man/Girl at the Bar/That's When She Started to Stop Loving You//Girl from Muskogee /I'd Rather Be Gone/The House of the Rising Sun	1969	3.75	7.50	15.00
—Jukebox issue; small hole, plays at 33 1/3 rpm					
❏ DL 734732 [PS]	To See an Angel Cry	1969	3.75	7.50	15.00
MGM					
❏ X-1623	(contents unknown)	1958	37.50	75.00	150.00
❏ X-1623 [PS]	It's Only Make Believe	1958	37.50	75.00	150.00
❏ X-1640	It's Only Make Believe/Hallelujah, I Love Her So/ /First Romance/Make Me Know You're Mine	1959	25.00	50.00	100.00
❏ X-1640 [PS]	Conway Twitty Sings, Volume 1	1959	25.00	50.00	100.00
❏ X-1641	(contents unknown)	1959	25.00	50.00	100.00
❏ X-1641 [PS]	Conway Twitty Sings, Volume 2	1959	25.00	50.00	100.00
❏ X-1642	(contents unknown)	1959	25.00	50.00	100.00
❏ X-1642 [PS]	Conway Twitty Sings, Volume 3	1959	25.00	50.00	100.00
❏ X-1678	Danny Boy/Heavenly//She's Mine/Blueberry Hill	1959	25.00	50.00	100.00
❏ X-1678 [PS]	Saturday Night with Conway Twitty, Volume 1	1959	25.00	50.00	100.00
❏ X-1679	(contents unknown)	1959	25.00	50.00	100.00
❏ X-1679 [PS]	Saturday Night with Conway Twitty, Volume 2	1959	25.00	50.00	100.00
❏ X-1680	(contents unknown)	1959	25.00	50.00	100.00
❏ X-1680 [PS]	Saturday Night with Conway Twitty, Volume 3	1959	25.00	50.00	100.00
❏ X-1701	(contents unknown)	1960	25.00	50.00	100.00
❏ X-1701 [PS]	Lonely Blue Boy	1960	25.00	50.00	100.00
Albums					
ACCORD					
❏ SN-7169	Early Favorites	1982	3.00	6.00	12.00
ALLEGIANCE					
❏ AV-5012	You Made Me What I Am	1983	3.75	7.50	15.00
DECCA					
❏ DL 4724 [M]	Conway Twitty Sings	1965	6.25	12.50	25.00
❏ DL 4828 [M]	Look Into My Teardrops	1966	6.25	12.50	25.00
❏ DL 4913 [M]	Conway Twitty Country	1967	7.50	15.00	30.00
❏ DL 4990 [M]	Here's Conway Twitty	1968	12.50	25.00	50.00
❏ DL 74724 [S]	Conway Twitty Sings	1965	7.50	15.00	30.00
❏ DL 74828 [S]	Look Into My Teardrops	1966	7.50	15.00	30.00
❏ DL 74913 [S]	Conway Twitty Country	1967	7.50	15.00	30.00
❏ DL 74990 [S]	Here's Conway Twitty	1968	7.50	15.00	30.00
❏ DL 75062	Next in Line	1968	6.25	12.50	25.00
❏ DL 75105	Darling, You Know I Wouldn't Lie	1968	5.00	10.00	20.00
❏ DL 75131	I Love You More Today	1969	5.00	10.00	20.00
❏ DL 75172	To See My Angel Cry	1970	5.00	10.00	20.00
❏ DL 75209	Hello Darlin'	1970	5.00	10.00	20.00
❏ DL 75248	Fifteen Years Ago	1970	5.00	10.00	20.00
❏ DL 75276	How Much More Can She Stand	1971	5.00	10.00	20.00
❏ DL 75292	I Wonder What She'll Think About Me Leaving	1971	5.00	10.00	20.00
❏ DL 75335	I Can't See Me Without You	1972	5.00	10.00	20.00
❏ DL 75352	Conway Twitty's Greatest Hits Vol. I	1972	5.00	10.00	20.00
❏ DL 75361	I Can't Stop Loving You/Last Date	1972	5.00	10.00	20.00
❏ ST-93776	How Much More Can She Stand	1971	6.25	12.50	25.00
—Capitol Record Club edition					
ELEKTRA					
❏ 60005	Southern Confort	1982	2.50	5.00	10.00
❏ 60115	#1 Classics, Volume 1	1982	2.50	5.00	10.00
❏ 60182	Dream Maker	1982	2.50	5.00	10.00
❏ 60209	#1 Classics, Volume 2	1982	2.50	5.00	10.00
HEARTLAND					
❏ HL-1088/9 [(2)]	The Very Best of Conway Twitty	1989	5.00	10.00	20.00
MCA					
❏ 18	To See My Angel Cry	1973	3.00	6.00	12.00
—Reissue of Decca 75172					
❏ 19	Hello Darlin'	1973	3.00	6.00	12.00
—Reissue of Decca 75209					
❏ 52	Conway Twitty's Greatest Hits	1973	3.00	6.00	12.00
—Reissue of Decca 75352					
❏ 53	I Can't Stop Loving You/Last Date	1973	3.00	6.00	12.00
—Reissue of Decca 75361					
❏ 303	She Needs Someone to Hold Her (When She Cries)	1973	3.75	7.50	15.00
❏ 359	You've Never Been This Far Before/ Baby's Gone	1973	3.75	7.50	15.00
❏ 376	Clinging to a Saving Hand	1973	15.00	30.00	60.00
❏ 406	Honky Tonk Angel	1974	3.75	7.50	15.00
❏ 441	I'm Not Through Loving You Yet	1974	3.75	7.50	15.00
❏ 469	Linda on My Mind	1975	3.75	7.50	15.00
❏ 625	High Priest of Country	197?	2.50	5.00	10.00
—Reissue of MCA 2144					
❏ 702	Conway	197?	2.50	5.00	10.00
—Reissue of MCA 3063					
❏ 2144	High Priest of Country Music	1975	3.75	7.50	15.00
❏ 2176	Twitty (This Time I've Hurt Her More Than She Loves Me)	1975	3.75	7.50	15.00
❏ 2206	Now and Then	1976	3.75	7.50	15.00
❏ 2235	Conway Twitty's Greatest Hits, Vol. 2	1976	3.75	7.50	15.00
❏ 2262	Play Guitar Play	1977	3.00	6.00	12.00
❏ 2293	I've Already Loved You in My Mind	1977	3.00	6.00	12.00
❏ 2328	Georgia Keeps Pullin' on My Ring	1978	3.00	6.00	12.00
❏ 2345	Conway Twitty's Greatest Hits, Vol. 1	1978	3.00	6.00	12.00
—Reissue of Decca 75352					
❏ 3043	The Very Best of Conway Twitty	1978	3.00	6.00	12.00
❏ 3063	Conway	1978	3.00	6.00	12.00
❏ 3086	Cross Winds	1979	3.00	6.00	12.00
❏ 3210	Heart and Soul	1980	3.00	6.00	12.00
❏ 5138	Rest Your Love on Me	1980	3.00	6.00	12.00
❏ 5204	Mr. T.	1981	3.00	6.00	12.00
❏ 5318	Number Ones	1982	3.00	6.00	12.00
❏ 5424	Classic Conway	1983	2.50	5.00	10.00
❏ 5700	Songwriter	1986	2.00	4.00	8.00
❏ 5817	A Night with Conway Twitty	1986	2.00	4.00	8.00
❏ 5969	Borderline	1987	2.00	4.00	8.00
❏ 37081	Georgia Keeps Pullin' on My Ring	197?	2.00	4.00	8.00
—Budget-line reissue					
❏ 37163	Cross Winds	197?	2.00	4.00	8.00
—Budget-line reissue					
❏ 37227	Heart and Soul	1983	2.00	4.00	8.00
—Budget-line reissue					
❏ 37228	Rest Your Love on Me	1983	2.00	4.00	8.00
—Budget-line reissue					
❏ 37229	Conway Twitty's Greatest Hits, Vol. 1	1983	2.00	4.00	8.00
—Budget-line reissue					
❏ 42115	Still in Your Dreams	1988	2.00	4.00	8.00
❏ 42297	House on Old Lonesome Road	1989	3.00	6.00	12.00
MCA CORAL					
❏ CB-20000	I'm So Used to Loving You	1973	3.00	6.00	12.00
METRO					
❏ M-512 [M]	It's Only Make Believe	1966	3.75	7.50	15.00
❏ MS-512 [S]	It's Only Make Believe	1966	5.00	10.00	20.00
MGM					
❏ GAS-110	Conway Twitty (Golden Archive Series)	1970	5.00	10.00	20.00
❏ E-3744 [M]	Conway Twitty Sings	1959	25.00	50.00	100.00
—Yellow label					
❏ E-3744 [M]	Conway Twitty Sings	196?	75.00	150.00	300.00
—Reissue with orange cover and a clean-cut photo of Conway					
❏ E-3744 [M]	Conway Twitty Sings	1960	10.00	20.00	40.00
—Black label					
❏ SE-3744 [S]	Conway Twitty Sings	1959	37.50	75.00	150.00
—Yellow label					
❏ SE-3744 [S]	Conway Twitty Sings	196?	75.00	150.00	300.00
—Reissue with orange cover and a clean-cut photo of Conway					
❏ SE-3744 [S]	Conway Twitty Sings	1960	12.50	25.00	50.00
—Black label					
❏ E-3786 [M]	Saturday Night with Conway Twitty	1960	17.50	35.00	70.00
❏ SE-3786 [S]	Saturday Night with Conway Twitty	1960	25.00	50.00	100.00
❏ E-3818 [M]	Lonely Blue Boy	1960	17.50	35.00	70.00
❏ SE-3818 [S]	Lonely Blue Boy	1960	25.00	50.00	100.00
❏ E-3849 [M]	Conway Twitty's Greatest Hits	1960	10.00	20.00	40.00
—Without poster					
❏ E-3849 [M]	Conway Twitty's Greatest Hits	1960	17.50	35.00	70.00
—With poster					
❏ SE-3849 [P]	Conway Twitty's Greatest Hits	1960	12.50	25.00	50.00
—Without poster					
❏ SE-3849 [P]	Conway Twitty's Greatest Hits	1960	20.00	40.00	80.00
—With poster					
❏ E-3907 [M]	The Rock and Roll Story	1961	12.50	25.00	50.00
❏ SE-3907 [S]	The Rock and Roll Story	1961	20.00	40.00	80.00
❏ E-3943 [M]	The Conway Twitty Touch	1961	12.50	25.00	50.00
❏ SE-3943 [S]	The Conway Twitty Touch	1961	20.00	40.00	80.00
❏ E-4019 [M]	Portrait of a Fool and Others	1962	10.00	20.00	40.00
❏ SE-4019 [S]	Portrait of a Fool and Others	1962	12.50	25.00	50.00
❏ E-4089 [M]	R & B '63	1963	10.00	20.00	40.00
❏ SE-4089 [S]	R & B '63	1963	12.50	25.00	50.00
❏ E-4217 [M]	Hit the Road	1964	6.25	12.50	25.00
❏ SE-4217 [S]	Hit the Road	1964	7.50	15.00	30.00
❏ SE-4650	You Can't Take the Country Out of Conway	1969	3.75	7.50	15.00
❏ SE-4799	Conway Twitty Hits	1971	3.75	7.50	15.00

Johnny Tillotson, "Talk Back Trembling Lips," MGM K12181, picture sleeve, $10-$20.

Pete Townshend, "Face the Face," Atco 7-99590, picture sleeve, $1-$3.

The Tradewinds, *Excursions,* Kama Sutra KLPS-8057, stereo LP, $15-30.

The Troggs, *Wild Thing,* Atco 33-193, mono LP, $25-$50.

The Turtles, "You Showed Me," White Whale 292, picture sleeve, $6-$12.

The Tymes, "So Much in Love," Parkway 871, picture sleeve, $15-$30.

T

Number	Title (A Side/B Side)	Yr	VG	VG+	NM
❏ SE-4837	Conway Twitty Sings the Blues	1972	3.75	7.50	15.00
❏ SES-4844 [(2)]	20 Great Hits by Conway Twitty	1973	4.50	9.00	18.00
PICKWICK					
❏ SPC-3360	Shake It Up	1973	3.00	6.00	12.00
TEE VEE					
❏ 1009	20 Certified #1 Hits	1978	3.75	7.50	15.00
WARNER BROS.					
❏ 23869	Lost in the Feeling	1983	2.50	5.00	10.00
❏ 23971	Merry Twismas	1983	5.00	10.00	20.00
❏ 25078	By Heart	1984	2.50	5.00	10.00
❏ 25170	Conway's Latest Greatest Hits	1984	2.50	5.00	10.00
❏ 25207	Don't Call Him a Cowboy	1985	2.50	5.00	10.00
❏ 25294	Chasin' Rainbows	1985	2.50	5.00	10.00
❏ 25406	Fallin' for You for Years	1986	2.50	5.00	10.00
❏ 25777	#1's — The Warner Bros. Years	1988	2.00	4.00	8.00
❏ 60115	#1 Classics, Volume 1	1983	2.00	4.00	8.00
—Reissue of Elektra LP					
❏ 60182	Dream Maker	1983	2.00	4.00	8.00
—Reissue of Elektra LP					
❏ 60209	#1 Classics, Volume 2	1983	2.00	4.00	8.00
—Reissue of Elektra LP					

TWITTY, CONWAY, AND LORETTA LYNN Also see each artist's individual listings.
45s
DECCA

Number	Title (A Side/B Side)	Yr	VG	VG+	NM
❏ 32776	After the Fire Is Gone/ The One I Can't Live Without	1971	—	3.50	7.00
❏ 32873	Lead Me On/Four Glass Walls	1971	—	3.50	7.00
MCA					
❏ 40079	Louisiana Woman, Mississippi Man/ Living Together Alone	1973	—	2.50	5.00
❏ 40251	As Soon As I Hang Up the Phone/ A Lifetime Before	1974	—	2.50	5.00
❏ 40283	Trouble in Paradise/We've Already Tasted Love	1974	—	2.50	5.00
❏ 40420	Feelin's/You Done Lost Your Baby	1975	—	2.50	5.00
❏ 40572	The Letter/God Bless America Again	1976	—	2.50	5.00
❏ 40728	The Bed I'm Dreaming On/ I Can't Love You Enough	1977	—	2.50	5.00
❏ 40920	You're the Reason Our Kids Are Ugly/ From Seven Until Ten	1978	—	2.50	5.00
❏ 41141	The Sadness of It All/You Know Just What I'd Do	1979	—	2.50	5.00
❏ 41232	Hit the Road Jack/It's True Love	1980	—	2.00	4.00
❏ 51050	Lovin' What Your Lovin' Does to Me/ Silent Partners	1981	—	2.00	4.00
❏ 51114	I Still Believe in Waltzes/Oh Honey	1981	—	2.00	4.00
❏ 53417	Making Believe/As Soon As I Hang Up the Phone (The Telephone Song)	1988	—	2.00	4.00
❏ 53610	Louisiana Woman, Mississippi Man/ After the Fire Is Gone	198?	—	—	3.00
—"Double Play" reissue					
❏ 60167	Lead Me On/After the Fire Is Gone	197?	—	2.00	4.00
—Reissue series; black label with rainbow					
❏ 60183	Louisiana Woman, Mississippi Man/ As Soon As I Hang Up the Phone	1976	—	2.00	4.00
—Reissue series; black label with rainbow					

Albums
DECCA

Number	Title	Yr	VG	VG+	NM
❏ DL 75251	We Only Make Believe	1971	5.00	10.00	20.00
❏ DL 75326	Lead Me On	1972	5.00	10.00	20.00
HEARTLAND					
❏ HL-1059/60 [(2)]	The Best of Conway and Loretta	1987	5.00	10.00	20.00
MCA					
❏ 8	We Only Make Believe	1973	3.00	6.00	12.00
—Reissue of Decca 75251					
❏ 9	Lead Me On	1973	3.00	6.00	12.00
—Reissue of Decca 75326					
❏ 335	Louisiana Woman, Mississippi Man	1973	3.75	7.50	15.00
❏ 427	Country Partners	1974	3.75	7.50	15.00
❏ 629	United Talent	198?	2.50	5.00	10.00
—Reissue of MCA 2209					
❏ 722	Honky Tonk Heroes	198?	2.50	5.00	10.00
—Reissue of MCA 2372					
❏ 723	Diamond Duet	198?	2.50	5.00	10.00
—Reissue of MCA 3190					
❏ 2143	Feelins'	1975	3.75	7.50	15.00
❏ 2209	United Talent	1976	3.75	7.50	15.00
❏ 2278	Dynamic Duo	1977	3.00	6.00	12.00
❏ 2354	Country Partners	1978	2.50	5.00	10.00
—Reissue of MCA 427					
❏ 2372	Honky Tonk Heroes	1978	3.00	6.00	12.00
❏ 3164	The Very Best of Loretta and Conway	1979	3.00	6.00	12.00
❏ 3190	Diamond Duet	1979	3.00	6.00	12.00
❏ 5178	Two's a Party	1981	3.00	6.00	12.00
❏ 37237	The Very Best of Loretta and Conway	1983	2.00	4.00	8.00
—Budget-line reissue					
❏ 42216	Making Believe	1988	2.00	4.00	8.00
MCA CORAL					
❏ CDL-8006	Never Ending Song of Love	1973	3.00	6.00	12.00

TWO CHAPS, THE With JAY BLACK, later of JAY AND THE AMERICANS.
45s
ATLANTIC

Number	Title (A Side/B Side)	Yr	VG	VG+	NM
❏ 1195	Forgive Me/No More	1958	7.50	15.00	30.00

2 OF CLUBS
45s
FRATERNITY

Number	Title (A Side/B Side)	Yr	VG	VG+	NM
❏ F972	Heart/My First Heartbreak	1966	2.50	5.00	10.00
❏ F975	Walk Tall/So Blue Is Fall	1966	3.00	6.00	12.00
❏ F975	Walk Tall Like a Man/So Blue Is Fall	1966	3.75	7.50	15.00
❏ F990	Let Me Walk with You/You Love Me	1967	2.50	5.00	10.00
❏ F994	River Deep — Mountain High/You Love Me	1967	3.75	7.50	15.00
❏ F999	Look Away/(B-side unknown)	1967	3.75	7.50	15.00

TYLER, FRANKIE See FRANKIE VALLI.

TYLER, JOEY
45s
REPRISE

Number	Title (A Side/B Side)	Yr	VG	VG+	NM
❏ 0269	All the Good Times Are Over/When You Got Nothin' Else, You Got the Blues	1964	2.50	5.00	10.00

TYLER, KIP
45s
CHALLENGE

Number	Title (A Side/B Side)	Yr	VG	VG+	NM
❏ 1014	She Got Eyes/Shadow Street	1957	7.50	15.00	30.00
❏ 59008	Jungle Hop/Ooh Yeah Baby	1958	10.00	20.00	40.00
EBB					
❏ 154	She's My Witch/Rumble Rock	1959	12.50	25.00	50.00
❏ 156	Oh Linda/Kali Lou	1959	12.50	25.00	50.00
GYRO DISC					
❏ 711	Surfer's Lament (Eternity)/Toledo	1963	12.50	25.00	50.00
❏ 711 [PS]	Surfer's Lament (Eternity)/Toledo	1963	25.00	50.00	100.00
IMPERIAL					
❏ 5641	Rocket 'Round the Universe/The Goblin Trot	1960	7.50	15.00	30.00

TYLER, WILLIE, AND LESTER
Albums
TAMLA

Number	Title	Yr	VG	VG+	NM
❏ TM-265 [M]	Hello Dummy	1965	50.00	100.00	200.00

TYMES, THE
12-Inch Singles
RCA

Number	Title (A Side/B Side)	Yr	VG	VG+	NM
❏ PD-11068	How Am I to Know/I'll Take You There	1977	3.00	6.00	12.00

45s
CAPITOL

Number	Title (A Side/B Side)	Yr	VG	VG+	NM
❏ 3440	When I Look Around Me/Smile a Tender Smile	1972	—	3.00	6.00
COLUMBIA					
❏ 44630	People/For Love of Ivy	1968	2.00	4.00	8.00
❏ 44799	God Bless the Child/The Love That You're Looking For	1969	—	3.00	6.00
❏ 44917	Find My Way/If You Love Me Baby	1969	—	3.00	6.00
❏ 45078	Love Child/Most Beautiful Married Lady	1970	—	3.00	6.00
❏ 45336	She's Gone/Someone to Watch Over Me	1971	—	3.00	6.00
MGM					
❏ 13536	Pretend/Street Talk	1966	5.00	10.00	20.00
❏ 13631	(Touch of) Baby/What Would I Do	1966	5.00	10.00	20.00
PARKWAY					
❏ 871	So Much in Love/Roscoe James McClain	1963	3.75	7.50	15.00
❏ 871	So in Love/Roscoe James McClain	1963	6.25	12.50	25.00
—Original title of A-side					
❏ 871 [PS]	So Much in Love/Roscoe James McClain	1963	7.50	15.00	30.00
❏ 884	Wonderful! Wonderful!/Come with Me to the Sea	1963	3.75	7.50	15.00
❏ 884 [PS]	Wonderful! Wonderful!/Come with Me to the Sea	1963	6.25	12.50	25.00
❏ 891	Somewhere/View from My Window	1963	3.75	7.50	15.00
❏ 891 [PS]	Somewhere/View from My Window	1963	6.25	12.50	25.00
❏ 908	To Each His Own/Wonderland of Love	1964	3.75	7.50	15.00
❏ 908 [PS]	To Each His Own/Wonderland of Love	1964	6.25	12.50	25.00
❏ 919	The Magic of Our Summer Love/ With All My Heart	1964	3.75	7.50	15.00
❏ 919 [PS]	The Magic of Our Summer Love/ With All My Heart	1964	6.25	12.50	25.00
❏ 924	Here She Comes/Malibu	1964	3.75	7.50	15.00
❏ 924 [PS]	Here She Comes/Malibu	1964	6.25	12.50	25.00
❏ 933	The Twelfth of Never/Here She Comes	1964	3.75	7.50	15.00
❏ 7039	Isle of Love/I'm Always Chasing Rainbows	1964	3.75	7.50	15.00
—Included as a bonus with album 7039					
RCA					
❏ PB-10862	Love's Illusion/Savannah Sunny Sunday	1976	—	2.00	4.00
❏ PB-11136	I'll Take You There/How Am I to Know (The Things a Girl in Love Should Know)	1977	—	2.00	4.00
❏ GB-12082	You Little Trustmaker/Ms. Grace	1980	—	—	—
—Unreleased?					
RCA VICTOR					
❏ PB-10022	You Little Trustmaker/The North Hills	1974	—	2.50	5.00
❏ PB-10128	Ms. Grace/The Crutch	1974	—	2.00	4.00
❏ PB-10244	Interloop/Someday, Somehow I'm Keeping You	1975	—	2.00	4.00
❏ PB-10422	God's Gonna Punish You/ If I Can't Make You Smile	1975	—	2.00	4.00
❏ GB-10493	You Little Trustmaker/The North Hills	1975	—	2.00	4.00
—Gold Standard Series					
❏ PB-10561	Good Morning Dear Lord/It's Cool	1976	—	2.00	4.00
❏ PB-10713	Goin' Through the Motions/Only Your Love	1976	—	2.00	4.00
WINCHESTER					
❏ 1002	These Foolish Things (Remind Me of You)/ This Time It's Love	1967	2.50	5.00	10.00

Albums
ABKCO

Number	Title	Yr	VG	VG+	NM
❏ 4228	The Best of Tymes	1973	3.00	6.00	12.00
COLUMBIA					
❏ CS 9778	People	1969	3.75	7.50	15.00
PARKWAY					
❏ P 7032 [M]	So Much in Love	1963	10.00	20.00	40.00
—With group standing in front-cover photo					
❏ P 7032 [M]	So Much in Love	1963	50.00	100.00	200.00
—With head-and-shoulders group photo on front cover					
❏ P 7038 [M]	The Sound of the Wonderful Tymes	1963	10.00	20.00	40.00
❏ SP 7038 [S]	The Sound of the Wonderful Tymes	1963	12.50	25.00	50.00
❏ P 7039 [M]	Somewhere	1964	12.50	25.00	50.00
—Includes bonus single 7039 (deduct 20 percent if missing)					
❏ P 7049 [M]	18 Greatest Hits	1964	10.00	20.00	40.00
RCA VICTOR					
❏ APL1-0727	Trustmaker	1974	3.00	6.00	12.00
❏ APL1-1835	Turning Point	1976	3.00	6.00	12.00
❏ APL1-2406	Diggin' Their Roots	1977	3.00	6.00	12.00

TYRANNOSAURUS REX See T. REX.

TYRELL, DANNY, AND THE CLEESHAYS
45s
EASTMAN

Number	Title (A Side/B Side)	Yr	VG	VG+	NM
❏ 784	You're Only Seventeen/Let's Walk, Let's Talk	1958	10.00	20.00	40.00

TYSON, ROY
45s
DOUBLE L

Number	Title (A Side/B Side)	Yr	VG	VG+	NM
❏ 723	Oh What a Night for Love/Not Too Young	1963	20.00	40.00	80.00
❏ 733	The Girl I Love/I Want to Be Your Boyfriend	1964	25.00	50.00	100.00

Number	Title (A Side/B Side)	Yr	VG	VG+	NM

U

U.K.'S, THE
45s
CAMEO
| ❏ 342 | Ever Faithful Ever True/Your Love Is All I Want | 1965 | 2.50 | 5.00 | 10.00 |

U.S. 1
45s
PRIVATE STOCK
| ❏ 45,045 | Bye Bye Baby/Creation | 1975 | — | 3.00 | 6.00 |

UBANS, THE
45s
RADIANT
| ❏ 102 | Gloria/On the Bridge | 1964 | 50.00 | 100.00 | 200.00 |

UFO
12-Inch Singles
CHRYSALIS
❏ CHS-5-PDJ [DJ]Try Me (3:25) (4:52)		1977	5.00	10.00	20.00
❏ CHS-28-PDJ [DJ]Lonely Heart (same on both sides)		1981	2.50	5.00	10.00
❏ VAS 2266 [DJ] This Time//Too Hot to Handle/Lights Out		1986	2.50	5.00	10.00
❏ VAS 2363 [DJ] Night Run/Blue		1986	3.00	6.00	12.00
45s
CHRYSALIS
❏ 2040	Doctor Doctor/Lipstick Traces	197?	—	3.00	6.00
❏ 2157	Too Hot to Handle/Electric Phase	1977	2.00	4.00	8.00
—Red vinyl					
❏ 2157 [PS]	Too Hot to Handle/Electric Phase	1977	2.50	5.00	10.00
❏ 2178	Try Me/Gettin' Ready	1977	—	2.50	5.00
❏ 2239	Cherry/You Don't Fool Me	1978	—	2.50	5.00
❏ 2263	Only You Can Rock Me/Ain't No Baby	1978	—	2.50	5.00
❏ 2308	Doctor Doctor/Lights Out	1979	—	2.50	5.00
❏ 2590	Back in My Life/You'll Get Love	1981	—	2.50	5.00
Albums
CHRYSALIS
❏ CHR 1059	Phenomenon	1974	3.75	7.50	15.00
—Green label					
❏ CHR 1059	Phenomenon	1977	3.00	6.00	12.00
—Fading blue label					
❏ CHR 1074	Force It	1975	3.00	6.00	12.00
❏ CHR 1103	No Heavy Petting	1976	3.00	6.00	12.00
❏ CHR 1127	Lights Out	1977	3.00	6.00	12.00
❏ CHR 1182	Obsession	1978	3.00	6.00	12.00
❏ CHR 1209 [(2)] Strangers in the Night		1979	3.75	7.50	15.00
❏ CHR 1239	No Place to Run	1980	3.00	6.00	12.00
❏ CHR 1307	The Wild, the Willing and the Innocent	1981	3.00	6.00	12.00
❏ CHR 1360	Mechanix	1982	3.00	6.00	12.00
❏ PV 41059	Phenomenon	1983	2.00	4.00	8.00
❏ PV 41074	Force It	1983	2.00	4.00	8.00
❏ PV 41103	No Heavy Petting	1983	2.00	4.00	8.00
❏ FV 41127	Lights Out	1983	2.00	4.00	8.00
❏ PV 41127	Lights Out	1986	2.00	4.00	8.00
—Reissue of FV 41127					
❏ PV 41182	Obsession	1983	2.00	4.00	8.00
❏ V2X 41209 [(2)]Strangers in the Night		1983	2.50	5.00	10.00
❏ PV 41239	No Place to Run	1983	2.00	4.00	8.00
❏ PV 41307	The Wild, the Willing and the Innocent	1983	2.00	4.00	8.00
❏ PV 41360	Mechanix	1983	2.00	4.00	8.00
❏ FV 41402	Making Contact	1983	2.50	5.00	10.00
❏ PV 41402	Making Contact	1986	2.00	4.00	8.00
—Reissue of FV 41402					
❏ BFV 41518	Misdemeanor	1986	2.50	5.00	10.00
❏ FV 41644	The Best of the Rest	1988	2.50	5.00	10.00
METAL BLADE/ENIGMA
| ❏ 7 73404 1 [EP] Ain't Misbehavin' | | 1989 | 3.00 | 6.00 | 12.00 |
RARE EARTH
| ❏ RS 624 | UFO 1 | 1971 | 6.25 | 12.50 | 25.00 |

UGGAMS, LESLIE
45s
ATLANTIC
❏ 2313	Don't You Care/Who Killed Teddy Bear	1965	3.75	7.50	15.00
❏ 2371	If My Friends Could See Me Now/ We Can Work It Out	1967	2.50	5.00	10.00
❏ 2397	Hallelujah Baby/My Own Morning	1967	2.50	5.00	10.00
❏ 2469	I (Who Have Nothing)/The House Built on Sand	1967	2.50	5.00	10.00
❏ 2524	River Deep, Mountain High/Land of Make Believe	1968	2.50	5.00	10.00
❏ 2675	Just to Satisfy You/That Old Sweet Roll (Hi-De-Ho)	1969	2.00	4.00	8.00
❏ 2698	Home/Save the Country	1969	2.00	4.00	8.00
❏ 2727	He Can Do It/Walk Him Up the Stairs	1970	2.00	4.00	8.00
COLUMBIA
❏ 41451	One More Sunrise (Morgen)/The Eyes of God	1959	3.00	6.00	12.00
❏ 41531	My Favorite Things/ Sixteen Going on Seventeen	1959	3.00	6.00	12.00
❏ 41564	Carefree Years/Lullaby of the Leaves	1960	2.50	5.00	10.00
❏ 41654	I Grew Up Last Night/I'm Just a Little Sparrow	1960	2.50	5.00	10.00
❏ 41798	Inherit the Wind/Love Is Like a Violin	1960	2.50	5.00	10.00
❏ 42055	He Doesn't Know/I Love Him	1961	2.50	5.00	10.00
❏ 42255	Get Happy/Birth of the Blues	1961	2.50	5.00	10.00
❏ 42611	Each and Ev'ry Day/ Is He the Only Man in the World	1962	2.50	5.00	10.00
❏ 4-42948	Here and Now/A Fortune in Pennies	1964	2.50	5.00	10.00
❏ 43012	A Legend in My Time/My Wish	1964	2.50	5.00	10.00
❏ 43064	Little Bird/This Is My Prayer	1964	2.50	5.00	10.00
❏ 4-43121	And I Love Him/Who Do You Think	1964	2.50	5.00	10.00
GORDY
| ❏ 7149 | I Want to Make It Easy on You/Two Shoes | 1976 | — | 3.00 | 6.00 |
MGM
❏ 11437	Easter Sunny Day/Percy the Pale Faced Bear	1953	5.00	10.00	20.00
—As "Lesley 'Uggams' Crayne"					
❏ 11626	My Stocking Is Empty/This Is Santa Claus	1953	5.00	10.00	20.00
—As "Leslie 'Uggams' Crayne"					
❏ 11676	My Candy Apple/Kickin' Up a Storm	1954	5.00	10.00	20.00
—As "Lesley 'Uggams' Crayne"					
❏ 11755	Ev'ry Little Piggy's Curley Tail/Palsy Walsy Land	1954	5.00	10.00	20.00
❏ 11868	Uncle Santa/The Fat, Fat Man	1954	5.00	10.00	20.00
❏ 11965	Meet My Friend, Mr. Sun/Did You Ever Dream	1955	3.75	7.50	15.00
Albums
ATLANTIC
❏ 8128 [M]	Time to Love	1967	3.75	7.50	15.00
❏ SD 8128 [S]	Time to Love	1967	5.00	10.00	20.00
❏ SD 8196	What's an Uggams	1968	3.75	7.50	15.00
❏ SD 8241	Just to Satisfy You	1969	3.75	7.50	15.00
COLUMBIA
❏ CL 1706 [M]	Leslie Uggams on TV	1962	3.75	7.50	15.00
❏ CL 1865 [M]	More Leslie Uggams on TV	1963	3.75	7.50	15.00
❏ CL 2071 [M]	So in Love	1963	3.75	7.50	15.00
❏ CS 8506 [S]	Leslie Uggams on TV	1962	5.00	10.00	20.00
❏ CS 8665 [S]	More Leslie Uggams on TV	1963	5.00	10.00	20.00
❏ CS 8871 [S]	So in Love	1963	5.00	10.00	20.00
❏ CS 9936	Leslie	1970	3.00	6.00	12.00
MOTOWN
| ❏ M6-846 | Leslie Uggams | 1975 | 3.00 | 6.00 | 12.00 |
SONDAY
| ❏ 8000 | Try to See It My Way | 1972 | 3.00 | 6.00 | 12.00 |

UGLYS, THE
45s
ABC-PARAMOUNT
❏ 10707	Wake Up My Mind/Ugly Blues	1965	3.00	6.00	12.00
❏ 10748	It's Alright/A Friend	1965	3.00	6.00	12.00
❏ 10773	Quiet Explosion/A Good Idea	1966	3.00	6.00	12.00

ULANO, SAM
45s
MGM
| ❏ SK-37 | Santa & The Doodle-Li-Boop/ The Story Of Santa Claus | 1954 | 2.50 | 5.00 | 10.00 |
| ❏ SK-37 [PS] | Santa & The Doodle-Li-Boop/ The Story Of Santa Claus | 1954 | 5.00 | 10.00 | 20.00 |

ULTIMATE SPINACH
45s
MGM
| ❏ 14023 | (Just Like) Romeo and Juliet/Some Days You Just Can't Win | 1969 | 3.00 | 6.00 | 12.00 |
Albums
MGM
❏ E-4518 [M]	Ultimate Spinach	1968	7.50	15.00	30.00
❏ SE-4518 [S]	Ultimate Spinach	1968	6.25	12.50	25.00
❏ E-4570 [M]	Behold & See	1968	12.50	25.00	50.00
—Mono is promo only (yellow label)					
❏ SE-4570 [S]	Behold & See	1968	6.25	12.50	25.00
❏ SE-4600	Ultimate Spinach	1969	6.25	12.50	25.00

ULTRA VIOLET
45s
CAPITOL
| ❏ 3743 | Shanghai Bill/La Vie En Rose | 1973 | — | 3.00 | 6.00 |
Albums
CAPITOL
| ❏ ST-11244 | Ultra Violet | 1973 | 6.25 | 12.50 | 25.00 |

UMILIANI, PIERO
45s
ARIEL
| ❏ 500 | Mah-Na Mah-Na/You Tried to Warn Me | 1969 | 3.00 | 6.00 | 12.00 |
—From the movie "Swedish Heaven and Hell"; Umiliani's name is only in parentheses on the label, making it appear as if he is merely the composer

UNBEATABLES, THE
45s
DAWN
| ❏ 552 | I Love Paris/What I Say | 1964 | 10.00 | 20.00 | 40.00 |
Albums
DAWN
| ❏ 5050 [M] | Live at Palisades Park | 1964 | 37.50 | 75.00 | 150.00 |

UNCHAINED MYNDS, THE
45s
BUDDAH
❏ 111	We Can't Go On This Way/Going Back to Miami	1969	3.75	7.50	15.00
❏ 119	Every Day/(B-side unknown)	1969	3.75	7.50	15.00
❏ 140	You, Me, and My Yo-Yo/Every Day	1970	3.75	7.50	15.00
TEEN TOWN
| ❏ 106 | We Can't Go On This Way/Going Back to Miami | 1969 | 10.00 | 20.00 | 40.00 |

UNCLE DOG
45s
MCA
| ❏ 40005 | River Road/Boogie with Me | 1973 | — | 2.50 | 5.00 |
Albums
MCA
| ❏ 302 | Old Hat | 1973 | 5.00 | 10.00 | 20.00 |

UNDERBEATS, THE
45s
BANGAR
| ❏ 00632 | Annie Do the Dog/Sweet Words of Love | 1964 | 15.00 | 30.00 | 60.00 |
| ❏ 00632 | Broken Arrow/Little Romance | 1964 | 15.00 | 30.00 | 60.00 |
GARRETT
| ❏ 4004 | Foot Stompin'/Route 66 | 1964 | 6.25 | 12.50 | 25.00 |
METROBEAT
| ❏ 4449 | Sweetest Girl in the World/ It's Gonna Rain Today | 1967 | 6.25 | 12.50 | 25.00 |

Number	Title (A Side/B Side)	Yr	VG	VG+	NM
SOMA					
❏ 1449	Book of Love/Darling Lorraine	1966	6.25	12.50	25.00
❏ 1458	I Can't Stand It/Shake It for Me	1966	5.00	10.00	20.00
TWIN-TOWN					
❏ 706	Jo Jo Gunne/Our Love	1965	7.50	15.00	30.00

UNDERDOGS, THE
45s

Number	Title (A Side/B Side)	Yr	VG	VG+	NM
HIDEOUT					
❏ 1001	The Man in the Glass/ Friday at the Hideout (Judy Be Mine)	1965	7.50	15.00	30.00
❏ 1004	Little Girl/Don't Pretend	1965	7.50	15.00	30.00
❏ 1011	Surprise Surprise/Get Down on Your Knees	1966	10.00	20.00	40.00
REPRISE					
❏ 0422	The Man in the Glass/Friday at the Hideout (Judy Be Mine)	1965	3.75	7.50	15.00
❏ 0446	Little Girl/Don't Pretend	1966	3.75	7.50	15.00
V.I.P.					
❏ 25040	Love's Gone Bad/Mo Jo Hanna	1966	6.25	12.50	25.00

UNDERGRADS, THE
Albums

Number	Title (A Side/B Side)	Yr	VG	VG+	NM
SOMERSET					
❏ P-21600 [M]	Bluegrass Hoot on Campus	1963	2.50	5.00	10.00
❏ SF-21600 [S]	Bluegrass Hoot on Campus	1963	3.00	6.00	12.00

UNDERGROUND, THE
45s

Number	Title (A Side/B Side)	Yr	VG	VG+	NM
MAINSTREAM					
❏ 660	Easy/Satisfy'n Sunday	1967	6.25	12.50	25.00
❏ 667	Get Him Out of Your Mind/Take Me Back	1967	6.25	12.50	25.00

UNDERGROUND SUNSHINE   Also see THE CHALLENGERS (4).
45s

Number	Title (A Side/B Side)	Yr	VG	VG+	NM
INTREPID					
❏ ITDJ-3 [DJ]	Don't Shut Me Out (mono/stereo)	1969	3.00	6.00	12.00
—Promo issue of 75012					
❏ 75002	Birthday/All I Want Is You	1969	3.00	6.00	12.00
❏ 75012	Don't Shut Me Out/Take Me, Break Me	1969	2.50	5.00	10.00
❏ 75019	Nine to Five (Ain't My Bag)/Rotten Woman Blues	1969	2.50	5.00	10.00
❏ 75029	Jesus Is Just Alright/Six O'Clock	1970	2.50	5.00	10.00
Albums					
INTREPID					
❏ IT-74003	Let There Be Light	1969	7.50	15.00	30.00

UNDERTAKERS, THE
45s

Number	Title (A Side/B Side)	Yr	VG	VG+	NM
PARKWAY					
❏ 909	Just a Little Bit/Stupidity	1964	3.00	6.00	12.00

UNDISPUTED TRUTH, THE
12-Inch Singles

Number	Title (A Side/B Side)	Yr	VG	VG+	NM
WHITFIELD					
❏ 8306	Let's Go Down to the Disco (9:10)/ You + Me = Love	1976	5.00	10.00	20.00
❏ 8783	Show Time (8:59)/Misunderstood	1979	3.75	7.50	15.00
45s					
GORDY					
❏ 7106	Save My Love for a Rainy Day/ Since I've Lost You	1971	2.00	4.00	8.00
❏ 7108	Smiling Faces Sometimes/ You Got the Love I Need	1971	—	3.00	6.00
❏ 7112	You Make Your Own Heaven and Hell Right Here on Earth/Ball of Confusion (That's What the World Is Today)	1971	—	3.00	6.00
❏ 7114	What It Is/California Soul	1972	—	3.00	6.00
❏ 7117	Papa Was a Rollin' Stone/Friendship Train	1972	—	3.00	6.00
❏ 7122	With a Little Help from My Friends/ Girl You're Alright	1972	—	3.00	6.00
❏ 7124	Mama I Got a Brand New Thing (Don't Say No)/ Gonna Keep On Tryin' Till I Win Your Love	1973	—	3.00	6.00
❏ 7130	Law of the Land/Just My Imagination (Running Away with Me)	1973	—	3.00	6.00
❏ 7134	Help Yourself/What's Going On	1974	—	3.00	6.00
❏ 7139	I'm a Fool for You/Girl's Alright with Me	1974	—	3.00	6.00
❏ 7140	Big John Is My Name/L'il Red Ridin' Hood	1974	—	3.00	6.00
❏ 7141	Earthquake Shake/Spaced Out	1975	—	—	—
—Unreleased					
❏ 7143	UFO's/Got to Get My Hands on Some Lovin'	1975	—	3.00	6.00
❏ 7145	Higher Than High/Spaced Out	1975	—	3.00	6.00
❏ 7147	Boogie Bump Boogie/ I Saw Her When You Met Her	1975	—	3.00	6.00
WHITFIELD					
❏ 8231	You + Me = Love/(Instrumental)	1976	—	3.00	6.00
❏ 8295	Let's Get Down to the Disco/Loose	1977	—	3.00	6.00
❏ 8362	Hole in the Wall/Sunshine	1977	—	3.00	6.00
❏ 8781	Show Time (Part 1)/(Part 2)	1979	—	3.00	6.00
❏ 8873	I Can't Get Enough of Your Love/Misunderstood	1979	—	3.00	6.00
Albums					
GORDY					
❏ G 955L	The Undisputed Truth	1971	6.25	12.50	25.00
❏ G5-959	Face to Face with the Truth	1972	5.00	10.00	20.00
❏ G5-963	Law of the Land	1973	5.00	10.00	20.00
❏ G6-968	Down to Earth	1974	5.00	10.00	20.00
❏ G6-970	Cosmic Truth	1975	5.00	10.00	20.00
❏ G6-972	Higher Than High	1975	5.00	10.00	20.00
WHITFIELD					
❏ BS 2967	Method to the Madness	1977	5.00	10.00	20.00
❏ BSK 3202	Smokin'	1979	3.75	7.50	15.00

UNFOLDING
Albums

Number	Title (A Side/B Side)	Yr	VG	VG+	NM
AUDIO FIDELITY					
❏ AFLP-2184 [M]	How to Blow Your Mind and Have a Freak-Out Party	1967	17.50	35.00	70.00
❏ AFSD-6184 [S]	How to Blow Your Mind and Have a Freak-Out Party	1967	25.00	50.00	100.00

UNFORGETTABLES, THE

Number	Title (A Side/B Side)	Yr	VG	VG+	NM
COLPIX					
❏ 192	It Hurts/Was It All Right	1961	7.50	15.00	30.00
PAMELA					
❏ 204	Oh Wishing Well/Daddy Must Be a Man	1961	75.00	150.00	300.00
❏ 204	Oh Wishing Well/Daddy Must Be a Man	1961	125.00	250.00	500.00
—Blue vinyl					
TITANIC					
❏ 5012	He'll Be Sorry/Oh There He Goes	1963	10.00	20.00	40.00

UNICORN
45s

Number	Title (A Side/B Side)	Yr	VG	VG+	NM
CAPITOL					
❏ 3954	Bog Trotter/Ooh, Mother	1974	—	2.50	5.00
❏ 3993	Blue Pine Trees/Electric Night	1974	—	2.50	5.00
Albums					
CAPITOL					
❏ ST-11334	Blue Pine Trees	1974	2.50	5.00	10.00
—Produced by David Gilmour (Pink Floyd)					
❏ ST-11453	Unicorn 2	1976	2.50	5.00	10.00
❏ ST-11692	One More Tomorrow	1977	2.50	5.00	10.00

UNIFICS, THE
45s

Number	Title (A Side/B Side)	Yr	VG	VG+	NM
KAPP					
❏ 935	Court of Love/Which One Should I Choose	1968	3.00	6.00	12.00
❏ 957	The Beginning of My End/Sentimental Man	1968	3.00	6.00	12.00
❏ 957 [PS]	The Beginning of My End/Sentimental Man	1968	3.75	7.50	15.00
❏ 985	It's a Groovy World!/Memories	1969	3.00	6.00	12.00
❏ 985 [PS]	It's a Groovy World!/Memories	1969	3.75	7.50	15.00
❏ 2026	Toshisumasu/It's All Over	1969	3.00	6.00	12.00
❏ 2058	Got to Get You/Memories	1969	3.00	6.00	12.00
Albums					
KAPP					
❏ KS-3582	Sittin' In at the Court of Love	1968	6.25	12.50	25.00

UNION GAP, THE   See GARY PUCKETT AND THE UNION GAP.

UNIQUE ECHOES, THE
45s

Number	Title (A Side/B Side)	Yr	VG	VG+	NM
SOUTHERN SOUND					
❏ 108	Zoom/Italian Twist	1962	12.50	25.00	50.00

UNIQUE TEENS, THE
45s

Number	Title (A Side/B Side)	Yr	VG	VG+	NM
DYNAMIC					
❏ 110	Whatcha Know Now/Run Fast	1959	7.50	15.00	30.00
HANOVER					
❏ 4510	Jeannie/At the Ball	1959	10.00	20.00	40.00
IVY					
❏ 112	Jeannie/At the Ball	1958	10.00	20.00	40.00

UNIQUES, THE (1)   Country singer Joe Stampley was a member of this group.
45s

Number	Title (A Side/B Side)	Yr	VG	VG+	NM
PARAMOUNT					
❏ 0017	Eunice/No One But You	1970	—	2.50	5.00
❏ 0058	Shadow of Love/Lazy Afternoon	1970	—	2.50	5.00
❏ 0116	Lucille/One Night with You	1971	—	2.50	5.00
❏ 0172	Will You Love Me Tomorrow/I Am a Gemini	1972	—	2.50	5.00
PAULA					
❏ 219	Not Too Long Ago/Fast Way of Living	1965	2.50	5.00	10.00
❏ 222	Too Good to Be True/Never Been in Love	1965	2.00	4.00	8.00
❏ 227	Lady's Man/Bolivar	1965	2.00	4.00	8.00
❏ 231	Strange/You Ain't Tuff	1966	2.00	4.00	8.00
❏ 238	All These Things/Tell Me What to Do	1966	2.00	4.00	8.00
❏ 245	Goodbye, So Long/Run and Hide	1966	2.00	4.00	8.00
❏ 255	Please Come Home for Christmas/ (Instrumental)	1966	3.00	6.00	12.00
❏ 264	Groovin' Out/Areba	1967	2.00	4.00	8.00
❏ 275	Every Now and Then (I Cry)/ Love Is a Precious Thing	1967	2.00	4.00	8.00
❏ 289	Go On and Leave/I'll Do Anything	1967	2.00	4.00	8.00
—B-side by University of Utah Chamber Choir					
❏ 299	It's All Over Now/All I Took Was Love	1968	—	3.00	6.00
❏ 307	It Hurts Me to Remember/I Sure Feel More (Like I Do Then I Did When I Got Here)	1968	—	3.00	6.00
❏ 313	How Lucky Can One Man Be/ You Don't Miss Your Water	1968	—	3.00	6.00
❏ 320	Sha-La Love/You Know (That I Love You)	1970	—	2.50	5.00
❏ 324	My Babe/Toys Are Made for Children	1970	—	2.50	5.00
❏ 332	All These Things/You Know That I Love You	1970	—	2.50	5.00
Albums					
PAULA					
❏ LP-2190 [M]	Uniquely Yours	1966	6.25	12.50	25.00
❏ LPS-2190 [S]	Uniquely Yours	1966	7.50	15.00	30.00
❏ LP-2194 [M]	Happening Now	1967	6.25	12.50	25.00
❏ LPS-2194 [S]	Happening Now	1967	7.50	15.00	30.00
❏ LP-2199 [M]	Playtime	1968	6.25	12.50	25.00
❏ LPS-2199 [S]	Playtime	1968	6.25	12.50	25.00
❏ LPS-2204	The Uniques	1969	6.25	12.50	25.00
❏ LPS-2208	Golden Hits	1970	6.25	12.50	25.00

UNIQUES, THE (2)
45s

Number	Title (A Side/B Side)	Yr	VG	VG+	NM
AMBER					
❏ 2004	Taboo/Ghost Riders in the Sky	1961	12.50	25.00	50.00
UNITED SOUTHERN					
❏ 104	Renegade/Malaguena	1961	75.00	15.00	30.00

UNIQUES, THE (3)
45s

Number	Title (A Side/B Side)	Yr	VG	VG+	NM
BANGAR					
❏ 00609	Baby Don't Cry/Little Angel	1967	5.00	10.00	20.00

Number	Title (A Side/B Side)	Yr	VG	VG+	NM
UNIQUES, THE (4)					
45s					
BLISS					
❏ 1004	I'm So Unhappy/I'm Confessin'	1961	125.00	250.00	500.00
END					
❏ 1012	Tell the Angels/Hey, Little Cupid	1958	62.50	125.00	250.00
FLIPPIN'					
❏ 202	Come Marry Me/Do You Remember	1959	12.50	25.00	50.00
GONE					
❏ 5113	I'm So Unhappy/It's Got to Come	1961	17.50	35.00	70.00
❏ 5113	I'm So Unhappy/I'm Confessin'	1961	50.00	100.00	200.00
MR. CEE					
❏ 100	Look at Me/Bossa Nova Cha Cha	1960	75.00	150.00	300.00
PRIDE					
❏ 1018	I'm So Unhappy/It's Got to Come	1960	62.50	125.00	250.00
TEE KAY					
❏ 112	One Million Miles Away/All at Once	1962	12.50	25.00	50.00
UNIQUES, THE (5)					
45s					
CAPITOL					
❏ 4949	Loving You/Blue Skies	1963	3.00	6.00	12.00
ROULETTE					
❏ 4528	Send Him to Me/This Little Boy of Mine	1963	5.00	10.00	20.00
UNIQUES, THE (6)					
45s					
DEMAND					
❏ 1994	Merry Christmas, Darling/I Wanna Chance	198?	2.00	4.00	8.00
—B-side by the Vows; green vinyl "collector's issue"					
❏ 2490	Times Change/Alright, OK, You Win	1964	12.50	25.00	50.00
❏ 2936	Merry Christmas Darling/Rockin' Rudolph	1963	20.00	40.00	80.00
❏ 3950	Merry Christmas Darling (And A Happy New Year Too)/Times Change	1963	12.50	25.00	50.00
DOT					
❏ 16533	Merry Christmas Darling/Times Change	1963	10.00	20.00	40.00
UNIQUES, THE (7)					
45s					
PEACOCK					
❏ 1677	Right Now/Somewhere	1957	7.50	15.00	30.00
❏ 1695	Mysterious/Picture of My Baby	1960	6.25	12.50	25.00
UNIQUES, THE (U)					
45s					
CLIFTON					
❏ 62	After New Year's Eve/Kiss, Kiss, Kiss	19??	2.00	4.00	8.00
LUCKY FOUR					
❏ 1024	Silvery Moon/Chocolate Bar	1962	50.00	100.00	200.00
UNIT FOUR PLUS TWO					
45s					
LONDON					
❏ 1009	I Was Only Playing Games/I Won't Let You Down	1966	3.00	6.00	12.00
❏ 9732	Sorrow and Pain/Woman from Liberia	1965	3.00	6.00	12.00
❏ 9751	Concrete and Clay/When I Fall in Love	1965	3.00	6.00	12.00
❏ 9751	Concrete and Clay/Wild as the Wind	1965	4.00	8.00	16.00
❏ 9761	You've Never Been in Love Like This Before/ Tell Somebody You Know	1965	3.00	6.00	12.00
❏ 9790	Stop Wasting Your Time/Hark	1965	3.00	6.00	12.00
Albums					
LONDON					
❏ PS 427 [P]	Unit Four Plus Two #1	1965	12.50	25.00	50.00
❏ LL 3427 [M]	Unit Four Plus Two #1	1965	10.00	20.00	40.00
UNITED FRUIT CO.					
45s					
LAURIE					
❏ 3408	On the Good Ship Lollipop/Sunshine Street	1967	2.50	5.00	10.00
UNITED STATES DOUBLE QUARTET THE TOKENS and The Kirby Stone Four.					
45s					
B.T. PUPPY					
❏ 524	Life Is Groovy/Split	1966	2.50	5.00	10.00
❏ 547	Walking Along-Happy Wanderer/ When I Lock My Door	1968	2.50	5.00	10.00
❏ 551	Do Re Mi/When I Lock My Door	1969	2.50	5.00	10.00
Albums					
B.T. PUPPY					
❏ BTS-1005	Life Is Groovy	1969	12.50	25.00	50.00
UNITED STATES OF AMERICA, THE					
Albums					
COLUMBIA					
❏ CL 2814 [M]	The United States of America	1968	25.00	50.00	100.00
—Mono is promo only					
❏ CS 9614 [S]	The United States of America	1968	10.00	20.00	40.00
—Without outer bag					
❏ CS 9614 [S]	The United States of America	1968	20.00	40.00	80.00
—With outer bag					
UNIVERSALS, THE Probably more than one group.					
45s					
ASCOT					
❏ 2124	Dear Ruth/Gotta Little Girl	1963	15.00	30.00	60.00
CORA-LEE					
❏ 501	The Picture/He's So Right	1958	10.00	20.00	40.00
FESTIVAL					
❏ 1601	Dreaming/Love Bound	1961	15.00	30.00	60.00
—No subtitle on A-side					
❏ 25001	Dreaming/Love Bound	1961	6.25	12.50	25.00
MARK-X					
❏ 7004	Teenage Love/Again	1957	50.00	100.00	200.00
MODERN					
❏ 1057	New Lease on Life/Without Friends	1968	2.50	5.00	10.00
SHEPHERD					
❏ 2200	A Love Only You Can Give/I'm in Love	1962	12.50	25.00	50.00

Number	Title (A Side/B Side)	Yr	VG	VG+	NM
SOUTHERN					
❏ 102	Dear Ruth/Prayer of Love	1963	12.50	25.00	50.00
Albums					
RELIC					
❏ 5006	Acapella Showcase	197?	2.50	5.00	10.00
UNKNOWN, THE					
45s					
AUTOGRAPH					
❏ 206	I Have Returned/Keep Talking, Baby	1960	10.00	20.00	40.00
UNKNOWNS, THE (1) Also see STEVE ALAIMO; MARK LINDSAY.					
45s					
PARROT					
❏ 307	Melody for an Unknown Girl/Keith's Song	1966	6.25	12.50	25.00
UNKNOWNS, THE (2)					
45s					
SHIELD					
❏ 7101	One More Chance/You and Me	196?	50.00	100.00	200.00
X-TRA					
❏ 102	One More Chance/You and Me	1957	250.00	500.00	1000.
UNKNOWNS, THE (U)					
45s					
MARLIN					
❏ 16008	Tighter/Young Enough to Cry	1966	6.25	12.50	25.00
UNLUV'D, THE					
45s					
MGM					
❏ K13903	I Got It Bad/Steadfastly	1968	3.00	6.00	12.00
PARKWAY					
❏ 138	Ain't Gonna Do You No Harm/An Exception to the Rule	1967	6.25	12.50	25.00
TRUE LOVE					
❏ 1000	Ain't Gonna Do You No Harm/An Exception to the Rule	1967	12.50	25.00	50.00
UNRELATED SEGMENTS, THE					
45s					
HANNA-BARBERA					
❏ 514	It's Unfair/Story of My Life	1967	5.00	10.00	20.00
LIBERTY					
❏ 55992	It's Gonna Rain/Where You Gonna Go	1967	6.25	12.50	25.00
❏ 56052	Cry, Cry, Cry/It's Not Fair	1968	10.00	20.00	40.00
UNTAMED, THE					
45s					
PLANET					
❏ 117	It's Not True/Gimme Gimme Some Shade	1966	3.00	6.00	12.00
—Also reported to be Planet 103; do both exist as U.S. editions?					
UNTOUCHABLES, THE At least two different groups.					
45s					
ALAN K					
❏ 6901	Little Mary/Funny What a Little Kiss Can Do	1962	50.00	100.00	200.00
DOT					
❏ 16306	Blues in the Night/Bondaru	1962	3.75	7.50	15.00
LIBERTY					
❏ 55335	You're on Top/Lovely Dee	1961	5.00	10.00	20.00
❏ 55423	Papa/Medicine Man	1962	5.00	10.00	20.00
MADISON					
❏ 128	Poor Boy Need a Preacher/New Fad	1960	6.25	12.50	25.00
❏ 134	Goodnight Sweetheart Goodnight/Vickie Lee	1960	6.25	12.50	25.00
❏ 139	Sixty Minute Man/Everybody's Laughin'	1960	6.25	12.50	25.00
❏ 147	Do Your Best/Raisin' Cain	1961	6.25	12.50	25.00
MCA/STIFF					
❏ 52725	I Spy (For the F.B.I.)/Freak in the Street	1985	—	2.00	4.00
❏ 52725 [PS]	I Spy (For the F.B.I.)/Freak in the Street	1985	—	2.00	4.00
NAU VOO					
❏ 809	Blue Chip Bounce (Part 1)/ Blue Chip Bounce (Part 2)	1960	3.75	7.50	15.00
WASP					
❏ 105	Don't Go, I'm Beggin'/Baby, Let's Wait	1967	6.25	12.50	25.00
UNUSUAL WE					
Albums					
PULSAR					
❏ 10608	Unusual We	1969	7.50	15.00	30.00
UPBEATS, THE					
45s					
JOY					
❏ 223	Oh What It Seemed to Be/ The Night We Both Said Goodbye	1958	6.25	12.50	25.00
❏ 227	Keep Cool Crazy Heart/ You're the One I Care For	1959	6.25	12.50	25.00
❏ 229	Satin Shoes/Teenie Weenie Bikini	1959	6.25	12.50	25.00
❏ 233	To Me You're a Song/Unbelievable Love	1959	6.25	12.50	25.00
PREP					
❏ 119	Never in My Life/I Don't Know	1957	7.50	15.00	30.00
❏ 131	Will You Be Mine?/My Last Frontier	1958	7.50	15.00	30.00
SWAN					
❏ 4010	Just Like in the Movies/My Foolish Heart	1958	6.25	12.50	25.00
UPCHURCH, PHIL					
45s					
BOYD					
❏ 3398	You Can't Sit Down Part 2/ You Can't Sit Down Part 1	1961	3.00	6.00	12.00
CADET					
❏ 5661	You Don't Know the Reason/I Don't Know	1970	—	3.00	6.00
KUDU					
❏ 926	You Got Style/Ave Maria	1975	—	2.50	5.00
—With Tennyson Stephens					
MARLIN					
❏ 3325	Strawberry Letter 23/(B-side unknown)	1978	—	2.00	4.00

Number	Title (A Side/B Side)	Yr	VG	VG+	NM
UNITED ARTISTS					
❏ 329	You Can't Sit Down Part 2/ You Can't Sit Down Part 1	1961	2.50	5.00	10.00
❏ 355	Pink Lollipop/Straw Hat	1961	2.50	5.00	10.00
❏ 385	The Hog/That's Where It Is	1961	2.50	5.00	10.00
❏ 417	Organ Grinder's Swing/The Persian	1962	2.50	5.00	10.00
❏ 488	The Stonewall/Flap Jack	1962	2.50	5.00	10.00
Albums					
BLUE THUMB					
❏ BTS-59	Lovin' Feelin'	1973	3.00	6.00	12.00
❏ BTS-6005 [(2)]	Darkness, Darkness	1971	5.00	10.00	20.00
BOYD					
❏ B-398 [M]	You Can't Sit Down	1961	20.00	40.00	80.00
❏ BS-398 [S]	You Can't Sit Down	1961	25.00	50.00	100.00
CADET					
❏ LPS-826	Upchurch	1969	3.75	7.50	15.00
❏ LPS-840	The Way I Feel	1970	3.75	7.50	15.00
JAM					
❏ 007	Free and Easy	198?	3.00	6.00	12.00
KUDU					
❏ 22	Phil Upchurch and Tennyson Stevens	1975	3.00	6.00	12.00
MARLIN					
❏ 2209	Phil Upchurch	1978	3.00	6.00	12.00
MILESTONE					
❏ MSP-9010	Feeling Blue	1968	3.75	7.50	15.00
UNITED ARTISTS					
❏ UAL-3162 [M]	You Can't Sit Down, Part 2	1961	7.50	15.00	30.00
❏ UAL-3175 [M]	Big Hit Dances	1962	6.25	12.50	25.00
❏ UAS-6162 [S]	You Can't Sit Down, Part 2	1961	10.00	20.00	40.00
❏ UAS-6175 [S]	Big Hit Dances	1962	7.50	15.00	30.00

UPFRONTS, THE
45s

Number	Title (A Side/B Side)	Yr	VG	VG+	NM
LUMMTONE					
❏ 103	It Took Time/Betty Lou and the Lions	1960	12.50	25.00	50.00
❏ 104	Too Far to Turn Around/Married Jive	1960	10.00	20.00	40.00
❏ 106	Why You Kiss Me/Little Girl	1961	12.50	25.00	50.00
❏ 107	Send Me Someone to Love Who Will Love Me/ Baby For Your Love	1961	7.50	15.00	30.00
—Black label					
❏ 107	Send Me Someone to Love Who Will Love Me/ Baby For Your Love	1961	12.50	25.00	50.00
—White label					
❏ 108	It Took Time/Baby For Your Love	1962	6.25	12.50	25.00
❏ 114	Do the Beetle/Most of the Pretty Girls	1964	15.00	30.00	60.00

UPSETTERS, THE
45s

Number	Title (A Side/B Side)	Yr	VG	VG+	NM
ABC					
❏ 11081	Tossin' and Turnin'/Always in the Wrong Place at the Wrong Time	1968	2.50	5.00	10.00
❏ 11120	Don't Be Cruel/Down Home	1968	2.50	5.00	10.00
AUTUMN					
❏ 4	Autumn's Here/Draggin' the Main	1964	6.25	12.50	25.00
FALCON					
❏ 1010	The Upsetter/The Strip	1958	5.00	10.00	20.00
FIRE					
❏ 1029	Jaywalking/Steppin' Out	1960	5.00	10.00	20.00
GEE					
❏ 1055	The Blues/Rollin' On	1960	5.00	10.00	20.00
HIT					
❏ 237	No Matter What Shape (Your Stomach's In)/ Barbara Ann	1966	2.00	4.00	8.00
—B-side by the Chellows					
LITTLE STAR					
❏ 123	Yes, It's Me/Every Night About This Time	1962	12.50	25.00	50.00
—With Little Richard					

UPTONES, THE
45s

Number	Title (A Side/B Side)	Yr	VG	VG+	NM
LUTE					
❏ 6225	No More/I'll Be There	1962	5.00	10.00	20.00
—Multicolor label					
❏ 6225	No More/I'll Be There	1962	7.50	15.00	30.00
—Black label					
❏ 6229	Be Mine/Dreamin'	1962	10.00	20.00	40.00
MAGNUM					
❏ 714	Dreaming/Wear My Ring	1963	5.00	10.00	20.00
WATTS					
❏ 1080	Dreaming/Wear My Ring	1963	7.50	15.00	30.00

URIAH HEEP
45s

Number	Title (A Side/B Side)	Yr	VG	VG+	NM
CHRYSALIS					
❏ 2274	Come Back to Me/Love or Nothing	1978	—	2.00	4.00
MERCURY					
❏ 73103	Gypsy/Real Turned On	1970	2.00	4.00	8.00
❏ 73145	Come Away Melinda/Wake Up	1970	2.00	4.00	8.00
❏ 73154	I Wanna Be Free/What Should Be Done	1971	2.00	4.00	8.00
❏ 73174	High Priestess/(B-side unknown)	1970	2.50	5.00	10.00
❏ 73243	Look at Yourself/Love Machine	1971	2.00	4.00	8.00
❏ 73271	Why/The Wizard	1971	2.00	4.00	8.00
❏ 73307	Easy Livin'/All My Life	1972	2.00	4.00	8.00
❏ 73349	Sweet Lorraine/Blind Eye	1972	—	3.00	6.00
❏ 73406	Tears in My Eyes/July Morning	1973	—	3.00	6.00
❏ 76177	That's the Way It Is/Son of a Bitch	1982	—	2.00	4.00
❏ 76177 [PS]	That's the Way It Is/Son of a Bitch	1982	—	2.50	5.00
WARNER BROS.					
❏ 7738	Stealin'/Sunshine	1973	—	2.50	5.00
❏ 7836	Something or Nothing/What Can I Do	1974	—	—	—
—Unreleased?					
❏ 8013	Something or Nothing/What Can I Do	1974	—	2.50	5.00
❏ 8132	Prima Dance/Stealin'	1975	—	2.50	5.00
❏ 8581	Masquerade/Free Me	1978	—	2.50	5.00
7-Inch Extended Plays					
WARNER BROS.					
❏ S 2724	Dreamer/One Day//If I Had the Time/Circus	1974	2.50	5.00	10.00
—Jukebox issue; small hole, plays at 33 1/3 rpm					
❏ S 2724 [PS]	Sweet Freedom	1974	2.50	5.00	10.00
—Part of "Little LP" series (LLP #230)					

Number	Title (A Side/B Side)	Yr	VG	VG+	NM
Albums					
CHRYSALIS					
❏ CHR 1204	Fallen Angel	1978	2.50	5.00	10.00
COLUMBIA					
❏ BFC 40132	Equator	1985	2.00	4.00	8.00
MERCURY					
❏ SRM-1-614	Look at Yourself	1971	2.50	5.00	10.00
❏ SRM-1-630	Demons and Wizards	1972	2.50	5.00	10.00
❏ SRM-1-652	The Magician's Birthday	1972	2.50	5.00	10.00
❏ SRM-1-1070	The Best of Uriah Heep	1976	2.50	5.00	10.00
❏ SRM-1-4057	Abominog	1982	2.00	4.00	8.00
❏ SRM-2-7503 [(2)]	Uriah Heep Live	1973	3.00	6.00	12.00
❏ SR-61294	Uriah Heep	1970	3.00	6.00	12.00
❏ SR-61319	Salisbury	1970	3.00	6.00	12.00
❏ 812313-1	Head First	1983	2.00	4.00	8.00
❏ 822476-1	The Best of Uriah Heep	1986	2.00	4.00	8.00
—Reissue of Mercury 1070					
WARNER BROS.					
❏ BS 2724	Sweet Freedom	1973	2.50	5.00	10.00
❏ W 2800	Wonderworld	1974	2.50	5.00	10.00
❏ BS 2869	Return to Fantasy	1975	2.50	5.00	10.00
❏ BS 2949	High and Mighty	1976	2.50	5.00	10.00
❏ BS 3013	Firefly	1977	2.50	5.00	10.00
❏ BSK 3145	Innocent Victim	1978	2.50	5.00	10.00

USHER, GARY   Also see THE TIMERS.
45s

Number	Title (A Side/B Side)	Yr	VG	VG+	NM
CAPITOL					
❏ 5128	The Beetle/Jody	1964	12.50	25.00	50.00
❏ 5193	Sacramento/That's the Way I Feel	1964	20.00	40.00	80.00
—Produced by Brian Wilson					
❏ 5403	It's a Lie/Jody	1965	12.50	25.00	50.00
DOT					
❏ 16518	Three Surfer Boys/Milky Way	1963	100.00	200.00	400.00
LAN-CET					
❏ 144	Tomorrow/Lies	1961	15.00	30.00	60.00
TITAN					
❏ 1716	Driven Insane/You're the Girl	1961	37.50	75.00	150.00

UTMOSTS, THE
45s

Number	Title (A Side/B Side)	Yr	VG	VG+	NM
PAN-OR					
❏ 1123	I Need You/Big Man	1962	30.00	60.00	120.00

UTOPIA   Also see TODD RUNDGREN.
12-Inch Singles

Number	Title (A Side/B Side)	Yr	VG	VG+	NM
NETWORK					
❏ 67935	Hammer in My Heart (same on both sides)	1983	3.75	7.50	15.00
—Probably promo only					
PASSPORT					
❏ 4004 [DJ]	Cry Baby +2	1984	2.50	5.00	10.00
WAX TRAX!					
❏ WAX-9099 [DJ]	Greater Than One (same on both sides)	1989	2.50	5.00	10.00
45s					
BEARSVILLE					
❏ 0317	Sunburst Finish/Communion with the Sun	1977	—	2.00	4.00
❏ 0321	Love Is the Answer/Marriage of Heaven and Hell	1977	—	2.00	4.00
❏ 29947	Junk Rock/Lysistrata	1982	—	2.50	5.00
❏ 49180	Set Me Free/Umbrella Man	1980	—	2.50	5.00
❏ 49247	Love Alone/Very Last Time	1980	—	2.00	4.00
❏ 49545	Second Nature/You Make Me Crazy	1980	—	2.00	4.00
❏ 49579	Always Late/I Just Want to Touch You	1980	—	2.00	4.00
❏ 50062	One World/Special Interest	1982	—	2.50	5.00
NETWORK					
❏ 69830	Hammer in My Heart/ I'm Looking at You But I'm Talking to Myself	1983	—	2.00	4.00
❏ 69859	Feet Don't Fail Me Now/There Goes My Inspiration	1982	—	2.00	4.00
PASSPORT					
❏ 7923	Cry Baby/Winston Smith Takes It on the Jaw	1984	—	2.00	4.00
❏ 7923 [PS]	Cry Baby/Winston Smith Takes It on the Jaw	1984	—	2.50	5.00
❏ 7927	Stand for Something/Mated	1985	—	2.00	4.00
Albums					
BEARSVILLE					
❏ BRK 3487	Deface the Music	1980	3.00	6.00	12.00
❏ BRK 3666	Swing to the Right	1982	3.00	6.00	12.00
❏ BR 6954	Todd Rundgren's Utopia	1974	3.00	6.00	12.00
❏ BR 6961	Todd Rundgren's Utopia/Another Live	1975	3.00	6.00	12.00
❏ BR 6965	RA	1977	3.00	6.00	12.00
❏ BRK 6970	Oops! Wrong Planet	1977	3.00	6.00	12.00
❏ BRK 6991	Adventures in Utopia	1979	3.00	6.00	12.00
NETWORK					
❏ 60183 [(2)]	Utopia	1982	3.75	7.50	15.00
—The second record has the same five songs on both sides					
PASSPORT					
❏ PB 6029	Oblivion	1984	2.50	5.00	10.00
❏ PB 6044	POV	1985	2.50	5.00	10.00
❏ PB 6053	Trivia	1986	2.50	5.00	10.00
RHINO					
❏ RNLP 70865	Todd Rundgren's Utopia	1987	2.00	4.00	8.00
❏ RNLP 70867	Todd Rundgren's Utopia/Another Live	1987	2.00	4.00	8.00
❏ RNLP 70869	RA	1987	2.00	4.00	8.00
❏ RNLP 70870	Oops! Wrong Planet	1987	2.00	4.00	8.00
❏ RNLP 70872	Adventures in Utopia	1987	2.00	4.00	8.00
❏ RNLP 70873	Deface the Music	1987	2.00	4.00	8.00
❏ RNLP 70875	Swing to the Right	1987	2.00	4.00	8.00
❏ R1-70892	Anthology (1974-1985)	1989	2.50	5.00	10.00

UTOPIANS, THE
45s

Number	Title (A Side/B Side)	Yr	VG	VG+	NM
IMPERIAL					
❏ 5861	Dutch Treat/Ain't No Such Thing	1962	7.50	15.00	30.00
❏ 5876	Along My Lonely Way/Hurry to Your Date	1962	100.00	200.00	400.00
❏ 5921	Let Love Come Later/Opera vs. the Blues	1963	6.25	12.50	25.00

UTOPIAS, THE
45s

Number	Title (A Side/B Side)	Yr	VG	VG+	NM
LASALLE					
❏ 0072	Girls Are Against Me/(B-side unknown)	196?	300.00	600.00	1200.

V

Number	Title (A Side/B Side)	Yr	VG	VG+	NM
V.I.P.'S					
45s					
BIG TOP					
❏ 100	Don't Pass Me By/You Ain't Good for Nothing	1965	3.00	6.00	12.00
❏ 518	You Pulled a Fast One/Flashback	1964	3.00	6.00	12.00
❏ 521	I'm On to You Baby/If He Wants Me	1964	3.00	6.00	12.00
CONGRESS					
❏ 211	My Girl Cried/Strange Little Girl	1964	3.75	7.50	15.00
V-EIGHTS, THE					
45s					
ABC-PARAMOUNT					
❏ 10201	Papa's Yellow Tie/My Heart	1961	5.00	10.00	20.00
MOST					
❏ 711/3	Pretty Girl/Please Come Back	1959	25.00	50.00	100.00
VIBRO					
❏ 4005	Papa's Yellow Tie/My Heart	1960	7.50	15.00	30.00
❏ 4007	Let's Take a Chance/Hot Water	1961	7.50	15.00	30.00
VACELS, THE Also see RICKY AND THE VACELS.					
45s					
KAMA SUTRA					
❏ 200	You're My Baby (And Don't You Forget It)/Hey Girl, Stop Leading Me On	1965	2.50	5.00	10.00
❏ 204	Can You Please Crawl Out Your Window/I'm Just a Poor Boy	1965	2.50	5.00	10.00
VAGRANTS, THE					
45s					
ATCO					
❏ 6473	Respect/I Love You Yes I Do	1967	3.75	7.50	15.00
❏ 6513	Beside the Sea/Sunny Summer Rain	1967	3.75	7.50	15.00
❏ 6552	And When It's Over/I Don't Need Your Lovin'	1968	3.75	7.50	15.00
SOUTHERN SOUND					
❏ 204	Oh, Those Eyes/You're Too Young	1966	6.25	12.50	25.00
VANGUARD					
❏ 35038	I Can't Make a Friend/Young Blues	1966	3.75	7.50	15.00
❏ 35042	Final Hour/Your Hasty Heart	1966	5.00	10.00	20.00
Albums					
ARISTA					
❏ AL-8459	The Great Lost Vagrants Album	1987	5.00	10.00	20.00
VAL-AIRES, THE Forerunner to THE VOGUES.					
45s					
CORAL					
❏ 62177	Laurie My Love/Which One Will It Be	1960	20.00	40.00	80.00
WILLETTE					
❏ 114	Laurie My Love/Which One Will It Be	1959	100.00	200.00	400.00
VAL-CHORDS, THE					
45s					
GAME TIME					
❏ 104	Candy Store Love/You're Laughing at Me	1957	25.00	50.00	100.00
—With sword logo					
❏ 104	Candy Store Love/You're Laughing at Me	1957	75.00	150.00	300.00
—With no sword logo					
VAL-TONES, THE					
45s					
DELUXE					
❏ 6084	Tender Darling/Siam Sam	1955	37.50	75.00	150.00
VALADIERS, THE					
45s					
GORDY					
❏ 7003	While I'm Away/Because I Love Her	1962	15.00	30.00	60.00
❏ 7013	I Found a Girl/You'll Be Sorry Someday	1963	15.00	30.00	60.00
MIRACLE					
❏ 6	Greeting (This Is Uncle Sam)/Take a Chance	1961	12.50	25.00	50.00
—With subtitle on A-side and 2:15 version of B-side					
❏ 6	Greetings/Take a Chance	1961	20.00	40.00	80.00
—With no subtitle on A-side and 2:23 version of B-side					
VALAQUONS, THE					
45s					
LAGUNA					
❏ 102	Teardrops/Madeleine	1964	50.00	100.00	200.00
RAYCO					
❏ 516	Jolly Green Giant/Diddy Bop	1965	7.50	15.00	30.00
TANGERINE					
❏ 951	I Wanna Woman/Window Shopping on Girl's Avenue	1965	6.25	12.50	25.00
VALE, JERRY					
45s					
BUDDAH					
❏ 591	Toot Toot Tootsie (Goodbye)/Now Is Forever	1978	—	2.00	4.00
COLUMBIA					
❏ 10042	If I Could Write a Song/Woman of the World	1974	—	2.00	4.00
❏ 31163 [S]	(titles unknown)	1961	2.50	5.00	10.00
❏ 31164 [S]	(titles unknown)	1961	2.50	5.00	10.00
❏ 31165 [S]	(titles unknown)	1961	2.50	5.00	10.00
❏ 31166 [S]	(titles unknown)	1961	2.50	5.00	10.00
❏ 31167 [S]	(titles unknown)	1961	2.50	5.00	10.00
❏ 31468 [S]	(titles unknown)	1962	2.50	5.00	10.00
❏ 31469 [S]	(titles unknown)	1962	2.50	5.00	10.00
❏ 31470 [S]	(titles unknown)	1962	2.50	5.00	10.00
❏ 31471 [S]	(titles unknown)	1962	2.50	5.00	10.00
❏ 31472 [S]	(titles unknown)	1962	2.50	5.00	10.00
—Anyone who can fill in these gaps -- the above 10 all are Columbia "Stereo 7" singles -- please let us know.					
❏ 39929	And No One Knows/You Can Never Give Me Back Your Heart	1953	5.00	10.00	20.00
❏ 39990	For Me/Tired of Waiting	1953	5.00	10.00	20.00
❏ 40058	Ask Me/A Tear, a Kiss, a Smile	1953	5.00	10.00	20.00
❏ 40131	Two Purple Shadows/And This Is My Beloved	1953	3.75	7.50	15.00
❏ 40201	The Ghost in the Vine/I Live Each Day	1954	3.75	7.50	15.00
❏ 40260	I'll Follow You/Go	1954	3.75	7.50	15.00
❏ 40322	Love Is a Circus/For You, My Love	1954	3.75	7.50	15.00
❏ 40404	A Million Moons Ago/Lolly Linger Longer	1955	3.75	7.50	15.00
❏ 40429	Hey Punchinello/I Live for Only You	1955	3.75	7.50	15.00
❏ 40463	When I Let You Go/And No One Knows	1955	3.75	7.50	15.00
❏ 40499	Only Beautiful/How Do I Love You	1955	3.75	7.50	15.00
❏ 40541	Magic Night/Heaven Came Down to Earth	1955	3.75	7.50	15.00
❏ 40584	Miracle in the Rain/Adelaide	1955	3.75	7.50	15.00
❏ 40634	Innamorata (Sweetheart)/Second Ending	1956	3.00	6.00	12.00
❏ 40710	You Don't Know Me/Enchanted	1956	3.00	6.00	12.00
❏ 4-40775	Mother Mine/Tell Me So	1956	3.00	6.00	12.00
❏ 40825	All Dressed Up with a Brand New Broken Heart/It Looks Like Love	1957	3.00	6.00	12.00
❏ 40880	Don't You Know Me Anymore/For You My Love	1957	3.00	6.00	12.00
❏ 40941	Love in the Afternoon/I'm Not Ashamed	1957	3.00	6.00	12.00
❏ 41010	Pretend You Don't See Her/The Spreading Chestnut	1957	3.00	6.00	12.00
❏ 41120	I Always Say/She	1958	2.50	5.00	10.00
❏ 41182	With You/Blue Tears	1958	2.50	5.00	10.00
❏ 41238	Go Chase a Moonbeam/Around the Clock	1958	2.50	5.00	10.00
❏ 41314	Me and My Shadow/A Warm Spot	1959	2.50	5.00	10.00
❏ 41373	Bella, Bella Sue/The Heart Has Won the Game	1959	2.50	5.00	10.00
❏ 41423	The Flame/The Moon Is My Pillow	1959	2.50	5.00	10.00
❏ 41503	Prima Donna/What Do I Care	1959	2.50	5.00	10.00
❏ 41594	Solitaire/Please Believe Me	1960	2.50	5.00	10.00
❏ 41681	If/The Dawn of Love	1960	2.50	5.00	10.00
❏ 41732	No Moon at All/Making Believe You're Here	1960	2.50	5.00	10.00
❏ 41823	Just Friends/To Belong	1960	2.50	5.00	10.00
❏ 41942	Camelot/Thirteen Girls Too Much	1961	2.50	5.00	10.00
❏ 42027	Al Di La/Thinking of Your Happiness	1961	2.50	5.00	10.00
❏ 42201	Another Time, Another Place/If He Leaves You	1961	2.00	4.00	8.00
❏ 42304	If Ever I Would Leave You/Who Knows	1962	2.00	4.00	8.00
❏ 42439	Ah, Camminare/One Paradise for Sale	1962	2.00	4.00	8.00
❏ 42508	My Geisha/It's My Way	1962	2.00	4.00	8.00
❏ 42637	From the Bottom of My Heart/Here's to Us	1962	2.00	4.00	8.00
❏ 42783	One More Blessing/Doin' What I Said I'd Never Do	1963	2.00	4.00	8.00
❏ 42826	Old Cape Cod/Theme for Young Lovers (Where Is My Someone)	1963	2.00	4.00	8.00
❏ 42872	Maria Elena/Mala Femina	1963	2.00	4.00	8.00
❏ 42951	The Peking Theme (So Little Time)/On and On	1964	2.00	4.00	8.00
❏ 42994	The Lights of Rome/As Sure As Night Must Fall	1964	2.00	4.00	8.00
❏ 43105	Love Goddess/Where Love Has Gone	1964	2.00	4.00	8.00
❏ 43181	Have You Looked Into Your Heart/Andiamo	1964	—	3.00	6.00
❏ 43232	For Mama/Ti Adora	1965	—	3.00	6.00
❏ 43252	Tears Keep On Falling/Now	1965	—	3.00	6.00
❏ 43337	Where Were You When I Needed You/I Don't Wanna Go Home	1965	—	3.00	6.00
❏ 43413	Deep in Your Heart/If It Isn't in Your Heart	1965	—	3.00	6.00
❏ 43473	Big Wide World/Ashamed	1965	—	3.00	6.00
❏ 43605	Less Than Tomorrow/This Day of Days	1966	—	3.00	6.00
❏ 43656	My Melancholy Baby/It's Magic	1966	—	3.00	6.00
❏ 43696	It'll Take a Little Time/Palermo	1966	—	3.00	6.00
❏ 43774	Dommage, Dommage (Too Bad, Too Bad)/Promises	1966	—	3.00	6.00
❏ 43895	Somewhere/I've Lost My Heart Again	1966	—	3.00	6.00
❏ 44027	Have You Seen the One I Love Go By/Signs	1967	—	2.50	5.00
❏ 44087	So Near, Yet So Far/Time Alone Will Tell	1967	—	2.50	5.00
❏ 44185	I Love New England/In the Back of My Heart	1967	—	2.50	5.00
❏ 44274	In Time/Blame It on Me	1967	—	2.50	5.00
❏ 44280	Santa Mouse/Silent Night, Holy Night	1967	—	3.00	6.00
❏ 44347	What a Wonderful World/Love Me the Way I Love You	1967	—	2.50	5.00
❏ 44432	Don't Tell My Heart to Stop Loving You/When I'm With You	1968	—	2.50	5.00
❏ 44512	My Love, Forgive Me/I Never Let a Day Go By	1968	—	2.50	5.00
❏ 44572	The Look of Love/With Pen in Hand	1968	—	2.50	5.00
❏ 44615	Till Now/That Girl Would Be So Happy	1968	—	2.50	5.00
❏ 44687	There's a Baby/Where Are They Now	1968	—	2.50	5.00
❏ 44753	Life/Congratulations, I Guess	1969	—	2.50	5.00
❏ 44823	Close to Cathy/Fa Fa Fa (Live for Today)	1969	—	2.50	5.00
❏ 44914	He Who Loves/Close to You	1969	—	2.50	5.00
❏ 44969	This Is My Life/What's Wrong with My World	1969	—	2.50	5.00
❏ 45043	Stay Awhile/It's All in the Game	1969	—	2.50	5.00
❏ 45118	Hello and Goodbye/Look Homeward Angel	1970	—	2.00	4.00
❏ 45188	I'l Never Fall in Love Again/Lovin' Time	1970	—	2.00	4.00
❏ 45216	I Climbed the Mountain/Love Never Goes Away	1970	—	2.00	4.00
❏ 45308	Point Me in the Direction of Albuquerque/Perfect Love	1971	—	2.50	5.00
❏ 45361	My Little Girl/Is It Asking Too Much	1971	—	2.00	4.00
❏ 45407	Which Way You Goin' Girl/Moonlight	1971	—	2.00	4.00
❏ 45463	Two Purple Shadows/I Found You	1971	—	2.00	4.00
❏ 45545	Pretend/Too Young	1972	—	2.00	4.00
❏ 45597	Smile/All I Ever Wanted	1972	—	2.00	4.00
❏ 45677	Mister Good Times/Till We Two Are One	1972	—	2.00	4.00
❏ 45797	He/If I Give My Heart to You	1973	—	2.00	4.00
❏ 45896	Mon Amour/The Circle Ends	1973	—	2.00	4.00
❏ 45992	Free As the Wind/Reason to Believe	1974	—	2.00	4.00
❏ JZSP 79175/6 [DJ]	Silent Night, Holy Night/Oh Holy Night	1963	2.50	5.00	10.00
❏ JZSP 111776 [DJ]	Blue Christmas (same on both sides)	1965	2.50	5.00	10.00
7-Inch Extended Plays					
COLUMBIA					
❏ B-2568	*Innamorata/Two Purple Shadows/Pretend You Don't See Her/And This Is My Beloved	1958	2.50	5.00	10.00
❏ B-2568 [PS]	Jerry Vale (Hall of Fame Series)	1958	2.50	5.00	10.00
❏ 7-9073 [PS]	Standing Ovation!	1964	2.50	5.00	10.00
❏ 7-9073 [S]	Hey, Look Me Over/Lulu's Back in Town/With a Song in My Heart/If I Had You/I'm Always Chasing Rainbows/Lonesome Road	1964	2.50	5.00	10.00
—33 1/3 rpm, small hole, "Special Coin Operator Release"					
❏ 7-9187 [PS]	There Goes My Heart	1965	2.50	5.00	10.00

Number	Title (A Side/B Side)	Yr	VG	VG+	NM
❏ 7-9187 [S]	There Goes My Heart/Sogni D'Oro (Dreams of Gold/Can't You See I'm Sorry//Without Saying a Word/No One Will Ever Know/Somebody Else Is Taking My Place	1965	2.50	5.00	10.00
—33 1/3 rpm, small hole, "Special Coin Operator Release"					
❏ B-11641	Sweet and Lovely/All of Me//Prisoner of Love/Just Friends	1958	2.50	5.00	10.00
❏ B-11641 [PS]	(title unknown)	1958	2.50	5.00	10.00

Albums
COLUMBIA

Number	Title (A Side/B Side)	Yr	VG	VG+	NM
❏ GP 16 [(2)]	With Love, Jerry Vale	1969	3.75	7.50	15.00
❏ CS 1021	Let It Be	1970	3.00	6.00	12.00
❏ CL 1114 [M]	I Remember Buddy	1958	3.75	7.50	15.00
❏ CL 1164 [M]	I Remember Russ	1958	3.75	7.50	15.00
❏ CL 1380 [M]	The Same Old Moon	1959	3.75	7.50	15.00
❏ CL 1529 [M]	Jerry Vale's Greatest Hits	1961	3.75	7.50	15.00
❏ CL 1797 [M]	I Have But One Heart	1962	3.00	6.00	12.00
❏ CL 1955 [M]	Arrividerci, Roma	1963	3.00	6.00	12.00
❏ CL 2043 [M]	The Language of Love	1963	3.00	6.00	12.00
❏ CL 2116 [M]	Till the End of Time	1964	3.00	6.00	12.00
❏ CL 2181 [M]	Be My Love	1964	3.00	6.00	12.00
❏ CL 2225 [M]	Christmas Greetings from Jerry Vale	1964	3.00	6.00	12.00
❏ CL 2273 [M]	Standing Ovation!	1965	3.00	6.00	12.00
❏ CL 2313 [M]	Have You Looked Into Your Heart	1965	3.00	6.00	12.00
❏ CL 2371 [M]	Moonlight Becomes You	1965	3.00	6.00	12.00
❏ CL 2387 [M]	There Goes My Heart	1965	3.00	6.00	12.00
❏ CL 2444 [M]	It's Magic	1966	3.00	6.00	12.00
❏ CL 2489 [M]	Great Moments on Broadway	1966	3.00	6.00	12.00
❏ CL 2530 [M]	Everybody Loves Somebody	1966	3.00	6.00	12.00
❏ CL 2583 [M]	The Impossible Dream	1967	3.00	6.00	12.00
❏ CL 2659 [M]	More Jerry Vale's Greatest Hits	1967	3.75	7.50	15.00
❏ CL 2684 [M]	Time Alone Will Tell	1967	3.00	6.00	12.00
❏ CL 2774 [M]	You Don't Have to Say You Love Me	1968	3.75	7.50	15.00
❏ CS 8016 [S]	I Remember Russ	1958	5.00	10.00	20.00
—Originals have red and black "6 eye" labels					
❏ CS 8069 [S]	I Remember Buddy	1959	5.00	10.00	20.00
—Originals have red and black "6 eye" labels					
❏ CS 8175 [S]	The Same Old Moon	1960	3.75	7.50	15.00
❏ CS 8597 [S]	I Have But One Heart	1962	3.75	7.50	15.00
❏ CS 8755 [S]	Arrividerci, Roma	1963	3.75	7.50	15.00
❏ CS 8778 [R]	Jerry Vale's Greatest Hits	1963	3.00	6.00	12.00
❏ CS 8843 [S]	The Language of Love	1963	3.75	7.50	15.00
❏ CS 8916 [S]	Till the End of Time	1964	3.75	7.50	15.00
❏ CS 8981 [S]	Be My Love	1964	3.75	7.50	15.00
❏ CS 9025 [S]	Christmas Greetings from Jerry Vale	1964	3.75	7.50	15.00
❏ CS 9073 [S]	Standing Ovation!	1965	3.75	7.50	15.00
❏ CS 9113 [S]	Have You Looked Into Your Heart	1965	3.75	7.50	15.00
❏ CS 9171 [S]	Moonlight Becomes You	1965	3.75	7.50	15.00
❏ CS 9187 [S]	There Goes My Heart	1965	3.75	7.50	15.00
❏ CS 9244 [S]	It's Magic	1966	3.75	7.50	15.00
❏ CS 9289 [S]	Great Moments on Broadway	1966	3.75	7.50	15.00
❏ CS 9383 [S]	The Impossible Dream	1967	3.75	7.50	15.00
❏ CS 9459 [S]	More Jerry Vale's Greatest Hits	1967	3.00	6.00	12.00
❏ CS 9484 [S]	Time Alone Will Tell	1967	3.75	7.50	15.00
❏ CS 9574 [S]	You Don't Have to Say You Love Me	1968	3.75	7.50	15.00
❏ CS 9634	I Hear a Rhapsody	1968	3.75	7.50	15.00
❏ CS 9694	This Guy's in Love with You	1968	3.75	7.50	15.00
❏ CS 9757	Till	1969	3.75	7.50	15.00
❏ CS 9838	Where's the Playground Susie?	1969	3.75	7.50	15.00
❏ CS 9982	Jerry Vale Sings 16 Greatest Hits of the 60's	1970	3.00	6.00	12.00
❏ C 30104	We've Only Just Begun	1971	2.50	5.00	10.00
❏ C 30389	The Italian Album	1970	2.50	5.00	10.00
❏ C 30799	I Don't Know How to Love Her	1971	2.50	5.00	10.00
❏ C 31147	Jerry Vale Sings the Great Hits of Nat King Cole	1972	3.00	6.00	12.00
❏ KG 31543 [(2)]	All-Time Greatest Hits	1972	3.00	6.00	12.00
❏ KC 31716	Alone Again (Naturally)	1972	2.50	5.00	10.00
❏ KG 31938 [(2)]	Great Italian Hits	1973	3.00	6.00	12.00
❏ KG 32083 [(2)]	Jerry Vale Sings the Great Love Songs	1973	3.00	6.00	12.00
❏ C 32238	Love Is a Many-Splendored Thing	1973	2.50	5.00	10.00
❏ KC 32454	Jerry Vale's World	1973	2.50	5.00	10.00
❏ KC 32829	Free As the Wind	1974	2.50	5.00	10.00
❏ CG 33615 [(2)]	The Italian Album/Arrividerci, Roma	1974	3.00	6.00	12.00

COLUMBIA LIMITED EDITION

Number	Title (A Side/B Side)	Yr	VG	VG+	NM
❏ LE 10058	Till	197?	2.50	5.00	10.00
—Reissue of 9757					
❏ LE 10164	Christmas Greetings from Jerry Vale	197?	2.50	5.00	10.00
—Reissue					

HARMONY

Number	Title (A Side/B Side)	Yr	VG	VG+	NM
❏ HS 11298	As Long As She Needs Me	1969	2.50	5.00	10.00
❏ HS 11376	Hey Look Me Over	1970	2.50	5.00	10.00
❏ KH 30345	Born Free	1971	2.50	5.00	10.00
❏ KH 30759	More	1971	2.50	5.00	10.00
❏ KH 32478	What a Wonderful World	1973	2.50	5.00	10.00

VALE, RICKY, AND THE SURFERS
Albums
STRAND

Number	Title (A Side/B Side)	Yr	VG	VG+	NM
❏ SL-1104 [M]	Everybody's Surfin'	1963	10.00	20.00	40.00
❏ SLS-1104 [S]	Everybody's Surfin'	1963	12.50	25.00	50.00

VALENS, RITCHIE
45s
DEL-FI

Number	Title (A Side/B Side)	Yr	VG	VG+	NM
❏ 1287	La Bamba '87/La Bamba	1987	—	2.50	5.00
❏ 4106	Come On, Let's Go/Framed	1958	20.00	40.00	80.00
❏ 4110	Donna/La Bamba	1958	7.50	15.00	30.00
—Light blue label					
❏ 4110	Donna/La Bamba	1958	10.00	20.00	40.00
—Green label					
❏ 4110	Donna/La Bamba	1958	17.50	35.00	70.00
—Blue/green/black label with circles					
❏ 4110	Donna/La Bamba	196?	3.75	7.50	15.00
—Black label with light blue sawtooth border					
❏ 4110	Donna/La Bamba	196?	6.25	12.50	25.00
—Light blue label with black sawtooth border					
❏ 4110	Donna/La Bamba	1958	10.00	20.00	40.00
—White label, similar in style to the green and light blue labels (probably not a promo)					

Number	Title (A Side/B Side)	Yr	VG	VG+	NM
❏ 4111	Fast Freight/Big Baby Blues	1959	10.00	20.00	40.00
—As "Ritchie Valens"					
❏ 4111	Fast Freight/Big Baby Blues	1959	12.50	25.00	50.00
—As "Arvee Allens"					
❏ 4114	That's My Little Susie/In a Turkish Town	1959	10.00	20.00	40.00
❏ 4114 [PS]	That's My Little Susie/In a Turkish Town	1959			
—Rumored to exist, but without conclusive evidence, we will delete this from future editions					
❏ 4117	Little Girl/We Belong Together	1959	7.50	15.00	30.00
❏ 4117 [PS]	Little Girl/We Belong Together	1959	25.00	50.00	100.00
❏ 4128	Stay Beside Me/Big Baby Blues	1959	6.25	12.50	25.00
❏ 4133	The Paddiwack Song/Cry, Cry, Cry	1960	6.25	12.50	25.00
❏ 51341 [DJ]	Come On Let's Go/La Bamba	1998	—	2.50	5.00
❏ 51341 [PS]	Come On Let's Go/La Bamba	1998	—	2.50	5.00
—Promotional issue in advance of box set; number is not on sleeve, but is on record					

LANA

Number	Title (A Side/B Side)	Yr	VG	VG+	NM
❏ 153	Donna/La Bamba	196?	2.00	4.00	8.00
—Oldies reissue					

LOST-NITE

Number	Title (A Side/B Side)	Yr	VG	VG+	NM
❏ 201	Donna/La Bamba	196?	—	3.00	6.00
—Reissue					
❏ 212	Come On Let's Go/Framed	196?	—	3.00	6.00
—Reissue					

7-Inch Extended Plays
DEL-FI

Number	Title (A Side/B Side)	Yr	VG	VG+	NM
❏ PR-1 [DJ]	La Bamba/We Belong Together// Donna/Framed	1960	37.50	75.00	150.00
❏ PR-1 [PS]	Ritchie Valens (Limited Valens Memorial Series)	1960	50.00	100.00	200.00
—Sleeve accompanying promo-only EP states "February Is Ritchie Valens Memorial Month"					
❏ DFEP-101	(contents unknown)	1959	37.50	75.00	150.00
❏ DFEP-101 [PS]	Ritchie Valens	1959	37.50	75.00	150.00
—Cardboard sleeve					
❏ DFEP-101 [PS]	Ritchie Valens	1959	37.50	75.00	150.00
—Paper sleeve					
❏ DFEP-111	(contents unknown)	1960	37.50	75.00	150.00
❏ DFEP-111 [PS]	Ritchie Valens	1960	37.50	75.00	150.00

Albums
DEL-FI

Number	Title (A Side/B Side)	Yr	VG	VG+	NM
❏ DFLP 1201 [M]	Ritchie Valens	1959	37.50	75.00	150.00
—Black label with "diamonds" border					
❏ DFLP 1201 [M]	Ritchie Valens	1959	62.50	125.00	250.00
—Blue label with black border					
❏ DFLP 1206 [M]	Ritchie	1959	37.50	75.00	150.00
❏ DFLP 1214 [M]	In Concert at Pacoima Jr. High	1960	62.50	125.00	250.00
❏ DFLP 1225 [M]	His Greatest Hits	1963	37.50	75.00	150.00
—White cover					
❏ DFLP 1225 [M]	His Greatest Hits	1963	87.50	175.00	350.00
—Black cover					
❏ DFLP 1247 [M]	His Greatest Hits, Volume 2	1965	37.50	75.00	150.00

GUEST STAR

Number	Title (A Side/B Side)	Yr	VG	VG+	NM
❏ GS-1469 [M]	The Original Ritchie Valens	1963	7.50	15.00	30.00
❏ GSS-1469 [R]	The Original Ritchie Valens	1963	5.00	10.00	20.00
❏ GS-1484 [M]	The Original La Bamba	1963	7.50	15.00	30.00
❏ GSS-1484 [R]	The Original La Bamba	1963	5.00	10.00	20.00

MGM

Number	Title (A Side/B Side)	Yr	VG	VG+	NM
❏ GAS-117	Ritchie Valens (Golden Archive Series)	1970	7.50	15.00	30.00

RHINO

Number	Title (A Side/B Side)	Yr	VG	VG+	NM
❏ RNDF-200	The Best of Ritchie Valens	1981	3.00	6.00	12.00
❏ RNBC-2798 [(3)]	The History of Ritchie Valens	198?	6.25	12.50	25.00
❏ RNLP-70178	The Best of Ritchie Valens (Golden Archive Series)	1987	2.50	5.00	10.00
❏ RNLP-70231	Ritchie Valens	1987	2.50	5.00	10.00
❏ RNLP-70232	Ritchie	1987	2.50	5.00	10.00
❏ RNLP-70233	In Concert at Pacoima Jr. High	1987	2.50	5.00	10.00

VALENS, RITCHIE / JERRY KOLE
Albums
CROWN

Number	Title (A Side/B Side)	Yr	VG	VG+	NM
❏ CLP-5336 [M]	Ritchie Valens and Jerry Kole	1963	7.50	15.00	30.00

VALENTE, CATERINA
45s
DECCA

Number	Title (A Side/B Side)	Yr	VG	VG+	NM
❏ 9-29394	Malaguena/Mambo from Chile	1954	3.00	6.00	12.00
❏ 9-29467	The Breeze and I (Andalucia)/Jalousie	1955	3.75	7.50	15.00
❏ 9-29570	Babalu/This Must Be Wrong	1955	3.00	6.00	12.00
❏ 9-29709	Fiesta Cubana/If Hearts Could Talk	1955	3.00	6.00	12.00
❏ 9-29760	Temptation/Siboney	1955	3.00	6.00	12.00
❏ 9-29846	The Way You Love Me/Similau	1956	2.50	5.00	10.00
❏ 9-29951	Granada/There But For the Grace of God Go I	1956	2.50	5.00	10.00
❏ 9-30025	I'll Remember April/Everytime We Say Goodbye	1956	2.50	5.00	10.00
❏ 9-30168	Nocturne for the Blues/Poinciana	1956	2.50	5.00	10.00
❏ 9-30401	Anna/El Cumbanchero	1957	2.50	5.00	10.00
❏ 9-30456	Baia/Take Me to Your Heart	1957	2.50	5.00	10.00
❏ 9-30629	Be Mine Tonight/Mine, Mine, Mine	1958	2.50	5.00	10.00
❏ 9-30689	All My Love/Kiss of Fire	1958	2.50	5.00	10.00
❏ 9-30778	Secret Love/Oho-Aha	1958	2.50	5.00	10.00
❏ 9-30978	Tipi Tipso/Mack the Knife	1959	2.50	5.00	10.00

LONDON

Number	Title (A Side/B Side)	Yr	VG	VG+	NM
❏ 1018	Melodie/Underbar, Wie Schon Der Abend War	1969	—	3.00	6.00
❏ 1913	Down By the Riverside/Sweetheart, My Darling, My Dear	196?	2.00	4.00	8.00
❏ 1968	Personalita/Sucu Sucu	196?	2.00	4.00	8.00
❏ 9609	Hindustan/Never Will I Marry	1963	2.00	4.00	8.00
❏ 9667	When in Rome/With a Song in My Heart	1964	2.00	4.00	8.00
❏ 10001	Dis-Moi Septembre/Un Petit Beguin	196?	2.00	4.00	8.00
❏ 10003	Don Quixote/Spell of Love	196?	2.00	4.00	8.00
❏ 10007	Peppermint Twist/Twistin' the Twist	1962	2.00	4.00	8.00
❏ 10011	Port-au-Prince/Corporation	1962	2.00	4.00	8.00
—With Silvio Francesco					
❏ 10015	One Note Samba/Recado	196?	2.00	4.00	8.00
❏ 10021	Always Together/La Malaguena	196?	2.00	4.00	8.00
❏ 10033	Ja, Ja, Java/My Hawaiian Melody	196?	2.00	4.00	8.00
❏ 10041	Hey There/Corcovado	196?	2.00	4.00	8.00
❏ 10047	Don't Lose Your Head/Will He Be There	196?	2.00	4.00	8.00

Number	Title (A Side/B Side)	Yr	VG	VG+	NM
LONDON PHASE 4					
❏ 90004	Be In (Hare Krishna)/O Meu Viol	1969	—	3.00	6.00
—With Edmundo Ros					
RCA VICTOR					
❏ 47-7525	Where/La Strada Del' Amore	1959	2.50	5.00	10.00
TELEFUNKEN					
❏ 4502	Ciao, Ciao, Bambina/Passion Flower	196?	2.50	5.00	10.00
❏ 4507	Gondoli, Gondola/Tango Italiano	1962	3.00	6.00	12.00
—Canadian issue only?					
Albums					
DECCA					
❏ DL 4035 [M]	More Schlagerparade	1959	6.25	12.50	25.00
❏ DL 4050 [M]	Caterina A La Carte	1959	6.25	12.50	25.00
❏ DL 4051 [M]	Arriba	1959	6.25	12.50	25.00
❏ DL 4052 [M]	Catarina: The Greatest in Any Language	1959	6.25	12.50	25.00
❏ DL 4504 [M]	Golden Favorites	1964	5.00	10.00	20.00
❏ DL 8203 [M]	The Hi-Fi Nightingale	1956	6.25	12.50	25.00
❏ DL 8436 [M]	Ole Caterina	1957	6.25	12.50	25.00
❏ DL 8440 [M]	Plenty Valente!	1957	6.25	12.50	25.00
❏ DL 8755 [M]	A Toast to the Girls	1958	6.25	12.50	25.00
❏ DL 8852 [M]	Schlagerparade	1958	5.00	10.00	20.00
❏ DL 74504 [R]	Golden Favorites	1964	3.00	6.00	12.00
LONDON					
❏ PS 275 [S]	I Wish You Love	196?	3.75	7.50	15.00
—With Stanley Black					
❏ PS 307 [S]	Strictly U.S.A.	196?	3.75	7.50	15.00
❏ PS 355 [S]	Songs I've Sung on the Perry Como Show	196?	3.75	7.50	15.00
❏ PS 362 [S]	I Happen to Like New York	196?	3.75	7.50	15.00
❏ PS 363 [S]	Valente and Violins	196?	3.75	7.50	15.00
❏ PS 441 [S]	Caterina Valente's Greatest Hits	1965	3.75	7.50	15.00
❏ PS 471 [S]	Go Latin!	196?	3.75	7.50	15.00
—With Silvio Francesco					
❏ PS 473 [S]	Intimate Valente	196?	3.75	7.50	15.00
❏ PS 536	Sweet Beat	1969	3.75	7.50	15.00
❏ LL 3275 [M]	I Wish You Love	196?	3.00	6.00	12.00
—With Stanley Black					
❏ LL 3307 [M]	Strictly U.S.A.	196?	3.00	6.00	12.00
❏ LL 3355 [M]	Songs I've Sung on the Perry Como Show	196?	3.00	6.00	12.00
❏ LL 3362 [M]	I Happen to Like New York	196?	3.00	6.00	12.00
❏ LL 3363 [M]	Valente and Violins	196?	3.00	6.00	12.00
❏ LL 3441 [M]	Caterina Valente's Greatest Hits	1965	3.00	6.00	12.00
❏ LL 3471 [M]	Go Latin!	196?	3.00	6.00	12.00
—With Silvio Francesco					
❏ LL 3473 [M]	Intimate Valente	196?	3.00	6.00	12.00
❏ TW 91198 [M]	Continental Favorites	196?	3.75	7.50	15.00
❏ TW 91253 [M]	Fire and Frenzy	196?	3.75	7.50	15.00
—With Edmundo Ros					
❏ TW 91260 [M]	Miss Personality	196?	3.75	7.50	15.00
❏ TW 91267 [M]	German Evergreens	196?	3.75	7.50	15.00
—With Silvio Francesco					
❏ TW 91292 [M]	South of the Border	196?	3.75	7.50	15.00
❏ ST-93108 [S]	Caterina Valente's Greatest Hits	196?	5.00	10.00	20.00
—Capitol Record Club edition					
❏ SW 99019 [S]	Fire and Frenzy	196?	5.00	10.00	20.00
—With Edmundo Ros					
❏ SW 99025 [S]	German Evergreens	196?	5.00	10.00	20.00
—With Silvio Francesco					
❏ SW 99292 [S]	South of the Border	196?	5.00	10.00	20.00
LONDON PHASE 4					
❏ SP-44125	Silk and Latin	197?	6.25	12.50	25.00
❏ SP-44181	Love	197?	6.25	12.50	25.00
PETERS INT'L.					
❏ PLD-7021	Golden Days	197?	3.00	6.00	12.00
❏ PLD-7046	Caterina Valente	197?	3.00	6.00	12.00
RCA VICTOR					
❏ LPM-2119 [M]	Classics with a Chaser	1960	5.00	10.00	20.00
❏ LSP-2119 [S]	Classics with a Chaser	1960	6.25	12.50	25.00
❏ LPM-2241 [M]	Superfonics	1961	5.00	10.00	20.00
❏ LSP-2241 [S]	Superfonics	1961	6.25	12.50	25.00

VALENTI, DINO Also see QUICKSILVER MESSENGER SERVICE.
45s

Number	Title (A Side/B Side)	Yr	VG	VG+	NM
ELEKTRA					
❏ 45012	Birdses/Don't Let It Down	1964	3.75	7.50	15.00
Albums					
EPIC					
❏ LN 24335 [M]	Dino Valenti	1967	5.00	10.00	20.00
❏ BN 26335 [S]	Dino Valenti	1967	5.00	10.00	20.00

VALENTI, JOHN
45s

Number	Title (A Side/B Side)	Yr	VG	VG+	NM
ARIOLA AMERICA					
❏ 7625	Anything You Want/That's the Way Life Goes	1976	—	3.00	6.00
❏ 7656	I Wrote This Song for You/Morning Song	1977	—	3.00	6.00
❏ 7663	I Love Her Too/Morning Song	1977	—	3.00	6.00
RAINTREE					
❏ 2204	Machines/Driving Back to You	1975	—	3.00	6.00
—As "John LiVigni"					
RCA VICTOR					
❏ PB-12160	That's the Way Love Goes/Who Will It Be	1981	—	2.50	5.00
❏ PB-12237	I Won't Change/Stephanie	1981	—	3.00	6.00

VALENTINE, HILTON Former member of THE ANIMALS.
Albums

Number	Title (A Side/B Side)	Yr	VG	VG+	NM
CAPITOL					
❏ ST-330	All in Your Head	1969	7.50	15.00	30.00

VALENTINE, PENNY
45s

Number	Title (A Side/B Side)	Yr	VG	VG+	NM
LIBERTY					
❏ 55774	I Want to Kiss Ringo Goodbye/Show Me the Way to Love You	1964	7.50	15.00	30.00

VALENTINES, THE (1)
45s

Number	Title (A Side/B Side)	Yr	VG	VG+	NM
BETHLEHEM					
❏ 3055	I'll Forget You/Yes, You Made It That Way	1962	6.25	12.50	25.00
KING					
❏ 5338	Please Don't Leave, Please Don't Go/That's It Man	1960	6.25	12.50	25.00

Number	Title (A Side/B Side)	Yr	VG	VG+	NM
❏ 5433	That's How I Feel/Hey Ruby	1960	6.25	12.50	25.00
❏ 5830	I Have Two Loves/Camping Out	1963	5.00	10.00	20.00
UNITED ARTISTS					
❏ 764	Alone in the Night/Mink Coats and Sneakers	1964	3.75	7.50	15.00

VALENTINES, THE (2)
45s

Number	Title (A Side/B Side)	Yr	VG	VG+	NM
OLD TOWN					
❏ 1009	Tonight Kathleen/Summer Love	1954	200.00	400.00	800.00
RAMA					
❏ 171	Lily Maebelle/Falling for You	1955	12.50	25.00	50.00
—Red label					
❏ 171	Lily Maebelle/Falling for You	1955	50.00	100.00	200.00
—Blue label					
❏ 181	I Love You Darling/Hand Me Down Love	1955	37.50	75.00	150.00
❏ 186	Christmas Prayer/K-I-S-S Me	1955	12.50	25.00	50.00
—Red label					
❏ 186	Christmas Prayer/K-I-S-S Me	1955	125.00	250.00	500.00
—Blue label					
❏ 196	Why/The Woo Woo Train	1956	12.50	25.00	50.00
—Red label					
❏ 196	Why/The Woo Woo Train	1956	25.00	50.00	100.00
—Blue label					
❏ 201	Twenty Minutes (Before the Hour)/I'll Never Let You Go	1956	25.00	50.00	100.00
❏ 208	Nature's Creation/My Story of Love	1956	25.00	50.00	100.00
❏ 228	Don't Say Goodnight/I Cried Oh, Oh	1957	50.00	100.00	200.00
ROULETTE					
❏ 58	Christmas Prayer/Nature's Creation	196?	2.50	5.00	10.00
—"Golden Goodies Series"					

VALENTINES, THE (3)
45s

Number	Title (A Side/B Side)	Yr	VG	VG+	NM
SOUND STAGE 7					
❏ 2646	I'm Alright Now/Gotta Get Yourself Together	1969	3.75	7.50	15.00
❏ 2663	If You Love Me/Breakaway	1970	3.00	6.00	12.00

VALENTINES, THE (U)
45s

Number	Title (A Side/B Side)	Yr	VG	VG+	NM
IONA					
❏ 1003	The Sock/Sixteen Senoritas	196?	3.75	7.50	15.00
LUDIX					
❏ 102	Johnny One Heart/Mama I Have Come Home	1962	5.00	10.00	20.00

VALENTINO, DANNY
45s

Number	Title (A Side/B Side)	Yr	VG	VG+	NM
MGM					
❏ K12835	Stampede/(You Gotta Be a) Music Man	1959	5.00	10.00	20.00
❏ K12881	Biology/A Million Tears	1960	3.75	7.50	15.00
❏ K12952	Pictures from the Past/Till the End of Forever	1960	3.75	7.50	15.00

VALENTINO, MARK
45s

Number	Title (A Side/B Side)	Yr	VG	VG+	NM
SWAN					
❏ 4121	The Push and Kick/Walking Alone	1962	3.75	7.50	15.00
❏ 4135	Hey You're Lookin' Good/Do It	1963	3.00	6.00	12.00
❏ 4142	Jivin' at the Drive-In/Part Time Job	1963	3.00	6.00	12.00
Albums					
SWAN					
❏ SLP-508 [M]	Mark Valentino	1963	12.50	25.00	50.00

VALENTINO, SAL Of THE BEAU BRUMMELS.
45s

Number	Title (A Side/B Side)	Yr	VG	VG+	NM
FALCO					
❏ 306	Lisa Marie/I Wanna Twist	1962	10.00	20.00	40.00
WARNER BROS.					
❏ 7268	An Added Attraction (Come and See Me)/Alligator Man	1969	2.50	5.00	10.00
❏ 7289	Friends and Lovers/Alligator Man	1969	2.50	5.00	10.00
❏ 7368	Silkie/Going for Rochelle	1970	2.50	5.00	10.00

VALENTINO AND THE LOVERS
45s

Number	Title (A Side/B Side)	Yr	VG	VG+	NM
DONNA					
❏ 1345	One Teardrop Too Late/I'm Gonna Love	1961	10.00	20.00	40.00

VALENTINOS, THE Also see BOBBY WOMACK.
45s

Number	Title (A Side/B Side)	Yr	VG	VG+	NM
ABKCO					
❏ 4044	It's All Over Now/Lookin' for a Love	197?	2.00	4.00	8.00
ASTRA					
❏ 1026	Lookin' for a Love/Somewhere There's a Girl	196?	2.50	5.00	10.00
—Reissue of Sar 132					
CHESS					
❏ 1952	Do It Right/What About Me	1966	3.00	6.00	12.00
❏ 1977	Let's Get Together/Sweeter Than the Day Before	1966	3.00	6.00	12.00
JUBILEE					
❏ 5636	Death of Love/Tired of Being Nobody	1968	2.50	5.00	10.00
❏ 5650	Two Lovers' History/You've Got the Kind of Love That's for Real	1969	2.50	5.00	10.00
SAR					
❏ 132	Lookin' for a Love/Somewhere There's a Girl	1962	5.00	10.00	20.00
❏ 137	I'll Make It Alright/Darling Come Back Home	1963	5.00	10.00	20.00
❏ 144	Baby, Lots of Luck/She's So Good to Me	1963	5.00	10.00	20.00
❏ 152	It's All Over Now/Tired of Living in the Country	1964	5.00	10.00	20.00
❏ 155	Bitter Dreams/Everybody Wants to Fall in Love	1964	3.75	7.50	15.00

VALENTYNE, RUDY
45s

Number	Title (A Side/B Side)	Yr	VG	VG+	NM
ROULETTE					
❏ 4610	Don't Ever Leave Me/I Won't Cry Anymore	1965	2.50	5.00	10.00
❏ 4618	When I Fall in Love/When I Was a Child	1965	2.00	4.00	8.00
❏ 4619	And Now/Ev'rything Beautiful	1965	2.00	4.00	8.00
❏ 4620	Who Can I Turn To/More Than This I Cannot Give	1965	2.00	4.00	8.00

Number	Title (A Side/B Side)	Yr	VG	VG+	NM
Albums					
ROULETTE					
❏ R-25299 [M]	And Now... Rudy Valentyne	1965	5.00	10.00	20.00
❏ SR-25299 [S]	And Now... Rudy Valentyne	1965	6.25	12.50	25.00
VALERY, DANA					
45s					
ABC					
❏ 11138	The Lamplighter's Psalm/Didn't I	1968	3.00	6.00	12.00
❏ 11161	A Girl Without Love/Happy Birthday to Me	1968	3.00	6.00	12.00
❏ 11214	Surround Yourself with Sorrow/Breakfast in Bed	1969	3.00	6.00	12.00
COLUMBIA					
❏ 44004	Having You Around/You Don't Know Where Your Interest Lies	1967	6.25	12.50	25.00
—With Paul Simon					
❏ 44301	Imagine/You	1967	3.00	6.00	12.00
❏ 44389	Zabadak/Having You Around	1967	3.00	6.00	12.00
LIBERTY					
❏ 56156	Clinging Vine/Get In Line Girl	1970	2.00	4.00	8.00
❏ 56209	Point of No Return/Put Your Hand in the Hand	1970	2.00	4.00	8.00
PHANTOM					
❏ HB-10566	Will You Love Me Tomorrow/I Never Had It So Good	1975	—	2.50	5.00
SCOTTI BROS.					
❏ 509	I Don't Want to Be Lonely/Rainbow Connection	1979	—	2.00	4.00
❏ 612	I Gave You My Love/Roses and Rainbows	1980	—	2.00	4.00
VALETS, THE					
45s					
JON					
❏ 4025	I Need Someone/When I Met You	1958	25.00	50.00	100.00
❏ 4219	Sherry/You and You Alone	1959	7.50	15.00	30.00
VULCAN					
❏ 135	Sherry/You and You Alone	1959	50.00	100.00	200.00
VALHALLA					
Albums					
UNITED ARTISTS					
❏ UAS-6730	Valhalla	1969	6.25	12.50	25.00
VALIANTS, THE (1)					
45s					
ANDEX					
❏ 4026	Please Wait My Love/Freida, Freida	1958	30.00	60.00	120.00
—Some copies were pressed with this label in error (Keen 4026 is the "correct" issue)					
KEEN					
❏ 4008	Temptation of My Heart/Freida, Freida	1958	12.50	25.00	50.00
❏ 4026	Please Wait My Love/Freida, Freida	1958	15.00	30.00	60.00
❏ 34004	This Is the Nite/Good Golly Miss Molly	1957	10.00	20.00	40.00
❏ 34007	Lover Lover/Walkin' Girl	1958	10.00	20.00	40.00
❏ 82120	This Is the Nite/Walkin' Girl	1960	5.00	10.00	20.00
SHAR-DEE					
❏ 703	Dear Cindy/Surprise	1959	10.00	20.00	40.00
—With London distribution credit on label					
❏ 703	Dear Cindy/Surprise	1959	30.00	60.00	120.00
—No mention of London distribution on label					
VALIANTS, THE (2)					
45s					
ALLSTAR					
❏ 3677	Jack the Ripper/(B-side unknown)	196?	5.00	10.00	20.00
VALIANTS, THE (3)					
45s					
DOT					
❏ 16884	I'll Return to You/Don't Make the Same Mistake	1966	3.00	6.00	12.00
VALIANTS, THE (4)					
45s					
FAIRLANE					
❏ 21007	Blue Jeans and a Pony Tail/See Saw	1961	5.00	10.00	20.00
IMPERIAL					
❏ 5843	Love Comes in Many Ways/You Are Sweeter Than Wine	1962	3.75	7.50	15.00
❏ 5915	Living in Paradise/I'm in a World of My Own	1963	3.75	7.50	15.00
KC					
❏ 108	Frankie's Angel/Are You Ready	1962	3.75	7.50	15.00
VALIANTS, THE (5)					
45s					
SPECK					
❏ 1001	Wedding Bells/Velma	1958	625.00	1250.	2500.
VALIANTS, THE (U)					
45s					
JOY					
❏ 235	Let Me Go Lover/Let Me Ride	1960	5.00	10.00	20.00
ROULETTE					
❏ 4510	Johnny Lonely/Eternal Triangle	1963	5.00	10.00	20.00
VALINO, JOE					
45s					
BAND BOX					
❏ 261	Turn Back the Dawn/Now	1961	2.50	5.00	10.00
CROSLEY					
❏ 216	Back to Your Eyes/Hidden Persuasion	1958	3.00	6.00	12.00
❏ 219	Game of Fools/Vesta La Giubba	1959	3.00	6.00	12.00
DEBUT					
❏ 143	Christmas Is Here/In Old Judea	1967	2.00	4.00	8.00
❏ 144	Vicki/Most Charming	1968	2.00	4.00	8.00
RCA VICTOR					
❏ 47-7535	Out of Darkness/Everything I Touched Turned to Gold	1959	2.50	5.00	10.00
❏ 47-7723	Garden of Eden/Caravan	1960	2.50	5.00	10.00
❏ AMAO-0132	Garden of Eden/Caravan	1973	—	2.50	5.00
—Gold Standard Series reissue					

Number	Title (A Side/B Side)	Yr	VG	VG+	NM
UNITED ARTISTS					
❏ 101	Legend of the Lost/Declaration of Love	1957	3.00	6.00	12.00
❏ 101 [PS]	Legend of the Lost/Declaration of Love	1957	5.00	10.00	20.00
❏ 119	God's Little Acre/I'm Happy with What I've Got	1958	3.00	6.00	12.00
VIK					
❏ 0204	Buckets of Love (Zoop Zoop Do U Ba)/Four Seasons	1956	3.00	6.00	12.00
❏ 0226	Garden of Eden/Caravan	1956	3.75	7.50	15.00
❏ 0257	The Wind in the Riggin'/In the Arms of My Love	1957	3.00	6.00	12.00
❏ 0275	I'll Be Good/Tears (That I Cry Over You)	1957	3.00	6.00	12.00
7-Inch Extended Plays					
VIK					
❏ EXA-223	(contents unknown)	1956	5.00	10.00	20.00
❏ EXA-223 [PS]	Garden of Eden	1956	5.00	10.00	20.00
VALJEAN					
45s					
CARLTON					
❏ 573	Theme from Ben Casey/Theme from Dr. Kildare	1962	2.50	5.00	10.00
❏ 573 [PS]	Theme from Ben Casey/Theme from Dr. Kildare	1962	5.00	10.00	20.00
❏ 576	Till There Was You/18th Variation	1962	2.50	5.00	10.00
❏ 576 [PS]	Till There Was You/18th Variation	1962	3.75	7.50	15.00
❏ 582	Mr. Mozart's Mash/Newsette	1962	2.50	5.00	10.00
❏ 586	For the Birds/Hungarian Hash	1963	2.00	4.00	8.00
Albums					
CARLTON					
❏ LP-143 [M]	The Theme from Ben Casey	1962	5.00	10.00	20.00
❏ STLP-143 [S]	The Theme from Ben Casey	1962	6.25	12.50	25.00
❏ LP-146 [M]	Mashin' the Classics	1963	5.00	10.00	20.00
❏ STLP-146 [S]	Mashin' the Classics	1963	6.25	12.50	25.00
VALLEY, JIM Of PAUL REVERE AND THE RAIDERS.					
45s					
DUNHILL					
❏ 4096	Try, Try, Try/Invitations	1967	3.00	6.00	12.00
❏ 4103	Go-Go Round/Maintain	1967	3.00	6.00	12.00
JERDEN					
❏ 814	I'm Real/There Is Love	196?	2.50	5.00	10.00
VALLI					
45s					
SCEPTER					
❏ 1233	Hurry Home to Me (Soldier Boy)/Jimmy's in a Hurry	1962	3.75	7.50	15.00
—With the Shirelles backing up					
VALLI, FRANKIE Includes records under numerous pseudonyms. Also see THE FOUR LOVERS; THE FOUR SEASONS.					
45s					
ATLANTIC					
❏ 89720	American Pop/Why	1983	—	2.00	4.00
—With Manhattan Transfer					
CAPITOL					
❏ B-5115	Can't Say No to You/You Make It Beautiful	1982	—	2.00	4.00
—With Cheryl Ladd					
❏ B-5115 [PS]	Can't Say No to You/You Make It Beautiful	1982	—	2.50	5.00
CINDY					
❏ 3012	Come Si Bella/Real (This Is Real)	1958	50.00	100.00	200.00
—As "Franke Valli and the Romans"					
CORONA					
❏ 1234	My Mother's Eyes/The Laugh's on Me	1953	500.00	1000.	1500.
—As "Frank Valley"					
DECCA					
❏ 30994	It May Be Wrong/Please Take a Chance	1959	50.00	100.00	200.00
—As "Frankie Vally"					
MCA					
❏ 41253	Doctor Dance/Where Did We Go Wrong	1980	—	2.50	5.00
—With Chris Forde					
MERCURY					
❏ 70381	Forgive and Forget/Somebody Else Took Her Home	1954	50.00	100.00	200.00
—As "Frankie Valley"; black label					
❏ 70381	Forgive and Forget/Somebody Else Took Her Home	1954	75.00	150.00	300.00
—As "Frankie Valley"; maroon label					
MOTOWN					
❏ 1251	You've Got Your Troubles/Listen to Yesterday	1973	3.00	6.00	12.00
❏ 1279	The Scalawag Song (And I Will Love You)/Listen to Yesterday	1973	3.00	6.00	12.00
MOWEST					
❏ 5011	Love Isn't Here/Poor Fool	1972	3.00	6.00	12.00
❏ 5025	The Night (mono/stereo)	1972	2.50	5.00	10.00
—Evidently, stock copies do not exist					
OKEH					
❏ 7103	I Go Ape/If You Care	1958	75.00	150.00	300.00
—As "Frankie Tyler"					
PHILIPS					
❏ DJP-16 [DJ]	My Mother's Eyes (mono/stereo)	1967	12.50	25.00	50.00
—Only issued as a promo; alternate number is 40460, but actual issue of 40460 is "C'mon Marianne" by the Four Seasons					
❏ 40407	The Proud One/Ivy	1966	2.50	5.00	10.00
❏ 40407 [PS]	The Proud One/Ivy	1966	3.75	7.50	15.00
❏ 40446	Can't Take My Eyes Off You/The Trouble with Me	1967	2.50	5.00	10.00
❏ 40446 [PS]	Can't Take My Eyes Off You/The Trouble with Me	1967	3.75	7.50	15.00
❏ 40484	I Make a Fool of Myself/September Rain (Here Comes the Rain)	1967	2.50	5.00	10.00
❏ 40484 [PS]	I Make a Fool of Myself/September Rain (Here Comes the Rain)	1967	3.75	7.50	15.00
❏ 40510	To Give (The Reason I Live)/Watch Where You Walk	1967	2.50	5.00	10.00
❏ 40510 [PS]	To Give (The Reason I Live)/Watch Where You Walk	1967	3.75	7.50	15.00
❏ 40622	The Girl I'll Never Know (Angels Never Fly This Low)/A Face Without a Name	1969	2.50	5.00	10.00

Number	Title (A Side/B Side)	Yr	VG	VG+	NM
❏ 40622 [PS]	The Girl I'll Never Know (Angels Never Fly This Low)/A Face Without a Name	1969	3.75	7.50	15.00
❏ 40661	You've Got Your Troubles/A Dream of Kings	1970	3.00	6.00	12.00
❏ 40680	Circles in the Sand/My Mother's Eyes	1970	2.50	5.00	10.00
PRIVATE STOCK					
❏ 45,003	My Eyes Adored You/Watch Where You Walk	1974	—	2.50	5.00
❏ 45,021	Swearin' to God/Why	1975	—	2.50	5.00
❏ 45,043	Our Day Will Come/You Can Bet	1975	—	2.50	5.00
❏ 45,074	Fallen Angel/Carrie (I Would Marry You)	1976	—	2.50	5.00
❏ 45,098	We're All Alone/You to Me Are Everything	1976	—	2.50	5.00
❏ 45,109	Boomerang/Look at the World, It's Changing	1976	—	2.50	5.00
❏ 45,140	Easily/What Good Am I Without You	1977	—	2.50	5.00
❏ 45,154	Second Thoughts/So She Says	1977	—	2.50	5.00
❏ 45,169	I Need You/I'm Gonna Love You	1977	—	2.50	5.00
❏ 45,180	I Could Have Loved You/Rainstorm	1978	—	2.50	5.00
RSO					
❏ 897	Grease/Grease (Instrumental)	1978	—	3.00	6.00
SMASH					
❏ 1995	The Sun Ain't Gonna Shine (Anymore)/This Is Goodbye	1965	2.50	5.00	10.00
❏ 2015	(You're Gonna) Hurt Yourself/Night Hawk	1965	3.75	7.50	15.00
—B-side by the Valli Boys					
❏ 2037	You're Ready Now/Cry for Me	1966	2.50	5.00	10.00
WARNER BROS.					
❏ 8670	No Love at All/Save Me, Save Me	1978	—	2.50	5.00
❏ 8734	Fancy Dancer/Needing You	1979	—	2.50	5.00
Albums					
MCA					
❏ 743	Heaven Above Me	1982	2.00	4.00	8.00
—Reissue of 5134					
❏ 756	The Very Best of Frankie Valli	1982	2.00	4.00	8.00
—Reissue of 3198					
❏ 3198	The Very Best of Frankie Valli	1980	2.50	5.00	10.00
❏ 5134	Heaven Above Me	1979	2.50	5.00	10.00
MOTOWN					
❏ M5-104V1	Motown Superstar Series, Vol. 4	1981	2.50	5.00	10.00
❏ M6-852	Inside You	1975	3.75	7.50	15.00
PHILIPS					
❏ PHM 200247 [M]	Frankie Valli — Solo	1967	10.00	20.00	40.00
❏ PHS 600247 [S]	Frankie Valli — Solo	1967	7.50	15.00	30.00
❏ PHS 600274	Timeless	1968	6.25	12.50	25.00
PRIVATE STOCK					
❏ PS-2000	Closeup	1975	3.00	6.00	12.00
❏ PS-2001	Frankie Valli Gold	1975	3.00	6.00	12.00
❏ PS-2006	Our Day Will Come	1975	3.00	6.00	12.00
❏ PS-2017	Valli	1976	3.00	6.00	12.00
❏ PS-7002	Lady Put the Light Out	1977	3.00	6.00	12.00
❏ PS-7012	Hits	1978	3.00	6.00	12.00
WARNER BROS.					
❏ BSK 3233	Frankie Valli…Is the Word	1978	2.50	5.00	10.00

VALLI, FRANKIE, AND THE FOUR SEASONS See THE FOUR SEASONS.

VALLI, JUNE
45s
ABC-PARAMOUNT

Number	Title (A Side/B Side)	Yr	VG	VG+	NM
❏ 10442	You Say You Wanna Be Around/Gather Your Dreams	1963	2.00	4.00	8.00
❏ 10467	Catch Myself Crying/Silly Girl	1963	2.00	4.00	8.00
MERCURY					
❏ 10029X45 [S]	Apple Green/Oh Why	1960	5.00	10.00	20.00
❏ 71332X45	Dance with Me/La Santa Venuta	1958	2.50	5.00	10.00
❏ 71382X45	The Wedding/Lunch Hour	1958	2.50	5.00	10.00
❏ 71422X45	The Answer to a Maiden's Prayer/In His Arms	1959	2.50	5.00	10.00
❏ 71461X45	An Anonymous Letter/Bygones	1959	2.50	5.00	10.00
❏ 71520X45	My Darling, My Darling/Shadows	1959	2.50	5.00	10.00
❏ 71588X45 [M]	Apple Green/Oh Why	1960	2.50	5.00	10.00
❏ 71653	I'll Step Aside/Looking at the World	1960	2.50	5.00	10.00
❏ 71688	Love in Bloom/Flittin' and a Flirtin'	1960	2.50	5.00	10.00
❏ 71729	Weep for Me Lover/Borrowed Kisses	1960	2.50	5.00	10.00
❏ 71750	Guess Things Happen That Way/Tell Him for Me	1961	2.50	5.00	10.00
❏ 71800	Come Back to Sorrento/The World We Love In	1961	2.50	5.00	10.00
❏ 71882	Everlastin'/So Long Loser	1961	2.50	5.00	10.00
RCA VICTOR					
❏ 47-4298	Always, Always/Now, Now, Now	1951	3.75	7.50	15.00
❏ 47-4388	Cry/The Three Bells	1951	3.75	7.50	15.00
❏ 47-4759	Strange Sensation/So Madly in Love	1952	3.75	7.50	15.00
❏ 47-4900	Taboo/Mighty Lonesome Feeling	1952	3.75	7.50	15.00
❏ 47-5017	Why Don't You Believe Me/A Shoulder to Weep On	1952	3.75	7.50	15.00
❏ 47-5177	Congratulations to Someone/Love and Hate	1953	3.75	7.50	15.00
❏ 47-5298	Brass Ring Love/Many Are the Times	1953	3.75	7.50	15.00
❏ 47-5368	Crying in the Chapel/Love Every Moment You Live	1953	3.75	7.50	15.00
❏ 47-5488	Mystery Street/Don't Forget to Write	1953	3.75	7.50	15.00
❏ 47-5653	The Gypsy Was Wrong/Old Shoes and a Bag of Rice	1954	3.75	7.50	15.00
❏ 47-5740	I Understand/Love, Tears and Kisses	1954	3.75	7.50	15.00
❏ 47-5837	Tell Me, Tell Me/Boy Wanted	1954	3.75	7.50	15.00
❏ 47-5924	Ole Pappy Time/Wrong, Wrong, Wrong	1954	3.75	7.50	15.00
❏ 47-5988	Young and Foolish/Tell It to Me Again	1955	3.75	7.50	15.00
❏ 47-6078	Unchained Melody/Tomorrow	1955	3.75	7.50	15.00
❏ 47-6215	Oh! My Love/A Kiss Like Yours	1955	3.75	7.50	15.00
❏ 47-6258	The Things They Say/Por Favor	1955	3.75	7.50	15.00
❏ 47-6331	Don't Tell Me Not to Love You/Oh! What a Day	1955	3.75	7.50	15.00
❏ 47-6402	Madonna in Blue/While There's Time	1956	3.00	6.00	12.00
❏ 47-6464	Sleepy Head/From the Wrong Side of Town	1956	3.00	6.00	12.00
❏ 47-6552	Shangri-La/I've Got Something in My Eye	1956	3.00	6.00	12.00
❏ 47-6662	Beauty Isn't Everything/Now	1956	3.00	6.00	12.00
❏ 47-6852	Will You Love Me Still/Strictly Sentimental	1957	3.00	6.00	12.00
❏ 47-7032	Baby Come Home/Open Your Arms	1957	3.00	6.00	12.00
UNITED ARTISTS					
❏ 466	Hush Little Baby/I'm Afraid	1962	2.00	4.00	8.00
❏ 490	I Forgot More Than You'll Ever Know/Is It Right or Wrong	1962	2.00	4.00	8.00

7-Inch Extended Plays
RCA VICTOR

Number	Title (A Side/B Side)	Yr	VG	VG+	NM
❏ EPA-667	Body and Soul/Don't Take Your Love from Me/Can't Help Lovin' Dat Man/But Not for Me	195?	3.00	6.00	12.00
❏ EPA-667 [PS]	Body and Soul	195?	3.00	6.00	12.00
Albums					
AUDIO FIDELITY					
❏ AFSD-6214 [S]	June Valli Today	1969	5.00	10.00	20.00
MERCURY					
❏ MG-20463 [M]	Do-It-Yourself Wedding Album	1959	3.75	7.50	15.00
❏ SR-60145 [S]	Do-It-Yourself Wedding Album	1959	5.00	10.00	20.00
RCA VICTOR					
❏ LPM-1120 [M]	The Torch	1955	10.00	20.00	40.00

VALOR, TONY
45s
MUSICTONE

Number	Title (A Side/B Side)	Yr	VG	VG+	NM
❏ 1119	There's a Story in My Heart/So Tenderly	1963	37.50	75.00	150.00

VALQUINS, THE
45s
GAITY

Number	Title (A Side/B Side)	Yr	VG	VG+	NM
❏ 161/2	My Dear/Falling Star	1959	200.00	400.00	800.00
❏ 161/2	My Dear/Falling Star	1959	500.00	1000.	1500.
—Red vinyl					

VALRAYS, THE
45s
PARKWAY

Number	Title (A Side/B Side)	Yr	VG	VG+	NM
❏ 880	Get A Board/Pee Wee	1963	7.50	15.00	30.00
❏ 904	Yo Me Pregunto/Tonky	1964	5.00	10.00	20.00

VALS, THE
45s
ASCOT

Number	Title (A Side/B Side)	Yr	VG	VG+	NM
❏ 2163	Too Late/I'm Stepping Out with My Memories	1964	7.50	15.00	30.00
UNIQUE LABORATORIES					
❏ (no #)	The Song of a Lover/Compensation Blues	1962	250.00	500.00	1000.

VALTONES, THE
45s
GEE

Number	Title (A Side/B Side)	Yr	VG	VG+	NM
❏ 1004	You Belong to My Heart/Have You Ever Met an Angel	1956	75.00	150.00	300.00

VALUMES, THE See THE VOLUMES.

VAMPIRES, THE
45s
CARROLL

Number	Title (A Side/B Side)	Yr	VG	VG+	NM
❏ 104	Why Didn't I Listen to Mother/Did Anybody Lose a Tear	1962	37.50	75.00	150.00
Albums					
UNITED ARTISTS					
❏ UAL-3378 [M]	The Vampires at the Monster Ball	1964	6.25	12.50	25.00
❏ UAS-6378 [S]	The Vampires at the Monster Ball	1964	7.50	15.00	30.00

VAN, HARVIE JUNE
45s
BRIAR

Number	Title (A Side/B Side)	Yr	VG	VG+	NM
❏ 121	Natividad (Nativity)/Dasher (With the Light Upon His Tail)	1961	5.00	10.00	20.00
KING					
❏ 1369	Can Can Skirt/My Sins of Yesterday	1954	6.25	12.50	25.00
❏ 1387	The Lights Are Growing Dim/I'm Jut Not That Kind	1954	5.00	10.00	20.00
❏ 1482	Don't Offer Me the Stars/Mama Don't Chase My Love Away	1955	5.00	10.00	20.00
❏ 1497	False or True/I Found Out	1955	5.00	10.00	20.00
RCA VICTOR					
❏ 47-7548	Butcher Boy/Leaving Woman Blues	1959	3.00	6.00	12.00
❏ 47-7668	When You Are Here/Poor Wildwood Flower	1960	3.00	6.00	12.00
❏ 47-7778	Johnny Darling/Little Wooden Man	1960	3.00	6.00	12.00
TODD					
❏ 1078	Biggest Broken Heart in Town/Good Morning Mr. Echo	1962	3.00	6.00	12.00

VAN DER GRAAF GENERATOR
45s
MERCURY

Number	Title (A Side/B Side)	Yr	VG	VG+	NM
❏ 72979	Necromancer/Afterwards	1969	5.00	10.00	20.00
Albums					
ABC DUNHILL					
❏ DS 50097	H to He Who Am the Only One	1971	3.75	7.50	15.00
CHARISMA					
❏ CAS-1051	Pawn Hearts	1971	3.75	7.50	15.00
MERCURY					
❏ SRM-1-1069	Godbluff	1975	3.00	6.00	12.00
❏ SRM-1-1096	Still Life	1976	3.00	6.00	12.00
❏ SRM-1-1116	World Record	1976	3.00	6.00	12.00
❏ SR-61238	The Aerosol Grey Machine	1969	25.00	50.00	100.00
PROBE					
❏ CPLP-4515	The Least We Can Do Is Wave to Each Other	1970	7.50	5.00	30.00
PVC					
❏ 9901 [(2)]	Vital	1979	3.75	7.50	15.00

VAN DERBUR, MARILYN
Albums
DECCA

Number	Title (A Side/B Side)	Yr	VG	VG+	NM
❏ DL 8770 [M]	Miss America	1958	10.00	20.00	40.00

VAN DYKE, CONNIE
45s
MOTOWN

Number	Title (A Side/B Side)	Yr	VG	VG+	NM
❏ 1041	Oh Freddie/It Hurt Me Too	1963	12.50	25.00	50.00
WHEELSVILLE					
❏ 112	Don't Do Nothin' I Wouldn't Do/The Words Won't Come	196?	37.50	75.00	150.00

Number	Title (A Side/B Side)	Yr	VG	VG+	NM
VAN DYKE, EARL, AND THE SOUL BROTHERS					
45s					
RENAISSANCE					
❏ 5000	September Song/(B-side unknown)	196?	18.75	37.50	75.00
SOUL					
❏ 35006	Soul Stomp/Hot 'N' Tot	1964	5.00	10.00	20.00
❏ 35009	All for You/Too Many Fish in the Sea	1965	200.00	400.00	800.00
❏ 35014	I Can't Help Myself/How Sweet It Is To Be Loved By You	1965	5.00	10.00	20.00
❏ 35018	The Flick (Part 1)/The Flick (Part 2)	1966	5.00	10.00	20.00
❏ 35028	6 x 6/There Is No Greater Love	1967	5.00	10.00	20.00
—By Earl Van Dyke and the Motown Brass					
❏ 35059	Runaway Child, Running Wild/Gonna Give Her All the Love I've Got	1969	5.00	10.00	20.00
Albums					
MOTOWN					
❏ M-631 [M]	The Motown Sound	1965	10.00	20.00	40.00
❏ MS-631 [S]	The Motown Sound	1965	12.50	25.00	50.00
SOUL					
❏ SS-715	The Earl of Funk	1970	10.00	20.00	40.00
VAN DYKE, LEROY					
45s					
ABC					
❏ 12070	Unfaithful Fools/ What Will You Do Now, Mrs. Jones	1975	—	2.00	4.00
ABC DOT					
❏ 17567	You Sure Look Good on My Pillow/Busted	1975	—	2.00	4.00
❏ 17597	Who's Gonna Run the Truck Stop in Tuba City When I'm Gone?/ There Ain't No Roses in My Bed	1975	—	2.00	4.00
❏ 17691	Texas Tea/Las Vegas Girl	1977	—	2.00	4.00
AUDIOGRAPH					
❏ 468	Here Today, Here Tomorrow/(B-side unknown)	1983	—	2.50	5.00
DECCA					
❏ 32756	Mister Professor/People Gonna Turn You Off	1970	—	3.00	6.00
❏ 32825	Birmingham/What Am I Gonna Tell Them Now	1971	—	3.00	6.00
❏ 32866	I Get Lonely When It Rains/Party Girl	1971	—	3.00	6.00
❏ 32933	I'd Rather Be Wantin' Love/My Mind Is On You	1972	—	3.00	6.00
❏ 32999	I'll Be Around/Yesterday Will Come Again Tonight	1972	—	3.00	6.00
❏ 33055	Untie Me/Sittin' In for Me	1973	—	3.00	6.00
DOT					
❏ 15503	Auctioneer/I Fell in Love with a Pony Tail	1956	3.75	7.50	15.00
—Second pressings have black labels					
❏ 15503	Auctioneer/I Fell in Love with a Pony Tail	1956	5.00	10.00	20.00
—Originals have maroon labels					
❏ 15561	The Pocket Book Song/Honky Tonk Song	1957	3.75	7.50	15.00
❏ 15652	One Heart/Everytime I Ask My Heart	1957	3.75	7.50	15.00
❏ 15698	Leather Jacket/My Good Mind Went Bad	1958	25.00	50.00	100.00
❏ 16299	Auctioneer/I Fell in Love with a Pony Tail	1961	2.50	5.00	10.00
KAPP					
❏ 908	Lonely Thing/One More Minute of Lonely	1968	—	3.00	6.00
❏ 931	You May Be Too Much for Memphis, Baby/ Road of Love	1968	—	3.00	6.00
❏ 951	Lonesome Is/The Long Drive Home	1968	—	3.00	6.00
❏ 983	Goin' Back to Boston/The Straw	1969	—	3.00	6.00
❏ 2021	Steal Away/This Beginning of a Man	1969	—	3.00	6.00
❏ 2054	Crack in the World/Try a Little Bit Harder	1969	—	3.00	6.00
❏ 2091	Belle-O/An Old Love Affair Now Showing	1970	—	3.00	6.00
MCA					
❏ 40114	I'm O.K., You're O.K./ Everytime Seems Like the First Time	1973	—	2.50	5.00
MERCURY					
❏ 71779	Faded Love/Big Man in a Big House	1961	3.00	6.00	12.00
❏ 71834	Walk On By/My World Is Caving In	1961	3.75	7.50	15.00
❏ 71926	If a Woman Answers (Hang Up the Phone)/A Broken Promise	1962	3.00	6.00	12.00
❏ 71988	The Life You Offered Me/Dim, Dark Corner	1962	3.00	6.00	12.00
❏ 72018	How Long Must You Keep Me a Secret/I Sat Back and Let It Happen	1962	3.00	6.00	12.00
❏ 72057	Black Cloud/Five Steps	1962	3.00	6.00	12.00
❏ 72097	Be a Good Girl/The Other Boys Are Talking	1963	3.00	6.00	12.00
❏ 72155	Wrong Side of the Track/ What Are the Lips of Janet	1963	3.00	6.00	12.00
❏ 72198	Happy to Be Unhappy/Now I Lay Me Down	1963	3.00	6.00	12.00
❏ 72232	Night People/Baby (Where Can You Be)	1964	2.50	5.00	10.00
❏ 72277	Afraid of a Heartbreak/Your Money	1964	2.50	5.00	10.00
❏ 72326	The South End of Town/ This Is Our Moment of Truth	1964	—	—	—
—Canceled					
❏ 72336	The South End of Town/ Anne of a Thousand Days	1964	—	—	—
—Canceled					
❏ 72360	Anne of a Thousand Days/Poor Guy	1964	2.50	5.00	10.00
PLANTATION					
❏ 170	Runaround Sue/House of the Rising Sun	1978	—	2.00	4.00
❏ 192	Don't Bite the Hand That Feeds You/ A Gay Ranchero	1978	—	2.00	4.00
SUN					
❏ 1146	Save Me a Seat by the Fire/Rev. Edmond Giles	1979	—	2.00	4.00
WARNER BROS.					
❏ 5650	It's All Over Now, Baby Blue/Just a State of Mind	1965	2.50	5.00	10.00
❏ 5692	Big Wide Wonderful World of Country/ Ol' Man Moses	1966	2.50	5.00	10.00
❏ 5807	(Now and Then There's) A Fool Such As I/You Couldn't Get My Love Back (If You Tried)	1966	2.50	5.00	10.00
❏ 5841	Roses from a Stranger/Before I Change My Mind	1966	2.00	4.00	8.00
❏ 7001	I've Never Been Loved/Less of Me	1967	2.00	4.00	8.00
❏ 7064	I'll Make It Up to You/What Am I Bid	1967	2.00	4.00	8.00
❏ 7155	Louisville/There's Always Tomorrow	1967	2.00	4.00	8.00
Albums					
DOT					
❏ DLP 3693 [M]	Auctioneer	1966	5.00	10.00	20.00

Number	Title (A Side/B Side)	Yr	VG	VG+	NM
HARMONY					
❏ HS 11308	I've Never Been Loved	196?	3.00	6.00	12.00
KAPP					
❏ KS-3571	Lonesome Is	1968	3.75	7.50	15.00
❏ KS-3605	Greatest Hits	1969	3.75	7.50	15.00
❏ KS-3607	Just a Closer Walk with Thee	1969	3.75	7.50	15.00
MCA					
❏ 145	Greatest Hits	1973	3.00	6.00	12.00
MERCURY					
❏ MG-20682 [M]	Walk On By	1962	5.00	10.00	20.00
❏ MG-20716 [M]	Movin' Van Dyke	1963	5.00	10.00	20.00
❏ MG-20802 [M]	The Great Hits of Leroy Van Dyke	1963	5.00	10.00	20.00
❏ MG-20922 [M]	Songs for Mom and Dad	1964	5.00	10.00	20.00
❏ MG-20950 [M]	Leroy Van Dyke at the Tradewinds	1964	5.00	10.00	20.00
❏ SR-60682 [S]	Walk On By	1962	6.25	12.50	25.00
❏ SR-60716 [S]	Movin' Van Dyke	1963	6.25	12.50	25.00
❏ SR-60802 [S]	The Great Hits of Leroy Van Dyke	1963	6.25	12.50	25.00
❏ SR-60922 [S]	Songs for Mom and Dad	1964	6.25	12.50	25.00
❏ SR-60950 [S]	Leroy Van Dyke at the Tradewinds	1964	6.25	12.50	25.00
PLANTATION					
❏ 516	Gospel Greats	1977	3.00	6.00	12.00
SUN					
❏ 131	Golden Hits	1974	3.00	6.00	12.00
WARNER BROS.					
❏ W 1618 [M]	The Leroy Van Dyke Show	1965	3.75	7.50	15.00
❏ WS 1618 [S]	The Leroy Van Dyke Show	1965	5.00	10.00	20.00
❏ W 1652 [M]	Country Hits	1966	3.75	7.50	15.00
❏ WS 1652 [S]	Country Hits	1966	5.00	10.00	20.00
WING					
❏ MGW-12302 [M]	Out of Love	196?	3.00	6.00	12.00
❏ MGW-12322 [M]	Movin'	196?	3.00	6.00	12.00
❏ SRW-16302 [S]	Out of Love	196?	3.75	7.50	15.00
❏ SRW-16322 [S]	Movin'	196?	3.75	7.50	15.00
VAN DYKE, REGGIE					
45s					
PARKWAY					
❏ 829	Sweetness/Happy Music	1961	3.75	7.50	15.00
VAN DYKES, THE (1)					
45s					
DELUXE					
❏ 6193	The Bells Are Ringing/The Meaning of Love	1960	6.25	12.50	25.00
DONNA					
❏ 1333	Gift of Love/Guardian Angel	1961	10.00	20.00	40.00
FELSTED					
❏ 8565	Once Upon a Dream/Dame Tu Corazon	1959	6.25	12.50	25.00
KING					
❏ 5158	The Bells Are Ringing/The Meaning of Love	1958	17.50	35.00	70.00
SPRING					
❏ 1113	Gift of Love/Guardian Angel	1961	30.00	60.00	120.00
VAN DYKES, THE (2)					
45s					
HUE					
❏ 6501	No Man Is an Island/I Won't Hold It Against You	1965	7.50	15.00	30.00
MALA					
❏ 520	No Man Is an Island/I Won't Hold It Against You	1965	3.75	7.50	15.00
❏ 530	I've Got to Go On Without You/ What Will I Do If I Lose You	1966	3.00	6.00	12.00
❏ 539	Never Let Me Go/I've Got to Find a Love	1966	3.00	6.00	12.00
❏ 549	You Need Confidence/You're Shakin' Me Up	1966	3.00	6.00	12.00
❏ 566	A Sunday Kind of Love/I'm So Happy	1967	5.00	10.00	20.00
❏ 584	Tears of Joy/Save My Love for a Rainy Day	1967	10.00	20.00	40.00
Albums					
BELL					
❏ 6004 [M]	Tellin' It Like It Is	1967	12.50	25.00	50.00
❏ S-6004 [S]	Tellin' It Like It Is	1967	15.00	30.00	60.00
VAN DYKES, THE (3)					
45s					
CO-OP					
❏ 515	Rich Girl/Miracle After Miracle	1967	5.00	10.00	20.00
❏ 516	Rock-a-Bye Girl/I'll Be By	1967	5.00	10.00	20.00
GREEN SEA					
❏ 101	Rich Girl/Again and Again	1965	10.00	20.00	40.00
❏ 105	Rock-a-Bye Girl/I'll Be By	1966	12.50	25.00	50.00
❏ 108	Miracle After Miracle/How Can I Forget Her	1966	10.00	20.00	40.00
VAN DYKES, THE (4)					
45s					
DECCA					
❏ 30654	The Fixer/Run Betty, Run	1958	10.00	20.00	40.00
❏ 30762	Come On Baby/Lambie Baby	1958	10.00	20.00	40.00
❏ 31036	Better Come Back to Me/ I Don't Know What to Do	1959	15.00	30.00	60.00
VAN DYKES, THE (U)					
45s					
ATLANTIC					
❏ 2161	King of Fools/Stupidity	1962	3.75	7.50	15.00
VAN EATEN, LON AND DERREK					
45s					
A&M					
❏ 1643	Wildfire/Music Lover	1974	—	2.50	5.00
—All A&M records as "Lon and Derrek"					
❏ 1662	Who Do You Outdo/ All You're Hungry For Is Love	1975	—	2.50	5.00
❏ 1696	The Harder You Pull... The Tighter It Gets/ Dancing in the Dark	1975	—	2.50	5.00
❏ 1845	Loving You/Baby It's You	1976	—	2.00	4.00
APPLE					
❏ 1845	Sweet Music/Song of Songs	1972	2.00	4.00	8.00
❏ 1845 [PS]	Sweet Music/Song of Songs	1972	2.50	5.00	10.00

Number	Title (A Side/B Side)	Yr	VG	VG+	NM
Albums					
A&M					
❑ SP-4507	Who Do You Outdo	1975	2.50	5.00	10.00
APPLE					
❑ SMAS-3390	Brother	1972	3.75	7.50	15.00
VAN LOAN, JOE					
45s					
FORD					
❑ 122	Autumn Leaves/Love Divided	1963	5.00	10.00	20.00
V-TONE					
❑ 200	Forever/Give Me Your Heart	1958	37.50	75.00	150.00
VAN ZANDT, ED					
45s					
HIT					
❑ 28	Little Diane/Devil Woman	1962	2.00	4.00	8.00
—B-side by Bill Murphy					
VAN ZANDT, TOWNES					
45s					
POPPY					
❑ XW170	Fraulein/Don't Let the Sunshine Fool You	1973	—	3.00	6.00
❑ XW238	Pancho and Lefty//(B-side unknown)	1973	2.50	5.00	10.00
❑ 506	Talking Karate Blues/Waiting Around to Die	1968	2.00	4.00	8.00
❑ 510	Second Lovers//(B-side unknown)	1968	2.00	4.00	8.00
❑ 90104	Come Tomorrow/Delta Momma Blues	1970	2.00	4.00	8.00
❑ 90108	Greensboro Woman/Stand-In	1971	2.00	4.00	8.00
❑ 90113	If I Needed You/Sunshine Boy	1971	2.00	4.00	8.00
❑ 90116	Honky Tonkin'/Snow Don't Fall	1972	2.00	4.00	8.00
TOMATO					
❑ 10003	Who Do You Love//(B-side unknown)	1977	—	2.50	5.00
❑ 10005	When She Don't Need Me/No Place to Fall	1978	—	2.50	5.00
Albums					
POPPY					
❑ PP-LA004-F	The Late Great Townes Van Zandt	1973	3.75	7.50	15.00
❑ PYS-5700	High, Low and In Between	1972	3.75	7.50	15.00
❑ PYS-40001	For the Sake of a Song	1968	6.25	12.50	25.00
❑ PYS-40004	Our Mother, The Mountain	1969	3.75	7.50	15.00
❑ PYS-40007	Townes Van Zandt	1969	3.75	7.50	15.00
❑ PYS-40012	Delta Momma Blues	1970	3.75	7.50	15.00
SUGAR HILL					
❑ SH-1020	At My Window	1987	2.50	5.00	10.00
❑ SH-1026	Live and Obscure	1989	2.50	5.00	10.00
TOMATO					
❑ 7001 [(2)]	Live at the Old Quarter, Houston, Texas	1977	3.75	7.50	15.00
❑ 7011	The Late Great Townes Van Zandt	1978	3.00	6.00	12.00
—Reissue of Poppy 004					
❑ 7012	High, Low and In Between	1978	3.00	6.00	12.00
—Reissue of Poppy 5700					
❑ 7013	Delta Momma Blues	1978	3.00	6.00	12.00
—Reissue of Poppy 40012					
❑ 7014	Townes Van Zandt	1978	3.00	6.00	12.00
—Reissue of Poppy 40007					
❑ 7015	Our Mother, The Mountain	1978	3.00	6.00	12.00
—Reissue of Poppy 40004					
❑ 7017	Flyin' Shoes	1978	3.00	6.00	12.00
VANCE, PAUL					
45s					
ROULETTE					
❑ 4420	Cleopatra/Sadie's Shawl	1962	2.50	5.00	10.00
SCEPTER					
❑ 12164	Dommage, Dommage (Too Bad, Too Bad)/Sexy	1966	2.00	4.00	8.00
❑ 12175	Ma Vie (My Life)/It Happens Every Day	1966	2.00	4.00	8.00
❑ 12191	Lonely People Can't Afford to Cry/Julie Knows	1967	2.00	4.00	8.00
❑ 12197	Don't Go/Julie Knows	1967	2.00	4.00	8.00
Albums					
SCEPTER					
❑ SPS-557 [S]	Ma Vie (My Life)	1966	5.00	10.00	20.00
❑ SRM-557 [M]	Ma Vie (My Life)	1966	3.75	7.50	15.00
VANGUARDS, THE (1)					
45s					
LAMP					
❑ 652	It's To Late for Love/ The Thought of Losing Your Love	1970	3.00	6.00	12.00
—Yes, the label misspelled the A-side					
❑ 653	Girl Go Away/Man Without Knowledge	1970	3.00	6.00	12.00
WHIZ					
❑ 612	Somebody Please/I Can't Use You Girl	1969	2.50	5.00	10.00
VANGUARDS, THE (2)					
45s					
DERBY					
❑ 854	Don't Let It Happen Again/So Live	1954	100.00	200.00	400.00
VANGUARDS, THE (3)					
45s					
IVY					
❑ 103	Moonlight/I'm Movin'	1958	10.00	20.00	40.00
—No mention of "Billy Butler's Orchestra"					
❑ 103	Moonlight/I'm Movin'	1958	30.00	60.00	120.00
—With mention of "Billy Butler's Orchestra"					
VANGUARDS, THE (4)					
45s					
WARNER BROS.					
❑ 5800	Girl/A Stranger in Your Town	1966	3.00	6.00	12.00
VANGUARDS, THE (U)					
45s					
DOT					
❑ 15791	Baby Doll/My Friend Mary Ann	1958	6.25	12.50	25.00

Number	Title (A Side/B Side)	Yr	VG	VG+	NM
VANILLA FUDGE					
45s					
ATCO					
❑ 6495	You Keep Me Hangin' On/Take Me for a Little While	1967	3.00	6.00	12.00
❑ 6554	The Look of Love/Where Is My Mind	1968	2.00	4.00	8.00
❑ 6590	You Keep Me Hangin' On/Come by Day, Come by Night	1968	2.50	5.00	10.00
❑ 6616	Take Me for a Little While/Thoughts	1968	2.00	4.00	8.00
❑ 6632	Season of the Witch (Part 1)/Season of the Witch (Part 2)	1968	2.00	4.00	8.00
❑ 6655	Good Good Lovin'/Shot Gun	1969	2.00	4.00	8.00
❑ 6679	People/Some Velvet Morning	1969	2.00	4.00	8.00
❑ 6703	Need Love/I Can't Make It Alone	1969	2.00	4.00	8.00
❑ 6728	Windmills of Your Mind/Lord in the Country	1970	—	3.00	6.00
❑ 99729	Mystery/The Stranger	1984	—	2.00	4.00
7-Inch Extended Plays					
ATCO					
❑ SP-4516 [DJ]	Eleanor Rigby-Part 1/You Keep Me Hanging On//Eleanor Rigby-Part 2/Ticket to Ride	1968	5.00	10.00	20.00
—Promo only, white label					
❑ SP-4516 [PS]	(title unknown)	1968	5.00	10.00	20.00
—Paper sleeve with above EP					
Albums					
ATCO					
❑ 33-224 [M]	Vanilla Fudge	1967	6.25	12.50	25.00
❑ SD 33-224 [S]	Vanilla Fudge	1967	5.00	10.00	20.00
—Purple and brown label					
❑ SD 33-224 [S]	Vanilla Fudge	1969	3.00	6.00	12.00
—Yellow label					
❑ SD 33-224	Vanilla Fudge	197?	2.00	4.00	8.00
—Any later label					
❑ 33-237 [M]	The Beat Goes On	1968	10.00	20.00	40.00
❑ SD 33-237	The Beat Goes On	1968	5.00	10.00	20.00
—Purple and brown label					
❑ SD 33-237	The Beat Goes On	1969	3.00	6.00	12.00
—Yellow label					
❑ SD 33-244	Renaissance	1968	5.00	10.00	20.00
—Purple and brown label					
❑ SD 33-244	Renaissance	1969	3.00	6.00	12.00
—Yellow label					
❑ SD 33-278	Near the Beginning	1969	3.75	7.50	15.00
❑ SD 33-303	Rock 'N' Roll	1969	3.75	7.50	15.00
❑ 90000	The Best of Vanilla Fudge	1982	2.50	5.00	10.00
❑ 90149	Mystery	1984	3.00	6.00	12.00
SUNDAZED					
❑ LP 5168 [M]	Vanilla Fudge	2004	3.00	6.00	12.00
—Reissue on 180-gram vinyl					
VANITY FARE					
45s					
BRENT					
❑ 7067	Peter Who (Peter Pan)/Salt Water Babies	1967	2.00	4.00	8.00
DJM					
❑ 70024	Where Did All the Good Times Go/Stand	1971	—	2.50	5.00
❑ 70029	Big Parade/Nowhere to Go	1971	—	2.50	5.00
PAGE ONE					
❑ 21007	I Live for the Sun/On the Other Side of Life	1969	—	3.00	6.00
❑ 21020	Highway of Dreams/Waiting for the Nightfall	1969	—	3.00	6.00
❑ 21027	Early in the Morning/You Made Me Love You	1969	2.00	4.00	8.00
❑ 21029	Hitchin' a Ride/Man Child	1970	2.00	4.00	8.00
❑ 21033	(I Remember) Summer Morning/Megowd (Something Tells Me)	1970	—	3.00	6.00
❑ 21036	Where Did All the Good Times Go/Stand	1970	—	3.50	7.00
SOMA					
❑ 5000	Hitchin' a Ride/Early in the Morning	197?	—	2.50	5.00
—Reissue					
20TH CENTURY					
❑ 2012	Rock and Roll Is Back/Making for the Sun	1973	—	2.50	5.00
❑ 2036	Down Home/Take It, Shake It, Break My Heart	1973	—	2.50	5.00
Albums					
PAGE ONE					
❑ 2502	Early in the Morning	1970	5.00	10.00	20.00
VANN, TEDDY					
45s					
CAPITOL					
❑ 5878	Theme from Coloredman/Introduction to the Adventures of Coloredman	1967	10.00	20.00	40.00
COLUMBIA					
❑ 4-41996	Lonely Crowd/I Was Born to Love You	1961	3.75	7.50	15.00
❑ 4-42145	The Rhythm & Blues Song/Soon One Morning	1961	3.75	7.50	15.00
END					
❑ 1059	There Is Someone/Sweetheart	1959	5.00	10.00	20.00
JUBILEE					
❑ 5424	River Keep Moving/Who Knows What Will Be Tomorrow	1962	3.75	7.50	15.00
ROULETTE					
❑ 4300	Do You Love Me/Young and Pretty Woman	1960	5.00	10.00	20.00
TRIPLE-X					
❑ 101	Cindy/I'm Waiting	1960	5.00	10.00	20.00
VANNELLI, GINO					
12-Inch Singles					
CBS ASSOCIATED					
❑ ZAS 2663 [DJ]	Wild Horses (same on both sides)	1987	2.00	4.00	8.00
❑ 06728	In the Name of Money (3 versions)	1987	—	3.00	6.00
HME					
❑ ZAS 2059 [DJ]	Black Cars (Dance Mix) (LP Version)	1985	2.00	4.00	8.00
❑ 05205	Black Cars (Dance Mix) (Instrumental) (LP Version)	1985	2.00	4.00	8.00
45s					
A&M					
❑ 1449	Granny Goodbye/Hollywood Holiday	1973	—	2.50	5.00
❑ 1467	Crazy Life/There's No Time	1973	—	2.50	5.00

Number	Title (A Side/B Side)	Yr	VG	VG+	NM
❑ 1614	People Gotta Move/Son of a New York Gun	1974	—	2.00	4.00
❑ 1652	Powerful People/Lady	1974	—	2.00	4.00
❑ 1732	Father and Son/Love Me Now	1975	—	2.00	4.00
❑ 1760	Gettin' High/Mama Coco	1975	—	2.00	4.00
❑ 1790	Keep On Walking/Love Is a Night	1976	—	2.00	4.00
❑ 1861	Love of My Life/Omens of Love	1976	—	2.00	4.00
❑ 1861 [PS]	Love of My Life/Omens of Love	1976	—	2.50	5.00
❑ 1879	Summers of My Life/Omens of Love	1976	—	2.00	4.00
❑ 1911	Fly Into This Night/Ugly Man	1977	—	2.00	4.00
❑ 2002	Feel the Fire (Valleys of Valhalla)/Black and Blue	1977	—	2.00	4.00
❑ 2025	One Night with You/Black and Blue	1978	—	2.00	4.00
❑ 2072	I Just Wanna Stop/ The Surest Things Can Change	1978	—	2.00	4.00
❑ 2072 [PS]	I Just Wanna Stop/ The Surest Things Can Change	1978	—	2.50	5.00
❑ 2114	Wheels of Life/Mardi Gras	1979	—	2.00	4.00
❑ 2114 [PS]	Wheels of Life/Mardi Gras	1979	—	2.50	5.00
❑ 2133	The River Must Flow/Mardi Gras	1979	—	2.00	4.00
ARISTA					
❑ 0588	Living Inside Myself/Stay with Me	1981	—	—	3.00
❑ 0588 [PS]	Living Inside Myself/Stay with Me	1981	—	2.00	4.00
❑ 0613	Nightwalker/ Sally She Says the Sweetest Things	1981	—	—	3.00
❑ 0613 [PS]	Nightwalker/ Sally She Says the Sweetest Things	1981	—	2.00	4.00
❑ 0664	The Longer You Wait/Bandito	1982	—	—	3.00
❑ 0664 [PS]	The Longer You Wait/Bandito	1982	—	2.00	4.00
CBS ASSOCIATED					
❑ 05586	Hurts to Be in Love/Here She Comes	1985	—	—	3.00
❑ 05586 [PS]	Hurts to Be in Love/Here She Comes	1985	—	—	3.00
❑ 06663	In the Name of Money/Shape Me Like a Man	1987	—	—	3.00
❑ 06699	Wild Horses/Shape Me Like a Man	1987	—	—	3.00
❑ 06699 [PS]	Wild Horses/Shape Me Like a Man	1987	—	—	3.00
HME					
❑ 04889	Black Cars/Imagination	1985	—	—	3.00
❑ 04889 [PS]	Black Cars/Imagination	1985	—	—	3.00
Albums					
A&M					
❑ SP-3112	The Gist of the Gemini	1981	2.00	4.00	8.00
—Reissue of 4596					
❑ SP-3120	Powerful People	1981	2.00	4.00	8.00
—Reissue of 3630					
❑ SP-3139	Crazy Life	1981	2.00	4.00	8.00
—Reissue of 4395					
❑ SP-3170	Brother to Brother	1981	2.00	4.00	8.00
—Reissue of 4722					
❑ SP-3260	The Best of Gino Vannelli	1982	2.00	4.00	8.00
—Reissue of 3729					
❑ SP-3630	Powerful People	1974	2.50	5.00	10.00
❑ SP-3729	The Best of Gino Vannelli	1981	2.50	5.00	10.00
❑ SP-4395	Crazy Life	1973	3.00	6.00	12.00
❑ SP-4533	Storm at Sunup	1975	2.50	5.00	10.00
❑ SP-4596	The Gist of the Gemini	1976	2.50	5.00	10.00
❑ SP-4664	A Pauper in Paradise	1977	2.50	5.00	10.00
❑ SP-4722	Brother to Brother	1978	2.50	5.00	10.00
ARISTA					
❑ AB 9539	Nightwalker	1981	2.50	5.00	10.00
CBS ASSOCIATED					
❑ BFZ 40337	Big Dreamers Never Sleep	1987	2.50	5.00	10.00
HME					
❑ FZ 40077	Black Cars	1985	2.50	5.00	10.00
MOBILE FIDELITY					
❑ 1-041	Powerful People	1980	5.00	10.00	20.00
—Audiophile vinyl					
NAUTILUS					
❑ NR-35	Brother to Brother	198?	6.25	12.50	25.00
—Audiophile vinyl					

VAQUEROS, THE
45s
AUDITION

Number	Title (A Side/B Side)	Yr	VG	VG+	NM
❑ 6102	Desert Wind/Echo	1964	12.50	25.00	50.00
BANGAR					
❑ 00647	Birds and Bees/80-Foot Wave	1964	10.00	20.00	40.00

VARE, RONNIE, AND THE INSPIRATIONS
45s
DELL

Number	Title (A Side/B Side)	Yr	VG	VG+	NM
❑ 5203	Let's Rock, Little Girl/Love Is Just for Two	1959	12.50	25.00	50.00

VAREEATIONS, THE
45s
DIONN

Number	Title (A Side/B Side)	Yr	VG	VG+	NM
❑ 506	The Time/Ssab-Bbrom	1968	3.75	7.50	15.00
❑ 510	Foolish One/It's the Loving Season	1969	3.75	7.50	15.00

VARISCO, PAUL, AND THE MILESTONES
45s
DATE

Number	Title (A Side/B Side)	Yr	VG	VG+	NM
❑ 2-1650	Gotta Have Love/Look Around You People	1969	2.00	4.00	8.00

VARNER, DON
45s
QUINCY

Number	Title (A Side/B Side)	Yr	VG	VG+	NM
❑ 8002	Tear Stained Face/Meet Me in the Church	1969	62.50	125.00	250.00
VEEP					
❑ 1296	Tear Stained Face/Meet Me in the Church	1969	50.00	100.00	200.00

VASEL, MARIANNE, AND ERICH STORZ
45s
MERCURY

Number	Title (A Side/B Side)	Yr	VG	VG+	NM
❑ 71286X45	The Little Train (Die Kleine Bimmelbahn)/ Sunny Lake Walk	1958	3.75	7.50	15.00

VAUGHAN, DENNY Also includes records as "Denny Vaughn."
45s
CORAL

Number	Title (A Side/B Side)	Yr	VG	VG+	NM
❑ 9-60316	Autumn Leaves/Patricia	1950	5.00	10.00	20.00
❑ 9-60321	A Marshmallow World/So Long, Sally	1950	5.00	10.00	20.00
❑ 9-60334	I Guess I'll Have to Dream the Rest/ Gee, But I'm Lonesome Tonight	1950	5.00	10.00	20.00
❑ 9-60355	If/Wait for Me	1951	5.00	10.00	20.00
❑ 9-60393	Too Young/I Love the Way You Say Goodnight	1951	5.00	10.00	20.00
❑ 9-60432	Love Tales/Mellow Mood	1951	5.00	10.00	20.00
❑ 9-60524	Do You Really Love Me?/I Want to Remember	1951	5.00	10.00	20.00
❑ 9-60531	Moonlight and Roses/Moonglow	1951	3.75	7.50	15.00
❑ 9-60532	Roses of Picardy/Moon Over Miami	1951	3.75	7.50	15.00
❑ 9-60533	Rose Room/The Moon Was Yellow	1951	3.75	7.50	15.00
❑ 9-60534	By the Light of the Silvery Moon/I'm Bringing a Red, Red Rose	1951	3.75	7.50	15.00
—The above four comprise a box set					
GLORY					
❑ 251	If You Believe/C'est Ca	1957	3.75	7.50	15.00
❑ 256	Wonderful, Wonderful/Since You Went Away	1957	3.75	7.50	15.00
❑ 261	Heart Beats/Once Again	1957	3.75	7.50	15.00
❑ 278	My Lost Love/Thoughts of You	1958	3.75	7.50	15.00
❑ 293	Lover's Lament/Ma Vleur D'Amor	1959	3.75	7.50	15.00
KAPP					
❑ 143	Walk Hand in Hand/Just Sing a Song	1956	3.75	7.50	15.00
—As "Denny Vaughn"					
Albums					
BEVERLY HILLS					
❑ BHS-19	Aberga-Denny	1969	3.75	7.50	15.00
CORAL					
❑ CRL 56038 [10]	Moonlight and Roses	1951	12.50	25.00	50.00

VAUGHAN, FRANKIE
45s
COLUMBIA

Number	Title (A Side/B Side)	Yr	VG	VG+	NM
❑ 41279	One Thing Led to Another/So Happy in Love	1958	3.75	7.50	15.00
❑ 41406	Honey Bunny Baby/Big Deal	1959	3.75	7.50	15.00
❑ 41480	Ain't Gonna Lead This Life No More/ Heart of a Man	1959	3.75	7.50	15.00
❑ 41537	The Very Very Young/If You Ever Fall in Love	1959	3.75	7.50	15.00
❑ 41638	Hey You with the Crazy Eyes/The Key	1960	3.75	7.50	15.00
❑ 41859	Do You Still Love Me/Milord	1960	3.75	7.50	15.00
EPIC					
❑ 9238	Pebble on the Beach/Isn't This a Lovely Evening	1957	3.75	7.50	15.00
❑ 9265	We're Not Alone/Can't Get Along Without You	1958	3.75	7.50	15.00
❑ 9273	Judy/Am I Wasting My Time with You	1958	4.00	8.00	16.00
MALA					
❑ 588	If I Didn't Care/So Tired	1968	—	3.00	6.00
❑ 12004	Nevertheless/Girl Talk	1968	—	3.00	6.00
PHILIPS					
❑ 40070	Hercules/I'm Gonna Clip Your Wings	1962	3.00	6.00	12.00
❑ 40349	Forgotten Man/Wait	1965	2.00	4.00	8.00
Albums					
PHILIPS					
❑ PHM 200006 [M]	Singin' Happy	1962	5.00	10.00	20.00
❑ PHS 600006 [S]	Singin' Happy	1962	6.25	12.50	25.00

VAUGHAN, SARAH
45s
ATLANTIC

Number	Title (A Side/B Side)	Yr	VG	VG+	NM
❑ 1012	It Might As Well Be Spring/You Go to My Head	1953	25.00	50.00	100.00
❑ 3835	Fool on the Hill/Get Back	1981	—	2.50	5.00
COLUMBIA					
❑ 1-199	Black Coffee/As You Desire Me	1949	10.00	20.00	40.00
—Microgroove 33 1/3 rpm single					
❑ 1-258 (?)	Tonight I Shall Sleep (With a Smile on My Face)/ While You're Gone	1949	10.00	20.00	40.00
—Microgroove 33 1/3 rpm single					
❑ 1-321	That Lucky Old Sun (Just Rolls Around Heaven All Day)/Make Believe (You Are Glad When You're Sorry)	1949	10.00	20.00	40.00
—Microgroove 33 1/3 rpm single					
❑ 1-385 (?)	Fool's Paradise/Lonely Girl	1949	10.00	20.00	40.00
—Microgroove 33 1/3 rpm single					
❑ 1-395 (?)	I Cried for You/You Say You Care	1950	10.00	20.00	40.00
—Microgroove 33 1/3 rpm single					
❑ 1-485	I'm Crazy to Love You/Summertime	1950	10.00	20.00	40.00
—Microgroove 33 1/3 rpm single					
❑ 1-679	Our Very Own/Don't Be Afraid	1950	10.00	20.00	40.00
—Microgroove 33 1/3 rpm single					
❑ 1-757 (?)	(I Love the Girl) I Love the Guy/Thinking of You	1950	10.00	20.00	40.00
—Microgroove 33 1/3 rpm single					
❑ 6-757 (?)	(I Love the Girl) I Love the Guy/Thinking of You	1950	7.50	15.00	30.00
❑ 1-830 (?)	Perdido/Whippa Whippa Woo	1950	10.00	20.00	40.00
—Microgroove 33 1/3 rpm single					
❑ 6-830 (?)	Perdido/Whippa Whippa Woo	1950	7.50	15.00	30.00
❑ 1-926	The Nearness of You/You're Mine You	1950	10.00	20.00	40.00
—Microgroove 33 1/3 rpm single					
❑ 6-926	The Nearness of You/You're Mine You	1950	7.50	15.00	30.00
❑ 4-38925	(I Love the Girl) I Love the Guy/Thinking of You	1950	6.25	12.50	25.00
❑ 4-39001	Perdido/Whippa Whippa Woo	1950	6.25	12.50	25.00
❑ 4-39071	The Nearness of You/You're Mine You	1950	6.25	12.50	25.00
❑ 4-39124	I'll Know/Gas Pipe Leaking	1950	6.25	12.50	25.00
❑ 4-39207	Ave Maria/A City Called Heaven	1951	6.25	12.50	25.00
❑ 4-39370	These Things I Offer You (For a Lifetime)/ Deep Purple	1951	6.25	12.50	25.00
❑ 4-39446	Vanity/My Reverie	1951	6.25	12.50	25.00
❑ 4-39494	After Hours/Out of Breath	1951	6.25	12.50	25.00
❑ 4-39576	I Ran All the Way Home/Just a Moment More	1951	6.25	12.50	25.00
❑ 4-39634	Pinky/A Miracle Happened	1952	5.00	10.00	20.00
❑ 4-39719	If Someone Had Told Me/Corner to Corner	1952	5.00	10.00	20.00
❑ 4-39789	Time to Go/Street of Dreams	1952	5.00	10.00	20.00
❑ 4-39839	Say You'll Wait for Me/My Tormented Heart	1952	5.00	10.00	20.00

Number	Title (A Side/B Side)	Yr	VG	VG+	NM
❏ 4-39873	Sinner or Saint/Mighty Lonesome Feeling	1952	5.00	10.00	20.00
❏ 4-39932	Lovers' Quarrel/I Confess	1953	5.00	10.00	20.00
❏ 4-39963	Spring Will Be a Little Late This Year/A Blues Serenade	1953	5.00	10.00	20.00
❏ 4-40041	Time/Linger Awhile	1953	5.00	10.00	20.00
MAINSTREAM					
❏ 5517	Imagine/Sweet Gingerbread Man	1971	—	2.50	5.00
❏ 5521	Pieces of Dreams/Once You've Been in Love	1972	—	2.50	5.00
❏ 5522	What Are You Doing the Rest of Your Life/The Summer Knows	1972	—	2.50	5.00
❏ 5523	Summer Me, Winter Me/The Story of a Frasier	1972	—	2.50	5.00
❏ 5527	And the Feeling's Good/Deep in the Night	1972	—	2.50	5.00
❏ 5533	Rainy Days and Mondays/Just a Little Lovin'	1973	—	2.50	5.00
❏ 5541	Send In the Clowns/(B-side unknown)	1973	—	2.50	5.00
❏ 5544	Alone Again (Naturally)/Run to Me	1973	—	2.50	5.00
❏ 5553	Do Away with April/I Need You More	1974	—	2.50	5.00
MERCURY					
❏ 10020 [S]	Smooth Operator/ Maybe It's Because (I Love You Too Much)	1959	5.00	10.00	20.00
❏ 70423x45	Ol' Devil Moon/Saturday	1954	3.75	7.50	15.00
❏ 70469x45	Make Yourself Comfortable/Idle Gossip	1954	3.75	7.50	15.00
❏ 70534x45	How Important Can It Be/ Waltzing Down the Aisle	1955	3.75	7.50	15.00
❏ 70595x45	Whatever Lola Wants/Oh Yeah	1955	3.75	7.50	15.00
❏ 70646x45	Experience Unnecessary/Slowly, With Feeling	1955	3.75	7.50	15.00
❏ 70693x45	Johnny, Be Smart/Hey Naughty Papa	1955	3.75	7.50	15.00
❏ 70727x45	C'est La Vie/Never	1955	3.75	7.50	15.00
❏ 70777x45	Mr. Wonderful/You Ought to Have a Wife	1956	3.00	6.00	12.00
❏ 70846x45	Hot and Cold Running Tears/That's Not the Kind of Love I Want	1956	3.00	6.00	12.00
❏ 70885x45	Fabulous Character/The Other Woman	1956	3.00	6.00	12.00
❏ 70947x45	It Happened Again/I Wanna Play House	1956	3.00	6.00	12.00
❏ 71020x45	The Banana Boat Song/I've Got a New Heartache	1956	3.00	6.00	12.00
❏ 71030x45	Leave It to Love/The Bashful Matador	1957	3.00	6.00	12.00
❏ 71085x45	Poor Butterfly/April Give Me One More Day	1957	3.00	6.00	12.00
❏ 71157x45	Band of Angels/Please Mr. Brown	1957	3.00	6.00	12.00
❏ 71235x45	Gone Train/Next Time Around	1957	3.00	6.00	12.00
❏ 71303	Padre/Spin the Bottle	1958	3.00	6.00	12.00
❏ 71326	What's So Bad About It/Too Much Too Soon	1958	3.00	6.00	12.00
❏ 71380	I Ain't Hurtin'/Everything I Do	1958	3.00	6.00	12.00
❏ 71407	Are You Certain/Cool Baby	1959	3.00	6.00	12.00
❏ 71433	Separate Ways/Careless	1959	3.00	6.00	12.00
❏ 71477	Broken-Hearted Melody/Misty	1959	3.00	6.00	12.00
❏ 71519 [M]	Smooth Operator/ Maybe It's Because (I Love You Too Much)	1959	3.00	6.00	12.00
❏ 71562	Eternally/You're My Baby	1960	3.00	6.00	12.00
❏ 71610	Some Other Spring/Our Waltz	1960	3.00	6.00	12.00
❏ 71642	Maybe You'll Be There/Doodlin'	1960	3.00	6.00	12.00
❏ 71669	For All We Know/The Rough Years	1960	3.00	6.00	12.00
❏ 71702	Close to You/Out of This World	1960	3.00	6.00	12.00
❏ 71742	If You Are But a Dream/Mary Contrary	1960	3.00	6.00	12.00
❏ 72249	Bluesette/You Got It Made	1964	2.50	5.00	10.00
❏ 72300	How's the World Treating You/Sole, Sole, Sole	1964	2.50	5.00	10.00
❏ 72381	The Other Side of Me/We Almost Made It	1965	2.00	4.00	8.00
❏ 72417	Pawn Broker/Bye Bye (Theme from Peter Gunn)	1965	2.00	4.00	8.00
❏ 72510	Darling/I'll Never Be Lonely Again	1965	2.00	4.00	8.00
❏ 72543	A Lover's Concerto/First Thing Every Morning	1966	2.00	4.00	8.00
❏ 72588	Everybody Loves Somebody/1-2-3	1966	2.00	4.00	8.00
MGM					
❏ K10705	Tenderly/I'll Wait and Pray	1950	7.50	15.00	30.00
❏ K10762	What a Difference A Day Made/ I Can't Get Started	1950	7.50	15.00	30.00
❏ K10819	I Cover the Waterfront/Don't Worry 'Bout Me	1950	7.50	15.00	30.00
❏ K10890	I'm Gonna Sit Right Down and Write Myself a Letter/I'm Through with Love	1951	6.25	12.50	25.00
❏ K11068	Don't Blame Me/If You Could See Me Now	1951	6.25	12.50	25.00
REMINGTON					
❏ R-45-1067	Interlude/Signing Off	195?	2.50	5.00	10.00
ROULETTE					
❏ 4285	Serenata/Let's	1960	2.50	5.00	10.00
❏ 4325	True Believer/What's the Use	1961	2.50	5.00	10.00
❏ 4359	April/Oh Lover	1961	2.50	5.00	10.00
❏ 4378	Untouchable/The Hills of Assisi	1961	2.50	5.00	10.00
❏ 4397	If Love Is Good to Me/A Great Day	1961	2.50	5.00	10.00
❏ 4413	One Mint Julep/ Mama (He Treats Your Daughter Mean)	1962	2.50	5.00	10.00
❏ 4482	Call Me Irresponsible/There'll Be Other Times	1963	2.00	4.00	8.00
❏ 4497	Once Upon a Summertime/Snowbound	1963	2.00	4.00	8.00
❏ 4516	What'll I Do/I Believe in You	1963	2.00	4.00	8.00
❏ 4547	The Wallflower Waltz/Only	1964	2.00	4.00	8.00
❏ 4604	A Taste of Honey/The Good Life	1965	2.00	4.00	8.00
❏ SSR-33-8047 [S]	When Your Lover Has Gone/I'm Gonna Laugh You Out of My Life	196?	3.75	7.50	15.00
—Small hole, plays at 33 1/3 rpm					
WARNER BROS.					
❏ 49890	Theme from "Sharkey's Machine"/Sharkey's Theme	1981	—	2.00	4.00
—B-side by Eddie Harris					
7-Inch Extended Plays					
COLUMBIA					
❏ B-2551	*Deep Purple/You're Mine, You/Street of Dreams/The Nearness of You	195?	5.00	10.00	20.00
❏ B-2551 [PS]	Sarah Vaughan (Hall of Fame Series)	195?	5.00	10.00	20.00
❏ B-2588	*Perdido/Linger Awhile/Time/Corner to Corner	1959	5.00	10.00	20.00
❏ B-2588 [PS]	Sarah Vaughan (Hall of Fame Series)	1959	5.00	10.00	20.00
❏ B-7452	Come Rain or Come Shine/Mean to Me//It Might As Well Be Spring/Can't Get Out of This Mood	195?	6.25	12.50	25.00
❏ B-7452 [PS]	Sarah Vaughan in Hi-Fi	195?	6.25	12.50	25.00
MERCURY					
❏ EP-1-3305	I'm in the Mood for Love/I Don't Know Why// Honey/Let's Put Out the Lights	195?	3.00	6.00	12.00
❏ EP-1-3305 [PS]	Songs by Sarah Vaughan	195?	3.00	6.00	12.00
MGM					
❏ X1019	(contents unknown)	1953	3.75	7.50	15.00
❏ X1019 [PS]	I've Got a Crush on You	1953	3.75	7.50	15.00

Number	Title (A Side/B Side)	Yr	VG	VG+	NM
❏ X1020	The Man I Love/Body and Soul//I Can Make You Love Me/Once in a While	1953	3.75	7.50	15.00
❏ X1020 [PS]	The Man I Love	1953	3.75	7.50	15.00
Albums					
ACCORD					
❏ SN-7195	Simply Divine	1981	2.50	5.00	10.00
ALLEGRO					
❏ 1592 [M]	Sarah Vaughan	1955	12.50	25.00	50.00
❏ 1608 [M]	Sarah Vaughan	1955	12.50	25.00	50.00
❏ 3080 [10]	Early Sarah	195?	20.00	40.00	80.00
ALLEGRO ELITE					
❏ 4106 [10]	Sarah Vaughan Sings	195?	7.50	15.00	30.00
ATLANTIC					
❏ SD 16037	Songs of the Beatles	1981	3.00	6.00	12.00
BRYLEN					
❏ BN 4411	Desires	198?	2.50	5.00	10.00
—Last name is misspelled "Vaughn"					
CBS MASTERWORKS					
❏ FM 37277	Gershwin Live!	1982	2.50	5.00	10.00
—With the Los Angeles Philharmonic Orchestra					
❏ FM 42519	Brazilian Romance	1987	2.50	5.00	10.00
COLUMBIA					
❏ CL 660 [M]	After Hours with Sarah Vaughan	1955	12.50	25.00	50.00
❏ CL 745 [M]	Sarah Vaughan in Hi-Fi	1956	12.50	25.00	50.00
❏ CL 914 [M]	Linger Awhile	1956	12.50	25.00	50.00
❏ CL 6133 [10]	Sarah Vaughan	1950	30.00	60.00	120.00
COLUMBIA SPECIAL PRODUCTS					
❏ P 13084	Sarah Vaughan in Hi-Fi	1976	2.50	5.00	10.00
—Reissue of Columbia 745					
❏ P 14364	Linger Awhile	1978	2.50	5.00	10.00
—Reissue of Columbia 914					
CONCORD					
❏ 3018 [M]	Sarah Vaughan Concert	1957	7.50	15.00	30.00
CORONET					
❏ 277	Sarah Vaughan Belts the Hits	196?	3.75	7.50	15.00
EMARCY					
❏ EMS-2-412 [(2)]	Sarah Vaughan Live	197?	3.00	6.00	12.00
❏ MG-26005 [10]	Images	1954	20.00	40.00	80.00
❏ MG-36004 [M]	Sarah Vaughan	1955	20.00	40.00	80.00
❏ MG-36058 [M]	In the Land of Hi-Fi	1956	20.00	40.00	80.00
❏ MG-36089 [M]	Sassy	1956	12.50	25.00	50.00
❏ MG-36109 [M]	Swingin' Easy	1957	12.50	25.00	50.00
❏ 814187-1 [(2)]	The George Gershwin Songbook	1983	3.00	6.00	12.00
❏ 824864-1	The Rodgers & Hart Songbook	1985	2.50	5.00	10.00
❏ 826454-1	In the Land of Hi-Fi	1986	2.50	5.00	10.00
—Reissue of 36058					
EVEREST ARCHIVE OF FOLK & JAZZ					
❏ 250	Sarah Vaughan	197?	2.50	5.00	10.00
❏ 271	Sarah Vaughan, Volume 2	1973	2.50	5.00	10.00
❏ 325	Sarah Vaughan, Volume 3	197?	2.50	5.00	10.00
FORUM					
❏ F-9034 [M]	Dreamy	196?	3.00	6.00	12.00
❏ SF-9034 [S]	Dreamy	196?	3.75	7.50	15.00
HARMONY					
❏ HL 7158 [M]	The Great Sarah Vaughan	196?	3.00	6.00	12.00
LION					
❏ L 70052 [M]	Tenderly	1958	6.25	12.50	25.00
MAINSTREAM					
❏ MRL 340	Time in My Life	1972	3.75	7.50	15.00
❏ MRL 361	Sarah Vaughan/Michel Legrand	1972	3.75	7.50	15.00
❏ MRL 379	Feelin' Good	1973	3.75	7.50	15.00
❏ MRL 404	Sarah Vaughan and the Jimmy Rowles Quintet	1974	3.75	7.50	15.00
❏ MRL 419	More Sarah Vaughan from Japan	1974	3.75	7.50	15.00
❏ MRL 2401 [(2)]	Sarah Vaughan "Live" In Japan	1973	5.00	10.00	20.00
MASTERSEAL					
❏ MS-55 [M]	Sarah Vaughan Sings	195?	6.25	12.50	25.00
MERCURY					
❏ MGP-2-100 [(2)M]	Great Songs from Hit Shows	1957	15.00	30.00	60.00
❏ MGP-2-101 [(2)M]	Sarah Vaughan Sings George Gershwin	1957	15.00	30.00	60.00
❏ MG-20094 [M]	Sarah Vaughan at the Blue Note	1956	10.00	20.00	40.00
❏ MG-20219 [M]	Wonderful Sarah	1957	10.00	20.00	40.00
❏ MG-20223 [M]	In a Romantic Mood	1957	10.00	20.00	40.00
❏ MG-20244 [M]	Great Songs from Hit Shows, Vol. 1	1958	7.50	15.00	30.00
❏ MG-20245 [M]	Great Songs from Hit Shows, Vol. 2	1958	7.50	15.00	30.00
❏ MG-20310 [M]	Sarah Vaughan Sings George Gershwin, Vol. 1	1958	7.50	15.00	30.00
❏ MG-20311 [M]	Sarah Vaughan Sings George Gershwin, Vol. 2	1958	7.50	15.00	30.00
❏ MG-20326 [M]	Sarah Vaughan and Her Trio at Mr. Kelly's	1958	10.00	20.00	40.00
❏ MG-20370 [M]	Vaughan and Violins	1958	10.00	20.00	40.00
❏ MG-20383 [M]	After Hours at the London House	1959	10.00	20.00	40.00
❏ MG-20438 [M]	The Magic of Sarah Vaughan	1959	7.50	15.00	30.00
❏ MG-20441 [M]	No 'Count Sarah	1959	7.50	15.00	30.00
❏ MG-20540 [M]	The Divine Sarah Vaughan	1960	6.25	12.50	25.00
❏ MG-20580 [M]	Close to You	1960	6.25	12.50	25.00
❏ MG-20617 [M]	My Heart Sings	1961	6.25	12.50	25.00
❏ MG-20645 [M]	Sarah Vaughan's Golden Hits	1961	5.00	10.00	20.00
❏ MG-20831 [M]	Sassy Swings the Tivoli	1962	5.00	10.00	20.00
❏ MG-20882 [M]	Vaughan with Voices	1963	5.00	10.00	20.00
❏ MG-20941 [M]	Viva Vaughan	1964	3.75	7.50	15.00
❏ MG-21009 [M]	Sarah Vaughan Sings the Mancini Songbook	1965	3.75	7.50	15.00
❏ MG-21069 [M]	Pop Artistry	1966	3.75	7.50	15.00
❏ MG-21079 [M]	The New Scene	1966	3.75	7.50	15.00
❏ MG-21116 [M]	Sassy Swings Again	1967	3.75	7.50	15.00
❏ MG-21122 [M]	It's a Man's World	1967	3.75	7.50	15.00
❏ MG-25188 [10]	Divine Sarah	1955	25.00	50.00	100.00
❏ MG-25213 [10]	The Divine Sarah Sings	1955	25.00	50.00	100.00
❏ SR-60038 [S]	After Hours at the London House	1959	10.00	20.00	40.00
❏ SR-60038 [S]	Vaughan and Violins	1959	10.00	20.00	40.00
❏ SR-60041 [S]	Great Songs from Hit Shows, Vol. 1	1959	10.00	20.00	40.00
❏ SR-60045 [S]	Sarah Vaughan Sings George Gershwin, Vol. 1	1959	10.00	20.00	40.00
❏ SR-60046 [S]	Sarah Vaughan Sings George Gershwin, Vol. 2	1959	10.00	20.00	40.00
❏ SR-60078 [S]	Great Songs from Hit Shows, Vol. 2	1959	10.00	20.00	40.00
❏ SR-60110 [S]	The Magic of Sarah Vaughan	1959	10.00	20.00	40.00
❏ SR-60116 [S]	No 'Count Sarah	1959	10.00	20.00	40.00
❏ SR-60240 [S]	Close to You	1960	7.50	15.00	30.00
❏ SR-60255 [S]	The Divine Sarah Vaughan	1960	7.50	15.00	30.00
❏ SR-60617 [S]	My Heart Sings	1961	7.50	15.00	30.00

Number	Title (A Side/B Side)	Yr	VG	VG+	NM
❏ SR-60645 [S]	Sarah Vaughan's Golden Hits	1961	6.25	12.50	25.00
—Original black label version					
❏ SR-60645 [S]	Sarah Vaughan's Golden Hits	1965	3.75	7.50	15.00
—Red label version with white "MERCURY" alone at top					
❏ SR-60645 [S]	Sarah Vaughan's Golden Hits	1968	3.00	6.00	12.00
—Red label with multiple Mercury logos along the label edge					
❏ SR-60831 [S]	Sassy Swings the Tivoli	1962	6.25	12.50	25.00
❏ SR-60882 [S]	Vaughan with Voices	1963	6.25	12.50	25.00
❏ SR-60941 [S]	Viva Vaughan	1964	5.00	10.00	20.00
❏ SR-61009 [S]	Sarah Vaughan Sings the Mancini Songbook	1965	5.00	10.00	20.00
❏ SR-61069 [S]	Pop Artistry	1966	5.00	10.00	20.00
❏ SR-61079 [S]	The New Scene	1966	5.00	10.00	20.00
❏ SR-61116 [S]	Sassy Swings Again	1967	5.00	10.00	20.00
❏ SR-61122 [S]	It's a Man's World	1967	5.00	10.00	20.00
❏ 826320-1 [(6)]	The Complete Sarah Vaughan on Mercury Vol. 1: Great Jazz years (1954-56)	1986	10.00	20.00	40.00
❏ 826327-1 [(5)]	The Complete Sarah Vaughan on Mercury Vol. 2: Great American Songs (1956-57)	1986	10.00	20.00	40.00
❏ 826333-1 [(6)]	The Complete Sarah Vaughan on Mercury Vol. 3: Great Show on Stage (1954-56)	1986	10.00	20.00	40.00
❏ 830721-1 [(4)]	The Complete Sarah Vaughan on Mercury Vol. 4 Part 1: Live in Europe (1963-64)	1987	10.00	20.00	40.00
❏ 830726-1 [(5)]	The Complete Sarah Vaughan on Mercury Vol. 4 Part 2: Sassy Swings Again	1987	10.00	20.00	40.00
METRO					
❏ M-539 [M]	Tenderly	1965	3.00	6.00	12.00
❏ MS-539 [S]	Tenderly	1965	3.75	7.50	15.00
MGM					
❏ E-165 [10]	Tenderly	1950	30.00	60.00	120.00
❏ E-544 [10]	Sarah Vaughan Sings	1951	30.00	60.00	120.00
❏ E-3274 [M]	My Kinda Love	1955	12.50	25.00	50.00
—Combination of two 10-inch LPs on one 12-inch LP					
MUSICRAFT					
❏ 504	Divine Sarah	197?	2.50	5.00	10.00
❏ MVS-2002	The Man I Love	1986	2.50	5.00	10.00
❏ MVS-2006	Lover Man	1986	2.50	5.00	10.00
PABLO					
❏ 2310821	How Long	1978	2.50	5.00	10.00
❏ 2310885	The Best of Sarah Vaughan	1983	2.50	5.00	10.00
❏ 2312101	I Love Brazil	1978	2.50	5.00	10.00
❏ 2312111	The Duke Ellington Songbook One	1979	2.50	5.00	10.00
❏ 2312116	The Duke Ellington Songbook Two	1980	2.50	5.00	10.00
❏ 2312125	Copacabana	1981	2.50	5.00	10.00
❏ 2405416	The Best of Sarah Vaughan	1990	2.50	5.00	10.00
PABLO TODAY					
❏ 2312137	Crazy and Mixed Up	1982	2.50	5.00	10.00
PALACE					
❏ 5191 [M]	Sarah Vaughan Sings	195?	6.25	12.50	25.00
PICKWICK					
❏ PCS-3035	Fabulous Sarah Vaughan	197?	2.50	5.00	10.00
REMINGTON					
❏ RLP-1024 [10]	Hot Jazz	1953	50.00	100.00	200.00
RIVERSIDE					
❏ RLP 2511 [10]	Sarah Vaughan Sings with John Kirby	1955	25.00	50.00	100.00
RONDO-LETTE					
❏ A-35 [M]	Songs of Broadway	1958	6.25	12.50	25.00
❏ A-53 [M]	Sarah Vaughan Sings	1959	6.25	12.50	25.00
ROULETTE					
❏ RE-103 [(2)]	Echoes of an Era: The Sarah Vaughan Years	197?	3.00	6.00	12.00
❏ K-105 [(2)M]	The Sarah Vaughan Years	196?	5.00	10.00	20.00
❏ SK-105 [(2)S]	The Sarah Vaughan Years	196?	7.50	15.00	30.00
❏ R 52046 [M]	Dreamy	1960	7.50	15.00	30.00
❏ SR 52046 [S]	Dreamy	1960	10.00	20.00	40.00
❏ R 52060 [M]	Divine One	1960	6.25	12.50	25.00
❏ SR 52060 [S]	Divine One	1960	7.50	15.00	30.00
❏ R 52070 [M]	After Hours	1961	6.25	12.50	25.00
❏ SR 52070 [S]	After Hours	1961	7.50	15.00	30.00
❏ R 52082 [M]	You're Mine	1962	6.25	12.50	25.00
❏ SR 52082 [S]	You're Mine	1962	7.50	15.00	30.00
—Black vinyl					
❏ SR 52082 [S]	You're Mine	1962	15.00	30.00	60.00
—Red vinyl					
❏ R 52091 [M]	Snowbound	1962	5.00	10.00	20.00
❏ SR 52091 [S]	Snowbound	1962	6.25	12.50	25.00
❏ R 52092 [M]	The Explosive Side of Sarah	1962	5.00	10.00	20.00
❏ SR 52092 [S]	The Explosive Side of Sarah	1962	6.25	12.50	25.00
❏ R 52100 [M]	Star Eyes	1963	3.75	7.50	15.00
❏ SR 52100 [S]	Star Eyes	1963	5.00	10.00	20.00
❏ R 52104 [M]	Lonely Hours	1963	3.75	7.50	15.00
❏ SR 52104 [S]	Lonely Hours	1963	5.00	10.00	20.00
❏ R 52109 [M]	The World of Sarah Vaughan	1964	3.75	7.50	15.00
❏ SR 52109 [S]	The World of Sarah Vaughan	1964	5.00	10.00	20.00
❏ R 52112 [M]	Sweet 'N Sassy	1964	3.75	7.50	15.00
❏ SR 52112 [S]	Sweet 'N Sassy	1964	5.00	10.00	20.00
❏ R 52116 [M]	Sarah Sings Soulfully	1965	3.75	7.50	15.00
❏ SR 52116 [S]	Sarah Sings Soulfully	1965	5.00	10.00	20.00
❏ R 52118 [M]	Sarah Plus Two	1965	3.75	7.50	15.00
❏ SR 52118 [S]	Sarah Plus Two	1965	5.00	10.00	20.00
❏ R 52123 [M]	Sarah Slightly Classical	1966	3.75	7.50	15.00
❏ SR 52123 [S]	Sarah Slightly Classical	1966	5.00	10.00	20.00
ROYALE					
❏ 18129 [10]	Sarah Vaughan and Orchestra	195?	7.50	15.00	30.00
❏ 18149 [10]	Sarah Vaughan and Orchestra	195?	7.50	15.00	30.00
—Includes recordings made on the Musicraft label in the 1940s					
SCEPTER					
❏ CTN-18029	The Best of Sarah Vaughan	1972	3.00	6.00	12.00
SPIN-O-RAMA					
❏ 73 [M]	Sweet, Sultry and Swinging	196?	10.00	20.00	40.00
❏ S-73 [S]	Sweet, Sultry and Swinging	196?	12.50	25.00	50.00
❏ 114 [M]	The Divine Sarah Vaughan	196?	10.00	20.00	40.00
❏ S-114 [S]	The Divine Sarah Vaughan	196?	12.50	25.00	50.00
TIME-LIFE					
❏ SLGD-09 [(2)]	Legendary Singers: Sarah Vaughan	1985	3.75	7.50	15.00
TRIP					
❏ 5501	Sarah Vaughan	197?	2.50	5.00	10.00
❏ 5517	Sassy	197?	2.50	5.00	10.00

Number	Title (A Side/B Side)	Yr	VG	VG+	NM
❏ 5523	In the Land of Hi-Fi	197?	2.50	5.00	10.00
❏ 5551	Swingin' Easy	197?	2.50	5.00	10.00
WING					
❏ MGW-12123 [M]	All Time Favorites	1963	3.00	6.00	12.00
❏ MGW-12280 [M]	The Magic of Sarah Vaughan	1964	3.00	6.00	12.00
❏ SRW-16123 [S]	All Time Favorites	1963	3.75	7.50	15.00
❏ SRW-16280 [S]	The Magic of Sarah Vaughan	1964	3.75	7.50	15.00

VAUGHAN, SARAH, AND COUNT BASIE

Albums

PABLO

Number	Title (A Side/B Side)	Yr	VG	VG+	NM
❏ 2312130	Send In the Clowns	1980	2.50	5.00	10.00
ROULETTE					
❏ SR 42018	Count Basie and Sarah Vaughan	1968	3.75	7.50	15.00
❏ R 52061 [M]	Count Basie and Sarah Vaughan	1960	6.25	12.50	25.00
❏ SR 52061 [S]	Count Basie and Sarah Vaughan	1960	7.50	15.00	30.00

VAUGHAN, SARAH, AND BILLY ECKSTINE Also see each artist's individual listings.

45s

MERCURY

Number	Title (A Side/B Side)	Yr	VG	VG+	NM
❏ 71122	Passing Strangers/The Door Is Open	1957	3.00	6.00	12.00
❏ 71393	Alexander's Ragtime Band/No Limit	1959	3.00	6.00	12.00

7-Inch Extended Plays

MGM

Number	Title (A Side/B Side)	Yr	VG	VG+	NM
❏ X1002	Dedicated to You/You're All I Need//Ev'ry Day/I Love You	195?	5.00	10.00	20.00
❏ X1002 [PS]	Dedicated to You	195?	5.00	10.00	20.00

Albums

EMARCY

Number	Title (A Side/B Side)	Yr	VG	VG+	NM
❏ 822526-1	The Irving Berlin Songbook	1984	2.50	5.00	10.00
LION					
❏ L-70088 [M]	Billy and Sarah	195?	6.25	12.50	25.00
MERCURY					
❏ MG-20316 [M]	Sarah Vaughan and Billy Eckstine Sing the Best of Irving Berlin	1959	7.50	15.00	30.00
❏ SR-60002 [S]	Sarah Vaughan and Billy Eckstine Sing the Best of Irving Berlin	1959	10.00	20.00	40.00

VAUGHAN, SARAH; DINAH WASHINGTON; JOE WILLIAMS

Albums

ROULETTE

Number	Title (A Side/B Side)	Yr	VG	VG+	NM
❏ R 52108 [M]	We Three	1964	3.75	7.50	15.00
❏ SR 52108 [S]	We Three	1964	5.00	10.00	20.00

VAUGHN, BILLY

45s

DOT

Number	Title (A Side/B Side)	Yr	VG	VG+	NM
❏ 225 [S]	Look for a Star/He'll Have to Go	1960	3.00	6.00	12.00
❏ 15247	Melody of Love/Joy Ride	1954	3.00	6.00	12.00
❏ 15347	Silver Moon/Baby o' Mine	1955	3.00	6.00	12.00
❏ 15374	The Waltz You Saved for Me/Billy Vaughn's Boogie	1955	3.00	6.00	12.00
❏ 15409	The Shifting, Whispering Sands (Part 1)/The Shifting, Whispering Sands (Part 2)	1955	3.00	6.00	12.00
❏ 15430	I'd Give a Million Tomorrows/Calico Cathy	1955	3.00	6.00	12.00
❏ 15444	A Theme from (The Three Penny Opera) "Moritat"/Little Boy Blue	1956	2.50	5.00	10.00
❏ 15454	Till I Waltz Again with You/Sleep	1956	2.50	5.00	10.00
❏ 15466	Angel, Angel/Autumn Concerto	1956	2.50	5.00	10.00
❏ 15479	Sweetheart Polka/The Left Bank	1956	2.50	5.00	10.00
❏ 15491	When the White Lilacs Bloom Again/Spanish Diary	1956	2.50	5.00	10.00
❏ 15506	Petticoats of Portugal/La La Colette	1956	2.50	5.00	10.00
❏ 15514	Sweet Leilani/Cradle Love Call	1956	2.50	5.00	10.00
❏ 15530	Sugar Blues/Pennsylvania Waltz	1957	2.50	5.00	10.00
❏ 15546	The Ship That Never Sailed/Song of the Nairobi Trio	1957	2.50	5.00	10.00
❏ 15575	Tell My Love/Ve'Borriquito	1957	2.50	5.00	10.00
❏ 15598	Johnny Tremain/Naughty Annette	1957	3.00	6.00	12.00
❏ 15661	Sail Along Silvery Moon/Raunchy	1957	2.00	4.00	8.00
❏ 15710	Tumbling Tumbleweeds/Trying	1958	2.00	4.00	8.00
❏ 15771	Singing Hills/Chimes of Arcady	1958	2.00	4.00	8.00
❏ 15795	La Paloma/Here Is My Love	1958	2.00	4.00	8.00
❏ 15836	Cimarron (Roll On)/You're My Baby Doll	1958	2.00	4.00	8.00
❏ 15836 [PS]	Cimarron (Roll On)/You're My Baby Doll	1958	3.00	6.00	12.00
❏ 15879	Blue Hawaii/Tico Tico	1958	2.00	4.00	8.00
❏ 15900	Hawaiian War Chant/Trade Winds	1959	2.00	4.00	8.00
❏ 15900 [PS]	Hawaiian War Chant/Trade Winds	1959	3.00	6.00	12.00
❏ 15936	Your Cheatin' Heart/Lights Out	1959	2.00	4.00	8.00
❏ 15976	Wabash Blues/Carnival in Paris	1959	2.00	4.00	8.00
❏ 15993	It's No Sin/After Hours	1959	2.00	4.00	8.00
❏ 16021	You're the Only Star (In My Blue Heaven)/Chop Stick	1959	2.00	4.00	8.00
❏ 16026	Melody of Love/Sail Along Silvery Moon	1960	—	3.00	6.00
—Reissue					
❏ 16030	The Shifting, Whispering Sands (Part 1)/The Shifting, Whispering Sands (Part 2)	1960	—	3.00	6.00
—Reissue					
❏ 16064	Skaters' Waltz/Beg Your Pardon	1960	2.00	4.00	8.00
❏ 16064 [PS]	Skaters' Waltz/Beg Your Pardon	1960	2.50	5.00	10.00
❏ 16106	Look for a Star/He'll Have to Go	1960	2.00	4.00	8.00
❏ 16121	Theme from The Apartment/(B-side unknown)	1960	2.00	4.00	8.00
❏ 16133	The Sundowners/Old Cape Cod	1960	2.00	4.00	8.00
❏ 16174	Wheels/Orange Blossom Special	1961	2.00	4.00	8.00
❏ 16220	Blue Tomorrow/Red Wing	1961	2.00	4.00	8.00
❏ 16245	Down Yonder/Born to Be with You	1961	2.00	4.00	8.00
❏ 16262	Berlin Melody/Come September	1961	2.00	4.00	8.00
❏ 16295	Everybody's Twisting Down in Mexico/Melody in the Night	1961	2.00	4.00	8.00
❏ 16329	Chapel by the Sea/One Love, One Heartache	1962	—	3.00	6.00
❏ 16359	Continental Melody/Born to Be with You	1962	—	3.00	6.00
❏ 16374	A Swingin' Safari/Indian Love Call	1962	2.00	4.00	8.00
❏ 16397	Blue Flame/Someone	1962	—	3.00	6.00
❏ 16417	Down Yonder/I'm Waitin'	1963	—	3.00	6.00
❏ 16436	Meditation (Meditacao)/Release Me	1963	—	3.00	6.00
❏ 16477	Happy Cowboy/Broken Date	1963	—	3.00	6.00
❏ 16484	Sukiyaki/Theme from A Summer Place	1963	—	3.00	6.00

Number	Title (A Side/B Side)	Yr	VG	VG+	NM
❏ 16522	Rag Mop/I'm Sorry	1963	—	3.00	6.00
❏ 16549	Cumberland County Feud/Chow Chow Amore	1963	—	3.00	6.00
❏ 16580	Boss/Blue Tango	1964	—	3.00	6.00
❏ 16604	One Rose/Lucky Duck	1964	—	3.00	6.00
❏ 16622	Guitar Song/Chianti Song	1964	—	3.00	6.00
❏ 16647	People/The World I Used to Know	1964	—	3.00	6.00
❏ 16664	Maybe/Pearly Shells	1964	—	3.00	6.00
❏ 16670	Song of Peace/Billy's Theme	1964	—	3.00	6.00
❏ 16686	There's a Star Spangled Banner Waving Somewhere/In the Ocean of Time	1965	—	3.00	6.00
❏ 16706	Mexican Pearls/Woodpecker	1965	—	3.00	6.00
❏ 16739	Making Other Plans/Our Dream of Love	1965	—	3.00	6.00
❏ 16762	Moon Over Naples/Tonight	1965	—	3.00	6.00
❏ 16774	Anniversary Song/Please	1965	—	3.00	6.00
❏ 16809	Michelle/Elaine	1965	—	3.00	6.00
❏ 16835	Mexican Shuffle/Organ Grinder's Swing	1966	—	2.50	5.00
❏ 16841	Things Go Better/James (Steady Does It)	1966	—	2.50	5.00
❏ 16883	Did You Ever Have to Make Up Your Mind/It's Over	1966	—	2.50	5.00
❏ 16900	Because They're Young/Buckaroo	1966	—	2.50	5.00
❏ 16924	Alfie/Lara's Theme	1966	—	2.50	5.00
❏ 16957	Tiny Bubbles/Too Many Hot Tacos	1966	—	2.50	5.00
❏ 16985	There Goes My Everything/Sweet Maria	1966	—	2.50	5.00
❏ 17000	That's Life/Pineapple Market	1967	—	2.50	5.00
❏ 17021	I Love You/Yellow Roses Mean Goodbye	1967	—	2.50	5.00
❏ 17054	Last Hearts of Kyoto/The Last Safari	1967	—	2.50	5.00
❏ 17074	Lolly/Moonlight Makes Memories	1968	—	2.50	5.00
❏ 17111	St. James Infirmary/Soulitude	1968	—	2.50	5.00
❏ 17214	You Win Again/No One Will Ever Know	1969	—	2.50	5.00
❏ 17215	A Mansion on the Hill/I've Got You on My Mind Again	1969		2.50	5.00
❏ 17229	The Windmills of Your Mind/The Way That I Live	1969	—	2.50	5.00
❏ 17295	True Grit/Odds and Ends	1969	—	2.50	5.00
❏ 17314	Color It Cool/On Days Like This	1969	—	2.50	5.00
❏ 17337	Coco/Always Mademoiselle	1970	—	2.00	4.00
❏ 17346	Come Saturday Morning/True Grit	1970	—	2.00	4.00
PARAMOUNT					
❏ 0036	Boulevard Saint/Michelle	1970	—	2.00	4.00
❏ 0073	Look What They've Done to My Song, Ma/Rooftops of Tokyo	1971	—	2.00	4.00
❏ 0156	Butterfly/To the End of This Day	1972	—	2.00	4.00

7-Inch Extended Plays

DOT

Number	Title (A Side/B Side)	Yr	VG	VG+	NM
❏ DEP 1066	La Paloma/Mexicali Rose//Estrellita/La Golondrina	195?	2.50	5.00	10.00
❏ DEP 1066 [PS]	Four by Billy Vaughn	195?	2.50	5.00	10.00
❏ DEP-1071	Canadian Sunset/Moonglow and Picnic//Fascination/Around the World	195?	2.50	5.00	10.00
❏ DEP-1071 [PS]	Billy Vaughn Plays Million Sellers	195?	2.50	5.00	10.00
❏ DEP-1072	Sail Along Silv'ry Moon/Jealous//Raunchy/I'm Getting Sentimental Over You	1958	2.50	5.00	10.00
❏ DEP-1072 [PS]	Sail Along Silv'ry Moon	1958	2.50	5.00	10.00
❏ DEP 1078	Hawaiian Paradise/Cocoanut Grove//Beyond the Reef/Hawaiian Wedding Song	195?	2.00	4.00	8.00
❏ DEP 1078 [PS]	Blue Hawaii	195?	2.00	4.00	8.00
❏ DEP 1095	Theme from A Summer Place/Tracy's Theme//Que Sera, Sera/Tammy	196?	2.00	4.00	8.00
❏ DEP 1095 [PS]	Theme from A Summer Place and Other Great Themes	196?	2.00	4.00	8.00

Albums

ABC

Number	Title (A Side/B Side)	Yr	VG	VG+	NM
❏ 4005	16 Great Performances	1974	2.50	5.00	10.00
DOT					
❏ DLP 3001 [M]	Sweet Music and Memories	1955	6.25	12.50	25.00
—Maroon label					
❏ DLP 3001 [M]	Sweet Music and Memories	1957	3.75	7.50	15.00
—Black label					
❏ DLP 3016 [M]	The Golden Instrumentals	1956	6.25	12.50	25.00
—Maroon label					
❏ DLP 3016 [M]	The Golden Instrumentals	1957	3.75	7.50	15.00
—Black label					
❏ DLP 3045 [M]	Instrumental Souvenirs	1957	3.75	7.50	15.00
❏ DLP 3064 [M]	Melodies in Gold	1957	3.75	7.50	15.00
❏ DLP 3086 [M]	Music for the Golden Hours	1958	3.75	7.50	15.00
❏ DLP 3100 [M]	Sail Along Silv'ry Moon	1958	3.75	7.50	15.00
❏ DLP 3119 [M]	Billy Vaughn Plays the Million Sellers	1958	3.75	7.50	15.00
❏ DLP 3140 [M]	La Paloma	1959	3.75	7.50	15.00
❏ DLP 3148 [M]	Christmas Carols	1958	3.75	7.50	15.00
❏ DLP 3156 [M]	Billy Vaughn Plays	1959	3.75	7.50	15.00
❏ DLP 3165 [M]	Blue Hawaii	1959	3.75	7.50	15.00
❏ DLP 3201 [M]	Golden Hits	1959	3.75	7.50	15.00
❏ DLP 3205 [M]	Golden Saxophones	1959	3.75	7.50	15.00
❏ DLP 3260 [M]	Billy Vaughn Plays Stephen Foster	1960	3.75	7.50	15.00
❏ DLP 3275 [M]	Linger Awhile	1960	3.75	7.50	15.00
❏ DLP 3276 [M]	Theme from A Summer Place	1960	3.75	7.50	15.00
❏ DLP 3280 [M]	Golden Waltzes	1961	3.75	7.50	15.00
❏ DLP 3288 [M]	Great Golden Hits	1960	3.75	7.50	15.00
❏ DLP 3322 [M]	Look for a Star	1960	3.75	7.50	15.00
❏ DLP 3349 [M]	Theme from The Sundowners	1960	3.75	7.50	15.00
❏ DLP 3366 [M]	Orange Blossom Special and Wheels	1961	3.75	7.50	15.00
❏ DLP 3396 [M]	Berlin Melody	1961	3.75	7.50	15.00
❏ DLP 3409 [M]	Greatest String Band Hits	1962	3.75	7.50	15.00
❏ DLP 3424 [M]	Chapel by the Sea	1962	3.75	7.50	15.00
❏ DLP 3442 [M]	The Shifting, Whispering Sands	1962	3.75	7.50	15.00
❏ DLP 3458 [M]	A Swingin' Safari	1962	3.75	7.50	15.00
❏ DLP 3497 [M]	1962's Greatest Hits	1963	3.00	6.00	12.00
❏ DLP 3523 [M]	Sukiyaki and 11 Hawaiian Hits	1963	3.00	6.00	12.00
❏ DLP 3540 [M]	Number One Hits, Vol. #1	1963	3.00	6.00	12.00
❏ DLP 3558 [M]	Greatest Boogie Woogie Hits	1963	3.00	6.00	12.00
❏ DLP 3559 [M]	Blue Velvet & 1963's Great Hits	1964	3.00	6.00	12.00
❏ DLP 3578 [M]	Forever	1964	3.00	6.00	12.00
❏ DLP 3593 [M]	Another Hit Album!	1964	3.00	6.00	12.00
❏ DLP 3605 [M]	Pearly Shells	1965	3.00	6.00	12.00
❏ DLP 3625 [M]	12 Golden Hits from Latin America	1965	3.00	6.00	12.00
❏ DLP 3628 [M]	Mexican Pearls	1965	3.00	6.00	12.00
❏ DLP 3654 [M]	Moon Over Naples	1965	3.00	6.00	12.00
❏ DLP 3679 [M]	Michelle	1966	3.00	6.00	12.00

Number	Title (A Side/B Side)	Yr	VG	VG+	NM
❏ DLP 3698 [M]	Great Country Hits	1966	3.00	6.00	12.00
❏ DLP 3751 [M]	Alfie	1966	3.00	6.00	12.00
❏ DLP 3782 [M]	Sweet Maria	1967	3.00	6.00	12.00
❏ DLP 3788 [M]	That's Life & Pineapple Market	1967	3.00	6.00	12.00
❏ DLP 3796 [M]	Josephine	1967	3.00	6.00	12.00
❏ DLP 3800 [M]	Billy Vaughn Presents Friends from Rio Playing "Something Stupid"	1967	3.00	6.00	12.00
❏ DLP 3811 [M]	Golden Hits/The Best of Billy Vaughn	1967	3.00	6.00	12.00
❏ DLP 3813 [M]	I Love You	1967	3.00	6.00	12.00
❏ DLP 3828 [M]	Ode to Billy Joe	1967	3.00	6.00	12.00
❏ DLP 5857	Quietly Wild	1968	2.50	5.00	10.00
❏ DLP 25001 [R]	Sweet Music and Memories	196?	2.50	5.00	10.00
❏ DLP 25016 [R]	The Golden Instrumentals	196?	2.50	5.00	10.00
❏ DLP 25064 [R]	Melodies in Gold	196?	2.50	5.00	10.00
❏ DLP 25086 [R]	Music for the Golden Hours	196?	2.50	5.00	10.00
❏ DLP 25100 [S]	Sail Along Silv'ry Moon	1959	5.00	10.00	20.00
❏ DLP 25119 [S]	Billy Vaughn Plays the Million Sellers	1959	5.00	10.00	20.00
❏ DLP 25140 [S]	La Paloma	1959	5.00	10.00	20.00
❏ DLP 25156 [S]	Billy Vaughn Plays	1959	5.00	10.00	20.00
❏ DLP 25165 [S]	Blue Hawaii	1959	5.00	10.00	20.00
❏ DLP 25201 [S]	Golden Hits	1959	5.00	10.00	20.00
❏ DLP 25205 [S]	Golden Saxophones	1959	5.00	10.00	20.00
❏ DLP 25260 [S]	Billy Vaughn Plays Stephen Foster	1960	5.00	10.00	20.00
❏ DLP 25275 [S]	Linger Awhile	1960	5.00	10.00	20.00
❏ DLP 25276 [S]	Theme from A Summer Place	1960	5.00	10.00	20.00
❏ DLP 25280 [S]	Golden Waltzes	1961	5.00	10.00	20.00
❏ DLP 25288 [S]	Great Golden Hits	1960	5.00	10.00	20.00
❏ DLP 25322 [S]	Look for a Star	1960	5.00	10.00	20.00
❏ DLP 25349 [S]	Theme from The Sundowners	1960	5.00	10.00	20.00
❏ DLP 25366 [S]	Orange Blossom Special and Wheels	1961	5.00	10.00	20.00
❏ DLP 25396 [S]	Berlin Melody	1961	5.00	10.00	20.00
❏ DLP 25409 [S]	Greatest String Band Hits	1962	5.00	10.00	20.00
❏ DLP 25424 [S]	Chapel by the Sea	1962	5.00	10.00	20.00
❏ DLP 25442 [S]	The Shifting, Whispering Sands	1962	5.00	10.00	20.00
❏ DLP 25458 [S]	A Swingin' Safari	1962	5.00	10.00	20.00
❏ DLP 25497 [S]	1962's Greatest Hits	1963	3.75	7.50	15.00
❏ DLP 25523 [S]	Sukiyaki and 11 Hawaiian Hits	1963	3.75	7.50	15.00
❏ DLP 25540 [S]	Number One Hits, Vol. #1	1963	3.75	7.50	15.00
❏ DLP 25558 [S]	Greatest Boogie Woogie Hits	1963	3.75	7.50	15.00
❏ DLP 25559 [S]	Blue Velvet & 1963's Great Hits	1964	3.75	7.50	15.00
❏ DLP 25578 [S]	Forever	1964	3.75	7.50	15.00
❏ DLP 25593 [S]	Another Hit Album!	1964	3.75	7.50	15.00
❏ DLP 25605 [S]	Pearly Shells	1965	3.75	7.50	15.00
❏ DLP 25625 [S]	12 Golden Hits from Latin America	1965	3.75	7.50	15.00
❏ DLP 25628 [S]	Mexican Pearls	1965	3.75	7.50	15.00
❏ DLP 25654 [S]	Moon Over Naples	1965	3.75	7.50	15.00
❏ DLP 25679 [S]	Michelle	1966	3.75	7.50	15.00
❏ DLP 25698 [S]	Great Country Hits	1966	3.75	7.50	15.00
❏ DLP 25751 [S]	Alfie	1966	3.75	7.50	15.00
❏ DLP 25782 [S]	Sweet Maria	1967	2.50	5.00	10.00
❏ DLP 25788 [S]	That's Life & Pineapple Market	1967	2.50	5.00	10.00
❏ DLP 25796 [S]	Josephine	1967	2.50	5.00	10.00
❏ DLP 25800 [S]	Billy Vaughn Presents Friends from Rio Playing "Something Stupid"	1967	2.50	5.00	10.00
❏ DLP 25811 [S]	Golden Hits/The Best of Billy Vaughn	1967	2.50	5.00	10.00
❏ DLP 25813 [S]	I Love You	1967	2.50	5.00	10.00
❏ DLP 25828 [S]	Ode to Billy Joe	1967	2.50	5.00	10.00
❏ DLP 25837	Pretty Country	1968	2.50	5.00	10.00
❏ DLP 25841	As Requested	1968	2.50	5.00	10.00
❏ DLP 25882	A Current Set of Standards	1968	2.50	5.00	10.00
❏ DLP-25897	Alone with Today	1968	2.50	5.00	10.00
❏ DLP 25899	Have Yourself a Merry Merry Christmas	1968	3.00	6.00	12.00
❏ DLP 25911	Nashville Saxophones	1969	2.50	5.00	10.00
❏ DLP 25937	The Windmills of Your Mind	1969	2.50	5.00	10.00
❏ DLP 25969	True Grit	1969	2.50	5.00	10.00
❏ DLP 25975	Winter World of Love	1970	2.50	5.00	10.00
❏ DLP 25985	Everything Is Beautiful	1970	2.50	5.00	10.00
HAMILTON					
❏ HLP 113 [M]	Golden Gems	196?	3.00	6.00	12.00
❏ HLP 147 [M]	Strauss Waltz Concert	196?	3.00	6.00	12.00
❏ HLP 162 [M]	Songs I Wrote	196?	3.00	6.00	12.00
❏ HLP 12113 [S]	Golden Gems	196?	3.00	6.00	12.00
❏ HLP 12147 [S]	Strauss Waltz Concert	196?	3.00	6.00	12.00
❏ HLP 12162 [S]	Songs I Wrote	196?	3.00	6.00	12.00
MCA					
❏ 801	La Paloma	198?	2.00	4.00	8.00
—Budget-line reissue					
❏ 4164 [(2)]	The Best of Billy Vaughn	198?	3.00	6.00	12.00
❏ 27018	Blue Hawaii	198?	2.00	4.00	8.00
—Budget-line reissue					
PARAMOUNT					
❏ PAS-1031 [(2)]	Billy Vaughn Plays His Greatest Hits	1974	3.00	6.00	12.00
❏ PAS-1033	Electrified	1974	2.50	5.00	10.00
❏ PAS-5032	Theme from Love Story	1971	2.50	5.00	10.00
❏ PAS-5037	I Don't Know How to Love Him	1971	2.50	5.00	10.00
❏ PAS-6025	An Old Fashioned Love Song	1972	2.50	5.00	10.00
❏ PAS-6035	Soundstage!	1972	2.50	5.00	10.00
❏ PAS-6044	Country's Greatest Hits	1973	2.50	5.00	10.00
PICKWICK					
❏ SPC-3093	Embraceable You	197?	2.50	5.00	10.00
❏ SPC-3146	Up, Up and Away	197?	2.50	5.00	10.00
❏ SPC-3213	Moon River	197?	2.50	5.00	10.00
RANWOOD					
❏ 7025 [(2)]	Billy Vaughn and His Orchestra Play 22 Greatest Hits	1982	3.00	6.00	12.00

VAUGHN, DENNY See DENNY VAUGHAN.

VAUGHN, YVONNE Later recorded as DONNA FARGO.

45s

DOT

Number	Title (A Side/B Side)	Yr	VG	VG+	NM
❏ 16751	Lonely Little Girl/When You Gonna Tell Her About Me	1965	37.50	75.00	150.00

Number	Title (A Side/B Side)	Yr	VG	VG+	NM

VEE, BOBBY
45s
COGNITO

Number	Title (A Side/B Side)	Yr	VG	VG+	NM
❑ 010	Tremble On/				
	Always Be Each Other's Best Friend	1981	—	2.50	5.00
LIBERTY					
❑ 54510	Devil or Angel/Rubber Ball	196?	—	3.00	6.00
❑ 54511	More Than I Can Say/Stayin' In	196?	—	3.00	6.00
❑ 54523	Take Good Care of My Baby/Please Don't Ask				
	About Barbara	196?	—	3.00	6.00
❑ 54524	Run to Him/Sharing You	196?	—	3.00	6.00
❑ 54536	The Night Has a Thousand Eyes/Charms	196?	—	3.00	6.00
❑ 54559	Come Back When You Grow Up/Beautiful				
	People	196?	—	3.00	6.00
—Records in the 54500s are from a reissue series					
❑ 55208	Suzie Baby/Flyin' High	1959	6.25	12.50	25.00
❑ 55234	What Do You Want/My Love Loves Me	1959	5.00	10.00	20.00
❑ 55251	Laurie/One Last Kiss	1960	3.75	7.50	15.00
❑ 55270	Devil or Angel/Since I Met You Baby	1960	5.00	10.00	20.00
❑ 55270 [PS]	Devil or Angel/Since I Met You Baby	1960	7.50	15.00	30.00
❑ 55287	Rubber Ball/Everyday	1960	5.00	10.00	20.00
❑ 55287 [PS]	Rubber Ball/Everyday	1960	7.50	15.00	30.00
❑ 55296	More Than I Can Say/Stayin' In	1961	3.75	7.50	15.00
❑ 55296 [PS]	More Than I Can Say/Stayin' In	1961	7.50	15.00	30.00
❑ 55325	How Many Tears/Baby Face	1961	3.75	7.50	15.00
❑ 55325 [PS]	How Many Tears/Baby Face	1961	7.50	15.00	30.00
❑ 55354	Take Good Care of My Baby/Bashful Bob	1961	3.75	7.50	15.00
❑ 55388	Run to Him/Walkin' with My Angel	1961	5.00	10.00	20.00
❑ 55419	Please Don't Ask About Barbara/				
	I Can't Say Goodbye	1962	3.75	7.50	15.00
❑ 55419 [PS]	Please Don't Ask About Barbara/				
	I Can't Say Goodbye	1962	6.25	12.50	25.00
❑ 55451	Sharing You/In My Baby's Eyes	1962	3.75	7.50	15.00
❑ 55479	Punish Her/Someday				
	(When I'm Gone from You)	1962	5.00	10.00	20.00
❑ 55479 [PS]	Punish Her/Someday				
	(When I'm Gone from You)	1962	7.50	15.00	30.00
—With the Crickets					
❑ 55517	A Not-So-Merry Christmas/Christmas Vacation	1962	7.50	15.00	30.00
—This record's existence has been questioned					
❑ 55521	The Night Has a Thousand Eyes/Anonymous				
	Phone Call	1962	3.00	6.00	12.00
❑ 55530	Charms/Bobby Tomorrow	1963	3.00	6.00	12.00
❑ 55530 [PS]	Charms/Bobby Tomorrow	1963	5.00	10.00	20.00
❑ 55581	Be True to Yourself/A Letter from Betty	1963	2.50	5.00	10.00
❑ 55581 [PS]	Be True to Yourself/A Letter from Betty	1963	5.00	10.00	20.00
❑ 55636	Yesterday and You (Armen's Theme)/				
	Never Love a Robin	1963	2.50	5.00	10.00
❑ 55654	Stranger in Your Arms/1963	1963	2.50	5.00	10.00
❑ 55654 [PS]	Stranger in Your Arms/1963	1963	5.00	10.00	20.00
❑ 55670	I'll Make You Mine/She's Sorry	1964	2.50	5.00	10.00
❑ 55700	Hickory, Dick and Doc/				
	I Wish You Were Mine Again	1964	2.50	5.00	10.00
❑ 55726	Where Is She/How to Make a Farewell	1964	2.50	5.00	10.00
❑ 55751	(There'll Come a Day When) Ev'ry Little Bit				
	Hurts/Pretend You Don't See Her	1964	2.50	5.00	10.00
❑ 55761	Cross My Heart/This Is the End	1965	2.00	4.00	8.00
❑ 55790	Keep On Trying/You Won't Forget Me	1965	2.00	4.00	8.00
❑ 55828	Run Like the Devil/Take a Look Around Us	1965	2.00	4.00	8.00
❑ 55843	The Story of My Life/High Coin	1965	2.00	4.00	8.00
❑ 55854	A Girl I Used to Know/Gone	1965	2.00	4.00	8.00
❑ 55877	Butterfly/Save a Love	1966	—	—	—
—Canceled?					
❑ 55877	Look at Me Girl/Save a Love	1966	2.00	4.00	8.00
❑ 55921	Before You Go/Here Today	1966	2.00	4.00	8.00
❑ 55964	Come Back When You Grow Up/Swahili				
	Serenade	1967	2.00	4.00	8.00
❑ 55964	Come Back When You Grow Up/				
	That's All There Is to That	1967	2.00	4.00	8.00
❑ 56009	Beautiful People/I May Be Gone	1967	2.00	4.00	8.00
❑ 56014	Maybe Just Today/You're a Big Girl Now	1968	—	3.00	6.00
❑ 56014 [PS]	Maybe Just Today/You're a Big Girl Now	1968	3.00	6.00	12.00
❑ 56033	Medley: My Girl-Hey Girl/Just Keep It Up	1968	—	3.00	6.00
❑ 56057	Do What You Gotta Do/Thank You	1968	—	3.00	6.00
❑ 56080	I'm Into Lookin' for Someone to Love Me/				
	Thank You	1968	—	3.00	6.00
❑ 56096	Jenny Come to Me/Santa Cruz	1969	—	3.00	6.00
❑ 56124	Let's Call It a Day Girl/				
	I'm Gonna Make It Up to You	1969	—	3.00	6.00
❑ 56149	Electric Trains and You/In and Out of Love	1969	—	3.00	6.00
❑ 56178	The Woman in My Life/No Obligations	1970	—	3.00	6.00
❑ 56208	Sweet Sweetheart/Rock and Roll Music and You	1970	—	3.00	6.00
SHADYBROOK					
❑ 45013	Saying Goodbye/(I'm) Lovin' You	1975	—	2.50	5.00
❑ 45026	You're Never Gonna Find Someone Like Me				
	(Long Version)/You're Never Gonna Find				
	Someone Like Me (Short Version)	1976	—	2.50	5.00
❑ 45030	It's Good to Be Here/If I Needed You	1976	—	2.50	5.00
SOMA					
❑ 1110	Suzie Baby/Flyin' High	1959	15.00	30.00	60.00
UNITED ARTISTS					
❑ 0020	Devil or Angel/Stayin' In	1973	—	2.00	4.00
❑ 0021	Rubber Ball/Punish Her	1973	—	2.00	4.00
❑ 0022	Take Good Care of My Baby/				
	Please Don't Ask About Barbara	1973	—	2.00	4.00
❑ 0023	Run to Him/Sharing You	1973	—	2.00	4.00
❑ 0024	The Night Has a Thousand Eyes/Charms	1973	—	2.00	4.00
❑ 0025	Come Back When You Grow Up/Beautiful				
	People	1973	—	2.00	4.00
—0020 through 0025 are "Silver Spotlight Series" reissues					
❑ XW199	Take Good Care of My Baby/Every Opportunity	1973	—	2.50	5.00
—As "Robert Thomas Velline"					
❑ XW1142	Well All Right/				
	Something Has Come Between Us	1978	—	2.50	5.00
❑ 50755	Signs/Something to Say	1971	—	2.50	5.00
❑ 50875	Sweet Sweetheart/Electric Trains and You	1972	—	2.50	5.00

7-Inch Extended Plays
LIBERTY

Number	Title (A Side/B Side)	Yr	VG	VG+	NM
❑ LSX-1006	Devil or Angel/One Last Kiss//				
	What Do You Want/My Love Loves Me	1960	12.50	25.00	50.00
❑ LSX-1006 [PS]	Devil or Angel	1960	12.50	25.00	50.00
❑ LSX-1010	(contents unknown)	1960	12.50	25.00	50.00
❑ LSX-1010 [PS]	Bobby Vee's Hits	1960	12.50	25.00	50.00
❑ LSX-1013	*Run to Him/Take Good Care of My Baby/				
	Walkin' with My Angel/How Many Tears	1961	12.50	25.00	50.00
❑ LSX-1013 [PS]	Bobby Vee	1961	12.50	25.00	50.00

Albums
LIBERTY

Number	Title (A Side/B Side)	Yr	VG	VG+	NM
❑ LRP-3165 [M]	Bobby Vee Sings Your Favorites	1960	12.50	25.00	50.00
❑ LRP-3181 [M]	Bobby Vee	1961	10.00	20.00	40.00
❑ LRP-3186 [M]	Bobby Vee With Strings and Things	1961	10.00	20.00	40.00
❑ LRP-3205 [M]	Bobby Vee Sings Hits of the Rockin' 50's	1961	10.00	20.00	40.00
❑ LRP-3211 [M]	Take Good Care of My Baby	1962	7.50	15.00	30.00
❑ LRP-3228 [M]	Bobby Vee Meets the Crickets	1962	10.00	20.00	40.00
❑ LRP-3232 [M]	A Bobby Vee Recording Session	1962	7.50	15.00	30.00
❑ LRP-3245 [M]	Bobby Vee's Golden Greats	1962	7.50	15.00	30.00
❑ LRP-3267 [M]	Merry Christmas from Bobby Vee	1962	7.50	15.00	30.00
❑ LRP-3285 [M]	The Night Has a Thousand Eyes	1963	7.50	15.00	30.00
❑ LRP-3289 [M]	Bobby Vee Meets the Ventures	1963	10.00	20.00	40.00
❑ LRP-3336 [M]	I Remember Buddy Holly	1963	10.00	20.00	40.00
❑ LRP-3352 [M]	Bobby Vee Sings the New Sound from England!	1964	6.25	12.50	25.00
❑ LRP-3385 [M]	30 Big Hits From the 60's	1964	6.25	12.50	25.00
❑ LRP-3393 [M]	Bobby Vee Live on Tour	1965	6.25	12.50	25.00
❑ LRP-3448 [M]	30 Big Hits From the 60's, Volume 2	1966	6.25	12.50	25.00
❑ LRP-3464 [M]	Bobby Vee's Golden Greats, Volume 2	1966	5.00	10.00	20.00
❑ LRP-3480 [M]	Look at Me Girl	1966	5.00	10.00	20.00
❑ LRP-3534 [M]	Come Back When You Grow Up	1967	5.00	10.00	20.00
❑ LST-3554 [M]	Just Today	1968	10.00	20.00	40.00
—Cover is stereo with "Audition Mono Not for Sale" sticker, but the label is regular stock mono					
❑ LST-7165 [S]	Bobby Vee Sings Your Favorites	1960	20.00	40.00	80.00
❑ LST-7181 [S]	Bobby Vee	1961	12.50	25.00	50.00
❑ LST-7186 [S]	Bobby Vee With Strings and Things	1961	12.50	25.00	50.00
❑ LST-7205 [S]	Bobby Vee Sings Hits of the Rockin' 50's	1961	12.50	25.00	50.00
❑ LST-7211 [S]	Take Good Care of My Baby	1962	10.00	20.00	40.00
❑ LST-7228 [S]	Bobby Vee Meets the Crickets	1962	12.50	25.00	50.00
❑ LST-7232 [S]	A Bobby Vee Recording Session	1962	10.00	20.00	40.00
❑ LST-7245 [S]	Bobby Vee's Golden Greats	1962	10.00	20.00	40.00
❑ LST-7267 [S]	Merry Christmas from Bobby Vee	1962	10.00	20.00	40.00
❑ LST-7285 [S]	The Night Has a Thousand Eyes	1963	10.00	20.00	40.00
❑ LST-7289 [S]	Bobby Vee Meets the Ventures	1963	12.50	25.00	50.00
❑ LST-7336 [S]	I Remember Buddy Holly	1963	12.50	25.00	50.00
❑ LST-7352 [S]	Bobby Vee Sings the New Sound from England!	1964	7.50	15.00	30.00
❑ LST-7385 [S]	30 Big Hits From the 60's	1964	7.50	15.00	30.00
❑ LST-7393 [S]	Bobby Vee Live on Tour	1965	7.50	15.00	30.00
❑ LST-7448 [S]	30 Big Hits From the 60's, Volume 2	1966	7.50	15.00	30.00
❑ LST-7464 [S]	Bobby Vee's Golden Greats, Volume 2	1966	6.25	12.50	25.00
❑ LST-7480 [S]	Look at Me Girl	1966	6.25	12.50	25.00
❑ LST-7534 [S]	Come Back When You Grow Up	1967	6.25	12.50	25.00
❑ LST-7554 [S]	Just Today	1968	6.25	12.50	25.00
❑ LST-7592	Do What You Gotta Do	1968	7.50	15.00	30.00
❑ LST-7612	Gates, Grills and Railings	1969	7.50	15.00	30.00
❑ LN-10223	I Remember Buddy Holly	198?	2.00	4.00	8.00
❑ LM-51008	Bobby Vee's Golden Greats	198?	2.00	4.00	8.00
SUNSET					
❑ SUM-1111 [M]	Bobby Vee	1966	2.50	5.00	10.00
❑ SUM-1162 [M]	A Forever Kind of Love	1967	2.50	5.00	10.00
❑ SUM-1186 [M]	The Christmas Album	1967	3.00	6.00	12.00
—Reissue of Liberty album with two fewer tracks					
❑ SUS-5111 [S]	Bobby Vee	1966	3.00	6.00	12.00
❑ SUS-5162 [S]	A Forever Kind of Love	1967	3.00	6.00	12.00
❑ SUS-5186 [S]	The Christmas Album	1967	3.00	6.00	12.00
UNITED ARTISTS					
❑ UA-LA025-G2 [(2)]	Legendary Masters Series	1973	75.00	150.00	300.00
—Withdrawn before release, but a few copies survived					
❑ UA-LA085-G	Robert Thomas Velline	1973	5.00	10.00	20.00
❑ UA-LA332-E	The Very Best of Bobby Vee	1975	3.00	6.00	12.00
❑ LT-1008	Bobby Vee's Golden Greats	1980	2.50	5.00	10.00
❑ UAS-5656	Nothin' Like a Sunny Day	1972	3.00	6.00	12.00

VEERS, RUSS
45s
TREND

Number	Title (A Side/B Side)	Yr	VG	VG+	NM
❑ 30010	Warm As Toast/The Answer	1958	125.00	250.00	500.00

VEGAS, PAT AND LOLLY Also see REDBONE.
45s
APOGEE

Number	Title (A Side/B Side)	Yr	VG	VG+	NM
❑ 101	Don't You Remember/The Robot Walk	1964	3.75	7.50	15.00
MERCURY					
❑ 72509	Walk On (Right Out of My Life)/Let's Get It On	1965	3.00	6.00	12.00
REPRISE					
❑ 20199	Boom Boom/Two Figures				
	(On the Wedding Cake)	1963	5.00	10.00	20.00

Albums
MERCURY

Number	Title (A Side/B Side)	Yr	VG	VG+	NM
❑ MG-21059 [M]	At the Haunted House	1966	7.50	15.00	30.00
❑ SR-61059 [S]	At the Haunted House	1966	10.00	20.00	40.00

VEJTABLES, THE
45s
AUTUMN

Number	Title (A Side/B Side)	Yr	VG	VG+	NM
❑ 15	I Still Love You/Anything	1965	3.00	6.00	12.00
❑ 23	The Last Thing on My Mind/Mansion of Texas	1965	3.00	6.00	12.00
UPTOWN					
❑ 741	Feel the Music/Shadows	1967	2.50	5.00	10.00

VEL-TONES, THE More than one group.
45s
COY

Number	Title (A Side/B Side)	Yr	VG	VG+	NM
❑ 101	Cal's Tune/Playboy	1959	1000.	1500.	2000.
GOLDWAX					
❑ 301	Darling/I Do	1966	3.75	7.50	15.00

Number	Title (A Side/B Side)	Yr	VG	VG+	NM
JIN					
❑ 107	Lover Blues/Take a Ride	1959	10.00	20.00	40.00
❑ 115	Jailbird/I'm Yours Now	1959	10.00	20.00	40.00
KAPP					
❑ 268	Cal's Tune/Playboy	1959	25.00	50.00	100.00
LOST-NITE					
❑ 103	Now/I Need You So	1961	25.00	50.00	100.00
MERCURY					
❑ 71526	Fool in Love/Someday	1959	7.50	15.00	30.00
SATELLITE					
❑ 100	Fool in Love/Someday	1959	25.00	50.00	100.00
VEL					
❑ 9178	Broken Heart/Please Say You'll Be True	1960	375.00	750.00	1500.
WEDGE					
❑ 1013	My Dear/I Want to Know	1964	50.00	100.00	200.00
ZARA					
❑ 901	Now/I Need You So	1960	20.00	40.00	80.00

VELAIRES, THE
45s

Number	Title (A Side/B Side)	Yr	VG	VG+	NM
JAMIE					
❑ 1198	Roll Over Beethoven/Brazil	1961	5.00	10.00	20.00
❑ 1203	Sticks and Stones/Dream	1961	3.75	7.50	15.00
❑ 1211	It's Almost Tomorrow/Ubangi Stomp	1962	3.75	7.50	15.00
❑ 1223	Memory Tree/Don't Wake Me Up	1962	3.75	7.50	15.00
PALMS					
❑ 726	Roll Over Beethoven/Brazil	1961	12.50	25.00	50.00
—As "The Flairs"					

VELEZ, MARTHA
45s

Number	Title (A Side/B Side)	Yr	VG	VG+	NM
MCA					
❑ 41244	What Becomes of the Brokenhearted/Wild Night in Paradise	1980	—	2.00	4.00
POLYDOR					
❑ 14158	Magic in His Hands/Black Rose	1973	—	3.00	6.00
SIRE					
❑ 722	Mockingbird/Aggravation	1975	—	2.50	5.00
—With Pete Wingfield					
❑ 727	Disco Night/Come On In	1976	—	2.50	5.00
❑ 735	Money Man/There You Are	1976	—	2.50	5.00
❑ 1010	When You Were Beautiful/Up to You	1977	—	2.50	5.00
❑ 4111	Tell Mama/Swamp Man	1969	2.50	5.00	10.00
Albums					
POLYDOR					
❑ PD 5034	Hypnotized	1972	3.75	7.50	15.00
SIRE					
❑ SR 6040	American Heartbeat	1977	2.50	5.00	10.00
❑ SES-7409	Matinee Weepers	1973	3.75	7.50	15.00
❑ SASD-7515	Escape from Babylon	1976	2.50	5.00	10.00
—Produced by Bob Marley					
❑ SES-97008	Fiends and Angels	1969	7.50	15.00	30.00

VELLS, THE Later recorded as MARTHA AND THE VANDELLAS.
45s

Number	Title (A Side/B Side)	Yr	VG	VG+	NM
MEL-O-DY					
❑ 103	There He Is At My Door/You'll Never Cherish a Love So True	1962	25.00	50.00	100.00

VELONS, THE
45s

Number	Title (A Side/B Side)	Yr	VG	VG+	NM
BJM					
❑ 6568	Summer Love/Why Don't You Write	1965	5.00	10.00	20.00
❑ 6569	That's What Love Can Do/That's All Right	1965	5.00	10.00	20.00
BLAST					
❑ 216	Shelly/From the Chapel	1964	25.00	50.00	100.00

VELOURS, THE
45s

Number	Title (A Side/B Side)	Yr	VG	VG+	NM
CLIFTON					
❑ 1987	Old Fashion Christmas/I Wish You Love	19??	—	3.00	6.00
CUB					
❑ 9014	Crazy Love/I'll Never Smile Again	1958	6.25	12.50	25.00
❑ 9029	Blue Velvet/Tired of Your Rock and Rollin'	1959	6.25	12.50	25.00
END					
❑ 1090	Lover Come Back/The Lonely One	1961	5.00	10.00	20.00
GOLDISC					
❑ 3012	Daddy Warbucks/Sweet Sixteen	1960	6.25	12.50	25.00
GONE					
❑ 5092	Can I Come Over Tonight/Where There's a Will (There's a Way)	1960	5.00	10.00	20.00
LOST-NITE					
❑ 391	My Love Come Back/Honey Drop	197?	—	2.50	5.00
—Reissue					
❑ 394	Can I Come Over Tonight/Where There's a Will (There's a Way)	197?	—	2.50	5.00
—Reissue					
❑ 400	This Could be the Night/Hands Across the Table	197?	—	2.50	5.00
—Reissue					
❑ 402	What You Do to Me/Romeo	197?	—	2.50	5.00
—Reissue					
MGM					
❑ 13780	Don't Pity Me/I'm Gonna Change	1967	7.50	15.00	30.00
ONYX					
❑ 501	My Love Come Back/Honey Drop	1956	50.00	100.00	200.00
❑ 508	What You Do to Me/Romeo	1957	200.00	400.00	800.00
❑ 512	Can I Come Over Tonight/Where There's a Will (There's a Way)	1957	50.00	100.00	200.00
❑ 515	This Could be the Night/Hands Across the Table	1957	30.00	60.00	120.00
❑ 520	Remember/Can I Walk You Home	1958	15.00	30.00	60.00
ORBIT					
❑ 9001	Remember/Can I Walk You Home	1958	12.50	25.00	50.00
RONA					
❑ 010	Woman for Me/(B-side unknown)	1966	6.25	12.50	25.00
STUDO					
❑ 9902	I Promise/Little Sweetheart	1959	12.50	25.00	50.00

VELVATONES, THE
45s

Number	Title (A Side/B Side)	Yr	VG	VG+	NM
METEOR					
❑ 5042	Real Gone Baby/Feeling Kinda Lonely	1957	50.00	100.00	200.00
NU KAT					
❑ 110	Impossible/I'm Leaving Home	1959	12.50	25.00	50.00

VELVELETTES, THE
45s

Number	Title (A Side/B Side)	Yr	VG	VG+	NM
I.P.G.					
❑ 1002	There He Goes/That's the Reason Why	1963	25.00	50.00	100.00
SOUL					
❑ 35025	These Things Will Keep Me Loving You/Since You've Been Loving Me	1966	5.00	10.00	20.00
V.I.P.					
❑ 25007	Needle in a Haystack/Should I Tell Them	1964	6.25	12.50	25.00
❑ 25013	He Was Realy Sayin' Somethin'/Throw a Farewell Kiss	1965	6.25	12.50	25.00
❑ 25017	I'm the Exception to the Rule/Lonely, Lonely Girl Am I	1965	5.00	10.00	20.00
❑ 25021	A Bird in the Hand (Is Worth Two in the Bush)/(B-side unknown)	1965	200.00	400.00	800.00
❑ 25030	A Bird in the Hand (Is Worth Two in the Bush)/Since You've Been Loving Me	1965	5.00	10.00	20.00
❑ 25034	These Things Will Keep Me Loving You/Since You've Been Loving Me	1966	7.50	15.00	30.00

VELVET, JIMMY Two different singers, both of whom also recorded as "Jimmy Velvit"! If someone can help us tell who's who, we'd really appreciate it.
45s

Number	Title (A Side/B Side)	Yr	VG	VG+	NM
ABC-PARAMOUNT					
❑ 10488	We Belong Together/History of Love	1963	5.00	10.00	20.00
❑ 10528	To the Aisle/Lonely, Lonely Night	1964	5.00	10.00	20.00
BELL					
❑ 692	Let Me Keep Your Love/Woman in Bloom	1967	2.00	4.00	8.00
CAMEO					
❑ 464	Take Me Tonight/Young Hearts	1967	6.25	12.50	25.00
CORREC-TONE					
❑ 102	When I Needed You/Bouquet of Flowers	1962	25.00	50.00	100.00
—As "James Velvet"; the Supremes sing backup					
CUB					
❑ 9100	Sometimes at Night/Look at Me	1961	3.75	7.50	15.00
❑ 9111	When I Needed You/Bouquet of Flowers	1962	3.75	7.50	15.00
DIVISION					
❑ 102	Sometimes at Night/Look at Me	1961	5.00	10.00	20.00
PHILIPS					
❑ 40285	It's Almost Tomorrow/Blue Eyes (Don't Run Away)	1965	5.00	10.00	20.00
❑ 40314	I Won't Be Back This Year/Young Hearts	1965	5.00	10.00	20.00
ROYAL AMERICAN					
❑ 286	It's You/A Woman	1968	2.00	4.00	8.00
❑ 291	Blue Velvet/Missing You	1969	2.00	4.00	8.00
STARTIME					
❑ 103	Wisdom of a Fool/Want to Be Loved	196?	3.00	6.00	12.00
TEAR DROP					
❑ 3353	Don't Go Near a Woman/Hey Nashville	196?	3.00	6.00	12.00
❑ 3395	Oh Lonesome Me-Detroit City/Crazy Arms	196?	3.00	6.00	12.00
—As "James Velvit"					
TOLLIE					
❑ 9037	Teen Angel/Mission Bell	1964	3.75	7.50	15.00
UNITED ARTISTS					
❑ 50272	Good Good Lovin'/Heart Breakin' Misery	1968	5.00	10.00	20.00
VELVET					
❑ 201	We Belong Together/You're Mine	1963	25.00	50.00	100.00
—As "Jimmy Velvit"					
VELVET TONE					
❑ 102	It's Almost Tomorrow/Young Hearts	1965	7.50	15.00	30.00
Albums					
UNITED ARTISTS					
❑ UAS-6653	A Touch of Velvet	1968	6.25	12.50	25.00
VELVET TONE					
❑ 501	A Touch of Velvet	1968	15.00	30.00	60.00

VELVET KEYS, THE
45s

Number	Title (A Side/B Side)	Yr	VG	VG+	NM
KING					
❑ 5090	My Baby's Gone/Let's Stay After School	1957	20.00	40.00	80.00
❑ 5109	Don't Take My Picture, Take Me/The Truth About Youth	1958	20.00	40.00	80.00

VELVET NIGHT
45s

Number	Title (A Side/B Side)	Yr	VG	VG+	NM
METROMEDIA					
❑ 110	Velvet Night/I'm Sure He'll Come Most Anytime	1969	2.00	4.00	8.00
Albums					
METROMEDIA					
❑ MD-1028	Velvet Night	1970	7.50	15.00	30.00

VELVET SOUNDS, THE
45s

Number	Title (A Side/B Side)	Yr	VG	VG+	NM
COSMOPOLITAN					
❑ 100/101	Silver Star/The Devil and the Stocker	1953	150.00	300.00	600.00
❑ 105/106	Pretty Darling/Who'll Take My Place	1953	100.00	200.00	400.00
❑ 530/531	Hanging Up Christmas Stockings/Sing A Song Of Christmas Cheer	1953	125.00	250.00	500.00

VELVET UNDERGROUND, THE Includes releases with NICO. Also see JOHN CALE; LOU REED.
12-Inch Singles

Number	Title (A Side/B Side)	Yr	VG	VG+	NM
VERVE					
❑ PRO 349-1 [DJ]	Foggy Notion/I Can't Stand It	1985	3.75	7.50	15.00
45s					
COTILLION					
❑ 44107	Who Loves the Sun/Oh, Sweet Nothin'	1971	75.00	150.00	300.00
❑ 44107 [DJ]	Who Loves the Sun (mono/stereo)	1971	25.00	50.00	100.00

Number	Title (A Side/B Side)	Yr	VG	VG+	NM

MGM
| ❏ 14057 | What Goes On/Jesus | 1969 | 75.00 | 150.00 | 300.00 |

—Existence of a stock copy of this record has been questioned.

| ❏ 14057 [DJ] | What Goes On/Jesus | 1969 | 50.00 | 100.00 | 200.00 |

VERVE
❏ 10427	All Tomorrow's Parties/I'll Be Your Mirror	1966	150.00	300.00	600.00
❏ 10427 [DJ]	All Tomorrow's Parties/I'll Be Your Mirror	1966	75.00	150.00	300.00
❏ 10427 [PS]	All Tomorrow's Parties/I'll Be Your Mirror	1966	2000.	4000.	8000.
❏ 10466	Femme Fatale/Sunday Morning	1966	100.00	200.00	400.00
❏ 10466 [DJ]	Femme Fatale/Sunday Morning	1966	75.00	150.00	300.00
❏ 10560	White Light/White Heat//Here She Comes Now	1967	75.00	150.00	300.00
❏ 10560 [DJ]	White Light/White Heat// I Heard Her Call My Name	1967	50.00	100.00	200.00

Albums

COTILLION
| ❏ SD 9034 | Loaded | 197? | 3.75 | 7.50 | 15.00 |

—Reissue with purplish label

| ❏ SD 9034 [DJ] | Loaded | 1970 | 18.75 | 37.50 | 75.00 |

—White label promo

| ❏ SD 9034 | Loaded | 1970 | 5.00 | 10.00 | 20.00 |

—Original pressing has a light blue label

| ❏ SD 9034 | Loaded | 198? | 3.00 | 6.00 | 12.00 |

—Reissue with purplish label and bar code on back cover

| ❏ SD 9500 | Live at Max's Kansas City | 197? | 3.75 | 7.50 | 15.00 |

—Reissue with purplish label

| ❏ SD 9500 [DJ] | Live at Max's Kansas City | 1972 | 18.75 | 37.50 | 75.00 |

—White label promo

| ❏ SD 9500 | Live at Max's Kansas City | 1972 | 5.00 | 10.00 | 20.00 |

—Original pressing has a light blue label

| ❏ SD 9500 | Live at Max's Kansas City | 198? | 3.00 | 6.00 | 12.00 |

—Reissue with purplish label and bar code on back cover

MERCURY
| ❏ SRM-2-7504 [(2)] | 1969 (Live) | 1974 | 3.75 | 7.50 | 15.00 |

—Reissues with Chicago skyline or black labels

| ❏ SRM-2-7504 [(2)] | 1969 (Live) | 1974 | 12.50 | 25.00 | 50.00 |

—Originals with red labels

MGM
❏ GAS-131	The Velvet Underground (Golden Archive Series)	1970	10.00	20.00	40.00
❏ SE-4617	The Velvet Underground	1969	12.50	25.00	50.00
❏ SE-4617 [DJ]	The Velvet Underground	1969	75.00	125.00	250.00

—Yellow label promo

| ❏ M3G 4950 | Archetypes | 1974 | 5.00 | 10.00 | 20.00 |

PRIDE
| ❏ 0022 | Lou Reed and the Velvet Underground | 1973 | 3.75 | 7.50 | 15.00 |

VERVE
| ❏ V-5008 [M] | The Velvet Underground and Nico | 1967 | 50.00 | 100.00 | 200.00 |

—Version 3: With peel-off banana peel, torso is airbrushed off the cover (deduct 50% if banana sticker removed)

| ❏ V-5008 [M] | The Velvet Underground and Nico | 1967 | 75.00 | 150.00 | 300.00 |

—Version 1: With peel-off banana peel, photo of band framed by a male torso (deduct 50% if banana sticker is gone)

| ❏ V-5008 [M] | The Velvet Underground and Nico | 1967 | 75.00 | 150.00 | 300.00 |

—Version 2: With peel-off banana peel, photo of torso obscured by a sticker (deduct 50% if stickers removed)

| ❏ V6-5008 [S] | The Velvet Underground and Nico | 1967 | 37.50 | 75.00 | 150.00 |

—Version 3: With peel-off banana peel, torso is airbrushed off the cover (deduct 50% if banana sticker removed)

| ❏ V6-5008 [S] | The Velvet Underground and Nico | 1967 | 50.00 | 100.00 | 200.00 |

—Version 1: With peel-off banana peel, photo of band framed by a male torso (deduct 50% if banana sticker is gone)

| ❏ V6-5008 [S] | The Velvet Underground and Nico | 1967 | 50.00 | 100.00 | 200.00 |

—Version 2: With peel-off banana peel, photo of torso obscured by a sticker (deduct 50% if stickers removed)

| ❏ V6-5008 [S] | The Velvet Underground and Nico | 1968 | 25.00 | 50.00 | 100.00 |

—Version 4: With unpeelable banana

| ❏ V-5046 [M] | White Light/White Heat | 1967 | 15.00 | 30.00 | 60.00 |

—Version 2: No "skeleton" on cover

| ❏ V-5046 [M] | White Light/White Heat | 1967 | 37.50 | 75.00 | 150.00 |

—Version 1: "Skeleton" cover -- a black-on-black skeleton is visible when cover is viewed at an angle

| ❏ V-5046 [M] | White Light/White Heat | 1967 | 75.00 | 150.00 | 300.00 |

—White label promo

| ❏ V6-5046 [S] | White Light/White Heat | 1967 | 10.00 | 20.00 | 40.00 |

—Version 2: No "skeleton" on cover

| ❏ V6-5046 [S] | White Light/White Heat | 1967 | 20.00 | 40.00 | 80.00 |

—Version 1: "Skeleton" cover -- a black-on-black skeleton is visible when cover is viewed at an angle

| ❏ V6-5046 [S] | White Light/White Heat | 1967 | 62.50 | 125.00 | 250.00 |

—Yellow label promo

| ❏ 815454-1 | The Velvet Underground | 1985 | 3.00 | 6.00 | 12.00 |

—Reissue of MGM SE-4617

| ❏ 823290-1 | The Velvet Underground and Nico | 1985 | 3.00 | 6.00 | 12.00 |

—Reissue of Verve V6-5008

| ❏ 823721-1 | VU | 1985 | 3.00 | 6.00 | 12.00 |
| ❏ 825119-1 | White Light/White Heat | 1985 | 3.00 | 6.00 | 12.00 |

—Reissue of Verve V6-5046

| ❏ 826284-1 [(2)] | 1969 (Live) | 1985 | 3.00 | 6.00 | 12.00 |

—Reissue of Mercury SRM-2-7504

| ❏ 829405-1 | Another View | 1986 | 3.00 | 6.00 | 12.00 |

VELVETEENS, THE
45s

GOLDEN ARTISTS
| ❏ 614 | I Feel Sorry for You Baby/Ching Bam Bah | 1965 | 2.50 | 5.00 | 10.00 |

LAURIE
| ❏ 3126 | I Thank You/Meant to Be | 1962 | 3.75 | 7.50 | 15.00 |

STARK
| ❏ 101 | Teen Prayer/Baby Baby | 1961 | 5.00 | 10.00 | 20.00 |

—Slightly altered A-side title

| ❏ 101 | The Teen Prayer/Baby Baby | 1961 | 7.50 | 15.00 | 30.00 |

—New A-side title

| ❏ 101 | Please Holy Father/Baby Baby | 1961 | 12.50 | 25.00 | 50.00 |

—Original title of A-side

| ❏ 105 | I Thank You/Meant to Be | 1962 | 6.25 | 12.50 | 25.00 |

VELVETEERS, THE
45s

SPITFIRE
| ❏ 15 | Tell Me You're Mine/Boo Wacka Boo | 1956 | 2000. | 3000. | 4000. |

VELVETIERS, THE
45s

RIC
| ❏ 958 | Oh Baby/Feelin' Right Saturday Night | 1958 | 75.00 | 150.00 | 300.00 |

VELVETONES, THE (1)
45s

ALADDIN
❏ 3372	Glory of Love/I Love Her So	1957	50.00	100.00	200.00
❏ 3391	I Found My Love/Melody of Love	1957	50.00	100.00	200.00
❏ 3463	My Every Thought/Little Girl I Love You So	1960	75.00	150.00	300.00

D
| ❏ 1049 | Come Back/Penalty of Love | 1959 | 37.50 | 75.00 | 150.00 |
| ❏ 1072 | Worried Over You/Space Man | 1959 | 25.00 | 50.00 | 100.00 |

DEB
| ❏ 1008 | Stars of Wonder/Who Took My Girl | 1959 | 37.50 | 75.00 | 150.00 |

IMPERIAL
| ❏ 5878 | The Glory of Love/I Love Her So | 1962 | 7.50 | 15.00 | 30.00 |
| ❏ 66020 | The Glory of Love/I Found My Love | 1964 | 3.75 | 7.50 | 15.00 |

VELVETONES, THE (2) Girl group.
45s

ASCOT
| ❏ 2117 | I Want Him So Bad/Yes I Will | 1962 | 3.75 | 7.50 | 15.00 |
| ❏ 2126 | Starry Eyed/I'm Ashamed | 1963 | 3.75 | 7.50 | 15.00 |

VELVETONES, THE (3)
45s

GARP
| ❏ 102 | Mister X/(B-side unknown) | 1965 | 15.00 | 30.00 | 60.00 |

—Black vinyl

| ❏ 102 | Mister X/(B-side unknown) | 1965 | 30.00 | 60.00 | 120.00 |

—Red vinyl

VELVETONES, THE (4)
45s

VERVE
| ❏ 10514 | What Can the Matter Be/Hairy Lumpty Bump | 1967 | 3.00 | 6.00 | 12.00 |

VELVETONES, THE (U) Could be group (3); could be someone completely different.
45s

GLENN
| ❏ 309 | Doheny Run/Static | 1965 | 7.50 | 15.00 | 30.00 |

VELVET
| ❏ 101 | Doheny Run/Static | 1965 | 17.50 | 35.00 | 70.00 |

VELVETS, THE (1)
45s

MONUMENT
❏ 435	That Lucky Old Sun/Time and Again	1961	7.50	15.00	30.00
❏ 441	Tonight (Could Be the Night)/Spring Fever	1961	7.50	15.00	30.00
❏ 448	Lana/Laugh	1961	7.50	15.00	30.00
❏ 458	The Love Express/Don't Let Him Take My Baby	1962	6.25	12.50	25.00
❏ 464	Let the Good Times Roll/The Lights Go On, The Lights Go Off	1962	6.25	12.50	25.00
❏ 810	Crying in the Chapel/Dawn	1963	5.00	10.00	20.00
❏ 836	Nightmare/Here Comes That Song Again	1964	5.00	10.00	20.00
❏ 861	If/Let the Fool Kiss You	1964	5.00	10.00	20.00
❏ 961	Baby the Magic Is Gone/Let the Fool Kiss You	1966	3.75	7.50	15.00
❏ 8917	Tonight (Could Be the Night)/That Lucky Old Sun (Just Rolls Around Heaven)	197?	—	2.50	5.00

—"Golden Series" reissue

VELVETS, THE (2)
45s

EVENT
| ❏ 4285 | I/At Last | 197? | 2.00 | 4.00 | 8.00 |

FURY
| ❏ 1012 | I-I-I (Love You So-So-So)/Dance Honey Dance | 1958 | 12.50 | 25.00 | 50.00 |

LOST-NITE
| ❏ 335 | They Tried/She's Gotta Grin | 197? | — | 2.50 | 5.00 |
| ❏ 341 | I/At Last | 197? | — | 2.50 | 5.00 |

—Reissue

| ❏ 345 | Tell Her/I Cried | 197? | — | 2.50 | 5.00 |

—Reissue

PILGRIM
| ❏ 706 | I/At Last | 1956 | 12.50 | 25.00 | 50.00 |
| ❏ 710 | Tell Her/I Cried | 1956 | 12.50 | 25.00 | 50.00 |

RED ROBIN
❏ 120	They Tried/She's Gotta Grin	1953	50.00	100.00	200.00
❏ 122	I/At Last	1953	37.50	75.00	150.00
❏ 127	Tell Her/I Cried	1954	37.50	75.00	150.00

VELVETS, THE (U) These could be by group (1).
45s

PLAID
| ❏ 101 | Everybody Knows/Hand Jivin' Baby | 1959 | 20.00 | 40.00 | 80.00 |

20TH FOX
| ❏ 165 | Happy Days Are Here Again/ If I Could Be with You | 1959 | 6.25 | 12.50 | 25.00 |

VENEERS, THE
45s

PRINCETON
| ❏ 102 | Believe Me (My Angel)/I | 1960 | 10.00 | 20.00 | 40.00 |

TREYCO
| ❏ 402 | With All My Love/Recipe of Love | 1963 | 3.75 | 7.50 | 15.00 |

VENET, NICK
45s

DECCA
| ❏ 31939 | Theme from "Out of Sight"/Camp Side | 1966 | 2.50 | 5.00 | 10.00 |

IMPERIAL
| ❏ 5522 | Love In Be-Bop Time/Honey Baby | 1958 | 5.00 | 10.00 | 20.00 |

Number	Title (A Side/B Side)	Yr	VG	VG+	NM
VENTRILLS, THE					
45s					
PARKWAY					
❑ 141	Alone in the Night/Confusion	1967	3.00	6.00	12.00
VENTURES, THE					
12-Inch Singles					
TRIDEX					
❑ 1245	Surfin' and Spyin'/Showdown at Newport	1981	5.00	10.00	20.00
45s					
BLUE HORIZON					
❑ 100	The Real McCoy/Cookies and Coke	1960	150.00	300.00	600.00
❑ 101	Walk-Don't Run/Home	1960	625.00	1250.	2500.
❑ 102	Hold Me, Thrill Me, Kiss Me/No Next Time	1960	50.00	100.00	200.00
—As "Scott Douglas and the Venture Quintet"					
DOLTON					
❑ 25	Walk — Don't Run/Home	1960	6.25	12.50	25.00
❑ 25X	Walk — Don't Run/The McCoy	1960	5.00	10.00	20.00
❑ 28	Perfidia/No Trespassing	1960	5.00	10.00	20.00
❑ 28 [PS]	Perfidia/No Trespassing	1960	12.50	25.00	50.00
❑ 32	Ram-Bunk-Shush/Lonely Heart	1961	5.00	10.00	20.00
❑ 41	Lullaby of the Leaves/Ginchy	1961	5.00	10.00	20.00
❑ 44	(Theme from) Silver City/Bluer Than Blue	1961	5.00	10.00	20.00
❑ 47	Blue Moon/Lady of Spain	1961	5.00	10.00	20.00
❑ 50	Yellow Jacket/Genesis	1962	5.00	10.00	20.00
❑ 55	Instant Mashed/My Bonnie	1962	5.00	10.00	20.00
❑ 60	Lolita Ya-Ya/Lucille	1962	5.00	10.00	20.00
❑ 67	The 2,000 Pound Bee (Part 1)/ The 2,000 Pound Bee (Part 2)	1962	5.00	10.00	20.00
❑ 68	El Cumbanchero/Skip To M'Limbo	1963	3.75	7.50	15.00
❑ 78	The Ninth Wave/Damaged Goods	1963	3.75	7.50	15.00
❑ 85	The Savage/The Chase	1963	3.75	7.50	15.00
❑ 91	Journey to the Stars/Walkin' with Pluto	1964	3.75	7.50	15.00
❑ 94	Fugitive/Scratchin'	1964	3.75	7.50	15.00
❑ 96	Walk... Don't Run '64/The Cruel Sea	1964	3.75	7.50	15.00
❑ 96 [PS]	Walk... Don't Run '64/The Cruel Sea	1964	7.50	15.00	30.00
❑ 300	Slaughter on Tenth Avenue/Rap City	1964	3.00	6.00	12.00
❑ 300 [PS]	Slaughter on Tenth Avenue/Rap City	1964	6.25	12.50	25.00
❑ 303	Diamond Head/Lonely Girl	1965	3.00	6.00	12.00
❑ 306	Pedal Pusher/The Swingin' Creeper	1965	3.00	6.00	12.00
❑ 308	Ten Seconds to Heaven/Bird Rockers	1965	3.00	6.00	12.00
❑ 311	La Bomba/Gemini	1965	3.00	6.00	12.00
❑ 312	Sleigh Ride/Snow Flakes	1965	3.75	7.50	15.00
❑ 316	Secret Agent Man/00-711	1966	3.00	6.00	12.00
❑ 320	Blue Star/Comin' Home Baby	1966	3.00	6.00	12.00
❑ 320 [PS]	Blue Star/Comin' Home Baby	1966	6.25	12.50	25.00
❑ 321	Arabesque/Ginza Lights	1966	3.00	6.00	12.00
❑ 323	Green Hornet Theme/Fuzzy and Wild	1966	3.00	6.00	12.00
❑ 323 [PS]	Green Hornet Theme/Fuzzy and Wild	1966	7.50	15.00	30.00
❑ 325	Penetration/Wild Thing	1966	3.00	6.00	12.00
❑ 325 [PS]	Penetration/Wild Thing	1966	6.25	12.50	25.00
❑ 327	Theme from "The Wild Angels"/Kickstand	1967	3.00	6.00	12.00
❑ S7-19770	Rudolph the Red-Nosed Reindeer/ Frosty (The Snow Man)	1997	—	—	3.00
—B-side by Jan and Dean on Liberty					
EMI					
❑ S7-18212	Jingle Bell Rock/Jingle Bells	1994	—	2.50	5.00
—Red vinyl					
❑ SPRO 19949 [DJ]Rudolf The Red-Nosed Reindeer/Depression	1994	—	2.50	5.00
—B-side by Johnny and the Dwellers					
❑ SPRO 19949 [PS]Rudolf The Red-Nosed Reindeer/Depression	1994	—	2.50	5.00
LIBERTY					
❑ 54518	Walk — Don't Run/Ram-Bunk-Shush	196?	—	3.00	6.00
❑ 54519	Perfidia/Blue Moon	196?	—	3.00	6.00
❑ 54557	Wipe Out/Secret Agent Man	196?	—	3.50	7.00
—Records in the 54500s are from a reissue series					
❑ 55967	Strawberry Fields Forever/Endless Dream	1967	2.00	4.00	8.00
❑ 55977	Theme from "Endless Summer"/Strawberry Fields Forever	1967	2.00	4.00	8.00
❑ 56007	On the Road/Mirrors and Shadows	1967	2.00	4.00	8.00
❑ 56019	Flights of Fantasy/Vibrations	1968	—	3.00	6.00
❑ 56044	Walk Don't Run-Land of 1000 Dances/Too Young to Know My Mind	1968	—	3.00	6.00
❑ 56068	Hawaii Five-O/Soul Breeze	1968	2.00	4.00	8.00
❑ 56115	Theme from A Summer Place/A Summer Love	1969	—	3.00	6.00
❑ 56153	Expo Seven-O/Swan Lake	1970	—	3.00	6.00
❑ 56169	The Wanderer/The Mercenary	1970	—	3.00	6.00
❑ 56189	Storefront Lawyers (Theme)/Kern County Line	1970	—	3.00	6.00
TRIDEX					
❑ 501	Surfin' and Spyin'/Rumble at Newport	1981	—	2.50	5.00
—A-side with Charlotte Caffey and Jane Wiedlin of the Go-Go's, who did their own version on an early single					
❑ 501 [PS]	Surfin' and Spyin'/Rumble at Newport	1981	—	2.50	5.00
UNITED ARTISTS					
❑ 0050	Walk—Don't Run/Ram-Bunk-Shush	1973	—	2.00	4.00
—0050, 0051 and 0052 are "Silver Spotlight Series" reissues					
❑ 0051	Perfidia/Telstar	1973	—	2.00	4.00
❑ 0052	Hawaii Five-O/Walk—Don't Run '64	1973	—	2.00	4.00
❑ XW207	Last Tango in Paris/Prima Vera	1973	—	3.00	6.00
❑ XW277	Skylab/The Little People	1973	—	3.00	6.00
❑ XW333	Also Sprach Zarathustra (2001)/The Cisco Kid	1973	—	3.00	6.00
❑ XW369	Main Theme from The Young and the Restless/ Eloise	1973	—	3.00	6.00
❑ XW392	Main Theme from The Young and the Restless/ Eloise	1974	—	3.00	6.00
❑ XW392 [PS]	Main Theme from The Young and the Restless/ Eloise	1974	2.00	4.00	8.00
❑ XW578	Theme from "Airport 1975"/ The Man with the Golden Gun	1974	—	3.00	6.00
❑ XW687	Superstar Revue (Part 1)/ Superstar Revue (Part 2)	1975	—	3.00	6.00
❑ XW784	Moonlight Serenade (Part 1)/ Moonlight Serenade (Part 2)	1976	2.00	4.00	8.00
—As "The New Ventures"					
❑ XW942	Theme from "Charlie's Angels"/ Theme from "Starsky and Hutch"	1977	2.00	4.00	8.00

Number	Title (A Side/B Side)	Yr	VG	VG+	NM
❑ XW1100	Walk Don't Run '77/Amanda's Theme	1977	—	3.00	6.00
❑ XW1161	Wipe Out/Nadia's Theme	1978	—	2.00	4.00
—Reissue					
❑ 50800	Indian Sun/Squaw Man	1971	—	3.00	6.00
❑ 50800 [PS]	Indian Sun/Squaw Man	1971	2.00	4.00	8.00
❑ 50851	Theme from "Shaft"/Tight Fit	1971	—	3.00	6.00
❑ 50872	Joy/Cherries Jubilee	1972	—	3.00	6.00
❑ 50903	Beethoven's Sonata in C# Minor/ Peter and the Wolf	1972	—	3.00	6.00
❑ 50925	Honky Tonk (Part 1)/Honky Tonk (Part 2)	1972	—	3.00	6.00
❑ 50989	Last Night/Ram-Bunk-Shush	1972	—	3.00	6.00
7-Inch Extended Plays					
DOLTON					
❑ BEP-503	Walk — Don't Run/The McCoy// Honky Tonk/Raunchy	1960	20.00	40.00	80.00
❑ BEP-503 [PS]	Walk — Don't Run	1960	20.00	40.00	80.00
❑ 4-8031	House of the Rising Sun/Night Train/Rap City// Walk Don't Run '64/One Mint Julep/The Creeper	1964	3.75	7.50	15.00
—Jukebox single, small hole, plays at 33 1/3 rpm					
❑ 4-8031 [PS]	Walk Don't Run '64	1964	3.75	7.50	15.00
Albums					
COMPLEAT					
❑ 672013-1	The Best of the Ventures	1986	2.50	5.00	10.00
DOLTON					
❑ BLP 2003 [M]	Walk Don't Run	1960	12.50	25.00	50.00
—Pale blue label with dolphins on top					
❑ BLP 2003 [M]	Walk Don't Run	1963	5.00	10.00	20.00
—Dark label, logo on left					
❑ BLP 2004 [M]	The Ventures	1961	12.50	25.00	50.00
—Pale blue label with dolphins on top					
❑ BLP 2004 [M]	The Ventures	1963	5.00	10.00	20.00
—Dark label, logo on left					
❑ BLP 2006 [M]	Another Smash!!!	1961	12.50	25.00	50.00
—Pale blue label with dolphins on top					
❑ BLP 2006 [M]	Another Smash!!!	1963	5.00	10.00	20.00
—Dark label, logo on left					
❑ BLP 2008 [M]	The Colorful Ventures	1961	12.50	25.00	50.00
—Pale blue label with dolphins on top					
❑ BLP 2008 [M]	The Colorful Ventures	1963	5.00	10.00	20.00
—Dark label, logo on left					
❑ BLP 2010 [M]	Twist with the Ventures	1962	12.50	25.00	50.00
—Pale blue label with dolphins on top					
❑ BLP 2010 [M]	Dance!	1963	5.00	10.00	20.00
—Dark label, logo on left; retitled version of "Twist with the Ventures"					
❑ BLP 2014 [M]	The Ventures' Twist Party, Vol. 2	1962	12.50	25.00	50.00
—Pale blue label with dolphins on top					
❑ BLP 2014 [M]	Dance with the Ventures	1963	5.00	10.00	20.00
—Dark label, logo on left' retitled version of "The Ventures' Twist Party, Vol. 2"					
❑ BLP 2016 [M]	Mashed Potatoes and Gravy	1962	7.50	15.00	30.00
❑ BLP 2016 [M]	Beach Party	1963	5.00	10.00	20.00
—Retitled version of "Mashed Potatoes and Gravy"					
❑ BLP 2017 [M]	Going to the Ventures Dance Party!	1962	7.50	15.00	30.00
❑ BLP 2019 [M]	The Ventures Play Telstar, The Lonely Bull	1962	7.50	15.00	30.00
❑ BLP 2022 [M]	Surfing	1963	6.25	12.50	25.00
❑ BLP 2023 [M]	The Ventures Play the Country Classics	1963	6.25	12.50	25.00
❑ BLP 2024 [M]	Let's Go!	1963	6.25	12.50	25.00
❑ BLP 2027 [M]	(The) Ventures in Space	1964	10.00	20.00	40.00
❑ BLP 2029 [M]	The Fabulous Ventures	1964	6.25	12.50	25.00
❑ BLP 2031 [M]	Walk, Don't Run, Vol. 2	1964	6.25	12.50	25.00
❑ BLP 2033 [M]	The Ventures Knock Me Out!	1965	6.25	12.50	25.00
❑ BLP 2035 [M]	The Ventures on Stage	1965	6.25	12.50	25.00
❑ BLP 2037 [M]	The Ventures A-Go-Go	1965	6.25	12.50	25.00
❑ BLP-2038 [M]	The Ventures' Christmas Album	1965	7.50	15.00	30.00
❑ BLP 2040 [M]	Where the Action Is	1966	5.00	10.00	20.00
❑ BLP 2042 [M]	The Ventures/Batman Theme	1966	7.50	15.00	30.00
❑ BLP 2045 [M]	Go with the Ventures!	1966	5.00	10.00	20.00
❑ BLP 2047 [M]	Wild Things!	1966	5.00	10.00	20.00
❑ BLP 2050 [M]	Guitar Freakout	1967	5.00	10.00	20.00
❑ BST 8003 [S]	Walk Don't Run	1960	15.00	30.00	60.00
—Pale blue label with dolphins on top					
❑ BST 8003 [S]	Walk Don't Run	1963	6.25	12.50	25.00
—Dark label, logo on left					
❑ BST 8004 [S]	The Ventures	1961	15.00	30.00	60.00
—Pale blue label with dolphins on top					
❑ BST 8004 [S]	The Ventures	1963	6.25	12.50	25.00
—Dark label, logo on left					
❑ BST 8006 [S]	Another Smash!!!	1961	15.00	30.00	60.00
—Pale blue label with dolphins on top					
❑ BST 8006 [S]	Another Smash!!!	1963	6.25	12.50	25.00
—Dark label, logo on left					
❑ BST 8008 [S]	The Colorful Ventures	1961	15.00	30.00	60.00
—Pale blue label with dolphins on top					
❑ BST 8008 [S]	The Colorful Ventures	1963	6.25	12.50	25.00
—Dark label, logo on left					
❑ BST 8010 [S]	Twist with the Ventures	1962	15.00	30.00	60.00
—Pale blue label with dolphins on top					
❑ BST 8010 [S]	Dance!	1963	6.25	12.50	25.00
—Dark label, logo on left; retitled version of "Twist with the Ventures"					
❑ BST 8014 [S]	The Ventures' Twist Party, Vol. 2	1962	15.00	30.00	60.00
—Pale blue label with dolphins on top					
❑ BST 8014 [S]	Dance with the Ventures	1963	6.25	12.50	25.00
—Dark label, logo on left' retitled version of "The Ventures' Twist Party, Vol. 2"					
❑ BST 8016 [S]	Mashed Potatoes and Gravy	1962	10.00	20.00	40.00
❑ BST 8016 [S]	Beach Party	1963	6.25	12.50	25.00
—Retitled version of "Mashed Potatoes and Gravy"					
❑ BST 8017 [S]	Going to the Ventures Dance Party!	1962	10.00	20.00	40.00
❑ BST 8019 [S]	The Ventures Play Telstar, The Lonely Bull	1962	10.00	20.00	40.00
❑ BST 8022 [S]	Surfing	1963	7.50	15.00	30.00
❑ BST 8023 [S]	The Ventures Play the Country Classics	1963	7.50	15.00	30.00
❑ BST 8024 [S]	Let's Go!	1963	7.50	15.00	30.00
❑ BST 8027 [S]	(The) Ventures in Space	1964	12.50	25.00	50.00
❑ BST 8029 [S]	The Fabulous Ventures	1964	7.50	15.00	30.00
❑ BST 8031 [S]	Walk, Don't Run, Vol. 2	1964	7.50	15.00	30.00
❑ BST 8033 [S]	The Ventures Knock Me Out!	1965	7.50	15.00	30.00
❑ BST 8035 [S]	The Ventures on Stage	1965	7.50	15.00	30.00
❑ BST 8037 [S]	The Ventures A-Go-Go	1965	7.50	15.00	30.00

Number	Title (A Side/B Side)	Yr	VG	VG+	NM
❏ BST-8038 [S]	The Ventures' Christmas Album	1965	5.00	10.00	20.00
❏ BST 8040 [S]	Where the Action Is	1966	6.25	2.50	25.00
❏ BST 8042 [S]	The Ventures/Batman Theme	1966	10.00	20.00	40.00
❏ BST 8045 [S]	Go with the Ventures!	1966	6.25	12.50	25.00
❏ BST 8047 [S]	Wild Things!	1966	6.25	12.50	25.00
❏ BST 8050 [S]	Guitar Freakout	1967	6.25	12.50	25.00
❏ BLP 16501 [M]	Play Guitar with the Ventures	1965	6.25	12.50	25.00
❏ BLP 16502 [M]	Play Guitar with the Ventures, Vol. 2	196?	6.25	12.50	25.00
❏ BLP 16503 [M]	Play Guitar with the Ventures, Vol. 3	196?	6.25	12.50	25.00
❏ BLP 16504 [M]	Play Guitar with the Ventures, Vol. 4	196?	6.25	12.50	25.00
❏ BST 16504 [S]	Play Guitar with the Ventures, Vol. 4	196?	7.50	15.00	30.00
❏ BST 17501 [S]	Play Guitar with the Ventures	1965	7.50	15.00	30.00
❏ BST 17502 [S]	Play Guitar with the Ventures, Vol. 2	196?	7.50	15.00	30.00
❏ BST 17503 [S]	Play Guitar with the Ventures, Vol. 3	196?	7.50	15.00	30.00
LIBERTY					
❏ LRP-2052 [M]	Super Psychedelics	1967	5.00	10.00	20.00
❏ LRP-2053 [M]	Golden Greats by the Ventures	1967	5.00	10.00	20.00
❏ LRP-2054 [M]	$1,000,000.00 Weekend	1967	5.00	10.00	20.00
❏ LRP-2055 [M]	Flights of Fancy	1968	7.50	15.00	30.00
❏ LST-8003	Walk Don't Run	1970	3.75	7.50	15.00
—Reissue of Dolton 8003 with new front cover, original back cover					
❏ LST-8003	Walk Don't Run	1970	5.00	10.00	20.00
—Reissue of Dolton 8003 with new front and back covers					
❏ LT-8003	Walk Don't Run	1981	2.00	4.00	8.00
❏ LST-8023	I Walk the Line and Other Giant Hits	1970	5.00	10.00	20.00
—Reissue of "The Ventures Play the Country Classics"					
❏ LST-8031	Walk, Don't Run, Vol. 2	1970	6.25	12.50	25.00
—Reissue of Dolton 8031 with new cover					
❏ LST-8050	Revolving Sounds	1970	7.50	15.00	30.00
—Reissue of "Guitar Freakout"					
❏ LST-8052 [S]	Super Psychedelics	1967	6.25	12.50	25.00
❏ LST-8052 [S]	Changing Times	1970	10.00	20.00	40.00
—Reissue of "Super Psychedelics"					
❏ LST-8053 [S]	Golden Greats by the Ventures	1967	5.00	10.00	20.00
❏ LTAO-8053	Golden Greats by the Ventures	1981	2.00	4.00	8.00
❏ LST-8054 [S]	$1,000,000.00 Weekend	1967	5.00	10.00	20.00
❏ LST-8055 [S]	Flights of Fancy	1968	5.00	10.00	20.00
❏ LST-8057	The Horse	1968	5.00	10.00	20.00
❏ LST-8057	On the Scene	1970	3.75	7.50	15.00
—Reissue of "The Horse"					
❏ LST-8059	Underground Fire	1969	5.00	10.00	20.00
❏ LST-8060	More Golden Greats	1970	3.75	7.50	15.00
❏ LST-8061	Hawaii Five-O	1969	3.75	7.50	15.00
❏ LST-8062	Swamp Rock	1969	3.75	7.50	15.00
❏ LN-10122	The Very Best of the Ventures	1981	2.00	4.00	8.00
❏ LN-10155	The Ventures Play Telstar, The Lonely Bull	1981	2.00	4.00	8.00
❏ LN-10156	The Ventures Play the Country Classics	1981	2.00	4.00	8.00
❏ LN-10188	Walk, Don't Run, Vol. 2	1984	2.00	4.00	8.00
❏ LN-10190	(The) Ventures in Space	1984	2.00	4.00	8.00
❏ LN-10203	The Ventures	1984	2.00	4.00	8.00
❏ LN-10224	TV Themes	1984	2.00	4.00	8.00
❏ LST-35000 [(2)]	The Ventures 10th Anniversary Album	1970	5.00	10.00	20.00
SUNSET					
❏ SUM-1160 [M]	The Guitar Genius of the Ventures	1967	3.00	6.00	12.00
❏ SUS-5160 [S]	The Guitar Genius of the Ventures	1967	3.75	7.50	15.00
❏ SUS-5270	Super Group	1969	3.00	6.00	12.00
UNITED ARTISTS					
❏ UXS-80 [(2)]	The Ventures	1971	3.75	7.50	15.00
❏ UA-LA147-G [(2)]	Only Hits	1973	3.75	7.50	15.00
❏ UA-LA217-E	The Jim Croce Songbook	1973	3.00	6.00	12.00
❏ UA-LA331-E	The Very Best of the Ventures	1974	3.00	6.00	12.00
❏ UA-LA586-F	Rocky Road	1976	3.00	6.00	12.00
❏ UA-LA717-F	TV Themes	1977	6.25	12.50	25.00
❏ UAS-5547	Theme from Shaft	1971	3.00	6.00	12.00
❏ UAS-5575	Joy/The Ventures Play the Classics	1972	3.00	6.00	12.00
❏ UAS-5649	Rock and Roll Forever	1972	3.00	6.00	12.00
❏ UAS-6796	New Testament	1971	3.00	6.00	12.00

VENUS, VIK
45s
BUDDAH

Number	Title (A Side/B Side)	Yr	VG	VG+	NM
❏ 118	Moonflight/Everybody's On Strike	1969	2.50	5.00	10.00
❏ 138	Moon Jack/Moon Welcome	1969	2.00	4.00	8.00

VERA, BILLY Includes records as "Billy and the Beaters."
45s
ALFA

Number	Title (A Side/B Side)	Yr	VG	VG+	NM
❏ 7002	I Can Take Care of Myself/Corner of the Night	1981	—	2.00	4.00
—As "Billy and the Beaters"					
❏ 7005	At This Moment/Someone Will School You, Someone Will Cool You	1981	—	2.50	5.00
❏ 7005 [PS]	At This Moment/Someone Will School You, Someone Will Cool You	1981	—	2.50	5.00
❏ 7012	Millie, Make Me Some Chili/Someone Will School You, Someone Will Cool You	1981	—	2.00	4.00
—As "Billy and the Beaters"					
❏ 7020	We Got It All/You Own It	1982	—	2.00	4.00
ATLANTIC					
❏ 2526	With Pen in Hand/Good Morning Blues	1968	2.00	4.00	8.00
❏ 2555	I've Been Loving You Too Long/Are You Coming to My Party	1968	2.00	4.00	8.00
❏ 2586	Julie/Time Doesn't Matter Anymore	1968	2.00	4.00	8.00
❏ 2628	Bible Salesman/Are You Coming to My Party	1969	—	3.00	6.00
❏ 2700	I've Never Been Loved Like This Before/J.W.'s Dream	1970	—	3.00	6.00
CAPITOL					
❏ B-44149	Between Like and Love/Heart Be Still	1988	—	—	3.00
❏ B-44149 [PS]	Between Like and Love/Heart Be Still	1988	—	—	3.00
❏ B-44200	Ronnie's Song/Between Like and Love	1988	—	—	3.00
MACOLA					
❏ 8912	She Ain't Johnnie/My Girl Josephine	1987	—	2.00	4.00
MIDLAND INT'L.					
❏ MB-10639	Back Door Man/Run and Tell the People	1976	—	2.50	5.00
❏ MB-10909	Private Clown/Billy, Meet Your Son	1977	—	2.50	5.00
❏ MB-11042	I've Had Enough/Something Like Nothing Before	1977	—	2.50	5.00
❏ 72014	She Ain't Johnnie/I've Had Enough	1977	—	2.50	5.00

Number	Title (A Side/B Side)	Yr	VG	VG+	NM
RHINO					
❏ 74403	At This Moment/Peanut Butter	1986	—	—	3.00
❏ 74403	At This Moment/I Can Take Care of Myself	1986	—	2.50	5.00
❏ 74404	I Can Take Care of Myself/Millie, Make Some Chili	1987	—	—	3.00
❏ 74404 [PS]	I Can Take Care of Myself/Millie, Make Some Chili	1987	—	2.50	5.00
❏ 74407	Hopeless Romantic/(B-side unknown)	1987	—	—	3.00
RUST					
❏ 5051	My Heart Cries/All My Love	1962	5.00	10.00	20.00
Albums					
ALFA					
❏ 10001	Billy and the Beaters	1981	3.75	7.50	15.00
❏ 10012	Billy Vera	1982	3.00	6.00	12.00
ATLANTIC					
❏ 8197 [M]	With Pen in Hand	1968	10.00	20.00	40.00
❏ SD 8197 [S]	With Pen in Hand	1968	6.25	12.50	25.00
CAPITOL					
❏ C1-46948	Retro Nuevo	1988	2.50	5.00	10.00
MACOLA					
❏ 0961	The Billy Vera Album	1987	2.50	5.00	10.00
—Reissue of Midsong Int'l. LP					
MIDSONG INT'L.					
❏ BKL1-2219	Out of the Darkness	1977	3.00	6.00	12.00
RHINO					
❏ RNLP 70185	The Atlantic Years	1987	2.50	5.00	10.00
❏ RNLP 70858	By Request — The Best of Billy Vera and the Beaters	1986	3.00	6.00	12.00
THUNDER					
❏ TVLP 0018	The Hollywood Sessions	1987	2.50	5.00	10.00

VERA, BILLY, AND JUDY CLAY
45s
ATLANTIC

Number	Title (A Side/B Side)	Yr	VG	VG+	NM
❏ 2445	Storybook Children/Really Together	1967	2.00	4.00	8.00
❏ 2480	Country Girl — City Man/So Good	1968	2.00	4.00	8.00
❏ 2515	Ever Since/When Do We Go	1968	2.00	4.00	8.00
❏ 2654	Tell It Like It Is/Reaching for the Moon	1969	—	3.00	6.00
Albums					
ATLANTIC					
❏ 8174 [M]	Storybook Children	1967	6.25	12.50	25.00
❏ SD 8174 [S]	Storybook Children	1967	7.50	15.00	30.00

VERA, RICKY, AND STEVE ALLEN
45s
CORAL

Number	Title (A Side/B Side)	Yr	VG	VG+	NM
❏ 61098	How Can Santa Come to Puerto Rico/Can I Wait Up for Santa Claus	1953	7.50	15.00	30.00

VERITY, JOHN, BAND
Albums
ABC DUNHILL

Number	Title (A Side/B Side)	Yr	VG	VG+	NM
❏ DSX-50170	The John Verity Band	1974	5.00	10.00	20.00

VERNE, LARRY
45s
ERA

Number	Title (A Side/B Side)	Yr	VG	VG+	NM
❏ 3024	Mr. Custer/Okefenokee Two-Step	1960	3.75	7.50	15.00
❏ 3034	Mister Livingston/Roller Coaster	1960	3.00	6.00	12.00
❏ 3034 [PS]	Mister Livingston/Roller Coaster	1960	6.25	12.50	25.00
❏ 3044	Abdul's Party/Tubby Tilly	1961	3.00	6.00	12.00
❏ 3051	Charlie at the Bat/Pow, Right in the Kisser	1961	3.00	6.00	12.00
❏ 3065	Beatnik/Speck	1961	3.00	6.00	12.00
❏ 3075	Hoo-Ha/I'm a Brave Little Soldier	1962	3.00	6.00	12.00
❏ 3091	The Coward Who Won the West/The Porcupine Patrol	1962	3.00	6.00	12.00
❏ 3139	Return of Mr. Custer/Running Through the Forest	1964	3.00	6.00	12.00
Albums					
ERA					
❏ 104 [M]	Mister Larry Verne	1961	15.00	30.00	60.00

VERNON, MARIE
45s
ALLIED

Number	Title (A Side/B Side)	Yr	VG	VG+	NM
❏ 5012	I Want You For Christmas/Christmas Tree Waltz	195?	3.75	7.50	15.00

VERNON GIRLS, THE
45s
CHALLENGE

Number	Title (A Side/B Side)	Yr	VG	VG+	NM
❏ 59234	We Love the Beatles/Hey Lover Boy	1964	7.50	15.00	30.00
❏ 59261	Only You Can Do It/Stupid Little Girl	1964	2.50	5.00	10.00

VERONICA Also see THE RONETTES; RONNIE SPECTOR.
45s
PHIL SPECTOR

Number	Title (A Side/B Side)	Yr	VG	VG+	NM
❏ 1	So Young/Larry L.	1964	50.00	100.00	200.00
❏ 2	Why Don't They Let Us Fall in Love/Chubby Danny D	1964	50.00	100.00	200.00
❏ 2	Why Can't They Let Us Fall in Love/Chubby Danny D	1964	150.00	300.00	600.00
—Note slightly different A-side title					

VERSATILES, THE More than one group.
45s
ATLANTIC

Number	Title (A Side/B Side)	Yr	VG	VG+	NM
❏ 2004	Passing By/Crying	1958	10.00	20.00	40.00
PEACOCK					
❏ 1910	White Cliffs of Dover/Just Words	1963	7.50	15.00	30.00
RAMCO					
❏ 3717	Blue Feeling/Just Pretending	1962	50.00	100.00	200.00
RO-CAL					
❏ 1002	I'll Whisper in Your Ear/Lundee Dundee	1960	25.00	50.00	100.00
SEA CREST					
❏ 6001	Lonely Boy/Moon Dawg	1964	6.25	12.50	25.00

Number	Title (A Side/B Side)	Yr	VG	VG+	NM
VERSATONES, THE Probably more than one group.					
45s					
ALL STAR					
❏ 501	Tight Skirt and Sweater/Bila	1958	10.00	20.00	40.00
ATLANTIC					
❏ 2211	Tight Skirt and Sweater/Bila	1963	5.00	10.00	20.00
FENWAY					
❏ 7001	Tight Skirt and Sweater/Bila	1960	6.25	12.50	25.00
LOST-NITE					
❏ 115	Tight Skirt and Sweater/Bila	196?	2.00	4.00	8.00
RCA VICTOR					
❏ 47-6917	Wait for Me/De Obeah Man	1957	3.75	7.50	15.00
❏ 47-6976	Lovely Teenage Girl/Bikini Baby	1957	3.75	7.50	15.00
Albums					
RCA VICTOR					
❏ LPM-1538 [M]	The Versatones	1957	25.00	50.00	100.00
VERTUES FOUR, THE					
45s					
SEA SEVEN					
❏ 22	Angel Baby/Uphill, Downhill	1963	10.00	20.00	40.00
VESPE, LITTLE JOE					
45s					
PARKWAY					
❏ 877	Caravan/Conservative Twist	1963	2.50	5.00	10.00
VESPERS, THE					
45s					
SWAN					
❏ 4156	Cupid/When I Walk with My Angel	1963	10.00	20.00	40.00
VESTELLES, THE					
45s					
DECCA					
❏ 9-30733	Come Home/Ditta Wa Do	1958	7.50	15.00	30.00
VETTES, THE With BRUCE JOHNSTON.					
45s					
MGM					
❏ 13186	Little Ford Ragtop/Happy Hodaddy (With Ragtop Caddy)	1963	12.50	25.00	50.00
Albums					
MGM					
❏ E-4193 [M]	Rev-Up	1963	25.00	50.00	100.00
❏ SE-4193 [S]	Rev-Up	1963	30.00	60.00	120.00
VIBES, THE (1)					
45s					
ABC-PARAMOUNT					
❏ 9810	Darling/Come Back Baby	1957	12.50	25.00	50.00
VIBES, THE (2) Probably the same group as THE VIBRANAIRES.					
45s					
AFTER HOURS					
❏ 105	Stop Torturing Me/Stop Jibing, Baby	1954	500.00	1000.	2000.
CHARIOT					
❏ 105	Stop Torturing Me/Stop Jibing, Baby	1954	375.00	750.00	1500.
VIBES, THE (3)					
45s					
ALLIED					
❏ 10006	What's Her Name/You Are	1958	15.00	30.00	60.00
❏ 10007	Misunderstood/Let the Old Folks Talk	1959	10.00	20.00	40.00
VIBES, THE (4)					
45s					
PERSPECTIVE					
❏ 5858	Pretty Baby (I Saw You Last Night)/Crying for You	1960	25.00	50.00	100.00
VIBES, THE (5)					
45s					
RAYNA					
❏ 103	You Got Me Crying/A Killer Came to Town	196?	10.00	20.00	40.00
VIBRA-SONICS, THE					
45s					
IDEAL					
❏ 94874	Thunder Storm/Drag Race	1964	12.50	25.00	50.00
VIBRANAIRES, THE Probably the same group as THE VIBES (2).					
45s					
AFTER HOURS					
❏ 103	Doll Face/Ooh, I Feel So Good	1954	625.00	1250.	2500.
CHARIOT					
❏ 103	Doll Face/Ooh, I Feel So Good	1954	500.00	1000.	2000.
VIBRATIONS, THE Also see THE JAYHAWKS; THE MARATHONS (1).					
45s					
ATLANTIC					
❏ 2204	Between Hello and Goodbye/ Lonesome Little Lonely Girl	1963	3.00	6.00	12.00
❏ 2221	My Girl Sloopy/Daddy Woo-Woo	1964	3.00	6.00	12.00
BET					
❏ 1	So Blue/Love Me Like You Should	1960	25.00	50.00	100.00
CHECKER					
❏ 954	So Blue/Love Me Like You Should	1960	7.50	15.00	30.00
❏ 961	Feel So Bad/Cave Man	1960	5.00	10.00	20.00
❏ 967	Doing the Slop/So Little Time	1961	5.00	10.00	20.00
❏ 969	The Watusi/Wallflower	1961	5.00	10.00	20.00
❏ 974	The Continental/The Junkeroo	1961	5.00	10.00	20.00
❏ 982	Don't Say Goodbye/Stranded in the Jungle	1961	5.00	10.00	20.00
❏ 987	All My Love Belongs to You/Stop Right Now	1961	10.00	20.00	40.00
❏ 990	Let's Pony Again/ What Made You Change Your Mind	1961	5.00	10.00	20.00
❏ 1002	Over the Rainbow/Oh, Cindy	1962	3.75	7.50	15.00
❏ 1011	The New Hully Gully/Anytime	1962	3.75	7.50	15.00
❏ 1022	Hamburgers on a Bun/If He Don't	1962	3.75	7.50	15.00
❏ 1038	Since I Fell for You/May the Best Man Win	1963	3.75	7.50	15.00
❏ 1061	Dancing Danny/(Instrumental)	1963	3.75	7.50	15.00
CHESS					
❏ 2151	Shake It Up/Make It Last	1974	—	3.00	6.00
EPIC					
❏ 10418	I Took an Overdose/Because You're Mine	1968	5.00	10.00	20.00
MANDALA					
❏ 2511	Ain't No Greens in Harlem/Wind-Up Toy	1972	—	3.00	6.00
❏ 2514	Man Overboard/(B-side unknown)	1972	—	3.00	6.00
NEPTUNE					
❏ 19	Expressway to Your Heart/Who's Gonna Help Me Now	1969	2.00	4.00	8.00
❏ 21	Smoke Signals/Who's Gonna Help Me Now	1970	2.00	4.00	8.00
❏ 28	Right On Brothers, Right On/ Surprise Party for Baby	1970	2.00	4.00	8.00
OKEH					
❏ 7205	Sloop Dance/Watusi Time	1964	3.00	6.00	12.00
❏ 7212	Hello Happiness/Keep On Keeping On	1965	3.00	6.00	12.00
❏ 7220	End Up Crying/Ain't Love That Way	1965	3.00	6.00	12.00
❏ 7228	Talkin' 'Bout Love/If You Only Knew	1965	3.00	6.00	12.00
❏ 7230	Misty/Finding Out the Hard Way	1965	3.00	6.00	12.00
❏ 7238	Gina/The Story of a Starry Night	1966	—	—	—
—Unreleased					
❏ 7241	Canadian Sunset/The Story of a Starry Night	1966	2.50	5.00	10.00
❏ 7249	Forgive and Forget/ Gonna Get Along Without You Now	1966	2.50	5.00	10.00
❏ 7257	And I Love Her/Soul a-Go-Go	1966	2.50	5.00	10.00
❏ 7276	Pick Me/You Better Beware	1967	2.50	5.00	10.00
❏ 7297	Together/Come To Yourself	1967	2.50	5.00	10.00
❏ 7311	Love in Them There Hills/Remember the Rain	1968	2.50	5.00	10.00
Albums					
CHECKER					
❏ LP-2978 [M]	The Watusi	1961	50.00	100.00	200.00
MANDALA					
❏ 3006	Taking a New Step	1972	5.00	10.00	20.00
OKEH					
❏ OKM-12111 [M]	Shout	1965	7.50	15.00	30.00
❏ OKM-12112 [M]	Misty	1966	7.50	15.00	30.00
❏ OKM-12114 [M]	New Vibrations	1967	7.50	15.00	30.00
❏ OKS-14111 [S]	Shout	1965	10.00	20.00	40.00
❏ OKS-14112 [S]	Misty	1966	10.00	20.00	40.00
❏ OKS-14114 [S]	New Vibrations	1967	10.00	20.00	40.00
❏ OKS-14129	The Vibrations' Greatest Hits	1969	7.50	15.00	30.00
VIC, PAUL AND BRUCE See THE CANADIAN BEADLES.					
VICEROYS, THE (1)					
45s					
ALADDIN					
❏ 3273	Please, Baby, Please/ I'm Yours As Long As I Live	1955	100.00	200.00	400.00
VICEROYS, THE (2)					
45s					
BETHLEHEM					
❏ 3045	Sea Green/Moasin'	1962	5.00	10.00	20.00
❏ 3045	Seagrams/Moasin'	1962	6.25	12.50	25.00
—Original A-side title					
❏ 3070	Joshin'/Buzz Bomb	1963	5.00	10.00	20.00
❏ 3070	The Fox/Buzz Bomb	1963	6.25	12.50	25.00
—Original A-side title					
❏ 3088	Not Too Much Twist/Tears on My Pillow	1965	5.00	10.00	20.00
VICEROYS, THE (3)					
45s					
BOLO					
❏ 736	Granny's Pad/Blues Bouquet	1962	3.00	6.00	12.00
❏ 739	Goin' Back to Granny's/Get Set	1963	3.00	6.00	12.00
❏ 743	Dartell Stomp/Granny's Medley	1964	2.50	5.00	10.00
❏ 749	Please, Please, Please/Tiger Shark	1964	2.50	5.00	10.00
❏ 750	Bacon Fat/Until	1965	2.50	5.00	10.00
❏ 754	That Sound/Tired of Waiting for You	1965	2.50	5.00	10.00
DOT					
❏ 16456	Granny's Pad/Blues Bouquet	1963	2.00	4.00	8.00
Albums					
BOLO					
❏ BLP-8000 [M]	The Viceroys at Granny's Pad	1963	10.00	20.00	40.00
VICEROYS, THE (4)					
45s					
LITTLE STAR					
❏ 107	I'm So Sorry (It's Ending with You)/ Uncle Sam Needs You	1961	37.50	75.00	150.00
ORIGINAL SOUND					
❏ 15	Dreamy Eyes/Ball 'N' Chain	1961	10.00	20.00	40.00
RAMCO					
❏ 3715	My Heart/I Need Your Love So Bad	1962	2000.00	3000.	4000.
SMASH					
❏ 1716	I'm So Sorry (It's Ending with You)/ Uncle Sam Needs You	1961	5.00	10.00	20.00
VICEROYS, THE (U)					
45s					
E'DEN					
❏ 9001	Don't Let Go/Down Beat Blues	1962	3.00	6.00	12.00
IMPERIAL					
❏ 66058	Death of an Angel/Earth Angel	1964	3.00	6.00	12.00
VICTORIALS, THE					
45s					
IMPERIAL					
❏ 5398	I Get That Feeling/The Prettiest Girl in the World	1956	12.50	25.00	50.00

Number	Title (A Side/B Side)	Yr	VG	VG+	NM

VICTORIANS, THE More than one group.
45s
ARNOLD
| ❑ 571 | Move In a Little Closer/Lovin' | 1963 | 5.00 | 10.00 | 20.00 |

BANG
| ❑ 550 | Merry-Go-Round/Wasn't the Summer Short | 1967 | 3.75 | 7.50 | 15.00 |

LIBERTY
❑ 55574	Climb Every Mountain/				
	What Makes Little Girls Cry	1963	5.00	10.00	20.00
❑ 55656	The Monkey Stroll/You're Invited to a Party	1964	3.75	7.50	15.00
❑ 55693	Happy Birthday Blues/Oh What a Night for Love	1964	3.75	7.50	15.00
❑ 55728	If I Loved You/The Monkey Stroll	1964	3.75	7.50	15.00

REPRISE
| ❑ 0434 | I Saw My Girl/Baby Toys | 1965 | 3.75 | 7.50 | 15.00 |

SAXONY
| ❑ 103 | Heartbreaking Moon/I'm Rollin' | 1956 | 125.00 | 250.00 | 500.00 |

SELMA
| ❑ 1002 | Wedding Bells/Please Say You Do | 1956 | 75.00 | 150.00 | 300.00 |

VICTORY FIVE, THE
45s
TERP
| ❑ 101 | I Never Knew/Swing Low | 1958 | 150.00 | 300.00 | 600.00 |
—All copies on colored vinyl

VIDALTONES, THE
45s
JOSIE
| ❑ 900 | Forever/Someone to Love | 1962 | 10.00 | 20.00 | 40.00 |

VIDELS, THE
45s
EARLY
| ❑ 702 | I Wish/Blow, Winds, Blow | 1960 | 100.00 | 200.00 | 400.00 |

JDS
| ❑ 5004 | Mr. Lonely/I'll Forget You | 1960 | 5.00 | 10.00 | 20.00 |
—Multicolor label
| ❑ 5004 | Mr. Lonely/I'll Forget You | 1960 | 7.50 | 15.00 | 30.00 |
—Gray label
| ❑ 5005 | She's Not Coming Home/ | | | | |
| | Now That Summer Is Here | 1960 | 5.00 | 10.00 | 20.00 |
—Multicolor label
| ❑ 5005 | She's Not Coming Home/ | | | | |
| | Now That Summer Is Here | 1960 | 7.50 | 15.00 | 30.00 |
—Gray label

KAPP
| ❑ 361 | Streets of Love/I'll Keep On Waiting | 1960 | 5.00 | 10.00 | 20.00 |
| ❑ 405 | A Letter from Ann/This Year's Mister New | 1961 | 10.00 | 20.00 | 40.00 |

MEDIEVAL
| ❑ 203 | Be My Girl/A Place in Your Heart | 1961 | 3.75 | 7.50 | 15.00 |

MUSICNOTE
| ❑ 117 | We Belong Together/It's All Over | 1963 | 12.50 | 25.00 | 50.00 |

RHODY
| ❑ 2000 | Be My Girl/A Place in Your Heart | 1959 | 12.50 | 25.00 | 50.00 |

TIC TAC TOE
| ❑ 5005 | She's Not Coming Home/ | | | | |
| | Now That Summer Is Here | 1962 | 12.50 | 25.00 | 50.00 |

VIDEOS, THE
45s
CASINO
| ❑ 102 | Trickle, Trickle/Moonglow You Know | 1958 | 5.00 | 10.00 | 20.00 |
—With playing cards on label
| ❑ 102 | Trickle, Trickle/Moonglow You Know | 1958 | 7.50 | 15.00 | 30.00 |
—"Casino" in normal print; no playing cards; no mention of distribution by Gone
| ❑ 102 | Trickle, Trickle/Moonglow You Know | 1958 | 12.50 | 25.00 | 50.00 |
—"Casino" in shadow print; no playing cards; no mention of distribution by Gone
| ❑ 102 | Trickle, Trickle/Moonglow You Know | 1961 | 6.25 | 12.50 | 25.00 |
—No playing cards; with distribution by Gone
| ❑ 105 | Love or Infatuation/ | | | | |
| | Shoo-Be-Doo-Be Cha Cha Cha | 1959 | 75.00 | 150.00 | 300.00 |

LOST-NITE
| ❑ 218 | Trickle, Trickle/Moonglow You Know | 196? | — | 2.50 | 5.00 |
—Reissue

VIGRASS AND OSBORNE With Gary Osborne, later a collaborator with Elton John.
45s
EPIC
| ❑ 50044 | Gypsy Woman/Haystacks | 1974 | — | 2.50 | 5.00 |

UNI
❑ 55330	Men of Learning/Forever Autumn	1972	—	3.00	6.00
❑ 55344	Virginia/Ballerina	1972	—	2.50	5.00
❑ 55355	Remember Pearl Harbor/Mister Deadline	1972	—	2.50	5.00

Albums
EPIC
| ❑ KE 33077 | Steppin' Out | 1975 | 3.00 | 6.00 | 12.00 |

UNI
| ❑ 73129 | Queues | 1971 | 3.75 | 7.50 | 15.00 |

VILLAGE SOUL CHOIR, THE
45s
ABBOTT
❑ 2010	The Cat Walk/The Country Walk	1970	2.50	5.00	10.00
❑ 2013	Love Everyday, Love Every Night/				
	(B-side unknown)	1970	2.50	5.00	10.00
❑ 2028	Sissy Football (Pt. 1)/(Pt. 2)	197?	3.75	7.50	15.00

VILLAGE STOMPERS, THE
45s
EPIC
❑ 9617	Washington Square/Turkish Delight	1963	2.00	4.00	8.00
❑ 9617 [PS]	Washington Square/Turkish Delight	1963	2.50	5.00	10.00
❑ 9655	Blue Grass/The La-Dee-La Song	1964	—	3.00	6.00
❑ 9655 [PS]	Blue Grass/The La-Dee-La Song	1964	2.00	4.00	8.00
❑ 9674	From Russia with Love/The Bridges of Budapest	1964	—	3.00	6.00
❑ 9702	Haunted House/Mozambique	1964	—	3.00	6.00

Number	Title (A Side/B Side)	Yr	VG	VG+	NM

❑ 9718	Oh, Marie/Lonesome Blues	1964	—	3.00	6.00
❑ 9740	Fiddler on the Roof/Moonlight on the Ganges	1964	—	3.00	6.00
❑ 9785	Brother, Can You Spare a Dime/Magic Horn	1965	—	3.00	6.00
❑ 9785 [PS]	Brother, Can You Spare a Dime/Magic Horn	1965	2.00	4.00	8.00
❑ 9824	Those Magnificant Men in Their Flying				
	Machines/Sweetwater Bay	1965	—	3.00	6.00
❑ 9868	The Bride of Bleecker Street/Call Me	1965	—	3.00	6.00
❑ 10017	Second Hand Rose/The Poet and the Prophet	1966	—	3.00	6.00
❑ 10106	Chopsticks/Wilkommen	1966	—	3.00	6.00
❑ 10142	Rose of Washington Square/				
	When I Tell You That I Love You	1967	—	3.00	6.00

Albums
EPIC
❑ LN 24078 [M]	Washington Square	1963	3.75	7.50	15.00
❑ LN 24090 [M]	More Sounds of Washington Square	1964	3.75	7.50	15.00
❑ LN 24109 [M]	Around the World with the Village Stompers	1964	3.00	6.00	12.00
❑ LN 24129 [M]	New Beat on Broadway!	1964	3.00	6.00	12.00
❑ LN 24161 [M]	Some Folk, a Bit of Country and a				
	Whole Lot of Dixie	1965	3.00	6.00	12.00
❑ LN 24180 [M]	A Taste of Honey	1965	3.00	6.00	12.00
❑ LN 24235 [M]	One More Time	1966	3.00	6.00	12.00
❑ LN 24318 [M]	The Village Stompers' Greatest Hits	1967	3.00	6.00	12.00
❑ BN 26078 [S]	Washington Square	1963	5.00	10.00	20.00
❑ BN 26090 [S]	More Sounds of Washington Square	1964	5.00	10.00	20.00
❑ BN 26109 [S]	Around the World with the Village Stompers	1964	3.75	7.50	15.00
❑ BN 26129 [S]	New Beat on Broadway!	1964	3.75	7.50	15.00
❑ BN 26161 [S]	Some Folk, a Bit of Country and a				
	Whole Lot of Dixie	1965	3.75	7.50	15.00
❑ BN 26180 [S]	A Taste of Honey	1965	3.75	7.50	15.00
❑ BN 26235 [S]	One More Time	1966	3.75	7.50	15.00
❑ BN 26318 [S]	The Village Stompers' Greatest Hits	1967	3.75	7.50	15.00

VILLAGE VOICES, THE See THE FOUR SEASONS.

VINCE AND THE WAIKIKI RUMBLERS
45s
BIG BEN
| ❑ 1003 | Waikiki Rumble/Pacifica | 1965 | 12.50 | 25.00 | 50.00 |

ZODIAC
| ❑ 1004 | Waikiki Rumble/Pacifica | 1965 | 20.00 | 40.00 | 80.00 |

VINCENT, GENE
45s
CAPITOL
| ❑ F3450 | Be-Bop-a-Lula/Woman Love | 1956 | 12.50 | 25.00 | 50.00 |
—With small Capitol logo; counterfeits exist on a white label with blue vinyl
| ❑ F3450 | Be-Bop-a-Lula/Woman Love | 1956 | 17.50 | 35.00 | 70.00 |
—With large Capitol logo
❑ F3530	Race with the Devil/Gonna Back Up, Baby	1956	10.00	20.00	40.00
❑ F3558	Bluejean Bop/Who Slapped John	1956	10.00	20.00	40.00
❑ F3617	Crazy Legs/Important Words	1956	12.50	25.00	50.00
❑ F3678	B-I-Bickey-Bi-Bo-Bo-Go/Five Days, Five Days	1957	12.50	25.00	50.00
❑ F3763	Lotta Lovin'/Wear My Ring	1957	12.50	25.00	50.00
❑ F3839	Dance to the Bop/I Got It	1957	7.50	15.00	30.00
❑ 3871	Be-Bop-a-Lula/Lotta Lovin'	1974	3.75	7.50	15.00
❑ F3874	Walkin' Home from School/I Gotta Baby	1958	10.00	20.00	40.00
❑ F3959	Baby Blue/True to You	1958	12.50	25.00	50.00
❑ F4010	Yes I Love You Baby/Rocky Road Blues	1958	10.00	20.00	40.00
❑ F4051	Little Lover/Git It	1958	10.00	20.00	40.00
❑ F4105	Say Mama/Be-Bop Boogie Boy	1958	12.50	25.00	50.00
❑ F4153	Over the Rainbow/Who's Pushin' Your Swing	1959	12.50	25.00	50.00
❑ F4237	The Night Is So Lonely/Right Now	1959	12.50	25.00	50.00
❑ F4237 [PS]	The Night Is So Lonely/Right Now	1959	500.00	1000.	2000.
❑ 4313	Wild Cat/Right Here on Earth	1959	12.50	25.00	50.00
❑ 4442	Pistol Packin' Mama/Anna Annabella	1960	10.00	20.00	40.00
❑ 4525	Mister Loneliness/If You Want My Lovin'	1961	6.25	12.50	25.00
❑ 4665	Lucy Star/Baby Don't Believe Him	1961	6.25	12.50	25.00

CHALLENGE
❑ 59337	Bird Doggin'/Ain't That Too Much	1966	5.00	10.00	20.00
❑ 59347	Lonely Street/I've Got My Eyes on You	1966	5.00	10.00	20.00
❑ 59365	Born to Be a Rolling Stone/Pickin' Poppies	1967	5.00	10.00	20.00

FOREVER
| ❑ 6001 | Story of the Rockers/Pickin' Poppies | 1969 | 12.50 | 25.00 | 50.00 |

KAMA SUTRA
| ❑ 514 | Sunshine/Geese | 1970 | 3.00 | 6.00 | 12.00 |
| ❑ 518 | High On Life/The Day the World Turned Blue | 1971 | 3.00 | 6.00 | 12.00 |

PLAYGROUND
| ❑ 100 | Story of the Rockers/Pickin' Poppies | 1968 | 50.00 | 100.00 | 200.00 |

7-Inch Extended Plays
CAPITOL
❑ EAP 1-764	Bluejean Bop/Jezebel//Jumps,				
	Giggles and Shouts/Ain't She Sweet	1957	37.50	75.00	150.00
❑ EAP 1-764 [PS]	Bluejean Bop! Part 1	1957	37.50	75.00	150.00
❑ EAP 2-764	*Who Slapped John/Wedding Bells/				
	Up a Lazy River/Bop Street	1957	37.50	75.00	150.00
❑ EAP 2-764 [PS]	Bluejean Bop! Part 2	1957	37.50	75.00	150.00
❑ EAP 3-764	*Jump Back, Honey, Jump Back/Waltz of the				
	Wind/I Flipped/Peg o' My Heart	1957	37.50	75.00	150.00
❑ EAP 3-764 [PS]	Bluejean Bop! Part 3	1957	37.50	75.00	150.00
❑ EAP 1-811	Red Blue Jeans and a Ponytail/You Told a Fib/				
	/Hold Me, Hug Me, Rock Me/				
	Unchained Melody	1957	37.50	75.00	150.00
❑ EAP 1-811 [PS]	Gene Vincent and the Blue Caps, Part 1	1957	37.50	75.00	150.00
❑ EAP 2-811	*Cruisin'/You Better Believe/Double Talkin'				
	Baby/Blues Stay Away from Me	1957	37.50	75.00	150.00
❑ EAP 2-811 [PS]	Gene Vincent and the Blue Caps, Part 2	1957	37.50	75.00	150.00
❑ EAP 3-811	*Pink Thunderbird/Pretty, Pretty Baby/				
	Cat Man/I Sure Miss You	1957	37.50	75.00	150.00
❑ EAP 3-811 [PS]	Gene Vincent and the Blue Caps, Part 3	1957	37.50	75.00	150.00
❑ EAP 1-970	*Frankie and Johnnie/In My Dreams/You'll				
	Never Walk Alone/Brand New Beat	1958	37.50	75.00	150.00
❑ EAP 1-970 [PS]	Gene Vincent Rocks!				
	And the Blue Caps Roll, Part 1	1958	37.50	75.00	150.00
❑ EAP 2-970	*By the Light of the Silvery Moon/Flea Brain/				
	Rollin' Danny/Your Cheatin' Heart	1958	37.50	75.00	150.00
❑ EAP 2-970 [PS]	Gene Vincent Rocks!				
	And the Blue Caps Roll, Part 2	1958	37.50	75.00	150.00

Number	Title (A Side/B Side)	Yr	VG	VG+	NM
❏ EAP 3-970	You Belong to Me/Time Will Bring You Everything//Should I Ever Love Again/ It's No Lie	1958	37.50	75.00	150.00
❏ EAP 3-970 [PS]	Gene Vincent Rocks! And the Blue Caps Roll, Part 3	1958	37.50	75.00	150.00
❏ EAP 1-985	Lovely Loretta/Dance to the Bop//Dance in the Street/Baby Blue	1958	50.00	100.00	200.00
❏ EAP 1-985 [PS]	Hot Rod Gang	1958	50.00	100.00	200.00
❏ EAP 1-1059	*Five Feet of Lovin'/The Wayward Wind/Somebody Help Me/Keep It a Secret	1958	37.50	75.00	150.00
❏ EAP 1-1059 [PS]	A Gene Vincent Record Date, Part 1	1958	37.50	75.00	150.00
❏ EAP 2-1059	Git It/Teenage Partner//Hey, Good Lookin'/I Can't Help It	1958	37.50	75.00	150.00
❏ EAP 2-1059 [PS]	A Gene Vincent Record Date, Part 2	1958	37.50	75.00	150.00
❏ EAP 3-1059	I Love You/Peace of Mind//Summertime/Look What You Gone and Done to Me	1958	37.50	75.00	150.00
❏ EAP 3-1059 [PS]	A Gene Vincent Record Date, Part 3	1958	37.50	75.00	150.00
NORTON					
❏ EP-076	My Love (In Love Again)/Lonesome Boy//The Night Is So Lonely/In My Dreams	1999	—	—	2.00
❏ EP-076 [PS]	Blue Gene	1999	—	—	2.00
Albums					
CAPITOL					
❏ DKAO-380 [R]	Gene Vincent's Greatest	1969	12.50	25.00	50.00
❏ SM-380 [R]	Gene Vincent's Greatest	197?	3.75	7.50	15.00
—Abridged reissue of DKAO-380					
❏ T 764 [M]	Bluejean Bop!	1957	100.00	200.00	400.00
—Turquoise label stock copy					
❏ T 764 [M]	Bluejean Bop!	1957	250.00	500.00	1000.
—Black label promo					
❏ T 764 [M]	Bluejean Bop!	1957	250.00	500.00	1000.
—Yellow label promo					
❏ T 811 [M]	Gene Vincent and the Blue Caps	1957	100.00	200.00	400.00
—Turquoise label stock copy					
❏ T 811 [M]	Gene Vincent and the Blue Caps	1957	250.00	500.00	1000.
—Black label promo					
❏ T 811 [M]	Gene Vincent and the Blue Caps	1957	250.00	500.00	1000.
—Yellow label promo					
❏ T 970 [M]	Gene Vincent Rocks! And the Blue Caps Roll	1958	100.00	200.00	400.00
—Turquoise label stock copy					
❏ T 970 [M]	Gene Vincent Rocks! And the Blue Caps Roll	1958	250.00	500.00	1000.
—Black label promo					
❏ T 970 [M]	Gene Vincent Rocks! And the Blue Caps Roll	1958	250.00	500.00	1000.
—Yellow label promo					
❏ T 1059 [M]	A Gene Vincent Record Date	1958	100.00	200.00	400.00
—Turquoise label stock copy					
❏ T 1059 [M]	A Gene Vincent Record Date	1958	250.00	500.00	1000.
—Black label promo					
❏ T 1059 [M]	A Gene Vincent Record Date	1958	250.00	500.00	1000.
—Yellow label promo					
❏ T 1207 [M]	Sounds Like Gene Vincent	1959	75.00	150.00	300.00
—Black label with colorband, Capitol logo at left					
❏ ST 1342 [S]	Crazy Times	1960	125.00	250.00	500.00
—Black label with colorband, Capitol logo at left					
❏ T 1342 [M]	Crazy Times	1960	75.00	150.00	300.00
—Black label with colorband, Capitol logo at left					
❏ SM-11287	The Bop That Just Won't Stop	1974	3.75	7.50	15.00
❏ N-16208	Gene Vincent's Greatest	198?	3.00	6.00	12.00
—Budget-line reissue					
❏ N-16209	The Bop That Just Won't Stop	198?	3.00	6.00	12.00
—Budget-line reissue					
DANDELION					
❏ 9-102	I'm Back and I'm Proud	1970	12.50	25.00	50.00
INTERMEDIA					
❏ QS-5074	Rockabilly Fever	198?	3.00	6.00	12.00
KAMA SUTRA					
❏ KSBS 2019	Gene Vincent	1970	12.50	25.00	50.00
❏ KSBS 2027	The Day the World Turned Blue	1971	12.50	25.00	50.00
ROLLIN' ROCK					
❏ 022	Forever	1981	3.75	7.50	15.00

VINCENT & PESCI The "Pesci" is future movie star Joe Pesci.

45s

Number	Title (A Side/B Side)	Yr	VG	VG+	NM
MAINSTREAM					
❏ 5531	Can You Fix The Way I Talk For Christmas?/Little People Blues	1972	2.50	5.00	10.00

VINEGAR JOE ROBERT PALMER was in this group.

45s

Number	Title (A Side/B Side)	Yr	VG	VG+	NM
ATCO					
❏ 6912	See the World/Circles	1973	2.00	4.00	8.00
❏ 6922	Whole Lotta Shakin' Goin' On/Rock 'n Roll Gypsies	1973	2.00	4.00	8.00
Albums					
ATCO					
❏ SD 7007	Vinegar Joe	1972	3.75	7.50	15.00
❏ SD 7016	Rock 'n Roll Gypsies	1973	3.75	7.50	15.00

VINSON, EDDIE "CLEANHEAD"

45s

Number	Title (A Side/B Side)	Yr	VG	VG+	NM
BETHLEHEM					
❏ 11097	Cherry Red/Kidney Stew	1961	5.00	10.00	20.00
BLUESWAY					
❏ 61005	Cadillac Blues/Old Maid Got Married	1967	3.00	6.00	12.00
KING					
❏ 4563	Good Bread Alley/I Need You Tonight	1952	15.00	30.00	60.00
❏ 4582	Lonesome Train/Person to Person	1952	15.00	30.00	60.00
❏ 6305	Person to Person/Cherry Red Blues	1970	—	3.00	6.00
MERCURY					
❏ 70334	Old Man Boogie/You Can't Have My Love No More	1954	50.00	100.00	200.00
❏ 70525	Anxious Heart/Suffer Fool	1954	30.00	60.00	120.00
❏ 70621	Tomorrow May Never Come/Big Chief Rain in the Face	1955	25.00	50.00	100.00
RIVERSIDE					
❏ 4512	Back Door Blues/Hold It	1962	5.00	10.00	20.00
Albums					
AAMCO					
❏ 312 [M]	Cleanhead's Back in Town	196?	10.00	20.00	40.00

Number	Title (A Side/B Side)	Yr	VG	VG+	NM
BETHLEHEM					
❏ BCP-5005 [M]	Eddie "Cleanhead" Vinson Sings	1957	25.00	50.00	100.00
❏ BCP-6036	Back in Town	1978	3.75	7.50	15.00
BLUESWAY					
❏ BL-6007 [M]	Cherry Red	1967	6.25	12.50	25.00
❏ BLS-6007 [S]	Cherry Red	1967	6.25	12.50	25.00
CIRCLE					
❏ CLP-57	Kidney Stew	1983	3.00	6.00	12.00
DELMARK					
❏ 631	Old Kidney Stew Is Fine	1980	3.00	6.00	12.00
FLYING DUTCHMAN					
❏ 31-1012	You Can't Make Love Alone	197?	3.75	7.50	15.00
KING					
❏ KS-1087	Cherry Red	1969	6.25	12.50	25.00
MUSE					
❏ MR-5116	The Clean Machine	1978	3.75	7.50	15.00
❏ MR-5208	Eddie "Cleanhead" Vinson and the Muse All-Stars: Live at Sandy's	1979	3.00	6.00	12.00
❏ MR-5243	Eddie "Cleanhead" Vinson and the Muse All-Stars: Hold It Right There	198?	3.00	6.00	12.00
❏ MR-5282	Cleanhead and Roomful of Blues	1982	3.00	6.00	12.00
❏ MR-5310	Eddie "Cleanhead" Vinson Sings the Blues	198?	3.00	6.00	12.00
PABLO					
❏ 2310866	I Want a Little Girl	198?	3.00	6.00	12.00
REGGIES					
❏ 1000	Rollin' Over the Devil	1981	3.00	6.00	12.00
RIVERSIDE					
❏ RLP-502 [M]	Back Door Blues	1965	10.00	20.00	40.00
❏ RLS-9502 [S]	Back Door Blues	1965	10.00	20.00	40.00

VINSON, EDDIE "CLEANHEAD"/JIMMY WITHERSPOON Also see each artist's individual listings.

Albums

Number	Title (A Side/B Side)	Yr	VG	VG+	NM
KING					
❏ 634 [M]	Battle of the Blues, Volume 3	1960	375.00	750.00	1500.

VINTON, BOBBY

45s

Number	Title (A Side/B Side)	Yr	VG	VG+	NM
ABC					
❏ 12022	My Melody of Love/I'll Be Loving You	1974	—	2.00	4.00
—Multi-colored label					
❏ 12022	My Melody of Love/I'll Be Loving You	1974	—	2.50	5.00
—Black label					
❏ 12056	Beer Barrel Polka/Dick and Jane	1974	—	2.00	4.00
❏ 12100	Wooden Heart/Polka Pose	1975	—	2.00	4.00
❏ 12131	My Gypsy Love/Midnight Show	1975	—	2.00	4.00
❏ 12178	Moonlight Serenade/Why Can't I Get Over You	1976	—	2.00	4.00
❏ 12186	Save Your Kisses for Me/Love Shine	1976	—	2.00	4.00
❏ 12229	Love Is the Reason/Nobody But Me	1976	—	2.00	4.00
❏ 12265	Only Love Can Break a Heart/Once More with Feeling	1977	—	2.00	4.00
❏ 12293	Hold Me, Thrill Me, Kiss Me/Her Name Is Love	1977	—	2.00	4.00
❏ 12308	All My Todays/Strike Up the Band for Love	1977	—	2.00	4.00
ALPINE					
❏ 50	First Impression/You'll Never Forget	1959	7.50	15.00	30.00
❏ 59	The Sheik/A Freshman and a Sophomore	1960	6.25	12.50	25.00
BOBBY VINTON					
❏ 100	Santa Must Be Polish/Santa Claus Is Coming to Town	1987	—	—	3.00
❏ 100 [PS]	Santa Must Be Polish/Santa Claus Is Coming to Town	1987	—	—	3.00
CURB					
❏ 10512	The Last Rose/Sealed with a Kiss	1988	—	—	3.00
❏ 10541	Please Tell Her That I Said Hello/Getting Used to Being Loved Again	1989	—	—	3.00
❏ 10560	It's Been One of Those Days/(Now and Then There's) A Fool Such As I	1989	—	—	3.00
❏ 76751	The Only Fire That Burns/What Did You Do with Your Old 45's	1990	—	2.00	4.00
DIAMOND					
❏ 121	I Love You the Way You Are/You're My Girl	1962	5.00	10.00	20.00
—B-side by Chuck and Johnny					
ELEKTRA					
❏ 45503	My First, My Only Love/Summerlove Sensation	1978	—	2.00	4.00
EPIC					
❏ 34-06537	Blue Velvet/Blue on Blue	1986	—	2.50	5.00
❏ 9417	Posin'/Tornado	1960	3.75	7.50	15.00
❏ 9440	Corrina, Corrina/Little Lonely One	1961	3.75	7.50	15.00
❏ 9469	Hip-Swinging, High-Stepping, Drum Majorette/Will I Ask Ya	1961	3.75	7.50	15.00
❏ 9509	Roses Are Red (My Love)/You and I	1962	3.00	6.00	12.00
❏ 9509 [PS]	Roses Are Red (My Love)/You and I	1962	3.75	7.50	15.00
—Bobby Vinton looks straight ahead, chin in hand					
❏ 9509 [PS]	Roses Are Red (My Love)/You and I	1962	3.75	7.50	15.00
—Bobby Vinton looks toward the lower right corner					
❏ 9532	Rain, Rain Go Away/Over and Over	1962	3.00	6.00	12.00
❏ 9532 [PS]	Rain, Rain Go Away/Over and Over	1962	3.75	7.50	15.00
❏ 9550	Excerpts from "Roses Are Red"	1962	3.00	6.00	12.00
❏ 9551	Excerpts from "Roses Are Red"	1962	3.00	6.00	12.00
❏ 9552	Excerpts from "Roses Are Red"	1962	3.00	6.00	12.00
❏ 9553	Excerpts from "Roses Are Red"	1962	3.00	6.00	12.00
❏ 9554	Excerpts from "Roses Are Red"	1962	3.00	6.00	12.00
❏ 9561	Trouble Is My Middle Name/Let's Kiss and Make Up	1962	2.50	5.00	10.00
❏ 9561 [PS]	Trouble Is My Middle Name/Let's Kiss and Make Up	1962	3.75	7.50	15.00
❏ 9577	Over the Mountain (Across the Sea)/Faded Pictures	1963	2.50	5.00	10.00
❏ 9577 [PS]	Over the Mountain (Across the Sea)/Faded Pictures	1963	3.75	7.50	15.00
❏ 9593	Blue on Blue/Those Little Things	1963	3.00	6.00	12.00
❏ 9593 [PS]	Blue on Blue/Those Little Things	1963	3.75	7.50	15.00
❏ 9614	Blue Velvet/Is There a Place (Where I Can Go)	1963	3.00	6.00	12.00
❏ 9614 [PS]	Blue Velvet/Is There a Place (Where I Can Go)	1963	3.75	7.50	15.00
❏ 9638	There! I've Said It Again/The Girl with the Bow in Her Hair	1963	3.00	6.00	12.00
❏ 9638 [PS]	There! I've Said It Again/The Girl with the Bow in Her Hair	1963	3.75	7.50	15.00

Number	Title (A Side/B Side)	Yr	VG	VG+	NM
❑ 9662	My Heart Belongs to Only You/Warm and Tender	1964	2.50	5.00	10.00
❑ 9662 [PS]	My Heart Belongs to Only You/Warm and Tender	1964	3.75	7.50	15.00
❑ 9687	Tell Me Why/Remembering	1964	2.00	4.00	8.00
❑ 9687 [PS]	Tell Me Why/Remembering	1964	3.75	7.50	15.00
❑ 9705	Clinging Vine/Imagination Is a Magic Dream	1964	2.00	4.00	8.00
❑ 9705 [PS]	Clinging Vine/Imagination Is a Magic Dream	1964	3.00	6.00	12.00
❑ 9730	Mr. Lonely/It's Better to Have Loved	1964	2.50	5.00	10.00
❑ 9730 [PS]	Mr. Lonely/It's Better to Have Loved	1964	3.00	6.00	12.00
❑ 9741	The Bell That Couldn't Jingle/Dearest Santa	1964	2.50	5.00	10.00
❑ 9768	Long Lonely Nights/Satin	1965	2.00	4.00	8.00
❑ 9768 [PS]	Long Lonely Nights/Satin	1965	3.00	6.00	12.00
❑ 9791	L-O-N-E-L-Y/Graduation Tears	1965	2.00	4.00	8.00
❑ 9791 [PS]	L-O-N-E-L-Y/Graduation Tears	1965	3.00	6.00	12.00
❑ 9814	Theme from "Harlow" (Lonely Girl)/If I Should Lose Your Love	1965	2.00	4.00	8.00
❑ 9814 [PS]	Theme from "Harlow" (Lonely Girl)/If I Should Lose Your Love	1965	3.00	6.00	12.00
❑ 9846	What Color (Is a Man)/Love or Infatuation	1965	2.00	4.00	8.00
❑ 9869	Satin Pillows/Careless	1965	2.00	4.00	8.00
❑ 9869 [PS]	Satin Pillows/Careless	1965	3.00	6.00	12.00
❑ 9894	Tears/Go Away Pain	1966	—	3.00	6.00
❑ 10014	Dum-De-Da/Blue Clarinet	1966	—	3.00	6.00
❑ 10014 [PS]	Dum-De-Da/Blue Clarinet	1966	2.50	5.00	10.00
❑ 10048	Petticoat White (Summer Sky Blue)/All the King's Horses	1966	—	3.00	6.00
❑ 10048 [PS]	Petticoat White (Summer Sky Blue)/All the King's Horses	1966	2.50	5.00	10.00
❑ 10090	Coming Home Soldier/Don't Let My Mary Go Around	1966	—	3.00	6.00
❑ 10090 [PS]	Coming Home Soldier/Don't Let My Mary Go Around	1966	2.50	5.00	10.00
❑ 10136	For He's a Jolly Good Fellow/Sweet Maria	1967	—	3.00	6.00
❑ 10136 [PS]	For He's a Jolly Good Fellow/Sweet Maria	1967	2.50	5.00	10.00
❑ 10168	Red Roses for Mom/College Town	1967	—	3.00	6.00
❑ 10228	Please Love Me Forever/Miss America	1967	2.00	4.00	8.00
❑ 10228 [PS]	Please Love Me Forever/Miss America	1967	2.50	5.00	10.00
❑ 10266	Just As Much As Ever/Another Memory	1967	—	3.00	6.00
❑ 10266 [PS]	Just As Much As Ever/Another Memory	1967	2.50	5.00	10.00
❑ 10305	Take Good Care of My Baby/Strange Sensations	1968	—	3.00	6.00
❑ 10305 [PS]	Take Good Care of My Baby/Strange Sensations	1968	2.50	5.00	10.00
❑ 10350	Halfway to Paradise/(My Little) Christie	1968	—	3.00	6.00
❑ 10350	Halfway to Paradise/(My Little) Kristie	1968	2.50	5.00	10.00
—Note variation in B-side spelling					
❑ 10350 [PS]	Halfway to Paradise/(My Little) Christie	1968	2.50	5.00	10.00
❑ 10397	I Love How You Love Me/Little Barefoot Boy	1968	—	3.00	6.00
❑ 10397 [PS]	I Love How You Love Me/Little Barefoot Boy	1968	2.50	5.00	10.00
❑ 10461	To Know You Is to Love You/The Beat of My Heart	1969	—	2.50	5.00
❑ 10461 [PS]	To Know You Is to Love You/The Beat of My Heart	1969	2.50	5.00	10.00
❑ 10485	The Days of Sand and Shovels/So Many Lonely Girls	1969	—	2.50	5.00
❑ 10485 [PS]	The Days of Sand and Shovels/So Many Lonely Girls	1969	2.50	5.00	10.00
❑ 10554	Where Is Love/For All We Know	1969	—	2.50	5.00
❑ 10576	My Elusive Dreams/Over and Over	1970	—	2.50	5.00
❑ 10576 [PS]	My Elusive Dreams/Over and Over	1970	2.50	5.00	10.00
❑ 10629	No Arms Can Ever Hold You/I've Got That Lovin' Feelin'	1970	—	2.50	5.00
❑ 10629 [PS]	No Arms Can Ever Hold You/I've Got That Lovin' Feelin'	1970	2.00	4.00	8.00
❑ 10651	Why Don't They Understand/Where Is Love	1970	—	2.50	5.00
❑ 10651 [PS]	Why Don't They Understand/Where Is Love	1970	2.00	4.00	8.00
❑ 10689	Christmas Eve in My Home Town/The Christmas Angel	1970	—	3.00	6.00
❑ 10711	She Loves Me/I'll Make You My Baby	1971	—	2.50	5.00
❑ 10736	And I Love You So/She Loves Me	1971	—	2.50	5.00
❑ 10790	A Little Bit of You/God Bless America	1971	—	2.50	5.00
❑ 10822	Every Day of My Life/You Can Do It to Me Anytime	1972	—	2.50	5.00
❑ 10822 [PS]	Every Day of My Life/You Can Do It to Me Anytime	1972	2.00	4.00	8.00
❑ 10861	Sealed with a Kiss/All My Life	1972	—	2.50	5.00
❑ 10861 [PS]	Sealed with a Kiss/All My Life	1972	2.00	4.00	8.00
❑ 10936	But I Do/When You Love	1972	—	2.50	5.00
❑ 10936 [PS]	But I Do/When You Love	1972	2.00	4.00	8.00
❑ 10980	I Love You the Way You Are/Hurt	1973	—	2.50	5.00
❑ 11038	Where Are the Children/I Can't Believe That It's All Over	1973	—	2.50	5.00
❑ 50080	Clinging Vine/I Can't Believe That It's All Over	1975	—	2.50	5.00
❑ 50169	Christmas Eve in My Home Town/The Christmas Angel	1975	—	2.50	5.00
LARC					
❑ 81019	You Are Love/Ghost of Another Man	1983	—	2.50	5.00
MELODY					
❑ 5001/2	Always in My Heart/Harlem Nocturne	1960	6.25	12.50	25.00
TAPESTRY					
❑ 001	Disco Polka (Pennsylvania Polka)/I Could Have Danced All Night	1979	—	2.00	4.00
❑ 002	Make Believe It's Your First Time/I Remember Loving You	1979	—	2.00	4.00
❑ 003	He/My First and Only Love	1980	—	2.00	4.00
❑ 005	It Was Nice to Know You John/Ain't That Lovin' You	1981	—	2.50	5.00
❑ 006	Let Me Love You, Goodbye/You Are Love	1981	—	2.00	4.00
❑ 007	Forever and Ever/Ain't That Lovin' You	1982	—	2.00	4.00
❑ 008	She Will Survive (Poland)/Love Is the Reason	1982	—	2.00	4.00
❑ 008 [PS]	She Will Survive (Poland)/Love Is the Reason	1982	—	2.50	5.00
❑ 010	It Hurts to Be in Love/Love Makes Everything Better	1985	—	2.00	4.00
❑ 013	What Did You Do with Your Old 45s/(B-side unknown)	1986	—	2.00	4.00
❑ 1986	Sweet Lady of Liberty (same on both sides)	1986	—	2.00	4.00
❑ 4009	Bed of Roses/I Know a Goodbye	1984	—	2.00	4.00

Number	Title (A Side/B Side)	Yr	VG	VG+	NM
7-Inch Extended Plays					
ABC					
❑ LLP-271	The Most Beautiful Girl/My Melody of Love/Never Ending Song of Love//You'll Never Know/Am I Losing You/Here in My Heart	1974	2.50	5.00	10.00
—Jukebox issue; small hole, plays at 33 1/3 rpm					
❑ LLP-271 [PS]	Melodies of Love	1974	2.50	5.00	10.00
EPIC					
❑ EG 7215	Silver Bells/White Christmas//O Holy Night/The Christmas Song	1963	2.50	5.00	10.00
❑ EG 7215 [PS]	Songs of Christmas	1963	2.50	5.00	10.00
❑ N7-26081	To Each His Own/You're Nobody 'Til Somebody Loves You/There! I've Said It Again// I Can Dream, Can't I?/Too Young/My Heart Belongs to Only You	196?	2.50	5.00	10.00
—Jukebox issue; small hole, plays at 33 1/3 rpm					
❑ N7-26081 [PS]	There! I've Said It Again	196?	2.50	5.00	10.00
❑ 5-26382	Take Good Care of My Baby/I Apologize/To Think You've Chosen Me//Sentimental Me/Serenade of the Bells/Forget Me Not	1968	2.50	5.00	10.00
—Jukebox issue; small hole, plays at 33 1/3 rpm					
❑ 5-26382 [PS]	Take Good Care of My Baby	1968	2.50	5.00	10.00
❑ 5-26437	If I Didn't Care/Shangri-La/It's No Sin//Why Don't You Believe Me/Together/Save the Last Dance for Me	1968	2.50	5.00	10.00
—Jukebox issue; small hole, plays at 33 1/3 rpm					
❑ 5-26437 [PS]	I Love How You Love Me	1968	2.50	5.00	10.00
❑ 7-31642	Our Day Will Come/Song Sung Blue/Come Softly to Me//Some Kind of Wonderful/Somebody's Breaking My Heart/I'm Leaving It Up to You	1972	2.50	5.00	10.00
—Jukebox issue; small hole, plays at 33 1/3 rpm					
❑ 7-31642 [PS]	Sealed with a Kiss	1972	2.50	5.00	10.00
Albums					
ABC					
❑ X-851	Melodies of Love	1974	2.50	5.00	10.00
❑ D-891	Heart of Hearts	1975	2.50	5.00	10.00
❑ D-924	The Bobby Vinton Show	1975	2.50	5.00	10.00
❑ D-957	Serenades of Love	1976	2.50	5.00	10.00
❑ AB-981	The Name Is Love	1977	2.50	5.00	10.00
COLUMBIA LIMITED EDITION					
❑ LE 10016	Big Ones	197?	2.50	5.00	10.00
❑ LE 10052	Please Love Me Forever	197?	2.50	5.00	10.00
❑ LE 10139	Roses Are Red	197?	2.50	5.00	10.00
❑ LE 10140	Blue Velvet	197?	2.50	5.00	10.00
—Reissue of Epic 26068					
COLUMBIA MUSICAL TREASURY					
❑ 6P 6035 [(6)]	The Bobby Vinton Treasury	197?	7.50	15.00	30.00
—"Columbia House" logo on upper right back cover					
EPIC					
❑ BN 579 [S]	Dancing at the Hop	1961	12.50	25.00	50.00
❑ BN 597 [S]	Young Man with a Big Band	1961	12.50	25.00	50.00
❑ LN 3727 [M]	Dancing at the Hop	1961	7.50	15.00	30.00
❑ LN 3780 [M]	Young Man with a Big Band	1961	7.50	15.00	30.00
❑ LN 24020 [M]	Roses Are Red	1962	3.75	7.50	15.00
❑ LN 24035 [M]	Bobby Vinton Sings the Big Ones	1962	3.75	7.50	15.00
❑ LN 24049 [M]	The Greatest Hits of the Greatest Groups	1963	3.75	7.50	15.00
❑ LN 24068 [M]	Blue Velvet	1963	3.75	7.50	15.00
—Retitled version of "Blue On Blue"					
❑ LN 24068 [M]	Blue On Blue	1963	6.25	12.50	25.00
—Stock copy on black vinyl					
❑ LN 24068 [M]	Blue On Blue	1963	37.50	75.00	150.00
—Promo only on blue vinyl					
❑ LN 24081 [M]	There! I've Said It Again	1964	3.75	7.50	15.00
❑ LN 24098 [M]	Bobby Vinton's Greatest Hits	1964	3.00	6.00	12.00
—Despite lower number, this came out after "Tell Me Why"					
❑ LN 24113 [M]	Tell Me Why	1964	3.00	6.00	12.00
❑ LN 24122 [M]	A Very Merry Christmas	1964	3.00	6.00	12.00
❑ LN 24136 [M]	Mr. Lonely	1965	3.00	6.00	12.00
❑ LN 24154 [M]	Bobby Vinton Sings for Lonely Nights	1965	3.00	6.00	12.00
❑ LN 24170 [M]	Drive-In Movie Time	1965	3.00	6.00	12.00
❑ LN 24182 [M]	Satin Pillows and Careless	1966	3.00	6.00	12.00
❑ LN 24187 [M]	More of Bobby Vinton's Greatest Hits	1966	3.00	6.00	12.00
❑ LN 24188 [M]	Country Boy	1966	3.00	6.00	12.00
❑ LN 24203 [M]	Live at the Copa	1967	3.00	6.00	12.00
❑ LN 24245 [M]	Bobby Vinton's Newest Hits	1967	3.00	6.00	12.00
❑ LN 24341 [M]	Please Love Me Forever	1967	3.75	7.50	15.00
❑ BN 26020 [S]	Roses Are Red	1962	5.00	10.00	20.00
❑ BN 26035 [S]	Bobby Vinton Sings the Big Ones	1962	5.00	10.00	20.00
❑ BN 26049 [S]	The Greatest Hits of the Greatest Groups	1963	5.00	10.00	20.00
❑ BN 26068 [S]	Blue Velvet	1963	5.00	10.00	20.00
—Retitled version of "Blue On Blue"					
❑ BN 26068 [S]	Blue On Blue	1963	7.50	15.00	30.00
❑ BN 26081 [S]	There! I've Said It Again	1964	5.00	10.00	20.00
❑ BN 26098 [S]	Bobby Vinton's Greatest Hits	1964	3.75	7.50	15.00
—Despite lower number, this came out after "Tell Me Why"					
❑ PE 26098	Bobby Vinton's Greatest Hits	198?	2.00	4.00	8.00
—Budget-line reissue					
❑ BN 26113 [S]	Tell Me Why	1964	3.75	7.50	15.00
❑ BN 26122 [S]	A Very Merry Christmas	1964	3.75	7.50	15.00
❑ BN 26136 [S]	Mr. Lonely	1965	3.75	7.50	15.00
❑ BN 26154 [S]	Bobby Vinton Sings for Lonely Nights	1965	3.75	7.50	15.00
❑ BN 26170 [S]	Drive-In Movie Time	1965	3.75	7.50	15.00
❑ BN 26182 [S]	Satin Pillows and Careless	1966	3.75	7.50	15.00
❑ BN 26187 [S]	More of Bobby Vinton's Greatest Hits	1966	3.75	7.50	15.00
❑ BN 26188 [S]	Country Boy	1966	3.75	7.50	15.00
❑ BN 26203 [S]	Live at the Copa	1967	3.75	7.50	15.00
❑ BN 26245 [S]	Bobby Vinton's Newest Hits	1967	3.75	7.50	15.00
❑ BN 26341 [S]	Please Love Me Forever	1967	3.75	7.50	15.00
❑ BN 26382	Take Good Care of My Baby	1968	3.75	7.50	15.00
❑ BN 26437	I Love How You Love Me	1968	3.75	7.50	15.00
❑ BN 26471	Vinton	1969	3.75	7.50	15.00
❑ BN 26503	Bobby Vinton's Greatest Hits of Love	1970	3.75	7.50	15.00
❑ BN 26540	My Elusive Dreams	1970	3.75	7.50	15.00
❑ KE 31286	Ev'ry Day of My Life	1972	3.00	6.00	12.00
❑ KEG 31487 [(2)]	Bobby Vinton's All-Time Greatest Hits	1972	3.75	7.50	15.00
❑ PEG 31487 [(2)]	Bobby Vinton's All-Time Greatest Hits	197?	3.00	6.00	12.00
—Reissue					
❑ KE 31642	Sealed with a Kiss	1972	3.00	6.00	12.00
❑ PE 32921	With Love	1974	2.50	5.00	10.00

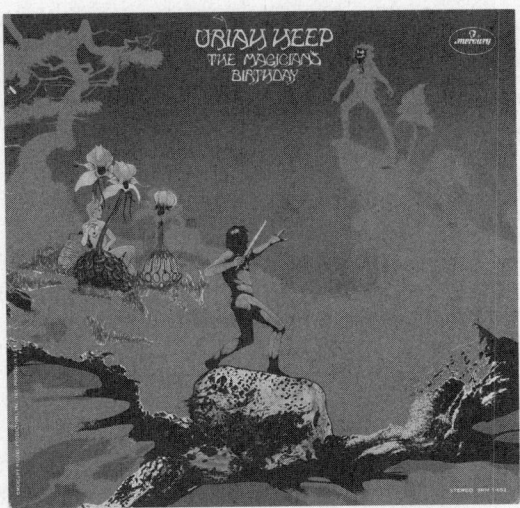

Uriah Heep, *The Magician's Birthday*, Mercury SRM-1-652, stereo LP, $5-$10.

Frankie Valli, "To Give (The Reason I Live)," Philips 40510, picture sleeve, $7.50-$15.

Sarah Vaughan, *The Divine Sarah*, Mercury MG 25188, 10-inch LP, $50-$100.

Bobby Vee, "Rubber Ball," Liberty 55287, picture sleeve, $15-$30.

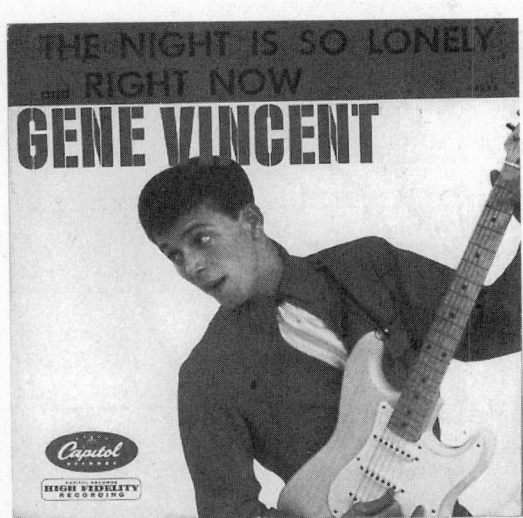

Gene Vincent, "The Night Is So Lonely," Capitol F4237, picture sleeve, $1,000-$2,000.

Bobby Vinton, "Mr. Lonely," Epic 5-9730, picture sleeve, $6-$12.

Number	Title (A Side/B Side)	Yr	VG	VG+	NM
☐ KEG 38468 [(2)]	Bobby Vinton Sings the Golden Decade of Love	1975	3.00	6.00	12.00
☐ KEG 33767 [(2)]	Greatest Hits/Greatest Hits of Love	1976	3.00	6.00	12.00
☐ JE 35605	Autumn Memories	1979	2.50	5.00	10.00
☐ JE 35998	Spring Sensations	1979	2.50	5.00	10.00
☐ JE 35999	Summer Serenade	1979	2.50	5.00	10.00
HARMONY					
☐ KH 11402	Vinton Sings Vinton.	197?	2.50	5.00	10.00
PICKWICK					
☐ SPC-3353	Melodies of Love	197?	2.00	4.00	8.00
TAPESTRY					
☐ TRS-1001 [EP]	Santa Must Be Polish	1987	2.50	5.00	10.00

VIPERS SKIFFLE GROUP, THE
45s
CAPITOL

Number	Title (A Side/B Side)	Yr	VG	VG+	NM
☐ F3673	Don't You Rock Me Daddy-O/10,000 Years Ago	1957	5.00	10.00	20.00
☐ F3711	Cumberland Gap/Maggie Mae	1957	3.75	7.50	15.00

VIRGIN INSANITY
Albums
FUNKY

Number	Title	Yr	VG	VG+	NM
☐ 71411	Illusions of the Maintenance Man	1970	50.00	100.00	200.00

VIRTUES, THE Includes records by "Frank Virtue" and "Frank Virtuoso."
45s
ABC-PARAMOUNT

Number	Title (A Side/B Side)	Yr	VG	VG+	NM
☐ 10071	Blues in the Cellar/Vaya Con Dios	1959	3.75	7.50	15.00
ARCADE					
☐ 135	Ooh You Gotta/I Make a Mistake	1955	7.50	15.00	30.00
—As "Frank Virtue"					
FAYETTE					
☐ 1626	Guitar Boogie Shuffle '65/Moon Maid	1965	3.75	7.50	15.00
HIGHLAND					
☐ 2505	Bye Bye Blues/Happy Guitar	1960	6.25	12.50	25.00
☐ 2505X	Bye Bye Blues/Strollin' Again	1960	6.25	12.50	25.00
HUNT					
☐ 324 [M]	Guitar Boogie Shuffle/Guitar in Orbit	1959	6.25	12.50	25.00
☐ S-324 [S]	Guitar Boogie Shuffle/Guitar in Orbit	1959	12.50	25.00	50.00
☐ 327	Flippin' In/Shufflin' Along	1959	5.00	10.00	20.00
☐ 328	Pickin' the Stroll/Virtue's Boogie Woogie	1959	5.00	10.00	20.00
☐ 329	Pony Walk/Virtue's Boogie Woogie	1959	5.00	10.00	20.00
☐ 331	Blues in the Cellar/Vaya Con Dios	1960	5.00	10.00	20.00
LIBERTY					
☐ 55706	Dream World/Move On	1964	3.00	6.00	12.00
—As "Frank Virtuoso"					
SURE					
☐ 501	Guitar Boogie Shuffle/Guitar in Orbit	1959	20.00	40.00	80.00
☐ 1733	Guitar Boogie Shuffle Twist/Guitar Boogie Stomp	1962	3.75	7.50	15.00
☐ 1779	Tel-Star Guitar/Jersey Bounce	1962	3.75	7.50	15.00
VIRNON					
☐ 603	Guitar Boogie Twist/Guitar Shimmy	1960	3.75	7.50	15.00
VIRTUE					
☐ 190	Cotton Candy/Love You	1966	2.50	5.00	10.00
☐ 2503	Guitar on the Wild Side/Meditation of the Soul	1970	—	3.00	6.00
WYNNE					
☐ 123	Highland Guitar/Pickin' Plankin' Boogie	1960	3.75	7.50	15.00
Albums					
FAYETTE					
☐ 1816 [M]	Frank Virtue and the Virtues	1964	10.00	20.00	40.00
—White cover					
☐ 1816 [M]	Frank Virtue and the Virtues	1964	15.00	30.00	60.00
—Blue cover					
STRAND					
☐ L-1061 [M]	Guitar Boogie Shuffle	1960	7.50	15.00	30.00
☐ SL-1061 [S]	Guitar Boogie Shuffle	1960	10.00	20.00	40.00
WYNNE					
☐ WLP-111 [M]	Guitar Boogie Shuffle	1960	30.00	60.00	120.00
☐ WLP-711 [S]	Guitar Boogie Shuffle	1960	45.00	90.00	180.00

VISCAYNES, THE Sylvester Stewart [Sly Stone] was a member.
45s
TROPO

Number	Title (A Side/B Side)	Yr	VG	VG+	NM
☐ 101	I Guess I'll Be/Stop What You're Doing.	1958	37.50	75.00	150.00
VPM					
☐ 1006	Yellow Moon/Heavenly Angel	1961	10.00	20.00	40.00

VISCOUNTS, THE (1)
45s
AMY

Number	Title (A Side/B Side)	Yr	VG	VG+	NM
☐ 940	Harlem Nocturne/Dig	1965	3.00	6.00	12.00
☐ 949	Night Train/When the Saints Go Marching In	1966	3.00	6.00	12.00
CORAL					
☐ 62490	Come, Come On Back/Off Shore	1966	2.50	5.00	10.00
☐ 62520	Moonlight in Vermont/Sweet Georgia Brown	1967	2.50	5.00	10.00
MADISON					
☐ 123	Harlem Nocturne/Dig	1959	6.25	12.50	25.00
☐ 129	The Touch/Chug-a-Lug	1960	3.75	7.50	15.00
☐ 133	Night Train/Summertime	1960	3.75	7.50	15.00
☐ 140	Wabash Blues/So Slow	1960	3.75	7.50	15.00
☐ 152	Shadrack/This Place	1961	3.75	7.50	15.00
☐ 159	Little Brown Jug/Opus One	1961	3.75	7.50	15.00
☐ 165	Drag Race/Sophisticated Lady	1961	3.75	7.50	15.00
MR. PEACOCK					
☐ 101	When Johnny Comes Marching Home/Mark's Mood	1961	3.00	6.00	12.00
☐ 107	The Continental Walk/Hully Gully	1962	3.00	6.00	12.00
☐ 112	Night Flight/A Girl Like You	1962	3.00	6.00	12.00
MR. PEEKE					
☐ 125	Night for Love/Ballin' the Jack	1963	3.00	6.00	12.00
Albums					
AMY					
☐ 8008 [M]	Harlem Nocturne	1965	10.00	20.00	40.00
☐ S-8008 [S]	Harlem Nocturne	1965	12.50	25.00	50.00
MADISON					
☐ 1001 [M]	The Viscounts	1960	50.00	100.00	200.00

VISCOUNTS, THE (2)
45s
MERCURY

Number	Title (A Side/B Side)	Yr	VG	VG+	NM
☐ 71073	My Girl/Raindrop	1957	10.00	20.00	40.00

VISION OF SUNSHINE
Albums
AVCO EMBASSY

Number	Title	Yr	VG	VG+	NM
☐ 33007	Vision of Sunshine	1970	7.50	15.00	30.00

VISIONS, THE Several different groups.
45s
BIG TOP

Number	Title (A Side/B Side)	Yr	VG	VG+	NM
☐ 3092	Tell Me You're Mine/All Through the Night	1961	5.00	10.00	20.00
☐ 3119	Secret Worlds of Tears/Swingin' Wedding	1962	5.00	10.00	20.00
BRUNSWICK					
☐ 55206	So Close/There'll Be No Next Time	1961	6.25	12.50	25.00
COED					
☐ 598	Down in My Heart/Tell Her Now	1964	3.00	6.00	12.00
ELGEY					
☐ 1003	Teenager's Life/Little Moon	1960	10.00	20.00	40.00
LOST-NITE					
☐ 102	Teenager's Life/Little Moon	196?	—	3.00	6.00
—Yellow label with "street lamp" logo					
☐ 102	Teenager's Life/Little Moon	1961	6.25	12.50	25.00
—Original pressing on pink label with no "street lamp" logo					
MERCURY					
☐ 72188	Oh Boy What a Girl/Tommy's Girl	1963	3.75	7.50	15.00
ORIGINAL SOUND					
☐ 32	Look at Me Now/Cigarette	1963	3.75	7.50	15.00
UNI					
☐ 55031	How Can I Be Down/Threshold of Love	1967	3.00	6.00	12.00
☐ 55042	Keepin' Your Eyes on the Sun/Small Town Commotion	1967	3.00	6.00	12.00
WARNER BROS.					
☐ 5898	Black and White Rainbow/Bulldog Cadillac	1967	2.50	5.00	10.00

VISITORS, THE (1)
45s
DAKAR

Number	Title (A Side/B Side)	Yr	VG	VG+	NM
☐ 603	I'm in Danger/Until You Came Along	1969	2.00	4.00	8.00
☐ 613	I'm Gonna Stay/Lonely One, Only Son	1969	2.00	4.00	8.00
TANGERINE					
☐ 1003	My Love Is Ready and Waiting/What About Me	1970	2.00	4.00	8.00
☐ 1010	Anytime Is the Right Time/Nevertheless	1970	2.00	4.00	8.00

VISITORS, THE (2)
45s
TOWER

Number	Title (A Side/B Side)	Yr	VG	VG+	NM
☐ 268	Theme from The Wild Angels/Is It Them or Me	1966	3.75	7.50	15.00

VISTAS, THE
45s
REBEL

Number	Title (A Side/B Side)	Yr	VG	VG+	NM
☐ 77755	Ghost Wave/Surfer's Minuet	1963	12.50	25.00	50.00
VENPRO					
☐ 1000	Ghost Wave/Surfer's Minuet	1963	20.00	40.00	80.00

VISUALS, THE
45s
POPLAR

Number	Title (A Side/B Side)	Yr	VG	VG+	NM
☐ 115	The Submarine Race/Maybe You	1962	10.00	20.00	40.00
☐ 117	My Juanita/A Girl, and a Dream	1963	12.50	25.00	50.00
☐ 121	Please Don't Be Mad at Me/Blue Enough to Cry	1963	75.00	150.00	300.00

VITALE, JOE
45s
ASYLUM

Number	Title (A Side/B Side)	Yr	VG	VG+	NM
☐ 47169	Never Gonna Leave You Alone/Theme from Cabin Weirdos	1981	—	2.00	4.00
☐ 47210	The Lady on the Rock (It's America)/Plantation Harbor	1981	—	2.00	4.00
☐ 47251	Man Gonna Love You/I'm Flyin'	1981	—	2.00	4.00
ATLANTIC					
☐ 3204	Roller Coaster Weekend/Take a Chance on Love	1974	—	2.00	4.00
☐ 3260	Two of Us/Shot 'Em Up	1975	—	2.00	4.00
Albums					
ASYLUM					
☐ 5E-529	Plantation Harbor	1981	2.50	5.00	10.00
ATLANTIC					
☐ SD 18114	Rollercoaster Weekend	1975	2.50	5.00	10.00

VITELLS, THE
45s
DECCA

Number	Title (A Side/B Side)	Yr	VG	VG+	NM
☐ 31362	Shirley/The Dip	1962	7.50	15.00	30.00

VITO, SONNY
45s
ABC-PARAMOUNT

Number	Title (A Side/B Side)	Yr	VG	VG+	NM
☐ 9958	Cameo Ring/Teen-Age Blues	1958	3.00	6.00	12.00
STRAND					
☐ 25045	An Angel Cries/Mister Groovy	1961	3.00	6.00	12.00

VITO AND THE SALUTATIONS
45s
APT

Number	Title (A Side/B Side)	Yr	VG	VG+	NM
☐ 25079	High Noon/Walkin'	1965	12.50	25.00	50.00
BOOM					
☐ 60020	Bring Back Yesterday/I Want You to Be My Baby	1966	5.00	10.00	20.00
CRYSTAL BALL					
☐ 105	Unchained Melody/So Much	1978	—	2.50	5.00
HAROLD					
☐ 5009	Gloria/Let's Untwist the Twist	1962	12.50	25.00	50.00
HERALD					
☐ 583	Unchained Melody/Hey Hey Baby	1963	7.50	15.00	30.00

Number	Title (A Side/B Side)	Yr	VG	VG+	NM
❑ 586	Eenie Meenie/Extraordinary Girl	1964	6.25	12.50	25.00
KRAM					
❑ 5002	Your Way/Hey, Hey Baby	1962	12.50	25.00	50.00
LOST-NITE					
❑ 429	Unchained Melody/Hey Hey Baby	197?	—	2.50	5.00
—Reissue					
RAYNA					
❑ 5009	Gloria/Let's Untwist the Twist	1962	12.50	25.00	50.00
RED BOY					
❑ 1001	So Wonderful (My Love)/I'd Best Be Going	1966	6.25	12.50	25.00
❑ 5009	Gloria/Let's Untwist the Twist	1962	7.50	15.00	30.00
REGINA					
❑ 1320	Get a Job/Girls I Know	1964	7.50	15.00	30.00
RUST					
❑ 5106	Can I Depend on You/Hello Dolly	1966	5.00	10.00	20.00
SANDBAG					
❑ 103	So Wonderful (My Love)/I'd Best Be Going	1966	5.00	10.00	20.00
WELLS					
❑ 1008	Can I Depend on You/Liverpool Bound	1964	6.25	12.50	25.00
❑ 1008	Can I Depend on You/Liverpool Bound	1964	12.50	25.00	50.00
—Yellow vinyl					
❑ 1010	The Banana Boat Song (Day-O)/ Don't Count on Me	1964	6.25	12.50	25.00

VOCALEERS, THE Possibly more than one group.
45s

Number	Title (A Side/B Side)	Yr	VG	VG+	NM
LOST-NITE					
❑ 333	Be True/Oh! Where	197?	—	2.50	5.00
—Reissue					
❑ 336	Is It a Dream/Hurry Home	197?	—	2.50	5.00
—Reissue					
❑ 339	I Walk Alone/How Soon	197?	—	2.50	5.00
—Reissue					
❑ 342	Will You Be True/Love You	197?	—	2.50	5.00
—Reissue					
❑ 346	Angel Face/Lovin' Baby	197?	—	2.50	5.00
—Reissue					
OLD TOWN					
❑ 1089	This Is the Night/Love and Devotion	1960	6.25	12.50	25.00
PARADISE					
❑ 113	I Need Your Love So Bad/ Have You Ever Loved Someone	1959	10.00	20.00	40.00
RED ROBIN					
❑ 113	Be True/Oh! Where	1953	150.00	300.00	600.00
❑ 114	Is It a Dream/Hurry Home	1953	75.00	150.00	300.00
❑ 119	I Walk Alone/How Soon	1953	100.00	200.00	400.00
❑ 125	Will You Be True/Love You	1954	75.00	150.00	300.00
❑ 132	Angel Face/Lovin' Baby	1954	75.00	150.00	300.00
TWISTIME					
❑ 11	Cootie Snap/A Golden Tear	1962	7.50	15.00	30.00
VEST					
❑ 832	Hear My Plea/The Night Is Quiet	1960	20.00	40.00	80.00

VOGUES, THE Also see THE VAL-AIRES.
45s

Number	Title (A Side/B Side)	Yr	VG	VG+	NM
ABC-PARAMOUNT					
❑ 10672	Big Man/Golden Locket	1965	5.00	10.00	20.00
ASTRA					
❑ 1029	You're the One/Goodnight My Love	1973	—	2.50	5.00
❑ 1030	Five O'Clock World/Land of Milk and Honey	1973	—	2.50	5.00
BELL					
❑ 991	Love Song/We're On Our Way	1971	—	2.50	5.00
❑ 45127	Take Time to Tell Her/I'll Be with You	1971	—	2.50	5.00
❑ 45158	An American Family/Gotta Have You Back	1971	—	2.50	5.00
BLUE STAR					
❑ 229	You're the One/Some Words	1965	6.25	12.50	25.00
CO & CE					
❑ 229	You're the One/Some Words	1965	3.00	6.00	12.00
❑ 232	Five O'Clock World/Nothing to Offer You	1965	3.00	6.00	12.00
❑ 234	Magic Town/Humpty Dumpty	1966	2.50	5.00	10.00
❑ 238	The Land of Milk and Honey/True Lovers	1966	2.50	5.00	10.00
❑ 240	Please Mr. Sun/Don't Blame the Rain	1966	2.50	5.00	10.00
❑ 242	That's the Tune/Midnight Dreams	1966	2.50	5.00	10.00
❑ 244	Take a Chance on My Heart/Summer Afternoon	1967	2.50	5.00	10.00
❑ 246	Brighter Days/Lovers of the World Unite	1967	2.50	5.00	10.00
MAINSTREAM					
❑ 5524	Need You/(B-side unknown)	1972	—	2.50	5.00
MGM					
❑ 13813	Brighter Days/Lovers of the World Unite	1967	2.00	4.00	8.00
REPRISE					
❑ 0663	I've Got You on My Mind/ Just What I've Been Looking For	1968	2.50	5.00	10.00
❑ 0686	Turn Around, Look at Me/Then	1968	2.00	4.00	8.00
❑ 0731	Turn Around, Look at Me/My Special Angel	1969	—	2.50	5.00
—"Back to Back Hits" series					
❑ 0736	No, Not Much/Earth Angel (Will You Be Mine)	1970	—	2.50	5.00
—"Back to Back Hits" series					
❑ 0741	Five O'Clock World/Magic Town	1970	—	3.00	6.00
—"Back to Back Hits" series; "Five O'Clock World" has overdubbed strings					
❑ 0766	My Special Angel/I Keep It Hid	1968	2.00	4.00	8.00
❑ 0788	Till/I Will	1968	2.00	4.00	8.00
❑ 0803	Woman Helping Man/No, Not Much	1969	—	3.00	6.00
❑ 0803	Woman Helping Man/I'll Know My Love	1969	2.00	4.00	8.00
❑ 0820	Earth Angel (Will You Be Mine)/P.S. I Love You	1969	—	3.00	6.00
❑ 0831	Moments to Remember/Once in a While	1969	—	3.00	6.00
❑ 0844	Green Fields/Easy to Say	1969	—	3.00	6.00
❑ 0856	See That Girl/If We Only Have Love	1969	—	3.00	6.00
❑ 0887	God Only Knows/Moody	1970	—	3.00	6.00
❑ 0909	Over the Rainbow/ Hey, That's No Way to Say Goodbye	1970	—	3.00	6.00
❑ 0931	50's Medley/Come Into My Arms	1970	—	3.00	6.00
❑ 0969	Since I Don't Have You/I Know You as a Woman	1970	—	3.00	6.00
20TH CENTURY					
❑ 2041	My Prayer/I've Got to Learn to Live Without You	1973	—	2.50	5.00
❑ 2060	Wonderful Summer/Guess Who	1973	—	2.50	5.00
❑ 2085	As Time Goes By/Prisoner of Love	1974	—	2.50	5.00

Albums

Number	Title (A Side/B Side)	Yr	VG	VG+	NM
CO & CE					
❑ LP-1229 [M]	Meet the Vogues	1965	12.50	25.00	50.00
❑ LP-1230 [M]	Five O'Clock World	1966	12.50	25.00	50.00
—Stereo pressings of these two albums are not known to exist!					
PICKWICK					
❑ SPC-3188 [R]	Five O'Clock World	1971	2.50	5.00	10.00
❑ SPC-3214 [R]	A Lover's Concerto	1971	2.50	5.00	10.00
REPRISE					
❑ RS 6314	Turn Around, Look at Me	1968	3.75	7.50	15.00
—With "W7" and "r:" logos on two-tone orange label					
❑ RS 6326	Till	1969	3.75	7.50	15.00
—With "W7" and "r:" logos on two-tone orange label					
❑ RS 6347	Memories	1969	3.75	7.50	15.00
—With "W7" and "r:" logos on two-tone orange label					
❑ RS 6371	The Vogues' Greatest Hits	1969	3.75	7.50	15.00
—With "W7" and "r:" logos on two-tone orange label					
❑ RS 6395	The Vogues Sing the Good Old Songs	1970	3.00	6.00	12.00
❑ ST-91559	Turn Around, Look at Me	1968	5.00	10.00	20.00
—Capitol Record Club edition					
❑ SW-93040	The Vogues' Greatest Hits	1970	5.00	10.00	20.00
—Capitol Record Club edition					
SSS INTERNATIONAL					
❑ 34	The Vogues' Greatest Hits	1977	2.50	5.00	10.00

VOGUES, THE (2) No relation to the more famous group above.
45s

Number	Title (A Side/B Side)	Yr	VG	VG+	NM
DOT					
❑ 15798	Love Is a Funny Little Game/Which Witch Doctor	1958	6.25	12.50	25.00
❑ 15859	Try, Baby. Try/Falling Star	1958	6.25	12.50	25.00

VOGUES, THE (U) Definitely not group (1); could be group (2).
45s

Number	Title (A Side/B Side)	Yr	VG	VG+	NM
CASCADE					
❑ 5908	Ev'ry Day, Ev'ry Night/Now I Lay Me Down to Cry	1959	5.00	10.00	20.00

VOICE MASTERS, THE LAMONT DOZIER and DAVID RUFFIN were originally in this group, though they did not appear on the later sides.
45s

Number	Title (A Side/B Side)	Yr	VG	VG+	NM
ANNA					
❑ 101	Hope and Pray/Oop's I'm Sorry	1959	50.00	100.00	200.00
❑ 102	Needed/Needed (For Lovers Only)	1959	50.00	100.00	200.00
BAMBOO					
❑ 103	You've Hurt Me Baby/If a Woman Catches a Fool	1968	6.25	12.50	25.00
❑ 105	Never Gonna Leave You/ If a Woman Catches a Fool	1969	3.75	7.50	15.00
❑ 113	Dance Right Into My Heart/ If a Woman Catches a Fool	1970	3.75	7.50	15.00
FRISCO					
❑ 15235	In Love in Vain/Two Lovers	196?	25.00	50.00	100.00

VOICES, THE
45s

Number	Title (A Side/B Side)	Yr	VG	VG+	NM
CASH					
❑ 1011	Why/Two Things I Love	1955	15.00	30.00	60.00
❑ 1014	Hey Now/My Love Grows Stronger	1955	15.00	30.00	60.00
❑ 1015	I Want to Be Ready/Takes Two to Make a Home	1955	15.00	30.00	60.00
❑ 1016	Santa Claus Boogie/Santa Claus Baby	1955	20.00	40.00	80.00
❑ 1016	Santa Claus Boogie/Santa Claus Baby	197?	—	2.50	5.00
—Reproduction					
SPECIALTY					
❑ 754	Santa Claus Boogie/Santa Claus Baby	197?	3.75	7.50	15.00
—Red vinyl					

VOICES OF EAST HARLEM, THE
45s

Number	Title (A Side/B Side)	Yr	VG	VG+	NM
ELEKTRA					
❑ 45753	Sit Yourself Down/Oxford Town	1971	—	3.00	6.00
❑ 45775	Angry/New York Lightning	1972	—	3.00	6.00
JUST SUNSHINE					
❑ 504	Giving Love/New Vibrations	1973	—	2.50	5.00
❑ 510	I Like Having You Around/Cashing In	1973	—	2.50	5.00
❑ 517	Can You Feel It/Wanted Dead or Alive	1974	—	2.50	5.00
Albums					
ELEKTRA					
❑ EKS-74080	Right On Be Free	1970	2.50	5.00	10.00
JUST SUNSHINE					
❑ 7	Voices of East Harlem	1973	2.50	5.00	10.00
❑ 3504	Can You Feel It?	1974	2.50	5.00	10.00

VOIGHT, WES
45s

Number	Title (A Side/B Side)	Yr	VG	VG+	NM
DELUXE					
❑ 6176	Midnight Blues/Another Guy's Line	1958	25.00	50.00	100.00
❑ 6180	I Want a Lover/Little Joan	1958	10.00	20.00	40.00
KING					
❑ 5211 [M]	I'm Loving It/Everything's the Same	1959	15.00	30.00	60.00
❑ S-5211 [S]	I'm Loving It/Everything's the Same	1959	50.00	100.00	200.00
❑ 5231 [M]	I'm Ready to Go Steady/ The Wind and the Cold Black Night	1959	10.00	20.00	40.00
❑ S-5231 [S]	I'm Ready to Go Steady/ The Wind and the Cold Black Night	1959	25.00	50.00	100.00

VOLCANICS, THE
45s

Number	Title (A Side/B Side)	Yr	VG	VG+	NM
PARKWAY					
❑ 149	Your Kind of Loving/But I Love Her	1967	3.75	7.50	15.00

VOLCANOES, THE
45s

Number	Title (A Side/B Side)	Yr	VG	VG+	NM
EPIC					
❑ 9490	Shotgun/Stardust	1962	3.00	6.00	12.00

VOLCANOS, THE Early version of THE TRAMMPS.
45s

Number	Title (A Side/B Side)	Yr	VG	VG+	NM
ARCTIC					
❑ 103	Make Your Move/Baby	1965	3.00	6.00	12.00
❑ 106	Storm Warning/Baby	1965	3.00	6.00	12.00
❑ 111	Help Wanted/Make Your Move	1965	3.00	6.00	12.00

Number	Title (A Side/B Side)	Yr	VG	VG+	NM
❑ 115	(It's Against the) Laws of Love/(Instrumental)	1965	3.00	6.00	12.00
—With correct song title as above					
❑ 115	(It's Against the) Rules of Love/(Instrumental)	1965	75.00	150.00	300.00
—With erroneous song title as above					
❑ 125	Lady's Man/Help Wanted	1966	2.50	5.00	10.00
❑ 128	You're Number 1/Make Your Move	1967	2.50	5.00	10.00

VOLK, VAL, AND THE MATCHED ACES
45s
ROCKET

Number	Title (A Side/B Side)	Yr	VG	VG+	NM
❑ 1050	A Rockin' Party Tonight/Spring Time Rock	195?	50.00	100.00	200.00

VOLUMES, THE
45s
AMERICAN ARTS

Number	Title (A Side/B Side)	Yr	VG	VG+	NM
❑ 6	Gotta Give Her Love/I Can't Live Without You	1964	7.50	15.00	30.00
❑ 18	I Just Can't Help Myself/One Way Lover	1965	7.50	15.00	30.00
CHEX					
❑ 1002	I Love You/Dreams	1962	6.25	12.50	25.00
—With "Nationally Dist. by Jay-Gee Rec. Co. Inc." on label					
❑ 1002	I Love You/Dreams	1962	10.00	20.00	40.00
—With no reference to Jay-Gee Records on label					
❑ 1002	I Love You/Dreams	1962	75.00	150.00	300.00
—With typographical error crediting "The Valumes"					
❑ 1005	Come Back Into My Heart/The Bell	1962	10.00	20.00	40.00
IMPACT					
❑ 1017	That Same Old Feeling/The Trouble I've Seen	1966	12.50	25.00	50.00
INFERNO					
❑ 2001	A Way to Love You/You Got It Baby	1967	5.00	10.00	20.00
❑ 2004	My Road Is the Right Road/My Kind of Girl	1967	5.00	10.00	20.00
❑ 5001	Ain't That Lovin' You/I Love You Baby	1968	5.00	10.00	20.00
JUBILEE					
❑ 5446	Sandra/Teenage Paradise	1963	5.00	10.00	20.00
❑ 5454	Our Song/Oh My Mother-in-Law	1963	5.00	10.00	20.00
KAREN					
❑ 1551	Am I Losing You/Ain't Gonna Give You Up	1970	2.00	4.00	8.00
OLD TOWN					
❑ 1154	Why/Monkey Hop	1964	6.25	12.50	25.00

VONDELLS, THE
45s
AIRTOWN CUSTOM

Number	Title (A Side/B Side)	Yr	VG	VG+	NM
❑ (# unknown)	Hey Girl You've Changed/(B-side unknown)	196?	375.00	750.00	1500.

VONNS, THE
45s
KING

Number	Title (A Side/B Side)	Yr	VG	VG+	NM
❑ 5793	Leave Us Alone/So Many Days	1963	5.00	10.00	20.00

VONTASTICS, THE
45s
CHESS

Number	Title (A Side/B Side)	Yr	VG	VG+	NM
❑ 2024	Why Must We Part/I Will Always Love You	1967	3.75	7.50	15.00
MOON SHOT					
❑ 4702	Lady Love/When My Baby Comes Back Home	1967	7.50	15.00	30.00
ST. LAWRENCE					
❑ 1007	Peace of Mind/No Love for Me	1966	3.75	7.50	15.00
❑ 1009	I Need You/Keep On Rolling	1966	5.00	10.00	20.00
❑ 1014	Day Tripper/My Baby	1966	5.00	10.00	20.00
❑ 1023	You Can Work It Out/Never Let Your Love Grow Cold	1967	3.75	7.50	15.00
SATELLITE					
❑ 2002	I'll Never Say Goodbye/Don't Mess Around	1965	30.00	60.00	120.00
TODDLIN' TOWN					
❑ 115	Let Me Down Easy/I'm the One You Need	1968	6.25	12.50	25.00

VOWS, THE
45s
MARKAY

Number	Title (A Side/B Side)	Yr	VG	VG+	NM
❑ 103	I Wanna Chance/Have You Heard	1962	10.00	20.00	40.00
—Black label					
❑ 103	I Wanna Chance/Have You Heard	1962	100.00	200.00	400.00
—Orange label					
RAN-DEE					
❑ 112	Girl in Red/Born with the Rhythm	196?	15.00	30.00	60.00
STA-SET					
❑ 402	Say You'll Be Mine/When a Boy Loves a Girl	1963	15.00	30.00	60.00
TAMARA					
❑ 506	The Things You Do to Me/Dottie	1963	10.00	20.00	40.00
❑ 760	Say You'll Be Mine/When a Boy Loves a Girl	1964	6.25	12.50	25.00
V.I.P.					
❑ 25016	Buttered Popcorn/Tell Me	1965	10.00	20.00	40.00

VOXPOPPERS, THE
45s
AMP 3

Number	Title (A Side/B Side)	Yr	VG	VG+	NM
❑ 1004	Wishing for Your Love/The Last Drag	1958	10.00	20.00	40.00
MERCURY					
❑ 71282	Wishing for Your Love/The Last Drag	1958	5.00	10.00	20.00
❑ 71315	Pony Tail/Ping Pong Baby	1958	5.00	10.00	20.00
POPLAR					
❑ 107	Come Back Little Girl/A Love to Last a Lifetime	1959	5.00	10.00	20.00
VERSAILLES					
❑ 200	Can't Understand It/A Blessing After All	1959	7.50	15.00	30.00
WARWICK					
❑ 589	Lonely for You/Helen Isn't Tellin'	1960	3.00	6.00	12.00
—As "Freddie and the Voxpoppers"					

7-Inch Extended Plays
MERCURY

Number	Title (A Side/B Side)	Yr	VG	VG+	NM
❑ EP 1-3391	Wishing for Your Love/The Last Drag//Stroll Roll/Guitar Stroll	1958	25.00	50.00	100.00
❑ EP 1-3391 [PS]	The Voxpoppers	1958	25.00	50.00	100.00

VY-DELLS, THE
45s
GARNET

Number	Title (A Side/B Side)	Yr	VG	VG+	NM
❑ 101	What I'm Gonna Do/Unknown	196?	25.00	50.00	100.00

W

WADE, ADAM
45s
COED

Number	Title (A Side/B Side)	Yr	VG	VG+	NM
❑ 520	Tell Her for Me/Don't Cry, My Love	1959	3.00	6.00	12.00
❑ 526	Ruby/Too Far	1960	3.00	6.00	12.00
❑ 530	I Can't Help It/I Had the Craziest Dream	1960	3.00	6.00	12.00
❑ 536	Speaking of Her/Black Out the Moon	1960	3.00	6.00	12.00
❑ 536 [PS]	Speaking of Her/Black Out the Moon	1960	5.00	10.00	20.00
❑ 539	For the Want of Your Love/In Pursuit of Happiness	1960	3.00	6.00	12.00
❑ 541	Gloria's Theme/Dreamy	1960	3.00	6.00	12.00
❑ 541 [PS]	Gloria's Theme/Dreamy	1960	3.75	7.50	15.00
❑ 546	Take Good Care of Her/Sleepy Time Gal	1961	2.50	5.00	10.00
❑ 546	Take Good Care of Her/Too Far	1961	3.00	6.00	12.00
❑ 550	The Writing on the Wall/Point of No Return	1961	2.50	5.00	10.00
❑ 550 [PS]	The Writing on the Wall/Point of No Return	1961	3.75	7.50	15.00
❑ 553	As If I Didn't Know/Playin' Around	1961	2.50	5.00	10.00
❑ 553 [PS]	As If I Didn't Know/Playin' Around	1961	3.75	7.50	15.00
❑ 556	Tonight I Won't Be There/Linda	1961	2.50	5.00	10.00
❑ 556 [PS]	Tonight I Won't Be There/Linda	1961	3.75	7.50	15.00
❑ 560	Cold Cold Winter/Preview of Paradise	1961	2.50	5.00	10.00
❑ 565	How Are Things in Lover's Lane/It's Good to Have You Back with Me	1962	2.50	5.00	10.00
❑ 566	Them There Eyes/Prisoner's Song	1962	3.75	7.50	15.00
❑ 567	Little Miss Lovely/For the First Time in My Life	1962	2.50	5.00	10.00
EPIC					
❑ 9521	I'm Climbin' (The Wall)/They Didn't Believe Me	1962	2.00	4.00	8.00
❑ 9521 [PS]	I'm Climbin' (The Wall)/They Didn't Believe Me	1962	6.25	12.50	25.00
❑ 9557	There'll Be No Teardrops Tonight/Here Comes the Pain	1962	2.00	4.00	8.00
❑ 9557 [PS]	There'll Be No Teardrops Tonight/Here Comes the Pain	1962	6.25	12.50	25.00
❑ 9566	Don't Let Me Cross Over/Rain from the Skies	1963	2.00	4.00	8.00
❑ 9590	Teenage Mona Lisa/Why Do We Have to Wait So Long	1963	2.00	4.00	8.00
❑ 9609	Let's Make the Most of a Beautiful Thing/Theme from "Irma La Douce" (Look Again)	1963	2.00	4.00	8.00
❑ 9639	Charade/Does Goodnight Mean Goodbye	1963	2.00	4.00	8.00
❑ 9659	Seven Loves for Seven Days/Whisper Away	1964	2.00	4.00	8.00
❑ 9686	Love Song from "Flight to Ashiya"/Pencil and Paper	1964	2.00	4.00	8.00
❑ 9752	Crying in the Chapel/Broken Hearted Stranger	1964	2.00	4.00	8.00
❑ 9771	It's Been a Long Time Comin'/A Lover's Question	1965	2.00	4.00	8.00
❑ 9808	Garden in the Rain/Play Some Music for Broken Hearts	1965	2.00	4.00	8.00
❑ 9840	Garden of Eden/Time for Dreams	1965	2.00	4.00	8.00
❑ 10024	How Can I Leave You/Solitude	1966	—	3.00	6.00
❑ 10112	A Man Alone/Wheels on the Highway	1966	—	3.00	6.00
KIRSHNER					
❑ 4272	Russell Never Had a Chance/Keeping Up with the Joneses	1977	—	2.00	4.00
REMEMBER					
❑ 7791	Half the World/My Time for Love	1969	—	3.00	6.00
WARNER BROS.					
❑ 7068	Julie on My Mind/With an Exception	1967	—	3.00	6.00
❑ 7179	Everybody Is Looking for That Someone/Maybe	1968	—	3.00	6.00
❑ 7225	Old Devil Woman/Rome	1968	—	3.00	6.00

Albums
COED

Number	Title (A Side/B Side)	Yr	VG	VG+	NM
❑ LPC-902 [M]	And Then Came Adam	1960	12.50	25.00	50.00
❑ LPCS-902 [S]	And Then Came Adam	1960	15.00	30.00	60.00
❑ LPC-903 [M]	Adam and Evening	1961	12.50	25.00	50.00
❑ LPCS-903 [S]	Adam and Evening	1961	15.00	30.00	60.00
EPIC					
❑ LN 24019 [M]	Adam Wade's Greatest Hits	1962	6.25	12.50	25.00
❑ LN 24026 [M]	One Is a Lonely Number	1962	6.25	12.50	25.00
❑ LN 24044 [M]	What Kind of Fool Am I?	1963	6.25	12.50	25.00
❑ LN 24056 [M]	A Very Good Year for Girls	1963	6.25	12.50	25.00
❑ BN 26019 [S]	Adam Wade's Greatest Hits	1962	7.50	15.00	30.00
❑ BN 26026 [S]	One Is a Lonely Number	1962	7.50	15.00	30.00
❑ BN 26044 [S]	What Kind of Fool Am I?	1963	7.50	15.00	30.00
❑ BN 26056 [S]	A Very Good Year for Girls	1963	7.50	15.00	30.00
KIRSHNER					
❑ PZ 34919	Adam Wade	1977	3.00	6.00	12.00

WADE, BILLY, AND THE 3 DEGREES
45s
ABC

Number	Title (A Side/B Side)	Yr	VG	VG+	NM
❑ 45-10991	Tear It Up (Part 1)/Tear It Up (Part 2)	1967	2.50	5.00	10.00

WADE, DON
45s
SAN

Number	Title (A Side/B Side)	Yr	VG	VG+	NM
❑ 206	Gone, Gone, Gone/(B-side unknown)	1958	75.00	150.00	300.00
❑ 207	Forever Yours/Oh Love	1958	7.50	15.00	30.00

WADE, RONNY
45s
KING

Number	Title (A Side/B Side)	Yr	VG	VG+	NM
❑ 5061	Gotta Make Her Mine/Let Me Cry	1957	20.00	40.00	80.00
❑ 5078	I Know But I'll Never Tell/I Never Fall in Love Again	1957	12.50	25.00	50.00
❑ 5099	Annie Don't Work/I'll Sail My Ship Alone	1958	12.50	25.00	50.00
❑ 5112	All I Want/A King and a Vow	1958	12.50	25.00	50.00

WADE AND DICK
45s
SUN

Number	Title (A Side/B Side)	Yr	VG	VG+	NM
❑ 269	Bop Bop Baby/Don't Need Your Lovin' Baby	1957	7.50	15.00	30.00

Number	Title (A Side/B Side)	Yr	VG	VG+	NM

WADSWORTH MANSION
45s
SUSSEX

Number	Title (A Side/B Side)	Yr	VG	VG+	NM
❏ 209	Sweet Mary/What's On Tonight	1970	—	3.00	6.00

—Later pressings have a short version of A-side

| ❏ 209 | Sweet Mary/What's On Tonight | 1970 | 2.00 | 4.00 | 8.00 |

—First pressings have a much longer version of A-side

❏ 215	Havin' Such a Good Time/				
	Michigan Harry Slaughter	1971	—	2.50	5.00
❏ 221	Nine on the Line/Queenie Dew	1971	—	2.50	5.00

Albums
SUSSEX

| ❏ SXBS-7008 | Wadsworth Mansion | 1971 | 5.00 | 10.00 | 20.00 |
| ❏ SXBS-7008 | Wadsworth Manison | 1971 | 6.25 | 12.50 | 25.00 |

—Some copies of this LP have the above typographical error

WAGNER, DANNY, AND KINDRED SOUL
45s
IMPERIAL

❏ 66305	I Lost a True Love/My Buddy	1968	7.50	15.00	30.00
❏ 66327	Harlem Shuffle/When Johnny Comes Marching				
	Home	1968	5.00	10.00	20.00

Albums
IMPERIAL

| ❏ LP-12405 | The Kindred Soul of Danny Wagner | 1968 | 7.50 | 15.00 | 30.00 |

WAGNER, DAVID See CROW.

WAGNER, DICK, AND THE FROSTS See THE FROST.

WAGONER, PORTER Also see PORTER WAGONER AND DOLLY PARTON.
45s
RCA

❏ PB-10803	When Lea Jane Sang/Storm of Love	1976	—	2.00	4.00
❏ PB-10974	I Haven't Learned a Thing/Hand Me Down My				
	Walking Cane	1977	—	2.00	4.00

—A-side with Merle Haggard

❏ PB-11186	Mountain Music/Natural Wonder	1977	—	2.00	4.00
❏ PB-11411	Ole Slew Foot/I'm Gonna Feed 'Em Now	1978	—	2.00	4.00
❏ PB-11491	I Want to Walk You Home/Old Love Letter	1979	—	2.00	4.00
❏ PB-11671	Everything I've Always Wanted/No Bed of Roses	1979	—	2.00	4.00
❏ PB-11771	Hold On Tight/Someone Just Like You	1979	—	2.00	4.00
❏ PB-11998	Is It Only 'Cause You're Lonely/				
	When She Was Mine	1980	—	2.00	4.00

RCA VICTOR

❏ 47-4996	Settin' the Woods on Fire/Headin' for a Weddin'	1952	7.50	15.00	30.00
❏ 47-5086	Takin' Chances/I Can't Live with You	1952	7.50	15.00	30.00
❏ 47-5215	That's It/Don't Play That Song	1953	6.25	12.50	25.00
❏ 47-5330	Trademark/A Beggar for Your Love	1953	6.25	12.50	25.00
❏ 47-5430	Bringing Home the Bacon/An Angel Made for				
	Love	1953	6.25	12.50	25.00
❏ 47-5527	Flame of Love/Dig That Crazy Moon	1953	6.25	12.50	25.00
❏ 47-5631	Trinidad/Bad News Travels Fast	1954	6.25	12.50	25.00
❏ 47-5754	Be Glad You Ain't Me/Love at First Sight	1954	6.25	12.50	25.00
❏ 47-5848	Company's Comin'/Tricks of the Trade	1954	6.25	12.50	25.00
❏ 47-6030	Hey, Maw/How Quick	1955	6.25	12.50	25.00
❏ 47-6105	A Satisfied Mind/Itchin' for My Baby	1955	5.00	10.00	20.00
❏ 47-6289	Eat, Drink and Be Merry (Tomorrow You'll Cry)/				
	Let's Squiggle	1955	5.00	10.00	20.00
❏ 47-6421	What Would You Do? (If Jesus Came to Your				
	House)/How Can You Refuse Him Now	1956	5.00	10.00	20.00
❏ 47-6494	Uncle Pen/How I've Tried	1956	5.00	10.00	20.00
❏ 47-6598	Tryin' to Forget the Blues/				
	I've Known You from Somewhere	1956	5.00	10.00	20.00
❏ 47-6803	I'm Day Dreamin' Tonight/I Should Be with You	1957	5.00	10.00	20.00
❏ 47-6844	Good Mornin', Neighbor/Who Will He Be	1957	5.00	10.00	20.00
❏ 47-6964	I Thought I Heard You Call My Name/Pay Day	1957	5.00	10.00	20.00
❏ 47-7073	Doll Face/Your Love	1957	5.00	10.00	20.00
❏ 47-7199	Tomorrow We'll Retire/				
	Heaven's Just a Prayer Away	1958	3.75	7.50	15.00
❏ 47-7279	Haven't You Heard/				
	Tell Her Lies and Feed Her Candy	1958	3.75	7.50	15.00
❏ 47-7374	Just Before Dawn/Dear Lonesome	1958	3.75	7.50	15.00
❏ 47-7457	Me and Fred and Joe and Bill/				
	Out of Sight, Out of Mind	1959	3.75	7.50	15.00
❏ 47-7532	I'm Gonna Sing/I Thought of God	1959	3.75	7.50	15.00
❏ 47-7568	The Battle of Little Big Horn/Our Song of Love	1959	3.75	7.50	15.00
❏ 47-7638	The Girl Who Didn't Need Love/				
	Your Kind of People	1959	3.75	7.50	15.00
❏ 47-7708	Legend of the Big Steeple/Wakin' Up the Crowd	1960	3.75	7.50	15.00
❏ 47-7770	Falling Again/An Old Log Cabin for Sale	1960	3.75	7.50	15.00
❏ 47-7837	Your Old Love Letters/Heartbreak Affair	1961	3.00	6.00	12.00
❏ 47-7901	Everything She Touches Gets the Blues/				
	Sugar Foot Rag	1961	3.00	6.00	12.00
❏ 47-7967	Misery Loves Company/I Cried Again	1961	3.00	6.00	12.00
❏ 47-8026	Cold Dark Waters/Ain't It Awful	1962	3.00	6.00	12.00
❏ 47-8105	I've Enjoyed As Much of This As I Can Stand/				
	One Way Ticket to the Blues	1962	3.00	6.00	12.00
❏ 47-8178	My Baby's Not Here (In Town Tonight)/In the				
	Shadows of the Wine	1963	3.00	6.00	12.00
❏ 47-8257	Howdy Neighbor Howdy/Fed Out	1963	3.00	6.00	12.00
❏ 47-8338	Sorrow on the Rocks/The Life of the Party	1964	3.00	6.00	12.00
❏ 47-8432	I'll Go Down Swinging/				
	Country Music Has Gone to Town	1964	3.00	6.00	12.00
❏ 47-8524	I'm Gonna Feed You Now/The Bride's Bouquet	1965	2.50	5.00	10.00
❏ 47-8622	Green, Green Grass of Home/Dooley	1965	2.50	5.00	10.00
❏ 47-8723	Skid Row Joe/Love Your Neighbor	1965	2.50	5.00	10.00
❏ 47-8800	I Just Came to Smell the Flowers/				
	I'm a Long Way from Home	1966	2.50	5.00	10.00
❏ 47-8882	I Dreamed I Saw America on Her Knees/				
	When I Reach That City	1966	2.50	5.00	10.00
❏ 47-8977	Old Slew-Foot/Let Me In	1966	2.50	5.00	10.00
❏ 47-9067	The Cold Hard Facts of Life/				
	You Can't Make a Heel Toe the Mark	1967	2.50	5.00	10.00
❏ 47-9243	Julie/Try Being Lonely	1967	2.50	5.00	10.00
❏ 47-9379	Woman Hungry/Out of the Silence				
	(Came a Song)	1967	2.50	5.00	10.00
❏ 47-9530	Be Proud of Your Man/Wino	1968	2.00	4.00	8.00
❏ 47-9651	The Carroll County Accident/				
	Sorrow Overtakes the Wine	1968	2.00	4.00	8.00
❏ 47-9802	You Got-Ta Have a License/Fairchild	1970	—	3.00	6.00
❏ 47-9811	Little Boy's Prayer/Roses Out of Season	1970	—	3.00	6.00
❏ 47-9895	Jim Johnson/One More Dime	1970	—	3.00	6.00
❏ 47-9939	The Last One to Touch Me/The Alley	1970	—	3.00	6.00
❏ 47-9979	Charley's Picture/As Simple As I Am	1971	—	3.00	6.00
❏ 48-1007	Be a Little Quieter/Watching	1971	—	3.00	6.00
❏ 74-0168	Big Wind/Tennessee Stud	1969	2.00	4.00	8.00
❏ 74-0267	When You're Hot You're Hot/The Answer Is Love	1969	2.00	4.00	8.00
❏ 74-0581	The Rubber Room/Late Love of Mine	1971	—	3.00	6.00
❏ 74-0648	What Ain't to Be, Just Might Happen/Little Bird	1972	—	3.00	6.00
❏ 74-0753	A World Without Music/Denise Mayree	1972	—	3.00	6.00
❏ 74-0820	Katy Did/Darlin' Debra Jean	1972	—	3.00	6.00
❏ 74-0923	Lightening the Load/Tomorrow Is Forever	1973	—	3.00	6.00
❏ 47-6697	Seeing Her Only Reminded Me of You/				
	A Good Time Was Had by All	1956	5.00	10.00	20.00
❏ 47-7158	Turn It Over in Your Mind/				
	As Long As I'm Dreaming	1958	3.75	7.50	15.00
❏ APBO-0013	Wake Up, Jacob/Stella, Dear Sweet Stella	1973	—	2.50	5.00
❏ APBO-0187	George Leory Chickashea/Cassie	1973	—	2.50	5.00
❏ APBO-0233	Tore Down/Nothing Between	1974	—	2.50	5.00
❏ APBO-0328	Highway Headin' South/Freda	1974	—	2.50	5.00
❏ PB-10124	Carolina Moonshiner/Not a Cloud in the Sky	1974	—	2.50	5.00
❏ PB-10281	It's My Time (To Say I Love You)/				
	Just for the Lonely Ones	1975	—	3.00	6.00
❏ PB-10411	Indian Creek/Thank You for the Happiness	1975	—	2.50	5.00

WARNER BROS.

❏ 29772	This Cowboy's Hat/She Don't Have a License to				
	Drive Me Up the Wall	1983	—	—	3.00
❏ 29875	Turn the Pencil Over/Texas Moonbeam Waltz	1982	—	2.00	4.00

—B-side by Johnny Gimble/Texas Swing Band

7-Inch Extended Plays
RCA VICTOR

❏ EPA-937	A Satisfied Mind/I Like Girls//Living in the Past/				
	Midnight	1956	6.25	12.50	25.00
❏ EPA-937 [PS]	Satisfied Mind	1956	6.25	12.50	25.00
❏ VLP 3389	My Baby Turns the Lights On Uptown/Dim				
	Lights, Thick Smoke and Loud Music/I'll Go				
	Down Swinging//My Friends Are Gonna Be				
	Strangers/Lovin' Lies/Sorrow on the Rocks	1965	3.75	7.50	15.00

—Jukebox issue; small hole, plays at 33 1/3 rpm

| ❏ VLP 3389 [PS] | The Thin Man from West Plains | 1965 | 3.75 | 7.50 | 15.00 |

Albums
ACCORD

| ❏ SN-7179 | Down Home Country | 1982 | 3.00 | 6.00 | 12.00 |

DOT/MCA

| ❏ 39053 | Porter Wagoner | 1986 | 2.50 | 5.00 | 10.00 |

RCA CAMDEN

❏ CAL-769 [M]	A Satisfied Mind	1963	3.00	6.00	12.00
❏ CAS-769(e) [R]	A Satisfied Mind	1963	2.50	5.00	10.00
❏ CAL-861 [M]	An Old Log Cabin for Sale	1965	3.00	6.00	12.00
❏ CAS-861 [S]	An Old Log Cabin for Sale	1965	3.00	6.00	12.00
❏ CAL-942 [M]	"Your Old Love Letters" And Other Country Hits	1966	3.00	6.00	12.00
❏ CAS-942 [S]	"Your Old Love Letters" And Other Country Hits	1966	3.00	6.00	12.00
❏ CAL-2116 [M]	I'm Day Dreamin' Tonight	1967	3.00	6.00	12.00
❏ CAS-2116 [S]	I'm Day Dreamin' Tonight	1967	3.00	6.00	12.00
❏ CAL-2191 [M]	Green, Green Grass of Home	1967	3.00	6.00	12.00
❏ CAS-2191 [S]	Green, Green Grass of Home	1967	3.00	6.00	12.00
❏ CAS-2321	Country Feeling	1968	3.00	6.00	12.00
❏ CAS-2409	Howdy Neighbor	1970	3.00	6.00	12.00
❏ CAS-2478	Porter Wagoner Country	1971	3.00	6.00	12.00
❏ CAS-2588	The Silent Kind	1972	3.00	6.00	12.00
❏ CXS-9010 [(2)]	Blue Moon of Kentucky	1971	3.75	7.50	15.00

RCA VICTOR

❏ APL1-0142	I'll Keep on Lovin' You	1973	3.75	7.50	15.00
❏ APL1-0346	The Farmer	1974	3.75	7.50	15.00
❏ APL1-0496	Tore Down	1974	3.75	7.50	15.00
❏ APL1-0713	Highway Headin' South	1974	3.75	7.50	15.00
❏ APL1-1056	Sing Love	1975	3.75	7.50	15.00
❏ ANL1-1213	The Best of Porter Wagoner	1975	3.00	6.00	12.00
❏ LPM-1358 [M]	A Satisfied Mind	1956	50.00	100.00	200.00
❏ AHL1-2432	Porter	1977	3.00	6.00	12.00
❏ LPM-2447 [M]	A Slice of Life — Songs Happy 'N' Sad	1962	6.25	12.50	25.00
❏ LSP-2447 [S]	A Slice of Life — Songs Happy 'N' Sad	1962	7.50	15.00	30.00
❏ LPM-2650 [M]	The Porter Wagoner Show	1963	6.25	12.50	25.00
❏ LSP-2650 [S]	The Porter Wagoner Show	1963	7.50	15.00	30.00
❏ LPM-2706 [M]	Y'All Come	1963	6.25	12.50	25.00
❏ LSP-2706 [S]	Y'All Come	1963	7.50	15.00	30.00
❏ LPM-2840 [M]	In Person	1964	6.25	12.50	25.00
❏ LSP-2840 [S]	In Person	1964	7.50	15.00	30.00
❏ LPM-2960 [M]	The Bluegrass Story	1964	5.00	10.00	20.00
❏ LSP-2960 [S]	The Bluegrass Story	1964	6.25	12.50	25.00
❏ LPM-3389 [M]	The Thin Man from West Plains	1965	5.00	10.00	20.00
❏ LSP-3389 [S]	The Thin Man from West Plains	1965	6.25	12.50	25.00
❏ LPM-3488 [M]	Grand Old Gospel	1966	6.25	12.50	25.00
❏ LSP-3488 [S]	Grand Old Gospel	1966	5.00	10.00	20.00
❏ LPM-3509 [M]	On the Road	1966	5.00	10.00	20.00
❏ LSP-3509 [S]	On the Road	1966	6.25	12.50	25.00
❏ LPM-3560 [M]	The Best of Porter Wagoner	1966	5.00	10.00	20.00
❏ LSP-3560 [S]	The Best of Porter Wagoner	1966	6.25	12.50	25.00
❏ LPM-3593 [M]	Confessions of a Broken Man	1966	5.00	10.00	20.00
❏ LSP-3593 [S]	Confessions of a Broken Man	1966	6.25	12.50	25.00
❏ LPM-3683 [M]	Soul of a Convict	1967	6.25	12.50	25.00
❏ LSP-3683 [S]	Soul of a Convict	1967	5.00	10.00	20.00
❏ LPM-3797 [M]	The Cold Hard Facts of Life	1967	6.25	12.50	25.00
❏ LSP-3797 [S]	The Cold Hard Facts of Life	1967	5.00	10.00	20.00
❏ LPM-3855 [M]	More Grand Old Gospel	1967	6.25	12.50	25.00
❏ LSP-3855 [S]	More Grand Old Gospel	1967	5.00	10.00	20.00
❏ LPM-3968 [M]	The Bottom of the Bottle	1968	25.00	50.00	100.00
❏ LSP-3968 [S]	The Bottom of the Bottle	1968	5.00	10.00	20.00
❏ LSP-4034	Gospel Country	1968	5.00	10.00	20.00
❏ LSP-4116	The Carroll County Accident	1969	5.00	10.00	20.00
❏ LSP-4181	Me and My Boys	1969	5.00	10.00	20.00
❏ LSP-4286	You Got-ta Have a License	1970	5.00	10.00	20.00
❏ LSP-4321	The Best of Porter Wagoner, Volume 2	1970	5.00	10.00	20.00
❏ LSP-4386	Down in the Alley	1970	5.00	10.00	20.00

Number	Title (A Side/B Side)	Yr	VG	VG+	NM
❑ LSP-4508	Simple As I Am	1971	5.00	10.00	20.00
❑ LSP-4586	Porter Wagoner Sings His Own	1971	3.75	7.50	15.00
❑ LSP-4661	What Ain't to Be	1972	3.75	7.50	15.00
❑ LSP-4734	Ballads of Love	1972	3.75	7.50	15.00
❑ LSP-4810	The Porter Wagoner Experience	1973	3.75	7.50	15.00
❑ AHL1-7000	Collector's Series	1985	2.50	5.00	10.00

WARNER BROS.

Number	Title (A Side/B Side)	Yr	VG	VG+	NM
❑ 23783	Viva Porter Wagoner!	1983	2.50	5.00	10.00

WAGONER, PORTER, AND SKEETER DAVIS Also see each artist's individual listings.
Albums

RCA VICTOR

Number	Title (A Side/B Side)	Yr	VG	VG+	NM
❑ LPM-2529 [M]	Porter Wagoner and Skeeter Davis Sing Duets	1962	6.25	12.50	25.00
❑ LSP-2529 [S]	Porter Wagoner and Skeeter Davis Sing Duets	1962	7.50	15.00	30.00

WAGONER, PORTER, AND DOLLY PARTON Also see each artist's individual listings.
45s

FREEDOM TRAIN

Number	Title (A Side/B Side)	Yr	VG	VG+	NM
❑ 5767	Here Comes the Freedom Train/ All Aboard America	1973	25.00	50.00	100.00

—B-side by Porter Wagoner solo; special promotional record for the American Freedom Train Foundation

RCA

Number	Title (A Side/B Side)	Yr	VG	VG+	NM
❑ PB-11983	Making Plans/Beneath the Sweet Magnolia Trees	1980	—	2.00	4.00
❑ PB-12119	If You Go, I'll Follow You/Hide Me Away	1980	—	2.00	4.00

RCA VICTOR

Number	Title (A Side/B Side)	Yr	VG	VG+	NM
❑ 47-9369	The Last Thing on My Mind/Love Is Worth Living	1967	2.00	4.00	8.00
❑ 47-9490	Holding On to Nothing/Just Between You and Me	1968	2.00	4.00	8.00
❑ 47-9577	We'll Get Ahead Someday/ Jeannie's Afraid of the Dark	1968	2.00	4.00	8.00
❑ 47-9799	Tomorrow Is Forever/Mandy Never Sleeps	1969	—	3.00	6.00
❑ 47-9875	Daddy Was An Old Time Preacher Man/Good Understanding	1970	—	3.00	6.00
❑ 47-9958	Better Move It On Home/Two of a Kind	1971	—	3.00	6.00
❑ 47-9994	The Right Combination/The Part of Loving You	1971	—	3.00	6.00
❑ 74-0104	Malena/Yours, Love	1969	—	3.00	6.00
❑ 74-0172	Always, Always/No Need to Hurry Home	1969	—	3.00	6.00
❑ 74-0247	Just Someone I Used to Know/ My Hands Are Tied	1969	—	3.00	6.00
❑ 74-0565	Burning the Midnight Oil/More Than Words Can Tell	1971	—	3.00	6.00
❑ 74-0675	Lost Forever in Your Kiss/The Fog Has Lifted	1972	—	2.50	5.00
❑ 74-0773	Together Always/Love's All Over	1972	—	2.50	5.00
❑ 74-0893	We Found It/Lord Have Mercy on Us	1973	—	2.50	5.00
❑ 74-0981	If Teardrops Were Pennies/Come to Me	1973	—	2.50	5.00
❑ PB-10010	Please Don't Stop Loving Me/Sounds of Nature	1974	—	2.00	4.00
❑ PB-10328	Say Forever You'll Be Mine/How Can I Help You Forgive Me	1975	—	2.00	4.00
❑ GB-10506	Please Don't Stop Loving Me/Sounds of Nature	1975	—	2.00	4.00

—Gold Standard Series

Number	Title (A Side/B Side)	Yr	VG	VG+	NM
❑ PB-10652	Is Forever Longer Than Always/If You Say I Can	1976	—	2.00	4.00
❑ GB-10675	Say Forever You'll Be Mine/ How Can I Help You Forgive Me	1976	—	2.00	4.00

—Gold Standard Series

Albums

PAIR

Number	Title (A Side/B Side)	Yr	VG	VG+	NM
❑ PDL1-1013 [(2)]	Sweet Harmony	1986	3.00	6.00	12.00

RCA VICTOR

Number	Title (A Side/B Side)	Yr	VG	VG+	NM
❑ APL1-0248	Love and Music	1973	3.75	7.50	15.00
❑ APL1-0646	Porter 'N' Dolly	1974	3.75	7.50	15.00
❑ APL1-1116	Say Forever	1975	3.75	7.50	15.00
❑ AHL1-3700	Porter Wagoner and Dolly Parton	1980	3.00	6.00	12.00
❑ LPM-3926 [M]	Just Between You and Me	1968	25.00	50.00	100.00
❑ LSP-3926 [S]	Just Between You and Me	1968	5.00	10.00	20.00
❑ LSP-4039	Just the Two of Us	1968	5.00	10.00	20.00
❑ LSP-4186	Always, Always	1969	5.00	10.00	20.00
❑ AYL1-4251	Porter Wagoner and Dolly Parton	1982	2.00	4.00	8.00

—"Best Buy Series" reissue

Number	Title (A Side/B Side)	Yr	VG	VG+	NM
❑ LSP-4305	Porter Wayne and Dolly Rebecca	1970	5.00	10.00	20.00
❑ LSP-4388	Once More	1970	5.00	10.00	20.00
❑ LSP-4490	Two of a Kind	1971	5.00	10.00	20.00
❑ AHL1-4556	The Best of Porter Wagoner and Dolly Parton	1983	2.50	5.00	10.00
❑ LSP-4556	The Best of Porter Wagoner and Dolly Parton	1971	5.00	10.00	20.00
❑ LSP-4628	The Right Combination/Burning the Midnight Oil	1972	3.75	7.50	15.00
❑ LSP-4761	Together Always	1972	3.75	7.50	15.00
❑ LSP-4841	We Found It	1973	3.75	7.50	15.00

WAIKIKIS, THE
45s

KAPP

Number	Title (A Side/B Side)	Yr	VG	VG+	NM
❑ KJB-30	Hawaii Tattoo/Tahiti Tamoure	1964	2.00	4.00	8.00
❑ KJB-52	Hawaii Honeymoon/Remember Boa-Boa	1965	2.00	4.00	8.00
❑ 891	Pearly Shells/Tiny Bubbles	1968	—	2.50	5.00

PALETTE

Number	Title (A Side/B Side)	Yr	VG	VG+	NM
❑ 5091	Hawaii Tattoo/Aloha Parade	1962	3.00	6.00	12.00
❑ 5109	Tikitiki Puki/Tanita Tamoure	1963	2.50	5.00	10.00

Albums

KAPP

Number	Title (A Side/B Side)	Yr	VG	VG+	NM
❑ KL-1366 [M]	Hawaii Tattoo	1964	3.75	7.50	15.00
❑ KL-1432 [M]	Hawaii Honeymoon	1965	3.75	7.50	15.00
❑ KL-1437 [M]	Beach Party	1965	3.75	7.50	15.00
❑ KL-1473 [M]	Lollipops and Roses	1966	3.75	7.50	15.00
❑ KL-1484 [M]	A Taste of Hawaii	1966	3.75	7.50	15.00
❑ KL-1555 [M]	Pearly Shells from Hawaii	1968	7.50	15.00	30.00

—White label promo in stereo cover, "Mono" sticker on front

Number	Title (A Side/B Side)	Yr	VG	VG+	NM
❑ KS-3366 [S]	Hawaii Tattoo	1964	5.00	10.00	20.00
❑ KS-3432 [S]	Hawaii Honeymoon	1965	5.00	10.00	20.00
❑ KS-3437 [S]	Beach Party	1965	5.00	10.00	20.00
❑ KS-3473 [S]	Lollipops and Roses	1966	5.00	10.00	20.00
❑ KS-3484 [S]	A Taste of Hawaii	1966	5.00	10.00	20.00
❑ KS-3555 [S]	Pearly Shells from Hawaii	1968	3.75	7.50	15.00
❑ KS-3575	Midnight Luau	1969	3.75	7.50	15.00
❑ KS-3593	Moonlight on Diamond Head	1969	3.75	7.50	15.00
❑ KS-3612	Greatest Hits	1970	3.00	6.00	12.00

MCA

Number	Title (A Side/B Side)	Yr	VG	VG+	NM
❑ 544	Pearly Shells from Hawaii	197?	2.50	5.00	10.00
❑ 547	Greatest Hits	197?	2.50	5.00	10.00

WAILERS, THE
45s

BELL

Number	Title (A Side/B Side)	Yr	VG	VG+	NM
❑ 694	Thinking Out Loud/You Can't Fly	1967	2.50	5.00	10.00

ETIQUETTE

Number	Title (A Side/B Side)	Yr	VG	VG+	NM
❑ 2	Mashi/Velva	1962	3.75	7.50	15.00
❑ 4	Stompin' Willie/Doin' the Seaside	1963	3.75	7.50	15.00
❑ 6	We're Goin' Surfin'/Shakedown	1963	3.75	7.50	15.00
❑ 7	Seattle/Party Time U.S.A.	1963	3.75	7.50	15.00
❑ 9	Tall Cool One/Frenzy	1964	3.75	7.50	15.00
❑ 12	You Better Believe It/Don't Take It So Hard	1965	3.75	7.50	15.00
❑ 15	You Weren't Using Your Head/Back to You	1965	3.75	7.50	15.00
❑ 19	Hang Up/Dirty Robber	1965	3.75	7.50	15.00
❑ 21	Out of Our Tree/I Got Me	1966	3.75	7.50	15.00
❑ 22	Christmas Spirit/Don't Believe in Christmas	1965	7.50	15.00	30.00

—B-side by the Sonics

Number	Title (A Side/B Side)	Yr	VG	VG+	NM
❑ 24	It's You Alone/Tears	1966	6.25	12.50	25.00

GOLDEN CREST

Number	Title (A Side/B Side)	Yr	VG	VG+	NM
❑ 375	Beat Guitar/Driftwood	19??	2.50	5.00	10.00
❑ 518	Tall Cool One/Roadrunner	1959	7.50	15.00	30.00

—Photo of group on label

Number	Title (A Side/B Side)	Yr	VG	VG+	NM
❑ 518	Tall Cool One/Roadrunner	1964	3.75	7.50	15.00

—No photo on label

Number	Title (A Side/B Side)	Yr	VG	VG+	NM
❑ 526	Mau-Mau/Dirty Robber	1959	6.25	12.50	25.00

—Photo of group on label

Number	Title (A Side/B Side)	Yr	VG	VG+	NM
❑ 526	Mau-Mau/Dirty Robber	1964	3.00	6.00	12.00

—No photo on label

Number	Title (A Side/B Side)	Yr	VG	VG+	NM
❑ 532	Wailin'/Shanghai'd	1960	6.25	12.50	25.00

—Photo of group on label

Number	Title (A Side/B Side)	Yr	VG	VG+	NM
❑ 532	Wailin'/Shanghai'd	1964	3.00	6.00	12.00

—No photo on label

Number	Title (A Side/B Side)	Yr	VG	VG+	NM
❑ 545	Lucille/Scratchin'	1960	6.25	12.50	25.00

—Photo of group on label

Number	Title (A Side/B Side)	Yr	VG	VG+	NM
❑ 545	Lucille/Scratchin'	1964	3.00	6.00	12.00

—No photo of group

Number	Title (A Side/B Side)	Yr	VG	VG+	NM
❑ 591	Mau-Mau/Beat Guitar	1964	2.50	5.00	10.00

IMPERIAL

Number	Title (A Side/B Side)	Yr	VG	VG+	NM
❑ 66028	Tall Cool One/Frenzy	1964	—	—	—

—Unreleased

Number	Title (A Side/B Side)	Yr	VG	VG+	NM
❑ 66045	Mashi/On the Rocks	1964	3.75	7.50	15.00

UNITED ARTISTS

Number	Title (A Side/B Side)	Yr	VG	VG+	NM
❑ 50026	Tears/It's You Alone	1966	2.50	5.00	10.00
❑ 50065	End of the Summer/Think Kindly Baby	1966	2.50	5.00	10.00
❑ 50110	Tears (Don't Have to Fall)/You Won't Lead Me On	1967	2.50	5.00	10.00

VIVA

Number	Title (A Side/B Side)	Yr	VG	VG+	NM
❑ 614	I'm Determined/I Don't Want to Follow You	1967	2.50	5.00	10.00

7-Inch Extended Plays

NORTON

Number	Title (A Side/B Side)	Yr	VG	VG+	NM
❑ EP-085	Scotch on the Rocks/Snake Pit//Dirty Robber/ High Wall	1999	—	—	2.00
❑ EP-085 [PS]	Scotch on the Rocks/Snake Pit//Dirty Robber/ High Wall	1999	—	—	2.00

—Custom yellow sleeve with center hole

Albums

BELL

Number	Title (A Side/B Side)	Yr	VG	VG+	NM
❑ 6016	Walk Thru the People	1969	7.50	15.00	30.00

ETIQUETTE

Number	Title (A Side/B Side)	Yr	VG	VG+	NM
❑ ALB-01 [M]	The Fabulous Wailers at the Castle	196?	25.00	50.00	100.00
❑ ALB-022 [M]	The Wailers and Company	196?	20.00	40.00	80.00
❑ ALB-023 [M]	Wailers, Wailers, Everywhere	196?	25.00	50.00	100.00
❑ ALB-026 [M]	Out of Our Tree	1966	25.00	50.00	100.00
❑ 22296/7 [(2)]	The Wailers and Their Greatest Hits	1979	6.25	12.50	25.00

GOLDEN CREST

Number	Title (A Side/B Side)	Yr	VG	VG+	NM
❑ CR-3075 [M]	Fabulous Wailers	1959	62.50	125.00	250.00

—Full-color photo on cover

Number	Title (A Side/B Side)	Yr	VG	VG+	NM
❑ CR-3075 [M]	Fabulous Wailers	196?	12.50	25.00	50.00

—Title, no photo, on cover

Number	Title (A Side/B Side)	Yr	VG	VG+	NM
❑ CR-3075 [M]	Fabulous Wailers	1962	25.00	50.00	100.00

—Black and white photo on cover

IMPERIAL

Number	Title (A Side/B Side)	Yr	VG	VG+	NM
❑ LP-9262 [M]	Tall Cool One	1964	12.50	25.00	50.00
❑ LP-12262 [S]	Tall Cool One	1964	20.00	40.00	80.00

UNITED ARTISTS

Number	Title (A Side/B Side)	Yr	VG	VG+	NM
❑ UAL-3557 [M]	Outburst!	1966	12.50	25.00	50.00
❑ UAS-6557 [S]	Outburst!	1966	20.00	40.00	80.00

WAILERS, THE (2)
45s

COLUMBIA

Number	Title (A Side/B Side)	Yr	VG	VG+	NM
❑ 40288	Hot Love/Stop the Clock	1954	30.00	60.00	120.00

WAINWRIGHT, LOUDON, III
45s

ARISTA

Number	Title (A Side/B Side)	Yr	VG	VG+	NM
❑ 0174	Bicentennial/Talking Big Apple '75	1976	—	2.50	5.00
❑ 0340	Final Exam/(B-side unknown)	1978	—	2.50	5.00

COLUMBIA

Number	Title (A Side/B Side)	Yr	VG	VG+	NM
❑ 45726	Dead Skunk/Needless to Say	1972	2.00	4.00	8.00

—Gray label

Number	Title (A Side/B Side)	Yr	VG	VG+	NM
❑ 45726	Dead Skunk/Needless to Say	1973	—	3.00	6.00

—Orange label

Number	Title (A Side/B Side)	Yr	VG	VG+	NM
❑ 45849	New Paint/Say That You Love Me	1973	—	2.50	5.00
❑ 45949	Down Drinking at the Bar/I Am the Way	1973	—	2.50	5.00
❑ 46064	Swimming Song/Bell Bottom Pants	1974	—	2.50	5.00

Albums

ARISTA

Number	Title (A Side/B Side)	Yr	VG	VG+	NM
❑ AL 4063	T Shirt	1976	3.00	6.00	12.00
❑ AB 4173	Final Exam	1978	3.00	6.00	12.00

ATLANTIC

Number	Title (A Side/B Side)	Yr	VG	VG+	NM
❑ SD 8260	Loudon Wainwright III	1970	5.00	10.00	20.00
❑ SD 8291	Album II	1971	5.00	10.00	20.00

COLUMBIA

Number	Title (A Side/B Side)	Yr	VG	VG+	NM
❑ KC 31462	Album III	1972	3.75	7.50	15.00
❑ PC 31462	Album III	198?	2.00	4.00	8.00

—Budget-line reissue

Number	Title (A Side/B Side)	Yr	VG	VG+	NM
❏ KC 32710	Attempted Mustache	1973	3.75	7.50	15.00
❏ PC 32710	Attempted Mustache	198?	2.00	4.00	8.00
—Budget-line reissue					
❏ PC 33369	Unrequited	1975	3.00	6.00	12.00
—No bar code on cover					
❏ PC 33369	Unrequited	198?	2.00	4.00	8.00
—Budget-line reissue with bar code					
ROUNDER					
❏ 3050	A Live One	1979	3.00	6.00	12.00
❏ 3076	Fame and Wealth	1983	3.00	6.00	12.00
❏ 3096	I'm Alright	1986	2.50	5.00	10.00
❏ 3106	More Love Songs	1987	2.50	5.00	10.00
SILVERTONE					
❏ 1203-1-J	Therapy	1989	3.00	6.00	12.00

WAITE, GENEVIEVE
Albums
PARAMOUR

Number	Title (A Side/B Side)	Yr	VG	VG+	NM
❏ 5088	Romance Is on the Rise	1974	6.25	12.50	25.00

WAITS, TOM
12-Inch Singles
ISLAND

Number	Title (A Side/B Side)	Yr	VG	VG+	NM
❏ 96750	Hang On St. Christopher (Extended Remix)/ (Instrumental)	1987	3.75	7.50	15.00

45s
ASYLUM

Number	Title (A Side/B Side)	Yr	VG	VG+	NM
❏ 11014	Ol' 55/(B-side unknown)	1973	—	3.00	6.00
❏ 45213	San Diego Serenade/ Diamonds on My Windshield	1974	—	2.50	5.00
❏ 45233	New Coat of Paint/Blue Skies	1975	—	2.50	5.00
❏ 45371	Step Right Up/The Piano Has Been Drinking	1976	—	2.50	5.00
❏ 45539	Red Shoes by the Drugstore/Somewhere	1978	—	2.50	5.00
❏ 47077	Jersey Girl/Heartattack and Vine	1980	2.00	4.00	8.00

Albums
ASYLUM

Number	Title (A Side/B Side)	Yr	VG	VG+	NM
❏ 6E-162	Blue Valentine	1978	2.50	5.00	10.00
❏ 6E-295	Heartattack and Vine	1980	2.50	5.00	10.00
❏ 7E-1015	The Heart of Saturday Night	1974	3.00	6.00	12.00
—Original "clouds" label, no Warner Communications logo					
❏ 7E-1015	The Heart of Saturday Night	1984	2.00	4.00	8.00
—Reissue with black and yellow label					
❏ 7E-1078	Small Change	1976	2.50	5.00	10.00
❏ 7E-1117	Foreign Affairs	1977	2.50	5.00	10.00
❏ 7E-2008 [(2)]	Nighthawks at the Diner	1975	3.00	6.00	12.00
❏ SD 5061	Closing Time	1973	3.00	6.00	12.00
ELEKTRA					
❏ 60416	Anthology of Tom Waits	1985	2.50	5.00	10.00
EPITAPH					
❏ 86547	Mule Variations	1999	3.00	6.00	12.00
ISLAND					
❏ 90095	Swordfishtrombone	1983	2.50	5.00	10.00
❏ 90299	Rain Dogs	1985	2.50	5.00	10.00
❏ 90572	Franks Wild Years	1987	2.50	5.00	10.00
❏ 90987	Big Time	1988	2.50	5.00	10.00

WAKEFIELD SUN
45s
MGM

Number	Title (A Side/B Side)	Yr	VG	VG+	NM
❏ 14028	When I See You/Get Out	1969	5.00	10.00	20.00
❏ 14072	Tryst on Love/Sing a Simple Song	1969	7.50	15.00	30.00

Albums
MGM

Number	Title (A Side/B Side)	Yr	VG	VG+	NM
❏ SE-4626	Wakefield Sun	1969	6.25	12.50	25.00

WAKELY, JIMMY
45s
ARTCO

Number	Title (A Side/B Side)	Yr	VG	VG+	NM
❏ 5012	If I Could Read Your Mind/Deep in the Heart of Texas	197?	—	3.00	6.00
CAPITOL					
❏ F929	Peter Cottontail/Mr. Easter Bunny	1950	5.00	10.00	20.00
❏ F1024	Under the Anheuser Bush/Home Town Rag	1950	5.00	10.00	20.00
❏ F1066	Sugar Plum Kisses/I Don't Have to Go to Heaven	1950	5.00	10.00	20.00
❏ F1151	Mona Lisa/Steppin' Out	1950	5.00	10.00	20.00
❏ F1240	Pot of Gold/Bandera Waltz	1950	5.00	10.00	20.00
❏ F1328	My Heart Cries for You/Music by the Angels	1950	5.00	10.00	20.00
❏ F1393	Beautiful Brown Eyes/At the Close of a Long Day	1951	5.00	10.00	20.00
❏ F1472	Did You Write a Letter to Your Sweetheart/Cryin' Just for Youq	1951	5.00	10.00	20.00
❏ F1534	Old Soldiers Never Die/I Like Wide Open Spaces	1951	5.00	10.00	20.00
❏ F1554	Don't Be Lonely//I'll Never Do a Thing	1951	5.00	10.00	20.00
❏ F1630	One Has My Name (The Other Has My Heart)/I Love You So Much It Hurts	1951	5.00	10.00	20.00
—Reissue of material first released on 78s					
❏ F1762	The Solid South/Another Fool Steps In	1951	5.00	10.00	20.00
❏ F1838	Each Step of the Way/Walk with the Lord	1951	5.00	10.00	20.00
❏ F1880	Keep a Light in Your Window/Won't You Ride in My Little Red Wagon	1951	5.00	10.00	20.00
❏ F1936	Missing in Action/Just a Little Waiting	1952	5.00	10.00	20.00
❏ F2028	Goodbye Little Girl/Love Song of the Waterfall	1952	5.00	10.00	20.00
❏ F2078	Forgive Me/Just Because	1952	5.00	10.00	20.00
❏ F2126	If You Would Only Be Mine/ My Heart Has Room for You	1952	5.00	10.00	20.00
❏ F2161	There's a Cloud in My Valley of Sunshine/ Four Legged Friend	1952	5.00	10.00	20.00
—B-side by Bob Hope					
❏ F2172	When I Say Goodnight/There's the Same Old Lovelight in Your Eyes	1952	5.00	10.00	20.00
❏ F2221	I Went to Your Wedding/Pale Moon	1952	5.00	10.00	20.00
❏ F2272	Rainbow at Midnight/When It's Harvest Time Sweet Angeline	1952	5.00	10.00	20.00
❏ F2380	Lorelei/If You Knew What It Meant to Be Lonesome	1953	5.00	10.00	20.00
❏ F2484	The Orchid Means Goodbye/ Out of Sight, Out of Mind	1953	5.00	10.00	20.00

Number	Title (A Side/B Side)	Yr	VG	VG+	NM
❏ F2626	You Took My Name/Pride	1953	5.00	10.00	20.00
❏ F2644	It's Christmas/Thanks	1953	5.00	10.00	20.00
❏ CCF 9004 [PS]	Christmas on the Range	1949	5.00	10.00	20.00
—Box for 3-record set (54-90014, 54-90015, 54-90016)					
❏ 54-90014	Silent Night/The First Nowell (The First Noel)	1949	5.00	10.00	20.00
❏ 54-90015	O Come All Ye Faithful/Joy to the World	1949	5.00	10.00	20.00
❏ 54-90016	It Came Upon a Midnight Clear/ O Little Town of Bethlehem	1949	5.00	10.00	20.00
—The above three are from "Album CCF-9004"					
❏ F90040	Christmas Polka/ If Santa Claus Could Bring You Back To Me	1949	6.25	12.50	25.00
CORAL					
❏ 9-61112	Red Deck of Cards/I've Had My Share of Tears	1953	5.00	10.00	20.00
❏ 9-61134	I Love You/I Stopped Livin'	1954	5.00	10.00	20.00
❏ 9-61143	Bimbo/Ain't She Sweet	1954	5.00	10.00	20.00
❏ 9-61175	Bright Eyed and Bushy Tailed/ Twilight Time in Tennessee	1954	5.00	10.00	20.00
—With Eileen Barton					
❏ 9-61220	Here Lies My Heart/It's Lonely on the Trail	1954	5.00	10.00	20.00
❏ 9-61276	You Took My Name/When I Stop Loving You	1954	5.00	10.00	20.00
❏ 9-61320	Let Me Go Lover/Let the Rest of the World Go By	1954	5.00	10.00	20.00
❏ 9-61324	Punch/This-a-Way, That-a-Way	1954	5.00	10.00	20.00
—With Eileen Barton					
❏ 9-61341	Let's Walk into the Future/ When He Grows Tired of You	1955	3.75	7.50	15.00
❏ 9-61389	Show Me the Way/ What God Hath Joined Together	1955	3.75	7.50	15.00
❏ 9-61392	Jim, Johnny and Jonas/Please Have Mercy (On a Fool Like Me)	1955	3.75	7.50	15.00
❏ 9-61428	Are You Mine?/Yellow Roses	1955	3.75	7.50	15.00
❏ 9-61460	Tattle Tale Blues/I'd Love to Live in Loveland	1955	3.75	7.50	15.00
❏ 9-61509	Steal a Penny from a Beggar/Keep No Secrets	1955	3.75	7.50	15.00
❏ 9-61706	His Name Was Dean/Giant	1956	6.25	12.50	25.00
❏ 9-61722	Jimmy, Jimmy/James Dean	1956	6.25	12.50	25.00
DECCA					
❏ 9-29756	Are You Satisfied/Mississippi Dreamboat	1955	3.75	7.50	15.00
❏ 9-29875	Folsom Prison Blues/ That's What the Lord Can Do	1956	3.75	7.50	15.00
❏ 9-29925	Goo Goo Da/Slow Down	1956	3.75	7.50	15.00
❏ 9-30019	The Lord's On My Side/Roundup for the Lord	1956	3.75	7.50	15.00
❏ 9-30270	Blue Nosed Mule/ The Hand That Swept the Stars	1957	3.75	7.50	15.00
❏ 9-30372	Tweedle-O-Twill/The Image of Me	1957	3.75	7.50	15.00
❏ 9-30524	Just a Boy and a Girl in Love/My Oh My	1957	3.75	7.50	15.00
—With Betsy Jones					
❏ 9-30632	Foreign Love Affair/The Blue Canadian Rockies	1958	3.75	7.50	15.00
❏ 31267	Blue Nosed Mule/Midnight Mule	1961	3.00	6.00	12.00
❏ 32271	Faded Love/Losing My Mind	1968	2.00	4.00	8.00
❏ 32324	Walking the Wet Streets/I Know How It Feels	1968	2.00	4.00	8.00
❏ 32381	Heartaches/I Gotta Have My Baby Back	1968	2.00	4.00	8.00
❏ 32459	I'll Steal Away in the Crowd/ My Life Was Filled with Love	1969	2.00	4.00	8.00
❏ 32539	Brotherly Love/I Haven't Lived Enough	1969	2.00	4.00	8.00
❏ 32595	I Wanta Go Home/My Sweet Lovin' Wife	1969	2.00	4.00	8.00
❏ 32649	Any Way That You Want Me/ That Silver-Haired Daddy of Mine	1970	2.00	4.00	8.00
❏ 32727	I'm Walkin' By/Peace in the World	1970	2.00	4.00	8.00
DOT					
❏ 16873	The Shelter of Your Arms/Look Back	1966	2.00	4.00	8.00
❏ 16986	Midnight Wind/Cowboy	1966	2.00	4.00	8.00
SHASTA					
❏ 104	Lonesome Lover/By the Waters of the Minnetonka	1958	3.00	6.00	12.00
❏ 105	I've Got a Secret/Tomorrow	1958	3.00	6.00	12.00
❏ 106	That's Santa Claus/Lonely Is the Hunter	1958	3.75	7.50	15.00
❏ 107	Slippin' Around/I Love You So Much It Hurts	1959	3.00	6.00	12.00
❏ 107 [PS]	Slippin' Around/I Love You So Much It Hurts	1959	6.25	12.50	25.00
❏ 110	When It's Springtime in Alaska/ Keeper of the Key	1959	3.00	6.00	12.00
❏ 113	I Know How It Feels/Out in the Cold	1959	3.00	6.00	12.00
❏ 119	Sugar Candy/You Came Along	1959	3.00	6.00	12.00
❏ 124	Swinging Jingle Bells/Silver Bells	1959	3.00	6.00	12.00
❏ 127	Hoot and Holler/I Heard an Angel	1960	2.50	5.00	10.00
❏ 128	My Heart Cries for You/Beautiful Brown Eyes	1960	2.50	5.00	10.00
❏ 137	Please Help Me, I'm Falling/One Has My Name (The Other Has My Heart)	1960	2.50	5.00	10.00
—With Jeanne McManus					
❏ 140	High School Romance/Quail Hunt	1960	2.50	5.00	10.00
❏ 143	Come to Me/Cowboy	1960	2.50	5.00	10.00
❏ 145	Snow Flakes/Wang Wang Blues	1961	2.50	5.00	10.00
❏ 150	Goodnight Irene/Please Don't Hurt Me Anymore	1961	2.50	5.00	10.00
❏ 155	Oklahoma Hills/Your Cheatin' Heart	196?	2.50	5.00	10.00
❏ 160	Tennessee Waltz/(B-side unknown)	196?	3.00	6.00	12.00
❏ 162	Cry Fool Cry/Keeper of the Key	196?	2.50	5.00	10.00
❏ 165	Signifying Signs of the Lord/ An Unfinished Prayer	196?	2.50	5.00	10.00
❏ 170	King's Airport/Magic Isle	196?	2.50	5.00	10.00
❏ 171	Cold, Cold Heart/Midnight Wind	196?	2.50	5.00	10.00
❏ 173	I Stopped Livin'/On and On	196?	2.50	5.00	10.00
❏ 176	Magic Isle/My Heart Cries for You	196?	2.50	5.00	10.00
❏ 177	Tomorrow/Lonely Is the Hunter	196?	2.50	5.00	10.00
❏ 178	Lonesome Guitar Man/You're Nobody 'Til Somebody Loves You	196?	2.50	5.00	10.00
❏ 179	Faded Love/Losin' My Mind	196?	2.50	5.00	10.00
❏ 201	Free from the Ghetto/ Just a Closer Walk with Thee	197?	—	3.00	6.00
❏ 206	Jesus Is Alive/Peace in the World	197?	—	3.00	6.00
❏ 207	How Can You Mend a Broken Heart/ Blue Moon of Kentucky	197?	—	3.00	6.00
❏ 209	Cimarron/Too Late	197?	—	3.00	6.00
❏ 210	Last Hour on Death Row/(B-side unknown)	197?	—	3.00	6.00
❏ 211	Goodbye Baby Goodbye/(B-side unknown)	197?	—	3.00	6.00
❏ 215	Ghost Riders in the Sky/ In a Hurry/In an Old Shanty Town	197?	—	3.00	6.00
❏ 216	A Tribute to Bob Wills/ Good Time Charlie's Got the Blues	197?	—	3.00	6.00
❏ 218	Corinna, Corinna/Stay a Little Longer	197?	—	3.50	7.00
❏ 219	Saturday's Heroes/I Could Be Beautiful	197?	—	3.00	6.00
SHASTONE					
❏ 103	High School Love/Puppy Love	1958	3.75	7.50	15.00

Number	Title (A Side/B Side)	Yr	VG	VG+	NM
Albums					
CAPITOL					
❏ H 4008 [10]	Songs of the West	195?	30.00	60.00	120.00
❏ H-9004 [10]	Christmas on the Range	1950	37.50	75.00	150.00
DECCA					
❏ DL 8409 [M]	Santa Fe Trail	1956	20.00	40.00	80.00
❏ DL 8680 [M]	Enter and Rest and Pray	1957	15.00	30.00	60.00
❏ DL 75077	Heartaches	1969	3.75	7.50	15.00
❏ DL 75192	Now and Then	1970	3.75	7.50	15.00
DOT					
❏ DLP-3711 [M]	Slippin' Around	1966	5.00	10.00	20.00
❏ DLP-3754 [M]	Christmas with Jimmy Wakely	1966	5.00	10.00	20.00
❏ DLP-25711 [S]	Slippin' Around	1966	6.25	12.50	25.00
❏ DLP-25734 [S]	Christmas with Jimmy Wakely	1966	6.25	12.50	25.00
MCA CORAL					
❏ 20033	Blue Shadows	1973	2.50	5.00	10.00
MCR					
❏ 1250	Jimmy Wakely Sings a Tribute to Bob Wills	1974	3.75	7.50	15.00
❏ 1254	Jimmy Wakely Revisits Country Western Swing with the Big Band Sound	1974	3.75	7.50	15.00
SHASTA					
❏ 501	Country Million Sellers	195?	3.75	7.50	15.00
❏ 502	Merry Christmas	1959	3.75	7.50	15.00
❏ 505	Jimmy Wakely Sings	196?	3.75	7.50	15.00
❏ 512	The Jimmy Wakely Family Show	196?	3.75	7.50	15.00
❏ 528	J.W. Country	196?	3.75	7.50	15.00
VOCALION					
❏ VL 73857	Here's Jimmy Wakely	1968	3.00	6.00	12.00
❏ VL 73904	Big Country Songs	1970	3.00	6.00	12.00

WAKEMAN, RICK Also see YES.

Number	Title (A Side/B Side)	Yr	VG	VG+	NM
45s					
A&M					
❏ 1430	Catherine/Anne	1973	—	2.50	5.00
❏ 1627	The Journey/The Return	1974	—	2.50	5.00
❏ 1635	The Battle/And Now a Word from Our Sponsor	1974	—	2.50	5.00
❏ 1708	Merlin the Magician/Sir Galahad	1975	—	2.50	5.00
❏ 1937	White Rock/After the Ball	1977	—	2.50	5.00
❏ 2010	The Birdman of Alcatraz/ And Now a Word from Our Sponsor	1978	—	2.50	5.00
Albums					
A&M					
❏ SP-3156	Journey to the Centre of the Earth	198?	2.00	4.00	8.00
—Budget-line reissue of 3621					
❏ SP-3229	The Six Wives of Henry VIII	1984	2.00	4.00	8.00
—Budget-line reissue of 4361					
❏ SP-3230	The Myths and Legends of King Arthur and the Knights of the Round Table	1984	2.00	4.00	8.00
—Budget-line reissue of 4515					
❏ SP-3621	Journey to the Centre of the Earth	1974	3.00	6.00	12.00
❏ SP-4361	The Six Wives of Henry VIII	1973	3.00	6.00	12.00
—Originals have brown labels					
❏ SP-4361	The Six Wives of Henry VIII	1974	2.50	5.00	10.00
—Silver label with "fading" A&M logo					
❏ SP-4515	The Myths and Legends of King Arthur and the Knights of the Round Table	1975	3.00	6.00	12.00
❏ SP-4583	No Earthly Connection	1976	3.00	6.00	12.00
❏ SP-4614	White Rock	1977	3.00	6.00	12.00
❏ SP-4660	Rick Wakeman's Criminal Record	1977	3.00	6.00	12.00
❏ SP-6501 [(2)]	Rhapsodies	1979	3.75	7.50	15.00
❏ QU-53621 [Q]	Journey to the Centre of the Earth	1974	6.25	12.50	25.00
❏ QU-54361 [Q]	The Six Wives of Henry VIII	1974	6.25	12.50	25.00
❏ QU-54515 [Q]	The Myths and Legends of King Arthur and the Knights of the Round Table	1975	6.25	12.50	25.00
MOBILE FIDELITY					
❏ 1-230	Journey to the Centre of the Earth	1995	5.00	10.00	20.00
—Audiophile vinyl					
SWEET THUNDER					
❏ 1	Journey to the Centre of the Earth	1981	12.50	25.00	50.00
—Audiophile vinyl					

WALCOS, THE

Number	Title (A Side/B Side)	Yr	VG	VG+	NM
45s					
DRUM					
❏ 011	Tell Me Why/Moonlight Rock	1959	25.00	50.00	100.00

WALES, HOWARD, AND JERRY GARCIA Also see JERRY GARCIA.

Number	Title (A Side/B Side)	Yr	VG	VG+	NM
45s					
DOUGLAS 7					
❏ ZS7 6501	South Side Strut/Uncle Martin's	1971	3.75	7.50	15.00
Albums					
DOUGLAS					
❏ Z 30589	Hooteroll	1971	10.00	20.00	40.00

WALKER, DAVID T.

Number	Title (A Side/B Side)	Yr	VG	VG+	NM
45s					
ODE					
❏ 66025	Hot Fun in the Summertime/I Want to Talk to You	1972	—	2.50	5.00
❏ 66037	Press On/Brother, Brother	1973	—	2.50	5.00
❏ 66042	I Got Work to Do/The Real T.	1974	—	2.50	5.00
❏ 66045	Loving You Is Sweeter Than Ever/Didn't I Blow Your Mind This Time	1974	—	2.50	5.00
❏ 66125	I Wish You Love/Oh Love	1976	—	2.50	5.00
REVUE					
❏ 11060	My Baby Loves Me/Can I Change My Mind	1969	—	3.00	6.00
❏ 11070	Watch Out Dynamite/Baby I Need Your Loving	1970	—	3.00	6.00
ZEA					
❏ 50005	Love Vibrations/(B-side unknown)	1970	—	2.50	5.00
Albums					
ODE					
❏ SP-77011	David T. Walker	1971	2.50	5.00	10.00
❏ SP-77020	Press On	1974	2.50	5.00	10.00
❏ SP-77035	On Love	1976	2.50	5.00	10.00
ZEA					
❏ 1000	Plum Happy	1970	3.75	7.50	15.00

WALKER, JERRY JEFF

Number	Title (A Side/B Side)	Yr	VG	VG+	NM
45s					
ATCO					
❏ 6594	Mr. Bojangles/Round and Round	1968	2.50	5.00	10.00
❏ 6767	I'm Gonna Tell on You/But For the Time	1970	—	3.00	6.00
ELEKTRA					
❏ 46016	Comfort and Crazy/ Eastern Ave. River Railway Blues	1979	—	2.00	4.00
MCA					
❏ 40054	L.A. Freeway/Charlie Dunn	1973	—	2.00	4.00
❏ 40167	Desperadoes Waitin' for a Train/Gettin' By	1973	—	2.00	4.00
❏ 40250	Sangria Wine/Hill Country Rain	1974	—	2.00	4.00
❏ 40389	Goodbye Easy Street/Salvation Army Band	1975	—	2.00	4.00
❏ 40487	Jaded Lover/I Love You	1975	—	2.00	4.00
❏ 40570	Dear John Letter Lounge/ It's a Good Night for Singing	1976	—	2.00	4.00
❏ 40622	(Looking for the) Heart of Saturday Night/Stoney	1976	—	2.00	4.00
❏ 40760	Mr. Bojangles/Don't It Make You Wanna Dance	1977	—	2.00	4.00
❏ 40822	Ro-Deo-Deo Cowboy/Leavin' Texas	1977	—	2.00	4.00
SOUTH COAST					
❏ 51146	Got Lucky Last Night/Maybe Mexico	1981	—	2.00	4.00
❏ 51215	Take It As It Comes/ She Knows Her Daddy Sings	1981	—	2.00	4.00
❏ 52122	Don't Think Twice, It's Alright/ Laying My Life on the Line	1982	—	2.00	4.00
TRIED & TRUE					
❏ 1690	I Feel Like Hank Williams Tonight/Mr. Bojangles	1989	—	2.50	5.00
❏ 1695	The Pickup Truck Song/ The Pickup Truck Song (Long Version)	1989	—	2.50	5.00
❏ 1698	Trashy Women/ I Feel Like Hank Williams Tonight	1989	—	2.50	5.00
Albums					
ATCO					
❏ SD 33-259	Mr. Bojangles	1968	6.25	12.50	25.00
❏ SD 33-297	Five Years Gone	1969	7.50	15.00	30.00
❏ SD 33-336	Bein' Free	1970	5.00	10.00	20.00
BAINBRIDGE					
❏ 6222	Mr. Bojangles	198?	2.50	5.00	10.00
DECCA					
❏ DL 75384	Jerry Jeff Walker	1972	3.75	7.50	15.00
ELEKTRA					
❏ 6E-163	Jerry Jeff	1978	2.50	5.00	10.00
❏ 6E-239	Too Old to Change	1980	2.50	5.00	10.00
MCA					
❏ 382	Viva Terlingua!	1973	2.50	5.00	10.00
❏ 450	Walker's Collectibles	1974	2.50	5.00	10.00
❏ 510	Jerry Jeff Walker	1975	2.50	5.00	10.00
—Reissue of Decca LP					
❏ 2156	Ridin' High	1975	2.50	5.00	10.00
❏ 2202	It's a Good Night for Singin'	1976	2.50	5.00	10.00
❏ 2350	Viva Terlingua!	1977	2.00	4.00	8.00
—Reissue of MCA 382					
❏ 2355	Walker's Collectibles	1977	2.00	4.00	8.00
—Reissue of MCA 450					
❏ 2358	Jerry Jeff Walker	1977	2.00	4.00	8.00
—Reissue of MCA 510					
❏ 3041	Contrary to Ordinary	1978	2.50	5.00	10.00
❏ 5128	The Best of Jerry Jeff Walker	1980	2.50	5.00	10.00
❏ 5355	Cowjazz	1983	2.50	5.00	10.00
❏ 6003 [(2)]	A Man Must Carry On	198?	2.50	5.00	10.00
—Budget-line reissue					
❏ 8013 [(2)]	A Man Must Carry On	1977	3.00	6.00	12.00
❏ 27026	It's a Good Night for Singin'	198?	2.00	4.00	8.00
—Budget-line reissue					
❏ 27027	Walker's Collectibles	198?	—	3.00	6.00
—Budget-line reissue					
❏ 37004	Jerry Jeff Walker	198?	—	3.00	6.00
—Budget-line reissue					
❏ 37005	Viva Terlingua!	198?	—	3.00	6.00
—Budget-line reissue					
❏ 37006	Ridin' High	198?	2.00	4.00	8.00
—Budget-line reissue					
❏ 37162	Contrary to Ordinary	198?	2.00	4.00	8.00
—Budget-line reissue					
SOUTHCOAST					
❏ 5199	Reunion	1981	2.50	5.00	10.00
VANGUARD					
❏ VSD-6521	Driftin' Way of Life	1969	5.00	10.00	20.00
❏ VMS-73124	Driftin' Way of Life	1985	2.00	4.00	8.00
—Reissue of 6521					

WALKER, JIMMIE

Number	Title (A Side/B Side)	Yr	VG	VG+	NM
Albums					
BUDDAH					
❏ BDS 5635	Dyn-O-Mite	1975	2.50	5.00	10.00

WALKER, JR., AND THE ALL STARS

Number	Title (A Side/B Side)	Yr	VG	VG+	NM
45s					
HARVEY					
❏ 113	Willie's Blues/Twist Lackawanna	1962	6.25	12.50	25.00
❏ 117	Cleo's Mood/Brain Washer	1963	5.00	10.00	20.00
❏ 119	Good Rockin'/Brain Washer	1963	5.00	10.00	20.00
MOTOWN					
❏ 1352	Country Boy/What Does It Take (To Win Your Love)	1975	—	2.50	5.00
❏ 1380	I'm So Glad/Hot Shot	1976	—	—	—
—Unreleased					
❏ 1689	Blow the House Down/Ball Baby	1983	—	2.00	4.00
SOUL					
❏ 35003	Monkey Jump/Satan's Blues	1964	3.75	7.50	15.00
❏ 35008	Shotgun/Hot Cha	1965	3.75	7.50	15.00
❏ 35008	Shot Gun/Hot Cha	1965	25.00	50.00	100.00
—Not only is the A-side title listed as two words, but the record is credited to "Jr. Walker and All The Stars"!					
❏ 35008 [PS]	Shotgun/Hot Cha	1965	6.25	12.50	25.00
❏ 35012	Do the Boomerang/Tune Up	1965	2.50	5.00	10.00

Number	Title (A Side/B Side)	Yr	VG	VG+	NM
❑ 35013	Shake and Fingerpop/Cleo's Back	1965	2.50	5.00	10.00
❑ 35015	(I'm a) Road Runner/Shoot Your Shot	1965	2.50	5.00	10.00
❑ 35017	Cleo's Mood/Baby You Know It Ain't Right	1966	2.00	4.00	8.00
❑ 35024	How Sweet It Is (To Be Loved By You)/ Nothing But Soul	1966	2.00	4.00	8.00
❑ 35024 [PS]	How Sweet It Is (To Be Loved By You)/ Nothing But Soul	1966	5.00	10.00	20.00
❑ 35026	Money (That's What I Want) Part I/Money (That's What I Want) Part II	1966	2.00	4.00	8.00
❑ 35030	Pucker Up Buttercup/Anyway You Wanna	1967	2.00	4.00	8.00
❑ 35036	Shoot Your Shot/Ain't That the Truth	1967	2.00	4.00	8.00
❑ 35041	Come See About Me/Sweet Soul	1967	2.00	4.00	8.00
❑ 35048	Hip City — Part 1/Hip City — Part 2	1968	2.00	4.00	8.00
❑ 35055	Home Cookin'/Mutiny	1969	2.00	4.00	8.00
❑ 35062	What Does It Take (To Win Your Love)/ Brainwasher — Part 1	1969	2.00	4.00	8.00
❑ 35067	These Eyes/Got to Find a Way to Win Maria Back	1969	—	3.00	6.00
❑ 35070	Gotta Hold On to This Feeling/Clinging to the Theory That She's Coming Back	1970	—	3.00	6.00
❑ 35073	Do You See My Love (For You Growing)/ Groove and More	1970	—	3.00	6.00
❑ 35081	Holly Holy/Carry Your Own Load	1970	—	3.00	6.00
❑ 35084	Take Me Girl, I'm Ready/ Right On Brothers and Sisters	1971	—	3.00	6.00
❑ 35090	Way Back Home/(Instrumental)	1971	—	3.00	6.00
❑ 35095	Walk in the Night/I Don't Want to Do Wrong	1972	—	3.00	6.00
❑ 35097	Groove Thang/Me and My Family	1972	—	3.00	6.00
❑ 35104	Gimme That Beat (Part 1)/ Gimme That Beat (Part 2)	1973	—	3.00	6.00
❑ 35106	I Don't Need No Reason/Country Boy	1973	—	3.00	6.00
❑ 35108	Peace and Understanding (Is Hard to Find)/ Soul Clappin'	1973	—	3.00	6.00
❑ 35110	Dancing Like They Do on Soul Train /I Ain't That Easy to Love	1973	—	3.00	6.00
❑ 35114 [DJ]	You Are the Sunshine of My Life/ Until You Come Back to Me	1974	—	—	—
—Unreleased					
❑ 35116	I'm So Glad/Soul Clappin'	1975	—	2.50	5.00
❑ 35118	Hot Shot/You're No Ordinary Woman	1976	—	2.50	5.00
❑ 35122	Whopper Bopper Show Stopper/Hard Love	1977	—	2.50	5.00
WHITFIELD					
❑ 8861	Back Street Boogie/Don't Let Me Go Away	1979	—	2.00	4.00
❑ 49052	Wishing on a Star/Hole in the Wall	1979	—	2.00	4.00
Albums					
MOTOWN					
❑ M5-105V1	Motown Superstar Series, Vol. 5	1981	2.50	5.00	10.00
❑ M5-141V1	Shotgun	1981	2.50	5.00	10.00
—Reissue of Soul 701					
❑ M5-208V1	Greatest Hits	1981	2.50	5.00	10.00
—Reissue of Soul 718					
❑ M7-786 [(2)]	Anthology	1974	5.00	10.00	20.00
❑ 5297 ML	All the Great Hits of Jr. Walker and the All Stars	1984	2.50	5.00	10.00
❑ 6053 ML	Blow the House Down	1983	2.50	5.00	10.00
PICKWICK					
❑ SPC-3391	Shotgun	197?	3.00	6.00	12.00
SOUL					
❑ 701 [M]	Shotgun	1965	5.00	10.00	20.00
—Purple swirl label with "Soul" at top					
❑ 701 [M]	Shotgun	1965	15.00	30.00	60.00
—Mostly white label with vertical "Soul" at left					
❑ SS-701 [S]	Shotgun	1965	7.50	15.00	30.00
❑ 702 [M]	Soul Session	1966	5.00	10.00	20.00
—Purple swirl label with "Soul" at top					
❑ 702 [M]	Soul Session	1966	15.00	30.00	60.00
—Mostly white label with vertical "Soul" at left					
❑ SS-702 [S]	Soul Session	1966	7.50	15.00	30.00
❑ 703 [M]	Road Runner	1966	5.00	10.00	20.00
❑ SS-703 [S]	Road Runner	1966	7.50	15.00	30.00
❑ 705 [M]	"Live"	1967	5.00	10.00	20.00
❑ SS-705 [S]	"Live"	1967	7.50	15.00	30.00
❑ SS-710	Home Cookin'	1969	5.00	10.00	20.00
❑ SS-718	Greatest Hits	1969	5.00	10.00	20.00
❑ SS-721	Gotta Hold on to This Feeling	1969	6.25	12.50	25.00
❑ SS-721	What Does It Take to Win Your Love	1970	5.00	10.00	20.00
—Retitled version of above					
❑ SS-726	A Gasssss	1970	3.75	7.50	15.00
❑ SS-732	Rainbow Funk	1971	3.75	7.50	15.00
❑ SS-733	Moody Jr.	1971	3.75	7.50	15.00
❑ SS-738	Peace and Understanding Is Hard to Find	1973	3.75	7.50	15.00
❑ S6-742	Jr. Walker and the All Stars	1973	—	—	—
—Canceled					
❑ S6-745	Hot Shot	1976	3.75	7.50	15.00
❑ S6-747	Sax Appeal	1976	3.75	7.50	15.00
❑ S6-748	Whopper Bopper Show Stopper	1977	3.75	7.50	15.00
❑ S7-750	Smooth	1978	3.75	7.50	15.00
WHITFIELD					
❑ WHK 3331	Back Street Boogie	1980	3.00	6.00	12.00

WALKER, T-BONE
45s

Number	Title (A Side/B Side)	Yr	VG	VG+	NM
ATLANTIC					
❑ 1045	Papa Ain't Salty/T-Bone Shuffle	1955	12.50	25.00	50.00
❑ 1074	Why Not/Play On Little Girl	1955	10.00	20.00	40.00
BLUESWAY					
❑ 61008	Confusion Blues/Every Night I Have to Cry	1967	2.00	4.00	8.00
CAPITOL					
❑ F799	Go Back to the One You Love/ On Your Way Blues	1950	37.50	75.00	150.00
❑ F944	Too Much Trouble Blues/ She's My Old Time Used to Be	1950	37.50	75.00	150.00
IMPERIAL					
❑ 5202	Street Walkin' Woman/The Blues Is a Woman	1952	100.00	200.00	400.00
—Note: T-Bone Walker records on Imperial before 5202 are unconfirmed on 45 rpm.					
❑ 5216	Blue Mood/Got No Use for You	1953	50.00	100.00	200.00
❑ 5228	Railroad Station Blues/Long Distance Blues	1953	50.00	100.00	200.00
❑ 5239	Party Girl/You're Here in the Dark	1953	75.00	150.00	300.00
❑ 5247	Everytime/Tell Me What's the Reason	1953	37.50	75.00	150.00

Number	Title (A Side/B Side)	Yr	VG	VG+	NM
❑ 5261	I'm About to Lose My Mind/I Miss You Baby	1954	25.00	50.00	100.00
❑ 5264	Pony Tail/When the Sun Goes Down	1954	20.00	40.00	80.00
❑ 5274	Vida Lee/My Baby Is Now on My Mind	1954	20.00	40.00	80.00
❑ 5284	Bye Bye Baby/Wanderin' Heart	1954	20.00	40.00	80.00
❑ 5299	Teenage Baby/Strugglin' Blues	1954	20.00	40.00	80.00
❑ 5311	Love Is Just a Gamble/High Society	1954	20.00	40.00	80.00
❑ 5330	I'll Understand/The Hard Way	1955	12.50	25.00	50.00
❑ 5384	You Don't Understand/Say! Pretty Baby	1956	12.50	25.00	50.00
❑ 5695	Travelin' Blues/Strollin' with Bones	1960	3.75	7.50	15.00
❑ 5832	Evil Hearted Woman/Life Is Too Short	1962	3.75	7.50	15.00
❑ 5962	Doin' Time/Cold, Cold Water	1963	3.00	6.00	12.00
JETSTREAM					
❑ 726	Reconsider Baby/I'm Not Your Fool Anymore	1966	2.50	5.00	10.00
❑ 730	T-Bone's Back/She's a Hit	1967	2.50	5.00	10.00
MODERN					
❑ 1004	Should I Let Her Go/Hey Hey Baby	1965	2.50	5.00	10.00
POST					
❑ 2002	I Get So Weary/Tell Me What's the Reason	1955	15.00	30.00	60.00
7-Inch Extended Plays					
CAPITOL					
❑ EAP 1-370	(contents unknown)	1953	50.00	100.00	200.00
❑ EAP 1-370 [PS]	Classics in Jazz	1953	50.00	100.00	200.00
Albums					
ATLANTIC					
❑ 8020 [M]	T-Bone Blues	1959	55.00	110.00	220.00
—Black label					
❑ 8020 [M]	T-Bone Blues	1960	17.50	35.00	70.00
—Red and purple label					
❑ SD 8256	T-Bone Blues	1970	5.00	10.00	20.00
BLUE NOTE					
❑ BN-LA533-H2 [(2)]	Classics	1975	5.00	10.00	20.00
BLUESTIME					
❑ 29004	Everyday I Have the Blues	1968	7.50	15.00	30.00
❑ 29010	Blue Rocks	1969	7.50	15.00	30.00
BLUESWAY					
❑ BLS-6008	Stormy Monday Blues	1968	7.50	15.00	30.00
—Reissue of Wet Soul LP?					
❑ BLS-6014	Funky Town	1968	7.50	15.00	30.00
❑ BLS-6058	Dirty Mistreater	1973	3.75	7.50	15.00
BRUNSWICK					
❑ BL 754126	The Truth	1968	7.50	15.00	30.00
CAPITOL					
❑ H 370 [10]	Classics in Jazz	1953	250.00	500.00	1000.
❑ T 370 [M]	Classics in Jazz	1953	75.00	150.00	300.00
❑ T 1958 [M]	Great Blues Vocal and Guitar	1963	37.50	75.00	150.00
—Black "The Star Line" label (existence of black colorband label not confirmed)					
DELMARK					
❑ D-633 [M]	I Want a Little Girl	1967	10.00	20.00	40.00
❑ DS-633 [S]	I Want a Little Girl	1967	12.50	25.00	50.00
IMPERIAL					
❑ LP-9098 [M]	T-Bone Walker Sings the Blues	1959	75.00	150.00	300.00
❑ LP-9116 [M]	Singing the Blues	1960	62.50	125.00	250.00
❑ LP-9146 [M]	I Get So Weary	1961	75.00	150.00	300.00
MOSAIC					
❑ MR9-130 [(9)]	The Complete Recordings of T-Bone Walker 1940-1954	199?	75.00	150.00	300.00
—Limited edition of 7,500					
POLYDOR					
❑ 24-4502	Good Feelin'	1972	3.75	7.50	15.00
❑ PD-5521	Fly Walker Airlines	1973	3.75	7.50	15.00
REPRISE					
❑ 2RS 6483 [(2)]	Very Rare	1973	5.00	10.00	20.00
WET SOUL					
❑ 1002	Stormy Monday Blues	1967	12.50	25.00	50.00

WALKER, WAYNE
45s

Number	Title (A Side/B Side)	Yr	VG	VG+	NM
ABC-PARAMOUNT					
❑ 9735	It's My Way/All I Can Do Is Cry	1956	15.00	30.00	60.00
BRUNSWICK					
❑ 55133	Little Ole You/What Kind of God Do You Think You Are	1959	10.00	20.00	40.00
COLUMBIA					
❑ 40905	A Teenage Love Affair/Whatever You Desire	1957	6.25	12.50	25.00
❑ 40979	Just a-Walkin' Around/Sands of Gold	1957	6.25	12.50	25.00
❑ 41042	Bo-Bo Sha Diddle Diddle/Come Away from His Arms	1957	6.25	12.50	25.00
❑ 41130	I'm Finally Free/It's Written in Your Arms	1958	6.25	12.50	25.00
CORAL					
❑ 62328	Battle of the Bulge/Reaching for the Impossible	1962	3.75	7.50	15.00
EVEREST					
❑ 19380	Love, Love, Love/Sweet Chains of Love	1960	3.75	7.50	15.00

WALKER BROTHERS, THE Also see SCOTT ENGEL.
45s

Number	Title (A Side/B Side)	Yr	VG	VG+	NM
KAY-Y					
❑ 66785	Beautiful Brown Eyes/Ninety-Seven	1960	12.50	25.00	50.00
SMASH					
❑ 1952	Doin' the Jerk/Pretty Girls Everywhere	1964	3.00	6.00	12.00
❑ 1976	Love Her/Seventh Dawn	1965	3.00	6.00	12.00
❑ 2000	Make It Easy on Yourself/But I Do	1965	3.75	7.50	15.00
❑ 2009	Make It Easy on Yourself/Doin' the Jerk	1965	3.00	6.00	12.00
❑ 2009 [PS]	Make It Easy on Yourself/Doin' the Jerk	1965	5.00	10.00	20.00
❑ 2016	My Ship Is Comin' In/You're All Around Me	1966	3.00	6.00	12.00
❑ 2016 [PS]	My Ship Is Comin' In/You're All Around Me	1966	5.00	10.00	20.00
❑ 2032	The Sun Ain't Gonna Shine (Anymore)/ After the Lights Go Out	1966	3.00	6.00	12.00
❑ 2048	(Baby) You Don't Have to Tell Me/ Young Man Cried	1966	3.00	6.00	12.00
❑ 2063	Another Tear Falls/Saddest Night in the World	1966	3.00	6.00	12.00
TOWER					
❑ 218	I Only Came to Dance with You/Greens	1966	3.00	6.00	12.00
Albums					
SMASH					
❑ MGS-27076 [M]	Introducing the Walker Brothers	1965	12.50	25.00	50.00
❑ MGS-27082 [M]	The Sun Ain't Gonna Shine (Anymore)	1966	10.00	20.00	40.00

Number	Title (A Side/B Side)	Yr	VG	VG+	NM
☐ SRS-67076 [R]	Introducing the Walker Brothers	1965	10.00	20.00	40.00
☐ SRS-67082 [P]	The Sun Ain't Gonna Shine (Anymore)	1966	12.50	25.00	50.00
—"The Sun Ain't Gonna Shine (Anymore)" and "When the Lights Go Out" are rechanneled.						
TOWER						
☐ ST 5026 [S]	I Only Came to Dance with You	1966	5.00	10.00	20.00
—As "Scott Engel and John Stewart"						
☐ T 5026 [M]	I Only Came to Dance with You	1966	3.75	7.50	15.00
—As "Scott Engel and John Stewart"						

WALLACE, BILLY
45s
DEB

Number	Title (A Side/B Side)	Yr	VG	VG+	NM
☐ 883	Wolf Call/(B-side unknown)	1957	37.50	75.00	150.00
☐ 1003	Don't Flirt with My Baby/You'll Never Cheat Me Anymore	1958	37.50	75.00	150.00
MERCURY						
☐ 70876	What'll I Do/That's My Reward	1956	50.00	100.00	200.00
☐ 70957	Mean Mistreating Baby/Burning the Wind	1956	75.00	150.00	300.00

WALLACE, JERRY
45s
ALLIED

Number	Title (A Side/B Side)	Yr	VG	VG+	NM
☐ 5015	Little Miss One/Petrillo	1954	12.50	25.00	50.00
—B-side by Eddie Oliver and the Oliver Twisters						
☐ 5019	That's What a Woman Can Do/I Hate to Go Home Alone	1954	10.00	20.00	40.00
☐ 5023	Runnin' After Love/Dixie Anna	1954	10.00	20.00	40.00
BMA						
☐ 7-002	I Miss You Already/At the End of a Rainbow	1977	—	2.50	5.00
☐ 7-005	I'll Promise You Tomorrow/You're on the Run	1977	—	2.50	5.00
☐ 8-006	At the End of a Rainbow/Looking for a Memory	1978	—	2.50	5.00
☐ 8-008	My Last Sad Song/Wickenburg Way	1978	—	2.50	5.00
CHALLENGE						
☐ 1003	Blue Jean Baby/Fool's Hall of Fame	1957	5.00	10.00	20.00
☐ 9107	Life's a Holiday/I Can See an Angel Walking	1961	3.00	6.00	12.00
☐ 9117	Eyes (Don't Give My Secrets Away)/Lonesome	1961	3.00	6.00	12.00
☐ 9130	Rollin' River/I Hang My Head and Cry	1961	3.00	6.00	12.00
☐ 9139	Little Miss Tease/Mr. Lonely	1962	3.00	6.00	12.00
☐ 9152	Here I Go/You'll Never Know	1962	3.00	6.00	12.00
☐ 9171	Shutters and Boards/Am I That Easy to Forget	1962	3.00	6.00	12.00
☐ 9185	Move Over/On a Merry-Go-Round	1963	3.00	6.00	12.00
☐ 9195	Just Walking in the Rain/San Francisco Mama	1963	3.00	6.00	12.00
☐ 59000	The Other Me/Good and Bad	1958	5.00	10.00	20.00
☐ 59013	How the Time Flies/With This Ring	1958	5.00	10.00	20.00
☐ 59027	Diamond Ring/All My Love Belongs to You	1958	5.00	10.00	20.00
☐ 59040	A Touch of Pink/Off Stage	1959	3.75	7.50	15.00
☐ 59047	Primrose Lane/By Your Side	1959	4.50	9.00	18.00
☐ 59060	Little Coco Palm/Mission Bell Blues	1959	3.75	7.50	15.00
☐ 59060 [PS]	Little Coco Palm/Mission Bell Blues	1959	10.00	20.00	40.00
☐ 59072	King of the Mountain/You're Singing Our Love Song to Somebody Else	1960	3.75	7.50	15.00
☐ 59082	Swingin' Down the Lane/Teardrops in the Rain	1960	3.75	7.50	15.00
☐ 59098	There She Goes/Angel on My Shoulder	1960	3.75	7.50	15.00
☐ 59205	Empty Arms Again/Bambola (My Darling One)	1963	3.00	6.00	12.00
☐ 59223	Auf Wiedersehn/If I Make It Through Today	1963	2.50	5.00	10.00
☐ 59246	In the Misty Moonlight/Even the Bad Times Are Good	1964	2.50	5.00	10.00
☐ 59246	In the Misty Moonlight/Cannon Ball	1964	3.75	7.50	15.00
—B-side by the Soul Surfers						
☐ 59265	Even the Bad Times Are Good/Spanish Guitars	1964	2.50	5.00	10.00
☐ 59278	You're Driving You Out of My Mind/Helpless	1965	2.50	5.00	10.00
CLASS						
☐ 502	Taj Mahal/Autumn Has Come and Gone	1955	6.25	12.50	25.00
DECCA						
☐ 32777	After You/She'll Remember	1971	—	3.50	7.00
☐ 32859	The Morning After/I Can't Take It Anymore	1971	—	3.50	7.00
☐ 32914	To Get to You/Time	1972	—	3.50	7.00
☐ 32989	If You Leave Me Tonight I'll Cry/What's He Doin' in My World	1972	—	3.50	7.00
☐ 33036	Do You Know What It's Like to Be Lonesome/Where Did He Come From	1972	—	3.50	7.00
DOOR KNOB						
☐ 116	You've Still Got Me/Now That Sandy's Gone	1979	—	2.50	5.00
☐ 127	Cling to Me/Paper Madonna	1980	—	2.50	5.00
☐ 134	If I Could Set My Love to Music/Cling to Me	1980	—	2.50	5.00
4 STAR						
☐ 1035	I Wanna Go to Heaven/After You	1978	—	2.50	5.00
☐ 1036	Yours Love/There She Goes	1979	—	2.50	5.00
GLENOLDEN						
☐ 159	Are You Ready/That's the Fool in Me	1968	—	3.00	6.00
LIBERTY						
☐ 55957	Runaway Boy/Dispossessed	1967	2.00	4.00	8.00
☐ 56001	This One's on the House/A New Sun Risin'	1967	2.00	4.00	8.00
☐ 56027	The Closest I Ever Came/That's What Fools Are For	1968	—	—	—
—Unreleased						
☐ 56028	Another Time, Another Place, Another World/That's What Fools Are For	1968	—	3.00	6.00
☐ 56059	Sweet Child of Sunshine/Our House on Paper	1968	—	3.00	6.00
☐ 56095	Temptation/Son	1969	—	3.00	6.00
☐ 56105	Venus/Soon We'll Be There	1969	—	3.00	6.00
☐ 56130	Swiss Cottage Place/With Aging	1969	—	3.00	6.00
☐ 56147	Honey Eyed Girl/Glory of My Girl	1969	—	3.00	6.00
☐ 56155	Even the Bad Times Are Good/For All We Know	1970	—	3.00	6.00
MCA						
☐ 40037	A Song Nobody Sings/Sound of Goodbye	1973	—	2.50	5.00
☐ 40111	Don't Give Up on Me/You Look Like Forever	1973	—	2.50	5.00
☐ 40183	Guess Who/All I Ever Want from You	1974	—	2.50	5.00
☐ 40248	My Wife's House/A Better Way to Say I Love You	1974	—	2.50	5.00
☐ 40321	Make Hay While the Sun Shines/I Wonder Whose Baby	1974	—	2.50	5.00
MERCURY						
☐ 70684	Taj Mahal/Autumn Has Come and Gone	1955	5.00	10.00	20.00
☐ 70758	The Greatest Magic of All/Walking in the Rain	1955	5.00	10.00	20.00
☐ 70812	One Night When Flowers Were Dancing/Gloria	1956	5.00	10.00	20.00
☐ 72246	In the Misty Moonlight/Even the Bad Times Are Good	1964	3.00	6.00	12.00
☐ 72258	Butterfly/Let the Tears Begin	1964	2.50	5.00	10.00

Number	Title (A Side/B Side)	Yr	VG	VG+	NM
☐ 72292	It's a Cotton Candy World/Keep a Lamp Burning	1964	2.50	5.00	10.00
☐ 72356	Careless Hands/San Francisco d'Assisi	1964	2.50	5.00	10.00
☐ 72406	Rainbow/Time	1965	2.50	5.00	10.00
☐ 72461	Life's Gone and Slipped Away/Twelve Little Roses	1965	2.50	5.00	10.00
☐ 72529	Diamonds and Horseshoes/Will the Pain Fade Away	1966	2.50	5.00	10.00
☐ 72589	Wallpaper Roses/Son of a Green Beret	1966	2.50	5.00	10.00
☐ 72619	Not That I Care/Release Me	1966	2.50	5.00	10.00
MGM						
☐ 14788	Comin' Home to You/The River St. Marie	1975	—	2.50	5.00
☐ 14809	Wanted Man/Your Love	1975	—	2.50	5.00
☐ 14832	Georgia Rain/In the Garden	1975	—	2.50	5.00
POLYDOR						
☐ 14322	The Fool I've Been Today/Jenny Angel	1976	—	2.00	4.00
TOPS						
☐ 369	P.S. I Love You/Vaya Con Dios (May God Be With You)	1953	10.00	20.00	40.00
—B-side by Betty Ford						
UNITED ARTISTS						
☐ XW239	Take Me As I Am/Touch Me	1973	—	2.50	5.00
☐ XW618	With Pen in Hand/All I Want Is You	1975	—	2.50	5.00
☐ 50971	Funny How Time Slips Away/Thanks to You for Loving Me	1972	—	2.50	5.00
WING						
☐ 90065	Eyes of Fire, Lips of Wine/Monkey See, Monkey Do	1956	5.00	10.00	20.00
Albums						
CHALLENGE						
☐ CHL 606 [M]	Just Jerry	1959	15.00	30.00	60.00
☐ CH 612 [M]	There She Goes	1961	7.50	15.00	30.00
☐ CHS 612 [S]	There She Goes	1961	10.00	20.00	40.00
☐ CH 616 [M]	Shutters and Boards	1962	7.50	15.00	30.00
☐ CHS 616 [S]	Shutters and Boards	1962	10.00	20.00	40.00
☐ CH 619 [M]	In the Misty Moonlight	1964	5.00	10.00	20.00
☐ CHS 619 [S]	In the Misty Moonlight	1964	6.25	12.50	25.00
☐ 2002	Greatest Hits	1969	3.75	7.50	15.00
DECCA						
☐ DL 75294	This Is Jerry Wallace	1971	3.75	7.50	15.00
☐ DL 75349	To Get to You	1972	3.75	7.50	15.00
LIBERTY						
☐ LRP-3545 [M]	This One's on the House	1967	10.00	20.00	40.00
—Stock copy inside stereo cover; "Audition Mono LP Not for Sale" sticker on front						
☐ LST-7545 [S]	This One's on the House	1967	5.00	10.00	20.00
☐ LST-7564	Another Time, Another World	1968	5.00	10.00	20.00
☐ LST-7597	Sweet Child of Sunshine	1968	5.00	10.00	20.00
MCA						
☐ 301	Do You Know What It's Like to Be Lonesome?	1973	3.00	6.00	12.00
☐ 366	Primrose Lane/Don't Give Up on Me	1973	3.00	6.00	12.00
☐ 408	For Wives and Lovers	1974	3.00	6.00	12.00
☐ 462	I Wonder Whose Baby (You Are Now)/Make Hay While the Sun Shines	1975	3.00	6.00	12.00
MERCURY						
☐ MG-21072 [M]	The Best of Jerry Wallace	1966	3.75	7.50	15.00
☐ SR-61072 [S]	The Best of Jerry Wallace	1966	5.00	10.00	20.00
MGM						
☐ M3G-4990	Greatest Hits	1975	2.50	5.00	10.00
☐ M3G-4995	Comin' Home to You	1976	3.00	6.00	12.00
☐ M3G-5007	Jerry Wallace	1976	2.50	5.00	10.00
SUNSET						
☐ SUS-5294	Primrose Lane	1969	3.00	6.00	12.00
UNITED ARTISTS						
☐ UXS-95 [(2)]	Jerry Wallace Superpak	1972	5.00	10.00	20.00

WALLACE, JIMMY
45s
ALPHA

Number	Title (A Side/B Side)	Yr	VG	VG+	NM
☐ 006	I'll Be Back/(B-side unknown)	196?	250.00	500.00	1000.

WALLACE, SONNY
45s
YUCCA

Number	Title (A Side/B Side)	Yr	VG	VG+	NM
☐ 127	Black Cadillac/If a Man Could See	1961	25.00	50.00	100.00

WALLER, GORDON Also see PETER AND GORDON.
45s
BELL

Number	Title (A Side/B Side)	Yr	VG	VG+	NM
☐ 794	The Lady in the Window/I Was a Boy When You Needed a Man	1969	2.00	4.00	8.00
☐ 882	Sunshine/You Gonna Hurt Yourself	1970	—	3.00	6.00
CAPITOL						
☐ 2346	Everyday/Because of a Woman	1968	2.00	4.00	8.00
☐ 5886	Speak for Me/Little Nonie	1967	2.00	4.00	8.00
Albums						
ABC						
☐ X-749	And Gordon	1972	3.75	7.50	15.00

WALLIS, RUTH
Albums
KING

Number	Title (A Side/B Side)	Yr	VG	VG+	NM
☐ 265-6 [10]	Rhumba Party	1952	30.00	60.00	120.00
☐ 265-9 [10]	House Party	1952	30.00	60.00	120.00
☐ 395-507 [M]	House Party	1956	25.00	50.00	100.00
☐ 904 [M]	Saucy Hit Parade	1964	7.50	15.00	30.00
☐ 986 [M]	Here's Looking Up Your Hatch	1966	7.50	15.00	30.00
☐ 987 [M]	Davy's Little Dinghy	1966	7.50	15.00	30.00
☐ 988 [M]	Marry Go Round	1966	7.50	15.00	30.00
☐ 989 [M]	Red Lights	1966	7.50	15.00	30.00
☐ 990 [M]	Ubangi Me	1966	7.50	15.00	30.00
☐ 991 [M]	Oil Man from Texas	1966	7.50	15.00	30.00
☐ 992 [M]	He Wants a Little…Pizza	1966	7.50	15.00	30.00
☐ 993 [M]	Bahama Mama	1966	7.50	15.00	30.00
WALLIS ORIGINAL						
☐ 2 [M]	Ruth Wallis	1957	10.00	20.00	40.00

Number	Title (A Side/B Side)	Yr	VG	VG+	NM

WALLS, TOM
45s
HIT
| ☐ 10 | Funny Way of Laughin'/PT 109 | 1962 | 2.00 | 4.00 | 8.00 |
—B-side by Johnny Keaton
| ☐ 20 | Speedy Gonzales/The Stripper | 1962 | 2.00 | 4.00 | 8.00 |
—B-side by the Music City Orchestra

WALLS, VAN
45s
ATLANTIC
| ☐ 980 | After Midnight/Blue Sender | 1952 | 25.00 | 50.00 | 100.00 |

WALSH, JOE Also see EAGLES; THE JAMES GANG (1).
12-Inch Singles
ABC
| ☐ SPDJ-46 [DJ] | Turn to Stone (same on both sides) | 1978 | 5.00 | 10.00 | 20.00 |
FULL MOON
| ☐ PRO-A-2038 [DJ] | Space Age Whiz Kids (same on both sides) | 1983 | — | 3.00 | 6.00 |
WARNER BROS.
☐ PRO-A-2340 [DJ]	Good Man Down (same on both sides)	1985	—	2.50	5.00
☐ PRO-A-2756 [DJ]	Radio Song (same on both sides)	1985	—	2.50	5.00
☐ PRO-A-2833 [DJ]	Malibu (same on both sides)	1985	—	2.50	5.00
45s
ABC
☐ 12115	Time Out/Help Me Through the Night	1975	—	2.50	5.00
☐ 12187	Walk Away/Help Me Through the Night	1976	—	2.50	5.00
☐ 12426	Rocky Mountain Way/Turn to Stone	1978	—	2.00	4.00
ABC DUNHILL
☐ 4327	I'll Tell the World About You/Mother Says	1972	—	2.50	5.00
☐ 4361	Rocky Mountain Way/Prayer	1973	—	2.50	5.00
☐ 4373	Meadows/Bookends	1973	—	2.50	5.00
☐ 15026	Turn to Stone/All Night Laundromat Blues	1974	—	2.50	5.00
ASYLUM
☐ 45493	Life's Been Good/Theme from Boat Weirdos	1978	—	2.00	4.00
☐ 45536	At the Station/Over and Over	1978	—	2.00	4.00
☐ 47144	A Life of Illusion/Rockets	1981	—	2.00	4.00
☐ 47197	Made Your Mind Up/Things	1981	—	2.00	4.00
EPIC
☐ 73843	Ordinary Average Guy/Alphabetical Order	1991	—	—	3.00
FULL MOON
☐ 69951	Waffle Stomp/Things	1982	—	2.00	4.00
☐ 69951 [PS]	Waffle Stomp/Things	1982	—	2.00	4.00
FULL MOON/ASYLUM
☐ 46639	All Night Long/Orange Blossom Special	1980	—	2.00	4.00
—B-side by Gilley's Urban Cowboy Band
| ☐ 46639 [PS] | All Night Long/Orange Blossom Special | 1980 | — | 2.50 | 5.00 |
WARNER BROS.
☐ 28225	In My Car/How Ya Doin'?	1987	—	—	3.00
☐ 28304	The Radio Song/How Ya Doin'?	1987	—	—	3.00
☐ 28304 [PS]	The Radio Song/How Ya Doin'?	1987	—	—	3.00
☐ 28910	Good Man Down/I Broke My Leg	1985	—	2.00	4.00
☐ 29454	I.L.B.T.'s/Love Letters	1983	—	2.00	4.00
☐ 29519	Here We Are Now/I Can Play That Rock and Roll	1983	—	2.00	4.00
☐ 29611	Space Age Whiz Kids/Theme from Island Weirdos	1983	—	2.00	4.00
☐ 29611 [PS]	Space Age Whiz Kids/Theme from Island Weirdos	1983	—	2.50	5.00
Albums
ABC
☐ ABCD-932	You Can't Argue with a Sick Mind	1976	2.50	5.00	10.00
☐ AA-1083	The Best of Joe Walsh	1978	2.50	5.00	10.00
—Also contains two James Gang tracks
ABC COMMAND
| ☐ QD-40016 [Q] | The Smoker You Drink, the Player You Get | 1974 | 5.00 | 10.00 | 20.00 |
| ☐ QD-40017 [Q] | So What | 1975 | — | — | — |
—Not released
ABC DUNHILL
| ☐ DS-50130 | Barnstorm | 1972 | 2.50 | 5.00 | 10.00 |
—Of the James Gang and the Eagles
| ☐ DS-50140 | The Smoker You Drink, the Player You Get | 1973 | 2.50 | 5.00 | 10.00 |
| ☐ DS-51071 | So What | 1974 | 2.50 | 5.00 | 10.00 |
ASYLUM
| ☐ 6E-141 | But Seriously, Folks… | 1978 | 2.50 | 5.00 | 10.00 |
| ☐ 5E-523 | There Goes the Neighborhood | 1981 | 2.00 | 4.00 | 8.00 |
MCA
| ☐ 37051 | You Can't Argue with a Sick Mind | 1979 | 2.00 | 4.00 | 8.00 |
—Reissue of ABC 932
| ☐ 37052 | The Best of Joe Walsh | 1979 | 2.00 | 4.00 | 8.00 |
—Reissue of ABC 1083
| ☐ 37053 | Barnstorm | 1979 | 2.00 | 4.00 | 8.00 |
—Reissue of ABC Dunhill 50130
| ☐ 37054 | The Smoker You Drink, the Player You Get | 1979 | 2.00 | 4.00 | 8.00 |
—Reissue of ABC Dunhill 50140
| ☐ 37055 | So What | 1979 | 2.00 | 4.00 | 8.00 |
—Reissue of ABC Dunhill 50171
WARNER BROS.
☐ 23884	You Bought It — You Name It	1983	2.00	4.00	8.00
☐ 25281	The Confessor	1985	2.00	4.00	8.00
☐ 25281 [DJ]	The Confessor	1985	3.75	7.50	15.00
—Promo only on Quiex II vinyl
| ☐ 25606 | Got Any Gum? | 1987 | 2.00 | 4.00 | 8.00 |

WALSTON, RAY
Albums
VEE JAY
| ☐ LP-1110 [M] | My Favorite Songs from "Mary Poppins" and Other Songs to Delight | 1965 | 6.25 | 12.50 | 25.00 |
| ☐ SR-1110 [S] | My Favorite Songs from "Mary Poppins" and Other Songs to Delight | 1965 | 7.50 | 15.00 | 30.00 |

WANDERERS, THE (1)
45s
CUB
| ☐ 9003 | A Teenage Quarrel/My Shining Hour | 1958 | 7.50 | 15.00 | 30.00 |

☐ 9019	Collecting Hearts/ Two Hearts on a Window Pane	1958	10.00	20.00	40.00
☐ 9023	Please/Shadrack, Meshack, and Abednego	1959	7.50	15.00	30.00
☐ 9035	Only When You're Lonely/I'm Not Ashamed	1959	7.50	15.00	30.00
☐ 9054	I Walked Through a Forest/ I'm Waiting for Green Pastures	1959	7.50	15.00	30.00
☐ 9075	I Need You More/I Could Make You Mine	1960	7.50	15.00	30.00
☐ 9089	For Your Love/Sally Goodheart	1961	7.50	15.00	30.00
☐ 9094	I'll Never Smile Again/A Little Too Long	1961	7.50	15.00	30.00
☐ 9099	She Wears My Ring/ Somebody Else's Sweetheart	1961	12.50	25.00	50.00
☐ 9109	There Is No Greater Love/As Time Goes By	1962	7.50	15.00	30.00
MGM
☐ 13082	There Is No Greater Love/As Time Goes By	1962	5.00	10.00	20.00
ONYX
☐ 518	Thinking of You/Great Jumpin' Catfish	1957	15.00	30.00	60.00
ORBIT
☐ 9003	A Teenage Quarrel/My Shining Hour	1958	15.00	30.00	60.00
SAVOY
☐ 1109	We Could Find Happiness/Holy Mae Ethel	1953	125.00	250.00	500.00
UNITED ARTISTS
☐ 570	After He Breaks Your Heart/Run, Run Senorita	1963	3.75	7.50	15.00
☐ 648	I'll Know/You Can't Run Away from Me	1963	7.50	15.00	30.00

WANDERERS, THE (2)
45s
PANAMA
| ☐ 3900 | Quiet Night/One Look | 1960 | 3.75 | 7.50 | 15.00 |

WANDERERS, THE (U) May be by group (1).
45s
GONE
| ☐ 5005 | Mask Off/My Lady Chocaonine | 1957 | 7.50 | 15.00 | 30.00 |

WANDERLEY, WALTER
45s
A&M
| ☐ 1023 | Surfboard/When It Was Done | 1969 | — | 3.00 | 6.00 |
GNP CRESCENDO
| ☐ 824 | Perpetual Motion Love/Monica | 197? | — | 2.00 | 4.00 |
TOWER
| ☐ 296 | You and I/What Do You Know About Me | 1966 | 2.00 | 4.00 | 8.00 |
| ☐ 334 | Brazilian Samba/Murmurio | 1967 | 2.00 | 4.00 | 8.00 |
VERVE
☐ 10421	Summer Samba (So Nice)/Call Me	1966	2.00	4.00	8.00
☐ 10456	Chaganca/Amanha	1966	2.00	4.00	8.00
☐ 10539	On the South Side of Chicago/Minha Saudade	1967	2.00	4.00	8.00
☐ 10579	Sensuous/Kee-Ka-Roo	1968	2.00	4.00	8.00
WORLD PACIFIC
☐ 77861	Jet Samba (Samba Do Aviao)/Sad Samba (Samba Triste)	1966	2.00	4.00	8.00
Albums
A&M
☐ SP-3018	When It Was Done	1969	3.00	6.00	12.00
☐ SP-3022	Moondreams	1969	3.00	6.00	12.00
CANYON
☐ 7711	Return of the Original Sound	196?	3.00	6.00	12.00
GNP CRESCENDO
☐ GNPS-2137	Brazil's Greatest Hits	197?	2.50	5.00	10.00
☐ GNPS-2142	Perpetual Motion Love	197?	2.50	5.00	10.00
MGM LATINO SERIES
☐ LAT 10010 [S]	Cheganca	197?	3.75	7.50	15.00
—Reissue of Verve V6-8676
PHILIPS
☐ PHM 200227 [M]	Brazilian Blend	1967	3.00	6.00	12.00
☐ PHM 200233 [M]	Organ-ized	1967	3.00	6.00	12.00
☐ PHS 600227 [S]	Brazilian Blend	1967	3.75	7.50	15.00
☐ PHS 600233 [S]	Organ-ized	1967	3.75	7.50	15.00
TOWER
☐ ST 5047 [S]	From Rio with Love	1966	3.75	7.50	15.00
☐ T 5047 [M]	From Rio with Love	1966	3.75	7.50	15.00
☐ ST 5058 [S]	Murmurio	1967	3.75	7.50	15.00
☐ T 5058 [M]	Murmurio	1967	3.75	7.50	15.00
VERVE
☐ V-8658 [M]	Rain Forest	1966	3.75	7.50	15.00
☐ V6-8658 [S]	Rain Forest	1966	5.00	10.00	20.00
☐ V-8676 [M]	Cheganca	1966	3.75	7.50	15.00
☐ V6-8676 [S]	Cheganca	1966	5.00	10.00	20.00
☐ V-8706 [M]	Batucada	1967	5.00	10.00	20.00
☐ V6-8706 [S]	Batucada	1967	3.75	7.50	15.00
☐ V-8739 [M]	Kee-Ka-Roo	1967	5.00	10.00	20.00
☐ V6-8739 [S]	Kee-Ka-Roo	1967	3.75	7.50	15.00
WORLD PACIFIC
☐ WP-1856 [M]	Samba So!	1967	5.00	10.00	20.00
☐ WP-1866 [M]	Quarteto Bossamba	1967	6.25	12.50	25.00
☐ ST-21856 [S]	Samba So!	1967	3.75	7.50	15.00
☐ ST-21866 [S]	Quarteto Bossamba	1967	3.75	7.50	15.00

WAR Also see ERIC BURDON AND WAR.
12-Inch Singles
AVENUE
| ☐ 76028 | Da Roof (3 versions) | 1994 | 2.00 | 4.00 | 8.00 |
LAX
| ☐ 02122 | Cinco de Mayo (7:29) (3:59) | 1981 | 2.50 | 5.00 | 10.00 |
PRIORITY
| ☐ VL-9364 | Low Rider '87 (Extended Version 7:45) (Radio Edit) (Instrumental) | 1987 | 3.75 | 7.50 | 15.00 |
| ☐ VL-9502 | Livin' in the Red (versions unknown) | 1987 | 3.00 | 6.00 | 12.00 |
RCA
☐ PD-13062	You Got the Power/Cinco de Mayo	1982	2.50	5.00	10.00
☐ PD-13239	Outlaw/I'm About Somebody	1982	2.50	5.00	10.00
☐ JD-13323 [DJ]	Just Because (same on both sides)	1982	2.00	4.00	8.00
☐ PD-13323	Just Because (Long Version)/ The Jungle (Medley)	1982	2.50	5.00	10.00
SISAPA
☐ 76707	Truth Be Known (4 versions)	1991	2.00	4.00	8.00

Number	Title (A Side/B Side)	Yr	VG	VG+	NM
UNITED ARTISTS					
❏ SP-184 [DJ]	Youngblood (Livin' in the Streets) (9:07)/Keep On Doin'	1978	3.75	7.50	15.00
45s					
BLUE NOTE					
❏ 1009	L.A. Sunshine/Slowly We Walk Together	1977	—	2.50	5.00
COCO PLUM					
❏ 2002	Groovin'/(Instrumental)	1985	—	2.00	4.00
LAX					
❏ 02120	Cinco de Mayo/Don't Let No One Get You Down	1981	—	2.50	5.00
MCA					
❏ 40820	Galaxy (Part 1)/Galaxy (Part 2)	1977	—	2.50	5.00
❏ 40820 [PS]	Galaxy (Part 1)/Galaxy (Part 2)	1977	—	3.00	6.00
❏ 40883	Hey Senorita/Sweet Fighting Lady	1978	—	2.50	5.00
❏ 40995	Good, Good Feelin'/Baby Face (She Said Do Do Do Do)	1979	—	2.50	5.00
❏ 41061	I'm the One Who Understands/ Corns & Calloues	1979	—	2.50	5.00
❏ 41158	Don't Take It Away/The Music Band 2 (We Are the Music Band)	1979	—	2.50	5.00
❏ 41209	I'll Be Around/The Music Band 2 (We Are the Music Band)	1980	—	2.50	5.00
RCA					
❏ PB-13061	You Got the Power/Cinco de Mayo	1982	—	2.00	4.00
❏ PB-13239	Outlaw/I'm About Somebody	1982	—	2.00	4.00
❏ PB-13322	Just Because/The Jungle (Medley)	1982	—	2.00	4.00
❏ JH-13426 [DJ]	Baby, It's Cold Outside (same on both sides)	1982	—	2.50	5.00
❏ PB-13544	Life (Is So Strange)/W.W. III	1983	—	2.00	4.00
UNITED ARTISTS					
❏ XW163	The Cisco Kid/Beetles in the Bog	1973	—	2.50	5.00
❏ XW281	Gypsy Man/Deliver the Word	1973	—	2.50	5.00
❏ XW350	Me and Baby Brother/In Your Eyes	1973	—	2.50	5.00
❏ XW432	Ballero/Slippin' Into Darkness	1974	—	2.50	5.00
❏ XW629	Why Can't We Be Friends?/In Mazatlin	1975	—	2.50	5.00
❏ XW629 [PS]	Why Can't We Be Friends?/In Mazatlin	1975	—	3.00	6.00
❏ XW706	Low Rider/So	1975	—	2.50	5.00
❏ XW706 [PS]	Low Rider/So	1975	—	3.00	6.00
❏ XW834	Summer/All Day Music	1976	—	2.50	5.00
❏ XW1213	Youngblood/(Instrumental)	1978	—	2.50	5.00
❏ XW1247	Sing a Happy Song/This Funky Music Makes You Feel Good	1978	—	2.50	5.00
❏ 50746	Lonely Feelin'/Sun Oh Sun	1971	2.00	4.00	8.00
❏ 50746 [PS]	Lonely Feelin'/Sun Oh Sun	1971	3.00	6.00	12.00
❏ 50815	All Day Music/Get Down	1971	2.00	4.00	8.00
❏ 50867	Slippin' Into Darkness/Happy Head	1971	—	3.00	6.00
❏ 50975	The World Is a Ghetto/Four Cornered Room	1972	—	3.00	6.00
7-Inch Extended Plays					
UNITED ARTISTS					
❏ SP-92 [DJ]	Where Was You At/City, Country, City//Beetles in the Bog/Four Cornered Room	1972	2.50	5.00	10.00
❏ SP-92 [PS]	Edited Versions from The World Is a Ghetto	1972	2.50	5.00	10.00
Albums					
AVENUE					
❏ R1 71706	Peace Sign	1994	3.75	7.50	15.00
BLUE NOTE					
❏ BN-LA690-G [(2)]	Platinum Jazz	1977	3.00	6.00	12.00
LAX					
❏ PW 37111	All Day Music	1981	2.50	5.00	10.00
—Reissue of United Artists 5546					
❏ PW 37112	The World Is a Ghetto	1981	2.50	5.00	10.00
—Reissue of United Artists 5652					
❏ PW 37113	Why Can't We Be Friends?	1981	2.50	5.00	10.00
—Reissue of United Artists 441					
MCA					
❏ 745	Galaxy	1983	2.00	4.00	8.00
—Reissue of MCA 3030					
❏ 747	The Music Band	1983	2.00	4.00	8.00
—Reissue of MCA 3085					
❏ 751	The Music Band 2	1983	2.00	4.00	8.00
—Reissue of MCA 3193					
❏ 3030	Galaxy	1977	2.50	5.00	10.00
❏ 3085	The Music Band	1979	2.50	5.00	10.00
❏ 3193	The Music Band 2	1979	2.50	5.00	10.00
❏ 5156	The Music Band Live	1980	2.50	5.00	10.00
❏ 5362	Best of the Music Band	1982	2.50	5.00	10.00
❏ 5411	Music Band Jazz	1983	2.50	5.00	10.00
PRIORITY					
❏ SL 9467	The Best of War…And More	1987	2.50	5.00	10.00
RCA VICTOR					
❏ AFL1-4208	Outlaw	1982	2.50	5.00	10.00
❏ AFL1-4598	Life (Is So Strange)	1983	2.50	5.00	10.00
UNITED ARTISTS					
❏ SP-103 [DJ]	Radio Free War	1974	6.25	12.50	25.00
—Promo only on blue vinyl					
❏ UA-LA128-F	Deliver the Word	1973	3.00	6.00	12.00
❏ UA-LA193-J [(2)]	War Live!	1974	3.75	7.50	15.00
❏ UA-LA441-G	Why Can't We Be Friends?	1975	2.50	5.00	10.00
❏ UA-LA648-G	Greatest Hits	1976	2.50	5.00	10.00
❏ UAS-5508	War	1971	3.75	7.50	15.00
❏ UAS-5546	All Day Music	1971	3.75	7.50	15.00
❏ UAS-5652	The World Is a Ghetto	1972	3.00	6.00	12.00

WAR BABIES, THE
45s

Number	Title (A Side/B Side)	Yr	VG	VG+	NM
UNI					
❏ 55164	War Baby/Together Forever	1969	2.00	4.00	8.00

WARD, BILLY, AND THE DOMINOES Also includes "The Dominoes."
45s

Number	Title (A Side/B Side)	Yr	VG	VG+	NM
ABC-PARAMOUNT					
❏ 10128	You're Mine/The World Is Waiting for the Sunrise	1960	5.00	10.00	20.00
❏ 10156	You/Gypsy	1960	5.00	10.00	20.00
DECCA					
❏ 29933	St. Therese of the Roses/ Home Is Where You Hang Your Hat	1956	7.50	15.00	30.00

Number	Title (A Side/B Side)	Yr	VG	VG+	NM
❏ 30043	Come On, Shake, Let's Crawl/ Will You Remember	1956	7.50	15.00	30.00
❏ 30149	Half a Love (Is Better Than None)/Evermore	1956	7.50	15.00	30.00
❏ 30199	Rock, Plymouth Rock/Till Kingdom Come	1957	7.50	15.00	30.00
❏ 30420	To Each His Own/ I Don't Stand a Ghost of a Chance	1957	7.50	15.00	30.00
❏ 30514	September Song/When the Saints Go Marching In	1957	7.50	15.00	30.00
FEDERAL					
❏ 12001	Do Something For Me/Chicken Blues	1951	200.00	400.00	800.00
—Note: Federal 12010 and 12016 were issued only on 78s					
❏ 12022AA	Sixty Minute Man/I Can't Escape from You	1951	125.00	250.00	500.00
❏ 12036	Heart to Heart/ Looking for a Man to Satisfy My Soul	1951	125.00	250.00	500.00
—With Little Esther					
❏ 12039	I Am with You/Weeping Willow Blues	1951	100.00	200.00	400.00
❏ 12059	That's What You're Doing to Me/When the Swallows Come Back to Capistrano	1952	100.00	200.00	400.00
❏ 12068AA	Have Mercy Baby/Deep Sea Blues	1952	62.50	125.00	250.00
❏ 12072	Love, Love, Love/ That's What You're Doing to Me	1952	50.00	100.00	200.00
❏ 12105	I'd Be Satisfied/No Room	1952	45.00	90.00	180.00
❏ 12106	I'm Lonely/Yours Forever	1952	45.00	90.00	180.00
❏ 12114	The Bells/Pedal Pushin' Papa	1952	50.00	100.00	200.00
❏ 12129	These Foolish Things Remind Me of You/ Don't Leave Me This Way	1953	75.00	150.00	300.00
—Green label, gold top					
❏ 12129	These Foolish Things Remind Me of You/ Don't Leave Me This Way	1954	25.00	50.00	100.00
—Green label, silver top					
❏ 12129	These Foolish Things Remind Me of You/ Don't Leave Me This Way	1955	7.50	15.00	30.00
—All-green label					
❏ 12139	You Can't Keep a Good Man Down/ Where Now Little Heart	1953	25.00	50.00	100.00
❏ 12162	Until the Real Thing Comes Along/My Baby's 3 D	1954	25.00	50.00	100.00
❏ 12178	Tootsie Roll/Move to the Outskirts of Town	1954	25.00	50.00	100.00
❏ 12184	Handwriting on the Wall/One Moment with You	1954	50.00	100.00	200.00
❏ 12193	Above Jacob's Ladder/Little Black Train	1954	12.50	25.00	50.00
❏ 12209	Can't Do Sixty No More/If I Never Get to Heaven	1955	25.00	50.00	100.00
❏ 12218	Love Me Now or Let Me Go/Cave Man	1955	12.50	25.00	50.00
❏ 12263	Bobby Sox Baby/How Long, How Long Blues	1956	12.50	25.00	50.00
❏ 12301	St. Louis Blues/One Moment with You	1957	12.50	25.00	50.00
❏ 12308	Have Mercy Baby/Love, Love, Love	1957	10.00	20.00	40.00
JUBLIEE					
❏ 5163	Gimme, Gimme, Gimme/Come to Me, Baby	1954	7.50	15.00	30.00
❏ 5213	Sweethearts on Parade/ Take Me Back to Heaven	1955	7.50	15.00	30.00
KING					
❏ 1280	Rags to Riches/Don't Ask Me	1953	12.50	25.00	50.00
❏ 1281	Christmas in Heaven/ Ringing In a Brand New Year	1953	25.00	50.00	100.00
❏ 1342	Tenderly/Little Lie	1954	12.50	25.00	50.00
❏ 1364	Three Coins in the Fountain/Lonesome Road	1954	12.50	25.00	50.00
❏ 1368	Little Things Mean a Lot/I Really Don't Want to Know	1954	10.00	20.00	40.00
❏ 1492	Learnin' the Blues/May I Never Love	1955	10.00	20.00	40.00
❏ 1502	Over the Rainbow/Give Me You	1955	10.00	20.00	40.00
❏ 5322	Sixty Minute Man/Have Mercy Baby	1960	5.00	10.00	20.00
❏ 5463	Lay It on the Line/ That's How You Know You're Growing Old	1961	5.00	10.00	20.00
❏ 6002	I'm Walking Behind You/This Love of Mine	1965	5.00	10.00	20.00
❏ 6016	O Holy Night/What Are You Doin' New Year's Eve	1965	5.00	10.00	20.00
LIBERTY					
❏ 55071	Star Dust/Lucinda	1957	6.25	12.50	25.00
❏ 55071 [PS]	Star Dust/Lucinda	1957	25.00	50.00	100.00
❏ 55099	Deep Purple/Do It Again	1957	6.25	12.50	25.00
❏ 55111	My Proudest Possession/Someone Greater Than I	1957	6.25	12.50	25.00
❏ 55126	Solitude/You Grow Sweeter As the Years Go By	1958	6.25	12.50	25.00
❏ 55136	Jennie Lee/Music, Maestro, Please	1958	6.25	12.50	25.00
❏ 55181	Please Don't Say No/Behave, Hula Girl	1959	6.25	12.50	25.00
RO-ZAN					
❏ 10001	Man in the Stain Glass Window/ My Fair Weather Friend	1961	5.00	10.00	20.00
UNITED ARTISTS					
❏ 0017	Stardust/These Foolish Things	1973	—	2.50	5.00
—"Silver Spotlight Series" reissue					
7-Inch Extended Plays					
DECCA					
❏ ED 2549	(contents unknown)	1958	50.00	100.00	200.00
❏ ED 2549 [PS]	Billy Ward and His Dominoes	1958	50.00	100.00	200.00
FEDERAL					
❏ 212	Sixty Minute Man/Do Something for Me//Have Mercy Baby/Don't Leave Me This Way	1956	25.00	50.00	100.00
—All-green label					
❏ 212	Sixty Minute Man/Do Something for Me//Have Mercy Baby/Don't Leave Me This Way	1956	100.00	200.00	400.00
—Green label, silver top					
❏ 212 [PS]	Billy Ward and His Dominoes, Vol. 1	1956	25.00	50.00	100.00
❏ 262	*The Bells/Pedal Pushin' Papa/I'd Be Satisfied/ That's What You're Doing to Me	1957	25.00	50.00	100.00
—All-green label					
❏ 262	*The Bells/Pedal Pushin' Papa/I'd Be Satisfied/ That's What You're Doing to Me	1957	100.00	200.00	400.00
—Green label, silver top					
❏ 262 [PS]	Billy Ward and His Dominoes, Vol. 2	1957	25.00	50.00	100.00
❏ 269	*These Foolish Things Remind Me of You/Rags to Riches/When the Swallows Come Back to Capistrano/Harbor Lights	1957	25.00	50.00	100.00
—All-green label					
❏ 269	*These Foolish Things Remind Me of You/Rags to Riches/When the Swallows Come Back to Capistrano/Harbor Lights	1957	100.00	200.00	400.00
—Green label, silver top					
❏ 269 [PS]	Billy Ward and His Dominoes Singing the All Time Hit Standards	1957	25.00	50.00	100.00

Number	Title (A Side/B Side)	Yr	VG	VG+	NM
LIBERTY					
❏ LEP-1-3056	(contents unknown)	1959	25.00	50.00	100.00
❏ LEP-1-3056 [PS]	Sea of Glass (Part One)	1959	25.00	50.00	100.00
❏ LEP-2-3056	Deep River/By and By//The House of the Lord/ The Lullaby Divine	1959	25.00	50.00	100.00
❏ LEP-2-3056 [PS]	Sea of Glass (Part 2)	1959	25.00	50.00	100.00
❏ LEP-3-3056	(contents unknown)	1959	25.00	50.00	100.00
❏ LEP-3-3056 [PS]	Sea of Glass (Part 3)	1959	25.00	50.00	100.00
❏ LEP-1-3083	Stardust/Eatin' and Sleepin'//Music, Maestro, Please/I'll Never Ask for More Than This	1959	25.00	50.00	100.00
❏ LEP-1-3083 [PS]	Yours Forever (Part One)	1959	25.00	50.00	100.00
❏ LEP-2-3083	Deep Purple/Lucinda//These Foolish Things/ Don't Say I Love You	1959	25.00	50.00	100.00
❏ LEP-2-3083 [PS]	Yours Forever (Part Two)	1959	25.00	50.00	100.00
❏ LEP-3-3083	Smoke Gets in Your Eyes/Do It Again//If You Please/Yours Forever	1959	25.00	50.00	100.00
❏ LEP-3-3083 [PS]	Yours Forever (Part Three)	1959	25.00	50.00	100.00
Albums					
DECCA					
❏ DL 8621 [M]	Billy Ward and the Dominoes	1958	50.00	100.00	200.00
FEDERAL					
❏ 295-94 [10]	Billy Ward and His Dominoes	1955	6000.	9500.	13000.
❏ 548 [M]	Billy Ward and His Dominoes	1958	375.00	750.00	1500.
❏ 559 [M]	Clyde McPhatter with Billy Ward and His Dominoes	1958	300.00	600.00	1200.
KING					
❏ 548 [M]	Billy Ward and His Dominoes	1958	—	—	—
—Unknown					
❏ 559 [M]	Clyde McPhatter with Billy Ward and His Dominoes	1958	150.00	300.00	600.00
—Yellow cover					
❏ 559 [M]	Clyde McPhatter with Billy Ward and His Dominoes	196?	75.00	150.00	300.00
—Pink cover					
❏ 733 [M]	Billy Ward and His Dominoes Featuring Clyde McPhatter and Jackie Wilson	1961	150.00	300.00	600.00
❏ 952 [M]	24 Songs	1966	12.50	25.00	50.00
❏ 5005	14 Hits	197?	3.00	6.00	12.00
❏ 5008	21 Hits	197?	3.00	6.00	12.00
LIBERTY					
❏ LRP-3056 [M]	Sea of Glass	1957	15.00	30.00	60.00
❏ LRP-3083 [M]	Yours Forever	1958	15.00	30.00	60.00
❏ LRP-3113 [M]	Pagan Love Song	1959	15.00	30.00	60.00
❏ LST-7113 [S]	Pagan Love Song	1959	25.00	50.00	100.00

WARD, BURT

45s

Number	Title (A Side/B Side)	Yr	VG	VG+	NM
MGM					
❏ 13632	Boy Wonder I Love You/Orange Colored Sky	1966	50.00	100.00	200.00

—Written and produced by Frank Zappa

WARD, HERB

45s

Number	Title (A Side/B Side)	Yr	VG	VG+	NM
ARGO					
❏ 5510	Strange Change/Why Do You Want to Leave	1965	20.00	40.00	80.00
RCA VICTOR					
❏ 47-9688	Honest to Goodness/If You Got to Leave Me	1968	15.00	30.00	60.00

WARD, JOE

45s

Number	Title (A Side/B Side)	Yr	VG	VG+	NM
GUSTO					
❏ 814	Nuttin' For Christmas/Christmas Time's A Coming	1979	—	2.00	4.00
—B-side by Mac Wiseman					
KING					
❏ 4854	Nuttin' for Xmas/Christmas Questions	1955	3.00	6.00	12.00
❏ 4897	Upsy Down Town/Mama Darling	1956	5.00	10.00	20.00
❏ 4931	Rock and Roll Merry-Go-Round/Freckle Face	1956	5.00	10.00	20.00

WARD, ROBIN

45s

Number	Title (A Side/B Side)	Yr	VG	VG+	NM
DOT					
❏ 16530	Wonderful Summer/Dream Boy	1963	3.00	6.00	12.00
❏ 16578	Winter's Here/Bobby	1963	2.50	5.00	10.00
❏ 16599	Johnny Come and Get Me/Where the Blue of the Night Meets the Gold of the Day	1964	5.00	10.00	20.00
❏ 16624	In His Car/Wishing	1964	6.25	12.50	25.00
Albums					
DOT					
❏ DLP 3555 [M]	Wonderful Summer	1963	50.00	100.00	200.00
❏ DLP 25555 [S]	Wonderful Summer	1963	75.00	150.00	300.00

WARD, SINGIN' SAMMY

45s

Number	Title (A Side/B Side)	Yr	VG	VG+	NM
MOTOWN					
❏ 1004	Lover/That's Why I Love You So Much	1960	10.00	20.00	40.00
—With Sherri Taylor					
SOUL					
❏ 35004	Bread Winner/You've Got to Change	1964	12.50	25.00	50.00
TAMLA					
❏ 54030	What Makes You Love Him/The Child Is Really Wild	1960	18.75	37.50	75.00
—With globe label					
❏ 54030	What Makes You Love Him/The Child Is Really Wild	1960	50.00	100.00	200.00
—With lines label					
❏ 54049	What Makes You Love Him/Don't Take It Away	1961	12.50	25.00	50.00
❏ 54057	Everybody Knew It/Big Joe Moe	1962	12.50	25.00	50.00
❏ 54071	Part Time Love/Someday Pretty Baby	1962	12.50	25.00	50.00

WARD, WALTER, AND THE CHALLENGERS Later recorded as THE OLYMPICS.

45s

Number	Title (A Side/B Side)	Yr	VG	VG+	NM
MELATONE					
❏ 1002	I Can Tell/The Mambo Beat	1957	100.00	200.00	400.00

WARDELL AND THE SULTANS

45s

Number	Title (A Side/B Side)	Yr	VG	VG+	NM
IMPERIAL					
❏ 5812	The Original Popeye/Dance Time	1962	5.00	10.00	20.00
❏ 5886	I Need Your Love/I'm Broke	1962	3.75	7.50	15.00

WARE, CURTIS, AND THE FOUR DO-MATICS

45s

Number	Title (A Side/B Side)	Yr	VG	VG+	NM
KAYBEE					
❏ 101	Flame in My Heart/Am I in Love	1961	125.00	250.00	500.00

WARE, EDDIE

45s

Number	Title (A Side/B Side)	Yr	VG	VG+	NM
STATES					
❏ 130	That's the Stuff I Like/Lonely Broken Heart	1954	30.00	60.00	120.00

WARING, FRED, AND THE PENNSYLVANIANS

45s

Number	Title (A Side/B Side)	Yr	VG	VG+	NM
CAPITOL					
❏ F3901	Christmas Was Meant for Children/I Heard the Bells on Christmas Day	1958	3.00	6.00	12.00
❏ F3993	Zorro/Din Skol Min Skol	1958	2.50	5.00	10.00
❏ 4289	Inch Worm/The Donkey Song	1959	2.00	4.00	8.00
DECCA					
❏ 9-67 [[4]]	'Twas the Night Before Christmas	1950	12.50	25.00	50.00
—Contains 4 records (23642, 23643, 23644, 23645) and box					
❏ 9-74 [[3]]	The Song of Christmas	1950	10.00	20.00	40.00
—Includes records and box					
❏ 9-97 [[4]]		195?	12.50	25.00	50.00
—Contains 4 records (27283, 27284, 27285, 27286) and box					
❏ 23642	Twas the Night Before Christmas (Part 1)/Twas the Night Before Christmas (Part 2)	1950	3.00	6.00	12.00
—Sides 1 and 2 of "Album No. 9-67"					
❏ 23643	Silent Night/Oh Gathering Clouds	1950	3.00	6.00	12.00
—Sides 3 and 4 of "Album No. 9-67"					
❏ 23644	Adeste Fideles/Cantique de Noel	1950	3.00	6.00	12.00
—Sides 5 and 6 of "Album No. 9-67"					
❏ 23645	The First Noel/O Little Town of Bethlehem//Carol of the Bells/Beautiful Saviour	1950	3.00	6.00	12.00
—Sides 7 and 8 of "Album No. 9-67"					
❏ 24500	White Christmas/Twelve Days Of Christmas	195?	3.00	6.00	12.00
—78 originally released in 1948					
❏ 24500	White Christmas/Twelve Days Of Christmas	1960	2.00	4.00	8.00
—Also known to exist on color bars label					
❏ 25698	Lollytoodum/On Top of Old Smoky	1966	—	2.50	5.00
❏ 27146	Ave Maria/The Rosary	1950	3.00	6.00	12.00
❏ 27147	The Bells of St. Mary's/In a Monastery Garden	1950	3.00	6.00	12.00
❏ 27148	The Lord's Prayer/Were You There When They Crucified My Lord	1950	3.00	6.00	12.00
❏ 27149	Faith of Our Fathers/Blest Be the Tie That Binds	1950	3.00	6.00	12.00
—The above four comprise a box set					
❏ 27150	A Cigarette, Sweet Music and You/So Beats My Heart for You	1950	3.00	6.00	12.00
❏ 27151	Remember/Day In-Day Out	1950	3.00	6.00	12.00
❏ 27152	Besame Mucho/Marcheta	1950	3.00	6.00	12.00
❏ 27153	Beyond the Blue Horizon/My Ideal	1950	3.00	6.00	12.00
—The above four comprise a box set					
❏ 27283	When Angels Sang Of Peace/The Christmas Song (Merry Christmas To You)	1950	3.00	6.00	12.00
—Sides 1 and 2 of "Album No. 9-97"					
❏ 27284	A Musical Christmas Card/O Christmas Tree// Kentucky Wassailsong/Parade Of The Wooden Soldiers	1950	3.00	6.00	12.00
—Sides 3 and 4 of "Album No. 9-97"					
❏ 27285	Heigh Ho the Holly/See Amid the Winter's Snow//Behold That Star/Carol of the Bells	1950	3.00	6.00	12.00
—Sides 5 and 6 of "Album No. 9-97"					
❏ 27286	Jingle Bells (Part 1)/Jingle Bells (Part 2)	1950	3.00	6.00	12.00
—Sides 7 and 8 of "Album No. 9-97"					
❏ 27291	Oklahoma!/The Surrey with the Fringe on Top	1950	3.00	6.00	12.00
❏ 27292	This Was A Real Nice Christmas/ You'll Never Walk Alone	1950	3.00	6.00	12.00
❏ 27292	You'll Never Walk Alone/ This Was a Real Nice Christmas	1950	3.00	6.00	12.00
❏ 27293	If I Loved You/What's the Use of Wond'rin'	1950	3.00	6.00	12.00
❏ 27294	Bali Ha'i/Some Enchanted Evening	1950	3.00	6.00	12.00
❏ 27295	A Wonderful Guy/People Will Say We're in Love	1950	3.00	6.00	12.00
❏ 27297	It Might As Well Be Spring/A Fellow Needs a Girl	1950	3.00	6.00	12.00
❏ 27454	No Man Is an Island/Worship	1951	3.00	6.00	12.00
❏ 27465	Palms/Before the Crucifix	1951	3.00	6.00	12.00
❏ 27480	The Place Where I Worship/A Home That's Filled with Love	1951	3.00	6.00	12.00
❏ 27496	Faithful/My Lost Melody	1951	3.00	6.00	12.00
❏ 27507	The Loveliest Night of the Year/ Tulips and Heather	1951	3.00	6.00	12.00
❏ 27581	Something Wonderful/Hello, Young Lovers	1951	3.00	6.00	12.00
❏ 27600	I Whistle a Happy Tune/We Kiss in the Shadows	1951	3.00	6.00	12.00
❏ 27855	Monastery Bells/A Little Foolish Pride	1951	3.00	6.00	12.00
❏ 27935	Remember Your Promise (Say the Bells of St. Thomas)/Two Sleepy People	1952	3.00	6.00	12.00
❏ 27964	You'll Never Walk Alone/Tulips and Heather	1952	3.00	6.00	12.00
❏ 27988	Heigh-Ho/Whistle While You Work	1952	3.00	6.00	12.00
❏ 28020	The Caissons Go Rolling Along/Army Air Corps	1952	3.00	6.00	12.00
❏ 28235	It Happened in Monterey/You	1952	3.00	6.00	12.00
❏ 28298	Peace in the Valley/Just a Closer Walk with Thee	1952	3.00	6.00	12.00
❏ 28305	My Gal Sal/I Do, I Do, I Do	1952	3.00	6.00	12.00
❏ 28400	Bibbidi-Bobbidi-Boo/Zip-a-Dee-Doo-Dah	1952	3.00	6.00	12.00
❏ 28401	When You Wish Upon a Star/One Song	1952	3.00	6.00	12.00
❏ 28402	Lavender Blue/Tico Tico	1952	3.00	6.00	12.00
❏ 28449	High Noon (Do Not Forsake Me)/ Outside of Heaven	1952	3.00	6.00	12.00
❏ 28512	God Bless America/Where in the World	1952	3.00	6.00	12.00
❏ 28527	Somebody Loves You/True, Be True, My Love	1953	2.50	5.00	10.00
❏ 28559	Mamie/Ike, Mr. President	1953	5.00	10.00	20.00
❏ 28600	One to Remember/Just a Dream of You Dear	1953	2.50	5.00	10.00
❏ 28970	Winter Wonderland/Snow, Snow	1953	3.00	6.00	12.00
❏ 29063	Easter Parade/Say It with Music	1954	2.50	5.00	10.00

Number	Title (A Side/B Side)	Yr	VG	VG+	NM
❏ 29192	My Friend/He Was There	1954	2.50	5.00	10.00
❏ 29304	Fanny/Restless Heart	1954	2.50	5.00	10.00
❏ 29305	Be Kind to Your Parents/I Have to Tell You	1954	2.50	5.00	10.00
❏ 29331	Without Love/Silk Stockings	1954	2.50	5.00	10.00
❏ 29351	Rudolph the Red-Nosed Reindeer/ Santa Claus Is Comin' to Town	1954	3.00	6.00	12.00
❏ 29451	We'll Go a Long Way Together/ He Was the Happiest	1955	2.50	5.00	10.00
❏ 29619	(I'll Be With You) In Apple Blossom Time/ Drug Store Cowboy	1955	2.50	5.00	10.00
❏ 30197	The Navy Hymn/Anchors Aweigh	1957	2.00	4.00	8.00
❏ 32323	Big Man/Kites Are Fun	1968	—	2.50	5.00
❏ 88023	A Visit From St. Nicholas Part 1/ A Visit From St. Nicholas Part 2	195?	3.00	6.00	12.00
❏ 88023 [PS]	A Visit From St. Nicholas Part 1/ A Visit From St. Nicholas Part 2	195?	5.00	10.00	20.00

REPRISE

Number	Title (A Side/B Side)	Yr	VG	VG+	NM
❏ 0315	It's Christmas Time Again/Christmas Candles	1964	3.00	6.00	12.00
—With Bing Crosby					
❏ 0316	The 12 Days of Christmas/ Do You Hear What I Hear	1964	2.50	5.00	10.00

7-Inch Extended Plays

CAPITOL

Number	Title (A Side/B Side)	Yr	VG	VG+	NM
❏ EAP 1-845	Whiffenpoof Song/So Beats My Heart for You/ Sleep//I Hear Music/Ol' Man River	1957	3.00	6.00	12.00
❏ EAP 1-845 [PS]	Fred Waring and the Pennsylvanians in Hi-Fi, Part 1	1957	3.00	6.00	12.00
❏ EAP 2-845	(contents unknown)	1957	3.00	6.00	12.00
❏ EAP 2-845 [PS]	Fred Waring and the Pennsylvanians in Hi-Fi, Part 2	1957	3.00	6.00	12.00
❏ EAP 3-845	(contents unknown)	1957	3.00	6.00	12.00
❏ EAP 3-845 [PS]	Fred Waring and the Pennsylvanians in Hi-Fi, Part 3	1957	3.00	6.00	12.00
❏ EAP 1-896	*Now Is the Caroling Season/We Three Kings/ Winter Wonderland/It Was a Night of Wonder/ White Christmas	1957	3.00	6.00	12.00
❏ EAP 1-896 [PS]	Now Is the Caroling Season, Part 1	1957	3.00	6.00	12.00
❏ EAP 2-896	O Christmas Tree/Silver Bells/Angels We Have Heard on High/In Sweetest Jubilee//I Heard the Bells on Christmas Day/ The Christmas Song	1957	3.00	6.00	12.00
❏ EAP 2-896 [PS]	Now Is the Caroling Season, Part 2	1957	3.00	6.00	12.00
❏ EAP 3-896	(contents unknown)	1957	3.00	6.00	12.00
❏ EAP 3-896 [PS]	Now Is the Caroling Season, Part 3	1957	3.00	6.00	12.00

DECCA

Number	Title (A Side/B Side)	Yr	VG	VG+	NM
❏ ED-548 [PS]	'Twas the Night Before Christmas	195?	3.00	6.00	12.00
—Cover for 2-EP set					
❏ ED 678 [PS]	Christmas Time	195?	2.50	5.00	10.00
—Cover for 2-EP set					
❏ ED 2007	Holiday for Strings/Prelude of the Bells// Jalousie/Hora Staccato	195?	3.00	6.00	12.00
❏ ED 2007 [PS]	Fred Waring and His Pennsylvanians, Vol. 1	195?	3.00	6.00	12.00
❏ ED 2038	Over the Rainbow/Stormy Weather//I Gotta Right to Sing the Blues/Let's Fall in Love	195?	3.00	6.00	12.00
❏ ED 2038 [PS]	Fred Waring and His Pennsylvanians, Vol. 2	195?	3.00	6.00	12.00
❏ ED 2039	(contents unknown)	195?	3.00	6.00	12.00
❏ ED 2039 [PS]	Fred Waring and the Pennsylvanians	195?	3.00	6.00	12.00
❏ ED 2198	The Holy City//The Palms/Before the Crucifix	195?	3.00	6.00	12.00
❏ ED 2198 [PS]	The Holy City	195?	3.00	6.00	12.00
❏ ED 2199	(contents unknown)	195?	3.00	6.00	12.00
❏ ED 2199 [PS]	Songs of Easter	195?	3.00	6.00	12.00
❏ ED 2546	The Night Before Christmas//It Came Upon the Midnight Clear/The First Noel-O Little Town of Bethlehem-Carol of the Bells	195?	3.00	6.00	12.00
❏ ED 2546 [PS]	Christmastime	195?	3.00	6.00	12.00
❏ ED 2656	(contents unknown)	195?	3.00	6.00	12.00
❏ ED 2656 [PS]	Christmas Songs	195?	3.00	6.00	12.00
❏ 91125	'Twas the Night Before Christmas// Silent Night/On Gathering Clouds	195?	3.00	6.00	12.00
—Part of 2-EP set ED 548					
❏ 91126	Adeste Fideles/Cantique de Noel//The First Noel-O LIttle Town of Bethlehem-Carol of the Bells//Beautiful Savior	195?	3.00	6.00	12.00
—Part of 2-EP set ED 548					
❏ 91224	I Believe/My Cathedral//One Little Candle/ No Man Is an Island	1954	2.50	5.00	10.00
—Part of 2-EP set ED 635					
❏ 91225	Somebody Bigger Than You and I/There'll Be Peace in the Valley for Me//He Was There/ You'll Never Walk Alone	1954	2.50	5.00	10.00
—Part of 2-EP set ED 635					
❏ 91329	When Angels Sang Of Peace/The Christmas Song//Medley: A Musical Christmas Card-O Christmas Tree-The Sleigh/Medley: Kentucky Wassail Song-Parade of the Wooden Soldiers	195?	2.50	5.00	10.00
—Part of 2-EP set ED 678					
❏ 91330	Medley: Heigh Ho The Holly-See Amid The Winter's Snow/Medley: Behold That Star-Carol Of The Bells//Jingle Bells	195?	2.50	5.00	10.00
—Part of 2-EP set ED 678					

Albums

CAPITOL

Number	Title (A Side/B Side)	Yr	VG	VG+	NM
❏ STBB-347 [(2)]	Christmas Magic	1969	3.75	7.50	15.00
—Collects ST 1260 and ST 1610 in one package (abridged); green label original					
❏ STBB-347 [(2)]	Christmas Magic	1972	3.00	6.00	12.00
—Orange label reissue					
❏ ST 896 [S]	Now Is the Caroling Season	1959	3.75	7.50	15.00
—Black colorband label, logo at left					
❏ ST 896 [S]	Now Is the Caroling Season	1962	3.00	6.00	12.00
—Black colorband label, logo at top					
❏ T 896 [M]	Now Is the Caroling Season	1957	5.00	10.00	20.00
—Originals have turquoise labels					
❏ T 896 [M]	Now Is the Caroling Season	1959	3.75	7.50	15.00
—Black colorband label, logo at left					
❏ T 896 [M]	Now Is the Caroling Season	1962	3.00	6.00	12.00
—Black colorband label, logo at top					
❏ ST 936 [S]	All Through the Night	1958	5.00	10.00	20.00

Number	Title (A Side/B Side)	Yr	VG	VG+	NM
❏ T 936 [M]	All Through the Night	1958	5.00	10.00	20.00
—Black colorband label, logo at left					
❏ ST 1260 [S]	The Sounds of Christmas	1959	5.00	10.00	20.00
—Originals have black label with colorband and "Capitol" logo at 9 o'clock					
❏ T 1260 [M]	The Sounds of Christmas	1959	3.75	7.50	15.00
—Black colorband label, logo at left					
❏ SM-1610	The Meaning of Christmas	197?	2.00	4.00	8.00
—Reissue of ST 1610 with same contents					
❏ ST 1610 [S]	The Meaning of Christmas	1961	5.00	10.00	20.00
❏ T 1610 [M]	The Meaning of Christmas	1961	3.75	7.50	15.00
❏ ST 2054 [S]	This I Believe	1964	3.75	7.50	15.00
❏ T 2054 [M]	This I Believe	1964	3.00	6.00	12.00
❏ ST 2625 [S]	The Best of Fred Waring and the Pennsylvanians	1967	3.75	7.50	15.00
❏ T 2625 [M]	The Best of Fred Waring and the Pennsylvanians	1967	3.00	6.00	12.00

CAPITOL CREATIVE PRODUCTS

Number	Title (A Side/B Side)	Yr	VG	VG+	NM
❏ L-6550 [M]	Fred Waring and the Pennsylvanians Sing of Faith, Home and Christmas	1967	3.75	7.50	15.00
—Compiled for the E.F. MacDonald Company, Dayton, Ohio					

CAPITOL PICKWICK SERIES

Number	Title (A Side/B Side)	Yr	VG	VG+	NM
❏ PC-3451 [M]	The Romantic Sound	196?	2.50	5.00	10.00
❏ SPC-3451 [S]	The Romantic Sound	196?	3.00	6.00	12.00
❏ PC-3454 [M]	Some Enchanted Evening	196?	2.50	5.00	10.00
❏ SPC-3454 [S]	Some Enchanted Evening	196?	3.00	6.00	12.00

DECCA

Number	Title (A Side/B Side)	Yr	VG	VG+	NM
❏ DBX 186 [(2)M]	The Best of Fred Waring	1965	3.75	7.50	15.00
❏ DL 4158 [M]	This Is My Country	1961	3.00	6.00	12.00
❏ DL 4234 [M]	Songs of Faith	1962	3.00	6.00	12.00
❏ DL 4345 [M]	God's Trombones	1962	3.00	6.00	12.00
❏ DL 4511 [M]	Song of Easter	1965	2.50	5.00	10.00
❏ DL 4753 [M]	Fred Waring Showcase	1966	2.50	5.00	10.00
❏ DL 4759 [M]	Magic Music	1966	2.50	5.00	10.00
❏ DL 4809 [M]	A-Caroling We Go	1966	3.00	6.00	12.00
❏ DL 4875 [M]	Barbershop Sing	1967	3.00	6.00	12.00
❏ DLP 5004 [10]	Jerome Kern Songs	1950	12.50	25.00	50.00
❏ DLP 5005 [10]	Cole Porter Songs	1950	12.50	25.00	50.00
❏ DLP 5009 [10]	Selections from Miss Liberty	1950	12.50	25.00	50.00
❏ DLP 5021 [10]	'Twas the Night Before Christmas	1950	12.50	25.00	50.00
❏ DLP 5036 [10]	Pleasure Time	1951	10.00	20.00	40.00
❏ DL 5061 [10]	Songs of Devotion, Vol. 1	1950	10.00	20.00	40.00
❏ DL 5062 [10]	Songs of Devotion, Vol. 2	1950	10.00	20.00	40.00
❏ DL 5141 [10]	This Is My Country	1950	10.00	20.00	40.00
❏ DL 5202 [10]	Columbia, the Gem of the Ocean (Patriotic and Service Songs)	1950	10.00	20.00	40.00
❏ DL 5292 [10]	Richard Rodgers and Oscar Hammerstein II Songs, Vol. 1	1950	10.00	20.00	40.00
❏ DL 5293 [10]	Richard Rodgers and Oscar Hammerstein II Songs, Vol. 2	1950	10.00	20.00	40.00
❏ DL 5295 [10]	Christmas Time	1950	10.00	20.00	40.00
❏ DXSB 7186 [(2)S]	The Best of Fred Waring	1965	3.75	7.50	15.00
❏ DL 8005 [M]	Listening Time	1950	10.00	20.00	40.00
❏ DL 8026 [M]	Program Time	1950	7.50	15.00	30.00
❏ DL 8033 [M]	Song of America	195?	10.00	20.00	40.00
❏ DL 8039 [M]	Songs of Faith, Vols. 1 and 2	195?	7.50	15.00	30.00
❏ DL 8047 [M]	God's Trombones and Other Spirituals	195?	7.50	15.00	30.00
❏ DL 8082 [M]	For Listening Only	1954	6.25	12.50	25.00
❏ DL 8084 [M]	Song of Christmas	1954	6.25	12.50	25.00
❏ DL 8110 [M]	Lullaby Time	1955	5.00	10.00	20.00
❏ DL 8111 [M]	Songs in Reverence	1955	5.00	10.00	20.00
❏ DL 8171 [M]	'Twas the Night Before Christmas	1955	5.00	10.00	20.00
❏ DL 8172 [M]	Christmas Time	1955	5.00	10.00	20.00
❏ DL 8222 [M]	College Memories	1956	3.75	7.50	15.00
❏ DL 8335 [M]	Harmonizin' the Old Songs	1956	3.75	7.50	15.00
❏ DL 8670 [M]	Songs of Devotion	1958	3.75	7.50	15.00
❏ DL 8708 [M]	Excerpts from Carousel and Oklahoma	1958	3.75	7.50	15.00
❏ DL 8709 [M]	Songs of Inspiration	1958	3.75	7.50	15.00
❏ DL 8710 [M]	Stars and Stripes Forever	1958	3.75	7.50	15.00
❏ DL 8829 [M]	Memorable Moments from Broadway Musicals	1959	3.75	7.50	15.00
❏ DL 9031 [M]	Hear, Hear	195?	3.75	7.50	15.00
❏ DL 74158 [S]	This Is My Country	1961	3.75	7.50	15.00
❏ DL 74234 [S]	Songs of Faith	1962	3.75	7.50	15.00
❏ DL 74345 [S]	God's Trombones	1962	3.75	7.50	15.00
❏ DL 74511 [S]	Song of Easter	1965	3.00	6.00	12.00
❏ DL 74753 [S]	Fred Waring Showcase	1966	3.00	6.00	12.00
❏ DL 74759 [S]	Magic Music	1966	3.00	6.00	12.00
❏ DL 74809 [S]	A-Caroling We Go	1966	3.75	7.50	15.00
❏ DL 74875 [S]	Barbershop Sing	1967	3.00	6.00	12.00
❏ DL 75007	Two Sides of Fred Waring and the Pennsylvanians	1968	3.00	6.00	12.00
❏ DL 78171 [R]	'Twas the Night Before Christmas	196?	3.00	6.00	12.00
❏ DL 78172 [R]	Christmas Time	196?	3.00	6.00	12.00

HARMONY

Number	Title (A Side/B Side)	Yr	VG	VG+	NM
❏ HS 11363	In Concert	1970	2.50	5.00	10.00

MCA

Number	Title (A Side/B Side)	Yr	VG	VG+	NM
❏ 193	This Is My Country	1973	2.00	4.00	8.00
—Reissue of Decca 74158					
❏ 207	God's Trombones	1973	2.00	4.00	8.00
—Reissue of Decca 74345					
❏ 4008 [(2)]	The Best of Fred Waring and the Pennsylvanians	1973	3.00	6.00	12.00
—Reissue of Decca 7186; black labels with rainbow					
❏ 15009	A-Caroling We Go	1973	2.50	5.00	10.00
—Reissue of DL 74809; black label with rainbow					
❏ 15009	A-Caroling We Go	1980	2.00	4.00	8.00
—Blue label with rainbow					
❏ 15011	Christmas Time	1973	2.50	5.00	10.00
—Reissue of DL 78172; black label with rainbow					
❏ 15011	Christmas Time	1980	2.00	4.00	8.00
—Blue label with rainbow					
❏ 15016	'Twas the Night Before Christmas	1973	2.50	5.00	10.00
—Reissue of DL 78171; black label with rainbow					
❏ 15016	'Twas the Night Before Christmas	1980	2.00	4.00	8.00
—Blue label with rainbow					

MEGA

Number	Title (A Side/B Side)	Yr	VG	VG+	NM
❏ 31-1005	Nashville	1971	2.50	5.00	10.00

Number	Title (A Side/B Side)	Yr	VG	VG+	NM
REPRISE					
❏ R 6137 [M]	To You...Forever	1964	3.00	6.00	12.00
❏ RS 6137 [S]	To You...Forever	1964	3.75	7.50	15.00
❏ R 6148 [M]	Fred Waring and the Pennsylvanians in Concert	1964	3.00	6.00	12.00
❏ RS 6148 [S]	Fred Waring and the Pennsylvanians in Concert	1964	3.75	7.50	15.00
STASH					
❏ 126	Memorial Album	1985	2.50	5.00	10.00

WARLOCKS, THE (1) Members of this group later joined ZZ TOP.

45s

Number	Title (A Side/B Side)	Yr	VG	VG+	NM
ARA					
❏ 1017	If You Really Want Me to Stay/Good Time Trippin'	1968	37.50	75.00	150.00

WARLOCKS, THE (2)

45s

Number	Title (A Side/B Side)	Yr	VG	VG+	NM
DECCA					
❏ 31806	I'll Go Crazy/Temper Tantrum	1965	5.00	10.00	20.00
WASHINGTON SQUARE					
❏ 2023	Hey Joe/Girl	1966	5.00	10.00	20.00

WARMEST SPRING, THE

45s

Number	Title (A Side/B Side)	Yr	VG	VG+	NM
PARKWAY					
❏ 985	Younger Girl/It Doesn't Matter Now	1966	2.50	5.00	10.00
❏ 985 [DJ]	Younger Girl	1966	5.00	10.00	20.00
—One-sided white label promo					
❏ 990	Suddenly (You Find Love)/Hard, Hard Girl	1966	2.50	5.00	10.00

WARNES, JENNIFER

45s

Number	Title (A Side/B Side)	Yr	VG	VG+	NM
ARISTA					
❏ 0223	Right Time of the Night/Daddy Don't Go	1976	—	2.50	5.00
❏ 0252	I'm Dreaming/Don't Lead Me On	1977	—	2.50	5.00
❏ 0430	I Know a Heartache When I See One/Frankie in the Rain	1979	—	2.00	4.00
❏ 0455	Don't Make Me Over/I'm Restless	1979	—	2.00	4.00
❏ 0497	When the Feeling Comes Around/Shot Through the Heart	1980	—	2.00	4.00
❏ 0611	Could It Be Love/I'm Restless	1982	—	2.00	4.00
❏ 0670	Come to Me/I'm Restless	1982	—	2.00	4.00
CASABLANCA					
❏ 814603-7	All the Right Moves/Theme — All the Right Moves	1983	—	2.00	4.00
—A-side with Chris Thompson; B-side by David Campbell					
CYPRESS					
❏ 661111-7	Ain't No Cure for Love/Famous Blue Raincoat	1986	—	2.00	4.00
❏ 661111-7 [PS]	Ain't No Cure for Love/Famous Blue Raincoat	1986	—	2.50	5.00
❏ 661115-7	First We Take Manhattan/Famous Blue Raincoat	1987	—	2.00	4.00
❏ 661115-7 [PS]	First We Take Manhattan/Famous Blue Raincoat	1987	—	2.00	4.00
PARROT					
❏ 324	Here, There and Everywhere/Sunny Day Blue	1968	3.00	6.00	12.00
❏ 328	Chelsea Morning/The Park	1969	2.50	5.00	10.00
❏ 333	I Am Waiting/The Leaves	1969	2.50	5.00	10.00
❏ 336	Easy to Be Hard/Let the Sunshine In	1969	2.50	5.00	10.00
❏ 343	We're Not Gonna Take It/The Weather's Better	1970	2.00	4.00	8.00
❏ 346	Old Folks/Cajun Train	1970	2.00	4.00	8.00
—All of the above as "Jennifer"					
REPRISE					
❏ 1070	Last Song/These Days	1972	2.00	4.00	8.00
—As "Jennifer"					
WARNER BROS.					
❏ 29593	Nights Are Forever/Kick the Can	1983	—	2.00	4.00

Albums

Number	Title (A Side/B Side)	Yr	VG	VG+	NM
ARISTA					
❏ AL 4062	Jennifer Warnes	1977	2.50	5.00	10.00
❏ AB 4217	Shot Through the Heart	1979	2.50	5.00	10.00
❏ AL 9560	The Best of Jennifer Warnes	1982	2.00	4.00	8.00
CYPRESS					
❏ 661111-1	Famous Blue Raincoat	1987	7.50	15.00	30.00
PARROT					
❏ PAS-71020	I Can Remember Anything	1968	5.00	10.00	20.00
—As "Jennifer"					
❏ PAS-71034	See Me	1970	5.00	10.00	20.00
—As "Jennifer"					
ROCK THE HOUSE					
❏ RTH 5052	Famous Blue Raincoat	1996	12.50	25.00	50.00
—Classic Records reissue					

WARREN, BEVERLY

45s

Number	Title (A Side/B Side)	Yr	VG	VG+	NM
B.T. PUPPY					
❏ 521	Would You Believe/So Glad You're My Baby	1966	2.50	5.00	10.00
❏ 526	He's So Fine/March	1967	2.50	5.00	10.00
RUST					
❏ 5098	Baby Hullabaloo/Let Me Get Close to You	1964	3.00	6.00	12.00
UNITED ARTISTS					
❏ 543	It Was Me Yesterday/Like a Million Years	1963	3.75	7.50	15.00

WARREN, BOBBY, FIVE

45s

Number	Title (A Side/B Side)	Yr	VG	VG+	NM
JORDAN					
❏ 119	Nite-Beat/Medicine Man	1960	10.00	20.00	40.00

WARREN, DOUG

45s

Number	Title (A Side/B Side)	Yr	VG	VG+	NM
IMAGE					
❏ 1011	Around Midnight/If the World Don't End Tomorrow	1960	10.00	20.00	40.00
❏ 1013	Ain't Gonna Wait No Longer/Ain't That Love	1960	7.50	15.00	30.00

WARREN, RUSTY

45s

Number	Title (A Side/B Side)	Yr	VG	VG+	NM
JUBILEE					
❏ 5473	Lil' Lizzy Beth/Life Is Really Worth Living	1964	3.00	6.00	12.00

Albums

Number	Title (A Side/B Side)	Yr	VG	VG+	NM
GNP CRESCENDO					
❏ 2079 [(2)]	Knockers Up!/Songs for Sinners	1975	3.75	7.50	15.00
❏ 2080 [(2)]	Rusty Warren Bounces Back/Sin-Sational	1975	3.75	7.50	15.00
❏ 2081	Rusty Warren Lays It on the Line	1975	3.00	6.00	12.00
❏ 2088	Knockers Up! '76	1976	3.00	6.00	12.00
❏ 2103	Bottoms Up!	1976	3.00	6.00	12.00
❏ 2114	Sexplosion	1977	3.00	6.00	12.00
JUBILEE					
❏ JLP 2024 [M]	Songs for Sinners	1960	6.25	12.50	25.00
❏ JLP 2029 [M]	Knockers Up!	1960	6.25	12.50	25.00
❏ JLP 2034 [M]	Sin-Sational	1961	6.25	12.50	25.00
❏ JGM 2039 [M]	Rusty Warren Bounces Back	1961	6.25	12.50	25.00
❏ JGM 2044 [M]	Rusty Warren in Orbit	1962	6.25	12.50	25.00
❏ JLP 2049 [M]	Banned in Boston?	1963	6.25	12.50	25.00
❏ JLP 2054 [M]	Sex-X-Ponent	1964	6.25	12.50	25.00
❏ JLP 2059 [M]	More Knockers Up!	1965	6.25	12.50	25.00
❏ JLP 2064 [M]	Rusty Rides Again	1966	6.25	12.50	25.00
❏ JGM 2069 [M]	Bottoms Up!	1967	5.00	10.00	20.00
❏ JGS 2069 [S]	Bottoms Up!	1967	5.00	10.00	20.00
❏ JGM 2074	Look What I've Got for You	1967	5.00	10.00	20.00
❏ JLP 5025 [M]	Portrait of Life	196?	5.00	10.00	20.00
❏ JLPS 5025 [S]	Portrait of Life	196?	5.00	10.00	20.00

WARWICK, DEE DEE

45s

Number	Title (A Side/B Side)	Yr	VG	VG+	NM
ATCO					
❏ 6754	Make Love to Me/She Didn't Know (She Kept On Talkin')	1970	—	3.00	6.00
❏ 6769	I'm Only Human/If This Was the Last Song	1970	—	3.00	6.00
❏ 6796	Cold Night in Georgia/Searchin'	1971	—	3.00	6.00
❏ 6810	Suspicious Minds/I'm Glad I'm a Woman	1971	—	3.00	6.00
❏ 6840	Everybody's Got to Believe in Somebody/Signed, Dee Dee	1971	—	3.00	6.00
BLUE ROCK					
❏ 4008	Do It with All Your Heart/Happiness	1965	2.50	5.00	10.00
❏ 4027	We're Doing Fine/I Want to Be with You	1965	2.50	5.00	10.00
❏ 4032	Baby I'm Yours/Gotta Get a Hold of Myself	1965	2.50	5.00	10.00
JUBILEE					
❏ 5459	You're No Good/Don't Call Me	1963	3.00	6.00	12.00
MERCURY					
❏ 72584	I Want to Be with You/Lover's Chant	1966	2.00	4.00	8.00
❏ 72638	I'm Gonna Make You Love Me/Yours Until Tomorrow	1966	2.00	4.00	8.00
❏ 72667	When Love Slips Away/House of Gold	1967	2.00	4.00	8.00
❏ 72710	Locked in Your Love/Alfie	1967	2.00	4.00	8.00
❏ 72738	Don't You Ever Give Up on Me/We've Got Everything Going for Us	1967	2.00	4.00	8.00
❏ 72788	Girls Need Love/It's Not Fair	1968	2.00	4.00	8.00
❏ 72834	I'll Be Better Off (Without You)/Monday, Monday	1968	2.00	4.00	8.00
❏ 72880	Foolish Fool/Thank You Girl	1969	2.00	4.00	8.00
❏ 72927	That's Not Love/It's Not Fair	1969	2.00	4.00	8.00
❏ 72940	Next Time (You Fall in Love)/Ring of Bright Water	1969	2.00	4.00	8.00
❏ 72966	I (Who Have Nothing)/Where Is That Rainbow	1969	2.00	4.00	8.00
PRIVATE STOCK					
❏ 45,011	Get Out of My Life/Funny How We Change Places	1975		2.50	5.00
❏ 45,033	This Time May Be My Last/Funny How We Change Places	1975		2.50	5.00
SUTRA					
❏ 134	Move with the World/The Way We Used to Be	1984	—	2.00	4.00
❏ 134 [PS]	Move with the World/The Way We Used to Be	1984	—	2.00	4.00

Albums

Number	Title (A Side/B Side)	Yr	VG	VG+	NM
ATCO					
❏ SD 33-337	Turnin' Around	1970	6.25	12.50	25.00
MERCURY					
❏ MG-21100 [M]	I Want to Be with You	1967	6.25	12.50	25.00
❏ SR-61100 [S]	I Want to Be with You	1967	6.25	12.50	25.00
❏ SR-61221	Foolish Fool	1968	6.25	12.50	25.00

WARWICK, DIONNE

12-Inch Singles

Number	Title (A Side/B Side)	Yr	VG	VG+	NM
ARISTA					
❏ ADP 9145 [DJ]	Got a Date (7:04) (4:07)	1983	2.00	4.00	8.00
RIVER NORTH					
❏ 51416 4686 1	What the World Needs Now Is Love (6 versions)	1998	2.50	5.00	10.00
—With the Hip-Hop Nation United					

45s

Number	Title (A Side/B Side)	Yr	VG	VG+	NM
ARISTA					
❏ 0419	I'll Never Love This Way Again/In Your Eyes	1979	—	2.00	4.00
❏ 0459	Deja Vu/All the Time	1979	—	2.00	4.00
❏ 0498	After You/Out of My Hands	1980	—	2.00	4.00
❏ 0527	No Night So Long/Reaching for the Sky	1980	—	2.00	4.00
❏ 0572	Easy Love/You Never Said Goodbye	1980	—	2.00	4.00
❏ 0602	Some Changes Are For Good/This Time Is Ours	1981	—	2.00	4.00
❏ 0630	There's a Long Road Ahead of Me/Medley of Hits	1981	—	2.00	4.00
❏ 0673	Friends in Love/What Is This	1982	—	2.00	4.00
—A-side with Johnny Mathis					
❏ 0701	For You/What Is This	1982	—	2.00	4.00
❏ 1015	Heartbreaker/I Can't See Anything But You	1982	—	2.00	4.00
❏ 1040	Take the Short Way Home/Just One More Night	1983	—	2.00	4.00
❏ 1067	All the Love in the World/You Are My Love	1983	—	—	—
—Unreleased?					
❏ 9032	All the Love in the World/You Are My Love	1983	—	2.00	4.00
❏ 9073	How Many Times Can We Say Goodbye/What Can a Miracle Do	1983	—	2.00	4.00
—With Luther Vandross					
❏ 9145	Got a Date/Two Ships Passing in the Night	1984	—	2.00	4.00
❏ 9281	Finder of Lost Loves/It's Love	1984	—	2.00	4.00
—A-side with Glen Jones					
❏ 9341	Run to Me/No Love in Sight	1985	—	—	3.00
—A-side with Barry Manilow					
❏ 9460	Whisper in the Dark/Extravagant Gestures	1986	—	—	3.00
❏ 9460 [PS]	Whisper in the Dark/Extravagant Gestures	1986	—	—	3.00

Number	Title (A Side/B Side)	Yr	VG	VG+	NM
❏ 9567	Love Power/In a World Such As This	1987	—	—	3.00
—A-side with Jeffrey Osborne					
❏ 9567 [PS]	Love Power/In a World Such As This	1987	—	—	3.00
❏ 9638	Reservations for Two/For Everything You Are	1987	—	—	3.00
—A-side with Kashif					
❏ 9638 [PS]	Reservations for Two/For Everything You Are	1987	—	—	3.00
❏ 9652	Another Chance for Love/Cry on Me	1987	—	—	3.00
—A-side with Howard Hewett					
❏ 9652 [PS]	Another Chance for Love/Cry on Me	1987	—	—	3.00
❏ 9901	Take Good Care of You and Me/Heartbreak of Love	1989	—	—	3.00
—A-side with Jeffrey Osborne; B-side with June Pointer					
❏ 9940	I Don't Need Another Love/Hertbreaker	1990	—	—	3.00
—A-side with the Spinners					
❏ 9940 [PS]	I Don't Need Another Love/Hertbreaker	1990	—	—	3.00
ATLANTIC					
❏ 3029	Then Came You/Just As Long As We Have Love	1974	—	3.00	6.00
—With the Spinners					
❏ 3202	Then Came You/Just As Long As We Have Love	1974	—	2.50	5.00
—With the Spinners					
MUSICOR					
❏ 6303	If I Ruled the World/Only Love Can Break a Heart	1977	—	2.50	5.00
RIVER NORTH					
❏ 163024-7	What the World Needs Now Is Love (same on both sides)	1998	—	2.00	4.00
—With the Hip-Hop Nation United					
SCEPTER					
❏ 1239	Don't Make Me Over/I Smiled Yesterday	1962	3.00	6.00	12.00
❏ 1247	This Empty Place/Wishin' and Hopin'	1963	3.00	6.00	12.00
❏ 1247 [PS]	This Empty Place/Wishin' and Hopin'	1963	5.00	10.00	20.00
❏ 1253	Make the Music Play/Please Make Him Love Me	1963	3.00	6.00	12.00
❏ 1262	Anyone Who Had a Heart/The Love of a Boy	1963	3.00	6.00	12.00
❏ 1274	Walk On By/Any Old Time of Day	1964	3.00	6.00	12.00
❏ 1282	You'll Never Get to Heaven (If You Break My Heart)/A House Is Not a Home	1964	2.50	5.00	10.00
❏ 1285	Reach Out for Me/How Many Days of Sadness	1964	2.50	5.00	10.00
❏ 1294	You Can Have Him/Is There Another Way to Love Him	1965	2.50	5.00	10.00
❏ 1298	Who Can I Turn To/Don't Say I Didn't Tell You Something	1965	2.50	5.00	10.00
❏ 12104	Here I Am/They Long to Be Close to You	1965	2.50	5.00	10.00
❏ 12111	Looking with My Eyes/Only the Strong, Only the Brave	1965	2.50	5.00	10.00
❏ 12122	Are You There (With Another Girl)/If I Ever Make You Cry	1965	2.50	5.00	10.00
❏ 12133	Message to Michael/Here Where There Is Love	1966	2.00	4.00	8.00
❏ 12153	Trains and Boats and Planes/Don't Go Breaking My Heart	1966	2.00	4.00	8.00
❏ 12167	I Just Don't Know What to Do with Myself/In Between the Heartaches	1966	2.00	4.00	8.00
❏ 12181	Another Night/Go with Love	1966	2.00	4.00	8.00
❏ 12187	Alfie/The Beginning of Loneliness	1967	2.00	4.00	8.00
❏ 12196	The Windows of the World/Walk Little Dolly	1967	2.00	4.00	8.00
❏ 12203	I Say a Little Prayer/(Theme from) Valley of the Dolls	1967	2.00	4.00	8.00
❏ 12216	Do You Know the Way to San Jose?/Let Me Be Lonely	1968	2.00	4.00	8.00
❏ 12226	Who Is Gonna Love Me?/(There's) Always Something There to Remind Me	1968	2.00	4.00	8.00
❏ 12231	Promises, Promises/Whoever You Are, I Love You	1968	—	3.50	7.00
❏ 12241	This Girl's In Love with You/Dream Sweet Dreamer	1969	—	3.50	7.00
❏ 12249	The April Fools/Slaves	1969	—	3.50	7.00
❏ 12256	Odds and Ends/As Long As There's an Apple Tree	1969	—	3.50	7.00
❏ 12262	You've Lost That Lovin' Feeling/Window Wishing	1969	—	3.50	7.00
❏ 12273	I'll Never Fall in Love Again/What the World Needs Now Is Love	1970	—	3.50	7.00
❏ 12276	Let Me Go to Him/Loneliness Remembers What Happiness Forgets	1970	—	3.00	6.00
❏ 12285	Paper Mache/The Wine Is Young	1970	—	3.00	6.00
❏ 12294	Make It Easy on Yourself/Knowing When to Leave	1970	—	3.00	6.00
❏ 12300	The Green Grass Starts to Grow/They Don't Give Medals to Yesterday's Heroes	1970	—	3.00	6.00
❏ 12309	Who Gets the Guy/Walk the Way You Talk	1971	—	3.00	6.00
❏ 12326	Amanda/He's Moving On	1971	—	3.00	6.00
❏ 12336	The Love of My Man/Hurts So Bad	1971	—	3.00	6.00
❏ 12346	Raindrops Keep Falling on My Head/Is There Another Way to Love You	1972	—	3.00	6.00
❏ 12352	I'm Your Puppet/Don't Make Me Over	1972	—	3.00	6.00
❏ 12383	Medley: Reach Out and Touch (Somebody's Hand)-All Kinds of People/The Good Life	1973	—	3.00	6.00
WARNER BROS.					
❏ 7560	If We Only Have Love/Close to You	1972	—	2.50	5.00
❏ 7669	Don't Let My Teardrops Bother TYou/I Think You Need Love	1973	—	2.50	5.00
❏ 7693	(I'm) Just Being Myself/You're Gonna Need Me	1973	—	2.50	5.00
❏ 8026	Sure Thing/Who Knows	1974	—	2.50	5.00
❏ 8088	Take it from Me/It's Magic	1975	—	2.50	5.00
❏ 8154	Once You Hit the Road/World of My Dreams	1975	—	2.50	5.00
❏ 8183	His House and Me/Ronnie Lee	1976	—	2.50	5.00
❏ 8280	I Didn't Mean to Love You/He's Not for You	1976	—	2.50	5.00
❏ 8419	Do You Believe in Love at First Sight/Do I Have to Cry	1977	—	2.50	5.00
❏ 8501	Keepin' My Head Above Water/Livin' It Up Is Startin' to Get Me Down	1977	—	2.50	5.00
❏ 8530	Don't Ever Take Your Love Away/Do I Have to Cry	1978	—	2.00	4.00

Number	Title (A Side/B Side)	Yr	VG	VG+	NM
7-Inch Extended Plays					
SCEPTER					
❏ SGS 565	Don't Make Me Over/Anyone Who Had a Heart/Wishin' and Hopin'//This Empty Place/(There's) Always Something There to Remind Me/Any Old Time of Day	1968	3.00	6.00	12.00
—Jukebox issue; small hole, plays at 33 1/3 rpm					
❏ SGS 565 [PS]	Dionne Warwick's Golden Hits, Part One	1968	3.00	6.00	12.00
❏ SGS 568	Do You Know the Way to San Jose/Let Me Be Lonely/As Long As There's an Apple Tree//(Theme from) Valley of the Dolls/Up, Up and Away/Where Would I Go	1968	3.00	6.00	12.00
—Jukebox issue; small hole, plays at 33 1/3 rpm					
❏ SGS 568 [PS]	Valley of the Dolls	1968	3.00	6.00	12.00
Albums					
ARISTA					
❏ AB 4230	Dionne	1979	2.50	5.00	10.00
❏ AL 8104	How Many Times Can We Say Goodbye	1983	2.50	5.00	10.00
❏ A2L 8111 [(2)]	Hot! Live and Otherwise	1983	2.50	5.00	10.00
—Budget-line reissue					
❏ AL 8262	Finder of Lost Loves	1985	2.50	5.00	10.00
❏ AL 8295	Dionne	1985	2.00	4.00	8.00
—Budget-line reissue					
❏ AL 8338	Heartbreaker	1985	2.00	4.00	8.00
—Budget-line reissue					
❏ AL 8358	Friends in Love	1985	2.00	4.00	8.00
—Budget-line reissue					
❏ AL 8398	Friends	1985	2.50	5.00	10.00
❏ AL 8446	Reservations for Two	1987	2.50	5.00	10.00
❏ AL 8540	Greatest Hits 1979-1990	1989	3.00	6.00	12.00
❏ AL 8573	Dionne Warwick Sings Cole Porter	1990	3.00	6.00	12.00
❏ A2L 8605 [(2)]	Hot! Live and Otherwise	1981	3.00	6.00	12.00
❏ AL 9526	No Night So Long	1980	2.50	5.00	10.00
❏ AL 9585	Friends in Love	1982	2.50	5.00	10.00
❏ AL 9609	Heartbreaker	1982	2.50	5.00	10.00
EVEREST					
❏ 4103	Dionne Warwick	1981	2.50	5.00	10.00
MOBILE FIDELITY					
❏ 2-098 [(2)]	Hot! Live and Otherwise	1982	7.50	15.00	30.00
—Audiophile vinyl					
MUSICOR					
❏ 2501	Only Love Can Break a Heart	1977	3.00	6.00	12.00
PAIR					
❏ PDL2-1043 [(2)]	The Dynamic Dionne Warwick	1986	3.00	6.00	12.00
❏ PDL2-1098 [(2)]	Masterpieces	1986	3.00	6.00	12.00
PICKWICK					
❏ PTP-2056 [(2)]	Alfie	1973	3.00	6.00	12.00
—As "Dionne Warwicke"					
RHINO					
❏ RNDA-1100 [(2)]	Anthology 1962-1971	1985	3.75	7.50	15.00
SCEPTER					
❏ S-508 [M]	Presenting Dionne Warwick	1963	3.75	7.50	15.00
❏ SS-508 [S]	Presenting Dionne Warwick	1963	5.00	10.00	20.00
❏ S-517 [M]	Anyone Who Had a Heart	1964	3.75	7.50	15.00
❏ SS-517 [S]	Anyone Who Had a Heart	1964	5.00	10.00	20.00
❏ LP-523 [M]	Make Way for Dionne Warwick	1964	3.75	7.50	15.00
❏ SPS-523 [S]	Make Way for Dionne Warwick	1964	5.00	10.00	20.00
❏ LP-528 [M]	The Sensitive Sound of Dionne Warwick	1965	3.75	7.50	15.00
❏ SPS-528 [S]	The Sensitive Sound of Dionne Warwick	1965	5.00	10.00	20.00
❏ SPS-531 [S]	Here I Am	1965	5.00	10.00	20.00
❏ SRM-531 [M]	Here I Am	1965	3.75	7.50	15.00
❏ SPS-534 [S]	Dionne Warwick in Paris	1966	3.75	7.50	15.00
❏ SRM-534 [M]	Dionne Warwick in Paris	1966	3.00	6.00	12.00
❏ SPS-555 [S]	Here Where There Is Love	1966	3.75	7.50	15.00
❏ SRM-555 [M]	Here Where There Is Love	1966	3.00	6.00	12.00
❏ SPS-559 [S]	On Stage and in the Movies	1967	3.75	7.50	15.00
❏ SRM-559 [M]	On Stage and in the Movies	1967	3.00	6.00	12.00
❏ SPS-563 [S]	The Windows of the World	1967	3.75	7.50	15.00
❏ SRM-563 [M]	The Windows of the World	1967	3.00	6.00	12.00
❏ SPS-565 [S]	Dionne Warwick's Golden Hits, Part One	1967	3.75	7.50	15.00
❏ SRM-565 [M]	Dionne Warwick's Golden Hits, Part One	1967	5.00	10.00	20.00
❏ SPS-567 [S]	The Magic of Believing	1968	5.00	10.00	20.00
❏ SRM-567 [M]	The Magic of Believing	1968	7.50	15.00	30.00
❏ SPS-568 [S]	Valley of the Dolls	1968	3.75	7.50	15.00
❏ SRM-568 [M]	Valley of the Dolls	1968	12.50	25.00	50.00
—May only exist as a white label promo					
❏ SPS-571	Promises, Promises	1968	3.75	7.50	15.00
❏ SPS-573	Soulful	1969	3.75	7.50	15.00
❏ SPS-575	Dionne Warwick's Greatest Motion Picture Hits	1969	3.75	7.50	15.00
❏ SPS-577	Dionne Warwick's Golden Hits, Part 2	1969	3.75	7.50	15.00
❏ SPS-581	I'll Never Fall in Love Again	1970	3.75	7.50	15.00
❏ SPS-587	Very Dionne	1970	3.75	7.50	15.00
❏ SPS 2-596 [(2)]	The Dionne Warwicke Story	1971	5.00	10.00	20.00
—As "Dionne Warwicke"					
❏ SPS-598 [(2)]	From Within	1972	5.00	10.00	20.00
—As "Dionne Warwicke"					
❏ P2M 5139 [(2)M]	Dionne!	1967	5.00	10.00	20.00
—Columbia Record Club exclusive					
❏ P2S 5140 [(2)S]	Dionne!	1967	5.00	10.00	20.00
—Columbia Record Club exclusive					
❏ ST-91010 [S]	Here Where There Is Love	1966	5.00	10.00	20.00
—Capitol Record Club edition					
❏ ST-91099 [S]	On Stage and in the Movies	1967	5.00	10.00	20.00
—Capitol Record Club edition					
SPRINGBOARD					
❏ SPS-4001	The Golden Voice of Dionne Warwicke	1972	2.50	5.00	10.00
—As "Dionne Warwicke"					
❏ SPS-4002	Dionne Warwicke Sings Her Very Best	1972	2.50	5.00	10.00
—As "Dionne Warwicke"					
❏ SPS-4003	One Hit After Another	1972	2.50	5.00	10.00
—As "Dionne Warwicke"					
❏ SPS-4032	Greatest Hits, Vol. 2	197?	2.50	5.00	10.00
TIME-LIFE					
❏ SLGD-18 [(2)]	Legendary Singers: Dionne Warwick	1987	3.75	7.50	15.00

Number	Title (A Side/B Side)	Yr	VG	VG+	NM
UNITED ARTISTS					
❑ UA-LA337-G	The Very Best of Dionne Warwicke	1974	3.00	6.00	12.00
—As "Dionne Warwicke"					
WARNER BROS.					
❑ BS 2585	Dionne	1971	3.00	6.00	12.00
—As "Dionne Warwicke"					
❑ BS 2658	Just Being Myself	1973	3.00	6.00	12.00
❑ BS 2846	Then Came You	1975	3.00	6.00	12.00
—As "Dionne Warwicke"					
❑ BS4 2846 [Q]	Then Came You	1975	5.00	10.00	20.00
—As "Dionne Warwicke"					
❑ BS 2893	Track of the Cat	1975	3.00	6.00	12.00
❑ BS 3119	Love at First Sight	1976	3.00	6.00	12.00

WASHINGTON, BABY Also includes records as "Justine Washington."

45s

Number	Title (A Side/B Side)	Yr	VG	VG+	NM
ABC-PARAMOUNT					
❑ 10223	My Time to Cry/Let Love Go By	1961	3.75	7.50	15.00
—As Jeanette "Baby" Washington					
❑ 10245	There You Go Again/Don't Cry, Foolish Heart	1961	3.75	7.50	15.00
AVI					
❑ 253	I Wanna Dance/I Can't Get Over Losing You	1978	—	2.50	5.00
—As Jeanette "Baby" Washington					
CHECKER					
❑ 918	I Hate to See You Go/Knock Yourself Out	1959	6.25	12.50	25.00
CHESS					
❑ 2099	Happy Birthday/Is It Worth It	1970	—	3.00	6.00
COTILLION					
❑ 44047	I Don't Know/I Can't Afford to Lose Him	1969	—	3.00	6.00
❑ 44065	Let Them Talk/I Love You Brother	1970	—	3.00	6.00
❑ 44086	Don't Let Me Lose This Dream/ I'm Good Enough for You	1970	—	3.00	6.00
J&S					
❑ 1604	There Must Be a Reason/ Congratulations Honey	1957	12.50	25.00	50.00
❑ 1632	I Hate to See You Go/Knock Yourself Out	1958	7.50	15.00	30.00
❑ 1656	Every Day/Smitty's Rock	1961	15.00	30.00	60.00
LIBERTY					
❑ 1393	Silent Night/Merry Christmas Baby	1980	—	2.50	5.00
—B-side by Charles Brown					
LOST-NITE					
❑ 256	That's How Heartaches Are Made/There He Is	196?	—	2.50	5.00
—Reissue					
MASTER 5					
❑ 3500	Can't Get Over Losing You/(B-side unknown)	1974	—	3.00	6.00
❑ 9103	Forever//(B-side unknown)	1973	—	3.00	6.00
—With Don Gardner					
❑ 9104	Just Can't Get You Out of My Mind/ (B-side unknown)	1973	—	3.00	6.00
❑ 9107	I've Got to Break Away/You (Just a Dream)	1973	—	3.00	6.00
NEPTUNE					
❑ 101	The Time/You Never Could Be Mine	1959	7.50	15.00	30.00
❑ 104	The Bells (On Our Wedding Day)/ (B-side unknown)	1959	7.50	15.00	30.00
❑ 107	Work Out/Let's Love in the Midnight	1960	7.50	15.00	30.00
❑ 120	Medicine Man/Tears Fall	1961	6.25	12.50	25.00
—As "Jeanette B. Washington"					
❑ 122	Nobody Cares (About Me)/(B-side unknown)	1961	6.25	12.50	25.00
—As "Jeanette (Baby) Washington"					
SUE					
❑ 104	The Clock/Standing on the Pier	1964	2.00	4.00	8.00
❑ 114	It'll Never Be Over for Me/Move On Drifter	1964	2.00	4.00	8.00
❑ 119	Your Fool/Run My Heart	1965	2.00	4.00	8.00
❑ 124	I Can't Wait Until I See My Baby/ Who's Going to Take Care of Me	1965	2.00	4.00	8.00
—As Justine Washington					
❑ 129	Only Those in Love/The Ballad of Bobby Dawn	1965	2.00	4.00	8.00
❑ 149	Silent Night/White Christmas	1967	5.00	10.00	20.00
❑ 150	Either You're With Me (Or Either You're Not)/ You Are What You Are	1967	3.75	7.50	15.00
❑ 764	Hey Lonely One/No Tears	1962	3.00	6.00	12.00
❑ 767	Handful of Memories/Careless Hands	1962	2.50	5.00	10.00
❑ 769	Hush Heart/I've Got a Feeling	1962	2.50	5.00	10.00
❑ 783	That's How Heartaches Are Made/There He Is	1963	2.50	5.00	10.00
❑ 790	Leave Me Alone/ You and the Night and the Music	1963	2.50	5.00	10.00
❑ 794	Hey Lonely One/Doodlin'	1963	2.50	5.00	10.00
❑ 797	I Can't Wait Until I See My Baby/Who's Going to Take Care of Me	1964	2.50	5.00	10.00
—As Justine Washington					
UNITED ARTISTS					
❑ 0143	That's How Heartaches Are Made/ Leave Me Alone	1973	—	2.50	5.00
—"Silver Spotlight Series" reissue					
VEEP					
❑ 1274	Silent Night/White Christmas	1967	5.00	10.00	20.00
❑ 1297	Think About the Good Times/ Hold Back the Dawn	1969	2.00	4.00	8.00

Albums

Number	Title (A Side/B Side)	Yr	VG	VG+	NM
AVI					
❑ 6038	I Wanna Dance	1978	2.50	5.00	10.00
COLLECTABLES					
❑ COL-5040	The Best of Baby Washington	198?	2.50	5.00	10.00
❑ COL-5108	Only Those in Love	198?	2.50	5.00	10.00
❑ COL-5124	That's How Heartaches Are Made	198?	2.50	5.00	10.00
SUE					
❑ LP-1014 [M]	That's How Heartaches Are Made	1963	37.50	75.00	150.00
❑ LP-1042 [M]	Only Those in Love	1965	37.50	75.00	150.00
❑ LPS-1042 [S]	Only Those in Love	1965	75.00	150.00	300.00
TRIP					
❑ 8009	The One and Only Baby Washington	1971	3.75	7.50	15.00
VEEP					
❑ VPS-16528	With You in Mind	1968	6.25	12.50	25.00

WASHINGTON, DINAH

45s

Number	Title (A Side/B Side)	Yr	VG	VG+	NM
MERCURY					
❑ 5488	Harbor Lights/I Cross My Fingers	1950	6.25	12.50	25.00
❑ 5503	Time Out for Tears/Only a Moment Ago	1950	6.25	12.50	25.00
❑ 5510	How Deep Is the Ocean/Harbor Lights	1950	6.25	12.50	25.00
❑ 5665	I'm a Fool/If You Don't Believe I'm Leaving	1951	6.25	12.50	25.00
❑ 5728	Cold, Cold Heart/Mixed Emotions	1951	6.25	12.50	25.00
❑ 5736	Just One More Chance/Baby Did You Hear	1951	6.25	12.50	25.00
❑ 5804	No Time for Blues/(B-side unknown)	1952	6.25	12.50	25.00
❑ 5842	I Can't Face the Music/Mad About the Boy	1952	6.25	12.50	25.00
❑ 5906	Stormy Weather/Make Believe Dreams	1952	6.25	12.50	25.00
❑ 8181	I Wanna Be Loved/Love with Misery	1950	10.00	20.00	40.00
—Note: Earlier Dinah Washington 45s in the Mercury 8000 series may exist					
❑ 8187	I'll Never Be Free/Big Deal	1950	6.25	12.50	25.00
❑ 8192	How Deep Is the Ocean/ Why Don't You Think Things Over	1950	6.25	12.50	25.00
❑ 8194	My Kind of Man/I Wanna Be Loved by You	1950	6.25	12.50	25.00
❑ 8195	It Isn't Fair/I'll Never Be Free	1950	6.25	12.50	25.00
❑ 8206	If I Loved You/My Kind of Man	1950	6.25	12.50	25.00
❑ 8207	Fast Movin' Mama/Juice Head Man of Mine	1950	6.25	12.50	25.00
❑ 8209	My Heart Cries for You/I Apologize	1951	6.25	12.50	25.00
❑ 8211	I Won't Cry Anymore/ Don't Say You're Sorry Again	1951	6.25	12.50	25.00
❑ 8231	Ain't Nobody's Bizness If I Do/Please Send Me Someone to Love	1951	6.25	12.50	25.00
❑ 8232	I'm So Lonely I Could Cry/Fine Fine Daddy	1951	6.25	12.50	25.00
❑ 8249	Saturday Night/Be Fair to Me	1951	6.25	12.50	25.00
❑ 8257	Hey Good Lookin'/Out in the Cold Again	1951	20.00	40.00	80.00
—With The Ravens					
❑ 8267	Wheel of Fortune/Tell Me Why	1952	6.25	12.50	25.00
❑ 8269	Trouble in Mind/New Blowtop Blues	1952	6.25	12.50	25.00
❑ 8292	Pillow Blues/Double Dealin' Daddy	1952	6.25	12.50	25.00
❑ 8294	My Song/Half As Much	1952	6.25	12.50	25.00
❑ 10008 [S]	What a Diff'rence a Day Made/Come On Home	1959	6.25	12.50	25.00
—The stereo title is listed differently on the stereo 45 than on the mono 45 (71435)					
❑ 70046	I Cried for You/Gambler's Blues	1953	6.25	12.50	25.00
❑ 70125	Ain't Nothing Good/You Let My Love Grow Old	1953	6.25	12.50	25.00
❑ 70175	My Lean Baby/Never Never	1953	6.25	12.50	25.00
❑ 70214	TV Is the Thing (This Year)/Fat Daddy	1953	6.25	12.50	25.00
❑ 70263	Silent Night/The Lord's Prayer	1953	6.25	12.50	25.00
❑ 70284	Since My Man Has Gone and Went/My Man's an Undertaker	1953	6.25	12.50	25.00
❑ 70329	Short John/Feel Like I Wanna Cry	1954	5.00	10.00	20.00
❑ 70336	Such a Night/Until Sunrise	1954	5.00	10.00	20.00
❑ 70392	(No, No, No) You Can't Love Two/ Big Long Slidin' Thing	1954	10.00	20.00	40.00
❑ 70439	I Don't Hurt Anymore/Dream	1954	5.00	10.00	20.00
❑ 70497	Teach Me Tonight/Wishing Well	1954	5.00	10.00	20.00
❑ 70537	That's All I Want from You/You Stay on My Mind	1955	5.00	10.00	20.00
❑ 70600	If It's the Last Thing I Do/I Diddie	1955	5.00	10.00	20.00
❑ 70653	I Hear Those Bells/The Cheat	1955	5.00	10.00	20.00
❑ 70694	I Concentrate on You/Not Without You	1955	5.00	10.00	20.00
❑ 70728	I'm Lost Without You Tonight/ You Might Have Told Me	1955	5.00	10.00	20.00
❑ 70776	The Show Must Go On/ I Just Couldn't Stand It No More	1956	3.75	7.50	15.00
❑ 70833	Let's Get Busy Too/Let's Go Around Together	1956	3.75	7.50	15.00
❑ 70868	Cat on a Hot Tin Roof/The First Time	1956	3.75	7.50	15.00
❑ 70906	Soft Winds/Tears to Burn	1956	3.75	7.50	15.00
❑ 70968	Relax, Max/The Kissing Way Home	1956	3.75	7.50	15.00
❑ 71018	All Because of You/To Love and Be Loved	1956	3.75	7.50	15.00
❑ 71043	You Let My Love Grow Old/I Know	1957	3.75	7.50	15.00
❑ 71087	Ain't Nobody Home/ I'm Gonna Keep My Eyes on You	1957	3.75	7.50	15.00
❑ 71220	Everybody Loves My Baby/Blues Down Home	1957	3.75	7.50	15.00
❑ 71317	Ring-a My Phone/Never Again	1958	3.75	7.50	15.00
❑ 71377	Make Me a Present of You/All of Me	1958	3.75	7.50	15.00
❑ 71435	What a Diff'rence a Day Makes/Come On Home	1959	3.75	7.50	15.00
❑ 71508	Unforgettable/Nothing in the World	1959	2.50	5.00	10.00
❑ 71557	Ol' Santa/The Light	1959	3.00	6.00	12.00
❑ 71560	It Could Happen to You/Age of Miracles	1960	2.50	5.00	10.00
❑ 71635	This Bitter Earth/I Understand	1960	2.50	5.00	10.00
❑ 71696	Love Walked In/I'm in Heaven Tonight	1960	2.50	5.00	10.00
❑ 71744	We Have Love/Looking Back	1960	2.50	5.00	10.00
❑ 71744 [PS]	We Have Love/Looking Back	1960	3.75	7.50	15.00
❑ 71778	Early Every Morning (Early Every Evening Too)/ Do You Want It That Way	1961	2.50	5.00	10.00
❑ 71778 [PS]	Early Every Morning (Early Every Evening Too)/ Do You Want It That Way	1961	3.75	7.50	15.00
❑ 71812	Our Love Is Here to Stay/ Congratulations to Someone	1961	2.50	5.00	10.00
❑ 71812 [PS]	Our Love Is Here to Stay/ Congratulations to Someone	1961	3.75	7.50	15.00
❑ 71876	September in the Rain/ Wake the Town and Tell the People	1961	2.50	5.00	10.00
❑ 71876 [PS]	September in the Rain/ Wake the Town and Tell the People	1961	3.75	7.50	15.00
❑ 71922	Tears and Laughter/If I Should Lose You	1962	2.50	5.00	10.00
❑ 71922 [PS]	Tears and Laughter/If I Should Lose You	1962	3.75	7.50	15.00
❑ 71958	Dream/Such a Night	1962	2.50	5.00	10.00
❑ 71958 [PS]	Dream/Such a Night	1962	3.75	7.50	15.00
❑ 72015	I Want to Be Loved/Am I Blue	1962	2.00	4.00	8.00
❑ 72015 [PS]	I Want to Be Loved/Am I Blue	1962	3.75	7.50	15.00
❑ 72040	Cold, Cold Heart/I Don't Hurt Anymore	1962	2.00	4.00	8.00
❑ 72040 [PS]	Cold, Cold Heart/I Don't Hurt Anymore	1962	3.75	7.50	15.00
ROULETTE					
❑ 4424	Where Are You/ You're Nobody 'Til Somebody Loves You	1962	2.00	4.00	8.00
❑ 4444	For All We Know/I Wouldn't Know (What to Do)	1962	2.00	4.00	8.00
❑ 4455	You're a Sweetheart/ It's a Mean Old Man's World	1962	2.00	4.00	8.00
❑ 4476	Romance in the Dark/No Hard Feelings	1963	2.00	4.00	8.00
❑ 4490	Soulsville/Let Me Be the First to Know	1963	2.00	4.00	8.00
❑ 4520	The Show Must Go On/ I'll Drown in My Own Tears	1963	2.00	4.00	8.00

Number	Title (A Side/B Side)	Yr	VG	VG+	NM
❏ 4534	That Sunday (That Summer)/ A Stranger on Earth	1963	2.00	4.00	8.00
❏ 4538	Call Me Irresponsible/Funny Thing	1963	2.00	4.00	8.00

7-Inch Extended Plays

EMARCY

Number	Title (A Side/B Side)	Yr	VG	VG+	NM
❏ EP 1-6054	(contents unknown)	195?	6.25	12.50	25.00
❏ EP-1-6054 [PS]	After Hours with Miss "D"	195?	6.25	12.50	25.00
❏ EP-1-6080	*Lover Come Back to Me/I've Got You Under My Skin/There Is No Greater Love	1955	6.25	12.50	25.00
❏ EP-1-6080 [PS]	Dinah Jams	1955	6.25	12.50	25.00
❏ EP-1-6082	You Go to My Head (Beginning)/(Conclusion)	1955	6.25	12.50	25.00
❏ EP-1-6082 [PS]	Jammin' with Dinah	1955	6.25	12.50	25.00

MERCURY

Number	Title (A Side/B Side)	Yr	VG	VG+	NM
❏ EP 1-3395	(contents unknown)	195?	5.00	10.00	20.00
❏ EP 1-3395 [PS]	Dinah Washington	195?	5.00	10.00	20.00
❏ EP 1-4035	(contents unknown)	195?	5.00	10.00	20.00
❏ EP 1-4035 [PS]	Dinah Washington	195?	5.00	10.00	20.00
❏ EP 1-4041	(contents unknown)	195?	5.00	10.00	20.00
❏ EP 1-4041 [PS]	For Lonely Lovers	195?	5.00	10.00	20.00

ROULETTE

Number	Title (A Side/B Side)	Yr	VG	VG+	NM
❏ SBG 269 [PS]	Dinah Washington	196?	3.75	7.50	15.00
❏ SBG 269 [S]	What's New/Somebody Else Is Taking My Place/ I'll Never Stop Loving You//He's My Guy/To Forget About You/That Old Feeling	196?	3.75	7.50	15.00

—Jukebox issue; smal hole, plays at 33 1/3 rpm

Albums

ACCORD

Number	Title (A Side/B Side)	Yr	VG	VG+	NM
❏ SN-7207	Retrospective	1982	2.50	5.00	10.00

COLLECTABLES

Number	Title (A Side/B Side)	Yr	VG	VG+	NM
❏ COL-5200	Golden Classics	1989	2.50	5.00	10.00

DELMARK

Number	Title (A Side/B Side)	Yr	VG	VG+	NM
❏ DL-451	Mellow Mama	1992	5.00	10.00	20.00

EMARCY

Number	Title (A Side/B Side)	Yr	VG	VG+	NM
❏ EMS-2-401 [(2)]	Jazz Sides	197?	3.75	7.50	15.00
❏ MG-26032 [10]	After Hours with Miss D	1954	30.00	60.00	120.00
❏ MG-36000 [M]	Dinah Jams	1955	12.50	25.00	50.00
❏ MG-36011 [M]	For Those in Love	1955	12.50	25.00	50.00
❏ MG-36028 [M]	After Hours with Miss D	1955	12.50	25.00	50.00

—Reissue of 26032

Number	Title (A Side/B Side)	Yr	VG	VG+	NM
❏ MG-36065 [M]	Dinah	1956	12.50	25.00	50.00
❏ MG-36073 [M]	In the Land of Hi-Fi	1956	12.50	25.00	50.00
❏ MG-36104 [M]	The Swingin' Miss "D"	1956	12.50	25.00	50.00
❏ MG-36119 [M]	Dinah Washington Sings Fats Waller	1957	12.50	25.00	50.00
❏ MG-36130 [M]	Dinah Washington Sings Bessie Smith	1957	12.50	25.00	50.00
❏ MG-36141 [M]	Newport '58	1958	10.00	20.00	40.00
❏ 814184-1 [(2)]	Slick Chick (On the Mellow Side)	1983	3.00	6.00	12.00
❏ 824883-1 [(2)]	Jazz Sides	198?	3.00	6.00	12.00

—Reissue of 401

Number	Title (A Side/B Side)	Yr	VG	VG+	NM
❏ 826453-1	In the Land of Hi-Fi	1986	2.50	5.00	10.00

EVEREST ARCHIVE OF FOLK & JAZZ

Number	Title (A Side/B Side)	Yr	VG	VG+	NM
❏ 297	Dinah Washington	197?	3.00	6.00	12.00

GRAND AWARD

Number	Title (A Side/B Side)	Yr	VG	VG+	NM
❏ GA 33-318 [M]	Dinah Washington Sings the Blues	1955	12.50	25.00	50.00

—Add 50% if removable wrap-around cover is still there

HARLEM HIT PARADE

Number	Title (A Side/B Side)	Yr	VG	VG+	NM
❏ 8002	Finer Dinah	197?	2.50	5.00	10.00

MERCURY

Number	Title (A Side/B Side)	Yr	VG	VG+	NM
❏ MGP-2-103 [(2)M]	This Is My Story	1963	6.25	12.50	25.00

—Combines 20788 and 20789 in one package

Number	Title (A Side/B Side)	Yr	VG	VG+	NM
❏ MGP-2-603 [(2)S]	This Is My Story	1963	7.50	15.00	30.00

—Combines 60788 and 60789 in one package

Number	Title (A Side/B Side)	Yr	VG	VG+	NM
❏ MG-20119 [M]	Music for a First Love	1957	12.50	25.00	50.00
❏ MG-20120 [M]	Music for Late Hours	1957	12.50	25.00	50.00
❏ MG-20247 [M]	The Best in Blues	1958	12.50	25.00	50.00
❏ MG-20439 [M]	The Queen	1959	7.50	15.00	30.00
❏ MG-20479 [M]	What a Diff'rence a Day Makes!	1960	7.50	15.00	30.00
❏ MG-20523 [M]	Newport '58	1960	7.50	15.00	30.00

—Reissue of EmArcy 36141

Number	Title (A Side/B Side)	Yr	VG	VG+	NM
❏ MG-20525 [M]	Dinah Washington Sings Fats Waller	1960	7.50	15.00	30.00

—Reissue of EmArcy 36119

Number	Title (A Side/B Side)	Yr	VG	VG+	NM
❏ MG-20572 [M]	Unforgettable	1961	6.25	12.50	25.00
❏ MG-20604 [M]	I Concentrate on You	1961	6.25	12.50	25.00
❏ MG-20614 [M]	For Lonely Lovers	1961	6.25	12.50	25.00
❏ MG-20638 [M]	September in the Rain	1961	6.25	12.50	25.00
❏ MG-20661 [M]	Tears and Laughter	1962	6.25	12.50	25.00
❏ MG-20729 [M]	I Wanna Be Loved	1962	6.25	12.50	25.00
❏ MG-20788 [M]	This Is My Story — Dinah Washington's Golden Hits, Volume 1	1963	3.75	7.50	15.00
❏ MG-20789 [M]	This Is My Story — Dinah Washington's Golden Hits, Volume 2	1963	3.75	7.50	15.00
❏ MG-20829 [M]	The Good Old Days	1963	3.75	7.50	15.00
❏ MG-20928 [M]	The Queen and Quincy	1965	3.75	7.50	15.00
❏ MG-21119 [M]	Dinah Discovered	1967	5.00	10.00	20.00
❏ MG-25060 [10]	Dinah Washington	1950	30.00	60.00	120.00
❏ MG-25138 [10]	Dynamic Dinah	1952	30.00	60.00	120.00
❏ MG-25140 [10]	Blazing Ballads	1952	30.00	60.00	120.00
❏ SR-60111 [S]	The Queen	1959	10.00	20.00	40.00
❏ SR-60158 [S]	What a Diff'rence a Day Makes!	1960	10.00	20.00	40.00
❏ SR-60200 [S]	Newport '58	1960	10.00	20.00	40.00
❏ SR-60202 [S]	Dinah Washington Sings Fats Waller	1960	10.00	20.00	40.00
❏ SR-60232 [S]	Unforgettable	1961	7.50	15.00	30.00
❏ SR-60604 [S]	I Concentrate on You	1961	7.50	15.00	30.00
❏ SR-60614 [S]	For Lonely Lovers	1961	7.50	15.00	30.00
❏ SR-60638 [S]	September in the Rain	1961	7.50	15.00	30.00
❏ SR-60661 [S]	Tears and Laughter	1962	7.50	15.00	30.00
❏ SR-60729 [S]	I Wanna Be Loved	1962	7.50	15.00	30.00
❏ SR-60788 [S]	This Is My Story — Dinah Washington's Golden Hits, Volume 1	1963	5.00	10.00	20.00
❏ SR-60789 [S]	This Is My Story — Dinah Washington's Golden Hits, Volume 2	1963	5.00	10.00	20.00
❏ SR-60829 [S]	The Good Old Days	1963	5.00	10.00	20.00
❏ SR-60928 [S]	The Queen and Quincy	1965	5.00	10.00	20.00
❏ SR-61119 [S]	Dinah Discovered	1967	3.75	7.50	15.00
❏ 818815-1	What a Diff'rence a Day Makes!	198?	2.00	4.00	8.00

—Reissue

Number	Title (A Side/B Side)	Yr	VG	VG+	NM
❏ 822867-1	This Is My Story — Dinah Washington's Golden Hits, Volume 1	1985	2.00	4.00	8.00

—Reissue

PICKWICK

Number	Title (A Side/B Side)	Yr	VG	VG+	NM
❏ SPC-3043	Dinah Washington	196?	2.50	5.00	10.00
❏ SPC-3230	I Don't Hurt Anymore	197?	2.50	5.00	10.00
❏ SPC-3536	Greatest Hits	197?	2.50	5.00	10.00

ROULETTE

Number	Title (A Side/B Side)	Yr	VG	VG+	NM
❏ RE 104 [(2)]	Echoes of an Era	196?	3.75	7.50	15.00
❏ RE 117 [(2)]	Queen of the Blues	1971	3.75	7.50	15.00
❏ RE 125 [(2)]	The Immortal Dinah Washington	1973	3.75	7.50	15.00
❏ R 25170 [M]	Dinah '62	1962	3.75	7.50	15.00
❏ SR 25170 [S]	Dinah '62	1962	5.00	10.00	20.00
❏ R 25180 [M]	In Love	1962	3.75	7.50	15.00
❏ SR 25180 [S]	In Love	1962	5.00	10.00	20.00
❏ R 25183 [M]	Drinking Again	1962	3.75	7.50	15.00
❏ SR 25183 [S]	Drinking Again	1962	5.00	10.00	20.00
❏ R 25189 [M]	Back to the Blues	1963	3.75	7.50	15.00
❏ SR 25189 [S]	Back to the Blues	1963	5.00	10.00	20.00
❏ R 25220 [M]	Dinah '63	1963	3.75	7.50	15.00
❏ SR 25220 [S]	Dinah '63	1963	5.00	10.00	20.00
❏ R 25244 [M]	In Tribute	1963	3.75	7.50	15.00
❏ SR 25244 [S]	In Tribute	1963	5.00	10.00	20.00
❏ R 25253 [M]	A Stranger on Earth	1964	3.75	7.50	15.00
❏ SR 25253 [S]	A Stranger on Earth	1964	5.00	10.00	20.00
❏ R 25269 [M]	Dinah Washington	1964	3.75	7.50	15.00
❏ SR 25269 [S]	Dinah Washington	1964	5.00	10.00	20.00
❏ R 25289 [M]	The Best of Dinah Washington	1965	3.75	7.50	15.00
❏ SR 25289 [S]	The Best of Dinah Washington	1965	5.00	10.00	20.00
❏ 42014	The Best of Dinah Washington	1968	3.00	6.00	12.00

—Reissue of 25289

TRIP

Number	Title (A Side/B Side)	Yr	VG	VG+	NM
❏ 5500	Dinah Jams	1973	2.50	5.00	10.00
❏ 5516	After Hours	1973	2.50	5.00	10.00
❏ 5524	Tears and Laughter	1974	2.50	5.00	10.00
❏ 5556	Dinah Washington Sings Bessie Smith	197?	2.50	5.00	10.00
❏ 5565	The Swingin' Miss D	197?	2.50	5.00	10.00
❏ TLX 9505 [(2)]	Sad Songs — Blue Songs	197?	3.00	6.00	12.00

VERVE

Number	Title (A Side/B Side)	Yr	VG	VG+	NM
❏ 818930-1	The Fats Waller Songbook	1984	2.50	5.00	10.00

WING

Number	Title (A Side/B Side)	Yr	VG	VG+	NM
❏ PKW-2-121 [(2)]	The Original Queen of Soul	1969	5.00	10.00	20.00
❏ MGW-12140 [M]	The Late Late Show	1963	3.00	6.00	12.00
❏ MGW-12271 [M]	Dinah Washington Sings Fats Waller	1964	3.00	6.00	12.00
❏ SRW-16140 [S]	The Late Late Show	1963	3.00	6.00	12.00
❏ SRW-16271 [S]	Dinah Washington Sings Fats Waller	1964	3.00	6.00	12.00
❏ SRW-16386	The Original Soul Sister	196?	3.00	6.00	12.00

WASHINGTON, DINAH, AND BROOK BENTON Also see each artist's individual listings.

45s

MERCURY

Number	Title (A Side/B Side)	Yr	VG	VG+	NM
❏ 71565	Baby (You Got What It Takes)/I Do	1960	3.75	7.50	15.00
❏ 71629	A Rockin' Good Way (To Mess Around and Fall in Love)/I Believe	1960	3.75	7.50	15.00
❏ 71629 [PS]	A Rockin' Good Way (To Mess Around and Fall in Love)/I Believe	1960	6.25	12.50	25.00

Albums

MERCURY

Number	Title (A Side/B Side)	Yr	VG	VG+	NM
❏ MG-20588 [M]	The Two of Us	1960	6.25	12.50	25.00
❏ SR-60244 [S]	The Two of Us	1960	7.50	15.00	30.00
❏ 824823-1	The Two of Us	1985	2.00	4.00	8.00

—Reissue

WASHINGTON, GINO

45s

ATAC

Number	Title (A Side/B Side)	Yr	VG	VG+	NM
❏ 101	Doin' the Popcorn/(B-side unknown)	1969	7.50	15.00	30.00
❏ 102	I'll Be Around/(B-side unknown)	1969	10.00	20.00	40.00
❏ 2830	Rat Race/(B-side unknown)	1969	7.50	15.00	30.00
❏ 7823	Like My Baby/(B-side unknown)	1969	10.00	20.00	40.00

CONGRESS

Number	Title (A Side/B Side)	Yr	VG	VG+	NM
❏ 269	Understanding/Water	1966	3.00	6.00	12.00
❏ 273	Beach Bash/Hi Hi Hazel	1966	3.00	6.00	12.00

CORREC-TONE

Number	Title (A Side/B Side)	Yr	VG	VG+	NM
❏ 503	Gino Is a Coward/Puppet on a String	1962	15.00	30.00	60.00

DJM

Number	Title (A Side/B Side)	Yr	VG	VG+	NM
❏ 1011	You Lovely Witch/Love Me, Love Me	1976	—	3.00	6.00

KAPP

Number	Title (A Side/B Side)	Yr	VG	VG+	NM
❏ 796	All I Need/Whatever Will Be, Will Be	1966	2.50	5.00	10.00

MALA

Number	Title (A Side/B Side)	Yr	VG	VG+	NM
❏ 12029	Like My Baby/I'll Be Around When You Want Me	1968	10.00	20.00	40.00

RIC-TIC

Number	Title (A Side/B Side)	Yr	VG	VG+	NM
❏ 100	Gino Is a Coward/Puppet on a String	1964	5.00	10.00	20.00

SIDRA

Number	Title (A Side/B Side)	Yr	VG	VG+	NM
❏ 9005	Romeo/Now You're Lonely	196?	6.25	12.50	25.00

SONBERT

Number	Title (A Side/B Side)	Yr	VG	VG+	NM
❏ 3770	Gino Is a Coward/Puppet on a String	1963	6.25	12.50	25.00

WAND

Number	Title (A Side/B Side)	Yr	VG	VG+	NM
❏ 147	Out of This World/Come Monkey with Me	1964	5.00	10.00	20.00

Albums

ATAC

Number	Title (A Side/B Side)	Yr	VG	VG+	NM
❏ 2730	Gino Washington's Golden Hits	1969	7.50	15.00	30.00

KAPP

Number	Title (A Side/B Side)	Yr	VG	VG+	NM
❏ KL-1415 [M]	Gino Washington's Ram Jam Band	1967	5.00	10.00	20.00
❏ KS-3415 [S]	Gino Washington's Ram Jam Band	1967	6.25	12.50	25.00

WATCHPOCKET

45s

TMI

Number	Title (A Side/B Side)	Yr	VG	VG+	NM
❏ 75-0100	Love Will Be the Answer/People All Around Me	1972	—	3.00	6.00
❏ ZS7 9005	Mammy Blue/(B-side unknown)	1971	—	3.50	7.00

Number	Title (A Side/B Side)	Yr	VG	VG+	NM

WATERS, MUDDY

45s
CHESS

Number	Title (A Side/B Side)	Yr	VG	VG+	NM
1509	All Night Long/Country Boy	1952	625.00	1250.	2500.

—Note: Muddy Waters records on Chess before 1509 are unconfirmed on 45 rpm

Number	Title (A Side/B Side)	Yr	VG	VG+	NM
1514	Please Have Mercy/Looking for My Baby	1952	200.00	400.00	800.00
1526	Standing Around Crying/Gone to Main St.	1952	175.00	350.00	700.00
1537	She's All Right/Sad, Sad Day	1953	100.00	200.00	400.00
1542	Who's Gonna Be Your Sweet Man/Turn the Lamp Down Low	1953	75.00	150.00	300.00
1550	Mad Love/Blow, Wind, Blow	1953	30.00	60.00	120.00
1560	I'm Your Hoochie Coochie Man/You're So Pretty	1954	25.00	50.00	100.00
1571	Just Make Love to Me/Oh Yeh!	1954	15.00	30.00	60.00
1579	I'm Ready/I Don't Know Why	1954	15.00	30.00	60.00
1585	Lovin' Man/I'm a Natural Born Lover	1955	12.50	25.00	50.00
1596	I Want to Be Loved/My Eyes Keep Me in Trouble	1955	12.50	25.00	50.00
1602	Manish Boy/Young Fashion Ways	1955	17.50	35.00	70.00
1612	Trouble, No More/Sugar Sweet	1955	20.00	40.00	80.00
1620	Forty Days and Forty Nights/All Aboard	1956	10.00	20.00	40.00
1630	Don't Go No Farther/Diamonds at Your Feet	1956	12.50	25.00	50.00
1644	I Got to Find My Baby/Just to Be with You	1956	10.00	20.00	40.00
1652	Got My Mojo Working/Rock Me	1957	12.50	25.00	50.00
1667	Good News/Come Home Baby	1957	7.50	15.00	30.00
1680	I Live the Life I Love/Evil	1958	7.50	15.00	30.00
1692	I Won't Go/She's Got It	1958	7.50	15.00	30.00
1704	Close to You/She's Nineteen Years Old	1958	7.50	15.00	30.00
1718	Mean Mistreater/Walking Thru the Park	1959	6.25	12.50	25.00
1724	Ooh Wee/Clouds in My Heart	1959	6.25	12.50	25.00
1733	Take the Bitter with the Sweet/She's Into Somethin'	1959	6.25	12.50	25.00
1739	Recipe for Love/Tell Me Baby	1959	6.25	12.50	25.00
1748	I Feel So Good/When I Get to Thinking	1960	6.25	12.50	25.00
1752	I'm Your Doctor/Ready Way Back	1960	6.25	12.50	25.00
1758	Love Affair/Look What You've Done	1960	6.25	12.50	25.00
1765	Tiger in Your Tank/Meanest Woman	1960	6.25	12.50	25.00
1774	Got My Mojo Working/Woman Wanted	1960	6.25	12.50	25.00
1796	Messin' with the Man/Lonesome Room Blues	1961	5.00	10.00	20.00
1819	Going Home/Tough Times	1962	5.00	10.00	20.00
1827	Muddy Waters Twist/You Shook Me	1962	6.25	12.50	25.00
1839	You Need Love/Little Brown Bird	1962	6.25	12.50	25.00
1862	Five Long Years/Twenty-Four Hours	1963	3.75	7.50	15.00
1895	The Same Thing/You Can't Lose What You Never Had	1964	3.75	7.50	15.00
1914	Short Dress Woman/My John the Conqueror	1964	3.75	7.50	15.00
1921	Put Me in Your Lay-A-Way/Still a Fool	1965	3.00	6.00	12.00
1937	My Dog Can't Bark/I Got a Rich Man's Woman	1965	3.00	6.00	12.00
1973	I'm Your Hoochie Coochie Man/Corrina, Corrina	1966	3.00	6.00	12.00
2018	When the Eagle Flies/Birdnest on the Ground	1967	2.50	5.00	10.00
2085	Going Home/I Feel So Good	1970	2.00	4.00	8.00
2107	Making Friends/Two Steps Forward	1971	2.00	4.00	8.00
2143	Garbage Man/Can't Get No Grindin'	1973	—	3.00	6.00

Albums
BLUE SKY

Number	Title (A Side/B Side)	Yr	VG	VG+	NM
PZ 34449	Hard Again	1977	3.00	6.00	12.00

—No bar code on cover

PZ 34449	Hard Again	198?	2.00	4.00	8.00

—Budget-line reissue with bar code

JZ 34928	I'm Ready	1978	3.00	6.00	12.00
PZ 34928	I'm Ready	198?	2.00	4.00	8.00

—Budget-line reissue

JZ 35712	Muddy "Missisiippi" Waters Live	1980	3.00	6.00	12.00
PZ 35712	Muddy "Missisiippi" Waters Live	198?	2.00	4.00	8.00

—Budget-line reissue

JZ 37064	King Bee	1981	3.00	6.00	12.00
PZ 37064	King Bee	198?	2.00	4.00	8.00

—Budget-line reissue

CADET CONCEPT

CS-314	Electric Mud	1968	6.25	12.50	25.00
CS-320	After the Rain	1969	6.25	12.50	25.00

CHESS

127 [(2)]	Fathers and Sons	1969	6.25	12.50	25.00
LP-1427 [DJ]	The Best of Muddy Waters	1957	500.00	1000.	1500.

—White label promo

LP-1427 [M]	The Best of Muddy Waters	1957	125.00	250.00	500.00

—Black label

LPS-1427 [R]	The Best of Muddy Waters	196?	3.00	6.00	12.00

—Black label

LP-1444 [DJ]	Muddy Waters Sings Big Bill	1960	250.00	500.00	1000.

—White label promo

LP-1444 [M]	Muddy Waters Sings Big Bill	1960	75.00	150.00	300.00
LPS-1444 [R]	Muddy Waters Sings Big Bill	196?	3.75	7.50	15.00

—Rechanneled stereo reissue

LP-1449 [M]	Muddy Waters at Newport	1962	30.00	60.00	120.00
LP-1483 [M]	Folk Singer	1964	30.00	60.00	120.00
LP-1501 [M]	The Real Folk Blues of Muddy Waters	1965	15.00	30.00	60.00
LP-1507 [M]	Muddy, Brass and Blues	1966	10.00	20.00	40.00
LPS-1507 [S]	Muddy, Brass and Blues	1966	12.50	25.00	50.00
LP-1511 [M]	More Real Folk Blues	1967	12.50	25.00	50.00
LPS-1511 [S]	More Real Folk Blues	1967	10.00	20.00	40.00
LP-1533 [M]	Blues from Big Bill's Copacabana	1968	12.50	25.00	50.00
LPS-1539	Sail On	1969	6.25	12.50	25.00
LPS-1553	They Call Me Muddy Waters	1971	5.00	10.00	20.00
CH-9101	Rolling Stone	1985	3.00	6.00	12.00
CH-9180	Rare and Unissued	1986	3.00	6.00	12.00
CH-9197	Muddy Waters Sings Big Bill	1986	2.50	5.00	10.00

—Reissue of 1444

CH-9198	Muddy Waters at Newport	1986	2.50	5.00	10.00

—Reissue of 1449

CH-9255	The Best of Muddy Waters	1987	2.50	5.00	10.00

—Reissue of 1427

CH-9261	Folk Singer	1987	2.50	5.00	10.00

—Reissue of 1483

CH-9274	The Real Folk Blues of Muddy Waters	1987	2.50	5.00	10.00

—Reissue of 1501

CH-9278	More Real Folk Blues	1988	2.50	5.00	10.00

—Reissue of 1511

Number	Title (A Side/B Side)	Yr	VG	VG+	NM
CH-9286	Muddy, Brass and the Blues	1989	2.50	5.00	10.00

—Reissue of 1507

CH-9291	Trouble No More: Singles 1955-1959	1989	3.00	6.00	12.00
CH-9298	The London Muddy Waters Sessions	1989	2.50	5.00	10.00

—Reissue of 60013

CH-9299	They Call Me Muddy Waters	1989	2.50	5.00	10.00

—Reissue of 1553

CH-9319	Can't Get No Grindin'	1990	2.50	5.00	10.00

—Reissue of 50023

CH-50012	Muddy Waters Live	1972	5.00	10.00	20.00
CH-50023	Can't Get No Grindin'	1973	5.00	10.00	20.00
2CH-50033 [(2)]	Fathers and Sons	1974	5.00	10.00	20.00

—Reissue of 127

CH-50035	The Muddy Waters Woodstock Album	1976	3.75	7.50	15.00
2CH-60006 [(2)]	McKinley Morganfield, A.K.A. Muddy Waters	1971	6.25	12.50	25.00
CH-60013	The London Muddy Waters Sessions	1972	5.00	10.00	20.00
CH-60026	London Revisited	1974	3.75	7.50	15.00
CH-60031	"Unk" in Funk	1975	3.75	7.50	15.00
CH6-80002 [(6)]	The Chess Box	1990	12.50	25.00	50.00

INTERMEDIA

QS-5071	Sweet Home Chicago	198?	2.50	5.00	10.00

MOBILE FIDELITY

1-201	Folk Singer	1994	6.25	12.50	25.00

—Audiophile vinyl

MUSE

MR-5008	Mud in Your Ear	198?	3.00	6.00	12.00

TESTAMENT

2210	Stovall's Plantation	197?	3.00	6.00	12.00

WATERS, MUDDY, AND HOWLIN' WOLF Also see each artist's individual listings.

Albums
CHESS

CH-9100	Muddy and The Wolf	1985	3.00	6.00	12.00

WATKINS, LOVELACE

45s
GROOVE

58-0016	Tender Love/Ma Cherie Au Revoir	1963	7.50	15.00	30.00
58-0016 [PS]	Tender Love/Ma Cherie Au Revoir	1963	20.00	40.00	80.00
58-0023	I Won't Believe It/He'[s Lookin' Out for the World	1963	7.50	15.00	30.00

MGM

12875	Hello Young Lovers/When I Fall in Love	1960	3.75	7.50	15.00

SUE

10-003	Who Am I/Dreams	1968	3.00	6.00	12.00

UNI

55211	Fool on the Hill/Je Vous Aime Beaucoup	1970	3.00	6.00	12.00

Albums
MGM

E-3831 [M]	The Voice of Lovelace Watkins	1960	6.25	12.50	25.00
SE-3831 [S]	The Voice of Lovelace Watkins	1960	10.00	20.00	40.00

WATSON, CLAYTON

45s
LAVENDER

2454	Everybody's Boppin'/Tall Skinny Annie	1958	100.00	200.00	400.00

WATSON, DOC Includes records by the father-son duo of "Doc and Merle Watson."

45s
POPPY

XW169	If I Needed You/Bonaparte's Retreat	1973	—	2.00	4.00

—With Merle Watson

XW276	Bottle of Wine/Corinna, Corinna	1973	—	2.00	4.00

—With Merle Watson

XW370	New Born King/Peace in the Valley	1973	—	2.00	4.00
XW414	Poor Boy Blues/Doc's Rag	1974	—	2.00	4.00

—With Merle Watson

90110	Freight Train Boogie/Going Down the Road Feeling Bad	1971	—	2.50	5.00
90114	Summertime/I Couldn't Believe It Was True	1972	—	2.50	5.00

—With Merle Watson

90119	New Born King/Peace in the Valley	1972	—	2.50	5.00

UNITED ARTISTS

XW713	Make Me a Pallet/Shady Grove	1975	—	2.00	4.00
XW824	I Can't Help But Wonder (Where I'm Bound)/Southbound Passenger Train	1976	—	2.00	4.00
XW894	Little Maggie/Cypress Grove Blues	1976	—	2.00	4.00
XW1020	My Creole Belle/Minglewood Blues	1977	—	2.00	4.00

—With Merle Watson

1231	Don't Think Twice, It's All Right/Under the Double Eagle	1978	—	2.00	4.00

—With Merle Watson

1275	All I Have to Do Is Dream/'Rangement Blues	1979	—	2.00	4.00

—With Merle Watson

VANGUARD

35079	Peach Picking Time in Georgia/Memphis Blues	1968	—	3.00	6.00

Albums
FLYING FISH

FF-252	Red Rocking Chair	1981	3.00	6.00	12.00
FF-301	Guitar Album	1983	3.00	6.00	12.00
FF-352	Pickin' the Blues	1985	2.50	5.00	10.00

FOLKWAYS

FA-2366 [M]	Doc Watson and Family	1963	6.25	12.50	25.00
FA-31021 [S]	Doc Watson and Family	196?	3.75	7.50	15.00

INTERMEDIA

QS-5031	Out in the Country	198?	3.00	6.00	12.00

LIBERTY

LWB-423	Memories	1981	3.00	6.00	12.00

—Reissue of United Artists 423

LW-601	Doc and the Boys	1981	2.50	5.00	10.00

—Reissue of United Artists 601

LT-887	Look Away!	1981	2.50	5.00	10.00

—Reissue of United Artists 887

LT-943	Live and Pickin'	1981	2.50	5.00	10.00

—Reissue of United Artists 943

LN-10027	Lonesome Road	1981	2.00	4.00	8.00

—Budget-line reissue

Number	Title (A Side/B Side)	Yr	VG	VG+	NM
POPPY					
❏ PP-LA022-F	Then and Now	1973	3.75	7.50	15.00
❏ PP-LA210-G	Two Days in November	1974	3.75	7.50	15.00
❏ PYS-5703	The Elementary Doc Watson	1972	3.75	7.50	15.00
SMITHSONIAN/FOLKWAYS					
❏ SF-40012	The Doc Watson Family	1990	3.00	6.00	12.00
—Reissue of Folkways LP					
SUGAR HILL					
❏ SH-3742	Down South	1985	2.50	5.00	10.00
❏ SH-3752	Riding the Midnight Train	1986	2.50	5.00	10.00
❏ SH-3759	Portrait	1987	2.50	5.00	10.00
UNITED ARTISTS					
❏ UA-LA423-G [(2)]	Memories	1975	3.75	7.50	15.00
❏ UA-LA601-G	Doc and the Boys	1976	3.00	6.00	12.00
❏ UA-LA725-G	Lonesome Road	1977	3.00	6.00	12.00
❏ UA-LA887-H	Look Away!	1978	3.00	6.00	12.00
❏ UA-LA943-H	Live and Pickin'	1979	3.00	6.00	12.00
VANGUARD					
❏ VSD-9/10 [(2)]	Doc Watson on Stage	1970	5.00	10.00	20.00
❏ VSD 45/46 [(2)]	The Essential Doc Watson	1973	5.00	10.00	20.00
❏ VSD 107/8 [(2)]	Old Timey Concert	1977	5.00	10.00	20.00
❏ VSD-6576	Ballads from Deep Gap	1971	3.75	7.50	15.00
❏ VRS-9152 [M]	Doc Watson	1964	5.00	10.00	20.00
❏ VRS-9170 [M]	Doc Watson and Son	1965	5.00	10.00	20.00
❏ VRS-9213 [M]	Southbound	1966	3.75	7.50	15.00
❏ VRS-9239 [M]	Home Again	1967	3.75	7.50	15.00
❏ VMS-73108	The Essential Doc Watson, Vol. 1	1985	2.50	5.00	10.00
❏ VMS-73121	The Essential Doc Watson, Vol. 2	1985	2.50	5.00	10.00
❏ VSD-79152 [S]	Doc Watson	1964	6.25	12.50	25.00
❏ VSD-79170 [S]	Doc Watson and Son	1965	6.25	12.50	25.00
❏ VSD-79213 [S]	Southbound	1966	5.00	10.00	20.00
❏ VSD-79239 [S]	Home Again	1967	5.00	10.00	20.00
❏ VSD-79276	Good Deal	1968	3.75	7.50	15.00

WATSON, JOHN L., AND THE HUMMELFUGS
45s
PARKWAY

Number	Title (A Side/B Side)	Yr	VG	VG+	NM
❏ 946	Lookin' for Love/I Only Came to Dance with You	1965	3.00	6.00	12.00

WATSON, JOHNNY "GUITAR"
45s

Number	Title (A Side/B Side)	Yr	VG	VG+	NM
A&M					
❏ 2383	Planet Funk/First Timothy Six	1981	—	2.00	4.00
❏ 2398	That's What Time It Is/First Timothy Six	1982	—	2.00	4.00
ARVEE					
❏ 5016	Untouchable/Johnny Guitar	1960	6.25	12.50	25.00
—As "Johnny Watson"					
CACTUS					
❏ 118	Let's Rock/(B-side unknown)	1959	37.50	75.00	150.00
CLASS					
❏ 246	The Bear/One More Kiss	1959	7.50	15.00	30.00
—As "Johnny Watson"					
DJM					
❏ 1013	I Need It/Since I Met You Baby	1976	—	2.50	5.00
❏ 1019	Superman Lover/We're No Exception	1976	—	2.50	5.00
❏ 1020	Ain't That a Bitch/Won't You Forgive Me Baby	1977	—	3.00	6.00
❏ 1020 [PS]	Ain't That a Bitch/Won't You Forgive Me Baby	1977	2.00	4.00	8.00
❏ 1024	A Real Mother for Ya/Nothing Left to Be Desired	1977	—	2.50	5.00
❏ 1029	Lover Jones/Tarzan	1977	—	2.50	5.00
❏ 1034	Love That Will Not Die/A Damn Shame	1978	—	2.50	5.00
❏ 1100	Virginia's Pretty Funky/The Institute	1978	—	2.50	5.00
—As "Watsonian Institute"					
❏ 1101	Gangster of Love/Guitar Disco	1978	—	2.50	5.00
❏ 1106	What the Hell Is This?/Can You Handle It	1979	—	2.50	5.00
❏ 1304	Love Jones/(B-side unknown)	1980	—	2.50	5.00
❏ 1305	Telephone Bill/(B-side unknown)	1980	—	2.50	5.00
FANTASY					
❏ 721	Like I'm Not Your Man/You Bring Love	1974	—	3.00	6.00
❏ 739	I Don't Want to Be a Lone Ranger/You Can Stay But the Noise Must Go	1975	—	3.00	6.00
❏ 752	It's Too Late/Tripping	1975	—	3.00	6.00
FEDERAL					
❏ 12120	Highway 60/No I Can't	1953	37.50	75.00	150.00
❏ 12131	Motor Head Baby/Sad Fool	1953	37.50	75.00	150.00
❏ 12143	I Got Eyes/Walkin' to My Baby	1953	37.50	75.00	150.00
❏ 12157	What's Going On?/Thinking	1953	37.50	75.00	150.00
❏ 12175	Half Pint of Whiskey/Space Guitar	1954	62.50	125.00	250.00
❏ 12183	Gettin' Drunk/You Can't Take It With You	1954	50.00	100.00	200.00
—All Federal 45s as "Young John Watson"					
KEEN					
❏ 3-4005	Gangster of Love/One Room Country Shack	1957	7.50	15.00	30.00
❏ 3-4023	Deana Baby/Honey	1957	7.50	15.00	30.00
KENT					
❏ 328	Those Lonely, Lonely Nights/(B-side unknown)	1959	5.00	10.00	20.00
KING					
❏ 5536	Posin'/Embraceable You	1961	5.00	10.00	20.00
❏ 5579	Broke and Lonely/Cuttin' In	1961	6.25	12.50	25.00
❏ 5607	The Nearness of You/I Just Want Me Some Love	1962	3.75	7.50	15.00
❏ 5666	What You Do to Me/Sweet Lovin' Mama	1962	3.75	7.50	15.00
❏ 5716	Cold, Cold Heart/That's the Chance You've Got to Take	1963	3.75	7.50	15.00
❏ 5774	Gangster of Love/In the Evening	1963	3.75	7.50	15.00
❏ 5833	I Say, I Love You/You Better Love Me	1964	3.75	7.50	15.00
OKEH					
❏ 7263	Keep On Lovin' You/South Like West	1966	3.00	6.00	12.00
❏ 7270	Hold On, I'm Comin'/Wolfman	1967	3.00	6.00	12.00
RPM					
❏ 423	Hot Little Mama/I Love to Love You	1955	12.50	25.00	50.00
❏ 431	Too Tired/Don't Touch Me	1955	12.50	25.00	50.00
❏ 436	Those Lonely, Lonely Nights/Someone Cares for Me	1955	10.00	20.00	40.00
❏ 447	Oh Baby/Give a Little	1955	10.00	20.00	40.00
❏ 455	Three Hours Past Midnight/Ruben	1956	10.00	20.00	40.00
❏ 471	She Moves Me/Love Me Baby	1956	10.00	20.00	40.00
VALLEY VUE					
❏ 769	Strike On Computers/(B-side unknown)	1984	—	2.50	5.00

Number	Title (A Side/B Side)	Yr	VG	VG+	NM
Albums					
A&M					
❏ SP-4880	That's What Time It Is	1981	2.50	5.00	10.00
CADET					
❏ LP-4056 [M]	I Cried for You	1967	6.25	12.50	25.00
❏ LPS-4056 [S]	I Cried for You	1967	7.50	15.00	30.00
CHESS					
❏ LP-1490 [M]	Blues Soul	1965	17.50	35.00	70.00
❏ LPS-1490 [S]	Blues Soul	1965	20.00	40.00	80.00
DJM					
❏ 3	Ain't That a Bitch	1976	2.50	5.00	10.00
❏ 7	A Real Mother for Ya	1977	2.50	5.00	10.00
❏ 13	Master Funk	1978	2.50	5.00	10.00
—As "Watsonian Institute"					
❏ 19	Giant	1978	2.50	5.00	10.00
❏ 24	What the Hell Is This?	1979	2.50	5.00	10.00
❏ 27	E.D.P. Extra Disco Perception	1979	2.50	5.00	10.00
—As "Watsonian Institute"					
❏ 31	Love Jones	1980	2.50	5.00	10.00
❏ 501	Johnny "Guitar" Watson and the Family Clone	1981	2.50	5.00	10.00
❏ 714	Funk Beyond the Call of Duty	1977	2.50	5.00	10.00
FANTASY					
❏ MPF-4503	Greatest Hits	1981	2.50	5.00	10.00
❏ 9437	Listen	1973	3.00	6.00	12.00
❏ 9484	I Don't Want to Be Alone Stranger	1975	3.00	6.00	12.00
KING					
❏ 857 [M]	Johnny Guitar Watson	1963	100.00	200.00	400.00
MCA					
❏ 5273	The Very Best of Johnny "Guitar" Watson	1981	2.50	5.00	10.00
OKEH					
❏ OKM 12118 [M]	Bad	1967	7.50	15.00	30.00
❏ OKM 12124 [M]	In the Fats Bag	1967	7.50	15.00	30.00
❏ OKS 14118 [S]	Bad	1967	10.00	20.00	40.00
❏ OKS 14124 [S]	In the Fats Bag	1967	10.00	20.00	40.00
POWER PAK					
❏ 306	Gangster of Love	1978	2.50	5.00	10.00

WATSON, JOHNNY "GUITAR", AND LARRY WILLIAMS
Also see each artist's individual listings.
45s

Number	Title (A Side/B Side)	Yr	VG	VG+	NM
OKEH					
❏ 7274	Mercy, Mercy, Mercy/A Quitter Never Wins	1967	2.50	5.00	10.00
❏ 7281	Two for the Price of One/Too Late	1967	2.50	5.00	10.00
❏ 7281 [PS]	Two for the Price of One/Too Late	1967	6.25	12.50	25.00
❏ 7300	Find Yourself Someone to Love/Nobody	1967	6.25	12.50	25.00
—Backed by Kaleidoscope					
Albums					
OKEH					
❏ OKM 12122 [M]	Two for the Price of One	1967	10.00	20.00	40.00
❏ OKS 14122 [S]	Two for the Price of One	1967	15.00	30.00	60.00

WATSONIAN INSTITUTE   See JOHNNY "GUITAR" WATSON.

WATTS, ALAN
Albums

Number	Title (A Side/B Side)	Yr	VG	VG+	NM
ASCENSION					
❏ (# unknown)	Dhyana: of the Art of Meditation, Vol. 1	1970	7.50	15.00	30.00
❏ (# unknown)	Dhyana: of the Art of Meditation, Vol. 2	1970	7.50	15.00	30.00
MEA					
❏ LP-1001 [M]	Haiku Poems	1962	12.50	25.00	50.00
❏ LP-1002 [M]	Zen and Senryu	1962	12.50	25.00	50.00
❏ LP-1007 [M]	This Is It	1962	15.00	30.00	60.00
TOGETHER					
❏ 1025	Why Not Now	1970	6.25	12.50	25.00
WARNER BROS.					
❏ W 1923	The Sounds of Hinduism	1968	6.25	12.50	25.00

WATTS, NOBLE
45s

Number	Title (A Side/B Side)	Yr	VG	VG+	NM
BATON					
❏ 246	Easy Going (Part 1)/Easy Going (Part 2)	1957	6.25	12.50	25.00
❏ 249	Hard Times (The Slop)/Midnite Flight	1957	3.75	7.50	15.00
❏ 249	The Slop/Midnite Flight	1957	6.25	12.50	25.00
❏ 251	Rickey Tick/Blast Off	1958	3.75	7.50	15.00
❏ 254	The Slide/Shakin'	1958	3.75	7.50	15.00
❏ 257	Great Times/The Creep	1958	3.75	7.50	15.00
❏ 266	Flap Jack/Hot Tamales	1959	3.75	7.50	15.00
BRUNSWICK					
❏ 55382	Thingamajig/F.L.A.	1968	2.00	4.00	8.00
CUB					
❏ 9078	The Beaver/Frog Hop	1960	3.00	6.00	12.00
DELUXE					
❏ 6066	Mashing Potatoes/Pig Ears and Rice	1954	7.50	15.00	30.00
ENJOY					
❏ 1008	Jookin'/What Ya Gonna Do	1963	3.00	6.00	12.00
SIR					
❏ 273	Boogie Woogie/Mashed Potatoes	1959	3.75	7.50	15.00

WATTS 103RD STREET RHYTHM BAND, THE   See CHARLES WRIGHT AND THE WATTS 103RD STREET RHYTHM BAND.

WAYLON AND JESSI   Also see JESSI COLTER; WAYLON JENNINGS.
45s

Number	Title (A Side/B Side)	Yr	VG	VG+	NM
RCA					
❏ PB-12176	Storms Never Last/I Ain't the One	1982	—	2.00	4.00
❏ PB-12245	Wild Side of Life/It Wasn't God Who Made Honky Tonk Angels	1982	—	2.00	4.00
RCA VICTOR					
❏ 47-9920	Suspicious Minds/I Ain't the One	1970	—	3.00	6.00
❏ 47-9992	Under Your Spell Again/Bridge Over Troubled Water	1971	—	3.00	6.00
❏ PB-10653	Suspicious Minds/I Ain't the One	1976	—	2.50	5.00
Albums					
RCA VICTOR					
❏ AAL1-3931	Leather and Lace	1981	2.50	5.00	10.00

Number	Title (A Side/B Side)	Yr	VG	VG+	NM

WAYLON AND WILLIE For convenience's sake, we've listed all the variations of their credits here, including "Willie Nelson and Waylon Jennings." Also see WAYLON JENNINGS; WILLIE NELSON.

45s
COLUMBIA

Number	Title (A Side/B Side)	Yr	VG	VG+	NM
❑ 04131	Take It to the Limit/Till I Gain Control Again	1983	—	2.00	4.00
❑ 04131 [PS]	Take It to the Limit/Till I Gain Control Again	1983	—	2.50	5.00

EPIC

| ❑ 73832 | If I Can Find a Clean Shirt/ Put Me on a Train Back to Texas | 1991 | — | — | 3.00 |
| ❑ 74024 | Tryin' to Outrun the Wind/The Makin's of a Song | 1991 | — | — | 3.00 |

RCA

| ❑ PB-11198 | Mammas Don't Let Your Babies Grow Up to Be Cowboys/I Can Get Off on You | 1978 | — | 2.00 | 4.00 |
| ❑ GB-11499 | Mammas Don't Let Your Babies Grow Up to Be Cowboys/Luckenbach, Texas (Back to the Basics of Love) | 1979 | — | 2.00 | 4.00 |

—Gold Standard Series

| ❑ GB-11996 | Mammas Don't Let Your Babies Grow Up to Be Cowboys/I Can Get Off on You | 1980 | — | — | 3.00 |

—Gold Standard Series

| ❑ PB-13073 | Just to Satisfy You/Get Naked With You | 1982 | — | 2.00 | 4.00 |
| ❑ PB-13319 | (Sittin' On) The Dock of the Bay/ Luckenbach, Texas | 1982 | — | 2.00 | 4.00 |

RCA VICTOR

| ❑ PB-10529 | Good Hearted Woman/Heaven or Hell | 1975 | — | 2.50 | 5.00 |

Albums
COLUMBIA

| ❑ FC 38562 | Take It to the Limit | 1983 | 2.50 | 5.00 | 10.00 |

RCA VICTOR

| ❑ AAL1-2686 | Waylon and Willie | 198? | 2.00 | 4.00 | 8.00 |

—Reissue with new prefix

| ❑ AFL1-2686 | Waylon and Willie | 1978 | 2.50 | 5.00 | 10.00 |
| ❑ AFL1-2686 [DJ] | Waylon and Willie | 1978 | 6.25 | 12.50 | 25.00 |

—Promo only on gold vinyl

| ❑ AHL1-4455 | WW II | 1982 | 2.50 | 5.00 | 10.00 |
| ❑ AYL1-5134 | Waylon and Willie | 198? | 2.00 | 4.00 | 8.00 |

—"Best Buy Series" reissue

| ❑ AYL1-5134 | WW II | 198? | 2.00 | 4.00 | 8.00 |

—"Best Buy Series" reissue

WAYLON AND WILLIE/WAYLON AND JESSI
45s
RCA

| ❑ GB-10928 | Good Hearted Woman/Suspicious Minds | 1977 | — | — | 3.00 |

—Gold Standard Series

WAYNE, ALVIS
45s
WESTPORT

| ❑ 132 | Swing Bop Boogie/Sleep, Rock-a-Roll Rock-a-Baby | 1956 | 50.00 | 100.00 | 200.00 |
| ❑ 138 | Don't Mean Maybe Baby/I'd Rather Be with You | 1957 | 37.50 | 75.00 | 150.00 |

—As "Tony Wayne"

| ❑ 138 | Don't Mean Maybe Baby/I'd Rather Be with You | 1958 | 25.00 | 50.00 | 100.00 |

—As "Alvis Wayne"

WAYNE, BERNIE
45s
ABC-PARAMOUNT

❑ 9664	Vanessa/Piff, Paff, Puff	1956	5.00	10.00	20.00
❑ 9679	You're Kinda Cute/ The Night Was Made for Dreamers	1956	5.00	10.00	20.00
❑ 9727	Shalimar/South of Saigon	1956	5.00	10.00	20.00
❑ 9752	Flirtango/Maracaibo	1956	5.00	10.00	20.00
❑ 9815	Leaky Faucet/Theme from "Abner the Baseball"	1957	5.00	10.00	20.00
❑ 9967	The Telegraph Operator and the Chorus Girl/ Cool Caballero	1958	5.00	10.00	20.00

HANOVER

| ❑ 4528 | Now/Chickie | 1960 | 5.00 | 10.00 | 20.00 |

IMPERIAL

| ❑ 5575 | The Whistling Pixie/Soft Shoe Rock | 1959 | 3.75 | 7.50 | 15.00 |

RUST

| ❑ 5063 | 38-24-38/Martinique | 1963 | 3.00 | 6.00 | 12.00 |

20TH CENTURY FOX

| ❑ 559 | Christmas Is Over/Christmas Is Over | 1964 | 2.00 | 4.00 | 8.00 |

—B-side by the Hushtones

WAYNE, BILLY
45s
FEDORA

| ❑ 1008 | Telegram/Heartbreak and Blues | 1962 | 6.25 | 12.50 | 25.00 |

HILLCREST

| ❑ 778 | I Love My Baby/Walkin' n' Strollin' | 1960 | 200.00 | 400.00 | 800.00 |

WAYNE, CARL, AND THE VIKINGS
45s
ABC-PARAMOUNT

| ❑ 10752 | Shimmy Shammy Jingle/My Girl | 1965 | 3.00 | 6.00 | 12.00 |

WAYNE, FARLEY
45s
HIT

| ❑ 18 | That's Old Fashioned/Wolverton Mountain | 1962 | 2.00 | 4.00 | 8.00 |

WAYNE, JOHN
45s
CASABLANCA

| ❑ 1002 | I Have Faith/The Prayer | 1979 | — | 3.00 | 6.00 |

Albums
RCA VICTOR

| ❑ AFL1-3484 | America, Why I Love Her | 1979 | 2.50 | 5.00 | 10.00 |

—Reissue of 4828

| ❑ AYL1-3959 | America, Why I Love Her | 1981 | 2.00 | 4.00 | 8.00 |

—"Best Buy Series" reissue

| ❑ LSP-4828 | America, Why I Love Her | 1973 | 6.25 | 12.50 | 25.00 |

WAYNE, THOMAS
45s
CAPEHART

| ❑ 5009 | Tragedy/No More, No More | 1961 | 7.50 | 15.00 | 30.00 |

CHALET

| ❑ 1054 | No One/You're Tearin' Down My Mind | 1969 | — | 3.00 | 6.00 |

FERNWOOD

❑ 106	You're the One That Done It/This Time	1958	75.00	150.00	300.00
❑ 109	Tragedy/Saturday Date	1959	7.50	15.00	30.00
❑ 111	Eternally/Scandalizing My Name	1959	7.50	15.00	30.00
❑ 113	Gonna Be Waitin'/Just Beyond	1959	7.50	15.00	30.00
❑ 120	Guilty of Love/Pancho Villa	1960	7.50	15.00	30.00
❑ 122	Girl Next Door/Because of You	1960	7.50	15.00	30.00
❑ 128	Tragedy/No More, No More	1961	7.50	15.00	30.00

MERCURY

| ❑ 71287 | You're the One That Done It/This Time | 1958 | 20.00 | 40.00 | 80.00 |
| ❑ 71454 | You're the One That Done It/This Time | 1959 | 10.00 | 20.00 | 40.00 |

PHILLIPS INT'L.

| ❑ 3577 | I've Got It Made/The Quiet Look | 1962 | 6.25 | 12.50 | 25.00 |

SANTO

| ❑ 9053 | Stop the River/Eighth Wonder of the World | 1962 | 6.25 | 12.50 | 25.00 |
| ❑ 9057 | Tragedy/Gonna Be Waiting | 1962 | 6.25 | 12.50 | 25.00 |

WAYNE AND DEE
45s
HIT

| ❑ 221 | I Got You Babe/Eve of Destruction | 1965 | 3.00 | 6.00 | 12.00 |

—B-side by the Roamers

WE FIVE
45s
A&M

| ❑ XMAS 1 [DJ] | My Favorite Things/The 12 Days Of Christmas | 1968 | 3.00 | 6.00 | 12.00 |

—B-side by the Baja Marimba Band

| ❑ XMAS 1 [PS] | My Favorite Things/The 12 Days Of Christmas | 1968 | 3.75 | 7.50 | 15.00 |

—B-side by the Baja Marimba Band

❑ 770	You Were On My Mind/Small World	1965	3.00	6.00	12.00
❑ 784	Let's Get Together/Cast Your Fate to the Wind	1965	2.00	4.00	8.00
❑ 793	You Let a Love Burn Out/ Somewhere Beyond the Sea	1966	2.00	4.00	8.00
❑ 800	Somewhere/There Stands the Door	1966	2.00	4.00	8.00
❑ 820	What's Goin' On/The First Time	1966	2.00	4.00	8.00
❑ 894	High Flying Bird/What Do I Do	1967	—	3.00	6.00
❑ 1072	Walk On By/It Really Doesn't Matter	1969	—	3.00	6.00

MGM

| ❑ 14618 | Seven Day Change/Natural Way | 1973 | — | 2.50 | 5.00 |

VAULT

| ❑ 964 | Never Goin' Back/Here Comes the Sun | 1970 | — | 3.00 | 6.00 |
| ❑ 969 | Catch the Wind/Oh, Lonesome Me | 1970 | — | 3.00 | 6.00 |

VERVE

| ❑ 10716 | Bandstand Dancer/Rejoice | 1973 | — | 2.50 | 5.00 |

Albums
A&M

❑ SP-111 [M]	You Were On My Mind	1965	3.75	7.50	15.00
❑ SP-138 [M]	Make Someone Happy	1967	5.00	10.00	20.00
❑ SP-4111 [S]	You Were On My Mind	1965	5.00	10.00	20.00
❑ SP-4138 [S]	Make Someone Happy	1967	3.75	7.50	15.00
❑ SP-4168	The Return of We Five	1969	3.75	7.50	15.00

VAULT

| ❑ 136 | Catch the Wind | 1970 | 3.75 | 7.50 | 15.00 |

WE TWO
45s
ABC

| ❑ 10930 | Magic Moments/Way Down Deep Inside | 1967 | 6.25 | 12.50 | 25.00 |

WEASELS, THE
Albums
WING

| ❑ MGW-12282 [M] | The Liverpool Beat | 1964 | 6.25 | 12.50 | 25.00 |
| ❑ SRW-16282 [S] | The Liverpool Beat | 1964 | 7.50 | 15.00 | 30.00 |

WEATHERLY, JIM
45s
ABC

❑ 12193	(Apples Won't Grow In) Colorado Snow/ To a Gentler Time	1976	—	2.50	5.00
❑ 12213	Gonna Shine It On Again/ People Some People Choose to Love	1976	—	2.50	5.00
❑ 12252	Storms of Troubled Times/(B-side unknown)	1977	—	2.50	5.00
❑ 12288	All That Keeps Me Going/ I Hope It Never Rains Like That Again	1977	—	2.50	5.00

BUDDAH

❑ 420	The Need to Be/Like Old Times Again	1974	—	2.50	5.00
❑ 420 [PS]	The Need to Be/Like Old Times Again	1974	—	3.00	6.00
❑ 444	I'll Still Love You/My First Day Without Her	1974	—	2.50	5.00
❑ 467	It Must Have Been the Rain/Mississippi	1975	—	2.50	5.00
❑ 505	What's One More Time/ How'd We Ever Get This Way	1975	—	2.50	5.00

ELEKTRA

❑ 46547	Smooth Sailin'/Let Me Love It Away	1979	—	2.00	4.00
❑ 46592	Gift from Missouri/All I Need to Know	1980	—	2.00	4.00
❑ 47027	Safe in the Arms of Your Love (Cold in the Streets)/All I Need to Know	1980	—	2.00	4.00
❑ 47096	Love That Went Away/(B-side unknown)	1980	—	2.00	4.00

RCA VICTOR

❑ 74-0822	Loving You Is Just an Old Habit/Between His Goodbye and My Hello	1972	—	3.00	6.00
❑ 74-0897	Old Kentucky Moon/Until Your Ship Comes In	1973	—	3.00	6.00
❑ 74-0949	Where Peaceful Waters Flow/ Like a First Time Thing	1973	—	3.00	6.00
❑ APBO-0020	Leavin' Dallas/It Must Be Love This Time	1973	—	2.50	5.00
❑ APBO-0153	Rebel Keeps On Rollin'/ Same Old Song and Dance	1973	—	2.50	5.00
❑ PB-10134	High on Love/Like a First Time Thing	1974	—	2.50	5.00

20TH CENTURY FOX

| ❑ 565 | I'm Gonna Make It/Wise Men Never Speak | 1965 | 3.75 | 7.50 | 15.00 |

Number	Title (A Side/B Side)	Yr	VG	VG+	NM
Albums					
ABC					
❑ ABCD-937	The People Some People Choose to Love	1976	2.50	5.00	10.00
❑ ABCD-982	Pictures and Rhymes	1977	2.50	5.00	10.00
BUDDAH					
❑ BDS-5608	The Songs of Jim Weatherly	1974	2.50	5.00	10.00
❑ BDS-5637	Magnolias & Misfits	1975	2.50	5.00	10.00
RCA VICTOR					
❑ APL1-0090	A Simpler Time	1973	3.00	6.00	12.00
❑ APL1-0267	Jim Weatherly	1974	3.00	6.00	12.00
❑ LSP-4747	Weatherly	1972	3.00	6.00	12.00

WEAVER, DENNIS
45s

Number	Title (A Side/B Side)	Yr	VG	VG+	NM
CASCADE					
❑ 5906	Girls (Wuz Made to Be Loved)/Michael Finnigan	1959	5.00	10.00	20.00
CENTURY CITY					
❑ 701	Days Like These/Cobwebs of Your Mind	1969	2.00	4.00	8.00
EVA					
❑ 103	The Apes/Chicken Mash	1963	3.00	6.00	12.00
IM'PRESS					
❑ 716	20th Century Man/No Name	1973	—	3.00	6.00
OVATION					
❑ 1056	Hubbardville Store/Prairie Dog Blues	1975	—	2.00	4.00
❑ 1056 [PS]	Hubbardville Store/Prairie Dog Blues	1975	—	2.50	5.00
WARNER BROS.					
❑ 5352	The Sinking of the Reuben James/Genesis Through Exodus	1963	3.75	7.50	15.00
Albums					
ABC					
❑ DP-847	People Songs	1974	3.00	6.00	12.00
IM'PRESS					
❑ 1614	Dennis Weaver	1972	3.75	7.50	15.00
OVATION					
❑ OVOD-1440	One More Road	1975	3.00	6.00	12.00

WEAVERS, THE   Also see PETE SEEGER.
45s

Number	Title (A Side/B Side)	Yr	VG	VG+	NM
DECCA					
❑ 9-284 [PS]	We Wish You a Merry Christmas	1951	3.75	7.50	15.00
—Empty box for 27783, 27817, 27818, 27819					
❑ 27053	Tzena, Tzena, Tzena/Around the World	1950	5.00	10.00	20.00
❑ 27077	Goodnight Irene/Tzena, Tzena, Tzena	1950	3.75	7.50	15.00
❑ 27332	The Roving Kind/(The Wreck of the) John B	1950	3.75	7.50	15.00
❑ 27376	So Long (It's Been Good to Know Yuh)/Lonesome Traveller	1951	3.75	7.50	15.00
❑ 9-27515	On Top of Old Smoky/Across the Wide Missouri	1951	5.00	10.00	20.00
—With Terry Gilkyson					
❑ 27670	Kisses Sweeter Than Wine/When the Saints Go Marching In	1951	3.75	7.50	15.00
❑ 27726	The Frozen Logger/Darling Corey	1951	3.75	7.50	15.00
❑ 27727	I Know Where I'm Going-Hush Little Baby/Suliram	1951	3.75	7.50	15.00
❑ 27728	Drinking Gourd/Easy Rider Blues	1951	3.75	7.50	15.00
❑ 27783	We Wish You a Merry Christmas/One for the Little Bitty Baby	1951	3.75	7.50	15.00
—Sides 1 and 2 of "Album No. 9-284"					
❑ 27817	The Seven Blessings of Mary/The Twelve Days of Christmas	1951	3.75	7.50	15.00
—Sides 3 and 4 of "Album No. 9-284"					
❑ 27818	Go Tell It on the Mountain/Poor Little Jesus	1951	3.75	7.50	15.00
—Sides 5 and 6 of "Album No. 9-284"					
❑ 27819	Lulloo Lullay-It's Almost Day/Burgundian Carol-God Rest Ye Merry Gentlemen	1951	3.75	7.50	15.00
—Sides 7 and 8 of "Album No. 9-284"					
❑ 27928	Wimoweh/Old Paint	1952	3.75	7.50	15.00
❑ 28054	Around the Corner (Beneath the Berry Tree)/The Gandy Dancer's Ball	1952	3.75	7.50	15.00
❑ 28228	Run Home to Ma-Ma/Hard Ain't It Hard	1952	3.75	7.50	15.00
❑ 28434	Clementine/True Love	1952	3.75	7.50	15.00
❑ 28542	Down in the Valley/The Bay of Mexico	1953	3.75	7.50	15.00
❑ 28637	Taking It Easy/Benoni	1953	3.75	7.50	15.00
❑ 28919	Rock Island Shuffle/Sylvia	1953	3.75	7.50	15.00
VANGUARD					
❑ 35001	Done Laid Around/Take This Letter	196?	3.00	6.00	12.00
❑ 35005	Aunt Rhodie/Bury Me Beneath the Willows	196?	3.00	6.00	12.00
❑ 35009	This Land Is Your Land/Aweigh, Santy Ano	196?	3.00	6.00	12.00
❑ 35010	On My Journey/The Sinking of the Reuben James	196?	3.00	6.00	12.00
❑ 35014	The Keeper/Twelve Gates to the City	196?	3.00	6.00	12.00
❑ 35015	Fight On/Rally Round the Flag	196?	3.00	6.00	12.00
7-Inch Extended Plays					
DECCA					
❑ ED 2015	*Goodnight Irene/Tzena, Tzena, Tzena/On Top of Old Smoky/So Long (It's Been Good to Know Yuh)	195?	12.50	25.00	50.00
❑ ED 2015 [PS]	The Weavers, Vol. 1	195?	12.50	25.00	50.00
Albums					
ANALOGUE PRODUCTIONS					
❑ 005	Reunion at Carnegie Hall, 1963	199?	7.50	15.00	30.00
—Audiophile vinyl					
DECCA					
❑ DXB 173 [(2)M]	The Best of the Weavers	1965	6.25	12.50	25.00
❑ DL 4277 [M]	Weavers' Gold	1962	5.00	10.00	20.00
❑ DL 5285 [10]	Folk Songs of America and Other Lands	1951	25.00	50.00	100.00
❑ DL-5373 [10]	We Wish You a Merry Christmas	1952	25.00	50.00	100.00
❑ DXSB 7173 [(2)R]	The Best of the Weavers	1965	5.00	10.00	20.00
❑ DL 8893 [M]	The Best of the Weavers	1959	10.00	20.00	40.00
—Black label, silver print					
❑ DL 8893 [M]	Folk Songs Made Famous by the Weavers	196?	5.00	10.00	20.00
❑ DL 8909 [M]	Folk Songs Around the World	1959	10.00	20.00	40.00
❑ DL 74277 [R]	Weavers' Gold	1962	3.75	7.50	15.00
❑ DL 75169 [R]	The Weavers' Greatest Hits	1971	3.00	6.00	12.00
❑ DL 78893 [R]	Folk Songs Made Famous by the Weavers	196?	3.75	7.50	15.00

Number	Title (A Side/B Side)	Yr	VG	VG+	NM
MCA					
❑ 4052 [(2)]	The Best of the Weavers	197?	3.75	7.50	15.00
—Reissue of Decca 7173; black rainbow labels					
❑ 4052 [(2)]	The Best of the Weavers	1980	3.00	6.00	12.00
—Blue rainbow labels					
VANGUARD					
❑ VSD-15/16 [(2)]	The Weavers' Greatest Hits	1971	3.75	7.50	15.00
❑ VSD 2022 [S]	Travelling on with the Weavers	1959	10.00	20.00	40.00
❑ VSD 2030 [S]	The Weavers at Home	1959	10.00	20.00	40.00
❑ VSD 2069 [S]	The Weavers at Carnegie Hall, Vol. 2	1960	10.00	20.00	40.00
❑ VSD 2101 [S]	Almanac	1961	10.00	20.00	40.00
❑ VSD 2150 [S]	Reunion at Carnegie Hall, 1963	1963	7.50	15.00	30.00
❑ SRV-3001 [(2)M]	The Weavers Song Bag	1967	5.00	10.00	20.00
❑ VRS-6533 [R]	The Weavers at Carnegie Hall	1970	3.00	6.00	12.00
❑ VRS-6537 [R]	The Weavers on Tour	1970	3.00	6.00	12.00
❑ VRS 9010 [M]	The Weavers at Carnegie Hall	1957	10.00	20.00	40.00
❑ VRS 9013 [M]	The Weavers on Tour	1957	10.00	20.00	40.00
❑ VRS 9024 [M]	The Weavers at Home	1959	7.50	15.00	30.00
❑ VRS 9043 [M]	Travelling on with the Weavers	1959	7.50	15.00	30.00
❑ VRS 9075 [M]	The Weavers at Carnegie Hall, Vol. 2	1960	7.50	15.00	30.00
❑ VRS 9100 [M]	Almanac	1961	7.50	15.00	30.00
❑ VRS 9130 [M]	Reunion at Carnegie Hall, 1963	1963	5.00	10.00	20.00
❑ VRS 9161 [M]	Reunion at Carnegie Hall, Part 2	1965	5.00	10.00	20.00
❑ SRV-73001 [(2)S]	The Weavers Song Bag	1967	6.25	12.50	25.00
❑ VMS-73101	The Weavers at Carnegie Hall	1984	2.00	4.00	8.00
—Reissue of 6533					
❑ VMS-73116	The Weavers on Tour	1985	2.00	4.00	8.00
—Reissue of 6537					
❑ VMS-73122	Classics	1985	2.50	5.00	10.00
❑ VSD 79161 [S]	Reunion at Carnegie Hall, Part 2	1965	7.50	15.00	30.00

WEB, THE
Albums

Number	Title (A Side/B Side)	Yr	VG	VG+	NM
DERAM					
❑ DES 18018	Fully Interlocking	1968	6.25	12.50	25.00

WEBB, BOOGIE BILL
45s

Number	Title (A Side/B Side)	Yr	VG	VG+	NM
IMPERIAL					
❑ 5257	Bad Dog/I Ain't For It	1953	62.50	125.00	250.00

WEBB, JACK
45s

Number	Title (A Side/B Side)	Yr	VG	VG+	NM
WARNER BROS.					
❑ 5003	Try a Little Tenderness/You'd Never Know the Old Place Now	1958	5.00	10.00	20.00
7-Inch Extended Plays					
RCA VICTOR					
❑ 547-0342	The Christmas Story (Part 1)/The Christmas Story (Part 4)	1953	7.50	15.00	30.00
❑ 547-0343	The Christmas Story (Part 2)/The Christmas Story (Part 3)	1953	7.50	15.00	30.00
❑ EPB 3199 [PS]	The Christmas Story	1953	10.00	20.00	40.00
—Cover for 2-EP set					
Albums					
RCA VICTOR					
❑ LPM-1126 [M]	Pete Kelly's Blues	1955	12.50	25.00	50.00
—Webb narrates; jazz combo plays					
❑ LPM-2053 [M]	Pete Kelly's Blues	1959	7.50	15.00	30.00
—Reissue of 1126					
❑ LSP-2053(e) [R]	Pete Kelly's Blues	1959	5.00	10.00	20.00
❑ LPM-3199 [10]	Dragnet — The Christmas Story	1954	37.50	75.00	150.00
WARNER BROS.					
❑ W 1207 [M]	You're My Girl	1958	7.50	15.00	30.00
❑ WS 1207 [S]	You're My Girl	1958	10.00	20.00	40.00
❑ WS 1207 [S]	You're My Girl	1958	10.00	20.00	40.00

WEBB, MORTI
45s

Number	Title (A Side/B Side)	Yr	VG	VG+	NM
HIT					
❑ 122	People/I Don't Want to Be Hurt Anymore	1964	2.00	4.00	8.00
—B-side by Leroy Jones					

WEBS, THE (1)   R&B group.
45s

Number	Title (A Side/B Side)	Yr	VG	VG+	NM
ATLANTIC					
❑ 2415	Let's Party/Keep Your Love Strong	1967	3.00	6.00	12.00
MGM					
❑ 13602	People Sure Act Funny/You Pretty Fool	1966	3.00	6.00	12.00
POPSIDE					
❑ 4593	This Thing Called Love/Tomorrow	1967	2.50	5.00	10.00
❑ 4595	Give In/It's So Hard to Break a Habit	1968	2.50	5.00	10.00
VERVE					
❑ 10610	We Belong Together/I Want You Back	1968	2.50	5.00	10.00

WEBS, THE (2)   BOBBY GOLDSBORO was in this group.
45s

Number	Title (A Side/B Side)	Yr	VG	VG+	NM
HEART					
❑ 333	Blue Skies/Lost (Cricket in My Ear)	1962	10.00	20.00	40.00
LITE					
❑ 9004	Blue Skies/Lost (Cricket in My Ear)	1962	5.00	10.00	20.00

WEBTONES, THE
45s

Number	Title (A Side/B Side)	Yr	VG	VG+	NM
MGM					
❑ 12724	My Lost Love/Walk, Talk and Kiss	1958	6.25	12.50	25.00

WECHTER, JULIUS   See BAJA MARIMBA BAND.

WEDGES, THE
Albums

Number	Title (A Side/B Side)	Yr	VG	VG+	NM
TIME					
❑ S-2090 [S]	Hang Ten (For Surfers Only)	1963	17.50	35.00	70.00
❑ 52090 [M]	Hang Ten (For Surfers Only)	1963	12.50	25.00	50.00

Number	Title (A Side/B Side)	Yr	VG	VG+	NM

WEIR, BOB Also see THE GRATEFUL DEAD.
45s
ARISTA
| ❏ 0315 | Bombs Away/Easy to Slip | 1978 | — | 3.00 | 6.00 |
| ❏ 0336 | I'll Be Doggone/Shade of Grey | 1978 | 3.00 | 6.00 | 12.00 |
—May be promo only
WARNER BROS.
| ❏ 7611 | One More Saturday Night/Cassidy | 1972 | 3.00 | 6.00 | 12.00 |
Albums
ARISTA
| ❏ AL 4155 | Heaven Help the Fool | 1978 | 2.50 | 5.00 | 10.00 |
| ❏ AL 8366 | Heaven Help the Fool | 1985 | 2.00 | 4.00 | 8.00 |
—Budget-line reissue
| ❏ AL 8367 | Bobby and the Midnites | 1985 | 2.00 | 4.00 | 8.00 |
—Budget-line reissue
| ❏ AL 9568 | Bobby and the Midnites | 1981 | 2.50 | 5.00 | 10.00 |
WARNER BROS.
| ❏ BS 2627 | Ace | 1972 | 7.50 | 15.00 | 30.00 |
—Black and white photo on back cover
| ❏ BS 2627 | Ace | 1972 | 10.00 | 20.00 | 40.00 |
—Color photo on back cover

WEIRD-OHS, THE
Albums
MERCURY
| ❏ MG-20976 [M] | The Sounds of the Weird-Ohs | 1964 | 37.50 | 75.00 | 150.00 |
| ❏ SR-60976 [S] | The Sounds of the Weird-Ohs | 1964 | 50.00 | 100.00 | 200.00 |

WEISBERG, TIM Also see DAN FOGELBERG.
45s
A&M
❏ 1318	Long Ago and Far Away/Hard Way to Go	1971	—	2.50	5.00
❏ 1330	Fog and Spice/For Those Who Never Dream	1972	—	2.50	5.00
❏ 1397	Our Thing/Tyme Cube	1972	—	2.50	5.00
❏ 1427	Killing Me Softly with His Song/Tibetan Silver	1973	—	2.50	5.00
❏ 1493	Do Dah/A Night for Crying	1973	—	2.50	5.00
❏ 1520	Streak-Out/A Night for Crying	1974	—	2.50	5.00
❏ 1680	Dion Blue/The Visit	1975	—	2.00	4.00
MCA
❏ 41036	Midsummer's Dream/Moonchild	1979	—	2.00	4.00
❏ 41307	I'm the Lucky One/Magic Lady	1980	—	2.00	4.00
❏ 51042	What's Going On/Page One	1981	—	2.00	4.00
❏ 51163	Sleep Walk/Paula	1981	—	2.00	4.00
UNITED ARTISTS
❏ XW933	Gonna Fly Now (Theme from "Rocky")/Just for Fun	1976	—	2.00	4.00
❏ XW1083	Cascade/Gene, Jean	1977	—	2.00	4.00
❏ 1227	Every Time I See Your Smile/So Good to Me	1978	—	2.00	4.00
Albums
A&M
❏ SP-3039	Tim Weisberg	1971	3.00	6.00	12.00
❏ SP-3045	Dreamspeaker	1973	2.50	5.00	10.00
❏ SP-3121	Tim Weisberg 4	198?	2.00	4.00	8.00
—Budget-line reissue
| ❏ SP-3261 | Smile/The Best of Tim Weisberg | 198? | 2.00 | 4.00 | 8.00 |
—Budget-line reissue
❏ SP-3658	Tim Weisberg 4	1974	2.50	5.00	10.00
❏ SP-4352	Hurtwood Edge	1972	3.00	6.00	12.00
❏ SP-4545	Listen to the City	1975	2.50	5.00	10.00
❏ SP-4600	Live at Last!	1976	2.50	5.00	10.00
❏ SP-4749	Smile/The Best of Tim Weisberg	1979	2.50	5.00	10.00
CYPRESS
❏ YL-0123	Outrageous Temptations	1989	3.00	6.00	12.00
❏ 661112-1	High Risk	1986	2.50	5.00	10.00
DESERT ROCK
❏ DR-001	High Risk	1985	3.75	7.50	15.00
LIBERTY
❏ LN-10029	Rotations	198?	2.00	4.00	8.00
—Budget-line reissue
| ❏ LN-10031 | The Tim Weisberg Band | 198? | 2.00 | 4.00 | 8.00 |
—Budget-line reissue
MCA
❏ 3084	Night-Rider!	1979	2.50	5.00	10.00
❏ 5125	Party of One	1980	2.50	5.00	10.00
❏ 5245	Travelin' Light	1981	2.50	5.00	10.00
NAUTILUS
❏ NR-7	Tip of the Weisberg	1980	7.50	15.00	30.00
—Audiophile vinyl
UNITED ARTISTS
| ❏ UA-LA773-G | The Tim Weisberg Band | 1977 | 2.50 | 5.00 | 10.00 |
| ❏ UA-LA857-H | Rotations | 1978 | 2.50 | 5.00 | 10.00 |

WEISSBERG, ERIC, AND MARSHALL BRICKMAN
Albums
ELEKTRA
| ❏ EKL-238 [M] | New Dimensions in Banjo and Bluegrass | 1963 | 5.00 | 10.00 | 20.00 |
| ❏ EKS-7238 [S] | New Dimensions in Banjo and Bluegrass | 1963 | 6.25 | 12.50 | 25.00 |
—Mandolin-player label
| ❏ EKS-7238 [S] | New Dimensions in Banjo and Bluegrass | 1967 | 5.00 | 10.00 | 20.00 |
—Tan label with large stylized "E" at top
| ❏ EKS-7238 [S] | New Dimensions in Banjo and Bluegrass | 1969 | 3.75 | 7.50 | 15.00 |
—Red label with large stylized "E" at top
| ❏ EKS-7238 [S] | New Dimensions in Banjo and Bluegrass | 1971 | 3.00 | 6.00 | 12.00 |
—Butterfly label
| ❏ EKS-7238 [S] | New Dimensions in Banjo and Bluegrass | 1980 | 2.50 | 5.00 | 10.00 |
—Red label with Warner Communications logo in lower right

WEISSBERG, ERIC, AND DELIVERANCE
45s
EPIC
| ❏ 50072 | Yakety Yak/Meadow Muffins | 1975 | — | 2.00 | 4.00 |
WARNER BROS.
| ❏ 7718 | Reuben's Train/Scalded Cat | 1973 | — | 2.00 | 4.00 |
| ❏ 7756 | Opening Day/Concrete Canyon Boogie | 1973 | — | 2.00 | 4.00 |

Albums
WARNER BROS.
| ❏ BS 2720 | Rural Free Delivery | 1973 | 2.50 | 5.00 | 10.00 |

WEISSBERG, ERIC, AND STEVE MANDELL
45s
WARNER BROS.
| ❏ 7659 | Dueling Banjos/End of a Dream | 1972 | — | 2.00 | 4.00 |
—Later pressings credit the musicians; "Dueling Banjos" time is 2:12
| ❏ 7659 | Dueling Banjos/End of a Dream | 1972 | 2.50 | 5.00 | 10.00 |
—A-side listed as "from the Warner Bros. motion picture Deliverance" with no artist mentioned on the B-side; "Dueling Banjos" time is 3:17
| ❏ 7659 | Dueling Banjos/End of a Dream | 1973 | — | 3.00 | 6.00 |
—A-side listed as "from the Warner Bros. motion picture Deliverance" with no artist mentioned on the B-side; "Dueling Banjos" time is 2:12
7-Inch Extended Plays
WARNER BROS.
| ❏ S 2683 | Eight More Miles to Louisville/Dueling Banjos/ Little Maggie//Pony Express/Buffalo Gals/ Eighth of January | 1973 | 2.50 | 5.00 | 10.00 |
—Jukebox issue; small hole, plays at 33 1/3 rpm
| ❏ S 2683 [PS] | Dueling Banjos | 1973 | 2.50 | 5.00 | 10.00 |
—Part of "Little LP" series (LLP #210)
Albums
WARNER BROS.
| ❏ BS 2683 | Dueling Banjos from Deliverance | 1973 | 2.00 | 4.00 | 8.00 |
—"Burbank" palm trees label
| ❏ BS 2683 | Dueling Banjos from Deliverance | 1973 | 2.50 | 5.00 | 10.00 |
—Except for the title song and "End of a Dream," this is actually a reissue of Elektra 7238; green label
| ❏ BS 2683 | Dueling Banjos from Deliverance | 1979 | — | 3.00 | 6.00 |
—Tan or white label

WELCH, LENNY
45s
ATCO
| ❏ 6894 | A Sunday Kind of Love/I Wish You Could Know Me | 1972 | — | 2.50 | 5.00 |
| ❏ 6915 | Goodnight My Love/Fancy Meeting You Here Baby | 1973 | — | 2.50 | 5.00 |
BIG TREE
| ❏ 16107 | Six Million Dollar Woman//(B-side unknown) | 1977 | — | 2.50 | 5.00 |
CADENCE
❏ 1373	You Don't Know Me/I Need Someone	1959	2.50	5.00	10.00
❏ 1386	Darlin'/Three Handed Woman	1960	2.50	5.00	10.00
❏ 1394	I'd Like to Know/Darlin'	1960	2.50	5.00	10.00
❏ 1399	Changa Rock/Boogie Cha Cha	1961	2.50	5.00	10.00
❏ 1416	It's Just Not That Easy/Mama Don't You Hit That Boy	1962	2.50	5.00	10.00
❏ 1422	Ebb Tide/Congratulations Baby	1962	5.00	10.00	20.00
—The A-side was the hit, but this is sought after for its group sound on the B-side
❏ 1428	A Taste of Honey/The Old Cathedral	1962	2.50	5.00	10.00
❏ 1439	Since I Fell for You/Are You Sincere	1963	3.00	6.00	12.00
❏ 1446	If You See My Love/Father Sebastian	1964	2.50	5.00	10.00
COLUMBIA
❏ 44007	Since I Fell for You/A Taste of Honey	1967	2.00	4.00	8.00
COMMONWEALTH UNITED
❏ 3004	Breaking Up Is Hard to Do/Get Mommy to Come Back Home	1969	—	3.00	6.00
❏ 3011	To Be Loved and Glory of Love/My Heart Won't Let Me	1970	—	3.00	6.00
DECCA
❏ 30637	Rocket to the Moon/My One Sincere	1958	3.00	6.00	12.00
❏ 30829	Blessing of Love/Last Star of the Evening	1959	3.00	6.00	12.00
KAPP
❏ 648	I'm Dreaming Again/My Fool of a Heart	1965	2.00	4.00	8.00
❏ 662	Darling Take Me Back/Time After Time	1965	2.00	4.00	8.00
❏ 689	Two Different Worlds/I'll Be There	1965	2.00	4.00	8.00
❏ 712	Run to My Lovin' Arms/Coronet Blue	1965	2.00	4.00	8.00
❏ 740	Rags to Riches/I Want to Worry (About Me)	1966	2.00	4.00	8.00
❏ 751	What Now My Love/Gonna Hear from Me	1966	2.00	4.00	8.00
❏ 761	Please Help Me I'm Falling/Just One Smile	1966	2.00	4.00	8.00
❏ 778	If You Love Me, Really Love Me/ Once Before I Die	1966	2.00	4.00	8.00
❏ 808	Until the Real Thing Comes Along/A Right to Cry	1967	2.00	4.00	8.00
❏ 827	Let's Start All Over Again/ Love Don't Live Here Anymore	1967	2.00	4.00	8.00
❏ 854	I'm Over You/Coronet Blue	1967	2.00	4.00	8.00
MAINSTREAM
❏ 5545	Since I Don't Have You/Right in the Next Room	1973	—	2.50	5.00
❏ 5554	Eyewitness News/I Need You More	1973	—	2.50	5.00
❏ 5560	A Hundred Pounds of Pain/The Iguana	1974	—	2.50	5.00
❏ 5561	When There's No Such Thing As Love/Minx	1974	—	2.50	5.00
MERCURY
❏ 72777	Darling Stay with Me/Wait a While Longer	1968	2.00	4.00	8.00
❏ 72811	Tennessee Waltz/He Who Loves	1968	2.00	4.00	8.00
❏ 72866	Halfway to Your Arms/You Can't Run Away	1968	2.00	4.00	8.00
Albums
CADENCE
| ❏ CLP 3068 [M] | Since I Fell for You | 1963 | 7.50 | 15.00 | 30.00 |
| ❏ CLP 25068 [S] | Since I Fell for You | 1963 | 12.50 | 25.00 | 50.00 |
COLUMBIA
| ❏ CL 2430 [M] | Since I Fell for You | 1965 | 5.00 | 10.00 | 20.00 |
—Reissue of Cadence 3068
| ❏ CS 9230 [S] | Since I Fell for You | 1965 | 7.50 | 15.00 | 30.00 |
—Reissue of Cadence 25068
KAPP
❏ KL-1457 [M]	Two Different Worlds	1965	3.75	7.50	15.00
❏ KL-1481 [M]	Rags to Riches	1966	3.75	7.50	15.00
❏ KL-1517 [M]	Lenny	1967	3.75	7.50	15.00
❏ KS-3457 [S]	Two Different Worlds	1965	5.00	10.00	20.00
❏ KS-3481 [S]	Rags to Riches	1966	5.00	10.00	20.00
❏ KS-3517 [S]	Lenny	1967	5.00	10.00	20.00

WELK, LAWRENCE Also see DICK KESNER; THE LENNON SISTERS. Because we've been asked about it, we'll note that the Dick Dale who sometimes appears in the credits of Welk records (45s, EPs and LPs) is a saxophone player and vocalist and not the surf guitarist.

45s

Number	Title (A Side/B Side)	Yr	VG	VG+	NM
(NO LABEL)					
☐ (no #)	Season's Greetings From Your Dodge Dealer	196?	2.00	4.00	8.00
—Cardboard record					
CORAL					
☐ 60405	Shenandoah Waltz/Metro Polka	1951	3.00	6.00	12.00
—Note: Earlier Lawrence Welk 45s on Coral may exist					
☐ 60444	Moonlight Bay/Boomp! Pa-Deedle Doodle	1951	3.00	6.00	12.00
☐ 60514	Sad and Lonely/Irving	1951	3.00	6.00	12.00
☐ 60516	Slow Drive/Moonlight Bay	1951	3.00	6.00	12.00
☐ 60517	Tell Me/Cuddle Up a Little Closer, Lovey Mine	1951	3.00	6.00	12.00
☐ 60518	Yoo Hoo/I'm Forever Blowing Bubbles	1951	3.00	6.00	12.00
☐ 60519	Every Little Moment/Till We Meet Again	1951.	3.00	6.00	12.00
☐ 60575	Sweetheart Waltz/I Wanna Say Hello	1951	3.00	6.00	12.00
☐ 60618	My Extraordinary Gal/Irene	1952	2.50	5.00	10.00
☐ 60619	Dolores/Emaline	1952	2.50	5.00	10.00
☐ 60620	Mary Lou/Annabelle	1952	2.50	5.00	10.00
☐ 60621	Louise/Sweet Eloise	1952	2.50	5.00	10.00
☐ 60630	Swingin' Down the Lane/You're Somebody	1952	2.50	5.00	10.00
☐ 60677	The Gandy Dancer's Ball/Ivory Rag	1952	2.50	5.00	10.00
☐ 60689	Bubbles in the Wine/Josephine	1952	3.75	7.50	15.00
☐ 60752	Dream House/Small Talk	1952	2.50	5.00	10.00
☐ 60784	Watermelon Weather/Busybody	1952	2.50	5.00	10.00
☐ 60806	Padam Padam (How It Echoes the Beat of My Heart)/Your Eyes So Lovely	1952	2.50	5.00	10.00
☐ 60813	Rustic Dance/Cocoanut Grove	1952	2.50	5.00	10.00
☐ 60828	Meet Mister Callaghan/Flirtation Waltz	1952	2.50	5.00	10.00
☐ 60893	Oh Happy Day/Your Mother and Mine	1952	2.50	5.00	10.00
☐ 60905	She Looked Down from Her Window/I'm Gonna Ring the Bell Tonight	1953	2.50	5.00	10.00
—Vocalist: Jack Smith					
☐ 60947	Minnie the Mermaid/Say It Isn't So	1953	2.50	5.00	10.00
☐ 60973	Ohio/It's Love	1953	2.50	5.00	10.00
☐ 60974	Canadian Capers/Did I Remember	1953	2.50	5.00	10.00
☐ 60975	Good Morning, Mr. Zip Zip Zip/Just Once Again	1953	2.50	5.00	10.00
☐ 60976	I'll See You in My Dreams/Peggy O'Neill	1953	2.50	5.00	10.00
☐ 60998	Bubbling Over/The La-De-Da Song	1953	2.50	5.00	10.00
☐ 61003	High Life Polka/Town and Country Polka	1953	2.50	5.00	10.00
☐ 61017	Hallejulah Brother/"O"	1953	2.50	5.00	10.00
☐ 61075	Ebb Tide/Beautiful Ohio	1953	2.50	5.00	10.00
☐ 61081	Angel on the Christmas Tree/Are My Ears On Straight	1953	3.75	7.50	15.00
—With Sara Berner					
☐ 61095	Christmas Carols (Part 1)/Christmas Carols (Part 2)	1953	3.00	6.00	12.00
☐ 61100	Joey's Theme/Coney Island	1953	2.50	5.00	10.00
☐ 61135	The Darktown Strutter's Ball/In the Mood	1954	2.50	5.00	10.00
☐ 61174	The Man with the Banjo/Until Sunrise	1954	2.50	5.00	10.00
☐ 61207	Nimble Fingers/Doll Dance	1954	2.50	5.00	10.00
—With Sara Berner					
☐ 61240	The Greatest Feeling in the World/Luxembourg Polka	1954	2.50	5.00	10.00
☐ 61318	At the Junior Prom/Home Again Blues	1954	2.50	5.00	10.00
☐ 61372	Elephant's Tango/Lazy Gondolier	1955	2.00	4.00	8.00
☐ 61387	I See God/Pray for Me	1955	2.00	4.00	8.00
☐ 61408	Hey, Mr. Banjo/Love Me or Leave Me	1955	2.00	4.00	8.00
☐ 61442	Ball of Fire/Go 'Way, Go 'Way	1955	2.00	4.00	8.00
☐ 61477	Wake the Town and Tell the People/I Hear Those Bells	1955	2.00	4.00	8.00
☐ 61508	Champagne Waltz/Musette	1955	2.00	4.00	8.00
☐ 61515	Bonnie Blue Gal/Sam the Old Accordian Man	1955	2.00	4.00	8.00
☐ 61524	It's Almost Tomorrow/Rice	1955	2.00	4.00	8.00
☐ 61574	Moritat (A Theme from the Threepenny Opera)/Stompin' at the Savoy	1956	2.00	4.00	8.00
☐ 61592	The Poor People of Paris/Nobody Knows But the Lord	1956	2.00	4.00	8.00
☐ 61595	Lisbon Antigua/Chain Gang	1956	2.00	4.00	8.00
☐ 61597	Mickey Mouse Mambo/Hi! to You	1956	3.00	6.00	12.00
☐ 61621	Practice, Practice What You Preach/What a Heavenly Night for Love	1956	2.00	4.00	8.00
☐ 61629	Helena Polka/Hot Pretzels	1956	2.00	4.00	8.00
☐ 61630	Jenny Lind/The Jolly Coppersmith	1956	2.00	4.00	8.00
☐ 61644	On the Street Where You Live/I Could Have Danced All Night	1956	2.00	4.00	8.00
☐ 61645	With a Little Bit of Luck/I've Grown Accustomed to Her Face	1956	2.00	4.00	8.00
☐ 61670	Weary Blues/In the Alps	1956	2.50	5.00	10.00
—With the McGuire Sisters					
☐ 61670 [PS]	Weary Blues/In the Alps	1956	3.75	7.50	15.00
☐ 61701	Tonight You Belong to Me/When the White Lilacs Bloom Again	1956	2.50	5.00	10.00
—With the Lennon Sisters					
☐ 61741	Around the World/Champagne Time	1956	2.00	4.00	8.00
☐ 61745	Ring Those Christmas Bells/Let's Have an Old-Fashioned Christmas	1956	2.50	5.00	10.00
☐ 61746	Christmas Waltz/Santa from Santa Fe	1956	3.00	6.00	12.00
—With the Lennon Sisters					
☐ 61765	Cinco Robles/Whispering Heart	1956	2.00	4.00	8.00
☐ 61783	McNamara's Band/Wild Colonial Boy	1957	2.00	4.00	8.00
☐ 61784	Dance Around a Stack of Barley/When Irish Eyes Are Smiling	1957	2.00	4.00	8.00
☐ 61786	Falling Star/It Was That Kiss	1957	2.00	4.00	8.00
☐ 61806	Ten Little Trees/The Bridge of Saint Lo	1957	2.00	4.00	8.00
☐ 61849	By the Bend of the River/Keyboard Serenade	1957	2.00	4.00	8.00
☐ 61870	Ricky-Dicky-Doo/To Be with You	1957	2.00	4.00	8.00
☐ 61893	Moon Love/We'll Be There	1957	2.00	4.00	8.00
☐ 61894	My Reverie/Fool Moon and Empty Arms	1957	2.00	4.00	8.00
☐ 61900	Lichtenstein Polka/You Know Too Much	1957	2.00	4.00	8.00
☐ 61914	Merry Christmas from Our House to Your House/Santa Claus Is Here Again	1957	3.00	6.00	12.00
—With the Lennon Sisters					
☐ 61937	One Note Polka/The Lovers on the Park Bench	1958	2.00	4.00	8.00
☐ 61958	I Want a Girl/When My Baby Smiles at Me	1958	2.00	4.00	8.00
☐ 62018	Walk with Me/Be Thankful	1958	2.00	4.00	8.00
☐ 62031	Mary Ann/Indiana Holiday	1958	2.00	4.00	8.00
☐ 62053	Outer Space Santa/All Around The Merry Christmas Tree	1958	3.00	6.00	12.00
—As "Lawrence Welk's Little Band"					
☐ 62056	Cha Cha Polka/I Never Should Have Let You Go	1958	2.00	4.00	8.00
☐ 62091	Gunsmoke/The Ballad of Paladin	1959	3.00	6.00	12.00
☐ 65511	Bubbles in the Wine/Josephine	196?	—	3.00	6.00
☐ 65517	Cocoanut Grove/Rustic Dance	196?	—	3.00	6.00
☐ 65523	Ave Maria/He'll Be There	196?	—	3.00	6.00
☐ 65541	Gold and Silver/Lichtenstein Polka	196?	—	3.00	6.00
☐ 65574	Pony Tail/The Wreck of the Old '88	196?	—	3.00	6.00
☐ 65604	I'll See You in My Dreams/Till We Meet Again	1966	—	2.50	5.00
☐ 98054 [DJ]	Christmas Carols (Part 1)/Christmas Carols (Part 2)	19??	2.00	4.00	8.00
—"Merry Christmas from Lawrence Welk" custom label					
DECCA					
☐ 23855	Beer Barrel Polka/Pennsylvania Polka	1950	2.50	5.00	10.00
—Reissue of 78; part of "Album No. 9-24"					
☐ 23857	Clarinet Polka/Pound Your Table Polka	1950	2.50	5.00	10.00
—Reissue of 78; part of "Album No. 9-24"					
☐ 23858	Barbara Polka/Friendly Tavern Polka	1950	2.50	5.00	10.00
—Reissue of 78; part of "Album No. 9-24"					
☐ 24442	Bubbles in the Wine/Kentucky Waltz	1950	5.00	10.00	20.00
—78 originally released in 1948; original 45 has black label with "rays" on either side of the word "Decca"					
☐ 24442	Bubbles in the Wine/Kentucky Waltz	1955	3.00	6.00	12.00
—Second 45 has star under "Decca"					
☐ 24442	Bubbles in the Wine/Kentucky Waltz	1960	2.00	4.00	8.00
—Third 45 has color bars on label					
DOT					
☐ 15924	The Swingin' Burglar/Bell Boogie	1959	2.00	4.00	8.00
—By "Lawrence Welk's Little Band"					
☐ 15967	Goodnight Sweetheart/This Night Is Young and You're So Beautiful	1959	2.00	4.00	8.00
—By "The Lawrence Welk Glee Club"					
☐ 15995	Every Night When You Say a Prayer/Thank the Lord for This Thanksgiving	1959	2.50	5.00	10.00
—With the Lennon Sisters					
☐ 16017	Christmas Moon/Peppy the Peppermint Bear	1959	3.00	6.00	12.00
—With the Lennon Sisters					
☐ 16062	Just Because/Tick-Tock Polka	1960	2.00	4.00	8.00
—With Myron Floren					
☐ 16063	Hour of Parting/Summer Set	1960	2.00	4.00	8.00
☐ 16114	It Started in Naples/I Get So Lonely (Oh Baby Mine)	1960	2.00	4.00	8.00
☐ 16145	Last Date/Remember Lolita	1960	—	3.00	6.00
☐ 16153	The Cradle to the Cross/Laura-Jean	1960	—	3.00	6.00
☐ 16161	Calcutta/My Grandfather's Clock	1960	2.00	4.00	8.00
☐ 16198	Theme from My Three Sons/Out of a Clear Blue Sky	1961	2.50	5.00	10.00
☐ 16222	Yellow Bird/Cruising Down the River	1961	—	3.00	6.00
☐ 16237	Riders in the Sky/My Love for You	1961	—	3.00	6.00
☐ 16285	You Gave Me Wings/A-One, a-Two, a-Cha Cha Cha	1961	—	3.00	6.00
☐ 16336	Runaway/Happy Love	1962	—	3.00	6.00
☐ 16364	Baby Elephant Walk/Theme from the Brothers Grimm	1962	2.00	4.00	8.00
☐ 16420	Zero-Zero/Night Theme	1962	—	3.00	6.00
☐ 16488	Scarlett O'Hara/Breakwater	1963	—	3.00	6.00
☐ 16526	Blue Velvet/Fiesta	1963	—	3.00	6.00
☐ 16582	Stockholm/Girl from Barbados	1964	—	3.00	6.00
☐ 16603	Hello, Dolly/Clair de Lune	1964	—	3.00	6.00
☐ 16620	Poodle Walk/Do I Need You	1964	—	3.00	6.00
☐ 16680	Sixteen Reasons/Little Things Mean a Lot	1964	—	3.00	6.00
☐ 16697	Apples and Bananas/Theme from "The Addams Family"	1965	2.00	4.00	8.00
☐ 16741	There's No One Like You/Schatzie	1965	—	3.00	6.00
☐ 16764	Down, Down, Down, Down/Jenny Dear	1965	—	3.00	6.00
☐ 16778	Summer Nights/La Bamba	1965	—	3.00	6.00
☐ 16794	Moonlight and Roses/Send Me the Pillow You Dream On	1965	—	3.00	6.00
☐ 16810	Currier and Ives/Tia-Juana	1965	—	3.00	6.00
☐ 16885	Wabash Cannonball/Tennessee Waltz	1966	—	2.50	5.00
☐ 16943	Family Affair/Tarzan (Tarzan's March)	1966	2.00	4.00	8.00
☐ 16981	Born Free/Winchester Cathedral	1966	—	2.50	5.00
☐ 17001	The Beat Goes On/Then You Can Tell Me Goodbye	1967	—	2.50	5.00
MERCURY					
☐ 5411	Doo-Wacka-Doo/Pizzacata	1950	3.75	7.50	15.00
—Note: Earlier Lawrence Welk 45s on Mercury may exist					
☐ 5419	Hoop-De-Dee/If You Can Get a Drum with a Boom, Boom, Boom	1950	3.75	7.50	15.00
☐ 5434	Dakota Polka/Windy River	1950	3.75	7.50	15.00
☐ 5440	Deep Freezer Dinah/Fancy Free	1950	3.75	7.50	15.00
☐ 5469	Mama's Samba/Skaters Waltz in Springtime	1950	3.75	7.50	15.00
—Vocalist: Roberta Linn					
☐ 5487	Petite Waltz/The Middle of a Riddle	1950	3.75	7.50	15.00
☐ 5518	Emilia Polka/Tinker Polka	1950	3.75	7.50	15.00
☐ 5519	Julida Polka/Laughing Polka	1950	3.75	7.50	15.00
☐ 5529	Tiger Rag/Military Polka	1950	3.75	7.50	15.00
☐ 5666	Bubbles in the Wine/Back Home in Illinois	1951	5.00	10.00	20.00
☐ 5735	Merry Christmas Polka/Julida Polka	1951	3.75	7.50	15.00
☐ 70065	Julinda Polka/Swiss Lullaby	1953	3.00	6.00	12.00
☐ 70149	Fiddle-Dee-Dee/Dancing Doll	1953	3.00	6.00	12.00
☐ 70734	Hoop-De-Dee/Bar Room Polka	1955	2.50	5.00	10.00
☐ 70735	Amilia Polka/Tinker Polka	1955	2.50	5.00	10.00
☐ 70736	Julida Polka/Military Polka	1955	2.50	5.00	10.00
☐ 70737	Dakota Polka/Kit Kat Polka	1955	2.50	5.00	10.00
☐ 70738	Merry Christmas Polka/Laughing Polka	1955	3.00	6.00	12.00
☐ 70739	Tiger Rag/Chopsticks Polka	1955	2.50	5.00	10.00
RANWOOD					
☐ 801	Green Tambourine/Watch What Happens	1968	—	2.00	4.00
☐ 814	Let's Make America What It Used to Be/To America with Love	1968	—	2.00	4.00
☐ 842	Galveston/Gentle on My Mind	1969	—	2.00	4.00
☐ 845	Land of Dreams/Chee Chee Kookaroo	1969	—	2.00	4.00
☐ 860	Jean/Spinning Wheel	1970	—	2.00	4.00

Number	Title (A Side/B Side)	Yr	VG	VG+	NM
❏ 865	Hello Dolly/Southtown U.S.A.	1970	—	2.00	4.00
❏ 874	Applause/Smiles	1970	—	2.00	4.00
❏ 888	Candida/Endlessly	1971	—	2.00	4.00
❏ 905	No, No, Nanette/Too Many Rings Around Rosie	1971	—	2.00	4.00
❏ 915	Theme from Summer of '42/Adios, Au Revoir, Auf Wiedersehn	1971	—	2.00	4.00
❏ 920	Melody of Love (Parody)/Melody of Love	1972	2.00	4.00	8.00
—With Bob Hudson (of Hudson and Landry) on A-side					
❏ 1039	Fantastic, That's You/Oh Harry	1975	—	—	3.00
—With Henry Questa					
❏ 1068	Nadia's Theme (The Young and the Restless)/Johnny's Theme	1976	—	—	3.00
❏ 1073	Keep Your Eyes on the Sparrow/Paloma Blanca	1977	—	—	3.00
❏ 1091	Christmas In Los Angeles/Carol Of The Bells	1980	—	2.00	4.00
—By "The Lawrence Welk Christmas Chorale"					

7-Inch Extended Plays

CORAL

Number	Title (A Side/B Side)	Yr	VG	VG+	NM
❏ EC 81007	Bubbles in the Wine/Josephine//12th Street Rag/Ivory Rag	195?	3.00	6.00	12.00
❏ EC 81007 [PS]	Dance Time	195?	3.00	6.00	12.00
❏ EC 81101	The Girl Friend/Margie//Marie/Sweet Sue, Just You	195?	2.50	5.00	10.00
❏ EC 81101 [PS]	(title unknown)	195?	2.50	5.00	10.00
❏ EC 81109	Liebesfreud/Liebeslied (Love's Sorrow)//Schon Rosmarin (Fair Rosemary)/Caprice Viennois	195?	2.50	5.00	10.00
❏ EC 81109 [PS]	(title unknown)	195?	2.50	5.00	10.00
❏ EC 81120	Malaguena/Lazy Gondolier//Blue Mirage/The Elephants Tango	195?	2.50	5.00	10.00
❏ EC 81120 [PS]	Yours for Dancing	195?	2.50	5.00	10.00
❏ EC 81133	I Could Have Danced All Night/I've Grown Accustomed to Her Face//On the Street Where You Live/With a Little Bit of Luck	1956	2.50	5.00	10.00
❏ EC 81133 [PS]	My Fair Lady	1956	2.50	5.00	10.00
❏ EC 81134 [PS]	Champagne Medley Time	195?	2.50	5.00	10.00
❏ EC 81134 [PS]	Say It With Music	195?	2.50	5.00	10.00
❏ EC 81146	(contents unknown)	195?	2.50	5.00	10.00
❏ EC 81146 [PS]	Pick-a-Polka	195?	2.50	5.00	10.00
❏ EC 81148	(contents unknown)	195?	2.50	5.00	10.00
❏ EC 81148 [PS]	Moments to Remember	195?	2.50	5.00	10.00
❏ EC 81154	(contents unknown)	195?	2.50	5.00	10.00
❏ EC 81154 [PS]	The Stars Visit Lawrence Welk	195?	2.50	5.00	10.00
❏ EC 81157	(a) Tenderly (b) When Your Hair Has Turned to Silver/(a) Cuban Love Song (b) Honolulu Eyes//(a) Alice Blue Gown (b) Ramona/(a) Three O'Clock in the Morning (b) Sleep	195?	2.50	5.00	10.00
❏ EC 81157 [PS]	Waltz with Lawrence Welk	195?	2.50	5.00	10.00
❏ EC 81160	(contents unknown)	195?	2.50	5.00	10.00
❏ EC 81160 [PS]	Champagne and Roses	195?	2.50	5.00	10.00
❏ EC 81171	(contents unknown)	195?	2.50	5.00	10.00
❏ EC 81171 [PS]	Champagne Dancing Party, Vol. I	195?	2.50	5.00	10.00
❏ EC 81172	(contents unknown)	195?	2.50	5.00	10.00
❏ EC 81172 [PS]	Champagne Dancing Party, Vol. II	195?	2.50	5.00	10.00
❏ EC 81180	All Around the Merry Christmas Tree/Merry Christmas from Our House to Your House//Outer Space Santa/Santa from Santa Fe	195?	2.50	5.00	10.00
❏ EC 81180 [PS]	Merry Christmas	195?	2.50	5.00	10.00
❏ EC 781181	Gunsmoke/Maverick//Ballad of Paladin/The Legend of Wyatt Earp	1959	3.75	7.50	15.00
—Stereo					
❏ EC 781181 [PS]	TV Western Theme Songs	1959	3.75	7.50	15.00
❏ EC 81502	Bubbles in the Wine/Cocoanut Grove//Metro Polka/Oh Happy Day	195?	2.50	5.00	10.00
❏ EC 81502 [PS]	Lawrence Welk	195?	2.50	5.00	10.00
❏ EC 82001 [PS]	Souvenir Album (Actually Recorded at the Aragon Ballroom)	195?	3.00	6.00	12.00
—Cover for 2-EP set (83000 and 83001)					
❏ EC 82005 [PS]	Nimble Fingers	195?	2.50	5.00	10.00
—Cover for 2-EP set (83006 and 83007)					
❏ EC 82026 [PS]	(title unknown)	195?	3.00	6.00	12.00
—Cover for 2-EP set (83056 and 83057)					
❏ EC 82027 [PS]	Say It With Music	1956	2.50	5.00	10.00
—Cover for 2-EP set (83058 and 83059)					
❏ EC 82032 [PS]	Jingle Bells	1956	3.00	6.00	12.00
—Cover for 2-EP set					
❏ 83000	Say It Isn't So/Minnie the Mermaid//Did I Remember/Canadian Capers	195?	2.50	5.00	10.00
—Part of 2-EP set EC 82001					
❏ 83001	Good Morning, Mr. Zip, Zip, Zip/Just Once Again//Peggy O'Neil/I'll See You in My Dreams	195?	2.50	5.00	10.00
—Part of 2-EP set EC 82001					
❏ 83006	Nimble Fingers/Flapperette//Nola/Dainty Miss	195?	2.50	5.00	10.00
—Part of 2-EP set EC 82005					
❏ 83007	Rag Doll/Doll Dance//The Wedding of the Painted Doll/Dancing Tambourine	195?	2.50	5.00	10.00
—Part of 2-EP set EC 82005					
❏ 83056	When Irish Eyes Are Smiling/My Heart Danced an Irish Jig//Irish Alphabet/McNamara's Band	1956	2.50	5.00	10.00
—Part of 2-EP set EC 82026					
❏ 83057	A Little Bit of Heaven (Shure They Call It Ireland)/Ireland Must Be Heaven For My Mother Came from There//Shamrocks, Shillelaghs and Shenanigans/Dance Aroun' a Stack of Barley	1956	2.50	5.00	10.00
—Part of 2-EP set EC 82026					
❏ 83058	Say It with Music/Tea for Two/Thou Swell/I Found a Million Dollar Baby in a Five and Ten Cent Store/Pretty Baby/Yes Sir, That's My Baby//Oh Lady Be Good/Somebody Loves Me/S'Wonderful/Sleepy Time Gal/My Blue Heaven/Doodle Doo Doo	1956	2.50	5.00	10.00
—Part of 2-EP set EC 82027					
❏ 83059	The Gypsy in My Soul/Exactly Like You/Anything Goes/Was That the Human Thing to Do/Cecilia/I Can't Believe It's True//Wabash Blues/September Song/Mood Indigo/Sympathy/L'Amour Toujours L'Amour (Love Everlasting)/Giannina Mia	1956	2.50	5.00	10.00
—Part of 2-EP set EC 82027					
❏ 83068	(contents unknown)	1956	2.50	5.00	10.00
—Part of 2-EP set EC 82032					

Number	Title (A Side/B Side)	Yr	VG	VG+	NM
❏ 83069	Santa Claus Is Comin' To Town/Winter Wonderland//Christmas Dreaming (A Little Early This Year)/The Twelve Gifts Of Christmas	1956	2.50	5.00	10.00
—Part of 2-EP set EC 82032					

DECCA

Number	Title (A Side/B Side)	Yr	VG	VG+	NM
❏ ED 2023	Bubbles in the Wine/Josephine//Kentucky Waltz/Canadian Capers	195?	3.00	6.00	12.00
❏ ED 2023 [PS]	Lawrence Welk, Vol. 1	195?	3.00	6.00	12.00
❏ ED 2568	(contents unknown)	195?	3.00	6.00	12.00
❏ ED 2568 [PS]	Polkas and Champagne	195?	3.00	6.00	12.00

Albums

CORAL

Number	Title	Yr	VG	VG+	NM
❏ 7CXSB 5 [(2)S]	The Best of Lawrence Welk	196?	3.75	7.50	15.00
❏ CXB 5 [(2)M]	The Best of Lawrence Welk	196?	5.00	10.00	20.00
❏ CRL 56043 [10]	On Moonlight Bay	195?	7.50	15.00	30.00
❏ CRL 56045 [10]	Songs About My Extraordinary Gal and Her Friends	195?	7.50	15.00	30.00
❏ CRL 56088 [10]	Souvenir Album	195?	7.50	15.00	30.00
❏ CRL 56101 [10]	Nimble Fingers	195?	7.50	15.00	30.00
❏ CRL 56120 [10]	Viennese Waltzes for Dancing	1954	7.50	15.00	30.00
❏ CRL 57011 [M]	Lawrence Welk and His Sparkling Strings	1955	5.00	10.00	20.00
❏ CRL 57023 [M]	Lawrence Welk Introduces the Girl Friends	1955	6.25	12.50	25.00
❏ CRL 57025 [M]	TV Favorites	1955	5.00	10.00	20.00
❏ CRL 57036 [M]	Shamrocks and Champagne	1955	5.00	10.00	20.00
❏ CRL 57038 [M]	Bubbles in the Wine	1956	5.00	10.00	20.00
❏ CRL 57041 [M]	Say It With Music	1956	5.00	10.00	20.00
❏ CRL 57066 [M]	Lawrence Welk at Madison Square Garden	1956	5.00	10.00	20.00
❏ CRL 57067 [M]	Pick-A-Polka!	1956	5.00	10.00	20.00
❏ CRL 57068 [M]	Moments to Remember	1956	5.00	10.00	20.00
❏ CRL 57078 [M]	Champagne Pops Parade	1956	5.00	10.00	20.00
❏ CRL 57093 [M]	Merry Christmas from Lawrence Welk	1956	5.00	10.00	20.00
❏ CRL 57111 [M]	Show Time	1957	5.00	10.00	20.00
❏ CRL 57113 [M]	The World's Finest Music	1957	5.00	10.00	20.00
❏ CRL 57119 [M]	Waltz with Lawrence Welk	1957	5.00	10.00	20.00
❏ CRL 57146 [M]	Lawrence Welk Plays Dixieland	1957	5.00	10.00	20.00
❏ CRL 57178 [M]	Nimble Fingers	1957	5.00	10.00	20.00
❏ CRL 57186 [M]	Jingle Bells	1957	5.00	10.00	20.00
❏ CRL 57191 [M]	Songs of Faith	1958	3.75	7.50	15.00
❏ CRL 57214 [M]	Lawrence Welk Presents Keyboard Kapers	1958	3.75	7.50	15.00
❏ CRL 57226 [M]	Champagne Dancing Party	1958	3.75	7.50	15.00
❏ CRL 57260 [M]	Lawrence Welk Featuring the Lennon Sisters	1959	3.75	7.50	15.00
❏ CRL 57262 [M]	Lawrence Welk Featuring Larry Hooper	1959	3.75	7.50	15.00
❏ CRL 57267 [M]	TV Western Theme Songs	1959	3.75	7.50	15.00
❏ CRL 57353 [M]	My Golden Favorites	1961	3.00	6.00	12.00
❏ CRL 57383 [M]	Lawrence Welk Showcase	1962	3.00	6.00	12.00
❏ CRL 57439 [M]	Songs Everybody Knows	1964	3.00	6.00	12.00
❏ CRL 757036 [R]	Shamrocks and Champagne	196?	3.00	6.00	12.00
❏ CRL 757041 [R]	Say It With Music	196?	3.00	6.00	12.00
❏ CRL 757067 [R]	Pick-A-Polka!	1959	3.00	6.00	12.00
❏ CRL 757093 [R]	Merry Christmas from Lawrence Welk	196?	3.00	6.00	12.00
❏ CRL 757113 [R]	The World's Finest Music	196?	3.00	6.00	12.00
❏ CRL 757186 [R]	Jingle Bells	196?	3.00	6.00	12.00
❏ CRL 757226 [S]	Champagne Dancing Party	1958	5.00	10.00	20.00
❏ CRL 757267 [S]	TV Western Theme Songs	1959	5.00	10.00	20.00
❏ CRL 757353 [S]	My Golden Favorites	1961	3.00	6.00	12.00
❏ CRL 757383 [S]	Lawrence Welk Showcase	1962	3.00	6.00	12.00
❏ CRL 757439 [S]	Songs Everybody Knows	1964	3.00	6.00	12.00

CORONET

Number	Title	Yr	VG	VG+	NM
❏ 275	Lawrence Welk and His Orchestra	196?	2.50	5.00	10.00

DECCA

Number	Title	Yr	VG	VG+	NM
❏ DL 8213 [M]	Lawrence Welk's Polka Party	1956	3.75	7.50	15.00
❏ DL 8323 [M]	Around We Go	1956	3.75	7.50	15.00
❏ DL 8324 [M]	Welktime	1956	3.75	7.50	15.00

DESIGN

Number	Title	Yr	VG	VG+	NM
❏ 200	Champagne Time	196?	2.50	5.00	10.00
❏ 912	Three of a Kind	196?	2.50	5.00	10.00

DOT

Number	Title	Yr	VG	VG+	NM
❏ DLP 3164 [M]	Mr. Music Maker	1959	3.00	6.00	12.00
❏ DLP 3200 [M]	The Voices and Strings of Lawrence Welk	1959	3.00	6.00	12.00
❏ DLP 3218 [M]	The Lawrence Welk Glee Club	1959	3.00	6.00	12.00
❏ DLP 3224 [M]	Dance with Lawrence Welk	1959	3.00	6.00	12.00
❏ DLP 3238 [M]	Lawrence Welk Presents Great American Composers	1960	2.50	5.00	10.00
❏ DLP 3247 [M]	Lawrence Welk Presents Great Overtures in Dance Time	1960	2.50	5.00	10.00
❏ DLP 3248 [M]	I'm Forever Blowing Bubbles	1960	2.50	5.00	10.00
❏ DLP 3251 [M]	Songs of the Islands	1960	2.50	5.00	10.00
❏ DLP 3274 [M]	Strictly for Dancing	1960	2.50	5.00	10.00
❏ DLP 3284 [M]	To Mother	1960	2.50	5.00	10.00
❏ DLP 3296 [M]	Sweet and Lovely	1960	2.50	5.00	10.00
❏ DLP 3302 [M]	Polkas	1960	2.50	5.00	10.00
❏ DLP 3317 [M]	Lawrence in Dixieland	1960	2.50	5.00	10.00
❏ DLP 3318 [M]	Double Shuffle	1960	2.50	5.00	10.00
❏ DLP 3342 [M]	The Champagne Music of Lawrence Welk	1960	2.50	5.00	10.00
❏ DLP 3350 [M]	Last Date	1960	2.50	5.00	10.00
❏ DLP 3359 [M]	Calcutta!	1961	2.50	5.00	10.00
❏ DLP 3389 [M]	Yellow Bird	1961	2.50	5.00	10.00
❏ DLP 3395 [M]	Diamond Jubilee	1961	2.50	5.00	10.00
❏ DLP 3397 [M]	Silent Night and 13 Other Best-Loved Christmas Songs	1961	3.00	6.00	12.00
❏ DLP 3412 [M]	Moon River	1961	2.50	5.00	10.00
❏ DLP 3428 [M]	Young World	1962	2.50	5.00	10.00
❏ DLP 3432 [M]	Sing-a-Long Party	1962	2.50	5.00	10.00
❏ DLP 3457 [M]	Baby Elephant Walk and Theme from The Brothers Grimm	1962	2.50	5.00	10.00
❏ DLP 3489 [M]	Bubbles in the Wine	1962	2.50	5.00	10.00
❏ DLP 3499 [M]	Waltz Time	1963	2.50	5.00	10.00
❏ DLP 3510 [M]	1963's Early Hits	1963	2.50	5.00	10.00
❏ DLP 3528 [M]	Scarlett O'Hara	1963	2.50	5.00	10.00
❏ DLP 3544 [M]	A Tribute to the All-Time Greats	1963	2.50	5.00	10.00
❏ DLP 3552 [M]	Wonderful! Wonderful!	1963	2.50	5.00	10.00
❏ DLP 3572 [M]	Early Hits of 1964	1964	2.50	5.00	10.00
❏ DLP 3591 [M]	The Lawrence Welk Television Show 10th Anniversary	1964	2.50	5.00	10.00
❏ DLP 3611 [M]	The Golden Millions	1964	2.50	5.00	10.00
❏ DLP 3616 [M]	My First of 1965	1965	2.50	5.00	10.00

Number	Title (A Side/B Side)	Yr	VG	VG+	NM
DLP 3629 [M]	Apples and Bananas	1965	2.50	5.00	10.00
DLP 3653 [M]	The Happy Wanderer	1966	2.50	5.00	10.00
DLP 3663 [M]	Today's Great Hits	1966	2.50	5.00	10.00
DLP 3688 [M]	Champagne on Broadway	1966	2.50	5.00	10.00
DLP 3774 [M]	Winchester Cathedral	1966	2.50	5.00	10.00
DLP 3779 [M]	Hymns We Love	1967	2.50	5.00	10.00
DLP 3790 [M]	Lawrence Welk's "Hits of Our Time"	1967	2.50	5.00	10.00
DLP 3812 [M]	Golden Hits/The Best of Lawrence Welk	1967	3.00	6.00	12.00
DLP 25164 [S]	Mr. Music Maker	1959	3.75	7.50	15.00
DLP 25200 [S]	Voices and Strings	1959	3.75	7.50	15.00
DLP 25218 [S]	The Lawrence Welk Glee Club	1959	3.75	7.50	15.00
DLP 25224 [S]	Dance with Lawrence Welk	1959	3.75	7.50	15.00
DLP 25238 [S]	Lawrence Welk Presents Great American Composers	1960	3.00	6.00	12.00
DLP 25247 [S]	Lawrence Welk Presents Great Overtures in Dance Time	1960	3.00	6.00	12.00
DLP 25248 [S]	I'm Forever Blowing Bubbles	1960	3.00	6.00	12.00
DLP 25251 [S]	Songs of the Islands	1960	3.00	6.00	12.00
DLP 25274 [S]	Strictly for Dancing	1960	3.00	6.00	12.00
DLP 25284 [S]	To Mother	1960	3.00	6.00	12.00
DLP 25296 [S]	Sweet and Lovely	1960	3.00	6.00	12.00
DLP 25302 [S]	Polkas	1960	3.00	6.00	12.00
DLP 25317 [S]	Lawrence in Dixieland	1960	3.00	6.00	12.00
DLP 25318 [S]	Double Shuffle	1960	3.00	6.00	12.00
DLP 25342 [S]	The Champagne Music of Lawrence Welk	1960	3.00	6.00	12.00
DLP 25350 [S]	Last Date	1960	3.00	6.00	12.00
DLP 25359 [S]	Calcutta!	1961	3.00	6.00	12.00
DLP 25389 [S]	Yellow Bird	1961	3.00	6.00	12.00
DLP 25395 [S]	Diamond Jubilee	1961	3.00	6.00	12.00
DLP 25397 [S]	Silent Night and 13 Other Best-Loved Christmas Songs	1961	3.75	7.50	15.00
DLP 25412 [S]	Moon River	1961	3.00	6.00	12.00
DLP 25428 [S]	Young World	1962	3.00	6.00	12.00
DLP 25432 [S]	Sing-a-Long Party	1962	3.00	6.00	12.00
DLP 25457 [S]	Baby Elephant Walk and Theme from The Brothers Grimm	1962	3.00	6.00	12.00
DLP 25489 [S]	Bubbles in the Wine	1962	3.00	6.00	12.00
DLP 25499 [S]	Waltz Time	1963	3.00	6.00	12.00
DLP 25510 [S]	1963's Early Hits	1963	3.00	6.00	12.00
DLP 25528 [S]	Scarlett O'Hara	1963	3.00	6.00	12.00
DLP 25544 [S]	A Tribute to the All-Time Greats	1963	3.00	6.00	12.00
DLP 25552 [S]	Wonderful! Wonderful!	1963	3.00	6.00	12.00
DLP 25572 [S]	Early Hits of 1964	1964	3.00	6.00	12.00
DLP 25591 [S]	The Lawrence Welk Television Show 10th Anniversary	1964	3.00	6.00	12.00
DLP 25611 [S]	The Golden Millions	1964	3.00	6.00	12.00
DLP 25616 [S]	My First of 1965	1965	3.00	6.00	12.00
DLP 25629 [S]	Apples and Bananas	1965	3.00	6.00	12.00
DLP 25653 [S]	The Happy Wanderer	1966	3.00	6.00	12.00
DLP 25663 [S]	Today's Great Hits	1966	3.00	6.00	12.00
DLP 25688 [S]	Champagne on Broadway	1966	3.00	6.00	12.00
DLP 25774 [S]	Winchester Cathedral	1966	3.00	6.00	12.00
DLP 25779 [S]	Hymns We Love	1967	3.00	6.00	12.00
DLP 25790 [S]	Lawrence Welk's "Hits of Our Time"	1967	3.00	6.00	12.00
DLP 25812 [S]	Golden Hits/The Best of Lawrence Welk	1967	2.50	5.00	10.00
HAMILTON					
HLP 152 [M]	Mary Poppins	1965	2.50	5.00	10.00
HLP 12152 [S]	Mary Poppins	1965	3.00	6.00	12.00
HARMONY					
HL 7394 [M]	Vintage Champagne	1966	3.00	6.00	12.00
HS 11194 [S]	Vintage Champagne	1966	3.00	6.00	12.00
HS 11301	Champagne Dance Party	1969	2.50	5.00	10.00
HEARTLAND					
1006	Musical Family Reunion	198?	2.50	5.00	10.00
MCA					
733	Polka and Waltz Time	197?	2.00	4.00	8.00
—Reissue of Vocalion 73670					
4026 [(2)]	The Best of Lawrence Welk, Volume 2	197?	3.00	6.00	12.00
4044 [(2)]	The Best of Lawrence Welk	197?	3.00	6.00	12.00
4104 [(2)]	The Best Polkas	197?	3.00	6.00	12.00
MCA CORAL					
20100	Champagne Music	197?	2.00	4.00	8.00
MERCURY					
MG-20092 [M]	Dance Party	1956	3.75	7.50	15.00
MISTLETOE					
MLP-1215	Christmas with Lawrence Welk	197?	2.50	5.00	10.00
PICKWICK					
SPC-1019	The Christmas Song	197?	2.50	5.00	10.00
—Reissue of Coral LP "Jingle Bells" with shuffled running order					
SPC-3070	Save the Last Dance for Me	196?	2.50	5.00	10.00
SPC-3092	I'll See You Again	196?	2.50	5.00	10.00
SPC-3116	You'll Never Walk Alone	196?	2.50	5.00	10.00
SPC-3143	If You Were the Only One	196?	2.50	5.00	10.00
SPC-3157	As Time Goes By	196?	2.50	5.00	10.00
SPC-3196	Love Is a Many-Splendored Thing	197?	2.50	5.00	10.00
SPC-3212	Blue Hawaii	197?	2.50	5.00	10.00
SPC-3252	Polkas!	197?	2.50	5.00	10.00
PREMIER					
9043	Lawrence Welk	196?	2.50	5.00	10.00
RANWOOD					
2000	Merry Christmas	197?	2.50	5.00	10.00
2004	Polkas	197?	2.00	4.00	8.00
—With Myron Floren					
2005	Moon River	197?	—	3.00	6.00
—Reissue of Ranwood 8016					
2006	Yellow Bird	197?	—	3.00	6.00
—Reissue of Ranwood 8021					
2007	Songs of the Islands	197?	—	3.00	6.00
—Reissue of Ranwood 8022					
2008	Waltz Time	197?	—	3.00	6.00
—Reissue of Ranwood 8025					
2009	Hymns We Love	197?	—	3.00	6.00
—Reissue of Ranwood 8042					
2010	Memories	197?	—	3.00	6.00
—Reissue of Ranwood 8044					
4100	On Tour, Volume 1	198?	2.00	4.00	8.00
4101	On Tour, Volume 2	198?	2.00	4.00	8.00
5001 [(2)]	Reminiscing	1972	3.00	6.00	12.00
5005 [(2)]	24 of the World's Greatest Polkas	197?	3.00	6.00	12.00
—With Myron Floren					
6001 [(2)]	Lawrence Welk and His Musical Family in Concert	1973	3.00	6.00	12.00
6002	Lawrence Welk and His Musical Family Celebrate 50 Years in Music	1974	2.50	5.00	10.00
7002 [(2)]	200 Years of American Music	1976	3.00	6.00	12.00
7004 [(2)]	22 Great Waltzes	1977	3.00	6.00	12.00
7009 [(2)]	22 Great Songs for Dancing	1978	3.00	6.00	12.00
7016 [(2)]	22 Great Songs for Easy Listening	198?	3.00	6.00	12.00
7023 [(2)]	22 All-Time Big Band Favorites	1983	3.00	6.00	12.00
7028 [(2)]	22 All-Time Favorite Waltzes	198?	3.00	6.00	12.00
7029 [(2)]	22 Merry Christmas Favorites	198?	3.00	6.00	12.00
8003	Love Is Blue	1968	2.50	5.00	10.00
8016	Moon River	1968	2.00	4.00	8.00
—Reissue of Dot 25412					
8017	Winchester Cathedral	1968	2.00	4.00	8.00
—Reissue of Dot 25774					
8020	Silent Night and 13 Other Best-Loved Christmas Songs	1968	2.00	4.00	8.00
—Reissue of Dot 25397					
8021	Yellow Bird	1968	2.00	4.00	8.00
—Reissue of Dot 25389					
8022	Songs of the Islands	1968	2.00	4.00	8.00
—Reissue of Dot 25251					
8023	The Champagne Music of Lawrence Welk	1968	2.00	4.00	8.00
—Reissue of Dot 25342					
8024	Calcutta!	1968	2.00	4.00	8.00
—Reissue of Dot 25359					
8025	Waltz Time	1968	2.00	4.00	8.00
—Reissue of Dot 25499					
8026	The Lawrence Welk Television Show	1968	2.00	4.00	8.00
—Reissue of Dot 25591					
8027	Country Music's Great Hits	1968	2.50	5.00	10.00
8028	Golden Hits/The Best of Lawrence Welk	1968	2.00	4.00	8.00
—Reissue of Dot 25812					
8030	To America with Love	1968	2.50	5.00	10.00
8034	The Lawrence Welk Singers and Orchestra	1968	2.50	5.00	10.00
8042	Hymns We Love	1968	2.00	4.00	8.00
—Reissue of Dot 25779					
8044	Memories	1969	2.50	5.00	10.00
8049	Galveston	1969	2.50	5.00	10.00
8053	Lawrence Welk Plays I Love You Truly and Other Songs of Love	1969	2.50	5.00	10.00
8060	Jean	1969	2.50	5.00	10.00
8068	The Golden 60's	1970	2.50	5.00	10.00
8077	The Big Band Sound	1970	2.50	5.00	10.00
8079	Champagne Strings	1970	2.50	5.00	10.00
8083	Candida	1970	2.50	5.00	10.00
8087	No, No, Nanette	1971	2.50	5.00	10.00
8091	Go Away Little Girl	1971	2.50	5.00	10.00
8109	(More of) The Big Band Sound	1972	2.50	5.00	10.00
8114	The Good Life	1973	2.50	5.00	10.00
8130	Lawrence Welk Plays From That's Entertainment	1974	2.50	5.00	10.00
8140	Most Requested TV Favorites	1974	2.50	5.00	10.00
8145	25 Years on Television	1975	2.50	5.00	10.00
8162	The Best of Lawrence Welk: 20 Great Hits	1976	2.50	5.00	10.00
8165	Nadia's Theme	1976	2.50	5.00	10.00
8183	My Personal Favorites	1978	2.50	5.00	10.00
8184	Hallelujah!	1978	2.50	5.00	10.00
8191	Remembering the Sweet and Swing Band Era, Vol. 1	1979	2.50	5.00	10.00
8192	Remembering the Sweet and Swing Band Era, Vol. 2	1979	2.50	5.00	10.00
8194	Lawrence Welk Plays Dixieland	1980	2.50	5.00	10.00
8195 [(2)]	Reminiscing, Vol. 2	1980	3.00	6.00	12.00
8201	Lawrence Welk Presents Anacani	1982	2.50	5.00	10.00
8210	Musical Memories with Lawrence Welk	1984	2.00	4.00	8.00
8211	Come Waltz with Me	1984	2.00	4.00	8.00
10001 [(2)]	Live at Lake Tahoe	1978	3.00	6.00	12.00
10002 [(2)]	The Sweet and Swing Band Era	1979	3.00	6.00	12.00
READER'S DIGEST					
RDA-07-A [(4)]	Merry Christmas from Lawrence Welk and His Champagne Music Makers	1970	6.25	12.50	25.00
RDA 95 [(6)]	Champagne Music Varieties	196?	6.25	12.50	25.00
RDA 156	Champagne Dance Time with Lawrence Welk	196?	2.50	5.00	10.00
SUNNYVALE					
SVL-1015	Silent Night and 13 Other Best-Loved Christmas Songs	1978	2.00	4.00	8.00
—Same contents as Dot 25397					
THOMAS					
20052	The Magic of Color-Glo	196?	3.00	6.00	12.00
VOCALION					
VL 3670 [M]	Polka and Waltz Time	196?	2.50	5.00	10.00
VL 3671 [M]	Lawrence Welk and His Champagne Music	196?	2.50	5.00	10.00
VL 3783 [M]	Lawrence Welk and His Champagne Music Makers Play for You	1967	3.00	6.00	12.00
VL 73670 [R]	Polka and Waltz Time	196?	2.50	5.00	10.00
VL 73671 [R]	Lawrence Welk and His Champagne Music	196?	2.50	5.00	10.00
VL 73783 [R]	Lawrence Welk and His Champagne Music Makers Play for You	1967	2.50	5.00	10.00
VL 73865	Champagne Polkas	1969	2.50	5.00	10.00
VL 73888	Til the End of Time	1969	2.50	5.00	10.00
VL 73921	Wonderful Music	1970	2.50	5.00	10.00
WING					
PKW-2-114 [(2)]	With a-One and a-Two	1969	3.75	7.50	15.00
MGW-12119 [M]	Dance Party	196?	3.00	6.00	12.00
MGW-12210 [M]	Music for Polka Lovers	196?	3.00	6.00	12.00
MGW-12214 [M]	Aragon Trianon Memories	196?	3.00	6.00	12.00
SRW-16210 [S]	Music for Polka Lovers	196?	2.50	5.00	10.00
SRW-16214 [R]	Aragon Trianon Memories	196?	2.50	5.00	10.00
SRW-16379	The Best of Welk	196?	2.50	5.00	10.00

Number	Title (A Side/B Side)	Yr	VG	VG+	NM
WELLER, FREDDY Also see PAUL REVERE AND THE RAIDERS.					
45s					
ABC DOT					
❑ 17554	Love You Back to Georgia/				
	Show Me the Way to Your Love	1975	—	2.50	5.00
❑ 17577	Stone Crazy/Still Making Love to You	1975	—	2.50	5.00
APT					
❑ 25096	Walk Away Slowly/				
	You Better Go Join the Campfire	1966	2.50	5.00	10.00
COLUMBIA					
❑ 10016	You're Not Getting Older (You're Getting Better)/				
	Are We Makin' Love	1974	—	2.00	4.00
❑ 10300	Ask Any Old Cheater Who Knows/				
	A Legend in My Home	1976	—	2.00	4.00
❑ 10352	Liquor, Love and Life/Celia Brown	1976	—	2.00	4.00
❑ 10411	Room 269/I Drank Myself Sober	1976	—	2.00	4.00
❑ 10482	Strawberry Curls/When You Were Mine	1977	—	2.00	4.00
❑ 10539	Merry-Go-Round/One Man Show	1977	—	2.00	4.00
❑ 10598	Nobody Cares But You/Love Doctor	1977	—	2.00	4.00
❑ 10682	Let Me Fall Back in Your Arms/Snuff Queens	1978	—	2.00	4.00
❑ 10769	Bar Wars/One of the Mysteries of Love	1978	—	2.00	4.00
❑ 10837	Love Got in the Way/You Win Again	1978	—	2.00	4.00
❑ 10890	Fantasy Island/Take a Little Bit	1979	—	2.00	4.00
❑ 10973	Nadine/Too Many Memories	1979	—	2.00	4.00
❑ 11044	That Run-Away Woman of Mine/Atlanta	1979	—	2.00	4.00
❑ 11149	Go for the Night/Two Makes One Wonderful	1979	—	2.00	4.00
❑ 11221	A Million Old Goodbyes/Sleep with Me	1980	—	2.00	4.00
❑ 11266	Lost in Austin/Explosion!	1980	—	2.00	4.00
❑ 11394	Still Your Fool/Tonight I'm Drinkin'	1980	—	2.00	4.00
❑ 44800	Games People Play/Home	1969	—	2.50	5.00
❑ 44916	These Are Not My People/Never Knew Julie	1969	—	2.50	5.00
❑ 45026	Down in the Boondocks/Amarillo, Texas	1969	—	2.50	5.00
❑ 45087	I Shook the Hand/We Gotta All Get Together	1970	—	2.50	5.00
❑ 45138	Listen to the Young Folks/That Little Boy	1970	—	3.00	6.00
❑ 45276	The Promised Land/Goodnight Sandy	1970	—	2.50	5.00
❑ 45388	Indian Lake/Over You	1971	—	2.50	5.00
❑ 45451	Another Night of Love/				
	Always Something Special	1971	—	2.50	5.00
❑ 45542	Ballad of a Hillbilly Singer/				
	Good Old-Fashioned Music	1972	—	2.50	5.00
❑ 45624	The Roadmaster/Who Do You Love	1972	—	2.50	5.00
❑ 45723	She Loves Me (Right Out of My Mind)/				
	Angel on My Shoulder	1972	—	2.50	5.00
❑ 45827	Too Much Monkey Business/It Sure Feels Good	1973	—	2.50	5.00
❑ 45902	The Perfect Stranger/Betty Ann and Shirley Cole	1973	—	2.50	5.00
❑ 45968	I've Just Got to Know (How Loving You Would				
	Be)/Georgia Girl	1973	—	2.50	5.00
❑ 46040	Sexy Lady/Bobby Crabtree's Grave	1974	—	2.50	5.00
DORE					
❑ 595	No One to Love/Mary, I'm Glad to See You	1961	3.75	7.50	15.00
Albums					
ABC DOT					
❑ DOSD-2026	Love You Back to Georgia	1975	3.00	6.00	12.00
COLUMBIA					
❑ CS 1036	Listen to the Young Folks	1970	3.75	7.50	15.00
❑ CS 9904	Games People Play/These Are Not My People	1969	3.75	7.50	15.00
❑ C 30638	Promised Land	1971	3.00	6.00	12.00
❑ KC 31769	Roadmaster	1972	3.00	6.00	12.00
❑ KC 32218	Too Much Monkey Business	1973	3.00	6.00	12.00
❑ KC 32958	Sexy Lady	1974	3.00	6.00	12.00
❑ KC 33883	Greatest Hits	1975	3.00	6.00	12.00
❑ KC 34244	Liquor, Love and Life	1976	2.50	5.00	10.00
❑ PC 34709	One Man Show	1977	2.50	5.00	10.00
❑ KC 35658	Love Got in the Way	1979	2.50	5.00	10.00
HARMONY					
❑ KH 31784	Country Collection	1972	2.50	5.00	10.00
WELLES, ORSON					
12-Inch Singles					
GNP CRESCENDO					
❑ 1206	I Know What It Is to Be Young/				
	Love Is a Lovely Word	1984	3.75	7.50	15.00
45s					
GNP CRESCENDO					
❑ 8345	I Know What It Is to Be Young/				
	Love Is a Lovely Word	1984	2.00	4.00	8.00
Albums					
AUDIO FIDELITY					
❑ W-90366	War of the Worlds	1964	3.75	7.50	15.00
—Capitol Record Club edition; same edited version as Audio Rarities LPA 2355					
AUDIO RARITIES					
❑ LPA 2355	War of the Worlds	1955	3.75	7.50	15.00
—Edited version of the October 30, 1938 Mercury Theatre radio broadcast					
EVOLUTION					
❑ 2 LPS 4001 [(2)]	War of the Worlds	1971	3.75	7.50	15.00
—Complete version of the October 30, 1938 Mercury Theatre radio broadcast					
LONGINES SYMPHONETTE					
❑ SY-5251	War of the Worlds	197?	3.75	7.50	15.00
—Complete version of the October 30, 1938 Mercury Theatre radio broadcast, but on one record					
MEDIARTS					
❑ 41-2	The Begatting of the President	1970	3.75	7.50	15.00
MURRAY HILL					
❑ S 44217 [(2)]	War of the Worlds	197?	3.00	6.00	12.00
—Complete version of the October 30, 1938 Mercury Theatre radio broadcast; reissue of Evolution LP					
UNITED ARTISTS					
❑ UAS-5521	The Begatting of the President	1971	3.00	6.00	12.00
—Reissue of Mediarts LP					
WELLINGTON, MARY SUE					
45s					
TUFF					
❑ 400	Spoiled/Save a Little Monkey	1964	2.00	4.00	8.00

Number	Title (A Side/B Side)	Yr	VG	VG+	NM
WELLINGTON, RUSTY					
45s					
ARCADE					
❑ 116	Dog-Gone It Baby, I'm in Love/				
	Every Precious Memory	1953	10.00	20.00	40.00
❑ 124	I Want a Little Lovin'/Slowly But Surely	1954	10.00	20.00	40.00
❑ 140	Blues from Tennessee/Jump Jump Honey	1955	10.00	20.00	40.00
❑ 144	The Convict and the Rose/				
	I Ain't A-Movin' On No More	1957	10.00	20.00	40.00
❑ 184	The Allegash/I've Been Away from You So Long	1965	3.75	7.50	15.00
❑ 185	Soft Shoulders/The Old Man	1966	3.75	7.50	15.00
❑ 191	Lonely Lips/Isle of Wild Roses	1967	3.75	7.50	15.00
MGM					
❑ 12581	Rocking Chair on the Moon/I Lost My Someone	1957	75.00	150.00	300.00
WELLS, BILLY, AND THE CRESCENTS					
45s					
RESERVE					
❑ 105	I Love Only You/Julie	1956	150.00	300.00	600.00
WELLS, DONNIE					
45s					
SCEPTER					
❑ 12119	Real Love/You've Got My Love	1965	6.25	12.50	25.00
WELLS, KITTY					
45s					
CAPRICORN					
❑ 0208	Too Much Love Between Us/What About You	1974	—	3.00	6.00
❑ 0226	I've Been Loving You Too Long/Too Stubborn	1975	—	3.00	6.00
❑ 0240	Anybody Out There Wanna Be a Daddy/				
	Somewhere Down the Road				
	(There's a Country Girl)	1975	—	3.00	6.00
❑ 0264	Mary Hartman, Mary Hartman/Nickel Candy Bar	1976	—	3,00	6.00
DECCA					
❑ 9-28232	It Wasn't God Who Made Honky Tonk Angels/I				
	Don't Want Your Money, I Want Your Time	1952	7.50	15.00	30.00
❑ 9-28432	I Heard the Juke Box Playing/				
	A Wedding Ring Ago	1952	6.25	12.50	25.00
❑ 9-28525	Divided by Two/The Things I Might Have Been	1953	6.25	12.50	25.00
❑ 9-28578	Paying for That Back Street Affair/				
	Crying Steel Guitar Waltz	1953	6.25	12.50	25.00
❑ 9-28666	You Said You Could Do Without Me/				
	Honky Tonk Waltz	1953	6.25	12.50	25.00
❑ 9-28753	I Don't Claim to Be an Angel/				
	The Life They Live in Songs	1953	6.25	12.50	25.00
❑ 9-28797	Hey Joe/My Cold Cold Heart Is Melted Now	1953	6.25	12.50	25.00
❑ 9-28931	Cheatin's a Sin/I Gave My Wedding Dress Away	1953	6.25	12.50	25.00
❑ 9-29023	Release Me/After Dark	1954	6.25	12.50	25.00
❑ 9-29134	You're Not Easy to Forget/He's Married to Me	1954	6.25	12.50	25.00
❑ 9-29313	Thou Shalt Not Steal/				
	I Hope My Divorce Is Never Granted	1954	6.25	12.50	25.00
❑ 9-29419	Makin' Believe/Whose Shoulder Will You Cry On	1955	5.00	10.00	20.00
❑ 9-29577	There's Poison in Your Heart/				
	I'm in Love with You	1955	5.00	10.00	20.00
❑ 9-29728	Lonely Side of Town/				
	I've Kissed You My Last Time	1955	5.00	10.00	20.00
❑ 9-29823	How Far Is Heaven/Dust on the Bible	1956	5.00	10.00	20.00
—A-side with Carol Sue					
❑ 9-29956	Searching (For Someone Like You)/				
	I'd Rather Stay Home	1956	5.00	10.00	20.00
❑ 9-30094	Repenting/I'm Counting on You	1956	5.00	10.00	20.00
❑ 9-30288	Three Ways (To Love You)/A Change of Heart	1957	3.75	7.50	15.00
❑ 9-30415	(I'll Always Be Your) Fraulein/What I Believe	1957	3.75	7.50	15.00
❑ 9-30551	I Can't Stop Loving You/She's No Angel	1958	3.75	7.50	15.00
❑ 9-30662	Jealousy/I Can't Help Wondering	1958	3.75	7.50	15.00
❑ 9-30736	Touch and Go Heart/He's Lost His Love for Me	1958	3.75	7.50	15.00
❑ 9-30804	Mommy for a Day/All the Time	1959	3.75	7.50	15.00
❑ 9-30890	Your Wild Life's Gonna Get You Down/You'll				
	Never Be Mine Again	1959	3.75	7.50	15.00
❑ 9-30987	Amigo's Guitar/Lonely Is a Word	1959	3.75	7.50	15.00
❑ 31065	Left to Right/Memory of Love	1960	3.75	7.50	15.00
❑ 31123	Carmel by the Sea/The Man I Used to Know	1960	3.00	6.00	12.00
❑ 31192	The Other Cheek/Fickle Fun	1961	3.00	6.00	12.00
❑ 31246	Heartbreak U.S.A./				
	There Must Be Another Way to Live	1961	3.00	6.00	12.00
❑ 31313	Day Into Night/Our Mansion Is a Prison Now	1961	3.00	6.00	12.00
❑ 31349	Unloved Unwanted/Au Revoir (Goodbye)	1962	3.00	6.00	12.00
❑ 31392	Will Your Lawyer Talk to God/The Big Let Down	1962	3.00	6.00	12.00
❑ 31422	We Missed You/Wicked World	1962	3.00	6.00	12.00
❑ 31441	Christmas Ain't Like Christmas Anymore/				
	Dancer (With the Light Upon His Tail)	1962	3.75	7.50	15.00
❑ 31457	Cold and Lonely (Is the Forecast for Tonight)/Is				
	It Asking Too Much	1963	2.50	5.00	10.00
❑ 31501	I Gave My Wedding Dress Away/				
	A Heartache for a Keepsake	1963	2.50	5.00	10.00
❑ 31580	This White Circle on My Finger/(I Didn't Have to)				
	Break Up Someone's Home	1964	2.50	5.00	10.00
❑ 31622	Password/I've Thought of Leaving You	1964	2.50	5.00	10.00
❑ 31705	I'll Repossess My Heart/Kill Him with Kindness	1964	2.50	5.00	10.00
❑ 31749	You Don't Hear/Six Lonely Hours	1965	2.50	5.00	10.00
❑ 31817	Meanwhile, Down at Joe's/Leavin' Town Tonight	1965	2.50	5.00	10.00
❑ 31881	A Woman Half My Age/When Your Little High				
	Horse Runs Down	1966	2.50	5.00	10.00
❑ 31957	It's All Over (But the Crying)/				
	You Left Your Mark on Me	1966	2.50	5.00	10.00
❑ 32024	Only Me and My Hairdresser Know/				
	A Woman Never Forgets	1966	2.50	5.00	10.00
❑ 32088	Love Makes the World Go Around/				
	I'm Just Not Smart	1967	2.00	4.00	8.00
❑ 32163	Queen of Honky Tonk Street/Wasting My Time	1967	2.00	4.00	8.00
❑ 32247	My Big Truck Drivin' Man/You Want Her Not Me	1967	2.00	4.00	8.00
❑ 32343	Gypsy King/When Hearts Grow Hard and Cold	1968	2.00	4.00	8.00
❑ 32389	Happiness Hill/You're No Angel Yourself	1968	2.00	4.00	8.00
❑ 32455	Guilty Street/Shape Up or Get Out	1969	2.00	4.00	8.00

W

Number	Title (A Side/B Side)	Yr	VG	VG+	NM
❏ 32455 [PS]	Guilty Street/Shape Up or Get Out	1969	5.00	10.00	20.00
—Her only known Decca picture sleeve					
❏ 32535	Just a Cheap Affair/Don't Call Me Your Darling	1969	2.00	4.00	8.00
❏ 32629	I Don't See What I Say/Gonna Find Me a Bluebird	1970	2.00	4.00	8.00
❏ 32700	Your Love Is the Way/It's Written All Over Your Face	1970	2.00	4.00	8.00
❏ 32763	I Love You/That Ain't a Woman's Way	1970	2.00	4.00	8.00
❏ 32795	They're Stepping All Over My Heart/Your Old Love Letters	1971	2.00	4.00	8.00
❏ 32840	Pledging My Love/Thank You for Loving Me	1971	2.00	4.00	8.00
❏ 32889	I'm the Wreck of Number Two/Reno Airport Nashville Plane	1971	2.00	4.00	8.00
❏ 32931	Sincerely/J.J. Sneed	1972	2.00	4.00	8.00
❏ 32976	A Bridge I Just Can't Burn/Love Is the Answer	1972	2.00	4.00	8.00
❏ 33016	I've Got Yesterday/Less Than a Lady	1972	2.00	4.00	8.00
❏ 33047	Full Grown Man/Every Step of the Way	1973	2.00	4.00	8.00
❏ 7-34185 [S]	Dasher (With the Light Upon His Tail)/C-H-R-I-S-T-M-A-S	1962	5.00	10.00	20.00
—Small hole, plays at 33 1/3 rpm					
❏ 7-34186 [S]	Santa's On His Way/(B-side unknown)	1962	5.00	10.00	20.00
—Small hole, plays at 33 1/3 rpm					
❏ 7-34187 [S]	titles unknown	1962	5.00	10.00	20.00
—Small hole, plays at 33 1/3 rpm					
❏ 7-34188 [S]	Rudolph the Red-Nosed Reindeer/Blue Christmas	1962	5.00	10.00	20.00
—Small hole, plays at 33 1/3 rpm					
❏ 7-34189 [S]	Ole Kris Kringle/(B-side unknown)	1962	5.00	10.00	20.00
—Small hole, plays at 33 1/3 rpm					
❏ 9-46409	Precious Memories/Gloryland March	1952	10.00	20.00	40.00
MCA					
❏ 40057	Easily Persuaded/It Doesn't Say	1973	—	3.00	6.00
❏ 40123	If I Was a Bottle/Mississippi Missus	1973	—	3.00	6.00
RCA VICTOR					
❏ 47-5539	Gathering Flowers for the Master's Banquet/Don't Wait for the Last Minute to Pray	1953	6.25	12.50	25.00
❏ 47-5686	Kiss Me/Why Fall So Slowly	1954	6.25	12.50	25.00
❏ 48-0084	Love or Hate/Don't Wait for the Last Minute to Pray	1949	15.00	30.00	60.00
—Originals on green vinyl					
❏ 48-0333	Make Up Your Mind/All Smiles Tonight	1950	12.50	25.00	50.00
—Originals on green vinyl					
❏ 48-0384	How Far Is Heaven/My Mother	1950	12.50	25.00	50.00
—Originals on green vinyl					
RUBOCA					
❏ 122	Thank You for the Roses/Loving You Was All I Ever Needed	1979	2.00	4.00	8.00
❏ 123	Old Milwaukee Talking/I Never Told Him I Loved Him	1979	2.00	4.00	8.00
❏ 124	I Can't Help It/I'll Hold You in My Heart	1980	2.00	4.00	8.00
7-Inch Extended Plays					
DECCA					
❏ ED 2163	It Wasn't God Who Made Honky Tonk Angels/The Things I Might Have Been//Paying for That Back Street Affair/I Don't Claim to Be an Angel	1955	6.25	12.50	25.00
❏ ED 2163 [PS]	Kitty Wells Sings	1955	6.25	12.50	25.00
❏ ED 2361	Makin' Believe/Release Me//I'm Too Lonely to Smile/Searching for a Soldier's Grave	1956	5.00	10.00	20.00
❏ ED 2361 [PS]	Kitty Wells' Country Hit Parade, Part 1	1956	5.00	10.00	20.00
❏ ED 2362	There's Poison in Your Heart/Whose Shoulder Will You Cry On//Cheatin's a Sin/I've Kissed You My Last Time	1956	5.00	10.00	20.00
❏ ED 2362 [PS]	Kitty Wells' Country Hit Parade, Vol. 2	1956	5.00	10.00	20.00
❏ ED 2363	(contents unknown)	1956	5.00	10.00	20.00
❏ ED 2363 [PS]	Kitty Wells' Country Hit Parade, Vol. 3	1956	5.00	10.00	20.00
❏ ED 2518	*Winner of Your Heart/Right or Wrong/Pace That Kills/Dancing with a Stranger	1957	5.00	10.00	20.00
❏ ED 2518 [PS]	Winner of Your Heart, Vol. 1	1957	5.00	10.00	20.00
❏ ED 2519	*Each Day/She's No Angel/Broken Marriage Vows/Change of Heart	1957	5.00	10.00	20.00
❏ ED 2519 [PS]	Winner of Your Heart, Vol. 2 (Change of Heart)	1957	5.00	10.00	20.00
❏ ED 2520	*Mansion on the Hill/Standing Room Only/I Guess I'll Go On Dreaming/Stubborn Heart	1957	5.00	10.00	20.00
❏ ED 2520 [PS]	Winner of Your Heart, Vol. 3 (Stubborn Heart)	1957	5.00	10.00	20.00
❏ ED 2584	That's Me Without You/Waltz of the Angels//Lonely Street/Love Me to Pieces	1958	5.00	10.00	20.00
❏ ED 2584 [PS]	Lonely Street	1958	5.00	10.00	20.00
❏ ED 2646 [M]	*Dust on the Bible/I Dreamed I Searched Heaven for You/Lonesome Valley/My Loved Ones Are Waiting for Me	1959	5.00	10.00	20.00
❏ ED 2646 [PS]	Dust on the Bible	1959	5.00	10.00	20.00
❏ ED 7-2646 [PS]	Dust on the Bible	1959	7.50	15.00	30.00
❏ ED 7-2646 [S]	Dust on the Bible/I Dreamed I Searched Heaven for You/Lonesome Valley/My Loved Ones Are Waiting for Me	1959	7.50	15.00	30.00
❏ ED 2677	*Sugartime/Dark Moon/Bonaparte's Retreat/When the Moon Comes Over the Mountain	1960	5.00	10.00	20.00
❏ ED 2677 [PS]	Kitty's Choice	1960	5.00	10.00	20.00
❏ ED 2684	*Seasons of My Heart/Lonely Is a Word/Send Me the Pillow You Dream On/Amigo's Guitar	1960	5.00	10.00	20.00
❏ ED 2684 [PS]	Seasons of My Heart	1960	5.00	10.00	20.00
❏ ED 2692	(contents unknown)	1961	5.00	10.00	20.00
❏ ED 2692 [PS]	Kitty Wells	1961	5.00	10.00	20.00
❏ ED 2699	*Heartbreak U.S.A./Heart to Heart Talk/This Old Heart/Cold, Cold Heart	1961	5.00	10.00	20.00
❏ ED 2699 [PS]	Heartbreak U.S.A.	1961	5.00	10.00	20.00
❏ ED 2710	(contents unknown)	1962	5.00	10.00	20.00
❏ ED 2710 [PS]	Kitty Wells	1962	5.00	10.00	20.00
❏ ED 2717	(contents unknown)	1962	5.00	10.00	20.00
❏ ED 2717 [PS]	Kitty Wells	1962	5.00	10.00	20.00
❏ ED 2732	*Will Your Lawyer Talk to God/The Big Let Down/I'm Couting on You/I've Got a New Heartache	1962	5.00	10.00	20.00
❏ ED 2732 [PS]	Kitty Wells	1962	5.00	10.00	20.00
❏ ED 2737	*Wicked World/We Missed You/Your Old Love Letters/Slowly	1963	5.00	10.00	20.00
❏ ED 2737 [PS]	Wicked World	1963	5.00	10.00	20.00

Number	Title (A Side/B Side)	Yr	VG	VG+	NM
❏ ED 2749	*I Can't Stop Loving You/All the Time/Your Wild Life's Gonna Get You Down/Hey Joe	1963	5.00	10.00	20.00
❏ ED 2749 [PS]	All the Time	1963	5.00	10.00	20.00
❏ ED 2763	*I Gave My Wedding Dress Away/A Heartache for a Keepsake/Cold and Lonely/Is It Asking Too Much	1963	5.00	10.00	20.00
❏ ED 2763 [PS]	Kitty Wells	1963	5.00	10.00	20.00
❏ ED 2777	*Talk Back Trembling Lips/Busted/Ring of Fire/Guilty	1964	6.25	12.50	25.00
❏ ED 2777 [PS]	Talk Back Trembling Lips	1964	6.25	12.50	25.00
❏ ED 2780	*Password/B.J. the D.J./Old Records/As Usual	1964	6.25	12.50	25.00
❏ ED 2780 [PS]	Password	1964	7.50	15.00	30.00
❏ ED 2781	(contents unknown)	1965	7.50	15.00	30.00
❏ ED 2781 [PS]	This White Circle	1965	7.50	15.00	30.00
❏ ED 2804	(contents unknown)	1965	7.50	15.00	30.00
❏ ED 2804 [PS]	Burning Memories	1965	7.50	15.00	30.00
❏ 7-34043	Dark Moon/Your Cheatin' Heart/Beautiful Brown Eyes//Jambalaya/Jealous Heart/My Happiness	196?	3.75	7.50	15.00
—Stereo jukebox issue; small hole, plays at 33 1/3 rpm					
❏ 7-34043 [PS]	Kitty's Choice	196?	3.75	7.50	15.00
❏ 7-34255	I've Thought of Leaving Too/As Usual/Begging to You//Password/This White Circle/Gonna Find Me a Bluebird	196?	3.75	7.50	15.00
—Stereo jukebox issue; small hole, plays at 33 1/3 rpm					
❏ 7-34255 [PS]	Country Music Time	196?	3.75	7.50	15.00
Albums					
DECCA					
❏ DXB 174 [(2)M]	The Kitty Wells Story	1963	7.50	15.00	30.00
❏ DL 4075 [M]	Seasons of My Heart	1961	7.50	15.00	30.00
❏ DL 4108 [M]	Kitty Wells' Golden Favorites	1961	7.50	15.00	30.00
❏ DL 4141 [M]	Heartbreak U.S.A.	1961	7.50	15.00	30.00
❏ DL 4197 [M]	Queen of Country Music	1962	7.50	15.00	30.00
❏ DL 4270 [M]	Singing on Sunday	1962	7.50	15.00	30.00
❏ DL 4349 [M]	Christmas Day with Kitty Wells	1962	6.25	12.50	25.00
❏ DL 4493 [M]	Especially for You	1964	6.25	12.50	25.00
❏ DL 4554 [M]	Country Music Time	1964	6.25	12.50	25.00
❏ DL 4612 [M]	Burning Memories	1965	6.25	12.50	25.00
❏ DL 4658 [M]	Lonesome Sad and Blue	1965	6.25	12.50	25.00
❏ DL 4679 [M]	Family Gospel Sing	1965	6.25	12.50	25.00
❏ DL 4741 [M]	Kitty Wells Sings Songs Made Famous by Jim Reeves	1966	6.25	12.50	25.00
❏ DL 4776 [M]	Country All the Way	1966	6.25	12.50	25.00
❏ DL 4831 [M]	The Kitty Wells Show	1966	6.25	12.50	25.00
❏ DL 4857 [M]	Love Makes the World Go Around	1967	7.50	15.00	30.00
❏ DL 4929 [M]	Queen of Honky Tonk Street	1967	10.00	20.00	40.00
❏ DL 5001 [M]	Kitty Wells' Greatest Hits	1968	12.50	25.00	50.00
—White label promo only					
❏ DXSB 7174 [(2)P]	The Kitty Wells Story	1963	10.00	20.00	40.00
❏ DL 8293 [M]	Kitty Wells' Country Hit Parade	1956	15.00	30.00	60.00
—Black label, silver print					
❏ DL 8293 [M]	Kitty Wells' Country Hit Parade	1961	7.50	15.00	30.00
—Black label with color bars					
❏ DL 8552 [M]	Winner of Your Heart	1957	15.00	30.00	60.00
—Black label, silver print					
❏ DL 8552 [M]	Winner of Your Heart	1961	7.50	15.00	30.00
—Black label with color bars					
❏ DL 8732 [M]	Lonely Street	1958	15.00	30.00	60.00
—Black label, silver print					
❏ DL 8732 [M]	Lonely Street	1961	7.50	15.00	30.00
—Black label with color bars					
❏ DL 8858 [M]	Dust on the Bible	1959	15.00	30.00	60.00
—Black label, silver print					
❏ DL 8858 [M]	Dust on the Bible	1961	7.50	15.00	30.00
—Black label with color bars					
❏ DL 8888 [M]	After Dark	1959	15.00	30.00	60.00
—Black label, silver print					
❏ DL 8888 [M]	After Dark	1961	7.50	15.00	30.00
—Black label with color bars					
❏ DL 8979 [M]	Kitty's Choice	1960	12.50	25.00	50.00
—Black label, silver print					
❏ DL 8979 [M]	Kitty's Choice	1961	6.25	12.50	25.00
—Black label with color bars					
❏ DL 74075 [S]	Seasons of My Heart	1961	10.00	20.00	40.00
❏ DL 74108 [R]	Kitty Wells' Golden Favorites	196?	5.00	10.00	20.00
❏ DL 74141 [S]	Heartbreak U.S.A.	1961	10.00	20.00	40.00
❏ DL 74197 [S]	Queen of Country Music	1962	10.00	20.00	40.00
❏ DL 74270 [S]	Singing on Sunday	1962	10.00	20.00	40.00
❏ DL 74349 [S]	Christmas Day with Kitty Wells	1962	7.50	15.00	30.00
❏ DL 74493 [S]	Especially for You	1964	7.50	15.00	30.00
❏ DL 74554 [S]	Country Music Time	1964	7.50	15.00	30.00
❏ DL 74612 [S]	Burning Memories	1965	7.50	15.00	30.00
❏ DL 74658 [S]	Lonesome Sad and Blue	1965	7.50	15.00	30.00
❏ DL 74679 [S]	Family Gospel Sing	1965	7.50	15.00	30.00
❏ DL 74741 [S]	Kitty Wells Sings Songs Made Famous by Jim Reeves	1966	7.50	15.00	30.00
❏ DL 74776 [S]	Country All the Way	1966	7.50	15.00	30.00
❏ DL 74831 [S]	The Kitty Wells Show	1966	7.50	15.00	30.00
❏ DL 74857 [S]	Love Makes the World Go Around	1967	7.50	15.00	30.00
❏ DL 74929 [S]	Queen of Honky Tonk Street	1967	6.25	12.50	25.00
❏ DL 74961	Kitty Wells Showcase	1968	6.25	12.50	25.00
❏ DL 75001 [S]	Kitty Wells' Greatest Hits	1968	6.25	12.50	25.00
❏ DL 75067	Cream of Country Hits	1968	6.25	12.50	25.00
❏ DL 75098	Guilty Street	1969	6.25	12.50	25.00
❏ DL 75164	Bouquet of Country Hits	1969	5.00	10.00	20.00
❏ DL 75221	Singin' 'Em Country	1970	5.00	10.00	20.00
❏ DL 75245	Your Love Is the Way	1970	5.00	10.00	20.00
❏ DL 75277	They're Stepping All Over My Heart	1971	5.00	10.00	20.00
❏ DL 75313	Pledging My Love	1971	5.00	10.00	20.00
❏ DL 75325	Heartwarming Gospel Songs	1972	5.00	10.00	20.00
❏ DL 75350	Sincerely	1972	5.00	10.00	20.00
❏ DL 75382	I've Got Yesterday	1972	5.00	10.00	20.00
❏ DL 78293 [R]	Kitty Wells' Country Hit Parade	196?	5.00	10.00	20.00
❏ DL 78552 [R]	Winner of Your Heart	196?	5.00	10.00	20.00
❏ DL 78732 [R]	Lonely Street	196?	5.00	10.00	20.00
❏ DL 78858 [R]	Dust on the Bible	196?	5.00	10.00	20.00

Number	Title (A Side/B Side)	Yr	VG	VG+	NM
❑ DL 78979 [S]	Kitty's Choice	1960	15.00	30.00	60.00
—Maroon label, silver print					
❑ DL 78979 [S]	Kitty's Choice	1961	7.50	15.00	30.00
—Black label with color bars					
❑ SW-94491	Sincerely	1972	6.25	12.50	25.00
—Capitol Record Club edition					

WELLS, KITTY, AND ROY DRUSKY
45s
DECCA

Number	Title (A Side/B Side)	Yr	VG	VG+	NM
❑ 31164	I Can't Tell My Heart That/When Do You Love Me	1960	3.00	6.00	12.00
❑ 31523	Another Chance to Fall in Love/My World's Losing You	1963	2.50	5.00	10.00

WELLS, KITTY, AND RED FOLEY Also see each artist's individual listings.
45s
DECCA

Number	Title (A Side/B Side)	Yr	VG	VG+	NM
❑ 9-29065	One by One/I'm a Stranger in My Home	1954	6.25	12.50	25.00
❑ 9-29228	Skinnie Minnie (Fishtart)/Thank You for Calling	1954	6.25	12.50	25.00
❑ 9-29390	As Long As I Live/Make Believe ('Til We Can Make It Come True)	1955	5.00	10.00	20.00
❑ 9-29740	You and Me/No One But You	1955	5.00	10.00	20.00
❑ 32126	Happiness Means You/Hello Number One	1967	2.00	4.00	8.00
❑ 32223	Living as Strangers/Loved and Wanted	1967	2.00	4.00	8.00
❑ 32427	Have I Told You Lately That I Love You?/We Need One More Chance	1968	2.00	4.00	8.00

7-Inch Extended Plays
DECCA

Number	Title (A Side/B Side)	Yr	VG	VG+	NM
❑ ED 2667	I'm a Stranger in My Home/One by One//As Long As I Live/Make Believe (Till We Can Make It Come True)	1959	6.25	12.50	25.00
❑ ED 2667 [PS]	Kitty Wells and Red Foley	1959	6.25	12.50	25.00
❑ 7-34297	One by One/Make Believe/As Long As I Live//You and Me/I'm a Stranger in My Home/No One But You	196?	6.25	12.50	25.00
—Jukebox issue; small hole, plays at 33 1/3 rpm					
❑ 7-34297 [PS]	Golden Favorites	196?	6.25	12.50	25.00

Albums
DECCA

Number	Title (A Side/B Side)	Yr	VG	VG+	NM
❑ DL 4109 [M]	Golden Favorites	1961	7.50	15.00	30.00
❑ DL 4906 [M]	Together Again	1967	7.50	15.00	30.00
❑ DL 74109 [S]	Golden Favorites	1961	10.00	20.00	40.00
❑ DL 74906 [S]	Together Again	1967	6.25	12.50	25.00

WELLS, KITTY, AND WEBB PIERCE Also see each artist's individual listings.
45s
DECCA

Number	Title (A Side/B Side)	Yr	VG	VG+	NM
❑ 9-30183	Oh So Many Years/Can You Find It in Your Heart	1957	3.75	7.50	15.00
❑ 9-30489	One Week Later/When I'm with You	1957	3.75	7.50	15.00
❑ 31663	Finally/He Made You for Me	1964	2.50	5.00	10.00

7-Inch Extended Plays
DECCA

Number	Title (A Side/B Side)	Yr	VG	VG+	NM
❑ ED 2666	*Oh So Many Years/One Week Later/When I'm With You/Can You Find It in Your Heart	1959	6.25	12.50	25.00
❑ ED 2666 [PS]	Kitty Wells and Webb Pierce	1959	6.25	12.50	25.00

WELLS, KITTY, AND JOHNNY WRIGHT
45s
DECCA

Number	Title (A Side/B Side)	Yr	VG	VG+	NM
❑ 32294	We'll Stick Together/Heartbreak Waltz	1968	2.00	4.00	8.00
❑ 32604	There Won't Be Any Tree This Christmas/White Christmas	1969	2.00	4.00	8.00

Albums
DECCA

Number	Title (A Side/B Side)	Yr	VG	VG+	NM
❑ DL 5028 [M]	We'll Stick Together	1968	12.50	25.00	50.00
—Mono appears to be white label promo only					
❑ DL 75028 [S]	We'll Stick Together	1968	6.25	12.50	25.00

WELLS, MARY Also see MARVIN GAYE AND MARY WELLS.
45s
ATCO

Number	Title (A Side/B Side)	Yr	VG	VG+	NM
❑ 6392	Dear Lover/Can't You See	1965	3.00	6.00	12.00
❑ 6423	Keep Me in Suspense/Such a Sweet Thing	1966	3.00	6.00	12.00
❑ 6436	Fancy Free/Me and My Baby	1966	3.00	6.00	12.00
❑ 6469	Coming Home/Hey You Set My Soul on Fire	1967	3.00	6.00	12.00

EPIC

Number	Title (A Side/B Side)	Yr	VG	VG+	NM
❑ 02664	Gigolo/I'm Changing My Ways	1982	—	2.00	4.00
❑ 02855	These Arms/Spend the Night With Me	1982	—	2.00	4.00

JUBILEE

Number	Title (A Side/B Side)	Yr	VG	VG+	NM
❑ 5621	The Doctor/Two Lovers' History	1968	3.75	7.50	15.00
❑ 5629	Can't Get Away From Your Love/A Woman in Love	1968	3.75	7.50	15.00
❑ 5639	Don't Look Back/500 Miles	1968	3.75	7.50	15.00
❑ 5676	Mind Reader/Never Give a Man the World	1969	3.00	6.00	12.00
❑ 5684	Dig the Way I Feel/Love Shooting Bandit	1969	3.00	6.00	12.00
❑ 5695	Sweet Love/It Must Be	1970	3.00	6.00	12.00
❑ 5718	Mr. Tough/Never Give a Man the World	1971	3.00	6.00	12.00

MOTOWN

Number	Title (A Side/B Side)	Yr	VG	VG+	NM
❑ 1003	Bye Bye Baby/Please Forgive Me	1960	12.50	25.00	50.00
❑ 1011	I Don't Want to Take a Chance/I'm Sorry	1961	5.00	10.00	20.00
—Blue "map" label					
❑ 1011	I Don't Want to Take a Chance/I'm Sorry	1961	7.50	15.00	30.00
—Pink "lines" label					
❑ 1011 [PS]	I Don't Want to Take a Chance/I'm Sorry	1961	20.00	40.00	80.00
❑ 1016	Strange Love/Come to Me	1961	5.00	10.00	20.00
❑ 1016 [PS]	Strange Love/Come to Me	1961	20.00	40.00	80.00
❑ 1024	The One Who Really Loves You/I'm Gonna Stay	1962	5.00	10.00	20.00
❑ 1024 [PS]	The One Who Really Loves You/I'm Gonna Stay	1962	20.00	40.00	80.00
❑ 1032	You Beat Me to the Punch/Old Love (Let's Try It Again)	1962	5.00	10.00	20.00
❑ 1032 [PS]	You Beat Me to the Punch/Old Love (Let's Try It Again)	1962	30.00	60.00	120.00
❑ 1035	Two Lovers/Operator	1962	5.00	10.00	20.00
❑ 1039	Laughing Boy/Two Wrongs Don't Make a Right	1963	5.00	10.00	20.00
❑ 1042	Your Old Stand By/What Love Has Joined Together	1963	5.00	10.00	20.00

Number	Title (A Side/B Side)	Yr	VG	VG+	NM
❑ 1048	You Lost the Sweetest Boy/What's Easy for Two Is So Hard for One	1963	5.00	10.00	20.00
❑ 1056	My Guy/Oh Little Boy (What Did You Do to Me)	1964	5.00	10.00	20.00
❑ 1061	When I'm Gone/Guarantee for a Lifetime	1964	150.00	300.00	600.00
❑ 1065	Whisper You Love Me/I'll Be Available	1964	—	—	—
—Unreleased?					

REPRISE

Number	Title (A Side/B Side)	Yr	VG	VG+	NM
❑ 1031	I Found What I Wanted/I See a Future in You	1971	2.50	5.00	10.00
❑ 1308	If You Can't Give Her Love (Give Her Up)/Cancel My Subscription	1974	2.50	5.00	10.00

20TH CENTURY FOX

Number	Title (A Side/B Side)	Yr	VG	VG+	NM
❑ 544	Ain't It the Truth/Stop Takin' Me for Granted	1964	3.75	7.50	15.00
❑ 555	Use Your Head/Everlovin' Boy	1965	3.75	7.50	15.00
❑ 570	Never, Never Leave Me?Why Don't You Let Yourself Go	1965	3.75	7.50	15.00
❑ 590	He's a Lover/I'm Learnin'	1965	3.75	7.50	15.00
❑ 590 [PS]	He's a Lover/I'm Learnin'	1965	7.50	15.00	30.00
❑ 6606	Me Without You/I'm Sorry	1965	3.75	7.50	15.00
❑ 6619	I Should Have Known Better/Please Please Me	1965	5.00	10.00	20.00

Albums
ALLEGIANCE

Number	Title (A Side/B Side)	Yr	VG	VG+	NM
❑ AV-444	The Old, the New, and the Best of Mary Wells	1984	2.50	5.00	10.00

ATCO

Number	Title (A Side/B Side)	Yr	VG	VG+	NM
❑ 33-199 [M]	Two Sides of Mary Wells	1966	6.25	12.50	25.00
❑ SD 33-199 [S]	Two Sides of Mary Wells	1966	7.50	15.00	30.00

EPIC

Number	Title (A Side/B Side)	Yr	VG	VG+	NM
❑ ARE 37540	In and Out of Love	1981	3.75	7.50	15.00

JUBILEE

Number	Title (A Side/B Side)	Yr	VG	VG+	NM
❑ JGS-8018	Servin' Up Some Soul	1968	6.25	12.50	25.00

MOTOWN

Number	Title (A Side/B Side)	Yr	VG	VG+	NM
❑ M5-161V1	Bye Bye Baby/I Don't Want to Take a Chance	1981	2.50	5.00	10.00
❑ M5-167V1	Mary Wells Sings My Guy	1981	2.50	5.00	10.00
❑ M5-221V1	Two Lovers	1981	2.50	5.00	10.00
❑ MLP-600 [M]	Bye Bye Baby/I Don't Want to Take a Chance	1961	75.00	150.00	300.00
—White label stock copy					
❑ MLP-600 [M]	Bye Bye Baby/I Don't Want to Take a Chance	1962	62.50	125.00	250.00
—With map; label address above the center hole					
❑ M 605 [M]	The One Who Really Loves You	1962	40.00	80.00	160.00
—With map; label address above the center hole					
❑ M 605 [M]	The One Who Really Loves You	1964	10.00	20.00	40.00
—With map; label address around lower part of label					
❑ M 607 [M]	Two Lovers and Other Great Hits	1963	30.00	60.00	120.00
—With map; label address above the center hole					
❑ M 607 [M]	Two Lovers and Other Great Hits	1964	10.00	20.00	40.00
—With map; label address around lower part of label					
❑ M 611 [M]	Recorded Live on Stage	1963	30.00	60.00	120.00
—With map; label address above the center hole					
❑ M 611 [M]	Recorded Live on Stage	1964	10.00	20.00	40.00
—With map; label address around lower part of label					
❑ M 612	Second Time Around	1963	—	—	—
—Canceled					
❑ M 616 [M]	Greatest Hits	1964	10.00	20.00	40.00
❑ MS 616 [S]	Greatest Hits	1964	10.00	20.00	40.00
❑ M 617 [M]	Mary Wells Sings My Guy	1964	12.50	25.00	50.00
❑ M 653 [M]	Vintage Stock	1967	12.50	25.00	50.00
❑ MS 653 [S]	Vintage Stock	1967	12.50	25.00	50.00
❑ 5233 ML	Greatest Hits	1982	2.50	5.00	10.00

MOVIETONE

Number	Title (A Side/B Side)	Yr	VG	VG+	NM
❑ 71010 [M]	Ooh	1966	6.25	12.50	25.00
❑ 72010 [S]	Ooh	1966	7.50	15.00	30.00

20TH FOX

Number	Title (A Side/B Side)	Yr	VG	VG+	NM
❑ TFM 3171 [M]	Mary Wells	1965	10.00	20.00	40.00
❑ TFM 3178 [M]	Love Songs to the Beatles	1965	20.00	40.00	80.00
❑ TFS 4171 [S]	Mary Wells	1965	15.00	30.00	60.00
❑ TFS 4178 [S]	Love Songs to the Beatles	1965	25.00	50.00	100.00
❑ ST-90790 [S]	Love Songs to the Beatles	1965	37.50	75.00	150.00
—Capitol Record Club edition					

WENDIGO
45s
SCEPTER

Number	Title (A Side/B Side)	Yr	VG	VG+	NM
❑ 12211	Gimmie Some Lovin' (Part 1)/Gimmie Some Lovin' (Part 2)	1968	3.00	6.00	12.00

WESLEY, FRED Also includes the J.B.'s.
45s
ATLANTIC

Number	Title (A Side/B Side)	Yr	VG	VG+	NM
❑ 3408	Up for the Down Stroke/When In Doubt	1977	—	2.50	5.00

KING

Number	Title (A Side/B Side)	Yr	VG	VG+	NM
❑ 6317	The Grunt (Part 1)/The Grunt (Part 2)	1970	2.50	5.00	10.00
—As "The J.B.'s"					
❑ 6333	These Are the J.B.'s (Part 1)/These Are the J.B.'s (Part 2)	1970	2.50	5.00	10.00
—As "The J.B.'s"					

PEOPLE

Number	Title (A Side/B Side)	Yr	VG	VG+	NM
❑ 602	Gimme Some More/The Rabbit Got the Gun	1972	—	3.00	6.00
—As "The J.B.'s"					
❑ 607	Pass the Peas/Hot Pants Road	1972	—	3.00	6.00
—As "The J.B.'s"					
❑ 610	Givin' Up Food for Funk (Part 1)/Givin' Up Food for Funk (Part 2)	1972	—	3.00	6.00
—As "The J.B.'s"					
❑ 614	Backstabbers/J.B. Shout	1972	—	3.00	6.00
❑ 616	If You Don't Get It the First Time/You Can Have Her Boogie	1973	—	3.00	6.00
❑ 617	Alone Again (Naturally)/Watermelon Man	1973	—	3.00	6.00
❑ 619	Sportin' Life/Dirty Harri	1973	—	3.00	6.00
❑ 621	Doing It to Death/Everybody Got Soul	1973	—	3.00	6.00
❑ 627	If You Don't Get It the First Time, Back Up and Try It Again, Party/You Can Have Watergate, Just Give Me Some Bucks and I'll Be Straight	1973	—	3.00	6.00
❑ 632	Same Beat - Part 1/Same Beat - Part 2	1974	—	3.00	6.00
❑ 638	Damn Right I Am Somebody-Part 1/Damn Right I Am Somebody-Part 2	1974	—	3.00	6.00
❑ 643	Rockin' Funky Watergate (Part 1)/Rockin' Funky Watergate (Part 2)	1974	—	3.00	6.00

Number	Title (A Side/B Side)	Yr	VG	VG+	NM
❏ 646	Little Boy Black/				
	Rockin' Funky Watergate (Part 2)	1974	—	3.00	6.00
❏ 648	Breakin' Bread/Funky Music Is My Style	1974	—	2.50	5.00
❏ 651	Makin' Love/Rice and Ribs	1975	—	2.50	5.00
❏ 654	Thank You for Lettin' Me Be Myself and Be Yours (Part 1)/Thank You for Lettin' Me Be Myself and Be Yours (Part 2)	1975	—	2.50	5.00
❏ 655	(It's Not the Express) It's the J.B.'s Monaurail, Part 1/(It's Not the Express) It's the J.B.'s Monaurail, Part 2	1975	—	2.50	5.00
❏ 660	Thank You for Lettin' Me Be Myself (Part 1)/Thank You for Lettin' Me Be Myself (Part 2)	1975	—	2.50	5.00
❏ 663	All Aboard the Funky Soul Train/Thank You for Lettin' Me Be Myself and You Be Yourself	1976	—	2.50	5.00
❏ 2502	My Brother (Part 1)/My Brother (Part 2)	1971	—	3.00	6.00

—As "The J.B.'s"

RSO/CURTOM

Number	Title	Yr	VG	VG+	NM
❏ 1037	House Party/I Make Music	1980	—	2.00	4.00

Albums
ATLANTIC

❏ SD 18214	A Blow for Me, A Toot to You	1977	3.00	6.00	12.00
❏ SD 19254	Say Blow by Blow Backwards	1979	3.00	6.00	12.00

PEOPLE

❏ PE-5601	Food for Thought	1972	20.00	40.00	80.00
❏ PE-5603	Doing It to Death	1973	20.00	40.00	80.00
❏ PE-6602	Damn Right I Am Somebody	1974	5.00	10.00	20.00
❏ PE-6604	Breakin' Bread	1974	5.00	10.00	20.00

WESLEY, GATE
45s
ATLANTIC

❏ 2319	Do the Batman/Do the Thing	1966	6.25	12.50	25.00

WEST
45s
EPIC

❏ 5-10335	Just Like Tom Thumb's Blues/Baby You Been On My Mind	1968	2.50	5.00	10.00
❏ 5-10378	Step by Step/Summer Flower	1968	2.00	4.00	8.00
❏ 5-10449	Peaceful Times/You Only Think You've Come Home	1969	2.00	4.00	8.00

Albums
EPIC

❏ BN 26380	West	1968	5.00	10.00	20.00
❏ BN 26433	Bridges	1969	5.00	10.00	20.00

WEST, DOTTIE Also see KENNY ROGERS AND DOTTIE WEST.
45s
ATLANTIC

❏ 2155	You Said I'd Never Love Again/I'll Pick Up My Heart (And Go Home)	1962	3.75	7.50	15.00

LIBERTY

❏ 1392	Are You Happy Baby/Right or Wrong	1980	—	—	3.00
❏ 1392 [PS]	Are You Happy Baby/Right or Wrong	1980	—	2.50	5.00
❏ 1404	What Are We Doin' in Love/Choosin' Means Losin'	1981	—	—	3.00

—Duet with Kenny Rogers, who is not credited on the label

❏ 1419	(I'm Gonna) Put You Back on the Rack/Sorry Seems to Be the Hardest Word	1981	—	—	3.00
❏ 1436	It's High Time/Don't Be Kind	1981	—	—	3.00
❏ 1451	You're Not Easy to Forget/Something's Missing	1982	—	—	3.00
❏ 1479	She Can't Get My Love Off the Bed/Hurt	1982	—	—	3.00
❏ 1490	If It Takes All Night/Try to Win a Friend	1982	—	—	3.00
❏ 1490 [PS]	If It Takes All Night/Try to Win a Friend	1982	—	2.00	4.00
❏ 1500	Tulsa Ballroom/A Woman in Love with You	1983	—	—	3.00
❏ 1506	The Night Love Let You Down/He's All I Need	1983	—	—	3.00

PERMIAN

❏ 82006	What's Good for the Goose (Is Good for the Gander)/Tell Me Again	1984	—	2.00	4.00
❏ 82007	Let Love Come Lookin' for You/Blue Fiddle Waltz	1984	—	2.00	4.00
❏ 82010	We Know Better Now/Let Love Come Lookin' for You	1985	—	2.00	4.00

RCA

❏ PB-12284	Once You Were Mine/Dream Baby (How Long Must I Dream)	1981	—	—	4.00

RCA VICTOR

❏ 47-8166	Touch Me/More Than I Meant To	1963	3.00	6.00	12.00
❏ 47-8225	Let Me Off at the Corner/I Wish You Wouldn't Do That	1963	2.50	5.00	10.00
❏ 47-8324	Love Is No Excuse/Look Who's Talking	1964	2.50	5.00	10.00

—With Jim Reeves

❏ 47-8374	Here Comes My Baby/(How Can I Face) These Heartaches Alone	1964	2.50	5.00	10.00
❏ 47-8467	Didn't I/In Its Own Little Way	1964	2.50	5.00	10.00
❏ 47-8525	Gettin' Married Has Made Us Strangers/It Just Takes Practice	1965	2.50	5.00	10.00
❏ 47-8615	No Sign of Living/Night Life	1965	2.50	5.00	10.00
❏ 47-8702	Before the Ring on Your Finger Turns Green/Wear Away	1965	2.50	5.00	10.00
❏ 47-8770	Would You Hold It Against Me/You're Just the Only World I Know	1965	2.00	4.00	8.00
❏ 47-8900	Mommy, Can I Still Call Him Daddy/Suffertime	1966	2.00	4.00	8.00
❏ 47-9011	What's Come Over My Baby/How Many Lifetimes Will It Take	1966	2.00	4.00	8.00
❏ 47-9118	Paper Mansions/Someone's Gotta Cry	1967	2.00	4.00	8.00
❏ 47-9267	Like a Fool/Everything's a Wreck	1967	2.00	4.00	8.00
❏ 47-9377	Childhood Places/No One	1967	2.00	4.00	8.00
❏ 47-9497	Country Girl/That's Where Our Love Must Be	1968	2.00	4.00	8.00
❏ 47-9604	Reno/My Heart Has Changed Its Mind	1968	2.00	4.00	8.00
❏ 47-9792	I Heard Our Song/Makin' Memories	1969	—	3.00	6.00
❏ 47-9834	Jack Daniels, Old Grand-Dad, Johnnie Walker and You/Long Black Limousine	1970	—	3.00	6.00
❏ 47-9872	It's Dawned on Me You're Gone/Love's Farewell	1970	—	3.00	6.00
❏ 47-9911	Forever Yours/Cold Hand of Fate	1970	—	3.00	6.00
❏ 47-9947	Slowly/Sweet Thang	1971	—	3.00	6.00

—With Jimmy Dean

Number	Title (A Side/B Side)	Yr	VG	VG+	NM
❏ 47-9957	Careless Hands/Only One Thing Left to Do	1971	—	3.00	6.00
❏ 47-9982	Lonely Is/Cancel Tomorrow	1971	—	3.00	6.00
❏ 48-1012	Six Weeks Every Summer (Christmas Every Day)/Wish I Didn't Love You Anymore	1971	—	2.50	5.00
❏ 74-0239	Clinging to My Baby's Hand/Don't Say a Word	1969	—	3.00	6.00
❏ 74-0601	Cold Hand of Fate/You're the Other Half of Me	1971	—	3.00	6.00
❏ 74-0711	I'm Only a Woman/Baby, I Tried	1972	—	2.50	5.00
❏ 74-0828	If It's All Right with You/Special Memory	1972	—	2.50	5.00
❏ 74-0930	Just What I've Been Looking For/Everything's a Wreck	1973	—	2.50	5.00
❏ APBO-0072	Country Sunshine/Wish I Didn't Love You Any More	1973	2.00	4.00	8.00
❏ APBO-0231	Last Time I Saw Him/Everybody Bring a Song	1974	—	2.50	5.00
❏ APBO-0321	House of Love/Love As Long As We Can	1974	—	2.50	5.00
❏ PB-10125	Lay Back Lover/Good Lovin' You	1974	—	2.50	5.00
❏ PB-10269	Rollin' in Your Sweet Sunshine/Carolina Cousins	1975	—	2.50	5.00
❏ PB-10553	Here Come the Flowers/He's Not for You	1976	—	2.50	5.00
❏ PB-10699	If I'm a Fool for Loving You/Home Made Love	1976	—	2.50	5.00

STARDAY

❏ 517	Angel on Paper/No Time Will I Ever	1960	5.00	10.00	20.00
❏ 547	I Lost, You Win, I'm Leavin'/I Should Start Runnin'	1961	5.00	10.00	20.00
❏ 574	My Big John/Men with Evil Hearts	1961	5.00	10.00	20.00
❏ 724	I'd Be Lying/Walking in the Dark	1965	2.50	5.00	10.00

UNITED ARTISTS

❏ XW898	When It's Just You and Me/We Love Each Other	1976	—	2.00	4.00
❏ XW946	Every Word I Write/We Love Each Other	1977	—	2.00	4.00
❏ XW1010	Tonight You Belong to Me/Tiny Fingers	1977	—	2.00	4.00
❏ XW1084	That's All I Wanted to Know/Who's Gonna Love Me Now	1977	—	2.00	4.00
❏ XW1209	Come See Me and Come Lonely/Decorate Your Conscience	1978	—	2.00	4.00
❏ XW1257	Reaching Out to Hold You/My Two Empty Arms	1978	—	2.00	4.00
❏ 1324	You Pick Me Up (And Put Me Down)/We Got Tonight	1979	—	2.00	4.00
❏ 1339	A Lesson in Leavin'/Love's So Easy for Two	1980	—	2.00	4.00
❏ 1352	Leavin' for Unbelievers/Blue As I Want To	1980	—	2.00	4.00

7-Inch Extended Plays
RCA VICTOR

❏ VLP 3587	Baby/Before the Ring on Your Finger Turns Green/Wear Away//Would You Hold It Against Me/Just Out of Reach/What's Come Over My Baby	1966	5.00	10.00	20.00

—Jukebox issue; small hole, plays at 33 1/3 rpm

❏ VLP 3587 [PS]	Suffering Time	1966	5.00	10.00	20.00

Albums
LIBERTY

❏ LT-740	When It's Just You and Me	1981	2.00	4.00	8.00

—Reissue of United Artists 740

❏ LT-860	Dottie	1981	2.00	4.00	8.00

—Reissue of United Artists 860

❏ LT-1000	Special Delivery	1981	2.00	4.00	8.00

—Reissue of United Artists 1000

❏ LT-1062	Wild West	1981	2.50	5.00	10.00
❏ LT-51114	High Times	1982	2.50	5.00	10.00
❏ LT-51129	Full Circle	1982	2.50	5.00	10.00
❏ LT-51145	New Horizons	1983	2.50	5.00	10.00
❏ LT-51155	Greatest Hits	1984	2.50	5.00	10.00

POWER PAK

❏ 274	Country Girl Singing Sensation	197?	2.50	5.00	10.00

RCA CAMDEN

❏ ACL1-0125	Would You Hold It Against Me	1973	2.50	5.00	10.00
❏ ACL1-0482	Loving You	1974	2.50	5.00	10.00
❏ CAL-2155 [M]	The Sound of Country Music	1967	3.75	7.50	15.00
❏ CAS-2155 [S]	The Sound of Country Music	1967	3.00	6.00	12.00
❏ CAS-2454	A Legend in My Time	1971	3.00	6.00	12.00

RCA VICTOR

❏ APD1-0151 [Q]	If It's All Right with You/Just What I've Been Looking For	1973	5.00	10.00	20.00
❏ APL1-0151	If It's All Right with You/Just What I've Been Looking For	1973	3.00	6.00	12.00
❏ APL1-0344	Country Sunshine	1973	3.00	6.00	12.00
❏ APL1-0543	House of Love	1974	3.00	6.00	12.00
❏ APL1-1041	Carolina Cousins	1975	3.00	6.00	12.00
❏ ANL1-2327	Country Sunshine	1977	2.50	5.00	10.00

—Reissue of APL1-0344

❏ LPM-3368 [M]	Here Comes My Baby	1965	6.25	12.50	25.00
❏ LSP-3368 [S]	Here Comes My Baby	1965	7.50	15.00	30.00
❏ LPM-3490 [M]	Dottie West Sings	1966	6.25	12.50	25.00
❏ LSP-3490 [S]	Dottie West Sings	1966	7.50	15.00	30.00
❏ LPM-3587 [M]	Suffer Time	1966	6.25	12.50	25.00
❏ LSP-3587 [S]	Suffer Time	1966	7.50	15.00	30.00
❏ LPM-3693 [M]	With All My Heart and Soul	1967	7.50	15.00	30.00
❏ LSP-3693 [S]	With All My Heart and Soul	1967	6.25	12.50	25.00
❏ LPM-3784 [M]	Dottie West Sings Sacred Ballads	1967	7.50	15.00	30.00
❏ LSP-3784 [S]	Dottie West Sings Sacred Ballads	1967	6.25	12.50	25.00
❏ LPM-3830 [M]	I'll Help You Forget Her	1967	7.50	15.00	30.00
❏ LSP-3830 [S]	I'll Help You Forget Her	1967	6.25	12.50	25.00
❏ LPM-3932 [M]	What I'm Cut Out to Be	1968	12.50	25.00	50.00
❏ LSP-3932 [S]	What I'm Cut Out to Be	1968	6.25	12.50	25.00
❏ LSP-4004	Country Girl	1968	6.25	12.50	25.00
❏ LSP-4095	Feminine Fancy	1969	5.00	10.00	20.00
❏ AHL1-4117	Once You Were Mine	1981	2.50	5.00	10.00
❏ LSP-4154	Dottie Sings Eddy	1969	5.00	10.00	20.00
❏ LSP-4276	Makin' Memories	1970	5.00	10.00	20.00
❏ AYL1-4302	Once You Were Mine	1982	2.00	4.00	8.00
❏ LSP-4332	Country and West	1970	5.00	10.00	20.00
❏ LSP-4433	Forever Yours	1970	5.00	10.00	20.00
❏ LSP-4482	Careless Hands	1971	3.75	7.50	15.00
❏ LSP-4606	Have You Heard	1971	3.75	7.50	15.00
❏ LSP-4704	I'm Only a Woman	1972	3.75	7.50	15.00
❏ LSP-4811	The Best of Dottie West	1973	3.75	7.50	15.00
❏ CPL1-7047	Collector's Series	1985	2.50	5.00	10.00

STARDAY

❏ SLP-302 [M]	Country Girl Singing Sensation	1964	10.00	20.00	40.00

UNITED ARTISTS

❏ UA-LA740-G	When It's Just You and Me	1977	2.50	5.00	10.00
❏ UA-LA860-G	Dottie	1978	2.50	5.00	10.00
❏ LT-1000	Special Delivery	1980	2.50	5.00	10.00

Number	Title (A Side/B Side)	Yr	VG	VG+	NM

WEST, DOTTIE, AND DON GIBSON Also see each artist's individual listings.
45s
RCA VICTOR

Number	Title (A Side/B Side)	Yr	VG	VG+	NM
❏ 47-9715	Rings of Gold/Final Examination	1969	—	3.00	6.00
❏ 47-9867	Till I Can't Take It Anymore/I Love You Because	1970	—	3.00	6.00
❏ 74-0178	Sweet Memories/How's the World Treating You	1969	—	3.00	6.00
❏ 74-0291	There's a Story (Goin' 'Round)/Lock, Stock and Teardrops	1969	—	3.00	6.00

Albums
RCA VICTOR

❏ LSP-4131	Dottie and Don	1969	5.00	10.00	20.00

WEST, LESLIE Also see MOUNTAIN; WEST, BRUCE & LAING.
12-Inch Singles
PASSPORT

❏ 6061 [DJ]	Love Is Forever (same on both sides)	1987	—	3.00	6.00

45s
PHANTOM

❏ ?B-10301	E.S.P./Don't Burn Me	1975	—	2.00	4.00

WINDFALL

❏ 530	This Wheel's On Fire/Dreams of Milk and Honey	1969	—	2.50	5.00
❏ 531	Blood of the Sun/Long Red	1969	—	2.50	5.00

7-Inch Extended Plays
PHANTOM

❏ JF-10424 [DJ]	Honey/Dear Prudence//Get It Up/The Setting Sun	1975	2.50	5.00	10.00

Albums
I.R.S.

❏ 82016	Alligator	1989	3.75	7.50	15.00

PASSPORT

❏ PB-6061	Theme	1987	3.00	6.00	12.00

PHANTOM

❏ BPL1-0954	The Great Fatsby	1975	3.00	6.00	12.00
❏ BPL1-1258	The Leslie West Band	1976	3.00	6.00	12.00

WINDFALL

❏ 4500	Mountain	1969	3.75	7.50	15.00

WEST, MAE
45s
DAGONET

❏ 6	Put the Loot in the Boot, Santa/With Love from Me to You	1966	3.75	7.50	15.00

DECCA

❏ 29452	Love Is the Greatest Thing/All of Me	1955	3.75	7.50	15.00
❏ 32738	The Sayings of Mae West/More Sayings of Mae West	1970	2.50	5.00	10.00

MGM

❏ 14491	Great Balls of Fire/Naked Ape	1973	2.00	4.00	8.00

TOWER

❏ 260	Day Tripper/Treat Him Right	1966	2.50	5.00	10.00
❏ 260 [PS]	Day Tripper/Treat Him Right	1966	5.00	10.00	20.00
❏ 261	Shakin' All Over/If You Gotta Go	1966	2.50	5.00	10.00
❏ 261 [PS]	Shakin' All Over/If You Gotta Go	1966	5.00	10.00	20.00

20TH CENTURY FOX

❏ 6718	Hard to Handle/You Gotta Taste All the Fruit	1968	2.50	5.00	10.00
❏ 6718 [PS]	Hard to Handle/You Gotta Taste All the Fruit	1968	6.25	12.50	25.00

Albums
DAGONET

❏ DG-4 [M]	Wild Christmas	1966	7.50	15.00	30.00
❏ DGS-4 [S]	Wild Christmas	1966	10.00	20.00	40.00

DECCA

❏ DL 9016 [M]	The Fabulous Mae West	1955	15.00	30.00	60.00
—All-black label with silver print					
❏ DL 9016 [M]	The Fabulous Mae West	1960	7.50	15.00	30.00
—Black label with colorband					
❏ DL 79016 [R]	The Fabulous Mae West	1960	3.75	7.50	15.00
❏ DL 79176	The Original Voice Tracks from Her Greatest Movies	1970	3.75	7.50	15.00

MCA

❏ 2053	The Fabulous Mae West	1974	3.00	6.00	12.00
—Reissue of Decca LP					

MEZZOTONE

❏ 1 [10]	Mae West Songs, Vol. 1	1952	25.00	50.00	100.00
❏ 2 [10]	Mae West Songs, Vol. 2	1952	25.00	50.00	100.00

MGM

❏ SE-4869	Great Balls of Fire	1972	5.00	10.00	20.00

ROUND

❏ RS-100	Under the Mistletoe with Mae West	1977	5.00	10.00	20.00

TOWER

❏ ST 5028 [S]	Way Out West	1966	10.00	20.00	40.00
❏ T 5028 [M]	Way Out West	1966	7.50	15.00	30.00

WEST, MARSHALL
45s
PARKWAY

❏ 878	This House Is Gonna Live/I Hurt Myself	1963	3.00	6.00	12.00

WEST, RED
45s
DOT

❏ 16268	Midnight Ride/Unforgiven	1961	5.00	10.00	20.00

JARO

❏ 77031	FBI Story/What Must I Do	1960	12.50	25.00	50.00

SANTO

❏ 9006	Bossa Nova Mamza/My Babe	1963	3.75	7.50	15.00

WEST, SONNY
45s
ATLANTIC

❏ 1174	Rave On!/Call On Cupid	1958	10.00	20.00	40.00

NOR VA JAK

❏ 1956	Rock-Ola Ruby/Sweet Rockin' Baby	1959	25.00	50.00	100.00
—As "Sonee West"					

WEST, BRUCE & LAING Also see JACK BRUCE; LESLIE WEST.
45s
WINDFALL

❏ 45751	Shake Ma Thing (Rollin' Jack)/The Doctor	1973	—	2.50	5.00
❏ 45829	Why Don'tcha/Mississippi Queen	1973	—	2.50	5.00

Albums
WINDFALL

❏ CQ 31929 [Q]	Why Dontcha	1972	5.00	10.00	20.00
❏ KC 31929	Why Dontcha	1972	3.00	6.00	12.00
❏ CQ 32216 [Q]	Whatever Turns You On	1973	5.00	10.00	20.00
❏ KC 32216	Whatever Turns You On	1973	3.00	6.00	12.00
❏ KC 32899	Live 'N' Kickin'	1974	3.00	6.00	12.00

WEST COAST POP ART EXPERIMENTAL BAND, THE
45s
AMOS

❏ 119	Free As a Bird/Where's My Daddy	1969	3.75	7.50	15.00

REPRISE

❏ 0552	Shifting Sands/1906	1967	6.25	12.50	25.00
❏ 0582	Help, I'm a Rock/Transparent Day	1967	6.25	12.50	25.00
❏ 0776	Smell of Incense/Unfree Child	1968	6.25	12.50	25.00

Albums
AMOS

❏ AAS-7004	Where's My Daddy	1969	12.50	25.00	50.00

FIFO

❏ M 101	West Coast Pop Art Experimental Band	1966	125.00	250.00	500.00
—With plain cardboard cover					
❏ M 101	West Coast Pop Art Experimental Band	1966	1000.	1500.	2000.
—With regular cover					

RAZZBERRY SAWFLY

❏ 800	West Coast Pop Art Experimental Band	1980	25.00	50.00	100.00
—Reissue of Fifo LP					

REPRISE

❏ R 6247 [M]	The West Coast Pop Art Experimental Band, Part One	1967	20.00	40.00	80.00
❏ RS 6247 [S]	The West Coast Pop Art Experimental Band, Part One	1967	25.00	50.00	100.00
❏ R 6270 [M]	The West Coast Pop Art Experimental Band, Vol. 2	1967	20.00	40.00	80.00
❏ RS 6270 [S]	The West Coast Pop Art Experimental Band, Vol. 2	1967	25.00	50.00	100.00
❏ R 6298 [M]	Vol. 3: A Child's Guide to Good and Evil	1968	50.00	100.00	200.00
—May exist only as a white label promo					
❏ RS 6298 [S]	Vol. 3: A Child's Guide to Good and Evil	1968	25.00	50.00	100.00

SUNDAZED

❏ LP 5036 [(2)]	West Coast Pop Art Experimental Band, Volume One	1997	3.75	7.50	15.00

WESTON, KIM Also see MARVIN GAYE AND KIM WESTON.
45s
ENTERPRISE

❏ 9101	Beautiful People/Goodness Gracious	1974	—	2.50	5.00

GORDY

❏ 7041	I'll Never See My Love Again/A Thrill a Moment	1965	5.00	10.00	20.00
❏ 7046	Take Me in Your Arms (Rock Me A Little While)/Don't Compare Me to Her	1965	5.00	10.00	20.00
❏ 7050	Helpless/A Love Like Yours (Don't Come Knocking Every Day)	1966	5.00	10.00	20.00

MGM

❏ 13720	I Got What You Need/Someone Like You	1967	5.00	10.00	20.00
❏ 13804	That's Groovy/Land of Tomorrow	1967	5.00	10.00	20.00
❏ 13881	Nobody/You're Just the Kind of Guy	1967	5.00	10.00	20.00
❏ 13927	Lift Every Voice and Sing/This Is America	1968	5.00	10.00	20.00
❏ 13928	The Impossible Dream/When Johnny Comes Marching Home	1968	3.75	7.50	15.00
❏ 13992	I Will Understand/Thankful	1968	3.75	7.50	15.00

PEOPLE

❏ 1001	Danger, Heartbreak Ahead/I'll Be Thinkin'	1970	2.50	5.00	10.00

PRIDE

❏ 1	Lift Every Voice and Sing/This Is America	1970	2.50	5.00	10.00

TAMLA

❏ 54076	It Should Have Been Me/Love Me All the Way	1963	12.50	25.00	50.00
❏ 54085	Just Loving You/Another Train Coming	1963	12.50	25.00	50.00
❏ 54100	Looking for the Right Guy/Feel Alright Tonight	1964	12.50	25.00	50.00
❏ 54100 [DJ]	Looking for the Right Guy	1964	18.75	37.50	75.00
—One-sided white-label promo (B-side blank)					
❏ 54106	A Little More Love/Go Ahead and Laugh	1964	25.00	50.00	100.00
❏ 54110	I'm Still Loving You/Go Ahead and Laugh	1964	15.00	30.00	60.00

VOLT

❏ 1502	If I Had My Way/Gonna Be Alright	1971	3.75	7.50	15.00
❏ 1503	Little By Little, Bit By Bit/(B-side unknown)	1971	3.75	7.50	15.00

Albums
MGM

❏ E-4477 [M]	For the First Time	1967	7.50	15.00	30.00
❏ SE-4477 [S]	For the First Time	1967	10.00	20.00	40.00
❏ SE-4561	This Is America	1968	10.00	20.00	40.00

VOLT

❏ VOS-6014	Kim, Kim, Kim	1971	6.25	12.50	25.00

WESTON, PAUL Also see JONATHAN AND DARLENE EDWARDS.
45s
CAPITOL

❏ F826	Fairy Tales/Am I Wasting My Time	1950	3.75	7.50	15.00
—Note: Earlier Paul Weston 45s on Capitol may exist					
❏ F833	Big Movie Show in the Sky/Little Gray House	1950	3.75	7.50	15.00
❏ F890	La Vie En Rose/Les Feviles Mortes	1950	3.75	7.50	15.00
❏ F918	Orchids in the Moonlight/I'll Be Seeing You	1950	3.75	7.50	15.00
❏ F949	Panama/Original Dixieland One-Step	1950	3.75	7.50	15.00
❏ F1022	I'll Get By/Blue Prelude	1950	3.75	7.50	15.00
❏ F1251	Autumn Leaves/No Other Love	1950	3.75	7.50	15.00
❏ F1495	Hot Canary/La Raspa	1951	3.75	7.50	15.00
❏ F1640	Deep Purple/Etude	1951	3.75	7.50	15.00
—Reissue of 78 rpm from 1948					
❏ F1670	Laura/Intermezzo	1951	3.75	7.50	15.00
—Reissue					
❏ 4350	The Thrill Is Gone/I Love You	1960	2.00	4.00	8.00

W

Number	Title (A Side/B Side)	Yr	VG	VG+	NM
COLUMBIA					
❏ 39000	So Long Sally/These Foolish Things	1950	3.75	7.50	15.00
❏ 39114	When You Return/In Your Arms	1950	3.75	7.50	15.00
❏ 39160	So Long/Across the Wide Missouri	1951	3.00	6.00	12.00
❏ 39210	Lonesome Gal/				
	Never Let the Sun Set on a Quarrel	1951	3.00	6.00	12.00
❏ 39424	Morningside/What Will I Tell	1951	3.00	6.00	12.00
❏ 39465	Bonne Nuit/Maybe It's Because	1951	3.00	6.00	12.00
❏ 39508	Stardust/When Your Lover Has Gone	1951	2.50	5.00	10.00
❏ 39509	Moon Song/Among My Souvenirs	1951	2.50	5.00	10.00
❏ 39510	Then I'll Be Tired of You/My Silent Love	1951	2.50	5.00	10.00
❏ 39511	Yesterdays/Under a Blanket of Blue	1951	2.50	5.00	10.00
—The above four comprise a box set					
❏ 39569	Story of Love/And So to Sleep	1951	3.00	6.00	12.00
❏ 39608	What'll I Do/One Night of Love	1951	2.50	5.00	10.00
❏ 39609	Wonderful One/Sweethearts	1951	2.50	5.00	10.00
❏ 39610	I'll Follow My Secret Heart/All Alone	1951	2.50	5.00	10.00
❏ 39611	Together/I'll See You Again	1951	2.50	5.00	10.00
—The above four comprise a box set					
❏ 39616	Charmaine/At Dawning	1951	3.00	6.00	12.00
❏ 39644	You Were Meant for Me/S'Posin'	1952	2.50	5.00	10.00
❏ 39645	This Can't Be Love/Why Shouldn't I?	1952	2.50	5.00	10.00
❏ 39646	Embraceable You/Pennies from Heaven	1952	2.50	5.00	10.00
❏ 39647	How High the Moon/Over the Rainbow	1952	2.50	5.00	10.00
—The above four comprise a box set					
❏ 39662	Charmaine/Jealousy (Jalousie)	1952	3.00	6.00	12.00
—B-side by Frankie Laine; part of a box set					
❏ 39666	Low in Lehigh Valley/Flapperette	1952	3.00	6.00	12.00
❏ 39736	So Help Me/Beautiful Ohio	1952	3.00	6.00	12.00
❏ 39864	Forgetting You/Wonderful Copenhagen	1952	3.00	6.00	12.00
❏ 39968	Anna/Dutch Treat	1953	3.00	6.00	12.00
❏ 40014	Shane/Gigi	1953	3.00	6.00	12.00
❏ 40086	You're the Right One/Planters Punch	1953	3.00	6.00	12.00
❏ 40152	Autumn in Rome/Indiscretion	1954	2.50	5.00	10.00
❏ 40237	The Bells of Notre Dame/I Went Out of My Way	1954	2.50	5.00	10.00
❏ 40292	Bimbo/Champagne Wine	1954	2.50	5.00	10.00
❏ 40359	The Song from Desiree/Maria, Maria, Maria	1954	3.00	6.00	12.00
❏ 40385	Tara's Theme/Love Letters	1954	3.00	6.00	12.00
❏ 40484	A Streetcar Named Desire/				
	For Whom the Bell Tolls	1955	3.00	6.00	12.00
❏ 40527	The Kentuckian Song/You and You Alone	1955	3.00	6.00	12.00
❏ 40561	Nice Work If You Can Get It/A Chance at Love	1955	2.50	5.00	10.00
❏ 40605	Memories of You/Naked Sea	1956	2.50	5.00	10.00
❏ 40675	Theme from My Foolish Heart/Infatuation	1956	2.50	5.00	10.00
❏ 40737	The Kentuckian Song/				
	Love Theme from "La Strada"	1956	2.50	5.00	10.00
❏ 40861	Ten Minutes Ago/Where Is Cinderella	1957	2.50	5.00	10.00
❏ 40876	Mardi Gras/Storyville	1957	2.50	5.00	10.00
❏ 40901	High Society/Riverfront Blues	1957	2.50	5.00	10.00
7-Inch Extended Plays					
COLUMBIA					
❏ B-293 [PS]	Melodies for a Sentimental Mood	195?	2.50	5.00	10.00
—Gatefold cover for 5-1085 and 5-1086					
❏ 5-1085	You Were Meant for Me/Over the Rainbow//Why				
	Shouldn't I/Embraceable You	195?	2.50	5.00	10.00
—Alternate numbers are "B-293-1" and "B-293-4"					
❏ 5-1086	S'Posin'/How High the Moon//This Can't Be				
	Love/Pennies from Heaven	195?	2.50	5.00	10.00
—Alternate numbers are "B-293-2" and "B-293-3"					
❏ 5-1327 (?)	I'm Yours/Charmaine//Beautiful Ohio/At				
	Dawning (I Love You)	195?	2.50	5.00	10.00
—Alternate number is B-1584					
❏ B-1584 [PS]	Paul Weston Spotlite	195?	2.50	5.00	10.00
❏ 5-1848	Autumn in Rome/Jennie's Song//The Song of				
	Bernadette/Love Letters	195?	2.50	5.00	10.00
—Alternate numbers are "B-369-1" and "B-369-4"					
❏ B-2569	*Tara's Theme/Infatuation/Anna/Stardust	195?	2.50	5.00	10.00
❏ B-2569 [PS]	Paul Weston (Hall of Fame Series)	195?	2.50	5.00	10.00
❏ B-7941	(contents unknown)	195?	2.50	5.00	10.00
❏ B-7941 [PS]	Love Music from Hollywood, Vol. 1	195?	2.50	5.00	10.00
❏ B-7942	Theme from "Spellbound"/Theme from "Odd				
	Man Out"//Theme from "King's Row"/Theme				
	from "Diane"	195?	2.50	5.00	10.00
❏ B-7942 [PS]	Love Music from Hollywood, Vol. 2	195?	2.50	5.00	10.00
❏ B-7943	Theme from "Now Voyager"/Theme from				
	"Wuthering Heights"//Theme from "Dark				
	Victory"/Theme from "Lost Horizon"	195?	2.50	5.00	10.00
❏ B-7943 [PS]	Love Music from Hollywood, Vol. 3	195?	2.50	5.00	10.00
❏ B-9091	*Moonlight Becomes You/But Not for Me/It				
	Never Entered My Mind/				
	I Remember You from Somewhere	1956	2.50	5.00	10.00
❏ B-9091 [PS]	Moonlight Becomes You, Vol. 1	1956	2.50	5.00	10.00
❏ B-9092	(contents unknown)	1956	2.50	5.00	10.00
❏ B-9092 [PS]	Moonlight Becomes You, Vol. 2	1956	2.50	5.00	10.00
❏ B-9093	(contents unknown)	1956	2.50	5.00	10.00
❏ B-9093 [PS]	Moonlight Becomes You, Vol. 3	1956	2.50	5.00	10.00
Albums					
CAPITOL					
❏ H 222 [10]	Music for Dreaming	195?	10.00	20.00	40.00
❏ T 1153 [M]	Floatin' Like a Feather	1959	3.00	6.00	12.00
❏ ST 1154 [S]	Music for Dreaming	1959	3.75	7.50	15.00
❏ T 1154 [M]	Music for Dreaming	1959	3.00	6.00	12.00
❏ ST 1192 [S]	Music for the Fireside	1959	3.75	7.50	15.00
❏ T 1192 [M]	Music for the Fireside	1959	3.00	6.00	12.00
❏ ST 1222 [S]	Music for Memories	1959	3.75	7.50	15.00
❏ T 1222 [M]	Music for Memories	1959	3.00	6.00	12.00
❏ ST 1563 [S]	Music for My Love	1961	3.75	7.50	15.00
❏ T 1563 [M]	Music for My Love	1961	3.00	6.00	12.00
❏ ST-91212	Romantic Reflections	196?	3.75	7.50	15.00
—Capitol Record Club exclusive					
COLUMBIA					
❏ CL 572 [M]	Caribbean Cruise	1955	3.75	7.50	15.00
❏ CL 693 [M]	Mood for 12	1955	3.75	7.50	15.00
❏ CL 794 [M]	Love Music from Hollywood	1956	3.75	7.50	15.00
❏ CL 879 [M]	Solo Mood	1956	3.75	7.50	15.00
❏ CL 909 [M]	Moonlight Becomes You	1956	3.75	7.50	15.00
❏ CL 977 [M]	Crescent City	1956	3.75	7.50	15.00

Number	Title (A Side/B Side)	Yr	VG	VG+	NM
❏ CL 1112 [M]	Hollywood	1958	3.75	7.50	15.00
❏ CL 6232 [10]	Whispers in the Dark	195?	10.00	20.00	40.00
CORINTHIAN					
❏ 107	Cinema Cameos	198?	2.00	4.00	8.00
❏ 109	Easy Jazz	198?	2.00	4.00	8.00
❏ 116	Crescent City	198?	2.00	4.00	8.00
HARMONY					
❏ KH 31578	Paul Weston Plays Jerome Kern	1972	2.50	5.00	10.00
❏ KH 31603	Paul Weston Plays Jerome Kern, Vol. 2	1972	2.50	5.00	10.00

WET WILLIE

Number	Title (A Side/B Side)	Yr	VG	VG+	NM
45s					
CAPRICORN					
❏ 0008	Shout Bamalama/Airport	1972	—	3.00	6.00
❏ 0022	Shout Bamalama/Airport	1973	—	3.00	6.00
❏ 0031	Country Side of Life/In Our Hearts	1973	—	3.00	6.00
❏ 0043	Keep On Smilin'/Soul Jones	1974	—	3.00	6.00
❏ 0052	Keep On Smilin'/Country Side of Life	1975	—	2.00	4.00
—"Back to Back Hits" reissue					
❏ 0206	Keep On Smilin'/Soul Jones	1974	—	2.00	4.00
❏ 0212	Country Side of Life/Don't Wait Too Long	1974	—	2.00	4.00
❏ 0224	Leona/Ain't He a Mess	1975	—	2.00	4.00
❏ 0231	Dixie Rock/She's My Lady	1975	—	2.00	4.00
❏ 0254	Everything That 'Cha Do (Will Come Back to				
	You)/Walkin' By Myself	1976	—	2.00	4.00
❏ 0260	Comic Book Hero/Baby Fat	1976	—	2.00	4.00
❏ 8020	Rock and Roll Band/Dirty Leg	1971	2.00	4.00	8.00
EPIC					
❏ 50478	Street Corner Serenade/We Got Lovin'	1977	—	2.00	4.00
❏ 50528	Let It Shine/Make You Feel Love Again	1978	—	2.00	4.00
❏ 50714	Weekend/Mr. Streamline	1979	—	2.00	4.00
❏ 50760	The Hard Way/Ramona	1979	—	2.00	4.00
Albums					
CAPRICORN					
❏ CP 0109	Wet Willie II	1972	3.00	6.00	12.00
❏ CP 0113	Drippin' Wet/Live	1973	3.00	6.00	12.00
❏ CP 0128	Keep on Smilin'	1974	2.50	5.00	10.00
❏ CP 0138	Wet Willie	1974	2.50	5.00	10.00
—Reissue of 861					
❏ CP 0149	Dixie Rock	1975	2.50	5.00	10.00
❏ CP 0166	The Wetter the Better	1976	2.50	5.00	10.00
❏ CP 0182	Left Coast Live	1977	2.50	5.00	10.00
❏ CP 0200	Greatest Hits	1978	2.50	5.00	10.00
❏ SD 861	Wet Willie	1971	3.75	7.50	15.00
EPIC					
❏ JE 34983	Manorisms	1977	2.50	5.00	10.00
❏ JE 35794	Which One's Willie?	1979	2.50	5.00	10.00

WHALEFEATHERS, THE

Number	Title (A Side/B Side)	Yr	VG	VG+	NM
Albums					
NASCO					
❏ 9003	The Whalefeathers Declare	1969	25.00	50.00	100.00
❏ 9005	The Whalefeathers	1970	25.00	50.00	100.00

WHAT FOUR, THE

Number	Title (A Side/B Side)	Yr	VG	VG+	NM
45s					
CAPITOL					
❏ 5449	Anything for a Laugh/				
	Baby Can't You Hear Me Call Your Name	1965	3.00	6.00	12.00
COLUMBIA					
❏ 43711	Baby, I Dig Love/It's Hard to Live on Promises	1966	3.00	6.00	12.00
DESTINATION					
❏ 633	We Could Be Happy/Where Love Can Go	1967	3.00	6.00	12.00
—As "What For"					
ESP-DISK'					
❏ 109	Our Love Should Last Forever/(B-side unknown)	1966	7.50	15.00	30.00
MERCURY					
❏ 72716	Dandelion Wine/				
	You're Wishin' I Was Someone Else	1967	6.25	12.50	25.00
—As "Whatt Four"					
REPRISE					
❏ 0387	Gemini 4/Night Surf	1965	6.25	12.50	25.00
TOWER					
❏ 404	Asparagus/Stop in the Name of Love	1968	3.00	6.00	12.00

WHAT-KNOTS, THE

Number	Title (A Side/B Side)	Yr	VG	VG+	NM
45s					
DIAL					
❏ 4067	I Ain't Dead Yet/Talkin' 'Bout Our Breakup	1967	6.25	12.50	25.00

WHEEL MEN, THE   GARY USHER was in this group.

Number	Title (A Side/B Side)	Yr	VG	VG+	NM
45s					
WARNER BROS.					
❏ 5480	Hon-Da Beach/School Is a Gas	1964	12.50	25.00	50.00

WHEELER, BILLY EDD

Number	Title (A Side/B Side)	Yr	VG	VG+	NM
45s					
CAPITOL					
❏ 4149	Humperdink (The Coon Huntin' Monkey)/				
	Baby Martin	1975	—	2.50	5.00
❏ 4231	The Hole (In Uncle Vincent's Wooden Leg)/				
	Dust Marks	1976	—	2.50	5.00
KAPP					
❏ 595	On the Outside (Lookin' In)/				
	The Right Foot in His World	1964	2.50	5.00	10.00
❏ 606	The Bachelor/Anne	1964	2.50	5.00	10.00
❏ 617	Ode to the Little Brown Shack Out Back/				
	Goin' Down to Town	1964	2.50	5.00	10.00
❏ 617	Ode to the Little Brown Shack Out Back/				
	Sister Sara	1964	2.50	5.00	10.00
❏ 655	Burning Bridges/Tonight I'm Singing Just for You	1965	2.00	4.00	8.00
❏ 670	Jackson/The Politician's Dog	1965	2.00	4.00	8.00
❏ 687	Hillbilly Bossa Nova/				
	The Waltz of Miss Sarah Green	1965	2.00	4.00	8.00
❏ 739	The Coming of the Roads/				
	The Doves of San Morey	1966	2.00	4.00	8.00
❏ 845	Half a Man/She	1967	2.00	4.00	8.00

Number	Title (A Side/B Side)	Yr	VG	VG+	NM
❏ 873	High Flying Bird/They Can't Put It Back	1967	2.00	4.00	8.00
❏ 928	I Ain't the Worryin' Kind/It's More Than Home	1968	2.00	4.00	8.00
NSD					
❏ 47	Mama's Going Down in the Mine/Time to Make Love	1980	—	2.50	5.00
❏ 84	Bald Headed Men/The Spinster and the Cowboy	1981	—	2.50	5.00
❏ 94	Daddy/Long Arm of the Law	1981	—	2.50	5.00
—With Rashell Richmond					
❏ 108	In Your Spanish Eyes/The Memory	1981	—	2.50	5.00
❏ 124	Pepsi/Chain Gang of Love	1982	—	2.50	5.00
RADIO CINEMA					
❏ 001	Duel Under the Snow/Ode to the Little Brown Shack Out Back	1979	2.00	4.00	8.00
RCA VICTOR					
❏ 47-9898	The Day After Tomorrow/Soon As Buddy Gets Home	1970	—	3.00	6.00
❏ 47-9943	Woman's Talkin' Liberation Blues/Little Lucy	1971	—	3.00	6.00
❏ 48-1001	Ode to a Critter/Sally	1971	—	3.00	6.00
❏ 74-0610	Plutebobelle/Gifts	1971	—	3.00	6.00
❏ 74-0656	Betty Bow Legs/Does Mel Tillis Really Stutter	1972	—	3.00	6.00
❏ 74-0739	200 Lbs. o' Slingin' Hound/The Hoedown	1972	—	3.00	6.00
❏ 74-0832	The Girl Who Loved the Man Who Robbed the Bank at Santa Fe/Gabriel's Horn	1972	—	3.00	6.00
❏ 74-0881	Gentle Big Man/Peter Gonzales	1973	—	3.00	6.00
UNITED ARTISTS					
❏ 50507	West Virginia Woman/One Stop	1969	—	3.50	7.00
❏ 50579	Fried Chicken and a Country Tune/One Excuse	1969	—	3.50	7.00
❏ 50583	Bow of Love/Young Billy Young	1969	—	3.50	7.00
❏ 50597	Coon Hunters/Fried Chicken and a Country Tune	1969	—	3.50	7.00
Albums					
FLYING FISH					
❏ FF-085	Wild Mountain Flowers	1979	3.00	6.00	12.00
FOLKWAYS					
❏ 31014	When Kentucky Had No Union Men	196?	5.00	10.00	20.00
KAPP					
❏ KL-1351 [M]	A New Bag of Songs Written and Sung by Billy Edd Wheeler	1964	3.75	7.50	15.00
❏ KL-1425 [M]	Memories of America/Ode to the Little Brown Shack Out Back	1965	3.75	7.50	15.00
❏ KL-1443 [M]	Wheeler Man	1965	3.75	7.50	15.00
❏ KL-1479 [M]	Goin' Town and Country	1966	3.75	7.50	15.00
❏ KL-1533 [M]	Paper Birds	1967	5.00	10.00	20.00
❏ KS-3351 [S]	A New Bag of Songs Written and Sung by Billy Edd Wheeler	1964	5.00	10.00	20.00
❏ KS-3425 [S]	Memories of America/Ode to the Little Brown Shack Out Back	1965	5.00	10.00	20.00
❏ KS-3443 [S]	Wheeler Man	1965	5.00	10.00	20.00
❏ KS-3479 [S]	Goin' Town and Country	1966	5.00	10.00	20.00
❏ KS-3533 [S]	Paper Birds	1967	3.75	7.50	15.00
❏ KS-3567	I Ain't the Worryin' Kind	1968	3.75	7.50	15.00
MONITOR					
❏ MF-354 [M]	Billy Edd U.S.A.	1961	7.50	15.00	30.00
❏ MF-367 [M]	Billy Edd and Bluegrass	1962	7.50	15.00	30.00
RCA VICTOR					
❏ LSP-4491	Love	1971	3.75	7.50	15.00
UNITED ARTISTS					
❏ UAS-6711	Nashville Zodiac	1969	3.75	7.50	15.00

WHEELER, MARY, AND THE KNIGHTS
45s

Number	Title (A Side/B Side)	Yr	VG	VG+	NM
ATOM					
❏ 701	A Falling Tear/I Feel in My Heart	196?	10.00	20.00	40.00

WHEELER, ONIE
45s

Number	Title (A Side/B Side)	Yr	VG	VG+	NM
CHARTA					
❏ 122	I Don't Believe We're Through/Pick Up the Pieces	1978	—	3.00	6.00
❏ 129	Lucie Ann's Song/I Don't Believe We're Through	1978	—	3.00	6.00
❏ 148	Onie's Bop/I'd Rather Scratch with the Chickens	1979	—	3.00	6.00
COLUMBIA					
❏ 4-21371	Little Mama/She Wiggled and Giggled	1955	5.00	10.00	20.00
❏ 4-21418	My Home Is Not a Home at All/That's What I Like	1955	5.00	10.00	20.00
❏ 4-21454	Cut It Out/I'm Satisfied with My Dreams	1955	5.00	10.00	20.00
❏ 4-21500	No I Don't Guess I Will/I Tried and I Tried	1956	5.00	10.00	20.00
❏ 4-21523	Onie's Bop/I Wanna Hold My Baby	1956	15.00	30.00	60.00
❏ 4-40707	A Beggar for Your Love/A Booger Gonna Getcha	1956	12.50	25.00	50.00
❏ 4-40911	Steppin' Out/Going Back to the City	1957	3.75	7.50	15.00
EPIC					
❏ 9540	What About Tomorrow/Sunnyland Farmer	1962	2.50	5.00	10.00
JAB					
❏ 9003	Just Leave Her to Me/Water Your Flower	1967	2.00	4.00	8.00
❏ 9013	Dirt Behind My Years/Burn Another Honky Tonk Down	1968	2.00	4.00	8.00
K-ARK					
❏ 606	Too Hot to Handle/I Need to Go Home	196?	3.75	7.50	15.00
❏ 617	You're Getting All Over Me/All Day, All Night, Always	196?	3.75	7.50	15.00
❏ 620	Go Home/I Saw Mother with God Last Night	196?	3.75	7.50	15.00
❏ 626	White Lightning Cherokee/Stubborn Heart	196?	3.75	7.50	15.00
❏ 671	Too Hot to Handle/I Need to Go Home	1966	2.50	5.00	10.00
❏ 856	Please Don't Plant Pretty Flowers/Which-A-Way, That-A-Way	197?	2.00	4.00	8.00
MUSICOR					
❏ 1096	I'm Gonna Hang My Britches Up/You're Too Good for Me	1965	2.50	5.00	10.00
❏ 1121	Her Porch Came Up to My Knees/Pretty Little Tomboy	1965	2.50	5.00	10.00
OKEH					
❏ 18022	When We All Get There/Run 'Em Off	1952	7.50	15.00	30.00
❏ 18026	Mother Prayed Loud in Her Sleep/A Million Years in Glory	195?	6.25	12.50	25.00
❏ 18037	Closing Time/I'll Swear You Don't Love Me	195?	6.25	12.50	25.00
❏ 18049	Love Me Like You Used to Do/Little Mama	195?	7.50	15.00	30.00

Number	Title (A Side/B Side)	Yr	VG	VG+	NM
❏ 18058	Would You Like to Wear a Crown/I Saw Mother with God Last Night	1954	6.25	12.50	25.00
RANWOOD					
❏ 1025	EIO (The Sawmill Man)/Train to Louisville	1975	—	3.00	6.00
ROYAL AMERICAN					
❏ 76	John's Been Shucking My Corn/Make 'Em All Go Home	1973	—	2.50	5.00
❏ 85	Shuckin' My Way to the Hall of Fame/I Can't Pass an Orchard	1973	—	2.50	5.00
STARDAY					
❏ 767	Mr. Free/Dancing	1966	2.50	5.00	10.00
❏ 785	Playing Tricks/I Closed My Book Last Night	1966	2.50	5.00	10.00
SUN					
❏ 315	Jump Right Out of This Jukebox/Tell 'Em Off	1959	7.50	15.00	30.00
UNITED ARTISTS					
❏ 716	Wanted for Robbery/Who Put Out the Fire	1964	3.00	6.00	12.00

WHEELERS, THE
45s

Number	Title (A Side/B Side)	Yr	VG	VG+	NM
CENCO					
❏ 107	Once I Had a Girl/Shine 'Em On	196?	15.00	30.00	60.00

WHEELS, BURT, AND THE SPEEDSTERS
Albums

Number	Title (A Side/B Side)	Yr	VG	VG+	NM
CORONET					
❏ CX-216 [M]	Sounds of the Big Racers	196?	6.25	12.50	25.00
❏ CXS-216 [S]	Sounds of the Big Racers	196?	7.50	15.00	30.00

WHEELS, THE (1) British group.
45s

Number	Title (A Side/B Side)	Yr	VG	VG+	NM
AURORA					
❏ 157	Bad Little Woman/Don't You Know	1966	6.25	12.50	25.00

WHEELS, THE (2)
45s

Number	Title (A Side/B Side)	Yr	VG	VG+	NM
FOLLY					
❏ 800	Clap Your Hands (Part 1)/Clap Your Hands (Part 2)	1959	3.75	7.50	15.00

WHEELS, THE (3)
45s

Number	Title (A Side/B Side)	Yr	VG	VG+	NM
IMPACT					
❏ 1029	Dancing in the Streets/A Taste of Money	1967	6.25	12.50	25.00

WHEELS, THE (4)
45s

Number	Title (A Side/B Side)	Yr	VG	VG+	NM
LOST-NITE					
❏ 109	My Heart's Desire/Let's Have a Ball	196?	2.00	4.00	8.00
PREMIUM					
❏ 405	My Heart's Desire/Let's Have a Ball	1956	15.00	30.00	60.00
❏ 408	Teasin' Heart/Loco	1956	20.00	40.00	80.00
❏ 410	I Can't Forget/How Could I Ever Leave Me	1956	37.50	75.00	150.00

WHEELS, THE (5)
45s

Number	Title (A Side/B Side)	Yr	VG	VG+	NM
ROULETTE					
❏ 4271	No One But You/I've Waited for a Lifetime	1960	5.00	10.00	20.00

WHEELS, THE (U)
45s

Number	Title (A Side/B Side)	Yr	VG	VG+	NM
TIME					
❏ 1003	Where Were You/So Young and So In Love	1958	20.00	40.00	80.00

WHIPPOORWILLS, THE
45s

Number	Title (A Side/B Side)	Yr	VG	VG+	NM
JOSIE					
❏ 892	Deep Within/Going to a Party	1961	15.00	30.00	60.00
VITA					
❏ 1005	Blue Raindrops/I Must Have Holes in My Head	195?	25.00	50.00	100.00

WHIPS, THE More than one group.
45s

Number	Title (A Side/B Side)	Yr	VG	VG+	NM
DORE					
❏ 502	Yes, Master/Rosie's Blues	1958	5.00	10.00	20.00
FLAIR					
❏ 1025	Pleadin' Heart/She Done Me Wrong	1954	200.00	400.00	800.00
MGM					
❏ 13401	Whip It on Me, Baby/First Dance Fear	1965	3.00	6.00	12.00

WHIRLERS, THE
45s

Number	Title (A Side/B Side)	Yr	VG	VG+	NM
PORT					
❏ 70025	Tonight and Forever/Magic Mirror	1961	5.00	10.00	20.00
WHIRLIN' DISC					
❏ 108	Tonight and Forever/Magic Mirror	1956	20.00	40.00	80.00

WHIRLWINDS, THE
45s

Number	Title (A Side/B Side)	Yr	VG	VG+	NM
GUYDEN					
❏ 2052	Angel Love/The Mountain	1961	7.50	15.00	30.00
PHILIPS					
❏ 40139	Heartbeat/At the Party	1963	31.25	62.50	125.00

WHISPERS, THE Well-known male R&B vocal group.
12-Inch Singles

Number	Title (A Side/B Side)	Yr	VG	VG+	NM
CAPITOL					
❏ SPRO 10230 [DJ]	Come On Home (Album Version) (Heavy D Remix)	1995	2.00	4.00	8.00
❏ V-15598	Innocent (Extended Mix) (Heat of the Heat Mix) (Midnight & You Mix) (Instrumental) (Whispers Groove)	1990	—	3.50	7.00
❏ V-15637	Is It Good to You (Fel the Heat Remix) (Feel the Heat Instrumental) (Midnight and You Remix) (Midnight and You Dub) (Whispers Jazzy Remix)	1990	—	3.50	7.00
❏ SPRO-79803 [DJ]	I Want 2B the 14U (same on both sides)	1991	2.00	4.00	8.00
SOLAR					
❏ ED 5017 [DJ]	Contagious (LP Version) (Edit Version)/Keep Your Love Around	1984	2.00	4.00	8.00

Number	Title (A Side/B Side)	Yr	VG	VG+	NM
❏ ED 5036 [DJ]	Some Kinda Lover (same on both sides)	1984	2.00	4.00	8.00
❏ ED 5055 [DJ]	Don't Keep Me Waiting (4:08) (4:36)	1985	2.50	5.00	10.00
❏ AS-11565 [DJ]	Emergency (4:18 stereo/4:18 mono)	1982	3.00	6.00	12.00
❏ YD-11591	Can't Do Without Love (5:22)				
	(same on both sides?)	1979	3.00	6.00	12.00
❏ YD-11895	And the Beat Goes On (7:30)/				
	Can You Do the Boogie (6:07)	1979	5.00	10.00	20.00
❏ YD-12052	Out the Box/Welcome Into My Dream	1980	3.00	6.00	12.00
❏ YD-12155	It's a Love Thing (unknown versions)	1980	3.75	7.50	15.00
❏ YD-12233	I Can Make It Better/Say You				
	(Would Love for Me Too)	1980	3.00	6.00	12.00
❏ YD-12299	This Kind of Lovin'/What Will I Do	1981	3.00	6.00	12.00
❏ 67930	Tonight (6:10)/Small Talkin' (4:06)	1983	2.50	5.00	10.00
❏ 67980	Love Is Where You Find It (5:20)/Say Yes	1982	2.50	5.00	10.00
❏ V-71153	Rock Steady (Vocal) (Instrumental)/				
	Are You Going My Way	1987	2.00	4.00	8.00
❏ V-71163	No Pain No Gain (7 versions)	1988	2.00	4.00	8.00
SOUL TRAIN					
❏ SD-10997	Make It with You/You Are Number One	1977	3.75	7.50	15.00
45s					
CANADIAN AMERICAN					
❏ 179	It's Rainin', It's Pourin'/Tomorrow's On Your Side	1964	7.50	15.00	30.00
CAPITOL					
❏ S7-18394	Make Sweet Love to Me/My Funny Valentine	1995	—	—	3.00
❏ S7-18727	Come On Home/Better Watch Your Heart	1995	—	—	3.00
❏ 7PRO-79170/215	Innocent (7" Edit)/(Club Edit)	1990	2.00	4.00	8.00
—Vinyl is promo only					
DORE					
❏ 724	It Only Hurts for a Little While/The Happy One	1964	6.25	12.50	25.00
❏ 729	Slow Jerk/Never Again	1965	5.00	10.00	20.00
❏ 735	The Dip/Weirdo	1965	5.00	10.00	20.00
❏ 740	As I Sit Here/Shake It, Shake It	1965	5.00	10.00	20.00
❏ 751	Doctor Love/Lonely Avenue	1966	5.00	10.00	20.00
❏ 758	Walkin' the Fat Man/				
	I Was Born When You Kissed Me	1966	5.00	10.00	20.00
❏ 768	Take a Lesson from the Teacher/				
	Claire De Looney	1966	5.00	10.00	20.00
❏ 792	You Got a Man on Your Hands/				
	You Can't Fight What's Right	1967	3.75	7.50	15.00
❏ 794	Needle in a Haystack/Waltz for You	1967	3.75	7.50	15.00
❏ 833	Never Again/I Was Born When You Kissed Me	1969	3.00	6.00	12.00
❏ 842	The Dip/It Only Hurts for a Little While	1970	2.50	5.00	10.00
FONTANA					
❏ 1564	My Long and Sleepless Night/Knowin'	1966	5.00	10.00	20.00
JANUS					
❏ 140	There's a Love for Everyone/It Sure Ain't Pretty	1970	—	3.00	6.00
❏ 150	Your Love Is So Doggone Good/Cracker Jack	1971	—	3.00	6.00
❏ 174	Can't Help But Love You/A Hopeless Situation	1971	—	3.00	6.00
❏ 184	I Only Meant to Wet My Feet/				
	You Fill My Life with Music	1972	—	3.00	6.00
❏ 200	Somebody Loves You/Can We Love Forever	1972	—	3.00	6.00
❏ 212	POW-MIA/Does She Care	1973	—	3.00	6.00
❏ 222	Feel Like Comin' Home/				
	I Love the Way You Make Me Feel	1973	—	3.00	6.00
❏ 231	A Mother for My Children/				
	What More Can a Girl Ask For	1973	—	3.00	6.00
❏ 238	Bingo/Once More with Feeling	1974	—	3.00	6.00
❏ 244	What More Can a Girl Ask For/Broken Home	1974	—	3.00	6.00
❏ 247	All I Ever Do (Is Dream of You)/				
	Here Comes Tomorrow	1975	—	3.00	6.00
❏ 253	You're What's Been Missing in My Life/				
	Given a Little Love	1975	—	3.00	6.00
SOLAR					
❏ YB-11246	(Let's Go) All the Way/Chocolate Girl	1978	—	2.00	4.00
❏ GB-11328	Living Together (In Sin)/One for the Money	1978	—	—	3.00
—Gold Standard Series					
❏ YB-11353	(Olivia) Lost and Turned Out/				
	Try and Make It Better	1978	—	2.00	4.00
❏ YB-11449	Happy Holidays to You/Try and Make It Better	1978	—	3.00	6.00
❏ YB-11590	Can't Do Without Love/Headlights	1979	—	2.00	4.00
❏ YB-11685	Homemade Lovin'/You'll Never Get Away	1979	—	2.00	4.00
❏ YB-11739	A Song for Donny/(Instrumental)	1979	—	2.00	4.00
❏ YB-11739 [PS]	A Song for Donny/(Instrumental)	1979	—	3.00	6.00
❏ YB-11894	And the Beat Goes On/Can You Do the Boogie	1980	—	2.00	4.00
❏ YB-11928	Lady/I Love You	1980	—	2.00	4.00
❏ GB-11977	(Let's Go) All the Way/Lost and Turned Out	1980	—	—	3.00
—Gold Standard Series					
❏ YB-12050	Out the Box/Welcome Into My Dream	1980	—	2.00	4.00
❏ YB-12154	It's a Love Thing/Girl I Need You	1981	—	2.00	4.00
❏ GB-12230	And the Beat Goes On/Lady	1981	—	—	3.00
—Gold Standard Series					
❏ YB-12232	I Can Make It Better/Say You				
	(Would Love for Me Too)	1981	—	2.00	4.00
❏ YB-12295	This Kind of Lovin'/What Will I Do	1981	—	2.00	4.00
❏ YB-13005	I'm the One for You/I'm Gonna Love You More	1981	—	2.00	4.00
❏ GB-13486	It's a Love Thing/Make That Move	1983	—	—	3.00
—Gold Standard Series; B-side by Shalamar					
❏ 47961	In the Raw/Small Talkin'	1982	—	2.00	4.00
❏ 48008	Emergency/Only You	1982	—	2.00	4.00
❏ 48008 [PS]	Emergency/Only You	1982	—	3.00	6.00
❏ 69639	Don't Keep Me Waiting/Suddenly	1985	—	2.00	4.00
❏ 69658	Some Kinda Lover/Never Too Late	1985	—	2.00	4.00
❏ 69683	Contagious/(B-side unknown)	1984	—	2.00	4.00
❏ 69809	This Time/Love for Real	1983	—	2.00	4.00
❏ 69827	Keep On Lovin' Me/Try It Again	1983	—	2.00	4.00
❏ 69842	Tonight/Small Talkin'	1983	—	2.00	4.00
❏ 69965	Love Is Where You Find It/Say Yes	1982	—	2.00	4.00
❏ B-70006	Rock Steady/Are You Going My Way	1987	—	—	3.00
❏ B-70012	Just Gets Better with Time/Say Yes	1987	—	—	3.00
❏ B-70017	In the Mood/(Instrumental)	1987	—	—	3.00
❏ B-70020	No Pain, No Gain/(Instrumental)	1988	—	—	3.00
SOUL CLOCK					
❏ 104	Great Day/I Can't See Myself Leaving	1969	2.50	5.00	10.00
❏ 107	The Time Will Come/Flying High	1969	2.50	5.00	10.00
❏ 109	What Will I Do/Remember	1969	2.50	5.00	10.00
❏ 1001	I Can Remember/Planets of Life	1970	2.00	4.00	8.00

Number	Title (A Side/B Side)	Yr	VG	VG+	NM
❏ 1004	Seems Like I Gotta Do Wrong/				
	Needle in a Haystack	1970	2.00	4.00	8.00
❏ 1005	I'm the One/You Must Be Doing All Right	1970	2.00	4.00	8.00
SOUL TRAIN					
❏ SB-10430	In Love Forever/Fairytale	1975	—	2.50	5.00
❏ SB-10628	(You're a) Special Part of My Life/Grove Street	1976	—	2.50	5.00
❏ SB-10700	One for the Money (Part 1)/One for the Money				
	(Part 2)	1976	—	2.50	5.00
❏ SB-10773	Living Together (In Sin)/I've Got a Feeling	1976	—	2.50	5.00
❏ SB-10878	You're Only As Good As You Think You Are/				
	Sounds Like a Love Song	1977	—	2.50	5.00
❏ SB-10996	Make It with You/You Are Number One	1977	—	2.50	5.00
❏ SB-11139	I'm Gonna Make You My Wife/				
	You Never Miss Your Water	1977	—	2.50	5.00
Albums					
ACCORD					
❏ SN-7100	I Can Remember	1981	2.50	5.00	10.00
ALLEGIANCE					
❏ AV-5004	Excellence	1985	2.50	5.00	10.00
CAPITOL					
❏ C1-92957	More of the Night	1990	3.00	6.00	12.00
DORE					
❏ 338	Shhh	197?	3.00	6.00	12.00
INTERMEDIA					
❏ QS-5075	Doctor Love	198?	2.50	5.00	10.00
JANUS					
❏ JLS-3041	The Whispers' Love Story	1972	12.50	25.00	50.00
❏ JLS-3046	Life and Breath	1973	10.00	20.00	40.00
❏ 7006	Bingo	1974	10.00	20.00	40.00
❏ 7013	Greatest Hits	1975	7.50	15.00	30.00
SOLAR					
❏ S-27	Love Is Where You Find It	1982	2.50	5.00	10.00
❏ BXL1-2270	Open Up Your Love	1978	3.00	6.00	12.00
—Reissue of Soul Train 2270					
❏ BXL1-2774	Headlights	1978	3.00	6.00	12.00
❏ BXL1-3105	Whisper in Your Ear	1979	3.00	6.00	12.00
❏ BXL1-3521	The Whspers	1979	3.00	6.00	12.00
❏ BXL1-3578	Imagination	1980	3.00	6.00	12.00
❏ AYL1-3839	Open Up Your Love	1981	2.00	4.00	8.00
—"Best Buy Series" reissue					
❏ BXL1-3976	This Kind of Lovin'	1981	3.00	6.00	12.00
❏ BXL1-4242	The Best of the Whispers	1982	3.00	6.00	12.00
❏ 60216	Love for Love	1983	2.50	5.00	10.00
❏ 60356	So Good	1984	2.50	5.00	10.00
❏ 60451	Happy Holidays to You	1985	3.00	6.00	12.00
❏ ST-72554	Just Gets Better with Time	1987	2.50	5.00	10.00
❏ PZ 75306	Vintage Whispers	1989	3.00	6.00	12.00
SOUL CLOCK					
❏ 22001	Planets of Life	1969	25.00	50.00	100.00
SOUL TRAIN					
❏ BVL1-1450	One for the Money	1976	3.75	7.50	15.00
❏ BVL1-2270	Open Up Your Love	1977	3.75	7.50	15.00

WHISPERS, THE (2)

45s

GOTHAM

Number	Title (A Side/B Side)	Yr	VG	VG+	NM
❏ 309	Fool Heart/Don't Fool with Lizzie	1953	62.50	125.00	250.00
❏ 312	Are You Sorry/We're Getting Married	1953	375.00	750.00	1500.

WHISPERS, THE (3)

45s

LAURIE

Number	Title (A Side/B Side)	Yr	VG	VG+	NM
❏ 3344	Here Comes Summer/If You Don't Care	1966	5.00	10.00	20.00

WHITCOMB, IAN

45s

JERDEN

Number	Title (A Side/B Side)	Yr	VG	VG+	NM
❏ 735	Soho/Bony Moronie	1964	3.75	7.50	15.00
❏ 747	This Sporting Life/Soho	1964	3.75	7.50	15.00
TOWER					
❏ 120	This Sporting Life/Fizz	1965	2.50	5.00	10.00
❏ 134	You Turn Me On (Turn On Song)/				
	Poor But Honest	1965	3.75	7.50	15.00
❏ 134	Turn On Song/Poor But Honest	1965	6.25	12.50	25.00
❏ 155	N-E-R-V-O-U-S!/The End	1965	2.50	5.00	10.00
❏ 170	18 Whitcomb St./Fizz	1965	2.50	5.00	10.00
❏ 189	No Tears for Johnny/Be My Baby	1966	2.50	5.00	10.00
❏ 192	High Blood Pressure/Good Hard Rock	1966	2.50	5.00	10.00
❏ 212	Lover's Prayer/				
	Your Baby Has Gone Down the Plug Hole	1966	2.50	5.00	10.00
❏ 251	You Won't See Me/				
	Please Don't Put Me on the Shelf	1966	2.50	5.00	10.00
❏ 274	Where Did Robinson Crusoe Go (With Friday on				
	Saturday Night)/Poor Little Bird	1966	3.00	6.00	12.00
❏ 274 [PS]	Where Did Robinson Crusoe Go (With Friday on				
	Saturday Night)/Poor Little Bird	1966	6.25	12.50	25.00
❏ 336	You Really Bent Me Out of Shape/				
	Rolling Home Georgeanne	1967	2.50	5.00	10.00
❏ 355	You Really Bent Me Out of Shape/				
	Rolling Home Georgeanne	1967	2.50	5.00	10.00
❏ 385	Groovy Day/Sally Sails the Sky	1967	2.50	5.00	10.00
❏ 385 [PS]	Groovy Day/Sally Sails the Sky	1967	10.00	20.00	40.00
UNITED ARTISTS					
❏ XW162	They Go Wild, Simply Wild Over Me/Yaaka Hula				
	Hickey Dula	1973	—	3.00	6.00
Albums					
AUDIOPHILE					
❏ AP-115	Treasures of Tin Pan Alley	197?	3.00	6.00	12.00
❏ AP-147	At the Ragtime Ball	1983	3.00	6.00	12.00
FIRST AMERICAN					
❏ 7704	Crooner Tunes	1979	2.50	5.00	10.00
❏ 7725	Red Hot "Blue Heaven"	1980	2.50	5.00	10.00
❏ 7729	The Rock and Roll Years	1981	2.50	5.00	10.00
❏ 7751	Instrumentals	1981	2.50	5.00	10.00
❏ 7789	In Hollywood	1982	2.50	5.00	10.00

Number	Title (A Side/B Side)	Yr	VG	VG+	NM
RHINO					
❑ RNLP-127	The Best of Ian Whitcomb (1964-1968)	1986	2.00	4.00	8.00
SIERRA					
❑ 8708	Pianomelt	1980	2.50	5.00	10.00
TOWER					
❑ DT 5004 [R]	You Turn Me On	1965	5.00	10.00	20.00
❑ T 5004 [M]	You Turn Me On	1965	6.25	12.50	25.00
❑ ST 5042 [S]	Mod, Mod Music Hall	1966	5.00	10.00	20.00
❑ T 5042 [M]	Mod, Mod Music Hall	1966	3.75	7.50	15.00
❑ ST 5071 [S]	Yellow Underground	1967	5.00	10.00	20.00
❑ T 5071 [M]	Yellow Underground	1967	3.75	7.50	15.00
❑ ST 5100	Sock Me Some Rock	1968	5.00	10.00	20.00
UNITED ARTISTS					
❑ UA-LA021-F	Under the Ragtime Moon	1972	2.50	5.00	10.00

WHITCOMB, IAN, AND DICK ZIMMERMAN
Albums

Number	Title (A Side/B Side)	Yr	VG	VG+	NM
AUDIOPHILE					
❑ AP-225	Steppin' Out	1987	2.50	5.00	10.00
STOMP OFF					
❑ SOS-1017	Don't Say Goodbye Miss Ragtime	198?	3.00	6.00	12.00
❑ SOS-1049	My Wife Is Dancing Mad	198?	3.00	6.00	12.00

WHITE, BARRY
12-Inch Singles

Number	Title (A Side/B Side)	Yr	VG	VG+	NM
A&M					
❑ 31458 1027 1	Come On (6 versions)	1995	2.00	4.00	8.00
❑ 31458 8375 1 [DJ]	Practice What You Preach (7 versions)	1994	2.00	4.00	8.00
❑ SP-12237	Sho You Right (Remix) (Instrumental)	1987	—	3.00	6.00
—Black vinyl					
❑ SP-12237 [DJ]	Sho You Right (Remix) (Instrumental)	1987	3.00	6.00	12.00
—White vinyl					
❑ SP-12317	Super Lover (3 versions)	1989	—	3.00	6.00
❑ SP-12327	I Wanna Do It Good to Ya (3 versions)	1989	2.00	4.00	8.00
❑ 18026 [DJ]	I Wanna Do It Good to Ya (5 versions)	1989	—	3.00	6.00
20TH CENTURY					
❑ TCD-88	I Love to Sing the Songs I Sing/(B-side unknown)	1979	3.00	6.00	12.00
❑ TCD-102	How Did You Know It Was Me?/(B-side unknown)	1979	3.00	6.00	12.00
UNLIMITED GOLD					
❑ AS 864 [DJ]	I Believe in Love (3:26) (8:01)	1980	2.50	5.00	10.00
❑ 1403	It Ain't Love, Baby (Until You Give It)/Hung Up in Your Love	1979	3.00	6.00	12.00
❑ AS 1509 [DJ]	Change (4:22) (7:04)	1982	2.50	5.00	10.00
❑ 02429	Louie Louie/Ghetto Letto	1981	2.50	5.00	10.00
❑ 03051	Change/I Like You, You Like Me	1982	2.50	5.00	10.00
❑ 03381	Passion (Long)/Passion (Short)	1982	2.50	5.00	10.00
❑ 03958	America/Life	1983	2.50	5.00	10.00
❑ 04099	Don't Let 'Em Blow Your Mind/Dreams	1983	2.50	5.00	10.00
❑ 70075	Mi Nueva Cancion (Love Makin' Music)/Ella Es Todo Para Mi (She's Everything to Me)	1981	5.00	10.00	20.00

45s

Number	Title (A Side/B Side)	Yr	VG	VG+	NM
A&M					
❑ 31458 0924 7	Practice What You Preach/Come On	1995	—	—	3.00
—Second pressing indeed contains these two songs					
❑ 31458 0924 7	Practice What You Preach/Come On	1995	—	2.50	5.00
—First pressing actually contains Lo-Key?'s "I Got a Thang 4 Ya!"/"Sweet On U," which are otherwise unavailable on 45. Can be identified without playing by checking the trail-off vinyl for a different number than that on the record.					
❑ 1203	Right Night/There's a Place (Where Love Never Ends)	1988	—	—	3.00
❑ 1459	Super Lover/I Wanna Do It Good to Ya	1989	—	—	3.00
❑ 75021 1511 7	When Will I See You Again/Goodnight My Love	1990	—	—	3.00
❑ 2943	Sho' You Right/You're What's On My Mind	1987	—	—	3.00
❑ 2943 [PS]	Sho' You Right/You're What's On My Mind	1987	—	—	3.00
❑ 3000	For Your Love (I'd Do Most Anything)/I'm Ready for Love	1987	—	—	3.00
❑ 3000 [PS]	For Your Love (I'd Do Most Anything)/I'm Ready for Love	1987	—	—	3.00
FARO					
❑ 613	Tracy/Flame of Love	1964	3.75	7.50	15.00
—B-side by the Atlantics					
20TH CENTURY					
❑ (no #) [PS]	"With Love from Barry White"	1975	5.00	10.00	20.00
—Pink and white sleeve issued with some stock copies of "What Am I Gonna Do with You"					
❑ 2018	I'm Gonna Love You Just a Little More Baby/Just a Little More Baby	1973	—	2.50	5.00
❑ 2042	I've Got So Much to Give/I've Got So Much to Give	1973	—	2.50	5.00
❑ 2058	Never Never Gonna Give Ya Up/No, I'm Never Gonna Give Ya Up	1973	—	2.50	5.00
❑ 2077	Honey Please Can't You See/Honey Please Can't You See	1974	—	2.50	5.00
❑ 2120	Can't Get Enough of Your Love, Babe/Just Not Enough	1974	—	2.50	5.00
❑ 2133	You're the First, the Last, My Everything/More Than Anything, You're My Everything	1974	—	2.50	5.00
❑ 2177	What Am I Gonna Do with You/What Am I Gonna Do with You, Baby	1975	—	2.50	5.00
❑ 2208	I'll Do for You Anything You Want Me To/Anything You Want Me To	1975	—	2.50	5.00
❑ 2265	Let the Music Play/(Instrumental)	1975	—	2.50	5.00
❑ 2277	You See the Trouble with Me/I'm So Blue When You Are Too	1976	—	2.50	5.00
❑ 2298	Baby, We Better Try to Get It Together/If You Know, Won't You Tell Me	1976	—	2.50	5.00
❑ 2309	Don't Make Me Wait Too Long/Can't You See It's Only You I Want	1976	—	2.50	5.00
❑ 2328	I'm Qualified to Satisfy You/(Instrumental)	1977	—	2.50	5.00
❑ 2350	It's Ecstasy When You Lay Down Next to Me/Never Thought I'd Fall in Love with You	1977	—	2.50	5.00
❑ 2361	Playing Your Game, Baby/Of All the Guys in the World	1977	—	2.50	5.00
❑ 2365	Oh What a Night for Dancing/You're So Good You're Bad	1978	—	2.50	5.00

Number	Title (A Side/B Side)	Yr	VG	VG+	NM
❑ 2380	Your Sweetness Is My Weakness/It's Only Love Doing Its Thing	1978	—	2.50	5.00
❑ 2395	Just the Way You Are/Now I'm Gonna Make Love to You	1979	—	2.50	5.00
❑ 2416	I Love to Sing the Songs I Sing/Oh Me Oh My	1979	—	2.50	5.00
❑ 2433	How Did You Know It Was Me?/Oh Me Oh My	1979	—	2.50	5.00
UNLIMITED GOLD					
❑ 1401	Any Fool Could See (You Were Meant for Me)/You're the One I Need	1979	—	2.00	4.00
❑ 1404	It Ain't Love, Babe (Until You Give It)/Hung Up in Your Love	1979	—	2.00	4.00
❑ 1411	Love Ain't Easy/I Found Love	1980	—	2.00	4.00
❑ 1415	Sheet Music/(Instrumental)	1980	—	2.00	4.00
❑ 1418	Love Makin' Music/Ella Es Todo Mi (She's Everything to Me)	1980	—	2.00	4.00
❑ 1420	I Believe in Love/You're the One I Need	1980	—	2.00	4.00
❑ 02425	Louie Louie/Ghetto Letto	1981	—	2.00	4.00
❑ 02580	Beware/Tell Me Who Do You Love	1981	—	2.00	4.00
❑ 02956	Change/I Like You, You Like Me	1982	—	2.00	4.00
❑ 03379	Passion/It's All About Love	1982	—	2.00	4.00
❑ 03957	America/Life	1983	—	2.00	4.00
❑ 04098	Don't Let 'Em Blow Your Mind/Dreams	1983	—	2.00	4.00
Albums					
A&M					
❑ SP-5154	The Right Night and Barry White	1987	2.50	5.00	10.00
❑ SP-5256	The Man Is Back!	1990	2.50	5.00	10.00
❑ 75021 5377 1	Put Me in Your Mix	1991	3.00	6.00	12.00
CASABLANCA					
❑ 822782-1	Barry White's Greatest Hits	1984	2.00	4.00	8.00
❑ 822783-1	Barry White's Greatest Hits, Volume 2	1984	2.00	4.00	8.00
SUPREMACY					
❑ SUP-8002	No Limit on Love	1974	3.00	6.00	12.00
—Compilation of older material					
20TH CENTURY					
❑ T-407	I've Got So Much to Give	1973	2.50	5.00	10.00
❑ T-423	Stone Gon'	1973	2.50	5.00	10.00
❑ T-444	Can't Get Enough	1974	2.50	5.00	10.00
❑ T-466	Just Another Way to Say I Love You	1975	2.50	5.00	10.00
❑ T-493	Barry White's Greatest Hits	1975	2.50	5.00	10.00
❑ T-502	Let the Music Play	1976	2.50	5.00	10.00
❑ T-516	Is This Whatcha Wont?	1976	2.50	5.00	10.00
❑ T-543	Barry White Sings for Someone You Love	1977	2.50	5.00	10.00
❑ T-571	Barry White The Man	1978	2.50	5.00	10.00
❑ T-590	I Love to Sing the Songs I Sing	1979	2.50	5.00	10.00
❑ T-599	Barry White's Greatest Hits, Volume 2	1981	2.50	5.00	10.00
UNLIMITED GOLD					
❑ JZ 35763	The Message Is Love	1979	2.50	5.00	10.00
❑ FZ 36208	Barry White's Sheet Music	1980	2.50	5.00	10.00
❑ Z2X 36957 [(2)]	The Best of Our Love	1981	3.00	6.00	12.00
❑ FZ 37176	Beware	1982	2.50	5.00	10.00
❑ FZ 38048	Change	1982	2.50	5.00	10.00
❑ FZ 38711	Dedicated	1983	2.50	5.00	10.00

WHITE, BARRY AND GLODEAN
45s

Number	Title (A Side/B Side)	Yr	VG	VG+	NM
UNLIMITED GOLD					
❑ 02087	I Want You/Our Theme (Part 1)	1981	—	2.00	4.00
❑ 02419	You're the Only One for Me/This Love	1981	—	2.00	4.00
❑ 70064	Didn't We Make It Happen, Baby/Our Theme (Part 2)	1981	—	2.00	4.00

Albums

Number	Title (A Side/B Side)	Yr	VG	VG+	NM
UNLIMITED GOLD					
❑ FZ 37054	Barry and Glodean White	1981	2.50	5.00	10.00

WHITE, BEN, AND THE DARCHAES
45s

Number	Title (A Side/B Side)	Yr	VG	VG+	NM
ALJON					
❑ 1247/8	Jocko Sent Me/Nationwide Stamps	1962	100.00	200.00	400.00

WHITE, JACK
45s

Number	Title (A Side/B Side)	Yr	VG	VG+	NM
HIT					
❑ 197	I've Got a Tiger by the Tail/Whisper Tell Me Sweetly	1965	2.00	4.00	8.00
—B-side by Connie Dee					
❑ 208	10 Little Bottles/Lonely Girl	1965	2.00	4.00	8.00
—B-side by Fred York					

WHITE, LENNY
45s

Number	Title (A Side/B Side)	Yr	VG	VG+	NM
NEMPEROR					
❑ 003	Chicken Fried Steak/(B-side unknown)	1975	—	2.00	4.00
❑ 012	Sweet Dreamer/(B-side unknown)	1976	—	2.00	4.00
Albums					
ELEKTRA					
❑ 6E-121	Adventures of Astral Pirates	1978	2.50	5.00	10.00
❑ 6E-164	Streamline	1978	2.50	5.00	10.00
❑ 6E-223	Best of Friends	1979	2.50	5.00	10.00
❑ 6E-304	Twennynine with Lenny White	1980	2.50	5.00	10.00
❑ 5E-551	Just Like Dreamin'	1981	2.50	5.00	10.00
NEMPEROR					
❑ SD 435	Venusian Summer	1975	3.00	6.00	12.00
❑ SD 441	Big City	1977	3.00	6.00	12.00

WHITE, TONY JOE
12-Inch Singles

Number	Title (A Side/B Side)	Yr	VG	VG+	NM
CASABLANCA					
❑ NBD 20218	I Get Off On It	1980	3.00	6.00	12.00
—B-side is blank					
45s					
ARISTA					
❑ 0376	We'll Live on Love/You and Me Baby	1978	—	2.00	4.00
❑ 0395	It Must Be Love/We'll Live on Love	1979	—	2.00	4.00
CASABLANCA					
❑ 2279	I Get Off on It/Feelin' Loose	1980	—	2.50	5.00
❑ 2304	Mamas Don't Let Your Cowboys Grow Up to Be Babies/Disco Blues	1980	—	2.50	5.00

W

Number	Title (A Side/B Side)	Yr	VG	VG+	NM
COLUMBIA					
❑ 38-03967	Swamp Rap/Living in the River City	1983	—	2.00	4.00
❑ 38-04134	The Lady in My Life/We Belong Together	1983	—	2.00	4.00
❑ 38-04356	We Belong Together/Naughty Lady	1984	—	2.00	4.00
❑ 38-04476	You Just Get Better All the Time/				
	Do You Have a Garter Belt	1984	—	2.00	4.00
❑ 38-04683	Nobody's Baby Tonight/Down by the Border	1984	—	2.00	4.00
MONUMENT					
❑ 1003	Georgia Pines/Ten More Miles to Louisiana	1967	2.00	4.00	8.00
❑ 1053	Watching the Trains Go By/Old Man Willie	1968	2.00	4.00	8.00
❑ 1070	I Protest/Man Can Only Stand So Much Pain	1968	2.00	4.00	8.00
❑ 1086	Soul Francisco/Whompt Out on You	1968	2.00	4.00	8.00
❑ 1104	Polk Salad Annie/Aspen Colorado	1968	2.50	5.00	10.00
❑ 1169	Roosevelt and Ira Lee (Night of the Mossacin)/				
	The Migrant	1969	—	3.00	6.00
—Some, if not all, of these have "Moccasin" misspelled as above					
❑ 1193	High Sheriff/Groupy Girl	1970	—	3.00	6.00
❑ 1206	Save Your Sugar for Me/My Friend	1970	—	3.00	6.00
❑ 1227	Old Man Willis/Scratch My Back	1970	—	3.00	6.00
20TH CENTURY					
❑ 2276	It Must Be Love/Susie-Q	1976	—	2.00	4.00
❑ 2322	Texas Woman/Hold On to Your Hiney	1976	—	2.00	4.00
WARNER BROS.					
❑ 7468	The Daddy/Voodoo Village	1971	—	2.50	5.00
❑ 7477	My Kind of Woman/I Just Walked Away	1971	—	2.50	5.00
❑ 7505	Lustful Earl and the Married Woman/				
	I Just Walked Away	1971	—	2.50	5.00
❑ 7523	Delta Love/That On the Road Look	1971	—	2.50	5.00
❑ 7591	Even Trolls Love Rock and Roll/				
	If I Ever Saw a Good Thing	1972	—	2.50	5.00
❑ 7607	I've Got a Thing About You, Baby/Gospel Singer	1972	—	2.50	5.00
❑ 7712	Backwoods Preacher Man/				
	Saturday Night in Oak Grove, La.	1973	—	2.50	5.00
❑ 7780	Love 'Tween You and Me/Sign of the Lion	1974	—	2.50	5.00
❑ 8042	Wishful Thinking/Don't Let the Door	1974	—	2.50	5.00
Albums					
CASABLANCA					
❑ NBLP 7233	Real Thang	1980	2.50	5.00	10.00
COLUMBIA					
❑ FC 38817	Dangerous	1983	2.50	5.00	10.00
MONUMENT					
❑ SLP-18114	Black and White	1969	3.75	7.50	15.00
❑ SLP-18133	…Continued	1969	3.75	7.50	15.00
❑ SLP-18142	Tony Joe	1970	3.75	7.50	15.00
20TH CENTURY					
❑ T-523	Eyes	1977	3.00	6.00	12.00
WARNER BROS.					
❑ WS 1900	Tony Joe White	1971	3.00	6.00	12.00
❑ BS 2580	The Train I'm On	1972	3.00	6.00	12.00
❑ BS 2708	Homemade Ice Cream	1973	3.00	6.00	12.00

WHITE LIGHT
Albums

Number	Title (A Side/B Side)	Yr	VG	VG+	NM
CENTURY					
❑ 39955	White Light	1968	75.00	150.00	300.00

WHITE PLAINS
45s

Number	Title (A Side/B Side)	Yr	VG	VG+	NM
DERAM					
❑ 85058	My Baby Loves Lovin'/Show Me Your Hand	1970	2.00	4.00	8.00
❑ 85066	Lovin' You Baby/Noises (In My Head)	1970	—	3.00	6.00
❑ 85072	Carolina's Coming Home/				
	Every Little Move She Makes	1971	—	3.00	6.00
❑ 85076	When You Are a King/				
	The World Gets Better with Love	1971	—	3.00	6.00
❑ 85080	I Can't Stop/Julie Anne	1972	—	3.00	6.00
❑ 85086	Step Into a Dream/Look to See	1973	—	3.00	6.00
❑ 85089	Does Anybody Know Where My Baby Is/Just for				
	a Change	1973	—	3.00	6.00
Albums					
DERAM					
❑ DES 18045	My Baby Loves Lovin'	1970	3.75	7.50	15.00

WHITE WITCH
45s

Number	Title (A Side/B Side)	Yr	VG	VG+	NM
CAPRICORN					
❑ 0012	And I'm Leaving/Parabrahm Greeting-				
	Dweller of the Threshold	1972	—	3.00	6.00
❑ 0016	Don't Close Your Mind/You're the One	1973	—	3.00	6.00
❑ 0023	Home Grown Girl/It's So Nice to Be Stoned	1973	—	3.00	6.00
❑ 0025	Home Grown Girl/Help Me Lord	1973	—	3.00	6.00
❑ 0080	Showdown/Walk On	1974	—	3.00	6.00
Albums					
CAPRICORN					
❑ CP 0107	White Witch	1973	6.25	12.50	25.00
❑ CP 0129	A Spiritual Greeting	1974	6.25	12.50	25.00

WHITEMAN, PAUL
45s

Number	Title (A Side/B Side)	Yr	VG	VG+	NM
CAPITOL					
❑ F1668	Travelin' Light/The General Jumped at Dawn	1951	5.00	10.00	20.00
—Reissue of 78 rpm hit from 1942					
❑ F2999	Wang Wang Blues/San	1954	2.50	5.00	10.00
CORAL					
❑ 61228	Whispering/You're Driving Me Crazy	1954	2.50	5.00	10.00
❑ 61254	I Love You/Japanese Sandman	1954	2.50	5.00	10.00
❑ 61273	Saw Your Eyes/There's a Small Hotel	1954	2.50	5.00	10.00
❑ 61336	Mississippi Mud/Then and Now	1955	2.50	5.00	10.00
❑ 61403	Three O'Clock in the Morning/Jukin'	1955	2.50	5.00	10.00
❑ 61516	Charleston/Black Bottom	1955	2.50	5.00	10.00
7-Inch Extended Plays					
CORAL					
❑ EC 81095	Japanese Sandman/I Love You//				
	O Me, O My, O You/Chicago	1954	3.00	6.00	12.00
❑ EC 81095 [PS]	All Time Dance Party, Vol. 2	1954	3.00	6.00	12.00

Number	Title (A Side/B Side)	Yr	VG	VG+	NM
Albums					
CAPITOL					
❑ T 622 [M]	Classics in Jazz	1955	12.50	25.00	50.00
❑ DT 1678 [R]	Paul Whiteman Conducts George Gershwin	1962	3.00	6.00	12.00
❑ T 1678 [M]	Paul Whiteman Conducts George Gershwin	1962	3.75	7.50	15.00
COLUMBIA					
❑ CL 2830 [M]	Paul Whiteman Featuring Bing Crosby	1968	3.75	7.50	15.00
CORAL					
❑ CRL 57021 [M]	The Great Gershwin	1955	5.00	10.00	20.00
GRAND AWARD					
❑ GA-208 SD [S]	Hawaiian Magic	1958	7.50	15.00	30.00
❑ GA-241 SD [S]	The Night I Played at 666 Fifth Ave.	1960	7.50	15.00	30.00
❑ GA-244 SD [S]	Cavalcade of Music	1960	7.50	15.00	30.00
❑ GA-33-351 [M]	Fiddle on Fire	195?	7.50	15.00	30.00
❑ GA-33-356 [M]	Hawaiian Magic	1958	5.00	10.00	20.00
❑ GA-33-409 [M]	The Night I Played at 666 Fifth Ave.	1960	5.00	10.00	20.00
❑ GA-33-412 [M]	Cavalcade of Music	1960	5.00	10.00	20.00
❑ GA-33-502 [M]	Great Whiteman Hits	195?	7.50	15.00	30.00
❑ GA-33-503 [M]	The Greatest Stars of My Life	195?	12.50	25.00	50.00
—In red velvet jacket					
❑ GA-33-901 [(2)M]	Paul Whiteman/50th Anniversary	1956	12.50	25.00	50.00
MARK 56					
❑ 761 [M]	Tribute to Gershwin 1936	197?	3.00	6.00	12.00
RCA VICTOR					
❑ LPV-555 [M]	Paul Whiteman, Volume 1	195?	3.75	7.50	15.00
SUNBEAM					
❑ 18 [M]	In Concert 1927-32	197?	3.00	6.00	12.00
"X"					
❑ LVA-3040 [10]	Paul Whiteman's Orchestra				
	Featuring Bix Beiderbecke	1955	20.00	40.00	80.00

WHITING, MARGARET
45s

Number	Title (A Side/B Side)	Yr	VG	VG+	NM
CAPITOL					
❑ 54-546	A Wonderful Guy/Younger Than Springtime	1949	6.25	12.50	25.00
—Note: Earlier Margaret Whiting 45s on Capitol may exist					
❑ 54-709	Dime a Dozen/Whirlwind	1949	6.25	12.50	25.00
❑ 54-724	It's a Most Unusual Day/St. Louis Blues	1949	6.25	12.50	25.00
❑ F809	You're An Old Smoothie/He's Funny That Way	1950	5.00	10.00	20.00
❑ F841	I Said My Pajamas				
	(And Put On My Pray'rs)/Be Mine	1950	5.00	10.00	20.00
❑ F851	Solid As a Rock/Sure Thing	1950	5.00	10.00	20.00
❑ F874	It Might As Well Be Spring/				
	How Deep Is the Ocean	1950	5.00	10.00	20.00
❑ F879	Come Rain or Come Shine/				
	Dream Peddler's Serenade	1950	5.00	10.00	20.00
❑ F934	My Foolish Heart/Stay with the Happy People	1950	5.00	10.00	20.00
❑ F1027	Razza-Ma-Tazz/I Gotta Get Out of the Habit	1950	5.00	10.00	20.00
❑ F1041	Shawl of Galway Gray/If You Were Only Mine	1950	5.00	10.00	20.00
❑ F1042	Blind Date/Home Cookin'	1950	7.50	15.00	30.00
—With Bob Hope					
❑ F1103	I Didn't Know What Time It Was/				
	This Can't Be Love	1950	5.00	10.00	20.00
❑ F1123	You're Mine You/I've Forgotten You	1950	5.00	10.00	20.00
❑ F1132	Let's Do It Again/Friendly Star	1950	5.00	10.00	20.00
❑ F1160	Don't Rock the Boat/I'm in Love with You	1950	3.75	7.50	15.00
—With Dean Martin					
❑ F1213	I've Never Been in Love Before/				
	The Best Things for You	1950	3.75	7.50	15.00
❑ F1309	Once You Find Your Guy/				
	Man Ain't Nothin' But a Nothin'	1950	3.75	7.50	15.00
❑ F1343	Over and Over and Over/The Moon Was Yellow	1950	3.75	7.50	15.00
❑ F1391	Faithful/Lonesome Gal	1951	3.75	7.50	15.00
❑ F1417	You Are One/Sing You Sinners	1951	3.75	7.50	15.00
❑ F1469	We Kiss in a Shadow/Make Man Love Me	1951	3.75	7.50	15.00
❑ F1491	Something Wonderful/Hello Young Lovers	1951	3.75	7.50	15.00
❑ F1566	Happy, Topper and Me/This Little Pig	1951	3.75	7.50	15.00
❑ F1585	Everlasting/The End of a Love Affair	1951	3.75	7.50	15.00
❑ F1645	It Might As Well Be Spring/How Deep Is the				
	Ocean	1951	3.75	7.50	15.00
—Reissue of 78 rpm hit of 1945					
❑ F1671	Moonlight in Vermont/My Ideal	1951	3.75	7.50	15.00
—Reissue					
❑ F1702	Good Morning, Mr. Echo/River Road Two-Step	1951	3.75	7.50	15.00
❑ F1784	And So to Sleep/Beer Barrel Polka	1951	3.75	7.50	15.00
❑ F1801	Bill/More More More	1951	3.75	7.50	15.00
❑ F1845	That's For Sure/If I Can Love You	1951	3.75	7.50	15.00
❑ F1939	Round and Round/Oops	1952	3.75	7.50	15.00
❑ F1984	Foggy River/Try Me One More Time	1952	3.75	7.50	15.00
❑ F2000	I'll Walk Alone/I Could Write a Book	1952	3.75	7.50	15.00
❑ F2177	Till We Meet Again/				
	The Gods Were Angry with Me	1952	3.75	7.50	15.00
❑ F2217	Alone Together/Outside of Heaven	1952	3.75	7.50	15.00
❑ F2292	Why Don't You Believe Me/				
	Come Back to Me Johnny	1952	3.75	7.50	15.00
❑ F2331	Singing Bells/Take Care My Love	1953	3.75	7.50	15.00
❑ F2489	Something Wonderful Happens/				
	Where Did He Go	1953	3.75	7.50	15.00
❑ F2550	Waltz to the Blues/C.O.D.	1953	3.75	7.50	15.00
❑ F2599	I Just Love You/The Night Holds No Fear	1953	3.75	7.50	15.00
❑ F2681	Kiss or Get Off the Spot/In the Still of the Night	1953	3.75	7.50	15.00
❑ F2717	I Speak to the Stars/It's Nice to Have You Home	1954	3.75	7.50	15.00
❑ F2853	Joey/Ask Me	1954	3.75	7.50	15.00
❑ F2869	How Long Has It Been/Affair of the Heart	1954	3.75	7.50	15.00
❑ F2913	All I Want Is All There Is And Then Some/				
	Can This Be Mine	1954	3.75	7.50	15.00
❑ F2996	My Son, My Son/My Own True Love	1954	3.75	7.50	15.00
❑ F3067	Stowaway/Allah Be Praised	1955	3.00	6.00	12.00
❑ F3189	Mama's Pearls/Man	1955	3.00	6.00	12.00
❑ F3232	Lover Lover/I Kiss You a Million Times	1955	3.00	6.00	12.00
❑ F3314	I Love a Mystery/Bidin' My Time	1956	3.00	6.00	12.00
❑ F3412	Second Time in Love/Old Enough	1956	3.00	6.00	12.00
❑ F3473	True Love/Haunting Love	1956	3.00	6.00	12.00
❑ F3509	Hello Young Lovers/We Kiss in a Shadow	1956	3.00	6.00	12.00
❑ F3586	The Money Tree/Maybe I Love Him	1956	3.00	6.00	12.00
❑ F3666	Tippy Toe/Spring in Maine	1957	3.00	6.00	12.00
❑ 4638	On Second Thought/Who Can You Can	1961	2.50	5.00	10.00

Number	Title (A Side/B Side)	Yr	VG	VG+	NM
DOT					
❑ 15583	Kill Me with Kisses/Speak for Yourself, John	1957	2.50	5.00	10.00
❑ 15680	I Can't Help It (If I'm Still in Love with You)/That's Why I Was Born	1957	2.50	5.00	10.00
❑ 15742	I'm So Lonely I Could Cry/Hot Spell	1958	2.50	5.00	10.00
❑ 15804	Just a Dream/Pretty-Eyed Baby	1958	2.50	5.00	10.00
❑ 15826	I Love You Because/The Waiting Game	1958	2.50	5.00	10.00
❑ 15931	I'm Alone Because I Love You/Top of the Moon	1959	2.50	5.00	10.00
❑ 15973	Half As Much/My Ideal	1959	2.50	5.00	10.00
LONDON					
❑ 101	The Wheel of Hurt/Nothing Lasts Forever	1966	—	3.00	6.00
❑ 106	Just Like a Man/World Inside Your Arms	1967	—	3.00	6.00
❑ 108	Only Love Can Break a Heart/Where Do I Stand	1967	—	3.00	6.00
❑ 115	I Almost Called Your Name/Let's Pretend	1968	—	3.00	6.00
❑ 119	I Hate to See Me Go/It Keeps Right On a Hurtin'	1968	—	3.00	6.00
❑ 122	Faithfully/Am I Losing You	1968	—	3.00	6.00
❑ 124	Maybe Just One More/Can't Get You Out of My Mind	1968	—	3.00	6.00
❑ 126	Love's the Only Answer/Where Was I	1969	—	3.00	6.00
❑ 128	Love Has a Way/At the End of the Ocean	1969	—	3.00	6.00
❑ 132	Theme from Z/Life Goes On	1970	—	2.50	5.00
❑ 137	Until It's Time for You to Go/I'll Tell Him Today	1970	—	2.50	5.00
VERVE					
❑ 10212	Why Was I Born/You Couldn't Be Cuter	1960	2.50	5.00	10.00
❑ 10230	Hey, Look Me Over/What's New at the Zoo	1960	2.50	5.00	10.00
—With Mel Torme					
7-Inch Extended Plays					
CAPITOL					
❑ EAP 1-410	*My Ideal/Moonlight in Vermont/A Tree in the Meadow/It Might As Well Be Spring	195?	3.75	7.50	15.00
❑ EAP 1-410 [PS]	Love Songs	195?	3.75	7.50	15.00
Albums					
AUDIOPHILE					
❑ AP-152	Too Marvelous for Words	198?	2.50	5.00	10.00
❑ AP-173	Come a Little Closer	198?	2.50	5.00	10.00
❑ AP-207	This Lady's in Love with You	1986	2.50	5.00	10.00
CAPITOL					
❑ H 163 [10]	South Pacific	1950	12.50	25.00	50.00
❑ H 209 [10]	Margaret Whiting Sings Rodgers and Hart	1950	12.50	25.00	50.00
❑ H 234 [10]	Songs	1950	12.50	25.00	50.00
❑ T 410 [M]	Love Songs	1954	10.00	20.00	40.00
❑ T 685 [M]	For the Starry-Eyed	1955	10.00	20.00	40.00
DOT					
❑ DLP 3072 [M]	Goin' Places	1957	6.25	12.50	25.00
❑ DLP 3113 [M]	Margaret	1958	3.75	7.50	15.00
❑ DLP 3176 [M]	Margaret Whiting's Great Hits	1959	3.75	7.50	15.00
❑ DLP 3235 [M]	Ten Top Hits	1960	3.75	7.50	15.00
❑ DLP 3337 [M]	Just a Dream	1960	3.75	7.50	15.00
❑ DLP 25113 [S]	Margaret	1958	5.00	10.00	20.00
❑ DLP 25176 [S]	Margaret Whiting's Great Hits	1959	5.00	10.00	20.00
❑ DLP 25235 [S]	Ten Top Hits	1960	5.00	10.00	20.00
❑ DLP 25337 [S]	Just a Dream	1960	5.00	10.00	20.00
HAMILTON					
❑ HLP 143 [M]	My Ideal	196?	3.00	6.00	12.00
❑ HLP 12143 [S]	My Ideal	196?	3.75	7.50	15.00
LONDON					
❑ PS 497 [S]	The Wheel of Hurt	1967	3.75	7.50	15.00
❑ PS 510 [S]	Maggie Isn't Margaret Anymore	1967	3.75	7.50	15.00
❑ PS 527	Pop Country	1968	3.75	7.50	15.00
❑ LL 3497 [M]	The Wheel of Hurt	1967	5.00	10.00	20.00
❑ LL 3510 [M]	Maggie Isn't Margaret Anymore	1967	5.00	10.00	20.00
MGM					
❑ E-4006 [M]	Past Midnight	1961	3.75	7.50	15.00
❑ SE-4006 [S]	Past Midnight	1961	5.00	10.00	20.00
VERVE					
❑ V-4038 [M]	The Jerome Kern Song Book	1960	3.75	7.50	15.00
❑ V6-4038 [S]	The Jerome Kern Song Book	1960	5.00	10.00	20.00

WHITING, MARGARET, AND JIMMY WAKELY

45s

Number	Title (A Side/B Side)	Yr	VG	VG+	NM
CAPITOL					
❑ F800	Broken Down Merry-Go-Round/The Gods Were Angry with Me	1950	5.00	10.00	20.00
❑ F960	Let's Go to Church (Next Sunday Morning)/Why Do You Say Those Things	1950	5.00	10.00	20.00
❑ F1065	Close Your Pretty Eyes/Fools' Paradise	1950	5.00	10.00	20.00
❑ F1234	A Bushel and a Peck/Beyond the Reef	1950	3.75	7.50	15.00
❑ F1255	Silver Bells/Christmas Candy	1950	5.00	10.00	20.00
❑ F1382	Easter Parade/Let's Go to Church	1951	5.00	10.00	20.00
❑ F1500	When You and I Were Young Maggie Blues/Till We Meet Again	1951	3.75	7.50	15.00
❑ F1555	Star of Hope/Why Am I Losing You	1951	3.75	7.50	15.00
❑ F1634	Slipping Around/Wedding Bells	1951	3.75	7.50	15.00
—Reissue of 78 rpm hits from 1948					
❑ F1816	Let's Live a Little/I Don't Want to Be Free	1951	3.75	7.50	15.00
❑ F1965	Give Me More, More, More/Let Old Mother Nature Have Her	1952	3.75	7.50	15.00
❑ F2402	Gomen Nasai/I Learned to Love You Too Late	1953	3.75	7.50	15.00
❑ F2528	My Heart Knows/When Love Goes Wrong	1953	3.75	7.50	15.00
❑ F2689	Tennessee Church Bells/There's a Silver Moon on Golden Gate	1953	3.75	7.50	15.00
❑ F3905	Silver Bells/Christmas Candy	1958	3.00	6.00	12.00
❑ 54-40224	Slipping Around/Wedding Bells	1949	10.00	20.00	40.00
❑ 54-40246	I'll Never Slip Around Again/Six Times a Week and Twice on Sunday	1949	7.50	15.00	30.00

7-Inch Extended Plays

Number	Title (A Side/B Side)	Yr	VG	VG+	NM
CAPITOL					
❑ EAP 1-403	Slipping Around/Wedding Bells//I'll Never Slip Around/Six Times a Week and Twice on Sundays	195?	5.00	10.00	20.00
❑ EAP 1-403 [PS]	Margaret Whiting and Jimmy Wakely Sing	195?	5.00	10.00	20.00

Albums

Number	Title (A Side/B Side)	Yr	VG	VG+	NM
HILLTOP					
❑ JM-6053 [M]	I'll Never Slip Around Again	196?	3.00	6.00	12.00
❑ JS-6053 [R]	I'll Never Slip Around Again	196?	3.00	6.00	12.00

WHITLEY, RAY (1) Cowboy singer; co-wrote "Back in the Saddle Again."

45s

Number	Title (A Side/B Side)	Yr	VG	VG+	NM
ARZEE					
❑ 128	Slightly on the Angel Side/Worlds Apart	197?	—	3.50	7.00

WHITLEY, RAY (2) Best known as a composer; wrote "What Kind of Fool (Do You Think I Am)" for the Tams, among many others.

45s

Number	Title (A Side/B Side)	Yr	VG	VG+	NM
APT					
❑ 25086	I'll Tell the Robin/Runaway	1965	3.00	6.00	12.00
ATTARACK					
❑ 103	Hey Girl Don't Bother Me/Everybody	196?	3.75	7.50	15.00
COLUMBIA					
❑ 4-43607	Just a Boy in Love/The End of My World	1966	2.50	5.00	10.00
❑ 4-43980	Here Today, Gone Tomorrow/Take Back Your Mind	1967	2.50	5.00	10.00
1-2-3					
❑ 1707	Don't Throw Your Love to the Wind/Underdose of Faith	1969	2.50	5.00	10.00
TRX					
❑ 5007	Gotta Go There/1983	1968	2.50	5.00	10.00
VEE JAY					
❑ 414	There Goes a Teardrop/I Wasn't Sure	1961	3.75	7.50	15.00
❑ 433	Yessiree, Yessiree/A Love We Can Have and Hold	1962	6.25	12.50	25.00
❑ 448	It Hurts/Deeper in Love	1962	3.75	7.50	15.00
❑ 521	Teenage Crush/Your Heartaches	1963	3.75	7.50	15.00

WHITLOCK, BOBBY

45s

Number	Title (A Side/B Side)	Yr	VG	VG+	NM
ABC DUNHILL					
❑ 4312	Song for Paula/Where There's a Will, There's a Way	1972	—	2.50	5.00
❑ 4318	Ease Your Pain/Satisfied	1972	—	2.50	5.00
❑ 4326	Hello L.A., Bye Bye Birmingham/Start All Over	1972	—	2.50	5.00
❑ 4332	Tell the Truth/You Came Along	1972	—	2.50	5.00
Albums					
ABC DUNHILL					
❑ DS-50121	Bobby Whitlock	1972	3.00	6.00	12.00
❑ DSX-50131	Raw Velvet	1972	3.00	6.00	12.00
CAPRICORN					
❑ CP 0160	One of a Kind	1975	2.50	5.00	10.00
❑ CP 0168	Rock Your Sox Off	1976	2.50	5.00	10.00

WHITMAN, SLIM

45s

Number	Title (A Side/B Side)	Yr	VG	VG+	NM
CLEVELAND INT'L.					
❑ 02402	Can't Help Falling in Love with You/Oh My Darlin' (I Love You)	1981	—	2.00	4.00
❑ 02544	If I Had My Life to Live Over/Flowers	1981	—	2.00	4.00
❑ 02779	My Melody of Love/Open Up Your Heart	1982	—	2.00	4.00
❑ 03370	Where Is the Christ in Christmas/Sleep My Child (All Through the Night)	1982	—	2.00	4.00
❑ 50912	When/Since You Went Away	1980	—	2.00	4.00
❑ 50946	That Silver-Haired Daddy of Mine/If I Could Only Dream	1980	—	2.00	4.00
❑ 50957	Where Is the Christ in Christmas/Sleep My Child (All Through the Night)	1980	—	2.00	4.00
❑ 50971	I Remember You/Where Do I Go from Here	1981	—	2.00	4.00
EPIC					
❑ 04358	Blue Memories/Cry Baby Heart	1983	—	2.00	4.00
❑ 04549	Four Walls/Tryin' to Outrun the Wind	1984	—	2.00	4.00
IMPERIAL					
❑ 5731	Remember Me/Just Call Me Lonesome	1961	2.50	5.00	10.00
❑ 5746	The Bells That Broke My Heart/I'd Climb the Highest Mountain	1961	2.50	5.00	10.00
❑ 5766	Once in a Lifetime/When I Call on You	1961	2.50	5.00	10.00
❑ 5778	The Old Spinning Wheel/In a Hundred Years	1961	2.50	5.00	10.00
❑ 5791	Yesterday's Love/It Sure Looks Lonesome Outside	1961	2.50	5.00	10.00
❑ 5821	Valley of Tears/Annie Laurie	1962	2.50	5.00	10.00
❑ 5859	I Forgot More Than You'll Ever Know (About Her)/Backward, Turn Backward	1962	2.50	5.00	10.00
❑ 5871	Blues Stay Away from Me/You Have My Heart	1962	2.50	5.00	10.00
❑ 5900	The Wayward Wind/Straight from Heaven	1962	2.50	5.00	10.00
❑ 5919	Love Letters in the Sand/You're the Only One	1963	2.50	5.00	10.00
❑ 5938	What'll I Do/So Long Mary	1963	2.50	5.00	10.00
❑ 5966	Broken Down Merry-Go-Round/Never	1963	2.50	5.00	10.00
❑ 5990	My Wild Irish Rose/Chime Bells	1963	2.50	5.00	10.00
❑ 8134	Love Song of the Waterfall/My Love's Growing Stale	1951	6.25	12.50	25.00
❑ 8144	Bandera Waltz/End of the World	1952	6.25	12.50	25.00
❑ 8147	Cold Empty Arms/In a Hundred Years or More	1952	6.25	12.50	25.00
❑ 8156	Indian Love Call/China Doll	1952	6.25	12.50	25.00
—Black vinyl					
❑ 8156	Indian Love Call/China Doll	1952	12.50	25.00	50.00
—Opaque red vinyl					
❑ 8163	By the Waters of the Winnetonka/An Amateur in Love	1952	6.25	12.50	25.00
❑ 8169	Keep It a Secret/My Heart Is Broken in Threes	1952	6.25	12.50	25.00
❑ 8180	How Can I Tell/All That I'm Asking Is Sympathy	1953	6.25	12.50	25.00
❑ 8189	Restless Heart/Song of the Old Water Wheel	1953	6.25	12.50	25.00
❑ 8194	Once Before/Have Mercy on Me	1953	6.25	12.50	25.00
❑ 8201	Danny Boy/There's a Rainbow in Every Teardrop	1953	6.25	12.50	25.00
❑ 8208	North Wind/Darlin' Don't Cry	1953	6.25	12.50	25.00
❑ 8223	Secret Love/Why	1954	5.00	10.00	20.00
❑ 8236	Rose-Marie/We Stood at the Altar	1954	5.00	10.00	20.00
❑ 8257	Beautiful Dreamer/Ride Away	1954	5.00	10.00	20.00
❑ 8267	Singing Hills/I Hate to See You Cry	1954	5.00	10.00	20.00
❑ 8281	Cattle Call/When I Grow Too Old to Dream	1954	5.00	10.00	20.00
❑ 8290	Roll On Silvery Moon/Haunted Hungry Heart	1955	5.00	10.00	20.00
❑ 8298	I'll Never Stop Loving You/I'll Never Take You Back Again	1955	5.00	10.00	20.00
❑ 8299	Song of the Wild/You Have My Heart	1955	5.00	10.00	20.00
❑ 8304	Tumbling Tumbleweeds/Tell Me	1955	5.00	10.00	20.00

Number	Title (A Side/B Side)	Yr	VG	VG+	NM
❏ 8305	I'm a Fool/Serenade	1956	5.00	10.00	20.00
❏ 8307	The Whiffenpoof Song/Dear Mary	1956	5.00	10.00	20.00
❏ 8308	Smoke Signals/Curtain of Tears	1956	5.00	10.00	20.00
❏ 8309	Careless Love/I Must Have Been Blind	1957	3.75	7.50	15.00
❏ 8310	I'll Take You Home Again Kathleen/				
	Lovesick Blues	1957	3.75	7.50	15.00
❏ 8312	Unchain My Heart/Hush-a-Bye	1957	3.75	7.50	15.00
❏ 8316	A Very Precious Love/Careless	1958	3.75	7.50	15.00
❏ 8317	Candy Kisses/Tormented	1958	3.75	7.50	15.00
❏ 8318	When It's Springtime in the Rockies/				
	Put Your Trust in Me	1958	3.75	7.50	15.00
❏ 8319	At the End of Nowhere/Wherever You Are	1958	3.75	7.50	15.00
❏ 8320	The Letter Edged in Black/I Never See Maggie	1959	3.75	7.50	15.00
❏ 8321	A Tree in the Meadow/What Kind of God	1959	3.75	7.50	15.00
❏ 8322	A Fool Such As I/The Prisoner's Song	1959	3.75	7.50	15.00
❏ 8323	Indian Love Call/Haunted Hungry Heart	1960	3.00	6.00	12.00
❏ 8326	Roll, River, Roll/Twilla Lee	1960	3.00	6.00	12.00
❏ 8327	Sunrise/I'll Walk with God	1960	3.00	6.00	12.00
❏ 8328	A Lonesome Heart/The Wind	1960	3.00	6.00	12.00
❏ 8329	Vaya Con Dios/Ramona	1960	3.00	6.00	12.00
❏ 66002	Maria Elena/Gortamona	1963	2.50	5.00	10.00
❏ 66012	Tell Me Pretty Words/Only You And You Alone	1964	2.00	4.00	8.00
❏ 66040	I'll Hold You in My Heart (Till I Can Hold You in				
	My Arms)/No Other Arms, No Other Lips	1964	2.00	4.00	8.00
❏ 66077	Love Song of the Waterfall/Virginia	1964	2.00	4.00	8.00
❏ 66103	Mansion on the Hill/Reminiscing	1965	2.00	4.00	8.00
❏ 66130	More Than Yesterday/La Golondrina	1965	2.00	4.00	8.00
❏ 66153	The Twelfth of Never/Straight from Heaven	1966	2.00	4.00	8.00
❏ 66181	I Remember You/Travelin' Man	1966	2.50	5.00	10.00
❏ 66212	One Dream/Jerry	1966	2.00	4.00	8.00
❏ 66226	What's This World a-Comin' To/You Bring Out				
	the Best in Me	1967	2.00	4.00	8.00
❏ 66248	I'm a Fool/North Wind	1967	2.00	4.00	8.00
❏ 66262	The Keeper of the Key/Broken Wings	1967	2.00	4.00	8.00
❏ 66283	Rainbows Are Back in Style/				
	How Could I Not Love You	1968	—	3.00	6.00
❏ 66311	Happy Street/My Heart Is In the Roses	1968	—	3.00	6.00
❏ 66337	Livin' On Lovin' (And Lovin' Livin' with You)/				
	Heaven Says Hello	1968	—	3.00	6.00
❏ 66358	My Happiness/Promises	1969	—	3.00	6.00
❏ 66384	Irresistible/Flower of Love	1969	—	3.00	6.00
❏ 66411	When You Were 16/Love Song of the Waterfall	1969	—	3.00	6.00
❏ 66441	Tomorrow Never Comes/Come Take My Hand	1970	—	3.00	6.00

RCA VICTOR

Number	Title (A Side/B Side)	Yr	VG	VG+	NM
❏ 47-5431	There's a Rainbow in Every Teardrop/I'm				
	Casting My Lasso	1953	6.25	12.50	25.00
❏ 47-5557	Birmingham Jail/Wabash Waltz	1953	6.25	12.50	25.00
❏ 47-5724	I'll Never Pass This Way Again/Please Paint a				
	Rose on the Garden Wall	1954	6.25	12.50	25.00
❏ 48-0069	Please Paint a Rose on the Garden Wall/Tears				
	Can Never Drown the Flame	1949	15.00	30.00	60.00
—Green vinyl					
❏ 48-0145	I'll Never Pass This Way Again/Birmingham Jail	1949	15.00	30.00	60.00
—Green vinyl					
❏ 48-0358	I'm Crying for You/Wabash Waltz	1950	15.00	30.00	60.00
—Green vinyl					

UNITED ARTISTS

Number	Title (A Side/B Side)	Yr	VG	VG+	NM
❏ 0138	Indian Love Call/China Doll	1973	—	2.00	4.00
—"Silver Spotlight Series" reissue					
❏ 0139	Rose Marie/Secret Love	1973	—	2.00	4.00
—"Silver Spotlight Series" reissue					
❏ XW178	Hold Me/So Close to Home	1973	—	2.50	5.00
❏ XW269	Where the Lilacs Grow/Something Beautiful	1973	—	2.50	5.00
❏ XW402	It's All in the Game/Make Believe	1974	—	2.50	5.00
❏ XW530	Happy Anniversary/What I Had with You	1974	—	2.00	4.00
❏ XW619	The Most Beautiful Girl/Foolish Question	1975	—	2.00	4.00
❏ XW690	Everything Leads Back to You/				
	I'm Beginning to Love You	1975	—	2.00	4.00
❏ XW731	Mexicali Rose/				
	As You Take a Walk Through My Mind	1975	—	2.00	4.00
❏ XW1022	Red River Valley/Somewhere My Love	1977	—	2.00	4.00
❏ 50697	Shutters and Boards/I Pretend	1970	—	2.50	5.00
❏ 50731	Guess Who/From Heaven to Heartache	1970	—	2.50	5.00
❏ 50775	Something Beautiful (To Remember)/Jerry	1971	—	2.50	5.00
❏ 50806	It's a Sin to Tell a Lie/That's Enough for Me	1971	—	2.50	5.00
❏ 50852	Loveliest Night of the Year/Near You	1971	—	2.50	5.00
❏ 50899	Little Drops of Silver/Tammy	1972	—	2.50	5.00
❏ 50952	(It's No) Sin/(B-side unknown)	1972	—	2.50	5.00

7-Inch Extended Plays

IMPERIAL

Number	Title (A Side/B Side)	Yr	VG	VG+	NM
❏ IMP 104	(contents unknown)	1954	12.50	25.00	50.00
❏ IMP 104 [PS]	America's Favorite Folk Artist	1954	12.50	25.00	50.00
❏ IMP-130	Love Song of the Waterfall/Bandera Waltz//				
	Beautiful Dreamer/Rose Marie	1956	10.00	20.00	40.00
❏ IMP-130 [PS]	Slim Whitman Singing…	1956	10.00	20.00	40.00
❏ IMP-131	In a Hundred Years or More/Why//Secret Love/				
	Singing Hills	1956	10.00	20.00	40.00
❏ IMP-131 [PS]	Songs by Slim Whitman	1956	10.00	20.00	40.00
❏ IMP-132	(contents unknown)	1956	10.00	20.00	40.00
❏ IMP-132 [PS]	Songs by Slim Whitman	1956	10.00	20.00	40.00
❏ IMP-133	When My Blue Moon Turns to Gold/Blue Eyes				
	Crying in the Rain//That Silver Haired Daddy				
	of Mine/A Petal from a Faded Rose	1956	10.00	20.00	40.00
❏ IMP-133 [PS]	Songs by Slim Whitman	1956	10.00	20.00	40.00
❏ IMP-134	(contents unknown)	1956	10.00	20.00	40.00
❏ IMP-134 [PS]	Songs by Slim Whitman	1956	10.00	20.00	40.00
❏ IMP-135	(contents unknown)	1956	10.00	20.00	40.00
❏ IMP-135 [PS]	Slim Whitman	1956	10.00	20.00	40.00
❏ IMP-136	(contents unknown)	1956	10.00	20.00	40.00
❏ IMP-136 [PS]	Songs by Slim Whitman	1956	10.00	20.00	40.00
❏ IMP-137	Roll On Silvery Moon/End of the World//Restless				
	Heart/There's a Rainbow in Every Teardrop	1956	10.00	20.00	40.00
❏ IMP-137 [PS]	Slim Whitman	1956	10.00	20.00	40.00

Albums

CLEVELAND INT'L.

Number	Title (A Side/B Side)	Yr	VG	VG+	NM
❏ AS99-875 [DJ]	Songs I Love to Sing	1980	7.50	15.00	30.00
—Promo-only picture disc					
❏ JE 36768	Songs I Love to Sing	1980	2.50	5.00	10.00
❏ JE 36847	Christmas with Slim Whitman	1980	3.00	6.00	12.00
❏ FE 37403	Mr. Songman	1982	2.50	5.00	10.00

COLUMBIA SPECIAL PRODUCTS

Number	Title (A Side/B Side)	Yr	VG	VG+	NM
❏ P 16323	Christmas with Slim Whitman	1981	2.50	5.00	10.00

EPIC

Number	Title (A Side/B Side)	Yr	VG	VG+	NM
❏ PE 36768	Songs I Love to Sing	198?	2.00	4.00	8.00
—Reissue of Cleveland Int'l. JE 36768					
❏ PE 36847	Christmas with Slim Whitman	1981	2.00	4.00	8.00
—Reissue of Cleveland Int'l. JE 36847					

IMPERIAL

Number	Title (A Side/B Side)	Yr	VG	VG+	NM
❏ LP-3004 [10]	America's Favorite Folk Artist	1954	150.00	300.00	600.00
❏ LP-9003 [M]	Favorites	1956	12.50	25.00	50.00
—Maroon label					
❏ LP-9003 [M]	Favorites	1958	7.50	15.00	30.00
—Black label with stars on top					
❏ LP-9003 [M]	Favorites	1964	5.00	10.00	20.00
—Black and pink label					
❏ LP-9003 [M]	Favorites	1966	3.75	7.50	15.00
—Black and green label					
❏ LP-9026 [M]	Slim Whitman Sings	1957	12.50	25.00	50.00
—Maroon label					
❏ LP-9026 [M]	Slim Whitman Sings	1958	7.50	15.00	30.00
—Black label with stars on top					
❏ LP-9026 [M]	Slim Whitman Sings	1964	5.00	10.00	20.00
—Black and pink label					
❏ LP-9026 [M]	Slim Whitman Sings	1966	3.75	7.50	15.00
—Black and green label					
❏ LP-9056 [M]	Slim Whitman Sings	1958	7.50	15.00	30.00
—Black label with stars on top					
❏ LP-9056 [M]	Slim Whitman Sings	1958	12.50	25.00	50.00
—Maroon label					
❏ LP-9056 [M]	Slim Whitman Sings	1964	5.00	10.00	20.00
—Black and pink label					
❏ LP-9056 [M]	Slim Whitman Sings	1966	3.75	7.50	15.00
—Black and green label					
❏ LP-9064 [M]	Slim Whitman Sings	1959	7.50	15.00	30.00
—Black label with stars on top					
❏ LP-9064 [M]	Slim Whitman Sings	1964	5.00	10.00	20.00
—Black and pink label					
❏ LP-9064 [M]	Slim Whitman Sings	1966	3.75	7.50	15.00
—Black and green label					
❏ LP-9088 [M]	I'll Walk with God	1960	7.50	15.00	30.00
—Black label with stars on top					
❏ LP-9088 [M]	I'll Walk with God	1964	5.00	10.00	20.00
—Black and pink label					
❏ LP-9088 [M]	I'll Walk with God	1966	3.75	7.50	15.00
—Black and green label					
❏ LP-9102 [M]	Million Record Hits	1960	7.50	15.00	30.00
—Black label with stars on top					
❏ LP-9102 [M]	Million Record Hits	1964	5.00	10.00	20.00
—Black and pink label					
❏ LP-9102 [M]	Million Record Hits	1966	3.75	7.50	15.00
—Black and green label					
❏ LP-9135 [M]	Slim Whitman's First Visit to Britain	1960	6.25	12.50	25.00
—Black label with stars on top					
❏ LP-9135 [M]	Slim Whitman's First Visit to Britain	1964	3.75	7.50	15.00
—Black and pink label					
❏ LP-9135 [M]	Slim Whitman's First Visit to Britain	1966	3.00	6.00	12.00
—Black and green label					
❏ LP-9137 [M]	Just Call Me Lonesome	1961	6.25	12.50	25.00
—Black label with stars on top					
❏ LP-9137 [M]	Just Call Me Lonesome	1964	3.75	7.50	15.00
—Black and pink label					
❏ LP-9137 [M]	Just Call Me Lonesome	1966	3.00	6.00	12.00
—Black and green label					
❏ LP-9156 [M]	Once in a Lifetime	1961	6.25	12.50	25.00
—Black label with stars on top					
❏ LP-9156 [M]	Once in a Lifetime	1964	3.75	7.50	15.00
—Black and pink label					
❏ LP-9156 [M]	Once in a Lifetime	1966	3.00	6.00	12.00
—Black and green label					
❏ LP-9163 [M]	Slim Whitman Sings Annie Laurie	1961	6.25	12.50	25.00
—Black label with stars on top					
❏ LP-9163 [M]	Slim Whitman Sings Annie Laurie	1964	3.75	7.50	15.00
—Black and pink label					
❏ LP-9163 [M]	Slim Whitman Sings Annie Laurie	1966	3.00	6.00	12.00
—Black and green label					
❏ LP-9171 [M]	Forever	1961	6.25	12.50	25.00
—Black label with stars on top					
❏ LP-9171 [M]	Forever	1964	3.75	7.50	15.00
—Black and pink label					
❏ LP-9171 [M]	Forever	1966	3.00	6.00	12.00
—Black and green label					
❏ LP-9194 [M]	Slim Whitman Sings	1962	6.25	12.50	25.00
—Black label with stars on top					
❏ LP-9194 [M]	Slim Whitman Sings	1964	3.75	7.50	15.00
—Black and pink label					
❏ LP-9194 [M]	Slim Whitman Sings	1966	3.00	6.00	12.00
—Black and green label					
❏ LP-9209 [M]	Heart Songs and Love Songs	1962	6.25	12.50	25.00
—Black label with stars on top					
❏ LP-9209 [M]	Heart Songs and Love Songs	1964	3.75	7.50	15.00
—Black and pink label					
❏ LP-9209 [M]	Heart Songs and Love Songs	1966	3.00	6.00	12.00
—Black and green label					
❏ LP-9226 [M]	I'm a Lonely Wanderer	1963	6.25	12.50	25.00
—Black label with stars on top					
❏ LP-9226 [M]	I'm a Lonely Wanderer	1964	3.75	7.50	15.00
—Black and pink label					
❏ LP-9226 [M]	I'm a Lonely Wanderer	1966	3.00	6.00	12.00
—Black and green label					
❏ LP-9235 [M]	Yodeling	1963	6.25	12.50	25.00
—Black label with stars on top					
❏ LP-9235 [M]	Yodeling	1964	3.75	7.50	15.00
—Black and pink label					

Number	Title (A Side/B Side)	Yr	VG	VG+	NM
❏ LP-9235 [M]	Yodeling	1966	3.00	6.00	12.00
—Black and green label					
❏ LP-9245 [M]	Irish Songs The Whitman Way	1963	6.25	12.50	25.00
—Black label with stars on top					
❏ LP-9245 [M]	Irish Songs The Whitman Way	1964	3.75	7.50	15.00
—Black and pink label					
❏ LP-9245 [M]	Irish Songs The Whitman Way	1966	3.00	6.00	12.00
—Black and green label					
❏ LP-9252 [M]	All-Time Favorites	1964	3.75	7.50	15.00
—Black and pink label					
❏ LP-9252 [M]	All-Time Favorites	1964	7.50	15.00	30.00
—Black label with stars on top					
❏ LP-9252 [M]	All-Time Favorites	1966	3.00	6.00	12.00
—Black and green label					
❏ LP-9268 [M]	Country Songs/City Hits	1964	3.75	7.50	15.00
—Black and pink label					
❏ LP-9268 [M]	Country Songs/City Hits	1966	3.00	6.00	12.00
—Black and green label					
❏ LP-9277 [M]	Love Song of the Waterfall	1964	3.75	7.50	15.00
—Black and pink label					
❏ LP-9277 [M]	Love Song of the Waterfall	1966	3.00	6.00	12.00
—Black and green label					
❏ LP-9288 [M]	Reminiscing	1965	3.75	7.50	15.00
—Black and pink label					
❏ LP-9288 [M]	Reminiscing	1966	3.00	6.00	12.00
—Black and green label					
❏ LP-9303 [M]	More Than Yesterday	1965	3.75	7.50	15.00
—Black and pink label					
❏ LP-9303 [M]	More Than Yesterday	1966	3.00	6.00	12.00
—Black and green label					
❏ LP-9308 [M]	God's Hand in Mine	1966	3.00	6.00	12.00
❏ LP-9313 [M]	A Travelin' Man	1966	3.00	6.00	12.00
❏ LP-9333 [M]	A Time for Love	1966	3.00	6.00	12.00
❏ LP-9342 [M]	15th Anniversary	1967	3.75	7.50	15.00
❏ LP-9356 [M]	Country Memories	1967	3.75	7.50	15.00
❏ LP-12032 [S]	I'll Walk with God	1959	10.00	20.00	40.00
—Black label with silver top					
❏ LP-12032 [S]	I'll Walk with God	1964	6.25	12.50	25.00
—Black and pink label					
❏ LP-12032 [S]	I'll Walk with God	1966	5.00	10.00	20.00
—Black and green label					
❏ LP-12077 [S]	Slim Whitman Sings Annie Laurie	1961	7.50	15.00	30.00
—Black label with silver top					
❏ LP-12077 [S]	Slim Whitman Sings Annie Laurie	1964	5.00	10.00	20.00
—Black and pink label					
❏ LP-12077 [S]	Slim Whitman Sings Annie Laurie	1966	3.75	7.50	15.00
—Black and green label					
❏ LP-12100 [R]	Slim Whitman	1964	3.75	7.50	15.00
—Black and pink label					
❏ LP-12100 [R]	Slim Whitman	1966	3.00	6.00	12.00
—Black and green label					
❏ LP-12102 [R]	Song of the Old Waterwheel	1964	3.75	7.50	15.00
—Black and pink label					
❏ LP-12102 [R]	Song of the Old Waterwheel	1966	3.00	6.00	12.00
—Black and green label					
❏ LP-12194 [S]	Slim Whitman Sings	1962	7.50	15.00	30.00
—Black label with silver top					
❏ LP-12194 [S]	Slim Whitman Sings	1964	5.00	10.00	20.00
—Black and pink label					
❏ LP-12194 [S]	Slim Whitman Sings	1966	3.75	7.50	15.00
—Black and green label					
❏ LP-12268 [S]	Country Songs/City Hits	1964	5.00	10.00	20.00
—Black and pink label					
❏ LP-12268 [S]	Country Songs/City Hits	1966	3.75	7.50	15.00
—Black and green label					
❏ LP-12277 [S]	Love Song of the Waterfall	1964	5.00	10.00	20.00
—Black and pink label					
❏ LP-12277 [S]	Love Song of the Waterfall	1966	3.75	7.50	15.00
—Black and green label					
❏ LP-12288 [S]	Reminiscing	1965	5.00	10.00	20.00
—Black and pink label					
❏ LP-12288 [S]	Reminiscing	1966	3.75	7.50	15.00
—Black and green label					
❏ LP-12303 [S]	More Than Yesterday	1965	5.00	10.00	20.00
—Black and pink label					
❏ LP-12303 [S]	More Than Yesterday	1966	3.75	7.50	15.00
—Black and green label					
❏ LP-12313 [S]	A Travelin' Man	1966	3.75	7.50	15.00
❏ LP-12333 [S]	A Time for Love	1966	3.75	7.50	15.00
❏ LP-12342 [S]	15th Anniversary	1967	3.00	6.00	12.00
❏ LP-12356 [S]	Country Memories	1967	3.00	6.00	12.00
❏ LP-12375	In Love, The Whitman Way	1968	3.00	6.00	12.00
❏ LP-12411	Happy Street	1969	3.00	6.00	12.00
❏ LP-12436	Slim	1969	3.00	6.00	12.00
❏ LP-12448	The Slim Whitman Christmas Album	1969	3.75	7.50	15.00
LIBERTY					
❏ LM-1005	The Very Best of Slim Whitman	1981	2.00	4.00	8.00
—Reissue of United Artists 1005					
❏ LM-1067	The Slim Whitman Christmas Album	1980	2.00	4.00	8.00
—Abridged reissue of Imperial 12448					
❏ SL-8128	All My Best	1981	3.00	6.00	12.00
—Mail-order album					
❏ LN-10033	Red River Valley	1981	2.00	4.00	8.00
—Budget-line reissue					
❏ LN-10123	Till We Meet Again	1981	2.00	4.00	8.00
—Budget-line reissue					
❏ LN-10124	Ghost Riders in the Sky	1981	2.00	4.00	8.00
—Budget-line reissue					
❏ LN-10125	The Best of Slim Whitman, Vol. 2	1981	2.00	4.00	8.00
—Budget-line reissue					
❏ LN-10152	God's Hand in Mine	1981	2.00	4.00	8.00
—Budget-line reissue					
❏ LN-10153	Country Songs/City Hits	1981	2.00	4.00	8.00
—Budget-line reissue					
PAIR					
❏ PDL2-1085 [(2)]	One of a Kind	1986	3.00	6.00	12.00

Number	Title (A Side/B Side)	Yr	VG	VG+	NM
PICKWICK					
❏ SPC-3590	Happy Anniversary	1978	2.50	5.00	10.00
RCA CAMDEN					
❏ CAL-954 [M]	Birmingham Jail	1966	5.00	10.00	20.00
❏ CAS-954(e) [R]	Birmingham Jail	1966	3.00	6.00	12.00
RCA VICTOR					
❏ LPM-3217 [10]	Slim Whitman Sings and Yodels	1954	75.00	150.00	300.00
❏ AYL1-3774	Birmingham Jail	1980	2.00	4.00	8.00
—"Best Buy Series" reissue					
SUNSET					
❏ SUM-1112 [M]	Unchain Your Heart	1966	3.00	6.00	12.00
❏ SUM-1167 [M]	Lonesome Heart	1967	3.00	6.00	12.00
❏ SUS-5112 [R]	Unchain Your Heart	1966	3.00	6.00	12.00
❏ SUS-5167 [R]	Lonesome Heart	1967	3.00	6.00	12.00
❏ SUS-5267	Slim Whitman	1969	3.00	6.00	12.00
❏ SUS-5320	Ramblin' Rose	1970	2.50	5.00	10.00
UNITED ARTISTS					
❏ UA-LA046-F	I'll See You When I Get There	1973	2.50	5.00	10.00
❏ UA-LA245-G	The Very Best of Slim Whitman	1974	2.50	5.00	10.00
❏ UA-LA319-G	Happy Anniversary	1974	2.50	5.00	10.00
❏ UA-LA386-E	The Very Best of Slim Whitman	1974	2.50	5.00	10.00
❏ UA-LA513-G	Everything Leads Back to You	1975	2.50	5.00	10.00
❏ UA-LA752-G	Red River Valley	1977	2.50	5.00	10.00
❏ UA-LA787-G	Home on the Range	1978	2.50	5.00	10.00
❏ LM-1005	The Very Best of Slim Whitman	1980	2.50	5.00	10.00
❏ UAS-6763	Tomorrow Never Comes	1970	3.00	6.00	12.00
❏ UAS-6783	Guess Who	1970	3.00	6.00	12.00
❏ UAS-6819	It's a Sin to Tell a Lie	1971	3.00	6.00	12.00
❏ UAS-6832	The Best of Slim Whitman	1972	3.00	6.00	12.00

WHITNEY SUNDAY
Albums
DECCA

Number	Title (A Side/B Side)	Yr	VG	VG+	NM
❏ DL 75239	Whitney Sunday	1970	5.00	10.00	20.00

WHITTAKER, ROGER
45s
CAPITOL NASHVILLE

Number	Title (A Side/B Side)	Yr	VG	VG+	NM
❏ 7PRO-79035	I'd Fall in Love Tonight (same on both sides)	1990	—	3.00	6.00
—Vinyl is promo only					
❏ 7PRO-79036	But She Loves Me (same on both sides)	1990	—	3.00	6.00
—Vinyl is promo only					
❏ 7PRO-79397	Take Away My Pain (same on both sides)	1990	—	3.00	6.00
—Vinyl is promo only					
MAIN STREET					
❏ 93016	I Love You Because/Eternally	1983	—	2.50	5.00
❏ 93018	There Goes My Everything//(B-side unknown)	1984	—	2.50	5.00
RCA					
❏ PB-10874	Here We Stand/Before She Breaks My Heart	1976	—	2.00	4.00
❏ PB-11218	Last Song/Sea Gull	1978	—	2.00	4.00
❏ PB-11300	Love Last Forever/If I Knew Just What to Say	1978	—	2.00	4.00
❏ PB-11760	You Are My Miracle/Blow Gentle Breeze	1979	—	2.00	4.00
❏ PB-11941	You Are My Miracle/Blow Gentle Breeze	1980	—	—	3.00
❏ PB-11966	Wishes/I Was Born	1980	—	—	3.00
❏ PB-12096	River Lady/Lighthouse	1980	—	—	—
—Unreleased					
❏ PB-12110	A Man Without Love/I Am But a Small Voice	1980	—	—	3.00
❏ PB-12165	Tall Dark Stranger/Goodbye	1981	—	—	3.00
❏ PB-12330	How Does It Feel/Moonshine	1981	—	—	3.00
❏ PB-13030	River Lady/Smooth Sailing	1981	—	—	3.00
❏ JB-13379 [DJ]	Too Beautiful to Cry/Together	1982	—	2.50	5.00
❏ PB-14043	Take a Little-Give a Little/Dover to Calais	1985	—	—	3.00
❏ PB-14147	My Silver Eagle/Chicago Girl	1985	—	—	3.00
❏ PB-14333	The Genius of Love/				
	Everybody's Got a Lonely Heart	1986	—	—	3.00
RCA VICTOR					
❏ 74-0320	New World in the Morning/Durham Town	1970	2.00	4.00	8.00
❏ 74-0355	I Don't Believe in It Anymore/I Should Have				
	Taken My Time	1970	—	3.00	6.00
❏ 74-0442	Why/Moonshine	1971	—	3.00	6.00
❏ 74-0501	The Mexican Whistler/What Love Is	1971	—	3.00	6.00
❏ PB-10356	I Don't Believe in It Anymore/				
	New World in the Morning	1975	—	2.00	4.00
❏ PB-10447	Durham Town (The Leaving)/Mexican Whistler	1975	—	2.00	4.00
❏ GB-10494	The Last Farewell/Paradise	1975	—	—	3.00
—Gold Standard Series					
❏ PB-10732	Summer Days/				
	The First Hello, The Last Goodbye	1976	—	2.00	4.00
❏ PB-50030	The Last Farewell/Paradise	1975	—	2.00	4.00
—Canadian number, but pressed and released in the U.S. as well					
UNIVERSAL					
❏ UVL-66010	Have I Told You Lately That I Love You/Just				
	Across the Rio Grande	1989	—	2.00	4.00
❏ UVL-66030	There Goes My Everything/				
	Love Still Means You to Me	1989	—	2.00	4.00

Albums
CAPITOL NASHVILLE

Number	Title (A Side/B Side)	Yr	VG	VG+	NM
❏ C1 594058	World's Most Beautiful Christmas Songs	1990	3.75	7.50	15.00
—Available on vinyl through Columbia House only					
PAIR					
❏ PDL2-1039 [(2)]	Golden Tones	1986	3.00	6.00	12.00
❏ PDL2-1111 [(2)]	Fire and Rain	1986	3.00	6.00	12.00
RCA VICTOR					
❏ AFL1-0078	Traveling with Roger Whittaker	1978	2.50	5.00	10.00
—Reissue of APL1-0078					
❏ APL1-0078	Traveling with Roger Whittaker	1973	3.75	7.50	15.00
❏ AFL1-0855	Last Farewell" and Other Hits, The	1978	2.50	5.00	10.00
—Reissue of APL1-0855					
❏ APL1-0855	Last Farewell" and Other Hits, The	1975	3.00	6.00	12.00
❏ AQL1-0855	Last Farewell" and Other Hits, The	198?	2.00	4.00	8.00
—Reissue of AFL1-0855					
❏ AFL1-1313	The Magical World of Roger Whittaker	1978	2.50	5.00	10.00
—Reissue of APL1-1313					
❏ APL1-1313	The Magical World of Roger Whittaker	1976	3.00	6.00	12.00
❏ ANL1-1405	Roger Whittaker	1976	3.00	6.00	12.00

Number	Title (A Side/B Side)	Yr	VG	VG+	NM
❑ AFL1-1853	Reflections of Love	1978	2.50	5.00	10.00
—Reissue of APL1-1853					
❑ APL1-1853	Reflections of Love	1976	3.00	6.00	12.00
❑ AFL1-2255	The Best of Roger Whittaker	1978	2.50	5.00	10.00
—Reissue of APL1-2255					
❑ APL1-2255	The Best of Roger Whittaker	1977	3.00	6.00	12.00
❑ AQL1-2255	The Best of Roger Whittaker	198?	2.00	4.00	8.00
❑ AFL1-2525	Folk Songs	1978	3.00	6.00	12.00
❑ AQL1-2525	Folk Songs	198?	2.50	5.00	10.00
—Reissue of AFL1-2525					
❑ ANL1-2933	The Roger Whittaker Christmas Album	1978	3.00	6.00	12.00
❑ AFL1-3077	Imagine	1978	3.00	6.00	12.00
❑ AQL1-3077	Imagine	198?	2.00	4.00	8.00
—Reissue of AFL1-3077					
❑ AFL1-3355	When I Need You	1979	2.50	5.00	10.00
❑ AFL1-3501	Mirrors of My Mind	1979	2.50	5.00	10.00
❑ AQL1-3501	Mirrors of My Mind	198?	2.00	4.00	8.00
—Reissue of AFL1-3501					
❑ AFL1-3518	Voyager	1980	2.50	5.00	10.00
❑ AQL1-3518	Voyager	198?	2.00	4.00	8.00
—Reissue of AFL1-3518					
❑ AYL1-3670	The Magical World of Roger Whittaker	1980	2.00	4.00	8.00
—"Best Buy Series" reissue					
❑ AFL1-3778	With Love	1980	2.50	5.00	10.00
❑ AYL1-3911	When I Need You	1981	2.00	4.00	8.00
—"Best Buy Series" reissue					
❑ AYL1-3946	A Special Kind of Man	1981	2.00	4.00	8.00
—"Best Buy Series" reissue					
❑ CPL2-4057 [(2)]	Live in Concert	1981	3.00	6.00	12.00
❑ AFL1-4129	Changes	1982	2.50	5.00	10.00
❑ AYL1-4177	I Don't Believe in It Any More	1982	2.00	4.00	8.00
—"Best Buy Series" reissue					
❑ AYL1-4178	New World in the Morning	1982	2.00	4.00	8.00
—"Best Buy Series" reissue					
❑ AFL1-4321	The Wind Beneath My Wings	1983	2.50	5.00	10.00
❑ AFL1-4340	New World in the Morning	1978	2.50	5.00	10.00
—Reissue of LSP-4340					
❑ LSP-4340	New World in the Morning	1970	3.75	7.50	15.00
❑ AFL1-4405	I Don't Believe in It Any More	1978	2.50	5.00	10.00
—Reissue of LSP-4405					
❑ LSP-4405	I Don't Believe in It Any More	1970	3.75	7.50	15.00
❑ AFL1-4505	A Special Kind of Man	1978	2.50	5.00	10.00
—Reissue of LSP-4505					
❑ LSP-4505	A Special Kind of Man	1971	3.75	7.50	15.00
❑ LSP-4652	Loose and Fiery	1972	3.75	7.50	15.00
❑ AYL1-5166	The Best of Roger Whittaker	1985	—	3.00	6.00
—"Best Buy Series" reissue					
❑ AFL1-5803	The Genius of Love	1986	2.50	5.00	10.00
❑ NFL1-8047	Take a Little — Give a Little	1985	2.50	5.00	10.00

WHO, THE Also see ROGER DALTREY; JOHN ENTWISTLE; KEITH MOON; PETE TOWNSHEND.

12-Inch Singles
MCA

Number	Title (A Side/B Side)	Yr	VG	VG+	NM
❑ L33-1257 [DJ]	Twist and Shout/I Can't Explain/My Generation	1984	2.50	5.00	10.00

WARNER BROS.

❑ PRO-A-938 [DJ]	You Better You Bet (LP Version) (Edited Version)	1981	2.50	5.00	10.00
❑ PRO-A-1065 [DJ]	Athena (same on both sides)	1982	2.00	4.00	8.00
❑ PRO-A-1087 [DJ]	Eminence Front (LP Version) (Edited Version)	1982	2.50	5.00	10.00

45s
ATCO

| ❑ 6409 | Substitute/Waltz for a Pig | 1966 | 12.50 | 25.00 | 50.00 |
| ❑ 6509 | Substitute/Waltz for a Pig | 1967 | 5.00 | 10.00 | 20.00 |

DECCA

❑ 31725	I Can't Explain/Bald Headed Woman	1965	7.50	15.00	30.00
❑ 31801	Anyway, Anyhow, Anywhere/Anytime You Want Me	1965	12.50	25.00	50.00
❑ 31877	My Generation/Out in the Street (You're Going to Know Me)	1965	7.50	15.00	30.00
❑ 31988	The Kids Are Alright/A Legal Matter	1966	7.50	15.00	30.00
❑ 32058	I'm a Boy/In the City	1966	7.50	15.00	30.00
❑ 32114	Happy Jack/Whiskey Man	1967	7.50	15.00	30.00
❑ 32114 [PS]	Happy Jack/Whiskey Man	1967	12.50	25.00	50.00
❑ 32156	Pictures of Lily/Doctor, Doctor	1967	5.00	10.00	20.00
❑ 32206	I Can See for Miles/Mary-Anne with the Shaky Hands	1967	5.00	10.00	20.00
❑ 32288	Call Me Lightning/Dr. Jeckyll & Mr. Hyde	1968	6.25	12.50	25.00
❑ 32362	Magic Bus/Someone's Coming	1968	3.75	7.50	15.00
❑ 732465	Pinball Wizard/Dogs Part Two	1969	2.50	5.00	10.00
❑ 732465 [PS]	Pinball Wizard/Dogs Part Two	1969	5.00	10.00	20.00
❑ 32519	I'm Free/We're Not Gonna Take It	1969	2.50	5.00	10.00
❑ 32670	The Seeker/Here for More	1970	3.00	6.00	12.00
❑ 32708	Summertime Blues/Heaven and Hell	1970	3.00	6.00	12.00
❑ 732729	See Me, Feel Me/Overture from Tommy	1970	3.00	6.00	12.00
—With custom gold label					
❑ 732729 [PS]	See Me, Feel Me/Overture from Tommy	1970	5.00	10.00	20.00
❑ 32737	Young Man (Blues)/Substitute	1970	62.50	125.00	250.00
—Stock copies do exist					
❑ 32737 [DJ]	Young Man (Blues)/Substitute	1970	37.50	75.00	150.00
❑ 32737 [PS]	Young Man (Blues)/Substitute	1970	125.00	250.00	500.00
❑ 32846	Won't Get Fooled Again/I Don't Even Know Myself	1971	2.50	5.00	10.00
❑ 32888	Behind Blue Eyes/My Wife	1971	2.50	5.00	10.00
❑ 32983	Join Together/Baby, Don't You Do It	1972	2.50	5.00	10.00
❑ 34444 [DJ]	Happy Jack (same on both sides)	1967	10.00	20.00	40.00
—Promo-only number, pink label					
❑ 34470 [DJ]	Pictures of Lily (same on both sides)	1967	10.00	20.00	40.00
—Promo-only number, pink label					
❑ 7-34610 [DJ]	Amazing Journey/The Acid Queen	1970	6.25	12.50	25.00
❑ 7-34610/3 [DJ]	Excerpts from Tommy	1970	50.00	100.00	200.00
—Promo-only four-record box set with box and 4-page insert. As the records are sometimes found separately, they are also priced individually below.					
❑ 7-34611 [DJ]	Go to the Mirror Boy/Tommy Can You Hear Me	1970	6.25	12.50	25.00
❑ 7-34612 [DJ]	Smash the Mirror/Sensation	1970	6.25	12.50	25.00
❑ 7-34613 [DJ]	Sally Simpson/I'm Free	1970	6.25	12.50	25.00

Number	Title (A Side/B Side)	Yr	VG	VG+	NM
MCA					
❑ L45-1809 [DJ]	Had Enough (same on both sides)	1978	2.50	5.00	10.00
❑ 40475	Squeeze Box/Success Story	1975	—	2.50	5.00
❑ 40475 [PS]	Squeeze Box/Success Story	1975	7.50	15.00	30.00
—Sleeve is promo only					
❑ 40603	Slip Kid/Dreaming from the Waist	1976	—	2.50	5.00
❑ 40948	Who Are You/Had Enough	1978	—	2.50	5.00
❑ 40948 [DJ]	Who Are You (Short 3:22)/(Long 6:11)	1978	2.50	5.00	10.00
—Promo only; the long version has two lines deleted from the LP version					
❑ 40978	Trick of the Light/9:05	1978	—	2.50	5.00
❑ 41053	Long Live Rock/My Wife	1979	—	2.50	5.00
❑ 60106	See Me, Feel Me/Overture from Tommy	1973	—	2.50	5.00
—Reissue; black label with rainbow					
❑ 60110	I Can't Explain/Bald Headed Woman	1973	—	2.50	5.00
—Reissue; black label with rainbow					
❑ 60174	Pinball Wizard/Dogs Part Two	1974	—	2.50	5.00
—Reissue; black label with rainbow					
❑ 60174	Pinball Wizard/Dogs Part Two	1980	—	—	3.00
—Reissue; blue label with rainbow					
MERCURY					
❑ DJ-570 [DJ]	I'm the Face/Zoot Suit	1980	—	2.50	5.00
❑ DJ-570 [PS]	I'm the Face/Zoot Suit	1980	—	2.50	5.00
—As "The High Numbers"					
POLYDOR					
❑ 2022	5:15/I'm One	1979	—	2.00	4.00
❑ 2022 [PS]	5:15/I'm One	1979	—	2.50	5.00
TRACK					
❑ 32983	Join Together/Baby, Don't You Do It	1972	5.00	10.00	20.00
—Later pressing than Decca 32983, but much scarcer					
❑ 33041	The Relay/Waspman	1972	2.50	5.00	10.00
❑ 40152	Love, Reign O'er Me/Water	1973	2.00	4.00	8.00
❑ 40182	The Real Me/I'm One	1974	2.00	4.00	8.00
❑ 40330	Postcard/Put the Money Down	1974	10.00	20.00	40.00
WARNER BROS.					
❑ 29731	It's Hard/Dangerous	1983	—	2.50	5.00
❑ 29814	Eminence Front/One at a Time	1983	—	2.50	5.00
❑ 29905	Athena/It's Your Turn	1982	—	2.00	4.00
❑ 29905 [PS]	Athena/It's Your Turn	1982	—	2.50	5.00
❑ 49698	You Better You Bet/Quiet One	1981	—	2.00	4.00
❑ 49698 [PS]	You Better You Bet/Quiet One	1981	—	2.50	5.00
❑ 49743	Don't Let Go the Coat/You	1981	—	2.00	4.00
Albums					
DECCA					
❑ DL 4664 [M]	The Who Sing My Generation	1966	25.00	50.00	100.00
❑ DL 4664 [M]	The Who Sing My Generation	1966	50.00	100.00	200.00
—White label promo					
❑ DL 4892 [M]	Happy Jack	1967	12.50	25.00	50.00
❑ DL 4892 [M]	Happy Jack	1967	37.50	75.00	150.00
—White label promo					
❑ DL 4950 [M]	The Who Sell Out	1967	25.00	50.00	100.00
❑ DL 4950 [M]	The Who Sell Out	1967	50.00	100.00	200.00
—White label promo with songs in the same order as the stock copy					
❑ DL 4950 [M]	The Who Sell Out	1967	75.00	150.00	300.00
—White label promo with side 1 banded for airplay and all the commercials on one side					
❑ DL 5064 [M]	Magic Bus — The Who on Tour	1968	50.00	100.00	200.00
—Promo only; no stock copies were released in mono					
❑ DXSW 7205 [(2)]	Tommy	1969	10.00	20.00	40.00
—With booklet					
❑ DXSW 7205 [(2)DJ]	Tommy	1969	50.00	100.00	200.00
—White label promo					
❑ DL 74664 [R]	The Who Sing My Generation	1966	15.00	30.00	60.00
❑ DL 74664 [R]	The Who Sing My Generation	1966	50.00	100.00	200.00
—White label promo					
❑ DL 74892 [P]	Happy Jack	1967	12.50	25.00	50.00
—All stereo except that "Happy Jack" and "Don't Look Away" are rechanneled					
❑ DL 74892 [P]	Happy Jack	1967	37.50	75.00	150.00
—White label promo					
❑ DL 74950 [S]	The Who Sell Out	1967	12.50	25.00	50.00
❑ DL 74950 [S]	The Who Sell Out	1967	62.50	125.00	250.00
—White label promo with songs in the same order as the stock copy					
❑ DL 74950 [S]	The Who Sell Out	1967	100.00	200.00	400.00
—White label promo with side 1 banded for airplay and all the commercials on one side					
❑ DL 75064 [P]	Magic Bus — The Who on Tour	1968	12.50	25.00	50.00
—All rechanneled except "Magic Bus" and "I Can't Reach You," which are true stereo					
❑ DL 75064 [P]	Magic Bus — The Who on Tour	1968	37.50	75.00	150.00
—White label promo					
❑ DL 79175	Live at Leeds	1970	10.00	20.00	40.00
—With gatefold cover and numerous inserts					
❑ DL 79182	Who's Next	1971	6.25	12.50	25.00
❑ DL 79184	Meaty Beaty Big and Bouncy	1971	7.50	15.00	30.00
—With poster (deduct 1/3 if missing)					
❑ DL 734586	The Who/The Strawberry Alarm Clock	1969	25.00	50.00	100.00
—Special Products release for Philco. One side has Who songs, the other, Strawberry Alarm Clock songs					
DIRECT DISC					
❑ SD 16610	Who Are You	1980	7.50	15.00	30.00
—Audiophile vinyl					
LIFE					
❑ DL 74664 [R]	The Who Sing My Generation	1967	37.50	75.00	150.00
MCA					
❑ 1496	Who's Greatest Hits	1987	2.00	4.00	8.00
❑ 1577	Live at Leeds	1988	2.00	4.00	8.00
❑ 1578	Meaty Beaty Big and Bouncy	1988	2.00	4.00	8.00
❑ 1579	The Who By Numbers	1988	2.00	4.00	8.00
❑ 1580	Who Are You	1988	2.00	4.00	8.00
❑ L33-1987 [DJ]	Who Are You	1978	6.25	12.50	25.00
—White label promo with sticker "Who Are You Edited for Broadcast" on cover -- the line "Who the fuck are you?" is deleted twice					
❑ 2022	Live at Leeds	1973	3.00	6.00	12.00
❑ 2023	Who's Next	1973	3.00	6.00	12.00
❑ 2025	Meaty Beaty Big and Bouncy	1973	3.00	6.00	12.00
❑ 2044 [R]	The Who Sing My Generation	1974	12.50	25.00	50.00
❑ 2045 [P]	Happy Jack	1974	12.50	25.00	50.00
❑ 2161	The Who By Numbers	1975	3.00	6.00	12.00
❑ 3023	Live at Leeds	1977	2.50	5.00	10.00
❑ 3024	Who's Next	1977	2.50	5.00	10.00

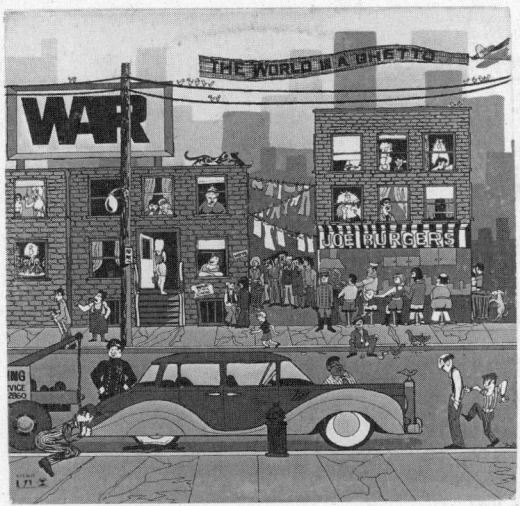

War, *The World Is a Ghetto*, United Artists UAS-5652, stereo LP, tan label, $6-$12.

Dionne Warwick, *Promises, Promises*, Scepter SPS-571, stereo LP, $7.50-$15.

Dinah Washington, *Dinah Washington Sings Fats Waller*, EmArcy MG-36119, mono LP, $25-$50.

Barry White, *Can't Get Enough*, 20th Century T-444, stereo LP, $5-$10.

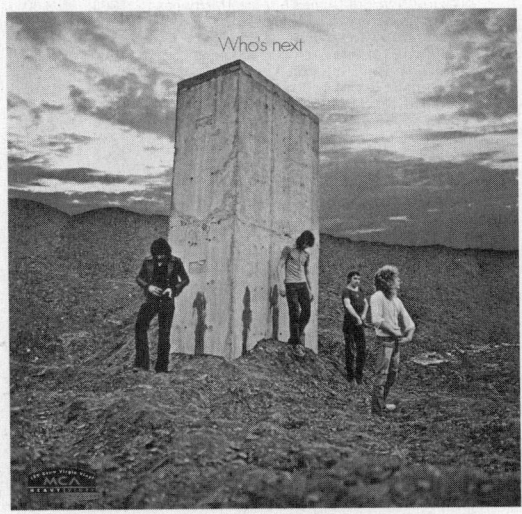

The Who, *Who's Next*, Decca DL 79182, stereo LP, $12.50-$25.

The Wilburn Brothers, *Carefree Moments*, Vocalion VL 3691, mono LP, $7.50-$15.

Number	Title (A Side/B Side)	Yr	VG	VG+	NM
❏ 3025	Meaty Beaty Big and Bouncy	1977	2.50	5.00	10.00
❏ 3026	The Who By Numbers	1977	2.50	5.00	10.00
❏ 3050	Who Are You	1978	2.50	5.00	10.00
❏ 2-4067 [(2)P]	A Quick One/The Who Sell Out	1976	5.00	10.00	20.00
—Black labels with rainbow					
❏ 2-4067 [(2)P]	A Quick One/The Who Sell Out	1978	3.75	7.50	15.00
—Tan labels					
❏ 2-4067 [(2)P]	A Quick One/The Who Sell Out	1980	3.00	6.00	12.00
—Blue labels with rainbow					
❏ 2-4068 [(2)P]	Magic Bus/The Who Sing My Generation	1976	5.00	10.00	20.00
—Black labels with rainbow					
❏ 2-4068 [(2)P]	Magic Bus/The Who Sing My Generation	1978	3.75	7.50	15.00
—Tan labels					
❏ 2-4068 [(2)P]	Magic Bus/The Who Sing My Generation	1980	3.00	6.00	12.00
—Blue labels with rainbow					
❏ 5220	Who's Next	1979	2.00	4.00	8.00
❏ 5408	Who's Greatest Hits	1983	2.00	4.00	8.00
❏ 5641	Who's Missing	1986	2.50	5.00	10.00
❏ 5712	Two's Missing	1987	2.50	5.00	10.00
❏ 6895 [(2)]	Quadrophenia	1980	2.50	5.00	10.00
❏ 6899 [(2)]	The Kids Are Alright	1980	2.50	5.00	10.00
—Early versions have number stamped in gold on cover with 11005 records. No difference in value.					
❏ 8018 [(2)]	Who's Last	1984	2.50	5.00	10.00
❏ 8031 [(2)]	Who's Better, Who's Best	1989	3.75	7.50	15.00
❏ 2-10004 [(2)]	Quadrophenia	1973	3.75	7.50	15.00
—Black labels with rainbow					
❏ 2-10004 [(2)]	Quadrophenia	1978	3.00	6.00	12.00
—Tan labels					
❏ 2-10005 [(2)]	Tommy	1973	3.75	7.50	15.00
—Black labels with rainbow					
❏ 2-10005 [(2)]	Tommy	1978	3.00	6.00	12.00
—Tan labels					
❏ 2-10005 [(2)]	Tommy	1980	2.50	5.00	10.00
—Blue labels with rainbow					
❏ 2-11005 [(2)]	The Kids Are Alright	1979	3.00	6.00	12.00
❏ 11164	Who's Next	1995	6.25	12.50	25.00
—"Heavy Vinyl" reissue on 180-gram vinyl with gatefold cover					
❏ 2-12001 [(2)]	Hooligans	1981	2.50	5.00	10.00
❏ 14950 [PD]	Who Are You	1978	3.75	7.50	15.00
—Picture disc					
❏ 3-19501 [(3)]	Join Together	1990	5.00	10.00	20.00
—Box set with booklet					
❏ 25986	It's Hard	1989	2.00	4.00	8.00
❏ 25987	Face Dances	1989	2.00	4.00	8.00
❏ 37000	Live at Leeds	1979	2.00	4.00	8.00
❏ 37001	Meaty Beaty Big and Bouncy	1979	2.00	4.00	8.00
❏ 37002	The Who By Numbers	1979	2.00	4.00	8.00
❏ 37003	Who Are You	1979	2.00	4.00	8.00
❏ 37169	Odds and Sods	1980	2.00	4.00	8.00
MOBILE FIDELITY					
❏ 1-115	Face Dances	1984	6.25	12.50	25.00
—Audiophile vinyl					
TRACK					
❏ 2126	Odds and Sods	1974	6.25	12.50	25.00
❏ 2-4067 [(2)P]	A Quick One/The Who Sell Out	1974	6.25	12.50	25.00
❏ 2-4068 [(2)P]	Magic Bus/The Who Sing My Generation	1974	6.25	12.50	25.00
❏ 2-10004 [(2)]	Quadrophenia	1973	5.00	10.00	20.00
WARNER BROS.					
❏ WBMS-116 [DJ]	Filling In the Gaps	1981	12.50	25.00	50.00
—With generic "Warner Bros. Music Show" cover					
❏ WBMS-116 [DJ]	Filling In the Gaps	1981	20.00	40.00	80.00
—With drawing on cover					
❏ HS 3516	Face Dances	1981	2.00	4.00	8.00
❏ 23731	It's Hard	1982	2.00	4.00	8.00
❏ 23731 [DJ]	It's Hard	1982	7.50	15.00	30.00
—Promo version on Quiex II vinyl					

WHOLE OATS See DARYL HALL AND JOHN OATES.

WHYTE BOOTS, THE
45s
PHILIPS

❏ 40422	Nightmare/Let No One Come Between Us	1967	20.00	40.00	80.00

WICHITA TRAIN WHISTLE, THE Produced by MICHAEL NESMITH.
45s
DOT

❏ 17152	Tapioca Tundra/Don't Cry Now	1968	3.75	7.50	15.00

Albums
DOT

❏ DLP-25861	Mike Nesmith Presents/The Wichita Train Whistle Sings	1968	7.50	15.00	30.00

WIER, RUSTY
45s
ABC

❏ 12019	Stoned, Slow and Rugged/Jeremiah Black	1974	—	3.00	6.00

BLACK HAT

❏ 102	Close Your Eyes/Kum-Back Bar and Grill	1987	—	3.00	6.00
❏ 103	(Lover of the) Other Side of the Hill/I Kept Thinkin' About You	1987	—	3.00	6.00

COLUMBIA

❏ 3-10445	I Think It's Time (I Learned How to Let Her Go)/Me and Daisy on the Run	1976	—	2.00	4.00

COMPLEAT

❏ 107	Don't It Make You Wanna Dance/You Gave Me a Reason	1983	—	2.50	5.00
❏ 121	Lone Star Lady/I Still Believe in You	1984	—	2.50	5.00

LONGHORN

❏ 101	(Lover of the) Other Side of the Hill/(B-side unknown)	1965	3.75	7.50	15.00

20TH CENTURY

❏ 2188	I Heard You Been Layin' My Old Lady (Apologies to Susie)/Aqua Dulce	1975	—	2.50	5.00
❏ 2219	Don't It Make You Wanna Dance/I Believe in the Way That You Love Me	1975	—	2.50	5.00
❏ 2273	I Don't Want to Lay This Guitar Down/Long and Lonesome Highway Blues	1976	—	2.50	5.00

Albums
ABC

❏ D-820	Stoned, Slow and Rugged	1974	3.00	6.00	12.00

COLUMBIA

❏ KC 34319	Black Hat Saloon	1976	2.50	5.00	10.00
❏ PC 34775	Stacked Deck	1977	2.50	5.00	10.00

MCA

❏ 820	Stoned, Slow and Rugged	1980	2.00	4.00	8.00
—Reissue of ABC 820					

20TH CENTURY

❏ T-469	Don't It Make You Wanna Dance?	1975	2.50	5.00	10.00
❏ T-495	Rusty Wier	1975	2.50	5.00	10.00

WIGGINS, JAY
45s
AMY

❏ 955	Sad Girl/No, Not Me	1966	2.50	5.00	10.00

I.P.G.

❏ 1008	Sad Girl/No, Not Me	196?	3.75	7.50	15.00
❏ 1015	Forgive Then Forget/My Lonely Girl	196?	3.00	6.00	12.00

LOST-NITE

❏ 258	Sad Girl/No, Not Me	196?	—	2.50	5.00
—Reissue					

WIGGINS, WALLY
45s
MERCURY

❏ 71645	I Need You/Maybe Someday	1960	20.00	40.00	80.00
❏ 71713	Maybelline/Sweeter Than Sweet	1960	5.00	10.00	20.00
❏ 71953	The Habit of Loving You/Little Old Lady Who Lives in a Shoe	1962	7.50	15.00	30.00

WIGWAM
45s
VERVE FORECAST

❏ 5114	Call Me on Your Telephone/Wishful Thinker	1970	2.00	4.00	8.00

Albums
VERVE FORECAST

❏ FTS-3089	Tombstone Valentine	1970	5.00	10.00	20.00

WILBURN BROTHERS, THE
45s
DECCA

❏ 29190	If You Love Me/A Little Time Out for Love	1954	5.00	10.00	20.00
❏ 29277	Carefree Moments/Let Me Be the First to Know	1954	5.00	10.00	20.00
❏ 29459	I Wanna Wanna Wanna/My Heart or My Mind	1955	5.00	10.00	20.00
❏ 29614	Temptation Go Away/Mixed-Up Medley	1955	5.00	10.00	20.00
❏ 29747	You're Not Play Love/Look Around, Take a Look at Me	1955	5.00	10.00	20.00
❏ 29887	I'm So in Love with You/Deep Elem Blues	1956	5.00	10.00	20.00
❏ 30087	Go Away with Me/Great Big Love	1956	5.00	10.00	20.00
❏ 30228	Nothing at All/I'm Setting You Free	1957	3.75	7.50	15.00
❏ 30428	I Close My Eyes/I Got Over the Blues	1957	3.75	7.50	15.00
❏ 30591	Oo Bop Sha Boom/My Baby Ain't My Baby No More	1958	7.50	15.00	30.00
❏ 30686	Cry Baby Cry/Till I'm the Only One	1958	3.75	7.50	15.00
❏ 30787	Which One Is to Blame/The Knoxville Girl	1958	3.75	7.50	15.00
❏ 30871	Somebody's Back in Town/I Love Everybody	1959	3.75	7.50	15.00
❏ 30968	A Woman's Intuition/A Town That Never Sleeps	1959	3.75	7.50	15.00
❏ 31062	Sentenced to Die/You Can't Take It With You	1960	3.00	6.00	12.00
❏ 31114	When Will You Know It/Big Heartbreak	1960	3.00	6.00	12.00
❏ 31152	The Best of All My Heartaches/Someone Else's Love	1960	3.00	6.00	12.00
❏ 31214	The Flame's Still Burning/The Legend of the Big River Train	1961	3.00	6.00	12.00
❏ 31276	Blue Blue Day/No Legal Right	1961	3.00	6.00	12.00
❏ 31333	Tag Along/Gift of the Blues	1961	3.00	6.00	12.00
❏ 31363	Trouble's Back in Town/Young But True Love	1962	3.00	6.00	12.00
❏ 31425	The Sound of Your Footsteps/Day After Day	1962	3.00	6.00	12.00
❏ 31464	Roll Muddy River/Not That I Care	1963	3.00	6.00	12.00
❏ 31520	Tell Her So/Here Comes a Million Memories	1963	3.00	6.00	12.00
❏ 31578	Hangin' Around/Never Alone	1964	2.50	5.00	10.00
❏ 31625	Impossible/I'll Take What's Left of Me	1964	2.50	5.00	10.00
❏ 31674	I'm Gonna Tie One On Tonight/Making Plans	1964	2.50	5.00	10.00
❏ 31764	I Had One Too Many/Left Out	1965	2.50	5.00	10.00
❏ 31819	It's Another World/My Day Won't Be Complete	1965	2.50	5.00	10.00
❏ 31894	Someone Before Me/Something About You	1966	2.50	5.00	10.00
❏ 31974	I Can't Keep Away from You/I'm Gonna Dress Up	1966	2.50	5.00	10.00
❏ 32038	Hurt Her Once for Me/Just to Be Where You Are	1966	2.50	5.00	10.00
❏ 32117	Roarin' Again/Go Mena Si (I'm Sorry)	1967	2.00	4.00	8.00
❏ 32169	Goody, Goody Gumdrop/You're Standing in the Way	1967	2.00	4.00	8.00
❏ 32225	I'm Leavin'/Wastin' My Time	1967	2.00	4.00	8.00
❏ 32292	Shakiest Gun in the West/She'll Walk All Over You	1968	2.00	4.00	8.00
❏ 32386	We Need a Lot More Happiness/If You're with Me	1968	2.00	4.00	8.00
❏ 32449	It Looks Like the Sun's Gonna Shine/Make My Heart Die Away	1969	2.00	4.00	8.00
❏ 32531	Signs Are Everywhere/Who Could Ask for More	1969	2.00	4.00	8.00
❏ 32597	Gift of the Blues/Tag Along	1969	2.00	4.00	8.00
❏ 32608	Little Johnny from Down the Street/Which Side's the Wrong Side	1970	2.00	4.00	8.00
❏ 32683	Lilacs in Winter/Country Boy (Sing Your Heart Out)	1970	2.00	4.00	8.00
❏ 32771	Little Eyes That Look at Me/I've Gotta Hang My Hat Up on the Wind	1971	2.00	4.00	8.00
❏ 32835	That She's Leaving Feeling/Everything I Am	1971	2.00	4.00	8.00
❏ 32909	The War Keeps Draggin' On/Bloomin' Fools	1971	2.00	4.00	8.00
❏ 32921	Arkansas/Santa Fe Rolls Royce	1972	2.00	4.00	8.00
❏ 32978	Opryland/Hard Times Have Been There	1972	2.00	4.00	8.00
❏ 33027	The City's Goin' Country/Minds of Lonely Men	1972	2.00	4.00	8.00
❏ 7-38215 [S]	Faded Love/The Great Speckled Bird	196?	3.75	7.50	15.00
—Jukebox issue; small hole, plays at 33 1/3 rpm					

MCA

❏ 40042	Simon Crutchfield's Grave/Treat the Dog Like a Dog	1973	—	2.50	5.00

Number	Title (A Side/B Side)	Yr	VG	VG+	NM
❑ 40264	There Must Be More to Love Than This/ You've Still Got a Place in My Heart	1974	—	2.50	5.00
❑ 40473	Country Honey/Milwaukee, You're in Trouble	1975	—	2.50	5.00
❑ 40577	Country Kind of Feeling/Goin' and Comin'	1975	—	2.50	5.00

SCORPION

Number	Title (A Side/B Side)	Yr	VG	VG+	NM
❑ 0558	Mama's Shoe Box/What a Way to Go	1978	—	2.00	4.00

7-Inch Extended Plays

DECCA

Number	Title (A Side/B Side)	Yr	VG	VG+	NM
❑ ED 2537	*That's When I Miss You/Cry, Cry Darling/I Know You Don't Love Me Anymore/Always Alone	1957	6.25	12.50	25.00
❑ ED 2537 [PS]	The Wilburn Brothers	1957	6.25	12.50	25.00
❑ ED 2551	*You Win Again/I'll Sail My Ship Alone/Don't Sweetheart Me/Time Changes Everything	1957	6.25	12.50	25.00
❑ ED 2551 [PS]	The Wilburn Brothers	1957	6.25	12.50	25.00
❑ ED 2588	*If It's Wrong to Love You/One Has My Name, The Other Has My Heart/You Can't Break the Chains of Love/Much Too Often	1958	5.00	10.00	20.00
❑ ED 2588 [PS]	The Wilburn Brothers	1958	5.00	10.00	20.00
❑ ED 2617	*Need Someone/A Boy's Faithful Friend/Faded Love/Great Speckled Bird	1959	5.00	10.00	20.00
❑ ED 2617 [PS]	Side by Side	1959	5.00	10.00	20.00
❑ ED 2681	*Never Be Anyone Else But You/Big Heartbreak/ Empty Arms/I Almost Lost My Mind	1960	5.00	10.00	20.00
❑ ED 2681 [PS]	Big Heartbreak	1960	5.00	10.00	20.00
❑ ED 2689	*When Will You Know It/A Town That Never Sleeps/Sentenced to Die/You Can't Take It With You	1961	5.00	10.00	20.00
❑ ED 2689 [PS]	The Wilburn Brothers	1961	5.00	10.00	20.00
❑ ED 2727	*Trouble's Back in Town/Young But True Love/ Roll On Buddy, Roll On/Michael	1962	5.00	10.00	20.00
❑ ED 2727 [PS]	Trouble's Back in Town	1962	5.00	10.00	20.00
❑ ED 2756	Which One Is to Blame/No Legal Right//Blue Blue Day/Day After Day	1963	5.00	10.00	20.00
❑ ED 2756 [PS]	The Wilburn Brothers	1963	5.00	10.00	20.00
❑ ED 2782	*Roll Muddy River/Talk Back Trembling Lips/ Hangin' Around/A Fool Never Learns	1964	6.25	12.50	25.00
❑ ED 2782 [PS]	Roll Muddy River	1964	6.25	12.50	25.00
❑ ED 2783	(contents unknown)	1964	6.25	12.50	25.00
❑ ED 2783 [PS]	Take Up Thy Cross	1964	6.25	12.50	25.00
❑ ED 2803	(contents unknown)	1965	6.25	12.50	25.00
❑ ED 2803 [PS]	I'm Gonna Tie One on Tonight	1965	6.25	12.50	25.00

Albums

DECCA

Number	Title (A Side/B Side)	Yr	VG	VG+	NM
❑ DL 4058 [M]	The Big Heartbreak	1960	7.50	15.00	30.00
❑ DL 4142 [M]	The Wilburn Brothers Sing	1961	7.50	15.00	30.00
❑ DL 4211 [M]	City Limits	1961	7.50	15.00	30.00
❑ DL 4225 [M]	Folk Songs	1962	5.00	10.00	20.00
❑ DL 4391 [M]	Trouble's Back in Town	1963	5.00	10.00	20.00
❑ DL 4464 [M]	Take Up Thy Cross	1964	5.00	10.00	20.00
❑ DL 4544 [M]	Never Alone	1964	5.00	10.00	20.00
❑ DL 4615 [M]	Country Gold	1965	5.00	10.00	20.00
❑ DL 4645 [M]	I'm Gonna Tie One on Tonight	1965	5.00	10.00	20.00
❑ DL 4721 [M]	The Wilburn Brothers Show	1966	15.00	30.00	60.00
—With guests Loretta Lynn, Ernest Tubb, Harold Morrison					
❑ DL 4764 [M]	Let's Go Country	1966	5.00	10.00	20.00
❑ DL 4824 [M]	Two for the Show	1967	6.25	12.50	25.00
❑ DL 4871 [M]	Cool	1967	7.50	15.00	30.00
❑ DL 4954 [M]	It's Another World	1968	10.00	20.00	40.00
❑ DL 8576 [M]	The Wilburn Brothers	1957	10.00	20.00	40.00
❑ DL 8774 [M]	Side by Side	1958	10.00	20.00	40.00
❑ DL 8959 [M]	Livin' in God's Country	1959	10.00	20.00	40.00
❑ DL 74058 [S]	The Big Heartbreak	1960	10.00	20.00	40.00
❑ DL 74142 [S]	The Wilburn Brothers Sing	1961	10.00	20.00	40.00
❑ DL 74211 [S]	City Limits	1961	10.00	20.00	40.00
❑ DL 74225 [S]	Folk Songs	1962	7.50	15.00	30.00
❑ DL 74391 [S]	Trouble's Back in Town	1963	7.50	15.00	30.00
❑ DL 74464 [S]	Take Up Thy Cross	1964	6.25	12.50	25.00
❑ DL 74544 [S]	Never Alone	1964	6.25	12.50	25.00
❑ DL 74615 [S]	Country Gold	1965	6.25	12.50	25.00
❑ DL 74645 [S]	I'm Gonna Tie One on Tonight	1965	6.25	12.50	25.00
❑ DL 74721 [S]	The Wilburn Brothers Show	1966	20.00	40.00	80.00
—With guests Loretta Lynn, Ernest Tubb, Harold Morrison					
❑ DL 74764 [S]	Let's Go Country	1966	6.25	12.50	25.00
❑ DL 74824 [S]	Two for the Show	1967	5.00	10.00	20.00
❑ DL 74871 [S]	Cool	1967	5.00	10.00	20.00
❑ DL 74954 [S]	It's Another World	1968	5.00	10.00	20.00
❑ DL 75173	Little Johnny from Down the Street	1970	5.00	10.00	20.00
❑ DL 75214	Sing Your Heart Out Country Boy	1971	5.00	10.00	20.00
❑ DL 75291	That She's Leaving Feeling	1972	5.00	10.00	20.00
❑ DL 78774 [S]	Side by Side	1959	15.00	30.00	60.00
❑ DL 78959 [S]	Livin' in God's Country	1959	15.00	30.00	60.00

KING

Number	Title (A Side/B Side)	Yr	VG	VG+	NM
❑ 746 [M]	The Wonderful Wilburn Brothers	1961	25.00	50.00	100.00

MCA

Number	Title (A Side/B Side)	Yr	VG	VG+	NM
❑ 4011 [(2)]	Portrait	197?	3.75	7.50	15.00

MCA CORAL

Number	Title (A Side/B Side)	Yr	VG	VG+	NM
❑ 20058	That Country Feeling	1973	2.50	5.00	10.00

VOCALION

Number	Title (A Side/B Side)	Yr	VG	VG+	NM
❑ VL 3691 [M]	Carefree Moments	1962	3.75	7.50	15.00
❑ VL 73691 [S]	Carefree Moments	1962	3.75	7.50	15.00
❑ VL 73876	That Country Feeling	197?	3.00	6.00	12.00
❑ VL 73889	I Walk the Line	197?	3.00	6.00	12.00

WILCOX THREE, THE

Albums

RCA CAMDEN

Number	Title (A Side/B Side)	Yr	VG	VG+	NM
❑ CAL-669 [M]	The Greatest Folk Songs Ever Sung	1961	5.00	10.00	20.00

WILD, JACK

45s

BUDDAH

Number	Title (A Side/B Side)	Yr	VG	VG+	NM
❑ 241	(Holy Moses) Everything's Coming Up Roses/ Bring Yourself Back to Me	1971	2.00	4.00	8.00

CAPITOL

Number	Title (A Side/B Side)	Yr	VG	VG+	NM
❑ 2742	Some Beautiful/A Picture of You	1970	—	3.00	6.00
❑ 2742 [PS]	Some Beautiful/A Picture of You	1970	3.00	6.00	12.00
❑ 2868	Wait for Summer/Melody	1970	—	3.00	6.00

Number	Title (A Side/B Side)	Yr	VG	VG+	NM

Albums

BUDDAH

Number	Title (A Side/B Side)	Yr	VG	VG+	NM
❑ BDS-5083	Everything's Coming Up Roses	1971	6.25	12.50	25.00
❑ BDS-5110	A Beautiful World	1972	6.25	12.50	25.00

CAPITOL

Number	Title (A Side/B Side)	Yr	VG	VG+	NM
❑ SKAO-545	The Jack Wild Album	1970	6.25	12.50	25.00

WILD BEES, THE

45s

RCA VICTOR

Number	Title (A Side/B Side)	Yr	VG	VG+	NM
❑ 47-7275	Doctor Rock/Bamboozled	1958	7.50	15.00	30.00

WILD BUTTER

45s

UNITED ARTISTS

Number	Title (A Side/B Side)	Yr	VG	VG+	NM
❑ 50688	Roxanna/Terribly Blind	1970	—	3.00	6.00

Albums

UNITED ARTISTS

Number	Title (A Side/B Side)	Yr	VG	VG+	NM
❑ UAS-6766	Wild Butter	1970	6.25	12.50	25.00

WILD-CATS, THE

45s

UNITED ARTISTS

Number	Title (A Side/B Side)	Yr	VG	VG+	NM
❑ 154	Gazachstahagen/Billy's Cha Cha	1958	6.25	12.50	25.00
❑ 169	Dancing Elephants/King Size Guitar	1959	6.25	12.50	25.00

Albums

UNITED ARTISTS

Number	Title (A Side/B Side)	Yr	VG	VG+	NM
❑ UAL-3031 [M]	Bandstand Record Hop	1958	12.50	25.00	50.00

WILD CHERRY

45s

A&M

Number	Title (A Side/B Side)	Yr	VG	VG+	NM
❑ 1656	Voodoo Doll/Because Your Love Is Mine	1974	—	2.50	5.00

EPIC

Number	Title (A Side/B Side)	Yr	VG	VG+	NM
❑ 50225	Play That Funky Music/The Lady Wants Your Money	1976	—	2.50	5.00
❑ 50306	Get It Up/Baby Don't You Know	1976	—	2.00	4.00
❑ 50362	Hot to Trot/Put Yourself in My Shoes	1977	—	2.00	4.00
❑ 50401	Are You Boogieing Around on Your Daddy/Hold On (With Strings)	1977	—	2.00	4.00
❑ 50500	Don't Stop, Get Off/I Love My Music	1978	—	2.00	4.00
❑ 50551	1-2-3 Kind of Love/Fools Fall in Love	1978	—	2.00	4.00
❑ 50619	This Old Heart of Mine (Is Weak for You)/Lana	1978	—	2.00	4.00
❑ 50702	Try a Piece of My Love/Take Me Back	1979	—	2.00	4.00

UNITED ARTISTS

Number	Title (A Side/B Side)	Yr	VG	VG+	NM
❑ XW217 [DJ]	Get Down (mono/stereo)	1973	—	2.50	5.00
—Stock copy not known to exist					

Albums

EPIC

Number	Title (A Side/B Side)	Yr	VG	VG+	NM
❑ PE 34195	Wild Cherry	1976	3.00	6.00	12.00
❑ PE 34462	Electrified Funk	1977	2.50	5.00	10.00
❑ JE 35011	I Love My Music	1978	2.50	5.00	10.00
❑ JE 35760	Only the Wild	1979	2.50	5.00	10.00

WILD COUNTRY See ALABAMA.

WILD MAN STEVE

Albums

DEALER'S CHOICE

Number	Title (A Side/B Side)	Yr	VG	VG+	NM
❑ 777	Is It Good Baby	198?	3.75	7.50	15.00
❑ 780	Did He Really Say That	198?	3.75	7.50	15.00

DICK-ER

Number	Title (A Side/B Side)	Yr	VG	VG+	NM
❑ D 70	Do Not Disturb	1972	5.00	10.00	20.00

LAFF

Number	Title (A Side/B Side)	Yr	VG	VG+	NM
❑ 181	Eatin' Ain't Cheatin'	1973	3.00	6.00	12.00
❑ 191	When You're Hot You're Hot	1976	3.00	6.00	12.00

RAW

Number	Title (A Side/B Side)	Yr	VG	VG+	NM
❑ 7000	My Man! Wild Man!	1969	3.75	7.50	15.00
❑ 7001	Wild! Wild! Wild! Wild!	1970	3.75	7.50	15.00
❑ 7002	King of Them All	1971	3.75	7.50	15.00

WILD ONES, THE (1)

45s

MAINLINE

Number	Title (A Side/B Side)	Yr	VG	VG+	NM
❑ 500	Caught in the Cookie Jar/Super Fox	1965	2.50	5.00	10.00

MALA

Number	Title (A Side/B Side)	Yr	VG	VG+	NM
❑ 564	High-Ho/Valerie	1967	2.00	4.00	8.00

UNITED ARTISTS

Number	Title (A Side/B Side)	Yr	VG	VG+	NM
❑ 947	Wild Thing/Just Can't Cry Anymore	1965	3.00	6.00	12.00
❑ 971	My Love/Lord Love a Duck	1966	2.50	5.00	10.00
❑ 971 [PS]	My Love/Lord Love a Duck	1966	3.75	7.50	15.00
❑ 50043	For Your Love (I Would Do Almost Anything)/ Never Givin' Up (On Your Love)	1966	2.50	5.00	10.00

Albums

UNITED ARTISTS

Number	Title (A Side/B Side)	Yr	VG	VG+	NM
❑ UAL-3450 [M]	The Arthur Sound	1965	6.25	12.50	25.00
❑ UAS-6450 [S]	The Arthur Sound	1965	7.50	15.00	30.00

WILD ONES, THE (2)

45s

SEARS

Number	Title (A Side/B Side)	Yr	VG	VG+	NM
❑ 2180	Come On Back/(Instrumental)	1966	2.50	5.00	10.00
❑ 2180 [PS]	Come On Back/(Instrumental)	1966	7.50	15.00	30.00

WILD ONES, THE (3)

45s

S.P.Q.R.

Number	Title (A Side/B Side)	Yr	VG	VG+	NM
❑ 3316	A Little Bit o' Soul/I've Been Crying	1964	6.25	12.50	25.00

WILD TURKEY

Albums

CHRYSALIS

Number	Title (A Side/B Side)	Yr	VG	VG+	NM
❑ CHR 1010	Turkey	1973	2.50	5.00	10.00

REPRISE

Number	Title (A Side/B Side)	Yr	VG	VG+	NM
❑ MS 2070	Battle Hymn	1972	3.00	6.00	12.00

W

Number	Title (A Side/B Side)	Yr	VG	VG+	NM

WILDCATS, THE (1)
45s
RCA VICTOR

Number	Title (A Side/B Side)	Yr	VG	VG+	NM
❏ 47-6386	Keep Talkin'/Beatin' on a Rug	1956	10.00	20.00	40.00

WILDCATS, THE (2) Actually THE BLOSSOMS.
45s
REPRISE

Number	Title (A Side/B Side)	Yr	VG	VG+	NM
❏ 0253	3625 Groovy Street/ What Are We Gonna Do in '64	1964	5.00	10.00	20.00

WILDE, MARTY
45s
BELL

Number	Title (A Side/B Side)	Yr	VG	VG+	NM
❏ 45603	All Night Girl/(B-side unknown)	1974	—	2.50	5.00

EPIC

Number	Title (A Side/B Side)	Yr	VG	VG+	NM
❏ 9291	My Lucky Love/Misery's Child	1958	3.75	7.50	15.00
❏ 9356	Bad Boy/Teenage Years	1960	3.00	6.00	12.00
❏ 9392	Little Girl/Your Seventeenth Spring	1960	3.00	6.00	12.00
❏ 9400	Angry/My Baby Is Gone (Stop This World)	1960	3.00	6.00	12.00
❏ 9424	The Part of a Fool/Forgotten Dreams	1960	—	—	—
—Unreleased?					

HERITAGE

Number	Title (A Side/B Side)	Yr	VG	VG+	NM
❏ 814	Abergavenny/Alice in Blue	1969	—	3.00	6.00
—As "Shannon"					
❏ 814 [PS]	Abergavenny/Alice in Blue	1969	2.50	5.00	10.00
—As "Shannon"					
❏ 819	Jesamine/Lullaby	1969	—	3.00	6.00
—As "Shannon"					

JAMIE

Number	Title (A Side/B Side)	Yr	VG	VG+	NM
❏ 1282	Kiss Me/My, What a Woman	1964	2.50	5.00	10.00

Albums
EPIC

Number	Title (A Side/B Side)	Yr	VG	VG+	NM
❏ BN 575 [S]	Wilde About Marty	1960	25.00	50.00	100.00
❏ LN 3686 [M]	Bad Boy	1960	20.00	40.00	80.00
❏ LN 3711 [M]	Wilde About Marty	1960	20.00	40.00	80.00

WILDERNESS ROAD
45s
COLUMBIA

Number	Title (A Side/B Side)	Yr	VG	VG+	NM
❏ 4-45565	Bounty Man/Dr. Morpho's Revenge	1972	2.00	4.00	8.00

Albums
COLUMBIA

Number	Title (A Side/B Side)	Yr	VG	VG+	NM
❏ C 31118	Wilderness Road	1972	5.00	10.00	20.00

REPRISE

Number	Title (A Side/B Side)	Yr	VG	VG+	NM
❏ MS 2125	Sold for the Prevention of Disease Only	1973	5.00	10.00	20.00

WILDING, BOBBY
45s
ABC-PARAMOUNT

Number	Title (A Side/B Side)	Yr	VG	VG+	NM
❏ 10275	Mama/You Give Me No Choice	1961	3.00	6.00	12.00

DCP

Number	Title (A Side/B Side)	Yr	VG	VG+	NM
❏ 1009	I Want to Be a Beatle/ Since I've Been Wearing My Hair Like a Beatle	1964	5.00	10.00	20.00
❏ 1106	I Want You/Too Young to Fall in Love	1964	3.00	6.00	12.00

MAY

Number	Title (A Side/B Side)	Yr	VG	VG+	NM
❏ 125	Slide (Part 1)/Slide (Part 2)	1962	3.00	6.00	12.00

WILDWOODS, THE Actually THE FIVE SATINS.
45s
CAPRICE

Number	Title (A Side/B Side)	Yr	VG	VG+	NM
❏ 101	When the Swallows Come Back to Capistrano/ Heart of Mine	1961	37.50	75.00	150.00

MAY

Number	Title (A Side/B Side)	Yr	VG	VG+	NM
❏ 106	Golden Sunset/Here Comes Big Ed	1961	7.50	15.00	30.00

WILEY, CHUCK
45s
JAX

Number	Title (A Side/B Side)	Yr	VG	VG+	NM
❏ 1004	I Love You So Much/I Begin to Miss You	1959	25.00	50.00	100.00

UNITED ARTISTS

Number	Title (A Side/B Side)	Yr	VG	VG+	NM
❏ 113	Tear It Up/Shake Up the Dance	1958	18.75	37.50	75.00
❏ 120	By My Side/Door to Door	1958	—	—	—
—Unreleased					

WILKENS, ARTIE, AND THE PALMS
45s
STATES

Number	Title (A Side/B Side)	Yr	VG	VG+	NM
❏ 157	Darling Patricia/Please Come Back	1956	150.00	300.00	600.00

WILKINSON TRI-CYCLE
Albums
DATE

Number	Title (A Side/B Side)	Yr	VG	VG+	NM
❏ TES 4016	Wilkinson Tri-Cycle	1969	10.00	20.00	40.00

WILLIAMS, ALAINE
45s
PARKWAY

Number	Title (A Side/B Side)	Yr	VG	VG+	NM
❏ 923	When Are We Getting Married/So This Is Goodbye	1964	5.00	10.00	20.00

WILLIAMS, ANDRE
45s
AVIN

Number	Title (A Side/B Side)	Yr	VG	VG+	NM
❏ 103	Rib Tips (Part 1)/Rib Tips (Part 2)	1965	3.00	6.00	12.00

CHECKER

Number	Title (A Side/B Side)	Yr	VG	VG+	NM
❏ 1187	The Stroke/Humpin' Bumpin' and Trumpin'	1967	3.00	6.00	12.00
❏ 1205	Cadillac Jack/Mrs. Mother USA	1968	3.00	6.00	12.00
❏ 1214	Do the Popcorn/It's Gonna Be Fine in '69	1969	3.00	6.00	12.00
❏ 1219	Girdle Up/(Instrumental)	1969	3.00	6.00	12.00

EPIC

Number	Title (A Side/B Side)	Yr	VG	VG+	NM
❏ 9196	Bacon Fat/Just Because of a Kiss	1956	6.25	12.50	25.00

FORTUNE

Number	Title (A Side/B Side)	Yr	VG	VG+	NM
❏ 824	Pulling Time/Going Down to Tia-Juana	1955	20.00	40.00	80.00
❏ 827	Mozelle/Just Want a Little Lovin'	1956	10.00	20.00	40.00
❏ 828	Bobby Jean/It's All Over	1956	10.00	20.00	40.00
❏ 831	Bacon Fat/Just Because of a Kiss	1956	7.50	15.00	30.00

Number	Title (A Side/B Side)	Yr	VG	VG+	NM
❏ 834	Mean Jean/You Are My Sunshine	1957	7.50	15.00	30.00
❏ 837	Jail Bait/My Tears	1957	20.00	40.00	80.00
❏ 839	Come On Baby/The Greasy Chicken	1957	7.50	15.00	30.00
—With Gino Park					
❏ 839	The Greasy Chicken/Please Pass the Biscuits	1957	15.00	30.00	60.00
—With Gino Park					
❏ 839	Don't Touch/Please Pass the Biscuits	1957	20.00	40.00	80.00
—With Gino Park					
❏ 842	My Last Dance with You/Hey! Country Girl	1958	7.50	15.00	30.00
❏ 847	Put a Chain on It/I'm All For You	1959	7.50	15.00	30.00
❏ 851	(Georgia May Is) Movin'/(Mmmm — Andre Williams Is) Movin'	1960	15.00	30.00	60.00
—With Gino Park					
❏ 856	Jail House Blues/I Still Love You	1960	7.50	15.00	30.00

MIRACLE

Number	Title (A Side/B Side)	Yr	VG	VG+	NM
❏ 4	Rosa Lee/Shoo Shoo	1960	300.00	600.00	1200.

NORTON

Number	Title (A Side/B Side)	Yr	VG	VG+	NM
❏ 45-069	Poor Mr. Santa (N-N-Naughty!)/ Poor Mr. Santa (N-n-nice!)	1997	—	—	2.00
❏ 45-069 [PS]	Poor Mr. Santa (N-N-Naughty!)/ Poor Mr. Santa (N-n-nice!)	1997	—	—	2.00

RIC-TIC

Number	Title (A Side/B Side)	Yr	VG	VG+	NM
❏ 124	You Got It And I Want It/I Can't Stop Crying	1967	6.25	12.50	25.00

RONALD

Number	Title (A Side/B Side)	Yr	VG	VG+	NM
❏ 1001	Please Give Me a Chance/(B-side unknown)	196?	6.25	12.50	25.00

SPORT

Number	Title (A Side/B Side)	Yr	VG	VG+	NM
❏ 105	Pearl Time/Soul Groove	1967	6.25	12.50	25.00

WINGATE

Number	Title (A Side/B Side)	Yr	VG	VG+	NM
❏ 014	Loose Juice/Sweet Little Pussycat	1966	3.75	7.50	15.00
❏ 021	Do It! (Part 1)/Do It! (Part 2)	1966	5.00	10.00	20.00

Albums
SDEG

Number	Title (A Side/B Side)	Yr	VG	VG+	NM
❏ 4020	Directly from the Streets	198?	2.50	5.00	10.00

WILLIAMS, ANDY
12-Inch Singles
COLUMBIA

Number	Title (A Side/B Side)	Yr	VG	VG+	NM
❏ AS 545 [DJ]	Love Story (Where Do I Begin) (Long Version) (Short Version)	1979	2.50	5.00	10.00
❏ 23-10953	Love Story (Where Do I Begin)/Love Theme from "Oliver's Story"	1979	3.75	7.50	15.00

45s
CADENCE

Number	Title (A Side/B Side)	Yr	VG	VG+	NM
❏ 1282	Christmas Is a Feeling in Your Heart/The Wind, The Sand and The Stars	1955	3.75	7.50	15.00
❏ 1288	Walk Hand in Hand/Not Anymore	1956	3.00	6.00	12.00
❏ 1297	Canadian Sunset/High Upon a Mountain	1956	3.00	6.00	12.00
❏ 1303	Baby Doll/Since I've Found My Baby	1956	3.00	6.00	12.00
❏ 1308	Butterfly/It Doesn't Take Very Long	1957	3.00	6.00	12.00
❏ 1323	I Like Your Kind of Love/Stop Teasin' Me	1957	3.00	6.00	12.00
❏ 1336	Lips of Wine/Straight from the Heart	1957	3.00	6.00	12.00
❏ 1340	Are You Sincere/Be Mine Tonight	1957	3.00	6.00	12.00
❏ 1351	Promise Me, Love/ Your Hand, Your Heart, Your Love	1958	2.50	5.00	10.00
❏ 1358	The Hawaiian Wedding Song/House of Bamboo	1958	2.50	5.00	10.00
❏ 1370	Lonely Street/Summer Love	1959	2.50	5.00	10.00
❏ 1374	The Village of St. Bernadette/ I'm So Lonesome I Could Cry	1959	2.50	5.00	10.00
❏ 1374 [PS]	The Village of St. Bernadette/ I'm So Lonesome I Could Cry	1959	3.75	7.50	15.00
❏ 1378	Wake Me When It's Over/We Have a Date	1960	2.50	5.00	10.00
❏ 1381	Do You Mind?/Dreamsville	1960	2.50	5.00	10.00
❏ 1389	In the Summertime (You Don't Want My Love)/ Don't Go to Strangers	1960	2.50	5.00	10.00
❏ 1389	You Don't Want My Love/Don't Go to Strangers	1960	3.00	6.00	12.00
❏ 1398	The Bilbao Song/How Wonderful to Know	1961	2.50	5.00	10.00
❏ 1433	Twilight Time/So Rare	1962	2.50	5.00	10.00
❏ 1447	Let It Be Me/Under Paris Skies	1964	2.50	5.00	10.00
❏ 2501 [S]	Unchained Melody/I'm So Alone	1960	3.75	7.50	15.00
❏ 2502 [S]	You Don't Know What Love Is/Say It Isn't So	1960	3.75	7.50	15.00

COLUMBIA

Number	Title (A Side/B Side)	Yr	VG	VG+	NM
❏ AE7 1108 [DJ]	It's the Most Wonderful Time of the Year/Kay Thompson's Jingle Bells	1976	2.50	5.00	10.00
—Special radio promo for Christmas Seals. Also contains public service announcements for Christmas Seals by Williams on each side.					
❏ AE7 1108 [PS]	It's the Most Wonderful Time of the Year/Kay Thompson's Jingle Bells	1976	2.50	5.00	10.00
❏ 10029	A Mi Esposa Con Amor (To My Wife with Love)/ Another Lonely Song	1974	—	2.00	4.00
❏ 10054	Christmas Present/The Lord's Prayer	1974	—	2.00	4.00
❏ 10054 [PS]	Christmas Present/The Lord's Prayer	1974	—	2.50	5.00
❏ 10078	Love Said Goodbye/One More Time	1974	—	2.00	4.00
❏ 10113	Cry Softly/You Lay So Easy on My Mind	1975	—	2.00	4.00
❏ 10144	Feelings/Quits	1975	—	2.00	4.00
❏ 10208	Sad Eyes/Quits	1975	—	2.00	4.00
❏ 10263	Tell It Like It Is/Goin' Through the Motions	1975	—	2.00	4.00
❏ 3-10471	Are You In There?/(Disco Version)	1977	—	2.00	4.00
❏ 3-10878	Love Theme from "Oliver's Story"/Everytime I See Laureen	1979	—	2.00	4.00
❏ 3-10952	Love Story (Where Do I Begin)/Love Theme from "Oliver's Story"	1979	—	2.00	4.00
❏ 1-11152	Jason/I'll Never Love Anyone Anymore	1979	—	2.00	4.00
❏ S7 31458 [S]	Love Is a Many-Splendored Thing/A Summer Place	1962	3.00	6.00	12.00
❏ S7 31459 [S]	Maria/Never on Sunday	1962	3.00	6.00	12.00
❏ S7 31460 [S]	The Exodus Song/Moon River	1962	3.00	6.00	12.00
❏ S7 31461 [S]	Tonight/The Second Time Around	1962	3.00	6.00	12.00
❏ S7 31462 [S]	It Might As Well Be Spring/Three Coins in the Fountain	1962	3.00	6.00	12.00
—The above five are "Stereo Seven" 33 1/3 rpm jukebox singles from set "JS 7-55" and the album "Moon River and Other Great Movie Themes"					
❏ 31495 [S]	(titles unknown)	1962	3.00	6.00	12.00
❏ 31496 [S]	(titles unknown)	1962	3.00	6.00	12.00
❏ 31497 [S]	(titles unknown)	1962	3.00	6.00	12.00
❏ 31498 [S]	(titles unknown)	1962	3.00	6.00	12.00
❏ 31499 [S]	(titles unknown)	1962	3.00	6.00	12.00

Number	Title (A Side/B Side)	Yr	VG	VG+	NM
❏ S7 31972 [S]	Canadian Sunset/Sing a Rainbow	1964	3.00	6.00	12.00
❏ S7 31973 [S]	Dream/Wives and Lovers	1964	3.00	6.00	12.00
❏ S7 31974 [S]	Pennies from Heaven/First Born	1964	3.00	6.00	12.00
❏ S7 31975 [S]	Noelle/Let It Be Me	1964	3.00	6.00	12.00
❏ S7 31976 [S]	(titles unknown)	1964	3.00	6.00	12.00

—*The above five are 33 1/3 rpm jukebox singles with small holes and are taken from the album "The Wonderful World of Andy Williams"*

Number	Title (A Side/B Side)	Yr	VG	VG+	NM
❏ 42199	Danny Boy/Fly by Night	1961	2.00	4.00	8.00
❏ 42199 [PS]	Danny Boy/Fly by Night	1961	3.00	6.00	12.00
❏ 42265	The Wonderful World of the Young/Help Me	1962	2.00	4.00	8.00
❏ 42265 [PS]	The Wonderful World of the Young/Help Me	1962	2.50	5.00	10.00
❏ 42451	Stranger on the Shore/I Want to Be Wanted	1962	2.00	4.00	8.00
❏ 42451 [PS]	Stranger on the Shore/I Want to Be Wanted	1962	2.50	5.00	10.00
❏ 42523	Don't You Believe It/Summertime	1962	2.00	4.00	8.00
❏ 42523 [PS]	Don't You Believe It/Summertime	1962	2.50	5.00	10.00
❏ 4-42674	Can't Get Used to Losing You/ Days of Wine and Roses	1963	2.00	4.00	8.00
❏ 4-42674 [DJ]	Can't Get Used to Losing You (same on both sides)	1963	3.75	7.50	15.00

—*Promo only on red vinyl*

Number	Title (A Side/B Side)	Yr	VG	VG+	NM
❏ 4-42674 [DJ]	Days of Wine and Roses (same on both sides)	1963	5.00	10.00	20.00

—*Promo only on yellow vinyl*

Number	Title (A Side/B Side)	Yr	VG	VG+	NM
❏ 4-42674 [PS]	Can't Get Used to Losing You/ Days of Wine and Roses	1963	2.50	5.00	10.00
❏ 42784	Hopeless/The Peking Theme (So Little Time)	1963	2.00	4.00	8.00
❏ 42894	The Christmas Song (Chestnuts Roasting On An Open Fire)/White Christmas	1963	2.00	4.00	8.00

—*Stock copy or black vinyl promo*

Number	Title (A Side/B Side)	Yr	VG	VG+	NM
❏ 42894 [DJ]	The Christmas Song (Chestnuts Roasting On An Open Fire)/White Christmas	1963	3.00	6.00	12.00

—*Promo only on green vinyl*

Number	Title (A Side/B Side)	Yr	VG	VG+	NM
❏ 42950	A Fool Never Learns/Charade	1963	2.00	4.00	8.00
❏ 43015	Wrong for Each Other/Madrigal	1964	—	3.00	6.00
❏ 43128	On the Street Where You Live/Almost There	1964	—	3.00	6.00
❏ 43180	Dear Heart/Emily	1964	—	3.00	6.00
❏ 43257	…And Roses and Roses/My Carousel	1965	—	3.00	6.00
❏ 43257 [PS]	…And Roses and Roses/My Carousel	1965	2.00	4.00	8.00
❏ 43358	Ain't It True/Loved One	1965	—	3.00	6.00
❏ 43456	I'll Remember You/Quiet Nights of Quiet Stars	1965	—	3.00	6.00
❏ 43458	Do You Hear What I Hear/ Some Children See Him	1965	2.00	4.00	8.00
❏ 43519	Bye Bye Blues/You're Gonna Hear from Me!	1966	—	3.00	6.00
❏ 43650	The Summer of Our Love/ How Can I Tell Her It's Over	1966	—	3.00	6.00
❏ 43737	In the Arms of Love/The Many Faces of Love	1966	—	3.00	6.00
❏ 44065	Music to Watch Girls By/The Face I Love	1967	—	2.50	5.00
❏ 44102	Born Free/Alfie	1967	2.50	5.00	10.00

—*Possibly yellow-label promo only*

Number	Title (A Side/B Side)	Yr	VG	VG+	NM
❏ 44202	More and More/I Want to Be Free	1967	—	2.50	5.00
❏ 44325	When I Look in Your Eyes/Holly	1967	—	2.50	5.00
❏ 44527	Sweet Memories/You Are Where Everything Is	1968	—	2.50	5.00
❏ 44650	Battle Hymn of the Republic/Ave Maria	1968	—	2.50	5.00
❏ 44650 [PS]	Battle Hymn of the Republic/Ave Maria	1968	—	3.00	6.00
❏ 44709	The Christmas Song (Chestnuts Roasting On An Open Fire)/It's The Most Wonderful Time Of The Year	1968	—	3.00	6.00
❏ 44818	Happy Heart/Our Last Goodbye	1969	—	2.50	5.00
❏ 44929	Live and Learn/You Are	1969	—	2.50	5.00
❏ 45003	What Am I Living For/A Woman's Way	1969	—	2.50	5.00
❏ 45094	Can't Help Falling in Love/Sweet Memories	1970	—	2.50	5.00
❏ 45175	One Day of Your Life/Long Time Blues	1970	—	2.50	5.00
❏ 45246	Whistling Away the Dark/Home Lovin' Man	1970	—	2.50	5.00
❏ 45317	(Where Do I Begin) Love Story/Something	1971	—	2.00	4.00
❏ 45434	You've Got a Friend/A Song for You	1971	—	2.00	4.00
❏ 45494	Help Me Make It Through the Night/Love Is All	1971	—	2.00	4.00
❏ 45531	The Last Time I Saw Her/ Music from Across the Way	1972	—	2.00	4.00
❏ 45533	Love Story (Spanish Version)/Music from Across the Way (Spanish Version)	1972	—	3.00	6.00
❏ 45579	Love Theme from "The Godfather" (Speak Softly Love)/Home for Thee	1972	—	2.00	4.00
❏ 45647	MacArthur Park/Amazing Grace	1972	—	2.00	4.00
❏ 45716	Who Was It?/Home Lovin' Man	1972	—	2.00	4.00
❏ 45757	Marmalade, Molenaisse and Honey/Who Was It	1973	—	2.00	4.00
❏ 45814	Last Tango in Paris/I'll Never Be the Same	1973	—	2.00	4.00
❏ 45936	Solitaire/My Love	1973	—	2.00	4.00
❏ 45985	Walk Right Back/Remember	1974	—	2.00	4.00

—*With Noelle*

Number	Title (A Side/B Side)	Yr	VG	VG+	NM
❏ 46049	Love's Theme/You're the Best Thing That's Ever Happened to Me	1974	—	2.00	4.00
❏ JZSP 76322/3 [DJ]	Away In A Manger/O Holy Night	1963	2.50	5.00	10.00
❏ JZSP 111911/2 [DJ]	Have Yourself A Merry Little Christmas/The Bells Of St. Mary's	1966	2.00	4.00	8.00

—*White label, black vinyl*

Number	Title (A Side/B Side)	Yr	VG	VG+	NM
❏ JZSP 111911/2 [DJ]	Have Yourself A Merry Little Christmas/The Bells Of St. Mary's	1966	2.00	4.00	8.00

—*Yellow label*

Number	Title (A Side/B Side)	Yr	VG	VG+	NM
❏ JZSP 111911/2 [DJ]	Have Yourself A Merry Little Christmas/The Bells Of St. Mary's	1966	3.75	7.50	15.00

—*White label, green vinyl*

MGM

Number	Title (A Side/B Side)	Yr	VG	VG+	NM
❏ 11076	Gentle Hands/From the Manger to the Cross	1951	6.25	12.50	25.00

"X"

Number	Title (A Side/B Side)	Yr	VG	VG+	NM
❏ 0036	Why Should I Cry Over You/ You Can't Buy Happiness	1954	5.00	10.00	20.00
❏ 0091	Now I Know/Here Comes That Dream Again	1955	5.00	10.00	20.00

7-Inch Extended Plays

CADENCE

Number	Title (A Side/B Side)	Yr	VG	VG+	NM
❏ CEP-103	*Canadian Sunset/Baby Doll/Butterfly/I Like Your Kind of Love	1957	3.00	6.00	12.00
❏ CEP-103 [PS]	Andy Williams	1957	3.00	6.00	12.00
❏ CEP-112	The Hawaiian Wedding Song/Sail Along Silv'ry Moon//Blue Hawaii/Sweet Leilani	1959	3.00	6.00	12.00
❏ CEP-112 [PS]	Andy Williams	1959	3.00	6.00	12.00
❏ CEP-116	It's All in the Game/My Happiness//Twilight Time/Love Letters in the Sand	1959	3.00	6.00	12.00
❏ CEP-116 [PS]	Two Time Winners	1959	3.00	6.00	12.00
❏ CEP-119	To You Sweetheart, Aloha/The Moon of Manakoora//I'll Weave a Lot of Stars for You/Beyond the Reef	1959	3.00	6.00	12.00
❏ CEP-119 [PS]	To You Sweetheart, Aloha	1959	3.00	6.00	12.00
❏ CEP-120	Aloha Oe/A Song of Old Hawaii//Song of the Islands/Love Song of Kalua	1959	3.00	6.00	12.00
❏ CEP-120 [PS]	Song of the Islands	1959	3.00	6.00	12.00

COLUMBIA

Number	Title (A Side/B Side)	Yr	VG	VG+	NM
❏ 7-8815	Falling in Love with Love/Days of Wine and Roses/I Left My Heart in San Francisco//Can't Get Used to Losing You/You Are My Sunshine/What Kind of Fool Am I?	196?	2.50	5.00	10.00

—*Jukebox issue; small hole, plays at 33 1/3*

Number	Title (A Side/B Side)	Yr	VG	VG+	NM
❏ 7-8815 [PS]	Days of Wine and Roses	196?	2.50	5.00	10.00
❏ 7-9138	Dear Heart/Red Roses for a Blue Lady/Who Can I Turn To//You're Nobody 'Til Somebody Loves You/Everybody Loves Somebody/I Can't Stop Loving You	1965	2.50	5.00	10.00

—*"Special Coin Operator Release"; small hole, plays at 33 1/3 rpm*

Number	Title (A Side/B Side)	Yr	VG	VG+	NM
❏ 7-9138 [PS]	Dear Heart	1965	2.50	5.00	10.00
❏ 7-9299	The Shadow of Your Smile/Try to Remember/Yesterday//Michelle/A Taste of Honey/Somewhere	1966	2.50	5.00	10.00

—*"Special Coin Operator Release"; small hole, plays at 33 1/3 rpm*

Number	Title (A Side/B Side)	Yr	VG	VG+	NM
❏ 7-9299 [PS]	The Shadow of Your Smile	1966	2.50	5.00	10.00

COLUMBIA SPECIAL PRODUCTS

Number	Title (A Side/B Side)	Yr	VG	VG+	NM
❏ CSM 679	A Taste of Honey/(Corcovado) Quiet Nights of Quiet Stars/Holly//You Are Where Everything Is/Noelle/May Each Day	1968	2.50	5.00	10.00

—*Small hole, plays at 33 1/3 rpm*

Number	Title (A Side/B Side)	Yr	VG	VG+	NM
❏ CSM 679 [PS]	Andy Williams	1968	3.75	7.50	15.00

—*"Produced Exclusively for Kentucky Fried Chicken Corp."*

Albums

ATCO

Number	Title (A Side/B Side)	Yr	VG	VG+	NM
❏ 90561	Close Enough for Love	1987	2.50	5.00	10.00

CADENCE

Number	Title (A Side/B Side)	Yr	VG	VG+	NM
❏ CLP 1018 [M]	Andy Williams	1957	12.50	25.00	50.00
❏ CLP 3002 [M]	Andy Williams	1958	12.50	25.00	50.00

—*Cover depicts Andy standing*

Number	Title (A Side/B Side)	Yr	VG	VG+	NM
❏ CLP 3002 [M]	Andy Williams	1960	5.00	10.00	20.00

—*Cover depicts Andy reclining*

Number	Title (A Side/B Side)	Yr	VG	VG+	NM
❏ CLP 3005 [M]	Andy Williams Sings Rodgers and Hammerstein	1958	10.00	20.00	40.00

—*Cover depicts a cafÉ scene*

Number	Title (A Side/B Side)	Yr	VG	VG+	NM
❏ CLP 3005 [M]	Andy Williams Sings Rodgers and Hammerstein	1960	5.00	10.00	20.00

—*Cover depicts a close-up of Andy's face*

Number	Title (A Side/B Side)	Yr	VG	VG+	NM
❏ CLP 3026 [M]	Two Time Winners	1959	5.00	10.00	20.00
❏ CLP 3027 [M]	Andy Williams Sings…Steve Allen	1959	5.00	10.00	20.00
❏ CLP 3029 [M]	To You Sweetheart, Aloha	1959	5.00	10.00	20.00
❏ CLP 3030 [M]	Lonely Street	1960	5.00	10.00	20.00
❏ CLP 3038 [M]	The Village of St. Bernadette	1960	5.00	10.00	20.00
❏ CLP 3047 [M]	Under Paris Skies	1961	5.00	10.00	20.00
❏ CLP 3054 [M]	Andy Williams' Best	1962	5.00	10.00	20.00
❏ CLP 3061 [M]	Million Seller Songs	1962	5.00	10.00	20.00
❏ CLP 25026 [S]	Two Time Winners	1959	7.50	15.00	30.00

—*Black vinyl*

Number	Title (A Side/B Side)	Yr	VG	VG+	NM
❏ CLP 25026 [S]	Two Time Winners	1959	20.00	40.00	80.00

—*Red vinyl*

Number	Title (A Side/B Side)	Yr	VG	VG+	NM
❏ CLP 25027 [R]	Andy Williams Sings…Steve Allen	1959	3.75	7.50	15.00
❏ CLP 25029 [S]	To You Sweetheart, Aloha	1959	7.50	15.00	30.00
❏ CLP 25030 [S]	Lonely Street	1960	7.50	15.00	30.00
❏ CLP 25038 [S]	The Village of St. Bernadette	1960	7.50	15.00	30.00
❏ CLP 25047 [S]	Under Paris Skies	1961	7.50	15.00	30.00
❏ CLP 25054 [S]	Andy Williams' Best	1962	6.25	12.50	25.00
❏ CLP 25061 [S]	Million Seller Songs	1962	6.25	12.50	25.00

CAPITOL

Number	Title (A Side/B Side)	Yr	VG	VG+	NM
❏ ST-12387	Greatest Love Classics	1984	2.50	5.00	10.00

COLUMBIA

Number	Title (A Side/B Side)	Yr	VG	VG+	NM
❏ GP 5 [(2)]	The Andy Williams Sound of Music	1969	5.00	10.00	20.00
❏ CL 1751 [M]	Danny Boy And Other Songs I Love to Sing	1962	3.75	7.50	15.00
❏ CL 1809 [M]	Moon River and Other Great Movie Themes	1962	3.00	6.00	12.00
❏ CL 1879 [M]	Warm and Willing	1962	3.00	6.00	12.00
❏ CL 2015 [M]	Days of Wine and Roses	1963	3.00	6.00	12.00
❏ CL 2087 [M]	The Andy Williams Christmas Album	1963	3.00	6.00	12.00
❏ CL 2137 [M]	The Wonderful World of Andy Williams	1964	3.00	6.00	12.00
❏ CL 2171 [M]	The Academy Award Winning "Call Me Irresponsible" and Other Hits Songs from the Movies	1964	3.00	6.00	12.00
❏ CL 2205 [M]	The Great Songs from "My Fair Lady" and Other Broadway Hits	1964	3.00	6.00	12.00
❏ CL 2323 [M]	Hawaiian Wedding Song	1965	3.00	6.00	12.00
❏ CL 2324 [M]	Canadian Sunset	1965	3.00	6.00	12.00

—*Reissue of Cadence 3029*

Number	Title (A Side/B Side)	Yr	VG	VG+	NM
❏ CL 2338 [M]	Dear Heart	1965	3.00	6.00	12.00
❏ CL 2383 [M]	Andy Williams' Newest Hits	1966	3.00	6.00	12.00
❏ CL 2420 [M]	Merry Christmas	1965	3.00	6.00	12.00
❏ CL 2499 [M]	The Shadow of Your Smile	1966	3.00	6.00	12.00
❏ CL 2533 [M]	In the Arms of Love	1967	3.00	6.00	12.00
❏ CL 2680 [M]	Born Free	1967	3.00	6.00	12.00
❏ CL 2766 [M]	Love, Andy	1967	3.75	7.50	15.00
❏ CS 2862 [M]	Honey	1968	5.00	10.00	20.00
❏ CS 8551 [S]	Danny Boy And Other Songs I Love to Sing	1962	5.00	10.00	20.00
❏ CS 8609 [S]	Moon River and Other Great Movie Themes	1962	3.75	7.50	15.00
❏ CS 8679 [S]	Warm and Willing	1962	3.75	7.50	15.00
❏ CS 8815 [S]	Days of Wine and Roses	1963	3.75	7.50	15.00
❏ CS 8887 [S]	The Andy Williams Christmas Album	1963	3.00	6.00	12.00
❏ CS 8937 [S]	The Wonderful World of Andy Williams	1964	3.75	7.50	15.00
❏ CS 8971 [S]	The Academy Award Winning "Call Me Irresponsible" and Other Hits Songs from the Movies	1964	3.75	7.50	15.00
❏ CS 9005 [S]	The Great Songs from "My Fair Lady" and Other Broadway Hits	1964	3.75	7.50	15.00
❏ CS 9123 [S]	Hawaiian Wedding Song	1965	3.75	7.50	15.00

—*Reissue of Cadence 25029*

Number	Title (A Side/B Side)	Yr	VG	VG+	NM
❏ CS 9124 [S]	Canadian Sunset	1965	3.75	7.50	15.00

—*Reissue of Cadence 25054*

Number	Title (A Side/B Side)	Yr	VG	VG+	NM
❏ CS 9138 [S]	Dear Heart	1965	3.75	7.50	15.00

Number	Title (A Side/B Side)	Yr	VG	VG+	NM
❏ CS 9183 [S]	Andy Williams' Newest Hits	1966	3.75	7.50	15.00
❏ CS 9220 [S]	Merry Christmas	1965	3.00	6.00	12.00
❏ CS 9299 [S]	The Shadow of Your Smile	1966	3.75	7.50	15.00
❏ CS 9333 [S]	In the Arms of Love	1967	3.75	7.50	15.00
❏ CS 9480 [S]	Born Free	1967	3.75	7.50	15.00
❏ CS 9566 [S]	Love, Andy	1967	3.00	6.00	12.00
❏ CS 9662 [S]	Honey	1968	3.00	6.00	12.00
❏ CS 9844	Happy Heart	1969	3.00	6.00	12.00
❏ CS 9896	Raindrops Keep Fallin' on My Head	1970	3.00	6.00	12.00
❏ CS 9922	Get Together with Andy Williams	1969	3.75	7.50	15.00

—The Osmonds appear on three tracks

Number	Title (A Side/B Side)	Yr	VG	VG+	NM
❏ KCS 9979	Andy Williams' Greatest Hits	1970	3.00	6.00	12.00
❏ KC 30105	The Andy Williams Show	1970	2.50	5.00	10.00
❏ CQ 30497 [Q]	Love Story	1972	3.75	7.50	15.00
❏ KC 30497	Love Story	1971	2.50	5.00	10.00
❏ CQ 30797 [Q]	You've Got a Friend	1971	3.75	7.50	15.00
❏ KC 30797	You've Got a Friend	1971	2.50	5.00	10.00
❏ CG 31064 [(2)]	The Impossible Dream	1971	3.75	7.50	15.00
❏ CQ 31303 [Q]	Love Theme from "The Godfather"	1972	3.75	7.50	15.00
❏ KC 31303	Love Theme from "The Godfather"	1972	2.50	5.00	10.00
❏ CQ 31625 [Q]	Alone Again (Naturally)	1972	3.75	7.50	15.00
❏ KC 31625	Alone Again (Naturally)	1972	2.50	5.00	10.00
❏ KC 32383	Solitaire	1973	2.50	5.00	10.00
❏ KC 32384	Andy Williams' Greatest Hits, Vol. 2	1973	2.50	5.00	10.00
❏ KC 32949	The Way We Were	1974	2.50	5.00	10.00
❏ C 33191	Christmas Present	1974	2.50	5.00	10.00
❏ KC 33234	You Lay So Easy on My Mind	1974	2.50	5.00	10.00
❏ PC 33563	The Other Side of Me	1975	2.50	5.00	10.00
❏ CG 33597 [(2)]	Love Story/Born Free	1975	3.00	6.00	12.00
❏ CG 33600 [(2)]	Moon River/Days of Wine and Roses	1975	3.00	6.00	12.00
❏ PC 34299	Andy	1976	2.50	5.00	10.00
❏ PCQ 34299 [Q]	Andy	1976	3.75	7.50	15.00

COLUMBIA SPECIAL PRODUCTS

Number	Title (A Side/B Side)	Yr	VG	VG+	NM
❏ CSS 966	Andy... & Company	1969	3.00	6.00	12.00

—Side 1 is Andy Williams; Side 2 has tracks by the Williams Brothers, Claudine Longet and the Osmond Brothers; sold only at Woolworth's

HARMONY

Number	Title (A Side/B Side)	Yr	VG	VG+	NM
❏ KH 30133	Andy Williams	1970	2.50	5.00	10.00

PAIR

Number	Title (A Side/B Side)	Yr	VG	VG+	NM
❏ PDL2-1103 [(2)]	The Best of Andy Williams	1986	3.00	6.00	12.00

TIME-LIFE

Number	Title (A Side/B Side)	Yr	VG	VG+	NM
❏ SLGD-11 [(2)]	Legendary Singers: Andy Williams	1986	3.75	7.50	15.00

WILLIAMS, BARRY "Greg Brady" of THE BRADY BUNCH.
45s
PARAMOUNT

Number	Title (A Side/B Side)	Yr	VG	VG+	NM
❏ 0122	Sweet Sweetheart/Sunny	1971	3.75	7.50	15.00
❏ 0122 [PS]	Sweet Sweetheart/Sunny	1971	5.00	10.00	20.00

WILLIAMS, BERNIE
45s
BELL

Number	Title (A Side/B Side)	Yr	VG	VG+	NM
❏ 768	Ever Again/Next to You	1969	300.00	600.00	1200.

WILLIAMS, BETTY
45s
HIT

Number	Title (A Side/B Side)	Yr	VG	VG+	NM
❏ 101	As Usual/The Boy Next Door	1964	2.00	4.00	8.00

—B-side by the Belles

WILLIAMS, BIG JOE
Albums
BLUESVILLE

Number	Title (A Side/B Side)	Yr	VG	VG+	NM
❏ BVLP-1056 [M]	Blues for 9 Strings	1962	25.00	50.00	100.00

—Blue label, silver print

| ❏ BVLP-1056 [M] | Blues for 9 Strings | 1964 | 6.25 | 12.50 | 25.00 |

—Blue label with trident logo

| ❏ BVLP-1067 [M] | Big Joe Williams at Folk City | 1963 | 25.00 | 50.00 | 100.00 |

—Blue label, silver print

| ❏ BVLP-1067 [M] | Big Joe Williams at Folk City | 1964 | 6.25 | 12.50 | 25.00 |

—Blue label with trident logo

| ❏ BVLP-1083 [M] | Studio Blues | 1964 | 6.25 | 12.50 | 25.00 |

—Blue label with trident logo

| ❏ BVLP-1083 [M] | Studio Blues | 1964 | 25.00 | 50.00 | 100.00 |

—Blue label, silver print

DELMARK

Number	Title (A Side/B Side)	Yr	VG	VG+	NM
❏ DL-604 [M]	Blues on Highway 49	1962	15.00	30.00	60.00
❏ DL-609 [M]	Starvin' Chain Blues	1966	6.25	12.50	25.00

FOLKWAYS

Number	Title (A Side/B Side)	Yr	VG	VG+	NM
❏ FA-3820 [M]	Mississippi's Big Joe Williams	1962	7.50	15.00	30.00
❏ FAS-3820 [R]	Mississippi's Big Joe Williams	1962	5.00	10.00	20.00

MILESTONE

Number	Title (A Side/B Side)	Yr	VG	VG+	NM
❏ 3001 [M]	Classic Delta Blues	1966	6.25	12.50	25.00

WILLIAMS, BILLY Also see THE CHARIOTEERS.
45s
CORAL

Number	Title (A Side/B Side)	Yr	VG	VG+	NM
❏ 61212	Sh-Boom (Life Could Be a Dream)/ Whenever Wherever	1954	3.00	6.00	12.00
❏ 61264	Love Me/The Honeydripper	1954	3.00	6.00	12.00
❏ 61346	Fools Rush In/He Follows She	1955	3.00	6.00	12.00
❏ 61462	Glory of Love/Wonderful, Wonderful One	1955	3.00	6.00	12.00
❏ 61498	Just a Little Bit More/Learning to Love	1955	3.00	6.00	12.00
❏ 61576	Cry Baby/A Crazy Little Place	1956	2.50	5.00	10.00
❏ 61639	Pray/You'll Reach Your Star	1956	2.50	5.00	10.00
❏ 61684	This Planet Earth/I Guess I'll Be On My Way	1956	2.50	5.00	10.00
❏ 61730	Shame, Shame, Shame/ Don't Cry on My Shoulder	1956	2.50	5.00	10.00
❏ 61751	Stormy/Follow Me	1956	2.50	5.00	10.00
❏ 61795	Butterfly/The Pied Piper	1957	2.50	5.00	10.00
❏ 61830	I'm Gonna Sit Right Down and Write Myself a Letter/Date with the Blues	1957	3.00	6.00	12.00
❏ 61886	Got a Date with an Angel/ The Lord Will Understand	1957	2.50	5.00	10.00
❏ 61932	Don't Let Go/Baby, Baby	1958	2.50	5.00	10.00
❏ 61961	There! I've Said It Again/Steppin' Out Tonight	1958	2.50	5.00	10.00
❏ 61999	I'll Get By/It's Prayin' Time	1958	2.50	5.00	10.00

Number	Title (A Side/B Side)	Yr	VG	VG+	NM
❏ 62029	It Hurts So Much/So Long	1958	2.50	5.00	10.00
❏ 62069	Nola/Tied to the Strings of Your Heart	1959	2.50	5.00	10.00
❏ 62101	Goodnight Irene/Red Hot Love	1959	2.50	5.00	10.00
❏ 62131	Go to Sleep, Go to Sleep, Go to Sleep/ Telephone Conversation	1959	2.00	4.00	8.00

—With Barbara McNair

Number	Title (A Side/B Side)	Yr	VG	VG+	NM
❏ 62140	Smack Dab in the Middle/I Wonder	1959	2.00	4.00	8.00
❏ 62218	I Cried for You/The Lover of All Lovers	1960	2.00	4.00	8.00
❏ 62230	Begin the Beguine/For You	1960	2.00	4.00	8.00
❏ 62438	Why Do I Love You So/Raise Your Hand	1964	—	3.00	6.00
❏ 62438	Why Do I Love You So/The Honeydripper	1964	—	3.00	6.00

MERCURY

Number	Title (A Side/B Side)	Yr	VG	VG+	NM
❏ 5866	Stay/Azure-Te (Paris Blues)	1952	3.75	7.50	15.00
❏ 5884	Who Knows/It's Best We Say Goodbye	1952	3.75	7.50	15.00
❏ 5902	That's What I'm Here For/Some Folks Do, Some Folks Don't	1952	3.75	7.50	15.00
❏ 70012	I Don't Know Why/Mad About 'Cha	1952	3.75	7.50	15.00
❏ 70094	Pour Me a Glass of Teardrops/It's a Miracle	1953	3.75	7.50	15.00
❏ 70180	This Side of Heaven/You're the One for Me	1953	3.75	7.50	15.00
❏ 70210	Why Do You Have to Go?/Cattle Call	1953	3.75	7.50	15.00
❏ 70271	If I Ever Get to Heaven/Ask Me No Questions	1953	3.75	7.50	15.00
❏ 70324	Invitation to Dance/I'll Close My Eyes	1954	3.75	7.50	15.00
❏ 70376	Go Home, Joe/You're the Only One I Adore	1954	3.75	7.50	15.00

MGM

Number	Title (A Side/B Side)	Yr	VG	VG+	NM
❏ 10764	Longing/I Didn't Slip	1950	5.00	10.00	20.00
❏ 10857	The Room I'm Sleeping In/Music by Angels	1950	5.00	10.00	20.00
❏ 10928	Gaucho Serenade/I Won't Cry Anymore	1951	3.75	7.50	15.00
❏ 10967	Pretty Eyed Baby/You Made Me Love You	1951	3.75	7.50	15.00
❏ 10998	Shang-Hai/A Wondrous Word	1951	3.75	7.50	15.00
❏ 11066	Sin/It's Over	1951	3.75	7.50	15.00
❏ 11117	I'll Never Find You/Busy Line	1951	3.75	7.50	15.00
❏ 11145	No Other Love/Callaway Went That-A-Way	1952	3.75	7.50	15.00
❏ 11172	Wheel of Fortune/What Can I Say	1952	3.75	7.50	15.00
❏ 11184	Confetti/Don't Grieve	1952	3.75	7.50	15.00
❏ 12537	Shang-Hai/Gaucho Serenade	1957	2.50	5.00	10.00

7-Inch Extended Plays
CORAL

Number	Title (A Side/B Side)	Yr	VG	VG+	NM
❏ EC 81164	*I'm Gonna Sit Right Down and Write Myself A Letter/Lucy Lou/The❏ Lord Will Understand (And Say "Well Done")/The Honeydripper	1957	3.00	6.00	12.00
❏ EC 81164 [PS]	(title unknown)	1957	3.00	6.00	12.00

Albums
CORAL

Number	Title (A Side/B Side)	Yr	VG	VG+	NM
❏ CRL 57184 [M]	Billy Williams	1957	15.00	30.00	60.00
❏ CRL 57251 [M]	Half Sweet, Half Beat	1959	12.50	25.00	50.00
❏ CRL 57343 [M]	The Billy Williams Revue	1960	12.50	25.00	50.00
❏ CRL 757251 [S]	Half Sweet, Half Beat	1959	20.00	40.00	80.00
❏ CRL 757343 [S]	The Billy Williams Revue	1960	15.00	30.00	60.00

MERCURY

Number	Title (A Side/B Side)	Yr	VG	VG+	NM
❏ MG 20317 [M]	Oh Yeah!	1958	15.00	30.00	60.00

MGM

Number	Title (A Side/B Side)	Yr	VG	VG+	NM
❏ E-3400 [M]	The Billy Williams Quartet	1957	15.00	30.00	60.00

WING

Number	Title (A Side/B Side)	Yr	VG	VG+	NM
❏ MGW-12131 [M]	Vote for Billy Williams	1959	10.00	20.00	40.00

WILLIAMS, BILLY DEE
Albums
PRESTIGE LIVELY ARTS

Number	Title (A Side/B Side)	Yr	VG	VG+	NM
❏ 30001 [M]	Let's Misbehave	1962	10.00	20.00	40.00

WILLIAMS, CORA/SHIRLEY HAVEN AND THE FOUR JACKS
45s
FEDERAL

Number	Title (A Side/B Side)	Yr	VG	VG+	NM
❏ 12079	I Ain't Coming Back Anymore/Sure Cure for the Blues	1952	150.00	300.00	600.00

WILLIAMS, DANNY
45s
UNITED ARTISTS

Number	Title (A Side/B Side)	Yr	VG	VG+	NM
❏ 348	Lonely/We Will Never Be As Young As This Again	1961	3.00	6.00	12.00
❏ 411	Jeannie/Weaver of Dreams	1962	3.00	6.00	12.00
❏ 480	Something's Gotta Give/Miracle of You	1962	3.00	6.00	12.00
❏ 493	Tears/Miracle of You	1962	3.00	6.00	12.00
❏ 601	More (Theme from Mondo Cane)/Rhapsody	1963	3.00	6.00	12.00
❏ 685	White on White/The Comedy Is Ended	1964	3.75	7.50	15.00
❏ 729	The Truth Hurts/Little Toy Balloon	1964	2.50	5.00	10.00
❏ 762	I Watched a Flower Grow/Forget Her, Forget Her	1964	2.50	5.00	10.00
❏ 825	How Soon/The Seventh Dawn	1965	2.50	5.00	10.00
❏ 860	All's Fair in Love and War/Masquerade	1965	2.50	5.00	10.00
❏ 959	The Stranger/I Can't Believe I'm Losing You	1965	2.50	5.00	10.00
❏ 50020	Blue on White/It's Not for Me to Say	1966	2.00	4.00	8.00

Albums
UNITED ARTISTS

Number	Title (A Side/B Side)	Yr	VG	VG+	NM
❏ UAL-3297 [M]	The Exciting Danny Williams	1963	3.75	7.50	15.00
❏ UAL-3359 [M]	White on White	1964	3.75	7.50	15.00
❏ UAL-3380 [M]	With You in Mind	1964	3.75	7.50	15.00
❏ UAL-3493 [M]	Magic Town	1966	3.75	7.50	15.00
❏ UAS-6297 [S]	The Exciting Danny Williams	1963	5.00	10.00	20.00
❏ UAS-6359 [S]	White on White	1964	5.00	10.00	20.00
❏ UAS-6380 [S]	With You in Mind	1964	5.00	10.00	20.00
❏ UAS-6493 [S]	Magic Town	1966	5.00	10.00	20.00

WILLIAMS, DENIECE
12-Inch Singles
ARC

Number	Title (A Side/B Side)	Yr	VG	VG+	NM
❏ 10991	I've Got the Next Dance/ When Love Comes Calling	1979	3.00	6.00	12.00
❏ 11141	I Found Love/Are You Thinking?	1979	3.00	6.00	12.00
❏ 60504	What Two Can Do/Suspicious	1981	—	2.00	4.00

COLUMBIA

Number	Title (A Side/B Side)	Yr	VG	VG+	NM
❏ AS 1838 [DJ]	Let's Hear It for the Boy (6:00) (3:34)	1984	3.75	7.50	15.00
❏ CAS 2688 [DJ]	Never Say Never (3 versions)	1987	—	3.00	6.00
❏ 04988	Let's Hear It for the Boy (6:00) (4:13)	1984	2.00	4.00	8.00
❏ 05043	Next Love (7:07)/(Instrumental)	1984	2.00	4.00	8.00
❏ 05918	Wiser and Weaker (6:15) (5:50 Instrumental)	1986	2.00	4.00	8.00
❏ 06929	I Confess (3 versions)	1987	—	3.00	6.00
❏ 10513	Free/It's Important to Me	1977	3.75	7.50	15.00

Number	Title (A Side/B Side)	Yr	VG	VG+	NM
45s					
ARC					
❏ 02108	It's Your Conscience/Sweet Surrender	1981	—	2.00	4.00
❏ 02406	Silly/My Melody	1981	—	2.00	4.00
❏ 02812	It's Gonna Take a Miracle/Part of Love	1982	—	2.00	4.00
❏ 03015	Waiting by the Hotline/Love Notes	1982	—	2.00	4.00
❏ 03242	It's Gonna Take a Miracle/Silly	1982	—	—	3.00
—Reissue					
❏ 03261	Waiting/How Does It Feel	1982	—	2.00	4.00
❏ 10971	I've Got the Next Dance/				
	When Love Comes Calling	1979	—	2.00	4.00
❏ 11063	I Found Love/Are You Thinking?	1979	—	2.00	4.00
COLUMBIA					
❏ AE7 1153 [DJ]	God Is Amazing/God Is Standing By	1977	2.00	4.00	8.00
—B-side by Johnnie Taylor; promo with "Suggested Christmas Programming" on label					
❏ 03807	Do What You Feel/Love, Peace and Unity	1983	—	2.00	4.00
❏ 03807 [PS]	Do What You Feel/Love, Peace and Unity	1983	—	2.00	4.00
❏ 04037	I'm So Proud/It's Okay	1983	—	2.00	4.00
❏ 04218	Heaven in Your Eyes/Love, Peace and Unity	1983	—	2.00	4.00
❏ 38-04417	Let's Hear It for the Boy/(Instrumental)	1984	—	—	3.00
❏ 38-04417 [PS]	Let's Hear It for the Boy/(Instrumental)	1984	—	2.00	4.00
❏ 04537	Next Love/Picking Up the Pieces	1984	—	—	3.00
❏ 04537 [PS]	Next Love/Picking Up the Pieces	1984	—	2.00	4.00
❏ 04641	Black Butterfly/Blind Dating	1984	—	—	3.00
❏ 06157	Wiser and Weaker/(Instrumental)	1986	—	—	3.00
❏ 06157 [PS]	Wiser and Weaker/(Instrumental)	1986	—	—	3.00
❏ 06318	Healing/I Feel the Night	1986	—	—	3.00
❏ 07021	Never Say Never/Love Finds You	1987	—	—	3.00
❏ 07021 [PS]	Never Say Never/Love Finds You	1987	—	—	3.00
❏ 07357	I Confess/(Instrumental)	1987	—	—	3.00
❏ 07633	Water Under the Bridge/Love Finds You	1987	—	—	3.00
❏ 07704	I Believe in You/(Instrumental)	1988	—	—	3.00
❏ 08014	I Can't Wait/(Instrumental)	1988	—	—	3.00
❏ 08014 [PS]	I Can't Wait/(Instrumental)	1988	—	—	3.00
❏ 08425	Let's Hear It for the Boy/(Instrumental)	1988	—	—	3.00
—Reissue					
❏ 08507	This Is As Good As It Gets/Don't Stop the Love	1988	—	—	3.00
❏ 10429	Free/'Cause You Love Me Baby	1976	—	2.50	5.00
❏ 10556	That's What Friends Are For/It's Important to Me	1977	—	2.50	5.00
❏ 10648	Baby, Baby My Love's All for You/Be Good to Me	1977	—	2.50	5.00
MCA					
❏ 53707	Every Moment/Do You Hear What I Hear?	1989	—	—	3.00
SPARROW					
❏ S7-18215	Do You Hear What I Hear/Silent Night	1994	—	2.50	5.00
—B-side by Bebe and Cece Winans; green vinyl					
TODDLIN' TOWN					
❏ 107	Love Is Tears/I'm Walkin' Away	1968	2.50	5.00	10.00
—As "Deniece Chandler"					
❏ 113	Hey Baby/Glorious Feeling	1968	2.50	5.00	10.00
—As "Deniece Chandler"; with Lee Sain					
❏ 118	I Don't Wanna Cry/Goodbye Cruel World	1969	2.50	5.00	10.00
❏ 127	Shy Boy/(B-side unknown)	1969	2.50	5.00	10.00
—As "Deniece Chandler"					
Albums					
ARC					
❏ AS 1432 [DJ]	Niecy	1982	6.25	12.50	25.00
—Promo-only picture disc					
❏ JC 35568	When Love Comes Calling	1979	2.50	5.00	10.00
❏ FC 37048	My Melody	1981	2.50	5.00	10.00
❏ PC 37048	My Melody	198?	2.00	4.00	8.00
—Budget-line reissue					
❏ FC 37952	Niecy	1982	2.50	5.00	10.00
❏ PC 37952	Niecy	198?	2.00	4.00	8.00
—Budget-line reissue					
❏ HC 47952	Niecy	1983	12.50	25.00	50.00
—Half-speed mastered edition					
COLUMBIA					
❏ PC 34242	This Is Niecy	1976	2.50	5.00	10.00
—No bar code on cover					
❏ PC 34242	This Is Niecy	198?	2.00	4.00	8.00
—Reissue with bar code on cover					
❏ JC 34911	Song Bird	1977	2.50	5.00	10.00
❏ PC 34911	Song Bird	198?	2.00	4.00	8.00
—Budget-line reissue					
❏ FC 38622	I'm So Proud	1983	2.50	5.00	10.00
❏ PC 38622	I'm So Proud	198?	2.00	4.00	8.00
—Budget-line reissue					
❏ FC 39366	Let's Hear It for the Boy	1984	2.50	5.00	10.00
❏ FC 40084	Hot on the Trail	1986	2.50	5.00	10.00
❏ FC 44322	As Good As It Gets	1989	2.50	5.00	10.00
MCA					
❏ 6338	Special Love	1989	2.50	5.00	10.00
SPARROW					
❏ SPR-1256	From the Beginning	1990	3.00	6.00	12.00
❏ ST-41039	So Glad I Know	1986	3.00	6.00	12.00

WILLIAMS, DON Also see EMMYLOU HARRIS; THE POZO-SECO SINGERS.

Number	Title (A Side/B Side)	Yr	VG	VG+	NM
45s					
ABC					
❏ 12332	I've Got a Winner in You/Overlookin' and				
	Underthinkin'	1978	—	2.00	4.00
❏ 12373	Rake and Ramblin' Man/Too Many Tears	1978	—	2.00	4.00
❏ 12425	Tulsa Time/When I'm With You	1978	—	2.50	5.00
❏ 12458	Lay Down Beside Me/				
	I Would Like to See You Again	1979	—	2.50	5.00
ABC DOT					
❏ 17531	The Ties That Bind/				
	Goodbye Isn't Really Good at All	1974	—	2.00	4.00
❏ 17550	You're My Best Friend/Where Are You	1975	—	2.00	4.00
❏ 17568	(Turn the Light And) Love Me Tonight/				
	Reason to Be	1975	—	2.00	4.00
❏ 17604	Till the Rivers All Run Dry/				
	Don't You Think It's Time	1976	—	2.00	4.00
❏ 17631	Say It Again/I Don't Want the Money	1976	—	2.00	4.00
❏ 17658	She Never Knew Me/Ramblin'	1976	—	2.00	4.00

Number	Title (A Side/B Side)	Yr	VG	VG+	NM
❏ 17683	Some Broken Hearts Never Mend/				
	I'll Forgive But I'll Never Forget	1977	—	2.00	4.00
❏ 17717	I'm Just a Country Boy/It's Gotta Be Magic	1977	—	2.00	4.00
CAPITOL					
❏ B-5526	We've Got a Good Fire Goin'/Shot Full of Love	1985	—	—	3.00
❏ B-5588	Heartbeat in the Darkness/Light in Your Eyes	1986	—	—	3.00
❏ B-5638	Then It's Love/It's About Time	1986	—	—	3.00
❏ B-5683	Senorita/Send Her Roses	1987	—	—	3.00
❏ B-44019	I'll Never Be in Love Again/Send Her Roses	1987	—	—	3.00
❏ B-44066	I Wouldn't Be a Man/Light in Your Eyes	1987	—	—	3.00
❏ B-44131	Another Place, Another Time/Running Out of				
	Reasons to Run	1988	—	—	3.00
❏ B-44216	Desperately/You Loved Me Through It All	1988	—	—	3.00
❏ B-44274	Old Coyote Town/You Loved Me Through It All	1988	—	—	3.00
DOT					
❏ 17516	I Wouldn't Want to Live If You Didn't Love Me/				
	Fly Away	1974	—	2.50	5.00
GIANT					
❏ 17126	Pretty Little Baby Child/				
	'Twas the Night Before Christmas	1998	—	—	3.00
JMI					
❏ 7	Don't You Believe/You Have a Star	1972	—	3.00	6.00
❏ 12	The Shelter of Your Eyes/Playin' Around	1972	—	3.00	6.00
❏ 24	Come Early Morning/Amanda	1973	—	3.00	6.00
❏ 32	Atta Way to Go/I Recall a Gypsy Woman	1973	—	3.00	6.00
❏ 36	We Should Be Together/Miller's Cave	1974	—	3.00	6.00
❏ 42	Down the Road I Go/				
	She's in Love with a Rodeo Man	1974	—	3.00	6.00
MCA					
❏ S45-1763 [DJ]	A Special Message from Don Williams For Your				
	Radio Station and Audience	1982	3.00	6.00	12.00
❏ 12458	Lay Down Beside Me/				
	I Would Like to See You Again	1979	—	—	3.00
—Reissue of ABC 12458					
❏ 41069	It Must Be Love/Not a Chance	1979	—	—	3.00
❏ 41155	Love Me Over Again/Circle Driveway	1979	—	—	3.00
❏ 41205	Good Ole Boys Like Me/We're All the Way	1980	—	—	3.00
❏ 41304	I Believe in You/It Only Rains on Me	1980	—	2.00	4.00
❏ 51065	Falling Again/				
	I Keep Putting Off Getting Over You	1981	—	—	3.00
❏ 51134	Miracles/I Don't Want to Love You	1981	—	—	3.00
❏ 51207	Lord, I Hope This Day Is Good/Smooth Talking				
	Baby	1981	—	—	3.00
❏ 52037	Listen to the Radio/Only Love	1982	—	—	3.00
❏ 52097	Mistakes/Fool, Fool Heart	1982	—	—	3.00
❏ 52152	If Hollywood Don't Need You/Help Yourselves				
	to Each Other	1982	—	—	3.00
❏ 52205	Love Is on a Roll/I'll Take Your Love Anytime	1983	—	—	3.00
❏ 52245	Nobody But You/If Love Gets There Before I Do	1983	—	—	3.00
❏ 52310	Stay Young/Pressure Makes Diamonds	1983	—	—	3.00
❏ 52389	That's the Thing About Love/I'm Still Looking for				
	You	1984	—	—	3.00
❏ 52448	Maggie's Dream/Leavin'	1984	—	—	3.00
❏ 52514	Walkin' a Broken Heart/True Blue Hearts	1984	—	—	3.00
❏ 52692	It's Time for Love/I'll Never Need Another You	1985	—	—	3.00
RCA					
❏ 2507-7-R	Maybe That's All It Takes/We're All the Way	1990	—	2.00	4.00
❏ 2677-7-R	Back in My Younger Days/Diamonds to Dust	1990	—	2.00	4.00
❏ 2745-7-R	True Love/Learn to Let It Go	1990	—	2.00	4.00
❏ 2820-7-R	Lord Have Mercy on a Country Boy/				
	Jamaica Farewell	1991	—	2.00	4.00
❏ 8867-7-R	One Good Well/Flowers Won't Grow				
	(In a Field of Stone)	1989	—	2.00	4.00
❏ 9017-7-R	I've Been Loved by the Best/				
	If You Love, Won't You Love Me	1989	—	2.00	4.00
❏ 9119-7-R	Just As Long As I Have You/Why Get Up	1989	—	2.00	4.00
❏ 62055	Donald and June/Come a Little Closer	1991	—	2.00	4.00
❏ 62180	Too Much Love/Back on the Street Again	1992	—	2.00	4.00
❏ 62220	It's Who You Love/The Old Trail	1992	—	2.00	4.00
❏ 62317	Catfish Bates/That Song About the River	1992	—	2.00	4.00
Albums					
ABC					
❏ AA-1069	Expressions	1978	3.00	6.00	12.00
ABC/DOT					
❏ DOSD-2004	Don Williams, Vol. III	1974	3.00	6.00	12.00
❏ DOSD-2014	Don Williams, Volume One	1974	3.00	6.00	12.00
—Reissue of JMI 4004					
❏ DOSD-2018	Don Williams, Vol. 2	1974	3.00	6.00	12.00
—Reissue of JMI 4006					
❏ DOSD-2021	You're My Best Friend	1975	3.00	6.00	12.00
❏ DO-2035	Greatest Hits	1975	3.00	6.00	12.00
❏ DO-2049	Harmony	1976	3.00	6.00	12.00
❏ DO-2064	Visions	1976	3.00	6.00	12.00
❏ DO-2088	I'm Just a Country Boy	1977	3.00	6.00	12.00
CAPITOL					
❏ ST-12440	New Moves	1987	2.00	4.00	8.00
❏ CLT-48034	Traces	1988	2.00	4.00	8.00
❏ C1-91444	Prime Cuts	1989	2.00	4.00	8.00
JMI					
❏ 4004	Don Williams, Volume One	1973	6.25	12.50	25.00
❏ 4006	Don Williams, Volume 2	1974	5.00	10.00	20.00
MCA					
❏ 1442	The Best of Don Williams, Vol. 3	1985	2.00	4.00	8.00
—Budget-line reissue					
❏ 3096	The Best of Don Williams, Vol. 2	1979	2.50	5.00	10.00
❏ 3192	Portrait	1980	2.50	5.00	10.00
❏ 3279	Expressions	1980	2.00	4.00	8.00
—Reissue of ABC 1069					
❏ 5133	I Believe in You	1980	2.50	5.00	10.00
❏ 5210	Especially for You	1981	2.50	5.00	10.00
❏ 5306	Listen to the Radio	1982	2.50	5.00	10.00
❏ 5407	Yellow Moon	1983	2.50	5.00	10.00
❏ 5465	The Best of Don Williams, Vol. 3	1984	2.50	5.00	10.00
❏ 5493	Café Carolina	1984	2.50	5.00	10.00
❏ 5671	The Best of Don Williams, Vol. 4	1985	2.50	5.00	10.00
❏ 5697	Don Williams Sings Bob McDill	1986	2.50	5.00	10.00

Number	Title (A Side/B Side)	Yr	VG	VG+	NM
❏ 5803	Lovers and Best Friends	1986	2.50	5.00	10.00
❏ 37135	Greatest Hits	198?	2.00	4.00	8.00
—Budget-line reissue					
❏ 37155	The Best of Don Williams, Vol. 2	198?	2.00	4.00	8.00
—Budget-line reissue					
❏ 37230	Visions	198?	2.00	4.00	8.00
—Budget-line reissue					
❏ 37231	Portrait	198?	2.00	4.00	8.00
—Budget-line reissue					
❏ 37232	I'm Just a Country Boy	198?	2.00	4.00	8.00
—Budget-line reissue					
❏ 37233	Especially for You	198?	2.00	4.00	8.00
—Budget-line reissue					
❏ 37234	I Believe in You	198?	2.00	4.00	8.00
—Budget-line reissue					
RCA					
❏ 9656-1-R	One Good Well	1989	2.50	5.00	10.00
❏ R 124814	True Love	1990	3.75	7.50	15.00
—BMG Music Service pressing; only US vinyl edition					

WILLIAMS, HANK

45s

MGM

Number	Title (A Side/B Side)	Yr	VG	VG+	NM
❏ KGC-107	Lovesick Blues/Your Cheatin' Heart	196?	2.50	5.00	10.00
❏ KGC-108	Hey Good Lookin'/Why Don't You Love Me	196?	2.50	5.00	10.00
❏ KGC-109	Honky Tonk Blues/Half as Much	196?	2.50	5.00	10.00
❏ KGC-110	Jambalaya/I'll Never Get Out of This World Alive	196?	2.50	5.00	10.00
❏ KGC-111	Kaw-Liga/Ramblin' Man	196?	2.50	5.00	10.00
❏ KGC-112	You Win Again/Moanin' the Blues	196?	2.50	5.00	10.00
❏ KGC-113	Cold, Cold Heart/I'm So Lonesome I Could Cry	196?	2.50	5.00	10.00
❏ KGC-127	My Bucket's Got a Hole in It/We Live in Two Different Worlds	196?	2.50	5.00	10.00
❏ KGC-128	I Can't Help It (If I'm Still in Love with You)/House of Gold	196?	2.50	5.00	10.00
❏ KGC-134	Long Gone Lonesome Blues/My Son Calls Another Man Daddy	196?	2.50	5.00	10.00
❏ KGC-142	Roly Poly/Just Waitin'	196?	2.50	5.00	10.00
—All of the above "KGC" singles are "Golden Circle Series" reissues; original editions have gold labels; later editions go for less					
❏ 8010	Lovesick Blues/Never Again (Will I Knock on Your Door)	1949	17.50	35.00	70.00
❏ K10033	Move It On Over/(Last Night) I Heard You Cryin' in Your Sleep	1950	12.50	25.00	50.00
—Yellow label; 78 first issued in 1947					
❏ K10171	Honky Tonkin'/I'll Be a Bachelor 'Til I Die	1950	12.50	25.00	50.00
—Yellow label; 78 first issued in 1948					
❏ K10328	Mansion on the Hill/I Can't Get You Off of My Mind	1950	12.50	25.00	50.00
—Yellow label; 78 first issued in 1949					
❏ K10352	Lovesick Blues/Never Again (Will I Knock on Your Door)	1950	12.50	25.00	50.00
—Reissue has original 45 rpm number in parentheses under this number					
❏ K10401	Wedding Bells/I've Just Told Mama Goodbye	1949	15.00	30.00	60.00
❏ 10434	Dear Brother/Lost on the River	1949	15.00	30.00	60.00
❏ 10461	Mind Your Own Business/There'll Be No Teardrops Tonight	1949	15.00	30.00	60.00
❏ 10506	You're Gonna Change (Or I'm Gonna Leave)/Lost Highway	1949	15.00	30.00	60.00
❏ 10560	My Bucket's Got a Hole In It/I'm So Lonesome I Could Cry	1949	15.00	30.00	60.00
❏ 10609	I Just Don't Like This Kind of Lovin'/May You Never Be Alone	1950	10.00	20.00	40.00
❏ 10630	Beyond the Sunset/The Funeral	1950	15.00	30.00	60.00
—As "Luke the Drifter"					
❏ 10645	Long Gone Lonesome Blues/My Son Calls Another Man Daddy	1950	10.00	20.00	40.00
❏ 10696	Why Don't You Love Me/A House Without Love	1950	10.00	20.00	40.00
❏ 10718	Everything's OK/Too Many Parties	1950	15.00	30.00	60.00
—As "Luke the Drifter"					
❏ 10760	They'll Never Take Her Love from Me/Why Should We Try Anymore	1950	10.00	20.00	40.00
❏ 10806	No, No, Joe/Help Me Understand	1950	15.00	30.00	60.00
—As "Luke the Drifter"					
❏ 10813	I Heard My Mother Praying for Me/Jesus Remembered Me	1950	12.50	25.00	50.00
❏ 10832	Moanin' the Blues/Nobody's Lonesome for Me	1950	10.00	20.00	40.00
❏ 10904	Cold, Cold Heart/Dear John	1951	7.50	15.00	30.00
❏ 10932	Just Waitin'/Men with Broken Hearts	1951	12.50	25.00	50.00
—As "Luke the Drifter"					
❏ 10961	I Can't Help It (If I'm Still in Love with You)/Howlin' at the Moon	1951	7.50	15.00	30.00
❏ 11000	Hey, Good Lookin'/My Heart Would Know	1951	7.50	15.00	30.00
❏ 11017	I Dreamed About Mama Last Night/I've Been Down That Road Before	1951	12.50	25.00	50.00
—As "Luke the Drifter"					
❏ 11054	Crazy Heart/Lonesome Whistle	1951	7.50	15.00	30.00
❏ 11083	Leave Us Women Alone/If You See My Baby	1951	10.00	20.00	40.00
❏ 11100	Baby, We're Really in Love/I'd Still Want You	1951	7.50	15.00	30.00
❏ 11120	Ramblin' Man/A Picture from Life's Other Side	1952	10.00	20.00	40.00
—As "Luke the Drifter"					
❏ 11160	Honky Tonk Blues/I'm Sorry for You My Friend	1952	7.50	15.00	30.00
❏ 11202	Half As Much/Let's Turn Back the Years	1952	7.50	15.00	30.00
❏ 11283	Jambalaya (On the Bayou)/Window Shopping	1952	7.50	15.00	30.00
❏ 11309	Be Careful of Stones That You Throw/Why Don't You Make Up Your Mind	1952	10.00	20.00	40.00
—As "Luke the Drifter"					
❏ 11318	Settin' the Woods On Fire/You Win Again	1952	7.50	15.00	30.00
❏ 11366	I'll Never Get Out of This World Alive/I Could Never Be Ashamed	1952	7.50	15.00	30.00
❏ 11416	Kaw-Liga/Your Cheatin' Heart	1953	7.50	15.00	30.00
❏ 11479	Take These Chains from My Heart/Ramblin' Man	1953	6.25	12.50	25.00
❏ 11533	I Won't Be Home No More/My Love for You	1953	6.25	12.50	25.00
❏ 11574	Weary Blues from Waitin'/I Can't Escape from You	1953	6.25	12.50	25.00
❏ 11628	Calling You/When God Comes and Gathers His Jewels	1953	6.25	12.50	25.00
❏ 11675	You Better Keep It on Your Mind/Low Down Blues	1954	6.25	12.50	25.00
❏ 11707	How Can You Refuse Him Now/A House of Gold	1954	6.25	12.50	25.00
❏ 11768	I Ain't Got Nothin' But Time/I'm Satisfied with You	1954	6.25	12.50	25.00
❏ 11861	Angel of Death/(I'm Gonna) Sing, Sing, Sing	1954	6.25	12.50	25.00
❏ 11928	Please Don't Let Me Love You/Faded Love and Winter's Roses	1955	6.25	12.50	25.00
❏ 11975	Message to My Mother/Mother Is Gone	1955	6.25	12.50	25.00
❏ 12029	A Teardrop on a Rose/Alone and Forsaken	1955	6.25	12.50	25.00
❏ 12077	Someday You'll Call My Name/The First Fall of Snow	1955	6.25	12.50	25.00
❏ 12127	The Battle of Armageddon/Thank God	1955	6.25	12.50	25.00
❏ 12185	California Zephyr/Thy Burdens Are Greater Than Mine	1956	6.25	12.50	25.00
❏ 12244	I Wish I Had a Nickel/There's No Room in My Heart	1956	6.25	12.50	25.00
❏ 12332	Blue Love (In My Heart)/Singing Waterfall	1956	6.25	12.50	25.00
❏ 12394	The Pale Horse and His Rider/A Home in Heaven	1956	5.00	10.00	20.00
—As "Hank and Audrey Williams"					
❏ 12438	Ready to Go Home/We're Getting Closer	1957	5.00	10.00	20.00
❏ 12484	Leave Me Alone with the Blues/With Tears in My Eyes	1957	5.00	10.00	20.00
❏ 12535	No One Will Ever Know/The Waltz of the Wind	1957	5.00	10.00	20.00
❏ 12611	Why Don't You Love Me/I Can't Help It (If I'm Still in Love with You)	1958	5.00	10.00	20.00
❏ 12635	We Live in Two Different Worlds/My Bucket's Got a Hole In It	1958	5.00	10.00	20.00
❏ 12727	Just Waitin'/Roly-Poly	1958	5.00	10.00	20.00
❏ 13305	Your Cheatin' Heart/Lovesick Blues	1964	3.00	6.00	12.00
❏ 13305 [PS]	Your Cheatin' Heart/Lovesick Blues	1964	5.00	10.00	20.00
❏ 13489	I'm So Lonesome I Could Cry/You Win Again	1966	3.00	6.00	12.00
❏ 13542	Kaw-Liga/Let's Turn Back the Years	1966	3.00	6.00	12.00
❏ 13630	There'll Be No Teardrops Tonight/They'll Never Take Her Love from Me	1966	3.00	6.00	12.00
❏ 13717	Long Gone Lonesome Blues/Hang On the Bell, Nellie	1967	3.00	6.00	12.00
❏ 14849	Why Don't You Love Me/Ramblin' Man	1976	—	3.00	6.00

7-Inch Extended Plays

MGM

Number	Title (A Side/B Side)	Yr	VG	VG+	NM
❏ X-168 [PS]	Moanin' the Blues	1953	10.00	20.00	40.00
—Cover with X-4041 and X-4042					
❏ X-202 [PS]	The Hank Williams Memorial Album	1953	10.00	20.00	40.00
—Cover with X-4102 and X-4103					
❏ X-242 [PS]	Honky Tonkin'	1954	10.00	20.00	40.00
—Cover for X4108 and X4109					
❏ X-243 [PS]	I Saw the Light	195?	10.00	20.00	40.00
—Cover with X-4110 and X-4111					
❏ X-1014	Crazy Heart/Baby We're Really in Love//My Heart Would Know/I Can't Help It (If I'm Still in Love with You)	1953	20.00	40.00	80.00
—Yellow label					
❏ X-1014 [PS]	Crazy Heart	1953	5.00	10.00	20.00
❏ X-1014	Crazy Heart/Baby We're Really in Love//My Heart Would Know/I Can't Help It (If I'm Still in Love with You)	1960	5.00	10.00	20.00
—Black label					
❏ X-1047	Pictures from Life's Other Side/Men with Broken Hearts//Help Me Understand/Too Many Parties (And Too Many Pals)	1954	15.00	30.00	60.00
—Yellow label					
❏ X-1047 [PS]	Hank Williams as Luke the Drifter	1954	5.00	10.00	20.00
❏ X-1047	Pictures from Life's Other Side/Men with Broken Hearts//Help Me Understand/Too Many Parties (And Too Many Pals)	1960	5.00	10.00	20.00
—Black label					
❏ X-1076	Move It On Over/Fly Trouble//Window Shopping/Pan American	1954	15.00	30.00	60.00
—Yellow label					
❏ X-1076 [PS]	Move It On Over	1954	5.00	10.00	20.00
❏ X-1076	Move It On Over/Fly Trouble//Window Shopping/Pan American	1960	5.00	10.00	20.00
—Black label					
❏ X-1082	There'll Be No Tear-Drops Tonight/You're Gonna Change (Or I'm Gonna Leave)//Nobody's Lonesome for Me/Mind Your Own Business	1954	15.00	30.00	60.00
❏ X-1082 [PS]	There'll Be No Teardrops Tonight	1954	5.00	10.00	20.00
❏ X-1082	There'll Be No Tear-Drops Tonight/You're Gonna Change (Or I'm Gonna Leave)//Nobody's Lonesome for Me/Mind Your Own Business	1960	5.00	10.00	20.00
—Black label					
❏ X-1101	I Saw the Light/Mansion on the Hill//Six More Miles/Wedding Bells	1955	15.00	30.00	60.00
—Yellow label					
❏ X-1101 [PS]	Hank Williams Sings	1955	5.00	10.00	20.00
❏ X-1101	I Saw the Light/Mansion on the Hill//Six More Miles/Wedding Bells	1960	5.00	10.00	20.00
—Black label					
❏ X-1102	Lost Highway/I've Just Told Mama Goodbye//Wealth Won't Save Your Soul/A House Without Love	1955	15.00	30.00	60.00
—Yellow label					
❏ X-1102 [PS]	Hank Williams Sings Vol. 2	1955	5.00	10.00	20.00
❏ X-1102	Lost Highway/I've Just Told Mama Goodbye//Wealth Won't Save Your Soul/A House Without Love	1960	5.00	10.00	20.00
—Black label					
❏ X-1135	Ramblin' Man/My Son Calls Another Man Daddy//I Can't Escape from You/Nobody's Lonesome for Me	1955	10.00	20.00	40.00
—Yellow label					
❏ X-1135 [PS]	Ramblin' Man Vol. 1	1955	3.75	7.50	15.00

Number	Title (A Side/B Side)	Yr	VG	VG+	NM
❏ X-1135	Ramblin' Man/My Son Calls Another Man Daddy//I Can't Escape from You/Nobody's Lonesome for Me	1960	3.75	7.50	15.00
—Black label					
❏ X-1136	Lonesome Whistle/I Jus' Don't Like This Kind of Livin'//Take These Chains from My Heart/Why Don't You Love Me?	1955	10.00	20.00	40.00
—Yellow label					
❏ X-1136 [PS]	Ramblin' Man Vol. 2	1955	3.75	7.50	15.00
❏ X-1136	Lonesome Whistle/I Jus' Don't Like This Kind of Livin'//Take These Chains from My Heart/Why Don't You Love Me?	1960	3.75	7.50	15.00
—Black label					
❏ X-1165	Why Don't You Make Up Your Mind/I've Been Down That Road Before//Just Waitin'/Everything's Okay	1955	10.00	20.00	40.00
—Yellow label					
❏ X-1165 [PS]	Luke the Drifter	1955	3.75	7.50	15.00
❏ X-1165	Why Don't You Make Up Your Mind/I've Been Down That Road Before//Just Waitin'/Everything's Okay	1960	3.75	7.50	15.00
—Black label					
❏ X-1215	Low Down Blues/Someday You'll Call My Name//Alone and Forsaken/Weary Blues From Waitin'	1956	10.00	20.00	40.00
—Yellow label					
❏ X-1215 [PS]	Moanin' the Blues Vol. 1	1956	3.75	7.50	15.00
❏ X-1215	Low Down Blues/Someday You'll Call My Name//Alone and Forsaken/Weary Blues From Waitin'	1960	3.75	7.50	15.00
—Black label					
❏ X-1216	Moanin' the Blues/I'm So Lonesome I Could Cry//My Sweet Love Ain't Around/Honky Tonk Blues	1956	10.00	20.00	40.00
—Yellow label					
❏ X-1216 [PS]	Moanin' the Blues Vol. 2	1956	3.75	7.50	15.00
❏ X-1216	Moanin' the Blues/I'm So Lonesome I Could Cry//My Sweet Love Ain't Around/Honky Tonk Blues	1960	3.75	7.50	15.00
—Black label					
❏ X-1217	Lovesick Blues/The Blues Come Around//I'm a Long Gone Daddy/Long Gone Lonesome Blues	1956	10.00	20.00	40.00
—Yellow label					
❏ X-1217 [PS]	Moanin' the Blues Vol. 3	1956	3.75	7.50	15.00
❏ X-1217	Lovesick Blues/The Blues Come Around//I'm a Long Gone Daddy/Long Gone Lonesome Blues	1960	3.75	7.50	15.00
—Black label					
❏ X-1218	I'm Gonna Sing/Message to My Mother//Thank God/The Angel of Death	1956	10.00	20.00	40.00
—Yellow label					
❏ X-1218 [PS]	I Saw the Light	1956	3.75	7.50	15.00
❏ X-1218	I'm Gonna Sing/Message to My Mother//Thank God/The Angel of Death	1960	3.75	7.50	15.00
—Black label					
❏ X-1235	*Honky Tonkin'/Mind Your Own Business/Rootie Tootie/I Ain't Got Nothing But Time	1956	10.00	20.00	40.00
—Yellow label					
❏ X-1235 [PS]	Honky Tonkin'	1956	3.75	7.50	15.00
❏ X-1235	*Honky Tonkin'/Mind Your Own Business/Rootie Tootie/I Ain't Got Nothing But Time	1960	3.75	7.50	15.00
—Black label					
❏ X-1317	Jambalaya (On the Bayou)/I Won't Be Home No More//Honky Tonk Blues/I'll Never Get Out of This World Alive	1957	10.00	20.00	40.00
—Yellow label					
❏ X-1317 [PS]	Honky Tonkin' Vol. 1	1957	3.75	7.50	15.00
❏ X-1317	Jambalaya (On the Bayou)/I Won't Be Home No More//Honky Tonk Blues/I'll Never Get Out of This World Alive	1960	3.75	7.50	15.00
—Black label					
❏ X-1318	Honky Tonkin'/Howlin' at the Moon//My Bucket's Got a Hole in It/Baby, We're Really in Love	1957	10.00	20.00	40.00
—Yellow label					
❏ X-1318 [PS]	Honky Tonkin' Vol. 2	1957	3.75	7.50	15.00
❏ X-1318	Honky Tonkin'/Howlin' at the Moon//My Bucket's Got a Hole in It/Baby, We're Really in Love	1960	3.75	7.50	15.00
—Black label					
❏ X-1319	Mind Your Own Business/Rootie Tootie//I Ain't Got Nothin' But Time/You Better Keep It on Your Mind	1957	10.00	20.00	40.00
—Yellow label					
❏ X-1319 [PS]	Honky Tonkin' Vol. 3	1957	3.75	7.50	15.00
❏ X-1319	Mind Your Own Business/Rootie Tootie//I Ain't Got Nothin' But Time/You Better Keep It on Your Mind	1960	3.75	7.50	15.00
—Black label					
❏ X-1491	Wedding Bells/May You Never Be Alone//Lost Highway/Why Should We Try Anymore	1958	7.50	5.00	30.00
—Yellow label					
❏ X-1491 [PS]	Sing Me a Blue Song Vol. 1	1958	3.75	7.50	15.00
❏ X-1491	Wedding Bells/May You Never Be Alone//Lost Highway/Why Should We Try Anymore	1960	3.75	7.50	15.00
—Black label					
❏ X-1492	I Heard You Crying in Your Sleep/Blue Love//Mansion on the Hill/They'll Never Take Her Love from Me	1958	7.50	15.00	30.00
—Yellow label					
❏ X-1492 [PS]	Sing Me a Blue Song Vol. 2	1958	3.75	7.50	15.00
❏ X-1492	I Heard You Crying in Your Sleep/Blue Love//Mansion on the Hill/They'll Never Take Her Love from Me	1960	3.75	7.50	15.00
—Black label					
❏ X-1493	I've Just Told Mama Goodbye/House Without Love//Six More Miles/Singing Waterfall	1958	7.50	15.00	30.00
—Yellow label					
❏ X-1493 [PS]	Sing Me a Blue Song Vol. 3	1958	3.75	7.50	15.00
❏ X-1493	I've Just Told Mama Goodbye/House Without Love//Six More Miles/Singing Waterfall	1960	3.75	7.50	15.00
—Black label					
❏ X-1554	There's No Room in My Heart/Waltz of the Wind//Pan American/With Tears in My Eyes	1958	7.50	15.00	30.00
—Yellow label					
❏ X-1554 [PS]	The Immortal Hank Williams Vol. 1	1958	3.75	7.50	15.00
❏ X-1554	There's No Room in My Heart/Waltz of the Wind//Pan American/With Tears in My Eyes	1960	3.75	7.50	15.00
—Black label					
❏ X-1555	I Wish I Had a Nickel/Fly Trouble//Please Don't Let Me Love You/I'm Satisfied with You	1958	7.50	15.00	30.00
—Yellow label					
❏ X-1555 [PS]	The Immortal Hank Williams Vol. 2	1958	3.75	7.50	15.00
❏ X-1555	I Wish I Had a Nickel/Fly Trouble//Please Don't Let Me Love You/I'm Satisfied with You	1960	3.75	7.50	15.00
—Black label					
❏ X-1556	No One Will Ever Know/Faded Love and Winter Roses//First Fall of Snow/California Zephyr	1958	7.50	15.00	30.00
—Yellow label					
❏ X-1556 [PS]	The Immortal Hank Williams Vol. 3	1958	3.75	7.50	15.00
❏ X-1556	No One Will Ever Know/Faded Love and Winter Roses//First Fall of Snow/California Zephyr	1960	3.75	7.50	15.00
—Black label					
❏ X-1612	Your Cheatin' Heart/Settin' the Woods on Fire//You Win Again/Hey, Good Lookin'	1959	7.50	15.00	30.00
—Yellow label					
❏ X-1612 [PS]	Hank Williams Memorial Album Vol. 1	1959	3.75	7.50	15.00
❏ X-1612	Your Cheatin' Heart/Settin' the Woods on Fire//You Win Again/Hey, Good Lookin'	1960	3.75	7.50	15.00
—Black label					
❏ X-1613	Cold, Cold Heart/Kaw-Liga//I Could Never Be Ashamed of You/Half As Much	1959	7.50	15.00	30.00
—Yellow label					
❏ X-1613 [PS]	Hank Williams Memorial Album Vol. 2	1959	3.75	7.50	15.00
❏ X-1613	Cold, Cold Heart/Kaw-Liga//I Could Never Be Ashamed of You/Half As Much	1960	3.75	7.50	15.00
—Black label					
❏ X-1636	Crazy Heart/Move It On Over//My Heart Would Know/I'm Sorry for You My Friend	1959	7.50	15.00	30.00
—Yellow label					
❏ X-1636 [PS]	Hank Williams Memorial Album Vol. 3	1959	3.75	7.50	15.00
❏ X-1636	Crazy Heart/Move It On Over//My Heart Would Know/I'm Sorry for You My Friend	1960	3.75	7.50	15.00
—Black label					
❏ X-1637	*I Can't Get You Off My Mind/I Don't Care (If Tomorrow Never Comes)/Dear John/My Love for You (Has Turned to Hate)	1959	3.75	7.50	15.00
—Black label					
❏ X-1637	*I Can't Get You Off My Mind/I Don't Care (If Tomorrow Never Comes)/Dear John/My Love for You (Has Turned to Hate)	1959	7.50	15.00	30.00
—Yellow label					
❏ X-1637 [PS]	The Unforgettable Hank Williams, Vol. 1	1959	3.75	7.50	15.00
❏ X-1638	(contents unknown)	1959	7.50	15.00	30.00
—Yellow label					
❏ X-1638 [PS]	The Unforgettable Hank Williams, Vol. 2	1959	3.75	7.50	15.00
❏ X-1638	(contents unknown)	1960	3.75	7.50	15.00
—Black label					
❏ X-1643	Pictures from Life's Other Side/Men with Broken Hearts//Help Me Understand/Too Many Parties and Too Many Pals	1959	7.50	15.00	30.00
—Yellow label					
❏ X-1643 [PS]	Hank Williams as Luke the Drifter	1959	3.75	7.50	15.00
❏ X-1643	Pictures from Life's Other Side/Men with Broken Hearts//Help Me Understand/Too Many Parties and Too Many Pals	1960	3.75	7.50	15.00
—Black label					
❏ X-1644	Be Careful of Stones That You Throw/I Dreamed About Mama Last Night//Funeral/Beyond the Sunset	1959	7.50	15.00	30.00
—Yellow label					
❏ X-1644 [PS]	Hank Williams as Luke the Drifter	1959	3.75	7.50	15.00
❏ X-1644	Be Careful of Stones That You Throw/I Dreamed About Mama Last Night//Funeral/Beyond the Sunset	1960	3.75	7.50	15.00
—Black label					
❏ X-1698	(contents unknown)	1960	3.75	7.50	15.00
❏ X-1698 [PS]	The Lonesome Sound of Hank Williams Vol. 1	1960	3.75	7.50	15.00
❏ X-1699	I'm Free at Last/Roly Poly//The Old Home/Rock My Cradle (Once Again)	1960	3.75	7.50	15.00
❏ X-1699 [PS]	The Lonesome Sound of Hank Williams Vol. 2	1960	3.75	7.50	15.00
❏ X-1700	(contents unknown)	1960	3.75	7.50	15.00
❏ X-1700 [PS]	The Lonesome Sound of Hank Williams Vol. 3	1960	3.75	7.50	15.00
❏ X-4041	Moanin' the Blues/I'm So Lonesome I Could Cry//My Sweet Love Ain't Around/Honky Tonk Blues	1953	10.00	20.00	40.00
—One record of "X168"					
❏ X-4042	Lovesick Blues/The Blues Come Around//I'm a Long Gone Daddy/Long Gone Lonesome Blues	1953	10.00	20.00	40.00
—One record of "X168"					
❏ X-4102	Your Cheatin' Heart/Settin' the Woods on Fire//You Win Again/Hey, Good Lookin'	1953	10.00	20.00	40.00
—One record of "X202"					
❏ X-4103	Cold, Cold Heart/Kaw-Liga//I Could Never Be Ashamed of You/Half As Much	1953	10.00	20.00	40.00
—One record of "X202"					
❏ X-4108	Honky Tonkin'/Howlin' at the Moon//My Bucket's Got a Hole in It/Baby, We're Really in Love	1954	10.00	20.00	40.00
—One record of "X242"					
❏ X-4109	Jambalaya (On the Bayou)/I Won't Be Home No More//Honky Tonk Blues/I'll Never Get Out of This World Alive	1954	10.00	20.00	40.00
—One record of "X242"					

Number	Title (A Side/B Side)	Yr	VG	VG+	NM
❏ X-4110	I Saw the Light/Calling You//Dear Brother/ "Wealth Won't Save Your Soul"	195?	10.00	20.00	40.00
—One record of "X243"					
❏ X-4111	How Can You Refuse Him Now/When God Comes and Gathers His Jewels//Just Remember Me/House of God	195?	10.00	20.00	40.00
—One record of "X243"					
❏ SLM-4377	I'm So Lonesome I Could Cry/You Win Again/ Kaw-Liga//Lovesick Blues/Let's Turn Back the Years/I'm Sorry for You, My Friend	1966	6.25	12.50	25.00
—Jukebox issue; small hole, plays at 33 1/3 rpm					
❏ SLM-4377 [PS]	The Legend Lives Anew — Hank Williams with Strings	1966	6.25	12.50	25.00
Albums					
COUNTRY MUSIC FOUNDATION					
❏ CMF-006	Just Me and My Guitar	198?	2.50	5.00	10.00
❏ CMF-007	The First Recordings	198?	2.50	5.00	10.00
METRO					
❏ M-509 [M]	Hank Williams	1966	5.00	10.00	20.00
❏ MS-509 [R]	Hank Williams	1966	3.00	6.00	12.00
❏ M-547 [M]	Mr. and Mrs. Hank Williams	1966	5.00	10.00	20.00
❏ MS-547 [R]	Mr. and Mrs. Hank Williams	1966	3.00	6.00	12.00
❏ M-602 [M]	The Immortal Hank Williams	1967	5.00	10.00	20.00
❏ MS-602 [R]	The Immortal Hank Williams	1967	3.00	6.00	12.00
MGM					
❏ 3E-2 [(3)M]	36 of His Greatest Hits	1957	50.00	100.00	200.00
—Yellow labels					
❏ 3E-2 [(3)M]	36 of His Greatest Hits	1960	25.00	50.00	100.00
—Black labels					
❏ 3E-4 [(3)M]	Hank Williams Sings 36 More of His Greatest Hits	1958	50.00	100.00	200.00
—Yellow labels					
❏ 3E-4 [(3)M]	Hank Williams Sings 36 More of His Greatest Hits	1960	25.00	50.00	100.00
—Black labels					
❏ E-107 [10]	Hank Williams Sings	1952	100.00	200.00	400.00
❏ E-168 [10]	Moanin' the Blues	1952	100.00	200.00	400.00
❏ E-202 [10]	Memorial Album	1953	100.00	200.00	400.00
❏ E-203 [10]	Hank Williams as Luke the Drifter	1953	100.00	200.00	400.00
❏ SE 240-2 [(2)]	24 Karat Hits	1969	6.25	12.50	25.00
❏ E-242 [10]	Honky Tonkin'	1954	100.00	200.00	400.00
❏ E-243 [10]	I Saw the Light	1954	100.00	200.00	400.00
❏ E-291 [10]	Ramblin' Man	1954	100.00	200.00	400.00
❏ PRO-912 [(3)DJ]	Reflections of Those Who Loved Him	1975	62.50	125.00	250.00
—Promo-only box set					
❏ E-3219 [M]	Ramblin' Man	1955	25.00	50.00	100.00
—Yellow label					
❏ E-3219 [M]	Ramblin' Man	1960	10.00	20.00	40.00
—Black label					
❏ E-3267 [M]	Hank Williams as Luke the Drifter	1955	25.00	50.00	100.00
—Yellow label					
❏ E-3267 [M]	Hank Williams as Luke the Drifter	1960	10.00	20.00	40.00
—Black label					
❏ E-3272 [M]	Memorial Album	1955	25.00	50.00	100.00
—Yellow label					
❏ E-3272 [M]	Memorial Album	1960	10.00	20.00	40.00
—Black label					
❏ E-3272 [M]	Memorial Album	1968	5.00	10.00	20.00
—Blue and gold label					
❏ E-3330 [M]	Moanin' the Blues	1956	25.00	50.00	100.00
—Yellow label					
❏ E-3330 [M]	Moanin' the Blues	1960	10.00	20.00	40.00
—Black label					
❏ E-3331 [M]	I Saw the Light	1956	50.00	100.00	200.00
—Yellow label; green cover					
❏ E-3331 [M]	I Saw the Light	1959	25.00	50.00	100.00
—Yellow label; church on cover					
❏ E-3331 [M]	I Saw the Light	1960	10.00	20.00	40.00
—Black label					
❏ SE-3331 [R]	I Saw the Light	1968	3.00	6.00	12.00
—Blue and gold label					
❏ E-3412 [M]	Honky Tonkin'	1957	25.00	50.00	100.00
—Yellow label					
❏ E-3412 [M]	Honky Tonkin'	1960	10.00	20.00	40.00
—Black label					
❏ E-3560 [M]	Sing Me a Blue Song	1957	25.00	50.00	100.00
—Yellow label					
❏ E-3560 [M]	Sing Me a Blue Song	1960	10.00	20.00	40.00
—Black label					
❏ E-3605 [M]	The Immortal Hank Williams	1958	25.00	50.00	100.00
—Yellow label					
❏ E-3605 [M]	The Immortal Hank Williams	1960	10.00	20.00	40.00
—Black label					
❏ E-3733 [M]	The Unforgettable Hank Williams	1959	25.00	50.00	100.00
—Yellow label					
❏ E-3733 [M]	The Unforgettable Hank Williams	1960	10.00	20.00	40.00
—Black label					
❏ SE-3733 [R]	The Unforgettable Hank Williams	1968	3.00	6.00	12.00
—Blue and gold label					
❏ E-3803 [M]	The Lonesome Sound of Hank Williams	1960	10.00	20.00	40.00
❏ E-3850 [M]	Wait for the Light to Shine	1960	10.00	20.00	40.00
❏ SE-3850 [R]	Wait for the Light to Shine	1968	3.00	6.00	12.00
—Blue and gold label					
❏ E-3918 [M]	Hank Williams' Greatest Hits	1961	10.00	20.00	40.00
❏ SE-3918 [R]	Hank Williams' Greatest Hits	1963	5.00	10.00	20.00
—Black label					
❏ SE-3918 [R]	Hank Williams' Greatest Hits	1968	3.00	6.00	12.00
—Blue and gold label					
❏ E-3923 [M]	Hank Williams Lives Again	1961	10.00	20.00	40.00
—Reissue of E-3272 with new title					
❏ SE-3923 [R]	Hank Williams Lives Again	1968	3.00	6.00	12.00
—Blue and gold label					
❏ E-3924 [M]	Let Me Sing a Blue Song	1961	10.00	20.00	40.00
—Reissue of E-3560					
❏ SE-3924 [R]	Let Me Sing a Blue Song	1968	3.00	6.00	12.00
—Blue and gold label					
❏ E-3925 [M]	Wanderin' Around	1961	10.00	20.00	40.00
—Reissue of E-3219					
❏ SE-3925 [R]	Wanderin' Around	1968	3.00	6.00	12.00
—Blue and gold label					
❏ E-3926 [M]	I'm Blue Inside	1961	10.00	20.00	40.00
—Reissue of E-3330					
❏ SE-3926 [R]	I'm Blue Inside	1968	3.00	6.00	12.00
—Blue and gold label					
❏ E-3927 [M]	Hank Williams as Luke the Drifter	1961	10.00	20.00	40.00
—Reissue of E-3267					
❏ SE-3927 [R]	Hank Williams as Luke the Drifter	1968	3.00	6.00	12.00
—Blue and gold label					
❏ E-3928 [M]	First, Last and Always	1961	10.00	20.00	40.00
—Reissue of E-3605					
❏ SE-3928 [R]	First, Last and Always	1968	3.00	6.00	12.00
—Blue and gold label					
❏ E-3955 [M]	The Spirit of Hank Williams	1961	10.00	20.00	40.00
❏ SE-3955 [R]	The Spirit of Hank Williams	1968	3.00	6.00	12.00
—Blue and gold label					
❏ E-3999 [M]	Hank Williams on Stage Recorded Live	1962	10.00	20.00	40.00
—Note revised title					
❏ E-3999 [R]	On Stage! Hank Williams Recorded Live	1962	15.00	30.00	60.00
❏ SE-3999 [R]	On Stage! Hank Williams Recorded Live	196?	5.00	10.00	20.00
—Black label					
❏ SE-3999 [R]	Hank Williams on Stage Recorded Live	1968	3.00	6.00	12.00
—Blue and gold label					
❏ E-4040 [M]	14 More of Hank Williams' Greatest Hits — Vol. II	1962	10.00	20.00	40.00
❏ SE-4040 [R]	14 More of Hank Williams' Greatest Hits — Vol. II	1963	3.75	7.50	15.00
—Black label					
❏ SE-4040 [R]	Hank Williams' Greatest Hits, Volume 2	1968	3.00	6.00	12.00
—Blue and gold label					
❏ E-4109 [M]	On Stage Volume II/Hank Williams	1963	10.00	20.00	40.00
❏ SE-4109 [R]	On Stage Volume II/Hank Williams	1963	5.00	10.00	20.00
—Black label					
❏ SE-4109 [R]	On Stage Volume II/Hank Williams	1968	3.00	6.00	12.00
—Blue and gold label					
❏ E-4138 [M]	Beyond the Sunset	1963	7.50	15.00	30.00
❏ SE-4138 [R]	Beyond the Sunset	1963	3.75	7.50	15.00
—Black label					
❏ E-4140 [M]	14 More of Hank Williams' Greatest Hits (Volume 3)	1963	7.50	15.00	30.00
❏ SE-4140 [R]	14 More of Hank Williams' Greatest Hits (Volume 3)	1963	3.75	7.50	15.00
—Black label					
❏ SE-4140 [R]	14 More of Hank Williams' Greatest Hits (Volume 3)	1968	3.00	6.00	12.00
—Blue and gold label					
❏ E-4168 [M]	The Very Best of Hank Williams	1963	7.50	15.00	30.00
❏ SE-4168 [R]	The Very Best of Hank Williams	1963	3.75	7.50	15.00
—Black label					
❏ SE-4168 [R]	The Very Best of Hank Williams	1968	3.00	6.00	12.00
—Blue and gold label					
❏ E-4227 [M]	The Very Best of Hank Williams, Volume 2	1964	7.50	15.00	30.00
❏ SE-4227 [R]	The Very Best of Hank Williams, Volume 2	1964	3.75	7.50	15.00
—Black label					
❏ SE-4227 [R]	The Very Best of Hank Williams, Volume 2	1968	3.00	6.00	12.00
—Blue and gold label					
❏ E-4254 [M]	Lost Highway (and Other Folk Ballads)	1964	10.00	20.00	40.00
❏ SE-4254 [R]	Lost Highway (and Other Folk Ballads)	1964	5.00	10.00	20.00
—Black label					
❏ SE-4254 [R]	Lost Highway (and Other Folk Ballads)	1968	3.00	6.00	12.00
—Blue and gold label					
❏ E-4267-4 [(4)M]	The Hank Williams Story	1965	15.00	30.00	60.00
❏ E-4300 [M]	Kaw-Liga and Other Humorous Songs	1965	7.50	15.00	30.00
❏ SE-4300 [R]	Kaw-Liga and Other Humorous Songs	1965	3.75	7.50	15.00
❏ SE-4300 [R]	Kaw-Liga and Other Humorous Songs	1968	3.00	6.00	12.00
—Blue and gold label					
❏ E-4377 [M]	The Legend Lives Anew — Hank Williams with Strings	1966	5.00	10.00	20.00
❏ SE-4377 [S]	The Legend Lives Anew — Hank Williams with Strings	1966	6.25	12.50	25.00
—Black label					
❏ SE-4377 [S]	The Legend Lives Anew — Hank Williams with Strings	1968	3.75	7.50	15.00
—Blue and gold label					
❏ E-4380 [M]	Movin' on — Luke the Drifter	1966	7.50	15.00	30.00
❏ SE-4380 [R]	Movin' on — Luke the Drifter	1968	3.00	6.00	12.00
—Blue and gold label					
❏ E-4429 [M]	More Hank Williams and Strings	1966	5.00	10.00	20.00
❏ SE-4429 [S]	More Hank Williams and Strings	1966	6.25	12.50	25.00
—Black label					
❏ SE-4429 [S]	More Hank Williams and Strings	1968	3.75	7.50	15.00
❏ E-4481 [M]	I Won't Be Home No More	1967	7.50	15.00	30.00
❏ SE-4481 [S]	I Won't Be Home No More	1967	5.00	10.00	20.00
—Black label					
❏ SE-4481 [S]	I Won't Be Home No More	1968	3.75	7.50	15.00
—Blue and gold label					
❏ E-4529 [M]	Hank Williams and Strings, Volume 3	1968	10.00	20.00	40.00
❏ SE-4529 [S]	Hank Williams and Strings, Volume 3	1968	5.00	10.00	20.00
❏ E-4576 [M]	Hank Williams in the Beginning	1968	10.00	20.00	40.00
❏ SE-4576 [R]	Hank Williams in the Beginning	1968	3.75	7.50	15.00
❏ SE-4651	Essential Hank Williams	1969	3.00	6.00	12.00
❏ SE-4680	Life to Legend	1970	3.00	6.00	12.00
❏ SE-4755-2 [(2)]	24 Greatest Hits	1971	3.75	7.50	15.00
❏ M3G-4954	Archetypes	1974	3.00	6.00	12.00
❏ MG-1-5019	Hank Williams, Sr., Live at the Grand Old Opry	1976	3.00	6.00	12.00
❏ MG-2-5401 [(2)]	24 Greatest Hits, Volume 2	197?	3.75	7.50	15.00
❏ ST-90511 [R]	The Very Best of Hank Williams	1965	5.00	10.00	20.00
—Capitol Record Club edition					
❏ T-90511 [M]	The Very Best of Hank Williams	1965	10.00	20.00	40.00
—Capitol Record Club edition					
❏ ST-90884 [R]	Movin' on — Luke the Drifter	1968	3.75	7.50	15.00
—Capitol Record Club edition; blue and gold label					
❏ ST-91115 [S]	The Legend Lives Anew — Hank Williams with Strings	1968	5.00	10.00	20.00
—Capitol Record Club edition; blue and gold label					
POLYDOR					
❏ 821233-1 [(2)]	40 Greatest Hits	1984	3.75	7.50	15.00
❏ 823291-1	Hank Williams' Greatest Hits	1984	2.00	4.00	8.00

Number	Title (A Side/B Side)	Yr	VG	VG+	NM
❏ 823292-1	The Very Best of Hank Williams	1984	2.00	4.00	8.00
❏ 823293-1 [(2)]	24 Greatest Hits	1984	3.00	6.00	12.00
❏ 823294-1 [(2)]	24 Greatest Hits, Volume 2	1984	3.00	6.00	12.00
❏ 823695-1	Rare Takes and Radio Cuts	1984	2.50	5.00	10.00
❏ 825531-1	On the Air	1985	2.50	5.00	10.00
❏ 825548-1	I Ain't Got Nothin' But Time	1985	2.50	5.00	10.00
❏ 825551-1	Lovesick Blues	1985	2.50	5.00	10.00
❏ 825554-1	Lost Highway	1986	2.50	5.00	10.00
❏ 825557-1	I'm So Lonesome I Could Cry	1986	2.50	5.00	10.00
❏ 831574-1	Beyond the Sunset	1987	2.50	5.00	10.00
❏ 831633-1	Long Gone Lonesome Blues	1987	2.50	5.00	10.00
❏ 831634-1	Hey, Good Lookin'	1987	2.50	5.00	10.00
❏ 833749-1	Let's Turn Back the Years	1988	2.50	5.00	10.00
❏ 833752-1	I Won't Be Home No More	1988	2.50	5.00	10.00

TIME-LIFE

Number	Title (A Side/B Side)	Yr	VG	VG+	NM
❏ TLCW-01 [(3)]	Country and Western Classics	1981	6.25	12.50	25.00
❏ STW-118	Country Music	1981	2.50	5.00	10.00

WILLIAMS, HANK /ROY ACUFF
Albums
LAMB AND LION

Number	Title (A Side/B Side)	Yr	VG	VG+	NM
❏ LL-706 [(3)]	Hank Williams, Sr./Roy Acuff "Collector's Item!"	197?	10.00	20.00	40.00

—Sides 1-4 are reissues of Hank Williams; side 5-6 are Roy Acuff

WILLIAMS, HANK, AND HANK WILLIAMS, JR. Also see each artist's individual listings.
Albums
MGM

Number	Title (A Side/B Side)	Yr	VG	VG+	NM
❏ E-4276 [M]	Father and Son	1965	5.00	10.00	20.00
❏ SE-4276 [S]	Father and Son	1965	6.25	12.50	25.00
❏ E-4378 [M]	Again	1966	5.00	10.00	20.00
❏ SE-4378 [S]	Again	1966	6.25	12.50	25.00
❏ 2SES-4865 [(2)]	Hank Williams: The Legend in Story and Song	1973	3.75	7.50	15.00
❏ M3HB 4975 [(2)]	Insights Into Hank Williams in Song and Story	1974	3.75	7.50	15.00

WILLIAMS, HANK, JR.
12-Inch Singles
WARNER BROS.

Number	Title (A Side/B Side)	Yr	VG	VG+	NM
❏ PRO-A-2088 [DJ]	Woman on the Run (same on both sides)	1983	2.00	4.00	8.00
❏ PRO-A-2662 [DJ]	My Name Is Bocephus (same on both sides)	1987	2.00	4.00	8.00

45s
CAPRICORN

Number	Title (A Side/B Side)	Yr	VG	VG+	NM
❏ 18486	Diamond Mine/Dirty Mind	1993	—	—	3.00
❏ 18614	Everything Comes Down to Money and Love/ S.O.B. I'm Tired	1993	—	—	3.00
❏ 18800	Lyin' Jukebox/Fax Me a Beer	1992	—	—	3.00
❏ 18923	Come On Over to the Country/Wild Weekend	1992	—	—	3.00
❏ 19023	Hotel Whiskey/The Count Song	1992	—	—	3.00

ELEKTRA

Number	Title (A Side/B Side)	Yr	VG	VG+	NM
❏ 46018	To Love Somebody/We Can Work It All Out	1979	—	2.50	5.00
❏ 46046	Family Tradition/Paying On Time	1979	—	2.50	5.00
❏ 46535	Whiskey Bent and Hell Bound/O.D.'d in Denver	1979	—	2.50	5.00
❏ 46593	Women I've Never Had/ Tired of Being Johnny B. Goode	1980	—	2.50	5.00
❏ 46636	Kaw-Liga/The American Way	1980	—	2.50	5.00
❏ 47012	If You Don't Like Hank Williams/Outlaw Women	1980	—	3.00	6.00
❏ 47016	Old Habits/Won't It Be Nice	1980	—	2.50	5.00
❏ 47102	Texas Women/You Can't Find Many Kisses	1981	—	2.50	5.00
❏ 47137	Dixie on My Mind/Ramblin' Man	1981	—	2.50	5.00
❏ 47191	All My Rowdy Friends (Have Settled Down)/ Everytime I Hear That Song	1981	—	2.50	5.00
❏ 47231 [DJ]	Little Drummer Boy/The Christmas Song	1981	2.00	4.00	8.00

—B-side by Sonny Curtis

Number	Title (A Side/B Side)	Yr	VG	VG+	NM
❏ 47257	A Country Boy Can Survive/Weatherman	1982	—	2.50	5.00
❏ 47462	Honky Tonkin'/High and Pressurized	1982	—	2.50	5.00
❏ 69846	Gonna Go Huntin' Tonight/Twodot, Montana	1983	—	2.00	4.00
❏ 69960	The American Dream/ If Heaven Ain't a Lot Like Dixie	1982	—	2.00	4.00

MCG CURB

Number	Title (A Side/B Side)	Yr	VG	VG+	NM
❏ 76932	I Ain't Goin' Peacefully/Greeted in Enid	1995	—	2.00	4.00
❏ 76948	Hog Wild/Wild Thing	1995	—	2.00	4.00

MGM

Number	Title (A Side/B Side)	Yr	VG	VG+	NM
❏ 13208	Long Gone Lonesome Blues/Doesn't Anybody Know My Name	1964	3.00	6.00	12.00
❏ 13208 [PS]	Long Gone Lonesome Blues/Doesn't Anybody Know My Name	1964	5.00	10.00	20.00
❏ 13253	Guess What, That's Right, She's Gone/Goin' Steady with the Blues	1964	3.00	6.00	12.00
❏ 13253 [PS]	Guess What, That's Right, She's Gone/Goin' Steady with the Blues	1964	6.25	12.50	25.00
❏ 13278	Endless Sleep/My Bucket's Got a Hole In It	1964	3.00	6.00	12.00
❏ 13318	I'm So Lonesome I Could Cry/Is It That Much Fun to Hurt Someone	1965	3.00	6.00	12.00
❏ 13318 [PS]	I'm So Lonesome I Could Cry/Is It That Much Fun to Hurt Someone	1965	5.00	10.00	20.00
❏ 13353	I Went to All That Trouble for Nothin'/Mule Skinner Blues	1965	3.00	6.00	12.00
❏ 13392	Pecos Jail/You're Ruinin' My Life	1965	3.00	6.00	12.00
❏ 13392 [PS]	Pecos Jail/You're Ruinin' My Life	1965	6.25	12.50	25.00
❏ 13443	Rainmaker/The River	1966	3.00	6.00	12.00
❏ 13504	Standing in the Shadows/ It's Written All Over Your Face	1966	3.00	6.00	12.00
❏ 13640	I Can't Take It No Longer/ You Can Hear a Tear Drop	1966	3.00	6.00	12.00
❏ 13730	I'm In No Condition/I'm Gonna Break Your Heart	1967	3.00	6.00	12.00
❏ 13782	Nobody's Child/The Next Best Thing to Nothing	1967	3.00	6.00	12.00
❏ 13857	I Wouldn't Change a Thing About You (But Your Name)/No Meaning and No End	1967	3.00	6.00	12.00
❏ 13922	The Old Ryman/ I Wonder Where You Are Tonight	1968	2.50	5.00	10.00
❏ 13968	It's All Over But the Crying/Rock in My Shoes	1968	2.50	5.00	10.00
❏ 14002	I Was With Red Foley (The Night He Passed Away)/On Trial	1968	3.00	6.00	12.00

—As "Luke the Drifter, Jr."

Number	Title (A Side/B Side)	Yr	VG	VG+	NM
❏ 14020	Custody/My Home Town Circle "R"	1968	3.00	6.00	12.00

—As "Luke the Drifter, Jr."

Number	Title (A Side/B Side)	Yr	VG	VG+	NM
❏ 14024	A Baby Again/Swim Across a Tear	1969	2.50	5.00	10.00
❏ 14047	Cajun Baby/My Heart Won't Let Me Go	1969	2.50	5.00	10.00

Number	Title (A Side/B Side)	Yr	VG	VG+	NM
❏ 14062	Be Careful of Stones That You Throw/ Book of Memories	1969	2.50	5.00	10.00

—As "Luke the Drifter, Jr."

Number	Title (A Side/B Side)	Yr	VG	VG+	NM
❏ 14077	I'd Rather Be Gone/Try, Try Again	1969	2.50	5.00	10.00
❏ 14095	Something to Think About/(There Must Be) A Better Way to Love	1969	2.50	5.00	10.00
❏ 14107	I Walked Out on Heaven/Your Love's One Thing	1970	2.00	4.00	8.00
❏ 14120	It Don't Take But One Mistake/Goin' Home	1970	2.00	4.00	8.00

—As "Luke the Drifter, Jr."

Number	Title (A Side/B Side)	Yr	VG	VG+	NM
❏ 14152	All for the Love of Sunshine/Ballad of the Moonshine	1970	2.00	4.00	8.00
❏ 14194	Rainin' in My Heart/A-Eee	1970	2.00	4.00	8.00
❏ 14240	I've Got a Right to Cry/Jesus Loved the Devil Out of Me	1971	2.00	4.00	8.00
❏ 14277	After All They All Used to Belong to Me/Happy Kind of Sadness	1971	2.00	4.00	8.00
❏ 14317	Ain't That a Shame/End of a Bad Day	1971	2.00	4.00	8.00
❏ 14371	Eleven Roses/Richmond Valley Breeze	1972	2.00	4.00	8.00
❏ 14421	Pride's Not Hard to Swallow/Hamburger Steak, Holiday Inn	1972	2.00	4.00	8.00
❏ 14486	After You/Knoxville Courthouse Blues	1973	—	3.00	6.00
❏ 14550	Hank/Hank (Part 2)	1973	—	3.00	6.00
❏ 14656	The Last Love Song/Those Tear Jerking Songs	1973	—	3.00	6.00
❏ 14700	Rainy Night in Georgia/Country Music in My Soul	1974	—	3.00	6.00
❏ 14731	I'll Think of Something/Country Music Lover	1974	—	3.00	6.00
❏ 14755	Angels Are Hard to Find/Getting Over You	1974	—	3.00	6.00
❏ 14794	Where He's Going, I've Already Gone/The Kind of Woman I've Got	1975	—	3.00	6.00
❏ 14813	The Same Old Story/Country Love	1975	—	3.00	6.00
❏ 14833	Stoned at the Jukebox/The Devil in the Bottle	1975	—	3.00	6.00
❏ 14845	Living Proof/Brothers of the Road	1976	—	3.00	6.00

VERVE

Number	Title (A Side/B Side)	Yr	VG	VG+	NM
❏ 10540	Meter Reader Maid/Just a Dream	1967	12.50	25.00	50.00

—As "Bocephus"

Number	Title (A Side/B Side)	Yr	VG	VG+	NM
❏ 10572	Mental Revenge/Splish Splash	1967	10.00	20.00	40.00

—As "Bocephus"

WARNER BROS.

Number	Title (A Side/B Side)	Yr	VG	VG+	NM
❏ PRO-S-3838 [DJ]	All My Rowdy Friends (Are Here on Monday Night) (same on both sides)	1989	3.75	7.50	15.00
❏ PRO-S-4492 [DJ]	Don't Give Us a Reason (same on both sides)	1990	2.00	4.00	8.00
❏ 8345	She's the Star (On the Stage of My Mind)/Call Me, Honey, Won't You	1977	—	2.50	5.00
❏ 8361	Mobile Boogie/She's the Star (On the Stage of My Mind)	1977	—	2.50	5.00
❏ 8410	I'm Not Responsible/(Honey, Won't You) Call Me	1977	—	2.50	5.00
❏ 8451	One Night Stands/I'm Not Responsible	1977	—	2.50	5.00
❏ 8507	Feelin' Better/Once and For All	1977	—	2.50	5.00
❏ 8549	The New South/Storms Never Last	1978	—	3.00	6.00
❏ 8564	You Love the Thunder/I Just Ain't Been Able	1978	—	2.50	5.00
❏ 8641	I Fought the Law/It's Different with You	1978	—	2.50	5.00
❏ 8715	Old Flame, New Fire/Payin' On Time	1978	—	2.50	5.00
❏ 19193	Angels Are Hard to Find/Hollywood Honeys	1991	—	—	3.00
❏ 19352	If It Will It Will/Won't It Be Nice	1991	—	—	3.00
❏ 19463	I Mean I Love You/Stoned at the Jukebox	1990	—	—	3.00
❏ 19542	Don't Give Us a Reason/U.S.A. Today	1990	—	—	3.00
❏ 19818	Man to Man/Whiskey Bent and Hell Bound	1990	—	—	3.00
❏ 19872	Good Friends, Good Whiskey, Good Lovin'/ Family Tradition	1990	—	—	3.00
❏ 19957	Ain't Nobody's Business/Big Mamou	1990	—	—	3.00
❏ 22945	Finders Keepers/What You Don't Know (Won't Hurt You)	1989	—	—	3.00
❏ 27584	There's a Tear in My Beer/ You Brought Me Down to Earth	1989	—	2.00	4.00

—A-side with Hank Williams Sr.

Number	Title (A Side/B Side)	Yr	VG	VG+	NM
❏ 27584 [PS]	There's a Tear in My Beer/ You Brought Me Down to Earth	1989	—	2.00	4.00
❏ 27722	Early in the Morning and Late at Night/ I'm Just a Man	1988	—	—	3.00
❏ 27722 [PS]	Early in the Morning and Late at Night I'm Just a Man	1988	—	2.00	4.00
❏ 27862	If the South Woulda Won/Wild Streak	1988	—	—	3.00
❏ 27862 [PS]	If the South Woulda Won/Wild Streak	1988	—	2.00	4.00
❏ 28120	Young Country/Buck Naked	1988	—	—	3.00
❏ 28120 [PS]	Young Country/Buck Naked	1988	—	2.00	4.00
❏ 28227	Heaven Can't Be Found/Doctor's Song	1987	—	—	3.00
❏ 28227 [PS]	Heaven Can't Be Found/Doctor's Song	1987	—	2.00	4.00
❏ 28369	Born to Boogie/What It Boils Down To	1987	—	—	3.00
❏ 28452	When Something Is Good (Why Does It Change)/Loving Instructor	1987	—	—	3.00
❏ 28581	Mind Your Own Business/My Name Is Bocephus	1986	—	2.00	4.00
❏ 28691	Country State of Mind/Fat Friends	1986	—	2.00	4.00
❏ 28794	Ain't Misbehavin'/I've Been Around	1986	—	2.00	4.00
❏ 28912	This Ain't Dallas/I Really Like Girls	1985	—	2.00	4.00
❏ 29022	I'm for Love/Lawyers, Guns and Money	1985	—	2.00	4.00
❏ 29095	Major Moves/Mr. Lincoln	1985	—	2.00	4.00
❏ 29184	All My Rowdy Friends Are Coming Over Tonight/ Video Blues		—	2.00	4.00
❏ 29253	Attitude Adjustment/Knoxville Courthouse Blues	1984	—	2.00	4.00
❏ 29382	Man of Steel/Now I Know How George Feels	1984	—	2.00	4.00
❏ 29500	Queen of My Heart/She Had Me	1983	—	2.00	4.00
❏ 29633	Leave Them Boys Alone/The Girl in the Front Row at Fort Worth	1983	—	2.00	4.00

7-Inch Extended Plays
MGM

Number	Title (A Side/B Side)	Yr	VG	VG+	NM
❏ SLM-4316	Cowpoke/Big Twenty/The Blizzard//Streets of Laredo/The River†	1966	3.75	7.50	15.00

—Jukebox issue; small hole, plays at 33 1/3 rpm

Number	Title (A Side/B Side)	Yr	VG	VG+	NM
❏ SLM-4316 [PS]	Ballads of the Hills and Plains	1966	3.75	7.50	15.00

Albums
CAPRICORN

Number	Title (A Side/B Side)	Yr	VG	VG+	NM
❏ W1-26806	Maverick	1992	5.00	10.00	20.00

—Columbia House edition (only U.S. vinyl release)

ELEKTRA

Number	Title (A Side/B Side)	Yr	VG	VG+	NM
❏ 6E-194	Family Tradition	1979	3.00	6.00	12.00
❏ 6E-237	Whiskey Bent and Hell Bound	1979	2.50	5.00	10.00
❏ 6E-278	Habits Old and New	1980	2.50	5.00	10.00

Number	Title (A Side/B Side)	Yr	VG	VG+	NM
❏ 6E-330	Rowdy	1981	2.50	5.00	10.00
❏ 5E-535	The Pressure Is On	1981	2.50	5.00	10.00
❏ 5E-538	One Night Stands	1982	2.50	5.00	10.00
—Reissue					
❏ 5E-539	The New South	1982	2.50	5.00	10.00
—Reissue					
❏ 60100	High Notes	1982	2.50	5.00	10.00
❏ 60193	Hank Williams, Jr.'s, Greatest Hits	1982	2.50	5.00	10.00
❏ 60223	Strong Stuff	1983	3.75	7.50	15.00
MGM					
❏ GAS-119	Hank Williams, Jr. (Golden Archive Series)	1970	3.75	7.50	15.00
❏ E-4213 [M]	Sings the Songs of Hank Williams	1964	5.00	10.00	20.00
❏ SE-4213 [S]	Sings the Songs of Hank Williams	1964	6.25	12.50	25.00
❏ E-4260 [M]	Your Cheatin' Heart	1964	5.00	10.00	20.00
❏ SE-4260 [S]	Your Cheatin' Heart	1964	6.25	12.50	25.00
❏ E-4316 [M]	Ballads of the Hills and Plains	1965	5.00	10.00	20.00
❏ SE-4316 [S]	Ballads of the Hills and Plains	1965	6.25	12.50	25.00
❏ E-4344 [M]	Blues My Name	1966	5.00	10.00	20.00
❏ SE-4344 [S]	Blues My Name	1966	6.25	12.50	25.00
❏ E-4391 [M]	Country Shadows	1966	5.00	10.00	20.00
❏ SE-4391 [S]	Country Shadows	1966	6.25	12.50	25.00
❏ E-4428 [M]	My Own Way	1967	5.00	10.00	20.00
❏ SE-4428 [S]	My Own Way	1967	6.25	12.50	25.00
❏ E-4513 [M]	The Best of Hank Williams, Jr.	1967	5.00	10.00	20.00
❏ SE-4513 [S]	The Best of Hank Williams, Jr.	1967	6.25	12.50	25.00
❏ E-4527 [M]	My Songs	1968	10.00	20.00	40.00
❏ SE-4527 [S]	My Songs	1968	6.25	12.50	25.00
❏ SE-4540	A Time to Sing	1968	6.25	12.50	25.00
❏ SE-4559	Luke the Drifter, Jr.	1969	5.00	10.00	20.00
❏ SE-4621	Songs My Father Left Me	1969	5.00	10.00	20.00
❏ SE-4632	Luke the Drifter, Jr. (Vol. 2)	1969	5.00	10.00	20.00
❏ SE-4644	Live at Cobo Hall, Detroit	1969	5.00	10.00	20.00
❏ SE-4656	Hank Williams, Jr.'s Greatest Hits	1970	3.75	7.50	15.00
❏ SE-4657	Sunday Morning	1970	3.75	7.50	15.00
❏ SE-4673	Luke the Drifter, Jr. (Vol. 3)	1970	3.75	7.50	15.00
❏ SE-4675	Hank Williams, Jr., Singing My Songs (Johnny Cash)	1970	3.75	7.50	15.00
❏ SE-4774	I've Got a Right to Cry/ They All Used to Belong to Me	1971	3.75	7.50	15.00
❏ SE-4798	Sweet Dreams	1972	3.00	6.00	12.00
—With the Mike Curb Congregation					
❏ SE-4822	Hank Williams, Jr.'s Greatest Hits, Volume 2	1972	3.00	6.00	12.00
❏ SE-4843	Eleven Roses	1972	3.00	6.00	12.00
❏ SE-4862	After You/Pride's Not Hard to Swallow	1973	3.00	6.00	12.00
❏ SE-4906	Just Pickin' — No Singin'	1973	3.00	6.00	12.00
❏ SE-4936	The Last Love Song	1973	3.00	6.00	12.00
❏ M3G-4971	Living Proof	1974	3.00	6.00	12.00
❏ M3G-4988	Bocephus	1974	3.00	6.00	12.00
❏ MG-1-5009	Hank Williams, Jr., and Friends	1975	10.00	20.00	40.00
❏ MG-1-5020	14 Greatest Hits	1976	3.00	6.00	12.00
❏ ST-90695 [S]	Blues My Name	1966	7.50	15.00	30.00
—Capitol Record Club edition					
❏ T-90695 [M]	Blues My Name	1966	6.25	12.50	25.00
—Capitol Record Club edition					
❏ T-90925 [M]	Country Shadows	1966	6.25	12.50	25.00
—Capitol Record Club edition					
PAIR					
❏ PDL2-1164 [(2)]	I'm Walkin'	1987	3.00	6.00	12.00
POLYDOR					
❏ 811902-1	Live at Cobo Hall, Detroit	1983	2.00	4.00	8.00
—Reissue					
❏ 811903-1	Hank Williams, Jr.'s Greatest Hits	1983	2.00	4.00	8.00
❏ 811906-1	Hank Williams, Jr.'s Greatest Hits, Volume 2	1983	2.00	4.00	8.00
❏ 825091-1	14 Greatest Hits	1985	2.00	4.00	8.00
❏ 831575-1	Hank Williams, Jr., and Friends	1987	3.00	6.00	12.00
❏ 833069-1	Blues My Name	1987	2.00	4.00	8.00
❏ 833070-1	Eleven Roses	1987	2.00	4.00	8.00
❏ 835132-1	Standing in the Shadows	1988	2.00	4.00	8.00
WARNER BROS.					
❏ 6E-194	Family Tradition	1983	2.00	4.00	8.00
❏ 6E-237	Whiskey Bent and Hell Bound	1983	2.00	4.00	8.00
❏ 6E-278	Habits Old and New	1983	2.00	4.00	8.00
❏ 6E-330	Rowdy	1983	2.00	4.00	8.00
❏ 5E-535	The Pressure Is On	1983	2.00	4.00	8.00
❏ 5E-538	One Night Stands	1983	2.00	4.00	8.00
❏ 5E-539	The New South	1983	2.00	4.00	8.00
❏ PRO-A-2092 [DJ]	The Hank Williams, Jr., Interview	1983	6.25	12.50	25.00
❏ BS 2988	One Night Stands	1977	3.00	6.00	12.00
❏ BS 3127	The New South	1977	3.00	6.00	12.00
❏ 23924	Man of Steel	1983	2.50	5.00	10.00
❏ 25088	Major Moves	1984	2.50	5.00	10.00
❏ 25267	Five-O	1985	2.50	5.00	10.00
❏ 25328	Greatest Hits — Volume 2	1985	2.00	4.00	8.00
❏ 25412	Montana Café	1986	2.00	4.00	8.00
❏ 25514 [(2)]	The Early Years	1984	3.00	6.00	12.00
❏ 25538	Hank "Live"	1987	2.00	4.00	8.00
❏ 25593	Born to Boogie	1987	2.00	4.00	8.00
❏ 25725	Wild Streak	1988	2.00	4.00	8.00
❏ 25834	Greatest Hits III	1989	2.00	4.00	8.00
❏ 26090	Lone Wolf	1990	3.00	6.00	12.00
❏ 60100	High Notes	1983	2.00	4.00	8.00
❏ 60193	Hank Williams, Jr.'s, Greatest Hits	1983	2.00	4.00	8.00
❏ 60223	Strong Stuff	1983	2.50	5.00	10.00
❏ R 120612	America (The Way I See It)	1990	5.00	10.00	20.00
—BMG Music Service edition (no regular vinyl release)					
❏ R 160351	Pure Hank	1991	5.00	10.00	20.00
—BMG Music Service edition (no regular vinyl release)					

WILLIAMS, HANK, JR., AND LOIS JOHNSON
45s
MGM

Number	Title (A Side/B Side)	Yr	VG	VG+	NM
❏ 14136	Removing the Shadow/Party People	1970	2.00	4.00	8.00
❏ 14164	So Sad (To Watch Good Love Go Bad)/ Let's Talk It Over Again	1970	2.00	4.00	8.00
❏ 14356	Send Me Some Lovin'/ What We Used to Hang On To	1972	2.00	4.00	8.00
❏ 14443	Whole Lotta Loving/ Why Should We Try Anymore	1972	2.00	4.00	8.00
Albums					
MGM					
❏ SE-4721	Removing the Shadow	1971	3.75	7.50	15.00
—The label has the word "Shadows" instead of "Shadow"					
❏ SE-4750	All for the Love of Sunshine	1971	5.00	10.00	20.00
❏ SE-4857	Send Me Some Lovin'/Whole Lotta Lovin'	1972	5.00	10.00	20.00

WILLIAMS, HERB
45s
MGM

Number	Title (A Side/B Side)	Yr	VG	VG+	NM
❏ 12431	Alimony Blues/Because You've Been Away	1957	5.00	10.00	20.00
—This record was erroneously listed in the past as a HANK Williams record					

WILLIAMS, JIM
45s
SUN

Number	Title (A Side/B Side)	Yr	VG	VG+	NM
❏ 270	Please Don't Cry Over Me/That Depends on You	1957	7.50	15.00	30.00

WILLIAMS, JIMMY
45s
ABC-PARAMOUNT

Number	Title (A Side/B Side)	Yr	VG	VG+	NM
❏ 10471	I Gave My Love a Cherry/Half Man	1963	3.00	6.00	12.00
❏ 10523	Green Pastures (23rd Psalm)/ I'm Strung Out Over You, Baby	1964	3.00	6.00	12.00
ATLANTIC					
❏ 2296	Walking on Air/I'm So Lost	1965	2.50	5.00	10.00
CUB					
❏ 9031	My Pledge and My Promise/Keep Me with You	1959	3.75	7.50	15.00
❏ 9039	C'mon Baby (What's Your Name)/ Don't Put It Off (Do It Now)	1959	3.75	7.50	15.00
DUB					
❏ 2842	You're Always Late/I Belong to You	1958	25.00	50.00	100.00
DYNO VOICE					
❏ 931	Mushroom City/Standing There	1969	2.00	4.00	8.00
HULL					
❏ 765	I Can't Help Falling in Love/Smile	1964	2.50	5.00	10.00
LIMELIGHT					
❏ 3038	Mrs. Cherry/Keoto'To	1964	2.50	5.00	10.00
MGM					
❏ 11938	No One Knows/These Blues Are Over You	1955	5.00	10.00	20.00
❏ 12262	Alpha and Omega/ Where Will I Shelter My Sheep	1956	5.00	10.00	20.00
❏ 12362	Throwing My Life Away/ We're Drifting Further Apart	1956	5.00	10.00	20.00
❏ 12596	You're the One/I'll Only Give My Love	1957	6.25	12.50	25.00
ORBIT					
❏ 9002	You're the One/I'll Only Give My Love	1958	3.75	7.50	15.00
ROULETTE					
❏ 4303	There Is No Doubt/What a Change	1960	3.75	7.50	15.00

WILLIAMS, LARRY Also see JOHNNY "GUITAR" WATSON AND LARRY WILLIAMS.
45s
BELL

Number	Title (A Side/B Side)	Yr	VG	VG+	NM
❏ 813	I Could Love You Baby/ Can't Find No Substitute for Love	1969	2.50	5.00	10.00
—With Johnny Watson					
CHESS					
❏ 1736	My Baby's Got Soul/Every Day I Wonder	1959	5.00	10.00	20.00
❏ 1745	Get Ready/Baby, Baby	1959	5.00	10.00	20.00
❏ 1761	I Wanna Know/Like a Gentle Man	1960	5.00	10.00	20.00
❏ 1764	Oh Baby/I Hear My Baby	1960	5.00	10.00	20.00
❏ 1805	Lawdy Mama/Fresh Out of Tears	1961	5.00	10.00	20.00
EL BAM					
❏ 69	Call on Me/Boss Lovin'	1965	3.00	6.00	12.00
FANTASY					
❏ 806	Doing the Best I Can (With What I Got)/ Gimme Some	1977	—	2.50	5.00
❏ 810	One Thing or the Other (Part 1)/One Thing or the Other (Part 2)	1977	—	2.50	5.00
❏ 841	The Resurrection of Funk/(B-side unknown)	1978	—	2.50	5.00
MERCURY					
❏ 72147	Woman/Can't Help Myself	1963	3.75	7.50	15.00
OKEH					
❏ 7259	This Old Heart (Is So Lonely)/ I'd Rather Fight Than Switch	1966	2.50	5.00	10.00
❏ 7280	I Am the One/You Ask for One Good Reason	1967	2.50	5.00	10.00
❏ 7294	Just Because/Boss Lovin'	1967	2.50	5.00	10.00
SMASH					
❏ 2035	Call on Me/Boss Lovin'	1966	3.00	6.00	12.00
SPECIALTY					
❏ 597	Just Because/Let Me Tell You Baby	1957	7.50	15.00	30.00
❏ 608	Short Fat Fannie/High School Dance	1957	10.00	20.00	40.00
❏ 608	Short Fat Fannie/High School Dance	1984	—	2.00	4.00
—Gold vinyl					
❏ 615	Bony Moronie/You Bug Me, Baby	1957	10.00	20.00	40.00
❏ 615	Bony Moronie/You Bug Me, Baby	1984	—	2.00	4.00
—Red vinyl					
❏ 626	Dizzy, Miss Lizzy/Slow Down	1958	10.00	20.00	40.00
❏ 626 [PS]	Dizzy, Miss Lizzy/Slow Down	1958	20.00	40.00	80.00
❏ 626	Dizzy, Miss Lizzy/Slow Down	1984	—	2.00	4.00
—Blue vinyl					
❏ 634	Hootchy-Koo/The Dummy	1958	6.25	12.50	25.00
❏ 634	Hootchy-Koo/The Dummy	1984	—	2.00	4.00
—Green vinyl					
❏ 647	I Was a Fool/Peaches and Cream	1958	6.25	12.50	25.00
❏ 658	Bad Boy/She Said "Yeah"	1959	7.50	15.00	30.00
❏ 658	Bad Boy/She Said "Yeah"	1984	—	2.00	4.00
—Orange vinyl					
❏ 665	Steal a Little Kiss/I Can't Stop Loving You	1959	6.25	12.50	25.00
❏ 677	Give Me Your Love/Teardrops	1959	6.25	12.50	25.00
❏ 682	Ting-a-Ling/Little Schoolgirl	1960	6.25	12.50	25.00
❏ 682	Ting-a-Ling/Little Schoolgirl	1984	—	2.00	4.00
—Gold vinyl					

Number	Title (A Side/B Side)	Yr	VG	VG+	NM
VENTURE					
❏ 622	Shake Your Body Girl/				
	Love I Can't Seem to Find It	1968	2.50	5.00	10.00
❏ 627	Wake Up (Nothing Comes to a Sleeper				
	But a Dream)/Love I Can't Seem to Find It	1968	2.50	5.00	10.00
Albums					
CHESS					
❏ LP-1457 [M]	Larry Williams	1961	50.00	100.00	200.00
OKEH					
❏ OKM-12123 [M]	Larry Williams' Greatest Hits	1967	7.50	15.00	30.00
❏ OKS-14123 [S]	Larry Williams' Greatest Hits	1967	10.00	20.00	40.00
SPECIALTY					
❏ SP-2109 [M]	Here's Larry Williams	1959	50.00	100.00	200.00
—Original pressing on thick vinyl with no copyright information on back cover					
❏ SP-2109 [M]	Here's Larry Williams	198?	2.50	5.00	10.00
—Reissue with thinner vinyl and copyright information on back					
❏ SP-7002 [(2)]	Bad Boy	1990	5.00	10.00	20.00
WILLIAMS, LENNY					
Albums					
ABC					
❏ AB-1023	Choosing You	1977	2.50	5.00	10.00
❏ AA-1073	Spark of Love	1978	2.50	5.00	10.00
MCA					
❏ 3155	Love Current	1979	2.50	5.00	10.00
❏ 5147	Let's Do It Today	1980	2.50	5.00	10.00
❏ 5253	Taking Chances	1982	2.50	5.00	10.00
MOTOWN					
❏ M6-843	Rise Sleeping Beauty	1975	3.00	6.00	12.00
WILLIAMS, LEONA					
45s					
ELEKTRA					
❏ 47114	I'm Almost Ready/The End of the World	1981	—	2.00	4.00
❏ 47162	You Can't Find Many Kisses/Guitar Pickin' Man	1981	—	2.00	4.00
❏ 47217	Always Late with Your Kisses/Startin' Today	1981	—	2.00	4.00
HICKORY					
❏ 1501	A Woman's Man/Ten Minutes Till Heartaches	1968	2.00	4.00	8.00
❏ 1511	Broadminded/Papa's Medicine Show	1968	2.00	4.00	8.00
❏ 1523	I Want Some More of This/They'll Never Take				
	His Love from Me	1968	2.00	4.00	8.00
❏ 1532	Once More/I Narrowed This Triangle				
	(Down to Two)	1969	2.00	4.00	8.00
❏ 1544	Baby, We're Really in Love/Circle of Love	1969	2.00	4.00	8.00
❏ 1555	Just Because of You/When I Stop Dreaming	1969	2.00	4.00	8.00
❏ 1565	This Ain't a Home No More/Yes Ma'am (He				
	Found Me in a Honky Tonk)	1970	2.00	4.00	8.00
❏ 1578	If I'd Only Listened to Mama and Dad/				
	Watch Her Go	1970	2.00	4.00	8.00
❏ 1590	Somewhere Inside/He's Just You Made Over	1971	2.00	4.00	8.00
❏ 1606	Country Girl with Hot Pants On/				
	Babe, Just for You	1971	2.00	4.00	8.00
❏ 1619	Country Music in My Soul/				
	The Boys and Lucy Brown	1972	—	3.50	7.00
❏ 1635	Happy Anniversary, Baby/				
	The Old Place Is Gone	1972	—	3.50	7.00
❏ 1650	Out of Hand/Gentleman on My Mind	1972	—	3.50	7.00
❏ 1662	A Woman's Life Is More Than Just a Man/				
	I'd Rather Die	1973	—	3.50	7.00
❏ 1670	Papa's Medicine Show/I Can't Tell My Heart That	1973	—	3.50	7.00
HICKORY/MGM					
❏ 304	Your Shoeshine Girl/Since I'm Not with the One				
	I Love (I'll Love the One I'm With)	1973	—	3.00	6.00
❏ 310	Anything Goes/I Spent a Week There Last Night	1973	—	3.00	6.00
❏ 315	I'm Not Supposed to Love You Anymore/Once				
	More	1974	—	3.00	6.00
MCA					
❏ 40515	If Anyone Ought to Know/I Wonder Where I'll				
	Find You At Tonight	1976	—	2.50	5.00
❏ 40557	Cotton-Eyed Joe/San Quentin	1976	—	2.50	5.00
❏ 40856	Mama I've Got to Go to Memphis/That Lonely				
	Unloved Wife Look	1978	—	2.50	5.00
❏ 40926	Rockin' Rollin' Stoned/Bright Morning Light	1978	—	2.50	5.00
❏ 40988	The Baby Song/Call Me Crazy Lady	1979	—	2.50	5.00
❏ 41006	Yes Ma'am (He Found Me in a Honky Tonk)/				
	Good Nights Make Good Mornings	1979	—	2.50	5.00
❏ 41196	Catchin' Crawfish/Any Port in a Storm	1980	—	2.50	5.00
MERCURY					
❏ 818946-7	Midnight Love/My First Night Away from Home	1984	—	2.00	4.00
RCA VICTOR					
❏ PB-10097	Just Like a Prayer/A Lifetime to Forget	1974	—	3.00	6.00
❏ PB-10300	Shape Up or Ship Out/				
	You Don't Love Me Like You Mean It	1975	—	3.00	6.00
Albums					
HICKORY					
❏ LPS-151	That Williams Girl	1971	3.75	7.50	15.00
❏ LPS-165	The Best of Leona Williams	1972	3.75	7.50	15.00
MCA					
❏ 2212	San Quentin's First Lady	1976	3.00	6.00	12.00
MERCURY					
❏ 822424-1	Someday When Things Are Good	1984	2.00	4.00	8.00
WILLIAMS, LESTER					
45s					
DUKE					
❏ 123	Let's Do It/Good Lovin' Baby	1954	12.50	25.00	50.00
❏ 131	Crazy 'Bout You Baby/Don't Take Your Love				
	from Me	1954	10.00	20.00	40.00
IMPERIAL					
❏ 5402	McDonald's Daughter/Daddy Loves You	1956	12.50	25.00	50.00
SPECIALTY					
❏ 422	I Can't Lose with the Stuff I Use/				
	My Home Ain't Here	1952	25.00	50.00	100.00
❏ 431	Let Me Tell You a Thing or Two/Tryin' to Forget	1952	37.50	75.00	150.00
❏ 437	Sweet Lovin' Daddy/Lost Gal	1952	37.50	75.00	150.00
❏ 450	Brand New Baby/				
	If I Knew How Much I Loved You	1953	25.00	50.00	100.00

Number	Title (A Side/B Side)	Yr	VG	VG+	NM
WILLIAMS, LEW					
45s					
IMPERIAL					
❏ 5394	Cat Talk/Gone Ape Man	1956	30.00	60.00	120.00
❏ 5411	Bop Bop Ba Doo Bop/Something I Said	1956	30.00	60.00	120.00
❏ 5429	Centipede/Abra Cadabra	1957	30.00	60.00	120.00
❏ 8306	Don't Mention My Name/I'll Play Your Game	1956	37.50	75.00	150.00
WILLIAMS, MASON					
45s					
MERCURY					
❏ 72603	Exciting Accident/Love Our Wine	1966	2.50	5.00	10.00
WARNER BROS.					
❏ 7190	Classical Gas/Long Time Blues	1968	—	3.00	6.00
❏ 7235	Baroque-a-Nova/Wanderlove	1968	—	2.50	5.00
❏ 7245	Cinderella Rockafella/Generatah-Oscillath	1968	—	2.50	5.00
❏ 7248	Saturday Night at the World/				
	One Minute Commercial	1968	—	2.50	5.00
❏ 7272	Greensleeves/13 Dollar Stella	1969	—	2.50	5.00
❏ 7301	Gift of Song/Major Thang	1969	—	2.50	5.00
❏ 7402	Find a Reason to Believe/Jose's Piece	1970	—	2.50	5.00
❏ 7513	Here I Am Again/Train Ride in G	1971	—	2.50	5.00
7-Inch Extended Plays					
WARNER BROS.					
❏ S 1729	Overture/All the Time/Baroque-a-Nova//She's				
	Gone Away/The Prince's Panties/				
	Long Time Blues	1968	2.50	5.00	10.00
—Jukebox issue; small hole, plays at 33 1/3 rpm					
❏ S 1729 [PS]	The Mason Williams' Phonograph Record	1968	2.50	5.00	10.00
Albums					
AMERICAN GRAMAPHONE					
❏ AG-800	Classical Gas	1987	2.50	5.00	10.00
—With Mannheim Steamroller					
EVEREST					
❏ 3265	Listening Matter	1969	3.00	6.00	12.00
FLYING FISH					
❏ FF-059	Fresh Fish	1978	2.50	5.00	10.00
VEE JAY					
❏ VJ-1103 [M]	Them Poems and Things	1964	5.00	10.00	20.00
❏ VJS-1103 [S]	Them Poems and Things	1964	6.25	12.50	25.00
WARNER BROS.					
❏ WS 1729	The Mason Williams Phonograph Record	1968	3.00	6.00	12.00
—Green label with "W7" logo					
❏ WS 1729	The Mason Williams Phonograph Record	1970	2.50	5.00	10.00
—Green label with "WB" logo					
❏ WS 1729	The Mason Williams Phonograph Record	1973	2.00	4.00	8.00
—"Burbank" palm trees label					
❏ WS 1729	The Mason Williams Phonograph Record	1979	—	3.00	6.00
—White or tan label					
❏ WS 1776	The Mason Williams Ear Show	1968	3.00	6.00	12.00
❏ WS 1788	Music by Mason Williams	1969	3.00	6.00	12.00
❏ WS 1838	Hand Made	1970	3.00	6.00	12.00
❏ WS 1941	Sharepickers	1971	3.00	6.00	12.00
WILLIAMS, MAURICE, AND THE ZODIACS Also see THE GLADIOLAS.					
45s					
ATLANTIC					
❏ 2199	Funny/Loneliness	1963	3.75	7.50	15.00
—As "The Zodiacs"					
❏ 2741	Sweetness/Whirlpool	1970	—	2.50	5.00
COLE					
❏ 100	Golly Gee/"I" Town	1959	12.50	25.00	50.00
❏ 101	Lover (Where Are You)/She's Mine	1959	10.00	20.00	40.00
DEESU					
❏ 302	Baby Baby/Being Without You	1967	5.00	10.00	20.00
❏ 304	May I/This Feeling	1967	5.00	10.00	20.00
❏ 307	Ooh Poo Pa Doo (Part 1)/				
	Ooh Poo Pa Doo (Part 2)	1967	5.00	10.00	20.00
❏ 309	Don't Ever Leave Me/Surely	1967	5.00	10.00	20.00
❏ 311	Don't Be Half Safe/How to Pick a Winner	1967	5.00	10.00	20.00
❏ 318	Stay '68 (Live Version)/Dance, Dance, Dance	1968	3.75	7.50	15.00
HERALD					
❏ 552	Stay/Do You Believe	1960	5.00	10.00	20.00
❏ 556	Always/I Remember	1961	3.75	7.50	15.00
❏ 559	Do I/Come Along	1961	3.75	7.50	15.00
❏ 563	Someday/Come and Get It	1961	3.75	7.50	15.00
❏ 565	Please/High Blood Pressure	1961	3.75	7.50	15.00
❏ 572	It's Alright/Here I Stand	1962	3.75	7.50	15.00
LOST-NITE					
❏ 413	Stay/Do You Believe	197?	—	2.50	5.00
—Reissue					
❏ 443	May I/Lollipop	197?	—	2.50	5.00
—Reissue					
RCA					
❏ 5363-7-R	Stay/She's Like the Wind	1987	—	—	3.00
—B-side by Patrick Swayze					
SCEPTER					
❏ 12113	Nobody Knows/I Know	1965	3.75	7.50	15.00
SEA HORN					
❏ 503	My Baby's Gone/Return	1964	3.75	7.50	15.00
SELWYN					
❏ 5121	Say Yeah/College Girl	1959	12.50	25.00	50.00
SPHERE SOUND					
❏ 707	So Fine/The Winds	1965	3.00	6.00	12.00
VEE JAY					
❏ 678	May I/Lollipop	1965	5.00	10.00	20.00
VEEP					
❏ 1294	My Reason for Living/The Four Corners	1969	2.00	4.00	8.00
Albums					
COLLECTABLES					
❏ COL-5021	The Best of Maurice Williams and the Zodiacs	198?	2.50	5.00	10.00
HERALD					
❏ HLP-1014 [M]	Stay	1961	125.00	250.00	500.00
RELIC					
❏ 5017	Greatest Hits	197?	3.75	7.50	15.00

Number	Title (A Side/B Side)	Yr	VG	VG+	NM
SNYDER					
❏ 5586 [M]	At the Beach	196?	25.00	50.00	100.00
SPHERE SOUND					
❏ SR-7007 [M]	Stay	1965	30.00	60.00	120.00
❏ SSR-7007 [R]	Stay	1965	20.00	40.00	80.00

WILLIAMS, OTIS, AND HIS CHARMS Also see THE CHARMS.
45s

Number	Title (A Side/B Side)	Yr	VG	VG+	NM
DELUXE					
❏ 6088	Miss the Love/Tell Me Now	1955	7.50	15.00	30.00
—As "Otis Williams and His New Group"					
❏ 6090	Gum Drop/Save Me, Save Me	1955	7.50	15.00	30.00
—As "Otis Williams and His New Group"					
❏ 6091	That's Your Mistake/Too Late I Learned	1955	7.50	15.00	30.00
❏ 6092	Rolling Home/Do Be You	1956	7.50	15.00	30.00
❏ 6093	Ivory Tower/In Paradise	1956	7.50	15.00	30.00
❏ 6095	One Night Only/It's All Over	1956	7.50	15.00	30.00
❏ 6097	I'd Like to Thank You Mr. D.J./Whirlwind	1956	7.50	15.00	30.00
❏ 6098	Gypsy Lady/I'll Remember You	1956	7.50	15.00	30.00
❏ 6105	Blues Stay Away from Me/Pardon Me	1957	6.25	12.50	25.00
❏ 6115	Walkin' After Midnight/I'm Waiting Just for You	1957	6.25	12.50	25.00
❏ 6130	Nowhere on Earth/No Got De Woman	1957	6.25	12.50	25.00
❏ 6137	Talking to Myself/One Kind Word from You	1957	6.25	12.50	25.00
❏ 6138	United/Don't Deny Me	1957	6.25	12.50	25.00
❏ 6149	Dynamite Darling/Well Oh Well	1957	6.25	12.50	25.00
❏ 6158	Could This Be Magic/Oh Julie	1958	6.25	12.50	25.00
❏ 6160	Let Some Love in Your Heart/Baby-O	1958	6.25	12.50	25.00
❏ 6165	Burnin' Lips/Red Hot Love (Do This Love)	1958	6.25	12.50	25.00
❏ 6174	Don't Wake Up the Kids/You'll Remain Forever	1958	6.25	12.50	25.00
❏ 6178	My Friends/The Secret	1958	6.25	12.50	25.00
❏ 6181	Pretty Little Things Called Girls/Welcome Home	1959	6.25	12.50	25.00
❏ 6183	My Prayer Tonight/Watch Dog	1959	6.25	12.50	25.00
❏ 6185	I Knew It All the Time/Tears of Happiness	1959	6.25	12.50	25.00
❏ 6186	In Paradise/Who Knows	1959	6.25	12.50	25.00
❏ 6187	Blues Stay Away from Me/				
	Funny What True Love Can Do	1959	6.25	12.50	25.00
KING					
❏ 5323	Chief Um (Take It Easy)/It's a Treat	1960	5.00	10.00	20.00
❏ 5332	Silver Star/Rickety Rickshaw Man	1960	5.00	10.00	20.00
❏ 5372	Image of a Girl/Wait a Minute Baby	1960	12.50	25.00	50.00
❏ 5389	The First Sign of Love/So Be It	1960	5.00	10.00	20.00
❏ 5421	Wait/And Take My Love	1960	5.00	10.00	20.00
❏ 5455	Little Turtle Dove/So Can I	1961	5.00	10.00	20.00
❏ 5497	Just Forget About Me/				
	You Know How Much I Care	1961	5.00	10.00	20.00
❏ 5527	Pardon Me/Panic	1961	5.00	10.00	20.00
❏ 5558	Two Hearts/The Secret	1961	5.00	10.00	20.00
❏ 5682	When We Get Together/Only Young Once	1962	3.75	7.50	15.00
❏ 5816	It Just Ain't Right/It'll Never Happen Again	1963	3.75	7.50	15.00
❏ 5880	Unchain My Heart/Friends Call Me a Fool	1964	3.75	7.50	15.00
❏ 6034	Bye Bye Baby/Please Believe in Me	1966	3.75	7.50	15.00
OKEH					
❏ 7225	Baby, You Turn Me On/				
	Love Don't Grow on Trees	1965	3.75	7.50	15.00
❏ 7235	I Fall to Pieces/Gotta Get Myself Together	1965	3.75	7.50	15.00
❏ 7248	I Got Loving/Welcome Home	1966	3.75	7.50	15.00
❏ 7261	Ain't Gonna Walk Your Dog No More/Your				
	Sweet Love (Rained Over Me)	1966	3.75	7.50	15.00
SCEPTER					
❏ 12376	Here Lie the Bones of Nellie Jones/				
	When You Turn On the Love	1973	2.00	4.00	8.00
STOP					
❏ 301	Begging to You/(B-side unknown)	1968	2.50	5.00	10.00
❏ 306	Begging to You/Everybody's Got a Song But Me	1968	2.50	5.00	10.00
❏ 346	Jesus Is a Soul Man/Make a Woman Feel Like				
	a Woman	1969	2.50	5.00	10.00
❏ 360	Ling, Ting, Tong/For the Love	1970	2.50	5.00	10.00
❏ 388	I Wanna Go Country/Rocky Top	1971	2.00	4.00	8.00
—As "Otis Williams and the Midnight Cowboys"					

7-Inch Extended Plays

Number	Title (A Side/B Side)	Yr	VG	VG+	NM
DELUXE					
❏ EP-385	*That's Your Mistake/Too Late I Learned/Miss				
	the Love/Gum Drop	1956	75.00	150.00	300.00
❏ EP-385	Otis Williams and His Charms	1956	75.00	150.00	300.00

Albums

Number	Title (A Side/B Side)	Yr	VG	VG+	NM
DELUXE					
❏ 570 [M]	Their All Time Hits	1957	250.00	500.00	1000.
KING					
❏ 570 [M]	Their All Time Hits	1957	150.00	300.00	600.00
❏ 614 [M]	This Is Otis Williams and His Charms	1959	100.00	200.00	400.00
STOP					
❏ STLP-1022	Otis Williams and the Midnight Cowboys	1971	6.25	12.50	25.00

WILLIAMS, PAUL
45s

Number	Title (A Side/B Side)	Yr	VG	VG+	NM
A&M					
❏ 1325	We've Only Just Begun/Waking Up Alone	1972	—	2.00	4.00
❏ 1356	My Love and I/I Never Had It So Good	1972	—	2.00	4.00
❏ 1409	I Won't Last a Day Without You/Little Girl	1973	—	2.00	4.00
❏ 1429	Lady in Waiting/Look What I Found	1973	—	2.00	4.00
❏ 1479	What Would They Say/Inspiration	1973	—	2.00	4.00
❏ 1525	That's What Friends Are For/Dream Away	1974	—	2.00	4.00
❏ 1659	A Little Bit of Love/Nice to Be Around	1975	—	2.00	4.00
❏ 1686	One More Angel/This Is Supposed to Be a Party	1975	—	2.00	4.00
❏ 1797	Don't Call It Love/Time and Tide	1976	—	2.00	4.00
❏ 1853	Even Better Than I Know Myself/Time and Tide	1976	—	2.00	4.00
❏ 1868	Bugsy Malone/Ordinary Fool	1976	—	2.00	4.00
❏ 1961	Love Theme from "A Star Is Born"/				
	Waking Up Alone	1977	—	2.00	4.00
PAID					
❏ 146	Making Believe/Oh, How I Miss You Tonight	1981	—	2.00	4.00
PORTRAIT					
❏ 70029	The Gift/A Little on the Windy Side	1979	—	2.00	4.00
REPRISE					
❏ 0903	Someday/Mornin' I'll Be Movin' On	1970	—	3.00	6.00

Albums

Number	Title (A Side/B Side)	Yr	VG	VG+	NM
A&M					
❏ SP-3131	Just an Old Fashioned Love Song	198?	2.00	4.00	8.00
—Budget-line reissue					
❏ SP-3606	Here Comes Inspiration	1974	2.50	5.00	10.00
❏ SP-3655	A Little Bit of Love	1974	2.50	5.00	10.00
❏ SP-4327	Just an Old Fashioned Love Song	1971	2.50	5.00	10.00
❏ SP-4367	Life Goes On	1972	2.50	5.00	10.00
❏ SP-4550	Ordinary Fool	1975	2.50	5.00	10.00
❏ SP-4701	Classics	1977	2.50	5.00	10.00
PORTRAIT					
❏ JR 35610	Windy Side	1979	2.50	5.00	10.00
REPRISE					
❏ RS 6401	Someday Man	1970	3.00	6.00	12.00

WILLIAMS, ROGER
45s

Number	Title (A Side/B Side)	Yr	VG	VG+	NM
KAPP					
❏ KJB-48	Try to Remember/(B-side unknown)	1965	—	3.00	6.00
❏ KJB-87	White Christmas/Winter Wonderland	196?	2.00	4.00	8.00
❏ 101	You'll Never Walk Alone/The Boy Next Door	1955	2.50	5.00	10.00
❏ 116	Autumn Leaves/Take Care	1955	2.50	5.00	10.00
❏ 116 [PS]	Autumn Leaves/Take Care	1955	5.00	10.00	20.00
❏ 127	Wanting You/Night Wind	1955	2.50	5.00	10.00
❏ 138	La Mer (Beyond the Sea)/Song of Devotion	1956	2.50	5.00	10.00
❏ 144	Hi-Lili, Hi-Lo/My Dream Sonata	1956	2.50	5.00	10.00
❏ 156	Tumbling Tumbleweeds				
	/I'll Always Walk with You	1956	2.50	5.00	10.00
❏ 161	Two Different Worlds/Nights in Verona	1956	2.50	5.00	10.00
—With Jane Morgan					
❏ 169	Anastasia/A Serenade for Joy	1956	2.50	5.00	10.00
❏ 175	Almost Paradise/For the First Time	1957	2.00	4.00	8.00
❏ 186	Moonlight Love/Every Little Movement	1957	2.00	4.00	8.00
❏ 197	Till/Big Town	1957	2.00	4.00	8.00
❏ 210	Arrividerci Roma/Sentimental Touch	1958	2.00	4.00	8.00
❏ 224	Indiscreet/Young and Warm and Wonderful	1958	2.00	4.00	8.00
❏ 233	Near You/Merry Widow Waltz	1958	2.00	4.00	8.00
❏ 246	The World Outside/Tchaikovsky Piano Concerto	1958	2.00	4.00	8.00
❏ 257	Dearer Than Dear/The Key to the Kingdom	1959	2.00	4.00	8.00
❏ 265	Mockin' Bird Hill/Memories Are Made of This	1959	2.00	4.00	8.00
❏ 299	Adeste Fideles/Hark the Herald Angels Sing	1959	2.50	5.00	10.00
❏ 300	Mary's Little Boy Child/Winter Wonderland	1959	2.50	5.00	10.00
❏ 301	Sunrise Serenade/Cool Water	1959	2.00	4.00	8.00
❏ 301 [PS]	Sunrise Serenade/Cool Water	1959	3.00	6.00	12.00
❏ 331	La Montana (If She Should Come to You)/				
	What Lies Over the Hill	1960	—	3.50	7.00
❏ 345	Little Rock Get Away/Riviera Concerto	1960	—	3.50	7.00
❏ 347	Temptation/Homesick for New England	1960	—	3.50	7.00
❏ 364	Maria Maria/I Get a Kick Out of You	1961	—	3.50	7.00
❏ 386	A Lover's Symphony/Song of the Rain	1961	—	3.50	7.00
❏ 408	Yellow Bird/Roger's Bumble Bee	1961	—	3.50	7.00
❏ 437	Maria/Even Tide	1961	—	3.50	7.00
❏ 437 [PS]	Maria/Even Tide	1961	3.00	6.00	12.00
❏ 440	Santa Claus, Santa Claus				
	(We Love You)/Jingle Bells	1961	2.50	5.00	10.00
❏ 447	Amor/Maria	1962	—	3.50	7.00
❏ 454	Intermezzo/Skaters' Waltz	1962	—	3.50	7.00
❏ 470	Hatari/On Top of Old Smoky	1962	—	3.50	7.00
❏ 479	Lorelei/Niagara Theme	1962	—	3.50	7.00
❏ 492	Theme from Mutiny on the Bounty/It's Now or				
	Never	1962	—	3.50	7.00
❏ 505	Cold, Cold Heart/San Antonio Rose	1963	—	3.00	6.00
❏ 522	Walking Alone/On the Trail	1963	—	3.00	6.00
❏ 533	Theme from "11th Hour"/Janie Is Her Name	1963	—	3.00	6.00
❏ 545	Danke Schoen/Look Again	1963	—	3.00	6.00
❏ 560	Cardinal/Walking Alone	1963	—	3.00	6.00
❏ 574	Felicia/Takewood Nocturne	1964	—	3.00	6.00
❏ 587	This Is My Prayer/Roger's Bumble Bee	1964	—	3.00	6.00
❏ 607	Lollipops and Roses/Whistlin'	1964	—	3.00	6.00
❏ 707	Autumn Leaves 1965/Autumn Leaves 1955	1965	—	3.00	6.00
❏ 738	Lara's Theme from "Dr. Zhivago"/Dulcinea	1966	—	3.00	6.00
❏ 767	Born Free/Jimmie's Train	1966	—	3.00	6.00
❏ 801	Sunrise, Sunset/Edelweiss	1966	—	2.50	5.00
❏ 821	Love Me Forever/Sweet Pea	1967	—	2.50	5.00
❏ 843	Tiny Bubbles/More Than a Miracle	1967	—	2.50	5.00
❏ 890	Spinning Song/Glory of Love	1968	—	2.50	5.00
❏ 907	The Impossible Dream/If You Go	1968	—	2.50	5.00
❏ 929	Who Killed Ezra Brymay/Marlena	1968	—	2.50	5.00
❏ 949	Elvira Madigan Theme/Only for Lovers	1968	—	2.50	5.00
❏ 975	Love Theme from La Strada/Gentle on My Mind	1969	—	2.50	5.00
❏ 995	Love Theme from Romeo and Juliet/				
	As Long As He Needs Me	1969	—	2.50	5.00
❏ 2007	Galveston/Mini Minuet	1969	—	2.00	4.00
❏ 2043	The Windmills of Your Mind/				
	Fill the World with Love	1969	—	2.00	4.00
❏ 2064	Let It Be Me/Fill the World with Love	1969	—	2.00	4.00
❏ 2078	The Lonely Ones/I'm a Believer	1970	—	2.00	4.00
❏ 2084	Suicide Is Painless/The Time for Love Is Anytime	1970	—	2.00	4.00
❏ 2106	Junk/Butterflies	1970	—	2.00	4.00
❏ 2110	America the Beautiful/Ain't No Mountain High				
	Enough	1970	—	2.00	4.00
❏ 2123	Theme from Love Story/For All We Know	1971	—	2.00	4.00
❏ 2135	Wandering Star/Your Song	1971	—	2.00	4.00
❏ 2140	Summer Knows/Your Song	1971	—	2.00	4.00
❏ 2148	How Can You Mend a Broken Heart/Bach Talk	1971	—	2.00	4.00
❏ 2165	Love Theme from The Godfather/				
	Life Is What You Name It	1972	—	2.00	4.00
❏ 2177	The Way of Love/Tchaikovsky '73	1972	—	2.00	4.00
❏ 2189	Lady Sings the Blues/Play Me	1972	—	2.00	4.00
MCA					
❏ 40044	Theme from "Baxter"/Rain Song	1973	—	—	3.00
❏ 40098	Tie a Yellow Ribbon Round the Ole Oak Tree/				
	Rain Song	1973	—	—	3.00
❏ 40155	Theme from "Exodus"/Hungarian Dance No. 5	1973	—	—	3.00
❏ 40185	Dark Lady/Solace	1974	—	—	3.00
❏ 40341	Theme from "Murder on the Orient Express"/				
	Half-Breed	1974	—	—	3.00

Number	Title (A Side/B Side)	Yr	VG	VG+	NM
❏ 40373	Theme from "The Young and the Restless"/ Melody to Dawn	1975	—	2.00	4.00
❏ 40451	Theme from "Rollerball"/Bolero	1975	—	—	3.00
❏ 40529	Country Comfort/Roger's Bumble Bee (Latter Day)	1976	—	—	3.00
❏ 40571	God Bless America/Grieg's You Know What By Roger You Know Who	1976	—	—	3.00
❏ 40625	Jesu Joy of Man's Desiring/ Cast Your Fate to the Wind	1976	—	—	3.00
❏ 40669	Main Title from "King Kong"/Love Song	1976	—	—	3.00
❏ 40725	Love Theme from "A Star Is Born"/ Theme from "Airport '77"	1977	—	—	3.00
❏ 40741	Theme from "New York, New York"/Me	1977	—	—	3.00
❏ 40845	You Light Up My Life/Candle on the Water	1977	—	—	3.00
❏ 40873	Verde (Green)/ How Can You Mend a Broken Heart	1978	—	—	3.00
WARNER BROS.					
❏ 49584	Somewhere in Time/Bee Side	1980	—	—	3.00
7-Inch Extended Plays					
KAPP					
❏ KE-708	Autumn Leaves/Take Care//Summertime/'Til Roses Cry	1955	2.00	4.00	8.00
❏ KE-708 [PS]	Roger Williams Plays	1955	2.00	4.00	8.00
❏ KE-710	You'll Never Walk Alone/The Boy Next Door// Moonlight in Vermont/There You Are	1956	2.00	4.00	8.00
❏ KE-710 [PS]	Roger Williams at the Piano	1956	2.00	4.00	8.00
❏ KE-714	*True Love/Because of You/Young at Heart/ Three Coins in the Fountain	195?	2.00	4.00	8.00
❏ KE-714 [PS]	Songs of the Fabulous Fifties 1	195?	2.00	4.00	8.00
❏ KE-715	(contents unknown)	195?	2.00	4.00	8.00
❏ KE-715 [PS]	Songs of the Fabulous Fifties 2	195?	2.00	4.00	8.00
❏ KE-716	(contents unknown)	195?	2.00	4.00	8.00
❏ KE-716 [PS]	Songs of the Fabulous Fifties 3	195?	2.00	4.00	8.00
❏ KE-717	*Tennessee Waltz/High Noon/ Blue Tango/Hey There	195?	2.00	4.00	8.00
❏ KE-717 [PS]	Songs of the Fabulous Fifties 4	195?	2.00	4.00	8.00
❏ KE-737	*Holiday for Strings/The Last Time I Saw Paris/ Anniversary Song/Some Enchanted Evening	195?	2.00	4.00	8.00
❏ KE-737 [PS]	Songs of the Fabulous Forties Vol. 1	195?	2.00	4.00	8.00
❏ KE-738	Buttons and Bows/Sunday, Monday or Always/ /Oh, What It Seemed to Be/ Zip-a-Dee Doo-Dah	1957	2.00	4.00	8.00
❏ KE-738 [PS]	Songs of the Fabulous Forties Vol. 2	1957	2.00	4.00	8.00
❏ KE-751	*Till/Marcheta/Always/The Merry Widow Waltz	1958	2.00	4.00	8.00
❏ KE-751 [PS]	Roger Williams	1958	2.00	4.00	8.00
❏ KE-753	April Love/Que Sera, Sera//Fascination/ Brahms' A Flat Waltz	1958	2.00	4.00	8.00
❏ KE-753 [PS]	(title unknown)	1958	2.00	4.00	8.00
❏ KE-754	Tammy/Oh, My Papa//Arrividerci Roma/ The High and the Mighty	1958	2.00	4.00	8.00
❏ KE-754 [PS]	(title unknown)	1958	2.00	4.00	8.00
Albums					
BAINBRIDGE					
❏ 6265	Somewhere in Time	1986	2.50	5.00	10.00
❏ 8002 [(2)]	Ivory Impact	1982	3.00	6.00	12.00
HOLIDAY					
❏ HDY 1927	Golden Christmas	1981	2.00	4.00	8.00
KAPP					
❏ KLE-1 [(3)M]	10th Anniversary/Limited Edition	1964	5.00	10.00	20.00
—Reissue of Kapp 1088, 1130 and 1172 in one package					
❏ SKLE-1 [(3)S]	10th Anniversary/Limited Edition	1964	6.25	12.50	25.00
❏ KW-900 [M]	Roger Williams Showcase	196?	3.00	6.00	12.00
❏ SKW-900 [S]	Roger Williams Showcase	196?	3.75	7.50	15.00
❏ KL-1003 [M]	The Boy Next Door	1955	6.25	12.50	25.00
—Maroon and silver (or blue and silver) labels					
❏ KL-1003 [M]	The Boy Next Door	1962	3.00	6.00	12.00
—Any later label variation					
❏ KL-1008 [M]	It's a Big, Wide, Wonderful World	1955	6.25	12.50	25.00
—Maroon and silver (or blue and silver) labels					
❏ KL-1008 [M]	It's a Big, Wide, Wonderful World	1962	3.00	6.00	12.00
—Any later label variation					
❏ KL-1012 [M]	Autumn Leaves	1956	5.00	10.00	20.00
—Retitled version of above; maroon and silver (or blue and silver) label					
❏ KL-1012 [M]	Roger Williams	1956	6.25	12.50	25.00
❏ KL-1012 [M]	Autumn Leaves	1962	3.00	6.00	12.00
—Any later label variation					
❏ KL-1031 [M]	Daydreams	1956	3.75	7.50	15.00
—Maroon and silver (or blue and silver) label					
❏ KL-1031 [M]	Daydreams	1962	3.00	6.00	12.00
—Any later label variation					
❏ KL-1040 [M]	Roger Williams Plays the Wonderful Music of the Masters	1956	3.75	7.50	15.00
—Maroon and silver (or blue and silver) label					
❏ KL-1040 [M]	Roger Williams Plays the Wonderful Music of the Masters	1962	3.00	6.00	12.00
—Any later label variation					
❏ KL-1042 [M]	Roger Williams Plays Christmas Songs	1956	3.75	7.50	15.00
—Maroon and silver label; unbanded					
❏ KL-1062 [M]	Roger Williams Plays Beautiful Waltzes	1957	3.75	7.50	15.00
—Maroon and silver (or blue and silver) label					
❏ KL-1062 [M]	Roger Williams Plays Beautiful Waltzes	1962	3.00	6.00	12.00
—Any later label variation					
❏ KL-1063 [M]	Almost Paradise	1957	3.75	7.50	15.00
—Maroon and silver (or blue and silver) label					
❏ KL-1063 [M]	Almost Paradise	1962	3.00	6.00	12.00
—Any later label variation					
❏ K-1081-S [S]	Till	1959	5.00	10.00	20.00
—Maroon and silver (or blue and silver) label					
❏ KL-1081 [M]	Till	1958	3.75	7.50	15.00
—Maroon and silver (or blue and silver) label					
❏ KL-1081 [M]	Till	1962	3.00	6.00	12.00
—Any later label variation					
❏ KS-1081 [S]	Till	1962	3.75	7.50	15.00
—Any later label variation					
❏ KL-1088 [M]	Roger Williams Plays Gershwin	1958	3.75	7.50	15.00
—Maroon and silver (or blue and silver) labels					

Number	Title (A Side/B Side)	Yr	VG	VG+	NM
❏ KL-1088 [M]	Roger Williams Plays Gershwin	1962	3.00	6.00	12.00
—Any later label variation					
❏ KL-1112 [M]	Near You	1959	3.75	7.50	15.00
—Maroon and silver (or blue and silver) labels					
❏ KL-1112 [M]	Near You	1962	3.00	6.00	12.00
❏ KS-1112 [S]	Near You	1959	5.00	10.00	20.00
—Maroon and silver (or blue and silver) labels					
❏ KS-1112 [S]	Near You	1962	3.75	7.50	15.00
—Any later label variation					
❏ KL-1130 [M]	More Songs of the Fabulous Fifties	1959	3.75	7.50	15.00
—Maroon and silver (or blue and silver) labels					
❏ KL-1130 [M]	More Songs of the Fabulous Fifties	1962	3.00	6.00	12.00
—Any later label variation					
❏ KL-1147 [M]	With These Hands	1959	3.75	7.50	15.00
—Maroon and silver (or blue and silver) labels					
❏ KL-1147 [M]	With These Hands	1962	3.00	6.00	12.00
—Any later label variation					
❏ KL-1164 [M]	Christmas Time	1959	3.75	7.50	15.00
—"Merry Christmas" silver, red and green label					
❏ KL-1164 [M]	Christmas Time	1962	3.00	6.00	12.00
—Any later label variation					
❏ KL-1172 [M]	Always	1960	3.75	7.50	15.00
—Maroon and silver (or blue and silver) labels					
❏ KL-1172 [M]	Always	1962	3.00	6.00	12.00
—Any later label variation					
❏ KL-1207 [M]	Songs of the Fabulous Forties, Volume 1	1960	3.00	6.00	12.00
❏ KL-1208 [M]	Songs of the Fabulous Forties, Volume 2	1960	3.00	6.00	12.00
❏ KL-1209 [M]	Songs of the Fabulous Fifties, Volume 1	1960	3.00	6.00	12.00
❏ KL-1210 [M]	Songs of the Fabulous Fifties, Volume 2	1960	3.00	6.00	12.00
❏ KL-1211 [M]	Songs of the Fabulous Century, Volume 1	1960	3.00	6.00	12.00
❏ KL-1212 [M]	Songs of the Fabulous Century, Volume 2	1960	3.00	6.00	12.00
❏ KL-1217 [M]	Temptation	1960	3.75	7.50	15.00
—Maroon and silver (or blue and silver) labels					
❏ KL-1217 [M]	Temptation	1962	3.00	6.00	12.00
—Any later label variation					
❏ KL-1222 [M]	Roger Williams Invites You to Dance	1961	3.75	7.50	15.00
❏ KL-1244 [M]	Yellow Bird	1961	3.75	7.50	15.00
❏ KL-1251 [M]	Songs of the Soaring '60s	1961	3.75	7.50	15.00
❏ KL-1260 [M]	Greatest Hits	1962	3.00	6.00	12.00
❏ KL-1266 [M]	Maria	1962	3.00	6.00	12.00
❏ KL-1290 [M]	Mr. Piano	1962	3.00	6.00	12.00
❏ KL-1305 [M]	Country Style	1963	3.00	6.00	12.00
❏ KL-1336 [M]	For You	1963	3.00	6.00	12.00
❏ KL-1354 [M]	The Solid Gold Steinway	1964	3.00	6.00	12.00
❏ KL-1395 [M]	Family Album of Hymns	1964	2.50	5.00	10.00
❏ KL-1406 [M]	Academy Award Winners	1964	2.50	5.00	10.00
❏ KL-1414 [M]	Roger Williams Plays the Hits	1965	2.50	5.00	10.00
❏ KL-1434 [M]	Summer Wind	1965	2.50	5.00	10.00
❏ KL-1452 [M]	Autumn Leaves — 1965	1965	2.50	5.00	10.00
❏ KL-1470 [M]	I'll Remember You	1966	2.50	5.00	10.00
❏ KL-1483 [M]	Academy Award Winners, Vol. 2	1966	2.50	5.00	10.00
❏ KL-1501 [M]	Born Free	1966	2.50	5.00	10.00
❏ KL-1512 [M]	Roger!	1967	2.50	5.00	10.00
❏ KL-1530 [M]	Roger Williams/Golden Hits	1967	3.00	6.00	12.00
❏ KS-3000 [S]	Waltzes in Stereo	1959	5.00	10.00	20.00
—Maroon and silver (or blue and silver) labels					
❏ KS-3000 [S]	Waltzes in Stereo	1962	3.75	7.50	15.00
—Any later label variation					
❏ KS-3013 [S]	More Songs of the Fabulous Fifties	1959	5.00	10.00	20.00
—Maroon and silver (or blue and silver) labels					
❏ KS-3013 [S]	More Songs of the Fabulous Fifties	1962	3.75	7.50	15.00
—Any later label variation					
❏ KS-3030 [S]	With These Hands	1959	5.00	10.00	20.00
—Maroon and silver (or blue and silver) labels					
❏ KS-3030 [S]	With These Hands	1962	3.75	7.50	15.00
—Any later label variation					
❏ KS-3048 [S]	Christmas Time	1959	5.00	10.00	20.00
❏ KS-3056 [S]	Always	1960	5.00	10.00	20.00
—Maroon and silver (or blue and silver) labels					
❏ KS-3056 [S]	Always	1962	3.75	7.50	15.00
—Any later label variation					
❏ KS-3164 [S]	Christmas Time	196?	3.00	6.00	12.00
—Reissue of KS-3048 (new cover, no gatefold)					
❏ KS-3207 [S]	Songs of the Fabulous Forties, Volume 1	1960	3.75	7.50	15.00
❏ KS-3208 [S]	Songs of the Fabulous Forties, Volume 2	1960	3.75	7.50	15.00
❏ KS-3209 [S]	Songs of the Fabulous Fifties, Volume 1	1960	3.75	7.50	15.00
❏ KS-3210 [S]	Songs of the Fabulous Fifties, Volume 2	1960	3.75	7.50	15.00
❏ KS-3211 [S]	Songs of the Fabulous Century, Volume 1	1960	3.75	7.50	15.00
❏ KS-3212 [S]	Songs of the Fabulous Century, Volume 2	1960	3.75	7.50	15.00
❏ KS-3217 [S]	Temptation	1960	5.00	10.00	20.00
❏ KS-3222 [S]	Roger Williams Invites You to Dance	1961	5.00	10.00	20.00
❏ KS-3244 [S]	Yellow Bird	1961	5.00	10.00	20.00
❏ KS-3251 [S]	Songs of the Soaring '60s	1961	5.00	10.00	20.00
❏ KS-3260 [S]	Greatest Hits	1962	3.75	7.50	15.00
❏ KS-3266 [S]	Maria	1962	3.75	7.50	15.00
❏ KS-3290 [S]	Mr. Piano	1962	3.75	7.50	15.00
❏ KS-3305 [S]	Country Style	1963	3.75	7.50	15.00
❏ KS-3336 [S]	For You	1963	3.75	7.50	15.00
❏ KS-3354 [S]	The Solid Gold Steinway	1964	3.75	7.50	15.00
❏ KS-3395 [S]	Family Album of Hymns	1964	3.00	6.00	12.00
❏ KS-3406 [S]	Academy Award Winners	1964	3.00	6.00	12.00
❏ KS-3414 [S]	Roger Williams Plays the Hits	1965	3.00	6.00	12.00
❏ KS-3434 [S]	Summer Wind	1965	3.00	6.00	12.00
❏ KS-3452 [S]	Autumn Leaves — 1965	1965	3.00	6.00	12.00
❏ KS-3470 [S]	I'll Remember You	1966	3.00	6.00	12.00
❏ KS-3483 [S]	Academy Award Winners, Vol. 2	1966	3.00	6.00	12.00
❏ KS-3501 [S]	Born Free	1966	3.00	6.00	12.00
❏ KS-3512 [S]	Roger!	1967	3.00	6.00	12.00
❏ KS-3530 [S]	Roger Williams/Golden Hits	1967	3.00	6.00	12.00
❏ KS-3549	Amore	1968	3.00	6.00	12.00
❏ KS-3550	More Than a Miracle	1968	3.00	6.00	12.00
❏ KS-3565	Only for Lovers	1969	3.00	6.00	12.00
❏ KS-3595	Happy Heart	1969	3.00	6.00	12.00
❏ KS-3610	Love Theme from "Romeo and Juliet"	1969	3.00	6.00	12.00
❏ KS-3629	Themes from Great Movies	1970	3.00	6.00	12.00
❏ KS-3638	Roger Williams/Golden Hits, Volume 2	1970	3.00	6.00	12.00

Number	Title (A Side/B Side)	Yr	VG	VG+	NM
❏ KS-3645	Love Story	1971	2.50	5.00	10.00
❏ KS-3650	Summer of '42	1971	2.50	5.00	10.00
❏ KS-3665	Love Theme from "The Godfather"	1972	2.50	5.00	10.00
❏ KS-3671	Play Me	1972	2.50	5.00	10.00
❏ KXL-5000 [(2)M]Songs of the Fabulous Fifties		1957	5.00	10.00	20.00
—Maroon and silver (or blue and silver) labels					
❏ KXL-5000 [(2)M]Songs of the Fabulous Fifties		1962	3.75	7.50	15.00
—Any later label variation					
❏ KXS-5000 [(2)S]Songs of the Fabulous Fifties		1959	6.25	12.50	25.00
—Maroon and silver (or blue and silver) labels					
❏ KXS-5000 [(2)S]Songs of the Fabulous Fifties		1962	5.00	10.00	20.00
—Any later label variation					
❏ KXL-5003 [(2)M]Songs of the Fabulous Forties		1957	5.00	10.00	20.00
—Maroon and silver (or blue and silver) labels					
❏ KXL-5003 [(2)M]Songs of the Fabulous Forties		1962	3.75	7.50	15.00
—Any later label variation					
❏ KXS-5003 [(2)S]Songs of the Fabulous Forties		1959	6.25	12.50	25.00
—Maroon and silver (or blue and silver) labels					
❏ KXS-5003 [(2)S]Songs of the Fabulous Forties		1962	5.00	10.00	20.00
—Any later label variation					
❏ KXL-5005 [(2)M]Songs of the Fabulous Century		195?	5.00	10.00	20.00
—Maroon and silver (or blue and silver) labels					
❏ KXL-5005 [(2)M]Songs of the Fabulous Century		1962	3.75	7.50	15.00
—Any later label variation					
❏ KXS-5005 [(2)S]Songs of the Fabulous Century		1959	6.25	12.50	25.00
—Maroon and silver (or blue and silver) labels					
❏ KXS-5005 [(2)S]Songs of the Fabulous Century		1962	5.00	10.00	20.00
—Any later label variation					
❏ KXL-5008 [(2)M]Tonight! Roger Williams at Town Hall		196?	5.00	10.00	20.00
❏ KXS-5008 [(2)S]Tonight! Roger Williams at Town Hall		196?	6.25	12.50	25.00
MCA					
❏ 63	Greatest Hits	1973	2.00	4.00	8.00
—Reissue of Kapp 3260					
❏ 64	Roger Williams/Golden Hits	1973	2.00	4.00	8.00
—Reissue of Kapp 3530					
❏ 68	Roger Williams/Golden Hits, Volume 2	1973	2.00	4.00	8.00
—Reissue of Kapp 3638					
❏ 71	Somewhere My Love	1973	2.00	4.00	8.00
—Retitled reissue of unknown Kapp LP					
❏ 76	Play Me	1973	2.00	4.00	8.00
—Reissue of Kapp 3671					
❏ 324	Last Tango in Paris	1973	2.50	5.00	10.00
❏ 378	Live	1973	2.50	5.00	10.00
❏ 403	The Way We Were	1974	2.50	5.00	10.00
❏ 438	I Honestly Love You	1974	2.50	5.00	10.00
❏ 539	Family Album of Hymns	1975	2.00	4.00	8.00
—Reissue of Kapp 3395					
❏ 542	Somewhere My Love	1975	—	3.00	6.00
—Reissue of MCA 71					
❏ 2175	Virtuoso	1975	2.50	5.00	10.00
❏ 2237	Nadia's Theme	1976	2.50	5.00	10.00
❏ 2279	Evergreen	1977	2.50	5.00	10.00
❏ 4106 [(2)]	The Best of Roger Williams	197?	3.00	6.00	12.00
❏ 5574	To Amadeus With Love	1985	2.50	5.00	10.00
❏ 15005	Christmas Time	197?	2.00	4.00	8.00
—Reissue of Kapp material					
❏ 20202	Autumn Leaves	198?	2.00	4.00	8.00
—Reissue of Kapp material					
PICKWICK					
❏ PTP-2086 [(2)]	Roger Williams at the Piano	197?	3.00	6.00	12.00
❏ SPC-3367	Spanish Eyes	197?	2.00	4.00	8.00
❏ SPC-3511	Sunrise, Sunset	197?	2.00	4.00	8.00
VOCALION					
❏ VL 73918	Moments to Remember	1970	2.50	5.00	10.00

WILLIAMS, TIMMY
45s
MALA

Number	Title (A Side/B Side)	Yr	VG	VG+	NM
❏ 515	Competition/Wipe Away Your Tears	1965	300.00	600.00	1200.

WILLIAMS, TONY Also see THE PLATTERS.
45s
DOT

Number	Title (A Side/B Side)	Yr	VG	VG+	NM
❏ 16806	Endless Street/Smoke, Drink, Play 21	1965	2.00	4.00	8.00
MERCURY					
❏ 71158	Let's Start All Over Again/When You Return	1957	5.00	10.00	20.00
❏ 71532	Charmaine/Peg o' My Heart	1959	5.00	10.00	20.00
PHILIPS					
❏ 40069	Chloe/Second Best	1962	2.50	5.00	10.00
❏ 40123	Twenty-Four Lonely Hours/Save Me	1963	2.50	5.00	10.00
❏ 40141	How Come/When I Had You	1963	2.50	5.00	10.00
REPRISE					
❏ 20019	Sleepless Nights/Movin' In	1961	3.75	7.50	15.00
❏ 20030	Miracle/My Prayer	1961	3.75	7.50	15.00
❏ 20067	Come Along Now/That's More Like It	1962	3.75	7.50	15.00
Albums					
MERCURY					
❏ MG-20454 [M]	A Girl Is a Girl Is a Girl	1959	10.00	20.00	40.00
❏ SR-60138 [S]	A Girl Is a Girl Is a Girl	1959	12.50	25.00	50.00
PHILIPS					
❏ PHM 200051 [M]The Magic Touch of Tony		1962	6.25	12.50	25.00
❏ PHS 600051 [S]The Magic Touch of Tony		1962	7.50	15.00	30.00
REPRISE					
❏ R-6006 [M]	His Greatest Hits	1961	6.25	12.50	25.00
❏ R9-6006 [S]	His Greatest Hits	1961	7.50	15.00	30.00

WILLIAMSON, SONNY BOY (1) The "original," born John Lee Williamson and murdered in 1948.
45s
RCA VICTOR

Number	Title (A Side/B Side)	Yr	VG	VG+	NM
❏ 50-0005	Little Girl/Bring Another Half a Pint	1949	75.00	150.00	300.00
—Orange vinyl					
❏ 50-0030	Southern Dream/I Love You For Myself	1949	75.00	150.00	300.00
—Orange vinyl					

Number	Title (A Side/B Side)	Yr	VG	VG+	NM
Albums					
BLUES CLASSICS					
❏ 3	Blues Classics by Sonny Boy Williamson	196?	6.25	12.50	25.00
❏ 20	Blues Classics by Sonny Boy Williamson, Vol. 2	196?	6.25	12.50	25.00
❏ BC 24	Blues Classics by Sonny Boy Williamson, Volume 3	196?	6.25	12.50	25.00

WILLIAMSON, SONNY BOY (2) Really Aleck Ford, also known as Alex "Rice" Miller, before taking the name of his predecessor.
45s
ACE

Number	Title (A Side/B Side)	Yr	VG	VG+	NM
❏ 511	Boppin' with Sonny/No Nights By Myself	1955	30.00	60.00	120.00
CHECKER					
❏ 824	Don't Start Me Talkin'/All My Love In Vain	1955	25.00	50.00	100.00
❏ 834	Let Me Explain/Your Imagination	1956	15.00	30.00	60.00
❏ 847	Keep It To Yourself/The Key to Your Door	1956	12.50	25.00	50.00
❏ 864	I Don't Know/Fattening Frogs for Snakes	1957	12.50	25.00	50.00
❏ 883	Born Blind/Ninety-Nine	1958	10.00	20.00	40.00
❏ 894	Your Funeral & My Trial/Wake Up, Baby	1958	10.00	20.00	40.00
❏ 910	Cross My Heart/Dissatisfied	1958	10.00	20.00	40.00
❏ 927	Let Your Conscience Be Your Guide/ Unseeing Eye	1959	10.00	20.00	40.00
❏ 943	The Goat/It's Sad to Be Alone	1960	7.50	15.00	30.00
❏ 956	Temperature 110/Lonesome Cabin	1960	7.50	15.00	30.00
❏ 963	Trust My Baby/Too Close Together	1960	7.50	15.00	30.00
❏ 975	The Hurt/Stop Right Now	1961	7.50	15.00	30.00
❏ 1003	One Way Out/Nine Below Zero	1962	7.50	15.00	30.00
❏ 1036	Bye Bye Bird/Help Me	1963	7.50	15.00	30.00
❏ 1065	Trying to Get Back on My Feet/Decoration Day	1963	7.50	15.00	30.00
❏ 1080	My Younger Days/I Want You Close to Me	1964	7.50	15.00	30.00
❏ 1134	Bring It On Home/Down Child	1966	6.25	12.50	25.00
TRUMPET					
❏ 144	West Memphis Blues/I Cross My Heart	1951	25.00	50.00	100.00
❏ 145	Sonny Boy's Christmas Blues/Pontiac Blues	195?	30.00	60.00	120.00
❏ 166	Nine Below Zero/Mighty Long Time	1952	25.00	50.00	100.00
❏ 167	Too Close Together/ She Brought Life Back to the Dead	1952	—	—	—
—Unreleased					
❏ 168	Stop Now Baby/Mr. Downchild	1952	25.00	50.00	100.00
❏ 212	Cat Hop/Too Close Together	1952	20.00	40.00	80.00
❏ 215	Gettin' Out of Time/ She Brought Life Back to the Dead	1952	20.00	40.00	80.00
❏ 216	Red Hot Kisses/Going in Your Direction	1952	20.00	40.00	80.00
❏ 228	From the Bottom/Empty Bedroom	1953	17.50	35.00	70.00
Albums					
ALLIGATOR					
❏ AL-4787	Keep It To Ourselves	1990	3.00	6.00	12.00
ARHOOLIE					
❏ 2020	King Biscuit Time	197?	3.00	6.00	12.00
CHECKER					
❏ LP-1437 [M]	Down and Out Blues	1959	80.00	160.00	320.00
CHESS					
❏ 2ACMB-206 [(2)]Sonny Boy Williamson		1976	5.00	10.00	20.00
—Reissue of 50027					
❏ CHV-417	One Way Out	1975	3.75	7.50	15.00
❏ LP-1503 [M]	The Real Folk Blues	1966	20.00	40.00	80.00
❏ LP-1509 [M]	More Real Folk Blues	1966	20.00	40.00	80.00
❏ LPS-1536	Bummer Road	1969	6.25	12.50	25.00
❏ CH-9116	One Way Out	198?	2.50	5.00	10.00
❏ CH-9257	Down and Out Blues	1988	2.50	5.00	10.00
❏ CH-9272	The Real Folk Blues	1988	2.50	5.00	10.00
❏ CH-9277	More Real Folk Blues	1988	2.50	5.00	10.00
❏ 2CH-50027 [(2)]This Is My Story		1972	6.25	12.50	25.00
GNP CRESCENDO					
❏ GNPS-10003	Sonny Boy Williamson in Chicago	198?	2.50	5.00	10.00
STORYVILLE					
❏ 4016	A Portrait in Blues	197?	3.00	6.00	12.00
❏ 4062	The Blues of Sonny Boy Williamson	197?	3.00	6.00	12.00

WILLIAMSON, SONNY BOY (2), AND THE YARDBIRDS
Albums
MERCURY

Number	Title (A Side/B Side)	Yr	VG	VG+	NM
❏ MG-21071 [M]	Sonny Boy Williamson and the Yardbirds	1965	20.00	40.00	80.00
❏ SR-61071 [R]	Sonny Boy Williamson and the Yardbirds	196?	6.25	12.50	25.00
—Later cover with cartoon artwork on the cover					
❏ SR-61071 [R]	Sonny Boy Williamson and the Yardbirds	1965	12.50	25.00	50.00
—First cover with a picture of the bluesman and the band					
❏ SR-61271 [R]	Eric Clapton and the Yardbirds Live with Sonny Boy Williamson	1970	5.00	10.00	20.00
—Reissue					

WILLIE AND THE WHEELS Still another creation of STEVE BARRI and P.F. SLOAN.
45s
DUNHILL

Number	Title (A Side/B Side)	Yr	VG	VG+	NM
❏ 4002	Skateboard Craze/Do What You Do	1965	10.00	20.00	40.00

WILLING, FOY, AND THE RIDERS OF THE PURPLE SAGE
45s
CAPITOL

Number	Title (A Side/B Side)	Yr	VG	VG+	NM
❏ F1070	Texas Blues/Sometime	1950	10.00	20.00	40.00
CHALLENGE					
❏ 1011	Cool Water/No One to Cry To	1958	5.00	10.00	20.00
DECCA					
❏ 9-46365	Detour/Address Unknown	1951	6.25	12.50	25.00
Albums					
CROWN					
❏ CST-582	Country & Western Favorites	196?	2.50	5.00	10.00
❏ CLP-5306 [M]	Cool Water	196?	3.00	6.00	12.00
CUSTOM					
❏ CS 1017	Cool, Cool Water	197?	2.50	5.00	10.00
JUBILEE					
❏ JL-5028 [M]	The New Sound of American Folk	1962	5.00	10.00	20.00

Number	Title (A Side/B Side)	Yr	VG	VG+	NM

WILLIS, CHUCK Also see THE ROYALS (2).
45s
ATLANTIC
❑ 1098	It's Too Late/Kansas City Woman	1956	6.25	12.50	25.00
❑ 1112	Juanita/Whatcha' Gonna Do When Your Baby Leaves You	1956	6.25	12.50	25.00
❑ 1130	C.C. Rider/Ease the Pain	1957	6.25	12.50	25.00
❑ 1148	Love Me, Cherry/That Train Has Gone	1957	6.25	12.50	25.00
❑ 1168	Betty and Dupree/My Crying Eyes	1958	6.25	12.50	25.00
❑ 1179	What Am I Living For/Hang Up My Rock And Roll Shoes	1958	7.50	15.00	30.00
❑ 1192	Thunder and Lightning/My Life	1958	5.00	10.00	20.00
❑ 2005	You'll Be My Love/Keep a-Driving	1958	5.00	10.00	20.00
❑ 2029	My Baby/Just One Kiss	1959	5.00	10.00	20.00
OKEH
❑ 6810	I Tried/I Rule My House	1951	25.00	50.00	100.00
❑ 6841	Let's Jump Tonight/It's Too Late Baby	1951	20.00	40.00	80.00
❑ 6873	Lud Mouth Lucy/Here I Come	1952	20.00	40.00	80.00
❑ 6905	My Story/Caldonia	1952	12.50	25.00	50.00
❑ 6930	Salty Tears/Wrong Lake to Catch a Fish	1953	12.50	25.00	50.00
❑ 6952	Going to the River/Baby Has Left Me Again	1953	12.50	25.00	50.00
❑ 6985	Don't Deceive Me/ I've Been Treated Wrong Too Long	1953	12.50	25.00	50.00
❑ 7004	My Baby's Coming Home/When My Day Is Over	1953	12.50	25.00	50.00
❑ 7015	You're Still My Baby/What's Your Name	1954	12.50	25.00	50.00
❑ 7029	I Feel So Bad/Need One More Chance	1954	15.00	30.00	60.00
❑ 7041	Change My Mind/My Heart's Been Broke Again	1954	10.00	20.00	40.00
❑ 7048	Give and Take/I've Been Away Too Long	1954	10.00	20.00	40.00
❑ 7051	Lawdy Miss Mary/Love-Struck	1955	10.00	20.00	40.00
❑ 7055	I Can Tell/One More Break	1955	10.00	20.00	40.00
❑ 7062	Search My Heart/Ring-Ding-Doo	1955	10.00	20.00	40.00
❑ 7067	Come On Home/It Were You	1956	10.00	20.00	40.00
❑ 7070	Two Spoons of Tears/Charged with Cheating	1956	10.00	20.00	40.00
7-Inch Extended Plays
ATLANTIC
❑ EP 591	Juanita/Whatcha' Gonna Do When Your Baby Leaves You//Kansas City Woman/It's Too Late	1957	50.00	100.00	200.00
❑ EP 591 [PS]	Chuck Willis	1957	50.00	100.00	200.00
❑ EP 609	C.C. Rider/Ease the Pain//That Train Has Gone/ Love Me, Cherry	1958	30.00	60.00	120.00
❑ EP 609 [PS]	Rock with Chuck Willis	1958	30.00	60.00	120.00
❑ EP 612	What Am I Living For/Hang Up My Rock and Roll Shoes//Betty and Dupree/My Crying Eyes	1958	37.50	75.00	150.00
❑ EP 612 [PS]	What Am I Living For	1958	50.00	100.00	200.00
EPIC
❑ 7070	(contents unknown)	1956	50.00	100.00	200.00
❑ 7070 [PS]	Chuck Willis Sings the Blues	1956	50.00	100.00	200.00
Albums
ATLANTIC
❑ 8018 [M]	The King of the Stroll	1958	75.00	150.00	300.00
—Black label					
❑ 8018 [M]	The King of the Stroll	1960	37.50	75.00	150.00
—Purple and orange label					
❑ 8079 [M]	I Remember Chuck Willis	1963	37.50	75.00	150.00
❑ SD 8079 [P]	I Remember Chuck Willis	1963	50.00	100.00	200.00
EPIC
❑ LN 3425 [M]	Chuck Willis Wails the Blues	1958	125.00	250.00	500.00
❑ LN 3728 [M]	A Tribute to Chuck Willis	1960	75.00	150.00	300.00

WILLIS, HAL
45s
ATHENS
| ❑ 704 | Crazy Little Mama/Walkin' Dream | 1958 | 37.50 | 75.00 | 150.00 |
ATLANTIC
| ❑ 1114 | Bop-A-Dee, Bop-A-Doo/My Pink Cadillac | 1956 | 50.00 | 100.00 | 200.00 |
DECCA
| ❑ 30949 | Poor Little Jimmy/That's the Way It Goes | 1959 | 3.00 | 6.00 | 12.00 |
MERCURY
| ❑ 71933 | Bayou Pierre/I Love You (Around the World) | 1962 | 3.00 | 6.00 | 12.00 |
SIMS
❑ 207	The Lumberjack/Dig Me a Hole	1964	3.00	6.00	12.00
❑ 224	The One I Love/What's Left of Me	1965	3.00	6.00	12.00
❑ 235	Klondike Mike/So Right But So Wrong	1965	3.00	6.00	12.00
❑ 243	Thumb and Shoes/Nopper the Topper	1965	3.00	6.00	12.00
❑ 250	Creole Rose/When It's Springtime in Alaska	1965	3.00	6.00	12.00
❑ 288	Doggin' in the U.S. Mail/The Battle of Viet Nam	1966	3.00	6.00	12.00
❑ 307	Parson from Paint Rock/Private Dick	1966	3.00	6.00	12.00

WILLOWS, THE (1)
45s
MELBA
❑ 102	Church Bells May Ring/Baby Tell Me	1956	25.00	50.00	100.00
❑ 102	Church Bells Are Ringing/Beby Tell Me	1956	75.00	150.00	300.00
—Original A-side title					
❑ 106	Do You Love Me/My Angel	1956	15.00	30.00	60.00
❑ 115	Little Darlin'/My Angel	1957	20.00	40.00	80.00

WILLOWS, THE (2)
45s
4-STAR
| ❑ 1753 | There's a Dance Goin' On/Now That I Have You | 1961 | 75.00 | 150.00 | 300.00 |

WILLOWS, THE (3)
45s
HEIDI
| ❑ 103 | It's Such a Shame/Tears in Your Eyes | 1964 | 3.75 | 7.50 | 15.00 |
| ❑ 107 | Sit by the Fire/Such a Night | 1965 | 3.75 | 7.50 | 15.00 |

WILLOWS, THE (4)
45s
MGM
| ❑ 13484 | Hurtin' All Over/My Kinda Guy | 1966 | 3.00 | 6.00 | 12.00 |
| ❑ 13714 | Snow Song/Outside the City | 1967 | 3.00 | 6.00 | 12.00 |

WILMER AND THE DUKES
45s
APHRODISIAC
❑ 260	Give Me One More Chance/Git It	1968	2.00	4.00	8.00
❑ 261	Heavy Time/I'm Free	1969	2.00	4.00	8.00
❑ 261 [PS]	Heavy Time/I'm Free	1969	3.00	6.00	12.00
❑ 262	Living in the U.S.A./Count on Me	1969	2.00	4.00	8.00
❑ 263	Get Out of My Life, Women/I Do Love You	1969	2.50	5.00	10.00
Albums
APHRODISIAC
❑ 6001	Wilmer and the Dukes	1969	5.00	10.00	20.00

WILSON, AL
45s
BELL
| ❑ 867 | Mississippi Woman/Sometimes a Man Must Cry | 1970 | — | 3.50 | 7.00 |
| ❑ 909 | You Do the Right Thing/Bachelor Man | 1970 | — | 3.50 | 7.00 |
CAROUSEL
| ❑ 30051 | I Hear You Knocking/Sugar Cane Girl | 1971 | — | 3.00 | 6.00 |
| ❑ 30052 | Falling/Bachelor Man | 1971 | — | 3.00 | 6.00 |
PLAYBOY
❑ 6062	I've Got a Feeling (We'll Be Seeing Each Other Again)/Be Concerned	1976	—	2.50	5.00
❑ 6076	Baby I Want Your Body/Stay with Me	1976	—	2.50	5.00
❑ 6076 [PS]	Baby I Want Your Body/Stay with Me	1976	—	3.00	6.00
❑ 6085	You Did It for Me/Differently	1976	—	2.50	5.00
ROADSHOW
❑ PB-11583	Count the Days/Is This the End	1979	—	2.00	4.00
❑ PB-11714	Earthquake/You Got It	1979	—	2.00	4.00
ROCKY ROAD
❑ 30060	Heavy Church/(B-side unknown)	1972	—	3.00	6.00
❑ 30067	Born on the Bayou/(B-side unknown)	1972	—	3.00	6.00
❑ 30073	Show and Tell/Listen to Me	1973	—	3.00	6.00
❑ 30076	Touch and Go/Settle Me Down	1974	—	3.00	6.00
❑ 30200	La La Peace Song/Keep On Loving You	1974	—	3.00	6.00
❑ 30202	I Won't Last a Day Without You-Let Me Be the One/Willoughbry Brook Road	1974	—	3.00	6.00
SOUL CITY
❑ 759	When You're Loved, You're Loved Too/ Who Could Be Lovin' You	1967	2.50	5.00	10.00
❑ 761	Do What You Gotta Do/Now I Know What Love Is	1968	2.00	4.00	8.00
❑ 767	The Snake/Getting Ready for Tomorrow	1968	2.00	4.00	8.00
❑ 771	Poor Side of Town/The Dolphins	1969	2.00	4.00	8.00
❑ 773	I Stand Accused/Shake Me, Wake Me	1969	2.00	4.00	8.00
❑ 775	Lodi/By the Time I Get to Phoenix	1969	2.00	4.00	8.00
WAND
❑ 1135	Help Me/(Instrumental)	1966	7.50	15.00	30.00
Albums
PLAYBOY
❑ PB 410	I've Got a Feeling	1976	3.00	6.00	12.00
❑ JZ 34744	I've Got a Feeling	1977	2.50	5.00	10.00
—Reissue of 410					
ROCKY ROAD
❑ RR-3600	Weighing In	1973	3.75	7.50	15.00
❑ RR-3601	Show and Tell	1973	3.75	7.50	15.00
❑ 3700	La La Peace Song	1974	3.75	7.50	15.00
SOUL CITY
❑ SCS-92006	Searching for the Dolphins	1969	6.25	12.50	25.00

WILSON, ANN, AND THE DAYBREAKS Ann Wilson was later with Heart.
45s
TOPAZ
| ❑ 1311 | Standin' Watchin' You/Wonder How I Managed | 1967 | 30.00 | 60.00 | 120.00 |
| ❑ 1312 | Through Eyes and Glass/ I'm Gonna Drink My Hurt Away | 1967 | 30.00 | 60.00 | 120.00 |

WILSON, BRIAN Also see THE BEACH BOYS.
45s
CAPITOL
| ❑ 5610 | Caroline, No/Summer Means New Love | 1966 | 6.25 | 12.50 | 25.00 |
| —Actually a Beach Boys recording released as a solo Brian record | | | | | |
GIANT
| ❑ 17216 | Your Imagination/Your Imagination (A Cappella) | 1998 | — | — | 3.00 |
SIRE
❑ 27694	Melt Away/Being with the One You Love	1988	5.00	10.00	20.00
❑ 27787 [DJ]	Night Time (same on both sides)	1988	7.50	15.00	30.00
—Stock copies not known to exist					
❑ 27787 [PS]	Night Time	1988	15.00	30.00	60.00
❑ 27814	Love and Mercy/ He Couldn't Get His Poor Old Body to Move	1988	2.50	5.00	10.00
—Promo copies go for 50% of this price					
❑ 27814 [PS]	Love and Mercy/ He Couldn't Get His Poor Old Body to Move	1988	—	2.50	5.00
—Accompanied both stock and promo copies					
❑ 28350	Let's Go to Heaven in My Car/Too Much Sugar	1987	2.50	5.00	10.00
—Promo copies go for 50% of this price					
❑ 28350 [PS]	Let's Go to Heaven in My Car/Too Much Sugar	1987	—	2.50	5.00
—Accompanied both stock and promo copies					
Albums
SIRE
❑ PRO-A-3248 [DJ]	Words and Music	1988	6.25	12.50	25.00
—Promo-only music and interview					
❑ 25669	Brian Wilson	1988	2.50	5.00	10.00

WILSON, BRIAN, AND MIKE LOVE Also see THE BEACH BOYS; BRIAN WILSON.
45s
BROTHER
| ❑ 1002 | Gettin' Hungry/Devoted to You | 1967 | 7.50 | 15.00 | 30.00 |

WILSON, CLARA
45s
HIT
❑ 62	Don't Say Nothin' Bad About My Baby/Pipeline	1963	2.00	4.00	8.00
—B-side by the Music City Five					
❑ 71	Easier Said Than Done/Surf City	1963	2.00	4.00	8.00
—B-side by Jimmy and Joe					
❑ 117	My Guy/Little Children	1964	2.00	4.00	8.00
—B-side by Ed Hardin					

Number	Title (A Side/B Side)	Yr	VG	VG+	NM

WILSON, CLARA, AND THE CLEFTONES
This Cleftones is no relation to the popular vocal group, as this is a studio girl group.

45s

HIT
| ❏ 55 | Our Day Will Come/The End of the World | 1963 | 2.00 | 4.00 | 8.00 |

—*As "Clara and the Cleftones"; B-side by Kathy Taylor*

| ❏ 65 | Foolish Little Girl/Da Doo Ron Ron | 1963 | 2.00 | 4.00 | 8.00 |

—*B-side by Alpha Zoe*

WILSON, FLIP
45s

LITTLE DAVID
❏ 721	Don't Fight the Feeling/Geraldine-Killer	1972	—	2.50	5.00
❏ 730	There Oughta Be a Law/Berries in Salinas	1975	—	2.50	5.00
❏ 8113	There Oughta Be a Law/Berries in Salinas	1975	—	2.00	4.00

Albums

ATLANTIC
| ❏ 8149 [M] | Cowboys and Colored People | 1967 | 6.25 | 12.50 | 25.00 |
| ❏ SD 8149 [S] | Cowboys and Colored People | 1967 | 3.75 | 7.50 | 15.00 |

—*Green and blue label*

| ❏ SD 8149 [S] | Cowboys and Colored People | 1969 | 3.00 | 6.00 | 12.00 |

—*Red and green label*

| ❏ SD 8179 | You Devil You | 1968 | 3.75 | 7.50 | 15.00 |

—*Green and blue label*

| ❏ SD 8179 | You Devil You | 1969 | 3.00 | 6.00 | 12.00 |

—*Red and green label*

IMPERIAL
| ❏ LP-9155 [M] | Flippin' | 1961 | 6.25 | 12.50 | 25.00 |

LITTLE DAVID
| ❏ LD 1000 | The Devil Made Me Buy This Dress | 1970 | 3.00 | 6.00 | 12.00 |
| ❏ LD 1001 [M] | Geraldine/Don't Fight the Feeling | 1972 | 6.25 | 12.50 | 25.00 |

—*White label promo only; sticker on cover says "Promotional DJ Copy Monaural Not for Sale"*

| ❏ LD 1001 [S] | Geraldine/Don't Fight the Feeling | 1972 | 3.00 | 6.00 | 12.00 |
| ❏ LD 2000 | The Flip Wilson Show | 1970 | 3.00 | 6.00 | 12.00 |

MINIT
| ❏ 24012 | Flippin' | 1968 | 3.75 | 7.50 | 15.00 |

—*Reissue of Imperial LP*

SCEPTER
| ❏ S-520 | Flip Wilson's Pot Luck | 1964 | 5.00 | 10.00 | 20.00 |

SPRINGBOARD
| ❏ SPB-4004 | Funny and Live at the Village Gate | 1972 | 3.00 | 6.00 | 12.00 |

—*Reissue of Scepter LP*

SUNSET
| ❏ SUS-5297 | Flipped Out | 1970 | 3.00 | 6.00 | 12.00 |

—*Reissue of Minit LP*

WILSON, FRANK
45s

SOUL
| ❏ 35019 | Do I Love You (Indeed I Do)/Sweeter As the Days Go By | 1966 | 10000. | 15000. | 20000. |

WILSON, HANK   See LEON RUSSELL.

WILSON, J. FRANK, AND THE CAVALIERS
45s

CHARAY
| ❏ 13 | Last Kiss '69/Black Car | 1969 | — | 3.00 | 6.00 |

JOSIE
| ❏ 923 | Last Kiss/That's How Much I Love You | 1964 | 3.00 | 6.00 | 12.00 |
| ❏ 924 | Tears of Happiness/Summertime | 1964 | 2.50 | 5.00 | 10.00 |

—*As "The Cavaliers"*

❏ 926	Hey Little One/Speak to Me	1964	2.50	5.00	10.00
❏ 929	Say It Now/Six Boys	1965	2.50	5.00	10.00
❏ 931	Dreams of a Fool/Open Your Eyes	1965	2.50	5.00	10.00
❏ 938	Forget Me Not/A White Sport Coat (And a Pink Carnation)	1965	2.50	5.00	10.00

LE CAM
| ❏ 722 | Last Kiss/Carla | 1964 | 7.50 | 15.00 | 30.00 |

SOLLY
| ❏ 927 | Me and My Teardrops/Unmarked and Uncovered with Sand | 1966 | 2.50 | 5.00 | 10.00 |

TAMARA
| ❏ 761 | Last Kiss/That's How Much I Love You | 1964 | 6.25 | 12.50 | 25.00 |

VIRGO
| ❏ 506 | Last Kiss/That's How Much I Love You | 1973 | — | 3.50 | 7.00 |

Albums

JOSIE
| ❏ JM-4006 [M] | Last Kiss | 1964 | 18.75 | 37.50 | 75.00 |
| ❏ JS-4006 [S] | Last Kiss | 1964 | 25.00 | 50.00 | 100.00 |

WILSON, JACKIE   Also see THE DOMINOES.
45s

BRUNSWICK
❏ 9-55024	Reet Petite (The Finest Girl You Ever Want to Meet)/By the Light of the Silvery Moon	1957	7.50	15.00	30.00
❏ 9-55052	To Be Loved/Come Back to Me	1958	6.25	12.50	25.00
❏ 9-55070	As Long As I Live/I'm Wanderin'	1958	6.25	12.50	25.00
❏ 9-55086	We Have Love/Singing a Song	1958	6.25	12.50	25.00
❏ 9-55105	Lonely Teardrops/In the Blue of Evening	1958	7.50	15.00	30.00
❏ 55121	That's Why (I Love You So)/Love Is All	1959	6.25	12.50	25.00
❏ 55121 [PS]	That's Why (I Love You So)/Love Is All	1959	15.00	30.00	60.00
❏ 55136	I'll Be Satisfied/Ask	1959	6.25	12.50	25.00
❏ 55149	You Better Know It/Never Go Away	1959	5.00	10.00	20.00
❏ 55165	Talk That Talk/Only You, Only Me	1959	5.00	10.00	20.00
❏ 55165 [PS]	Talk That Talk/Only You, Only Me	1959	15.00	30.00	60.00
❏ 55166	Night/Doggin' Around	196?	2.50	5.00	10.00

—*Black label, color-bar arrow (reissue pressing)*

| ❏ 55166 | Night/Doggin' Around | 1960 | 3.75 | 7.50 | 15.00 |

—*Orange label (standard pressing)*

| ❏ 55166 | Night/Doggin' Around | 1960 | 10.00 | 20.00 | 40.00 |

—*Maroon label (scarce original)*

❏ 55166 [PS]	Night/Doggin' Around	1960	12.50	25.00	50.00
❏ 55167	(You Were Made for) All My Love/A Woman, A Lover, A Friend	1960	5.00	10.00	20.00
❏ 55170	Alone at Last/Am I the Man	1960	5.00	10.00	20.00

❏ 55170 [PS]	Alone at Last/Am I the Man	1960	12.50	25.00	50.00
❏ 55201	My Empty Arms/The Tear of the Year	1961	3.75	7.50	15.00
❏ 55201 [PS]	My Empty Arms/The Tear of the Year	1961	10.00	20.00	40.00
❏ 55208	Please Tell Me Why/Your One and Only Love	1961	3.75	7.50	15.00
❏ 55216	I'm Comin' On Back to You/Lonely Life	1961	3.75	7.50	15.00
❏ 55219	Years from Now/You Don't Know What It Means	1961	3.75	7.50	15.00
❏ 55220	The Way I Am/My Heart Belongs to Only You	1961	3.75	7.50	15.00
❏ 55220 [PS]	The Way I Am/My Heart Belongs to Only You	1961	10.00	20.00	40.00
❏ 55221	The Greatest Hurt/There'll Be No Next Time	1962	3.75	7.50	15.00
❏ 55221 [PS]	The Greatest Hurt/There'll Be No Next Time	1962	10.00	20.00	40.00
❏ 55224	I Found Love/There's Nothing Like Love	1962	3.00	6.00	12.00

—*With Linda Hopkins*

❏ 55225	Hearts/Sing (And Tell the Blues So Long)	1962	3.75	7.50	15.00
❏ 55229	I Just Can't Help It/My Tale of Woe	1962	3.75	7.50	15.00
❏ 55233	Forever and a Day/Baby That's All	1962	3.75	7.50	15.00
❏ 55236	What Good Am I Without You/A Girl Named Tamiko	1962	3.75	7.50	15.00
❏ 55236 [PS]	What Good Am I Without You/A Girl Named Tamiko	1962	7.50	15.00	30.00
❏ 55239	Baby Workout/I'm Going Crazy	1963	5.00	10.00	20.00
❏ 55243	Shake a Hand/Say I Do	1963	3.00	6.00	12.00

—*With Linda Hopkins*

❏ 55246	Shake! Shake! Shake!/He's a Fool	1963	3.00	6.00	12.00
❏ 55250	Baby Get It (And Don't Quit It)/The New Breed	1963	3.00	6.00	12.00
❏ 55254	Silent Night/Oh Holy Night	1963	3.75	7.50	15.00
❏ 55260	Haunted House/I'm Travelin' On	1964	2.50	5.00	10.00
❏ 55263	Call Her Up/The Kickapoo	1964	2.50	5.00	10.00
❏ 55266	Big Boss Line/Be My Girl	1964	2.50	5.00	10.00
❏ 55269	Squeeze Her-Tease Her (But Love Her)/Give Me Back My Heart	1964	2.50	5.00	10.00
❏ 55273	Watch Out/She's All Right	1964	2.50	5.00	10.00
❏ 55277	Danny Boy/Soul Time	1965	2.00	4.00	8.00
❏ 55278	Yes Indeed/When the Saints Go Marching In	1965	2.00	4.00	8.00

—*With Linda Hopkins*

❏ 55280	No Pity (In the Naked City)/I'm So Lonely	1965	2.00	4.00	8.00
❏ 55283	I Believe I'll Love On/Lonely Teardrops	1965	2.00	4.00	8.00
❏ 55287	Think Twice/Please Don't Hurt Me	1965	2.00	4.00	8.00

—*With LaVern Baker*

❏ 55289	I've Got to Get Back/3 Days, 1 Hour, 30 Minutes	1966	2.00	4.00	8.00
❏ 55290	Soul Galore/Brand New Things	1966	2.00	4.00	8.00
❏ 55294	I Believe/Be My Love	1966	2.00	4.00	8.00
❏ 55300	Whispers (Gettin' Louder)/The Fairest of Them All	1966	2.00	4.00	8.00
❏ 55309	I Don't Want to Lose You/Just Be Sincere	1967	2.00	4.00	8.00
❏ 55321	I've Lost You/Those Heartaches	1967	2.00	4.00	8.00
❏ 55336	(Your Love Keeps Lifting Me) Higher and Higher/I'm the One to Do It	1967	2.50	5.00	10.00
❏ 55354	Since You Showed Me How to Be Happy/The Who Who Song	1967	2.00	4.00	8.00
❏ 55365	For Your Precious Love/Uptight	1968	2.00	4.00	8.00
❏ 55373	Chain Gang/Funky Broadway	1968	2.00	4.00	8.00
❏ 55381	I Get the Sweetest Feeling/Nothing But Heartaches	1968	2.00	4.00	8.00
❏ 55392	For Once in My Life/You Brought About a Change in Me	1968	2.00	4.00	8.00
❏ 55402	I Still Love You/Hum De Dum De Do	1969	2.00	4.00	8.00
❏ 55418	Helpless/Do It the Right Way	1969	2.00	4.00	8.00
❏ 55423	With These Hands/Why Don't You (Do Your Thing)	1969	2.00	4.00	8.00
❏ 55435	Let This Be a Letter (To My Baby)/Didn't I	1970	—	3.00	6.00
❏ 55435 [PS]	Let This Be a Letter (To My Baby)/Didn't I	1970	3.00	6.00	12.00
❏ 55443	(I Can Feel Those Vibrations) This Love Is Real/Love Uprising	1970	—	3.00	6.00
❏ 55449	This Guy's in Love with You/Say You Will	1971	—	3.00	6.00
❏ 55454	Say You Will/(B-side unknown)	1971	—	3.00	6.00
❏ 55461	Love Is Funny That Way/Try It Again	1971	—	3.00	6.00
❏ 55467	You Got Me Walking/The Mountain	1972	—	3.00	6.00
❏ 55475	The Girl Turned Me On/Forever and a Day	1972	—	3.00	6.00
❏ 55480	What a Lovely Way/You Left the Fire Burning	1972	—	3.00	6.00
❏ 55490	Beautiful Day/What 'Cha Gonna Do About Love	1973	—	3.00	6.00
❏ 55495	Because of You/Go Away	1973	—	3.00	6.00
❏ 55499	Sing a Little Song/No More Goodbyes	1973	—	3.00	6.00
❏ 55504	It's All Over/Shake a Leg	1973	—	3.00	6.00
❏ 55522	Don't Burn No Bridges/(Instrumental)	1975	—	3.00	6.00

—*With the Chi-Lites*

| ❏ 55536 | Nobody But You/I've Learned About Life | 1977 | — | 3.00 | 6.00 |
| ❏ 7-78002 [S] | (You Were Made) For All My Love/One Kiss | 196? | 10.00 | 20.00 | 40.00 |

—*Jukebox issue; small hole, plays at 33 1/3 rpm*

COLUMBIA
| ❏ 38-07329 | Reet Petite/You Better Know It | 1987 | — | 2.50 | 5.00 |
| ❏ 38-07329 [PS] | Reet Petite/You Better Know It | 1987 | — | 2.50 | 5.00 |

7-Inch Extended Plays

BRUNSWICK
❏ EB 71040	To Be Loved/Reet Petite//Danny Boy/As Long As I Live	1959	15.00	30.00	60.00
❏ EB 71040 [PS]	The Versatile Jackie Wilson	1959	15.00	30.00	60.00
❏ EB 71042	Lonely Teardrops/It's Too Bad We Had to Say Goodbye//Someone to Need Me/Joke	1960	15.00	30.00	60.00
❏ EB 71042 [PS]	Jumpin' Jack	1960	15.00	30.00	60.00
❏ EB 71045 [M]	That's Why/Love Is All//You Better Know It/Each Time	1960	15.00	30.00	60.00
❏ EB 71045 [PS]	That's Why (I Love You So)	1960	15.00	30.00	60.00
❏ EB 71046	Talk That Talk/Ask//I'll Be Satisfied/Wishing Well	1960	15.00	30.00	60.00
❏ EB 71046 [PS]	Talk That Talk	1960	15.00	30.00	60.00
❏ EB 71047	(contents unknown)	1960	15.00	30.00	60.00
❏ EB 71047 [PS]	Mr. Excitement	1960	15.00	30.00	60.00
❏ EB 71048	So Much/Only You, Only Me//Happiness/Magic of Love	1960	15.00	30.00	60.00
❏ EB 71048 [PS]	Jackie Wilson	1960	15.00	30.00	60.00
❏ EB 71049	Night/Doggin' Around//All My Love/A Woman, a Lover, a Friend	1960	15.00	30.00	60.00
❏ EB 71049 [PS]	Jackie Wilson	1960	15.00	30.00	60.00
❏ EB 71101	The Greatest Hurt/I Don't Know You Anymore//Tear of the Year/There'll Be No Next Time	1962	15.00	30.00	60.00
❏ EB 71101 [PS]	Jackie Wilson	1962	15.00	30.00	60.00
❏ EB 71102	I Just Can't Help It/My Tale of Woe//Bad News Travels Fast/You Ought to Be Ashamed	1962	15.00	30.00	60.00
❏ EB 71102 [PS]	Jackie Wilson	1962	15.00	30.00	60.00

Number	Title (A Side/B Side)	Yr	VG	VG+	NM
❏ EB 71103	Baby Workout/Say You Will//Kickapoo/ Yeah Yeah Yeah	1963	15.00	30.00	60.00
❏ EB 71103 [PS]	Baby Workout	1963	15.00	30.00	60.00
❏ EB 71104	(contents unknown)	1963	15.00	30.00	60.00
❏ EB 71104 [PS]	Shake a Hand	1963	15.00	30.00	60.00
❏ 7-78009	No Pity (In the Naked City)/Mama of My Song/ Soul Time//Danny Boy/She's All Right/No Time Out	196?	12.50	25.00	50.00
—Jukebox issue; small hole, plays at 33 1/3 rpm						
❏ 7-78009 [PS]	Soul Time	196?	12.50	25.00	50.00
❏ EB 771045	That's Why/Love Is All//You Better Know It/Each Time	1960	20.00	40.00	80.00
❏ EB 771045 [PS]	That's Why (I Love You So)	1960	20.00	40.00	80.00

Albums
BRUNSWICK

Number	Title (A Side/B Side)	Yr	VG	VG+	NM
❏ BL 54042 [M]	He's So Fine	1959	30.00	60.00	120.00
—All-black label						
❏ BL 54042 [M]	He's So Fine	1964	6.25	12.50	25.00
—Black label with color bars						
❏ BL 54045 [M]	Lonely Teardrops	1959	37.50	75.00	150.00
—All-black label						
❏ BL 54045 [M]	Lonely Teardrops	1964	6.25	12.50	25.00
—Black label with color bars						
❏ BL 54050 [M]	So Much	1960	25.00	50.00	100.00
—All-black label						
❏ BL 54050 [M]	So Much	1964	5.00	10.00	20.00
—Black label with color bars						
❏ BL 54055 [M]	Jackie Sings the Blues	1960	37.50	75.00	150.00
—All-black label						
❏ BL 54055 [M]	Jackie Sings the Blues	1964	5.00	10.00	20.00
—Black label with color bars						
❏ BL 54058 [M]	My Golden Favorites	1960	15.00	30.00	60.00
—All-black label						
❏ BL 54058 [M]	My Golden Favorites	1964	6.25	12.50	25.00
—Black label with color bars						
❏ BL 54059 [M]	A Woman, a Lover, a Friend	1961	12.50	25.00	50.00
—All-black label						
❏ BL 54059 [M]	A Woman, a Lover, a Friend	1964	5.00	10.00	20.00
—Black label with color bars						
❏ BL 54100 [M]	You Ain't Heard Nothin' Yet	1961	12.50	25.00	50.00
—All-black label						
❏ BL 54100 [M]	You Ain't Heard Nothin' Yet	1964	5.00	10.00	20.00
—Black label with color bars						
❏ BL 54101 [M]	By Special Request	1961	12.50	25.00	50.00
—All-black label						
❏ BL 54101 [M]	By Special Request	1964	5.00	10.00	20.00
—Black label with color bars						
❏ BL 54105 [M]	Body and Soul	1962	12.50	25.00	50.00
—All-black label						
❏ BL 54105 [M]	Body and Soul	1964	5.00	10.00	20.00
—Black label with color bars						
❏ BL 54106 [M]	The World's Greatest Melodies	1962	12.50	25.00	50.00
—All-black label						
❏ BL 54106 [M]	The World's Greatest Melodies	1964	5.00	10.00	20.00
—Black label with color bars						
❏ BL 54108 [M]	Jackie Wilson at the Copa	1962	12.50	25.00	50.00
—All-black label						
❏ BL 54108 [M]	Jackie Wilson at the Copa	1964	5.00	10.00	20.00
—Black label with color bars						
❏ BL 54110 [M]	Baby Workout	1963	5.00	10.00	20.00
—Black label with color bars						
❏ BL 54110 [M]	Baby Workout	1963	12.50	25.00	50.00
—All-black label						
❏ BL 54112 [M]	Merry Christmas from Jackie Wilson	1963	7.50	15.00	30.00
❏ BL 54113 [M]	Shake a Hand	1964	6.25	12.50	25.00
❏ BL 54115 [M]	My Golden Favorites, Volume 2	1964	6.25	12.50	25.00
❏ BL 54117 [M]	Somethin' Else	1964	6.25	12.50	25.00
❏ BL 54118 [M]	Soul Time	1965	6.25	12.50	25.00
❏ BL 54119 [M]	Spotlight on Jackie	1965	6.25	12.50	25.00
❏ BL 54120 [M]	Soul Galore	1966	6.25	12.50	25.00
❏ BL 54122 [M]	Whispers	1966	6.25	12.50	25.00
❏ BL 54130 [M]	Higher and Higher	1967	6.25	12.50	25.00
❏ BL 54134 [M]	Manufacturers of Soul	1968	12.50	25.00	50.00
—With Count Basie						
❏ BL 54138 [M]	I Get the Sweetest Feeling	1968	25.00	50.00	100.00
—Yellow label promo only; "Monaural" sticker over the word "Stereo" on cover						
❏ BL 754050 [S]	So Much	1960	37.50	75.00	150.00
—All-black label						
❏ BL 754050 [S]	So Much	1964	6.25	12.50	25.00
—Black label with color bars						
❏ BL 754055 [S]	Jackie Sings the Blues	1960	50.00	100.00	200.00
—All-black label						
❏ BL 754055 [S]	Jackie Sings the Blues	1964	6.25	12.50	25.00
—Black label with color bars						
❏ BL 754059 [S]	A Woman, a Lover, a Friend	1961	20.00	40.00	80.00
—All-black label						
❏ BL 754059 [S]	A Woman, a Lover, a Friend	1964	6.25	12.50	25.00
—Black label with color bars						
❏ BL 754100 [S]	You Ain't Heard Nothin' Yet	1961	20.00	40.00	80.00
—All-black label						
❏ BL 754100 [S]	You Ain't Heard Nothin' Yet	1964	6.25	12.50	25.00
—Black label with color bars						
❏ BL 754101 [S]	By Special Request	1961	20.00	40.00	80.00
—All-black label						
❏ BL 754101 [S]	By Special Request	1964	6.25	12.50	25.00
—Black label with color bars						
❏ BL 754105 [S]	Body and Soul	1962	20.00	40.00	80.00
—All-black label						
❏ BL 754105 [S]	Body and Soul	1964	6.25	12.50	25.00
—Black label with color bars						
❏ BL 754106 [S]	The World's Greatest Melodies	1962	20.00	40.00	80.00
—All-black label						
❏ BL 754106 [S]	The World's Greatest Melodies	1964	6.25	12.50	25.00
—Black label with color bars						
❏ BL 754108 [S]	Jackie Wilson at the Copa	1962	20.00	40.00	80.00
—All-black label						

Number	Title (A Side/B Side)	Yr	VG	VG+	NM
❏ BL 754108 [S]	Jackie Wilson at the Copa	1964	6.25	12.50	25.00
—Black label with color bars						
❏ BL 754110 [S]	Baby Workout	1963	6.25	12.50	25.00
—Black label with color bars						
❏ BL 754110 [S]	Baby Workout	1963	20.00	40.00	80.00
—All-black label						
❏ BL 754112 [S]	Merry Christmas from Jackie Wilson	1963	10.00	20.00	40.00
❏ BL 754113 [S]	Shake a Hand	1964	7.50	15.00	30.00
❏ BL 754115 [S]	My Golden Favorites, Volume 2	1964	7.50	15.00	30.00
❏ BL 754117 [S]	Somethin' Else	1964	7.50	15.00	30.00
❏ BL 754118 [S]	Soul Time	1965	7.50	15.00	30.00
❏ BL 754119 [S]	Spotlight on Jackie	1965	7.50	15.00	30.00
❏ BL 754120 [S]	Soul Galore	1966	7.50	15.00	30.00
❏ BL 754122 [S]	Whispers	1966	7.50	15.00	30.00
❏ BL 754130 [S]	Higher and Higher	1967	7.50	15.00	30.00
❏ BL 754134 [S]	Manufacturers of Soul	1968	5.00	10.00	20.00
—With Count Basie						
❏ BL 754138 [S]	I Get the Sweetest Feeling	1968	5.00	10.00	20.00
❏ BL 754140	Jackie Wilson's Greatest Hits	1969	5.00	10.00	20.00
❏ BL 754154	Do Your Thing	1969	5.00	10.00	20.00
❏ BL 754158	It's All a Part of Love	1970	5.00	10.00	20.00
❏ BL 754167	This Love Is Real	1971	5.00	10.00	20.00
❏ BL 754172	You Got Me Walking	1971	5.00	10.00	20.00
❏ BL 754185	Beautiful Day	1972	3.75	7.50	15.00
❏ BL 754199	Nowstalgia	1974	3.75	7.50	15.00
❏ BL 754212	Nobody But You	1977	3.75	7.50	15.00

COLUMBIA

Number	Title (A Side/B Side)	Yr	VG	VG+	NM
❏ FC 40866	Reet Petite: The Best of Jackie Wilson	1987	3.00	6.00	12.00

EPIC

Number	Title (A Side/B Side)	Yr	VG	VG+	NM
❏ EG 38623 [(2)]	The Jackie Wilson Story	1983	5.00	10.00	20.00
❏ PE 39408	The Jackie Wilson Story, Vol. 2	1985	3.00	6.00	12.00
❏ PE 39408	The Jackie Wilson Story, Vol. 2	198?	2.00	4.00	8.00
—Budget-line reissue						

RHINO

Number	Title (A Side/B Side)	Yr	VG	VG+	NM
❏ RNLP-70230	Through the Years: A Collection of Rare Album Tracks and Single Sides	1987	3.00	6.00	12.00

WILSON, MARTY
45s
DECCA

Number	Title (A Side/B Side)	Yr	VG	VG+	NM
❏ 30544	Super Sonic/I'm All Woke Up	1958	7.50	15.00	30.00
❏ 30644	Po-Go/Hey Eula	1958	7.50	15.00	30.00

TEL

❏ 1008	Stroll Me/Hot Foot	1959	6.25	12.50	25.00

WILSON, MURRY Father of Brian, Carl and Dennis Wilson of the Beach Boys.
45s
CAPITOL

Number	Title (A Side/B Side)	Yr	VG	VG+	NM
❏ 2063	Leaves/Plumber's Tune	1967	3.00	6.00	12.00

Albums
CAPITOL

❏ ST 2819 [S]	The Many Moods of Murry Wilson	1967	12.50	25.00	50.00
❏ T 2819 [M]	The Many Moods of Murry Wilson	1967	15.00	30.00	60.00

WILSON, NANCY
45s
CAPITOL

Number	Title (A Side/B Side)	Yr	VG	VG+	NM
❏ 2061	Ode to Billie Joe/ I'm Always Drunk in San Francisco	1967	—	3.00	6.00
❏ 2136	Face It Girl, It's Over/The End of Our Love	1968	—	3.00	6.00
❏ 2283	Peace of Mind/This Bitter Earth	1968	—	3.00	6.00
❏ 2361	In a Long White Room/Only Love	1968	—	3.00	6.00
❏ 2422	You'd Better Go/I'm Your Special Fool	1969	—	3.00	6.00
❏ 2555	Got It Together/One Soft Night	1969	—	3.00	6.00
❏ 2644	Can't Take My Eyes Off You/Do You Know Why	1969	—	3.00	6.00
❏ 2749	Waitin' for Charlie to Come Home/ Words and Music	1970	—	3.00	6.00
❏ 2831	This Girl Is a Woman Now/Trip with Me	1970	—	3.00	6.00
❏ 2934	Now I'm a Woman/The Real Me	1970	—	3.00	6.00
❏ 3212	The Greatest Performance of My Life/ Everybody Knows	1971	—	3.00	6.00
❏ 3956	Streetrunner/Ocean of Love	1974	—	2.50	5.00
❏ 3973	You're As Right As Rain/ There'll Always Be Forever	1974	—	2.50	5.00
❏ 4117	He Called Me Baby/Like a Circle Never Stops	1975	—	2.50	5.00
❏ 4189	Don't Let Me Be Lonely Tonight/Happy Tears	1975	—	2.50	5.00
❏ 4284	Now/This Mother's Daughter	1976	—	2.00	4.00
❏ 4359	In My Loneliness (When We Were One)/He Never Had It So Good	1976	—	2.00	4.00
❏ 4476	I've Never Been to Me/Here It Comes	1977	—	2.00	4.00
❏ 4509	My Foolish Heart/Seventh Son	1961	3.75	7.50	15.00
❏ 4558	Next Time You See Him/Give Him Love	1961	2.50	5.00	10.00
❏ 4578	I'm Gonna Let Ya/Light	1978	—	2.00	4.00
❏ 4647	The Verdict/Guess Who I Saw Today	1961	2.50	5.00	10.00
❏ 4741	Life, Love and Harmony/Open Up Your Heart and Take Me In	1979	—	2.00	4.00
❏ 4801	Sunshine/This Is Our Song	1979	—	2.00	4.00
❏ 4816	Put On a Happy Face/ You Don't Know What Love Is	1962	2.00	4.00	8.00
❏ 4839	Welcome Home/Let's Hold On to Love	1980	—	2.00	4.00
❏ 4926	You Can Have Him/A Lot of Livin' to Do	1963	2.00	4.00	8.00
❏ 4991	Tell Me the Truth/My Sweet Thing	1963	2.00	4.00	8.00
❏ 5084	That's What I Want for Christmas/What Are You Doing New Year's Eve	1963	2.50	5.00	10.00
❏ 5133	Don't Rain on My Parade/The Grass Is Greener	1964	2.00	4.00	8.00
❏ 5198	(You Don't Know) How Glad I Am/ Never Less Than Yesterday	1964	—	3.50	7.00
❏ 5254	I Wanna Be with You/It's Time for Me	1964	—	3.50	7.00
❏ 5319	And Satisfy/Take What I Have	1964	—	3.50	7.00
❏ 5340	Don't Come Running Back to Me/ Love Has Many Faces	1965	—	3.50	7.00
❏ 5340 [PS]	Don't Come Running Back to Me/ Love Has Many Faces	1965	3.00	6.00	12.00
❏ 5408	The Best Is Yet to Come/Welcome, Welcome	1965	—	3.50	7.00
❏ 5455	Where Does That Leave Me/Gentle Is My Love	1965	—	3.50	7.00
❏ 5515	I'll Only Miss Him When I Think of Him/ Afterthoughts	1965	—	3.50	7.00

Number	Title (A Side/B Side)	Yr	VG	VG+	NM
❏ 5564	No One Else But You/Have a Heart	1966	—	3.50	7.00
❏ 5639	The Power of Love/Rain Sometime	1966	—	3.50	7.00
❏ 5673	Uptight (Everything's Alright)/ You've Got Your Troubles	1966	—	3.50	7.00
❏ 5720	Go Away/That Special Way	1966	—	3.50	7.00
❏ 5771	Love Can Do Anything/I'll Make a Man of the Man	1966	—	3.50	7.00
❏ 5841	In the Dark/Ten Years of Tears	1967	—	3.50	7.00
❏ 5935	Don't Look Over Your Shoulder/ But Only Sometimes	1967	—	3.50	7.00
❏ 6275	That's What I Want for Christmas/ What Are You Doing New Year's Eve	197?	—	2.50	5.00
—Starline reissue					
❏ S7-19763	That's What I Want for Christmas/ What Are You Doing New Year's Eve	1997	—	—	3.00
COLUMBIA					
❏ 07037	Forbidden Lover/A Song for You	1987	—	—	3.00
❏ 08058	Quiet Fire/The Power, The Glory	1988	—	—	3.00

7-Inch Extended Plays
CAPITOL

Number	Title (A Side/B Side)	Yr	VG	VG+	NM
❏ SXA-2351 [PS]	Gentle Is My Love	1965	2.50	5.00	10.00
❏ SXA-2351 [S]	Who Can I Turn To/Gentle Is My Love/There Will Never Be Another You//Funnier Than Funny/ More/If Ever I Would Leave You	1965	2.50	5.00	10.00
—33 1/3 rpm, small hole					
❏ SU-2555 [PS]	Tender Loving Care	1966	2.50	5.00	10.00
❏ SU-2555 [S]	Don't Go to Strangers/Like Someone in Love/ Tender Loving Care/Gee Baby, Ain't I Good to You/Close Your Eyes/As You Desire Me	1966	2.50	5.00	10.00
—33 1/3 rpm, small hole					

Albums
CAPITOL

Number	Title (A Side/B Side)	Yr	VG	VG+	NM
❏ ST-148	Nancy	1969	3.75	7.50	15.00
❏ ST-234	Son of a Preacher Man	1969	3.75	7.50	15.00
❏ SWBB-256 [(2)]	Close-Up	1969	5.00	10.00	20.00
—Combines 1828 and 1934 into one package					
❏ ST-353	Hurt So Bad	1969	3.75	7.50	15.00
❏ ST-429	Can't Take My Eyes Off You	1970	3.75	7.50	15.00
❏ ST-541	Now I'm a Woman	1970	3.75	7.50	15.00
❏ STBB-727 [(2)]	For Once in My Life/Who Can I Turn To	1971	5.00	10.00	20.00
❏ ST-763	The Right to Love	1971	3.75	7.50	15.00
—Retitled reissue of 2757					
❏ SM-798	But Beautiful	197?	2.50	5.00	10.00
—Reissue					
❏ ST-798	But Beautiful	1971	3.75	7.50	15.00
❏ ST-842	Kaleidoscope	1971	3.75	7.50	15.00
❏ ST 1319 [S]	Like in Love	1960	5.00	10.00	20.00
—Black label with colorband, Capitol logo on top					
❏ ST 1319 [S]	Like in Love	1960	7.50	15.00	30.00
—Black label with colorband, Capitol logo on left					
❏ T 1319 [M]	Like in Love	1960	3.75	7.50	15.00
—Black label with colorband, Capitol logo on top					
❏ T 1319 [M]	Like in Love	1960	6.25	12.50	25.00
—Black label with colorband, Capitol logo on left					
❏ ST 1440 [S]	Something Wonderful	1960	5.00	10.00	20.00
—Black label with colorband, Capitol logo on top					
❏ ST 1440 [S]	Something Wonderful	1960	7.50	15.00	30.00
—Black label with colorband, Capitol logo on left					
❏ T 1440 [M]	Something Wonderful	1960	3.75	7.50	15.00
—Black label with colorband, Capitol logo on top					
❏ T 1440 [M]	Something Wonderful	1960	6.25	12.50	25.00
—Black label with colorband, Capitol logo on left					
❏ SM-1524 [S]	The Swingin's Mutual	1976	2.50	5.00	10.00
—With George Shearing; reissue					
❏ ST 1524 [S]	The Swingin's Mutual	1961	5.00	10.00	20.00
—Black label with colorband, Capitol logo on top					
❏ ST 1524 [S]	The Swingin's Mutual	1961	7.50	15.00	30.00
—Black label with colorband, Capitol logo on left					
❏ T 1524 [M]	The Swingin's Mutual	1961	3.75	7.50	15.00
—Black label with colorband, Capitol logo on top					
❏ T 1524 [M]	The Swingin's Mutual	1961	6.25	12.50	25.00
—Black label with colorband, Capitol logo on left					
❏ ST 1767 [S]	Hello Young Lovers	1962	6.25	12.50	25.00
❏ T 1767 [M]	Hello Young Lovers	1962	5.00	10.00	20.00
❏ SM-1828	Broadway My Way	197?	2.50	5.00	10.00
—Reissue					
❏ ST 1828 [S]	Broadway My Way	1963	5.00	10.00	20.00
❏ T 1828 [M]	Broadway My Way	1963	3.75	7.50	15.00
❏ SM-1934	Hollywood My Way	197?	2.50	5.00	10.00
—Reissue					
❏ ST 1934 [S]	Hollywood My Way	1963	5.00	10.00	20.00
❏ T 1934 [M]	Hollywood My Way	1963	3.75		7.50
❏ ST 2012 [S]	Yesterday's Love Songs/Today's Blues	1964	5.00	10.00	20.00
❏ T 2012 [M]	Yesterday's Love Songs/Today's Blues	1964	3.75	7.50	15.00
❏ ST 2082 [S]	Today, Tomorrow, Forever	1964	5.00	10.00	20.00
❏ T 2082 [M]	Today, Tomorrow, Forever	1964	3.75	7.50	15.00
❏ KAO 2136 [M]	The Nancy Wilson Show!	1965	3.75	7.50	15.00
❏ SKAO 2136 [S]	The Nancy Wilson Show!	1965	5.00	10.00	20.00
❏ ST 2155 [S]	How Glad I Am	1964	5.00	10.00	20.00
❏ T 2155 [M]	How Glad I Am	1964	3.75	7.50	15.00
❏ ST 2321 [S]	Today — My Way	1965	5.00	10.00	20.00
❏ T 2321 [M]	Today — My Way	1965	3.75	7.50	15.00
❏ ST 2351 [S]	Gentle Is My Love	1965	5.00	10.00	20.00
❏ T 2351 [M]	Gentle Is My Love	1965	3.75	7.50	15.00
❏ ST 2433 [S]	From Broadway with Love	1966	5.00	10.00	20.00
❏ T 2433 [M]	From Broadway with Love	1966	3.75	7.50	15.00
❏ SM-2495	A Touch of Today	197?	2.50	5.00	10.00
—Reissue					
❏ ST 2495 [S]	A Touch of Today	1966	5.00	10.00	20.00
❏ T 2495 [M]	A Touch of Today	1966	3.75	7.50	15.00
❏ ST 2555 [S]	Tender Loving Care	1966	5.00	10.00	20.00
❏ T 2555 [M]	Tender Loving Care	1966	3.75	7.50	15.00
❏ ST 2634 [S]	Nancy — Naturally	1967	5.00	10.00	20.00
❏ T 2634 [M]	Nancy — Naturally	1967	3.75	7.50	15.00
❏ ST 2712 [S]	Just for Now	1967	5.00	10.00	20.00
❏ T 2712 [M]	Just for Now	1967	3.75	7.50	15.00
❏ ST 2757 [S]	Lush Life	1967	3.75	7.50	15.00
❏ T 2757 [M]	Lush Life	1967	5.00	10.00	20.00

Number	Title (A Side/B Side)	Yr	VG	VG+	NM
❏ ST 2844 [S]	Welcome to My Love	1968	3.75	7.50	15.00
❏ T 2844 [M]	Welcome to My Love	1968	6.25	12.50	25.00
❏ ST 2909	Easy	1968	3.75	7.50	15.00
❏ SKAO 2947	The Best of Nancy Wilson	1968	3.75	7.50	15.00
❏ ST 2970	The Sound of Nancy Wilson	1968	3.75	7.50	15.00
❏ SY-4575	Broadway My Way	197?	2.50	5.00	10.00
—Odd reissue					
❏ ST-11131	I Know I Love Him	1972	3.00	6.00	12.00
❏ ST-11317	All in Love Is Fair	1974	3.00	6.00	12.00
❏ ST-11386	Come Get to This	1975	3.00	6.00	12.00
❏ ST-11518	This Mother's Daughter	1976	3.00	6.00	12.00
❏ ST-11659	I've Never Been to Me	1977	3.00	6.00	12.00
❏ SM-11767	How Glad I Am	1978	2.50	5.00	10.00
—Reissue of 2155					
❏ SMAS-11786	Music on My Mind	1978	3.00	6.00	12.00
❏ SM-11802	Easy	1978	2.50	5.00	10.00
—Reissue of 2909					
❏ SM-11819	Come Get to This	1978	2.50	5.00	10.00
—Reissue of 11386					
❏ SM-11884	Nancy — Naturally	1979	2.50	5.00	10.00
—Reissue of 2634					
❏ ST-11943	Life, Love and Happiness	1979	3.00	6.00	12.00
❏ SM-12031	Can't Take My Eyes Off You	1980	2.50	5.00	10.00
—Reissue of 429					
❏ ST-12055	Take My Love	1980	3.00	6.00	12.00
❏ SN-16128	The Best of Nancy Wilson	198?	2.00	4.00	8.00
—Budget-line reissue					
COLUMBIA					
❏ FC 40330	Keep You Satisfied	1986	2.50	5.00	10.00
❏ FC 40787	Forbidden Lover	1987	2.50	5.00	10.00
❏ FC 44464	Nancy Now!	1989	2.50	5.00	10.00
PAUSA					
❏ PR-9041	Nancy — Naturally	1985	2.50	5.00	10.00
PICKWICK					
❏ SPC-3273	Goin' Out of My Head	197?	2.50	5.00	10.00
❏ SPC-3348	The Good Life	197?	2.50	5.00	10.00

WILSON, NANCY, AND CANNONBALL ADDERLEY
45s
CAPITOL

Number	Title (A Side/B Side)	Yr	VG	VG+	NM
❏ 4693	Save Your Love for Me/Never Will I Marry	1962	2.00	4.00	8.00

Albums
CAPITOL

Number	Title (A Side/B Side)	Yr	VG	VG+	NM
❏ SM-1657	Nancy Wilson/Cannonball Adderley	197?	2.50	5.00	10.00
—Reissue					
❏ ST 1657 [S]	Nancy Wilson/Cannonball Adderley	1962	5.00	10.00	20.00
—Black label with colorband, Capitol logo on top					
❏ ST 1657 [S]	Nancy Wilson/Cannonball Adderley	1962	7.50	15.00	30.00
—Black label with colorband, Capitol logo on left					
❏ T 1657 [M]	Nancy Wilson/Cannonball Adderley	1962	3.75	7.50	15.00
—Black label with colorband, Capitol logo on top					
❏ T 1657 [M]	Nancy Wilson/Cannonball Adderley	1962	6.25	12.50	25.00
—Black label with colorband, Capitol logo on left					

WILSON, PEANUTS
45s
BRUNSWICK

Number	Title (A Side/B Side)	Yr	VG	VG+	NM
❏ 55039	Cast Iron Arm/You've Got Love	1957	37.50	75.00	150.00

WILSON, SONNY
45s
CANDIX

Number	Title (A Side/B Side)	Yr	VG	VG+	NM
❏ 327	I Ain't Givin' Up Nothin'/Troubled Time	1962	5.00	10.00	20.00

SUN

Number	Title (A Side/B Side)	Yr	VG	VG+	NM
❏ 341	The Great Pretender/I'm Gonna Take a Walk	1960	5.00	10.00	20.00

WILSON, TED
45s
SIERRA

Number	Title (A Side/B Side)	Yr	VG	VG+	NM
❏ 267	I Can't Take No More/(B-side unknown)	196?	375.00	750.00	1500.

WILSON, WALLY
45s
SABRE

Number	Title (A Side/B Side)	Yr	VG	VG+	NM
❏ 106	If You Don't Love Me/The Hunt	1954	150.00	300.00	600.00

WIMBERLEY, MAGGIE SUE
45s
SUN

Number	Title (A Side/B Side)	Yr	VG	VG+	NM
❏ 229	Daydreams Come True/How Long	1956	15.00	30.00	60.00

WINCHELL, DANNY
45s
MGM

Number	Title (A Side/B Side)	Yr	VG	VG+	NM
❏ 11335	Carolina in the Morning/There Goes My Heart	1952	7.50	15.00	30.00

RECORTE

Number	Title (A Side/B Side)	Yr	VG	VG+	NM
❏ 406	Jeannie/Beware You've Fallen in Love	1959	10.00	20.00	40.00
❏ 410	We're Gonna Have a Rockin' Party/Don't Say You're Sorry	1959	12.50	25.00	50.00
❏ 415	Come Back Baby/I've Chosen You	1959	10.00	20.00	40.00

WINCHESTER, JESSE
45s
AMPEX

Number	Title (A Side/B Side)	Yr	VG	VG+	NM
❏ 11004	Yankee Lady/That's the Touch I Like	1970	—	3.00	6.00
❏ 11018	Quiet About It/Biloxi	1970	—	3.00	6.00

BEARSVILLE

Number	Title (A Side/B Side)	Yr	VG	VG+	NM
❏ 0311	The Brand New Tennessee Waltz/ Let the Rough Side Drag	1976	—	2.00	4.00
❏ 0314	Everybody Knows But Me/Damned If You Do	1976	—	2.00	4.00
❏ 0318	Nothing But a Breeze/Twigs and Seeds	1977	—	2.00	4.00
❏ 0320	Rhumba Man/Twigs and Seeds	1977	—	2.00	4.00
❏ 0332	Sassy/Wintry Feeling	1978	—	2.00	4.00
❏ 49711	Say What/If Only	1981	—	2.00	4.00
❏ 49781	Baby Blue/Sure Enough	1981	—	2.00	4.00

Number	Title (A Side/B Side)	Yr	VG	VG+	NM
Albums					
AMPEX					
❏ A 10104	Jesse Winchester	1970	5.00	10.00	20.00
BEARSVILLE					
❏ PRO 560 [DJ]	The Jesse Winchester Radio Show	1976	10.00	20.00	40.00
❏ PRO-A-693 [(2)DJ]	Live at the Bijou Café Plus a Live Interview				
	at Media College in Montreal	1977	10.00	20.00	40.00
❏ BR 2045	Jesse Winchester	1971	3.75	7.50	15.00
—Reissue of Ampex LP					
❏ BR 2102	Third Down, 110 to Go	1972	3.75	7.50	15.00
❏ BR 6953	Learn to Love It	1974	3.00	6.00	12.00
❏ BR 6964	Let the Rough Side Drag	1976	3.00	6.00	12.00
❏ BR 6968	Nothing But a Breeze	1977	2.50	5.00	10.00
❏ BRK 6984	A Touch on the Rainy Side	1978	2.50	5.00	10.00
❏ BRK 6989	Talk Memphis	1981	2.50	5.00	10.00
RHINO					
❏ R1-70085	The Best of Jesse Winchester	1989	2.50	5.00	10.00
❏ RNLP-70885	Jesse Winchester	1988	2.50	5.00	10.00
❏ RNLP-70886	Third Down, 110 to Go	1988	2.50	5.00	10.00
SUGAR HILL					
❏ SH-1023	Humour Me	1988	3.00	6.00	12.00

WIND   TONY ORLANDO was in this group.
45s
FORWARD

Number	Title (A Side/B Side)	Yr	VG	VG+	NM
❏ 152	Groovin' with Mr. Bloe/Are You Nuts?	1970	—	2.50	5.00
—As "Cool Heat"					
LIFE					
❏ 200	Make Believe/Groovin' with Mr. Bloe	1969	—	2.50	5.00
❏ 202	Teeny Bopper/I'll Hold Out My Hand	1969	—	2.50	5.00
❏ 203	Groovin' with Mr. Bloe/Are You Nuts?	1970	—	3.00	6.00
—As "Cool Heat"					
Albums					
LIFE					
❏ LLPS-2000	Make Believe	1969	5.00	10.00	20.00

WIND HARP, THE
Albums
UNITED ARTISTS

Number	Title (A Side/B Side)	Yr	VG	VG+	NM
❏ UAS-9963 [(2)]	Song from the Hill	1972	5.00	10.00	20.00

WIND IN THE WILLOWS, THE   With Debbie Harry, later of Blondie.
45s
CAPITOL

Number	Title (A Side/B Side)	Yr	VG	VG+	NM
❏ 2274	Uptown Girl/Moments Spent	1968	5.00	10.00	20.00
Albums					
CAPITOL					
❏ SKAO 2956	The Wind in the Willows	1968	12.50	25.00	50.00

WINDSORS, THE (1)
45s
ABC-PARAMOUNT

Number	Title (A Side/B Side)	Yr	VG	VG+	NM
❏ 10563	Keep Away/Fingers and Thumbs	1964	3.75	7.50	15.00

WINDSORS, THE (2)
45s
BACK BEAT

Number	Title (A Side/B Side)	Yr	VG	VG+	NM
❏ 506	My Gloria/Cool Seabreeze	1958	4000.	6000.	8000.

WINDSORS, THE (U)
45s
UNITED ARTISTS

Number	Title (A Side/B Side)	Yr	VG	VG+	NM
❏ 128	Saki Rock/Caramba	1958	5.00	10.00	20.00
WIG WAG					
❏ 203	Carol Ann/Keep Me from Crying	1959	50.00	100.00	200.00

WINE, TONI
45s
ATCO

Number	Title (A Side/B Side)	Yr	VG	VG+	NM
❏ 6736	Sisters in Sorrow/Take a Little Time Out for Love	1970	—	3.00	6.00
COLPIX					
❏ 715	My Boyfriend's Coming Home for Christmas/				
	What a Pity	1963	3.75	7.50	15.00
❏ 732	I Love That Boy/The Thirteenth Hour	1964	3.00	6.00	12.00
❏ 742	A Boy Like You/Funny Little Heart	1964	3.00	6.00	12.00
❏ 756	Only Fools/A Girl Is Not a Girl	1964	3.00	6.00	12.00
SENATE					
❏ 2104	River Deep, Mountain High/Toni's Tune	1967	2.50	5.00	10.00

WINGFIELD, PETE   Also see OLYMPIC RUNNERS.
45s
ISLAND

Number	Title (A Side/B Side)	Yr	VG	VG+	NM
❏ 026	Eighteen with a Bullet/Shadow of a Doubt	1975	—	2.50	5.00
—Second pressing: Mostly black label with Island logo at bottom					
❏ 026	Eighteen with a Bullet/Shadow of a Doubt	1975	2.00	4.00	8.00
—First pressing: Mostly yellow label with island scene					
❏ 051	Lovin' As You Wanna Be/Please	1975	—	2.00	4.00
❏ 065	Scratchy 45's/A Whole Pot of Jelly (For a Little				
	Slice of Toast)	1976	—	2.00	4.00
Albums					
ISLAND					
❏ ILPS 9333	Breakfast Special	1975	3.00	6.00	12.00

WINGS   See PAUL McCARTNEY.

WINKLEY AND NUTLEY
45s
MK

Number	Title (A Side/B Side)	Yr	VG	VG+	NM
❏ 101	Report to the Nation (Part 1)/				
	Report to the Nation (Part 2)	1960	5.00	10.00	20.00

WINSTON, GEORGE
45s
WINDHAM HILL

Number	Title (A Side/B Side)	Yr	VG	VG+	NM
❏ WS-0005	Variations on the Kanon by Johann Pachelbel/				
	Carol of the Bells	1984	—	2.50	5.00

Number	Title (A Side/B Side)	Yr	VG	VG+	NM
❏ WS-0005 [PS]	Variations on the Kanon by Johann Pachelbel/				
	Carol of the Bells	1984	—	2.50	5.00
Albums					
LOST LAKE ARTS					
❏ LL-0081	Ballads and Blues 1972	1981	2.50	5.00	10.00
—Reissue of Takoma recordings					
TAKOMA					
❏ 9016	Piano Solos	1973	3.75	7.50	15.00
WINDHAM HILL					
❏ C-1012	Autumn	1980	3.00	6.00	12.00
—Original issue					
❏ WH-1012	Autumn	1984	2.50	5.00	10.00
—Reissue with A&M distribution					
❏ C-1019	Winter Into Spring	1982	3.00	6.00	12.00
—Original issue					
❏ WH-1019	Winter Into Spring	1984	2.50	5.00	10.00
—Reissue, distributed by A&M Records					
❏ C-1025	December	1982	3.75	7.50	15.00
—NOT distributed by A&M Records; "December" in black letters					
❏ WH-1025	December	1984	2.50	5.00	10.00
—Distributed by A&M Records; "December" in raised white letters					

WINSTON, HATTIE
45s
PARKWAY

Number	Title (A Side/B Side)	Yr	VG	VG+	NM
❏ 928	Pictures Don't Lie/Please Write Back to Me	1964	5.00	10.00	20.00
❏ 956	Pass Me By/Pictures Don't Lie	1965	20.00	40.00	80.00

WINSTONS, THE
45s
METROMEDIA

Number	Title (A Side/B Side)	Yr	VG	VG+	NM
❏ 117	Color Him Father/Amen, Brother	1969	2.00	4.00	8.00
❏ 142	Love of the Common People/Wheel of Fortune	1969	—	3.00	6.00
❏ 151	Birds of a Feather/The Greatest Love	1969	—	3.00	6.00
Albums					
METROMEDIA					
❏ MD-1010	Color Him Father	1969	12.50	25.00	50.00

WINTER, EDGAR
45s
BLUE SKY

Number	Title (A Side/B Side)	Yr	VG	VG+	NM
❏ 2758	One Day Tomorrow/Jasmine Nightdream	1975	—	2.00	4.00
❏ 2761	Outa Control/I Always Wanted You	1975	—	2.00	4.00
❏ 2762	Cool Dance/People Music	1975	—	2.00	4.00
❏ 2763	Diamond Eyes/Infinite Peace in Rhythm	1976	—	2.00	4.00
❏ 2769	Stickin' It Out/Puttin' It Back	1977	—	2.00	4.00
❏ 2780	Forever in Love/It's Your Life to Live	1979	—	2.00	4.00
❏ 2786	Above and Beyond/(Instrumental)	1980	—	2.00	4.00
❏ 70068	Love Is Everywhere/Everyday Man	1981	—	2.00	4.00
EPIC					
❏ JBQ 506 [Q]	Frankenstein/Free Ride	1973	2.50	5.00	10.00
—"Special Coin Operator Release" in quadraphonic; contains single edit of "Frankenstein" and					
unknown version of "Free Ride"					
❏ 10618	Tobacco Road/Now Is the Time	1970	2.00	4.00	8.00
❏ 10740	Good Morning Music/Where Would I Be	1971	2.00	4.00	8.00
❏ 10750	Where Would I Be/Feeling Like a Woman	1971	—	3.00	6.00
—B-side by Patsy Sledd					
❏ 10762	Give It Everything You've Got/You Were My				
	Light	1971	—	3.00	6.00
❏ 10788	Keep Playin' That Rock 'N' Roll/Dying to Live	1971	—	3.00	6.00
❏ 10855	I Can't Turn You Loose/Cool Fool	1972	—	3.00	6.00
❏ 10903	Free Ride/Catchin' Up	1972	2.00	4.00	8.00
❏ 10922	Round and Round/Catchin' Up	1972	2.00	4.00	8.00
❏ 10945	Frankenstein/Hangin' Around	1973	2.00	4.00	8.00
❏ 10967	Frankenstein/Undercover Man	1973	—	2.00	4.00
—Orange label					
❏ 10967	Frankenstein/Undercover Man	1973	—	3.00	6.00
—Yellow label					
❏ 11024	Free Ride/When It Comes	1973	—	2.00	4.00
❏ 11069	Hangin' Around/We All Had a Real Good Time	1973	—	2.00	4.00
❏ 11143	River's Risin'/Animal	1974	—	2.00	4.00
❏ 50034	Easy Street/Do Like Me	1974	—	2.00	4.00
❏ 50060	Miracle of Love/Someone Take My Heart Away	1975	—	2.00	4.00
Albums					
BLUE SKY					
❏ PZ 33483	Jasmine Nightdreams	1975	3.00	6.00	12.00
❏ PZQ 33483 [Q]	Jasmine Nightdreams	1975	5.00	10.00	20.00
❏ PZ 33798	The Edgar Winter Group with Rick Derringer	1975	3.00	6.00	12.00
❏ PZQ 33798 [Q]	The Edgar Winter Group with Rick Derringer	1975	5.00	10.00	20.00
❏ PZ 34858	Re-Cycled	1977	3.00	6.00	12.00
❏ JZ 35989	The Edger Winter Album	1979	3.00	6.00	12.00
❏ JZ 36494	Standing on Rock	1981	3.00	6.00	12.00
EPIC					
❏ BN 26503	Entrance	1970	3.75	7.50	15.00
—Yellow label					
❏ BN 26503	Entrance	1973	3.00	6.00	12.00
—Orange label					
❏ E 30512	Edgar Winter's White Trash	1971	3.75	7.50	15.00
—Yellow label					
❏ KE 30512	Edgar Winter's White Trash	1973	3.00	6.00	12.00
—Orange label					
❏ PE 30512	Edgar Winter's White Trash	1985	2.00	4.00	8.00
—Budget-line reissue; dark blue label					
❏ EG 31249 [(2)]	Roadwork	1987	2.50	5.00	10.00
—Budget-line reissue; dark blue labels					
❏ KEG 31249 [(2)]	Roadwork	1972	5.00	10.00	20.00
—Yellow labels					
❏ KEG 31249 [(2)]	Roadwork	1973	3.75	7.50	15.00
—Orange labels					
❏ EQ 31584 [Q]	They Only Come Out at Night	1973	6.25	12.50	25.00
❏ KE 31584	They Only Come Out at Night	1972	3.75	7.50	15.00
—Yellow label					
❏ KE 31584	They Only Come Out at Night	1973	3.00	6.00	12.00
—Orange label					
❏ PE 31584	They Only Come Out at Night	197?	2.50	5.00	10.00
—Reissue with new prefix; orange label					

Number	Title (A Side/B Side)	Yr	VG	VG+	NM
❑ PE 31584	They Only Come Out at Night	1979	2.00	4.00	8.00
—Budget-line reissue; dark blue label					
❑ PE 32461	Shock Treatment	1974	3.75	7.50	15.00
—Orange label					
❑ PE 32461	Shock Treatment	1985	2.00	4.00	8.00
—Budget-line reissue; dark blue label					
❑ PEQ 32461 [Q]	Shock Treatment	1974	6.25	12.50	25.00
❑ BG 33770 [(2)]	Entrance/White Trash	1975	3.75	7.50	15.00
—Combines 26503 and 30512 into one package					
RHINO					
❑ R1-70709	Mission Earth	1989	3.00	6.00	12.00
❑ R1-70895	The Edger Winter Collection	1989	2.50	5.00	10.00

WINTER, JOHNNY   Also see JOHNNY AND THE JAMMERS.

45s

ATLANTIC

Number	Title (A Side/B Side)	Yr	VG	VG+	NM
❑ 2248	Gangster of Love/Eternally	1964	2.50	5.00	10.00
BLUE SKY					
❑ 2754	Raised on Rock/Pick Up on My Mojo	1974	—	2.00	4.00
❑ 2756	Golden Olden Days of Rock 'N' Roll/Stranger	1975	—	2.00	4.00
BUDDAH					
❑ 168	Out of Sight/Bad News	1970	2.50	5.00	10.00
COLUMBIA					
❑ 44900	I'll Drown in My Tears/I'm Yours and I'm Here	1969	—	2.50	5.00
❑ 45058	Johnny B. Goode/I'm Not Sure	1969	—	2.50	5.00
❑ 45260	Rock and Roll Hoochie Koo/21st Century Man	1970	—	2.50	5.00
❑ 45368	Jumpin' Jack Flash/Good Morning, Little Schoolgirl	1971	—	2.50	5.00
❑ 45860	Silver Train/Rock and Roll	1973	—	2.50	5.00
❑ 45899	Can't You Feel It/Rock and Roll	1973	—	2.50	5.00
❑ 46006	Bad Luck Situation/Stone County	1974	—	2.50	5.00
❑ 46036	Boney Moroney/Hurtin' So Bad	1974	—	2.50	5.00
FROLIC					
❑ 501	That's What Love Does/Shed So Many Tears	1962	12.50	25.00	50.00
❑ 503	Voo Doo Twist/Ease My Pain	1962	25.00	50.00	100.00
❑ 509	Gangster of Love/Eternally	1963	12.50	25.00	50.00
❑ 512	Gone for Bad/I Won't Believe It	1963	15.00	30.00	60.00
GRT					
❑ 9	Gangster of Love/Roadrunner	1969	2.00	4.00	8.00
IMPERIAL					
❑ 66376	Forty-Four/Rollin' & Tumblin'	1969	2.00	4.00	8.00
MGM					
❑ 13380	Gone for Bad/I Won't Believe It	1965	2.00	4.00	8.00
PACEMAKER					
❑ 243	Leavin' Blues/Birds Can't Row Boats	1966	5.00	10.00	20.00
TODD					
❑ 1084	Road Runner/The Guy You Left Behind	1963	5.00	10.00	20.00

Albums

ACCORD

Number	Title (A Side/B Side)	Yr	VG	VG+	NM
❑ SN-7135	Ready for Winter	1981	2.50	5.00	10.00
ALLIGATOR					
❑ 4735	Guitar Slinger	1984	2.50	5.00	10.00
❑ 4742	Serious Business	1985	2.50	5.00	10.00
❑ 4748	Third Degree	1986	2.50	5.00	10.00
BLUE SKY					
❑ PZ 33292	John Dawson Winter III	1974	3.00	6.00	12.00
❑ PZQ 33292 [Q]	John Dawson Winter III	1974	5.00	10.00	20.00
❑ PZ 33944	Captured Live!	1976	3.00	6.00	12.00
—No bar code on cover					
❑ PZ 33944	Captured Live	198?	2.00	4.00	8.00
—Budget-line reissue with bar code on cover					
❑ PZ 34813	Nothin' But the Blues	1977	3.00	6.00	12.00
—No bar code on cover					
❑ PZ 34813	Nothin' But the Blues	198?	2.00	4.00	8.00
—Budget-line reissue with bar code on cover					
❑ JZ 35475	White, Hot and Blue	1978	3.00	6.00	12.00
❑ JZ 36343	Raisin' Cain	1980	3.00	6.00	12.00
BUDDAH					
❑ BDS-7513	First Winter	1969	5.00	10.00	20.00
COLUMBIA					
❑ CS 9826	Johnny Winter	1969	5.00	10.00	20.00
—"360 Sound" label					
❑ CS 9826	Johnny Winter	1970	3.00	6.00	12.00
—Orange label					
❑ PC 9826	Johnny Winter	198?	2.00	4.00	8.00
—Budget-line reissue					
❑ KCS 9947 [(2)]	Second Winter	1969	6.25	12.50	25.00
—"360 Sound" labels; record 2 has music on only one side (other side is blank)					
❑ KCS 9947 [(2)]	Second Winter	1970	3.75	7.50	15.00
—Orange labels					
❑ PC 9947 [(2)]	Second Winter	198?	2.50	5.00	10.00
—Budget-line reissue					
❑ C 30221	Johnny Winter And	1970	3.00	6.00	12.00
—Orange labels					
❑ C 30221	Johnny Winter And	1970	5.00	10.00	20.00
—"360 Sound" label					
❑ PC 30221	Johnny Winter And	198?	2.00	4.00	8.00
—Budget-line reissue					
❑ C 30475	Live/Johnny Winter And	1971	3.75	7.50	15.00
❑ PC 30475	Live/Johnny Winter And	198?	2.00	4.00	8.00
—Budget-line reissue					
❑ CQ 32188 [Q]	Still Alive and Well	1973	6.25	12.50	25.00
❑ KC 32188	Still Alive and Well	1973	3.75	7.50	15.00
❑ PC 32188	Still Alive and Well	198?	2.00	4.00	8.00
—Budget-line reissue					
❑ CQ 32715 [Q]	Saints and Sinners	1974	6.25	12.50	25.00
❑ KC 32715	Saints and Sinners	1974	3.75	7.50	15.00
❑ PC 32715	Saints and Sinners	197?	2.00	4.00	8.00
—Budget-line reissue					
❑ CG 33651 [(2)]	Johnny Winter And//Live/Johnny Winter And	1975	3.75	7.50	15.00
GRT					
❑ 10010	The Johnny Winter Story	1969	5.00	10.00	20.00
IMPERIAL					
❑ LP-12431	The Progressive Blues Experiment	1969	12.50	25.00	50.00
JANUS					
❑ 3008	About Blues	1970	5.00	10.00	20.00

Number	Title (A Side/B Side)	Yr	VG	VG+	NM
❑ 3023	Early Times	1970	6.25	12.50	25.00
❑ 3056 [(2)]	Before the Storm	197?	5.00	10.00	20.00
LIBERTY					
❑ LN-10294	The Progressive Blues Experiment	1986	2.50	5.00	10.00
—Reissue of Imperial LP					
MCA/VOYAGER					
❑ 42241	The Winter of '88	1988	2.50	5.00	10.00
SONOBEAT					
❑ RS-1002	The Progressive Blues Experiment	1968	75.00	150.00	300.00
—Released in plain white cardboard jacket					
UNITED ARTISTS					
❑ UA-LA139-F	Austin, Tex.	1974	3.75	7.50	15.00

WINTER, JOHNNY AND EDGAR   Also see each artist's individual listings.

45s

BLUE SKY

Number	Title (A Side/B Side)	Yr	VG	VG+	NM
❑ 2764	Soul Man/Let the Good Times Roll	1976	—	2.00	4.00

Albums

BLUE SKY

Number	Title (A Side/B Side)	Yr	VG	VG+	NM
❑ ASZ 242 [DJ]	Johnny and Edgar Winter Discuss Together	1976	6.25	12.50	25.00
—Promo-only interview album					
❑ PZ 34033	Together	1976	3.00	6.00	12.00

WINTER, PAUL

45s

A&M

Number	Title (A Side/B Side)	Yr	VG	VG+	NM
❑ 1058	Both Sides Now/Little Train of the Caipira	1969	—	3.00	6.00
—As "The Winter Consort"					
❑ 1182	Mr. Bojangles/Jenny	1970	—	2.50	5.00
❑ 1986	Icarus/Jenny	1977	—	2.00	4.00
COLUMBIA					
❑ 42627	Maria Nobody/Journey to Recife	1962	2.00	4.00	8.00
EPIC					
❑ 10928	Icarus/Minuet	1972	—	2.00	4.00

Albums

A&M

Number	Title (A Side/B Side)	Yr	VG	VG+	NM
❑ SP-4170	The Winter Consort	1968	3.75	7.50	15.00
❑ SP-4207	Something in the Wind	1969	3.75	7.50	15.00
❑ SP-4279	The Road	1970	3.75	7.50	15.00
❑ SP-4653	Earthdance	1977	3.00	6.00	12.00
❑ SP-4698	Common Ground	1978	3.00	6.00	12.00
COLUMBIA					
❑ CL 1925 [M]	Jazz Meets the Bossa Nova	1962	3.75	7.50	15.00
❑ CL 1997 [M]	Jazz Premiere: Washington	1963	3.75	7.50	15.00
❑ CL 2064 [M]	New Jazz on Campus	1963	3.75	7.50	15.00
❑ CL 2155 [M]	Jazz Meets the Folk Song	1964	3.75	7.50	15.00
❑ CL 2272 [M]	The Sound of Ipanema	1965	3.75	7.50	15.00
❑ CL 2315 [M]	Rio	1965	3.75	7.50	15.00
❑ CS 8725 [S]	Jazz Meets the Bossa Nova	1962	5.00	10.00	20.00
❑ CS 8797 [S]	Jazz Premiere: Washington	1963	5.00	10.00	20.00
❑ CS 8864 [S]	New Jazz on Campus	1963	5.00	10.00	20.00
❑ CS 8955 [S]	Jazz Meets the Folk Song	1964	5.00	10.00	20.00
❑ CS 9072 [S]	The Sound of Ipanema	1965	5.00	10.00	20.00
❑ CS 9115 [S]	Rio	1965	5.00	10.00	20.00
EPIC					
❑ KE 31643	Icarus	1972	3.00	6.00	12.00
❑ PE 31643	Icarus	197?	2.50	5.00	10.00
—Reissue					
LIVING MUSIC					
❑ LM-0001 [(2)]	Callings	198?	3.75	7.50	15.00
—Reissue of LMR-1					
❑ LMR-1 [(2)]	Callings	1981	5.00	10.00	20.00
—With 20-page booklet					
❑ LMR-2 [(2)]	Missa Gaia/Earth Mass	1983	5.00	10.00	20.00
❑ LM-0003	Sun Singer	198?	2.50	5.00	10.00
—Reissue of LMR-3					
❑ LMR-3	Sun Singer	1984	3.00	6.00	12.00
❑ LM-0004	Icarus	198?	2.50	5.00	10.00
—Reissue of LMR-4					
❑ LMR-4	Icarus	1985	3.00	6.00	12.00
—Reissue of Epic LP					
❑ LMR-5	Concert for the Earth Live at the United Nations	1985	3.00	6.00	12.00
❑ LMR-6	Canyon	1986	3.00	6.00	12.00
❑ LM-0012	Wintersong	1986	2.50	5.00	10.00
❑ LM-0015	Earthbeat	1987	2.50	5.00	10.00

WINTERS, JONATHAN

Albums

COLUMBIA

Number	Title (A Side/B Side)	Yr	VG	VG+	NM
❑ CL 2811 [M]	Jonathan Winters Wings It!	1968	6.25	12.50	25.00
❑ CS 9611 [S]	Jonathan Winters Wings It!	1968	3.75	7.50	15.00
❑ CS 9799	Stuff 'N' Nonsense	1969	3.75	7.50	15.00
❑ KG 31985 [(2)]	Jonathan Winters Laughs Live	1972	5.00	10.00	20.00
—Reissue of 9611 and 9799 in one package					
❑ PG 31985 [(2)]	Jonathan Winters Laughs Live	197?	3.00	6.00	12.00
—Reissue with new prefix					
VERVE					
❑ MGVS-6099 [S]	The Wonderful World of Jonathan Winters	1960	6.25	12.50	25.00
❑ MGVS-6155 [S]	Down to Earth	1960	6.25	12.50	25.00
❑ MGV-15009 [M]	The Wonderful World of Jonathan Winters	1960	6.25	12.50	25.00
❑ V-15009 [M]	The Wonderful World of Jonathan Winters	1961	5.00	10.00	20.00
❑ V6-15009 [S]	The Wonderful World of Jonathan Winters	1961	5.00	10.00	20.00
—Reissue of 6099					
❑ MGV-15011 [M]	Down to Earth	1960	6.25	12.50	25.00
❑ V-15011 [M]	Down to Earth	1961	5.00	10.00	20.00
❑ V6-15011 [S]	Down to Earth	1961	5.00	10.00	20.00
—Reissue of 6155					
❑ V-15025 [M]	Here's Jonathan	1961	6.25	12.50	25.00
❑ V6-15025 [S]	Here's Jonathan	1961	6.25	12.50	25.00
❑ V-15032 [M]	Another Day, Another World	1962	6.25	12.50	25.00
❑ V6-15032 [R]	Another Day, Another World	196?	3.00	6.00	12.00
❑ V-15035 [M]	Humor As Seen Through the Eyes of Jonathan Winters	1963	6.25	12.50	25.00
❑ V6-15035 [S]	Humor As Seen Through the Eyes of Jonathan Winters	1963	6.25	12.50	25.00
❑ V-15037 [M]	Whistle Stopping with Jonathan Winters	1964	5.00	10.00	20.00

Number	Title (A Side/B Side)	Yr	VG	VG+	NM
❏ V6-15037 [R]	Whistle Stopping with Jonathan Winters	196?	3.00	6.00	12.00
❏ V-15041 [M]	Jonathan Winters' Mad, Mad, Mad, Mad World	1964	5.00	10.00	20.00
❏ V6-15041 [R]	Jonathan Winters' Mad, Mad, Mad, Mad World	196?	3.00	6.00	12.00
❏ V-15047 [M]	Great Moments in Comedy	1965	5.00	10.00	20.00
❏ V6-15047 [R]	Great Moments in Comedy	196?	3.00	6.00	12.00
❏ V-15052 [M]	The Best of Frickert and Suggins	1966	5.00	10.00	20.00
❏ V6-15052 [R]	The Best of Frickert and Suggins	196?	3.00	6.00	12.00
❏ V-15057 [M]	Movies Are Better Than Ever	1967	5.00	10.00	20.00
❏ V6-15057 [R]	Movies Are Better Than Ever	196?	3.00	6.00	12.00

WINWOOD, STEVE Also see BLIND FAITH; THE SPENCER DAVIS GROUP; TRAFFIC.

12-Inch Singles
ISLAND

Number	Title (A Side/B Side)	Yr	VG	VG+	NM
❏ PRO-A-1054 [DJ]	Still in the Game (same on both sides)	1982	2.00	4.00	8.00
❏ PRO-A-2562 [DJ]	Freedom Overspill (Edit) (LP Version)	1986	—	3.00	6.00
❏ PRO-A-2908 [DJ]	Talking Back to the Night (same on both sides)	1987	—	3.00	6.00
❏ 20537	Freedom Overspill (2 versions)/Higher Love/ + 1	1986	2.00	4.00	8.00

VIRGIN

Number	Title (A Side/B Side)	Yr	VG	VG+	NM
❏ 2637 [DJ]	Hearts on Fire (Remix) (LP Version)	1988	—	3.00	6.00
❏ 96620	Don't You Know What the Night Can Do? (Extended)/(Instrumental)	1988	2.00	4.00	8.00

45s
ISLAND

Number	Title (A Side/B Side)	Yr	VG	VG+	NM
❏ 091	Time Is Running Out/Hold On	1977	—	2.50	5.00
❏ 28122	Talking Back to the Night/There's a River	1988	—	2.00	4.00
❏ 28122 [PS]	Talking Back to the Night/There's a River	1988	—	2.00	4.00
❏ 28231	Valerie/Talking Back to the Night (Instrumental)	1987	—	—	3.00
❏ 28231 [PS]	Valerie/Talking Back to the Night (Instrumental)	1987	—	—	3.00
❏ 28472	Back in the High Life Again/Night Train	1987	—	—	3.00
❏ 28472 [PS]	Back in the High Life Again/Night Train	1987	—	—	3.00
❏ 28498	The Finer Things/Night Train	1987	—	—	3.00
❏ 28498 [PS]	The Finer Things/Night Train	1987	—	—	3.00
❏ 28595	Freedom Overspill/Help Me Angel	1986	—	—	3.00
❏ 28595 [PS]	Freedom Overspill/Help Me Angel	1986	—	—	3.00
❏ 28710	Higher Love/And I Go	1986	—	—	3.00
❏ 28710 [PS]	Higher Love/And I Go	1986	—	—	3.00
❏ 29879	Valerie/Slowdown	1982	—	2.50	5.00
❏ 29940	Still in the Game/Dust	1982	—	2.00	4.00
❏ 49656	While You See a Chance/Vacant Chair	1981	—	2.00	4.00
❏ 49656 [PS]	While You See a Chance/Vacant Chair	1981	—	2.50	5.00
❏ 49726	Arc of a Diver/Dust	1981	—	2.00	4.00
❏ 49726 [PS]	Arc of a Diver/Dust	1981	—	2.50	5.00
❏ 49773	Night Train (Part 1)/Night Train (Part 2)	1981	—	2.00	4.00

VIRGIN

Number	Title (A Side/B Side)	Yr	VG	VG+	NM
❏ 98892	One and Only Man/(instrumental)	1990	—	—	3.00
❏ 99234	Hearts On Fire (7" Remix)/(Instrumental)	1989	—	—	3.00
❏ 99234 [PS]	Hearts On Fire (7" Remix)/(Instrumental)	1989	—	—	3.00
❏ 99261	Holding On/(Instrumental)	1988	—	—	3.00
❏ 99261 [PS]	Holding On/(Instrumental)	1988	—	—	3.00
❏ 99290	Don't You Know What the Night Can Do/(Instrumental)	1988	—	—	3.00
❏ 99290 [PS]	Don't You Know What the Night Can Do/(Instrumental)	1988	—	—	3.00
❏ 99326	Roll With It/The Morning Side	1988	—	—	3.00
❏ 99326 [PS]	Roll With It/The Morning Side	1988	—	—	3.00

Albums
ISLAND

Number	Title (A Side/B Side)	Yr	VG	VG+	NM
❏ ILPS 9387	Go	1976	3.00	6.00	12.00

—With Stomo Yamashita and Michael Shrieve

Number	Title (A Side/B Side)	Yr	VG	VG+	NM
❏ ILPS 9494	Steve Winwood	1977	2.50	5.00	10.00
❏ ILPS 9576	Arc of a Diver	1981	2.50	5.00	10.00
❏ ILPS 9777	Talking Back to the Night	1982	2.50	5.00	10.00
❏ 25448	Back in the High Life	1986	2.00	4.00	8.00
❏ 25660	Chronicles	1987	2.00	4.00	8.00

SPRINGBOARD

Number	Title (A Side/B Side)	Yr	VG	VG+	NM
❏ SPB-4040	Winwood & Friends	197?	2.00	4.00	8.00

—Budget release with Winwood material on Side 1 and a collection of Jeff Beck, Yardbirds, Long John Baldry and Jack Bruce/Ginger Baker material on Side 2

UNITED ARTISTS

Number	Title (A Side/B Side)	Yr	VG	VG+	NM
❏ UAS-9950 [(2)]	Winwood	1971	3.75	7.50	15.00

—Without booklet

Number	Title (A Side/B Side)	Yr	VG	VG+	NM
❏ UAS-9950 [(2)]	Winwood	1971	6.25	12.50	25.00

—Collection of tracks Winwood recorded with the Spencer Davis Group, Traffic and Blind Faith; with booklet

VIRGIN

Number	Title (A Side/B Side)	Yr	VG	VG+	NM
❏ 90946	Roll With It	1988	2.00	4.00	8.00
❏ 91405	Refugees of the Heart	1990	3.75	7.50	15.00

WISDOM, BILLY
45s
OUT-A-SITE

Number	Title (A Side/B Side)	Yr	VG	VG+	NM
❏ 11	Handwriting on the Wall/(B-side unknown)	196?	1000.	1750.	2500.

WISDOMS, THE
45s
GAITY

Number	Title (A Side/B Side)	Yr	VG	VG+	NM
❏ 169	Two Hearts Make One Love/Lost in Dreams	1959	150.00	300.00	600.00

WISHBONE ASH
45s
ATLANTIC

Number	Title (A Side/B Side)	Yr	VG	VG+	NM
❏ 3381	Lorelei/(B-side unknown)	1977	—	2.50	5.00

DECCA

Number	Title (A Side/B Side)	Yr	VG	VG+	NM
❏ 32826	Blind Eye/Queen of Torture	1971	2.00	4.00	8.00
❏ 32902	Jail Bait/Vas Dis	1971	2.00	4.00	8.00
❏ 33004	Blowin' Free/No Easy Road	1972	2.00	4.00	8.00

MCA

Number	Title (A Side/B Side)	Yr	VG	VG+	NM
❏ 40041	Rock and Roll Widow/No Easy Road	1973	—	3.00	6.00
❏ 40362	Persephone/Silver Shoes	1975	—	3.00	6.00
❏ 40829	Front Page News/Goodbye Baby, Hello Friends	1977	—	2.00	4.00

Albums
ATLANTIC

Number	Title (A Side/B Side)	Yr	VG	VG+	NM
❏ SD 18164	Locked In	1976	2.50	5.00	10.00
❏ SD 18200	New England	1976	2.50	5.00	10.00

DECCA

Number	Title (A Side/B Side)	Yr	VG	VG+	NM
❏ DL 75249	Wishbone Ash	1971	3.75	7.50	15.00
❏ DL 75295	Pilgrimage	1971	3.75	7.50	15.00
❏ DL 75437	Argus	1972	3.75	7.50	15.00

FANTASY

Number	Title (A Side/B Side)	Yr	VG	VG+	NM
❏ 9629	Twin Barrels Burning	1983	2.50	5.00	10.00

I.R.S.

Number	Title (A Side/B Side)	Yr	VG	VG+	NM
❏ 42101	Nouveau Calls	1988	3.00	6.00	12.00
❏ 82006	Here to Hear	1989	3.00	6.00	12.00

MCA

Number	Title (A Side/B Side)	Yr	VG	VG+	NM
❏ 36	Pilgrimage	1973	3.00	6.00	12.00

—Reissue of Decca 75295

Number	Title (A Side/B Side)	Yr	VG	VG+	NM
❏ 49	Argus	1973	3.00	6.00	12.00

—Reissue of Decca 75437

Number	Title (A Side/B Side)	Yr	VG	VG+	NM
❏ 327	Wishbone Four	1973	3.00	6.00	12.00
❏ 464	There's the Rub	1974	3.00	6.00	12.00
❏ 769	No Smoke Without Fire	198?	2.00	4.00	8.00

—Reissue

Number	Title (A Side/B Side)	Yr	VG	VG+	NM
❏ 770	Just Testing	198?	2.00	4.00	8.00

—Reissue

Number	Title (A Side/B Side)	Yr	VG	VG+	NM
❏ 786	Wishbone Four	198?	2.00	4.00	8.00

—Reissue

Number	Title (A Side/B Side)	Yr	VG	VG+	NM
❏ 787	Argus	198?	2.00	4.00	8.00

—Reissue

Number	Title (A Side/B Side)	Yr	VG	VG+	NM
❏ 2311	Front Page News	1977	2.50	5.00	10.00
❏ 2343	Wishbone Ash	1978	2.50	5.00	10.00

—Reissue of Decca 75249

Number	Title (A Side/B Side)	Yr	VG	VG+	NM
❏ 2344	Argus	1978	2.50	5.00	10.00

—Reissue of MCA 49

Number	Title (A Side/B Side)	Yr	VG	VG+	NM
❏ 2348	Wishbone Four	1978	2.50	5.00	10.00

—Reissue of MCA 327

Number	Title (A Side/B Side)	Yr	VG	VG+	NM
❏ 3060	No Smoke Without Fire	1978	2.50	5.00	10.00
❏ 3221	Just Testing	1980	2.50	5.00	10.00
❏ 5283	Hot Ash	1981	2.50	5.00	10.00
❏ 8006 [(2)]	Live Dates	1973	3.75	7.50	15.00

WITHERS, BILL
12-Inch Singles
COLUMBIA

Number	Title (A Side/B Side)	Yr	VG	VG+	NM
❏ CAS 2112 [DJ]	Something That Turns You On (same on both sides)	1985	2.00	4.00	8.00

45s
COLUMBIA

Number	Title (A Side/B Side)	Yr	VG	VG+	NM
❏ 02071	I Want to Spend the Night/Memories Are That Way	1981	—	2.00	4.00
❏ 02651	USA/Paint Your Pretty Picture	1981	—	2.00	4.00
❏ 02651 [PS]	USA/Paint Your Pretty Picture	1981	—	2.50	5.00
❏ 04841	Oh Yeah!/Just Like the First Time	1985	—	2.00	4.00
❏ 05424	Something That Turns You On/You Tried to Find a Love	1985	—	2.00	4.00
❏ 05424 [PS]	Something That Turns You On/You Tried to Find a Love	1985	—	2.00	4.00
❏ 05675	We Could Be Sweet Lovers/You Just Can't Smile It Away	1985	—	2.00	4.00
❏ 10255	Make Love to Your Mind/I Love You Dawn	1975	—	2.50	5.00
❏ 10308	I Wish You Well/She's Lonely	1976	—	2.50	5.00
❏ 10357	Family Table/Hello Like Before	1976	—	2.50	5.00
❏ 10420	If I Didn't Mean You Well/My Imagination	1976	—	2.50	5.00
❏ 10459	Close to Me/I'll Be with You	1976	—	2.50	5.00
❏ 10627	Lovely Day/It Ain't Because of Me Baby	1977	—	2.50	5.00
❏ 10702	Lovely Night for Dancing/I Want to Spend the Night	1978	—	2.50	5.00
❏ 10892	Don't It Make It Better/Love Is	1979	—	2.00	4.00
❏ 10958	You Got the Stuff/Look to Each Other for Love	1979	—	2.00	4.00

SUSSEX

Number	Title (A Side/B Side)	Yr	VG	VG+	NM
❏ 219	Ain't No Sunshine/Harlem	1971	—	3.00	6.00
❏ 227	Grandma's Hands/Sweet Wanomi	1971	—	2.50	5.00
❏ 227 [DJ]	Grandma's Hands (with Monologue)/(without Monologue)	1971	2.50	5.00	10.00
❏ 235	Lean On Me/Better Off Dead	1972	—	3.00	6.00
❏ 241	Use Me/Let Me in Your Life	1972	—	2.50	5.00
❏ 247	Let Us Love/The Gift of Giving	1972	—	2.50	5.00
❏ 247 [PS]	Let Us Love/The Gift of Giving	1972	2.00	4.00	8.00
❏ 250	Kissing My Love/I Don't Know	1973	—	2.50	5.00
❏ 257	Friend of Mine/Lonely Town, Lonely Street	1973	—	2.50	5.00
❏ 513	The Same Love That Made Me Laugh/Make a Smile for Me	1974	—	2.50	5.00
❏ 518	You/Stories	1974	—	2.50	5.00
❏ 629	Heartbreak Road/Ruby Lee	1974	—	2.50	5.00
❏ 638	Who Is He (And What Is He to You?)/Harlem	1975	—	2.50	5.00

Albums
COLUMBIA

Number	Title (A Side/B Side)	Yr	VG	VG+	NM
❏ PC 33704	Making Music	1975	2.50	5.00	10.00
❏ PC 34327	Naked and Warm	1976	2.50	5.00	10.00
❏ JC 34903	Menagerie	1977	2.50	5.00	10.00
❏ JC 35596	'Bout Love	1979	2.50	5.00	10.00
❏ JC 36877	The Best of Bill Withers	1981	—	—	—

—Canceled?

Number	Title (A Side/B Side)	Yr	VG	VG+	NM
❏ FC 37199	Bill Withers' Greatest Hits	1981	2.50	5.00	10.00

—Re-release of 36877 with "Just the Two of Us" added

Number	Title (A Side/B Side)	Yr	VG	VG+	NM
❏ FC 39887	Watching You Watching Me	1985	2.50	5.00	10.00
❏ PC 40177	Still Bill	1985	2.00	4.00	8.00

—Reissue of Sussex 7014

Number	Title (A Side/B Side)	Yr	VG	VG+	NM
❏ PC 40178	Just As I Am	1985	2.00	4.00	8.00

—Reissue of Sussex 7006

SUSSEX

Number	Title (A Side/B Side)	Yr	VG	VG+	NM
❏ SXBS-7006	Just As I Am	1971	5.00	10.00	20.00
❏ SXBS-7014	Still Bill	1972	5.00	10.00	20.00
❏ SXBS-7025-2 [(2)]	Bill Withers Live at Carnegie Hall	1973	5.00	10.00	20.00
❏ SUX-8032	+'Justments	1974	3.75	7.50	15.00
❏ SUX-8037	The Best of Bill Withers	1975	3.75	7.50	15.00

WITHERSPOON, JIMMY
45s
ABC

Number	Title (A Side/B Side)	Yr	VG	VG+	NM
❏ 11288	Handbags and Gladrags/Stay with Me Baby	1971	—	3.00	6.00

BLUE NOTE

Number	Title (A Side/B Side)	Yr	VG	VG+	NM
❏ XW716	Pearly Whites/Sign on the Building	1975	—	2.50	5.00

BLUESWAY

Number	Title (A Side/B Side)	Yr	VG	VG+	NM
❏ 61028	Just a Dream/I Don't Know	1969	—	3.00	6.00

Number	Title (A Side/B Side)	Yr	VG	VG+	NM
CAPITOL					
❏ 3998	Love Is a Five Letter Word/Other Side of Love	1974	—	2.50	5.00
CHECKER					
❏ 798	Big Daddy/When the Lights Go Out	1954	7.50	15.00	30.00
❏ 810	Time Brings About a Change/Waiting for Your Return	1955	7.50	15.00	30.00
❏ 826	It Ain't No Secret/Why Do I Love You Like I Do	1955	7.50	15.00	30.00
FEDERAL					
❏ 12095	Foolish Prayer/Two Little Girls	1952	7.50	15.00	30.00
❏ 12099	Lucille/Blues in Trouble	1952	7.50	15.00	30.00
❏ 12107	Don't Tell Me Now/Corn Whiskey	1952	7.50	15.00	30.00
❏ 12118	Jay's Blues (Part 1)/Jay's Blues (Part 2)	1953	7.50	15.00	30.00
❏ 12128	One Fine Gal/Back Home	1953	7.50	15.00	30.00
❏ 12138	Back Door Blues/Last Mile	1953	7.50	15.00	30.00
❏ 12155	Fast Women and Sloe Gin/Miss Mistreater	1953	7.50	15.00	30.00
❏ 12156	Sad Life/Move Me Baby	1953	12.50	25.00	50.00
—With the Lamplighters					
❏ 12173	24 Sad Hours/Just for You	1954	7.50	15.00	30.00
❏ 12180	It/Highway to Happiness	1954	7.50	15.00	30.00
❏ 12189	Oh Boy/I Done Told You	1954	7.50	15.00	30.00
GNP CRESCENDO					
❏ 156	Ain't Nobody's Business/No Rollin' Blues	1959	3.00	6.00	12.00
HIFI					
❏ 594	Everytime I Feel the Spirit/ Oh Mary Don't You Weep	1960	3.00	6.00	12.00
KENT					
❏ 4551	Ain't Nobody's Business (Part 1)/ Ain't Nobody's Business (Part 2)	1971	—	3.00	6.00
KING					
❏ 5997	Foolish Prayer/Two Little Girls	1965	2.50	5.00	10.00
MODERN					
❏ 857	The Wind Is Blowin'/My Baby Make a Change	1952	10.00	20.00	40.00
—Note: Earlier Jimmy Witherspoon 45s on Modern are not known to exist					
❏ 877	Love My Baby/Daddy Pinocchio	1952	10.00	20.00	40.00
❏ 895	Baby Baby/Slow Your Speed	1953	10.00	20.00	40.00
❏ 903	Each Step of the Way/Let Jesus Fix It for You	1953	10.00	20.00	40.00
❏ 909	Oh Mother, Dear Mother/I'll Be Right On Down	1953	10.00	20.00	40.00
PACIFIC JAZZ					
❏ 327	Ain't Nobody's Business/Times Have Changed	1961	2.50	5.00	10.00
PRESTIGE					
❏ 266	One Scotch, One Bourbon, One Beer/ Baby, Baby, Baby	196?	2.50	5.00	10.00
❏ 274	Mean Ole Frisco/Sail On Little Girl	196?	2.50	5.00	10.00
❏ 291	Goin' to Chicago Blues/You Made You Love You	196?	2.50	5.00	10.00
❏ 298	I Had a Dream/S.K. Blues	1963	2.50	5.00	10.00
❏ 307	Money's Gettin' Cheaper/Ever In	1963	2.50	5.00	10.00
❏ 340	I Never Will Marry/Happy Blues	1964	2.50	5.00	10.00
❏ 341	Some of My Best Friends Are the Blues/ You're Next	1964	2.50	5.00	10.00
❏ 358	Come On and Walk with Me/ Two Hearts Are Better Than One	196?	2.00	4.00	8.00
❏ 378	Love Me Right/ Make This Heart of Mine Smile Again	196?	2.00	4.00	8.00
❏ 402	I Never Thought I'd See the Day/ If There Wasn't Any You	196?	2.00	4.00	8.00
RCA VICTOR					
❏ 47-6977	Ain't Nobody's Business/Who Baby Who	1957	5.00	10.00	20.00
❏ 47-7377	Confessin' the Blues/ Ooo Wee, Then the Lights Go Out	1958	5.00	10.00	20.00
REPRISE					
❏ 0275	Key to the Highway/ I'd Rather Drink Muddy Water	1964	2.00	4.00	8.00
❏ 20013	The Masquerade Is Over/I Don't Know	1961	2.50	5.00	10.00
❏ 20029	Warm Your Heart/Hey Mrs. Jones	1961	2.50	5.00	10.00
VEE JAY					
❏ 322	Everything But You/I Know, I Know	1959	3.00	6.00	12.00
VERVE					
❏ 10439	It's All Over But the Crying/My Blue Tears	1966	2.00	4.00	8.00
❏ 10495	Fast Forty Blues/My Baby Quit Me	1967	2.00	4.00	8.00
WORLD PACIFIC					
❏ 814	Ain't Nobody's Business/ There's Good Rockin' Tonight	1960	3.00	6.00	12.00
Albums					
ABC					
❏ 717	Handbags and Gladrags	1970	6.25	12.50	25.00
ANALOGUE PRODUCTIONS					
❏ APR 3008	Evenin' Blues	199?	3.75	7.50	15.00
BLUE NOTE					
❏ BN-LA534-G	Spoonful	1976	3.00	6.00	12.00
BLUESWAY					
❏ BLS-6026	Blues Singer	1969	6.25	12.50	25.00
❏ BLS-6040	Hunh	1970	6.25	12.50	25.00
❏ BLS-6051	The Best of Jimmy Witherspoon	1970	6.25	12.50	25.00
CAPITOL					
❏ ST-11360	Love Is a Five Letter Word	1975	3.00	6.00	12.00
CHESS					
❏ CH-93003	Spoon So Easy: The Chess Years	1990	3.00	6.00	12.00
CONSTELLATION					
❏ CM 1422 [M]	Take This Hammer	1964	12.50	25.00	50.00
❏ CMS 1422 [R]	Take This Hammer	1964	7.50	15.00	30.00
CROWN					
❏ CST-215 [S]	Jimmy Witherspoon Sings the Blues	1961	25.00	50.00	100.00
—Black vinyl; this value assumes that this is in true stereo, as the red vinyl version is, but this has not been confirmed					
❏ CST-215 [S]	Jimmy Witherspoon Sings the Blues	1961	37.50	75.00	150.00
—Red vinyl; contrary to prior reports, this album -- at least the red vinyl version -- is in true stereo!					
❏ CLP-5156 [M]	Jimmy Witherspoon	1959	20.00	40.00	80.00
—Black label, silver print					
❏ CLP-5156 [M]	Jimmy Witherspoon	1961	6.25	12.50	25.00
—Gray label, black print					
❏ CLP-5192 [M]	Jimmy Witherspoon Sings the Blues	1959	20.00	40.00	80.00
—Black label, silver print					
❏ CLP-5192 [M]	Jimmy Witherspoon Sings the Blues	1961	6.25	12.50	25.00
—Gray label, black print					

Number	Title (A Side/B Side)	Yr	VG	VG+	NM
FANTASY					
❏ OBC-511	Evenin' Blues	1988	3.00	6.00	12.00
—Reissue of Prestige 7300					
❏ OBC-527	Baby, Baby, Baby	1990	3.00	6.00	12.00
—Reissue of Prestige 7290					
❏ 9660	Rockin' L.A.	1989	3.00	6.00	12.00
❏ 24701 [(2)]	The 'Spoon Concerts	1972	5.00	10.00	20.00
HIFI					
❏ R-421 [M]	At the Monterey Jazz Festival	1959	25.00	50.00	100.00
❏ SR-421 [S]	At the Monterey Jazz Festival	1959	15.00	30.00	60.00
❏ R-422 [M]	Feelin' the Spirit	1959	25.00	50.00	100.00
❏ SR-422 [S]	Feelin' the Spirit	1959	15.00	30.00	60.00
❏ R-426 [M]	Jimmy Witherspoon at the Renaissance	1959	25.00	50.00	100.00
❏ SR-426 [S]	Jimmy Witherspoon at the Renaissance	1959	15.00	30.00	60.00
JAZZ MAN					
❏ 5013	Jimmy Witherspoon Sings the Blues	1980	3.00	6.00	12.00
LAX					
❏ PW 37115	Love Is a Five Letter Word	1981	2.50	5.00	10.00
—Reissue of Capitol LP					
MUSE					
❏ MR-5288	Jimmy Witherspoon Sings the Blues	1983	2.50	5.00	10.00
❏ MR-5327	Midnight Lady Called the Blues	1986	2.50	5.00	10.00
PRESTIGE					
❏ PRLP-7290 [M]	Baby, Baby, Baby	1963	10.00	20.00	40.00
❏ PRST-7290 [S]	Baby, Baby, Baby	1963	10.00	20.00	40.00
❏ PRLP-7300 [M]	Evenin' Blues	1964	10.00	20.00	40.00
❏ PRST-7300 [S]	Evenin' Blues	1964	10.00	20.00	40.00
❏ PRLP-7314 [M]	Blues Around the Clock	1964	10.00	20.00	40.00
❏ PRST-7314 [S]	Blues Around the Clock	1964	10.00	20.00	40.00
❏ PRLP-7327 [M]	Blue Spoon	1964	10.00	20.00	40.00
❏ PRST-7327 [S]	Blue Spoon	1964	10.00	20.00	40.00
❏ PRLP-7356 [M]	Some of My Best Friends Are the Blues	1965	6.25	12.50	25.00
❏ PRST-7356 [S]	Some of My Best Friends Are the Blues	1965	6.25	12.50	25.00
❏ PRLP-7418 [M]	Spoon in London	1966	6.25	12.50	25.00
❏ PRST-7418 [S]	Spoon in London	1966	6.25	12.50	25.00
❏ PRLP-7475 [M]	Blues for Easy Livers	1967	6.25	12.50	25.00
❏ PRST-7475 [S]	Blues for Easy Livers	1967	5.00	10.00	20.00
❏ PRST-7713	The Best of Jimmy Witherspoon	1969	5.00	10.00	20.00
❏ 7855	Mean Old Frisco	1974	3.75	7.50	15.00
RCA VICTOR					
❏ ANL1-1048	Goin' to Kansas City Blues	1976	2.50	5.00	10.00
—Reissue					
❏ LPM-1639 [M]	Goin' to Kansas City Blues	1957	25.00	50.00	100.00
REPRISE					
❏ R-2008 [M]	Spoon	1961	10.00	20.00	40.00
❏ R9-2008 [S]	Spoon	1961	15.00	30.00	60.00
❏ R-6012 [M]	Hey, Mrs. Jones	1961	10.00	20.00	40.00
❏ R9-6012 [S]	Hey, Mrs. Jones	1961	15.00	30.00	60.00
❏ R-6059 [M]	Roots	1962	10.00	20.00	40.00
❏ R9-6059 [S]	Roots	1962	15.00	30.00	60.00
UNITED					
❏ 7715	A Spoonful of Blues	197?	3.00	6.00	12.00
VERVE					
❏ V-5007 [M]	Blue Point of View	1966	5.00	10.00	20.00
❏ V6-5007 [S]	Blue Point of View	1966	6.25	12.50	25.00
❏ V-5030 [M]	Blues Is Now	1967	6.25	12.50	25.00
❏ V6-5030 [S]	Blues Is Now	1967	5.00	10.00	20.00
❏ V-5050 [M]	A Spoonful of Soul	1968	7.50	15.00	30.00
❏ V6-5050 [S]	A Spoonful of Soul	1968	5.00	10.00	20.00
WORLD PACIFIC					
❏ WP-1267 [M]	Singin' the Blues	1959	25.00	50.00	100.00
❏ WP-1402 [M]	There's Good Rockin' Tonight	1961	15.00	30.00	60.00
—Reissue of 1267					

WITHERSPOON, JIMMY, AND RICHARD "GROOVE" HOLMES
Albums

Number	Title (A Side/B Side)	Yr	VG	VG+	NM
OLYMPIC GOLD MEDAL					
❏ 7107	Groovin' and Spoonin'	1974	3.00	6.00	12.00
SURREY					
❏ S-1106 [M]	Blues for Spoon and Groove	1965	6.25	12.50	25.00
❏ SS-1106 [S]	Blues for Spoon and Groove	1965	7.50	15.00	30.00

WITHERSPOON, JIMMY, AND GERRY MULLIGAN
Albums

Number	Title (A Side/B Side)	Yr	VG	VG+	NM
EVEREST ARCHIVE OF FOLK & JAZZ					
❏ 264	Jimmy Witherspoon and Gerry Mulligan	197?	3.00	6.00	12.00

WITHERSPOON, JIMMY, AND BEN WEBSTER
Albums

Number	Title (A Side/B Side)	Yr	VG	VG+	NM
VERVE					
❏ V6-8835	Previously Unreleased Recordings	197?	3.75	7.50	15.00

WIZARDS FROM KANSAS, THE
Albums

Number	Title (A Side/B Side)	Yr	VG	VG+	NM
MERCURY					
❏ SR-61309	The Wizards from Kansas	1970	50.00	100.00	200.00

WOLFE, DANNY
45s

Number	Title (A Side/B Side)	Yr	VG	VG+	NM
DOT					
❏ 15591	Pretty Blue Jean Baby/Once with You	1957	10.00	20.00	40.00
❏ 15667	Let's Flat Get It/I'm Glad I Waited	1957	15.00	30.00	60.00
❏ 15715	I'd Rather Be Lucky/Pucker Paint	1958	10.00	20.00	40.00

WOMACK, BOBBY Also see THE VALENTINOS.
12-Inch Singles

Number	Title (A Side/B Side)	Yr	VG	VG+	NM
MCA					
❏ L33-17104 [DJ]	Gypsy Woman/Whatever Happened to the Times? (2 versions)	1986	2.00	4.00	8.00
❏ 23688	(I Wanna) Make Love to You/Whatever Happened to the Times?	1986	2.00	4.00	8.00
❏ 23795	Living in a Box (3 versions)	1987	—	3.00	6.00
❏ 23827	Outside Myself (3 versions)	1988	—	3.00	6.00
SOLAR					
❏ ZAS 1923 [DJ]	Save the Children (3 versions)	1989	2.00	4.00	8.00

45s

ARISTA

Number	Title (A Side/B Side)	Yr	VG	VG+	NM
0421	How Could You Break My Heart/I Honestly Love You	1979	—	2.00	4.00
0446	The Roads of Life/Give It Up	1979	—	2.00	4.00

ATLANTIC

Number	Title (A Side/B Side)	Yr	VG	VG+	NM
2388	Night Train/It's Karate Time	1967	2.50	5.00	10.00

BEVERLY GLEN

Number	Title (A Side/B Side)	Yr	VG	VG+	NM
2000	If You Think You're Lonely Now/Secrets	1981	—	2.00	4.00
2001	Where Do We Go from Here/Just My Imagination	1982	—	2.00	4.00
2012	Love Has Finally Come at Last/American Dream	1984	—	2.00	4.00
—With Patti LaBelle					
2014	Tell Me Why/Through the Eyes of a Child	1984	—	2.00	4.00
—B-side with Patti LaBelle					
2018	It Takes a Lot of Strength to Say Goodbye/Who's Foolin' Who	1984	—	2.00	4.00
—A-side with Patti LaBelle					
2021	Someday We'll All Be Free/I Wish I Had Someone to Go Home To	1985	—	2.00	4.00
2023	I'm So Proud/Searching for My Love	1985	—	2.00	4.00

CHECKER

Number	Title (A Side/B Side)	Yr	VG	VG+	NM
1122	Lonesome Man/I Found a True Love	1965	3.75	7.50	15.00

COLUMBIA

Number	Title (A Side/B Side)	Yr	VG	VG+	NM
10437	Home Is Where the Heart Is/We've Only Just Begun	1976	—	2.50	5.00
10493	Standing in the Safety Zone/A Change Is Gonna Come	1977	—	2.50	5.00
10672	Trust Your Heart/When Love Begins, Friendship Ends	1978	—	2.50	5.00
10732	Wind It Up/Stop Before We Start	1978	—	2.50	5.00

LIBERTY

Number	Title (A Side/B Side)	Yr	VG	VG+	NM
56186	I'm Gonna Forget About You/Don't Look Back	1970	2.00	4.00	8.00
56206	Something/Everybody's Talkin'	1970	2.00	4.00	8.00

MCA

Number	Title (A Side/B Side)	Yr	VG	VG+	NM
52624	I Wish He Didn't Trust Me So Much/Got to Be with You Tonight	1985	—	2.00	4.00
52624 [PS]	I Wish He Didn't Trust Me So Much/Got to Be with You Tonight	1985	—	2.00	4.00
52709	Let Me Kiss It Where It Hurts/Check It Out	1985	—	2.00	4.00
52793	Gypsy Woman/What Evert Happened to the Times	1986	—	—	3.00
52955	(I Wanna) Make Love to You/The Launch	1986	—	—	3.00
52955 [PS]	(I Wanna) Make Love to You/The Launch	1986	—	—	3.00
53190	Living in a Box/I Can't Stay Mad	1987	—	—	3.00
53263	Outside Myself/A Woman Likes to Hear Than	1988	—	—	3.00

MINIT

Number	Title (A Side/B Side)	Yr	VG	VG+	NM
32024	Baby, I Can't Stand It/Trust Me	1967	2.50	5.00	10.00
32030	Somebody Special/Broadway Walk	1967	2.50	5.00	10.00
32037	What Is This/What You Gonna Do (When Your Love Is Gone)	1968	2.50	5.00	10.00
32048	Fly Me to the Moon/Take Me	1968	2.50	5.00	10.00
32055	California Dreamin'/Baby, You Oughta Think It Over	1968	2.50	5.00	10.00
32059	I Left My Heart in San Francisco/Love, The Time Is Now	1969	2.00	4.00	8.00
32071	It's Gonna Rain/Thank You	1969	2.00	4.00	8.00
32081	How I Miss You Baby/Tried and Convicted	1969	2.00	4.00	8.00
32093	More Than I Can Stand/Arkansas State Prison	1970	2.00	4.00	8.00

SOLAR

Number	Title (A Side/B Side)	Yr	VG	VG+	NM
74006	Save the Children/(Instrumental)	1989	—	—	3.00

THE RIGHT STUFF

Number	Title (A Side/B Side)	Yr	VG	VG+	NM
58815	Dear Santa Claus/Dear Santa Claus (Kids Version)	1999	—	—	3.00

UNITED ARTISTS

Number	Title (A Side/B Side)	Yr	VG	VG+	NM
0123	That's the Way I Feel About Cha/Woman's Gotta Have It	1973	—	2.00	4.00
—"Silver Spotlight Series" reissue					
XW196	Across 110th Street/Hang On In There	1973	—	2.50	5.00
XW255	Nobody Wants You When You're Down and Out/I'm Thru Trying to Prove My Love	1973	—	2.50	5.00
XW375	Lookin' for a Love/Let It Hang Out	1973	—	2.50	5.00
XW439	You're Welcome, Stop On By/I Don't Want to Be Hurt	1974	—	2.50	5.00
XW525	Lookin' for a Love/Nobody Wants You When You're Down and Out	1974	—	2.00	4.00
—Reissue					
XW526	Harry Hippie/Sweet Caroline	1974	—	2.00	4.00
—Reissue					
XW527	California Dreamin'/Fly Me to the Moon	1974	—	2.50	5.00
XW561	I Don't Know/Yes, Jesus Loves Me	1974	—	2.50	5.00
XW621	Check It Out/Interlude No. 2	1975	—	2.50	5.00
XW674	It's All Over Now/Git It	1975	—	2.50	5.00
XW735	Where There's a Will, There's a Way/Everything's Gonna Be Alright	1975	—	2.50	5.00
XW763	Daylight/Trust Me	1976	—	2.50	5.00
XW804	I Feel a Groove Comin' On/Trust Me	1976	—	2.50	5.00
50773	The Preacher/More Than I Can Stand	1971	—	3.00	6.00
50816	Communication/Fire and Rain	1971	—	3.00	6.00
50847	That's the Way I Feel About 'Cha/Come L'Amore	1971	—	3.00	6.00
50902	Woman's Gotta Have It/Give It Back	1972	—	3.00	6.00
50946	Harry Hippie/Sweet Caroline (Good Times Never Seemed So Good)	1972	—	3.00	6.00
50988 [DJ]	Harry Hippie (mono/stereo)	1972	2.00	4.00	8.00
—Apparently, no stock copy exists					

Albums

ARISTA

Number	Title	Yr	VG	VG+	NM
AB 4222	Roads of Life	1979	2.50	5.00	10.00

BEVERLY GLEN

Number	Title	Yr	VG	VG+	NM
10000	The Poet	1981	2.50	5.00	10.00
10003	The Poet II	1984	2.50	5.00	10.00

COLUMBIA

Number	Title	Yr	VG	VG+	NM
PC 34384	Home Is Where the Heart Is	1977	2.50	5.00	10.00
JC 35083	Pieces	1978	2.50	5.00	10.00

LIBERTY

Number	Title	Yr	VG	VG+	NM
LST-7645	The Womack "Live"	1971	3.00	6.00	12.00
LN-10171	Bobby Womack's Greatest Hits	198?	2.00	4.00	8.00
—Budget-line reissue of United Artists 346					

MCA

Number	Title	Yr	VG	VG+	NM
5617	So Many Rivers	1985	2.00	4.00	8.00

MINIT

Number	Title	Yr	VG	VG+	NM
24014	Fly Me to the Moon	1968	7.50	15.00	30.00
24027	My Prescription	1969	7.50	15.00	30.00

UNITED ARTISTS

Number	Title	Yr	VG	VG+	NM
UA-LA043-F	Facts of Life	1973	3.00	6.00	12.00
UA-LA199-G	Lookin' for a Love Again	1974	3.00	6.00	12.00
UA-LA346-G	Bobby Womack's Greatest Hits	1974	3.00	6.00	12.00
UA-LA353-G	I Don't Know What the World Is Coming To	1975	3.00	6.00	12.00
UA-LA544-G	Safety Zone	1975	3.00	6.00	12.00
UA-LA638-G	B.W. Goes C and W	1976	3.00	6.00	12.00
LM-1002	Understanding	1980	2.00	4.00	8.00
—Reissue of 5577					
UAS-5225	Across 110th Street	1972	3.00	6.00	12.00
UAS-5539	Communication	1971	3.00	6.00	12.00
UAS-5577	Understanding	1972	3.00	6.00	12.00

WOMB

45s

DOT

Number	Title (A Side/B Side)	Yr	VG	VG+	NM
17250	Hang On/My Baby Thinks About the Good Things	1969	3.00	6.00	12.00

Albums

DOT

Number	Title	Yr	VG	VG+	NM
DLP-25933	Womb	1969	5.00	10.00	20.00
DLP-25959	Overdub	1969	5.00	10.00	20.00

WOMBLES, THE

45s

COLUMBIA

Number	Title (A Side/B Side)	Yr	VG	VG+	NM
10013	Wombling Summer Party/Wimbledon Sunset	1974	—	2.00	4.00
10033	Remember You're a Womble/The Wellington Womble	1974	—	2.00	4.00

EPIC

Number	Title (A Side/B Side)	Yr	VG	VG+	NM
11119	Wombling Song/Wombles Everywhere	1974	—	2.50	5.00

Albums

COLUMBIA

Number	Title	Yr	VG	VG+	NM
KC 33140	Remember You're a Womble	1974	3.00	6.00	12.00

WOMENFOLK, THE

45s

RCA VICTOR

Number	Title (A Side/B Side)	Yr	VG	VG+	NM
47-8301	Little Boxes/Love Came a-Tricklin' Down	1964	2.00	4.00	8.00
47-8562	My Heart Tells Me to Believe/The Way I Feel	1965	2.00	4.00	8.00
47-8782	The Last Thing on My Mind/Meditation	1966	2.00	4.00	8.00

Albums — RCA VICTOR

Number	Title	Yr	VG	VG+	NM
LPM-2832 [M]	The Womenfolk	1964	3.00	6.00	12.00
LSP-2832 [S]	The Womenfolk	1964	3.75	7.50	15.00
LPM-2919 [M]	Never Underestimate the Power of the Womenfolk	1964	3.00	6.00	12.00
LSP-2919 [S]	Never Underestimate the Power of the Womenfolk	1964	3.75	7.50	15.00
LPM-2991 [M]	The Womenfolk at the Hungry I	1965	3.00	6.00	12.00
LSP-2991 [S]	The Womenfolk at the Hungry I	1965	3.75	7.50	15.00
LPM-3527 [M]	Man Oh Man	1966	3.00	6.00	12.00
LSP-3527 [S]	Man Oh Man	1966	3.75	7.50	15.00

WONDER, STEVIE Also see PAUL McCARTNEY AND STEVIE WONDER.

12-Inch Singles

MOTOWN

Number	Title (A Side/B Side)	Yr	VG	VG+	NM
PR 161 [DJ]	Love Light in Flight (Special 12" Version 6:30)(Instrumental 7:38)	1984	2.50	5.00	10.00
L33-1065 [DJ]	Keep Our Love Alive/(Instrumental)	1990	2.00	4.00	8.00
L33-1093 [DJ]	Gotta Have You (3 versions)	1991	2.50	5.00	10.00
37463 1215 1 [DJ]	Tomorrow Robins Will Sing (7 versions)	1995	2.50	5.00	10.00
37463 1261 1 [DJ]	For Your Love (Single Version) (LP Version)(Instrumental) (A Cappella)	1995	2.50	5.00	10.00
37463 1482 1 [DJ]	Kiss Lonely Goodbye (6 versions)	1996	3.75	7.50	15.00
L33-1602 [DJ]	Fun Day (Edit) (LP) (Instrumental)	1991	2.50	5.00	10.00
L33-1690 [DJ]	Fun Day (8 versions)	1991	3.00	6.00	12.00
4517 MG	Happy Birthday/Martin Luther King: Excerpts from His Speeches	1984	20.00	40.00	80.00
4527 MG	Don't Drive Drunk (12" Version 8:18)(Instrumental 8:27)/Did I Hear You Say You Love Me (8:27)	1984	2.00	4.00	8.00
4593 MG	Skeletons (6:43)/(Instrumental)	1987	2.00	4.00	8.00
MOT-4616	My Eyes Don't Cry (Extended Version 6:30)(Radio Edit 5:18) (Dub Mix 7:21)	1988	2.00	4.00	8.00
MOT-4626	With Each Beat of My Heart (LP) (Edit)(Instrumental)	1988	2.00	4.00	8.00
MOT12-4665	Keep Our Love Alive/(Instrumental)	1990	2.00	4.00	8.00
MOT12-4759	Gotta Have You (3 versions)/Feeding Off the Love of the Land	1991	2.50	5.00	10.00
L33-17755 [DJ]	With Each Beat of My Heart (LP) (Edit)(Instrumental)	1987	2.00	4.00	8.00

TAMLA

Number	Title (A Side/B Side)	Yr	VG	VG+	NM
PR 61 [DJ]	A Seed's a Star-Tree Medley/Power Flower//Black Orchid/Outside My Window	1979	5.00	10.00	20.00
—Promo-only sampler for "Journey Through the Secret Life of Plants"					
PR 76 [DJ]	Master Blaster (Jammin') (6:11)/Master Blaster (Dub) (6:27)	1980	17.50	35.00	70.00
PR 77 [DJ]	I Ain't Gonna Stand For It/All I Do/Did I Hear You Say You Love Me	1980	15.00	30.00	60.00
—Promo-only sampler for "Hotter Than July"					
PR 98/99 [(2)DJ]	Do I Do (10:27)(Instrumental 10:27)//Front Line (6:01) (Instrumental 6:01)	1982	6.25	12.50	25.00
—Two-record promo set					
PR 186 [DJ]	Land of La La (8:40)/(Instrumental)	1986	2.00	4.00	8.00
4548 TG	Part Time Lover (12-Inch Vocal Version 8:20)(12-Inch Instrumental 8:20)	1985	2.50	5.00	10.00
4553 TG	Go Home (12" Version 9:22)/(Radio Edit of 12" Version 6:26) (Instrumental 8:36)	1985	2.50	5.00	10.00

45s

GORDY

Number	Title (A Side/B Side)	Yr	VG	VG+	NM
❑ 7076	Alfie/More Than a Dream	1968	6.25	12.50	25.00

—As "Eivets Rednow" (read it backwards)

MOTOWN

Number	Title (A Side/B Side)	Yr	VG	VG+	NM
❑ 1745	I Just Called to Say I Love You/(Instrumental)	1984	—	—	3.00
❑ 1745 [PS]	I Just Called to Say I Love You/(Instrumental)	1984	10.00	20.00	40.00

—Sleeve is labeled promo only, though it has been found on the (very) occasional stock copy

❑ 1769	Love Light in Flight/It's More Than You	1984	—	—	3.00
❑ 1769 [PS]	Love Light in Flight/It's More Than You	1984	—	2.00	4.00
❑ 1907	Skeletons/(Instrumental)	1987	—	—	3.00
❑ 1907 [PS]	Skeletons/(Instrumental)	1987	—	2.00	4.00
❑ 1919	You Will Know/(Instrumental)	1988	—	—	3.00
❑ 1919 [DJ]	You Will Know/You Will Know-Stevie Wonder Interview	1988	—	3.00	6.00

—Promo-only release

❑ 1919 [PS]	You Will Know/(Instrumental)	1988	—	2.00	4.00
❑ 1919 [PS]	You Will Know/You Will Know-Stevie Wonder Interview	1988	—	3.00	6.00

—Only the promo sleeve mentions the interview

❑ 1946	My Eyes Don't Cry/(Instrumental)	1988	—	—	3.00
❑ 1946 [PS]	My Eyes Don't Cry/(Instrumental)	1988	—	—	3.00
❑ 1953	With Each Beat of My Heart/(Instrumental)	1989	—	—	3.00
❑ 1990	Keep Our Love Alive/(Instrumental)	1990	—	2.50	5.00
❑ 2081	Gotta Have You/Feeding Off the Love of the Land	1991	—	2.00	4.00
❑ 2127	Fun Day/(Instrumental)	1991	—	2.00	4.00
❑ 2143	These Three Words (same on both sides)	1991	—	2.00	4.00
❑ 860310-7	For Your Love/(Instrumental)	1995	—	2.00	4.00
❑ 860418-7	Tomorrow Robins Will Sing/For Your Love	1995	—	2.00	4.00

MOTOWN YESTERYEAR

❑ Y 620F	I Wish/Sir Duke	1978	—	—	3.00

—Reissue

| ❑ Y 621F | Another Star/As | 1978 | — | — | 3.00 |

—Reissue

| ❑ Y 646F | Master Blaster (Jammin')/Master Blaster (Dub) | 1982 | — | — | 3.00 |

—Reissue

| ❑ Y 647F | I Ain't Gonna Stand For It/Lately | 1982 | — | — | 3.00 |

—Reissue

| ❑ Y 657F | That Girl/Do I Do | 1983 | — | — | 3.00 |

—Reissue

| ❑ Y 684F | I Just Called to Say I Love You/Love Light in Flight | 1985 | — | — | 3.00 |

—Reissue

| ❑ Y 685F | Don't Drive Drunk/(Instrumental) | 1985 | — | — | 3.00 |

—First U.S. edition of this song on 45

TAMLA

❑ 1602	That Girl/All I Do	1982	—	2.00	4.00
❑ 1612	Do I Do/Rocket Love	1982	—	2.00	4.00
❑ 1639	Ribbon in the Sky/Black Orchid	1982	—	2.00	4.00
❑ 1639 [PS]	Ribbon in the Sky/Black Orchid	1982	—	2.00	4.00
❑ 1808	Part-Time Lover/(Instrumental)	1985	—	—	3.00
❑ 1808 [PS]	Part-Time Lover/(Instrumental)	1985	—	2.00	4.00
❑ 1817	Go Home/(Instrumental)	1985	—	—	3.00
❑ 1817 [PS]	Go Home/(Instrumental)	1985	—	2.00	4.00
❑ 1832	Overjoyed/(Instrumental)	1986	—	—	3.00
❑ 1832 [PS]	Overjoyed/(Instrumental)	1986	—	2.00	4.00
❑ 1846	Land of La La/(Instrumental)	1986	—	—	3.00
❑ 1846 [PS]	Land of La La/(Instrumental)	1986	—	2.00	4.00
❑ 54061	I Call It Pretty Music But The Old People Call It the Blues (Part 1)/I Call It Pretty Music But The Old People Call It the Blues (Part 2)	1962	7.50	15.00	30.00
❑ 54061 [PS]	I Call It Pretty Music But The Old People Call It the Blues (Part 1)/I Call It Pretty Music But The Old People Call It the Blues (Part 2)	1962	20.00	40.00	80.00
❑ 54070	Little Water Boy/La La La La La	1962	6.25	12.50	25.00
❑ 54074	Contract on Love/Sunset	1963	6.25	12.50	25.00
❑ 54080	Fingertips — Pt. 2/Fingertips — Pt. 1	1963	5.00	10.00	20.00
❑ 54080 [PS]	Fingertips — Pt. 2/Fingertips — Pt. 1	1963	12.50	25.00	50.00
❑ 54086	Workout Stevie, Workout/Monkey Talk	1963	3.75	7.50	15.00
❑ 54090	Castles in the Sand/Thank You (For Loving Me All the Way)	1964	3.75	7.50	15.00

—Up to and including this, as "Little Stevie Wonder"

❑ 54096	Hey Harmonica Man/This Little Girl	1964	3.75	7.50	15.00
❑ 54096 [PS]	Hey Harmonica Man/This Little Girl	1964	10.00	20.00	40.00
❑ 54103	Sad Boy/Happy Street	1964	5.00	10.00	20.00
❑ 54108	Pretty Little Angel/Tears in Vain	1964	—	—	—

—Unreleased

❑ 54114	Kiss Me Baby/Tears in Vain	1965	3.00	6.00	12.00
❑ 54119	High Heel Sneakers/Music Talk	1965	3.00	6.00	12.00
❑ 54119	High Heel Sneakers/Funny How Time Slips Away	1965	5.00	10.00	20.00
❑ 54124	Uptight (Everything's Alright)/Purple Rain Drops	1965	3.75	7.50	15.00
❑ 54130	Nothing's Too Good for My Baby/With a Child's Heart	1966	3.00	6.00	12.00
❑ 54136	Blowin' in the Wind/Ain't That Asking for Trouble	1966	3.00	6.00	12.00
❑ 54136 [PS]	Blowin' in the Wind/Ain't That Asking for Trouble	1966	6.25	12.50	25.00
❑ 54139	A Place in the Sun/Sylvia	1966	3.00	6.00	12.00
❑ 54139 [PS]	A Place in the Sun/Sylvia	1966	6.25	12.50	25.00
❑ 54142	Some Day at Christmas/The Miracles of Christmas	1966	3.75	7.50	15.00
❑ 54147	Travlin' Man/Hey Love	1967	2.50	5.00	10.00
❑ 54151	I Was Made to Love Her/Hold Me	1967	2.50	5.00	10.00
❑ 54157	I'm Wondering/Every Time I See You I Go Wild	1967	2.50	5.00	10.00
❑ 54165	Shoo-Be-Doo-Be-Doo-Da-Day/Why Don't You Lead Me to Love	1968	2.00	4.00	8.00
❑ 54168	You Met Your Match/My Girl	1968	2.00	4.00	8.00
❑ 54174	For Once in My Life/Angie Girl	1968	2.00	4.00	8.00
❑ 54180	My Cherie Amour/Don't Know Why I Love You	1969	2.00	4.00	8.00

—Re-release with A and B side switched and new title on B-side

❑ 54180	I Don't Know Why/My Cherie Amour	1969	2.50	5.00	10.00
❑ 54188	Yester-Me, Yester-You, Yesterday/I'd Be a Fool Right Now	1969	2.00	4.00	8.00
❑ 54191	Never Had a Dream Come True/Somebody Knows, Somebody Cares	1970	—	3.00	6.00
❑ 54196	Signed, Sealed, Delivered, I'm Yours/I'm More Than Happy	1970	—	3.00	6.00

Number	Title (A Side/B Side)	Yr	VG	VG+	NM
❑ 54200	Heaven Help Us All/I Gotta Have a Song	1970	—	3.00	6.00
❑ 54202	We Can Work It Out/Never Dreamed You'd Leave in Summer	1971	—	3.00	6.00
❑ 54208	If You Really Love Me/Think of Me As Your Soldier	1971	—	3.00	6.00
❑ 54214	What Christmas Means to Me/Bedtime for Toys	1971	—	3.00	6.00
❑ 54216	Superwoman (Where Were You When I Needed You)/I Love Every Little Thing About You	1972	—	3.00	6.00
❑ 54223	Keep On Running/Evil	1972	—	3.00	6.00
❑ 54226	Superstition/You've Got It Bad Girl	1972	—	2.50	5.00
❑ 54232	You Are the Sunshine of My Life/Tuesday Heartbreak	1973	—	2.50	5.00
❑ 54235	Higher Ground/Too High	1973	—	2.50	5.00
❑ 54242	Living for the City/Visions	1973	—	2.50	5.00
❑ 54245	Don't You Worry 'Bout a Thing/Blame It on the Sun	1974	—	2.50	5.00
❑ 54252	You Haven't Done Nothin'/Big Brother	1974	—	2.50	5.00
❑ 54254	Boogie On Reggae Woman/Seems So Long	1974	—	2.50	5.00

—With correct spelling of A-side

| ❑ 54254 | Boogie On Raggae Woman/Seems So Long | 1974 | — | 3.00 | 6.00 |

—With incorrect spelling of A-side

❑ 54274	I Wish/You and I	1976	—	2.50	5.00
❑ 54281	Sir Duke/He's Misstra Know-It-All	1977	—	2.50	5.00
❑ 54281 [PS]	Sir Duke/He's Misstra Know-It-All	1977	2.50	5.00	10.00
❑ 54286	Another Star/Creepin'	1977	—	2.50	5.00
❑ 54291	As/Contusion	1977	—	2.50	5.00
❑ 54303	Send One Your Love/(Instrumental)	1979	—	2.00	4.00
❑ 54303 [PS]	Send One Your Love/(Instrumental)	1979	—	3.00	6.00
❑ 54308	Outside My Window/Same Old Story	1980	—	2.00	4.00
❑ 54308 [PS]	Outside My Window/Same Old Story	1980	—	3.00	6.00
❑ 54317	Master Blaster (Jammin')/(Instrumental)	1980	—	2.00	4.00
❑ 54317 [PS]	Master Blaster (Jammin')/(Instrumental)	1980	—	3.00	6.00
❑ 54320	I Ain't Gonna Stand For It/Knocks Me Off My Feet	1980	—	2.00	4.00
❑ 54323	Lately/If It's Magic	1981	—	2.00	4.00
❑ 54328	Did I Hear You Say You Love Me/As If You Read My Mind	1981	—	2.00	4.00
❑ 54331	Happy Birthday/(Instrumental)	1981	—	—	—

—Canceled

TOPPS/MOTOWN

❑ 8	Fingertips Part 2	1967	18.75	37.50	75.00

—Cardboard record

| ❑ 10 | Uptight (Everything's Alright) | 1967 | 18.75 | 37.50 | 75.00 |

—Cardboard record

7-Inch Extended Plays

TAMLA

❑ T 340EP	Saturn/Ebony Eyes//All Day Sucker/Easy Goin' Evening	1976	—	2.00	4.00

—Called "A Something's Extra for Songs in the Key of Life," this was issued with the 2-LP set of the same name and is sometimes found separately, though it was never sold separately; not issued with picture sleeve

Albums

GORDY

❑ GS 932	Eivets Rednow	1968	7.50	15.00	30.00

—As "Eivets Rednow"

JOBETE

| ❑ JSA-6253 [DJ] | The Wonder of Stevie | 1988 | 5.00 | 10.00 | 20.00 |

—Publisher's demo with excerpts of 105 (!) Stevie Wonder songs

MOTOWN

❑ M5-131V1	Recorded Live/Little Stevie Wonder/The 12 Year Old Genius	1981	3.00	6.00	12.00

—Reissue of Tamla 240

| ❑ M5-150V1 | With a Song in My Heart | 1981 | 3.00 | 6.00 | 12.00 |

—Reissue of Tamla 250

| ❑ M5-166V1 | Down to Earth | 1981 | 3.00 | 6.00 | 12.00 |

—Reissue of Tamla 272

| ❑ M5-173V1 | Tribute to Uncle Ray | 1981 | 3.00 | 6.00 | 12.00 |

—Reissue of Tamla 232

| ❑ M5-176V1 | Signed, Sealed and Delivered | 1981 | 3.00 | 6.00 | 12.00 |

—Reissue of Tamla 304

| ❑ M5-179V1 | My Cherie Amour | 1981 | 3.00 | 6.00 | 12.00 |

—Reissue of Tamla 296

| ❑ M5-183V1 | Up-Tight Everything's Alright | 1981 | 3.00 | 6.00 | 12.00 |

—Reissue of Tamla 268

| ❑ M5-219V1 | The Jazz Soul of Little Stevie | 1981 | 3.00 | 6.00 | 12.00 |

—Reissue of Tamla 233

| ❑ 31453 0238-1 [(2)DJ] | Conversation Peace | 1995 | 6.25 | 12.50 | 25.00 |

—Vinyl is promo only; white cover with custom sticker

| ❑ M9-804A3 [(3)] | Looking Back | 1977 | 6.25 | 12.50 | 25.00 |

—Withdrawn after Stevie Wonder objected to its release

| ❑ 5255 ML | Someday at Christmas | 1982 | 2.50 | 5.00 | 10.00 |

—Reissue of Tamla 281

| ❑ 6108 ML | The Woman in Red | 1984 | 2.50 | 5.00 | 10.00 |

—With sticker at top proclaiming "New Stevie Wonder Album"

| ❑ 6108 ML | The Woman in Red | 1984 | 3.00 | 6.00 | 12.00 |

—With no sticker proclaiming "New Stevie Wonder Album"

❑ 6248 ML	Characters	1987	2.50	5.00	10.00
❑ 6291 ML	Music from the Movie Jungle Fever	1991	5.00	10.00	20.00

TAMLA

❑ T 232 [M]	Tribute to Uncle Ray	1962	37.50	75.00	150.00
❑ T 233 [M]	The Jazz Soul of Little Stevie	1962	37.50	75.00	150.00
❑ T 240 [M]	Recorded Live/Little Stevie Wonder/The 12 Year Old Genius	1963	30.00	60.00	120.00

—The above three LPs as "Little Stevie Wonder"

| ❑ T 248 [M] | Workout Stevie, Workout | 1963 | 250.00 | 500.00 | 1000. |

—Canceled; test pressings or acetates may exist

❑ T 250 [M]	With a Song in My Heart	1964	20.00	40.00	80.00
❑ T 255 [M]	Stevie at the Beach	1964	20.00	40.00	80.00
❑ T 268 [M]	Up-Tight Everything's Alright	1966	6.25	12.50	25.00
❑ TS 268 [S]	Up-Tight Everything's Alright	1966	7.50	15.00	30.00
❑ T 272 [M]	Down to Earth	1966	5.00	10.00	20.00
❑ TS 272 [S]	Down to Earth	1966	6.25	12.50	25.00
❑ T 279 [M]	I Was Made to Love Her	1967	5.00	10.00	20.00
❑ TS 279 [S]	I Was Made to Love Her	1967	6.25	12.50	25.00
❑ T 281 [M]	Someday at Christmas	1967	7.50	15.00	30.00
❑ TS 281 [S]	Someday at Christmas	1967	10.00	20.00	40.00
❑ T 282 [M]	Greatest Hits	1968	7.50	15.00	30.00
❑ TS 282 [S]	Greatest Hits	1968	5.00	10.00	20.00

Number	Title (A Side/B Side)	Yr	VG	VG+	NM
❑ TS 291	For Once in My Life	1968	5.00	10.00	20.00
❑ TS 296	My Cherie Amour	1969	5.00	10.00	20.00
❑ TS 298	Stevie Wonder Live	1970	5.00	10.00	20.00
❑ TS 304	Signed Sealed and Delivered	1970	5.00	10.00	20.00
❑ TS 308	Where I'm Coming From	1971	5.00	10.00	20.00
❑ T 313L	Stevie Wonder's Greatest Hits Vol. 2	1971	5.00	10.00	20.00
—Some, if not all, LP covers have the title mis-punctuated as "Stevie Wonders' Greatest Hits Vol. 2"					
❑ T 314L	Music of My Mind	1972	5.00	10.00	20.00
❑ T 319L	Talking Book	1972	3.75	7.50	15.00
—Original pressings have a braille note on cover					
❑ T 319L	Talking Book	1973	2.50	5.00	10.00
—No braille note on cover					
❑ T 326L	Innervisions	1973	3.75	7.50	15.00
❑ T6-332S1	Fulfillingness' First Finale	1974	3.75	7.50	15.00
❑ T13-340C2 [(2)]	Songs in the Key of Life	1976	5.00	10.00	20.00
—With booklet and bonus 7-inch EP (deduct 25% if missing)					
❑ T7-362R1	Someday at Christmas	1978	5.00	10.00	20.00
—Unusual reissue of 281					
❑ T13-371C2 [(2)]	Journey Through the Secret Life of Plants	1979	3.75	7.50	15.00
❑ T8-373S1	Hotter Than July	1980	3.00	6.00	12.00
❑ 6002 TL2 [(2)]	Stevie Wonder's Original Musiquarium I	1982	3.75	7.50	15.00
❑ 6134 TL	In Square Circle	1985	2.50	5.00	10.00

WONDER, STEVIE, AND MICHAEL JACKSON Also see each artist's individual listings.
12-Inch Singles
MOTOWN

Number	Title (A Side/B Side)	Yr	VG	VG+	NM
❑ 4606 MG	Get It (6:44) (Instrumental 6:47)	1988	2.00	4.00	8.00

45s
MOTOWN

Number	Title (A Side/B Side)	Yr	VG	VG+	NM
❑ 1930	Get It/(Instrumental)	1988	—	—	3.00
❑ 1930 [PS]	Get It/(Instrumental)	1988	—	—	3.00

WONDER WHO?, THE See THE FOUR SEASONS.

WONDERETTES, THE
45s
ENTERPRISE

Number	Title (A Side/B Side)	Yr	VG	VG+	NM
❑ 5025	Love's Got a Hold on Me/Work Out Fine	1964	6.25	12.50	25.00

RUBY

Number	Title (A Side/B Side)	Yr	VG	VG+	NM
❑ 5065	I Feel Strange/Wait Until Tonight	1965	10.00	20.00	40.00

UNITED ARTISTS

Number	Title (A Side/B Side)	Yr	VG	VG+	NM
❑ 944	I Feel Strange/Wait Until Tonight	1965	6.25	12.50	25.00
❑ 997	Mend My Broken Heart/And If I Had My Way	1966	5.00	10.00	20.00

—By "Rose St. John and the Wonderettes"
VEEP

Number	Title (A Side/B Side)	Yr	VG	VG+	NM
❑ 1231	Fool Don't Laugh/I Know the Meeting	1966	6.25	12.50	25.00

—As "Rose St. John and the Wonderettes"

WOOD, ANITA
45s
SUN

Number	Title (A Side/B Side)	Yr	VG	VG+	NM
❑ 361	I'll Wait Forever/I Can't Show How I Feel	1961	7.50	15.00	30.00

WOOD, BOBBY
45s
CHALLENGE

Number	Title (A Side/B Side)	Yr	VG	VG+	NM
❑ 9160	The Day After Forever/Everybody's Searchin'	1962	2.50	5.00	10.00

CINNAMON

Number	Title (A Side/B Side)	Yr	VG	VG+	NM
❑ 790	I'm a Fool for Loving You/Secret Love Affair	1974	—	2.00	4.00

JOY

Number	Title (A Side/B Side)	Yr	VG	VG+	NM
❑ 277	I Still Hurt/Just the Same	1963	2.50	5.00	10.00
❑ 279	Do Darlin' (Do Remember Me)/That's All I Need	1963	2.50	5.00	10.00
❑ 285	If I'm a Fool for Loving You/My Heart Went Boing! Boing! Boing!	1964	2.50	5.00	10.00
❑ 288	That's All I Need to Know/This Time	1964	2.50	5.00	10.00
❑ 291	So Cruel/I'd Do It Again	1964	2.50	5.00	10.00
❑ 295	Bed of Roses/Show Me	1965	2.00	4.00	8.00
❑ 298	Human Emotions/When a Lonely Boy Meets a Lonely Girl	1965	2.00	4.00	8.00
❑ 301	Fool's Paradise/What Am I Gonna Tell Myself	1965	2.00	4.00	8.00

LUCKY ELEVEN

Number	Title (A Side/B Side)	Yr	VG	VG+	NM
❑ 361	One Day Behind/Sound of Sadness	1973	—	2.50	5.00

MALA

Number	Title (A Side/B Side)	Yr	VG	VG+	NM
❑ 526	My Special Angel/I'd Rather Forgive You	1966	2.00	4.00	8.00

MGM

Number	Title (A Side/B Side)	Yr	VG	VG+	NM
❑ 13729	My Last Date (With You)/Everybody's Baby	1967	—	3.00	6.00
❑ 13797	Break My Mind/This Thing Called Love	1967	—	3.00	6.00
❑ 13912	Is That All There Is To It/Say It's Not You	1968	—	3.00	6.00
❑ 13952	Mary/Big Buildup	1968	—	3.00	6.00
❑ 14051	(Margie's at the) Lincoln Park Inn/I'm the Name of Her Game	1969	—	3.00	6.00

SUN

Number	Title (A Side/B Side)	Yr	VG	VG+	NM
❑ 369 [DJ]	Everybody's Searchin'/Human Emotions	1961	200.00	400.00	600.00

—No stock copies known; should one be discovered, it would be worth much more
Albums
JOY

Number	Title (A Side/B Side)	Yr	VG	VG+	NM
❑ JL 1001 [M]	Bobby Wood	1964	10.00	20.00	40.00

WOOD, BRENTON
45s
BRENT

Number	Title (A Side/B Side)	Yr	VG	VG+	NM
❑ 7052	Good Lovin'/I Want to Love	1966	3.75	7.50	15.00
❑ 7057	Cross the Bridge/Sweet Molly Malone	1966	6.25	12.50	25.00
❑ 7068	I Want Love/Sweet Molly Malone	1967	2.50	5.00	10.00

CREAM

Number	Title (A Side/B Side)	Yr	VG	VG+	NM
❑ 7602	All That Jazz/Bless Your Little Heart	1976	—	2.00	4.00
❑ 7716	Come Softly to Me/You're Everything I Need	1977	—	2.00	4.00
❑ 7720	Number One/(B-side unknown)	1977	—	2.00	4.00
❑ 7833	Let's Get Crazy Together/Love Is Free	1978	—	2.00	4.00

DOUBLE SHOT

Number	Title (A Side/B Side)	Yr	VG	VG+	NM
❑ 111	The Oogum Boogum Song/I Like the Way You Love Me	1967	2.50	5.00	10.00
❑ 116	Gimme Little Sign/I Think You've Got Your Fools Mixed Up	1967	2.50	5.00	10.00
❑ 121	Baby You Got It/Catch You on the Rebound	1967	2.00	4.00	8.00
❑ 126	Lovey Dovey Kinda Lovin'/Two-Time Loser	1968	2.00	4.00	8.00
❑ 130	Some Got It, Some Don't/Me and You	1968	2.00	4.00	8.00

Number	Title (A Side/B Side)	Yr	VG	VG+	NM
❑ 135	Trouble/It's Just a Game, Love	1968	2.00	4.00	8.00
❑ 137	Where Are You/A Change Is Gonna Come	1969	2.00	4.00	8.00
❑ 142	Whoop It On Me/Take a Chance	1969	2.00	4.00	8.00
❑ 147	Can You Dig It/Great Big Bubble of Love	1970	—	3.00	6.00
❑ 150	Bogaloosa, Lousiana/I Need Your Love So Bad	1970	—	3.00	6.00
❑ 156	Sad Little Song/Who But a Fool	1971	—	3.00	6.00

MIDGET

Number	Title (A Side/B Side)	Yr	VG	VG+	NM
❑ 101	Rainin' Love/All That Jazz	197?	—	2.50	5.00

PHILCO-FORD

Number	Title (A Side/B Side)	Yr	VG	VG+	NM
❑ HP-38	Gimme Little Sign/Oogum Boogum	1969	5.00	10.00	20.00

—4-inch plastic "Hip Pocket Record" with color sleeve
PROPHESY

Number	Title (A Side/B Side)	Yr	VG	VG+	NM
❑ 3002	Sticky Boom Boom Too Cold (Part 1)/Sticky Boom Boom Too Cold (Part 2)	1973	—	2.50	5.00
❑ 3003	Another Saturday Night/(B-side unknown)	1973	—	2.50	5.00

WAND

Number	Title (A Side/B Side)	Yr	VG	VG+	NM
❑ 145	Mr. Schemer/Hide-A-Way	1963	10.00	20.00	40.00

WARNER BROS.

Number	Title (A Side/B Side)	Yr	VG	VG+	NM
❑ 8079	All That Jazz/Rainin' Love	1975	—	2.50	5.00
❑ 8144	Better Believe It/It Only Makes Me Want It More	1975	—	2.50	5.00

Albums
BRENT

Number	Title (A Side/B Side)	Yr	VG	VG+	NM
❑ S-100 [S]	Introducing Brenton Wood! Boogaloo	1967	15.00	30.00	60.00
—Four tracks by Brenton Wood, six by other artists					
❑ 5100 [M]	Introducing Brenton Wood! Boogaloo	1967	10.00	20.00	40.00

CREAM

Number	Title (A Side/B Side)	Yr	VG	VG+	NM
❑ 1006	Come Softly	1977	3.75	7.50	15.00

DOUBLE SHOT

Number	Title (A Side/B Side)	Yr	VG	VG+	NM
❑ 1002 [M]	Oogum Boogum	1967	6.25	12.50	25.00
❑ 1003 [M]	Baby You Got It	1967	6.25	12.50	25.00
❑ 5002 [S]	Oogum Boogum	1967	7.50	15.00	30.00
❑ 5003 [S]	Baby You Got It	1967	7.50	15.00	30.00
—Black vinyl					
❑ 5003 [S]	Baby You Got It	1967	50.00	100.00	200.00
—Multi-color vinyl					

RHINO

Number	Title (A Side/B Side)	Yr	VG	VG+	NM
❑ RNLP-70223	The Best of Brenton Wood	1986	2.50	5.00	10.00

WOOD, MARTY
45s
HIT

Number	Title (A Side/B Side)	Yr	VG	VG+	NM
❑ 67	18 Yellow Roses/I Love You Because	1963	2.00	4.00	8.00
❑ 128	Tears and Roses/My Boy Lollipop	1964	2.00	4.00	8.00
—B-side by Connie Dee					
❑ 140	In the Misty Moonlight/G.T.O.	1964	2.00	4.00	8.00
—B-side by the Roamers					
❑ 162	Right or Wrong/Just Give Me Time	1964	2.00	4.00	8.00
—B-side by Bobby and Buddy					
❑ 177	You're Nobody Till Somebody Loves You/Speaking of Broken Hearts	1965	2.00	4.00	8.00
—B-side by John Preston					
❑ 200	Send Me the Pillow You Dream On/You Can't Trust a Friend	1965	2.00	4.00	8.00
—B-side by Lisa French					

WOOD, MITCH
45s
HIT

Number	Title (A Side/B Side)	Yr	VG	VG+	NM
❑ 92	500 Miles Away from Home/Walking Proud	1963	2.00	4.00	8.00

—B-side by John Preston

WOOD, RONNIE Also see FACES; THE ROLLING STONES.
45s
COLUMBIA

Number	Title (A Side/B Side)	Yr	VG	VG+	NM
❑ 1-11014	Seven Days/Breakin' My Heart	1979	—	3.00	6.00

WARNER BROS.

Number	Title (A Side/B Side)	Yr	VG	VG+	NM
❑ 8036	Breathe on Me/I Can Feel the Fire	1974	—	3.00	6.00
❑ 8131	I Got a Feeling/If You Don't Want My Love	1975	—	3.00	6.00

Albums
COLUMBIA

Number	Title (A Side/B Side)	Yr	VG	VG+	NM
❑ JC 35702	Gimme Some Neck	1979	3.75	7.50	15.00
❑ PC 35702	Gimme Some Neck	198?	2.00	4.00	8.00
—Budget-line reissue					
❑ FC 37473	1234	1981	3.75	7.50	15.00

WARNER BROS.

Number	Title (A Side/B Side)	Yr	VG	VG+	NM
❑ BS 2819	I've Got My Own Album to Do	1974	5.00	10.00	20.00
❑ BS 2872	Now Look	1975	3.75	7.50	15.00

WOOD, ROY Also see ELECTRIC LIGHT ORCHESTRA; THE MOVE.
45s
UNITED ARTISTS

Number	Title (A Side/B Side)	Yr	VG	VG+	NM
❑ XW160	Ball Park Incident/Carlsberg Special	1973	—	2.50	5.00
—As "Wizzard/Roy Wood"					
❑ XW272	See My Baby Jive/Bend Over Beethoven	1973	—	2.50	5.00
❑ XW320	Dear Elaine/Song of Praise	1973	—	2.50	5.00
❑ XW394	Forever/Woodbe	1974	—	2.50	5.00
❑ XW792	Any Old Time Will Do/Why Does Such a Pretty Girl Sing Those Sad Songs	1976	—	2.00	4.00

Albums
TOWNHOUSE

Number	Title (A Side/B Side)	Yr	VG	VG+	NM
❑ SN-7127	One Man Band	1981	3.00	6.00	12.00

UNITED ARTISTS

Number	Title (A Side/B Side)	Yr	VG	VG+	NM
❑ (# unknown) [DJ]	Boulders Folder	1973	10.00	20.00	40.00
—Promo version of 168 in 13x13 folder with press kit and postcards					
❑ UA-LA042-F	Wizzard's Brew	1973	2.50	5.00	10.00
❑ UA-LA168-F	Boulders	1973	2.50	5.00	10.00
❑ UA-LA219-G	Introducing Eddy and the Falcons	1974	2.50	5.00	10.00
❑ UA-LA575-G	Mustard	1976	2.50	5.00	10.00

WARNER BROS.

Number	Title (A Side/B Side)	Yr	VG	VG+	NM
❑ BS 3065	Super Active Wizzo	1977	2.50	5.00	10.00
❑ BSK 3247	On the Road Again	1979	2.50	5.00	10.00

Number	Title (A Side/B Side)	Yr	VG	VG+	NM
WOODBURY, WOODY					
Albums					
STEREODDITIES					
❑ BITOA	Booze Is the Only Answer	1961	10.00	20.00	40.00
—With record, paperback book and smaller booklets					
❑ MW 1	Woody Woodbury Looks at Love and Life	1960	6.25	12.50	25.00
❑ MW 2	Woody Woodbury's Laughing Room	1960	6.25	12.50	25.00
❑ MW 3	Woody Woodbury's Concert in Comedy	1961	6.25	12.50	25.00
❑ MW 4	Woody Woodbury's Saloonatics	1961	6.25	12.50	25.00
❑ MW 5	The Spice Is Right	1962	6.25	12.50	25.00
❑ MW 6	The Best of Woody Woodbury	1963	5.00	10.00	20.00
❑ MW 7	Through the Keyhole	1964	5.00	10.00	20.00
WOODS, BENNIE					
45s					
ATLAS					
❑ 1040	I Cross My Fingers/Wheel Baby Wheel	1955	125.00	250.00	500.00
—As "Bennie Woods and Rockin' Townies"					
❑ 1040	I Cross My Fingers/Wheel Baby Wheel	1955	200.00	400.00	800.00
—As "Bennie Woods and the Five Dukes"					
WOODS, BILLY					
45s					
DOT					
❑ 16053	Falling Rain/Friendly Mr. Wendley	1960	10.00	20.00	40.00
SUSSEX					
❑ 213	Let Me Make You Happy/That Was the Love That Was	1971	375.00	750.00	1500.
VERVE					
❑ 10451	I Don't Want to Lose Your Love/No One to Blame	1966	12.50	25.00	50.00
❑ 10484	I Found Satisfaction/If I Could Only See	1967	12.50	25.00	50.00
WOODS, DANNY					
45s					
HIT					
❑ 188	No Arms Can Ever Hold You/Swinging Spiritual	1965	2.00	4.00	8.00
—B-side by William Randolph					
WOODS, DONALD					
45s					
ALADDIN					
❑ 3412	Memories of an Angel/That Much of Your Love	1958	7.50	15.00	30.00
FLIP					
❑ 306	Death of an Angel/Man from Utopia	1955	10.00	20.00	40.00
WOODS, KENNI					
45s					
PHILIPS					
❑ 40112	Can't He Take a Hint/That Guy Is Mine	1963	2.50	5.00	10.00
❑ 40156	Back with My Baby/Do You Really Love Me	1963	2.50	5.00	10.00
WOODS, MARTY					
45s					
HIT					
❑ 248	Secret Agent Man/Time Won't Let Me	1966	2.00	4.00	8.00
—B-side by the Chellows					
WOODS, MICKEY					
45s					
TAMLA					
❑ 54039	They Rode Through the Valley/Poor Sam Jones	1961	12.50	25.00	50.00
❑ 54052	Please Mr. Kennedy/(They Call Me) Cupid	1962	10.00	20.00	40.00
WOODY, DON					
45s					
DECCA					
❑ 30277	You're Barking Up the Wrong Tree/Bird-Dog	1957	25.00	50.00	100.00
WOOFERS, THE					
Albums					
WYNCOTE					
❑ SW 9011 [S]	Dragsville	1964	12.50	25.00	50.00
❑ W 9011 [M]	Dragsville	1964	10.00	20.00	40.00
WOOLERY, CHUCK Also see THE AVANT-GARDE.					
45s					
COLUMBIA					
❑ 45017	I've Been Wrong/Soft Velvet Love	1969	—	3.00	6.00
❑ 45135	Heaven Here on Earth/Pleasure of Her Company	1970	—	3.00	6.00
❑ 45224	Your Name Is Woman/Soft Velvet Love	1970	—	3.00	6.00
❑ 45224 [PS]	Your Name Is Woman/Soft Velvet Love	1970	3.75	7.50	15.00
❑ 45274	Hey, Baby/Soft Velvet Love	1970	—	3.00	6.00
EPIC					
❑ 50897	The Greatest Love Affair/Heroes and Lovers	1980	—	2.00	4.00
RCA VICTOR					
❑ 74-0554	Deja Vu/Forgive My Heart	1971	—	2.50	5.00
❑ 74-0703	Kiss Me Three Times/If Only	1972	—	2.50	5.00
❑ 74-0771	Time and Time Again/Pen of a Poet	1972	—	2.50	5.00
❑ 74-0865	Forgive My Heart/Love Me, Love Me	1973	—	2.50	5.00
WARNER BROS.					
❑ 8381	Painted Lady/Growing Up in a Country Way	1977	—	2.50	5.00
WOOLEY, SHEB Includes records by his comedic alter ego, "Ben Colder."					
45s					
BLUE BONNET					
❑ 124	Wooley's Polka/Lazy Mary	1954	17.50	35.00	70.00
❑ 125	Peeping Thru the Keyhole/Time Won't Heal an Achin' Heart	1954	17.50	35.00	70.00
❑ 130	Too Long with the Wrong Mama/Your Papa Ain't Steppin' Anymore	1954	15.00	30.00	60.00
MGM					
❑ 10697	Mule Boogie/Changing Your Name	1950	7.50	15.00	30.00
❑ 10960	Hoot Owl Boogie/Country Kisses	1951	7.50	15.00	30.00
❑ 11059	Over the Barrel/Air Castles	1951	7.50	15.00	30.00
❑ 11180	Backroom Boogie/Down in the Toolies	1952	7.50	15.00	30.00
❑ 11272	You're the Cat's Meow/Wha' Happened to Me Baby	1952	7.50	15.00	30.00
❑ 11308	A Cowboy Had Ought to Be Single/You Never Can Tell	1952	7.50	15.00	30.00
❑ 11403	Heart Bound in Chains/Freight Train Cinders	1953	6.25	12.50	25.00
❑ 11580	Love Is a Merry-Go-Round/Texas Tango	1953	6.25	12.50	25.00
❑ 11640	Goodbye Texas, Hello Tennessee/I'll Rerturn the Letters	1953	6.25	12.50	25.00
❑ 11665	Don't Stop Kissing Me Goodnight/Knew I Had Lost	1954	5.00	10.00	20.00
❑ 11717	Blue Guitar/Panama Pete	1954	5.00	10.00	20.00
❑ 11792	White Lightnin'/Fool About You	1954	5.00	10.00	20.00
❑ 11836	Hillbilly Mambo/I Go Outta My Mind	1954	5.00	10.00	20.00
❑ 11910	38-24-35/I Flipped	1955	3.75	7.50	15.00
❑ 11976	Speak of the Devil/Love at First Sight	1955	3.75	7.50	15.00
❑ 12048	Listening to Your Footsteps/Love Is a Prayer	1955	3.75	7.50	15.00
❑ 12060	It Takes a Heap of Livin'/Listen for Your Footsteps	1955	3.75	7.50	15.00
❑ 12114	Are You Satisfied/Humdinger	1955	3.75	7.50	15.00
❑ 12202	The Birth of the Rock 'N' Roll/A King or a Clown	1956	3.75	7.50	15.00
❑ 12260	You Can Do It/Do I Remember?	1956	3.75	7.50	15.00
❑ 12328	First Day of School/The Lonely Man	1956	3.75	7.50	15.00
❑ 12382	Honey I'm Lonesome/Let the Big Winds Blow	1956	3.75	7.50	15.00
❑ 12467	Plenty of Love/I Won't Come Back	1957	3.00	6.00	12.00
❑ 12541	Recipe for Love/I'm Too Young	1957	3.00	6.00	12.00
❑ 12584	So Close to Heaven/I Found Me An Angel	1957	3.00	6.00	12.00
❑ 12651	The Purple People Eater/I Can't Believe You're Mine	1958	4.50	9.00	18.00
❑ 12704	The Chase/Monkey Jive	1958	3.00	6.00	12.00
❑ 12733	Santa and the Purple People Eater/Star of Love	1958	5.00	10.00	20.00
❑ 12733 [PS]	Santa and the Purple People Eater/Star of Love	1958	10.00	20.00	40.00
❑ 12743	Cherry Street/Star of Love	1958	3.00	6.00	12.00
❑ 12778	More/Deep Goes the Love	1959	2.50	5.00	10.00
❑ 12781	Sweet Chile/More	1959	2.50	5.00	10.00
❑ 12817	Careless Hands/Pigmy Love	1959	2.50	5.00	10.00
❑ 12851	Love Like Mine/Josie	1959	2.50	5.00	10.00
❑ 12853	It's Almost Time/Roughneck	1959	2.50	5.00	10.00
❑ 12882	Luke the Spook/My Only Treasure	1960	2.50	5.00	10.00
❑ 12931	Taste of Ashes/Reach for the Moon	1960	2.50	5.00	10.00
❑ 13013	Skin Tight, Pin Striped, Pink Pedal Pushers/Till the End of the World	1961	2.50	5.00	10.00
❑ 13013 [PS]	Skin Tight, Pin Striped, Pink Pedal Pushers/Till the End of the World	1961	10.00	20.00	40.00
❑ 13046	That's My Pa/Meet Mr. Lonely	1961	2.50	5.00	10.00
❑ 13065	Laughin' the Blues/Somebody Please	1962	2.50	5.00	10.00
❑ 13079	That's My Ma/Land of No Love	1962	2.50	5.00	10.00
❑ 13094	The Leged of Echo Mountain/Give That Ball to Willie B	1962	2.50	5.00	10.00
❑ 13104	Don't Go Near the Eskimos/Louisiana Trapper	1962	2.50	5.00	10.00
—As "Ben Colder"					
❑ 13122	Hello Wall No. 2/Shudders and Screams	1963	2.50	5.00	10.00
—As "Ben Colder"					
❑ 13125	Little Bitty Bilbo Abernathy Nathan Allen Quincy Jones/Daddy Kiss and Make It Well	1963	2.50	5.00	10.00
❑ 13147	Still No. 2/Goin' Surfin'	1963	3.75	7.50	15.00
—As "Ben Colder"					
❑ 13152	Buildin' a Railroad/Cowboy Hero	1963	2.50	5.00	10.00
❑ 13166	Old Rag Joe/Hootenanny Hoot	1963	2.50	5.00	10.00
❑ 13166 [PS]	Old Rag Joe/Hootenanny Hoot	1963	10.00	20.00	40.00
❑ 13167	Detroit City No. 2/Ring of Smoke	1963	2.50	5.00	10.00
—As "Ben Colder"					
❑ 13195	Papa's Ole Fiddle/She Called Me Baby	1963	2.50	5.00	10.00
❑ 13197	I Walk the Line No. 2/Talk Back Blubberin' Lips	1963	2.50	5.00	10.00
—As "Ben Colder"					
❑ 13241	Blue Guitar/Natchez Landing	1964	2.00	4.00	8.00
❑ 13262	TV Westerns/Dobro's Catchin' On Again (And I'm Gonna Be a Star)	1964	2.00	4.00	8.00
—As "Ben Colder"					
❑ 13294	Wild and Wooley, Big Unruly Me/Sittin' and Thinkin'	1964	2.00	4.00	8.00
❑ 13351	Silver (The Wonder Horse)/Blistered	1965	2.00	4.00	8.00
❑ 13395	Big Land/Sally's Arms	1965	2.00	4.00	8.00
❑ 13444	Make the World Go Away No. 2/May the Bird of Paradise Fly Up Your Snoot	1966	2.00	4.00	8.00
—As "Ben Colder"					
❑ 13477	Buba Hoo Boba Dee/I'll Leave the Singin' to the Bluebirds	1966	2.00	4.00	8.00
❑ 13556	Tonight's the Night My Angel's Halo Fell/Anchors Aweigh	1966	2.00	4.00	8.00
❑ 13590	Almost Persuaded No. 2/A Packet of Pencils	1966	2.00	4.00	8.00
—As "Ben Colder"					
❑ 13668	There Goes My Everything No. 2/Great Men Repeat Themselves	1967	2.00	4.00	8.00
—As "Ben Colder"					
❑ 13705	Letter to Daddy/Draggin' the River	1967	2.00	4.00	8.00
❑ 13771	The Purple People Eater No. 2/Undertaker's Love Lament	1967	2.00	4.00	8.00
—As "Ben Colder"					
❑ 13806	Number One on the Survey/Big Ole, Good Ole Girl	1967	2.00	4.00	8.00
❑ 13827	The Love-In/Wildwood Flower on the Autoharp	1967	2.00	4.00	8.00
❑ 13897	Ain't It Funny How Wine Sips Away/The Doo-Hickey Song	1968	2.00	4.00	8.00
—As "Ben Colder"					
❑ 13914	By the Time I Get to Phoenix No. 2/Skip a Rope No. 2	1968	2.00	4.00	8.00
—As "Ben Colder"					
❑ 13938	Make 'Em Laugh/Tie a Tiger Down	1968	—	3.00	6.00
❑ 13997	Harper Valley P.T.A. (Later That Same Day)/Folsom Prison Blues No. 1 1/2	1968	2.50	5.00	10.00
—As "Ben Colder"					
❑ 14005	That Girl I Remember Loving You	1968	—	3.00	6.00
❑ 14015	Little Green Apples No. 2/It's Such a Pretty World Tonight	1968	2.00	4.00	8.00
—As "Ben Colder"					
❑ 14044	Ode to the Little Shack Out Back/You're a Real Good Friend	1969	—	3.00	6.00
—As "Ben Colder"					

Number	Title (A Side/B Side)	Yr	VG	VG+	NM
❑ 14065	The Carroll County Accident No. 2/His Lincoln's Parked at Margie's Again	1969	—	3.00	6.00
—As "Ben Colder"					
❑ 14070	The Recipient/Big Ole, Good Ole Girl	1969	—	3.00	6.00
❑ 14076	Ruby Please Bring Your Love to Town/Yet	1969	—	3.00	6.00
—As "Ben Colder"					
❑ 14085	One Man Band/You Still Turn Me On	1969	—	3.00	6.00
❑ 14111	Big Sweet John/Games People Play	1970	—	3.00	6.00
—As "Ben Colder"					
❑ 14123	Daddy's Home/The Will	1970	—	3.00	6.00
❑ 14133	Tennessee Bird Talk/What Is Youth	1970	—	3.00	6.00
—As "Ben Colder"					
❑ 14165	One of Them Roarin' Songs/I Don't Belong in Her Arms	1970	—	3.00	6.00
❑ 14209	Fifteen Beers Ago/Sunday Mornin' Fallin' Down	1970	—	3.00	6.00
—As "Ben Colder"					
❑ 14247	Help Me Fake It Through the Night/Rose Garden	1971	—	3.00	6.00
—As "Ben Colder"					
❑ 14287	Goodbye Wabash Cannonball/Joy	1971	—	3.00	6.00
❑ 14327	Easy Loving No. 2/Sing a Drinkin' Song	1971	—	3.00	6.00
❑ 14384	Life Is a Fountain/Somebody Gonna Come Along	1972	—	3.00	6.00
❑ 14420	The Unhappiest Squirrel in the Whole U.S.A./Runnin' Bare	1972	—	2.50	5.00
—As "Ben Colder"					
❑ 14444	A Kick in the Head/Personality	1972	—	3.00	6.00
❑ 14471	Glossy 8 x 10/Moontan	1972	—	2.50	5.00
—As "Ben Colder"					
❑ 14610	Early in the Morning/Getting High on Love	1973	—	3.00	6.00
❑ 14639	Behind Cloe's Door/Satin Sheets	1973	—	2.50	5.00
—As "Ben Colder"					
❑ 14647	The Purple People Eater/I Can't Believe You're Mine	1973	2.50	5.00	10.00
SCORPION					
❑ 0556	Lucille No. 2/Senior Citizen's Lament	1978	—	2.00	4.00
—As "Ben Colder"					
SUNBIRD					
❑ 104	The Rambler/Amazania	1979	—	2.00	4.00
❑ 109	Flower of the County (Censored Version)/Flower of the County (Uncensored Version)	1980	—	2.00	4.00
—As "Ben Colder"					
❑ 7566	The Belly Button Song/Jack Hammer Man	1981	—	2.00	4.00
Albums					
MGM					
❑ GAS-139	Ben Colder (Golden Archive Series)	1970	3.75	7.50	15.00
—As "Ben Colder"					
❑ E-3299 [M]	Sheb Wooley	1956	37.50	75.00	150.00
❑ E-3904 [M]	Songs from the Days of Rawhide	1961	10.00	20.00	40.00
❑ SE-3904 [S]	Songs from the Days of Rawhide	1961	12.50	25.00	50.00
❑ E-4026 [M]	That's My Ma and That's My Pa	1962	7.50	15.00	30.00
❑ SE-4026 [S]	That's My Ma and That's My Pa	1962	10.00	20.00	40.00
❑ E-4117 [M]	Spoofing the Big Ones	1961	10.00	20.00	40.00
❑ SE-4117 [S]	Spoofing the Big Ones	1961	12.50	25.00	50.00
—MGM 4117 as "Ben Colder"					
❑ E-4136 [M]	Tales of How the West Was Won	1963	7.50	15.00	30.00
❑ SE-4136 [S]	Tales of How the West Was Won	1963	10.00	20.00	40.00
❑ E-4173 [M]	Ben Colder	1963	7.50	15.00	30.00
❑ SE-4173 [S]	Ben Colder	1963	10.00	20.00	40.00
—MGM 4173 as "Ben Colder"					
❑ E-4275 [M]	The Very Best of Sheb Wooley	1965	5.00	10.00	20.00
❑ SE-4275 [S]	The Very Best of Sheb Wooley	1965	6.25	12.50	25.00
❑ E-4325 [M]	It's a Big Land	1965	5.00	10.00	20.00
❑ SE-4325 [S]	It's a Big Land	1965	6.25	12.50	25.00
❑ E-4421 [M]	Big Ben Strikes Again	1967	5.00	10.00	20.00
❑ SE-4421 [S]	Big Ben Strikes Again	1967	5.00	10.00	20.00
—MGM 4421 as "Ben Colder"					
❑ E-4482 [M]	Wine, Women and Song	1967	5.00	10.00	20.00
❑ SE-4482 [S]	Wine, Women and Song	1967	5.00	10.00	20.00
—MGM 4482 as "Ben Colder"					
❑ SE-4530	The Best of Ben Colder	1968	5.00	10.00	20.00
—As "Ben Colder"					
❑ SE-4614	Harper Valley P.T.A.	1968	5.00	10.00	20.00
—As "Ben Colder"					
❑ SE-4615	Warm and Wooley	1969	5.00	10.00	20.00
❑ SE-4629	Have One On	1969	3.75	7.50	15.00
—As "Ben Colder"					
❑ SE-4674	Wild Again	1970	3.75	7.50	15.00
❑ SE-4758	Live and Loaded	1971	3.75	7.50	15.00
—As "Ben Colder"					
❑ SE-4807	Warming Up to Colder	1972	3.75	7.50	15.00
—As "Ben Colder"					
❑ SE-4876	The Wacky World of Ben Colder	1973	3.75	7.50	15.00
—As "Ben Colder"					

WORLD OF OZ, THE

45s

Number	Title (A Side/B Side)	Yr	VG	VG+	NM
DERAM					
❑ 85029	The Muffin Man/Peter's Birthday	1968	2.50	5.00	10.00
❑ 85034	King Croesus/Jack	1968	2.50	5.00	10.00
❑ 85043	Mandy-Ann/Beside the Fire	1969	2.50	5.00	10.00
Albums					
DERAM					
❑ DES 18022	The World of Oz	1969	12.50	25.00	50.00

WOULD

Albums

Number	Title (A Side/B Side)	Yr	VG	VG+	NM
PERCEPTION					
❑ 24	Would	1972	7.50	15.00	30.00

WRAY, LINK

45s

Number	Title (A Side/B Side)	Yr	VG	VG+	NM
CADENCE					
❑ 1347	Rumble/The Swag	1958	10.00	20.00	40.00
EPIC					
❑ 9300	Raw-Hide/Dixie-Doodle	1958	6.25	12.50	25.00
❑ 9321	Comanche/Lillian	1959	6.25	12.50	25.00
❑ 9343	Rendezvous/Slinky	1959	6.25	12.50	25.00
❑ 9343 [PS]	Rendezvous/Slinky	1959	62.50	125.00	250.00
❑ 9361	Trail of the Lonesome Pine/Golden Strings	1960	6.25	12.50	25.00
❑ 9419	Mary Ann/Ain't That Lovin' You Baby	1960	6.25	12.50	25.00
❑ 9454	El Toro/Tijuana	1961	6.25	12.50	25.00
HEAVY					
❑ 101	Rumble '68/Blow Your Mind	1968	3.75	7.50	15.00
KAY					
❑ 3690	I Sez Baby/(B-side unknown)	1958	25.00	50.00	100.00
MALA					
❑ 458	There's a Hole in the Middle of the Moon/Dancing Party	1963	5.00	10.00	20.00
MR. G.					
❑ 820	Rumble '69/Mind Blower	1969	2.50	5.00	10.00
NORTON					
❑ (no #) [PS]	Link Wray and the Wraymen	199?	—	—	2.00
—Custom sleeve with large hole to reveal the record label. The same generic sleeve was issued with each of 801-810.					
❑ 801	Jack the Ripper/Bo Diddley	199?	—	—	3.00
❑ 802	Ace of Spades/Fat Back	199?	—	—	3.00
❑ 803	Hidden Charms/Five and Ten	199?	—	—	3.00
❑ 804	The Black Widow/Mustang	199?	—	—	3.00
❑ 805	Run Chicken Run/Scatter	199?	—	—	3.00
❑ 806	Branded/Law of the Jungle	199?	—	—	3.00
❑ 807	Deuces Wild/The Sweeper	199?	—	—	3.00
❑ 808	The Shadow Knows/Hang On	199?	—	—	3.00
❑ 809	Good Rockin' Tonight/Soul Train	199?	—	—	3.00
❑ 810	Batman Theme/Zip Code	199?	—	—	3.00
OKEH					
❑ 7166	Rumble Mambo/Ham Bone	1963	5.00	10.00	20.00
—B-side by Red Saunders					
❑ 7282	Rumble Mambo/Ham Bone	1967	3.75	7.50	15.00
—B-side by Red Saunders					
POLYDOR					
❑ 14084	Fire and Brimstone/June Box Mama	1970	2.00	4.00	8.00
❑ 14096	Fallin' Rain/Juke Box Mama	1971	2.00	4.00	8.00
❑ 14188	Shine the Light/Lawdy Miss Clawdy	1973	—	3.00	6.00
❑ 14256	I Got to Ramble/She's That Kind of Woman	1974	—	3.00	6.00
RUMBLE					
❑ 1000	Jack the Ripper/The Stranger	1961	10.00	20.00	40.00
SWAN					
❑ 4137	Jack the Ripper/The Black Widow	1963	5.00	10.00	20.00
❑ 4154	Weekend/Turnpike U.S.A.	1963	5.00	10.00	20.00
❑ 4163	Run Chicken Run/The Sweeper	1963	5.00	10.00	20.00
❑ 4171	The Shadow Knows/My Alberta	1964	5.00	10.00	20.00
❑ 4187	Deuces Wild/Summer Dream	1964	5.00	10.00	20.00
❑ 4201	Good Rockin' Tonight/I'll Do Anything for You	1965	6.25	12.50	25.00
❑ 4211	Branded/Hang On	1965	5.00	10.00	20.00
❑ 4232	Girl from the North Country/You Hurt Me So	1965	5.00	10.00	20.00
❑ 4239	The Fuzz/Ace of Spades	1966	5.00	10.00	20.00
❑ 4244	Batman Theme/Alone	1966	6.25	12.50	25.00
❑ 4261	Ace of Spades/Hidden Charms	1966	6.25	12.50	25.00
❑ 4284	Jack the Ripper/I'll Do Anything for You	1967	3.75	7.50	15.00
TRANS ATLAS					
❑ 687	Big City Stomp/Poppin' Popeye	1962	5.00	10.00	20.00
Albums					
EPIC					
❑ LN 3661 [M]	Link Wray and the Wraymen	1960	62.50	125.00	250.00
NORTON					
❑ 210	Hillbilly Wolf (Missing Links Vol. 1)	199?	2.50	5.00	10.00
❑ 211	Big City After Dark (Missing Links Vol. 2)	199?	2.50	5.00	10.00
❑ 212	Some Kinda Nut (Missing Links Vol. 3)	199?	2.50	5.00	10.00
❑ 253	Streets of Chicago (Missing Links Vol. 4)	1995	2.50	5.00	10.00
POLYDOR					
❑ 24-4064	Link Wray	1971	5.00	10.00	20.00
❑ PD-5047	Be What You Want To	1972	5.00	10.00	20.00
❑ PD-6025	The Link Wray Rumble	1974	5.00	10.00	20.00
RECORD FACTORY					
❑ 1929	Yesterday and Today	1969	20.00	40.00	80.00
SWAN					
❑ SLP-510 [M]	Jack the Ripper	1963	37.50	75.00	150.00
VERMILLION					
❑ 1924 [M]	Great Guitar Hits	196?	20.00	40.00	80.00
❑ 1925 [M]	Link Wray Sings and Plays Guitar	196?	20.00	40.00	80.00
VISA					
❑ 7009	Bullshot	1979	3.00	6.00	12.00
❑ 7010	Live at the Paradiso	1980	3.00	6.00	12.00

WRENS, THE

45s

Number	Title (A Side/B Side)	Yr	VG	VG+	NM
RAMA					
❑ 53	Love's Something That's Made for Two/Beggin' for Love	1955	375.00	750.00	1500.
❑ 65	Come Back My Love/Beggin' for Love	1955	37.50	75.00	150.00
❑ 65	Come Back My Love/Eleven Roses	1955	100.00	200.00	400.00
❑ 110	Love's Something That's Made for Two/Eleven Roses	1955	75.00	150.00	300.00
❑ 174	Hey Girl/Serenade of the Bells	1955	100.00	200.00	400.00
❑ 184	I Won't Come to Your Wedding/What Makes You Do the Things That You Do	1956	100.00	200.00	400.00
❑ 194	C'est La Vie/C'est La Vie	1956	100.00	200.00	400.00
—B-side by Jimmy Wright and His Orchestra					

WRIGHT, BETTY

12-Inch Singles

Number	Title (A Side/B Side)	Yr	VG	VG+	NM
FIRST STRING					
❑ 268	I Can (2 versions)/Music Street	1986	2.50	5.00	10.00
JAMAICA					
❑ 9002	One Step Up, Two Steps Back (9:52) (7:57 Dub)	1984	2.00	4.00	8.00
❑ 9004	Sinderella (6:30) (5:28)	1985	2.00	4.00	8.00
MS. B.					
❑ 1217	From Pain to Joy (Project Mix)/From Pain to Joy (Project Mix with Rap)	1989	2.00	4.00	8.00

Number	Title (A Side/B Side)	Yr	VG	VG+	NM
❏ 1230	We Down (5 versions)	1989	2.00	4.00	8.00
T.K. DISCO					
❏ 125	Lovin' Is Really My Game (2 versions)	1979	3.00	6.00	12.00
VISION					
❏ 7005	After the Pain (6:56)/After the Pain (Project Mix)	1988	2.00	4.00	8.00
45s					
ALSTON					
❏ 3711	Shoorah! Shoorah!/Tonight Is the Night	1974	—	2.50	5.00
❏ 3713	Where Is the Love/				
	My Baby Ain't My Baby Anymore	1975	—	2.50	5.00
❏ 3715	Ooola La/To Love and Be Loved	1975	—	2.50	5.00
❏ 3718	Slip and Do It/I Think I Better Think About It	1975	—	2.50	5.00
❏ 3719	Everybody Was Rockin'/Show Your Girl	1976	—	2.50	5.00
❏ 3722	If I Ever Do Wrong/Rock On Baby, Rock On	1976	—	2.50	5.00
❏ 3725	Life/If I Was a Kid.	1976	—	2.50	5.00
❏ 3734	You Can't See for Lookin'/				
	Sometime Kind of Thing	1977	—	2.50	5.00
❏ 3736	Man of Mine/Sweet	1978	—	2.50	5.00
❏ 3740	Tonight Is the Night (Part 1)/				
	Tonight Is the Night (Part 2)	1978	—	2.50	5.00
❏ 3745	Lovin' Is Really My Game/A Song for You	1979	—	2.50	5.00
❏ 3747	My Love Is/I Believe It's Love	1979	—	2.50	5.00
❏ 3749	Thank You for the Many Things You've Done/				
	Child of the Man	1979	—	2.50	5.00
❏ 4569	Girls Can't Do What the Guys Do/				
	Sweet Lovin' Daddy	1968	2.00	4.00	8.00
❏ 4571	He's Bad Bad Bad/Watch Out, Love	1968	2.00	4.00	8.00
❏ 4573	The Best Girls Don't Always Win/Circle of				
	Heartbreaks	1969	2.00	4.00	8.00
❏ 4575	The Wrong Girl/The Joy of Becoming a Woman	1969	2.00	4.00	8.00
❏ 4580	I'm Not Free Hearted/				
	A Woman Was Made for One Man	1969	2.00	4.00	8.00
❏ 4581	Soldier Boy/A Woman Was Made for One Man	1969	2.00	4.00	8.00
❏ 4587	Pure Love/If You Ain't Got It	1970	—	3.50	7.00
❏ 4589	I Found That Guy/If You Love Like I Love You	1970	—	3.50	7.00
❏ 4594	I Love the Way You Love/When We Get				
	Together Again	1971	—	3.50	7.00
❏ 4601	Clean Up Woman/I'll Love You Forever	1971	—	3.00	6.00
❏ 4609	If You Love Me Like You Say You Love Me/I'm				
	Gettin' Tired Baby	1972	—	3.00	6.00
❏ 4611	Is It You Girl/Crying in My Sleep	1972	—	3.00	6.00
❏ 4614	Baby Sitter/Outside Woman	1972	—	3.00	6.00
❏ 4617	It's Hard to Stop (Doing Something When It's				
	Good to You)/Who'll Be the Fool	1973	—	3.00	6.00
❏ 4619	Let Me Be Your Lovemaker/Jealous Man	1973	—	3.00	6.00
❏ 4620	It's Bad for Me to See You/				
	One Thing Leads to Another	1974	—	3.00	6.00
❏ 4622	Secretary/Value Your Love	1974	—	3.00	6.00
EPIC					
❏ 02143	I Like Your Loving/Body Slang	1981	—	2.00	4.00
❏ 02521	Goodbye Him Hello You/Make Me Love the Rain	1981	—	2.00	4.00
❏ 03523	He's Older Now/Special Love	1983	—	2.00	4.00
❏ 03954	Burning Desire/Show Me	1983	—	2.00	4.00
❏ 51009	What Are We Gonna Do About It/I Believe in You	1981	—	2.00	4.00
FIRST STRING					
❏ 965	Pain/(B-side unknown)	1985	—	2.00	4.00
❏ 968	The Sun Don't Shine/Music Street	1986	—	2.00	4.00
JAMAICA					
❏ 3	One Step Up, Two Steps Back/				
	(B-side unknown)	1984	—	2.00	4.00
MS. B.					
❏ 4501	No Pain, No Gain/(Instrumental)	1988	—	2.00	4.00
❏ 4503	After the Pain/Love Days	1988	—	2.00	4.00
❏ 4504	A Christmas To Remember/2nd Chapter Of The				
	Book Of Mathew	1988	—	—	3.00
❏ 4505	From Pain to Joy/				
	From Pain to Joy (The Project Mix)	1989	—	2.00	4.00
❏ 4508	Quiet Storm/We Down	1989	—	2.00	4.00
Albums					
ALSTON					
❏ SD 33-388	I Love the Way You Love	1972	3.75	7.50	15.00
❏ 4400	Danger High Voltage	1974	3.00	6.00	12.00
❏ 4406	This Time for Real	1977	3.00	6.00	12.00
❏ 4408	Betty Wright Live	1978	3.00	6.00	12.00
❏ 4410	Betty Travelin' in the Wright Circle	1979	3.00	6.00	12.00
❏ SD 7026	Hard to Stop	1973	3.75	7.50	15.00
ATCO					
❏ SD 33-260	My First Time Around	1968	6.25	12.50	25.00
COLLECTABLES					
❏ COL-5118	Golden Classics	198?	2.50	5.00	10.00
EPIC					
❏ JE 36879	Betty Wright	1981	2.50	5.00	10.00
❏ FE 38558	Wright Back at You	1983	2.50	5.00	10.00
FANTASY					
❏ 9644	Sevens	1986	2.50	5.00	10.00
MS. B.					
❏ 3301	Mother Wit	1988	2.50	5.00	10.00
❏ 3318	Passion and Compassion	198?	3.75	7.50	15.00

WRIGHT, CHARLES, AND THE WATTS 103RD STREET RHYTHM BAND

45s

Number	Title (A Side/B Side)	Yr	VG	VG+	NM
ABC					
❏ 12127	Is It Real/One Lie	1975	—	2.00	4.00
—Charles Wright solo					
ABC DUNHILL					
❏ 4363	Liberated Lady/You Threw It All Away	1973	—	2.00	4.00
❏ 4364	(Well I'm) Doing What Cums Naturally Part 1/				
	Part 2	1973	—	2.00	4.00
❏ 4381	The Weight of Hate/You Threw It All Away	1974	—	2.00	4.00
❏ 15027	Don't Rush Tomorrow/Is It Real	1974	—	2.00	4.00
KEYMEN					
❏ 108	Spreadin' Honey/Charlie	1967	2.50	5.00	10.00
—As "The Watts 103rd Street Rhythm Band"					
WARNER BROS.					
❏ 7175	Brown Sugar/Caesar's Palace	1968	2.50	5.00	10.00
—Through 7298, as "The Watts 103rd Street Rhythm Band"					

Number	Title (A Side/B Side)	Yr	VG	VG+	NM
❏ 7222	Bottomless/65 Bars and a Taste of Soul	1968	2.50	5.00	10.00
❏ 7250	Do Your Thing/A Dance, a Kiss, and a Song	1969	2.00	4.00	8.00
❏ 7298	Till You Get Enough/Light My Fire	1969	2.00	4.00	8.00
❏ 7338	Must Be Your Thing/Comment	1969	—	3.00	6.00
❏ 7365	Love Land/Sorry Charlie	1970	—	3.00	6.00
❏ 7417	Express Yourself/Living on Borrowed Time	1970	—	3.00	6.00
❏ 7475	Your Love (Means Everything to Me)/				
	What Can You Bring Me	1971	—	2.50	5.00
❏ 7504	Nobody/Wine	1971	—	2.50	5.00
❏ 7577	I've Got Love/Let's Make Love — Not War	1972	—	2.50	5.00
❏ 7600	Soul Train/Run Judy Run	1972	—	2.50	5.00
❏ 7630	Here Comes the Sun/				
	You Gotta Know Whatcha Doin'	1972	—	2.50	5.00
Albums					
ABC					
❏ D-887	Lil' Encouragement	1975	3.00	6.00	12.00
ABC DUNHILL					
❏ DS-50162 [(2)]	Doin' What Comes Naturally	1973	3.75	7.50	15.00
❏ DS-50187	Ninety Day Cycle People	1974	3.00	6.00	12.00
WARNER BROS.					
❏ WS 1741	The Watts 103rd Street Rhythm Band	1968	5.00	10.00	20.00
❏ WS 1761	Together	1969	5.00	10.00	20.00
—Green label with "W7" logo					
❏ WS 1761	Together	1970	3.75	7.50	15.00
—Green label with "WB" logo					
❏ WS 1801	In the Jungle, Babe	1969	5.00	10.00	20.00
—Green label with "W7" logo					
❏ WS 1801	In the Jungle, Babe	1970	3.75	7.50	15.00
—Green label with "WB" logo					
❏ WS 1864	Express Yourself	1970	3.75	7.50	15.00
❏ WS 1904	You're So Beautiful	1971	3.75	7.50	15.00
❏ BS 2620	Rhythm and Poetry	1972	3.75	7.50	15.00
—Green label with "WB" logo					
❏ BS 2620	Rhythm and Poetry	1973	3.00	6.00	12.00
—"Burbank" palm-trees logo					

WRIGHT, GARY Also see SPOOKY TOOTH.

45s

Number	Title (A Side/B Side)	Yr	VG	VG+	NM
A&M					
❏ 1228	Over You Now/Get On the Right Road	1970	—	2.50	5.00
❏ 1267	Stand for Our Rights/I Can't See the Reason	1971	—	2.50	5.00
❏ 1319	Love to Survive/Fascinating Things	1972	—	2.50	5.00
❏ 1344	Two-Faced Man/I Know	1972	—	2.50	5.00
WARNER BROS.					
❏ 8143	Love Is Alive/Much Higher	1975	—	2.00	4.00
—Reissued in 1976 with the same number					
❏ 8167	Dream Weaver/Let It Out	1975	—	2.00	4.00
❏ 8250	Made to Love You/Power of Love	1976	—	2.00	4.00
❏ 8331	Phantom Writer/Child of Light	1977	—	2.00	4.00
❏ 8383	Empty Inside/Water Sign	1977	—	2.00	4.00
❏ 8426	Light of Smiles/Silent Fury	1977	—	2.00	4.00
❏ 8548	Something Very Special/Starry Eyed	1978	—	2.00	4.00
❏ 8598	Can't Get Above Losing You/Starry Eyed	1978	—	2.00	4.00
❏ 8809	Follow Next to You/				
	I'm the One Who'll Be At Your Side	1979	—	2.00	4.00
❏ 49769	Really Wanna Know You/More Than a				
	Heartache	1981	—	2.00	4.00
❏ 49836	Comin' Apart/Heartbeat	1981	—	2.00	4.00
❏ 49879	Got the Feelin'/Close to You	1981	—	2.00	4.00
Albums					
A&M					
❏ SP-3528 [(2)]	That Was Only Yesterday	1976	3.75	7.50	15.00
—By "Gary Wright/Spooky Tooth"					
❏ SP-4277	Extraction	1970	3.75	7.50	15.00
❏ SP-4296	Footprint	1971	3.75	7.50	15.00
CYPRESS					
❏ 0111	Who I Am	1988	3.00	6.00	12.00
WARNER BROS.					
❏ BS 2868	The Dream Weaver	1975	2.50	5.00	10.00
❏ BS 2951	The Light of Smiles	1976	2.50	5.00	10.00
❏ BSK 3137	Touch and Gone	1977	2.50	5.00	10.00
❏ BSK 3244	Headin' Home	1979	2.50	5.00	10.00
❏ BSK 3511	The Right Place	1981	2.50	5.00	10.00

WRIGHT, O.V.

45s

Number	Title (A Side/B Side)	Yr	VG	VG+	NM
ABC					
❏ 12119	What More Can I Do (To Prove My Love to You)/				
	Henpecked Man	1975	—	3.00	6.00
❏ 12154	Nobody But You/Slow and Easy	1976	—	3.00	6.00
BACK BEAT					
❏ 544	Don't Want to Sit Down/Can't Find True Love	1965	2.50	5.00	10.00
❏ 548	You're Gonna Make Me Cry/Monkey Dog	1965	2.50	5.00	10.00
❏ 551	I'm In Your Corner/Poor Boy	1965	2.50	5.00	10.00
❏ 558	Gone for Good/How Long Baby	1966	2.50	5.00	10.00
❏ 580	Eight Men, Four Women/Fed Up with the Blues	1967	2.00	4.00	8.00
❏ 583	Heartaches-Heartaches/Treasured Moments	1967	2.00	4.00	8.00
❏ 586	What About You/				
	What Did You Tell This Girl of Mine	1967	2.00	4.00	8.00
❏ 591	Oh Baby Mine/Working Your Game	1968	2.00	4.00	8.00
❏ 597	I Want Everyone to Know/				
	I'm Gonna Forget About You	1968	2.00	4.00	8.00
❏ 604	Missing You/This Must Be Real	1969	2.00	4.00	8.00
❏ 607	I'll Take Care of You/Why Not Give Me a Chance	1969	2.00	4.00	8.00
❏ 611	Love the Way You Love/Blowin' in the Wind	1970	2.00	4.00	8.00
❏ 615	Ace of Spade/Afflicted	1970	2.00	4.00	8.00
❏ 620	When You Took Your Love from Me/				
	I Was Born All Over	1971	—	3.00	6.00
❏ 622	A Nickel and a Nail/Pledging My Love	1971	—	3.00	6.00
❏ 625	He Made Woman for Man/				
	Don't Let My Baby Ride	1972	—	3.00	6.00
❏ 626	Drowning on Dry Land/				
	I'm Gonna Forget About You	1973	—	3.00	6.00
❏ 628	I'd Rather Be (Blind, Cripple and Crazy)/				
	Please Forgive Me	1973	—	3.00	6.00
❏ 631	I've Been Searching/I'm Going Home	1974	—	3.00	6.00
❏ 5103	I'm In Your Corner/Poor Boy	1974	—	3.00	6.00

Andy Williams, *Moon River and Other Great Movie Themes*, Columbia CS 8609, stereo LP, "360 Sound Stereo" in black on label, $7.50-$15.

Hank Williams, *Hank Williams As Luke the Drifter*, MGM E-3267, mono LP, yellow label, $50-$100.

Jackie Wilson, *Body and Soul*, Brunswick BL 54105, mono LP, all-black label, $25-$50.

Jonathan Winters, *The Best of Maude Frickert and Elwood P. Suggins,* Verve V 15052, mono LP, $10-$20.

Stevie Wonder, *Recorded Live/Little Stevie Wonder/The 12 Year Old Genius*, Tamla T 240, mono LP, $60-$120.

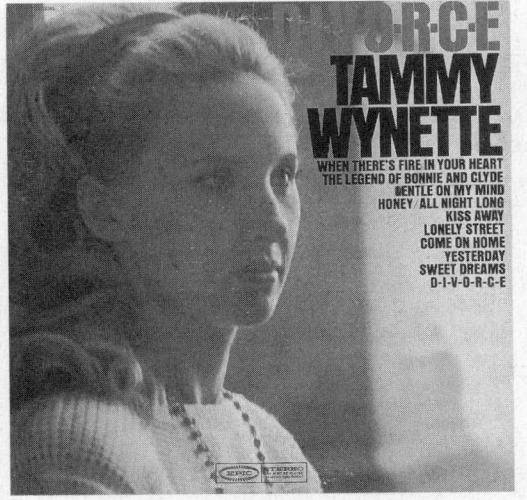

Tammy Wynette, *D-I-V-O-R-C-E,* Epic BN 26392, stereo LP, $10-$20.

Number	Title (A Side/B Side)	Yr	VG	VG+	NM
GOLDWAX					
❏ 106	That's How Strong My Love Is/				
	There Goes My Used to Be	1964	3.00	6.00	12.00
HI					
❏ 2315	Rhymes/Without You	1976	—	3.00	6.00
❏ 77501	Into Something (Can't Shake Loose)/				
	The Time We Have	1977	—	3.00	6.00
❏ 77506	Precious, Precious/You Gotta Have Love	1977	—	3.00	6.00
❏ 78514	I Don't Do Windows/I Feel Love Growin'	1978	—	3.00	6.00
❏ 78521	No Easy Way to Say Goodbye/Bottom Line	1978	—	3.00	6.00
❏ 79531	We're Still Together/I Don't Know Why	1979	—	3.00	6.00
Albums					
BACK BEAT					
❏ 61 [M]	If It's Only for Tonight	1965	25.00	50.00	100.00
❏ S-61 [S]	If It's Only for Tonight	1965	37.50	75.00	150.00
❏ 66	Eight Men, Four Women	1968	15.00	30.00	60.00
❏ 67	Nucleus of Soul	1969	15.00	30.00	60.00
❏ 70	A Nickel and a Nail and Ace of Spade	1971	15.00	30.00	60.00
❏ 72	Memphis Unlimited	1973	12.50	25.00	50.00
HI					
❏ 6001	Into Something	1977	6.25	12.50	25.00
❏ 6008	Bottom Line	1978	6.25	12.50	25.00
❏ 6011	We're Still Together	1979	6.25	12.50	25.00
WRIGHT, RANDY					
45s					
ATLANTIC					
❏ 1115	What My Heart Didn't Know/Snake in the Grass	1956	5.00	10.00	20.00
WRIGHT, RITA Later recorded as SYREETA.					
45s					
GORDY					
❏ 7064	I Can't Give Back the Love I Feel for You/				
	Something on My Mind	1967	2.50	5.00	10.00
WRIGHT, RUBY (1)					
45s					
CANDEE					
❏ 502	This Is Christmas/(B-side unknown)	196?	5.00	10.00	20.00
COLUMBIA					
❏ 4-41807	Wasn't the Summer Short/Fooled	1960	5.00	10.00	20.00
FRATERNITY					
❏ 787	Let's Light the Christmas Tree/				
	Merry Merry Christmas	1957	3.75	7.50	15.00
KING					
❏ 1249	You Walked Out of My Dreams/				
	I Only Have One Lifetime	1953	7.50	15.00	30.00
❏ 1288	Santa's Little Sleigh Bells/Toodle Oo To You	1953	7.50	15.00	30.00
❏ 1293	Boy You Got Yourself a Girl/Bimbo	1953	6.25	12.50	25.00
❏ 1305	Tennessee Churchbells/				
	I Had the Funniest Feeling	1954	6.25	12.50	25.00
❏ 1411	God Loves You Child/What Have They Told You	1954	6.25	12.50	25.00
❏ 4850	Do You Believe/I Fall in Love with You Every Day	1955	5.00	10.00	20.00
❏ 4870	Rummy Dumb Bunny/Don't Take Me for Granted	1956	5.00	10.00	20.00
❏ 5192	Three Stars/I Only Have One Lifetime	1959	5.00	10.00	20.00
❏ 5208	Goodbye, Jimmy, Goodbye/				
	Don't Take Me for Granted	1959	5.00	10.00	20.00
❏ 5225	Don't Take Me for Granted/				
	I Only Have One Lifetime	1959	5.00	10.00	20.00
❏ 5261	Sweet Night of Love/You're Just a Flower from				
	an Old Bouquet	1959	5.00	10.00	20.00
❏ 5297	Free-Hearted/When You're Away	1959	5.00	10.00	20.00
7-Inch Extended Plays					
CANDEE					
❏ EP-50-50	Christmas Is a Birthday Time//Have A Merry				
	Merry Merry Merry Christmas/The Happy Time	196?	2.00	4.00	8.00
—B-side by Ruth Lyons					
WRIGHT, RUBY (2)					
45s					
EPIC					
❏ 5-10055	A New Place to Hang Your Hat/A Kick in the				
	Conscience	1966	2.50	5.00	10.00
❏ 5-10150	(I Can Find) A Better Deal Than That/Everything,				
	All the Time	1967	2.50	5.00	10.00
WRIGHT, SONNY (1) R&B singer, formerly with THE DIAMONDS (2).					
45s					
ATLANTIC					
❏ 45-2045	Heaven Help Me/Lullaby with a Beat	1960	7.50	15.00	30.00
WRIGHT, SONNY (2)					
45s					
COLUMBIA					
❏ 4-44320	Leftover Love/Running Drunk	1967	2.00	4.00	8.00
❏ 4-44496	Pain Remover/Hung to Another Man	1968	2.00	4.00	8.00
COUNTRY INT'L.					
❏ 178	Don't Leave Without Taking Your Silver/(B-side				
	unknown)	1982	—	2.50	5.00
❏ 184	The Ride/Don't Leave Without Taking Your				
	Silver	198?	—	2.50	5.00
CUTLASS					
❏ 126	Gettin' Ready to Die/Here Comes a Million	197?	—	3.00	6.00
❏ 814	Truck Driver's Hymn/Hangout for a Hasbeen	197?	—	3.00	6.00
DOOR KNOB					
❏ 040	Motel Mourning/When I Start Drinking	1977	—	2.50	5.00
❏ 057	Same Old Highway/Motel Mourning	1978	—	2.50	5.00
❏ 100	You Make Me Feel Brand New/If This Isn't It	1979	—	2.50	5.00
❏ 128	Molly (And the Texas Rain)/It Wasn't Me Who				
	Said I Owned a Gold Mine	1980	—	2.50	5.00
KAPP					
❏ 2009	I Love You, Loretta Lynn/Rose	1969	2.50	5.00	10.00
❏ 2040	Hung Over/The Trash You Threw Away	1969	2.00	4.00	8.00
❏ 2090	My Long Gone Reason/				
	Mama Didn't Bend the Twig	1970	2.00	4.00	8.00
PARTHENON					
❏ 002	Gotta Swim the Mississippi/99 Years	198?	—	3.00	6.00
❏ 008	I'll Build Her Up/You're Leaving Me for Him	198?	—	3.00	6.00

Number	Title (A Side/B Side)	Yr	VG	VG+	NM
Albums					
KAPP					
❏ KS-3614	I Love You, Loretta Lynn	1968	5.00	10.00	20.00
WRIGLEY, BETTY					
45s					
HIT					
❏ 141	Selfish One/Save It for Me	1964	2.00	4.00	8.00
—B-side by the Roamers					
WRITIS, ARTHUR, AND THE NAGGING PAINS					
45s					
REPRISE					
❏ 0589	Say What/Welcome to San Francisco	1967	2.50	5.00	10.00
WYATT, GENE					
45s					
DOLLIE					
❏ 502	Fightin' for the Free Land/				
	Searching for a New Love Affair	1966	2.50	5.00	10.00
EBB					
❏ 123	Love Fever/Lover Boy	1957	25.00	50.00	100.00
LUCKY SEVEN					
❏ 101	Prettiest Girl at the Dance/Music and Arithmetic	1959	15.00	30.00	60.00
MERCURY					
❏ 72752	I Stole the Flowers/I'm a One Woman Man	1967	2.50	5.00	10.00
PAULA					
❏ 308	I Just Ain't Got (As Much As He's Got Going for				
	Me)/Chains Around My Heart	1968	2.50	5.00	10.00
❏ 1206	Little Liza Jane/Country Music Peyton Place	1968	2.50	5.00	10.00
❏ 1211	My Story of Love/Evangeline	1969	2.50	5.00	10.00
❏ 1216	Milk and Honey Memories/Failure of T Crop	1969	2.50	5.00	10.00
❏ 1223	Twelve Men/Back Door of My Mind	1970	2.00	4.00	8.00
❏ 1224	Go Together/As Long As I Live	1970	2.00	4.00	8.00
WYMAN, BILL Also see THE ROLLING STONES.					
12-Inch Singles					
A&M					
❏ SP-12041	(Si Si) Je Suis Un Rock Star (2 versions)/				
	Rio de Janeiro	1981	3.75	7.50	15.00
—Red label					
❏ SP-12041	(Si Si) Je Suis Un Rock Star (2 versions)/				
	Rio de Janeiro	1981	10.00	20.00	40.00
—Silver label					
45s					
A&M					
❏ 2367	(Si Si) Je Suis Un Rock Star/Rio De Janeiro	1981	—	2.50	5.00
❏ 2367 [PS]	(Si Si) Je Suis Un Rock Star/Rio De Janeiro	1981	2.50	5.00	10.00
ROLLING STONES					
❏ 19111	White Lightning/I Wanna Get Me a Gun	1974	—	2.50	5.00
❏ 19119	A Quarter to Three/Soul Satisfying	1975	—	2.50	5.00
❏ 19303	Apache Woman/Soul Satisfying	1975	—	2.50	5.00
Albums					
ROLLING STONES					
❏ COC 59102	Monkey Grip	1974	3.75	7.50	15.00
❏ COC 79100	Monkey Grip	1974	3.00	6.00	12.00
—Reissue of 59102					
❏ QD 79100 [Q]	Monkey Grip	1974	5.00	10.00	20.00
❏ COC 79103	Stone Alone	1976	3.00	6.00	12.00
❏ QD 79103 [Q]	Stone Alone	1976	5.00	10.00	20.00
WYNDER K. FROG					
45s					
UNITED ARTISTS					
❏ 50156	The Green Door/Dancing Frog	1967	—	3.00	6.00
❏ 50320	I'm a Man/Oh Mary	1968	—	3.00	6.00
❏ 50453	Jumpin' Jack Flash/I Feel So Bad	1968	—	3.00	6.00
Albums					
UNITED ARTISTS					
❏ UAS-5740	Into the Fire	1971	3.00	6.00	12.00
❏ UAS-6695	Out of the Frying Pan	1970	3.00	6.00	12.00
WYNETTE, TAMMY Also see DAVID HOUSTON AND TAMMY WYNETTE; GEORGE JONES AND TAMMY WYNETTE.					
45s					
COLUMBIA					
❏ 77294	Silver Threads and Golden Needles/Let Her Fly	1993	—	—	3.00
—With Dolly Parton and Loretta Lynn					
EPIC					
❏ AS 60 [DJ]	White Christmas/One Happy Christmas	1973	2.00	4.00	8.00
—1973 Christmas Seals promotional record					
❏ AS 60 [PS]	White Christmas/One Happy Christmas	1973	2.50	5.00	10.00
❏ 02439	Crying in the Rain/Bring Back My Baby to Me	1981	—	2.00	4.00
❏ 02770	Another Chance/What's It Like to Be a Woman	1982	—	2.00	4.00
❏ 03064	You Still Get To Me in My Dreams/If I Didn't Have				
	a Heart	1982	—	2.00	4.00
❏ 03384	A Good Night's Love/I'm Going On with				
	Everything Gone	1982	—	2.00	4.00
❏ 03811	I Just Heard a Heart Break				
	(And I'm So Afraid It's Mine)/Back to the Wall	1983	—	2.00	4.00
❏ 03971	Unwed Fathers				
	/I'm So Afraid That I'd Live Through It	1983	—	2.00	4.00
❏ 04101	Still in the Ring/Midnight Love	1983	—	2.00	4.00
❏ 04467	Lonely Heart/(I'm Not) A Candle in the Wind	1984	—	—	3.00
❏ 05399	You Can Lead a Heart to Love (But You Can't				
	Make It Fall)/He Talks to Me	1985	—	—	3.00
❏ 06263	Alive and Well/I'll Be Thinking of You	1986	—	—	3.00
❏ 07226	Your Love/I Wasn't Meant to Live My Life Alone	1987	—	—	3.00
❏ 07635	Talkin' to Myself Again/A Slow Burning Fire	1987	—	—	3.00
❏ 07788	Beneath a Painted Sky/				
	Some Things Will Never Change	1988	—	—	3.00
❏ 5-10095	Apartment No. 9/I'm Not Mine to Give	1966	2.50	5.00	10.00
❏ 5-10134	Your Good Girl's Gonna Go Bad/				
	Send Me No Roses	1967	2.00	4.00	8.00
❏ 5-10211	I Don't Wanna Play House/Soakin' Wet	1967	2.00	4.00	8.00
❏ 5-10269	Take Me to Your World/Good	1967	2.00	4.00	8.00

Number	Title (A Side/B Side)	Yr	VG	VG+	NM
❏ 5-10315	D-I-V-O-R-C-E/Don't Make It Now	1968	2.00	4.00	8.00
❏ 5-10398	Stand By Your Man/I Stayed Long Enough	1968	2.50	5.00	10.00
❏ 5-10462	Singing My Song/Too Far Gone	1969	—	3.00	6.00
❏ 5-10462 [PS]	Singing My Song/Too Far Gone	1969	2.50	5.00	10.00
❏ 5-10512	The Ways to Love a Man/Still Around	1969	—	3.00	6.00
❏ 5-10571	I'll See Him Through/Enough of a Woman	1970	—	3.00	6.00
❏ 5-10612	He Loves Me All the Way/ One Last Night Together	1970	—	3.00	6.00
❏ 5-10653	Run, Woman, Run/My Daddy Doll	1970	—	3.00	6.00
❏ 5-10687	The Wonders You Perform/Gentle Shepherd	1970	—	3.00	6.00
❏ 5-10690	One Happy Christmas/(Merry Christmas) We Must Be Having One	1970	2.00	4.00	8.00
❏ 5-10707	We Sure Can Love Each Other/Fun	1971	—	3.00	6.00
❏ 5-10759	Good Lovin' (Makes It Right)/ I Love You, Mr. Jones	1971	—	3.00	6.00
❏ 5-10818	Bedtime Story/Reach Out Your Hand	1971	—	3.00	6.00
❏ 5-10856	Reach Out Your Hand/Love's the Answer	1972	—	3.00	6.00
❏ 5-10909	My Man/Things I Love to Do	1972	—	3.00	6.00
❏ 5-10940	'Til I Get It Right/The Bridge of Love	1973	—	3.00	6.00
❏ 5-10969	Kids Say the Darnedest Things/I Wish I Had a Mommy Like You	1973	—	3.00	6.00
❏ 5-11044	One Final Stand/Crying Steel Guitar	1973	—	—	—
—Canceled?					
❏ 5-11079	Another Lonely Song/ The Only Time I'm Really Me	1973	—	3.00	6.00
❏ 50008	Woman to Woman/Love Me Forever	1974	—	2.50	5.00
❏ 50071	(You Make Me Want to Be) A Mother/ I'm Not a Has-Been	1975	—	2.50	5.00
❏ 50145	I Still Believe in Fairy Tales/ Your Memory's Gone to Rest	1975	—	2.50	5.00
❏ 50196	'Til I Can Make It on My Own/ Love Is Something Good for Everybody	1976	—	2.50	5.00
❏ 50264	You and Me/When Love Was All We Had	1976	—	2.50	5.00
❏ 50349	(Let's Get Together) One Last Time/Hardly a Day Goes By	1977	—	2.50	5.00
❏ 50450	One of a Kind/Loving You, I Do	1977	—	2.50	5.00
❏ 50538	I'd Like to See Jesus (On the Midnight Special)/ Love Doesn't Always Come (On the Night It's Needed)	1978	—	2.50	5.00
❏ 50574	Womanhood/50 Words or Less	1978	—	2.50	5.00
❏ 50661	They Call It Making Love/Let Me Be Me	1979	—	2.50	5.00
❏ 50722	No One Else in the World/ Mama, Your Little Girl Fell	1979	—	2.50	5.00
❏ 50868	He Was There (When I Needed You)/Only the Names Have Been Changed	1980	—	2.50	5.00
❏ 50915	Starting Over/I'll Be Thinking of You	1980	—	2.50	5.00
❏ 51011	Cowboys Don't Shoot Straight (Like They Used To)/You Brought Me Back	1981	—	2.00	4.00
❏ 68570	Next to You/When a Girl Becomes a Wife	1989	—	—	3.00
❏ 68894	Thank the Cowboy for the Ride/We Called It Everything But Quits	1989	—	—	3.00
❏ 73427	Let's Call It a Day Today/ When a Girl Becomes a Wife	1990	—	2.00	4.00
❏ 73579	I'm Turning You Loose/Just a Minute There	1990	—	2.00	4.00
❏ 73656	What Goes with Blue/Let's Call It a Day Today	1991	—	2.00	4.00
❏ 73958	We're Strangers Again/If You Were the Friend	1991	—	2.00	4.00
—A-side with Randy Travis					

7-Inch Extended Plays

EPIC

Number	Title (A Side/B Side)	Yr	VG	VG+	NM
❏ 5-26392	D-I-V-O-R-C-E/Kiss Away/Lonely Street// Honey/Sweet Dreams/Yesterday	1968	3.00	6.00	12.00
—Jukebox issue; small hole, plays at 33 1/3 rpm					
❏ 5-26392 [PS]	D-I-V-O-R-C-E	1968	3.00	6.00	12.00
❏ 5-26451	Stand By Your Man/It's My Way/I Stayed Long Enough//My Arms Stay Open Late/I've Learned/Cry, Cry Again	1969	3.00	6.00	12.00
—Jukebox issue; small hole, plays at 33 1/3 rpm					
❏ 5-26451 [PS]	Stand By Your Man	1969	3.00	6.00	12.00
❏ 5-30213	I Wish I Had a Mommy Like You/He's Still My Man/Playin' Around with Love//True and Lasting Love/ I Never Once Stopped Loving You/The Lovin' Kind	1970	3.00	6.00	12.00
—Jukebox issue; small hole, plays at 33 1/3 rpm					
❏ 5-30213 [PS]	The First Lady	1970	3.00	6.00	12.00

Albums

COLUMBIA LIMITED EDITION

Number	Title (A Side/B Side)	Yr	VG	VG+	NM
❏ LE 10049	The First Lady	197?	3.00	6.00	12.00
❏ LE 10193	The Ways to Love a Man	197?	3.00	6.00	12.00
❏ LE 10194	Tammy's Touch	197?	3.00	6.00	12.00
❏ LE 10195	We Sure Can Love Each Other	197?	3.00	6.00	12.00

COLUMBIA SPECIAL PRODUCTS

Number	Title (A Side/B Side)	Yr	VG	VG+	NM
❏ P 11228	Take Me to Your World	1973	3.00	6.00	12.00
❏ P 11519	Your Good Girl's Gonna Go Bad	1973	3.00	6.00	12.00

Number	Title (A Side/B Side)	Yr	VG	VG+	NM
❏ P 13256	The Ways to Love a Man	1976	3.00	6.00	12.00
❏ P 13259	My Man	1976	3.00	6.00	12.00
❏ P 13261	Bedtime Story	1976	3.00	6.00	12.00
❏ P 13611	Twenty Big Hits of Tammy Wynette	197?	3.75	7.50	15.00

EPIC

Number	Title (A Side/B Side)	Yr	VG	VG+	NM
❏ EGP 503 [(2)]	The World of Tammy Wynette	1970	6.25	12.50	25.00
❏ LN 24305 [M]	Your Good Girl's Gonna Go Bad	1967	7.50	15.00	30.00
❏ LN 24353 [M]	Take Me to Your World/I Don't Wanna Play House	1968	10.00	20.00	40.00
—May exist only as a white label promo					
❏ LN 24392 [M]	D-I-V-O-R-C-E	1968	12.50	25.00	50.00
—This has been confirmed to exist on yellow label stock copies					
❏ BN 26305 [S]	Your Good Girl's Gonna Go Bad	1967	5.00	10.00	20.00
❏ BN 26353 [S]	Take Me to Your World/ I Don't Wanna Play House	1968	5.00	10.00	20.00
❏ BN 26392 [S]	D-I-V-O-R-C-E	1968	5.00	10.00	20.00
❏ BN 26423	Inspiration	1969	5.00	10.00	20.00
❏ BN 26451	Stand By Your Man	1969	5.00	10.00	20.00
❏ BN 26486	Tammy's Greatest Hits	1969	5.00	10.00	20.00
❏ PE 26486	Tammy's Greatest Hits	198?	2.00	4.00	8.00
—Budget-line reissue					
❏ BN 26519	The Ways to Love a Man	1970	5.00	10.00	20.00
❏ BN 26549	Tammy's Touch	1970	5.00	10.00	20.00
❏ E 30213	The First Lady	1970	5.00	10.00	20.00
❏ E 30343	Christmas with Tammy	1970	5.00	10.00	20.00
❏ KEG 30358 [(2)]	The First Songs of the First Lady	1970	5.00	10.00	20.00
❏ E 30658	We Sure Can Love Each Other	1971	5.00	10.00	20.00
❏ EQ 30658 [Q]	We Sure Can Love Each Other	1972	7.50	15.00	30.00
❏ E 30733	Tammy's Greatest Hits, Volume II	1971	5.00	10.00	20.00
❏ PE 30733	Tammy's Greatest Hits, Volume II	198?	2.00	4.00	8.00
—Budget-line reissue					
❏ KE 31285	Bedtime Story	1972	3.75	7.50	15.00
❏ KE 31717	My Man	1972	3.75	7.50	15.00
❏ KE 31937	Kids Say the Darndest Things	1973	3.75	7.50	15.00
❏ KE 32745	Another Lonely Song	1974	3.00	6.00	12.00
❏ KE 33246	Woman to Woman	1975	3.00	6.00	12.00
❏ KE 33396	Tammy's Greatest Hits, Volume III	1975	3.00	6.00	12.00
❏ PE 33396	Tammy's Greatest Hits, Volume III	198?	2.00	4.00	8.00
—Budget-line reissue					
❏ KE 33582	I Still Believe in Fairy Tales	1975	3.00	6.00	12.00
❏ BG 33773 [(2)]	Stand By Your Man/Bedtime Story	1976	3.75	7.50	15.00
❏ PE 34075	'Til I Can Make It on My Own	1976	3.00	6.00	12.00
❏ PE 34289	You and Me	1976	3.00	6.00	12.00
❏ PE 34694	Let's Get Together One Last Time	1977	3.00	6.00	12.00
❏ KE 35044	One of a Kind	1977	3.00	6.00	12.00
❏ KE 35442	Womanhood	1978	3.00	6.00	12.00
❏ KE 35630	Tammy's Greatest Hits, Volume IV	1978	3.00	6.00	12.00
❏ KE 36013	Just Tammy	1979	3.00	6.00	12.00
❏ JE 36485	Only Lonely Sometimes	1980	2.50	5.00	10.00
❏ FE 37104	You Brought Me Back	1981	2.50	5.00	10.00
❏ FE 37344	Encore	1981	2.50	5.00	10.00
❏ PE 37344	Encore	198?	2.00	4.00	8.00
—Budget-line reissue					
❏ FE 37980	Soft Touch	1982	2.50	5.00	10.00
❏ FE 38312	Biggest Hits	1984	2.50	5.00	10.00
❏ FE 38372	Good Love and Heartbreak	1983	2.50	5.00	10.00
❏ FE 38744	Even the Strong Get Lonely	1983	2.50	5.00	10.00
❏ FE 39971	Sometimes When We Touch	1985	2.50	5.00	10.00
❏ EG 40625 [(2)]	Anniversary: 20 Years of Hits	1987	3.75	7.50	15.00
❏ FE 40832	Higher Ground	1987	2.50	5.00	10.00
❏ FE 44498	Next to You	1989	3.00	6.00	12.00

HARMONY

Number	Title (A Side/B Side)	Yr	VG	VG+	NM
❏ KH 30096	Send Me No Roses	1970	3.00	6.00	12.00
❏ KH 30914	Just a Matter of Time	1971	3.00	6.00	12.00

PAIR

Number	Title (A Side/B Side)	Yr	VG	VG+	NM
❏ PDL2-1073 [(2)]	From the Bottom of My Heart	1986	3.00	6.00	12.00

TIME-LIFE

Number	Title (A Side/B Side)	Yr	VG	VG+	NM
❏ STW-116	Country Music	1981	3.00	6.00	12.00

WYNTER, MARK

45s

ARLEN

Number	Title (A Side/B Side)	Yr	VG	VG+	NM
❏ 744	Running to You/Don't Cry	1964	3.00	6.00	12.00

GUYDEN

Number	Title (A Side/B Side)	Yr	VG	VG+	NM
❏ 2115	Answer Me/Only You	1964	2.50	5.00	10.00

LONDON

Number	Title (A Side/B Side)	Yr	VG	VG+	NM
❏ 1973	Dream Girl/Two Little Girls	1961	3.75	7.50	15.00
❏ 1997	Exclusively Yours/Warm and Willing	1961	3.75	7.50	15.00
❏ 9522	Heaven's Plan/You Are Everything	1962	3.75	7.50	15.00

SCEPTER

Number	Title (A Side/B Side)	Yr	VG	VG+	NM
❏ 1299	Am I Living in a Dream/ Can I Get to Know You Better	1965	2.50	5.00	10.00

X

Number	Title (A Side/B Side)	Yr	VG	VG+	NM

X-CELLENTS, THE
45s
SMASH

Number	Title (A Side/B Side)	Yr	VG	VG+	NM
❏ 1996	Hey Little Willie/I'll Always Be On Your Side	1965	5.00	10.00	20.00

X-CITERS UNLIMITED
45s
ABC

Number	Title (A Side/B Side)	Yr	VG	VG+	NM
❏ 11029	Soul to Fillie Joe/Hang On Sloopy	1967	2.50	5.00	10.00

X. LINCOLN
45s
DOT

Number	Title (A Side/B Side)	Yr	VG	VG+	NM
❏ 17101	In the Freedom of My Mind/What Am I Gonna Do Now	1968	2.50	5.00	10.00
❏ 17170	Anywhere I Happen to Be/You're Everything	1968	2.50	5.00	10.00
❏ 17267	You're My Heaven/Mama Was a Proper Lady	1969	2.50	5.00	10.00

X-TREMES, THE
45s
STAR TREK

Number	Title (A Side/B Side)	Yr	VG	VG+	NM
❏ 1221	Substitute/Facts of Life	1966	6.25	12.50	25.00

XIT
45s
MOTOWN

Number	Title (A Side/B Side)	Yr	VG	VG+	NM
❏ 1304	I Need Your Love (Git It To Me)/Movin' from the City	1974	2.00	4.00	8.00
❏ 1320	Renegade/Cement Prairie	1974	2.00	4.00	8.00

RARE EARTH

Number	Title (A Side/B Side)	Yr	VG	VG+	NM
❏ 5044	Nihaa Shil Hozho (I Am Happy About You)/End	1972	2.50	5.00	10.00
❏ 5055	Reservation of Education/Color Nature Gone	1973	2.50	5.00	10.00

Albums
CANYON

Number	Title (A Side/B Side)	Yr	VG	VG+	NM
❏ 7114	Entrance	197?	12.50	25.00	50.00
❏ 7121	Relocation	197?	10.00	20.00	40.00

RARE EARTH

Number	Title (A Side/B Side)	Yr	VG	VG+	NM
❏ R-536	Plight of the Redman	1972	7.50	15.00	30.00
❏ R-545	Silent Warrior	1973	7.50	15.00	30.00

WARRIOR

Number	Title (A Side/B Side)	Yr	VG	VG+	NM
❏ WAR 49	Plight of the Redman	1981	3.75	7.50	15.00

—Reissue of Rare Earth 536

Y

YA HO WA 13
Albums
HIGHER KEY

Number	Title (A Side/B Side)	Yr	VG	VG+	NM
❏ 3301	Kohoutek	1973	75.00	150.00	300.00
❏ 3302	Contraction	1974	125.00	250.00	500.00
❏ 3303	Expansion	1974	125.00	250.00	500.00
❏ 3304	All or Nothing at All	1974	100.00	200.00	400.00

—Above 4 as "Father Yod and the Spirit of '76"

Number	Title (A Side/B Side)	Yr	VG	VG+	NM
❏ 3305	Ya Ho Wa 13	1974	125.00	250.00	500.00
❏ 3306	The Savage Sons of Ya Ho Wa	1974	100.00	200.00	400.00
❏ 3307	Penetration: An Aquarian Symphony	1974	100.00	200.00	400.00
❏ 3308 [(2)]	I'm Gonna Take You Home	1975	200.00	400.00	800.00
❏ 3309	To the Principles for the Children	1975	200.00	400.00	800.00

YANCY DERRINGER
Albums
HEMISPHERE

Number	Title (A Side/B Side)	Yr	VG	VG+	NM
❏ H-15104	Openers	1975	12.50	25.00	50.00

YANKEE DOLLAR, THE
45s
DOT

Number	Title (A Side/B Side)	Yr	VG	VG+	NM
❏ 17123	City Sidewalks/Sanctuary	1968	3.75	7.50	15.00
❏ 17155	Live and Let Live/Sanctuary	1968	3.75	7.50	15.00
❏ 17213	Mucky Truckee River/Reflections of a Shattered Mind	1969	3.75	7.50	15.00

Albums
DOT

Number	Title (A Side/B Side)	Yr	VG	VG+	NM
❏ DLP-25874	The Yankee Dollar	1968	30.00	60.00	120.00

YANOVSKY, ZALMAN   Also see THE LOVIN' SPOONFUL.
45s
BUDDAH

Number	Title (A Side/B Side)	Yr	VG	VG+	NM
❏ 12	As Long As You're Here/Ereh Er'uoy Sa Gnol Sa	1967	2.50	5.00	10.00
❏ 12 [PS]	As Long As You're Here/Ereh Er'uoy Sa Gnol Sa	1967	7.50	15.00	30.00

Albums
BUDDAH

Number	Title (A Side/B Side)	Yr	VG	VG+	NM
❏ BDS-5019	Alive and Well in Argentina	1968	10.00	20.00	40.00

KAMA SUTRA

Number	Title (A Side/B Side)	Yr	VG	VG+	NM
❏ KSBS-2030	Alive and Well in Argentina	1971	5.00	10.00	20.00

YARBROUGH, GLENN   Also see THE LIMELITERS.
45s
PRIDE

Number	Title (A Side/B Side)	Yr	VG	VG+	NM
❏ 1020	Back Roads/(B-side unknown)	1972	—	2.50	5.00

RCA VICTOR

Number	Title (A Side/B Side)	Yr	VG	VG+	NM
❏ 47-8366	The Honey Wind Blows/San Francisco Bay Blues	1964	2.00	4.00	8.00
❏ 47-8447	An Acre of Gal to a Foot of Ground/Jenny's Gone And I Don't Care	1964	2.00	4.00	8.00
❏ 47-8498	Baby the Rain Must Fall/I've Been to Town	1965	2.50	5.00	10.00
❏ 47-8498 [PS]	Baby the Rain Must Fall/I've Been to Town	1965	3.75	7.50	15.00
❏ 47-8619	It's Gonna Be Fine/She	1965	2.00	4.00	8.00
❏ 47-8745	Ain't No Way/You Can't Ever Go Home Again	1965	2.00	4.00	8.00
❏ 47-8796	Lonely Things/Changing Way No. 2	1966	—	3.00	6.00
❏ 47-9019	Spin, Spin/Love Are Wine	1966	—	3.00	6.00

Number	Title (A Side/B Side)	Yr	VG	VG+	NM
❏ 47-9187	Golden Under the Sun/Gently Here Beside Me	1967	—	3.00	6.00
❏ 47-9309	Honey and Wine/Ain't You Glad You're Livin', Joe	1967	—	3.00	6.00
❏ 47-9452	A Face in the Crown/Times Gone By	1968	—	3.00	6.00

STANYAN

Number	Title (A Side/B Side)	Yr	VG	VG+	NM
❏ 34	Simple Christmas/A Hand To Hold At Christmas	1974	—	2.50	5.00

—B-side by Rod McKuen

STAX

Number	Title (A Side/B Side)	Yr	VG	VG+	NM
❏ 0185	I See America/Holy Creation	1973	—	2.50	5.00
❏ 0204	Everybody's Reaching Out for Someone/Freedom to Stay	1974	—	2.50	5.00
❏ 0225	Ride This Road/Mary Makes Magic	1974	—	2.50	5.00

WARNER BROS.

Number	Title (A Side/B Side)	Yr	VG	VG+	NM
❏ 7196	Downtown L.A./Until You Happened to Pass By	1968	—	3.00	6.00
❏ 7247	Let Me Choose Life/I'll Catch the Sun	1968	—	3.00	6.00
❏ 7269	Somehow, Someway (I'm Gonna Get to You)/Child of the Night Time	1969	—	3.00	6.00
❏ 7335	(Don't Let the Sun Shine On You) In Tulsa/Wisconsin	1969	—	3.00	6.00
❏ 7382	Goodbye Girl/Sunshine Fields of Love	1970	—	2.50	5.00
❏ 7427	I Wish I Knew How It Would Feel to Be Free/Jubilee	1970	—	2.50	5.00
❏ 7448	Gentle Hearts and Gentle People/A Friend of Jesus	1970	—	2.50	5.00
❏ 7478	Lonesome Cities/Ivy That Clings to the Wall	1971	—	2.50	5.00

Albums
ELEKTRA

Number	Title (A Side/B Side)	Yr	VG	VG+	NM
❏ EKL-135 [M]	Here We Go, Baby	1957	10.00	20.00	40.00

FIRST AMERICAN

Number	Title (A Side/B Side)	Yr	VG	VG+	NM
❏ 7766	Just a Little Love	1981	2.50	5.00	10.00

RCA VICTOR

Number	Title (A Side/B Side)	Yr	VG	VG+	NM
❏ ANL1-2138	Baby the Rain Must Fall	1977	2.50	5.00	10.00

—Reissue of LSP-3422

Number	Title (A Side/B Side)	Yr	VG	VG+	NM
❏ LPM-2905 [M]	One More Round	1964	3.75	7.50	15.00
❏ LSP-2905 [S]	One More Round	1964	5.00	10.00	20.00
❏ LPM-3301 [M]	Come Share My Life	1965	3.75	7.50	15.00
❏ LSP-3301 [S]	Come Share My Life	1965	5.00	10.00	20.00
❏ LPM-3422 [M]	Baby the Rain Must Fall	1965	3.00	6.00	12.00
❏ LSP-3422 [S]	Baby the Rain Must Fall	1965	3.75	7.50	15.00
❏ LPM-3472 [M]	It's Gonna Be Fine	1965	3.00	6.00	12.00
❏ LSP-3472 [S]	It's Gonna Be Fine	1965	3.75	7.50	15.00
❏ LPM-3539 [M]	The Lonely Things	1966	3.00	6.00	12.00
❏ LSP-3539 [S]	The Lonely Things	1966	3.75	7.50	15.00
❏ LPM-3661 [M]	Live at the Hungry I	1966	3.00	6.00	12.00
❏ LSP-3661 [S]	Live at the Hungry I	1966	3.75	7.50	15.00
❏ LPM-3801 [M]	For Emily, Whenever I May Find Her	1967	3.75	7.50	15.00
❏ LSP-3801 [S]	For Emily, Whenever I May Find Her	1967	3.75	7.50	15.00
❏ LPM-3860 [M]	Honey and Wine	1967	5.00	10.00	20.00
❏ LSP-3860 [S]	Honey and Wine	1967	3.75	7.50	15.00
❏ LPM-3951 [M]	The Bitter and the Sweet	1968	7.50	15.00	30.00
❏ LSP-3951 [S]	The Bitter and the Sweet	1968	3.75	7.50	15.00
❏ LSP-4047	We Survived the Madness	1968	3.75	7.50	15.00
❏ LSP-4349	The Best of Glenn Yarbrough	1970	3.00	6.00	12.00
❏ VPS-6018 [(2)]	Glenn Yarbrough Sings the Rod McKuen Songbook	1969	3.75	7.50	15.00

STAX

Number	Title (A Side/B Side)	Yr	VG	VG+	NM
❏ STX-5506	My Sweet Lady	1975	2.50	5.00	10.00

TRADITION

Number	Title (A Side/B Side)	Yr	VG	VG+	NM
❏ 1019 [M]	Come Sit By My Side	195?	5.00	10.00	20.00
❏ 2054	The Best of Glenn Yarbrough	1967	3.75	7.50	15.00
❏ 2095	Looking Back	1970	3.00	6.00	12.00

WARNER BROS.

Number	Title (A Side/B Side)	Yr	VG	VG+	NM
❏ WS 1736	Each of Us Alone: Glenn Yarbrough Sings the Words and Music of Rod McKuen	1968	3.00	6.00	12.00
❏ WS 1782	Somehow, Someway	1969	3.00	6.00	12.00
❏ WS 1817	Yarbrough Country	1969	3.00	6.00	12.00
❏ WS 1832	Let Me Choose Life	1969	3.00	6.00	12.00
❏ WS 1876	Jubilee	1970	3.00	6.00	12.00
❏ WS 1911	Bend Down and Touch Me	1971	3.00	6.00	12.00

YARDBIRDS, THE   Also see JEFF BECK; ERIC CLAPTON; JIMMY PAGE; KEITH RELF; SONNY BOY WILLIAMSON (2). Ex-members of the group formed LED ZEPPELIN and RENAISSANCE.
45s
EPIC

Number	Title (A Side/B Side)	Yr	VG	VG+	NM
❏ 5-9709	I Wish You Could/I Ain't Got You	1964			

—Unreleased?

Number	Title (A Side/B Side)	Yr	VG	VG+	NM
❏ 5-9709	I Wish You Could/A Certain Girl	1964	10.00	20.00	40.00

—With typographical error on A-side

Number	Title (A Side/B Side)	Yr	VG	VG+	NM
❏ 5-9709	I Wish You Would/A Certain Girl	1964	12.50	25.00	50.00

—With correct A-side title; also includes "Radio Station Copy" versions, some of which were used as giveaways in stores

Number	Title (A Side/B Side)	Yr	VG	VG+	NM
❏ 5-9709 [PS]	I Wish You Could/A Certain Girl	1964	200.00	400.00	800.00

—Promo-only picture sleeve used by Esquire Socks, Burlington, N.C.; the back of the sleeve advertises "Denim Tones" by Esquire Socks; some copies of the sleeve also contain an insert, through which a store could order multiple copies of the Yardbirds record for use as a giveaway in the store (double the value if included)

Number	Title (A Side/B Side)	Yr	VG	VG+	NM
❏ 5-9790	For Your Love/Got to Hurry	1965	3.75	7.50	15.00
❏ 5-9823	Heart Full of Soul/Steeled Blues	1965	3.75	7.50	15.00
❏ 5-9823 [PS]	Heart Full of Soul/Steeled Blues	1965	12.50	25.00	50.00
❏ 5-9857	I'm a Man/Still I'm Sad	1965	3.75	7.50	15.00
❏ 5-9881	Shapes of Things/I'm Not Talking	1966	3.75	7.50	15.00
❏ 5-10006	New York City Blues/You're a Better Man Than I	1966	—	—	—

—Unreleased

Number	Title (A Side/B Side)	Yr	VG	VG+	NM
❏ 5-10006	Shapes of Things/New York City Blues	1966	5.00	10.00	20.00
❏ 5-10035	Over Under Sideways Down/Jeff's Boogie	1966	3.75	7.50	15.00
❏ 5-10035 [PS]	Over Under Sideways Down/Jeff's Boogie	1966	12.50	25.00	50.00
❏ 5-10094	Happenings Ten Years Time Ago/Psycho Daisies	1966	—	—	—

—Unreleased

Number	Title (A Side/B Side)	Yr	VG	VG+	NM
❏ 5-10094	Happenings Ten Years Time Ago/The Nazz Are Blue	1966	3.75	7.50	15.00
❏ 5-10094 [PS]	Happenings Ten Years Time Ago/The Nazz Are Blue	1966	12.50	25.00	50.00
❏ 5-10156	Little Games/Puzzles	1967	5.00	10.00	20.00
❏ 5-10204	Ha Ha Said the Clown/Tinker, Tailor, Soldier, Sailor	1967	5.00	10.00	20.00

Number	Title (A Side/B Side)	Yr	VG	VG+	NM
❏ 5-10248	Ten Little Indians/Drinking Muddy Water	1967	5.00	10.00	20.00
❏ 5-10303	Goodnight Sweet Josephine/Think About It	1968	12.50	25.00	50.00

Albums

ACCORD

Number	Title (A Side/B Side)	Yr	VG	VG+	NM
❏ SN-7143 [S]	For Your Love	1981	2.00	4.00	8.00
❏ SN-7237 [R]	Having a Rave Up with the Yardbirds	1981	2.00	4.00	8.00

COLUMBIA SPECIAL PRODUCTS

❏ P 13311 [S]	Live Yardbirds Featuring Jimmy Page	1976	20.00	40.00	80.00

COMPLEAT

❏ CPL-2-2002 [(2)]	A Compleat Collection	1984	3.00	6.00	12.00

EPIC

❏ LN 24167 [DJ]	For Your Love	1965	100.00	200.00	400.00
—White label promo					
❏ LN 24167 [M]	For Your Love	1965	75.00	150.00	300.00
❏ LN 24177 [DJ]	Having a Rave Up with the Yardbirds	1965	100.00	200.00	400.00
—White label promo					
❏ LN 24177 [M]	Having a Rave Up with the Yardbirds	1965	20.00	40.00	80.00
❏ LN 24210 [DJ]	Over Under Sideways Down	1966	100.00	200.00	400.00
—White label promo					
❏ LN 24210 [M]	Over Under Sideways Down	1966	15.00	30.00	60.00
❏ LN 24246 [DJ]	The Yardbirds' Greatest Hits	1966	75.00	150.00	300.00
—White label promo					
❏ LN 24246 [M]	The Yardbirds' Greatest Hits	1966	12.50	25.00	50.00
❏ LN 24313 [DJ]	Little Games	1967	75.00	150.00	300.00
❏ LN 24313 [M]	Little Games	1967	20.00	40.00	80.00
—Some copies with this number are stereo; look for the "XSB" prefix before the master number					
❏ BN 26167 [P]	For Your Love	1965	50.00	100.00	200.00
—The album is in true stereo except for "Sweet Music"					
❏ BN 26177 [R]	Having a Rave Up with the Yardbirds	1965	12.50	25.00	50.00
❏ BN 26177 [R]	Having a Rave Up with the Yardbirds	1973	7.50	15.00	30.00
—Reissue with orange label					
❏ BN 26210 [P]	Over Under Sideways Down	1966	20.00	40.00	80.00
—"Over Under Sideways Down" is rechanneled					
❏ BN 26246 [P]	The Yardbirds' Greatest Hits	1966	7.50	15.00	30.00
❏ BN 26313 [S]	Little Games	1967	12.50	25.00	50.00
❏ EG 30135 [(2)]	The Yardbirds Featuring Performances by Jeff Beck, Eric Clapton, Jimmy Page	1970	12.50	25.00	50.00
❏ E 30615 [S]	Live Yardbirds Featuring Jimmy Page	1971	20.00	40.00	80.00
❏ PE 34490 [P]	Yardbirds Favorites	1977	2.50	5.00	10.00
❏ PE 34491 [P]	Great Hits	1977	2.50	5.00	10.00
❏ FE 38455	Yardbirds (Roger the Engineer)	1982	7.50	15.00	30.00
❏ HE 48455	Yardbirds (Roger the Engineer)	1982	62.50	125.00	250.00
—"Half-Speed Mastered" edition					

PAIR

❏ PDL2-1151 [(2)]	Best of British Rock	1988	3.00	6.00	12.00

RHINO

❏ RNDF 253 [PD]	Afternoon Tea	1982	3.75	7.50	15.00
❏ RNLP 70128 [M]	Greatest Hits, Volume 1: 1964-1966	1986	2.00	4.00	8.00
❏ RNLP 70189 [M]	Five Live Yardbirds	1986	2.00	4.00	8.00

SPRINGBOARD

❏ SPB-4036 [R]	Eric Clapton and the Yardbirds	1972	2.50	5.00	10.00
❏ SPB-4039 [R]	Shapes of Things	1972	2.50	5.00	10.00

SUNDAZED

❏ LP 5181	Live! Blueswailing July '64	2004	3.00	6.00	12.00

YARROW, PETER Also see PETER, PAUL AND MARY.

45s

WARNER BROS.

Number	Title (A Side/B Side)	Yr	VG	VG+	NM
❏ 7236	Don't Remind Me Now of Time/Teenage Fair	1968	2.00	4.00	8.00
—B-side by Rosko					
❏ 7567	Don't Ever Take Away My Freedom/Greenwood	1972	—	2.50	5.00
❏ 7587	Weave Me the Sunshine/Wings of Time	1972	—	2.50	5.00
❏ 7761	Old Father Time/Isn't That So	1973	—	2.00	4.00
❏ 8114	Wanderin'/Another Chain Unbound	1975	—	2.00	4.00

Albums

WARNER BROS.

❏ BS 2599	Peter	1972	3.00	6.00	12.00
❏ BS 2730	That's Enough for Me	1973	3.00	6.00	12.00
❏ BS 2860	Hard Times	1975	3.00	6.00	12.00
❏ BS 2891	Peter Yarrow	1975	3.00	6.00	12.00

YATES, BILL

45s

SUN

❏ 390	Stop, Wait and Listen/Don't Step on My Dog	1964	3.75	7.50	15.00
❏ 397	Carleen/Too Late to Right My Wrong	1965	3.75	7.50	15.00
❏ 399	Big Big World/I Dropped My M & M's	1966	3.75	7.50	15.00

YATES, TOMMY

45s

VERVE

❏ 10556	Darling, Something's Gotta Give/If You're Looking for a Fool	1967	6.25	12.50	25.00

YELLOW BALLOON, THE

45s

CANTERBURY

❏ 508	Yellow Balloon/Noollab Wolley	1967	3.00	6.00	12.00
❏ 513	Good Feeling Time/I've Got a Feeling for Love	1967	2.50	5.00	10.00
❏ 516	Stained Glass Window/Can't Get Enough of Your Love	1967	2.50	5.00	10.00

Albums

CANTERBURY

❏ CLPM-1502 [M]	The Yellow Balloon	1967	6.25	12.50	25.00
❏ CLPS-1502 [S]	The Yellow Balloon	1967	7.50	15.00	30.00

YELLOW PAYGES, THE

45s

SHOWPLACE

❏ 216	Sleeping Minds/Never See the Good in Me	1967	7.50	15.00	30.00
❏ 217	Love in the Making/Jezebel	1967	5.00	10.00	20.00

UNI

❏ .212/3	Finger Poppin' Party/Moonfire	1970	5.00	10.00	20.00
—Though not marked as such, this appears to be a promo; no regular Uni number; both sides have custom labels					
❏ 55043	Our Time Is Running Out/Sweet Sunrise	1967	3.75	7.50	15.00

Number	Title (A Side/B Side)	Yr	VG	VG+	NM
❏ 55072	Judge Carter/Childhood Friends	1968	3.75	7.50	15.00
❏ 55089	You're Just What I Was Looking For Today/Crowd Pleaser	1968	3.75	7.50	15.00
❏ 55107	The Two of Us/Never Put Away My Love for You	1969	3.75	7.50	15.00
❏ 55153	Would You Mind If I Loved You/Vanilla on My Mind	1969	3.75	7.50	15.00
❏ 55176	Slow Down/Fresco Annie	1969	3.75	7.50	15.00
❏ 55192	Little Women/Follow the Bouncing Ball	1970	3.75	7.50	15.00
❏ 55225	I'm a Man/Home Again	1970	3.75	7.50	15.00

Albums

UNI

❏ 73045	The Yellow Payges, Volume 1	1969	7.50	15.00	30.00

YELVINGTON, MALCOLM

45s

SUN

❏ 211	Drinkin' Wine Spo-Dee-O-Dee/Just Rolling Along	1954	25.00	50.00	100.00
❏ 246	Rockin' with My Baby/It's Me Baby	1956	25.00	50.00	100.00

YES Also see STEVE HOWE; RICK WAKEMAN.

12-Inch Singles

ATCO

Number	Title (A Side/B Side)	Yr	VG	VG+	NM
❏ PR 529 [DJ]	Owner of a Lonely Heart (Edit)/Owner of a Lonely Heart (LP Version)	1983	3.00	6.00	12.00
❏ PR 587 [DJ]	Leave It (3 versions)	1984	2.00	4.00	8.00
❏ PR 796 [DJ]	Hold On (Edit 5:10)/(LP Version 6:50)	1985	3.00	6.00	12.00
❏ PR 1133 [DJ]	Rhythm of Love (3 versions)	1987	2.50	5.00	10.00
❏ PR 2088 [DJ]	Love Will Find a Way (Edit)/Love Will Find a Way (LP Version)	1987	3.00	6.00	12.00
❏ 96722	Rhythm of Love (3 versions)/City of Love (Live Edit)	1987	2.50	5.00	10.00
❏ 96964	Leave It (3 versions)	1984	2.00	4.00	8.00
❏ 96976	Owner of a Lonely Heart (Special Red & Blue Dance Version)/(Edit)/Our Song	1983	3.00	6.00	12.00

45s

ARISTA

❏ 2218	Lift Me Up/Give and Take	1991	—	2.00	4.00

ATCO

❏ 99419	Rhythm of Love/City of Love	1987	—	—	3.00
❏ 99419 [PS]	Rhythm of Love/City of Love	1987	—	—	3.00
❏ 99449	Love Will Find a Way/Holy Lamb	1987	—	—	3.00
❏ 99449 [PS]	Love Will Find a Way/Holy Lamb	1987	—	—	3.00
❏ 99745	It Can Happen/It Can Happen (Live)	1984	—	—	3.00
❏ 99745 [PS]	It Can Happen/It Can Happen (Live)	1984	—	—	3.00
❏ 99787	Leave It/Leave It (Acapella)	1984	—	—	3.00
❏ 99787 [PS]	Leave It/Leave It (Acapella)	1984	—	—	3.00
❏ 99817	Owner of a Lonely Heart/Our Song	1983	—	—	3.00
❏ 99817 [PS]	Owner of a Lonely Heart/Our Song	1983	—	—	3.00

ATLANTIC

❏ 2709	Every Little Thing/Sweetness	1970	—	3.00	6.00
❏ 2819	Your Move/Clap	1971	—	2.50	5.00
❏ 2854	Roundabout/Long Distance Runaround	1972	—	2.50	5.00
❏ 2854 [DJ]	Roundabout (mono/stereo)	1972	25.00	50.00	100.00
—Promo only on yellow vinyl					
❏ 2899	America/Total Mass Retain	1972	—	2.50	5.00
❏ 2920	And You And I (Part 1)/And You And I (Part 2)	1972	—	2.50	5.00
❏ 3242	Sound Chaser/Soon	1975	—	2.50	5.00
❏ 3416	Awaken (Part 1)/Wonderful Stories	1977	—	2.50	5.00
❏ 3534	Don't Kill the Whale/Release, Release	1978	—	2.50	5.00
❏ 3767	Into the Lens/Does It Really Happen	1980	—	2.50	5.00
❏ 3801	Run Through the Light/White Car	1981	—	2.50	5.00

Albums

ARISTA

❏ AL 8643	Union	1991	5.00	10.00	20.00
—U.S. vinyl available only through Columbia House					

ATCO

❏ 90125	90125	1983	2.00	4.00	8.00
❏ 90474	9012Live: The Solos	1985	2.00	4.00	8.00
❏ 90522	Big Generator	1987	2.00	4.00	8.00

ATLANTIC

❏ SD 3-100 [(3)]	Yessongs	1973	4.50	9.00	18.00
❏ PR 260 [DJ]	Yes Solo LP Sampler	1976	6.25	12.50	25.00
❏ PR 285 [DJ]	Yes Music: An Evening with Jon Anderson	1977	12.50	25.00	50.00
❏ SD 2-510 [(2)]	Yesshows	1980	3.00	6.00	12.00
❏ SD 2-908 [(2)]	Tales from Topographic Oceans	1974	3.75	7.50	15.00
❏ SD 2-908 [(2)DJ]	Tales from Topographic Oceans	1974	7.50	15.00	30.00
—Promo copies banded for airplay					
❏ SD 7211	Fragile	1972	3.00	6.00	12.00
❏ 7244 [DJ]	Close to the Edge	1972	12.50	25.00	50.00
—White label mono copies banded for airplay					
❏ SD 7244	Close to the Edge	1972	3.00	6.00	12.00
❏ SD 8243	Yes	1969	3.00	6.00	12.00
❏ SD 8273	Time and a Word	1970	3.00	6.00	12.00
❏ 8283 [M]	The Yes Album	1971	10.00	20.00	40.00
—White label promo only; "DJ Copy Monaural" sticker on cover					
❏ SD 8283	The Yes Album	1971	3.00	6.00	12.00
❏ SD 16019	Drama	1980	2.50	5.00	10.00
❏ SD 18103	Yesterdays	1975	2.50	5.00	10.00
❏ SD 18122	Relayer	1974	2.50	5.00	10.00
❏ SD 18122 [DJ]	Relayer	1974	5.00	10.00	20.00
—Promo copies banded for airplay					
❏ SD 19106	Going for the One	1977	2.50	5.00	10.00
❏ SD 19131	The Yes Album	1977	2.00	4.00	8.00
❏ SD 19132	Fragile	1977	2.00	4.00	8.00
❏ SD 19133	Close to the Edge	1977	2.00	4.00	8.00
❏ SD 19134	Yesterdays	1977	2.00	4.00	8.00
❏ SD 19135	Relayer	1977	2.00	4.00	8.00
❏ SD 19202	Tormato	1978	2.50	5.00	10.00
❏ SD 19320	Classic Yes	1982	2.50	5.00	10.00
—With bonus single missing					
❏ SD 19320	Classic Yes	1982	3.75	7.50	15.00
—Original copies include a bonus 7-inch promo single					

MOBILE FIDELITY

❏ 1-077	Close to the Edge	1982	15.00	30.00	60.00
—Audiophile vinyl					

Number	Title (A Side/B Side)	Yr	VG	VG+	NM

RHINO
- ❏ R1-73788 — The Yes Album — 2003 — 3.75 — 7.50 — 15.00
—Reissue on 180-gram vinyl

YESTER, JERRY Also see THE LOVIN' SPOONFUL.
45s
DUNHILL
- ❏ 4042 — The Sound of Summer Showers/ Ashes Have Turned — 1966 — 2.50 — 5.00 — 10.00
- ❏ 4061 — I Can Live Without You/Garden of Imagining — 1967 — 2.50 — 5.00 — 10.00

YESTERDAY'S FOLK
Albums
BUDDAH
- ❏ BDS-5035 — U.S. 69 — 1969 — 5.00 — 10.00 — 20.00

YETTI-MEN, THE / THE UPPA TRIO
Albums
KAL
- ❏ KB-4348 — The Yetti-Men/The Uppa Trio — 1967 — 200.00 — 400.00 — 600.00

YORK, BETTY
45s
HIT
- ❏ 174 — Downtown/Have You Been There — 1965 — 2.00 — 4.00 — 8.00
—B-side by the Chords (2)
- ❏ 238 — My Love/Michelle — 1966 — 2.50 — 5.00 — 10.00
—B-side by Bobby and Buddy

YORK, FRED
45s
HIT
- ❏ 29 — Send Me the Pillow You Dream On/ Ramblin' Rose — 1962 — 2.00 — 4.00 — 8.00
—B-side by Frank Clark
- ❏ 43 — Go Away Little Girl/My Coloring Book — 1962 — 2.00 — 4.00 — 8.00
—B-side by Connie Landers
- ❏ 59 — Don't Be Afraid Little Darling/ Puff the Magic Dragon — 1963 — 2.00 — 4.00 — 8.00
—B-side by Jimmy, Joe and Betty
- ❏ 82 — Blue Velvet/You Can Never Stop Me Loving You — 1963 — 2.00 — 4.00 — 8.00
—B-side by Bill Austin
- ❏ 96 — There! I've Said It Again/ You Don't Have to Be a Baby to Cry — 1963 — 2.00 — 4.00 — 8.00
—B-side by the Belles
- ❏ 104 — A Fool Never Learns/I Want to Hold Your Hand — 1964 — 3.00 — 6.00 — 12.00
—B-side by the Doodles
- ❏ 113 — White on White/Can't Buy Me Love — 1964 — 3.00 — 6.00 — 12.00
—B-side by the Beagles
- ❏ 139 — Clinging Vine/A Broken Hearted Fool Like Me — 1964 — 2.00 — 4.00 — 8.00
- ❏ 157 — Pay It No Mind/Ask Me — 1964 — 2.00 — 4.00 — 8.00
—B-side by Ed Hardin
- ❏ 163 — Mr. Lonely/Two Plus Two — 1964 — 2.00 — 4.00 — 8.00
—B-side by the Chords (2)
- ❏ 179 — My Love, Forgive Me/Anything — 1965 — 2.00 — 4.00 — 8.00
—B-side by Joanie Key
- ❏ 204 — The Race Is On/Uptown, Downtown — 1965 — 2.00 — 4.00 — 8.00
- ❏ 208 — Lonely Girl/10 Little Bottles — 1965 — 2.00 — 4.00 — 8.00
—B-side by Jack White
- ❏ 239 — Lightnin' Strikes/Crying Time — 1966 — 2.00 — 4.00 — 8.00
—B-side by Leroy Jones
- ❏ 249 — A Sign of the Times/ I'm So Lonesome I Could Cry — 1966 — 2.00 — 4.00 — 8.00
—B-side by Leroy Jones
- ❏ 253 — Rhapsody in the Rain/Sloop John B — 1966 — 3.00 — 6.00 — 12.00
—B-side by the Jalopy Five

YORK, RUSTY
45s
CAPITOL
- ❏ 4663 — That's What I Need/Just Like You — 1961 — 3.75 — 7.50 — 15.00
CHESS
- ❏ 1730 — Sugaree/Red Rooster — 1959 — 5.00 — 10.00 — 20.00
GAYLORD
- ❏ 6428 — Sally Was a Good Old Girl/I Might Just Walk Right Back Again — 1962 — 3.75 — 7.50 — 15.00
KING
- ❏ 5103 — Peggy Sue/Shake 'Em Up Baby — 1958 — 6.25 — 12.50 — 25.00
- ❏ 5511 — Love Struck/Goodnight Cincinnati, Good Morning Tennessee — 1961 — 3.75 — 7.50 — 15.00
- ❏ 5587 — Tramblin'/Tore Up Over You — 1961 — 3.75 — 7.50 — 15.00
NOTE
- ❏ 10021 — Sugaree/Red Rooster — 1959 — 6.25 — 12.50 — 25.00
P.J.
- ❏ 100 — Sugaree/Red Rooster — 1959 — 7.50 — 15.00 — 30.00
SAGE AND SAND
- ❏ 266 — Sadie May/Margaret Ann — 1960 — 5.00 — 10.00 — 20.00

YOST, DENNIS, AND THE CLASSICS IV See CLASSICS IV.

YOUNG, BARRY
45s
COLUMBIA
- ❏ 43584 — A Heart Without a Home/He'll Have to Go — 1966 — 2.00 — 4.00 — 8.00
- ❏ 43723 — I Love You So Much It Hurts/Cryin' Street — 1966 — 2.00 — 4.00 — 8.00
DOT
- ❏ 16756 — One Has My Name (The Other Has My Heart)/ Show Me the Way — 1965 — 2.50 — 5.00 — 10.00
- ❏ 16819 — Since You Have Gone from Me/ Nashville, Tennessee — 1966 — 2.00 — 4.00 — 8.00
Albums
DOT
- ❏ DLP 3672 [M] — One Has My Name — 1965 — 5.00 — 10.00 — 20.00
- ❏ DLP 25672 [S] — One Has My Name — 1965 — 6.25 — 12.50 — 25.00

YOUNG, BOBBY
45s
GUYDEN
- ❏ 2087 — To Each His Own/The Only Girl for Me — 1963 — 62.50 — 125.00 — 250.00

YOUNG, CATHY
45s
MAINSTREAM
- ❏ 703 — Spoonful/Circus — 1969 — 3.75 — 7.50 — 15.00
Albums
MAINSTREAM
- ❏ S-6121 — A Spoonful of Cathy Young — 1968 — 10.00 — 20.00 — 40.00

YOUNG, COLIN Formerly of THE FOUNDATIONS.
45s
UNI
- ❏ 55286 — You're No Good/Amy Time at All — 1971 — — — 3.00 — 6.00

YOUNG, DONNY See JOHNNY PAYCHECK.

YOUNG, FARON
45s
CAPITOL
- ❏ F2039 — Tattle Tale Tears/Have I Waited Too Long — 1952 — 10.00 — 20.00 — 40.00
- ❏ F2133 — Foolish Pride/I Knew You When — 1952 — 7.50 — 15.00 — 30.00
- ❏ F2171 — Saving My Tears/What Can I Do with My Sorrow — 1952 — 7.50 — 15.00 — 30.00
- ❏ F2299 — Goin' Steady/Just Out of Reach (Of My Two Open Arms) — 1952 — 6.25 — 12.50 — 25.00
- ❏ F2461 — I Can't Wait (For the Sun to Go Down)/What's the Use to Love You — 1953 — 6.25 — 12.50 — 25.00
- ❏ F2570 — That's What I'd Do for You/Baby My Heart — 1953 — 6.25 — 12.50 — 25.00
- ❏ F2629 — You're an Angel on My Christmas Tree/I'm Gonna Tell Santa Claus on You — 1953 — 7.50 — 15.00 — 30.00
- ❏ F2690 — Just Married/I Hardly Knew It Was You — 1953 — 6.25 — 12.50 — 25.00
- ❏ F2780 — They Made Me Fall in Love with You/ You're Right — 1954 — 6.25 — 12.50 — 25.00
- ❏ F2859 — A Place for Girls Like You/ In the Chapel in the Moonlight — 1954 — 6.25 — 12.50 — 25.00
- ❏ F2953 — If You Ain't Lovin' (You Ain't Livin')/ If That's the Fashion — 1954 — 6.25 — 12.50 — 25.00
- ❏ F3056 — Live Fast, Love Hard, Die Young/ Forgive Me, Dear — 1955 — 6.25 — 12.50 — 25.00
- ❏ F3107 — Where Could I Go/God Bless God — 1955 — 6.25 — 12.50 — 25.00
- ❏ F3169 — All Right/Go Back You Fool — 1955 — 6.25 — 12.50 — 25.00
- ❏ F3258 — It's a Great Life (If You Don't Weaken)/For the Love of a Woman Like You — 1955 — 6.25 — 12.50 — 25.00
- ❏ F3369 — You're Still Mine/I've Got Five Dollars and It's Saturday Night — 1956 — 5.00 — 10.00 — 20.00
- ❏ F3443 — Sweet Dreams/Until I Met You — 1956 — 5.00 — 10.00 — 20.00
- ❏ F3549 — Turn Her Down/I'll Be Satisfied with Love — 1956 — 5.00 — 10.00 — 20.00
- ❏ F3611 — I Miss You Already (And You're Not Even Gone)/ I'm Gonna Live Some Before I Die — 1957 — 5.00 — 10.00 — 20.00
- ❏ F3696 — The Shrine of St. Cecilia/He Was There — 1957 — 5.00 — 10.00 — 20.00
- ❏ F3753 — Love Has Finally Come My Way/ Moonlight Mountain — 1957 — 5.00 — 10.00 — 20.00
- ❏ F3805 — Vacation's Over/Honey Stop — 1957 — 5.00 — 10.00 — 20.00
- ❏ F3855 — The Locket/Snowball — 1957 — 5.00 — 10.00 — 20.00
- ❏ F3898 — Rosalie/I Can't Dance — 1958 — 5.00 — 10.00 — 20.00
- ❏ F3982 — Alone with You/Every Time I'm Kissing You — 1958 — 5.00 — 10.00 — 20.00
- ❏ F4050 — That's the Way I Feel/I Hate Myself — 1958 — 5.00 — 10.00 — 20.00
- ❏ F4113 — A Long Time Ago/Last Night at a Party — 1959 — 5.00 — 10.00 — 20.00
- ❏ F4164 — That's the Way It's Gotta Be/ We're Talking It Over — 1959 — 5.00 — 10.00 — 20.00
- ❏ F4233 — Country Girl/I Hear You Talkin' — 1959 — 5.00 — 10.00 — 20.00
- ❏ F4291 — Riverboat/Face to the Wall — 1959 — 5.00 — 10.00 — 20.00
- ❏ 4351 — Your Old Used to Be/ I'll Be Alright (In the Morning) — 1960 — 3.75 — 7.50 — 15.00
- ❏ 4410 — There's Not Any Like You Left/ is She All You Thought She'd Be — 1960 — 3.75 — 7.50 — 15.00
- ❏ 4463 — Forget the Past/A World So Full of Love — 1960 — 3.75 — 7.50 — 15.00
- ❏ 4533 — Hello Walls/Congratulations — 1961 — 3.75 — 7.50 — 15.00
- ❏ 4616 — Backtrack/I Can't Find the Time — 1961 — 3.75 — 7.50 — 15.00
- ❏ 4616 [PS] — Backtrack/I Can't Find the Time — 1961 — 7.50 — 15.00 — 30.00
- ❏ 4696 — Three Days/I Let It Slip Away — 1962 — 3.75 — 7.50 — 15.00
- ❏ 4696 [PS] — Three Days/I Let It Slip Away — 1962 — 7.50 — 15.00 — 30.00
- ❏ 4754 — The Comeback/Over Lonely and Under Kissed — 1962 — 3.75 — 7.50 — 15.00
- ❏ 4868 — Down by the River/Safely in Love Again — 1962 — 3.75 — 7.50 — 15.00
MCA
- ❏ 41004 — The Great Chicago Fire/Old Songs — 1979 — — — 2.50 — 5.00
- ❏ 41046 — That Over Thirty Look/Second Hand Emotion — 1979 — — — 2.00 — 4.00
- ❏ 41177 — (If I'd Only Known) It Was the Last Time/ Free and Easy — 1980 — — — 2.00 — 4.00
- ❏ 41292 — Tearjoint/I May Lose You Tomorrow — 1980 — — — 2.00 — 4.00
- ❏ 51088 — Until the Bitter End/Motel with No Phone — 1981 — — — 2.00 — 4.00
- ❏ 51176 — Pull Up a Pillow/ Ain't Your Memory Got No Pride at All — 1981 — — — 2.00 — 4.00
MERCURY
- ❏ 55019 — Loving Here and Living There and Lying In Between/City Lights — 1978 — — — 3.00 — 6.00
- ❏ 72085 — The Yellow Bandana/ How Much I Must Have Loved You — 1963 — 3.00 — 6.00 — 12.00
- ❏ 72114 — Nightmare/I've Come to Say Goodbye — 1963 — 3.00 — 6.00 — 12.00
- ❏ 72167 — We've Got Something in Common/ Think About the Old Days — 1963 — 3.00 — 6.00 — 12.00
- ❏ 72201 — You'll Drive Me Back (Into Her Arms Again)/ What Will I Tell My Darling — 1963 — 3.00 — 6.00 — 12.00
- ❏ 72271 — Rhinestones/Old Courthouse — 1964 — 3.00 — 6.00 — 12.00
- ❏ 72313 — My Friend on the Right/ The World's Greatest Love — 1964 — 3.00 — 6.00 — 12.00
- ❏ 72375 — Walk Tall/Heartbreak Valley — 1965 — 2.50 — 5.00 — 10.00
- ❏ 72375 — Walk Tall/The Weakness of a Man — 1965 — 2.50 — 5.00 — 10.00
- ❏ 72440 — Nothing Left to Lose/Dingaka (The Witch Doctor) — 1965 — 2.50 — 5.00 — 10.00
- ❏ 72490 — My Dreams/You Had a Call — 1965 — 2.50 — 5.00 — 10.00
- ❏ 72576 — Sweet Love and Happiness/ You Don't Treat Me Right — 1966 — 2.50 — 5.00 — 10.00
- ❏ 72617 — Unmitigated Gall/Some of Your Memories (Hurt Me All of the Time) — 1966 — 2.50 — 5.00 — 10.00

Number	Title (A Side/B Side)	Yr	VG	VG+	NM
❑ 72656	I Guess I Had Too Much to Dream Last Night/I				
	Just Don't Know How to Say No	1967	2.50	5.00	10.00
❑ 72728	Wonderful World of Women/All I Can Stand	1967	2.50	5.00	10.00
❑ 72774	She Went a Little Bit Farther/Stay, Love	1968	2.00	4.00	8.00
❑ 72774 [PS]	She Went a Little Bit Farther/Stay, Love	1968	3.75	7.50	15.00
❑ 72827	I Just Came to Get My Baby/				
	Missing You Is All I Did Today	1968	2.00	4.00	8.00
❑ 72889	I've Got Precious Memories/				
	You Stayed Just Long Enough	1969	2.00	4.00	8.00
❑ 72936	Wine Me Up/				
	That's Where My Baby Feels at Home	1969	2.00	4.00	8.00
❑ 72983	Your Time's Comin'/Painted Girls and Wine	1969	2.00	4.00	8.00
❑ 73018	Occasional Wife/The Guns of Johnny Rondo	1970	—	3.50	7.00
❑ 73065	If I Ever Fall in Love (With a Honky Tonk Girl)/				
	A Bunch of Young Ideas	1970	—	3.50	7.00
❑ 73112	Goin' Steady/That's My Way	1970	—	3.50	7.00
❑ 73191	Step Aside/Seems Like I'm Always Leaving	1971	—	3.50	7.00
❑ 73220	Leavin' and Sayin' Goodbye/				
	She Was the Color of Love	1971	—	3.50	7.00
❑ 73250	It's Four in the Morning/It's Not the Miles	1971	—	3.50	7.00
❑ 73308	This Little Girl of Mine/It Hurts So Good	1972	—	3.50	7.00
❑ 73337	A Woman's Touch/It's Four in the Morning	1972	—	3.50	7.00
❑ 73359	She Fights That Lovin' Feeling/I'm in Love with				
	Everything	1973	—	3.50	7.00
❑ 73403	Just What I Had in Mind/All at Once It's Forever	1973	—	3.50	7.00
❑ 73464	Some Kind of a Woman/Again Today	1974	—	3.50	7.00
❑ 73500	The Wrong in Loving You/				
	Almost Dawn in Denver	1974	—	3.50	7.00
❑ 73633	Another You/God's Been Good to Me	1974	—	3.00	6.00
❑ 73692	Here I Am in Dallas/				
	Too Much of Not Enough of You	1975	—	3.00	6.00
❑ 73731	Feel Again/Some Old Rainy Mornin'	1975	—	3.00	6.00
❑ 73782	I'd Just Be Fool Enough/				
	What You See Is What You Get	1976	—	3.00	6.00
❑ 73847	(The Worst You Ever Gave Me Was) The Best				
	I Ever Had/You Get the Feelin'	1976	—	3.00	6.00
❑ 73925	Crutches/The Last Goodbye	1977	—	3.00	6.00

STEP ONE

Number	Title (A Side/B Side)	Yr	VG	VG+	NM
❑ 390	Stop and Take the Time/Misty Morning Rain	1988	—	2.50	5.00
❑ 397	Here's to You/				
	You're Just Another Beer Drinking Song	1989	—	2.50	5.00
❑ 408	After the Lovin'/Let Me Walk	1989	—	2.50	5.00
❑ 414	Baxter Hill/A Waste of Love	1990	—	2.50	5.00
❑ 429	Just an Ol' Heartache/(B-side unknown)	1991	—	2.50	5.00
❑ 436	Memories That Last/A Whole Lot of You	1991	—	2.50	5.00
—With Ray Price					
❑ 440	Too Big to Fight/Now She's in Paris	1992	—	2.50	5.00
❑ 455	White Christmas/The Christmas Song	1992	—	3.00	6.00
—Red vinyl					

7-Inch Extended Plays

CAPITOL

Number	Title (A Side/B Side)	Yr	VG	VG+	NM
❑ EAP 1-450	Goin' Steady/Tattle Tale Tears//Saving My				
	Tears (For Tomorrow)/I Knew You When	1954	7.50	15.00	30.00
❑ EAP 1-450 [PS]	Goin' Steady with Faron Young	1954	7.50	15.00	30.00
❑ EAP 1-611	(contents unknown)	1956	7.50	15.00	30.00
❑ EAP 1-611 [PS]	Faron Young	1956	7.50	15.00	30.00
❑ EAP 1-778	Sweethearts or Strangers/Your Cheatin' Heart/				
	/Shame on You/I Can't Tell My Heart	1957	6.25	12.50	25.00
❑ EAP 1-778 [PS]	Sweethearts or Strangers, Part 1	1957	6.25	12.50	25.00
❑ EAP 2-778	You Call Everybody Darlin'/Better Things Than				
	These//Worried Mind/I'll Be Yours	1957	6.25	12.50	25.00
❑ EAP 2-778 [PS]	Sweethearts or Strangers, Part 2	1957	6.25	12.50	25.00
❑ EAP 3-778	I'm a Poor Boy/I Can't Help It//You Are My				
	Sunshine/That's What It's Like to Be				
	Lonesome	1957	6.25	12.50	25.00
❑ EAP 3-778 [PS]	Sweethearts or Strangers, Part 3	1957	6.25	12.50	25.00
❑ EAP 1-869	(contents unknown)	1957	6.25	12.50	25.00
❑ EAP 1-869 [PS]	The Shrine of St. Cecilia	1957	6.25	12.50	25.00
❑ EAP 1-921	(contents unknown)	1958	5.00	10.00	20.00
❑ EAP 1-921 [PS]	Country Music Holiday, Part 1	1958	5.00	10.00	20.00
❑ EAP 2-921	(contents unknown)	1958	5.00	10.00	20.00
❑ EAP 2-921 [PS]	Country Music Holiday, Part 2	1958	5.00	10.00	20.00
❑ EAP 3-921	(contents unknown)	1958	5.00	10.00	20.00
❑ EAP 3-921 [PS]	Country Music Holiday, Part 3	1958	5.00	10.00	20.00
❑ EAP 1-1096	(contents unknown)	1959	5.00	10.00	20.00
❑ EAP 1-1096 [PS]	This Is Faron Young, Part 1	1959	5.00	10.00	20.00
❑ EAP 2-1096	(contents unknown)	1959	5.00	10.00	20.00
❑ EAP 2-1096 [PS]	This Is Faron Young, Part 2	1959	5.00	10.00	20.00
❑ EAP 3-1096	(contents unknown)	1959	5.00	10.00	20.00
❑ EAP 3-1096 [PS]	This Is Faron Young, Part 3	1959	5.00	10.00	20.00
❑ EAP 1-1185	(contents unknown)	1959	5.00	10.00	20.00
❑ EAP 1-1185 [PS]	My Garden of Prayer, Part 1	1959	5.00	10.00	20.00
❑ EAP 2-1185	(contents unknown)	1959	5.00	10.00	20.00
❑ EAP 2-1185 [PS]	My Garden of Prayer, Part 2	1959	5.00	10.00	20.00
❑ EAP 3-1185	(contents unknown)	1959	5.00	10.00	20.00
❑ EAP 3-1185 [PS]	My Garden of Prayer, Part 3	1959	5.00	10.00	20.00
❑ EAP 1-1245	(contents unknown)	1959	5.00	10.00	20.00
❑ EAP 1-1245 [PS]	Talk About Hits, Part 1	1959	5.00	10.00	20.00
❑ EAP 2-1245	(contents unknown)	1959	5.00	10.00	20.00
❑ EAP 2-1245 [PS]	Talk About Hits, Part 2	1959	5.00	10.00	20.00
❑ EAP 3-1245	(contents unknown)	1959	5.00	10.00	20.00
❑ EAP 3-1245 [PS]	Talk About Hits, Part 3	1959	5.00	10.00	20.00

Albums

ALLEGIANCE

Number	Title (A Side/B Side)	Yr	VG	VG+	NM
❑ AV-5008	The Sheriff	198?	2.50	5.00	10.00

CAPITOL

Number	Title (A Side/B Side)	Yr	VG	VG+	NM
❑ T 778 [M]	Sweethearts or Strangers	1957	15.00	30.00	60.00
—Turquoise or gray label					
❑ T 778 [M]	Sweethearts or Strangers	1959	6.25	12.50	25.00
—Black colorband label, logo at left					
❑ T 1004 [M]	The Object of My Affection	1958	12.50	25.00	50.00
❑ T 1096 [M]	This Is Faron Young	1959	12.50	25.00	50.00
❑ T 1185 [M]	My Garden of Prayer	1959	10.00	20.00	40.00
❑ ST 1245 [S]	Talk About Hits	1959	10.00	20.00	40.00
❑ T 1245 [M]	Talk About Hits	1959	7.50	15.00	30.00
❑ ST 1450 [S]	The Best of Faron Young	1960	10.00	20.00	40.00
❑ T 1450 [M]	The Best of Faron Young	1960	7.50	15.00	30.00

Number	Title (A Side/B Side)	Yr	VG	VG+	NM
❑ ST 1528 [S]	Hello Walls	1961	10.00	20.00	40.00
❑ T 1528 [M]	Hello Walls	1961	7.50	15.00	30.00
❑ ST 1634 [S]	The Young Approach	1961	10.00	20.00	40.00
❑ T 1634 [M]	The Young Approach	1961	7.50	15.00	30.00
❑ DT 1876 [P]	The All-Time Great Hits of Faron Young	1963	5.00	10.00	20.00
❑ T 1876 [M]	The All-Time Great Hits of Faron Young	1963	6.25	12.50	25.00
❑ DT 2037 [R]	Faron Young's Memory Lane	1964	5.00	10.00	20.00
❑ T 2037 [M]	Faron Young's Memory Lane	1964	6.25	12.50	25.00
❑ ST 2307 [S]	Falling in Love	1965	6.25	12.50	25.00
❑ T 2307 [M]	Falling in Love	1965	5.00	10.00	20.00
❑ DT 2536 [R]	If You Ain't Lovin' You Ain't Livin'	1966	5.00	10.00	20.00
❑ T 2536 [M]	If You Ain't Lovin' You Ain't Livin'	1966	6.25	12.50	25.00

HILLTOP

Number	Title (A Side/B Side)	Yr	VG	VG+	NM
❑ JM-6037 [M]	Faron Young	1966	3.75	7.50	15.00
❑ JS-6037 [S]	Faron Young	1966	3.00	6.00	12.00
❑ JS-6073	I'll Be Yours	1968	3.00	6.00	12.00

MARY CARTER

Number	Title (A Side/B Side)	Yr	VG	VG+	NM
❑ MC 1000 [M]	Faron Young Sings on Stage for Mary Carter				
	Paints	196?	15.00	30.00	60.00
—Promotional item for sponsor of The Faron Young Show					

MCA

Number	Title (A Side/B Side)	Yr	VG	VG+	NM
❑ 757	Chapter Two	198?	2.00	4.00	8.00
—Budget-line reissue of 3092					
❑ 3092	Chapter Two	1979	3.00	6.00	12.00
❑ 3212	Free and Easy	1980	3.00	6.00	12.00

MERCURY

Number	Title (A Side/B Side)	Yr	VG	VG+	NM
❑ SRM-1-674	Just What I Had in Mind	1973	3.75	7.50	15.00
❑ SRM-1-698	Faron Young Sings "Some Kind of a Woman"	1974	3.75	7.50	15.00
❑ SRM-1-1016	A Man and His Music	1974	3.00	6.00	12.00
❑ SRM-1-1075	I'd Just Be Fool Enough	1976	3.00	6.00	12.00
❑ SRM-1-1130	The Best of Faron Young, Vol. 2	1977	3.00	6.00	12.00
❑ SRM-1-5005	Young Feelin'	1978	3.00	6.00	12.00
❑ MG 20785 [M]	This Is Faron	1963	5.00	10.00	20.00
❑ MG 20840 [M]	Faron Young Aims at the West	1963	5.00	10.00	20.00
❑ MG 20896 [M]	Story Songs for Country Folks	1964	5.00	10.00	20.00
❑ MG 20931 [M]	Country Dance Favorites	1964	5.00	10.00	20.00
❑ MG 20971 [M]	Story Songs of Mountains and Valleys	1965	5.00	10.00	20.00
❑ MG 21007 [M]	Pen and Paper	1965	5.00	10.00	20.00
❑ MG 21047 [M]	Faron Young's Greatest Hits	1965	5.00	10.00	20.00
❑ MG 21058 [M]	Faron Young Sings the Best of Jim Reeves	1966	5.00	10.00	20.00
❑ MG 21110 [M]	Unmitigated Gall	1967	6.25	12.50	25.00
❑ SR 60785 [S]	This Is Faron	1963	6.25	12.50	25.00
❑ SR 60840 [S]	Faron Young Aims at the West	1963	6.25	12.50	25.00
❑ SR 60896 [S]	Story Songs for Country Folks	1964	6.25	12.50	25.00
❑ SR 60931 [S]	Country Dance Favorites	1964	6.25	12.50	25.00
❑ SR 60971 [S]	Story Songs of Mountains and Valleys	1965	6.25	12.50	25.00
❑ SR 61007 [S]	Pen and Paper	1965	6.25	12.50	25.00
❑ SR 61047 [S]	Faron Young's Greatest Hits	1965	6.25	12.50	25.00
❑ SR 61058 [S]	Faron Young Sings the Best of Jim Reeves	1966	6.25	12.50	25.00
❑ SR 61110 [S]	Unmitigated Gall	1967	5.00	10.00	20.00
❑ SR 61143	Greatest Hits Vol. 2	1968	5.00	10.00	20.00
❑ SR 61174	Here's Faron Young	1968	5.00	10.00	20.00
❑ SR 61212	I've Got Precious Memories	1969	5.00	10.00	20.00
❑ SR 61241	Wine Me Up	1969	5.00	10.00	20.00
❑ SR 61267	The Best of Faron Young	1970	5.00	10.00	20.00
❑ SR 61275	Faron Young Sings "Occasional Wife" and "If I				
	Ever Fall in Love with a Honky Tonk Girl"	1970	5.00	10.00	20.00
❑ SR 61337	Step Aside	1971	5.00	10.00	20.00
❑ SR 61354	Faron Young Sings "Leavin' and Sayin'				
	Goodbye"	1971	3.75	7.50	15.00
❑ SR 61359	It's Four in the Morning	1972	3.75	7.50	15.00
—Revised title to reflect the hit?					
❑ SR 61359	Evening	1972	5.00	10.00	20.00
—Original title?					
❑ SR 61364	Faron Young Sings This Little Girl of Mine	1972	3.75	7.50	15.00
❑ SR 61376	This Time the Hurtin's on Me	1973	3.75	7.50	15.00

PICCADILLY

Number	Title (A Side/B Side)	Yr	VG	VG+	NM
❑ 3547	Hello Walls	198?	2.50	5.00	10.00

SEARS

Number	Title (A Side/B Side)	Yr	VG	VG+	NM
❑ SPS-124	Candy Kisses	1969	6.25	12.50	25.00

SESAC

Number	Title (A Side/B Side)	Yr	VG	VG+	NM
❑ (# unknown) [DJ]	Church Songs	196?	20.00	40.00	80.00

TOWER

Number	Title (A Side/B Side)	Yr	VG	VG+	NM
❑ DT 5022 [R]	It's a Great Life	1966	3.00	6.00	12.00
❑ T 5022 [M]	It's a Great Life	1966	5.00	10.00	20.00
❑ DT 5121	The World of Faron Young	1968	3.75	7.50	15.00

YOUNG, GEORGIE
45s

CAMEO

Number	Title (A Side/B Side)	Yr	VG	VG+	NM
❑ 150	Nine More Miles/The Sneak	1958	6.25	12.50	25.00
❑ 166	Feels So Good/Two Weeks with Pay	1959	5.00	10.00	20.00
❑ 168	Georgie Porgie/Where Is Your Heart	1959	5.00	10.00	20.00

CHANCELLOR

Number	Title (A Side/B Side)	Yr	VG	VG+	NM
❑ 1066	Autumn Lovers/Indian Summer	1960	3.75	7.50	15.00
❑ 1069	Birdland Hully Gully/Marie	1961	3.75	7.50	15.00

COLUMBIA

Number	Title (A Side/B Side)	Yr	VG	VG+	NM
❑ 42773	Supercar/Chicken Scratch	1963	7.50	15.00	30.00

FORTUNE

Number	Title (A Side/B Side)	Yr	VG	VG+	NM
❑ 524	Shakin' Shelley/Buggin' Baby	1957	6.25	12.50	25.00

MERCURY

Number	Title (A Side/B Side)	Yr	VG	VG+	NM
❑ 71259	Can't Stop Me/Come Back to Me	1958	20.00	40.00	80.00

PARKWAY

Number	Title (A Side/B Side)	Yr	VG	VG+	NM
❑ 809	Gold Rush/That's Tough	1960	5.00	10.00	20.00

SWAN

Number	Title (A Side/B Side)	Yr	VG	VG+	NM
❑ 4059	Yogi/By George	1960	3.75	7.50	15.00

YOUNG, JACK AND SHERRY
45s

HIT

Number	Title (A Side/B Side)	Yr	VG	VG+	NM
❑ 296	Jackson/Don't Sleep in the Subway	1967	2.00	4.00	8.00
—B-side by Kathy Shannon					

YOUNG, JESSE COLIN Also see THE YOUNGBLOODS.
45s

ELEKTRA

Number	Title (A Side/B Side)	Yr	VG	VG+	NM
❑ 45530	Rave On/Maui Sunrise	1978	—	2.00	4.00
❑ 46026	Sanctuary/City Boy	1979	—	2.00	4.00

Number	Title (A Side/B Side)	Yr	VG	VG+	NM
WARNER BROS.					
❏ 7404	Peace Song/Pretty in the Fair	1970	—	3.00	6.00
❏ 7581	Good Times/Peace Song	1972	—	2.50	5.00
❏ 7581 [PS]	Good Times/Peace Song	1972	2.50	5.00	10.00
❏ 7618	It's a Lovely Day/Sweet Little Child	1972	—	2.50	5.00
❏ 7749	Evenin'/Morning Sun	1973	—	2.50	5.00
❏ 7816	Cuckoo/Light Shine	1974	—	2.50	5.00
❏ 8053	Susan/Barbados	1974	—	2.50	5.00
❏ 8106	Songbird/'Til You Come Back Home	1975	—	2.50	5.00
❏ 8129	Sugar Babe/Motorhome	1975	—	2.50	5.00
❏ 8225	Sunlight/Peace Song	1976	—	2.50	5.00
❏ 8352	Love on the Wing/(B-side unknown)	1977	—	2.50	5.00
❏ 8398	Fool/Higher and Higher	1977	—	2.50	5.00
Albums					
CAPITOL					
❏ T 2070 [M]	The Soul of a City Boy	1964	12.50	25.00	50.00
❏ ST-11267	The Soul of a City Boy	1974	3.00	6.00	12.00
—Reissue of 2070					
❏ N-16129	The Soul of a City Boy	1981	2.00	4.00	8.00
—Budget-line reissue					
CYPRESS					
❏ 0103	The Highway Is for Heroes	1987	2.50	5.00	10.00
ELEKTRA					
❏ 6E-157	American Dreams	1978	2.50	5.00	10.00
MERCURY					
❏ MG 21005 [M]	Young Blood	1965	7.50	15.00	30.00
❏ SR 61005 [S]	Young Blood	1965	10.00	20.00	40.00
RACCOON					
❏ BS 2588	Together	1972	3.00	6.00	12.00
WARNER BROS.					
❏ BS 2734	Song for Juli	1973	2.50	5.00	10.00
❏ BS 2790	Light Shine	1974	2.50	5.00	10.00
❏ BS 2845	Songbird	1975	2.50	5.00	10.00
❏ BS 2913	On the Road	1976	2.50	5.00	10.00
❏ BS 3033	Love on the Wing	1977	2.50	5.00	10.00

YOUNG, KATHY, AND THE INNOCENTS Also see THE INNOCENTS.

45s

Number	Title (A Side/B Side)	Yr	VG	VG+	NM
INDIGO					
❏ 108	A Thousand Stars/Eddie My Darling	1960	7.50	15.00	30.00
❏ 115	Happy Birthday Blues/Someone to Love	1961	5.00	10.00	20.00
❏ 115 [PS]	Happy Birthday Blues/Someone to Love	1961	12.50	25.00	50.00
❏ 121	Our Parents Talked It Over/Just As Though You Were Here	1961	5.00	10.00	20.00
❏ 125	Magic Is the Night/Du Du'nt Du	1961	5.00	10.00	20.00
❏ 125 [PS]	Magic Is the Night/Du Du'nt Du	1961	12.50	25.00	50.00
❏ 137	Baby, Oh Baby/The Great Pretender	1961	5.00	10.00	20.00
❏ 141	Time/Dee Dee Di Oh	1962	5.00	10.00	20.00
❏ 146	Lonely Blue Nights/I'll Hang My Letters Out to Dry	1962	5.00	10.00	20.00
❏ 147	Send Her Away/Dream Awhile	1962	5.00	10.00	20.00
MONOGRAM					
❏ 506	Dreamboy/I'll Love That Man	1962	5.00	10.00	20.00
PORT					
❏ 3025	A Thousand Stars/Eddie My Darling	196?	—	2.50	5.00
STARFIRE					
❏ 112	Sparkle and Shine/Please Love Me Forever	1979	—	2.50	5.00
7-Inch Extended Plays					
INDIGO					
❏ 1001	Sparkle and Shine/Eddie My Darling//Happy Birthday Blues/Angel on My Shoulder	1961	50.00	100.00	200.00
❏ 1001 [PS]	Kathy Young	1961	50.00	100.00	200.00
Albums					
INDIGO					
❏ LP-504 [M]	The Sound of Kathy Young	1961	75.00	150.00	300.00

YOUNG, LEON

45s

Number	Title (A Side/B Side)	Yr	VG	VG+	NM
ATCO					
❏ 6274	Sea Winds/Spinning Jenny	1963	2.00	4.00	8.00
❏ 6301	John, Paul, George and Ringo/Westward Ho	1964	3.00	6.00	12.00
Albums					
ATCO					
❏ 33-163 [M]	Liverpool Sound for Strings	1964	6.25	12.50	25.00
❏ SD 33-163 [S]	Liverpool Sound for Strings	1964	7.50	15.00	30.00

YOUNG, NEIL Also see BUFFALO SPRINGFIELD; CROSBY, STILLS, NASH AND YOUNG; THE STILLS-YOUNG BAND.

12-Inch Singles

Number	Title (A Side/B Side)	Yr	VG	VG+	NM
GEFFEN					
❏ PRO-A-2373 [DJ]	Get Back to the Country (Long)/Get Back to the Country (Short)	1985	2.50	5.00	10.00
❏ PRO-A-2528 [DJ]	Weight of the World (same on both sides)	1986	2.50	5.00	10.00
❏ PRO-A-2623 [DJ]	People on the Street (same on both sides)	1986	2.50	5.00	10.00
❏ PRO-A-2811 [DJ]	Too Lonely (Remix Edit) (same on both sides)	1987	2.50	5.00	10.00
REPRISE					
❏ PRO2-901 [DJ]	Hawks & Doves/Union Man	1980	2.50	5.00	10.00
—Blue vinyl					
❏ 49895	Southern Pacific/Motor City	1982	2.50	5.00	10.00
—Black vinyl, triangle-shaped					
❏ 49895	Southern Pacific/Motor City	1982	2.50	5.00	10.00
—Red vinyl, triangle-shaped					
❏ 49895	Southern Pacific/Motor City	1982	50.00	100.00	200.00
—Green vinyl, triangle-shaped					
❏ 49895	Southern Pacific/Motor City	1982	75.00	150.00	300.00
—Picture disc, triangle-shaped					
45s					
GEFFEN					
❏ 28196	Mideast Vacation/Long Walk Home	1987	—	—	3.00
❏ 28623	Weight of the World/Pressure	1986	—	—	3.00
❏ 28623 [PS]	Weight of the World/Pressure	1986	—	—	3.00
❏ 28753	Old Ways/Once an Angel	1986	—	—	3.00
❏ 28883	Get Back to the Country/Misfits	1985	—	—	3.00
❏ 29433	Cry, Cry, Cry/Payola Blues	1983	—	2.00	4.00
❏ 29574	Wonderin'/Payola Blues	1983	—	2.00	4.00
❏ 29574 [PS]	Wonderin'/Payola Blues	1983	—	2.00	4.00

Number	Title (A Side/B Side)	Yr	VG	VG+	NM
❏ 29707	Mr. Soul/Mr. Soul	1983	—	2.00	4.00
❏ 29887	Little Thing Called Love/We Are In Control	1982	—	2.00	4.00
❏ 29887 [PS]	Little Thing Called Love/We Are In Control	1982	—	2.00	4.00
REPRISE					
❏ 0746	Only Love Can Break Your Heart/Cinnamon Girl	1971	—	—	3.00
—"Back to Back Hits" release					
❏ 0785	The Loner/Sugar Mountain	1968	30.00	60.00	120.00
❏ 0819	Everyone Knows This Is Nowhere/The Emperor of Wyoming	1969	25.00	50.00	100.00
❏ 0819 [DJ]	Everyone Knows This Is Nowhere/The Emperor of Wyoming	1969	7.50	15.00	30.00
—Standard version of A-side, with "RE-1" in trail-off wax					
❏ 0819 [DJ]	Everyone Knows This Is Nowhere/The Emperor of Wyoming	1969	125.00	250.00	500.00
—Alternate acoustic version of A-side					
❏ 0836	Down By the River/(When You're On the) Losing End	1969	12.50	25.00	50.00
❏ 0861	Oh, Lonesome Me/Sugar Mountain	1969	12.50	25.00	50.00
❏ 0898	I've Been Waiting for You/Oh, Lonesome Me	1970	12.50	25.00	50.00
❏ 0911	Cinnamon Girl/Sugar Mountain	1970	—	2.50	5.00
❏ 0958	Only Love Can Break Your Heart/Birds	1970	—	2.50	5.00
❏ 0992	When You Dance I Can Really Love/Sugar Mountain	1971	—	2.50	5.00
❏ 1023	Brave Belt/Rock and Roll Band	1971	—	2.50	5.00
—With Graham Nash					
❏ 1065	Heart of Gold/Sugar Mountain	1971	—	2.00	4.00
—Without reference to "Harvest" LP on label					
❏ 1065	Heart of Gold/Sugar Mountain	1971	—	2.50	5.00
—With reference to "Harvest" LP on label					
❏ 1084	Old Man/The Needle and the Damage Done	1972	—	2.00	4.00
❏ 1099	War Song/The Needle and the Damage Done	1972	—	2.00	4.00
—With Graham Nash					
❏ 1152	Heart of Gold/Old Man	1972	—	—	3.00
—"Back to Back Hits" release					
❏ 1184	Time Fades Away/The Last Train to Tulsa (Live)	1973	2.50	5.00	10.00
❏ 1209	Walk On/For the Turnstiles	1974	—	2.00	4.00
❏ 1209 [DJ]	Walk On (same on both sides)	1974	2.50	5.00	10.00
—Large hole					
❏ 1209 [DJ]	Walk On (same on both sides)	1974	3.75	7.50	15.00
—Small hole					
❏ 1344	Lookin' for a Love/Sugar Mountain	1976	—	2.00	4.00
❏ 1350	Drive Back/Stupid Girl	1976	—	2.00	4.00
❏ 1390	Hey Baby/Homegrown	1977	—	2.00	4.00
❏ 1391	Like a Hurricane/Hold Back the Tears	1978	—	2.00	4.00
❏ 1393	Sugar Mountain/The Needle and the Damage Done	1978	—	2.00	4.00
❏ 1395	Comes a Time/Motorcycle Mama	1978	—	2.00	4.00
❏ 1395 [PS]	Comes a Time/Motorcycle Mama	1978	—	2.00	4.00
❏ 1396	Four Strong Winds/Human Highway	1979	—	2.00	4.00
❏ 18685	Harvest Moon/Old King	1992	—	2.00	4.00
❏ 22776	Rockin' in the Free World/Rockin' in the Free World (Live)	1989	—	2.00	4.00
❏ 22776 [DJ]	Rockin' in the Free World (same on both sides)	1989	2.50	5.00	10.00
❏ 22776 [PS]	Rockin' in the Free World/Rockin' in the Free World (Live)	1989	—	2.00	4.00
❏ 27848	This Note's For You (LP Version)/This Note's For You (Edited Live Version)	1988	—	2.00	4.00
❏ 27848 [PS]	This Note's For You (LP Version)/This Note's For You (Edited Live Version)	1988	—	2.00	4.00
❏ 27908	Ten Men Workin'/I'm Goin'	1988	—	—	3.00
❏ 27908 [PS]	Ten Men Workin'/I'm Goin'	1988	2.00	4.00	8.00
❏ 49031	Rust Never Sleeps (Hey Hey, My My [Into the Black]/Rust Never Sleeps (My My, Hey Hey [Out of the Blue])	1979	—	2.00	4.00
❏ 49031 [PS]	Rust Never Sleeps (Hey Hey, My My [Into the Black]/Rust Never Sleeps (My My, Hey Hey [Out of the Blue])	1979	2.50	5.00	10.00
❏ 49189	The Loner/Cinnamon Girl	1980	—	2.00	4.00
❏ 49555	Hawks and Doves/Union Man	1980	—	—	3.00
❏ 49555 [PS]	Hawks and Doves/Union Man	1980	—	—	3.00
❏ 49641	Stayin' Power/Captain America	1980	—	—	3.00
❏ 49870	Southern Pacific/Motor City	1981	—	—	3.00
❏ 50014	Opera Star/Surfer Joe and Moe the Sleaze	1982	—	—	3.00
7-Inch Extended Plays					
REPRISE					
❏ SR 2032	Old Man/The Needle and the Damage Done/Heart of Gold//Harvest/Alabama	1972	5.00	10.00	20.00
—Jukebox issue; small hole, plays at 33 1/3 rpm					
❏ SR 2032 [PS]	Harvest	1972	5.00	10.00	20.00
—Part of "Little LP" series (LLP #183)					
Albums					
GEFFEN					
❏ GHS 2018	Trans	1982	2.50	5.00	10.00
—Later pressings have neither sticker nor title of absent song					
❏ GHS 2018	Trans	1982	3.75	7.50	15.00
—First pressings have a sticker on rear cover explaining the absence of "If You've Got Love"					
❏ GHS 2018 [DJ]	Trans	1982	5.00	10.00	20.00
—Promo on Quiex II audiophile vinyl					
❏ GHS 4013	Everybody's Rockin'	1983	2.50	5.00	10.00
❏ GHS 4013	Everybody's Rockin'	1983	5.00	10.00	20.00
—Promo on Quiex II audiophile vinyl					
❏ GHS 24068	Old Ways	1985	3.00	6.00	12.00
❏ GHS 24109	Landing on Water	1986	3.00	6.00	12.00
❏ GHS 24154	Life	1987	3.00	6.00	12.00
❏ R 134125	Landing on Water	1986	3.75	7.50	15.00
—RCA Music Service edition					
❏ R 144439	Life	1987	3.75	7.50	15.00
—BMG Direct Marketing edition					
❏ R 163233	Old Ways	1985	3.75	7.50	15.00
—RCA Music Service edition					
MOBILE FIDELITY					
❏ 1-252	Old Ways	1996	5.00	10.00	20.00
—Audiophile vinyl					
NAUTILUS					
❏ NR-44	Harvest	1982	37.50	75.00	150.00
—Audiophile vinyl					

Number	Title (A Side/B Side)	Yr	VG	VG+	NM

REPRISE

Number	Title (A Side/B Side)	Yr	VG	VG+	NM
❏ MS 2032	Harvest	1972	2.50	5.00	10.00
❏ MS 2032	Harvest	1972	3.75	7.50	15.00

—First pressings have textured cover and lyric insert

❏ M 2151 [M]	Time Fades Away	1973	25.00	50.00	100.00

—Special mono pressing for radio stations only

❏ MS 2151	Time Fades Away	1973	2.50	5.00	10.00
❏ MS 2151 [S]	Time Fades Away	1973	50.00	100.00	200.00

—With a cardboard inner sleeve, withdrawn after the earliest pressing

❏ R 2180	On the Beach	1974	5.00	10.00	20.00
❏ MS 2221	Tonight's the Night	1975	2.50	5.00	10.00
❏ MS 2242	Zuma	1975	2.50	5.00	10.00
❏ 3RS 2257 [(3)]	Decade	1977	5.00	10.00	20.00
❏ 3RS 2257 [(3)DJ]	Decade	1977	125.00	250.00	500.00

—Test pressing; "Campaigner" contains extra verse deleted from the final version

❏ MSK 2261	American Stars 'N' Bars	1977	2.50	5.00	10.00
❏ MSK 2266	Comes A Time	1978	2.50	5.00	10.00

—With "Peace of Mind" as the last song on side 1. Covers can list either "Lotta Love" or "Peace of Mind."

❏ MSK 2266	Comes A Time	1978	18.75	37.50	75.00

—With "Lotta Love" listed and playing as the last song on side 1

❏ MSK 2266 [DJ]	Give to the Wind	1978	250.00	500.00	1000.

—Test pressing; plain white jacket with inserts and STOCK COPY LABEL. Title changed to "Comes A Time" for commercial release.

❏ MSK 2277	Harvest	1978	2.00	4.00	8.00

—Brown "Reprise" label; new number

❏ MSK 2282	Everybody Knows This Is Nowhere	1978	2.00	4.00	8.00

—Brown "Reprise" label; new number

❏ MSK 2283	After the Gold Rush	1978	10.00	20.00	40.00

—Contains remixed extended version of "When You Dance I Can Really Love." Title on cover in red, "RE 2" in trail-off vinyl

❏ HS 2295	Rust Never Sleeps	1979	2.50	5.00	10.00
❏ 2RX 2296 [(2)]	Live Rust	1979	3.75	7.50	15.00
❏ HS 2297	Hawks and Doves	1980	2.50	5.00	10.00
❏ HS 2304	Re-Ac-Tor	1981	2.50	5.00	10.00
❏ RS 6317	Neil Young	1968	50.00	100.00	200.00

—Brown and orange "Reprise/W7" label, no name on front cover, no "RE-1" in trail-off wax

❏ RS 6317	Neil Young	1969	15.00	30.00	60.00

—Re-release: Brown and orange "Reprise/W7" label, no name on front cover, four tracks remixed ("RE 1" in trail-off wax)

❏ RS 6317	Neil Young	1970	3.75	7.50	15.00

—Reissue: Brown "Reprise" label, Neil Young's name is now on front cover

❏ RS 6349	Everybody Knows This Is Nowhere	1969	7.50	15.00	30.00

—Brown and orange "Reprise/W7" label

❏ RS 6349 [DJ]	Everybody Knows This Is Nowhere	1969	18.75	37.50	75.00

—White label promo

❏ RS 6349	Everybody Knows This Is Nowhere	1970	3.75	7.50	15.00

—Brown "Reprise" label

❏ RS 6383	After the Gold Rush	1970	2.50	5.00	10.00

—Brown "Reprise" label

❏ RS 6383	After the Gold Rush	1970	3.75	7.50	15.00

—Brown and orange label; all photos correct

❏ RS 6383	After the Gold Rush	1970	8.75	17.50	35.00

—Brown and orange label; photo of Neil Young appears erroneously printed upside down in gatefold

❏ RS 6383	After the Gold Rush	1970	10.00	20.00	40.00

—Brown and orange label; photo of Marc Bolan (of T. Rex) appears erroneously in gatefold

❏ 2XS 6480 [(2)]	Journey Through the Past (Soundtrack)	1972	5.00	10.00	20.00
❏ 25719	This Note's for You	1988	3.00	6.00	12.00
❏ 25899	Freedom	1989	3.75	7.50	15.00
❏ 26315	Ragged Glory	1990	5.00	10.00	20.00
❏ 45749 [(2)]	Sleeps with Angels	1994	3.75	7.50	15.00
❏ 45934 [(2)]	Mirror Ball	1995	3.75	7.50	15.00

—With Pearl Jam (uncredited)

❏ 46291 [(2)]	Broken Arrow	1996	3.75	7.50	15.00
❏ 46652 [(2)]	Year of the Horse	1997	3.75	7.50	15.00
❏ SMAS-94285	Harvest	1972	6.25	12.50	25.00

—Capitol Record Club edition

❏ R 113998	Harvest	1972	3.00	6.00	12.00

—RCA Music Service edition

❏ R 154182	This Note's for You	1987	3.00	6.00	12.00

—BMG Direct Marketing edition

VAPOR

❏ 46171 [(2)]	Dead Man (Soundtrack)	1996	3.00	6.00	12.00

WARNER BROS.

❏ WBMS-107 [DJ]	The Warner Bros. Music Show	1979	12.50	25.00	50.00

—Promo-only interview album

YOUNG, SHERRY
45s
HIT

❏ 206	Goldfinger/Something's Happened	1965	2.00	4.00	8.00

—B-side by Fred Hess

❏ 274	Single Girl/Sugar Town	1966	2.00	4.00	8.00

—B-side by Connie Dee

YOUNG AMERICANS, THE
45s
ABC

❏ 10940	Born to Be with You/One by One	1967	—	3.00	6.00
❏ 10977	Beautiful, Beautiful World/Little Girl	1967	—	3.00	6.00
❏ 10998	Here I Am (Billy Guy)/As Quiet As It's Kept	1967	—	3.00	6.00
❏ 11044	Happiness/Oh, What a Lovely Day	1968	—	3.00	6.00
❏ 11220	On the Blue Cloud Sky/Blackberry Organ	1969	—	3.00	6.00

Albums
ABC

❏ 586 [M]	While We're Young	1967	3.75	7.50	15.00
❏ S-586 [S]	While We're Young	1967	3.00	6.00	12.00
❏ S-626	The Wonderful World of the Young	1968	3.00	6.00	12.00
❏ S-659	Time for Livin'	1969	3.00	6.00	12.00

YOUNG BROTHERS, THE
45s
SOUL POWER

❏ 21267	What's Your Name/(B-side unknown)	196?	250.00	500.00	1000.

Number	Title (A Side/B Side)	Yr	VG	VG+	NM

YOUNG GENERATION, THE With Janis Siegel, pre-MANHATTAN TRANSFER.
45s
RED BIRD

❏ 10-065	Hideaway/Hymn of Love	1966	3.75	7.50	15.00

YOUNG-HOLT UNLIMITED
45s
BRUNSWICK

❏ 55305	Wack Wack/This Little Light of Mine	1966	2.00	4.00	8.00

—As "The Young-Holt Trio"

❏ 55317	Ain't There Something Money Can't Buy/Mellow Yellow	1967	2.00	4.00	8.00

—As "The Young-Holt Trio"

❏ 55338	The Beat Goes On/Doin' the Thing	1967	2.00	4.00	8.00

—As "The Young-Holt Trio"

❏ 55356	Dig Her Walk/You Gimmie Thum	1967	2.00	4.00	8.00
❏ 55374	Soul Sister/Give It Up	1968	2.00	4.00	8.00
❏ 55391	Soulful Strut/Country Slicker Joe	1968	2.00	4.00	8.00
❏ 55400	Who's Making Love/Just Ain't No Love	1969	—	3.00	6.00
❏ 55410	Just a Melody/Young and Holtful	1969	—	3.00	6.00
❏ 55417	Straight Ahead/California Montage	1969	—	3.00	6.00
❏ 55420	Soulful Samba/Horoscope	1969	—	3.00	6.00

COTILLION

❏ 44092	Mellow Dreaming/Got to Get My Baby Back Home	1970	—	2.50	5.00
❏ 44111	Luv Bugg/Wah Wah Man	1971	—	2.50	5.00
❏ 44120	Hot Pants/I'll Be There	1971	—	2.50	5.00

PAULA

❏ 380	Superfly/Give Me Your Love	1973	—	2.50	5.00
❏ 382	Could It Be I'm Falling in Love/HeyPancho	1973	—	2.50	5.00

Albums
ATLANTIC

❏ SD 1634	Oh Girl	1973	3.00	6.00	12.00

BRUNSWICK

❏ BL 54121 [M]	Wack-Wack	1966	5.00	10.00	20.00

—As "Young-Holt Trio"

❏ BL 54125 [M]	On Stage	1967	5.00	10.00	20.00

—As "Young-Holt Trio"

❏ BL 54128 [M]	The Beat Goes On	1967	7.50	15.00	30.00
❏ BL 754121 [S]	Wack-Wack	1966	5.00	10.00	20.00

—As "Young-Holt Trio"

❏ BL 754125 [S]	On Stage	1967	5.00	10.00	20.00

—As "Young-Holt Trio"

❏ BL 754128 [S]	The Beat Goes On	1967	5.00	10.00	20.00
❏ BL 754141	Funky But!	1968	5.00	10.00	20.00
❏ BL 754144	Soulful Strut	1968	3.75	7.50	15.00
❏ BL 754150	Just a Melody	1969	3.75	7.50	15.00

CADET

❏ LP-791 [M]	Feature Spot	1967	7.50	15.00	30.00
❏ LPS-791 [S]	Feature Spot	1967	5.00	10.00	20.00

—As "Eldee Young and Red Holt (of the Ramsey Lewis Trio)"

COTILLION

❏ SD 18001	Mellow Dreamin'	1971	3.00	6.00	12.00
❏ SD 18004	Born Again	1972	3.00	6.00	12.00

PAULA

❏ LPS-4002	Super Fly	1973	5.00	10.00	20.00

YOUNG LADS, THE
45s
FELICE

❏ 712	Graduation Kiss/Night After Night	1963	25.00	50.00	100.00

NEIL

❏ 100	Moonlight/I'm in Love	1956	17.50	35.00	70.00

YOUNG LIONS, THE (U)
45s
DOT

❏ 16172	Little Girl/It Would Be	1960	12.50	25.00	50.00

YOUNG RASCALS, THE See THE RASCALS.

YOUNG WORLD SINGERS, THE
45s
DECCA

❏ 31660	Ringo for President/Like That	1964	3.00	6.00	12.00

YOUNGBLOODS, THE Also see JESSE COLIN YOUNG.
45s
MERCURY

❏ 72583	Sometimes/Rider	1966	5.00	10.00	20.00

—As "Jesse Colin and the Youngbloods"

❏ 73068	Sometimes/Rider	1969	2.50	5.00	10.00

RCA VICTOR

❏ 47-9015	Grizzly Bear/Tears Are Falling	1966	2.50	5.00	10.00
❏ 47-9142	Merry-Go-Round/Foolin' Around (The Waltz)	1967	2.50	5.00	10.00
❏ 47-9222	The Wine Song/Euphoria	1967	2.50	5.00	10.00
❏ 47-9264	Get Together/All My Dreams Blue	1967	3.75	7.50	15.00
❏ 47-9360	Fool Me/I Can Tell	1967	2.50	5.00	10.00
❏ 47-9424	Dreamer's Dream/Quicksand	1967	2.50	5.00	10.00
❏ 47-9752	Get Together/Beautiful	1969	2.00	4.00	8.00
❏ 74-0129	On Sir Francis Drake/Darkness, Darkness	1969	2.00	4.00	8.00
❏ 74-0270	Sunlight/Trillium	1969	2.00	4.00	8.00
❏ 74-0342	On Sir Francis Drake/Darkness, Darkness	1970	—	3.50	7.00
❏ 74-0380	On Sir Francis Drake/Darkness, Darkness	1970	—	3.00	6.00
❏ 74-0465	Reason to Believe/Sunlight	1971	—	3.00	6.00

WARNER BROS.

❏ 7445	Hippie from Olema/Misty Roses	1970	—	2.50	5.00
❏ 7499	It's a Lovely Day/Ice Bag	1971	—	2.50	5.00
❏ 7563	Will the Circle Be Unbroken/Light Shine	1972	—	2.50	5.00
❏ 7639	Dreamboat/Kind Hearted Woman	1972	—	2.50	5.00
❏ 7660	Running Bear/Kind Hearted Woman	1972	—	2.50	5.00

Albums
MERCURY

❏ SR-61273	Two Trips	1970	6.25	12.50	25.00

—Gold border on cover

Number	Title (A Side/B Side)	Yr	VG	VG+	NM
❑ SR-61273	Two Trips	1971	5.00	10.00	20.00
—Red border on cover					
RACCOON					
❑ WS 1878	Rock Festival	1970	3.00	6.00	12.00
❑ BS 2563	Ride the Wind	1971	3.00	6.00	12.00
❑ BS 2566	Good and Dusty	1971	3.00	6.00	12.00
❑ BS 2653	High on a Ridge Top	1972	3.00	6.00	12.00
RCA VICTOR					
❑ AYL1-3680	The Best of the Youngbloods	1980	2.00	4.00	8.00
—"Best Buy Series" reissue					
❑ LPM-3724 [M]	The Youngbloods	1967	10.00	20.00	40.00
❑ LSP-3724 [S]	The Youngbloods	1967	6.25	12.50	25.00
❑ LSP-3724	Get Together	1969	3.75	7.50	15.00
—Retitled version of "The Youngbloods"					
❑ LPM-3865 [M]	Earth Music	1968	12.50	25.00	50.00
❑ LSP-3865 [S]	Earth Music	1968	6.25	12.50	25.00
❑ AFL1-4150	Elephant Mountain	1977	2.50	5.00	10.00
—Reissue of LSP-4150					
❑ LSP-4150	Elephant Mountain	1969	3.75	7.50	15.00
—Orange label					
❑ LSP-4150	Elephant Mountain	1975	3.00	6.00	12.00
—Tan label					
❑ AFL1-4399	The Best of the Youngbloods	1977	2.50	5.00	10.00
—Reissue of LSP-4399					
❑ LSP-4399	The Best of the Youngbloods	1970	3.75	7.50	15.00
❑ LSP-4561	Sunlight	1971	3.00	6.00	12.00
❑ VPS-6051 [(2)]	This Is the Youngbloods	1972	3.75	7.50	15.00

YOUNGTONES, THE
45s
BRUNSWICK

Number	Title (A Side/B Side)	Yr	VG	VG+	NM
❑ 55089	Come On Baby/Oh Tell Me	1958	15.00	30.00	60.00

YUM YUM KIDS, THE
Albums
MGM

Number	Title (A Side/B Side)	Yr	VG	VG+	NM
❑ E-4396 [M]	Yummy in Your Tummy	1966	3.75	7.50	15.00
❑ SE-4396 [S]	Yummy in Your Tummy	1966	5.00	10.00	20.00

YUM YUMS, THE
45s
ABC-PARAMOUNT

Number	Title (A Side/B Side)	Yr	VG	VG+	NM
❑ 10697	Looky, Looky (What I Got)/Gonna Be a Big Thing	1965	5.00	10.00	20.00

YURO, TIMI
45s
LIBERTY

Number	Title (A Side/B Side)	Yr	VG	VG+	NM
❑ 55343	Hurt/I Apologize	1961	3.75	7.50	15.00
❑ 55375	Smile/She Really Loves You	1961	3.00	6.00	12.00
❑ 55400	I Believe/A Mother's Love	1961	2.50	5.00	10.00
—With Johnnie Ray					
❑ 55410	Let Me Call You Sweetheart/Satan Never Sleeps	1962	2.50	5.00	10.00
❑ 55432	I Know (I Love You)/Count Everything	1962	2.50	5.00	10.00
❑ 55469	What's a Matter Baby (Is It Hurting You)/Thirteenth Hour	1962	3.00	6.00	12.00
❑ 55519	The Love of a Boy/I Ain't Gonna Cry No More	1962	2.50	5.00	10.00
❑ 55551	Insult to Injury/Talkin' About Hurt	1963	—	—	—
—Unreleased					
❑ 55552	Insult to Injury/Just About the Time	1963	2.50	5.00	10.00
❑ 55587	Make the World Go Away/Look Down	1963	2.50	5.00	10.00
❑ 55634	Gotta Travel On/Down in the Valley	1963	2.50	5.00	10.00
❑ 55665	Call Me/Permanently Lonely	1964	2.00	4.00	8.00
❑ 55701	A Legend in My Time/Should I Ever Love Again	1964	2.00	4.00	8.00
❑ 55747	I'm Movin' On (Part 1)/I'm Movin' On (Part 2)	1964	2.00	4.00	8.00
❑ 56049	Wrong/Something Bad on My Mind	1968	—	3.00	6.00
❑ 56061	I Must Have Been Out of My Head/Interlude	1968	—	3.00	6.00
MERCURY					
❑ 72316	If/The Masquerade Is Over	1964	2.00	4.00	8.00
❑ 72355	I Got It Bad and That Ain't Good/Johnny	1964	2.00	4.00	8.00
❑ 72391	Could This Be Magic/You Can Have Him	1965	2.00	4.00	8.00
❑ 72431	Can't Stop Running Away/Get Out of My Life	1965	2.00	4.00	8.00
❑ 72478	Big Mistake/Teardrops Till Dawn	1965	2.00	4.00	8.00
❑ 72515	Once a Day/Pretend	1966	2.00	4.00	8.00
❑ 72601	Don't Keep Me Lonely Too Long/You Took My Happy Away	1966	2.00	4.00	8.00
❑ 72628	Turn the World Around the Other Way/Just a Ribbon	1966	2.00	4.00	8.00
❑ 72674	Why Not Now/Cuttin' In	1967	2.00	4.00	8.00
PLAYBOY					
❑ 6050	Southern Lady/Lovin' You Is All I Ever Had	1975	—	2.50	5.00
UNITED ARTISTS					
❑ 0042	Hurt/What's a Matter Baby (Is It Hurting You)	1973	—	2.00	4.00
—"Silver Spotlight Series" reissue					

Albums
LIBERTY

Number	Title (A Side/B Side)	Yr	VG	VG+	NM
❑ LRP-3208 [M]	Hurt	1961	10.00	20.00	40.00
❑ LRP-3212 [M]	Soul	1962	3.75	7.50	15.00
❑ LRP-3234 [M]	Let Me Call You Sweetheart	1962	3.75	7.50	15.00
❑ LRP-3263 [M]	What's a Matter Baby?	1963	3.75	7.50	15.00
❑ LRP-3286 [M]	The Best of Timi Yuro	1963	3.75	7.50	15.00
❑ LRP-3319 [M]	Make the World Go Away	1963	3.75	7.50	15.00
❑ LST-7208 [S]	Hurt	1961	12.50	25.00	50.00
❑ LST-7212 [S]	Soul	1962	5.00	10.00	20.00
❑ LST-7234 [S]	Let Me Call You Sweetheart	1962	5.00	10.00	20.00
❑ LST-7263 [S]	What's a Matter Baby?	1963	5.00	10.00	20.00
❑ LST-7286 [S]	The Best of Timi Yuro	1963	5.00	10.00	20.00
❑ LST-7319 [S]	Make the World Go Away	1963	5.00	10.00	20.00
❑ LST-7594	Something Bad on My Mind	1968	3.00	6.00	12.00
MERCURY					
❑ MG-20963 [M]	The Amazing Timi Yuro	1964	3.00	6.00	12.00
❑ SR-60963 [S]	The Amazing Timi Yuro	1964	3.75	7.50	15.00
SUNSET					
❑ SUM-1107 [M]	Timi Yuro	1966	2.50	5.00	10.00
❑ SUS-5107 [S]	Timi Yuro	1966	3.00	6.00	12.00
UNITED ARTISTS					
❑ UA-LA429-E	The Very Best of Timi Yuro	1974	3.00	6.00	12.00

Z

ZABACH, FLORIAN
45s
CADENCE

Number	Title (A Side/B Side)	Yr	VG	VG+	NM
❑ 1406	Oceans of Love/Theme from "Carnival"	1961	2.00	4.00	8.00
DECCA					
❑ 9-27509	The Hot Canary/Jalousie	1951	3.75	7.50	15.00
❑ 9-27614	Tea for Two/Running After the Rails	1951	3.75	7.50	15.00
❑ 9-27729	The Waltzing Cat/The Whistler and His Dog	1951	3.75	7.50	15.00
❑ 9-27775	Ida (Sweet as Apple Cider)/Cold Turkey	1951	3.75	7.50	15.00
❑ 9-28090	The Happy Whistler/Jazz Legato-Jazz Pizzicato	1952	3.75	7.50	15.00
❑ 9-28646	Red Canary/April in Portugal	1953	3.75	7.50	15.00
❑ 9-28781	Red Wing/Pussy Footin'	1953	3.75	7.50	15.00
❑ 9-28916	The Funny Fiddle/Plink, Plank, Plunk	1953	3.75	7.50	15.00
❑ 9-29047	Callaghan's Monkey/Solfaggio	1954	3.75	7.50	15.00
❑ 9-29497	Nocturne/Poeme by Fibich	1955	3.00	6.00	12.00
MERCURY					
❑ 70936X45	When the White Lilacs Bloom Again/Fiddler's Boogie	1956	3.00	6.00	12.00
❑ 70975X45	Petticoats of Portugal/Rainbow Trail	1956	3.00	6.00	12.00
❑ 71213X45	Runaway Romance/Two Tickets to Guantanamo	1957	3.00	6.00	12.00

7-Inch Extended Plays
DECCA

Number	Title (A Side/B Side)	Yr	VG	VG+	NM
❑ ED 2154	The Hot Canary/Jalousie//Tea for Two/The Whistler and His Dog	195?	3.00	6.00	12.00
❑ ED 2154 [PS]	The Hot Canary	195?	3.00	6.00	12.00

Albums
DECCA

Number	Title (A Side/B Side)	Yr	VG	VG+	NM
❑ DL 4425 [M]	The Hot Canary	196?	3.75	7.50	15.00
❑ DL 5367 [10]	The Hot Canary	1951	12.50	25.00	50.00
❑ DL 8086 [M]	Hour of Love	195?	6.25	12.50	25.00
—Black label, silver print					
❑ DL 8158 [M]	Dream of Romance	195?	6.25	12.50	25.00
—Black label, silver print					
❑ DL 8239 [M]	Hi-Fi Fiddle	195?	6.25	12.50	25.00
—Black label, silver print					
MERCURY					
❑ MG 20305 [M]	Till the End of Time	1958	3.75	7.50	15.00
❑ MG 20436 [M]	It's Easy to Dance with Florian Zabach	1959	5.00	10.00	20.00
❑ SR 60084 [S]	Till the End of Time	1958	5.00	10.00	20.00
❑ SR 60107 [S]	It's Easy to Dance with Florian Zabach	1959	6.25	12.50	25.00
VOCALION					
❑ VL 3701 [M]	String Along	196?	3.00	6.00	12.00
WING					
❑ MGW 12172 [M]	Golden Strings	196?	3.00	6.00	12.00
❑ MGW 12245 [M]	Till the End of Time	196?	3.00	6.00	12.00
❑ SRW 16172 [S]	Golden Strings	196?	3.75	7.50	15.00
❑ SRW 16245 [S]	Till the End of Time	196?	3.75	7.50	15.00

ZACHARIAS, HELMUT
45s
CAPITOL

Number	Title (A Side/B Side)	Yr	VG	VG+	NM
❑ 2415	Respect/Hurdy Gurdy Man	1969	—	3.00	6.00
DECCA					
❑ 9-29632	Under the Linden Tree/Waltzes from "The Merry Widow"	1955	3.00	6.00	12.00
❑ 9-29849	China-Boogie/The Big Bell and the Little Bell	1956	3.00	6.00	12.00
❑ 9-30039	When the White Lilacs Bloom Again/Blue Blues	1956	3.00	6.00	12.00
❑ 9-30102	Spanish Violins/The Whistler and His Dog	1956	2.50	5.00	10.00
❑ 9-30795	Crazy Violins/The Tipsy Piano	1958	2.50	5.00	10.00
❑ 9-31101	La Montana/Mare Nostrum	1960	2.00	4.00	8.00
❑ 31259	Tres Jolie/Innocence Abroad	1961	2.00	4.00	8.00
❑ 31296	Bermuda Shorts/Adios My Love	1961	2.00	4.00	8.00
❑ 31715	Tokyo Melody/Teatime in Tokyo	1964	2.00	4.00	8.00

Albums
CAPITOL

Number	Title (A Side/B Side)	Yr	VG	VG+	NM
❑ ST-150	Zacharias Plays the Hits	1969	3.00	6.00	12.00
DECCA					
❑ DL 4083 [M]	Themes	196?	3.00	6.00	12.00
❑ DL 8089 [M]	Wine, Women and Waltzes	195?	3.75	7.50	15.00
❑ DL 8150 [M]	Holiday in Vienna	195?	3.75	7.50	15.00
❑ DL 8382 [M]	A Million Strings	195?	3.75	7.50	15.00
❑ DL 8431 [M]	Magic Violins	195?	3.75	7.50	15.00
❑ DL 8594 [M]	Strings, Moonlight and You	195?	3.75	7.50	15.00
❑ DL 8753 [M]	Smorgasbord for Strings	195?	3.75	7.50	15.00
❑ DL 8822 [M]	Hi-Fi Fiddler's Delight	195?	3.75	7.50	15.00
❑ DL 8926 [M]	2,000,000 Strings	1960	3.00	6.00	12.00
❑ DL 8949 [M]	Romantic Strings	1960	3.00	6.00	12.00
❑ DL 8982 [M]	Rendezvous for Strings	1960	3.00	6.00	12.00
❑ DL 8985 [M]	Strauss Waltzes	1960	3.00	6.00	12.00
❑ DL 74083 [S]	Themes	196?	3.75	7.50	15.00
❑ DL 78926 [S]	2,000,000 Strings	1960	3.75	7.50	15.00
❑ DL 78949 [S]	Romantic Strings	1960	3.75	7.50	15.00
❑ DL 78982 [S]	Rendezvous for Strings	1960	3.75	7.50	15.00
❑ DL 78985 [S]	Strauss Waltzes	1960	3.75	7.50	15.00
PHILIPS					
❑ PHM 200053 [M]	A Violin Sings	196?	3.00	6.00	12.00
❑ PHS 600053 [S]	A Violin Sings	196?	3.75	7.50	15.00
RCA VICTOR					
❑ LPM-3597 [M]	Pop Goes Baroque	1966	3.00	6.00	12.00
❑ LSP-3597 [S]	Pop Goes Baroque	1966	3.75	7.50	15.00

ZACHARIAS AND THE TREE PEOPLE
45s
VIKING

Number	Title (A Side/B Side)	Yr	VG	VG+	NM
❑ 1004	We're All Paul Bearers (Part 1)/We're All Paul Bearers (Part 2)	1969	5.00	10.00	20.00

ZACHERLE, JOHN

45s

CAMEO

Number	Title (A Side/B Side)	Yr	VG	VG+	NM
❏ 130	Dinner with Drac (Part 1)/ Dinner with Drac (Part 2)	1958	7.50	15.00	30.00
—Orange label					
❏ 130	Igor/Dinner with Drac	1958	10.00	20.00	40.00
❏ 130	Dinner with Drac (Part 1)/ Dinner with Drac (Part 2)	1960	5.00	10.00	20.00
—Red and black label					
❏ 139	Lunch with Mother Goose/82 Tombstones	1958	7.50	15.00	30.00
❏ 145	I Was a Teenage Caveman/Dummy Doll	1958	7.50	15.00	30.00

COLPIX

Number	Title (A Side/B Side)	Yr	VG	VG+	NM
❏ 743	Monsters Have Problems Too/Hello Dolly	1964	6.25	12.50	25.00

PARKWAY

Number	Title (A Side/B Side)	Yr	VG	VG+	NM
❏ 853	Dinner with Drac/Hurry Bury Baby	1962	6.25	12.50	25.00
❏ 885	Clementine/Surfboard 109	1963	6.25	12.50	25.00
—As "Zacherley"					
❏ 888	Scarey Tales from Mother Goose/ Monster Monkey	1963	6.25	12.50	25.00
—As "Zacherley"					

Albums

ELEKTRA

Number	Title (A Side/B Side)	Yr	VG	VG+	NM
❏ EKL-190 [M]	Spook Along with Zacherle	1960	15.00	30.00	60.00
❏ EKS-7190 [S]	Spook Along with Zacherle	1960	20.00	40.00	80.00

PARKWAY

Number	Title (A Side/B Side)	Yr	VG	VG+	NM
❏ P 7018 [M]	Monster Mash	1962	15.00	30.00	60.00
❏ P 7023 [M]	Scary Tales	1963	15.00	30.00	60.00

ZACK, EDDIE

45s

COLUMBIA

Number	Title (A Side/B Side)	Yr	VG	VG+	NM
❏ 4-21148	Little Donkey/ You Knew Men When You Were Lonely	1953	10.00	20.00	40.00

DECCA

Number	Title (A Side/B Side)	Yr	VG	VG+	NM
❏ 9-28082	Call of the Mountains/Words	1952	10.00	20.00	40.00
❏ 9-28329	Draggin' the Bow/Lights Out	1952	10.00	20.00	40.00
❏ 9-46245	Dill Pickles/That Silver Haired Daddy of Mine	1950	10.00	20.00	40.00
❏ 9-46284	Land Beyond the Sun/Heaven's TV Screen	1951	10.00	20.00	40.00
❏ 9-46302	Beautiful Brown Eyes/Shenandoah Waltz	1951	10.00	20.00	40.00
❏ 9-46330	The Clouds Will Soon Roll By/ You Remind Me of So Much	1951	10.00	20.00	40.00

ZACK, EDDIE, AND COUSIN RICHIE

45s

COLUMBIA

Number	Title (A Side/B Side)	Yr	VG	VG+	NM
❏ 4-21199	I've Lost Again/I Never Saw Her Again	1954	12.50	25.00	50.00
❏ 4-21261	Positively No Dancing/Dancing Country Style	1954	12.50	25.00	50.00
❏ 4-21307	You're Out of My Sight/Cryin' Tears	1954	37.50	75.00	150.00
❏ 4-21387	Rocky Road Blues/Lover, Lover	1955	37.50	75.00	150.00
❏ 4-21441	I'm Gonna Rock and Roll/Foolish Me	1955	37.50	75.00	150.00

ZAGER AND EVANS

45s

RCA VICTOR

Number	Title (A Side/B Side)	Yr	VG	VG+	NM
❏ 47-9816	Help One Man Today/Year 32	1969	—	2.50	5.00
❏ 74-0174	In the Year 2525 (Exordium & Terminus)/Little Kids	1969	—	3.00	6.00
❏ 74-0246	Mr. Turnkey/Cary Lynn Jones	1969	—	2.50	5.00
❏ 74-0299	Listen to the People/ She Never Sleeps Beside Me	1969	—	2.50	5.00
❏ 74-0359	Plastic Park/Crutches	1970	—	2.50	5.00

TRUTH

Number	Title (A Side/B Side)	Yr	VG	VG+	NM
❏ (# unknown)	In the Year 2525 (Exordium & Terminus)/ Little Kids	1967	5.00	10.00	20.00

VANGUARD

Number	Title (A Side/B Side)	Yr	VG	VG+	NM
❏ 35125	Hydra 15,000/I Am	1971	—	2.50	5.00
❏ 35125 [PS]	Hydra 15,000/I Am	1971	5.00	10.00	20.00

Albums

RCA VICTOR

Number	Title (A Side/B Side)	Yr	VG	VG+	NM
❏ ANL1-1077	2525 (Exordium and Terminus)	1975	2.50	5.00	10.00
—Reissue of 4214					
❏ LSP-4214	2525 (Exordium and Terminus)	1969	5.00	10.00	20.00
❏ LSP-4302	Zager and Evans	1970	5.00	10.00	20.00

VANGUARD

Number	Title (A Side/B Side)	Yr	VG	VG+	NM
❏ VSD-6568	Food for the Mind	1971	3.75	7.50	15.00

WHITE WHALE

Number	Title (A Side/B Side)	Yr	VG	VG+	NM
❏ WWS-7123	The Early Writings of Zager and Evans (And Others)	1969	5.00	10.00	20.00

—Actually doesn't contain any music by Zager or Evans, but only songs they wrote; it remains here as it's usually considered a "Zager and Evans" LP

ZAHND, RICKY, AND THE BLUE JEANERS

45s

COLUMBIA

Number	Title (A Side/B Side)	Yr	VG	VG+	NM
❏ 4-263	(I'm Getting) Nuttin' For Christmas/Something Barked On Christmas Morning	1955	3.75	7.50	15.00
—Yellow-label Children's Series edition					
❏ 40576	(I'm Getting) Nuttin' For Christmas/Something Barked On Christmas Morning	1955	3.75	7.50	15.00
❏ 40670	My Church Is My Palace/ You Got to Go to Church	1956	3.00	6.00	12.00

ZANIES, THE

45s

DORE

Number	Title (A Side/B Side)	Yr	VG	VG+	NM
❏ 509	The Blob/Do You Dig Me, Mr. Pygmy	1958	6.25	12.50	25.00
❏ 515	The Mad Scientist/She's a Winner	1958	6.25	12.50	25.00
❏ 597	It's Lovely/Saxophone Safari	1961	5.00	10.00	20.00
❏ 632	Rockin' Chopin/Frustration	1962	5.00	10.00	20.00
❏ 638	London Rock/Stalled	1962	5.00	10.00	20.00
❏ 647	Sleepwalker/Alexander's Ragtime Band	1962	5.00	10.00	20.00
❏ 655	Comin' Down the Track/Hello Jackie	1962	5.00	10.00	20.00
❏ 658	Russian Roulette/Caught in a Ringer1	1963	5.00	10.00	20.00
❏ 683	Chicken Surfer/London Rick	1963	5.00	10.00	20.00
❏ 705	Slinky/Camel Walk	1964	3.75	7.50	15.00

Number	Title (A Side/B Side)	Yr	VG	VG+	NM
❏ 734	Bless 'Em All/Last Dance at the Prom	1965	3.75	7.50	15.00
❏ 853	Will the Real Dr. Frankenstein Please Stand Up/ Frankenstein's Laboratory	1971	3.75	7.50	15.00
❏ 875	Do the 1-2-3/Mr. President-to-Be	1972	2.50	5.00	10.00
❏ 889	Let Out a Scream (Part 1)/ Let Out a Scream (Part 2)	1973	2.00	4.00	8.00
❏ 893	Flakey/(Instrumental)	1974	—	3.00	6.00
❏ 900	Los Angeles, Los Angeles/Let Out a Scream	1974	—	3.00	6.00
❏ 912	Frustration/Roller Coaster	1975	—	2.50	5.00
❏ 920	Old Man River/Los Angeles, Los Angeles	1976	—	2.50	5.00
❏ 957	Janie for President/Los Angeles, Los Angeles	1980	—	2.00	4.00
❏ 959	The Song of the Masochist/Special	1980	—	2.00	4.00
❏ 959	The Song of the Masochist/What Is a One	1980	—	2.00	4.00
❏ 959	What Is a One/Louie's Market	1980	—	2.00	4.00
❏ 962	Curvacious Cora and Carlos Condo/Percolator	1980	—	2.00	4.00
❏ 963	I Love Life, Men, Candy and Paree/I Love Life, Men, Candy and Paree (X-Rated Adult Version)	1981	—	2.00	4.00
❏ 968	From Peanuts to Jelly Beans/ For He's a Jolly Good Fellow	1981	—	2.00	4.00
❏ 974	I Hate Baseball/Dancing with Ronnie Cey	1982	—	2.50	5.00
—With "A. Player"					
❏ 975	Just Another Day in L.A./I'll Be Waiting	1983	—	2.00	4.00
❏ 978	Is There An Echo in the Joint/Doin' the Head	1983	—	2.00	4.00
❏ 979	Gesundheit/Darlin' Come Back	1983	—	2.00	4.00
❏ 980	The Raiders, the Steelers, the Cowboys and Bills (same on both sides)	1984	—	2.00	4.00
❏ 1015	Politics, Religion, and Sin (Part 1)/ Politics, Religion, and Sin (Part 2)	198?	—	2.00	4.00

Albums

DORE

Number	Title (A Side/B Side)	Yr	VG	VG+	NM
❏ 321	The Zanies	1969	7.50	15.00	30.00
❏ 337	The Zanies	1979	3.75	7.50	15.00

ZAPPA, FRANK

Includes his work leading The Mothers of Invention. The label credit, if other than "Frank Zappa," is listed under each record. Also see BABY RAY AND THE FERNS; BOB GUY.

12-Inch Singles

BARKING PUMPKIN

Number	Title (A Side/B Side)	Yr	VG	VG+	NM
❏ 4W9-02616	Goblin Girl/Pink Napkins	1982	7.50	15.00	30.00
—Picture disc					
❏ 4W9-03069	Valley Girl/You Are What You Is	1982	3.75	7.50	15.00
—Sleeve credit is "Frank and Moon Zappa"					

ZAPPA

Number	Title (A Side/B Side)	Yr	VG	VG+	NM
❏ MK 107 [DJ]	Joe's Garage/Central Scrutinizer	1979	10.00	20.00	40.00

45s

BARKING PUMPKIN

Number	Title (A Side/B Side)	Yr	VG	VG+	NM
❏ WS9-02972	Valley Girl/You Are What You Is	1982	—	—	3.00
❏ WS9-02972 [PS]	Valley Girl/You Are What You Is	1982	—	3.50	7.00
—Sleeve credited to "Frank and Moon Zappa"					

BIZARRE

Number	Title (A Side/B Side)	Yr	VG	VG+	NM
❏ 0840	My Guitar/Dog Breath	1969	12.50	25.00	50.00
—The Mothers of Invention					
❏ 0889	Peaches En Regalia/Little Umbrellas	1970	12.50	25.00	50.00
❏ 0892	WPLJ/My Guitar	1970	12.50	25.00	50.00
—The Mothers of Invention					
❏ 0967	Tell Me You Love Me/Would You Go All the Way for the U.S.A.?	1970	12.50	25.00	50.00
❏ 1027	Tears Began to Fall/Junior Mintz Boogie	1971	12.50	25.00	50.00
—Junior Mintz					
❏ 1052	Tears Began to Fall/Junior Mintz Boogie	1971	12.50	25.00	50.00
—Frank Zappa and The Mothers of Invention					
❏ 1127	Cletus Awreetus-Awrightus/Eat That Question	1972	8.75	17.50	35.00
—The Mothers					

DISCREET

Number	Title (A Side/B Side)	Yr	VG	VG+	NM
❏ PRO 586 [DJ]	Uncle Remus/Cozmik Debris	1974	5.00	10.00	20.00
❏ 1180	I'm the Slime/Montana	1973	6.25	12.50	25.00
—The Mothers					
❏ 1312	Don't Eat the Yellow Snow/Cosmic Debris	1974	3.75	7.50	15.00

UNITED ARTISTS

Number	Title (A Side/B Side)	Yr	VG	VG+	NM
❏ 50857	Magic Fingers/Daddy, Daddy, Daddy	1971	12.50	25.00	50.00

VERVE

Number	Title (A Side/B Side)	Yr	VG	VG+	NM
❏ 10418	How Could I Be Such a Fool/Help I'm a Rock (3rd Movement: It Can't Happen Here)	1966	50.00	100.00	200.00
—The Mothers of Invention					
❏ 10418 [DJ]	How Could I Be Such a Fool/Help I'm a Rock (3rd Movement: It Can't Happen Here)	1966	25.00	50.00	100.00
—The Mothers of Invention					
❏ 10458	Who Are the Brain Police/ Trouble Comin' Every Day	1966	50.00	100.00	200.00
—The Mothers of Invention					
❏ 10458 [DJ]	Who Are the Brain Police/ Trouble Comin' Every Day	1966	25.00	50.00	100.00
—The Mothers of Invention					
❏ 10513	Why Don't You Do Me Right/Big Leg Emma	1967	50.00	100.00	200.00
—The Mothers of Invention					
❏ 10513 [DJ]	Why Don't You Do Me Right/Big Leg Emma	1967	25.00	50.00	100.00
—The Mothers of Invention					
❏ 10570	Mother People/Lonely Little Girl	1967	50.00	100.00	200.00
—The Mothers of Invention					
❏ 10570 [DJ]	Mother People/Lonely Little Girl	1967	25.00	50.00	100.00
—The Mothers of Invention					
❏ 10632	Jelly Roll Gum Drop/Any Way the Wind Blows	1968	37.50	75.00	150.00
—Ruben & The Jets					
❏ 10632	Jelly Roll Gum Drop/Deseri	1968	37.50	75.00	150.00
—Ruben & The Jets					
❏ 10632 [DJ]	Jelly Roll Gum Drop/Any Way the Wind Blows	1968	18.75	37.50	75.00
—Ruben & The Jets					
❏ 10632 [DJ]	Jelly Roll Gum Drop/Deseri	1968	18.75	37.50	75.00
—Ruben & The Jets					

WARNER BROS.

Number	Title (A Side/B Side)	Yr	VG	VG+	NM
❏ 8296	Find Her Finer/Zoot Allures	1976	6.25	12.50	25.00
❏ 8342	Disco Boy/Miss Pinky	1977	6.25	12.50	25.00

ZAPPA

Number	Title (A Side/B Side)	Yr	VG	VG+	NM
❏ Z-10	Dancin' Fool/Baby Snakes	1979	2.50	5.00	10.00
❏ ZRP-21 [DJ]	I Don't Wanna Get Drafted (Stereo)/(Mono)	1980	3.75	7.50	15.00
—Sold at Zappa concerts around 1980					

Z

Number	Title (A Side/B Side)	Yr	VG	VG+	NM
❑ Z-31	Joe's Garage/Central Scrutinizer	1979	5.00	10.00	20.00
❑ ZR 1001	I Don't Wanna Get Drafted/				
	Ancient Armaments (Live)	1980	—	2.00	4.00
❑ ZR 1001 [PS]	I Don't Wanna Get Drafted/				
	Ancient Armaments (Live)	1980	2.50	5.00	10.00

Albums
ANGEL

❑ DS-38170	Boulez Conducts Zappa: The Perfect Stranger	1983	3.00	6.00	12.00

BARKING PUMPKIN

❑ 7X4-1	The Old Masters Sampler	1984	6.25	12.50	25.00
❑ AS 995 [DJ]	Tinsel Town Rebellion	1981	5.00	10.00	20.00
—Promo-only sampler					
❑ BPR-1111	Shut Up 'N' Play Yer Guitar	1981	5.00	10.00	20.00
—Mail-order item only					
❑ BPR-1112	Shut Up 'N' Play Yer Guitar Some More	1981	5.00	10.00	20.00
—Mail-order item only					
❑ BPR-1113	Return of the Son of Shut Up 'N' Play Yer Guitar	1981	5.00	10.00	20.00
—Mail-order item only					
❑ BPRP-1114 [PD]	Zappa	1982	3.75	7.50	15.00
—Picture disc with two songs					
❑ BPRP-1115 [PD]	Baby Snakes	1983	3.75	7.50	15.00
—Picture disc					
❑ AS 1294 [DJ]	You Are What You Is Special Clean Cuts Edition	1981	5.00	10.00	20.00
❑ 7777 [(8)]	The Old Masters, Box 1	1984	15.00	30.00	60.00
—Boxed set					
❑ 8888 [(8)]	The Old Masters, Box 2	1986	15.00	30.00	60.00
—Another boxed set					
❑ 8888X	The Old Masters Sampler 2	1986	6.25	12.50	25.00
❑ 9999 [(8)]	The Old Masters, Box 3	1987	15.00	30.00	60.00
—Still another boxed set					
❑ PW2 37336 [(2)]	Tinsel Town Rebellion	1981	5.00	10.00	20.00
❑ PW2 37537 [(2)]	You Are What You Is	1981	5.00	10.00	20.00
❑ FW 38066	Ship Arriving Too Late to Save a Drowning Witch	1982	3.00	6.00	12.00
❑ W3X-38289 [(3)]	Shut Up 'N' Play Yer Guitar	1982	6.25	12.50	25.00
—Box set containing all three "Shut Up 'N' Play Yer Guitar" albums					
❑ FW 38403	Man from Utopia	1983	3.00	6.00	12.00
❑ FW 38820	London Symphony Orchestra	1983	3.00	6.00	12.00
❑ SVBO-74200 [(2)]	Them Or Us	1984	3.75	7.50	15.00
❑ SWCO-74201 [(3)]	Thing-Fish	1984	5.00	10.00	20.00
❑ ST-74202	Francesco Zappa	1985	2.50	5.00	10.00
❑ ST-74203	Frank Zappa Meets the Mothers of Prevention	1985	2.50	5.00	10.00
❑ ST-74205	Jazz from Hell	1986	2.50	5.00	10.00
❑ 74206 [(3)]	Joe's Garage, Acts 1, 2 and 3	1986	12.50	25.00	50.00
—Box set, two gatefolds, with insert					
❑ SJ-74207	London Symphony Orchestra, Volume 2	1987	2.50	5.00	10.00
❑ D1-74212 [(2)]	Guitar	1988	2.50	5.00	10.00
❑ D1-74213 [(3)]	You Can't Do That on Stage Anymore Sampler	1988	2.50	5.00	10.00
❑ R1 74213	You Can't Do That on Stage Anymore Sampler	1988	3.00	6.00	12.00
❑ D1-74217 [(3)]	You Can't Do That on Stage Anymore Vol. 2	1988	2.50	5.00	10.00
❑ D1-74218	Broadway the Hard Way	1988	2.50	5.00	10.00

BIZARRE

❑ MS-2024 [(2)]	Uncle Meat	1969	8.75	17.50	35.00
—Originals come with a booklet; blue label					
❑ MS-2024 [(2)]	Uncle Meat	1973	5.00	10.00	20.00
—Reissue with brown Reprise label					
❑ MS-2028	Weasels Ripped My Flesh	1970	6.25	12.50	25.00
—Blue label original					
❑ MS-2028	Weasels Ripped My Flesh	1973	3.75	7.50	15.00
—Reissue with brown Reprise label					
❑ MS 2030 [DJ]	Chunga's Revenge	1970	12.50	25.00	50.00
—White label promo					
❑ MS-2030	Chunga's Revenge	1970	6.25	12.50	25.00
—Blue label original					
❑ MS-2030	Chunga's Revenge	1973	3.75	7.50	15.00
—Reissue with brown Reprise label					
❑ MS-2042	Fillmore East, June 1971	1971	6.25	12.50	25.00
—Blue label original					
❑ MS-2042	Fillmore East, June 1971	1973	2.75	7.50	15.00
—Reissue with brown Reprise label					
❑ MS 2075	Just Another Band from L.A.	1972	6.25	12.50	25.00
—Blue label original					
❑ MS 2075	Just Another Band from L.A.	1973	3.75	7.50	15.00
—Reissue with brown Reprise label					
❑ MS 2093	The Grand Wazoo	1972	6.25	12.50	25.00
—Blue label original					
❑ MS 2093	The Grand Wazoo	1973	3.75	7.50	15.00
—Reissue with brown Reprise label					
❑ MS 2094	Waka/Jawaka	1972	6.25	12.50	25.00
—Blue label original					
❑ MS 2094	Waka/Jawaka	1973	3.75	7.50	15.00
—Reissue with brown Reprise label					
❑ RS-6356	Hot Rats	1969	12.50	25.00	50.00
—Blue label original					
❑ RS-6356	Hot Rats	1973	3.75	7.50	15.00
—Reissue with brown Reprise label					
❑ RS-6370	Burnt Weenie Sandwich	1970	6.25	12.50	25.00
—Blue label original; with booklet					
❑ RS-6370	Burnt Weenie Sandwich	1973	3.75	7.50	15.00
—Reissue with brown Reprise label					

COLUMBIA

❑ (no #) [(4)DJ]	Lather	1977	187.50	375.00	750.00
—Test pressing only; parts of this LP are on DSK 2291, 2292 and 2294; released as a whole only after Zappa's death, with vinyl only coming out in Japan					

DISCREET

❑ MS 2149	Over-Nite Sensation	1973	5.00	10.00	20.00
❑ MS4 2149 [Q]	Over-Nite Sensation	1973	10.00	20.00	40.00
❑ DS 2175	Apostrophe (')	1974	3.75	7.50	15.00
❑ DS 2175	Apostrophe (')	1974	12.50	25.00	50.00
—White label promo					
❑ DS4 2175 [Q]	Apostrophe (')	1974	8.75	17.50	35.00
❑ 2DS 2202 [(2)]	Roxy and Elsewhere	1974	6.25	12.50	25.00
❑ DS 2216	One Size Fits All	1975	3.75	7.50	15.00
❑ DS 2234	Bongo Fury	1975	3.75	7.50	15.00
❑ DSK 2288	Over-Nite Sensation	1977	3.00	6.00	12.00
—Reissue of DiscReet 2149 with new number					

Number	Title (A Side/B Side)	Yr	VG	VG+	NM
❑ DSK 2289	Apostrophe (')	1977	3.00	6.00	12.00
—Reissue with new number					
❑ 2D 2290 [(2)]	Zappa in New York	1978	5.00	10.00	20.00
❑ 2D 2290 [(2)]	Zappa in New York	1978	62.50	125.00	250.00
—Stock copy with "Punky's Whips" erroneously listed on jacket					
❑ 2D 2290 [(2)DJ]	Zappa in New York	1978	100.00	200.00	400.00
—Test pressing with "Punky's Whips"					
❑ DSK 2291	Studio Tan	1978	3.75	7.50	15.00
❑ DSK 2292	Sleep Dirt	1978	3.75	7.50	15.00
❑ DSK 2294	Orchestral Favorites	1978	3.75	7.50	15.00

FOO-EEE

❑ R1-70372 [(11)]	Beat the Boots #2	1992	25.00	50.00	100.00
—Legitimate box-set release by Rhino of 11 bootlegged concerts					
❑ R1-70907 [(10)]	Beat the Boots	1991	25.00	50.00	100.00
—Legitimate box-set release by Rhino of eight bootlegged concerts					

MCA

❑ 4183 [(2)]	200 Motels (movie soundtrack)	1986	3.75	7.50	15.00
—Reissue					

MGM

❑ GAS-112	The Mothers of Invention	1970	12.50	25.00	50.00
❑ GAS-112 [DJ]	The Mothers of Invention	1970	25.00	50.00	100.00
—Yellow label promo					
❑ SE-4754	The Worst of the Mothers	1971	12.50	25.00	50.00
❑ SE-4754 [DJ]	The Worst of the Mothers	1971	37.50	75.00	150.00
—Yellow label promo					

RHINO/DEL-FI

❑ RNEP-604	Rare Meat: The Early Productions of Frank Zappa	1984	10.00	20.00	40.00
—With original cover					

RYKO ANALOGUE

❑ RALP 10503	We're Only in It for the Money	1995	—	6.00	12.00
—Vinyl reissue; Frank Zappa/The Mothers of Invention					
❑ RALP 40500 [(2)]	Strictly Commercial: The Best of Frank Zappa	1995	5.00	10.00	20.00
—Issued with obi					

UNITED ARTISTS

❑ UAS-9956 [(2)]	200 Motels (movie soundtrack)	1971	12.50	25.00	50.00

VERVE

❑ V-5005-2 [(2)M]	Freak Out!	1966	37.50	75.00	150.00
—Cover version 2: Has no blurb inside on getting a map of "freak-out hot spots"					
❑ V-5005-2 [(2)M]	Freak Out!	1966	50.00	100.00	200.00
—Cover version 1: Has blurb on inside gatefold on how to get a map of "freak-out hot spots" in L.A.					
❑ V-5005-2 [(2)M]	Freak Out!	1966	100.00	200.00	400.00
—White label promo					
❑ V6-5005-2 [(2)S]	Freak Out!	1966	15.00	30.00	60.00
—Cover version 2: Has no blurb inside on getting a map of "freak-out hot spots"					
❑ V6-5005-2 [(2)S]	Freak Out!	1966	20.00	40.00	80.00
—Cover version 1: Has blurb on inside gatefold on how to get a map of "freak-out hot spots" in L.A.					
❑ V6-5005-2 [(2)S]	Freak Out!	1966	75.00	150.00	300.00
—Yellow label promo					
❑ V-5013 [M]	Absolutely Free	1967	30.00	60.00	120.00
❑ V-5013 [M]	Absolutely Free	1967	50.00	100.00	200.00
—White label promo					
❑ V6-5013 [S]	Absolutely Free	1967	15.00	30.00	60.00
❑ V-5045 [M]	We're Only in It for the Money	1968	37.50	75.00	150.00
—With sheet of cut-outs a la "Sgt. Pepper's Lonely Hearts Club Band"					
❑ V-5045 [M]	We're Only in It for the Money	1968	75.00	150.00	300.00
—White label promo					
❑ V6-5045 [S]	We're Only in It for the Money	1968	15.00	30.00	60.00
—Un-censored version, with cut-outs					
❑ V6-5045 [S]	We're Only in It for the Money	1968	37.50	75.00	150.00
—Censored version: the songs "Who Needs the Peace Corps?" and "Let's Make the Water Turn Black" have lines deleted					
❑ V6-5055	Cruising with Ruben and the Jets	1968	15.00	30.00	60.00
❑ V6-5055 [DJ]	Cruising with Ruben and the Jets	1968	37.50	75.00	150.00
—Yellow label promo					
❑ V6-5068	Mothermania — The Best of the Mothers	1969	18.75	37.50	75.00
❑ V6-5068 [DJ]	Mothermania — The Best of the Mothers	1969	37.50	75.00	150.00
—Yellow label promo					
❑ V6-5074	The XXXX of the Mothers	1969	12.50	25.00	50.00
❑ V6-5074 [DJ]	The XXXX of the Mothers	1969	37.50	75.00	150.00
—Yellow label promo					
❑ V-8741 [M]	Lumpy Gravy	1968	75.00	150.00	300.00
—Yellow label promo; no stock copies were issued in mono					
❑ V6-8741	Lumpy Gravy	1968	12.50	25.00	50.00
❑ V6-8741 [DJ]	Lumpy Gravy	1968	50.00	100.00	200.00
—Yellow label promo					

WARNER BROS.

❑ BS-2970	Zoot Allures	1976	3.75	7.50	15.00

ZAPPA

❑ MK-78 [DJ]	Sheik Yerbouti Clean Cuts	1979	8.75	17.50	35.00
❑ MK-129 [DJ]	Joe's Garage Acts I, II and III Sampler	1980	8.75	17.50	35.00
❑ SRZ-2-1501 [(2)]	Sheik Yerbouti	1979	5.00	10.00	20.00
❑ SRZ-2-1502 [(2)]	Joe's Garage, Acts II and III	1980	5.00	10.00	20.00
❑ SRZ-1-1603	Joe's Garage, Act I	1979	3.75	7.50	15.00

ZAVARONI, LENA

45s
STAX

❑ 0206	Ma! (He's Making Eyes at Me)/Rock-a-Bye Your Baby with a Dixie Melody	1974	—	3.00	6.00

Albums
STAX

❑ STS-5511	Ma! He's Making Eyes at Me	1974	3.00	6.00	12.00

ZAZU

Albums
WOODEN NICKEL

❑ BWL1-0791	Zazu	1975	5.00	10.00	20.00

ZEBRA, THE

45s
BLUE THUMB

❑ 109	Christmas Morning (Part 1)/ Christmas Morning (Part 2)	1969	2.50	5.00	10.00

Number	Title (A Side/B Side)	Yr	VG	VG+	NM
PHILIPS					
❏ 40535	Groovy Personality/Miss Ann (Ain't That Kind of Man)	1968	3.00	6.00	12.00
WHITE WHALE					
❏ 305	Bring Me to My Knees/(B-side unknown)	1969	2.50	5.00	10.00

ZEBULONS, THE
45s

Number	Title (A Side/B Side)	Yr	VG	VG+	NM
CUB					
❏ 9069	Falling Water/Wo-Ho-La-Tee-Da	1960	15.00	30.00	60.00

ZEE, TOMMY
45s

Number	Title (A Side/B Side)	Yr	VG	VG+	NM
AMY					
❏ 815	Rebecca, Remember/Worlds Apart	1961	10.00	20.00	40.00

ZEKLEY, GARY Also see THE YELLOW BALLOON.
45s

Number	Title (A Side/B Side)	Yr	VG	VG+	NM
AVA					
❏ 151	Vagabond/When I Go to Sleep	1963	10.00	20.00	40.00

—With Dean Torrence on backing vocals

ZELLA, DANNY
45s

Number	Title (A Side/B Side)	Yr	VG	VG+	NM
DIAL					
❏ 100	Sapphire/You Made Me Blue	1959	50.00	100.00	200.00
FOX					
❏ F # 1	Black Saxs/Wicked Ruby	1959	7.50	15.00	30.00
❏ ZTSC 10056/7	Black Saxs/Wicked Ruby	1959	7.50	15.00	30.00

—Some copies of this 45 do not have a catalog number; these are the master numbers of each side

Number	Title (A Side/B Side)	Yr	VG	VG+	NM
RED ROCKET					
❏ 475	Black Saxs/Wicked Ruby	1959	10.00	20.00	40.00

ZENITHS, THE
Albums

Number	Title (A Side/B Side)	Yr	VG	VG+	NM
ATLANTIC					
❏ 8043 [M]	Makin' the Scene	1960	25.00	50.00	100.00
❏ SD 8043 [S]	Makin' the Scene	1960	37.50	75.00	150.00

ZENTNER, SI
45s

Number	Title (A Side/B Side)	Yr	VG	VG+	NM
LIBERTY					
❏ 55204	Sock Hop/Two Guitars	1959	2.50	5.00	10.00
❏ 55240	Armen's Theme/The Swinging Eye	1960	2.50	5.00	10.00
❏ 55374	Up a Lazy River/Shufflin' Blues	1961	2.00	4.00	8.00
❏ 55408	Hollywood Twist/Nice 'N Easy	1962	2.00	4.00	8.00
❏ 55420 [DJ]	The Goulash (Shufflin' Blues)	1962	3.75	7.50	15.00

—One-sided promo-only release

Number	Title (A Side/B Side)	Yr	VG	VG+	NM
❏ 55476	Shadrack/Boogie Woogie Maxine	1962	2.00	4.00	8.00
❏ 55499	Desafinado/Elephant's Tango	1962	2.00	4.00	8.00
❏ 55538	Waltz in Jazz Time/A La Mode	1963	2.00	4.00	8.00
❏ 55609	Broken Date/Fink	1963	2.00	4.00	8.00
❏ 55648	James Bond Theme/Classes de Cha-Cha	1963	2.50	5.00	10.00
❏ 55675	I'm Getting Sentimental Over You/ Sentimental Journey	1964	2.00	4.00	8.00
❏ 55683	From Russia with Love/James Bond Theme	1964	2.50	5.00	10.00
❏ 55941	Warning Shot/Mona Lisa	1967	—	3.00	6.00
❏ 55955	Dear John/Haven't Been to Church	1967	—	3.00	6.00
RCA VICTOR					
❏ 47-8454	Theme from Max/Spanish Rice	1964	—	3.00	6.00
❏ 47-8550	Dear Heart/In a Little Spanish Town	1965	—	3.00	6.00
❏ 47-8634	Fat Cat/My Devotion	1965	—	3.00	6.00
❏ 47-8779	Baby, Take Another Bow/Mr. Nashville	1966	—	3.00	6.00

7-Inch Extended Plays

Number	Title (A Side/B Side)	Yr	VG	VG+	NM
RCA VICTOR					
❏ VLP 3484	You Were Meant for Me/Fly Me to the Moon (In Other Words)/Don't Blame Me//Put Your Head on My Shoulder/You're Nobody 'Til Somebody Loves You/Soft Sound of Love	1966	2.50	5.00	10.00

—Jukebox issue; small hole, plays at 33 1/3 rpm

Number	Title (A Side/B Side)	Yr	VG	VG+	NM
❏ VLP 3484 [PS]	Put Your Head on My Shoulder	1966	2.50	5.00	10.00
SESAC					
❏ AD-78	Oatmeal Stomp/Hollow Horse Hoedown//All-American Scramble/Tigertail	196?	3.00	6.00	12.00
❏ AD-78 [PS]	Tigertail	196?	3.00	6.00	12.00

Albums

Number	Title (A Side/B Side)	Yr	VG	VG+	NM
LIBERTY					
❏ LRP-3197 [M]	Big Band Plays the Big Hits	1961	3.00	6.00	12.00
❏ LRP-3216 [M]	Up a Lazy River (Big Band Plays the Big Hits: Vol. 2)	1962	3.00	6.00	12.00
❏ LRP-3247 [M]	The Stripper and Other Big Band Hits	1962	3.00	6.00	12.00
❏ LRP-3273 [M]	Desafinado	1963	3.00	6.00	12.00
❏ LRP-3284 [M]	Waltz in Jazz Time	1963	3.00	6.00	12.00
❏ LRP-3326 [M]	More	1963	3.00	6.00	12.00
❏ LRP-3350 [M]	Big Big Band Hits	1964	3.00	6.00	12.00
❏ LRP-3353 [M]	From Russia with Love	1964	3.00	6.00	12.00
❏ LRP-3457 [M]	The Best of Si Zentner	1966	3.00	6.00	12.00
❏ LST-7197 [S]	Big Band Plays the Big Hits	1961	3.75	7.50	15.00
❏ LST-7216 [S]	Up a Lazy River (Big Band Plays the Big Hits: Vol. 2)	1962	3.75	7.50	15.00
❏ LST-7247 [S]	The Stripper and Other Big Band Hits	1962	3.75	7.50	15.00
❏ LST-7273 [S]	Desafinado	1963	3.75	7.50	15.00
❏ LST-7284 [S]	Waltz in Jazz Time	1963	3.75	7.50	15.00
❏ LST-7326 [S]	More	1963	3.75	7.50	15.00
❏ LST-7350 [S]	Big Big Band Hits	1964	3.75	7.50	15.00
❏ LST-7353 [S]	From Russia with Love	1964	3.75	7.50	15.00
❏ LST-7457 [S]	The Best of Si Zentner	1966	3.00	6.00	12.00
❏ LMM-13009 [M]	A Great Band with Great Voices	1961	3.00	6.00	12.00
❏ LMM-13017 [M]	A Great Band with Great Voices Swing the Great Voices of the Great Bands	1962	3.00	6.00	12.00
❏ LSS-14009 [S]	A Great Band with Great Voices	1961	3.75	7.50	15.00
❏ LSS-14017 [S]	A Great Band with Great Voices Swing the Great Voices of the Great Bands	1962	3.75	7.50	15.00
SMASH					
❏ MGS-27007 [M]	Presenting Si Zentner	1961	3.75	7.50	15.00
❏ MGS-27013 [M]	Swing Fever	1962	3.75	7.50	15.00
❏ SRS-67007 [S]	Presenting Si Zentner	1961	5.00	10.00	20.00
❏ SRS-67013 [S]	Swing Fever	1962	5.00	10.00	20.00

Number	Title (A Side/B Side)	Yr	VG	VG+	NM
SUNSET					
❏ SUM-1110 [M]	Big Band Brilliance	196?	2.50	5.00	10.00
❏ SUS-5110 [S]	Big Band Brilliance	196?	3.00	6.00	12.00

ZENTNER, SI AND MARTIN DENNY Also see each artist's individual listings.
Albums

Number	Title (A Side/B Side)	Yr	VG	VG+	NM
LIBERTY					
❏ LMM-13020 [M]	Exotica Suite	1962	3.75	7.50	15.00
❏ LSS-14020 [S]	Exotica Suite	1962	5.00	10.00	20.00

ZEPHYR Also see TOMMY BOLIN.
45s

Number	Title (A Side/B Side)	Yr	VG	VG+	NM
PROBE					
❏ 475	Sail On/Cross the River	1970	3.00	6.00	12.00
WARNER BROS.					
❏ 7444	Going Back to Colorado/Radio Song	1970	2.50	5.00	10.00

Albums

Number	Title (A Side/B Side)	Yr	VG	VG+	NM
PROBE					
❏ 4510	Zephyr	1969	12.50	25.00	50.00
WARNER BROS.					
❏ WS 1897	Goin' Back to Colorado	1971	10.00	20.00	40.00
❏ BS 2603	Sunset Ride	1972	5.00	10.00	20.00

ZEPHYRS, THE
45s

Number	Title (A Side/B Side)	Yr	VG	VG+	NM
ROTATE					
❏ 5006	She's Lost You/There's Something About You	1965	3.75	7.50	15.00
❏ 5009	Let Me Love You Baby/Wonder What I'm Gonna Do	1965	3.75	7.50	15.00

ZERFAS
Albums

Number	Title (A Side/B Side)	Yr	VG	VG+	NM
700 WEST					
❏ 730710	Zerfas	1973	200.00	400.00	800.00

ZEROES, THE
45s

Number	Title (A Side/B Side)	Yr	VG	VG+	NM
TY-TEX					
❏ 105	Flossie Mae/Twisting with Crazee Babee	1963	50.00	100.00	200.00

ZEVON, WARREN
12-Inch Singles

Number	Title (A Side/B Side)	Yr	VG	VG+	NM
ASYLUM					
❏ AS 11386 [DJ]	Werewolves of London/Roland the Headless Thompson Gunner	1978	7.50	15.00	30.00

—Promo-only picture disc

Number	Title (A Side/B Side)	Yr	VG	VG+	NM
❏ AS 11395 [DJ]	Nighttime in the Switching Yard (same on both sides?)	1978	7.50	15.00	30.00
VIRGIN					
❏ DMD 1053 [DJ]	Leave My Monkey Alone (10:31) (5:45) (5:51)	1987	2.00	4.00	8.00
❏ PR 2062 [DJ]	Detox Mansion/Leave My Monkey Alone	1987	2.00	4.00	8.00
❏ PR 2133 [DJ]	Boom Boom Mancini (same on both sides)	1987	2.00	4.00	8.00
❏ PR 2216 [DJ]	Reconsider Me (same on both sides)	1988	2.00	4.00	8.00
❏ 96762	Leave My Monkey Alone (10:31) (5:45) (5:51)	1987	2.00	4.00	8.00

45s

Number	Title (A Side/B Side)	Yr	VG	VG+	NM
ASYLUM					
❏ 45356	Hasten Down the Wind/Mohammad's Radio	1976	2.00	4.00	8.00
❏ 45472	Werewolves of London/Roland the Headless Thompson Gunner	1978	—	2.50	5.00
❏ 45498	Lawyers, Guns and Money/Vera Cruz	1978	—	3.00	6.00
❏ 45526	Johnny Strikes Up the Band/Night Time in the Switching Yard	1978	—	3.00	6.00
❏ 46610	A Certain Girl/Empty-Handed Heart	1980	—	2.00	4.00
❏ 46641	Gorilla, You're a Desperado/Jungle Work	1980	—	2.00	4.00
❏ 47118	Lawyers, Guns and Money/Down on My Luck	1981	—	2.00	4.00
❏ 69509	Werewolves of London/Jesus Mentioned	1986	—	2.50	5.00
❏ 69946	Let Nothing Come Between You/ The Hula Hula Boys	1982	—	2.00	4.00
❏ 69966	Looking for the Next Best Thing/ The Hula Hula Boys	1982	—	2.50	5.00
ELEKTRA					
❏ 45091	Werewolves of London/ Lawyers, Guns and Money	1979	—	2.00	4.00

—"Spun Gold" reissue series

Number	Title (A Side/B Side)	Yr	VG	VG+	NM
VIRGIN					
❏ 99370	Reconsider Me/Factory	1988	—	—	3.00
❏ 99370 [PS]	Reconsider Me/Factory	1988	—	—	3.00
❏ 99440	Leave My Monkey Alone/(Latin Rascals Dub)	1987	—	—	3.00
❏ 99440 [PS]	Leave My Monkey Alone/(Latin Rascals Dub)	1987	—	—	3.00

Albums

Number	Title (A Side/B Side)	Yr	VG	VG+	NM
ASYLUM					
❏ 6E-118	Excitable Boy	1978	2.50	5.00	10.00
❏ 5E-509	Bad Luck Streak in Dancing School	1979	2.50	5.00	10.00
❏ 5E-519	Stand in the Fire	1980	2.50	5.00	10.00
❏ 7E-1060	Warren Zevon	1976	2.50	5.00	10.00
❏ 60159	The Envoy	1982	2.50	5.00	10.00
❏ 60503	A Quiet Normal Life: The Best of Warren Zevon	1987	2.50	5.00	10.00
IMPERIAL					
❏ LP-12456	Wanted Dead or Alive	1970	7.50	15.00	30.00

—As "Zevon"

Number	Title (A Side/B Side)	Yr	VG	VG+	NM
PICKWICK					
❏ SPC-3715	Wanted Dead or Alive	1979	3.75	7.50	15.00

—Reissue of Imperial album

Number	Title (A Side/B Side)	Yr	VG	VG+	NM
VIRGIN					
❏ 90603	Sentimental Hygiene	1987	2.50	5.00	10.00
❏ 91068	Transverse City	1989	2.50	5.00	10.00

ZILL, PAT
45s

Number	Title (A Side/B Side)	Yr	VG	VG+	NM
BIG ADD					
❏ 3151	Big Man, Big House/Little Lies	196?	2.50	5.00	10.00
BIG C					
❏ 119	Air Mail to Heaven/Two Empty Arms	1962	3.75	7.50	15.00
BOONE					
❏ 1031	All I Have to Do Is Wait/ Heartaches by the Number	1965	2.50	5.00	10.00

Z

Number	Title (A Side/B Side)	Yr	VG	VG+	NM
CAROL					
❏ 109	It Don't Mean a Thing to Me/I Took the Blues Out	196?	2.50	5.00	10.00
DOLEJO					
❏ 1002	The Fool/Pretend	196?	2.50	5.00	10.00
ERA					
❏ 3108	The Key's in the Mailbox/I Couldn't See My Heart Before My Eyes	1963	3.00	6.00	12.00
INDIGO					
❏ 119	Pick Me Up on Your Way Down/La Marida	1961	3.75	7.50	15.00
❏ 126	Bouquet of Roses/Hold Tight	1961	3.75	7.50	15.00
QCA					
❏ 403	Glory of Love/ Let's Say Goodbye Like We Said Hello	197?	2.00	4.00	8.00
SAND					
❏ 336	Pick Me Up on Your Way Down/La Marida	1961	5.00	10.00	20.00
SIMS					
❏ 234	The Key's in the Mailbox/ I Couldn't See My Heart Before My Eyes	1965	2.50	5.00	10.00
STOP					
❏ 236	The Things You Should Do/Lonesome 7-7203	1969	2.00	4.00	8.00

ZIMMERMAN, GEORGE, AND THE THRILLS
45s

Number	Title (A Side/B Side)	Yr	VG	VG+	NM
JAB					
❏ 103	Whose Baby Are You/ I Ain't Got the Money to Pay for This Drink	1956	100.00	200.00	400.00

ZINE, BEN
45s

Number	Title (A Side/B Side)	Yr	VG	VG+	NM
PARKWAY					
❏ 994	Village of Tears/ What the Heck's the Hanky Panky	1966	20.00	40.00	80.00

ZIP AND THE ZIPPERS
45s

Number	Title (A Side/B Side)	Yr	VG	VG+	NM
PAGEANT					
❏ 607	Where You Goin' Little Boy/Gig	1963	6.25	12.50	25.00

ZIP CODES, THE
45s

Number	Title (A Side/B Side)	Yr	VG	VG+	NM
LIBERTY					
❏ 55703	Run, Little Mustang/Fancy Filly from Detroit City	1964	7.50	15.00	30.00
Albums					
LIBERTY					
❏ LRP-3367 [M]	Mustang	1964	37.50	75.00	150.00
❏ LST-7367 [S]	Mustang	1964	50.00	100.00	200.00

ZIRCONS, THE   Could be as many as four different groups.
45s

Number	Title (A Side/B Side)	Yr	VG	VG+	NM
AMBER					
❏ 851	One Summer Night/The Lone Stranger	1966	3.75	7.50	15.00
BAGDAD					
❏ 1007	Going Places/Surfing in the Sunset	1963	20.00	40.00	80.00
CAPITOL					
❏ 2667	Finders Keepers/You Ain't Comin' Back	1969	10.00	20.00	40.00
COOL SOUND					
❏ 1030	Silver Bells/You Are My Sunshine	1964	7.50	15.00	30.00
DOT					
❏ 15724	Only One Love/I Need It	1958	5.00	10.00	20.00
FEDERAL					
❏ 12452	No Twistin' on Sunday/Mama Wants to Drive	1962	5.00	10.00	20.00
❏ 12478	Get Up and Go to School/Mr. Jones	1962	5.00	10.00	20.00
HEIGH HO					
❏ 607	Where There's a Will/Don't Put Off for Tomorrow	1967	10.00	20.00	40.00
❏ 608/9	I Couldn't Stop Crying/Sit Down Girl	1967	10.00	20.00	40.00
❏ 645/6	Go On and Cry/Was It Meant to Be This Way	1967	10.00	20.00	40.00
MELLOMOOD					
❏ 1000	Lonely Way/Your Way	1963	5.00	10.00	20.00
OLD TIMER					
❏ 603	Stormy Weather/Sincerely	1964	3.75	7.50	15.00
SIAMESE					
❏ 403	Stormy Weather/Sincerely	1964	3.00	6.00	12.00
WINSTON					
❏ 1020	I Need It/Only One Love	1957	15.00	30.00	60.00
❏ 1022	Crazy Crazy/Return My Love	1958	20.00	40.00	80.00
Albums					
SNOWFLAKE					
❏ 1003	The Crown Kings of Acappella	196?	15.00	30.00	60.00

ZODIACS, THE   See MAURICE WILLIAMS AND THE ZODIACS.

ZOE, ALPHA
45s

Number	Title (A Side/B Side)	Yr	VG	VG+	NM
HIT					
❏ 31	You Beat Me to the Punch/Patches	1962	2.00	4.00	8.00
—B-side by Mitch Lucas					
❏ 41	Keep Your Hands Off My Baby/You Are My Sunshine	1962	2.00	4.00	8.00
—B-side by Leroy Jones and Lucille Johns					
❏ 44	Everybody Loves a Lover/Love Came to Me	1962	2.00	4.00	8.00
—B-side by Ed Hardin					
❏ 54	Let's Turkey Trot/One Broken Heart for Sale	1963	2.00	4.00	8.00
—B-side by Ed Hardin					
❏ 65	Da Doo Ron Ron/Foolish Little Girl	1963	2.00	4.00	8.00
—B-side by Clara Wilson and the Cleftones					
❏ 70	Hello Stranger/Sukiyaki	1963	2.00	4.00	8.00
—B-side by the Music City Chorus and Orchestra Featuring Samayami					
❏ 229	A Lover's Concerto/Keep On Dancing	1965	5.00	10.00	20.00
—B-side by the Gentrys					

ZOMBIES, THE   Also see ARGENT; COLIN BLUNSTONE.
45s

Number	Title (A Side/B Side)	Yr	VG	VG+	NM
COLUMBIA					
❏ 44363	Care of Cell 44/Maybe After He's Gone	1967	12.50	25.00	50.00

Number	Title (A Side/B Side)	Yr	VG	VG+	NM
DATE					
❏ 2-1203	Time of the Season/Imagine the Swan	1970	—	2.50	5.00
—"Hall of Fame" series					
❏ 1604	Time of the Season/I'll Call You Mine	1968	5.00	10.00	20.00
❏ 1612	Butcher's Tale (Western Front 1914)/ This Will Be Our Year	1968	2.50	5.00	10.00
❏ 1628	Time of the Season/Friends of Mine	1968	3.00	6.00	12.00
❏ 1644	Imagine the Swan/Conversation of Floral Street	1969	2.50	5.00	10.00
❏ 1648	If It Don't Work Out/Don't Cry for Me	1969	2.50	5.00	10.00
EPIC					
❏ 11145	Time of the Season/Imagine the Swan	1974	—	2.50	5.00
PARROT					
❏ 3004	Indication/How We Were Before	1966	2.50	5.00	10.00
❏ 9695	She's Not There/You Make Me Feel So Good	1964	3.75	7.50	15.00
❏ 9723	Tell Her No/Leave Me Be	1965	3.75	7.50	15.00
❏ 9723 [PS]	Tell Her No/Leave Me Be	1965	7.50	15.00	30.00
❏ 9747	She's Coming Home/I Must Move	1965	3.00	6.00	12.00
❏ 9747 [PS]	She's Coming Home/I Must Move	1965	7.50	15.00	30.00
❏ 9769	I Want You Back Again/Once Upon a Time	1965	3.00	6.00	12.00
❏ 9786	I Love You/Whenever You're Ready	1965	3.00	6.00	12.00
❏ 9797	Just Out of Reach/Remember You	1965	3.00	6.00	12.00
❏ 9821	Don't Go Away/Is This the Dream	1966	3.00	6.00	12.00
Albums					
DATE					
❏ TES-4013	Odessey and Oracle	1968	7.50	15.00	30.00
—With no mention of "Time of the Season" on front cover					
❏ TES-4013	Odessey and Oracle	1969	5.00	10.00	20.00
—With "Time of the Season" mentioned on front cover					
EPIC					
❏ KEG 32861 [(2)B]	Time of the Zombies	1974	5.00	10.00	20.00
—Record 1 is mono; Record 2 is stereo; orange labels					
❏ PEG 32861 [(2)B]	Time of the Zombies	1979	3.75	7.50	15.00
—Later edition with blue labels					
LONDON					
❏ PS 557 [P]	Early Days	1969	5.00	10.00	20.00
—All tracks in true stereo except "Tell Her No"					
PARROT					
❏ PA 61001 [M]	The Zombies	1965	15.00	30.00	60.00
❏ PAS 71001 [R]	The Zombies	1965	10.00	20.00	40.00
RHINO					
❏ RNLP-120	Live on the BBC, 1965-67	1985	2.50	5.00	10.00
❏ RNLP 70186 [S]	Odessy and Oracle	1986	2.00	4.00	8.00

ZOO, THE (1)
45s

Number	Title (A Side/B Side)	Yr	VG	VG+	NM
SUNBURST					
❏ 775	One Night Man/(Standing On) The Sunset Strip	1968	2.50	5.00	10.00
Albums					
MERCURY					
❏ SR-61300	The Zoo	1970	5.00	10.00	20.00
SUNBURST					
❏ 7500	The Zoo Presents the Chocolate Moose	1968	12.50	25.00	50.00

ZOO, THE (U)   Could be group (1).
45s

Number	Title (A Side/B Side)	Yr	VG	VG+	NM
PARKWAY					
❏ 147	Good Day Sunshine/ Where Have All the Good Times Gone	1967	3.00	6.00	12.00

ZZ TOP   Also see MOVING SIDEWALKS.
12-Inch Singles

Number	Title (A Side/B Side)	Yr	VG	VG+	NM
WARNER BROS.					
❏ PRO-A-877 [DJ]	Cheap Sunglasses (LP Version)/(Live Version)	1979	5.00	10.00	20.00
❏ PRO-A-2011 [DJ]	Gimme All Your Lovin/Got Me Under Pressure	1983	3.75	7.50	15.00
❏ PRO-A-2052 [DJ]	Sharp Dressed Man	1983	3.75	7.50	15.00
❏ PRO-A-2094 [DJ]	TV Dinners (same on both sides)	1983	3.75	7.50	15.00
❏ PRO-A-2124 [DJ]	Legs (Remix 4:31) (same on both sides)	1984	3.75	7.50	15.00
❏ PRO-A-2146 [DJ]	Legs (Special Dance Mix) (same on both sides)	1983	3.00	6.00	12.00
❏ PRO-A-2365 [DJ]	Sleeping Bag (same on both sides)	1985	—	3.50	7.00
❏ PRO-A-2404 [DJ]	Can't Stop Rockin' (3:01) (same on both sides)	1985	2.50	5.00	10.00
❏ PRO-A-2407 [DJ]	Stages (3:32) (same on both sides)	1985	—	3.50	7.00
❏ PRO-A-2432 [DJ]	Delirious (3:41) (same on both sides)	1985	2.00	4.00	8.00
❏ PRO-A-2456 [DJ]	Rough Boy (same on both sides)	1985	2.00	4.00	8.00
❏ PRO-A-2494 [DJ]	Woke Up with Wood (same on both sides)	1986	2.00	4.00	8.00
❏ PRO-A-2529 [DJ]	Velcro Fly (Extended Mix) (Dub Version)	1985	2.00	4.00	8.00
❏ PRO-A-5483 [DJ]	Viva Las Vegas (5:11) (8:36)	1992	3.00	6.00	12.00
❏ 20207	Legs (Special Dance Mix)/La Grange	1984	2.00	4.00	8.00
❏ 20395	Sleeping Bag (Extended Version)/Party on the Patio	1985	2.50	5.00	10.00
❏ 20524	Velcro Fly (Extended Mix) (Dub Mix)/Woke Up with Wood	1985	2.00	4.00	8.00
❏ 21840	Give It Up (2,800 Mile Remix 6:24) (2,800 Mile Dub 5:51) (D.O.R. Remix 6:39) (D.O.R. Dub 5:30)/Concrete and Steel	1990	—	3.50	7.00
45s					
LONDON					
❏ 45-131	Salt Lick/Miller's Farm	1970	2.50	5.00	10.00
❏ 45-138	Neighbor, Neighbor/(Somebody Else Been) Shakin' Your Tree	1970	2.50	5.00	10.00
❏ 45-179	Francene/Francene (Spanish)	1972	2.50	5.00	10.00
❏ 45-203	La Grange/Just Got Paid	1973	2.00	4.00	8.00
❏ 5N-220	Tush/Blue Jean Blues	1975	2.00	4.00	8.00
❏ 5N-220 [PS]	Tush/Blue Jean Blues	1975	3.00	6.00	12.00
❏ 5N-241	It's Only Love/Asleep in the Desert	1976	2.00	4.00	8.00
❏ 5N-241 [PS]	It's Only Love/Asleep in the Desert	1976	2.50	5.00	10.00
❏ 5N-251	Arrested for Driving While Blind/It's Only Love	1977	—	3.50	7.00
❏ 5N-252	Enjoy and Get It On/El Diablo	1977	2.50	5.00	10.00
RCA					
❏ 62812	Breakaway/Pincushion	1994	—	2.00	4.00
❏ 62928	Fuzzbox Voodoo/Girl in a T-Shirt	1994	—	2.00	4.00
SCAT					
❏ 500	Salt Lick/Miller's Farm	1969	50.00	100.00	200.00

Yes, *Union*, Arista AL 8643, stereo LP, Columbia House edition, $10-$20.

Kathy Young, *The Sound of Kathy Young,* Indigo LP-504, mono LP, $150-$300.

Neil Young, "Rockin' in the Free World," Reprise 22776, picture sleeve, $2-$4.

The Mothers of Invention (Frank Zappa), *Freak Out!,* Verve V6-5005-2, stereo LP, 2-record set, with liner note mentioning "Freak-Out Hot Spots," $40-$80.

The Zombies, *Odessey and Oracle,* Date TES-4013, stereo LP, cover as pictured, $15-$30.

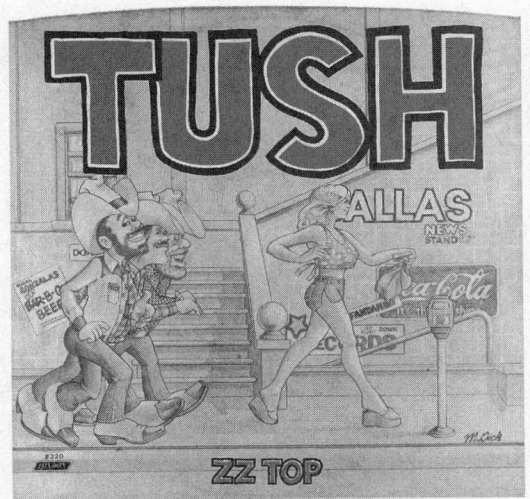

ZZ Top, "Tush," London 5N-220, picture sleeve, $6-$12.

Number	Title (A Side/B Side)	Yr	VG	VG+	NM
WARNER BROS.					
❏ 18979	Viva Las Vegas/2000 Blues	1992	—	2.00	4.00
❏ 19812	Doubleback/Planet of Women	1990	—	—	3.00
❏ 19812 [PS]	Doubleback/Planet of Women	1990	—	3.00	6.00
❏ 28650	Velcro Fly/Woke Up with Wood	1986	—	—	3.00
❏ 28733	Rough Boy/Delirious	1986	—	—	3.00
❏ 28733 [PS]	Rough Boy/Delirious	1986	—	—	3.00
❏ 28810	Stages/Can't Stop Rockin'	1986	—	—	3.00
❏ 28810 [PS]	Stages/Can't Stop Rockin'	1986	—	—	3.00
❏ 28884	Sleeping Bag/Party on the Patio	1985	—	—	3.00
❏ 28884 [PS]	Sleeping Bag/Party on the Patio	1985	—	—	3.00
❏ 29272	Legs/Bad Girl	1984	—	2.00	4.00
❏ 29272 [PS]	Legs/Bad Girl	1984	—	2.00	4.00
❏ 29576	Sharp Dressed Man/I Got the Six	1983	—	2.00	4.00
❏ 29693	Gimme All Your Lovin'/				
	If I Could Only Flag Her Down	1983	—	2.00	4.00
❏ 29693 [PS]	Gimme All Your Lovin'/				
	If I Could Only Flag Her Down	1983	—	2.50	5.00
❏ 49163	I Thank You/Fool for Your Stockings	1980	—	2.00	4.00
❏ 49220	Cheap Sunglasses/Esther Be the One	1980	—	2.00	4.00
❏ 49782	Leila/Don't Tease Me	1981	—	2.00	4.00
❏ 49865	Tube Snake Boogie/Heaven, Hell or Houston	1981	—	2.50	5.00
Albums					
LONDON					
❏ PS 584	ZZ Top's First Album	1971	3.00	6.00	12.00

Number	Title (A Side/B Side)	Yr	VG	VG+	NM
❏ PS 612	Rio Grande Mud	1972	3.00	6.00	12.00
❏ XPS 631	Tres Hombres	1973	3.00	6.00	12.00
❏ PS 656	Fandango!	1975	3.00	6.00	12.00
❏ PS 680	Tejas	1977	3.00	6.00	12.00
❏ PS 706	The Best of ZZ Top	1977	3.00	6.00	12.00
❏ PS-X-1001 [DJ]	Takin' Texas to the People	1976	12.50	25.00	50.00
WARNER BROS.					
❏ BSK 3268	ZZ Top's First Album	1979	2.00	4.00	8.00
❏ BSK 3269	Rio Grande Mud	1979	2.00	4.00	8.00
❏ BSK 3270	Tres Hombres	1979	2.00	4.00	8.00
❏ BSK 3271	Fandango!	1979	2.00	4.00	8.00
❏ BSK 3272	Tejas	1979	2.00	4.00	8.00
❏ BSK 3273	The Best of ZZ Top	1979	2.00	4.00	8.00
❏ HS 3361	Deguello	1979	2.50	5.00	10.00
❏ BSK 3593	El Loco	1981	2.50	5.00	10.00
❏ 23774	Eliminator	1983	2.00	4.00	8.00
❏ 25342	Afterburner	1985	2.00	4.00	8.00
❏ 26265	Recycler	1990	3.75	7.50	15.00
❏ 26846	Greatest Hits	1992	5.00	10.00	20.00
—U.S. vinyl available only through Columbia House					

ZZEBRA

Albums

POLYDOR

Number	Title (A Side/B Side)	Yr	VG	VG+	NM
❏ PD-6043	Panic	1975	3.00	6.00	12.00

Number	Title	Yr	VG	VG+	NM

ORIGINAL CAST RECORDINGS

ALL AMERICAN
❏ Columbia Masterworks KOS 2160 [S]		1962	7.50	15.00	30.00
❏ Columbia Masterworks KOL 5760 [M]		1962	6.25	12.50	25.00

ANKLES AWEIGHT
❏ Decca DL 9025 [M]		1955	10.00	20.00	40.00

ANNIE GET YOUR GUN
❏ Decca DL 8001 [M]		1949	12.50	25.00	50.00
—Original LP issue of the Broadway cast					
❏ Decca DL 9018 [M]		1955	10.00	20.00	40.00
—Early reissue of DL 8001; black label with silver print					
❏ Decca DL 79018 [R]		196?	3.00	6.00	12.00
❏ RCA Victor LOC-1124 [M]		1966	3.00	6.00	12.00
❏ RCA Victor LSO-1124 [S]		1966	3.75	7.50	15.00
—Revival cast; black label, dog on top, "Stereo Dynagroove" at bottom					
❏ RCA Victor LSO-1124 [S]		1969	2.50	5.00	10.00
—Revival cast; orange, tan or black "dog near top" label					

ANYA
❏ United Artists UAL-4133 [M]		1965	5.00	10.00	20.00
❏ United Artists UAS-5133 [S]		1965	12.50	25.00	50.00

APPLAUSE
❏ ABC ABCS-OC-11		1970	5.00	10.00	20.00

THE APPLE TREE
❏ Columbia Masterworks KOS 3020 [S]		1966	6.25	12.50	25.00
❏ Columbia Masterworks KOL 6620 [M]		1966	5.00	10.00	20.00

ARABIAN NIGHTS
❏ Decca DL 9013 [M]		1954	20.00	40.00	80.00

THE ATHENIAN TOUCH
❏ Broadway East OCM-101 [M]		1964	37.50	75.00	150.00
❏ Broadway East OCS-101 [S]		1964	50.00	100.00	200.00

BAJOUR
❏ Columbia Masterworks KOS 2700 [S]		1964	7.50	15.00	30.00
❏ Columbia Masterworks KOL 6300 [M]		1964	6.25	12.50	25.00

BAKER STREET (A MUSICAL ADVENTURE OF SHERLOCK HOLMES)
❏ MGM E-7000 [M]		1965	6.25	12.50	25.00
❏ MGM SE-7000 [S]		1965	7.50	15.00	30.00

A BALLAD FOR BIMSHIRE
❏ London AM 48002 [M]		1963	10.00	20.00	40.00
❏ London AMS 78002 [S]		1963	20.00	40.00	80.00

THE BALLAD OF BABY DOE
❏ MGM 3GC-1 [(3)M]		1958	37.50	75.00	150.00
—Box set					

THE BAND WAGON
❏ "X" LVA-1001 [M]		1955	17.50	35.00	70.00

BELLS ARE RINGING
❏ Columbia Masterworks OS 2006 [S]		1959	6.25	12.50	25.00
—Re-recording in stereo of OL 5170					
❏ Columbia Masterworks OL 5170 [M]		1957	7.50	15.00	30.00
—Gray and black label with six "eye" logos					

BEN FRANKLIN IN PARIS
❏ Capitol SVAS 2191 [S]		1964	7.50	15.00	30.00
❏ Capitol VAS 2191 [M]		1964	6.25	12.50	25.00

BEST FOOT FORWARD
❏ Cadence CLP-4012 [M]		1963	5.00	10.00	20.00
❏ Cadence CLP-24012 [S]		1963	7.50	15.00	30.00
—1963 revival of 1941 play					

BEYOND THE FRINGE
❏ Capitol SW 1792 [S]		1962	7.50	15.00	30.00
❏ Capitol W 1792 [M]		1962	6.25	12.50	25.00

BEYOND THE FRINGE '64
❏ Capitol SW 2072 [S]		1964	6.25	12.50	25.00
❏ Capitol W 2072 [M]		1964	5.00	10.00	20.00

THE BOY FRIEND
❏ RCA Victor LOC-1018 [M]		1954	7.50	15.00	30.00
—Originals have green labels					

THE BOYS IN THE BAND
❏ A&M SP-6001 [(2)]		1969	6.25	12.50	25.00

BRAVO, GIOVANNI
❏ Columbia Masterworks KOS 2200 [S]		1962	5.00	10.00	20.00
❏ Columbia Masterworks KOL 5800 [M]		1962	3.75	7.50	15.00

BRIGADOON
❏ RCA Victor LOC-1001 [M]		195?	5.00	10.00	20.00
—Photos of kilted dancers on front cover; black "Long Play" label					

❏ RCA Victor LOC-1001 [M]		1951	7.50	15.00	30.00
—Green front cover; green label					
❏ RCA Victor LOC-1001 [M]		1963	3.75	7.50	15.00
—Drawing of kilted dancers on front cover; black "Mono" label					
❏ RCA Victor LSO-1001(e) [R]		1963	3.00	6.00	12.00
—Black label, dog on top					

BY JUPITER
❏ RCA Victor LOC-1137 [M]		1967	10.00	20.00	40.00
❏ RCA Victor LSO-1137 [S]		1967	18.75	37.50	75.00
—Above is by a revival cast					

BY THE BEAUTIFUL SEA
❏ Capitol S 531 [M]		1954	17.50	35.00	70.00

BYE BYE BIRDIE
❏ Columbia Masterworks KOS 2025 [S]		1960	7.50	15.00	30.00
—Gray and black label with six "eye" logos; with gatefold cover					
❏ Columbia Masterworks OS 2025 [S]		196?	6.25	12.50	25.00
—Gray and black label with six "eye" logos; with regular cover					
❏ Columbia Masterworks KOL 5510 [M]		1960	6.25	12.50	25.00
—Gray and black label with six "eye" logos; with gatefold cover					
❏ Columbia Masterworks OL 5510 [M]		196?	5.00	10.00	20.00
—Gray and black label with six "eye" logos; with regular cover					

CABARET
❏ Columbia Masterworks KOS 3040 [S]		1966	5.00	10.00	20.00
❏ Columbia Masterworks KOL 6640 [M]		1966	3.75	7.50	15.00

CABIN IN THE SKY
❏ Capitol SW 2073 [S]		1964	12.50	25.00	50.00
—Above is by a revival cast					
❏ Capitol W 2073 [M]		1964	7.50	15.00	30.00

CALL ME MADAM
❏ RCA Victor LOC-1000 [M]		1950	20.00	40.00	80.00
—Dinah Shore sings Ethel Merman's part for contractual reasons, otherwise it's by the entire original cast					

CAMELOT
❏ Columbia Masterworks KOS 2031 [S]		1960	6.25	12.50	25.00
—Gray and black label with six "eye" logos; gatefold cover					
❏ Columbia Masterworks KOL 5620 [M]		1960	5.00	10.00	20.00
—Gray and black label with six "eye" logos					

CAN-CAN
❏ Capitol DW 452 [R]		196?	3.00	6.00	12.00
❏ Capitol S 452 [M]		1953	6.25	12.50	25.00
—Originals have red labels with Capitol logo at top					
❏ Capitol W 452 [M]		195?	3.75	7.50	15.00

CANTERBURY TALES
❏ Capitol SW-229		1969	6.25	12.50	25.00

CAPTAIN JINKS OF THE HORSE MARINES
❏ RCA Victor ARL2-1727 [(2)]		1975	7.50	15.00	30.00
—Box set					

CARMEN JONES
❏ Decca DL 8014 [M]		1949	10.00	20.00	40.00
—Black label, gold print					
❏ Decca DL 9021 [M]		1955	5.00	10.00	20.00
—Reissue of 8014; black label, silver print					

CARNIVAL
❏ MGM E-3946 [M]		1961	5.00	10.00	20.00
❏ MGM SE-3946 [S]		1961	6.25	12.50	25.00
—Black label					
❏ MGM SE-3946 [S]		1968	2.50	5.00	10.00
—Blue and gold label					

CAROUSEL
❏ Command RS 33-843 [M]		1962	3.75	7.50	15.00
—Studio cast					
❏ Command RS-843 SD [M]		1962	5.00	10.00	20.00
—Studio cast witrh Alfred Drake and Roberta Peters, and Enoch Light's orchestra					
❏ Decca DL 8003 [M]		1949	10.00	20.00	40.00
—Original LP issue of the Broadway cast					
❏ Decca DL 9020 [M]		1955	7.50	15.00	30.00
—Early reissue of DL 8003; black label with silver print					
❏ Decca DL 79020 [R]		196?	2.50	5.00	10.00
❏ MCA 1627 [R]		198?	2.00	4.00	8.00
—Reissue of MCA 37093					
❏ MCA 2033 [R]		1973	2.00	4.00	8.00
—Reissue of Decca 79020; black label with rainbow					
❏ MCA 37093 [R]		1980	2.00	4.00	8.00
—Reissue of MCA 2033					

CHRISTINE
❏ Columbia Masterworks OS 2026 [S]		1960	25.00	50.00	100.00
❏ Columbia Masterworks OL 5520 [M]		1960	15.00	30.00	60.00

CINDY
❏ ABC-Paramount ABC-OC-2 [M]		1964	7.50	15.00	30.00
❏ ABC-Paramount ABC-OCS-2 [S]		1964	12.50	25.00	50.00

Number Title	Yr	VG	VG+	NM
CLARA (BEG, BORROW OR STEAL)				
❑ Commentary CYN-02 [M]	1960	15.00	30.00	60.00
CLOWNAROUND				
❑ RCA Victor LSP-4741	1972	62.50	125.00	250.00
CLUB 15				
❑ Decca DL 5155 [10]	1949	15.00	30.00	60.00
THE COACH WITH THE SIX INSIDES				
❑ ESP-Disk' 1019 [M]	1967	6.25	12.50	25.00
COCO				
❑ Paramount PMS-1002	1969	6.25	12.50	25.00
THE COMMITTEE				
❑ Reprise F-2023 [M]	1964	7.50	15.00	30.00
❑ Reprise FS-2023 [S]	1964	10.00	20.00	40.00
COMPANY				
❑ Columbia Masterworks OS 3550	1970	3.00	6.00	12.00
❑ Columbia Masterworks SQ 30993 [Q]	1971	7.50	15.00	30.00
—Quadraphonic version has substantially different mixes than the original stereo LP				
THE CRADLE WILL ROCK				
❑ MGM E-4289-2 [(2)M]	1964	6.25	12.50	25.00
❑ MGM SE-4289-2 [(2)S]	1964	7.50	15.00	30.00
—The above is by a revival cast				
THE CRITIC				
❑ Decca DL 9154 [M]	1967	5.00	10.00	20.00
❑ Decca DL 79154 [S]	1967	5.00	10.00	20.00
CRY FOR US ALL				
❑ Project 3 TS-1000 SD	1970	10.00	20.00	40.00
DAMES AT SEA				
❑ Columbia Masterworks OS 3550	1969	5.00	10.00	20.00
DAMN YANKEES				
❑ RCA Victor LOC-1021 [M]	195?	5.00	10.00	20.00
—Orange cover				
❑ RCA Victor LOC-1021 [M]	1955	7.50	15.00	30.00
—Green cover				
❑ RCA Victor LSO-1021(e) [R]	1965	3.75	7.50	15.00
—Black label, dog on top, "Stereo Electronically Reprocessed" at bottom				
THE DANCERS OF BALI				
❑ Columbia Masterworks ML 4618 [M]	1952	10.00	20.00	40.00
DARLING OF THE DAY				
❑ RCA Victor LOC-1149 [M]	1968	10.00	20.00	40.00
❑ RCA Victor LSO-1149 [S]	1968	15.00	30.00	60.00
DEAR WORLD				
❑ Columbia Masterworks BOS 3260	1969	5.00	10.00	20.00
DEATH OF A SALESMAN				
❑ Decca DX 102 [(2)M]	1951	10.00	20.00	40.00
—Two-record boxed set with contents of 9007 and 9008				
DEATH OF A SALESMAN (PART 1)				
❑ Decca DL 9006 [M]	1951	6.25	12.50	25.00
—Black label, gold print				
DEATH OF A SALESMAN (PART 2)				
❑ Decca DL 9007 [M]	1951	6.25	12.50	25.00
—Black label, gold print				
DESTRY RIDES AGAIN				
❑ Decca DL 9075 [M]	1959	7.50	15.00	30.00
❑ Decca DL 79075 [S]	1959	10.00	20.00	40.00
DO I HEAR A WALTZ?				
❑ Columbia Masterworks KOS 2770 [S]	1965	5.00	10.00	20.00
❑ Columbia Masterworks KOL 6370 [M]	1965	3.75	7.50	15.00
DO RE MI				
❑ RCA Victor LOC-1105 [M]	1965	3.75	7.50	15.00
—Reissue of 2002 with standard red cover				
❑ RCA Victor LSO-1105 [S]	1965	5.00	10.00	20.00
—Reissue of 2002 with standard red cover				
❑ RCA Victor LOCD-2002 [M]	1961	7.50	15.00	30.00
—In black box with orange sleeve				
❑ RCA Victor LSOD-2002 [S]	1961	10.00	20.00	40.00
—In black box with orange sleeve				
DOCTOR SELAVY'S MAGIC THEATRE				
❑ United Artists UA-LA196-G	1974	7.50	15.00	30.00
DONNYBROOK!				
❑ Kapp KD-8500-S [S]	1961	6.25	12.50	25.00
❑ Kapp KDL-8500 [M]	1961	5.00	10.00	20.00
DRESSED TO THE NINES				
❑ MGM E-3914 [M]	1960	6.25	12.50	25.00
❑ MGM SE-3914 [S]	1960	10.00	20.00	40.00
THE EARL OF RUSTON				
❑ Capitol ST-465	1971	10.00	20.00	40.00
ERNEST IN LOVE				
❑ Columbia Masterworks OS 2027 [S]	1960	25.00	50.00	100.00
❑ Columbia Masterworks OL 5530 [M]	1960	15.00	30.00	60.00
AN EVENING WITH RICHARD NIXON				
❑ Ode SP-77015	1972	7.50	15.00	30.00
FADE OUT-FADE IN				
❑ ABC-Paramount ABC-OC-3 [M]	1964	6.25	12.50	25.00
❑ ABC-Paramount ABCS-OC-3 [S]	1964	7.50	15.00	30.00
A FAMILY AFFAIR				
❑ United Artists UAL-4099 [M]	1962	7.50	15.00	30.00
❑ United Artists UAS-5099 [S]	1962	12.50	25.00	50.00
FANNY				
❑ RCA Victor LOC-1015 [M]	1954	6.25	12.50	25.00
—"Long Play" on label				
❑ RCA Victor LOC-1015 [M]	196?	3.75	7.50	15.00
—"Mono" on label				
❑ RCA Victor LSO-1015(e) [R]	196?	3.00	6.00	12.00
—"Stereo Electronically Reprocessed" on label				
THE FANTASTICKS				
❑ MGM E-3872 [M]	196?	2.50	5.00	10.00
—White gatefold cover				
❑ MGM E-3872 [M]	1963	5.00	10.00	20.00
—Original non-gatefold cover				
❑ MGM SE-3872 [S]	196?	2.50	5.00	10.00
—Black gatefold cover				
❑ MGM SE-3872 [S]	196?	3.00	6.00	12.00
—White gatefold cover				
❑ MGM SE-3872 [S]	1963	6.25	12.50	25.00
—Original non-gatefold cover				
FIDDLER ON THE ROOF				
❑ RCA Victor LOC-1093 [M]	1964	3.75	7.50	15.00
❑ RCA Victor LSO-1093 [S]	1964	5.00	10.00	20.00
—Black label, dog on top				
FINIAN'S RAINBOW				
❑ Columbia Masterworks OS 2080 [R]	1963	3.00	6.00	12.00
❑ Columbia Masterworks ML 4062 [M]	1948	7.50	15.00	30.00
—Original cover with no photo; green label				
❑ Columbia Masterworks OL 4062 [M]	196?	3.00	6.00	12.00
—Reissue cover, either pink or green; gray label				
❑ RCA Victor LOC-1057 [M]	1960	2.50	5.00	10.00
—Revival cast; cover shows co-stars hiding in the trees				
❑ RCA Victor LOC-1057 [M]	1960	3.00	6.00	12.00
—Revival cast; "pot of gold" cover				
❑ RCA Victor LSO-1057 [S]	1960	3.00	6.00	12.00
—Revival cast; cover shows co-stars hiding in the trees				
❑ RCA Victor LSO-1057 [S]	1960	3.75	7.50	15.00
—Revival cast; "pot of gold" cover				
FIORELLO!				
❑ Capitol SWAO 1321 [S]	1959	6.25	12.50	25.00
❑ Capitol WAO 1321 [M]	1959	5.00	10.00	20.00
FIRST IMPRESSIONS				
❑ Columbia Masterworks OS 2014 [S]	1959	15.00	30.00	60.00
❑ Columbia Masterworks OL 5400 [M]	1959	7.50	15.00	30.00
FLAHOOLEY				
❑ Capitol S 284 [M]	1951	37.50	75.00	150.00
FLORA, THE RED MENACE				
❑ RCA Victor LOC-1111 [M]	1965	6.25	12.50	25.00
❑ RCA Victor LSO-1111 [S]	1965	7.50	15.00	30.00
FLOWER DRUM SONG				
❑ Columbia Masterworks OS 2009 [S]	1958	6.25	12.50	25.00
—Gray and black label with six "eye" logos				
❑ Columbia Masterworks OL 5350 [M]	1958	5.00	10.00	20.00
—Gray and black label with six "eye" logos				
FLY BLACKBIRD				
❑ Mercury OCM-2206 [M]	1962	7.50	15.00	30.00
❑ Mercury OCS-6206 [S]	1962	15.00	30.00	60.00
FUNNY GIRL				
❑ Capitol STAO 2059 [S]	196?	3.00	6.00	12.00
—Only Barbra Streisand is pictured on the back cover				
❑ Capitol SVAS 2059 [S]	1964	5.00	10.00	20.00
—Both Barbra Streisand and Sydney Chaplin are pictured on the back cover				
❑ Capitol VAS 2059 [M]	1964	3.75	7.50	15.00
A FUNNY THING HAPPENED ON THE WAY TO THE FORUM				
❑ Capitol SWAO 1717 [S]	1962	5.00	10.00	20.00
—Gatefold cover				
❑ Capitol WAO 1717 [M]	1962	3.75	7.50	15.00
—Gatefold cover				

Number	Title	Yr	VG	VG+	NM

THE GAY LIFE
- ❏ Capitol SWAO 1560 [S] — 1961 — 12.50 — 25.00 — 50.00
- ❏ Capitol WAO 1560 [M] — 1961 — 6.25 — 12.50 — 25.00

GENTLEMEN PREFER BLONDES
- ❏ Columbia Masterworks OS 2310 [R] — 1963 — 2.50 — 5.00 — 10.00
  —Gray label
- ❏ Columbia Masterworks ML 4290 [M] — 1949 — 6.25 — 12.50 — 25.00
  —Original with green label
- ❏ Columbia Masterworks OL 4290 [M] — 196? — 3.75 — 7.50 — 15.00
  —Reissue with new prefix and various gray labels
- ❏ Columbia Masterworks S 32610 [R] — 1973 — 2.00 — 4.00 — 8.00

GEORGE M!
- ❏ Columbia Masterworks KOS 3200 [S] — 1968 — 5.00 — 10.00 — 20.00
- ❏ Columbia Masterworks KOL 6800 [M] — 1968 — 7.50 — 15.00 — 30.00

THE GIRL IN PINK TIGHTS
- ❏ Columbia Masterworks ML 4890 [M] — 1954 — 15.00 — 30.00 — 60.00

THE GIRL WHO CAME TO SUPPER
- ❏ Columbia Masterworks KOS 2420 [S] — 1963 — 7.50 — 15.00 — 30.00
- ❏ Columbia Masterworks KOL 6020 [M] — 1963 — 6.25 — 12.50 — 25.00

GIVE 'EM HELL, HARRY!
- ❏ United Artists UA-LA540-H2 [(2)] — 1975 — 5.00 — 10.00 — 20.00

THE GOLDEN APPLE
- ❏ RCA Victor LOC-1014 [M] — 1954 — 25.00 — 50.00 — 100.00

GOLDEN BOY
- ❏ Capitol SVAS 2124 [S] — 1964 — 7.50 — 15.00 — 30.00
- ❏ Capitol VAS 2124 [M] — 1964 — 6.25 — 12.50 — 25.00

GOLDILOCKS
- ❏ Columbia Masterworks OS 2007 [S] — 1958 — 15.00 — 30.00 — 60.00
- ❏ Columbia Masterworks OL 5340 [M] — 1958 — 6.25 — 12.50 — 25.00

GOODTIME CHARLEY
- ❏ RCA Victor ARL1-1011 — 1975 — 7.50 — 15.00 — 30.00

GREASE
- ❏ MGM 1SE-34 — 1972 — 3.00 — 6.00 — 12.00

THE GREAT WALTZ
- ❏ Capitol SVAS 2426 [S] — 1965 — 6.25 — 12.50 — 25.00
- ❏ Capitol VAS 2426 [M] — 1965 — 5.00 — 10.00 — 20.00

GREENWICH VILLAGE U.S.A.
- ❏ 20th Fox TCF-105-2 [(2)M] — 1960 — 15.00 — 30.00 — 60.00
  —With complete show
- ❏ 20th Fox TCF-105-2S [(2)S] — 1960 — 25.00 — 50.00 — 100.00
  —With complete show
- ❏ 20th Fox FOX-4005 [M] — 1960 — 10.00 — 20.00 — 40.00
  —With excerpts from the show
- ❏ 20th Fox SFX-4005 [S] — 1960 — 12.50 — 25.00 — 50.00
  —With excerpts from the show

GREENWILLOW
- ❏ RCA Victor LOC-2001 [M] — 1960 — 5.00 — 10.00 — 20.00
- ❏ RCA Victor LSO-2001 [S] — 1960 — 12.50 — 25.00 — 50.00

GUYS AND DOLLS
- ❏ Decca DL 8036 [M] — 1950 — 7.50 — 15.00 — 30.00
- ❏ Decca DL 9023 [M] — 1955 — 5.00 — 10.00 — 20.00
  —Reissue of 8036
- ❏ Decca DL 79023 [R] — 196? — 3.00 — 6.00 — 12.00
- ❏ MCA 2034 — 1973 — 2.50 — 5.00 — 10.00
  —Reissue of 79023

GYPSY
- ❏ Columbia Masterworks OS 2017 [S] — 1959 — 6.25 — 12.50 — 25.00
  —Original covers are white with drawings
- ❏ Columbia Masterworks OS 2017 [S] — 1962 — 3.75 — 7.50 — 15.00
  —Reissue covers are brown with show photos
- ❏ Columbia Masterworks OL 5420 [M] — 1959 — 5.00 — 10.00 — 20.00
  —Original covers are white with drawings
- ❏ Columbia Masterworks OL 5420 [M] — 1962 — 3.00 — 6.00 — 12.00
  —Reissue covers are brown with show photos

HAIR
- ❏ Atco SD 7002 — 1969 — 6.25 — 12.50 — 25.00
  —Original London cast
- ❏ Philips PHS 600329 — 1969 — 6.25 — 12.50 — 25.00
  —Original French cast
- ❏ RCA Victor ABD1-0245 [Q] — 1973 — 5.00 — 10.00 — 20.00
  —Broadway cast; quadraphonic remix
- ❏ RCA Victor ANL1-0986 — 1974 — 2.50 — 5.00 — 10.00
  —Off-Broadway cast; reissue with new number
- ❏ RCA Victor LOC-1143 [M] — 1967 — 3.75 — 7.50 — 15.00
  —Off-Broadway cast
- ❏ RCA Victor LSO-1143 [S] — 1967 — 3.00 — 6.00 — 12.00
  —Off-Broadway cast; black label, dog at top, "Stereo" at bottom
- ❏ RCA Victor LOC-1150 [M] — 1968 — 7.50 — 15.00 — 30.00
  —Broadway cast
- ❏ RCA Victor LSO-1150 [S] — 1968 — 2.50 — 5.00 — 10.00
  —Broadway cast; orange label
- ❏ RCA Victor LSO-1150 [S] — 1968 — 5.00 — 10.00 — 20.00
  —Broadway cast; black label, dog on top, "Stereo" at bottom

HALF A SIXPENCE
- ❏ RCA Victor LOC-1110 [M] — 1965 — 5.00 — 10.00 — 20.00
- ❏ RCA Victor LSO-1110 [S] — 1965 — 6.25 — 12.50 — 25.00

HALF PAST WEDNESDAY
- ❏ Columbia CL 1917 [M] — 1962 — 7.50 — 15.00 — 30.00
- ❏ Columbia CS 8717 [S] — 1962 — 10.00 — 20.00 — 40.00

HAMLET
- ❏ Columbia Masterworks DOL 302 [(4)M] — 1964 — 6.25 — 12.50 — 25.00
  —Boxed set with entire play (Broadway revival)
- ❏ Columbia Masterworks DOS 702 [(4)S] — 1964 — 6.25 — 12.50 — 25.00
  —Boxed set with entire play (Broadway revival)
- ❏ Columbia Masterworks OS 2620 [S] — 1964 — 3.75 — 7.50 — 15.00
  —Highlights from the box set
- ❏ Columbia Masterworks OL 6220 [M] — 1964 — 3.75 — 7.50 — 15.00
  —Highlights from the box set

THE HAPPIEST GIRL IN THE WORLD
- ❏ Columbia Masterworks KOS 2050 [S] — 1961 — 10.00 — 20.00 — 40.00
  —Second covers are white
- ❏ Columbia Masterworks KOS 2050 [S] — 1961 — 15.00 — 30.00 — 60.00
  —Original covers are yellow
- ❏ Columbia Masterworks KOL 5650 [M] — 1961 — 7.50 — 15.00 — 30.00
  —Second covers are white
- ❏ Columbia Masterworks KOL 5650 [M] — 1961 — 10.00 — 20.00 — 40.00
  —Original covers are yellow

HAPPY HUNTING
- ❏ RCA Victor LOC-1026 [M] — 1956 — 10.00 — 20.00 — 40.00

HEAR! HEAR!
- ❏ Decca DL 9031 [M] — 1955 — 12.50 — 25.00 — 50.00

HELLO, DOLLY!
- ❏ RCA Victor LOCD-1087 [M] — 1964 — 3.75 — 7.50 — 15.00
  —New back cover is in color and has a photo of Carol Channing; "RE" is on cover
- ❏ RCA Victor LOCD-1087 [M] — 1964 — 6.25 — 12.50 — 25.00
  —Original cover is black and white on back and spotlights "Come and Be My Butterfly"; this song was deleted from the show, so the cover was changed
- ❏ RCA Victor LSOD-1087 [S] — 1964 — 5.00 — 10.00 — 20.00
  —New back cover is in color and has a photo of Carol Channing; "RE" is on cover; black label, dog on top
- ❏ RCA Victor LSOD-1087 [S] — 1964 — 7.50 — 15.00 — 30.00
  —Original cover is black and white on back and spotlights "Come and Be My Butterfly"; this song was deleted from the show, so the cover was changed
- ❏ RCA Victor LSOD-1087 [S] — 1969 — 2.50 — 5.00 — 10.00
  —Orange or tan label

HENRY, SWEET HENRY
- ❏ ABC ABC-OC-4 [M] — 1967 — 7.50 — 15.00 — 30.00
- ❏ ABC ABCS-OC-4 [S] — 1967 — 12.50 — 25.00 — 50.00

HERE'S LOVE
- ❏ Columbia Masterworks KOS 2400 [S] — 1963 — 10.00 — 20.00 — 40.00
- ❏ Columbia Masterworks KOL 6000 [M] — 1963 — 7.50 — 15.00 — 30.00

HIGH BUTTON SHOES
- ❏ RCA Camden CAL-457 [M] — 1958 — 7.50 — 15.00 — 30.00
- ❏ RCA Victor LOC-1107 [M] — 1964 — 10.00 — 20.00 — 40.00
- ❏ RCA Victor LSO-1107 [R] — 1964 — 7.50 — 15.00 — 30.00

HIGH SPIRITS
- ❏ ABC-Paramount ABC-OC-1 [M] — 1964 — 6.25 — 12.50 — 25.00
- ❏ ABC-Paramount ABCS-OC-1 [S] — 1964 — 7.50 — 15.00 — 30.00

HOUSE OF FLOWERS
- ❏ Columbia Masterworks ML 4969 [M] — 1954 — 10.00 — 20.00 — 40.00
  —Blue label original
- ❏ United Artists UAS-5180 — 1968 — 10.00 — 20.00 — 40.00
  —Revival cast

HOW NOW, DOW JONES
- ❏ RCA Victor LOC-1142 [M] — 1967 — 6.25 — 12.50 — 25.00
- ❏ RCA Victor LSO-1142 [S] — 1967 — 7.50 — 15.00 — 30.00

HOW TO SUCCEED IN BUSINESS WITHOUT REALLY TRYING
- ❏ RCA Victor LOC-1066 [M] — 1961 — 5.00 — 10.00 — 20.00
- ❏ RCA Victor LSO-1066 [S] — 1961 — 6.25 — 12.50 — 25.00
  —Black label, dog on top
- ❏ RCA Victor LSO-1066 [S] — 1969 — 2.50 — 5.00 — 10.00
  —Orange or tan label

HUGHIE
- ❏ Columbia Masterworks OS 2760 [S] — 1965 — 7.50 — 15.00 — 30.00
- ❏ Columbia Masterworks OL 6260 [M] — 1965 — 6.25 — 12.50 — 25.00

I CAN GET IT FOR YOU WHOLESALE
- ❏ Columbia Masterworks KOS 2180 [S] — 1962 — 7.50 — 15.00 — 30.00
- ❏ Columbia Masterworks KOL 5780 [M] — 1962 — 6.25 — 12.50 — 25.00

I DO! I DO!
- ❏ RCA Victor LOC-1128 [M] — 1966 — 3.75 — 7.50 — 15.00
- ❏ RCA Victor LSO-1128 [S] — 1966 — 5.00 — 10.00 — 20.00
  —Black label, dog on top

Number	Title	Yr	VG	VG+	NM

I HAD A BALL

❏ Mercury OCM-2210 [M]		1964	5.00	10.00	20.00
❏ Mercury OCM-2210 [(2)M]		1964	10.00	20.00	40.00
—Promo-only two-record set with bonus interview record MGD-2-24					
❏ Mercury OCS-6210 [S]		1964	6.25	12.50	25.00

ICE FOLLIES

❏ Dot DLP-3757 [M]		1967	6.25	12.50	25.00
❏ Dot DLP-25757 [S]		1967	7.50	15.00	30.00

ILLYA DARLING

❏ United Artists UAL-8901 [M]		1967	5.00	10.00	20.00
❏ United Artists UAS-9901 [S]		1967	5.00	10.00	20.00

IRMA LA DOUCE

❏ Columbia Masterworks OS 2029 [S]		1960	6.25	12.50	25.00
❏ Columbia Masterworks OL 5560 [M]		1960	5.00	10.00	20.00

J.B.

❏ RCA Victor LD-6075 [(2)M]		1959	15.00	30.00	60.00
❏ RCA Victor LDS-6075 [(2)S]		1959	17.50	35.00	70.00

JACQUES BREL IS ALIVE AND WELL AND LIVING IN PARIS

❏ Columbia Masterworks D2S 779 [(2)]		1968	5.00	10.00	20.00
—Box set; gray "360 Sound" labels					

JENNIE

❏ RCA Victor LOC-1083 [M]		1963	6.25	12.50	25.00
❏ RCA Victor LSO-1083 [S]		1963	12.50	25.00	50.00

JESUS CHRIST SUPERSTAR

❏ Decca DL 71503		1971	5.00	10.00	20.00
—From the Broadway production; also see listings for this title in the VARIOUS ARTISTS COLLECTIONS sections.					
❏ MCA 5000		1973	3.00	6.00	12.00
—From the Broadway production; reissue					

JOSEPH AND THE AMAZING TECHNICOLOR DREAMCOAT

❏ Scepter SPS-588X		1968	5.00	10.00	20.00
—With gatefold cover and libretto					
❏ Scepter SMAS-93738		197?	6.25	12.50	25.00
—Capitol Record Club edition					

JOY

❏ RCA Victor LSO-1166		1970	5.00	10.00	20.00

JUNO

❏ Columbia Masterworks OS 2013 [S]		1959	17.50	35.00	70.00
❏ Columbia Masterworks OL 5380 [M]		1959	10.00	20.00	40.00

KEAN

❏ Columbia Masterworks KSO 2120 [S]		1961	10.00	20.00	40.00
❏ Columbia Masterworks KOL 5720 [M]		1961	7.50	15.00	30.00

THE KING AND I

❏ Decca DL 9008 [M]		195?	3.00	6.00	12.00
—Drawing of Gertrude Lawrence and Yul Brynner on cover, with title on two lines					
❏ Decca DL 9008 [M]		195?	10.00	20.00	40.00
—Drawing of Gertrude Lawrence and Yul Brynner on cover, with title on three lines					
❏ Decca DL 9008 [M]		1951	6.25	12.50	25.00
—Black label, gold print					
❏ Decca DL 79008 [R]		196?	2.50	5.00	10.00

KWAMINA

❏ Capitol SW 1645 [S]		1962	12.50	25.00	50.00
❏ Capitol W 1645 [M]		1962	7.50	15.00	30.00

THE LADY'S NOT FOR BURNING

❏ Decca DL 9508 /9 [(2)M]		1951	12.50	25.00	50.00
—Oversize box set					

LAGINAPPE '59 PRESENTS BE MY GUEST

❏ (no label) XCTV-10303 [M]		1959	62.50	125.00	250.00
—Custom pressing for New Trier High School, Illinois. Collectible because the future Ann-Margret sings one track on the LP!					

LET IT RIDE

❏ RCA Victor LOC-1064 [M]		1961	5.00	10.00	20.00
❏ RCA Victor LSO-1064 [S]		1961	10.00	20.00	40.00

LI'L ABNER

❏ Columbia Masterworks OL 5150 [M]		1956	7.50	15.00	30.00

LITTLE ME

❏ RCA Victor LOC-1078 [M]		1962	5.00	10.00	20.00
❏ RCA Victor LSO-1078 [S]		1962	6.25	12.50	25.00

LOOK MA, I'M DANCIN'!

❏ Decca DL 5231 [M]		1950	25.00	50.00	100.00

LORELEI

❏ MGM M3G-55		1974	7.50	15.00	30.00
—Second version, recorded with Broadway cast					
❏ Verve MV-5097-OC		1974	6.25	12.50	25.00
—First version, recorded before the show hit Broadway					

LOST IN THE STARS

❏ Decca DL 8028 [M]		1949	12.50	25.00	50.00
❏ Decca DL 9120 [M]		1965	3.75	7.50	15.00
—Reissue of 8028					

THE MAD SHOW

❏ Columbia Masterworks OS 2930 [S]		1965	25.00	50.00	100.00
❏ Columbia Masterworks OL 6530 [M]		1965	12.50	25.00	50.00

MAGGIE FLYNN

❏ RCA Victor LSOD-2009		1968	5.00	10.00	20.00
❏ RCA Victor LSOD-2009		1968	6.25	12.50	25.00

THE MAGIC SHOW

❏ Bell 9003		1974	5.00	10.00	20.00

MAKE A WISH

❏ RCA Victor LOC-1002 [M]		1951	37.50	75.00	150.00

MAME

❏ Columbia Masterworks KOS 3000 [S]		1966	5.00	10.00	20.00
—Gray label with "360 Sound Stereo"					
❏ Columbia Masterworks KOS 3000 [S]		1970	3.00	6.00	12.00
—Olive label with orange "Columbia" around outside					
❏ Columbia Masterworks KOL 6600 [M]		1966	3.75	7.50	15.00

MAN OF LA MANCHA

❏ Kapp KRL-4505 [M]		1965	3.75	7.50	15.00
❏ Kapp KRS-4505 [S]		1965	5.00	10.00	20.00

MARK TWAIN TONIGHT!

❏ Columbia Masterworks OS 2019 [S]		1959	3.75	7.50	15.00
❏ Columbia Masterworks OL 5440 [M]		1959	3.00	6.00	12.00

ME AND JULIET

❏ RCA Victor LOC-1012 [M]		1953	17.50	35.00	70.00

MEDEA

❏ Decca DLP 9000 [M]		1949	7.50	15.00	30.00

MEGILLA OF ITZIG MANGER

❏ Columbia Masterworks OS 3270		1968	10.00	20.00	40.00

THE MERRY WIDOW

❏ RCA Victor LOC-1094 [M]		1964	5.00	10.00	20.00
❏ RCA Victor LSO-1094 [S]		1964	6.25	12.50	25.00

MEXICAN HAYRIDE

❏ Decca DL 5232 [10]		1950	30.00	60.00	120.00

MILK AND HONEY

❏ RCA Victor LOC-1065 [M]		1961	5.00	10.00	20.00
—With picture of Tommy Rall and two dancers on front cover					
❏ RCA Victor LOC-1065 [M]		1961	6.25	12.50	25.00
—With only credits (no picture) on front cover					
❏ RCA Victor LSO-1065 [S]		1961	6.25	12.50	25.00
—With picture of Tommy Rall and two dancers on front cover					
❏ RCA Victor LSO-1065 [S]		1961	7.50	15.00	30.00
—With only credits (no picture) on front cover					

MISS LIBERTY

❏ Columbia Masterworks ML 4220 [M]		1949	7.50	15.00	30.00
—Originals have green labels					

THE MOST HAPPY FELLA

❏ Columbia Masterworks O3L 240 [(3)M]		1956	12.50	25.00	50.00
—Box set with entire show					
❏ Columbia Masterworks OS 2330 [R]		196?	3.75	7.50	15.00
❏ Columbia Masterworks OL 5118 [M]		1956	7.50	15.00	30.00
—Gray and black label with six "eye" logos					

MR. PRESIDENT

❏ Columbia Masterworks KOS 2270 [S]		1962	7.50	15.00	30.00
—Gatefold with shiny silver cover					
❏ Columbia Masterworks KOL 5870 [M]		1962	5.00	10.00	20.00
—Gatefold with shiny silver cover					

MR. WONDERFUL

❏ Decca DL 9032 [M]		1956	12.50	25.00	50.00

MRS. PATTERSON

❏ RCA Victor LOC-1017 [M]		1954	37.50	75.00	150.00

THE MUSIC MAN

❏ Capitol SW 990 [S]		196?	3.75	7.50	15.00
—Regular cover with photo of Robert Preston as Harold Hill					
❏ Capitol SWAO 990 [S]		1957	6.25	12.50	25.00
—Gatefold cover, white with credits and drawing on front; gray label					
❏ Capitol W 990 [M]		196?	3.00	6.00	12.00
—Regular cover with photo of Robert Preston as Harold Hill					
❏ Capitol WAO 990 [M]		1957	5.00	10.00	20.00
—Gatefold cover, white with credits and drawing on front; gray label					

MY FAIR LADY

❏ Columbia Masterworks OS 2015 [S]		1959	3.00	6.00	12.00
—Gray label, "Stereo" at bottom; original London cast					

Number Title	Yr	VG	VG+	NM
❑ Columbia Masterworks OS 2015 [S]	1959	5.00	10.00	20.00
—Gray and black label with six "eye" logos; original London cast				
❑ Columbia Masterworks PS 2015 [S]	198?	—	3.00	6.00
—Budget-line reissue with new prefix				
❑ Columbia Masterworks OL 5090 [M]	1956	2.50	5.00	10.00
—Gray label, "Mono" at bottom				
❑ Columbia Masterworks OL 5090 [M]	1956	6.25	12.50	25.00
—Gray and black label with six "eye" logos				
❑ Columbia Masterworks OL 5090 [M]	1963	3.75	7.50	15.00
—Gray label with "Guaranteed High Fidelity" at bottom				

MY PEOPLE

❑ Contact C-1 [M]	1966	5.00	10.00	20.00
❑ Contact CS-1 [S]	1966	6.25	12.50	25.00

THE NERVOUS SET

❑ Columbia Masterworks OS 2018 [S]	1959	15.00	30.00	60.00
❑ Columbia Masterworks OL 5430 [M]	1959	7.50	15.00	30.00

NEW FACES OF 1952

❑ RCA Victor LOC-1008 [M]	1952	6.25	12.50	25.00

NEW FACES OF 1956

❑ RCA Victor LOC-1025 [M]	1956	12.50	25.00	50.00

NEW FACES OF 1968

❑ Warner Bros. BS 2551	1968	7.50	15.00	30.00

THE NEW GIRL IN TOWN

❑ RCA Victor LOC-1027 [M]	1957	5.00	10.00	20.00
❑ RCA Victor LSO-1027 [S]	1958	12.50	25.00	50.00
❑ RCA Victor LOC-1106 [M]	1965	5.00	10.00	20.00
❑ RCA Victor LSC-1106 [S]	1965	7.50	15.00	30.00

THE NINA, THE PINTA AND THE SANTA MARIA

❑ Dot DLP-9009 [M]	1960	10.00	20.00	40.00
❑ Dot DLP-29009 [S]	1960	12.50	25.00	50.00

NO STRINGS

❑ Capitol O 1695 [M]	1962	5.00	10.00	20.00
❑ Capitol SO 1695 [S]	1962	10.00	20.00	40.00

OF THEE I SING

❑ Capitol S 350 [M]	1952	37.50	75.00	150.00

OH, KAY!

❑ 20th Fox FOX-4003 [M]	1960	6.25	12.50	25.00
❑ 20th Fox SFX-4003 [S]	1960	12.50	25.00	50.00

OKLAHOMA!

❑ Decca DLP 8000 [M]	1949	7.50	15.00	30.00
—Black label, gold print; the first 12-inch LP on Decca				
❑ Decca DL 9017 [M]	1955	5.00	10.00	20.00
—Reissue of 8000				
❑ Decca DL 9017 [M]	196?	5.00	10.00	20.00
—Reissue with new cover art				
❑ Decca DL 79017 [R]	196?	3.75	7.50	15.00
❑ Decca DL 79017 [R]	1968	5.00	10.00	20.00
—Special 25th Anniversary edition; cover has yellow drawing, inner sleeve has liner notes				
❑ MCA 2030	1973	2.00	4.00	8.00
—Reissue of 79017; black label with rainbow				
❑ MCA 37096	198?	2.00	4.00	8.00
—Reissue of 2030				

OLIVER!

❑ RCA Victor LOCD-2004 [M]	1962	3.75	7.50	15.00
❑ RCA Victor LSOD-2004 [S]	1962	5.00	10.00	20.00

ON A CLEAR DAY YOU CAN SEE FOREVER

❑ RCA Victor LOCD-2006 [M]	1965	5.00	10.00	20.00
❑ RCA Victor LSOD-2006 [S]	1965	6.25	12.50	25.00

ON YOUR TOES

❑ Decca DL 9015 [M]	1954	18.75	37.50	75.00

ONCE UPON A MATTRESS

❑ Kapp KDL-7004 [M]	1959	6.25	12.50	25.00
❑ Kapp KDL-7004-S [S]	1959	7.50	15.00	30.00

110 IN THE SHADE

❑ RCA Victor LOC-1085 [M]	1963	6.25	12.50	25.00
❑ RCA Victor LSO-1085 [S]	1963	10.00	20.00	40.00

ONE TOUCH OF VENUS

❑ Decca DL 9122 [M]	1965	6.25	12.50	25.00
❑ Decca DL 79122 [R]	1965	6.25	12.50	25.00

OVER HERE!

❑ Columbia Masterworks KS 32961	1974	5.00	10.00	20.00
❑ Columbia Masterworks SQ 32961 [Q]	1974	7.50	15.00	30.00

PAINT YOUR WAGON

❑ RCA Victor LOC-1006 [M]	1951	6.25	12.50	25.00
—Green label				
❑ RCA Victor LOC-1006 [M]	1955	5.00	10.00	20.00
—Black label, dog on top, "Long Play" at bottom				

Number Title	Yr	VG	VG+	NM
❑ RCA Victor LOC-1006 [M]	1965	3.75	7.50	15.00
—Black label, dog on top, "Mono" at bottom				
❑ RCA Victor LSO-1006 [R]	1965	3.00	6.00	12.00
—Black label, dog on top				
❑ RCA Victor LSO-1006 [R]	1969	2.50	5.00	10.00
—Orange or tan label				

PARADE

❑ Kapp KDL-7005 [M]	1960	50.00	100.00	200.00
❑ Kapp KDS-7005 [S]	1960	62.50	125.00	250.00

PARIS '90

❑ Columbia Masterworks ML 4619 [M]	1952	37.50	75.00	150.00

PEACE

❑ Metromedia MP-33001	1969	7.50	15.00	30.00

PETER PAN

❑ RCA Victor LOC-1019 [M]	1954	10.00	20.00	40.00
❑ RCA Victor LSO-1019 [R]	196?	3.00	6.00	12.00
❑ RCA Victor AYL1-3762 [R]	1980	2.00	4.00	8.00

PIPE DREAM

❑ RCA Victor LOC-1023 [M]	1955	12.50	25.00	50.00
—Without "Special Advance Edition" sticker on cover				
❑ RCA Victor LOC-1023 [M]	1955	17.50	35.00	70.00
—With "Special Advance Edition" sticker on cover				

PLAIN AND FANCY

❑ Capitol S 603 [M]	1955	6.25	12.50	25.00
—Red label				

PLAYGIRLS

❑ Warner Bros. W 1530 [M]	1964	6.25	12.50	25.00
❑ Warner Bros. WS 1530 [S]	1964	7.50	15.00	30.00

PORGY AND BESS

❑ Decca DL 7006 [10]	1950	7.50	15.00	30.00
—Reissue of material first released on 78s				
❑ Decca DL 8042 [M]	1950	7.50	15.00	30.00
❑ Decca DL 9024 [M]	1955	6.25	12.50	25.00
—Reissue of 8042; drawing of Catfish Row on cover				
❑ Decca DL 9024 [M]	196?	3.75	7.50	15.00
—Photo of cast members on cover				
❑ Decca DL 79024 [R]	196?	2.50	5.00	10.00
—Photo of cast members on cover				
❑ MCA 1631 [R]	198?	—	3.00	6.00
—Reissue of 2035				
❑ MCA 2035 [R]	1973	2.00	4.00	8.00
—Reissue of 79024; black label with rainbow				

THE PREMISE

❑ Vanguard VRS-9092 [M]	1960	10.00	20.00	40.00

PURLIE

❑ Ampex A-40101	1970	7.50	15.00	30.00

RASHOMON

❑ Carlton LPX-5000 [M]	1959	6.25	12.50	25.00
❑ Carlton STLPX-5000 [S]	1959	7.50	15.00	30.00
—Not actually the original cast recording, but the play's incidental music				

REDHEAD

❑ RCA Victor LOC-1048 [M]	1959	5.00	10.00	20.00
❑ RCA Victor LSO-1048 [S]	1959	12.50	25.00	50.00
—Without "Essie's Vision"				
❑ RCA Victor LOC-1104 [M]	1959	3.75	7.50	15.00
—Reissue of 1048				
❑ RCA Victor LSO-1104 [S]	1965	6.25	12.50	25.00
—Reissue adds "Essie's Vision" to stereo version				

THE RIVER WIND

❑ London AM-48001 [M]	1962	10.00	20.00	40.00
❑ London AMS-78001 [S]	1962	20.00	40.00	80.00

THE ROAR OF THE GREASEPAINT — THE SMELL OF THE CROWD

❑ RCA Victor LOC-1109 [M]	1965	3.75	7.50	15.00
❑ RCA Victor LOC-1109 [S]	1965	5.00	10.00	20.00

THE ROTHSCHILDS

❑ Columbia Masterworks S 30337	1970	6.25	12.50	25.00

SAIL AWAY

❑ Capitol SWAO 1643 [S]	1961	7.50	15.00	30.00
❑ Capitol WAO 1643 [M]	1961	5.00	10.00	20.00

SARATOGA

❑ RCA Victor LOC-1051 [M]	1959	6.25	12.50	25.00
❑ RCA Victor LSO-1051 [S]	1959	12.50	25.00	50.00

SAY, DARLING

❑ RCA Victor LOC-1045 [M]	1958	10.00	20.00	40.00
❑ RCA Victor LSO-1045 [S]	1958	15.00	30.00	60.00

SEVENTEEN

❑ RCA Victor LOC-1003 [M]	1951	37.50	75.00	150.00

Number Title	Yr	VG	VG+	NM
1776				
❑ Columbia Masterworks BOS 3310	1969	3.00	6.00	12.00
—Revised (correct) edition has Rex Everhart shown as Ben Franklin in credits and synopsis				
❑ Columbia Masterworks BOS 3310	1969	7.50	15.00	30.00
—The first edition has Howard DaSilva shown as Ben Franklin in credits and synopsis, though he does not appear on the LP				
SEVENTH HEAVEN				
❑ Decca DL 9001 [M]	1955	37.50	75.00	150.00
70 GIRLS, 70				
❑ Columbia Masterworks S 30589	1971	12.50	25.00	50.00
SHE LOVES ME				
❑ MGM E 4118OC-2 [(2)M]	1963	10.00	20.00	40.00
❑ MGM SE 4118OC-2 [(2)S]	1963	12.50	25.00	50.00
SHOW BIZ (FROM VAUDE TO VIDEO)				
❑ RCA Victor LOC-1011 [M]	1954	10.00	20.00	40.00
SHOW BOAT				
❑ Columbia Masterworks ML 4058 [M]	1948	6.25	12.50	25.00
—From the 1946 revival; paper envelope jacket with its opening on top				
❑ Columbia Masterworks OL 4058 [M]	195?	5.00	10.00	20.00
—From the 1946 revival; reissue of ML 4058				
SHOW GIRL				
❑ Roulette R-80001 [M]	1961	5.00	10.00	20.00
❑ Roulette SR-80001 [S]	1961	6.25	12.50	25.00
SILK STOCKINGS				
❑ RCA Victor LOC-1016 [M]	1955	10.00	20.00	40.00
❑ RCA Victor LOC-1102 [M]	1965	5.00	10.00	20.00
—Reissue; regular cover				
❑ RCA Victor LSO-1102 [R]	1965	5.00	10.00	20.00
SIMPLY HEAVENLY				
❑ Columbia Masterworks OL 5240 [M]	1957	6.25	12.50	25.00
SING OUT, SWEET LAND!				
❑ Decca DL 4304 [M]	1963	5.00	10.00	20.00
❑ Decca DL 8023 [M]	1950	12.50	25.00	50.00
❑ Decca DL 74304 [R]	1963	5.00	10.00	20.00
SKYSCRAPER				
❑ Capitol SVAS 2422 [S]	1965	6.25	12.50	25.00
❑ Capitol VAS 2422 [M]	1965	5.00	10.00	20.00
SONDHEIM: A MUSICAL TRIBUTE				
❑ Warner Bros. 2WS 2705 [(2)]	1973	5.00	10.00	20.00
SONG OF NORWAY				
❑ Columbia CL 1328 [M]	1959	5.00	10.00	20.00
—1958 revival cast				
❑ Columbia CS 8135 [S]	1959	12.50	25.00	50.00
—1958 revival cast				
❑ Decca DL 8002 [M]	1949	7.50	15.00	30.00
❑ Decca DL 9019 [M]	1955	5.00	10.00	20.00
❑ Decca DL 79019 [R]	196?	3.00	6.00	12.00
❑ MCA 2032 [R]	1973	2.50	5.00	10.00
—Reissue of 79019; black label with rainbow				
THE SOUND OF MUSIC				
❑ Capitol DT 91034 [M]	1966	3.00	6.00	12.00
—Original London cast; Capitol Record Club exclusive				
❑ Columbia Masterworks KOS 2020 [S]	1959	3.00	6.00	12.00
—Gray label with "360 Sound Stereo" at bottom				
❑ Columbia Masterworks KOS 2020 [S]	1959	6.25	12.50	25.00
—Gray and black label with six "eye" logos				
❑ Columbia Masterworks KOL 5450 [M]	1959	5.00	10.00	20.00
—Gray and black label with six "eye" logos				
❑ Columbia Masterworks KOL 5450 [M]	1963	3.00	6.00	12.00
—Gray label with "Guaranteed High Fidelity" or "360 Sound Mono" on label				
❑ Columbia Masterworks S 32601 [S]	1973	2.50	5.00	10.00
—Reissue of 2020				
SOUTH PACIFIC				
❑ Columbia Masterworks OS 2040 [R]	196?	2.50	5.00	10.00
—Gray label with "360 Sound Stereo"				
❑ Columbia Masterworks ML 4180 [M]	1949	6.25	12.50	25.00
—Green or blue label; large anchor on front cover				
❑ Columbia Masterworks OL 4180 [M]	195?	3.00	6.00	12.00
—Gray and black label with six "eye" logos; glossy gatefold cover with Ezio Pinza and Mary Martin pictured				
❑ Columbia Masterworks OL 4180 [M]	195?	3.75	7.50	15.00
—Gray and black label with six "eye" logos; large anchor on front cover				
❑ Columbia Masterworks OL 4180 [M]	1963	2.50	5.00	10.00
—Gray label with "Guaranteed High Fidelity" or "360 Sound Mono"				
❑ Columbia Masterworks S 32604 [R]	1973	2.00	4.00	8.00
—Reissue of 2040				
ST. LOUIS WOMAN				
❑ Capitol L 355 [10]	1952	20.00	40.00	80.00
STOP THE WORLD-I WANT TO GET OFF				
❑ London AM 58001 [M]	1962	3.75	7.50	15.00
❑ London AMS 88001 [S]	1962	5.00	10.00	20.00

Number Title	Yr	VG	VG+	NM
STREET SCENE				
❑ Columbia Masterworks ML 4139 [M]	1949	7.50	15.00	30.00
—Paper envelope jacket with its opening on top				
THE SUBJECT WAS ROSES				
❑ Columbia Masterworks DOL 308 [(3)M]	1964	5.00	10.00	20.00
❑ Columbia Masterworks DOS 708 [(3)S]	1964	7.50	15.00	30.00
SUBWAYS ARE FOR SLEEPING				
❑ Columbia Masterworks KOS 2130 [S]	1962	10.00	20.00	40.00
❑ Columbia Masterworks KOL 5730 [M]	1962	6.25	12.50	25.00
THE SURVIVAL OF ST. JOAN				
❑ Paramount PAS-9000 [(2)]	1971	6.25	12.50	25.00
SWEET CHARITY				
❑ Columbia Masterworks KOS 2900 [S]	1966	5.00	10.00	20.00
❑ Columbia Masterworks KOL 6500 [M]	1966	3.75	7.50	15.00
TAKE ME ALONG				
❑ RCA Victor LOC-1050 [M]	1959	3.75	7.50	15.00
❑ RCA Victor LSO-1050 [S]	1959	5.00	10.00	20.00
—Black label				
TAMALPAIS EXCHANGE				
❑ Atlantic SD 8263	1970	7.50	15.00	30.00
TAROT				
❑ United Artists UAS-5563	1970	5.00	10.00	20.00
TENDERLOIN				
❑ Capitol SWAO 1492 [S]	1960	10.00	20.00	40.00
—With program				
❑ Capitol WAO 1492 [M]	1960	6.25	12.50	25.00
—With program				
TEVYA AND HIS DAUGHTERS				
❑ Columbia Masterworks OL 5225 [M]	1957	7.50	15.00	30.00
TEXAS, LI'L DARLIN'				
❑ Decca DL 5188 [10]	1950	20.00	40.00	80.00
THIS IS THE ARMY				
❑ Decca DL 5108 [10]	1950	25.00	50.00	100.00
THIS WAS BURLESQUE				
❑ Roulette R-25185 [M]	1962	6.25	12.50	25.00
❑ Roulette SR-25186 [S]	1962	7.50	15.00	30.00
THREE TO MAKE MUSIC				
❑ RCA Victor LPM-2012 [M]	1958	6.25	12.50	25.00
❑ RCA Victor LSP-2012 [S]	1958	7.50	15.00	30.00
THREE WISHES FOR JAMIE				
❑ Capitol S 317 [M]	1952	30.00	60.00	120.00
THE THREEPENNY OPERA				
❑ MGM E-3121 [M]	1954	6.25	12.50	25.00
—Revival cast; yellow label				
❑ MGM E-3121 [M]	1959	3.75	7.50	15.00
—Revival cast; black label				
❑ MGM SE-3121 [R]	196?	3.00	6.00	12.00
—Revival cast; rechanneled stereo				
❑ Polydor 820260-1	198?	2.00	4.00	8.00
—Revival cast; reissue				
TIME CHANGES				
❑ ABC ABCS-681	1969	7.50	15.00	30.00
A TIME FOR SINGING				
❑ Warner Bros. W 1639 [M]	1966	10.00	20.00	40.00
❑ Warner Bros. WS 1639 [S]	1966	15.00	30.00	60.00
A TIME REMEMBERED				
❑ Mercury MG-20380 [M]	1957	6.25	12.50	25.00
❑ Mercury SR-60023 [S]	1957	10.00	20.00	40.00
—Music from the dramatic play				
TO BROADWAY WITH LOVE				
❑ Columbia Masterworks OS 2630 [S]	1964	12.50	25.00	50.00
❑ Columbia Masterworks OL 6030 [M]	1964	6.25	12.50	25.00
TOP BANANA				
❑ Capitol S 308 [M]	1952	25.00	50.00	100.00
TOVARICH				
❑ Capitol STAO 1940 [S]	1963	7.50	15.00	30.00
❑ Capitol TAO 1940 [M]	1963	5.00	10.00	20.00
A TREE GROWS IN BROOKLYN				
❑ Columbia Masterworks ML 4405 [M]	1951	7.50	15.00	30.00
—Blue label				
TWO BY TWO				
❑ Columbia Masterworks S 30338	1970	5.00	10.00	20.00

Number Title	Yr	VG	VG+	NM
TWO ON THE AISLE				
❏ Decca DL 8040 [M]	1951	25.00	50.00	100.00
—Black label, gold print				
❏ Decca DL 8040 [M]	1955	15.00	30.00	60.00
—Black label, silver print				
❏ Decca DL 8040 [M]	196?	15.00	30.00	60.00
—Black label with color bars				
TWO'S COMPANY				
❏ RCA Victor LOC-1009 [M]	1952	25.00	50.00	100.00
THE UNSINKABLE MOLLY BROWN				
❏ Capitol SWAO 1509 [S]	1960	6.25	12.50	25.00
❏ Capitol WAO 1509 [M]	1960	5.00	10.00	20.00
UP IN CENTRAL PARK				
❏ Decca DL 8016 [M]	1950	10.00	20.00	40.00
—Black label, gold print				
❏ Decca DL 8016 [M]	1955	7.50	15.00	30.00
—Black label, silver print				
WAITING FOR GODOT				
❏ Columbia Masterworks O2L 238 [(2)M]	1956	7.50	15.00	30.00
WEST SIDE STORY				
❏ Columbia Masterworks OS 2001 [S]	1958	7.50	15.00	30.00
—Gray and black label with six "eye" logos				
❏ Columbia Masterworks OS 2001 [S]	1963	3.75	7.50	15.00
—Gray label with "360 Sound Stereo"				
❏ Columbia Masterworks OL 5230 [M]	1958	6.25	12.50	25.00
—Gray and black label with six "eye" logos				
❏ Columbia Masterworks OL 5230 [M]	1963	3.00	6.00	12.00
—Gray label with "Guaranteed High Fidelity" or "360 Sound Mono"				
❏ Columbia Masterworks S 32603 [S]	1973	2.50	5.00	10.00
—Reissue with new number				
WHAT MAKES SAMMY RUN?				
❏ Columbia Masterworks KSO 2440 [S]	1964	10.00	20.00	40.00
❏ Columbia Masterworks KOL 6040 [M]	1964	7.50	15.00	30.00
WILDCAT				
❏ RCA Victor LOC-1060 [M]	1961	6.25	12.50	25.00
❏ RCA Victor LSO-1060 [S]	1961	10.00	20.00	40.00
WISH YOU WERE HERE				
❏ RCA Victor LOC-1007 [M]	1952	15.00	30.00	60.00
WONDERFUL TOWN				
❏ Decca DL 9010 [M]	1953	7.50	15.00	30.00
—Black label, gold print				
YOU'RE A GOOD MAN, CHARLIE BROWN				
❏ MGM 1E-9 [M]	1967	5.00	10.00	20.00
❏ MGM S1E-9 [S]	1967	5.00	10.00	20.00
YOUR OWN THING				
❏ RCA Victor LOC-1148 [M]	1968	6.25	12.50	25.00
❏ RCA Victor LSO-1148 [S]	1968	5.00	10.00	20.00
ZORBA				
❏ Capitol SO-118	1969	5.00	10.00	20.00

SOUNDTRACKS

Number Title	Yr	VG	VG+	NM
AARON SLICK FROM PUNKIN CRICK				
❏ RCA Victor LPM-3006 [10]	1952	37.50	75.00	150.00
ADVENTURES IN PARADISE				
❏ ABC-Paramount ABC-329 [M]	1960	7.50	15.00	30.00
❏ ABC-Paramount ABCS-329 [S]	1960	10.00	20.00	40.00
ADVISE AND CONSENT				
❏ RCA Victor LOC-1068 [M]	1962	7.50	15.00	30.00
❏ RCA Victor LSO-1068 [S]	1962	15.00	30.00	60.00
AN AFFAIR TO REMEMBER				
❏ Columbia CL 1013 [M]	1957	10.00	20.00	40.00
AFRICA ADDIO				
❏ United Artists UAL-4141 [M]	1966	5.00	10.00	20.00
❏ United Artists UAS-5141 [S]	1966	6.25	12.50	25.00
THE AGONY AND THE ECSTASY				
❏ Capitol MAS 2427 [M]	1965	15.00	30.00	60.00
❏ Capitol SMAS 2427 [S]	1965	20.00	40.00	80.00
AIRPORT				
❏ Decca DL 79173	1970	6.25	12.50	25.00
ALAKAZAM THE GREAT				
❏ Vee Jay LP-6000 [M]	1961	20.00	40.00	80.00
THE ALAMO				
❏ Columbia CL 1558 [M]	1960	5.00	10.00	20.00
❏ Columbia CS 8358 [S]	1960	6.25	12.50	25.00
ALBERT PECKINPAW'S REVENGE				
❏ Sidewalk ST 5907 [S]	1967	7.50	15.00	30.00
❏ Sidewalk T 5907 [M]	1967	7.50	15.00	30.00
ALEXANDER				
❏ Polydor 24-7001	1970	10.00	20.00	40.00
ALEXANDER THE GREAT				
❏ Mercury MG-20148 [M]	1956	62.50	125.00	250.00
ALFIE				
❏ ABC Impulse! AS-9111 [S]	1968	3.75	7.50	15.00
❏ Impulse! A-9111 [M]	1966	7.50	15.00	30.00
❏ Impulse! AS-9111 [S]	1966	7.50	15.00	30.00
ALIKI, MY LOVE				
❏ Fontana MGF-27523 [M]	1963	6.25	12.50	25.00
❏ Fontana SRF-67523 [S]	1963	7.50	15.00	30.00
ALL NIGHT LONG				
❏ Epic LA 16032 [M]	1962	10.00	20.00	40.00
❏ Epic BA 17032 [S]	1962	12.50	25.00	50.00
ALL THE LOVING COUPLES				
❏ GNP Crescendo GNPS-2051	1969	10.00	20.00	40.00
ALL THE RIGHT NOISES				
❏ Buddah BDS-5132	1971	7.50	15.00	30.00
AMERICA, AMERICA				
❏ Warner Bros. W 1527 [M]	1963	5.00	10.00	20.00
❏ Warner Bros. WS 1527 [S]	1963	6.25	12.50	25.00
AN AMERICAN IN PARIS				
❏ MGM E-93 [10]	1951	10.00	20.00	40.00
THE AMOROUS ADVENTURES OF MOLL FLANDERS				
❏ RCA Victor LOC-1113 [M]	1965	10.00	20.00	40.00
❏ RCA Victor LSO-1113 [S]	1965	20.00	40.00	80.00
ANASTASIA				
❏ Decca DL 8460 [M]	1956	7.50	15.00	30.00
ANATOMY OF A MURDER				
❏ Columbia CL 1360 [M]	1959	10.00	20.00	40.00
❏ Columbia CS 8166 [S]	1959	12.50	25.00	50.00
AND GOD CREATED WOMAN				
❏ Decca DL 8685 [M]	1957	30.00	60.00	120.00
THE ANDROMEDA STRAIN				
❏ Kapp KRS-5513	1971	10.00	20.00	40.00
—Regular cover				
❏ Kapp KRS-5513	1971	25.00	50.00	100.00
—Hexagonal cover glued onto silver cardboard				
ANGEL, ANGEL, DOWN WE GO				
❏ Tower ST-5161	1970	6.25	12.50	25.00

Number Title	Yr	VG	VG+	NM
ANGELS DIE HARD				
❏ Uni 73091	1971	7.50	15.00	30.00
ANGELS FROM HELL				
❏ Tower ST 5128	1968	15.00	30.00	60.00
THE ANONYMOUS VENETIAN				
❏ United Artists UAS-5218	1971	7.50	15.00	30.00
ANOTHER TIME, ANOTHER PLACE				
❏ Columbia CL 1180 [M]	1958	10.00	20.00	40.00
ANY WEDNESDAY				
❏ Warner Bros. W 1669 [M]	1966	6.25	12.50	25.00
❏ Warner Bros. WS 1669 [S]	1966	10.00	20.00	40.00
THE APARTMENT				
❏ United Artists UAL-3105 [M]	1960	7.50	15.00	30.00
❏ United Artists UAS-6105 [S]	1960	10.00	20.00	40.00
APRIL LOVE				
❏ Dot DLP-9000 [M]	1957	5.00	10.00	20.00
ARMS AND THE GIRL				
❏ Decca DL 5200 [10]	1950	25.00	50.00	100.00
AROUND THE WORLD IN 80 DAYS				
❏ Decca DL 9046 [M]	1957	6.25	12.50	25.00
—Black label, silver print				
❏ Decca DL 79046 [S]	1959	10.00	20.00	40.00
—Maroon label, silver print; cover has "Full Stereo" banner				
❏ Decca DL 79046 [S]	196?	3.00	6.00	12.00
—Black label with color bars				
❏ Decca SW-94840 [S]	1972	3.75	7.50	15.00
—Capitol Record Club edition				
❏ MCA 2062 [S]	1973	2.50	5.00	10.00
—Reissue of 79046; black label with rainbow				
❏ MCA 37086 [S]	198?	2.00	4.00	8.00
—Reissue of 2062				
AROUND THE WORLD UNDER THE SEA				
❏ Monument MLP-8050 [M]	1966	7.50	15.00	30.00
❏ Monument SLP-18050 [S]	1966	12.50	25.00	50.00
ARRIVIDERCI, BABY!				
❏ RCA Victor LOC-1132 [M]	1966	5.00	10.00	20.00
❏ RCA Victor LSO-1132 [S]	1966	10.00	20.00	40.00
AT LONG LAST LOVE				
❏ RCA Victor ABL2-0967 [(2)]	1975	5.00	10.00	20.00
ATHENA				
❏ Mercury MG-25202 [10]	1954	37.50	75.00	150.00
BABES IN TOYLAND				
❏ Buena Vista BV-4022 [M]	1961	7.50	15.00	30.00
❏ Buena Vista STER-4022 [S]	1961	10.00	20.00	40.00
BABY DOLL				
❏ Columbia CL 958 [M]	195?	12.50	25.00	50.00
—No ads for LPs on back cover				
❏ Columbia CL 958 [M]	1956	15.00	30.00	60.00
—Ads for other Columbia LPs on back cover				
BABY FACE NELSON				
❏ Jubilee JLP-2021 [M]	1957	30.00	60.00	120.00
BABY, THE RAIN MUST FALL				
❏ Ava A-53 [M]	1965	10.00	20.00	40.00
❏ Ava AS-53 [S]	1965	12.50	25.00	50.00
❏ Mainstream S-6056 [S]	1965	10.00	20.00	40.00
—Reissue of Ava AS-53				
❏ Mainstream 56056 [M]	1965	7.50	15.00	30.00
—Reissue of Ava A-53				
BACK STREET				
❏ Decca DL 9097 [M]	1961	10.00	20.00	40.00
❏ Decca DL 79097 [S]	1961	20.00	40.00	80.00
THE BAD SEED				
❏ RCA Victor LPM-1395 [M]	1956	75.00	150.00	300.00
BAND OF ANGELS				
❏ RCA Victor LPM-1557 [M]	1957	25.00	50.00	100.00
THE BAND WAGON				
❏ MGM E-3051 [M]	1953	7.50	15.00	30.00
—Yellow label				
❏ MGM E-3051 [M]	1960	5.00	10.00	20.00
—Black label				
BARABBAS				
❏ Colpix CP 510 [M]	1962	10.00	20.00	40.00
❏ Colpix SCP 510 [S]	1962	20.00	40.00	80.00

Number Title	Yr	VG	VG+	NM
BARBARELLA				
❏ Dyno Voice DV-31908	1968	12.50	25.00	50.00
THE BARBARIAN AND THE GEISHA				
❏ 20th Fox FOX-3004 [M]	1958	62.50	125.00	250.00
BAREFOOT ADVENTURE				
❏ Pacific Jazz PJ-35 [M]	1961	10.00	20.00	40.00
❏ Pacific Jazz ST-35 [S]	1961	15.00	30.00	60.00
BAREFOOT IN THE PARK				
❏ Dot DLP-3803 [M]	1967	5.00	10.00	20.00
❏ Dot DLP-25803 [S]	1967	7.50	15.00	30.00
THE BARKLEYS OF BROADWAY				
❏ MGM E-503 [10]	1949	20.00	40.00	80.00
BATTLE OF THE BULGE				
❏ Warner Bros. W 1617 [M]	1965	10.00	20.00	40.00
❏ Warner Bros. WS 1617 [S]	1965	10.00	20.00	40.00
BEACH BLANKET BINGO				
❏ Capitol ST 2323 [S]	1965	15.00	30.00	60.00
❏ Capitol T 2323 [M]	1965	7.50	15.00	30.00
BEAU JAMES				
❏ Imperial LP-9041 [M]	1957	10.00	20.00	40.00
BECKET				
❏ Decca DL 9117 [M]	1964	7.50	15.00	30.00
❏ Decca DL 79117 [S]	1964	12.50	25.00	50.00
BEDAZZLED				
❏ London MS-82009	1967	20.00	40.00	80.00
BEHOLD A PALE HORSE				
❏ Colpix CP 519 [M]	1964	12.50	25.00	50.00
❏ Colpix SCP 519 [S]	1964	17.50	35.00	70.00
BELL, BOOK AND CANDLE				
❏ Colpix CP 502 [M]	1959	15.00	30.00	60.00
BELLS ARE RINGING				
❏ Capitol SW 1435 [S]	1960	7.50	15.00	30.00
❏ Capitol W 1435 [M]	1960	6.25	12.50	25.00
BEN-HUR				
❏ MGM 1E1 [M]	1959	10.00	20.00	40.00
—Boxed edition with hardcover book				
❏ MGM 1E1 [M]	196?	3.00	6.00	12.00
—Gatefold cover, no book				
❏ MGM S-1E1 [S]	1959	12.50	25.00	50.00
—Boxed edition with hardcover book				
❏ MGM S-1E1 [S]	196?	2.50	5.00	10.00
—Gatefold cover, no book; blue and gold label				
❏ MGM S-1E1 [S]	196?	3.75	7.50	15.00
—Gatefold cover, no book; black label				
BENEATH THE PLANET OF THE APES				
❏ Amos AAS-8001	1970	10.00	20.00	40.00
BEYOND THE GREAT WALL				
❏ Capitol T 10401 [M]	1965	12.50	25.00	50.00
BEYOND THE VALLEY OF THE DOLLS				
❏ 20th Century Fox TFS-4211	1970	50.00	100.00	200.00
THE BIBLE				
❏ 20th Century Fox TF-3184 [M]	1966	5.00	10.00	20.00
❏ 20th Century Fox TFS-4184 [S]	1966	7.50	15.00	30.00
THE BIG COUNTRY				
❏ United Artists UAL-4004 [M]	1958	6.25	12.50	25.00
❏ United Artists UAS-5004 [S]	1958	12.50	25.00	50.00
THE BIG GUNDOWN				
❏ United Artists UAS-5190	1967	10.00	20.00	40.00
THE BIGGEST BUNDLE OF THEM ALL				
❏ MGM E-4446 [M]	1967	5.00	10.00	20.00
❏ MGM SE-4446 [S]	1967	6.25	12.50	25.00
BILLIE				
❏ United Artists UAL-4131 [M]	1965	5.00	10.00	20.00
❏ United Artists UAS-5131 [S]	1965	6.25	12.50	25.00
THE BILLION DOLLAR BRAIN				
❏ United Artists UAL-4174 [M]	1967	3.75	7.50	15.00
❏ United Artists UAS-5174 [S]	1967	5.00	10.00	20.00
BILLY JACK				
❏ Warner Bros. BJS-1001	1973	3.75	7.50	15.00
—Reissue; "Burbank" palm trees label				
❏ Warner Bros. WS 1926	1971	6.25	12.50	25.00
—Original; green "WB" label				

Number Title	Yr	VG	VG+	NM
THE BIRD WITH THE CRYSTAL PLUMAGE				
❏ Capitol ST-642	1970	25.00	50.00	100.00
BLACK GIRL				
❏ Fantasy F-9420	1973	17.50	35.00	70.00
THE BLACK ORCHID				
❏ Dot DLP-3178 [M]	1959	10.00	20.00	40.00
❏ Dot SLP-25178 [S]	1959	12.50	25.00	50.00
BLACK ORPHEUS				
❏ Epic LN 3672 [M]	1959	10.00	20.00	40.00
❏ Fontana MGF-27520 [M]	1963	5.00	10.00	20.00
❏ Fontana SRF-67520 [R]	1963	3.75	7.50	15.00
BLACKBIRDS OF 1928				
❏ Columbia Masterworks OL 6770 [M]	1968	3.75	7.50	15.00
❏ Revue 1 [M]	196?	7.50	15.00	30.00
❏ Sutton SSU-270 [R]	196?	3.00	6.00	12.00
❏ Sutton SU-270 [M]	196?	5.00	10.00	20.00
BLACULA				
❏ RCA Victor LSP-4806	1972	15.00	30.00	60.00
BLESS THE BEASTS AND CHILDREN				
❏ A&M SP-4322	1971	6.25	12.50	25.00
BLOOD AND SAND				
❏ Decca DL 5380 [10]	1952	20.00	40.00	80.00
BLOOMER GIRL				
❏ Decca DL 8015 [M]	1950	7.50	15.00	30.00
BLOW-UP				
❏ MGM E-4447 [M]	1967	10.00	20.00	40.00
❏ MGM SE-4447 [S]	1967	12.50	25.00	50.00
THE BLUE MAX				
❏ Mainstream S-6081 [S]	1966	20.00	40.00	80.00
❏ Mainstream 56081 [M]	1966	10.00	20.00	40.00
BOBO				
❏ Warner Bros. W 1711 [M]	1967	5.00	10.00	20.00
❏ Warner Bros. WS 1711 [S]	1967	5.00	10.00	20.00
BOEING, BOEING				
❏ RCA Victor LOC-1121 [M]	1965	6.25	12.50	25.00
❏ RCA Victor LSO-1121 [S]	1965	7.50	15.00	30.00
BONNIE AND CLYDE				
❏ Warner Bros. W 1742 [M]	1968	10.00	20.00	40.00
❏ Warner Bros. WS 1742 [S]	1968	6.25	12.50	25.00
—Originals have green labels with "W7" logo in a square at top				
❏ Warner Bros. ST-91414 [S]	1968	7.50	15.00	30.00
—Capitol Record Club issue				
BORA, BORA				
❏ American Int'l. STA-1029	1970	7.50	15.00	30.00
BORN FREE				
❏ MGM E-4368 [M]	1966	3.75	7.50	15.00
❏ MGM SE-4368 [S]	1966	5.00	10.00	20.00
BORSALINO				
❏ Paramount PAS-5019	1970	7.50	15.00	30.00
THE BOY FRIEND				
❏ MGM 1SE-32	1971	5.00	10.00	20.00
A BOY NAMED CHARLIE BROWN				
❏ Columbia Masterworks OS 3500	1970	5.00	10.00	20.00
BOY ON A DOLPHIN				
❏ Decca DL 8580 [M]	1957	15.00	30.00	60.00
—Black label with silver print, or pink label with black print (promo)				
❏ Decca DL 8580 [M]	196?	5.00	10.00	20.00
—Black label with color bars				
THE BOYS FROM SYRACUSE				
❏ Capitol STAO 1933 [S]	1963	7.50	15.00	30.00
❏ Capitol TAO 1933 [M]	1963	6.25	12.50	25.00
THE BRAVE ONE				
❏ Decca DL 8344 [M]	1956	10.00	20.00	40.00
BROTHER ON THE RUN				
❏ Perception PLP-45	1973	10.00	20.00	40.00
BUCCANEER				
❏ Columbia CL 1278 [M]	1958	6.25	12.50	25.00
❏ Columbia CS 8096 [S]	1958	10.00	20.00	40.00
BULLITT				
❏ Warner Bros. WS 1777	1968	15.00	30.00	60.00

Number Title	Yr	VG	VG+	NM
BUNDLE OF JOY				
❏ RCA Victor LPM-1399 [M]	1956	10.00	20.00	40.00
BUNNY LAKE IS MISSING				
❏ RCA Victor LOC-1115 [M]	1965	10.00	20.00	40.00
❏ RCA Victor LSO-1115 [S]	1965	17.50	35.00	70.00
BUNNY O'HARE				
❏ American Int'l. STA-1041	1971	5.00	10.00	20.00
BUONA SERA, MRS. CAMPBELL				
❏ United Artists UAS-5192	1969	7.50	15.00	30.00
THE BURGLARS				
❏ Bell 1105	1971	10.00	20.00	40.00
BUTTERFIELD-8				
❏ MGM E-3952 [M]	1960	5.00	10.00	20.00
❏ MGM SE-3952 [S]	1960	6.25	12.50	25.00
BYE BYE BIRDIE				
❏ RCA Victor LOC-1081 [M]	196?	3.75	7.50	15.00
—Third cover with Ann-Margret on front and with credits underneath				
❏ RCA Victor LOC-1081 [M]	196?	5.00	10.00	20.00
—Second cover with Ann-Margret on front, but with no credits underneath				
❏ RCA Victor LOC-1081 [M]	1963	6.25	12.50	25.00
—First cover without Ann-Margret on the front				
❏ RCA Victor LSO-1081 [S]	196?	5.00	10.00	20.00
—Third cover with Ann-Margret on front and with credits underneath				
❏ RCA Victor LSO-1081 [S]	196?	6.25	12.50	25.00
—Second cover with Ann-Margret on front, but with no credits underneath				
❏ RCA Victor LSO-1081 [S]	1963	7.50	15.00	30.00
—First cover without Ann-Margret on the front				
C'MON, LET'S LIVE A LITTLE				
❏ Liberty LRP-3430 [M]	1966	6.25	12.50	25.00
❏ Liberty LST-7430 [S]	1966	7.50	15.00	30.00
CABARET				
❏ ABC ABCD-752	1972	5.00	10.00	20.00
❏ MCA 37125	198?	2.00	4.00	8.00
—Reissue; blue label with rainbow				
THE CAINE MUTINY				
❏ RCA Victor LOC-1013 [M]	1954	4000.	7000.	10000.
❏ RCA Victor LOC-1013 [M]	1993	50.00	100.00	200.00
—Very limited edition (100 copies) reproduction of the original LP				
CALL ME MADAM				
❏ Decca DL 5465 [10]	1953	12.50	25.00	50.00
CALL ME MISTER				
❏ Decca DLP 7005 [10]	1950	25.00	50.00	100.00
CAMELOT				
❏ Warner Bros. B 1712 [M]	1967	6.25	12.50	25.00
❏ Warner Bros. BS 1712 [S]	1967	5.00	10.00	20.00
—Gold label original				
❏ Warner Bros. BS 1712 [S]	1968	3.75	7.50	15.00
—Green label, "W7" box logo at top				
❏ Warner Bros. BS 1712 [S]	1970	3.00	6.00	12.00
—Green label, "WB" shield logo at top				
❏ Warner Bros. BS 1712 [S]	1973	2.50	5.00	10.00
—"Burbank" palm trees label				
❏ Warner Bros. BSK 3102 [S]	1977	2.00	4.00	8.00
—Reissue with new number				
❏ Warner Bros. SW-91347	1968	6.25	12.50	25.00
—Capitol Record Club edition				
CAN-CAN				
❏ Capitol SW 1301 [S]	1960	7.50	15.00	30.00
❏ Capitol W 1301 [M]	1960	5.00	10.00	20.00
CANDY				
❏ ABC ABCS-OC-9	1968	7.50	15.00	30.00
THE CARDINAL				
❏ RCA Victor LOC-1084 [M]	1963	10.00	20.00	40.00
❏ RCA Victor LSO-1084 [S]	1963	15.00	30.00	60.00
THE CARETAKERS				
❏ Ava A-31 [M]	1963	5.00	10.00	20.00
❏ Ava AS-31 [S]	1963	6.25	12.50	25.00
CAROUSEL				
❏ Capitol SW 694 [S]	1962	5.00	10.00	20.00
—Black colorband label				
❏ Capitol SW 694 [S]	1969	3.75	7.50	15.00
—Lime green label				
❏ Capitol SW 694 [S]	1973	3.00	6.00	12.00
—Orange label				
❏ Capitol W 694 [M]	1956	7.50	15.00	30.00
—Gray label				
❏ Capitol W 694 [M]	1959	5.00	10.00	20.00
—Black colorband label, logo at left				
❏ Capitol W 694 [M]	1962	3.75	7.50	15.00
—Black colorband label, logo at top				

Number Title	Yr	VG	VG+	NM
THE CARPETBAGGERS				
❏ Ava A-45 [M]	1964	7.50	15.00	30.00
❏ Ava AS-45 [S]	1964	10.00	20.00	40.00
CARRY IT ON				
❏ Vanguard VSD-79313	1971	6.25	12.50	25.00
CASINO ROYALE				
❏ Colgems COMO-5005 [M]	1967	7.50	15.00	30.00
❏ Colgems COSO-5005 [S]	1967	25.00	50.00	100.00
❏ Colgems COSO-5005-45 [(4)]	199?	10.00	20.00	40.00
—Classic Records reissue on four 12-inch 45 rpm records				
A CERTAIN SMILE				
❏ Columbia CL 1194 [M]	1958	10.00	20.00	40.00
❏ Columbia CS 8068 [S]	1958	20.00	40.00	80.00
THE CHAIRMAN				
❏ Tetragrammaton T-5007	1969	7.50	15.00	30.00
CHARLOTTE'S WEB				
❏ Paramount PAS-1008	1973	7.50	15.00	30.00
THE CHASE				
❏ Columbia Masterworks OS 2960 [S]	1966	15.00	30.00	60.00
❏ Columbia Masterworks OL 6560 [M]	1966	10.00	20.00	40.00
CHINATOWN				
❏ ABC ABDP-848	1974	10.00	20.00	40.00
CHITTY CHITTY BANG BANG				
❏ United Artists UAS-5188	1968	6.25	12.50	25.00
THE CHRISTMAS THAT ALMOST WASN'T				
❏ RCA Camden CAL-1086 [M]	1966	6.25	12.50	25.00
❏ RCA Camden CAS-1086 [S]	1966	10.00	20.00	40.00
CINDERELLA				
❏ Disneyland DQ-1207 [M]	1959	10.00	20.00	40.00
—Second issue, white back cover with ads for nine other LPs				
❏ Disneyland DQ-1207 [M]	1963	7.50	15.00	30.00
—Third issue, pink back cover				
❏ Disneyland WDL-4007 [M]	1957	50.00	100.00	200.00
—Original issue, gatefold cover				
CINDERFELLA				
❏ Dot DLP-8001 [M]	1960	15.00	30.00	60.00
❏ Dot SLP-38001 [S]	1960	25.00	50.00	100.00
—Gatefold cover with many extras including game board, spinner, booklet, music stand.				
CLEOPATRA				
❏ 20th Century Fox FXG-5008 [M]	1963	7.50	15.00	30.00
❏ 20th Century Fox SXG-5008 [S]	1963	10.00	20.00	40.00
CLEOPATRA JONES				
❏ Warner Bros. BS 2719	1973	7.50	15.00	30.00
THE CLOWNS				
❏ Columbia S 30772	1971	10.00	20.00	40.00
COFFY				
❏ Polydor PD-5048	1973	25.00	50.00	100.00
THE COLLECTOR				
❏ Mainstream S-6053 [S]	1965	12.50	25.00	50.00
❏ Mainstream 56053 [M]	1965	7.50	15.00	30.00
COLLEGE CONFIDENTIAL				
❏ Chancellor CHL-5016 [M]	1960	10.00	20.00	40.00
❏ Chancellor CHLS-5016 [S]	1960	12.50	25.00	50.00
COMANCHE				
❏ Coral CRL 57046 [M]	1956	100.00	200.00	400.00
COME BACK CHARLESTON BLUE				
❏ Atco SD 7010	1972	7.50	15.00	30.00
COME BLOW YOUR HORN				
❏ Reprise R-6071 [M]	1963	7.50	15.00	30.00
❏ Reprise R9-6071 [S]	1963	12.50	25.00	50.00
COMETOGETHER				
❏ Apple SW-3377	1971	5.00	10.00	20.00
THE CONNECTION				
❏ Charlie Parker PLP-806 [M]	1962	7.50	15.00	30.00
❏ Charlie Parker PLP-806S [S]	1962	10.00	20.00	40.00
❏ Felsted 2512 [S]	1960	75.00	150.00	300.00
❏ Felsted 7512 [M]	1960	50.00	100.00	200.00
COOL WORLD				
❏ Philips PHM 200138 [M]	1964	12.50	25.00	50.00
❏ Philips PHS 600138 [S]	1964	20.00	40.00	80.00
COOLEY HIGH				
❏ Motown M7-840 R2 [(2)]	1975	5.00	10.00	20.00

Number Title	Yr	VG	VG+	NM
THE CORRUPT ONES				
❏ United Artists UAL-4158 [M]	1967	10.00	20.00	40.00
❏ United Artists UAS-5158 [S]	1967	10.00	20.00	40.00
COTTON COMES TO HARLEM				
❏ United Artists UAS-5211	1970	7.50	15.00	30.00
THE COURT JESTER				
❏ Decca DL 8212 [M]	1956	17.50	35.00	70.00
—Black label, silver print, or pink label, black print promo copy				
❏ Decca DL 8212 [M]	196?	7.50	15.00	30.00
—Black label with color bars				
THE COWBOY				
❏ Decca DL 8684 [M]	1958	15.00	30.00	60.00
—Black label, silver print, or pink label, black print promo copy				
❏ Decca DL 8684 [M]	196?	5.00	10.00	20.00
—Black label with color bars				
CRIME IN THE STREETS				
❏ Decca DL 8376 [M]	1956	15.00	30.00	60.00
—Black label, silver print, or pink label, black print promo copy				
❏ Decca DL 8376 [S]	196?	7.50	15.00	30.00
—Black label with color bars				
THE CROSS AND THE SWITCHBLADE				
❏ Light LS-5550	1970	7.50	15.00	30.00
CUSTER OF THE WEST				
❏ ABC ABC-OC-5 [M]	1968	20.00	40.00	80.00
❏ ABC ABCS-OC-5 [S]	1968	25.00	50.00	100.00
CYCLE SAVAGES				
❏ American Int'l. STA-1033	1970	7.50	15.00	30.00
CYRANO DE BERGERAC				
❏ Capitol S 283 [M]	1951	7.50	15.00	30.00
—Originals have red labels with Capitol logo at top				
DAKTARI				
❏ Leo the Lion CH-1043 [M]	1967	5.00	10.00	20.00
❏ MGM CH-1043 [M]	1967	5.00	10.00	20.00
DAMN THE DEFIANT!				
❏ Colpix CP 511 [M]	1962	7.50	15.00	30.00
❏ Colpix SCP 511 [S]	1962	15.00	30.00	60.00
DAMN YANKEES				
❏ RCA Victor LOC-1047 [M]	1958	10.00	20.00	40.00
—Original pressing with "Long Play" on label				
THE DAMNED				
❏ Warner Bros. WS 1829	1969	7.50	15.00	30.00
THE DARK OF THE SUN				
❏ MGM SE-4544	1968	10.00	20.00	40.00
DARLING LILI				
❏ RCA Victor LSPX-1000	1969	5.00	10.00	20.00
DAY OF ANGER				
❏ RCA Victor LSO-1165	1969	5.00	10.00	20.00
THE DAY OF THE DOLPHIN				
❏ Avco AV-11014	1973	6.25	12.50	25.00
THE DAY THE FISH CAME OUT				
❏ 20th Century Fox TF-3194 [M]	1967	7.50	15.00	30.00
❏ 20th Century Fox TFS-4194 [S]	1967	10.00	20.00	40.00
DAYDREAMER				
❏ Columbia Masterworks OS 2940 [S]	1966	10.00	20.00	40.00
❏ Columbia Masterworks OL 6540 [M]	1966	7.50	15.00	30.00
DE SADE				
❏ Tower ST-5170	1969	7.50	15.00	30.00
DEADFALL				
❏ 20th Century Fox S-4203	1968	15.00	30.00	60.00
THE DEADLY AFFAIR				
❏ Verve V-8679 [M]	1966	6.25	12.50	25.00
❏ Verve V6-8679 [S]	1966	7.50	15.00	30.00
DEAR JOHN				
❏ Dunhill OCD-55001 [M]	1966	5.00	10.00	20.00
❏ Dunhill OCDS-55001 [S]	1966	6.25	12.50	25.00
DEEP IN MY HEART				
❏ MGM E-3153 [M]	1955	10.00	20.00	40.00
❏ MGM E-3153 [M]	1955	12.50	25.00	50.00
DESIRE UNDER THE ELMS				
❏ Dot DLP-3095 [M]	1958	25.00	50.00	100.00

Original Cast, *Flower Drum Song*, Columbia Masterworks OL 5350, mono LP, gray and black label with six "eye" logos, $10-$20.

Original Cast, *The Gay Life,* Capitol SWAO 1560, stereo LP, $25-$50.

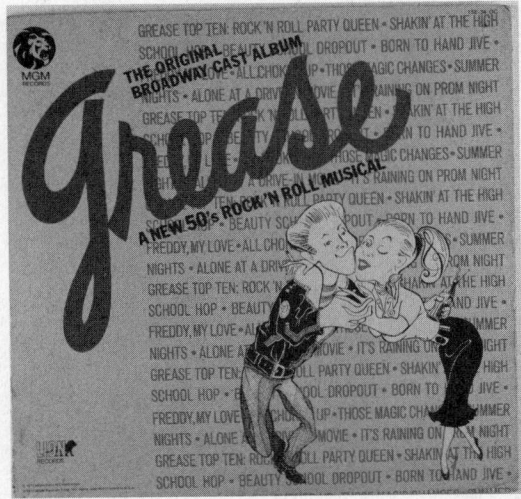

Original Cast, *Grease,* MGM 1SE-34, stereo LP, $6-$12.

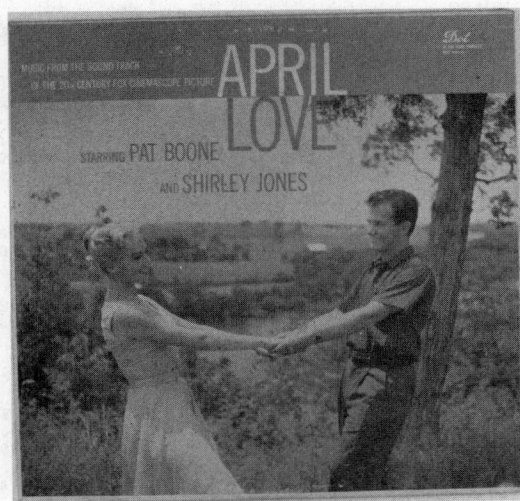

Soundtrack, *April Love,* Dot DLP-9000, mono LP, $10-$20.

Soundtrack, *Damn the Defiant!,* Colpix CP-511, mono LP, $15-$30.

Soundtrack, *The Graduate*, Columbia Masterworks OS 3108, stereo LP, gray label with "360 Sound Stereo," $6-$12.

Number	Title	Yr	VG	VG+	NM
DESTINATION MOON					
Columbia CL 6151 [10]		1950	30.00	60.00	120.00
Omega OL-3 [M]		1959	10.00	20.00	40.00
Omega OSL-3 [S]		196?	20.00	40.00	80.00
THE DEVIL AT 4 O'CLOCK					
Colpix CP 509 [M]		1962	10.00	20.00	40.00
Colpix SCP 509 [S]		1962	17.50	35.00	70.00
THE DEVIL IN MISS JONES					
Janus JLS-3059		1973	6.25	12.50	25.00
THE DEVIL'S BRIGADE					
United Artists UAS-6654		1968	5.00	10.00	20.00
DIAMOND HEAD					
Colpix CP-440 [M]		1963	7.50	15.00	30.00
Colpix SCP 440 [S]		1963	15.00	30.00	60.00
DIAMONDS ARE FOREVER					
United Artists UA-LA301-G		1974	3.00	6.00	12.00
—Reissue of 5520					
United Artists UAS-5520		1971	5.00	10.00	20.00
THE DIARY OF ANNE FRANK					
20th Fox FOX-3012 [M]		1959	12.50	25.00	50.00
20th Fox SFX-3012 [S]		1959	20.00	40.00	80.00
DIRTY GAME					
Laurie LLP-2034 [M]		1966	6.25	12.50	25.00
Laurie SLP-2034 [S]		1966	7.50	15.00	30.00
DIVORCE AMERICAN STYLE					
United Artists UAL-4163 [M]		1967	5.00	10.00	20.00
United Artists UAS-5163 [S]		1967	5.00	10.00	20.00
DIVORCE ITALIAN STYLE					
United Artists UAL-4106 [M]		1962	10.00	20.00	40.00
United Artists UAS-5106 [S]		1962	12.50	25.00	50.00
DOCTOR DOLITTLE					
20th Century Fox TCF-5101 [M]		1967	5.00	10.00	20.00
20th Century Fox TCS-5101 [S]		1967	5.00	10.00	20.00
DOCTOR GOLDFOOT AND THE GIRL BOMBS					
Tower DT 5053 [R]		1966	6.25	12.50	25.00
Tower T 5053 [M]		1966	5.00	10.00	20.00
DOCTOR ZHIVAGO					
MCA 39042		198?	2.00	4.00	8.00
—Reissue					
MGM 1E-6 [M]		1965	3.75	7.50	15.00
MGM S1E-6 ST [S]		1965	5.00	10.00	20.00
MGM SWAE-90620 [S]		1965	5.00	10.00	20.00
—Capitol Record Club issue					
A DOG OF FLANDERS					
20th Fox FOX-3026 [M]		1959	20.00	40.00	80.00
20th Fox SFX-3026 [S]		1959	75.00	150.00	300.00
$ (DOLLARS)					
Reprise MS 2051		1971	5.00	10.00	20.00
DON'T MAKE WAVES					
MGM E-4483 [M]		1967	7.50	15.00	30.00
MGM SE-4483 [S]		1967	7.50	15.00	30.00
DR. NO					
Liberty LT-50275		1981	2.00	4.00	8.00
—Reissue of United Artists 275					
United Artists UA-LA275-G		1974	2.50	5.00	10.00
—Reissue of 5108					
United Artists UAL-4108 [M]		1963	10.00	20.00	40.00
United Artists UAS-5108 [S]		1963	12.50	25.00	50.00
DR. PHIBES					
American Int'l. A-1040		1971	15.00	30.00	60.00
DRANGO					
Liberty LRP-3036 [M]		1957	37.50	75.00	150.00
A DREAM OF KINGS					
National General NG-1000		1969	7.50	15.00	30.00
DUCK, YOU SUCKER					
United Artists UAS-5221		1972	10.00	20.00	40.00
DUEL AT DIABLO					
United Artists UAL-4139 [M]		1966	6.25	12.50	25.00
United Artists UAS-5139 [S]		1966	7.50	15.00	30.00
DUMBO					
Disneyland 1204 [M]		197?	2.50	5.00	10.00
—Fourth issue, yellow rainbow label, flying Dumbo on back cover					
Disneyland DQ-1204 [M]		1959	6.25	12.50	25.00
—Second issue, back cover has ads for nine other LPs					

Number	Title	Yr	VG	VG+	NM
Disneyland DQ-1204 [M]		1963	3.75	7.50	15.00
—Third issue, four black & white photos on back cover					
Disneyland WDL-4013 [M]		1957	50.00	100.00	200.00
—Original issue, gatefold cover					
Disneyland ST-4904 [M]		1963	50.00	100.00	200.00
—Special issue with pop-up figures in gatefold					
THE DUNWICH HORROR					
American Int'l. STA-1028		1970	10.00	20.00	40.00
EAST SIDE, WEST SIDE					
Columbia CL 2123 [M]		1963	7.50	15.00	30.00
Columbia CS 8923 [S]		1963	10.00	20.00	40.00
EASTER PARADE					
MGM E-502 [10]		1950	20.00	40.00	80.00
EASY RIDER					
ABC Dunhill DSX-50063		1969	6.25	12.50	25.00
ECCO					
Warner Bros. W 1600 [M]		1965	6.25	12.50	25.00
Warner Bros. WS 1600 [S]		1965	7.50	15.00	30.00
THE EDDY DUCHIN STORY					
Decca DL 8289 [M]		1956	10.00	20.00	40.00
—Original cover with Tyrone Power and Kim Novak at a piano					
Decca DL 8289 [M]		1959	5.00	10.00	20.00
—Reissue cover with Tyrone Power and Kim Novak kissing					
Decca DL 9121 [M]		196?	3.00	6.00	12.00
—Reissue of 8289					
Decca DL 78289 [S]		1959	6.25	12.50	25.00
—Maroon label, silver print, "Full Stereo" on front cover					
Decca DL 79121 [S]		196?	3.75	7.50	15.00
—Reissue of 78289					
MCA 2041		1973	2.50	5.00	10.00
—Reissue of 79121; black label with rainbow					
MCA 37088		198?	2.00	4.00	8.00
—Reissue of 2041					
THE EDUCATION OF SONNY CARSON					
Paramount PAS-1045		1974	5.00	10.00	20.00
THE EGYPTIAN					
Decca DL 9014 [M]		1954	15.00	30.00	60.00
Decca DL 79014 [R]		196?	5.00	10.00	20.00
EL CID					
MGM E-3977 [M]		1962	10.00	20.00	40.00
MGM SE-3977 [S]		1962	12.50	25.00	50.00
EL DORADO					
Epic FLM-13114 [M]		1967	12.50	25.00	50.00
Epic LFS-15114 [S]		1967	17.50	35.00	70.00
EL TOPO					
Apple SWAO-3388		1972	10.00	20.00	40.00
ELECTRA GLIDE IN BLUE					
United Artists UA-LA062-H [(2)]		1973	10.00	20.00	40.00
—With booklet and two posters					
ELEPHANT STEPS					
Columbia Masterwords M2X 33044 [(2)]		1975	5.00	10.00	20.00
ELMER GANTRY					
United Artists UAL-4069 [M]		1960	10.00	20.00	40.00
United Artists UAS-5069 [S]		1960	12.50	25.00	50.00
ENTER THE DRAGON					
Warner Bros. BS 2727		1973	15.00	30.00	60.00
EVERYTHING I HAVE IS YOURS					
MGM E-187 [10]		1953	10.00	20.00	40.00
EXODUS					
RCA Victor LOC-1058 [M]		1960	5.00	10.00	20.00
—"Long Play" on label					
RCA Victor LSO-1058 [S]		1960	6.25	12.50	25.00
—"Living Stereo" on label					
THE EXORCIST					
Warner Bros. W 2774		1974	7.50	15.00	30.00
A FACE IN THE CROWD					
Capitol W 872 [M]		1957	12.50	25.00	50.00
THE FALL OF THE ROMAN EMPIRE					
Columbia Masterworks OS 2460 [S]		1964	15.00	30.00	60.00
Columbia Masterworks OL 6060 [M]		1964	10.00	20.00	40.00
THE FAMILY WAY					
London M 76007 [M]		1967	25.00	50.00	100.00
—No promo sticker on front cover (deduct 20 percent for promo)					
London ST 82007 [S]		1967	30.00	60.00	120.00
—No promo sticker on front cover (deduct 20 percent for promo)					

Number	Title	Yr	VG	VG+	NM
FANNY					
❏ Warner Bros. W 1416 [M]		1961	6.25	12.50	25.00
❏ Warner Bros. WS 1416 [S]		1961	7.50	15.00	30.00
FANTASIA					
❏ Buena Vista 101 [(2)S]		1982	5.00	10.00	20.00
—*Stereo reissue, two records, no booklet*					
❏ Buena Vista STER-101 [(3)S]		1961	10.00	20.00	40.00
—*First stereo issue, black and yellow rainbow labels, includes 24-page booklet*					
❏ Buena Vista WDX-101 [(3)M]		1961	7.50	15.00	30.00
—*Second issue, blue labels, includes 24-page booklet*					
❏ Disneyland WDX-101 [(3)]		1957	15.00	30.00	60.00
—*Original issue, maroon/red labels, includes 24-page booklet*					
FANTASIA: NIGHT ON BALD MOUNTAIN; PASTORAL SYMPHONY; AVE MARIA					
❏ Disneyland STER-4101C [S]		1958	7.50	15.00	30.00
❏ Disneyland WDL-4101C [M]		1958	5.00	10.00	20.00
FANTASIA: RITE OF SPRING; TOCCATA AND FUGUE					
❏ Disneyland STER-4101A [S]		1959	7.50	15.00	30.00
❏ Disneyland WDL-4101A [M]		1958	5.00	10.00	20.00
FANTASIA: THE NUTCRACKER SUITE; DANCE OF THE HOURS					
❏ Disneyland STER-4101B [S]		1959	7.50	15.00	30.00
❏ Disneyland WDL-4101B [M]		1958	5.00	10.00	20.00
THE FANTASTIC PLASTIC MACHINE					
❏ Epic BN 26469		1969	6.25	12.50	25.00
FAR FROM THE MADDING CROWD					
❏ MGM 1E-11 [M]		1967	3.75	7.50	15.00
❏ MGM S1E-11 [S]		1967	6.25	12.50	25.00
A FAREWELL TO ARMS					
❏ Capitol W 918 [M]		1957	12.50	25.00	50.00
THE FASTEST GUITAR ALIVE					
❏ MGM SE-4475		1968	7.50	15.00	30.00
FATHOM					
❏ 20th Century Fox TFM-4195 [M]		1967	10.00	20.00	40.00
❏ 20th Century Fox TFS-4195 [S]		1967	12.50	25.00	50.00
FELLINI SATYRICON					
❏ United Artists UAS-5208		1969	7.50	15.00	30.00
FELLINI'S ROMA					
❏ United Artists UA-LA052-F		1972	7.50	15.00	30.00
THE FEMALE PRISONER					
❏ Columbia Masterworks OS 3320		1969	7.50	15.00	30.00
FIDDLER ON THE ROOF					
❏ United Artists UAS-10900 [(2)]		1971	5.00	10.00	20.00
—*With booklet*					
55 DAYS AT PEKING					
❏ Columbia CL 2028 [M]		1963	10.00	20.00	40.00
❏ Columbia CS 8828 [S]		1963	17.50	35.00	70.00
THE FIGHTER					
❏ Decca DL 5414 [10]		1952	20.00	40.00	80.00
FINIAN'S RAINBOW					
❏ Warner Bros. BS 2550		1968	5.00	10.00	20.00
FIRE DOWN BELOW					
❏ Decca DL 8597 [M]		1957	17.50	35.00	70.00
A FISTFUL OF DOLLARS					
❏ RCA Victor LOC-1135 [M]		1967	5.00	10.00	20.00
❏ RCA Victor LSO-1135 [S]		1967	7.50	15.00	30.00
—*Black label, dog on top*					
❏ RCA Victor LSO-1135 [S]		1969	3.00	6.00	12.00
—*Orange label, tan label, or black label with dog at 1 o'clock*					
FITZWILLY					
❏ United Artists UAL-4173 [M]		1967	5.00	10.00	20.00
❏ United Artists UAS-5173 [S]		1967	6.25	12.50	25.00
FIVE EASY PIECES					
❏ Epic KE 30456		1971	6.25	12.50	25.00
THE FIVE PENNIES					
❏ Dot DLP-9500 [M]		1959	6.25	12.50	25.00
❏ Dot DLP-29500 [S]		1959	12.50	25.00	50.00
A FLEA IN HER EAR					
❏ 20th Century Fox TFS-4200		1968	7.50	15.00	30.00
FLOWER DRUM SONG					
❏ Decca DL 9098 [M]		1961	5.00	10.00	20.00
❏ Decca DL 79098 [S]		1961	6.25	12.50	25.00
❏ MCA 2069		1973	2.50	5.00	10.00
—*Reissue; black label with rainbow*					
FOLIES BERGERE					
❏ Decca DL 8571 [M]		1958	6.25	12.50	25.00
FOLLOW ME					
❏ Uni 73056		1969	7.50	15.00	30.00
FOR A FEW DOLLARS MORE					
❏ United Artists UAL-3608 [M]		1967	5.00	10.00	20.00
❏ United Artists UAS-6608 [S]		1967	6.25	12.50	25.00
FOR LOVE OF IVY					
❏ ABC SOC-7		1968	6.25	12.50	25.00
FOR THE FIRST TIME					
❏ RCA Victor Red Seal LM-2338 [M]		1959	3.75	7.50	15.00
❏ RCA Victor Red Seal LSC-2338 [S]		1959	5.00	10.00	20.00
—*"Shaded dog" and smaller "RCA Victor" lettering*					
❏ RCA Victor Red Seal LSC-2338 [S]		1965	3.75	7.50	15.00
—*"White dog" and larger "RCA Victor" lettering*					
❏ RCA Victor Red Seal LSC-2338 [S]		1969	3.00	6.00	12.00
—*Red label, no dog*					
40 POUNDS OF TROUBLE					
❏ Mercury MG-20784 [M]		1963	7.50	15.00	30.00
❏ Mercury SR-60784 [S]		1963	10.00	20.00	40.00
THE FOUR HORSEMEN OF THE APOCALYPSE					
❏ MGM E-3993 [M]		1962	5.00	10.00	20.00
❏ MGM SE-3993 [S]		1962	6.25	12.50	25.00
FOUR IN THE MORNING					
❏ Roulette OS 805 [M]		1966	10.00	20.00	40.00
❏ Roulette OSS 805 [S]		1966	12.50	25.00	50.00
THE FOX					
❏ Warner Bros. W 1738 [M]		1968	10.00	20.00	40.00
❏ Warner Bros. WS 1738 [S]		1968	6.25	12.50	25.00
FOXY BROWN					
❏ Motown M7-811		1974	5.00	10.00	20.00
FRANCIS OF ASSISI					
❏ 20th Fox FOX-3053 [M]		1961	50.00	100.00	200.00
❏ 20th Fox SFX-3053 [S]		1961	62.50	125.00	250.00
THE FRENCH LINE					
❏ Mercury MG-25182 [10]		1954	20.00	40.00	80.00
FRIENDLY PERSUASION					
❏ RKO Unique LP-110 [M]		1956	18.75	37.50	75.00
FRITZ THE CAT					
❏ Fantasy F-9406		1972	7.50	15.00	30.00
FROM RUSSIA WITH LOVE					
❏ United Artists UAL-4114 [M]		1964	5.00	10.00	20.00
❏ United Artists UAS-5114 [S]		1964	6.25	12.50	25.00
THE FUGITIVE KIND					
❏ United Artists UAL-4065 [M]		1959	12.50	25.00	50.00
❏ United Artists UAS-5065 [S]		1959	17.50	35.00	70.00
FUNERAL IN BERLIN					
❏ RCA Victor LOC-1136 [M]		1966	7.50	15.00	30.00
❏ RCA Victor LSO-1136 [S]		1966	12.50	25.00	50.00
FUNNY GIRL					
❏ Columbia Masterworks BOS 3220		1968	3.00	6.00	12.00
—*Gray "360 Sound" label; record is removed from inside the gatefold; liner notes on a tan background*					
❏ Columbia Masterworks BOS 3220		1968	3.75	7.50	15.00
—*Gray "360 Sound" label; record is removed from inside the gatefold; liner notes on a black background*					
❏ Columbia Masterworks BOS 3220		1970	2.50	5.00	10.00
—*Olive label with "Columbia" encircling the edge*					
❏ Columbia Masterworks SQ 30992 [Q]		1971	10.00	20.00	40.00
A FUNNY THING HAPPENED ON THE WAY TO THE FORUM					
❏ United Artists UA-LA284-G		1974	2.50	5.00	10.00
—*Reissue of 5144*					
❏ United Artists UAL-4144 [M]		1966	3.00	6.00	12.00
❏ United Artists UAS-5144 [S]		1966	3.75	7.50	15.00
GAILY, GAILY					
❏ United Artists UAS 5202		1969	6.25	12.50	25.00
THE GAME IS OVER					
❏ Atco 33-205 [M]		1967	5.00	10.00	20.00
❏ Atco SD 33-205 [S]		1967	6.25	12.50	25.00
THE GAMES					
❏ Viking LPS-105		1970	50.00	100.00	200.00
GAY PURR-EE					
❏ Warner Bros. B 1479 [M]		1963	5.00	10.00	20.00
❏ Warner Bros. BS 1479 [S]		1963	7.50	15.00	30.00

Number Title	Yr	VG	VG+	NM
GEISHA BOY				
❑ Jubilee JGS-1096 [S]	1959	20.00	40.00	80.00
❑ Jubilee JLP-1096 [M]	1958	12.50	25.00	50.00
THE GENE KRUPA STORY				
❑ Verve MGVS-6105 [S]	1959	25.00	50.00	100.00
—Original issue				
❑ Verve MGV-15010 [M]	1959	12.50	25.00	50.00
❑ Verve V-15010 [M]	1961	5.00	10.00	20.00
❑ Verve V6-15010 [S]	1963	20.00	40.00	80.00
—Early reissue				
GENGHIS KHAN				
❑ Liberty LRP-3412 [M]	1965	10.00	20.00	40.00
❑ Liberty LST-7412 [S]	1965	15.00	30.00	60.00
THE GENTLE RAIN				
❑ Mercury MG-21016 [M]	1966	5.00	10.00	20.00
❑ Mercury SR-61016 [S]	1966	6.25	12.50	25.00
GENTLEMEN MARRY BRUNETTES				
❑ Coral CRL 57013 [M]	1955	17.50	35.00	70.00
GENTLEMEN PREFER BLONDES				
❑ MGM E-208 [M]	1953	30.00	60.00	120.00
GET YOURSELF A COLLEGE GIRL				
❑ MGM E-4273 [M]	1965	5.00	10.00	20.00
❑ MGM SE-4273 [S]	1965	10.00	20.00	40.00
GETTING STRAIGHT				
❑ Colgems COSO-5010	1970	7.50	15.00	30.00
GIANT				
❑ Capitol DW 773 [R]	196?	3.00	6.00	12.00
❑ Capitol W 773 [M]	1956	10.00	20.00	40.00
—Turquoise or gray label				
❑ Capitol W 773 [M]	1959	6.25	12.50	25.00
—Black colorband label, logo at left				
❑ Capitol W 773 [M]	1962	3.75	7.50	15.00
—Black colorband label, logo at top				
GIDGET GOES HAWAIIAN				
❑ Colpix CP 418 [M]	1961	12.50	25.00	50.00
GIGI				
❑ MGM E-3641 [M]	1958	5.00	10.00	20.00
—Yellow label				
❑ MGM E-3641 [M]	1960	3.00	6.00	12.00
—Black label				
❑ MGM SE-3641 [S]	1959	6.25	12.50	25.00
—Yellow label				
❑ MGM SE-3641 [S]	1960	3.75	7.50	15.00
—Black label				
❑ MGM SE-3641 [S]	1968	3.00	6.00	12.00
—Blue and gold label				
❑ MGM SW 90523 [S]	1965	3.75	7.50	15.00
❑ MGM W 90523 [M]	1965	3.00	6.00	12.00
—Capitol Record Club edition				
GIGOT				
❑ Capitol SW 1754 [S]	1962	10.00	20.00	40.00
❑ Capitol W 1754 [M]	1962	7.50	15.00	30.00
THE GIRL IN THE BIKINI				
❑ Poplar PLP 33-1002 [M]	1952	100.00	200.00	400.00
THE GIRL MOST LIKELY				
❑ Capitol W 930 [M]	1957	15.00	30.00	60.00
GIRL ON A MOTORCYCLE				
❑ Tetragrammaton T-5000	1969	7.50	15.00	30.00
THE GLENN MILLER STORY				
❑ Decca DL 5519 [10]	1954	10.00	20.00	40.00
❑ Decca DL 8226 [M]	1956	7.50	15.00	30.00
❑ Decca DL 9123 [M]	196?	5.00	10.00	20.00
—Reissue of 8226				
❑ Decca DL 79123 [R]	196?	3.75	7.50	15.00
❑ MCA 1624	198?	3.75	7.50	15.00
—This reissue is a bit more desirable because it was issued in true stereo				
❑ MCA 2036	1973	2.50	5.00	10.00
THE GLORY STOMPERS				
❑ Sidewalk DT 5910 [R]	1968	12.50	25.00	50.00
GO, GO, GO WORLD				
❑ Musicor MM-2059 [M]	1965	10.00	20.00	40.00
❑ Musicor MS-3059 [S]	1965	15.00	30.00	60.00
GO, JOHNNY, GO!				
❑ (no label) (no number) [DJ]	1959	250.00	500.00	1000.
—Only exists as a promo				
GOD'S LITTLE ACRE				
❑ United Artists UAL-4002 [M]	1958	37.50	75.00	150.00

Number Title	Yr	VG	VG+	NM
THE GODFATHER				
❑ Paramount PAS-1003	1972	5.00	10.00	20.00
—Original cover with triple gatefold				
THE GODFATHER PART II				
❑ ABC ABDP-856	1975	5.00	10.00	20.00
GOLD				
❑ ABC ABCD-855	1975	7.50	15.00	30.00
GOLDEN BOY				
❑ Colpix CP-478 [M]	1964	5.00	10.00	20.00
❑ Colpix SCP-478 [S]	1964	6.25	12.50	25.00
THE GOLDEN BREED				
❑ Capitol ST 2886	1967	7.50	15.00	30.00
THE GOLDEN COACH				
❑ MGM E-3111 [M]	1954	37.50	75.00	150.00
THE GOLDEN SCREW				
❑ Atco 33-208 [M]	1967	7.50	15.00	30.00
❑ Atco SD 33-208 [S]	1967	10.00	20.00	40.00
GOLDFINGER				
❑ United Artists UAL-4117 [M]	1964	3.75	7.50	15.00
❑ United Artists UAS-5117 [S]	1964	5.00	10.00	20.00
GOLIATH AND THE BARBARIANS				
❑ American Int'l. 1001-M [M]	1960	10.00	20.00	40.00
❑ American Int'l. 1001-S [S]	1960	17.50	35.00	70.00
GONE WITH THE WAVE				
❑ Colpix CP-492 [M]	1965	10.00	20.00	40.00
❑ Colpix SCP-492 [S]	1965	15.00	30.00	60.00
GONE WITH THE WIND				
❑ MGM 1E-10 [M]	1967	5.00	10.00	20.00
—Gatefold edition with 32-page booklet				
❑ MGM S1E-10 [S]	1967	5.00	10.00	20.00
—Gatefold edition with 32-page booklet				
GOOD NEWS				
❑ MGM E-504 [10]	1950	12.50	25.00	50.00
GOODBYE AGAIN				
❑ United Artists UAL-4091 [M]	1961	7.50	15.00	30.00
❑ United Artists UAS-5091 [S]	1961	10.00	20.00	40.00
GOODBYE, CHARLIE				
❑ 20th Century Fox TFM-3165 [M]	1964	6.25	12.50	25.00
❑ 20th Century Fox TFS-4165 [S]	1964	7.50	15.00	30.00
GOODBYE, MR. CHIPS				
❑ MCA 39006	1986	2.00	4.00	8.00
—Reissue				
❑ MGM 1SE-19	1969	5.00	10.00	20.00
GORDON'S WAR				
❑ Buddah BDS-5137	1973	10.00	20.00	40.00
THE GOSPEL ACCORDING TO ST. MATTHEW				
❑ Mainstream S-4000 [S]	1966	25.00	50.00	100.00
❑ Mainstream 54000 [M]	1966	6.25	12.50	25.00
GOYA				
❑ Decca DL 8236 [M]	1959	37.50	75.00	150.00
GRAND PRIX				
❑ MGM 1E-8 [M]	1967	5.00	10.00	20.00
❑ MGM 1SE-8 [S]	1967	6.25	12.50	25.00
THE GREAT ESCAPE				
❑ United Artists UAL-4107 [M]	1963	6.25	12.50	25.00
❑ United Artists UAS-5107 [S]	1963	7.50	15.00	30.00
THE GREAT GATSBY				
❑ Paramount 2-3001 [(2)]	1974	5.00	10.00	20.00
THE GREATEST SHOW ON EARTH				
❑ RCA Victor LPM-3018 [10]	1952	50.00	100.00	200.00
THE GREATEST STORY EVER TOLD				
❑ United Artists UAL-4120 [M]	1965	6.25	12.50	25.00
❑ United Artists UAS-5120 [S]	1965	7.50	15.00	30.00
GROUNDS FOR MARRIAGE				
❑ MGM E-536 [M]	1950	20.00	40.00	80.00
GUESS WHO'S COMING TO DINNER				
❑ Colgems COM-108 [M]	1968	7.50	15.00	30.00
❑ Colgems COS-108 [S]	1968	7.50	15.00	30.00
GULLIVER'S TRAVELS BEYOND THE MOON				
❑ Mainstream S-4001 [S]	1965	10.00	20.00	40.00
❑ Mainstream 54001 [M]	1965	7.50	15.00	30.00

Number Title	Yr	VG	VG+	NM
GUNS FOR SAN SEBASTIAN				
❏ MGM SE-4565	1968	15.00	30.00	60.00
THE GUNS OF NAVARONE				
❏ Columbia CL 1655 [M]	1961	5.00	10.00	20.00
❏ Columbia CS 8455 [S]	1961	12.50	25.00	50.00
GURU				
❏ RCA Victor LSO-1158	1969	5.00	10.00	20.00
GYPSY				
❏ Warner Bros. B 1480 [M]	1962	5.00	10.00	20.00
❏ Warner Bros. BS 1480 [S]	1962	7.50	15.00	30.00
GYPSY GIRL				
❏ Mainstream S-6090 [S]	1966	10.00	20.00	40.00
❏ Mainstream 56090 [M]	1966	7.50	15.00	30.00
HALLELUJAH THE HILLS				
❏ Fontana MGF-27524 [M]	1964	6.25	12.50	25.00
❏ Fontana SRF-67524 [S]	1964	7.50	15.00	30.00
THE HALLELUJAH TRAIL				
❏ United Artists UAL-4127 [M]	1965	5.00	10.00	20.00
❏ United Artists UAS-5127 [S]	1965	6.25	12.50	25.00
HAMMERHEAD				
❏ Colgems COS-110	1968	10.00	20.00	40.00
HAMMERSMITH IS OUT				
❏ Capitol SW-861	1972	7.50	15.00	30.00
HANG 'EM HIGH				
❏ United Artists UAS-5179	1968	6.25	12.50	25.00
THE HAPPENING				
❏ Colgems COMO-5006 [M]	1967	7.50	15.00	30.00
❏ Colgems COSO-5006 [S]	1967	12.50	25.00	50.00
THE HAPPIEST MILLIONAIRE				
❏ Buena Vista BV-5001 [M]	1967	3.75	7.50	15.00
❏ Buena Vista STER-5001 [S]	1967	5.00	10.00	20.00
THE HARD RIDE				
❏ Paramount PAS-6005	1971	7.50	15.00	30.00
HARPER				
❏ Mainstream S-6078 [S]	1966	6.25	12.50	25.00
❏ Mainstream 56078 [M]	1966	5.00	10.00	20.00
THE HARRAD EXPERIMENT				
❏ Capitol ST-11182	1973	6.25	12.50	25.00
HARRAD SUMMER				
❏ Capitol ST-11338	1974	6.25	12.50	25.00
HAWAII				
❏ United Artists UAL-4143 [M]	1966	5.00	10.00	20.00
❏ United Artists UAS-5143 [S]	1966	6.25	12.50	25.00
❏ United Artists SW-90935 [S]	1966	7.50	15.00	30.00
—Capitol Record Club issue				
THE HEART IS A LONELY HUNTER				
❏ Warner Bros. WS 1759	1968	7.50	15.00	30.00
HEAVY TRAFFIC				
❏ Fantasy F-9436	1973	6.25	12.50	25.00
THE HELEN MORGAN STORY				
❏ RCA Victor LOC-1030 [M]	1957	15.00	30.00	60.00
HELL TO ETERNITY				
❏ Warwick W 2030 [M]	1960	30.00	60.00	120.00
❏ Warwick WST 2030 [S]	1960	50.00	100.00	200.00
HELL UP IN HARLEM				
❏ Motown M 802V1	1974	7.50	15.00	30.00
HELL'S ANGELS '69				
❏ Capitol SKAO-303	1969	6.25	12.50	25.00
HELL'S ANGELS ON WHEELS				
❏ Smash MGS-27094 [M]	1967	6.25	12.50	25.00
❏ Smash SRS-67094 [S]	1967	7.50	15.00	30.00
HELL'S BELLS				
❏ Sidewalk ST 5919	1969	7.50	15.00	30.00
HELLCATS				
❏ Tower ST 5124	1968	7.50	15.00	30.00
HELLO-GOODBYE				
❏ 20th Century Fox S-4210	1970	10.00	20.00	40.00
HEMINGWAY'S ADVENTURES OF A YOUNG MAN				
❏ RCA Victor LOC-1074 [M]	1962	10.00	20.00	40.00
❏ RCA Victor LSO-1074 [S]	1962	17.50	35.00	70.00

Number Title	Yr	VG	VG+	NM
THE HERO				
❏ Capitol SW-11098	1972	5.00	10.00	20.00
HEROES OF TELEMARK				
❏ Mainstream S-6064 [S]	1965	7.50	15.00	30.00
❏ Mainstream 56064 [M]	1965	5.00	10.00	20.00
HEY THERE, IT'S YOGI BEAR!				
❏ Colpix CP-472 [M]	1964	12.50	25.00	50.00
❏ Colpix SCP-472 [S]	1964	20.00	40.00	80.00
HEY, LET'S TWIST				
❏ Roulette R-25168 [M]	1962	6.25	12.50	25.00
❏ Roulette SR-25168 [S]	1962	7.50	15.00	30.00
HIGH SOCIETY				
❏ Capitol SW 750 [S]	1959	7.50	15.00	30.00
—Black colorband label, logo at left				
❏ Capitol SW 750 [S]	1962	5.00	10.00	20.00
—Black colorband label, logo at top				
❏ Capitol W 750 [M]	1956	7.50	15.00	30.00
—Gray label original				
❏ Capitol W 750 [M]	1959	5.00	10.00	20.00
—Black colorband label, logo at left				
❏ Capitol W 750 [M]	1962	3.75	7.50	15.00
—Black colorband label, logo at top				
HOLIDAY INN				
❏ Decca DL 4256	1962	6.25	12.50	25.00
HOOTENANNY HOOT				
❏ MGM E-4172 [M]	1963	5.00	10.00	20.00
❏ MGM SE-4172 [S]	1963	6.25	12.50	25.00
THE HORSE SOLDIERS				
❏ United Artists UAL-4035 [M]	1959	15.00	30.00	60.00
❏ United Artists UAS-5035 [S]	1959	37.50	75.00	150.00
THE HORSEMEN				
❏ Sunflower SNF-5007	1971	10.00	20.00	40.00
THE HOT ROCK				
❏ Prophesy SD 8055	1972	5.00	10.00	20.00
HOT ROD RUMBLE				
❏ Liberty LRP-3048 [M]	1957	37.50	75.00	150.00
HOTEL PARADISO				
❏ MGM E-4419 [M]	1966	5.00	10.00	20.00
❏ MGM SE-4419 [S]	1966	6.25	12.50	25.00
THE HOUR OF THE GUN				
❏ United Artists UAL-4166 [M]	1967	10.00	20.00	40.00
❏ United Artists UAS-5166 [S]	1967	17.50	35.00	70.00
A HOUSE IS NOT A HOME				
❏ Ava A-50 [M]	1964	6.25	12.50	25.00
❏ Ava AS-50 [S]	1964	7.50	15.00	30.00
HOUSEBOAT				
❏ Columbia CL 1222 [M]	1958	12.50	25.00	50.00
HOW SWEET IT IS				
❏ RCA Victor LSP-4037	1968	5.00	10.00	20.00
HOW THE WEST WAS WON				
❏ MGM 1E-5 [M]	1963	3.75	7.50	15.00
❏ MGM 1SE-5 [S]	1963	5.00	10.00	20.00
HOW TO MURDER YOUR WIFE				
❏ United Artists UAL-4119 [M]	1965	3.75	7.50	15.00
❏ United Artists UAS-5119 [S]	1965	5.00	10.00	20.00
HOW TO SAVE A MARRIAGE AND RUIN YOUR LIFE				
❏ Columbia Masterworks OS 3140	1968	5.00	10.00	20.00
HOW TO STEAL A MILLION				
❏ 20th Century Fox TFM-3183 [M]	1966	10.00	20.00	40.00
❏ 20th Century Fox TFS-4183 [S]	1966	12.50	25.00	50.00
HOW TO STUFF A WILD BIKINI				
❏ Wand 671 [M]	1965	7.50	15.00	30.00
❏ Wand S-671 [S]	1965	10.00	20.00	40.00
HOW TO SUCCEED IN BUSINESS WITHOUT REALLY TRYING				
❏ United Artists UAL-4151 [M]	1967	5.00	10.00	20.00
❏ United Artists UAS-5151 [S]	1967	6.25	12.50	25.00
HURRY SUNDOWN				
❏ RCA Victor LOC-1133 [M]	1967	7.50	15.00	30.00
❏ RCA Victor LSO-1133 [S]	1967	10.00	20.00	40.00
THE HUSTLER				
❏ Kapp KL-1264 [M]	1961	15.00	30.00	60.00
❏ Kapp KS-3264 [S]	1961	30.00	60.00	120.00

Number Title	Yr	VG	VG+	NM
I LOVE MELVIN				
❑ MGM E-190 [10]	1953	12.50	25.00	50.00
I NEVER SANG FOR MY FATHER				
❑ Bell 1204	1970	10.00	20.00	40.00
I WANT TO LIVE				
❑ United Artists UXL 1 [(2)M]	1958	15.00	30.00	60.00
—Combines 4005 and 4006 into one package				
❑ United Artists UXS 51 [(2)S]	1958	20.00	40.00	80.00
—Combines 5005 and 5006 into one package				
❑ United Artists UAL-4005 [M]	1958	6.25	12.50	25.00
—Orchestral music by Johnny Mandel				
❑ United Artists UAS-4005 [S]	1958	10.00	20.00	40.00
—Orchestral music by Johnny Mandel				
❑ United Artists UAL-4006 [M]	1958	7.50	15.00	30.00
—Jazz music by Gerry Mulligan, Shelly Manne and Art Farmer				
❑ United Artists UAS-4006 [S]	1958	10.00	20.00	40.00
—Jazz music by Gerry Mulligan, Shelly Mann and Art Farmer				
I'LL NEVER FORGET WHAT'S 'IS NAME				
❑ Decca DL 9163 [M]	1967	6.25	12.50	25.00
❑ Decca DL 79163 [S]	1967	7.50	15.00	30.00
ICE STATION ZEBRA				
❑ MGM S1E-14 ST	1968	10.00	20.00	40.00
IF HE HOLLERS, LET HIM GO				
❑ Tower ST 5152	1968	10.00	20.00	40.00
IMITATION OF LIFE				
❑ Decca DL 8879 [M]	1959	12.50	25.00	50.00
❑ Decca DL 78879 [S]	1959	20.00	40.00	80.00
IN HARM'S WAY				
❑ RCA Victor LOC-1100 [M]	1965	10.00	20.00	40.00
❑ RCA Victor LSO-1100 [S]	1965	20.00	40.00	80.00
IN LIKE FLINT				
❑ 20th Century Fox 4193 [M]	1967	10.00	20.00	40.00
❑ 20th Century Fox S-4193 [S]	1967	20.00	40.00	80.00
IN SEARCH OF THE CASTAWAYS				
❑ Disneyland ST-3916 [M]	1962	17.50	35.00	70.00
IN THE GOOD OLD SUMMERTIME				
❑ MGM E-169 [10]	1949	25.00	50.00	100.00
IN THE HEAT OF THE NIGHT				
❑ United Artists UAL-4160 [M]	1967	3.75	7.50	15.00
❑ United Artists UAS-5160 [S]	1967	5.00	10.00	20.00
THE INDISCRETION OF AN AMERICAN WIFE				
❑ Columbia CL 6277 [10]	1954	20.00	40.00	80.00
THE INN OF THE SIXTH HAPPINESS				
❑ 20th Century Fox FOX-3011 [M]	1958	12.50	25.00	50.00
❑ 20th Century Fox SFX-3011 [S]	1958	17.50	35.00	70.00
INSIDE DAISY CLOVER				
❑ Warner Bros. W 1616 [M]	1965	5.00	10.00	20.00
❑ Warner Bros. WS 1616 [S]	1965	7.50	15.00	30.00
INSPECTOR CLOUSEAU				
❑ United Artists UAS-5186	1968	7.50	15.00	30.00
INTERLUDE				
❑ Colgems COSO-5007	1968	10.00	20.00	40.00
THE INTERNS				
❑ Colpix CP 427 [M]	1962	7.50	15.00	30.00
❑ Colpix SCP 427 [S]	1962	10.00	20.00	40.00
INVITATION TO THE DANCE				
❑ MGM E-3207 [M]	1956	12.50	25.00	50.00
THE IPCRESS FILE				
❑ Decca DL 9124 [M]	1965	7.50	15.00	30.00
❑ Decca DL 79124 [S]	1965	10.00	20.00	40.00
IRMA LA DOUCE				
❑ United Artists UAL-4109 [M]	1963	5.00	10.00	20.00
❑ United Artists UAS-5109 [S]	1963	6.25	12.50	25.00
IS PARIS BURNING?				
❑ Columbia Masterworks OS 3030 [S]	1966	10.00	20.00	40.00
❑ Columbia Masterworks OL 6630 [M]	1966	7.50	15.00	30.00
THE ISLAND AT THE TOP OF THE WORLD				
❑ Disneyland ST-3814	1974	6.25	12.50	25.00
ISLAND IN THE SKY				
❑ Decca DL 7029 [10]	1953	75.00	150.00	300.00
IT STARTED IN NAPLES				
❑ Dot DLP-3324 [M]	1960	15.00	30.00	60.00
❑ Dot DLP-25324 [S]	1960	25.00	50.00	100.00

Number Title	Yr	VG	VG+	NM
IT'S A MAD, MAD, MAD, MAD WORLD				
❑ United Artists UA-LA276-G	1974	2.50	5.00	10.00
—Reissue of 5110				
❑ United Artists UAL-4110 [M]	1963	5.00	10.00	20.00
❑ United Artists UAS-5110 [S]	1963	6.25	12.50	25.00
IT'S ALWAYS FAIR WEATHER				
❑ MGM E-3241 [M]	1955	12.50	25.00	50.00
THE ITALIAN JOB				
❑ Paramount PAS-5007	1969	10.00	20.00	40.00
JACK THE RIPPER				
❑ RCA Victor LPM-2199 [M]	1960	7.50	15.00	30.00
❑ RCA Victor LSP-2199 [S]	1960	12.50	25.00	50.00
JAMBOREE!				
❑ Warner Bros. (no #) [M]	1957	300.00	600.00	1200.
—Album has been counterfeited. Originals have front cover slicks and back cover notes printed on the cardboard, and the records have "Jam 1" and "Jam 2" stamped (not etched) in the dead wax.				
THE JAMES DEAN STORY				
❑ Capitol W 881 [M]	1957	15.00	30.00	60.00
❑ Kimberly 2016 [M]	1960	10.00	20.00	40.00
❑ Kimberly 11016 [S]	1960	12.50	25.00	50.00
—Reissue of World Pacific 2005				
❑ World Pacific P-2005 [M]	1958	25.00	50.00	100.00
JAWS				
❑ MCA 2087	1975	5.00	10.00	20.00
JEREMIAH JOHNSON				
❑ Warner Bros. BS 2902	1972	5.00	10.00	20.00
—Green label				
JESSICA				
❑ United Artists UAL-4096 [M]	1962	5.00	10.00	20.00
❑ United Artists UAS-5096 [S]	1962	6.25	12.50	25.00
THE JOE LOUIS STORY				
❑ MGM E-221 [10]	1953	20.00	40.00	80.00
JOHN PAUL JONES				
❑ Warner Bros. W 1293 [M]	1959	15.00	30.00	60.00
❑ Warner Bros. WS 1293 [S]	1959	30.00	60.00	120.00
JOHNNY COOL				
❑ United Artists UAL-4111 [M]	1963	5.00	10.00	20.00
❑ United Artists UAS-5111 [S]	1963	6.25	12.50	25.00
JOHNNY TREMAIN				
❑ Disneyland WDL-4014 [M]	1957	12.50	25.00	50.00
JUD				
❑ Ampex A-50101	1971	5.00	10.00	20.00
JUDGMENT AT NUREMBERG				
❑ United Artists UAL-4095 [M]	1961	5.00	10.00	20.00
❑ United Artists UAS-5095 [S]	1961	12.50	25.00	50.00
JUDITH				
❑ RCA Victor LOC-1119 [M]	1966	3.75	7.50	15.00
❑ RCA Victor LSO-1119 [S]	1966	7.50	15.00	30.00
JULIET OF THE SPIRITS				
❑ Mainstream S-6062 [S]	1965	15.00	30.00	60.00
❑ Mainstream 56062 [M]	1965	6.25	12.50	25.00
JULIUS CAESAR				
❑ MGM E-3033 [M]	1953	10.00	20.00	40.00
JUMBO (BILLY ROSE'S)				
❑ Columbia Masterworks OS 2260 [S]	1962	7.50	15.00	30.00
❑ Columbia Masterworks OL 5860 [M]	1962	5.00	10.00	20.00
THE JUNGLE BOOK				
❑ Buena Vista BV-4041 [M]	1967	3.75	7.50	15.00
❑ Buena Vista STER-4041 [S]	1967	6.25	12.50	25.00
JUSTINE				
❑ Monument SLP-18123	1969	7.50	15.00	30.00
KALEIDOSCOPE				
❑ Warner Bros. W 1663 [M]	1966	5.00	10.00	20.00
❑ Warner Bros. WS 1663 [S]	1966	6.25	12.50	25.00
KELLY'S HEROES				
❑ MGM S1E-23	1970	7.50	15.00	30.00
THE KEY				
❑ Columbia CL 1185 [M]	1958	20.00	40.00	80.00
KILLERS THREE				
❑ Tower ST-5141	1968	5.00	10.00	20.00

Number Title	Yr	VG	VG+	NM
THE KING AND I				
❑ Capitol SW 740 [S]	1959	5.00	10.00	20.00
—Black colorband label, logo at left				
❑ Capitol SW 740 [S]	1962	3.75	7.50	15.00
—Black colorband label, logo at top				
❑ Capitol SW 740 [S]	1969	3.00	6.00	12.00
—Lime green label				
❑ Capitol SW 740 [S]	1973	2.50	5.00	10.00
—Orange label				
❑ Capitol W 740 [M]	1956	6.25	12.50	25.00
—Gray label				
❑ Capitol W 740 [M]	1959	3.75	7.50	15.00
—Black colorband label, logo at left				
❑ Capitol W 740 [M]	1962	3.00	6.00	12.00
—Black colorband label, logo at top				
KING KONG				
❑ Reprise MS 2260	1976	5.00	10.00	20.00
KING OF KINGS				
❑ MGM 1E-2 [M]	1961	3.75	7.50	15.00
—Standard cover				
❑ MGM 1E-2 [M]	1961	7.50	15.00	30.00
—Boxed version with hardbound book and four 8x10 photos				
❑ MGM S1E-2 [S]	1961	5.00	10.00	20.00
—Standard cover				
❑ MGM S1E-2 [S]	1961	10.00	20.00	40.00
—Boxed version with hardbound book and four 8x10 photos				
KING RAT				
❑ Mainstream S-6061 [S]	1965	12.50	25.00	50.00
❑ Mainstream 56061 [M]	1965	7.50	15.00	30.00
KINGS GO FORTH				
❑ Capitol W 1063 [M]	1958	37.50	75.00	150.00
KISMET				
❑ Metro M-526 [M]	1965	3.00	6.00	12.00
—Reissue of MGM E-3281 with one fewer track				
❑ Metro MS-526 [R]	1955	2.50	5.00	10.00
—Rechanneled reissue of MGM E-3281 with one fewer track				
❑ MGM E-3281 [M]	1955	5.00	10.00	20.00
—Yellow label				
❑ MGM E-3281 [M]	1960	3.75	7.50	15.00
—Black label				
KISS ME, KATE				
❑ Metro M-525 [M]	1965	3.00	6.00	12.00
—Reissue of MGM 3077, but with only 10 songs				
❑ Metro MS-525 [R]	1965	2.50	5.00	10.00
—Rechanneled reissue of MGM 3077, but with only 10 songs				
❑ MGM E-3077 [M]	1953	5.00	10.00	20.00
—Yellow label				
❑ MGM E-3077 [M]	1959	3.75	7.50	15.00
—Black label				
KWAMINA				
❑ Mercury MG-20654 [M]	1961	6.25	12.50	25.00
❑ Mercury SR-60654 [S]	1961	7.50	15.00	30.00
LADY AND THE TRAMP				
❑ Decca DL 5557 [10]	1955	15.00	30.00	60.00
❑ Decca DL 8462 [M]	1957	17.50	35.00	70.00
THE LANDLORD				
❑ United Artists UAS-5209	1970	5.00	10.00	20.00
THE LAST OF THE SECRET AGENTS				
❑ Dot DLP-3714 [M]	1966	5.00	10.00	20.00
❑ Dot DLP-25714 [S]	1966	6.25	12.50	25.00
THE LAST RUN				
❑ MGM 1SE-30	1971	6.25	12.50	25.00
LAST SUMMER				
❑ Warner Bros. WS 1791	1969	5.00	10.00	20.00
THE LAST VALLEY				
❑ ABC-Dunhill DSX-50102	1971	10.00	20.00	40.00
LAWRENCE OF ARABIA				
❑ Arista ABM-4009	1975	2.50	5.00	10.00
—Reissue of Bell 1205				
❑ Bell 1205	1971	2.50	5.00	10.00
—Reissue of Colgems COSO-5004				
❑ Colgems COMO-5004 [M]	1967	3.00	6.00	12.00
—Reissue of Colpix CP-514				
❑ Colgems COSO-5004 [S]	1967	3.75	7.50	15.00
—Reissue of Colpix SCP-514				
❑ Colpix CP-514 [M]	1962	5.00	10.00	20.00
❑ Colpix SCP-514 [S]	1962	7.50	15.00	30.00
LENNY				
❑ United Artists UA-LA359-H [(2)]	1974	5.00	10.00	20.00
THE LEOPARD				
❑ 20th Century Fox FXG-5015 [M]	1963	7.50	15.00	30.00
❑ 20th Century Fox SXG-5015 [S]	1963	10.00	20.00	40.00

Number Title	Yr	VG	VG+	NM
LES LIAISONS DANGEREUSES				
❑ Charlie Parker PLP-813 [M]	1962	6.25	12.50	25.00
❑ Charlie Parker PLP-813S [S]	1962	7.50	15.00	30.00
❑ Epic LA 16022 [M]	1961	10.00	20.00	40.00
❑ Epic BA 17022 [S]	1961	7.50	15.00	30.00
❑ Fontana MGF-27539 [M]	1965	5.00	10.00	20.00
❑ Fontana SRF-67539 [R]	1965	3.75	7.50	15.00
LET THE GOOD TIMES ROLL				
❑ Bell 9002 [(2)]	1973	6.25	12.50	25.00
LET'S MAKE LOVE				
❑ Columbia CL 1527 [M]	1960	7.50	15.00	30.00
❑ Columbia CS 8327 [S]	1960	12.50	25.00	50.00
LI'L ABNER				
❑ Columbia Masterworks OS 2021 [S]	1959	10.00	20.00	40.00
—Credits within photo				
❑ Columbia Masterworks OS 2021 [S]	196?	6.25	12.50	25.00
—Credits in red strip at bottom of photo				
❑ Columbia Masterworks OL 5460 [M]	1959	7.50	15.00	30.00
—Credits within photo				
❑ Columbia Masterworks OL 5460 [M]	196?	5.00	10.00	20.00
—Credits in red strip at bottom of photo				
THE LIFE AND TIMES OF JUDGE ROY BEAN				
❑ Columbia Masterworks S 31948	1972	6.25	12.50	25.00
LIGHT FANTASTIC				
❑ 20th Century Fox FXG-5016 [M]	1963	5.00	10.00	20.00
❑ 20th Century Fox SXG-5016 [S]	1963	6.25	12.50	25.00
LILIES OF THE FIELD				
❑ Epic LN 24094 [M]	1964	5.00	10.00	20.00
❑ Epic BN 26094 [S]	1964	7.50	15.00	30.00
THE LION				
❑ London M-76001 [M]	1962	100.00	200.00	400.00
THE LION IN WINTER				
❑ Columbia Masterworks OS 3250	1969	5.00	10.00	20.00
LITTLE BIG MAN				
❑ Columbia Masterworks S 30545	1970	5.00	10.00	20.00
LIVE AND LET DIE				
❑ United Artists UA-LA100-G	1973	2.50	5.00	10.00
—Tan label; cover corner is clipped				
❑ United Artists UA-LA100-G	1973	5.00	10.00	20.00
—Tan label; cover corner is not clipped off				
❑ United Artists SWAO-95120	1973	7.50	15.00	30.00
—Longines (formerly Capitol) Record Club edition				
LIVE FOR LIFE				
❑ United Artists UAL-4165 [M]	1967	5.00	10.00	20.00
❑ United Artists UAS-5165 [S]	1967	5.00	10.00	20.00
THE LIVELY SET				
❑ Decca DL 9119 [M]	1964	7.50	15.00	30.00
❑ Decca DL 79119 [S]	1964	10.00	20.00	40.00
LOLITA				
❑ MGM E-4050 [M]	1962	5.00	10.00	20.00
❑ MGM SE-4050 [S]	1962	7.50	15.00	30.00
THE LOLLIPOP COVER				
❑ Mainstream S-6067 [S]	1966	7.50	15.00	30.00
❑ Mainstream 56067 [M]	1966	5.00	10.00	20.00
THE LONG HOT SUMMER				
❑ Roulette R-25026 [M]	1958	18.75	37.50	75.00
LONG JOHN SILVER				
❑ RCA Victor LPM-3279 [10]	1954	75.00	150.00	300.00
THE LONG SHIPS				
❑ Colpix CP-517 [M]	1964	12.50	25.00	50.00
❑ Colpix SCP-517 [S]	1964	15.00	30.00	60.00
THE LONGEST DAY				
❑ 20th Century Fox FXG-5007 [M]	1962	5.00	10.00	20.00
❑ 20th Century Fox SXG-5007 [S]	1962	6.25	12.50	25.00
LORD JIM				
❑ Colpix CP-521 [M]	1965	6.25	12.50	25.00
❑ Colpix SCP-521 [S]	1965	10.00	20.00	40.00
LORD LOVE A DUCK				
❑ United Artists UAL-4137 [M]	1966	5.00	10.00	20.00
❑ United Artists UAS-5137 [S]	1966	6.25	12.50	25.00
THE LORDS OF FLATBUSH				
❑ ABC ABCD-828	1974	7.50	15.00	30.00
A LOSS OF INNOCENCE				
❑ Colpix CP-508 [M]	1961	10.00	20.00	40.00

Number Title	Yr	VG	VG+	NM
THE LOST CONTINENT				
❏ MGM E-3635 [M]	1957	50.00	100.00	200.00
LOVE IN 4 DIMENSIONS				
❏ Request RLP-8090 [M]	1966	6.25	12.50	25.00
❏ Request SRLP-8090 [S]	1966	7.50	15.00	30.00
LOVE LIFE				
❏ Heritage 600 [M]	195?	15.00	30.00	60.00
LOVERS AND OTHER STRANGERS				
❏ ABC ABCS-OC-15	1970	5.00	10.00	20.00
❏ ABC SW-93479	1971	6.25	12.50	25.00
—Capitol Record Club edition				
M*A*S*H				
❏ Columbia Masterworks OS 3520	1970	5.00	10.00	20.00
—Original copies do not have the theme song done by Ahmad Jamal				
❏ Columbia Masterworks S 32753	1973	2.50	5.00	10.00
—Reissue with the movie's theme performed by Ahmad Jamal				
THE MAD ADVENTURES OF RABBI JACOB				
❏ London PS 652	1974	2.50	5.00	10.00
—Cover has cut-out markings (usually a hole punch or a cut-off corner)				
❏ London PS 652	1974	5.00	10.00	20.00
—Cover is intact with no cut-out markings				
MADAME BOVARY				
❏ MGM E-3507 [M]	195?	37.50	75.00	150.00
THE MAGIC CHRISTIAN				
❏ Commonwealth United CU-6004	1970	6.25	12.50	25.00
MAGNIFICENT OBSESSION				
❏ Decca DL 8078 [M]	1954	15.00	30.00	60.00
—Black label, gold print				
❏ Decca DL 8078 [M]	1955	12.50	25.00	50.00
—Black label, silver print				
❏ Decca DL 8078 [M]	196?	7.50	15.00	30.00
—Black label with color bars				
MAJOR DUNDEE				
❏ Columbia Masterworks OS 2780 [S]	1965	7.50	15.00	30.00
❏ Columbia Masterworks OL 6380 [M]	1965	5.00	10.00	20.00
MALAMONDO				
❏ Epic LN 24126 [M]	1964	7.50	15.00	30.00
❏ Epic BN 26126 [S]	1964	10.00	20.00	40.00
MAME				
❏ Warner Bros. PRO 580 [DJ]	1973	12.50	25.00	50.00
—Promo-only gatefold edition with Lucille Ball in Christmas hat on the cover				
❏ Warner Bros. W 2773	1974	3.75	7.50	15.00
A MAN AND A WOMAN (UN HOMME ET UNE FEMME)				
❏ United Artists UAL-4147 [M]	1966	3.75	7.50	15.00
❏ United Artists UAS-5147 [S]	1966	5.00	10.00	20.00
❏ United Artists SW-91032 [S]	1967	6.25	12.50	25.00
—Capitol Record Club edition				
A MAN CALLED ADAM				
❏ Reprise R 6180 [M]	1966	3.75	7.50	15.00
❏ Reprise RS 6180 [S]	1966	5.00	10.00	20.00
A MAN CALLED DAGGER				
❏ MGM E-4516 [M]	1967	3.75	7.50	15.00
❏ MGM SE-4516 [S]	1967	5.00	10.00	20.00
A MAN CALLED FLINTSTONE				
❏ Hanna-Barbera HLP-2055 [M]	1967	25.00	50.00	100.00
A MAN COULD GET KILLED				
❏ Decca DL 4750 [M]	1966	3.75	7.50	15.00
❏ Decca DL 74750 [S]	1966	5.00	10.00	20.00
A MAN FOR ALL SEASONS				
❏ RCA Victor VDM-116 [(2)M]	1966	7.50	15.00	30.00
MAN FROM SHAFT				
❏ MGM SE-4836	1972	7.50	15.00	30.00
MAN IN THE MIDDLE				
❏ 20th Century Fox TFM-3128 [M]	1965	7.50	15.00	30.00
❏ 20th Century Fox TFS-4128 [S]	1965	12.50	25.00	50.00
THE MAN OF A THOUSAND FACES				
❏ Decca DL 8623 [M]	1957	12.50	25.00	50.00
—Black label, silver print, or pink label, black print promos				
❏ Decca DL 8623 [M]	196?	7.50	15.00	30.00
—Black label with color bars				
MAN OF LA MANCHA				
❏ United Artists UAS-9906	1972	2.50	5.00	10.00
—Cover has cut-out marking such as a cut-off corner				
❏ United Artists UAS-9906	1972	5.00	10.00	20.00
—Cover is intact with no cut corners				

Number Title	Yr	VG	VG+	NM
THE MAN WHO WOULD BE KING				
❏ Capitol SW-11474	1975	5.00	10.00	20.00
THE MAN WITH THE GOLDEN ARM				
❏ Decca DL 8257 [M]	1956	10.00	20.00	40.00
❏ Decca DL 78257 [R]	196?	5.00	10.00	20.00
❏ MCA 2043 [R]	1973	2.50	5.00	10.00
—Reissue of Decca 78257; black label with rainbow				
THE MAN WITH THE GOLDEN GUN				
❏ United Artists UA-LA358-G	1974	5.00	10.00	20.00
MARACAIBO				
❏ Decca DL 8756 [M]	1958	10.00	20.00	40.00
—Black label, silver print, or pink label, black print promos				
❏ Decca DL 8756 [M]	196?	5.00	10.00	20.00
—Black label with color bars				
MARCO THE MAGNIFICENT				
❏ Columbia Masterworks OS 2870 [S]	1966	10.00	20.00	40.00
❏ Columbia Masterworks OL 6470 [M]	1966	6.25	12.50	25.00
MARJORIE MORNINGSTAR				
❏ RCA Victor LOC-1044 [M]	1958	10.00	20.00	40.00
—"RE" next to label number				
❏ RCA Victor LOC-1044 [M]	1958	15.00	30.00	60.00
—"An Original Soundtrack Recording" on spine				
MARRY ME, MARRY ME				
❏ RCA Victor LSO-1160	1969	5.00	10.00	20.00
MARY POPPINS				
❏ Buena Vista BV-4026 [M]	1964	3.00	6.00	12.00
—Originals have gatefold covers				
❏ Buena Vista STER-4026 [S]	1964	3.75	7.50	15.00
—Originals have gatefold covers				
❏ Buena Vista STER-5005 [S]	1973	2.50	5.00	10.00
—Reissue with new number and no gatefold				
❏ RCA Victor COP-111 [M]	1964	3.75	7.50	15.00
—With gatefold; RCA Record Club edition				
❏ RCA Victor CSO-111 [S]	1964	5.00	10.00	20.00
—With gatefold; RCA Record Club edition				
MARY, QUEEN OF SCOTS				
❏ Decca DL 79186	1972	7.50	15.00	30.00
MASTER OF THE WORLD				
❏ Vee Jay LP-4000 [M]	1961	6.25	12.50	25.00
❏ Vee Jay SR-4000 [S]	1961	10.00	20.00	40.00
MCLINTOCK!				
❏ United Artists UAL-4112 [M]	1963	15.00	30.00	60.00
❏ United Artists UAS-5112 [S]	1963	20.00	40.00	80.00
ME AND THE COLONEL				
❏ RCA Victor LOC-1046 [M]	1958	12.50	25.00	50.00
MEDITERRANEAN HOLIDAY				
❏ London M-76003 [M]	1964	12.50	25.00	50.00
❏ London MS-82003 [S]	1964	20.00	40.00	80.00
MEET ME IN ST. LOUIS				
❏ Decca DL 8498 [M]	1957	7.50	15.00	30.00
—LP reissue of 78 rpm album from 1944; B-side of LP is "The Harvey Girls."				
MEMORIES AUX BRUXELLES				
❏ Carlton LP-112 [M]	1959	6.25	12.50	25.00
❏ Carlton LP-12112 [S]	1959	10.00	20.00	40.00
MEN IN WAR				
❏ Imperial LP-9032 W [M]	1957	37.50	75.00	150.00
MERRY ANDREW				
❏ Capitol T 1016 [M]	1958	12.50	25.00	50.00
MICKEY ONE				
❏ MGM E-4312 [M]	1965	5.00	10.00	20.00
❏ MGM SE-4312 [S]	1965	6.25	12.50	25.00
MIDNIGHT COWBOY				
❏ United Artists UAS-5198	1969	5.00	10.00	20.00
A MILANESE STORY				
❏ Atlantic 1388 [M]	1962	5.00	10.00	20.00
❏ Atlantic SD 1388 [S]	1962	6.25	12.50	25.00
THE MINX				
❏ Amsterdam 12007	1970	30.00	60.00	120.00
THE MISFITS				
❏ United Artists UA-LA273-G [S]	1974	3.00	6.00	12.00
—Reissue of 5087				
❏ United Artists UAL-4087 [M]	1961	12.50	25.00	50.00
❏ United Artists UAS-5087 [S]	1961	25.00	50.00	100.00

Number Title	Yr	VG	VG+	NM
MISS SADIE THOMPSON				
❑ Mercury MG-20123 [M]	1956	37.50	75.00	150.00
❑ Mercury MG-25181 [10]	1954	18.75	37.50	75.00
MOBY DICK				
❑ RCA Victor LPM-1247 [M]	1956	30.00	60.00	120.00
MODERN TIMES				
❑ United Artists UAL-4049 [M]	1959	6.25	12.50	25.00
❑ United Artists UAS-5049 [R]	196?	5.00	10.00	20.00
MODESTY BLAISE				
❑ 20th Century Fox TFM-3182 [M]	1966	7.50	15.00	30.00
❑ 20th Century Fox TFS-4182 [S]	1966	12.50	25.00	50.00
MONDO CANE				
❑ United Artists UAL-4105 [M]	1963	3.75	7.50	15.00
❑ United Artists UAS-5105 [S]	1963	5.00	10.00	20.00
MONDO CANE NO. 2				
❑ 20th Century Fox TFM-3147 [M]	1964	7.50	15.00	30.00
❑ 20th Century Fox TFS-4147 [S]	1964	10.00	20.00	40.00
THE MOON SPINNERS				
❑ Buena Vista BV-3323 [M]	1964	10.00	20.00	40.00
MR. BUDDWING				
❑ Verve V-8638 [M]	1965	3.75	7.50	15.00
❑ Verve V6-8638 [S]	1965	6.25	12.50	25.00
MR. MAGOO: 1001 ARABIAN NIGHTS				
❑ Colpix CP-410 [M]	1959	12.50	25.00	50.00
❑ Colpix SCP-410 [S]	1959	37.50	75.00	150.00
MURDER INC.				
❑ Canadian American CALP-1003 [M]	1960	25.00	50.00	100.00
MUSCLE BEACH PARTY PLUS MERLIN JONES AND THE SCRAMBLED EGGHEAD				
❑ Buena Vista BV-3314 [M]	1964	15.00	30.00	60.00
❑ Buena Vista STER-3314 [S]	1964	30.00	60.00	120.00
THE MUSIC MAN				
❑ Warner Bros. B 1459 [M]	1962	3.75	7.50	15.00
❑ Warner Bros. BS 1459 [S]	1962	5.00	10.00	20.00
—Gold label originals				
❑ Warner Bros. BS 1459 [S]	1968	3.00	6.00	12.00
—Green label with "W7" box logo at top				
❑ Warner Bros. BS 1459 [S]	1970	2.50	5.00	10.00
—Green label with "WB" shield logo at top				
❑ Warner Bros. BS 1459 [S]	1973	2.00	4.00	8.00
—"Burbank" palm trees label or later white label				
MUTINY ON THE BOUNTY				
❑ MCA 25007	1986	2.00	4.00	8.00
—Reissue of MGM 1SE-4				
❑ MGM 1E-4 [M]	196?	3.00	6.00	12.00
—Standard cover				
❑ MGM 1E-4 [M]	1962	7.50	15.00	30.00
—Boxed set with book and painting				
❑ MGM S1E-4 [S]	196?	3.75	7.50	15.00
—Standard cover				
❑ MGM S1E-4 [S]	1962	10.00	20.00	40.00
—Boxed set with book and painting				
MY FAIR LADY				
❑ Columbia Masterworks KOS 2600 [S]	1964	3.75	7.50	15.00
❑ Columbia Masterworks KOL 8000 [M]	1964	3.00	6.00	12.00
MY GEISHA				
❑ RCA Victor LOC-1070 [M]	1962	12.50	25.00	50.00
❑ RCA Victor LSO-1070 [S]	1962	25.00	50.00	100.00
MY SIDE OF THE MOUNTAIN				
❑ Capitol ST-245	1969	6.25	12.50	25.00
MY WILD IRISH ROSE				
❑ RCA Victor LPM-3036 [10]	1952	10.00	20.00	40.00
NAKED ANGELS				
❑ Straight STS-1056	1969	6.25	12.50	25.00
THE NAKED MAJA				
❑ United Artists UAL-4031 [M]	1959	7.50	15.00	30.00
❑ United Artists UAS-5031 [S]	1959	10.00	20.00	40.00
NANCY GOES TO RIO				
❑ MGM E-508 [10]	1950	15.00	30.00	60.00
NASHVILLE				
❑ ABC ABCD-893	1975	5.00	10.00	20.00
NAVAJO JOE				
❑ United Artists UA-LA292-G	1974	6.25	12.50	25.00
NED KELLY				
❑ United Artists UA-LA300-G	1974	3.00	6.00	12.00
—Reissue of 5213				
❑ United Artists UAS-5213	1970	6.25	12.50	25.00
NEVADA SMITH				
❑ Dot DLP-3718 [M]	1966	6.25	12.50	25.00
❑ Dot DLP-25718 [S]	1966	10.00	20.00	40.00
NEVER ON SUNDAY				
❑ United Artists UAL-4070 [M]	1960	3.75	7.50	15.00
❑ United Artists UAS-5070 [S]	1960	5.00	10.00	20.00
❑ United Artists SW-90834 [S]	196?	5.00	10.00	20.00
—Capitol Record Club edition				
THE NEW INTERNS				
❑ Colpix CP-473 [M]	1964	7.50	15.00	30.00
❑ Colpix SCP-473 [S]	1964	10.00	20.00	40.00
A NEW KIND OF LOVE				
❑ Mercury MG-20859 [M]	1963	3.75	7.50	15.00
❑ Mercury SR-60859 [S]	1963	5.00	10.00	20.00
THE NEW MESSIAH				
❑ Columbia KC 31713	1972	5.00	10.00	20.00
NICHOLAS AND ALEXANDRA				
❑ Bell 1103	1971	6.25	12.50	25.00
NIGHT OF THE GENERALS				
❑ Colgems COMO-5002 [M]	1967	10.00	20.00	40.00
❑ Colgems COSO-5002 [S]	1967	17.50	35.00	70.00
THE NIGHT OF THE HUNTER				
❑ RCA Victor LPM-1136 [M]	1955	62.50	125.00	250.00
NINE HOURS TO RAMA				
❑ London M-76002 [M]	1963	75.00	150.00	300.00
NO WAY TO TREAT A LADY				
❑ Dot DLP-25846	1968	6.25	12.50	25.00
NOT WITH MY WIFE, YOU DON'T				
❑ Warner Bros. W 1668 [M]	1966	3.75	7.50	15.00
❑ Warner Bros. WS 1668 [S]	1966	5.00	10.00	20.00
NOTHING BUT THE BEST				
❑ Colpix CP-477 [M]	1964	5.00	10.00	20.00
❑ Colpix SCP-477 [S]	1964	6.25	12.50	25.00
A NUN'S STORY				
❑ Warner Bros. B 1306 [M]	1959	15.00	30.00	60.00
❑ Warner Bros. BS 1306 [S]	1959	25.00	50.00	100.00
THE ODD COUPLE				
❑ Dot DLP-25862	1968	5.00	10.00	20.00
ODDS AGAINST TOMORROW				
❑ United Artists UAL-4061 [M]	1959	7.50	15.00	30.00
❑ United Artists UAS-5061 [S]	1959	12.50	25.00	50.00
OF LOVE AND DESIRE				
❑ 20th Century Fox FXG-5014 [M]	1963	6.25	12.50	25.00
❑ 20th Century Fox SXG-5014 [S]	1963	7.50	15.00	30.00
OH DAD, POOR DAD, MAMMA'S HUNG YOU IN THE CLOSET AND I'M FEELIN' SO SAD				
❑ RCA Victor LPM-3750 [M]	1967	5.00	10.00	20.00
❑ RCA Victor LSP-3750 [S]	1967	6.25	12.50	25.00
OH, ROSALINDA!				
❑ Mercury MG-20145 [M]	1957	12.50	25.00	50.00
OIL TOWN, U.S.A.				
❑ RCA Victor LFM-2000 [10]	1953	15.00	30.00	60.00
OKLAHOMA!				
❑ Capitol SWAO 595 [S]	1959	5.00	10.00	20.00
—Black colorband label, logo at left				
❑ Capitol SWAO 595 [S]	1962	3.75	7.50	15.00
—Black colorband label, logo at top				
❑ Capitol SWAO 595 [S]	1969	3.00	6.00	12.00
—Lime green label				
❑ Capitol SWAO 595 [S]	1973	2.50	5.00	10.00
—Orange label				
❑ Capitol WAO 595 [M]	1955	6.25	12.50	25.00
—Purple or dark red label				
❑ Capitol WAO 595 [M]	1956	5.00	10.00	20.00
—Gray label				
❑ Capitol WAO 595 [M]	1959	3.75	7.50	15.00
—Black colorband label, logo at left				
❑ Capitol WAO 595 [M]	1962	3.00	6.00	12.00
—Black colorband label, logo at top				
THE OLD MAN AND THE SEA				
❑ Columbia CL 1183 [M]	1958	7.50	15.00	30.00
❑ Columbia CS 8013 [S]	1958	15.00	30.00	60.00

Number Title	Yr	VG	VG+	NM
OLD YELLER				
❏ Disneyland 1024 [M]	1974	6.25	12.50	25.00
—Reissue with no prefix				
❏ Disneyland WDL-1024 [M]	1960	10.00	20.00	40.00
—Second edition				
❏ Disneyland WDL-3024 [M]	1957	12.50	25.00	50.00
—First edition				
ON HER MAJESTY'S SECRET SERVICE				
❏ United Artists UA-LA299-G	1974	3.00	6.00	12.00
—Reissue of 5204				
❏ United Artists UAS-5204	1969	5.00	10.00	20.00
ON THE BEACH				
❏ Roulette R-25098 [M]	1959	20.00	40.00	80.00
❏ Roulette SR-25098 [S]	1959	37.50	75.00	150.00
ONCE UPON A TIME IN THE WEST				
❏ RCA Victor LSP-4736	1969	7.50	15.00	30.00
THE ONE AND ONLY, GENUINE, ORIGINAL FAMILY BAND				
❏ Buena Vista BV-5002 [M]	1968	3.75	7.50	15.00
❏ Buena Vista STER-5002 [S]	1968	5.00	10.00	20.00
ONE FLEW OVER THE CUCKOO'S NEST				
❏ Fantasy MPF-4531	198?	2.50	5.00	10.00
—Budget-line reissue of 9500				
❏ Fantasy F-9500	1975	5.00	10.00	20.00
101 DALMATIONS				
❏ Disneyland DQ-1308 [M]	1966	5.00	10.00	20.00
❏ Disneyland ST-1908 [M]	1960	6.25	12.50	25.00
❏ Disneyland ST-3931 [M]	1965	10.00	20.00	40.00
❏ Disneyland ST-4903 [M]	1963	37.50	75.00	150.00
—Gatefold cover with pop-up scene in center				
THE ONE-EYED JACKS				
❏ Liberty LOM-16001 [M]	1961	7.50	15.00	30.00
❏ Liberty LOS-17001 [S]	1961	12.50	25.00	50.00
THE OPTIMISTS				
❏ Paramount PAS-1015	1973	7.50	15.00	30.00
ORCHESTRA WIVES				
❏ RCA Victor LPT-3065 [10]	1954	15.00	30.00	60.00
THE OSCAR				
❏ Columbia Masterworks OS 2950 [S]	1966	6.25	12.50	25.00
❏ Columbia Masterworks OL 6550 [M]	1966	5.00	10.00	20.00
OTLEY				
❏ Colgems COS-112	1969	7.50	15.00	30.00
OUR MAN FLINT				
❏ 20th Century Fox TFM-3179 [M]	1966	10.00	20.00	40.00
❏ 20th Century Fox TFS-4179 [S]	1966	15.00	30.00	60.00
OUT OF SIGHT				
❏ Decca DL 4751 [M]	1966	5.00	10.00	20.00
❏ Decca DL 74751 [S]	1966	6.25	12.50	25.00
THE OUTLAW RIDERS				
❏ MGM 1SE-26	1970	5.00	10.00	20.00
PAGAN LOVE SONG				
❏ MGM E-534 [M]	1950	10.00	20.00	40.00
PAINT YOUR WAGON				
❏ Paramount PMS-1001	1969	5.00	10.00	20.00
—With booklet				
THE PAJAMA GAME				
❏ Columbia Masterworks OL 5210 [M]	1957	7.50	15.00	30.00
—Gray and black label with six "eye" logos				
PAL JOEY				
❏ Capitol DW 912 [R]	196?	2.50	5.00	10.00
—Black colorband label				
❏ Capitol W 912 [M]	1957	5.00	10.00	20.00
—Gray label				
❏ Capitol W 912 [M]	1959	3.75	7.50	15.00
—Black colorband label, logo at left				
❏ Capitol W 912 [M]	1962	3.00	6.00	12.00
—Black colorband label, logo on top				
PANIC BUTTON				
❏ Musicor MM-2026 [M]	1964	20.00	40.00	80.00
❏ Musicor MS-3026 [S]	1964	30.00	60.00	120.00
PAPER MOON				
❏ Paramount PAS-1012	1973	5.00	10.00	20.00
PAPER TIGER				
❏ Capitol SW-11475	1975	5.00	10.00	20.00

Number Title	Yr	VG	VG+	NM
PAPILLON				
❏ Capitol ST-11260	1973	5.00	10.00	20.00
THE PARENT TRAP!				
❏ Buena Vista BV-3309 [M]	1961	10.00	20.00	40.00
❏ Buena Vista STER-3309 [S]	1961	15.00	30.00	60.00
—B-side of the above two: Camerata Conducts Themes from Great Motion Pictures				
PARIS BLUES				
❏ United Artists UAL-4092 [M]	1961	6.25	12.50	25.00
❏ United Artists UAS-5092 [S]	1961	7.50	15.00	30.00
PARIS HOLIDAY				
❏ United Artists UAL-4001 [M]	1958	12.50	25.00	50.00
PARIS WHEN IT SIZZLES				
❏ Reprise R 6113 [M]	1964	6.25	12.50	25.00
❏ Reprise RS 6113 [S]	1964	10.00	20.00	40.00
PARRISH				
❏ Warner Bros. W 1413 [M]	1961	7.50	15.00	30.00
❏ Warner Bros. WS 1413 [S]	1961	20.00	40.00	80.00
—B-side of the above two: Popular Piano Concertos by George Greeley				
A PATCH OF BLUE				
❏ Mainstream S-6068 [S]	1965	6.25	12.50	25.00
❏ Mainstream 56068 [M]	1965	5.00	10.00	20.00
❏ Mainstream ST-90805 [S]	1965	7.50	15.00	30.00
—Capitol Record Club edition				
PATTON				
❏ 20th Century Fox S-4208	1970	5.00	10.00	20.00
PENELOPE				
❏ MGM E-4426 [M]	1966	5.00	10.00	20.00
❏ MGM SE-4426 [S]	1966	7.50	15.00	30.00
PENTHOUSE				
❏ United Artists UAL-4170 [M]	1967	5.00	10.00	20.00
❏ United Artists UAS-5170 [S]	1967	5.00	10.00	20.00
THE PEOPLE NEXT DOOR				
❏ Avco AV-11002	1970	6.25	12.50	25.00
PEPE				
❏ Colpix CP-507 [M]	1960	5.00	10.00	20.00
❏ Colpix SCP-507 [S]	1960	6.25	12.50	25.00
PERFORMANCE				
❏ Warner Bros. WS 1846	1970	375.00	750.00	1500.
—Original issue; has a completely different cover to the more common 2554				
❏ Warner Bros. BS 2554	1970	5.00	10.00	20.00
—Second issue				
PETE KELLY'S BLUES				
❏ Columbia CL 690 [M]	1955	10.00	20.00	40.00
❏ Decca DL 8166 [M]	1955	12.50	25.00	50.00
—Black label, silver print				
PETULIA				
❏ Warner Bros. WS 1755	1968	6.25	12.50	25.00
PEYTON PLACE				
❏ RCA Victor LOC-1042 [M]	1958	7.50	15.00	30.00
—"Long Play" at bottom of label				
❏ RCA Victor LOC-1042 [M]	1965	6.25	12.50	25.00
—"Monaural" at bottom of label				
❏ RCA Victor LSO-1042 [S]	1958	25.00	50.00	100.00
—"Living Stereo" at bottom of label				
❏ RCA Victor LSO-1042 [S]	1965	15.00	30.00	60.00
—"Stereo" at bottom of label				
PHAEDRA				
❏ United Artists UAL-4102 [M]	1962	5.00	10.00	20.00
❏ United Artists UAS-5102 [S]	1962	7.50	15.00	30.00
PICNIC				
❏ Decca DL 8320 [M]	1956	7.50	15.00	30.00
—Black label, silver print				
❏ Decca DL 8320 [M]	196?	3.75	7.50	15.00
—Black label with color bars				
❏ Decca DL 78320 [S]	1959	7.50	15.00	30.00
—Maroon or all-black label				
❏ Decca DL 78320 [S]	196?	3.75	7.50	15.00
—Black label with color bars				
❏ MCA 2049	1973	2.50	5.00	10.00
—Reissue of Decca 78320; black label with rainbow				
PINOCCHIO				
❏ Disneyland DQ-1202 [M]	1959	7.50	15.00	30.00
—Second edition				
❏ Disneyland DQ-1202MO [M]	1963	5.00	10.00	20.00
—Third edition				
❏ Disneyland WDL-4002 [M]	1956	62.50	125.00	250.00
—Original edition				
❏ Disneyland ST-4905 [M]	1963	37.50	75.00	150.00
—Gatefold cover with pop-up center graphics				

Number Title	Yr	VG	VG+	NM
THE PIRATE				
❑ MGM E-21 [10]	1951	17.50	35.00	70.00
PLANET OF THE APES				
❑ Project 3 PR-5023 SD	1968	5.00	10.00	20.00
—Regular cover				
❑ Project 3 PR-5023 SD	1968	7.50	15.00	30.00
—Gatefold cover				
THE PLEASURE SEEKERS				
❑ RCA Victor LOC-1101 [M]	1964	12.50	25.00	50.00
❑ RCA Victor LSO-1101 [S]	1964	25.00	50.00	100.00
POLLYANNA				
❑ Disneyland DQ-1307 [M]	1967	6.25	12.50	25.00
❑ Disneyland ST-1906 [M]	1960	12.50	25.00	50.00
PORGY AND BESS				
❑ Columbia Masterworks OS 2016 [S]	1959	5.00	10.00	20.00
❑ Columbia Masterworks OL 5410 [M]	1959	3.75	7.50	15.00
PRETTY BOY FLOYD				
❑ Audio Fidelity AFLP-1936 [M]	1960	15.00	30.00	60.00
❑ Audio Fidelity AFSD-5936 [S]	1960	20.00	40.00	80.00
THE PRIDE AND THE PASSION				
❑ Capitol W 873 [M]	1957	15.00	30.00	60.00
THE PRISONER OF ZENDA				
❑ United Artists UA-LA374-G	1974	5.00	10.00	20.00
PRIVATE HELL 36				
❑ Coral CRL 56122 [10]	1954	25.00	50.00	100.00
THE PRODUCERS				
❑ RCA Victor ANL1-1132	1975	2.50	5.00	10.00
—Reissue of LSP-4008				
❑ RCA Victor LPM-4008 [M]	1968	12.50	25.00	50.00
❑ RCA Victor LSP-4008 [S]	1968	7.50	15.00	30.00
THE PROFESSIONALS				
❑ Colgems COMO-5001 [M]	1966	15.00	30.00	60.00
❑ Colgems COSO-5001 [S]	1966	37.50	75.00	150.00
A PROMISE AT DAWN				
❑ Polydor 24-5502	1970	7.50	15.00	30.00
THE PROPER TIME				
❑ Contemporary M-3587 [M]	1960	7.50	15.00	30.00
❑ Contemporary S-7587 [S]	1960	10.00	20.00	40.00
PRUDENCE AND THE PILL				
❑ 20th Century Fox S-4199	1968	5.00	10.00	20.00
THE QUIET MAN				
❑ Decca DL 5411 [10]	1952	30.00	60.00	120.00
THE QUILLER MEMORANDUM				
❑ Columbia Masterworks OS 3060 [S]	1966	15.00	30.00	60.00
❑ Columbia Masterworks OL 6660 [M]	1966	7.50	15.00	30.00
QUO VADIS?				
❑ MGM E-103 [10]	1951	10.00	20.00	40.00
—Music soundtrack only				
❑ MGM E-134 [(2)10]	1951	15.00	30.00	60.00
—Box set of two discs; includes dialogue				
❑ MGM E-3524 [M]	1957	6.25	12.50	25.00
—Yellow label; has both music and dialogue				
THE RAILWAY CHILDREN				
❑ Capitol SW-871	1972	5.00	10.00	20.00
THE RAINMAKER				
❑ RCA Victor LPM-1434 [M]	1956	25.00	50.00	100.00
RAINTREE COUNTY				
❑ RCA Victor LOC-1038 [M]	1958	7.50	15.00	30.00
❑ RCA Victor LSO-1038 [S]	1958	12.50	25.00	50.00
❑ RCA Victor LOC-6000 [(2)M]	1957	30.00	60.00	120.00
THE RAT RACE				
❑ Dot DLP-3306 [M]	1960	10.00	20.00	40.00
❑ Dot DLP-25306 [S]	1960	12.50	25.00	50.00
RED GARTERS				
❑ Columbia CL 6282 [10]	1954	12.50	25.00	50.00
THE RED PONY				
❑ Columbia Masterworks ML 5983 [M]	196?	6.25	12.50	25.00
❑ Columbia Masterworks MS 6583 [R]	196?	6.25	12.50	25.00
THE RED TENT				
❑ Paramount PAS-6019	1971	6.25	12.50	25.00
THE REPORTER				
❑ Columbia CL 2269 [M]	1963	7.50	15.00	30.00
❑ Columbia CS 9069 [S]	1963	10.00	20.00	40.00
RETURN TO PARADISE				
❑ Decca DL 5489 [10]	1953	50.00	100.00	200.00
THE REVOLUTION				
❑ United Artists UA-LA296-G	1974	3.00	6.00	12.00
—Reissue of 5185				
❑ United Artists UAS-5185	1968	6.25	12.50	25.00
RHAPSODY OF STEEL				
❑ U.S. Steel JB-502/3	1958	25.00	50.00	100.00
RICH, YOUNG AND PRETTY				
❑ MGM E-86 [10]	1951	10.00	20.00	40.00
RIDER ON THE RAIN				
❑ Capitol ST-584	1970	6.25	12.50	25.00
RIOT ON SUNSET STRIP				
❑ Tower DT 5065 [R]	1967	6.25	12.50	25.00
❑ Tower T 5065 [M]	1967	5.00	10.00	20.00
ROAD TO HONG KONG				
❑ Liberty LOM-16002 [M]	1962	5.00	10.00	20.00
❑ Liberty LOS-17002 [S]	1962	10.00	20.00	40.00
THE ROBE				
❑ Decca DL 9012 [M]	1953	7.50	15.00	30.00
—Maroon label				
❑ Decca DL 79012 [R]	196?	3.00	6.00	12.00
❑ MCA 1529	198?	2.00	4.00	8.00
—Reissue of MCA 2052				
❑ MCA 2052	1973	2.50	5.00	10.00
—Reissue of Decca 79012; black label with rainbow				
ROBIN AND THE SEVEN HOODS				
❑ Reprise F 2021 [M]	1964	12.50	25.00	50.00
❑ Reprise FS 2021 [S]	1964	15.00	30.00	60.00
ROBIN HOOD				
❑ Disneyland ST-3810	1973	6.25	12.50	25.00
ROCK ALL NIGHT				
❑ Mercury MG-20293 [M]	1957	25.00	50.00	100.00
ROCK, PRETTY BABY				
❑ Decca DL 8429 [M]	1957	30.00	60.00	120.00
—Black label, silver print; also includes pink label promo				
❑ Decca DL 8429 [M]	196?	7.50	15.00	30.00
—Black label with color bars				
ROCK, ROCK, ROCK				
❑ (no label) (no #) [M]	1958	375.00	750.00	1500.
—Demo version, 20 tracks				
❑ Chess LP-1425 [M]	1958	50.00	100.00	200.00
ROMANCE OF A HORSETHIEF				
❑ Allied Artists AAS-110-100	1971	12.50	25.00	50.00
ROME ADVENTURE				
❑ Warner Bros. W 1458 [M]	1962	5.00	10.00	20.00
❑ Warner Bros. WS 1458 [S]	1962	6.25	12.50	25.00
ROMEO AND JULIET				
❑ Capitol SWDR-289 [(4)]	1969	7.50	15.00	30.00
—From the 1968 Franco Zeffirelli remake; contains dialogue and music				
❑ Capitol ST-400	1970	3.75	7.50	15.00
—From the 1968 Franco Zeffirelli remake; edited version of 289				
❑ Capitol ST-2993	1968	3.00	6.00	12.00
—From the 1968 Franco Zeffirelli remake; contains the music; black label with colorband				
❑ Epic LC 3126 [M]	1954	15.00	30.00	60.00
❑ Epic FLM 13104 [M]	1966	7.50	15.00	30.00
—Reissue of 3126				
❑ Epic FLS 15104 [R]	1966	6.25	12.50	25.00
ROOTS OF HEAVEN				
❑ 20th Fox FOX-3005 [M]	1958	75.00	150.00	300.00
ROSE MARIE				
❑ MGM E-229 [10]	1954	10.00	20.00	40.00
THE ROSE TATTOO				
❑ Columbia CL 727 [M]	1955	12.50	25.00	50.00
ROSEMARY'S BABY				
❑ Dot DLP-25875	1968	5.00	10.00	20.00
THE ROYAL WEDDING				
❑ MGM E-543 [10]	1951	12.50	25.00	50.00
THE RULING CLASS				
❑ Avco AV-11003	1972	6.25	12.50	25.00
THE RUN OF THE ARROW				
❑ Decca DL 8620 [M]	1957	15.00	30.00	60.00
—Black label, silver print, or pink label, black print promo				
❑ Decca DL 8620 [M]	196?	7.50	15.00	30.00
—Black label with color bars				

Number Title	Yr	VG	VG+	NM
RUN WILD, RUN FREE				
☐ SGC SD 5003	1969	5.00	10.00	20.00
RUN, ANGEL, RUN				
☐ Epic BN 26474	1969	5.00	10.00	20.00
RYAN'S DAUGHTER				
☐ MGM 1SE-27	1970	6.25	12.50	25.00
SACCO AND VANZETTI				
☐ RCA Victor LSP-4612	1971	5.00	10.00	20.00
THE SACRED IDOL				
☐ Capitol ST 1293 [S]	1960	7.50	15.00	30.00
☐ Capitol T 1293 [M]	1960	6.25	12.50	25.00
SAINT JOAN				
☐ Capitol W 865 [M]	1957	7.50	15.00	30.00
SALLAH				
☐ Philips PHM 200177 [M]	1965	5.00	10.00	20.00
☐ Philips PHS 600177 [S]	1965	6.25	12.50	25.00
SALOME				
☐ Decca DL 6026 [10]	1953	30.00	60.00	120.00
SAMSON AND DELILAH				
☐ Decca DL 6007 [10]	1952	15.00	30.00	60.00
THE SAND CASTLE				
☐ Columbia CL 1455 [M]	1961	3.75	7.50	15.00
☐ Columbia CS 8249 [S]	1961	5.00	10.00	20.00
THE SAND PEBBLES				
☐ 20th Century Fox 3189 [M]	1966	7.50	15.00	30.00
☐ 20th Century Fox S-4189 [S]	1966	12.50	25.00	50.00
THE SANDPIPER				
☐ Mercury MG-21032 [M]	1965	6.25	12.50	25.00
☐ Mercury SR-61032 [S]	1965	7.50	15.00	30.00
SANTA AND THE 3 BEARS				
☐ Mr. Pickwick SPC 1501	196?	5.00	10.00	20.00
—With "Santa" cutout intact				
SATAN IN HIGH HEELS				
☐ Charlie Parker PLP-406 [M]	1962	7.50	15.00	30.00
—Standard cover				
☐ Charlie Parker PLP-406 [M]	1962	12.50	25.00	50.00
—Gatefold cover				
☐ Charlie Parker PLP-406S [S]	1962	10.00	20.00	40.00
—Standard cover				
☐ Charlie Parker PLP-406S [S]	1962	15.00	30.00	60.00
—Gatefold cover				
SATAN'S SADISTS				
☐ Smash SRS-67127	1969	7.50	15.00	30.00
THE SAVAGE SEVEN				
☐ Atco 33-245 [M]	1968	7.50	15.00	30.00
☐ Atco SD 33-245 [S]	1968	7.50	15.00	30.00
SAVAGE WILD				
☐ American Int'l. STA-1032	1970	5.00	10.00	20.00
SAY ONE FOR ME				
☐ Columbia CL 1337 [M]	1959	10.00	20.00	40.00
☐ Columbia CS 8147 [S]	1959	20.00	40.00	80.00
SAYONARA				
☐ RCA Victor LOC-1041 [M]	1957	12.50	25.00	50.00
☐ RCA Victor LSO-1041 [S]	1957	17.50	35.00	70.00
THE SCALPHUNTERS				
☐ United Artists UAL-4176 [M]	1968	7.50	15.00	30.00
☐ United Artists UAS-5176 [S]	1968	10.00	20.00	40.00
SCENT OF MYSTERY				
☐ Ramrod ST-6001 [S]	1960	25.00	50.00	100.00
☐ Ramrod T-6001 [M]	1960	12.50	25.00	50.00
SCROOGE				
☐ Columbia Masterworks S 30258	1970	7.50	15.00	30.00
SEARCH FOR PARADISE				
☐ RCA Victor LOC-1034 [M]	1957	10.00	20.00	40.00
SEASIDE SWINGERS				
☐ Mercury MG-21031 [M]	1965	5.00	10.00	20.00
☐ Mercury SR-61031 [S]	1965	6.25	12.50	25.00
SEBASTIAN				
☐ Dot DLP-3845 [M]	1968	12.50	25.00	50.00
☐ Dot DLP-25845 [S]	1968	5.00	10.00	20.00

Number Title	Yr	VG	VG+	NM
THE SECRET OF SANTA VITTORIA				
☐ United Artists UAS-5200	1969	7.50	15.00	30.00
SERGEANTS 3				
☐ Reprise R-2013 [M]	1962	7.50	15.00	30.00
☐ Reprise RS-2013 [S]	1962	12.50	25.00	50.00
SERPICO				
☐ Paramount PAS-1016	1973	6.25	12.50	25.00
SEVEN BRIDES FOR SEVEN BROTHERS				
☐ MGM E-244 [10]	1954	10.00	20.00	40.00
SEVEN GOLDEN MEN				
☐ United Artists UAS-5193	1969	6.25	12.50	25.00
THE SEVEN LITTLE FOYS				
☐ RCA Victor LPM-3275 [10]	1955	17.50	35.00	70.00
1776				
☐ Columbia S 31741	1972	5.00	10.00	20.00
THE 7TH DAWN				
☐ United Artists UAL-4115 [M]	1964	7.50	15.00	30.00
☐ United Artists UAS-5115 [S]	1964	10.00	20.00	40.00
THE 7TH VOYAGE OF SINBAD				
☐ Colpix CP-504 [M]	1958	50.00	100.00	200.00
SEX AND THE SINGLE GIRL				
☐ Warner Bros. W 1572 [M]	1964	3.75	7.50	15.00
☐ Warner Bros. WS 1572 [S]	1964	5.00	10.00	20.00
SHAFT IN AFRICA				
☐ ABC ABCX-793	1973	7.50	15.00	30.00
SHAFT'S BIG SCORE				
☐ MGM 1SE-36	1972	7.50	15.00	30.00
SHAKE HANDS WITH THE DEVIL				
☐ United Artists UAL-4043 [M]	1959	7.50	15.00	30.00
☐ United Artists UAS-5043 [S]	1959	12.50	25.00	50.00
SHALAKO				
☐ Philips PHS 600286	1968	7.50	15.00	30.00
SHEBA BABY				
☐ Buddah BDS-5634	1975	7.50	15.00	30.00
SHENANDOAH				
☐ Decca DL 9125 [M]	1965	7.50	15.00	30.00
☐ Decca DL 79125 [S]	1965	10.00	20.00	40.00
THE SHOP ON MAIN STREET				
☐ Mainstream S-6082 [S]	1966	10.00	20.00	40.00
☐ Mainstream 56082 [M]	1966	6.25	12.50	25.00
SHOW BOAT				
☐ MGM E-559 [10]	1951	7.50	15.00	30.00
THE SICILIAN CLAN				
☐ 20th Century Fox S-4209	1970	12.50	25.00	50.00
THE SIDEHACKERS				
☐ Amaret ST-5004	1969	5.00	10.00	20.00
THE SILENCERS				
☐ RCA Victor LOC-1120 [M]	1966	7.50	15.00	30.00
☐ RCA Victor LSO-1120 [S]	1966	12.50	25.00	50.00
SILENT RUNNING				
☐ Decca DL 79188	1972	10.00	20.00	40.00
SILK STOCKINGS				
☐ MGM E-3542 [M]	1957	7.50	15.00	30.00
SINGIN' IN THE RAIN				
☐ MCA 39044	198?	2.50	5.00	10.00
☐ Metro M-599 [M]	1966	3.75	7.50	15.00
—Reissue of MGM LP				
☐ Metro MS-599 [R]	1966	3.00	6.00	12.00
☐ MGM E-113 [10]	1952	7.50	15.00	30.00
SINGLE ROOM FURNISHED				
☐ Sidewalk ST-5917	1968	10.00	20.00	40.00
THE 633 SQUADRON				
☐ United Artists UA-LA305-G	1974	6.25	12.50	25.00
SKATEDANCER				
☐ Mira LP-3004 [M]	1966	5.00	10.00	20.00
☐ Mira LPS-3004 [S]	1966	6.25	12.50	25.00

Number Title	Yr	VG	VG+	NM
SKI ON THE WILD SIDE				
❏ MGM E-4439 [M]	1967	7.50	15.00	30.00
❏ MGM SE-4439 [S]	1967	12.50	25.00	50.00
SLAUGHTER ON 10TH AVENUE				
❏ Decca DL 8657 [M]	1957	6.25	12.50	25.00
—Black label, silver print				
❏ Decca DL 8657 [M]	1960	3.00	6.00	12.00
—Black label with color bars				
❏ Decca DL 78657 [S]	1957	7.50	15.00	30.00
—Black label, silver print				
❏ Decca DL 78657 [S]	1960	3.75	7.50	15.00
—Black label with color bars				
SLAUGHTERHOUSE-FIVE				
❏ Columbia Masterworks S 31333	1972	6.25	12.50	25.00
THE SLAVE TRADE IN THE WORLD TODAY				
❏ London M-76006 [M]	1964	50.00	100.00	200.00
SLAVES				
❏ Skye SK-11	1969	6.25	12.50	25.00
SLEEPING BEAUTY				
❏ Disneyland STER-4018 [S]	1959	10.00	20.00	40.00
❏ Disneyland WDL-4018 [M]	1959	7.50	15.00	30.00
❏ Disneyland STER-4036 [S]	1970	5.00	10.00	20.00
—Reissue of STER-4018				
SLEUTH				
❏ Columbia Masterworks S 32154	1973	5.00	10.00	20.00
SLIPPERY WHEN WET				
❏ World Pacific WP-1265 [M]	1959	12.50	25.00	50.00
A SMASHING TIME				
❏ ABC ABC-OC-6 [M]	1967	5.00	10.00	20.00
❏ ABC ABCS-OC-6 [S]	1967	6.25	12.50	25.00
❏ ABC SW-91399 [S]	1967	6.25	12.50	25.00
—Capitol Record Club edition				
SNOOPY COME HOME				
❏ Columbia Masterworks S 31451	1972	5.00	10.00	20.00
THE SNOW QUEEN				
❏ Decca DL 8977 [M]	1959	10.00	20.00	40.00
❏ Decca DL 78977 [S]	1959	15.00	30.00	60.00
SNOW WHITE AND THE SEVEN DWARFS				
❏ Buena Vista 102 [(3)]	1975	12.50	25.00	50.00
—Entire movie on three LPs; TV mail-order item				
❏ Disneyland DQ-1201 [M]	1959	12.50	25.00	50.00
—Reissue of 4005; whirlpool-like designs on cover				
❏ Disneyland DQ-1201 [M]	1968	6.25	12.50	25.00
—Reissue; with same cover as 4005, but no gatefold				
❏ Disneyland WDL-4005 [M]	1956	50.00	100.00	200.00
—Gatefold cover				
SNOW WHITE AND THE THREE STOOGES				
❏ Columbia CL 1650 [M]	1961	15.00	30.00	60.00
❏ Columbia CS 8450 [S]	1961	25.00	50.00	100.00
SO THIS IS LOVE				
❏ RCA Victor LOC-3000 [10]	1953	20.00	40.00	80.00
SO THIS IS PARIS				
❏ Decca DL 5553 [10]	1955	12.50	25.00	50.00
SODOM AND GOMORRAH				
❏ RCA Victor LOC-1076 [M]	1963	20.00	40.00	80.00
❏ RCA Victor LSO-1076 [S]	1963	25.00	50.00	100.00
SOL MADRID				
❏ MGM SE-4541 ST	1968	7.50	15.00	30.00
SOLOMON AND SHEBA				
❏ United Artists UAL-4051 [M]	1959	6.25	12.50	25.00
—Second, regular cover				
❏ United Artists UAL-4051 [M]	1959	12.50	25.00	50.00
—First cover with silky finish				
❏ United Artists UAS-5051 [S]	1959	15.00	30.00	60.00
—Second, regular cover				
❏ United Artists UAS-5051 [S]	1959	30.00	60.00	120.00
—First cover with silky finish				
SOME CAME RUNNING				
❏ Capitol SW 1109 [S]	1958	20.00	40.00	80.00
❏ Capitol W 1109 [M]	1958	7.50	15.00	30.00
SOME LIKE IT HOT				
❏ United Artists UA-LA272-G	1974	3.00	6.00	12.00
—Reissue of 5030				
❏ United Artists UAL-4030 [M]	1959	12.50	25.00	50.00
❏ United Artists UAS-5030 [S]	1959	18.75	37.50	75.00

Number Title	Yr	VG	VG+	NM
SOMEBODY LOVES ME				
❏ RCA Victor LPM-3097 [10]	1952	12.50	25.00	50.00
SONG OF THE SOUTH				
❏ Disneyland WDL-4001 [M]	1956	75.00	150.00	300.00
—Yellow label (first pressing)				
❏ Disneyland WDL-4001 [M]	1957	50.00	100.00	200.00
—Red/maroon label (second pressing)				
SONG OF THE SOUTH (UNCLE REMUS)				
❏ Disneyland DQ-1205 [M]	1959	6.25	12.50	25.00
SONG WITHOUT END				
❏ Colpix CP-506 [M]	1960	5.00	10.00	20.00
❏ Colpix SCP-506 [S]	1960	6.25	12.50	25.00
THE SONS OF KATIE ELDER				
❏ Columbia Masterworks OS 2820 [S]	1965	25.00	50.00	100.00
❏ Columbia Masterworks OL 6420 [M]	1965	12.50	25.00	50.00
THE SOUL OF NIGGER CHARLEY				
❏ MGM 1SE-46	1973	5.00	10.00	20.00
THE SOUND AND THE FURY				
❏ Decca DL 8885 [M]	1959	7.50	15.00	30.00
❏ Decca DL 78885 [S]	1959	17.50	35.00	70.00
THE SOUND OF MUSIC				
❏ RCA Victor LOCD-2005 [M]	1965	3.00	6.00	12.00
—With booklet; back cover lists "I Have Confidence" correctly				
❏ RCA Victor LOCD-2005 [M]	1965	3.75	7.50	15.00
—With booklet; back cover lists "I Have Confidence" as "I Have Confidence in Me"				
❏ RCA Victor LSOD-2005 [S]	1965	3.75	7.50	15.00
—With booklet; back cover lists "I Have Confidence" correctly				
❏ RCA Victor LSOD-2005 [S]	1965	5.00	10.00	20.00
—With booklet; back cover lists "I Have Confidence" as "I Have Confidence in Me"				
❏ RCA Victor LSOD-2005 [S]	1969	3.00	6.00	12.00
—No booklet; gatefold cover, record comes out from inside; orange or tan label				
❏ RCA Victor LSOD-2005 [S]	1977	2.50	5.00	10.00
—Gatefold cover, record comes out from outside; black label with dog at 1 o'clock				
SOUTH PACIFIC				
❏ RCA Victor LOC-1032 [M]	1958	5.00	10.00	20.00
—"Long Play" on label; no "Academy Award Winner" on front cover				
❏ RCA Victor LOC-1032 [M]	196?	3.00	6.00	12.00
—"Long Play" or "Mono" on label; with "Academy Award Winner" on front cover				
❏ RCA Victor LSO-1032 [S]	1958	3.00	6.00	12.00
—Orange label				
❏ RCA Victor LSO-1032 [S]	1958	6.25	12.50	25.00
—"Living Stereo" on label; no "Academy Award Winner" on front cover				
❏ RCA Victor LSO-1032 [S]	196?	3.75	7.50	15.00
—"Living Stereo" or "Stereo" on black label; with "Academy Award Winner" on front cover				
❏ RCA Victor LOCD-2000 [M]	1958	10.00	20.00	40.00
—Gatefold cover with photos inside				
SOUTHERN STAR				
❏ Colgems COSO-5009	1969	15.00	30.00	60.00
A SPANISH AFFAIR				
❏ Dot DLP-3078 [M]	1958	25.00	50.00	100.00
SPARTACUS				
❏ Decca DL 9092 [M]	1960	5.00	10.00	20.00
—Black label, silver print				
❏ Decca DL 9092 [M]	1961	3.00	6.00	12.00
—Black label with color bars				
❏ Decca DL 79092 [S]	1960	6.25	12.50	25.00
—Maroon label, silver print				
❏ Decca DL 79092 [S]	1961	3.75	7.50	15.00
—Black label with color bars				
❏ MCA 2068	1973	3.00	6.00	12.00
—Reissue of 79092; black label with rainbow				
THE SPIRIT OF ST. LOUIS				
❏ RCA Victor LPM-1472 [M]	1957	12.50	25.00	50.00
THE SPY WHO CAME IN FROM THE COLD				
❏ RCA Victor LOC-1118 [M]	1965	5.00	10.00	20.00
❏ RCA Victor LSO-1118 [S]	1965	10.00	20.00	40.00
THE SPY WITH A COLD NOSE				
❏ Columbia Masterworks OS 3070 [S]	1966	7.50	15.00	30.00
❏ Columbia Masterworks OL 6670 [M]	1966	5.00	10.00	20.00
ST. LOUIS BLUES				
❏ Capitol W 993 [M]	1958	12.50	25.00	50.00
—Turquoise or gray label				
❏ Capitol W 993 [M]	1959	6.25	12.50	25.00
—Black colorband label, logo at left				
❏ Capitol W 993 [M]	196?	5.00	10.00	20.00
—Black colorband label, logo at top				
ST. LOUIS WOMAN				
❏ Capitol L 355 [10]	1955	20.00	40.00	80.00
STAGECOACH				
❏ Mainstream S-6077 [S]	1966	7.50	15.00	30.00
❏ Mainstream 56077 [M]	1966	5.00	10.00	20.00

Number Title	Yr	VG	VG+	NM
☐ Mainstream ST-90802 [S]	1966	7.50	15.00	30.00
—Capitol Record Club edition				
☐ Mainstream T-90802 [M]	1966	6.25	12.50	25.00
—Capitol Record Club edition				
STAR!				
☐ 20th Century Fox DTCS-5102	1968	5.00	10.00	20.00
THE STARS AND STRIPES FOREVER				
☐ MGM E-176 [10]	1952	7.50	15.00	30.00
STATE FAIR				
☐ Dot DLP-9011 [M]	1962	6.25	12.50	25.00
☐ Dot DLP-29011 [S]	1962	7.50	15.00	30.00
THE STERILE CUCKOO				
☐ Paramount PAS-5009	1970	5.00	10.00	20.00
STILETTO				
☐ Columbia Masterworks OS 3360	1969	5.00	10.00	20.00
THE STING				
☐ MCA 390	1973	3.00	6.00	12.00
—Original edition				
THE STRANGE ONE				
☐ Coral CRL 57132 [M]	1957	17.50	35.00	70.00
THE STRAWBERRY STATEMENT				
☐ MGM 2SE-14 [(2)]	1970	6.25	12.50	25.00
A STREETCAR NAMED DESIRE				
☐ Capitol L 289 [10]	1951	12.50	25.00	50.00
A STUDY IN TERROR				
☐ Roulette OS-801 [M]	1965	10.00	20.00	40.00
☐ Roulette OSS-801 [S]	1965	20.00	40.00	80.00
THE SUBTERRANEANS				
☐ MGM E-3812 ST [M]	1960	10.00	20.00	40.00
☐ MGM SE-3812 ST [S]	1960	20.00	40.00	80.00
SUMMER AND SMOKE				
☐ RCA Victor LOC-1067 [M]	1961	12.50	25.00	50.00
☐ RCA Victor LSO-1067 [S]	1961	17.50	35.00	70.00
SUMMER HOLIDAY				
☐ Epic LN 24063 [M]	1963	6.25	12.50	25.00
☐ Epic BN 26063 [S]	1963	7.50	15.00	30.00
SUMMER LOVE				
☐ Decca DL 8714 [M]	1958	15.00	30.00	60.00
—Black label, silver print, or pink label, black print promo				
☐ Decca DL 8714 [M]	196?	7.50	15.00	30.00
—Black label with color bars				
SUMMER MAGIC				
☐ Buena Vista BV-4025 [M]	1963	10.00	20.00	40.00
☐ Buena Vista STER-4025 [S]	1963	15.00	30.00	60.00
SUMMER STOCK				
☐ MGM E-519 [10]	1950	10.00	20.00	40.00
THE SUN ALSO RISES				
☐ Kapp KDL-7001 [M]	1957	15.00	30.00	60.00
SUN VALLEY SERENADE				
☐ RCA Victor LPT-3064 [10]	1954	15.00	30.00	60.00
THE SUNNY SIDE OF THE STREET				
☐ Mercury MG-25100 [10]	1951	15.00	30.00	60.00
SURF PARTY				
☐ 20th Century Fox TFM-3131 [M]	1964	6.25	12.50	25.00
☐ 20th Century Fox TFS-4131 [S]	1964	7.50	15.00	30.00
THE SWAN				
☐ MGM E-3399 [M]	1956	17.50	35.00	70.00
SWEDISH HEAVEN AND HELL				
☐ Ariel ARS-15000	1969	6.25	12.50	25.00
SWEET CHARITY				
☐ Decca DL 71502	1969	5.00	10.00	20.00
SWEET LOVE, BITTER				
☐ ABC Impulse! AS-9141 [S]	1968	3.75	7.50	15.00
☐ Impulse! A-9141 [M]	1967	10.00	20.00	40.00
☐ Impulse! AS-9141 [S]	1967	7.50	15.00	30.00
THE SWEET RIDE				
☐ 20th Century Fox S-4198	1968	5.00	10.00	20.00
THE SWEET SMELL OF SUCCESS				
☐ Decca DL 8610 [M]	1957	15.00	30.00	60.00

Number Title	Yr	VG	VG+	NM
SWEET SWEETBACK'S BADASSSSSS SONG				
☐ Stax STS-3001	1971	7.50	15.00	30.00
SWEPT AWAY				
☐ Peters International PLD 1005	1957	10.00	20.00	40.00
THE SWIMMER				
☐ Columbia Masterworks OS 3210	1968	6.25	12.50	25.00
SWINGER'S PARADISE				
☐ Epic LN 24145 [M]	1965	5.00	10.00	20.00
☐ Epic BN 26145 [S]	1965	6.25	12.50	25.00
A SWINGIN' SUMMER				
☐ Hanna-Barbera HLP-8500 [M]	1966	6.25	12.50	25.00
☐ Hanna-Barbera HST-9500 [S]	1966	7.50	15.00	30.00
SYLVIA				
☐ Mercury MG-21004 [M]	1965	5.00	10.00	20.00
☐ Mercury SR-61004 [S]	1965	7.50	15.00	30.00
TARAS BULBA				
☐ United Artists UAL-4100 [M]	1962	7.50	15.00	30.00
☐ United Artists UAS-5100 [S]	1962	12.50	25.00	50.00
TEENAGE REBELLION				
☐ Sidewalk ST-5903 [S]	1967	6.25	12.50	25.00
☐ Sidewalk T-5903 [M]	1967	5.00	10.00	20.00
TELL ME THAT YOU LOVE ME, JUNIE MOON				
☐ Columbia Masterworks OS 3540	1970	5.00	10.00	20.00
THE TEN COMMANDMENTS				
☐ Dot DLP-3054 [M]	1956	10.00	20.00	40.00
☐ Dot DLP-25054 [S]	1959	6.25	12.50	25.00
—Re-recording of the original soundtrack in stereo				
☐ Paramount PAS-1006 [(2)]	1973	5.00	10.00	20.00
—Reissue of Dot 25054				
TENDER IS THE NIGHT				
☐ 20th Century Fox FOX-3054 [M]	1962	37.50	75.00	150.00
☐ 20th Century Fox SFX-3054 [S]	1962	50.00	100.00	200.00
THE TENTH VICTIM				
☐ Mainstream S-6071 [S]	1965	12.50	25.00	50.00
☐ Mainstream 56071 [M]	1965	10.00	20.00	40.00
THAT DARN CAT				
☐ Buena Vista BV-3334 [M]	1965	5.00	10.00	20.00
☐ Buena Vista STER-3334 [S]	1965	6.25	12.50	25.00
THAT MAN IN ISTANBUL				
☐ Mainstream S-6072 [S]	1966	6.25	12.50	25.00
☐ Mainstream 56072 [M]	1966	5.00	10.00	20.00
THERE'S NO BUSINESS LIKE SHOW BUSINESS				
☐ Decca DL 8091 [M]	1954	7.50	15.00	30.00
—Black label with silver print				
☐ Decca DL 8091 [M]	196?	5.00	10.00	20.00
—Black label with color bars				
THEY SHOOT HORSES, DON'T THEY?				
☐ ABC ABCS-OC-10	1969	5.00	10.00	20.00
THIS COULD BE THE NIGHT				
☐ MGM E-3530 [M]	1957	12.50	25.00	50.00
THIS EARTH IS MINE				
☐ Decca DL 8915 [M]	1959	20.00	40.00	80.00
☐ Decca DL 78915 [S]	1959	25.00	50.00	100.00
THIS PROPERTY IS CONDEMNED				
☐ Verve V-8664 [M]	1966	5.00	10.00	20.00
☐ Verve V6-8664 [S]	1966	7.50	15.00	30.00
THE THOMAS CROWN AFFAIR				
☐ United Artists UA-LA295-G	1974	3.00	6.00	12.00
—Reissue of 5182				
☐ United Artists UAS-5182	1968	5.00	10.00	20.00
THOROUGHLY MODERN MILLIE				
☐ Decca DL 1500 [M]	1967	5.00	10.00	20.00
—With bound-in booklet				
☐ Decca DL 71500 [S]	1967	5.00	10.00	20.00
—With bound-in booklet				
THOSE GLORIOUS MGM MUSICALS: DEEP IN MY HEART/WORDS AND MUSIC				
☐ MGM 2-SES-54-ST [(2)]	1973	5.00	10.00	20.00
THOSE GLORIOUS MGM MUSICALS: EVERYTHING I HAVE IS YOURS/ SUMMER STOCK/I LOVE MELVIN				
☐ MGM 2-SES-52-ST [(2)]	1973	5.00	10.00	20.00

Number	Title	Yr	VG	VG+	NM
THOSE GLORIOUS MGM MUSICALS: GOOD NEWS/IN THE GOOD OLD SUMMERTIME/TWO WEEKS WITH LOVE					
☐ MGM 2-SES-49-ST [(2)]		1973	5.00	10.00	20.00
THOSE GLORIOUS MGM MUSICALS: LOVELY TO LOOK AT/ BRIGADOON					
☐ MGM 2-SES-50-ST [(2)]		1973	5.00	10.00	20.00
THOSE GLORIOUS MGM MUSICALS: NANCY GOES TO RIO/RICH, YOUNG AND PRETTY/ROYAL WEDDING					
☐ MGM 2-SES-53-ST [(2)]		1973	5.00	10.00	20.00
THOSE GLORIOUS MGM MUSICALS: ROSE MARIE/SEVN BRIDES FOR SEVEN BROTHERS					
☐ MGM 2-SES-41-ST [(2)]		1973	5.00	10.00	20.00
THOSE GLORIOUS MGM MUSICALS: SHOW BOAT/ANNIE GET YOUR GUN					
☐ MGM 2-SES-42-ST [(2)]		1973	5.00	10.00	20.00
THOSE GLORIOUS MGM MUSICALS: SINGIN' IN THE RAIN/EASTER PARADE					
☐ MGM 2-SES-40-ST [(2)]		1973	5.00	10.00	20.00
THOSE GLORIOUS MGM MUSICALS: THE BAND WAGON/KISS ME, KATE					
☐ MGM 2-SES-44-ST [(2)]		1973	5.00	10.00	20.00
THOSE GLORIOUS MGM MUSICALS: THE BARKLEYS OF BROADWAY/LES GIRLS					
☐ MGM 2-SES-51-ST [(2)]		1973	5.00	10.00	20.00
THOSE GLORIOUS MGM MUSICALS: THE PIRATE/PAGAN LOVE SONG/HIT THE DECK					
☐ MGM 2-SES-43-ST [(2)]		1973	10.00	20.00	40.00
THOSE GLORIOUS MGM MUSICALS: TILL THE CLOUDS ROLL BY/ THREE LITTLE WORDS					
☐ MGM 2-SES-45-ST [(2)]		1973	5.00	10.00	20.00
THREE BITES OF THE APPLE					
☐ MGM E-4444 [M]		1967	6.25	12.50	25.00
☐ MGM SE-4444 [S]		1967	5.00	10.00	20.00
THREE FOR THE SHOW					
☐ Mercury MG-25204 [M]		1955	15.00	30.00	60.00
THREE IN THE ATTIC					
☐ Sidewalk ST-5918		1968	7.50	15.00	30.00
THREE LITTLE WORDS					
☐ MGM E-516 [10]		1959	15.00	30.00	60.00
THE THREE WORLDS OF GULLIVER					
☐ Colpix CP-414 [M]		1960	15.00	30.00	60.00
THE THREEPENNY OPERA					
☐ RCA Victor LOC-1086 [M]		1964	3.75	7.50	15.00
—Reissue cover: White background, orange drawing, Sammy Davis Jr. in foreground, "RE" at bottom					
☐ RCA Victor LOC-1086 [M]		1964	37.50	75.00	150.00
—With rare original cover: White background, pink and black drawing, characters underneath					
☐ RCA Victor LSO-1086 [S]		1964	5.00	10.00	20.00
—Reissue cover: White background, orange drawing, Sammy Davis Jr. in foreground, "RE" at bottom					
☐ RCA Victor LSO-1086 [S]		1964	50.00	100.00	200.00
—With rare original cover: White background, pink and black drawing, characters underneath					
THUNDER ALLEY					
☐ Sidewalk ST-5902 [S]		1967	6.25	12.50	25.00
☐ Sidewalk T-5902 [M]		1967	5.00	10.00	20.00
THUNDERBALL					
☐ United Artists UAL-4132 [M]		1965	5.00	10.00	20.00
☐ United Artists UAS-5132 [S]		1965	7.50	15.00	30.00
☐ United Artists SW-90820 [S]		1965	10.00	20.00	40.00
—Capitol Record Club edition					
TICK...TICK...TICK					
☐ MGM SE-4667 [M]		1970	6.25	12.50	25.00
TILL THE CLOUDS ROLL BY					
☐ Metro M-578 [M]		1966	3.00	6.00	12.00
—Reissue of MGM 501					
☐ Metro MS-578 [R]		1966	2.50	5.00	10.00
☐ MGM E-501 [10]		1950	12.50	25.00	50.00
A TIME TO LOVE AND A TIME TO DIE					
☐ Decca DL 8778 [M]		1958	25.00	50.00	100.00
TO BED... OR NOT TO BED					
☐ London M-76005 [M]		1963	10.00	20.00	40.00
TO KILL A MOCKINGBIRD					
☐ Ava A-20 [M]		1962	6.25	12.50	25.00
☐ Ava AS-20 [S]		1962	7.50	15.00	30.00
TO SIR, WITH LOVE					
☐ Fontana MGF-27569 [M]		1967	5.00	10.00	20.00
☐ Fontana SRF-67569 [S]		1967	6.25	12.50	25.00
TOKYO OLYMPIAD					
☐ Monument MLP-8046 [M]		1966	3.75	7.50	15.00
☐ Monument SLP-18046 [S]		1966	5.00	10.00	20.00
TOM JONES					
☐ United Artists UAL-4113 [M]		1963	5.00	10.00	20.00
☐ United Artists UAS-5113 [S]		1963	6.25	12.50	25.00
TOM SAWYER					
☐ United Artists UA-LA057-F		1973	5.00	10.00	20.00
TOMMY					
☐ Polydor PD 2-9502 [(2)]		1975	5.00	10.00	20.00
TOO MUCH TOO SOON					
☐ Mercury MG-20381 [M]		1958	7.50	15.00	30.00
☐ Mercury SR-60019 [S]		1958	20.00	40.00	80.00
TOPKAPI					
☐ United Artists UAL-4118 [M]		1964	5.00	10.00	20.00
☐ United Artists UAS-5118 [M]		1964	7.50	15.00	30.00
THE TOUCHABLES					
☐ 20th Century Fox S-4206		1969	5.00	10.00	20.00
THE TRAIN					
☐ United Artists UAL-4122 [M]		1965	5.00	10.00	20.00
☐ United Artists UAS-5122 [S]		1965	10.00	20.00	40.00
THE TRAP					
☐ Atco 33-204 [M]		1966	10.00	20.00	40.00
☐ Atco SD 33-204 [S]		1966	17.50	35.00	70.00
TRAPEZE					
☐ Columbia CL 870 [M]		1956	6.25	12.50	25.00
THE TRAPP FAMILY					
☐ 20th Fox FOX-3044 [M]		1961	6.25	12.50	25.00
☐ 20th Fox STX-3044 [S]		1961	10.00	20.00	40.00
THE TREASURE OF SAN GENNARO					
☐ Buddah BDS-5011		1968	10.00	20.00	40.00
THE TRIP					
☐ Sidewalk ST-5908 [S]		1967	10.00	20.00	40.00
☐ Sidewalk T-5908 [M]		1967	7.50	15.00	30.00
TRIPLE CROSS					
☐ United Artists UAL-4162 [M]		1967	5.00	10.00	20.00
☐ United Artists UAS-5162 [S]		1967	7.50	15.00	30.00
THE TROUBLE WITH ANGELS					
☐ Mainstream S-6073 [S]		1966	20.00	40.00	80.00
☐ Mainstream 56073 [M]		1966	10.00	20.00	40.00
TRUE GRIT					
☐ Capitol ST-263		1969	7.50	15.00	30.00
☐ Capitol ST-8-0263		1969	10.00	20.00	40.00
—Capitol Record Club edition					
TRUE LIFE ADVENTURES					
☐ Disneyland WDL-4011 [M]		1957	17.50	35.00	70.00
THE TRUE STORY OF THE CIVIL WAR					
☐ Coral CRL 59100 [M]		1958	20.00	40.00	80.00
TWO MULES FOR SISTER SARA					
☐ Kapp KRS-5512		1970	6.25	12.50	25.00
TWO WEEKS WITH LOVE					
☐ MGM E-530 [10]		1950	10.00	20.00	40.00
ULYSSES					
☐ RCA Victor LOC-1138 [M]		1967	6.25	12.50	25.00
☐ RCA Victor LSO-1138 [S]		1967	7.50	15.00	30.00
THE UMBRELLAS OF CHERBOURG (LES PARAPLUIES DE CHERBOURG)					
☐ Philips PCC 216 [M]		1965	5.00	10.00	20.00
☐ Philips PCC 616 [S]		1965	7.50	15.00	30.00
UNCLE TOM'S CABIN					
☐ Philips PHS 600272		1968	10.00	20.00	40.00
THE UNFORGIVEN					
☐ United Artists UAL-4068 [M]		1960	10.00	20.00	40.00
☐ United Artists UAS-5068 [S]		1960	17.50	35.00	70.00

Number Title	Yr	VG	VG+	NM
THE UNSINKABLE MOLLY BROWN				
❏ MGM E-4232 [M]	1964	3.75	7.50	15.00
❏ MGM SE-4232 [S]	1964	5.00	10.00	20.00
❏ MGM SW-90048 [S]	1964	3.75	7.50	15.00
—Capitol Record Club edition				
❏ MGM W-90048 [M]	1964	3.00	6.00	12.00
—Capitol Record Club edition				
UP IN THE CELLAR				
❏ American Int'l. A-1036	1970	5.00	10.00	20.00
UP THE DOWN STAIRCASE				
❏ United Artists UAL-4169 [M]	1967	5.00	10.00	20.00
❏ United Artists UAS-5169 [S]	1967	10.00	20.00	40.00
UP THE JUNCTION				
❏ Mercury SR-61159	1968	6.25	12.50	25.00
THE V.I.P.S				
❏ MGM E-4184 [M]	1963	5.00	10.00	20.00
❏ MGM SE-4184 [S]	1963	6.25	12.50	25.00
—Music by Bill Evans				
VALLEY OF THE DOLLS				
❏ 20th Century Fox TF-4196 [M]	1968	7.50	15.00	30.00
❏ 20th Century Fox TFS-4196 [S]	1968	7.50	15.00	30.00
❏ 20th Century Fox SW-91374 [S]	1968	7.50	15.00	30.00
—Capitol Record Club edition				
THE VANISHING POINT				
❏ Amos AAS-8002	1971	5.00	10.00	20.00
THE VANISHING PRAIRIE				
❏ Columbia CL 6332 [10]	1954	20.00	40.00	80.00
VERTIGO				
❏ Mercury MG-20384 [M]	1958	37.50	75.00	150.00
THE VICTORS				
❏ Colpix CP-516 [M]	1963	5.00	10.00	20.00
❏ Colpix SCP-516 [S]	1963	7.50	15.00	30.00
THE VIKINGS				
❏ United Artists UAL-4003 [M]	1958	7.50	15.00	30.00
❏ United Artists UAS-5003 [S]	1958	10.00	20.00	40.00
VILLA RIDES!				
❏ Dot DLP-25870	1968	10.00	20.00	40.00
VIVA MARIA!				
❏ United Artists UAL-4135 [M]	1965	5.00	10.00	20.00
❏ United Artists UAS-5135 [S]	1965	7.50	15.00	30.00
VIVA MAX!				
❏ RCA Victor LSP-4275	1969	5.00	10.00	20.00
THE VIXEN				
❏ Beverly Hills BHS-22	1968	12.50	25.00	50.00
VOYAGE EN BALLON				
❏ Philips PHM 200029 [M]	1960	7.50	15.00	30.00
❏ Philips PHS 600029 [S]	1960	10.00	20.00	40.00
W.W. AND THE DIXIE DANCEKINGS				
❏ 20th Century ST-103	1975	6.25	12.50	25.00
WALK DON'T RUN				
❏ Mainstream S-6080 [S]	1966	10.00	20.00	40.00
❏ Mainstream 56080 [M]	1966	5.00	10.00	20.00
WALK ON THE WILD SIDE				
❏ Ava A-4-ST [M]	1962	5.00	10.00	20.00
❏ Ava AS-4-ST [S]	1962	10.00	20.00	40.00
❏ Choreo A-4-ST [M]	1962	7.50	15.00	30.00
❏ Choreo AS-4-ST [S]	1962	12.50	25.00	50.00
WAR AND PEACE				
❏ Columbia CL 930 [M]	1956	6.25	12.50	25.00
❏ Melodiya/Capitol SWAO 2918	1968	10.00	20.00	40.00
THE WAR LORD				
❏ Decca DL 9149 [M]	1965	6.25	12.50	25.00
❏ Decca DL 79149 [S]	1965	12.50	25.00	50.00
WARNING SHOT				
❏ Liberty LRP-3498 [M]	1967	7.50	15.00	30.00
❏ Liberty LST-7498 [S]	1967	10.00	20.00	40.00
WATERLOO				
❏ Paramount PAS-6003	1971	7.50	15.00	30.00
❏ Paramount SW-93703	1971	7.50	15.00	30.00
—Capitol Record Club edition				
WATERMELON MAN				
❏ Beverly Hills BHS-26	1970	7.50	15.00	30.00

Number Title	Yr	VG	VG+	NM
WAY...WAY OUT				
❏ 20th Century Fox 3192 [M]	1966	7.50	15.00	30.00
❏ 20th Century Fox S-4192 [S]	1966	10.00	20.00	40.00
WEDDING IN MONACO				
❏ Mercury MG-20149 [M]	1956	62.50	125.00	250.00
WEST SIDE STORY				
❏ Columbia Masterworks OS 2070 [S]	196?	3.00	6.00	12.00
—Regular cover; gray "360 Sound Stereo" label				
❏ Columbia Masterworks OS 2070 [S]	1961	6.25	12.50	25.00
—Originals have gatefold covers and gray and black labels with six "eye" logos				
❏ Columbia Masterworks OS 2070 [S]	1963	3.75	7.50	15.00
—Gatefold cover; gray "360 Sound Stereo" label				
❏ Columbia Masterworks OS 2070 [S]	1971	2.50	5.00	10.00
—Regular cover; olive label with "Columbia" continuously around edge				
❏ Columbia Masterworks OL 5670 [M]	196?	2.50	5.00	10.00
—Regular cover; gray "360 Sound Stereo" label				
❏ Columbia Masterworks OL 5670 [M]	1961	5.00	10.00	20.00
—Originals have gatefold covers and gray and black labels with six "eye" logos				
❏ Columbia Masterworks OL 5670 [M]	1963	3.00	6.00	12.00
—Gatefold cover; gray "360 Sound Stereo" label				
WHAT A WAY TO GO!				
❏ 20th Century Fox TFM-3143 [M]	1964	5.00	10.00	20.00
❏ 20th Century Fox TFS-4143 [S]	1964	10.00	20.00	40.00
WHAT'S NEW PUSSYCAT?				
❏ United Artists UA-LA278-G	1974	3.00	6.00	12.00
—Reissue of 5128				
❏ United Artists UAL-4128 [M]	1965	5.00	10.00	20.00
❏ United Artists UAS-5128 [S]	1965	6.25	12.50	25.00
WHEN THE BOYS MEET THE GIRLS				
❏ MGM E-4334 [M]	1965	3.75	7.50	15.00
❏ MGM SE-4334 [S]	1965	7.50	15.00	30.00
WHERE EAGLES DARE				
❏ MGM S1E-16 ST	1969	7.50	15.00	30.00
WHERE'S JACK?				
❏ Paramount PAS-5005	1969	6.25	12.50	25.00
WHERE'S POPPA?				
❏ United Artists UAS-5216	1970	6.25	12.50	25.00
THE WHISPERERS				
❏ United Artists UAL-4161 [M]	1967	5.00	10.00	20.00
❏ United Artists UAS-5161 [S]	1967	7.50	15.00	30.00
WHITE CHRISTMAS				
❏ Decca DL 8083	1954	12.50	25.00	50.00
WHO'S AFRAID OF VIRGINIA WOOLF?				
❏ Warner Bros. B 1656 [M]	1966	6.25	12.50	25.00
❏ Warner Bros. BS 1656 [S]	1966	7.50	15.00	30.00
❏ Warner Bros. 2B 1657 [(2)M]	1966	10.00	20.00	40.00
—Above (1657) is the complete film, not just the music and some dialogue				
THE WILD BUNCH				
❏ Warner Bros. WS 1814	1969	25.00	50.00	100.00
THE WILD EYE				
❏ RCA Victor LSP-4003	1968	6.25	12.50	25.00
WILD IN THE STREETS				
❏ Tower SKAO 5099	1968	7.50	15.00	30.00
WILD IS THE WIND				
❏ Columbia CL 1090 [M]	1957	6.25	12.50	25.00
WILD ON THE BEACH				
❏ RCA Victor LPM-3441 [M]	1965	6.25	12.50	25.00
❏ RCA Victor LSP-3441 [S]	1965	10.00	20.00	40.00
THE WILD ONE				
❏ Decca DL 5515 [10]	1954	20.00	40.00	80.00
❏ Decca DL 8349 [M]	1956	10.00	20.00	40.00
THE WILD RACERS				
❏ Sidewalk ST-5914	1968	6.25	12.50	25.00
WILD WHEELS				
❏ RCA Victor LSO-1156	1969	5.00	10.00	20.00
WILD, WILD WINTER				
❏ Decca DL 4699 [M]	1966	5.00	10.00	20.00
❏ Decca DL 74699 [S]	1966	7.50	15.00	30.00
WILLIE DYNAMITE				
❏ MCA 393	1974	5.00	10.00	20.00
WILLY WONKA AND THE CHOCOLATE FACTORY				
❏ Paramount PAS-6012	1971	10.00	20.00	40.00

Number Title	Yr	VG	VG+	NM
WITH A SONG IN MY HEART				
❑ Capitol L 309 [10]	1952	10.00	20.00	40.00
❑ Capitol T 309 [M]	195?	6.25	12.50	25.00
THE WIZARD OF OZ				
❑ MGM E-3464 [M]	1956	12.50	25.00	50.00
—Yellow label				
❑ MGM E-3996 [M]	1962	3.75	7.50	15.00
—Gatefold cover, black label				
❑ MGM SE-3996 [R]	196?	3.75	7.50	15.00
—Gatefold cover, black label				
WOMEN OF THE WORLD				
❑ Decca DL 9112 [M]	1963	5.00	10.00	20.00
❑ Decca DL 79112 [S]	1963	7.50	15.00	30.00
WONDERFUL COUNTRY				
❑ United Artists UAL-4050 [M]	1959	12.50	25.00	50.00
❑ United Artists UAS-5050 [S]	1959	25.00	50.00	100.00
WONDERFUL TO BE YOUNG				
❑ Dot DLP-3474 [M]	1962	6.25	12.50	25.00
❑ Dot DLP-25474 [S]	1962	10.00	20.00	40.00
THE WONDERFUL WORLD OF THE BROTHERS GRIMM				
❑ MGM 1E-3 [M]	1962	6.25	12.50	25.00
—With box and hardback book				
❑ MGM S1E-3 [S]	1962	10.00	20.00	40.00
—With box and hardback book				
WORDS AND MUSIC				
❑ Metro M-580 [M]	1966	3.00	6.00	12.00
❑ Metro MS-580 [R]	1966	2.50	5.00	10.00
❑ MGM E-505 [10]	1950	12.50	25.00	50.00
THE WORLD OF SUZIE WONG				
❑ RCA Victor LOC-1059 [M]	1960	5.00	10.00	20.00
❑ RCA Victor LSO-1059 [S]	1960	12.50	25.00	50.00
WRITTEN ON THE WIND				
❑ Decca DL 8424 [M]	1956	10.00	20.00	40.00
—Black label, silver print, or pink label, black print promo				
❑ Decca DL 8424 [M]	196?	5.00	10.00	20.00
—Black label with color bars				
THE WRONG BOX				
❑ Mainstream S-6088 [S]	1966	37.50	75.00	150.00
❑ Mainstream 56088 [M]	1966	25.00	50.00	100.00
WUTHERING HEIGHTS				
❑ American Int'l. A-1039	1971	7.50	15.00	30.00
THE YELLOW CANARY				
❑ Verve V-8548 [M]	1963	5.00	10.00	20.00
❑ Verve V6-8548 [S]	1963	6.25	12.50	25.00
THE YELLOW ROLLS-ROYCE				
❑ MGM E-4292 [M]	1965	5.00	10.00	20.00
❑ MGM SE-4292 [S]	1965	7.50	15.00	30.00
❑ MGM ST 90424 [S]	1965	3.75	7.50	15.00
—Capitol Record Club edition				
❑ MGM T 90424 [M]	1965	3.75	7.50	15.00
—Capitol Record Club edition				
YESTERDAY, TODAY AND TOMORROW				
❑ Warner Bros. W 1552 [M]	1964	10.00	20.00	40.00
❑ Warner Bros. WS 1552 [S]	1964	12.50	25.00	50.00

Number Title	Yr	VG	VG+	NM
YOJIMBO				
❑ MGM E-4096 [M]	1962	25.00	50.00	100.00
❑ MGM SE-4096 [S]	1962	37.50	75.00	150.00
YOU ARE WHAT YOU EAT				
❑ Columbia Masterworks OS 3240	1968	5.00	10.00	20.00
YOU ONLY LIVE TWICE				
❑ United Artists UA-LA289-G	1974	3.00	6.00	12.00
—Reissue of 5155				
❑ United Artists UAL-4155 [M]	1967	5.00	10.00	20.00
❑ United Artists UAS-5155 [S]	1967	6.25	12.50	25.00
YOUNG BILLY YOUNG				
❑ United Artists UAS-5199	1969	6.25	12.50	25.00
YOUNG FRANKENSTEIN				
❑ ABC ABCD-870	1975	5.00	10.00	20.00
THE YOUNG GIRLS OF ROCHEFORT				
❑ Philips PCC 2-226 [(2)M]	1968	5.00	10.00	20.00
❑ Philips PCC 2-626 [(2)S]	1968	7.50	15.00	30.00
THE YOUNG LIONS				
❑ Decca DL 8719 [M]	1958	7.50	15.00	30.00
❑ Decca DL 78719 [S]	1958	20.00	40.00	80.00
YOUNG LOVERS				
❑ Columbia Masterworks OS 2510 [S]	1964	6.25	12.50	25.00
❑ Columbia Masterworks OL 7010 [M]	1964	5.00	10.00	20.00
YOUNG MAN WITH A HORN				
❑ Columbia CL 582 [M]	1950	7.50	15.00	30.00
❑ Columbia CL 6106 [10]	1950	12.50	25.00	50.00
THE YOUNG SAVAGES				
❑ Columbia CL 1672 [M]	1961	7.50	15.00	30.00
❑ Columbia CS 8472 [S]	1961	25.00	50.00	100.00
YOUNG WINSTON				
❑ Angel SFO-36901	1972	6.25	12.50	25.00
YOURS, MINE AND OURS				
❑ United Artists UAS-5181	1968	5.00	10.00	20.00
Z				
❑ Columbia Masterworks OS 3370	1970	5.00	10.00	20.00
ZABRISKIE POINT				
❑ MGM SE-4468	1970	5.00	10.00	20.00
ZACHARIAH				
❑ ABC ABCS-OC-13	1970	6.25	12.50	25.00
ZORBA THE GREEK				
❑ 20th Century T-903	1973	3.00	6.00	12.00
—Reissue of 20th Century Fox 4167				
❑ 20th Century Fox TFM-3167 [M]	1965	5.00	10.00	20.00
❑ 20th Century Fox TFS-4167 [S]	1965	6.25	12.50	25.00
ZULU				
❑ United Artists UAL-4116 [M]	1964	10.00	20.00	40.00
❑ United Artists UAS-5116 [S]	1964	17.50	35.00	70.00

Number	Title	Yr	VG	VG+	NM

TELEVISION RECORDS

THE ADDAMS FAMILY

❏ RCA Victor LPM-3421 [M]	1965	20.00	40.00	80.00
❏ RCA Victor LSP-3421 [S]	1965	37.50	75.00	150.00

AFRICA

❏ MGM E-4462 [M]	1967	12.50	25.00	50.00
❏ MGM SE-4462 [S]	1967	15.00	30.00	60.00

THE AGE OF TELEVISION — A CHRONICLE OF THE FIRST 25 YEARS

❏ RCA Victor LL-8	1972	5.00	10.00	20.00

—With booklet

❏ Warner Bros. BS 2670	1972	7.50	15.00	30.00

—With booklet; this version seems to be much rarer than the RCA issue

ALADDIN

❏ Columbia CL 1117 [M]	1958	12.50	25.00	50.00

ALICE THROUGH THE LOOKING GLASS

❏ RCA Victor LOC-1130 [M]	1966	6.25	12.50	25.00
❏ RCA Victor LSO-1130 [S]	1966	7.50	15.00	30.00

AMAHL AND THE NIGHT VISITORS

❏ RCA Red Seal LM-1701 [10]	1952	12.50	25.00	50.00

—Soundtrack of the 1951 NBC-TV production

❏ RCA Red Seal LM-1701 [M]	1952	10.00	20.00	40.00

—Soundtrack of the 1951 NBC-TV production; 12-inch record in box with booklet

❏ RCA Red Seal LM-2762 [M]	1964	3.75	7.50	15.00

—Soundtrack of the 1963 NBC Opera Company TV production

❏ RCA Red Seal LSC-2762 [S]	1964	3.75	7.50	15.00

—Large "RCA Victor" and dog at top of label

❏ RCA Red Seal LSC-2762 [S]	1969	3.00	6.00	12.00

—Stereo reissue on red label without dog; no bar code on back cover

ANDROCLES AND THE LION

❏ RCA Victor LOC-1141 [M]	1967	6.25	12.50	25.00
❏ RCA Victor LSO-1141 [S]	1967	6.25	12.50	25.00

ANNIE GET YOUR GUN

❏ Capitol W 913 [M]	1957	7.50	15.00	30.00

—Los Angeles/San Francisco production aired on NBC-TV

AT HOME WITH THE MUNSTERS

❏ Golden LP-139 [M]	1964	50.00	100.00	200.00

ATOM ANT IN MUSCLE MAGIC

❏ Hanna-Barbera HLP-2041 [M]	1966	37.50	75.00	150.00

THE AVENGERS

❏ Hanna-Barbera HLP-8506 [M]	1966	15.00	30.00	60.00
❏ Hanna-Barbera HST-9506 [S]	1966	20.00	40.00	80.00

BATMAN

❏ 20th Century Fox TFM-3180 [M]	1966	15.00	30.00	60.00
❏ 20th Century Fox TFS-4180 [S]	1966	25.00	50.00	100.00

THE BEVERLY HILLBILLIES

❏ Columbia CL 2402 [M]	1965	10.00	20.00	40.00
❏ Columbia CS 9202 [S]	1965	15.00	30.00	60.00

THE BIG VALLEY

❏ ABC-Paramount ABC-527 [M]	1965	10.00	20.00	40.00
❏ ABC-Paramount ABCS-527 [S]	1965	12.50	25.00	50.00

THE BORN LOSERS

❏ Tower DT 5082 [R]	1967	5.00	10.00	20.00
❏ Tower T 5082 [M]	1967	6.25	12.50	25.00

THE BORROWERS

❏ Stanyan SRQ-4014 [Q]	1973	12.50	25.00	50.00

BOURBON STREET BEAT

❏ Warner Bros. W 1321 [M]	1960	6.25	12.50	25.00
❏ Warner Bros. WS 1321 [S]	1960	7.50	15.00	30.00

BRIGADOON

❏ Columbia Special Products CSM 385	1968	5.00	10.00	20.00

—Sold through the mail by broadcast sponsor Armstrong

BURKE'S LAW

❏ Liberty LRP-3374 [M]	1964	15.00	30.00	60.00
❏ Liberty LST-7374 [S]	1964	20.00	40.00	80.00

CAROUSEL

❏ Columbia Special Products CSM 479	1969	5.00	10.00	20.00

—Sold through the mail by broadcast sponsor Armstrong

CHECKMATE

❏ Columbia CL 1591 [M]	1960	10.00	20.00	40.00
❏ Columbia CS 8391 [S]	1960	15.00	30.00	60.00

CINDERELLA

❏ Columbia Masterworks OS 2005 [S]	1959	10.00	20.00	40.00

—Stage presentation for TV starring Julie Andrews

❏ Columbia Masterworks OS 2730 [S]	1965	7.50	15.00	30.00

—Stage presentation for TV starring Lesley-Ann Warren

❏ Columbia Masterworks OL 5190 [M]	1957	7.50	15.00	30.00
❏ Columbia Masterworks OL 6330 [M]	1965	6.25	12.50	25.00

THE COMING OF CHRIST

❏ Decca DL 9093 [M]	1960	10.00	20.00	40.00
❏ Decca DL 79093 [S]	1960	12.50	25.00	50.00

THE CRICKET ON THE HEARTH

❏ RCA Victor LOC-1140 [M]	1967	5.00	10.00	20.00
❏ RCA Victor LSO-1140 [S]	1967	7.50	15.00	30.00

DANGER

❏ MGM E-111 [10]	1951	30.00	60.00	120.00

THE DANGEROUS CHRISTMAS OF RED RIDING HOOD

❏ ABC-Paramount ABC-536 [M]	1965	3.75	7.50	15.00
❏ ABC-Paramount ABCS-536 [S]	1965	6.25	12.50	25.00

DARK SHADOWS

❏ Philips PHS 600314	1969	7.50	15.00	30.00

—With poster

DAVID COPPERFIELD

❏ GRT 10008	1970	37.50	75.00	150.00

DENNIS THE MENACE SONGS

❏ Golden LP-59 [M]	1960	20.00	40.00	80.00

—Black label original

DOGGIE DADDY TELLS AUGGY DOGGIE THE STORY OF PINOCCHIO

❏ Hanna-Barbera HLP-2028 [M]	1965	25.00	50.00	100.00

EAST SIDE, WEST SIDE

❏ Columbia CL 2123 [M]	1963	7.50	15.00	30.00
❏ Columbia CS 8923 [S]	1963	10.00	20.00	40.00

ELEVEN AGAINST THE ICE

❏ RCA Victor LPM-1618 [M]	1958	15.00	30.00	60.00

ELIZABETH TAYLOR IN LONDON

❏ Colpix CP 459 [M]	1963	7.50	15.00	30.00
❏ Colpix SCP 459 [S]	1963	12.50	25.00	50.00

EXCITING HONG KONG

❏ ABC-Paramount ABC-367 [M]	1961	10.00	20.00	40.00
❏ ABC-Paramount ABCS-367 [S]	1961	12.50	25.00	50.00

FELIX THE CAT

❏ Cricket CR-28 [M]	1958	25.00	50.00	100.00

FENWICK

❏ Fenwick FLP-621	1968	5.00	10.00	20.00

—Soundtrack to TV special; packaged in oversize (13 1/2 x 13 1/2) sleeve with color cartoon booklet; made especially for Motorola

THE FLINTSTONES

❏ Colpix CP-302 [M]	1961	50.00	100.00	200.00

THE FLINTSTONES AND JOSE JIMENEZ IN THE TIME MACHINE

❏ Hanna-Barbera HLP-2052 [M]	1966	20.00	40.00	80.00

THE FLINTSTONES IN S.A.S.F.A.T.P.O.G.O.B.S.O.A.L.T.

❏ Hanna-Barbera HLP-2047 [M]	1966	25.00	50.00	100.00

THE FLINTSTONES' FLIP FABLES: GOLDI-ROCKS AND THE THREE BEAROSAURUSES

❏ Hanna-Barbera HLP-2021 [M]	1965	25.00	50.00	100.00

THE FORD 50TH ANNIVERSARY TELEVISION SHOW

❏ Decca DL 7027 [10]	1953	10.00	20.00	40.00

FOUR ADVENTURES OF ZORRO

❏ Disneyland WDA-3601 [M]	1958	20.00	40.00	80.00

—Gatefold with booklet

FRED FLINTSTONE AND BARNEY RUBBLE SING SONGS FROM MARY POPPINS

❏ Hanna-Barbera HLP-2035 [M]	1965	25.00	50.00	100.00

FROSTY THE SNOWMAN

❏ MGM SE-4733	1970	15.00	30.00	60.00

GENERAL ELECTRIC THEATER

❏ Columbia CL 1395 [M]	1959	10.00	20.00	40.00
❏ Columbia CS 8190 [S]	1959	12.50	25.00	50.00

GENERAL MOTORS' 50TH ANNIVERSARY SHOW

❏ RCA Victor LOC-1037 [M]	1958	25.00	50.00	100.00

GET SMART

❏ United Artists UAL-3533 [M]	1965	10.00	20.00	40.00
❏ United Artists UAS-6566 [S]	1965	15.00	30.00	60.00

Number Title	Yr	VG	VG+	NM
THE GIFT OF LOVE				
☐ Columbia CL 1113 [M]	1958	7.50	15.00	30.00
THE GIFT OF THE MAGI				
☐ United Artists UAL-4013 [M]	1959	10.00	20.00	40.00
☐ United Artists UAS-5103 [S]	1959	12.50	25.00	50.00
THE GIRL FROM U.N.C.L.E.				
☐ MGM E-4410 [M]	1966	10.00	20.00	40.00
☐ MGM SE-4410 [S]	1966	15.00	30.00	60.00
GOOFY'S TV SPECTACULAR				
☐ Disneyland DQ-1252 [M]	1964	5.00	10.00	20.00
THE GREEN HORNET				
☐ 20th Century Fox S-3186 [S]	1966	62.50	125.00	250.00
☐ 20th Century Fox TF-3186 [M]	1966	50.00	100.00	200.00
HANS BRINKER				
☐ Dot DLP-9001 [M]	1958	10.00	20.00	40.00
HANSEL AND GRETEL STARRING THE FLINTSTONES				
☐ Hanna-Barbera HLP-2038 [M]	1965	25.00	50.00	100.00
HAWAII FIVE-O				
☐ Capitol ST-410	1969	10.00	20.00	40.00
HAWAIIAN EYE				
☐ Warner Bros. W 1355 [M]	1959	7.50	15.00	30.00
☐ Warner Bros. WS 1355 [S]	1959	10.00	20.00	40.00
HECTOR, THE STOWAWAY PUP				
☐ Disneyland ST-1921 [M]	1964	7.50	15.00	30.00
HEIDI				
☐ Capitol SKAO 2995	1968	10.00	20.00	40.00
HENNESSEY				
☐ Signature 1049 [M]	1959	15.00	30.00	60.00
☐ Signature SS-1049 [S]	1959	20.00	40.00	80.00
HERE COMES HUCKLEBERRY HOUND				
☐ Colpix CP-207 [M]	1961	45.00	90.00	180.00
HEY THERE, IT'S YOGI BEAR				
☐ Golden LP-124 [M]	1964	10.00	20.00	40.00
HIGH TOR				
☐ Decca DL 8272 [M]	1956	100.00	200.00	400.00
THE HILLBILLY BEARS IN HILLBILLY SHINDIG				
☐ Hanna-Barbera HLP-2044 [M]	1966	37.50	75.00	150.00
HOGAN'S HEROES SING THE BEST OF WWII				
☐ Sunset SUM-1137 [M]	1967	7.50	15.00	30.00
☐ Sunset SUS-5137 [S]	1967	10.00	20.00	40.00
HONEY WEST				
☐ ABC-Paramount ABC-532 [M]	1965	10.00	20.00	40.00
☐ ABC-Paramount ABCS-532 [S]	1965	12.50	25.00	50.00
HOW THE GRINCH STOLE CHRISTMAS				
☐ Leo LE-901 [M]	1966	12.50	25.00	50.00
☐ Leo LES-901 [S]	1966	17.50	35.00	70.00
HOWL ALONG WITH HUCKLEBERRY HOUND AND YOGI BEAR				
☐ Golden LP-55 [M]	1959	37.50	75.00	150.00
—Black label original				
HUCKLEBERRY HOUND AND THE GHOST SHIP				
☐ Colpix CP-210 [M]	1962	25.00	50.00	100.00
HUCKLEBERRY HOUND FOR PRESIDENT				
☐ Golden LP-60 [M]	1960	25.00	50.00	100.00
—Black label original				
HUCKLEBERRY HOUND TELLS STORIES OF UNCLE REMUS				
☐ Hanna-Barbera HLP-2022 [M]	1965	25.00	50.00	100.00
HUCKLEBERRY HOUND, THE GREAT KELLOGG'S TV SHOW				
☐ Colpix CP-202 [M]	1959	50.00	100.00	200.00
I SPY				
☐ Warner Bros. W 1637 [M]	1965	7.50	15.00	30.00
☐ Warner Bros. WS 1637 [S]	1965	10.00	20.00	40.00
I SPY, VOLUME 2				
☐ Capitol ST 2839	1968	7.50	15.00	30.00
IT'S HOWDY DOODY TIME				
☐ RCA Victor LSP-4546	1971	6.25	12.50	25.00
JAMES BOMB STARRING SUPER SNOOPER AND BLABBER MOUSE				
☐ Hanna-Barbera HLP-2036 [M]	1965	25.00	50.00	100.00
JANE EYRE				
☐ Capitol SW-749	1971	7.50	15.00	30.00

Number Title	Yr	VG	VG+	NM
THE JETSONS				
☐ Colpix CP-213 [M]	1962	62.50	125.00	250.00
☐ Golden LP-98 [M]	1963	50.00	100.00	200.00
—Red cover original				
☐ Golden LP-98 [M]	1964	30.00	60.00	120.00
—Blue cover reissue				
THE JETSONS IN FIRST FAMILY ON THE MOON				
☐ Hanna-Barbera HLP-2037 [M]	1965	37.50	75.00	150.00
THE JIMMY DURANTE TV SHOW				
☐ Royale 1812 [10]	1955	25.00	50.00	100.00
JONNY QUEST IN 20,000 LEAGUES UNDER THE SEA				
☐ Hanna-Barbera HLP-2030 [M]	1965	37.50	75.00	150.00
KING KONG				
☐ Golden LP-151 [M]	1965	10.00	20.00	40.00
KISS ME, KATE				
☐ Columbia Special Products CSS 645	1968	6.25	12.50	25.00
—Sold through the mail by broadcast sponsor Armstrong				
A LOOK AT MONACO				
☐ Columbia CL 2019 [M]	1963	12.50	25.00	50.00
☐ Columbia CS 8819 [R]	1963	12.50	25.00	50.00
LOVE, AMERICAN STYLE				
☐ Capitol ST-11250	1973	10.00	20.00	40.00
MAGILLA GORILLA AND HIS PALS				
☐ Golden LP-120 [M]	1964	12.50	25.00	50.00
MAGILLA GORILLA TELLS OGEE THE STORY OF ALICE IN WONDERLAND				
☐ Hanna-Barbera HLP-2024 [M]	1965	25.00	50.00	100.00
THE MAN FROM INTERPOL				
☐ Top Rank RM-327 [M]	1962	12.50	25.00	50.00
☐ Top Rank RS-627 [S]	1962	15.00	30.00	60.00
THE MAN FROM U.N.C.L.E.				
☐ RCA Victor LPM-3475 [M]	1965	15.00	30.00	60.00
☐ RCA Victor LSP-3475 [S]	1965	20.00	40.00	80.00
THE MAN FROM U.N.C.L.E. VOLUME 2				
☐ RCA Victor LPM-3574	1966	10.00	20.00	40.00
☐ RCA Victor LSP-3574	1966	12.50	25.00	50.00
MARK TWAIN TONIGHT!				
☐ Columbia Masterworks OS 3080 [S]	1967	5.00	10.00	20.00
☐ Columbia Masterworks OL 6680 [M]	1967	3.75	7.50	15.00
MERRY CHRISTMAS FROM KUKLA, FRAN AND OLLIE				
☐ Decca DL 8192 [M]	1955	20.00	40.00	80.00
MICKEY MOUSE CLUB MOUSEKEDANCES AND OTHER MOUSEKETEER FAVORITES				
☐ Disneyland DQ-1362 [M]	1974	5.00	10.00	20.00
—With booklet				
☐ Disneyland STER-1362 [S]	1974	6.25	12.50	25.00
—With booklet				
MICKEY MOUSE CLUB SONG HITS				
☐ Disneyland ST-3815	1975	10.00	20.00	40.00
—With 16-page photo album				
MICKEY MOUSE CLUB: 27 NEW SONGS FROM THE MICKEY MOUSE CLUB TV SHOW				
☐ Mickey Mouse Club MM-14	1958	12.50	25.00	50.00
MICKEY MOUSE CLUB: A WALT DISNEY SONG FEST				
☐ Mickey Mouse Club MM-20	1958	10.00	20.00	40.00
MICKEY MOUSE CLUB: FUN WITH MUSIC — 30 FAVORITE DISNEY SONGS				
☐ Disneyland DQ-1209 [M]	1959	6.25	12.50	25.00
MICKEY MOUSE CLUB: HOLIDAYS WITH THE MOUSEKETEERS (A SONG FOR EVERY HOLIDAY)				
☐ Mickey Mouse Club MM-22	1958	10.00	20.00	40.00
MICKEY MOUSE CLUB: HOW TO BE A MOUSEKETEER				
☐ Disneyland ST-3918	1962	10.00	20.00	40.00
MICKEY MOUSE CLUB: MOUSEKETEERS TALENT ROUNDUP				
☐ Mickey Mouse Club MM-16	1958	10.00	20.00	40.00
MICKEY MOUSE CLUB: MUSICAL HIGHLIGHTS FROM THE MICKEY MOUSE CLUB				
☐ Disneyland DQ-1227 [M]	1962	7.50	15.00	30.00
MICKEY MOUSE CLUB: MUSICAL HIGHLIGHTS FROM THE MICKEY MOUSE CLUB TV SHOW				
☐ Mickey Mouse Club MM-12	1958	20.00	40.00	80.00

Number / Title	Yr	VG	VG+	NM
MICKEY MOUSE CLUB: SONGS FROM ANNETTE AND OTHER WALT DISNEY SERIALS				
☐ Mickey Mouse Club MM-24	1958	30.00	60.00	120.00
MICKEY MOUSE CLUB: SONGS FROM THE MICKEY MOUSE CLUB SERIALS				
☐ Disneyland DQ-1229 [M]	1962	10.00	20.00	40.00
MICKEY MOUSE CLUB: WE'RE THE MOUSEKETEERS				
☐ Mickey Mouse Club MM-18	1957	10.00	20.00	40.00
THE MIGHTY HERCULES				
☐ Golden LP-109 [M]	1963	50.00	100.00	200.00
MIKADO				
☐ Columbia Masterworks OS 2022 [S]	1960	25.00	50.00	100.00
☐ Columbia Masterworks OL 5480 [M]	1960	7.50	15.00	30.00
THE MISADVENTURES OF DENNIS THE MENACE				
☐ Colpix CP-204 [M]	1960	50.00	100.00	200.00
MR. BROADWAY				
☐ RCA Victor LPM-1520 [M]	1957	7.50	15.00	30.00
MR. ED, THE TALKING HORSE				
☐ Colpix CP-209 [M]	1962	75.00	150.00	300.00
MR. ED: STRAIGHT FROM THE HORSE'S MOUTH				
☐ Golden LP-88 [M]	1962	50.00	100.00	200.00
MR. JINKS, PIXIE AND DIXIE				
☐ Colpix CP-208 [M]	1961	25.00	50.00	100.00
THE MUNSTERS				
☐ Decca DL 4588 [M]	1964	15.00	30.00	60.00
☐ Decca DL 74588 [S]	1964	25.00	50.00	100.00
THE MUSIC FROM M SQUAD				
☐ RCA Victor LPM-2062 [M]	1959	7.50	15.00	30.00
☐ RCA Victor LSP-2062 [S]	1959	10.00	20.00	40.00
THE MUSIC FROM MARLBORO COUNTRY				
☐ United Artists SP-107	1967	12.50	25.00	50.00
MUSIC FROM SHUBERT ALLEY				
☐ Sinclair OSS-2250 [M]	1959	10.00	20.00	40.00
—From the NBC TV program, November 13, 1959				
NAKED CITY — A MUSICAL PORTRAIT				
☐ Colpix CP-505 [M]	1958	10.00	20.00	40.00
☐ Colpix SCP-505 [S]	1959	15.00	30.00	60.00
OF THEE I SING				
☐ Columbia S 31763	1972	5.00	10.00	20.00
THE OFFICIAL ALBUM OF NBC'S BAT MASTERSON				
☐ Sea Horse/Chancellor CSH-7002 [M]	1960	20.00	40.00	80.00
ON THE FLIP SIDE				
☐ Decca DL 4836	1966	6.25	12.50	25.00
☐ Decca DL 74836 [S]	1966	7.50	15.00	30.00
ONE STEP BEYOND				
☐ Decca DL 8970 [M]	1960	7.50	15.00	30.00
☐ Decca DL 78970 [S]	1960	10.00	20.00	40.00
ORIGINAL AMATEUR HOUR 25TH ANNIVERSARY ALBUM				
☐ United Artists UXL 2 [(2)M]	1960	10.00	20.00	40.00
THE ORIGINAL TV ADVENTURES OF KING KONG				
☐ Epic LN 24231 [M]	1966	6.25	12.50	25.00
☐ Epic BN 26231 [S]	1966	7.50	15.00	30.00
THE OTHER WORLD OF WINSTON CHURCHILL				
☐ Mercury MG-21033 [M]	1965	7.50	15.00	30.00
☐ Mercury SR-61033 [S]	1965	10.00	20.00	40.00
OZZIE AND HARRIET				
☐ Imperial LP-9049 [M]	1957	50.00	100.00	200.00
PEYTON PLACE				
☐ Epic LN 24147 [M]	1965	7.50	15.00	30.00
☐ Epic BN 26147 [S]	1965	10.00	20.00	40.00
THE PIED PIPER OF HAMELIN				
☐ RCA Victor LPM-1563 [M]	1957	12.50	25.00	50.00
PINOCCHIO				
☐ Columbia CL 1055 [M]	1957	10.00	20.00	40.00
PIXIE AND DIXIE WITH MR. JINKS TELL THE STORY OF CINDERELLA				
☐ Hanna-Barbera HLP-2025 [M]	1965	25.00	50.00	100.00
PRECIOUS PUPP IN HOT ROD GRANNY				
☐ Hanna-Barbera HLP-2045 [M]	1966	37.50	75.00	150.00
QUICK DRAW MCGRAW				
☐ Colpix CP-203 [M]	1960	20.00	40.00	80.00
QUICK DRAW MCGRAW AND HUCKLEBERRY HOUND				
☐ Golden LP-51 [M]	1959	37.50	75.00	150.00
—Black label original				
QUICK DRAW MCGRAW: THE TREASURE OF SARAH'S MATTRESS				
☐ Colpix CP-211 [M]	1962	30.00	60.00	120.00
THE REPORTER				
☐ Columbia CL 2269 [M]	1964	7.50	15.00	30.00
☐ Columbia CS 9069 [S]	1964	10.00	20.00	40.00
RICHARD DIAMOND				
☐ EmArcy MG-36162 [M]	1959	12.50	25.00	50.00
☐ EmArcy SR-80045 [S]	1959	20.00	40.00	80.00
THE RISE AND FALL OF THE THIRD REICH				
☐ MGM 1SE-12	1968	7.50	15.00	30.00
ROBIN HOOD STARRING TOP CAT				
☐ Hanna-Barbera HLP-2031 [M]	1965	25.00	50.00	100.00
ROCKY AND HIS FRIENDS				
☐ Golden LP-64 [M]	1961	50.00	100.00	200.00
—Gold label original				
THE ROGUES				
☐ RCA Victor LPM-2976 [M]	1964	5.00	10.00	20.00
☐ RCA Victor LSP-2976 [S]	1964	7.50	15.00	30.00
RUDOLPH THE RED-NOSED REINDEER				
☐ Decca DL 4815 [M]	1964	15.00	30.00	60.00
☐ Decca DL 34327 [M]	1965	10.00	20.00	40.00
—Same as DL 4815; custom products reissue				
☐ Decca DL 74815 [S]	1964	20.00	40.00	80.00
☐ MCA 15003	1973	5.00	10.00	20.00
—Reissue; black rainbow label				
RUFF AND READY ADVENTURES IN SPACE				
☐ Colpix CP-201 [M]	1959	50.00	100.00	200.00
RUGGLES OF RED GAP				
☐ Verve MGV-15000 [M]	1957	12.50	25.00	50.00
THE SAINT				
☐ RCA Victor LPM-3631 [M]	1966	30.00	60.00	120.00
☐ RCA Victor LSP-3631 [S]	1966	50.00	100.00	200.00
SANTA CLAUS IS COMIN' TO TOWN				
☐ MGM SE-4732	1970	15.00	30.00	60.00
SATINS AND SPURS				
☐ Capitol L 547 [10]	1954	17.50	35.00	70.00
SECRET AGENT				
☐ RCA Victor LPM-3630 [M]	1966	62.50	125.00	250.00
☐ RCA Victor LSP-3630 [S]	1966	62.50	125.00	250.00
—With incorrect title, "Danger Man," on label				
☐ RCA Victor LSP-3630 [S]	1966	75.00	150.00	300.00
—With correct title on label				
SECRET AGENT MEETS THE SAINT				
☐ RCA Victor LPM-3467 [M]	1965	50.00	100.00	200.00
☐ RCA Victor LSP-3467 [S]	1965	55.00	110.00	220.00
—Music from both TV shows; pre-dates the individual albums				
SECRET SQUIRREL AND MOROCCO MOLE IN SUPER SPY				
☐ Hanna-Barbera HLP-2046 [M]	1966	37.50	75.00	150.00
77 SUNSET STRIP				
☐ Warner Bros. W 1289 [M]	1959	7.50	15.00	30.00
☐ Warner Bros. WS 1289 [S]	1959	10.00	20.00	40.00
SHOTGUN SLADE				
☐ Mercury MG-20575 [M]	1960	10.00	20.00	40.00
☐ Mercury SR-60235 [S]	1960	15.00	30.00	60.00
SINBAD JR. IN TREASURE ISLAND				
☐ Hanna-Barbera HLP-2039 [M]	1965	30.00	60.00	120.00
67 MELODY LANE				
☐ Columbia CL 724 [M]	1955	7.50	15.00	30.00
SNAGGLEPUSS TELLS THE STORY OF THE WIZARD OF OZ				
☐ Hanna-Barbera HLP-2026 [M]	1965	25.00	50.00	100.00
SONGS OF THE FLINTSTONES				
☐ Golden LP-66 [M]	1961	62.50	125.00	250.00
—Gold label original				
SONGS OF YOGI BEAR AND HIS PALS				
☐ Golden LP-70 [M]	1961	20.00	40.00	80.00
—Gold label original				
THE SOUND OF JAZZ				
☐ Columbia CL 1098 [M]	1958	6.25	12.50	25.00
☐ Columbia CS 8040 [S]	1958	10.00	20.00	40.00

Number Title	Yr	VG	VG+	NM

SPACE: 1999
❏ RCA Victor ABL1-1422 — 1975 — 5.00 — 10.00 — 20.00

SQUIDDLEY DIDDLEY IN SURFIN' SAFARI
❏ Hanna-Barbera HLP-2043 [M] — 1966 — 37.50 — 75.00 — 150.00

STACCATO (MUSIC FROM JOHNNY STACCATO)
❏ Capitol ST 1287 [S] — 1959 — 12.50 — 25.00 — 50.00
❏ Capitol T 1287 [M] — 1959 — 7.50 — 15.00 — 30.00

THE STINGIEST MAN IN TOWN
❏ Columbia CL 950 — 1956 — 5.00 — 10.00 — 20.00
—Music from a television play first aired on The Alcoa Hour
❏ Columbia Special Products P 12637 — 1975 — 2.50 — 5.00 — 10.00
—Reissue of Columbia LP; same contents

SUPER SNOOPER AND BLABBER MOUSE IN MONSTER SHINDIG
❏ Hanna-Barbera HLP-2020 [M] — 1965 — 25.00 — 50.00 — 100.00

THRILLER
❏ Time S-2034 [S] — 1960 — 10.00 — 20.00 — 40.00
❏ Time 52034 [M] — 1960 — 7.50 — 15.00 — 30.00

TOM SAWYER
❏ Decca DL 8432 [M] — 1957 — 10.00 — 20.00 — 40.00
—First aired on the U.S. Steel Hour, starring Jimmy Boyd

TOP CAT
❏ Colpix CP-212 [M] — 1963 — 75.00 — 150.00 — 300.00

TOUCHE TURTLE AND DUM-DUM IN THE RELUCTANT DRAGON
❏ Hanna-Barbera HLP-2029 [M] — 1965 — 25.00 — 50.00 — 100.00

THE UNTOUCHABLES
❏ Capitol ST 1430 [S] — 1960 — 12.50 — 25.00 — 50.00
❏ Capitol T 1430 [M] — 1960 — 10.00 — 20.00 — 40.00

UP WITH PEOPLE!
❏ Pace 1101 — 1965 — 5.00 — 10.00 — 20.00
—Among the many people on this LP is a young Glenn Close (first name misspelled "Gleen")

THE VALIANT YEARS
❏ ABC-Paramount ABC-387 [M] — 1962 — 7.50 — 15.00 — 30.00
❏ ABC-Paramount ABCS-387 [S] — 1962 — 10.00 — 20.00 — 40.00

VICTORY AT SEA
❏ RCA Victor LM-1779 [M] — 1954 — 6.25 — 12.50 — 25.00
—Original recording
❏ RCA Victor LM-2335 [M] — 1959 — 5.00 — 10.00 — 20.00
—Re-recording of 1779
❏ RCA Victor LSC-2335 [S] — 1959 — 5.00 — 10.00 — 20.00
—Re-recording of 1779 in stereo

VICTORY AT SEA, VOL. 2
❏ RCA Victor LM-2226 [M] — 1958 — 5.00 — 10.00 — 20.00
❏ RCA Victor LSC-2226 [S] — 1958 — 6.25 — 12.50 — 25.00
—Original with "shaded dog" label

VICTORY AT SEA, VOL. 3
❏ RCA Victor LM-2523 [M] — 1961 — 5.00 — 10.00 — 20.00
❏ RCA Victor LSC-2523 [S] — 1961 — 6.25 — 12.50 — 25.00

WAGON TRAIN
❏ Mercury MG-20502 [M] — 1959 — 12.50 — 25.00 — 50.00
❏ Mercury SR-60179 [S] — 1959 — 20.00 — 40.00 — 80.00

WALT DISNEY'S WONDERFUL WORLD OF COLOR
❏ Disneyland DQ-1245 [M] — 1963 — 7.50 — 15.00 — 30.00

WIDE, WIDE WORLD
❏ RCA Victor LPM-1280 [M] — 1956 — 10.00 — 20.00 — 40.00

WILMA FLINTSTONE TELLS THE STORY OF BAMBI
❏ Hanna-Barbera HLP-2027 [M] — 1965 — 25.00 — 50.00 — 100.00

WINSOME WITCH IN IT'S MAGIC
❏ Hanna-Barbera HLP-2042 [M] — 1966 — 37.50 — 75.00 — 150.00

WONDERFUL TOWN
❏ Columbia Masterworks OS 2008 [S] — 1958 — 6.25 — 12.50 — 25.00
❏ Columbia Masterworks OL 5360 [M] — 1958 — 5.00 — 10.00 — 20.00

YOGI BEAR AND BOO-BOO
❏ Colpix CP-205 [M] — 1961 — 30.00 — 60.00 — 120.00

YOGI BEAR AND BOO-BOO TELL STORIES OF LITTLE RED RIDING HOOD AND JACK AND THE BEANSTALK
❏ Hanna-Barbera HLP-2023 [M] — 1965 — 25.00 — 50.00 — 100.00

YOGI BEAR AND THE THREE STOOGES IN THE MAD, MAD, DR. NO-NO
❏ Hanna-Barbera HLP-2050 [M] — 1966 — 25.00 — 50.00 — 100.00

YOGI BEAR: HOW TO BE A BETTER THAN AVERAGE CHILD
❏ Golden LP-90 [M] — 1962 — 20.00 — 40.00 — 80.00

VARIOUS ARTISTS COLLECTIONS

ACCENT ON PIANO
❏ Urania UJLP-1207 [M] — 1955 — 7.50 — 15.00 — 30.00

ACCENT ON TROMBONE
❏ Urania UJLP-1205 [M] — 1955 — 7.50 — 15.00 — 30.00

ADD-A-PART JAZZ
❏ Columbia CL 908 [M] — 1956 — 6.25 — 12.50 — 25.00

THE ADVANCE GUARD OF THE '40S
❏ EmArcy MG-36016 [M] — 1955 — 12.50 — 25.00 — 50.00

AFRO SUMMIT
❏ BASF 20675 — 197? — 5.00 — 10.00 — 20.00

AFRO-COOL
❏ GNP Crescendo GNP-48 [M] — 1959 — 5.00 — 10.00 — 20.00

AFTER HOUR JAZZ
❏ Epic LN (# unk) [M] — 1955 — 7.50 — 15.00 — 30.00

AFTER HOURS
❏ King 395-528 [M] — 1956 — 125.00 — 250.00 — 500.00

AFTER HOURS BLUES, 1949
❏ Biograph 12010 — 1969 — 3.00 — 6.00 — 12.00

AIN'T THAT GOOD NEWS
❏ Specialty SPS-2115 — 1969 — 5.00 — 10.00 — 20.00

ALAN FREED'S GOLDEN PICS
❏ End LP-313 [M] — 1961 — 15.00 — 30.00 — 60.00

ALAN FREED'S MEMORY LANE
❏ End LP-314 [M] — 1962 — 15.00 — 30.00 — 60.00

ALAN FREED'S TOP 15
❏ End LP-315 [M] — 1962 — 15.00 — 30.00 — 60.00
❏ Roulette SR 42042 [R] — 1970 — 3.75 — 7.50 — 15.00
—Reissue of End LP-315

ALL DAY LONG
❏ Prestige PRLP-7081 [M] — 1957 — 25.00 — 50.00 — 100.00
—Reissued as Prestige 7277

ALL GIRL MILLION SELLERS
❏ Ascot AM-13007 [M] — 1964 — 10.00 — 20.00 — 40.00
❏ Ascot AS-16007 [P] — 1964 — 10.00 — 20.00 — 40.00

ALL MEAT
❏ Warner Bros. PRO 604 [(2)] — 1975 — 5.00 — 10.00 — 20.00

ALL NIGHT LONG
❏ Prestige PRLP-7073 [M] — 1957 — 25.00 — 50.00 — 100.00
—Reissued as Prestige 7289

ALL SINGING — ALL TALKING — ALL ROCKING
❏ Warner Bros. PRO 573 [(2)] — 1973 — 6.25 — 12.50 — 25.00

ALL STAR JAZZ
❏ Halo 50223 [M] — 195? — 7.50 — 15.00 — 30.00

ALL STAR ROCK AND ROLL REVUE
❏ King 395-513 [M] — 1956 — 100.00 — 200.00 — 400.00
❏ King 638 [M] — 1959 — 50.00 — 100.00 — 200.00
—Reissue of King 395-513

ALL STAR SESSIONS
❏ Capitol M-11031 — 1973 — 3.00 — 6.00 — 12.00

ALL STAR TRIBUTE TO TATUM
❏ American Recording Society G-424 [M] — 1957 — 7.50 — 15.00 — 30.00

ALL THE HITS BY ALL THE STARS
❏ Parkway P 7013 [M] — 1962 — 10.00 — 20.00 — 40.00

ALL THE HITS BY ALL THE STARS, VOL. 2
❏ Parkway P 7016 [M] — 1963 — 7.50 — 15.00 — 30.00

ALL THE STARS' BIGGEST HITS
❏ Parkway P-7033 [M] — 1963 — 12.50 — 25.00 — 50.00
—With "pull-off pix" still intact on cover

ALL THE STARS' BIGGEST HITS, VOLUME 2
❏ Parkway P-7034 [M] — 1963 — 12.50 — 25.00 — 50.00
—With "pull-off pix" still intact on cover

ALL THESE THINGS
❏ Instant LP-71000 — 1969 — 7.50 — 15.00 — 30.00

ALL TIME COUNTRY AND WESTERN HITS
❏ King 537 [M] — 1956 — 37.50 — 75.00 — 150.00
❏ King 710 [M] — 1961 — 25.00 — 50.00 — 100.00
—Not a reissue of King 537, but a different collection

Number Title	Yr	VG	VG+	NM
ALL TIME HIT SACRED AND GOSPEL SONGS				
☐ King 1023 [M]	1967	7.50	15.00	30.00
ALL-STAR DATES				
☐ RCA Victor LPT-21 [10]	1951	12.50	25.00	50.00
ALL-TIME CHRISTMAS FAVORITES				
☐ Capitol Special Markets SL-6931	1973	3.00	6.00	12.00
—Sold only at Sylvania dealers				
ALTERNATIVES				
☐ Warner Bros. BS 1873	1970	3.00	6.00	12.00
ALTO ALTITUDE				
☐ EmArcy MG-36018 [M]	1955	12.50	25.00	50.00
ALTO SAXES				
☐ Norgran MGN-1035 [M]	1955	20.00	40.00	80.00
☐ Verve MGV-8126 [M]	1957	7.50	15.00	30.00
☐ Verve V-8126 [M]	1961	5.00	10.00	20.00
ALTO SUMMIT				
☐ Prestige PRLP-7684	1969	3.75	7.50	15.00
THE AMAZING METS				
☐ Buddah 1969	1969	6.25	12.50	25.00
AMERICA'S GREATEST JAZZMEN PLAY COLE PORTER				
☐ Moodsville MVLP-34 [M]	1963	10.00	20.00	40.00
—Green label				
☐ Moodsville MVLP-34 [M]	1965	5.00	10.00	20.00
—Blue label, trident logo at right				
☐ Moodsville MVST-34 [S]	1963	10.00	20.00	40.00
—Green label				
☐ Moodsville MVST-34 [S]	1965	5.00	10.00	20.00
—Blue label, trident logo at right				
AMERICA'S GREATEST JAZZMEN PLAY GEORGE GERSHWIN				
☐ Moodsville MVLP-33 [M]	1963	10.00	20.00	40.00
—Green label				
☐ Moodsville MVLP-33 [M]	1965	5.00	10.00	20.00
—Blue label, trident logo at right				
☐ Moodsville MVST-33 [S]	1963	10.00	20.00	40.00
—Green label				
☐ Moodsville MVST-33 [S]	1965	5.00	10.00	20.00
—Blue label, trident logo at right				
AMERICA'S GREATEST JAZZMEN PLAY RICHARD RODGERS				
☐ Moodsville MVLP-35 [M]	1963	10.00	20.00	40.00
—Green label				
☐ Moodsville MVLP-35 [M]	1965	5.00	10.00	20.00
—Blue label, trident logo at right				
☐ Moodsville MVST-35 [S]	1963	10.00	20.00	40.00
—Green label				
☐ Moodsville MVST-35 [S]	1965	5.00	10.00	20.00
—Blue label, trident logo at right				
AMERICA'S GREATEST JAZZMEN PLAY THE BROADWAY SCENE				
☐ Moodsville MVLP-38 [M]	1963	10.00	20.00	40.00
—Green label				
☐ Moodsville MVLP-38 [M]	1965	5.00	10.00	20.00
—Blue label, trident logo at right				
☐ Moodsville MVST-38 [S]	1963	10.00	20.00	40.00
—Green label				
☐ Moodsville MVST-38 [S]	1965	5.00	10.00	20.00
—Blue label, trident logo at right				
AMERICAN FOLK BLUES FESTIVAL				
☐ Excello LPS-8029	1972	5.00	10.00	20.00
☐ Exodus EX-302 [M]	1966	5.00	10.00	20.00
☐ Exodus EXS-302 [S]	1966	6.25	12.50	25.00
AMERICAN JAZZ FESTIVAL AT NEWPORT '56, NO. 1				
☐ Columbia CL 931 [M]		—	—	—
—See LOUIS ARMSTRONG.				
AMERICAN JAZZ FESTIVAL AT NEWPORT '56, NO. 2				
☐ Columbia CL 932 [M]		—	—	—
—See DAVE BRUBECK.				
AMERICAN JAZZ FESTIVAL AT NEWPORT '56, NO. 3				
☐ Columbia CL 933 [M]		—	—	—
—See DUKE ELLINGTON.				
AMERICAN JAZZ FESTIVAL AT NEWPORT '56, NO. 4				
☐ Columbia CL 934 [M]		—	—	—
—See DUKE ELLINGTON.				
AMERICANS ABROAD, VOL. 1				
☐ Pax LP-6009 [10]	1955	10.00	20.00	40.00
AMERICANS ABROAD, VOL. 2				
☐ Pax LP-6015 [10]	1955	10.00	20.00	40.00
AMERICANS IN EUROPE, VOL. 1				
☐ ABC Impulse! AS-36 [S]	1968	3.00	6.00	12.00
☐ Impulse! A-36 [M]	1963	5.00	10.00	20.00
☐ Impulse! AS-36 [S]	1963	6.25	12.50	25.00

Number Title	Yr	VG	VG+	NM
AMERICANS IN EUROPE, VOL. 2				
☐ ABC Impulse! AS-37 [S]	1968	3.00	6.00	12.00
☐ Impulse! A-37 [M]	1963	5.00	10.00	20.00
☐ Impulse! AS-37 [S]	1963	6.25	12.50	25.00
THE ANATOMY OF IMPROVISATION				
☐ Verve MGV-8230 [M]	1958	7.50	15.00	30.00
☐ Verve V-8230 [M]	1961	5.00	10.00	20.00
ANOTHER MONDAY NIGHT AT BIRDLAND				
☐ Roulette R 52022 [M]	1959	7.50	15.00	30.00
☐ Roulette SR 52022 [S]	1959	7.50	15.00	30.00
AN ANTHOLOGY OF BRITISH BLUES, VOL. 1				
☐ Immediate Z12 52006	1968	7.50	15.00	30.00
AN ANTHOLOGY OF BRITISH BLUES, VOL. 2				
☐ Immediate Z12 52014	1968	7.50	15.00	30.00
AN ANTHOLOGY OF CALIFORNIA MUSIC				
☐ Jazz: West Coast JWC-500 [M]	1955	37.50	75.00	150.00
AN ANTHOLOGY OF CALIFORNIA MUSIC, VOL. 2				
☐ Jazz: West Coast JWC-501 [M]	1956	37.50	75.00	150.00
APOLLO SATURDAY NIGHT				
☐ Atco 33-159 [M]	1964	10.00	20.00	40.00
☐ Atco SD 33-159 [S]	1964	12.50	25.00	50.00
APPETIZERS				
☐ Warner Bros. PRO 569 [(2)]	1973	6.25	12.50	25.00
APPROVED BY 10,000,000				
☐ Teem LP-5004 [M]	196?	7.50	15.00	30.00
AROUND THE CHRISTMAS TREE				
☐ Decca DL 38170 [M]	196?	3.00	6.00	12.00
THE ART OF JAZZ PIANO				
☐ Epic LN 3295 [M]	1956	7.50	15.00	30.00
THE ART OF THE BALLAD				
☐ Verve VSP-17 [M]	1966	3.75	7.50	15.00
☐ Verve VSPS-17 [R]	1966	2.50	5.00	10.00
THE ART OF THE BALLAD 2				
☐ Verve VSP-38 [M]	1966	3.75	7.50	15.00
☐ Verve VSPS-38 [R]	1966	2.50	5.00	10.00
ASSORTED FLAVORS OF PACIFIC JAZZ				
☐ Pacific Jazz HFS-1 [M]	1956	12.50	25.00	50.00
AT THE HOOTENANNY				
☐ Kapp KL-1330 [M]	1963	5.00	10.00	20.00
☐ Kapp KS-3330 [S]	1963	6.25	12.50	25.00
AT THE HOOTENANNY, VOL. 2				
☐ Kapp KL-1343 [M]	1963	5.00	10.00	20.00
☐ Kapp KS-3343 [S]	1963	6.25	12.50	25.00
AT THE HOOTENANNY, VOL. 3				
☐ Kapp KL-1344 [M]	1963	5.00	10.00	20.00
☐ Kapp KS-3344 [S]	1963	6.25	12.50	25.00
AUTOBIOGRAPHY IN JAZZ				
☐ Debut DEB-198 [M]	1955	37.50	75.00	150.00
AWARD ALBUM JAZZ VOCALS				
☐ Bethlehem BCP-6060 [M]	1961	6.25	12.50	25.00
BACKGROUNDS OF JAZZ, VOL. 1: THE JUG BANDS				
☐ "X" LX-3009 [10]	1954	20.00	40.00	80.00
BACKGROUNDS OF JAZZ, VOL. 2: COUNTRY & URBAN BLUES				
☐ "X" LVA-3016 [10]	1954	20.00	40.00	80.00
BACKGROUNDS OF JAZZ, VOL. 3: KINGS OF THE BLUES				
☐ "X" LVA-3032 [10]	1955	20.00	40.00	80.00
BACKWOOD BLUES				
☐ Riverside RLP-1039 [10]	1954	20.00	40.00	80.00
BALLADS AND BREAKDOWNS OF THE GOLDEN ERA				
☐ Columbia CS 9660	1968	5.00	10.00	20.00
BALLROOM BANDSTAND				
☐ Columbia CL 611 [M]	1955	6.25	12.50	25.00
BANG AND SHOUT SUPER HITS				
☐ Bang BLPS-220 [P]	1969	5.00	10.00	20.00
BANJO COUNTRY STYLE				
☐ Audio Lab AL-1569 [M]	1962	20.00	40.00	80.00

Number	Title	Yr	VG	VG+	NM
BARGAIN DAY					
☐ EmArcy MG-36087 [M]		1956	10.00	20.00	40.00
BARREL HOUSE PIANO					
☐ Brunswick BL 58022 [10]		1951	15.00	30.00	60.00
A BARREL OF OLDIES					
☐ Del-Fi DFLP-1219 [M]		1961	12.50	25.00	50.00
BARRY MANN AND CYNTHIA WEIL: SOLID GOLD					
☐ Screen Gems/Columbia CPL-712 [DJ]		1975	5.00	10.00	20.00
—Promo-only compilation of oldies sent to radio to spur airplay on songs owned by this publishing house					
THE BASS					
☐ ABC Impulse! AS-9284 [(3)]		197?	5.00	10.00	20.00
BATTLE OF BANDS					
☐ Capitol H 235 [10]		1950	12.50	25.00	50.00
BATTLE OF JAZZ, VOL. 3					
☐ Brunswick BL 58039 [10]		1953	12.50	25.00	50.00
BATTLE OF THE BIG BANDS					
☐ Capitol T 667 [M]		1956	7.50	15.00	30.00
BATTLE OF THE GROUPS					
☐ End LP-305 [M]		1960	15.00	30.00	60.00
BATTLE OF THE GROUPS, VOLUME 2					
☐ End LP-309 [M]		1960	15.00	30.00	60.00
BATTLE OF THE SAXES-TENOR ALL STARS					
☐ EmArcy MG-36023 [M]		1955	12.50	25.00	50.00
BE OUR GUEST					
☐ Gene Norman GNP-20 [M]		1955	6.25	12.50	25.00
THE BE-BOP ERA					
☐ RCA Victor LPV-519		1965	5.00	10.00	20.00
BE-BOP SINGERS					
☐ Prestige PRST-7828		1971	3.00	6.00	12.00
THE BELLS OF CHRISTMAS					
☐ Book-of-the-Month Club 90-5677 [(3)]		1973	5.00	10.00	20.00
—Sold through Book-of-the-Month Records; secondary number is "P3 11972"					
BEST COAST JAZZ					
☐ EmArcy MG-36039 [M]		1955	20.00	40.00	80.00
BEST FROM THE WEST: MODERN SOUNDS FROM CALIFORNIA, VOL. 1					
☐ Blue Note BLP-5059 [10]		1955	50.00	100.00	200.00
BEST FROM THE WEST: MODERN SOUNDS FROM CALIFORNIA, VOL. 2					
☐ Blue Note BLP-5060 [10]		1955	50.00	100.00	200.00
THE BEST OF ARGO JAZZ					
☐ Argo ALPS-1 [M]		1961	7.50	15.00	30.00
THE BEST OF BLUE NOTE, VOL. 1					
☐ Blue Note BST-84429 [(2)]		197?	5.00	10.00	20.00
THE BEST OF BLUE NOTE, VOL. 2					
☐ Blue Note BST-84433 [(2)]		197?	5.00	10.00	20.00
THE BEST OF CHRISTMAS					
☐ Capitol STBB 2979 [(2)]		1968	5.00	10.00	20.00
THE BEST OF DIXIELAND					
☐ RCA Victor LPM-2982 [M]		1965	5.00	10.00	20.00
☐ RCA Victor LSP-2982 [R]		1965	3.00	6.00	12.00
BEST OF RHYTHM AND BLUES					
☐ Jubilee JLP-1014 [M]		1956	37.50	75.00	150.00
—Blue label, black vinyl					
☐ Jubilee JLP-1014 [M]		1956	50.00	100.00	200.00
—Pink label, black vinyl					
☐ Jubilee JLP-1014 [M]		1956	125.00	250.00	500.00
—Pink label, red vinyl					
THE BEST OF RHYTHM AND BLUES					
☐ Warwick W 2026 [M]		1961	20.00	40.00	80.00
BEST OF THE BIG NAME BANDS					
☐ RCA Camden CAL-368 [M]		1958	6.25	12.50	25.00
BEST OF THE BLUES, VOLUME 1					
☐ Imperial LP-9257 [M]		1964	6.25	12.50	25.00
☐ Imperial LP-12257 [R]		1964	5.00	10.00	20.00

Number	Title	Yr	VG	VG+	NM
BEST OF THE BLUES, VOLUME 2					
☐ Imperial LP-9259 [M]		1964	6.25	12.50	25.00
☐ Imperial LP-12259 [R]		1964	5.00	10.00	20.00
BEST OF THE GREAT SONGS OF CHRISTMAS (ALBUM 10)					
☐ Columbia Special Products CSS 1478		1970	3.00	6.00	12.00
—Sold only at Goodyear tire dealers					
BEST OF THE MUSICAL SOUNDS OF CHRISTMAS					
☐ Capitol Creative Products SL-6713		1971	3.00	6.00	12.00
THE BEST OF THE R AND B GROUPS					
☐ Warwick W 2025 [M]		1961	25.00	50.00	100.00
BEST OF THE SOUNDTRACKS					
☐ Tower ST-5148		1969	6.25	12.50	25.00
THE BEST VOCAL GROUPS IN ROCK 'N' ROLL					
☐ Dooto DL-224 [M]		1957	25.00	50.00	100.00
—Yellow label					
☐ Dooto DL-224 [M]		196?	7.50	15.00	30.00
—Multi-color label					
BETHLEHEM'S BEST					
☐ Bethlehem EXLP-6 [(3)M]		1958	17.50	35.00	70.00
—Box set of 82, 83, and 84					
BETHLEHEM'S BEST, VOLUME 1					
☐ Bethlehem BCP-82 [M]		1958	7.50	15.00	30.00
BETHLEHEM'S BEST, VOLUME 2					
☐ Bethlehem BCP-83 [M]		1958	7.50	15.00	30.00
BETHLEHEM'S BEST, VOLUME 3					
☐ Bethlehem BCP-84 [M]		1958	7.50	15.00	30.00
BETHLEHEM'S GRAB BAG					
☐ Bethlehem EXLP-2 [M]		1958	10.00	20.00	40.00
THE BIG BALL					
☐ Warner Bros. PRO 358 [(2)]		1970	6.25	12.50	25.00
—Originals have green labels					
BIG BAND CONTRAST					
☐ Bethlehem BCP-6037 [M]		1960	7.50	15.00	30.00
BIG BAND JAZZ					
☐ Brunswick BL 58050 [10]		1953	12.50	25.00	50.00
BIG BAND STEREO					
☐ Capitol SW 1055 [S]		1959	6.25	12.50	25.00
BIG BANDS					
☐ Capitol STFL-293 [(6)]		1969	7.50	15.00	30.00
—One album each by Les Brown, Glen Gray, Duke Ellington, Benny Goodman, Harry James and Woody Herman					
THE BIG BANDS 1933					
☐ Prestige PRLP-7645		1969	3.75	7.50	15.00
BIG BANDS UPTOWN, VOL. 1					
☐ Decca DL 79242		1969	3.00	6.00	12.00
BIG BANDS' GREATEST HITS					
☐ Columbia CG 30009 [(2)]		197?	3.00	6.00	12.00
—"CG" prefix is a reissue of "G"					
☐ Columbia G 30009 [(2)]		1970	3.75	7.50	15.00
—Orange labels					
☐ Columbia G 30009 [(2)]		1970	5.00	10.00	20.00
—Red "360 Sound" labels					
BIG BANDS' GREATEST HITS, VOL. 2					
☐ Columbia CG 31213 [(2)]		197?	3.00	6.00	12.00
—"CG" prefix is a reissue of "G"					
☐ Columbia G 31213 [(2)]		1972	3.75	7.50	15.00
BIG COUNTRY HITS					
☐ Pickwick JS-6166		1975	7.50	15.00	30.00
THE BIG HITS					
☐ Columbia CL 1353 [M]		1959	7.50	15.00	30.00
☐ Columbia CS 8161 [S]		1959	10.00	20.00	40.00
THE BIG HITS OF MID-AMERICA					
☐ Soma MG-1245 [M]		1965	20.00	40.00	80.00
THE BIG HITS OF MID-AMERICA, VOLUME 2					
☐ Soma MG-1246 [M]		1965	20.00	40.00	80.00
BIG NAME DIXIE					
☐ Score SLP-4024 [M]		1958	12.50	25.00	50.00
THE BIG ONES FROM DUKE AND PEACOCK RECORDS					
☐ Peacock PLP-2000 [M]		1967	5.00	10.00	20.00

Number	Title	Yr	VG	VG+	NM
THE BIG SOUNDS OF THE DRAGS!					
☐ Capitol ST 2001 [S]		1963	6.25	12.50	25.00
☐ Capitol T 2001 [M]		1963	5.00	10.00	20.00
BIG SUR FESTIVAL/ONE HAND CLAPPING					
☐ Columbia KC 31138		1972	5.00	10.00	20.00
BIG SURF HITS					
☐ Del-Fi DFLP-1249 [M]		1964	12.50	25.00	50.00
☐ Del-Fi DFST-1249 [S]		1964	18.75	37.50	75.00
BILLIE HOLIDAY REVISITED					
☐ Mainstream MRL-409		197?	3.00	6.00	12.00
BIRD'S NIGHT — THE MUSIC OF CHARLIE PARKER					
☐ Savoy MG-12138 [M]		1958	12.50	25.00	50.00
BIRDLAND ALL STARS AT CARNEGIE HALL					
☐ Roulette RE-127 [(2)]		197?	3.00	6.00	12.00
THE BIRDLAND STARS ON TOUR, VOL. 1					
☐ RCA Victor LPM-1327 [M]		1956	10.00	20.00	40.00
THE BIRDLAND STARS ON TOUR, VOL. 2					
☐ RCA Victor LPM-1328 [M]		1956	10.00	20.00	40.00
THE BIRDLAND STORY					
☐ Roulette RB-2 [(2)M]		1961	10.00	20.00	40.00
☐ Roulette SRB-2 [(2)S]		1961	10.00	20.00	40.00
THE BIRTH OF BOP, VOL. 1					
☐ Savoy MG-9022 [10]		1953	37.50	75.00	150.00
THE BIRTH OF BOP, VOL. 2					
☐ Savoy MG-9023 [10]		1953	37.50	75.00	150.00
THE BIRTH OF BOP, VOL. 3					
☐ Savoy MG-9024 [10]		1953	37.50	75.00	150.00
THE BIRTH OF BOP, VOL. 4					
☐ Savoy MG-9025 [10]		1953	37.50	75.00	150.00
THE BIRTH OF BOP, VOL. 5					
☐ Savoy MG-9026 [10]		1953	37.50	75.00	150.00
BIRTH OF SOUL					
☐ Decca DL 79245		1969	3.00	6.00	12.00
BLACK AND WHITE RAGTIME, 1921-39					
☐ Biograph 12047		197?	3.00	6.00	12.00
BLOWIN' SESSIONS					
☐ Blue Note BN-LA521-H2 [(2)]		1975	5.00	10.00	20.00
BLOWOUT AT MARDI GRAS					
☐ Cook LP-1084 [M]		1955	10.00	20.00	40.00
BLUE NOTE CLASSICS					
☐ Blue Note B-6509 [M]		1969	3.75	7.50	15.00
BLUE RIBBON COUNTRY					
☐ Capitol STBB 2969 [(2)]		1968	6.25	12.50	25.00
BLUE RIBBON COUNTRY, VOL. 2					
☐ Capitol STBB-217 [(2)]		1969	6.25	12.50	25.00
THE BLUES					
☐ Vee Jay VJS-2-1007 [(2)]		1974	5.00	10.00	20.00
☐ Vee Jay LP-1020 [M]		1960	10.00	20.00	40.00
BLUES 'N' FOLK					
☐ Bethlehem BCP-6071 [M]		1963	15.00	30.00	60.00
BLUES FOR TOMORROW					
☐ Riverside RLP 12-243 [M]		1957	10.00	20.00	40.00
BLUES FROM BIG BILL'S COPACABANA					
☐ Chess LP 1533 [M]		1969	6.25	12.50	25.00
—Possibly a reissue of "Folk Festival of the Blues," Argo 4031					
THE BLUES IN MODERN JAZZ					
☐ Atlantic 1337 [M]		1961	5.00	10.00	20.00
—Multicolor label, white "fan" logo at right					
☐ Atlantic 1337 [M]		1963	3.75	7.50	15.00
—Multicolor label, black "fan" logo at right					
☐ Atlantic SD 1337 [R]		1969	3.00	6.00	12.00
THE BLUES IN STEREO					
☐ World Pacific ST-1021 [S]		1959	7.50	15.00	30.00
BLUES LIVE IN BATON ROUGE					
☐ Excello LPS-8021		1971	6.25	12.50	25.00
THE BLUES PROJECT					
☐ Elektra EKL-264 [M]		1964	6.25	12.50	25.00
☐ Elektra EKS-7264 [S]		1964	7.50	15.00	30.00
—No relation to the band of the same name; on one track, Bob Dylan plays piano under the name "Bob Landy"					

Number	Title	Yr	VG	VG+	NM
BLUES THAT GAVE AMERICA SOUL					
☐ ABC Duke DLPX-82 [S]		1974	3.75	7.50	15.00
☐ Duke DLP-82 [M]		1966	5.00	10.00	20.00
☐ Duke DLPS-82 [S]		1966	6.25	12.50	25.00
BLUES UPTOWN: URBAN BLUES, VOLUME 1					
☐ Imperial LP-94002		1968	5.00	10.00	20.00
THE BLUES, VOL. 2					
☐ Pacific Jazz JWC-502 [M]		1956	12.50	25.00	50.00
☐ World Pacific JWC-502 [M]		1958	10.00	20.00	40.00
THE BLUES, VOL. 2: HAVE BLUES, WILL TRAVEL					
☐ World Pacific JWC-509 [M]		1958	10.00	20.00	40.00
THE BLUES, VOL. 3: BLOWIN' THE BLUES					
☐ World Pacific JWC-512 [M]		1958	10.00	20.00	40.00
☐ World Pacific ST-1029 [S]		1959	7.50	15.00	30.00
THE BLUES, VOLUME 1					
☐ Argo LP-4026 [M]		1963	6.25	12.50	25.00
THE BLUES, VOLUME 2					
☐ Argo LP-4027 [M]		1963	6.25	12.50	25.00
THE BLUES, VOLUME 3					
☐ Argo LP-4034 [M]		1964	6.25	12.50	25.00
THE BLUES, VOLUME 4					
☐ Argo LP-4042 [M]		1964	6.25	12.50	25.00
THE BLUES, VOLUME 5					
☐ Cadet LP-4051 [M]		1966	6.25	12.50	25.00
BLUESVILLE					
☐ Bethlehem BCP-6038 [M]		1960	7.50	15.00	30.00
BODY AND SOUL					
☐ RCA Victor LPV-501		1964	5.00	10.00	20.00
BONING UP ON 'BONES					
☐ EmArcy MG-36038 [M]		1955	12.50	25.00	50.00
BOOGIE WOOGIE					
☐ Decca DL 5248 [10]		1950	12.50	25.00	50.00
BOOGIE WOOGIE KINGS AND QUEENS					
☐ Decca DL 5249 [10]		1950	12.50	25.00	50.00
BOOGIE WOOGIE PIANO					
☐ Brunswick BL 58018 [10]		1950	15.00	30.00	60.00
BOOGIE WOOGIE PIANOS					
☐ Columbia KC 32708		197?	2.50	5.00	10.00
BOOTY					
☐ Mainstream MRL-413		197?	3.00	6.00	12.00
BOPPIN'					
☐ Jubilee JGM-1118 [M]		1960	37.50	75.00	150.00
BOSS GOLDIES — SOUNDS FROM THE GROOVEYARD					
☐ Columbia CL 2559 [M]		1966	5.00	10.00	20.00
☐ Columbia CS 9339 [S]		1966	6.25	12.50	25.00
BOY MEETS GIRL					
☐ Stax STS 2-2024 [(2)]		1969	5.00	10.00	20.00
THE BRIGHTEST STARS OF CHRISTMAS					
☐ RCA Special Products DPL1-0086		1974	5.00	10.00	20.00
—Sold only at JCPenney department stores					
BRITISH FESTIVAL OF JAZZ CONCERT					
☐ Decca DL 5422 [10]		1952	12.50	25.00	50.00
BRITISH JAZZ FESTIVAL					
☐ Decca DL 5424 [10]		1952	12.50	25.00	50.00
BRUNSWICK'S GREATEST HITS					
☐ Brunswick BL 754186		1973	5.00	10.00	20.00
BUBBLE GUM MUSIC IS THE NAKED TRUTH, VOLUME 1					
☐ Buddah BDA 5032		1969	6.25	12.50	25.00
BUDDAH'S 360 DEGREE DIAL-A-HIT					
☐ Buddah BDA 5039		1969	7.50	15.00	30.00
—With rotating wheel under the front LP cover					
A BUMPER CROP OF ALL STARS					
☐ King 753 [M]		1961	25.00	50.00	100.00
BUNCH OF GOODIES					
☐ Chess LP 1441 [DJ]		1960	150.00	300.00	600.00
—Multi-color splash vinyl					

Number	Title	Yr	VG	VG+	NM
❏ Chess LP 1441 [M]		1960	30.00	60.00	120.00
—Black vinyl					

BURBANK

Number	Title	Yr	VG	VG+	NM
❏ Warner Bros. PRO 529 [(2)]		1972	6.25	12.50	25.00
—Originals have green labels					

BURBANK'S GREATEST HITS

Number	Title	Yr	VG	VG+	NM
❏ Warner Bros. PRO 548		1973	5.00	10.00	20.00

BUSHKIN-SAFRANSKI-WILSON GROUPS

Number	Title	Yr	VG	VG+	NM
❏ Allegro 1590 [10]		1955	12.50	25.00	50.00

BYE BYE BIRDIE

Number	Title	Yr	VG	VG+	NM
❏ Colpix CP-454 [M]		1963	20.00	40.00	80.00
❏ Colpix SCP-454 [S]		1963	25.00	50.00	100.00
—Studio version performed by Paul Petersen, Shelley Fabares, James Darren, the Marcels and others					

CARLOAD O' HITS

Number	Title	Yr	VG	VG+	NM
❏ Muse M-500 [M]		1959	50.00	100.00	200.00

A CARNIVAL OF SONGS

Number	Title	Yr	VG	VG+	NM
❏ King 819 [M]		1963	25.00	50.00	100.00

CAROLS AND CANDLELIGHT

Number	Title	Yr	VG	VG+	NM
❏ Columbia Special Products P 12525		1974	2.50	5.00	10.00
—Sold only at Goodyear tire dealers					

THE CATS

Number	Title	Yr	VG	VG+	NM
❏ New Jazz NJLP-8217 [M]		1959	20.00	40.00	80.00
—Purple label					
❏ New Jazz NJLP-8217 [M]		1965	7.50	15.00	30.00
—Blue label, trident logo at right					

CATS AND JAMMER KIDS

Number	Title	Yr	VG	VG+	NM
❏ Angel ANG-60007 [10]		1955	12.50	25.00	50.00

CATS VS. CHICKS

Number	Title	Yr	VG	VG+	NM
❏ MGM E-255 [10]		1954	12.50	25.00	50.00

CBS TWO-FERS ARE GREAT MUSICAL VALUES!

Number	Title	Yr	VG	VG+	NM
❏ CBS A2S 143/4 [(2)DJ]		1975	5.00	10.00	20.00

CHA CHA CHA CARNIVAL

Number	Title	Yr	VG	VG+	NM
❏ Forum F 9051 [M]		196?	2.50	5.00	10.00
❏ Forum FS 9051 [S]		196?	3.00	6.00	12.00
—Caney; Neil Lewis; Joe Lustig; Machito; Tito Puente; Tito Rodriguez; Pete Terrace					

CHARLIE PARKER 10TH MEMORIAL CONCERT

Number	Title	Yr	VG	VG+	NM
❏ Limelight LM-82017 [M]		1965	3.75	7.50	15.00
❏ Limelight LS-86017 [S]		1965	5.00	10.00	20.00

CHARLIE PARKER MEMORIAL CONCERT

Number	Title	Yr	VG	VG+	NM
❏ Cadet 2CA-60002 [(2)]		1971	5.00	10.00	20.00

CHART BUSTERS '62

Number	Title	Yr	VG	VG+	NM
❏ Capitol ST 1837 [S]		1963	10.00	20.00	40.00
❏ Capitol T 1837 [M]		1963	7.50	15.00	30.00

CHARTBUSTERS, VOL. 2

Number	Title	Yr	VG	VG+	NM
❏ Capitol ST 1945 [S]		1963	10.00	20.00	40.00
❏ Capitol T 1945 [M]		1963	7.50	15.00	30.00

CHARTBUSTERS, VOL. 3

Number	Title	Yr	VG	VG+	NM
❏ Capitol ST 2006 [S]		1963	10.00	20.00	40.00
❏ Capitol T 2006 [M]		1963	7.50	15.00	30.00

CHARTBUSTERS, VOL. 4

Number	Title	Yr	VG	VG+	NM
❏ Capitol ST 2094 [S]		1964	15.00	30.00	60.00
❏ Capitol T 2094 [M]		1964	10.00	20.00	40.00

CHICAGO / AUSTIN HIGH SCHOOL

Number	Title	Yr	VG	VG+	NM
❏ RCA Victor LPM-1508 [M]		1957	7.50	15.00	30.00

CHICAGO AND ALL THAT JAZZ!

Number	Title	Yr	VG	VG+	NM
❏ Verve V-8441 [M]		1961	6.25	12.50	25.00
❏ Verve V6-8441 [S]		1962	7.50	15.00	30.00

CHICAGO BLUES ANTHOLOGY

Number	Title	Yr	VG	VG+	NM
❏ Chess 2CH-60012 [(2)]		1972	5.00	10.00	20.00

CHICAGO JAZZ ALBUM

Number	Title	Yr	VG	VG+	NM
❏ Decca DL 8029 [M]		1954	10.00	20.00	40.00

CHICAGO JAZZ, 1923-29

Number	Title	Yr	VG	VG+	NM
❏ Biograph 12005		1968	3.00	6.00	12.00

CHICAGO JAZZ, VOLUME 2, 1925-29

Number	Title	Yr	VG	VG+	NM
❏ Biograph 12043		197?	3.00	6.00	12.00

CHICAGO SOUTH SIDE

Number	Title	Yr	VG	VG+	NM
❏ Historical 10		1968	2.50	5.00	10.00

CHICAGO SOUTH SIDE, VOL. 2

Number	Title	Yr	VG	VG+	NM
❏ Historical 30		1969	2.50	5.00	10.00

CHICAGO'S BOSS TENORS

Number	Title	Yr	VG	VG+	NM
❏ Chess CHV-414		1970	3.75	7.50	15.00

CHICAGO: THE LIVING LEGENDS, VOL. 1

Number	Title	Yr	VG	VG+	NM
❏ Riverside RLP-389 [M]		196?	5.00	10.00	20.00
❏ Riverside RS-9389 [R]		196?	3.00	6.00	12.00

CHICAGO: THE LIVING LEGENDS, VOL. 2

Number	Title	Yr	VG	VG+	NM
❏ Riverside RLP-390 [M]		196?	5.00	10.00	20.00
❏ Riverside RS-9390 [R]		196?	3.00	6.00	12.00

THE CHICAGOANS

Number	Title	Yr	VG	VG+	NM
❏ Decca DL 79231		1968	3.00	6.00	12.00

A CHILD'S CHRISTMAS

Number	Title	Yr	VG	VG+	NM
❏ Harmony HS 14563		197?	3.00	6.00	12.00

CHRISTMAS — A GIFT OF MUSIC

Number	Title	Yr	VG	VG+	NM
❏ Capitol Special Markets SL-6687		197?	3.00	6.00	12.00
—Reissue of "Zenith Presents Chrisrmas, A Gift of Music, Vol. 4" with almost identical cover					

CHRISTMAS — THE SEASON OF MUSIC

Number	Title	Yr	VG	VG+	NM
❏ Capitol Creative Products SL-6679		1970	3.00	6.00	12.00
—Reissue of "Zenith Presents Christmas, A Gift of Music, Vol. 3" with almost identical cover					

THE CHRISTMAS ALBUM

Number	Title	Yr	VG	VG+	NM
❏ Columbia G 30763 [(2)]		1972	3.75	7.50	15.00

CHRISTMAS AMERICA

Number	Title	Yr	VG	VG+	NM
❏ Capitol Special Markets SL-6884		1973	3.00	6.00	12.00
—Sold only at Firestone tire dealers (add 50% for sticker that says "Season's Greetings Firestone")					

CHRISTMAS AMERICA, ALBUM TWO

Number	Title	Yr	VG	VG+	NM
❏ Capitol Special Markets SL-6950		1974	3.00	6.00	12.00
—Sold only at Firestone tire dealers (add 50% for sticker that says "Season's Greetings Firestone")					

CHRISTMAS AS IT HAPPENED

Number	Title	Yr	VG	VG+	NM
❏ Mennonite Hour TR4H-5299/5300 [DJ]		1966	3.00	6.00	12.00
—"A series of seven 'newscasts' of the memorable events leading up to the birth of Jesus Christ"; tracks have locked grooves; possibly issued without a cover					

CHRISTMAS AT HOME

Number	Title	Yr	VG	VG+	NM
❏ Capitol Creative Products SL-6530		1967	3.00	6.00	12.00

CHRISTMAS AT OUR HOUSE

Number	Title	Yr	VG	VG+	NM
❏ Impact R 3381		1975	3.00	6.00	12.00
—Also contains narration by John T. Benson					

CHRISTMAS CAROUSEL

Number	Title	Yr	VG	VG+	NM
❏ Capitol SQBE-94406 [(2)]		1972	3.75	7.50	15.00
—Available only through the Capitol Record Club					

CHRISTMAS CHORUS

Number	Title	Yr	VG	VG+	NM
❏ Columbia Special Products CSS 932/3 [(2)]		1969	3.75	7.50	15.00
—Produced for NORM/A Step Ahead					

CHRISTMAS CLASSICS 1963

Number	Title	Yr	VG	VG+	NM
❏ E.F. MacDonald EFMX-63		1963	5.00	10.00	20.00
—Special album done by the E.F. MacDonald Company, Dayton, Ohio					

CHRISTMAS DAY IN THE COUNTRY

Number	Title	Yr	VG	VG+	NM
❏ Columbia Special Products P 11887		1973	2.50	5.00	10.00

CHRISTMAS DAY WITH COLONEL SANDERS

Number	Title	Yr	VG	VG+	NM
❏ RCA Victor PRS-274		1968	5.00	10.00	20.00
—Sold only at Kentucky Fried Chicken restaurants					

CHRISTMAS EVE WITH COLONEL SANDERS

Number	Title	Yr	VG	VG+	NM
❏ RCA Victor PRS-256		1967	5.00	10.00	20.00
—Sold only at Kentucky Fried Chicken restaurants					

CHRISTMAS FAVORITES

Number	Title	Yr	VG	VG+	NM
❏ RCA Victor PR-115-A [M]		1961	3.75	7.50	15.00
—Sold only at Acme markets (Mid-Atlantic states)					

A CHRISTMAS FESTIVAL

Number	Title	Yr	VG	VG+	NM
❏ RCA Record Club CCS-0145 [(2)]		1970	3.75	7.50	15.00

A CHRISTMAS FESTIVAL OF SONGS AND CAROLS

Number	Title	Yr	VG	VG+	NM
❏ RCA Victor PRM-170 [M]		1964	3.00	6.00	12.00
—Sold only at JCPenney department stores					
❏ RCA Victor PRS-170 [S]		1964	3.75	7.50	15.00
—Sold only at JCPenney department stores					

A CHRISTMAS FESTIVAL OF SONGS AND CAROLS, VOLUME 2

Number	Title	Yr	VG	VG+	NM
❏ RCA Victor PRM-195 [M]		1965	3.00	6.00	12.00
—Sold only at JCPenney department stores					
❏ RCA Victor PRS-195 [S]		1965	3.75	7.50	15.00
—Sold only at JCPenney department stores					

CHRISTMAS GIFT 'RAP

Number	Title	Yr	VG	VG+	NM
❏ Motown MS-725		1970	5.00	10.00	20.00
—Reissue of "Merry Christmas from Motown," MS-681					

Number	Title	Yr	VG	VG+	NM

A CHRISTMAS GIFT FOR YOU FROM PHILLES RECORDS

Number	Title	Yr	VG	VG+	NM
❏ Philles PHLP-4005 [M]		1963	37.50	75.00	150.00

—*First edition of this group of songs; blue and black labels*

| ❏ Philles PHLP-4005 [M] | | 1964 | 20.00 | 40.00 | 80.00 |

—*Second edition of this group of songs; yellow and red labels; both first and second editions have "Marshmellow [sic] World" typo on front cover; also see PHIL SPECTOR'S CHRISTMAS ALBUM*

CHRISTMAS GREETINGS

| ❏ Columbia Special Products CSS 1433 | | 1970 | 2.50 | 5.00 | 10.00 |
| ❏ Columbia Special Products CSS 1499 | | 1970 | 2.50 | 5.00 | 10.00 |

—*Sold only at A&P grocery stores*

CHRISTMAS GREETINGS FROM NASHVILLE

| ❏ RCA Victor APL1-0262 | | 1973 | 3.00 | 6.00 | 12.00 |

CHRISTMAS GREETINGS, VOL. 2

| ❏ Columbia Special Products C 10399 | | 1971 | 2.50 | 5.00 | 10.00 |

—*Sold only at A&P grocery stores*

CHRISTMAS GREETINGS, VOL. 3

| ❏ Columbia Special Products P 11383 | | 1972 | 2.50 | 5.00 | 10.00 |

—*Sold only at A&P grocery stores*

CHRISTMAS GREETINGS, VOL. 4

| ❏ Columbia Special Products P 11987 | | 1973 | 3.00 | 6.00 | 12.00 |

—*Sold only at A&P grocery stores*

CHRISTMAS HITS FROM WARNER BROS.

| ❏ Warner Bros. 8467/8 [DJ] | | 1959 | 12.50 | 25.00 | 50.00 |

CHRISTMAS IN CALIFORNIA

| ❏ RCA Victor PRS-276 | | 1968 | 3.00 | 6.00 | 12.00 |

—*Available only from Bank of America*

CHRISTMAS IN ENGLAND

| ❏ Capitol T 10097 [M] | | 195? | 3.75 | 7.50 | 15.00 |

CHRISTMAS IN ITALY

| ❏ Capitol SM-10093 [R] | | 197? | 2.50 | 5.00 | 10.00 |
| ❏ Capitol T 10093 [M] | | 196? | 3.75 | 7.50 | 15.00 |

CHRISTMAS IN NEW YORK

| ❏ RCA Victor PRM-257 [M] | | 1967 | 3.00 | 6.00 | 12.00 |
| ❏ RCA Victor PRS-257 [S] | | 1967 | 3.75 | 7.50 | 15.00 |

CHRISTMAS IN NEW YORK VOLUME 2

| ❏ RCA Victor PRS-270 | | 1968 | 3.00 | 6.00 | 12.00 |

CHRISTMAS IN NORWAY

| ❏ Capitol T 10377 [M] | | 196? | 3.75 | 7.50 | 15.00 |

CHRISTMAS IN SAN FRANCISCO

| ❏ Embarcadero Center EC-101 | | 1974 | 3.75 | 7.50 | 15.00 |

—*Featuring members of the San Francisco, Oakland ans San Jose Symphonies, the San Francisco and Western Operas, etc.; not all tracks have artists identified*

CHRISTMAS IN THE AIR

| ❏ RCA Special Products DPL1-0133 | | 1975 | 2.50 | 5.00 | 10.00 |

CHRISTMAS IS...

| ❏ Columbia Special Products P 11417 | | 1972 | 3.00 | 6.00 | 12.00 |

—*Sold only at Goodyear tire dealers*

A CHRISTMAS MUSIC FESTIVAL

| ❏ Capitol Creative Products SL-6688 | | 1970 | 2.50 | 5.00 | 10.00 |

CHRISTMAS NIGHT IN BETHLEHEM: THE MIDNIGHT CEREMONY AT ST. CATHERINE'S CHURCH

| ❏ ABC Dunhill DS-55002 | | 1968 | 3.75 | 7.50 | 15.00 |

—*Recording of the 1967 midnight Mass in the Holy Land; with 24-page booklet*

CHRISTMAS PROGRAMMING FROM RCA VICTOR

| ❏ RCA Victor SP-33-66 [DJ] | | 1959 | 250.00 | 500.00 | 1000. |

—*Promo-only collection; has been counterfeited, but originals have color covers*

THE CHRISTMAS SONG AND OTHER FAVORITES

| ❏ Columbia Special Products P 12446 | | 1974 | 2.50 | 5.00 | 10.00 |

THE CHRISTMAS SOUND OF MUSIC

| ❏ Capitol Special Markets SL-6996 | | 1975 | 2.50 | 5.00 | 10.00 |

THE CHRISTMAS SOUNDS OF MUSIC

| ❏ Capitol Creative Products SL-6643 | | 1969 | 3.00 | 6.00 | 12.00 |

—*Sold only at B.F. Goodrich tire dealers*

CHRISTMAS STARS: SUTHERLAND/TEBALDI/PRICE SING BEST LOVED CHRISTMAS FAVORITES

| ❏ London OS 26408 | | 1974 | 3.00 | 6.00 | 12.00 |

CHRISTMAS STOCKING

| ❏ Capitol NP 90494 [M] | | 1965 | 3.75 | 7.50 | 15.00 |

—*Available only through the Capitol Record Club*

| ❏ Capitol SNP 90494 [S] | | 1965 | 3.75 | 7.50 | 15.00 |

—*Available only through the Capitol Record Club*

CHRISTMAS THROUGH THE YEARS

| ❏ MCA Special Markets DL 734596 | | 197? | 3.00 | 6.00 | 12.00 |

—*Produced for First Financial Marketing Group*

CHRISTMAS TIME

| ❏ Decca DL 34037 [M] | | 196? | 3.75 | 7.50 | 15.00 |

CHRISTMAS TRIMMINGS

| ❏ Columbia Special Products P 12795 | | 1975 | 2.50 | 5.00 | 10.00 |

CHRISTMAS WITH ANDY WILLIAMS AND THE WILLIAMS BROTHERS

| ❏ Columbia Special Products C 10105 | | 1971 | 2.50 | 5.00 | 10.00 |

CHRISTMAS WITH COLONEL SANDERS

| ❏ RCA Victor PRS-291 | | 1969 | 5.00 | 10.00 | 20.00 |

—*Sold only at Kentucky Fried Chicken restaurants*

CHRISTMAS WITH EDDY ARNOLD/CHRISTMAS WITH HENRY MANCINI

| ❏ RCA Special Products DPL1-0079 | | 1974 | 3.00 | 6.00 | 12.00 |

CHRISTMAS WITH GLEN CAMPBELL AND THE HOLLYWOOD POPS ORCHESTRA

| ❏ Capitol Creative Products SL-6699 | | 1971 | 3.00 | 6.00 | 12.00 |
| ❏ Capitol Special Markets SL-6699 | | 197? | 2.50 | 5.00 | 10.00 |

—*Reissue on renamed label*

CHRISTMAS WITH JOHNNY MATHIS AND PERCY FAITH

| ❏ Columbia Special Products P 11805 | | 1973 | 2.50 | 5.00 | 10.00 |

CHRISTMAS WITH JULIE ANDREWS (FEATURING THE YULETIDE CHORISTERS)

| ❏ RCA Victor PRS-290 | | 1969 | 3.00 | 6.00 | 12.00 |

CHRISTMAS WITH NAT KING COLE AND FRED WARING & THE PENNSYLVANIANS

| ❏ Capitol Special Markets SL-6883 | | 197? | 2.50 | 5.00 | 10.00 |

CHRISTMAS WITH THE STARS

| ❏ Capitol Special Markets SL-6931 | | 1973 | 2.50 | 5.00 | 10.00 |

CHRISTMASTIME IN CAROL AND SONG

❏ RCA Victor PRM-271 [M]		1968	5.00	10.00	20.00
❏ RCA Victor PRS-271 [S]		1968	3.00	6.00	12.00
❏ RCA Victor PRS-289		1969	3.00	6.00	12.00

CLAMBAKE ON BOURBON STREET

| ❏ Cook LP-1085 [10] | | 1955 | 12.50 | 25.00 | 50.00 |

CLASSIC BLUES ACCOMPANISTS

| ❏ Riverside RLP-1052 [10] | | 1955 | 20.00 | 40.00 | 80.00 |

THE CLASSIC COLLECTION — TRADITIONAL: THE GREAT JAZZ MEN/VOL. 1

| ❏ Dot DLP-25878 | | 1968 | 3.75 | 7.50 | 15.00 |

CLASSIC JAZZ PIANO STYLES

| ❏ RCA Victor LPV-544 [M] | | 1967 | 5.00 | 10.00 | 20.00 |

CLASSICS IN JAZZ

| ❏ Capitol T 320 [M] | | 1954 | 7.50 | 15.00 | 30.00 |

CLASSICS IN JAZZ: COOL AND QUIET

| ❏ Capitol H 371 [10] | | 1953 | 12.50 | 25.00 | 50.00 |

CLASSICS IN JAZZ: DIXIELAND STYLISTS

| ❏ Capitol H 321 [10] | | 1952 | 12.50 | 25.00 | 50.00 |

CLASSICS IN JAZZ: SMALL COMBOS

| ❏ Capitol H 322 [10] | | 1952 | 12.50 | 25.00 | 50.00 |

CLAY COLE PRESENTS BLASTS FROM THE PAST

| ❏ Blast BLP 6803 [M] | | 196? | 12.50 | 25.00 | 50.00 |

CLAY COLE'S BIN OF ORIGINAL GOLDEN OLDIES

| ❏ Jubilee JGM-5026 [M] | | 1964 | 25.00 | 50.00 | 100.00 |

A COLLECTION OF 16 ORIGINAL BIG HITS, VOLUME 10

| ❏ Motown MS 684 | | 1969 | 5.00 | 10.00 | 20.00 |

A COLLECTION OF 16 ORIGINAL BIG HITS, VOLUME 11

| ❏ Motown MS 693 | | 1969 | 5.00 | 10.00 | 20.00 |

A COLLECTION OF 16 ORIGINAL BIG HITS, VOLUME 3

| ❏ Motown MS 624 [S] | | 1966 | 6.25 | 12.50 | 25.00 |

A COLLECTION OF 16 ORIGINAL BIG HITS, VOLUME 5

| ❏ Motown MS 651 [S] | | 1966 | 5.00 | 10.00 | 20.00 |

A COLLECTION OF 16 ORIGINAL BIG HITS, VOLUME 6

| ❏ Motown M 655 [M] | | 1967 | 5.00 | 10.00 | 20.00 |
| ❏ Motown MS 655 [S] | | 1967 | 5.00 | 10.00 | 20.00 |

Number Title	Yr	VG	VG+	NM
A COLLECTION OF 16 ORIGINAL BIG HITS, VOLUME 7				
❏ Motown M 661 [M]	1967	5.00	10.00	20.00
❏ Motown MS 661 [S]	1967	5.00	10.00	20.00
A COLLECTION OF 16 ORIGINAL BIG HITS, VOLUME 8				
❏ Motown M 666 [M]	1967	5.00	10.00	20.00
❏ Motown MS 666 [S]	1967	5.00	10.00	20.00
A COLLECTION OF 16 ORIGINAL BIG HITS, VOLUME 9				
❏ Motown MS 668	1968	5.00	10.00	20.00
COLLECTORS ITEMS, VOL. 2				
❏ Riverside RLP-1040 [10]	1954	20.00	40.00	80.00
COLLECTORS' CHOICE				
❏ Verve V-8408 [M]	1961	—	—	—
—Canceled				
COLLECTORS' ITEMS, 1922-30				
❏ Historical 11	1967	2.50	5.00	10.00
COLLECTORS' ITEMS, 1925-29				
❏ Historical 20	1968	2.50	5.00	10.00
COLLEGE ALBUM				
❏ Verve MGV-8341 [M]	1959	—	—	—
—Canceled				
COLLEGE JAZZ: DIXIELAND				
❏ Columbia CL 736 [M]	1956	5.00	10.00	20.00
COLOR ME OBG: STATION WDRC				
❏ Roulette R 25347 [M]	1967	5.00	10.00	20.00
COLORADO JAZZ PARTY				
❏ BASF 25099 [(2)]	197?	5.00	10.00	20.00
COLUMBIA JAZZ FESTIVAL				
❏ Columbia JJ-1 [M]	1959	6.25	12.50	25.00
COMBO JAZZ				
❏ Jazztone J-1221 [M]	1956	7.50	15.00	30.00
COME CLOSER TO GOD				
❏ Vee Jay LP-5061 [M]	1964	7.50	15.00	30.00
COMPARATIVE BLUES				
❏ Jazztone J-1258 [M]	1957	7.50	15.00	30.00
COMPOSERS AT PLAY: HAROLD ARLEN AND COLE PORTER				
❏ "X" LVA-1003 [M]	1955	10.00	20.00	40.00
THE COMPOSITIONS OF BENNY GOLSON				
❏ Riverside RLP-3505 [M]	1962	3.75	7.50	15.00
❏ Riverside RS-93505 [S]	1962	5.00	10.00	20.00
THE COMPOSITIONS OF BOBBY TIMMONS				
❏ Riverside RLP-3512 [M]	1962	3.75	7.50	15.00
❏ Riverside RS-93512 [S]	1962	5.00	10.00	20.00
THE COMPOSITIONS OF CHARLIE PARKER				
❏ Riverside RLP-3506 [M]	1962	3.75	7.50	15.00
❏ Riverside RS-93506 [S]	1962	5.00	10.00	20.00
THE COMPOSITIONS OF COLE PORTER				
❏ Riverside RM-3515 [M]	1963	3.75	7.50	15.00
❏ Riverside RS-93515 [S]	1963	5.00	10.00	20.00
THE COMPOSITIONS OF DIZZY GILLESPIE				
❏ Riverside RLP-3508 [M]	1962	3.75	7.50	15.00
❏ Riverside RS-93508 [S]	1962	5.00	10.00	20.00
THE COMPOSITIONS OF DUKE ELLINGTON				
❏ Riverside RLP-3507 [M]	1962	3.75	7.50	15.00
❏ Riverside RS-93507 [S]	1962	5.00	10.00	20.00
THE COMPOSITIONS OF DUKE ELLINGTON, VOL. 2				
❏ Riverside RLP-3510 [M]	1962	3.75	7.50	15.00
❏ Riverside RS-93510 [S]	1962	5.00	10.00	20.00
THE COMPOSITIONS OF GEORGE GERSHWIN				
❏ Riverside RM-3517 [M]	1963	3.75	7.50	15.00
❏ Riverside RS-93517 [S]	1963	5.00	10.00	20.00
THE COMPOSITIONS OF HAROLD ARLEN				
❏ Riverside RM-3518 [M]	1963	3.75	7.50	15.00
❏ Riverside RS-93518 [S]	1963	5.00	10.00	20.00
THE COMPOSITIONS OF HORACE SILVER				
❏ Riverside RLP-3509 [M]	1962	3.75	7.50	15.00
❏ Riverside RS-93509 [S]	1962	5.00	10.00	20.00
THE COMPOSITIONS OF IRVING BERLIN				
❏ Riverside RM-3519 [M]	1963	3.75	7.50	15.00
❏ Riverside RS-93519 [S]	1963	5.00	10.00	20.00

Number Title	Yr	VG	VG+	NM
THE COMPOSITIONS OF JEROME KERN				
❏ Riverside RM-3516 [M]	1963	3.75	7.50	15.00
❏ Riverside RS-93516 [S]	1963	5.00	10.00	20.00
COMPOSITIONS OF LIONEL HAMPTON				
❏ Crown CLP-5107 [M]	195?	6.25	12.50	25.00
THE COMPOSITIONS OF MILES DAVIS				
❏ Riverside RLP-3504 [M]	1962	3.75	7.50	15.00
❏ Riverside RS-93504 [S]	1962	5.00	10.00	20.00
THE COMPOSITIONS OF RICHARD RODGERS				
❏ Riverside RM-3514 [M]	1963	3.75	7.50	15.00
❏ Riverside RS-93514 [S]	1963	5.00	10.00	20.00
THE COMPOSITIONS OF TADD DAMERON				
❏ Riverside RLP-3511 [M]	1962	3.75	7.50	15.00
❏ Riverside RS-93511 [S]	1962	5.00	10.00	20.00
THE COMPOSITIONS OF THELONIOUS MONK				
❏ Riverside RLP-3503 [M]	1962	3.75	7.50	15.00
❏ Riverside RS-93503 [S]	1962	5.00	10.00	20.00
CONCEPTION				
❏ Prestige PRLP-7013 [M]	1956	25.00	50.00	100.00
CONCERT IN JAZZ				
❏ Tops L-1532 [M]	1958	5.00	10.00	20.00
CONCERT JAZZ				
❏ Brunswick BL 54027 [M]	1956	7.50	15.00	30.00
COOL AND CAREFREE				
❏ Columbia Special Products CSP 119 [M]	1963	3.00	6.00	12.00
—Sold only by Carrier air conditioner dealers				
COOL EUROPE				
❏ MGM E-3157 [M]	1955	7.50	15.00	30.00
COOL GABRIELS				
❏ Groove LG-1003 [M]	1956	15.00	30.00	60.00
COOL JAZZ				
❏ Seeco CELP-465 [M]	1960	5.00	10.00	20.00
COOL JAZZ FROM HOLLAND				
❏ Epic LN 1126 [10]	1955	10.00	20.00	40.00
COOLIN'				
❏ New Jazz NJLP-8216 [M]	1959	15.00	30.00	60.00
—Purple label				
❏ New Jazz NJLP-8216 [M]	1965	7.50	15.00	30.00
—Blue label, trident logo at right				
THE CORE OF JAZZ				
❏ MGM SE-4737	1970	3.00	6.00	12.00
COUNTRY & WESTERN CLASSICS 1955				
❏ Economic Consultants 1955	1973	5.00	10.00	20.00
COUNTRY & WESTERN CLASSICS 1956				
❏ Economic Consultants 1956	1973	5.00	10.00	20.00
COUNTRY & WESTERN CLASSICS 1957				
❏ Economic Consultants 1957	1973	5.00	10.00	20.00
COUNTRY & WESTERN CLASSICS 1958				
❏ Economic Consultants 1958	1973	5.00	10.00	20.00
COUNTRY AND WESTERN JAMBOREE				
❏ King 697 [M]	1961	37.50	75.00	150.00
COUNTRY CHRISTMAS				
❏ Columbia CS 9888	1968	3.75	7.50	15.00
❏ King 811 [M]	1962	25.00	50.00	100.00
❏ Monument SLP-18125	1969	5.00	10.00	20.00
A COUNTRY CHRISTMAS				
❏ Columbia Special Products CSS 1434	1970	3.00	6.00	12.00
COUNTRY CHRISTMAS FAVORITES				
❏ Columbia Special Products C 10876	1972	2.50	5.00	10.00
COUNTRY FAIR				
❏ Capitol SWBB-562 [(2)]	1970	6.25	12.50	25.00
COUNTRY HOLIDAY				
❏ Columbia Musical Treasury DS 467	1968	3.75	7.50	15.00
COUNTRY MUSIC BY THE WAYSIDE				
❏ Wayside 1013	1968	5.00	10.00	20.00
COUNTRY MUSIC HOOTENANNY				
❏ Capitol ST 2009 [S]	1963	7.50	15.00	30.00
❏ Capitol T 2009 [M]	1963	6.25	12.50	25.00

Number Title	Yr	VG	VG+	NM
COUNTRY MUSIC STAR SPECTACULAR				
❑ Hickory LPM-116 [M]	1963	6.25	12.50	25.00
THE COUNTRY SIDE OF CHRISTMAS/ALL-TIME FAVORITES IN THE TRADITIONAL STYLE				
❑ Capitol Creative Products SL-6586	1968	3.00	6.00	12.00
COUNTRY SPECIAL				
❑ Capitol STBB-402 [(2)]	1969	6.25	12.50	25.00
A COUNTRY STYLE CHRISTMAS				
❑ Columbia Musical Treasury 3P 6316 [(3)]	1975	3.75	7.50	15.00
CRITICS' CHOICE				
❑ Dawn DLP-1123 [M]	1958	20.00	40.00	80.00
CRUISIN'				
❑ Jazzland JLP-7 [M]	1960	6.25	12.50	25.00
❑ Jazzland JLP-97 [S]	1960	7.50	15.00	30.00
D'OES CRAZY OLDIES				
❑ Oldies 33 OL-8007 [M]	1964	6.25	12.50	25.00
DANCE BAND HITS				
❑ RCA Victor LPT-2 [10]	1951	10.00	20.00	40.00
DANCE DISCOTHEQUE				
❑ Decca DL 4556 [M]	1964	3.75	7.50	15.00
❑ Decca DL 74556 [S]	1964	5.00	10.00	20.00
DANCE ON THE WILD SIDE				
❑ Chancellor CHL-5028 [M]	1962	6.25	12.50	25.00
❑ Chancellor CHLS-5028 [S]	1962	7.50	15.00	30.00
DANCE THE ROCK & ROLL				
❑ Atlantic 8013 [M]	1957	20.00	40.00	80.00
DANCE TO THE BANDS				
❑ Capitol TBO 727 [(2)M]	1956	10.00	20.00	40.00
❑ Capitol T 977 [M]	1958	5.00	10.00	20.00
DANCE TUNES FROM THE VAULT, VOLUME 2				
❑ Chess LP 1476 [M]	1962	10.00	20.00	40.00
DANCE, BE HAPPY!				
❑ Columbia CL 967 [M]	1957	5.00	10.00	20.00
DANCING WITH THE STARS				
❑ Epic LN 3136 [M]	1955	7.50	15.00	30.00
DARK MUDDY BOTTOM BLUES				
❑ Specialty SPS-2149	1971	5.00	10.00	20.00
DAS IS JAZZ!				
❑ Decca DL 8229 [M]	1956	7.50	15.00	30.00
A DATE WITH GREATNESS				
❑ Imperial LP-9188A [M]	1962	12.50	25.00	50.00
—Features Aladdin tracks by Coleman Hawkins, Howard McGhee and Lester Young				
❑ Imperial LP-12188A [R]	1962	6.25	12.50	25.00
A DATE WITH RIVERSIDE				
❑ Riverside S-4 [M]	195?	10.00	20.00	40.00
A DAY IN THE COUNTRY				
❑ Audio Lab AL-1519 [M]	1959	20.00	40.00	80.00
DAYS OF WINE AND VINYL				
❑ Warner Bros. PRO 540 [(2)]	1973	7.50	15.00	30.00
DECADE OF JAZZ, VOLUME 1, 1939-49				
❑ Blue Note BN-LA158-G2 [(2)]	1974	3.75	7.50	15.00
DECADE OF JAZZ, VOLUME 2, 1949-59				
❑ Blue Note BN-LA159-G2 [(2)]	1974	3.75	7.50	15.00
DECADE OF JAZZ, VOLUME 3, 1959-69				
❑ Blue Note BN-LA160-G2 [(2)]	1974	3.75	7.50	15.00
DEEP EAR				
❑ Warner Bros. PRO 591 [(2)]	1974	6.25	12.50	25.00
THE DEFINITIVE JAZZ SCENE, VOL. 1				
❑ ABC Impulse! AS-99 [S]	1968	3.00	6.00	12.00
❑ Impulse! A-99 [M]	1966	3.75	7.50	15.00
❑ Impulse! AS-99 [S]	1966	5.00	10.00	20.00
THE DEFINITIVE JAZZ SCENE, VOL. 2				
❑ ABC Impulse! AS-100 [S]	1968	3.00	6.00	12.00
❑ Impulse! A-100 [M]	1966	3.75	7.50	15.00
❑ Impulse! AS-100 [S]	1966	5.00	10.00	20.00
THE DEFINITIVE JAZZ SCENE, VOL. 3				
❑ ABC Impulse! AS-9101 [S]	1968	3.00	6.00	12.00
❑ Impulse! A-9101 [M]	1966	3.75	7.50	15.00
❑ Impulse! AS-9101 [S]	1966	5.00	10.00	20.00

Number Title	Yr	VG	VG+	NM
DEL-FI ALBUM SAMPLER				
❑ Del-Fi (no #) [DJ]	1959	125.00	250.00	500.00
—Green vinyl, promo only, with paper sleeve				
DEL-FI RECORD HOP				
❑ Del-Fi DFLP-1210 [M]	1959	20.00	40.00	80.00
DEMAND PERFORMANCES				
❑ Monument MLP-8010 [M]	1963	6.25	12.50	25.00
❑ Monument SLP-18010 [S]	1963	10.00	20.00	40.00
DEMONSTRATION RECORD — DISC JOCKEYS — JAN.-FEB. 1955				
❑ Capitol PRO-213 [DJ]	1955	10.00	20.00	40.00
DIAL A HIT				
❑ Bell 6030	1969	5.00	10.00	20.00
DICK CLARK: 20 YEARS OF ROCK N' ROLL				
❑ Buddah BDS 5133 [(2)]	1973	5.00	10.00	20.00
—Gatefold cover with booklet and bonus 7-inch cardboard record				
❑ Buddah BDS 5133 [(2)]	1974	2.50	5.00	10.00
—With none of the extras				
DISCO-TEEN '66				
❑ Columbia Record Club D 155 [M]	1966	5.00	10.00	20.00
❑ Columbia Record Club DS 155 [S]	1966	12.50	25.00	50.00
—Sought-after for its otherwise unavailable extended stereo mix of Bob Dylan's "Positively 4th Street"				
DISCOTHEQUE AU GO GO				
❑ Design DLP-194 [M]	1964	3.00	6.00	12.00
—Cover calls this "Johnny Rivers Discotheque Au Go Go," but only one Johnny Rivers song is on the LP				
❑ Design SDLP-194 [R]	1964	2.50	5.00	10.00
—Cover calls this "Johnny Rivers Discotheque Au Go Go," but only one Johnny Rivers song is on the LP				
DISPLAY CASE #10				
❑ Warner Bros. PRO 542 [(3)]	1973	7.50	15.00	30.00
DISPLAY CASE #8				
❑ Warner Bros. PRO 532 [(2)]	1972	7.50	15.00	30.00
DISPLAY CASE #9				
❑ Warner Bros. PRO 538 [(2)]	1972	7.50	15.00	30.00
DIXIE LAND U.S.A.				
❑ Promenade 2134 [M]	195?	3.75	7.50	15.00
DIXIE, LONDON STYLE				
❑ London LL 1337 [M]	1956	5.00	10.00	20.00
DIXIELAND — NEW ORLEANS				
❑ Mainstream S-6003 [R]	1965	3.00	6.00	12.00
❑ Mainstream 56003 [M]	1965	6.25	2.50	25.00
DIXIELAND AT CARNEGIE HALL				
❑ Forum F-9011 [M]	196?	5.00	10.00	20.00
❑ Forum SF-9011 [S]	196?	6.25	12.50	25.00
❑ Roulette R 25038 [M]	1958	7.50	15.00	30.00
—Originals have a black label				
❑ Roulette R 25038 [M]	1959	5.00	10.00	20.00
—Second pressings have a white label with colored spokes				
DIXIELAND AT ITS BEST				
❑ RCA Camden CAL-838 [M]	1964	3.00	6.00	12.00
❑ RCA Camden CAS-838 [R]	1964	2.50	5.00	10.00
DIXIELAND AT JAZZ, LTD.				
❑ Atlantic 1261 [M]	1957	10.00	20.00	40.00
—Black label				
❑ Atlantic 1261 [M]	1961	6.25	12.50	25.00
—Multicolor label, white "fan" logo at right				
DIXIELAND AT JAZZ, LTD., VOL. 1				
❑ Atlantic ALS-139 [10]	1952	15.00	30.00	60.00
DIXIELAND AT JAZZ, LTD., VOL. 2				
❑ Atlantic ALS-140 [10]	1952	15.00	30.00	60.00
DIXIELAND CLASSICS				
❑ Jazztone J-1216 [M]	1956	7.50	15.00	30.00
DIXIELAND CONTRASTS				
❑ Jazzman LJ-334 [M]	1954	7.50	15.00	30.00
DIXIELAND DETOUR				
❑ Capitol H 312 [10]	1952	—	—	—
—See PEE WEE HUNT.				
DIXIELAND FESTIVAL, VOL. 1				
❑ Vik LX-1057 [M]	1956	7.50	15.00	30.00
DIXIELAND HITS				
❑ Swingville SVLP-2040 [M]	1962	10.00	20.00	40.00
—Purple label				

Number	Title	Yr	VG	VG+	NM
❑ Swingville SVLP-2040 [M]		1965	5.00	10.00	20.00
—Blue label, trident logo at right					

DIXIELAND IN OLD NEW ORLEANS
❑ Golden Crest GC-3021 [M]		1958	5.00	10.00	20.00

DIXIELAND JAZZ
❑ Audiophile XL-325 [M]		1954	7.50	15.00	30.00
❑ Audiophile XL-330 [M]		1954	7.50	15.00	30.00
❑ Grand Award GA 33-310 [M]		1955	6.25	12.50	25.00
—Without wrap-around outer cover					
❑ Grand Award GA 33-310 [M]		1955	15.00	30.00	60.00
—With wrap-around outer cover					

DIXIELAND JAZZ GEMS
❑ Commodore FL-20010 [10]		1950	12.50	25.00	50.00

DIXIELAND MAIN STREAM
❑ Savoy MG-12213 [M]		196?	5.00	10.00	20.00

DIXIELAND RHYTHM KINGS
❑ Paradox LP-6002 [10]		1951	12.50	25.00	50.00

DIXIELAND SERIES, VOL. 1
❑ Savoy MG-15005 [10]		1952	20.00	40.00	80.00

DIXIELAND SERIES, VOL. 2
❑ Savoy MG-15009 [10]		1952	20.00	40.00	80.00

DIXIELAND VS. BIRDLAND
❑ MGM E-231 [10]		1954	12.50	25.00	50.00

DIZZY ATMOSPHERE
❑ Specialty LP-2110 [M]		1957	10.00	20.00	40.00

DOO WOP
❑ Specialty SPS-2114		1969	5.00	10.00	20.00

DOUBLE BARREL JAZZ
❑ Bethlehem BCP-87 [M]		1958	7.50	15.00	30.00

DOWN BEAT CRITICS POLL WINNERS
❑ Clef MGC-742 [M]		1955	—	—	—
—Canceled					

DOWN BEAT JAZZ CONCERT
❑ Dot DLP-9003 [M]		1958	7.50	15.00	30.00
❑ Dot DLP-29003 [S]		1958	6.25	12.50	25.00

DOWN BEAT JAZZ CONCERT, VOL. 2
❑ Dot DLP-3188 [M]		1959	7.50	15.00	30.00
❑ Dot DLP-25188 [S]		1959	6.25	12.50	25.00

DOWN BEAT'S HALL OF FAME, VOL. 1
❑ Verve MGV-8320 [M]		1959	12.50	25.00	50.00
❑ Verve V-8320 [M]		1961	5.00	10.00	20.00

DOWN HOME STOMP: RURAL BLUES, VOLUME 3
❑ Imperial LP-94006		1968	5.00	10.00	20.00

DREAMING ON THE RIVER TO NEW ORLEANS
❑ Southland SLP-238		1963	3.75	7.50	15.00

THE DRUMS
❑ ABC Impulse! AS-9272 [(3)]		197?	5.00	10.00	20.00

DRUMS ON FIRE
❑ World Pacific WP-1247 [M]		1958	10.00	20.00	40.00

THE DUTCH EXPLOSION
❑ White Whale WWS-7130		1970	7.50	15.00	30.00

DYNAMITE
❑ K-Tel TU 2360		1974	2.50	5.00	10.00

EARLY AND RARE: CLASSIC JAZZ "COLLECTORS ITEMS"
❑ Riverside RLP 12-134 [M]		1957	10.00	20.00	40.00

EARLY JAZZ GREATS, VOL. 1
❑ Jazztone J-1249 [M]		1957	7.50	15.00	30.00

EARLY JAZZ GREATS, VOL. 2
❑ Jazztone J-1252 [M]		1957	7.50	15.00	30.00

EARTHY!
❑ Prestige PRLP-7102 [M]		1957	25.00	50.00	100.00

THE EAST COAST JAZZ SCENE, VOL. 1
❑ Coral CRL 57035 [M]		1956	12.50	25.00	50.00

EASY LISTENING
❑ Audiophile AP-27 [M]		1953	7.50	15.00	30.00
❑ Audiophile AP-38 [M]		1953	7.50	15.00	30.00
❑ Audiophile XL-327 [M]		1954	7.50	15.00	30.00

ECHOES OF NEW ORLEANS
❑ Southland SLP-239		1963	3.75	7.50	15.00

EIGHT WAYS TO JAZZ
❑ Riverside RLP 12-272 [M]		1958	7.50	15.00	30.00

18 ALL TIME COUNTRY AND WESTERN HITS
❑ King 1027 [M]		1968	7.50	15.00	30.00

18 ALL TIME RHYTHM 'N' BLUES HITS
❑ King 1026 [M]		1968	7.50	15.00	30.00

18 KING-SIZE COUNTRY HITS
❑ Columbia CL 2668 [M]		1967	5.00	10.00	20.00
❑ Columbia CS 9468 [R]		1967	5.00	10.00	20.00

18 KING-SIZE RHYTHM AND BLUES HITS
❑ Columbia CL 2667 [M]		1967	7.50	15.00	30.00
❑ Columbia CS 9467 [R]		1967	5.00	10.00	20.00

ELEKTRA'S BEST, VOLUME 1: 1966-1968
❑ Elektra EB-1 [(2)]		1969	6.25	12.50	25.00
—Promo only, red labels					

ENCYCLOPEDIA OF JAZZ IN THE '60'S, VOL. 1
❑ Verve V-8677 [M]		1966	3.75	7.50	15.00
❑ Verve V6-8677 [S]		1966	5.00	10.00	20.00

THE ENCYCLOPEDIA OF JAZZ ON RECORDS
❑ Decca DXF 140 [(4)M]		1957	25.00	50.00	100.00
—Box set; individually issued as Decca 8398, 8399, 8400 and 8401					

THE ENCYCLOPEDIA OF JAZZ ON RECORDS, VOL. 1: JAZZ OF THE TWENTIES
❑ Decca DL 8398 [M]		1957	5.00	10.00	20.00

THE ENCYCLOPEDIA OF JAZZ ON RECORDS, VOL. 2: JAZZ OF THE THIRTIES
❑ Decca DL 8399 [M]		1957	5.00	10.00	20.00

THE ENCYCLOPEDIA OF JAZZ ON RECORDS, VOL. 3: JAZZ OF THE FORTIES
❑ Decca DL 8400 [M]		1957	5.00	10.00	20.00

THE ENCYCLOPEDIA OF JAZZ ON RECORDS, VOL. 4: JAZZ OF THE FIFTIES
❑ Decca DL 8401 [M]		1957	5.00	10.00	20.00

END OF AN ERA: RHYTHM 'N' BLUES, VOLUME 1
❑ Imperial LP-94003		1968	5.00	10.00	20.00

ENERGY ESSENTIALS
❑ ABC Impulse! ASD-9228 [(3)]		197?	5.00	10.00	20.00

ENGLAND'S GREATEST HIT MAKERS
❑ London PS 430 [R]		1965	5.00	10.00	20.00
❑ London LL 3430 [M]		1965	6.25	12.50	25.00

ENGLAND'S GREATEST HITS
❑ Fontana MGF 27570 [M]		1967	10.00	20.00	40.00
—Without poster					
❑ Fontana MGF 27570 [M]		1967	12.50	25.00	50.00
—With poster					
❑ Fontana SRF 67570 [R]		1967	5.00	10.00	20.00
—Without poster					
❑ Fontana SRF 67570 [R]		1967	7.50	15.00	30.00
—With poster					

ERA OF THE CLARINET
❑ Mainstream S-6011 [R]		1965	3.00	6.00	12.00
❑ Mainstream 56011 [M]		1965	6.25	12.50	25.00

ESCAPADE REVIEWS THE JAZZ SCENE
❑ Liberty SL-9005 [M]		1957	7.50	15.00	30.00

ESCAPE
❑ Gene Norman GNP-27 [M]		1958	6.25	12.50	25.00

ESQUIRE'S ALL-AMERICAN HOT JAZZ
❑ RCA Victor LPV-544 [M]		1967	5.00	10.00	20.00

ESQUIRE'S WORLD OF JAZZ
❑ Capitol STBO 1970 [(2)S]		1963	5.00	10.00	20.00
❑ Capitol TBO 1970 [(2)M]		1963	5.00	10.00	20.00

THE ESSENTIAL JAZZ VOCALS
❑ Verve V-8505 [M]		1963	5.00	10.00	20.00
❑ Verve V6-8505 [S]		1963	6.25	12.50	25.00

AN EVENING OF JAZZ
❑ Norgran MGN-1065 [M]		1956	20.00	40.00	80.00
❑ Verve MGV-8155 [M]		1957	7.50	15.00	30.00
❑ Verve V-8155 [M]		1961	5.00	10.00	20.00

Number Title	Yr	VG	VG+	NM
EVERYBODY'S FAVORITE BLUES				
❑ King 875 [M]	1963	17.50	35.00	70.00
EVERYBODY'S GONE SURFIN'				
❑ Parkway P-7035 [M]	1963	12.50	25.00	50.00
THE EXCELLO STORY				
❑ Excello LPS-8025 [(2)]	1972	6.25	12.50	25.00
THE EXCITING NEW LIVERPOOL SOUND				
❑ Columbia CL 2172 [M]	1964	7.50	15.00	30.00
EXPLOSIVE!				
❑ Liberty MM-412 [DJ]	1962	12.50	25.00	50.00
—Promo-only release				
FABULOUS FAVORITES OF OUR TIME				
❑ Liberty LRP-3223 [M]	1962	5.00	10.00	20.00
❑ Liberty LST-7223 [S]	1962	6.25	12.50	25.00
FAMILY CHRISTMAS FAVORITES FROM BING CROSBY AND THE COLUMBUS BOYCHOIR				
❑ Decca DL 34487	1967	3.75	7.50	15.00
—Sold only at Safeway grocery stores				
FAMILY PORTRAIT				
❑ A&M SP-19002	1968	5.00	10.00	20.00
FANFARE OF HITS				
❑ Argo LP-656 [M]	1960	6.25	12.50	25.00
FAVORITE CHRISTMAS CAROLS FROM THE VOICE OF FIRESTONE				
❑ Firestone MLP 7005 [M]	1962	3.75	7.50	15.00
—Sold only at Firestone tire dealers; actually Volume 1 of the "Firestone Presents..." series				
FAVORITE SACRED SONGS				
❑ King 556 [M]	1956	37.50	75.00	150.00
THE FEMININE TOUCH				
❑ Decca DL 5486 [10]	1953	12.50	25.00	50.00
❑ Decca DL 8316 [M]	1956	7.50	15.00	30.00
15 FAVORITES				
❑ Hickory LPM-105 [M]	1962	6.25	12.50	25.00
15 GOLDEN HITS				
❑ United Artists UAL-3192 [M]	1962	6.25	12.50	25.00
❑ United Artists UAS-6192 [S]	1962	7.50	15.00	30.00
15 HITS: THE ORIGINAL RECORDINGS (THE ORIGINAL HITS, VOLUME 5)				
❑ Liberty LRP-3235 [M]	1962	5.00	10.00	20.00
FIFTEEN STAR SAXOPHONES				
❑ Bethlehem BCP-6035 [M]	1959	7.50	15.00	30.00
FIFTY CHRISTMAS FAVORITES				
❑ RCA Camden CXS-9025 [(2)]	1972	3.75	7.50	15.00
50 YEARS OF FILM				
❑ Warner Bros. 3XX 2737 [(3)]	1973	6.25	12.50	25.00
—Box set with 60-page booklet				
50 YEARS OF FILM MUSIC				
❑ Warner Bros. 3XX 2736 [(3)]	1973	6.25	12.50	25.00
—Box set with 28-page booklet				
50 YEARS OF JAZZ GREATS				
❑ Columbia Musical Treasury P3S 5932 [(3)]	197?	5.00	10.00	20.00
52ND STREET JAZZ				
❑ Waldorf Music Hall MH 33-148 [10]	195?	25.00	50.00	100.00
FILL YOUR HEAD WITH JAZZ				
❑ Columbia G 30217 [(2)]	1971	3.75	7.50	15.00
FILLET OF SOUL				
❑ Stax STS 3021	1972	5.00	10.00	20.00
FILM MUSIC FROM FRANCE				
❑ Philips PHM 200071 [M]	1962	5.00	10.00	20.00
❑ Philips PHS 600071 [S]	1962	7.50	15.00	30.00
FINK ALONG WITH MAD				
❑ Big Top 12-1306 [M]	1962	25.00	50.00	100.00
FIRESTONE PRESENTS YOUR CHRISTMAS FAVORITES, VOLUME 3				
❑ Firestone MLP 7008 [M]	1964	3.75	7.50	15.00
—Sold only at Firestone tire dealers				
❑ Firestone SLP 7008 [S]	1964	4.00	8.00	16.00
—Sold only at Firestone tire dealers				

Number Title	Yr	VG	VG+	NM
FIRESTONE PRESENTS YOUR CHRISTMAS FAVORITES, VOLUME 7				
❑ Firestone CSLP 7015	1968	3.00	6.00	12.00
—Sold only at Firestone tire dealers				
FIRESTONE PRESENTS YOUR FAVORITE CHRISTMAS CAROLS, VOLUME 2				
❑ Firestone MLP 7006 [M]	1963	3.75	7.50	15.00
—Sold only at Firestone tire dealers				
❑ Firestone SLP 7006 [S]	1963	4.00	8.00	16.00
—Sold only at Firestone tire dealers				
FIRESTONE PRESENTS YOUR FAVORITE CHRISTMAS MUSIC, VOLUME 4				
❑ Firestone MLP 7011 [M]	1965	3.00	6.00	12.00
—Sold only at Firestone tire dealers				
❑ Firestone SLP 7011 [S]	1965	3.75	7.50	15.00
—Sold only at Firestone tire dealers				
FIRESTONE PRESENTS YOUR FAVORITE CHRISTMAS MUSIC, VOLUME 5				
❑ Firestone MLP 7012 [M]	1966	3.00	6.00	12.00
—Sold only at Firestone tire dealers				
❑ Firestone SLP 7012 [S]	1966	3.75	7.50	15.00
—Sold only at Firestone tire dealers				
FIRESTONE PRESENTS YOUR FAVORITE CHRISTMAS MUSIC, VOLUME 6				
❑ Firestone MLP 7014 [M]	1967	2.50	5.00	10.00
—Sold only at Firestone tire dealers				
❑ Firestone SLP 7014 [S]	1967	3.00	6.00	12.00
—Sold only at Firestone tire dealers				
FIRST ALBUM OF JAZZ				
❑ Folkways FP-712 [10]	1951	12.50	25.00	50.00
FIRST CHRISTMAS RECORD FOR CHILDREN				
❑ Harmony HS 14554	197?	3.00	6.00	12.00
THE FIRST GREAT ROCK FESTIVALS OF THE SEVENTIES: ISLE OF WIGHT/ATLANTA POP FESTIVAL				
❑ Columbia G3X 30805 [(3)]	1971	6.25	12.50	25.00
FIVE FEET OF SWING				
❑ Decca DL 8045 [M]	1954	10.00	20.00	40.00
5-STRING BANJO PICKIN' AND SINGIN'				
❑ King 994 [M]	1966	10.00	20.00	40.00
THE FOLK BOX				
❑ Elektra EKL-9001 [(4)]	1964	12.50	25.00	50.00
FOLK FESTIVAL				
❑ Elektra SMP 2 [M]	1956	7.50	15.00	30.00
FOLK FESTIVAL OF THE BLUES				
❑ Argo LP-4031 [M]	1964	10.00	20.00	40.00
FOLK POPS 'N JAZZ SAMPLER				
❑ Elektra SMP 3 [M]	1957	6.25	12.50	25.00
FOLK SAMPLER FIVE				
❑ Elektra SMP 5 [M]	196?	6.25	12.50	25.00
THE FOLK SCENE				
❑ Elektra SMP 6 [M]	196?	6.25	12.50	25.00
FOLKSONG '65				
❑ Elektra SMP 8 [M]	1965	5.00	10.00	20.00
❑ Elektra S 78 [S]	1965	6.25	12.50	25.00
FOOTNOTES TO JAZZ, VOL. 2: ANATOMY OF A JAZZ COMPOSITION				
❑ Folkways FP-31 [10]	1951	12.50	25.00	50.00
FOOTPRINTS IN TIME				
❑ White Whale WWS-7125	1970	6.25	12.50	25.00
FOR A MUSICAL MERRY CHRISTMAS				
❑ RCA Victor PR-149A [M]	1963	3.00	6.00	12.00
—Sold only at Acme Markets (Mid-Atlantic states)				
❑ RCA Victor PRM-163 [M]	1964	3.00	6.00	12.00
—Sold at B.F. Goodrich dealers				
❑ RCA Victor PRS-163(e) [S]	1964	3.00	6.00	12.00
—Sold at B.F. Goodrich dealers				
FOR A MUSICAL MERRY CHRISTMAS, VOL. TWO				
❑ RCA Victor PRM 189 [M]	1965	3.00	6.00	12.00
—Sold at B.F. Goodrich dealers				
❑ RCA Victor PRS 189 [S]	1965	3.75	7.50	15.00
—Sold at B.F. Goodrich tire dealers				
FOR A MUSICAL MERRY CHRISTMAS, VOLUME 3				
❑ RCA Victor PRM-221 [M]	1966	3.00	6.00	12.00
—Sold at B.F. Goodrich dealers				

Number / Title	Yr	VG	VG+	NM
❏ RCA Victor PRS-221 [S]	1966	3.75	7.50	15.00
—Sold at B.F. Goodrich dealers				
FOR A MUSICAL MERRY CHRISTMAS, VOLUME 4				
❏ RCA Victor PRS-253	1967	3.00	6.00	12.00
—Sold at B.F. Goodrich dealers				
FOR DANCERS ONLY				
❏ Epic LN 3120 [M]	1955	7.50	15.00	30.00
FOR JAZZ LOVERS				
❏ EmArcy MG-36086 [M]	1956	10.00	20.00	40.00
FOR TWISTERS ONLY				
❏ Ace LP-1020 [M]	1962	17.50	35.00	70.00
THE FORCE				
❏ Warner Bros. PRO 593	1974	5.00	10.00	20.00
❏ Warner Bros. PRO 596 [(2)]	1974	6.25	12.50	25.00
FORD HOOTENANNY				
❏ RCA Victor PRM-152 [M]	1964	5.00	10.00	20.00
—Sold only at Ford dealers				
FORGOTTEN MILLION SELLERS				
❏ King 792 [M]	1962	25.00	50.00	100.00
FORTY GOSPEL GREATS				
❏ Vee Jay VJS-2-19000 [(2)]	1975	6.25	12.50	25.00
FOUR ALTOS				
❏ Prestige PRLP-7116 [M]	1957	25.00	50.00	100.00
FOUR FRENCH HORNS				
❏ Savoy MG-12173 [M]	1961	12.50	25.00	50.00
THE FOUR MOST GUITARS				
❏ ABC-Paramount ABC-109 [M]	1956	7.50	15.00	30.00
❏ Paramount LP-109 [10]	1954	15.00	30.00	60.00
THE FOUR ROSES DANCE PARTY				
❏ Columbia Special Products XTV 68933/4 [M]	1961	3.75	7.50	15.00
FOUR TO GO				
❏ Columbia CL 2018 [M]	1963	5.00	10.00	20.00
❏ Columbia CS 8818 [S]	1963	3.75	7.50	15.00
14 GOLDEN RECORDINGS FROM THE HISTORIC VAULTS OF DUKE-PEACOCK RECORDS				
❏ ABC ABCX-784	1973	5.00	10.00	20.00
14 GOLDEN RECORDINGS FROM THE HISTORIC VAULTS OF DUKE-PEACOCK RECORDS, VOLUME 2				
❏ ABC ABCX-789	1973	5.00	10.00	20.00
14 GREAT ALL TIME C&W WALTZES				
❏ King 890 [M]	1964	17.50	35.00	70.00
14 HIT FLASHBACKS FROM THE GOLDEN GROUP ERA				
❏ King 893 [M]	1964	17.50	35.00	70.00
14 MORE NEWIES BUT GOODIES				
❏ Mercury MG-20493 [M]	1960	7.50	15.00	30.00
❏ Mercury SR-60241 [S]	1960	10.00	20.00	40.00
14 NEWIES BUT GOODIES				
❏ Mercury MG-20493 [M]	1960	7.50	15.00	30.00
❏ Mercury SR-60172 [S]	1960	10.00	20.00	40.00
14 OF THE WORLD'S BEST-LOVED CHRISTMAS SONGS				
❏ Columbia Special Products CSP 122 [M]	1963	3.75	7.50	15.00
—Sold only at Walgreens drug stores. Title on record is "Music of Christmas"; number on record is "XTV 88672" on Side 1, "XTV 88673" on Side 2				
FRANK BULL AND GENE NORMAN PRESENT DIXIELAND JUBILEE				
❏ Decca DL 7022 [10]	1952	12.50	25.00	50.00
FRENCH TOAST				
❏ Angel ANG-60009 [10]	1956	12.50	25.00	50.00
FROM DAVID FROST AND BILLY TAYLOR...MERRY CHRISTMAS				
❏ Bell 6053	1970	3.75	7.50	15.00
FROM UNDER THE CHRISTMAS TREE				
❏ Capitol Creative Products SL-6589	1968	3.00	6.00	12.00
FUNKY BLUES NO. 2				
❏ American Recording Society G-404 [M]	1956	7.50	15.00	30.00
GARDEN OF DELIGHTS				
❏ Elektra S3 10 [(3)]	1971	5.00	10.00	20.00
—Butterfly labels, possibly promo only				
GARY MOORE PRESENTS "MY KIND OF MUSIC"				
❏ Columbia CL 717 [M]	1956	6.25	12.50	25.00

Number / Title	Yr	VG	VG+	NM
GEMS OF JAZZ, VOL. 1				
❏ Decca DL 5133 [10]	1950	12.50	25.00	50.00
❏ Decca DL 8039 [M]	1954	10.00	20.00	40.00
GEMS OF JAZZ, VOL. 2				
❏ Decca DL 5134 [10]	1950	12.50	25.00	50.00
❏ Decca DL 8040 [M]	1954	10.00	20.00	40.00
GEMS OF JAZZ, VOL. 3				
❏ Decca DL 5383 [10]	1952	12.50	25.00	50.00
❏ Decca DL 8041 [M]	1954	10.00	20.00	40.00
GEMS OF JAZZ, VOL. 4				
❏ Decca DL 5384 [10]	1952	12.50	25.00	50.00
❏ Decca DL 8042 [M]	1954	10.00	20.00	40.00
GEMS OF JAZZ, VOL. 5				
❏ Decca DL 8043 [M]	1954	10.00	20.00	40.00
GENE NORMAN PRESENTS JUST JAZZ				
❏ RCA Victor LPM-3102 [10]	1953	12.50	25.00	50.00
GERRY GOFFIN AND CAROLE KING: SOLID GOLD				
❏ Screen Gems/Columbia CPL-713 [DJ]	1975	5.00	10.00	20.00
—Promo-only compilation of oldies sent to radio to spur airplay on songs owned by this publishing house				
GET IT TOGETHER				
❏ Mainstream MRL-350	197?	3.00	6.00	12.00
GIANTS OF BOOGIE WOOGIE				
❏ Riverside RLP 12-106 [M]	1956	10.00	20.00	40.00
GIANTS OF JAZZ				
❏ American Recording Society G-401 [M]	1956	7.50	15.00	30.00
THE GIANTS OF JAZZ				
❏ Columbia CL 1970 [M]	1963	7.50	15.00	30.00
GIANTS OF JAZZ ORGAN				
❏ King 837 [M]	1963	30.00	60.00	120.00
GIANTS OF JAZZ VOL. 2				
❏ American Recording Society G-444 [M]	1957	7.50	15.00	30.00
GIANTS OF SMALL BAND SWING, VOL. 1				
❏ Riverside RLP 12-143 [M]	1957	10.00	20.00	40.00
GIANTS OF SMALL BAND SWING, VOL. 2				
❏ Riverside RLP 12-145 [M]	1957	10.00	20.00	40.00
THE GIFT OF CHRISTMAS				
❏ Columbia Special Products C 10018	1971	3.00	6.00	12.00
—Sold only at Ace hardware stores (sticker on lower right front cover)				
❏ Columbia Special Products P 11648	1973	2.50	5.00	10.00
—Same contents and order as "The Gift of Christmas," C 10018; oddly, the record calls this "The Gift of Christmas -- Volume II"!				
THE GIFT OF CHRISTMAS, VOLUME I				
❏ Columbia Special Products CSS 706	1968	3.00	6.00	12.00
—Produced for First Financial Marketing Group				
THE GIRLS SING				
❏ Savoy MG-12220 [M]	196?	5.00	10.00	20.00
THE GLORY OF CHRISTMAS				
❏ Columbia Musical Treasury P3S 5356 [(3)]	196?	3.75	7.50	15.00
—Performed by anonymous musicians				
GOIN' UP THE COUNTRY: RURAL BLUES, VOLUME 1				
❏ Imperial LP-94000	1968	5.00	10.00	20.00
GOLD HITS				
❏ Warwick W 2008 [M]	1959	20.00	40.00	80.00
—Reissue of "Goodies But Oldies, Volume 2"; this title still appears on the label				
GOLD SOUL				
❏ Stax STS 2031	1970	5.00	10.00	20.00
THE GOLDEN AGE OF RHYTHM AND BLUES				
❏ Chess 2CH-50030 [(2)]	1972	6.25	12.50	25.00
GOLDEN ECHOES				
❏ Arvee A-433 [M]	1962	6.25	12.50	25.00
❏ Arvee SA-433 [S]	1962	7.50	15.00	30.00
GOLDEN ENCORES				
❏ Cadence CLP-3043 [M]	1960	10.00	20.00	40.00
THE GOLDEN ERA OF JAZZ, VOL. 1				
❏ Savoy MG-15015 [10]	1952	20.00	40.00	80.00
THE GOLDEN ERA OF JAZZ, VOL. 2				
❏ Savoy MG-15018 [10]	1952	20.00	40.00	80.00

Number Title	Yr	VG	VG+	NM
GOLDEN GASSERS				
☐ Chess LP 1458 USA [M]	1961	30.00	60.00	120.00
—National version; see listings in this section under "KYA," "Murray the K" and "WAMO" for regional releases				
THE GOLDEN GLOW OF CHRISTMAS				
☐ Columbia Special Products C 10925	1972	3.00	6.00	12.00
—Sold only at JCPenney department stores				
GOLDEN GOODIES OF 1963, VOL. 18				
☐ Roulette R 25247 [M]	1964	5.00	10.00	20.00
GOLDEN GOODIES, VOL. 1				
☐ Roulette R 25207 [M]	1963	6.25	12.50	25.00
GOLDEN GOODIES, VOL. 2				
☐ Roulette R 25210 [M]	1963	6.25	12.50	25.00
GOLDEN GOODIES, VOL. 3				
☐ Roulette R 25218 [M]	1963	6.25	12.50	25.00
GOLDEN GOODIES, VOL. 4: GOODIES FOR A DANCE PARTY				
☐ Roulette R 25209 [M]	1963	6.25	12.50	25.00
GOLDEN GOODIES, VOL. 5				
☐ Roulette R 25215 [M]	1963	6.25	12.50	25.00
GOLDEN GOODIES, VOL. 6				
☐ Roulette R 25216 [M]	1963	6.25	12.50	25.00
GOLDEN GOODIES, VOL. 7				
☐ Roulette R 25212 [M]	1963	6.25	12.50	25.00
GOLDEN GOODIES, VOL. 8				
☐ Roulette R 25214 [M]	1963	6.25	12.50	25.00
GOLDEN GOODIES, VOL. 9				
☐ Roulette R 25213 [M]	1963	6.25	12.50	25.00
GOLDEN GOODIES, VOL. 10				
☐ Roulette R 25217 [M]	1963	6.25	12.50	25.00
GOLDEN GOODIES, VOL. 11				
☐ Roulette R 25219 [M]	1963	6.25	12.50	25.00
GOLDEN GOODIES, VOL. 12				
☐ Roulette R 25211 [M]	1963	6.25	12.50	25.00
GOLDEN GOODIES, VOL. 14				
☐ Roulette R 25239 [M]	1964	5.00	10.00	20.00
GOLDEN GOODIES, VOL. 15				
☐ Roulette R 25240 [M]	1964	5.00	10.00	20.00
GOLDEN GOODIES, VOL. 16				
☐ Roulette R 25241 [M]	1964	5.00	10.00	20.00
GOLDEN GOODIES, VOL. 17				
☐ Roulette R 25242 [M]	1964	5.00	10.00	20.00
GOLDEN GREATS				
☐ Liberty LRP-3500 [M]	1967	3.75	7.50	15.00
☐ Liberty LST-7500 [P]	1967	5.00	10.00	20.00
THE GOLDEN GROUPS				
☐ Specialty SPS-2155	1972	5.00	10.00	20.00
GOLDEN HITS FROM THE GANG AT BANG				
☐ Bang BLP-215 [M]	1967	5.00	10.00	20.00
☐ Bang BLPS-215 [P]	1967	6.25	12.50	25.00
GOLDEN INSTRUMENTALS				
☐ Dot DLP-3820 [M]	1967	6.25	12.50	25.00
☐ Dot DLP-25820 [S]	1967	6.25	12.50	25.00
GOLDEN JAZZ INTRSUMENTALS				
☐ Bethlehem BCP-6065 [M]	1962	6.25	12.50	25.00
GOLDEN MOMENTS IN COUNTRY AND WESTERN MUSIC				
☐ Capitol SQBO-90985 [(2)S]	196?	5.00	10.00	20.00
—Capitol Record Club exclusive				
GOLDEN SOUVENIRS				
☐ United Artists UAL-3317 [M]	1963	6.25	12.50	25.00
☐ United Artists UAS-6317 [S]	1963	7.50	15.00	30.00
GOLDEN TEEN HITS				
☐ Liberty L-5505 [M]	1962	10.00	20.00	40.00
GOLDEN TREASURE CHEST				
☐ United Artists UAL-3314 [M]	1963	6.25	12.50	25.00
☐ United Artists UAS-6314 [S]	1963	7.50	15.00	30.00
GONE BUT NOT FORGOTTEN				
☐ Class LP-5004 [M]	1959	25.00	50.00	100.00
☐ Rendezvous M-1314 [M]	196?	10.00	20.00	40.00
—Reissue of Class 5004				

Number Title	Yr	VG	VG+	NM
GOOD GUY JACK SPECTOR PRESENTS 22 ORIGINAL WINNERS				
☐ Roulette R 25254 [M]	1964	5.00	10.00	20.00
THE GOOD OLD 50'S				
☐ Atco 33-118 [M]	1960	15.00	30.00	60.00
GOODIES BUT OLDIES VOLUME 2				
☐ Warwick W 2008 [M]	1959	30.00	60.00	120.00
—Original title of LP appears on both cover and label; reissued as "Gold Hits" -- and there was no Volume 1!				
GOOFY GREATS				
☐ K-Tel NU 9030 [(2)]	1975	3.00	6.00	12.00
GOSPEL HOOTENANNY				
☐ Imperial LP-9240 [M]	1963	5.00	10.00	20.00
☐ Imperial LP-12240 [S]	1963	6.25	12.50	25.00
GOSPEL STARS IN CONCERT				
☐ Specialty SPS-2153	1971	5.00	10.00	20.00
GRAFFITI GOLD				
☐ Vee Jay VJS-2-9000 [(2)]	1974	5.00	10.00	20.00
THE GREAT BAND ERA				
☐ Reader's Digest RD-25 [(10)M]	1965	5.00	10.00	20.00
—Box set with flip-open top				
☐ Reader's Digest RD-25 [(10)R]	1965	3.75	7.50	15.00
—Box set with flip-open top				
THE GREAT BANDS				
☐ Columbia Musical Treasury P2M 5267 [(2)]	1968	5.00	10.00	20.00
GREAT BLUES				
☐ Riverside RLP-1074 [10]	1955	20.00	40.00	80.00
GREAT BLUES SINGERS				
☐ Riverside RLP 12-121 [M]	1957	10.00	20.00	40.00
THE GREAT BLUES SINGERS				
☐ Riverside RLP-1032 [10]	1954	20.00	40.00	80.00
THE GREAT GROUP GOODIES				
☐ Atco 33-143 [M]	1962	20.00	40.00	80.00
GREAT GROUP OLDIES				
☐ Oldies 33 OL-8003 [M]	1963	6.25	12.50	25.00
GREAT GROUP OLDIES, VOL. 2				
☐ Oldies 33 OL-8006 [M]	1964	6.25	12.50	25.00
GREAT GROUPS, GREAT RECORDS				
☐ Laurie LLP-2010 [M]	1961	7.50	15.00	30.00
GREAT GUITARS OF JAZZ				
☐ MGM SE-4691	1970	3.00	6.00	12.00
THE GREAT HITS OF 1964 AND SOME GOLDEN OLDIES				
☐ Vee Jay LP-1112 [M]	1965	7.50	15.00	30.00
—Not known to exist in stereo				
GREAT INSTRUMENTAL R&B HITS				
☐ Imperial LP-9271 [M]	1964	6.25	12.50	25.00
☐ Imperial LP-12271 [R]	1964	5.00	10.00	20.00
GREAT JAZZ				
☐ Rondo-lette A-31 [M]	195?	6.25	12.50	25.00
GREAT JAZZ BRASS				
☐ RCA Camden CAL-383 [M]	1958	6.25	12.50	25.00
GREAT JAZZ PIANISTS				
☐ RCA Camden CAL-328 [M]	1958	6.25	12.50	25.00
GREAT JAZZ PIANISTS OF OUR TIME				
☐ RCA Camden CAL-882 [M]	1965	3.75	7.50	15.00
☐ RCA Camden CAS-882 [R]	1965	2.50	5.00	10.00
GREAT JAZZ REEDS				
☐ RCA Camden CAL-339 [M]	1958	6.25	12.50	25.00
THE GREAT JAZZ SINGERS				
☐ Halo 50269 [M]	1957	3.75	7.50	15.00
GREAT MOTION PICTURE THEMES				
☐ United Artists UAL-3122 [M]	1960	3.75	7.50	15.00
☐ United Artists UAS-6122 [S]	1960	5.00	10.00	20.00
GREAT MOTION PICTURE THEMES (MORE ORIGINAL SOUND TRACKS AND HIT MUSIC)				
☐ United Artists UAL-3158 [M]	1961	3.75	7.50	15.00
☐ United Artists UAS-6158 [S]	1961	5.00	10.00	20.00

Number / Title	Yr	VG	VG+	NM
THE GREAT SONGS OF CHRISTMAS				
❑ Columbia Special Products XTV 69406/7 [M]	1961	3.75	7.50	15.00
—Sold only at Goodyear tire dealers				
❑ Columbia Special Products XTV 69406/7 [M]	1962	3.00	6.00	12.00
—Reissue with no reference to Goodyear on the cover				
THE GREAT SONGS OF CHRISTMAS, ALBUM TWO				
❑ Columbia Special Products XTV 86100/1 [M]	1962	3.75	7.50	15.00
—Sold only at Goodyear tire dealers				
THE GREAT SONGS OF CHRISTMAS, ALBUM THREE				
❑ Columbia Special Products CSP 117 [M]	1963	3.75	7.50	15.00
—Sold only at Goodyear tire dealers. The number listed is on the jacket; on the record, the number is "XTV 86656" on Side 1 and "XTV 86657" on Side 2				
THE GREAT SONGS OF CHRISTMAS, ALBUM FOUR				
❑ Columbia Special Products CSP 155M [M]	1964	3.75	7.50	15.00
—Sold only at Goodyear tire dealers				
❑ Columbia Special Products CSP 155S [S]	1964	4.50	9.00	18.00
—Sold only at Goodyear tire dealers				
THE GREAT SONGS OF CHRISTMAS, ALBUM FIVE				
❑ Columbia Special Products CSP 238M [M]	1965	3.00	6.00	12.00
—Sold only at Goodyear tire dealers				
❑ Columbia Special Products CSP 238S [S]	1965	3.75	7.50	15.00
—Sold only at Goodyear tire dealers				
THE GREAT SONGS OF CHRISTMAS, ALBUM SIX				
❑ Columbia Special Products CSM 388 [M]	1966	3.00	6.00	12.00
—Sold only at Goodyear tire dealers				
❑ Columbia Special Products CSS 388 [S]	1966	3.75	7.50	15.00
—Sold only at Goodyear tire dealers				
THE GREAT SONGS OF CHRISTMAS, ALBUM SEVEN				
❑ Columbia Special Products CSS 547	1967	3.00	6.00	12.00
—Sold only at Goodyear tire dealers				
GREAT SONGS OF CHRISTMAS, ALBUM EIGHT				
❑ Columbia Special Products CSS 888	1968	3.00	6.00	12.00
—Sold only at Goodyear tire dealers				
GREAT SONGS OF CHRISTMAS, ALBUM NINE				
❑ Columbia Special Products CSS 1033	1969	3.00	6.00	12.00
—Sold only at Goodyear tire dealers; version 1 has a 10 1/2-inch flap on right inner gatefold (part of record is exposed)				
❑ Columbia Special Products CSS 1033	1969	3.00	6.00	12.00
—Sold only at Goodyear tire dealers; version 2 has a 12 1/4-inch flap on right inner gatefold (record is completely covered)				
THE GREAT SOUL HITS				
❑ Brunswick BL 54129 [M]	1968	6.25	12.50	25.00
❑ Brunswick BL 754129 [S]	1968	3.75	7.50	15.00
THE GREAT SWING BANDS				
❑ Jazztone J-1245 [M]	1957	7.50	15.00	30.00
GREAT SWING BANDS OF THE FORTIES				
❑ Audio Lab AL-1530 [M]	1959	20.00	40.00	80.00
THE GREAT TENOR JAZZMEN				
❑ Allegro 1634 [M]	195?	10.00	20.00	40.00
GREAT TRUMPET ARTISTS				
❑ RCA Victor LPT-26 [10]	1951	12.50	25.00	50.00
❑ RCA Victor LPT-35 [10]	1952	12.50	25.00	50.00
THE GREATEST 15 HITS ON ACE RECORDS				
❑ Ace LP-1012 [M]	1960	17.50	35.00	70.00
GREATEST COUNTRY AND WESTERN HITS NO. 3				
❑ Columbia CL 1816 [M]	1962	5.00	10.00	20.00
❑ Columbia CS 8616 [S]	1962	6.25	12.50	25.00
GREATEST COUNTRY AND WESTERN HITS NO. 4				
❑ Columbia CL 2081 [M]	1963	5.00	10.00	20.00
❑ Columbia CS 8881 [S]	1963	6.25	12.50	25.00
THE GREATEST GOLDEN GOODIES				
❑ Laurie LLP-2014 [M]	1962	7.50	15.00	30.00
❑ Laurie SLP-2014 [R]	196?	3.75	7.50	15.00
GREATEST GOSPEL SONGS OF OUR TIMES				
❑ Vee Jay LP-5043 [M]	1963	7.50	15.00	30.00
GREATEST GOSPEL SONGS, VOLUME 1				
❑ Specialty SPS-2144	1970	5.00	10.00	20.00
GREATEST GOSPEL SONGS, VOLUME 2				
❑ Specialty SPS-2145	1970	5.00	10.00	20.00
GREATEST HITS				
❑ Harmony HL 7255 [M]	1960	3.75	7.50	15.00
THE GREATEST HITS FROM ENGLAND				
❑ Parrot PA 61010 [M]	1967	6.25	12.50	25.00
❑ Parrot PAS 71010 [R]	1967	5.00	10.00	20.00
THE GREATEST HITS FROM ENGLAND, VOLUME 2				
❑ Parrot PA 61017 [M]	1968	6.25	12.50	25.00
❑ Parrot PAS 71017 [R]	1968	5.00	10.00	20.00
THE GREATEST NAMES IN JAZZ				
❑ Verve PR2-3 [(3)]	196?	5.00	10.00	20.00
—Box set				
THE GREATEST ROCK & ROLL				
❑ Atlantic 8001 [M]	1956	30.00	60.00	120.00
THE GREATEST SONGS OF WOODY GUTHRIE				
❑ Vanguard VSD-35/36 [(2)]	1972	3.75	7.50	15.00
THE GREATEST TEENAGE HITS OF ALL TIME!				
❑ Teem LP-5003 [M]	196?	7.50	15.00	30.00
GREATEST WESTERN HITS				
❑ Columbia CL 1257 [M]	1959	7.50	15.00	30.00
❑ Columbia CS 8776 [R]	1963	5.00	10.00	20.00
GREATEST WESTERN HITS NO. 2				
❑ Columbia CL 1408 [M]	1960	7.50	15.00	30.00
❑ Columbia CS 8777 [R]	1963	5.00	10.00	20.00
GRETSCH DRUM NIGHT AT BIRDLAND				
❑ Roulette R 52049 [M]	1960	7.50	15.00	30.00
❑ Roulette SR 52049 [S]	1960	7.50	15.00	30.00
GRETSCH DRUM NIGHT, VOLUME 2				
❑ Roulette R 52067 [M]	1961	7.50	15.00	30.00
❑ Roulette SR 52067 [S]	1961	7.50	15.00	30.00
GROOVY GOODIES				
❑ Colpix CP-466 [M]	1964	20.00	40.00	80.00
❑ Colpix SCP-466 [S]	1964	25.00	50.00	100.00
GROUP OF GOODIES				
❑ Chess LP 1478 [M]	1963	12.50	25.00	50.00
❑ Chess LPS 1478 [R]	196?	5.00	10.00	20.00
GROUP OF GOODIES, VOLUME 2				
❑ Chess LP 1491 [M]	1965	12.50	25.00	50.00
GUARANTEED TO PLEASE				
❑ Teem LP-5002 [M]	196?	7.50	15.00	30.00
GUIDE TO JAZZ				
❑ RCA Victor LPM-1393 [M]	1956	7.50	15.00	30.00
GUITAR BOOGIE				
❑ Pickwick ACL-7041	197?	2.50	5.00	10.00
—Reissue of RCA Victor LSP-4624(e)				
❑ RCA Victor AYL1-3768(e)	1980	2.00	4.00	8.00
—Another reissue of RCA Victor LSP-4624(e)				
❑ RCA Victor LSP-4624(e)	1971	3.75	7.50	15.00
—Includes tracks by Eric Clapton, Eric Clapton and Jimmy Page, The Allstars Featuring Jeff Beck, The Allstars Featuring Jimmy Page; orange label original				
GUITAR PLAYERS				
❑ Mainstream MRL-410	197?	3.00	6.00	12.00
HANDFUL OF COOL JAZZ				
❑ Bethlehem BCP-90 [M]	1959	7.50	15.00	30.00
HAPPY HOLIDAYS				
❑ Columbia Special Products CSP 242 [M]	1965	3.75	7.50	15.00
—Sold only at True Value Hardware stores				
HAPPY HOLIDAYS, VOLUME II				
❑ Columbia Special Products CSM 348 [M]	1966	3.75	7.50	15.00
—Sold only at True Value Hardware stores				
❑ Columbia Special Products CSS 348 [S]	1966	3.00	6.00	12.00
—Sold only at True Value Hardware stores				
HAPPY HOLIDAYS, VOL. III				
❑ RCA Victor PRS-255	1967	3.75	7.50	15.00
—Sold only at True Value Hardware stores				
HAPPY HOLIDAYS, VOLUME IV				
❑ RCA Victor PRS-267	1968	3.75	7.50	15.00
—Sold only at True Value Hardware stores				
HAPPY HOLIDAYS, VOL. 5				
❑ Capitol Creative Products SL-6627	1969	3.00	6.00	12.00
—Sold only at True Value Hardware stores				
HAPPY HOLIDAYS, ALBUM 6				
❑ Capitol Creative Products SL-6669	1970	3.00	6.00	12.00
—Sold only at True Value Hardware stores				
HAPPY HOLIDAYS, ALBUM SEVEN				
❑ Capitol Creative Products SL-6730	1971	3.00	6.00	12.00
—Sold only at True Value Hardware stores				

Number	Title	Yr	VG	VG+	NM

HAPPY HOLIDAYS, ALBUM 8
❑ Columbia Special Products C 11086 — 1972 — 2.50 — 5.00 — 10.00
—*Sold only at True Value Hardware stores*

HAPPY HOLIDAYS, ALBUM NINE
❑ Columbia Special Products P 11793 — 1973 — 2.50 — 5.00 — 10.00
—*Sold only at True Value Hardware stores*

HAPPY HOLIDAYS, ALBUM 10
❑ Columbia Special Products P 12344 — 1974 — 2.50 — 5.00 — 10.00
—*Sold only at True Value Hardware stores*

HAPPY HOLLY DAYS
❑ Capitol Creative Products SL-6654 — 1969 — 3.00 — 6.00 — 12.00
❑ Capitol Creative Products SL-6761 — 1971 — 2.50 — 5.00 — 10.00

HAPPY JAZZ
❑ Jazztone J-1215 [M] — 1956 — 7.50 — 15.00 — 30.00

HARD GOODS
❑ Warner Bros. PRO 583 [(2)] — 1974 — 6.25 — 12.50 — 25.00

THE HARD SWING
❑ Pacific Jazz JWC-508 [M] — 1957 — 12.50 — 25.00 — 50.00
❑ World Pacific JWC-508 [M] — 1958 — 10.00 — 20.00 — 40.00

HARLEM JAZZ 1930
❑ Brunswick BL 58024 [10] — 1951 — 12.50 — 25.00 — 50.00

HAVE A HAPPY HOLIDAY
❑ Columbia Special Products CSS 1432 — 1970 — 2.50 — 5.00 — 10.00

HAVE A JEWISH CHRISTMAS...?
❑ Tower T-5081 [M] — 1967 — 3.75 — 7.50 — 15.00
—*Comedy sketches narrated by Lennie Weinrib and acted by Christine Nelson, Benny Rubin, Reginald X. Carlisle and Naomi Lewis*

HAVE YOURSELF A MERRY LITTLE CHRISTMAS
❑ Reprise 50001 [M] — 1963 — 6.25 — 12.50 — 25.00
—*Red and green cover with ornaments at top; titled on back cover "Top Hollywood Stars Want You to..."*
❑ Reprise R 50001 [M] — 1963 — 6.25 — 12.50 — 25.00
—*Christmas tree cover; titled "Frank Sinatra and His Friends Want You to..."*
❑ Reprise R 50001 [M] — 1963 — 6.25 — 12.50 — 25.00
—*Wreath cover; titled on back cover "Top Hollywood Stars Want You to..."*
❑ Reprise R9-50001 [S] — 1963 — 7.50 — 15.00 — 30.00
—*Christmas tree cover; titled "Frank Sinatra and His Friends Want You to..."; stereo version of above*

HAVING A BALL
❑ End LP-302 [M] — 1958 — 125.00 — 250.00 — 500.00
—*Original cover with groups pictured on a record*

HEAVY HEADS
❑ Chess LP 1522 [M] — 1967 — 6.25 — 12.50 — 25.00
❑ Chess LPS 1522 [P] — 1967 — 6.25 — 12.50 — 25.00

HEAVY HEADS, VOYAGE 2
❑ Chess LP 1528 [M] — 1969 — 5.00 — 10.00 — 20.00

HEAVY HITS!
❑ Columbia CS 9840 — 1969 — 3.75 — 7.50 — 15.00

HEAVY METAL (SUPERSTARS OF THE 70S, VOLUME 2)
❑ Warner Special Products SP-2001 — 1974 — 5.00 — 10.00 — 20.00

HEAVY SOUNDS
❑ Columbia CS 9952 — 1970 — 3.75 — 7.50 — 15.00

HENRY MANCINI SELECTS GREAT SONGS OF CHRISTMAS
❑ RCA Special Products DPL1-0148 — 1975 — 2.50 — 5.00 — 10.00
—*Sold only at Goodyear tire dealers*

HERALD THE BEAT
❑ Herald HLP-0110 [M] — 195? — 37.50 — 75.00 — 150.00
—*Yellow label*
❑ Herald HLP-0110 [M] — 1957 — 75.00 — 150.00 — 300.00
—*Black label*

HERE ARE THE HITS!
❑ Fire FLP-100 [M] — 1959 — 100.00 — 200.00 — 400.00
—*Reissued as "Memory Lane, Hits by the Original Groups" with the same label and number*

HERE COME THE GIRLS
❑ Verve MGV-2036 [M] — 1956 — 10.00 — 20.00 — 40.00
❑ Verve V-2036 [M] — 1961 — 5.00 — 10.00 — 20.00

HERE COME THE SWINGING BANDS
❑ Verve MGV-8207 [M] — 1957 — 7.50 — 15.00 — 30.00
❑ Verve V-8207 [M] — 1961 — 5.00 — 10.00 — 20.00

HI-FI JAZZ
❑ Brunswick BL 58058 [10] — 1954 — 12.50 — 25.00 — 50.00

HI-FI JAZZ SESSION
❑ Masterseal MSLP 5013 [M] — 1957 — 6.25 — 12.50 — 25.00

A HI-FI SALUTE TO THE GREAT ONES
❑ MGM E-3325 [M] — 1956 — 7.50 — 15.00 — 30.00

A HI-FI SALUTE TO THE GREAT ONES, VOL. 2
❑ MGM E-3354 [M] — 1956 — 7.50 — 15.00 — 30.00

HILLBILLY HOUSE PARTY
❑ Imperial LP-9214 [M] — 1963 — 6.25 — 12.50 — 25.00
❑ Imperial LP-12214 [R] — 1963 — 5.00 — 10.00 — 20.00

HISTORIC JAZZ CONCERT AT MUSIC INN
❑ Atlantic 1298 [M] — 1958 — 10.00 — 20.00 — 40.00
—*Black label*
❑ Atlantic 1298 [M] — 1961 — 6.25 — 12.50 — 25.00
—*Multicolor label, white "fan" logo at right*
❑ Atlantic 1298 [M] — 1963 — 5.00 — 10.00 — 20.00
—*Multicolor label, black "fan" logo at right*

HISTORY OF BRITISH BLUES, VOLUME 1
❑ Sire SASH-3701 [(2)] — 1973 — 5.00 — 10.00 — 20.00

HISTORY OF BRITISH ROCK
❑ Sire SASH-3702 [(2)] — 1974 — 5.00 — 10.00 — 20.00

HISTORY OF BRITISH ROCK, VOLUME 2
❑ Sire SASH-3705 [(2)] — 1974 — 5.00 — 10.00 — 20.00

HISTORY OF BRITISH ROCK, VOLUME 3
❑ Sire SASH-3712 [(2)] — 1975 — 5.00 — 10.00 — 20.00

HISTORY OF CLASSIC JAZZ
❑ Riverside SDP-11 [(5)M] — 1956 — 75.00 — 150.00 — 300.00
—*Five-record set in leatherette album with booklet; records were available separately as Riverside 112, 113, 114, 115 and 116.*

HISTORY OF CLASSIC JAZZ, VOL. 1
❑ Riverside RLP 12-112 [M] — 1957 — 10.00 — 20.00 — 40.00

HISTORY OF CLASSIC JAZZ, VOL. 2
❑ Riverside RLP 12-113 [M] — 1957 — 10.00 — 20.00 — 40.00

HISTORY OF CLASSIC JAZZ, VOL. 3
❑ Riverside RLP 12-114 [M] — 1957 — 10.00 — 20.00 — 40.00

HISTORY OF CLASSIC JAZZ, VOL. 4
❑ Riverside RLP 12-115 [M] — 1957 — 10.00 — 20.00 — 40.00

HISTORY OF CLASSIC JAZZ, VOL. 5
❑ Riverside RLP 12-116 [M] — 1957 — 10.00 — 20.00 — 40.00

HISTORY OF JAZZ, VOL. 1: NEW ORLEANS ORIGINS
❑ Capitol T 793 [M] — 1956 — 6.25 — 12.50 — 25.00

HISTORY OF JAZZ, VOL. 1: THE SOLID SOUTH
❑ Capitol H 239 [10] — 1950 — 12.50 — 25.00 — 50.00

HISTORY OF JAZZ, VOL. 2: THE GOLDEN ERA
❑ Capitol H 240 [10] — 1950 — 12.50 — 25.00 — 50.00

HISTORY OF JAZZ, VOL. 2: THE TURBULENT '20S
❑ Capitol T 794 [M] — 1956 — 6.25 — 12.50 — 25.00

HISTORY OF JAZZ, VOL. 3: EVERYBODY SWINGS
❑ Capitol T 795 [M] — 1956 — 6.25 — 12.50 — 25.00

HISTORY OF JAZZ, VOL. 3: THEN CAME SWING
❑ Capitol H 241 [10] — 1950 — 12.50 — 25.00 — 50.00

HISTORY OF JAZZ, VOL. 4: ENTER THE COOL
❑ Capitol H 242 [10] — 1950 — 12.50 — 25.00 — 50.00
❑ Capitol T 796 [M] — 1956 — 6.25 — 12.50 — 25.00

HISTORY OF RHYTHM & BLUES, VOLUME 1/THE ROOTS 1947-52
❑ Atlantic SD 8161 — 1968 — 5.00 — 10.00 — 20.00

HISTORY OF RHYTHM & BLUES, VOLUME 2/THE GOLDEN YEARS 1953-55
❑ Atlantic 8162 [M] — 1968 — 10.00 — 20.00 — 40.00
❑ Atlantic SD 8162 [S] — 1968 — 5.00 — 10.00 — 20.00

HISTORY OF RHYTHM & BLUES, VOLUME 3/ROCK & ROLL 1956-57
❑ Atlantic SD 8163 — 1968 — 5.00 — 10.00 — 20.00

HISTORY OF RHYTHM & BLUES, VOLUME 4/THE BIG BEAT 1958-60
❑ Atlantic SD 8164 — 1968 — 5.00 — 10.00 — 20.00

HISTORY OF RHYTHM & BLUES, VOLUME 5/THE BEAT GOES ON, 1961-62
❑ Atlantic 8193 [M] — 1968 — 10.00 — 20.00 — 40.00
—*Mono is promo only; "DJ Copy Monaural" sticker on front cover*
❑ Atlantic SD 8193 [S] — 1968 — 5.00 — 10.00 — 20.00

THE HIT MAKERS AND THEIR RECORD BREAKERS
❑ King 737 [M] — 1961 — 25.00 — 50.00 — 100.00

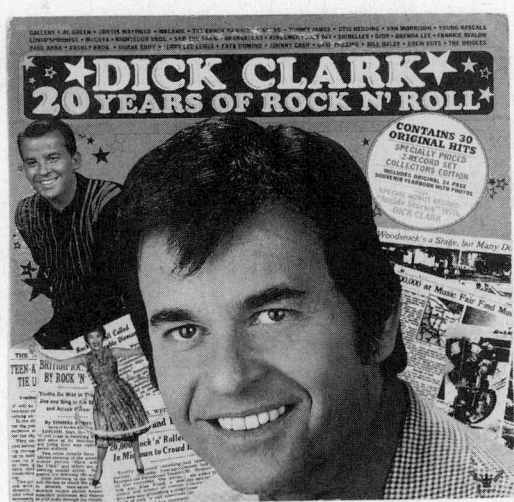

Various Artists, *Dick Clark – 20 Years of Rock n' Roll,* Buddah BDS 5133, two stereo LPs, gatefold with booklet and bonus cardboard record, $10-$20.

Various Artists, *Disco Teen '66,* Columbia Record Club DS 155, stereo LP, $25-$50.

Various Artists, *Great Songs of Christmas, Album Eight,* Columbia Special Products CSS 888, made for Goodyear tire stores, stereo LP, $6-$12.

Various Artists, *The Greatest Hits from England,* Parrot PAS-71010, stereo LP, $10-$20.

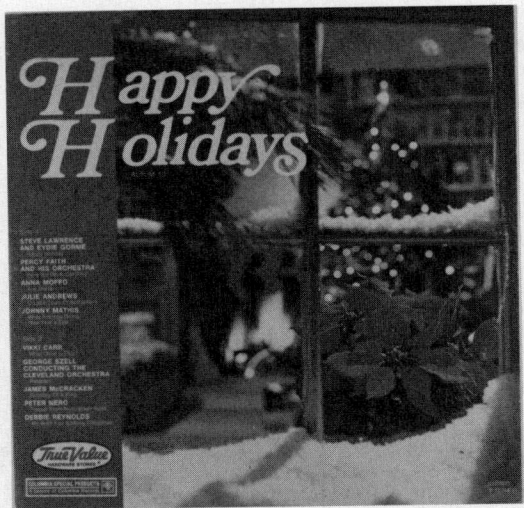

Various Artists, *Happy Holidays Album 10,* Columbia Special Products P 12344, made for True Value Hardware stores, stereo LP, $5-$10.

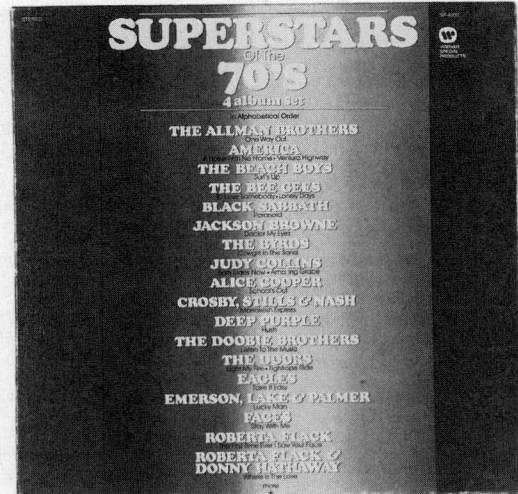

Various Artists, *Superstars of the 70's,* Warner Special Products SP-4000, four stereo LPs, with pamphlet of liner notes, $20-$40.

Number	Title	Yr	VG	VG+	NM

HIT SOUNDS OF MERRIE MELODIES
❑ Warner Bros. PRO 550 [(2)] — 1973 — 6.25 — 12.50 — 25.00

THE HITS ARE ON VERVE
❑ Verve V-201 [M] — 1964 — 3.75 — 7.50 — 15.00
❑ Verve V6-201 [S] — 1964 — 5.00 — 10.00 — 20.00

HITS FROM THE SOUTH PRESENTED BY NICK CHARLES
❑ Stax 702 [M] — 1962 — 25.00 — 50.00 — 100.00
—*Has the same number as "Walk Right In" by Gus Cannon, but this LP doesn't have any mention of Atlantic distribution*

HITS I FORGOT TO BUY
❑ Swan SLP-512 [M] — 1963 — 12.50 — 25.00 — 50.00

HITS OF THE HOPS
❑ Warner Bros. W 1448 [M] — 1962 — 7.50 — 15.00 — 30.00
❑ Warner Bros. WS 1448 [S] — 1962 — 10.00 — 20.00 — 40.00

HITS THAT JUMPED
❑ Checker LP 2975 [M] — 1959 — 30.00 — 60.00 — 120.00

HITSVILLE
❑ Coral CRL 57269 [M] — 1959 — 20.00 — 40.00 — 80.00
❑ Coral CRL 757269 [S] — 1959 — 25.00 — 50.00 — 100.00

HITSVILLE U.S.A.
❑ Imperial LP-9084 [M] — 1959 — 10.00 — 20.00 — 40.00

HITSVILLE U.S.A., VOLUME 2
❑ Imperial LP-9099 [M] — 1960 — 10.00 — 20.00 — 40.00

HOLIDAY IN SAX
❑ EmArcy MG-26019 [10] — 1954 — 20.00 — 40.00 — 80.00

HOLIDAY IN TRUMPET
❑ EmArcy MG-26015 [10] — 1954 — 20.00 — 40.00 — 80.00

HOLIDAY MAGIC
❑ Capitol Creative Products SL-6728 — 1971 — 3.00 — 6.00 — 12.00
❑ Capitol Special Markets SL-6728 — 197? — 2.50 — 5.00 — 10.00
—*Same as above, but reissue on renamed label*

HOME FOR CHRISTMAS
❑ Columbia Musical Treasury P3S 5608 [(3)] — 1971 — 3.75 — 7.50 — 15.00

HOME FOR THE HOLIDAYS
❑ Columbia Special Products P 12014 — 1973 — 2.50 — 5.00 — 10.00
—*Sold only at Big N discount department store*

HOME OF THE BLUES
❑ Minit LP-0001 [M] — 1961 — 12.50 — 25.00 — 50.00

HOME OF THE BLUES, VOLUME 2
❑ Minit LP-0004 [M] — 1963 — 12.50 — 25.00 — 50.00
❑ Minit LP-24004 [R] — 1964 — 5.00 — 10.00 — 20.00
❑ Minit LP-40004 [M] — 1964 — 6.25 — 12.50 — 25.00
—*Reissue of 0004*

HOMESPUN HUMOR
❑ King 726 [M] — 1961 — 25.00 — 50.00 — 100.00

HOT CANARIES
❑ Columbia CL 2534 [10] — 1954 — 7.50 — 15.00 — 30.00

HOT CLARINETS
❑ Historical 25 — 1969 — 2.50 — 5.00 — 10.00

THE HOT ONES
❑ Columbia Special Products CSP-107 [M] — 1963 — 5.00 — 10.00 — 20.00
—*Available only from Johnson Sea Horse boat dealers*

HOT PIANOS
❑ Historical 29 — 1969 — 2.50 — 5.00 — 10.00

HOT PLATTERS
❑ Warner Bros. PRO 474 [(2)] — 1971 — 6.25 — 12.50 — 25.00
—*Originals have green labels*

HOT TRUMPETS
❑ Historical 28 — 1969 — 2.50 — 5.00 — 10.00

HOT VS. COOL: A BATTLE OF JAZZ
❑ MGM E-211 [10] — 1953 — 12.50 — 25.00 — 50.00

HOUSE RENT PARTY
❑ Savoy MG-12199 [M] — 1961 — 12.50 — 25.00 — 50.00

HOW HIGH THE MOON
❑ Clef MGC-Vol. 1 [M] — 1955 — 12.50 — 25.00 — 50.00
—*Reissue of 608*
❑ Clef MGC-608 [M] — 1955 — 10.00 — 20.00 — 40.00
—*Reissue of Mercury 608*
❑ Mercury MGC-Vol. 1 [10] — 1951 — 15.00 — 30.00 — 60.00
—*Reissue of 35001*

❑ Mercury MGC-608 [M] — 1953 — 20.00 — 40.00 — 80.00
—*Reissue of Vol. 1*
❑ Mercury MG-35001 [10] — 1950 — 20.00 — 40.00 — 80.00
❑ Verve MGV-Vol. 1 [M] — 1957 — 7.50 — 15.00 — 30.00
—*Reissue of 12-inch Clef Vol. 1*

HOW THE GRINCH STOLE CHRISTMAS
❑ Random House/Scholastic 0-394-05008-8 — 1975 — 3.75 — 7.50 — 15.00
—*Not the original soundtrack, but placed here to avoid confusion (we hope). B-side is a condensation of Folkways FC-7750 (1956).*

HUM-N-STRUM: THE BEST OF FOLK AND COUNTRY
❑ Columbia Special Products CSP 309 [M] — 1966 — 3.75 — 7.50 — 15.00
—*For General Electric*

HYMNS OF FAITH
❑ Colpix CP-408 [M] — 1959 — 7.50 — 15.00 — 30.00

I DIDN'T KNOW THEY STILL MADE RECORDS LIKE THIS
❑ Warner Bros. PRO 608 [(2)] — 1975 — 5.00 — 10.00 — 20.00

I DIG ROCK AND ROLL
❑ Score SLP-4002 [M] — 1957 — 50.00 — 100.00 — 200.00
—*Reissue of "Rock & Roll with Rhythm & Blues," Aladdin 710*

I LIKE JAZZ!
❑ Columbia JZ 1 [M] — 1955 — 7.50 — 15.00 — 30.00

I'M WILD ABOUT MY LOVIN'
❑ Historical 32 — 1969 — 2.50 — 5.00 — 10.00

IMAGINE THE JOYS OF CHRISTMAS. PRESENTED BY SYLVANIA.
❑ Capitol Creative Products SL-6700 — 1971 — 3.00 — 6.00 — 12.00
—*Sold only at Sylvania dealers; label calls this "A Sylvania Christmas"*

IMPERIAL MOVES
❑ Imperial MM-428 [DJ] — 1966 — 10.00 — 20.00 — 40.00

IMPERIAL SAMPLER
❑ Imperial DJLP-1 [10] — 195? — 25.00 — 50.00 — 100.00
—*Promo-only item*

IMPULSE ARTISTS ON TOUR
❑ ABC Impulse! AS-9264 — 197? — 3.00 — 6.00 — 12.00

IMPULSIVELY!
❑ ABC Impulse! AS-9266 [(2)] — 197? — 3.75 — 7.50 — 15.00

IN CONCERT
❑ RCA Victor CPL2-1014 [(2)] — 1975 — 5.00 — 10.00 — 20.00

IN LOVING MEMORY
❑ Motown M 642 [DJ] — 1969 — 125.00 — 250.00 — 500.00
—*With custom silver cover; Loucye Gordy Wakefield Scholarship Fund benefit giveaway*
❑ Motown M 642 [M] — 1968 — 37.50 — 75.00 — 150.00
—*With song titles on cover*
❑ Motown M 642 [M] — 1968 — 62.50 — 125.00 — 250.00
—*Without song titles on cover*
❑ Motown MS 642 [S] — 1968 — 37.50 — 75.00 — 150.00
—*With song titles on cover*
❑ Motown MS 642 [S] — 1968 — 62.50 — 125.00 — 250.00
—*Without song titles on cover*

INCENSE AND OLDIES
❑ Buddah BDS 5014 — 1969 — 5.00 — 10.00 — 20.00

INFORMAL SESSION AT SQUIRREL'S BY THE SONS OF BIX
❑ Paramount LP-104 [(2)10] — 1954 — 20.00 — 40.00 — 80.00

THE INSTRUMENTAL CHRISTMAS FAVORITES
❑ Capitol STBB-349 [(2)] — 1969 — 3.75 — 7.50 — 15.00

INSTRUMENTAL GOLDEN GOODIES, VOL. 13
❑ Roulette R 25238 [M] — 1964 — 5.00 — 10.00 — 20.00

INTERCOLLEGIATE MUSIC FESTIVAL, VOL. 1
❑ ABC Impulse! AS-9145 [S] — 1968 — 3.00 — 6.00 — 12.00
❑ Impulse! A-9145 [M] — 1967 — 5.00 — 10.00 — 20.00
❑ Impulse! AS-9145 [S] — 1967 — 3.75 — 7.50 — 15.00

INTERNATIONAL JAZZ WORKSHOP
❑ EmArcy MGE-26002 [M] — 1964 — 6.25 — 12.50 — 25.00
❑ EmArcy SRE-66002 [S] — 1964 — 7.50 — 15.00 — 30.00

INTERPLAY FOR TWO TRUMPETS AND TWO TENORS
❑ Prestige PRLP-7112 [M] — 1957 — 25.00 — 50.00 — 100.00

INTRODUCTION TO JAZZ
❑ Decca DL 8244 [M] — 1956 — 7.50 — 15.00 — 30.00

INTRODUCTION TO RARE EARTH RECORDS
❑ Rare Earth RS-505 to 509 [(5)DJ] — 1969 — 50.00 — 100.00 — 200.00
—*Promo-only box set with rounded top; contains the first five LPs on the Rare Earth label*

IRREPRESSIBLE IMPULSES
❑ ABC Impulse! IMP-1972 — 1972 — 3.75 — 7.50 — 15.00

Number	Title	Yr	VG	VG+	NM
ISLES OF JAZZ					
☐ Discovery DL-2010 [10]		1954	12.50	25.00	50.00
IT'S CHRISTMAS					
☐ Columbia Special Products C 10040		1971	3.00	6.00	12.00
IT'S CHRISTMASTIME!					
☐ Columbia Special Products CSM 429 [M]		1966	3.00	6.00	12.00
—Sold only at A&P grocery stores					
IT'S DANCE TIME					
☐ Cameo C-1068 [M]		1964	7.50	15.00	30.00
ITALIAN JAZZ STARS					
☐ Angel ANG-60001 [10]		1955	12.50	25.00	50.00
IVY LEAGUE JAZZ					
☐ Decca DL 8282 [M]		1956	7.50	15.00	30.00
☐ Golden Crest GC-3039 [M]		1958	5.00	10.00	20.00
JACKPOT OF HITS					
☐ Apollo LP-490 [M]		1959	37.50	75.00	150.00
JAM SESSION					
☐ Clef MGC-4001/7 [(7)M]		1953	75.00	150.00	300.00
—Boxed set containing 4001-4007					
☐ EmArcy MG-36002 [M]		1954	12.50	25.00	50.00
JAM SESSION #1					
☐ Clef MGC-601 [M]		1954	10.00	20.00	40.00
☐ Clef MGC-651 [M]		1955	10.00	20.00	40.00
—Reissue of 4001					
☐ Clef MGC-4001 [M]		1953	12.50	25.00	50.00
☐ Mercury MGC-601 [M]		1953	20.00	40.00	80.00
☐ Verve MGV-8049 [M]		1956	7.50	15.00	30.00
—Reissue of Clef 651					
JAM SESSION #2					
☐ Clef MGC-602 [M]		1954	10.00	20.00	40.00
☐ Clef MGC-652 [M]		1955	10.00	20.00	40.00
—Reissue of 4002					
☐ Clef MGC-4002 [M]		1953	12.50	25.00	50.00
☐ Mercury MGC-602 [M]		1953	20.00	40.00	80.00
☐ Verve MGV-8050 [M]		1956	7.50	15.00	30.00
—Reissue of Clef 652					
JAM SESSION #3					
☐ Clef MGC-653 [M]		1955	10.00	20.00	40.00
—Reissue of 4003					
☐ Clef MGC-4003 [M]		1953	12.50	25.00	50.00
☐ Verve MGV-8051 [M]		1956	7.50	15.00	30.00
—Reissue of Clef 653					
JAM SESSION #4					
☐ Clef MGC-654 [M]		1955	10.00	20.00	40.00
—Reissue of 4004					
☐ Clef MGC-4004 [M]		1953	12.50	25.00	50.00
☐ Verve MGV-8052 [M]		1956	7.50	15.00	30.00
—Reissue of Clef 654					
JAM SESSION #5					
☐ Clef MGC-655 [M]		1955	10.00	20.00	40.00
—Reissue of 4005					
☐ Clef MGC-4005 [M]		1953	12.50	25.00	50.00
☐ Verve MGV-8053 [M]		1956	7.50	15.00	30.00
—Reissue of Clef 655					
JAM SESSION #6					
☐ Clef MGC-656 [M]		1955	10.00	20.00	40.00
—Reissue of 4006					
☐ Clef MGC-4006 [M]		1953	12.50	25.00	50.00
☐ Verve MGV-8054 [M]		1956	7.50	15.00	30.00
—Reissue of Clef 656					
JAM SESSION #7					
☐ Clef MGC-677 [M]		1955	10.00	20.00	40.00
☐ Verve MGV-8062 [M]		1957	7.50	15.00	30.00
—Reissue of Clef 677					
JAM SESSION #8					
☐ Clef MGC-711 [M]		1955	10.00	20.00	40.00
☐ Verve MGV-8094 [M]		1957	7.50	15.00	30.00
—Reissue of Clef 711					
JAM SESSION #9					
☐ Verve MGV-8196 [M]		1957	7.50	15.00	30.00
JAM SESSION AT CARNEGIE HALL					
☐ Columbia CL 557 [M]		1954	7.50	15.00	30.00
JAM SESSION AT COMMODORE					
☐ Commodore FL-30006 [M]		1951	10.00	20.00	40.00
JAM SESSION COAST TO COAST					
☐ Columbia CL 547 [M]		1954	7.50	1.00	30.00

Number	Title	Yr	VG	VG+	NM
JAMES BOND — 10TH ANNIVERSARY					
☐ United Artists UXS-91 [(2)]		1972	7.50	15.00	30.00
THE JATP ALL STARS: HOW HIGH THE MOON					
☐ Verve VSP-15 [M]		1966	3.75	7.50	15.00
☐ Verve VSPS-15 [R]		1966	2.50	5.00	10.00
THE JATP ALL STARS: PERDIDO					
☐ Verve VSP-16 [M]		1966	3.75	7.50	15.00
☐ Verve VSPS-16 [R]		1966	2.50	5.00	10.00
THE JATP ALL-STARS AT THE OPERA HOUSE					
☐ Verve MGVS-6029 [S]		1960	7.50	15.00	30.00
☐ Verve MGV-8267 [M]		1958	10.00	20.00	40.00
☐ Verve V-8267 [M]		1961	5.00	10.00	20.00
☐ Verve V6-8267 [S]		1961	3.75	7.50	15.00
☐ Verve MGV-8284 [M]		1959	—	—	—
—Canceled					
☐ Verve V-8489 [M]		1962	6.25	12.50	25.00
☐ Verve V6-8489 [S]		1962	7.50	15.00	30.00
THE JATP ALL-STARS: FUNKY BLUES					
☐ Verve V-8486 [M]		1962	6.25	12.50	25.00
☐ Verve V6-8486 [S]		1962	7.50	15.00	30.00
JAZZ					
☐ Halo 50242 [M]		1957	3.75	7.50	15.00
☐ Mainstream MRL-408		197?	3.00	6.00	12.00
☐ Royale 1883 [10]		195?	7.50	15.00	30.00
JAZZ — WEST COAST VOL. III					
☐ Jazztone J-1274 [M]		195?	7.50	15.00	30.00
JAZZ A LA MIDNIGHT					
☐ Jazztone J-1282 [M]		1957	7.50	15.00	30.00
JAZZ A LA MOOD					
☐ Jazztone J-1254 [M]		1957	7.50	15.00	30.00
JAZZ AMERICANA					
☐ Tampa TP-11 [M]		1957	25.00	50.00	100.00
—Colored vinyl					
☐ Tampa TP-11 [M]		1958	10.00	20.00	40.00
—Black vinyl					
JAZZ ANTHOLOGY OF WEST COAST JAZZ					
☐ Jazztone J-1243 [M]		1957	7.50	15.00	30.00
JAZZ AT CARNEGIE HALL					
☐ Arco AL-4 [10]		1950	20.00	40.00	80.00
☐ Mercury MG-35002 [10]		1950	20.00	40.00	80.00
—Reissue of Arco 4					
JAZZ AT CARNEGIE HALL, VOLUME 2					
☐ Arco AL-8 [10]		195?	20.00	40.00	80.00
JAZZ AT COLUMBIA — COLLECTORS ITEMS					
☐ Columbia CB-16 [M]		195?	5.00	10.00	20.00
—Columbia Record Club "bonus record" in generic sleeve with die-cut circle in middle					
JAZZ AT COLUMBIA — DIXIELAND					
☐ Columbia CB-8 [M]		195?	5.00	10.00	20.00
—Columbia Record Club "bonus record" in generic sleeve with die-cut circle in middle					
JAZZ AT JAZZ LTD.					
☐ Atlantic 1338 [M]		1961	6.25	12.50	25.00
—Multicolor label, white "fan" logo at right					
JAZZ AT PRESERVATION HALL					
☐ Atlantic 1408 [M]		1964	3.00	6.00	12.00
☐ Atlantic SD 1408 [S]		1964	3.75	7.50	15.00
JAZZ AT PRESERVATION HALL, VOL. 2					
☐ Atlantic 1409 [M]		1964	3.00	6.00	12.00
☐ Atlantic SD 1409 [S]		1964	3.75	7.50	15.00
JAZZ AT PRESERVATION HALL, VOL. 3					
☐ Atlantic 1410 [M]		1964	3.00	6.00	12.00
☐ Atlantic SD 1410 [S]		1964	3.75	7.50	15.00
JAZZ AT STORYVILLE					
☐ Paradox LP-6003 [10]		1951	12.50	25.00	50.00
☐ Savoy MG-15001 [10]		1952	20.00	40.00	80.00
☐ Savoy MG-15014 [10]		1952	20.00	40.00	80.00
☐ Storyville STLP-319 [10]		1955	20.00	40.00	80.00
JAZZ AT STORYVILLE, VOL. 2					
☐ Savoy MG-15016 [10]		1952	20.00	40.00	80.00
JAZZ AT STORYVILLE, VOL. 3					
☐ Savoy MG-15019 [10]		1953	20.00	40.00	80.00
JAZZ AT STORYVILLE, VOL. 4					
☐ Savoy MG-15020 [10]		1953	20.00	40.00	80.00

Number	Title	Yr	VG	VG+	NM

JAZZ AT THE BOSTON ARTS FESTIVAL
- ❑ Storyville STLP-311 [10] — 1954 — 20.00 — 40.00 — 80.00

JAZZ AT THE HOLLYWOOD BOWL
- ❑ Verve MGV-8231-2 [(2)M] — 1958 — 12.50 — 25.00 — 50.00
- ❑ Verve V-8231-2 [(2)M] — 1961 — 6.25 — 12.50 — 25.00

JAZZ AT THE PHILHARMONIC
- ❑ Stinson SLP-23 [10] — 195? — 20.00 — 40.00 — 80.00
- —*Black vinyl*
- ❑ Stinson SLP-23 [10] — 195? — 20.00 — 40.00 — 80.00
- —*Opaque red vinyl*
- ❑ Stinson SLP-23 [10] — 1950 — 30.00 — 60.00 — 120.00
- —*See-through red vinyl; the first pressing of the first volume to be issued*
- ❑ Stinson SLP-23 [M] — 195? — 5.00 — 10.00 — 20.00

JAZZ AT THE PHILHARMONIC ALL STARS
- ❑ American Recording Society G-416 [M] — 1957 — 7.50 — 15.00 — 30.00

JAZZ AT THE PHILHARMONIC IN EUROPE
- ❑ Verve V6-8823 [(2)] — 197? — 5.00 — 10.00 — 20.00

JAZZ AT THE PHILHARMONIC IN EUROPE, VOL. 1
- ❑ Verve V-8539 [M] — 1963 — 5.00 — 10.00 — 20.00
- ❑ Verve V6-8539 [S] — 1963 — 6.25 — 12.50 — 25.00

JAZZ AT THE PHILHARMONIC IN EUROPE, VOL. 2
- ❑ Verve V-8540 [M] — 1963 — 5.00 — 10.00 — 20.00
- ❑ Verve V6-8540 [S] — 1963 — 6.25 — 12.50 — 25.00

JAZZ AT THE PHILHARMONIC IN EUROPE, VOL. 3
- ❑ Verve V-8541 [M] — 1963 — 5.00 — 10.00 — 20.00
- ❑ Verve V6-8541 [S] — 1963 — 6.25 — 12.50 — 25.00

JAZZ AT THE PHILHARMONIC IN EUROPE, VOL. 4
- ❑ Verve V-8542 [M] — 1963 — 5.00 — 10.00 — 20.00
- ❑ Verve V6-8542 [S] — 1963 — 6.25 — 12.50 — 25.00

JAZZ AT THE PHILHARMONIC, NEW VOLUME 2
- ❑ Clef MGC-Vol. 2 [M] — 1955 — 12.50 — 25.00 — 50.00
- —*Side 1 is the 10-inch Vol. 2; Side 2 is the 10-inch Vol. 3*

JAZZ AT THE PHILHARMONIC, NEW VOLUME 3
- ❑ Clef MGC-Vol. 3 [M] — 1955 — 12.50 — 25.00 — 50.00
- —*Side 1 is the 10-inch Vol. 4; Side 2 is the 10-inch Vol. 5*

JAZZ AT THE PHILHARMONIC, NEW VOLUME 4
- ❑ Clef MGC-Vol. 4 [M] — 1955 — 12.50 — 25.00 — 50.00
- —*Combines the 10-inch Vol. 6 and Vol. 14 on one record*

JAZZ AT THE PHILHARMONIC, NEW VOLUME 5
- ❑ Clef MGC-Vol. 5 [M] — 1955 — 12.50 — 25.00 — 50.00
- —*Combines the 10-inch Vol. 7, 10 and 11 on one record*

JAZZ AT THE PHILHARMONIC, NEW VOLUME 6
- ❑ Clef MGC-Vol. 6 [M] — 1955 — 12.50 — 25.00 — 50.00
- —*Combines the 10-inch Vol. 8 and Vol. 9 on one record*

JAZZ AT THE PHILHARMONIC, NEW VOLUME 7
- ❑ Clef MGC-Vol. 7 [M] — 1955 — 12.50 — 25.00 — 50.00
- —*Combines the 10-inch Vol. 12 and 13 on one record*

JAZZ AT THE PHILHARMONIC, VOL. 2
- ❑ Verve MGV-Vol. 2 [M] — 1957 — 7.50 — 15.00 — 30.00
- —*Reissue of 12-inch Clef Vol. 2*

JAZZ AT THE PHILHARMONIC, VOL. 3
- ❑ Verve MGV-Vol. 3 [M] — 1957 — 7.50 — 15.00 — 30.00
- —*Reissue of 12-inch Clef Vol. 3*

JAZZ AT THE PHILHARMONIC, VOL. 4
- ❑ Verve MGV-Vol. 4 [M] — 1957 — 7.50 — 15.00 — 30.00
- —*Reissue of 12-inch Clef Vol. 4*

JAZZ AT THE PHILHARMONIC, VOL. 5
- ❑ Verve MGV-Vol. 5 [M] — 1957 — 7.50 — 15.00 — 30.00
- —*Reissue of 12-inch Clef Vol. 5*

JAZZ AT THE PHILHARMONIC, VOL. 6
- ❑ Verve MGV-Vol. 6 [M] — 1957 — 7.50 — 15.00 — 30.00
- —*Reissue of 12-inch Clef Vol. 6*

JAZZ AT THE PHILHARMONIC, VOL. 7
- ❑ Verve MGV-Vol. 7 [M] — 1957 — 7.50 — 15.00 — 30.00
- —*Reissue of 12-inch Clef Vol. 7*

JAZZ AT THE PHILHARMONIC, VOL. 8
- ❑ Verve MGV-Vol. 8 [(3)M] — 1957 — 15.00 — 30.00 — 60.00
- —*Reissue of Clef Vol. 15*

JAZZ AT THE PHILHARMONIC, VOL. 9
- ❑ Verve MGV-Vol. 9 [(3)M] — 1957 — 15.00 — 30.00 — 60.00
- —*Reissue of Clef Vol. 16*

Number	Title	Yr	VG	VG+	NM

JAZZ AT THE PHILHARMONIC, VOL. 10
- ❑ Verve MGV-Vol. 10 [(3)M] — 1957 — 15.00 — 30.00 — 60.00
- —*Reissue of Clef Vol. 17*

JAZZ AT THE PHILHARMONIC, VOL. 11
- ❑ Verve MGV-Vol. 11 [(3)M] — 1957 — 15.00 — 30.00 — 60.00
- —*Reissue of Clef Vol. 18*

JAZZ AT THE PHILHARMONIC, VOL. 12
- ❑ Verve MGV-Vol. 12 [(2)M] — 195? — — — —
- —*Advertised, but unreleased?*

JAZZ AT THE PHILHARMONIC, VOLUME 2
- ❑ Arco AL-1 [10] — 1950 — 20.00 — 40.00 — 80.00
- ❑ Clef MGC-Vol. 2 [10] — 1953 — 15.00 — 30.00 — 60.00
- —*Reissue of Mercury Vol. 2*
- ❑ Mercury MGC-Vol. 2 [10] — 1951 — 15.00 — 30.00 — 60.00
- —*Reissue of 35003*
- ❑ Mercury MG-35003 [10] — 1950 — 20.00 — 40.00 — 80.00
- —*Reissue of Arco 1*

JAZZ AT THE PHILHARMONIC, VOLUME 3
- ❑ Arco AL-2 [10] — 1950 — 20.00 — 40.00 — 80.00
- ❑ Clef MGC-Vol. 3 [10] — 1953 — 15.00 — 30.00 — 60.00
- —*Reissue of Mercury Vol. 3*
- ❑ Mercury MGC-Vol. 3 [10] — 1951 — 15.00 — 30.00 — 60.00
- —*Reissue of 35004*
- ❑ Mercury MG-35004 [10] — 1950 — 20.00 — 40.00 — 80.00
- —*Reissue of Arco 2*

JAZZ AT THE PHILHARMONIC, VOLUME 4
- ❑ Clef MGC-Vol. 4 [10] — 1953 — 15.00 — 30.00 — 60.00
- —*Reissue of Mercury Vol. 4*
- ❑ Mercury MGC-Vol. 4 [10] — 1951 — 15.00 — 30.00 — 60.00
- —*Reissue of 35005*
- ❑ Mercury MG-35005 [10] — 1950 — 20.00 — 40.00 — 80.00

JAZZ AT THE PHILHARMONIC, VOLUME 5
- ❑ Clef MGC-Vol. 5 [10] — 1953 — 15.00 — 30.00 — 60.00
- —*Reissue of Mercury Vol. 5*
- ❑ Mercury MGC-Vol. 5 [10] — 1951 — 15.00 — 30.00 — 60.00
- —*Reissue of 35006*
- ❑ Mercury MG-35006 [10] — 1950 — 20.00 — 40.00 — 80.00

JAZZ AT THE PHILHARMONIC, VOLUME 6
- ❑ Clef MGC-Vol. 6 [10] — 1953 — 15.00 — 30.00 — 60.00
- —*Reissue of Mercury Vol. 6*
- ❑ Mercury MGC-Vol. 6 [10] — 1951 — 15.00 — 30.00 — 60.00
- —*Reissue of 35007*
- ❑ Mercury MG-35007 [10] — 1950 — 20.00 — 40.00 — 80.00

JAZZ AT THE PHILHARMONIC, VOLUME 7
- ❑ Clef MGC-Vol. 7 [10] — 1953 — 15.00 — 30.00 — 60.00
- —*Reissue of Mercury Vol. 7*
- ❑ Mercury MGC-Vol. 7 [10] — 1951 — 15.00 — 30.00 — 60.00
- —*Reissue of 35008*
- ❑ Mercury MG-35008 [10] — 1950 — 20.00 — 40.00 — 80.00

JAZZ AT THE PHILHARMONIC, VOLUME 8
- ❑ Clef MGC-Vol. 8 [10] — 1953 — 15.00 — 30.00 — 60.00
- —*Reissue of Mercury Vol. 8*
- ❑ Mercury MGC-Vol. 8 [10] — 1951 — 15.00 — 30.00 — 60.00
- —*Reissue of 35000*
- ❑ Mercury MG-35000 [10] — 1950 — 20.00 — 40.00 — 80.00

JAZZ AT THE PHILHARMONIC, VOLUME 9
- ❑ Clef MGC-Vol. 9 [10] — 1953 — 15.00 — 30.00 — 60.00
- —*Reissue of Mercury Vol. 9*
- ❑ Mercury MGC-Vol. 9 [10] — 1951 — 15.00 — 30.00 — 60.00
- —*Reissue of 35009*
- ❑ Mercury MG-35009 [10] — 1950 — 20.00 — 40.00 — 80.00

JAZZ AT THE PHILHARMONIC, VOLUME 10
- ❑ Clef MGC-Vol. 10 [10] — 1953 — 15.00 — 30.00 — 60.00
- —*Reissue of Mercury Vol. 10*
- ❑ Mercury MGC-Vol. 10 [10] — 1951 — 15.00 — 30.00 — 60.00
- —*Reissue of 35010*
- ❑ Mercury MG-35010 [10] — 1950 — 25.00 — 50.00 — 100.00

JAZZ AT THE PHILHARMONIC, VOLUME 11
- ❑ Clef MGC-Vol. 11 [10] — 1953 — 15.00 — 30.00 — 60.00
- —*Reissue of Mercury Vol. 11*
- ❑ Mercury MGC-Vol. 11 [10] — 1951 — 15.00 — 30.00 — 60.00
- —*Reissue of 35011*
- ❑ Mercury MG-35011 [10] — 1950 — 20.00 — 40.00 — 80.00

JAZZ AT THE PHILHARMONIC, VOLUME 12
- ❑ Clef MGC-Vol. 12 [10] — 1953 — 15.00 — 30.00 — 60.00
- —*Reissue of Mercury Vol. 12*
- ❑ Mercury MGC-Vol. 12 [10] — 1951 — 15.00 — 30.00 — 60.00

JAZZ AT THE PHILHARMONIC, VOLUME 13
- ❑ Clef MGC-Vol. 13 [10] — 1953 — 15.00 — 30.00 — 60.00
- —*Reissue of Mercury Vol. 13*
- ❑ Mercury MGC-Vol. 13 [10] — 1951 — 15.00 — 30.00 — 60.00

Number Title	Yr	VG	VG+	NM
JAZZ AT THE PHILHARMONIC, VOLUME 14				
❏ Clef MGC-Vol. 14 [10]	1953	15.00	30.00	60.00
—Reissue of Mercury Vol. 14				
❏ Mercury MGC-Vol. 14 [10]	1951	15.00	30.00	60.00
JAZZ AT THE PHILHARMONIC, VOLUME 15				
❏ Clef MGC-Vol. 15 [10]	1953	15.00	30.00	60.00
—Reissue of Mercury Vol. 15				
❏ Clef MGC-Vol. 15 [(3)M]	1954	20.00	40.00	80.00
—Boxed set of new material with program				
❏ Mercury MGC-Vol. 15 [10]	1951	15.00	30.00	60.00
JAZZ AT THE PHILHARMONIC, VOLUME 16				
❏ Clef MGC-Vol. 16 [(3)M]	1954	20.00	40.00	80.00
—Boxed set of new material with program				
JAZZ AT THE PHILHARMONIC, VOLUME 17				
❏ Clef MGC-Vol. 17 [(3)M]	1955	20.00	40.00	80.00
—Boxed set of new material with photo booklet				
JAZZ AT THE PHILHARMONIC, VOLUME 18				
❏ Clef MGC-Vol. 18 [(3)M]	1955	20.00	40.00	80.00
—Boxed set of new material with booklet				
JAZZ BAND BALL				
❏ Good Time Jazz L-12005 [M]	1954	5.00	10.00	20.00
JAZZ BANDS 1926-30				
❏ Historical 16	1967	2.50	5.00	10.00
JAZZ CITY PRESENTS				
❏ Bethlehem BCP-80 [M]	1957	7.50	15.00	30.00
JAZZ COMMITTEE FOR LATIN AMERICAN AFFAIRS				
❏ FM LP-303 [M]	1963	12.50	25.00	50.00
JAZZ CONCERT				
❏ Jazztone J-1219 [M]	1956	7.50	15.00	30.00
❏ Mercury MGJC-1 [(2)M]	1953	30.00	60.00	120.00
—Combines 601 and 602 in a box				
❏ Norgran MGN-3501-2 [(2)M]	1956	30.00	60.00	120.00
—Reissue of Mercury MGJC-1				
JAZZ CONCERT WEST COAST				
❏ Savoy MG-12012 [M]	1955	20.00	40.00	80.00
❏ Savoy MG-12196 [M]	1961	12.50	25.00	50.00
JAZZ CONFIDENTIAL				
❏ Crown CLP-5056 [M]	1959	5.00	10.00	20.00
JAZZ CORNUCOPIA				
❏ Coral CRL 57149 [M]	1958	7.50	15.00	30.00
JAZZ CRITICS' CHOICE: GREAT JAZZ CRITICS CHOOSE HISTORIC PERFORMANCES				
❏ Columbia CL 2126 [M]	1964	3.00	6.00	12.00
JAZZ DANCE				
❏ Jaguar JP-801 [10]	1954	12.50	25.00	50.00
JAZZ DUPLEX				
❏ Pax LP-6006 [10]	1954	7.50	15.00	30.00
JAZZ FESTIVAL				
❏ Imperial LP-9233 [M]	1963	5.00	10.00	20.00
❏ Imperial LP-12233 [S]	1963	6.25	12.50	25.00
❏ Kapp KS-1 [M]	1956	5.00	10.00	20.00
JAZZ FESTIVAL IN HI-FI: NEAR IN AND FAR OUT				
❏ Warner Bros. W 1281 [M]	1959	6.25	12.50	25.00
JAZZ FESTIVAL IN STEREO: NEAR IN AND FAR OUT				
❏ Warner Bros. WS 1281 [S]	1959	7.50	15.00	30.00
JAZZ FESTIVAL, VOLUME 2				
❏ Imperial LP-9238 [M]	1963	5.00	10.00	20.00
❏ Imperial LP-12238 [S]	1963	6.25	12.50	25.00
JAZZ FOR A SUNDAY AFTERNOON				
❏ Solid State SS-18027	1968	3.75	7.50	15.00
JAZZ FOR A SUNDAY AFTERNOON, VOL. 2				
❏ Solid State SS-18028	1968	3.75	7.50	15.00
JAZZ FOR A SUNDAY AFTERNOON, VOL. 3				
❏ Solid State SS-18037	1968	3.75	7.50	15.00
JAZZ FOR A SUNDAY AFTERNOON, VOL. 4				
❏ Solid State SS-18052	1969	3.75	7.50	15.00
JAZZ FOR ART'S SAKE				
❏ Dotted Eighth 101 [M]	195?	10.00	20.00	40.00
JAZZ FOR HI-FI LOVERS				
❏ Dawn DLP-1124 [M]	1958	20.00	40.00	80.00
JAZZ FOR LOVERS				
❏ Riverside RLP 12-244 [M]	1957	10.00	20.00	40.00
JAZZ FOR PEOPLE WHO HATE JAZZ				
❏ RCA Victor LJM-1008 [M]	1954	12.50	25.00	50.00
JAZZ FOR SURF-NIKS				
❏ Bethlehem BCP-6073 [M]	1961	7.50	15.00	30.00
JAZZ FROM DOWN UNDER				
❏ Jaguar JP-803 [10]	1954	12.50	25.00	50.00
JAZZ FROM NEW YORK, 1928-32				
❏ Historical 33	1969	2.50	5.00	10.00
JAZZ FROM SWEDEN				
❏ Discovery DL-2002 [10]	1953	12.50	25.00	50.00
JAZZ GIANTS				
❏ Biograph 3002	196?	3.00	6.00	12.00
THE JAZZ GIANTS				
❏ Norgran MGN-1056 [M]	1956	20.00	40.00	80.00
THE JAZZ GIANTS '56				
❏ Verve MGV-8146 [M]	1957	7.50	15.00	30.00
❏ Verve V-8146 [M]	1961	5.00	10.00	20.00
JAZZ GIANTS '58				
❏ Verve MGV-8248 [M]	1958	12.50	25.00	50.00
❏ Verve V-8248 [M]	1961	6.25	12.50	25.00
JAZZ GIANTS, VOL. 1				
❏ EmArcy MG-36048 [M]	1955	10.00	20.00	40.00
JAZZ GIANTS, VOL. 2: THE PIANO PLAYERS				
❏ EmArcy MG-36049 [M]	1955	10.00	20.00	40.00
JAZZ GIANTS, VOL. 3: REEDS, PART 1				
❏ EmArcy MG-36050 [M]	1955	10.00	20.00	40.00
JAZZ GIANTS, VOL. 3: REEDS, PART 2				
❏ EmArcy MG-36051 [M]	1955	10.00	20.00	40.00
JAZZ GIANTS, VOL. 4: FOLK BLUES				
❏ EmArcy MG-36052 [M]	1955	10.00	20.00	40.00
JAZZ GIANTS, VOL. 5: BRASS				
❏ EmArcy MG-36053 [M]	1955	10.00	20.00	40.00
JAZZ GIANTS, VOL. 6: MODERN SWEDES				
❏ EmArcy MG-36054 [M]	1955	10.00	20.00	40.00
JAZZ GIANTS, VOL. 7: DIXIELAND				
❏ EmArcy MG-36055 [M]	1955	10.00	20.00	40.00
JAZZ GIANTS, VOL. 8: DRUM ROLE				
❏ EmArcy MG-36071 [M]	1956	10.00	20.00	40.00
JAZZ GOES TO BROADWAY				
❏ Kapp KL-1007 [M]	1956	5.00	10.00	20.00
JAZZ GREATS				
❏ Tops L-1508 [M]	1958	5.00	10.00	20.00
JAZZ GREATS!				
❏ Allegro 737 [M]	1958	7.50	15.00	30.00
JAZZ HALL OF FAME, VOL. 2				
❏ Design DLP-113 [M]	196?	5.00	10.00	20.00
A JAZZ HOLIDAY				
❏ MCA MCA2-4018 [(2)]	1973	3.75	7.50	15.00
—Black label with rainbow				
THE JAZZ HOUR				
❏ Savoy MG-12126 [M]	1957	12.50	25.00	50.00
JAZZ IN HOLLYWOOD				
❏ Liberty LJH-6001 [M]	1955	7.50	15.00	30.00
JAZZ IN TRANSITION				
❏ Transition TRLP-30 [M]	1956	50.00	100.00	200.00
—With booklet (deduct 1/4 if missing)				
JAZZ INTERPLAY				
❏ Prestige PRLP-7341 [(2)M]	1964	10.00	20.00	40.00
❏ Prestige PRLP-7341 [(2)R]	1964	6.25	12.50	25.00
JAZZ IS BUSTING OUT ALL OVER				
❏ Savoy MG-12123 [M]	1957	12.50	25.00	50.00
JAZZ JAMBOREE				
❏ Halo 50229 [M]	1957	5.00	10.00	20.00

Number	Title	Yr	VG	VG+	NM
JAZZ LAB					
❏ Starlite ST-7003 [M]		1955	12.50	25.00	50.00
THE JAZZ LIFE					
❏ Candid CD-8019 [M]		1960	10.00	20.00	40.00
❏ Candid CS-9019 [S]		1960	7.50	15.00	30.00
JAZZ LTD.					
❏ Regal LP-11 [10]		1951	12.50	25.00	50.00
THE JAZZ MAKERS					
❏ Columbia CL 1036 [M]		1957	5.00	10.00	20.00
JAZZ MONTAGE					
❏ Liberty LRP-3292 [M]		1963	3.75	7.50	15.00
❏ Liberty LST-7292 [S]		1963	5.00	10.00	20.00
JAZZ MUSIC FOR BIRDS					
❏ Bethlehem BCP-6039 [M]		1959	7.50	15.00	30.00
JAZZ MUSIC FOR PEOPLE WHO DON'T CARE ABOUT MONEY					
❏ Bethlehem BCP-88 [M]		1958	7.50	15.00	30.00
JAZZ ODYSSEY: THE SOUND OF CHICAGO					
❏ Columbia C3L 32 [(3)M]		1964	10.00	20.00	40.00
JAZZ ODYSSEY: THE SOUND OF HARLEM					
❏ Columbia C3L 33 [(3)M]		1964	10.00	20.00	40.00
JAZZ ODYSSEY: THE SOUND OF NEW ORLEANS					
❏ Columbia C3L 30 [(3)M]		1964	10.00	20.00	40.00
JAZZ OF THE FORTIES, VOL. 1					
❏ Folkways FJ-2841		197?	3.00	6.00	12.00
JAZZ OF THE ROARING 20'S					
❏ Riverside RLP 12-801 [M]		195?	12.50	25.00	50.00
JAZZ OF THE ROARING TWENTIES: DANCE MUSIC OF THE CHARLESTON ERA					
❏ Riverside RLP 12-108 [M]		1956	10.00	20.00	40.00
JAZZ OF THE SIXTIES					
❏ Vee Jay VJS-2-1008 [(2)]		1974	5.00	10.00	20.00
JAZZ OF TWO DECADES					
❏ EmArcy DEM-2 [M]		1956	10.00	20.00	40.00
JAZZ OFF THE AIR, VOL. 1					
❏ Esoteric ESJ-2 [10]		1952	20.00	40.00	80.00
JAZZ OFF THE AIR, VOL. 2					
❏ Esoteric ESJ-3 [10]		1952	20.00	40.00	80.00
JAZZ OMNIBUS					
❏ Columbia CL 1020 [M]		1957	5.00	10.00	20.00
JAZZ ON THE AIR					
❏ Brunswick BL 58048 [10]		1953	12.50	25.00	50.00
JAZZ ON THE SCREEN					
❏ Fontana MGF-27532 [M]		1965	7.50	15.00	30.00
❏ Fontana SRF-67532 [S]		1965	10.00	20.00	40.00
JAZZ PIANISTS GALORE					
❏ Jazz: West Coast JWC-506 [M]		1956	37.50	75.00	150.00
THE JAZZ PIANO					
❏ RCA Victor LPM-3499 [M]		1966	5.00	10.00	20.00
❏ RCA Victor LSP-3499 [S]		1966	6.25	12.50	25.00
A JAZZ PIANO ANTHOLOGY					
❏ Columbia PG 32355 [(2)]		197?	3.75	7.50	15.00
JAZZ PIANO GREATS					
❏ Folkways FJ-2852		197?	3.00	6.00	12.00
JAZZ PIONEERS 1933-36					
❏ Prestige PRLP-7647		1969	3.75	7.50	15.00
JAZZ POLL WINNERS					
❏ Columbia CL 1610 [M]		1960	5.00	10.00	20.00
JAZZ POTPOURRI					
❏ Audiophile AP-24 [M]		1953	7.50	15.00	30.00
THE JAZZ ROUND					
❏ Verve VSP-24 [M]		1966	3.75	7.50	15.00
❏ Verve VSPS-24 [R]		1966	2.50	5.00	10.00
A JAZZ SALUTE TO FREEDOM					
❏ Core 100 [(2)M]		196?	6.25	12.50	25.00
THE JAZZ SCENE					
❏ American Recording Society G-419 [M]		1957	7.50	15.00	30.00
❏ Clef MGC-674 [M]		1955	10.00	20.00	40.00
—Reissue of 4007					
❏ Clef MGC-4007 [M]		1953	12.50	25.00	50.00
❏ Clef Special Edition (no #) [(2)10]		1953	25.00	50.00	100.00
—Two 10-inch LPs in box. Buyers had the option of purchasing a collection of photos that had been used in the original 78 rpm album; add another 50 percent if these photos are included					
❏ Verve MGV-8060 [M]		1957	7.50	15.00	30.00
—Reissue of Clef 674					
❏ Verve V-8060 [M]		1961	5.00	10.00	20.00
JAZZ SET					
❏ Columbia Special Products CSP-217M [M]		1965	3.00	6.00	12.00
❏ Columbia Special Products CSP-217S [S]		1965	2.50	5.00	10.00
—Special item for Zenith					
JAZZ SOUL OF "CLEOPATRA"					
❏ New Jazz NJLP-8292 [M]		1962	10.00	20.00	40.00
—Purple label					
❏ New Jazz NJLP-8292 [M]		1965	5.00	10.00	20.00
—Blue label, trident logo at right					
THE JAZZ SOUND					
❏ Columbia Special Products CSP 298 [M]		1966	2.50	5.00	10.00
JAZZ SOUTH PACIFIC					
❏ Regent MG-6001 [M]		1956	12.50	25.00	50.00
❏ Savoy MG-12205 [M]		196?	5.00	10.00	20.00
THE JAZZ STORY					
❏ Coral CJE-100 [(3)M]		195?	25.00	50.00	100.00
—Box set; narrated by Steve Allen					
JAZZ SUPER HITS					
❏ Atlantic SD 1528		1969	6.25	12.50	25.00
JAZZ SUPER HITS, VOL. 2					
❏ Atlantic SD 1559		1970	5.00	10.00	20.00
JAZZ SURPRISE					
❏ Crown CLP-5008 [M]		1957	5.00	10.00	20.00
JAZZ SWINGS BROADWAY					
❏ Pacific Jazz PJM-404 [M]		1956	12.50	25.00	50.00
❏ World Pacific PJM-404 [M]		1958	10.00	20.00	40.00
JAZZ TIME U.S.A. — VOLUME 1					
❏ Brunswick BL 54000 [M]		1952	7.50	15.00	30.00
JAZZ TIME U.S.A. — VOLUME 2					
❏ Brunswick BL 54001 [M]		1953	7.50	15.00	30.00
JAZZ TIME U.S.A. — VOLUME 3					
❏ Brunswick BL 54002 [M]		1954	7.50	15.00	30.00
JAZZ VARIATIONS, VOL. 1					
❏ Stinson SLP-20 [10]		195?	15.00	30.00	60.00
❏ Stinson SLP-20 [M]		196?	6.25	12.50	25.00
JAZZ VARIATIONS, VOL. 2					
❏ Stinson SLP-29 [M]		196?	6.25	12.50	25.00
JAZZ VIOLINS OF THE 40S					
❏ Folkways FJ-2854		197?	3.00	6.00	12.00
JAZZ VOCALS AWARD ALBUM					
❏ Bethlehem BCP-6068 [M]		1963	6.25	12.50	25.00
JAZZ WEST COAST, VOL. 1					
❏ Pacific Jazz JWC-500 [M]		1956	12.50	25.00	50.00
❏ World Pacific JWC-500 [M]		1958	10.00	20.00	40.00
JAZZ WEST COAST, VOL. 2					
❏ Pacific Jazz JWC-501 [M]		1956	12.50	25.00	50.00
❏ World Pacific JWC-501 [M]		1958	10.00	20.00	40.00
JAZZ WEST COAST, VOL. 3					
❏ Pacific Jazz JWC-507 [M]		1957	12.50	25.00	50.00
❏ World Pacific JWC-507 [M]		1958	10.00	20.00	40.00
JAZZ WEST COAST, VOL. 4					
❏ World Pacific JWC-510 [M]		1958	10.00	20.00	40.00
❏ World Pacific ST-1009 [S]		1959	7.50	15.00	30.00
JAZZ WEST COAST, VOL. 5					
❏ World Pacific JWC-511 [M]		1958	10.00	20.00	40.00
THE JAZZ WORLD					
❏ Columbia Special Products CSS 524 [S]		1967	2.50	5.00	10.00
JAZZ, VOL. 1: THE SOUTH					
❏ Folkways FP-53/4 [M]		1951	6.25	12.50	25.00
❏ Folkways FJ-2801 [M]		197?	3.00	6.00	12.00

Number Title	Yr	VG	VG+	NM

JAZZ, VOL. 2: THE BLUES

❑ Folkways FP-55/6 [M]	1951	6.25	12.50	25.00
❑ Folkways FJ-2802 [M]	197?	3.00	6.00	12.00

JAZZ, VOL. 3: NEW ORLEANS

❑ Folkways FP-57/8 [M]	1951	6.25	12.50	25.00
❑ Folkways FJ-2803 [M]	197?	3.00	6.00	12.00

JAZZ, VOL. 4: JAZZ SINGERS

❑ Folkways FP-59/60 [M]	1951	6.25	12.50	25.00
❑ Folkways FJ-2804 [M]	197?	3.00	6.00	12.00

JAZZ, VOL. 5: CHICAGO

❑ Folkways FP-63/4 [M]	1951	6.25	12.50	25.00
❑ Folkways FJ-2805 [M]	197?	3.00	6.00	12.00

JAZZ, VOL. 6: CHICAGO #2

❑ Folkways FP-65/6 [M]	1951	6.25	12.50	25.00
❑ Folkways FJ-2806 [M]	197?	3.00	6.00	12.00

JAZZ, VOL. 7: NEW YORK 1922-1934

❑ Folkways FP-67/8 [M]	1951	6.25	12.50	25.00
❑ Folkways FJ-2807 [M]	197?	3.00	6.00	12.00

JAZZ, VOL. 8: BIG BANDS BEFORE 1938

❑ Folkways FP-69/70 [M]	1951	6.25	12.50	25.00
❑ Folkways FJ-2808 [M]	197?	3.00	6.00	12.00

JAZZ, VOL. 9: PIANO

❑ Folkways FP-71/2 [M]	1951	6.25	12.50	25.00
❑ Folkways FJ-2809 [M]	197?	3.00	6.00	12.00

JAZZ, VOL. 10: BOOGIE WOOGIE, JUMP, KANSAS CITY

❑ Folkways FP-73/4 [M]	1951	6.25	12.50	25.00
❑ Folkways FJ-2810 [M]	197?	3.00	6.00	12.00

JAZZ, VOL. 11: ADDENDA

❑ Folkways FP-75/6 [M]	1951	6.25	12.50	25.00
❑ Folkways FJ-2811 [M]	197?	3.00	6.00	12.00

JAZZMEN — DETROIT

❑ Savoy MG-12083 [M]	1956	20.00	40.00	80.00

JAZZTONE SAMPLER

❑ Jazztone J-SPEC-100 [10]	1955	12.50	25.00	50.00
—With booklet				

JAZZVILLE, VOL. 1

❑ Dawn DLP-1101 [M]	1956	20.00	40.00	80.00

JESUS CHRIST SUPERSTAR

❑ Decca DXA 7206 [(2)]	1970	7.50	15.00	30.00
—Box set with booklet				
❑ Decca DXSA 7206 [(2)]	1970	6.25	12.50	25.00
—Gatefold cover with booklet				
❑ Decca MCA 2-10000 [(2)]	1973	3.00	6.00	12.00
—Gatefold cover with booklet; reissue; same custom labels as Decca issue				
❑ MCA 10000 [(2)]	197?	3.00	6.00	12.00
—Gatefold cover with booklet; reissue; generic MCA labels				

JINGLE BELL JAZZ

❑ Columbia CL 1893 [M]	1962	5.00	10.00	20.00
❑ Columbia CS 8693 [S]	1962	3.75	7.50	15.00
❑ Harmony KH 32529	1973	3.00	6.00	12.00
—Reissue of CS 8693 with one track changed				

JOHN COLTRANE IN THE WINNER'S CIRCLE

❑ Bethlehem BCP-6066 [M]	1961	6.25	12.50	25.00
—Reissue of 6024 with new title				

JOHN HAMMOND PRESENTS "FROM SPIRITUALS TO SWING" AT CARNEGIE HALL 1938

❑ Vanguard VRS-8523 [M]	1959	10.00	20.00	40.00

JOHN HAMMOND PRESENTS "FROM SPIRITUALS TO SWING" AT CARNEGIE HALL 1939

❑ Vanguard VRS-8524 [M]	1959	10.00	20.00	40.00

THE JOY OF CHRISTMAS

❑ Capitol SP 8693	1968	3.00	6.00	12.00
❑ Capitol Creative Products SL-6580	1968	3.00	6.00	12.00
❑ Columbia Special Products P 12042	1973	3.00	6.00	12.00
—Sold only at Strawbridge & Clothier stores (Philadelphia area)				
❑ RCA Victor PRM-197 [M]	1965	3.75	7.50	15.00
—Created for the National Tea Company				
❑ RCA Victor PRS-429	1972	3.00	6.00	12.00

THE JOY OF CHRISTMAS, FEATURING MARTY ROBBINS AND HIS FRIENDS

❑ Columbia Special Products C 11087	1972	3.75	7.50	15.00

THE JOY OF CHRISTMAS, VOLUME II

❑ RCA Victor PRM-230 [M]	1966	3.75	7.50	15.00
—Created for the National Tea Company				
❑ RCA Victor PRM-230-A [M]	1966	3.75	7.50	15.00
—Sold only at Acme markets (Mid-Atlantic area); same contents as PRM-230				

Number Title	Yr	VG	VG+	NM

JOY TO THE WORLD

❑ Columbia Special Products P 11647	1973	2.50	5.00	10.00

THE JOYFUL SOUND OF CHRISTMAS

❑ RCA Record Club CSP-0601 [(2)]	1969	5.00	10.00	20.00
—Available only through the RCA Record Club				

JOYOUS CHRISTMAS, VOLUME 2

❑ Columbia Special Products CSS 808	1968	3.00	6.00	12.00
—Produced for the Beneficial Finance System				

JOYOUS CHRISTMAS, VOLUME 4

❑ Columbia Special Products CSS 1485	1970	3.00	6.00	12.00
—Produced for the Beneficial Finance System				

JOYOUS CHRISTMAS, VOLUME V

❑ Columbia Special Products C 10398	1971	2.50	5.00	10.00
—Produced for the Beneficial Finance System				

JOYOUS CHRISTMAS, VOLUME 6

❑ Columbia Special Products C 11083	1972	2.50	5.00	10.00
—Produced for the Beneficial Finance System				

JOYOUS MUSIC FOR CHRISTMAS TIME

❑ Reader's Digest RD 45-M [(4)M]	1963	5.00	10.00	20.00
❑ Reader's Digest RD 45-S [(4)S]	1963	5.00	10.00	20.00
—Available only through Reader's Digest magazine by mail order				

JOYOUS NOEL

❑ Reader's Digest RDA-57A [(4)]	1966	5.00	10.00	20.00
—Available only through Reader's Digest magazine by mail order				

THE JOYOUS SONGS OF CHRISTMAS

❑ Columbia Special Products C 10400	1971	2.50	5.00	10.00
—Sold only at Goodyear tire dealers				

JOYS OF CHRISTMAS

❑ Capitol Creative Products SL-6610	1969	3.00	6.00	12.00
❑ Capitol Special Markets SL-6610	197?	2.50	5.00	10.00
—Reissue with revised label name				

JUBILEE MONAURAL SAMPLER: VOCALS AND INSTRUMENTALS

❑ Jubilee MSJLP-803 [M]	1959	7.50	15.00	30.00

JUBILEE STEREOSONIC VOCAL SAMPLER, VOLUME 2

❑ Jubilee SSJLP-802 [S]	1959	10.00	20.00	40.00

JUBILEE SURPRISE PARTY

❑ Jubilee JGM-1107 [M]	1959	37.50	75.00	150.00
❑ Jubilee JGS-1107 [S]	1959	50.00	100.00	200.00

JUST FOUR LAUGHS VOLUME I

❑ Scepter SPS 5104	1972	3.00	6.00	12.00
—Contains routines by Bill Cosby, Dick Gregory, Redd Foxx and Flip Wilson				

JUST FOUR LAUGHS VOLUME II

❑ Scepter SPS 5105	1972	3.00	6.00	12.00
—Contains routines by Bill Cosby, Dick Gregory, Redd Foxx and Flip Wilson				

JUST JAZZ

❑ Imperial LP-9246 [M]	1963	5.00	10.00	20.00
❑ Imperial LP-12246 [S]	1963	6.25	12.50	25.00

K-BOX DUSTY DISCS

❑ Roulette R 25338 [M]	1966	5.00	10.00	20.00

KANSAS CITY IN THE '30S

❑ Capitol T 1057 [M]	1958	6.25	12.50	25.00

KANSAS CITY JAZZ

❑ Decca DL 8044 [M]	1954	10.00	20.00	40.00

KANSAS CITY PIANO

❑ Decca DL 9226 [M]	1967	7.50	15.00	30.00
❑ Decca DL 79226 [R]	1967	3.00	6.00	12.00

KATS KARAVAN (OLD FAVORITES WITH JIM LOWE)

❑ Vee Jay LP-100 [M]	1957	12.50	25.00	50.00
—Gold label, black print				

KBIG CHOICES

❑ World Pacific KBIG-1 [S]	1964	6.25	12.50	25.00

KEYBOARD KINGS

❑ MGM E-100 [10]	1951	12.50	25.00	50.00

KEYBOARD KINGS OF JAZZ

❑ RCA Victor LPT-4 [10]	1951	10.00	20.00	40.00

KGFJ SOUNDS OF SUCCESS

❑ Roulette R 25349 [M]	1967	5.00	10.00	20.00

KINGS OF CLASSIC JAZZ

❑ Riverside RLP 12-131 [M]	1957	10.00	20.00	40.00

Number / Title	Yr	VG	VG+	NM
KINGS OF THE KEYBOARD				
☐ American Recording Society G-406 [M]	1956	7.50	15.00	30.00
THE KINGS SING THE BLUES				
☐ Teem LP-5005 [M]	196?	7.50	15.00	30.00
KNOW YOUR JAZZ				
☐ ABC-Paramount ABC-115 [M]	1956	7.50	15.00	30.00
KPOI'S BATTLE OF THE SURFING BANDS				
☐ Del-Fi DFLP-1235 [M]	1964	15.00	30.00	60.00
☐ Del-Fi DFST-1235 [S]	1964	25.00	50.00	100.00
—Honolulu version of the above LP				
KTLA'S BATTLE OF THE SURFING BANDS				
☐ Del-Fi DFLP-1235 [M]	1964	12.50	25.00	50.00
☐ Del-Fi DFST-1235 [S]	1964	20.00	40.00	80.00
—Los Angeles version of the above LP				
KYA GOLDEN GATE GREATS				
☐ Chess LP 1458 SF [M]	1961	37.50	75.00	150.00
—San Francisco version of "Golden Gassers," Chess 1458				
KYA'S BATTLE OF THE SURFING BANDS				
☐ Del-Fi DFLP-1235 [M]	1964	12.50	25.00	50.00
☐ Del-Fi DFST-1235 [S]	1964	20.00	40.00	80.00
—San Francisco version of the above LP, with slightly different contents				
KYA'S MEMORIES OF THE COW PALACE				
☐ Autumn LP 101 [M]	1963	17.50	35.00	70.00
LATE MUSIC, VOLUME I				
☐ Columbia CL 541 [M]	1954	6.25	12.50	25.00
LATE MUSIC, VOLUME II				
☐ Columbia CL 542 [M]	1954	6.25	12.50	25.00
LATE MUSIC, VOLUME III				
☐ Columbia CL 543 [M]	1954	6.25	12.50	25.00
LAURIE GOLDEN GOODIES				
☐ Laurie LLP-2041 [M]	1967	3.75	7.50	15.00
☐ Laurie SLLP-2041 [P]	1967	6.25	12.50	25.00
LEONARD FEATHER'S ENCYCLOPEDIA OF JAZZ OF THE '60S: BLUES BAG				
☐ Vee Jay LP-2506 [M]	1964	5.00	10.00	20.00
LEONARD FEATHER'S ENCYCLOPEDIA OF JAZZ, VOLUME ONE: GIANTS OF THE SAXOPHONE				
☐ Vee Jay LP-2501 [M]	1964	5.00	10.00	20.00
☐ Vee Jay VJS-2501 [S]	1964	6.25	12.50	25.00
LET'S CELEBRATE CHRISTMAS				
☐ Capitol Special Markets SL-6923	1973	3.00	6.00	12.00
LET'S HAVE A DANCE PARTY				
☐ Ace LP-1019 [M]	1961	17.50	35.00	70.00
LET'S SING ABOUT FREEDOM				
☐ Vee Jay LP-5044 [M]	1963	7.50	15.00	30.00
LIBERTY PREMIER SERIES SPECTACULAR				
☐ Liberty L-5504 [M]	1962	5.00	10.00	20.00
☐ Liberty S-6604 [S]	1962	7.50	15.00	30.00
LIBERTY PROUDLY PRESENTS STEREO — THE VISUAL SOUND				
☐ Liberty LST-100 [S]	1959	10.00	20.00	40.00
THE LIFE TREASURY OF CHRISTMAS MUSIC				
☐ Project/Capitol TL 100 [M]	1963	5.00	10.00	20.00
—Designed as a supplement to the Life Book of Christmas; selections performed by anonymous chorus and orchestra and Boy Choristers from the Church of the Transfiguration (NY)				
LIGHTS OUT SAN FRANCISCO				
☐ Blue Thumb BT 6004	1970	6.25	12.50	25.00
LIKE 'ER RED HOT				
☐ ABC Duke DLPX-73 [M]	1974	3.75	7.50	15.00
☐ Duke DLP-73 [M]	196?	7.50	15.00	30.00
—Green label, "Distributed by ABC-Dunhill"				
☐ Duke DLP-73 [M]	196?	12.50	25.00	50.00
—Orange label				
☐ Duke DLP-73 [M]	1960	30.00	60.00	120.00
—Purple and yellow label				
LISTEN TO OUR STORY				
☐ Brunswick BL 59001 [10]	1950	15.00	30.00	60.00
A LITTLE ROCK AND ROLL FOR EVERYBODY				
☐ Audio Lab AL-1567 [M]	1960	50.00	100.00	200.00
THE LITTLEST ANGEL/LULLABY OF CHRISTMAS				
☐ Decca DLP 8009 [M]	1949	10.00	20.00	40.00

Number / Title	Yr	VG	VG+	NM
LIVE AT BILL GRAHAM'S FILLMORE WEST				
☐ Columbia CS 9893	1969	3.75	7.50	15.00
LIVE AT THE WHISKEY A-GO-GO				
☐ Vee Jay LP-1100 [M]	1964	7.50	15.00	30.00
—Not known to exist in stereo				
THE LIVELY SOUND OF UNIVERSITY				
☐ Capitol Custom (no #) [M]	1966	5.00	10.00	20.00
—"Mustang Sweepstakes Prize Winner" on front cover				
LOADED				
☐ Savoy MG-12074 [M]	1956	12.50	25.00	50.00
LONDON BROIL				
☐ Angel ANG-60004 [10]	1955	12.50	25.00	50.00
A LOOK AT YESTERDAY				
☐ Mainstream S-6025 [R]	1965	3.00	6.00	12.00
☐ Mainstream 56025 [M]	1965	6.25	12.50	25.00
LOOK WHO'S SURFIN' NOW!				
☐ King 882 [M]	1964	37.50	75.00	150.00
LOONEY TUNES AND MERRIE MELODIES				
☐ Warner Bros. PRO 423 [(3)]	1970	25.00	50.00	100.00
—Box set with booklet of liner notes; originals have green labels				
A LOT OF YARN BUT A WELL-KNITTED JAZZ ALBUM				
☐ Bethlehem BCP-91 [M]	1958	7.50	15.00	30.00
LOVE THOSE GOODIES				
☐ Checker LP 2973 [DJ]	1959	125.00	250.00	500.00
—White label, multi-color splash vinyl				
☐ Checker LP 2973 [M]	1959	30.00	60.00	120.00
LULLABY OF BIRDLAND				
☐ RCA Victor LPM-1146 [M]	1955	12.50	25.00	50.00
LUSTY MOODS				
☐ Moodsville MVLP-37 [M]	1963	10.00	20.00	40.00
—Green label				
☐ Moodsville MVLP-37 [M]	1965	5.00	10.00	20.00
—Blue label, trident logo at right				
☐ Moodsville MVST-37 [S]	1963	10.00	20.00	40.00
—Green label				
☐ Moodsville MVST-37 [S]	1965	5.00	10.00	20.00
—Blue label, trident logo at right				
☐ New Jazz NJLP-8319 [M]	1963	—	—	—
—Canceled				
☐ Status ST-8319 [M]	1965	7.50	15.00	30.00
MAD "TWISTS" ROCK 'N' ROLL				
☐ Big Top 12-1305 [M]	1962	25.00	50.00	100.00
THE MAGIC HORN				
☐ RCA Victor LPM-1332 [M]	1956	10.00	20.00	40.00
THE MAGIC OF CHRISTMAS				
☐ Capitol SWBB-93810 [(2)]	1971	3.75	7.50	15.00
—Available only through the Capitol Record Club				
☐ Columbia Musical Treasury P2M 5245	196?	3.75	7.50	15.00
—No artists mentioned				
☐ Columbia Musical Treasury P3S 5806 [(3)]	1972	5.00	10.00	20.00
THE MAGIC OF CHRISTMAS WITH CHILDREN				
☐ Capitol Creative Products L 6517 [M]	196?	3.75	7.50	15.00
—Sold only at Safeway stores (In Association with Jon M. Huntsman Inc., Continental Production Company)				
MAGNAVOX ALBUM OF CHRISTMAS MUSIC				
☐ Columbia Special Products CSQ 11093 [Q]	1972	5.00	10.00	20.00
—Sold only at Magnavox dealers; yes, this is in quadraphonic!				
MAGNAVOX PRESENTS A REPRISE OF GREAT HITS				
☐ Reprise PRO 578	1973	2.50	5.00	10.00
MAHALIA (JACKSON) AND FRIENDS AT CHRISTMASTIME				
☐ Columbia Special Products P 11804	1973	3.00	6.00	12.00
—Side 2 is all rechanneled stereo; Side 1 is true stereo				
MAMBO JAZZ				
☐ Prestige PRLP-135 [10]	1952	37.50	75.00	150.00
THE MAN WITH A HORN				
☐ Decca DL 5191 [10]	1950	12.50	25.00	50.00
THE MANY FACES OF THE BLUES				
☐ Savoy MG-12125 [M]	1957	12.50	25.00	50.00
THE MANY MOODS OF CHRISTMAS				
☐ Columbia Special Products P 12013	1973	3.00	6.00	12.00
—Sold only at Goodyear tire dealers				
☐ RCA Special Products DPL1-0085	1974	2.50	5.00	10.00

Number Title	Yr	VG	VG+	NM
MAR Y SOL				
❑ Atco SD-2-705 [(2)]	1972	3.75	7.50	15.00
THE MELLOW MOODS				
❑ RCA Victor LPM-1365 [M]	1956	10.00	20.00	40.00
MELLOW THE MOOD/JAZZ IN A MELLOW MOOD				
❑ Blue Note BLP-5001 [10]	1951	50.00	100.00	200.00
MEMORABLE SESSIONS IN JAZZ				
❑ Blue Note BLP-5026 [10]	1953	50.00	100.00	200.00
MEMORIES ARE MADE OF HITS				
❑ Liberty LRP-3200 [M]	1961	6.25	12.50	25.00
—Reissued as "The Original Hits, Volume 4"				
MEMORY LANE, HITS BY THE ORIGINAL GROUPS				
❑ Fire FLP-100 [M]	1959	50.00	100.00	200.00
—Reissue of "Here Are the Hits!" with the same label and number				
MEMPHIS COUNTRY				
❑ Sun 120	1970	3.75	7.50	15.00
MEMPHIS GOLD				
❑ Stax 710 [M]	1966	6.25	12.50	25.00
❑ Stax S710 [S]	1966	7.50	15.00	30.00
MEMPHIS GOLD VOLUME 2				
❑ Stax 726 [M]	1967	5.00	10.00	20.00
❑ Stax S726 [S]	1967	6.25	12.50	25.00
MEMPHIS MILLIONS				
❑ Stax STS 3023	1973	3.75	7.50	15.00
MERRY CHRISTMAS				
❑ Columbia Musical Treasury 3P 6306 [(3)]	1975	3.75	7.50	15.00
❑ Coral CRL 56080 [10]	1952	20.00	40.00	80.00
❑ RCA Victor PRS-168	1964	3.75	7.50	15.00
MERRY CHRISTMAS BABY (CHRISTMAS MUSIC FOR YOUNG LOVERS)				
❑ Hollywood HLP 501 [M]	1956	30.00	60.00	120.00
MERRY CHRISTMAS FROM CORAL RECORDS				
❑ Coral CRL 57355 [M]	1960	5.00	10.00	20.00
MERRY CHRISTMAS FROM MOTOWN				
❑ Motown MS-681	1968	7.50	15.00	30.00
MERRY CHRISTMAS FROM SESAME STREET				
❑ CRA CTW 25516	1975	3.00	6.00	12.00
MERRY CHRISTMAS FROM...				
❑ King 680 [M]	1959	50.00	100.00	200.00
MERRY CHRISTMAS MUSIC/CHRISTMAS FAVORITES				
❑ Plymouth P12-59 [M]	1952	5.00	10.00	20.00
—Artists not mentioned on jacket or label				
MERRY CHRISTMAS TO YOU				
❑ Capitol T 9030 [M]	1955	12.50	25.00	50.00
MERRY CHRISTMAS WITH NAT KING COLE/FRED WARING AND THE PENNSYLVANIANS				
❑ Capitol Special Markets SL-6883	1973	2.50	5.00	10.00
A MERRY MERRY CHRISTMAS				
❑ Columbia Special Products CSP 161	1964	3.75	7.50	15.00
—Number on record is "XTV 86094" on Side 1 and "XTV 86095" on Side 2				
METRONOME ALL STARS 1956				
❑ Clef MGC-743 [M]	1956	10.00	20.00	40.00
❑ Verve MGV-8030 [M]	1957	10.00	20.00	40.00
❑ Verve V-8030 [M]	1961	5.00	10.00	20.00
METRONOME ALL-STARS				
❑ Harmony HL 7044 [M]	1957	6.25	12.50	25.00
❑ RCA Camden CAL-426 [M]	1958	6.25	12.50	25.00
THE METRONOME ALL-STARS				
❑ Columbia CL 2528 [10]	1954	7.50	15.00	30.00
MGM RECORDS PARADE OF STARS				
❑ MGM NP 90569 [M]	1965	5.00	10.00	20.00
—Capitol Record Club sampler of 12 MGM artists and soundtracks				
MICKEY MOST PRESENTS BRITISH GO-GO				
❑ MGM E 4306 [M]	1965	7.50	15.00	30.00
❑ MGM SE 4306 [R]	1965	7.50	15.00	30.00
MICKEY MOST PRESENTS ENGLISH IN-GROUPS				
❑ Metro M-577 [M]	1966	5.00	10.00	20.00
❑ Metro MS-577 [R]	1966	5.00	10.00	20.00

Number Title	Yr	VG	VG+	NM
MIDDLE OF THE ROAD				
❑ Warner Bros. PRO 525 [(2)]	1972	7.50	15.00	30.00
—Originals have green labels				
MIDNIGHT JAZZ AT CARNEGIE HALL				
❑ Verve MGV-8189-2 [(2)M]	1957	12.50	25.00	50.00
❑ Verve V-8189-2 [(2)M]	1961	6.25	12.50	25.00
A MILLION OR MORE				
❑ ABC-Paramount ABC-216 [M]	1959	20.00	40.00	80.00
MILLION SELLER DANCE HITS				
❑ Parkway P-7028 [M]	1963	7.50	15.00	30.00
THE MILLION-AIRS				
❑ Coral CRL 57310 [M]	1959	6.25	12.50	25.00
THE MODERN IDIOM				
❑ Capitol H 325 [10]	1952	12.50	25.00	50.00
MODERN JAZZ				
❑ London LL 1185 [M]	1955	5.00	10.00	20.00
❑ Tops L-1521 [M]	1958	5.00	10.00	20.00
MODERN JAZZ CONCERT				
❑ Adventures in Sound WL-127 [M]	1958	10.00	20.00	40.00
MODERN JAZZ FESTIVAL				
❑ Harmony HL 7196 [M]	1958	5.00	10.00	20.00
MODERN JAZZ GALLERY				
❑ Kapp KXL-5001 [M]	195?	5.00	10.00	20.00
MODERN JAZZ GREATS				
❑ Crown CLP-5212 [M]	196?	3.75	7.50	15.00
MODERN JAZZ GREATS, VOL. 2				
❑ Crown CLP-5220 [M]	196?	3.75	7.50	15.00
MODERN JAZZ HALL OF FAME				
❑ Design DLP-29 [M]	196?	3.00	6.00	12.00
❑ Design DLPS-29 [R]	196?	2.00	4.00	8.00
MODERN JAZZ PIANO				
❑ RCA Camden CAL-384 [M]	1958	6.25	12.50	25.00
MODERN JAZZ SPECTACULAR				
❑ Jazztone J-1231 [M]	1956	7.50	15.00	30.00
MODERN JAZZ TRUMPETS				
❑ Prestige PRLP-113 [10]	1951	50.00	100.00	200.00
MODERN MOODS				
❑ Moodsville MVLP-2 [M]	1961	10.00	20.00	40.00
—Green label				
❑ Moodsville MVLP-2 [M]	1965	5.00	10.00	20.00
—Blue label, trident logo at right				
MONARCH ALL STAR JAZZ, VOL. 1				
❑ Monarch LP-201 [10]	1952	12.50	25.00	50.00
MONARCH ALL STAR JAZZ, VOL. 2				
❑ Monarch LP-202 [10]	1952	12.50	25.00	50.00
MONARCH ALL STAR JAZZ, VOL. 3				
❑ Monarch LP-203 [10]	1952	12.50	25.00	50.00
MONARCH ALL STAR JAZZ, VOL. 4				
❑ Monarch LP-204 [10]	1952	12.50	25.00	50.00
MONARCH ALL STAR JAZZ, VOL. 5				
❑ Monarch LP-205 [10]	1952	12.50	25.00	50.00
MONDAY NIGHT AT BIRDLAND				
❑ Roulette R 52015 [M]	1958	7.50	15.00	30.00
❑ Roulette SR 52015 [S]	1959	7.50	15.00	30.00
MONTAGE				
❑ Savoy MG-12029 [M]	1955	20.00	40.00	80.00
MONTGOMERY WARD PRESENTS A CHRISTMAS TO REMEMBER				
❑ Capitol Creative Products SL-6573	1968	3.00	6.00	12.00
—Sold only at Montgomery Ward stores				
MONTGOMERY WARD PRESENTS A CHRISTMAS TO REMEMBER VOL. 2				
❑ Capitol Creative Products SL-6610	1969	3.00	6.00	12.00
—Sold only at Montgomery Ward stores				
MONTGOMERY WARD PRESENTS A CHRISTMAS TO REMEMBER VOL. 3				
❑ Capitol Creative Products SL-6681	1970	2.50	5.00	10.00
—Sold only at Montgomery Ward stores				

Number Title	Yr	VG	VG+	NM
MONTGOMERY WARD PRESENTS CHRISTMAS FAVORITES				
❑ Montgomery Ward W-101	1965	3.75	7.50	15.00
—No artists mentioned on label or jacket				
MONUMENTAL COUNTRY HITS				
❑ Monument SLP-18095	1968	5.00	10.00	20.00
MONUMENTAL POP HITS				
❑ Monument SLP-18096	1968	5.00	10.00	20.00
MOOD IN BLUE				
❑ Urania UJLP-1209 [M]	1955	7.50	15.00	30.00
MOOD TO BE WOOED				
❑ Cadet LP-784 [M]	1967	5.00	10.00	20.00
❑ Cadet LPS-784 [S]	1967	3.75	7.50	15.00
MORE DRUMS ON FIRE				
❑ World Pacific ST-1022 [S]	1960	7.50	15.00	30.00
❑ World Pacific WP-1261 [M]	1960	10.00	20.00	40.00
MORE FOR YOUR MONEY				
❑ Bell 6009	1968	5.00	10.00	20.00
MORE GOLD HITS, VOLUME 2				
❑ Warwick W 2044 [M]	1961	20.00	40.00	80.00
MORE GOLDEN GREATS				
❑ Liberty LRP-3548 [M]	1967	5.00	10.00	20.00
❑ Liberty LST-7548 [P]	1967	3.75	7.50	15.00
MORE GREAT HITS OF 1964 AND OTHER GOLDEN GOODIES				
❑ Vee Jay LP-1136 [M]	1965	7.50	15.00	30.00
—Not known to exist in stereo				
MORE LIVE ECHOES OF THE SWINGING BANDS				
❑ RCA Victor LPM-1983 [M]	1959	10.00	20.00	40.00
❑ RCA Victor LSP-1983 [S]	1959	12.50	25.00	50.00
MORE SOLID GOLD PROGRAMMING				
❑ Screen Gems/Columbia CPL-716/7 [(2)DJ]	1975	7.50	15.00	30.00
—Promo-only compilation of oldies sent to radio to spur airplay on songs owned by this publishing house; contains three Beatles recordings				
THE MOST				
❑ Forum Circle FC-9079 [M]	1963	3.00	6.00	12.00
❑ Forum Circle FCS-9079 [S]	1963	3.00	6.00	12.00
THE MOST OF THE TWIST				
❑ Roulette R 25176 [M]	1962	6.25	12.50	25.00
—Originals have a white label with colored spokes				
THE MOST, VOLUME 1				
❑ Roulette R 52050 [M]	1960	5.00	10.00	20.00
❑ Roulette SR 52050 [S]	1960	6.25	12.50	25.00
THE MOST, VOLUME 2				
❑ Roulette R 52053 [M]	1960	5.00	10.00	20.00
❑ Roulette SR 52053 [S]	1960	6.25	12.50	25.00
THE MOST, VOLUME 3				
❑ Roulette R 52057 [M]	1961	5.00	10.00	20.00
❑ Roulette SR 52057 [S]	1961	6.25	12.50	25.00
THE MOST, VOLUME 4				
❑ Roulette R 52062 [M]	1961	5.00	10.00	20.00
❑ Roulette SR 52062 [S]	1961	6.25	12.50	25.00
THE MOST, VOLUME 5				
❑ Roulette R 52075 [M]	1961	5.00	10.00	20.00
❑ Roulette SR 52075 [S]	1961	6.25	12.50	25.00
MOTOR CITY SCENE				
❑ Bethlehem BCP-6056 [M]	1961	12.50	25.00	50.00
THE MOTOR-TOWN REVIEW, VOL. 1				
❑ Motown MT 609 [M]	1963	10.00	20.00	40.00
THE MOTOR-TOWN REVIEW, VOL. 2				
❑ Motown MT 615 [M]	1964	7.50	15.00	30.00
THE MOTORTOWN REVIEW IN PARIS				
❑ Tamla T 264 [M]	1965	6.25	12.50	25.00
❑ Tamla TS 264 [S]	1965	7.50	15.00	30.00
THE MOTORTOWN REVUE LIVE!				
❑ Motown MS-688	1969	6.25	12.50	25.00
MOTOWN AT THE HOLLYWOOD PALACE				
❑ Motown MS 703	1970	3.75	7.50	15.00
❑ Motown MS-703	1970	3.75	7.50	15.00
MOTOWN CHARTBUSTERS, VOLUME 1				
❑ Motown MS-707	1970	3.75	7.50	15.00
MOTOWN CHARTBUSTERS, VOLUME 2				
❑ Motown MS-715	1970	3.75	7.50	15.00
A MOTOWN CHRISTMAS				
❑ Motown M-795V2 [(2)]	1973	5.00	10.00	20.00
MOTOWN SPECIAL				
❑ Motown M 603 [M]	1962	20.00	40.00	80.00
THE MOTOWN STORY: THE FIRST DECADE				
❑ Motown MS-726 [(5)]	1971	7.50	15.00	30.00
MOTOWN WINNER'S CIRCLE: #1 HITS, VOL. 1				
❑ Gordy GS-935	1969	6.25	12.50	25.00
MOTOWN WINNER'S CIRCLE: #1 HITS, VOL. 2				
❑ Gordy GS-936	1969	6.25	12.50	25.00
MOTOWN WINNER'S CIRCLE: #1 HITS, VOL. 3				
❑ Gordy GS-943	1969	6.25	12.50	25.00
MOTOWN WINNER'S CIRCLE: #1 HITS, VOL. 4				
❑ Gordy GS-946	1969	6.25	12.50	25.00
MOTOWN WINNER'S CIRCLE: #1 HITS, VOL. 5				
❑ Gordy GS-950	1970	6.25	12.50	25.00
MOUNTAIN FROLIC				
❑ Brunswick BL 59000 [10]	1950	15.00	30.00	60.00
MURRAY THE "K'S" SING ALONG WITH THE ORIGINAL GOLDEN GASSERS				
❑ Roulette R 25159 [M]	1961	7.50	15.00	30.00
MURRAY THE K — LIVE FROM THE BROOKLYN FOX				
❑ KFM 1001 [M]	1963	10.00	20.00	40.00
MURRAY THE K PRESENTS GOLDEN GASSERS FOR A DANCE PARTY				
❑ Roulette R 25192 [M]	1962	6.25	12.50	25.00
MURRAY THE K PRESENTS GOLDEN GASSERS FOR HAND HOLDERS				
❑ Roulette R 25191 [M]	1962	6.25	12.50	25.00
MURRAY THE K'S BLASTS FROM THE PAST				
❑ Chess LP 1461 [M]	1961	10.00	20.00	40.00
MURRAY THE K'S GASSERS FOR SUBMARINE RACE WATCHERS				
❑ Chess LP 1470 [M]	1962	10.00	20.00	40.00
MURRAY THE K'S GOLDEN GASSERS				
❑ Chess LP 1458 NYC [M]	1961	37.50	75.00	150.00
—New York version of "Golden Gassers," Chess 1458				
MURRAY THE K'S NINETEEN-SIXTY TWO BOSS GOLDEN GASSERS				
❑ Scepter SP-510 [M]	1963	5.00	10.00	20.00
❑ Scepter SPS-510 [P]	1963	6.25	12.50	25.00
MUSIC BOX				
❑ A&M SP-19006	196?	3.00	6.00	12.00
—Created for BankAmericard				
MUSIC FOR THE BOY FRIEND...HE REALLY DIGS JAZZ				
❑ Decca DL 8314 [M]	1956	7.50	15.00	30.00
MUSIC FROM THE DANCING YEARS				
❑ RCA Victor PR-112 [M]	1961	3.75	7.50	15.00
—Created for Dole Pineapple				
MUSIC FROM THE SOUTH, VOL. 1: COUNTRY BRASS BANDS				
❑ Folkways FA-2650 [M]	195?	5.00	10.00	20.00
THE MUSIC OF NEW ORLEANS, VOL. 1				
❑ Folkways FA-2461 [M]	1959	5.00	10.00	20.00
THE MUSIC OF NEW ORLEANS, VOL. 2				
❑ Folkways FA-2462 [M]	1959	5.00	10.00	20.00
THE MUSIC OF NEW ORLEANS, VOL. 3: DANCE HALLS				
❑ Folkways FA-2463 [M]	1959	5.00	10.00	20.00
THE MUSIC OF NEW ORLEANS, VOL. 4: THE BIRTH OF JAZZ				
❑ Folkways FA-2464 [M]	1959	5.00	10.00	20.00
THE MUSIC OF NEW ORLEANS, VOL. 5: NEW ORLEANS JAZZ				
❑ Folkways FA-2465 [M]	1959	5.00	10.00	20.00
THE MUSIC PEOPLE				
❑ Columbia C3X 31280 [(3)]	1972	6.25	12.50	25.00
MUSIC TO READ JAMES BOND BY				
❑ United Artists UAL-3415 [M]	1965	5.00	10.00	20.00
❑ United Artists UAS-6415 [S]	1965	6.25	12.50	25.00

Number / Title	Yr	VG	VG+	NM
MUSIC TO READ JAMES BOND BY, VOL. 2				
❏ United Artists UAL-3541 [M]	1966	5.00	10.00	20.00
❏ United Artists UAS-6541 [S]	1966	6.25	12.50	25.00
MUSIC TO TRIM YOUR TREE BY				
❏ RCA Victor PRM 225 [M]	1966	3.00	6.00	12.00
❏ RCA Victor PRS 225 [S]	1966	3.75	7.50	15.00
A MUSICAL HISTORY OF JAZZ				
❏ Grand Award GA 33-322 [M]	1955	5.00	10.00	20.00
MY FAIR LADY				
❏ New Jazz NJLP-8315 [M]	1963	—	—	—
—Canceled				
❏ Status ST-8315 [M]	1965	7.50	15.00	30.00
MY SON THE SURF NUT				
❏ Capitol ST 1939 [S]	1963	15.00	30.00	60.00
❏ Capitol T 1939 [M]	1963	12.50	25.00	50.00
THE NAMES OF DIXIELAND				
❏ Baronet B-108 [M]	195?	5.00	10.00	20.00
NASCAR GOES COUNTRY				
❏ MCA 474	1975	7.50	15.00	30.00
NASHVILLE BANDSTAND				
❏ King 813 [M]	1962	25.00	50.00	100.00
NASHVILLE BANDSTAND, VOLUME 2				
❏ King 847 [M]	1963	20.00	40.00	80.00
NATIVE NEW ORLEANS JAZZ				
❏ Dot DLP-3009 [M]	1956	7.50	15.00	30.00
NEW BLUE HORNS				
❏ Riverside RLP 12-294 [M]	1958	7.50	15.00	30.00
NEW CHAMBER JAZZ				
❏ Epic LN 1124 [10]	1955	7.50	15.00	30.00
NEW FACES AT NEWPORT				
❏ Metrojazz E-1005 [M]	1959	10.00	20.00	40.00
❏ Metrojazz SE-1005 [S]	1959	7.50	15.00	30.00
NEW ORLEANS BOUNCE: URBAN BLUES, VOLUME 2				
❏ Imperial LP-94004	1968	5.00	10.00	20.00
NEW ORLEANS DIXIELAND				
❏ Southland SLP-216 [M]	1955	6.25	12.50	25.00
NEW ORLEANS ENCORE				
❏ Riverside RLP-2503 [10]	1954	20.00	40.00	80.00
NEW ORLEANS EXPRESS				
❏ EmArcy MG-36022 [M]	1955	12.50	25.00	50.00
NEW ORLEANS HORNS				
❏ Riverside RLP-1005 [10]	1953	20.00	40.00	80.00
NEW ORLEANS JAZZ				
❏ Decca DL 5483 [10]	1953	12.50	25.00	50.00
❏ Decca DL 8283 [M]	1956	7.50	15.00	30.00
NEW ORLEANS JAZZ BABIES				
❏ Southland SLP-214 [M]	1955	6.25	12.50	25.00
NEW ORLEANS JAZZ KINGS				
❏ Southland SLP-217 [M]	1955	6.25	12.50	25.00
NEW ORLEANS JAZZ STARS				
❏ Southland SLP-211 [M]	1955	6.25	12.50	25.00
NEW ORLEANS LEGENDS				
❏ Riverside RLP 12-119 [M]	1957	10.00	20.00	40.00
NEW ORLEANS REVIVAL				
❏ Riverside RLP-1047 [10]	1954	20.00	40.00	80.00
NEW ORLEANS STYLE				
❏ "X" LVA-3029 [10]	1954	20.00	40.00	80.00
NEW ORLEANS TO LOS ANGELES				
❏ Southland SLP-215 [M]	1955	6.25	12.50	25.00
NEW ORLEANS, OUR HOME TOWN				
❏ Imperial LP-9260 [M]	1964	6.25	12.50	25.00
❏ Imperial LP-12260 [R]	1964	5.00	10.00	20.00
NEW ORLEANS: THE LIVING LEGENDS				
❏ Riverside RLP-356/7 [(2)M]	196?	12.50	25.00	50.00
—Two records in gatefold jacket				
NEW ORLEANS: THE LIVING LEGENDS, VOL. 1				
❏ Riverside RLP-356 [M]	196?	5.00	10.00	20.00
❏ Riverside RS-9356 [R]	196?	3.00	6.00	12.00

Number / Title	Yr	VG	VG+	NM
NEW ORLEANS: THE LIVING LEGENDS, VOL. 2				
❏ Riverside RLP-357 [M]	196?	5.00	10.00	20.00
❏ Riverside RS-9357 [R]	196?	3.00	6.00	12.00
NEW SOUNDS FROM SWEDEN, VOL. 1: THE DARING YOUNG SWEDES				
❏ Prestige PRLP-119 [10]	1951	50.00	100.00	200.00
THE NEW SPIRIT OF CAPITOL				
❏ Capitol SNP-6	1970	3.00	6.00	12.00
NEW VOICES				
❏ Dawn DLP-1125 [M]	1956	20.00	40.00	80.00
THE NEW WAVE IN JAZZ				
❏ ABC Impulse! AS-90 [S]	1968	3.00	6.00	12.00
❏ Impulse! A-90 [M]	1966	3.75	7.50	15.00
❏ Impulse! AS-90 [S]	1966	5.00	10.00	20.00
NEW YORK JAZZ OF THE TWENTIES				
❏ Riverside RLP-1048 [10]	1954	20.00	40.00	80.00
NEWPORT JAZZ FESTIVAL				
❏ RCA Victor LPM-3369 [M]	1965	3.75	7.50	15.00
❏ RCA Victor LSP-3369 [S]	1965	5.00	10.00	20.00
NEWPORT JAZZ FESTIVAL ALL STARS				
❏ Atlantic SD 1331 [S]	1961	7.50	15.00	30.00
—Multicolor label, white "fan" logo at right				
NEWPORT JAZZ FESTIVAL ALL-STARS				
❏ Atlantic 1331 [M]	1961	6.25	12.50	25.00
—Multicolor label, white "fan" logo at right				
A NIGHT AT EDDIE CONDON'S				
❏ Decca DL 8281 [M]	1956	7.50	15.00	30.00
A NIGHT AT THE BOULEVARD				
❏ Felsted FL-7503 [M]	1960	10.00	20.00	40.00
THE 1969 WARNER/REPRISE RECORD SHOW				
❏ Warner Bros. PRO 336 [(2)]	1969	7.50	15.00	30.00
—Originals have "W7" logos on labels				
❏ Warner Bros. PRO 336 [(2)]	197?	3.75	7.50	15.00
—With "WB" logos on labels				
THE 1969 WARNER/REPRISE SONGBOOK				
❏ Warner Bros. PRO 331 [(2)]	1969	7.50	15.00	30.00
—The first of the famous Warner/Reprise "Loss Leaders" mail-order series; originals have "W7" logos on labels				
❏ Warner Bros. PRO 331 [(2)]	197?	3.75	7.50	15.00
—With "WB" logos on labels				
THE NITTY GRITTY				
❏ Vee Jay LP-1084 [M]	1964	7.50	15.00	30.00
—Not known to exist in stereo				
NO 'COUNT				
❏ Savoy MG-12078 [M]	1956	15.00	30.00	60.00
NO ENERGY CRISIS				
❏ ABC Impulse! AS-9267 [(2)]	1974	5.00	10.00	20.00
NO SOUR GRAPES, JUST PURE JAZZ				
❏ Bethlehem BCP-92 [M]	1958	7.50	15.00	30.00
NON DAIRY CREAMER				
❏ Warner Bros. PRO 443	1971	6.25	12.50	25.00
—Originals have green labels				
NORMAN GRANZ JAZZ CONCERT				
❏ Norgran MGN-2501 [M]	1954	20.00	40.00	80.00
❏ Norgran MGN-2502 [M]	1954	20.00	40.00	80.00
NOTHING CHEESY ABOUT THIS JAZZ				
❏ Bethlehem BCP-85 [M]	1958	7.50	15.00	30.00
NOVA SCOTIA FOLK SONGS				
❏ Elektra EKL-23 [10]	1954	10.00	20.00	40.00
NUGGETS				
❏ Elektra 7E-2006 [(2)]	1972	10.00	20.00	40.00
O. HENRY'S THE GIFT OF THE MAGI				
❏ E.F. MacDonald EFMX-62	1962	5.00	10.00	20.00
—Special album done by the E.F. MacDonald Company, Dayton, Ohio				
OCTOBER '61 POP SAMPLER				
❏ RCA Victor SPS-33-141 [DJ]	1961	150.00	300.00	600.00
—Promo-only collection.				
OCTOBER 1960 POPULAR STEREO SAMPLER				
❏ RCA Victor SPS-33-96 [DJ]	1960	150.00	300.00	600.00
—Promo-only collection				

Number	Title	Yr	VG	VG+	NM

OCTOBER CHRISTMAS SAMPLER 59-40-41
❑ RCA Victor SPS-33-54 [DJ] — 1959 — 150.00 — 300.00 — 600.00
—Promo-only collection

OLD 'N GOLDEN
❑ Jamie JLPS-3031 — 1968 — 5.00 — 10.00 — 20.00

OLD AND HEAVY GOLD 1955
❑ Economic Consultants 1955 — 1973 — 5.00 — 10.00 — 20.00

OLD AND HEAVY GOLD 1956
❑ Economic Consultants 1956 — 1973 — 7.50 — 15.00 — 30.00

OLD AND HEAVY GOLD 1957
❑ Economic Consultants 1957 — 1973 — 7.50 — 15.00 — 30.00

OLD AND HEAVY GOLD 1958
❑ Economic Consultants 1958 — 1973 — 7.50 — 15.00 — 30.00

OLD AND HEAVY GOLD 1959
❑ Economic Consultants 1959 — 1973 — 5.00 — 10.00 — 20.00

OLD AND HEAVY GOLD 1960
❑ Economic Consultants 1960 — 1973 — 7.50 — 15.00 — 30.00

OLD AND HEAVY GOLD 1961
❑ Economic Consultants 1961 — 1973 — 7.50 — 15.00 — 30.00

OLD AND HEAVY GOLD 1962
❑ Economic Consultants 1962 — 1973 — 7.50 — 15.00 — 30.00

OLD AND HEAVY GOLD 1963
❑ Economic Consultants 1963 — 1973 — 5.00 — 10.00 — 20.00

OLD AND HEAVY GOLD 1964
❑ Economic Consultants 1964 — 1973 — 5.00 — 10.00 — 20.00
—Original magazine ads claimed that six Beatles tracks would appear on this LP; they were replaced before release

OLD AND HEAVY GOLD 1965
❑ Economic Consultants 1965 — 1973 — 5.00 — 10.00 — 20.00
—Original magazine ads claimed that three Beatles tracks would appear on this LP; they were replaced before release

OLD AND HEAVY GOLD 1966
❑ Economic Consultants 1966 — 1973 — 5.00 — 10.00 — 20.00

OLD AND HEAVY GOLD 1967
❑ Economic Consultants 1967 — 1973 — 5.00 — 10.00 — 20.00
—Original magazine ads claimed that a Beatles track would appear on this LP; it was replaced with another track before release

OLD AND HEAVY GOLD 1968
❑ Economic Consultants 1968 — 1973 — 5.00 — 10.00 — 20.00
—Original magazine ads claimed that a Beatles track would appear on this LP; it was replaced with another track before release

OLD AND HEAVY GOLD 1969
❑ Economic Consultants 1969 — 1973 — 5.00 — 10.00 — 20.00
—Original magazine ads claimed that a Beatles track would appear on this LP; it was replaced with another track before release

OLD AND HEAVY GOLD 1970
❑ Economic Consultants 1970 — 1973 — 5.00 — 10.00 — 20.00
—Original magazine ads claimed that a Beatles track would appear on this LP; it was replaced with another track before release

OLD AND HEAVY GOLD 1971
❑ Economic Consultants 1971 — 1973 — 5.00 — 10.00 — 20.00
—Original magazine ads claimed that a Paul McCartney track would appear on this LP; it was replaced with another track before release

OLD TIME BANJO PROJECT
❑ Elektra EKL-276 [M] — 1964 — 5.00 — 10.00 — 20.00
❑ Elektra EKS-7276 [S] — 1964 — 6.25 — 12.50 — 25.00

OLDIES BUT GOODIES
❑ Original Sound LPM-5001 [M] — 1959 — 12.50 — 25.00 — 50.00
—Original pressing with no reference to other volumes on the back cover
❑ Original Sound LPM-5001 [M] — 1960s — 3.00 — 6.00 — 12.00
—Later editions with later volumes in the series on the back cover

OLDIES BUT GOODIES, VOL. 2
❑ Original Sound LPM-5003 [M] — 1960 — 10.00 — 20.00 — 40.00
—Original pressing with no reference to later volumes on the back cover
❑ Original Sound LPM-5003 [M] — 1960s — 3.00 — 6.00 — 12.00
—Later editions with later volumes in the series on the back cover

OLDIES BUT GOODIES, VOL. 3
❑ Original Sound LPM-5004 [M] — 1960s — 3.00 — 6.00 — 12.00
—Later editions with later volumes in the series on the back cover
❑ Original Sound LPM-5004 [M] — 1961 — 7.50 — 15.00 — 30.00
—Original pressing with no reference to later volumes on the back cover

OLDIES BUT GOODIES, VOL. 4
❑ Original Sound LPM-5005 [M] — 1960s — 3.00 — 6.00 — 12.00
—Later editions with later volumes in the series on the back cover
❑ Original Sound LPM-5005 [M] — 1962 — 7.50 — 15.00 — 30.00
—Original pressing with no reference to later volumes on the back cover

OLDIES BUT GOODIES, VOL. 5
❑ Original Sound LPM-5007 [M] — 1960s — 3.00 — 6.00 — 12.00
—Later editions with later volumes in the series on the back cover
❑ Original Sound LPM-5007 [M] — 1963 — 5.00 — 10.00 — 20.00
—Original pressing with no reference to later volumes on the back cover

OLDIES BUT GOODIES, VOL. 6
❑ Original Sound LPM-5011 [M] — 1960s — 3.00 — 6.00 — 12.00
—Later editions with later volumes in the series on the back cover
❑ Original Sound LPM-5011 [M] — 1963 — 5.00 — 10.00 — 20.00
—Original pressing with no reference to later volumes on the back cover

OLDIES BUT GOODIES, VOL. 7
❑ Original Sound LPM-5012 [M] — 1960s — 3.00 — 6.00 — 12.00
—Later editions with later volumes in the series on the back cover
❑ Original Sound LPM-5012 [M] — 1964 — 5.00 — 10.00 — 20.00
—Original pressing with no reference to later volumes on the back cover

OLDIES BUT GOODIES, VOL. 8
❑ Original Sound LPM-5014 [M] — 1960s — 2.50 — 5.00 — 10.00
—Later editions with later volumes in the series on the back cover
❑ Original Sound LPM-5014 [M] — 1966 — 3.75 — 7.50 — 15.00
—Original pressing with no reference to later volumes on the back cover

OLDIES BY THE DOZEN
❑ Parkway P-7035 [M] — 1963 — 7.50 — 15.00 — 30.00

OLDIES BY THE DOZEN, VOLUME 2
❑ Parkway P-7041 [M] — 1964 — 12.50 — 25.00 — 50.00
—With bonus 45 of "The Twist" by Chubby Checker on on side and "Mashed Potato Time" by Dee Dee Sharp on the other; deduct 40 percent if missing

OLDIES DANCE PARTY, VOLUME 1
❑ Oldies 33 OL-8001 [M] — 1963 — 5.00 — 10.00 — 20.00

OLDIES DANCE PARTY, VOLUME 2
❑ Oldies 33 OL-8002 [M] — 1963 — 5.00 — 10.00 — 20.00

OLDIES IN HI-FI
❑ Chess LP 1439 [DJ] — 1959 — 150.00 — 300.00 — 600.00
—Multi-color splash vinyl
❑ Chess LP 1439 [M] — 1959 — 75.00 — 150.00 — 300.00
—Black vinyl

OLIO
❑ Prestige PRLP-7084 [M] — 1957 — 25.00 — 50.00 — 100.00

ON-THE-ROAD JAZZ
❑ Riverside RLP 12-127 [M] — 1957 — 10.00 — 20.00 — 40.00

ONE DOZEN GOLDIES
❑ Carlton LP 12-121 [M] — 1960 — 12.50 — 25.00 — 50.00

ONE WORLD JAZZ
❑ Adventures in Sound WL-162 [M] — 1959 — 12.50 — 25.00 — 50.00
❑ Adventures in Sound WS-314 [S] — 1959 — 10.00 — 20.00 — 40.00

OPUS DE BLUES
❑ Savoy MG-12142 [M] — 1959 — 15.00 — 30.00 — 60.00

OPUS DE JAZZ
❑ Savoy MG-12036 [M] — 1955 — 20.00 — 40.00 — 80.00

OPUS IN SWING
❑ Savoy MG-12085 [M] — 1956 — 15.00 — 30.00 — 60.00

THE ORCHESTRA "HOUSE OF SOUND"
❑ Brunswick BL 54003 [M] — 1954 — 7.50 — 15.00 — 30.00

THE ORGAN PLAYS MUSIC FOR A MERRY CHRISTMAS
❑ Reader's Digest RDA 42-A [(4)] — 1966 — 5.00 — 10.00 — 20.00
—Available only through Reader's Digest magazine by mail order

ORIGINAL BLUE NOTE JAZZ, VOL. 1
❑ Blue Note B-6504 — 1969 — 5.00 — 10.00 — 20.00

ORIGINAL BLUE NOTE JAZZ, VOL. 2
❑ Blue Note B-6506 — 1970 — 5.00 — 10.00 — 20.00

THE ORIGINAL COUNTRY HITS #1
❑ Liberty LRP-3305 [M] — 1963 — 5.00 — 10.00 — 20.00

THE ORIGINAL COUNTRY HITS #2
❑ Liberty LRP-3345 [M] — 1964 — 5.00 — 10.00 — 20.00

THE ORIGINAL COUNTRY HITS #3
❑ Liberty LRP-3382 [M] — 1964 — 5.00 — 10.00 — 20.00

Number	Title	Yr	VG	VG+	NM

ORIGINAL GOLDEN BLUES GREATS, VOL. 1
❏ Liberty LST-7572 [R] — 1968 — 3.00 — 6.00 — 12.00
—Reissue of "The Original R&B Hits, Volume 1," Liberty 3381, in rechanneled stereo

ORIGINAL GOLDEN COUNTRY GREATS, VOLUME 1
❏ Liberty LST-7569 [R] — 1968 — 3.00 — 6.00 — 12.00
—Reissue of "The Original Country Hits #1," Liberty 3305, in rechanneled stereo

ORIGINAL GOLDEN COUNTRY GREATS, VOLUME 2
❏ Liberty LST-7570 [R] — 1968 — 3.00 — 6.00 — 12.00
—Reissue of "The Original Country Hits #2," Liberty 3345, in rechanneled stereo

ORIGINAL GOLDEN COUNTRY GREATS, VOLUME 3
❏ Liberty LST-7571 [R] — 1968 — 3.00 — 6.00 — 12.00
—Reissue of "The Original Country Hits #3," Liberty 3382, in rechanneled stereo

ORIGINAL GOLDEN GREATS, VOLUME 3
❏ Liberty LST-7573 [R] — 1968 — 3.00 — 6.00 — 12.00
—Reissue of "The Original Hits, Volume 7," Liberty 3274, in rechanneled stereo

ORIGINAL GOLDEN GREATS, VOLUME 4
❏ Liberty LST-7574 [R] — 1968 — 3.00 — 6.00 — 12.00
—Only one track, "Surf City" by Jan and Dean, is true stereo

ORIGINAL GOLDEN GREATS, VOLUME 5
❏ Liberty LST-7575 [R] — 1968 — 3.00 — 6.00 — 12.00
—Three tracks are in true stereo: "Hurt" (Timi Yuro), "Tower of Strength" (Gene McDaniels) and "The Night Has a Thousand Eyes" (Bobby Vee)

ORIGINAL GOLDEN GREATS, VOLUME 6
❏ Liberty LST-7576 [R] — 1968 — 3.00 — 6.00 — 12.00
—Four tracks are in true stereo

ORIGINAL GOLDEN GREATS, VOLUME 7
❏ Liberty LST-7577 [R] — 1968 — 3.00 — 6.00 — 12.00
—Three tracks are in true stereo

ORIGINAL GOLDEN GREATS, VOLUME 8
❏ Liberty LST-7578 [R] — 1968 — 3.00 — 6.00 — 12.00

ORIGINAL GOLDEN GREATS, VOLUME 9
❏ Liberty LST-7579 [R] — 1968 — 3.00 — 6.00 — 12.00

ORIGINAL GOLDEN GREATS, VOLUME 10
❏ Liberty LST-7619 — 1969 — 3.75 — 7.50 — 15.00

ORIGINAL GOLDIES FROM THE FABULOUS '50S, VOLUME 1
❏ Josie JM-4002 [M] — 1963 — 15.00 — 30.00 — 60.00

ORIGINAL GOLDIES FROM THE FABULOUS '50S, VOLUME 2
❏ Josie JM-4003 [M] — 1963 — 15.00 — 30.00 — 60.00

ORIGINAL GOLDIES FROM THE FABULOUS '50S, VOLUME 3
❏ Josie JM-4004 [M] — 1963 — 15.00 — 30.00 — 60.00

ORIGINAL HIT RECORDS
❏ Roulette R 25106 [M] — 1960 — 7.50 — 15.00 — 30.00
—Originals have a white label with colored spokes

THE ORIGINAL HITS, PAST & PRESENT
❏ Liberty LRP-3178 [M] — 1960 — 5.00 — 10.00 — 20.00

THE ORIGINAL HITS, VOLUME 10
❏ Liberty LRP-3344 [M] — 1964 — 5.00 — 10.00 — 20.00

THE ORIGINAL HITS, VOLUME 11
❏ Liberty LRP-3418 [M] — 1965 — 5.00 — 10.00 — 20.00
❏ Liberty LST-7418 [P] — 1965 — 5.00 — 10.00 — 20.00

THE ORIGINAL HITS, VOLUME 3: PAST & PRESENT
❏ Liberty LRP-3187 [M] — 1961 — 5.00 — 10.00 — 20.00

THE ORIGINAL HITS, VOLUME 4
❏ Liberty LRP-3200 [M] — 1962 — 5.00 — 10.00 — 20.00
—Reissue of "Memories Are Made of Hits"; for "The Original Hits, Volume 5," see "15 Hits: The Original Recordings"

THE ORIGINAL HITS, VOLUME 6
❏ Liberty LRP-3260 [M] — 1962 — 5.00 — 10.00 — 20.00

THE ORIGINAL HITS, VOLUME 7: ALL-TIME HIT INSTRUMENTALS
❏ Liberty LRP-3274 [M] — 1963 — 5.00 — 10.00 — 20.00

THE ORIGINAL HITS, VOLUME 8
❏ Liberty LRP-3288 [M] — 1963 — 5.00 — 10.00 — 20.00

THE ORIGINAL HITS, VOLUME 9
❏ Liberty LRP-3325 [M] — 1963 — 5.00 — 10.00 — 20.00

THE ORIGINAL HITS, VOLUME TWO: PAST & PRESENT
❏ Liberty LRP-3180 [M] — 1961 — 5.00 — 10.00 — 20.00

THE ORIGINAL HOOTENANNY
❏ Crestview CRV 806 [M] — 1963 — 5.00 — 10.00 — 20.00
❏ Crestview CRS 7806 [S] — 1963 — 6.25 — 12.50 — 25.00

ORIGINAL MEMPHIS ROCK AND ROLL, VOLUME 1
❏ Sun 116 — 1970 — 5.00 — 10.00 — 20.00

ORIGINAL MOTION PICTURE HIT THEMES
❏ United Artists UAL-3197 [M] — 1962 — 3.75 — 7.50 — 15.00
❏ United Artists UAS-6197 [S] — 1962 — 5.00 — 10.00 — 20.00

THE ORIGINAL R&B HITS, VOLUME 1
❏ Liberty LRP-3381 [M] — 1964 — 5.00 — 10.00 — 20.00

ORIGINAL ROCK OLDIES, VOLUME 1
❏ Specialty SPS-2129 — 1970 — 5.00 — 10.00 — 20.00

ORIGINAL ROCK OLDIES, VOLUME 2
❏ Specialty SPS-2130 — 1970 — 5.00 — 10.00 — 20.00

THE ORIGINAL SOUND OF THE 20'S
❏ Columbia C3L 35 [(3)] — 1965 — 10.00 — 20.00 — 40.00

ORIGINAL SURFIN' HITS
❏ GNP Crescendo GNP-84 [M] — 1963 — 10.00 — 20.00 — 40.00
—With bonus photos; deduct 25-50 percent if missing
❏ GNP Crescendo GNPS-84 [S] — 1963 — 12.50 — 25.00 — 50.00
—With bonus photos; deduct 25-50 percent if missing

OUR BEST
❏ Clef MGC-639 [M] — 1955 — 12.50 — 25.00 — 50.00
❏ Norgran MGN-1021 [M] — 1955 — 20.00 — 40.00 — 80.00

OUR BEST TO YOU
❏ Everlast ELP-201 [M] — 1960 — 50.00 — 100.00 — 200.00

OUR SIGNIFICANT HITS
❏ Specialty SP-2112 [M] — 1960 — 30.00 — 60.00 — 120.00
—Gold and black label

OUR SINGING HERITAGE, VOL. 1
❏ Elektra EKL-151 [M] — 1958 — 6.25 — 12.50 — 25.00

OUR SINGING HERITAGE, VOL. 2
❏ Elektra EKL-152 [M] — 1958 — 6.25 — 12.50 — 25.00

OUTSTANDING JAZZ COMPOSITIONS OF THE 20TH CENTURY
❏ Columbia C2L 31 [(2)M] — 1964 — 5.00 — 10.00 — 20.00

A PACKAGE OF 16 BIG HITS
❏ Motown MS 614 [S] — 1966 — 7.50 — 15.00 — 30.00
—No "package" on cover; contains alternate stereo versions of "Please Mr. Postman" by the Marvelettes and "Do You Love Me" by the Contours
❏ Motown MT 614 [M] — 1964 — 25.00 — 50.00 — 100.00
—"Package" cover
❏ Motown MT 614 [M] — 1966 — 5.00 — 10.00 — 20.00
—No "package" on cover

PAJAMA PARTY
❏ Forum F-9006 [M] — 196? — 7.50 — 15.00 — 30.00
—Reissue of Roulette 25021
❏ Forum SF-9006 [R] — 196? — 5.00 — 10.00 — 20.00
❏ Gee GLP-703 [M] — 1959 — — — —
—Canceled; released as Roulette R-25021 instead
❏ Roulette R 25021 [M] — 1958 — 10.00 — 20.00 — 40.00
—Originals have a black label
❏ Roulette R 25021 [M] — 1959 — 6.25 — 12.50 — 25.00
—Second pressings have a white label with colored spokes
❏ Roulette SR 25021 [R] — 196? — 3.00 — 6.00 — 12.00

PANORAMA OF BRITISH JAZZ
❏ Discovery DL-2001 [10] — 1953 — 12.50 — 25.00 — 50.00

PARTY AFTER HOURS
❏ Aladdin LP-703 [10] — 1950 — 1000. — 2000. — 4000.
—Black vinyl
❏ Aladdin LP-703 [10] — 1950 — 2000. — 4000. — 8000.
—Red vinyl

PEACE ON EARTH
❏ Capitol S?B?-585 [(2)] — 1970 — 3.75 — 7.50 — 15.00

PERCUSSION UNABRIDGED
❏ Kimberly 2022 [M] — 1963 — 5.00 — 10.00 — 20.00
❏ Kimberly 11022 [S] — 1963 — 6.25 — 12.50 — 25.00

PERFECT FOR DANCING: ALL TEMPOS
❏ RCA Victor LPM-1072 [M] — 1954 — 7.50 — 15.00 — 30.00

PERFECT FOR DANCING: FOX TROTS
❏ RCA Victor LPM-1070 [M] — 1954 — 7.50 — 15.00 — 30.00

PERFECT FOR DANCING: JITTERBUG OR LINDY
❏ RCA Victor LPM-1071 [M] — 1954 — 7.50 — 15.00 — 30.00

PERIOD'S JAZZ DIGEST
❏ Period SPL-302 [M] — 1956 — 12.50 — 25.00 — 50.00

PERIOD'S JAZZ DIGEST VOL. 2
❏ Period SPL-304 [M] — 1955 — 12.50 — 25.00 — 50.00

Number Title	Yr	VG	VG+	NM
PETAL PUSHERS				
❏ Chess LP 1520 [M]	1967	6.25	12.50	25.00
❏ Chess LPS 1520 [S]	1967	6.25	12.50	25.00
THE PHIL SPECTOR SPECTACULAR				
❏ Philles PHLP 100 [DJ]	1972	375.00	750.00	1500.
—Not issued with cover				
PHIL SPECTOR'S CHRISTMAS ALBUM				
❏ Apple SW 3400 [M]	1972	7.50	15.00	30.00
—Reissue of A CHRSTMAS GIFT FOR YOU FROM PHILLES RECORDS; third edition of this group of songs; completely different cover with Phil Spector dressed as Santa Claus and wearing a "Back to Mono" button				
❏ Warner/Spector SP 9103 [S]	1974	5.00	10.00	20.00
—Fourth edition of this group of songs; similar cover to third edition; despite the cover's "Authentic Mono" statement and Phil Spector-as-Santa Claus' "Back to Mono" button, this album is in true stereo!				
PHIL SPECTOR'S GREATEST HITS				
❏ Warner/Spector 2SP 9104 [(2)]	1977	10.00	20.00	40.00
THE PHILCO ALBUM OF HOLIDAY MUSIC				
❏ Columbia Special Products CSM 431	1966	3.75	7.50	15.00
—Sold only at Philco dealers				
PIANISTS GALORE				
❏ Pacific Jazz JWC-506 [M]	1957	12.50	25.00	50.00
❏ World Pacific JWC-506 [M]	1958	10.00	20.00	40.00
PIANO ARTISTRY				
❏ Audiophile AP-28 [M]	1953	7.50	15.00	30.00
PIANO INTERPRETATIONS				
❏ Norgran MGN-1036 [M]	1955	20.00	40.00	80.00
❏ Verve MGV-8125 [M]	1957	7.50	15.00	30.00
❏ Verve V-8125 [M]	1961	5.00	10.00	20.00
PIANO JAZZ, VOLUME 1				
❏ Brunswick BL 54014 [M]	1955	7.50	15.00	30.00
PIANO JAZZ, VOLUME 2				
❏ Brunswick BL 54015 [M]	1955	7.50	15.00	30.00
PIANO MODERN				
❏ Verve VSP-13 [M]	1966	3.75	7.50	15.00
❏ Verve VSPS-13 [R]	1966	2.50	5.00	10.00
PIANO MUSIC FOR PARTIES				
❏ Columbia CL 603 [M]	1955	6.25	12.50	25.00
PIANO MUSIC FOR TWO				
❏ Columbia CL 602 [M]	1955	6.25	12.50	25.00
PIANO ROLL HALL OF FAME				
❏ Sounds 1202	196?	3.00	6.00	12.00
PIANO ROLL TRANSCRIPTIONS				
❏ Riverside RLP 12-110 [M]	1956	10.00	20.00	40.00
❏ Riverside RLP 12-126 [M]	1957	10.00	20.00	40.00
PIANO STYLISTS				
❏ Capitol H 323 [10]	1952	12.50	25.00	50.00
PIANO VARIATIONS				
❏ King 540 [M]	1956	37.50	75.00	150.00
PICK HITS OF THE RADIO GOOD GUYS				
❏ Laurie LLP-2021 [M]	1963	7.50	15.00	30.00
❏ Laurie SLP-2021 [R]	196?	3.75	7.50	15.00
PICK HITS OF THE RADIO GOOD GUYS, VOLUME 2				
❏ Laurie LLP-2026 [M]	1964	6.25	12.50	25.00
❏ Laurie SLP-2026 [R]	196?	3.75	7.50	15.00
PICK UP THE BEAT				
❏ Epic LN 3127 [M]	1955	7.50	15.00	30.00
PIONEERS OF BOOGIE WOOGIE				
❏ Riverside RLP-1009 [10]	1953	20.00	40.00	80.00
PIONEERS OF BOOGIE WOOGIE, VOL. 2				
❏ Riverside RLP-1034 [10]	1954	20.00	40.00	80.00
PLAYBOY ALL STARS VOLUME 1				
❏ Playboy PB-1957 [(2)M]	1957	10.00	20.00	40.00
PLAYBOY ALL STARS VOLUME 2				
❏ Playboy PB-1958 [(2)M]	1958	10.00	20.00	40.00
PLAYBOY ALL STARS VOLUME 3				
❏ Playboy PB-1959 [(3)M]	1959	15.00	30.00	60.00
PLAZA HOUSE PRESENTS MUSIC HALL				
❏ Capitol Creative Products SL-6719	1971	3.00	6.00	12.00
—One side by Merle Haggard; one side by Sonny James				

Number Title	Yr	VG	VG+	NM
POLKAS				
❏ Audio Lab AL-1543 [M]	1959	10.00	20.00	40.00
POP HIT PARTY				
❏ Columbia CL 1237 [M]	195?	5.00	10.00	20.00
POP ORIGINS				
❏ Chess LP 1544 [M]	1969	6.25	12.50	25.00
POP PARADE				
❏ MGM E-194 [10]	1953	12.50	25.00	50.00
POPULAR FAVORITES				
❏ Columbia CL 6057 [10]	1949	10.00	20.00	40.00
THE POPULAR GOLD ALBUM				
❏ Capitol T 972 [M]	1958	7.50	15.00	30.00
PORGY AND BESS				
❏ Bethlehem EXLP-1 [(3)M]	1956	17.50	35.00	70.00
❏ Bethlehem BCP-6040 [M]	1959	7.50	15.00	30.00
PORTRAITS IN JAZZ				
❏ Reprise R-6084 [M]	1963	3.00	6.00	12.00
❏ Reprise R9-6084 [S]	1963	3.75	7.50	15.00
A POT OF FLOWERS				
❏ Mainstream S-6100 [S]	1967	25.00	50.00	100.00
❏ Mainstream 56100 [M]	1967	20.00	40.00	80.00
POT OF GOLDEN GOODIES				
❏ Herald HLP-1015 [M]	1962	37.50	75.00	150.00
A POTPOURRI OF JAZZ				
❏ Verve MGV-2032 [M]	1956	10.00	20.00	40.00
❏ Verve V-2032 [M]	1961	5.00	10.00	20.00
PRESTIGE GROOVY GOODIES, VOL. 1				
❏ Prestige PRLP-7298 [M]	1964	7.50	15.00	30.00
❏ Prestige PRST-7298 [R]	1964	5.00	10.00	20.00
PRIMITIVE PIANO				
❏ Tone 1 [M]	195?	7.50	15.00	30.00
PROGRESSIVE PIANO				
❏ RCA Victor LJM-3001 [10]	1952	12.50	25.00	50.00
THE PROGRESSIVES				
❏ Columbia CG 31574 [(2)]	197?	3.00	6.00	12.00
—"CG" prefix is a reissue of "KG"				
❏ Columbia KG 31574 [(2)]	1973	5.00	10.00	20.00
RADAR BLUES				
❏ King KLP-1050 [M]	1969	7.50	15.00	30.00
RADIO SMASH FLASHBACKS: DRIVE TIME				
❏ Laurie LLP-2028 [M]	1964	6.25	12.50	25.00
❏ Laurie SLP-2028 [R]	196?	3.75	7.50	15.00
RADIO SMASH FLASHBACKS: PRIME TIME				
❏ Laurie LLP-2029 [M]	1964	6.25	12.50	25.00
❏ Laurie SLP-2029 [R]	196?	3.75	7.50	15.00
RAGTIME PIANO ROLL, VOL. 1				
❏ Riverside RLP-1006 [10]	1953	25.00	50.00	100.00
RAGTIME PIANO ROLL, VOL. 2				
❏ Riverside RLP-1025 [10]	1954	20.00	40.00	80.00
RAGTIME PIANO ROLL, VOL. 3				
❏ Riverside RLP-1049 [10]	1954	20.00	40.00	80.00
RAGTIMERS' IMMORTAL PERFORMANCES				
❏ RCA Victor LPT-1000 [M]	1954	7.50	15.00	30.00
RAILROAD SONGS				
❏ King 869 [M]	1963	17.50	35.00	70.00
RARE BANDS OF THE 20S, VOL. 1				
❏ Historical ASC-3	1966	3.00	6.00	12.00
RARE BANDS OF THE 20S, VOL. 2				
❏ Historical ASC-6	1966	3.00	6.00	12.00
RARE BANDS OF THE 20S, VOL. 3				
❏ Historical ASC-7	1966	3.00	6.00	12.00
RARE VERTICAL JAZZ				
❏ Historical ASC-8	1966	3.00	6.00	12.00
THE RCA VICTOR ENCYCLOPEDIA OF RECORDED JAZZ, ALBUM 1				
❏ RCA Victor LEJ-1 [10]	1956	10.00	20.00	40.00
THE RCA VICTOR ENCYCLOPEDIA OF RECORDED JAZZ, ALBUM 2				
❏ RCA Victor LEJ-2 [10]	1956	10.00	20.00	40.00

Number / Title	Yr	VG	VG+	NM
THE RCA VICTOR ENCYCLOPEDIA OF RECORDED JAZZ, ALBUM 3				
❏ RCA Victor LEJ-3 [10]	1956	10.00	20.00	40.00
THE RCA VICTOR ENCYCLOPEDIA OF RECORDED JAZZ, ALBUM 4				
❏ RCA Victor LEJ-4 [10]	1956	10.00	20.00	40.00
THE RCA VICTOR ENCYCLOPEDIA OF RECORDED JAZZ, ALBUM 5				
❏ RCA Victor LEJ-5 [10]	1956	10.00	20.00	40.00
THE RCA VICTOR ENCYCLOPEDIA OF RECORDED JAZZ, ALBUM 6				
❏ RCA Victor LEJ-6 [10]	1956	10.00	20.00	40.00
THE RCA VICTOR ENCYCLOPEDIA OF RECORDED JAZZ, ALBUM 7				
❏ RCA Victor LEJ-7 [10]	1956	10.00	20.00	40.00
THE RCA VICTOR ENCYCLOPEDIA OF RECORDED JAZZ, ALBUM 8				
❏ RCA Victor LEJ-8 [10]	1956	10.00	20.00	40.00
THE RCA VICTOR ENCYCLOPEDIA OF RECORDED JAZZ, ALBUM 9				
❏ RCA Victor LEJ-9 [10]	1956	10.00	20.00	40.00
THE RCA VICTOR ENCYCLOPEDIA OF RECORDED JAZZ, ALBUM 10				
❏ RCA Victor LEJ-10 [10]	1956	10.00	20.00	40.00
THE RCA VICTOR ENCYCLOPEDIA OF RECORDED JAZZ, ALBUM 11				
❏ RCA Victor LEJ-11 [10]	1956	10.00	20.00	40.00
THE RCA VICTOR ENCYCLOPEDIA OF RECORDED JAZZ, ALBUM 12				
❏ RCA Victor LEJ-12 [10]	1956	10.00	20.00	40.00
RCA VICTOR PRESENTS MUSIC FOR THE TWELVE DAYS OF CHRISTMAS				
❏ RCA Victor PRS-188 [S]	1965	3.00	6.00	12.00
THE REAL AMBASSADORS				
❏ Columbia OS 2250 [S]	1962	6.25	12.50	25.00
❏ Columbia CL 5850 [M]	1962	5.00	10.00	20.00
THE REAL BLUES				
❏ Excello LPS-8011 [R]	1969	5.00	10.00	20.00
RECORD HOP				
❏ Decca DL 8067 [M]	1955	7.50	15.00	30.00
RECORDED IN NEW ORLEANS, VOL. 1				
❏ Good Time Jazz L-12019 [M]	1955	5.00	10.00	20.00
RECORDED IN NEW ORLEANS, VOL. 2				
❏ Good Time Jazz L-12020 [M]	1955	5.00	10.00	20.00
RECORDED ON LOCATION AT THE FIVE SPORT CAFE IN NEW YORK CITY...A MEMORIAL CONCERT DEDICATED TO THE MUSIC OF CHARLIE PARKER				
❏ Signal S-1204 [M]	1957	30.00	60.00	120.00
RED BIRD GOLDIES				
❏ Red Bird LP 20-102 [M]	1965	20.00	40.00	80.00
RED HOT AND BLUE JAZZ				
❏ Waldorf Music Hall MH 33-141 [10]	195?	50.00	100.00	200.00
RELAXED SAXOPHONE MOODS				
❏ Prestige PRLP-141 [10]	1953	25.00	50.00	100.00
REMEMBER HOW GREAT, VOLUME 1				
❏ Roulette SR 42027 [R]	1968	3.00	6.00	12.00
REMEMBER HOW GREAT, VOLUME 2				
❏ Roulette SR 42028 [R]	1968	3.00	6.00	12.00
REMEMBER HOW GREAT, VOLUME 3				
❏ Roulette SR 42029 [R]	1968	3.00	6.00	12.00
REMEMBER HOW GREAT, VOLUME 4				
❏ Roulette SR 42031 [R]	1969	3.00	6.00	12.00
REMEMBER HOW GREAT, VOLUME 5				
❏ Roulette SR 42032 [R]	1969	3.00	6.00	12.00
REMEMBER THE OLDIES				
❏ Argo LP-649 [M]	1963	10.00	20.00	40.00
❏ Argo LP-649 [M]	1963	100.00	200.00	400.00
—Multi-color splash vinyl; white label promo				
REQUESTED BY YOU				
❏ Columbia CL 607 [M]	1955	6.25	12.50	25.00
RHYTHM & BLUES				
❏ RCA Camden CAL-371 [M]	1958	6.25	12.50	25.00
RHYTHM AND BLUES				
❏ Savoy MG-15008 [10]	1952	20.00	40.00	80.00
RHYTHM PLUS ONE				
❏ Epic LN 3297 [M]	1956	7.50	15.00	30.00
THE RHYTHM SECTION				
❏ Epic LN 3271 [M]	1956	7.50	15.00	30.00
RHYTHM, BLUES AND BOOGIE-WOOGIE				
❏ Decca DL 4011 [M]	1960	7.50	15.00	30.00
RICHARD NADER/LET THE GOOD TIMES ROLL				
❏ Bell 9002 [(2)]	1973	5.00	10.00	20.00
RINGSIDE AT CONDON'S				
❏ Savoy MG-15029 [10]	1954	20.00	40.00	80.00
RINGSIDE AT CONDON'S VOL. 2				
❏ Savoy MG-15030 [10]	1954	20.00	40.00	80.00
RIVERBOAT JAZZ				
❏ Brunswick BL 58026 [10]	1951	12.50	25.00	50.00
RIVERSIDE DRIVE				
❏ Riverside RLP 12-267 [M]	1958	7.50	15.00	30.00
RIVERSIDE MODERN JAZZ SAMPLER				
❏ Riverside S-3 [M]	1956	10.00	20.00	40.00
ROBERT W. SARNOFF — 25 YEARS OF RCA LEADERSHIP				
❏ RCA Victor RWS-0001 [DJ]	1973	1000.	1500.	2000.
—Souvenir record handed out at Sarnoff's retirement party				
ROCK & ROLL FOREVER				
❏ Atlantic 1239 [M]	1956	37.50	75.00	150.00
ROCK & ROLL WITH RHYTHM & BLUES				
❏ Aladdin LP-710 [M]	195?	375.00	750.00	1500.
ROCK 'N' ROLL SOCK HOP				
❏ Score SLP-4018 [M]	1958	50.00	100.00	200.00
ROCK AND ROLL BANDSTAND				
❏ Roulette R 25093 [M]	1959	7.50	15.00	30.00
—Originals have a white label with colored spokes				
ROCK AND ROLL DANCE PARTY				
❏ King 536 [M]	1956	75.00	150.00	300.00
❏ RPM LRP-3001	195?	125.00	250.00	500.00
ROCK AND ROLL RECORD HOP				
❏ Roulette R 25059 [M]	1959	7.50	15.00	30.00
—Originals have a white label with colored spokes				
ROCK AND ROLL REVUE, VOLUME 2				
❏ King 654 [M]	1959	37.50	75.00	150.00
ROCK AND ROLL VS. RHYTHM AND BLUES				
❏ Dooto DTL-223 [M]	1957	25.00	50.00	100.00
ROCK N' ROLL JAMBOREE				
❏ End LP-302 [M]	1959	30.00	60.00	120.00
—Second cover and title with puppet and a guitar				
ROCK'S GREATEST HITS				
❏ Columbia GP 11 [(2)]	1969	5.00	10.00	20.00
ROCK-A-BALLADS				
❏ Cadence CLP-3041 [M]	1960	10.00	20.00	40.00
ROCK-A-HITS				
❏ Cadence CLP-3042 [M]	1960	10.00	20.00	40.00
ROCK-O-RAMA				
❏ Abkco AB 4222 [(2)]	1972	5.00	10.00	20.00
ROCK-O-RAMA, VOLUME 2				
❏ Abkco AB 4223 [(2)]	1972	5.00	10.00	20.00
A ROCKIN' CHRISTMAS				
❏ Columbia Special Products P 12445	1974	3.75	7.50	15.00
ROCKIN' SLUMBER PARTY				
❏ Famous LP-501 [M]	1961	7.50	15.00	30.00
ROCKIN' TOGETHER				
❏ Atco 33-103 [M]	1958	25.00	50.00	100.00
RODGERS AND HART GEMS				
❏ Pacific Jazz JWC-504 [M]	1956	12.50	25.00	50.00
❏ World Pacific JWC-504 [M]	1958	10.00	20.00	40.00
RONCO PRESENTS A CHRISTMAS GIFT				
❏ Ronco/CSP P 12430	1974	3.75	7.50	15.00
—Gatefold with pop-up manger scene				

Number / Title	Yr	VG	VG+	NM
RONCO PRESENTS A CHRISTMAS PRESENT				
☐ Ronco/CSP P 11772	1973	3.75	7.50	15.00
—Gatefold with pop-up North Pole scene				
ROOST 5TH ANNIVERSARY ALBUM				
☐ Roost RST-1201 [M]	1955	12.50	25.00	50.00
ROOTS OF BRITISH ROCK				
☐ Sire SASH-3711 [(2)]	1975	5.00	10.00	20.00
ROULETTE PRESENTS A DEMONSTRATION OF THE NEW DIMENSIONAL SOUND OF DYNAMIC STEREO				
☐ Roulette SR-100 [S]	1958	7.50	15.00	30.00
RUMBLE				
☐ Jubilee JGM-1114 [M]	1959	37.50	75.00	150.00
SATURDAY NIGHT AT THE UPTOWN				
☐ Atlantic 8101 [M]	1964	6.25	12.50	25.00
☐ Atlantic SD 8101 [S]	1964	7.50	15.00	30.00
SATURDAY NIGHT FUNCTION: RURAL BLUES, VOLUME 2				
☐ Imperial LP-94001	1968	5.00	10.00	20.00
SATURDAY NIGHT MOOD				
☐ Columbia CL 599 [M]	1954	6.25	12.50	25.00
THE SAX SECTION				
☐ Epic LN 3278 [M]	1956	10.00	20.00	40.00
SAX STYLISTS				
☐ Capitol H 328 [10]	1952	12.50	25.00	50.00
SAXES, INC.				
☐ Warner Bros. W 1336 [M]	1959	6.25	12.50	25.00
☐ Warner Bros. WS 1336 [S]	1959	10.00	20.00	40.00
SAXOMANIAC				
☐ Apollo LP-477 [M]	1958	25.00	50.00	100.00
THE SAXOPHONE				
☐ ABC Impulse! AS-9253 [(3)]	197?	5.00	10.00	20.00
SAXOPHONE REVOLT				
☐ Riverside RLP 12-284 [M]	1958	37.50	75.00	150.00
SCHLAGERS!				
☐ Warner Bros. PRO 359 [(2)]	1970	7.50	15.00	30.00
—Originals have green labels				
A SCRAPBOOK OF BRITISH JAZZ, 1926-1956				
☐ London LL 1444 [M]	1956	5.00	10.00	20.00
SEASON'S GREETINGS FROM BARBRA STREISAND...AND FRIENDS				
☐ Columbia Special Products CSS 1075	1969	5.00	10.00	20.00
—Created exclusively for Maxwell House Coffee				
SEASONS GREETINGS (A CHRISTMAS FESTIVAL OF STARS)				
☐ Columbia CL 1394 [M]	1959	5.00	10.00	20.00
☐ Columbia CS 8189 [S]	1959	6.25	12.50	25.00
SECOND SESSION AT SQUIRREL'S				
☐ Paramount LP-108 [10]	1954	15.00	30.00	60.00
SELECTIONS FROM APRIL 1956 ALBUMS FOR RADIO-TV PROGRAM USE				
☐ Capitol PRO-252/3 [DJ]	1956	10.00	20.00	40.00
SELECTIONS FROM FEBRUARY 1956 POPULAR ALBUMS FOR RADIO-TV PROGRAM USE				
☐ Capitol PRO-240/1 [DJ]	1956	10.00	20.00	40.00
SELECTIONS FROM JANUARY 1956 ALBUMS FOR RADIO-TV PROGRAM USE				
☐ Capitol PRO-238/9 [DJ]	1956	10.00	20.00	40.00
SELECTIONS FROM MARCH 1956 ALBUMS FOR RADIO-TV PROGRAM USE				
☐ Capitol PRO-246/7 [DJ]	1956	10.00	20.00	40.00
SELECTIONS FROM THE VINTAGE SERIES				
☐ RCA Victor SP-33-322 [DJ]	196?	3.75	7.50	15.00
—Promo-only sampler from albums issued in the LPV-500 series				
SESSION AT MIDNIGHT				
☐ Capitol T 707 [M]	1956	7.50	15.00	30.00
SESSION AT RIVERSIDE				
☐ Capitol T 761 [M]	1956	7.50	15.00	30.00
THE SEVEN AGES OF JAZZ				
☐ Metrojazz 2-E-1009 [(2)M]	1959	15.00	30.00	60.00
☐ Metrojazz 2-SE-1009 [(2)S]	1959	12.50	25.00	50.00

Number / Title	Yr	VG	VG+	NM
SHADES OF GOSPEL SOUL				
☐ Motown MS-701	1970	3.75	7.50	15.00
SHADES OF NEW ORLEANS				
☐ Southland SLP-240	1963	3.75	7.50	15.00
SHOUTIN', SWINGIN' AND MAKIN' LOVE				
☐ Chess CHV-412	1970	3.75	7.50	15.00
SHUT DOWN				
☐ Capitol DT 1918 [R]	1963	10.00	20.00	40.00
☐ Capitol T 1918 [M]	1963	10.00	20.00	40.00
SHUT DOWNS AND HILL CLIMBS				
☐ Liberty LRP-3366 [M]	1964	10.00	20.00	40.00
☐ Liberty LST-7366 [S]	1964	12.50	25.00	50.00
THE SINATRA FAMILY WISH YOU A MERRY CHRISTMAS				
☐ Reprise FS-1026	1969	12.50	25.00	50.00
SING A SONG OF SOUL				
☐ Checker LP 2998 [M]	1966	20.00	40.00	80.00
☐ Checker LPS 2998 [S]	1966	25.00	50.00	100.00
THE SINGER-SONGWRITER PROJECT				
☐ Elektra EKL-299 [M]	1965	5.00	10.00	20.00
—With 11 tracks, though the label and cover claim there are 13				
☐ Elektra EKL-299 [M]	1965	6.25	12.50	25.00
—With 13 tracks				
☐ Elektra EKS-7299 [S]	1965	5.00	10.00	20.00
—With 11 tracks, though the label and cover claim there are 13				
☐ Elektra EKS-7299 [S]	1965	7.50	15.00	30.00
—With 13 tracks				
SINGIN' AND SWINGIN'				
☐ Savoy MG-12217 [M]	196?	5.00	10.00	20.00
SITTIN' IN				
☐ Verve MGV-8225 [M]	1958	12.50	25.00	50.00
☐ Verve V-8225 [M]	1961	6.25	12.50	25.00
16 GOODIES — BLASTS FROM THE PAST				
☐ Blast BLP-6803 [M]	1964	10.00	20.00	40.00
16 ORIGINAL BIG HITS, VOLUME 2				
☐ Tamla TM 256 [M]	1964	5.00	10.00	20.00
16 ORIGINAL BIG HITS, VOLUME 3				
☐ Motown MT 624 [M]	1965	5.00	10.00	20.00
16 ORIGINAL BIG HITS, VOLUME 4				
☐ Motown M 633 [M]	1965	3.75	7.50	15.00
☐ Motown MS 633 [S]	1965	5.00	10.00	20.00
16 ORIGINAL BIG HITS, VOLUME 5				
☐ Motown M 651 [M]	1966	3.75	7.50	15.00
60 YEARS OF MUSIC AMERICA LOVES BEST				
☐ RCA Victor LM-6074 [(2)]	1959	7.50	15.00	30.00
60 YEARS OF MUSIC AMERICA LOVES BEST, VOLUME II				
☐ RCA Victor LM-6088 [(2)]	1960	7.50	15.00	30.00
60 YEARS OF MUSIC AMERICA LOVES BEST, VOLUME III (POPULAR)				
☐ RCA Victor LOP-1509	1961	5.00	10.00	20.00
$64,000 JAZZ				
☐ Columbia CL 777 [M]	1955	12.50	25.00	50.00
A SLICE OF LEMON				
☐ Columbia Special Products CSM-389 [M]	1966	6.25	12.50	25.00
—Manufactured for Dr. Pepper; contains a spoken-word introduction by Dick Clark, plus tracks by Bob Dylan, Simon & Garfunkel, the Dave Clark Five, the Brothers Four, Percy Faith, Dave Brubeck, the New Christy Minstrels, Tony Bennett and Doris Day				
SMALL COMBO HITS				
☐ RCA Victor LPT-3 [10]	1951	10.00	20.00	40.00
SMART, LUSCIOUS, BEAUTIFUL				
☐ Bethlehem BCP-6034 [M]	1960	7.50	15.00	30.00
THE SMITHSONIAN COLLECTION OF CLASSIC JAZZ				
☐ Smithsonian/CSP P6 11891 [(6)]	1973	12.50	25.00	50.00
SMOKE RINGS				
☐ RCA Victor LPT-13 [10]	1951	10.00	20.00	40.00
SOFT PEDAL				
☐ Columbia CL 2511 [10]	1954	7.50	15.00	30.00
SOLID GOLD HITS				
☐ Imperial LP-9230 [M]	1963	6.25	12.50	25.00
☐ Imperial LP-12230 [R]	1963	5.00	10.00	20.00

Number Title	Yr	VG	VG+	NM
SOLID GOLD PROGRAMMING				
❑ Screen Gems/Columbia CPL-711 [DJ]	1975	5.00	10.00	20.00
—*Promo-only compilation of oldies sent to radio to spur airplay on songs owned by this publishing house*				
❑ Screen Gems/Columbia CPL-715 [DJ]	1975	5.00	10.00	20.00
—*Same concept as above album, but completely different contents, and mostly in stereo*				
SOLID GOLD SONGS INSTRUMENTALLY				
❑ Screen Gems/Columbia CPL-714 [DJ]	1975	5.00	10.00	20.00
—*Promo-only compilation of oldies sent to radio to spur airplay on songs owned by this publishing house*				
SOLID GOLD SOUL				
❑ Atlantic 8116 [M]	1966	3.75	7.50	15.00
❑ Atlantic SD 8116 [S]	1966	5.00	10.00	20.00
SOLID STATE DEMONSTRATION RECORD				
❑ Solid State SS 93 [DJ]	1966	3.75	7.50	15.00
—*Sampler from six Solid State LP releases*				
SOLO FLIGHT				
❑ Pacific Jazz JWC-505 [M]	1956	12.50	25.00	50.00
❑ World Pacific JWC-505 [M]	1958	10.00	20.00	40.00
SOLO SPOTLIGHTS				
❑ King 745 [M]	1961	25.00	50.00	100.00
SOME LIKE IT COOL				
❑ United Artists SX-71 [S]	1959	10.00	20.00	40.00
❑ United Artists X-71 [M]	1959	10.00	20.00	40.00
SOMETHING FESTIVE!				
❑ A&M SP-19003	1968	3.75	7.50	15.00
—*Sold only at B.F. Goodrich tire dealers*				
SOMETHING FOR BOTH EARS				
❑ World Pacific HFS-2 [S]	1958	10.00	20.00	40.00
—*Stereo sampler*				
SOMETHING NEW, SOMETHING BLUE				
❑ Columbia CL 1388 [M]	1959	5.00	10.00	20.00
SONGS BY RODGERS AND HART AND JOHNNY GREEN				
❑ Discovery DL-3014 [10]	1951	12.50	25.00	50.00
SONGS FOR A SUMMER NIGHT				
❑ Columbia PM 2 [(2)M]	1963	5.00	10.00	20.00
❑ Columbia PMS 2 [(2)S]	1963	6.25	12.50	25.00
SONGS FOR CHRISTMAS — THE OLD AND THE NEW				
❑ RCA Victor PR-132-A [M]	1962	3.75	7.50	15.00
—*Sold only at Jewel food stores*				
SONGS FOR THE CHRISTMAS SEASON				
❑ Capitol Creative Products SL-6541	1967	3.00	6.00	12.00
SONGS OF FAITH				
❑ Audio Lab AL-1504 [M]	1959	20.00	40.00	80.00
SONGS OF FAITH VOLUME 2				
❑ Audio Lab AL-1523 [M]	1959	20.00	40.00	80.00
SONGS OF RIVERS, OCEANS AND SEAS				
❑ King 871 [M]	1963	17.50	35.00	70.00
SONGS OF THE HILLS				
❑ Audio Lab AL-1515 [M]	1959	20.00	40.00	80.00
SOUL CHRISTMAS				
❑ Atco SD 33-269	1968	7.50	15.00	30.00
SOUL EXPLOSION				
❑ Stax STS 2-2007 [(2)]	1969	5.00	10.00	20.00
SOUL JAZZ GIANTS				
❑ Prestige PRST-7791	1970	3.75	7.50	15.00
SOUL JAZZ, VOL. 1				
❑ Bluesville BVLP-1009 [M]	1960	12.50	25.00	50.00
—*Blue label, silver print*				
❑ Bluesville BVLP-1009 [M]	1965	6.25	12.50	25.00
—*Blue label, trident logo at right*				
SOUL JAZZ, VOL. 2				
❑ Bluesville BVLP-1010 [M]	1960	12.50	25.00	50.00
—*Blue label, silver print*				
❑ Bluesville BVLP-1010 [M]	1965	6.25	12.50	25.00
—*Blue label, trident logo at right*				
SOUL MEETING SATURDAY NIGHT HOOTENANNY STYLE				
❑ Vee Jay LP-1074 [M]	1963	7.50	15.00	30.00
—*Not known to exist in stereo*				
THE SOUL OF JAZZ				
❑ Riverside S-5 [M]	1957	10.00	20.00	40.00
❑ World Wide MGS-20002 [S]	1958	20.00	40.00	80.00

Number Title	Yr	VG	VG+	NM
THE SOUL OF JAZZ PERCUSSION				
❑ Warwick W 5003 [M]	1961	7.50	15.00	30.00
❑ Warwick W 5003ST [S]	1961	10.00	20.00	40.00
THE SOUL OF JAZZ PIANO				
❑ Riverside 9S-7 [S]	196?	7.50	15.00	30.00
SOUL OLDIES VOLUME I				
❑ Unart M 20022 [M]	1967	3.75	7.50	15.00
❑ Unart S 21022 [S]	1967	3.00	6.00	12.00
SOUL OLDIES VOLUME II				
❑ Unart M 20023 [M]	1967	3.75	7.50	15.00
❑ Unart S 21023 [S]	1967	3.00	6.00	12.00
SOULED OUT				
❑ Chess LPS 1546 [S]	1969	12.50	25.00	50.00
SOULFUL OLDIES				
❑ Oldies 33 OL-8005 [M]	1964	6.25	12.50	25.00
THE SOUND OF BIG BAND JAZZ IN HI-FI				
❑ World Pacific WP-1257 [M]	1960	10.00	20.00	40.00
THE SOUND OF BIG BAND JAZZ IN STEREO				
❑ World Pacific ST-1015 [S]	1960	7.50	15.00	30.00
THE SOUND OF CHRISTMAS				
❑ Capitol Creative Products SL-6515 [S]	1966	3.00	6.00	12.00
THE SOUND OF CHRISTMAS, VOL. 2				
❑ Capitol Creative Products SL-6534	1967	3.00	6.00	12.00
THE SOUND OF CHRISTMAS, VOL. 3				
❑ Capitol Creative Products SL-6680	1970	3.00	6.00	12.00
THE SOUND OF GENIUS				
❑ Columbia Masterworks SGM 1 [(2)M]	1963	5.00	10.00	20.00
❑ Columbia Masterworks SGS 1 [(2)S]	1963	6.25	12.50	25.00
THE SOUND OF JAZZ				
❑ Columbia CL 1098 [M]	1957	5.00	10.00	20.00
SOUNDS OF CHRISTMAS				
❑ Columbia Special Products P 12474	1974	3.00	6.00	12.00
—*Sold only through Amway dealers*				
THE SOUNDS OF CHRISTMAS				
❑ Capitol STBB-93245 [(2)]	1970	3.75	7.50	15.00
—*Available only through the Capitol Record Club*				
❑ MCA Special Markets DL 734735	197?	3.00	6.00	12.00
SOUNDS OF SUCCESS				
❑ Jamie JLP-3017 [M]	1961	6.25	12.50	25.00
❑ Jamie JLPS-3017 [S]	1961	7.50	15.00	30.00
SOUTH SIDE JAZZ				
❑ Chess CHV-415	1971	3.00	6.00	12.00
SOUTHERN MEETIN'				
❑ Kimberly 2017 [M]	1963	5.00	10.00	20.00
❑ Kimberly 11017 [S]	1963	6.25	12.50	25.00
SOUVENIR/PROGRAMMING RECORD — DEALERS/DISC JOCKEYS — OCT.-NOV. 1955				
❑ Capitol PRO-232 [DJ]	1955	10.00	20.00	40.00
THE SPANISH SIDE OF JAZZ				
❑ Roulette SR-42001	1968	5.00	10.00	20.00
SPECIAL CHRISTMAS LP FOR DISC JOCKEYS				
❑ Capitol PRO-201 [DJ]	1954	12.50	25.00	50.00
SPIN TIME WITH LIBERTY				
❑ Liberty MM-417 [DJ]	1962	12.50	25.00	50.00
—*Promo-only release*				
THE SPIRIT OF CHRISTMAS				
❑ Capitol Creative Products SL-6516	1966	3.75	7.50	15.00
❑ Columbia Musical Treasury DS 453	1968	3.00	6.00	12.00
—*Columbia Record Club exclusive*				
❑ Columbia Special Products CSP 249 [M]	1965	3.75	7.50	15.00
—*Sold only at A&P grocery stores*				
❑ Columbia Special Products P 11403	1972	2.50	5.00	10.00
—*Sold only by The Treasury family store and supermarket*				
THE SPIRIT OF CHRISTMAS, VOLUME II				
❑ Columbia Special Products CSS 889	1969	3.00	6.00	12.00
—*Distributed by TG&Y*				
THE SPIRIT OF CHRISTMAS, VOLUME III				
❑ Columbia Special Products CSS 1463	1970	3.00	6.00	12.00

Number Title	Yr	VG	VG+	NM

SPIRITUALS
☐ King 951 [M] — 1966 — 12.50 — 25.00 — 50.00
—Reissue of "Spirituals, Volume 5," King 576

SPIRITUALS TO SWING: JOHN HAMMOND'S 30TH ANNIVERSARY CONCERT 1967
☐ Columbia CG 30776 [(2)] — 197? — 3.00 — 6.00 — 12.00
—"CG" prefix is a reissue of "G"
☐ Columbia G 30776 [(2)] — 1971 — 3.75 — 7.50 — 15.00

SPIRITUALS, VOLUME 5
☐ King 576 [M] — 1957 — 37.50 — 75.00 — 150.00

STABLE MATES
☐ Savoy MG-12115 [M] — 1957 — 12.50 — 25.00 — 50.00

STARS FOR A SUMMER NIGHT
☐ Columbia PM 1 [(2)M] — 1961 — 6.25 — 12.50 — 25.00
☐ Columbia PMS 1 [(2)S] — 1961 — 7.50 — 15.00 — 30.00

THE STARS OF HEE HAW
☐ Capitol ST-437 — 1970 — 5.00 — 10.00 — 20.00

STARS OF JAZZ '61
☐ Jazzland JLP-1001 [M] — 1961 — 6.25 — 12.50 — 25.00

STARS OF THE APOLLO
☐ Columbia CG 30788 [(2)] — 197? — 3.00 — 6.00 — 12.00
—"CG" prefix is a reissue of "G"
☐ Columbia G 30788 [(2)] — 1971 — 3.75 — 7.50 — 15.00

STARS OF THE GRAND OLE OPRY 1926-1974
☐ RCA Victor CPL2-0466 [(2)] — 1974 — 5.00 — 10.00 — 20.00

THE STAX/VOLT REVUE — LIVE IN LONDON
☐ Stax 721 [M] — 1967 — 5.00 — 10.00 — 20.00
☐ Stax S721 [S] — 1967 — 6.25 — 12.50 — 25.00

THE STAX/VOLT REVUE — LIVE IN LONDON, VOLUME 2
☐ Stax 722 [M] — 1967 — 5.00 — 10.00 — 20.00
☐ Stax S722 [S] — 1967 — 6.25 — 12.50 — 25.00

STAX…ONCE YOU'VE BEEN THERE, YOU KNOW YOU'RE HOME
☐ Stax STS 1 [(2)DJ] — 1971 — 10.00 — 20.00 — 40.00
—Promo only in blank white gatefold cover

STAY IN SCHOOL — DON'T BE A DROP OUT
☐ Stax A-11 [DJ] — 1967 — 125.00 — 250.00 — 500.00

STEREOSONIC JUBILEE SAMPLER, VOLUME 1
☐ Jubilee SSJLP-801 [S] — 1959 — 10.00 — 20.00 — 40.00

STERLING BALL 1971
☐ Motown M 739 [DJ] — 1971 — 62.50 — 125.00 — 250.00
—Loucye Gordy Wakefield Scholarship Fund benefit giveaway

STILL MORE GOLD HITS, VOLUME 3
☐ Warwick W 2048 [M] — 1962 — 20.00 — 40.00 — 80.00

STRETCHING OUT
☐ United Artists UAL-4023 [M] — 1959 — 30.00 — 60.00 — 120.00
☐ United Artists UAS-5023 [S] — 1959 — 25.00 — 50.00 — 100.00

STRICTLY BEBOP
☐ Capitol M-11059 — 1973 — 3.00 — 6.00 — 12.00

STRICTLY FROM DIXIE
☐ MGM E-3262 [M] — 1956 — 7.50 — 15.00 — 30.00

THE STRING BAND PROJECT
☐ Elektra EKL-292 [M] — 1965 — 5.00 — 10.00 — 20.00
☐ Elektra EKS-7292 [S] — 1965 — 6.25 — 12.50 — 25.00

A STRING OF SWINGIN' PEARLS
☐ RCA Victor LPM-1373 [M] — 1956 — 7.50 — 15.00 — 30.00

SUMMER SOUVENIRS
☐ Bell 6035 — 1969 — 5.00 — 10.00 — 20.00

SUMMIT MEETING
☐ Vee Jay LP-3026 [M] — 1961 — 5.00 — 10.00 — 20.00
☐ Vee Jay SR-3026 [S] — 1961 — 6.25 — 12.50 — 25.00

SUN'S GOLD HITS
☐ Sun LP-1250 [M] — 1961 — 50.00 — 100.00 — 200.00

SUNDAY MORNING
☐ Vee Jay LP-5016 [M] — 1961 — 7.50 — 15.00 — 30.00

SUPER GOLDEN HITS
☐ Jubilee JGS-8019 — 1968 — 25.00 — 50.00 — 100.00
—Despite the stereo prefix, this LP is mono

SUPER GOLDEN HITS, VOLUME 2
☐ Jubilee JGS-8023 — 1969 — 25.00 — 50.00 — 100.00
—Reissue of "Clay Cole's Bin of Original Golden Oldies," Jubilee 5026; again, despite the stereo prefix, this LP is mono

THE SUPER GROUPS
☐ Atco SD 33-279 — 1969 — 5.00 — 10.00 — 20.00

THE SUPER GROUPS FROM HOLLAND
☐ White Whale WWS-7129 — 1970 — 6.25 — 12.50 — 25.00

THE SUPER HITS, VOL. 2
☐ Atlantic SD 8188 — 1968 — 5.00 — 10.00 — 20.00

THE SUPER HITS, VOL. 3
☐ Atlantic SD 8203 — 1968 — 5.00 — 10.00 — 20.00

THE SUPER HITS, VOL. 4
☐ Atlantic SD 8224 — 1969 — 5.00 — 10.00 — 20.00

THE SUPER HITS, VOL. 5
☐ Atlantic SD 8274 — 1970 — 5.00 — 10.00 — 20.00

SUPER OLDIES/VOL. 1
☐ Capitol ST 2562 [S] — 1966 — 6.25 — 12.50 — 25.00
☐ Capitol T 2562 [M] — 1966 — 5.00 — 10.00 — 20.00

SUPER OLDIES/VOL. 2
☐ Capitol ST 2565 [S] — 1966 — 6.25 — 12.50 — 25.00
☐ Capitol T 2565 [M] — 1966 — 5.00 — 10.00 — 20.00

SUPER OLDIES/VOL. 3
☐ Capitol STBB 2910 [(2)] — 1968 — 5.00 — 10.00 — 20.00

SUPER OLDIES/VOL. 4
☐ Capitol STBB-149 [(2)] — 1969 — 5.00 — 10.00 — 20.00

SUPER OLDIES/VOL. 5
☐ Capitol STBB-216 [(2)] — 1969 — 5.00 — 10.00 — 20.00

SUPER ROCK
☐ Columbia G 30121 [(2)] — 1970 — 3.75 — 7.50 — 15.00

THE SUPER SOUL-DEES
☐ Capitol ST 2798 [S] — 1967 — 5.00 — 10.00 — 20.00
☐ Capitol T 2798 [M] — 1967 — 5.00 — 10.00 — 20.00

THE SUPER SOUL-DEES, VOL. 2
☐ Capitol STBB-2911 [(2)] — 1968 — 5.00 — 10.00 — 20.00

THE SUPER SOUL-DEES, VOL. 3
☐ Capitol STBB-178 [(2)] — 1969 — 5.00 — 10.00 — 20.00

SUPERSTARS OF THE '70S
☐ Warner Special Products SP-4000 [(4)] — 1973 — 10.00 — 20.00 — 40.00
—Box set with booklet of liner notes

SURF'S UP AT BANZAI PIPELINE
☐ Northridge NM-101 [M] — 1963 — 50.00 — 100.00 — 200.00
—Original pressing of LP reissued on Reprise
☐ Reprise R 6094 [M] — 1963 — 25.00 — 50.00 — 100.00
☐ Reprise RS 6094 [S] — 1963 — 37.50 — 75.00 — 150.00

SURFIN' ON WAVE NINE
☐ King 855 [M] — 1963 — 20.00 — 40.00 — 80.00

SWAMP BLUES VOLUME 1
☐ Excello LPS-8015 [R] — 1970 — 5.00 — 10.00 — 20.00

SWAMP BLUES VOLUME 2
☐ Excello LPS-8016 [R] — 1970 — 5.00 — 10.00 — 20.00

SWEDES FROM JAZZVILLE
☐ Epic LN 3309 [M] — 1957 — 12.50 — 25.00 — 50.00

SWEDISH PASTRY
☐ Discovery DL-2008 [10] — 1954 — 12.50 — 25.00 — 50.00

SWEET 'N GREASY: RHYTHM 'N' BLUES, VOLUME 2
☐ Imperial LP-94005 — 1968 — 5.00 — 10.00 — 20.00

SWEET ADELINES MEDALIST QUARTETS OF 1958
☐ Cadence CLP-3018 [M] — 1959 — 10.00 — 20.00 — 40.00

SWEET ADELINES MEDALISTS OF 1957
☐ Cadence CLP-3009 [M] — 1958 — 10.00 — 20.00 — 40.00

SWING 1946
☐ Prestige PRLP-7604 — 1969 — 3.75 — 7.50 — 15.00

SWING AGAIN!
☐ Capitol DT 1386 [R] — 196? — 3.00 — 6.00 — 12.00
☐ Capitol T 1386 [M] — 1960 — 5.00 — 10.00 — 20.00

Number Title	Yr	VG	VG+	NM
SWING BILLIES				
❏ Audio Lab AL-1546 [M]	1960	30.00	60.00	120.00
SWING BILLIES VOLUME 2				
❏ Audio Lab AL-1566 [M]	1960	30.00	60.00	120.00
SWING CLASSICS 1935				
❏ Prestige PRLP-7646	1969	3.75	7.50	15.00
THE SWING ERA, VOL. 1				
❏ "X" LVA-3030 [10]	1955	20.00	40.00	80.00
SWING GOES DIXIE				
❏ American Recording Society G-420 [M]	1957	7.50	15.00	30.00
SWING GUITARS				
❏ Norgran MGN-1033 [M]	1955	20.00	40.00	80.00
❏ Verve MGV-8124 [M]	1957	7.50	15.00	30.00
❏ Verve V-8124 [M]	1961	5.00	10.00	20.00
SWING HI, SWING LO				
❏ Blue Note BLP-5027 [10]	1953	50.00	100.00	200.00
❏ Blue Note B-6507 [M]	1969	3.75	7.50	15.00
SWING LIGHTLY				
❏ Jazztone J-1265 [M]	1957	7.50	15.00	30.00
SWING POTPOURRI				
❏ Audiophile AP-23 [M]	1953	7.50	15.00	30.00
SWING... NOT SPRING!				
❏ Savoy MG-12062 [M]	1956	12.50	25.00	50.00
A SWINGIN' GIG				
❏ Tampa TP-2 [M]	1957	25.00	50.00	100.00
—Colored vinyl				
❏ Tampa TP-2 [M]	1958	10.00	20.00	40.00
—Black vinyl				
SWINGIN' LIKE SIXTY, VOL. 1				
❏ World Pacific ST-1289 [S]	1960	7.50	15.00	30.00
SWINGIN' LIKE SIXTY, VOL. 2				
❏ World Pacific ST-1290 [S]	1960	7.50	15.00	30.00
SWINGIN' LIKE SIXTY, VOL. 3				
❏ World Pacific ST-1291 [S]	1960	7.50	15.00	30.00
SWINGIN' SOUNDS				
❏ Columbia Special Products XTV 82030 [M]	1962	6.25	12.50	25.00
—Issued for the W.A. Sheaffer Pen Co.				
SWINGIN': BIG BAND SWING AND JAZZ FROM THE 1930S AND 1940S				
❏ Folkways FJ-2861	1986	3.00	6.00	12.00
SWINGING BROADWAY				
❏ Kimberly 2024 [M]	1963	5.00	10.00	20.00
❏ Kimberly 11024 [S]	1963	6.25	12.50	25.00
SWINGING FOR THE KING				
❏ Mercury MG-20133 [M]	1956	12.50	25.00	50.00
SWINGING SOUNDTRACK				
❏ Kimberly 2016 [M]	1963	5.00	10.00	20.00
❏ Kimberly 11016 [S]	1963	6.25	12.50	25.00
THE SWINGVILLE ALL-STARS				
❏ Swingville SVLP-2010 [M]	1960	10.00	20.00	40.00
—Purple label				
❏ Swingville SVLP-2010 [M]	1965	5.00	10.00	20.00
—Blue label, trident logo at right				
SWITCHED ON BLUES				
❏ Soul SS-720	1969	37.50	75.00	150.00
TAKE THE LIBERTY				
❏ Liberty MM-427 [DJ]	1966	10.00	20.00	40.00
TAMLA SPECIAL #1				
❏ Tamla TM 224 [M]	1962	37.50	75.00	150.00
—White label				
❏ Tamla TM 224 [M]	1963	17.50	35.00	70.00
—Yellow label				
TEEN DELIGHTS				
❏ Vee Jay LP-1021 [M]	1960	7.50	15.00	30.00
TEEN DELIGHTS, VOLUME 2				
❏ Vee Jay LP-1036 [M]	1961	7.50	15.00	30.00
THE TEEN SOUND				
❏ Columbia Special Products CSS 523	1967	3.00	6.00	12.00

Number Title	Yr	VG	VG+	NM
TEENAGE PARTY				
❏ Gee GLP-702 [M]	1958	50.00	100.00	200.00
—Red label				
❏ Gee GLP-702 [M]	196?	15.00	30.00	60.00
—Gray label				
TEENSVILLE				
❏ Liberty L-5503 [M]	1962	10.00	20.00	40.00
TENNESSEE				
❏ Design DLP-611 [M]	1962	5.00	10.00	20.00
TENOR CONCLAVE				
❏ Prestige PRLP-7074 [M]	1957	25.00	50.00	100.00
—Reissued as Prestige 7249; see JOHN COLTRANE.				
TENOR JAZZ				
❏ Mercury MG-20016 [10]	1950	25.00	50.00	100.00
—Issued in a paper sleeve				
TENOR SAX				
❏ Concord 3012 [M]	195?	10.00	20.00	40.00
TENOR SAX SOLOS, VOL. 1				
❏ Savoy MG-9008 [10]	1952	37.50	75.00	150.00
TENOR SAX SOLOS, VOL. 2				
❏ Savoy MG-9013 [10]	1952	37.50	75.00	150.00
TENOR SAX SOLOS, VOL. 3				
❏ Savoy MG-9021 [10]	1953	37.50	75.00	150.00
TENOR SAXES				
❏ Norgran MGN-1034 [M]	1955	20.00	40.00	80.00
❏ Verve MGV-8127 [M]	1957	7.50	15.00	30.00
❏ Verve V-8127 [M]	1961	5.00	10.00	20.00
TENORS ANYONE?				
❏ Dawn DLP-1126 [M]	1958	20.00	40.00	80.00
TERRITORY BANDS 1926-31				
❏ Historical 26	1969	2.50	5.00	10.00
TERRITORY BANDS 1929-33				
❏ Historical 24	1968	2.50	5.00	10.00
THAT CHRISTMAS FEELING				
❏ Columbia Special Products P 11853	1973	3.00	6.00	12.00
—Sold only at JCPenney department stores				
THAT CHRISTMAS FEELING!				
❏ Columbia Special Products CSS 1429	1970	2.50	5.00	10.00
THEME SONGS				
❏ Columbia CL 6016 [10]	1949	10.00	20.00	40.00
❏ RCA Victor LPT-1 [10]	1951	10.00	20.00	40.00
THEMES LIKE OLD TIMES				
❏ Viva 36018 [(2)]	1969	5.00	10.00	20.00
THESAURUS OF CLASSIC JAZZ				
❏ Columbia C4L 18 [(4)]	1961	12.50	25.00	50.00
A THIRD SESSION AT SQUIRREL'S				
❏ Paramount LP-110 [10]	1954	15.00	30.00	60.00
30 FAVORITE SONGS OF CHRISTMAS WITH CHIMES AND CHORUS				
❏ Disneyland DQ-1329 [M]	1963	5.00	10.00	20.00
—Performed by anonymous musicians				
THIS COULD LEAD TO LOVE				
❏ Riverside RLP 12-808 [M]	195?	12.50	25.00	50.00
THIS IS CHRISTMAS				
❏ RCA Victor VPS-6046 [(2)]	1971	3.75	7.50	15.00
THIS IS HOW IT ALL BEGAN: THE SPECIALTY STORY, VOLUME 1				
❏ Specialty SPS-2117	1970	5.00	10.00	20.00
THIS IS HOW IT ALL BEGAN: THE SPECIALTY STORY, VOLUME 2				
❏ Specialty SPS-2118	1970	5.00	10.00	20.00
THIS IS SOUL				
❏ Atlantic 8170 [M]	1968	10.00	20.00	40.00
❏ Atlantic SD 8170 [S]	1968	5.00	10.00	20.00
THIS IS STEREO				
❏ Liberty LST-101 [S]	1960	10.00	20.00	40.00
—Black vinyl				
❏ Liberty LST-101 [S]	1960	30.00	60.00	120.00
—Red vinyl				
THIS IS THE BIG BAND ERA				
❏ RCA Victor VPM-6043 [(2)]	197?	3.75	7.50	15.00

Number Title	Yr	VG	VG+	NM
THIS IS THE BLUES				
❏ Kimberly 2020 [M]	1963	5.00	10.00	20.00
❏ Kimberly 11020 [S]	1963	6.25	12.50	25.00
THIS IS THE BLUES, VOL. 1				
❏ Pacific Jazz PJ-13 [M]	1961	7.50	15.00	30.00
THIS IS THE BLUES, VOL. 2				
❏ Pacific Jazz PJ-30 [M]	1962	6.25	12.50	25.00
❏ Pacific Jazz ST-30 [M]	1962	7.50	15.00	30.00
THREADS OF GLORY — 200 YEARS OF AMERICA IN WORDS & MUSIC				
❏ London Phase 4 6SP 14000 [(6)]	1975	7.50	15.00	30.00
THREE DECADES OF MUSIC, 1939-49, VOL. 1				
❏ Blue Note BST-89902 [(2)]	1969	6.25	12.50	25.00
THREE DECADES OF MUSIC, 1949-59, VOL. 1				
❏ Blue Note BST-89903 [(2)]	1969	6.25	12.50	25.00
THREE DECADES OF MUSIC, 1959-69, VOL. 1				
❏ Blue Note BST-89904 [(2)]	1969	6.25	12.50	25.00
THREE ROADS TO JAZZ				
❏ American Recording Society LP-100 [M]	1956	7.50	15.00	30.00
A TIME FOR PRAYER				
❏ Audio Lab AL-1518 [M]	1959	20.00	40.00	80.00
'TIS THE SEASON				
❏ Columbia Special Products C 10874	1972	2.50	5.00	10.00
TODAY'S HITS				
❏ Philles PHLP 4004 [M]	1963	100.00	200.00	400.00
—First pressings have blue and black labels				
❏ Philles PHLP 4004 [M]	1964	50.00	100.00	200.00
—Second pressings have yellow and red labels				
TOGETHER				
❏ Warner Bros. PRO 486	1972	5.00	10.00	20.00
—Originals have green labels				
TOGETHER AT CHRISTMAS (READER'S DIGEST FAMILY ALBUM OF CHRISTMAS MUSIC)				
❏ Reader's Digest RDA 151-A [(5)]	1974	5.00	10.00	20.00
—Available only through Reader's Digest magazine by mail order				
TOMORROW'S HITS				
❏ Vee Jay LP-1042 [M]	1962	7.50	15.00	30.00
TOP HITS OF '54 VOLUME II				
❏ Capitol H 9119 [10]	1954	12.50	25.00	50.00
TOP R&B ARTISTS SING COUNTRY SONGS				
❏ King 884 [M]	1964	20.00	40.00	80.00
TOWN HALL CONCERT				
❏ Mainstream S-6004 [R]	1965	3.00	6.00	12.00
❏ Mainstream 56004 [M]	1965	6.25	12.50	25.00
TRADITIONAL CHRISTMAS SONGS				
❏ Audio Lab AL-1517 [M]	1959	20.00	40.00	80.00
TRADITIONAL JAZZ				
❏ London LL 1242 [M]	1955	5.00	10.00	20.00
TRADITIONAL JAZZ AT THE ROYAL FESTIVAL HALL				
❏ London LL 1184 [M]	1955	5.00	10.00	20.00
TREASURE ALBUM				
❏ Hickory LPS-154	1970	10.00	20.00	40.00
TREASURE CHEST GOODIES				
❏ Stax 703 [M]	1963	10.00	20.00	40.00
—National version of "Hits from the South Presented by Nick Charles" with rearranged contents				
TREASURE CHEST OF HITS				
❏ Swan LP-501 [M]	1960	20.00	40.00	80.00
A TREASURE CHEST OF SONG HITS				
❏ Columbia CL 613 [M]	1955	6.25	12.50	25.00
TREASURE TUNES FROM THE VAULT (AS ADVERTISED ON WLS)				
❏ Chess LP 1474 [M]	1962	10.00	20.00	40.00
A TREASURY OF CHRISTMAS				
❏ Columbia Record Club P4S 5022 [(4)]	1965	7.50	15.00	30.00
A TREASURY OF GOLDEN CHRISTMAS SONGS				
❏ Vee Jay LP-5045 [M]	1963	7.50	15.00	30.00

Number Title	Yr	VG	VG+	NM
TRIBUTE TO CHARLIE PARKER FROM THE NEWPORT JAZZ FESTIVAL				
❏ RCA Victor LPM-3738 [M]	1967	7.50	15.00	30.00
❏ RCA Victor LSP-3738 [S]	1967	5.00	10.00	20.00
TROMBONE BAND STAND				
❏ Bethlehem BCP-6036 [M]	1960	7.50	15.00	30.00
TROMBONE SCENE				
❏ Vik LX-1087 [M]	1957	7.50	15.00	30.00
TROMBONES				
❏ Savoy MG-12086 [M]	1956	15.00	30.00	60.00
THE TROMBONES, INC.				
❏ Warner Bros. W 1272 [M]	1959	6.25	12.50	25.00
❏ Warner Bros. WS 1272 [S]	1959	7.50	15.00	30.00
TRUCK DRIVER SONGS				
❏ King 866 [M]	1963	17.50	35.00	70.00
TRUMPET BLUES 1925-29				
❏ Historical 27	1969	2.50	5.00	10.00
TRUMPET INTERLUDE				
❏ EmArcy MG-36017 [M]	1955	12.50	25.00	50.00
TRUMPET STYLISTS				
❏ Capitol H 326 [10]	1952	12.50	25.00	50.00
TRUMPETER'S HOLIDAY				
❏ Epic LN 3252 [M]	1956	7.50	15.00	30.00
TRUMPETS ALL OUT				
❏ Savoy MG-12096 [M]	1957	15.00	30.00	60.00
TUNES TO BE REMEMBERED				
❏ Excello LP-8001 [M]	1960	37.50	75.00	150.00
—Original cover is green with black records that list the title and artist of each selection				
TURN BACK THE CLOCK				
❏ King 859 [M]	1963	17.50	35.00	70.00
THE 12 GREATEST OLDIES IN THE WHOLE WORLD, EVER				
❏ Parkway P-7031 [M]	1963	7.50	15.00	30.00
12 MILLION SELLERS				
❏ Forum F-9057 [M]	1963	5.00	10.00	20.00
❏ Forum SF-9057 [R]	1963	3.75	7.50	15.00
12 + 3 = 15 HITS				
❏ End LP 310 [M]	1961	15.00	30.00	60.00
12 SONGS OF CHRISTMAS				
❏ Reprise F-2022 [M]	1964	5.00	10.00	20.00
❏ Reprise FS-2022 [S]	1964	3.75	7.50	15.00
12 TOP TEEN DANCES 1961-1962				
❏ Cameo C-1016 [M]	1962	7.50	15.00	30.00
20 ALL TIME NO. 1 HITS				
❏ Roulette R 25290 [M]	1965	5.00	10.00	20.00
❏ Roulette SR 25290 [R]	1965	3.00	6.00	12.00
20 BIG BOSS FAVORITES: 10 GREAT HITS OF 1964 — 10 GREAT OLDIES HITS				
❏ Roulette R 25304 [M]	1965	5.00	10.00	20.00
❏ Roulette SR 25304 [R]	1965	3.75	7.50	15.00
—Of the 20 tracks, only "Laugh, Laugh" by the Beau Brummels and "El Watusi" by Ray Barretto are true stereo				
20 ORIGINAL WINNERS OF 1964				
❏ Roulette R 25293 [M]	1965	5.00	10.00	20.00
❏ Roulette SR 25293 [R]	1965	3.00	6.00	12.00
20 ORIGINAL WINNERS, VOLUME 1				
❏ Roulette R 25249 [M]	1964	5.00	10.00	20.00
20 ORIGINAL WINNERS, VOLUME 2				
❏ Roulette R 25251 [M]	1964	5.00	10.00	20.00
20 ORIGINAL WINNERS, VOLUME 3				
❏ Roulette R 25263 [M]	1965	5.00	10.00	20.00
20 ORIGINAL WINNERS, VOLUME 4				
❏ Roulette R 25264 [M]	1965	5.00	10.00	20.00
20 SOULFUL OLDIES, VOLUME 1				
❏ Vee Jay VJVS-1001 [R]	1972	5.00	10.00	20.00
20 SOULFUL OLDIES, VOLUME 2				
❏ Vee Jay VJVS-1002 [R]	1972	5.00	10.00	20.00

Number Title	Yr	VG	VG+	NM
20 SOULFUL OLDIES, VOLUME 3				
❑ Vee Jay VJVS-1003 [R]	1972	5.00	10.00	20.00
20 SOULFUL OLDIES, VOLUME 4				
❑ Vee Jay VJVS-73-1006/7 [R]	1973	5.00	10.00	20.00
20 SOULFUL OLDIES, VOLUME 5				
❑ Vee Jay VJVS-73-1008/9 [R]	1973	5.00	10.00	20.00
20 SOULFUL OLDIES, VOLUME 6				
❑ Vee Jay VJVS-73-1010/11 [R]	1973	5.00	10.00	20.00
24 KARAT GOLD FOR GROOVIN'				
❑ Verve V6-6654 [(2)]	1968	5.00	10.00	20.00
24 SACRED SONGS				
❑ King 965 [M]	1966	12.50	25.00	50.00
25 YEARS OF C&W HITS				
❑ King 1006 [M]	1966	7.50	15.00	30.00
25 YEARS OF COUNTRY AND WESTERN SACRED SONGS				
❑ King 807 [M]	1962	25.00	50.00	100.00
25 YEARS OF POPULAR MUSIC				
❑ King 1008 [M]	1966	7.50	15.00	30.00
25 YEARS OF R&B HITS				
❑ King 1004 [M]	1966	7.50	15.00	30.00
25 YEARS OF R&B HITS, VOLUME 1				
❑ King 725 [M]	1961	25.00	50.00	100.00
25 YEARS OF R&B HITS, VOLUME 2				
❑ King 749 [M]	1961	25.00	50.00	100.00
TWISTIN' ALL NIGHT LONG				
❑ Swan LP-506 [M]	1962	30.00	60.00	120.00
THE UNAVAILABLE 16				
❑ Vee Jay LP-1051 [M]	1962	10.00	20.00	40.00
UNDER ONE ROOF				
❑ EmArcy MG-36088 [M]	1956	10.00	20.00	40.00
UNDERGROUND GOLD				
❑ Liberty LST-7625	1969	3.75	7.50	15.00
UNEXPURGATED JAZZ				
❑ Audiophile AP-43 [M]	1953	7.50	15.00	30.00
UNFORGETTABLE OLDIES				
❑ Unart M 20014 [M]	1967	3.75	7.50	15.00
❑ Unart S 21014 [S]	1967	3.00	6.00	12.00
UNFORGETTABLE OLDIES — VOLUME II				
❑ Unart M 20027 [M]	1968	3.75	7.50	15.00
❑ Unart S 21027 [S]	1968	3.00	6.00	12.00
UNFORGETTABLE PERFORMANCES BY THE JAZZ IMMORTALS				
❑ Dot DLP-3444 [M]	196?	3.00	6.00	12.00
UP SWING				
❑ RCA Victor LPT-12 [10]	1951	10.00	20.00	40.00
UPRIGHT AND LOWDOWN				
❑ Columbia CL 685 [M]	1955	5.00	10.00	20.00
A VARIETY OF COUNTRY SACRED SONGS				
❑ Audio Lab AL-1557 [M]	1960	15.00	30.00	60.00
THE VERVE COMPENDIUM OF JAZZ, NO. 1				
❑ Verve MGV-8194 [M]	1957	7.50	15.00	30.00
❑ Verve V-8194 [M]	1961	5.00	10.00	20.00
THE VERVE COMPENDIUM OF JAZZ, NO. 2				
❑ Verve MGV-8195 [M]	1957	7.50	15.00	30.00
❑ Verve V-8195 [M]	1961	5.00	10.00	20.00
A VERY MERRY CHRISTMAS				
❑ Columbia Special Products CSS 563	1967	5.00	10.00	20.00
—Sold only at Grants stores				
A VERY MERRY CHRISTMAS, VOLUME TWO				
❑ Columbia Special Products CSS 788	1968	3.00	6.00	12.00
—Sold only at Grants stores				
A VERY MERRY CHRISTMAS, VOLUME 3				
❑ Columbia Special Products CSS 997	1969	3.00	6.00	12.00
—Sold only at Grants stores				
A VERY MERRY CHRISTMAS, VOLUME IV				
❑ Columbia Special Products CSS 1464	1970	3.75	7.50	15.00
—Sold only at Grants stores				

Number Title	Yr	VG	VG+	NM
A VERY MERRY CHRISTMAS, VOLUME 5				
❑ RCA Special Products PRS-343	1971	2.50	5.00	10.00
—Sold only at Grants stores				
A VERY MERRY CHRISTMAS, VOLUME VI				
❑ RCA Special Products PRS-427	1972	2.50	5.00	10.00
—Sold only at Grants stores				
A VERY MERRY CHRISTMAS, VOLUME VII				
❑ RCA Special Products DPL1-0049	1973	2.50	5.00	10.00
—Sold only at Grants stores				
A VERY MERRY CHRISTMAS, VOLUME VIII				
❑ Capitol Special Markets SL-6954	1974	2.50	5.00	10.00
—Sold only at Grants stores				
A VERY MERRY CHRISTMAS TO ALL				
❑ Columbia Special Products CSP 159	1964	3.75	7.50	15.00
—Sold only at Acme markets (Mid-Atlantic states)				
VERY SAXY				
❑ Prestige PRLP-7167 [M]	1959	15.00	30.00	60.00
❑ Prestige PRST-7790	1971	5.00	10.00	20.00
—Reissue of 7167				
VICEROY CIGARETTES CAMPUS JAZZ FESTIVAL				
❑ RCA Custom KO7P-1544 [M]	1959	7.50	15.00	30.00
—Available thoruigh Viceroy cigarettes				
THE VIOLIN SUMMIT				
❑ Prestige PRLP-7631	1969	3.75	7.50	15.00
VOICES OF HAITI				
❑ Elektra EKL-5 [10]	1953	10.00	20.00	40.00
VOODOO DRUMS IN HI-FI				
❑ Atlantic 1296 [M]	1958	10.00	20.00	40.00
—Black label				
❑ Atlantic 1296 [M]	1961	6.25	12.50	25.00
—Multicolor label, white "fan" logo at right				
❑ Atlantic 1296 [M]	1963	5.00	10.00	20.00
—Multicolor label, black "fan" logo at right				
WALKIN' BY MYSELF				
❑ Chess LP 1446 [M]	1960	20.00	40.00	80.00
THE WALTONS' CHRISTMAS ALBUM				
❑ Columbia KC 33193	1974	3.75	7.50	15.00
—Only one of the actors who appeared on the show appears on the album, thus it's listed here under Various Artists rather than Soundtracks or Television Albums				
WAMO'S GOLDEN GASSERS				
❑ Chess LP 1458 PGH [M]	1961	37.50	75.00	150.00
—Pittsburgh version of "Golden Gassers," Chess 1458				
THE WARNER/REPRISE RADIO SHOW				
❑ Warner Bros. PRO 463	1971	6.25	12.50	25.00
—Originals have green labels				
WASHBOARD RHYTHM KINGS, VOL. 1				
❑ "X" LVA-3021 [10]	1954	20.00	40.00	80.00
WE CUT THIS ALBUM FOR BREAD				
❑ Bethlehem BCP-86 [M]	1958	7.50	15.00	30.00
WE LIKE BANDS				
❑ Coral CRL 57229 [M]	195?	3.00	6.00	12.00
WE LIKE BOYS/GREAT BOY OLDIES				
❑ Oldies 33 OL-8004 [M]	1964	6.25	12.50	25.00
WE SING THE BLUES				
❑ Minit LP-0003 [M]	1962	12.50	25.00	50.00
WE WISH YOU A MERRY CHRISTMAS				
❑ Harmony KH 31536	1972	2.50	5.00	10.00
❑ RCA Victor PRS-277 [Picture Sleeve]	1968	2.50	5.00	10.00
—Sleeve says the number is "68-1968"				
❑ Warner Bros. W 1337 [M]	1960	6.25	12.50	25.00
❑ Warner Bros. WS 1337 [S]	1960	7.50	15.00	30.00
WE'VE BUILT A JAZZ ALBUM FOR YOU				
❑ Bethlehem BCP-89 [M]	1958	7.50	15.00	30.00
WEST COAST JAZZ, VOL. 2				
❑ Jazztone J-(# unk) [M]	1957	7.50	15.00	30.00
WEST COAST VS. EAST COAST				
❑ MGM E-3390 [M]	1956	7.50	15.00	30.00
WESTERN SWING				
❑ King 876 [M]	1963	17.50	35.00	70.00
WFUN GOOD GUYS				
❑ Roulette R 25273 [M]	1965	5.00	10.00	20.00

Number	Title	Yr	VG	VG+	NM
WHAT'S NEW? ON CAPITOL STEREO, VOL. 1					
❑ Capitol SN-1 [S]		1959	6.25	12.50	25.00
WHAT'S SHAKIN'					
❑ Elektra EKL-4002 [M]		1966	10.00	20.00	40.00
—Deduct 25 percent if booklet is missing					
❑ Elektra EKS-74002 [S]		1966	12.50	25.00	50.00
—Deduct 25 percent if booklet is missing					
WHEELIN' AND DEALIN'					
❑ Prestige PRLP-7131 [M]		1957	25.00	50.00	100.00
—Reissued as Status 8327; see JOHN COLTRANE.					
WHK GOOD GUYS					
❑ Roulette R 25295 [M]		1965	5.00	10.00	20.00
THE WHO'S WHO OF COUNTRY AND WESTERN MUSIC					
❑ Capitol ST 2538 [S]		1966	5.00	10.00	20.00
❑ Capitol T 2538 [M]		1966	5.00	10.00	20.00
THE WHOLE BURBANK CATALOG					
❑ Warner Bros. PRO 512 [(2)]		1972	5.00	10.00	20.00
—Originals have green labels					
A WHOLE LOT OF BLOWIN'					
❑ Audio Lab AL-1539 [M]		1959	15.00	30.00	60.00
WHOPPERS					
❑ Jubilee JGM-1119 [M]		1960	25.00	50.00	100.00
—Reissue of "Best of Rhythm and Blues," Jubilee 1014					
THE WIDE, WIDE WORLD OF JAZZ					
❑ RCA Victor LPM-1325 [M]		1956	7.50	15.00	30.00
WILD WILDWOOD RECORDED LIVE					
❑ Chancellor CHL-5017 [M]		1960	6.25	12.50	25.00
❑ Chancellor CHLS-5017 [S]		1960	7.50	15.00	30.00
WILDFLOWERS: NEW YORK LOFT JAZZ 1					
❑ Douglas 7045		1976	3.00	6.00	12.00
WILDFLOWERS: NEW YORK LOFT JAZZ 2					
❑ Douglas 7046		1976	3.00	6.00	12.00
WILDFLOWERS: NEW YORK LOFT JAZZ 3					
❑ Douglas 7047		1976	3.00	6.00	12.00
WILDFLOWERS: NEW YORK LOFT JAZZ 4					
❑ Douglas 7048		1976	3.00	6.00	12.00
WILDFLOWERS: NEW YORK LOFT JAZZ 5					
❑ Douglas 7049		1976	3.00	6.00	12.00
WING LIVELY GUYS					
❑ Roulette R 25307 [M]		1965	5.00	10.00	20.00
WINNER'S CIRCLE					
❑ Bethlehem BCP-6024 [M]		1958	10.00	20.00	40.00
WINNERS ALL! THE DOWN BEAT JAZZ POLL '64					
❑ Verve V-8579 [M]		1964	5.00	10.00	20.00
❑ Verve V6-8579 [S]		1964	6.25	12.50	25.00
WINNERS CIRCLE LIMITED EDITION					
❑ Columbia GB-4 [M]		1959	6.25	12.50	25.00
WINTER'S WARMTH					
❑ Columbia Special Products CSP 315/6 [(2)]		1965	3.75	7.50	15.00
—Produced for NORM/A Step Ahead					
WISHING YOU A MERRY CHRISTMAS					
❑ RCA Victor LSP-4793		1972	3.00	6.00	12.00
WMAK JET SET-22 WINNERS					
❑ Roulette R 25291 [M]		1965	5.00	10.00	20.00
WOL SOUL BROTHERS					
❑ Roulette R 25337 [M]		1966	5.00	10.00	20.00
—Same LP as "WWIN Astro Jocks"					
THE WOMEN IN JAZZ					
❑ Storyville STLP-916 [M]		1956	12.50	25.00	50.00
WONDERFUL MEMORIES FROM THE FAMILY PRAYER BOOK					
❑ Vee Jay LP-5066 [M]		1964	7.50	15.00	30.00
THE WONDERFUL WORLD OF CHRISTMAS					
❑ Capitol Special Markets SL-8000		1975	3.00	6.00	12.00
—Sold only at Firestone tire dealers (add 50% for sticker that says "Season's Greetings Firestone")					
WONDROUS WINTER					
❑ Columbia Special Products CSS 708/9 [(2)]		1968	3.75	7.50	15.00
—Produced for NORM/A Step Ahead					
WOODSTOCK					
❑ Cotillion SD 3-500 [(3)]		1970	5.00	10.00	20.00
—Pale blue labels					

Number	Title	Yr	VG	VG+	NM
WOODSTOCK TWO					
❑ Cotillion SD 2-400 [(2)]		1971	5.00	10.00	20.00
THE WORKS					
❑ Warner Bros. PRO 610 [(2)]		1975	6.25	12.50	25.00
A WORLD OF BLUES					
❑ Imperial LP-9210		1963	7.50	15.00	30.00
❑ Imperial LP-12210 [R]		1963	5.00	10.00	20.00
THE WORLD OF COUNTRY MUSIC					
❑ Capitol NPB-5 [(3)]		1965	7.50	15.00	30.00
THE WORLD OF SWING					
❑ Columbia KG 32945 [(2)]		1974	3.75	7.50	15.00
THE WORLD'S GREATEST MUSIC SERIES 'POP' — JAZZ					
❑ Artia-Parliament WGM(S)-2A [(5)S]		196?	15.00	30.00	60.00
❑ Artia-Parliament WGM-2A [(5)M]		196?	12.50	25.00	50.00
❑ Artia-Parliament WGM 2AB [(10)]		196?	25.00	50.00	100.00
—Box set of material from the Roulette label; also issued as two five-record boxes					
❑ Artia-Parliament WGM 2B [(5)]		196?	12.50	25.00	50.00
—Second of two five-record sets					
WWIN ASTRO JOCKS					
❑ Roulette R 25337 [M]		1966	5.00	10.00	20.00
—Same LP as "WOL Soul Brothers"					
YESTERDAY					
❑ Mainstream MRL-364		197?	3.00	6.00	12.00
YOU'VE GOT TO HEAR IT TO BELIEVE IT					
❑ Solid State SS-94		1966	5.00	10.00	20.00
THE YOUNG AT BOP					
❑ EmArcy MG-26001 [10]		1954	20.00	40.00	80.00
THE YOUNG ONES OF JAZZ					
❑ EmArcy MG-36085 [M]		1956	10.00	20.00	40.00
YOUR FAVORITE GROUPS AND THEIR GOLDEN GOODIES, VOL. 19					
❑ Roulette R 25248 [M]		1964	5.00	10.00	20.00
YOUR FAVORITE SINGING GROUPS					
❑ Hull 1002 [M]		1962	375.00	750.00	1500.
YOUR INTRODUCTION TO THE SOUND OF THE 'SIXTIES					
❑ Liberty MM-403 [DJ]		1960	7.50	15.00	30.00
—Promo-only release					
YOUR OLD FAVORITES ON OLD TOWN					
❑ Old Town LP-101 [M]		1959	50.00	100.00	200.00
YOURS					
❑ Harmony HL 7042 [M]		1957	5.00	10.00	20.00
ZENITH PRESENTS ALL STAR HOOTENANNY					
❑ Columbia Special Products CSP 149 [M]		1963	12.50	25.00	50.00
—With three early Bob Dylan tracks credited to "Bobby Dylan." Also has tracks by Pete Seeger (2), Orriel Smith (2) and The Clancy Brothers with Tommy Makem (3)					
ZENITH PRESENTS CHRISTMAS, A GIFT OF MUSIC					
❑ Capitol Creative Products SL-6544 [S]		1967	3.00	6.00	12.00
—Sold only at Zenith dealers					
ZENITH PRESENTS CHRISTMAS, A GIFT OF MUSIC VOL. 2					
❑ Columbia Special Products CSS 834		1968	3.00	6.00	12.00
—Sold only at Zenith dealers					
ZENITH PRESENTS CHRISTMAS, A GIFT OF MUSIC VOL. 3					
❑ Capitol Creative Products SL-6659		1969	3.00	6.00	12.00
—Sold only at Zenith dealers; reissued as "Christmas -- The Season of Music" for general release					
ZENITH PRESENTS CHRISTMAS, A GIFT OF MUSIC VOL. 4					
❑ Capitol Creative Products SL-6687		1970	3.00	6.00	12.00
—Sold only at Zenith dealers; reissued as "Christmas -- A Gift of Music" for general release					
ZENITH PRESENTS CHRISTMAS, A GIFT OF MUSIC VOL. 5					
❑ Columbia Special Products C 10395		1971	2.50	5.00	10.00
—Sold only at Zenith dealers					
ZENITH PRESENTS CHRISTMAS, A GIFT OF MUSIC, VOL. 6 (THE CHRISTMAS HIT PARADE)					
❑ Longines Symphonette SYS 5562		1972	2.50	5.00	10.00
—Sold only at Zenith dealers					
ZENITH PRESENTS HOOTENANNY SPECIAL					
❑ Columbia Special Products CSP 216M [M]		1965	6.25	12.50	25.00
❑ Columbia Special Products CSP 216S [S]		1965	7.50	151.00	30.00
ZENITH SALUTES THE SWINGIN' BANDS					
❑ Columbia Special Products CSS 525 [M]		1967	3.75	7.50	15.00
—Available from Zenith dealers					
ZIG ZAG FESTIVAL					
❑ Mercury SRD-2-29 [DJ]		1970	6.25	12.50	25.00